Webster's New Collegiate Dictionary 150th Anniversary Edition

The G. & C. Merriam Company
1831-1981

WEBSTER'S
New
Collegiate
Dictionary

WEBSTER'S

New Collegiate Dictionary

G. & C. MERRIAM COMPANY
Springfield, Massachusetts, U.S.A.

Library of Congress Cataloging in Publication Data
Main entry under title:

Webster's new collegiate dictionary.

Editions for 1898–1948 have title: Webster's collegiate dictionary.
Includes index.
1. English language—Dictionaries.
PE1628.W4M4   1981   423   80-25144
ISBN 0-87779-408-1
ISBN 0-87779-409-x (indexed)
ISBN 0-87779-410-3 (deluxe)

Made in the United States of America

424344RMcN80

Contents

Preface

Webster's New Collegiate Dictionary is a completely new volume in the Merriam-Webster series of dictionaries. It is a general dictionary edited for use in school or college, in the office, and in the home—in short, wherever information about English words is likely to be sought. The average user should rarely have occasion to look for information about the vocabulary of present-day English that is not available within these pages.

The first Merriam-Webster Collegiate appeared in 1898 and quickly won the esteem of student and general reader. A second edition was published in 1910, and subsequent editions came out in 1916, 1931, 1936, 1949, and 1963. This eighth in the series incorporates the best of the time-tested features of its predecessors and introduces new features designed to add to its usefulness. Its more than 1500 pages make it the most comprehensive Merriam-Webster Collegiate ever published.

The heart of Webster's New Collegiate Dictionary is the more than 1300 pages given over to the A–Z vocabulary. The information there set down derives not only from the 10,000,000 citations which were available to the editors of Webster's Third New International Dictionary and the 1963 Collegiate but also from the considerably more than 1,000,000 citations collected since the publication of these books. Thus each entry is based on a constantly updated file of actual English usage.

Those entries known to be trademarks or service marks are so labeled and are treated in accordance with a formula approved by the United States Trademark Association. No entry in this dictionary, however, should be regarded as affecting the validity of any trademark or service mark.

A noteworthy feature of the vocabulary section is the nearly 900 pictorial illustrations, many of which were drawn especially for this book. These illustrations were selected not simply for their decorative function but particularly for their value in clarifying definitions.

The front matter—those pages preceding the A–Z vocabulary—contains two important sections. The Explanatory Notes should be read by every user of the dictionary since a thorough understanding of the information contained in them will contribute markedly to the value of this book. And all users of the dictionary are urged to read the lucid essay on the English language which was written for this Collegiate by Professor W. Nelson Francis of Brown University.

The back matter—those pages following the A–Z vocabulary—contains several sections that dictionary users have long found helpful. These include more than five hundred Foreign Words and Phrases that occur frequently in English texts but that have not become part of the English vocabulary; several thousand proper names that are entered under the separate headings Biographical Names and Geographical Names; and a list of the Colleges and Universities of the United States and Canada. There is also a Handbook of Style in which various stylistic conventions (as of punctuation and capitalization) are concisely summarized.

Webster's New Collegiate Dictionary has been edited by the trained staff of the G. & C. Merriam Co. It is the result of a collaborative effort, and it would be invidious to single out particular editors for special mention. At the same time, it would be ungracious to observe the anonymity which is often the lot of the present-day lexicographer, and so a list of those who contributed substantially to the completion of this book is printed below.

Webster's New Collegiate Dictionary is the product of a company that has been publishing dictionaries for more than 125 years. It is offered to the user with the conviction that it will serve him well.

Henry Bosley Woolf
Editor in Chief

Editorial Staff

Editor in Chief

Henry Bosley Woolf

Senior Editors

Edward Artin • F. Stuart Crawford
• E. Ward Gilman • Mairé Weir Kay
• Roger W. Pease, Jr.

Associate Editors

Robert D. Copeland • Grace A. Kellogg
• Hubert P. Kelsey • James G. Lowe
• George M. Sears

Assistant Editors

William Parr Black • Kathryn K. Flynn
• Dolores R. Harris • Laverne W. King
• Kerry W. Metz • Trudy A. Perkins
• James E. Shea, Jr. • Anne H. Soukhanov
• Raymond R. Wilson

Editorial Assistants

Dwight H. Day, Jr. • Philip B. Dickinson
• Kathleen M. Doherty • L. Aimee Garn
• Peter B. Kent

Editorial Consultants

Charlotte A. Bridgman • Philip W. Cummings
• Philip B. Gove

Librarian

Marion D. Ware

Departmental Secretary

Hazel O. Lord

Head of Typing Room

Evelyn G. Summers

Clerks and Typists

Maude L. Barnes • Esther L. Gauthier
• Mildred A. Lindsay • Maureen E. McCartney
• Mildred M. McWha • Catherine T. Meaney
• Frances W. Muldrew • Mildred C. Paquette
• Genevieve M. Sherry • Francine A. Socha

Left column labels	Dictionary entries

angle brackets
PAGE 16a

antonym
PAGE 18a

binomial
PAGE 18a

boldface colon
PAGE 17a

boldface type
PAGE 10a

capitalization label
PAGE 14a

centered periods
PAGE 10a

cognate cross-reference
PAGE 18a

cutback inflected forms
PAGE 13a

definition
PAGE 17a

directional cross-reference
PAGE 18a

equal variant
PAGE 11a

etymology
PAGE 14a

functional label
PAGE 12a

homographs
PAGE 10a

illustrative quotation
PAGE 16a

inflected forms
PAGES 12a, 13a

inflectional cross-reference
PAGE 18a

lightface type
PAGE 10a

lowercase
PAGE 14a

main entry
PAGE 10a

major stress
PAGE 11a

---

pachy·der·ma·tous \ˌpak-i-'dər-mət-əs\ *adj* [deriv. of Gk *pachys* + *dermat-*, *derma* skin] **1** : of or relating to the pachyderms **2 a** : THICK, THICKENED <~ SKIN> **b** : CALLOUS, INSENSITIVE — **pachy·der·ma·tous·ly** *adv*

pam·per \'pam-pər\ *vt* **pam·pered; pam·per·ing** \-p(ə-)riŋ\ [ME *pamperen*, prob. of D origin; akin to Flem *pamperen* to pamper] **1** *archaic* : to cram with rich food : GLUT **2 a** : to treat with extreme or excessive care and attention <~ed their guests> **b** : GRATIFY, HUMOR <enabled him to ~ his wanderlust —*New Yorker*> *syn* see INDULGE, *ant* chasten — **pam·per·er** \-pər-ər\ *n*

pa·pa·ya \pə-'pī-ə\ *n* [Sp, of AmerInd origin; akin to Otomac *papai*] : a tropical American tree *Carica papaya* of the family Caricaceae, the papaya family) with large oblong yellow edible fruit; *also* : its fruit

²**paper** *vb* **pa·pered; pa·per·ing** \'pā-p(ə-)riŋ\ *vt* **1** *archaic* : to put down or describe in writing **2** : to fold or enclose in paper **3** : to cover or line with paper; *esp* : to apply wallpaper to **4** : to fill by giving out free passes <~ the theater for opening night> **5** : to cover (an area) with advertising bills, circulars, or posters ~ *vi* : to hang wallpaper — **pa·per·er** \-pər-ər\ *n*

paper tiger *n* : one that is outwardly powerful or dangerous but inwardly weak or ineffectual <necessary to show that the . . . military presence was not a *paper tiger* —Kaye Whiteman>

²**Paphian** *n* **1** : a native or inhabitant of Paphos **2** *often not cap* : PROSTITUTE

pap·il·lo·ma \ˌpap-ə-'lō-mə\ *n, pl* **-mas** *or* **-ma·ta** \-mət-ə\ **1** : a benign tumor (as a wart) due to overgrowth of epithelial tissue on papillae of vascular connective tissue (as of the skin) **2** : an epithelial tumor caused by a virus — **pap·il·lo·ma·tous** \-'lō-mət-əs\ *adj*

par·a·lyse *Brit var of* PARALYZE

pa·ram·e·ter·ize \pə-'ram-ət-ə-ˌrīz\ *or* **pa·ram·e·trize** \-'ram-ə-ˌtrīz\ *vt* **-ter·ized** *or* **-trized; -ter·iz·ing** *or* **-triz·ing** : to express in terms of parameters — **pa·ram·e·ter·iza·tion** \-ram-ət-ə-rə-'zā-shən, -ə-ˌtrə-'zā-\ *or* **pa·ram·e·tri·za·tion** \-ə-ˌtrə-'zā-\ *n*

pa·rang \'pär-ˌaŋ\ *n* [Malay] : a short sword, cleaver, or machete common in Malaysia and Indonesia

parasympathetic nervous system *n* : the part of the autonomic nervous system that contains chiefly cholinergic fibers, that tends to induce secretion, to increase the tone and contractility of smooth muscle, and to cause the dilatation of blood vessels, and that consists of a cranial and a sacral part — compare SYMPATHETIC NERVOUS SYSTEM

ped·dler *or* **ped·lar** \'ped-lər\ *n* : one who peddles: as **a** : one who offers merchandise (as fresh produce) for sale along the street or from door to door **b** : one who deals in or promotes something intangible (as a personal asset or an idea) <influence ~s>

¹**pe·des·tri·an** \pə-'des-trē-ən\ *adj* [L *pedestr-, pedester*, lit., going on foot, fr. *pedes* one going on foot, fr. *ped-, pes* foot — more at FOOT] **1** : COMMONPLACE, UNIMAGINATIVE **2 a** : going or performed on foot **b** : of, relating to, or designed for walking <a ~ mall>

peg leg *n* **1** [*peg*] : an artificial leg; *esp* : one fitted at the knee

¹**pen·i·tent** \-tənt\ *adj* [ME, fr. MF, fr. L *paenitent-, paenitens*, fr. prp. of *paenitēre* to be sorry; akin to L *paene* almost — more at PATIENT] : feeling or expressing humble or regretful pain or sorrow for sins or offenses : REPENTANT — **pen·i·tent·ly** *adv*

²**penitent** *n* **1** : a person who repents of sin **2** : a person under church censure but admitted to penance esp. under the direction of a confessor

per·cent·age \pər-'sent-ij\ *n* **1** : a part of a whole expressed in hundredths **2 a** : a share of winnings or profits **b** : ADVANTAGE, PROFIT <no ~ in going around looking like an old sack of laundry —Wallace Stegner> **3** : an indeterminate part : PROPORTION **4 a** : PROBABILITY **b** : favorable odds

per·jure \'pər-jər\ *vt* **per·jured; per·jur·ing** \'pərj-(ə-)riŋ\ [MF *perjurer*, fr. L *perjurare*, fr. *per-* to destruction, to the bad + *jurare* to swear — more at PER-, JURY] **1** *obs* : to cause to commit perjury **2** : to make a perjurer of (oneself)

pies *pl of* PI *or of* PIE

⁴**pile** *vb* **piled; pil·ing** *vt* **1** : to lay or place in a pile : STACK **2** : to heap in abundance : LOAD <*piled* potatoes on his plate> ~ *vi* **1** : to form a pile : ACCUMULATE **2** : to move or press forward in or as if in a mass : CROWD <*piled* into a car>

pile driver *n* **1** : a machine for driving down piles with a pile hammer or a steam or air hammer **2** : an operator of a pile driver

pil·grim \'pil-grəm\ *n* [ME, fr. OF *peligrin*, fr. LL *pelegrinus*, alter. of L *peregrinus* foreigner, fr. *peregrinus* foreign, fr. *pereger* being abroad, fr. *per* through + *agr-, ager* land — more at FOR, ACRE] **1** : one who journeys in foreign lands : WAYFARER **2** : one who travels to a shrine or holy place as a devotee **3** *cap* : one of the English colonists settling at Plymouth in 1620

pinch·beck \'pinch-ˌbek\ *n* [Christopher *Pinchbeck* †1732 E watchmaker] **1** : an alloy of copper and zinc used esp. to imitate gold in jewelry **2** : something counterfeit or spurious — **pinch·beck** *adj*

8a

Explanatory Chart

pin·cush·ion \'pin-ˌkush-ən\ *n* : a small cushion in which pins may be stuck ready for use

²**pine** *n* *often attrib* [ME, fr. OF *pin*, fr. L *pinus*; akin to Gk *pitys* pine, L *opimus* fat — more at FAT] **1** : any of a *genus* (*Pinus* of the family Pinaceae, the pine family) of coniferous evergreen trees which have slender elongated needles and some of which are valuable timber trees or ornamentals **2** : the straight-grained white or yellow usu. durable and resinous wood of a pine varying from extreme softness in the white pine to hardness in the longleaf pine **3** : any of various Australian coniferous trees (as of the genera *Callitris, Araucaria,* or *Cupressus*) **4** : PINEAPPLE — **piny** *or* **pin·ey** \'pī-nē\ *adj*

post·card \'pōs(t)-ˌkard\ *n* **1** : a card on which a message may be written for mailing without an envelope and to which the sender must affix a stamp **2** : POSTAL CARD 1

post–free \'pōs(t)-'frē\ *adj, chiefly Brit* : POSTPAID

post·mas·ter \-ˌmas-tər\ *n* **1** : one who has charge of a post office **2** : one who has charge of a station for the accommodation of travelers or who supplies post-horses — **post·mas·ter·ship** \-ˌship\ *n*

²**private** *n* **1** *archaic* : one not in public office **2** *obs* : PRIVACY **3 a** : a person of low rank in various organizations (as a police or fire department) **b** : an enlisted man of the lowest rank in the marine corps or of one of the two lowest ranks in the army — **in private** : not openly or in public

pro·gram·mer *also* **pro·gram·er** \'prō-ˌgram-ər, -grə-mər\ *n* : one that programs: as **a** : one that prepares and tests programs for mechanisms **b** : a person or device that programs a mechanism **c** : one that prepares educational programs

pro·jec·tor \prə-'jek-tər\ *n* **1** : one that plans a project; *specif* : PROMOTER **2** : one that projects: as **a** : a device for projecting a beam of light **b** : an optical instrument for projecting an image upon a surface **c** : a machine for projecting motion pictures on a screen **3** : an imagined line from an object to a surface along which projection takes place

pro·jet \prō-'zhā, 'prō-\ *n, pl* **projets** \-'zhā(z), -ˌzhā(z)\ [F, fr. MF *pourjet*] **1** : PLAN *esp* : a draft of a proposed measure or treaty **2** : a projected or proposed design

pro·mote \prə-'mōt\ *vt* **pro·mot·ed; pro·mot·ing** [L *promotus,* pp. of *promovēre,* lit., to move forward, fr. *pro-* forward + *movēre* to move] **1 a** : to advance in station, rank, or honor : RAISE **b** : to change (a pawn) into a piece in chess by moving to the eighth rank **c** : to advance (a student) from one grade to the next higher grade **2 a** : to contribute to the growth or prosperity of : FURTHER <~ international understanding> **b** : to help bring (as an enterprise) into being : LAUNCH **c** : to present (merchandise) for public acceptance through advertising and publicity **3** *slang* : to get possession of by doubtful means or by ingenuity *syn* see ADVANCE *ant* impede

proph·et \'präf-ət\ *n* [ME *prophete,* fr. OF, fr. L *propheta,* fr. Gk *prophētēs,* fr. *pro* for + *phanai* to speak — more at FOR, BAN] **1** : one who utters divinely inspired revelations; *specif, often cap* : the writer of one of the prophetic books of the Old Testament **2** : one gifted with more than ordinary spiritual and moral insight; *esp* : an inspired poet **3** : one who foretells future events : PREDICTOR <a weather ~> **4** : an effective or leading spokesman for a cause, doctrine, or group <he is first the student and then the ~ of power —Alfred Kazin> **5** *Christian Science* **a** : a spiritual seer **b** : disappearance of material sense before the conscious facts of spiritual Truth — **proph·et·ess** \-ət-əs\ *n*

pro·rate \(')prō-'rāt\ *vb* **pro·rat·ed; pro·rat·ing** [*pro rata*] *vt* : to divide, distribute, or assess proportionately ~ *vi* : to make a pro rata distribution

pro·spec·tive \prə-'spek-tiv *also* 'prä-, prō-', prä-'\ *adj* **1** : likely to come about : EXPECTED <the ~ benefits of this law> **2** : likely to be or become <a ~ mother> — **pro·spec·tive·ly** *adv*

pun·gent \-jənt\ *adj* [L *pungent-, pungens,* prp. of *pungere* to prick, sting; akin to L *pugnus* fist, *pugnare* to fight, Gk *pygmē* fist] **1** : having a stiff and sharp point <~ leaves> **2** : sharply painful; *also* : POIGNANT **3 a** : marked by a sharp incisive quality : CAUSTIC <a ~ denunciation> **b** : being to the point : highly expressive <~ prose> **4** : causing a sharp or irritating sensation; *esp* : ACRID — **pun·gent·ly** *adv*

syn PUNGENT, PIQUANT, POIGNANT, RACY *shared meaning element* : sharp and stimulating to the mind or senses *ant* bland

pur·blind \'pər-ˌblind\ *adj* [ME *pur blind,* fr. *pur* purely, wholly, fr. *pur* pure] **1 a** *obs* : wholly blind **b** : partly blind **2** : lacking in vision, insight, or understanding : OBTUSE — **pur·blind·ly** \-ˌblīn-(d)lē\ *adv* — **pur·blind·ness** \-ˌblīn(d)-nəs\ *n*

pur·dah \'pərd-ə\ *n* [Hindi *parda,* lit., curtain, screen, veil] : seclusion of women from public observation among Muslims and some Hindus esp. in India

Py·ram·i·don \pə-'ram-ə-ˌdän\ *n, trademark — used for aminopyrine*

pyre \'pī(ə)r\ *n* [L *pyra,* fr. Gk, fr. *pyr* fire — more at FIRE] : a combustible heap for burning a dead body as a funeral rite; *broadly* : a pile of material to be burned <a ~ of dead leaves>

minor stress	*PAGE 11a*
often attrib	*PAGE 14a*
pronunciation	*PAGES 11a, 12a*
regional label	*PAGE 16a*
run-on entry (undefined)	*PAGE 11a*
run-on entry (defined)	*PAGE 11a*
secondary variant	*PAGE 11a*
sense divider	*PAGE 17a*
sense letter	*PAGE 17a*
sense numeral	*PAGE 17a*
small capitals	*PAGE 18a*
stylistic label	*PAGE 16a*
subject label	*PAGE 16a*
swung dash (boldface)	*PAGE 12a*
swung dash (lightface)	*PAGE 16a*
synonymous cross-reference	*PAGES 18a, 19a*
synonym list	*PAGE 19a*
temporal label	*PAGES 15a, 16a*
uppercase	*PAGE 14a*
usage note	*PAGES 16a, 17a*
verbal illustration	*PAGE 16a*

Explanatory Notes

Entries

A boldface letter or a combination of such letters set flush with the left-hand margin of each column of type is a main entry. The main entry may consist of letters set solid, of letters joined by a hyphen, or of letters separated by one or more spaces:

> **teach** ... *vb*
>
> **teach–in** ... *n*
>
> **teaching fellow** *n*

The material in lightface type that follows each main entry on the same line and on succeeding indented lines explains and justifies its inclusion in the dictionary.

The main entries follow one another in alphabetical order letter by letter: *book of account* follows *bookmobile*. Those containing an Arabic numeral are alphabetized as if the numeral were spelled out: *3-D* comes between *three-color* and *three-decker*. Those derived from proper names beginning with abbreviated forms of *Mac-* are alphabetized as if spelled *mac-*: *McCoy* comes after *macaroon* and before *mace*. Those that often begin with the abbreviation *St.* in common usage have the abbreviation spelled out: *Saint Martin's summer*.

A pair of guide words is printed at the top of each page. These indicate that the entries falling alphabetically between the words at the top of the outer column of each page are found on that page.

The guide words are the alphabetically first and usually the alphabetically last entries on the page:

acacia ● acceptable

Occasionally the last printed entry is not the alphabetically last entry. On page 237, for example, *connective tissue* is the last printed entry, but *connectivity*, run on at the first homograph *connective*, is the alphabetically last entry and is therefore the second guide word. The alphabetically last entry is not used, however, if it follows alphabetically the first guide word on the succeeding page. Thus on page 124 *bonder* is not a guide word because it follows alphabetically the entry *bonded*, which is the first guide word on page 125. Any boldface word—a main entry with definition, a variant, an inflected form, a defined or undefined run-on, or an entry in a list of self-explanatory words—may be used as a guide word.

When one main entry has exactly the same written form as another, the two are distinguished by superscript numerals preceding each word:

> [1]**man** ... *n*   [1]**quail** ... *n*
>
> [2]**man** *vt*   [2]**quail** *vb*

Sometimes such homographs are related: the two entries *man* are derived from the same root. Sometimes there is no relationship: the two entries *quail* are unrelated

beyond the accident of spelling. The order of homographs is usually historical: the one first used in English is entered first.

Words precede word elements made up of the same letters; solid compounds precede hyphened compounds; hyphened compounds precede open compounds; and lowercase entries precede those with an initial capital:

> **mini** ... *n*
>
> **mini-** *comb form*
>
> **work·up** ... *n*
>
> **work–up** ... *n*
>
> **work up** ... *vt*
>
> **ti·ta·nia** ... *n*
>
> **Ti·ta·nia** ... *n*

The centered periods within entry words indicate division points at which a hyphen may be put at the end of a line of print or writing. Thus the noun *re·frig·er·a·tor* may be ended on one line with:

> re-
> refrig-
> refriger-
> refrigera-

and continued on the next with:

> *frigerator*
> *erator*
> *ator*
> *tor*

Centered periods are not shown after a single initial letter or before a single terminal letter because printers seldom cut off a single letter:

> **aplomb** ... *n*
>
> **hoary** ... *adj*
>
> **idea** ... *n*

Nor are they shown at second and succeeding homographs unless these differ among themselves:

> [1]**mas·ter** ... *n*   [1]**till·er**
>
> [2]**master** ... *vt*   [2]**till·er**
>
> [3]**master** *adj*   [3]**til·ler**

There are acceptable alternative end-of-line divisions just as there are acceptable variant spellings and pronunciations. It is, for example, all but impossible to produce a convincing argument that either of the divisions *aus·ter·i·ty*, *au·ster·i·ty* is better than the other. But space cannot be taken for entries like *aus·ter·i·ty* or *au·ster·i·ty*, and *au·s·ter·i·ty* would likely be confusing to many. No more than one division is, therefore, shown for any entry in this dictionary.

Many words have two or more common pronunciation variants, and the same end-of-line division is not always appropriate for each of them. The division *pi·an·ist*, for example, best fits the variant \pē-'an-əst\ whereas the division *pi·a·nist* best fits the variant \'pē-ə-nəst\. In instances like this, the division falling farthest to the left is used, regardless of the order of the pronunciations:

pi·a·nist \pē-'an-əst, 'pē-ə-nəst\

When a main entry is followed by the word *or* and another spelling, the two spellings are equal variants. Both are standard, and either one may be used according to personal inclination:

the·ater *or* **the·atre**

If two variants joined by *or* are out of alphabetical order, they remain equal variants. The one printed first is, however, slightly more common than the second:

coun·sel·or *or* **coun·sel·lor**

When another spelling is joined to the main entry by the word *also*, the spelling after *also* is a secondary variant and occurs less frequently than the first:

lov·able *also* **love·able**

Secondary variants belong to standard usage and may be used according to personal inclination. If there are two secondary variants, the second is joined to the first by *or*. Once the word *also* is used to signal a secondary variant, all following variants are joined by *or*:

¹Shake·spear·ean *or* **Shake·spear·ian** *also*

Shak·sper·ean *or* **Shak·sper·ian**

Variants whose spelling places them alphabetically more than a column away from the main entry are entered at their own alphabetical places and usually not at the main entry:

Cha·nu·kah ... *var of* HANUKKAH

rime, rimer, rimester *var of* RHYME, RHYMER, RHYMESTER

Variants having a usage label appear only at their own alphabetical places:

fla·vour *chiefly Brit var of* FLAVOR

agin ... *dial var of* AGAINST

To show all the stylings that are found for English compounds would require space that can be better used for other information. So this dictionary limits itself to a single styling for a compound:

week·end

red–eye

high school

When a compound is widely used and one styling predominates, that styling is shown. When a compound is uncommon or when the evidence indicates that two or three stylings are approximately equal in frequency, the styling shown is based on the analogy of parallel compounds.

A main entry may be followed by one or more derivatives or by a homograph with a different functional label. These are run-on entries. Each is introduced by a lightface dash and each has a functional label. They are not defined, however, since their meanings are readily derivable from the meaning of the root word:

²question *vt* ... — **ques·tion·er** *n*

¹fun·ny ... *adj* ... — **fun·ni·ly** ... *adv* — **fun·ni·ness** ... *n*

mu·tant ... *adj* ... — **mutant** *n*

A main entry may be followed by one or more phrases containing the entry word or an inflected form of it.

These are also run-on entries. Each is introduced by a lightface dash but there is no functional label. They are, however, defined since their meanings are more than the sum of the meanings of their elements:

¹call ... *vb* ... — **call one's bluff :** ...

²mend *n* ... — **on the mend :** ...

Defined phrases of this sort are run on at the entry constituting the first major element in the phrase. When there are variants, however, the run-on appears at the entry constituting the first major invariable element in the phrase:

¹clock ... *n* ... — **kill the clock** *or* **run out the clock :** ...

¹seed ... *n* ... — **go to seed** *or* **run to seed :** ...

Attention is called to the definition of *vocabulary entry* on page 1301. The term *dictionary entry* includes all vocabulary entries as well as all boldface entries in the separate sections of the back matter headed "Foreign Words and Phrases," "Biographical Names," "Geographical Names," and "Colleges and Universities."

Pronunciation

The matter between a pair of reversed virgules \ \ following the entry word indicates the pronunciation. The symbols used are explained in the chart printed inside the front and back covers of this dictionary and on page 32a. For a detailed discussion of these symbols and related matters, the serious student is referred to "A Guide to Pronunciation" in Webster's Third New International Dictionary.

A hyphen is used in the pronunciation to show syllabic division. These hyphens sometimes coincide with the centered periods in the entry word that indicate end-of-line division; sometimes they do not:

dis·cov·er \dis-'kəv-ər\

¹met·ric \'me-trik\

A high-set mark ' indicates major (primary) stress or accent; a low-set mark ˌ indicates minor (secondary) stress or accent:

rough·neck \'rəf-ˌnek\

The stress mark stands at the beginning of the syllable that receives the stress.

The presence of variant pronunciations indicates that not all educated speakers pronounce words the same way. A second-place variant is not to be regarded as less acceptable than the pronunciation that is given first. It may, in fact, be used by as many educated speakers as the first variant, but the requirements of the printed page are such that one must precede the other:

apri·cot \'ap-rə-ˌkät, 'ā-prə-\

for·eign \'fòr-ən, 'fär-\

A variant that is appreciably less common than the preceding variant is preceded by the word *also*:

col·league \'käl-ˌēg *also* -ig\

Sometimes a regional label precedes a variant:

¹great \'grāt, *South also* 'gre(ə)t\

Symbols enclosed by parentheses represent elements that are present in the pronunciation of some speakers but are absent from the pronunciation of other speakers, elements that are present in some but absent from other utterances of the same speaker, or elements whose presence or absence is uncertain:

hap·pen ... *vi* ... **hap·pen·ing** \'hap-(ə-)niŋ\

sat·is·fac·to·ry \ˌsat-əs-'fak-t(ə-)rē\

re·sponse \ri-'spän(t)s\

Thus, the parentheses at *happening* mean that there are some who pronounce the \ə\ between \p\ and \n\ and others who do not pronounce it.

When a main entry has less than a full pronunciation, the missing part is to be supplied from a pronunciation in a preceding entry or within the same pair of reversed virgules:

cham·pi·on·ship \-ˌship\

Ma·dei·ra \mə-'dir-ə, -'der-\

The pronunciation of the first three syllables of *championship* is found at the main entry *champion*:

¹cham·pi·on \'cham-pē-ən\

The hyphens before and after \'der\ in the pronunciation of *Madeira* indicate that both the first and the last parts of the pronunciation are to be taken from the immediately preceding pronunciation.

In general, no pronunciation is indicated for open compounds consisting of two or more English words that have own-place entry:

kangaroo court *n*

Only the first entry in a sequence of numbered homographs is given a pronunciation if their pronunciations are the same:

¹re·ward \ri-'wó(ə)rd\

²reward

Pronunciations are shown for obsolete words only if they occur in Shakespeare:

clois·tress \'klói-strəs\ *n, obs*

The pronunciation of unpronounced derivatives and compounds run on at a main entry is a combination of the pronunciation at the main entry and the pronunciation of the suffix or final element as given at its alphabetical place in the vocabulary:

— oval·ness *n*

— over one's head

Thus, the pronunciation of *ovalness* is the sum of the pronunciations given at *oval* and *-ness*; that of *over one's head*, the sum of the pronunciation of the three elements that make up the phrase.

Partial pronunciations are usually shown when two or more variants have a part in common. When a variation of stress is involved, a partial pronunciation may be terminated at the stress mark which stands at the beginning of a syllable not shown:

di·verse \dī-'vərs, də-', 'dī-ˌ\

an·cho·vy \'an-ˌchō-vē, an-'\

In some cases the pronunciation of a word or compound shows no major (primary) stress. One such class of words includes those that occur in main entries only as elements of an open compound. The stress shown for these words is the usual stress in the compound and may be less than major (primary):

clum·ber spaniel \ˌkləm-bər-\

In other contexts the word may have major (primary) stress, as in "Is that spaniel a clumber?"

Functional Labels

An italic label indicating a part of speech or some other functional classification follows the pronunciation or, if no pronunciation is given, the main entry. The eight traditional parts of speech are indicated as follows:

de·cep·tive ... *adj*		**war·den** ... *n*	
hap·pi·ly ... *adv*		**of** ... *prep*	
be·cause ... *conj*		**they** ... *pron*	
hey ... *interj*		**re·lax** ... *vb*	

If a verb is both transitive and intransitive, the labels *vt* and *vi* introduce the subdivisions:

pen·e·trate ... *vb* ... *vt* ... ~ *vi*

A boldface swung dash ~ is used to stand for the main entry (as *penetrate*) and separate the subdivisions of the verb. If there is no subdivision, *vt* or *vi* takes the place of *vb*:

in·fect ... *vt*

²vacation *vi*

Labeling a verb as transitive, however, does not preclude occasional intransitive use (as in absolute constructions).

Other italicized labels used to indicate functional classifications that are not traditional parts of speech are:

alt ... *abbr*	**-ness** ... *n suffix*
tele- *or* **tel-** *comb form*	**-ize** ... *vb suffix*
-onym ... *n comb form*	**Fe** *symbol*
-gen·ic ... *adj comb form*	**Fris·bee** ... *trademark*
¹pro- *prefix*	**must** ... *verbal auxiliary*
Air Express *service mark*	**whoa** ... *vb imper*
¹-ic ... *adj suffix*	**me·seems** ... *vb impersonal*
²-ly *adv suffix*	

Two functional labels are sometimes combined:

zilch ... *adj or n*

¹le·ga·to ... *adv or adj*

Inflected Forms

NOUNS

The plurals of nouns are shown in this dictionary when suffixation brings about a change of final *-y* to *-i-*, when the noun ends in a consonant plus *-o* or in *-ey*, when the noun ends in *-oo*, when the noun has an irregular plural or a zero plural or a foreign plural, when the noun is a compound that pluralizes any element but the last, when the noun has variant plurals, and when it is believed that the dictionary user might have reasonable doubts about the spelling of the plural or when the plural is spelled in a way contrary to expectations:

²fly *n, pl* **flies**

to·ma·to ... *n, pl* **-toes**

val·ley ... *n, pl* **valleys**

²boo *n, pl* **boos**

¹mouse ... *n, pl* **mice**

sheep ... *n, pl* **sheep**

alum·nus ... *n, pl* **-ni**

moth·er–in–law ... *n, pl* **mothers–in–law**

¹seed ... *n, pl* **seed** *or* **seeds**

¹pi ... *n, pl* **pis**

³dry *n, pl* **drys**

Cutback inflected forms are used when the noun has three or more syllables:

an·i·mos·i·ty ... *n, pl* **-ties**

The plurals of nouns are usually not shown when the base word is unchanged by suffixation, when the noun is a compound whose second element is readily recognizable as a regular free form entered at its own place, or when the noun is unlikely to occur in the plural:

¹cat ... *n*

¹church ... *n*

gad·fly ... *n*

al·che·my ... *n*

Nouns that are plural in form and that regularly occur in plural construction are labeled *n pl*:

en·vi·rons ... *n pl*

Nouns that are plural in form but that are not always construed as plurals are appropriately labeled:

ge·net·ics ... *n pl but sing in constr*

forty winks *n pl but sing or pl in constr*

A noun that is singular in construction takes a singular verb when it is used as a subject; a noun that is plural in construction takes a plural verb when it is used as a subject.

VERBS

The principal parts of verbs are shown in this dictionary when suffixation brings about a doubling of a final consonant or an elision of a final *-e* or a change of final *-y* to *-i-*, when final *-c* changes to *-ck* in suffixation, when the verb ends in *-ey*, when the inflection is irregular, when there are variant inflected forms, and when it is believed that the dictionary user might have reasonable doubts about the spelling of an inflected form or when the inflected form is spelled in a way contrary to expectations:

³brag *vb* **bragged; brag·ging**

¹blame ... *vt* **blamed; blam·ing**

¹spy ... *vb* **spied; spy·ing**

²pic·nic ... *vi* **pic·nicked; pic·nick·ing**

²volley *vb* **vol·leyed; vol·ley·ing**

³ring *vb* **rang** ...; **rung** ...; **ring·ing**

⁴bias *vt* **bi·ased** *or* **bi·assed; bi·as·ing** *or* **bi·as·sing**

²visa *vt* **vi·saed** ...; **vi·sa·ing**

²chagrin *vt* **cha·grined** ...; **cha·grin·ing**

The principal parts of a regularly inflected verb are shown when it is desirable to indicate the pronunciation of one of the inflected forms:

³spell *vb* **spelled \'speld, 'spelt\; spell·ing**

²but·ton ... *vb* **but·toned; but·ton·ing \'bət-niŋ, -ᵊn-iŋ**

Cutback inflected forms are often used when the verb has three or more syllables, when it is a disyllable that ends in *-l* and has variant spellings, and when it is a compound whose second element is readily recognized as an irregular verb:

de·i·fy ... *vt* **-fied; -fy·ing**

²carol *vb* **-oled** *or* **-olled; -ol·ing** *or* **-ol·ling**

with·draw *vb* **-drew** ...; **-drawn** ...; **-draw·ing**

The principal parts of verbs are usually not shown when the base word is unchanged by suffixation or when the verb is a compound whose second element is readily recognizable as a regular free form entered at its own place:

⁴halt ... *vi*

dis·sat·is·fy ... *vb*

ADJECTIVES & ADVERBS

The comparative and superlative forms of adjectives and adverbs are shown in this dictionary when suffixation brings about a doubling of a final consonant or an elision of a final *-e* or a change of final *-y* to *-i-*, when the word ends in *-ey*, when the inflection is irregular, and when there are variant inflected forms:

¹red ... *adj* **red·der; red·dest**

¹bare ... *adj* **bar·er; bar·est**

¹heavy ... *adj* **heavi·er; -est**

¹ear·ly ... *adv* **ear·li·er; -est**

hom·ey *also* **homy** ... *adj* **hom·i·er; -est**

¹good ... *adj* **bet·ter** ...; **best**

²ill ... *adv* **worse; worst**

¹shy ... *adj* **shi·er** *or* **shy·er** ...; **shi·est** *or* **shy·est**

Adjectives and adverbs of two or more syllables are usually cut back:

come·ly ... *adj* **come·li·er; -est**

²easy *adv* **eas·i·er; -est**

The comparative and superlative forms of regularly inflected adjectives and adverbs are shown when it is desirable to indicate the pronunciation of the inflected forms:

¹long \'lȯŋ *adj* **lon·ger \'lȯŋ-ger\; lon·gest \'lȯŋ-gəst**

The inclusion of inflected forms in *-er* and *-est* at adjective and adverb entries means nothing more about the use of *more* and *most* with these adjectives and adverbs than that their comparative and superlative degrees may be expressed in either way: *lazier* or *more lazy*; *laziest* or *most lazy*.

At a few adjective entries only the superlative form is shown:

mere ... *adj* **mer·est**

The absence of the comparative form indicates that there is no evidence of its use.

The comparative and superlative forms of adjectives and adverbs are not shown when the base word is unchanged by suffixation or when the word is a compound whose second element is readily recognizable as a regular free form entered at its own place:

¹full ... *adj*

un·lucky ... *adj*

The comparative and superlative forms of adverbs are not shown when they are identical with the inflected forms of a preceding adjective homograph:

¹hot ... *adj* **hot·ter; hot·test**

²hot *adv*

Inflected forms are not shown at undefined run-ons or at some entries bearing a limiting label:

Jac·o·bin ... *n* ... — **jac·o·bin·ize** ... *vt*

²lampoon *vt* ... — **lam·poon·ery** ... *n*

¹net ... *n* ... — **net·ty** ... *adj*

²cote ... *vt* ... *obs* : to pass by

crouse ... *adj* ... *chiefly Scot* : BRISK, LIVELY

Capitalization

Most entries in this dictionary begin with a lowercase letter. A few of these have an italicized label *often cap*, which indicates that the word is as likely to be capitalized as not, that it is as acceptable with an uppercase initial as it is with one in lowercase. Some entries begin with an uppercase letter, which indicates that the word is usually capitalized. The absence of an initial capital or of an *often cap* label indicates that the word is not ordinarily capitalized:

> **mas·sive** ... *adj*
>
> **an·gli·cize** ... *vt* ... *often cap*
>
> **Swiss** ... *n*

The capitalization of entries that are open or hyphened compounds is similarly indicated by the form of the entry or by an italicized label:

> **ice cream** ... *n*
>
> **¹french fry** *vt, often cap 1st F*
>
> **neo–im·pres·sion·ism** ... *n, often cap N&I*
>
> **non–Com·mu·nist** ... *adj*
>
> **Irish setter** *n*
>
> **Memorial Day** *n*

A word that is capitalized in some senses and lowercase in others shows variations from the form of the main entry by the use of italicized labels at the appropriate senses:

> **Gyp·sy** ... *n* ... **3** *not cap*
>
> **Sal·va·tion·ist** ... *n* ... **2** *often not cap*
>
> **¹mass** ... *n* ... **1** *cap*
>
> **es·tab·lish·ment** ... *n* ... **2** ... **b** *often cap*

Attributive Nouns

The italicized label *often attrib* placed after the functional label *n* indicates that the noun is often used as an adjective equivalent in attributive position before another noun:

> **ap·ple** ... *n, often attrib*
>
> **¹dog** ... *n, often attrib*

Examples of the attributive use of these nouns are *apple pie* and *dog license*.

While any noun may occasionally be used attributively, the label *often attrib* is limited to those having broad attributive use. This label is not used when an adjective homograph (as *iron* or *paper*) is entered. And it is not used at open compounds (as *X ray*) that may be used attributively with an inserted hyphen (as in *X-ray therapy*).

Etymology

The matter in boldface square brackets preceding the definition is the etymology. Meanings given in roman type within these brackets are not definitions of the entry, but are meanings of the Middle English, Old English, or non-English words within the brackets.

The etymology traces a vocabulary entry as far back as possible in English (as to Old English), tells from what language and in what form it came into English, and (except in the case of such words outside the general vocabulary of English as *dacha* and *talipot*) traces the pre-English source as far back as possible. These etyma are printed in italics.

The etymology usually gives the Middle English and the Old English forms of words in the following style:

> **¹reed** ... *n* [ME *rede,* fr. OE *hrēod* ...]
>
> **¹hate** ... *n* [ME, fr. OE *hete* ...]

An etymology in which a word is traced back to Middle English but not to Old English indicates that the word is found in Middle English but not in those texts that have survived from the Old English period:

> **¹clog** ... *n* [ME *clogge* short thick piece of wood]
>
> **¹rub** ... *vb* [ME *rubben;* akin to Icel *rubba* to scrape]

An etymology in which a word is traced back directly to Old English with no intervening mention of Middle English indicates that the word has not survived continuously from Old English times to the present. Rather, it died out after the Old English period and has been revived in modern times:

> **Geat** ... *n* [OE *Gēat*]
>
> **thegn** ... *n* [OE ...]

The etymology gives the language from which words borrowed into English have come. It also gives the form or a transliteration of the word in that language if the form differs from that in English:

> **¹fes·ti·val** ... *adj* [ME, fr. MF, fr. L *festivus* festive]
>
> **linn** ... *n* [ScGael *linne* pool]
>
> **¹school** ... *n* [ME *scole,* fr. OE *scōl,* fr. L *schola* ...]
>
> **smor·gas·bord** ... *n* [Sw *smörgåsbord* ...]

In a few cases the expression "deriv. of" replaces the more usual "fr." This expression indicates that one or more intermediate steps have been omitted in tracing the derivation of the form preceding the expression from the form following it:

> **gal·ley** ... *n* [... OF *galie,* deriv. of MGk *galea*]

An etymology is not usually given for a word created in English by the combination of existing constituents or by functional shift. This indicates that the identity of the constituents is expected to be self-evident to the user:

> **like·ness** ... *n* **1** : the quality or state of being like
>
> **tone–deaf** ... *adj* : relatively insensitive to differences in musical pitch
>
> **tooth·paste** ... *n* : a paste for cleaning the teeth
>
> **profit system** *n* : FREE ENTERPRISE
>
> **²wheel** *vi* **1** : to turn on or as if on an axis ...

In the case of a family of words obviously related to a common English word but differing from it by containing various easily recognizable suffixes, an etymology is usually given only at the base word, even though some of the derivatives may have been formed in a language other than English:

> **¹im·mor·tal** ... *adj* [ME, fr. L *immortalis* ...] **1** : exempt from death
>
> **im·mor·tal·i·ty** ... *n* : the quality or state of being immortal

The word *immortality* was actually borrowed into Middle English (via Middle French) from Latin *immortalitas*.

Much of the technical vocabulary of the sciences and

other specialized studies consists of words or word elements that are current in two or more languages, with only such slight modifications as are necessary to adapt them to the structure of the individual language in each case. Many words and word elements of this kind have become sufficiently a part of the general vocabulary of English as to require entry in an abridged dictionary. Because of the vast extent of the relevant published material in many languages and in many scientific and other specialized fields, it is impracticable to ascertain the language of origin of every such term. Yet it would not be accurate to formulate a statement about the origin of any such term in a way that could be interpreted as implying that it was coined in English. Accordingly, whenever a term that is entered in this dictionary belongs recognizably to this class of internationally current terms and whenever no positive evidence is at hand to show that it was coined in English, the etymology recognizes its international status and the possibility that it originated elsewhere than in English by use of the label ISV (for International Scientific Vocabulary):

> **meg·a·watt** ... *n* [ISV]
>
> **phy·lo·ge·net·ic** ... *adj* [ISV, fr. NL *phylogenesis* ...]
>
> ¹**-ol** ... *n suffix* [ISV, fr. *alcohol*]

An etymology beginning with the name of a language (including ME or OE) and not giving the foreign (or Middle English or Old English) form indicates that this form is the same as that of the entry word:

> ¹**tan·go** ... *n* ... [AmerSp]
>
> ¹**po·grom** ... *n* [Yiddish, fr. Russ ...]
>
> ¹**gang** ... *n* [ME, fr. OE ...]

An etymology beginning with the name of a language (including ME or OE) and not giving the foreign (or Middle English or Old English) meaning indicates that this meaning is the same as that expressed in the first definition in the entry:

> **vig·or·ous** ... *adj* [ME, fr. MF, fr. OF, fr. *vigor*] **1 :** possessing vigor

When an entry word is derived from an earlier Modern English word that is not entered in this dictionary, the meaning of such a word is given in parentheses:

> ³**press** *vb* [alter. of obs. *prest* (to enlist by giving pay in advance)]

Small superscript figures following words or syllables in an etymology refer to the tone of the word or syllable which they follow. They are, accordingly, used only with forms cited from tone languages:

> **chow mein** ... *n* [Chin (Pek) *ch'ao*³ *mien*¹, fr. *ch'ao*³ to fry + *mien*⁴ dough]
>
> ¹**voo·doo** ... *n* ... [LaF *voudou*, of African origin; akin to Ewe *vo*¹*du*³ tutelary deity, demon]

When the source of a word appearing as a main entry is unknown, the expression "origin unknown" is usually used. Only in rare and exceptional circumstances (as with some ethnic names) does the absence of an etymology mean that it has not been possible to furnish any informative etymology. More often, it means that no etymology is believed to be necessary. This is the case, for instance, with most of the entries identified as variants and with many derivatives.

When a word has been traced back to the earliest language in which it is attested, and if this is an Indo-European language, selected cognates in other Indo-European languages (especially Old High German, Latin, and Greek) are usually given:

> ¹**one** ... *adj* [ME *on*, fr. OE *ān;* akin to OHG *ein* one, L *unus* (OL *oinos*), Skt *eka*]

> **equine** ... *adj* [L *equinus*, fr. *equus* horse; akin to OE *eoh* horse, Gk *hippos*]

Sometimes, however, to avoid space-consuming repetition, the expression "more at" directs the user to another entry where the cognates are given:

> ²**thought** *n* [ME, fr. OE *thōht;* akin to OE *thencan* to think — more at THINK]

Besides the use of "akin to" to denote an ordinary cognate relationship, some etymologies make special use of "akin to" as part of a longer formula "of— origin; akin to—." This formula indicates that a word was borrowed from some language belonging to a group of languages whose name is inserted in the blank before the word *origin*, that it is impossible to say that the word in question is a borrowing of a particular attested word in a particular language of the source group, and that the form cited in the blank after the expression *akin to* is a cognate of the word in question as attested within the source group:

> ¹**ca·noe** ... *n* [F, fr. NL *canoa*, fr. Sp, fr. Arawakan, of Cariban origin; akin to Galibi *canaoua*]
>
> ²**cant** *n* [ME, prob. fr. MD or ONF; MD, edge, corner, fr. ONF, fr. L *canthus, cantus* iron tire, perh. of Celt origin; akin to W *cant* rim; akin to Gk *kanthos* corner of the eye]

This last example shows the two contrasting uses of "akin to." The word cited immediately after "of Celt origin; akin to" is a Celtic cognate of the presumed Celtic source word from which the Latin word was borrowed. The word cited after the second "akin to" is a further cognate from another Indo-European language.

When the origin of a word is traced to the name of a person or place not further identified, additional information may be found in the Biographical Names or Geographical Names section in the back matter:

> **new·ton** ... *n* [Sir Isaac *Newton*]
>
> **cal·i·co** ... *n* ... [*Calicut*, India]

Usage

Three types of status labels are used in this dictionary —temporal, regional, and stylistic—to signal that a word or a sense of a word is not part of the standard vocabulary of English.

The temporal label *obs* for "obsolete" means that there is no evidence of use since 1755:

> **egal** ... *adj* ... *obs*
>
> **har·di·ment** ... *n* ... **2** *obs*

The label *obs* is a comment on the word being defined. When a thing, as distinguished from the word used to designate it, is obsolete, appropriate orientation is usually given in the definition:

> ¹**cat·a·pult** ... *n* ... **1 :** an ancient military device for hurling missiles
>
> ²**ruff** *n* ... **1 :** a wheel-shaped stiff collar worn by men and women of the late 16th and early 17th centuries

The temporal label *archaic* means that a word or sense once in common use is found today only sporadically or in special contexts:

> **eft·soons** ... *adv* ... *archaic*
>
> ²**tender** ... *vt* ... **2** *archaic*

A word or sense limited in use to a specific region of the U.S. has a label that corresponds loosely to one of the areas defined in Hans Kurath's *Word Geography of the Eastern United States*. The adverb *chiefly* precedes a label when the word has some currency outside the specified region, and a double label is used to indicate considerable currency in each of two specific regions:

> ban·nock ... *n* ...   2 *NewEng*
>
> ban·quette ... *n* ...   1 ...   b *South*
>
> cal·cu·late ... *vt* ...   3 *chiefly North*
>
> can·ti·na ... *n* ...   1 *Southwest*
>
> em·bar·ca·de·ro ... *n* ... *West*
>
> goo·ber ... *n* ... *South & Midland*
>
> jolt–wag·on ... *n, Midland*
>
> ¹pot·latch ... *n* ...   2 *Northwest*

Words current in all regions of the U.S. have no label.

A word or sense limited in use to one of the other countries of the English-speaking world has an appropriate regional label:

> bairn ... *n* ... *chiefly Scot*
>
> be·gor·ra ... *interj* ... *Irish*
>
> bil·la·bong ... *n* ...   1 *Austral*
>
> com·man·do ... *n* ...   1 *So Afr*
>
> corn flour *n, Brit*
>
> foot·ball ... *n*   1 ...   e *Canad*
>
> ³gang *vi* ... *Scot*
>
> gar·ron ... *n* ... *Scot & Irish*

The label *dial* for "dialect" indicates that the pattern of use of a word or sense is too complex for summary labeling: it usually includes several regional varieties of American English or of American and British English:

> crit·ter ... *n* ... *dial*

The label *dial Brit* indicates currency in several dialects of the British Commonwealth; *dial Eng* indicates currency in one or more provincial dialects of England:

> ¹lair ... *n* ...   1 *dial Brit*
>
> few·trils ... *n* ... *dial Eng*

The stylistic label *slang* is used with words or senses that are especially appropriate in contexts of extreme informality, that usually have a currency not limited to a particular region or area of interest, and that are composed typically of shortened forms or extravagant or facetious figures of speech:

> clip joint *n*   1 *slang* : a place of public entertainment (as a nightclub) that makes a practice of defrauding patrons (as by overcharging)
>
> horn·swog·gle ... *vt* ... *slang* : BAMBOOZLE, HOAX
>
> ¹prof ... *n, slang* : PROFESSOR

There is no satisfactory objective test for slang, especially with reference to a word out of context. No word, in fact, is invariably slang, and many standard words can be given slang applications.

The stylistic label *nonstand* for "nonstandard" is used for a few words or senses that are disapproved by many but that have some currency in reputable contexts:

> ir·re·gard·less ... *adv* ... *nonstand*
>
> ¹lay ... *vi* ...   2 *nonstand*

The stylistic label *substand* for "substandard" is used for those words or senses that conform to a widespread pattern of usage that differs in choice of word or form from that of the prestige group of the community:

> ain't ...   2 *substand*
>
> learn ... *vt* ...   2 a *substand*

A subject label or guide phrase is sometimes used to indicate the specific application of a word or sense:

> ape·ri·od·ic ... *adj* ...   3 *cryptology*
>
> hemi·he·dral ... *adj* ... *of a crystal*
>
> lose ... *vi* ...   3 *of a timepiece*

In general, however, subject orientation is given in the definition:

> Gun·ther ... *n* ... : a Burgundian king and husband of Brunhild in Germanic legend
>
> blitz ... *n* ...   2 b : a rush of the passer by the defensive linebackers in football

Definitions are sometimes followed by verbal illustrations that show a typical use of the word in context. These illustrations are enclosed in angle brackets, and the word being illustrated is usually replaced by a lightface swung dash. The swung dash stands for the boldface entry word, and it may be followed by an italicized suffix:

> large–print ... *adj* ... <~ books>
>
> ³low *adj* ...   11 ... <had a ~ opinion of him>
>
> ²mess ... *vi* ...   4 c ... <~ing in other people's affairs>
>
> proud ... *adj* ...   2 b ... <the ~*est* moment in her life>

The swung dash is not used when the form of the boldface entry word is changed in suffixation, and it is not used for open compounds:

> ¹dare ... *vt* ...   1 a ... <*dared* him to jump>
>
> upper hand *n* ... <was determined not to let his opponent get the *upper hand*>

Illustrative quotations are also used to show words in typical contexts:

> ¹with·in ... *adv*   2 ... <search ~ for a creative impulse — Kingman Brewster, Jr.>

Omissions in quotations are indicated by suspension points:

> ¹jog ... *vi* ...   1 : < his ... holster *jogging* against his hip —Thomas Williams>

Definitions are sometimes followed by usage notes that give supplementary information about such matters as idiom, syntax, semantic relationship, and status. A usage note is introduced by a lightface dash:

> ¹stead ... *n* ...   2 : ... — used chiefly in the phrase *to stand one in good stead*
>
> ³zero *vt* ...   2 a : ... — usu. used with *in*
>
> ad·e·noid ... *n* ... : ... — usu. used in pl.
>
> ¹guide ... *n* ...   3 : ... — used esp. in commands
>
> ¹pi·a·nis·si·mo ... *adv or adj* ... : ... — used as a direction in music
>
> dick ... *n* ...   2 : ... — usu. considered vulgar
>
> Po·lack ... *n* ...   2 : ... — usu. used disparagingly

Two or more usage notes are separated by a semicolon:

> ²cat ... *vi* ... — often used with *around;* often considered vulgar

Sometimes a usage note is used in place of a definition. Some function words (as conjunctions and prepositions) have little or no semantic content; most interjections express feelings but are otherwise untranslatable into meaning; and some other words (as oaths and honorific titles) are more amenable to comment than to definition:

¹if ... *conj* ... **3** — used as a function word to introduce an exclamation expressing a wish

¹for ... *prep* ... **9** — used as a function word to indicate duration of time or extent of space

²ouch *interj* ... — used esp. to express sudden pain

³gad *interj* ... — used as a mild oath

¹lord ... *n* ... **4** — used as a British title

Sense Division

A boldface colon is used in this dictionary to introduce a definition:

deb·u·tante ... *n* ... : a young woman making her formal entrance into society

It is also used to separate two or more definitions of a single sense:

²imitation *adj* : resembling something else that is usu. genuine and of better quality : not real

Boldface Arabic numerals separate the senses of a word that has more than one sense:

²quiz *vt* ... **1** : to make fun of : MOCK **2** : to look at inquisitively **3** : to question closely

Boldface lowercase letters separate the subsenses of a word:

¹pack ... *n* ... **2 a** : the contents of a bundle **b** : a large amount or number : HEAP **c** : a full set of playing cards

Lightface numerals in parentheses indicate a further division of subsenses:

¹re·treat ... *n* ... **1 a** (1) : an act or process of withdrawing ... (2) : the process of receding ... **b** (1) : the usu. forced withdrawal of troops ... (2) : a signal for retreating ...

A lightface colon following a definition and immediately preceding two or more subsenses indicates that the subsenses are subsumed by the preceding definition:

huge ... *adj* ... : very large or extensive: as **a** : of great size or area **b** : great in scale or degree ... **c** : great in scope or character

¹pe·cu·liar ... *adj* ... **3** : different from the usual or normal: **a** : SPECIAL, PARTICULAR **b** : CURIOUS **c** : ECCENTRIC, QUEER

The word *as* may or may not follow the lightface colon. Its presence (as at *huge*) indicates that the following subsenses are typical or significant examples. Its absence (as at *peculiar*) indicates that the subsenses which follow are exhaustive.

The system of separating the various senses of a word by numerals and letters is a lexical convenience. It reflects something of their semantic relationship, but it does not evaluate senses or set up a hierarchy of importance among them.

Sometimes a particular semantic relationship between senses is suggested by the use of one of four italic sense dividers: *esp*, *specif*, *also*, or *broadly*.

The sense divider *esp* (for *especially*) is used to introduce the most common meaning subsumed in the more general preceding definition:

chick ... *n* **1 a** : CHICKEN; *esp* : one newly hatched

The sense divider *specif* (for *specifically*) is used to introduce a common but highly restricted meaning subsumed in the more general preceding definition:

²pitcher *n* : one that pitches; *specif* : the player that pitches in a game of baseball

The sense divider *also* is used to introduce a meaning that is closely related to but may be considered less important than the preceding sense:

Mo·selle ... *n* ... a white table wine made in the valley of the Moselle; *also* : a similar wine made elsewhere

The sense divider *broadly* is used to introduce an extended or wider meaning of the preceding definition:

bull's-eye ... *n* ... **3 b** : a shot that hits the bull's-eye; *broadly* : something that precisely attains a desired end

The order of senses is historical: the sense known to have been first used in English is entered first. This is not to be taken to mean, however, that each sense of a multisense word developed from the immediately preceding sense. It is altogether possible that sense 1 of a word has given rise to sense 2 and sense 2 to sense 3, but frequently sense 2 and sense 3 may have arisen independently of one another from sense 1.

Information coming between the entry word and the first definition of a multisense word applies to all senses and subsenses. Information applicable only to some senses or subsenses is given between the appropriate boldface numeral or letter and the symbolic colon:

ole·in ... *n* ... **2** *also* **ole·ine** \-ən, -₁ēn\

cru·ci·fix·ion ... *n* ... **1 a** ... **b** *cap*

¹tile ... *n* ... **1** *pl* **tiles** *or* **tile a** : ...

²palm *n* ... **3** [L *palmus*, fr. *palma*]

When an italicized label or guide phrase follows a boldface numeral, the label or phrase applies only to that specific numbered sense and its subsenses. It does not apply to any other boldface numbered senses:

ro·ta ... *n* ... **1** *chiefly Brit* : ... **2** *cap* ...

ro·man·ti·cism ... *n* **1** : ... **2** *often cap* **a** (1) : ... (2) : ... **b** : ...

At *rota*, the *chiefly Brit* label applies to sense **1** but not to sense **2**. The *cap* label applies to sense **2** but not to sense **1**.

At *romanticism*, the *often cap* label applies to all the subsenses of sense **2** but not to sense **1**.

When an italicized label or guide phrase follows a boldface letter, the label or phrase applies only to that specific lettered sense and its subsenses. It does not apply to any other boldface lettered senses:

¹hearse ... *n* ... **2 a** *archaic* : ... **b** *obs*

The *archaic* label applies to sense **2a** but not to sense **2b**. The *obs* label applies to sense **2b** but not to sense **2a**.

When an italicized label or guide phrase follows a parenthesized numeral, the label or phrase applies only to that specific numbered sense:

¹mat·ter ... *n* ... **1** ... **h** (1) *obs* : REASON, CAUSE

The *obs* label applies to sense **1h** (1) and to no other subsenses of the word.

Names of Plants & Animals

An entry that defines the name of a plant or animal (as peach or lion) is a taxonomic entry. Such entries employ in part a formal codified vocabulary of New Latin names—taxa—that has been developed and used by biologists in accordance with international codes of botanical and of zoological nomenclature for the purpose of identifying and indicating the relationships of plants and animals. Names of taxa higher than the genus (as class, order, and family) are capitalized plural nouns which are often used with singular verbs and which are not abbreviated in normal use.

The genus is the fundamental taxon. It names a group of closely related kinds of plants (as *Prunus*, which includes the wild and cultivated cherries, apricots, peaches, and almonds) or animals (as *Felis*, which includes domestic and wild cats, lions, tigers, and cougars). It is a capitalized singular noun.

Each organism has one—and only one—correct name under these codes. The name for a species—the binomial or species name—consists of a singular capitalized genus name combined with an uncapitalized specific epithet. The name for a variety or subspecies—the trinomial, variety name, or subspecies name—adds a similar varietal or subspecific epithet. Thus the cultivated cabbage (*Brassica oleracea capitata*), the cauliflower (*Brassica oleracea botrytis*), and the brussels sprout (*Brassica oleracea gemmifera*) belong to the same species (*Brassica oleracea*) of cole.

Taxa in this dictionary are enclosed in parentheses and usually come immediately after the primary orienting noun. Genus names as well as binomials and trinomials are italicized, but names of taxa above the genus are not italicized:

ba·sid·io·my·cete ... *n* ... : any of a large class (Basidio-mycetes) of higher fungi having septate hyphae, bearing spores on a basidium, and including rusts, smuts, mushrooms, and puffballs

rob·in ... *n* **1 a** : a small European thrush (*Erithacus rubecola*) resembling a warbler and having a brownish olive back and yellowish red throat and breast **b** : any of various Old World songbirds that are related to or resemble the European robin **2** : a large No. American thrush (*Turdus migratorius*) with olivaceous gray upperparts, blackish head and tail, black and whitish streaked throat, and chiefly dull reddish breast and underparts

Taxa are used in this dictionary to provide precise technical identifications through which defined terms may be pursued in technical writing. Because of their specialized nature, however, taxa do not have separate entries.

Taxonomic entries are usually oriented indirectly to higher taxa by other vernaculars (as by *alga* at *seaweed* or *thrush* at *robin*) or by technical adjectives (as by *composite* at *daisy*, *leguminous* at *pea*, or *teleost* at *perch*). Among the higher plants, except the composites and legumes and a few obscure tropical groups, such orientation is by a vernacular family name that is linked at the corresponding taxonomic entry to its technical equivalent:

beech ... *n* ... : any of a genus (*Fagus* of the family Fagaceae, the beech family) of hardwood trees with smooth gray bark and small edible nuts; *also* : its wood

oak ... *n* ... **1 a** : a tree or shrub (genera *Quercus* or *Lithocarpus*) of the beech family that produces a rounded one-seeded thin-shelled nut surrounded at the base by an indurated cup

A genus name may be abbreviated to its initial letter when it is used more than once in senses not separated by a boldface number:

nas·tur·tium ... *n* ... : any of a genus (*Tropaeolum* of the family Tropaeolaceae, the nasturtium family) of herbs with showy spurred flowers and pungent seeds; *esp* : either of two widely cultivated ornamentals (*T. majus* and *T. minus*)

Cross-Reference

Four different kinds of cross-references are used in this dictionary: directional, synonymous, cognate, and inflectional. In each instance the cross-reference is readily recognized by the lightface small capitals in which it is printed.

A cross-reference following a lightface dash and beginning with *see* or *compare* is a directional cross-reference. It directs the dictionary user to look elsewhere for further information. A *compare* cross-reference is regularly appended to a definition; a *see* cross-reference may stand alone:

plea ... *n* ... **2** ... **a** ... — compare DEMURRER

¹**scru·ple** ... *n* ... **1** —see WEIGHT table

A cross-reference immediately following a boldface colon is a synonymous cross-reference. It may stand alone as the only definitional matter for an entry or for a sense or subsense of an entry; it may follow an analytical definition; it may be one of two synonymous cross-references separated by a comma:

mul·ti·syl·lab·ic ... *adj* : POLYSYLLABIC

drain·age ... *n* ... **2** : a device for draining : DRAIN

drip·py ... *adj* ... **1** : RAINY, DRIZZLY

A synonymous cross-reference indicates that a definition at the entry cross-referred to can be substituted as a definition for the entry or the sense or subsense in which the cross-reference appears.

A cross-reference following an italic *var of* is a cognate cross-reference:

fiord *var of* FJORD

Sometimes a cognate cross-reference has a limiting label preceding *var of* as a specific indication that the variant is not standard English:

mair ... *chiefly Scot var of* MORE

quare ... *dial var of* ¹QUEER

sher·ris ... *archaic var of* SHERRY

A cross-reference following an italic label that identifies an entry as an inflected form of a noun, of an adjective or adverb, or of a verb is an inflectional cross-reference. Inflectional cross-references appear only when the inflected form falls at least a column away from the entry cross-referred to:

mice *pl of* MOUSE

sang *past of* SING

Synonyms & Antonyms

Synonymous words believed to be of interest to the dictionary user are listed in groups following the entry of one of the words in the group. (See, for example, *talkative* on page 1180.) They are signaled by an indented boldface italic **syn**. They are followed by a brief statement of their common denotation which is called the "shared meaning element" and by a list of antonyms which is identified by a prefixed boldface italic **ant** and is specific to the first member of the group.

Synonymous words believed to present special problems to the dictionary user are similarly listed and are, further, clearly discriminated and illustrated in an accompanying paragraph. (See, for example, ¹*gaudy* on page 471.)

When a word is included in a synonym list, the main entry of that word is followed by a run-on **syn** see— which refers to the entry where the synonym list may be found. Where appropriate, the run-on is followed by **ant** and any antonyms specific to the word. (See, for example, *facetious* on page 406.)

make recognizable the meaningful elements of new words that are not well enough established in the language to warrant dictionary entry.

Combining Forms, Prefixes & Suffixes

An entry that begins or ends with a hyphen is a word element that forms part of an English compound:

self- *comb form*

-l·o·gy ... *n comb form* ... <phraseo*logy*>

-lyze ... *vb comb form* ... <electro*lyze*>

pre- *prefix* ... <*pre*historic>

[1]**-er** ... *adj suffix or adv suffix* ... <hott*er*> <dri*er*>

-ism ... *n suffix* ... <barbarian*ism*>

-fy ... *vb suffix* ... <citi*fy*>

Combining forms, prefixes, and suffixes are entered in this dictionary for three reasons: to make easier the writing of etymologies of words in which these word elements occur over and over again; to make understandable the meaning of many undefined run-ons which for reasons of space would be omitted if they had to be given etymologies and definitions; and to

Lists of Undefined Words

Lists of undefined words occur after the entries of the prefixes **non-**, **re-**, and **un-**. These words are not defined because they are self-explanatory: their meanings are simply the sum of a meaning of the prefix combined with a meaning of the root word.

Abbreviations & Symbols

Abbreviations and symbols for chemical elements are included as main entries in the vocabulary:

acct *abbr*

Au *symbol*

Abbreviations have been normalized to one form. In practice, however, there is considerable variation in the use of periods and in capitalization (as *mph*, *m.p.h.*, *Mph*, and *MPH*), and stylings other than those given in this dictionary are often acceptable.

Abbreviations regularly used in this dictionary are listed separately on page 31a.

Symbols that are not capable of being alphabetized are included in a separate section of the back matter headed "Signs and Symbols."

The English Language and Its History

W. Nelson Francis
Professor of Linguistics and English
Brown University

English is undoubtedly the most important of the world's languages at the present time. In number of speakers it ranks second,[1] with approximately 275 million native speakers, compared with 610 million native speakers of Mandarin Chinese. Spanish comes next, with 210 million, followed by Russian with 140 million and Hindi-Urdu and Arabic with 130 million each. Importance is not measured only by numbers, however. The uses to which a language is put and the extent of its international exposure are at least as important as the sheer bulk of native speakers. The worldwide use of English in diplomacy, commerce, and science is evidence of its importance in this regard, and serves to explain why many millions around the world find it desirable and sometimes necessary to learn it as a second language.

It is not the intrinsic superiority of English over other languages that has made it the premier world language. If it is richer in vocabulary, more flexible in grammar, and more expressive than other languages (and some would question at least the last two of these claims), these qualities are the results, not the causes, of its importance in the world. Simply stated, what makes a language important is the importance of the people who use it and the uses to which they put it. Since the eighteenth century, speakers of English—at first from the British Isles and later from America and the dominions—have played a dominant role in colonial expansion, industrial and technological development, and world politics. The position of English in the world is the direct result of the history of those who speak it.

What is modern English, this great world language, like? Before we can answer that question at all meaningfully, we must deal with the broader questions What is a language like? and What qualities, if any, are shared by all languages, regardless of their relative prominence or obscurity? These are questions which are central to the study called linguistics. They cannot be completely answered by linguistics in its present state; probably they will never be completely answered. But linguistics has progressed sufficiently so that partial answers, dealing with the larger aspects of the questions, can be tentatively suggested. Like the answers put forward by most sciences, these are subject to revision in the future as new insights and new techniques are brought to bear and new minds take up the old problems from new angles. All we can say is that this is what we know, or think we know, now.

In the first place, language is a uniquely human possession, at least in that little corner of the universe that we know about. All races, tribes, and families of men have language; no animals do. Some people might question the second of these statements,

since we know that animals communicate with one another by sounds. But when we identify the particular qualities of genuine language, we discover that animal communication systems are different in several fundamental ways. Why this is so, when we share so much of our anatomy, physiology, and psychology with the animals, especially the apes and monkeys, science cannot yet clearly explain. It seems to be largely due to the structure of our brains, though other physical differences, especially in the anatomy of the throat and mouth, may have something to do with it. Much research is going on now in the attempt to answer this question. Meanwhile it is certainly a deeply ingrained part of our human nature to consider language as belonging to man alone. There is something a bit eerie about those animals, mostly birds, which can be taught to mimic the sounds of language. All the stories, whether fables, fairy tales, or fantasies, that endow animals with speech also give them other human qualities as well, so that they cease to be animals and become humans in disguise. On the other hand, we find it hard to imagine a human society lacking language. None has ever been found. If there still are tribes unknown to us living in isolation in Amazonian jungles, we are confident that they have language.

It is paradoxical that in spite of this universality of language among humans it still must be learned afresh by each individual person. There is considerable debate among linguists and psychologists as to how much of our linguistic ability we inherit and how much we have to learn from others. A conservative position would be that we inherit a remarkable aptitude for learning language, or at least one language, together with a very strong motivation to learn it early in life. Some linguists go much farther, as far as to maintain that we inherit not only an aptitude and a desire to learn, but actually a good part of the underlying system that is much the same in all languages. In any case, three conditions meet together to allow us to learn a language rapidly and successfully while we are still very young children: aptitude, strong motivation, and exposure to older people actually using language as they go about their lives. All normal children seem to have the first two of these; the third supplies the input which decides what particular language, or sometimes languages, we learn. It is thus a factor of our heredity that we are able and eager to learn a language, and an accident of our environment that the language we learn is English or French or some other of the three thousand or so living languages. The normal circumstance is to learn the language surrounding us in early childhood and to speak it the rest of our lives; it is our NATIVE SPEECH or MOTHER TONGUE. Occasionally the environment is such that the child learns two mother tongues at the same time and is thus a native bilingual. Even more rarely, the child

1 According to figures compiled by the Center for Applied Linguistics, Arlington, Va., in 1976.

may begin with one native speech but switch to another at such an early age that he forgets the first one completely. Whatever the situation, it is wholly a result of the environment. Most people are monolingual native speakers simply because most families and communities are homogeneously monolingual.

The fact that every normal human learns whatever language he happens to be surrounded by in childhood and that the amount of time and effort expended in this learning seems to be about the same for all languages suggests that languages must be essentially similar in their general form, however different they may be in details. Linguistics supports this supposition. It is possible to list a large number of qualities as being characteristic of language in general and hence of all known languages. Linguists call these LANGUAGE UNIVERSALS.

In the first place, languages are very versatile and adaptable. Their versatility is shown by the fact that all kinds of people, from scholars and mystics to laborers and mechanics, can make use of the same language to carry on their work, their social life, their thoughts, and their recreations. There are differences between the ways in which these different groups use their language, but it is at bottom the same means of communication. Another sign of the versatility of language is the fact that speakers are constantly saying new things that they never heard before, and others understand their utterances with equal ease, often without even realizing that they are new. This is one of the great differences between language proper and the pseudolanguages used by animals. So far as we know, all animal communications consist of a relatively short list of utterances which cannot be changed, expanded, or used in new and different ways. An animal "language", then, is rather like one of those little pocket phrase books for travelers. Even if he memorizes the book, the traveler is restricted to the immediate practical needs covered by the repertory of messages in the book. He can ask the way to his hotel or the price of a souvenir, but he can't comment very effectively on the sunset or describe the way things are in his hometown. And if something he says moves a speaker of the language to engage in real conversation, the traveler is lost. But two speakers of the same language, even though they may be very different in background, experience, education, and personality, can find a way to talk about anything they want to, using sentences that were never printed in any phrase book because nobody ever used them before.

The adaptability of language is related to its versatility. Like other human institutions, a language is adjusted by long use to the particular needs of the people and the society that use it. When these needs change, the language also changes, usually much more rapidly than most other institutions. This is why it is that in 1500 years—a relatively short space of time in human history—English has changed from the language of a rough, warlike, rather savage, agrarian, tribal society like that of the Anglo-Saxons to the typical language of the most complicated technological civilization yet developed on earth. It has always been easily adjusted to meet the new needs put upon it by a new religion, a new social system, an age of worldwide exploration, conquest, and colonization, and a series of political, agricultural, industrial, scientific, technological, and electronic revolutions. Other languages have done the same, and the process is going on today as the peoples of many different cultures around the world cope with the problem of adapting to Western society. Here again language shows itself fundamentally different from the communication systems of animals. A group of animals transplanted from their natural habitat to a new and different one do not devise new cries to deal with the new circumstances. They have only their little phrase book of specific and unalterable utterances, many of which are irrelevant to their new condition.

The versatility and adaptability that characterize all languages, as well as the fact that they all can be learned readily by any people, come from their organization or structure. Basically a language consists of four main parts or systems, each of which has its own organization while also being related to the others. First, and certainly most obvious in a dictionary like this one, is the VOCABULARY or LEXICON, a relatively large collection of words and word parts. Then there is the GRAMMAR, a set of rules governing the ways in which items from the lexicon can be combined into larger units. These words and sentences are related to the vast variety of things, events, and ideas that we talk about by a system of meanings, a SEMANTIC SYSTEM. Finally a tightly organized system of sound patterns, which linguists call the PHONOLOGY, controls the way in which the strings of words put in order according to the grammar are translated into sounds that can be spoken and heard. All languages have these four parts. Many languages, including English, have a fifth part, a WRITING SYSTEM, which supplies an alternative, visual way in which the ordered strings of words can be expressed. Unlike the other four systems, which seem to be as old as language itself, writing is a relatively new invention, probably not more than 6000 years old. Usually it is a kind of visual imitation of the phonology, using about the same number of units and following the same patterns of arrangement, though some writing systems—notably the Chinese—are based directly on the words themselves, rather than on the way they sound.

The vocabulary is the most loosely organized of the systems of language, and hence the one most open to change. It is relatively easy to add a new word to it. There are three requirements: first a need, second an inventive person, and third a group of speakers to pick up the new word and use it. The need may be of various kinds, the most obvious of which is some new element in the culture that must be named. Thus when lysergic acid diethylamide, which had been known to chemists under that ponderous name for some time, began to be used widely as a hallucinogenic drug, its name became shortened to LSD. There was also a need for a word to describe the people who use it. They could have been called *lysergic acid diethylamide users* or *LSD addicts,* but the inventiveness of some anonymous word coiner came up with *acidhead,* neatly combining a quality of the substance itself with the part of the body affected. Since the group that took up this term consisted chiefly of the drug users themselves and their associates on the fringes of society, the new word was at first considered slang, but it has now been used so widely that it has become an item in the regular vocabulary of English. Its future, like that of most slang words as well as many words in the more respectable part of the vocabulary, is in doubt, for social, not linguistic, reasons. If the use of LSD turns out to be a passing fad, the term will die out with the practice, and a future generation will find it as quaint as the present one finds outmoded expressions of the twenties, like *lounge lizard* and *flapper.*

The need may be of other kinds as well. Sometimes words acquire associations with unpleasant, antisocial, or otherwise undesirable ideas or experiences, so that people become reluctant to use them. There is then a need for a substitute that people find innocuous enough to use in ordinary conversation. Men who work on the land were once called *villains* in English (ultimately from the Latin word *villa* 'farm'); now they are called *farm labourers* or even *agricultural labourers* in England and *farmhands* in the United States. Sometimes the need is for more controllable precision, as in technical and scientific language. Thus linguists coined the word *phoneme* when the older *speech-sound* turned out to be too general and vague. Or the need may be for vocabulary items that identify the speaker with a particular social group. The special vocabularies of sailors, surfers, skiers, airplane pilots, and hundreds of other groups are full of terms which in a way serve the need for precision, but also serve to show that the speaker is "in" and to mystify and exclude those who are "out". Often these terms have perfectly good synonyms in the regular vocabulary. This is an old social use of language. Shakespeare makes amusing use of it when he shows that Prince Hal got along so well with the tavern *drawers* (waiters) that they taught him their "in" language. As the Prince puts it:

They call drinking deep, dying scarlet; and when you breathe in your watering, they cry 'hem!' and bid you play it off. To conclude, I am so good a proficient in one quarter of an hour that I can drink with any tinker in his own language during my life. [1 Henry IV, II.iv]

The sources of new vocabulary items are many and varied and may change in popularity from one period to another or from one language to another. Very commonly the new words are not new at all in form, but are simply new uses of established words, such as the modern *acid* for *LSD* or Prince Hal's *dying scarlet* for drinking deep. Commonly also new combinations of old words or word parts are put together into what linguists call COMPOUNDS. The term *acidhead* is an example using whole words. The newly popular *astronaut* uses two word parts, originally from Greek, which are already familiar through their appearance in words like *astronomy* and *nautical*. Once a new word is established, a whole family of new words can be made out of it by the process of DERIVATION, the adding on of prefixes and suffixes primarily to change the grammatical function of the word. Thus as soon as English had *psychiatry* (ultimately from Greek elements meaning 'soul' and 'doctor'), the related *psychiatrist* and *psychiatric* were easily added. In English, as in many languages which at some time in their history have been in contact with one or more other languages, it is common to get new words by BORROWING. This is the process which accounts for the fact that a large majority of the words in the English lexicon are ultimately Latin or French. These four —transferred meaning, compounding, derivation, and borrowing—are the major ways in which a language gets new words. There are several minor ways as well, among which may be mentioned CLIPPING (as in *mini* from *miniskirt*, itself a compound), BLENDS (as in *brunch* from *breakfast* plus *lunch*), IMITATIONS (as in the verb *whiz*), ACRONYMS (as in *NASA* from *National Aeronautics and Space Administration*), ABBREVIATIONS (as in *emcee* and *deejay* for *master of ceremonies* and *disc jockey*), and COINAGES (*boondoggle, quark*). The last are the rarest of all, at least in English. We seem to resist the idea of making up a word completely afresh, without any reference to words already in existence.

Just as new words keep coming into the language, so old ones keep going out of use and eventually out of memory. The usual reason is that the things they refer to are no longer talked about; the generation born since World War II does not know words like *stuka* and *panzer*, which refer to modes of warfare that are no longer employed. Sometimes, however, an old word will be replaced by a new one for no apparent reason, as in the case of *eme*, the Old English word replaced by its French synonym *uncle*. These processes are natural ones, too, common to all languages. As the great lexicographer Samuel Johnson said, in answer to Swift's wish that words should

be prevented from becoming obsolete, "But what makes a word obsolete, more than general agreement to forbear it? and how shall it be continued, when it conveys an offensive idea, or recalled again into the mouths of mankind, when it has once by disuse become unfamiliar, and by unfamiliarity unpleasing." [from Preface to *A Dictionary of the English Language,* 1755]

The other part of the central core of a language is its grammar. The largest and most complicated vocabulary would be of little value without a grammar to control the ways in which words can be put together to make larger constructions. Without a grammar the lexicon is only a list of separate items, like the entries in this dictionary. Many of these words can be used alone to make brief messages, but mostly they depend on being combined with other words to make utterances worth saying or listening to. Nor is it enough simply to put words alongside each other, in the fashion of the classic "Me Tarzan you Jane." Any sentence in this essay, any definition in this dictionary, will illustrate how complex and how delicate are the conventions governing combinations of words. They are not just strung along like beads in a necklace; they are fitted together into interlocking arrangements as intricate as the works of a watch. A change in the relationships of the parts usually changes the whole utterance: consider the difference between *Rats are our enemies* and *Our enemies are rats.* The words are the same but the messages are different.

There are various ways we can look at the grammar of a language. One analogy might be the rules of such a game as chess. The basic rules of chess are quite simple. There are only six kinds of pieces, each of which has the privilege of moving in a particular way. When certain combinations occur, certain moves are obligatory. Otherwise the player has many options each time it is his turn to move. As they move in turn, the two players construct a series of patterns on the board which is not like any series either of them has seen before. In the same way the words of a language are classified as belonging to certain classes, traditionally called PARTS OF SPEECH. The functions of these are different, just as the moves of the chess pieces are. Nouns can be subjects and objects, adjectives are modifiers, pronouns substitute for nouns, and so on. The rules are more complicated than those of chess, but not so complicated that they cannot be learned by a five-year-old child. Just as the chess players create a new game, unlike any other played in the past, so the speaker is constantly making up new sentences, many —perhaps most—of which are unlike any he ever heard or spoke in the past. The secret is in the fact that the grammar rules may be applied in many different combinations, some of them over and over, as sentences are created. Here is the major difference between animal communication and human language. Animal communication, again like the traveler's phrase book, has little or no grammar. Neither the animal nor the traveler has the power to use rules in new combinations to make original utterances. When we consider this fact, we realize that grammar is one of the greatest of all human inventions.

Another way of looking at grammar is to consider it as a set of patterns of behavior which the person using the language has somehow built into his mental structure. These patterns are sometimes called rules, but they are rules in a different sense from the rules of a game. These latter are imposed from the outside and consciously learned. But the rules of grammar, particularly those of the native language, are, as it were, invented by the child as he learns the language; they are largely unconscious, self-invented, and self-imposed. Only if he should happen to study formal grammar much later in life will the speaker encounter explicit formulations of these rules, and even then he may not recognize them. It seems rather paradoxical that many people find the study of grammar difficult, when all it is is an attempt to formulate what they themselves invented when they were children!

When grammar is looked at in this way, it is easy to see why it is much less subject to change than is vocabulary. The grammar rules are a closely integrated system, so that if a change is made in one part it may affect many other parts of the system. The vocabulary, on the other hand, is like the population of a city, where individuals may be born and die, or move in from outside, with only minor effects on the whole organization. As we shall see when we retrace the history of English, there have been a good many changes in the grammar of English, but they have occurred very slowly and gradually over a long period of time. In many of its aspects English grammar is still much like that of German, although the two languages, once the same, diverged and went their separate ways two thousand years ago.

The third major system of language is the sound system, or phonology. It is important because it controls the principal channel through which we send messages back and forth to each other. No matter how large a person's vocabulary and how carefully constructed his sentences, he would not be able to communicate normally if he did not know how to turn them into the modulated flow of sound we call speech. Underlying this continuous flow is a tightly organized system, which depends on our ability to make and to recognize sounds that contrast with one another. Thus for the middle part of *pit* we make a sound which is clearly different from the middle sounds of *pat* and *pot*. Similarly we contrast the first part of *pit* with the first part of *bit* or *nit*, and the last part with the last part of *pick*. There doesn't happen to be an English word *pid*, but if there were we would never confuse it with *pit* or *bid* or *pod*. There are normally only 25 to 50 of these contrasting sound units in a language (30 to 40 in English, depending on the dialect), but they are enough to permit us to give each word its characteristic shape. There are, of course, many cases of HOMOPHONES (words that sound alike) like *doe* and *dough*, but we are seldom confused by these because they usually appear in different contexts.

In addition to these contrasting units, which linguists call PHONEMES, each language has quite rigorous rules about how they may be combined in syllables and words. They cannot be strung along in any and all possible combinations. In a language like Hawaiian, for example, each syllable must be either just a vowel or a single consonant followed by a vowel. The few Hawaiian words and names we all know illustrate this rule: *hula, aloha, Honolulu, Waikiki*. In contrast, English syllables have only one vowel or diphthong but may have as many as three consonants before it and three after, as in *splints*. But the rules governing which consonants may be used are quite strict. For example, if there are three at the beginning of a word, the first must be *s*, the second *p, t,* or *k*, and the third *r, l, w,* or *y* (remember we are talking about sounds, not spellings). If you will look in the *s*-section of this dictionary, you will find how closely this rule is followed; the only words that break this rule are recent borrowings from other languages, and even these are usually changed to fit the English pattern.

A third part of the sound system concerns not the individual sounds but the features of rhythm, accent, and even musical pitch which are part of the flow of speech. Since most of these are related to whole clauses and sentences, rather than individual words, they are not given much attention in a dictionary, which deals primarily with single words. But an important exception is STRESS, which in English is a feature of individual words. The rules for assigning stress to the correct syllables of an English word are quite rigorous, and the native speaker of English knows them as he knows the rules of grammar. But there are some doubtful cases, such as *contemplative, hospitable,* and *altimeter,* for which we turn to the dictionary.

Because of its tight structure, the phonological system of a language does not usually change very much or very fast. Such changes as do occur usually affect the minor details of pronunciation, rather than the underlying system of contrasts. But this may change also, by the addition or disappearance of phonemes, by changes in the combining rules, or in the rules of stress. Thus Chaucer's English of six hundred years ago had a frictional sound made in the back of the mouth, as in modern German *Nacht,* and the ancestor of our word *courage* had three syllables with the stress on the second \kù-ˈrä-jə\.

As has been already noted, writing systems are comparatively recent innovations, as compared to the venerable antiquity of language itself with its basic systems of vocabulary, grammar, and phonology. The human race got along for several hundred thousand years with only the channel of speech through which to communicate verbal messages. But when societies became so complex that their essential records could no longer be kept in the memories of men and when they found it necessary to transmit at a distance messages that could not be entrusted safely to the memory of a messenger, various modes of writing were invented. The earliest of these seem to have been based on the word as a unit, and made use of a separate symbol or CHARACTER, originally a conventionalized picture, for each word. The Chinese system is still based on this principle, with some modifications. Systems of this sort have certain advantages, the chief of which is that they are largely independent of pronunciation. In fact, the Chinese system is used by a number of different languages, so that people who cannot understand one another's speech can communicate by writing. But the disadvantage of having to invent and learn to read and draw thousands of characters to represent the vocabulary of a language led people to devise new types of writing systems, based on the phonological structure, which, as we have seen, has many fewer units than the vocabulary and was already in full development as a channel of communication. At first the syllable was used as the unit to be represented. Symbols representing syllables could be strung along in the same order as the syllables of speech, usually with some additional indication as to where the boundaries between words fell. Finally the phoneme became the unit to be represented, and the ALPHABET was born. Most present-day writing systems are alphabetic, though because of accidents of history they have departed more or less from the principle of consistently representing each phoneme by a single character. Alphabets are rather readily adaptable to other languages besides those for which they were originally developed. Thus our Roman alphabet, originally devised for Latin, has been adopted by most of the languages of western Europe and the New World. Other familiar alphabets are the Cyrillic, used for Russian and other Slavic languages; the Arabic, used also for Persian and Urdu and formerly for Turkish; the Hebrew, also used for Yiddish; the Devanagari of India; and the Greek.

Alphabetic writing systems resemble phonological systems in that they have a relatively small number of units and a set of rules, sometimes quite elaborate, governing the ways in which the units may and may not be combined. Some of these rules are, as might be expected, simply reflections of the rules of the phonology. But others belong to the writing systems themselves. In English, for example, though we have many words ending in the sounds of *v* and *j*, there is a strong rule, with very few exceptions, against ending a word with either of these letters. Instead we write *-ge* or *-dge* for a final *j*-sound and *-ve* for a final *v*-sound. There is also a rule against doubling these letters, and *k* as well, even for the usual purpose of indicating that the preceding vowel is short. So we write *liver, flicker,* and *badger,* instead of the more consistent *livver, flikker, bajjer*.[2] It is these rules, which are known unconsciously by all literate users of English, that give English its characteristic look on the page. Combinations like *zdenek, lliiji,* and *mbau* simply don't look English, while *flace, crasp,* and *splick* could very well represent English words, though they don't happen to. In short, our system, for all its inconsistencies, is indeed a system and one which most people can learn to use easily and accurately. But it is also true that checking on spelling is one of the most common reasons for using the dictionary.

The semantic system has been left to the last partly because we know least about it in a formal way. It is probably not obvious to the ordinary observer that there is such a system. Everyone knows that meaning is an important part of language, but somehow they feel that words and sentences represent meaning directly, without the intervention of another formal system. But a little thought about how language works, and especially some comparisons of how different languages convey similar facts and ideas, leads us to the conclusion that there is a quite elaborate formally structured system between the infinite variety of the outside world and our ways of talking about it. Take the question of measurements. English, like the other languages in the western European tradition, has an elaborate system of ways of describing the size of things in terms of abstract standard units that can be counted, added, subtracted, multiplied, and divided. If asked how big a book or a desk is, we think of applying a ruler to it and giving the answer in inches or feet and fractions of these units. The whole repertory of miles, pounds, pints, cubic feet, acres, and all the rest is based on this underlying assumption that numerically manipulable standard units are the way to measure things. We are so committed to this way of measuring that we can hardly imagine any other. But many cultures, and the languages associated with them, measure distance in terms of time; two localities may be "two days' journey" apart. According to our system, one 20-mile stretch across country is equal to another, though the first may be across a level plain and the other across rough broken country or through a jungle. Another system might find these two not equal at all; the first might be "half a day's walk" and the second "two days' walk."[3]

Another illustration of the formal structuring of meanings, also taken from the general area of measurements, is the description of dimensions. In English we do this with pairs of words signifying opposite poles of measurement along a certain line, such as *tall : short* and *far : near.* Furthermore we have two sets of these, one set in which the line of measurement is related to a fixed point, often but not always that of the observer or speaker, and another set in which the line of measurement is related rather to the shape of the object being measured. Thus the first set has three main pairs: *far* and *near* (measured along a line extending from the observer in a specified direction), *high* and *low* (measured along a vertical line perpendicular to the observer's line of sight), *wide* and *narrow* (measured along a horizontal line perpendicular to the observer's line of sight). The second set has more dimensions—at least five—but they are still signified by pairs of opposed words: *large* (*big*) and *small* (*little*), *long* and *short, tall* and *short, deep* and *shallow, wide* (*broad*) and *narrow, thick* and *thin.* A further interesting point about English is that in each of these pairs one, which is somehow the larger one, is chosen for giving a neutral measurement or asking a neutral question about one of the dimensions. We say "The door is three feet *wide,*" "The water is three feet *deep,*" or "How *tall* is John?" rather than "The door is three feet *narrow,*" "The water is three feet *shallow,*" or "How *short* is John?" We would say the latter if someone else had already said "John is quite short," and even then the answer would be "He is only five feet *tall.*" Similarly we choose the larger dimension for the neutral nouns describing these dimensions: the *length* of the journey, the *height* of the building, the *depth* of the water. There are also nouns for the small dimensions, but they are all what linguists would call SEMANTICALLY MARKED. Note that the "*shortness* of the journey," "the *lowness* of the building," "the *shallowness* of the water" all convey special meanings beyond a mere neutral indication of dimension. It is clear that systems like these are not merely parts of the natural world; they impose a structural framework on the natural world which makes it easier to talk about it. This is what we mean by speaking of a semantic system that is part of language.

The relationships among these various systems are quite complex, but they may be suggested in a diagram such as this:

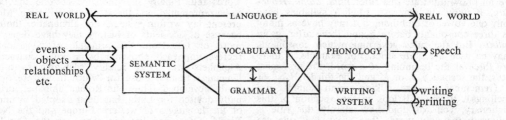

2 A few violations of this rule are beginning to appear, usually in slang, dialectal, and humorous words like *flivver* and *yakking.*

3 One unit of distance in terms of time that we do use is the *light-year.* But since the speed of light is constant, this is still an abstract standard: it is simply easier to say "one light-year" than "5,878,000,000,000 miles."

Here we see language, which is inside the minds of people, in contact with the outside world in two places, which scientists might call *interfaces*. At one end the semantic system sorts out, classifies, and arranges the jumble of events, objects, and relationships fed in by the outside world. At the other, the phonology and the writing system give instructions which control the actual performance of the speaker or writer. Within language itself, the internal structures of the various parts, as well as the relationships among them, are very complicated. It is the function of the dictionary to give information about many of these. Thus the main entries, in giving the correct spelling, indicate the relationship between the vocabulary and the writing system. Pronunciation cues indicate the relationship between vocabulary and phonology; definitions, that between vocabulary and the semantic system and sometimes between the semantic system and the real world. Each word is also classified under one or more parts of speech, which suggests the relationship between vocabulary and grammar. Thus the dictionary, centering on the vocabulary, also involves all the other parts of language.

The History of English

Language, like all other aspects of human culture, is constantly changing. This is implied in a good deal that is said above. Certainly the adaptability of language is one of the major sources of change; as the circumstances and needs of the speakers of a language change, they change the language to meet them. This is particularly apparent in vocabulary, where change is easiest to observe and most rapid. There are many words in this dictionary which were not included in Webster's Third New International Dictionary, published only twelve years ago. Less obviously, there are words now considered obsolete that were in current use not many decades ago. It is, of course, harder to decide that a word has left the vocabulary than that one has joined it, because the old words are enshrined in the older books even though people may not use them in speech. Hence the vocabulary, and the dictionary that reports it, has a category of ARCHAIC words—museum specimens, no longer completely alive, but still needed in special ways.

Change goes on in other parts of the language as well, though it is harder to observe. Anyone who has lived a moderately long life is not using exactly the same grammar and pronunciation that he learned as a child, though he himself is usually unaware of the changes that have taken place. These changes usually happen so slowly and gradually that they are imperceptible to the people in whose language they occur. It is only when we look back over a period of a century or more that language begins to look a little old-fashioned. Until recently it has not been possible to compare a person's pronunciation at various ages, as well as to observe what changes take place across the generations. Modern means of voice recording will make this possible in the future.

In order to see how the old-fashioned quality of language ultimately changes to complete unintelligibility if we go far enough back in time, let us take a retrospective trip into the older stages of English, making stops every two hundred years or so. The passages which will be used for illustration are all quite formal documents—in all cases but one they are public notices or proclamations—so that their kind of language is the kind that changes most slowly. Slang, informal conversation, personal letters, are all more unstable and changeable than the formal language of laws, legal documents, public announcements, and royal proclamations, which tends to retain archaic vocabulary and to some extent grammar as well. Yet we shall see that when we go back as far as five and a half centuries, even this conservative formal language becomes quite strange.

Our first example is from a document which is—or at least ought to be—familiar to all Americans: the Declaration of Independence, 1776.

Prudence, indeed, will dictate that Governments long established should not be changed for light and transient causes; and accordingly all experience hath shewn, that mankind are more disposed to suffer, while evils are sufferable, than to right themselves by abolishing the forms to which they are accustomed. But when a long train of abuses and usurpations, pursuing invariably the same Object, evinces a design to reduce them under absolute Despotism, it is their right, it is their duty, to throw off such Government, and to provide new Guards for their future security.—Such has been the patient sufferance of these Colonies; and such is now the necessity which constrains them to alter their former Systems of Government. The history of the present King of Great Britain is a history of repeated injuries and usurpations, all having in direct object the establishment of an absolute Tyranny over these States.

Probably what strikes the twentieth-century reader of this passage first is its extreme formality. It may even take a bit of study to realize that "the forms to which they are accustomed" means what we would more informally express as "the type of government they are used to," and we would feel easier with "the need that forces them to change the government" than we do with "the necessity which constrains them to alter their former Systems of Government." The more formal passages are still quite possible in modern English, however. It is rather a matter of style than age which makes them seem a bit out-of-date to us. The same may be said of the fact that the subjects of a good many of the sentences are abstract qualities: "Prudence . . . will dictate," "experience hath shewn," "necessity . . . constrains"—it is as though the actors in the drama were these abstractions, rather than people. But this is a characteristic feature of eighteenth-century style, which helps to emphasize that the only actual person mentioned is the villain, "the present King of Great Britain."

When we look a bit more closely, however, we find some features of vocabulary and grammar that are indeed old-fashioned to the point of being archaic. Words like *suffer, train, reduce,* and *object* are used in ways and with meanings that present-day writers would not use; we would be more likely to say *endure, series* or *succession, subject,* and *aim.* In grammar we note the form *hath*, which was already archaic in 1776, the treatment of *mankind* as a plural noun (*mankind are*), and the unusual word order of *Governments long established and pursuing invariably the same Object.* And *shew,* a variant spelling of *show,* long ago passed from common use.

What these various matters of style, vocabulary, and grammar add up to is a slight feeling of strangeness that can be a barrier to full understanding. The cautious reader might feel the need to go to the dictionary to check such words as *transient* and *suffer*. Nor would he expect the modern Congress, no matter how formal the situation, to produce a document quite like this. But he can still accept it as essentially his own language.

We go back another hundred and fifty years for the next example, a selection from a pamphlet written by John Winthrop and others of the Puritan pioneers from their ship, the *Arbella,* which was just about to set out across the ocean to establish Boston and the other settlements of the Massachusetts Bay Colony. The year is 1630, and the document bears a long and quaint title, *The Humble Request of His Maiesties loyall Subjects, the Governour and the Company late gone for New-England; To the rest of their Brethren, in and of the Church of England. For the obtaining of their Prayers and the removall of suspitions, and misconstructions of their Intentions.* Like many seventeenth-century titles, this one is really a summary of what the little pamphlet is about. The colonists are writing to those they are leaving behind, asking for understanding of their motives in leaving their country and their church to set up new settlements and a new church in the New World.

If any there be, who through want of cleare intelligence of our course, or tendernesse of affection towards us, cannot conceive so well of our way as we could desire, we would intreat such not to despise us, nor to desert us in their prayers & affections, but to consider rather, that they are so much the more bound to expresse the bowels of their compassion towards us, remembring alwaies that both Nature and Grace, doth ever binde us to relieve and rescue with our utmost & speediest power, such as are deare unto us, when wee conceive them to be running uncomfortable hazards.

What goodnes you shall extend to us in this or any other Christian kindnesse, wee your Brethren in CHRIST IESVS shall labour to repay in what dutie wee are or shall be able to performe, promising so farre as God shall enable us to give him no rest on your behalfes, wishing our heads and hearts may be as fountaines of teares for your everlasting welfare, when wee shall be in our poore Cottages in the wildernesse, . . .

Certainly one thing that strikes us here is the complexity of the sentences. The whole passage of 182 words comprises only two sentences; actually the second sentence has been broken off before its end, and runs on in the original for 23 more words. In spite of this, however, its tone is more personal and less abstract than that of the Declaration; the actors are people ("wee" and "you") rather than abstractions like "Prudence" and "necessity". Perhaps because of this more familiar tone, the vocabulary presents relatively few problems, though even in the first clause we realize that *want, intelligence,* and *affection* are being used in senses no longer current today—we would say *lack, understanding* or *knowledge,* and *feeling* (note that we now use just the word *affection* to mean what is here expressed by *tendernesse of affection*).

In other matters, however, the passage clearly declares itself as older than the Declaration. Even the spelling, which in our day is strictly standardized, is different, particularly in the matter of putting a final -e onto a good many words which we end with a consonant: *cleare, expresse, binde, deare, farre,* etc. Other spellings which are no longer current are *alwaies, wee,* and *dutie.* But it is probably the combination of grammatical complexity and archaic turns of phrase that gives the passage its antique flavor. A modern translation of the first sentence might go somewhat like this:

If there are any people who, either because of lack of understanding of what we are doing or because of their fondness for us, do not approve our actions as highly as we would like them to, we ask them not to despise us or to give up praying for us and loving us. Instead, they should realize that they have a greater obligation to show us their affection and understanding. They should remember that it is both natural and moral to do our best to help save those we love when we think they are taking dangerous risks.

Here the original sentence of 105 words has been broken up into three sentences, much of the complicated sentence-structure has been simplified, and quaint turns of phrase like "the bowels of their compassion" have been put into ordinary modern English. Though the reader may miss the old-fashioned flavor of the original, it is safe to say he is clearer about what is being said.

In spite of the fact that the second of these passages is 340 years old, both of them fall into what linguists call the Modern English period. Our next example, however, goes back another two centuries into what we call Middle English. It is "A Crye Made for a Commune Passage Toward Hareflieu," actually a proclamation issued in the name of King Henry V for the assembling of supplies in support of his invasion of France in 1415.

Be ther proclamacioun made, that alle manere of men, marchauntz, artificers, or other, of what estat, degre, or condicioun, that euere they be, that willen toward oure liege lorde the kyng, beyng atte harflewe in the costes of Normandye, that god him spede, with corne, brede, mele, or flour, wyne, ale, or biere, fyssh, flessh or any other viteille, clothe, lynnen, wollen or eny merchaundise, shertys, breches, doublettys, hosen, shone, or eny other manere ware of armure, artilrye, or of othere stuffe, lette hem apparaille and make redy betwen this and to-day seuenyght their bodyes, goodes, merchaundyses, ware, stoffure, viteille, what that euer it be; and in the mene while come to the Mair, and he shall dispose and assigne theym redy shippyng and passage vnto the forseide costes. [Text from Chambers & Daunt, *A Book of London English 1384–1425,* Oxford, 1931]

The first thing that the modern reader notices about this passage is undoubtedly the spelling. Just about half the running words are spelled differently from their modern forms. When we consider individual words, the difference is even more striking: only 29 of the 83 different words in the passage are spelled as in modern English. This certainly contributes to the superficial strangeness of the passage, but a closer look reveals that this in itself does not constitute a serious barrier to understanding, since most if not all of the words are easily identified in spite of their different spellings. In most cases the spellings conform to the general rules of modern English, the difference being in the alternatives chosen: thus *spede, mele,* and *mene* are perfectly possible modern spellings but they don't happen to be the accepted ways of spelling *speed, meal,* and *mean.* Some spellings, however, seem to indicate pronunciation differences. Thus *shertys* and *doublettys* for *shirts* and *doublets,* and perhaps *costes* for *coasts,* suggest that the plural ending in these words which end in *-t* was a full syllable, as it is to this day in some regional dialects where *posts* is pronounced as if spelled *postiz.*

Looking at the vocabulary of the proclamation, we find that once we get past the spelling so that we can identify the words, virtually all of them are still current in English. In fact, only *stoffure* ("material used for furnishing, supply, or outfit") is listed as completely obsolete by the Oxford English Dictionary. Nobody wears a *doublet* ("a quilted undergarment reinforced by rings of mail and worn under armor") nowadays, but the word turns up in enough historical fiction to be entered unlabeled in *Webster's Third New International Dictionary.* (The thing, not the word, is obsolete.) And *seue-nyght,* which appears in the same dictionary under its later form *sennight,* is labeled archaic and illustrated by quotations from the seventeenth and eighteenth centuries. Some might wonder at *viteille,* but in its later form *victuals* it is still occasionally used.

It is another matter, however, when we consider the meanings of the words. A large number of them, including some of the most familiar ones, are used in senses that are either quite infrequent or impossible in modern English. Among these we might list *manere* ('kind'), *artificers* ('craftsmen'), *estat* ('rank'), *spede* ('help, prosper'), *artilrye* ('arms, munitions'), *appuraille* ('prepare'), *to-day seuenyght* ('a week from today'), *dispose* ('order'). Since these are some of the key words in the passage, to give them their usual modern meanings would distort its total meaning quite badly. Once again we are reminded that changes in the meanings of words that remain in the language are probably more important in their effect than the coming in of new words or the passing away of old ones.

Another fact about the vocabulary that we become aware of in studying this passage is that there are two major sources of English words: native English and borrowed Romance. We are reminded that for about two centuries before this proclamation was written it had been quite common for writers and speakers of English, many of whom also knew and used French, to slip French words into their English. Many of these words were taken up by others and eventually naturalized in English. In this passage 23 of the 83 different words, or about 30%, are from French. They include *proclamacioun, manere, marchauntz, artificers, estat, degre, con-dicioun,* and so on down to *passage* and *costes.* The native words make up 70% of the vocabulary but 77% of the running words, since many of them are the little grammatical words that are frequently repeated, like *that, and, or, the,* and *other.* Some, however, are important "content" words like *lorde, kyng, corne, ale, fyssh, wollen,* and *shertys.* Since the language of the proclamation is legalistic and hence rather repetitious, we sometimes find a native word and its French synonym coupled together, as in *appuraille and make redy* or *shippyng and passage.* But this is probably accidental, since other repetitive strings may be all French words (*dispose and assigne*) or mixed (*goodes, merchaun-dyses, ware*—native, French, native). It is of some interest to compare the percentages of native and French words in this passage with that in our most recent example, the selection from the Declaration of Independence, in which 48% are native, 42% French, and 9% direct from Latin. Obviously the habit of borrowing continued during the period of three and a half centuries between Henry V and our founding fathers.

The grammar, too, of this passage is more than a bit strange to the modern reader. The opening phrase is impossible in modern English, even of the most formal sort; we would have to say "Let there be made a proclamation" or more likely "Let it be proclaimed". Modern English has made a whole new set of indefinite pronouns by tacking *ever* onto *who, which,* and *what;* here, as in *of what estat . . . that euere they be,* the *ever* is still a separate adverb. Plural forms like *hosen* and *shone* have gone out; *hose* has become a sort of plural without a singular, like *trousers* and *scissors,* while *shone* has adopted the regular plural ending and become *shoes.* In sum, while the passage is clearly English, the modern reader inexperienced in the Middle English of Chaucer and his contemporaries has difficulties in reading it.

These difficulties increase considerably when we go back another century and a half to 1258. Here is part of a proclamation by another King Henry, the Third, in which he confirms his acceptance of the Provisions of Oxford, a document which a group of barons had forced him to sign in much the same way the Magna Carta had been extracted from King John forty-odd years earlier.

Henri, þurȝ Godes fultume King on Englene-loande, Lhoauerd on Yrloande, Duk on Normandi, on Aquitaine, and Eorl on Aniow, send igretinge to alle hise holde, ilærde and ileawede, on Hunten-doneschire. Þæt witen ȝe wel alle þæt we willen and vnnen þæt, þæt vre rædesmen alle, oþer þe moare dæl of heom, þæt beoþ ichosen þurȝ us and þurȝ þæt loandes folk on vre kune-riche, habbeþ idon and shullen don in þe worþ-nesse of Gode and on vre treowþe, for þe freme of þe loande þurȝ þe besiȝte of þan toforeniseide redesmen, beo stedefæst and ilestinde in alle þinge a buten ænde. And we hoaten alle vre treowe in þe treowþe þæt heo vs oȝen, þæt heo stedefæstliche healden and swerien to healden and to werien þo isetnesses þæt beon imakede and beon to makien, þurȝ þan toforeniseide rædesmen, oþer þurȝ þe moare dæl of heom, alswo alse hit is biforen iseid; and þæt æhc oþer helpe þæt for to done bi þan ilche oþe aȝenes alle men riȝt for to done and to foangen. [Text from Dickins & Wilson, *Early Middle English Texts,* Cambridge, 1951]

One surprising thing about this document is that it is in English at all, rather than in French, which was the official language of the government at this time. Actually it was promulgated in French as well; the parallel English version is probably the result of a contemporary nationalistic movement to restore English to official use. In any case, the modern reader probably finds the English version as difficult as he would the French. A modern translation might go somewhat as follows:

Henry, by the grace of God King of England, Lord of Ireland, Duke of Normandy and Aquitaine, and Earl of Anjou, sends greetings to all his subjects, both clerical and lay, in Huntingdon-shire. You are all to know well that we will and agree that whatever all our councillors, or the majority of them, who have been chosen by us and by the common people in our kingdom have done and shall do, to the honor of God and in fidelity to us, for the benefit of the country by the wisdom of the said councillors, is to be firm and lasting in all respects without end. And we command all our faithful followers by the loyalty that they owe to us to hold firmly and swear to hold and to defend the provisions that have been made and are to be made by the aforesaid councillors, or the majority of them, as is stated above; and [we further command] them to help one another to do so, by virtue of that same oath—to render justice to and receive it from all men.

Once again, spelling is the first obstacle to the

modern reader who attempts to interpret the original. For one thing, there are three strange letters in the alphabet: þ, called 'thorn', which stands for the sounds now spelled *th;* ȝ, called 'yogh', which represents consonantal *y* at the beginning of a word or medially before a stressed vowel, *gh* at the end of a word or before another consonant, and *w* between vowels; and æ, called 'ash', which spells the vowel of modern English *hat.* With these clues it is easier to see that þurȝ is our word *through* or *thorough,* ȝe is the pronoun *ye,* an archaic form of *you,* riȝt is *right,* oȝen is *owe* or *own,* and þæt is *that.* A few more hints help a bit more, such as that *u* and *v* are used interchangeably for both the vowel *u* and the consonant *v,* with *v* appearing at the beginnings of words and *u* in the middle, so that vre is *ure* (= *our*); and that *oa* is used to spell an *aw*-type of vowel, as it still is in one word, *broad.*

But even if the spelling were to be completely converted to modern forms, we would still have difficulties with words. A major reason for this is that, although the proclamation was written nearly two centuries after the Norman Conquest, it comes before the great influx of French words into the language. In fact, the same nationalistic motives mentioned above may have led the writer (quite possibly the translator, since it is likely that the French version was written first) to consciously avoid using any French words at all. In any case, except for the title *Duk,* the king's given name *Henri,* and the names of the three French provinces where he claimed feudal title—*Normandi, Aquitaine,* and *Aniow*—there are no French words at all in this selection. Instead, the proclamation frequently uses Old English words and phrases that have since been replaced by French synonyms and hence have become obsolete. Some of these, with their modern equivalents, are:

þurȝ Godes fultume	through God's help
holde	subjects, vassals
vnnen	agree
rædesmen	councillors, advisors
moare dæl	larger part, majority
þæt loandes folk	the common people
freme	benefit
hoaten	command
treowþe	loyalty, fidelity
werien	defend, protect
isetnesses	agreements, provisions
foangen	receive

With the exception of *protect* and *defend,* which were taken directly from Latin, and the native word *help,* all the words in the right-hand column are of French origin. It is obvious that what amounted to a virtual revolution in the English vocabulary, especially its more formal layers, took place in the century and a half between Henry III and Henry V.

In grammar as well we find forms and constructions that are no longer current, though here the change has been more gradual. We may observe, for example, the contrast between the ending *-ing,* which marks verbal nouns, and *-ind,* which marks present participles, as in the words *igretinge* and *ilestinde.* At a somewhat later date, this distinction, which still prevails in modern German, was lost, and the *-ing* ending came to be used for both. This is in a way unfortunate since it can lead to ambiguity, as in *pursuing girls may be fun*—which can mean either 'the pursuit of girls' (verbal noun) or 'girls who pursue' (participle). Another grammatical marker that has since disappeared is the prefix *i-,* descended from an earlier *ge-,* which frequently appears with past participles, as in *idon, imakede,* and *iseid.* This prefix *ge-* has also survived in modern German. For the most part the word order is not far different from that

of modern English, as comparison of the original with the translation will show. But word order such as *ælc oþer helpe þæt for to done* ('each the other help that for to do'), with two instances of the direct object coming before the verb, has to be changed to *each help the other to do that* to accord with modern grammar.

All these things—strange spelling, often reflecting a quite different pronunciation, obsolete words, and grammatical differences—add up to making the language of this passage seem like a foreign language, though paradoxically its freedom from French words makes it very pure English for its time. By the time we take another giant step backward, this time of nearly two and a half centuries, we are indeed dealing with an almost wholly unfamiliar language, in spite of the fact that we can trace an unbroken tradition of nearly a thousand years down to our own time. Linguists call this language OLD ENGLISH or ANGLO-SAXON. Here is part of another royal document, a writ, dated 1020, of King Cnut (or Canute, as he is more commonly known), a Danish Viking who was king of England for twenty years (1016–35) and of Denmark and Norway for shorter periods. He had just returned to England from a successful expedition to Denmark to make good his claim to the throne there, and put out this writ to reassure the English people of his intent to keep the peace. As a Dane, it is quite likely that he did not himself speak English, but had this document written by some clerk of his household. Also, in spite of his pagan background he had become a Christian, a fact which he emphasizes strongly in this document.

Cnut cyning gret his arcebiscopas and his leodbiscopas and Þurcyl eorl and ealle his eorlas and ealne his þeodscype, twelfhynde and twyhynde, gehadode and læwede, on Englalande freondlice. And ic cyðe eow, þæt ic wylle beon hold hlaford and unswicende to godes gerihtum and to rihtre woroldlage.

Ic nam me to gemynde þa gewritu and þa word, þe se arcebiscop Lyfing me fram þam papan brohte of Rome, þæt ic scolde æghwær godes lof upp aræran and unriht alecgan and full frið wyrcean be ðære mihte, þe me god syllan wolde.

Nu ne wandode ic na minum sceattum, þa hwile þe eow unfrið on handa stod: nu ic mid godes fultume þæt totwæmde mid minum scattum. Þa cydde man me, þæt us mara hearm to fundode, þonne us wel licode: and þa for ic me sylf mid þam mannum þe me mid foron into Denmearcon, þe eow mæst hearm of com: and þæt hæbbe mid godes fultume forene forfangen, þæt eow næfre heonon forð þanon nan unfrið to ne cymð, þa hwile þe ge me rihtlice healdað and min lif byð. [Text from Kaiser, *Medieval English,* Berlin, 1958]

There is no doubt about this being virtually as strange as a foreign language. Only a few words—mostly pronouns and other function words—look like their modern descendants: *his, and, on, to, me, us, into.* There is another new character, ð, called 'edh', which is in variation with þ as a means of writing the sounds we spell with *th.* Even a full understanding of the spelling conventions would not help the modern reader very much. He cannot understand it without a translation, which might go as follows:

Canute the king greets his archbishops and his provincial bishops and Earl Thurcyl and all his earls and all his people, rich and poor, ordained and lay, in England, in friendly fashion. And I assure you that I wish to be a gracious lord and devoted to the laws of God and to just human law.

I have remembered the writs and the words that Archbishop Lyfing brought me from the Pope of Rome, [to the effect] that I should in all ways support the praise of God and put down injustice and promote perfect peace to the extent of the strength that God would grant me.

I have never spared my wealth as long as discord was among you; now with God's help I have dispersed it [discord] with my wealth. When I was informed that more affliction had come upon us than we could put up with, then I went myself to Denmark with those men who caused you the most injury; and with God's help I have now seen to it that from this time on no breach of the peace will ever come to you from that source, so long as you obey me properly and my life endures.

With the exception of the ecclesiastical titles *arcebiscop* and *leodbiscop* and the Danish names Cnut and Thurcyl, the vocabulary here is totally English. Many of the words have survived into modern English, with changes in spelling that reflect changes in pronunciation: *cyning* (*king*), *hlaford* (*lord*), *brohte* (*brought*), *scolde* (*should*), *licode* (*liked*), *rihtlice* (*rightly*), etc. But many have become obsolete during the nine and a half centuries since this was written: *þeodscype* ('people'), *cyðe*, past *cydde* ('make known'), *unswicende* ('unyielding'), *lof* ('praise'), *frið* ('peace'), *wandode*, from *wandian* ('hesitate, omit'), etc. Of the 96 different words in the passage, 31 are now obsolete and 7 more have undergone rather drastic changes of meaning, so that even if the reader knew enough about Old English spelling to recognize the survivors, he would have to go to a dictionary of Old English for the meanings of 40% of the words.

In terms of grammar also, this English of 1020 shows more clearly its affiliation with the other Germanic languages. As in modern German, not only nouns but adjectives and even the definite article are INFLECTED; that is, they have special endings indicating the case, number, and sometimes gender. Some examples illustrating this:

se arcebiscop	'the archbishop'	masculine singular nominative
þam papan	'the pope'	masculine singular dative
ðære mihte	'the might'	feminine singular dative
þa gewritu	'the writs'	neuter plural accusative
þam mannum	'the men'	masculine plural dative
ealle his eorlas	'all his earls'	masculine plural accusative
ealne his þeodscype	'all his people'	masculine singular accusative
min lif	'my life'	neuter singular nominative
minum sceattum	'my treasures'	masculine plural dative

Verbs also have inflections, many of which have survived into modern English. We still have the distinction between STRONG verbs—those that form the past tense by changing the stem vowel—and WEAK verbs —those that add an ending containing a *d* or *t*.[4] The following are some forms from this passage illustrating these two types:

Strong past tense forms
  nam, from niman, 'take'
  stod, from standan, 'stand'
  for (sing.) and foron (plural) from faran, 'go, travel'
  com, from cuman, 'come'

Weak past tense forms
  brohte, from bringan, 'bring'
  wandode, from wandian, 'omit, neglect'
  totwæmde, from totwæman, 'break up, scatter'
  cydde, from cyðan, 'proclaim, make known'

In another important grammatical feature, the order of the elements in constructions, this passage shows many differences from modern English. In fact, only the subject-verb-object order of main clauses, as in *Cnut cyning gret his arcebiscopas,* is the same as ours. This is inverted if an adverb begins the sentence, as in *þa for ic* 'then went I.' This inversion survives today with only a few adverbs, such as *never* and *seldom.* The order in subordinate clauses, however, is quite different from ours. Here the rule is that the verb comes at the end of the clause, which makes the other elements come in an order that seems very unnatural to us, especially when it is combined with the practice of putting prepositions after their objects, often with other elements in between. All this is illustrated by *þe eow mæst hearm of com* ('whom to you most harm from came') and *þæt eow næfre heonon forð þanon nan unfrið to ne cymð* ('that you never hence forth thence no war to not comes'), where *eow* is the object of the preposition *to,* which doesn't come until seven words later. This last clause also illustrates the manner of emphasizing negation by multiple negative forms, which is still common in substandard speech ("I ain't never had no luck") but is generally considered unacceptable in standard English.

Many more points of difference could be found by further analysis of this passage, but this is enough to show that when we trace English back as much as two-thirds of its 1500-year history we discover that it has many of the features which we associate with a foreign language. In fact, we could only continue our backward journey by means of written texts about three centuries farther. After that we would come to a time when English was rarely or never written down, and we would have to depend on the various ingenious indirect methods which philologists use to reconstruct the unwritten early stages of the history of a language. By these methods we could push our horizon back to the time, about the beginning of the Christian era, when English was not a separate language at all but simply one of the dialects of the common Germanic language of northern Europe. By even more ingenious methods, involving comparison with other language families like Celtic, Slavic, Indic, Latin, and Greek, we can go back another two or three thousand years and draw hypothetical inferences about the common Indo-European tongue from which most of the languages of Europe ultimately derive. That is as far as we can go. Tens, perhaps hundreds, of thousands of years of the history of our language are irretrievably lost in the mists of time.

4 Some weak verbs such as *deal—dealt* and *creep—crept* also show vowel change in the past, but this is due to vowel shortening in Middle English, much later than the vowel shifts in strong verbs which go back to Proto-Germanic.

TABULAR HISTORY OF THE ENGLISH LANGUAGE

Date & Period	Historical Events	Linguistic Events
About 3000 B.C. Proto-Indo-European	Neolithic Age. Indo-Europeans living in north central Europe.	Indo-European undifferentiated, except dialectally.
3000–500 B.C. Indo-European Proto-Germanic	Extensive migrations of Indo-European speakers to India, Greece, and western Europe.	Differentiation of Indo-European language families, including Germanic. Earliest documents in Sanskrit, Greek, etc.
500–0 B.C. Germanic	Celts in Britain. Contact of Roman Empire with Germanic peoples.	Germanic undifferentiated except dialectally. First borrowings from Latin.
0–300 A.D. West Germanic	Expansion and power of Roman Empire. Romanization of Britain. Growth and migrations of Germanic tribes.	Differentiation of West, North, and East branches of Germanic. Continued Latin borrowings.
300–500 Proto Old English	Breakup of Roman Empire. Anglo-Saxon invasions of Britain.	Beginnings of differentiation of Vulgar Latin. Emergence of Old English. Contact with Celts. Oldest Germanic documents (Gothic Bible c. 350).
500–700 Early Old English	Conversion of Anglo-Saxons. Northumbrian culture. Earliest surviving literature.	Borrowings from Latin and occasionally Celtic. Increased diversity of dialects. Adoption of alphabet.
700–1000 Old English	Danish and Norse raids and invasions. Alfred and the political ascendancy of Wessex. Establishment of the Danelaw. Cynewulf, Aelfric, and other writers.	West Saxon dominant dialect. More Latin borrowings. Development of Old French and other Romance languages.
1000–1150 Late Old English	Viking raids; Danish kings of England. Norman Conquest. Replacement of native ruling class by French speakers.	Extensive borrowings from Norse, especially in the North. French the official language. English "submerged". Further differentiation of dialects.
1150–1300 Early Middle English	Gradual loss of continental possessions of English kings. Continued dominance of French speakers in politics, law, church. Beginnings of revival of literature in English.	Breakdown and loss of Old English inflections. Extensive phonological and syntactic changes. Borrowings from French (Anglo-Norman).
1300–1475 Middle English	Hundred Years' War. Growth of nationalism; decay of feudalism. Chaucer, Gower, Langland, "Gawain Poet", Wyclif. Mystery and Morality plays.	Emergence of English (dialect of London) as the standard literary and official language. Extensive borrowings from French.
1475–1650 Early Modern English	Caxton and printing. Renaissance humanism: revived study of Greek and Latin classics. Spenser, Shakespeare, Milton, biblical translations. Age of discovery and exploration.	Great vowel shift and loss of final -e. Beginning of standardized spelling. Extensive borrowings from Latin, some from Greek. Changes in grammar, especially verb system.
1650–1800 Later Modern English	Settlement of America and growth of British Empire. Opening of India and the Orient. Beginnings of industrial and scientific revolutions. Augustan age and Enlightenment.	Development of American and other colonial dialects. Spread of English around the world; borrowings from many languages. Johnson's Dictionary. Prescriptive grammarians (Lowth).
1800– Recent and Present- Day English	Independence and expansion of U.S. General education and literacy. Acceleration of scientific, industrial, and technological research and development. Journalism, telephone, radio, motion pictures, television.	Growth of scientific and technical vocabularies. English as dominant world language. Development of linguistics. Oxford, Century, and Merriam-Webster dictionaries. Extensive study and teaching of grammar.

Abbreviations in This Work

A.&M.	Agricultural and Mechanical	*criminol*	criminologist	*LGk*	Late Greek	*physiol*	physiologist
ab	about	*d*	died	*LHeb*	Late Hebrew	*pl*	plural
abbr	abbreviation	*D*	Dutch	*lit*	literally, literary	*Pol*	Polish
abl	ablative	*Dan*	Danish	*Lith*	Lithuanian	*polit*	political, politician
Acad	Academy	*dat*	dative	*LL*	Late Latin		
acc	accusative	*dau*	daughter	*long*	longitude	*pop*	population
act	active	*def*	definite	*m*	miles	*Port*	Portuguese
A.D.	anno Domini	*deriv*	derivative	*manuf*	manufacturer	*pp*	past participle
adj	adjective	*dial*	dialect	*masc*	masculine	*prec*	preceding
adv	adverb	*dim*	diminutive	*math*	mathematician	*prep*	preposition
AF	Anglo-French	*disc*	discovered	*MBret*	Middle Breton	*pres*	present, president
AFB	Air Force Base	*Dor*	Doric	*MD*	Middle Dutch		
Afrik	Afrikaans	*dram*	dramatist	*ME*	Middle English	*prob*	probably
Agric	Agriculture	*Du*	Dutch	*Mech*	Mechanical	*pron*	pronoun, pronunciation
Alb	Albanian	*DV*	Douay Version	*Med*	Medical		
alter	alteration	*e*	eastern	*Mex*	Mexican, Mexico	*pronunc*	pronunciation
Am	America, American	*E*	east, eastern, English	*MexSp*	Mexican Spanish	*Prov*	Provençal
				MF	Middle French	*prp*	present participle
Amer	American	*econ*	economist	*MFlem*	Middle Flemish		
AmerF	American French	*Ed*	Education	*MGk*	Middle Greek	*Pruss*	Prussian
AmerInd	American Indian	*educ*	educator	*MHG*	Middle High German	*pseud*	pseudonym
		EGmc	East Germanic			*psychol*	psychologist
AmerSp	American Spanish	*Egypt*	Egyptian	*mil*	military	*R.C.*	Roman Catholic
anc	ancient, anciently	*emp*	emperor	*min*	minister		
ant	antonym	*Eng*	England, English	*MIr*	Middle Irish	*redupl*	reduplication
anthropol	anthropologist, anthropology	*equiv*	equivalent	*ML*	Medieval Latin	*refl*	reflexive
		Esk	Eskimo	*MLG*	Middle Low German	*rel*	relative
aor	aorist	*esp*	especially	*modif*	modification	*resp*	respectively
Ar	Arabic	*est*	estimated	*MPer*	Middle Persian	*rev*	revolution
Arab	Arabian	*Eth*	Ethiopic	*MS*	manuscript	*Rom*	Roman
Aram	Aramaic	*ethnol*	ethnologist	*mt*	mountain	*RSV*	Revised Standard Version
archaeol	archaeologist	*F*	Fahrenheit, French	*Mt*	Mount		
Arm	Armenian	*fem*	feminine	*MW*	Middle Welsh	*Rum*	Rumanian
art	article	*Finn*	Finnish	*n*	northern, noun	*Russ*	Russian
Assyr	Assyrian	*fl*	flourished	*N*	north, northern	*S*	south, southern
astron	astronomer, astronomy	*Flem*	Flemish	*naut*	nautical	*Sc*	Scotch, Scots
		fr	from	*NE*	New England	*Scand*	Scandinavian
attrib	attributive	*Fr*	France, French	*neut*	neuter	*ScGael*	Scottish Gaelic
atty	attorney	*freq*	frequentative	*NewEng*	New England	*Sch*	School
aug	augmentative	*Fris*	Frisian	*NGk*	New Greek	*Scot*	Scotland, Scottish
Austral	Australian	*ft*	feet	*NGmc*	North Germanic		
Av	Avestan	*fut*	future	*NHeb*	New Hebrew	*secy*	secretary
AV	Authorized Version	*G*	German	*NL*	New Latin	*Sem*	Seminary, Semitic
b	born	*Gael*	Gaelic	*nom*	nominative		
Bab	Babylonian	*gen*	general, genitive	*nonstand*	nonstandard	*Serb*	Serbian
bacteriol	bacteriologist	*Ger*	German	*Norw*	Norwegian	*Shak*	Shakespeare
B.C.	before Christ, British Columbia	*Gk*	Greek	*nov*	novelist	*sing*	singular
		Gmc	Germanic	*n pl*	noun plural	*Skt*	Sanskrit
Belg	Belgian	*Goth*	Gothic	*obs*	obsolete	*Slav*	Slavic
Beng	Bengali	*gov*	governor	*OCatal*	Old Catalan	*So Afr*	South Africa
bib	biblical	*govt*	government	*occas*	occasionally	*sociol*	sociologist
biochem	biochemist	*Gr Brit*	Great Britain	*OE*	Old English	*Sp, Span*	Spanish
Braz	Brazilian	*Heb*	Hebrew	*OF*	Old French	*specif*	specifically
Bret	Breton	*hist*	historian	*OFris*	Old Frisian	*spp*	species
Brit	Britain, British	*Hitt*	Hittite	*OHG*	Old High German	*St*	Saint
bro	brother	*Hung*	Hungarian	*OIr*	Old Irish	*Ste*	Sainte
Bulg	Bulgarian	*I*	island	*OIt*	Old Italian	*subj*	subjunctive
C	centigrade, College	*Icel*	Icelandic	*OL*	Old Latin	*substand*	substandard
		IE	Indo-European	*ON*	Old Norse	*superl*	superlative
Canad	Canadian	*imit*	imitative	*ONF*	Old North French	*Sw, Swed*	Swedish
CanF	Canadian French	*imper*	imperative			*syn*	synonym, synonymy
		incho	inchoative	*OPer*	Old Persian		
Cant	Cantonese	*indef*	indefinite	*OPg*	Old Portuguese	*Syr*	Syriac
cap	capital, capitalized	*indic*	indicative	*OProv*	Old Provençal	*Tag*	Tagalog
		infin	infinitive	*OPruss*	Old Prussian	*Tech*	Technology
Catal	Catalan	*Inst*	Institute	*orig*	originally	*theol*	theologian
caus	causative	*instr*	instrumental	*ORuss*	Old Russian	*Theol*	Theological
Celt	Celtic	*intens*	intensive	*OS*	Old Saxon	*Toch*	Tocharian
cen	central	*interj*	interjection	*OSlav*	Old Slavic	*trans*	translation
cent	century	*interrog*	interrogative	*OSp*	Old Spanish	*treas*	treasury
chem	chemist	*Ion*	Ionic	*OW*	Old Welsh	*Turk*	Turkish
Chin	Chinese	*Ir*	Irish	*PaG*	Pennsylvania German	*U*	University
comb	combining	*IrGael*	Irish Gaelic			*usu*	usually
Comm	Community	*irreg*	irregular	*part*	participle	*var*	variant
compar	comparative	*ISV*	International Scientific Vocabulary	*pass*	passive	*vb*	verb
Confed	Confederate			*Pek*	Pekingese	*vi*	verb intransitive
conj	conjugation, conjunction	*It, Ital*	Italian	*Per, Pers*	Persian		
		Jap	Japanese	*perf*	perfect	*VL*	Vulgar Latin
		Jav	Javanese	*perh*	perhaps	*voc*	vocative
constr	construction	*L*	Latin	*pers*	person	*vt*	verb transitive
contr	contraction	*LaF*	Louisiana French	*Pg*	Portuguese	*W*	Welsh, west, western
Copt	Coptic	*lat*	latitude	*philos*	philosopher		
Corn	Cornish	*Lat*	Latin	*PhilSp*	Philippine Spanish	*WGmc*	West Germanic
		LG	Low German			*zool*	zoologist

Pronunciation Symbols

ə .....**ba**nana, c**o**llide, **a**but

ˈə, ˌə .....h**u**mdr**u**m, ab**u**t

ᵊ .....immediately preceding \l\, \n\, \m\, \ŋ\, as in battle, mitten, eaten, and sometimes cap and bells \-ᵊm-\, lock and key \-ᵊŋ-\; immediately following \l\, \m\, \r\, as often in French table, prisme, titre

ər .....**oper**ation, furth**er**, urg**er**

ˈər-, ˈə-r .....as in two different pronunciations of hurry \ˈhər-ē, ˈhə-rē\

a .....m**a**t, m**a**p, m**a**d, g**a**g, sn**a**p, p**a**tch

ā .....d**ay**, f**a**de, d**a**te, **a**orta, dr**a**pe, c**a**pe

ä .....b**o**ther, c**o**t, and, with most American speakers, f**a**ther, c**a**rt

à .....f**a**ther as pronounced by speakers who do not rhyme it with b**o**ther

au̇ .....n**ow**, l**ou**d, **ou**t

b .....**b**a**b**y, ri**b**

ch .....**ch**in, na**t**ure \ˈnā-chər\ (actually, this sound is \t\ + \sh\)

d .....**d**i**d**, a**dd**er

e .....b**e**t, b**e**d, p**e**ck

ˈē, ˌē .....b**ea**t, nos**e**bl**ee**d, **e**venly, **e**asy

ē .....**ea**sy, m**ea**ly

f .....**f**i**f**ty, cu**ff**

g .....**g**o, bi**g**, **g**ift

h .....**h**at, a**h**ead

hw .....**wh**ale as pronounced by those who do not have the same pronunciation for both *whale* and *wail*

i .....t**i**p, b**a**nish, act**i**ve

ī .....s**i**te, s**i**de, b**uy**, tr**i**pe (actually, this sound is \ä\ + \i\, or \à\ + \i\)

j .....**j**ob, **g**em, e**dg**e, **j**oin, **j**u**dg**e (actually, this sound is \d\ + \zh\)

k .....**k**in, coo**k**, a**ch**e

k̲ .....German i**ch**, Bu**ch**

l̄ .....**l**i**l**y, poo**l**

m .....**m**ur**m**ur, di**m**, ny**m**ph

n .....**n**o, ow**n**

ⁿ .....indicates that a preceding vowel or diphthong is pronounced with the nasal passages open, as in French *un bon vin blanc* \œⁿ-bōⁿ-vaⁿ-blä̱ⁿ\

ŋ .....si**ng** \ˈsiŋ\, si**ng**er \ˈsiŋ-ər\, fi**ng**er \ˈfiŋ-gər\, i**n**k \ˈiŋk\

ō .....b**o**ne, kn**ow**, b**eau**

ȯ .....s**aw**, **a**ll, gn**aw**

œ .....French b**oeu**f, German H**ö**lle

ō̅e̅ .....French f**eu**, German H**ö**hle

ȯi .....c**oi**n, destr**oy**, s**aw**ing

p .....**p**e**pp**er, li**p**

r .....**r**ed, ca**r**, **r**a**r**ity

s .....**s**ource, le**ss**

sh .....with nothing between, as in **sh**y, mi**ss**ion, ma**ch**ine, **s**pe**c**ial (actually, this is a single sound, not two); with a hyphen between, two sounds as in death's-head \ˈdeths-ˌhed\

t .....**t**ie, a**tt**ack

th .....with nothing between, as in **th**in, e**th**er (actually, this is a single sound, not two); with a hyphen between, two sounds as in knighthood \ˈnīt-ˌhu̇d\

t̲h̲ .....**th**en, ei**th**er, **th**is (actually, this is a single sound, not two)

ü .....r**u**le, y**ou**th, uni**o**n \ˈyün-yən\, few \ˈfyü\

u̇ .....p**u**ll, w**oo**d, b**oo**k, curable \ˈkyu̇r-ə-bəl\

ue .....German f**ü**llen, h**ü**bsch

u̅e̅ .....French r**u**e, German f**ü**hlen

v .....**v**i**v**id, gi**v**e

w .....**w**e, a**w**ay; in some words having final \(ˌ)ō\ a variant \ə-w\ occurs before vowels, as in \ˈfäl-ə-wiŋ\, covered by the variant \ə(-w)\ at the entry word

y .....**y**ard, **y**oung, cue \ˈkyü\, union \ˈyün-yən\

ʸ .....indicates that during the articulation of the sound represented by the preceding character the front of the tongue has substantially the position it has for the articulation of the first sound of *yard*, as in French *digne* \dēnʸ\

yü .....**you**th, uni**o**n, c**ue**, f**ew**, m**u**te

yu̇ .....c**u**rable, f**u**ry

z .....**z**one, rai**s**e

zh .....with nothing between, as in vi**s**ion, a**z**ure \ˈazh-ər\ (actually, this is a single sound, not two); with a hyphen between, two sounds as in gazehound \ˈgāz-ˌhau̇nd\

\ .....slant line used in pairs to mark the beginning and end of a transcription: \ˈpen\

ˈ .....mark preceding a syllable with primary (strongest) stress: \ˈpen-mən-ˌship\

ˌ .....mark preceding a syllable with secondary (next-strongest) stress: \ˈpen-mən-ˌship\

- .....mark of syllable division

( ) .....indicate that what is symbolized between is present in some utterances but not in others: *factory* \ˈfak-t(ə-)rē\

A Dictionary of the English Language

¹**a** \'ā\ *n, pl* **a's** *or* **as** \'āz\ *often cap, often attrib* **1 a** : the 1st letter of the English alphabet **b** : a graphic representation of this letter **c** : a speech counterpart of orthographic *a* **2** : the 6th tone of a C-major scale **3** : a graphic device for reproducing the letter *a* **4** : one designated *a* esp. as the 1st in order or class **5 a** : a grade rating a student's work as superior in quality **b** : one graded or rated with an A **6** : something shaped like the letter A

²**a** \ə, (')ā\ *indefinite article* [ME, fr. OE *ān* one — more at ONE] **1** — used as a function word before singular nouns when the referent is unspecified ⟨*a* man overboard⟩ and before number collectives and some numbers ⟨*a* dozen⟩ ; used before words with an initial consonant sound **2** : the same ⟨birds of *a* feather⟩ ⟨swords all of *a* length⟩ **3 a** : used as a function word before a singular noun followed by a restrictive modifier ⟨*a* man who was here yesterday⟩ **b** : ANY ⟨*a* man who is sick can't work⟩ **c** — used as a function word before a mass noun to denote a particular type or instance ⟨*a* bronze made in ancient times⟩ ⟨glucose is *a* simple sugar⟩

³**a** \ə\ *prep* [ME, fr. OE *a-, an, on*] **1** *chiefly dial* : ON, IN, AT **2** : in, to, or for each ⟨twice *a* week⟩ ⟨five dollars *a* dozen⟩ — used before words with an initial consonant sound

⁴**a** \ə\ *vb* [ME, contr. of *have*] *archaic* : HAVE ⟨I might *a* had husbands afore now — John Bunyan⟩

⁵**a** \ə\ *prep* [ME, by contr.] : OF — often attached to the preceding word ⟨kinda⟩ ⟨lotta⟩

⁶**a** *abbr, often cap* **1** absent **2** acceleration **3** ace **4** acre **5** adult **6** alto **7** ampere **8** anode **9** answer **10** ante **11** anterior **12** are **13** area **14** author

A *symbol* angstrom unit

¹**a-** \ə\ *prefix* [ME, fr. OE] **1** : on : in : at ⟨abed⟩ **2** : in (such) a state or condition ⟨afire⟩ **3** : in (such) a manner ⟨aloud⟩ **4** : in the act or process of ⟨gone a-hunting⟩ ⟨atingle⟩

²**a-** \(')ā *also* (')a *or* (')ä *or* **an-** \(')an\ *prefix* [L & Gk; L, fr. Gk — more at UN-] : not : without ⟨asexual⟩ — *a-* before consonants other than *h* and sometimes even before *h*, *an-* before vowels and usu. before *h* ⟨achromatic⟩ ⟨ahistorical⟩ ⟨anastigmatic⟩ ⟨anharmonic⟩

-a- *comb form* [ISV] : replacing carbon esp. in a ring ⟨aza-⟩

-a \ə\ *n suffix* [NL, fr. -a (as in *magnesia*)] : OXIDE ⟨thoria⟩

aa *abbr* ana

AA *abbr* **1** Alcoholics Anonymous **2** antiaircraft **3** associate in arts **4** author's alterations

AAA *abbr* **1** Agricultural Adjustment Administration **2** American Automobile Association

AAAL *abbr* American Academy of Arts and Letters

AAAS \ˌtrip-ə-(ˌ)lā-'es\ *abbr* American Association for the Advancement of Science

AACS *abbr* Airways and Air Communications Service

AAGO *abbr* Associate, American Guild of Organists

aah \'ä, often prolonged and/or followed by ə\ *vi* : to exclaim in amazement, joy, or surprise ⟨one finds oneself oohing and ~*ing* over the exciting new TV commercials — Walter Goodman⟩ — **aah** *n*

A and M *abbr* **1** agricultural and mechanical **2** ancient and modern

A and R *abbr* artists and repertory

AAR *abbr* against all risks

aard·vark \'ärd-ˌvärk\ *n* [obs. Afrik, fr. Afrik *aard* earth + *vark* pig] : a large burrowing nocturnal African mammal (*Orycteropus afer* of the order Tubulidentata) that has an extensile tongue, powerful claws, large ears, and heavy tail and feeds on ants and termites

aard·wolf \-ˌwu̇lf\ *n* [Afrik, fr. *aard* + *wolf*] : a maned striped mammal (*Proteles cristata*) of southern and eastern Africa that resembles the related hyenas and feeds chiefly on carrion and insects

Aar·on \'ar-ən, 'er-\ *n* [LL, fr. Gk *Aarōn*, fr. Heb *Ahărōn*] : a brother of Moses and high priest of the Hebrews

Aa·ron·ic \a-'rän-ik, e-\ *adj* **1** : of or stemming from Aaron **2** : of or relating to the lower order of the Mormon priesthood

AAS *abbr* associate in applied science

AAU *abbr* Amateur Athletic Union

AAUN *abbr* American Association for the United Nations

AAUP *abbr* American Association of University Professors

AAUW *abbr* American Association of University Women

¹**Ab** \'äb, 'äv, 'ȯv\ *n* [Heb *Ābh*]: the 11th month of the civil year or the 5th month of the ecclesiastical year in the Jewish calendar — see MONTH table

²**Ab** *abbr* abortion

AB *abbr* **1** able-bodied seaman **2** airborne **3** airman basic **4** [NL *artium baccalaureus*] bachelor of arts

ab- *prefix* [ME, fr. OF & L; OF, fr. L *ab-, abs-, a-*, fr. *ab, a* — more at OF]: from : away : off ⟨abaxial⟩ ⟨abstrict⟩

aba \ə-'bä, ä-'bä\ *n* [Ar '*abā*'] **1** : a fabric woven from the hair of camels or goats **2** : a loose sleeveless outer garment worn by Arabs

ABA *abbr* **1** American Bankers Association **2** American Bar Association **3** American Basketball Association **4** American Booksellers Association

ab·a·ca \ˌab-ə-'kä\ *n* [Sp *abacá*, fr. Tag *abaká*] **1** : a fiber obtained from the leafstalk of a banana (*Musa textilis*) native to the Philippines — called also Manila hemp **2** : the plant that yields abaca

aback \ə-'bak\ *adv* **1** *archaic* : BACKWARD, BACK **2** : in a position to catch the wind upon the forward surface of a square sail **3** : by surprise : UNAWARES ⟨was taken ~ by her sharp retort⟩

abac·te·ri·al \ˌā-(ˌ)bak-'tir-ē-əl\ *adj* : not caused by or characterized by the presence of bacteria ⟨an ~ inflammation⟩

aba·cus \'ab-ə-kəs, ə-'bak-əs\ *n, pl* **aba·ci** \'ab-ə-ˌsī, -ˌkē\ *or* **aba·cus·es** [L, fr. Gk *abax, abax*, lit., slab] **1** : a slab that forms the uppermost member or division of the capital of a column **2** : an instrument for performing calculations by sliding counters along rods or in grooves

abacus 2

¹**abaft** \ə-'baft\ *adv* [¹*a-* + *baft* (aft)] : toward or at the stern : AFT

²**abaft** *prep* : to the rear of; *specif* : toward the stern from

ab·a·lo·ne \ˌab-ə-'lō-nē\ *n* [AmerSp *abulón*] : any of a genus (*Haliotis*) of rock-clinging gastropod mollusks that have a flattened shell slightly spiral in form, lined with mother-of-pearl, and with a row of apertures along its outer edge

¹**aban·don** \ə-'ban-dən\ *vt* [ME *abandounen*, fr. MF *abandoner*, fr. *abandon*, n., surrender, fr. *a bandon* in one's power] **1** : to give up with the intent of never again claiming a right or interest in **2** : to withdraw from often in the face of danger or encroachment ⟨~ ship⟩ **3** : to withdraw protection, support, or help from **4** : to give (oneself) over unrestrainedly to a feeling or emotion **5 a** : to cease from maintaining, practicing, or using ⟨immigrants slow to ~ their native language⟩ **b** : to cease intending or attempting to perform ⟨~ed their attempts to escape⟩ — **aban·don·er** *n* — **aban·don·ment** \-dən-mənt\ *n*

syn **1** ABANDON, DESERT, FORSAKE *shared meaning element* : to give up completely. ABANDON tends to suggest complete disinterest in the fate of what is given up ⟨abandon an old car⟩ ⟨abandon a too difficult task⟩ DESERT implies a relationship (as of occupancy or guardianship); it can suggest desolation ⟨deserted farms growing up to brush⟩ or culpability ⟨soldiers who desert their posts⟩ FORSAKE implies a breaking of a close association by repudiation or renunciation ⟨young men forsake their parents to form families of their own⟩ *ant* reclaim

2 see RELINQUISH *ant* cherish (as hopes), restrain (oneself)

²**abandon** *n* **1** : a thorough yielding to natural impulses **2** : ENTHUSIASM, EXUBERANCE *syn* see UNCONSTRAINT

aban·doned \ə-'ban-dənd\ *adj* **1** : given up : FORSAKEN **2** : wholly free from restraint

à bas \ä-'bä\ [F] : down with ⟨*à bas* the profiteers⟩

abase \ə-'bās\ *vt* **abased; abas·ing** [ME *abassen*, fr. MF *abaisser*, fr. *a-* (fr. L *ad-*) + (assumed) VL *bassiare* to lower] **1** *archaic* : to lower physically **2** : to lower in rank, office, prestige, or esteem — **abase·ment** \-'bā-smənt\ *n*

syn ABASE, DEMEAN, DEBASE, DEGRADE, HUMBLE, HUMILIATE *shared meaning element* : to lessen in dignity or status *ant* exalt, extol

abash \ə-'bash\ *vt* [ME *abaishen*, fr. (assumed) MF *abaiss-, abair* to astonish, alter. of MF *esbair*, fr. *ex-* + *baer* to yawn — more at

ə abut	ᵊ kitten	ər further	a back	ā bake
				ä cot, cart
au̇ out	ch chin	e less	ē easy	g gift	i trip	ī life
j joke	ŋ sing	ō flow	ȯ flaw	ȯi coin	th thin	t̶h̶ this
ü loot	u̇ foot	y yet	yü few	yu̇ furious	zh vision

ABEYANCE] : to destroy the self-possession or self-confidence of : DISCONCERT ***syn*** see EMBARRASS ***ant*** embolden, reassure — **abash·ment** \-mənt\ *n*

abate \ə-'bāt\ *vb* **abat·ed; abat·ing** [ME *abaten,* fr. OF *abattre* to beat down — more at REBATE] *vt* **1** : to put an end to : NULLIFY ⟨~ a nuisance⟩ **2 a** : to reduce in degree or intensity : MODERATE **b** : to reduce in value or amount : make less esp. by way of relief ⟨~ a tax⟩ **3** : DEDUCT, OMIT ⟨~ part of the price⟩ **4 a** : to beat down or cut away so as to leave a figure in relief **b** *obs* : BLUNT **5** : DEPRIVE ~ *vi* **1** : to decrease in force or intensity **2 a** : to become defeated or become null or void **b** : to decrease in amount or value — **abat·er** *n*

syn **1** see DECREASE ***ant*** augment, accelerate (*as speed*), intensify (*as hopes, a fever*)

2 ABATE, SUBSIDE, WANE, EBB *shared meaning element* : to die down in force or intensity ***ant*** rise, revive

abate·ment \ə-'bāt-mənt\ *n* **1** : the act or process of abating : the state of being abated **2** : an amount abated; *esp* : a deduction from the full amount of a tax

ab·a·tis \'ab-ə-ˌtē, 'ab-ət-əs\ *n, pl* **ab·a·tis** \'ab-ə-ˌtēz\ *or* **ab·a·tis·es** \-ət-ə-səz\ [F, fr. *abattre*] : a defensive obstacle formed by felled trees with sharpened branches facing the enemy

A battery *n* : a battery used to heat the filaments or cathode heaters of electron tubes

ab·at·toir \'ab-ə-ˌtwär\ *n* [F, fr. *abattre*] : SLAUGHTERHOUSE

ab·ax·i·al \(')a-'bak-sē-əl\ *adj* : situated out of or directed away from the axis

ab·ba·cy \'ab-ə-sē\ *n, pl* **-cies** [ME *abbatie,* fr. LL *abbatia*] : the office, dignity, jurisdiction, or tenure of an abbot

Ab·bas·id \ə-'bas-əd, 'ab-ə-səd\ *n* : a member of a dynasty of caliphs ruling the Muslim Empire (750–1258) and claiming descent from Abbas the uncle of Muhammad

ab·ba·tial \ə-'bā-shəl, a-\ *adj* : of or relating to an abbot, abbess, or abbey

ab·bé \a-'bā, 'ab-ˌā\ *n* [F, fr. LL *abbat-, abbas*] : a member of the French secular clergy in major or minor orders — used as a title

ab·bess \'ab-əs\ *n* [ME *abbesse,* fr. OF, fr. LL *abbatissa,* fem. of *abbat-, abbas*] : a woman who is the superior of a convent of nuns

Abbe·vil·li·an \ˌab-(ə-)'vil-ē-ən\ *adj* [*Abbeville, France*] : of or relating to an early lower Paleolithic culture characterized by bifacial stone hand axes

ab·bey \'ab-ē\ *n, pl* **abbeys** [ME, fr. OF *abaïe,* fr. LL *abbatia* abbey, fr. *abbat-, abbas*] **1 a** : a monastery ruled by an abbot **b** : a convent ruled by an abbess **2** : an abbey church

ab·bot \'ab-ət\ *n* [ME *abbod,* fr. OE, fr. LL *abbat-, abbas,* fr. LGk *abbas,* fr. Aram *abbā* father] : the superior of a monastery for men

ab·bre·vi·ate \ə-'brē-vē-ˌāt\ *vt* **-at·ed; -at·ing** [ME *abbreviaten,* fr. LL *abbreviatus,* pp. of *abbreviare* — more at ABRIDGE] : to make briefer; *esp* : to reduce to a shorter form intended to stand for the whole ***syn*** see SHORTEN ***ant*** lengthen — **ab·bre·vi·a·tor** \-ˌāt-ər\ *n*

ab·bre·vi·a·tion \ə-ˌbrē-vē-'ā-shən\ *n* **1** : the act or result of abbreviating : ABRIDGMENT **2** : a shortened form of a written word or phrase used in place of the whole ⟨*amt* is an ~ for *amount*⟩

[1]**ABC** \ˌā-(ˌ)bē-'sē\ *n, pl* **ABC's** *or* **ABCs** \-'sēz\ **1** : ALPHABET — usu. used in pl. **2 a** : the rudiments of reading, writing, and spelling — usu. used in pl. **b** : the rudiments of a subject

[2]**ABC** *abbr* **1** American Bowling Congress **2** American Broadcasting Company **3** Australian Broadcasting Company

ABCD *abbr* accelerated business collection and delivery

ABC powers *n pl, often cap P* : Argentina, Brazil, and Chile

ABC soil *n* : a soil that has a well-differentiated profile with distinct A-, B-, and C-horizons

abd *or* **abdom** *abbr* abdomen; abdominal

ABD *abbr* all but dissertation

Ab·di·as \ab-'dī-əs\ *n* [LL, fr. Gk] : OBADIAH

ab·di·cate \'ab-di-ˌkāt\ *vb* **-cat·ed; -cat·ing** [L *abdicatus,* pp. of *abdicare,* fr. *ab-* + *dicare* to proclaim — more at DICTION] *vt* : to relinquish (as sovereign power) formally ~ *vi* : to renounce a throne, high office, dignity, or function — **ab·di·ca·ble** \-kə-bəl\ *adj* — **ab·di·ca·tion** \ˌab-di-'kā-shən\ *n* — **ab·di·ca·tor** \'ab-di-ˌkāt-ər\ *n*

syn ABDICATE, RENOUNCE, RESIGN *shared meaning element* : to give up formally or definitely ***ant*** assume (*as power, office*), usurp

ab·do·men \'ab-də-mən, ab-'dō-mən\ *n* [MF & L; MF, fr. L] **1** : the part of the body between the thorax and the pelvis; *also* : the cavity of this part of the trunk containing the chief viscera **2** : the posterior section of the body behind the thorax in an arthropod — see INSECT illustration — **ab·dom·i·nal** \ab-'däm-ən-ᵊl\ *adj* — **ab·dom·i·nal·ly** \-ē\ *adv*

ab·duce \ab-'d(y)üs\ *vt* **ab·duced; ab·duc·ing** [L *abducere*] : ABDUCT

ab·du·cens \ab-'d(y)ü-ˌsenz\ *n, pl* **ab·du·cen·tes** \ˌab-d(y)ù-'sent-(ˌ)ēz\ : ABDUCENS NERVE

abducens nerve *n* [NL *abducent; abducens,* fr. L, prp.] : either of the 6th pair of cranial nerves which are motor nerves that supply muscles of the eye — called also *abducent nerve*

ab·du·cent \ab-'d(y)üs-ᵊnt\ *adj* [L *abducent-, abducens,* prp. of *abducere*] : serving to abduct ⟨an ~ muscle⟩

ab·duct \ab-'dəkt\ *vt* [L *abductus,* pp. of *abducere,* lit., to lead away, fr. *ab-* + *ducere* to lead — more at TOW] **1** : to carry off (as a person) by force **2** : to draw away (as a limb) from a position near or parallel to the median axis of the body; *also* : to move (similar parts) apart — **ab·duc·tor** \-'dək-tər\ *n*

ab·duc·tion \ab-'dək-shən\ *n* **1** : the action of abducting : the condition of being abducted **2** : the unlawful carrying away of a woman for marriage or intercourse

abeam \ə-'bēm\ *adv or adj* : on a line at right angles to a ship's keel

[1]**abe·ce·dar·i·an** \ˌā-bē-(ˌ)sē-'der-ē-ən\ *n* [ME *abecedary,* fr. ML *abecedarium* alphabet, fr. LL, neut. of *abecedarius* of the alphabet, fr. the letters *a* + *b* + *c* + *d*] : one learning the rudiments of something (as the alphabet)

[2]**abecedarian** *adj* **1 a** : of or relating to the alphabet **b** : alphabetically arranged **2** : RUDIMENTARY

abed \ə-'bed\ *adv or adj* : in bed

Abel \'ā-bəl\ *n* [LL, fr. Gk, fr. Heb *Hebhel*] : a son of Adam and Eve killed by his brother Cain

Abe·li·an \ə-'bē-lē-ən\ *adj* [Niels *Abel* †1829 Norw. mathematician] : COMMUTATIVE 2 ⟨~ group⟩ ⟨~ ring⟩

abel·mosk \'ā-bəl-ˌmäsk\ *n* [deriv. of Ar *abū -l- misk* father of the musk] : a bushy herb (*Hibiscus moschatus*) of the mallow family native to tropical Asia and the East Indies whose musky seeds are used in perfumery and in flavoring coffee

Ab·er·deen An·gus \ˌab-ər-ˌdē-'naŋ-gəs\ *n* [*Aberdeen & Angus,* counties in Scotland] : any of a breed of black hornless beef cattle originating in Scotland

[1]**ab·er·rant** \a-'ber-ənt\ *adj* [L *aberrant-, aberrans,* prp. of *aberrare* to go astray, fr. *ab-* + *errare* to wander, err] **1** : straying from the right or normal way **2** : deviating from the usual or natural type : ATYPICAL — **ab·er·rance** \-ən(t)s\ *n* — **ab·er·ran·cy** \-ən-sē\ *n* — **ab·er·rant·ly** *adv*

[2]**aberrant** *n* **1** : an aberrant natural group, individual, or structure **2** : a person whose behavior departs substantially from the standard

ab·er·rat·ed \'ab-ə-ˌrāt-əd\ *adj* [L *aberratus*] : ABERRANT

ab·er·ra·tion \ˌab-ə-'rā-shən\ *n* [L *aberratus,* pp. of *aberrare*] **1** : the act of being aberrant esp. from a moral standard or normal state **2** : failure of a mirror, refracting surface, or lens to produce exact point-to-point correspondence between an object and its image **3** : unsoundness or disorder of the mind **4** : a small periodic change of apparent position in celestial bodies due to the combined effect of the motion of light and the motion of the observer **5** : an aberrant organ or individual : SPORT 5 — **ab·er·ra·tion·al** \-shnəl, -shən-ᵊl\ *adj*

abet \ə-'bet\ *vt* **abet·ted; abet·ting** [ME *abetten,* fr. MF *abeter,* fr. OF, fr. *a-* (fr. L *ad-*) + *beter* to bait, of Gmc origin; akin to OE *bǣtan* to bait] **1** : to actively second and encourage (an activity or plan) : FORWARD **2** : to assist or support in the achievement of a purpose ⟨*abetted* the cause of justice⟩ ***syn*** see INCITE ***ant*** deter — **abet·ment** \-mənt\ *n* — **abet·tor** *or* **abet·ter** \-'bet-ər\ *n*

abey·ance \ə-'bā-ən(t)s\ *n* [MF *abeance* expectation, fr. *abaer* to desire, fr. *a-* + *baer* to yawn, fr. ML *batare*] **1** : a lapse in succession during which there is no person in whom a title is vested **2** : temporary inactivity : SUSPENSION

abey·ant \-ənt\ *adj* [back-formation fr. *abeyance*] : being in abeyance ***syn*** see LATENT ***ant*** operative, active

ab·hor \əb-'hò(ə)r, ab-\ *vt* **ab·horred; ab·hor·ring** [ME *abhorren,* fr. L *abhorrēre,* fr. *ab-* + *horrēre* to shudder — more at HORROR] **1** : to regard with extreme repugnance : LOATHE **2** : to turn aside or keep away from esp. in scorn or shuddering fear : REJECT ⟨the university should ~ mediocrity — Walter Moberly⟩

syn see HATE ***ant*** admire (*as people or deeds*), enjoy (*things which are a matter of taste*) — **ab·hor·rer** \-'hòr-ər\ *n*

ab·hor·rence \əb-'hòr-ən(t)s, -'här-\ *n* **1 a** : the act or state of abhorring **b** : the feeling of one who abhors **2** : one that is abhorred

ab·hor·rent \-ənt\ *adj* [L *abhorrent-, abhorrens,* prp. of *abhorrēre*] **1 a** *archaic* : strongly opposed **b** : feeling or showing abhorrence **2** : not agreeable : CONTRARY ⟨a notion ~ to their philosophy⟩ **3** : being so repugnant as to stir up positive antagonism ⟨acts ~ to every right-minded person⟩ ***syn*** see REPUGNANT ***ant*** congenial — **ab·hor·rent·ly** *adv*

Abib \ä-'vēv\ *n* [Heb Ābhībh, lit., ear of grain] : the 1st month of the ancient Hebrew calendar corresponding to Nisan

abid·ance \ə-'bīd-ᵊn(t)s\ *n* **1** : an act or state of abiding : CONTINUANCE **2** : COMPLIANCE ⟨~ by the rules⟩

abide \ə-'bīd\ *vb* **abode** \-'bōd\ *or* **abid·ed; abid·ing** [ME *abiden,* fr. OE *ābīdan,* fr. *ā-,* perfective prefix + *bīdan* to bide; akin to OHG *ir-,* perfective prefix] *vt* **1** *archaic* : to wait for : AWAIT **2 a** : to endure without yielding : WITHSTAND **b** : to bear patiently : TOLERATE ⟨cannot ~ such bigots⟩ **3** : to accept without objection ~ *vi* **1** : to remain stable or fixed in a state **2** : to continue in a place : SOJOURN ***syn*** see STAY, CONTINUE, BEAR — **abid·er** *n* — **abide by 1** : to conform to **2** : to acquiesce in

abid·ing \ə-'bīd-iŋ\ *adj* : ENDURING, CONTINUING ⟨an ~ interest in nature⟩ — **abid·ing·ly** \-iŋ-lē\ *adv*

ab·i·gail \'ab-ə-ˌgāl\ *n* [*Abigail,* servant in *The Scornful Lady,* a play by Francis Beaumont & John Fletcher] : a lady's personal maid

abil·i·ty \ə-'bil-ət-ē\ *n, pl* **-ties** [ME *abilite,* fr. MF *habilité,* fr. L *habilitat-, habilitas,* fr. *habilis* apt, skillful — more at ABLE] **1 a** : the quality or state of being able; *esp* : physical, mental, or legal power to perform **b** : competence in doing : SKILL **2** : natural talent or acquired proficiency : APTITUDE ⟨children whose *abilities* warrant higher education⟩

-abil·i·ty *also* **-ibil·i·ty** \ə-'bil-ət-ē\ *n suffix* [ME *-abilite, -ibilite,* fr. MF *-abilité, -ibilité,* fr. L *-abilitas, -ibilitas,* fr. *-abilis, -ibilis,* -able + *-tas* -ty] : capacity, fitness, or tendency to act or be acted on in a (specified) way ⟨ensil*ability*⟩

ab in·i·tio \ˌab-ə-'nish-ē-ˌō\ *adv* [L] : from the beginning

abio·gen·e·sis \ˌā-ˌbī-ō-'jen-ə-səs\ *n* [NL, fr. [2]*a-* + *bio-* + L *genesis*] : the origination of living from lifeless matter — **abio·ge·net·ic** \-ō-jə-'net-ik\ *or* **abio·ge·net·i·cal** \-i-kəl\ *adj* — **abio·ge·net·i·cal·ly** \-k(ə-)lē\ *adv* — **abi·og·e·nist** \ˌā-(ˌ)bī-'äj-ə-nəst\ *n*

abi·o·log·i·cal \ˌā-ˌbī-ə-'läj-i-kəl\ *adj* : not biological; *esp* : not involving or produced by organisms ⟨~ synthesis of amino acids⟩ — **abi·o·log·i·cal·ly** \-i-k(ə-)lē\ *adv*

abi·ot·ic \ˌā-(ˌ)bī-'ät-ik\ *adj* : not biotic : ABIOLOGICAL — **abi·ot·i·cal·ly** \-i-k(ə-)lē\ *adv*

ab·ject \'ab-ˌjekt, ab-'\ *adj* [ME, fr. L *abjectus,* fr. pp. of *abicere* to cast off, fr. *ab-* + *jacere* to throw — more at JET] **1** : sunk to or existing in a low state or condition ⟨to lowest pitch of ~ fortune thou art fallen —John Milton⟩ **2 a** : cast down in spirit : SERVILE, SPIRITLESS ⟨a man made ~ by suffering⟩ **b** : showing utter hopelessness or resignation ⟨~ surrender⟩ **3** : expressing or offered in a humble and often ingratiating spirit ⟨~ flattery⟩ ⟨an ~ apology⟩ ***syn*** see MEAN ***ant*** exalted (*as in rank or mood*), imperious (*as in manner*) — **ab·ject·ly** \'ab-ˌjek-(t)lē, ab-'\ *adv* — **ab·ject·ness** \-ˌjek(t)-nəs, -'jek(t)-\ *n*

ab·jec·tion \ab-ˈjek-shən\ *n* **1 :** a low or downcast state **:** DEGRADATION **2 :** the act of making abject **:** HUMBLING, REJECTION ⟨I protest . . . this vile ~ of youth to age — G. B. Shaw⟩
ab·ju·ra·tion \ˌab-jə-ˈrā-shən\ *n* **1 :** the act or process of abjuring **2 :** an oath of abjuring
ab·jure \ab-ˈju̇(ə)r\ *vt* **ab·jured; ab·jur·ing** [ME *abjuren,* fr. MF or L; MF *abjurer,* fr. L *abjurare,* fr. *ab-* + *jurare* to swear — more at JURY] **1 a :** to renounce upon oath **b :** to reject solemnly **2 :** to abstain from **:** AVOID ⟨~ extravagance⟩ — **ab·jur·er** *n*
syn ABJURE, RENOUNCE, FORSWEAR, RECANT, RETRACT *shared meaning element* **:** to withdraw a vow or a given word ***ant*** pledge (*as allegiance, a vow*), elect (*as a way of life, an end*)
abl *abbr* ablative
ab·late \a-ˈblāt\ *vb* **ab·lat·ed; ab·lat·ing** [L *ablatus* (suppletive pp. of *auferre* to remove, fr. *au-* away + *ferre* to carry), fr. *ab-* + *latus,* suppletive pp. of *ferre* — more at UKASE, BEAR, TOLERATE] *vt* **:** to remove by cutting, erosion, melting, evaporation, or vaporization ~ *vi* **:** to become ablated
ab·la·tion \a-ˈblā-shən\ *n* **:** the process of ablating: as **a :** surgical removal **b :** removal of a part (as the outside of a nose cone) by melting or vaporization
1**ab·la·tive** \ˈab-lət-iv\ *adj* **:** of, relating to, or constituting a grammatical case expressing typically the relations of separation and source and also frequently such relations as cause or instrument — **ablative** *n*
2**ab·la·tive** \a-ˈblāt-iv\ *adj* **1 :** of or relating to ablation **2 :** tending to ablate ⟨~ material on a nose cone⟩ — **ab·la·tive·ly** *adv*
ablative absolute \ˌab-lət-iv-\ *n* **:** a construction in Latin in which a noun or pronoun and its adjunct both in the ablative case form together an adverbial phrase expressing generally the time, cause, or an attendant circumstance of an action
ab·laut \ˈäp-ˌlau̇t, ˈab-\ *n* [G, fr. *ab* away from + *laut* sound] **:** a systematic variation of vowels in the same root or affix or in related roots or affixes esp. in the Indo-European languages that is usu. paralleled by differences in use or meaning (as in *sing, sang, sung, song*)
ablaze \ə-ˈblāz\ *adj or adv* **1 :** being on fire **2 :** having radiant light or bright color **:** GLOWING ⟨his face all ~ with excitement — Bram Stoker⟩
able \ˈā-bəl\ *adj* **abler** \-b(ə-)lər\; **ablest** \-b(ə-)ləst\ [ME, fr. MF, fr. L *habilis* apt, fr. *habēre* to have — more at HABIT] **1 a :** having sufficient power, skill, or resources to accomplish an object **b :** susceptible to action or treatment **2 :** marked by intelligence, knowledge, skill, or competence
syn ABLE, CAPABLE, COMPETENT, QUALIFIED *shared meaning element* **:** having power or fitness (as for work or a way of life) ***ant*** inept, unable
-able *also* **-ible** \ə-bəl\ *adj suffix* [ME, fr. OF, fr. L *-abilis, -ibilis,* fr. *-a-, -i-,* verb stem vowels + *-bilis* capable or worthy of] **1 :** capable of, fit for, or worthy of (being so acted upon or toward) — chiefly in adjectives derived from verbs ⟨break*able*⟩ ⟨collect*ible*⟩ **2 :** tending, given, or liable to ⟨knowledge*able*⟩ ⟨perish*able*⟩
able-bod·ied \ˌā-bəl-ˈbäd-ēd\ *adj* **:** having a sound strong body
able-bodied seaman *n* **:** ABLE SEAMAN
able seaman *n* **:** an experienced deck-department seaman qualified to perform routine duties at sea
abloom \ə-ˈblüm\ *adj* **:** abounding with blooms **:** BLOOMING ⟨parks ~ with roses⟩
ab·lut·ed \ə-ˈblüt-əd, a-\ *adj* [back-formation fr. *ablution*] **:** washed clean
ab·lu·tion \ə-ˈblü-shən, a-ˈblü-\ *n* [ME, fr. MF or L; MF, fr. L *ablution-, ablutio,* fr. *ablutus,* pp. of *abluere* to wash away, fr. *ab-* + *lavere* to wash — more at LYE] **1 :** the washing of one's body or part of it (as in a religious rite) **2** *pl* **:** a building housing bathing and toilet facilities on a military base — **ab·lu·tion·ary** \-shə-ˌner-ē\ *adj*
ably \ˈā-blē\ *adv* **:** in an able manner
ABM \ˌā-(ˌ)bē-ˈem\ *n* **:** ANTIBALLISTIC MISSILE
abn *abbr* airborne
Ab·na·ki \ab-ˈnäk-ē\ *n, pl* **Abnaki** *or* **Abnakis** **1 :** a member of an Amerindian people of Maine and southern Quebec **2 :** an Algonquian language of the Abnaki and Penobscot peoples
ab·ne·gate \ˈab-ni-ˌgāt\ *vt* **-gat·ed; -gat·ing** [back-formation fr. *abnegation*] **1 :** SURRENDER, RELINQUISH ⟨*abnegated* his powers⟩ **2 :** DENY, RENOUNCE ⟨*abnegated* his God⟩ — **ab·ne·ga·tor** \-ˌgāt-ər\ *n*
ab·ne·ga·tion \ˌab-ni-ˈgā-shən\ *n* [LL *abnegation-, abnegatio,* fr. L *abnegatus,* pp. of *abnegare* to refute, fr. *ab-* + *negare* to deny — more at NEGATE] **:** DENIAL; *esp* **:** SELF-DENIAL
1**ab·nor·mal** \(ˈ)ab-ˈnȯr-məl\ *adj* [F *anormal,* fr. ML *anormalis,* fr. L *a-* + LL *normalis* normal] **1 :** deviating from the normal or average; *esp* **:** markedly irregular ⟨~ behavior⟩ **2 :** characterized by mental deficiency or disorder ⟨~ children⟩ — **ab·nor·mal·ly** \-mə-lē\ *adv*
2**abnormal** *n* **:** an abnormal person
ab·nor·mal·i·ty \ˌab-nər-ˈmal-ət-ē, -(ˌ)nȯr-\ *n, pl* **-ties** **1 :** the quality or state of being abnormal **2 :** something abnormal
abnormal psychology *n* **:** the psychology of mental and behavioral disorder **:** PSYCHOPATHOLOGY
abo \ˈab-(ˌ)ō\ *n, pl* **ab·os** *Austral* **:** ABORIGINE
1**aboard** \ə-ˈbō(ə)rd, -ˈbȯ(ə)rd\ *adv or adj* **1 :** on, onto, or within a car, ship, or airplane **2 :** ALONGSIDE **3** *baseball* **:** on base
2**aboard** *prep* **:** ON, ONTO, WITHIN ⟨go ~ ship⟩ ⟨~ a plane⟩
abode \ə-ˈbōd\ *n* [ME *abod,* fr. *abiden* to abide] **1** *obs* **:** WAIT, DELAY **2 :** a temporary stay **:** SOJOURN **3 :** the place where one abides **:** HOME
aboil \ə-ˈbȯi(ə)l\ *adj or adv* **1 :** being at the boiling point **:** BOILING **2 :** intensely excited or stirred up ⟨the meeting was ~ with controversy⟩
abol·ish \ə-ˈbäl-ish\ *vt* [ME *abolisshen,* fr. MF *aboliss-,* stem of *abolir,* fr. L *abolēre,* prob. back-formation fr. *abolescere* to disappear, fr. *ab-* + *-olescere* (as in *adolescere* to grow up) — more at ADULT] **1 :** to do away with wholly **:** ANNUL **2 :** to destroy completely — **abol·ish·able** \-ə-bəl\ *adj* — **abol·ish·er** *n* — **abol·ish·ment** \-mənt\ *n*
syn ABOLISH, ANNIHILATE, EXTINGUISH *shared meaning element* **:** to make nonexistent or wholly ineffective or inactive ***ant*** establish
ab·o·li·tion \ˌab-ə-ˈlish-ən\ *n* [MF, fr. L *abolition-, abolitio,* fr. *abolitus,* pp. of *abolēre*] **1 :** the act of abolishing **:** the state of being abolished **2 :** the abolishing of slavery — **ab·o·li·tion·ary** \-ˈlish-ə-ˌner-ē\ *adj*
ab·o·li·tion·ism \-ˈlish-ə-ˌniz-əm\ *n* **:** principles or measures fostering abolition esp. of slavery — **ab·o·li·tion·ist** \-ˈlish-(ə-)nəst\ *n or adj*
ab·oma·sum \ˌab-ō-ˈmā-səm\ *n, pl* **-sa** \-sə\ [NL, fr. L *ab-* + *omasum* tripe of a bullock] **:** the fourth or true digestive stomach of a ruminant — **ab·oma·sal** \-səl\ *adj*
A-bomb \ˈā-ˌbäm\ *n* **:** ATOM BOMB — **A-bomb** *vb*
abom·i·na·ble \ə-ˈbäm-(ə-)nə-bəl\ *adj* **1 :** worthy of or causing disgust or hatred **:** DETESTABLE ⟨the ~ treatment of the poor⟩ **2 :** quite disagreeable or unpleasant ⟨~ weather⟩ — **abom·i·na·bly** \-blē\ *adv*
abominable snow·man \-ˈsnō-mən, -ˌman\ *n, often cap A&S* **:** a mysterious animal reported as existing in the high Himalayas and usu. thought to be a bear — called also *yeti*
abom·i·nate \ə-ˈbäm-ə-ˌnāt\ *vt* **-nat·ed; -nat·ing** [L *abominatus,* pp. of *abominari,* lit., to deprecate as an ill omen, fr. *ab-* + *omin-, omen* omen] **:** to hate or loathe intensely **:** ABHOR ***syn*** see HATE ***ant*** esteem, enjoy — **abom·i·na·tor** \-ˌnāt-ər\ *n*
abom·i·na·tion \ə-ˌbäm-ə-ˈnā-shən\ *n* **1 :** something abominable **2 :** extreme disgust and hatred **:** LOATHING
ab·oral \(ˈ)a-ˈbōr-əl, -ˈbȯr-\ *adj* **:** situated opposite to or away from the mouth — **ab·oral·ly** \-ə-lē\ *adv*
1**ab·orig·i·nal** \ˌab-ə-ˈrij-nəl, -ən-ᵊl\ *adj* **1 :** being the first of its kind present in a region and often primitive in comparison with more advanced types **2 :** of or relating to aborigines ***syn*** see NATIVE — **ab·orig·i·nal·ly** \-ē\ *adv*
2**aboriginal** *n* **:** ABORIGINE; *specif* **:** an Australian aborigine
ab·orig·i·ne \ˌab-ə-ˈrij-ə-(ˌ)nē\ *n* [L *aborigines,* pl., fr. *ab origine* from the beginning] **1 :** an aboriginal inhabitant esp. as contrasted with an invading or colonizing people **2** *pl* **:** the original fauna and flora of a geographical area
aborn·ing \ə-ˈbȯ(ə)r-niŋ\ *adv* [1*a-* + E dial. *borning* (birth)] **:** while being born or produced ⟨a resolution that died ~⟩
1**abort** \ə-ˈbȯ(ə)rt\ *vb* [L *abortare,* fr. *abortus,* pp. of *aboriri* to miscarry, fr. *ab-* + *oriri* to rise, be born — more at RISE] *vi* **1 :** to bring forth premature or stillborn offspring **2 :** to become checked in development so as to remain rudimentary or to shrink away ~ *vt* **1 a :** to give birth to prematurely **b :** to terminate the pregnancy of before term **2 a :** to terminate prematurely **:** CANCEL ⟨~ a project⟩ ⟨~ a spaceflight⟩ **b :** to stop in the early stages ⟨~ a disease⟩ — **abort·er** *n*
2**abort** *n* **:** the premature termination of the flight of an aircraft on a combat or bombing mission; *also* **:** such termination of an action, procedure, or mission relating to a rocket or spacecraft ⟨a launch ~⟩
abor·ti·fa·cient \ə-ˌbȯrt-ə-ˈfā-shənt\ *adj* **:** inducing abortion — **abortifacient** *n*
abor·tion \ə-ˈbȯr-shən\ *n* **1 :** the expulsion of a nonviable fetus: as **a :** spontaneous expulsion of a human fetus during the first 12 weeks of gestation — compare MISCARRIAGE **b :** induced abortion **2 :** MONSTROSITY **3 a :** arrest of development (as of a part or process) resulting in imperfection **b :** a result of such arrest
abor·tion·ist \-sh(ə-)nəst\ *n* **:** a producer of abortions
abor·tive \ə-ˈbȯrt-iv\ *adj* **1** *obs* **:** prematurely born **2 :** FRUITLESS, UNSUCCESSFUL **3 :** imperfectly formed or developed **4 :** tending to cut short — **abor·tive·ly** *adv* — **abor·tive·ness** *n*
ABO system \ˌā-(ˌ)bē-ˈō-\ *n* **:** the basic system of antigens of human blood behaving in heredity as an allelic unit to produce any of the four blood groups A, B, AB, or O — called also *ABO group*
abound \ə-ˈbau̇nd\ *vi* [ME *abounden,* fr. MF *abonder,* fr. L *abundare,* fr. *ab-* + *unda* wave — more at WATER] **1 :** to be present in large numbers or in great quantity **:** be prevalent **2 :** to become copiously supplied ⟨the old edition *~ed* in . . . coloured pictures — *Times Lit. Supp.*⟩ ⟨institutions ~ with evidence of his success — *Johns Hopkins Mag.*⟩
1**about** \ə-ˈbau̇t\ *adv* [ME, fr. OE *abūtan,* fr. 1*a-* + *būtan* outside — more at BUT] **1 :** on all sides **:** AROUND **2 a :** in rotation **b :** around the outside **3 a :** APPROXIMATELY **b :** ALMOST ⟨~ starved⟩ **4 :** here and there **5 :** in the vicinity **:** NEAR **6 :** in succession **:** ALTERNATELY ⟨turn ~ is fair play⟩ **7 :** in the opposite direction ⟨face ~⟩ ⟨the other way ~⟩
2**about** *prep* **1 :** on every side of **:** AROUND **2 a :** in the immediate neighborhood of **:** NEAR **b :** on or near the person of **c :** in the makeup of ⟨a mature wisdom ~ him⟩ **d :** at the command of ⟨has his wits ~ him⟩ **3 a :** engaged in **b :** on the verge of ⟨~ to join the army⟩ **4 :** with regard to **:** CONCERNING **5 :** over or in different parts of **6** — used with the negative to express intention or determination ⟨is not ~ to quit⟩
3**about** *adj* **1 :** moving from place to place; *specif* **:** out of bed **2 :** AROUND 2
about-face \ə-ˈbau̇t-ˈfās\ *n* [fr. the imper. phrase *about face*] **1 :** a 180° turn to the right from the position of attention **2 :** a reversal of direction **3 :** a reversal of attitude or point of view — **about-face** *vi*
1**above** \ə-ˈbəv\ *adv* [ME, fr. OE *abufan,* fr. *a-* + *bufan* above, fr. *be-* + *ufan* above; akin to OE *ofer* over] **1 a :** in the sky **:** OVERHEAD **b :** in or to heaven **2 a :** in or to a higher place **b :** higher on the same page or on a preceding page **c :** UPSTAIRS **3**

ə abut	ᵊ kitten	ər further	a back	ā bake	ä cot, cart
au̇ out	ch chin	e less	ē easy	g gift	i trip
ī life					
j joke	ŋ sing	ō flow	ȯ flaw	ȯi coin	th thin
t͟h this					
ü loot	u̇ foot	y yet	yü few	yu̇ furious	zh vision

: in or to a higher rank or number ⟨30 and ~⟩ **4** *archaic* : in addition : BESIDES **5** : UPSTAGE

[2]**above** *prep* **1** : in or to a higher place than : OVER **2 a** : superior to (as in rank, quality, or degree) **b** : out of reach of **c** : in preference to **d** : too proud or honorable to stoop to **3** : exceeding in number, quantity, or size : more than

[3]**above** *n, pl* **above 1 a** : something that is above **b** : a person whose name is written above **2 a** : a higher authority **b** : HEAVEN

[4]**above** *adj* : written or discussed higher on the same page or on a preceding page

above all *adv* : before every other consideration : ESPECIALLY

[1]**above·board** \ə-ˈbəv-ˌbō(ə)rd, -ˌbȯ(ə)rd\ *adv* [fr. the difficulty of cheating at cards when the hands are above the table] : in a straightforward manner : OPENLY

[2]**aboveboard** *adj* : free from all traces of deceit or duplicity ***syn*** see STRAIGHTFORWARD ***ant*** underhand, underhanded

above·ground \ə-ˈbəv-ˌgrau̇nd\ *adj* **1** : located on or above the surface of the ground **2** : existing, produced, or published by or within the establishment ⟨~ movies⟩

ab ovo \a-ˈbō-(ˌ)vō\ *adv* [L, lit., from the egg] : from the beginning

abp *abbr* archbishop

abr *abbr* abridged; abridgment

ab·ra·ca·dab·ra \ˌab-rə-kə-ˈdab-rə\ *n* [LL] **1** : a magical charm or incantation used to ward off calamity **2** : unintelligible language

abrad·ant \ə-ˈbrād-ᵊnt\ *n* : ABRASIVE

abrade \ə-ˈbrād\ *vb* **abrad·ed; abrad·ing** [L *abradere* to scrape off, fr. *ab-* + *radere* to scrape — more at RAT] *vt* **1 a** : to rub or wear away esp. by friction : ERODE **b** : to irritate or roughen by rubbing **2** : to wear down in spirit : IRRITATE, WEARY ~ *vi* : to undergo abrasion — **abrad·able** \-ˈbrād-ə-bəl\ *adj* — **abrad·er** *n*

Abra·ham \ˈā-brə-ˌham\ *n* [LL, fr. Gk *Abraam*, fr. Heb *ʼAbhrāhām*] : an Old Testament patriarch and founder of the Hebrew people

abra·sion \ə-ˈbrā-zhən\ *n* [ML *abrasion-, abrasio*, fr. L *abrasus*, pp. of *abradere*] **1 a** : a wearing, grinding, or rubbing away by friction **b** : IRRITATION **2** : an abraded area of the skin or mucous membrane

[1]**abra·sive** \ə-ˈbrā-siv, -ziv\ *adj* **1** : tending to abrade **2** : causing irritation ⟨~ manners⟩ — **abra·sive·ly** *adv* — **abra·sive·ness** *n*

[2]**abrasive** *n* : a substance (as emery or pumice) used for abrading, smoothing, or polishing

ab·re·act \ˌab-rē-ˈakt\ *vt* [part trans. of G *abreagieren*, fr. *ab* away from + *reagieren* to react] : to release (a repressed or forgotten emotion) by or as if by verbalization esp. in psychoanalysis — **ab·re·ac·tion** \-ˈak-shən\ *n*

abreast \ə-ˈbrest\ *adv or adj* **1** : beside one another with bodies in line ⟨columns of men five ~⟩ **2** : up to a particular standard or level esp. of knowledge of recent developments ⟨keeps ~ of the latest trends⟩

abridge \ə-ˈbrij\ *vt* **abridged; abridg·ing** [ME *abregen*, fr. MF *abregier*, fr. LL *abbreviare*, fr. L *ad-* + *brevis* short — more at BRIEF] **1 a** *archaic* : DEPRIVE **b** : to reduce in scope : DIMINISH ⟨attempts to ~ the right of free speech⟩ **2** : to shorten in duration or extent ⟨modern transportation that ~s distance⟩ **3** : to shorten by omission of words without sacrifice of sense : CONDENSE ***syn*** see SHORTEN ***ant*** expand, extend — **abridg·er** *n*

abridg·ment *or* **abridge·ment** \ə-ˈbrij-mənt\ *n* **1** : the action of abridging : the state of being abridged **2** : a shortened form of a work retaining the general sense and unity of the original

syn ABRIDGMENT, ABSTRACT, SYNOPSIS, CONSPECTUS, EPITOME *shared meaning element* : a shorter version of a larger work or treatment ***ant*** expansion

abroach \ə-ˈbrōch\ *adv or adj* **1** : in a condition for letting out a liquid (as wine) ⟨a cask set ~⟩ **2** : in action or agitation : ASTIR ⟨mischiefs that I set ~ —Shak.⟩

abroad \ə-ˈbrȯd\ *adv or adj* **1** : over a wide area : WIDELY **2** : away from one's home **3** : beyond the boundaries of one's country **4** : in wide circulation : ABOUT **5** : wide of the mark : ASTRAY

ab·ro·gate \ˈab-rə-ˌgāt\ *vt* **-gat·ed; -gat·ing** [L *abrogatus*, pp. of *abrogare*, fr. *ab-* + *rogare* to ask, propose a law — more at RIGHT] **1** : to abolish by authoritative action : ANNUL **2** : to do away with ***syn*** see NULLIFY ***ant*** establish, fix (*as a right or custom*) — **ab·ro·ga·tion** \ˌab-rə-ˈgā-shən\ *n*

abrupt \ə-ˈbrəpt\ *adj* [L *abruptus*, fr. pp. of *abrumpere* to break off, fr. *ab-* + *rumpere* to break — more at REAVE] **1 a** : broken off **b** : suddenly terminating as if cut or broken off ⟨~ plant filaments⟩ **2 a** : occurring without warning : UNEXPECTED ⟨~ weather changes⟩ **b** : unceremoniously curt ⟨an ~ manner⟩ **c** : marked by sudden changes in subject matter : DISCONNECTED **3** : rising or dropping sharply as if broken off ⟨a high ~ bank bounded the stream⟩ ***syn* 1** see STEEP **2** see PRECIPITATE ***ant*** deliberate, leisurely — **abrupt·ly** \ə-ˈbrəp-(t)lē\ *adv* — **abrupt·ness** \ə-ˈbrəp(t)-nəs\ *n*

abrup·tion \ə-ˈbrəp-shən\ *n* : a sudden breaking off or away

abs *abbr* **1** absolute **2** abstract

ABS *abbr* American Bible Society

ab·scess \ˈab-ˌses\ *n* [L *abscessus*, lit., act of going away, fr. *abscessus*, pp. of *abscedere* to go away, fr. *abs-, ab-* + *cedere* to go — more at CEDE] : a localized collection of pus surrounded by inflamed tissue — **ab·scessed** \-ˌsest\ *adj*

ab·scise \ab-ˈsīz\ *vb* **ab·scised; ab·scis·ing** [L *abscisus*, pp. of *abscidere*, fr. *abs-* + *caedere* to cut — more at CONCISE] *vt* : to cut off by abscission ~ *vi* : to separate by abscission

ab·scis·ic acid \ˌab-ˌsiz-ik-, -ˌsis-\ *n* [*abscision* (var. of *abscission*) + *-ic*] : a plant hormone $C_{15}H_{20}O_4$ that is widespread in nature and is made synthetically and that typically promotes leaf abscission and dormancy and has an inhibitory effect on cell elongation — called also *abscisin II, dormin*

ab·sci·sin *also* **ab·scis·sin** \ˈab-sə-sən, ab-ˈsis-ᵊn\ *n* [*abscision, abscission* + *-in*] : any of a group of plant regulatory substances orig. found in young cotton bolls that tend to promote leaf abscission and inhibit various growth processes — compare ABSCISIC ACID

ab·scis·sa \ab-ˈsis-ə\ *n, pl* **abscissas** *also* **ab·scis·sae** \-ˈsis-(ˌ)ē\ [NL, fr. L, fem. of *abscissus*, pp. of *abscindere* to cut off, fr. *ab-* + *scindere* to cut — more at SHED] : the horizontal coordinate of a point in a plane Cartesian coordinate system obtained by measuring parallel to the x-axis — compare ORDINATE

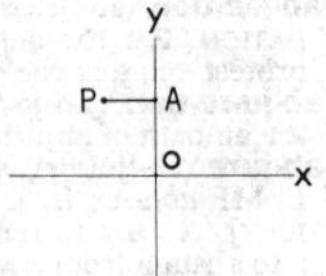

AP abscissa of point *P*

ab·scis·sion \ab-ˈsizh-ən\ *n* [L *abscission-, abscissio*, fr. *abscissus*] **1** : the act or process of cutting off : REMOVAL **2** : the natural separation of flowers, fruit, or leaves from plants at a special separation layer

ab·scond \ab-ˈskänd\ *vi* [L *abscondere* to hide away, fr. *abs-* + *condere* to store up, conceal — more at CONDIMENT] : to depart secretly and hide oneself — **ab·scond·er** *n*

ab·sence \ˈab-sən(t)s\ *n* **1** : the state of being absent **2** : the period of time that one is absent **3** : WANT, LACK ⟨an ~ of detail⟩ **4** : inattention to present surroundings or occurrences ⟨~ of mind⟩

[1]**ab·sent** \ˈab-sənt\ *adj* [ME, fr. MF, fr. L *absent-, absens*, prp. of *abesse* to be absent, fr. *ab-* + *esse* to be — more at IS] **1** : not present or attending : MISSING **2** : not existing : LACKING ⟨danger in a situation where power is ~ —M. H. Trytten⟩ **3** : INATTENTIVE, PREOCCUPIED — **ab·sent·ly** *adv*

[2]**ab·sent** \ab-ˈsent\ *vt* : to keep (oneself) away

ab·sen·tee \ˌab-sən-ˈtē\ *n* : one that is absent or that absents himself; *specif* : a proprietor that lives away from his estate or business — **absentee** *adj*

absentee ballot *n* : a ballot submitted (as by mail) in advance of an election by a voter who is unable to be present at the polls

ab·sen·tee·ism \ˌab-sən-ˈtē-ˌiz-əm\ *n* **1** : prolonged absence of an owner from his property **2** : chronic absence from duty (as work)

absentee voter *n* : a registered voter who is permitted to vote by absentee ballot

ab·sent·mind·ed \ˌab-sənt-ˈmīn-dəd\ *adj* : lost in thought and unaware of one's surroundings or action : PREOCCUPIED; *also* : given to absence of mind — **ab·sent·mind·ed·ly** *adv* — **ab·sent·mind·ed·ness** *n*

absent without leave *adj* : absent without authority from one's place of duty in the armed forces

ab·sinthe *or* **ab·sinth** \ˈab-ˌsin(t)th\ *n* [F *absinthe*, fr. L *absinthium*, fr. Gk *apsinthion*] **1** : WORMWOOD 1; *esp* : a common European wormwood (*Artemisia absinthium*) **2** : a green liqueur flavored with wormwood or a substitute, anise, and other aromatics

ab·so·lute \ˈab-sə-ˌlüt, ˌab-sə-ˈ\ *adj* [ME *absolut*, fr. L *absolutus*, fr. pp. of *absolvere* to set free, absolve] **1 a** : free from imperfection : PERFECT **b** : free or relatively free from mixture : PURE ⟨~ alcohol⟩ **c** : OUTRIGHT, UNMITIGATED ⟨an ~ lie⟩ **2** : being, governed by, or characteristic of a ruler or authority completely free from constitutional or other restraint **3 a** : standing apart from a normal or usual syntactical relation with other words or sentence elements ⟨the ~ construction *this being the case* in the sentence "this being the case, let us go"⟩ **b** *of an adjective or possessive pronoun* : standing alone without a modified substantive ⟨*blind* in "help the blind" and *ours* in "your work and ours" are ~⟩ **c** *of a verb* : having no object in the particular construction under consideration though normally transitive ⟨*kill* in "if looks could kill" is an ~ verb⟩ **4** : having no restriction, exception, or qualification ⟨an ~ requirement⟩ ⟨~ freedom⟩ **5** : POSITIVE, UNQUESTIONABLE ⟨~ proof⟩ **6 a** : independent of arbitrary standards of measurement **b** : relating to or derived in the simplest manner from the fundamental units of length, mass, and time ⟨~ electric units⟩ **c** : relating to the absolute-temperature scale ⟨10° ~⟩ **7** : FUNDAMENTAL, ULTIMATE ⟨~ knowledge⟩ **8** : perfectly embodying the nature of a thing ⟨~ justice⟩ **9** : being self-sufficient and free of external references or relationships ⟨an ~ term in logic⟩ ⟨~ music⟩ **10** : measuring or representing the distance from an aircraft to the ground or water beneath — **absolute** *n* — **ab·so·lute·ly** *adv* — **ab·so·lute·ness** *n*

absolute ceiling *n* : the maximum height above sea level at which a particular airplane can maintain horizontal flight under standard air conditions — called also *ceiling*

absolute humidity *n* : the amount of water vapor present in a unit volume of air

absolute magnitude *n* : the intrinsic luminosity of a celestial body (as a star) if viewed from a distance of 10 parsecs

absolute pitch *n* **1** : the position of a tone in a standard scale independently determined by its rate of vibration **2** : the ability to sing or name a note asked for or heard

absolute scale *n* : a temperature scale based on absolute zero

absolute space *n* : SPACE 4b

absolute temperature *n* : temperature measured on the absolute scale

absolute value *n* **1** : the numerical value of a real number irrespective of sign **2** : the positive square root of the sum of the squares of the real and imaginary parts of a complex number

absolute zero *n* : a hypothetical temperature characterized by complete absence of heat and equivalent to approximately −273.15°C or −459.67°F

ab·so·lu·tion \ˌab-sə-ˈlü-shən\ *n* : the act of absolving; *specif* : a remission of sins pronounced by a priest (as in the sacrament of penance)

ab·so·lut·ism \ˈab-sə-ˌlüt-ˌiz-əm\ *n* **1 a** : a political theory that absolute power should be vested in one or more rulers **b** : government by an absolute ruler or authority : DESPOTISM **2** : advocacy of a rule by absolute standards or principles **3** : an absolute standard or principle — **ab·so·lut·ist** \-ˌlüt-əst\ *n or adj* — **ab·so·lu·tis·tic** \ˌab-sə-(ˌ)lü-ˈtis-tik\ *adj*

ab·so·lut·ize \ˈab-sə-ˌlüt-ˌīz\ *vt* **-ized; -iz·ing** : to make absolute : convert into an absolute

ab·solve \əb-ˈzälv, -ˈsälv, -ˈzȯlv, -ˈsȯlv\ *vt* **ab·solved; ab·solv·ing** [ME *absolven*, fr. L *absolvere*, fr. *ab-* + *solvere* to loosen — more at

SOLVE] **1 :** to set free from an obligation or the consequences of guilt **2 :** to remit (a sin) by absolution — **ab·solv·er** *n*

ab·sorb \əb-ˈsȯ(ə)rb, -ˈzȯ(ə)rb\ *vt* [MF *absorber,* fr. L *absorbēre,* fr. *ab-* + *sorbēre* to suck up; akin to Gk *rhophein* to suck up] **1 :** to take in and make part of an existent whole ⟨the capacity of China to ~ invaders⟩ **2 a :** to suck up or take up ⟨a sponge ~*s* water⟩ ⟨charcoal ~*s* gas⟩ ⟨plant roots ~ water⟩ **b :** to take in ⟨convictions ~*ed* in youth —M. R. Cohen⟩ **3 :** to engage or engross wholly ⟨~*ed* in thought⟩ **4 a :** to receive without recoil or echo ⟨provided with a sound-*absorbing* surface⟩ **b :** to transform (radiant energy) into a different form usu. with a resulting rise in temperature ⟨the earth ~*s* the sun's rays⟩ **5 :** to take over (a cost) — **ab·sorb·abil·i·ty** \əb-ˌsȯr-bə-ˈbil-ət-ē, -ˌzȯr-\ *n* — **ab·sorb·able** \əb-ˈsȯr-bə-bəl, -ˈzȯr-\ *adj* — **ab·sorb·er** *n*

syn* 1** ABSORB, IMBIBE, ASSIMILATE *shared meaning element* : to take in and incorporate something (as into the substance or mind) ***ant dissipate (*as time, energies*)

2 see MONOPOLIZE

ab·sor·bance \əb-ˈsȯr-bən(t)s, -ˈzȯr-\ *n* : ABSORBENCY 2

ab·sor·ben·cy \əb-ˈsȯr-bən-sē, -ˈzȯr-\ *n, pl* **-cies 1 :** the quality or state of being absorbent **2** *or* **ab·sor·ban·cy :** the ability of a layer of a substance to absorb radiation expressed mathematically as the negative common logarithm of transmittance

ab·sor·bent *also* **ab·sor·bant** \-bənt\ *adj* [L *absorbent-, absorbens,* prp. of *absorbēre*] : able to absorb ⟨as ~ as a sponge⟩ — **absorbent** *also* **absorbant** *n*

ab·sorb·ing *adj* : fully taking one's attention : ENGROSSING ⟨an ~ novel⟩ — **ab·sorb·ing·ly** \-biŋ-lē\ *adv*

ab·sorp·tance \əb-ˈsȯrp-tən(t)s, -ˈzȯrp-\ *n* [*absorption* + *-ance*] : the ratio of the radiant energy absorbed by a body to that incident upon it

ab·sorp·tion \əb-ˈsȯrp-shən, -ˈzȯrp-\ *n* [F & L; F, fr. L *absorption-, absorptio,* fr. *absorptus,* pp. of *absorbēre*] **1 a :** the process of absorbing or of being absorbed — compare ADSORPTION **b :** interception of radiant energy or sound waves **2 :** entire occupation of the mind ⟨~ in his work⟩ — **ab·sorp·tion·al** \-shnəl, -shən-ᵊl\ *adj* — **ab·sorp·tive** \-tiv\ *adj*

ab·stain \əb-ˈstān\ *vi* [ME *absteinen,* fr. MF *abstenir,* fr. L *abstinēre,* fr. *abs-, ab-* + *tenēre* to hold — more at THIN] : to refrain deliberately and often with an effort of self-denial from an action or practice ***syn*** see REFRAIN — **ab·stain·er** *n*

ab·ste·mi·ous \ab-ˈstē-mē-əs\ *adj* [L *abstemius,* fr. *abs-* + *temetum* mead; akin to L *tenebrae* darkness — more at TEMERITY] **1 :** sparing esp. in eating or drinking **2 :** sparingly used or indulged in ⟨~ diet⟩ — **ab·ste·mi·ous·ly** *adv*

ab·sten·tion \əb-ˈsten-chən\ *n* [LL *abstention-, abstentio,* fr. L *abstentus,* pp. of *abstinēre*] : the act or practice of abstaining — **ab·sten·tious** \-chəs\ *adj*

ab·sti·nence \ˈab-stə-nən(t)s\ *n* [ME, fr. OF, fr. L *abstinentia,* fr. *abstinent-, abstinens,* prp. of *abstinēre*] **1 :** voluntary forbearance esp. from indulgence of appetite or from eating some foods : ABSTENTION **2 :** habitual abstaining from intoxicating beverages — **ab·sti·nent** \-nənt\ *adj* — **ab·sti·nent·ly** *adv*

abstr *abbr* abstract

[1]**ab·stract** \ab-ˈstrakt, ˈab-ˌ\ *adj* [ML *abstractus,* fr. L, pp. of *abstrahere* to draw away, fr. *abs-, ab-* + *trahere* to draw — more at DRAW] **1 a :** disassociated from any specific instance ⟨~ entity⟩ **b :** difficult to understand : ABSTRUSE ⟨~ problems⟩ **c :** IDEAL ⟨~ justice⟩ **d :** insufficiently factual : FORMAL ⟨possessed only an ~ right⟩ **2 :** expressing a quality apart from an object ⟨the word *poem* is concrete, *poetry* is ~⟩ **3 a :** dealing with a subject in its abstract aspects : THEORETICAL ⟨~ science⟩ **b :** IMPERSONAL, DETACHED ⟨the ~ compassion of a surgeon —*Time*⟩ **4 :** having only intrinsic form with little or no attempt at pictorial representation ⟨~ painting⟩ — **ab·stract·ly** \ab-ˈstrak-(t)lē, ˈab-ˌ\ *adv* — **ab·stract·ness** \ab-ˈstrak(t)-nəs, ˈab-ˌ\ *n*

[2]**ab·stract** \ˈab-ˌstrakt, *in sense 2 also* ab-ˈ\ *n* [ME, fr. L *abstractus*] **1 :** a summary of points (as of a writing) usu. presented in skeletal form **2 :** an abstract thing or state **3 :** ABSTRACTION 4 ***syn*** see ABRIDGMENT ***ant*** amplification

[3]**ab·stract** \ab-ˈstrakt, ˈab-ˌ, *in sense 3 usu* ˈab-ˌ\ *vt* **1 :** REMOVE, SEPARATE **2 :** to consider apart from application to a particular instance **3 :** to make an abstract of : SUMMARIZE **4 :** to draw away the attention of **5 :** STEAL, PURLOIN ~ *vi* : to make an abstraction — **ab·stract·able** \-ˈstrak-tə-bəl, -ˌstrak-\ *adj* — **ab·strac·tor** *or* **ab·stract·er** \-tər\ *n*

ab·stract·ed \ab-ˈstrak-təd, ˈab-ˌ\ *adj* : PREOCCUPIED, ABSENT-MINDED ⟨the ~ look of a professor⟩ — **ab·stract·ed·ly** *adv* — **ab·stract·ed·ness** *n*

abstract expressionism *n* : art in which the artist attempts to convey his attitudes and emotions through nonrepresentational means — **abstract expressionist** *n*

ab·strac·tion \ab-ˈstrak-shən\ *n* **1 a :** the act or process of abstracting : the state of being abstracted **b :** an abstract idea or term **2 :** absence of mind **3 :** abstract quality or character **4 :** an abstract composition or creation in art — **ab·strac·tion·al** \-shnəl, -shən-ᵊl\ *adj* — **ab·strac·tive** \ab-ˈstrak-tiv, ˈab-ˌ\ *adj*

ab·strac·tion·ism \ab-ˈstrak-shə-ˌniz-əm\ *n* : the principles or practice of creating abstract art — **ab·strac·tion·ist** \-sh(ə-)nəst\ *adj or n*

abstract of title : a summary statement of the successive conveyances and other facts on which a person's title to a piece of land rests

ab·strict \ab-ˈstrikt\ *vt* [*ab-* + L *strictus,* pp. of *stringere* to draw tight — more at STRAIN] : to cut off in or as if in abstriction

ab·stric·tion \-ˈstrik-shən\ *n* : the formation of spores by the cutting off of portions of the sporophore through the growth of septa

ab·struse \əb-ˈstrüs, ab-\ *adj* [L *abstrusus,* fr. pp. of *abstrudere* to conceal, fr. *abs-, ab-* + *trudere* to push — more at THREAT] : difficult to comprehend : RECONDITE ⟨the ~ calculations of mathematicians⟩ — **ab·struse·ly** *adv* — **ab·struse·ness** *n*

ab·stru·si·ty \-ˈstrü-sət-ē\ *n, pl* **-ties 1 :** the quality or state of being abstruse : ABSTRUSENESS **2 :** something that is abstruse

[1]**ab·surd** \əb-ˈsərd, -ˈzərd\ *adj* [MF *absurde,* fr. L *absurdus,* fr. *ab-* + *surdus* deaf, stupid — more at SURD] **1 :** ridiculously unreasonable, unsound, or incongruous **2 :** having no rational or orderly relationship to man's life : MEANINGLESS; *also* : lacking order or value **3 :** dealing with the absurd or with absurdism — **ab·surd·ly** *adv* — **ab·surd·ness** *n*

[2]**absurd** *n* : the state or condition in which man exists in an irrational and meaningless universe and in which man's life has no meaning outside his own existence

ab·surd·ism \-ˌiz-əm\ *n* : a philosophy based on the belief that man exists in an irrational and meaningless universe and that his search for order brings him into conflict with his universe — compare EXISTENTIALISM — **ab·surd·ist** \-əst\ *n or adj*

ab·sur·di·ty \əb-ˈsərd-ət-ē, -ˈzərd-\ *n, pl* **-ties 1 :** the quality or state of being absurd : ABSURDNESS **2 :** something that is absurd

absurd theater *n* : THEATER OF THE ABSURD

abub·ble \ə-ˈbəb-əl\ *adj* **1 :** being in the process of bubbling : EFFERVESCENT **2 :** being in a state of agitated activity or motion : ASTIR

abuild·ing \ə-ˈbil-diŋ\ *adj* : being in the process of building or of being built

abun·dance \ə-ˈbən-dən(t)s\ *n* **1 :** an ample quantity : PROFUSION **2 :** AFFLUENCE, WEALTH **3 :** relative degree of plentifulness ⟨low ~*s* of uranium and thorium —H. C. Urey⟩

abun·dant \-dənt\ *adj* [ME, fr. MF, fr. L *abundant-, abundans,* prp. of *abundare* to abound] **1 a :** marked by great plenty (as of resources) ⟨a fair and ~ land⟩ **b :** amply supplied : ABOUNDING ⟨~ with fly life and other natural trout food —Alexander MacDonald⟩ **2 :** occurring in abundance ⟨~ rainfall⟩ ***syn*** see PLENTIFUL ***ant*** scarce — **abun·dant·ly** *adv*

abundant year *n* : PERFECT YEAR

[1]**abuse** \ə-ˈbyüz\ *vt* **abused; abus·ing** [ME *abusen,* fr. MF *abuser,* fr. L *abusus,* pp. of *abuti,* fr. *ab-* + *uti* to use — more at USE] **1 :** to attack in words : REVILE **2** *obs* : DECEIVE **3 :** to put to a wrong or improper use ⟨~ a privilege⟩ **4 :** to use so as to injure or damage : MALTREAT ⟨~ a dog⟩ — **abus·able** \-ˈbyü-zə-bəl\ *adj* — **abus·er** *n*

[2]**abuse** \ə-ˈbyüs\ *n* **1 :** a corrupt practice or custom **2 :** improper use or treatment : MISUSE ⟨drug ~⟩ **3** *obs* : a deceitful act : DECEPTION **4 :** abusive language **5 :** physical maltreatment

syn ABUSE, VITUPERATION, INVECTIVE, OBLOQUY, SCURRILITY, BILLINGSGATE *shared meaning element* : vehemently expressed condemnation or disapproval ***ant*** adulation

abu·sive \ə-ˈbyü-siv, -ziv\ *adj* **1 :** characterized by wrong or improper use or action : CORRUPT ⟨~ financial practices⟩ **2 a :** characterized by or serving for verbal abuse **b :** physically injurious ⟨received ~ treatment⟩ — **abu·sive·ly** *adv* — **abu·sive·ness** *n*

abut \ə-ˈbət\ *vb* **abut·ted; abut·ting** [ME *abutten,* partly fr. OF *aboter* to border on, fr. *a-* (fr. L *ad-*) + *bout* blow, end, fr. *boter* to strike; partly fr. OF *abuter* to come to an end, fr. *a-* + *but* end, aim — more at [1]BUTT, [3]BUTT] *vi* **1 :** to touch along a border or with a projecting part ⟨land ~*s* on the road⟩ **2 a :** to terminate at a point of contact **b :** to lean for support ~ *vt* **1 :** to border on : TOUCH **2 :** to cause to abut — **abut·ter** *n*

abu·ti·lon \ə-ˈbyüt-ᵊl-ˌän\ *n* [NL, genus name, fr. Ar *awbūtīlūn* abutilon] : any of a genus (*Abutilon*) of plants of the mallow family with usu. lobed leaves and showy solitary bell-shaped flowers

abut·ment \ə-ˈbət-mənt\ *n* **1 :** the place at which abutting occurs **2 a :** the part of a structure that directly receives thrust or pressure (as of an arch) **b :** an anchorage for the cables of a suspension bridge or aerial railway

abut·tals \ə-ˈbət-ᵊlz\ *n pl* : the boundaries of lands with respect to adjacent lands

abut·ting *adj* : that abuts or serves as an abutment : ADJOINING, BORDERING ***syn*** see ADJACENT

abuzz \ə-ˈbəz\ *adj* : filled or resounding with or as if with a buzzing sound ⟨a lake ~ with outboards⟩ ⟨a town ~ with excitement⟩

aby *or* **abye** \ə-ˈbī\ *vt* [ME *abien,* fr. OE *ābycgan,* fr. *ā-* + *bycgan* to buy — more at ABIDE, BUY] *archaic* : to suffer a penalty for

abysm \ə-ˈbiz-əm\ *n* [ME *abime,* fr. OF *abisme,* modif. of LL *abyssus*] : ABYSS ⟨the dark backward and ~ of time —Shak.⟩

abys·mal \ə-ˈbiz-məl\ *adj* **1 a :** having immense or fathomless extension downward, backward, or inward ⟨an ~ cliff⟩ **b :** immeasurably great : PROFOUND ⟨~ ignorance⟩ ⟨the ~ sufferings of the dispossessed⟩ **2 :** ABYSSAL ***syn*** see DEEP — **abys·mal·ly** \-mə-lē\ *adv*

abyss \ə-ˈbis\ *n* [ME *abissus,* fr. LL *abyssus,* fr. Gk *abyssos,* fr. *abyssos* bottomless, fr. *a-* + *byssos* depth; akin to Gk *bathys* deep — more at BATHY-] **1 :** the bottomless gulf, pit, or chaos of the old cosmogonies **2 a :** an immeasurably deep gulf or great space **b :** intellectual or spiritual profundity

abys·sal \ə-ˈbis-əl\ *adj* **1 :** UNFATHOMABLE a **2 :** of or relating to the bottom waters of the ocean depths

Ab·ys·sin·i·an cat \ˌab-ə-ˌsin-ē-ən-, -ˌsin-yən-\ *n* [*Abyssinia,* kingdom in Africa] : any of a breed of small slender cats of African origin with short brownish hair ticked with darker color

ac *abbr* **1** account **2** money of account

[1]**Ac** *abbr* altocumulus

[2]**Ac** *symbol* actinium

AC *abbr* **1** alternating current **2** [L *ante Christum*] before Christ **3** [L *ante cibum*] before meals **4** area code **5** athletic club

ac- — see AD-

-ac \ˌak, *in a few words* ik *or* ək\ *n suffix* [NL *-acus* of or relating to, fr. Gk *-akos*] : one affected with ⟨nostalgiac⟩

ə abut	ᵊ kitten	ər further	a back	ā bake	ä cot, cart
au̇ out	ch chin	e less	ē easy	g gift	i trip	ī life
j joke	ŋ sing	ō flow	ȯ flaw	ȯi coin	th thin	t͟h this
ü loot	u̇ foot	y yet	yü few	yu̇ furious	zh vision

aca·cia \ə-ˈkā-shə\ *n* [NL, genus name, fr. L, acacia tree, fr. Gk *akakia* shittah] **1 :** any of a genus (*Acacia*) of woody leguminous plants of warm regions with leaves pinnate or reduced to phyllodes and white or yellow flower clusters **2 :** GUM ARABIC

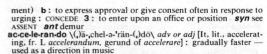

acacia 1

acad *abbr* academic; academy

ac·a·deme \ˈak-ə-ˌdēm\ *n* [irreg. fr. NL *academia*] **1 a :** a place of instruction : SCHOOL **b :** the academic environment **c** (1) **:** the academic community (2) **:** academic life **2 :** ACADEMIC; *esp* **:** PEDANT

ac·a·de·mia \ˌak-ə-ˈdē-mē-ə\ *n* [NL, fr. L, academy] **:** ACADEME 1c

[1]**ac·a·dem·ic** \ˌak-ə-ˈdem-ik\ *also* **ac·a·dem·i·cal** \-i-kəl\ *adj* **1 a :** of, relating to, or associated with an academy or school esp. of higher learning **b :** of or relating to performance in academic courses **c :** very learned but inexperienced in practical matters ⟨~ thinkers⟩ **d :** based on formal study esp. at an institution of higher learning **2 :** of or relating to literary or art rather than technical or professional studies **3 :** conforming to the traditions or rules of a school (as of literature or art) or an official academy **:** CONVENTIONAL **4 a :** theoretical without having an immediate or practical bearing : ABSTRACT ⟨an ~ question⟩ **b :** having no practical or useful significance ***syn*** see PEDANTIC, THEORETICAL — **ac·a·dem·i·cal·ly** \ik-(ə-)lē\ *adv*

[2]**academic** *n* **1 :** a member of an institution of learning **2 :** one who is academic in background, outlook, or methods

academic freedom *n* **:** freedom to teach or to learn without interference (as by government officials)

ac·a·de·mi·cian \ˌak-əd-ə-ˈmish-ən, ə-ˌkad-ə-\ *n* **1 a :** a member of an academy for promoting science, art, or literature **b :** a follower of an artistic or philosophical tradition or a promoter of its ideas **2 :** ACADEMIC

ac·a·dem·i·cism \ˌak-ə-ˈdem-ə-ˌsiz-əm\ *also* **acad·e·mism** \ə-ˈkad-ə-ˌmiz-əm\ *n* **1 :** the doctrines of Plato's Academy; *specif* **:** the skeptical doctrines of the later Academy holding that nothing can be known — compare PYRRHONISM **2 :** purely speculative thoughts and attitudes

academic year *n* **:** the annual period of sessions of an educational institution usu. beginning in September and ending in June

acad·e·my \ə-ˈkad-ə-mē\ *n, pl* **-mies** [L *academia*, fr. Gk *Akadēmeia*, fr. *Akadēmeia*, gymnasium where Plato taught, fr. *Akadēmos* Attic mythological hero] **1** *cap* **a :** the school for advanced education founded by Plato **b :** the philosophical doctrines associated with Plato's Academy: (1) **:** PLATONISM (2) **:** ACADEMICISM **2 a :** a school usu. above the elementary level; *esp* **:** a private high school **b :** a high school or college in which special subjects or skills are taught **c :** higher education ⟨the functions of the ~ in modern society⟩ **3 :** a society of learned persons organized to advance art, science, or literature **4 :** a body of established opinion in a particular field widely accepted as authoritative

Aca·di·an \ə-ˈkād-ē-ən\ *n* **1 :** a native or inhabitant of Acadia **2 a :** a Louisianian descended from French-speaking immigrants from Acadia **b :** a dialect of French spoken by Acadians — **Acadian** *adj*

AC and U *abbr* Association of Colleges and Universities

acanth- *or* **acantho-** *comb form* [NL, fr. Gk *akanth-*, *akantho-*, fr. *akantha;* akin to ON *ögn* awn — more at AWN] **:** thorn : spine ⟨*acanth*ous⟩ ⟨*acantho*cephalan⟩

acan·tho·ceph·a·lan \ə-ˌkan(t)-thə-ˈsef-ə-lən\ *n* [deriv. of *acanth-* + Gk *kephalē* head — more at CEPHALIC] **:** any of a group (Acanthocephala) of intestinal worms with a hooked proboscis that as adults lack a digestive tract and absorb food through the body wall — **acanthocephalan** *adj*

ac·an·thop·ter·yg·i·an \ˌak-ən-ˌthäp-tə-ˈrij-ē-ən\ *n* [deriv. of *acanth-* + Gk *pteryg-*, *pteryx* wing, fin — more at PTERYGOID] **:** any of a major division (Acanthopterygii) of teleost fishes including most spiny-finned fishes (as basses, perches, and mackerels) and some soft-finned fishes — **acanthopterygian** *adj*

acan·thus \ə-ˈkan(t)-thəs\ *n, pl* **acan·thus·es** *also* **acan·thi** \-ˈkan-ˌthī\ [NL, genus name, fr. Gk *akanthos*, an acanthus, fr. *akantha*] **1 :** any of a genus (*Acanthus* of the family Acanthaceae, the acanthus family) of prickly herbs of the Mediterranean region **2 :** an ornamentation (as in a Corinthian capital) representing or suggesting the leaves of the acanthus

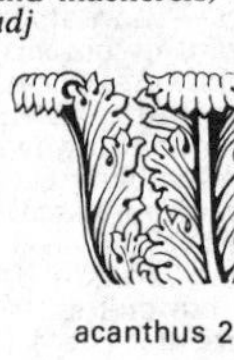

acanthus 2

a cap·pel·la *also* **a ca·pel·la** \ˌäk-ə-ˈpel-ə\ *adv or adj* [It *a cappella* in chapel style] **:** without instrumental accompaniment

ac·a·ri·a·sis \ˌak-ə-ˈrī-ə-səs\ *n* **:** infestation with or disease caused by mites

ac·a·rid \ˈak-ə-rəd\ *n* **:** any of an order (Acarina) of arachnids including the mites and ticks; *esp* **:** a typical mite (family Acaridae) — **acarid** *adj*

ac·a·roid resin \ˌak-ə-ˌrȯid-\ *n* [NL *acaroides*] **:** an alcohol-soluble resin from Australian grass trees

acar·pel·ous *or* **acar·pel·lous** \(ˈ)ā-ˈkär-pə-ləs\ *adj* **:** having no carpels

ac·a·rus \ˈak-ə-rəs\ *n, pl* **-ri** \-ˌrī\ [NL, genus name, fr. Gk *akari*, a mite] **:** MITE; *esp* **:** one of a formerly extensive genus (*Acarus*)

acat·a·lec·tic \(ˌ)ā-ˌkat-ᵊl-ˈek-tik\ *adj* [LL *acatalecticus*, fr. *acatalectus*, fr. Gk *akatalēktos*, fr. *a-* + *katalēgein* to leave off — more at CATALECTIC] **:** not catalectic ⟨~ verse⟩ — **acatalectic** *n*

acau·les·cent \ˌā-kȯ-ˈles-ᵊnt\ *adj* [*a-* + L *caulis* stem — more at HOLE] **:** having no stem or appearing to have none — **acau·les·cence** \-ᵊn(t)s\ *n*

acc *abbr* accusative

ACC *abbr* Air Coordinating Committee

ac·cede \ak-ˈsēd\ *vi* **ac·ced·ed; ac·ced·ing** [ME *acceden*, fr. L *accedere* to go to, be added, fr. *ad-* + *cedere* to go — more at CEDE] **1** *archaic* **:** APPROACH **2 a :** to become a party (as to an agreement) **b :** to express approval or give consent often in response to urging : CONCEDE **3 :** to enter upon an office or position ***syn*** see ASSENT ***ant*** demur

ac·ce·le·ran·do \(ˌ)ä-ˌchel-ə-ˈrän-(ˌ)dō\ *adv or adj* [It, lit., accelerating, fr. L *accelerandum*, gerund of *accelerare*] **:** gradually faster — used as a direction in music

ac·cel·er·ate \ik-ˈsel-ə-ˌrāt, ak-\ *vb* **-at·ed; -at·ing** [L *acceleratus*, pp. of *accelerare*, fr. *ad-* + *celer* swift — more at CELERITY] *vt* **1 :** to bring about at an earlier time **2 :** to cause to move faster; *also* **:** to cause to undergo acceleration **3 a :** to hasten the progress or development of **b :** to cause to grow : INCREASE ⟨~ food production⟩ **4 a :** to enable (a student) to complete a course in less than usual time **b :** to speed up (a course of study) ~ *vi* **1 a :** to move faster : gain speed **b :** GROW, INCREASE ⟨believed inflation was *accelerating*⟩ **2 :** to follow a speeded-up educational program — **ac·cel·er·at·ing·ly** \-ˌrāt-iŋ-lē\ *adv*

ac·cel·er·a·tion \ik-ˌsel-ə-ˈrā-shən, (ˌ)ak-\ *n* **1 :** the act or process of accelerating : the state of being accelerated **2 :** change of velocity; *also* **:** the rate of this change

acceleration of gravity : the acceleration of a freely falling body under the influence of gravity expressed as the rate of increase of velocity per unit of time with the value at sea level in latitude 45 degrees being 980.616 centimeters per second per second

acceleration principle *n* **:** a theory in economics: an increase or decrease in income induces a corresponding but magnified change in investment

ac·cel·er·a·tive \ik-ˈsel-ə-ˌrāt-iv, ak-\ *adj* **:** of, relating to, or tending to cause acceleration : ACCELERATING

ac·cel·er·a·tor \ik-ˈsel-ə-ˌrāt-ər, ak-\ *n* **:** one that accelerates: as **a :** a muscle or nerve that speeds the performance of an action **b :** a device for increasing the speed of a motor vehicle engine; *esp* **:** a foot-operated throttle that varies the supply of fuel-air mixture to the combustion chamber **c :** a substance that speeds a chemical reaction **d :** an apparatus for imparting high velocities to charged particles (as electrons)

ac·cel·er·om·e·ter \ik-ˌsel-ə-ˈräm-ət-ər, ak-\ *n* [ISV *accelera*tion + *-o-* + *-meter*] **:** an instrument for measuring acceleration or for detecting and measuring vibrations

[1]**ac·cent** \ˈak-ˌsent\ *n* [MF, fr. L *accentus*, fr. *ad-* + *cantus* song, fr. *cantus*, pp. of *canere* to sing — more at CHANT] **1 :** a distinctive manner of expression: as **a :** the inflection, tone, or choice of words taken to be unique in or highly characteristic of an individual — usu. used in pl. **b :** speech habits typical of the natives or residents of a region or of any other group **2 :** an articulative effort giving prominence to one syllable over adjacent syllables; *also* **:** the prominence thus given a syllable **3 :** rhythmically significant stress on the syllables of a verse usu. at regular intervals **4** *archaic* **:** UTTERANCE **5 a :** a mark (as ´, ˋ, ˆ) used in writing or printing to indicate a specific sound value, stress, or pitch, to distinguish words otherwise identically spelled, or to indicate that an ordinarily mute vowel should be pronounced **b :** an accented letter **6 a :** greater stress given to one musical tone than to its neighbors **b** (1) **:** the principle of regularly recurring stresses which serve to distribute a succession of pulses into measures (2) **:** special emphasis placed exceptionally upon tones not subject to such accent **c :** ACCENT MARK 2 **7 a :** emphasis laid on a part of an artistic design or composition **b :** an emphasized detail or area; *esp* **:** a small detail in sharp contrast with its surroundings **c :** a substance or object used for emphasis **8 :** a mark placed to the right of a letter or number and usu. slightly above it: **a** (1) **:** a double prime (2) **:** PRIME **b :** a mark used singly with numbers to denote minutes and doubly to denote seconds of time or to denote minutes and seconds of an angle or arc **c :** a mark used singly with numbers to denote feet and doubly to denote inches **9 :** special concern or attention : EMPHASIS ⟨an ~ on youth⟩ — **ac·cent·less** \-ləs\ *adj*

[2]**ac·cent** \ˈak-ˌsent, ak-ˈ\ *vt* **1 a :** to pronounce with accent : STRESS **b :** to mark with a written or printed accent **2 :** to give prominence to : make more prominent

accent mark *n* **1 :** ACCENT 5a, 8 **2 a :** a symbol used to indicate musical stress **b :** a mark placed after a letter designating a note of music to indicate in which octave the note occurs

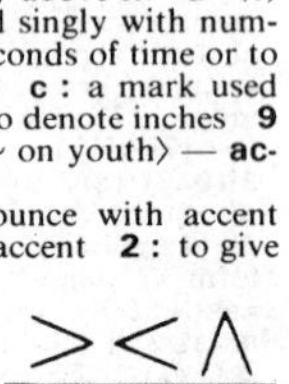

accent mark 2a

ac·cen·tu·al \ak-ˈsench-(ə-)wəl\ *adj* [L *accentus*] **:** of, relating to, or characterized by accent; *specif* **:** based on accent rather than on quantity or syllabic recurrence — **ac·cen·tu·al·ly** \-ē\ *adv*

ac·cen·tu·ate \ak-ˈsen-chə-ˌwāt, ik-\ *vt* **-at·ed; -at·ing** [ML *accentuatus*, pp. of *accentuare*, fr. L *accentus*] **:** ACCENT, EMPHASIZE — **ac·cen·tu·a·tion** \(ˌ)ak-ˌsen-chə-ˈwā-shən, ik-\ *n*

ac·cept \ik-ˈsept, ak-\ *vb* [ME *accepten*, fr. MF *accepter*, fr. L *acceptare*, fr. *acceptus*, pp. of *accipere* to receive, fr. *ad-* + *capere* to take — more at HEAVE] *vt* **1 a :** to receive with consent ⟨~ a gift⟩ **b :** to be able or designed to take or hold (something applied) ⟨a surface that will not ~ ink⟩ **2 :** to give admittance or approval to ⟨~ her as one of the group⟩ **3 a :** to endure without protest ⟨~ poor living conditions⟩ **b :** to regard as proper, normal, or inevitable ⟨the idea of universal education is widely ~*ed*⟩ **c :** to receive as true ⟨refused to ~ the hypothesis⟩ **d :** to receive into the mind : UNDERSTAND ⟨users of a language ~ words to mean certain things⟩ **4 a :** to make a favorable response to ⟨~ an offer⟩ **b :** to undertake the responsibility of ⟨~ a job⟩ **5 :** to assume an obligation to pay **6 :** to receive (a legislative report) officially ~ *vi* **:** to receive favorably something offered — usu. used with *of* ***syn*** see RECEIVE — **ac·cept·ing·ly** \-ˈsep-tiŋ-lē\ *adv* — **ac·cept·ing·ness** \-iŋ-nəs\ *n*

ac·cept·able \ik-ˈsep-tə-bəl, ak-\ *adj* **1 :** capable or worthy of being accepted ⟨no compromise would be ~⟩ **2 a :** WELCOME, PLEASING ⟨compliments are always ~⟩ **b :** barely satisfactory or adequate ⟨performances varied from excellent to ~⟩ — **ac·cept-**

abil·i·ty \ik-ˌsep-tə-'bil-ət-ē, (ˌ)ak-\ *n* — **ac·cept·able·ness** \ik-'sep-tə-bəl-nəs, ak-\ *n* — **ac·cept·ably** \-blē\ *adv*
ac·cep·tance \ik-'sep-tən(t)s, ak-\ *n* **1** : the act of accepting : APPROVAL **2** : the quality or state of being accepted or acceptable **3** : an agreeing either expressly or by conduct to the act or offer of another so that a contract is concluded and the parties become legally bound **4 a** : the act of accepting a time draft or bill of exchange for payment when due according to the specified terms **b** : an accepted draft or bill of exchange **5** : ACCEPTATION 2
ac·cep·tant \-tənt\ *adj* : willing to accept : RECEPTIVE
ac·cep·ta·tion \ˌak-ˌsep-'tā-shən\ *n* **1** : ACCEPTANCE; *esp* : favorable reception or approval **2** : a generally accepted meaning of a word or understanding of a concept ***syn*** see MEANING
ac·cept·ed *adj* : generally approved or used — **ac·cept·ed·ly** *adv*
ac·cept·er \ik-'sep-tər, ak-\ *n* **1** : one that accepts **2** : ACCEPTOR 2
ac·cep·tive \ak-'sep-tiv\ *adj* **1** : RECEPTIVE **2** : ACCEPTABLE
ac·cep·tor \ik-'sep-tər, ak-\ *n* **1** : ACCEPTER 1 **2** : one that accepts an order or a bill of exchange **3** : a compound, atom, or elementary particle capable of combining with another entity (as an atom, radical, or elementary particle) — compare DONOR 3a
[1]ac·cess \'ak-ˌses\ *n* [ME, fr. MF & L; MF *acces* arrival, fr. L *accessus* approach, fr. *accessus*, pp. of *accedere* to approach — more at ACCEDE] **1 a** : ONSET 2 **b** : a fit of intense feeling : OUTBURST **2 a** : permission, liberty, or ability to enter, approach, communicate with, or pass to and from **b** : freedom or ability to obtain or make use of **c** : a way or means of access **d** : the action of going to or reaching **3** : an increase by addition
[2]access *vt* : to get at : gain access to ⟨accumulator and index registers can be ~*ed* by the programmer — *Datamation*⟩
ac·ces·si·ble \ik-'ses-ə-bəl, ak-\ *adj* **1** : usable for access **2 a** : capable of being reached ⟨~ by rail⟩ **b** : easy to get along with ⟨~ people⟩ **3** : capable of being influenced : OPEN **4** : capable of being used or seen — **ac·ces·si·bil·i·ty** \ik-ˌses-ə-'bil-ət-ē, ak-\ *n* — **ac·ces·si·ble·ness** \ik-'ses-ə-bəl-nəs, ak-\ *n* — **ac·ces·si·bly** \-blē\ *adv*
[1]ac·ces·sion \ik-'sesh-ən, ak-\ *n* **1** : something added : ACQUISITION **2 a** : the act of becoming joined : ADHERENCE **b** : the act by which one nation becomes party to an agreement already in force between other powers **3 a** : increase by something added **b** : acquisition of additional property by growth, increase, or other addition to existing property **4** : the act of assenting or agreeing **5 a** : an act of coming near or to : APPROACH, ADMITTANCE **b** : the act of coming to high office or a position of honor or power **6** : a sudden fit or outburst : ACCESS — **ac·ces·sion·al** \-'sesh-nəl, -ən-ᵊl\ *adj*
[2]accession *vt* : to record in order of acquisition
ac·ces·so·ri·al \ˌak-sə-'sōr-ē-əl, -'sȯr-\ *adj* **1** : of or relating to an accessory ⟨~ liability⟩ **2** : of, relating to, or constituting an accession : SUPPLEMENTARY ⟨~ services⟩
ac·ces·so·rize \ik-'ses-ə-ˌrīz, ak-\ *vb* **-rized; -riz·ing** *vt* : to furnish with accessories ~ *vi* : to wear clothing accessories
[1]ac·ces·so·ry *also* **ac·ces·sa·ry** \ik-'ses-(ə-)rē, ak-\ *n, pl* **-ries** **1 a** : a thing of secondary or subordinate importance : ADJUNCT **b** : an object or device not essential in itself but adding to the beauty, convenience, or effectiveness of something else ⟨auto *accessories*⟩ ⟨clothing *accessories*⟩ **2 a** : a person not actually or constructively present but contributing as an assistant or instigator to the commission of an offense — called also *accessory before the fact* **b** : one who knowing that a crime has been committed aids or shelters the offender with intent to defeat justice — called also *accessory after the fact*
[2]accessory *adj* **1** : aiding or contributing in a secondary way : SUPPLEMENTARY **2** : assisting as a subordinate; *esp* : contributing to a crime but not as the chief agent **3** : present in a minor amount and not essential as a constituent ⟨an ~ mineral in a rock⟩
accessory fruit *n* : a fruit (as the apple) of which a conspicuous part consists of tissue other than that of the ripened ovary
accessory nerve *n* : either of a pair of motor nerves that are the 11th cranial nerves of higher vertebrates, arise from the medulla and the upper part of the spinal cord, and supply chiefly the pharynx and muscles of the upper chest, back, and shoulders
accessory shoe *n* : SHOE 5b
access road *n* : a road that provides access to a particular area
access time *n* : the time lag between the time stored information (as in a computer) is requested and the time it is delivered
ac·ciac·ca·tu·ra \(ˌ)ä-ˌchäk-ə-'tu̇r-ə\ *n* [It, lit., crushing] : a discordant note sounded with a principal note or chord and immediately released
ac·ci·dence \'ak-səd-ən(t)s, -sə-ˌden(t)s\ *n* [L *accidentia* inflections of words, nonessential qualities, pl. of *accident-, accidens*, n.] : a part of grammar that deals with inflections
ac·ci·dent \'ak-səd-ənt, -sə-ˌdent\ *n* [ME, fr. MF, fr. L *accident-, accidens* nonessential quality, chance, fr. prp. of *accidere* to happen, fr. *ad-* + *cadere* to fall — more at CHANCE] **1 a** : an event occurring by chance or arising from unknown causes **b** : lack of intention or necessity : CHANCE ⟨met by ~ rather than by design⟩ **2 a** : an unfortunate event resulting from carelessness, unawareness, ignorance, or a combination of causes **b** : an unexpected happening causing loss or injury which is not due to any fault or misconduct on the part of the person injured but from the consequences of which he may be entitled to some legal relief **3** : a nonessential property of an entity or circumstance ⟨the ~ of appearance⟩ **4** : an irregularity of a surface (as of the moon)
[1]ac·ci·den·tal \ˌak-sə-'dent-ᵊl\ *adj* **1** : arising from extrinsic causes : NONESSENTIAL **2 a** : occurring unexpectedly or by chance **b** : happening without intent or through carelessness and often with unfortunate results — **ac·ci·den·tal·ly** \-'dent-lē, -ᵊl-ē\ *also* **ac·ci·dent·ly** \-'dent-lē\ *adv* — **ac·ci·den·tal·ness** \-'dent-ᵊl-nəs\ *n*
syn **1** ACCIDENTAL, FORTUITOUS, CONTINGENT, CASUAL *shared meaning element* : happening by chance ***ant*** planned
2 ACCIDENTAL, INCIDENTAL, ADVENTITIOUS *shared meaning element* : not part of the real or essential element of something ***ant*** essential
[2]accidental *n* **1** : a nonessential property **2 a** : a chromatically altered note (as a sharp or flat) foreign to a key indicated by a signature **b** : a prefixed sign indicating an accidental
accident insurance *n* : insurance against loss through accidental bodily injury to the insured
accident–prone *adj* **1** : having a greater than average number of accidents **2** : having personality traits that predispose to accidents
ac·cip·i·ter \ak-'sip-ət-ər\ *n* [NL, genus name, fr. L, hawk] : any of a genus (*Accipiter*) of medium-sized short-winged long-legged hawks with low darting flight; *broadly* : a hawk (as of the family Accipitridae, the accipiter family) of similar appearance or habit of flight — **ac·cip·i·trine** \-'sip-ə-ˌtrīn\ *adj or n*
[1]ac·claim \ə-'klām\ *vb* [L *acclamare*, lit., to shout at, fr. *ad-* + *clamare* to shout — more at CLAIM] *vt* **1** : APPLAUD, PRAISE **2** : to declare by acclamation ~ *vi* : to shout praise or applause — **ac·claim·er** *n*
[2]acclaim *n* **1** : the act of acclaiming **2** : PRAISE, APPLAUSE
ac·cla·ma·tion \ˌak-lə-'mā-shən\ *n* [L *acclamation-, acclamatio*, fr. *acclamatus*, pp. of *acclamare*] **1** : a loud eager expression of approval, praise, or assent **2** : an overwhelming affirmative vote by cheers, shouts, or applause rather than by ballot
ac·cli·mate \'ak-lə-ˌmāt, ə-'klī-mət\ *vb* **-mat·ed; -mat·ing** [F *acclimater*, fr. *a-* (fr. L *ad-*) + *climat* climate] : ACCLIMATIZE
ac·cli·ma·tion \ˌak-lə-'mā-shən, -ˌlī-\ *n* : acclimatization esp. under controlled (as laboratory) conditions
ac·cli·ma·ti·za·tion \ə-ˌklī-mət-ə-'zā-shən\ *n* : the process or result of acclimatizing
ac·cli·ma·tize \ə-'klī-mə-ˌtīz\ *vb* **-tized; -tiz·ing** *vt* : to adapt to a new temperature, altitude, climate, environment, or situation ~ *vi* : to become acclimatized — **ac·cli·ma·tiz·er** *n*
ac·cliv·i·ty \ə-'kliv-ət-ē, a-\ *n, pl* **-ties** [L *acclivitas*, fr. *acclivis* ascending, fr. *ad-* + *clivus* slope — more at DECLIVITY] : an ascending slope (as of a hill)
ac·co·lade \'ak-ə-ˌlād\ *n* [F, fr. *accoler* to embrace, fr. (assumed) VL *accollare*, fr. L *ad-* + *collum* neck — more at COLLAR] **1** : a ceremonial embrace **2 a** : a ceremony or salute to mark the conferring of knighthood **b** : a ceremony marking the recognition of special merit **3 a** : a mark of acknowledgment : AWARD **b** : an expression of praise **4** : a brace or a line used in music to join two or more staffs carrying simultaneous parts
ac·com·mo·date \ə-'käm-ə-ˌdāt\ *vb* **-dat·ed; -dat·ing** [L *accommodatus*, pp. of *accommodare*, fr. *ad-* + *commodare* to make fit, fr. *commodus* suitable — more at COMMODE] *vt* **1** : to make fit, suitable, or congruous **2** : to bring into agreement or concord : RECONCILE **3** : to furnish with something desired, needed, or suited: **a** : to grant a loan to esp. without security **b** : to provide with lodgings : HOUSE **4 a** : to make room for **b** : to hold without crowding or inconvenience **5** : to give consideration to : allow for ⟨~ the special interests of various groups⟩ ~ *vi* : to adapt oneself; *also* : to undergo visual accommodation ***syn*** **1** see ADAPT ***ant*** constrain **2** see OBLIGE ***ant*** incommode — **ac·com·mo·da·tive** \-ˌdāt-iv\ *adj* — **ac·com·mo·da·tive·ness** *n*
ac·com·mo·dat·ing *adj* : HELPFUL, OBLIGING — **ac·com·mo·dat·ing·ly** \-ˌdāt-iŋ-lē\ *adv*
ac·com·mo·da·tion \ə-ˌkäm-ə-'dā-shən\ *n* **1** : something supplied for convenience or to satisfy a need: as **a** : lodging, food, and services or seat, berth, or other space occupied together with services available — usu. used in pl. ⟨tourist ~*s* on the boat⟩ ⟨overnight ~*s*⟩ **b** : a public conveyance (as a train) that stops at all or nearly all points **c** : LOAN **2** : the act of accommodating : the state of being accommodated: as **a** : the provision of what is needed or desired for convenience **b** : ADAPTATION, ADJUSTMENT **c** : an adjustment of differences : SETTLEMENT **d** : the automatic adjustment of the eye for seeing at different distances effected chiefly by changes in the convexity of the crystalline lens; *also* : the range over which such adjustment is possible — **ac·com·mo·da·tion·al** \-shnəl, -shən-ᵊl\ *adj*
accommodation ladder *n* : a light ladder or stairway hung over the side of a ship for ascending from or descending to small boats
accommodation paper *n* : a bill, draft, or note made, drawn, accepted, or endorsed by one person for another without consideration to enable that other to raise money or obtain credit
ac·com·mo·da·tor \ə-'käm-ə-ˌdāt-ər\ *n* : one that accommodates; *esp* : a part-time or special-occasion domestic worker
ac·com·pa·ni·ment \ə-'kəmp-(ə-)nē-mənt\ *n* **1** : a subordinate instrumental or vocal part designed to support or complement a principal voice or instrument **2 a** : an addition (as an ornament) intended to give completeness or symmetry : COMPLEMENT **b** : an accompanying situation or occurrence : CONCOMITANT
ac·com·pa·nist \ə-'kəmp-(ə-)nəst\ *n* : one (as a pianist) who plays an accompaniment
ac·com·pa·ny \ə-'kəmp-(ə-)nē\ *vb* **-nied; -ny·ing** [ME *accompanien*, fr. MF *acompaignier*, fr. *a-* (fr. L *ad-*) + *compaing* companion, fr. LL *companio*] *vt* **1** : to go with or attend as an associate or companion **2** : to perform an accompaniment to or for **3 a** : to cause to be in association ⟨*accompanied* his advice with a warning⟩ **b** : to be in association with ⟨the pictures that ~ the text⟩ ~ *vi* : to perform an accompaniment
syn ACCOMPANY, ATTEND, ESCORT *shared meaning element* : to go along with

ə abut	ᵊ kitten	ər further	a back	ā bake	ä cot, cart
au̇ out	ch chin	e less	ē easy	g gift	i trip	ī life
j joke	ŋ sing	ō flow	ȯ flaw	ȯi coin	th thin	t͟h this
ü loot	u̇ foot	y yet	yü few	yu̇ furious	zh vision

ac·com·plice \ə-'käm-pləs, -'kəm-\ *n* [alter. (fr. incorrect division of *a complice*) of *complice*] : one associated with another esp. in wrongdoing
ac·com·plish \ə-'käm-plish, -'kəm-\ *vt* [ME *accomplisshen*, fr. MF *acompliss-*, stem of *acomplir*, fr. (assumed) VL *accomplēre*, fr. L *ad-* + *complēre* to fill up — more at COMPLETE] **1** : to bring to a successful conclusion : carry to completion ⟨when they had ~*ed* their journey⟩ ⟨I hope to ~ much more today⟩ **2** : to attain to (a measure of time or distance) : COVER ⟨at that rate will ~ only half the distance⟩ **3** *archaic* **a** : to equip thoroughly **b** : PERFECT ***syn*** see PERFORM — **ac·com·plish·able** \-ə-bəl\ *adj* — **ac·com·plish·er** *n*
ac·com·plished *adj* **1** : COMPLETED, EFFECTED ⟨an ~ fact⟩ **2 a** : complete in acquirements as the result of practice or training ⟨an ~ dancer⟩ **b** : having many social accomplishments
ac·com·plish·ment \ə-'käm-plish-mənt, -'kəm-\ *n* **1** : the act of accomplishing : COMPLETION **2** : something accomplished : ACHIEVEMENT **3 a** : a quality or ability equipping one for society **b** : a special skill or ability acquired by training or practice
[1]**ac·cord** \ə-'kȯ(ə)rd\ *vb* [ME *accorden*, fr. OF *acorder*, fr. (assumed) VL *accordare*, fr. L *ad-* + *cord-*, *cor* heart — more at HEART] *vt* **1** : to bring into agreement : RECONCILE **2 a** : to grant as suitable or proper **b** : to allow as a concession **c** : to confer something on as an award **d** : to assign as a portion ~ *vi* **1** *archaic* : to arrive at an agreement **2** *obs* : to give consent **3** : to exhibit perfect fitness in a relationship or association : adjust or fit harmoniously ***syn* 1** see AGREE ***ant*** conflict **2** see GRANT ***ant*** withhold
[2]**accord** *n* [ME, fr. OF *acort*, fr. *acorder*] **1 a** : AGREEMENT, CONFORMITY ⟨acted in ~ with the company's policy⟩ **b** : a formal act of agreement : TREATY **2** : balanced interrelationship : HARMONY **3** *obs* : ASSENT **4** : voluntary or spontaneous impulse to act ⟨gave generously of their own ~⟩
ac·cor·dance \ə-'kȯrd-ᵊn(t)s\ *n* **1** : AGREEMENT, CONFORMITY ⟨in ~ with a rule⟩ **2** : the act of granting
ac·cor·dant \-ᵊnt\ *adj* **1** : CONSONANT, AGREEING **2** : HARMONIOUS, CORRESPONDENT — **ac·cor·dant·ly** *adv*
ac·cord·ing as *conj* **1** : in accord with the way in which **2 a** : depending on how **b** : depending on whether : IF
ac·cord·ing·ly \ə-'kȯrd-iŋ-lē\ *adv* **1** : in accordance : CORRESPONDINGLY **2** : CONSEQUENTLY, SO
according to *prep* **1** : in conformity with **2** : as stated or attested by **3** : depending on
[1]**ac·cor·di·on** \ə-'kȯrd-ē-ən\ *n* [G *akkordion*, fr. *akkord* chord, fr. F *accord*, fr. OF *acort*] : a portable keyboard wind instrument in which the wind is forced past free reeds by means of a hand-operated bellows — **ac·cor·di·on·ist** \-ē-ə-nəst\ *n*
[2]**accordion** *adj* : folding or creased or hinged to fold like an accordion ⟨an ~ pleat⟩ ⟨an ~ door⟩
ac·cost \ə-'kȯst, -'käst\ *vt* [MF *accoster*, deriv. of L *ad-* + *costa* rib, side — more at COAST] : to approach and speak to often in a challenging or aggressive way

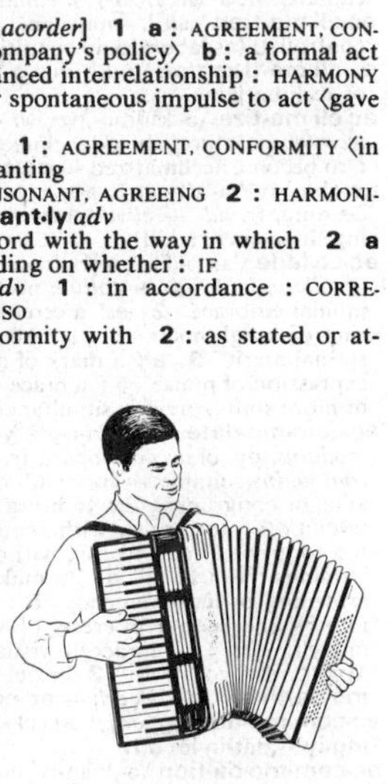
accordion

ac·couche·ment \,a-,küsh-'mäⁿ, ə-'küsh-,\ *n* [F] : LYING-IN; *esp* : PARTURITION
ac·cou·cheur \,a-,kü-'shər\ *n* [F] : one that assists at a birth ⟨without President Truman as ~ there would have been no Israel —B. C. Crum⟩; *esp* : OBSTETRICIAN
[1]**ac·count** \ə-'kaůnt\ *n* **1** *archaic* : RECKONING, COMPUTATION **2 a** : a record of debit and credit entries chronologically posted to a ledger page to cover transactions involving a particular item or a particular person or concern **b** : a statement of transactions during a fiscal period **3** : a collection of items to be balanced — usu. used in pl. **4** : a statement explaining one's conduct **5 a** : a periodically rendered calculation listing charged purchases and credits ⟨a grocery ~⟩ **b** : the patronage involved in establishing or maintaining an account : BUSINESS⟨glad to get that customer's ~⟩ **6 a** : VALUE, IMPORTANCE ⟨a man of no ~⟩ **b** : ESTEEM, JUDGMENT ⟨he stands high in their ~⟩ **7** : PROFIT, ADVANTAGE ⟨turned his wit to good ~⟩ **8 a** : a statement or exposition of reasons, causes, grounds, or motives ⟨no satisfactory ~ of these phenomena⟩ **b** : a reason for an action : BASIS ⟨on all ~*s* you must do it⟩ **c** : careful thought : CONSIDERATION ⟨left nothing out of ~⟩ **9** : a statement of facts or events : RELATION ⟨a newspaper ~⟩ **10** : HEARSAY, REPORT — usu. used in pl. ⟨by all ~*s* a rich man⟩ **11** : a sum of money or its equivalent deposited in the common cash of a bank and subject to withdrawal by the depositor — **on account of** : for the sake of : by reason of : because of — **on no account** : under no circumstances — **on one's own account 1** : on one's own behalf **2** : at one's own risk **3** : by oneself : on one's own
[2]**account** *vb* [ME *accounten*, fr. MF *acompter*, fr. *a-* (fr. L *ad-*) + *compter* to count] *vt* **1** : to probe into : ANALYZE **2** : to think of as : CONSIDER ⟨~*s* himself lucky⟩ ~ *vi* **1** : to furnish a justifying analysis or explanation — used with *for* **2 a** : to be the sole or primary factor — used with *for* **b** : to bring about the capture, death, or destruction of something ⟨~*ed* for two rabbits⟩
ac·count·able \ə-'kaůnt-ə-bəl\ *adj* **1** : subject to giving an account : ANSWERABLE **2** : capable of being accounted for : EXPLAINABLE — **ac·count·abil·i·ty** \-,kaůnt-ə-'bil-ət-ē\ *n* — **ac·count·able·ness** \-'kaůnt-ə-bəl-nəs\ *n* — **ac·count·ably** \-blē\ *adv*
ac·coun·tan·cy \ə-'kaůnt-ᵊn-sē\ *n* : the profession or practice of accounting
ac·coun·tant \ə-'kaůnt-ᵊnt\ *n* **1** : one that gives an account or is accountable **2** : one who is skilled in the practice of accounting or who is in charge of public or private accounts — **ac·coun·tant·ship** \-ᵊn(t)-,ship\ *n*
account book *n* : a book in which accounts are kept : LEDGER
account executive *n* : a business executive (as in an advertising agency) responsible for the management of a client's account
ac·count·ing \ə-'kaůnt-iŋ\ *n* **1** : the system of recording and summarizing business and financial transactions in books and analyzing, verifying, and reporting the results; *also* : the principles and procedures of accounting **2 a** : practical application of accounting **b** : an instance of applying the principles and procedures of accounting
accounting machine *n* : a business machine that is key-operated or uses stored data (as punch cards) and that tabulates, adds, subtracts, or totals
account payable *n, pl* **accounts payable** : the balance due to a creditor on a current account
account receivable *n, pl* **accounts receivable** : a balance due from a debtor on a current account
ac·cou·tre *or* **ac·cou·ter** \ə-'küt-ər\ *vt* **-cou·tred** *or* **-cou·tered; -cou·tring** *or* **-cou·ter·ing** \-'küt-ə-riŋ, -'kü-triŋ\ [F *accoutrer*, fr. MF *acoustrer*, fr. *a-* + *costure* seam, fr. (assumed) VL *consutura*, fr. L *consutus*, pp. of *consuere* to sew together, fr. *com-* + *suere* to sew — more at SEW] : to provide with equipment or furnishings : OUTFIT ***syn*** see FURNISH
ac·cou·tre·ment *or* **ac·cou·ter·ment** \ə-'kü-trə-mənt, -'küt-ər-mənt\ *n* **1** : the act of accoutering : the state of being accoutered **2 a** : an article of equipment or dress esp. when used as an accessory **b** : EQUIPMENT, TRAPPINGS; *specif* : a soldier's outfit usu. not including clothes and weapons — usu. used in pl. **3** : an identifying and often superficial characteristic
ac·cred·it \ə-'kred-ət\ *vt* [F *accréditer*, fr. *ad-* + *crédit* credit] **1** : to consider or recognize as outstanding **2** : to give official authorization to or approval of: **a** : to provide with credentials; *esp* : to send (an envoy) with letters of authorization **b** : to recognize or vouch for as conforming with a standard **c** : to recognize (an educational institution) as maintaining standards that qualify the graduates for admission to higher or more specialized institutions or for professional practice **3** : CREDIT ***syn*** see APPROVE — **ac·cred·i·table** \-ə-bəl\ *adj* — **ac·cred·i·ta·tion** \ə-,kred-ə-'tā-shən\ *n*
ac·crete \ə-'krēt\ *vb* **ac·cret·ed; ac·cret·ing** [back-formation fr. *accretion*] *vi* : to grow or become attached by accretion ~ *vt* : to cause to adhere or become attached : ACCUMULATE
ac·cre·tion \ə-'krē-shən\ *n* [L *accretion-*, *accretio*, fr. *accretus*, pp. of *accrescere* — more at ACCRUE] **1** : the process of growth or enlargement: as **a** : increase by external addition or accumulation (as by adhesion of external parts or particles) **b** : the increase of land by the gradual or imperceptible action of natural forces **2** : a product of accretion; *esp* : an extraneous addition ⟨~*s* of grime⟩ **3** : coherence of separate particles : CONCRETION — **ac·cre·tion·ary** \-shə-,ner-ē\ *adj* — **ac·cre·tive** \ə-'krēt-iv\ *adj*
ac·cru·al \ə-'krü-əl\ *n* **1** : the action or process of accruing **2** : something that accrues or has accrued
ac·crue \ə-'krü\ *vb* **ac·crued; ac·cru·ing** [ME *acreuen*, prob. fr. MF *acreue* increase, fr. *acreistre* to increase, fr. L *accrescere*, fr. *ad-* + *crescere* to grow — more at CRESCENT] *vi* **1** : to come into existence as a legally enforceable claim **2** : to come by way of increase or addition : arise as a growth or a result **3** : to be periodically accumulated whether as an increase or a decrease ~ *vt* : COLLECT, ACCUMULATE — **ac·cru·able** \-'krü-ə-bəl\ *adj* — **ac·crue·ment** \-'krü-mənt\ *n*
acct *abbr* account; accountant
ac·cul·tur·ate \ə-'kəl-chə-,rāt\ *vt* **-at·ed; -at·ing** [back-formation fr. *acculturation*] : to change through acculturation
ac·cul·tur·a·tion \ə-,kəl-chə-'rā-shən\ *n* **1** : cultural modification of an individual, group, or people through prolonged and continuous interaction involving intercultural exchange and borrowing with a different culture; *esp* : modification in a primitive culture resulting from contact with an advanced society **2** : the process beginning at infancy by which a human being acquires the culture of his society — **ac·cul·tur·a·tion·al** \-shnəl, -shən-ᵊl\ *adj* — **ac·cul·tur·a·tive** \ə-'kəl-chə-,rāt-iv\ *adj*
ac·cu·mu·late \ə-'kyü-myə-,lāt\ *vb* **-lat·ed; -lat·ing** [L *accumulatus*, pp. of *accumulare*, fr. *ad-* + *cumulare* to heap up — more at CUMULATE] *vt* **1** : to heap or pile up : AMASS ⟨~ a fortune⟩ **2** : COLLECT, GATHER ⟨a composer *accumulating* one award after another⟩ ~ *vi* : to increase in quantity or number
ac·cu·mu·la·tion \ə-,kyü-myə-'lā-shən\ *n* **1** : the action or process of accumulating : the state of being or having accumulated **2** : increase or growth by addition esp. when continuous or repeated ⟨~ of interest⟩ **3** : something that has accumulated or has been accumulated
ac·cu·mu·la·tive \ə-'kyü-myə-,lāt-iv, -lət-\ *adj* **1** : CUMULATIVE ⟨an age of rapid and ~ change⟩ **2** : tending or given to accumulation — **ac·cu·mu·la·tive·ly** *adv* — **ac·cu·mu·la·tive·ness** *n*
ac·cu·mu·la·tor \ə-'kyü-myə-,lāt-ər\ *n* : one that accumulates: as **a** : SHOCK ABSORBER **b** *Brit* : STORAGE CELL **c** : a part (as in a computer) where numbers are totaled or stored
ac·cu·ra·cy \'ak-yə-rə-sē\ *n, pl* **-cies** **1** : freedom from mistake or error : CORRECTNESS **2 a** : conformity to truth or to a standard or model : EXACTNESS **b** : degree of conformity of a measure to a standard or a true value
ac·cu·rate \'ak-yə-rət\ *adj* [L *accuratus*, fr. pp. of *accurare* to take care of, fr. *ad-* + *cura* care — more at CURE] **1** : free from error esp. as the result of care ⟨~ methods⟩ **2** : conforming exactly to truth or to a standard : EXACT ⟨~ instruments⟩ ***syn*** see CORRECT ***ant*** inaccurate — **ac·cu·rate·ly** \-yə-rət-lē, -yərt-\ *adv* — **ac·cu·rate·ness** \-yə-nət-nəs\ *n*
ac·cursed \ə-'kərst, -'kər-səd\ *or* **ac·curst** \ə-'kərst\ *adj* [ME *acursed*, fr. pp. of *acursen* to consign to destruction with a curse, fr. *a-* (fr. OE *ā*, perfective prefix) + *cursen* to curse — more at ABIDE] **1** : being under a curse **2** : DAMNABLE — **ac·curs·ed·ly** \-'kər-səd-lē\ *adv* — **ac·curs·ed·ness** \-'kər-səd-nəs\ *n*
accus *abbr* accusative
ac·cus·al \ə-'kyü-zəl\ *n* : ACCUSATION

ac·cu·sa·tion \ˌak-yə-ˈzā-shən\ *n* **1** : the act of accusing : the state or fact of being accused **2** : a charge of wrongdoing

¹ac·cu·sa·tive \ə-ˈkyü-zət-iv\ *adj* [ME, fr. MF or L; MF *accusatif,* fr. L *accusativus,* fr. *accusatus,* pp. of *accusare*] **1** : of, relating to, or being the grammatical case that marks the direct object of a verb or the object of any of several prepositions **2** : ACCUSATORY

²accusative *n* : the accusative case of a language : a form in the accusative case

ac·cu·sa·to·ry \ə-ˈkyü-zə-ˌtōr-ē, -ˌtȯr-\ *adj* : containing or expressing accusation : ACCUSING

ac·cuse \ə-ˈkyüz\ *vb* **ac·cused; ac·cus·ing** [ME *accusen,* fr. OF *acuser,* fr. L *accusare* to call to account, fr. *ad-* + *causa* lawsuit, cause] *vt* **1** : to charge with a fault or offense : BLAME **2** : to charge with an offense judicially or by a public process ~ *vi* : to bring an accusation — **ac·cus·er** \ə-ˈkyü-zər\ *n* — **ac·cus·ing·ly** \-ˈkyü-ziŋ-lē\ *adv*

ac·cused *n, pl* **accused** : one charged with an offense; *esp* : the defendant in a criminal case

ac·cus·tom \ə-ˈkəs-təm\ *vt* [ME *accustomen,* fr. MF *acostumer,* fr. *a-* (fr. L *ad-*) + *costume* custom] : to make familiar through use or experience — **ac·cus·tom·ation** \-ˌkəs-tə-ˈmā-shən\ *n*

ac·cus·tomed \ə-ˈkəs-təmd\ *adj* **1** : familiar through use or experience : often used or practiced ⟨her ~ cheerfulness⟩ **2** : being in the habit or custom ⟨~ to making decisions⟩ ***syn*** see USUAL ***ant*** unaccustomed — **ac·cus·tomed·ness** \-təm(d)-nəs\ *n*

AC/DC \ˈā-(ˌ)sē-ˈdē-(ˌ)sē\ *adj* [fr. the likening of a bisexual person to an electrical appliance which can operate on either alternating or direct current] : BISEXUAL 1b

¹ace \ˈās\ *n* [ME *as,* fr. OF, fr. L, unit, a copper coin] **1 a** : a die face marked with one spot **b** : a playing card marked in its center with one large pip **c** : a domino end marked with one spot **2** : a very small amount or degree : PARTICLE **3** : a score made by a single stroke; *specif* : a point scored on a shot (as a service in tennis or handball) that an opponent fails to touch **4** : a golf score of one stroke on a hole; *also* : a hole made in one stroke **5** : a combat pilot who has brought down at least five enemy airplanes **6** : one that excels at something — **ace in the hole 1** : an ace dealt face down to a player (as in stud poker) and not exposed until the showdown **2** : an effective and decisive argument or resource held in reserve — **within an ace of** : on the point of : very near to ⟨came *within an ace of* winning⟩

²ace *vt* **aced; ac·ing 1** : to score an ace against (an opponent) **2** : to make (a hole in golf) in one stroke

³ace *adj* : of first or high rank or quality

ACE *abbr* American Council on Education

-a·ce·ae \ˈā-sē-ˌē\ *n pl suffix* [NL, fr. L, fem. pl. of *-aceus* -aceous] : plants of the nature of ⟨Rosaceae⟩ — in names of families of plants; formerly in names of orders of plants

ace·dia \ə-ˈsēd-ē-ə\ *n* [LL, fr. Gk *akēdeia,* fr. *a-* + *kēdos* care, grief — more at HATE] : APATHY, BOREDOM

acel·da·ma \ə-ˈsel-də-mə\ *n* [fr. *Aceldama,* field bought by Judas with the money received for betraying Christ (Acts 1:18–19), fr. Gk *Akeldama,* fr. Aram *ḥăqēl dĕmā,* lit., field of blood] **1** : a place of bloodshed **2** : a place associated with evil

acel·lu·lar \(ˈ)ā-ˈsel-yə-lər\ *adj* : containing no cells : not divided into cells

acen·tric \(ˈ)ā-ˈsen-trik\ *adj* : lacking a centromere ⟨~ chromosomes⟩

-a·ceous \ˈā-shəs\ *adj suffix* [L *-aceus*] **1 a** : characterized by : full of ⟨set*aceous*⟩ **b** : consisting of ⟨carbon*aceous*⟩ : having the nature or form of ⟨tuff*aceous*⟩ **2 a** : of or relating to a group of animals typified by (such) a form ⟨cet*aceous*⟩ or characterized by (such) a feature ⟨crust*aceous*⟩ **b** : of or relating to a plant family typified by (such) a genus ⟨ros*aceous*⟩

aceph·a·lous \(ˈ)ā-ˈsef-ə-ləs, ə-ˈsef-\ *adj* [Gk *akephalos,* fr. *a-* + *kephalē* head — more at CEPHALIC] **1** : lacking a head or having the head reduced **2** : lacking a governing head or chief

ace·quia \ə-ˈsā-kē-ə, ä-\ *n* [Sp, fr. Ar *as-sāqiyah* the irrigation stream] *Southwest* : an irrigation ditch or canal

acerb \ə-ˈsərb, a-\ *adj* [F or L; F *acerbe,* fr. L *acerbus,* fr. *acer*] : acid in temper, mood, or tone

ac·er·bate \ˈas-ər-ˌbāt\ *vt* **-bat·ed; -bat·ing** : IRRITATE, EXASPERATE

acer·bic \ə-ˈsər-bik\ *adj* : ACERB — **acer·bi·cal·ly** \-bi-k(ə-)lē\ *adv*

acer·bi·ty \ə-ˈsər-bət-ē\ *n, pl* **-ties** : acidity of manner or mood ***syn*** see ACRIMONY ***ant*** mellowness

ac·er·o·la \ˌas-ə-ˈrō-lə\ *n* [Amer Sp, fr. Sp, fruit of a shrub (*Crataegus azarolus*), fr. Ar *az-zuʿrūr*] : a West Indian shrub (genus *Malpighia*) with mildly acid cherrylike fruits very rich in vitamin C

ac·er·ose \ˈas-ə-ˌrōs\ *adj* [L *acer* sharp — more at EDGE] : shaped like a needle ⟨~ leaves⟩

acer·vate \ə-ˈsər-vət, ˈas-ər-ˌvāt\ *adj* [L *acervatus,* pp. of *acervare* to heap up, fr. *acervus* heap] : growing in heaps or closely compacted clusters — **acer·vate·ly** *adv* — **ac·er·va·tion** \ˌas-ər-vā-shən\ *n*

acet- *or* **aceto-** *comb form* [F & L; F *acét-,* fr. L *acet-,* fr. *acetum*] : acetic acid : acetic ⟨*acetyl*⟩

ac·e·tab·u·lar·ia \ˌas-ə-ˌtab-yə-ˈlar-ē-ə, -ˈler-\ *n* [NL, genus name, fr. L *acetabulum* vinegar cup] : a large single-celled green alga (genus *Acetabularia*) of warm seas that resembles a small mushroom in form

ac·e·tab·u·lum \-ˈtab-yə-ləm\ *n, pl* **-lums** *or* **-la** \-lə\ [L, lit., vinegar cup, fr. *acetum* vinegar] **1 a** : the cup-shaped socket in the hipbone **b** : the cavity by which the leg of an insect articulates with the body **2** : a sucker of an invertebrate (as a trematode or leech) — **ac·e·tab·u·lar** \-lər\ *adj*

ac·e·tal \ˈas-ə-ˌtal\ *n* [G *azetal,* fr. *azet-* acet- + *al*kohol alcohol] : any of various compounds characterized by the grouping $C(OR)_2$ and obtained esp. by heating aldehydes or ketones with alcohols

ac·et·al·de·hyde \ˌas-ə-ˈtal-də-ˌhīd\ *n* [ISV] : a colorless volatile water-soluble liquid aldehyde C_2H_4O used chiefly in organic synthesis

acet·amide \ə-ˈset-ə-ˌmīd, ˌas-ət-ˈam-ˌīd\ *n* [G *azetamid,* fr. *azet-* + *amid* amide] : a white crystalline amide C_2H_5NO of acetic acid used esp. as a solvent and in organic synthesis

acet·amin·o·phen \ə-ˌsēt-ə-ˈmin-ə-fən, ˌas-ət-\ *n* [*acet-* + *amin-* + *phenol*] : a crystalline compound $C_8H_9NO_2$ that is a hydroxy derivative of acetanilide and is used in chemical synthesis and in medicine to relieve pain and fever

ac·et·an·i·lide *or* **ac·et·an·i·lid** \ˌas-ə-ˈtan-ᵊl-ˌīd, -ᵊl-əd\ *n* [ISV] : a white crystalline compound C_8H_9NO that is derived from aniline and acetic acid and is used esp. to check pain or fever

ac·e·tate \ˈas-ə-ˌtāt\ *n* **1** : a salt or ester of acetic acid **2** : cellulose acetate or one of its products **3** : a phonograph recording disk made of an acetate or coated with cellulose acetate

ace·tic \ə-ˈsēt-ik\ *adj* [prob. fr. F *acétique,* fr. L *acetum* vinegar, fr. *acēre* to be sour, fr. *acer* sharp — more at EDGE] : of, relating to, or producing acetic acid or vinegar

acetic acid *n* : a colorless pungent liquid acid $C_2H_4O_2$ that is the chief acid of vinegar and that is used esp. in synthesis (as of plastics)

ace·ti·fy \ə-ˈsēt-ə-ˌfī, -ˈset-\ *vt* **-fied; -fy·ing** : to turn into acetic acid or vinegar — **ace·ti·fi·ca·tion** \-ˌsēt-ə-fə-ˈkā-shən, -ˌset-\ *n* — **ace·ti·fi·er** \ˈsēt-ə-ˌfī(-ə)r, -ˈset-\ *n*

ace·to·ace·tic acid \ˌas-ə-tō-ə-ˌsēt-ik-, ə-ˌsēt-ō-\ *n* [part trans. of G *azetessigsäure,* fr. *azet-* acet- + *essigsäure* acetic acid] : an unstable acid $C_4H_6O_3$ found in abnormal urine

ac·e·tone \ˈas-ə-ˌtōn\ *n* [G *azeton,* fr. L *acetum*] : a volatile fragrant flammable liquid ketone C_3H_6O used chiefly as a solvent and in organic synthesis and found abnormally in urine — **ac·e·ton·ic** \ˌas-ə-ˈtän-ik\ *adj*

ace·to·phe·net·i·din \ˌas-ə-ˌtō-fə-ˈnet-əd-ən, ə-ˌsēt-ō-\ *n* [ISV] : a white crystalline compound $C_{10}H_{13}NO_2$ that is used to ease pain or fever

ace·tous \ə-ˈsēt-əs\ *adj* : relating to or producing vinegar; *also* : SOUR, VINEGARY

ace·tyl \ə-ˈsēt-ᵊl, ˈas-ət-\ *n* : the radical CH_3CO of acetic acid

acet·y·late \ə-ˈset-ᵊl-ˌāt\ *vt* **-lat·ed; -lat·ing** : to introduce the acetyl radical into (a compound) — **acet·y·la·tion** \-ˌset-ᵊl-ˈā-shən\ *n* — **acet·y·la·tive** \-ˈset-ᵊl-ˌāt-iv\ *adj*

ace·tyl·cho·line \ə-ˌsēt-ᵊl-ˈkō-ˌlēn\ *n* [ISV] : a compound $C_7H_{17}NO_3$ released at autonomic nerve endings, active in the transmission of the nerve impulse, and formed enzymatically in the tissues from choline — **ace·tyl·cho·lin·ic** \-kō-ˈlin-ik\ *adj*

ace·tyl·cho·lin·es·ter·ase \-ˌkō-lə-ˈnes-tə-ˌrās, -ˌrāz\ *n* [*acetylcholine* + *esterase*] : an enzyme that promotes the hydrolysis of acetylcholine

ace·tyl-coA \ə-ˌsēt-ᵊl-ˌkō-ˈā\ *n* : ACETYL COENZYME A

acetyl coenzyme A *n* : a compound $C_{25}H_{38}N_7O_{17}P_3S$ formed as an intermediate in metabolism and active as a coenzyme in biological acetylations

acet·y·lene \ə-ˈset-ᵊl-ən, -ᵊl-ˌēn\ *n* : a colorless gaseous hydrocarbon $HC{\equiv}CH$ made esp. by the action of water on calcium carbide and used chiefly in organic synthesis and as a fuel (as in welding and soldering) — **acet·y·le·nic** \ə-ˌset-ᵊl-ˈē-nik, -ˈen-ik\ *adj*

ace·tyl·sa·lic·y·late \ə-ˌsēt-ᵊl-sə-ˈlis-ə-ˌlāt\ *n* : a salt or ester of acetylsalicylic acid

ace·tyl·sal·i·cyl·ic acid \ə-ˈsēt-ᵊl-ˌsal-ə-ˌsil-ik-\ *n* [ISV] : ASPIRIN 1

Acha·tes \ə-ˈkāt-əz\ *n* [L] **1** : a faithful companion of Aeneas in Vergil's *Aeneid* **2** : a faithful friend

¹ache \ˈāk\ *vi* **ached; ach·ing** [ME *aken,* fr. OE *acan;* akin to LG *äken* to hurt] **1 a** : to suffer a usu. dull persistent pain **b** : to become distressed or disturbed (as with anxiety or regret) **c** : to feel compassion **2** : to become filled with painful yearning — **ach·ing·ly** \ˈā-kiŋ-lē\ *adv*

²ache *n* **1** : a usu. dull persistent pain **2** : a condition marked by aching

achene \ə-ˈkēn\ *n* [NL *achaenium,* fr. *a-* + Gk *chainein* to yawn — more at YAWN] : a small dry indehiscent one-seeded fruit developing from a simple ovary and usu. having a thin pericarp attached to the seed at only one point — **ache·ni·al** \ə-ˈkē-nē-əl\ *adj*

Ach·er·on \ˈak-ə-ˌrän, -rən\ *n* [Gk *Acherōn*] : a river in Hades

Acheu·le·an *or* **Acheu·li·an** \ə-ˈshü-lē-ən\ *adj* [F *Acheuléen,* fr. St. *Acheul,* near Amiens, France] : of or relating to a lower Paleolithic culture characterized by bifacial tools with round cutting edges

à che·val \ˌäsh-ə-ˈväl\ *adv* [F, lit., on horseback] **1** : with a leg on each side : ASTRIDE **2** : in such a way as to straddle a line on the layout of a game of chance (as roulette) or be split between two numbers, cards, or events

achieve \ə-ˈchēv\ *vb* **achieved; achiev·ing** [ME *acheven,* fr. MF *achever* to finish, fr. *a-* (fr. L *ad-*) + *chief* end, head — more at CHIEF] *vt* **1** : to carry out successfully : ACCOMPLISH ⟨~ a low unemployment rate⟩ **2** : to get as the result of exertion : WIN ⟨~ greatness⟩ ~ *vi* : to attain a desired end or aim ***syn*** see PERFORM, REACH — **achiev·able** \-ˈchē-və-bəl\ *adj* — **achiev·er** *n*

achieve·ment \ə-ˈchēv-mənt\ *n* **1** : the act of achieving : successful completion : ACCOMPLISHMENT **2 a** : a result brought about by resolve, persistence, or endeavor **b** : a great or heroic deed **3** : the quality and quantity of a student's work ***syn*** see FEAT

Achil·les \ə-ˈkil-ēz\ *n* [L, fr. Gk *Achilleus*] : the greatest warrior among the Greeks at Troy and slayer of Hector

Achilles' heel *n* [fr. the story that Achilles was vulnerable only in the heel] : a vulnerable point

Achilles tendon *n* : the strong tendon joining the muscles in the calf of the leg to the bone of the heel

achla·myd·e·ous \ˌak-lə-ˈmid-ē-əs, ˌā-klə-\ *adj* [*a-* + Gk *chlamyd-, chlamys* mantle] : lacking both calyx and corolla

achlor·hyd·ria \ˌā-ˌklōr-ˈhid-rē-ə, -ˌklȯr-\ *n* [NL, fr. *a-* + *chlor*ine + *hydro*gen] : absence of hydrochloric acid from the gastric juice — **achlor·hy·dric** \-ˈhid-rik, -ˈhī-drik\ *adj*

ə abut	ᵊ kitten	ər further	a back	ā bake	ä cot, cart
aù out	ch chin	e less	ē easy	g gift	i trip	ī life
j joke	ŋ sing	ō flow	ȯ flaw	ȯi coin	th thin	t͟h this
ü loot	ù foot	y yet	yü few	yù furious	zh vision

achon·drite \(')ä-'kän-,drīt\ n : a stony meteorite without rounded grains — achon·drit·ic \,ä-,kän-'drit-ik\ adj

achon·dro·pla·sia \,ä-,kän-drə-'plā-zh(ē-)ə\ n [NL] : failure of normal development of cartilage resulting in dwarfism — achon·dro·plas·tic \-'plas-tik\ adj

ach·ro·mat \'ak-rə-,mat\ n : ACHROMATIC LENS

achromat- or achromato- comb form [Gk achrōmatos colorless, fr. a- + chrōmat-, chrōma color — more at CHROMATIC] : achromatic ⟨achromatism⟩

ach·ro·mat·ic \,ak-rə-'mat-ik\ adj 1 : refracting light without dispersing into its constituent colors : giving images practically free from extraneous colors ⟨an ~ telescope⟩ 2 : not readily colored by the usual staining agents 3 : possessing no hue : being black, gray, or white : NEUTRAL 4 : being without accidentals or modulation : DIATONIC — ach·ro·mat·i·cal·ly \-i-k(ə-)lē\ adv — ach·ro·ma·tic·i·ty \,ak-rō-mə-'tis-ət-ē\ n — achro·ma·tize \(')ä-'krō-mə-,tīz, a-\ vt

achromatic lens n : a lens made by combining lenses of different glasses having different focal powers so that the light emerging from the lens forms an image practically free from unwanted colors

CROWN GLASS
FLINT GLASS
achromatic lens

achro·ma·tism \(')ä-'krō-mə-,tiz-əm, a-\ n : the quality or state of being achromatic

achy \'ā-kē\ adj ach·i·er; ach·i·est : afflicted with aches — ach·i·ness n

acic·u·la \ə-'sik-yə-lə\ n, pl -lae \-,lē\ or -las [NL, fr. LL, ornamental pin — more at AGLET] : a needlelike spine, bristle, or crystal — acic·u·lar \-lər\ adj — acic·u·late \-lət, -,lāt\ adj

¹ac·id \'as-əd\ adj [F or L; F acide, fr. L acidus, fr. acēre to be sour — more at ACETIC] 1 a : sour, sharp, or biting to the taste b : sharp, biting, or sour in manner, disposition, or nature ⟨an ~ individual⟩ c : sharply clear, discerning, or pointed ⟨an ~ wit⟩ d : piercingly intense and often jarring ⟨~ yellow⟩ 2 a : of, relating to, or being an acid; also : having the reactions or characteristics of an acid ⟨~ soil⟩ ⟨an ~ solution⟩ b : of salts and esters : derived by partial exchange of replaceable hydrogen ⟨~ sodium carbonate NaHCO₃⟩ c : marked by or resulting from an abnormally high concentration of acid ⟨~ indigestion⟩ 3 : relating to or made by a process (as in making steel) in which the furnace is lined with acidic material and an acidic slag is used 4 : rich in silica ⟨~ rocks⟩ syn see SOUR ant sweet, alkaline — ac·id·ly adv — ac·id·ness n

²acid n 1 : a sour substance; specif : any of various typically water-soluble and sour compounds that are capable of reacting with a base to form a salt, that redden litmus, that are hydrogen-containing molecules or ions able to give up a proton to a base, or that are substances able to accept an unshared pair of electrons from a base 2 : something incisive, biting, or sarcastic ⟨a social satire dripping with ~⟩ 3 : LSD

ac·id-fast \'as-əd-,fast\ adj : not easily decolorized by acids

ac·id·head \-,hed\ n : an individual who uses LSD

acid·ic \ə-'sid-ik, a-\ adj 1 : acid-forming 2 : ACID

acid·i·fi·er \ə-'sid-ə-,fī(-ə)r\ n : one that acidifies; esp : a substance used to increase soil acidity

acid·i·fy \-,fī\ vb -fied; -fy·ing vt 1 : to make acid 2 : to convert into an acid ~ vi : to become acid — acid·i·fi·ca·tion \-,sid-ə-fə-'kā-shən\ n

ac·i·dim·e·ter \,as-ə-'dim-ət-ər\ n : an apparatus for measuring the strength or the amount of acid present in a solution — acid·i·met·ric \ə-,sid-ə-'me-trik\ adj — ac·i·dim·e·try \,as-ə-'dim-ə-trē\ n

acid·i·ty \ə-'sid-ət-ē\ n, pl -ties 1 : the quality, state, or degree of being acid : TARTNESS 2 : the quality or state of being excessively or abnormally acid

acid·o·phile \ə-'sid-ə-,fil\ or acid·o·phil \-,fil\ n : an acidophilic substance, tissue, or organism

ac·i·do·phil·ic \,as-ə-dō-'fil-ik\ adj 1 : staining readily with acid stains 2 : preferring or thriving in a relatively acid environment

ac·i·doph·i·lus milk \,as-ə-,däf-(ə-)ləs-\ n [NL Lactobacillus acidophilus, lit., acidophilic Lactobacillus] : milk fermented by any of several bacteria and used therapeutically to change the intestinal flora

ac·i·do·sis \,as-ə-'dō-səs\ n : an abnormal state of reduced alkalinity of the blood and of the body tissues — ac·i·dot·ic \-'dät-ik\ adj

acid phosphatase n : a phosphatase (as the phosphomonoesterase from the prostate gland) active in acid medium

acid rock n : rock music with lyrics having cryptic reference to a drug (as LSD)

acid test n : a severe or crucial test

acid·u·late \ə-'sij-ə-,lāt\ vt -lat·ed; -lat·ing [L acidulus] : to make acid or slightly acid — acid·u·la·tion \-,sij-ə-'lā-shən\ n

acid·u·lent \ə-'sij-ə-lənt\ adj [F acidulant, fr. prp. of aciduler to acidulate, fr L acidulus] : ACIDULOUS

acid·u·lous \ə-'sij-ə-ləs\ adj [L acidulus sourish, fr. acidus] : somewhat acid in taste or manner : HARSH syn see SOUR ant saccharine

ac·i·nar \'as-ə-nər, -,när\ adj : of, relating to, or comprising an acinus ⟨pancreatic ~ cells⟩

ac·i·nus \'as-ə-nəs\ n, pl -ni \-,nī\ [NL, fr. L, berry, berry seed] : one of the small sacs in a racemose gland lined with secreting cells — ac·i·nous \-nəs\ adj

ack abbr acknowledge; acknowledgment

ack–ack \'ak-,ak\ n [Brit. signalmen's telephone pron. of AA, abbr. of antiaircraft] : an antiaircraft gun; also : antiaircraft fire

ac·knowl·edge \ik-'näl-ij, ak-\ vt -edged; -edg·ing [ac- (as in accord) + knowledge] 1 : to own or admit knowledge of or agreement with 2 : to recognize the rights, authority, or status of 3 a : to express gratitude or obligation for b : to take notice of c : to make known the receipt of 4 : to recognize as genuine or valid ⟨~ a debt⟩ — ac·knowl·edge·able \ə-'sä-bəl\ adj

syn ACKNOWLEDGE, ADMIT, OWN, AVOW, CONFESS shared meaning element : to disclose against one's will or inclination. ACKNOWLEDGE implies the disclosure of what has been or might have been withheld ⟨acknowledge a fault⟩ ADMIT often stresses reluctance in

disclosing or conceding ⟨at last the government ... admitted its mistake — which governments seldom do — Willa Cather⟩ OWN applies especially to acknowledgment of something in close relation to oneself ⟨finally owned that he was responsible⟩ AVOW implies open or bold declaration of what one might be expected to be silent about ⟨had an avowed hostility to his family⟩ CONFESS usually applies to something felt to be wrong; thus, one admits an error but confesses a crime. In less specific use it may imply no more than deference to the opinion of another ⟨I confess that I don't follow your reasoning⟩ ant deny

ac·knowl·edged \-ijd\ adj : generally recognized, accepted, or admitted — ac·knowl·edg·ed·ly \-ij-(ə-)dlē\ adv

ac·knowl·edg·ment also ac·knowl·edge·ment \ik-'näl-ij-mənt, ak-\ n 1 a : the act of acknowledging b : recognition or favorable notice of an act or achievement 2 : a thing done or given in recognition of something received 3 : a declaration or avowal of one's act or of a fact to give it legal validity

aclin·ic line \(,)ā-,klin-ik-\ n [²a- + clinic] : an imaginary line roughly parallel to the geographical equator and passing through those points where a magnetic needle has no dip

ACLS abbr American Council of Learned Societies

ACLU abbr American Civil Liberties Union

ACM abbr Association for Computing Machinery

ac·me \'ak-mē\ n [Gk akmē point, highest point — more at EDGE] : the highest point or stage; esp : one that represents perfection of the thing expressed ⟨he was the ~ of courtesy⟩ syn see SUMMIT

ac·ne \'ak-nē\ n [Gk aknē eruption of the face, MS var. of akmē, lit., point] : a disorder of the skin caused by inflammation of the skin glands and hair follicles; specif : one found chiefly in adolescents and marked by pimples esp. on the face — ac·ned \-nēd\ adj

acock \ə-'käk\ adj or adv : being in a cocked position ⟨a dog listening with ears ~⟩

acold \ə-'kōld\ adj [ME] archaic : COLD, CHILLED ⟨the owl, for all his feathers, was ~ —John Keats⟩

ac·o·lyte \'ak-ə-,līt\ n [ME acolite, fr. OF & ML; OF, fr. ML acoluthus, fr. MGk akolouthos, fr. Gk, adj., following, fr. a-, ha- (akin to Gk homos same) + keleuthos path — more at SAME] 1 : one who assists the clergyman in a liturgical service by performing minor duties 2 : one who attends or assists : FOLLOWER ⟨helped by his admiring ~s⟩

ac·o·nite \'ak-ə-,nīt\ n 1 : ACONITUM 1; esp : a common monkshood (Aconitum napellus) 2 : the dried tuberous root of a monkshood (Aconitum napellus) formerly used as a sedative

ac·o·ni·tum \,ak-ə-'nit-əm\ n [NL, genus name, fr. L aconitum, fr. Gk akoniton] 1 : any of a genus (Aconitum) of usu. bluish flowered poisonous herbs of the buttercup family — compare MONKSHOOD, WOLFSBANE 2 : ACONITE 2

acorn \'ā-,kó(ə)rn, -,kərn\ n [ME akern, fr. OE æcern; akin to MHG ackeran acorns collectively, Russ yagoda berry] : the nut of the oak usu. seated in or surrounded by a hard woody cupule of indurated bracts

acorns

acorn squash n : an acorn-shaped dark green winter squash with a ridged surface and sweet yellow to orange flesh

acorn tube n : a very small vacuum tube that resembles an acorn in shape and is used at extremely high frequencies

acorn worm n : any of a group (Enteropneusta) of burrowing wormlike marine animals having an acorn-shaped proboscis and usu. classed with the chordates

acous·tic \ə-'kü-stik\ adj [Gk akoustikos of hearing, fr. akouein to hear — more at HEAR] 1 : of or relating to the sense or organs of hearing, to sound, or to the science of sounds ⟨~ apparatus of the ear⟩ ⟨~ energy⟩; as a : deadening or absorbing sound ⟨~ tile⟩ b : operated by or utilizing sound waves 2 : of, relating to, or being a musical instrument whose sound is not electronically modified — acous·ti·cal \-sti-kəl\ adj — acous·ti·cal·ly \-k(ə-)lē\ adv

ac·ous·ti·cian \,ak-,ü-'stish-ən, ə-,kü-\ n : a specialist in acoustics

acous·tics \ə-'kü-stiks\ n pl but sing or pl in constr 1 : a science that deals with the production, control, transmission, reception, and effects of sound 2 also acoustic : the sum of the qualities that determine the value of an enclosure (as an auditorium) as to distinct hearing

ACP abbr American College of Physicians

acpt abbr acceptance

ac·quaint \ə-'kwānt\ vt [ME aquainten, fr. OF acointier, fr. ML accognitare, fr. LL accognitus, pp. of accognoscere to know perfectly, fr. L ad- + cognoscere to know — more at COGNITION] 1 : to cause to know personally ⟨was ~ed with the mayor⟩ 2 : to make familiar : cause to know firsthand syn see INFORM

ac·quain·tance \ə-'kwānt-ⁿ(t)s\ n 1 a : personal knowledge : FAMILIARITY b : the state of being acquainted 2 a : the persons with whom one is acquainted ⟨should auld ~ be forgot — Robert Burns⟩ b : a person whom one knows but who is not a particularly close friend — ac·quain·tance·ship \-,ship\ n

ac·qui·esce \,ak-wē-'es\ vi -esced; -esc·ing [F acquiescer, fr. L acquiescere, fr. ad- + quiescere to be quiet — more at QUIET] : to accept or comply tacitly or passively syn see ASSENT ant object

ac·qui·es·cence \,ak-wē-'es-ⁿn(t)s\ n 1 : the act of acquiescing : the state of being acquiescent 2 : an instance of acquiescing

ac·qui·es·cent \,ak-wē-'es-ⁿnt\ adj [L acquiescent-, acquiescens, prp. of acquiescere] : inclined to acquiesce : ACQUIESCING — ac·qui·es·cent·ly adv

ac·quir·able \ə-'kwī-rə-bəl\ adj : capable of being acquired

ac·quire \ə-'kwī(ə)r\ vt ac·quired; ac·quir·ing [ME aqueren, fr. MF aquerre, fr. L acquirere, fr. ad- + quaerere to seek, obtain] 1 : to get as one's own: a : to come into possession or control of often by unspecified means b : to come to have as a new or additional characteristic, trait, or ability (as by sustained effort or through environmental forces) ⟨~ fluency in French⟩ ⟨bacteria that ~ tolerance to antibiotics⟩ 2 : to locate and hold (a desired object) in a detector ⟨ ~ a target by radar⟩ ***syn*** see GET ***ant*** forfeit

ac·quire·ment \ə-ˈkwī(ə)r-mənt\ *n* **1** : the act of acquiring **2** : an attainment of mind or body usu. resulting from continued endeavor

ac·qui·si·tion \ˌak-wə-ˈzish-ən\ *n* [ME *acquisicioun,* fr. MF or L; MF *acquisition,* fr. L *acquisition-, acquisitio,* fr. *acquisitus,* pp. of *acquirere*] **1** : the act of acquiring **2** : something acquired or gained **3** : the acquiring of library materials (as books and periodicals) by purchase, exchange, or gift — **ac·qui·si·tion·al** \-shnəl, -shən-ᵊl\ *adj* — **ac·quis·i·tor** \ə-ˈkwiz-ət-ər\ *n*

ac·quis·i·tive \ə-ˈkwiz-ət-iv\ *adj* : strongly desirous of acquiring and possessing ***syn*** see COVETOUS ***ant*** sacrificing, abnegating — **ac·quis·i·tive·ly** *adv* — **ac·quis·i·tive·ness** *n*

ac·quit \ə-ˈkwit\ *vt* **ac·quit·ted; ac·quit·ting** [ME *aquiten,* fr. OF *aquiter,* fr. *a-* (fr. L *ad-*) + *quite* free of — more at QUIT] **1 a** *archaic* : to pay off (as a claim or debt) **b** *obs* : REPAY, REQUITE **2** : to discharge completely (as from an obligation or accusation) ⟨the court *acquitted* the prisoner⟩ **3** : to conduct (oneself) satisfactorily esp. under stress ⟨the recruits *acquitted* themselves like veterans⟩ ***syn*** see BEHAVE — **ac·quit·ter** *n*

ac·quit·tal \ə-ˈkwit-ᵊl\ *n* : a setting free from the charge of an offense by verdict, sentence, or other legal process

ac·quit·tance \ə-ˈkwit-ᵊn(t)s\ *n* : a document evidencing a discharge from an obligation; *esp* : a receipt in full

acr- *or* **acro-** *comb form* [MF or Gk; MF *acro-,* fr. Gk *akr-, akro-,* fr. *akros* topmost, extreme; akin to Gk *akmē* point — more at EDGE] **1** : beginning : end : tip ⟨*acro*nym⟩ **2 a** : top : peak : summit ⟨*acro*dont⟩ **b** : height ⟨*acro*phobia⟩ **c** : extremity of the body ⟨*acro*cyanosis⟩

ac·ra·sin \ˈak-rə-sən\ *n* [NL *Acrasia,* genus of fungi related to the slime molds + *-in*] : a substance and esp. cyclic AMP secreted by the individual cells of a slime mold and causing them to aggregate into a multicellular mass

acre \ˈā-kər\ *n* [ME, fr. OE *æcer;* akin to OHG *ackar* field, L *ager,* Gk *agros,* L *agere* to drive — more at AGENT] **1 a** *archaic* : a field esp. of arable or pasture land **b** *pl* : LANDS, ESTATE **2** : any of various units of area; *esp* : a unit in the U.S. and England equal to 160 square rods ⟨a lake of 9 ~*s*⟩ — see WEIGHT table **3** : a broad expanse or great quantity ⟨~*s* of time devoted to trivia⟩

acre·age \ˈā-k(ə-)rij\ *n* : area in acres : ACRES

acre–foot \ˈā-kər-ˈfu̇t\ *n* : the volume (as of irrigation water) that would cover one acre to a depth of one foot

acre–inch \ˈā-kə-ˈrinch\ *n* : one twelfth of an acre-foot

ac·rid \ˈak-rəd\ *adj* [modif. of L *acr-, acer* sharp — more at EDGE] **1** : sharp and harsh or unpleasantly pungent in taste or odor : IRRITATING, CORROSIVE **2** : deeply or violently bitter : ACRIMONIOUS ⟨an ~ denunciation⟩ — **acrid·i·ty** \a-ˈkrid-ət-ē, ə-\ *n* — **ac·rid·ly** \ˈak-rəd-lē\ *adv* — **ac·rid·ness** *n*

ac·ri·dine \ˈak-rə-ˌdēn\ *n* : a colorless crystalline compound $C_{13}H_9N$ occurring in coal tar and important as the parent compound of dyes and pharmaceuticals

ac·ri·fla·vine \ˌak-rə-ˈflā-ˌvēn, -vən\ *n* [*acridine* + *flavine*] : a yellow dye $C_{14}H_{14}N_3Cl$ used as an antiseptic esp. for wounds

Ac·ri·lan \ˈak-rə-ˌlan, -lən\ *trademark* — used for an acrylic fiber

ac·ri·mo·ni·ous \ˌak-rə-ˈmō-nē-əs\ *adj* : caustic, biting, or rancorous esp. in feeling, language, or manner ⟨an ~ dispute⟩ — **ac·ri·mo·ni·ous·ly** *adv* — **ac·ri·mo·ni·ous·ness** *n*

ac·ri·mo·ny \ˈak-rə-ˌmō-nē\ *n, pl* **-nies** [MF or L; MF *acrimonie,* fr. L *acrimonia,* fr. *acr-, acer*] : harsh or biting sharpness esp. of words, manner, or disposition

syn ACRIMONY, ACERBITY, ASPERITY *shared meaning element* : temper or language marked by angry irritation ***ant*** suavity

ac·ro·bat \ˈak-rə-ˌbat\ *n* [F & Gk; F *acrobate,* fr. Gk *akrobatēs,* fr. *akrobatos* walking up high, fr. *akros* + *bainein* to go — more at COME] **1** : one that performs gymnastic feats requiring skillful control of the body **2** : one adept at swiftly changing his position or viewpoint ⟨a political ~⟩ — **ac·ro·bat·ic** \ˌak-rə-ˈbat-ik\ *adj* — **ac·ro·bat·i·cal·ly** \-i-k(ə-)lē\ *adv*

ac·ro·bat·ics \ˌak-rə-ˈbat-iks\ *n pl but sing or pl in constr* **1** : the art, performance, or activity of an acrobat **2** : a spectacular, showy, or startling performance involving great agility

ac·ro·car·pous \ˌak-rō-ˈkär-pəs\ *adj* [NL *acrocarpus,* fr. Gk *akrokarpos* bearing fruit at the top, fr. *akr-* acr- + *-karpos* -carpous] *of a moss* : having the archegonia and hence the capsules terminal on the stem

ac·ro·cen·tric \-ˈsen-trik\ *adj* [*acr-* + *-centric*] : having the centromere situated so that one chromosomal arm is much shorter than the other — **acrocentric** *n*

ac·ro·dont \ˈak-rə-ˌdänt\ *adj* **1** *of teeth* : consolidated with the summit of the alveolar ridge without sockets **2** : having acrodont teeth

acro·le·in \ə-ˈkrō-lē-ən\ *n* [ISV *acr-* (fr. L *acr-, acer*) + L *olēre* to smell — more at ODOR] : a colorless irritant pungent liquid aldehyde C_3H_4O obtained by dehydration of glycerol or destructive distillation of fats

ac·ro·meg·a·ly \ˌak-rō-ˈmeg-ə-lē\ *n* [F *acromégalie,* fr. *acr-* + Gk *megal-, megas* large — more at MUCH] : chronic hyperpituitarism marked by progressive enlargement of hands, feet, and face — **ac·ro·me·gal·ic** \-mə-ˈgal-ik\ *adj or n*

ac·ro·nym \ˈak-rə-ˌnim\ *n* [*acr-* + *-onym* (as in *homonym*)] : a word (as *radar or snafu*) formed from the initial letter or letters of each of the successive parts or major parts of a compound term — **ac·ro·nym·ic** \ˌak-rə-ˈnim-ik\ *adj* — **ac·ro·nym·i·cal·ly** \-i-k(ə-)lē\ *adv*

acrop·e·tal \ə-ˈkräp-ət-ᵊl, a-\ *adj* [*acr-* + *-petal* (as in *centripetal*)] : proceeding from the base toward the apex or from below upward — **acrop·e·tal·ly** \-ᵊl-ē\ *adv*

ac·ro·pho·bia \ˌak-rə-ˈfō-bē-ə\ *n* [NL] : abnormal dread of being at a great height

acrop·o·lis \ə-ˈkräp-ə-ləs\ *n* [Gk *akropolis,* fr. *akr-* acr- + *polis* city — more at POLICE] : the upper fortified part of an ancient Greek city (as Athens)

¹across \ə-ˈkrȯs\ *adv* [ME *acros,* fr. AF *an crois,* fr. *an* in (fr. L *in*) + *crois* cross, fr. L *crux* — more at IN, CROSS] **1** : in a position reaching from one side to the other : CROSSWISE **2** : to or on the opposite side **3** : so as to be understandable, acceptable, or successful : OVER ⟨get an argument ~⟩

²across *prep* **1 a** : from one side to the opposite side of : OVER, THROUGH ⟨swam ~ the river⟩ **b** : on the opposite side of ⟨lives ~ the street from us⟩ **2** : so as to intersect or pass through at an angle ⟨sawed ~ the grain of the wood⟩ **3** : into transitory contact with ⟨ran ~ an old friend in the store⟩

³across *adj* : being in a crossed position

across–the–board *adj* **1** : placed in combination to win, place, or show ⟨an ~ racing bet⟩ **2** : embracing or affecting all classes or categories : BLANKET ⟨an ~ pay raise⟩

acros·tic \ə-ˈkrȯs-tik, -ˈkräs-\ *n* [MF & Gk; MF *acrostiche,* fr. Gk *akrostichis,* fr. *akr-* acr- + *stichos* line; akin to *steichein* to go — more at STAIR] **1** : a composition usu. in verse in which sets of letters (as the initial or final letters of the lines) taken in order form a word or phrase or a regular sequence of letters of the alphabet **2** : ACRONYM **3** : a series of words of equal length arranged to read the same horizontally or vertically — **acrostic** *also* **acros·ti·cal** \-ti-kəl\ *adj* — **acros·ti·cal·ly** \-ti-k(ə-)lē\ *adv*

ACRR *abbr* American Council on Race Relations

ac·ry·late \ˈak-rə-ˌlāt\ *n* **1** : a salt or ester of acrylic acid **2** : ACRYLIC RESIN

¹acryl·ic \ə-ˈkril-ik\ *adj* [ISV *acr*olein + *-yl* + *-ic*] : of or relating to acrylic acid or its derivatives ⟨~ polymers⟩

²acrylic *n* **1 a** : ACRYLIC RESIN **b** : a paint in which the vehicle is an acrylic resin **c** : a painting done in an acrylic resin **2** : ACRYLIC FIBER

acrylic acid *n* : an unsaturated liquid acid $C_3H_4O_2$ that is obtained by synthesis and that polymerizes readily to form useful products (as constituents for varnishes and lacquers)

acrylic fiber *n* : a quick-drying synthetic textile fiber made by polymerization of acrylonitrile usu. with other monomers

acrylic resin *n* : a glassy thermoplastic made by polymerizing acrylic or methacrylic acid or a derivative of either and used for cast and molded parts or as coatings and adhesives

ac·ry·lo·ni·trile \ˌak-rə-lō-ˈnī-trəl, -ˌtrēl\ *n* : a colorless volatile flammable liquid nitrile C_3H_3N used chiefly in organic synthesis and for polymerization

ACS *abbr* **1** American Chemical Society **2** American College of Surgeons

¹act \ˈakt\ *n* [ME, partly fr. L *actus* doing, act, fr. *actus,* pp. of *agere* to drive, do; partly fr. L *actum* thing done, record, fr. neut. of *actus,* pp. — more at AGENT] **1 a** : a thing done : DEED **b** : something done voluntarily **2** : a state of real existence rather than possibility **3** : the formal product of a legislative body : STATUTE; *also* : a decision or determination of a sovereign, a legislative council, or a court of justice **4** : the process of doing **5** *often cap* : a formal record of something done or transacted **6 a** : one of the principal divisions of a theatrical work (as a play or opera) **b** : one of the successive parts or performances in a variety show or circus **7** : a display of affected behavior : PRETENSE ***syn*** see ACTION

²act *vt* **1** *obs* : ACTUATE, ANIMATE **2 a** : to represent or perform by action esp. on the stage **b** : FEIGN, SIMULATE **c** : IMPERSONATE **3** : to play the part of as if in a play ⟨~ the man of the world⟩ **4** : to behave in a manner suitable to ⟨~ your age⟩ ~ *vi* **1 a** : to perform on the stage **b** : to behave as if performing on the stage : PRETEND **2** : to take action : MOVE ⟨think before ~*ing*⟩ ⟨~*ed* favorably on the recommendation⟩ **3** : to conduct oneself : BEHAVE ⟨~ like a fool⟩ **4** : to perform a specified function : SERVE ⟨trees ~*ing* as a windbreak⟩ **5** : to produce an effect : WORK ⟨wait for a medicine to ~ ⟩ **6** *of a play* : to be capable of being performed ⟨the play ~*s* well⟩ **7** : to give a decision or award — **act·abil·i·ty** \ˌak-tə-ˈbil-ət-ē\ *n* — **act·able** \ˈak-tə-bəl\ *adj*

³act *abbr* **1** active **2** actor **3** actual

ACT *abbr* **1** American College Test **2** Association of Classroom Teachers **3** Australian Capital Territory

Ac·tae·on \ak-ˈtē-ən\ *n* [L, fr. Gk *Aktaiōn*] : a hunter turned into a stag and killed by his own hounds for having seen Artemis bathing

actg *abbr* acting

ACTH \ˌā-ˌsē-(ˌ)tē-ˈāch\ *n* [*a*drenocortico*t*rophic *h*ormone] : ADRENOCORTICOTROPHIC HORMONE

ac·tin \ˈak-tən\ *n* [ISV, fr. L *actus*] : a protein of muscle that is active in muscular contraction

actin- *or* **actini-** *or* **actino-** *comb form* [NL, ray, fr. Gk *aktin-, aktino-,* fr. *aktin-, aktis;* akin to OE *ūhte* morning twilight, L *noct-, nox* night — more at NIGHT] **1 a** : having a radiate form ⟨*Actino*myces⟩ **b** : actinian ⟨*actini*form⟩ **2 a** : actinic ⟨*actin*ium⟩ **b** : actinic radiation (as X rays) ⟨*actino*therapy⟩

¹act·ing \ˈak-tiŋ\ *adj* **1** : holding a temporary rank or position : performing services temporarily ⟨~ president⟩ **2 a** : suitable for stage performance ⟨an ~ play⟩ **b** : prepared with directions for actors ⟨an ~ text of a play⟩

²acting *n* : the art or practice of representing a character on a stage or before cameras

ac·tin·ia \ak-ˈtin-ē-ə\ *n, pl* **-i·ae** \-ē-ˌē\ *or* **-i·as** [NL, fr. Gk *aktin-, aktis*] : SEA ANEMONE; *also* : a related animal — **ac·tin·i·an** \-ē-ən\ *adj or n*

ac·tin·ic \ak-ˈtin-ik\ *adj* : of, relating to, or exhibiting actinism — **ac·tin·i·cal·ly** \-i-k(ə-)lē\ *adv*

actinic ray *n* : a radiation having marked photochemical action

ac·ti·nide \ˈak-tə-ˌnīd\ *n* [ISV] : any element in a series of elements of increasing atomic numbers beginning with actinium (89) or

ə abut ᵊ kitten ər further a back ā bake ä cot, cart
au̇ out ch chin e less ē easy g gift i trip ī life
j joke ŋ sing ō flow ȯ flaw ȯi coin th thin t͟h this
ü loot u̇ foot y yet yü few yu̇ furious zh vision

thorium (90) and ending with element of atomic number 103 — see PERIODIC TABLE table
ac·ti·nism \'ak-tə-ˌniz-əm\ *n* : the property of radiant energy esp. in the visible and ultraviolet spectral regions by which chemical changes are produced
ac·tin·i·um \ak-'tin-ē-əm\ *n* [NL] : a radioactive trivalent metallic element that resembles lanthanum in chemical properties and that is found esp. in pitchblende — see ELEMENT table
ac·tin·o·lite \ak-'tin-ᵊl-ˌīt\ *n* : a bright or grayish green amphibole occurring in fibrous, radiated, or columnar forms
ac·ti·nom·e·ter \ˌak-tə-'näm-ət-ər\ *n* **1** : an instrument for measuring the direct heating power of the sun's rays **2** : an instrument for measuring the actinic power of radiant energy or for determining photographic exposure to be given — **ac·ti·no·me·tric** \-nō-'me-trik\ *adj* — **ac·ti·nom·e·try** \-'näm-ə-trē\ *n*
ac·ti·no·mor·phic \ˌak-tə-nō-'mȯr-fik\ *also* **ac·ti·no·mor·phous** \-fəs\ *adj* [ISV] : being radially symmetrical and capable of division into essentially symmetrical halves by any longitudinal plane passing through the axis — **ac·ti·no·mor·phy** \'ak-tə-nō-ˌmȯr-fē\ *n*
ac·ti·no·my·ces \ˌak-tə-nō-'mī-ˌsēz\ *n, pl* **actinomyces** [NL, genus name, fr. *actin-* + Gk *mykēt-, mykēs* fungus; akin to Gk *myxa* mucus — more at MUCUS] : any of a genus (*Actinomyces*) of filamentous bacteria including both soil-inhabiting saprophytes and disease-producing parasites — **ac·ti·no·my·ce·tal** \-mī-'sēt-ᵊl\ *adj*
ac·ti·no·my·cete \ˌak-tə-nō-'mī-ˌsēt, -mī-'sēt\ *n* [deriv. of Gk *aktin-, aktis* + *mykēt-, mykēs*] : any of an order (Actinomycetales) of filamentous or rod-shaped bacteria including the actinomyces and streptomyces — **ac·ti·no·my·ce·tous** \-mī-'sēt-əs\ *adj*
ac·ti·no·my·cin \ˌak-tə-nō-'mīs-ᵊn\ *n* : any of various red or yellow-red mostly toxic polypeptide antibiotics isolated from soil bacteria (esp. *Streptomyces antibioticus*)
ac·ti·no·my·co·sis \ˌak-tə-nō-mī-'kō-səs\ *n* : infection with or disease caused by actinomycetes; *esp.* : a chronic disease of cattle, swine, and man characterized by hard granulomatous masses usu. in mouth and jaw — **ac·ti·no·my·cot·ic** \-'kät-ik\ *adj*
ac·ti·non \'ak-tə-ˌnän\ *n* [NL, fr. *actinium*] : a gaseous radioactive isotope of radon that has a half-life of about 4 seconds
ac·ti·no·ura·ni·um \ˌak-tə-nō-yu̇-'rā-nē-əm\ *n* [NL, fr. *actinium* + *uranium*] : the uranium isotope of mass 235
ac·ti·no·zo·an \ˌ-nō-'zō-ən\ *n* [*actin-* + Gk *zōion* animal; akin to Gk *zōē* life — more at QUICK] : ANTHOZOAN — **actinozoan** *adj*
ac·tion \'ak-shən\ *n* **1** : a proceeding in a court of justice by which one demands or enforces one's right **2** : the bringing about of an alteration by force or through a natural agency **3** : the manner or method of performing: **a** : the deportment of an actor or speaker or his expression by means of attitude, voice, and gesture **b** : the style of movement of the feet and legs (as of a horse) **c** : a function of the body or one of its parts **4** : an act of will **5 a** : a thing accomplished usu. over a period of time, in stages, or with the possibility of repetition ⟨an ~, the product and expression of exerted force —Thomas Carlyle⟩ **b** *pl* : BEHAVIOR, CONDUCT ⟨somber ~*s*⟩ **c** : INITIATIVE, ENTERPRISE ⟨a man of ~⟩ **6 a** (1) : an engagement between troops or ships (2) : combat in war ⟨gallantry in ~⟩ **b** (1) : an event or series of events forming a literary composition (2) : the unfolding of the events of a drama or work of fiction : PLOT (3) : the movement of incidents in a plot **c** : the combination of circumstances that constitute the subject matter of a painting or sculpture **7 a** : an operating mechanism **b** : the manner in which a mechanism operates **8 a** : the price movement and trading volume of a commodity, security, or market **b** : the process of betting including the offering and acceptance of a bet and determination of a winner **9** : the most vigorous, productive, or exciting activity in a particular field, area, or group ⟨they itch to go where the ~ is —D. J. Henahan⟩
syn **1** ACTION, ACT, DEED *shared meaning element* : something done or effected
2 see BATTLE
ac·tion·able \'ak-sh(ə-)nə-bəl\ *adj* : subject to or affording ground for an action or suit at law — **ac·tion·ably** \-blē\ *adv*
ac·tion·less \'ak-shən-ləs\ *adj* : marked by inaction : IMMOBILE
action painting *n* : abstract expressionism marked esp. by the use of spontaneous techniques (as dribbling, splattering, or smearing)
action potential *n* : a recorded change in potential (as between the inside of a nerve cell and the extracellular medium) during activity of a cell or tissue
ac·ti·vate \'ak-tə-ˌvāt\ *vb* **-vat·ed; -vat·ing** *vt* : to make active or more active: as **a** (1) : to make (as molecules) reactive or more reactive (2) : to convert (as a provitamin) into a biologically active derivative **b** : to make (a substance) radioactive, luminescent, photosensitive, or photoconductive **c** : to treat (as carbon or alumina) esp. so as to improve adsorptive properties **d** : to aerate (sewage) so as to favor the growth of organisms that decompose organic matter **e** (1) : to set up or formally institute (as a military unit) with the necessary personnel and equipment **e** (2) : to put (an individual or unit) on active duty ~ *vi* : to become active ***syn*** see VITALIZE ***ant*** arrest — **ac·ti·va·tion** \ˌak-tə-'vā-shən\ *n* — **ac·ti·va·tor** \'ak-tə-ˌvāt-ər\ *n*
activated carbon *n* : a highly adsorbent powdered or granular carbon made usu. by carbonization and chemical activation and used chiefly for purifying by adsorption — called also *activated charcoal*
activation analysis *n* : analysis to determine chemical elements in a material by bombarding it with neutrons to produce radioactive atoms whose radiations are characteristic of the elements present
ac·tive \'ak-tiv\ *adj* [ME, fr. MF or L; MF *actif,* fr. L *activus,* fr. *actus,* pp. of *agere* to drive, do — more at AGENT] **1** : characterized by action rather than by contemplation or speculation **2** : productive of action or movement **3 a** *of a verb form or voice* : asserting that the person or thing represented by the grammatical subject performs the action represented by the verb ⟨*hits* in "he hits the ball" is ~⟩ **b** : expressing action as distinct from mere existence or state **4** : quick in physical movement : LIVELY **5** : marked by vigorous activity : BUSY ⟨the stock market was ~⟩ **6** : requiring vigorous action or exertion ⟨~ sports⟩ **7** : having practical operation or results : EFFECTIVE ⟨an ~ law⟩ **8 a** : disposed to action : ENERGETIC ⟨~ interest⟩ **b** : engaged in an action or activity : PARTICIPATING ⟨an ~ club member⟩ **9** : engaged in full-time service esp. in the armed forces ⟨~ duty⟩ **10** : marked by present operation, transaction, movement, or use ⟨~ account⟩ **11 a** : capable of acting or reacting : ACTIVATED ⟨~ nitrogen⟩ ⟨~ charcoal⟩ **b** : tending to progress or to cause degeneration ⟨~ tuberculosis⟩ **c** : exhibiting optical activity **12** : still eligible to win the pot in poker **13** : moving down the line : visiting in the set — used of couples in contredanses or square dances — **active** *n* — **ac·tive·ly** *adv* — **ac·tive·ness** *n*
active immunity *n* : usu. long-lasting immunity that is acquired through production of antibodies within the organism in response to the presence of antigens — compare PASSIVE IMMUNITY
active transport *n* : movement of a chemical substance by the expenditure of energy through a gradient (as across a cell membrane) in concentration or electrical potential and opposite to the direction of normal diffusion
ac·tiv·ism \'ak-ti-ˌviz-əm\ *n* : a doctrine or practice that emphasizes direct vigorous action (as a mass demonstration) in support of or opposition to one side of a controversial issue — **ac·tiv·ist** \-vəst\ *n or adj* — **ac·tiv·is·tic** \ˌak-ti-'vis-tik\ *adj*
ac·tiv·i·ty \ak-'tiv-ət-ē\ *n, pl* **-ties** **1** : the quality or state of being active **2** : vigorous or energetic action : LIVELINESS **3** : natural or normal function: as **a** : a process (as digestion) that an organism carries on or participates in by virtue of being alive **b** : similar process actually or potentially involving mental function; *specif* : an educational procedure designed to stimulate learning by firsthand experience **4** : an active force **5 a** : a pursuit in which a person is active **b** : a form of organized, supervised, often extracurricular recreation **6** : an organizational unit for performing a specific function; *also* : its function or duties
act of God : an extraordinary interruption by a natural cause (as a flood or earthquake) of the usual course of events that experience, prescience, or care cannot reasonably foresee or prevent
ac·to·my·o·sin \ˌak-tə-'mī-ə-sən\ *n* [ISV *actin* + *-o-* + *myosin*] : a viscous contractile complex of actin and myosin concerned together with ATP in muscular contraction
ac·tor \'ak-tər\ *n* **1** : one that acts : DOER **2 a** : one who represents a character in a dramatic production **b** : a theatrical performer **c** : one that behaves as if acting a part **3** : one that takes part in any affair : PARTICIPANT — **ac·tor·ish** \-tə-rish\ *adj* — **ac·tress** \-trəs\ *n*
act out *vt* **1 a** : to represent in action ⟨children *act out* what they read⟩ **b** : to translate into action ⟨unwilling to *act out* their beliefs⟩ **2** : to express (repressed or unconscious impulses) in overt behavior without awareness or insight esp. during psychoanalytic investigation
Acts \'akts\ *n pl but sing in constr* : a book in the New Testament narrating the beginnings of the Church — called also *Acts of the Apostles;* see BIBLE table
ac·tu·al \'ak-ch(ə-w)əl, 'aksh-wəl\ *adj* [ME *actuel,* fr. MF, fr. LL *actualis,* fr. L *actus* act] **1** *obs* : ACTIVE **2 a** : existing in act and not merely potentially **b** : existing in fact or reality ⟨~ and imagined conditions⟩ **c** : not false or apparent ⟨~ costs⟩ **3** : existing or occurring at the time : CURRENT ⟨caught in the ~ commission of a crime⟩ ***syn*** see REAL ***ant*** ideal, imaginary
actual cash value *n* : the amount necessary to replace or restore lost, stolen, or damaged property (as an automobile)
ac·tu·al·i·ty \ˌak-chə-'wal-ət-ē\ *n, pl* **-ties** **1** : the quality or state of being actual **2** : something that is actual : FACT, REALITY ⟨possible risks which have been seized upon as *actualities* —T. S. Eliot⟩
ac·tu·al·ize \'ak-ch(ə-w)ə-ˌlīz, 'aksh-wə-\ *vb* **-ized; -iz·ing** *vt* : to make actual ~ *vi* : to become actual — **ac·tu·al·iza·tion** \ˌak-ch(ə-w)ə-lə-'zā-shən, ˌaksh-wə-\ *n*
ac·tu·al·ly \'ak-ch(ə-w)ə-lē, 'aksh-(wə-)lē\ *adv* **1** : in act or in fact : REALLY ⟨nominally but not ~ independent —Karl Loewenstein⟩ **2** : at the present moment ⟨the party ~ in power⟩ **3** : in point of fact : in truth ⟨she ~ spoke Latin⟩
ac·tu·ar·i·al \ˌak-chə-'wer-ē-əl\ *adj* **1** : of or relating to actuaries **2** : relating to statistical calculation esp. of life expectancy — **ac·tu·ar·i·al·ly** \-ē-ə-lē\ *adv*
ac·tu·ary \'ak-chə-ˌwer-ē\ *n, pl* **-ar·ies** [L *actuarius* shorthand writer, fr. *actum* record — more at ACT] **1** *obs* : CLERK, REGISTRAR **2** : one who calculates insurance and annuity premiums, reserves, and dividends
ac·tu·ate \'ak-chə-ˌwāt\ *vt* **-at·ed; -at·ing** [ML *actuatus,* pp. of *actuare,* fr. L *actus* act] **1** : to put into mechanical action or motion **2** : to move to action ***syn*** see MOVE — **ac·tu·a·tion** \ˌak-chə-'wā-shən\ *n*
ac·tu·a·tor \'ak-chə-ˌwāt-ər\ *n* : one that actuates; *specif* : a mechanism for moving or controlling something indirectly instead of by hand
act up *vi* **1** : to act in a way different from that which is normal or expected: as **a** : to behave in an unruly, recalcitrant, or capricious manner **b** : to show off **c** : to function improperly ⟨this typewriter is *acting up* again⟩ **2** : to become active or acute after being quiescent ⟨her rheumatism started to *act up*⟩
acu·ity \ə-'kyü-ət-ē\ *n, pl* **-ities** [MF *acuité,* fr. OF *agüeté,* fr. *agu* sharp, fr. L *acutus*] : keenness of perception : SHARPNESS
acu·le·ate \ə-'kyü-lē-ət\ *adj* [L *aculeatus* having stings, fr. *aculeus,* dim. of *acus*] : having a sting ⟨~ insects⟩
acu·men \ə-'kyü-mən\ *n* [L *acumin-, acumen,* lit., point, fr. *acuere*] : keenness and depth of perception, discernment, or discrimination esp. in practical matters : SHREWDNESS ***syn*** see DISCERNMENT
[1]**acu·mi·nate** \ə-'kyü-mə-nət\ *adj* : tapering to a slender point : POINTED
[2]**acu·mi·nate** \-ˌnāt\ *vb* **-nat·ed; -nat·ing** *vt* : to make sharp or acute ~ *vi* : to taper or come to a point — **acu·mi·na·tion** \ə-ˌkyü-mə-'nā-shən\ *n*
acu·punc·ture \'ak-yu̇-ˌpəŋ(k)-chər\ *n* [L *acus* + E *puncture*] : an orig. Chinese practice of puncturing the body (as with needles) to cure disease or relieve pain

acute \ə-'kyüt\ *adj* **acut·er; acut·est** [L *acutus,* pp. of *acuere* to sharpen, fr. *acus* needle; akin to L *acer* sharp — more at EDGE] **1** : ending in a sharp point: as **a** : being or forming an angle measuring less than 90 degrees ⟨~ angle⟩ **b** : composed of acute angles ⟨~ triangle⟩ **2 a** : marked by keen discernment or intellectual perception esp. of subtle distinctions : PENETRATING ⟨an ~ thinker⟩ **b** : responsive to slight impressions or stimuli ⟨~ observer⟩ **3** : of a kind to act keenly on the senses; *esp* : characterized by sharpness or severity ⟨~ pain⟩ **4 a** : having a sudden onset, sharp rise, and short course ⟨~ disease⟩ **b** : lasting a short time ⟨~ experiments⟩ **5** : seriously demanding urgent attention ⟨an ~ housing shortage⟩ **6 a** *of an accent mark* : having the form ´ **b** : marked with an acute accent **c** : of the variety indicated by an acute accent — **acute·ly** *adv* — **acute·ness** *n*

syn **1** see SHARP ***ant*** obtuse

2 ACUTE, CRITICAL, CRUCIAL *shared meaning element* : full of uncertainty as to outcome ***ant*** chronic

ACV *abbr* **1** actual cash value **2** air-cushion vehicle

acy·clic \(')ā-'sī-klik, -'sik-lik\ *adj* **1** : not cyclic; *esp* : not disposed in cycles or whorls **2** : having an open-chain structure; *esp* : ALIPHATIC ⟨an ~ compound⟩

ac·yl \'as-əl\ *n* [ISV, fr. *acid*] : a radical derived usu. from an organic acid by removal of the hydroxyl from all acid groups

¹ad \'ad\ *n* : ADVERTISEMENT 2

²ad *n* : ADVANTAGE 4

AD *abbr* **1** active duty **2** after date **3** air-dried **4** anno Domini — often printed in small capitals **5** assembly district

ad- *or* **ac-** *or* **af-** *or* **ag-** *or* **al-** *or* **ap-** *or* **as-** *or* **at-** *prefix* [ME, fr. MF, OF & L; MF, fr. OF, fr. L, fr. *ad* — more at AT] **1** : to : toward — usu. *ac-* before *c, k,* or *q* ⟨*ac*culturation⟩ and *af-* before *f* and *ag-* before *g* ⟨*ag*grade⟩ and *al-* before *l* ⟨*al*literation⟩ and *ap-* before *p* ⟨*ap*proximal⟩ and *as-* before *s* ⟨*as*suasive⟩ and *at-* before *t* ⟨*at*tune⟩ and *ad-* before other sounds but sometimes *ad-* even before one of the listed consonants ⟨*ad*sorb⟩ **2** : near : adjacent to — in this sense always in the form *ad-* ⟨*ad*renal⟩

-ad \,ad, əd\ *adv suffix* [L *ad*] : in the direction of : toward ⟨cephal*ad*⟩

ADA *abbr* **1** American Dental Association **2** Americans for Democratic Action **3** average daily attendance

ad·age \'ad-ij\ *n* [MF, fr. L *adagium,* fr. *ad-* + *-agium* (akin to *aio* I say); akin to Gk *ē* he spoke] : a saying often in metaphorical form that embodies a common observation

¹ada·gio \ə-'däj-(ē-,)ō, -'däzh-\ *adv or adj* [It, fr. *ad* to + *agio* ease] : in an easy graceful manner : SLOWLY — used chiefly as a direction in music

²adagio *n, pl* **-gios** **1** : a musical composition or movement in adagio tempo **2** : a ballet duet by a man and woman or a mixed trio displaying difficult feats of balance, lifting, or spinning

¹Ad·am \'ad-əm\ *n* [ME, fr. LL, fr. Gk, fr. Heb *Ādhām*] **1** : the first man and father by Eve of Cain and Abel **2** : the unregenerate nature of man — used esp. in the phrase *the old Adam* — **Adam·ic** \ə-'dam-ik\ *or* **Adam·i·cal** \-i-kəl\ *adj*

²Adam *adj* [Robert *Adam* †1792 & James *Adam* †1794 Sc designers] : of or relating to an 18th century style of furniture characterized by straight lines, surface decoration, and conventional designs (as festooned garlands and medallions)

ad·a·mance \'ad-ə-mən(t)s\ *n* : ADAMANCY

ad·a·man·cy \-mən-sē\ *n* [²*adamant* + *-cy*] : unyielding quality : OBSTINACY

adam–and–eve \,ad-ə-mən-'(d)ēv\ *n* : PUTTYROOT

¹ad·a·mant \'ad-ə-mənt *also* -,mant\ *n* [ME, fr. OF, fr. L *adamant-, adamas* hardest metal, diamond, fr. Gk] **1** : a stone (as a diamond) formerly believed to be of impenetrable hardness **2** : an unbreakable or extremely hard substance

²adamant *adj* : unshakable or immovable esp. in opposition : UNYIELDING ***syn*** see INFLEXIBLE ***ant*** yielding — **ad·a·mant·ly** *adv*

ad·a·man·tine \,ad-ə-'man-,tēn, -,tīn, -'mant-ᵊn\ *adj* [ME, fr. L *adamantinus,* fr. Gk *adamantinos,* fr. *adamant-, adamas*] **1** : made of or having the quality of adamant **2** : rigidly firm : UNYIELDING **3** : resembling the diamond in hardness or luster

Adam's apple *n* : the projection in the front of the neck formed by the largest cartilage of the larynx — see LARYNX illustration

Adam's needle *n* : any of several yuccas

adapt \ə-'dapt\ *vb* [F or L; F *adapter,* fr. L *adaptare,* fr. *ad-* + *aptare* to fit, fr. *aptus* apt, fit] *vt* : to make fit (as for a specific or new use or situation) often by modification ~ *vi* : to become adapted — **adapt·ed·ness** *n*

syn ADAPT, ADJUST, ACCOMMODATE, CONFORM, RECONCILE *shared meaning element* : to bring one into correspondence with another ***ant*** unfit

adapt·able \ə-'dap-tə-bəl\ *adj* : capable of being adapted : SUITABLE ***syn*** see PLASTIC ***ant*** inadaptable, unadaptable — **adapt·abil·i·ty** \-,dap-tə-'bil-ət-ē\ *n*

ad·ap·ta·tion \,ad-,ap-'tā-shən, -əp-\ *n* **1** : the act or process of adapting : the state of being adapted **2** : adjustment to environmental conditions: as **a** : adjustment of a sense organ to the intensity or quality of stimulation **b** : modification of an organism or its parts that makes it more fit for existence under the conditions of its environment **3** : something that is adapted; *specif* : a composition rewritten into a new form — **ad·ap·ta·tion·al** \-shnəl, -shən-ᵊl\ *adj* — **ad·ap·ta·tion·al·ly** \-ē\ *adv*

adapt·er *also* **adap·tor** \ə-'dap-tər\ *n* **1** : one that adapts **2 a** : a device for connecting two parts (as of different diameters) of an apparatus **b** : an attachment for adapting apparatus for uses not orig. intended

adap·tion \ə-'dap-shən\ *n* : ADAPTATION

adap·tive \ə-'dap-tiv\ *adj* : showing or having a capacity for or tendency toward adaptation — **adap·tive·ly** *adv* — **adap·tive·ness** *n* — **ad·ap·tiv·i·ty** \,ad-,ap-'tiv-ət-ē\ *n*

Adar \ä-'där\ *n* [ME, fr. Heb *Adhār*] : the 6th month of the civil year or the 12th month of the ecclesiastical year in the Jewish calendar — see MONTH table

Adar She·ni \ä-,där-shā-'nē\ *n* [Heb *Ădhār Shēnī* second Adar] : VEADAR

ad·ax·i·al \(')a-'dak-sē-əl\ *adj* : situated on the same side as or facing the axis (as of an organ)

ADC *abbr* **1** aide-de-camp **2** Aid to Dependent Children **3** Air Defense Command **4** assistant division commander

add \'ad\ *vb* [ME *adden,* fr. L *addere,* fr. *ad-* + *-dere* to put — more at DO] *vt* **1** : to join or unite so as to bring about an increase or improvement ⟨~*s* 60 acres to his land⟩ ⟨wine ~*s* a creative touch to cooking⟩ **2** : to say further : APPEND **3** : to combine (numbers) into an equivalent simple quantity or number **4** : to include as a member of a group ⟨don't forget to ~ me in⟩ ~ *vi* **1 a** : to perform addition **b** : to come together or unite by addition **2 a** : to serve as an addition ⟨the movie will ~ to his fame⟩ **b** : to make an addition : ENLARGE — **add·able** *or* **add·ible** \'ad-ə-bəl\ *adj*

ADD *abbr* American Dialect Dictionary

ad·dax \'ad-,aks\ *n, pl* **ad·dax·es** [L] : a large light-colored antelope (*Addax nasomaculata*) of No. Africa, Arabia, and Syria

ad·dend \'ad-,end, ə-'dend\ *n* [short for *addendum*] : a number to be added to another

ad·den·dum \ə-'den-dəm\ *n, pl* **-da** \-də\ [L, neut. of *addendus,* gerundive of *addere*] **1** : a thing added : ADDITION **2** : a supplement to a book — often used in pl. but sing. in constr.

¹ad·der \'ad-ər\ *n* [ME, alter. (by incorrect division of *a naddre*) of *naddre,* fr. OE *nǣdre;* akin to OHG *nātara* adder, L *natrix* water snake] **1** : the common venomous viper (*Vipera berus*) of Europe; *broadly* : a terrestrial viper (family Viperidae) **2** : any of several No. American snakes (as the hognose snakes) that are harmless but are popularly believed to be venomous

²add·er \'ad-ər\ *n* : one that adds; *esp* : a device (as in a computer) that performs addition

ad·der's–tongue \'ad-ərz-,təŋ\ *n* **1** : a fern (genus *Ophioglossum,* family Ophioglossaceae) whose fruiting spike resembles a serpent's tongue **2** : DOGTOOTH VIOLET

¹ad·dict \ə-'dikt\ *vt* [L *addictus,* pp. of *addicere* to favor, fr. *ad-* + *dicere* to say — more at DICTION] **1** : to devote or surrender (oneself) to something habitually or obsessively ⟨~*ed* to gambling⟩ **2** : to cause (a person) to become physiologically dependent upon a drug

²ad·dict \'ad-(,)ikt\ *n* **1** : one who is addicted to a drug **2** : DEVOTEE 2 ⟨a detective novel ~⟩

ad·dic·tion \ə-'dik-shən\ *n* **1** : the quality or state of being addicted ⟨~ to reading⟩ **2** : compulsive physiological need for a habit-forming drug (as heroin) — compare HABITUATION

ad·dic·tive \ə-'dik-tiv\ *adj* : causing or characterized by addiction

Ad·di·son's disease \'ad-ə-sənz-\ *n* [Thomas *Addison* †1860 E physician] : a destructive disease marked by deficient secretion of the adrenal cortical hormone and characterized by extreme weakness, loss of weight, low blood pressure, gastrointestinal disturbances, and brownish pigmentation of the skin and mucous membranes

ad·di·tion \ə-'dish-ən\ *n* [ME, fr. MF, fr. L *addition-, additio,* fr. *additus,* pp. of *addere*] **1** : the result of adding : INCREASE **2** : the act or process of adding; *esp* : the operation of combining numbers so as to obtain an equivalent simple quantity **3** : a part added (as to a building or residential section) **4** : direct chemical combination of substances into a single product — **in addition** : ¹BESIDES, ALSO — **in addition to** : over and above

ad·di·tion·al \ə-'dish-nəl, -'dish-ən-ᵊl\ *adj* : existing by way of addition : ADDED — **ad·di·tion·al·ly** \-ē\ *adv*

¹ad·di·tive \'ad-ət-iv\ *adj* **1** : of, relating to, or characterized by addition **2** : produced by addition — **ad·di·tive·ly** *adv* — **ad·di·tiv·i·ty** \,ad-ə-'tiv-ət-ē\ *n*

²additive *n* : a substance added to another in relatively small amounts to impart or improve desirable properties or suppress undesirable properties ⟨food ~*s*⟩

additive identity *n* : an identity element (as 0 in the group of whole numbers under the operation of addition) that in a given mathematical system leaves unchanged any element to which it is added

additive inverse *n* : a number of opposite sign with respect to a given number so that addition of the two numbers gives zero ⟨the *additive inverse* of 4 is −4⟩

¹ad·dle \'ad-ᵊl\ *adj* [ME *adel* filth, fr. OE *adela;* akin to MLG *adele* liquid manure] **1** *of an egg* : ROTTEN **2** : CONFUSED, MUDDLED

²addle *vb* **ad·dled; ad·dling** \'ad-liŋ, -ᵊl-iŋ\ *vt* : to throw into confusion : CONFOUND ~ *vi* **1** : to become rotten : SPOIL **2** : to become confused

ad·dle·pat·ed \,ad-ᵊl-'pāt-əd\ *adj* **1** : being mixed up : CONFUSED **2** : ECCENTRIC

addn *abbr* addition

addnl *abbr* additional

¹ad·dress \ə-'dres\ *vb* [ME *adressen,* fr. MF *adresser,* fr. *a-* (fr. L *ad-*) + *dresser* to arrange — more at DRESS] *vt* **1** *archaic* **a** : DIRECT, AIM **b** : to direct to go : SEND **2** *archaic* : to make ready; *esp* : DRESS **3 a** : to direct the efforts or attention of (oneself) ⟨will ~ himself to the problem⟩ **b** : to deal with : TREAT ⟨intrigued by the chance to ~ important issues — I. L. Horowitz⟩ **4 a** : to communicate directly ⟨~*es* his thanks to his host⟩ **b** : to speak or write directly to; *esp* : to deliver a formal speech to **5 a** : to mark directions for delivery on ⟨~ a letter⟩ **b** : to consign to the care of another (as an agent or factor) **6** : to greet by a prescribed form **7** : to adjust the club preparatory to hitting (a golf ball) ~ *vi, obs* : to direct one's speech or attentions — **ad·dress·er** *n*

²ad·dress \ə-'dres, *for 5 & 7 & less often 4 also* 'ad-,res\ *n* **1** : dutiful and courteous attention esp. in courtship — usu. used in pl. **2 a** : readiness and capability for dealing (as with a person or problem) skillfully and smoothly : ADROITNESS **b** *obs* : a making ready; *also* : a state of preparedness **3 a** : manner of bearing onself ⟨a man of rude ~⟩ **b** : manner of speaking or singing : DELIVERY **4** : a formal communication; *esp* : a prepared speech delivered to a special audience or on a special occasion **5 a** : a place where a person or organization may be communicated with **b** : directions for delivery on the outside of an object (as a letter or package) **c** : the designation of place of delivery placed between the heading and salutation on a business letter **6** : a preparatory position of the player and club in golf **7** : a location (as in the memory of a computer) where particular information is stored; *also* : the digits that identify such a location ***syn*** see TACT ***ant*** maladroitness

ad·dress·able \ə-'dres-ə-bəl\ *adj* : accessible through an address ⟨~ registers in a computer⟩

ad·dress·ee \ˌad-ˌres-'ē, ə-ˌdres-'ē\ *n* : one to whom something is addressed

ad·duce \ə-'d(y)üs\ *vt* **ad·duced; ad·duc·ing** [L *adducere,* lit., to lead to, fr. *ad-* + *ducere* to lead — more at TOW] : to offer as example, reason, or proof in discussion or analysis — **ad·duc·er** *n*

syn ADDUCE, CITE, ADVANCE, ALLEGE *shared meaning element* : to bring forward (as in explanation, proof, or demonstration)

1ad·duct \ə-'dəkt, a-\ *vt* [L *adductus,* pp. of *adducere*] : to draw (as a limb) toward or past the median axis of the body; *also* : to bring together (similar parts) ⟨~ the fingers⟩ — **ad·duc·tive** \-'dək-tiv\ *adj*

2ad·duct \'ad-ˌəkt\ *n* [G *addukt,* fr. L *adductus*] : a chemical addition product

ad·duc·tion \ə-'dək-shən, a-\ *n* **1** : the action of adducting : the state of being adducted **2** : the act or action of adducing or bringing forward

ad·duc·tor \-'dək-tər\ *n* [NL, fr. L, one that draws to, fr. *adductus*] **1** : a muscle that draws a part toward the median line of the body or toward the axis of an extremity **2** : a muscle that closes the valves of a bivalve mollusk

add up *vi* **1** : AMOUNT — used with *to* ⟨the play *adds up* to a lot of laughs⟩ **2** : to come to the expected total ⟨the bill doesn't *add up*⟩ ~ *vt* : to form an opinion of ⟨*added* him *up* at a glance⟩

-ade \'ād\ *n suffix* [ME, fr. MF, fr. OProv *-ada,* fr. LL *-ata,* fr. L, fem. of *-atus* -ate] **1** : act : action ⟨block*ade*⟩ **2** : product; *esp* : sweet drink ⟨lime*ade*⟩

Adé·lie penguin \ə-ˌdā-lē-\ *n* [*Adélie* Coast, Antarctica] : a small antarctic penguin (*Pygoscelis adeliae*) — called also *Adélie*

-adel·phous \ə-'del-fəs\ *adj comb form* [prob. fr. NL *-adelphus,* fr. Gk *adelphos* brother, fr. *ha-, a-* (akin to *homos* same) + *delphys* womb — more at SAME, DOLPHIN] : having (such or so many) stamen fascicles ⟨mon*adelphous*⟩

aden- *or* **adeno-** *comb form* [NL, fr. Gk, fr. *aden-, adēn;* akin to L *inguen* groin, Gk *nephros* kidney — more at NEPHRITIS] : gland ⟨*aden*itis⟩

ad·e·nine \'ad-ᵊn-ˌēn\ *n* [ISV, fr. its presence in glandular tissue] : a purine base $C_5H_3N_4NH_2$ that codes hereditary information in the genetic code in DNA and RNA — compare CYTOSINE, GUANINE, THYMINE, URACIL

ad·e·ni·tis \ˌad-ᵊn-'īt-əs\ *n* [NL] : inflammation of one or more lymph nodes

ad·e·no·car·ci·no·ma \ˌad-ᵊn-(ˌ)ō-ˌkärs-ᵊn-'ō-mə\ *n* [NL] : a malignant tumor originating in glandular epithelium — **ad·e·no·car·ci·no·ma·tous** \-mət-əs\ *adj*

ad·e·no·hy·poph·y·sis \-hī-'päf-ə-səs\ *n, pl* **-y·ses** \-ə-ˌsēz\ [NL] : the anterior glandular lobe of the pituitary gland — **ad·e·no·hy·poph·y·se·al** \-(ˌ)hī-ˌpäf-ə-'sē-əl\ *or* **ad·e·no·hy·po·phys·i·al** \-ˌhī-pə-'fiz-ē-əl\ *adj*

ad·e·noid \'ad-ᵊn-ˌȯid, 'ad-ˌnȯid\ *n* [Gk *adenoeidēs* glandular, fr. *adēn*] : an enlarged mass of lymphoid tissue at the back of the pharynx characteristically obstructing breathing — usu. used in pl. — **adenoid** *adj*

ad·e·noi·dal \ˌad-ᵊn-'ȯid-ᵊl\ *adj* **1** : of or relating to the adenoids **2** : typical or suggestive of one affected with abnormally enlarged adenoids ⟨an ~ tenor⟩ ⟨~ breathing⟩

ad·e·no·ma \ˌad-ᵊn-'ō-mə\ *n, pl* **-nomas** *or* **-no·ma·ta** \-mət-ə\ [NL *adenomat-, adenoma*] : a benign tumor of a glandular structure or of glandular origin — **ad·e·no·ma·tous** \-mət-əs\ *adj*

aden·o·sine \ə-'den-ə-ˌsēn\ *n* [ISV, blend of *adenine* & *ribose*] : a nucleoside $C_{10}H_{13}N_5O_4$ that is a constituent of ribonucleic acid yielding adenine and ribose on hydrolysis

adenosine diphosphate *n* : ADP

adenosine mo·no·phos·phate \-ˌmän-ə-'fäs-ˌfāt, -ˌmō-nə-\ *n* **1** : AMP **2** : CYCLIC AMP

adenosine tri·phos·pha·tase \-trī-'fäs-fə-ˌtās, -ˌtāz\ *n* : ATPASE

adenosine tri·phos·phate \-trī-'fäs-ˌfāt\ *n* : ATP

ad·e·no·vi·rus \ˌad-ᵊn-ō-'vī-rəs\ *n* [*adenoid* + *-o-* + *virus*] : any of a group of DNA-containing viruses orig. identified in human adenoid tissue, causing respiratory diseases (as catarrh), and including some capable of inducing malignant tumors in experimental animals — **ad·e·no·vi·ral** \-rəl\ *adj*

ad·e·nyl \'ad-ᵊn-ˌil\ *n* : an univalent radical $C_5H_4N_5$ derived from adenine

adenyl cy·clase \-'sī-ˌklās, -ˌklāz\ *n* : an enzyme that catalyzes the formation of cyclic AMP from ATP

ad·e·nyl·ic acid \ˌad-ᵊn-ˌil-ik-\ *n* : a nucleotide $C_{10}H_{14}N_5O_7P$ formed by partial hydrolysis of RNA or ATP

1ad·ept \'ad-ˌept\ *n* [NL, *adeptus,* alchemist who has attained the knowledge of how to change base metals into gold, fr. L, pp. of *adipisci* to attain, fr. *ad-* + *apisci* to reach — more at APT] : a highly skilled or well-trained individual : EXPERT ⟨an ~ at chess⟩

2adept \ə-'dept\ *adj* : thoroughly proficient : EXPERT ***syn*** see PROFICIENT ***ant*** inadept, inept, bungling — **adept·ly** \-'dep-(t)lē\ *adv* — **adept·ness** \-'dep(t)-nəs\ *n*

ad·e·qua·cy \'ad-i-kwə-sē\ *n, pl* **-cies** : the quality or state of being adequate

ad·e·quate \-kwət\ *adj* [L *adaequatus,* pp. of *adaequare* to make equal, fr. *ad-* + *aequare* to equal — more at EQUATE] **1 a** : sufficient for a specific requirement ⟨~ taxation of goods⟩; *esp* : barely sufficient or satisfactory ⟨her first performance was merely ~⟩ **2** : lawfully and reasonably sufficient ***syn*** see SUFFICIENT ***ant*** inadequate — **ad·e·quate·ly** *adv* — **ad·e·quate·ness** *n*

ad eun·dem \ˌad-ē-'ən-dəm\ *or* **ad eundem gra·dum** \-'grād-əm\ *adv or adj* [NL *ad eundem gradum*] : to, in, or of the same rank — used esp. of the honorary granting of academic standing or a degree by a university to one whose actual work was done elsewhere

1à deux \ä-'də(r), ȧ-dœ\ *adj* [F] : involving two people esp. in private ⟨a cozy evening *à deux*⟩

2à deux *adv* : privately or intimately with only two present ⟨dining *à deux*⟩

ADF *abbr* automatic direction finder

ADH *abbr* antidiuretic hormone

ad·here \ad-'hi(ə)r, əd-\ *vb* **ad·hered; ad·her·ing** [MF or L; MF *adhérer,* fr. L *adhaerēre,* fr. *ad-* + *haerēre* to stick — more at HESITATE] *vi* **1** : to give support or maintain loyalty **2** *obs* : to be consistent : ACCORD **3** : to hold fast or stick by or as if by gluing, suction, grasping, or fusing **4** : to bind oneself to observance ~ *vt* : to cause to stick fast ***syn*** see STICK

ad·her·ence \-'hir-ən(t)s\ *n* **1** : the act, action, or quality of adhering **2** : steady or faithful attachment : FIDELITY

syn ADHERENCE, ADHESION *shared meaning element* : a sticking to or together ***ant*** nonadherence

ad·her·end \-'hi(ə)r-ˌend, ˌad-ˌhi(ə)r-'\ *n* [*adhere* + *-end* (as in *addend*)] **1** : the surface to which an adhesive adheres **2** : one of the bodies held to another by an adhesive

1ad·her·ent \ad-'hir-ənt, əd-\ *adj* [ME, fr. MF or L; MF *adhérent,* fr. L *adhaerent-, adhaerens,* prp. of *adhaerēre*] **1** : able or tending to adhere **2** : connected or associated with esp. by contract **3** : ADNATE — **ad·her·ent·ly** *adv*

2adherent *n* : one that adheres: as **a** : a follower of a leader, party, or profession **b** : a believer in or advocate esp. of a particular idea or church ***syn*** see FOLLOWER ***ant*** renegade

ad·he·sion \ad-'hē-zhən, əd-\ *n* [F or L; F *adhésion,* fr. L *adhaesion-, adhaesio,* fr. *adhaesus,* pp. of *adhaerēre*] **1** : steady or firm attachment : ADHERENCE **2** : the action or state of adhering; *specif* : a union of bodily parts by growth **3** : tissues abnormally united by fibrous tissue resulting from an inflammatory process **4** : agreement to join **5** : the molecular attraction exerted between the surfaces of bodies in contact ***syn*** see ADHERENCE ***ant*** nonadhesion — **ad·he·sion·al** \-'hēzh-nəl, -'hē-zhən-ᵊl\ *adj*

1ad·he·sive \-'hē-siv, -ziv\ *adj* **1** : tending to remain in association or memory **2** : tending to adhere or cause adherence **3** : prepared for adhering : STICKY — **ad·he·sive·ly** *adv* — **ad·he·sive·ness** *n*

2adhesive *n* **1** : an adhesive substance (as glue or cement) **2** : a postage stamp with a gummed back

adhesive tape *n* : tape coated on one side with an adhesive mixture; *esp* : one used for covering wounds

1ad hoc \(ˈ)ad-'häk, -'hōk\ *adv* [L, for this] : for the particular end or case at hand without consideration of wider application

2ad hoc *adj* : concerned with a particular end or purpose ⟨an *ad hoc* investigating committee⟩

1ad ho·mi·nem \(ˈ)ad-'häm-ə-ˌnem\ *adj* [NL, lit., to the man] **1** : appealing to a person's feelings or prejudices rather than his intellect **2** : marked by an attack on an opponent's character rather than by an answer to his contentions

2ad hominem *adv* : in an ad hominem manner ⟨was arguing *ad hominem*⟩

adi·a·bat·ic \ˌad-ē-ə-'bat-ik, ˌā-ˌdī-ə-\ *adj* [Gk *adiabatos* impassable, fr. *a-* + *diabatos* passable, fr. *diabainein* to go across, fr. *dia-* + *bainein* to go — more at COME] : occurring without loss or gain of heat ⟨~ expansion of a body of air⟩ — **adi·a·bat·i·cal·ly** \-i-k(ə-)lē\ *adv*

adieu \ə-'d(y)ü\ *n, pl* **adieus** *or* **adieux** \ə-'d(y)üz\ [ME, fr. MF, fr. *a* (fr. L *ad*) + *Dieu* God, fr. L *Deus* — more at AT, DEITY] : FAREWELL — often used interjectionally

ad in·fi·ni·tum \ˌad-ˌin-fə-'nīt-əm\ *adv or adj* [L] : without end or limit

ad int *abbr* ad interim

1ad in·ter·im \(ˈ)ad-'in-tə-rəm, -ˌrim\ *adv* [L] : for the intervening time : TEMPORARILY

2ad interim *adj* : made or serving ad interim

adi·os \ˌad-ē-'ōs, ˌäd-\ *interj* [Sp *adiós,* fr. *a* (fr. L *ad*) + *Dios* God, fr. L *Deus*] — used to express farewell

ad·i·pose \'ad-ə-ˌpōs\ *adj* [NL *adiposus,* fr. L *adip-, adeps* fat, fr. Gk *aleipha;* akin to Gk *lipos* fat — more at LEAVE] : of or relating to animal fat : FATTY — **ad·i·pos·i·ty** \ˌad-ə-'päs-ət-ē\ *n*

adipose tissue *n* : connective tissue in which fat is stored and which has the cells distended by droplets of fat

ad·it \'ad-ət\ *n* [L *aditus* approach, fr. *aditus,* pp. of *adire* to go to, fr. *ad-* + *ire* to go — more at ISSUE] : a nearly horizontal passage from the surface in a mine

ADIZ *abbr* air defense identification zone

adj *abbr* **1** adjective **2** adjunct **3** adjustment **4** adjutant

ad·ja·cen·cy \ə-'jās-ᵊn-sē\ *n, pl* **-cies** **1** : something that is adjacent **2** : the quality or state of being adjacent : CONTIGUITY

ad·ja·cent \ə-'jās-ᵊnt\ *adj* [ME, fr. MF or L; MF, fr. L *adjacent-, adjacens,* prp. of *adjacēre* to lie near, fr. *ad-* + *jacēre* to lie; akin to L *jacere* to throw — more at JET] **1 a** : not distant : NEARBY ⟨the city and ~ suburbs⟩ **b** : having a common border ⟨~ lots⟩ **c** : immediately preceding or following **2** *of two angles* : having the vertex and one side in common — **ad·ja·cent·ly** *adv*

syn ADJACENT, ADJOINING, CONTIGUOUS, ABUTTING, CONTERMINOUS *shared meaning element* : being in proximity ***ant*** nonadjacent

ad·jec·ti·val \ˌaj-ik-'tī-vəl\ *adj* **1** : ADJECTIVE **2** : characterized by the use of adjectives — **ad·jec·ti·val·ly** \-və-lē\ *adv*

1ad·jec·tive \'aj-ik-tiv\ *adj* [ME, fr. MF or LL; MF *adjectif,* fr. LL *adjectivus,* fr. L *adjectus,* pp. of *adjicere* to throw to, fr. *ad-* + *jacere* to throw — more at JET] **1** : of, relating to, or functioning as an adjective ⟨an ~ clause⟩ **2** : not standing by itself : DEPENDENT **3** : requiring or employing a mordant ⟨~ dyes⟩ **4** : PROCEDURAL ⟨~ law⟩ — **ad·jec·tive·ly** *adv*

2adjective *n* : a word belonging to one of the major form classes in any of numerous languages and typically serving as a modifier of a noun to denote a quality of the thing named, to indicate its quantity or extent, or to specify a thing as distinct from something else

ad·join \ə-ˈjȯin\ *vb* [ME *adjoinen*, fr. MF *adjoindre*, fr. L *adjungere*, fr. *ad-* + *jungere* to join — more at YOKE] *vt* **1** : to add or attach by joining **2** : to lie next to or in contact with ~ *vi* : to be close to or in contact with one another

ad·join·ing *adj* : touching or bounding at a point or line ***syn*** see ADJACENT ***ant*** detached, disjoined

ad·joint \ˈaj-ˌȯint\ *n* [F, fr. pp. of *adjoindre* to adjoin] : the transpose of a matrix in which each element is replaced by its cofactor

ad·journ \ə-ˈjərn\ *vb* [ME *ajournen*, fr. MF *ajourner*, fr. *a-* (fr. L *ad-*) + *jour* day — more at JOURNEY] *vt* : to suspend indefinitely or until a later stated time ~ *vi* **1** : to suspend a session to another time or place or indefinitely **2** : to move to another place

syn ADJOURN, PROROGUE, DISSOLVE *shared meaning element* : to terminate the activities of (as a legislature)

ad·journ·ment \-mənt\ *n* **1** : the act of adjourning **2** : the state or interval of being adjourned

ad·judge \ə-ˈjəj\ *vt* **ad·judged; ad·judg·ing** [ME *ajugen*, fr. MF *ajugier*, fr. L *adjudicare*, fr. *ad-* + *judicare* to judge — more at JUDGE] **1 a** : to decide or rule upon as a judge : ADJUDICATE **b** : to pronounce judicially : RULE **2** *archaic* : SENTENCE, CONDEMN **3** : to hold or pronounce to be : DEEM ⟨~ the book a success⟩ **4** : to award or grant judicially in a case of controversy

ad·ju·di·cate \ə-ˈjüd-i-ˌkāt\ *vb* **-cat·ed; -cat·ing** [L *adjudicatus*, pp. of *adjudicare*] *vt* : to settle judicially ~ *vi* : to act as judge — **ad·ju·di·ca·tive** \-ˌkāt-iv, -kət-\ *adj* — **ad·ju·di·ca·tor** \-ˌkāt-ər\ *n*

ad·ju·di·ca·tion \ə-ˌjüd-i-ˈkā-shən\ *n* **1** : the act or process of adjudicating **2 a** : a judicial decision or sentence **b** : a decree in bankruptcy — **ad·ju·di·ca·to·ry** \-ˈjüd-i-kə-ˌtōr-ē, -ˌtȯr-\ *adj*

1ad·junct \ˈaj-ˌəŋ(k)t\ *n* [L *adjunctum*, fr. neut. of *adjunctus*, pp. of *adjungere*] **1** : something joined or added to another thing but not essentially a part of it **2** : a word or word group that qualifies or completes the meaning of another word or other words and is not itself one of the principal structural elements in its sentence **3** : a person associated with or assisting another — **ad·junc·tive** \a-ˈjəŋ(k)-tiv\ *adj*

2adjunct *adj* **1** : added or joined as an accompanying object or circumstance **2** : attached in a subordinate or temporary capacity to a staff ⟨an ~ psychiatrist⟩ — **ad·junct·ly** \ˈaj-ˌəŋ(k)-tlē, -ˌəŋ-klē\ *adv*

ad·junc·tion \a-ˈjəŋ(k)-shən\ *n* : the act or process of adjoining

ad·ju·ra·tion \ˌaj-ə-ˈrā-shən\ *n* **1** : a solemn oath **2** : an earnest or solemn urging or advising — **ad·jur·a·to·ry** \ə-ˈju̇r-ə-ˌtōr-ē, -ˌtȯr-\ *adj*

ad·jure \ə-ˈju̇(ə)r\ *vt* **ad·jured; ad·jur·ing** [ME *adjuren*, fr. MF & L; MF *ajurer*, fr. L *adjurare*, fr. *ad-* + *jurare* to swear — more at JURY] **1** : to charge or command solemnly under or as if under oath or penalty of a curse **2** : to entreat or advise earnestly ***syn*** see BEG

ad·just \ə-ˈjəst\ *vb* [F *ajuster*, fr. *a-* + *juste* exact, just] *vt* **1 a** : to bring to a more satisfactory state: (1) : SETTLE, RESOLVE (2) : RECTIFY **b** : to make correspondent or conformable : ADAPT **c** : to bring the parts of to a true or more effective relative position ⟨~ a carburetor⟩ **2** : to reduce to a system : REGULATE **3** : to determine the amount to be paid under an insurance policy in settlement of (a loss) ~ *vi* **1** : to adapt or conform oneself (as to climate, food, or new working hours) **2** : to achieve mental and behavioral balance between one's own needs and the demands of others ***syn*** see ADAPT — **adjust·abil·i·ty** \-ˌjəs-tə-ˈbil-ət-ē\ *n* — **ad·just·able** \-ˈjəs-tə-bəl\ *adj* — **adjus·tive** \-ˈjəs-tiv\ *adj*

ad·just·ed *adj* **1** : accommodated to suit a particular set of circumstances or requirements **2** : having achieved a harmonious relationship with the environment or with other individuals ⟨a well-*adjusted* schoolchild⟩

ad·just·er *also* **ad·jus·tor** \ə-ˈjəs-tər\ *n* : one that adjusts; *esp* : an insurance agent who investigates personal or property damage and makes estimates for effecting settlements

ad·just·ment \ə-ˈjəs(t)-mənt\ *n* **1** : the act or process of adjusting **2** : a settlement of a claim or debt in a case in which the amount involved is uncertain or in which full payment is not made **3** : the state of being adjusted **4** : a means (as a mechanism) by which things are adjusted one to another **5** : a correction or modification to reflect actual conditions — **ad·just·men·tal** \ə-ˌjəs(t)-ˈment-ᵊl, ˌaj-ˌəs(t)-\ *adj*

ad·ju·tan·cy \ˈaj-ət-ən-sē\ *n* : the office or rank of an adjutant

ad·ju·tant \ˈaj-ət-ənt\ *n* [L *adjutant-*, *adjutans*, prp. of *adjutare* to help — more at AID] **1** : a staff officer in the army, air force, or marine corps who assists the commanding officer and is responsible esp. for correspondence **2** : one who helps : ASSISTANT

adjutant general *n*, *pl* **adjutants general** **1** : the chief administrative officer of an army who is responsible esp. for the administration and preservation of personnel records **2** : the chief administrative officer of a major military unit (as a division or corps)

1ad·ju·vant \ˈaj-ə-vənt\ *adj* [F or L; F, fr. L *adjuvant-*, *adjuvans*, prp. of *adjuvare* to aid — more at AID] : serving to aid or contribute : AUXILIARY

2adjuvant *n* : one that helps or facilitates; *esp* : something that enhances the effectiveness of medical treatment

Ad·le·ri·an \äd-ˈlir-ē-ən, ad-\ *adj* [Alfred *Adler* †1937 Austrian psychiatrist] : of, relating to, or being a theory and technique of psychotherapy emphasizing the importance of feelings of inferiority, a will to power, and overcompensation in neurotic processes

1ad–lib \ˈad-ˈlib\ *adj* [*ad lib*] : spoken, composed, or performed without preparation

2ad–lib *vb* **ad–libbed; ad–lib·bing** *vt* : to deliver spontaneously ~ *vi* : to improvise esp. lines or a speech — **ad–lib** *n*

ad lib *adv* [NL *ad libitum*] **1** : in accordance with one's wishes **2** : without restraint or limit

1ad li·bi·tum \(ˈ)ad-ˈlib-ət-əm\ *adv* [NL, in accordance with desire] : ad lib ⟨rats fed ~⟩

2ad libitum *adj* : omissible according to a performer's wishes — used as a direction in music; compare OBBLIGATO

ad loc *abbr* [L *ad locum*] to or at the place

adm *abbr* administration; administrative

ADM *abbr* admiral

ad·man \ˈad-ˌman\ *n* : one who writes, solicits, or places advertisements

ad·mass \ˈad-ˌmas\ *adj* [*advertising* + *mass*] *chiefly Brit* : of, relating to, or characteristic of a society that devotes itself chiefly to the production, promotion, and consumption of material goods

ad·mea·sure \ad-ˈmezh-ər, -ˈmā-zhər\ *vt* **-sured; -sur·ing** [ME *amesuren*, fr. MF *amesurer*, fr. *a-* (fr. L *ad-*) + *mesurer* to measure] : to determine the proper share of : APPORTION

ad·mea·sure·ment \-ˈmezh-ər-mənt, -ˈmā-zhər-\ *n* **1** : determination and apportionment of shares **2** : determination or comparison of dimensions **3** : DIMENSIONS, SIZE

Ad·me·tus \ad-ˈmēt-əs\ *n* [L, fr. Gk *Admētos*] : a king of Pherae who was saved from his fated death by the substitution of his wife Alcestis

admin *abbr* administration

ad·min·is·ter \əd-ˈmin-ə-stər\ *vb* **ad·min·is·tered; ad·min·is·ter·ing** \-st(ə-)riŋ\ [ME *administren*, fr. MF *administrer*, fr. L *administrare*, fr. *ad-* + *ministrare* to serve, fr. *minister* servant — more at MINISTER] *vt* **1** : to manage or supervise the execution, use, or conduct of ⟨~ a trust fund⟩ **2 a** : to mete out : DISPENSE ⟨~ punishment⟩ **b** : to give ritually ⟨~ the last rites⟩ **c** : to give remedially ⟨~ a dose of medicine⟩ ~ *vi* **1** : to perform the office of administrator **2** : to furnish a benefit : MINISTER ⟨~ to his ailing friend⟩ **3** : to manage affairs ***syn*** see EXECUTE — **ad·min·is·tra·ble** \-strə-bəl\ *adj* — **ad·min·is·trant** \-strənt\ *n*

ad·min·is·trate \-ˌstrāt\ *vt* **-trat·ed; -trat·ing** [L *administratus*, pp. of *administrare*] : ADMINISTER

ad·min·is·tra·tion \əd-ˌmin-ə-ˈstrā-shən, (ˌ)ad-\ *n* **1** : the act or process of administering **2** : performance of executive duties : MANAGEMENT **3** : the execution of public affairs as distinguished from policymaking **4 a** : a body of persons who administer **b** *cap* : a group constituting the political executive in a presidential government **c** : a governmental agency or board **5** : the term of office of an administrative officer or body — **ad·min·is·tra·tion·al** \-shnəl, -shən-ᵊl\ *adj* — **ad·min·is·tra·tion·ist** \-sh(ə-)nəst\ *n*

ad·min·is·tra·tive \əd-ˌmin-ə-ˌstrāt-iv, -strət-\ *adj* : of or relating to administration or an administration : EXECUTIVE — **ad·min·is·tra·tive·ly** *adv*

administrative county *n* : a British local administrative unit often not coincident with an older county

administrative law *n* : law dealing with the establishment, duties, and powers of and available remedies against authorized agencies in the executive branch of the government

ad·min·is·tra·tor \əd-ˈmin-ə-ˌstrāt-ər\ *n* **1** : a person legally vested with the right of administration of an estate **2 a** : one that administers esp. business, school, or governmental affairs **b** : a priest appointed to administer a diocese or parish temporarily

ad·min·is·tra·trix \-ˌmin-ə-ˈstrā-triks\ *n*, *pl* **-tra·tri·ces** \-ˈstrā-trə-ˌsēz\ [NL] : a female administrator esp. of an estate

ad·mi·ra·ble \ˈad-m(ə-)rə-bəl\ *adj* **1** *obs* : exciting wonder : SURPRISING **2** : deserving the highest esteem : EXCELLENT — **ad·mi·ra·bil·i·ty** \ˌad-m(ə-)rə-ˈbil-ət-ē\ *n* — **ad·mi·ra·ble·ness** \ˈad-m(ə-)rə-bəl-nəs\ *n* — **ad·mi·ra·bly** \-blē\ *adv*

ad·mi·ral \ˈad-m(ə-)rəl\ *n* [ME, fr. MF *amiral* admiral & ML *admiralis* emir, *admirallus* admiral, fr. Ar *amīr -al-* commander of the (as in *amīr-al-bahr* commander of the sea)] **1** *archaic* : the commander in chief of a navy **2 a** : FLAG OFFICER **b** : a commissioned officer in the navy or coast guard who ranks above a vice admiral and whose insignia is four stars — compare GENERAL **3** *archaic* : FLAGSHIP **4** : any of several brightly colored butterflies (family Nymphalidae)

admiral of the fleet : the highest-ranking officer of the British navy

ad·mi·ral·ty \ˈad-m(ə-)rəl-tē\ *n* **1** *cap* : the executive department or officers formerly having general authority over British naval affairs **2** : the court having jurisdiction of maritime questions; *also* : the system of law administered by admiralty courts

Admiralty mile *n* : NAUTICAL MILE a

ad·mi·ra·tion \ˌad-mə-ˈrā-shən\ *n* **1** *archaic* : WONDER **2** : an object of admiring esteem **3 a** : a feeling of delighted or astonished approbation **b** : the act or process of regarding with admiration

ad·mire \əd-ˈmī(ə)r\ *vt* **ad·mired; ad·mir·ing** [MF *admirer*, fr. L *admirari*, fr. *ad-* + *mirari* to wonder — more at SMILE] **1** *archaic* : to marvel at **2** : to regard with admiration **3** : to think highly of often in a somewhat impersonal manner ⟨~ a man's capacity for work⟩ ***syn*** see REGARD ***ant*** abhor — **ad·mir·er** *n* — **ad·mir·ing·ly** \-ˈmī-riŋ-lē\ *adv*

ad·mis·si·ble \əd-ˈmis-ə-bəl\ *adj* [F, fr. ML *admissibilis*, fr. L *admissus*, pp. of *admittere*] **1** : capable of being allowed or conceded : PERMISSIBLE ⟨behavior that was hardly ~⟩ **2** : capable or worthy of being admitted ⟨foreign products ~ to a domestic market⟩ — **ad·mis·si·bil·i·ty** \-ˌmis-ə-ˈbil-ət-ē\ *n*

ad·mis·sion \əd-ˈmish-ən\ *n* **1 a** : the granting of an argument or position not fully proved **b** : acknowledgment that a fact or statement is true **2 a** : the act or process of admitting **b** : the state or privilege of being admitted **c** : a fee paid at or for admission ***syn*** see ADMITTANCE — **ad·mis·sive** \-ˈmis-iv\ *adj*

ad·mit \əd-ˈmit\ *vb* **ad·mit·ted; ad·mit·ting** [ME *admitten*, fr. L *admittere*, fr. *ad-* + *mittere* to send — more at SMITE] *vt* **1 a** : to allow scope for : PERMIT **b** : to concede as true or valid ⟨compelled to ~ his failure⟩ **2** : to allow entry (as to a place, fellowship, or privilege) ⟨each ticket ~s two persons⟩ ⟨*admitted* to the university⟩ ~ *vi* **1** : to give entrance or access **2 a** : ALLOW,

ə abut	ᵊ kitten	ər further	a back	ā bake	ä cot, cart	
au̇ out	ch chin	e less	ē easy	g gift	i trip	ī life
j joke	ŋ sing	ō flow	ȯ flaw	ȯi coin	th thin	<u>th</u> this
ü loot	u̇ foot	y yet	yü few	yu̇ furious	zh vision	

PERMIT ⟨this order ∼s of two interpretations⟩ **b** : to make acknowledgment — used with *to* **syn** 1 see RECEIVE **ant** eject, expel **2** see ACKNOWLEDGE **ant** gainsay, disdain — **ad·mit·ted·ly** \-'mit-əd-lē\ *adv*

ad·mit·tance \əd-'mit-ᵊn(t)s\ *n* **1** : permission to enter a place : ENTRANCE **2** : the reciprocal of the impedance of a circuit
syn ADMITTANCE, ADMISSION *shared meaning element* : permitted entry

ad·mix \ad-'miks\ *vt* [back-formation fr. obs. *admixt* mingled (with), fr. ME, fr. L *admixtus*] : MINGLE, BLEND

ad·mix·ture \ad-'miks-chər\ *n* [L *admixtus*, pp. of *admiscēre* to mix with, fr. *ad-* + *miscēre* to mix — more at MIX] **1 a** : the act of mixing **b** : the fact of being mixed **2 a** : something added by mixing **b** : a product of mixing : MIXTURE

ad·mon·ish \ad-'män-ish\ *vt* [ME *admonesten*, fr. MF *admonester*, fr. (assumed) VL *admonestare*, alter. of L *admonēre* to warn, fr. *ad-* + *monēre* to warn — more at MIND] **1 a** : to indicate duties or obligations to **b** : to express warning or disapproval to esp. in a gentle, earnest, or solicitous manner **2** : to give friendly earnest advice or encouragement to **syn** see REPROVE — **ad·mon·ish·er** *n* — **ad·mon·ish·ing·ly** \-ish-iŋ-lē\ *adv* — **ad·mon·ish·ment** \-mənt\ *n*

ad·mo·ni·tion \,ad-mə-'nish-ən\ *n* [ME *amonicioun*, fr. MF *amonition*, fr. L *admonition-, admonitio*, fr. *admonitus*, pp. of *admonēre*] **1** : gentle or friendly reproof **2** : counsel or warning against fault or oversight

ad·mon·i·to·ry \əd-'män-ə-,tōr-ē, -,tȯr-\ *adj* : expressing admonition : WARNING — **ad·mon·i·to·ri·ly** \-,män-ə-'tōr-ə-lē, -'tȯr-\ *adv*

admrx *abbr* administratrix

ad·nate \'ad-,nāt\ *adj* [L *adgnatus*, pp. of *adgnasci* to grow on, fr. *ad-* + *nasci* to be born — more at NATION] : grown to a usu. unlike part esp. along a margin ⟨a calyx ∼ to the ovary⟩ — **ad·na·tion** \ad-'nā-shən\ *n*

ad nau·se·am \ad-'nȯ-zē-əm\ *adv* [L] : to a sickening degree

ad·nexa \ad-'nek-sə\ *n pl* [NL, fr. L *annexa*, neut. pl. of *annexus*, pp. of *annectere* to bind to — more at ANNEX] : conjoined, subordinate, or associated anatomic parts; *specif* : the embryonic membranes and other temporary structures of the embryo — **ad·nex·al** \-səl\ *adj*

ado \ə-'dü\ *n* [ME, fr. *at do*, fr. *at* + *don, do* to do] **1** : fussy bustling excitement : TO-DO **2** : time-wasting bother over trivial details ⟨wrote the paper without further ∼⟩ **3** : TROUBLE, DIFFICULTY **syn** see STIR

adobe \ə-'dō-bē\ *n* [Sp, fr. Ar *at-tub* the brick, fr. Copt *tōbe* brick] **1** : a brick or building material of sun-dried earth and straw **2** : a heavy clay used in making adobe bricks; *broadly* : alluvial or playa clay in desert or arid regions **3** : a structure made of adobe bricks

ad·o·les·cence \,ad-ᵊl-'es-ᵊn(t)s\ *n* **1** : the state or process of growing up **2** : the period of life from puberty to maturity terminating legally at the age of majority

¹**ad·o·les·cent** \-ᵊnt\ *n* [F, fr. L *adolescent-, adolescens*, prp. of *adolescere* to grow up — more at ADULT] : one that is in the state of adolescence

²**adolescent** *adj* : of, relating to, or being in adolescence — **ad·o·les·cent·ly** *adv*

Ado·nai \,äd-ə-'nȯi, -'nī\ *n* [Heb *'ādhōnāy*] — used as a name of the God of the Hebrews

Ado·nis \ə-'dän-əs, -'dō-nəs\ *n* [L, fr. Gk *Adōnis*] : a youth loved by Aphrodite, killed at hunting by a wild boar, and restored to Aphrodite from Hades

adopt \ə-'däpt\ *vt* [MF or L; MF *adopter*, fr. L *adoptare*, fr. *ad-* + *optare* to choose — more at OPTION] **1** : to take by choice into a relationship; *specif* : to take voluntarily (a child of other parents) as one's own child **2** : to take up and practice or use as one's own ⟨∼ another's mannerisms⟩ **3** : to accept formally and put into effect ⟨∼ a constitutional amendment⟩ **4** : to choose (a textbook) for required study in a course — **adopt·abil·i·ty** \ə-,däp-tə-'bil-ət-ē\ *n* — **adopt·able** \-'däp-tə-bəl\ *adj* — **adopt·er** *n*
syn ADOPT, EMBRACE, ESPOUSE *shared meaning element* : to take (as an opinion, policy, or practice) as one's own **ant** repudiate, discard

adopt·ee \ə-,däp-'tē\ *n* : one that is adopted

adop·tion \ə-'däp-shən\ *n* : the act of adopting : the state of being adopted

adop·tion·ism *or* **adop·tian·ism** \-shə-,niz-əm\ *n, often cap* : the doctrine that Jesus of Nazareth became the Son of God by adoption — **adop·tion·ist** \-sh(ə-)nəst\ *n, often cap*

adop·tive \ə-'däp-tiv\ *adj* **1** : of or relating to adoption **2** : made or acquired by adoption ⟨the ∼ father⟩ **3** : tending to adopt — **adop·tive·ly** *adv*

ador·able \ə-'dōr-ə-bəl, -'dȯr-\ *adj* **1** : worthy of being adored **2** : extremely charming ⟨an ∼ child⟩ — **ador·abil·i·ty** \-,dōr-ə-'bil-ət-ē, -,dȯr-\ *n* — **ador·able·ness** \-'dōr-ə-bəl-nəs, -'dȯr-\ *n* — **ador·ably** \-blē\ *adv*

ad·o·ra·tion \,ad-ə-'rā-shən\ *n* : the act of adoring : the state of being adored

adore \ə-'dō(ə)r, -'dȯ(ə)r\ *vt* **adored; ador·ing** [MF *adorer*, fr. L *adorare*, fr. *ad-* + *orare* to speak, pray — more at ORATION] **1** : to worship or honor as a deity or as divine **2** : to regard with reverent admiration and devotion ⟨at 40 he still *adored* his father⟩ **3** : to be extremely fond of ⟨always ∼s a good time⟩ **syn** see REVERE **ant** blaspheme — **ador·er** *n*

adorn \ə-'dō(ə)rn\ *vt* [ME *adornen*, fr. MF *adorner*, fr. L *adornare*, fr. *ad-* + *ornare* to furnish — more at ORNATE] : to decorate esp. with ornaments
syn ADORN, DECORATE, ORNAMENT, EMBELLISH, BEAUTIFY, DECK, GARNISH *shared meaning element* : to add something to for the purpose of making more attractive **ant** disfigure

adorn·ment \-mənt\ *n* **1** : the action of adorning : the state of being adorned **2** : something that adorns

adoze \ə-'dōz\ *adv or adj* : in a state of dozing

¹**ADP** \,ā-,dē-'pē, ə-'dē-,pē\ *n* [adenosine diphosphate] : an ester of adenosine that is reversibly converted to ATP for the storing of

energy by the addition of a high-energy phosphate group — called also *adenosine diphosphate*

²**ADP** *abbr* automatic data processing

¹**ad rem** \(')ad-'rem\ *adv* [L, to the thing] : to the point : RELEVANTLY

²**ad rem** *adj* : relevant to the point or purpose

adren- *or* **adreno-** *comb form* [*adrenal*] **1** : adrenal glands ⟨adrenocortical⟩ **2** : adrenaline ⟨adrenergic⟩

¹**ad·re·nal** \ə-'drēn-ᵊl\ *adj* **1** : adjacent to the kidneys **2** : of, relating to, or derived from adrenal glands or secretion — **ad·re·nal·ly** \-ᵊl-ē\ *adv*

²**adrenal** *n* : ADRENAL GLAND

ad·re·nal·ec·to·my \ə-,drēn-ᵊl-'ek-tə-mē\ *n* : surgical removal of one or both adrenal glands — **ad·re·nal·ec·to·mized** \-,mīzd\ *adj*

adrenal gland *n* : either of a pair of complex endocrine organs near the anterior medial border of the kidney consisting of a mesodermal cortex that produces steroids like sex hormones and hormones concerned esp. with metabolic functions and an ectodermal medulla that produces adrenaline — called also *adrenal*

Adren·a·lin \ə-'dren-ᵊl-ən\ *trademark* — used for a preparation of levorotatory epinephrine

adren·a·line \ə-'dren-ᵊl-ən\ *n* : EPINEPHRINE

ad·ren·er·gic \,ad-rə-'nər-jik\ *adj* [adren- + Gk *ergon* work — more at WORK] **1** : liberating or activated by adrenaline or a substance like adrenaline ⟨an ∼ nerve⟩ **2** : resembling adrenaline

ad·re·no·cor·ti·cal \ə-,drē-nō-'kȯrt-i-kəl\ *adj* : of, relating to, or derived from the cortex of the adrenal glands

ad·re·no·cor·ti·co·ste·roid \ə-'drē-nō-,kȯrt-i-kō-'sti(ə)r-,ȯid *also* -'ste)r-\ *n* : a steroid obtained from or resembling or having physiological effects like those of the adrenal cortex

ad·re·no·cor·ti·co·tro·phic \ə-'drē-nō-,kȯrt-i-kō-'trō-fik\ *or* **adre·no·cor·ti·co·trop·ic** \-'träp-ik\ *adj* : acting on or stimulating the adrenal cortex

adrenocorticotrophic hormone *n* : a protein hormone of the anterior lobe of the pituitary gland that stimulates the adrenal cortex — called also *ACTH*

ad·re·no·cor·ti·co·tro·phin \-'trō-fən\ *n* : ADRENOCORTICOTROPHIC HORMONE

adrift \ə-'drift\ *adv or adj* **1** : without motive power and without anchor or mooring **2** : without guidance or purpose

adroit \ə-'drȯit\ *adj* [F, fr. *à droit* properly] **1** : dexterous in the use of the hands **2** : marked by shrewdness, craft, or resourcefulness in coping with difficulty or danger **syn** **1** see DEXTEROUS **ant** maladroit **2** see CLEVER **ant** stolid — **adroit·ly** *adv* — **adroit·ness** *n*

ad·sci·ti·tious \,ad-sə-'tish-əs\ *adj* [L *adscitus*, fr. pp. of *adsciscere* to receive, fr. *ad-* + *sciscere* to accept, fr. *scire* to know — more at SCIENCE] : derived or acquired from something extrinsic

ad·sorb \ad-'sȯ(ə)rb, -'zȯ(ə)rb\ *vb* [*ad-* + *-sorb* (as in *absorb*)] *vt* : to take up and hold by adsorption ∼ *vi* : to become adsorbed — **ad·sorb·able** \-'sȯr-bə-bəl, -'zȯr-\ *adj*

ad·sor·bate \ad-'sȯr-bət, -'zȯr-, -,bāt\ *n* : an adsorbed substance

ad·sor·bent \-bənt\ *adj* : having the capacity or tendency to adsorb — **adsorbent** *n*

ad·sorp·tion \ad-'sȯrp-shən, -'zȯrp-\ *n* [irreg. fr. *adsorb*] : the adhesion in an extremely thin layer of molecules (as of gases, solutes, or liquids) to the surfaces of solid bodies or liquids with which they are in contact — compare ABSORPTION — **ad·sorp·tive** \-'sȯrp-tiv, -'zȯrp-\ *adj*

ad·u·lar·ia \,aj-ə-'lar-ē-ə, -'ler-\ *n* [It *adularia*, fr. F *adulaire*, fr. *Adula*, Swiss mountain group] : a transparent or translucent orthoclase

ad·u·late \'aj-ə-,lāt\ *vt* **-lat·ed; -lat·ing** [back-formation fr. *adulation*, fr. ME, fr. MF, fr. L *adulation-, adulatio*, fr. *adulatus*, pp. of *adulari* to flatter] : to flatter or admire excessively or slavishly — **ad·u·la·tion** \,aj-ə-'lā-shən\ *n* — **ad·u·la·tor** \'aj-ə-,lāt-ər\ *n* — **ad·u·la·to·ry** \-lə-,tōr-ē, -,tȯr-\ *adj*

¹**adult** \ə-'dəlt, 'ad-,əlt\ *adj* [L *adultus*, pp. of *adolescere* to grow up, fr. *ad-* + *-olescere* (fr. *alescere* to grow) — more at OLD] **1** : fully developed and mature : GROWN-UP **2 a** : of, relating to, or befitting adults ⟨an ∼ approach to a problem⟩ **b** : restricted to adults ⟨∼ movies⟩ **syn** see MATURE **ant** juvenile, puerile — **adulthood** \ə-'dəlt-,hu̇d\ *n* — **adult·like** \ə-'dəlt-,līk\ *adj* — **adult·ly** \ə-'dəlt-lē, 'ad-,əlt-\ *adv* — **adult·ness** \-'dəlt-nəs, 'ad-,əlt-\ *n*

²**adult** *n* : one that is adult; *esp* : a human being after an age (as 21) specified by law

adult education *n* : lecture or correspondence courses for adults usu. not otherwise engaged in formal study

adul·ter·ant \ə-'dəl-t(ə-)rənt\ *n* : an adulterating substance or agent — **adulterant** *adj*

¹**adul·ter·ate** \ə-'dəl-tə-,rāt\ *vt* **-at·ed; -at·ing** [L *adulteratus*, pp. of *adulterare*, fr. *ad-* + *alter* other — more at ELSE] : to corrupt, debase, or make impure by the addition of a foreign or inferior substance; *esp* : to prepare for sale by replacing more valuable with less valuable or inert ingredients — **adul·ter·a·tor** \-,rāt-ər\ *n*

²**adul·ter·ate** \ə-'dəl-t(ə-)rət\ *adj* **1** : tainted with adultery : ADULTEROUS **2** : being adulterated : SPURIOUS

adul·ter·a·tion \ə-,dəl-tə-'rā-shən\ *n* **1** : the process of adulterating : the condition of being adulterated **2** : an adulterated product

adul·ter·er \ə-'dəl-tər-ər\ *n* : one that commits adultery; *esp* : a man who commits adultery

adul·ter·ess \ə-'dəl-t(ə-)rəs\ *n* : a woman who commits adultery

adul·ter·ine \ə-'dəl-tə-,rīn, -,rēn\ *adj* **1 a** : marked by adulteration : SPURIOUS **b** : ILLEGAL **2** : born of adultery

adul·ter·ous \ə-'dəl-t(ə-)rəs\ *adj* : relating to, characterized by, or given to adultery — **adul·ter·ous·ly** *adv*

adul·tery \ə-'dəl-t(ə-)rē\ *n, pl* **-ter·ies** [ME, alter. of *avoutrie*, fr. MF, fr. L *adulterium*, fr. *adulter* adulterer, back-formation fr. *adulterare*] : voluntary sexual intercourse between a married man and someone other than his wife or a married woman and someone other than her husband; *also* : an act of adultery

ad·um·brate \'ad-əm-,brāt, a-'dəm-\ *vt* **-brat·ed; -brat·ing** [L *adumbratus*, pp. of *adumbrare*, fr. *ad-* + *umbra* shadow — more at

UMBRAGE] **1** : to foreshadow vaguely : INTIMATE **2 a** : to give a sketchy representation or outline of **b** : to suggest or disclose partially **3** : OVERSHADOW, OBSCURE — **ad·um·bra·tion** \ˌad-(ˌ)əm-ˈbrā-shən\ *n* — **ad·um·bra·tive** \a-ˈdəm-brət-iv\ *adj* — **ad·um·bra·tive·ly** *adv*

adust \ə-ˈdəst\ *adj* [ME, fr. L *adustus*, pp. of *adurere* to set fire to, fr. *ad-* + *urere* to burn — more at EMBER] **1** : SCORCHED, BURNED **2** *archaic* : of a sunburned appearance **3** *archaic* : of a gloomy appearance or disposition

adv *abbr* **1** adverb **2** [L *adversus*] against **3** advertisement; advertising **4** advisory

ad val *abbr* ad valorem

ad va·lo·rem \ˌad-və-ˈlōr-əm, -ˈlȯr-\ *adj* [L, according to the value] : imposed at a rate percent of the value as stated in an invoice ⟨*ad valorem* tax on goods⟩

1ad·vance \əd-ˈvan(t)s\ *vb* **ad·vanced; ad·vanc·ing** [ME *advauncen*, fr. OF *avancier*, fr. (assumed) VL *abantiare*, fr. L *abante* before, fr. *ab-* + *ante* before — more at ANTE-] *vt* **1** : to bring or move forward **2** : to accelerate the growth or progress of **3** : to raise to a higher rank **4** : to supply or furnish in expectation of repayment **5** *archaic* : to lift up : RAISE **6 a** : to bring forward in time; *esp* : to make earlier ⟨~ the date of the meeting⟩ **b** : to place later in time **7** : to bring for notice, consideration, or acceptance : PROPOSE **8** : to raise in rate : INCREASE ⟨~ the rent⟩ ~ *vi* **1** : to move forward : PROCEED **2** : to make progress : INCREASE ⟨~ in age⟩ **3** : to rise in rank, position, or importance **4** : to rise in rate or price — **ad·vanc·er** *n*
syn 1 ADVANCE, PROMOTE, FORWARD, FURTHER *shared meaning element* : to help to move ahead **ant** retard, check
2 see ADDUCE

2advance *n* **1** : a moving forward **2 a** : progress in development : IMPROVEMENT ⟨an ~ in medical technique⟩ **b** : a progressive step ⟨the job meant a personal ~ forward⟩ **3** : a rise in price, value, or amount **4** : a first step or approach made : OFFER ⟨her attitude discouraged all ~*s*⟩ **5** : a provision of something (as money or goods) before a return is received; *also* : the money or goods supplied — **in advance** : before a deadline or an anticipated event — **in advance of** : ahead of

3advance *adj* **1** : made, sent, or furnished ahead of time ⟨an ~ payment⟩ **2** : going or situated before ⟨an ~ party of soldiers⟩

ad·vanced *adj* **1** : far on in time or course ⟨a man ~ in years⟩ **2 a** : beyond the elementary or introductory ⟨~ chemistry⟩ **b** : being beyond others in progress or development ⟨an ~ country⟩

advanced degree *n* : a university degree (as a master's or doctor's degree) higher than a bachelor's

advance man *n* **1** : a business representative (as of a theatrical company) who makes necessary arrangements for the public appearance of the company — called also *advance agent* **2** : an aide (as of a political candidate) who makes a security check or handles publicity in advance of his employer's personal appearances

ad·vance·ment \əd-ˈvan(t)-smənt\ *n* **1** : the action of advancing : the state of being advanced: **a** : promotion or elevation to a higher rank or position **b** : progression to a higher stage of development **2** : an advance of money or value

1ad·van·tage \əd-ˈvant-ij\ *n* [ME *avantage*, fr. MF, fr. *avant* before, fr. L *abante*] **1** : superiority of position or condition ⟨higher ground gave the enemy the ~⟩ **2 a** : BENEFIT, GAIN; *esp* : benefit resulting from some course of action ⟨a mistake which turned out to his ~⟩ **b** *obs* : INTEREST 3a **3** : a factor or circumstance of benefit to its possessor ⟨lacked the ~*s* of an education⟩ **4** : the first point won in tennis after deuce; *also* : the score for it — **to advantage** : so as to produce a favorable impression or effect

2advantage *vt* **-taged; -tag·ing** : to give an advantage to : BENEFIT

ad·van·ta·geous \ˌad-ˌvan-ˈtā-jəs, -vən-\ *adj* : giving an advantage : FAVORABLE **syn** see BENEFICIAL **ant** disadvantageous — **ad·van·ta·geous·ly** *adv* — **ad·van·ta·geous·ness** *n*

ad·vec·tion \ad-ˈvek-shən\ *n* [L *advection-, advectio* act of bringing, fr. *advectus*, pp. of *advehere* to carry to, fr. *ad-* + *vehere* to carry — more at WAY] : the horizontal movement of a mass of air that causes changes in temperature or in other physical properties of the air — **ad·vec·tive** \-ˈvek-tiv\ *adj*

Ad·vent \ˈad-ˌvent\ *n* [ME, fr. ML *adventus*, fr. L, arrival, fr. *adventus*, pp.] **1** : the period beginning four Sundays before Christmas and observed by some Christians as a season of prayer and fasting **2 a** : the coming of Christ at the Incarnation **b** : SECOND COMING **3** *not cap* : ARRIVAL, COMING ⟨the ~ of spring⟩

Ad·vent·ism \ˈad-ˌvent-ˌiz-əm\ *n* **1** : the doctrine that the second coming of Christ and the end of the world are near at hand **2** : the principles and practices of Seventh-Day Adventists — **Ad·vent·ist** \əd-ˈvent-əst, ad-ˈ, ˈad-ˌ\ *adj or n*

ad·ven·ti·tia \ˌad-vən-ˈtish-ə, -(ˌ)ven-\ *n* [NL, alter. of L *adventicia*, neut. pl. of *adventicius* coming from outside, fr. *adventus*, pp.] : an external chiefly connective tissue covering of an organ; *esp* : the external coat of a blood vessel — **ad·ven·ti·tial** \-əl\ *adj*

ad·ven·ti·tious \ˌad-vən-ˈtish-əs, -(ˌ)ven-\ *adj* [L *adventicius*] **1** : added from another source and not inherent or innate **2** : arising or occurring sporadically or in other than the usual location ⟨~ buds⟩ **syn** see ACCIDENTAL **ant** inherent — **ad·ven·ti·tious·ly** *adv* — **ad·ven·ti·tious·ness** *n*

ad·ven·tive \ad-ˈvent-iv\ *adj* **1** : introduced but not fully naturalized **2** : ADVENTITIOUS 2 — **adventive** *n* — **ad·ven·tive·ly** *adv*

Advent Sunday *n* : the first Sunday in Advent

1ad·ven·ture \əd-ˈven-chər\ *n* [ME *aventure*, fr. OF, fr. (assumed) VL *adventura*, fr. L *adventus*, pp. of *advenire* to arrive, fr. *ad-* + *venire* to come — more at COME] **1 a** : an undertaking involving danger and unknown risks **b** : the encountering of risks ⟨the spirit of ~⟩ **2** : an exciting or remarkable experience ⟨an ~ in exotic dining⟩ **3** : an enterprise involving financial risk

2adventure *vb* **ad·ven·tured; ad·ven·tur·ing** \-ˈvench-(ə-)riŋ\ *vt* **1** : to expose to danger or loss : VENTURE **2** : to venture upon : TRY ~ *vi* **1** : to proceed despite danger or risk **2** : to take the risk

ad·ven·tur·er \əd-ˈvench-(ə-)rər\ *n* **1** : one that adventures: as **a** : SOLDIER OF FORTUNE **b** : one that engages in risky commercial enterprises for profit **2** : one who seeks unmerited wealth or position esp. by playing on the credulity or prejudice of others

ad·ven·ture·some \əd-ˈven-chər-səm\ *adj* : inclined to take risks : VENTURESOME — **ad·ven·ture·some·ness** *n*

ad·ven·tur·ess \əd-ˈvench-(ə-)rəs\ *n* : a female adventurer; *esp* : a woman who seeks position or livelihood by questionable means

ad·ven·tur·ism \əd-ˈven-chə-ˌriz-əm\ *n* : ill-considered or rash improvisation or experimentation esp. in politics or foreign affairs in the absence or in defiance of consistent plans or principles — **ad·ven·tur·ist** \-ˈvench-(ə-)rəst\ *n* — **ad·ven·tur·is·tic** \-ˌven-chə-ˈris-tik\ *adj*

ad·ven·tur·ous \əd-ˈvench-(ə-)rəs\ *adj* **1** : disposed to seek adventure or to cope with the new and unknown ⟨an ~ explorer⟩ **2** : characterized by unknown dangers and risks ⟨an ~ journey⟩ — **ad·ven·tur·ous·ly** *adv* — **ad·ven·tur·ous·ness** *n*
syn ADVENTUROUS, VENTURESOME, DARING, DAREDEVIL, RASH, RECKLESS, FOOLHARDY *shared meaning element* : exposing oneself to danger beyond what is called for by duty or courage **ant** cautious

1ad·verb \ˈad-ˌvərb\ *n* [MF *adverbe*, fr. L *adverbium*, fr. *ad-* + *verbum* word — more at WORD] : a word belonging to one of the major form classes in any of numerous languages, typically serving as a modifier of a verb, an adjective, another adverb, a preposition, a phrase, a clause, or a sentence, and expressing some relation of manner or quality, place, time, degree, number, cause, opposition, affirmation, or denial

2adverb *adj* : ADVERBIAL

ad·ver·bi·al \ad-ˈvər-bē-əl\ *adj* : of, relating to, or having the function of an adverb — **adverbial** *n* — **ad·ver·bi·al·ly** \-ə-lē\ *adv*

ad ver·bum \(ˈ)ad-ˈvər-bəm\ *adv* [L] : to a word : VERBATIM

1ad·ver·sary \ˈad-və(r)-ˌser-ē\ *n, pl* **-sar·ies** : one that contends with, opposes, or resists : ENEMY **syn** see OPPONENT — **ad·ver·sari·ness** *n*

2adversary *adj* **1** : of, relating to, or involving an adversary **2** : having or involving antagonistic parties or interests ⟨divorce can be an ~ proceeding⟩

ad·ver·sa·tive \əd-ˈvər-sət-iv, ad-\ *adj* : expressing antithesis, opposition, or adverse circumstance ⟨the ~ conjunction *but*⟩ — **ad·versative** *n* — **ad·ver·sa·tive·ly** *adv*

ad·verse \ad-ˈvərs, ˈad-ˌ\ *adj* [ME, fr. MF *advers*, fr. L *adversus*, pp. of *advertere*] **1** : acting against or in a contrary direction : HOSTILE ⟨hindered by ~ winds⟩ **2** : opposed to one's interests : UNFAVORABLE ⟨an ~ verdict⟩ **3** *archaic* : opposite in position — **ad·verse·ly** *adv* — **ad·verse·ness** *n*
syn ADVERSE, INIMICAL, ANTAGONISTIC, COUNTER, COUNTERACTIVE *shared meaning element* : so opposed as to cause often harmful interference **ant** propitious

ad·ver·si·ty \ad-ˈvər-sət-ē\ *n, pl* **-ties** **1** : a condition of suffering, destitution, or affliction **2** : a calamitous or disastrous experience **syn** see MISFORTUNE **ant** prosperity

1ad·vert \ad-ˈvərt\ *vi* [ME *adverten*, fr. MF & L; MF *advertir*, fr. L *advertere*, fr. *ad-* + *vertere* to turn — more at WORTH] **1** : to pay heed or attention **2** : to make a usu. slight or glancing reference : refer casually (as by interpolation) **syn** see REFER

2ad·vert \ˈad-ˌvərt\ *n, chiefly Brit* : ADVERTISEMENT

ad·ver·tence \ad-ˈvərt-ᵊns\ *n* **1** : the action or process of adverting : ATTENTION **2** : ADVERTENCY 1

ad·ver·ten·cy \-ᵊn-sē\ *n, pl* **-cies** **1** : the quality or state of being advertent : HEEDFULNESS **2** : ADVERTENCE 1

ad·ver·tent \-ᵊnt\ *adj* [L *advertent-, advertens*, prp. of *advertere*] : giving attention : HEEDFUL — **ad·ver·tent·ly** *adv*

ad·ver·tise \ˈad-vər-ˌtīz\ *vb* **-tised; -tis·ing** [ME *advertisen*, fr. MF *advertiss-*, stem of *advertir*] *vt* **1** : to make something known to : NOTIFY **2 a** : to make publicly and generally known ⟨*advertising* their readiness to make concessions⟩ **b** : to announce publicly esp. by a printed notice or a broadcast **c** : to call public attention to esp. by emphasizing desirable qualities so as to arouse a desire to buy or patronize ~ *vi* : to issue or sponsor advertising ⟨~ for a secretary⟩ **syn** see DECLARE — **ad·ver·tis·er** *n*

ad·ver·tise·ment \ˌad-vər-ˈtīz-mənt; əd-ˈvərt-əz-mənt, -ə-smənt\ *n* **1** : the act or process of advertising **2** : a public notice; *esp* : one published in the press or broadcast over the air

ad·ver·tis·ing *n* **1** : the action of calling something to the attention of the public esp. by paid announcements **2** : ADVERTISEMENTS ⟨the magazine contains much ~⟩ **3** : the business of preparing advertisements for publication or broadcast

ad·vice \əd-ˈvīs\ *n* [ME, fr. OF *avis* opinion, prob. fr. the phrase *ce m'est a vis* that appears to me, part trans. of L *mihi visum est* it seemed so to me, I decided] **1** : recommendation regarding a decision or course of conduct : COUNSEL ⟨he shall have power, by and with the ~ and consent of the Senate, to make treaties — *U.S. Constitution*⟩ **2** : information or notice given : INTELLIGENCE — usu. used in pl. **3** : an official notice concerning a business transaction ⟨a remittance ~⟩

ad·vis·able \əd-ˈvī-zə-bəl\ *adj* : fit to be advised or done : PRUDENT **syn** see EXPEDIENT **ant** inadvisable — **ad·vis·abil·i·ty** \-ˌvī-zə-ˈbil-ət-ē\ *n* — **ad·vis·able·ness** \-ˈvī-zə-bəl-nəs\ *n* — **ad·vis·ably** \-blē\ *adv*

ad·vise \əd-ˈvīz\ *vb* **ad·vised; ad·vis·ing** [MF *advisen*, fr. OF *aviser*, fr. *avis*] *vt* **1 a** : to give advice to : COUNSEL ⟨~ her to try a drier climate⟩ **b** : CAUTION, WARN ⟨~ him of the danger⟩ **c** : RECOMMEND ⟨~ prudence⟩ **2** : to give information or notice to : INFORM ⟨~ his friends of his marriage⟩ ~ *vi* **1** : to give advice ⟨~ on legal matters⟩ **2** : to take counsel : CONSULT ⟨~ with one's parents⟩ — **ad·vis·er** *or* **ad·vi·sor** \-ˈvī-zər\ *n*

ad·vised \əd-ˈvīzd\ *adj* : thought out : CONSIDERED — usu. used in combination ⟨ill-*advised* plans⟩ — **ad·vis·ed·ly** \-ˈvī-zəd-lē\ *adv*
ad·vis·ee \əd-ˌvī-ˈzē\ *n* : one that is advised
ad·vise·ment \əd-ˈvīz-mənt\ *n* : careful consideration : DELIBERATION
[1]**ad·vi·so·ry** \əd-ˈvīz-(ə-)rē\ *adj* **1** : having or exercising power to advise **2** : containing or giving advice
[2]**advisory** *n, pl* **-ries** : a report giving information (as on the weather)
ad·vo·ca·cy \ˈad-və-kə-sē\ *n* : the act or process of advocating : SUPPORT
[1]**ad·vo·cate** \ˈad-və-kət, -ˌkāt\ *n* [ME *advocat*, fr. MF, fr. L *advocatus*, fr. pp. of *advocare* to summon, fr. *ad-* + *vocare* to call — more at VOICE] **1** : one that pleads the cause of another; *specif* : one that pleads the cause of another before a tribunal or judicial court ⟨the ~ for the defense⟩ **2** : one that defends or maintains a cause or proposal
[2]**ad·vo·cate** \-ˌkāt\ *vt* **-cat·ed; -cat·ing** : to plead in favor of ***syn*** see SUPPORT — **ad·vo·ca·tion** \ˌad-və-ˈkā-shən\ *n* — **ad·vo·ca·tive** \ˈad-və-ˌkāt-iv\ *adj* — **ad·vo·ca·tor** \-ˌkāt-ər\ *n*
ad·vow·son \əd-ˈvau̇z-ᵊn\ *n* [ME, fr. OF *avoueson*, fr. ML *advocation-, advocatio*, fr. L, act of calling, fr. *advocatus*, pp.] : the right in English law of presenting a nominee to a vacant ecclesiastical benefice
advt *abbr* advertisement
ady·nam·ic \ˌā(ˌ)dī-ˈnam-ik, ˌad-ə-ˈnam-\ *adj* [Gk *adynamia* lack of strength, fr. *a-* + *dynamis* power, fr. *dynasthai* to be able] : characterized by or causing a loss of strength or function
ad·y·tum \ˈad-ə-təm\ *n, pl* **-ta** \-tə\ [L, fr. Gk *adyton*, neut. of *adytos* not to be entered, fr. *a-* + *dyein* to enter; akin to Skt *upā-du* to put on] : the innermost sanctuary in an ancient temple open only to priests : SANCTUM
adz *or* **adze** \ˈadz\ *n* [ME *adse*, fr. OE *adesa*] : a cutting tool that has a thin arched blade set at right angles to the handle and is used chiefly for shaping wood

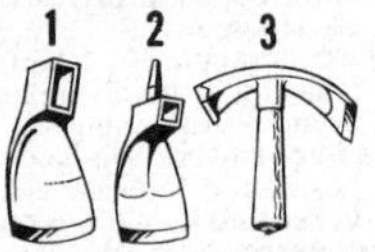

adzes: *1* carpenter's with flat head, *2* shipwright's with spur, *3* cooper's

ae \ˈā\ *adj* [ME (northern dial.) *a*, alter. of *an*] *chiefly Scot* : ONE
Ae·a·cus \ˈē-ə-kəs\ *n* [L, fr. Gk *Aiakos*] : a son of Zeus who was given the Myrmidons as followers and became on his death a judge of the underworld
AEC *abbr* Atomic Energy Commission
ae·cio·spore \ˈē-s(h)ē-ə-ˌspō(ə)r, -ˌspȯ(ə)r\ *n* : one of the spores arranged within an aecium in a series like a chain
ae·ci·um \ˈē-s(h)ē-əm\ *n, pl* **-cia** \-s(h)ē-ə\ [NL, fr. Gk *aikia* assault, fr. *aeikēs* unseemly, fr. *a-* + *eikōs* seemly, fr. participle of *eikenai* to seem] : the fruiting body of a rust fungus in which the first binucleate spores are usu. produced — **ae·cial** \-sh(ē-)əl\ *adj*
aë·des \ā-ˈēd-(ˌ)ēz\ *n, pl* **aëdes** [NL, genus name, fr. Gk *aēdēs* unpleasant, fr. *a-* + *ēdos* pleasure; akin to Gk *hēdys* sweet — more at SWEET] : any of a genus (*Aëdes*) of mosquitoes including the vector of yellow fever, dengue, and other diseases — see MOSQUITO illustration — **ae·dine** \-ˈē-ˌdīn\ *adj*
ae·dile \ˈē-ˌdīl\ *n* [L *aedilis*, fr. *aedes* temple — more at EDIFY] : an official in ancient Rome in charge of public works and games, police, and the grain supply
AEF *abbr* American Expeditionary Force
Ae·ge·an \i-ˈjē-ən\ *adj* [L *Aegaeus*, fr. Gk *Aigaios*] **1** : of or relating to the arm of the Mediterranean sea east of Greece **2** : of or relating to the chiefly Bronze Age civilization of the islands of the Aegean sea and the countries adjacent to it
ae·gis \ˈē-jəs\ *n* [L, fr. Gk *aigis* goatskin, perh. fr. *aig-, aix* goat; akin to Arm *aic* goat] **1** : a shield or breastplate emblematic of majesty that was orig. associated chiefly with Zeus but later mainly with Athena **2** : PROTECTION ⟨under the ~ of the law⟩ **3** : AUSPICES, SPONSORSHIP ⟨under the ~ of the education department⟩
Ae·gis·thus \i-ˈjis-thəs\ *n* [L, fr. Gk *Aigisthos*] : a lover of the married Clytemnestra slain with her by her son Orestes
-aemia — see -EMIA
Ae·ne·as \i-ˈnē-əs\ *n* [L, fr. Gk *Aineias*] : a son of Anchises and Aphrodite, defender of Troy, and hero of Vergil's *Aeneid*
Aeneo·lith·ic \ā-ˌē-nē-ō-ˈlith-ik\ *adj* [L *aeneus* of copper or bronze, fr. *aes* copper, bronze — more at ORE] : of or relating to a transitional period between the Neolithic and Bronze ages in which some copper was used
[1]**ae·o·lian** \ē-ˈō-lē-ən, -ˈōl-yən\ *adj* **1** *often cap* : of or relating to Aeolus **2** : giving forth or marked by a moaning or sighing sound or musical tone produced by or as if by the wind
[2]**aeolian** *var of* EOLIAN
[1]**Ae·o·lian** \ē-ˈō-lē-ən, -ˈōl-yən\ *adj* : of or relating to Aeolis or its inhabitants
[2]**Aeolian** *n* **1** : a member of a group of Greek peoples of Thessaly and Boeotia that colonized Lesbos and the adjacent coast of Asia Minor **2** : AEOLIC
aeolian harp *n* : a box-shaped musical instrument having stretched strings usu. tuned in unison on which the wind produces varying harmonics over the same fundamental tone
[1]**Ae·ol·ic** \ē-ˈäl-ik\ *adj* : AEOLIAN
[2]**Aeolic** *n* : a group of ancient Greek dialects used by the Aeolians
ae·o·lo·trop·ic \ˌē-ə-lō-ˈträp-ik\ *adj* [Gk *aiolos* variegated] : ANISOTROPIC 1 — **ae·o·lot·ro·py** \-ˈlä-trə-pē\ *n*
Ae·o·lus \ˈē-ə-ləs\ *n* [L, fr. Gk *Aiolos*] : the Greek god of the winds
ae·on \ˈē-ən, ˈē-ˌän\ *n* [L, fr. Gk *aiōn* — more at AYE] **1** : an immeasurably or indefinitely long period of time : AGE **2** : a unit of time equal to one billion years — used in geology
ae·o·ni·an \ē-ˈō-nē-ən\ *or* **ae·on·ic** \-ˈän-ik\ *adj* : lasting for an immeasurably or indefinitely long period of time
ae·py·or·nis \ˌē-pē-ˈȯr-nəs\ *n* [NL, genus name, fr. Gk *aipys* high + *ornis* bird — more at ERNE] : any of a group (genus *Aepyornis* or order Aepyornithiformes) of gigantic ratite birds known only from remains found in Madagascar
aeq *abbr* [L *aequalis*] equal
aer- *or* **aero-** *comb form* [ME *aero-*, fr. MF, fr. L, fr. Gk *aer-, aero-*, fr. *aēr*] **1 a** : air : atmosphere ⟨*aer*ate⟩ ⟨*aero*biology⟩ **b** : aerial and ⟨*aero*marine⟩ **2** : gas ⟨*aero*sol⟩ **3** : aviation ⟨*aero*drome⟩
aer·ate \ˈa(-ə)r-ˌāt, ˈe(-ə)r-\ *vt* **aer·at·ed; aer·at·ing** **1** : to supply (the blood) with oxygen by respiration **2** : to supply or impregnate (as the soil or a liquid) with air **3 a** : to combine or charge with a gas (as carbon dioxide) **b** : to make effervescent — **aer·a·tion** \ˌa(-ə)r-ˈā-shən, ˌe(-ə)r-\ *n*
aer·a·tor \ˈa(-ə)r-ˌāt-ər, ˈe(-ə)r-\ *n* : one that aerates; *esp* : an apparatus for aerating something (as sewage)
aer·en·chy·ma \ˌa(ə)r-ˈeŋ-kə-mə, ˌe(ə)r-\ *n* [NL] : the spongy modified cork tissue of many aquatic plants that facilitates gaseous exchange and maintains buoyancy
[1]**ae·ri·al** \ˈar-ē-əl, ˈer-, ā-ˈir-ē-əl\ *adj* [L *aerius*, fr. Gk *aerios*, fr. *aēr*] **1 a** : of, relating to, or occurring in the air or atmosphere **b** : consisting of air ⟨~ particles⟩ **c** : existing or growing in the air rather than in the ground or in water **d** : LOFTY ⟨~ spires⟩ **e** : operating or operated overhead on elevated cables or rails ⟨an ~ railroad⟩ **2** : suggestive of air: as **a** : lacking substance : THIN ⟨fine and ~ distinctions⟩ **b** : IMAGINARY, ETHEREAL ⟨visions of ~ joy — P. B. Shelley⟩ **3 a** : of or relating to aircraft ⟨~ navigation⟩ **b** : designed for use in, taken from, or operating from or against aircraft ⟨~ photo⟩ **c** : effected by means of aircraft ⟨~ transportation⟩ **4** : of, relating to, or gained by the forward pass in football — **ae·ri·al·ly** \-ə-lē\ *adv*
[2]**aer·i·al** \ˈar-ē-əl, ˈer-\ *n* **1** : ANTENNA 2 **2** : FORWARD PASS
ae·ri·al·ist \ˈar-ē-ə-ləst, ˈer-, ā-ˈir-\ *n* : one that performs feats in the air or above the ground esp. on the flying trapeze
aerial ladder *n* : a mechanically operated extensible ladder usu. mounted on a fire truck
aerial perspective *n* : the expression of space in painting by gradation of color and distinctness
ae·rie \ˈa(ə)r-ē, ˈe(ə)r-, ˈi(ə)r-, ˈā-(ə-)rē\ *n* [ML *aerea*, fr. OF *aire*, fr. L *area* area, feeding place for animals] **1** : the nest of a bird on a cliff or a mountaintop **2** *obs* : a brood of birds of prey **3** : a dwelling on a height
[1]**aero** \ˈa(-ə)r-(ˌ)ō, ˈe(-ə)r-\ *adj* [*aero-*] **1** : of or relating to aircraft or aeronautics ⟨an ~ engine⟩ **2** : designed for aerial use ⟨an ~ lens⟩
[2]**aero** *abbr* aeronautical; aeronautics
aero- — see AER-
aero·bal·lis·tics \ˌar-ō-bə-ˈlis-tiks, ˌer-\ *n pl but sing or pl in constr* : the ballistics of the flight of missiles and projectiles in the atmosphere — **aero·bal·lis·tic** \-tik\ *adj*
aer·o·bat·ics \ˌar-ə-ˈbat-iks, ˌer-\ *n pl but sing or pl in constr* [blend of *aer-* and *acrobatics*] : spectacular flying feats and maneuvers (as rolls and dives) — **aer·o·bat·ic** \-ik\ *adj*
aer·obe \ˈa(-ə)r-ˌōb, ˈe(-ə)r-\ *n* [F *aérobie*, fr. *aér-* aer- + *-bie* (fr. Gk *bios* life) — more at QUICK] : an organism (as a bacterium) that lives only in the presence of oxygen
aer·o·bic \ˌa(-ə)r-ˈrō-bik, ˌe(-ə)r-\ *adj* **1** : living, active, or occurring only in the presence of oxygen ⟨~ respiration⟩ **2** : of, relating to, or induced by aerobes — **aer·o·bi·cal·ly** \-bi-k(ə-)lē\ *adv*
aero·bi·ol·o·gy \ˌar-ō-bī-ˈäl-ə-jē\ *n* [*aer-* + *biology*] : the science dealing with the occurrence, transportation, and effects of airborne microorganisms or biological objects (as viruses, pollen, or plant spores) — **aero·bi·o·log·i·cal** \-ˌbī-ə-ˈläj-i-kəl\ *adj* — **aero·bi·o·log·i·cal·ly** \-k(ə-)lē\ *adv*
aero·bi·o·sis \ˌar-ō-bī-ˈō-səs, ˌer-, -bē-\ *n, pl* **-o·ses** \-ˌsēz\ : life in the presence of air or oxygen — **aero·bi·ot·ic** \-ˈät-ik\ *adj* — **aero·bi·ot·i·cal·ly** \-i-k(ə-)lē\ *adv*
aero·drome \ˈar-ə-ˌdrōm, ˈer-\ *n, chiefly Brit* : AIRFIELD, AIRPORT
aero·dy·nam·i·cist \-ˈnam-ə-səst\ *n* : one who specializes in aerodynamics
aero·dy·nam·ics \ˌar-ō-dī-ˈnam-iks, ˌer-\ *n pl but sing or pl in constr* : a branch of dynamics that deals with the motion of air and other gaseous fluids and with the forces acting on bodies in motion relative to such fluids — **aero·dy·nam·ic** \-ik\ *or* **aero·dy·nam·i·cal** \-i-kəl\ *adj* — **aero·dy·nam·i·cal·ly** \-i-k(ə-)lē\ *adv*
aero·dyne \ˈar-ə-ˌdīn, ˈer-\ *n* [*aerodynamic*] : a heavier-than-air aircraft that derives its lift in flight from forces resulting from its motion through the air
aero·em·bo·lism \ˌar-ō-ˈem-bə-ˌliz-əm, ˌer-\ *n* **1** : a gaseous embolism **2** : a condition equivalent to caisson disease caused by rapid ascent to high altitudes and resulting exposure to rapidly lowered air pressure — called also *air bends*
aero·gram *or* **aero·gramme** \ˈar-ə-ˌgram, ˈer-\ *n* : AIR LETTER 2
aer·og·ra·pher \ˌa(-ə)r-ˈräg-rə-fər, ˌe(-ə)r-\ *n* : a navy warrant officer who observes and forecasts weather and surf conditions
aer·og·ra·phy \-fē\ *n* : METEOROLOGY
aer·o·lite \ˈar-ə-ˌlīt, ˈer-\ *also* **aero·lith** \-ˌlith\ *n* : a stony meteorite — **aer·o·lit·ic** \ˌar-ə-ˈlit-ik, ˌer-\ *adj*
aer·ol·o·gy \ˌa(-ə)r-ˈäl-ə-jē, ˌe(-ə)r-\ *n* **1** : METEOROLOGY **2** : a branch of meteorology that deals esp. with the air — **aer·o·log·i·cal** \ˌar-ə-ˈläj-i-kəl, ˌer-\ *adj* — **aer·ol·o·gist** \ˌa(-ə)r-ˈäl-ə-jəst, ˌe(-ə)r-\ *n*
aero·mag·net·ic \ˌar-ō-mag-ˈnet-ik, ˌer-\ *adj* : of, relating to, or derived from a study of the earth's magnetic field esp. from the air ⟨an ~ survey⟩
aero·me·chan·ics \-mə-ˈkan-iks\ *n pl but sing or pl in constr* : mechanics that deals with the equilibrium and motion of gases and of solid bodies immersed in them
aero·med·i·cine \-ˈmed-ə-sən\ *n* : a branch of medicine that deals with the diseases and disturbances arising from flying and the associated physiological and psychological problems — **aero·med·i·cal** \-ˈmed-i-kəl\ *adj*
aero·me·te·or·o·graph \ˌar-ō-ˌmēt-ē-ˈȯr-ə-ˌgraf, ˌer-\ *n* : METEOROGRAPH; *esp* : one adapted for use on an airplane
aer·om·e·ter \ˌa(-ə)r-ˈäm-ət-ər, ˌe(-ə)r-\ *n* [prob. fr. F *aéromètre*, fr. *aér-* + *mètre* -meter] : an instrument for ascertaining the weight or density of air or other gases

aero·naut \ˈar-ə-ˌnȯt, ˈer-, -ˌnät\ *n* [F *aéronaute,* fr. *aér-* aer- + Gk *nautēs* sailor — more at NAUTICAL] **:** one that operates or travels in an airship or balloon

aero·nau·tics \ˌar-ə-ˈnȯt-iks\ *n pl but sing in constr* **1 :** a science dealing with the operation of aircraft **2 :** the art or science of flight — **aero·nau·ti·cal** \-i-kəl\ *or* **aero·nau·tic** \-ik\ *adj* — **aero·nau·ti·cal·ly** \-i-k(ə-)lē\ *adv*

aero·neu·ro·sis \ˌar-ō-n(y)u̇-ˈrō-səs, ˌer-\ *n* **:** a functional nervous disorder of airmen caused by emotional stress and characterized by physical symptoms (as restlessness, abdominal pains, and diarrhea)

aer·on·o·my \ˌa(-ə)r-ˈän-ə-mē, ˌe(-ə)r-\ *n* **:** a science that deals with the physics and chemistry of the upper atmosphere — **aer·on·o·mer** \-mər\ *n* — **aer·o·nom·ic** \ˌar-ə-ˈnäm-ik\ *or* **aer·o·nom·i·cal** \-i-kəl\ *adj* — **aer·o·nom·ics** \-iks\ *n pl but sing in constr* — **aer·on·o·mist** \ˌa(-ə)r-ˈän-ə-məst, ˌe(-ə)r-\ *n*

aero·pause \ˈar-ō-ˌpȯz, ˈer-\ *n* **:** the level above the earth's surface where the atmosphere becomes ineffective for human and aircraft functions

aero·plane \ˈar-ə-ˌplān, ˈer-\ *chiefly Brit var of* AIRPLANE

aero·sol \ˈar-ə-ˌsäl, ˈer-, -ˌsȯl\ *n* **1 :** a suspension of fine solid or liquid particles in gas ⟨smoke, fog, and mist are ~*s*⟩ **2 :** a substance (as an insecticide or cosmetic) dispensed from a pressurized container as an aerosol; *also* **:** the container for this

aero·sol·ize \-ˌīz\ *vt* **-ized; -iz·ing :** to disperse as an aerosol — **aero·sol·iza·tion** \ˌar-ə-ˌsäl-ə-ˈzā-shən, -ˌsȯl-\ *n*

[1]aero·space \ˈar-ō-ˌspās, ˈer-\ *n* **1 :** space comprising the earth's atmosphere and the space beyond **2 :** a physical science that deals with aerospace **3 :** the aerospace industry

[2]aerospace *adj* **:** of or relating to aerospace, to vehicles used in aerospace or the manufacture of such vehicles, or to travel in aerospace ⟨~ research⟩ ⟨~ profits⟩ ⟨~ medicine⟩

aero·sphere \ˈar-ō-ˌsfi(ə)r, ˈer-\ *n* [F *aérosphère,* fr. *aér-* aer- + *sphère* sphere, fr. L *sphaera*] **:** the body of air around the earth

aero·stat \-ˌstat\ *n* [F *aérostat,* fr. *aér-* + *-stat*] **:** an aircraft that embodies one or more containers filled with a gas lighter than air and that is supported chiefly by buoyancy derived from the surrounding air

aero·stat·ics \ˌar-ō-ˈstat-iks, ˌer-\ *n pl but sing or pl in constr* [modif. of NL *aerostatica,* fr. *aer-* + *statica* statics] **:** a branch of statics that deals with the equilibrium of gaseous fluids and of solid bodies immersed in them

aero·ther·mo·dy·nam·ics \-ˌthər-mə-(ˌ)dī-ˈnam-iks\ *n pl but sing or pl in constr* **:** the thermodynamics of gases and esp. of air

[1]aery \ˈa(ə)r-ē, ˈe(ə)r-ē, ˈā-ə-rē\ *adj* **aer·i·er; -est** [L *aerius* — more at AERIAL] **:** having an aerial quality **:** ETHEREAL ⟨~ visions⟩ — **aer·i·ly** \ˈar-ə-lē, ˈer-\ *adv*

[2]aery *like* AERIE\ *var of* AERIE

Aes·cu·la·pi·an \ˌes-kyə-ˈlā-pē-ən\ *adj* [*Aesculapius,* Greco-Roman god of medicine, fr. L, fr. Gk *Asklēpios*] **:** of or relating to Aesculapius or the healing art **:** MEDICAL

Ae·sir \ˈā-ˌsi(ə)r\ *n pl* [ON *Æsir,* pl. of *āss* god] **:** the principal race of Norse gods

Ae·so·pi·an \ē-ˈsō-pē-ən\ *also* **Ae·sop·ic** \-ˈsäp-ik\ *adj* **1 :** of, relating to, or characteristic of Aesop or his fables **2 :** conveying an innocent meaning to an outsider but a concealed meaning to an informed member of a conspiracy or underground movement ⟨~ language⟩

aesthesio- — see ESTHESIO-

aes·thete \ˈes-ˌthēt\ *n* [back-formation fr. *aesthetic*] **:** one having or affecting sensitivity to the beautiful esp. in art

aes·thet·ic \es-ˈthet-ik, is-\ *adj* [G *ästhetisch,* fr. NL *aestheticus,* fr. Gk *aisthētikos* of sense perception, fr. *aisthanesthai* to perceive — more at AUDIBLE] **1 a :** of, relating to, or dealing with aesthetics or the beautiful ⟨~ theories⟩ **b :** ARTISTIC ⟨a work of ~ value⟩ **2 :** appreciative of, responsive to, or zealous about the beautiful — **aes·thet·i·cal** \-i-kəl\ *adj* — **aes·thet·i·cal·ly** \-i-k(ə-)lē\ *adv*

aesthetic distance *n* **:** the frame of reference that an artist creates by the use of technical devices in and around the work of art to differentiate it psychologically from reality

aes·the·ti·cian \ˌes-thə-ˈtish-ən\ *n* **:** a specialist in aesthetics

aes·thet·i·cism \es-ˈthet-ə-ˌsiz-əm, is-\ *n* **1 a :** a doctrine that the principles of beauty are basic to other and esp. moral principles **b :** the advocacy of artistic and aesthetic autonomy **2 :** devotion to or emphasis on beauty or the cultivation of the arts

aes·thet·ics \-ˈthet-iks\ *n pl but sing or pl in constr, also* **aes·thet·ic** \-ik\ **1 :** a branch of philosophy dealing with the nature of the beautiful and with judgments concerning beauty **2 :** the description and explanation of artistic phenomena and aesthetic experience by means of other sciences (as psychology, sociology, ethnology, or history) **3 :** a particular philosophical theory or conception of art or beauty

aes·ti·val \ˈes-tə-vəl\ *adj* [ME *estival,* fr. MF or L; MF, fr. L *aestivalis,* fr. *aestivus* of summer, fr. *aestas* summer — more at EDIFY] **:** of or relating to the summer

aes·ti·vate \-ˌvāt\ *vi* **-vat·ed; -vat·ing 1 :** to spend the summer usu. at one place **2 :** to pass the summer in a state of torpor — compare HIBERNATE

aes·ti·va·tion \ˌes-tə-ˈvā-shən\ *n* **1 :** the state of one that aestivates **2 :** the disposition or method of arrangement of floral parts in a bud

aet *or* **aetat** *abbr* [L *aetatis*] of age; aged

ae·ti·ol·o·gy *var of* ETIOLOGY

af *abbr* affix

AF *abbr* **1** air force **2** audio frequency

af- — see AD-

AFAM *abbr* Ancient Free and Accepted Masons

[1]afar \ə-ˈfär\ *adv* [ME *afer,* fr. *on fer* at a distance and *of fer* from a distance] **:** from, to, or at a great distance ⟨roamed ~⟩

[2]afar *n* **:** a great distance ⟨saw him from ~⟩

AFB *abbr* air force base

AFC *abbr* **1** American Football Conference **2** automatic frequency control

A1C *abbr* airman first class

AFDC *abbr* Aid to Families with Dependent Children

afeard *or* **afeared** \ə-ˈfi(ə)rd\ *adj* [ME *afered,* fr. OE *āfǣred,* pp. of *āfǣran* to frighten, fr. *ā-,* perfective prefix + *fǣran* to frighten — more at ABIDE, FEAR] *dial* **:** AFRAID

aff *abbr* affirmative

af·fa·ble \ˈaf-ə-bəl\ *adj* [MF, fr. L *affabilis,* fr. *affari* to speak to, fr. *ad-* + *fari* to speak — more at BAN] **1 :** being pleasant and at ease in talking to others **2 :** characterized by ease and friendliness ***syn*** see GRACIOUS ***ant*** reserved — **af·fa·bil·i·ty** \ˌaf-ə-ˈbil-ət-ē\ *n* — **af·fa·bly** \-blē\ *adv*

af·fair \ə-ˈfa(ə)r, -ˈfe(ə)r\ *n* [ME & MF; ME *affaire,* fr. MF, fr. *a faire* to do] **1 a** *pl* **:** commercial, professional, or public business **b :** MATTER, CONCERN **2 :** a procedure, action, or occasion only vaguely specified; *also* **:** an object or collection of objects only vaguely specified ⟨his house was a 2-story ~⟩ **3** *also* **af·faire a :** a romantic or passionate attachment typically of limited duration **:** LIAISON 1b **b :** a matter occasioning public anxiety, controversy, or scandal **:** CASE

[1]af·fect \ˈaf-ˌekt\ *n* [L *affectus,* fr. *affectus,* pp.] **1** *obs* **:** FEELING, AFFECTION **2 :** the conscious subjective aspect of an emotion considered apart from bodily changes

[2]af·fect \ə-ˈfekt, a-\ *vb* [MF & L; MF *affecter,* fr. L *affectare,* fr. *affectus,* pp. of *afficere* to influence, fr. *ad-* + *facere* to do — more at DO] *vt* **1** *archaic* **:** to aim at **2 a** *archaic* **:** to have affection for **b :** to be given to **:** FANCY ⟨~ flashy clothes⟩ **3 :** to make a display of liking or using **:** CULTIVATE ⟨~ a worldly manner⟩ **4 :** to put on a pretense of **:** FEIGN ⟨~ indifference, though deeply hurt⟩ **5 :** to tend toward ⟨drops of water ~ roundness⟩ **6 :** FREQUENT ~ *vi, obs* **:** INCLINE 2 ***syn*** see ASSUME

[3]affect *vt* **:** to produce an effect upon: as **a :** to produce a material influence upon or alteration in ⟨paralysis ~*ed* his limbs⟩ **b :** to act upon (as a person or his mind or his feelings) so as to effect a response **:** INFLUENCE — **af·fect·abil·i·ty** \-ˌfek-tə-ˈbil-ət-ē\ *n* — **af·fect·able** \-ˈfek-tə-bəl\ *adj*

syn AFFECT, INFLUENCE, TOUCH, IMPRESS, STRIKE, SWAY *shared meaning element* **:** to produce or have an effect upon. AFFECT implies the action of a stimulus that can produce a response or reaction ⟨the sight *affected* her to tears⟩ INFLUENCE implies a force that brings about a change (as in nature or behavior) ⟨our beliefs are *influenced* by our upbringing⟩ ⟨a drug that *influences* growth rates⟩ TOUCH may carry a vivid suggestion of close contact and may connote stirring, arousing, or harming ⟨plants *touched* by frost⟩ ⟨his emotions were *touched* by her distress⟩ IMPRESS stresses the depth and persistence of the effect ⟨only one of the plans *impressed* him⟩ STRIKE, similar to but weaker than *impress,* may convey the notion of sudden sharp perception or appreciation ⟨*struck* by the solemnity of the occasion⟩ SWAY implies the acting of influences that are not resisted or are irresistible, with resulting change in character or course of action ⟨he is *swayed* by fashion, by suggestion, by transient moods —H. L. Mencken⟩

af·fec·ta·tion \ˌaf-ˌek-ˈtā-shən\ *n* **1** *obs* **:** a striving after **2 a :** the act of taking on or displaying an attitude or mode of behavior not natural to oneself or not genuinely felt **b :** speech or conduct not natural to oneself **:** ARTIFICIALITY ***syn*** see POSE

af·fect·ed \ə-ˈfek-təd, a-\ *adj* **1 :** INCLINED, DISPOSED ⟨was well ~ toward her⟩ **2 a :** given to affection **b :** assumed artificially or falsely **:** PRETENDED ⟨an ~ interest in art⟩ — **af·fect·ed·ly** *adv* — **af·fect·ed·ness** *n*

af·fect·ing \ə-ˈfek-tiŋ, a-\ *adj* **:** evoking a strong emotional response ***syn*** see MOVING — **af·fect·ing·ly** \-tiŋ-lē\ *adv*

[1]af·fec·tion \ə-ˈfek-shən\ *n* [ME, fr. MF *affection,* fr. L *affection-, affectio,* fr. *affectus,* pp.] **1 :** a moderate feeling or emotion **2 :** tender attachment **:** FONDNESS ⟨she had a deep ~ for her parents⟩ **3** *obs* **:** PARTIALITY, PREJUDICE **4 :** the feeling aspect (as in pleasure or displeasure) of consciousness **5 a :** PROPENSITY, DISPOSITION **b** *archaic* **:** AFFECTATION 2 ***syn*** see FEELING — **af·fec·tion·less** \-ləs\ *adj*

[2]affection *n* **1 :** the action of affecting **:** the state of being affected **2 a (1) :** a bodily condition **(2) :** DISEASE, MALADY **b :** ATTRIBUTE ⟨shape and weight are ~*s* of bodies⟩

af·fec·tion·al \ə-ˈfek-shnəl, -shən-ᵊl\ *adj* **:** of or relating to the affections — **af·fec·tion·al·ly** \-ē\ *adv*

af·fec·tion·ate \ə-ˈfek-sh(ə-)nət\ *adj* **1** *obs* **:** mentally or emotionally affected or inclined **2 :** having affection or warm regard **:** LOVING **3 :** proceeding from affection **:** TENDER ⟨~ care⟩ — **af·fec·tion·ate·ly** *adv*

af·fec·tioned \-shənd\ *adj, archaic* **:** having a tendency, disposition, or inclination **:** DISPOSED

af·fec·tive \a-ˈfek-tiv\ *adj* **1 :** relating to, arising from, or influencing feelings or emotions **:** EMOTIONAL ⟨~ disorders⟩ **2 :** expressing emotion ⟨~ language⟩ — **af·fec·tive·ly** *adv* — **af·fec·tiv·i·ty** \ˌaf-ˌek-ˈtiv-ət-ē\ *n*

af·fect·less \ˈaf-ˌek-tləs, a-ˈfek-\ *adj* **:** UNFEELING ⟨a ruthless ~ society⟩ — **af·fect·less·ness** *n*

af·fen·pin·scher \ˈaf-ən-ˌpin-chər\ *n* [G, fr. *affe* monkey + *pinscher,* a breed of hunting dog] **:** any of a breed of small dogs with a stiff red, gray, or black coat, pointed ears, and bushy eyebrows, chin tuft, and mustache

af·fer·ent \ˈaf-ə-rənt, -ˌer-ənt\ *adj* [L *afferent-, afferens,* prp. of *afferre* to bring to, fr. *ad-* + *ferre* to bear — more at BEAR] **:** bearing or conducting inward; *specif* **:** conveying impulses toward a nerve center — compare EFFERENT — **af·fer·ent·ly** *adv*

[1]af·fi·ance \ə-ˈfī-ən(t)s\ *n* [ME, fr. MF, fr. *affier* to pledge, trust, fr. ML *affidare* to pledge, fr. L *ad-* + (assumed) VL *fidare* to trust — more at FIANCÉ] *archaic* **:** TRUST, CONFIDENCE

[2]affiance *vt* **-anced; -anc·ing :** to solemnly promise (oneself or another) in marriage **:** BETROTH

ə abut	ᵊ kitten	ər further	a back	ā bake	ä cot, cart
au̇ out	ch chin	e less	ē easy	g gift	i trip
ī life	j joke	ŋ sing	ō flow	ȯ flaw	ȯi coin
th thin	t͟h this	ü loot	u̇ foot	y yet	yü few
yu̇ furious	zh vision				

af·fi·ant \ə-ˈfī-ənt\ *n* [MF, fr. prp. of *affier*] : one that swears to an affidavit; *broadly* : DEPONENT
af·fi·cio·na·do *var of* AFICIONADO
af·fi·da·vit \ˌaf-ə-ˈdā-vət\ *n* [ML, he has made an oath, fr. *affidare*] : a sworn statement in writing made esp. under oath or on affirmation before an authorized magistrate or officer
1af·fil·i·ate \ə-ˈfil-ē-ˌāt\ *vb* **-at·ed; -at·ing** [ML *affiliatus,* pp. of *affiliare* to adopt as a son, fr. L *ad-* + *filius* son — more at FEMININE] *vt* **1 a** : to bring or receive into close connection as a member or branch **b** : to associate as a member ⟨~*s* himself with the local club⟩ **2** : to trace the origin of ~ *vi* : to connect or associate oneself : COMBINE — **af·fil·i·a·tion** \-ˌfil-ē-ˈā-shən\ *n*
2af·fil·i·ate \ə-ˈfil-ē-ət\ *n* : an affiliated person or organization; *specif* : a company effectively controlled by another or associated with others under common ownership or control
af·fil·i·at·ed \-ē-ˌāt-əd\ *adj* : closely associated with another typically in a dependent or subordinate position ⟨the university and its ~ medical school⟩ ***syn*** see RELATED
1af·fine \a-ˈfīn, ə-\ *n* [MF *affin,* fr. L *affinis,* fr. *affinis* related] : a relative by marriage
2affine *adj* [L *affinis,* adj.] : of, relating to, or being a transformation (as a translation, a rotation, or a uniform stretching) that carries straight lines into straight lines and parallel lines into parallel lines but may alter distance between points and angles between lines ⟨~ geometry⟩ — **af·fine·ly** *adv*
af·fined \a-ˈfīnd, ə-\ *adj* **1** : joined in a close relationship : CONNECTED **2** : bound by obligation
af·fin·i·ty \ə-ˈfin-ət-ē\ *n, pl* **-ties** [ME *affinite,* fr. MF or L; MF *afinité,* fr. L *affinitas,* fr. *affinis* bordering on, related by marriage, fr. *ad-* + *finis* end, border] **1** : relationship by marriage **2 a** : sympathy marked by community of interest : KINSHIP **b** : ATTRACTION; *esp* : an attractive force between substances or particles that causes them to enter into and remain in chemical combination **c** : a person esp. of the opposite sex having a particular attraction for one **3 a** : likeness based on relationship or causal connection **b** : a relation between biological groups involving resemblance in structural plan and indicating community of origin ***syn*** see ATTRACTION, LIKENESS
af·firm \ə-ˈfərm\ *vb* [ME *affermen,* fr. MF *afermer,* fr. L *affirmare,* fr. *ad-* + *firmare* to make firm, fr. *firmus* firm — more at FIRM] *vt* **1 a** : VALIDATE, CONFIRM **b** : to state positively **2** : to assert (as a judgment or decree) as valid or confirmed **3** : to express dedication to ⟨~ life by refusing to kill⟩ ~ *vi* **1** : to testify or declare by affirmation **2** : to uphold a judgment or decree of a lower court ***syn*** see ASSERT ***ant*** deny — **af·firm·able** \ə-ˈfər-mə-bəl\ *adj* — **af·fir·mance** \ə-ˈfər-mən(t)s\ *n*
af·fir·ma·tion \ˌaf-ər-ˈmā-shən\ *n* **1 a** : the act of affirming **b** : something affirmed : a positive assertion **2** : a solemn declaration made under the penalties of perjury by a person who conscientiously declines taking an oath
1af·fir·ma·tive \ə-ˈfər-mət-iv\ *adj* **1** : asserting a predicate of a subject **2** : asserting that the fact is so **3** : POSITIVE ⟨~ approach⟩ **4** : favoring or supporting a proposition or motion — **af·fir·ma·tive·ly** *adv*
2affirmative *n* **1** : an expression (as the word *yes*) of affirmation or assent **2** : an affirmative proposition **3** : the side that upholds the proposition stated in a debate
1af·fix \ə-ˈfiks, a-\ *vt* [ML *affixare,* fr. L *affixus,* pp. of *affigere* to fasten to, fr. *ad-* + *figere* to fasten — more at DIKE] **1** : to attach physically ⟨~ a stamp to a letter⟩ **2** : to attach in any way : ADD, APPEND ⟨~ a signature to a document⟩ **3** : IMPRESS ⟨~*ed* his seal⟩ ***syn*** see FASTEN ***ant*** detach — **af·fix·able** \-ˈfik-sə-bəl\ *adj* — **af·fix·a·tion** \ˌaf-ˌik-ˈsā-shən\ *n* — **af·fix·ment** \ə-ˈfik-smənt, a-\ *n*
2af·fix \ˈaf-ˌiks\ *n* **1** : a sound or sequence of sounds or a letter or sequence of letters occurring as a bound form attached to the beginning or end of a word, base, or phrase or inserted within a word or base and serving to produce a derivative word or an inflectional form **2** : APPENDAGE — **af·fix·al** \-ˌik-səl\ *or* **af·fix·i·al** \a-ˈfik-sē-əl\ *adj*
af·fla·tus \ə-ˈflāt-əs, a-\ *n* [L, act of blowing or breathing on, fr. *afflatus,* pp. of *afflare* to blow on, fr. *ad-* + *flare* to blow — more at BLOW] : a divine imparting of knowledge or power : INSPIRATION
af·flict \ə-ˈflikt\ *vt* [ME *afflicten,* fr. L *afflictus,* pp. of *affligere* to cast down, fr. *ad-* + *fligere* to strike — more at PROFLIGATE] **1** *obs* **a** : HUMBLE **b** : OVERTHROW **2 a** : to distress so severely as to cause persistent suffering or anguish **b** : TROUBLE, INJURE
syn AFFLICT, TRY, TORMENT, TORTURE, RACK *shared meaning element* : to inflict on one something (as suffering, disease, or embarrassment) that he finds hard to bear ***ant*** comfort
af·flic·tion \ə-ˈflik-shən\ *n* **1** : the state of being afflicted **2 a** : the cause of persistent pain or distress **b** : great suffering
af·flic·tive \ə-ˈflik-tiv\ adj : causing affliction : DISTRESSING, TROUBLESOME — **af·flic·tive·ly** *adv*
af·flu·ence \ˈaf-ˌlü-ən(t)s *also* a-ˈflü- *or* ə-\ *n* **1 a** : an abundant flow or supply : PROFUSION **b** : abundance of property : WEALTH **2** : a flowing to or toward a point : INFLUX
af·flu·en·cy \-ən-sē\ *n, pl* **-cies** : AFFLUENCE
1af·flu·ent \-ənt\ *adj* [ME, fr. MF, fr. L *affluent-, affluens,* prp. of *affluere* to flow to, flow abundantly, fr. *ad-* + *fluere* to flow — more at FLUID] **1 a** : flowing in abundance : COPIOUS **b** : having a generously sufficient and typically increasing supply of material possessions ⟨our ~ society⟩ **2** : flowing toward ***syn*** see RICH ***ant*** impecunious, straitened — **af·flu·ent·ly** *adv*
2affluent *n* **1** : a tributary stream **2** : an affluent person
af·flux \ˈaf-ˌləks\ *n* [F or L; F, fr. L *affluxus,* pp. of *affluere*] : AFFLUENCE 2
af·ford \ə-ˈfō(ə)rd, -ˈfȯ(ə)rd\ *vt* [ME *aforthen,* fr. OE *geforthian* to carry out, fr. *ge-,* perfective prefix + *forthian* to carry out, fr. *forth* — more at CO-, FORTH] **1 a** : to manage to bear without serious detriment ⟨you can't ~ to neglect your health⟩ **b** : to be able to bear the cost of ⟨he can't ~ to be out of work long⟩ ⟨~ a new coat⟩ **2 a** : to have the capacity for providing esp. to one who seeks ⟨her letters ~ no clue to her intentions⟩ **b** : to make available or give forth as a consequence of nature : provide naturally or inevitably ⟨the sun ~*s* warmth to the earth⟩ ⟨the roof ~*ed* a fine view⟩ ***syn*** see GIVE — **af·ford·able** \-ˈfōrd-ə-bəl, -ˈfȯrd-\ *adj*
af·for·est \a-ˈfȯr-əst, -ˈfär-\ *vt* [ML *afforestare,* fr. L *ad-* + ML *forestis* forest — more at FOREST] : to establish forest cover on — **af·for·es·ta·tion** \(ˌ)a-ˌfȯr-ə-ˈstā-shən, -ˌfär-\ *n*
1af·fray \ə-ˈfrā\ *n* [ME, fr. MF, fr. *affreer* to startle] : FRAY, BRAWL
2affray *vt* [ME *affraien,* fr. MF *affreer*] *archaic* : STARTLE, FRIGHTEN
af·fri·cate \ˈaf-ri-kət\ *n* [prob. fr. G *affrikata,* fr. L *affricata,* fem. of *affricatus,* pp. of *affricare* to rub against, fr. *ad-* + *fricare* to rub — more at FRICTION] : a stop and its immediately following release through the articulatory position for a continuant nonsyllabic consonant (as the \t\ and \sh\ that are the constituents of the \ch\ in *why choose*) — **af·fric·a·tive** \a-ˈfrik-ət-iv, ə-\ *n or adj*
af·fri·ca·tion \ˌaf-rə-ˈkā-shən\ *n* : conversion (as of a simple stop sound) into an affricate
1af·fright \ə-ˈfrīt\ *vt* [fr. ME *afyrht, afright* frightened, fr. OE *āfyrht, pp. of āfyrhtan* to frighten, fr. *ā-,* perfective prefix + *fyrhtan* to fear; akin to OE *fyrhto* fright — more at ABIDE, FRIGHT] : FRIGHTEN, ALARM
2affright *n* : sudden and great fear : TERROR
1af·front \ə-ˈfrənt\ *vt* [ME *afronten,* fr. MF *afronter* to defy, fr. (assumed) VL *affrontare,* fr. L *ad-* + *front-, frons* forehead — more at FRONT] **1** : to insult esp. to the face by behavior or language **2 a** : to face in defiance : CONFRONT ⟨~ death⟩ **b** *obs* : to encounter face to face **3** : to appear directly before ***syn*** see OFFEND
2affront *n* **1** : a deliberate offense : INSULT ⟨an ~ to his dignity⟩ **2** *obs* : a hostile encounter
afft *abbr* affidavit
af·fu·sion \a-ˈfyü-zhən\ *n* [LL *affusion-, affusio,* fr. L *affusus,* pp. of *affundere* to pour on, fr. *ad-* + *fundere* to pour — more at FOUND] : an act of pouring a liquid on (as in baptism)
Af·ghan \ˈaf-ˌgan *also* -gən\ *n* [Pashto *afghānī*] **1** : a native or inhabitant of Afghanistan **2** : PASHTO **3** *not cap* : a blanket or shawl of colored wool knitted or crocheted in strips or squares **4** *not cap* : a Turkoman carpet of large size and long pile woven in geometric designs **5** : AFGHAN HOUND — **Afghan** *adj*
Afghan hound *n* : a tall slim swift hunting dog native to the Near East with a coat of silky thick hair and a long silky topknot
af·ghani \af-ˈgan-ē, -ˈgän-\ *n* [Pashto *afghānī,* lit., Afghan] — see MONEY table
afi·cio·na·da \ə-ˌfish(-ē)-ə-ˈnäd-ə, -ˌfis-ē-, -ˌfē-sē-, -ˈnäd-(ˌ)ä\ *n* [Sp, fem. of *aficionado*] : a female aficionado ⟨card-playing ~*s*⟩
afi·cio·na·do \-ˈnäd-(ˌ)ō\ *n, pl* **-dos** [Sp, fr. pp. of *aficionar* to inspire affection, fr. *afición* affection, fr. L *affection-, affectio* — more at AFFECTION] : DEVOTEE, FAN ⟨~*s* of the bullfight⟩ ⟨movie ~*s*⟩
afield \ə-ˈfē(ə)ld\ *adv or adj* **1** : to, in, or on the field ⟨was weak at bat but strong ~⟩ **2** : away from home : ABROAD **3** : out of the way : ASTRAY ⟨irrelevant remarks that carried us far ~⟩
AFIPS *abbr* American Federation of Information Processing Societies
afire \ə-ˈfī(ə)r\ *adj or adv* : being on fire : BLAZING ⟨set the house ~⟩
AFL *abbr* American Football League
aflame \ə-ˈflām\ *adj or adv* : AFIRE
af·la·tox·in \ˌaf-lə-ˈtäk-sən\ *n* [NL *Aspergillus flavus,* species of mold + E *toxin*] : any of several mycotoxins that are produced esp. in corn or oilseed meals by molds (as *Aspergillus flavus*) and are suspected of being carcinogenic
AFL–CIO *abbr* American Federation of Labor and Congress of Industrial Organizations
afloat \ə-ˈflōt\ *adj or adv* [ME *aflot,* fr. OE *on flot,* fr. *on* + *flot,* fr. *flot* deep water, sea; akin to OE *flēotan* to float — more at FLEET] **1 a** : borne on or as if on the water : FLOATING **b** : at sea **2** : free of difficulties : SELF-SUFFICIENT ⟨the inheritance kept them ~ for years⟩ **3 a** : circulating about : RUMORED ⟨nasty stories were ~⟩ **b** : ADRIFT
aflut·ter \ə-ˈflət-ər\ *adj* **1** : being in a flutter : FLUTTERING **2** : nervously excited **3** : filled with or marked by the presence of fluttering things ⟨roofs ~ with flags⟩
afoot \ə-ˈfu̇t\ *adv or adj* **1** : on foot **2** : in the process of development : under way ⟨something out of the ordinary was ~ — Hamilton Basso⟩
afore \ə-ˈfō(ə)r, -ˈfȯ(ə)r\ *adv or conj or prep* [ME, fr. OE *onforan,* fr. *on* + *foran* before — more at BEFORE] *chiefly dial* : BEFORE
afore·men·tioned \-ˈmen-chənd\ *adj* : mentioned previously
afore·said \-ˌsed\ *adj* : said or named before or above
afore·thought \-ˌthȯt\ *adj* : previously in mind : PREMEDITATED, DELIBERATE ⟨with malice ~⟩
a for·ti·o·ri \ˌä-ˌfȯrt-ē-ˈō-rē; ˌā-ˌfȯrt-ē-ˈō(ə)r-ˌī, -ˈō(ə)r-ē; -ē-ˈȯ(ə)r-\ *adv* [NL, lit., from the stronger (argument)] : with greater reason or more convincing force — used in drawing a conclusion that is inferred to be even more certain than another ⟨the man of prejudice is, *a fortiori,* a man of limited mental vision⟩
afoul of \ə-ˈfau̇l-əv\ *prep* **1** : in or into collision or entanglement with **2** : in or into conflict with
Afr *abbr* Africa; African
Afr- *or* **Afro-** *comb form* [L, *Afr-, Afer*] : African ⟨*Afr*american⟩ : African and ⟨*Afro*-Asiatic⟩
afraid \ə-ˈfrād, *South also* ə-ˈfre(ə)d\ *adj* [ME *affraied,* fr. pp. of *affraien* to frighten — more at AFFRAY] **1** : filled with fear or apprehension ⟨~ of machines⟩ ⟨~ for his job⟩ **2** : filled with concern or regret over an unwanted situation ⟨I'm ~ I won't be able to go⟩ **3** : having a dislike for something : DISINCLINED, RELUCTANT ⟨~ of hard work⟩ ***syn*** see FEARFUL ***ant*** unafraid, sanguine
A–frame \ˈā-ˌfrām\ *n* : a building typically having triangular front and rear walls and a roof reaching to the ground
afreet *or* **afrit** \ˈaf-ˌrēt, ə-ˈfrēt\ *n* [Ar *ʽifrīt*] : a powerful evil jinn, demon, or monstrous giant in Arabic mythology
afresh \ə-ˈfresh\ *adv* : from a fresh beginning : ANEW, AGAIN
Af·ri·can \ˈaf-ri-kən\ *n* **1** : a native or inhabitant of Africa **2** : an individual of immediate or remote African ancestry; *esp* : NEGRO — **African** *adj* — **Af·ri·can·ness** \-kən-nəs\ *n*

Af·ri·can·der *or* **Af·ri·kan·der** \,af-ri-'kan-dər\ *n* [Afrik *Afrikaner, Afrikaander*, lit., Afrikaner] : any of a breed of tall red large= horned humped southern African cattle used chiefly for meat or draft

Af·ri·can·ism \'af-ri-kə-,niz-əm\ *n* **1** : a characteristic feature (as a custom or belief) of African culture **2** : a characteristic feature of an African language occurring in a non-African language **3** : allegiance to the traditions, interests, or ideals of Africa

Af·ri·can·ist \-nəst\ *n* : a specialist in African languages or cultures

Af·ri·can·ize \-,nīz\ *vt* **-ized; -iz·ing** **1** : to cause to acquire a distinctively African trait **2** : to bring under the control or the cultural or civil supremacy of Africans and esp. Negroes **3** : to replace (a non-African) with an African — **Af·ri·can·iza·tion** \,af-ri-kə-nə-'zā-shən\ *n*

African mahogany *n* : MAHOGANY 1b

African violet *n* : any of several tropical African plants (esp. *Saintpaulia ionantha*) of the gloxinia family widely grown as houseplants for their velvety fleshy leaves and showy purple, pink, or white flowers

¹Af·ri·kaans \,af-ri-'kän(t)s, -'känz, 'af-ri-,\ *n* [Afrik, fr. *afrikaans*, adj., African, fr. obs. Afrik *afrikanisch*, fr. L *africanus*] : a language developed from 17th century Dutch that is one of the official languages of the Republic of So. Africa

²Afrikaans *adj* : of or relating to Afrikaners or Afrikaans

Af·ri·ka·ner \,af-ri-'kän-ər\ *n* [Afrik, lit., African, fr. L *africanus*] : a So. African native of European descent; *esp* : an Afrikaans= speaking descendant of the 17th century Dutch settlers

¹Af·ro \'af-(,)rō\ *adj* [prob. fr. *Afro-American*] : having the hair shaped into a round bushy mass

²Afro *n, pl* **Afros** : an Afro hairstyle

Af·ro-Amer·i·can \,af-rō-ə-'mer-ə-kən\ *n* : an American of African and esp. of Negroid descent — **Afro–American** *adj*

Af·ro-Asi·at·ic languages \,af-rō-,ā-z(h)ē-,at-ik- *also* -shē-\ *n pl* : a family of languages widely distributed over southwestern Asia and northern Africa comprising the Semitic, Egyptian, Berber, Cushitic, and Chad subfamilies

¹aft \'aft\ *adv* [ME *afte* back, fr. OE *æftan* from behind, behind; akin to OE *æfter*] : near, toward, or in the stern of a ship or the tail of an aircraft : ABAFT ⟨called all hands ∼⟩

²aft *adj* : REARWARD. **⁴AFTER** 2 ⟨the ∼ decks⟩

³aft *Scot var of* OFT

⁴aft *abbr* afternoon

AFT *abbr* American Federation of Teachers

Afro

¹af·ter \'af-tər\ *adv* [ME, fr. OE *æfter* after] : following in time or place : AFTERWARD, BEHIND, LATER ⟨we arrived shortly ∼⟩ ⟨returned 20 years ∼⟩

²after *prep* **1 a** : behind in place **b** (1) : subsequent to in time or order (2) : subsequent to and in view of ⟨∼ all our advice⟩ **2** — used as a function word to indicate the object of a stated or implied action ⟨go ∼ gold⟩ **3** : so as to resemble: as **a** : in accordance with **b** : with the name of or a name derived from that of **c** : in the characteristic manner of **d** : in imitation of

³after *conj* : subsequently to the time when

⁴after *adj* **1** : later in time : SUBSEQUENT ⟨in ∼ years⟩ **2** : located toward the rear and esp. toward the stern of a ship or tail of an aircraft

⁵after *n* : AFTERNOON

after all *adv* : in spite of considerations to the contrary : NEVERTHELESS ⟨decided to take the train *after all*⟩

af·ter·birth \'af-tər-,bərth\ *n* : the placenta and fetal membranes that are expelled after delivery

af·ter·burn·er \-,bər-nər\ *n* **1** : an auxiliary burner attached to the tail pipe of a turbojet engine for injecting fuel into the hot exhaust gases and burning it to provide extra thrust **2** : a device for burning or catalytically destroying unburned or partially burned carbon compounds in exhaust (as from an automobile)

af·ter·care \-,ke(ə)r, -,ka(ə)r\ *n* : the care, treatment, help, or supervision given to persons discharged from an institution (as a hospital or prison)

af·ter·clap \-,klap\ *n* : an unexpected damaging or unsettling event following a supposedly closed affair

af·ter·damp \-,damp\ *n* : a toxic gas mixture remaining after an explosion of firedamp in mines

af·ter·deck \-,dek\ *n* : the part of a deck abaft midships

af·ter·ef·fect \'af-tə-rə-,fekt\ *n* : an effect that follows its cause after an interval

af·ter·glow \'af-tər-,glō\ *n* **1** : a glow remaining where a light has disappeared **2** : a reflection of past splendor, success, or emotion

af·ter–hours \,af-tə-'raú(-ə)rz\ *adj* **1** : engaged in after closing time ⟨∼ drinking⟩ **2** : operating after a legal or conventional closing time ⟨an ∼ nightclub⟩

af·ter·im·age \'af-tə-,rim-ij\ *n* : a usu. visual sensation occurring after stimulation by its external cause has ceased

af·ter·life \'af-tər-,līf\ *n* **1** : an existence after death **2** : a later period in one's life

af·ter·math \-,math\ *n* [⁴*after* + *math* (mowing, crop)] **1** : a second-growth crop — called also *rowen* **2** : CONSEQUENCE, RESULT ⟨stricken with guilt as an ∼ of the accident⟩ **3** : the period immediately following a usu. ruinous event ⟨in the ∼ of the war⟩

af·ter·most \-,mōst\ *adj* : nearest the stern of a ship : farthest aft

af·ter·noon \,af-tər-'nün\ *n* **1** : the part of day between noon and sunset **2** : a relatively late period (as of time or life) ⟨in the ∼ of the 19th century⟩ — **afternoon** *adj*

af·ter·noons \-'nünz\ *adv* : in the afternoon repeatedly : on any afternoon

af·ter·piece \'af-tər-,pēs\ *n* : a short usu. comic entertainment performed after a play

af·ters \'af-tərz\ *n pl, Brit* : DESSERT

af·ter–shave \'af-tər-,shāv\ *n* : a usu. scented lotion for use on the face after shaving

af·ter·taste \-,tāst\ *n* : persistence of a sensation (as of flavor or an emotion) after the stimulating agent or experience has gone

af·ter–tax \'af-tər-,taks\ *adj* : remaining after payment of taxes and esp. of income tax ⟨an ∼ profit⟩

af·ter·thought \-,thöt\ *n* **1** : an idea occurring later **2** : a part, feature, or device not thought of originally

af·ter·time \-,tīm\ *n* : FUTURE

af·ter·ward \'af-tə(r)-wərd\ *or* **af·ter·wards** \-wərdz\ *adv* : at a later or succeeding time : SUBSEQUENTLY, THEREAFTER

af·ter·word \-,wərd\ *n* : EPILOGUE 1

af·ter·world \-,wərld\ *n* : a future world : a world after death

Ag *symbol* [L *argentum*] silver

AG *abbr* **1** adjutant general **2** attorney general

ag- — see AD-

Aga·da \ə-'gäd-ə, -'gód-\ *var of* HAGGADAH

again \ə-'gen, -'gin, -'gān\ *adv* [ME, opposite, again, fr. OE *ongēan* opposite, back, fr. *on* + *gēn, gēan* still, again; akin to OE *gēan*-against, OHG *gegin* against, toward] **1** : in return : BACK ⟨swore he would pay him ∼ when he was able —Shak.⟩ **2** : another time : once more : ANEW ⟨I shall not look upon his like ∼ —Shak.⟩ **3** : on the other hand ⟨he might go, and ∼ he might not⟩ **4** : in addition : BESIDES ⟨∼, there is another matter to consider⟩

again and again *adv* : OFTEN, REPEATEDLY

¹against \ə-'gen(t)st, -'gin(t)st, -gān(t)st\ *prep* [ME, alter. of *againes*, fr. *again*] **1 a** : directly opposite : FACING **b** *obs* : exposed to **2 a** : in opposition or hostility to **b** : unfavorable to **c** : as a defense or protection from **3** : compared or contrasted with **4** : in preparation or provision for **5 a** : in the direction of and into contact with **b** : in contact with **6** : in a direction opposite to the motion or course of : counter to **7 a** : as a counterbalance to **b** : in exchange for **c** : as a charge on **8** : before the background of

²against *conj, archaic* : in preparation for the time when ⟨throw on another log of wood ∼ father comes home —Charles Dickens⟩

Ag·a·mem·non \,ag-ə-'mem-,nän, -nən\ *n* [L, fr. Gk *Agamemnōn*] : a king of Mycenae who was the leader of the Greeks in the Trojan War

aga·mete \,ā-gə-'mēt, (')ā-'gam-,ēt\ *n* [ISV, fr. Gk *agametos* unmarried, fr. *a-* + *gamein* to marry — more at GAMETE] : an asexual reproductive cell

agam·ic \(')ā-'gam-ik\ *adj* [Gk *agamos* unmarried, fr. *a-* + *gamos* marriage — more at BIGAMY] : ASEXUAL, PARTHENOGENETIC — **agam·i·cal·ly** \-i-k(ə-)lē\ *adv*

agam·ma·glob·u·lin·emia \,ā-,gam-ə-,gläb-yə-lə-'nē-mē-ə\ *n* [NL, fr. *a-* + ISV *gamma globulin* + NL *-emia*] : a condition in which the body forms few or no gamma globulins or antibodies — **agam·ma·glob·u·lin·emic** \-'nē-mik\ *adj*

aga·mo·sper·my \(')ā-'gam-ə-,spər-mē, 'ag-ə-mō-,spər-\ *n* [Gk *agamos* + E *-spermy*] : APOGAMY; *specif* : apogamy in which sexual union is not completed and the embryo is produced from the innermost layer of the integument of the female gametophyte

ag·a·pan·thus \,ag-ə-'pan(t)-thəs\ *n* [NL, genus name, fr. Gk *agapē* + *anthos* flower — more at ANTHOLOGY] : any of several African plants (genus *Agapanthus*) of the lily family cultivated for their umbels of showy blue or purple flowers

¹agape \ə-'gäp *also* -'gap\ *adj or adv* **1** : wide open : GAPING **2** : being in a state of wonder

²aga·pe \ä-'gä-(,)pā, 'äg-ə-,pā\ *n* [LL, fr. Gk *agapē*, lit., love] **1** : LOVE 4a **2** : LOVE FEAST — **aga·pe·ic** \,äg-ə-'pā-ik\ *adj* — **aga·pe·i·cal·ly** \-'pā-ə-k(ə-)lē\ *adv*

agar \'äg-,är\ *n* [Malay *agar-agar*] **1** : a gelatinous colloidal extractive of a red alga (as of the genera *Gelidium, Gracilaria*, and *Eucheuma*) used esp. in culture media or as a gelling and stabilizing agent in foods **2** : a culture medium containing agar

agar–agar \,äg-,är-'äg-,är\ *n* [Malay] : AGAR

aga·ric \'ag-ə-rik, ə-'gar-ik\ *n* [L *agaricum*, a fungus, fr. Gk *agarikon*] **1 a** : any of several pore fungi (genus *Fomes*) used esp. in the preparation of punk **b** : the dried fruiting body of a fungus (*F. officinalis*) formerly used in medicine **2** : any of a family (Agaricaceae) of fungi with the sporophore usu. resembling an umbrella and with numerous lamellae on the underside of the cap

ag·ate \'ag-ət\ *n, often attrib* [MF, fr. L *achates*, fr. Gk *achatēs*] **1** : a fine-grained variegated chalcedony having its colors arranged in stripes, blended in clouds, or showing mosslike forms **2** : something made of or fitted with agate: as **a** : a drawplate used by gold-wire drawers **b** : a bookbinder's burnisher **c** : a playing marble of agate **3** : a size of type approximately 5½ point

agate line *n* : a space one column wide and ¹/₁₄ inch deep used as a unit of measurement in classified advertising

ag·ate·ware \'ag-ət-,wa(ə)r, -,we(ə)r\ *n* **1** : pottery veined and mottled to resemble agate **2** : an enameled iron or steel ware for household utensils

aga·ve \ə-'gäv-ē\ *n* [NL *Agave*, genus name, fr. L, a daughter of Cadmus, fr. Gk *Agauē*] : any of a genus (*Agave*) of plants of the amaryllis family having spiny-margined leaves and flowers in tall spreading panicles and including some cultivated for their fiber or for ornament

agaze \ə-'gāz\ *adj* : engaged in the act of gazing

AGC *abbr* advanced graduate certificate

agcy *abbr* agency

ə abut	³ kitten	ər further	a back	ā bake	ä cot, cart
aú out	ch chin	e less	ē easy	g gift	i trip ī life
j joke	ŋ sing	ō flow	ò flaw	òi coin	th thin th̲ this
ü loot	ú foot	y yet	yü few	yú furious	zh vision

[1]**age** \ˈāj\ *n* [ME, fr. OF *aage,* fr. (assumed) VL *aetaticum,* fr. L *aetat-, aetas,* fr. *aevum* lifetime — more at AYE] **1 a :** the part of an existence extending from the beginning to any given time ⟨a boy 10 years of ~⟩ **b :** LIFETIME **c :** the time of life at which some particular qualification, power, or capacity arises or rests ⟨the voting ~ is 18⟩; *specif* **:** MAJORITY **d :** one of the stages of life **e :** an advanced stage of life **2 a :** the period contemporary with a person's lifetime or with his active life **b :** GENERATION **c :** a long time — usu. used in pl. ⟨haven't seen him in ~*s*⟩ **3 :** a period of time dominated by a central figure or prominent feature ⟨the ~ of Pericles⟩: as **a :** a period in history or human progress ⟨the ~ of reptiles⟩ ⟨the ~ of exploration⟩ **b :** a cultural period marked by the prominence of a particular item ⟨entering the atomic ~⟩ **c :** a division of geologic time that is usu. shorter than an epoch **4 :** an individual's development measured in terms of the years requisite for like development of an average individual ***syn*** see PERIOD

agave

[2]**age** *vb* **aged; ag·ing** *or* **age·ing** *vi* **1 :** to become old : show the effects or the characteristics of increasing age **2 a :** to acquire a desirable quality by standing undisturbed for some time ⟨after flour is milled it ~*s* —S. C. Prescott & B. E. Proctor⟩ **b :** to become mellow or mature : RIPEN ⟨this cheese has *aged* for nearly two years⟩ ~ *vt* **1 :** to cause to become old **2 :** to bring to a state fit for use or to maturity

-age \ij\ *n suffix* [ME, fr. OF, fr. L *-aticum*] **1 :** aggregate : collection ⟨track*age*⟩ **2 a :** action : process ⟨haul*age*⟩ **b :** cumulative result of ⟨break*age*⟩ **c :** rate of ⟨dos*age*⟩ **3 :** house or place of ⟨orphan*age*⟩ **4 :** state : rank ⟨peon*age*⟩ **5 :** fee : charge ⟨post*age*⟩

aged \ˈā-jəd, ˈājd; ˈājd *for 1b*\ *adj* **1 :** grown old: as **a :** of an advanced age **b :** having attained a specified age ⟨a man ~ 40 years⟩ **c :** well advanced toward reduction to base level — used of topographic features **2 :** typical of old age — **aged·ness** \ˈā-jəd-nəs\ *n*

age–group \ˈāj-ˌgrüp\ *n* **:** a segment of a population that is of approximately the same age or is within a specified range of ages

age·ism \ˈā-(ˌ)jiz-əm\ *n* **:** prejudice or discrimination against a particular age-group and esp. against the elderly — **age·ist** \-jist\ *adj*

age·less \ˈāj-ləs\ *adj* **1 :** not growing old or showing the effects of age **2 :** TIMELESS, ETERNAL ⟨~ truths⟩ — **age·less·ly** *adv* — **age·less·ness** *n*

age·long \ˈāj-ˌlȯŋ\ *adj* **:** lasting for an age : EVERLASTING

age–mate \-ˌmāt\ *n* **:** one who is of approximately the same age as another

agen·cy \ˈā-jən-sē\ *n, pl* **-cies 1 :** the capacity, condition, or state of acting or of exerting power : OPERATION **2 :** a person or thing through which power is exerted or an end is achieved : INSTRUMENTALITY ⟨communicated through the ~ of his ambassador⟩ **3 a :** the office or function of an agent **b :** the relationship between a principal and his agent **4 :** an establishment engaged in doing business for another ⟨an advertising ~⟩ **5 :** an administrative division (as of a government) ⟨the ~ for consumer protection⟩

agency shop *n* **:** a shop in which the union serves as the agent for and receives dues and assessments from all employees in the bargaining unit regardless of union membership

agen·da \ə-ˈjen-də\ *n* [L, neut. pl. of *agendum,* gerundive of *agere*] **:** a list, outline, or plan of things to be considered or done ⟨~*s* of faculty meetings⟩ — **agen·da·less** \-də-ləs\ *adj*

agen·dum \-dəm\ *n, pl* **-da** \-də\ *or* **-dums** [L] **1 :** AGENDA **2 :** an item on an agenda

agene \ˈā-ˌjēn\ *n* [fr. *Agene,* a trademark] **:** the trichloride of nitrogen

agen·e·sis \(ˈ)ā-ˈjen-ə-səs\ *n* [NL] **:** lack or failure of development (as of a body part)

age·nize \ˈā-jə-ˌnīz\ *vt* **-nized; -niz·ing :** to treat (flour) with nitrogen trichloride

agent \ˈā-jənt\ *n* [ME, fr. ML *agent-, agens,* fr. L, prp. of *agere* to drive, lead, act, do; akin to ON *aka* to travel in a vehicle, Gk *agein* to drive, lead] **1 a :** something that produces or is capable of producing an effect : an active or efficient cause **b :** a chemically, physically, or biologically active principle **2 :** one that acts or exerts power **3 :** a person responsible for his acts **4 :** a means or instrument by which a guiding intelligence achieves a result **5 :** one who acts for or in the place of another by authority from him: as **a :** a representative, emissary, or official of a government ⟨crown ~⟩ ⟨secret-service ~⟩ **b :** one engaged in undercover activities (as espionage) : SPY ⟨secret ~⟩ ***syn*** see MEAN

agent–general *n, pl* **agents–general :** a chief agent; *specif* **:** the representative in England of a British dominion

agent pro·vo·ca·teur \ˈäzh-ˌäⁿ-prō-ˌväk-ə-ˈtər, ˈā-jənt-\ *n, pl* **agents provocateurs** \ˈäzh-ˌäⁿ-prō-ˌväk-ə-ˈtər, ˈā-jən(t)s-prō-\ [F, lit., provoking agent] **:** one employed to associate himself with members of a group or with suspected persons and by pretended sympathy with their aims or attitudes to incite them to some action that will make them liable to apprehension and punishment

agent·ry \ˈā-jən-trē\ *n, pl* **-ries :** the office, duties, or activities of an agent

age of consent : the age at which one is legally competent to give consent (as to marriage)

age of reason 1 : a period characterized by a prevailing belief in the use of reason; *esp* **:** the 18th century in England and France **2 :** the time of life when one begins to be able to distinguish right from wrong

age–old \ˈā-ˈjōld\ *adj* **:** having existed for ages : ANCIENT

ag·er·a·tum \ˌaj-ə-ˈrāt-əm\ *n, pl* **-tums** [NL, genus name, fr. Gk *agēratos* ageless, fr. *a-* + *gēras* old age — more at CORN] **:** any of a large genus (*Ageratum*) of tropical American composite herbs often cultivated for their small showy heads of blue or white flowers; *also* **:** any of several related blue-flowered plants (genus *Eupatorium*)

Ag·ge·us \a-ˈgē-əs\ *n* [LL *Aggaeus,* fr. Gk *Aggaois,* fr. Heb *Ḥaggai*] **:** HAGGAI

[1]**ag·gie** \ˈag-ē\ *n* [agate + *-ie*] **:** a playing marble; *specif* **:** AGATE 2c

[2]**aggie** *n, often cap* [agricultural + *-ie*] **:** an agricultural school or college; *also* **:** a student at such an institution

ag·gior·na·men·to \ə-ˌjȯr-nə-ˈmen-(ˌ)tō\ *n, pl* **-tos** [It, fr. *aggiornare* to bring up to date, fr. *a* to (fr. L *ad-*) + *giorno* day, fr. LL *diurnum* day — more at JOURNEY] **:** a bringing up to date : MODERNIZATION ⟨dedicated to the ~ of the church⟩

[1]**ag·glom·er·ate** \ə-ˈgläm-ə-ˌrāt\ *vt* **-at·ed; -at·ing** [L *agglomeratus,* pp. of *agglomerare* to heap up, join, fr. *ad-* + *glomer-, glomus* ball — more at CLAM] **:** to gather into a ball, mass, or cluster

[2]**ag·glom·er·ate** \-rət\ *adj* **:** gathered into a ball, mass, or cluster; *specif* **:** clustered or growing together but not coherent ⟨an ~ flower head⟩

[3]**ag·glom·er·ate** \-rət\ *n* **1 :** a jumbled mass or collection **2 :** a rock composed of volcanic fragments of various sizes and degrees of angularity

ag·glom·er·a·tion \ə-ˌgläm-ə-ˈrā-shən\ *n* **1 :** the action or process of collecting in a mass **2 :** a heap or cluster of disparate elements ⟨urban ~*s* knit together by the new railways —*Times Lit. Supp.*⟩ — **ag·glom·er·a·tive** \-ˈgläm-ə-ˌrāt-iv\ *adj*

ag·glu·ti·na·bil·i·ty \ə-ˌglüt-ᵊn-ə-ˈbil-ət-ē\ *n* **:** capacity (as of red blood cells) to be agglutinated

[1]**ag·glu·ti·nate** \ə-ˈglüt-ᵊn-ət\ *adj* **:** AGGLUTINATIVE 2

[2]**ag·glu·ti·nate** \-ᵊn-ˌāt\ *vb* **-nat·ed; -nat·ing** [L *agglutinatus,* pp. of *agglutinare* to glue to, fr. *ad-* + *glutinare* to glue, fr. *glutin-, gluten* glue — more at GLUTEN] *vt* **1 :** to cause to adhere : FASTEN **2 :** to combine into a compound : attach to a base as an affix **3 :** to cause to undergo agglutination ~ *vi* **1 :** to unite or combine into a group or mass **2 :** to form words by agglutination

ag·glu·ti·na·tion \ə-ˌglüt-ᵊn-ˈā-shən\ *n* **1 :** the action or process of agglutinating **2 :** a mass or group formed by the union of separate elements **3 :** the formation of derivational or inflectional words by putting together constituents of which each expresses a single definite meaning **4 :** a reaction in which particles (as red blood cells or bacteria) suspended in a liquid collect into clumps and which occurs esp. as a serologic response to a specific antibody

ag·glu·ti·na·tive \ə-ˈglüt-ᵊn-ˌāt-iv, -ət-\ *adj* **1 :** ADHESIVE **2 :** characterized by agglutination

ag·glu·ti·nin \ə-ˈglüt-ᵊn-ən\ *n* [ISV *agglutination* + *-in*] **:** a substance (as an antibody) producing agglutination

ag·glu·ti·no·gen \ə-ˈglüt-ᵊn-ə-jən\ *n* [*agglutinin* + *-o-* + *-gen*] **:** an antigen whose presence results in the formation of an agglutinin — **ag·glu·ti·no·gen·ic** \-ˌglüt-ᵊn-ə-ˈjen-ik\ *adj*

ag·gra·da·tion \ˌag-rə-ˈdā-shən\ *n* **:** a modification of the earth's surface in the direction of uniformity of grade by deposition

ag·grade \ə-ˈgrād\ *vt* [*ad-* + *grade*] **:** to fill with detrital material

ag·gran·dize \ə-ˈgran-ˌdīz, ˈag-rən-\ *vt* **-dized; -diz·ing** [F *agrandiss-,* stem of *agrandir,* fr. *a-* (fr. L *ad-*) + *grandir* to increase, fr. L *grandire,* fr. *grandis* great] **1 :** to make great or greater : INCREASE, ENLARGE **2 :** to make appear great or greater : praise highly ⟨*aggrandized* the one and disparaged the other⟩ **3 :** to enhance the power, wealth, position, or reputation of ⟨exploited the situation to ~ himself⟩ — **ag·gran·dize·ment** \ə-ˈgran-dəz-mənt, -ˌdīz-; ˌag-rən-ˈdīz-\ *n* — **ag·gran·diz·er** \ə-ˈgran-ˌdī-zər, ˈag-rən-\ *n*

ag·gra·vate \ˈag-rə-ˌvāt\ *vt* **-vat·ed; -vat·ing** [L *aggravatus,* pp. of *aggravare* to make heavier, fr. *ad-* + *gravare* to burden, fr. *gravis* heavy — more at GRIEVE] **1** *obs* **a :** to make heavy : BURDEN **b :** INCREASE **2 :** to make worse, more serious, or more severe : intensify unpleasantly ⟨problems have been *aggravated* by neglect⟩ **3 a :** to rouse to displeasure or anger by usu. persistent and often petty goading **b :** to produce inflammation in ***syn* 1** see INTENSIFY ***ant*** alleviate **2** see IRRITATE

aggravated assault *n* **:** an assault that is more serious than a common assault: as **a :** an assault combined with an intent to commit a crime **b :** any of various assaults so defined by statute

ag·gra·va·tion \ˌag-rə-ˈvā-shən\ *n* **1 :** the act, action, or result of aggravating; *esp* **:** an increasing in seriousness or severity **2 :** an act or circumstance that intensifies or makes worse **3 :** IRRITATION, PROVOCATION

[1]**ag·gre·gate** \ˈag-ri-gət\ *adj* [ME *aggregat,* fr. L *aggregatus,* pp. of *aggregare* to add to, fr. *ad-* + *greg-, grex* flock — more at GREGARIOUS] **:** formed by the collection of units or particles into a body, mass, or amount : COLLECTIVE: as **a** (1) **:** clustered in a dense mass or head ⟨an ~ flower⟩ **a** (2) **:** formed from the several ovaries of a single flower **b :** composed of mineral crystals of one or more kinds or of mineral rock fragments **c :** taking all units as a whole : TOTAL ⟨~ earnings⟩ ⟨~ sales⟩ — **ag·gre·gate·ly** *adv* — **ag·gre·gate·ness** *n*

[2]**ag·gre·gate** \-ˌgāt\ *vt* **-gat·ed; -gat·ing 1 :** to collect or gather into a mass or whole **2 :** to amount in the aggregate to : TOTAL

[3]**ag·gre·gate** \-gət\ *n* **1 :** a mass or body of units or parts somewhat loosely associated with one another **2 :** the whole sum or amount : SUM TOTAL **3 a :** an aggregate rock **b :** any of several hard inert materials (as sand, gravel, or slag) used for mixing with a cementing material to form concrete, mortar, or plaster **c :** a clustered mass of individual soil particles varied in shape, ranging in size from a microscopic granule to a small crumb, and considered the basic structural unit of soil **4 :** SET 19 — **in the aggregate :** considered as a whole : COLLECTIVELY ⟨knowledge of . . . man *in the aggregate* rather as an individual person —G. B. Dearing⟩

ag·gre·ga·tion \ˌag-ri-ˈgā-shən\ *n* **1 a :** the collecting of units or parts into a mass or whole **b :** the condition of being so collected

2 : a group, body, or mass composed of many distinct parts — **ag·gre·ga·tion·al** \-shnəl, -shən-ᵊl\ *adj*

ag·gre·ga·tive \'ag-ri-,gāt-iv\ *adj* **1 :** tending to aggregate **2 :** of or relating to an aggregate — **ag·gre·ga·tive·ly** *adv*

ag·gress \ə-'gres\ *vi* **:** to commit aggression **:** act aggressively ⟨westerners even ~*ed* against one another —A. E. Stevenson †1965⟩

ag·gres·sion \ə-'gresh-ən\ *n* [L *aggressus,* pp. of *aggredi* to attack, fr. *ad-* + *gradi* to step, go — more at GRADE] **1 :** a forceful action or procedure (as an unprovoked attack) esp. when intended to dominate or master **2 :** the practice of making attacks or encroachments; *esp* **:** unprovoked violation by one country of the territorial integrity of another **3 :** hostile, injurious, or destructive behavior or outlook esp. when caused by frustration

ag·gres·sive \ə-'gres-iv\ *adj* **1 a :** tending toward or practicing aggression ⟨~ behavior⟩ **b :** marked by combative readiness ⟨an ~ fighter⟩ **2 a :** marked by driving forceful energy or initiative **:** ENTERPRISING ⟨an ~ salesman⟩ **b :** marked by obtrusive energy — **ag·gres·sive·ly** *adv* — **ag·gres·sive·ness** *n* — **ag·gres·siv·i·ty** \,ag-,re-'siv-ət-ē\ *n*

syn AGGRESSIVE, MILITANT, ASSERTIVE, SELF-ASSERTIVE, PUSHING *shared meaning element* **:** conspicuously or obtrusively active or energetic

ag·gres·sor \ə-'gres-ər\ *n* **:** one that commits or practices aggression

ag·grieve \ə-'grēv\ *vt* **ag·grieved; ag·griev·ing** [ME *agreven,* fr. MF *agrever,* fr. L *aggravare* to make heavier] **1 :** to give pain or trouble to **:** DISTRESS **2 :** to inflict injury on

ag·grieved \ə-'grēvd\ *adj* **1 :** troubled or distressed in spirit **2 a :** showing or expressing grief, injury, or offense ⟨an ~ plea⟩ **b :** suffering from an infringement or denial of legal rights ⟨~ minority groups⟩ — **ag·griev·ed·ly** \-'grē-vəd-lē\ *adv*

Aghan \ə-'gän\ *n* [Hindi, fr. Skt *Agrahāyaṇa*] **:** a month of the Hindu year — see MONTH table

aghast \ə-'gast\ *adj* [ME *agast,* fr. pp. of *agasten* to frighten, fr. *a-* (perfective prefix) + *gasten* to frighten — more at ABIDE, GAST] **:** struck with terror, amazement, or horror **:** SHOCKED ⟨were ~ when they heard of his defection⟩

ag·ile \'aj-əl\ *adj* [MF, fr. L *agilis,* fr. *agere* to drive, act — more at AGENT] **1 :** marked by ready ability to move with quick easy grace **2 :** mentally quick and resourceful — **ag·ile·ly** \-ə(l)-lē\ *adv*

syn AGILE, NIMBLE, BRISK, SPRY *shared meaning element* **:** acting or moving with easy alacrity ***ant*** torpid

agil·i·ty \ə-'jil-ət-ē\ *n, pl* **-ties :** the quality or state of being agile **:** NIMBLENESS, DEXTERITY ⟨played with increasing ~⟩

agin \ə-'gin\ *dial var of* AGAINST

aging *pres part of* AGE

agin·ner \ə-'gin-ər\ *n* [*agin* + *-er*] *slang* **:** one who opposes change

agio \'aj-(ē-,)ō\ *n, pl* **agios** [It, alter. of It dial. *lajjē,* fr. MGk *allagion* exchange, fr. Gk *allagē* exchange, fr. *allos* other — more at ELSE] **:** a premium or percentage paid for the exchange of one currency for another; *also* **:** the premium or discount on foreign bills of exchange

ag·i·tate \'aj-ə-,tāt\ *vb* **-tat·ed; -tat·ing** [L *agitatus,* pp. of *agitare,* freq. of *agere* to drive — more at AGENT] *vt* **1 a** *obs* **:** to give motion to **b :** to move with an irregular, rapid, or violent action ⟨the storm *agitated* the sea⟩ **2 :** to excite and often trouble the mind or feelings of **:** DISTURB **3 a :** to discuss excitedly and earnestly **b :** to stir up public discussion of ~ *vi* **:** to attempt to arouse public feeling ⟨*agitated* for better schools⟩ ***syn* 1** see SHAKE **2** see DISCOMPOSE ***ant*** calm, tranquilize — **ag·i·tat·ed·ly** *adv* — **ag·i·ta·tion** \,aj-ə-'tā-shən\ *n* — **ag·i·ta·tion·al** \-shnəl, -shən-ᵊl\ *adj*

ag·i·ta·tive \'aj-ə-,tāt-iv\ *adj* **:** causing or tending to cause agitation

ag·i·ta·to \,aj-ə-'tät-(,)ō\ *adv or adj* [It, lit., agitated, fr. L *agitatus*] **:** in a restless and agitated manner — used as a direction in music

ag·i·ta·tor \'aj-ə-,tāt-ər\ *n* **:** one that agitates: as **a :** one who stirs up public feeling on controversial issues ⟨political ~*s*⟩ **b :** a device or an apparatus for stirring or shaking

ag·it·prop \'aj-ət-,präp\ *n* [Russ, office of agitation and propaganda, fr. *agitatsiya* agitation + *propaganda*] **:** political and esp. pro-communist propaganda promulgated esp. in literature, drama, music, or art — **agitprop** *adj*

Aglaia \ə-'glī-ə, -'glā-(y)ə\ *n* [L, fr. Gk] **:** one of the three Graces

aglare \ə-'gla(ə)r, -'gle(ə)r\ *adj* **:** GLARING ⟨his eyes ~ with fury⟩ ⟨buildings ~ in the sunlight⟩

agleam \ə-'glēm\ *adj* **:** reflecting light by gleaming

ag·let \'ag-lət\ *n* [ME *aglet,* fr. MF *aguillette, aiguillette,* dim. of *aguille, aiguille* needle, fr. LL *acicula, acucula* ornamental pin, dim. of L *acus* needle, pin — more at ACUTE] **1 :** the plain or ornamental tag covering the ends of a lace or point **2 :** any of various ornamental studs, cords, or pins worn on clothing

agley \ə-'glā, -'glē, -'glī\ *adv* [Sc, lit., squintingly, fr. 1*a-* + *gley* to squint] *chiefly Scot* **:** AWRY, WRONG ⟨the best-laid schemes o' mice an' men gang aft ~ —Robert Burns⟩

aglit·ter \ə-'glit-ər\ *adj* **:** reflecting light by glittering

aglow \ə-'glō\ *adj* **:** radiant with warmth or excitement

agly·con \ag-'lī-,kän\ *or* **agly·cone** \-,kōn\ *n* [ISV *a-* (fr. Gk *ha-,* together) + *glyc-* + *-on, -one*] **:** an organic compound (as a phenol or alcohol) combined with the sugar portion of a glycoside

ag·nail \'ag-,nāl\ *n* [ME, corn on the foot or toe, fr. OE *angnægl,* fr. *ang-* (akin to *enge* tight, painful) + *nægl* metal nail — more at ANGER, NAIL] **:** a sore or inflammation about a fingernail or toenail; *also* **:** HANGNAIL

1ag·nate \'ag-,nāt\ *n* [L *agnatus,* fr. pp. of *agnasci* to be born in addition to, fr. *ad-* + *nasci* to be born — more at NATION] **1 :** a relative whose kinship is traceable exclusively through males **2 :** a paternal kinsman

2agnate *adj* **1 :** related through male descent or on the father's side **2 :** ALLIED, AKIN — **ag·nat·ic** \ag-'nat-ik\ *adj* — **ag·nat·i·cal·ly** \-i-k(ə-)lē\ *adv* — **ag·na·tion** \-'nā-shən\ *n*

Ag·ne·an \'äg-nē-ən\ *n* [*Agni,* ancient kingdom in Turkestan] **:** TOCHARIAN A

ag·nize \ag-'nīz\ *vt* **ag·nized; ag·niz·ing** [L *agnoscere* to acknowledge (fr. *ad-* + *noscere* to know) + E *-ize* (as in *recognize*) — more at KNOW] *archaic* **:** RECOGNIZE, ACKNOWLEDGE

ag·no·men \ag-'nō-mən\ *n, pl* **-nom·i·na** \-'näm-ə-nə\ *or* **-no·mens** [L, irreg. fr. *ad-* + *nomen* name — more at NAME] **:** an additional cognomen given to a person by the ancient Romans (as in honor of some achievement)

1ag·nos·tic \ag-'näs-tik, əg-\ *n* [Gk *agnōstos* unknown, unknowable, fr. *a-* + *gnōstos* known, fr. *gignōskein* to know — more at KNOW] **:** one who holds the view that any ultimate reality (as God) is unknown and prob. unknowable ***syn*** see ATHEIST — **ag·nos·ti·cism** \-tə-,siz-əm\ *n*

2agnostic *adj* **1 :** of, relating to, or being an agnostic or the beliefs of agnostics **2 :** NONCOMMITTAL, UNDOGMATIC

Ag·nus Dei \,äg-,nùs-'dā(-,ē), ,än-,yüs-; ,ag-nəs-'dē-,ī\ *n* [ME, fr. LL, lamb of God, fr. its opening words] **1 :** a liturgical prayer addressed to Christ as Savior **2 :** an image of a lamb often with a halo and a banner and cross as a symbol of Christ

Agnus Dei 2

ago \ə-'gō\ *adj or adv* [ME *agon, ago,* fr. pp. of *agon* to pass away, fr. OE *āgān,* fr. *ā-* (perfective prefix) + *gān* to go — more at ABIDE, GO] **:** earlier than the present time ⟨10 years ~⟩

agog \ə-'gäg\ *adj* [MF *en gogues* in mirth] **:** full of intense interest or excitement **:** EAGER ⟨the . . . court was ~ with gossip, scandal and intrigue —*Times Lit. Supp.*⟩

1a–go–go \ä-'gō-(,)gō\ *n* [*Whisky à Gogo,* cafe and discotheque in Paris, France, from F *à gogo* galore, fr. MF] **1 :** DISCOTHEQUE **2 :** a usu. small intimate nightclub for dancing to live music and esp. rock'n'roll

2a–go–go *adj* **:** GO-GO

-a·gogue \ə-,gäg\ *n comb form* [F & NL; F, fr. LL *-agogus* promoting the expulsion of, fr. Gk *-agōgos,* fr. *agein* to lead; NL *-agogon,* fr. Gk, neut. of *-agōgos* — more at AGENT] **:** substance that promotes the secretion or expulsion of ⟨emmen*agogue*⟩

agon \'äg-,än, ä-'gōn\ *n* [Gk *agōn*] **:** CONTEST, CONFLICT; *specif* **:** the dramatic conflict between the chief characters in a literary work

ag·o·nal \'ag-ən-ᵊl\ *adj* **:** of, relating to, or associated with agony and esp. the death agony

agone \ə-'gon *also* -'gän\ *adj or adv, archaic* **:** AGO

agon·ic \(')ā-'gän-ik, ə-\ *adj* [Gk *agōnos* without angle, fr. *a-* + *gōnia* angle — more at -GON] **1 :** not forming an angle **2 :** being an imaginary line passing through points where there is no magnetic declination and where a freely suspended magnetic needle indicates true north

ag·o·nist \'ag-ə-nəst\ *n* [LL *agonista* competitor, fr. Gk *agōnistēs,* fr. *agōnizesthai* to contend, fr. *agōn*] **1 :** one that is engaged in a struggle **2** [back-formation fr. *antagonist*] **:** a muscle that is checked and controlled by the opposing simultaneous contraction of another muscle

ag·o·nis·tic \,ag-ə-'nis-tik\ *adj* **1 :** of or relating to the athletic contests of ancient Greece **2 :** ARGUMENTATIVE **3 :** striving for effect **:** STRAINED **4 :** of, relating to, or being aggressive or defensive social interaction (as fighting, fleeing, or submitting) between individuals usu. of the same species — **ag·o·nis·ti·cal** \-ti-kəl\ *adj* — **ag·o·nis·ti·cal·ly** \-k(ə-)lē\ *adv*

ag·o·nize \'ag-ə-,nīz\ *vb* **-nized; -niz·ing** *vt* **:** to cause to suffer agony **:** TORTURE ~ *vi* **1 :** to suffer agony, torture, or anguish ⟨~*s* over every decision⟩ **2 :** STRUGGLE

ag·o·nized *adj* **:** characterized by, suffering, or expressing agony

ag·o·niz·ing *adj* **:** causing agony **:** PAINFUL ⟨an ~ reappraisal of his policies⟩ — **ag·o·niz·ing·ly** \-,nī-ziŋ-lē\ *adv*

ag·o·ny \'ag-ə-nē\ *n, pl* **-nies** [ME *agonie,* fr. LL *agonia,* fr. Gk *agōnia* struggle, anguish, fr. *agōn* gathering, contest for a prize, fr. *agein* to lead, celebrate — more at AGENT] **1 a :** intense pain of mind or body **:** ANGUISH, TORTURE **b :** the struggle that precedes death **2 :** a violent struggle or contest **3 :** a strong sudden display (as of joy or delight) **:** OUTBURST ***syn*** see DISTRESS

agony column *n* **:** a newspaper column of personal advertisements relating esp. to missing relatives or friends

1ag·o·ra \'ag-ə-rə\ *n, pl* **-ras** *or* **-rae** \-,rē, -,rī\ [Gk — more at GREGARIOUS] **:** a gathering place; *esp* **:** the marketplace in ancient Greece

2ago·ra \,äg-ə-'rä\ *n, pl* **ago·rot** \-'rōt\ [N Heb *ăgōrāh,* fr. Heb, a small coin] — see *pound* at MONEY table

ag·o·ra·pho·bia \,ag-ə-rə-'fō-bē-ə\ *n* [NL, fr. Gk *agora* + NL *phobia*] **:** abnormal fear of crossing or of being in open spaces — **ag·o·ra·pho·bi·ac** \-'fō-bē-,ak\ *n* — **ag·o·ra·pho·bic** \-'fō-bik, -'fäb-ik\ *adj*

agou·ti \ə-'güt-ē\ *n* [F, fr. Sp. *agutí,* fr. Guarani] **1 :** a tropical American rodent (genus *Dasyprocta* or *Myoprocta*) about the size of a rabbit **2 :** a grizzled color of fur resulting from the barring of each hair in several alternate dark and light bands

agr *or* **agric** *abbr* agricultural; agriculture

agrafe *or* **agraffe** \ə-'graf\ *n* [F *agrafe*] **:** a hook-and-loop fastening; *esp* **:** an ornamental clasp used on armor or costumes

agran·u·lo·cyte \(')ā-'gran-yə-lō-,sīt\ *n* **:** a leukocyte without cytoplasmic granules

agran·u·lo·cy·to·sis \,ā-,gran-yə-lō-,sī-'tō-səs\ *n* **:** a destructive condition marked by severe decrease in blood granulocytes and often associated with the use of certain drugs

ag·ra·pha \'ag-rə-fə\ *n pl* [Gk, neut. pl. of *agraphos* unwritten, fr. *a-* + *graphein* to write — more at CARVE] **:** sayings of Jesus not in the

ə abut ᵊ kitten ər further a back ā bake ä cot, cart
aù out ch chin e less ē easy g gift i trip ī life
j joke ŋ sing ō flow ȯ flaw ȯi coin th thin th this
ü loot ù foot y yet yü few yù furious zh vision

canonical gospels but found in other New Testament or early Christian writings

agraph·ia \(ˈ)ā-ˈgraf-ē-ə\ *n* [NL, fr. 2*a-* + Gk *graphein* to write] : the pathologic loss of the ability to write

1**agrar·i·an** \ə-ˈgrer-ē-ən, -ˈgrar-\ *adj* [L *agrarius*, fr. *agr-, ager* field — more at ACRE] **1 :** of or relating to fields or lands or their tenure **2 a :** of, relating to, or characteristic of the farmer or his way of life **b :** organized or designed to promote agricultural interests ⟨an ~ political party⟩ ⟨~ reforms⟩

2**agrarian** *n* **:** a member of an agrarian party or movement

agrar·i·an·ism \-ē-ə-ˌniz-əm\ *n* **:** a social or political movement designed to bring about land reforms or to improve the economic status of the farmer

agree \ə-ˈgrē\ *vb* **agreed; agree·ing** [ME *agreen*, fr. MF *agreer*, fr. *a-* (fr. L *ad-*) + *gre* will, pleasure, fr. L *gratum*, neut. of *gratus* pleasing, agreeable — more at GRACE] *vt* **1 :** ADMIT, CONCEDE **2 :** to settle on by common consent : ARRANGE ~ *vi* **1 :** to accept or concede something (as the views or wishes of another) typically after resolving points of disagreement **2 a :** to achieve or be in harmony (as of opinion, feeling, or purpose) **b :** to get along together **c :** to come to terms **3 a :** to be similar : CORRESPOND ⟨both copies ~⟩ **b :** to be consistent ⟨the story ~*s* with the facts⟩ **4 :** to be fitting, pleasing, or healthful : SUIT ⟨this climate ~*s* with him⟩ **5 :** to have an inflectional form denoting identity or a regular correspondence other than identity in a grammatical category (as gender, number, case, or person)

syn **1** see ASSENT ***ant*** protest (*against*), differ (*with*)

2 AGREE, CONCUR, COINCIDE *shared meaning element* **:** to come into or be in harmony regarding a matter of opinion. AGREE implies complete accord usually attained by discussion and adjustment of differences ⟨on some points we all can *agree*⟩ CONCUR tends to suggest cooperative thinking or acting toward an end ⟨for the creation of a masterwork of literature two powers must *concur*, the power of the man and the power of the moment —Matthew Arnold⟩ but sometimes implies no more than approval (as of a decision reached by others). COINCIDE, used more often of opinions, judgments, wishes, or interests than of people, implies an agreement amounting to identity ⟨their wishes *coincide* exactly with my desire⟩ ***ant*** differ, disagree

3 AGREE, SQUARE, CONFORM, ACCORD, COMPORT, HARMONIZE, CORRESPOND *shared meaning element* **:** to go or exist together without conflict or incongruity ***ant*** differ (*from*)

agree·able \ə-ˈgrē-ə-bəl\ *adj* **1 :** pleasing to the mind or senses esp. as according well with one's tastes or needs ⟨an ~ companion⟩ ⟨an ~ change⟩ **2 :** ready or willing to agree or consent **3 :** being in harmony : CONSONANT ***syn*** see PLEASANT ***ant*** disagreeable — **agree·abil·i·ty** \-ˌgrē-ə-ˈbil-ət-ē\ *n* — **agree·able·ness** \-ˈgrē-ə-bəl-nəs\ *n* — **agree·ably** \-blē\ *adv*

agree·ment \ə-ˈgrē-mənt\ *n* **1 a :** the act or fact of agreeing **b :** harmony of opinion, action, or character : CONCORD **2 a :** an arrangement as to a course of action **b :** COMPACT, TREATY **3 a :** a contract duly executed and legally binding **b :** the language or instrument embodying such a contract

ag·ri·busi·ness \ˈag-rə-ˌbiz-nəs, -nəz\ *n* [*agriculture* + *business*] **:** a combination of the producing operations of a farm, the manufacture and distribution of farm equipment and supplies, and the processing, storage, and distribution of farm commodities

ag·ri·cul·tur·al \ˌag-ri-ˈkəlch-(ə-)rəl\ *adj* **:** of, relating to, used in, or concerned with agriculture — **ag·ri·cul·tur·al·ly** \-ē\ *adv*

ag·ri·cul·ture \ˈag-ri-ˌkəl-chər\ *n* [F, fr. L *agricultura*, fr. *ager* field + *cultura* cultivation — more at ACRE, CULTURE] **:** the science or art of cultivating the soil, producing crops, and raising livestock and in varying degrees the preparation of these products for man's use and their disposal (as by marketing) : FARMING — **ag·ri·cul·tur·ist** \ˌag-ri-ˈkəlch-(ə-)rəst\ *or* **ag·ri·cul·tur·al·ist** \-(ə-)rə-ləst\ *n*

ag·ri·mo·ny \ˈag-rə-ˌmō-nē\ *n, pl* **-nies** [ME, fr. MF & L; MF *aigremoine*, fr. L *agrimonia*, MS var. of *argemonia*, fr. Gk *argemōnē*] **:** a common yellow-flowered herb (genus *Agrimonia*) of the rose family having toothed leaves and fruits like burs; *also* **:** any of several similar or related plants

ag·ri·ol·o·gy \ˌag-rē-ˈäl-ə-jē\ *n* [Gk *agrios* wild, fr. *agros* field, country] **:** the comparative study of the customs of nonliterate peoples

agro- *comb form* [F, fr. Gk, fr. *agros* field — more at ACRE] **1 :** of or belonging to fields or soil : agricultural ⟨*agro*logy⟩ **2 :** agricultural and ⟨*agro*-industrial⟩

ag·ro·bi·ol·o·gy \ˌag-rō-bī-ˈäl-ə-jē\ *n* **:** the study of plant nutrition and growth and crop production in relation to soil management — **ag·ro·bi·o·log·ic** \-ˌbī-ə-ˈläj-ik\ *or* **ag·ro·bi·o·log·i·cal** \-i-kəl\ *adj* — **ag·ro·bi·o·log·i·cal·ly** \-i-k(ə-)lē\ *adv*

ag·ro–in·dus·tri·al \ˌag-rō-in-ˈdəs-trē-əl\ *adj* **:** of or relating to production (as of power for industry and water for irrigation) for both industrial and agricultural purposes

agrol·o·gy \ə-ˈgräl-ə-jē\ *n* [ISV] **:** a branch of agriculture dealing with soils esp. in relation to crops — **ag·ro·log·ic** \ˌag-rə-ˈläj-ik\ *or* **ag·ro·log·i·cal** \-ˈläj-i-kəl\ *adj* — **ag·ro·log·i·cal·ly** \-i-k(ə-)lē\ *adv* — **agrol·o·gist** \ə-ˈgräl-ə-jəst\ *n*

agron·o·my \ə-ˈgrän-ə-mē\ *n* [prob. fr. F *agronomie*, fr. *agro-* + *-nomie* -nomy] **:** a branch of agriculture dealing with field-crop production and soil management — **ag·ro·nom·ic** \ˌag-rə-ˈnäm-ik\ *or* **ag·ro·nom·i·cal** \ˌag-rə-ˈnäm-i-kəl\ *adj* — **ag·ro·nom·i·cal·ly** \-i-k(ə-)lē\ *adv* — **agron·o·mist** \ə-ˈgrän-ə-məst\ *n*

aground \ə-ˈgrau̇nd\ *adv or adj* **1 :** on or onto the shore or the bottom of a body of water ⟨a ship run ~⟩ **2 :** on the ground ⟨planes aloft and ~⟩

agt *abbr* agent

ague \ˈā-(ˌ)gyü\ *n* [ME, fr. MF *aguë*, fr. ML (*febris*) *acuta*, lit., sharp fever, fr. L, fem. of *acutus* sharp — more at ACUTE] **1 :** a fever (as malaria) marked by paroxysms of chills, fever, and sweating that recur at regular intervals **2 :** a fit of shivering : CHILL — **agu·ish** \ˈā-ˌgyü-ish\ *adj* — **agu·ish·ly** *adv*

ah \ˈä\ *interj* [ME] — used to express delight, relief, regret, or contempt

AH *abbr* **1** ampere-hour **2** anno hegirae **3** arts and humanities

aha \ä-ˈhä\ *interj* [ME] — used to express surprise, triumph, or derision

AHA *abbr* American Historical Association

ahead \ə-ˈhed\ *adv or adj* **1 a :** in a forward direction or position : FORWARD **b :** in front **2 :** in, into, or for the future ⟨plan ~⟩ ⟨the years ~⟩ **3 :** in or toward a more advantageous position ⟨helped others to get ~⟩ **4 :** at or to an earlier time : in advance ⟨make payments ~⟩

ahead of *prep* **1 :** in front or advance of **2 :** in excess of : ABOVE

ahim·sa \ə-ˈhim-ˌsä\ *n* [Skt *ahiṁsā* noninjury] **:** the Hindu and Buddhist doctrine of refraining from harming any living being

ahis·tor·i·cal \ˌā-his-ˈtȯr-i-kəl, -ˈtär-\ *or* **ahis·tor·ic** \-ik\ *adj* **:** not concerned with or related to history, historical development, or tradition ⟨the ~ attitudes of the radicals⟩

AHL *abbr* American Hockey League

ahold \ə-ˈhōld\ *n* [prob. fr. the phrase *a hold*] **:** HOLD ⟨if you could get ~ of a representative who . . . would come along —Norman Mailer⟩

A–horizon *n* **:** the outer dark-colored layer of a soil profile consisting largely of partly disintegrated organic debris

ahoy \ə-ˈhȯi\ *interj* [*a-* (as in *aha*) + *hoy*] — used in hailing ⟨ship ~⟩

Ah·ri·man \ˈär-i-mən, -ˌmän\ *n* [Per, modif. of Av *aṅrō mainyuš* hostile spirit] **:** Ahura Mazda's antagonist who is a spirit of darkness and evil in Zoroastrianism

Ahu·ra Maz·da \ə-ˌhu̇r-ə-ˈmaz-də, ä-ˌhu̇r-\ *n* [Av *Ahuramazda*, lit., wise god] **:** the Supreme Being represented as a deity of goodness and light in Zoroastrianism

ai \ˈī, ä-ˈē\ *n* [Pg *ai* or Sp *aí*, fr. Tupi *ai*] **:** a sloth (genus *Bradypus*) with three claws on each front foot

AI *abbr* **1** ad interim **2** airborne intercept **3** air interception

AIA *abbr* American Institute of Architects

Ai·as \ˈī-əs\ *n* [Gk] **:** AJAX

ai·blins \ˈā-blənz\ *adv* [*able* + *-lings*, *-lins* -lings] *chiefly Scot* **:** PERHAPS

AIChE *abbr* American Institute of Chemical Engineers

1**aid** \ˈād\ *vb* [ME *eyden*, fr. MF *aider*, fr. L *adjutare*, fr. *adjutus*, pp. of *adjuvare*, fr. *ad-* + *juvare* to help] *vt* **:** to provide with what is useful or necessary in achieving an end ~ *vi* **:** to give assistance ***syn*** see HELP ***ant*** injure — **aid·er** *n*

2**aid** *n* **1 :** a subsidy granted to the king by the English parliament until the 18th century for an extraordinary purpose **2 a :** the act of helping **b :** help given : ASSISTANCE; *specif* **:** tangible means of assistance (as money or supplies) **3 a :** an assisting person or group — compare AIDE **b :** something by which assistance is given : an assisting device ⟨an ~ to understanding⟩ ⟨a visual ~⟩; *specif* : HEARING AID **4 :** a tribute paid by a vassal to his lord

AID *abbr* Agency for International Development

aide \ˈād\ *n* [short for *aide-de-camp*] **:** a person who acts as an assistant; *specif* **:** a military officer acting as assistant to a superior

aide–de–camp \ˌād-di-ˈkamp, -ˈkäⁿ\ *n, pl* **aides–de–camp** \ˌād(z)-di-\ [F *aide de camp*, lit., camp assistant] **:** a military aide

aide–mé·moire \ˌād-mām-ˈwär\ *n, pl* **aide–mémoire** [F, fr. *aider* to aid + *mémoire* memory] **1 :** an aid to the memory; *esp* **:** a mnemonic device **2 :** a written summary or outline of important items of a proposed agreement or diplomatic communication : MEMORANDUM

aid·man \ˈād-ˌman\ *n* **:** an army medical corpsman attached to a field unit

ai·grette \ā-ˈgret, ˈā-ˌ\ *n* [F] **1 :** a spray of feathers (as of the egret) for the head **2 :** a spray of gems worn on a hat or in the hair

ai·guille \ā-ˈgwē(ə)l, -ˈgwē\ *n* [F, lit., needle — more at AGLET] **1 :** a sharp-pointed pinnacle of rock **2 :** an instrument for boring holes in stone or other masonry materials

ai·guil·lette \ˌā-gwi-ˈlet\ *n* [F — more at AGLET] **:** AGLET; *specif* **:** a shoulder cord worn by designated military aides — compare FOURRAGÈRE

ai·ki·do \ˌī-ki-ˈdō\ *n* [Jap *aikidō*, fr. *ai-* together, mutual + *ki* spirit + *dō* art] **:** a Japanese art of self-defense employing locks and holds and utilizing the principle of nonresistance to cause an opponent's own momentum to work against him

ail \ˈā(ə)l\ *vb* [ME *eilen*, fr. OE *eglan*; akin to MLG *egelen* to annoy] *vt* **:** to give physical or emotional pain, discomfort, or trouble to ~ *vi* **:** to have something the matter; *esp* **:** to suffer ill health ***syn*** see TROUBLE

ai·lan·thus \ā-ˈlan(t)-thəs\ *n* [NL, genus name, fr. Amboinese *ai lanto*, lit., tree (of) heaven] **:** any of a small Asiatic genus (*Ailanthus* of the family Simaroubaceae, the ailanthus family) of chiefly tropical trees and shrubs with bitter bark, pinnate leaves, and terminal panicles of ill-scented greenish flowers

ai·le·ron \ˈā-lə-ˌrän\ *n* [F, fr. dim. of *aile* wing] **:** a movable part of an airplane wing or a movable airfoil external to the wing at the trailing edge for imparting a rolling motion and thus providing lateral control —see AIRPLANE illustration

ail·ment \ˈā(ə)l-mənt\ *n* **1 :** a bodily disorder or chronic disease **2 :** UNREST, UNEASINESS

ai·lu·ro·phile \ī-ˈlu̇r-ə-ˌfīl, ā-\ *n* [Gk *ailouros* cat] **:** a cat fancier : a lover of cats

ai·lu·ro·phobe \-ˌfōb\ *n* [Gk *ailouros* cat] **:** one who hates or fears cats

1**aim** \ˈām\ *vb* [ME *aimen*, fr. MF *aesmer* & *esmer*; MF *aesmer*, fr. OF, fr. *a-* (fr. L *ad-*) + *esmer* to estimate, fr. L *aestimare* — more at ESTEEM] *vi* **1 :** to direct a course; *specif* **:** to point a weapon at an object **2 :** ASPIRE, INTEND ⟨~*s* to reform the government⟩ ~ *vt* **1** *obs* **:** GUESS, CONJECTURE **2 a :** POINT **b :** to direct to or toward a specified object or goal

2**aim** *n* **1** *obs* **:** MARK, TARGET **2 a :** the pointing of a weapon at a mark **b :** the ability to hit a target ⟨his ~ was deadly⟩ **c :** a weapon's accuracy or effectiveness **3** *obs* **a :** CONJECTURE, GUESS **b :** the directing of effort toward a goal **4 :** a clearly directed intent or purpose ***syn*** see INTENTION — **aim·less** \-ləs\ *adj* — **aim·less·ly** *adv* — **aim·less·ness** *n*

ain \ˈān\ *adj* [prob. fr. ON *eiginn*] *Scot* **:** OWN

ain't \'ānt\ [prob. contr. of *are not*] **1 a** : are not **b** : is not **c** : am not — though disapproved by many and more common in less educated speech, used orally in most parts of the U.S. by many educated speakers esp. in the phrase *ain't I* **2** *substand* **a** : have not **b** : has not

Ai·nu \'ī-(,)nü\ *n, pl* **Ainu** *or* **Ainus** [Ainu, lit., man] **1** : a member of an indigenous Caucasoid people of Japan **2** : the language of the Ainu people

¹**air** \'a(ə)r, 'e(ə)r\ *n, often attrib* [ME, fr. OF, fr. L *aer*, fr. Gk *aēr*] **1 a** : the mixture of invisible odorless tasteless gases (as nitrogen and oxygen) that surrounds the earth **b** : a light breeze **c** *archaic* : BREATH **2 a** : empty space **b** : NOTHINGNESS ⟨vanished into thin ~⟩ **c** : a sudden severance of relations ⟨she gave him the ~⟩ **3** : COMPRESSED AIR **4 a** (1) : AIRCRAFT ⟨go by ~⟩ (2) : AVIATION ⟨~ safety⟩ ⟨~ rights⟩ (3) : AIR FORCE ⟨~ headquarters⟩ **b** : the medium of transmission of radio waves; *also* : RADIO, TELEVISION ⟨went on the ~⟩ **5** : public utterance ⟨he gave ~ to his opinion⟩ **6 a** : the look, appearance, or bearing of a person esp. as expressive of some personal quality or emotion : DEMEANOR ⟨an ~ of dignity⟩ **b** : an artificial or affected manner : HAUGHTINESS ⟨to put on ~s⟩ **c** : outward appearance of a thing ⟨an ~ of luxury⟩ **d** : a surrounding or pervading influence : ATMOSPHERE ⟨an ~ of mystery⟩ **7** [prob. trans. of It *aria*] **a** *Elizabethan & Jacobean music* : an accompanied song or melody in usu. strophic form **b** : the chief voice part or melody in choral music **c** : TUNE, MELODY **8** : a football offense utilizing primarily the forward pass ⟨behind by three touchdowns and forced to take to the ~⟩ *syn* see POSE — **air·less** \-ləs\ *adj* — **air·less·ness** *n* — **up in the air** : not yet settled

²**air** *vt* **1** : to expose to the air for drying, purifying, or refreshing : VENTILATE — often used with *out* **2** : to expose to public view or bring to public notice **3** : to transmit by radio or television ⟨~ a program⟩ ~ *vi* : to become exposed to the open air *syn* see EXPRESS

air bag *n* : an automatically inflating bag in front of riders in an automobile to protect them from pitching forward into solid parts in case of an accident

air base *n* : a base of operations for military aircraft

air bends *n pl* : AEROEMBOLISM 2

air bladder *n* : a sac containing gas and esp. air; *esp* : a hydrostatic organ present in most fishes that serves as an accessory respiratory organ

air·borne \'a(ə)r-,bō(ə)rn, 'e(ə)r-, -,bó(ə)rn\ *adj* **1** : supported wholly by aerodynamic and aerostatic forces **2** : transported by air

air brake *n* **1** : a brake operated by a piston driven by compressed air **2** : a surface (as an aileron) that may be projected into the airstream for lowering the speed of an airplane

air·brush \-,brəsh\ *n* : an atomizer for applying by compressed air a fine spray (as of paint or liquid color) — **airbrush** *vt*

air·burst \-,bərst\ *n* : the burst of a shell or bomb in the air

air·bus \-,bəs\ *n* : a short-range or medium-range subsonic jet passenger airplane

air cavalry *n* **1** : an army component that is transported in air vehicles and carries out the traditional cavalry missions of reconnaissance and security **2** : an army component organized for sustained ground combat and esp. equipped and adapted for transportation in air vehicles

air chief marshal *n* : a commissioned officer in the British air force who ranks with a general in the army

air coach *n* : a passenger airliner offering service at less than first-class rates usu. with curtailed accommodations

air commodore *n* : a commissioned officer in the British air force who ranks with a brigadier in the army

air–con·di·tion \,a(ə)r-kən-'dish-ən, ,e(ə)r-\ *vt* [back-formation fr. *air conditioning*] : to equip (as a building) with an apparatus for washing air and controlling its humidity and temperature; *also* : to subject (air) to these processes — **air con·di·tion·er** \-'dish-(ə-)nər\ *n*

air–cool \'a(ə)r-'kül, 'e(ə)r-\ *vt* [back-formation fr. *air-cooled & air cooling*] : to cool the cylinders of (an internal-combustion engine) by air without the use of an intermediate medium

air·craft \'a(ə)r-,kraft, 'e(ə)r-\ *n, pl* **aircraft** *often attrib* : a weight-carrying structure for navigation of the air that is supported either by its own buoyancy or by the dynamic action of the air against its surfaces

aircraft carrier *n* : a warship with a flight deck on which airplanes can be launched and landed

air·crew \'a(ə)r-,krü, 'e(ə)r-\ *n* : the crew manning an airplane

air–cushion vehicle *n* : GROUND-EFFECT MACHINE

air·drome \'a(ə)r-,drōm, 'e(ə)r-\ *n* [alter. of *aerodrome*] : AIRPORT

air·drop \-,dräp\ *n* : delivery of cargo or personnel by parachute from an airplane in flight — **air–drop** *vt* — **air–drop·pa·ble** \-,dräp-ə-bəl\ *adj*

air–dry \-'drī\ *adj* : dry to such a degree that no further moisture is given up on exposure to air

Aire·dale terrier \,a(ə)r-,dāl-, ,e(ə)r-\ *n* [*Airedale*, valley of the Aire river, England] : any of a breed of large terriers with a hard wiry coat that is dark on the back and sides and tan elsewhere — called also *Airedale*

Air Express *service mark* — used for package transport by air

air·field \'a(ə)r-,fēld, 'e(ə)r-\ *n* **1** : the landing field of an airport **2** : AIRPORT

air·flow \-,flō\ *n* : the motion of air (as around parts of an airplane in flight) relative to the surface of a body immersed in it

air·foil \-,fȯil\ *n* : a body (as an airplane wing or propeller blade) designed to provide a desired reaction force when in motion relative to the surrounding air

air force *n* **1** : the military organization of a nation for air warfare **2** : a unit of the U.S. Air Force higher than a division and lower than a command

air·frame \-,frām\ *n* [*aircraft* + *frame*] : the structure of an airplane or rocket without the power plant

air·freight \-'frāt\ *n* : freight transport by air in volume; *also* : the charge for this service — **airfreight** *vt*

air·glow \-,glō\ *n* : light that is observed esp. during the night, that originates in the high atmosphere, and that is associated with photochemical reactions of gases caused by solar radiation

air gun *n* **1** : a rifle from which a projectile is propelled by compressed air **2** : any of various hand tools that work by compressed air; *esp* : AIRBRUSH

air·head \-,hed\ *n* ['air + -head (as in *beachhead*)] : an area in hostile territory secured usu. by airborne troops for further use in bringing in troops and materiel by air

air hole *n* **1** : a hole to admit or discharge air **b** : a spot not frozen over in ice **2** : AIR POCKET

air·ing \'a(ə)r-iŋ, 'e(ə)r-\ *n* **1** : exposure to air or heat for drying or freshening **2** : exposure to or exercise in the open air esp. to promote health or fitness **3** : exposure to public view or notice **4** : a radio or television broadcast

air lane *n* : a path customarily followed by airplanes

air letter *n* **1** : an airmail letter **2** : a sheet of airmail stationery that can be folded and sealed with the message inside and the address outside

air·lift \'a(ə)r-,lift, 'e(ə)r-\ *n* : a system of transporting cargo or passengers by aircraft usu. to an otherwise inaccessible area — **airlift** *vt*

air·line \-,līn\ *n* : an air transportation system including its equipment, routes, operating personnel, and management

air line *n* : a straight line through the air between two points : BEELINE

air·lin·er \-,lī-nər\ *n* : an airplane operated by an airline

air lock *n* **1** : an intermediate chamber between the outer air and the working chamber of a pneumatic caisson; *also* : a similar intermediate chamber **2** : a stoppage of flow caused by air being in a part where liquid ought to circulate

air·mail \'a(ə)r-,māl, 'e(ə)r-\ *vt* : to send by airmail

air·mail \'a(ə)r-,māl, 'e(ə)r-, -,māl\ *n* : the system of transporting mail by aircraft; *also* : the mail thus transported — **airmail** *vt*

air·man \-mən\ *n* **1** : an enlisted man in the air force: as **a** : an enlisted man of one of the three ranks below sergeant **b** : an enlisted man ranking above an airman basic and below an airman first class **2** : a civilian or military pilot, aviator, or aviation technician

airman basic *n* : an enlisted man of the lowest rank in the air force

airman first class *n* : an enlisted man in the air force ranking above an airman and below a sergeant

air·man·ship \'a(ə)r-mən-,ship, 'e(ə)r-\ *n* : skill in piloting or navigating airplanes

air marshal *n* : a commissioned officer in the British air force who ranks with a lieutenant general in the army

air mass *n* : a body of air extending hundreds or thousands of miles horizontally and sometimes as high as the stratosphere and maintaining as it travels nearly uniform conditions of temperature and humidity at any given level

air mattress *n* : MATTRESS 1b

Air Medal *n* : a U.S. military decoration awarded for meritorious achievement while participating in an aerial flight

air mile *n* : a mile in air navigation; *specif* : a unit equal to 6076.1154 feet

air–mind·ed \'a(ə)r-'mīn-dəd, 'e(ə)r-\ *adj* : interested in aviation or in air travel — **air–mind·ed·ness** *n*

air·mo·bile \-,mō-bəl, -,bēl, -,bil\ *adj* [*air* + ¹*mobile*] : of, relating to, or being a military unit whose members are transported to combat areas usu. by helicopter

air·park \-,pärk\ *n* : a small airport usu. near an industrial area

air piracy *n* : the hijacking of a flying airplane : SKYJACKING

air·plane \-,plān, 'e(ə)r-\ *n* [alter. of *aeroplane*, prob. fr. LGk *aeroplanos* wandering in air, fr. Gk *aer-* + *planos* wandering, fr. *planasthai* to wander — more at PLANET] : a fixed-wing aircraft heavier than air that is driven by a screw propeller or by a high-velocity jet and supported by the dynamic reaction of the air against its wings

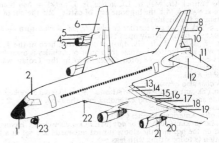

airplane: *1* weather radar, *2* cockpit, *3* jet engine, *4* engine pod, *5* pylon, *6* swept-back wing, *7* vertical stabilizer, *8* rudder, *9, 10* tabs, *11* elevator, *12* horizontal stabilizer, *13* inboard flap, *14* inboard spoiler, *15, 16* tabs, *17* aileron, *18* outboard flap, *19* outboard spoiler, *20* sound suppressor, *21* thrust reverser, *22* cabin air intake, *23* nose landing gear

air plant n **1** : EPIPHYTE **2** : a plant (genus *Kalanchoe*) that propagates new plants from the leaves

air pocket n : a condition of the atmosphere (as a local down current) that causes an airplane to drop suddenly

air police n : the military police of an air force

air·port \'a(ə)r-,pō(ə)rt, 'e(ə)r-, -,pó(ə)rt\ n : a tract of land or water that is maintained for the landing and takeoff of aircraft and for receiving and discharging passengers and cargo and that usu. has facilities for the shelter, supply, and repair of planes

air·post \-'pōst\ n : AIRMAIL

air power n : the military strength of a nation's air force

air pump n : a pump for exhausting air from a closed space or for compressing air or forcing it through other apparatus

air raid n : an attack by armed airplanes on a surface target

air right n : a property right to the space above a surface area or object

air sac n **1** : one of the air-filled spaces in the body of a bird connected with the air passages of the lungs **2** : ALVEOLUS 1b **3** : a thin-walled dilation of a trachea occurring in many insects

air·screw \'a(ə)r-,skrü, 'e(ə)r-\ n **1** : a screw propeller designed to operate in air **2** *Brit* : an airplane propeller

air·ship \-,ship\ n : a lighter-than-air aircraft having propulsion and steering systems

air·sick \-,sik\ adj : affected with motion sickness associated with flying — **air·sick·ness** n

air·space \-,spās\ n : the space lying above the earth or above a certain area of land or water; esp : the space lying above a nation and coming under its jurisdiction

air·speed \-,spēd\ n : the speed (as of an airplane) with relation to the air — compare GROUND SPEED

air·stream \-,strēm\ n : a current of air; specif : AIRFLOW

air strike n : an air attack

air·strip \-,strip\ n : a runway without normal air base or airport facilities

¹airt \'ärt, 'ert\ n [ME art, fr. ScGael àird] chiefly Scot : compass point : DIRECTION

²airt vt, chiefly Scot : DIRECT, GUIDE

air·tight \'a(ə)r-'tīt, 'e(ə)r-\ adj **1** : impermeable to air or nearly so **2 a** : having no noticeable weakness, flaw, or loophole ⟨an ~ argument⟩ **b** : permitting no opportunity for an opponent to score ⟨an ~ defense⟩ — **air·tight·ness** n

air-to-air \,a(ə)rt-ə-'(w)a(ə)r, ,e(ə)rt-ə-'(w)e(ə)r\ adj : launched from one airplane in flight at another : involving aircraft in flight ⟨~ rockets⟩ ⟨~ combat⟩

air vice-marshal n : a commissioned officer in the British air force who ranks with a major general in the army

air·wave \'a(ə)r-,wāv, 'e(ə)r-\ n **1** : the medium of radio and television transmission — usu. used in pl. **2** : AIRWAY 4

air·way \-,wā\ n **1** : a passage for a current of air (as in a mine or to the lungs) **2** : a designated route along which airplanes fly from airport to airport; esp : such a route equipped with navigational aids **3** : AIRLINE **4** : a channel of a designated radio frequency for broadcasting or other radio communication

air·wor·thy \-,wər-thē\ adj : fit for operation in the air ⟨an ~ airplane⟩ — **air·wor·thi·ness** n

airy \'a(ə)r-ē, 'e(ə)r-\ adj **air·i·er; -est 1 a** : of or relating to air : ATMOSPHERIC **b** : high in the air : LOFTY ⟨~ perches⟩ **c** : performed in air : AERIAL ⟨~ leaps⟩ **2** : UNREAL, ILLUSORY ⟨~ romances⟩ **3 a** : being light and graceful in movement or manner : SPRIGHTLY, VIVACIOUS **b** : ETHEREAL **4** : open to the free circulation of air : BREEZY **5** : AFFECTED, PROUD ⟨~ condescension⟩

aisle \'ī(ə)l\ n [ME ile, fr. MF aile wing, fr. L ala; akin to OE eaxl shoulder, L axilla armpit — more at AXIS] **1** : the side of a church nave separated by piers from the nave proper — see BASILICA illustration **2 a** : a passage (as in a theater) separating sections of seats **b** : a passage in a store or warehouse) for inside traffic

ait \'āt\ n [ME, alter. of OE īegeoth, fr. īg island — more at ISLAND] Brit : a little island

aitch \'āch\ n [F hache, fr. (assumed) VL hacca] : the letter h

aitch·bone \'āch-,bōn\ n [ME hachbon, alter. (resulting from incorrect division of a nachebon) of (assumed) ME nachebon, fr. ME nache buttock (fr. MF, fr. LL natica, fr. L natis) + bon bone — more at NATES] **1** : the hipbone esp. of cattle **2** : the cut of beef containing the aitchbone

ajar \ə-'jär\ adj or adv [earlier on char, fr. on + char turn — more at CHARE] : being slightly open ⟨a door ~⟩

Ajax \'ā-,jaks\ n [L, fr. Gk Aias] **1** : a Greek hero in the Trojan War who kills himself because the armor of Achilles is awarded to Odysseus **2** : a fleet-footed Greek hero in the Trojan war — called also Ajax the Less

AK abbr Alaska

AKA abbr also known as

Akan \'äk-,än\ n, pl **Akan** or **Akans 1** : a language spoken over a wide area in Ghana and extending into the Ivory Coast **2** : the Akan-speaking peoples

AKC abbr American Kennel Club

akim·bo \ə-'kim-(,)bō\ adj or adv [ME in kenebowe] **1** : having the hand on the hip and the elbow turned outward **2** : set in a bent position ⟨a tailor sitting with legs ~⟩

akin \ə-'kin\ adj **1** : related by blood : descended from a common ancestor or prototype **2** : essentially similar, related, or compatible syn see SIMILAR ant alien

Ak·ka·di·an \ə-'kād-ē-ən\ n **1** : a Semitic inhabitant of central Mesopotamia before 2000 B.C. **2** : an ancient Semitic language of Mesopotamia used from about the 28th to the 1st century B.C. — **Akkadian** adj

ak·va·vit \'äk-wə-,vēt, 'äk-vä-\ var of AQUAVIT

Al symbol aluminum

AL abbr **1** Alabama **2** American League **3** American Legion

al- — see AD-

¹-al \əl, ²l\ adj suffix [ME, fr. OF & L; OF, fr. L -alis] : of, relating to, or characterized by ⟨directional⟩ ⟨fictional⟩

²-al n suffix [ME -aille, fr. OF, fr. L -alia, neut. pl. of -alis] : action : process ⟨rehearsal⟩

³-al \,al, ,ól, əl, ²l\ n suffix [F, fr. alcool alcohol, fr. ML alcohol] **1** : aldehyde ⟨butanal⟩ **2** : acetal ⟨butyral⟩

ala \'ā-lə\ n, pl **alae** \-,lē\ [L — more at AISLE] : a wing or a winglike anatomic process or part — **alar** \'ā-lər\ adj — **ala·ry** \-lə-rē\ adj

à la or **à la** \al-ə, ,äl-ə, ,äl-(,)ä\ prep [F à la] : in the manner of

Ala abbr Alabama

ALA abbr **1** American Library Association **2** Automobile Legal Association

al·a·bas·ter \'al-ə-,bas-tər\ n [ME alabastre, fr. MF, fr. L alabaster vase of alabaster, fr. Gk alabastros] **1** : a compact fine-textured usu. white and translucent gypsum often carved into vases and ornaments **2** : a hard compact calcite or aragonite that is translucent and sometimes banded — **alabaster** or **al·a·bas·trine** \,al-ə-'bas-trən\ adj

à la carte \,al-ə-'kärt, ,äl-\ adv or adj [F à la carte by the bill of fare] : according to a menu that prices each item separately

alack \ə-'lak\ interj [ME] archaic — used to express sorrow or regret

alac·ri·ty \ə-'lak-rət-ē\ n [L alacritas, fr. alacr-, alacer lively, eager; akin to OE & OHG ellen zeal] : promptness in response : cheerful readiness ⟨accepted the invitation with ~⟩ syn see CELERITY ant languor — **alac·ri·tous** \-rət-əs\ adj

Alad·din \ə-'lad-²n\ n : a youth in the Arabian Nights' Entertainments who comes into possession of a magic lamp

al·a·me·da \,al-ə-'mēd-ə, -'mäd-\ n [Sp, fr. álamo poplar] : a public promenade bordered with trees

à la mode \,al-ə-'mōd, ,äl-\ adj [F à la mode according to the fashion] **1** : FASHIONABLE, STYLISH **2** : topped with ice cream

al·a·nine \'al-ə-,nēn\ n [G alanin, irreg. fr. aldehyd aldehyde] : a white crystalline amino acid $C_3H_7NO_2$ formed esp. by the hydrolysis of proteins

al·a·nyl \'al-ə-,nil\ n [ISV alanine + -yl] : an acyl radical of alanine

¹alarm \ə-'lärm\ also **ala·rum** \-'lär-əm, -'lar-\ n [ME alarme, alarom, fr. MF alarme, fr. OIt all'arme, lit., to the weapon] **1** usu **alarum**, obs : a call to arms ⟨the angry trumpet sounds ~ —Shak.⟩ **2** : a signal (as a loud noise or flashing light) that warns or alerts; also : a device that signals ⟨set the ~ to wake me at seven⟩ **3** : sudden sharp apprehension and fear resulting from the perception of imminent danger **4** : a warning notice syn see FEAR ant assurance, composure

²alarm also **alarum** vt **1** : to give warning to **2** : to strike with fear **3** : DISTURB, EXCITE — **alarm·ing·ly** \-'lär-min-lē\ adv

alarm clock n : a clock that can be set to sound an alarm at a desired time

alarm·ism \ə-'lär-,miz-əm\ n : the often unwarranted exciting of fears or warning of danger — **alarm·ist** \-məst\ n or adj

alarm reaction n : the complex of reactions of an organism to stress (as by increased hormonal activity)

alarums and excursions n pl **1** : martial sounds and the movement of soldiers across the stage — used as a stage direction in Elizabethan drama **2** : clamor, excitement, and feverish or disordered activity

alas \ə-'las\ interj [ME, fr. OF, fr. a ah + las weary, fr. L lassus — more at LET] — used to express unhappiness, pity, or concern

Alas·kan malamute \ə-,las-kən-\ n : any of a breed of powerful heavy-coated deep-chested dogs of Alaskan origin with erect ears, heavily cushioned feet, and plumy tail

Alas·ka time \ə-'las-kə-\ n : the time of the 10th time zone west of Greenwich that includes central Alaska

alate \'ā-,lāt\ also **alat·ed** \-,lāt-əd\ adj [L alatus, fr. ala] : having wings or a winglike part — **ala·tion** \ā-'lā-shən\ n

alb \'alb\ n [ME albe, fr. OE, fr. ML alba, fr. L, fem. of albus white] : a full-length white linen ecclesiastical vestment with long sleeves that is gathered at the waist with a cincture — see VESTMENT illustration

Alb abbr Albania; Albanian

al·ba·core \'al-bə-,kō(ə)r, -,kó(ə)r\ n, pl -**core** or -**cores** [Pg albacor, fr. Ar al-bakūrah the albacore] **1** : a large pelagic tuna (Thunnus alalunga) with long pectoral fins that is a source of canned tuna; broadly : any of various tunas (as a bonito) **2** : any of several carangid fishes

Al·ba·nian \al-'bā-nē-ən, -nyən also ól-\ n **1** : a native or inhabitant of Albania **2** : the Indo-European language of the Albanian people — see INDO-EUROPEAN LANGUAGES table — **Albanian** adj

al·ba·tross \'al-bə-,trós, -,träs\ n, pl -**tross** or -**tross·es** [prob. alter. of alcatras (water bird), fr. Pg or Sp alcatraz pelican] **1** : any of various large webfooted seabirds (family Diomedeidae) that are related to the petrels and include the largest seabirds **2 a** : something that causes persistent deep concern or anxiety **b** : something that makes accomplishment particularly difficult

albatross

al·be·do \al-'bēd-(,)ō\ n, pl -**dos** [LL, whiteness, fr. L albus] : reflective power; specif : the fraction of incident light or electromagnetic radiation that is reflected by a surface or body (as the moon or a cloud)

al·be·it \ól-'bē-ət, al-\ conj [ME, lit., all though it be] : conceding the fact that : even though syn see THOUGH

Al·bi·gen·ses \,al-bə-'jen-,sēz\ n pl [ML, pl. of Albigensis, lit., inhabitant of Albi, fr. Albiga (Albi), France] : members of a Catharistic sect of southern France between the 11th and 13th centuries — **Al·bi·gen·sian** \-'jen-chən, -'jen(t)-sē-ən\ adj or n — **Al·bi·gen·sian·ism** \-,iz-əm\ n

al·bi·nism \'al-bə-,niz-əm, al-'bī-\ n : the condition of an albino

al·bi·no \al-'bī-(,)nō\ n, pl -**nos** [Pg, fr. Sp, fr. albo white, fr. L albus] : an organism exhibiting deficient pigmentation; esp : a human being or lower animal that is congenitally deficient in pigment and usu. has a milky or translucent skin, white or colorless hair, and eyes with pink or blue iris and deep-red pupil — **al·bin·ic** \-ˈbin-ik\ *adj*

al·bi·not·ic \ˌal-bə-ˈnät-ik\ *adj* [*albino* + *-tic* (as in *melanotic*)] **1** : of, relating to, or affected with albinism **2** : tending toward albinism

Al·bi·on \ˈal-bē-ən\ *n* [L] **1** : Great Britain **2** : England

al·bite \ˈal-ˌbīt\ *n* [Sw *albit*, fr. L *albus*] : a triclinic usu. white feldspar consisting of a sodium aluminum silicate $NaAlSi_3O_8$ — **al·bit·ic** \al-ˈbit-ik\ *adj*

al·bum \ˈal-bəm\ *n* [L, a white tablet, fr. neut. of *albus*] **1 a** : a book with blank pages used for making a collection (as of autographs, stamps, or photographs) **b** : a paperboard container for a phonograph record : JACKET **c** : one or more long-playing phonograph records or tape recordings produced as a single unit ⟨a 2-record ~⟩ **2** : a collection usu. in book form of literary selections, musical compositions, or pictures : ANTHOLOGY

al·bu·men \al-ˈbyü-mən\ *n* [L, fr. *albus*] **1** : the white of an egg — see EGG illustration **2** : ALBUMIN

al·bu·min \al-ˈbyü-mən\ *n* [ISV *albumen* + *-in*] : any of numerous simple heat-coagulable water-soluble proteins that occur in blood plasma or serum, muscle, the whites of eggs, milk, and other animal substances and in many plant tissues and fluids

1**al·bu·min·oid** \-mə-ˌnȯid\ *adj* : resembling albumin : PROTEIN

2**albuminoid** *n* **1** : PROTEIN **2** : SCLEROPROTEIN

al·bu·min·ous \al-ˈbyü-mə-nəs\ *adj* : relating to, containing, or having the properties of albumen or albumin

al·bu·min·uria \(ˌ)al-ˌbyü-mə-ˈn(y)u̇r-ē-ə\ *n* [NL] : the presence of albumin in the urine often symptomatic of kidney disease — **al·bu·min·uric** \-ˈn(y)u̇(ə)r-ik\ *adj*

al·bu·mose \ˈal-byə-ˌmōs, -ˌmōz\ *n* [F, fr. *albumine* albumen + *-ose*] : any of various products of enzymatic protein hydrolysis

al·bur·num \al-ˈbər-nəm\ *n* [L, fr. *albus* white] : SAPWOOD

alc *abbr* alcohol

al·ca·ic \al-ˈkā-ik\ *adj, often cap* [LL *Alcaicus* of Alcaeus, fr. Gk *Alkaïkos*, fr. *Alkaios* Alcaeus, *fl ab* 600 B.C. Gk poet] : relating to or written in a verse or strophe marked by complicated variation of a dominant iambic pattern — **alcaic** *n*

al·cai·de *or* **al·cay·de** \al-ˈkīd-ē\ *n* [Sp *alcaide*, fr. Ar *al-qāʼid* the captain] : a commander of a castle or fortress (as among Spaniards, Portuguese, or Moors)

al·cal·de \al-ˈkäl-dē\ *n* [Sp, fr. Ar *al-qāḍī* the judge] : the chief administrative and judicial officer of a Spanish town

al·ca·zar \al-ˈkäz-ər, -ˈkaz-\ *n* [Sp *alcázar*, fr. Ar *al-qaṣr* the castle] : a Spanish fortress or palace

Al·ces·tis \al-ˈses-təs\ *n* [L, fr. Gk *Alkēstis*] : the wife of Admetus who dies for her husband and is restored to him by Hercules

al·che·mist \ˈal-kə-məst\ *n* : one who studies or practices alchemy — **al·che·mis·tic** \ˌal-kə-ˈmis-tik\ *or* **al·che·mis·ti·cal** \-ti-kəl\ *adj*

al·che·mize \ˈal-kə-ˌmīz\ *vt* **-mized; -miz·ing** : to change by alchemy : TRANSMUTE

al·che·my \ˈal-kə-mē\ *n* [ME *alkamie, alquemie*, fr. MF or ML; MF *alquemie*, fr. ML *alchymia*, fr. Ar *al-kīmiyā'*, fr. *al* the + *kīmiyā'* alchemy, fr. LGk *chēmeia*] **1** : a medieval chemical science and speculative philosophy aiming to achieve the transmutation of the base metals into gold, the discovery of a universal cure for disease, and the discovery of a means of indefinitely prolonging life **2** : a power or process of transforming something common into something precious — **al·chem·ic** \al-ˈkem-ik\ *or* **al·chem·i·cal** \-i-kəl\ *adj* — **al·chem·i·cal·ly** \-i-k(ə-)lē\ *adv*

Alc·me·ne \alk-ˈmē-nē\ *n* [Gk *Alkmēnē*] : the mother of Hercules by Zeus in the form of her husband Amphitryon

al·co·hol \ˈal-kə-ˌhȯl\ *n* [NL, fr. ML, powdered antimony, fr. OSp, fr. Ar *al-kuḥul* the powdered antimony] **1** : a colorless volatile flammable liquid C_2H_6O that is the intoxicating agent in fermented and distilled liquors and is used also as a solvent — called also *ethyl alcohol* **2** : any of various compounds that are analogous to ethyl alcohol in constitution and that are hydroxyl derivatives of hydrocarbons **3** : liquor (as whiskey) containing alcohol

1**al·co·hol·ic** \ˌal-kə-ˈhȯl-ik, -ˈhäl-\ *adj* **1 a** : of, relating to, or caused by alcohol **b** : containing alcohol **2** : affected with alcoholism — **al·co·hol·i·cal·ly** \-i-k(ə-)lē\ *adv*

2**alcoholic** *n* : one affected with alcoholism

al·co·hol·ism \ˈal-kə-ˌhȯ-ˌliz-əm\ *n* **1** : continued excessive or compulsive use of alcoholic drinks **2** : poisoning by alcohol; *esp* : a complex chronic psychological and nutritional disorder associated with excessive and usu. compulsive drinking

al·co·hol·ize \-ˌlīz\ *vt* **-ized; -iz·ing** : to treat or saturate with alcohol

al·co·hol·om·e·ter \ˌal-kə-ˌhȯ-ˈläm-ət-ər\ *n* [F *alcoolomètre*, fr. *alcool* alcohol + *-o-* + *-mètre* -meter] : a device for determining the alcoholic strength of liquids — **al·co·hol·om·e·try** \-ˈläm-ə-trē\ *n*

Al·co·ran \ˌal-kə-ˈran\ *n* [ME, fr. MF or ML; MF & ML, fr. Ar *al-qur'ān*, lit., the reading] *archaic* : KORAN

al·cove \ˈal-ˌkōv\ *n* [F *alcôve*, fr. Sp *alcoba*, fr. Ar *al-qubbah* the arch] **1 a** : a small recessed section of a room : NOOK **b** : an arched opening (as in a wall) : NICHE **2** : SUMMERHOUSE — **al·coved** \-ˌkōvd\ *adj*

Al·cy·o·ne \al-ˈsī-ə-(ˌ)nē\ *n* [L, fr. Gk *Alkyonē*] : the brightest star in the Pleiades

ald *abbr* alderman

Al·deb·a·ran \al-ˈdeb-ə-rən\ *n* [Ar *al-dabarān*, lit., the follower] : a red star of the first magnitude that is seen in the eye of Taurus and is the brightest star in the Hyades

al·de·hyde \ˈal-də-ˌhīd\ *n* [G *aldehyd*, fr. NL *al. dehyd.*, abbr. of *alcohol dehydrogenatum* dehydrogenated alcohol] : ACETALDEHYDE; *broadly* : any of various highly reactive compounds typified by acetaldehyde and characterized by the group CHO — **al·de·hy·dic** \ˌal-də-ˈhīd-ik\ *adj*

al·der \ˈȯl-dər\ *n* [ME, fr. OE *alor*; akin to OHG *elira* alder, L *alnus*] : any of a genus (*Alnus*) of toothed-leaved trees or shrubs of the birch family growing in moist ground and having wood used by turners and bark used in dyeing and tanning

al·der·man \ˈȯl-dər-mən\ *n* [ME, fr. OE *ealdorman*, fr. *ealdor* parent (fr. *eald* old) + *man* — more at OLD] **1** : a person governing a kingdom, district, or shire as viceroy for an Anglo-Saxon king **2** : a magistrate ranking next below the mayor in an English or Irish city or borough **3** : a member of a city legislative body — **al·der·man·ic** \ˌȯl-dər-ˈman-ik\ *adj*

al·dol \ˈal-ˌdȯl, -ˌdōl\ *n* [ISV *aldehyde* + *-ol*] : a colorless beta-hydroxy aldehyde $C_4H_8O_2$ used esp. in organic synthesis; *broadly* : any of various similar aldehydes — **al·dol·iza·tion** \ˌal-ˌdȯ-lə-ˈzā-shən, -ˌdō-\ *n*

al·dol·ase \ˈal-də-ˌlās, -ˌlāz\ *n* [*aldol* + *-ase*] : a crystalline enzyme that occurs widely in living systems and catalyzes reversibly the cleavage of a fructose ester into triose sugars

al·dose \ˈal-ˌdōs, -ˌdōz\ *n* [ISV *ald*ehyde + *-ose*] : a sugar containing one aldehyde group per molecule

al·do·ste·rone \al-ˈdäs-tə-ˌrōn, ˌal-dō-stə-ˈrōn\ *n* [*ald*ehyde + *-o-* + *ster*ol + *-one*] : a steroid hormone $C_{13}H_{16}N_2O$ of the adrenal cortex that functions in the regulation of the salt and water balance of the body

al·do·ste·ron·ism \-ˌrō-ˌniz-əm, -ˈrō-\ *n* : a condition that is characterized by excessive production and excretion of aldosterone and typically by loss of body potassium, muscular weakness, and elevated blood pressure

al·drin \ˈȯl-drən, ˈal-\ *n* [Kurt *Alder* †1958 G chemist + E *-in*] : an exceedingly poisonous cyclodiene insecticide $C_{12}H_6Cl_6$

ale \ˈā(ə)l\ *n* [ME, fr. OE *ealu*; akin to ON *öl* ale, L *alumen* alum] **1** : a fermented liquor brewed esp. by rapid fermentation from an infusion of malt with the addition of hops **2** : an English country festival at which ale is the principal beverage

ale·a·tor·ic \ˌā-lē-ə-ˈtȯr-ik, -ˈtär-\ *adj* [L *aleatorius* of a gambler] : improvisatory or random in character ⟨~ music⟩

ale·a·to·ry \ˈā-lē-ə-ˌtȯr-ē, -ˌtȯr-\ *adj* [L *aleatorius* of a gambler, fr. *aleator* gambler, fr. *alea* a dice game] **1** : depending on an uncertain event or contingency as to both profit and loss ⟨an ~ contract⟩ **2** : relating to luck and esp. to bad luck **3** : ALEATORIC

alee \ə-ˈlē\ *adv* : on or toward the lee — compare AWEATHER

ale·house \ˈā(ə)l-ˌhau̇s\ *n* : a place where ale is sold to be drunk on the premises

Al·e·man·nic \ˌal-ə-ˈman-ik\ *n* [LL *alemanni*, of Gmc origin; akin to Goth *alamans* totality of people] : the group of dialects of German spoken in Alsace, Switzerland, and southwestern Germany

alem·bic \ə-ˈlem-bik\ *n* [ME, fr. MF & ML; MF *alambic* & ML *alembicum*, fr. Ar *al-anbīq*, fr. *al* the + *anbīq* still, fr. LGk *ambik-, ambix* alembic, fr. Gk, cap of a still] **1** : an apparatus formerly used in distillation **2** : something that refines or transmutes as if by distillation ⟨philosophy . . . filtered through the ~ of Plato's mind — B. T. Shropshire⟩

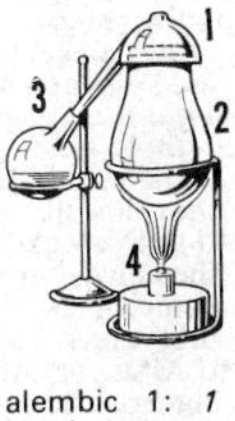

alembic 1: *1* head, *2* cucurbit, *3* receiver, *4* lamp

aleph \ˈäl-ˌef, -əf\ *n* [Heb *āleph*, prob. fr. *eleph* ox] : the 1st letter of the Hebrew alphabet — see ALPHABET table

aleph–null \-ˈnəl\ *n* : the cardinal number of the set of all integers which is the smallest transfinite cardinal number

1**alert** \ə-ˈlərt\ *adj* [It *all' erta*, lit., on the ascent] **1 a** : watchful and prompt to meet danger or emergency **b** : quick to perceive and act **2** : ACTIVE, BRISK ***syn* 1** see WATCHFUL ***ant*** supine **2** see INTELLIGENT — **alert·ly** *adv* — **alert·ness** *n*

2**alert** *n* **1** : an alarm or other signal of danger **2** : the state of readiness of those warned by an alert **3** : the period during which an alert is in effect — **on the alert** : on the lookout esp. for danger or opportunity

3**alert** *vt* : to call to a state of readiness : WARN

-a·les \ˈā-(ˌ)lēz\ *n pl suffix* [NL, fr. L, pl. of *-alis* -al] : plants consisting of or related to — in the names of taxonomic orders

al·eu·rone \ˈal-yə-ˌrōn\ *n* [G *aleuron*, fr. Gk, flour; akin to Arm *ałam* I grind] : protein matter in the form of minute granules or grains occurring in seeds in endosperm or in a special peripheral layer — **al·eu·ron·ic** \ˌal-yə-ˈrän-ik\ *adj*

Aleut \ə-ˈlüt\ *n* [Russ] **1** : a member of a people of the Aleutian and Shumagin islands and the western part of Alaska peninsula **2** : the language of the Aleuts

al·e·vin \ˈal-ə-vən\ *n* [F, fr. OF, fr. *alever* to lift up, rear (offspring), fr. L *allevare*, fr. *ad-* + *levare* to raise — more at LEVER] : a young fish; *esp* : the newly hatched salmon when still attached to the yolk sac

1**ale·wife** \ˈā(ə)l-ˌwīf\ *n* : a woman who keeps an alehouse

2**alewife** *n* : a food fish (*Alosa pseudoharengus*) of the herring family (Clupeidae) very abundant on the Atlantic coast; *also* : any of several related fishes (as the menhaden)

al·ex·an·der \ˌal-ig-ˈzan-dər, ˌel-\ *n, often cap* : an iced cocktail made from crème de cacao, sweet cream, and gin or brandy

Al·ex·an·dri·an \ˌal-ig-ˈzan-drē-ən, ˌel-\ *adj* **1** : of or relating to Alexander the Great **2** : HELLENISTIC

al·ex·an·drine \-ˈzan-drən\ *n, often cap* [MF *alexandrin*, adj., fr. *Alexandre* Alexander the Great †323 B.C. king of Macedonia; fr. its use in a poem on Alexander] : a line of verse of 12 syllables consisting regularly of 6 iambics with a caesura after the 3d iambic — **alexandrine** *adj*

al·ex·an·drite \-ˈzan-ˌdrīt\ *n* [G *alexandrit*, fr. *Alexander I* †1825 Russ emperor] : a grass-green chrysoberyl that shows a red color by transmitted or artificial light

ə abut ᵊ kitten ər further a back ā bake ä cot, cart
au̇ out ch chin e less ē easy g gift i trip ī life
j joke ŋ sing ō flow ȯ flaw ȯi coin th thin th this
ü loot u̇ foot y yet yü few yu̇ furious zh vision

alex·ia \ə-ˈlek-sē-ə\ *n* [NL, fr. *a-* + Gk *lexis* speech, fr. *legein* to speak — more at LEGEND] : aphasia characterized by loss of ability to read

Al·fa \ˈal-fə\ — a communications code word for the letter *a*

al·fal·fa \al-ˈfal-fə\ *n* [Sp, modif. of Ar dial. *al-fasfaṣah* the alfalfa] : a deep-rooted European leguminous plant (*Medicago sativa*) widely grown for hay and forage

al·fil·a·ria \(ˌ)al-ˌfil-ə-ˈrē-ə\ *n* [AmerSp *alfilerillo*, fr. Sp, dim. of *alfiler* pin, modif. of Ar *al-khilāl* the thorn] : a European weed (*Erodium cicutarium*) of the geranium family grown for forage in western America

al·for·ja \al-ˈfȯr-(ˌ)hä\ *n* [Sp, fr. Ar *al-khurj*] *West* : SADDLEBAG

al·fres·co \al-ˈfres-(ˌ)kō\ *adj or adv* [It] : taking place in the open air ⟨an ~ lunch⟩

alg *abbr* algebra

alg- *or* **algo-** *comb form* [NL, fr. Gk *alg-*, fr. *algos*] : pain ⟨*algophobia*⟩

al·ga \ˈal-gə\ *n, pl* **al·gae** \ˈal-(ˌ)jē\ *also* **algas** [L, seaweed] : any of a group (Algae) of chiefly aquatic nonvascular plants (as seaweeds, pond scums, and stoneworts) with chlorophyll often masked by a brown or red pigment — **al·gal** \-gəl\ *adj* — **al·goid** \-ˌgȯid\ *adj*

al·gar·ro·ba \ˌal-gə-ˈrō-bə\ *n* [Sp, fr. Ar *al-kharrūbah* the carob] **1** : CAROB **2** [MexSp, fr. Sp] : MESQUITE; *also* : its pods

al·ge·bra \ˈal-jə-brə\ *n* [ML, fr. Ar *al-jabr*, lit., the reduction] **1 a** : a generalization of arithmetic in which letters representing numbers are combined according to the rules of arithmetic **b** : a treatise on algebra **2** : LINEAR ALGEBRA 2 **3** : a logical or set calculus — **al·ge·bra·ist** \-ˌbrā-əst\ *n*

al·ge·bra·ic \ˌal-jə-ˈbrā-ik\ *adj* **1** : relating to, involving, or according to the laws of algebra **2** : involving only a finite number of repetitions of addition, subtraction, multiplication, division, extraction of roots, and raising to powers ⟨~ equation⟩ — compare TRANSCENDENTAL — **al·ge·bra·i·cal·ly** \-ˈbrā-ə-k(ə-)lē\ *adv*

algebraic number *n* : a root of an algebraic equation with rational coefficients

Al·ger·ish \ˈal-jə-rish\ *adj* : of, relating to, or characteristic of the works of Horatio Alger in which success is achieved through self-reliance and hard work

-al·gia \ˈal-j(ē-)ə\ *n comb form* [Gk, fr. *algos*] : pain ⟨neur*algia*⟩

al·gi·cide \ˈal-jə-ˌsīd\ *n* [*alga* + *-i-* + *-cide*] : an agent used to kill algae — **al·gi·cid·al** \ˌal-jə-ˈsīd-ᵊl\ *adj*

al·gid \ˈal-jəd\ *adj* [L *algidus*, fr. *algēre* to feel cold; akin to Icel *elgur* slush] : CHILL, COLD — **al·gid·i·ty** \al-ˈjid-ət-ē\ *n*

al·gin \ˈal-jən\ *n* : any of various colloidal substances from marine brown algae: as **a** : ALGINIC ACID **b** : a soluble salt of alginic acid used esp. as a stabilizer or emulsifier

al·gi·nate \ˈal-jə-ˌnāt\ *n* : a salt of alginic acid

al·gin·ic acid \(ˌ)al-ˌjin-ik-\ *n* [ISV *algin* + *-ic*] : an insoluble colloidal acid $(C_6H_8O_6)_n$ that in the form of its salts is a constituent of the cell walls of brown algae

Al·gol \ˈal-ˌgäl, -ˌgȯl\ *n* [Ar *al-ghūl*, lit., the ghoul] : a binary star in the constellation Perseus whose larger component revolves about and eclipses the smaller brighter star causing periodic variation in brightness

AL·GOL *or* **Al·gol** \ˈal-ˌgäl, -ˌgȯl\ *n* [*algo*rithmic *l*anguage] : an algebraic and logical language for programming a computer

al·go·lag·nia \ˌal-gō-ˈlag-nē-ə\ *n* [NL, fr. *alg-* + Gk *lagneia* lust] : pleasure in inflicting or suffering pain — **al·go·lag·nic** \-nik\ *adj* — **al·go·lag·nist** \-nəst\ *n*

al·gol·o·gy \al-ˈgäl-ə-jē\ *n* : the study or science of algae — **al·go·log·i·cal** \ˌal-gə-ˈläj-i-kəl\ *adj* — **al·go·log·i·cal·ly** \-k(ə-)lē\ *adv* — **al·gol·o·gist** \al-ˈgäl-ə-jəst\ *n*

al·gom·e·ter \al-ˈgäm-ət-ər\ *n* : an instrument for measuring the smallest pressure that induces pain — **al·go·met·ric** \ˌal-gə-ˈme-trik\ *or* **al·go·met·ri·cal** \-tri-kəl\ *adj* — **al·gom·e·try** \al-ˈgäm-ə-trē\ *n*

Al·gon·ki·an \al-ˈgäŋ-kē-ən\ *adj* : PROTEROZOIC

Al·gon·qui·an \al-ˈgän-kwē-ən, -ˈgäŋ-\ *or* **Al·gon·quin** \-kwən\ *or* **Al·gon·ki·an** \-ˈgäŋ-kē-ən\ *or* **Al·gon·kin** \-ˈgäŋ-kən\ *n* [CanF *Algonquin*] **1** : an Amerindian people of the Ottawa river valley **2** *usu Algonquin* : a dialect of Ojibwa **3** *usu Algonquian* : a stock of Indian languages spoken from Labrador to Carolina and westward to the Great Plains **4** *usu Algonquian* : a member of the Amerindian peoples speaking Algonquian languages **5** *Algonkian* : the Algonkian era or system or group of systems

al·go·pho·bia \ˌal-gə-ˈfō-bē-ə\ *n* [NL] : morbid fear of pain

al·go·rithm \ˈal-gə-ˌrith-əm\ *n* [alter. of ME *algorisme*, fr. OF & ML; OF, fr. ML *algorismus*, fr. Ar *al-khuwārizmi*, *fr. al-Khuwārizmi fl* 825 A.D. Arab mathematician] : a procedure for solving a mathematical problem (as of finding the greatest common divisor) in a finite number of steps that frequently involves repetition of an operation; *broadly* : a step-by-step procedure for solving a problem or accomplishing some end — **al·go·rith·mic** \ˌal-gə-ˈrith-mik\ *adj*

Al·ham·bra \al-ˈham-brə\ *n* [Sp, fr. Ar *al-ḥamrā'* the red house] : the palace of the Moorish kings at Granada, Spain

Al·ham·bra·ic \ˌal-ˌham-ˈbrā-ik\ *adj* : ALHAMBRESQUE

Al·ham·bresque \ˌal-ˌham-ˈbresk\ *adj* : made or decorated after the fanciful style of the ornamentation in the Alhambra

ali- *comb form* [L, fr. *ala* — more at AISLE] : wing ⟨*aliform*⟩

1alias \ˈā-lē-əs, ˈāl-yəs\ *adv* [L, otherwise, fr. *alius* other — more at ELSE] : otherwise called : otherwise known as

2alias *n* : an assumed name

Ali Ba·ba \ˌal-ē-ˈbäb-ə\ *n* : a woodcutter in the *Arabian Nights' Entertainments* who enters the cave of the Forty Thieves by using the password *Sesame*

1al·i·bi \ˈal-ə-ˌbī\ *n* [L, elsewhere, fr. *alius*] **1** : the plea of having been at the time of the commission of an act elsewhere than at the place of commission; *also* : the fact or state of having been elsewhere at the time **2** : a plausible excuse usu. intended to avert blame or punishment (as for failure or negligence) ***syn*** see APOLOGY

2alibi *vb* **-bied; -bi·ing** *vi* : to offer an excuse ~ *vt* : to exonerate by an alibi

ali·cy·clic \ˌal-ə-ˈsī-klik, -ˈsik-lik\ *adj* [ISV *aliphatic* + *cyclic*] : combining the properties of aliphatic and cyclic compounds

al·i·dade \ˈal-ə-ˌdād\ *n* [ME *allidatha*, fr. ML *alhidada*, fr. Ar *al-'idadah* the revolving radius of a circle] : a rule equipped with simple or telescopic sights and used for determination of direction: as **a** : a part of an astrolabe **b** : a part of a surveying instrument consisting of the telescope and its attachments

1alien \ˈā-lē-ən, ˈāl-yən\ *adj* [ME, fr. OF, fr. L *alienus*, fr. *alius*] **1 a** : belonging or relating to another person, place, or thing : STRANGE **b** : relating, belonging, or owing allegiance to another country or government : FOREIGN **2** : differing in nature or character typically to the point of incompatibility ***syn*** see EXTRINSIC ***ant*** akin, assimilable — **alienly** *adv* — **alien·ness** \-lē-ən-nəs, -yən-nəs\ *n*

2alien *n* **1** : a person of another family, race, or nation **2** : a foreign-born resident who has not been naturalized and is still a subject or citizen of a foreign country; *broadly* : a foreign-born citizen

3alien *vt* **1** : ALIENATE, ESTRANGE **2** : to make over (as property)

alien·able \ˈāl-yə-nə-bəl, ˈā-lē-ə-nə-\ *adj* : transferable to the ownership of another — **alien·abil·i·ty** \ˌāl-yə-nə-ˈbil-ət-ē, ˌā-lē-ə-nə-\ *n*

alien·age \ˈāl-yə-nij, ˈā-lē-ə-nij\ *n* : the status of an alien

alien·ate \ˈā-lē-ə-ˌnāt, ˈāl-yə-\ *vt* **-at·ed; -at·ing** **1** : to convey or transfer (as property or a right) usu. by a specific act rather than the due course of law **2** : to make unfriendly, hostile, or indifferent where attachment formerly existed **3** : to cause to be withdrawn or diverted ***syn*** **1** see TRANSFER **2** see ESTRANGE ***ant*** unite, reunite — **alien·ator** \-ˌnāt-ər\ *n*

alien·ation \ˌā-lē-ə-ˈnā-shən, ˌāl-yə-\ *n* **1** : a conveyance of property to another **2** : a withdrawing or separation of a person or his affections from an object or position of former attachment : ISOLATION, EXILE ⟨~ . . . from the values of one's society and family — S. L. Halleck⟩

alien·ee \-ˈnē\ *n* : one to whom property is transferred

alien·ism \ˈā-lē-ə-ˌniz-əm, ˈāl-yə-\ *n* : ALIENAGE

alien·ist \-nəst\ *n* [F *aliéniste*, fr. *aliéné* insane, fr. L *alienatus*, pp. of *alienare* to estrange, fr. *alienus*] : one that treats diseases of the mind; *esp* : a specialist in legal aspects of psychiatry

alien·or \ˌā-lē-ə-ˈnȯ(ə)r, ˌāl-yə-\ *n* : one who transfers property to another

ali·form \ˈā-lə-ˌfȯrm, ˈal-ə-\ *adj* : having winglike extensions : wing-shaped ⟨~ parenchyma of wood⟩

1alight \ə-ˈlīt\ *vi* **alight·ed** *also* **alit** \ə-ˈlit\; **alight·ing** [ME *alighten*, fr. OE *ālīhtan*, fr. *ā-* (perfective prefix) + *līhtan* to alight — more at ABIDE, LIGHT] **1** : to come down from something: as **a** : DISMOUNT **b** : DEPLANE **2** : to descend from the air and settle : LAND **3** *archaic* : to come by chance — **alight·ment** *n*

2alight *adj* **1** *chiefly Brit* : being on fire **2** : lighted up : ILLUMINATED

align *also* **aline** \ə-ˈlīn\ *vb* [F *aligner*, fr. OF, fr. *a-* (fr. L *ad-*) + *ligne* line, fr. L *linea*] *vt* **1** : to bring into line or alignment **2** : to array on the side of or against a party or cause ~ *vi* **1** : to get or fall into line **2** : to be in or come into precise adjustment or correct relative position ***syn*** see LINE — **align·er** *n*

align·ment *also* **aline·ment** \ə-ˈlīn-mənt\ *n* **1** : the act of aligning or state of being aligned; *esp* : the proper positioning or state of adjustment of parts (as of a mechanical or electronic device) in relation to each other **2 a** : a forming in line **b** : the line thus formed **3** : the ground plan (as of a railroad or fieldwork) in distinction from the profile **4** : an arrangement of groups or forces in relation to one another ⟨sectional ~s within the political party⟩

1alike \ə-ˈlīk\ *adj* [ME *ilik* (alter. of *ilich*) & *alik*, alter. of OE *onlīc*, fr. *on* + *līc* body — more at LIKE] : exhibiting close resemblance without being identical ⟨~ in their beliefs⟩ ***syn*** see SIMILAR ***ant*** different — **alike·ness** *n*

2alike *adv* : in the same manner, form, or degree : EQUALLY ⟨was denounced by teachers and students ~⟩

1al·i·ment \ˈal-ə-mənt\ *n* [ME, fr. L *alimentum*, fr. *alere* to nourish — more at OLD] : FOOD, NUTRIMENT; *also* : SUSTENANCE

2al·i·ment \-ˌment\ *vt* : to give aliment to : NOURISH, SUSTAIN

al·i·men·ta·ry \ˌal-ə-ˈment-ə-rē, -ˈmen-trē\ *adj* **1** : of or relating to nourishment or nutrition **2** : furnishing sustenance or maintenance

alimentary canal *n* : the tubular passage that extends from mouth to anus and functions in digestion and absorption of food and elimination of residual waste

al·i·men·ta·tion \ˌal-ə-mən-ˈtā-shən, -ˌmen-\ *n* : the act or process of affording nutriment; *also* : the state or mode of being nourished — **al·i·men·ta·tive** \ˌal-ə-ˈment-ət-iv\ *adj*

al·i·mo·ny \ˈal-ə-ˌmō-nē\ *n, pl* **-nies** [L *alimonia* sustenance, fr. *alere*] **1** : the means of living : MAINTENANCE **2** : an allowance made to one spouse by the other for support pending or after legal separation or divorce

A-line \ˈā-ˌlīn\ *adj* : having a flared bottom and a close-fitting top — used of a garment ⟨an ~ skirt⟩

Al·i·oth \ˈal-ē-ˌäth, -ˌōth\ *n* [Ar *alyat* fat tail of a sheep] : a star of the second magnitude in the handle of the Big Dipper

al·i·phat·ic \ˌal-ə-ˈfat-ik\ *adj* [ISV, fr. Gk *aleiphat-*, *aleiphar* oil, fr. *aleiphein* to smear; akin to Gk *lipos* fat — more at LEAVE] : of, relating to, or derived from fat; *specif* : belonging to a group of organic compounds having an open-chain structure and consisting of the paraffin, olefin, and acetylene hydrocarbons and their derivatives

al·i·quot \ˈal-ə-ˌkwät, -kwət\ *adj* [ML *aliquotus*, fr. L *aliquot* some, several, fr. *alius* other + *quot* how many — more at ELSE, QUOTA] **1** : contained an exact number of times in something else — used of a divisor or part ⟨5 is an ~ part of 15⟩ ⟨an ~ portion of a solution⟩ **2** : FRACTIONAL ⟨an ~ part of invested capital⟩ — **aliquot** *n*

alive \ə-ˈlīv\ *adj* [ME, fr. OE *on līfe*, fr. *on* + *līf* life] **1** : having life : not dead or inanimate **2** : still in existence, force, or operation : ACTIVE ⟨kept hope ~⟩ **3** : knowing or realizing the existence of : SENSITIVE ⟨~ to the danger⟩ **4** : marked by alertness, activity, or briskness **5** : marked by much life, animation, or activity : SWARMING **6** — used as an intensive following the noun ⟨the proudest boy ~⟩ ***syn*** **1** see LIVING ***ant*** dead, defunct **2** see AWARE ***ant*** blind (*to*) — **alive·ness** *n*

ali·yah \ä-ˈlē-(ˌ)yä\ *n* [NHeb *ʽaliyāh*, fr. Heb, ascent] **1** : the action of going up or of being called to the reading desk of the synagogue to read from the Scriptures **2** : the immigration of Jews to Israel

aliz·a·rin \ə-ˈliz-ə-rən\ *n* [prob. fr. F *alizarine*] **1** : an orange or red crystalline compound $C_{14}H_8O_4$ formerly prepared from madder and now made synthetically and used esp. to dye Turkey reds and in making red pigments **2** : any of various acid, mordant, and solvent dyes derived like alizarin proper from anthraquinone

alk *abbr* alkaline

al·ka·hest \ˈal-kə-ˌhest\ *n* [NL *alchahest*] : the universal solvent believed by the alchemists to exist — **al·ka·hes·tic** \ˌal-kə-ˈhes-tik\ *adj*

al·ka·les·cence \ˌal-kə-ˈles-ᵊn(t)s\ *n* : the property or degree of being alkaline — **al·ka·les·cent** \-ᵊnt\ *adj*

al·ka·li \ˈal-kə-ˌlī\ *n, pl* **-lies** *or* **-lis** [ME, fr. ML, fr. Ar *al-qili* the ashes of the plant saltwort] **1** : a soluble salt obtained from the ashes of plants and consisting largely of potassium or sodium carbonate; *broadly* : a substance (as a hydroxide or carbonate of an alkali metal) having marked basic properties — compare BASE 7 **2** : ALKALI METAL **3** : a soluble salt or a mixture of soluble salts present in some soils of arid regions in quantity detrimental to agriculture

al·ka·li·fy \al-ˈkal-ə-ˌfī, ˈal-kə-lə-\ *vb* **-fied; -fy·ing** *vt* : to convert or change into an alkali : make alkaline ~ *vi* : to become alkaline

alkali metal *n* : any of the univalent mostly basic metals of group I of the periodic table comprising lithium, sodium, potassium, rubidium, cesium, and francium

al·ka·lim·e·ter \ˌal-kə-ˈlim-ət-ər\ *n* [F *alcalimètre*, fr. *alcali* alkali + *-mètre* -meter] : an apparatus for measuring the strength or the amount of alkali in a mixture or solution — **al·ka·lim·e·try** \-ˈlim-ə-trē\ *n*

al·ka·line \ˈal-kə-lən, -ˌlīn\ *adj* : of, relating to, or having the properties of an alkali; *esp* : having a pH of more than 7 — **al·ka·lin·i·ty** \ˌal-kə-ˈlin-ət-ē\ *n*

alkaline earth *n* **1** : an oxide of any of several bivalent strongly basic metals comprising calcium, strontium, and barium and sometimes also magnesium, radium, or less often beryllium **2** : ALKALINE-EARTH METAL

alkaline–earth metal *n* : any of the metals whose oxides are the alkaline earths

alkaline phosphatase *n* : a phosphatase (as the phosphomonoesterase from blood plasma or milk) active in alkaline medium

al·ka·lin·ize \ˈal-kə-lə-ˌnīz\ *vt* **-ized; -iz·ing** : to make alkaline — **al·ka·lin·iza·tion** \ˌal-kə-ˌlin-ə-ˈzā-shən, -lə-nə-\ *n*

al·ka·loid \ˈal-kə-ˌlȯid\ *n* : any of numerous usu. colorless, complex, and bitter organic bases (as morphine or codeine) containing nitrogen and usu. oxygen that occur esp. in seed plants — **al·ka·loi·dal** \ˌal-kə-ˈlȯid-ᵊl\ *adj*

al·ka·lo·sis \ˌal-kə-ˈlō-səs\ *n* : a condition of increased alkalinity of the blood and tissues

al·ka·net \ˈal-kə-ˌnet\ *n* [ME, fr. OSp *alcaneta*, dim. of *alcana* henna shrub, fr. ML *alchanna*, fr. Ar *al-ḥinnāʼ* the henna] **1 a** : a European plant (*Alkanna tinctoria*) of the borage family; *also* : its root **b** : a red dyestuff prepared from the root **2** : BUGLOSS

alk·oxy \ˈal-ˌkäk-sē\ *adj* [ISV *alkyl* + *oxygen*] : of, relating to, or containing a univalent radical composed of an alkyl group united with oxygen

alky *abbr* alkalinity

al·kyd \ˈal-kəd\ *n* [blend of *alkyl* and *acid*] : any of numerous thermoplastic or thermosetting synthetic resins made by heating polyhydroxy alcohols with polybasic acids or their anhydrides and used esp. for protective coatings

al·kyl \ˈal-kəl\ *n* [prob. fr. G, fr. *alkohol* alcohol, fr. ML *alcohol*] **1 a** : a univalent aliphatic radical C_nH_{2n+1} (as methyl) **b** : any univalent aliphatic, aromatic-aliphatic, or alicyclic hydrocarbon radical **2** : a compound of alkyl radicals with a metal — **al·kyl·ic** \al-ˈkil-ik\ *adj*

al·kyl·ate \ˈal-kə-ˌlāt\ *vt* **-at·ed; -at·ing** : to introduce one or more alkyl groups into (a compound)

al·kyl·ation \ˌal-kə-ˈlā-shən\ *n* : the act or process of alkylating esp. for producing high-octane fuel

[1]all \ˈȯl\ *adj* [ME *all, al*, fr. OE *eall*; akin to OHG *al* all] **1 a** : the whole amount or quantity of ⟨sat up ~ night⟩ **b** : as much as possible ⟨spoke in ~ seriousness⟩ **2 a** : every member or individual component of ⟨~ men will go⟩ ⟨~ five children were present⟩ **b** — used in logic as a verbalized equivalent of the universal quantifier **3** : the whole number or sum of ⟨~ the angles of a triangle are equal to two right angles⟩ **4** : EVERY ⟨~ manner of hardship⟩ **5** : any whatever ⟨beyond ~ doubt⟩ **6** : nothing but : ONLY: **a** : completely taken up with, given to, or absorbed by ⟨became ~ attention⟩ **b** : having or seeming to have (some physical feature) in conspicuous excess or prominence ⟨~ thumbs⟩ **c** : paying full attention with ⟨~ ears⟩ **7** *dial* : used up : entirely consumed — used esp. of food and drink **8** : being more than one person or thing — **all the** : as much of . . . as : as much of a . . . as ⟨*all the* home I ever had⟩

[2]all *adv* **1** : WHOLLY, ALTOGETHER ⟨sat ~ alone⟩ — often used as an intensive ⟨~ out of proportion⟩ **2** *obs* : EXCLUSIVELY, ONLY **3** *archaic* : JUST **4** : so much ⟨~ the better for it⟩ **5** : for each side : APIECE ⟨the score is two ~⟩

[3]all *pron* **1** : the whole number, quantity, or amount : TOTALITY ⟨~ that I have⟩ ⟨~ of us⟩ ⟨~ of the books⟩ **2** : EVERYBODY, EVERYTHING ⟨sacrificed ~ for love⟩ — **all in all** : on the whole : generally ⟨*all in all*, things might have been worse⟩ — **at all** : in any way — usu. used with a negative ⟨no good *at all*⟩

[4]all *n* : the whole of one's possessions or of what one prizes ⟨gave his ~ for the cause⟩

all- *or* **allo-** *comb form* [Gk, fr. *allos* other — more at ELSE] **1** : other : different : atypical ⟨*allo*gamous⟩ ⟨*allo*merism⟩ **2** *allo-* : isomeric form or variety of (a specified chemical compound) **3** *allo-* : being one of a group whose members together constitute a structural unit esp. of a language ⟨*allo*phone⟩

[1]al·la breve \ˌal-ə-ˈbrev, ˌäl-ə-ˈbrev-(ˌ)ā\ *adv or adj* [It, lit., according to the breve] : in duple or quadruple time with the beat represented by the half note

[2]alla breve *n* : the sign marking a piece or passage to be played alla breve; *also* : a passage so marked

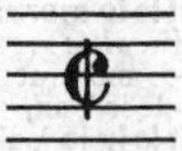

alla breve

Al·lah \ˈal-ə, ä-ˈlä\ *n* [Ar *allāh*] : the Supreme Being of the Muslims

[1]all–Amer·i·can \ˌȯ-lə-ˈmer-ə-kən\ *adj* **1** : composed wholly of American elements **2** : representative of the ideals of the U.S. ⟨an ~ boy⟩ **3 a** : selected (as by a poll of journalists) as one of the best in the U.S. in a particular category at a particular time ⟨an ~ quarterback⟩ **b** : made up of all-American participants ⟨an ~ basketball team⟩ **4** : of or relating to the American nations as a group

[2]all–American *n* : one (as an athlete) that is voted all-American

al·lan·to·is \ə-ˈlant-ə-wəs\ *n, pl* **al·lan·to·ides** \ˌal-ən-ˈtō-ə-ˌdēz, ˌal-ˌan-\ [NL, deriv. of Gk *allant-, allas* sausage] : a vascular fetal membrane of reptiles, birds, or mammals that is formed as a pouch from the hindgut and that in placental mammals is intimately associated with the chorion in formation of the placenta — **al·lan·to·ic** \ˌal-ən-ˈtō-ik, ˌal-ˌan-\ *adj*

al·lar·gan·do \ˌäl-är-ˈgän-(ˌ)dō\ *adj or adv* [It, widening, verbal of *allargare* to widen, fr. *al-* (fr. L *ad-*) + *largare* to widen] : becoming gradually broader with the same or greater volume — used as a direction in music

all–around \ˌȯ-lə-ˈrau̇nd\ *adj* **1** : competent in many fields ⟨an ~ man of letters⟩ **2** : having general utility **3** : considered in or encompassing all aspects : INCLUSIVE ⟨the best ~ recording of the work to date⟩ ⟨good nature and ~ competence —G. H. Soule⟩ ***syn*** see VERSATILE

al·lay \ə-ˈlā\ *vb* [ME *alayen*, fr. OE *ālecgan*, fr. *ā-* (perfective prefix) + *lecgan* to lay — more at ABIDE, LAY] *vt* **1** : to subdue or reduce in intensity or severity : ALLEVIATE ⟨wishing for a breeze to ~ the summer heat⟩ **2** : to make quiet : CALM ~ *vi, obs* : to diminish in strength : SUBSIDE ***syn*** see RELIEVE ***ant*** intensify

all but *adv* : very nearly : ALMOST ⟨he *all but* disappeared from public notice⟩

all clear *n* : a signal that a danger has passed

all–day \ˌȯl-ˌdā\ *adj* : lasting for, occupying, or appearing throughout an entire day ⟨an ~ trip⟩

al·le·ga·tion \ˌal-i-ˈgā-shən\ *n* **1** : the act of alleging **2** : a positive assertion; *specif* : a statement by a party to a legal action of what he undertakes to prove **3** : an assertion unsupported and by implication regarded as unsupportable ⟨vague ~s of misconduct⟩

al·lege \ə-ˈlej\ *vt* **al·leged; al·leg·ing** [ME *alleggen*, fr. OF *alleguer*, fr. L *allegare* to dispatch, cite, fr. *ad-* + *legare* to depute — more at LEGATE] **1** : to assert without proof or before proving ⟨the newspaper ~s the mayor's guilt⟩ **2** *archaic* : to adduce or bring forward as a source or authority **3** : to bring forward as a reason or excuse ***syn*** see ADDUCE ***ant*** contravene, traverse

al·leged \ə-ˈlejd, -ˈlej-əd\ *adj* **1** : asserted to be true or to exist : AVOWED ⟨an ~ miracle⟩ **2** : questionably true or of a specified kind : SO-CALLED ⟨bought an ~ antique vase⟩ — **al·leg·ed·ly** \-ˈlej-əd-lē\ *adv*

Al·le·ghe·ny spurge \ˌal-ə-ˌgā-nē- *also* ˌgen-ē\ *n* [*Allegheny* mts., U.S.A.] : a low herb or subshrub (*Pachysandra procumbens*) of the box family widely grown as a ground cover

al·le·giance \ə-ˈlē-jən(t)s\ *n* [ME *allegeaunce*, modif. of MF *ligeance*, fr. OF, fr. *lige* liege] **1 a** : the obligation of a feudal vassal to his liege lord **b** (1) : the fidelity owed by a subject or citizen to his sovereign or government (2) : the obligation of an alien to the government under which he resides **2** : devotion or loyalty to a person, group, or cause ***syn*** see FIDELITY ***ant*** treachery, treason

al·le·giant \-jənt\ *adj* : giving allegiance : LOYAL

al·le·gor·i·cal \ˌal-ə-ˈgȯr-i-kəl, -ˈgär-\ *adj* **1** : of, relating to, or having the characteristics of allegory **2** : having hidden spiritual meaning that transcends the literal sense of a sacred text — **al·le·gor·i·cal·ly** \-k(ə-)lē\ *adv* — **al·le·gor·i·cal·ness** \-kəl-nəs\ *n*

al·le·go·rist \ˈal-ə-ˌgōr-əst, -ˌgȯr-\ *n* : a writer of allegory

al·le·go·ri·za·tion \ˌal-ə-ˌgōr-ə-ˈzā-shən, -ˌgȯr-, -gər-\ *n* : allegorical representation or interpretation

al·le·go·rize \ˈal-ə-ˌgōr-ˌīz, -ˌgȯr-, -gər-\ *vb* **-rized; -riz·ing** *vt* **1** : to make into allegory **2** : to treat or explain as allegory ~ *vi* **1** : to give allegorical explanations **2** : to compose or use allegory — **al·le·go·riz·er** *n*

al·le·go·ry \ˈal-ə-ˌgōr-ē, -ˌgȯr-\ *n, pl* **-ries** [ME *allegorie*, fr. L *allegoria*, fr. Gk *allēgoria*, fr. *allēgorein* to speak figuratively, fr. *allos* other + *-agorein* to speak publicly, fr. *agora* assembly — more at ELSE, GREGARIOUS] **1 a** : the expression by means of symbolic fictional figures and actions of truths or generalizations about human existence **b** : an instance (as in a story or painting) of such expression **2** : a symbolic representation : EMBLEM

[1]al·le·gret·to \ˌal-ə-ˈgret-(ˌ)ō, ˌäl-\ *adv or adj* [It, fr. *allegro*] : faster than andante but not so fast as allegro — used as a direction in music

[2]allegretto *n, pl* **-tos** : a musical composition or movement in allegretto tempo

[1]al·le·gro \ə-ˈleg-(ˌ)rō, -ˈlā-(ˌ)grō\ *adv or adj* [It, merry, fr. (assumed) VL *alecrus* lively, alter. of L *alacr-, alacer* — more at ALACRITY] : in a brisk lively manner — used as a direction in music

[2]allegro *n, pl* **-gros** : a musical composition or movement in allegro tempo

ə abut	ᵊ kitten	ər further	a back	ā bake	ä cot, cart
au̇ out	ch chin	e less	ē easy	g gift	i trip
ī life	j joke	ŋ sing	ō flow	ȯ flaw	ȯi coin
th thin	t͟h this	ü loot	u̇ foot	y yet	yü few
yu̇ furious	zh vision				

al·lele \ə-ˈlē(ə)l\ *n* [G *allel,* short for *allelomorph*] **1 :** either of a pair of alternative Mendelian characters (as smooth and wrinkled seed in the pea) **2 :** one of a group of genes that occur alternatively at a given locus — **al·le·lic** \-ˈlē-lik, -ˈlel-ik\ *adj* — **al·lel·ism** \-ˈlē(ə)l-ˌiz-əm, -ˈlel-ˌiz-\ *n*

al·le·lo·morph \ə-ˈlel-ə-ˌmȯrf, -ˈlē-lə-\ *n* [Gk *allēlōn* of each other (fr. *allos . . . allos* one . . . the other, fr. *allos* other) + *morphē* form — more at ELSE] **:** ALLELE — **al·le·lo·mor·phic** \ə-ˌlel-ə-ˈmȯr-fik, -ˌlē-lə-\ *adj* — **al·le·lo·mor·phism** \ə-ˈlel-ə-ˌmȯr-ˌfiz-əm, -ˈlē-lə-\ *n*

al·le·lu·ia \ˌal-ə-ˈlü-yə\ *interj* [ME, fr. LL, fr. Gk *allēlouia,* fr. Heb *halălūyāh* praise ye Jehovah] **:** HALLELUJAH

al·le·mande \ˈal-ə-ˌman(d), -mən, -ˌmänd\ *n, often cap* [F, fr. fem. of *allemand* German] **1 a :** a 17th and 18th century court dance developed in France from a German folk dance **b :** a dance step with arms interlaced **2 :** a musical composition or movement in moderate tempo and duple or quadruple time

all–em·brac·ing \ˌȯ-lim-ˈbrā-siŋ\ *adj* **:** COMPLETE, SWEEPING ⟨an ~ charity toward his fellowmen⟩

al·ler·gen \ˈal-ər-jən\ *n* **:** a substance that induces allergy — **al·ler·gen·ic** \ˌal-ər-ˈjen-ik\ *adj*

al·ler·gic \ə-ˈlər-jik\ *adj* **1 :** of, relating to, inducing, or affected by allergy **2 :** disagreeably sensitive **:** ANTIPATHETIC ⟨~ to marriage⟩

al·ler·gist \ˈal-ər-jəst\ *n* **:** a specialist in allergy

al·ler·gy \ˈal-ər-jē\ *n, pl* **-gies** [G *allergie,* fr. *all-* + Gk *ergon* work — more at WORK] **1 :** altered bodily reactivity (as anaphylaxis) to an antigen in response to a first exposure ⟨his bee-venom ~ may render a second sting fatal⟩ **2 :** exaggerated or pathological reaction (as by sneezing, respiratory embarrassment, itching, or skin rashes) to substances, situations, or physical states that are without comparable effect on the average individual **3 :** medical practice concerned with allergies **4 :** a feeling of antipathy or repugnance

al·le·thrin \ˈal-ə-thrən\ *n* [*allyl* + *pyrethrin*] **:** a light yellow viscous oily synthetic insecticide $C_{19}H_{26}O_3$ used esp. in household aerosols

al·le·vi·ate \ə-ˈlē-vē-ˌāt\ *vt* **-at·ed; -at·ing** [LL *alleviatus,* pp. of *alleviare,* fr. L *ad-* + *levis* light — more at LIGHT] **:** RELIEVE, LESSEN: as **a :** to make (as suffering) more bearable ⟨her sympathy *alleviated* his distress⟩ **b :** to partially remove or correct ***syn*** see RELIEVE ***ant*** aggravate — **al·le·vi·a·tion** \-ˌlē-vē-ˈā-shən\ *n* — **al·le·vi·a·tor** \-ˈlē-vē-ˌāt-ər\ *n*

al·le·vi·a·tive \ə-ˈlē-vē-ˌāt-iv\ *or* **al·le·vi·a·to·ry** \-vē-ə-ˌtōr-ē, -ˌtȯr-\ *adj* **:** tending to alleviate **:** PALLIATIVE

¹al·ley \ˈal-ē\ *n, pl* **alleys** [ME, fr. MF *alee,* fr. OF, fr. *aler* to go, modif. of L *ambulare* to walk] **1 :** a garden or park walk bordered by trees or bushes **2 a** (1) **:** a grassed enclosure for bowling or skittles (2) **:** a hardwood lane for bowling; *also* **:** a room or building housing a group of such lanes **b :** the space on each side of a tennis doubles court between the sideline and the service sideline **3 :** a narrow street; *esp* **:** a thoroughfare through the middle of a block giving access to the rear of lots or buildings — **up one's alley** *also* **down one's alley :** suited to one's own tastes or abilities

²alley *n, pl* **alleys** [by shortening and alter. fr. *alabaster*] **:** a playing marble; *esp* **:** one of superior quality

al·ley·way \ˈal-ē-ˌwā\ *n* **1 :** a narrow passageway **2 :** ALLEY 3

All Fools' Day *n* **:** APRIL FOOLS' DAY

all fours *n pl* **1 a :** all four legs of a quadruped **b :** the two legs and two arms of a person when used to support the body **2** *sing in constr* **:** any of various card games in which points are scored for the high trump, low trump, jack of trumps, and game

all get–out \ˌȯl-get-ˈau̇t, -git-\ *n* **:** the utmost conceivable degree — used in comparisons to suggest something superlative ⟨is handsome as *all get-out* and has a deft way with the ladies — John McCarten⟩

all hail *interj* — used to express greeting, welcome, or acclamation

All·hal·lows \ȯl-ˈhal-(ˌ)ōz, -əz\ *n, pl* **Allhallows** [short for *All Hallows' Day*] **:** ALL SAINTS' DAY

all·heal \ˈȯl-ˌhēl\ *n* **:** any of several plants (as valerian or self-heal) used esp. in folk medicine

al·li·a·ceous \ˌal-ē-ˈā-shəs\ *adj* [L *allium*] **:** resembling garlic or onion esp. in smell or taste

al·li·ance \ə-ˈlī-ən(t)s\ *n* **1 a :** the state of being allied **:** the action of allying **b :** a bond or connection between families, states, parties, or individuals ⟨a closer ~ between government and industry⟩ **2 :** an association to further the common interests of the members; *specif* **:** a confederation of nations by formal treaty **3 :** union by relationship in qualities **:** AFFINITY **4 :** a treaty of alliance

al·lied \ə-ˈlīd, ˈal-ˌīd\ *adj* **1 :** having or being in close association **:** CONNECTED ⟨a strong personal pride ~ with the utmost probity⟩ ⟨two families ~ by marriage⟩ **2 :** joined in alliance by compact or treaty; *specif, cap* **:** of or relating to the nations united against the Central European powers in World War I or those united against the Axis powers in World War II **3 a :** related esp. by common properties or qualities ⟨heraldry and ~ subjects⟩ **b :** related genetically ***syn*** see RELATED

al·li·ga·tor \ˈal-ə-ˌgāt-ər\ *n* [Sp *el lagarto* the lizard, fr. *el* the (fr. L *ille* that) + *lagarto* lizard, fr. (assumed) VL *lacartus,* fr. L *lacertus, lacerta* — more at LARIAT, LIZARD] **1 a :** either of two crocodilians (genus *Alligator*) having broad heads not tapering to the snout and a special pocket in the upper jaw for reception of the enlarged lower fourth tooth **b :** CROCODILIAN **2 :** leather made from alligator hide

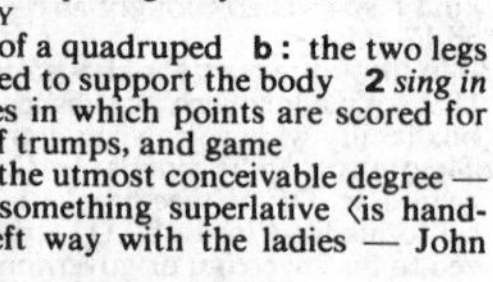

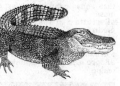

alligator 1a

alligator pear *n* **:** AVOCADO

alligator snapper *n* **:** a snapping turtle (*Macrochelys temminckii*) of the rivers of the Gulf states that may reach nearly 150 pounds in weight and 5 feet in length

all–im·por·tant \ˌȯ-lim-ˈpȯrt-ᵊnt, -ənt\ *adj* **:** of very great or greatest importance ⟨an ~ question⟩

all–in·clu·sive \ˌȯ-lin-ˈklü-siv, -ziv\ *adj* **:** including everything ⟨a broader and more nearly ~ view⟩ — **all–in·clu·sive·ness** *n*

al·lit·er·ate \ə-ˈlit-ə-ˌrāt\ *vb* **-at·ed; -at·ing** [back-formation fr. *alliteration*] *vi* **1 :** to form an alliteration **2 :** to write or speak alliteratively ~ *vt* **:** to arrange or place so as to make alliteration ⟨~ syllables in a sentence⟩

al·lit·er·a·tion \ə-ˌlit-ə-ˈrā-shən\ *n* [*ad-* + L *littera* letter] **:** the repetition of usu. initial consonant sounds in two or more neighboring words or syllables (as *w*ild and *w*oolly, *thr*eatening *thr*ongs) — called also *head rhyme, initial rhyme*

al·lit·er·a·tive \ə-ˈlit-ə-ˌrāt-iv, -rət-\ *adj* **:** of, relating to, or marked by alliteration — **al·lit·er·a·tive·ly** *adv*

al·li·um \ˈal-ē-əm\ *n* [NL, genus name, fr. L, garlic] **:** any of a large genus (*Allium*) of bulbous herbs of the lily family including the onion, garlic, chive, leek, and shallot

all–night \ˌȯl-ˌnīt\ *adj* **1 :** lasting throughout the night ⟨an ~ poker game⟩ **2 :** open throughout the night ⟨an ~ diner⟩

allo *abbr* allegro

allo- — see ALL-

al·lo·ca·ble \ˈal-ə-kə-bəl\ *adj* **1 :** capable of being allocated **2 :** assignable in accounting to a particular account or to a particular period of time

al·lo·cate \ˈal-ə-ˌkāt\ *vt* **-cat·ed; -cat·ing** [ML *allocatus,* pp. of *allocare,* fr. L *ad-* + *locare* to place, fr. *locus* place — more at STALL] **1 :** to apportion for a specific purpose or to particular persons or things **:** DISTRIBUTE ⟨~ tasks among human and automated components⟩ **2 :** to set apart or earmark **:** DESIGNATE ⟨~ a section of the building for special research purposes⟩ ***syn*** see ALLOT — **al·lo·cat·able** \-ˌkāt-ə-bəl\ *adj* — **al·lo·ca·tion** \ˌal-ə-ˈkā-shən\ *n* — **al·lo·ca·tor** \ˈal-ə-ˌkāt-ər\ *n*

al·lo·cu·tion \ˌal-ə-ˈkyü-shən\ *n* [L *allocution-, allocutio,* fr. *allocutus,* pp. of *alloqui* to speak to, fr. *ad-* + *loqui* to speak] **:** a formal speech; *esp* **:** an authoritative or hortatory address

al·log·a·mous \ə-ˈläg-ə-məs\ *adj* **:** reproducing by cross-fertilization — **al·log·a·my** \-mē\ *n*

al·lo·ge·ne·ic \ˌal-ō-jə-ˈnē-ik\ *adj* [*all-* + *-geneic* (as in *syngeneic*)] **:** sufficiently unlike genetically to interact antigenically

al·lo·graft \ˈal-ə-ˌgraft\ *n* **:** a homograft between allogeneic individuals

al·lo·graph \ˈal-ə-ˌgraf\ *n* **1 :** a letter of an alphabet in a particular shape (as A or a) **2 :** a letter or combination of letters that is one of several ways of representing one phoneme (as *pp* in *hopping* representing the phoneme *p*) — **al·lo·graph·ic** \ˌal-ə-ˈgraf-ik\ *adj*

al·lom·er·ism \ə-ˈläm-ə-ˌriz-əm\ *n* **:** variability in chemical constitution without variation in crystalline form — **al·lom·er·ous** \-rəs\ *adj*

al·lom·e·try \ə-ˈläm-ə-trē\ *n* **:** relative growth of a part in relation to an entire organism; *also* **:** the measure and study of such growth — **al·lo·me·tric** \ˌal-ə-ˈme-trik\ *adj*

¹al·lo·morph \ˈal-ə-ˌmȯrf\ *n* [ISV] **1 :** any of two or more distinct crystalline forms of the same substance **2 :** a pseudomorph that has undergone change or substitution of material — **al·lo·mor·phic** \ˌal-ə-ˈmȯr-fik\ *adj* — **al·lo·mor·phism** \ˈal-ə-ˌmȯr-ˌfiz-əm\ *n*

²allomorph *n* [*allo-* + *morph*eme] **:** one of two or more forms that a morpheme has at different points in the language ⟨the *-es* \əz\ of *dishes,* the *-s* \z\ of *dreams,* the *-s* \s\ of *traps,* the *-en* \ən\ of *oxen,* the vowel modification distinguishing *teeth* from *tooth,* and the zero suffix of *sheep* in *those sheep* are ~s of the same morpheme⟩ — **al·lo·mor·phic** \ˌal-ə-ˈmȯr-fik\ *adj* — **al·lo·mor·phism** \ˈal-ə-ˌmȯr-ˌfiz-əm\ *n*

al·longe \a-ˈlōⁿzh\ *n* [F, lit., lengthening] **:** RIDER 2a

al·lo·path \ˈal-ə-ˌpath\ *n* **:** one who practices allopathy

al·lop·a·thy \ə-ˈläp-ə-thē\ *n* [G *allopathie,* fr. *all-* + *-pathie* -pathy] **1 :** a system of medical practice that combats disease (as gonorrhea) by treatments (as by exciting nonspecific inflammation through the injection of silver nitrate) that produce effects different from those produced by the disease treated **2 :** a system of medical practice making use of all measures proved of value in treatment of disease **:** conventional medicine exclusive of homeopathy — **al·lo·path·ic** \ˌal-ə-ˈpath-ik\ *adj* — **al·lo·path·i·cal·ly** \-i-k(ə-)lē\ *adv*

al·lo·pat·ric \ˌal-ə-ˈpa-trik\ *adj* [*all-* + Gk *patra* fatherland, fr. *patēr* father — more at FATHER] **:** occurring in different areas or in isolation ⟨~ speciation⟩ — **al·lo·pat·ri·cal·ly** \-tri-k(ə-)lē\ *adv* — **al·lop·a·try** \ə-ˈläp-ə-trē\ *n*

al·lo·phane \ˈal-ə-ˌfān\ *n* [Gk *allophanēs* appearing otherwise, fr. *all-* + *phainesthai* to appear, pass. of *phainein* to show — more at FANCY] **:** an amorphous translucent mineral of various colors often occurring in incrustations or stalactite forms and consisting of a hydrous aluminum silicate

al·lo·phone \ˈal-ə-ˌfōn\ *n* [*allo-* + *phone*] **:** one of two or more variants of the same phoneme ⟨the aspirated *p* of *pin* and the nonaspirated *p* of *spin* are ~s of the phoneme *p*⟩ — **al·lo·phon·ic** \ˌal-ə-ˈfän-ik\ *adj*

al·lo·pu·ri·nol \ˌal-ō-ˈpyu̇r-ə-ˌnȯl, -ˌnōl\ *n* [*all-* + *purine* + *-ol*] **:** a drug $C_5H_4N_4O$ used to promote excretion of uric acid

all–or–none \ˌȯ-lər-ˈnən\ *adj* **:** marked either by entire or complete operation or effect or by none at all ⟨~ response of a nerve cell⟩

all–or–noth·ing \-ˈnəth-iŋ\ *adj* **1 :** ALL-OR-NONE **2 a :** accepting no less than everything ⟨he's an ~ perfectionist⟩ **b :** risking everything ⟨playing an ~ game⟩

al·lo·ste·ric \ˌal-ə-ˈster-ik, -ˈsti(ə)r-\ *adj* [*all-* + *steric*] **:** of, relating to, or being change (as inhibition) in enzyme activity caused by alteration of an enzyme at a point other than its enzymatically active site — **al·lo·ste·ri·cal·ly** \-i-k(ə-)lē\ *adv*

al·lot \ə-ˈlät\ *vt* **al·lot·ted; al·lot·ting** [ME *alotten,* fr. MF *aloter,* fr. *a-* (fr. L *ad-*) + *lot,* of Gmc origin; akin to OE *hlot* lot] **1 :** to assign as a share or portion ⟨~ 10 minutes for the speech⟩ **2 :** to distribute by or as if by lot ⟨~ hotel rooms to members of the delegation⟩ — **al·lot·ter** *n*

syn ALLOT, ASSIGN, APPORTION, ALLOCATE *shared meaning element* **:** to give as a share, portion, role, or lot

al·lot·ment \ə-ˈlät-mənt\ *n* **1 :** the act of allotting : APPORTIONMENT **2 :** something that is allotted

al·lo·trans·plant \ˌal-ō-tran(t)s-ˈplant\ *vt* : to transplant as a homograft — **al·lo·trans·plant** \-ˈtran(t)s-ˌ\ *n* — **al·lo·trans·plan·ta·tion** \-ˌtran(t)s-ˌplan-ˈtā-shən\ *n*

al·lo·trope \ˈal-ə-ˌtrōp\ *n* [ISV, back-formation fr. *allotropy*] : a form showing allotropy — **al·lo·trop·ic** \ˌal-ə-ˈträp-ik\ *adj* — **al·lo·trop·i·cal·ly** \-i-k(ə-)lē\ *adv*

al·lot·ro·py \ə-ˈlä-trə-pē\ *n, pl* **-pies** : the existence of a substance and esp. an element in two or more different forms (as of crystals) usu. in the same phase

all' ot·ta·va \ˌal-ə-ˈtäv-ə, ˌäl-ō-\ *adv or adj* [It, at the octave] : OTTAVA

al·lot·tee \ə-ˌlät-ˈē\ *n* : one to whom an allotment is made

al·lo·type \ˈal-ə-ˌtīp\ *n* : an isoantigenic immunoglobulin — **al·lo·typ·ic** \ˌal-ə-ˈtip-ik\ *adj* — **al·lo·typ·i·cal·ly** \-i-k(ə-)lē\ *adv* — **al·lo·typy** \ˈal-ə-ˌtī-pē\ *n*

all–out \ˈȯ-ˈlau̇t\ *adj* : made with maximum effort : THOROUGHGOING ⟨an ~ effort to win the contest⟩

all out *adv* : with full determination or enthusiasm : with maximum effort — used chiefly in the phrase *go all out*

1all·over \ˈȯ-ˌlō-vər\ *adj* : covering the whole extent or surface ⟨a sweater with an ~ pattern⟩

2allover *n* **1 :** an embroidered, printed, or lace fabric with a design covering most of the surface **2 :** a pattern or design in which a single unit is repeated so as to cover an entire surface

all over *adv* **1 :** over the whole extent ⟨decorated *all over* with a flower pattern⟩ **2 :** EVERYWHERE ⟨looked *all over* for the missing book⟩ **3 :** in every respect : THOROUGHLY ⟨she is her mother *all over*⟩

all–overs \ˈȯ-ˌlō-vərz\ *n pl, chiefly South & Midland* : a feeling of nervousness : FIDGETS ⟨I don't like such stories . . . they give me the ~ — J. C. Harris⟩

al·low \ə-ˈlau̇\ *vb* [ME *allowen,* fr. MF *alouer* to place, (fr. ML *allocare*) & *allouer* to approve, fr. L *adlaudare* to extol, fr. *ad-* + *laudare* to praise — more at ALLOCATE, LAUD] *vt* **1 a :** to assign as a share or suitable amount (as of time or money) ⟨~ an hour for lunch⟩ **b :** to reckon as a deduction or an addition ⟨~ a gallon for leakage⟩ **2 :** ADMIT, CONCEDE ⟨must ~ that money causes problems in marriage⟩ **3 a :** PERMIT ⟨doesn't ~ people to smoke in his home⟩ **b :** to forbear or neglect to restrain or prevent ⟨~ the dog to roam⟩ **4** *dial* **a :** to be of the opinion : THINK **b :** INTEND, PLAN ~ *vi* **1 :** to make a possibility : ADMIT — used with *of* ⟨evidence that ~*s* of only one conclusion⟩ **2 :** to make allowance — used with *for* ⟨~ for expansion⟩ **3** *dial* : SUPPOSE, CONSIDER ***syn*** see LET ***ant*** inhibit

al·low·able \ə-ˈlau̇-ə-bəl\ *adj* : PERMISSIBLE — **al·low·able·ness** *n* — **al·low·ably** \-blē\ *adv*

1al·low·ance \ə-ˈlau̇-ən(t)s\ *n* **1 a :** a share or portion allotted or granted **b :** a sum granted as a reimbursement or bounty or for expenses ⟨salary includes cost-of-living ~⟩; *esp* : a sum regularly provided for personal or household expenses ⟨each child has an ~⟩ **c :** a fixed or available amount ⟨provide an ~ of time for recreation⟩ **d :** a reduction from a list price or stated price ⟨a trade-in ~⟩ **2 :** an imposed handicap (as in a race) **3 :** an allowed dimensional difference between mating parts of a machine **4 :** the act of allowing : PERMISSION **5 :** the taking into account of mitigating circumstances or contingencies ***syn*** see RATION

2allowance *vt* **-anced; -anc·ing 1 :** to put on a fixed allowance (as of food and drink) **2 :** to supply in a fixed or regular quantity

al·low·ed·ly \ə-ˈlau̇-əd-lē\ *adv* : by allowance : ADMITTEDLY

al·lox·an \ə-ˈläk-sən\ *n* [G, fr. *all*antoin, a chemical found in the allantoic membrane of cows + *ox*alsäure oxalic acid + *-an*] : a crystalline compound $C_4H_2N_2O_4$ causing diabetes mellitus when injected into experimental animals; *also* : one of its similarly acting derivatives

1al·loy \ˈal-ˌȯi, ə-ˈlȯi\ *n* [MF *aloi,* fr. *aloier* to combine, fr. L *alligare* to bind — more at ALLY] **1 :** the degree of mixture with base metals : FINENESS **2 :** a substance composed of two or more metals or of a metal and a nonmetal intimately united usu. by being fused together and dissolving in each other when molten; *also* : the state of union of the components **3** *archaic* : a metal mixed with a more valuable metal to give durability or some other desired quality **4 a :** an admixture that lessens value **b :** an impairing alien element **5 :** a compound, mixture, or union of different things : AMALGAM ⟨an ethnic ~ of many peoples⟩

2al·loy \ə-ˈlȯi, ˈal-ˌȯi\ *vt* **1 :** to reduce the purity of by mixing with a less valuable metal **2 :** to mix so as to form an alloy **3 a :** to impair or debase by admixture **b :** TEMPER, MODERATE ~ *vi* : to lend itself to being alloyed ⟨iron ~*s* well⟩

all–pow·er·ful \ˈȯl-ˈpau̇(-ə)r-fəl\ *adj* : having complete or sole power

all–pur·pose \-ˈpər-pəs\ *adj* : suited for many purposes or uses

1all right \(ˈ)ȯl-ˈrīt, *esp for 2* ˈȯl-ˌ\ *adv* **1 :** well enough ⟨does *all right* in school⟩ **2 :** very well : YES ⟨*all right,* let's go⟩ **3 :** beyond doubt : CERTAINLY ⟨he has pneumonia *all right*⟩

2all right \(ˈ)ȯl-ˈ\ *adj* **1 :** SATISFACTORY ⟨the film is *all right* for children⟩ **2 :** SAFE, WELL ⟨he was ill but he's *all right* now⟩ **3 :** AGREEABLE, PLEASING — usu. used as a generalized term of approval

all–round \ˈȯl-ˈrau̇nd\ *var of* ALL-AROUND

All Saints' Day *n* : November 1 observed in Western liturgical churches as a Christian feast in honor of all the saints

all·seed \ˈȯl-ˌsēd\ *n* : any of several many-seeded plants (as knotgrass)

All Souls' Day *n* : November 2 observed as a day of prayer for the souls of the faithful departed

all·spice \ˈȯl-ˌspīs\ *n* **1 :** the berry of a West Indian tree (*Pimenta dioica*) of the myrtle family; *also* : the allspice tree **2 :** a mildly pungent and aromatic spice prepared from allspice berries

1all–star \ˌȯl-ˈstär\ *adj* : composed wholly or chiefly of stars or of outstanding performers or participants ⟨an ~ cast⟩

2all–star \ˈȯl-ˌstär\ *n* : a member of an all-star team ⟨major league ~*s*⟩

all that \(ˈ)ȯl-ˈthat\ *adv* : to an indicated or suggested extent or degree : SO ⟨didn't take his threats *all that* seriously⟩

all the same *adv* : NEVERTHELESS ⟨she was very tired but enjoyed the play *all the same*⟩

all–time \ˌȯl-ˌtīm\ *adj* **1 :** FULL-TIME **2 :** exceeding all others of all time ⟨an ~ best seller⟩

all told *adv* : with everything taken into account : in all

al·lude \ə-ˈlüd\ *vi* **al·lud·ed; al·lud·ing** [L *alludere,* lit., to play with, fr. *ad-* + *ludere* to play — more at LUDICROUS] : to make indirect reference ***syn*** see REFER

1al·lure \ə-ˈlu̇(ə)r\ *vt* **al·lured; al·lur·ing** [ME *aluren,* fr. MF *alurer,* fr. OF, fr. *a-* (fr. L *ad-*) + *loire* lure — more at LURE] : to entice by charm or attraction ***syn*** see ATTRACT ***ant*** repel — **al·lure·ment** \-ˈlu̇(ə)r-mənt\ *n*

2allure *n* : power of attraction or fascination : CHARM

al·lu·sion \ə-ˈlü-zhən\ *n* [LL *allusion-, allusio,* fr. L *allusus,* pp. of *alludere*] **1 :** the act of alluding or hinting at **2 :** an implied or indirect reference esp. when used in literature; *also* : the use of such references — **al·lu·sive** \-ˈlü-siv, -ziv\ *adj* — **al·lu·sive·ly** *adv* — **al·lu·sive·ness** *n*

1al·lu·vi·al \ə-ˈlü-vē-əl\ *adj* : relating to, composed of, or found in alluvium ⟨~ soil⟩ ⟨~ diamonds⟩

2alluvial *n* : an alluvial deposit

alluvial fan *n* : the alluvial deposit of a stream where it issues from a gorge upon a plain or of a tributary stream at its junction with the main stream

al·lu·vi·on \ə-ˈlü-vē-ən\ *n* [L *alluvion-, alluvio,* fr. *alluere* to wash against, fr. *ad-* + *lavere* to wash — more at LYE] **1 :** the wash or flow of water against a shore **2 :** FLOOD, INUNDATION **3 :** ALLUVIUM **4 :** an accession to land by the gradual addition of matter (as by deposit of alluvium) that then belongs to the owner of the land to which it is added; *also* : the land so added

al·lu·vi·um \-vē-əm\ *n, pl* **-vi·ums** *or* **-via** \-vē-ə\ [LL, neut. of *alluvius* alluvial, fr. L *alluere*] : clay, silt, sand, gravel, or similar detrital material deposited by running water

1al·ly \ə-ˈlī, ˈal-ˌī\ *vb* **al·lied; al·ly·ing** [ME *allien,* fr OF *alier,* fr. L *alligare* to bind to, fr. *ad-* + *ligare* to bind — more at LIGATURE] *vt* **1 :** to unite or form a connection between : ASSOCIATE ⟨*allied* himself with a wealthy family by marriage⟩ **2 :** to connect or form a relation between (as by likeness or compatibility) : RELATE ~ *vi* : to form or enter into an alliance

2al·ly \ˈal-ˌī, ə-ˈlī\ n, *pl* **allies 1 :** a plant or animal linked to another by genetic or evolutionary relationship **2 :** a sovereign or state associated with another by treaty or league **3 :** one that is associated with another as a helper : AUXILIARY

-al·ly \(ə-)lē\ *adv suffix* [1*-al* + *-ly*] : 2-LY ⟨terrific*ally*⟩ — in adverbs formed from adjectives in *-ic* with no alternative form in *-ical*

al·lyl \ˈal-əl\ *n* [ISV, fr. L *allium* garlic] : an unsaturated univalent radical C_3H_5 compounds of which are found in the oils of garlic and mustard — **al·lyl·ic** \ə-ˈlil-ik, a-\ *adj*

al·ma·gest \ˈal-mə-ˌjest\ *n* [ME *almageste,* fr. MF & ML, fr. Ar *al-majusti* the almagest, fr. *al* the + Gk *megistē,* fem. of *megistos,* superl. of *megas* great — more at MUCH] : any of several early medieval treatises on a branch of knowledge

al·ma ma·ter \ˌal-mə-ˈmät-ər\ *n* [L, fostering mother] **1 :** a school, college, or university which one has attended or from which one has graduated **2 :** the song or hymn of a school, college, or university

al·ma·nac \ˈȯl-mə-ˌnak, ˈal-\ *n* [ME *almenak,* fr. ML *almanach,* prob. fr. Ar *al-manākh* the almanac] **1 :** a publication containing astronomical and meteorological data arranged according to the days, weeks, and months of a given year and often including a miscellany of other information **2 :** a usu. annual publication containing statistical, tabular, and general information

al·man·dine \ˈal-mən-ˌdēn\ *n* [ME *alabandine,* fr. ML *alabandina,* fr. *Alabanda* ancient city in Asia Minor] **1 :** ALMANDITE **2 :** a violet variety of the ruby spinel or sapphire **3 :** the purple Indian garnet

al·man·dite \ˈal-mən-ˌdīt\ *n* [alter. of *almandine*] : a deep red garnet consisting of an iron aluminum silicate $Fe_3Al_2(SiO_4)_3$

1al·mighty \ȯl-ˈmīt-ē\ *adj* [ME, fr. OE *ealmihtig,* fr. *eall* all + *mihtig* mighty] **1** *often cap* : having absolute power over all ⟨*Almighty* God⟩ **2 :** relatively unlimited in power **3 :** great in magnitude or seriousness — **al·mighti·ness** *n, often cap*

2almighty *adv* : to a great degree : EXTREMELY ⟨although he did not precisely starve, he was ~ hungry — W. A. Swanberg⟩

Almighty *n* : GOD 1 — used with *the*

al·mond \ˈäm-ənd, ˈam-; ˈal-mənd\ *n* [ME *almande,* fr. OF, fr. LL *amandula,* alter. of L *amygdala,* fr. Gk *amygdalē*] **1 a :** a small tree (*Prunus amygdalus*) of the rose family with flowers and young fruit resembling those of the peach **b :** the drupaceous fruit of the almond; *esp* : its ellipsoidal edible kernel used as a nut **2 :** any of several fruits similar to the almond; *also* : the trees producing them

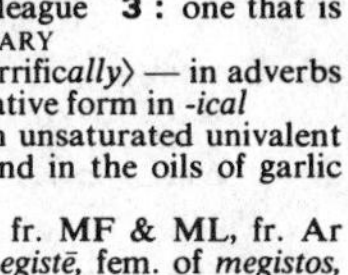

almonds 1b

al·mond–eyed \ˌäm-ən-ˈdīd, ˌam-; ˌal-mən-\ *adj* : having narrow slant almond-shaped eyes

almond green *n* : a variable color averaging a moderate yellowish green

al·mo·ner \ˈal-mə-nər, ˈäm-ə-\ *n* [ME *almoiner,* fr. OF *almosnier,* fr. *almosne* alms, fr. LL *eleemosyna*] **1 :** one who distributes alms **2** *Brit* : a social-service worker in a hospital

al·most \ˈȯl-ˌmōst, ȯl-ˈ\ *adv* [ME, fr. OE *ealmǣst,* fr. *eall* + *mǣst* most] : very nearly but not exactly or entirely

ə abut ᵊ kitten ər further a back ā bake ä cot, cart
au̇ out ch chin e less ē easy g gift i trip ī life
j joke ŋ sing ō flow ȯ flaw ȯi coin th thin th this
ü loot u̇ foot y yet yü few yu̇ furious zh vision

ALPHABET TABLE

Showing the letters of five non-Roman alphabets and the transliterations used in the etymologies

HEBREW[1,4]

Letter	Name	Translit.
א	aleph	' [2]
ב	beth	b, bh
ג	gimel	g, gh
ד	daleth	d, dh
ה	he	h
ו	waw	w
ז	zayin	z
ח	heth	ḥ
ט	teth	ṭ
י	yod	y
כ ך	kaph	k, kh
ל	lamed	l
מ ם	mem	m
נ ן	nun	n
ס	samekh	s
ע	ayin	'
פ ף	pe	p, ph
צ ץ	sadhe	ṣ
ק	qoph	q
ר	resh	r
שׂ	sin	ś
שׁ	shin	sh
ת	taw	t, th

ARABIC[3,4]

Forms	Name	Translit.
ا ـا	alif	[5]
ب بـ ـبـ ـب	bā	b
ت تـ ـتـ ـت	tā	t
ث ثـ ـثـ ـث	thā	th
ج جـ ـجـ ـج	jīm	j
ح حـ ـحـ ـح	ḥā	ḥ
خ خـ ـخـ ـخ	khā	kh
د ـد	dāl	d
ذ ـذ	dhāl	dh
ر ـر	rā	r
ز ـز	zāy	z
س سـ ـسـ ـس	sīn	s
ش شـ ـشـ ـش	shīn	sh
ص صـ ـصـ ـص	ṣād	ṣ
ض ضـ ـضـ ـض	ḍād	ḍ
ط طـ ـطـ ـط	ṭā	ṭ
ظ ظـ ـظـ ـظ	ẓā	ẓ
ع عـ ـعـ ـع	'ayn	'
غ غـ ـغـ ـغ	ghayn	gh
ف فـ ـفـ ـف	fā	f
ق قـ ـقـ ـق	qāf	q
ك كـ ـكـ ـك	kāf	k
ل لـ ـلـ ـل	lām	l
م مـ ـمـ ـم	mīm	m
ن نـ ـنـ ـن	nūn	n
ه هـ ـهـ ـه	hā	h [6]
و ـو	wāw	w
ي يـ ـيـ ـي	yā	y

GREEK[7]

Letter	Name	Translit.
Α α	alpha	a
Β β	beta	b
Γ γ	gamma	g, n
Δ δ	delta	d
Ε ε	epsilon	e
Ζ ζ	zeta	z
Η η	eta	ē
Θ θ	theta	th
Ι ι	iota	i
Κ κ	kappa	k
Λ λ	lambda	l
Μ μ	mu	m
Ν ν	nu	n
Ξ ξ	xi	x
Ο ο	omicron	o
Π π	pi	p
Ρ ρ	rho	r, rh
Σ σ ς	sigma	s
Τ τ	tau	t
Υ υ	upsilon	y, u
Φ φ	phi	ph
Χ χ	chi	ch
Ψ ψ	psi	ps
Ω ω	omega	ō

RUSSIAN[8]

Letter	Translit.
А а	a
Б б	b
В в	v
Г г	g
Д д	d
Е е	e
Ж ж	zh
З з	z
И и Й й	i, ĭ
К к	k
Л л	l
М м	m
Н н	n
О о	o
П п	p
Р р	r
С с	s
Т т	t
У у	u
Ф ф	f
Х х	kh
Ц ц	ts
Ч ч	ch
Ш ш	sh
Щ щ	shch
Ъ ъ[9]	"
Ы ы	y
Ь ь[10]	'
Э э	e
Ю ю	yu
Я я	ya

SANSKRIT[11]

Letter	Translit.	Letter	Translit.
अ	a	ञ	ñ
आ	ā	ट	ṭ
इ	i	ठ	th
ई	ī	ड	ḍ
उ	u	ढ	ḍh
ऊ	ū	ण	ṇ
ऋ	ṛ	त	t
ॠ	ṝ	थ	th
ऌ	ḷ	द	d
ॡ	ḹ	ध	dh
ए	e	न	n
ऐ	ai	प	p
ओ	o	फ	ph
औ	au	ब	b
ं	ṃ	भ	bh
:	ḥ	म	m
क	k	य	y
ख	kh	र	r
ग	g	ल	l
घ	gh	व	v
ङ	ṅ	श	ś
च	c	ष	ṣ
छ	ch	स	s
ज	j	ह	h
झ	jh		

1 See ALEPH, BETH, etc., in the vocabulary. Where two forms of a letter are given, the one at the right is the form used at the end of a word. 2 Not represented in transliteration when initial. 3 The left column shows the form of each Arabic letter that is used when it stands alone, the second column its form when it is joined to the preceding letter, the third column its form when it is joined to both the preceding and the following letter, and the right column its form when it is joined to the following letter only. In the names of the Arabic letters, ā, ī, and ū respectively are pronounced like a in *father*, i in *machine*, u in *rude*. 4 Hebrew and Arabic are written from right to left. The Hebrew and Arabic letters are all primarily consonants; a few of them are also used secondarily to represent certain vowels, but full indication of vowels, when provided at all, is by means of a system of dots or strokes adjacent to the consonantal characters. 5 Alif represents no sound in itself, but is used principally as an indicator of the presence of a glottal stop (transliterated ' medially and finally; not represented in transliteration when initial) and as the sign of a long a. 6 When ة has two dots above it (ة), it is called *tā marbūta*, and if it immediately precedes a vowel, is transliterated t instead of h. 7 See ALPHA, BETA, GAMMA, etc., in the vocabulary. The letter gamma is transliterated n only before velars; the letter upsilon is transliterated u only as the final element in diphthongs. 8 See CYRILLIC in the vocabulary. 9 This sign indicates that the immediately preceding consonant is not palatalized even though immediately followed by a palatal vowel. 10 This sign indicates that the immediately preceding consonant is palatalized even though not immediately followed by a palatal vowel. 11 The alphabet shown here is the Devanagari. When vowels are combined with preceding consonants they are indicated by various strokes or hooks instead of by the signs here given, or, in the case of short a, not written at all. Thus the character क represents ka; the character का, kā; the character कि, ki; the character की, kī; the character कु, ku; the character कू, kū; the character कृ, kṛ; the character कॄ, kṝ; the character के, ke; the character कै, kai; the character को, ko; the character कौ, kau; and the character क्, k without any following vowel. There are also many compound characters representing combinations of two or more consonants.

alms \'ämz, 'älmz\ n, pl **alms** [ME almesse, almes, fr. OE ælmesse, ælmes; akin to OHG alamuosan alms; both fr. a prehistoric WGmc word borrowed fr. LL eleemosyna alms, fr. Gk eleēmosynē pity, alms, fr. eleēmōn merciful, fr. eleos pity] **1** archaic : CHARITY **2** : something (as money or food) given freely to relieve the poor — **alms-giv-er** \-,giv-ər\ n — **alms-giv-ing** \-,giv-iŋ\ n

alms-house \-,haús\ n **1** Brit : a privately financed home for the poor **2** archaic : POORHOUSE

alms-man \-mən\ n : a recipient of alms

al-ni-co \'al-ni-,kō\ n [aluminum + nickel + cobalt] : a powerful permanent-magnet alloy containing iron, nickel, aluminum, and one or more of the elements cobalt, copper, and titanium

al-oe \'al-(,)ō\ n [ME, fr. LL, fr. L, dried juice of aloe leaves, fr. Gk aloē dried juice of aloe leaves] **1** pl : the fragrant wood of an East Indian tree (Aquilaria agallocha) of the mezereon family **2** a : any of a large genus (Aloe) of succulent chiefly southern African plants of the lily family with basal leaves and spicate flowers **b** : the dried juice of the leaves of various aloes used as a purgative and tonic — usu. used in pl. but sing. in constr. **3** : any of a genus (Furcraea) of American plants of the amaryllis family somewhat like the African aloes

¹aloft \ə-'lóft\ adv [ME, fr. ON ā lopt, fr. ā on, in + lopt air — more at ON, LOFT] **1** : at or to a great height **2** : in the air; esp : in flight (as in an airplane) (meals served ∼) **3** : at, on, or to the masthead or the higher rigging

²aloft prep : on top of : ABOVE (bright signs ∼ hotels)

alog-i-cal \(')ā-'läj-i-kəl\ adj : being outside the bounds of that to which logic can apply — **alog-i-cal-ly** \-k(ə-)lē\ adv

alo-ha \ə-'lō-(h)ə, ä-, -,(h)ä\ interj [Hawaiian, fr. aloha love] — used as a greeting or farewell

aloha shirt n : a loose brightly colored Hawaiian sport shirt

al-o-in \'al-ə-wən\ n : a bitter yellow crystalline cathartic obtained from the aloe

¹alone \ə-'lōn\ adj [ME, fr. al all + one one] **1** : separated from others : ISOLATED **2** : exclusive of anyone or anything else : ONLY **3** a : considered without reference to any other (the children ∼ would eat that much) **b** : INCOMPARABLE, UNIQUE (∼ in his ability to solve fiscal problems) — **alone-ness** \-'lōn-nəs\ n

syn ALONE, SOLITARY, LONELY, LONESOME, LONE, LORN, FORLORN, DESOLATE shared meaning element : isolated from others. ALONE stresses the objective fact of being by oneself with slighter notion of emotional involvement than most of the remaining terms (everyone needs to be alone sometimes) SOLITARY may indicate isolation as a chosen course (glorying in the calm of her solitary life) but more often it suggests sadness and a sense of loss (left solitary by the death of his wife) LONELY adds to solitary a suggestion of longing for companionship (felt lonely and forsaken) LONESOME heightens the implication of dreariness and longing (an only child often leads a lonesome life) LONE may replace lonely or lonesome but typically is as objective as alone (a lone robin pecking at the lawn) LORN suggests recent separation or bereavement (when lorn lovers sit and droop — W. M. Praed) FORLORN stresses dejection, woe, and listlessness at separation from one held dear (a forlorn lost child) DESOLATE implies a sharp and poignant sense of loneliness ant accompanied

²alone adv **1** : SOLELY, EXCLUSIVELY **2** : without aid or support

¹along \ə-'lóŋ\ prep [ME, fr. OE andlang, fr. and- against + lang long — more at ANTE] **1** : in a line parallel with the length and direction of **2** : in the course of **3** : in accordance with : IN

²along adv **1** : FORWARD, ON (move ∼) **2** : from one to another (word was passed ∼) **3** a : as a companion (brought his wife ∼) **b** : in association — used with with (work ∼ with colleagues) **4** : at or to an advanced point (plans are far ∼) **5** : in addition : ALSO — often used with with (a bill came ∼ with the package) **6** : at hand : as a necessary or useful item (had his gun ∼) **7** : on hand : THERE (tell him I'll be ∼ to see him) — **all along** : all the time (knew the truth all along)

along of prep [ME ilong on, fr. OE gelang on, fr. ge-, associative prefix + lang — more at CO-] dial : because of

along-shore \ə-'lóŋ-'shō(ə)r, -'shó(ə)r\ adv or adj : along the shore or coast (walked ∼) (∼ currents)

¹along-side \-,sīd\ adv **1** : along the side : in parallel position **2** : at the side : close by (a guard with a prisoner ∼)

²alongside prep : side by side with; specif : parallel to

alongside of prep : ALONGSIDE

¹aloof \ə-'lüf\ adv [obs. aloof (to windward)] : at a distance : out of involvement

²aloof adj : removed or distant in interest or feeling : RESERVED syn see INDIFFERENT ant familiar, close — **aloof-ly** adv — **aloof-ness** n

al-o-pe-cia \,al-ə-'pē-sh(ē-)ə\ n [ME allopicia, fr. L alopecia, fr. Gk alōpekia, fr. alōpek-, alōpēx fox — more at VULPINE] : loss of hair, wool, or feathers : BALDNESS — **al-o-pe-cic** \-'pē-sik\ adj

aloud \ə-'laúd\ adv [ME, fr. ¹a- + loud] **1** archaic : in a loud manner : LOUDLY **2** : with the speaking voice

alow \ə-'lō\ adv [ME, fr. ¹a- + low] : BELOW (∼ in the ship's hold)

alp \'alp\ n [back-formation fr. Alps, mountain system of Europe] **1** : a high rugged mountain **2** : something suggesting an alp in height, size, or ruggedness

al-pa-ca \al-'pak-ə\ n [Sp, fr. Aymara allpaca] **1** : a mammal with fine long woolly hair that is domesticated in Peru and is prob. a variety of the guanaco **2** a : wool of the alpaca **b** (1) : a thin cloth made of or containing this wool (2) : a rayon or cotton imitation of this cloth

al-pen-glow \'al-pən-,glō\ n [prob. part trans. of G Alpenglühen, fr. Alpen Alps + glühen glow] : a reddish glow seen near sunset or sunrise on the summits of mountains

alpaca 1

al-pen-stock \'al-pən-,stäk\ n [G, fr. Alpen + stock staff] : a long iron-pointed staff used in mountain climbing

al-pes-trine \al-'pes-trən\ adj [ML alpestris mountainous, fr. L Alpes Alps] : growing at high elevations but not above the timberline : SUBALPINE

¹al-pha \'al-fə\ n [ME, fr. L, fr. Gk, of Sem origin; akin to Heb āleph aleph] **1** : the 1st letter of the Greek alphabet — see ALPHABET table **2** : something that is first : BEGINNING **3** : the chief or brightest star of a constellation

²alpha or α- adj **1** : closest in the structure of an organic molecule to a particular group or atom (α-substitution) (α-naphthol)

³alpha adj : ALPHABETIC

al-pha-ad-ren-er-gic \'al-fə-,ad-rə-'nər-jik\ adj : of, relating to, or being an alpha-receptor (∼ blocking action)

alpha and omega n [fr. the fact that alpha and omega are respectively the first and last letters of the Greek alphabet] **1** : the beginning and ending **2** : the principal element

al-pha-bet \'al-fə-,bet, -bət\ n [ME alphabete, fr. LL alphabetum, fr. Gk alphabētos, fr. alpha + bēta beta] **1** a : a set of letters or other characters with which one or more languages are written esp. if arranged in a customary order **b** : a system of signs or signals that serve as equivalents for letters **2** : RUDIMENTS, ELEMENTS

al-pha-bet-ic \,al-fə-'bet-ik\ or **al-pha-bet-i-cal** \-i-kəl\ adj **1** : of, relating to, or employing an alphabet **2** : arranged in the order of the letters of the alphabet — **al-pha-bet-i-cal-ly** \-i-k(ə-)lē\ adv

al-pha-bet-iza-tion \,al-fə-,bet-ə-'zā-shən\ n **1** : the act or process of alphabetizing **2** : an alphabetically arranged series, list, or file

al-pha-bet-ize \'al-fə-bə-,tīz\ vt **-ized; -iz-ing** **1** : to furnish with an alphabet **2** : to arrange alphabetically — **al-pha-bet-iz-er** n

alpha globulin n [ISV] : any of several globulins of plasma or serum that have at alkaline pH the greatest electrophoretic mobility next to albumin — compare BETA GLOBULIN, GAMMA GLOBULIN

al-pha-he-lix \,al-fə-'hē-liks\ n : the coiled structural arrangement of many proteins consisting of a single spiral amino-acid chain that is stabilized by hydrogen bonds

alpha iron n : the form of iron stable below 910°C

al-pha-mer-ic \,al-fə-'mer-ik\ or **al-pha-mer-i-cal** \-i-kəl\ adj [alphabet + numeric, numerical] : ALPHANUMERIC

al-pha-nu-mer-ic \-,n(y)ü-'mer-ik\ also **al-pha-nu-mer-i-cal** adj [alphabet + numeric, numerical] **1** : consisting of both letters and numbers and other symbols (as punctuation marks and mathematical symbols) as well (an ∼ code); also : being a character in an alphanumeric system **2** : capable of using alphanumeric characters (an ∼ computer) — **al-pha-nu-mer-i-cal-ly** \-i-k(ə-)lē\ adv

alpha particle n : a positively charged nuclear particle identical with the nucleus of a helium atom that consists of two protons and two neutrons and is ejected at high speed in certain radioactive transformations

alpha privative n : the prefix a- or an- expressing negation in Greek and in English

alpha ray n **1** : an alpha particle moving at high speed (as in radioactive emission) **2** : a stream of alpha particles — called also alpha radiation

al-pha-re-cep-tor \'al-fə-ri-,sep-tər\ n : a receptor that is associated with vasoconstriction, relaxation of intestinal muscle, and contraction of the nictitating membrane, iris dilator muscle, splenic smooth muscle, and muscular layer of the wall of the uterus — called also alpha-adrenergic receptor

Al-phe-us \al-'fē-əs\ n [L, fr. Gk Alpheios] : a Greek river-god who pursues the nymph Arethusa and is finally united with her

al-pine \'al-,pīn\ n **1** : a plant native to alpine or boreal regions that is often grown for ornament **2** cap : a person possessing Alpine physical characteristics

Alpine adj **1** often not cap : of, relating to, or resembling the Alps or any mountains **2** often not cap : of, relating to, or growing in the biogeographic zone including the elevated slopes above timberline **3** : of or relating to a type of stocky broad-headed white men of medium height with brown hair or eyes often regarded as constituting a branch of the Caucasian race **4** : of or relating to competitive ski events consisting of slalom and downhill racing — compare NORDIC

al-pin-ism \'al-pə-,niz-əm\ n, often cap : mountain climbing in the Alps or other high mountains — **al-pin-ist** \-nəst\ n

al-ready \ól-'red-ē\ adv [ME al redy, fr. al redy, adj., wholly ready, fr. al all + redy ready] : prior to a specified or implied past, present, or future time : by this time : PREVIOUSLY (he had ∼ left when I called)

al-right \(')ól-'rīt, 'ól-,\ adv or adj [ME, fr. al + right] : ALL RIGHT (the first two years of the medical school were ∼ — Gertrude Stein)

Al-sa-tian \al-'sā-shən\ n [ML Alsatia Alsace] : GERMAN SHEPHERD

al-sike clover \,al-,sak-, -,sīk-\ n [Alsike, Sweden] : a European perennial clover (Trifolium hybridum) much used as a forage plant

al-so \'ól-(,)sō\ adv [ME, fr. OE eallswā, fr. eall all + swā so — more at SO] **1** : LIKEWISE l **2** : in addition : TOO

al-so-ran \-,ran\ n **1** : a horse or dog that finishes out of the money in a race **2** : a contestant that does not win **3** : one that is competitively of little importance (was just an ∼ in the scramble for . . . privileges — C. A. Buss)

alt abbr **1** alternate **2** altitude **3** alto

Alta abbr Alberta

Al-ta-ic \al-'tā-ik\ adj **1** : of or relating to the Altai mountains **2** : of, relating to, or constituting a language family comprising the Turkic, Tungusic, and Mongolic subfamilies

Al·tair \al-'tī(ə)r, -'ta(ə)r, -'te(ə)r, 'al-,\ *n* [Ar *al-ṭā'ir*, lit., the flier] : the first magnitude star Alpha (α) Aquilae
al·tar \'ȯl-tər\ *n, often attrib* [ME *alter*, fr. OE *altar*, fr. L *altare*; akin to L *adolēre* to burn up] **1** : a usu. raised structure or place on which sacrifices are offered or incense is burned in worship **2** : a table on which the eucharistic elements are consecrated or which serves as a center of worship or ritual — see BASILICA illustration
altar boy *n* : a boy who assists the celebrant in a liturgical service
altar call *n* : an appeal by an evangelist to worshipers to come forward to signify their decision to commit their lives to Christ
altar of repose *often cap A&R* : REPOSITORY 2
al·tar·piece \'ȯl-tər-,pēs\ *n* : a work of art that decorates the space above and behind an altar
altar rail *n* : a railing in front of an altar separating the chancel from the body of the church
altar stone *n* : a stone slab with a compartment containing the relics of martyrs that forms an essential part of a Roman Catholic altar
alt·az·i·muth \(')al-'taz-(ə-)məth\ *n* [ISV *altitude* + *azimuth*] : a telescope mounted so that it can swing horizontally and vertically; *also* : any of several other similarly mounted instruments
al·ter \'ȯl-tər\ *vb* **al·tered; al·ter·ing** \-t(ə-)riŋ\ [ME *alteren*, fr. MF *alterer*, fr. ML *alterare*, fr. L *alter* other (of two); akin to L *alius* other — more at ELSE] *vt* **1** : to make different without changing into something else **2** : CASTRATE, SPAY ~ *vi* : to become different *syn* see CHANGE *ant* fix — **al·ter·abil·i·ty** \,ȯl-t(ə-)rə-'bil-ət-ē\ *n* — **al·ter·able** \'ȯl-t(ə-)rə-bəl\ *adj* — **al·ter·ably** \-blē\ *adv* — **al·ter·er** \-tər-ər\ *n*
al·ter·ation \,ȯl-tə-'rā-shən\ *n* **1** : the act or process of altering : the state of being altered **2** : the result of altering : MODIFICATION
al·ter·ative \'ȯl-tə-,rāt-iv, -rət-\ *n* : a drug used empirically to alter favorably the course of an ailment
al·ter·cate \'ȯl-tər-,kāt\ *vi* **-cat·ed; -cat·ing** [L *altercatus*, pp. of *altercari*, fr. *alter*] : to dispute angrily or noisily : WRANGLE
al·ter·ca·tion \,ȯl-tər-'kā-shən\ *n* : a noisy heated angry dispute; *also* : noisy controversy *syn* see QUARREL
al·ter ego \,ȯl-tə-'rē-(,)gō *also* -'reg-(,)ō\ *n* [L, lit., second I] : a second self; *esp* : a trusted friend
[1]**al·ter·nate** \'ȯl-tər-nət *also* 'al-\ *adj* [L *alternatus*, pp. of *alternare*, fr. *alternus* alternate, fr. *alter*] **1** : occurring or succeeding by turns ⟨a day of ~ sunshine and rain⟩ **2 a** : arranged first on one side and then on the other at different levels or points along an axial line ⟨~ leaves⟩ — compare OPPOSITE **b** : arranged one above or alongside the other **3** : every other : every second ⟨he works on ~ days⟩ **4** : constituting an alternative ⟨took the ~ route home⟩ *syn* see INTERMITTENT *ant* consecutive — **al·ter·nate·ly** *adv*
[2]**al·ter·nate** \-,nāt\ *vb* **-nat·ed; -nat·ing** *vt* **1** : to perform by turns or in succession **2** : to cause to alternate ~ *vi* : to change from one to another repeatedly ⟨storms *alternated* with sunshine⟩
[3]**al·ter·nate** \-nət\ *n* **1** : ALTERNATIVE **2** : one that substitutes for or alternates with another
alternate angle *n* : one of a pair of angles on opposite sides of a transversal at its intersection with two other lines: **a** : one of a pair of angles inside the two intersected lines — called also *alternate interior angle* **b** : one of a pair of angles outside the two intersected lines — called also *alternate exterior angle*
alternating current *n* : an electric current that reverses its direction at regularly recurring intervals — abbr. *AC*
alternating group *n* : a permutation group whose elements comprise those permutations of *n* objects which can be formed from the original order by making consecutively an even number of interchanges of pairs of objects
al·ter·na·tion \,ȯl-tər-'nā-shən *also* ,al-\ *n* **1 a** : the act or process of alternating or causing to alternate **b** : alternating occurrence : SUCCESSION **2** : DISJUNCTION 2a **3** : the occurrence of different allomorphs or allophones
alternation of generations : the occurrence of two or more forms differently produced in the life cycle of a plant or animal usu. involving the regular alternation of a sexual with an asexual generation but not infrequently consisting of alternation of a dioecious generation with one or more parthenogenetic generations
[1]**al·ter·na·tive** \ȯl-'tər-nət-iv, al-\ *adj* **1** : offering or expressing a choice ⟨several ~ plans⟩ **2** : ALTERNATE — **al·ter·na·tive·ly** *adv* — **al·ter·na·tive·ness** *n*
[2]**alternative** *n* **1 a** : a proposition or situation offering a choice between two or more things only one of which may be chosen **b** : an opportunity for deciding between two or more courses or propositions **2** : one of two or more things, courses, or propositions to be chosen *syn* see CHOICE
al·ter·na·tor \'ȯl-tər-,nāt-ər *also* 'al-\ *n* : an electric generator for producing alternating current
al·thaea *or* **al·thea** \al-'thē-ə\ *n* [L *althaea* marsh mallow, fr. Gk *althaia*] **1** : ROSE OF SHARON 2 **2** : a hollyhock or related plant (genus *Althaea*)
alt·horn \'alt-,hȯ(ə)rn\ *n* [G, fr. *alt* alto + *horn* horn] : an alto saxhorn
al·though *also* **al·tho** \ȯl-'t͟hō\ *conj* [ME *although*, fr. *al* all + *though*] : in spite of the fact that : even though *syn* see THOUGH
al·tim·e·ter \al-'tim-ət-ər, 'al-tə-,mēt-ər\ *n* [L *altus* + E *-meter*] : an instrument for measuring altitude; *specif* : an aneroid barometer designed to register changes in atmospheric pressure accompanying changes in altitude — **al·tim·e·try** \al-'tim-ə-trē\ *n*
al·ti·pla·no \,al-ti-'plän-(,)ō\ *n, pl* **-nos** [AmerSp, fr. L *altus* + *planum* plain] : a high plateau or plain : TABLELAND
al·ti·tude \'al-tə-,t(y)üd\ *n* [ME, fr. L *altitudo* height, depth, fr. *altus* high, deep — more at OLD] **1 a** : the angular elevation of a celestial object above the horizon **b** : the vertical elevation of an object above sea level **c** : the perpendicular distance from a vertex of a geometric figure to the opposite side or from a side or face to a parallel side or face; *esp* : the altitude on a base **2** : the highest level of a quality or feeling ⟨the ~ of passion⟩ **3 a** : vertical distance or extent **b** : position at a height **c** : an elevated region : EMINENCE — usu. used in pl. *syn* see HEIGHT — **al·ti·tu·di·nal** \,al-tə-'t(y)üd-nəl, -ᵊn-əl\ *adj* — **al·ti·tu·di·nous** \-'t(y)üd-nəs, -ᵊn-əs\ *adj*
altitude sickness *n* : the effects (as nosebleed or nausea) of oxygen deficiency in the blood and tissues developed in rarefied air at high altitudes
[1]**al·to** \'al-(,)tō\ *n, pl* **altos** [It, lit., high, fr. L *altus*] **1 a** : COUNTERTENOR **b** : CONTRALTO **2** : the second highest part in 4-part harmony **3** : a member of a family of instruments having a range lower than that of the treble or soprano
[2]**alto** *adj* : relating to or having the range or part of an alto
al·to·cu·mu·lus \,al-tō-'kyü-myə-ləs\ *n, pl* **-li** \-,lī, -,lē\ [NL, fr. L *altus* + NL *-o-* + *cumulus*] : a fleecy cloud formation consisting of large whitish globular cloudlets with shaded portions — see CLOUD illustration
[1]**al·to·geth·er** \,ȯl-tə-'get͟h-ər\ *adv* [ME *altogedere*, fr. *al* all + *togedere* together] **1** : WHOLLY, THOROUGHLY ⟨an ~ different problem⟩ **2** : in all : all told **3** : on the whole : in the main
[2]**altogether** *n* : NUDE — used with *the* ⟨posed in the ~⟩
al·to–re·lie·vo *or* **al·to–ri·lie·vo** \,al-(,)tō-ri-'lē-(,)vō, ,äl-(,)tō-rēl-'yä-(,)vō\ *n, pl* **alto–relievos** *or* **al·to–ri·lie·vi** \,äl-(,)tō-rēl-'yä-(,)vē\ [It *altorilievo*] **1** : HIGH RELIEF **2** : a sculpture in high relief
al·to·stra·tus \,al-tō-'strāt-əs, -'strat-\ *n, pl* **-ti** \-,ī\ [NL, fr. L *altus* + NL *-o-* + *stratus*] : a cloud formation similar to cirrostratus but darker and at a lower level — see CLOUD illustration
al·tri·cial \al-'trish-əl\ *adj* [L *altric-*, *altrix* fem. of *altor* one who nourishes, fr. *altus* pp. of *alere* to nourish — more at OLD] : having the young hatched in a very immature and helpless condition so as to require care for some time — compare PRECOCIAL
al·tru·ism \'al-trü-,iz-əm\ *n* [F *altruisme*, fr. *autrui* other people, fr. OF, oblique case form of *autre* other, fr. L *alter*] : unselfish regard for or devotion to the welfare of others — **al·tru·ist** \-trü-əst\ *n* — **al·tru·is·tic** \,al-trü-'is-tik\ *adj* — **al·tru·is·ti·cal·ly** \-ti-k(ə-)lē\ *adv*
al·u·la \'al-yə-lə\ *n, pl* **-lae** \-,lē, -,lī\ [NL, fr. L, dim. of *ala* wing — more at AISLE] : BASTARD WING — **al·u·lar** \-lər\ *adj*
al·um \'al-əm\ *n* [ME, fr. MF *alum*, *alun*, fr. L *alumen* — more at ALE] **1** : a potassium aluminum sulfate $KAl(SO_4)_2.12H_2O$ or an ammonium aluminum sulfate $NH_4Al(SO_4)_2.12H_2O$ used esp. as an emetic and as an astringent and styptic **2** : any of various double salts isomorphous with potash alum **3** : ALUMINUM SULFATE
alu·mi·na \ə-'lü-mə-nə\ *n* [NL, fr. L *alumin-*, *alumen* alum] : aluminum oxide Al_2O_3 occurring native as corundum and in hydrated forms (as in bauxite)
alu·mi·nate \-nət\ *n* : a compound of alumina with a metallic oxide
alu·mi·nif·er·ous \ə-,lü-mə-'nif-(ə-)rəs\ *adj* : containing alum or aluminum
al·u·min·i·um \,al-yə-'min-ē-əm\ *n* [NL, fr. *alumina*] *chiefly Brit* : ALUMINUM
alu·mi·nize \ə-'lü-mə-,nīz\ *vt* **-nized; -niz·ing** : to treat or coat with aluminum
alu·mi·no·sil·i·cate \ə-,lü-mə-nō-'sil-ə-,kāt, -'sil-i-kət\ *n* [L *alumin-*, *alumen* + *-o-* + ISV *silicate*] : a combined silicate and aluminate
alu·mi·nous \ə-'lü-mə-nəs\ *adj* : of, relating to, or containing alum or aluminum
alu·mi·num \ə-'lü-mə-nəm\ *n, often attrib* [NL, fr. *alumina*] : a bluish silver-white malleable ductile light trivalent metallic element with good electrical and thermal conductivity, high reflectivity, and resistance to oxidation that is the most abundant metal in the earth's crust occurring always in combination — see ELEMENT table
aluminum sulfate *n* : a colorless salt $Al_2(SO_4)_3$ usu. made by treating bauxite with sulfuric acid and used in making paper, in water purification, and in tanning
alum·na \ə-'ləm-nə\ *n, pl* **-nae** \-(,)nē\ [L, fem. of *alumnus*] : a girl or woman who has attended or has graduated from a particular school, college, or university
alum·nus \ə-'ləm-nəs\ *n, pl* **-ni** \-,nī\ [L, foster son, pupil, fr. *alere* to nourish — more at OLD] **1** : one who has attended or has graduated from a particular school, college, or university **2** : one who is a former member, employee, contributor, or inmate ⟨former juvenile delinquent, hoodlum, ~ of reform schools — *Newsweek*⟩
al·um·root \'al-əm-,rüt, -,ru̇t\ *n* **1** : any of several No. American herbs (genus *Heuchera*) of the saxifrage family; *esp* : one (*H. americana*) with an astringent root **2** : WILD GERANIUM 1
al·u·nite \'al-(y)ə-,nīt\ *n* [F, fr. *alun* alum] : a mineral $K(AlO)_3(SO_4)_2.3H_2O$ consisting of a hydrous potassium aluminum sulfate and occurring in massive form or in rhombohedral crystals
al·ve·o·lar \al-'vē-ə-lər\ *adj* **1** : of, relating to, resembling, or having alveoli **2** : of, relating to, or constituting the part of the jaws where the teeth arise, the air cells of the lungs, or glands with secretory cells about a central space **3** : articulated with the tip of the tongue touching or near the teethridge — **al·ve·o·lar·ly** *adv*
al·ve·o·late \-lət\ *adj* : pitted like a honeycomb — **al·ve·o·la·tion** \(,)al-,vē-ə-'lā-shən\ *n*
al·ve·o·lus \al-'vē-ə-ləs\ *n, pl* **-li** \-,lī, -(,)lē\ [NL, fr. L, dim. of *alveus* cavity, hollow, fr. *alvus* belly; akin to ON *hvannjōli* stalk of angelica, Gk *aulos*, a reed instrument] **1** : a small cavity or pit: as **a** : a socket for a tooth **b** : an air cell of the lungs **c** : an acinus of a compound gland **d** : a cell or compartment of a honeycomb **2** : TEETHRIDGE
alw *abbr* allowance
al·way \'ȯl-(,)wā\ *adv* [ME] *archaic* : ALWAYS
al·ways \'ȯl-wēz, -wəz, -(,)wāz\ *adv* [ME *alway*, *alwayes*, fr. OE *ealne weg*, lit., all the way, fr. *ealne* (acc. of *eall* all) + *weg* (acc.) way — more at WAY] **1** : at all times : INVARIABLY **2** : FOREVER, PERPETUALLY **3** : at any rate : in any event ⟨as a last resort one can ~ work⟩
Al·yce clover \,al-əs-\ *n* [prob. by folk etymology fr. NL *Alysicarpus*, genus name, fr. Gk *halysis* chain + *karpos* fruit] : a low spreading annual Old World legume (*Alysicarpus vaginalis*) used in the southern U.S. as a cover crop and for hay and pasturage

alys·sum \ə-ˈlis-əm\ *n* [NL, fr. Gk *alysson,* plant believed to cure rabies, fr. neut. of *alyssos* curing rabies, fr. *a-* + *lyssa* rabies] **1** : any of a genus (*Alyssum*) of Old World herbs of the mustard family with small yellow racemose flowers **2** : SWEET ALYSSUM
am [ME, fr. OE *eom;* akin to ON *em* am, L *sum,* Gk *eimi,* OE *is* is] *pres 1st sing of* BE
1Am *abbr* America; American
2Am *symbol* americium
AM *abbr* **1** airmail **2** Air Medal **3** amplitude modulation **4** [L *anno mundi*] in the year of the world — often printed in small capitals **5** ante meridiem **6** [NL *artium magister*] master of arts
ama \ˈäm-(ˌ)ä\ *n, pl* **amas** *or* **ama** [Jap] : a Japanese diver esp. for pearls
AMA *abbr* American Medical Association
amah \ˈäm-(ˌ)ä\ *n* [Pg *ama* wet nurse, fr. ML *amma*] : an Oriental female servant; *esp* : a Chinese nurse
amain \ə-ˈmān\ *adv* **1** : with all one's might ⟨down came the storm, and smote ~ the vessel — H. W. Longfellow⟩ **2 a** : at full speed **b** : in great haste **3** : to a high degree : EXCEEDINGLY ⟨they whom I favour thrive in wealth ~ — John Milton⟩
Ama·le·kite \ˈam-ə-ˌlek-ˌīt, ə-ˈmal-ə-ˌkīt\ *n* [Heb *ʽĀmālēqī,* pl. fr. *ʽĀmālēq* Amalek, grandson of Esau] : a member of an ancient nomadic people living south of Canaan
amal·gam \ə-ˈmal-gəm\ *n* [ME *amalgame,* fr. MF, fr. ML *amalgama*] **1** : an alloy of mercury with another metal that is solid or liquid at room temperature according to the proportion of mercury present and is used esp. in making tooth cements **2** : a mixture of different elements
amal·gam·ate \-gə-ˌmāt\ *vt* **-at·ed; -at·ing** : to unite in or as if in an amalgam; *esp* : to merge into a single body ***syn*** see MIX — **amal·gam·ator** \-ˌmāt-ər\ *n*
amal·gam·ation \ə-ˌmal-gə-ˈmā-shən\ *n* **1 a** : the action or process of amalgamating : UNITING **b** : the state of being amalgamated **2** : the result of amalgamating : AMALGAM **3** : CONSOLIDATION, MERGER ⟨~ of two corporations⟩ — **amal·gam·ative** \-ˈmal-gə-ˌmāt-iv\ *adj*
am·a·ni·ta \ˌam-ə-ˈnīt-ə, -ˈnēt-\ *n* [NL, genus name, fr. Gk *amanitai,* pl., a kind of fungus] : any of various mostly poisonous white-spored fungi (genus *Amanita*) with the volva separate from the cap
aman·ta·dine \ə-ˈmant-ə-ˌdēn\ *n* [ISV *adamantane* ($C_{10}H_{16}$) + *amine*] : an antiviral drug used esp. to prevent infection (as by an influenza virus) by interfering with virus penetration into host cells
aman·u·en·sis \ə-ˌman-yə-ˈwen(t)-səs\ *n, pl* **-en·ses** \-(ˌ)sēz\ [L, fr. (*servus*) *a manu* slave with secretarial duties] : one employed to write from dictation or to copy manuscript
am·a·ranth \ˈam-ə-ˌran(t)th\ *n* [L *amarantus,* a flower, fr. Gk *amaranton,* fr. neut. of *amarantos* unfading, fr. *a-* + *marainein* to waste away — more at SMART] **1** : a flower that never fades **2** : any of a large genus (*Amaranthus* of the family Amaranthaceae, the amaranth family) of coarse herbs including pigweeds and various forms cultivated for their showy flowers **3** : a dark reddish purple
am·a·ran·thine \ˌam-ə-ˈran(t)-thən, -ˈran-ˌthīn\ *adj* **1 a** : of or relating to an amaranth **b** : that does not fade : UNDYING **2** : of the color amaranth
am·a·ryl·lis \ˌam-ə-ˈril-əs\ *n* [NL, genus name, prob. fr. L, name of a shepherdess in Vergil's *Eclogues*] : any of a genus (*Amaryllis* of the family Amaryllidaceae, the amaryllis family) of bulbous African herbs with showy umbellate flowers; *also* : a plant of any of several related genera (as *Hippeastrum* or *Sprekelia*)
amass \ə-ˈmas\ *vb* [MF *amasser,* fr. OF, fr. *a-* (fr. L *ad-*) + *masser* to gather into a mass, fr. *masse* mass] *vt* **1** : to collect for oneself : ACCUMULATE ⟨~ a great fortune⟩ **2** : to collect into a mass : GATHER ⟨~ the wool into a large ball⟩ ~ *vi* : to come together : ASSEMBLE — **amass·er** *n* — **amass·ment** \-mənt\ *n*
am·a·teur \ˈam-ə-ˌtər, -ət-ər, -ə-ˌt(y)u̇(ə)r, -ə-ˌchu̇(ə)r, -ə-chər\ *n* [F, fr. L *amator* lover, fr. *amatus,* pp. of *amare* to love] **1** : DEVOTEE, ADMIRER **2** : one who engages in a pursuit, study, science, or sport as a pastime rather than as a profession **3** : one lacking in experience and competence in an art or science — **amateur** *adj* — **am·a·teur·ish** \ˌam-ə-ˈtər-ish, -ˈt(y)u̇(ə)r-\ *adj* — **am·a·teur·ish·ly** *adv* — **am·a·teur·ish·ness** *n* — **am·a·teur·ism** \ˈam-ə-ˌtər-ˌiz-əm, -ət-ə-ˌriz-, -ə-ˌt(y)u̇(ə)r-ˌiz-, -ˌchu̇(ə)r-ˌiz-, -chə-ˌriz-\ *n*
syn AMATEUR, DILETTANTE, DABBLER, TYRO *shared meaning element* : one who follows a pursuit without attaining proficiency or professional status ***ant*** professional, expert
Ama·ti \ä-ˈmät-ē,ə-\ *n, pl* **Amatis** : a violin made by a member of the Amati family of Cremona
am·a·tive \ˈam-ət-iv\ *adj* [ML *amativus,* fr. L *amatus*] : disposed or disposing to love : AMOROUS — **am·a·tive·ly** *adv* — **am·a·tive·ness** *n*
am·a·tol \ˈam-ə-ˌtȯl, -ˌtäl, -ˌtōl\ *n* [ISV *ammonium* + connective *-a-* + trinitro*tol*uene] : an explosive consisting of ammonium nitrate and trinitrotoluene
am·a·to·ry \ˈam-ə-ˌtōr-ē, -ˌtȯr-\ *adj* : of, relating to, or expressing sexual love
am·au·ro·sis \ˌam-ȯ-ˈrō-səs\ *n, pl* **-ro·ses** \-ˌsēz\ [NL, fr. Gk *amaurōsis,* lit., dimming, fr. *amauroun* to dim, fr. *amauros* dim] : decay of sight occurring without perceptible external change — **am·au·rot·ic** \-ˈrät-ik\ *adj*
1amaze \ə-ˈmāz\ *vb* **amazed; amaz·ing** [ME *amasen,* fr. OE *āmasian,* fr. *ā-* (perfective prefix) + (assumed) *masian* to confuse — more at ABIDE] *vt* **1** *obs* : BEWILDER, PERPLEX **2** : to fill with wonder : ASTOUND ~ *vi* : to show or cause astonishment ⟨his calmness continues to ~⟩ ***syn*** see SURPRISE — **amaz·ing·ly** \-ˈmā-ziŋ-lē\ *adv*
2amaze *n* : AMAZEMENT
amaze·ment \ə-ˈmāz-mənt\ *n* **1** *obs* : CONSTERNATION, BEWILDERMENT **2** : the quality or state of being amazed
am·a·zon \ˈam-ə-ˌzän, -ə-zən\ *n* [ME, fr. L, fr. Gk *Amazōn*] **1** *cap* : a member of a race of female warriors repeatedly warring with the Greeks of classical mythology **2** : a tall strong masculine woman
Am·a·zo·nian \ˌam-ə-ˈzō-nē-ən, -nyən\ *adj* **1 a** : relating to, resembling, or befitting an Amazon **b** *not cap* : MASCULINE, WARLIKE ⟨an *amazonian* woman⟩ **2** : of or relating to the Amazon river or its valley
am·a·zon·ite \ˈam-ə-zə-ˌnīt\ *n* [*Amazon* river] : an apple-green or bluish-green microcline
am·a·zon·stone \-zən-ˌstōn\ *n* : AMAZONITE
amb *abbr* ambassador
am·bage \ˈam-bij\ *n, pl* **am·ba·ges** \am-ˈbā-(ˌ)jēz, ˈam-bij-əz\ [back-formation fr. ME *ambages,* fr. MF or L; MF, fr. L, fr. *ambi-* + *agere* to drive — more at AGENT] **1** *archaic* : AMBIGUITY, CIRCUMLOCUTION — usu. used in pl. **2** *pl, archaic* : indirect ways or proceedings — **am·ba·gious** \am-ˈbā-jəs\ *adj*
am·bas·sa·dor \am-ˈbas-əd-ər, əm-, im-\ *n* [ME *ambassadour,* fr. MF *ambassadeur,* of Gmc origin; akin to OHG *ambaht* service] **1** : an official envoy; *esp* : a diplomatic agent of the highest rank accredited to a foreign government or sovereign as the resident representative of his own government or sovereign or appointed for a special and often temporary diplomatic assignment **2 a** : an authorized representative or messenger **b** : an unofficial representative ⟨travelers abroad should be ~s of goodwill⟩ — **am·bas·sa·do·ri·al** \-ˌbas-ə-ˈdōr-ē-əl, -ˈdȯr-\ *adj* — **am·bas·sa·dor·ship** \-ˈbas-əd-ər-ˌship\ *n*
ambassador–at–large *n, pl* **ambassadors–at–large** : a minister of the highest rank not accredited to a particular foreign government or sovereign
am·bas·sa·dress \am-ˈbas-ə-drəs, əm-, im-\ *n* **1** : a female ambassador **2** : the wife of an ambassador
am·beer \ˈam-ˌbi(ə)r\ *n* [prob. alter. of *amber;* fr. its color] *chiefly South & Midland* : TOBACCO JUICE
1am·ber \ˈam-bər\ *n* [ME *ambre,* fr. MF, fr. ML *ambra,* fr. Ar *ʽanbar* ambergris] **1** : a hard yellowish to brownish translucent fossil resin that takes a fine polish and is used chiefly in making ornamental objects (as beads) **2** : a variable color averaging a dark orange yellow
2amber *adj* **1** : consisting of amber **2** : resembling amber; *esp* : having the color amber
am·ber·gris \ˈam-bər-ˌgris, -ˌgrēs\ *n* [ME *ambregris,* fr. MF *ambre gris,* fr. *ambre* + *gris* gray — more at GRIZZLE] : a waxy substance found floating in or on the shores of tropical waters, believed to originate in the intestines of the sperm whale, and used in perfumery as a fixative
am·ber·jack \-ˌjak\ *n* [fr. its color] : any of several carangid fishes (genus *Seriola*); *esp* : a large vigorous sport fish (*S. dumerili*) of the western Atlantic
ambi- *prefix* [L *ambi-, amb-* both, around; akin to L *ambo* both, Gk *amphō* both, *amphi* around — more at BY] : both ⟨*ambi*valent⟩
am·bi·dex·ter·i·ty \ˌam-bi-(ˌ)dek-ˈster-ət-ē\ *n* : the quality or state of being ambidextrous
am·bi·dex·trous \ˌam-bi-ˈdek-strəs\ *adj* [LL *ambidexter,* fr. L *ambi-* + *dexter*] **1** : using both hands with equal ease **2** : unusually skillful : VERSATILE **3** : characterized by duplicity : DOUBLE-DEALING — **am·bi·dex·trous·ly** *adv*
am·bi·ence *or* **am·bi·ance** \ˈam-bē-ən(t)s, äⁿ-byäⁿs\ *n* [F *ambiance,* fr. *ambiant* ambient] : a surrounding or pervading atmosphere : ENVIRONMENT
1am·bi·ent \ˈam-bē-ənt\ *adj* [L *ambient-, ambiens,* prp. of *ambire* to go around, fr. *ambi-* + *ire* to go — more at ISSUE] : surrounding on all sides : ENCOMPASSING
2ambient *n* : an encompassing atmosphere : ENVIRONMENT
am·bi·gu·ity \ˌam-bə-ˈgyü-ət-ē\ *n, pl* **-ities** **1 a** : the quality or state of being ambiguous in meaning ⟨~ is often a feature of poetry⟩ **b** : an ambiguous word or expression **2** : UNCERTAINTY ⟨the basic ~ of her self-image⟩
am·big·u·ous \am-ˈbig-yə-wəs\ *adj* [L *ambiguus,* fr. *ambigere* to wander about, fr. *ambi-* + *agere* to drive — more at AGENT] **1 a** : doubtful or uncertain esp. from obscurity or indistinctness ⟨eyes of an ~ color⟩ **b** : INEXPLICABLE **2** : capable of being understood in two or more possible senses ***syn*** see OBSCURE ***ant*** explicit — **am·big·u·ous·ly** *adv* — **am·big·u·ous·ness** *n*
am·bi·sex·trous \ˌam-bi-ˈsek-strəs\ *adj* [alter. (influenced by *ambidextrous*) of *ambisexual* (common to both sexes)] **1** : not distinguishable as male or female ⟨~ clothing⟩ **2** : including males and females ⟨an ~ party⟩
am·bit \ˈam-bət\ *n* [ME, fr. L *ambitus,* fr. *ambitus,* pp. of *ambire*] **1** : CIRCUIT, COMPASS **2** : the bounds or limits of a place or district **3** : a sphere of action, expression, or influence : SCOPE
1am·bi·tion \am-ˈbish-ən\ *n* [ME, fr. MF or L; MF, fr. L *ambition-, ambitio,* lit., going around, fr. *ambitus,* pp.] **1 a** : an ardent desire for rank, fame, or power **b** : desire to achieve a particular end **2** : the object of ambition **3** : a desire for activity or exertion ⟨felt sick and had no ~⟩ — **am·bi·tion·less** \-ləs\ *adj*
syn AMBITION, ASPIRATION, PRETENSION *shared meaning element* : strong desire for advancement or success
2ambition *vt* : to have as one's ambition : DESIRE
am·bi·tious \am-ˈbish-əs\ *adj* **1 a** : having or controlled by ambition **b** : having a desire to achieve a particular goal : ASPIRING **2** : resulting from, characterized by, or showing ambition — **am·bi·tious·ly** *adv* — **am·bi·tious·ness** *n*
am·biv·a·lence \am-ˈbiv-ə-lən(t)s\ *n* [ISV] **1** : simultaneous attraction toward and repulsion from an object, person, or action **2 a** : continual fluctuation (as between one thing and its opposite) **b** : uncertainty as to which approach to follow — **am·biv·a·lent** \-lənt\ *adj* — **am·biv·a·lent·ly** *adv*
am·bi·ver·sion \ˌam-bi-ˈvər-zhən, -shən\ *n* [*ambi-* + *-version* (as in *introversion*)] : the personality configuration of an ambivert — **am·bi·ver·sive** \-ˈvər-siv, -ziv\ *adj*

ə abut	ᵊ kitten	ər further	a back	ā bake	ä cot, cart
au̇ out	ch chin	e less	ē easy	g gift	i trip	ī life
j joke	ŋ sing	ō flow	ȯ flaw	ȯi coin	th thin	t͟h this
ü loot	u̇ foot	y yet	yü few	yu̇ furious	zh vision

am·bi·vert \'am-bi-,vərt\ n [ambi- + -vert (as in introvert)] : a person having characteristics of both extrovert and introvert

¹am·ble \'am-bəl\ vi am·bled; am·bling \-b(ə-)liŋ\ [ME amblen, fr. MF ambler, fr. L ambulare to walk] : to go at or as if at an amble — SAUNTER — am·bler \-b(ə-)lər\ n

²amble n **1 a** : an easy gait of a horse in which the legs on the same side of the body move together **b** : ⁷RACK b **2** : an easy gait **3** : a leisurely walk

am·blyg·o·nite \am-'blig-ə-,nīt\ n [G amblygonit, fr. Gk amblygōnios obtuse-angled, fr. amblys blunt, dull + gōnia angle; akin to L molere to grind — more at MEAL, -GON] : a mineral (Li,Na)AlPO₄(F,OH) consisting of basic lithium aluminum phosphate commonly containing sodium and fluorine and occurring in white cleavable masses

am·bly·opia \,am-blē-'ō-pē-ə\ n [NL, fr. Gk amblyōpia, fr. amblys + -ōpia -opia] : dimness of sight without apparent change in the eye structures associated esp. with toxic effects or dietary deficiencies — **am·bly·opic** \-'ōpik, -'äp-ik\ adj

am·bo·cep·tor \'am-bō-,sep-tər\ n [ISV ambi- + receptor] : the lytic antibody used in complement-fixation tests

Am·boi·nese \,am-bȯ(i)-'nēz, -'nēs, am-'bȯi-\ or **Am·bo·nese** \,am-bə-'nēz, -'nēs\ n, pl **Amboinese** or **Ambonese** [Amboina (Ambon) + -ese] **1** : a native or inhabitant of Ambon **2** : the language of the people of Ambon

am·boy·na or **am·boi·na** \am-'bȯi-nə\ n [Amboina, Moluccas, Indonesia] : a mottled curly-grained wood of a leguminous tree (Pterocarpus indicus) of southeastern Asia

am·bro·sia \am-'brō-zh(ē-)ə\ n [L, fr. Gk, lit., immortality, fr. ambrotos immortal, fr. a- + -mbrotos (akin to brotos mortal) — more at MURDER] **1 a** : the food of the Greek and Roman gods **b** : the ointment or perfume of the gods **2** : something extremely pleasing to taste or smell **3** : a dessert made of oranges and shredded coconut — **am·bro·sial** \-zh(ē-)əl\ adj — **am·bro·sial·ly** \-ē\ adv

am·bro·type \'am-brə-,tīp\ n [Gk ambrotos + E type] : a positive picture made of a photographic negative on glass backed by a dark surface

am·bry \'am-brē\ \'äm-rē, 'ȯm-\ n, pl **ambries** [ME armarie, fr. OF, fr. L armarium, fr. arma weapons — more at ARM] **1** : a recess in a church wall (as for holding sacramental vessels) **2** dial chiefly Brit : PANTRY

ambs·ace \'äm-,zās\ n [ME ambes as, fr. OF, fr. ambes both + as aces] archaic : the lowest throw at dice; also : something worthless or unlucky

am·bu·la·crum \,am-byə-'lak-rəm, -'lāk-\ n, pl **-cra** \-rə\ [NL, fr. L, alley, fr. ambulare to walk] : one of the radial areas of echinoderms along which run the principal nerves, blood vessels, and elements of the water-vascular system — **am·bu·la·cral** \-rəl\ adj

am·bu·lance \'am-byə-lən(t)s\ n [F, field hospital, fr. ambulant itinerant, fr. L ambulant-, ambulans, prp. of ambulare] : a vehicle equipped for transporting the injured or sick

ambulance chaser n : a lawyer or lawyer's agent who incites accident victims to sue for damages — **ambulance chasing** n

am·bu·lant \'am-byə-lənt\ adj : moving about : AMBULATORY

am·bu·late \-,lāt\ vi **-lat·ed; -lat·ing** [L ambulatus, pp. of ambulare] : to move from place to place : WALK — **am·bu·la·tion** \,am-byə-'lā-shən\ n

¹am·bu·la·to·ry \'am-byə-lə-,tōr-ē, -,tȯr-\ adj **1** : of, relating to, or adapted to walking; also : occurring while walking **2** : moving from place to place : ITINERANT **3** : capable of being altered ⟨a will is ~ until the testator's death⟩ **4 a** : able to walk about and not bedridden **b** : involving an individual who is able to walk about ⟨~ medical care⟩ — **am·bu·la·to·ri·ly** \,am-byə-lə-'tōr-ə-lē, -'tȯr-\ adv

²ambulatory n, pl **-ries** : a sheltered place (as in a cloister or church) for walking

am·bus·cade \'am-bə-,skād, ,am-bə-\ n [MF embuscade, modif. of OIt imboscata, fr. imboscare to place in ambush, fr. in (fr. L) + bosco forest, perh. of Gmc origin; akin to OHG busc forest — more at IN, BUSH] : AMBUSH — **ambuscade** vi — **am·bus·cad·er** n

¹am·bush \'am-,bu̇sh\ vb [ME embushen, fr. OF embuschier, fr. en in (fr. L in) + busche stick of firewood] vt **1** : to station in ambush **2** : to attack from an ambush : WAYLAY ~ vi : to lie in wait : LURK syn see SURPRISE — **am·bush·er** n — **am·bush·ment** \-mənt\ n

²ambush n **1** : a trap in which concealed persons lie in wait to attack by surprise **2** : the persons stationed in ambush; also : their concealed position

amdt abbr amendment

ameba, ameban, amebic, ameboid var of AMOEBA, AMOEBAN, AMOEBIC, AMOEBOID

ame·bi·a·sis \,am-i-'bī-ə-səs\ n : infection with or disease caused by amoebas

ame·bic dysentery \ə-,mē-bik-\ n : acute intestinal amebiasis of man caused by an amoeba (Endamoeba histolytica) and marked by dysentery, griping pain, and erosion of the intestinal wall

amebocyte var of AMOEBOCYTE

âme dam·née \äm-dä-nā\ n, pl **âmes damnées** \äm-dä-nā(z)\ [F, lit., damned soul] : a willing tool of another person

ameer var of EMIR

ame·lio·rate \ə-'mēl-yə-,rāt, -'mē-lē-ə-\ vb **-rat·ed; -rat·ing** [alter. of meliorate] vt : to make better or more tolerable ~ vi : to grow better syn see IMPROVE ant worsen, deteriorate — **ame·lio·ra·tion** \-,mēl-yə-'rā-shən, -,mē-lē-ə-\ n — **ame·lio·ra·tive** \'mēl-yə-,rāt-iv, -'mē-lē-ə-\ adj — **ame·lio·ra·tor** \-,rāt-ər\ n — **ame·lio·ra·to·ry** \-rə-,tōr-ē, -,tȯr-\ adj

amen \(')ä-'men, (')ā-; 'ä- when sung\ interj [ME, fr. OE, fr. LL, fr. Gk amēn, fr. Heb āmēn] — used to express solemn ratification (as of an expression of faith) or hearty approval (as of an assertion)

ame·na·ble \ə-'mē-nə-bəl, -'men-ə-\ adj [prob. fr. (assumed) AF, fr. MF amener to lead up, fr. OF, fr. a- (fr. L ad-) + mener to lead, fr. L minare to drive, fr. minari to threaten — more at MOUNT] **1** : liable to be brought to account : ANSWERABLE ⟨citizens ~ to the law⟩ **2 a** : capable of submission (as to judgment or test) ⟨the

data is ~ to analysis⟩ **b** : readily brought to yield or submit : TRACTABLE ⟨a child ~ to discipline⟩ syn see OBEDIENT ant recalcitrant, refractory — **ame·na·bil·i·ty** \-,mē-nə-'bil-ət-ē, -,men-ə-\ n — **ame·na·bly** \-'mē-nə-blē, -'men-ə-\ adv

amen corner \,ä-,men-\ n : a conspicuous corner in a church occupied by fervent worshipers

amend \ə-'mend\ vb [ME amenden, fr. OF amender, modif. of L emendare, fr. e, ex out + menda fault; akin to L mendax lying, mendicus beggar, Skt mindā physical defect] vt **1** : to put right; specif : to make emendations in (as a text) **2 a** : to change or modify for the better : IMPROVE ⟨~ the situation⟩ **b** : to alter esp. in phraseology; specif : to alter formally by modification, deletion, or addition ⟨~ the constitution⟩ ~ vi : to reform oneself syn see CORRECT ant debase, impair — **amend·able** \-'men-də-bəl\ adj — **amend·er** n

amen·da·to·ry \ə-'men-də-,tōr-ē, -,tȯr-\ adj [amend + -atory (as in emendatory)] : CORRECTIVE

amend·ment \ə-'men(d)-mənt\ n **1** : the act of amending esp. for the better : CORRECTION **2** : a substance that aids plant growth indirectly by improving the condition of the soil **3 a** : the process of amending by parliamentary or constitutional procedure **b** : an alteration proposed or effected by this process ⟨the 18th ~⟩

amends \ə-'men(d)z\ n pl but sing or pl in constr [ME amendes, fr. OF, pl. of amende reparation, fr. amender] : compensation for a loss or injury : RECOMPENSE

ame·ni·ty \ə-'men-ət-ē, -'mē-nət-\ n, pl **-ties** [ME amenite, fr. L amoenitat-, amoenitas, fr. amoenus pleasant] **1 a** : the quality of being pleasant or agreeable **b** (1) : the attractiveness and value of real estate or of a residential structure (2) : a feature conducive to such attractiveness and value **2** : something that conduces to material comfort or convenience **3** : something (as a conventional social gesture) that conduces to smoothness or pleasantness of social intercourse

amen·or·rhea \,ā-,men-ə-'rē-ə, ,äm-,en-\ n [NL, fr. a- + Gk mēn month + NL -o- + -rrhea — more at MOON] : abnormal absence or suppression of the menstrual discharge — **amen·or·rhe·ic** \-'rē-ik\ adj

ament \'am-ənt, 'ā-mənt\ n [NL amentum, fr. L, thong, strap] : an indeterminate spicate inflorescence (as in the willow) bearing scaly bracts and apetalous unisexual flowers — **amen·ta·ceous** \,am-ən-'tā-shəs, ,ā-mən-\ adj — **amen·tif·er·ous** \-'tif-(ə-)rəs\ adj

amen·tia \(')ā-'men-ch(ē-)ə, (')ä-\ n [NL, fr. L, madness, fr. ament-, amens mad, fr. a- (fr. ab-) + ment-, mens mind — more at MIND] : mental deficiency; specif : a condition of lack of development of intellectual capacity

Amer abbr America; American

Am·er·asian \,am-ə-'rā-zhən, -shən\ n [American + Asian] : a person of mixed American and Asian descent; esp : one whose mother is Asian and whose father is American

staminate ament

amerce \ə-'mərs\ vt **amerced; amerc·ing** [ME amercien, fr. AF amercier, fr. OF a merci at (one's) mercy] : to punish by a fine whose amount is fixed by the court; broadly : PUNISH — **amerce·ment** \-'mər-smənt\ n — **amer·cia·ble** \-'mər-sē-ə-bəl, -'mər-shə-bəl\ adj

¹Amer·i·can \ə-'mer-ə-kən\ n **1** : an Indian of No. America or So. America **2** : a native or inhabitant of No. America or So. America **3** : a citizen of the U.S.

²American adj **1** : of or relating to America **2** : of or relating to the U.S. or its possessions or original territory **3** : of or relating to the division of mankind that comprises the Indians of No. America and So. America — **Amer·i·can·ness** \-kən-nəs\ n

Amer·i·ca·na \ə-,mer-ə-'kan-ə, -'kän-, -'kä-nə\ n pl : materials concerning or characteristic of America, its civilization, or its culture; also : a collection of such materials

American chameleon n : a lizard (Anolis carolinensis) of the southeastern U.S.

American cheese n : a process cheese made from American cheddar cheese

American dream n : an American social ideal that stresses egalitarianism and esp. material prosperity

American elm n : a large elm (Ulmus americana) with gradually spreading branches and pendulous branchlets that is common in eastern No. America

American English n : the native language of most inhabitants of the U.S. — used esp. with the implication that it is clearly distinguishable from British English yet not so divergent as to be a separate language

American foxhound n : any of an American breed of foxhounds that are smaller than the English foxhound but with longer ears and that have a dense hard glossy coat usu. of black, tan, and white, straight forelegs, and powerful hindquarters

American Indian n : a member of any of the aboriginal peoples of the western hemisphere except usu. the Eskimos constituting one of the divisions of the Mongoloid race

American Indian Day n : the fourth Friday in September observed in honor of the American Indian

Amer·i·can·ism \ə-'mer-ə-kə-,niz-əm\ n **1** : a characteristic feature of American English esp. as contrasted with British English **2** : attachment or allegiance to the traditions, interests, or ideals of the U.S. **3 a** : a custom or trait peculiar to America **b** : the political principles and practices essential to American national culture

Amer·i·can·ist \-kə-nəst\ n **1** : a specialist in the languages or cultures of the aboriginal inhabitants of America **2** : a specialist in American culture or history

American ivy n : VIRGINIA CREEPER

Amer·i·can·iza·tion \ə-,mer-ə-kə-nə-'zā-shən\ n **1** : the act or process of Americanizing **2** : instruction of foreigners (as immigrants) in English and in U.S. history, government, and culture

Amer·i·can·ize \ə-'mer-ə-kə-ˌnīz\ *vb* **-ized; -iz·ing** *vt* : to cause to acquire or conform to American characteristics ~ *vi* : to acquire or conform to American traits
American plan *n* : a hotel plan whereby the daily rates cover the costs of the room and meals — compare EUROPEAN PLAN
American saddle horse *n* : a 3-gaited or 5-gaited saddle horse of a breed developed chiefly in Kentucky from Thoroughbreds and native stock
American Standard Version *n* : an American version of the Bible based on the Revised Version and published in 1901 — called also *American Revised Version*
American trotter *n* : STANDARDBRED
American water spaniel *n* : a medium-sized spaniel of American origin with a thick curly chocolate or liver-colored coat
am·er·i·ci·um \ˌam-ə-'ris(h)-ē-əm\ *n* [NL, fr. *America* + NL *-ium*] : a radioactive metallic element produced by bombardment of plutonium with high-energy neutrons — see ELEMENT table
Amerind *abbr* American Indian
Am·er·in·di·an \ˌam-ə-'rin-dē-ən\ *n* [*American* + *Indian*] : AMERICAN INDIAN — **Am·er·ind** \'am-ə-ˌrind\ *n* — **Amerindian** *adj* — **Am·er·in·dic** \ˌam-ə-'rin-dik\ *adj*
âmes damnées *pl of* ÂME DAMNÉE
am·e·thop·ter·in \ˌam-ə-'thäp-tə-rən\ *n* [*amin-* + *meth-* + *pteroic acid* + *-in*] : METHOTREXATE
am·e·thyst \'am-ə-thəst, -(ˌ)thist\ *n* [ME *amatiste*, fr. OF & L; OF, fr. L *amethystus*, fr. Gk *amethystos*, lit., remedy against drunkenness, fr. *a-* + *methyein* to be drunk, fr. *methy* wine — more at MEAD] **1 a** : a clear purple or bluish violet variety of crystallized quartz that is much used as a jeweler's stone **b** : a deep purple variety of corundum **2** : a variable color averaging a moderate purple — **am·e·thys·tine** \ˌam-ə-'this-tən\ *adj*
am·e·tro·pia \ˌam-ə-'trō-pē-ə\ *n* [NL, fr. Gk *ametros* without measure (fr. *a-* + *metron* measure) + NL *-opia* — more at MEASURE] : an abnormal refractive condition of the eye in which images fail to focus upon the retina — **am·e·tro·pic** \-'trō-pik, -'träp-ik\ *adj*
AMG *abbr* allied military government
Am·har·ic \am-'har-ik\ *n* : the Semitic language that is the official language of Ethiopia — **Amharic** *adj*
ami·a·ble \'ā-mē-ə-bəl\ *adj* [ME, fr. MF, fr. LL *amicabilis* friendly, fr. L *amicus* friend; akin to L *amare* to love] **1** *archaic* : PLEASING, ADMIRABLE **2 a** : generally agreeable ⟨an ~ musical comedy⟩ **b** : having a friendly, sociable, and congenial disposition — **ami·a·bil·i·ty** \ˌā-mē-ə-'bil-ət-ē\ *n* — **ami·a·ble·ness** \'ā-mē-ə-bəl-nəs\ *n* — **ami·a·bly** \-blē\ *adv*
syn AMIABLE, GOOD-NATURED, OBLIGING, COMPLAISANT *shared meaning element* : having or showing a will to please ***ant*** unamiable
am·i·an·thus \ˌam-ē-'an(t)-thəs\ *or* **am·i·an·tus** \-'ant-əs\ *n* [L *amiantus*, fr. Gk *amiantos*, fr. *amiantos* unpolluted, fr. *a-* + *miainein* to pollute] : fine silky asbestos
am·i·ca·ble \'am-i-kə-bəl\ *adj* [ME, fr. LL *amicabilis*] : characterized by friendly goodwill : PEACEABLE — **am·i·ca·bil·i·ty** \ˌam-i-kə-'bil-ət-ē\ *n* — **am·i·ca·ble·ness** \'am-i-kə-bəl-nəs\ *n* — **am·i·ca·bly** \-blē\ *adv*
syn AMICABLE, NEIGHBORLY, FRIENDLY *shared meaning element* : exhibiting goodwill and an absence of antagonism ***ant*** antagonistic
am·ice \'am-əs\ *n* [ME *amis*, prob. fr. MF, pl. of *amit*, fr. ML *amictus*, fr. L, cloak, fr. *amictus*, pp. of *amicire* to wrap around, fr. *am-*, *amb-* around + *jacere* to throw — more at AMBI-, JET] : a liturgical vestment made of an oblong piece of cloth usu. of white linen and worn about the neck and shoulders and partly under the alb — see VESTMENT illustration
ami·cus cu·ri·ae \ə-ˌmē-kə-'sk(y)ůr-ē-ˌī\ *n, pl* **ami·ci curiae** \-ˌmē-(ˌ)kē-'k(y)ůr-\ [NL, lit., friend of the court] : one (as a professional person or organization) that is not a party to a particular litigation but that is permitted by the court to advise it in respect to some matter of law that directly affects the case in question
amid \ə-'mid\ *or* **amidst** \-'midst, -'mitst\ *prep* [*amid* fr. ME *amidde*, fr. OE *onmiddan*, fr. *on* + *middan*, dat. of *midde* mid; *amidst* fr. ME *amiddes*, fr. *amidde* + *-es* -s] **1** : in or into the middle of : AMONG **2** : DURING
amid- *or* **amido-** *comb form* [ISV, fr. *amide*] **1** : containing the group NH_2 characteristic of amides united to a radical of acid character ⟨*amido*sulfuric⟩ **2** : AMIN- ⟨*amido*phenol⟩
am·i·dase \'am-ə-ˌdās, -ˌdāz\ *n* [ISV *amide* + *-ase*] : an enzyme that hydrolyzes acid amides usu. with the liberation of ammonia
am·ide \'am-ˌīd, -əd\ *n* [ISV, fr. NL *ammonia*] : a compound resulting from replacement of an atom of hydrogen in ammonia by an element or radical or of one or more atoms of hydrogen in ammonia by univalent acid radicals — compare IMIDE — **amid·ic** \ə-'mid-ik, a-\ *adj*
ami·do \ə-'mēd-(ˌ)ō, 'am-ə-ˌdō\ *adj* [*amid-*] **1** : relating to or containing the group NH_2 or a substituted group NHR or NR_2 united to a radical of acid character — compare AMINO **2** : AMINO
am·i·dol \'am-ə-ˌdȯl, -ˌdōl\ *n* [G, fr. *Amidol*, a trademark] : a colorless crystalline salt $C_6H_8N_2O.2HCl$ used chiefly as a photographic developer
amid·ships \ə-'mid-ˌships\ *adv* **1** : in or toward the part of a ship midway between the bow and the stern **2** : in or toward the middle
ami·go \ə-'mē-(ˌ)gō, ä-\ *n, pl* **-gos** [Sp, fr. L *amicus* — more at AMIABLE] : FRIEND
amin- *or* **amino-** *comb form* [ISV, fr. *amine*] : containing the group NH_2 united to a radical other than an acid radical ⟨*amino*benzoic acid⟩
amine \ə-'mēn, 'am-ˌēn\ *n* [ISV, fr. NL *ammonia*] **1** : any of various basic compounds derived from ammonia by replacement of hydrogen by one or more univalent hydrocarbon radicals **2** : a compound containing one or more halogen atoms attached to nitrogen — **ami·nic** \ə-'mē-nik, a-, -'min-ik\ *adj*
ami·no \ə-'mē-(ˌ)nō\ *adj* [*amin-*] : relating to or containing the group NH_2 or a substituted group NHR or NR_2 united to a radical other than an acid radical — compare AMIDO
amino acid *n* : an amphoteric organic acid containing the amino group NH_2; *esp* : any of the alpha-amino acids that are the chief components of proteins and are synthesized by living cells or are obtained as essential components of the diet
ami·no·ac·id·uria \ə-ˌmē-nō-ˌas-ə-'d(y)ůr-ē-ə\ *n* [NL] : a condition in which one or more amino acids are excreted in excessive amounts
ami·no·ben·zo·ic acid \ə-ˌmē-nō-ben-ˌzō-ik-\ *n* [ISV] : any of three crystalline derivatives $C_7H_7NO_2$ of benzoic acid of which the yellowish para-substituted acid is a growth factor of the vitamin B complex and of folic acids
amino nitrogen *n* : nitrogen occurring as a constituent of the amino group
am·i·noph·yl·line \ˌam-ə-'näf-ə-lən\ *n* [*amin-* + *theophylline*] : a compound of theophylline and the diamine of ethylene that has various medical and veterinary uses
ami·no·py·rine \ə-ˌmē-nō-'pī(ə)r-ˌēn\ *n* [ISV, fr. *amin-* + *antipyrine*] : a white crystalline compound $C_{13}H_{17}N_3O$ formerly much used to relieve pain and fever but now largely curtailed because of the association of fatal agranulocytosis with its abuse
ami·no·sal·i·cyl·ic acid \ə-ˌmē-nō-ˌsal-ə-ˌsil-ik-\ *n* : any of four isomeric derivatives $C_7H_8O_3N$ of salicylic acid that have a single amino group; *esp* : PARA-AMINOSALICYLIC ACID
ami·no·trans·fer·ase \-'tran(t)s-fə-ˌrās, -ˌrāz\ *n* : TRANSAMINASE
ami·no·tri·azole \ə-ˌmē-nō-'trī-ə-ˌzōl\ *n* [*amin-* + *triazole*] : AMITROLE
amir *var of* EMIR
Amish \'äm-ish, 'am-, 'ām-\ *adj* [prob. fr. G *amisch*, fr. Jacob *Amman* or *Amen fl* 1693 Swiss Mennonite bishop] : of or relating to a strict sect of Mennonite followers of Amman that settled in America chiefly in the 18th century — **Amish** *n*
[1]**amiss** \ə-'mis\ *adv* **1 a** : in a mistaken way : WRONGLY ⟨if you think he is guilty, you judge ~⟩ **b** : ASTRAY ⟨something had gone ~⟩ **2** : in a faulty way : IMPERFECTLY
[2]**amiss** *adj* **1** : not being in accordance with right order **2** : FAULTY, IMPERFECT **3** : out of place in given circumstances — usu. used with a negative ⟨a few pertinent remarks may not be ~ here⟩
ami·to·sis \ˌā-mī-'tō-səs\ *n* [NL, fr. [2]a- + *mitosis*] : cell division by simple cleavage of the nucleus and division of the cytoplasm without spindle formation or appearance of chromosomes — **ami·tot·ic** \-'tät-ik\ *adj* — **ami·tot·i·cal·ly** \-i-k(ə-)lē\ *adv*
am·i·trip·ty·line \ˌam-ə-'trip-tə-ˌlēn\ *n* [origin unknown] : an antidepressant drug $C_{20}H_{23}N$
am·i·trole \'am-ə-ˌtrōl\ *n* [*amin-* + *triazole*] : a systemic herbicide $C_2H_4N_4$ used in areas other than food croplands
am·i·ty \'am-ət-ē\ *n, pl* **-ties** [ME *amite*, fr. MF *amité*, fr. ML *amicitas*, fr. L *amicus* friend — more at AMIABLE] : FRIENDSHIP; *esp* : friendly relations between nations
am·me·ter \'am-ˌēt-ər\ *n* [*ampere* + *-meter*] : an instrument for measuring electric current in amperes
am·mine \'am-ˌēn, a-'mēn\ *n* [ISV *ammonia* + *-ine*] **1** : a molecule of ammonia as it exists in a coordination complex ⟨hex-*ammine*-cobalt chloride $CoN_6H_{18}Cl_3$⟩ **2** : an ammino compound
am·mi·no \'am-ə-ˌnō, a-'mē-(ˌ)nō\ *adj* [ISV *ammino-*, fr. *ammine*] : of, relating to, or being an ammine
am·mo \'am-(ˌ)ō\ *n* [by shortening & alter.] : AMMUNITION
am·mo·nia \ə-'mō-nyə\ *n* [NL, fr. L *sal ammoniacus* sal ammoniac, lit., salt of Ammon, fr. Gk *ammōniakos* of Ammon, fr. *Ammōn* Ammon, Amen, an Egyptian god near one of whose temples it was prepared] **1** : a pungent colorless gaseous alkaline compound of nitrogen and hydrogen NH_3 that is very soluble in water and can easily be condensed to a liquid by cold and pressure **2** : AMMONIA WATER
am·mo·ni·ac \ə-'mō-nē-ˌak\ *n* [ME & L; ME, fr. L *ammoniacum*, fr. Gk *ammōniakon*, fr. neut. of *ammōniakos* of Ammon] : the aromatic gum resin of a Persian herb (*Dorema ammoniacum*) of the carrot family used as an expectorant and stimulant and in plasters
am·mo·ni·a·cal \ˌam-ə-'nī-ə-kəl\ *or* **am·mo·ni·ac** \ə-'mō-nē-ˌak\ *adj* : of, relating to, containing, or having the properties of ammonia
am·mo·ni·ate \ə-'mō-nē-ˌāt\ *vt* **-at·ed; -at·ing** **1** : to combine or impregnate with ammonia or an ammonium compound **2** : to subject to ammonification — **am·mo·ni·a·tion** \-ˌmō-nē-'ā-shən\ *n*
ammonia water *n* : a water solution of ammonia
am·mo·ni·fi·ca·tion \ə-ˌmän-ə-fə-'kā-shən, -ˌmō-nə-\ *n* **1** : the act or process of ammoniating **2** : decomposition with production of ammonia or ammonium compounds esp. by the action of bacteria on nitrogenous organic matter — **am·mo·ni·fi·er** \-'män-ə-ˌfī(-ə)r, nə-\ *n* — **am·mo·ni·fy** \-ˌfī\ *vb*
am·mo·nite \'am-ə-ˌnīt\ *n* [NL *ammonites*, fr. L *cornu Ammonis*, lit., horn of Ammon] : any of numerous flat spiral fossil shells of cephalopods (order Ammonoidea) esp. abundant in the Mesozoic age — **am·mo·nit·ic** \ˌam-ə-'nit-ik\ *adj*
Am·mon·ite \'am-ə-ˌnīt\ *n* [LL *Ammonites*, fr. Heb *'Ammōn*, Ammon (son of Lot), descendant of Ammon] : a member of a Semitic people who in Old Testament times lived east of the Jordan between the Jabbok and the Arnon — **Ammonite** *adj*
am·mo·ni·um \ə-'mō-nē-əm\ *n* [NL, fr. *ammonia*] : an ion NH_4^+ or radical NH_4 derived from ammonia by combination with a hydrogen ion or atom and known in compounds (as salts) that resemble in properties the compounds of the alkali metals and in organic compounds (as quaternary ammonium compounds)
ammonium carbonate *n* : a carbonate of ammonium; *specif* : the commercial mixture of the bicarbonate and carbamate used esp. in smelling salts

ə abut ᵊ kitten ər further a back ā bake ä cot, cart
aů out ch chin e less ē easy g gift i trip ī life
j joke ŋ sing ō flow ȯ flaw ȯi coin th thin t͟h this
ü loot ů foot y yet yü few yů furious zh vision

ammonium chloride *n* **:** a white crystalline volatile salt NH_4Cl that is used in dry cells and as an expectorant — called also *sal ammoniac*

ammonium cyanate *n* **:** an inorganic white crystalline salt N_5H_4OC that can be converted into organic urea

ammonium hydroxide *n* **:** a weakly basic compound NH_5O that is formed when ammonia dissolves in water and that exists only in solution

ammonium nitrate *n* **:** a colorless crystalline salt $N_2H_4O_3$ used in explosives and fertilizers

ammonium phosphate *n* **:** a phosphate of ammonium; *esp* **:** a white crystalline compound $N_2H_9PO_4$ used esp. as a fertilizer and as a fire retardant

ammonium sulfate *n* **:** a colorless crystalline salt $N_2H_8SO_4$ used chiefly as a fertilizer

am·mo·noid \'am-ə-ˌnȯid\ *n* **:** AMMONITE

am·mu·ni·tion \ˌam-yə-'nish-ən\ *n* [obs. F *amunition,* fr. MF, alter. of *munition*] **1 a :** the projectiles with their fuzes, propelling charges, and primers fired from guns **b :** explosive military items (as grenades or bombs) **2 :** material for use in attacking or defending a position ⟨derived their critical ~ from . . . Aristotelian doctrines — R. A. Hall *b*1911⟩

Amn *abbr* airman

am·ne·sia \am-'nē-zhə\ *n* [NL, fr. Gk *amnēsia* forgetfulness, prob. alter. of *amnēstia*] **1 :** loss of memory due usu. to brain injury, shock, fatigue, repression, or illness **2 :** a gap in one's memory — **am·ne·si·ac** \-z(h)ē-ˌak\ *or* **am·ne·sic** \-zik, -sik\ *adj or n* — **am·nes·tic** \-'nes-tik\ *adj*

am·nes·ty \'am-nə-stē\ *n, pl* **-ties** [Gk *amnēstia* forgetfulness, fr. *amnēstos* forgotten, fr. *a-* + *mnasthai* to remember — more at MIND] **:** the act of an authority (as a government) by which pardon is granted to a large group of individuals — **amnesty** *vt*

am·nio·cen·te·sis \ˌam-nē-ō-(ˌ)sen-'tē-səs\ *n* [NL, fr. *amnion* + *centesis* puncture, fr. Gk *kentesis,* fr. *kentein* to prick — more at CENTER] **:** the surgical insertion of a hollow needle through the abdominal wall and uterus of a pregnant female esp. to obtain amniotic fluid for the determination of sex or chromosomal abnormality

am·ni·on \'am-nē-ˌän, -ən\ *n, pl* **amnions** *or* **am·nia** \-nē-ə\ [NL, fr. Gk, caul, prob. fr. dim. of *amnos* lamb — more at YEAN] **1 :** a thin membrane forming a closed sac about the embryos of reptiles, birds, and mammals and containing a serous fluid in which the embryo is immersed **2 :** a membrane analogous to the amnion and occurring in various invertebrates — **am·ni·ote** \-nē-ˌōt\ *adj or n* — **am·ni·ot·ic** \ˌam-nē-'ät-ik\ *adj*

amo·bar·bi·tal \ˌam-ō-'bär-bə-ˌtȯl\ *n* [*amyl* + *-o-* + *barbital*] **:** a barbiturate $C_{11}H_{18}N_2O_3$ used as a hypnotic and sedative; *also* **:** its sodium salt

amoe·ba \ə-'mē-bə\ *n, pl* **-bas** *or* **-bae** \-(ˌ)bē\ [NL, genus name, fr. Gk *amoibē* change, fr. *ameibein* to change — more at MIGRATE] **:** any of a large genus (*Amoeba*) of naked rhizopod protozoans with lobed and never anastomosing pseudopodia and without permanent organelles or supporting structures that are widely distributed in fresh and salt water and moist terrestrial situations; *broadly* **:** a naked rhizopod or other amoeboid protozoan — **amoe·bic** \-bik\ *also* **amoe·ban** \-bən\ *adj*

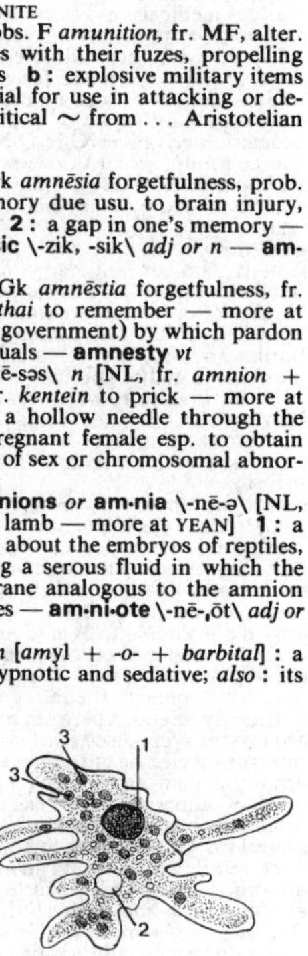

amoeba: *1* nucleus, *2* contractile vacuole, *3* food vacuoles

am·oe·bi·a·sis *var of* AMEBIASIS

amoe·bo·cyte \ə-'mē-bə-ˌsīt\ *n* **:** a cell (as a phagocyte) having amoeboid form or movements

amoe·boid \-ˌbȯid\ *adj* **:** resembling an amoeba specif. in moving or changing in shape by means of protoplasmic flow

¹amok \ə-'mək, -'mäk\ *adv* [Malay *amok*] **1 :** in a murderously frenzied state **2 a :** in a violently raging manner ⟨a virus that had run ~⟩ **b :** in an undisciplined or faulty manner

²amok *adj* **:** possessed with a murderous or violently uncontrollable frenzy

³amok *n* **:** a murderous frenzy that occurs chiefly among Malays

amo·le \ə-'mō-lē\ *n* [Sp. fr. Nahuatl *amolli* soap] **:** a plant part (as a root) possessing detergent properties and serving as a substitute for soap; *also* **:** a plant so used

among \ə-'məŋ\ *also* **amongst** \-'məŋ(k)st\ *prep* [*among* fr. ME, fr. OE *on gemonge,* fr. *on* + *gemonge,* dat. of *gemong* crowd, fr. *ge-* (associative prefix) + *-mong* (akin to OE *mengan* to mix); *amongst* fr. ME *amonges,* fr. *among* + *-es* -s — more at CO-, MINGLE] **1 :** in or through the midst of **:** surrounded by **2 :** in company or association with ⟨living ~ artists⟩ **3 :** by or through the aggregate of ⟨discontent ~ the poor⟩ **4 :** in the number or class of ⟨wittiest ~ poets⟩ ⟨~ other things he was president of his college class⟩ **5 :** in shares to each of ⟨divided ~ the heirs⟩ **6 a :** through the reciprocal acts of ⟨quarrel ~ themselves⟩ **b :** through the joint action of ⟨made a fortune ~ themselves⟩

amon·til·la·do \ə-ˌmän-tə-'läd-(ˌ)ō, -ti(l)-'yäth-(ˌ)ō\ *n, pl* **-dos** [Sp, fr. *a* to + *montilla* a wine from Montilla, Spain] **:** a pale dry sherry

amor·al \(')ā-'mȯr-əl, (')a-, -'mär-\ *adj* **1 a :** being neither moral nor immoral; *specif* **:** lying outside the sphere to which moral judgments apply **b :** lacking moral sensibility ⟨infants are ~⟩ **2 :** being outside or beyond the moral order or a particular code of morals ⟨~ customs⟩ ***syn*** see IMMORAL — **amor·al·ism** \-ə-ˌliz-əm\ *n* — **amo·ral·i·ty** \ˌā-mə-'ral-ət-ē, ˌa-, -(ˌ)mȯ-\ *n* — **amor·al·ly** \(')ā-'mȯr-ə-lē, (')a-, -'mär-\ *adv*

amo·ret·to \ˌam-ə-'ret-(ˌ)ō, ˌäm-\ *n, pl* **-ti** \-(ˌ)ē\ *or* **amorettos** [It, dim. of *amore* love, cupid, fr. L *amor*] **:** CUPID, CHERUB 2

am·or·ist \'am-ə-rəst\ *n* **1 :** a devotee of love and esp. sexual love **:** GALLANT **2 :** one that writes about romantic love — **am·or·is·tic** \ˌam-ə-'ris-tik\ *adj*

Am·o·rite \'am-ə-ˌrīt\ *n* [Heb *Ĕmōrī*] **:** a member of one of various Semitic peoples living in Mesopotamia, Syria, and Palestine during the 3d and 2d millennia B.C. — **Amorite** *adj*

am·o·rous \'am-(ə-)rəs\ *adj* [ME, fr. MF, fr. ML *amorosus,* fr. L *amor* love, fr. *amare* to love] **1 :** strongly moved by love and esp. sexual love ⟨~ women⟩ **2 :** being in love **:** ENAMORED — usu. used with *of* ⟨~ of the girl⟩ **3 a :** indicative of love ⟨received ~ glances from her partner⟩ **b :** of or relating to love ⟨an ~ novel⟩ — **am·o·rous·ly** *adv* — **am·o·rous·ness** *n*

amor·phism \ə-'mȯr-ˌfiz-əm\ *n* **:** amorphous quality

amor·phous \-fəs\ *adj* [Gk *amorphos,* fr. *a-* + *morphē* form] **1 a :** having no definite form **:** SHAPELESS ⟨an ~ cloud mass⟩ **b :** being without definite character or nature **:** UNCLASSIFIABLE **c :** lacking organization or unity **2 :** having no real or apparent crystalline form **:** UNCRYSTALLIZED ⟨an ~ mineral⟩ — **amor·phous·ly** *adv* — **amor·phous·ness** *n*

amort \ə-'mȯ(ə)rt\ *adj* [short for *all-a-mort,* by folk etymology fr. MF *a la mort* to the death] *archaic* **:** being at the point of death

am·or·ti·za·tion \ˌam-ərt-ə-'zā-shən *also* ə-ˌmȯrt-\ *n* **1 :** the act or process of amortizing **2 :** the result of amortizing

am·or·tize \'am-ər-ˌtīz *also* ə-'mȯr-\ *vt* **-tized; -tiz·ing** [ME *amortisen* to deaden, alienate in mortmain, modif. of MF *amortiss-,* stem of *amortir,* fr. (assumed) VL *admortire* to deaden, fr. L *ad-* + *mort-, mors* death — more at MURDER] **:** to provide for the gradual extinguishment of (as a mortgage) usu. by contribution to a sinking fund at the time of each periodic interest payment — **am·or·tiz·able** \-ˌtī-zə-bəl\ *adj*

Amos \'ā-məs\ *n* [Heb *'Āmōs*] **1 :** a Hebrew prophet of the 8th century B.C. **2 :** a prophetic book of canonical Jewish and Christian Scripture — see BIBLE table

¹amount \ə-'mau̇nt\ *vi* [ME *amounten,* fr. OF *amonter,* fr. *amont* upward, fr. *a-* (fr. L *ad-*) + *mont* mountain — more at MOUNT] **1 :** to add up ⟨the bill ~s to $10⟩ **2 :** to be equivalent ⟨acts that ~ to treason⟩

²amount *n* **1 :** the total number or quantity **:** AGGREGATE **2 a :** the whole effect, significance, or import **b :** the quantity at hand or under consideration ⟨has an enormous ~ of energy⟩ **3 :** a principal sum and the interest on it

amour \ə-'mu̇(ə)r, ä-, a-\ *n* [ME, love, affection, fr. OF, fr. OProv *amor,* fr. L, fr. *amare* to love] **:** a usu. illicit love affair

amour pro·pre \ˌam-ˌu̇r-'prōprᵊ, ˌäm-, -'prȯprᵊ\ *n* [F *amour-propre,* lit., love of oneself] **:** SELF-ESTEEM

Amoy \ä-'mȯi, a-, ə-\ *n* **:** the dialect of Chinese spoken in and near Amoy in southeastern China

amp *abbr* ampere

AMP \ˌā-ˌem-'pē\ *n* [*a*denosine *m*ono*p*hosphate] **:** a mononucleotide of adenine $C_{10}H_{12}N_5O_3H_2PO_4$ that was orig. isolated from mammalian muscle and is reversibly convertible to ADP and ATP in metabolic reactions — called also *adenosine monophosphate;* compare CYCLIC AMP

am·per·age \'am-p(ə-)rij, -ˌpi(ə)r-ij\ *n* **:** the strength of a current of electricity expressed in amperes

am·pere \'am-ˌpi(ə)r *also* -ˌpe(ə)r\ *n* [André M. *Ampère* †1836 F physicist] **1 :** the practical mks unit of electric current that is equivalent to a flow of one coulomb per second or to the steady current produced by one volt applied across a resistance of one ohm **2 :** a unit of electric current equal to a constant current that when maintained in two straight parallel conductors of infinite length and negligible circular sections one meter apart in a vacuum produces between the conductors a force equal to 2×10^{-7} newton per meter of length

ampere-hour *n* **:** a unit quantity of electricity equal to the quantity carried past any point of a circuit in one hour by a steady current of one ampere

ampere-turn *n* **:** the mks unit of magnetomotive force equal to the magnetomotive force around a path that links with one turn of wire carrying an electric current of one ampere

am·per·sand \'am-pər-ˌsand\ *n* [alter. of *and* (&)*per se and,* lit., (the character) & by itself (is the word) *and*] **:** a character typically & standing for the word *and*

am·phet·amine \am-'fet-ə-ˌmēn, -mən\ *n* [ISV *a*lpha + *m*ethyl + *phe*n- + e*t*hyl + *amine*] **1 :** a compound $C_9H_{13}N$ used esp. as an inhalant and in solution as a spray in head colds and hay fever **2 :** any of various derivatives of amphetamine used as stimulants for the central nervous system: as **a :** a white crystalline compound $C_{18}H_{28}N_2O_4S$ — called also *amphetamine sulfate* **b :** a compound consisting of the dextrorotatory form of amphetamine sulfate — called also *dextroamphetamine*

amphi- *or* **amph-** *prefix* [L *amphi-* around, on both sides, fr. Gk *amphi-, amph-,* fr. *amphi* — more at AMBI-] **:** on both sides **:** of both kinds **:** both ⟨*amphi*biotic⟩ ⟨*amphi*stylar⟩

am·phib·ia \am-'fib-ē-ə\ *n pl* **:** AMPHIBIANS

am·phib·i·an \-ē-ən\ *n* [deriv. of Gk *amphibion* amphibious being, fr. neut. of *amphibios*] **1 :** an amphibious organism; *esp* **:** any of a class (Amphibia) of cold-blooded vertebrates (as frogs, toads, or newts) intermediate in many characters between fishes and reptiles and having gilled aquatic larvae and air-breathing adults **2 :** an airplane designed to take off from and land on either land or water **3 :** a flat-bottomed vehicle that moves on tracks having finlike extensions by means of which it is propelled on land or water — **amphibian** *adj*

am·phib·i·ous \am-'fib-ē-əs\ *adj* [Gk *amphibios,* lit., living a double life, fr. *amphi-* + *bios* mode of life — more at QUICK] **1 :** able to live both on land and in water ⟨~ plants⟩ **2 a :** relating to or adapted for both land and water ⟨~ vehicles⟩ **b :** executed by coordinated action of land, sea, and air forces organized for invasion; *also* **:** trained or organized for such action ⟨~ forces⟩ **3 :** combining two characteristics — **am·phib·i·ous·ly** *adv* — **am·phib·i·ous·ness** *n*

am·phi·bole \'am(p)-fə-ˌbōl\ *n* [F, fr. LL *amphibolus,* fr. Gk *amphibolos* ambiguous fr. *amphiballein* to throw round, doubt, fr. *amphi-* + *ballein* to throw — more at DEVIL] **1 :** HORNBLENDE **2 :** any of a group of minerals $A_2B_5(Si, Al)_8O_{22}(OH)_2$ with like crystal structures usu. containing three groups of metal ions

am·phib·o·lite \am-'fib-ə-ˌlīt\ *n* : a usu. metamorphic rock consisting essentially of amphibole — **am·phib·o·lit·ic** \(ˌ)am-ˌfib-ə-'lit-ik\ *adj*

am·phi·brach \'am(p)-fə-ˌbrak\ *n* [L *amphibrachys*, fr. Gk, lit., short at both ends, fr. *amphi-* + *brachys* short — more at BRIEF] : a metrical foot consisting of a long syllable between two short syllables in quantitative verse or of a stressed syllable between two unstressed syllables in accentual verse ⟨*romantic* is an accentual ∼⟩ — **am·phi·brach·ic** \ˌam(p)-fə-'brak-ik\ *adj*

am·phic·ty·o·ny \am-'fik-tē-ə-nē\ *n, pl* **-nies** [Gk *amphiktyonia*] : an association of neighboring states in ancient Greece to defend a common religious center; *broadly* : an association of neighboring states for their common interest — **am·phic·ty·on·ic** \(ˌ)am-ˌfik-tē-'än-ik\ *adj*

am·phi·dip·loid \ˌam(p)-fi-'dip-ˌlȯid\ *adj, of an interspecific hybrid* : having a complete diploid chromosome set from each parent strain — **amphidiploid** *n* — **am·phi·dip·loi·dy** \-ˌdip-ˌlȯid-ē\ *n*

am·phi·ma·cer \am-'fim-ə-sər\ *n* [L *amphimacer*, fr. Gk *amphimakros*, lit., long at both ends, fr. *amphi-* + *makros* long — more at MEAGER] : a metrical foot consisting of a short syllable between two long syllables in quantitative verse or of an unstressed syllable between two stressed syllables in accentual verse ⟨*twenty-two* is an accentual ∼⟩

am·phi·mic·tic \ˌam(p)-fi-'mik-tik\ *adj* [ISV *amphi-* + Gk *miktos* blended, fr. *mignynai*] : capable of interbreeding freely and of producing fertile offspring — **am·phi·mic·ti·cal·ly** \-ti-k(ə-)lē\ *adv*

am·phi·mix·is \-'mik-səs\ *n, pl* **-mix·es** \-ˌsēz\ [NL, fr. *amphi-* + Gk *mixis* mingling, fr. *mignynai* to mix — more at MIX] : the union of germ cells in sexual reproduction

Am·phi·on \am-'fī-ən\ *n* [L, fr. Gk *Amphiōn*] : a musician who built the walls of Thebes by charming the stones into place with his lyre

am·phi·ox·us \ˌam(p)-fē-'äk-səs\ *n, pl* **-oxi** \-ˌsī\ *or* **-ox·us·es** [NL, fr. *amphi-* + Gk *oxys* sharp] : any of a genus (*Branchiostoma*) of lancelets; *broadly* : LANCELET

am·phi·ploid \'am(p)-fi-ˌplȯid\ *adj, of an interspecific hybrid* : having at least one complete diploid set of chromosomes derived from each ancestral species — **amphiploid** *n* — **am·phi·ploi·dy** \-ˌplȯid-ē\ *n*

am·phi·pod \-ˌpäd\ *n* [deriv. of Gk *amphi-* + *pod-, pous* foot — more at FOOT] : any of a large group (Amphipoda) of small crustaceans (as the sand flea) with a laterally compressed body — **amphipod** *adj*

am·phi·pro·style \ˌam(p)-fi-'prō-ˌstīl\ *adj* [L *amphiprostylos*, fr. Gk, fr. *amphi-* + *prostylos* having pillars in front, fr. *pro-* + *stylos* pillar — more at STEER] : having columns at each end only ⟨an ∼ building⟩ — **amphiprostyle** *n*

am·phis·bae·na \ˌam(p)-fəs-'bē-nə\ *n* [L, fr. Gk *amphisbaina*, fr. *amphis* on both sides (fr. *amphi* around) + *bainein* to walk, go — more at BY, COME] : a serpent in classical mythology having a head at each end and capable of moving in either direction — **am·phis·bae·nic** \-nik\ *adj*

am·phi·sty·lar \ˌam(p)-fi-'stī-lər\ *adj* : having columns at both ends or on both sides ⟨an ∼ building⟩

am·phi·the·ater \'am(p)-fə-ˌthē-ət-ər\ *n* [L *amphitheatrum*, fr. Gk *amphitheatron*, fr. *amphi-* + *theatron* theater] 1 : an oval or circular building with rising tiers of seats ranged about an open space and used in ancient Rome esp. for contests and spectacles 2 a : a very large auditorium b : a room with a gallery from which doctors and students may observe surgical operations c : a rising gallery in a modern theater d : a flat or gently sloping area surrounded by abrupt slopes 3 : a place of public games or contests — **am·phi·the·at·ric** \ˌam(p)-fə-thē-'a-trik\ *or* **am·phi·the·at·ri·cal** \-tri-kəl\ *adj* — **am·phi·the·at·ri·cal·ly** \-tri-k(ə-)lē\ *adv*

am·phit·ro·pous \am-'fi-trə-pəs\ *adj* : having the ovule inverted but with the attachment near the middle of one side

Am·phit·ry·on \am-'fi-trē-ən\ *n* [Gk *Amphitryōn*] : the husband of Alcmene

am·pho·ra \'am(p)-fə-rə\ *n, pl* **-rae** \-ˌrē, -ˌrī\ *or* **-ras** [L, modif. of Gk *amphoreus, amphiphoreus*, fr. *amphi-* + *phoreus* bearer, fr. *pherein* to bear — more at BEAR] 1 : an ancient Greek jar or vase with a large oval body, narrow cylindrical neck, and two handles that rise almost to the level of the mouth 2 : a 2-handled vessel shaped like an amphora

am·pho·ter·ic \ˌam(p)-fə-'ter-ik\ *adj* [ISV, fr. Gk *amphoteros* each of two, fr. *amphō* both — more at AMBI-] : partly one and partly the other; *specif* : capable of reacting chemically either as an acid or as a base

am·pho·ter·i·cin \-'ter-ə-sən\ *n* [*amphoteric* + *-in*] : either of two antibiotic drugs obtained from a soil actinomycete (*Streptomyces nodosus*); *esp* : the one useful against deep-seated and systemic fungal infections — called also *amphotericin B*

amp hr *abbr* ampere-hour

am·pi·cil·lin \ˌam-pə-'sil-ən\ *n* [*amin-* + *penicillin*] : an antibiotic of the penicillin group that is effective against gram-negative bacteria

am·ple \'am-pəl\ *adj* **am·pler** \-p(ə-)lər\; **am·plest** \-p(ə-)ləst\ [MF, fr. L *amplus*] 1 : generous or more than adequate in size, scope, or capacity ⟨there was room for an ∼ garden⟩ 2 : generously sufficient to satisfy a requirement or need ⟨they had ∼ money for the trip⟩ 3 : BUXOM, PORTLY ⟨an ∼ figure⟩ *syn* 1 see SPACIOUS 2 see PLENTIFUL *ant* meager, scant — **am·ple·ness** \-pəl-nəs\ *n* — **am·ply** \-plē\ *adv*

am·plex·i·caul \am-'plek-sə-ˌkȯl\ *adj* [NL *amplexicaulis*, fr. L *amplexus* (pp. of *amplecti* to entwine, fr. *ambi-* + *plectere* to braid) + *-i-* + *caulis* stem — more at HOLE] *of a leaf* : sessile with the base or stipules surrounding the stem

am·plex·us \am-'plek-səs\ *n* [NL, fr. L, embrace, fr. *amplexus*, pp.] : the mating embrace of a frog or toad during which eggs are shed into the water and there fertilized

am·pli·dyne \'am-plə-ˌdīn\ *n* [*amplifier* + Gk *dynamis* power — more at DYNAMIC] : a direct-current generator that by the use of compensating coils and a short circuit across two of its brushes precisely controls a large power output whenever a small power input is varied in the field winding of the generator

am·pli·fi·ca·tion \ˌam-plə-fə-'kā-shən\ *n* 1 : an act, example, or product of amplifying 2 a : the particulars by which a statement is expanded b : an expanded statement

am·pli·fi·er \'am-plə-ˌfī(-ə)r\ *n* : one that amplifies; *specif* : a device usu. employing electron tubes or transistors to obtain amplification of voltage, current, or power

am·pli·fy \-ˌfī\ *vb* **-fied; -fy·ing** [ME *amplifien*, fr. MF *amplifier*, fr. L *amplificare*, fr. *amplus*] *vt* 1 : to expand (as a statement) by the use of detail or illustration or by closer analysis 2 : to make larger or greater (as in amount, importance, or intensity) : INCREASE 3 : to utilize (an input of power) so as to obtain an output of greater magnitude through the relay action of a transducer ∼ *vi* : to expand one's remarks or ideas *syn* see EXPAND *ant* abridge, condense

am·pli·tude \-ˌt(y)üd\ *n* 1 : the quality or state of being ample : FULLNESS 2 : the extent or range of a quality, property, process, or phenomenon: as a : the extent of a vibratory movement (as of a pendulum) measured from the mean position to an extreme b : the maximum departure of the value of an alternating current or wave from the average value 3 : the arc of the horizon between the true east or west point and the foot of the vertical circle passing through any star or object

amplitude modulation *n* 1 : modulation of the amplitude of a radio carrier wave in accordance with the strength of the audio or other signal 2 : a broadcasting system using amplitude modulation — abbr. *AM*; compare FREQUENCY MODULATION

am·pul *or* **am·pule** *or* **am·poule** \'am-ˌpyü(ə)l, -ˌpül\ *n* [ME *ampulle* flask, fr. OE & OF; OE *ampulle* & OF *ampoule*, fr. L *ampulla*] 1 : a hermetically sealed small bulbous glass vessel that is used to hold a solution for hypodermic injection 2 : a vial resembling an ampul

am·pul·la \am-'púl-ə, -'pəl-\ *n, pl* **-lae** \-(ˌ)ē, -ˌī\ [ME, fr. OE, fr. L, dim. of *amphora*] 1 : a glass or earthenware flask with a globular body and two handles used esp. by the ancient Romans to hold ointment, perfume, or wine 2 : a saccular anatomic swelling or pouch — **am·pul·lar** \-ər\ *adj*

am·pu·tate \'am-pyə-ˌtāt\ *vt* **-tat·ed; -tat·ing** [L *amputatus*, pp. of *amputare*, fr. *am-, amb-* around + *putare* to cut, prune — more at AMBI-, PAVE] : to cut or lop off; *esp* : to cut (as a limb) from the body — **am·pu·ta·tion** \ˌam-pyə-'tā-shən\ *n* — **am·pu·ta·tor** \'am-pyə-ˌtāt-ər\ *n*

am·pu·tee \ˌam-pyə-'tē\ *n* : one that has had a limb amputated

AMS *abbr* Agricultural Marketing Service

amt *abbr* amount

am·trac *or* **am·track** \'am-ˌtrak\ *n* [*amphibious* + *tractor*] : AMPHIBIAN 3

AMU *abbr* atomic mass unit

amuck \ə-'mək\ *var of* AMOK

am·u·let \'am-yə-lət\ *n* [L *amuletum*] : a charm (as an ornament) often inscribed with a magic incantation or symbol to protect the wearer against evil (as disease or witchcraft) or to aid him *syn* see FETISH

amuse \ə-'myüz\ *vb* **amused; amus·ing** [MF *amuser*, fr. OF, fr. *a-* (fr. L *ad-*) + *muser* to muse] *vt* 1 a *archaic* : to divert the attention so as to deceive : BEMUSE b *obs* : to occupy the attention of : ABSORB c *obs* : DISTRACT, BEWILDER 2 a : to entertain or occupy in a light, playful, or pleasant manner ⟨∼ the child with a story⟩ b : to appeal to the sense of humor of ⟨the joke doesn't ∼ me⟩ ∼ *vi, obs* : MUSE — **amus·ed·ly** \-'myü-zəd-lē\ *adv* — **amus·er** *n*

syn AMUSE, DIVERT, ENTERTAIN *shared meaning element* : to pass or cause to pass one's time pleasantly *ant* bore

amuse·ment \ə-'myüz-mənt\ *n* 1 : a means of amusing or entertaining ⟨what are her favorite ∼s⟩ 2 : the condition of being amused ⟨his ∼ knew no bounds⟩ 3 : pleasurable diversion : ENTERTAINMENT ⟨plays the piano for ∼⟩

amusement park *n* : a commercially operated park with various devices for entertainment and booths for the sale of food and drink

amus·ing \ə-'myü-ziŋ\ *adj* : giving amusement : DIVERTING — **amus·ing·ly** \-ziŋ-lē\ *adv* — **amus·ing·ness** *n*

amu·sive \ə-'myü-ziv, -siv\ *adj* : tending to amuse or arouse mirth : AMUSING

AMVETS \'am-ˌvets\ *abbr* American Veterans (of World War II)

amyg·da·la \ə-'mig-də-lə\ *n, pl* **-lae** \-ˌlē, -ˌlī\ [NL, fr. L, almond, fr. Gk *amygdalē*] : an almond-shaped mass of gray matter in the roof of a lateral ventricle of the brain

amyg·da·lin \-lən\ *n* [NL *Amygdalus*, genus name, fr. LL, almond tree, fr. Gk *amygdalos*; akin to Gk *amygdalē*] : a white crystalline cyanogenetic glucoside $C_{20}H_{27}NO_{11}$ found esp. in the bitter almond (*Amygdalus communis amara*)

¹**amyg·da·loid** \-ˌlȯid\ *n* [Gk *amygdaloeidēs*, adj.] : an igneous and usu. volcanic rock orig. containing small cavities filled with deposits of different minerals (as chalcedony or calcite) — **amyg·da·loi·dal** \-ˌmig-də-'lȯid-ªl\ *adj*

²**amygdaloid** *adj* [Gk *amygdaloeidēs*, fr. *amygdalē* almond] 1 : almond-shaped 2 : of or relating to an amygdala

am·yl \'am-əl\ *n* [blend of *amyl-* and *-yl*] : a univalent hydrocarbon radical C_5H_{11} that occurs in various isomeric forms and is derived from pentane — called also *pentyl*

amyl- *or* **amylo-** *comb form* [LL *amyl-*, fr. L *amylum*, fr. Gk *amylon*, fr. neut. of *amylos* not ground at the mill, fr. *a-* + *mylē* mill — more at MEAL] : starch ⟨*amylase*⟩

am·y·la·ceous \ˌam-ə-'lā-shəs\ *adj* : of, relating to, or having the characteristics of starch : STARCHY

---

amyl acetate *n* : BANANA OIL 1

amyl alcohol *n* : any of eight isomeric alcohols $C_5H_{12}O$ used esp. as solvents and in making esters; *also* : either of two commercially produced mixtures of amyl alcohols obtained from fusel oil or derived from pentanes and used esp. as solvents

am·y·lase \ˈam-ə-ˌlās, -ˌlāz\ *n* : any of the enzymes (as amylopsin) that accelerate the hydrolysis of starch and glycogen or their intermediate hydrolysis products

1am·y·loid \-ˌlȯid\ *or* **am·y·loi·dal** \ˌam-ə-ˈlȯid-ᵊl\ *adj* : resembling or containing amylum

2amyloid *n* **1** : a nonnitrogenous starchy food **2** : a waxy translucent substance consisting of protein in combination with polysaccharides that is deposited in some animal organs under abnormal conditions

am·y·loid·osis \ˌam-ə-ˌlȯi-ˈdō-səs\ *n* [NL] : a condition characterized by the deposition of amyloid in organs or tissues of the animal body

am·y·lol·y·sis \ˌam-ə-ˈläl-ə-səs\ *n* [NL] : the conversion of starch into soluble products (as dextrins and sugars) esp. by enzymes — **am·y·lo·lyt·ic** \-lō-ˈlit-ik\ *adj*

am·y·lo·pec·tin \ˌam-ə-lō-ˈpek-tən\ *n* : a component of starch that has a high molecular weight and branched structure and does not tend to gel in aqueous solutions

am·y·lop·sin \ˌam-ə-ˈläp-sən\ *n* [*amyl-* + *-psin* (as in *trypsin*)] : the amylase of the pancreatic juice

am·y·lose \ˈam-ə-ˌlōs, -ˌlōz\ *n* **1** : any of various polysaccharides (as starch or cellulose) **2** : a component of starch characterized by its straight chains of glucose units and by the tendency of its aqueous solutions to set to a stiff gel **3** : any of various compounds $(C_6H_{10}O_5)_x$ obtained by the hydrolysis of starch

am·y·lum \-ləm\ *n* [L — more at AMYL-] : STARCH

amyo·to·nia \ˌā-ˌmī-ə-ˈtō-nē-ə\ *n* [NL] : deficiency of muscle tone

1an \ən, (ˈ)an\ *indefinite article* [ME, fr. OE *ān* one — more at ONE] : 2A — used (1) usu. in speech and writing before words beginning with a vowel sound ⟨*an* oak⟩ ⟨*an* hour⟩ ⟨*an* X ray⟩; (2) usu. in speech and less often in writing before *h*-initial words with an initial unstressed syllable in which \h\ is often lost after *an* ⟨*an* historian⟩; (3) sometimes esp. in England before words whose initial letter is a vowel and whose initial sound is a consonant ⟨*an* unique occurrence⟩ ⟨such *an* one⟩

2an \ən, an\ *prep* : 3A 2 — used usu. before words with an initial vowel sound ⟨once *an* afternoon⟩ ⟨fifty cents *an* hour⟩

3an *or* **an'** *conj* **1** *see* AND\ : AND **2** \(ˈ)an\ *archaic* : IF

4an *abbr* annum

an- — see A-

1-an *or* **-ian** *also* **-ean** *n suffix* [-*an* & -*ian* fr. ME -*an*, -*ian*, fr. OF & L; OF -*ien*, fr. L -*ianus*, fr. -*i*- + -*anus*, fr. -*anus*, adj. suffix; -*ean* fr. such words as *Mediterranean, European*] **1** : one that is of or relating to ⟨Americ*an*⟩ ⟨Boston*ian*⟩ **2** : one skilled in or specializing in ⟨phonetic*ian*⟩

2-an *or* **-ian** *also* **-ean** *adj suffix* **1** : of or belonging to ⟨Americ*an*⟩ ⟨Florid*ian*⟩ **2** : characteristic of : resembling ⟨Mozart*ean*⟩

3-an *n suffix* [ISV -*an*, -*ane*, alter. of -*ene*, -*ine*, & -*one*] **1** : unsaturated carbon compound ⟨tol*an*⟩ **2** : anhydride of a carbohydrate ⟨dextr*an*⟩

1ana \ˈan-ə\ *adv* [ME, fr. ML, fr. Gk, at the rate of, lit., up] : of each an equal quantity — used in prescriptions

2ana \ˈan-ə, ˈän-ə, ˈā-nə\ *n, pl* **ana** *or* **anas** [-*ana*] **1** : a collection of the memorable sayings of a person **2** : a collection of anecdotes or interesting information about a person or a place

ANA *abbr* **1** American Newspaper Association **2** American Nurses Association **3** Association of National Advertisers

ana- *or* **an-** *prefix* [L, fr. Gk, up, back, again, fr. *ana* up — more at ON] **1** : up : upward ⟨*ana*bolism⟩ **2** : back : backward ⟨*ana*tropous⟩

-ana \ˈan-ə, ˈän-ə, ˈā-nə\ *or* **-i·ana** \ē-ˈ\ *n pl suffix* [NL, fr. L, neut. pl. of -*anus* -an & -*ianus* -ian] : collected items of information esp. anecdotal or bibliographical concerning ⟨Americ*ana*⟩ ⟨Johnson*iana*⟩

ana·bap·tism \ˌan-ə-ˈbap-ˌtiz-əm\ *n* [NL *anabaptismus*, fr. LGk *anabaptismos* rebaptism, fr. *anabaptizein* to rebaptize, fr. *ana-* again + *baptizein* to baptize] **1** *cap* **a** : the doctrine or practices of the Anabaptists **b** : the Anabaptist movement **2** : the baptism of one previously baptized

Ana·bap·tist \-ˈbap-təst\ *n* : a Protestant sectarian of a radical movement arising in Zurich in 1524 and advocating the baptism and church membership of adult believers only, nonresistance, and the separation of church and state — **Anabaptist** *adj*

anab·a·sis \ə-ˈnab-ə-səs\ *n, pl* **-a·ses** \-ˌsēz\ [Gk, inland march, fr. *anabainein* to go up or inland, fr. *ana-* + *bainein* to go — more at COME] **1** : a going or marching up : ADVANCE; *esp* : a military advance **2** [fr. the retreat of Gk mercenaries in Asia Minor described in the *Anabasis* of Xenophon] : a difficult and dangerous military retreat

an·a·bat·ic \ˌan-ə-ˈbat-ik\ *adj* [Gk *anabatos*, verbal of *anabainein*] : moving upward : RISING ⟨an ~ wind⟩

ana·bi·o·sis \ˌan-ə-bī-ˈō-səs, -bē-\ *n, pl* **-o·ses** \-ˈō-ˌsēz\ [NL, fr. Gk *anabiōsis* return to life, fr. *anabioun* to return to life, fr. *ana-* + *bios* life — more at QUICK] : a state of suspended animation induced in some organisms by desiccation — **ana·bi·ot·ic** \-ˈät-ik\ *adj*

anab·o·lism \ə-ˈnab-ə-ˌliz-əm\ *n* [ISV *ana-* + *-bolism* (as in *metabolism*)] : the constructive part of metabolism concerned esp. with macromolecular synthesis — **an·a·bo·lic** \ˌan-ə-ˈbäl-ik\ *adj*

anach·ro·nism \ə-ˈnak-rə-ˌniz-əm\ *n* [prob. fr. MGk *anachronismos*, fr. *anachronizesthai* to be an anachronism, fr. LGk *anachronizein* to be late, fr. Gk *ana-* + *chronos* time] **1** : an error in chronology; *esp* : a chronological misplacing of persons, events, objects, or customs in regard to each other **2** : a person or a thing that is chronologically out of place; *esp* : one from a former age that is incongruous in the present — **anach·ro·nis·tic** \ə-ˌnak-rə-ˈnis-tik\ *also* **ana·chron·ic** \ˌan-ə-ˈkrän-ik\ *or* **anach·ro·nous** \ə-ˈnak-rə-nəs\ *adj* — **anach·ro·nis·ti·cal·ly** \ə-ˌnak-rə-ˈnis-ti-k(ə-)lē\ *also* **anach·ro·nous·ly** *adv*

an·a·clit·ic \ˌan-ə-ˈklit-ik\ *adj* [Gk *anaklitos*, verbal of *anaklinein* to lean upon, fr. *ana-* + *klinein* to lean — more at LEAN] : characterized by dependence of libido on a nonsexual instinct

an·a·co·lu·thon \ˌan-ə-kə-ˈlü-ˌthän\ *n, pl* **-tha** \-thə\ *or* **-thons** [LL, fr. LGk *anakolouthon* inconsistency in logic, fr. Gk, neut. of *anakolouthos*, inconsistent, fr. *an-* + *akolouthos* following, fr. *ha-*, *a-* together + *keleuthos* path; akin to Gk *hama* together — more at SAME] : syntactical inconsistency or incoherence within a sentence; *esp* : the shift from one construction to another (as in "you really ought — well, do it your own way") — **an·a·co·lu·thic** \-thik\ *adj* — **an·a·co·lu·thi·cal·ly** \-thi-k(ə-)lē\ *adv*

an·a·con·da \ˌan-ə-ˈkän-də\ *n* [prob. modif. of Sinhalese *henakandayā*, a slender green snake] : a large semiaquatic snake (*Eunectes murinus*) of the boa family of tropical So. America that crushes its prey in its coils; *broadly* : a large constricting snake

anac·re·on·tic \ə-ˌnak-rē-ˈänt-ik\ *n* : a poem in the manner of Anacreon; *esp* : a drinking song or light lyric

Anacreontic *adj* [L *anacreonticus*, fr. *Anacreont-*, *Anacreon* Anacreon, fr. Gk *Anakreont-*, *Anakreōn*] **1** : of, relating to, or resembling the poetry of Anacreon **2** : convivial or amatory in tone or theme

an·a·cru·sis \ˌan-ə-ˈkrü-səs\ *n, pl* **-cru·ses** \-ˌsēz\ [NL, fr. Gk *anakrousis* beginning of a song, fr. *anakrouein* to begin a song, fr. *ana-* + *krouein* to strike, beat; akin to Lith *krušti* to stamp] **1** : one or more syllables at the beginning of a line of poetry that are regarded as preliminary to and not a part of the metrical pattern **2** : UPBEAT; *specif* : one or more notes or tones preceding the first downbeat of a musical phrase

ana·cul·ture \ˈan-ə-ˌkəl-chər\ *n* [ISV] : a mixed bacterial culture; *esp* : one used in the preparation of autogenous vaccines

an·a·dem \ˈan-ə-ˌdem\ *n* [L *anadema*, fr. Gk *anadēma*, fr. *anadein* to wreathe, fr. *ana-* + *dein* to bind — more at DIADEM] *archaic* : a wreath for the head : GARLAND

ana·di·plo·sis \ˌan-əd-ə-ˈplō-səs, ˌan-ə-(ˌ)dī-ˈplō-\ *n, pl* **-plo·ses** \-ˌsēz\ [LL, fr. Gk *anadiplōsis*, lit., repetition, fr. *anadiploun* to double, fr. *ana-* + *diploun* to double — more at DIPLOMA] : repetition of a prominent and usu. the last word in one phrase or clause at the beginning of the next (as in "rely on his honor — honor such as his?")

anad·ro·mous \ə-ˈnad-rə-məs\ *adj* [Gk *anadromos* running upward, fr. *anadramein* to run upward, fr. *ana-* + *dramein* to run — more at DROMEDARY] : ascending rivers from the sea for breeding ⟨shad are ~⟩

anae·mia, anae·mic *var of* ANEMIA, ANEMIC

an·aer·obe \ˈan-ə-ˌrōb; (ˈ)an-ˈa(-ə)r-ˌōb, -ˈe(-ə)r-\ *n* [ISV] : an anaerobic organism

an·aer·o·bic \ˌan-ə-ˈrō-bik; ˌan-ˌa(-ə)r-ˈō-, -ˌe(-ə)r-\ *adj* **1** : living, active, or occurring in the absence of free oxygen ⟨~ respiration⟩ **2** : relating to or induced by anaerobes — **an·aer·o·bi·cal·ly** \-bi-k(ə-)lē\ *adv*

an·aero·bi·o·sis \ˌan-ə-rō-(ˌ)bī-ˈō-səs, -bē-; ˌan-ˌa(-ə)r-ō-, -ˌe(-ə)r-\ *n pl* **-o·ses** \-ˈō-ˌsēz\ : life in the absence of air or free oxygen

an·aes·the·sia, an·aes·thet·ic *var of* ANESTHESIA, ANESTHETIC

ana·glyph \ˈan-ə-ˌglif\ *n* [LL *anaglyphus* embossed, fr. Gk *anaglyphos*, fr. *anaglyphein* to emboss, fr. *ana-* + *glyphein* to carve — more at CLEAVE] **1** : a sculptured, chased, or embossed ornament worked in low relief **2** : a stereoscopic motion or still picture in which the right component of a composite image usu. red in color is superposed on the left component in a contrasting color to produce a three-dimensional effect when viewed through correspondingly colored filters in the form of spectacles — **ana·glyph·ic** \ˌan-ə-ˈglif-ik\ *adj*

an·a·go·ge *or* **an·a·go·gy** \ˈan-ə-ˌgō-jē\ *n, pl* **-ges** *or* **-gies** [LL *anagoge*, fr. LGk *anagōgē*, fr. Gk, reference, fr. *anagein* to refer, fr. *ana-* + *agein* to lead — more at AGENT] : interpretation of a word, passage, or text (as of Scripture or poetry) that finds beyond the literal, allegorical, and moral senses a fourth and ultimate spiritual or mystical sense — **an·a·gog·ic** \ˌan-ə-ˈgäj-ik\ *or* **an·a·gog·i·cal** \-i-kəl\ *adj* — **an·a·gog·i·cal·ly** \-i-k(ə-)lē\ *adv*

1ana·gram \ˈan-ə-ˌgram\ *n* [prob. fr. MF *anagramme*, fr. NL *anagrammat-*, *anagramma*, modif. of Gk *anagrammatismos*, fr. *anagrammatizein* to transpose letters, fr. *ana-* + *grammat-*, *gramma* letter — more at GRAM] **1** : a word or phrase made by transposing the letters of another word or phrase **2** *pl but sing in constr* : a game in which words are formed by rearranging the letters of other words or by arranging letters taken (as from a stock of cards or blocks) at random — **ana·gram·mat·ic** \ˌan-ə-grə-ˈmat-ik\ *or* **ana·gram·mat·i·cal** \-i-kəl\ *adj* — **ana·gram·mat·i·cal·ly** \-i-k(ə-)lē\ *adv*

2anagram *vt* **-grammed; -gram·ming** **1** : ANAGRAMMATIZE **2** : to rearrange (the letters of a text) in order to discover a hidden message

ana·gram·ma·tize \ˌan-ə-ˈgram-ə-ˌtīz\ *vt* **-tized; -tiz·ing** : to transpose (as letters in a word) so as to form an anagram — **ana·gram·ma·ti·za·tion** \-ˌgram-ət-ə-ˈzā-shən\ *n*

1anal \ˈān-ᵊl\ *adj* **1** : of, relating to, or situated near the anus **2** **a** : of, relating to, or characterized by the stage of psychosexual development in psychoanalytic theory during which the child is concerned esp. with its feces **b** : of, relating to, or characterized by personality traits (as parsimony, meticulousness, and ill humor) considered typical of fixation at the anal stage of development — **anal·ly** \-ᵊl-ē\ *adv*

2anal *abbr* **1** analogy **2** analysis; analytic

anal·cime \ə-ˈnal-ˌsēm\ *n* [F, fr. Gk *analkimos* weak, fr. *an-* + *alkimos* strong, fr. *alkē* strength] : a white or slightly colored mineral $NaAlSi_2O_6.H_2O$ occurring in various igneous rocks massive or in crystals — **anal·ci·mic** \-ˌnal-ˈsē-mik, -ˈsim-ik\ *adj*

anal·cite \ə-ˈnal-ˌsīt\ *n* : ANALCIME

an·a·lects \ˈan-ᵊl-ˌek(t)s\ *also* **an·a·lec·ta** \ˌan-ᵊl-ˈek-tə\ *n pl* [NL *analecta*, fr. Gk *analekta*, neut. pl. of *analektos*, verbal of *analegein* to collect, fr. *ana-* + *legein* to gather — more at LEGEND] : selected miscellaneous written passages

an·a·lem·ma \ˌan-ə-ˈlem-ə\ *n* [L, sundial on a pedestal, fr. Gk *analēmma*, lofty structure, sundial, fr. *analambanein* to take up, fr.

ana- + *lambanein* to take — more at LATCH] : a graduated scale having the shape of a figure 8 and showing the sun's declination and the equation of time for each day of the year — **an·a·lem·mat·ic** \-lə-'mat-ik, -lə-\ *adj*

an·a·lep·tic \ˌan-ᵊl-'ep-tik\ *adj* [Gk *analēptikos*, fr. *analambanein* to take up, restore] : RESTORATIVE; *esp* : stimulant to the central nervous system — **analeptic** *n*

an·al·ge·sia \ˌan-ᵊl-'jē-zhə, -z(h)ē-ə\ *n* [NL, fr. Gk *analgēsia*, fr. *an-* + *algēsis* sense of pain, fr. *algein* to suffer pain, fr. *algos* pain] : insensibility to pain without loss of consciousness — **an·al·ge·sic** \-'jē-zik, -sik\ *adj or n* — **an·al·get·ic** \-'jet-ik\ *adj or n*

anal·i·ty \ā-'nal-ət-ē\ *n, pl* **-ties** : the psychological state or quality of being anal

analog *also* **analogue** \'an-ᵊl-ˌȯg, -ˌäg\ *adj* : of or relating to an analog computer

analog computer *n* : a computer that operates with numbers represented by directly measurable quantities (as voltages or rotations) — compare DIGITAL COMPUTER, HYBRID COMPUTER

an·a·log·i·cal \ˌan-ᵊl-'äj-i-kəl\ *also* **an·a·log·ic** \-ik\ *adj* **1** : of, relating to, or based on analogy **2** : expressing or implying analogy — **an·a·log·i·cal·ly** \-i-k(ə-)lē\ *adv*

anal·o·gist \ə-'nal-ə-jəst\ *n* : one who searches for or reasons from analogies

anal·o·gize \-ˌjīz\ *vb* **-gized; -giz·ing** *vi* : to use or exhibit analogy ~ *vt* : to compare by analogy

anal·o·gous \ə-'nal-ə-gəs\ *adj* [L *analogus*, fr. Gk *analogos*, lit., proportionate, fr. *ana-* + *logos* reason, ratio, fr. *legein* to gather, speak — more at LEGEND] **1** : showing an analogy or a likeness that permits one to draw an analogy : COMPARABLE **2** : being or related to as an analogue ***syn*** see SIMILAR — **anal·o·gous·ly** *adv* — **anal·o·gous·ness** *n*

analogue *or* **an·a·log** \'an-ᵊl-ˌȯg, -ˌäg\ *n* [F *analogue*, fr. *analogue* analogous, fr. Gk *analogos*] **1** : something that is analogous or similar to something else **2** : an organ similar in function to an organ of another animal or plant but different in structure and origin **3** : a chemical compound structurally similar to another but differing often by a single element of the same valence and group of the periodic table as the element it replaces ***syn*** see PARALLEL

anal·o·gy \ə-'nal-ə-jē\ *n, pl* **-gies** **1** : inference that if two or more things agree with one another in some respects they will prob. agree in others **2** : resemblance in some particulars between things otherwise unlike : SIMILARITY **3** : correspondence between the members of pairs or sets of linguistic forms that serves as a basis for the creation of another form **4** : correspondence in function between anatomical parts of different structure and origin — compare HOMOLOGY ***syn*** see LIKENESS

analogy test *n* : a reasoning test that requires the person tested to supply the missing term in a proportion (as *darkness* in the proportion *day:light::night: . . .*)

an·al·pha·bet \(ˈ)an-'al-fə-ˌbet, -bət\ *n* [Gk *analphabētos* not knowing the alphabet, fr. *an-* + *alphabētos* alphabet] : one who cannot read : ILLITERATE — **an·al·pha·bet·ic** \ˌan-ˌal-fə-'bet-ik\ *adj or n* — **an·al·pha·bet·ism** \(ˈ)an-'al-fə-bə-ˌtiz-əm\ *n*

anal·y·sand \ə-'nal-ə-ˌsand\ *n* [*analyse* + *-and* (as in *multiplicand*)] : one who is undergoing psychoanalysis

an·a·lyse *chiefly Brit var of* ANALYZE

anal·y·sis \ə-'nal-ə-səs\ *n, pl* **-y·ses** \-ˌsēz\ [NL, fr. Gk, fr. *analyein* to break up, fr. *ana-* + *lyein* to loosen — more at LOSE] **1** : separation of a whole into its component parts **2 a** : an examination of a complex, its elements, and their relations **b** : a statement of such an analysis **3** : the use of function words instead of inflectional forms as a characteristic device of a language **4 a** : the identification or separation of ingredients of a substance **b** : a statement of the constituents of a mixture **5 a** : proof of a mathematical proposition by assuming the result and deducing a valid statement by a series of reversible steps **b** (1) : a branch of mathematics concerned mainly with functions and limits (2) : CALCULUS 3b **6 a** : a method in philosophy of resolving complex expressions into simpler or more basic ones **b** : clarification of an expression by an elucidation of its use in discourse **7** : PSYCHOANALYSIS

analysis of variance : analysis of variation in an experimental outcome and esp. of a statistical variance in order to determine the contributions of given factors or variables to the variance

analysis si·tus \-'sīt-əs, -'sēt-; -'sī-ˌtüs, -'sē-\ *n* [NL, lit., analysis of situation] : TOPOLOGY 2a

an·a·lyst \'an-ᵊl-əst\ *n* [prob. fr. *analyze*] **1** : a person who analyzes or who is skilled in analysis **2** : PSYCHOANALYST **3** : SYSTEMS ANALYST

an·a·lyt·ic \ˌan-ᵊl-'it-ik\ *adj* [LL *analyticus*, fr. Gk *analytikos*, fr. *analyein*] **1** : of or relating to analysis or analytics; *esp* : separating something into component parts or constituent elements **2** : skilled in or using analysis esp. in thinking or reasoning ⟨a keenly ~ man⟩ **3** : not synthetic; *esp* : logically necessary : TAUTOLOGOUS ⟨an ~ truth⟩ **4** : characterized by analysis rather than inflection ⟨~ languages⟩ **5** : PSYCHOANALYTIC **6** : treated or treatable by or using the methods of algebra and calculus **7 a** *of a function of a real variable* : capable of being expanded in a Taylor's series in powers of $x - h$ in some neighborhood of the point h **b** *of a function of a complex variable* : differentiable at every point in some neighborhood of a given point or points ***syn*** see LOGICAL — **an·a·lyt·i·cal** \-i-kəl\ *adj* — **an·a·lyt·i·cal·ly** \-i-k(ə-)lē\ *adv* — **an·a·ly·tic·i·ty** \ˌan-ᵊl-ə-'tis-ət-ē\ *n*

analytic geometry *n* : the study of geometric properties by means of algebraic operations upon symbols defined in terms of a coordinate system — called also *coordinate geometry*

analytic philosophy *n* : PHILOSOPHICAL ANALYSIS

an·a·lyt·ics \ˌan-ᵊl-'it-iks\ *n pl but sing or pl in constr* : the method of logical analysis

an·a·ly·za·tion \ˌan-ᵊl-ə-'zā-shən\ *n* : ANALYSIS

an·a·lyze \'an-ᵊl-ˌīz\ *vt* **-lyzed; -lyz·ing** [prob. irreg. fr. *analysis*] **1** : to study or determine the nature and relationship of the parts of by analysis ⟨~ a traffic pattern⟩ **2** : to subject to scientific or grammatical analysis **3** : PSYCHOANALYZE — **an·a·lyz·abil·i·ty** \ˌan-ᵊl-ˌī-zə-'bil-ət-ē\ *n* — **an·a·lyz·able** \'an-ᵊl-ˌī-zə-bəl\ *adj*

syn ANALYZE, RESOLVE, DISSECT, BREAK DOWN *shared meaning element* : to divide a complex whole into its component parts or constituent elements ***ant*** compose, compound, construct

an·am·ne·sis \ˌan-ˌam-'nē-səs\ *n, pl* **-ne·ses** \-ˌsēz\ [NL, fr. Gk *anamnēsis*, fr. *anamimnēskesthai* to remember, fr. *ana-* + *mimnēskesthai* to remember — more at MIND] **1** : a recalling to mind : REMINISCENCE **2** : a preliminary case history of a medical or psychiatric patient

an·am·nes·tic \-'nes-tik\ *adj* [Gk *anamnēstikos* easily recalled, fr. *anamimnēskesthai*] **1** : of or relating to an anamnesis **2** : of or relating to a secondary response to an immunogenic substance after serum antibodies can no longer be detected in the blood — **an·am·nes·ti·cal·ly** \-ti-k(ə-)lē\ *adv*

ana·mor·phic \ˌan-ə-'mȯr-fik\ *adj* [NL *anamorphosis* distorted optical image] : producing or having different magnification of the image in each of two perpendicular directions — used of an optical device or its image

An·a·ni·as \ˌan-ə-'nī-əs\ *n* [Gk, prob. fr. Heb *Ḥănanyāh*] **1** : an early Christian struck dead for lying about his donation to the church **2** : a Christian of Damascus who baptized Paul **3** : LIAR

an·a·pest \'an-ə-ˌpest\ *n* [L *anapaestus*, fr. Gk *anapaistos*, lit., struck back (a dactyl reversed), fr. (assumed) Gk *anapaiein* to strike back, fr. Gk *ana-* + *paiein* to strike] **1** : a metrical foot consisting of two short syllables followed by one long syllable or of two unstressed syllables followed by one stressed syllable (as *unabridged*) — compare DACTYL **2** : a verse written in anapests — **an·a·pes·tic** \ˌan-ə-'pes-tik\ *adj or n*

ana·phase \'an-ə-ˌfāz\ *n* [ISV] : the stage of mitosis and meiosis in which the chromosomes move toward the poles of the spindle — **ana·pha·sic** \ˌan-ə-'fā-zik\ *adj*

anaph·o·ra \ə-'naf-ə-rə\ *n* [LL, fr. LGk, fr. Gk, act of carrying back, reference fr. *anapherein* to carry back, refer, fr. *ana-* + *pherein* to carry — more at BEAR] **1** : repetition of a word or phrase at the beginning of two or more successive clauses or verses esp. for rhetorical or poetic effect — compare EPISTROPHE **2** : use of a grammatical substitute (as a pronoun or a pro-verb) to refer to a preceding word or group of words

an·a·phor·ic \ˌan-ə-'fȯr-ik, -'fär-\ *adj* : referring to a preceding word or group of words ⟨the ~ *does* in "she dances better than he does"⟩

an·aph·ro·di·sia \ˌan-ˌaf-rə-'dizh-(ē-)ə\ *n* [NL, fr. *a-* + Gk *aphrodisios* sexual — more at APHRODISIAC] : absence or impairment of sexual desire — **an·aph·ro·dis·i·ac** \-'diz-ē-ˌak\ *adj or n*

ana·phy·lac·tic \ˌan-ə-fə-'lak-tik\ *adj* : of, relating to, affected by, or causing anaphylaxis ⟨~ shock⟩ — **ana·phy·lac·ti·cal·ly** \-ti-k(ə-)lē\ *adv*

ana·phy·lac·toid \-'lak-ˌtȯid\ *adj* : resembling anaphylaxis

ana·phy·lax·is \-'lak-səs\ *n, pl* **-lax·es** \-ˌsēz\ [NL, fr. *ana-* + *-phylaxis* (as in *prophylaxis*)] : hypersensitivity (as to foreign proteins or drugs) resulting from sensitization following prior contact with the causative agent

an·a·pla·sia \ˌan-ə-'plā-zh(ē-)ə\ *n* [NL] : reversion of cells to a more primitive or undifferentiated form — **an·a·plas·tic** \-'plas-tik\ *adj*

an·arch \'an-ˌärk\ *n* [back-formation fr. *anarchy*] : a leader or advocate of revolt or anarchy

an·ar·chic \a-'när-kik, ə-\ *adj* **1 a** : of, relating to, or advocating anarchy **b** : likely to bring about anarchy ⟨~ violence⟩ **2** : lacking order, regularity, or definiteness ⟨~ art forms⟩

an·ar·chism \'an-ər-ˌkiz-əm, -ˌär-\ *n* **1** : a political theory holding all forms of governmental authority to be unnecessary and undesirable and advocating a society based on voluntary cooperation and free association of individuals and groups **2** : the advocacy or practice of anarchistic principles

an·ar·chist \'an-ər-kəst, -ˌär-\ *n* **1** : one who rebels against any authority, established order, or ruling power **2** : one who believes in, advocates, or promotes anarchism or anarchy; *esp* : one who uses violent means to overthrow the established order — **anarchist** *or* **an·ar·chis·tic** \ˌan-ər-'kis-tik, -(ˌ)är-\ *adj*

an·ar·cho–syn·di·cal·ism \a-ˌnär-kō-'sin-di-kə-ˌliz-əm, ˌan-ər-kō-\ *n* : SYNDICALISM — **an·ar·cho–syn·di·cal·ist** \-kə-ləst\ *n or adj*

an·ar·chy \'an-ər-kē, -ˌär-\ *n* [ML *anarchia*, fr. Gk, fr. *anarchos* having no ruler, fr. *an-* + *archos* ruler — more at ARCH-] **1 a** : absence of government **b** : a state of lawlessness or political disorder due to the absence of governmental authority **c** : a utopian society made up of individuals who have no government and who enjoy complete freedom **2** : absence of order : DISORDER **3** : ANARCHISM

an·ar·thria \a-'när-thrē-ə\ *n* [NL, fr. Gk *anarthros* inarticulate, fr. *an-* + *arthron* joint — more at ARTHR-] : inability to articulate words as a result of brain lesion

an·a·sar·ca \ˌan-ə-'sär-kə\ *n* [NL, fr. *ana-* + Gk *sark-*, *sarx* flesh — more at SARCASM] : edema with accumulation of serum in the connective tissue — **ana·sar·cous** \-kəs\ *adj*

an·astig·mat \a-'nas-tig-ˌmat, ˌan-ə-'stig-\ *n* [G, back-formation fr. *anastigmatisch* anastigmatic] : an anastigmatic lens

an·astig·mat·ic \ˌan-ə-(ˌ)stig-'mat-ik, ˌan-ˌas-tig-\ *adj* [ISV] : not astigmatic — used esp. of lenses that are able to form approximately point images of object points

anas·to·mose \ə-'nas-tə-ˌmōz, -ˌmōs\ *vb* **-mosed; -mos·ing** [prob. back-formation fr. *anastomosis*] *vt* : to connect or join by anastomosis ~ *vi* : to communicate by anastomosis

anas·to·mo·sis \ə-ˌnas-tə-'mō-səs\ *n, pl* **-mo·ses** \-ˌsēz\ [LL, fr. Gk *anastomōsis*, fr. *anastomoun* to provide with an outlet, fr. *ana-* +

ə abut ᵊ kitten ər further a back ā bake ä cot, cart
aů out ch chin e less ē easy g gift i trip ī life
j joke ŋ sing ō flow ȯ flaw ȯi coin th thin t͟h this
ü loot u̇ foot y yet yü few yu̇ furious zh vision

stoma mouth, opening — more at STOMACH] **1 :** the union of parts or branches (as of streams, blood vessels, or leaf veins) so as to intercommunicate : INOSCULATION **2 :** a product of anastomosis : NETWORK — **anas·to·mot·ic** \-ˈmät-ik\ *adj*

anas·tro·phe \ə-ˈnas-trə-(ˌ)fē\ *n* [ML, fr. Gk *anastrophē,* lit., turning back, fr. *anastrephein* to turn back, fr. *ana-* + *strephein* to turn — more at STROPHE] : inversion of the usual syntactical order of words for rhetorical effect — compare HYSTERON PROTERON

anat *abbr* anatomical; anatomy

an·a·tase \ˈan-ə-ˌtās, -ˌtāz\ *n* [F, fr. Gk *anatasis* extension, fr. *anateinein* to extend, fr. *ana-* + *teinein* to stretch — more at THIN] : a tetragonal titanium dioxide used esp. as a white pigment

anath·e·ma \ə-ˈnath-ə-mə\ *n* [LL *anathemat-, anathema,* fr. Gk, thing devoted to evil, curse, fr. *anatithenai* to set up, dedicate, fr. *ana-* + *tithenai* to place, set — more at DO] **1 a :** a ban or curse solemnly pronounced by ecclesiastical authority and accompanied by excommunication **b :** the denunciation of something as accursed **c :** a vigorous denunciation : CURSE **2 a :** one that is cursed by ecclesiastical authority **b :** one that is intensely disliked or loathed ⟨men whose names were ~ —Thomas Wolfe⟩

anath·e·ma·tize \-ˌtīz\ *vt* **-tized; -tiz·ing :** to pronounce an anathema upon ***syn*** see EXECRATE

An·a·to·lian \ˌan-ə-ˈtō-lē-ən, -ˈtōl-yən\ *n* **1 :** a native or inhabitant of Anatolia and specif. of the western plateau lands of Turkey in Asia **2 :** a branch of the Indo-European language family that includes a group of extinct languages of ancient Anatolia — see INDO-EUROPEAN LANGUAGES table — **Anatolian** *adj*

an·a·tom·i·co- \ˌan-ə-ˈtäm-i-(ˌ)kō\ *or* **anat·o·mo-** \ə-ˈnat-ə-(ˌ)mō\ *comb form* : anatomical and : anatomical ⟨*anatomico*pathological⟩ ⟨*anatomo*clinical⟩

anat·o·mist \ə-ˈnat-ə-məst\ *n* **1 :** a student of anatomy; *esp* : one skilled in dissection **2 :** one who analyzes minutely and critically ⟨an ~ of urban society⟩

anat·o·mize \-ˌmīz\ *vt* **-mized; -miz·ing 1 :** to cut in pieces in order to display or examine the structure and use of the parts : DISSECT **2 :** ANALYZE

anat·o·my \ə-ˈnat-ə-mē\ *n, pl* **-mies** [LL *anatomia* dissection, fr. Gk *anatomē,* fr. *anatemnein* to dissect, fr. *ana-* + *temnein* to cut — more at TOME] **1 :** a branch of morphology that deals with the structure of organisms **2 :** a treatise on anatomic science or art **3 :** the art of separating the parts of an animal or plant in order to ascertain their position, relations, structure, and function : DISSECTION **4** *obs* **:** a body dissected or to be dissected **5 :** structural makeup esp. of an organism or any of its parts **6 :** a separating or dividing into parts for detailed examination : ANALYSIS **7 a** (1) : SKELETON (2) : MUMMY **b :** the human body — **an·a·tom·ic** \ˌan-ə-ˈtäm-ik\ *or* **an·a·tom·i·cal** \-i-kəl\ *adj* — **an·a·tom·i·cal·ly** \-i-k(ə-)lē\ *adv*

ana·tox·in \ˌan-ə-ˈtäk-sən\ *n* [ISV *ana-* + *toxin*] : TOXOID

anat·ro·pous \ə-ˈna-trə-pəs\ *adj* : having the ovule inverted so that the micropyle is bent down to the funiculus to which the body of the ovule is united

anc *abbr* ancient

-ance \ən(t)s, ᵊn(t)s\ *n suffix* [ME, fr. OF, fr. L *-antia,* fr. *-ant-, -ans* -ant + *-ia* -y] **1 :** action or process ⟨further*ance*⟩ : instance of an action or process ⟨perform*ance*⟩ **2 :** quality or state : instance of a quality or state ⟨protuber*ance*⟩ **3 :** amount or degree ⟨conduc*tance*⟩

an·ces·tor \ˈan-ˌses-tər\ *n* [ME *ancestre,* fr. OF, fr. L *antecessor* one that goes before, fr. *antecessus,* pp. of *antecedere* to go before, fr. *ante-* + *cedere* to go — more at CEDE] **1 a :** one from whom a person is descended and who is usu. more remote in the line of descent than a grandparent **b :** FOREFATHER 2 **2 :** FORERUNNER, PROTOTYPE **3 :** a progenitor of a more recent or existing species or group — **an·ces·tress** \-trəs\ *n*

ancestor worship *n* : the custom of venerating deceased ancestors who are considered still a part of the family and whose spirits are believed to have the power of intervention in the affairs of the living

an·ces·tral \an-ˈses-trəl\ *adj* : of, relating to, or inherited from an ancestor ⟨~ estates⟩ — **an·ces·tral·ly** \-trə-lē\ *adv*

an·ces·try \ˈan-ˌses-trē\ *n* **1 :** line of descent : LINEAGE; *specif* : honorable, noble, or aristocratic descent **2 :** persons initiating or comprising a line of descent : ANCESTORS

An·chi·ses \an-ˈkī-(ˌ)sēz, aŋ-\ *n* [L, fr. Gk *Anchisēs*] : the father of Aeneas rescued by his son from the burning city of Troy

1**an·chor** \ˈaŋ-kər\ *n, often attrib* [ME *ancre,* fr. OE *ancor,* fr. L *anchora,* fr. Gk *ankyra;* akin to L *uncus* hook — more at ANGLE] **1 :** a device usu. of metal attached to a ship or boat by a cable and cast overboard to hold it in a particular place by means of a fluke that digs into the bottom **2 :** a reliable support : MAINSTAY **3 :** something that serves to hold an object firmly **4 :** an object shaped like a ship's anchor **5 :** ANCHORMAN **6** *pl, slang* **:** the brakes of a motor vehicle — **an·chor·less** \-ləs\ *adj*

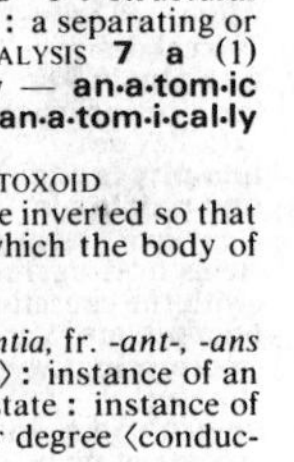

anchor 1: *1* ring, *2* stock, *3* shank, *4* bill, *5* fluke, *6* arm, *7* throat, *8* crown

2**anchor** *vb* **an·chored; an·chor·ing** \-k(ə-)riŋ\ *vt* **1 :** to hold in place in the water by an anchor **2 :** to secure firmly : FIX **3 :** to serve as an anchorman on ⟨~*ing* a television interview program —Charles Mandel⟩ ~ *vi* **1 :** to cast anchor **2 :** to become fixed

an·chor·age \ˈaŋ-k(ə-)rij\ *n* **1 a :** the act of anchoring : the condition of lying at anchor **b :** a place where vessels anchor : a place suitable for anchoring **2 :** a means of securing : a source of reassurance ⟨this ~ of Christian hope —T. O. Wedel⟩ **3 :** something that provides a secure hold

an·cho·ress \ˈaŋ-k(ə-)rəs\ *or* **an·cress** \-krəs\ *n* [ME *ankeresse,* fr. *anker* hermit, fr. OE *ancor,* fr. OIr *anchara,* fr. LL *anachoreta*] : a female anchorite

an·cho·rite \ˈaŋ-kə-ˌrīt\ *also* **an·cho·ret** \-ˌret\ *n* [ME, fr. ML *anchorita,* alter. of LL *anachoreta,* fr. LGk *anachōrētēs,* fr. Gk *anachōrein* to withdraw, fr. *ana-* + *chōrein* to make room, fr. *chōros* place; akin to Gk *chēros* left, bereaved — more at HEIR] : one who lives in seclusion usu. for religious reasons — **an·cho·rit·ic** \ˌaŋ-kə-ˈrit-ik\ *adj* — **an·cho·rit·i·cal·ly** \-i-k(ə-)lē\ *adv*

an·chor·man \ˈaŋ-kər-ˌman\ *n* **1 :** one who is last: as **a :** the member of a team who competes last ⟨the ~ on a relay team⟩ **b :** one who has the lowest scholastic standing in his graduating class **2 :** a broadcaster who coordinates the related activities of other usu. remotely located broadcasters so as to produce a coherent program **3 :** MODERATOR 2c

an·cho·vy \ˈan-ˌchō-vē, an-ˈ\ *n, pl* **-vies** *or* **-vy** [Sp *anchova*] : any of numerous small fishes (family Engraulidae) resembling herrings; *esp* : a common Mediterranean fish (*Engraulis encrasicholus*) used esp. for making sauces and relishes

an·cien ré·gime \äⁿs-yaⁿ-rā-zhēm\ *n* [F, lit., old regime] **1 :** the political and social system of France before the Revolution of 1789 **2 :** a system or mode no longer prevailing

1**an·cient** \ˈān-shənt, -chənt, ˈāŋ(k)-shənt\ *adj* [ME *ancien,* fr. MF, fr. (assumed) VL *anteanus,* fr. L *ante* before — more at ANTE-] **1 :** having had an existence of many years **2 :** of or relating to a remote period, to a time early in history, or to those living in such a period or time; *specif* : of or relating to the historical period beginning with the earliest known civilizations and extending to the fall of the western Roman Empire in 476 **3 :** having the qualities of age or long existence: **a :** VENERABLE **b :** OLD-FASHIONED, ANTIQUE ***syn*** see OLD ***ant*** modern — **an·cient·ness** *n*

2**ancient** *n* **1 :** an aged living being ⟨a penniless ~⟩ **2 :** one who lived in ancient times: **a** *pl* **:** the civilized people of antiquity; *esp* : those of the classical nations **b :** one of the classical authors ⟨Plutarch and other ~*s*⟩ **3 :** an ancient coin

3**ancient** *n* [alter. of *ensign*] **1** *archaic* **:** ENSIGN, STANDARD, FLAG **2** *obs* **:** the bearer of an ensign

ancient history *n* **1 :** the history of ancient times **2 :** knowledge or information (as of something in the recent past) that is widespread and has lost its initial freshness or importance : common knowledge

an·cient·ly *adv* : in ancient times : long ago

an·cient·ry \-rē\ *n* : ANTIQUITY, ANCIENTNESS

an·cil·la \an-ˈsil-ə\ *n, pl* **-lae** \-(ˌ)ē\ [L, female servant] : AID, HELPER

an·cil·lary \ˈan(t)-sə-ˌler-ē, *esp Brit* an-ˈsil-ə-rē\ *adj* **1 :** SUBORDINATE, SUBSIDIARY ⟨the main factory and its ~ plants⟩ **2 :** AUXILIARY, SUPPLEMENTARY ⟨the need for ~ evidence⟩ — **ancillary** *n*

an·con \ˈaŋ-ˌkän\ *n, pl* **an·co·nes** \aŋ-ˈkō-nēz\ [L, fr. Gk *ankōn* elbow; akin to L *uncus* hook] : a bracket, elbow, or console used as an architectural support

-an·cy \ən-sē, ᵊn-\ *n suffix* [L *-antia* — more at -ANCE] : quality or state ⟨piqu*ancy*⟩

an·cy·lo·sto·mi·a·sis \ˌaŋ-ki-lō-stə-ˈmī-ə-səs, ˌan(t)-sə-\ *n, pl* **-a·ses** \-ˌsēz\ [NL, fr. *Ancylostoma,* genus of hookworms, fr. Gk *ankylos* hooked + *stoma* mouth; akin to L *incus* hook — more at ANGLE, STOMACH] : infestation with or disease caused by hookworms; *esp* : a lethargic anemic state in man due to blood loss through the feeding of hookworms in the small intestine

and \ən(d), (ˈ)an(d), *usu* ᵊn(d) *after* t, d, s *or* z, *often* ᵊm *after* p *or* b, *sometimes* ᵊŋ *after* k *or* g\ *conj* [ME, fr. OE; akin to OHG *unti* and] **1 —** used as a function word to indicate connection or addition esp. of items within the same class or type; used to join sentence elements of the same grammatical rank or function **2 —** used as a function word to express logical modification, consequence, antithesis, or supplementary explanation **3** *obs* **:** IF **4 —** used in logic as a sentential connective that forms a complex sentence which is true only if both constituent sentences are true — compare CONJUNCTION — **and how** \ˈand-ˈhau̇\ — used to emphasize the preceding idea — **and so forth** \ən-ˈsō-ˌfōrth, -ˌfȯrth\ **1 :** and others or more of the same or similar kind **2 :** further in the same or similar manner **3 :** and the rest **4 :** and other things — **and so on** \ən-ˈsō-ˌȯn, -ˌän\ : and so forth

AND \ˈand\ *n* : a logical operator equivalent to the sentential connective *and* ⟨~ gate in a computer⟩

an·da·lu·site \ˌan-də-ˈlü-ˌsīt\ *n* [F *andalousite,* fr. *Andalousie* Andalusia, region in Spain] : a mineral Al_2SiO_5 consisting of a silicate of aluminum usu. in thick nearly square orthorhombic prisms of various colors

1**an·dan·te** \än-ˈdän-(ˌ)tā, -ˈdänt-ē; an-ˈdant-ē\ *adv or adj* [It, lit., going, prp. of *andare* to go] : moderately slow — used as a direction in music

2**andante** *n* : a musical composition or movement in andante tempo

1**an·dan·ti·no** \ˌän-ˌdän-ˈtē-(ˌ)nō\ *adv or adj* [It dim. of *andante*] : slightly faster than andante — used as a direction in music

2**andantino** *n, pl* **-nos :** a musical composition or movement in andantino tempo

an·des·ite \ˈan-di-ˌzīt\ *n* [G *andesit,* fr. *Andes*] : an extrusive usu. dark grayish rock consisting essentially of oligoclase or feldspar — **an·des·it·ic** \ˌan-di-ˈzit-ik\ *adj*

and·iron \ˈan-ˌdī(-ə)rn\ *n* [ME *aundiren,* modif. of OF *andier*] : one of a pair of metal supports for firewood used on a hearth and made of a horizontal bar mounted on short legs with usu. a vertical shaft surmounting the front end

and/or \ˈan-ˈdȯ(ə)r\ *conj* — used as a function word to indicate that two words or expressions are to be taken together or individually

andr- *or* **andro-** *comb form* [MF, fr. L, fr. Gk, fr. *andr-, anēr* man (male); akin to Oscan *ner* man, Skt *nr,* OIr *nert* strength] **1 :** man ⟨*andro*phobia⟩ **2 :** male ⟨*andro*ecium⟩

an·dra·dite \an-ˈdräd-ˌīt, ˈan-drə-ˌdīt\ *n* [José B. de *Andrada* e Silva †1838 Brazilian geologist] : a garnet $Ca_3Fe_2(SiO_4)_3$ of any of various colors ranging from yellow and green to brown and black

An·dro·cles \ˈan-drə-ˌklēz\ *n* [L, fr. Gk *Androklēs*] : a fabled Roman slave spared in the arena by a lion from whose foot he had years before extracted a thorn

an·droe·ci·um \an-ˈdrē-s(h)ē-əm\ *n, pl* **-cia** \-s(h)ē-ə\ [NL, fr. *andr-* + Gk *oikion,* dim of *oikos* house — more at VICINITY] : the aggregate of microsporophylls in the flower of a seed plant

an·dro·gen \'an-drə-jən\ *n* [ISV] : a male sex hormone (as testosterone) — **an·dro·gen·ic** \ˌan-drə-'jen-ik\ *adj*

an·drog·y·nous \an-'dräj-ə-nəs\ *adj* [L *androgynus* hermaphrodite, fr. Gk *androgynos*, fr. *andr-* + *gynē* woman — more at QUEEN] **1** : having the characteristics or nature of both male and female **2** : bearing both staminate and pistillate flowers in the same cluster with the male flowers uppermost — **an·drog·y·ny** \-nē\ *n*

an·droid \'an-ˌdrȯid\ *n* [LGk *androeidēs* manlike, fr. Gk *andr-* + *-oeidēs* -oid] : an automaton with a human form

An·drom·a·che \an-'dräm-ə-(ˌ)kē\ *n* [L, fr. Gk *Andromachē*] : the wife of Hector

An·drom·e·da \an-'dräm-əd-ə\ *n* [L, fr. Gk *Andromedē*] **1** : an Ethiopian princess of classical mythology rescued from a monster by her future husband Perseus **2** [L (gen. *Andromedae*)] : a northern constellation directly south of Cassiopeia between Pegasus and Perseus

an·dros·ter·one \an-'dräs-tə-ˌrōn\ *n* [ISV *andr-* + *sterol* + *-one*] : an androgenic hormone that is a hydroxy ketone $C_{19}H_{30}O_2$ and is found in human male and female urine

-an·drous \'an-drəs\ *adj comb form* [NL *-andrus*, fr. Gk *-andros* having (such or so many) men, fr. *andr-*, *anēr*] : having (such or so many) stamens ⟨mon*androus*⟩

ane \'ān\ *adj or n or pron, chiefly Scot* : ONE

-ane \ˌān\ *n suffix* [ISV *-an*, *-ane*, alter. of *-ene*, *-ine*, & *-one*] **1** : [3]-AN 1 ⟨tol*ane*⟩ **2** : saturated or completely hydrogenated carbon compound (as a hydrocarbon) ⟨meth*ane*⟩

an·ec·dot·age \'an-ik-ˌdōt-ij\ *n* : the telling of anecdotes; *also* : ANECDOTES

an·ec·dot·al \ˌan-ik-'dōt-ᵊl\ *adj* **1** : relating to, characteristic of, or containing anecdotes **2** : having the form or style of anecdotes **3** : depicting an anecdote ⟨~ art⟩ — **an·ec·dot·al·ly** \-ᵊl-ē\ *adv*

an·ec·dote \'an-ik-ˌdōt\ *n* [F, fr. Gk *anekdota* unpublished items, fr. neut. pl. of *anekdotos* unpublished, fr. *a-* + *ekdidonai* to publish, fr. *ex* out + *didonai* to give — more at EX-, DATE] : a usu. short narrative of an interesting, amusing, or biographical incident

an·ec·dot·ic \ˌan-ik-'dät-ik\ *or* **an·ec·dot·i·cal** \-'dät-i-kəl\ *adj* **1** : ANECDOTAL **2** : given to or skilled in telling anecdotes — **an·ec·dot·i·cal·ly** \-'dät-i-k(ə-)lē\ *adv*

an·ec·dot·ist \'an-ik-ˌdōt-əst\ *or* **an·ec·dot·al·ist** \ˌan-ik-'dōt-ᵊl-əst\ *n* : one who is given to or is skilled in telling anecdotes

an·echo·ic \ˌan-i-'kō-ik\ *adj* : free from echoes and reverberations ⟨an ~ chamber⟩

anem- *or* **anemo-** *comb form* [prob. fr. F *anémo-*, fr. Gk *anem-*, *anemo-*, fr. *anemos* — more at ANIMATE] : wind ⟨*anemo*meter⟩

ane·mia \ə-'nē-mē-ə\ *n* [NL, fr. Gk *anaimia* bloodlessness, fr. *a-* + *-aimia* -emia] **1** **a** : a condition in which the blood is deficient in red blood cells, in hemoglobin, or in total volume **b** : ISCHEMIA **2** : lack of vitality — **ane·mic** \ə-'nē-mik\ *adj* — **ane·mi·cal·ly** \-mi-k(ə-)lē\ *adv*

anemo·graph \ə-'nem-ə-ˌgraf\ *n* : a recording anemometer — **anemo·graph·ic** \-ˌnem-ə-'graf-ik\ *adj*

an·e·mom·e·ter \ˌan-ə-'mäm-ət-ər\ *n* : an instrument for measuring and indicating the force or speed of the wind — **an·e·mo·met·ric** \ˌan-ə-mō-'me-trik\ *also* **an·e·mo·met·ri·cal** \-tri-kəl\ *adj*

an·e·mom·e·try \ˌan-ə-'mäm-ə-trē\ *n* : the act or process of ascertaining the force, speed, and direction of wind

anem·o·ne \ə-'nem-ə-nē\ *n* [L, fr. Gk *anemōnē*] **1** : any of a large genus (*Anemone*) of the buttercup family having lobed or divided leaves and showy flowers without petals but with conspicuous often colored sepals **2** : SEA ANEMONE

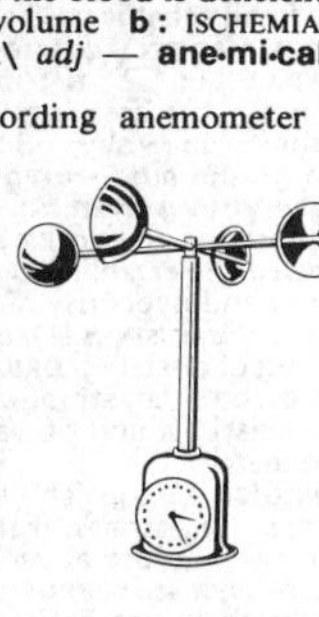

anemometer

an·e·moph·i·lous \ˌan-ə-'mäf-ə-ləs\ *adj* : normally wind-pollinated — **an·e·moph·i·ly** \-lē\ *n*

anent \ə-'nent\ *prep* [ME *onevent*, *anent*, fr. OE *on efen* alongside, fr. *on* + *efen* even] : ABOUT, CONCERNING

an·er·oid \'an-ə-ˌrȯid\ *adj* [F *anéroïde*, fr. Gk *a-* + LGk *nēron* water, fr. Gk, neut. of *nearos*, *nēros* fresh; akin to Gk *neos* new — more at NEW] : containing no liquid or actuated without the use of liquid ⟨an ~ manometer⟩

aneroid barometer *n* : a barometer in which the action of atmospheric pressure in bending a metallic surface is made to move a pointer

an·es·the·sia \ˌan-əs-'thē-zhə\ *n* [NL, fr. Gk *anaisthēsia* insensibility, fr. *a-* + *aisthēsis* perception, fr. *aisthanesthai* to perceive — more at AUDIBLE] : loss of sensation with or without loss of consciousness

an·es·the·si·ol·o·gist \-ˌthē-zē-'äl-ə-jəst\ *n* : ANESTHETIST; *specif* : a physician specializing in anesthesiology

an·es·the·si·ol·o·gy \-jē\ *n* : a branch of medical science dealing with anesthesia and anesthetics

[1]**an·es·thet·ic** \ˌan-əs-'thet-ik\ *adj* **1** : of, relating to, or capable of producing anesthesia **2** : lacking awareness or sensitivity ⟨unmoved and quite ~ to his presence —S. J. Perelman⟩ — **an·es·thet·i·cal·ly** \-i-k(ə-)lē\ *adv*

[2]**anesthetic** *n* **1** : a substance that produces anesthesia **2** : something that brings relief : PALLIATIVE

anes·the·tist \ə-'nes-thət-əst\ *n* : one who administers anesthetics

anes·the·tize \-thə-ˌtīz\ *vt* **-tized; -tiz·ing** : to subject to anesthesia

an·es·trous \(ˈ)an-'es-trəs\ *adj* **1** : not exhibiting estrus **2** : of or relating to anestrus

an·es·trus \-trəs\ *n* [NL, fr. *a-* + *estrus*] : the period of sexual quiescence between two periods of sexual activity in cyclically breeding mammals

an·eu·ploid \'an-yu̇-ˌplȯid\ *adj* [*an-* + *euploid*] : having or being a chromosome number that is not an exact multiple of the usu. haploid number — **aneuploid** *n* — **an·eu·ploi·dy** \-ˌplȯid-ē\ *n*

an·eu·rysm *also* **an·eu·rism** \'an-yə-ˌriz-əm\ *n* [Gk *aneurysma* fr. *aneurynein* to dilate, fr. *ana-* + *eurynein* to stretch, fr. *eurys* wide — more at EURY-] : a permanent abnormal blood-filled dilatation of a blood vessel resulting from disease of the vessel wall — **an·eu·rys·mal** \ˌan-yə-'riz-məl\ *adj*

anew \ə-'n(y)ü\ *adv* [ME *of newe*, fr. OE *of nīwe*, fr. *of* + *nīwe* new] **1** : for an additional time : AFRESH **2** : in a new or different form

an·frac·tu·os·i·ty \(ˌ)an-ˌfrak-chə-'wäs-ət-ē\ *n, pl* **-ties** **1** : the quality or state of being anfractuous **2** : a winding channel or course; *esp* : an intricate path or process (as of the mind)

an·frac·tu·ous \an-'frak-chə-wəs\ *adj* [F *anfractueux*, fr. LL *anfractuosus*, fr. L *anfractus* coil, bend, fr. *anfractus* crooked, fr. *an-* (fr. *ambi-* around) + *fractus*, pp. of *frangere* to break — more at AMBI-, BREAK] : full of windings and intricate turnings : TORTUOUS

Ang *abbr* Anglesey

an·ga·ry \'aŋ-gə-rē\ *n* [LL *angaria* service to a lord, fr. Gk *angareia* compulsory public service, fr. *angaros* Persian courier] : the right in international law of a belligerent to seize, use, or destroy property of neutrals

an·gel \'ān-jəl\ *n* [ME, fr. OF *angele*, fr. LL *angelus*, fr. Gk *angelos*, lit., messenger] **1** **a** : a spiritual being superior to man in power and intelligence; *specif* : one in the lowest rank in the Dionysian hierarchy **b** *pl* : an order of angels —see CELESTIAL HIERARCHY **2** : an attendant spirit or guardian **3** : a white-robed winged figure of human form in fine art **4** : MESSENGER, HARBINGER ⟨~ of death⟩ **5** : a person believed to resemble an angel **6** *Christian Science* : a message originating from God in his aspects of Truth and Love **7** : one (as a backer of a theatrical venture) who aids or supports with money or influence — **an·gel·ic** \an-'jel-ik\ *or* **an·gel·i·cal** \-i-kəl\ *adj* — **an·gel·i·cal·ly** \-i-k(ə-)lē\ *adv*

an·gel·fish \'ān-jəl-ˌfish\ *n* **1** : any of several compressed bright-colored teleost fishes (family Chaetodontidae) of warm seas **2** : SCALARE

angel food cake *n* : a usu. white sponge cake made of flour, sugar, and whites of eggs

an·gel·i·ca \an-'jel-i-kə\ *n* [NL, genus name, fr. ML, fr. LL, fem. of *angelicus* angelic, fr. LGk *angelikos*, of a messenger, fr. Gk, fr. *angelos*] **1** : any of a genus (*Angelica*) of herbs of the carrot family; *esp* : a biennial (*A. archangelica*) whose roots and fruit furnish a flavoring oil **2** *cap* : a sweet dessert wine produced in California

angelica tree *n* : HERCULES'-CLUB 1

An·ge·lus \'an-jə-ləs\ *n* [ML, fr. LL, angel; fr. the first word of the opening versicle] **1** : a devotion of the Western church that commemorates the Incarnation and is said morning, noon, and evenings **2** : a bell announcing the time for the Angelus

[1]**an·ger** \'aŋ-gər\ *n* [ME, affliction, anger, fr. ON *angr* grief; akin to OE *enge* narrow, L *angere* to strangle, Gk *anchein*] **1** : a strong feeling of displeasure and usu. of antagonism **2** : RAGE 2 — **an·ger·less** \-ləs\ *adj*

syn ANGER, IRE, RAGE, FURY, INDIGNATION, WRATH *shared meaning element* : emotional excitement induced by intense displeasure. ANGER, the most general term, names the reaction but in itself conveys nothing about intensity or justification or manifestation of the emotional state ⟨tried to hide his *anger*⟩ ⟨Moses' *anger* waxed hot —Exod 32:19 (AV)⟩ IRE, more frequent in literary contexts, may suggest greater intensity than *anger*, often with an evident display of feeling ⟨cheeks flushed dark with *ire*⟩ RAGE suggests loss of self-control from violence of emotion ⟨screaming with *rage*⟩ FURY is overmastering destructive rage merging on madness ⟨in his *fury* made sudden decisions which would prove utterly disastrous —W. L. Shirer⟩ INDIGNATION stresses righteous anger at what one considers unfair, mean, or shameful ⟨behavior that caused general *indignation*⟩ WRATH may imply either rage or indignation but is likely to suggest a desire or intent to revenge or punish ⟨rose in his *wrath* and struck his tormentor to the floor⟩

ant pleasure, gratification, forbearance

[2]**anger** *vb* **an·gered; an·ger·ing** \-g(ə-)riŋ\ *vt* : to make angry ~ *vi* : to become angry

An·ge·vin \'an-jə-vən\ *adj* [F, fr. OF, fr. ML *andegavinus*, fr. *Andegavia* Anjou] : of, relating to, or characteristic of Anjou or the Plantagenets — **Angevin** *n*

angi- *or* **angio-** *comb form* [NL, fr. Gk *angei-*, *angeio-*, fr. *angeion* vessel, blood vessel, dim. of *angos* vessel] **1** : blood or lymph vessel : blood vessels and ⟨*angi*oma⟩ ⟨*angio*cardiography⟩ **2** : seed vessel ⟨*angio*carpous⟩

an·gi·na \an-'jī-nə, 'an-jə-\ *n* [L, quinsy, fr. *angere*] : a disease marked by spasmodic attacks of intense suffocative pain: as **a** : a severe inflammatory or ulcerated condition of the mouth or throat **b** : ANGINA PECTORIS — **an·gi·nal** \an-'jīn-ᵊl, 'an-jən-\ *adj* — **an·gi·nose** \'an-jə-ˌnōs\ *adj*

angina pec·to·ris \-'pek-t(ə-)rəs\ *n* [NL, lit., angina of the chest] : a disease marked by brief paroxysmal attacks of chest pain precipitated by deficient oxygenation of the heart muscles

an·gio·car·di·og·ra·phy \ˌan-jē-ō-ˌkärd-ē-'äg-rə-fē\ *n* : the roentgenographic visualization of the heart and its blood vessels after injection of a radiopaque substance — **an·gio·car·dio·graph·ic** \-ē-ə-'graf-ik\ *adj*

an·gio·car·pous \ˌan-jē-ō-'kär-pəs\ *or* **an·gio·car·pic** \-pik\ *adj* : having or being fruit enclosed within an external covering — **an·gio·car·py** \'an-jē-ō-ˌkär-pē\ *n*

an·gi·og·ra·phy \ˌan-jē-'äg-rə-fē\ *n* : the roentgenographic visualization of the blood vessels after injection of a radiopaque substance — **an·gio·graph·ic** \ˌan-jē-ə-'graf-ik\ *adj*

an·gi·ol·o·gy \ˌan-jē-'äl-ə-jē\ *n* : the study of blood vessels and lymphatics

an·gi·o·ma \ˌan-jē-'ō-mə\ *n* : a tumor composed chiefly of blood vessels or lymph vessels — **an·gi·o·ma·tous** \-mət-əs\ *adj*

an·gio·sperm \'an-jē-ə-ˌspərm\ *n* [deriv. of NL *angi-* + Gk *sperma* seed — more at SPERM] : any of a class (Angiospermae) of vascular

ə abut ᵊ kitten ər further a back ā bake ä cot, cart
au̇ out ch chin e less ē easy g gift i trip ī life
j joke ŋ sing ō flow ȯ flaw ȯi coin th thin th this
ü loot u̇ foot y yet yü few yu̇ furious zh vision

plants (as orchids or roses) having the seeds in a closed ovary — **an·gio·sper·mous** \ˌan-jē-ə-ˈspər-məs\ *adj*
an·gio·ten·sin \ˌan-jē-ō-ˈten(t)-sən\ *n* [*angi-* + hyper*tension* + *-in*] : either of two forms of a kinin of which one has marked vasoconstrictive action; *also* : a synthetic amide of the active form used to treat some forms of hypotension
an·gio·ten·sin·ase \-sə-ˌnās, -ˌnāz\ *n* : any of several enzymes in the blood that hydrolyze angiotensin
Angl *abbr* Anglican
¹an·gle \ˈaŋ-gəl\ *n* [ME, fr. MF, fr. L *angulus;* akin to OE *anclēow* ankle] **1** : a corner whether constituting a projecting part or a partially enclosed space ⟨they sheltered in an ~ of the building⟩ **2 a** : the figure formed by two lines extending from the same point or by two surfaces diverging from the same line **b** : a measure of the amount of turning necessary to bring one line or plane into coincidence with or parallel to another **3 a** : the precise viewpoint from which something is observed or considered; *also* : the aspect seen from such an angle **b** (1) : a special approach, point of attack, or technique for accomplishing an objective (2) : an often improper or illicit method of obtaining advantage ⟨he always had an ~ to beat the other fellow⟩ **4** : a sharply divergent course ⟨the road went off at an ~⟩ **5** : a position to the side of an opponent in football from which a player may block his opponent more effectively or without penalty — usu. used in the phrases *get an angle* or *have an angle* ***syn*** see PHASE — **an·gled** \-gəld\ *adj*

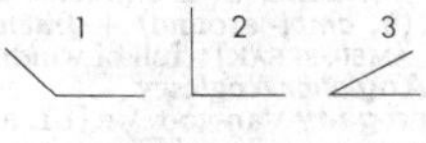

angles 2a: *1* obtuse, *2* right, *3* acute

²angle *vb* **an·gled; an·gling** \-g(ə-)liŋ\ *vt* **1** : to turn, move, or direct at an angle **2** : to present (as a news story) from a particular or prejudiced point of view : SLANT ~ *vi* : to turn or proceed at an angle
³angle *vi* **an·gled; an·gling** \-g(ə-)liŋ\ [ME *angelen,* fr. *angel* fishhook, fr. OE, fr. *anga* hook; akin to OHG *ango* hook, L *uncus,* Gk *onkos* barbed hook, *ankos* glen] **1** : to fish with a hook **2** : to use artful means to attain an objective ⟨*angled* for an invitation⟩
angle bracket *n* : BRACKET 3b
An·gle·doz·er \ˈaŋ-gəl-ˌdō-zər\ *trademark* — used for a tractor-driven pusher and scraper with the blade at an angle for pushing material to one side
angle iron *n* **1** : an iron cleat for joining parts of a structure at an angle **2** : a piece of structural steel rolled with an L-shaped section
angle of attack : the acute angle between the direction of the relative wind and the chord of an airfoil
angle of depression : the angle formed by the line of sight and the horizontal plane for an object below the horizontal
angle of elevation : the angle formed by the line of sight and the horizontal plane for an object above the horizontal
angle of incidence : the angle that a line (as a ray of light) falling on a surface makes with a perpendicular to the surface at the point of incidence
angle of reflection : the angle between a reflected ray and the normal drawn at the point of incidence to a reflecting surface
angle of refraction : the angle between a refracted ray and the normal drawn at the point of incidence to the interface at which refraction occurs
an·gler \ˈaŋ-glər\ *n* **1** : one that angles **2** : any of several pediculate fishes; *esp* : one (*Lophius piscatorius*) having a large flattened head and wide mouth with a lure on the head and fleshy mouth appendages used to attract smaller fishes as prey
An·gles \ˈaŋ-gəlz\ *n pl* [L *Angli,* of Gmc origin; akin to OE *Engle* Angles] : a Germanic people that invaded England along with the Saxons and Jutes in the 5th century A.D. and merged with them to form the Anglo-Saxon peoples
angle shot *n* : a picture taken with the camera pointed at an angle from the horizontal
an·gle·site \ˈaŋ-gəl-ˌsīt, -glə-\ *n* [F *anglésite,* fr. *Anglesey* island, Wales] : a mineral $PbSO_4$ consisting of lead sulfate formed by the oxidation of galena
an·gle·worm \ˈaŋ-gəl-ˌwərm\ *n* : EARTHWORM
An·gli·an \ˈaŋ-glē-ən\ *n* **1** : a member of the Angles **2** : the Old English dialects of Mercia and Northumbria — **Anglian** *adj*
An·gli·can \ˈaŋ-gli-kən\ *adj* [ML *anglicanus,* fr. *anglicus* English, fr. LL *Angli* English people, fr. L, Angles] **1** : of or relating to the established episcopal Church of England and churches of similar faith and order in communion with it **2** : of or relating to England or the English nation — **Anglican** *n* — **An·gli·can·ism** \-kə-ˌniz-əm\ *n*
an·gli·ce \ˈaŋ-glə-(ˌ)sē\ *adv, often cap* [ML, adv. of *anglicus*] : in English; *esp* : in readily understood English ⟨the city of Napoli, ~ Naples⟩
an·gli·cism \ˈaŋ-glə-ˌsiz-əm\ *n, often cap* [ML *anglicus* English] **1** : a characteristic feature of English occurring in another language **2** : adherence or attachment to English customs or ideas
An·gli·cist \ˈaŋ-glə-səst\ *n* : a specialist in English linguistics
an·gli·cize \ˈaŋ-glə-ˌsīz\ *vt* **-cized; -ciz·ing** *often cap* **1** : to make English in quality or characteristics **2** : to adapt (a foreign word or phrase) to English usage; *esp* : to borrow into English without alteration of form or spelling and with or without change in pronunciation — **an·gli·ci·za·tion** \ˌaŋ-glə-sə-ˈzā-shən\ *n, often cap*
an·gling \ˈaŋ-gliŋ\ *n* : the act of one who angles; *esp* : the act or sport of fishing with hook and line
An·glist \ˈaŋ-gləst\ *n* : ANGLICIST
An·glo \ˈaŋ-(ˌ)glō\ *n, pl* **Anglos** [in sense 2, fr. MexSp, fr. Sp *anglo-americano* Anglo-American] **1** : ANGLO-AMERICAN **2** : a Caucasian inhabitant of the U.S. of non-Latin extraction — **Anglo** *adj*
Anglo- *comb form* [NL, fr. LL *Angli*] **1** : English ⟨*Anglo*-Norman⟩ **2** : English and ⟨*Anglo*-Japanese⟩
An·glo–Amer·i·can \ˌaŋ-glō-ə-ˈmer-ə-kən\ *n* **1** : an inhabitant of the U.S. of English origin or descent **2** : a North American whose native language is English and whose culture is of English origin — **Anglo–American** *adj*
An·glo–Cath·o·lic \-ˈkath-(ə-)lik\ *adj* : of or relating to a High Church movement in Anglicanism emphasizing its continuity with historic Catholicism and fostering Catholic dogmatic and liturgical traditions — **Anglo–Catholic** *n* — **An·glo–Cathol·i·cism** \-kə-ˈthäl-ə-ˌsiz-əm\ *n*
An·glo–French \-ˈfrench\ *n* : the French language used in medieval England
An·glo–Nor·man \-ˈnȯr-mən\ *n* **1** : one of the Normans living in England after the Conquest **2** : the form of Anglo-French used by Anglo-Normans
an·glo·phile \ˈaŋ-glə-ˌfīl\ *also* **an·glo·phil** \-ˌfil\ *n, often cap* [F, fr. *anglo-* + *-phile*] : one who greatly admires or favors England and things English — **an·glo·phil·ic** \ˌaŋ-glə-ˈfil-ik\ *adj, often cap* — **an·gloph·i·lism** \aŋ-ˈgläf-ə-ˌliz-əm\ *n, often cap* — **an·gloph·i·ly** \aŋ-ˈgläf-ə-lē\ *n*
an·glo·phil·ia \ˌaŋ-glə-ˈfil-ē-ə\ *n, often cap* : excessive admiration of or partiality for England or English ways — **an·glo·phil·i·ac** \-ē-ˌak\ *adj, often cap*
an·glo·phobe \ˈaŋ-glə-ˌfōb\ *n, often cap* [prob. fr. F, fr. *anglo-* + *-phobe*] : one who is averse to England and things English — **an·glo·pho·bia** \ˌaŋ-glə-ˈfō-bē-ə\ *n, often cap* — **an·glo·pho·bic** \-bik\ *adj, often cap*
an·glo·phone \ˈaŋ-glə-ˌfōn\ *adj, often cap* : consisting of or belonging to an English-speaking population — **Anglophone** *n*
An·glo–Sax·on \ˌaŋ-glō-ˈsak-sən\ *n* [NL *Anglo-Saxones,* pl., alter. of ML *Angli Saxones,* fr. L *Angli* Angles + LL *Saxones* Saxons] **1** : a member of the Germanic peoples conquering England in the 5th century A.D. and forming the ruling class until the Norman conquest — compare ANGLES, JUTE, SAXON **2** : ENGLISHMAN; *specif* : a person descended from the Anglo-Saxons **3** : OLD ENGLISH 1 **4** : direct plain English — **Anglo–Saxon** *adj*
an·go·ra \aŋ-ˈgōr-ə, an-, -ˈgȯr-\ *n* **1** : the hair of the Angora rabbit or Angora goat — called also *angora wool* **2** : a yarn of Angora rabbit hair used esp. for knitting **3** *cap* **a** : ANGORA CAT **b** : ANGORA GOAT **c** : ANGORA RABBIT
Angora cat *n* [*Angora* (Ankara), Turkey] : a long-haired domestic cat
Angora goat *n* : any of a breed or variety of the domestic goat raised for its long silky hair which is the true mohair
Angora rabbit *n* : a long-haired usu. white rabbit with red eyes that is raised for fine wool
an·gos·tu·ra bark \ˌaŋ-gə-ˈst(y)u̇r-ə-\ *n* [*Angostura* (now Ciudad Bolívar), Venezuela] : the aromatic bitter bark of either of two So. American trees (*Galipea officinalis* and *Cusparia trifoliata*) of the rue family that is used as a tonic and antipyretic
an·gry \ˈaŋ-grē\ *adj* **an·gri·er; -est** **1** : feeling or showing anger : WRATHFUL **2 a** : indicative of or proceeding from anger ⟨~ words⟩ **b** : seeming to show anger or to threaten in an angry manner ⟨an ~ sky⟩ **3** : painfully inflamed ⟨an ~ rash⟩ — **an·gri·ly** \-grə-lē\ *adv* — **an·gri·ness** \-grē-nəs\ *n*
angry young man *n* : one of a group of mid-20th century British authors whose works express the bitterness of the lower classes toward the established sociopolitical system and toward the mediocrity and hypocrisy of the middle and upper classes
angst \ˈäŋ(k)st\ *n* [Dan & G; Dan, fr. G; akin to L *angustus*] : a feeling of anxiety : DREAD
ang·strom \ˈaŋ-strəm *also* ˈȯŋ-\ *n* [Anders J. *Ångström* †1874 Sw physicist] : a unit of wavelength of light equal to one ten-billionth of a meter
¹an·guish \ˈaŋ-gwish\ *n* [ME *angwisshe,* fr. OF *angoisse,* fr. L *angustiae,* pl., straits, distress fr. *angustus* narrow; akin to OE *enge* narrow — more at ANGER] : extreme pain or distress of body or mind ***syn*** see SORROW ***ant*** relief
²anguish *vi* : to suffer intense pain or sorrow ~ *vt* : to cause to suffer anguish or distress
an·guished *adj* **1** : suffering anguish : TORMENTED ⟨the ~ martyrs⟩ **2** : expressing anguish : AGONIZED ⟨~ cries⟩
an·gu·lar \ˈaŋ-gyə-lər\ *adj* [MF or L; MF *angulaire,* fr. L *angularis,* fr. *angulus* angle] **1 a** : having one or more angles **b** : forming an angle : sharp-cornered **2** : measured by an angle ⟨~ distance⟩ **3 a** : stiff in character or manner **b** : having the bones prominent from lack of plumpness — **an·gu·lar·ly** *adv*
an·gu·lar·i·ty \ˌaŋ-gyə-ˈlar-ət-ē\ *n, pl* **-ties** **1** : the quality of being angular **2** *pl* : angular outlines or characteristics
angular momentum *n* : a vector quantity that is the measure of the intensity of rotational motion, that is equal in classical physics to the product of the angular velocity of a rotating body or system and its moment of inertia with respect to the rotation axis, and that is directed along the rotation axis
angular velocity *n* : the time rate of change of angular position that has direction and sense such that the motion appears clockwise to one looking in the direction of the vector
an·gu·la·tion \ˌaŋ-gyə-ˈlā-shən\ *n* **1** : the action of making angular **2** : an angular position, formation, or shape
An·gus \ˈaŋ-gəs\ *n* [*Angus,* county in Scotland] : ABERDEEN ANGUS
an·hin·ga \an-ˈhiŋ-gə\ *n* [Pg, fr. Tupi] : SNAKEBIRD; *esp* : WATER TURKEY
anhyd *abbr* anhydrous
an·hy·dride \(ˈ)an-ˈhī-ˌdrīd\ *n* : a compound derived from another (as an acid) by removal of the elements of water
an·hy·drite \-ˌdrīt\ *n* [G *anhydrit,* fr. Gk *anydros*] : a mineral $CaSO_4$ consisting of an anhydrous calcium sulfate that is usu. massive and white or slightly colored
an·hy·drous \-drəs\ *adj* [Gk *anydros,* fr. *a-* + *hydōr* water — more at WATER] : free from water and esp. water of crystallization
ani \ä-ˈnē\ *n* [Sp *aní,* or Pg *ani,* fr. Tupi *anî*] : any of several black cuckoos (genus *Crotophaga*) of the warmer parts of America
anile \ˈan-ˌīl, ˈā-ˌnīl\ *adj* [L *anilis,* fr. *anus* old woman; akin to OHG *ano* grandfather] : of or resembling a doddering old woman; *esp* : SENILE — **anil·i·ty** \a-ˈnil-ət-ē, ā-, ə-\ *n*
an·i·line \ˈan-ᵊl-ən\ *n* [G *anilin,* fr. *anil* indigo, fr. F, fr. Pg, fr. Ar *an-nīl* the indigo plant, fr. Skt *nīlī* indigo, fr. fem. of *nīla* dark blue]

: an oily liquid poisonous amine $C_6H_5NH_2$ obtained esp. by the reduction of nitrobenzene and used chiefly in organic synthesis (as of dyes)

aniline dye *n* : a dye made by the use of aniline or one chemically related to such a dye; *broadly* : a synthetic organic dye

ani·lin·gus \ˌā-ni-ˈliŋ-gəs\ *or* **ani·linc·tus** \-ˈliŋ(k)-təs\ *n* [NL, fr. *anus* + *-i-* + *-lingus, -linctus* (as in *cunnilingus, cunnilinctus*)] : erotic stimulation achieved by contact between mouth and anus

an·i·ma \ˈan-ə-mə\ n [NL, fr. L, soul] : an individual's true inner self that in the analytic psychology of C. G. Jung reflects archetypal ideals of conduct; *esp* : an inner feminine part of the male personality — compare PERSONA 2

an·i·mad·ver·sion \ˌan-ə-ˌmad-ˈvər-zhən, -məd-, -ˈvər-shən\ *n* [L *animadversion-, animadversio,* fr. *animadversus,* pp. of *animadvertere*] **1** : a critical and usu. censorious remark **2** : adverse and typically ill-natured or unfair criticism
syn ANIMADVERSION, STRICTURE, ASPERSION, REFLECTION *shared meaning element* : adverse criticism *ant* commendation

an·i·mad·vert \-ˈvərt\ *vb* [L *animadvertere* to pay attention to, censure, fr. *animum advertere,* lit., to turn the mind to] *vt, archaic* : NOTICE, OBSERVE ~ *vi* : to make an animadversion *syn* see REMARK

[1]an·i·mal \ˈan-ə-məl\ *n* [L, fr. *animale,* neut. of *animalis* animate, fr. *anima* soul] **1** : any of a kingdom (Animalia) of living beings typically differing from plants in capacity for spontaneous movement and rapid motor response to stimulation **2 a** : one of the lower animals as distinguished from man **b** : MAMMAL **3** : a human being considered chiefly with regard to his physical nature **4** : ANIMALITY 2 — **an·i·mal·like** \-məl-ˌ(l)īk\ *adj* — **an·i·mal·ness** \-məl-nəs\ *n*

[2]animal *adj* **1** : of, relating to, or derived from animals **2 a** : of or relating to the physical or sentient as contrasted with the intellectual or rational **b** : SENSUAL, FLESHLY **3** : of or relating to the animal pole of an egg or to the part from which ectoderm normally develops *syn* see CARNAL *ant* rational — **an·i·mal·ly** \-mə-lē\ *adv*

animal cracker *n* : a small animal-shaped cracker

an·i·mal·cule \ˌan-ə-ˈmal-(ˌ)kyü(ə)l\ *or* **an·i·mal·cu·lum** \-ˈmal-kyə-ləm\ *n, pl* **-cules** *or* **-cu·la** \-kyə-lə\ [NL *animalculum,* dim. of L *animal*] : a minute usu. microscopic organism — **an·i·mal·cu·lar** \-kyə-lər\ *adj*

animal heat *n* : heat produced in the body of a living animal by functional chemical and physical activities

animal husbandry *n* : a branch of agriculture concerned with the production and care of domestic animals

an·i·mal·ism \ˈan-ə-mə-ˌliz-əm\ *n* **1 a** (1) : the qualities typical of animals; *esp* : buoyant health and uninhibited vitality (2) : the exercise of these qualities **b** : preoccupation with the satisfaction of physical drives or wants **2** : a theory that human beings are nothing more than animals — **an·i·mal·ist** \-mə-ləst\ *n* — **an·i·mal·is·tic** \ˌan-ə-mə-ˈlis-tik\ *adj*

an·i·mal·i·ty \ˌan-ə-ˈmal-ət-ē\ *n* **1** : ANIMALISM 1a (1) **2 a** : the state of being an animal **b** : animal nature **3** : the animal world

an·i·mal·ize \ˈan-ə-mə-ˌlīz\ *vt* **-ized; -iz·ing** **1** : to represent in animal form **2 a** : BRUTALIZE ⟨men *animalized* by the war⟩ **b** : SENSUALIZE ⟨*animalized* by passion⟩ — **an·i·mal·iza·tion** \ˌan-ə-mə-lə-ˈzā-shən\ *n*

animal kingdom *n* : the one of the three basic groups of natural objects that includes all living and extinct animals — compare MINERAL KINGDOM, PLANT KINGDOM

animal magnetism *n* : a force held to reside in some individuals by which a strong quasi-hypnotic influence can be exerted

animal pole *n* : the point on the surface of an egg that is diametrically opposite to the vegetal pole and usu. marks the most active part of the protoplasm or the part containing least yolk

animal spirits *n pl* : vivacity arising from physical health and energy

animal starch *n* : GLYCOGEN

[1]an·i·mate \ˈan-ə-mət\ *adj* [ME, fr. L *animatus,* pp. of *animare* to give life to, fr. *anima* breath, soul; akin to OE *ōthian* to breathe, L *animus* spirit, mind, courage, Gk *anemos* wind] **1 a** : possessing life : ALIVE **b** : of the kind or class of which life is a characteristic ⟨all ~ creation⟩ **2** : of or relating to animal life as opposed to plant life **3** : full of life : ANIMATED *syn* see LIVING *ant* inanimate — **an·i·mate·ly** *adv* — **an·i·mate·ness** *n*

[2]an·i·mate \-ˌmāt\ *vt* **-mat·ed; -mat·ing** **1** : to give spirit and support to : ENCOURAGE **2 a** : to give life to **b** : to give vigor and zest to **3** : to move to action **4 a** : to make or design in such a way that apparently spontaneous lifelike movement is effected **b** : to produce in the form of an animated cartoon *syn* see QUICKEN

an·i·mat·ed \-ˌmāt-əd\ *adj* **1 a** : endowed with life or the qualities of life : ALIVE ⟨viruses that can behave as ~ bodies or inert crystals⟩ **b** : full of movement and activity **c** : full of vigor and spirit : VIVACIOUS ⟨an ~ discussion⟩ **2** : having the appearance of something alive **3** : made in the form of an animated cartoon *syn* **1** see LIVING *ant* inert **2** see LIVELY — **an·i·mat·ed·ly** *adv*

animated cartoon *n* **1** : a motion picture made from a series of drawings simulating motion by means of slight progressive changes **2** : ANIMATION 2a

an·i·ma·tion \ˌan-ə-ˈmā-shən\ *n* **1** : the act of animating : the state of being animate or animated **2 a** : a motion picture made by photographing successive positions of inanimate objects (as puppets or mechanical parts) **b** : ANIMATED CARTOON 1 **3** : the preparation of animated cartoons

an·i·ma·to \ˌan-ə-ˈmät-(ˌ)ō\ *adv or adj* [It, fr. L *animatus*] : with animation — used as a direction in music

an·i·ma·tor \ˈan-ə-ˌmāt-ər\ *n* : one that contributes to the production of an animated cartoon

an·i·mism \ˈan-ə-ˌmiz-əm\ *n* [G *animismus,* fr. L *anima* soul] **1** : a doctrine that the soul is the vital principle of organic development **2** : attribution of conscious life to nature or natural objects **3** : belief in the existence of spirits separable from bodies — **an·i·mist** \-məst\ *n* — **an·i·mis·tic** \ˌan-ə-ˈmis-tik\ *adj*

an·i·mos·i·ty \ˌan-ə-ˈmäs-ət-ē\ *n, pl* **-ties** [ME *animosite,* fr. MF or LL; MF *animosité,* fr. LL *animositat-, animositas,* fr. L *animosus* spirited, fr. *animus*] : ill will or resentment tending toward active hostility *syn* see ENMITY

an·i·mus \ˈan-ə-məs\ *n* [L, spirit, mind, courage, anger] **1** : basic attitude or governing spirit : DISPOSITION, INTENTION **2** : a usu. prejudiced and often spiteful or malevolent ill will **3** : an inner masculine part of the female personality in the analytic psychology of C. G. Jung *syn* see ENMITY *ant* favor

an·ion \ˈan-ˌī-ən\ *n* [Gk, neut. of *aniōn,* prp. of *anienai* to go up, fr. *ana-* + *ienai* to go — more at ISSUE] : the ion in an electrolyzed solution that migrates to the anode; *broadly* : a negatively charged ion

an·ion·ic \ˌan-(ˌ)ī-ˈän-ik\ *adj* **1** : of or relating to anions **2** : characterized by an active and esp. surface-active anion — **an·ion·i·cal·ly** \-i-k(ə-)lē\ *adv*

anis- *or* **aniso-** *comb form* [NL, fr. Gk, fr. *anisos,* fr. *a-* + *isos* equal] : unequal ⟨*aniseikonia*⟩ ⟨*anisodactylous*⟩

an·ise \ˈan-əs\ *n* [ME *anis,* fr. OF, fr. L *anisum,* fr. Gk *annēson, anison*] : an herb (*Pimpinella anisum*) of the carrot family having carminative and aromatic seeds; *also* : ANISEED

ani·seed \ˈan-ə(s)-ˌsēd\ *n* [ME *anis seed,* fr. *anis* + *seed*] : the seed of anise often used as a flavoring in cordials and in cooking

an·is·ei·ko·nia \ˌan-ˌī-ˌsī-ˈkō-nē-ə\ *n* [NL, fr. *anis-* + Gk *eikōn* image — more at ICON] : a defect of binocular vision in which the two retinal images of an object differ in size — **an·is·ei·kon·ic** \-ˈkän-ik\ *adj*

an·is·ette \ˌan-ə-ˈset, -ˈzet\ *n* [F, fr. *anis*] : a usu. colorless sweet liqueur flavored with aniseed

an·isog·a·mous \ˌan-(ˌ)ī-ˈsäg-ə-məs\ *also* **an·iso·gam·ic** \-ˌī-sə-ˈgam-ik\ *adj* : characterized by fusion of heterogamous gametes or of individuals that usu. differ chiefly in size ⟨~ reproduction⟩ — **an·isog·a·my** \-(ˌ)ī-ˈsäg-ə-mē\ *n*

an·iso·me·tro·pia \ˌan-ˌī-sə-mə-ˈtrō-pē-ə\ *n* [NL, fr. Gk *anisometros* of unequal measure (fr. *anis-* + *metron* measure) + NL *-opia* — more at MEASURE] : unequal refractive power in the two eyes — **an·iso·me·tro·pic** \-ˈträp-ik, -ˈtrō-pik\ *adj*

an·iso·trop·ic \ˌan-ˌī-sə-ˈträp-ik\ *adj* **1** : exhibiting properties with different values when measured along axes in different directions ⟨an ~ crystal⟩ **2** : assuming different positions in response to external stimuli — **an·iso·trop·i·cal·ly** \-i-k(ə-)lē\ *adv* — **an·isot·ro·py** \-(ˌ)ī-ˈsä-trə-pē\ *or* **an·isot·ro·pism** \-ˌpiz-əm\ *n*

an·ker·ite \ˈaŋ-kə-ˌrīt\ *n* [G *ankerit,* fr. M. J. *Anker* †1843 Austrian mineralogist] : a dolomitic iron-containing mineral $Ca(Fe,Mg,Mn)(CO_3)_2$

ankh \ˈäŋk\ *n* [Egypt *ʿnh*] : a cross having a loop for its upper vertical arm and serving esp. in ancient Egypt as an emblem of life

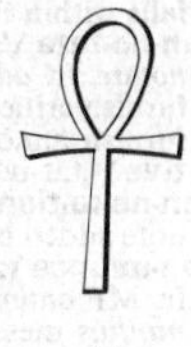
ankh

an·kle \ˈaŋ-kəl\ *n* [ME *ankel,* fr. OE *anclēow;* akin to OHG *anchlāo* ankle, L *angulus* angle] **1** : the joint between the foot and the leg; *also* : the region of this joint **2** : the joint between the cannon bone and pastern (as in the horse)

an·kle·bone \ˌaŋ-kəl-ˈbōn, ˈaŋ-kəl-ˌ\ *n* : TALUS 1

an·klet \ˈaŋ-klət\ *n* **1** : something (as an ornament) worn around the ankle **2** : a short sock reaching slightly above the ankle **3** : a woman's or child's low shoe having one or more ankle straps

an·ky·lose \ˈaŋ-ki-ˌlōs, -ˌlōz\ *vb* **-losed; -los·ing** [back-formation fr. *ankylosis*] *vt* : to unite or stiffen by ankylosis ~ *vi* : to undergo ankylosis

an·ky·lo·sis \ˌaŋ-ki-ˈlō-səs\ *n, pl* **-lo·ses** \-ˌsēz\ [NL, fr. Gk *ankylōsis,* fr. *ankyloun* to make crooked, fr. *ankylos* crooked; akin to L *uncus* hooked — more at ANGLE] **1** : stiffness or fixation of a joint by disease or surgery **2** : union of separate bones or hard parts to form a single bone or part — **an·ky·lot·ic** \-ˈlät-ik\ *adj*

an·la·ge \ˈän-ˌläg-ə\ *n, pl* **-gen** \-ən\ *also* **-ges** \-əz\ [G, lit., act of laying on] : the foundation of a subsequent development; *specif* : the first recognizable commencement of a developing part or organ in an embryo

ann *abbr* **1** annals **2** annual

an·na \ˈän-ə\ *n* [Hindi *ānā*] **1** : a former monetary unit of Burma, India, and Pakistan equal to $^1/_{16}$ rupee **2** : a coin representing one anna

an·nal·ist \ˈan-ᵊl-əst\ *n* : a writer of annals : HISTORIAN — **an·nal·is·tic** \ˌan-ᵊl-ˈis-tik\ *adj*

an·nals \ˈan-ᵊlz\ *n pl* [L *annales,* fr. pl. of *annalis* yearly — more at ANNUAL] **1** : a record of events arranged in yearly sequence **2** : historical records : CHRONICLES **3** : records of the activities of an organization *syn* see HISTORY

An·nam·ese \ˌan-ə-ˈmēz, -ˈmēs\ *n, pl* **Annamese** [*Annam,* region of Vietnam] **1 a** : a Mongolian people inhabiting Vietnam **b** *or* **An·nam·ite** \ˈan-ə-ˌmīt\ : a member of this people **2** : the language of the Annamese people : VIETNAMESE — **Annamese** *adj* — **Annamite** *adj*

an·nat·to \ə-ˈnät-(ˌ)ō\ *n* [of Cariban origin; akin to Galibi *annoto* tree producing annatto] : a yellowish red dyestuff made from the pulp around the seeds of a tropical tree (*Bixa orellana,* family Bixaceae)

an·neal \ə-ˈnē(ə)l\ *vt* [ME *anelen,* fr. OE *onǣlan,* fr. *on* + *ǣlan* to set on fire, burn, fr. *āl* fire; akin to OE *ād* funeral pyre — more at EDIFY] **1** : to heat (as glass) in order to fix laid-on colors **2** : to heat and then cool (as steel or glass) usu. for softening and making less brittle **3** : STRENGTHEN, TOUGHEN

an·ne·lid \ˈan-ᵊl-əd\ *n* [deriv. of L *anellus* little ring — more at ANNULET] : any of a phylum (Annelida) of coelomate and usu. elon-

ə abut	ᵊ kitten	ər further	a back	ā bake	ä cot, cart
aů out	ch chin	e less	ē easy	g gift	i trip
j joke	ŋ sing	ō flow	ȯ flaw	ȯi coin	th thin
ü loot	ů foot	y yet	yü few	yů furious	zh vision

ī life · th this

gated segmented invertebrates (as earthworms, various marine worms, and leeches) — **annelid** *adj* — **an·nel·i·dan** \ə-'nel-əd-ᵊn, a-\ *adj or n*

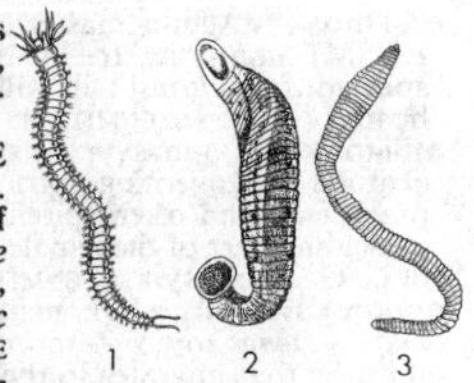
1 2 3
annelid: *1* nereis, *2* leech, *3* earthworm

[1]an·nex \ə-'neks, 'an-,eks\ *vt* [ME *annexen,* fr. MF *annexer,* fr. OF, fr. *annexe* joined, fr. L *annexus,* pp. of *annectere* to bind to, fr. *ad-* + *nectere* to bind] **1 :** to attach as a quality, consequence, or condition **2** *archaic* **:** to join together materially **:** UNITE **3 :** SUBJOIN, APPEND **4 :** to incorporate (a country or other territory) within the domain of a state **5 :** to obtain or take for oneself — **an·nex·ation** \,an-,ek-'sā-shən\ *n* — **an·nex·ation·al** \-shnəl, -shən-ᵊl\ *adj* — **an·nex·ation·ist** \-sh(ə-)nəst\ *n*

[2]an·nex \'an-,eks, -iks\ *n* **:** something annexed or appended: as **a :** an added stipulation or statement **:** APPENDIX **b :** a subsidiary or supplementary structure **:** WING

an·nexe \'an-,eks, -iks\ *chiefly Brit var of* [2]ANNEX

An·nie Oak·ley \,an-ē-'ō-klē\ *n, pl* **Annie Oakleys** [*Annie Oakley* †1926 Am markswoman; fr. the resemblance of a punched pass to a playing card with bullet holes through the spots] **:** a free ticket (as to a theater)

an·ni·hi·late \ə-'nī-ə-,lāt\ *vb* **-lat·ed; -lat·ing** [LL *annihilatus,* pp. of *annihilare* to reduce to nothing, fr. L *ad-* + *nihil* nothing — more at NIL] *vt* **1 a :** to cause to be of no effect **:** NULLIFY **b :** to destroy the substance or force of **2 :** to regard as of no consequence **3 :** to cause to cease to exist **4 a :** to destroy a considerable part of ⟨the army was *annihilated*⟩ **b :** to vanquish completely **:** ROUT ~ *vi* **:** to cease to exist **:** VANISH — used of a particle and its antiparticle upon coming together **syn** see ABOLISH — **an·ni·hi·la·tion** \-,nī-ə-'lā-shən\ *n* — **an·ni·hi·la·tive** \-'nī-ə-,lāt-iv\ *adj* — **an·ni·hi·la·tor** \-,lāt-ər\ *n* — **an·ni·hi·la·to·ry** \-'nī-ə-lə-,tōr-ē, -,tȯr-\ *adj*

an·ni·ver·sa·ry \,an-ə-'vərs-(ə-)rē\ *n, pl* **-ries** *often attrib* [ME *anniversarie,* fr. ML *anniversarium,* fr. L, neut. of *anniversarius* returning annually, fr. *annus* year + *versus,* pp. of *vertere* to turn — more at ANNUAL, WORTH] **1 :** the annual recurrence of a date marking a notable event **2 :** the celebration of an anniversary

an·no Do·mi·ni \,an-(,)ō-'däm-ə-nē, -'dō-mə-, -,nī\ *adv, often cap A* [ML, in the year of the Lord] — used to indicate that a time division falls within the Christian era

an·no he·gi·rae \-hi-'jī(ə)r-(,)ē, -'hej-ə-,rē\ *adv, often cap A&H* [NL, in the year of the Hegira] — used to indicate that a time division falls within the Muslim era

an·no·tate \'an-ə-,tāt\ *vb* **-tat·ed; -tat·ing** [L *annotatus,* pp. of *annotare,* fr. *ad-* + *notare* to mark — more at NOTE] *vi* **:** to make or furnish critical or explanatory notes or comment ~ *vt* **:** to make or furnish annotations for (a literary work or subject) — **an·no·ta·tive** \-,tāt-iv\ *adj* — **an·no·ta·tor** \-,tāt-ər\ *n*

an·no·ta·tion \,an-ə-'tā-shən\ *n* **1 :** the act of annotating **2 :** a note added by way of comment or explanation

an·nounce \ə-'nau̇n(t)s\ *vb* **-nounced; -nounc·ing** [ME *announcen,* fr. MF *annoncer,* fr. L *annuntiare,* fr. *ad-* + *nuntiare* to report, fr. *nuntius* messenger] *vt* **1 :** to make known publicly **:** PROCLAIM ⟨*announced* their engagement⟩ **2 a :** to give notice of the arrival, presence, or readiness of ⟨~ dinner⟩ **b :** to indicate beforehand **:** FORETELL **3 :** to serve as an announcer of ~ *vi* **1 :** to serve as an announcer **2 :** to declare one's candidacy **:** give one's political support **syn** see DECLARE

an·nounce·ment \ə-'nau̇n(t)-smənt\ *n* **1 :** the act of announcing or of being announced **2 :** a public notification or declaration **3 :** a piece of formal stationery designed for a social or business announcement

an·nounc·er \ə-'nau̇n(t)-sər\ *n* **:** one that announces; *esp* **:** one that introduces television or radio programs, makes commercial announcements, reads news summaries, and gives station identification

an·noy \ə-'nȯi\ *vb* [ME *anoien,* fr. OF *enuier,* fr. LL *inodiare* to make loathsome, fr. L *in* + *odium* hatred — more at ODIUM] *vt* **1 :** to disturb or irritate esp. by repeated acts **:** VEX **2 :** to harass esp. by quick and brief attacks ~ *vi* **:** to be a source of annoyance — **an·noy·er** *n*

syn 1 ANNOY, VEX, IRK, BOTHER *shared meaning element* **:** to disturb and nervously upset a person **ant** soothe
2 see WORRY

an·noy·ance \ə-'nȯi-ən(t)s\ *n* **1 :** the act of annoying or of being annoyed **2 :** the state or feeling of being annoyed **:** VEXATION **3 :** a source of vexation or irritation **:** NUISANCE

an·noy·ing *adj* **:** causing vexation **:** IRRITATING — **an·noy·ing·ly** \-iŋ-lē\ *adv*

[1]an·nu·al \'an-yə(-wə)l\ *adj* [ME, fr. MF & LL; MF *annuel,* fr. LL *annualis,* blend of L *annuus* yearly (fr. *annus* year) and L *annalis* yearly (fr. *annus* year); akin to Goth *athnam* (dat. pl.) years, Skt *atati* he walks, goes] **1 :** covering the period of a year ⟨~ rainfall⟩ **2 :** occurring or performed once a year **:** YEARLY ⟨an ~ reunion⟩ **3 :** completing the life cycle in one growing season — **an·nu·al·ly** \-ē\ *adv*

[2]annual *n* **1 :** a publication appearing yearly **2 :** an event that occurs yearly **3 :** something that lasts one year or season; *specif* **:** an annual plant

annual ring *n* **:** the layer of wood produced by a single year's growth of a woody plant

an·nu·itant \ə-'n(y)ü-ət-ənt\ *n* **:** a beneficiary of an annuity

an·nu·ity \ə-'n(y)ü-ət-ē\ *n, pl* **-ities** [ME *annuite,* fr. MF *annuité,* fr. ML *annuitat-, annuitas,* fr. L *annuus* yearly] **1 :** an amount payable yearly or at other regular intervals **2 :** the right to receive or the obligation to pay an annuity **3 :** a contract or agreement providing for the payment of an annuity

an·nul \ə-'nəl\ *vt* **an·nulled; an·nul·ling** [ME *annullen,* fr. MF *annuller,* fr. LL *annullare,* fr. L *ad-* + *nullus* not any — more at NULL] **1 :** to reduce to nothing **:** OBLITERATE **2 :** to make ineffective or inoperative **:** NEUTRALIZE ⟨~ the drug's effect⟩ **3 :** to declare or make legally invalid or void ⟨wants his marriage *annulled*⟩ **syn** see NULLIFY

an·nu·lar \'an-yə-lər\ *adj* [MF or L; MF *annulaire,* fr. L *annularis,* fr. *annulus*] **:** of, relating to, or forming a ring — **an·nu·lar·i·ty** \,an-yə-'lar-ət-ē\ *n* — **an·nu·lar·ly** \'an-yə-lər-lē\ *adv*

annular eclipse *n* **:** an eclipse in which a thin outer ring of the sun's disk is not covered by the apparently smaller dark disk of the moon

an·nu·late \'an-yə-lət, -,lāt\ *or* **an·nu·lat·ed** \-,lāt-əd\ *adj* **:** furnished with or composed of rings **:** RINGED — **an·nu·late·ly** *adv*

an·nu·la·tion \,an-yə-'lā-shən\ *n* **:** formation of rings; *also* **:** RING

an·nu·let \'an-yə-lət\ *n* [modif. of MF *annelet,* dim. of *anel,* fr. L *anellus,* dim. of *annulus*] **1 :** a little ring **2 :** a small architectural molding or ridge forming a ring

an·nul·ment \ə-'nəl-mənt\ *n* **1 :** the act of annulling or of being annulled **2 :** a judicial pronouncement declaring a marriage invalid

an·nu·lus \'an-yə-ləs\ *n, pl* **-li** \-,lī, -lē\ *also* **-lus·es** [L, dim. of *anus* ring, anus — more at ANUS] **1 :** RING **2 :** a part, structure, or marking resembling a ring; as **a :** a line of cells around a fern sporangium that ruptures the sporangium by contracting **b :** a growth ring (as on the scale of a fish) that is used in estimating age

an·nun·ci·ate \ə-'nən(t)-sē-,āt\ *vt* **-at·ed; -at·ing :** ANNOUNCE

an·nun·ci·a·tion \ə-,nən(t)-sē-'ā-shən\ *n* [ME *annunciacioun,* fr. MF *anunciation,* fr. LL *annuntiation-, annuntiatio,* fr. L *annuntiatus,* pp. of *annuntiare* — more at ANNOUNCE] **1 :** the act of announcing or of being announced **:** ANNOUNCEMENT **2** *cap* **:** March 25 observed as a church festival in commemoration of the announcement of the Incarnation to the Virgin Mary

an·nun·ci·a·tor \ə-'nən(t)-sē-,āt-ər\ *n* **:** one that annunciates; *specif* **:** a usu. electrically controlled signal board or indicator — **an·nun·ci·a·to·ry** \-sē-ə-,tōr-ē, -,tȯr-\ *adj*

an·nus mi·ra·bi·lis \,an-ə-smə-'räb-ə-ləs, ,än-\ *n, pl* **an·ni mi·ra·bi·les** \'an-,ī-mə-'räb-ə-,lēz, 'än-(,)ē-mə-'räb-ə-,lās\ [NL] **:** wonderful year — used of an esp. notable year

an·ode \'an-,ōd\ *n* [Gk *anodos* way up, fr. *ana-* + *hodos* way — more at CEDE] **1 :** the positive terminal of an electrolytic cell — compare CATHODE **2 :** the negative terminal of a primary cell or of a storage battery that is delivering current **3 :** the electron-collecting electrode of an electron tube — **an·od·ic** \a-'näd-ik\ *or* **an·od·al** \-'nōd-ᵊl\ *adj* — **an·od·i·cal·ly** \-i-k(ə-)lē\ *or* **an·od·al·ly** \-ᵊl-ē\ *adv*

an·od·ize \'an-ə-,dīz\ *vt* **-ized; -iz·ing :** to subject (a metal) to electrolytic action as the anode of a cell in order to coat with a protective or decorative film — **an·od·iza·tion** \,an-,ōd-ə-'zā-shən, -əd-\ *n*

[1]an·o·dyne \'an-ə-,dīn\ *adj* [L *anodynos,* fr. Gk *anōdynos,* fr. *a-* + *odynē* pain; akin to OE *etan* to eat] **:** serving to assuage pain

[2]anodyne *n* **1 :** a drug that allays pain **2 :** something that soothes, calms, or comforts ⟨the ~ of bridge, a comfortable book, or sport — Harrison Smith⟩ — **an·o·dyn·ic** \,an-ə-'din-ik\ *adj*

anoint \ə-'nȯint\ *vt* [ME *anointen,* fr. MF *enoint,* pp. of *enoindre,* fr. L *inunguere,* fr. *in-* + *unguere* to smear — more at OINTMENT] **1 :** to smear or rub with oil or an oily substance **2 a :** to apply oil to as a sacred rite esp. for consecration **b :** to designate as if through the rite of anointment **:** CONSECRATE — **anoint·er** *n* — **anoint·ment** \-mənt\ *n*

anom·a·lis·tic \ə-,näm-ə-'lis-tik\ *adj* **:** of or relating to the astronomical anomaly — **anom·a·lis·ti·cal** \-ti-kəl\ *adj*

anom·a·lous \ə-'näm-ə-ləs\ *adj* [LL *anomalus,* fr. Gk *anōmalos,* lit., uneven, fr. *a-* + *homalos* even, fr. *homos* same — more at SAME] **1 :** deviating from a general rule, method, or analogy **:** ABNORMAL **2 :** being out of keeping with accepted notions of fitness or order; *also* **:** inconsistent with what would naturally be expected **syn** see IRREGULAR — **anom·a·lous·ly** *adv* — **anom·a·lous·ness** *n*

anom·a·ly \ə-'näm-ə-lē\ *n, pl* **-lies 1 :** the angular distance of a planet from its perihelion as seen from the sun **2 :** deviation from the common rule **:** IRREGULARITY **3 :** something anomalous; *esp* **:** something that deviates in excess of normal variation **syn** see PARADOX

an·o·mie *or* **an·o·my** \'an-ə-mē\ *n* [F *anomie,* fr. Gk *anomia* lawlessness, fr. *anomos* lawless, fr. *a-* + *nomos* law, fr. *nemein* to distribute — more at NIMBLE] **:** a state of society in which normative standards of conduct and belief are weak or lacking; *also* **:** a similar condition in an individual commonly characterized by disorientation, anxiety, and isolation — **ano·mic** \ə-'näm-ik, -'nō-mik\ *adj*

[1]anon \ə-'nän\ *adv* [ME, fr. OE *on ān,* fr. *on* in + *ān* one — more at ON, ONE] **1** *obs* **:** at once **:** IMMEDIATELY **2** *archaic* **:** SOON, PRESENTLY **3 :** after a while **:** LATER

[2]anon *abbr* anonymous; anonymously

an·o·nym \'an-ə-,nim\ *n* **1 :** one who is anonymous **2 :** PSEUDONYM

an·o·nym·i·ty \,an-ə-'nim-ət-ē\ *n, pl* **-ties 1 :** the quality or state of being anonymous **2 :** one that is anonymous

anon·y·mous \ə-'nän-ə-məs\ *adj* [LL *anonymus,* fr. Gk *anōnymos,* fr. *a-* + *onyma* name — more at NAME] **1 :** having or giving no name ⟨an ~ author⟩ **2 :** of unknown or unnamed origin ⟨~ gifts⟩ **3 :** marked by lack of individuality or personality ⟨the gray ~ streets — William Styron⟩ — **anon·y·mous·ly** *adv* — **anon·y·mous·ness** *n*

anoph·e·les \ə-'näf-ə-,lēz\ *n* [NL, genus name, fr. Gk *anōphelēs* useless, fr. *a-* + *ophelos* advantage, help; akin to OE *ō-* behind, OHG *ā-*, Skt *ā-* toward and to Skt *phalam* fruit, profit] **:** any of a genus (*Anopheles*) of mosquitoes that includes all mosquitoes which transmit malaria to man — see MOSQUITO illustration — **anoph·e·line** \-,līn\ *adj or n*

an·o·rak \'an-ə-,rak\ *n* [Greenland Esk *ánorâq*] **:** PARKA

an·o·rec·tic \,an-ə-'rek-tik\ *or* **an·o·ret·ic** \-'ret-ik\ *adj* [Gk *anorektos,* fr. *an-* [2]a- + *oregein* to reach after] **1 :** lacking appetite **2 :** causing loss of appetite

an·orex·ia \,an-ə-'rek-sē-ə\ *n* [NL, fr. Gk, fr. *a-* + *orexis* appetite, fr. *oregein* to stretch out, reach after — more at RIGHT] **:** loss of appetite esp. when prolonged — **an·orexi·gen·ic** \,an-ə-,rek-sə-'jen-ik\ *adj*

an·or·thite \ə-'nȯr-ˌthīt\ n [F, fr. a- + Gk orthos straight — more at ARDUOUS] : a white, grayish, or reddish feldspar CaAl₂Si₂O₈ occurring in many igneous rocks — **an·or·thit·ic** \ˌan-ȯr-'thit-ik\ adj

an·or·tho·site \ə-'nȯr-thə-ˌsīt\ n [F anorthose, a feldspar, fr. a- + Gk orthos] : a granular plutonic igneous rock composed almost exclusively of a soda-lime feldspar (as labradorite)

an·os·mia \a-'näz-mē-ə\ n [NL, fr. a- + Gk osmē smell — more at ODOR] : loss or impairment of the sense of smell — **an·os·mic** \-mik-ˌad\

¹an·oth·er \ə-'nəth-ər\ adj 1 : different or distinct from the one first considered 〈the same scene viewed from ~ angle〉 2 : some other : LATER 〈do it ~ time〉 3 : being one more in addition to one or more of the same kind : NEW 〈have ~ piece of pie〉

²another pron 1 : an additional one : one more 2 : one that is different from the first or present one 3 : one of a group of unspecified or indefinite things

anoth·er-guess \ə-'nəth-ər-ˌges\ adj [alter. of anothergates, fr. ¹another + gate] archaic : of another sort

an·ovu·lant \a-'näv-yə-lənt, -'nōv-\ n [²a- + ovulate + -ant] : a drug that suppresses ovulation — **anovulant** adj

an·ovu·la·to·ry \(')an-'äv-yə-lə,tōr-ē, -'ōv-, -,tȯr-\ adj [²a- + ovulate + -ory] 1 : not involving or associated with ovulation 〈~ bleeding〉 2 : suppressing ovulation

an·ox·emia \ˌan-ˌäk-'sē-mē-ə\ n [NL] : a condition of subnormal oxygenation of the arterial blood — **an·ox·emic** \-mik\ adj

an·ox·ia \a-'näk-sē-ə\ n [NL] : hypoxia esp. of such severity as to result in permanent damage — **an·ox·ic** \-sik\ adj

ans abbr answer

an·ser·ine \'an(t)-sə-ˌrīn\ adj [L anserinus, fr. anser goose — more at GOOSE] : of, relating to, or resembling a goose

¹an·swer \'an(t)-sər\ n [ME, fr. OE andswaru; akin to ON andsvar answer; both fr. a prehistoric WGmc-NGmc compound whose first constituent is represented by OE and- against, and whose second constituent is akin to OE swerian to swear — more at ANTE-] 1 a : something spoken or written in reply to a question b : a correct response 2 a : a reply to a charge : DEFENSE b : a rejoinder made by the defendant in an equity case in reply to the charges made by the complainant in his bill 3 : something done in response 〈his only ~ was to walk out〉 4 : a solution of a problem 〈the ~ to a chess problem〉

²answer vb **an·swered; an·swer·ing** \'an(t)s-(ə-)riŋ\ vi 1 : to speak or write in reply 2 a : to be or make oneself responsible or accountable b : to make amends : ATONE 3 : to be in conformity or correspondence 〈~ed to the description〉 4 : to act in response to an action performed elsewhere or by another 5 : to be adequate : SERVE ~ vt 1 a : to speak or write in reply to b : to say or write by way of reply 2 : to reply in rebuttal, justification, or explanation 3 a : to correspond to b : to be adequate or usable for : serve the purpose of often in a temporary or expedient manner 4 obs : to atone for 5 : to act in response to 6 : to offer a solution for; esp : SOLVE — **an·swer·er** \'an(t)-sər-ər\ n

syn 1 ANSWER, RESPOND, REPLY, REJOIN, RETORT shared meaning element : to say or write or do something in return
2 see SATISFY

an·swer·able \'an(t)s-(ə-)rə-bəl\ adj 1 : liable to be called to account : RESPONSIBLE 2 archaic : SUITABLE, ADEQUATE 3 archaic : ACCORDANT, CORRESPONDING 4 : capable of being refuted

answering service n : a commercial service that answers telephone calls for its clients

¹ant \'ant\ n [ME ante, emete, fr. OE æmette; akin to OHG āmeiza ant] : any of a family (Formicidae) of colonial hymenopterous insects with a complex social organization and various castes performing special duties

²ant abbr 1 antenna 2 antonym

Ant abbr 1 Antarctica 2 Antrim

ant- — see ANTI-

ants: 1 winged male, 2 worker

¹-ant \ənt, ²nt\ n suffix [ME, fr. OF, fr. -ant, prp. suffix, fr. L -ant, -ans, prp. suffix of first conjugation, fr. -a- (stem vowel of first conjugation) + -nt-, -ns, prp. suffix; akin to OE -nde, prp. suffix, Gk -nt-, -n, part. suffix] 1 a : one that performs (a specified action) : personal or impersonal agent 〈claimant〉 〈coolant〉 b : thing that promotes (a specified action or process) 〈expectorant〉 2 : one connected with 〈annuitant〉 3 : thing that is acted upon (in a specified manner) 〈inhalant〉

²-ant adj suffix 1 : performing (a specified action) or being (in a specified condition) 〈somnambulant〉 2 : promoting (a specified action or process) 〈expectorant〉

an·ta \'ant-ə\ n, pl antas or an·tae \'an-ˌtē, -ˌtī\ [L; akin to ON ōnd anteroom] : a pier produced by thickening a wall at its termination

ANTA abbr American National Theater and Academy

ant·ac·id \(')ant-'as-əd\ adj : counteractive of acidity — **antacid** n

An·tae·an \an-'tē-ən\ adj [Antaeus, a giant overcome by Hercules] 1 : having superhuman strength : MAMMOTH

A, A antas

an·tag·o·nism \an-'tag-ə-,niz-əm\ n 1 a : actively expressed opposition, hostility, or antipathy 〈~ between factions〉 b : opposition of a conflicting force, tendency, or principle 〈the ~ of democracy to dictatorship〉 2 : opposition in physiological action; esp : interaction of two or more substances such that the action of any one of them on living cells or tissues is lessened **syn** see ENMITY **ant** accord, comity

an·tag·o·nist \-nəst\ n 1 : one that opposes another esp. in combat : ADVERSARY 2 : an agent of physiological antagonism: as a : a muscle that contracts with and limits the action of an agonist with which it is paired — called also antagonistic muscle b : a drug that opposes the action of another **syn** see OPPONENT

an·tag·o·nis·tic \(ˌ)an-ˌtag-ə-'nis-tik\ adj : characterized by or resulting from antagonism : OPPOSING **syn** see ADVERSE **ant** favoring, favorable — **an·tag·o·nis·ti·cal·ly** \-ti-k(ə-)lē\ adv

an·tag·o·nize \an-'tag-ə-ˌnīz\ vt -**nized; -niz·ing** [Gk antagōnizesthai, fr. anti- + agōnizesthai to struggle, fr. agōn contest — more at AGONY] 1 : to act in opposition to : COUNTERACT 2 : to incur or provoke the hostility of **syn** see OPPOSE

ant·arc·tic \(')ant-'ärk-tik, -'ärt-ik\ adj, often cap [ME antartik, fr. L antarcticus, fr. Gk antarktikos, fr. anti- + arktikos arctic] : of or relating to the south pole or to the region near it

antarctic circle n, often cap A&C : the parallel of latitude that is approximately 66¹/₂ degrees south of the equator and that circumscribes the southern frigid zone

An·tar·es \an-'ta(ə)r-(ˌ)ēz, -'te(ə)r-\ n [Gk Antarēs] : a giant red star of very low density that is the brightest star in Scorpio

ant bear n : a large anteater (Myrmecophaga jubata) of So. America with shaggy gray fur, a black band across the breast, and a white stripe on the shoulder

ant cow n : an aphid from which ants obtain honeydew

ant bear

¹an·te \'ant-ē\ n [ante-] 1 : a poker stake usu. put up before the deal to build the pot 〈the dealer called for a dollar ~〉 2 : an amount paid : PRICE 〈these improvements would raise the ~〉

²ante vt **an·ted; an·te·ing** : to put up (an ante); also : PAY, PRODUCE — often used with up

ante- prefix [ME, fr. L, fr. ante before, in front of; akin to OE and- against, Gk anti before, against — more at END] 1 a : prior : earlier 〈antetype〉 b : anterior : forward 〈anteroom〉 2 a : prior to : earlier than 〈antediluvian〉 b : in front of 〈antechoir〉

ant·eat·er \'ant-ˌēt-ər\ n : any of several mammals that feed largely or entirely on ants: as a : an edentate with a long narrow snout, a long tongue, and enormous salivary glands b : ECHIDNA c : AARDVARK

an·te·bel·lum \ˌant-i-'bel-əm\ adj [L ante bellum before the war] : existing before a war; esp : existing before the Civil War 〈an ~ brick mansion〉

an·te·cede \ˌant-ə-'sēd\ vt -**ced·ed; -ced·ing** [L antecedere, fr. ante- + cedere to go — more at CEDE] : PRECEDE

an·te·ced·ence \-'sēd-²n(t)s\ n : PRIORITY, PRECEDENCE

¹an·te·ced·ent \ˌant-ə-'sēd-²nt\ n [ME, fr. ML & L ML antecedent-, antecedens, fr. L, logical antecedent, lit., one that goes before, fr. neut. of antecedent-, antecedens, prp. of antecedere] 1 : a substantive word, phrase, or clause referred to by a pronoun (as John in "I saw John and spoke to him"); broadly : a word or group of words replaced and referred to by a substitute 2 : the conditional element in a proposition (as if A in "if A, then B") 3 : the first term of a mathematical ratio 4 a : a preceding event, condition, or cause b pl : the significant events, conditions, and traits of one's earlier life 5 a : a predecessor in a series; esp : a model or stimulus for later developments b pl : ANCESTORS, PARENTS **syn** see CAUSE

²antecedent adj 1 : prior in time or order 2 : causally or logically prior **syn** see PRECEDING **ant** subsequent, consequent — **an·te·ced·ent·ly** adv

an·te·ces·sor \ˌant-i-'ses-ər\ n [ME antecessour, fr. L antecessor — more at ANCESTOR] : one that goes before : PREDECESSOR

an·te·cham·ber \'ant-i-ˌchām-bər\ n [F antichambre, fr. MF, fr. It anti- (fr. L ante-) + MF chambre room — more at CHAMBER] : ANTEROOM

an·te·choir \'ant-i-ˌkwī(ə)r\ n : a space enclosed or reserved for the clergy and choristers at the entrance to a choir

¹an·te·date \'ant-i-ˌdāt\ n : a date assigned to an event or document earlier than the actual date of the event or document

²an·te·date \'ant-i-ˌdāt, ˌant-i-'\ vt 1 a : to date as of a time prior to that of execution b : to assign to a date prior to that of actual occurrence 2 archaic : ANTICIPATE 3 : to precede in time

an·te·di·lu·vi·an \ˌant-i-də-'lü-vē-ən, -ˌ)di-\ adj [ante- + L diluvium flood — more at DELUGE] 1 : of or relating to the period before the flood described in the Bible 2 : made, evolved, or developed a long time ago : ANTIQUATED 〈an ~ automobile〉 — **antediluvian** n

an·te·fix \'ant-i-ˌfiks\ n [L antefixum, fr. neut. of antefixus, pp. of antefigere to fasten before, fr. ante- + figere to fasten — more at DIKE] 1 : an ornament at the eaves of a classical building concealing the ends of the joint tiles of the roof 2 : an ornament of the molding of a classic cornice — **an·te·fix·al** \ˌant-i-'fik-səl\ adj

an·te·lope \'ant-²l-ˌōp\ n, pl -lope or -lopes [ME, fabulous heraldic beast, prob. fr. MF antelop savage animal with sawlike horns, fr. ML anthalopus, fr. LGk antholop-, antholops] 1 a : any of various Old World ruminant mammals (family Bovidae) that differ from the true oxen esp. in lighter racier build and horns directed upward and backward b : PRONGHORN 2 : leather from antelope hide

an·te me·ri·di·em \ˌant-i-mə-'rid-ē-əm, -ē-,em\ adj [L] : being before noon — abbr. a.m.

an·te·mor·tem \-'mȯrt-əm\ adj [L ante mortem] : preceding death

an·te·na·tal \-'nāt-²l\ adj : of or relating to an unborn child : PRENATAL; also : occurring during pregnancy

an·ten·na \an-'ten-ə\ n, pl -nae \-(ˌ)ē\ or -nas [ML, fr. L, sail yard] 1 : a movable segmented organ of sensation on the head of insects, myriapods, and crustaceans — see INSECT illustration 2 pl anten-

nas : a usu. metallic device (as a rod or wire) for radiating or receiving radio waves — **an·ten·nal** \-'ten-ᵊl\ *adj*
an·ten·nule \an-'ten-(,)yü(ə)l\ *n* : a small antenna or similar appendage
an·te·pen·di·um \,ant-i-'pen-dē-əm\ *n, pl* **-di·ums; -dia** \-dē-ə\ [ML, fr. L *ante-* + *pendēre* to hang — more at PENDANT] : a hanging for the front of an altar, pulpit, or lectern
an·te·pe·nult \,ant-i-'pē-,nəlt, -pi-'\ *also* **an·te·pen·ul·ti·ma** \-pi-'nəl-tə-mə\ *n* [LL *antepaenultima,* fem. of *antepaenultimus* preceding the next to last, fr. L *ante-* + *paenultimus* penultimate] : the 3d syllable of a word counting from the end (as *cu* in *accumulate*) — **an·te·pen·ul·ti·mate** \-pi-'nəl-tə-mət\ *adj or n*
an·te·ri·or \an-'tir-ē-ər\ *adj* [L, compar. of *ante* before — more at ANTE-] **1 a** : situated before or toward the front **b** : ABAXIAL **2 a** : coming before in time : ANTECEDENT **b** : logically prior ***syn*** see PRECEDING ***ant*** posterior — **an·te·ri·or·ly** *adv*
an·tero- \,ant-ə-(,)rō\ *comb form* [NL, fr. L *anterior*] : anterior ⟨*antero*parietal⟩ : anterior and ⟨*antero*lateral⟩ : from front to ⟨*antero*posterior⟩
an·te·room \'ant-i-,rüm, -,ru̇m\ *n* : an outer room that leads to another usu. more important room and that is often used as a waiting room
anth- — see ANTI-
an·the·lion \ant-'hēl-yən, an-'thēl-\ *n, pl* **-lia** \-yə\ *or* **-lions** [Gk *anthēlion,* fr. neut. of *anthēlios* opposite the sun, fr. *anti-* + *hēlios* sun — more at SOLAR] : a somewhat bright white spot appearing on the parhelic circle opposite the sun
an·thel·min·tic \,ant-,hel-'mint-ik, ,an-,thel-\ *adj* [*anti-* + Gk *helminth-, helmis* worm — more at HELMINTH] : expelling or destroying parasitic worms esp. of the intestine — **anthelmintic** *n*
an·them \'an(t)-thəm\ *n* [ME *antem,* fr. OE *antefn,* fr. LL *antiphona,* fr. LGk *antiphōna,* pl. of *antiphōnon,* fr. Gk, neut. of *antiphōnos* responsive, fr. *anti-* + *phōnē* sound — more at BAN] **1 a** : a psalm or hymn sung antiphonally or responsively **b** : a sacred vocal composition with words usu. from the Scriptures **2** : a song or hymn of praise or gladness
an·the·mi·on \an-'thē-mē-ən\ *n, pl* **-mia** \-mē-ə\ [Gk, fr. dim. of *anthemon* flower, fr. *anthos* — more at ANTHOLOGY] : an ornament of floral or foliated forms arranged in a radiating cluster but always flat (as in relief sculpture or in painting)
an·ther \'an(t)-thər\ *n* [NL *anthera,* fr. L, medicine made fr. flowers, fr. Gk *anthēra,* fr. fem. of *anthēros* flowery, fr. *anthos*] : the part of a stamen that develops and contains pollen and is usu. borne on a stalk — see FLOWER illustration — **an·ther·al** \-thə-rəl\ *adj*
an·ther·id·i·um \,an(t)-thə-'rid-ē-əm\ *n, pl* **-id·ia** \-ē-ə\ [NL, fr. *anthera*] : the male reproductive organ of a cryptogamous plant — **an·ther·id·i·al** \-ē-əl\ *adj*
an·the·sis \an-'thē-səs\ *n* [NL, fr. Gk *anthēsis* bloom, fr. *anthein* to flower, fr. *anthos*] : the action or period of opening of a flower
ant·hill \'ant-,hil\ *n* : a mound thrown up by ants or termites in digging their nest
an·tho·cy·a·nin \,an(t)-thə-'sī-ə-nən\ *also* **an·tho·cy·an** \-'sī-ən, -,an\ *n* [Gk *anthos* + *kyanos* dark blue] : any of various soluble glycoside pigments producing blue to red coloring in flowers and plants
an·thol·o·gist \an-'thäl-ə-jəst\ *n* : a compiler of an anthology
an·thol·o·gize \-,jīz\ *vt* **-gized; -giz·ing** : to compile or publish in an anthology — **an·thol·o·giz·er** \-,jī-zər\ *n*
an·thol·o·gy \an-'thäl-ə-jē\ *n, pl* **-gies** [NL *anthologia* collection of epigrams, fr. MGk, fr. Gk, flower gathering, fr. *anthos* flower + *logia* collecting, fr. *legein* to gather; akin to Skt *andha* herb — more at LEGEND] : a collection of selected literary pieces or passages
an·thoph·a·gous \an-'thäf-ə-gəs\ *adj* [Gk *anthos* + E *-phagous*] : feeding on flowers — **an·thoph·a·gy** \-ə-jē\ *n*
an·tho·zo·an \,an(t)-thə-'zō-ən\ *n* [deriv. of Gk *anthos* + *zōion* animal; akin to Gk *zōē* life — more at QUICK] : any of a class (Anthozoa) of marine coelenterates (as the corals and sea anemones) having polyps with radial partitions — **anthozoan** *adj*
an·thra·cene \'an(t)-thrə-,sēn\ *n* : a crystalline cyclic hydrocarbon $C_{14}H_{10}$ obtained from coal-tar distillation
an·thra·cite \'an(t)-thrə-,sīt\ *n* [Gk *anthrakitis,* fr. *anthrak-, anthrax* coal] : a hard natural coal of high luster differing from bituminous coal in containing little volatile matter — **an·thra·cit·ic** \,an(t)-thrə-'sit-ik\ *adj*
an·thrac·nose \an-'thrak-,nōs\ *n* [F, fr. Gk *anthrak-, anthrax* + *nosos* disease] : any of numerous destructive plant diseases caused by imperfect fungi and characterized by often dark sunken lesions or blisters
an·thra·ni·late \an-'thran-ᵊl-,āt, ,an-thrə-'nil-,āt\ *n* : a salt or ester of anthranilic acid
an·thra·nil·ic acid \,an(t)-thrə-,nil-ik-\ *n* [ISV *anthracene* + *aniline*] : a crystalline acid $NH_2C_6H_4COOH$ used as an intermediate in the manufacture of dyes (as indigo), pharmaceuticals, and perfumes
an·thra·qui·none \,an(t)-thrə-kwin-'ōn, -'kwin-,ōn\ *n* [prob. fr. F, fr. *anthracene* + *quinone*] : a yellow crystalline ketone $C_{14}H_8O_2$ derived from anthracene and used esp. in the manufacture of dyes
an·thrax \'an-,thraks\ *n* [ME *antrax* carbuncle, fr. L *anthrax,* fr. Gk, coal, carbuncle] : an infectious disease of warm-blooded animals (as cattle and sheep) caused by a spore-forming bacterium (*Bacillus anthracis*), transmissible to man esp. by the handling of infected products (as hair), and characterized by external ulcerating nodules or by lesions in the lungs
anthrop *abbr* anthropological; anthropology
anthrop- *or* **anthropo-** *comb form* [L *anthropo-,* fr. Gk *anthrōp-, anthrōpo-,* fr. *anthrōpos*] : human being ⟨*anthropo*genesis⟩
an·throp·ic \an-'thräp-ik\ *or* **an·throp·i·cal** \-i-kəl\ *adj* [Gk *anthrōpikos,* fr. *anthrōpos*] : of or relating to mankind or the period of man's existence on earth
an·thro·po·cen·tric \,an(t)-thrə-pə-'sen-trik\ *adj* **1** : considering man to be the most significant entity of the universe **2** : interpreting or regarding the world in terms of human values and experiences — **an·thro·po·cen·tri·cal·ly** \-tri-k(ə-)lē\ *adv* — **an·thro·po·cen·tric·i·ty** \-pō-(,)sen-'tris-ət-ē\ *n*
an·thro·po·gen·e·sis \,an(t)-thrə-pə-'jen-ə-səs\ *n* [NL, fr. *anthrop-* + L *genesis*] : the study of the origin and development of man — **an·thro·po·ge·net·ic** \-(,)pō-jə-'net-ik\ *adj*
an·thro·po·gen·ic \-pə-'jen-ik\ *adj* : of, relating to, or influenced by the impact of man on nature ⟨~ ecosystems⟩
an·thro·pog·ra·phy \,an(t)-thrə-'päg-rə-fē\ *n* : a branch of anthropology dealing with the distribution of man as distinguished by physical character, language, institutions, and customs
¹an·thro·poid \'an(t)-thrə-,pȯid\ *adj* [Gk *anthrōpoeidēs,* fr. *anthrōpos*] **1** : resembling man **2** : resembling an ape ⟨~ gangsters⟩
²anthropoid *n* : any of several large tailless semierect apes (family Pongidae)
anthropoid ape *n* : APE 1b
an·thro·pol·o·gy \,an(t)-thrə-'päl-ə-jē\ *n* [NL *anthropologia,* fr. *anthrop-* + *-logia* -logy] **1** : the science of man; *esp* : the study of man in relation to distribution, origin, classification, and relationship of races, physical character, environmental and social relations, and culture **2** : teaching about the origin, nature, and destiny of man esp. from the perspective of his relation to God — **an·thro·po·log·i·cal** \-pə-'läj-i-kəl\ *adj* — **an·thro·po·log·i·cal·ly** \-i-k(ə-)lē\ *adv* — **an·thro·pol·o·gist** \,an(t)-thrə-'päl-ə-jəst\ *n*
an·thro·pom·e·try \,an(t)-thrə-'päm-ə-trē\ *n* [F *anthropométrie,* fr. *anthrop-* + *-métrie* -metry] : the study of human body measurements esp. on a comparative basis — **an·thro·po·met·ric** \-pə-'me-trik\ *or* **an·thro·po·met·ri·cal** \-tri-kəl\ *adj* — **an·thro·po·met·ri·cal·ly** \-tri-k(ə-)lē\ *adv*
an·thro·po·mor·phic \,an(t)-thrə-pə-'mȯr-fik\ *adj* [LL, *anthropomorphus* of human form, fr. Gk *anthrōpomorphos,* fr. *anthrōp-* + *-morphos* -morphous] **1** : described or thought of as having a human form or human attributes ⟨~ deities⟩ **2** : ascribing human characteristics to nonhuman things ⟨~ supernaturalism⟩ — **an·thro·po·mor·phi·cal·ly** \-fi-k(ə-)lē\ *adv*
an·thro·po·mor·phism \-,fiz-əm\ *n* : an interpretation of what is not human or personal in terms of human or personal characteristics : HUMANIZATION — **an·thro·po·mor·phist** \-fəst\ *n*
an·thro·po·mor·phize \-,fīz\ *vt* **-phized; -phiz·ing** : to attribute human form or personality to
an·thro·po·pa·thism \,an(t)-thrə-'päp-ə-,thiz-əm, -pō-'path-,iz-\ *n* [LGk *anthrōpopatheia* humanity, fr. Gk *anthrōpopathēs* having human feelings, fr. *anthrōp-* + *pathos* experience — more at PATHOS] : the ascription of human feelings to something not human
an·thro·poph·a·gous \,an(t)-thrə-'päf-ə-gəs\ *adj* : feeding on human flesh — **an·thro·poph·a·gy** \-ə-jē\ *n*
an·thro·poph·a·gus \-ə-gəs\ *n, pl* **-a·gi** \-ə-,gī, -,jī, -,gē\ [L, fr. Gk *anthrōpophagos,* fr. *anthrōp-* + *-phagos* -phagous] : MAN-EATER, CANNIBAL
an·thro·pos·o·phy \,an(t)-thrə-'päs-ə-fē\ *n* : a 20th century religious system growing out of theosophy and centering on man rather than God
¹an·ti \'an-,tī, 'ant-ē\ *n, pl* **antis** [*anti-*] : one that is opposed
²anti *prep* : opposed to : AGAINST
anti- *or* **ant-** *or* **anth-** *prefix* [*anti-* fr. ME, fr. OF & L; OF, fr. L, against, fr. Gk, fr. *anti-; ant-* fr. ME, fr. L, against, fr. Gk, fr. *anti; anth-* fr. L, against, fr. Gk, fr. *anti* — more at ANTE-] **1 a** : of the same kind but situated opposite, exerting energy in the opposite direction, or pursuing an opposite policy ⟨*anti*clinal⟩ **b** : one that is opposite in kind to ⟨*anti*climax⟩ **2 a** : opposing or hostile to in opinion, sympathy, or practice ⟨*anti*-Semite⟩ **b** : opposing in effect or activity ⟨*ant*acid⟩ ⟨*anti*catalyst⟩ **3** : combating or defending against ⟨*anti*aircraft⟩ ⟨*anti*missile⟩
¹an·ti·air·craft \,ant-ē-'a(ə)r-,kraft, -'e(ə)r-\ *adj* : designed for or concerned with defense against air attack
²antiaircraft *n* : an antiaircraft weapon
an·ti·anx·i·ety \,ant-ē-(,)aŋ-'zī-ət-ē\ *adj* : tending to prevent or relieve anxiety ⟨~ drugs⟩
an·ti·ar·rhyth·mic \,ant-ē-(,)ā-'rith-mik, ,an-,tī-\ *adj* : tending to prevent or relieve arrhythmia ⟨an ~ agent⟩
an·ti·art \-'ärt\ *n* : art based on premises antithetical to traditional or popular art forms; *specif* : DADA
an·ti·au·thor·i·tar·i·an \-ō-,thär-ə-'ter-ē-ən, -ə-,thär-, -,thȯr-\ *adj* : opposing or hostile to authoritarians or authoritarianism — **an·ti·au·thor·i·tar·i·an·ism** \-,iz-əm\ *n*
an·ti·aux·in \-'ȯk-sən\ *n* : a plant substance that opposes or suppresses the natural effect of an auxin
an·ti·bac·te·ri·al \,ant-i-bak-'tir-ē-əl, ,an-,tī-\ *adj* : directed or effective against bacteria
an·ti·bal·lis·tic missile \,ant-i-bə-,lis-tik-, ,an-,tī-\ *n* : a missile for intercepting and destroying ballistic missiles
an·ti·bi·o·sis \-bī-'ō-səs, -bē-\ *n* [NL] : antagonistic association between organisms to the detriment of one of them or between one organism and a metabolic product of another
¹an·ti·bi·ot·ic \-bī-'ät-ik, -bē-\ *adj* **1** : tending to prevent, inhibit, or destroy life **2** : of or relating to antibiosis or antibiotics — **an·ti·bi·ot·i·cal·ly** \-i-k(ə-)lē\ *adv*
²antibiotic *n* : a substance produced by a microorganism and able in dilute solution to inhibit or kill another microorganism
an·ti·black \-'blak\ *adj* : opposed or hostile to people belonging to the Negro race ⟨his ~ attitude⟩ — **an·ti·black·ism** \-,iz-əm\ *n*
an·ti·body \'ant-i-,bäd-ē\ *n* : any of the body globulins that combine specifically with antigens and neutralize toxins, agglutinate bacteria or cells, and precipitate soluble antigens
¹an·tic \'ant-ik\ *n* **1** : a ludicrous act or action : CAPER ⟨childish ~s⟩ **2** *archaic* : a performer of a grotesque or ludicrous part : BUFFOON
²antic *adj* [It *antico* ancient, fr. L *antiquus* — more at ANTIQUE] **1** *archaic* : GROTESQUE, BIZARRE **2 a** : characterized by clownish extravagance or absurdity **b** : whimsically gay : FROLICSOME — **an·ti·cal·ly** \-i-k(ə-)lē\ *adv*
an·ti·can·cer \,ant-i-'kan(t)-sər, ,an-,tī-\ *also* **an·ti·can·cer·ous** \-'kan(t)s-(ə-)rəs\ *adj* : used or effective against cancer ⟨~ drugs⟩

an·ti·cat·a·lyst \-'kat-ᵊl-əst\ *n* **1 :** an agent that retards a chemical reaction **2 :** a catalytic poison
an·ti·cho·lin·er·gic \-ˌkō-lə-'nər-jik\ *adj* **:** opposing or annulling the physiologic action of acetylcholine — **anticholinergic** *n*
an·ti·cho·lin·es·ter·ase \-'nes-tə-ˌrās, -ˌrāz\ *n* **:** a substance that inhibits a cholinesterase by combination with it
An·ti·christ \'ant-i-ˌkrīst\ *n* [ME *anticrist,* fr. OF & LL; OF, fr. LL *Antichristus,* fr. Gk *Antichristos,* fr. *anti-* + *Christos* Christ] **1 :** one who denies or opposes Christ; *specif* **:** a great antagonist expected to fill the world with wickedness but to be conquered forever by Christ at his second coming **2 :** a false Christ
an·tic·i·pant \an-'tis-ə-pənt\ *adj* **:** EXPECTANT, ANTICIPATING — usu. used with *of* — **anticipant** *n*
an·tic·i·pate \an-'tis-ə-ˌpāt\ *vb* **-pat·ed; -pat·ing** [L *anticipatus,* pp. of *anticipare,* fr. *ante-* + *-cipare* (fr. *capere* to take) — more at HEAVE] *vt* **1 :** to give advance thought, discussion, or treatment to **2 :** to meet (an obligation) before a due date **3 :** to foresee and deal with in advance **:** FORESTALL **4 :** to use or expend in advance of actual possession **5 :** to act before (another) often so as to check or counter **6 :** to look forward to as certain **:** EXPECT ~ *vi* **:** to speak or write in knowledge or expectation of later matter ***syn*** see FORESEE — **an·tic·i·pat·able** \-ˌpāt-ə-bəl\ *adj* — **an·tic·i·pa·tor** \-ˌpāt-ər\ *n*
an·tic·i·pa·tion \(ˌ)an-ˌtis-ə-'pā-shən\ *n* **1 :** the use of money before it is available; *esp* **:** the taking or alienation of the income of a trust estate before it is due **2 a :** a prior action that takes into account or forestalls a later action **b :** the act of looking forward; *specif* **:** pleasurable expectation **3 a :** visualization of a future event or state **b :** an object or form that anticipates a later type **4 :** the early sounding of one or more tones of a succeeding chord to form a temporary dissonance — compare SUSPENSION ***syn*** see PROSPECT
an·tic·i·pa·tive \an-'tis-ə-ˌpāt-iv, -pət-\ *adj* **:** given to or engaged in anticipation — **an·tic·i·pa·tive·ly** *adv*
an·tic·i·pa·to·ry \an-'tis-ə-pə-ˌtōr-ē, -ˌtȯr-\ *adj* **:** characterized by anticipation **:** ANTICIPATING
an·ti·cler·i·cal \ˌant-i-'kler-i-kəl, ˌan-ˌtī-\ *adj* **:** opposed to clericalism or to the interference or influence of the clergy in secular affairs — **anticlerical** *n* — **an·ti·cler·i·cal·ism** \-kə-ˌliz-əm\ *n* — **an·ti·cler·i·cal·ist** \-ləst\ *n*
an·ti·cli·mac·tic \ˌant-i-klī-'mak-tik\ *also* **an·ti·cli·mac·ti·cal** \-ti-kəl\ *adj* **:** of, relating to, or marked by anticlimax — **an·ti·cli·mac·ti·cal·ly** \-ti-k(ə-)lē\ *adv*
an·ti·cli·max \-'klī-ˌmaks\ *n* **1 :** the usu. sudden transition in writing or speaking from a significant idea to a trivial or ludicrous idea; *also* **:** an instance of this transition **2 :** an event (as at the end of a series) that is strikingly less important than what has preceded it
an·ti·cli·nal \-'klīn-ᵊl\ *adj* [*anti-* + Gk *klinein* to lean — more at LEAN] **:** inclining in opposite directions; *specif* **:** of or relating to a geological anticline
an·ti·cline \'ant-i-ˌklīn\ *n* [back-formation fr. *anticlinal*] **:** an arch of stratified rock in which the layers bend downward in opposite directions from the crest — compare SYNCLINE

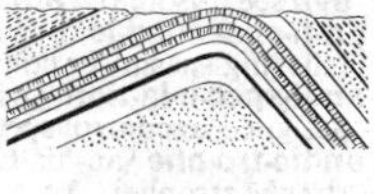
cross section of strata showing anticline

an·ti·clock·wise \ˌant-i-'kläk-ˌwīz, ˌan-ˌtī-\ *adj or adv* **:** COUNTERCLOCKWISE
an·ti·co·ag·u·lant \-kō-'ag-yə-lənt\ *n* **:** a substance that hinders the clotting of blood
an·ti·co·ag·u·late \-ˌlāt\ *vt* [back-formation fr. *anticoagulant*] **:** to hinder the clotting of the blood of esp. by treatment with an anticoagulant — **an·ti·co·ag·u·la·tion** \-ˌag-yə-'lā-shən\ *n*
an·ti·co·don \-'kō-ˌdän\ *n* [*anti-* + *codon*] **:** a triplet of nucleotide bases in transfer RNA that is believed to identify the amino acid carried and to bind to a complementary codon in messenger RNA during protein synthesis at a ribosome
an·ti·con·vul·sant \-kən-'vəl-sənt\ *or* **an·ti·con·vul·sive** \-siv\ *adj* **:** used or tending to control or prevent convulsions (as in epilepsy) — **anticonvulsant** *n*
an·ti·cy·clone \ˌant-i-'sī-ˌklōn\ *n* **1 :** a system of winds that rotates about a center of high atmospheric pressure clockwise in the northern hemisphere and counterclockwise in the southern, that usu. advances at 20 to 30 miles per hour, and that usu. has a diameter of 1500 to 2500 miles **2 :** HIGH 2 — **an·ti·cy·clon·ic** \-sī-'klän-ik\ *adj*
an·ti·de·pres·sant \ˌant-i-di-'pres-ᵊnt, ˌan-ˌtī-\ *or* **an·ti·de·pres·sive** \-'pres-iv\ *adj* **:** used or tending to relieve or prevent psychic depression — **antidepressant** *n*
an·ti·de·riv·a·tive \-di-'riv-ət-iv\ *n* **:** INDEFINITE INTEGRAL
an·ti·di·uret·ic \ˌant-i-ˌdī-yü-'ret-ik\ *n* **:** a substance that tends to check or oppose excretion of urine — **antidiuretic** *adj*
antidiuretic hormone *n* **:** VASOPRESSIN
an·ti·dot·al \ˌant-i-'dōt-ᵊl\ *adj* **:** of, relating to, or acting as an antidote — **an·ti·dot·al·ly** \-ᵊl-ē\ *adv*
an·ti·dote \'ant-i-ˌdōt\ *n* [ME *antidot,* fr. L *antidotum,* fr. Gk *antidotos,* fr. fem. of *antidotos* given as an antidote, fr. *antididonai* to give as an antidote, fr. *anti-* + *didonai* to give — more at DATE] **1 :** a remedy to counteract the effects of poison **2 :** something that relieves, prevents, or counteracts ⟨an ~ to the mechanization of our society⟩
an·ti·elec·tron \ˌant-ē-ə-'lek-ˌträn, ˌan-ˌtī-\ *n* **:** POSITRON
an·ti·en·zyme \-'en-ˌzīm\ *n* **:** an inhibitor of enzyme action; *esp* **:** one produced by living cells
an·ti·es·tab·lish·ment \-is-'tab-lish-mənt\ *adj* **:** opposed or hostile to the social, political, economic, or moral principles of a ruling class (as of a nation)
an·ti–fed·er·al·ist \ˌant-i-'fed-(ə-)rə-ləst, ˌan-ˌtī-\ *n, often cap A & F* **:** a member of the group that opposed the adoption of the U.S. Constitution
an·ti·fer·til·i·ty \-fər-'til-ət-ē\ *adj* **:** capable of or tending to reduce or destroy fertility **:** CONTRACEPTIVE ⟨~ agents⟩
an·ti·foul·ing \-'fau̇-liŋ\ *adj* **:** intended to prevent fouling of underwater structures (as the bottoms of ships) ⟨~ paint⟩
an·ti·freeze \'ant-i-ˌfrēz\ *n* **:** a substance added to a liquid (as the water in an automobile engine) to lower its freezing point
an·ti·fun·gal \ˌant-i-'fəŋ-gəl, ˌan-ˌtī-\ *adj* **:** used or effective against fungi **:** FUNGICIDAL ⟨~ drugs⟩
an·ti·gen \'ant-i-jən\ *n* [ISV] **:** a usu. protein or carbohydrate substance (as a toxin or enzyme) that when introduced into the body stimulates the production of an antibody — **an·ti·gen·ic** \ˌant-i-'jen-ik\ *adj* — **an·ti·gen·i·cal·ly** \-i-k(ə-)lē\ *adv* — **an·ti·ge·nic·i·ty** \-jə-'nis-ət-ē\ *n*
an·ti·glob·u·lin \ˌant-i-'gläb-yə-lən, ˌan-ˌtī-\ *n* **:** an antibody that combines with and precipitates globulin
An·tig·o·ne \an-'tig-ə-(ˌ)nē\ *n* [Gk *Antigonē*] **:** a daughter of Oedipus and Jocasta who buries her brother Polynices' body against the order of her uncle Creon
[1]**an·ti·grav·i·ty** \ˌant-i-'grav-ət-ē, ˌan-ˌtī-\ *adj* **:** reducing or canceling the effect of gravity or protecting against it
[2]**antigravity** *n* **:** a hypothetical effect resulting from cancellation or reduction of a gravitational field
an·ti·he·mo·phil·ic \ˌant-i-ˌhē-mə-'fil-ik, ˌan-ˌtī-\ *adj* **:** counteracting the bleeding tendency in hemophilia
an·ti·he·ro \'ant-i-ˌhē-(ˌ)rō, 'an-ˌtī, -ˌhi(ə)r-(ˌ)ō\ *n* **:** a protagonist who is notably lacking in heroic qualities (as courage or unselfishness) — **an·ti·he·ro·ic** \ˌant-i-hi-'rō-ik, ˌan-ˌtī-\ *adj*
an·ti·his·ta·mine \ˌant-i-'his-tə-ˌmēn, ˌan-ˌtī-, -mən\ *n* **:** any of various compounds that counteract histamine in the body and that are used for treating allergic reactions and cold symptoms — **an·ti·his·ta·min·ic** \-ˌhis-tə-'min-ik\ *adj or n*
an·ti·hu·man \ˌant-i-'hyü-mən, ˌan-ˌtī-, -'yü-\ *adj* **:** acting or being against man; *esp* **:** reacting strongly with human antigens
an·ti·hy·per·ten·sive \-ˌhī-pər-'ten(t)-siv\ *n* **:** a substance that is effective against high blood pressure — **antihypertensive** *adj*
an·ti–in·flam·ma·to·ry \ˌant-ē-in-'flam-ə-ˌtōr-ē, ˌan-ˌtī-, -ˌtȯr-\ *adj* **:** counteracting inflammation
an·ti·knock \ˌant-i-'näk\ *n* **:** a substance used as a fuel or fuel additive to prevent knocking in an internal-combustion engine
an·ti·leu·ke·mic \ˌant-i-lü-'kē-mik, ˌan-ˌtī-\ *adj* **:** counteracting the effects of leukemia
an·ti·lit·ter \-'lit-ər\ *adj* **:** serving to prevent or discourage the littering of public areas ⟨~ laws⟩
antilog *abbr* antilogarithm
an·ti·log·a·rithm \ˌant-i-'lȯg-ə-ˌrith-əm, ˌan-ˌtī-, -'läg-\ *n* **:** the number corresponding to a given logarithm
an·ti·lym·pho·cyte serum \-'lim(p)-fə-ˌsīt-\ *n* **:** a serum used for suppressing graft rejection caused by lymphocyte-controlled immune responses in organ or tissue transplant recipients
an·ti·lym·pho·cyt·ic serum \ˌant-i-ˌlim-fə-ˌsit-ik-, ˌan-ˌtī-\ *n* **:** ANTILYMPHOCYTE SERUM
an·ti·ma·cas·sar \ˌant-i-mə-'kas-ər\ *n* [*anti-* + *Macassar* (*oil*) (a hairdressing)] **:** a cover to protect the back or arms of furniture
an·ti·mag·net·ic \ˌant-i-mag-'net-ik, ˌan-ˌtī-\ *adj, of a watch* **:** having a balance unit composed of alloys that will not remain magnetized
an·ti·ma·lar·i·al \-mə-'ler-ē-əl\ *adj* **:** serving to prevent, check, or cure malaria — **antimalarial** *n*
an·ti·mat·ter \'ant-i-ˌmat-ər\ *n* **:** matter composed of the counterparts of ordinary matter, antiprotons instead of protons, positrons instead of electrons, and antineutrons instead of neutrons
an·ti·me·tab·o·lite \ˌant-i-mə-'tab-ə-ˌlīt, ˌan-ˌtī-\ *n* **:** a substance that replaces or inhibits the utilization of a metabolite
an·ti·mi·cro·bi·al \ˌant-i-mī-'krō-bē-əl\ *adj* **:** destroying or inhibiting the growth of microorganisms — **antimicrobial** *n*
an·ti·mis·sile missile \ˌant-i-'mis-əl-, ˌan-ˌtī-; *chiefly Brit* ˌant-i-'mis-ˌīl-\ *n* **:** ANTIBALLISTIC MISSILE
an·ti·mi·tot·ic \ˌant-i-mī-'tät-ik\ *adj* **:** inhibiting or disrupting mitosis ⟨~ agents⟩ ⟨~ activity⟩ — **antimitotic** *n*
an·ti·mo·ni·al \ˌant-ə-'mō-nē-əl\ *adj* **:** of, relating to, or containing antimony — **antimonial** *n*
an·ti·mon·ic \-'män-ik\ *adj* **:** of, relating to, or derived from antimony with a valence of five
an·ti·mo·ni·ous \-'mō-nē-əs\ *adj* **:** of, relating to, or derived from antimony with a valence of three
an·ti·mo·ny \'ant-ə-ˌmō-nē\ *n* [ME *antimonie,* fr. ML *antimonium*] **1 :** STIBNITE **2 :** a trivalent and pentavalent metalloid commonly metallic silvery white, crystalline, and brittle element that is used esp. as a constituent of alloys and in medicine — see ELEMENT table
an·ti·my·cin A \ˌant-i-ˌmīs-ᵊn-'ā\ *n* [*anti-* + *myc-* + *-in*] **:** a crystalline antibiotic $C_{28}H_{40}N_2O_9$ used esp. as a fungicide, insecticide, and miticide — called also *antimycin*
an·ti·neo·plas·tic \ˌant-i-ˌnē-ə-'plas-tik, ˌan-ˌtī-\ *adj* **:** inhibiting or preventing the growth and spread of neoplasms or malignant cells
an·ti·neu·tri·no \-n(y)ü-'trē-(ˌ)nō\ *n* **:** the antiparticle of the neutrino
an·ti·neu·tron \-'n(y)ü-ˌträn\ *n* **:** an uncharged particle of mass equal to that of the neutron but having a magnetic moment in the opposite direction
ant·ing \'ant-iŋ\ *n* **:** the deliberate placing by some passerine birds of living ants among the feathers
an·ti·node \'ant-i-ˌnōd, 'an-ˌtī-\ *n* [ISV] **:** a region of maximum amplitude situated between adjacent nodes in a vibrating body — **an·ti·nod·al** \ˌant-i-'nōd-ᵊl, ˌan-ˌtī-\ *adj*
an·ti·no·mi·an \ˌant-i-'nō-mē-ən\ *n* [ML *antinomus,* fr. L *anti-* + Gk *nomos* law] **1 :** one who holds that under the gospel dispensation of grace the moral law is of no use or obligation because faith alone is necessary to salvation **2 :** one who rejects a socially es-

ə abut	ᵊ kitten	ər further	a back	ā bake	ä cot, cart
au̇ out	ch chin	e less	ē easy	g gift	i trip	ī life
j joke	ŋ sing	ō flow	ȯ flaw	ȯi coin	th thin	th this
ü loot	u̇ foot	y yet	yü few	yu̇ furious	zh vision

tablished morality — **antinomian** *adj* — **an·ti·no·mi·an·ism** \-mē-ə-ˌniz-əm\ *n*

an·tin·o·my \an-ˈtin-ə-mē\ *n, pl* **-mies** [G *antinomie,* fr. L *antinomia* conflict of laws, fr. Gk, fr. *anti-* + *nomos* law — more at NIMBLE] **1** : a contradiction between two apparently equally valid principles or between inferences correctly drawn from such principles **2** : conflict (as of principles, ideas, or aspirations) insoluble in the light of available knowledge ***syn*** see PARADOX

an·ti·nov·el \ˈant-i-ˌnäv-əl, ˈan-ˌtī-\ *n* : a work of fiction that lacks most or all of the traditional features of the novel — **an·ti·nov·el·ist** \-ˌnäv-(ə-)ləst\ *n*

an·ti·nu·cle·on \ˌant-i-ˈn(y)ü-klē-ˌän, ˌan-ˌtī-\ *n* : the antiparticle of the nucleon

an·ti·ox·i·dant \ˌant-ē-ˈäk-səd-ənt, ˌan-ˌtī-\ *n* : a substance that opposes oxidation or inhibits reactions promoted by oxygen or peroxides — **antioxidant** *adj*

an·ti·par·a·sit·ic \ˌant-i-ˌpar-ə-ˈsit-ik, ˌan-ˌtī-\ *adj* : acting against parasites

an·ti·par·ti·cle \ˈant-i-ˌpärt-i-kəl, ˈan-ˌtī-\ *n* : an elementary particle identical to another elementary particle in mass but opposite to it in electric and magnetic properties that when brought together with its counterpart produces mutual annihilation

an·ti·pas·to \ˌant-i-ˈpas-(ˌ)tō, ˌänt-i-ˈpäs-\ *n, pl* **-tos** [It, fr. *anti-* (fr. L *ante-*) + *pasto* food, fr. L *pastus,* fr. *pastus,* pp. of *pascere* to feed — more at FOOD] : HORS D'OEUVRE

an·ti·pa·thet·ic \ˌant-i-pə-ˈthet-ik\ *adj* **1** : having a natural aversion ⟨a person ~ to violence⟩ **2** : arousing or showing antipathy — **an·ti·pa·thet·i·cal·ly** \-i-k(ə-)lē\ *adv*

an·tip·a·thy \an-ˈtip-ə-thē\ *n, pl* **-thies** [L *antipathia,* fr. Gk *antipatheia,* fr. *antipathēs* of opposite feelings, fr. *anti-* + *pathos* experience — more at PATHOS] **1** *obs* : opposition in feeling **2** : settled aversion or dislike : DISTASTE **3** : an object of aversion ***syn*** see ENMITY ***ant*** taste *(for),* affection *(for)*

an·ti·pe·ri·od·ic \-ˌpir-ē-ˈäd-ik\ *adj* [ISV] : preventing periodic returns of disease — **antiperiodic** *n*

an·ti·per·son·nel \ˌant-i-ˌpərs-ᵊn-ˈel, ˌan-ˌtī-\ *adj* : designed for use against military personnel ⟨an ~ mine⟩

an·ti·per·spi·rant \-ˈpər-sp(ə-)rənt\ *n* : a cosmetic preparation used to check excessive perspiration

an·ti·phlo·gis·tic \-flə-ˈjis-tik\ *adj* : counteracting inflammation — **antiphlogistic** *n*

an·ti·phon \ˈant-ə-fən, -ˌfän\ *n* [LL *antiphona* — more at ANTHEM] **1** : a psalm, anthem, or verse sung responsively **2** : a verse usu. from Scripture said or sung before and after a canticle, psalm, or psalm verse as part of the liturgy

[1]**an·tiph·o·nal** \an-ˈtif-ən-ᵊl\ *n* : ANTIPHONARY

[2]**antiphonal** *adj* : of or relating to an antiphon or antiphony — **an·tiph·o·nal·ly** \-ᵊl-ē\ *adv*

an·tiph·o·nary \an-ˈtif-ə-ˌner-ē\ *n, pl* **-nar·ies** **1** : a book containing a collection of antiphons **2** : a book containing the choral parts of the Divine Office

an·tiph·o·ny \an-ˈtif-ə-nē\ *n, pl* **-nies** : responsive alternation between two groups esp. of singers

an·tiph·ra·sis \an-ˈtif-rə-səs\ *n, pl* **-ra·ses** \-ˌsēz\ [LL, fr. Gk, fr. *anti-* + *phrasis* diction — more at PHRASE] : the usu. ironic or humorous use of words in senses opposite to the generally accepted meanings ⟨"the child is a giant of 3 feet 4 inches" is an example of ~⟩

[1]**an·tip·o·dal** \an-ˈtip-əd-ᵊl\ *adj* **1** : of or relating to the antipodes; *specif* : situated at the opposite side of the earth or moon ⟨an ~ meridian⟩ ⟨an ~ continent⟩ **2** : diametrically opposite ⟨an ~ point on a sphere⟩ **3** : OPPOSED

[2]**antipodal** *n* : any of three cells in the female gametophyte of most angiosperms that are grouped at the end of the embryo sac farthest from the micropyle

an·ti·pode \ˈant-ə-ˌpōd\ *n, pl* **an·tip·o·des** \an-ˈtip-ə-ˌdēz\ [ME *antipodes,* pl., persons dwelling at opposite points on the globe, fr. L, fr. Gk, fr. pl. of *antipod-, antipous* with feet opposite, fr. *anti-* + *pod-, pous* foot — more at FOOT] **1** : the parts of the earth diametrically opposite — usu. used in pl. **2** : the exact opposite or contrary — **an·tip·o·de·an** \(ˌ)an-ˌtip-ə-ˈdē-ən\ *adj*

an·ti·po·et·ic \ˌant-i-pō-ˈet-ik, ˌan-ˌtī-\ *adj* : of, relating to, or characterized by opposition to traditional poetic technique or style

an·ti·pol·lu·tion \-pə-ˈlü-shən\ *adj* : designed to prevent, reduce, or eliminate pollution ⟨~ laws⟩ — **antipollution** *n*

an·ti·pope \ˈant-i-ˌpōp\ *n* [MF *antipape,* fr. ML *antipapa,* fr. *anti-* + *papa* pope] : one elected or claiming to be pope in opposition to the pope canonically chosen

an·ti·pov·er·ty \ˌant-i-ˈpäv-ərt-ē, ˌan-ˌtī-\ *adj* : of or relating to action designed to relieve poverty ⟨~ programs⟩

an·ti·pro·ton \-ˈprō-ˌtän\ *n* : the antiparticle of the proton

an·ti·psy·chot·ic \ˌant-i-sī-ˈkät-ik\ *adj* : tending to alleviate psychosis or psychotic states ⟨an ~ drug⟩ — **antipsychotic** *n*

an·ti·py·ret·ic \-pī-ˈret-ik\ *n* : an agent that reduces fever — **antipyretic** *adj*

an·ti·py·rine \-ˈpī(ə)r-ˌēn\ *n* [fr. *Antipyrine,* a trademark] : a white crystalline compound $C_{11}H_{12}N_2O$ used to relieve fever, pain, or rheumatism

antiq *abbr* antiquarian; antiquary

[1]**an·ti·quar·i·an** \ˌant-ə-ˈkwer-ē-ən\ *n* : one who collects or studies antiquities

[2]**antiquarian** *adj* **1** : of or relating to antiquarians or antiquities **2** : dealing in old or rare books — **an·ti·quar·i·an·ism** \-ē-ə-ˌniz-əm\ *n*

an·ti·quary \ˈant-ə-ˌkwer-ē\ *n, pl* **-quar·ies** : ANTIQUARIAN

an·ti·quate \ˈant-ə-ˌkwāt\ *vt* **-quat·ed; -quat·ing** [LL *antiquatus,* pp. of *antiquare,* fr. L *antiquus*] : to make old or obsolete — **an·ti·qua·tion** \ˌant-ə-ˈkwā-shən\ *n*

an·ti·quat·ed *adj* **1** : OBSOLETE ⟨a calendar becomes ~ —A. L. Kroeber⟩ **2** : outmoded or discredited by reason of age : being out of style or fashion ⟨~ methods of farming⟩ **3** : advanced in age ***syn*** see OLD ***ant*** modish

[1]**an·tique** \an-ˈtēk\ *adj* [MF, fr. L *antiquus,* fr. *ante* before — more at ANTE-] **1** : existing since ancient or former times : belonging to antiquity ⟨a few of the ~ virtues still persist⟩ **2** : belonging to earlier times : ANCIENT ⟨ruins of an ~ city⟩ **3** **a** : being in the style or fashion of former times ⟨~ manners and graces⟩ **b** : made in or representative of the work of an earlier period ⟨~ mirrors⟩; *also* : being an antique **4** : selling or exhibiting antiques ⟨an ~ show⟩ ***syn*** see OLD ***ant*** modern, current

[2]**antique** *n* **1** : a relic or object of ancient times or of an earlier period than the present **2** : a work of art, piece of furniture, or decorative object made at an earlier period and according to various customs laws at least 100 years ago

[3]**antique** *vt* **-tiqued; -tiquing** : to finish or refinish in antique style : give an appearance of age to

an·tiq·ui·ty \an-ˈtik-wət-ē\ *n, pl* **-ties** **1** : ancient times; *esp* : those before the Middle Ages **2** : the quality of being ancient **3** *pl* **a** : relics or monuments (as coins, statues, or buildings) of ancient times **b** : matters relating to the life or culture of ancient times **4** : the people of ancient times

an·ti·rac·ism \ˌant-i-ˈrā-ˌsiz-əm, ˌan-ˌtī- *also* -ˌshiz-\ *n* : adherence to the view that racism is a social evil

an·ti·rheu·mat·ic \-rü-ˈmat-ik\ *adj* : alleviating or preventing rheumatism — **antirheumatic** *n*

an·tir·rhi·num \ˌant-ə-ˈrī-nəm\ *n* [NL, genus name, fr. L, snapdragon, fr. Gk *antirrhinon,* fr. *anti-* like (fr. *anti* against, equivalent to) + *rhin-, rhis* nose — more at ANTI-] : any of a large genus (*Antirrhinum*) of herbs (as the snapdragon) of the figwort family with bright-colored irregular flowers

antis *pl of* ANTI

an·ti–Sem·i·tism \ˌant-i-ˈsem-ə-ˌtiz-əm, ˌan-ˌtī-\ *n* : hostility toward or discrimination against Jews as a religious or racial group — **an·ti–Se·mit·ic** \-sə-ˈmit-ik\ *adj* — **an·ti–Sem·ite** \-ˈsem-ˌīt\ *n*

an·ti·sep·sis \ˌant-ə-ˈsep-səs\ *n* : the inhibiting of the growth and multiplication of microorganisms by antiseptic means

[1]**an·ti·sep·tic** \ˌant-ə-ˈsep-tik\ *adj* [*anti-* + Gk *sēptikos* putrefying, septic] **1** **a** : opposing sepsis, putrefaction, or decay; *esp* : preventing or arresting the growth of microorganisms (as on living tissue) **b** : acting or protecting like an antiseptic **2** : relating to or characterized by the use of antiseptics **3** **a** : scrupulously clean : ASEPTIC **b** : extremely neat or orderly; *esp* : neat to the point of being bare or uninteresting **c** : free from what is held to be contaminating **4** : IMPERSONAL, DETACHED; *esp* : coldly impersonal ⟨"acceptable losses on the battlefield" is another ~ phrase⟩ — **an·ti·sep·ti·cal·ly** \-ti-k(ə-)lē\ *adv*

[2]**antiseptic** *n* : a substance that checks the growth or action of microorganisms esp. in or on living tissue; *also* : GERMICIDE

an·ti·se·rum \ˈant-i-ˌsir-əm, ˈan-ˌtī-, -ˌser-\ *n* [ISV] : a serum containing antibodies

an·ti·slav·ery \ˌant-i-ˈslāv-(ə-)rē, ˌan-ˌtī-\ *n* : opposition to slavery

an·ti·smog \-ˈsmäg *also* -ˈsmȯg\ *adj* : designed to reduce pollutants contributing to the formation of smog ⟨~ devices for automobiles⟩

an·ti·so·cial \-ˈsō-shəl\ *adj* **1** : hostile or harmful to organized society; *esp* : being or marked by behavior deviating sharply from the social norm **2** : averse to the society of others : UNSOCIABLE ***syn*** see UNSOCIAL ***ant*** social

an·ti·spas·mod·ic \-spaz-ˈmäd-ik\ *adj* : capable of preventing or relieving spasms or convulsions — **antispasmodic** *n*

an·ti·spec·u·la·tion \-ˌspek-yə-ˈlā-shən\ *adj* : directed against or designed to control speculation

an·tis·tro·phe \an-ˈtis-trə-(ˌ)fē\ *n* [LL, fr. Gk *antistrophē,* fr. *anti-* + *strophē* strophe] **1** : a returning movement in Greek choral dance exactly answering to a previous strophe; *specif* : the part of a choral song delivered during this movement **2** **a** : the repetition of words in reversed order **b** : the repetition of a word or phrase at the end of successive clauses — **an·ti·stroph·ic** \ˌant-ə-ˈsträf-ik\ *adj* — **an·ti·stroph·i·cal·ly** \-i-k(ə-)lē\ *adv*

an·ti·sub·ma·rine \ˌant-i-ˈsəb-mə-ˌrēn, ˌan-ˌtī-, -ˌsəb-mə-ˈ\ *adj* : designed or waged to destroy submarines ⟨an ~ gun⟩ ⟨~ warfare⟩

an·ti·sym·met·ric \-sə-ˈme-trik\ *adj* : relating to or being a relation (as "is a subset of") that implies equality of any two quantities for which it holds in both directions ⟨the relation *R* is ~ if *aRb* and *bRa* implies $a = b$⟩

an·ti·tank \-ˈtaŋk\ *adj* : designed to destroy or check tanks ⟨an ~ gun⟩

an·tith·e·sis \an-ˈtith-ə-səs\ *n, pl* **-e·ses** \-ˌsēz\ [LL, fr. Gk, lit., opposition, fr. *antitithenai* to oppose, fr. *anti-* + *tithenai* to set — more at DO] **1** **a** (1) : the rhetorical contrast of ideas by means of parallel arrangements of words, clauses, or sentences (as in "action, not words" or "they promised freedom and provided slavery") (2) : OPPOSITION, CONTRAST ⟨the ~ of prose and verse⟩ **b** (1) : the second of two opposing constituents of an antithesis (2) : the direct opposite **2** : the second stage of a dialectic process

an·ti·thet·i·cal \ˌant-ə-ˈthet-i-kəl\ *or* **an·ti·thet·ic** \-ˈthet-ik\ *adj* **1** : constituting or marked by antithesis **2** : being in direct and unequivocal opposition ***syn*** see OPPOSITE — **an·ti·thet·i·cal·ly** \-i-k(ə-)lē\ *adv*

an·ti·thy·roid \ˌant-i-ˈthī-ˌrȯid\ *adj* : able to counteract excessive thyroid activity

an·ti·tox·ic \-ˈtäk-sik\ *adj* **1** : counteracting poison **2** : of, relating to, or being an antitoxin

an·ti·tox·in \ˌant-i-ˈtäk-sən\ *n* [ISV] : an antibody formed in the body as a result of the introduction of a toxin and capable of neutralizing the specific toxin that stimulated its production and produced commercially in animals by injection of a toxin or toxoid (as of human disease) with the resulting serum being used to counteract the toxin in other individuals; *also* : a serum containing antitoxins

an·ti·trades \ˈant-i-ˌtrādz, ˈan-ˌtī-\ *n pl* **1** : the prevailing westerly winds of middle latitudes **2** : the westerly winds above the trade winds

an·ti·trust \ˌant-i-ˈtrəst, ˌan-ˌtī-\ *adj* : of or relating to legislation or opposition to trusts or combinations; *specif* : consisting of laws to protect trade and commerce from unlawful restraints and monopolies or unfair business practices

an·ti·trust·er \-ˈtrəs-tər\ *n* : one who advocates or enforces antitrust provisions of the law

an·ti·tu·ber·cu·lous \-t(y)u̇-ˈbər-kyə-ləs\ *also* **an·ti·tu·ber·cu·lar** \-ˈbər-kyə-lər\ *adj*: used or effective against tuberculosis

an·ti·tu·mor \-ˈt(y)ü-mər\ *also* **an·ti·tu·mor·al** \-mə-rəl\ *adj* : ANTICANCER

an·ti·tus·sive \-ˈtəs-iv\ *adj* : tending or having the power to control or prevent cough — **antitussive** *n*

an·ti–uto·pia \ˌant-i-yu̇-ˈtō-pē-ə, ˌan-ˌtī-\ *n* : a place, state, or condition of social, political, and economic discord

¹an·ti–uto·pi·an \-pē-ən\ *adj* : of, relating to, or having the characteristics of an anti-utopia

²anti–utopian *n* : one that believes in or predicts an anti-utopia

an·ti·ven·in \ˌant-i-ˈven-ən, ˌan-ˌtī-\ *n* [ISV] : an antitoxin to a venom : an antiserum containing such antitoxin

an·ti·vi·ral \ˌan-ti-ˈvī-rəl\ *adj* : acting to make a virus ineffective

an·ti·vi·ta·min \ˈant-i-ˌvīt-ə-mən\ *n* : a substance that makes a vitamin ineffective

an·ti·white \ˌant-i-ˈhwīt, ˌan-ˌtī-, -ˈwīt\ *adj* : opposed or hostile to people belonging to a light-skinned race ⟨~ propaganda⟩ — **an·ti·whit·ism** \-ˈhwīt-ˌiz-əm, -ˈwīt-\ *n*

ant·ler \ˈant-lər\ *n* [ME *aunteler,* fr. MF *antoillier,* fr. (assumed) VL *anteoculare,* fr. neut. of *anteocularis* located before the eye, fr. L *ante-* + *oculus* eye — more at EYE] : the solid deciduous horn of an animal of the deer family; *also* : a branch of this horn — **ant·lered** \-lərd\ *adj*

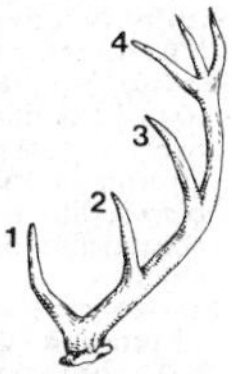

antlers: *1* brow antler, *2* bay antler, *3* royal antler, *4* surroyal

ant lion *n* : any of various neuropterous insects (as of the genus *Myrmeleon*) having a long-jawed larva that digs a conical pit in which it lies in wait to catch insects (as ants) on which it feeds

An·to·ni·an \an-ˈtō-nē-ən\ *n* [L *Antonius* Anthony] : a member of one of several monastic communities (as the Armenian Antonians) that follow a rule derived from St. Anthony

ant·onym \ˈant-ə-ˌnim\ *n* : a word of opposite meaning ⟨the usual ~ of *good* is *bad,* of *hot* is *cold*⟩ — **ant·onym·ic** \ˌant-ə-ˈnim-ik\ *adj* — **an·ton·y·mous** \an-ˈtän-ə-məs\ *adj* — **an·ton·y·my** \-mē\ *n*

an·tre \ˈant-ər\ *n* [F, fr. L *antrum*]: CAVE 1

an·trorse \ˈan-ˌtrȯ(ə)rs\ *adj* [NL *antrorsus,* irreg. fr. L *anterior* + *-orsus* (as in *dextrorsus* toward the right) — more at DEXTRORSE] : directed forward or upward — **an·trorse·ly** *adv*

an·trum \ˈan-trəm\ *n, pl* **an·tra** \-trə\ [LL, fr. L, cave, fr. Gk *antron*]: the cavity of a hollow organ or a sinus — **an·tral** \-trəl\ *adj*

an·uran \ə-ˈn(y)u̇r-ən, a-\ *adj or n* [deriv. of *a-* + Gk *oura* tail — more at SQUIRREL]: SALIENTIAN

an·uria \ə-ˈn(y)u̇r-ē-ə, a-\ *n* [NL] : absence or defective excretion of urine — **an·uric** \-ˈn(y)u̇r-ik\ *adj*

an·urous \ə-ˈn(y)u̇r-əs, a-\ *adj*: having no tail

anus \ˈā-nəs\ *n* [L; akin to OIr *ãinne* anus] : the posterior opening of the alimentary canal

an·vil \ˈan-vəl\ *n* [ME *anfilt,* fr. OE; akin to OHG *anafalz* anvil; both fr. a prehistoric WGmc compound whose first constituent is represented by OE *an* on, and whose second constituent is akin to Sw dial. *filta* to beat; akin to L *pellere* to beat — more at ON, FELT] **1** : a heavy usu. steel-faced iron block on which metal is shaped (as by hand hammering) **2** : INCUS

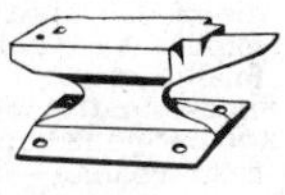

anvil 1

anx·i·ety \aŋ-ˈzī-ət-ē\ *n, pl* **-eties** [L *anxietas,* fr. *anxius*] **1 a** : painful or apprehensive uneasiness of mind usu. over an impending or anticipated ill **b** : fearful concern or interest **c** : a cause of anxiety **2** : an abnormal and overwhelming sense of apprehension and fear often marked by physiological signs (as sweating, tension, and increased pulse), by doubt concerning the reality and nature of the threat, and by self-doubt about one's capacity to cope with it ***syn*** see CARE ***ant*** security

anx·ious \ˈaŋ(k)-shəs\ *adj* [L *anxius;* akin to L *angere* to strangle, distress — more at ANGER] **1** : characterized by extreme uneasiness of mind or brooding fear about some contingency : WORRIED **2** : characterized by, resulting from, or causing anxiety : WORRYING **3** : ardently or earnestly wishing ***syn*** see EAGER ***ant*** loath — **anx·ious·ly** *adv* — **anx·ious·ness** *n*

¹any \ˈen-ē\ *adj* [ME, fr. OE *ǣnig;* akin to OHG *einag* any, OE *ān* one — more at ONE] **1** : one or some indiscriminately of whatever kind: **a** : one or another taken at random ⟨ask ~ man you meet⟩ **b** : EVERY — used to indicate one selected without restriction ⟨~ child would know that⟩ **2** : one, some, or all indiscriminately of whatever quantity: **a** : one or more — used to indicate an undetermined number or amount ⟨have you ~ money⟩ **b** : ALL — used to indicate a maximum or whole ⟨needs ~ help he can get⟩ **c** : a or some without reference to quantity or extent **3 a** : unmeasured or unlimited in amount, number, or extent ⟨~ quantity you desire⟩ **b** : appreciably large or extended ⟨could not endure it ~ length of time⟩

²any *pron, sing or pl in constr* **1** : any person or persons : ANYBODY **2 a** : any thing or things **b** : any part, quantity, or number

³any *adv* : to any extent or degree : at all ⟨was never ~ good⟩

any·body \-ˌbäd-ē, -bəd-\ *pron* : any person : ANYONE

any·how \-ˌhau̇\ *adv* **1 a** : in any manner whatever **b** : in a haphazard manner **2 a** : at any rate **b** : in any event

any·more \ˌen-ē-ˈmō(ə)r, -ˈmȯ(ə)r\ *adv* : at the present time : NOW — usu. used in a negative context

any·one \-(ˌ)wən\ *pron* : any person at all : ANYBODY

any·place \-ˌplās\ *adv* : in any place : ANYWHERE

¹any·thing \-ˌthiŋ\ *pron* : any thing whatever

²anything *adv* : at all

any·time \ˈen-ē-ˌtīm\ *adv* : at any time whatever

any·way \-ˌwā\ *adv* **1** : ANYWISE **2** : in any case : ANYHOW

any·ways \-ˌwāz\ *adv* **1** *archaic* : ANYWISE **2** *chiefly dial* : in any case

¹any·where \-ˌ(h)we(ə)r, -ˌ(h)wa(ə)r, -(h)wər\ *adv* **1** : at, in, or to any place or point **2** : at all : to any extent **3** — used as a function word to indicate limits of variation ⟨~ from 40 to 60 students⟩

²anywhere *n* : any place

any·wise \ˈen-ē-ˌwīz\ *adv* : in any way whatever : at all

An·zac \ˈan-ˌzak\ *n* [*A*ustralian and *N*ew *Z*ealand *A*rmy *C*orps] : a soldier from Australia or New Zealand

AO *abbr* **1** account of **2** and others

AOH *abbr* Ancient Order of Hibernians

A–OK \ˌā-(ˌ)ō-ˈkā\ *adv or adj* : very definitely OK

A 1 \ˈā-ˈwən\ *adj* **1** : having the highest possible classification — used of a ship **2** : of the finest quality : FIRST-RATE

aor *abbr* aorist

ao·rist \ˈā-ə-rəst, ˈe-ə-\ *n* [LL & Gk; LL *aoristos,* fr. Gk, fr. *aoristos* undefined, fr. *a-* + *horistos* definable, fr. *horizein* to define — more at HORIZON] : an inflectional form of a verb typically denoting simple occurrence of an action without reference to its completeness, duration, or repetition — **aorist** *or* **ao·ris·tic** \ˌā-ə-ˈris-tik, ˌe-ə-\ *adj* — **ao·ris·ti·cal·ly** \-ti-k(ə-)lē\ *adv*

aort- *or* **aorto-** *comb form* : aorta : aortic and ⟨*aorto*esophageal⟩

aor·ta \ā-ˈȯrt-ə\ *n, pl* **-tas** *or* **-tae** \-ē\ [NL, fr. Gk *aortē,* fr. *aeirein* to lift] : the great trunk artery that carries blood from the heart to be distributed by branch arteries through the body — see HEART illustration — **aor·tal** \-ˈȯrt-ᵊl\ *adj* — **aor·tic** \-ˈȯrt-ik\ *adj*

aortic arch *n* : one of the arterial branches in vertebrate embryos that exist in a series of pairs with one on each side of the embryo, connect the ventral arterial system lying anterior to the heart to the dorsal arterial system above the alimentary tract, and persist in adult fishes but are reduced or much modified in the adult of higher forms

aor·tog·ra·phy \ˌā-ˌȯr-ˈtäg-rə-fē\ *n* : arteriography of the aorta — **aor·to·graph·ic** \(ˌ)ā-ˌȯrt-ə-ˈgraf-ik\ *adj*

aou·dad \ˈau̇-ˌdad, ˈä-u̇-\ *n* [F, fr. Berber *audad*] : a wild sheep (*Ammotragus lervia*) of No. Africa

à ou·trance \ˌä-ˌü-ˈträⁿs\ *adv* [F]: to the limit : UNSPARINGLY

ap *abbr* **1** apostle **2** apothecaries'

AP *abbr* **1** additional premium **2** airplane **3** American plan **4** antipersonnel **5** arithmetic progression **6** armor-piercing **7** Associated Press **8** author's proof

¹ap- — see AD-

²ap- — see APO-

APA *abbr* **1** American Philological Association **2** American Philosophical Association **3** American Psychiatric Association **4** American Psychological Association

apace \ə-ˈpās\ *adv* [ME, prob. fr. MF *à pas* on step] **1** : at a quick pace : SWIFTLY **2** : ABREAST — used with *of* or *with*

Apache \ə-ˈpach-ē, *in sense 3* ə-ˈpash\ *n, pl* **Apache** *or* **Apach·es** \-ˈpach-ēz, -ˈpash(-əz)\ [Sp] **1 a** : a group of Amerindian peoples of the southwestern U.S. **b** : a member of any of these peoples **2** : any of the Athapaskan languages of the Apache people **3** *not cap* [F, fr. *Apache* Apache Indian] **a** : a member of a gang of criminals esp. in Paris **b** : RUFFIAN

ap·a·nage *var of* APPANAGE

ap·a·re·jo \ˌap-ə-ˈrā-(ˌ)(h)ō\ *n, pl* **-jos** [AmerSp] : a packsaddle of stuffed leather or canvas

¹apart \ə-ˈpärt\ *adv* [ME, fr. MF *a part,* lit., to the side] **1 a** : at a little distance ⟨tried to keep ~ from the family squabbles⟩ **b** : away from one another in space or time ⟨towns 20 miles ~⟩ **2 a** : as a separate unit : INDEPENDENTLY ⟨viewed ~, his arguments were unsound⟩ **b** : so as to separate one from another ⟨found it hard to tell the twins ~⟩ **3** : excluded from consideration : ASIDE ⟨a few blemishes ~, the novel is excellent⟩ **4** : in or into two or more parts : to pieces ⟨had to take the engine ~⟩

²apart *adj* **1** : SEPARATE, ISOLATED **2** : holding different opinions : DIVIDED — **apart·ness** *n*

apart from *prep* : other than : BESIDES

apart·heid \ə-ˈpär-ˌtāt, -ˌtīt\ *n* [Afrik, lit., separateness] : racial segregation; *specif* : a policy of segregation and political and economic discrimination against non-European groups in the Republic of So. Africa

apart·ment \ə-ˈpärt-mənt\ *n* [F *appartement,* fr. It *appartamento*] **1** : a room or set of rooms fitted esp. with housekeeping facilities and used as a dwelling **2** : a building made up of individual dwelling units — **apart·men·tal** \ə-ˌpärt-ˈment-ᵊl\ *adj*

apartment hotel *n* : an apartment house containing suites equipped for housekeeping purposes and in addition furnished rooms and dining service for transient and permanent guests

apartment house *n* : a building containing separate residential apartments — called also *apartment building*

ap·a·thet·ic \ˌap-ə-ˈthet-ik\ *adj* **1** : having or showing little or no feeling or emotion : SPIRITLESS **2** : having little or no interest or concern : INDIFFERENT ***syn*** see IMPASSIVE ***ant*** alert — **ap·a·thet·i·cal·ly** \-i-k(ə-)lē\ *adv*

ap·a·thy \ˈap-ə-thē\ *n* [Gk *apatheia,* fr. *apathēs* without feeling, fr. *a-* + *pathos* emotion — more at PATHOS] **1** : lack of feeling or emotion : IMPASSIVENESS **2** : lack of interest or concern : INDIFFERENCE

ap·a·tite \ˈap-ə-ˌtīt\ *n* [G *apatit,* fr. Gk *apatē* deceit] : any of a group of calcium phosphate minerals of the approximate general formula $Ca_5(F,Cl,OH,{}^1/_2CO_3)(PO_4)_3$ occurring variously as hexagonal crystals, as granular masses, or in fine-grained masses as the chief constituent of phosphate rock and of bones and teeth; *specif* : calcium phosphate fluoride $Ca_5F(PO_4)_3$

APB *abbr* all points bulletin

¹ape \ˈāp\ *n* [ME, fr. OE *apa;* akin to OHG *affo* ape] **1 a** : MONKEY; *esp* : one of the larger tailless or short-tailed Old World forms

ə abut	ᵊ kitten	ər further	a back	ā bake	ä cot, cart
au̇ out	ch chin	e less	ē easy	g gift	i trip ī life
j joke	ŋ sing	ō flow	ȯ flaw	ȯi coin	th thin th this
ü loot	u̇ foot	y yet	yü few	yu̇ furious	zh vision

b : any of a family (Pongidae) of large semierect primates (as the chimpanzee or gorilla) — called also *anthropoid ape* **2 a** : MIMIC **b** : a large uncouth person — **ape·like** \ˈā-ˌplīk\ *adj*
[2]ape *vt* **aped; ap·ing** : to copy closely but often clumsily and ineptly ⟨servants *aping* the ways of their betters⟩ ***syn*** see COPY — **ap·er** *n*
apeak \ə-ˈpēk\ *adj or adv* [alter. of earlier *apike*, prob. fr. *a-* + *pike*] : being in a vertical position ⟨with oars ~⟩
ape–man \ˈāp-ˈman, -ˌman\ *n* : a primate (as pithecanthropus) intermediate in character between Homo sapiens and the higher apes
aper·çu \á-per-sǖ, ˌap-ər-ˈsü\ *n, pl* **aperçus** \-sǖ(z), -ˈsüz\ [F] **1** : an immediate impression; *esp* : INSIGHT 2 **2** : a brief survey or sketch : OUTLINE
ape·ri·ent \ə-ˈpir-ē-ənt\ *adj* [L *aperient-, aperiens*, prp. of *aperire*] : gently moving the bowels : LAXATIVE — **aperient** *n*
ape·ri·od·ic \ˌā-ˌpir-ē-ˈäd-ik\ *adj* **1** : of irregular occurrence ⟨~ floods⟩ **2** : not having periodic vibrations : not oscillatory **3** *cryptology* : not repeating or not repeating with a short or easily discoverable period ⟨an ~ key⟩ — **ape·ri·od·i·cal·ly** \-i-k(ə-)lē\ *adv* — **ape·ri·o·dic·i·ty** \-ē-ə-ˈdis-ət-ē\ *n*
aper·i·tif \ˌäp-ˌer-ə-ˈtēf, ə-ˈper-ə-ˌ\ *n* [F *apéritif* aperient, aperitif, fr. MF *aperitif*, adj., aperient, fr. ML *aperitivus*, irreg. fr. L *aperire*] : an alcoholic drink taken before a meal as an appetizer
ap·er·ture \ˈap-ə(r)-ˌchu̇(ə)r, -chər, -ˌt(y)u̇(ə)r\ *n* [ME, fr. L *apertura*, fr. *apertus*, pp. of *aperire* to open — more at WEIR] **1** : an opening or open space : HOLE **2 a** : the opening in a photographic lens that admits the light **b** : the diameter of the stop in an optical system that determines the diameter of the bundle of rays traversing the instrument **c** : the diameter of the objective lens or mirror of a telescope
syn APERTURE, INTERSTICE, ORIFICE *shared meaning element* : an opening allowing passage through or in and out
apet·al·ous \(ˈ)ā-ˈpet-ᵊl-əs\ *adj* : having no petals — **apet·aly** \-ᵊl-ē\ *n*
apex \ˈā-ˌpeks\ *n, pl* **apex·es** *or* **api·ces** \ˈā-pə-ˌsēz, ˈap-ə-\ [L] **1 a** : the uppermost point : VERTEX ⟨the ~ of a mountain⟩ **b** : the narrowed or pointed end : TIP ⟨the ~ of the tongue⟩ **2** : the highest or culminating point ⟨the ~ of his career⟩ ***syn*** see SUMMIT
aphaer·e·sis *or* **apher·e·sis** \ə-ˈfer-ə-səs\ *n, pl* **-e·ses** \-ˌsēz\ [LL, fr. Gk *aphairesis*, lit., taking off, fr. *aphairein* to take away, fr. *apo-* + *hairein* to take] : the loss of one or more sounds or letters at the beginning of a word (as in *round* for *around* and *coon* for *raccoon*) — **aph·ae·ret·ic** \ˌaf-ə-ˈret-ik\ *adj*
aph·a·nite \ˈaf-ə-ˌnīt\ *n* [F, fr. Gk *aphanēs* invisible, fr. *a-* + *phainesthai* to appear — more at PHENOMENON] : a dark rock of such close texture that its separate grains are invisible to the naked eye — **aph·a·nit·ic** \ˌaf-ə-ˈnit-ik\ *adj*
apha·sia \ə-ˈfā-zh(ē-)ə\ *n* [NL, fr. Gk, fr. *a-* + *-phasia*] : loss or impairment of the power to use words usu. resulting from a brain lesion — **apha·si·ac** \-zē-ˌak\ *adj* — **apha·sic** \-zik\ *n or adj*
aph·elion \a-ˈfēl-yən\ *n, pl* **-elia** \-yə\ [NL, fr. *apo-* + Gk *hēlios* sun — more at SOLAR] : the point of a planet's or comet's orbit most distant from the sun — compare PERIHELION
aph·e·sis \ˈaf-ə-səs\ *n, pl* **-e·ses** \-ˌsēz\ [NL, fr. Gk, release, fr. *aphienai* to let go, fr. *apo-* + *hienai* to send — more at JET] : aphaeresis consisting of the loss of a short unaccented vowel (as in *lone* for *alone*) — **aphet·ic** \ə-ˈfet-ik\ *adj* — **aphet·i·cal·ly** \-i-k(ə-)lē\ *adv*
aphid \ˈā-fəd, ˈaf-əd\ *n* : any of numerous small sluggish homopterous insects (superfamily Aphidoidea) that suck the juices of plants
aphis \ˈā-fəs, ˈaf-əs\ *n, pl* **aphi·des** \ˈā-fə-ˌdēz, ˈaf-ə-\ [NL *Aphid-, Aphis*, genus name] : an aphid of a common genus (*Aphis*); *broadly* : APHID
aphis lion *n* : any of several insect larvae (as a lacewing or ladybug larva) that feed on aphids
aph·o·late \ˈaf-ə-ˌlāt\ *n* [prob. fr. *az-* + *pho*sphine + *-late* (of unknown origin)] : a chemosterilant esp. effective in controlling houseflies
apho·nia \(ˈ)ā-ˈfō-nē-ə\ *n* [NL, fr. Gk *aphōnia*, fr. *aphōnos* voiceless, fr. *a-* + *phōnē* sound — more at BAN] : loss of voice and of all but whispered speech — **apho·nic** \-ˈfän-ik, -ˈfō-nik\ *adj*
aph·o·rism \ˈaf-ə-ˌriz-əm\ *n* [MF *aphorisme*, fr. LL *aphorismus*, fr. Gk *aphorismos* definition, aphorism, fr. *aphorizein* to define, fr. *apo-* + *horizein* to bound — more at HORIZON] **1** : a concise statement of a principle **2** : a terse formulation of a truth or sentiment : ADAGE — **aph·o·rist** \-rəst\ *n* — **aph·o·ris·tic** \ˌaf-ə-ˈris-tik\ *adj* — **aph·o·ris·ti·cal·ly** \-ti-k(ə-)lē\ *adv*
aph·o·rize \ˈaf-ə-ˌrīz\ *vi* **-rized; -riz·ing** : to write or speak in or as if in aphorisms
apho·tic \(ˈ)ā-ˈfōt-ik\ *adj* : lacking light ⟨the ~ zone in the ocean⟩
aph·ro·dis·i·ac \ˌaf-rə-ˈdiz-ē-ˌak\ *adj* [Gk *aphrodisiakos* sexual, fr. *aphrodisia* sexual pleasures, fr. neut. pl. of *aphrodisios* of Aphrodite, fr. *Aphroditē*] : exciting sexual desire — **aphrodisiac** *n* — **aph·ro·di·si·a·cal** \ˌaf-rəd-ə-ˈzī-ə-kəl, -ˈsī-\ *adj*
Aph·ro·di·te \ˌaf-rə-ˈdīt-ē\ *n* [Gk *Aphroditē*] : the Greek goddess of love and beauty — compare VENUS
aphyl·lous \(ˈ)ā-ˈfil-əs\ *adj* [Gk *aphyllos*, fr. *a-* + *phyllon* leaf — more at BLADE] : not having foliage leaves — **aphyl·ly** \ˈā-ˌfil-ē\ *n*
API *abbr* **1** air position indicator **2** American Petroleum Institute
api·an \ˈā-pē-ən\ *adj* [L *apianus*, fr. *apis*] : of or relating to bees
api·ar·i·an \ˌā-pē-ˈer-ē-ən\ *adj* : of or relating to beekeeping or bees
api·a·rist \ˈā-pē-ə-rəst, -pē-ˌer-əst\ *n* : BEEKEEPER
api·ary \ˈā-pē-ˌer-ē\ *n, pl* **-ar·ies** [L *apiarium*, fr. *apis* bee] : a place where bees are kept; *esp* : a collection of hives or colonies of bees kept for their honey
api·cal \ˈā-pi-kəl *also* ˈap-i-\ *adj* [prob. fr. NL *apicalis*, fr. L *apic-, apex*] **1** : of, relating to, or situated at an apex **2** : of, relating to, or formed with the tip of the tongue ⟨*n, l*, and *r* are ~ consonants⟩ — **api·cal·ly** \-k(ə-)lē\ *adv*
apical dominance *n* : inhibition of the growth of lateral buds by the terminal bud of a shoot
apic·u·late \ə-ˈpik-yə-lət, ā-\ *adj* [NL *apiculus*, dim. of L *apic-, apex*] : ending abruptly in a small distinct point ⟨an ~ leaf⟩
api·cul·ture \ˈā-pə-ˌkəl-chər\ *n* [prob. fr. F, fr. L *apis* bee + F *culture*] : the keeping of bees esp. on a large scale — **api·cul·tur·al** \ˌā-pə-ˈkəlch(-ə)-rəl\ *adj* — **api·cul·tur·ist** \-rəst\ *n*
apiece \ə-ˈpēs\ *adv* : for each one : INDIVIDUALLY
Apis \ˈā-pəs\ *n* [L, fr. Gk, fr. Egypt *ḥp*] : a sacred bull worshiped by the ancient Egyptians
ap·ish \ˈā-pish\ *adj* : resembling an ape: as **a** : given to slavish imitation **b** : extremely silly or affected — **ap·ish·ly** *adv* — **ap·ish·ness** *n*
apla·cen·tal \ˌā-plə-ˈsent-ᵊl\ *adj* : having or developing no placenta
ap·la·nat·ic \ˌap-lə-ˈnat-ik\ *adj* [*a-* + Gk *planasthai* to wander — more at PLANET] : free from or corrected for spherical aberration ⟨an ~ lens⟩
apla·sia \(ˈ)ā-ˈplā-zh(ē-)ə, ə-\ *n* [NL, fr. [2]*a-* + *-plasia*] : incomplete or faulty development of an organ or part — **aplas·tic** \(ˈ)ā-ˈplas-tik\ *adj*
[1]aplen·ty \ə-ˈplent-ē\ *adj* : being in plenty or abundance ⟨money ~ for all his needs⟩
[2]aplenty *adv* **1** : in abundance : PLENTIFULLY **2** : very much : EXTREMELY ⟨scared ~⟩
ap·lite \ˈap-ˌlīt\ *n* [prob. fr. G *aplit*, fr. Gk *haploos* simple — more at HAPL-] : a fine-grained light-colored granite consisting almost entirely of quartz and feldspar — **ap·lit·ic** \a-ˈplit-ik\ *adj*
aplomb \ə-ˈpläm, -ˈpləm\ *n* [F, lit., perpendicularity, fr. MF, fr. *a plomb*, lit., according to the plummet] : complete and confident composure or self-assurance : POISE ***syn*** see CONFIDENCE ***ant*** shyness
ap·nea *or* **ap·noea** \ˈap-nē-ə\ *n* [NL] **1** : transient cessation of respiration **2** : ASPHYXIA — **ap·ne·ic** \-nē-ik\ *adj*
APO *abbr* army post office
apo- *or* **ap-** *prefix* [ME, fr. MF & L; MF, fr. L, fr. Gk, fr. *apo* — more at OF] **1** : away from : off ⟨*aph*elion⟩ **2** : detached : separate ⟨*apo*carpous⟩ **3** : formed from : related to ⟨*apo*morphine⟩
Apoc *abbr* **1** Apocalypse **2** Apocrypha; apocryphal
apoc·a·lypse \ə-ˈpäk-ə-ˌlips\ *n* [ME, revelation, Revelation, fr. LL *apocalypsis*, fr. Gk *apokalypsis*, fr. *apokalyptein* to uncover, fr. *apo-* + *kalyptein* to cover — more at HELL] **1 a** : one of the Jewish and Christian writings of 200 B.C. to A.D. 150 marked by pseudonymity, symbolic imagery, and the expectation of an imminent cosmic cataclysm in which God destroys the ruling powers of evil and raises the righteous to life in a messianic kingdom **b** *cap* : REVELATION 2 **2** : something viewed as a prophetic revelation
apoc·a·lyp·tic \ə-ˌpäk-ə-ˈlip-tik\ *also* **apoc·a·lyp·ti·cal** \-ti-kəl\ *adj* **1** : of, relating to, or resembling an apocalypse **2** : forecasting the ultimate destiny of the world : PROPHETIC **3** : foreboding imminent disaster or final doom : TERRIBLE **4** : wildly unrestrained in making predictions : GRANDIOSE **5** : ultimately decisive : CLIMACTIC — **apoc·a·lyp·ti·cal·ly** \-ti-k(ə-)lē\ *adv*
apoc·a·lyp·ti·cism \-tə-ˌsiz-əm\ *or* **apoc·a·lyp·tism** \ə-ˈpäk-ə-ˌlip-ˌtiz-əm\ *n* : apocalyptic expectation; *esp* : a doctrine concerning an imminent end of the world and an ensuing general resurrection and final judgment
apoc·a·lyp·tist \ə-ˈpäk-ə-ˌlip-təst\ *n* : the writer of an apocalypse
apo·car·pous \ˌap-ə-ˈkär-pəs\ *adj* : having the carpels of the gynoecium separate — **apo·car·py** \ˈap-ə-ˌkär-pē\ *n*
apo·chro·mat·ic \ˌap-ə-krō-ˈmat-ik\ *adj* [ISV] : free from chromatic and spherical aberration ⟨an ~ lens⟩
apoc·o·pe \ə-ˈpäk-ə-(ˌ)pē\ *n* [LL, fr. Gk *apokopē*, lit., cutting off, fr. *apokoptein* to cut off, fr. *apo-* + *koptein* to cut — more at CAPON] : the loss of one or more sounds or letters at the end of a word (as in *sing* from Old English *singan*)
apo·crine \ˈap-ə-krən, -ˌkrīn, -ˌkrēn\ *adj* [ISV *apo-* + Gk *krinein* to separate — more at CERTAIN] : producing a secretion by separation of part of the cytoplasm of the secreting cells
apoc·ry·pha \ə-ˈpäk-rə-fə\ *n pl but sing or pl in constr* [ML, fr. LL, neut. pl. of *apocryphus* secret, not canonical, fr. Gk *apokryphos* obscure, fr. *apokryptein* to hide away, fr. *apo-* + *kryptein* to hide — more at CRYPT] **1** : writings or statements of dubious authenticity **2** *cap* **a** : books included in the Septuagint and Vulgate but excluded from the Jewish and Protestant canons of the Old Testament — see BIBLE table **b** : early Christian writings not included in the New Testament
apoc·ry·phal \-fəl\ *adj* **1** *often cap* : of or resembling the Apocrypha **2** : of doubtful authenticity : SPURIOUS ***syn*** see FICTITIOUS — **apoc·ry·phal·ly** \-fə-lē\ *adv* — **apoc·ry·phal·ness** *n*
apo·cyn·thi·on \ˌap-ə-ˈsin(t)-thē-ən\ *n* [NL, fr. *apo-* + *Cynthia*] : APOLUNE
ap·o·dal \ˈap-əd-ᵊl\ *or* **ap·o·dous** \-əd-əs\ *adj* [Gk *apod-, apous*, fr. *a-* + *pod-, pous* foot — more at FOOT] : having no feet or analogous appendages ⟨eels are ~⟩
apo·dic·tic \ˌap-ə-ˈdik-tik\ *also* **apo·deic·tic** \-ˈdīk-tik\ *adj* [L *apodicticus*, fr. Gk *apodeiktikos*, fr. *apodeiknynai* to demonstrate, fr. *apo-* + *deiknynai* to show — more at DICTION] : expressing or of the nature of necessary truth or absolute certainty — **apo·dic·ti·cal·ly** \-ti-k(ə-)lē\ *adv*
apod·o·sis \ə-ˈpäd-ə-səs\ *n, pl* **-o·ses** \-ˌsēz\ [NL, fr. Gk, fr. *apodidonai* to give back, deliver, fr. *apo-* + *didonai* to give — more at DATE] : the main clause of a conditional sentence — compare PROTASIS
apo·en·zyme \ˌap-ō-ˈen-ˌzīm\ *n* [ISV] : a protein that forms an active enzyme system by combination with a coenzyme and determines the specificity of this system for a substrate
apog·a·my \ə-ˈpäg-ə-mē\ *n* [ISV] : development of a sporophyte from a gametophyte without fertilization — **apo·gam·ic** \ˌap-ə-ˈgam-ik\ *or* **apog·a·mous** \ə'päg-ə-məs\ *adj*
apo·gee \ˈap-ə-(ˌ)jē\ *n* [F *apogée*, fr. NL *apogaeum*, fr. Gk *apogaion*, fr. neut. of *apogeios, apogaios* far from the earth, fr. *apo-* + *gē* earth] **1** : the point in the orbit of a satellite of the earth or of a vehicle orbiting the earth that is at the greatest distance from the center of the earth; *also* : the point farthest from a planet or a satellite (as the moon) reached by an object orbiting it — compare PERIGEE **2**

: the farthest or highest point : CULMINATION ⟨Aegean civilization reached its ~ in Crete⟩ — **apo·ge·an** \ˌap-ə-ˈjē-ən\ *adj*

apolit·i·cal \ˌā-pə-ˈlit-i-kəl\ *adj* **1** : having an aversion for or no interest or involvement in political affairs **2** : having no political significance — **apolit·i·cal·ly** \-k(ə-)lē\ *adv*

Ap·ol·lin·i·an \ˌap-ə-ˈlin-ē-ən\ *adj* : APOLLONIAN

Apol·lo \ə-ˈpäl-(ˌ)ō\ *n* [L *Apollin-, Apollo,* fr. Gk *Apollōn*] : the Greek god and in later times the Roman god of sunlight, prophecy, music, and poetry

Ap·ol·lo·ni·an \ˌap-ə-ˈlō-nē-ən\ *adj* **1** : of, relating to, or resembling the god Apollo **2** : harmonious, measured, ordered, or balanced in character

Apol·lyon \ə-ˈpäl-yən, -ˈpäl-ē-ən\ *n* [Gk *Apollyōn*] : the angel of the bottomless pit in the Book of Revelation

¹apol·o·get·ic \ə-ˌpäl-ə-ˈjet-ik\ *adj* [Gk *apologētikos,* fr. *apologeisthai* to defend, fr. *apo-* + *logos* speech] **1 a** : offered in defense or vindication ⟨the ~ writings of the early Christians⟩ **b** : offered by way of excuse or apology ⟨an ~ smile⟩ **2** : regretfully acknowledging fault or failure : CONTRITE ⟨was most ~ about his mistake⟩ — **apol·o·get·i·cal·ly** \-i-k(ə-)lē\ *adv*

²apologetic *n* : APOLOGETICS

apol·o·get·ics \-iks\ *n pl but sing or pl in constr* **1** : systematic argumentative discourse in defense (as of a doctrine) **2** : a branch of theology devoted to the defense of the divine origin and authority of Christianity

ap·o·lo·gia \ˌap-ə-ˈlō-j(ē-)ə\ *n* [LL] : a defense esp. of one's opinions, position, or actions ⟨the finest ~ or explanation of what drives a man to devote his life to pure mathematics —*Brit. Book News*⟩ ***syn*** see APOLOGY

apol·o·gist \ə-ˈpäl-ə-jəst\ *n* : one who speaks or writes in defense of a faith, a cause, or an institution

apol·o·gize \-ˌjīz\ *vi* **-gized; -giz·ing** : to make an apology — **apol·o·giz·er** *n*

ap·o·logue \ˈap-ə-ˌlȯg, -ˌläg\ *n* [F, fr. L *apologus,* fr. Gk *apologos,* fr. *apo-* + *logos* speech, narrative] : an allegorical narrative usu. intended to convey a moral

apol·o·gy \ə-ˈpäl-ə-jē\ *n, pl* **-gies** [MF or LL; MF *apologie,* fr. LL *apologia,* fr. Gk, fr. *apo-* + *logos* speech — more at LEGEND] **1 a** : a formal justification : DEFENSE **b** : EXCUSE 2a **2** : an admission of error or discourtesy accompanied by an expression of regret **3** : a poor substitute : MAKESHIFT

syn APOLOGY, APOLOGIA, EXCUSE, PLEA, PRETEXT, ALIBI *shared meaning element* : matter offered in explanation or defense (as of an act, a policy, or a view). APOLOGY usually applies to an expression of regret for a mistake or wrong with implied admission of guilt or fault and with or without reference to palliating circumstances ⟨said by way of *apology* that he would have met them if he could⟩ Sometimes *apology,* like APOLOGIA, implies not admission of guilt or regret but a desire to clear the grounds for some course, belief, or position ⟨the speech was an effective *apology* for his foreign policy⟩ EXCUSE implies an intent to avoid or remove blame or censure ⟨used his illness as an *excuse* for missing the meeting⟩ PLEA stresses argument or appeal for understanding or sympathy or mercy ⟨their *pleas* for help were ignored⟩ PRETEXT suggests subterfuge and the offering of false reasons or motives in excuse or explanation ⟨used any *pretext* to get out of work⟩ ALIBI implies a desire to shift blame or evade punishment and imputes plausibility rather than truth to the explanation offered ⟨his *alibi* failed to stand scrutiny⟩

apo·lune \ˈap-ə-ˌlün\ *n* [*apo-* + L *luna* moon — more at LUNAR] : the point in the path of a body orbiting the moon that is farthest from the center of the moon — compare PERILUNE

apo·mict \ˈap-ə-ˌmikt\ *n* [prob. back-formation fr. ISV *apomictic,* fr. *apo-* + Gk *mignynai* to mix — more at MIX] : one produced or reproducing by apomixis — **apo·mic·tic** \ˌap-ə-ˈmik-tik\ *adj* — **apo·mic·ti·cal·ly** \-ti-k(ə-)lē\ *adv*

apo·mix·is \ˌap-ə-ˈmik-səs\ *n, pl* **-mix·es** \-ˌsēz\ [NL, fr. *apo-* + Gk *mixis* act of mixing, fr. *mignynai*] : reproduction (as apogamy or parthenogenesis) involving specialized generative tissues but not dependent on fertilization

apo·mor·phine \ˌap-ə-ˈmȯr-ˌfēn\ *n* [ISV] : an artificial crystalline alkaloid $C_{17}H_{17}NO_2$ from morphine with a powerful emetic action

apo·neu·ro·sis \ˌap-ə-n(y)u̇-ˈrō-səs\ *n* [NL, fr. Gk *aponeurōsis,* fr. *aponeurousthai* to pass into a tendon, fr. *apo-* + *neuron* sinew — more at NERVE] : any of the thicker and denser of the deep fasciae that cover, invest, and form the terminations and attachments of various muscles and differ from tendons in being flat and thin — **apo·neu·rot·ic** \-ˈrät-ik\ *adj*

apo·phyl·lite \ˌap-ə-ˈfil-ˌīt, ə-ˈpäf-ə-ˌlīt\ *n* [F, fr. *apo-* + Gk *phyllon* leaf] : a mineral $KCa_4Si_8O_{20}(F,OH).8H_2O$ composed of a hydrous potassium calcium silicate related to the zeolites and usu. found in transparent square prisms or white or grayish masses

apoph·y·sis \ə-ˈpäf-ə-səs\ *n, pl* **-y·ses** \-ˌsēz\ [NL, fr. Gk, fr. *apo-* + *phyein* to bring forth — more at BE] : an expanded or projecting part esp. of an organism — **apoph·y·se·al** \-ˌpäf-ə-ˈsē-əl\ *adj*

ap·o·plec·tic \ˌap-ə-ˈplek-tik\ *adj* [F or LL; F *apoplectique,* fr. LL *apoplecticus,* fr. Gk *apoplēktikos,* fr. *apoplēssein*] **1** : of, relating to, or causing apoplexy **2** : affected with, inclined to, or showing symptoms of apoplexy **3** : of a kind to cause apoplexy; *esp* : highly excited ⟨flew into an ~ rage⟩ — **ap·o·plec·ti·cal·ly** \-ti-k(ə-)lē\ *adv*

ap·o·plexy \ˈap-ə-ˌplek-sē\ *n* [ME *apoplexie,* fr. MF & LL; MF, fr. LL *apoplexia,* fr. Gk *apoplēxia,* fr. *apoplēssein* to cripple by a stroke, fr. *apo-* + *plēssein* to strike — more at PLAINT] : sudden diminution or loss of consciousness, sensation, and voluntary motion caused by rupture or obstruction (as by a clot) of an artery of the brain

aport \ə-ˈpō(ə)rt, -ˈpȯ(ə)rt\ *adv* : on or toward the left side of a ship ⟨put the helm hard ~⟩

apo·se·le·ne \ˌap-ō-sə-ˈlē-nē\ *n* [ISV *apo-* + Gk *selēnē* moon — more at SELENIUM] : APOLUNE

apo·se·mat·ic \ˌap-ə-si-ˈmat-ik\ *adj* : being conspicuous and serving to warn ⟨~ coloration⟩ — **apo·se·mat·i·cal·ly** \-i-k(ə-)lē\ *adv*

ap·o·si·o·pe·sis \ˌap-ə-ˌsī-ə-ˈpē-səs\ *n, pl* **-pe·ses** \-ˌsēz\ [LL, fr. Gk *aposiōpēsis,* fr. *aposiōpan* to be quite silent, fr. *apo-* + *siōpan* to be silent, fr. *siōpē* silence] : the leaving of a thought incomplete usu. by a sudden breaking off (as in "his behavior was — but I blush to mention that") — **ap·o·si·o·pet·ic** \-ˈpet-ik\ *adj*

apos·ta·sy \ə-ˈpäs-tə-sē\ *n, pl* **-sies** [ME *apostasie,* fr. LL *apostasia,* fr. Gk, lit., revolt, fr. *aphistasthai* to revolt, fr. *apo-* + *histasthai* to stand — more at STAND] **1** : renunciation of a religious faith **2** : abandonment of a previous loyalty : DEFECTION

apos·tate \ə-ˈpäs-ˌtāt, -tət\ *n* : one who commits apostasy — **apos·tate** *adj*

apos·ta·tize \ə-ˈpäs-tə-ˌtīz\ *vi* **-tized; -tiz·ing** : to commit apostasy

a pos·te·ri·o·ri \ˌä-(ˌ)pō-ˌstir-ē-ˈō(ə)r-ē, -ˌster-; ˌā-(ˌ)pä-ˌstir-ē-ˈō(ə)r-ˌī, -(ˌ)pō-, -ˈō(ə)r-ē; -ˈȯ(ə)r-\ *adj* [L, lit., from the latter] **1** : INDUCTIVE **2** : relating to or derived by reasoning from observed facts — compare A PRIORI — **a posteriori** *adv*

apos·tle \ə-ˈpäs-əl\ *n* [ME, fr. OF & OE; OF *apostle* & OE *apostol,* fr. LL *apostolus,* fr. Gk *apostolos,* fr. *apostellein* to send away, fr. *apo-* + *stellein* to send — more at STALL] **1** : one sent on a mission: as **a** : one of an authoritative New Testament group sent out to preach the gospel and made up esp. of Christ's 12 original disciples and Paul **b** : the first prominent Christian missionary to a region or group **2 a** : one who initiates a great moral reform or who first advocates an important belief or system **b** : an ardent supporter : ADHERENT ⟨an ~ of liberal tolerance⟩ **3** : the highest ecclesiastical official in some church organizations **4** : one of a Mormon administrative council of 12 men — **apos·tle·ship** \-ˌship\ *n*

Apostles' Creed *n* : a Christian statement of belief ascribed to the Twelve Apostles and used esp. in public worship

apos·to·late \ə-ˈpäs-tə-ˌlāt, -lət\ *n* [LL *apostolatus,* fr. *apostolus*] **1** : the office or mission of an apostle **2** : an association of persons dedicated to the propagation of a religion or a doctrine

ap·os·tol·ic \ˌap-ə-ˈstäl-ik\ *adj* **1 a** : of or relating to an apostle **b** : of, relating to, or conforming to the teachings of the New Testament apostles **2 a** : of or relating to a succession of spiritual authority from the apostles held (as by Roman Catholics, Anglicans, and Eastern Orthodox) to be perpetuated by successive ordinations of bishops and to be necessary for the validity of sacraments and orders **b** : PAPAL — **apos·to·lic·i·ty** \ə-ˌpäs-tə-ˈlis-ət-ē\ *n*

apostolic delegate *n* : an ecclesiastical representative of the Holy See in a country that has no formal diplomatic relations with it

Apostolic Father *n* : a church father of the first or second century A.D.

¹apos·tro·phe \ə-ˈpäs-trə-(ˌ)fē\ *n* [L, fr. Gk *apostrophē,* lit., act of turning away, fr. *apostrephein* to turn away, fr. *apo-* + *strephein* to turn — more at STROPHE] : the addressing of a usu. absent person or a usu. personified thing rhetorically ⟨Carlyle's "O Liberty, what things are done in thy name!" is an example of ~⟩ — **ap·os·troph·ic** \ˌap-ə-ˈsträf-ik\ *adj*

²apostrophe *n* [MF & LL; MF, fr. LL *apostrophus,* fr. Gk *apostrophos,* fr. *apostrophos* turned away, fr. *apostrephein*] : a mark ' used to indicate the omission of letters or figures, the possessive case, or the plural of letters or figures — **apostrophic** *adj*

apos·tro·phize \ə-ˈpäs-trə-ˌfīz\ *vb* **-phized; -phiz·ing** *vt* : to address by or in apostrophe ~ *vi* : to make use of apostrophe

apothecaries' measure *n* : a measure of capacity used chiefly by pharmacists — see WEIGHT table

apothecaries' weight *n* : a system of weights used chiefly by pharmacists — see WEIGHT table

apoth·e·cary \ə-ˈpäth-ə-ˌker-ē\ *n, pl* **-car·ies** [ME *apothecarie,* fr. ML *apothecarius,* fr. LL, shopkeeper, fr. L *apotheca* storehouse, fr. Gk *apothēkē,* fr. *apotithenai* to put away, fr. *apo-* + *tithenai* to put — more at DO] **1** : one who prepares and sells drugs or compounds for medicinal purposes **2** : PHARMACY

apo·the·ci·um \-ˈthē-s(h)ē-əm\ *n, pl* **-cia** \-s(h)ē-ə\ [NL, fr. L *apotheca*] : a spore-bearing structure in many lichens and fungi consisting of a discoid or cupped body bearing asci on the exposed flat or concave surface — **apo·the·cial** \-sh(ē-)əl, -sē-əl\ *adj*

ap·o·thegm \ˈap-ə-ˌthem\ *n* [Gk *apophthegmat-, apophthegma,* fr. *apophthengesthai* to speak out, fr. *apo-* + *phthengesthai* to utter] : a short, pithy, and instructive saying or formulation : APHORISM — **ap·o·theg·mat·ic** \ˌap-ə-theg-ˈmat-ik\ *or* **ap·o·theg·mat·i·cal** \-i-kəl\ *adj* — **ap·o·theg·mat·i·cal·ly** \-i-k(ə-)lē\ *adv*

ap·o·them \ˈap-ə-ˌthem\ *n* [ISV *apo-* + *-them* (fr. Gk *thema* something laid down, theme)] : the perpendicular from the center of a regular polygon to one of the sides

apo·the·o·sis \ə-ˌpäth-ē-ˈō-səs, ˌap-ə-ˈthē-ə-səs\ *n, pl* **-o·ses** \-ˌsēz\ [LL, fr. Gk *apotheōsis,* fr. *apotheoun* to deify, fr. *apo-* + *theos* god] **1** : elevation to divine status : DEIFICATION **2** : the perfect example : QUINTESSENCE ⟨she is the ~ of womanhood⟩ — **apo·the·o·size** \ˌap-ə-ˈthē-ə-ˌsīz, ə-ˈpäth-ē-ə-\ *vt*

apo·tro·pa·ic \ˌap-ə-trō-ˈpā-ik\ *adj* [Gk *apotropaios,* fr. *apotrepein* to avert, fr. *apo-* + *trepein* to turn — more at TROPE] : designed to avert evil ⟨an ~ ritual⟩ — **apo·tro·pa·i·cal·ly** \-ˈpā-ə-k(ə-)lē\ *adv*

app *abbr* **1** apparatus **2** appendix

ap·pall *also* **ap·pal** \ə-ˈpȯl\ *vb* **ap·palled; ap·pall·ing** [ME *appallen,* fr. MF *apalir,* fr. OF, fr. *a-* (fr. L *ad-*) + *palir* to grow pale, fr. L *pallescere,* incho. of *pallēre* to be pale — more at FALLOW] *vi, obs* : WEAKEN, FAIL ~ *vt* : to overcome with consternation, shock, or dismay ***syn*** see DISMAY ***ant*** nerve, embolden

ap·pall·ing *adj* : inspiring horror, dismay, or disgust ⟨living under ~ conditions⟩ ***syn*** see FEARFUL ***ant*** reassuring — **ap·pall·ing·ly** \-ˈpȯ-liŋ-lē\ *adv*

ə abut	ᵊ kitten	ər further	a back	ā bake	ä cot, cart	
au̇ out	ch chin	e less	ē easy	g gift	i trip	ī life
j joke	ŋ sing	ō flow	ȯ flaw	ȯi coin	th thin	th this
ü loot	u̇ foot	y yet	yü few	yu̇ furious	zh vision	

Ap·pa·loo·sa \ˌap-ə-ˈlü-sə\ *n* [prob. fr. *Palouse,* an Indian people of Wash. and Idaho] : a rugged saddle horse of a breed developed in western No. America that has a mottled skin, vertically striped hooves, and a blotched or dotted patch of white hair over the rump and loins

ap·pa·nage \ˈap-ə-nij\ *n* [F *apanage,* fr. OF, fr. *apaner* to provide for a younger offspring, fr. OProv *apanar* to support, fr. *a-* (fr. L *ad-*) + *pan* bread, fr. L *panis* — more at FOOD] **1 a :** a grant (as of land or revenue) made by a sovereign or a legislative body to a dependent member of the royal family or a principal liege man **b :** a property or privilege appropriated to or by a person as his share **2 :** a rightful endowment or adjunct

ap·pa·rat \ˈap-ə-ˌrat, ˌäp-ə-ˈrät\ *n* [Russ] : APPARATUS 2

ap·pa·ra·tchik \ˌäp-ə-ˈräch-ik\ *n, pl* **-ratchiks** *or* **-ra·tchi·ki** \-ˈräch-ə-(ˌ)kē\ [Russ, fr. *apparat*] : a member of a Communist apparat

ap·pa·ra·tus \ˌap-ə-ˈrat-əs, -ˈrāt-\ *n, pl* **-tus·es** *or* **-tus** [L, fr. *apparatus,* pp. of *apparare* to prepare, fr. *ad-* + *parare* to prepare — more at PARE] **1 a :** a set of materials or equipment designed for a particular use **b :** an instrument or appliance designed for a specific operation **c :** a group of organs having a common function **2 :** the functional machinery by means of which a systematized activity is carried out; *esp* **:** the organization of a political party or an underground movement

[1]**ap·par·el** \ə-ˈpar-əl\ *vt* **-eled** *or* **-elled; -el·ing** *or* **-el·ling** [ME *apparaillen,* fr. OF *apareillier* to prepare, fr. (assumed) VL *appariculare,* irreg. fr. L *apparare*] **1 :** to put clothes on : DRESS **2 :** ADORN, EMBELLISH

[2]**apparel** *n* **1 :** the equipment (as sails and rigging) of a ship **2 :** personal attire : CLOTHING **3 :** something that clothes or adorns ⟨the bright ~ of spring⟩

ap·par·ent \ə-ˈpar-ənt, -ˈper-\ *adj* [ME, fr. OF *aparent,* fr. L *apparent-, apparens,* prp. of *apparēre* to appear] **1 :** open to view : VISIBLE **2 :** clear or manifest to the understanding **3 :** appearing as actual to the eye or mind **4 :** having an indefeasible right to succeed to a title or estate **5 :** manifest to the senses or mind as real or true on the basis of evidence that may or may not be factually valid ⟨his ~ absorption was belied by his rigid pose⟩ — **ap·par·ent·ly** \-ˈpar(-ə)nt-lē, -ˈper(-ə)nt-\ *adv* — **ap·par·ent·ness** \-ˈpar-ənt-nəs, -ˈper-\ *n*

syn **1** APPARENT, ILLUSORY, ILLUSIONARY, SEEMING, OSTENSIBLE *shared meaning element* : not actually being what it appears to be ***ant*** real

2 see EVIDENT ***ant*** unintelligible

apparent time *n* : the time of day indicated by the hour angle of the sun or by a sundial

ap·pa·ri·tion \ˌap-ə-ˈrish-ən\ *n* [ME *apparicioun,* fr. LL *apparition-, apparitio* appearance, fr. L *apparitus,* pp. of *apparēre*] **1 a :** an unusual or unexpected sight : PHENOMENON **b :** a ghostly figure **2 :** the act of becoming visible : APPEARANCE — **ap·pa·ri·tion·al** \-ˈrish-nəl, -ən-ᵊl\ *adj*

ap·par·i·tor \ə-ˈpar-ət-ər\ *n* [L, fr. *apparitus*] : an official formerly sent to carry out the orders of a magistrate, judge, or court

[1]**ap·peal** \ə-ˈpē(ə)l\ *n* **1 :** a legal proceeding by which a case is brought from a lower to a higher court for rehearing **2 :** a criminal accusation **3 a :** an application (as to a recognized authority) for corroboration, vindication, or decision **b :** an earnest plea : ENTREATY **4 :** the power of arousing a sympathetic response : ATTRACTION ⟨movies had a great ~ for him⟩

[2]**appeal** *vb* [ME *appelen* to accuse, appeal, fr. MF *apeler,* fr. L *appellare,* fr. *appellere* to drive to, fr. *ad-* + *pellere* to drive — more at FELT] *vt* **1 :** to charge with a crime : ACCUSE **2 :** to take proceedings to have (a case) reheard in a higher court ~ *vi* **1 :** to take a case to a higher court for rehearing **2 :** to call upon another for corroboration, vindication, or decision **3 :** to make an earnest request **4 :** to arouse a sympathetic response — **ap·peal·abil·i·ty** \-ˌpē-lə-ˈbil-ət-ē\ *n* — **ap·peal·able** \-ˈpē-lə-bəl\ *adj* — **ap·peal·er** *n*

ap·peal·ing \ə-ˈpē-liŋ\ *adj* **1 :** having appeal : PLEASING **2 :** marked by earnest entreaty : IMPLORING — **ap·peal·ing·ly** \-liŋ-lē\ *adv*

ap·pear \ə-ˈpi(ə)r\ *vi* [ME *apperen,* fr. OF *aparoir,* fr. L *apparēre,* fr. *ad-* + *parēre* to show oneself; akin to Gk *peparein* to display] **1 a :** to be or come in sight ⟨the sun ~s on the horizon⟩ **b :** to show up ⟨~s promptly at eight each day⟩ **2 :** to come formally before an authoritative body ⟨must ~ in court today⟩ **3 :** to have an outward aspect ⟨~s happy enough⟩ **4 :** to become evident or manifest ⟨there ~s growing evidence to the contrary⟩ **5 :** to come into public view ⟨first ~ed on a television variety show⟩ **6 :** to come into existence ⟨man ~s late in the evolutionary chain⟩ ***syn*** see SEEM

ap·pear·ance \ə-ˈpir-ən(t)s\ *n* **1 a :** the act, action, or process of appearing **b :** the coming into court of a party in an action or his attorney **2 a :** outward aspect : LOOK ⟨had a fierce ~⟩ **b :** external show : SEMBLANCE ⟨although hostile, he tried to preserve an ~ of neutrality⟩ **c** *pl* **:** outward indication ⟨would do anything to keep up ~s⟩ **3 a :** a sense impression or aspect of a thing ⟨the blue of distant hills is only an ~⟩ **b :** the world of sensible phenomena **4 a :** something that appears : PHENOMENON **b :** an instance of appearing : OCCURRENCE

ap·pease \ə-ˈpēz\ *vt* **ap·peased; ap·peas·ing** [ME *appesen,* fr. OF *apaisier,* fr. *a-* (fr. L *ad-*) + *pais* peace — more at PEACE] **1 :** to bring to a state of peace or quiet : CALM **2 :** to cause to subside : ALLAY ⟨~ his hunger⟩ **3 :** PACIFY, CONCILIATE; *esp* **:** to buy off (an aggressor) by concessions usu. at the sacrifice of principles — **ap·peas·able** \-ˈpē-zə-bəl\ *adj* — **ap·pease·ment** \ə-ˈpēz-mənt\ *n* — **ap·peas·er** *n*

[1]**ap·pel·lant** \ə-ˈpel-ənt\ *adj* : of or relating to an appeal : APPELLATE

[2]**appellant** *n* : one that appeals; *specif* **:** one that appeals from a judicial decision or decree

ap·pel·late \ə-ˈpel-ət\ *adj* [L *appellatus,* pp. of *appellare*] : of, relating to, or recognizing appeals; *specif* **:** having the power to review the judgment of another tribunal ⟨an ~ court⟩

ap·pel·la·tion \ˌap-ə-ˈlā-shən\ *n* **1** *archaic* **:** the act of calling by a name **2 :** an identifying name or title : DESIGNATION

ap·pel·la·tive \ə-ˈpel-ət-iv\ *adj* **1 :** of or relating to a common noun **2 :** of, relating to, or inclined to the giving of names — **appel·la·tive** *n* — **ap·pel·la·tive·ly** *adv*

ap·pel·lee \ˌap-ə-ˈlē\ *n* : one against whom an appeal is taken

ap·pend \ə-ˈpend\ *vt* [F *appendre,* fr. LL *appendere,* fr. L, to weigh, fr. *ad-* + *pendere* to weigh — more at PENDANT] **1 :** ATTACH, AFFIX **2 :** to add as a supplement or appendix (as in a book)

ap·pend·age \ə-ˈpen-dij\ *n* **1 :** an adjunct to something larger or more important : APPURTENANCE **2 :** a dependent or subordinate person **3 :** a subordinate or derivative body part; *esp* **:** a limb or analogous part (as a seta)

ap·pen·dant \ə-ˈpen-dənt\ *adj* **1 :** associated as an attendant circumstance **2 :** belonging as a right — used of annexed land in English law **3 :** attached as an appendage ⟨a seal ~ to a document⟩ — **appendant** *n*

ap·pen·dec·to·my \ˌap-ən-ˈdek-tə-mē\ *n, pl* **-mies** [L *appendic-, appendix* + E *-ectomy*] : surgical removal of the vermiform appendix

ap·pen·di·ci·tis \ə-ˌpen-də-ˈsīt-əs\ *n* : inflammation of the vermiform appendix

ap·pen·dic·u·lar \ˌap-ən-ˈdik-yə-lər\ *adj* : of or relating to an appendage and esp. a limb ⟨the ~ skeleton⟩

ap·pen·dix \ə-ˈpen-diks\ *n, pl* **-dix·es** *or* **-di·ces** \-də-ˌsēz\ [L *appendic-, appendix,* fr. *appendere*] **1 a :** APPENDAGE **b :** supplementary material usu. attached at the end of a piece of writing **2 :** a bodily outgrowth or process; *specif* **:** VERMIFORM APPENDIX

ap·per·ceive \ˌap-ər-ˈsēv\ *vt* **-ceived; -ceiv·ing** [ME *apperceiven,* fr. OF *aperceivre,* fr. *a-* (fr. L *ad-*) + *perceivre* to perceive] : to have apperception of

ap·per·cep·tion \-ˈsep-shən\ *n* [F *aperception,* fr. *apercevoir*] **1 :** introspective self-consciousness **2 :** mental perception; *esp* **:** the process of understanding something perceived in terms of previous experience ***syn*** see RECOGNITION — **ap·per·cep·tive** \-ˈsep-tiv\ *adj*

ap·per·tain \ˌap-ər-ˈtān\ *vi* [ME *apperteinen,* fr. MF *apartenir,* fr. LL *appertinēre,* fr. L *ad-* + *pertinēre* to belong — more at PERTAIN] : to belong or be connected as a rightful part or attribute : PERTAIN

ap·pe·tence \ˈap-ət-ən(t)s\ *n* : APPETENCY

ap·pe·ten·cy \ˈap-ət-ən-sē\ *n, pl* **-cies** [L *appetentia,* fr. *appetent-, appetens,* prp. of *appetere*] **1 :** a fixed and strong desire : APPETITE **2 :** a natural affinity (as between chemicals) — **ap·pe·tent** \-ənt\ *adj*

ap·pe·tite \ˈap-ə-ˌtīt\ *n* [ME *apetit,* fr. MF, fr. L *appetitus,* fr. *appetitus,* pp. of *appetere* to strive after, fr. *ad-* + *petere* to go to — more at FEATHER] **1 :** one of the instinctive desires necessary to keep up organic life; *esp* **:** the desire to eat **2 a :** an inherent craving ⟨an insatiable ~ for work⟩ **b :** TASTE, PREFERENCE ⟨the cultural ~s of the time —J. D. Hart⟩ — **ap·pe·ti·tive** \-ˌtīt-iv\ *adj*

ap·pe·tiz·er \ˈap-ə-ˌtī-zər\ *n* : a food or drink that stimulates the appetite and is usu. served before a meal

ap·pe·tiz·ing \-ˌtī-ziŋ\ *adj* : appealing to the appetite esp. in appearance or aroma ***syn*** see PALATABLE ***ant*** unappetizing — **ap·pe·tiz·ing·ly** \-ziŋ-lē\ *adv*

Ap·pi·an Way \ˌap-ē-ən-\ *n* [*Appius* Claudius Caecus *fl* 300 B.C. Roman statesman] : an ancient paved highway extending from Rome to Brundisium

appl *abbr* applied

ap·plaud \ə-ˈplȯd\ *vb* [MF or L; MF *applaudir,* fr. L *applaudere,* fr. *ad-* + *plaudere* to applaud] *vi* **:** to express approval esp. by clapping the hands ~ *vt* **1 :** to express approval of : PRAISE ⟨~ her efforts to lose weight⟩ **2 :** to show approval of esp. by clapping the hands — **ap·plaud·able** \-ə-bəl\ *adj* — **ap·plaud·ably** \-blē\ *adv* — **ap·plaud·er** *n*

ap·plause \ə-ˈplȯz\ *n* [ML *applausus,* fr. L, clashing noise, fr. *applausus,* pp. of *applaudere*] **1 :** approval publicly expressed (as by clapping the hands) **2 :** marked commendation : ACCLAIM ⟨the kind of ~ every really creative writer wants—Robert Tallant⟩

ap·ple \ˈap-əl\ *n, often attrib* [ME *appel,* fr. OE *æppel;* akin to OHG *apful* apple, OSlav *ablŭko*] **1 :** the fleshy usu. rounded and red or yellow edible pome fruit of a tree (genus *Malus*) of the rose family; *also* **:** an apple tree **2 :** a fruit or other vegetable production suggestive of an apple — **apple of one's eye :** one that is highly cherished ⟨his daughter is the *apple of his eye*⟩

ap·ple·jack \-ˌjak\ *n* : brandy distilled from cider; *also* **:** an alcoholic beverage traditionally made by freezing hard cider

apple maggot *n* : a two-winged fly (*Rhagoletis pomonella*) whose larva burrows in and feeds esp. on apples

ap·ple–pie \ˌap-əl-ˌpī\ *adj* **1 :** EXCELLENT, PERFECT ⟨~ order⟩ **2 :** of, relating to, or characterized by traditionally American values (as honesty or simplicity) ⟨is the epitome of ~ wholesomeness⟩

ap·ple–pol·ish \ˈap-əl-ˌpäl-ish\ *vb* [fr. the traditional practice of schoolchildren bringing a shiny apple as a gift to their teacher] *vi* **:** to attempt to ingratiate oneself : TOADY ~ *vt* **:** to curry favor with (as by flattery) — **ap·ple–pol·ish·er** *n*

Ap·ple·ton layer \ˌap-əl-tən-, -əlt-ᵊn-\ *n* [Sir Edward *Appleton* †1965 E physicist] : F LAYER

ap·pli·ance \ə-ˈplī-ən(t)s\ *n* **1 :** an act of applying **2 a :** a piece of equipment for adapting a tool or machine to a special purpose : ATTACHMENT **b :** an instrument or device designed for a particular use; *specif* **:** a household or office device (as a stove, fan, or refrigerator) operated by gas or electric current **3** *obs* **:** COMPLIANCE

ap·pli·ca·ble \ˈap-li-kə-bəl *also* ə-ˈplik-ə-\ *adj* : capable of or suitable for being applied : APPROPRIATE ⟨there are several statutes ~ to the case⟩ ***syn*** see RELEVANT ***ant*** inapplicable — **ap·pli·ca·bil·i·ty** \ˌap-li-kə-ˈbil-ət-ē *also* ə-ˌplik-ə-\ *n*

ap·pli·cant \ˈap-li-kənt\ *n* : one who applies ⟨a job ~⟩

ap·pli·ca·tion \ˌap-lə-ˈkā-shən\ *n* [ME *applicacioun,* fr. L *application-, applicatio* inclination, fr. *applicatus,* pp. of *applicare*] **1 :** an act of applying: **a** (1) **:** an act of putting to use ⟨~ of new techniques⟩ (2) **:** a use to which something is put ⟨new ~s for old remedies⟩ **b :** an act of administering or superposing ⟨~ of paint to a house⟩ **c :** assiduous attention ⟨succeeds by ~ to his studies⟩ **2 a :** REQUEST, PETITION ⟨an ~ for financial aid⟩ **b :** a form used in making a request **3 :** the practical inference to be derived from a discourse (as a moral tale) **4 :** a medicated or protective layer or material ⟨an oily ~ for dry skin⟩ **5 :** capacity for practical use ⟨words of varied ~⟩

ap·pli·ca·tive \'ap-lə-ˌkāt-iv, ə-'plik-ət-\ *adj* **1 :** APPLICABLE, PRACTICAL **2 :** put to use : APPLIED — **ap·pli·ca·tive·ly** *adv*

ap·pli·ca·tor \'ap-lə-ˌkāt-ər\ *n* : one that applies; *specif* : a device for applying a substance (as medicine or polish)

ap·pli·ca·to·ry \'ap-li-kə-ˌtōr-ē, -ˌtȯr-, ə-'plik-ə-\ *adj* : capable of being applied

ap·plied \ə-'plīd\ *adj* : put to practical use; *esp* : applying general principles to solve definite problems ⟨~ sciences⟩

¹ap·pli·qué \ˌap-lə-'kā\ *n* [F, pp. of *appliquer* to put on, fr. L *applicare*] : a cutout decoration fastened to a larger piece of material

²appliqué *vt* **-quéd; -qué·ing :** to apply (as a decoration or ornament) to a larger surface : OVERLAY

ap·ply \ə-'plī\ *vb* **ap·plied; ap·ply·ing** [ME *applien,* fr. MF *aplier,* fr. L *applicare,* fr. *ad-* + *plicare* to fold — more at PLY] *vt* **1 a :** to put to use esp. for some practical purpose ⟨*applies* pressure to get what he wants⟩ **b :** to bring into action ⟨~ the brakes⟩ **c :** to lay or spread on ⟨~ varnish to a table⟩ **d :** to put into operation or effect ⟨~ a law⟩ **2 :** to employ diligently or with close attention ⟨should ~ himself to his work⟩ ~ *vi* **1 :** to have relevance or a valid connection ⟨this rule *applies* to freshmen only⟩ **2 :** to make an appeal or request esp. in the form of a written application ⟨~ for a job⟩ — **ap·pli·er** \-'plī(-ə)r\ *n*

ap·pog·gia·tu·ra \ə-ˌpäj-ə-'tu̇r-ə\ *n* [It, lit., support] : an embellishing note or tone preceding an essential melodic note or tone and usu. written as a note of smaller size

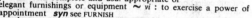

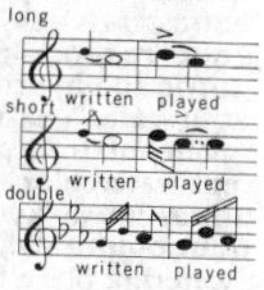
long
short
double
written
played
written
played
written
played
appoggiatura

ap·point \ə-'pȯint\ *vb* [ME *appointen,* fr. MF *apointier* to arrange, fr. *a-* (fr. L *ad-*) + *point*] *vt* **1 a :** to fix or set offically ⟨~ a trial date⟩ **b :** to name officially ⟨will ~ him director of the program⟩ **c** *archaic* **:** ARRANGE **d :** to determine the disposition of (an estate) to someone by virtue of a power of appointment **2 :** to provide with complete and usu. appropriate or elegant furnishings or equipment ~ *vi* : to exercise a power of appointment ***syn*** see FURNISH

ap·poin·tee \ə-ˌpȯin-'tē, ˌa-\ *n* **1 :** one who is appointed **2 :** one to whom an estate is appointed

ap·point·ive \ə-'pȯint-iv\ *adj* : of, relating to, or filled by appointment ⟨an ~ office⟩

ap·point·ment \ə-'pȯint-mənt\ *n* **1 a :** an act of appointing : DESIGNATION **b :** the designation by virtue of a vested power of a person to enjoy an estate **2 :** a nonelective office or position ⟨holds an academic ~⟩ **3 :** an arrangement for a meeting : ENGAGEMENT **4 :** EQUIPMENT, FURNISHINGS — usu. used in pl.

ap·por·tion \ə-'pōr-shən, -'pȯr-\ *vt* **ap·por·tioned; ap·por·tion·ing** \-sh(ə-)niŋ\ [MF *apportionner,* fr. *a-* (fr. L *ad-*) + *portionner* to portion] : to divide and share out according to a plan; *esp* : to make a proportionate division or distribution of ***syn*** see ALLOT

ap·por·tion·ment \-shən-mənt\ *n* : an act or result of apportioning; *esp* : the apportioning of representatives or taxes among the states according to U.S. law

ap·pose \a-'pōz\ *vt* **ap·posed; ap·pos·ing** [MF *aposer,* fr. OF, fr. *a-* + *poser* to put — more at POSE] **1** *archaic* **:** to put before : apply (one thing) to another **2 :** to place in juxtaposition or proximity

ap·po·site \'ap-ə-zət\ *adj* [L *appositus,* fr. pp. of *apponere* to place near, fr. *ad-* + *ponere* to put — more at POSITION] : highly pertinent or appropriate : APT ***syn*** see RELEVANT ***ant*** inapposite, inapt — **ap·po·site·ly** *adv* — **ap·po·site·ness** *n*

ap·po·si·tion \ˌap-ə-'zish-ən\ *n* **1 a :** a grammatical construction in which two usu. adjacent nouns having the same referent stand in the same syntactical relation to the rest of a sentence (as *the poet* and *Burns* in "a biography of the poet Burns") **b :** the relation of one of such a pair of nouns or noun equivalents to the other **2 a :** an act or instance of apposing; *specif* : the deposition of successive layers upon those already present (as in cell walls) **b :** the state of being apposed — **ap·po·si·tion·al** \-'zish-nəl, -ən-ᵊl\ *adj* — **ap·po·si·tion·al·ly** \-ē\ *adv*

ap·pos·i·tive \ə-'päz-ət-iv, a-\ *adj* : of, relating to, or standing in grammatical apposition — **appositive** *n* — **ap·pos·i·tive·ly** *adv*

ap·prais·al \ə-'prā-zəl\ *n* : an act or instance of appraising; *esp* : a valuation of property by the estimate of an authorized person

ap·praise \ə-'prāz\ *vt* **ap·praised; ap·prais·ing** [ME *appreisen,* fr. MF *aprisier* to apprize] **1 :** to set a value on : estimate the amount of **2 :** to evaluate the worth, significance, or status of; *esp* : to give an expert judgment of the value or merit of ***syn*** see ESTIMATE — **ap·praise·ment** \-'prāz-mənt\ *n* — **ap·prais·er** *n* — **ap·prais·ing** *adj* — **ap·prais·ing·ly** \-'prā-ziŋ-lē\ *adv*

ap·pre·cia·ble \ə-'prē-shə-bəl\ *adj* : capable of being perceived or measured ***syn*** see PERCEPTIBLE ***ant*** inappreciable — **ap·pre·cia·bly** \-blē\ *adv*

ap·pre·ci·ate \ə-'prē-shē-ˌāt\ *vb* **-at·ed; -at·ing** [LL *appretiatus,* pp. of *appretiare,* fr. L *ad-* + *pretium* price — more at PRICE] *vt* **1 a :** to grasp the nature, worth, quality, or significance of ⟨can't ~ the difference between right and wrong⟩ **b :** to value or admire highly ⟨think no one ~*s* his endeavors⟩ **c :** to judge with heightened perception or understanding : be fully aware of ⟨must experience it to ~ it⟩ **d :** to recognize with gratitude ⟨certainly ~*s* your kindness⟩ **2 :** to increase the value of ~ *vi* : to increase in number or value — **ap·pre·ci·a·tor** \-ˌāt-ər\ *n* — **ap·pre·cia·to·ry** \-shə-ˌtōr-ē, -ˌtȯr-\ *adj*

syn* 1** see UNDERSTAND ***ant depreciate

2 APPRECIATE, VALUE, PRIZE, TREASURE, CHERISH *shared meaning element* : to hold in high esteem ***ant*** despise

ap·pre·ci·a·tion \ə-ˌprē-shē-'ā-shən\ *n* **1 a :** sensitive awareness; *esp* : recognition of aesthetic values **b :** JUDGMENT, EVALUATION; *esp* : a favorable critical estimate **c :** an expression of admiration, approval, or gratitude **2 :** increase in value

ap·pre·cia·tive \ə-'prē-shət-iv *also* -shē-ˌāt-\ *adj* : having or showing appreciation — **ap·pre·cia·tive·ly** *adv* — **ap·pre·cia·tive·ness** *n*

ap·pre·hend \ˌap-ri-'hend\ *vb* [ME *apprehenden,* fr. L *apprehendere,* lit., to seize, fr. *ad-* + *prehendere* to seize — more at PREHENSILE] *vt* **1 :** ARREST, SEIZE ⟨~ a thief⟩ **2 a :** to become aware of : PERCEIVE **b :** to anticipate esp. with anxiety, dread, or fear **3 :** to grasp with the understanding : recognize the meaning of ~ *vi* : UNDERSTAND, GRASP ***syn*** see FORESEE

ap·pre·hen·si·ble \ˌap-ri-'hen(t)-sə-bəl\ *adj* : capable of being apprehended — **ap·pre·hen·si·bly** \-blē\ *adv*

ap·pre·hen·sion \ˌap-ri-'hen-chən\ *n* [ME, fr. LL *apprehension-, apprehensio,* fr. L *apprehensus,* pp. of *apprehendere*] **1 a :** the act or power of perceiving or comprehending ⟨a man of dull ~⟩ **b :** the result of apprehending mentally : CONCEPTION ⟨according to popular ~⟩ **2 :** seizure by legal process : ARREST **3 :** suspicion or fear esp. of future evil : FOREBODING

ap·pre·hen·sive \-'hen(t)-siv\ *adj* **1 :** capable of apprehending or quick to do so : DISCERNING **2 :** having apprehension : COGNIZANT **3 :** viewing the future with anxiety or alarm ***syn*** see FEARFUL ***ant*** confident — **ap·pre·hen·sive·ly** *adv* — **ap·pre·hen·sive·ness** *n*

¹ap·pren·tice \ə-'prent-əs\ *n* [ME *aprentis,* fr. MF, fr. OF, fr. *aprendre* to learn, fr. L *apprendere, apprehendere*] **1 a :** one bound by indenture to serve another for a prescribed period with a view to learning an art or trade **b :** one who is learning by practical experience under skilled workers a trade, art, or calling **2 :** an inexperienced person : NOVICE ⟨an ~ in cooking⟩ — **ap·pren·tice·ship** \-ə(sh)-ˌship, -əs-ˌship\ *n*

²apprentice *vt* **-ticed; -tic·ing :** to set at work as an apprentice; *esp* : to bind to an apprenticeship by contract or indenture

ap·pressed \a-'prest\ *adj* [L *appressus,* pp. of *apprimere* to press to, fr. *ad-* + *premere* to press — more at PRESS] : pressed close to or lying flat against something ⟨leaves ~ against the stem⟩

ap·prise \ə-'prīz\ *vt* **ap·prised; ap·pris·ing** [F *appris,* pp. of *apprendre* to learn, teach, fr. OF *aprendre*] : to give notice to : TELL ***syn*** see INFORM

ap·prize \ə-'prīz\ *vt* **ap·prized; ap·priz·ing** [ME *apprisen,* fr. MF *aprisier,* fr. OF, fr. *a-* (fr. L *ad-*) + *prisier* to appraise — more at PRIZE] : VALUE, APPRECIATE

¹ap·proach \ə-'prōch\ *vb* [ME *approchen,* fr. OF *aprochier,* fr. LL *appropiare,* fr. L *ad-* + *prope* near; akin to L *pro* before — more at FOR] *vt* **1 a :** to draw closer to : NEAR ⟨~ the podium⟩ **b :** to come very near to : be almost the same as ⟨its mathematics ~*es* mysticism —Theodore Sturgeon⟩ **2 a :** to make advances to esp. in order to create a desired result ⟨was ~*ed* by several Broadway producers⟩ **b :** to take preliminary steps toward accomplishment or full knowledge or experience of ⟨~ the subject with an open mind⟩ ~ *vi* **1 :** to draw nearer ⟨dawn ~*es*⟩ **2 :** to make an approach in golf ***syn*** see MATCH

²approach *n* **1 a :** an act or instance of approaching ⟨the ~ of summer⟩ **b :** APPROXIMATION ⟨in this book he makes his closest ~ to greatness⟩ **2 a :** the taking of preliminary steps toward a particular purpose ⟨experimenting with new lines of ~⟩ **b :** a particular manner of taking such steps ⟨a highly individual ~ to language⟩ **3 :** a means of access : AVENUE **4 a :** a golf shot from the fairway toward the green **b :** the steps taken by a bowler before he delivers the ball; *also* : the part of the alley behind the foul line from which the bowler delivers the ball

ap·proach·able \ə-'prō-chə-bəl\ *adj* : capable of being approached : ACCESSIBLE; *specif* : easy to meet or deal with — **ap·proach·abil·i·ty** \-ˌprō-chə-'bil-ət-ē\ *n*

ap·pro·bate \'ap-rə-ˌbāt\ *vt* **-bat·ed; -bat·ing** [ME *approbaten,* fr. L *approbatus,* pp. of *approbare*] : APPROVE, SANCTION — **ap·pro·ba·to·ry** \'ap-rə-bə-ˌtōr-ē, ə-'prō-bə-, -ˌtȯr-\ *adj*

ap·pro·ba·tion \ˌap-rə-'bā-shən\ *n* **1** *obs* **:** PROOF **2 a :** an act of approving formally or officially **b :** COMMENDATION, PRAISE

¹ap·pro·pri·ate \ə-'prō-prē-ˌāt\ *vt* **-at·ed; -at·ing** [ME *appropriaten,* fr. LL *appropriatus,* pp. of *appropriare,* fr. L *ad-* + *proprius* own] **1 :** to take exclusive possession of : ANNEX ⟨no one should ~ a common benefit⟩ **2 :** to set apart for or assign to a particular purpose or use ⟨~ money for the research program⟩ **3 :** to take or make use of without authority or right — **ap·pro·pri·a·ble** \-prē-ə-bəl\ *adj* — **ap·pro·pri·a·tor** \-prē-ˌāt-ər\ *n*

syn APPROPRIATE, PREEMPT, ARROGATE, CONFISCATE *shared meaning element* : to seize high-handedly

²ap·pro·pri·ate \ə-'prō-prē-ət\ *adj* : especially suitable or compatible : FITTING ***syn*** see FIT ***ant*** inappropriate — **ap·pro·pri·ate·ly** *adv* — **ap·pro·pri·ate·ness** *n*

ap·pro·pri·a·tion \ə-ˌprō-prē-'ā-shən\ *n* **1 :** an act or instance of appropriating **2 :** something that has been appropriated; *specif* : money set aside by formal action for a specific use — **ap·pro·pri·a·tive** \-'prō-prē-ˌāt-iv\ *adj*

ap·prov·able \ə-'prü-və-bəl\ *adj* : capable of being approved — **ap·prov·ably** \-blē\ *adv*

ap·prov·al \ə-'prü-vəl\ *n* : an act or instance of approving : APPROBATION — **on approval :** subject to a prospective buyer's acceptance or refusal ⟨took the suit home *on approval*⟩

ap·prove \ə-'prüv\ *vb* **ap·proved; ap·prov·ing** [ME *approven,* fr. OF *aprover,* fr. L *approbare,* fr. *ad-* + *probare* to prove — more at PROVE] *vt* **1** *obs* **:** PROVE, ATTEST **2 :** to have or express a favorable opinion of ⟨couldn't ~ his conduct⟩ **3 a :** to accept as satisfactory ⟨hopes he will ~ the date of the meeting⟩ **b :** to give formal or official sanction to : RATIFY ⟨Congress *approved* the proposed budget⟩ ~ *vi* : to take a favorable view ⟨doesn't ~ of fighting⟩ — **ap·prov·ing·ly** \-'prü-viŋ-lē\ *adv*

ə abut	ᵊ kitten	ər further	a back	ā bake	ä cot, cart
au̇ out	ch chin	e less	ē easy	g gift	i trip	ī life
j joke	ŋ sing	ō flow	ȯ flaw	ȯi coin	th thin	t͟h this
ü loot	u̇ foot	y yet	yü few	yu̇ furious	zh vision

syn APPROVE, ENDORSE, SANCTION, ACCREDIT, CERTIFY *shared meaning element* : to hold or express a favorable opinion **ant** disapprove
approved school *n, Brit* : a school for juvenile delinquents
approx *abbr* approximate; approximately
¹ap·prox·i·mate \ə-'präk-sə-mət\ *adj* [LL *approximatus,* pp. of *approximare* to come near, fr. L *ad-* + *proximare* to come near — more at PROXIMATE] **1** : nearly correct or exact **2** : located close together ⟨~ leaves⟩ — **ap·prox·i·mate·ly** *adv*
²ap·prox·i·mate \-,māt\ *vb* **-mat·ed; -mat·ing** *vt* **1 a** : to bring near or close **b** : to bring (cut edges of tissue) together **2** : to come near to or be close to in position, value or characteristics ⟨a child tries to ~ his parents' speech⟩ ~ *vi* : to come close
ap·prox·i·ma·tion \ə-,präk-sə-'mā-shən\ *n* **1** : the act or process of drawing together **2** : the quality or state of being close or near ⟨an ~ to the truth⟩ **3** : something that is approximate; *esp* : a mathematical quantity that is close in value to but not the same as a desired quantity — **ap·prox·i·ma·tive** \-'präk-sə-,māt-iv\ *adj* — **ap·prox·i·ma·tive·ly** *adv*
appt *abbr* appoint; appointed; appointment
apptd *abbr* appointed
ap·pur·te·nance \ə-'pərt-nən(t)s, -ᵊn-ən(t)s\ *n* **1** : an incidental right (as a right-of-way) attached to a principal property right and passing in possession with it **2** : a subordinate part or adjunct ⟨the ~ of welcome is fashion and ceremony—Shak.⟩ **3** *pl* : accessory objects : APPARATUS
ap·pur·te·nant \ə-'pərt-nənt, -ᵊn-ənt\ *adj* [ME *apertenant,* fr. MF, fr. OF, prp. of *apartenir* to belong — more at APPERTAIN] **1** : constituting a legal accompaniment **2** : AUXILIARY, ACCESSORY — **appurtenant** *n*
Apr *abbr* April
aprax·ia \(')ā-'prak-sē-ə\ *n* [NL, fr. Gk, inaction, fr. *a-* + *praxis* action, fr. *prassein* to do — more at PRACTICAL] : loss or impairment of the ability to execute complex coordinated movements — **aprac·tic** \-'prak-tik\ *or* **aprax·ic** \-'prak-sik\ *adj*
après-ski \,äp-,rä-'skē, ,ap-\ *n* [F *après* after + *ski* ski, skiing] : social activity (as at a ski lodge) after a day's skiing — **après-ski** *adj*
apri·cot \'ap-rə-,kät, 'ā-prə-\ *n, often attrib* [alter. of earlier *abrecock,* deriv. of Ar *al-birqūq* the apricot] **1 a** : the oval orange-colored fruit of a temperate-zone tree (*Prunus armeniaca*) resembling the related peach and plum in flavor **b** : a tree that bears apricots **2** : a variable color averaging a moderate orange
April \'ā-prəl\ *n* [ME, fr. OF & L; OF *avrill,* fr. L *Aprilis*] : the 4th month of the Gregorian calendar
April fool *n* : the butt of a joke or trick played on April Fools' Day; *also* : such a joke or trick
April Fools' Day *n* : April 1 characteristically marked by the playing of practical jokes
a pri·o·ri \,ä-prē-'ō(ə)r-ē, ap-rē-; ,ā-(,)prī-'ō(ə)r-,ī, ,ä-prē-'ō(ə)r-ē; -'ó(ə)r-\ *adj* [L, from the former] **1 a** : DEDUCTIVE **b** : relating to or derived by reasoning from self-evident propositions — compare A POSTERIORI **c** : presupposed by experience **2** : being without examination or analysis : PRESUMPTIVE — **a priori** *adv* — **apri·or·i·ty** \-'ór-ət-ē\ *n*
apron \'ā-prən, -pərn\ *n, often attrib* [ME, alter. (resulting fr. incorrect division of *a napron*) of *napron,* fr. MF *naperon,* dim. of *nape* cloth, modif. of L *mappa* napkin — more at MAP] **1** : a garment usu. of cloth, plastic, or leather usu. tied around the waist and used to protect clothing or adorn a costume **2** : something that suggests or resembles an apron in shape, position, or use: as **a** : the lower member under the sill of the interior casing of a window **b** : an upward or downward vertical extension of a sink or lavatory **c** : a piece of waterproof cloth spread out (as before the seat of a vehicle) as a protection from rain or mud **d** : a covering (as of sheet metal) for protecting parts of machinery **e** : an endless belt for carrying material **f** : an extensive fan-shaped deposit of detritus **g** : the part of the stage in front of the proscenium arch **h** : the area along the waterfront edge of a pier or wharf **i** : a shield (as of concrete, planking, or brushwood) along the bank of a river, along a seawall, or below a dam **j** : the extensive paved part of an airport immediately adjacent to the terminal area or hangars
apron string *n* : the string of an apron — usu. used in pl. as a symbol of dominance or complete control ⟨though 40 years old he was still tied to his mother's *apron strings*⟩
¹ap·ro·pos \,ap-rə-'pō, 'ap-rə-,\ *adv* [F *à propos,* lit., to the purpose] **1** : at an opportune time : SEASONABLY **2** : by the way
²apropos *adj* : being both relevant and opportune **syn** see RELEVANT
³apropos *prep* : apropos of
apropos of *prep* : with regard to : CONCERNING
apse \'aps\ *n* [ML & L; ML *apsis,* fr. L] **1** : a projecting part of a building (as a church) that is usu. semicircular in plan and vaulted — see BASILICA illustration **2** : APSIS 1
ap·si·dal \'ap-səd-ᵊl\ *adj* : of or relating to an apse
ap·sis \'ap-səs\ *n, pl* **ap·si·des** \-sə-,dēz\ [NL *apsid-, apsis,* fr. L, arch, orbit, fr. Gk *hapsid-, hapsis,* fr. *haptein* to fasten] **1** : the point in an astronomical orbit at which the distance of the body from the center of attraction is either greatest or least **2** : APSE 1
¹apt \'apt\ *adj* [ME, fr. L *aptus,* lit., fastened, fr. pp. of *apere* to fasten; akin to L *apisci* to reach, *apud* near, Skt *āpta* fit] **1** : unusually fitted or qualified : READY ⟨proved an ~ tool in the hands of the conspirators⟩ **2 a** : having a tendency : LIKELY ⟨plants ~ to suffer from drought⟩ **b** : ordinarily disposed : INCLINED ⟨~ to accept what is plausible as true⟩ **3** : suited to a purpose; *esp* : being to the point ⟨an ~ quotation⟩ **4** : keenly intelligent and responsive **syn 1** see FIT **ant** inapt, inept **2** see QUICK — **apt·ly** \'ap-(t)lē\ *adv* — **apt·ness** \'ap(t)-nəs\ *n*
²apt *abbr* **1** apartment **2** aptitude
ap·ter·ous \'ap-tə-rəs\ *adj* [Gk *apteros,* fr. *a-* + *pteron* wing — more at FEATHER] : lacking wings ⟨~ insects⟩
ap·ter·yx \'ap-tə-riks\ *n* [NL, fr. *a-* + Gk *pteryx* wing; akin to Gk *pteron*] : KIWI
ap·ti·tude \'ap-tə-,t(y)üd\ *n* **1** : capacity for learning : APTNESS **2 a** : INCLINATION, TENDENCY **b** : a natural ability : TALENT **3** : general suitability **syn** see GIFT — **ap·ti·tu·di·nal** \,ap-tə-'t(y)üd-nəl, -ᵊn-əl\ *adj* — **ap·ti·tu·di·nal·ly** \-ē\ *adv*
ap·y·rase \'ap-ə-,rās, -,rāz\ *n* [adenosine + *py*rophosphate + *-ase*] : any of several enzymes that hydrolyze ATP with the liberation of phosphate
aq *abbr* aqua; aqueous
aqua \'ak-wə, 'äk-\ *n, pl* **aquae** \'ak-(,)wē, 'äk-,wī\ *or* **aquas** [L— more at ISLAND] **1** : WATER; *esp* : an aqueous solution (as of a volatile substance) **2** : a light greenish blue color
aqua·cade \'ak-wə-,kād, 'äk-\ *n* [*Aquacade,* a water entertainment spectacle orig. at Cleveland, Ohio (1937)] : a water spectacle that consists usu. of exhibitions of swimming and diving with musical accompaniment
Aqua·dag \-,dag\ *trademark* — used for a colloidal suspension of fine particles of graphite in water for use as a lubricant
aqua·for·tis \,ak-wə-'fört-əs, ,äk-\ *n* [NL *aqua fortis,* lit., strong water] : NITRIC ACID
aqua·lung·er \'ak-wə-,ləŋ-ər, 'äk-\ *n* [fr. *Aqua-lung,* a trademark] : SCUBA DIVER
aqua·ma·rine \,ak-wə-mə-'rēn, ,äk-\ *n* [NL *aqua marina,* fr. L, sea water] **1** : a transparent beryl that is blue, blue-green, or green in color **2** : a pale blue to light greenish blue
aqua·naut \'ak-wə-,nöt, 'äk-\ *n* [L *aqua* + E *-naut* (as in *aeronaut*)] : a scuba diver who lives and operates both inside and outside an underwater shelter for an extended period
aqua·plane \'ak-wə-,plān, 'äk-\ *n* : a board towed behind a speeding motorboat and ridden by a person standing on it — **aquaplane** *vi* — **aqua·plan·er** *n*
aqua pu·ra \,ak-wə-'pyür-ə, ,äk-\ *n* [L] : pure water
aqua re·gia \-'rē-j(ē-)ə\ *n* [NL, lit., royal water] : a mixture of nitric and hydrochloric acids that dissolves gold or platinum
aqua·relle \,ak-wə-'rel, ,äk-\ *n* [F, fr. obs. It *acquarella* (now *acquerello*), fr. *acqua* water, fr. L *aqua*] : a drawing usu. in transparent watercolor — **aqua·rell·ist** \-'rel-əst\ *n*
aquar·ist \ə-'kwar-əst, -'kwer-\ *n* : one who keeps an aquarium
aquar·i·um \ə-'kwar-ē-əm, -'kwer-\ *n, pl* **-i·ums** *or* **-ia** \-ē-ə\ [L, watering place for cattle, fr. neut. of *aquarius* of water, fr. *aqua*] **1** : a container (as a glass tank) or an artificial pond in which living aquatic animals or plants are kept **2** : an establishment where aquatic collections of living organisms are kept and exhibited
Aquar·i·us \-ē-əs\ *n* [L (gen. *Aquarii*), lit., water carrier] **1** : a constellation south of Pegasus pictured as a man pouring water **2 a** : the 11th sign of the zodiac in astrology — see ZODIAC table **b** : one born under this sign
¹aquat·ic \ə-'kwät-ik, -'kwat-\ *adj* **1** : growing or living in or frequenting water **2** : taking place in or on water ⟨~ sports⟩ — **aquat·i·cal·ly** \-i-k(ə-)lē\ *adv*
²aquatic *n* **1** : an aquatic animal or plant **2** *pl but sing or pl in constr* : water sports
aqua·tint \'ak-wə-,tint, 'äk-\ *n* [It *acqua tinta* dyed water] : a method of etching a printing plate so that tones similar to watercolor washes can be reproduced; *also* : a print made from a plate so etched — **aquatint** *vt* — **aqua·tint·er** *n* — **aqua·tint·ist** \-əst\ *n*
aqua·vit \'äk-wə-,vēt\ *n* [Sw, Dan & Norw *akvavit,* fr. ML *aqua vitae*] : a clear Scandinavian liquor flavored with caraway seeds
aqua vi·tae \,ak-wə-'vīt-ē, ,äk-\ *n* [ME, fr. ML, lit., water of life] **1** : ALCOHOL **2** : a strong alcoholic liquor
aq·ue·duct \'ak-wə-,dəkt\ *n* [L *aquaeductus,* fr. *aquae* (gen. of *aqua*) + *ductus* act of leading — more at DUCT] **1 a** : a conduit for water; *esp* : one for carrying a large quantity of flowing water **b** : a structure for conveying a canal over a river or hollow **2** : a canal or passage in a part or organ
aque·ous \'ā-kwē-əs, 'ak-wē-\ *adj* [ML *aqueus,* fr. L *aqua*] **1 a** : of, relating to, or resembling water **b** : made from, with, or by water **2** : of or relating to the aqueous humor — **aque·ous·ly** *adv*
aqueous humor *n* : a limpid fluid occupying the space between the crystalline lens and the cornea of the eye
aqui·cul·ture *or* **aqua·cul·ture** \'ak-wə-,kəl-chər, 'äk-\ *n* [L *aqua* + E *-culture* (as in *agriculture*)] **1** : the cultivation of the natural produce of water **2** : HYDROPONICS — **aqui·cul·tur·al** \,ak-wə-'kəlch-(ə-)rəl, ,äk-\ *adj*
aqui·fer \'ak-wə-fər, 'äk-\ *n* [NL, fr. L *aqua* + *-fer*] : a water-bearing stratum of permeable rock, sand, or gravel — **aquif·er·ous** \a-'kwif-ə-rəs, ä-\ *adj*
Aq·ui·la \'ak-wə-lə\ *n* [L (gen. *Aquilae*), lit., eagle] : a northern constellation in the Milky Way southerly from Lyra and Cygnus
aq·ui·le·gia \,ak-wə-'lē-j(ē-)ə\ *n* [NL] : COLUMBINE
aq·ui·line \'ak-wə-,līn, -lən\ *adj* [L *aquilinus,* fr. *aquila* eagle] **1** : of, relating to, or resembling an eagle **2** : curving like an eagle's beak ⟨an ~ nose⟩ — **aq·ui·lin·i·ty** \,ak-wə-'lin-ət-ē\ *n*
aquiv·er \ə-'kwiv-ər\ *adj* : marked by trembling or quivering ⟨all ~ with excitement⟩
¹ar \'är\ *n* [ME] : the letter *r*
²ar *abbr* arrival; arrive
Ar *symbol* argon
AR *abbr* **1** acknowledgment of receipt **2** all rail **3** all risks **4** annual return **5** Arkansas **6** army regulation **7** autonomous republic
-ar \ər *also* ,är\ *adj suffix* [ME, fr. L *-aris,* alter. of *-alis* -al] : of or relating to ⟨molecul*ar*⟩ : being ⟨spectacul*ar*⟩ : resembling ⟨oracul*ar*⟩
¹Ar·ab \'ar-əb, *in sense 2 often* 'ā-,rab\ *n* [ME, fr. L *Arabus, Arabs,* fr. Gk *Arab-, Araps,* fr. Ar *'Arab*] **1 a** : a member of the Semitic people of the Arabian peninsula **b** : a member of an Arabic-speaking people **2** *not cap* : STREET ARAB **3** : a horse of the stock used by the natives of Arabia and adjacent regions; *specif* : a horse of a breed noted for its graceful build, speed, intelligence, and spirit — **Arab** *adj*
²Arab *abbr* Arabian; Arabic
¹ar·a·besque \,ar-ə-'besk\ *adj* [F, fr. It *arabesco* Arabian in fashion, fr. *Arabo* Arab, fr. L *Arabus*] : of, relating to, or being in the style of arabesque

[2]**arabesque** *n* **1 :** an ornament or style that employs flower, foliage, or fruit and sometimes animal and figural outlines to produce an intricate pattern of interlaced lines **2 :** a posture in ballet in which the body is bent forward from the hip on one leg with the corresponding arm extended forward and the other arm and leg backward **3 :** a contrived intricate pattern of verbal expression ⟨~s of alliteration —C. E. Montague⟩

arabesque 1

Ara·bi·an coffee \ə-ˌrā-bē-ən-\ *n* **:** COFFEE TREE 1a
Arabian horse *n* **:** ARAB 3
[1]**Ar·a·bic** \ˈar-ə-bik\ *adj* **1 :** of, relating to, or characteristic of Arabia or the Arabs **2 :** of, relating to, or constituting Arabic **3 :** expressed in or utilizing Arabic numerals
[2]**Arabic** *n* **:** a Semitic language orig. of the Arabs of the Hejaz and Nejd that is now the prevailing speech of Arabia, Jordan, Lebanon, Syria, Iraq, Egypt, and parts of northern Africa
Arabic alphabet *n* **:** the alphabet of 28 letters derived from the Aramaic which is used for writing Arabic and also with adaptations for numerous other languages of Asia, Africa, and Europe of peoples professing the Muslim religion
arab·i·cize \ə-ˈrab-ə-ˌsīz\ *vt* **-cized; -ciz·ing** *often cap* **1 :** to adapt (a language or elements of a language) to the phonetic or structural pattern of Arabic **2 :** ARABIZE 1
Arabic numeral *n* **:** one of the number symbols 0, 1, 2, 3, 4, 5, 6, 7, 8, 9 — see NUMBER table
arab·i·nose \ə-ˈrab-ə-ˌnōs, -ˌnōz\ *n* [ISV *arabin* (the solid principle in gum arabic, fr. *gum arabic* + *-in*) + *-ose*] **:** a crystalline aldose sugar $C_5H_{10}O_5$ of the pentose class
ara·bi·no·side \ˌar-ə-ˈbin-ə-ˌsīd, ə-ˈrab-ə-nō-ˌsīd\ *n* **:** a glycoside that yields arabinose on hydrolysis
Ar·ab·ist \ˈar-ə-bəst\ *n* **:** a specialist in the Arabic language or in Arabic culture
ar·ab·ize \ˈar-ə-ˌbīz\ *vt* **-ized; -iz·ing** *often cap* **1 a :** to cause to acquire Arabic customs, manners, speech, or outlook **b :** to modify (a racial or national stock) by an admixture of Arab blood **2 :** ARABICIZE 1
[1]**ar·a·ble** \ˈar-ə-bəl\ *adj* [MF or L; MF, fr. L *arabilis,* fr. *arare* to plow; akin to OE *erian* to plow, Gk *aroun*] **:** fit for or cultivated by plowing or tillage — **ar·a·bil·i·ty** \ˌar-ə-ˈbil-ət-ē\ *n*
[2]**arable** *n* **:** land that is tilled or tillable
arach·nid \ə-ˈrak-nəd, -ˌnid\ *n* [deriv. of Gk *arachnē* spider] **:** any of a class (Arachnida) of arthropods comprising mostly air-breathing invertebrates, including the spiders and scorpions, mites, and ticks, and having a segmented body divided into two regions of which the anterior bears four pairs of legs but no antennae — **arachnid** *adj*
[1]**arach·noid** \ə-ˈrak-ˌnȯid\ *n* [NL *arachnoides,* fr. Gk *arachnoeidēs,* like a cobweb, fr. *arachnē* spider, spider's web] **:** a thin membrane of the brain and spinal cord that lies between the dura mater and the pia mater
[2]**arachnoid** *adj* **1 :** of or relating to the arachnoid ⟨the ~ membrane⟩ **2 :** covered with or composed of soft loose hairs or fibers
[3]**arachnoid** *adj* [deriv. of Gk *arachnē*] **:** resembling or related to the arachnids
ara·go·nite \ə-ˈrag-ə-ˌnīt, ˈar-ə-gə-\ *n* [G *aragonit,* fr. *Aragon,* Spain] **:** a mineral $CaCO_3$ consisting like calcite of calcium carbonate but differing from calcite in its orthorhombic crystallization, greater density, and less distinct cleavage — **ara·go·nit·ic** \ə-ˌrag-ə-ˈnit-ik, ˌar-ə-gə-\ *adj*
Ar·a·mae·an \ˌar-ə-ˈmē-ən\ *n* [L *Aramaeus,* fr. Gk *Aramaios,* fr. Heb *ʼĂrām* Aram, ancient name for Syria] **1 :** a member of a Semitic people of the second millennium B.C. in Syria and Upper Mesopotamia **2 :** ARAMAIC — **Aramaean** *adj*
Ar·a·ma·ic \ˌar-ə-ˈmā-ik\ *n* **:** a Semitic language known since the ninth century B.C. as the speech of the Aramaeans and later used extensively in southwest Asia as a commercial and governmental language and adopted as their customary speech by various non-Aramaean peoples including the Jews after the Babylonian exile
Aramaic alphabet *n* **1 :** an extinct North Semitic alphabet dating from the ninth century B.C. which was for several centuries the commercial alphabet of southwest Asia and the parent of other alphabets (as Syriac and Arabic) **2 :** the square Hebrew alphabet as distinguished from the early Hebrew alphabet
ara·ne·id \ə-ˈrā-nē-əd, ˌar-ə-ˈ\ *n* [deriv. of L *aranea* spider] **:** SPIDER 1 — **ar·a·ne·idal** \ˌar-ə-ˈnē-əd-ᵊl\ *adj* — **ar·a·ne·idan** \-əd-ᵊn\ *adj or n*
Arap·a·ho *or* **Arap·a·hoe** \ə-ˈrap-ə-ˌhō\ *n, pl* **Arapaho** *or* **Arapahos** *or* **Arapahoe** *or* **Arapahoes :** a member of an Amerindian people of the plains region ranging from Saskatchewan and Manitoba to New Mexico and Texas
ar·a·pai·ma \ˌar-ə-ˈpī-mə\ *n* [Pg & Sp, of Tupian origin; akin to Mura *uarapâinu* pirarucu] **:** PIRARUCU
ar·a·ro·ba \ˌar-ə-ˈrō-bə\ *n* [Pg, of Tupian origin; akin to Tupi *araribá,* a Brazilian tree] **:** GOA POWDER
Arau·ca·ni·an \ə-ˌrau̇-ˈkän-ē-ən, ˌar-ˌȯ-ˈkän-\ *also* **Arau·can** \ə-ˈrau̇-kən\ *n* [Sp *araucano,* fr. *Arauco,* province in Chile] **1 :** a member of a group of Indian peoples of south central Chile and adjacent regions of Argentina **2 :** the language of the Araucanian people that constitutes an independent language family — **Araucanian** *adj*
ar·au·car·ia \ˌar-ˌȯ-ˈkar-ē-ə\ *n* [NL, genus name, fr. *Arauco*] **:** any of a genus (*Araucaria*) of So. American or Australian trees of the pine family — **ar·au·car·i·an** \-ē-ən\ *adj*
Ar·a·wak \ˈar-ə-ˌwäk\ *n, pl* **Arawak** *or* **Arawaks 1 :** a member of an American Indian people of the Arawakan group now living chiefly along the coast of Guyana **2 :** the language of the Arawak people
Ar·a·wak·an \ˌar-ə-ˈwäk-ən\ *n, pl* **Arawakan** *or* **Arawakans 1 :** a member of a group of Indian peoples of South America and the West Indies **2 :** the language family of the Arawakan peoples

ar·ba·lest *or* **ar·ba·list** \ˈär-bə-ləst\ *n* [ME *arblast,* fr. OE, fr. OF *arbaleste,* fr. LL *arcuballista,* fr. L *arcus* bow + *ballista* — more at ARROW] **:** CROSSBOW; *esp* **:** a medieval military weapon with a steel bow used to throw balls, stones, and quarrels — **ar·ba·lest·er** \-ˌles-tər\ *n*
ar·bi·ter \ˈär-bət-ər\ *n* [ME *arbitre,* fr. MF, fr. L *arbitr-, arbiter*] **1 :** a person with power to decide a dispute **:** JUDGE **2 :** a person or agency having absolute power of judging and determining
arbiter el·e·gan·ti·a·rum \-ˌel-ə-ˌgan-shē-ˈar-əm, -ˈer-\ *n* [L, arbiter of refinements] **:** one who prescribes, rules on, or is a recognized authority on matters of social behavior and taste
ar·bi·tra·ble \ˈär-bə-trə-bəl, är-ˈbi-\ *adj* **:** subject to decision by arbitration
[1]**ar·bi·trage** \ˈär-bə-ˌträzh\ *n* [F, fr. MF, arbitration, fr. OF, fr. *arbitrer* to render judgment, fr. L *arbitrari,* fr. *arbitr-, arbiter*] **:** simultaneous purchase and sale of the same or equivalent security in order to profit from price discrepancies
[2]**arbitrage** *vi* **-traged; -trag·ing :** to engage in arbitrage
ar·bi·tra·geur \ˌär-bə-(ˌ)trä-ˈzhər\ *or* **ar·bi·trag·er** \ˈär-bə-ˌträzh-ər\ *n* [F *arbitrageur,* fr. *arbitrage* + *eur* -or] **:** one that practices arbitrage
ar·bi·tral \ˈär-bə-trəl\ *adj* **:** of or relating to arbiters or arbitration
ar·bit·ra·ment \är-ˈbi-trə-mənt\ *n* [ME, fr. MF *arbitrement,* fr. *arbitrer*] **1** *archaic* **:** the right or power of deciding **2 :** the settling of a dispute by an arbiter **:** ARBITRATION **3 :** the judgment given by an arbitrator
ar·bi·trary \ˈär-bə-ˌtrer-ē\ *adj* **1 :** depending on choice or discretion; *specif* **:** determinable by decision of a judge or tribunal **2 a :** arising from will or caprice **b :** selected at random and without reason **3 :** DESPOTIC, TYRANNICAL ⟨~ rule⟩ — **ar·bi·trari·ly** \ˌär-bə-ˈtrer-ə-lē\ *adv* — **ar·bi·trari·ness** \ˈär-bə-ˌtrer-ē-nəs\ *n*
ar·bi·trate \ˈär-bə-ˌtrāt\ *vb* **-trat·ed; -trat·ing** *vi* **:** to act as arbitrator ⟨a committee appointed to ~ between the company and the union⟩ ~ *vt* **1 :** to act as arbiter upon **2 :** to submit or refer for decision to an arbiter ⟨agreed to ~ their differences⟩ **3** *archaic* **:** DECIDE, DETERMINE — **ar·bi·tra·tive** \-ˌtrāt-iv\ *adj*
ar·bi·tra·tion \ˌär-bə-ˈtrā-shən\ *n* **:** the act of arbitrating; *esp* **:** the hearing and determination of a case in controversy by a person chosen by the parties or appointed under statutory authority — **ar·bi·tra·tion·al** \-shnəl, -shən-ᵊl\ *adj*
ar·bi·tra·tor \ˈär-bə-ˌtrāt-ər\ *n* **1 :** a person chosen to settle differences between two parties in controversy **2 :** ARBITER
[1]**ar·bor** \ˈär-bər\ *n* [ME *erber* plot of grass, arbor, fr. OF *herbier* plot of grass, fr. *herbe* herb, grass] **:** a bower of vines or branches or of latticework covered with climbing shrubs or vines
[2]**arbor** *n* [L, tree, shaft] **1 a :** a main shaft or beam **b :** a spindle or axle of a wheel **c :** a shaft on which a revolving cutting tool is mounted **d :** a spindle on a cutting machine that holds the work to be cut **2** *pl* **ar·bo·res** \ˈär-bə-ˌrēz\ **:** a tree as distinguished from a shrub
Arbor Day *n* [L *arbor* tree] **:** a day designated for planting trees
ar·bo·re·al \är-ˈbōr-ē-əl, -ˈbȯr-\ *adj* [L *arboreus* of a tree, fr. *arbor*] **1 :** of, relating to, or resembling a tree **2 :** inhabiting or frequenting trees ⟨~ monkeys⟩ — **ar·bo·re·al·ly** \-ə-lē\ *adv*
ar·bo·re·ous \-ē-əs\ *adj* **1 :** WOODED **2 :** ARBOREAL ⟨an ~ palm⟩ ⟨an ~ bird⟩
ar·bo·res·cence \ˌär-bə-ˈres-ᵊn(t)s\ *n* **:** the condition of being arborescent
ar·bo·res·cent \-ᵊnt\ *adj* **:** resembling a tree in properties, growth, structure, or appearance — **ar·bo·res·cent·ly** *adv*
ar·bo·re·tum \ˌär-bə-ˈrēt-əm\ *n, pl* **-retums** *or* **-re·ta** \-ˈrēt-ə\ [NL, fr. L, place grown with trees, fr. *arbor*] **:** a place where trees, shrubs, and herbaceous plants are cultivated for scientific and educational purposes
ar·bo·ri·cul·ture \ˈär-bə-rə-ˌkəl-chər; är-ˈbōr-ə-, -ˈbȯr-\ *n* [[2]*arbor* + *-i-* + *culture*] **:** the cultivation of trees and shrubs esp. for ornament — **ar·bo·ri·cul·tur·ist** \ˌär-bə-rə-ˈkəlch-(ə-)rəst; är-ˌbōr-ə-, -ˌbȯr-\ *n*
ar·bor·ist \ˈär-bə-rəst\ *n* **:** a specialist in the care and maintenance of trees
ar·bo·ri·za·tion \ˌär-bə-rə-ˈzā-shən\ *n* **:** formation of or into an arborescent figure or arrangement; *also* **:** such a figure or arrangement
ar·bo·rize \ˈär-bə-ˌrīz\ *vi* **-rized; -riz·ing :** to branch freely and repeatedly
ar·bor·vi·tae \ˌär-bər-ˈvīt-ē\ *n* [NL *arbor vitae,* lit., tree of life] **:** any of various evergreen trees (esp. genus *Thuja*) of the pine family that usu. have closely overlapping or compressed scale leaves and are often grown for ornament and in hedges
ar·bour *chiefly Brit var of* ARBOR
ar·bo·vi·rus \ˌär-bə-ˈvī-rəs\ *n* [*ar*thropod-*bo*rne *virus*] **:** any of various viruses transmitted by arthropods and including the causative agents of encephalitis, yellow fever, and dengue
ar·bu·tus \är-ˈbyüt-əs\ *n* [NL, genus name, fr. L, strawberry tree] **1 :** any of a genus (*Arbutus*) of shrubs and trees of the heath family with white or pink flowers and scarlet berries **2 :** a trailing plant (*Epigaea repens*) of the heath family that occurs in eastern No. America and bears fragrant pinkish flowers in early spring
[1]**arc** \ˈärk\ *n* [ME *ark,* fr. MF *arc* bow, fr. L *arcus* bow, arch, arc — more at ARROW] **1 :** the apparent path described above and below the horizon by a celestial body (as the sun) **2 :** something arched or curved **3 :** a sustained luminous discharge of electricity across a gap in a circuit or between electrodes; *also* **:** ARC LAMP **4 :** a continuous portion (as of a circle or ellipse) of a curved line
[2]**arc** *vi* **1 :** to form an electric arc **2 :** to follow an arc-shaped course

ə abut ᵊ kitten ər further a back ā bake ä cot, cart
au̇ out ch chin e less ē easy g gift i trip ī life
j joke ŋ sing ō flow ȯ flaw ȯi coin th thin th this
ü loot u̇ foot y yet yü few yu̇ furious zh vision

³arc adj [arc sine arc or angle (corresponding to the) sine (of so many degrees)] : INVERSE 2 — used with the trigonometric functions and hyperbolic functions (~ sine)

ARC abbr American Red Cross

ar-cade \är-'kād\ n [F, fr. It arcata, fr. arco arch, fr. L arcus] 1 : a long arched building or gallery 2 : an arched covered passageway or avenue (as between shops) 3 : a series of arches with their columns or piers

ar-cad-ed \-'kād-əd\ adj : formed in or furnished or decorated with arches or arcades

ar-ca-dia \är-'kād-ē-ə\ n, often cap [Arcadia, region of ancient Greece frequently chosen as background for pastoral poetry] : a region or scene of simple pleasure and quiet

Ar-ca-di-an \är-'kād-ē-ən\ n 1 often not cap : a person who lives a simple quiet life 2 : a native or inhabitant of Arcadia 3 : the dialect of ancient Greek used in Arcadia — arcadian adj, often cap

ar-cad-ing \är-'kād-iŋ\ n : a series of arches or arcades in the construction or decoration esp. of a building

Ar-ca-dy \'är-kəd-ē\ n : ARCADIA

ar-cane \är-'kān\ adj [L arcanus] : known or knowable only to one having the key : SECRET (~ rites) syn see MYSTERIOUS

ar-ca-num \är-'kā-nəm\ n, pl -na \-nə\ [L, fr. neut. of arcanus secret, fr. arca chest — more at ARK] 1 : mysterious knowledge known only to the initiate 2 : ELIXIR 1

arc cosecant n : the inverse function to the cosecant (if y is the cosecant of θ, then θ is the arc cosecant of y) — symbol arc csc or csc⁻¹

arc cosine n : the inverse function to the cosine (if y is the cosine of θ, then θ is the arc cosine of y) — symbol arc cos or cos⁻¹

arc cotangent n : the inverse function to the cotangent (if y is the cotangent of θ, then θ is the arc cotangent of y) — symbol arc cot or cot⁻¹

¹arch \'ärch\ n [ME arche, fr. OF, fr. (assumed) VL arca, fr. L arcus — more at ARROW] 1 : a typically curved structural member spanning an opening and serving as a support (as for the wall or other weight above the opening) 2 a : something resembling an arch in form or function; esp : either of two vaulted portions of the bony structure of the foot that impart elasticity to it b : a curvature having the form of an arch : ARCHWAY

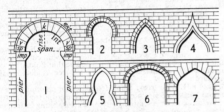

arches 1: 1 round: imp impost, sp springer, v voussoir, k keystone, ext extrados, int intrados, 2 horseshoe, 3 lancet, 4 ogee, 5 trefoil, 6 basket-handle, 7 Tudor

²arch vt 1 : to cover or provide with an arch 2 : to form or bend into an arch ~ vi 1 : to form an arch 2 : to take an arch-shaped course

³arch adj [arch-] 1 : PRINCIPAL, CHIEF (an arch-villain) 2 [arch- (as in archrogue) a : cleverly sly and alert b : playfully saucy syn see SAUCY — arch-ly adv — arch-ness n

⁴arch abbr 1 archaic 2 archery 3 architect; architectural; architecture

¹arch- prefix [ME arche-, arch-, fr. OE & OF; OE arce-, fr. LL arch- & L archi-; OF arch-, fr. LL arch- & L archi-; fr. Gk arch-, archi-, fr. archein to begin, rule; akin to Gk archē beginning, rule, archos ruler] 1 : chief : principal (archenemy) 2 : extreme : most fully embodying the qualities of his or its kind (archrogue)

²arch- — see ARCHI-

¹arch \'ärk, in a few words also ərk\ n comb form [ME -arche, fr. OF & L & L; OF -arche, fr. LL -archa, fr. L -arches, -archus, fr. Gk -archēs, -archos, fr. archein] : ruler : leader (matriarch)

²arch \'ärk\ adj comb form [prob. fr. G, fr. Gk archē beginning] : having (such) a point or (so many) points of origin (endarch)

archae- or archaeo- also archeo- comb form [Gk archaio-, fr. archaios ancient, fr. archē beginning] : ancient : primitive (Archaeopteryx) (Archeozoic)

ar-chae-ol-o-gist or ar-che-ol-o-gist \är-kē-'äl-ə-jəst\ n : a specialist in archaeology

ar-chae-ol-o-gy or ar-che-ol-o-gy \-jē\ n [F archéologie, fr. LL archaeologia antiquarian lore, fr. Gk archaiologia, fr. archaio- + -logia -logy] 1 : the scientific study of material remains (as fossil relics, artifacts, and monuments) of past human life and activities 2 : remains of the culture of a people : ANTIQUITIES — ar-chae-o-log-i-cal \-kē-ə-'läj-i-kəl\ adj — ar-chae-o-log-i-cal-ly \-k(ə-)lē\ adv

ar-chae-op-ter-yx \är-kē-'äp-tə-riks\ n [NL, genus name, fr. archae- + Gk pteryx wing; akin to Gk pteron wing — more at FEATHER] : a primitive bird (genus Archaeopteryx) of the Upper Jurassic period of Europe with reptilian characteristics

ar-chae-or-nis \är-kē-'or-nəs\ n [NL, genus name, fr. archae- + Gk ornis bird — more at ERNE] : any of a genus (Archaeornis) of Upper Jurassic toothed birds

ar-cha-ic \är-'kā-ik\ adj [F or Gk; F archaïque, fr. Gk archaïkos, fr. archaios] 1 : of, relating to, or characteristic of an earlier or more primitive time : ANTIQUATED (~ legal traditions) 2 : having the characteristics of the language of the past and surviving chiefly in specialized uses 3 : surviving from an earlier period; specif : typical of a previously dominant evolutionary stage syn see OLD ant up-to-date — ar-cha-i-cal-ly \-i-k(ə-)lē\ adv

archaic smile n : an expression that resembles a smile and is characteristic of early Greek sculpture

ar-cha-ism \'är-kē-,iz-əm, -,()kā-,iz-\ n [NL archaïsmus, fr. Gk archaïsmos, fr. archaios] 1 : the use of archaic diction or style 2 : an instance of archaic usage 3 : something that is outmoded or old-fashioned (judicial ~) — ar-cha-ist \-əst\ n — ar-cha-is-tic \,är-kē-'is-tik, -,()kā-\ adj — ar-cha-ize \'är-kē-,īz, -,()kā-\ vb

arch-an-gel \'är-,kān-jəl\ n [ME, fr. OF or LL; OF archangele, fr. LL archangelus, fr. Gk archangelos, fr. arch- + angelos angel] 1 : a chief angel 2 pl : an order of angels — see CELESTIAL HIERARCHY — arch-an-gel-ic \,är-(,)kan-'jel-ik\ adj

arch-bish-op \(')ärch-'bish-əp\ n [ME, fr. OE arcebiscop, fr. LL archiepiscopus, fr. LGk archiepiskopos, fr. archi- + episkopos bishop — more at BISHOP] : a bishop at the head of an ecclesiastical province or one of equivalent honorary rank — arch-bish-op-ric \-ə-(,)prik\ n

arch-dea-con \(')ärch-'dē-kən\ n [ME archedeken, fr. OE arcediacon, fr. LL archidiaconus, fr. LGk archi- + diakonos deacon] : a clergyman having the duty of assisting a diocesan bishop in ceremonial functions or administrative work — arch-dea-con-ate \-kə-nət\ n

arch-dea-con-ry \-kən-rē\ n, pl -ries : the district or residence of an archdeacon

arch-di-o-cese \(')ärch-'dī-ə-səs, -,sēz, -,sēs\ n : the diocese of an archbishop — arch-di-oc-e-san \,ärch-dī-'äs-ə-sən\ adj

arch-du-cal \(')ärch-'d(y)ü-kəl\ adj [F archiducal, fr. archiduc] : of or relating to an archduke or archduchy

arch-duch-ess \'ärch-,dəch-əs\ n [F archiduchesse, fem. of archiduc archduke, fr. MF archeduc] 1 : the wife or widow of an archduke 2 : a woman having in her own right a rank equal to that of an archduke

arch-duchy \-'dəch-ē\ n [F archiduché, fr. MF archeduché, fr. archeduc arch- + duché duchy] : the territory of an archduke or archduchess

arch-duke \-'d(y)ük\ n [MF archeduc, fr. arche- arch- + duc duke] 1 : a sovereign prince 2 : a prince of the imperial family of Austria — arch-duke-dom \-dəm\ n

Ar-che-an or Ar-chae-an \är-'kē-ən\ adj [Gk archaios] : of, relating to, or being the earlier part of the Precambrian era or the oldest known group of rocks; also : PRECAMBRIAN — Archean n

arched \'ärcht\ adj : made with, formed in, or covered with an arch (an ~ beam) (an ~ door)

ar-che-go-ni-al \,är-ki-'gō-nē-əl\ adj : of or relating to an archegonium; also : ARCHEGONIATE

¹ar-che-go-ni-ate \-nē-ət\ adj : bearing archegonia

²archegoniate n : a plant (as a moss, fern, horsetail, or club moss) that bears archegonia

ar-che-go-ni-um \-nē-əm\ n, pl -nia \-nē-ə\ [NL, fr. Gk archegonos originator, fr. archein to begin + gonos procreation; akin to Gk gignesthai to be born — more at ARCH-, KIN] : the flask-shaped female sex organ of mosses, ferns, and some gymnosperms

arch-en-e-my \(')är-'chen-ə-mē\ n, pl -mies : a principal enemy

arch-en-ter-on \är-'kent-ə-,rän, -rən\ n [NL] : the cavity of the gastrula of an embryo

archeol abbr archeology

Ar-cheo-zo-ic also Ar-chaeo-zo-ic \,är-kē-ə-'zō-ik\ adj : of, relating to, or being the earliest era of geological history; also : relating to the system of rocks formed in this era — see GEOLOGIC TIME table — Archeozoic n

ar-cher \'är-chər\ n [ME, fr. OF, fr. LL arcarius, alter. of arcuarius, fr. arcuarius of a bow, fr. L arcus bow — more at ARROW] 1 : one who uses a bow and arrow — called also bowman 2 cap : SAGITTARIUS

ar-chery \'ärch-(ə-)rē\ n 1 : the art, practice, or skill of shooting with bow and arrow 2 : an archer's weapons 3 : a body of archers

ar-che-spore \'är-ki-,spō(ə)r, -,spȯ(ə)r\ or ar-che-spo-ri-um \,är-ki-'spȯr-ē-əm, -'spȯr-\ n, pl -spores or -spo-ria \-ē-ə\ [NL archesporium, fr. arche- (as in archegonium) + -sporium (fr. spora spore)] : the cell or group of cells from which spore mother cells develop — ar-che-spo-ri-al \,är-ki-'spȯr-ē-əl, -'spȯr-\ adj

ar-che-type \'är-ki-,tīp\ n [L archetypum, fr. Gk archetypon, fr. neut. of archetypos archetypal, fr. archein + typos type] 1 : the original pattern or model of which all things of the same type are representations or copies : PROTOTYPE 2 : IDEA 1a 3 : an inherited idea or mode of thought in the psychology of C. G. Jung that is derived from the experience of the race and is present in the unconscious of the individual — ar-che-typ-al \,är-ki-'tī-pəl\ or ar-che-typ-i-cal \-'tip-i-kəl\ adj — ar-che-typ-al-ly \-pə-lē\ or ar-che-typ-i-cal-ly \-i-k(ə-)lē\ adv

arch-fiend \(')ärch-'fēnd\ n : a chief fiend; esp : SATAN

archi- or arch- prefix [F or L; F, fr. L, fr. Gk — more at ARCH-] 1 : chief : principal (archiblast) 2 : primitive : original : primary (archenteron) (archicarp)

ar-chi-carp \'är-ki-,kärp\ n : the female sex organ in ascomycetous fungi consisting usu. of a filamentous trichogyne and a basal fertile ascogonium

ar-chi-di-ac-o-nal \,är-ki-dī-'ak-ən-³l\ adj [LL archidiaconus archdeacon] : of or relating to an archdeacon

ar-chi-epis-co-pal \,är-kē-ə-'pis-kə-pəl\ adj [ML archiepiscopalis, fr. LL archiepiscopus archbishop — more at ARCHBISHOP] : of or relating to an archbishop — ar-chi-epis-co-pal-ly \-pə-lē\ adv — ar-chi-epis-co-pate \-pət, -,pāt\ n

ar-chil \'är-chəl\ n [ME orchell] 1 : a violet dye obtained from lichens (genera Roccella and Lecanora) 2 : a plant that yields archil

ar-chi-man-drite \,är-kə-'man-,drīt\ n [LL archimandrites, fr. LGk archimandritēs, fr. Gk archi- + LGk mandra monastery, fr. Gk, fold, pen] : a dignitary in an Eastern church ranking below a bishop; specif : the superior of a large monastery or group of monasteries

Ar-chi-me-des' screw \,är-kə-,mēd-ēz-\ n : a device made of a tube bent spirally around an axis or of a broad-threaded screw encased by a cylinder and used to raise water

ar·chi·pe·lag·ic \ˌär-kə-pə-ˈlaj-ik, ˌär-chə-\ *adj* : of, relating to, or located in an archipelago

ar·chi·pel·a·go \ˌär-kə-ˈpel-ə-ˌgō, ˌär-chə-\ *n, pl* **-goes** *or* **-gos** [*Archipelago* Aegean sea, fr. It *Arcipelago,* lit., chief sea, fr. *arci-* (fr. L *archi-*) + Gk *pelagos* sea — more at FLAKE] **1** : an expanse of water with many scattered islands **2** : a group of islands

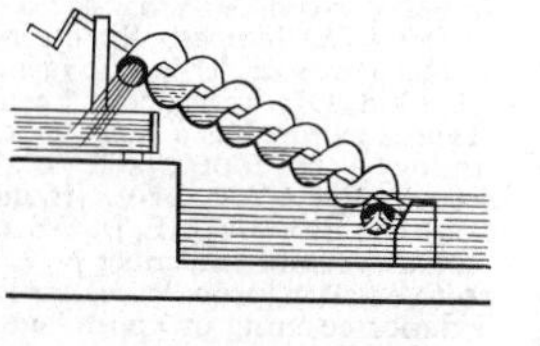
Archimedes' screw

ar·chi·tect \ˈär-kə-ˌtekt\ *n* [MF *architecte,* fr. L *architectus,* fr. Gk *architektōn* master builder, fr. *archi-* + *tektōn* builder, carpenter — more at TECHNICAL] **1** : one who designs buildings and superintends their construction **2** : one who plans and achieves a difficult objective ⟨the great ~ of the military victory —*Time*⟩

ar·chi·tec·ton·ic \ˌär-kə-ˌtek-ˈtän-ik\ *adj* [L *architectonicus,* fr. Gk *architektonikos,* fr. *architektōn*] **1** : of, relating to, or according with the principles of architecture : ARCHITECTURAL **2** : resembling architecture in structure or organization — **ar·chi·tec·ton·i·cal·ly** \-i-k(ə-)lē\ *adv*

ar·chi·tec·ton·ics \-ˈtän-iks\ *n pl but sing or pl in constr, also* **ar·chi·tec·ton·ic** \-ik\ **1** : the science of architecture **2 a** : the structural design of an entity **b** : the system of structure

ar·chi·tec·tur·al \ˌär-kə-ˈtek-chə-rəl, -ˈtek-shrəl\ *adj* : of, relating to, or conforming to the rules of architecture — **ar·chi·tec·tur·al·ly** \-ē\ *adv*

ar·chi·tec·ture \ˈär-kə-ˌtek-chər\ *n* **1** : the art or science of building; *specif* : the art or practice of designing and building structures and esp. habitable ones **2** : formation or construction as or as if as the result of conscious act **3** : architectural product or work **4** : a method or style of building

ar·chi·trave \ˈär-kə-ˌtrāv\ *n* [MF, fr. OIt, fr. *archi-* + *trave* beam, fr. L *trabs* — more at THORP] **1** : the lowest division of an entablature resting in classical architecture immediately on the capital of the column — see ENTABLATURE illustration **2** : the molding around a rectangular opening (as a door)

ar·chi·val \är-ˈkī-vəl\ *adj* : relating to, contained in, or constituting archives

¹ar·chive \ˈär-ˌkīv\ *n* [F & L; F, fr. L *archivum,* fr. Gk *archeion* government house (in pl., official documents), fr. *archē* rule, government — more at ARCH-] : a place in which public records or historical documents are preserved; *also* : the material preserved — often used in pl.

²archive *vt* **ar·chived; ar·chiv·ing** : to file or collect (as records or documents) in an archive or other repository

ar·chi·vist \ˈär-kə-vəst, -ˌkī-\ *n* : a person in charge of archives

ar·chi·volt \ˈär-kə-ˌvōlt\ *n* [It *archivolto,* fr. ML *archivoltum*] : an ornamental molding around an arch corresponding to an architrave

ar·chon \ˈär-ˌkän, -kən\ *n* [L, fr. Gk *archōn,* fr. prp. of *archein*] **1** : a chief magistrate in ancient Athens **2** : a presiding officer

arch·priest \(ˈ)ärch-ˈprēst\ *n* : a priest who occupies a preeminent position

arch·way \ˈärch-ˌwā\ *n* : a way or passage under an arch; *also* : an arch over a passage

-ar·chy \ˌär-kē, *in a few words also* ər-kē\ *n comb form* [ME *-archie,* fr. MF, fr. L *-archia,* fr. Gk, fr. *archein* to rule — more at ARCH-] : rule : government ⟨squire*archy*⟩

arc lamp *n* : an electric lamp that produces light by an arc made when a current passes between two incandescent electrodes surrounded by gas — called also *arc light*

ar·co \ˈär-(ˌ)kō\ *adv or adj* [It, fr. *arco* bow, fr. L *arcus*] : with the bow — usu. used as a direction in music for players of stringed instruments; compare PIZZICATO

arc secant *n* : the inverse function to the secant ⟨if y is the secant of θ, then θ is the *arc secant of* y⟩ — symbol *arc sec or* sec^{-1}

arc sine *n* : the inverse function to the sine ⟨if y is the sine of θ, then θ is the *arc sine of* y⟩ — symbol *arc sin or* sin^{-1}

arc tangent *n* : the inverse function to the tangent ⟨if y is the tangent of θ, then θ is the *arc tangent of* y⟩ — symbol *arc tan or* tan^{-1}

¹arc·tic \ˈärk-tik, ˈärt-ik\ *adj* [ME *artik,* fr. L *arcticus,* fr. Gk *arktikos,* fr. *arktos* bear, Ursa Major, north; akin to L *ursus* bear] **1** *often cap* : of or relating to the region around the north pole to approximately 65° N **2 a** : bitter cold : FRIGID **b** : cold in temper or mood ⟨an ~ smile⟩ — **arc·ti·cal·ly** \-(t)i-k(ə-)lē\ *adv*

²arc·tic \ˈärt-ik, ˈärk-tik\ *n* : a rubber overshoe reaching to the ankle or above

arctic circle *n, often cap A&C* : the parallel of latitude that is approximately 66½ degrees north of the equator and that circumscribes the northern frigid zone

Arc·tu·rus \ärk-ˈt(y)u̇r-əs\ *n* [L, fr. Gk *Arktouros,* lit., bear watcher] : a giant fixed star of the first magnitude in Boötes

ar·cu·ate \ˈär-kyə-wət, -ˌwāt\ *adj* [L *arcuatus,* pp. of *arcuare* to bend like a bow, fr. *arcus* bow] : curved like a bow ⟨an ~ cloud⟩ ⟨an ~ view of a leaf⟩ — **ar·cu·ate·ly** *adv*

-ard \ərd\ *also* **-art** \ərt\ *n suffix* [ME, fr. OF, of Gmc origin; akin to OHG *-hart* (in personal names such as *Gērhart* Gerard), OE *heard* hard] : one that is characterized by performing some action, possessing some quality, or being associated with some thing esp. conspicuously or excessively ⟨bragg*art*⟩ ⟨dull*ard*⟩ ⟨poll*ard*⟩

ar·deb \ˈär-ˌdeb\ *n* [Ar *ardabb, irdabb*] : any of numerous Egyptian units of capacity; *esp* : the customs unit equal to 5.44 imperial or 5.619 U.S. bushels

ar·dent \ˈärd-ᵊnt\ *adj* [ME, fr. MF, fr. L *ardent-, ardens* prp. of *ardēre*] **1** : characterized by warmth of feeling typically expressed in eager zealous support or activity **2** : FIERY, HOT ⟨an ~ sun⟩ **3** : SHINING, GLOWING ⟨~ eyes⟩ ***syn*** see IMPASSIONED ***ant*** cool — **ar·den·cy** \-ᵊn-sē\ *n* — **ar·dent·ly** *adv*

ardent spirits *n pl* : strong distilled liquors

ar·dor \ˈärd-ər\ *n* [ME *ardour,* fr. MF & L; MF, fr. L *ardor,* fr. *ardēre* to burn; akin to OHG *essa* forge, L *aridus* dry] **1 a** : an often restless or transitory warmth of feeling ⟨the sudden ~ *s* of youth⟩ **b** : extreme vigor or energy : INTENSITY **c** : ZEAL, LOYALTY **2** : strong or burning heat ***syn*** see PASSION

ar·dour *chiefly Brit var of* ARDOR

ar·du·ous \ˈärj-(ə-)wəs\ *adj* [L *arduus* high, steep, difficult; akin to ON *ǫrthigr* high, steep, Gk *orthos* straight] **1 a** : hard to accomplish or achieve : DIFFICULT ⟨years of ~ training⟩ **b** : marked by great labor or effort : STRENUOUS ⟨a life of ~ toil —A. C. Cole⟩ **2** : hard to climb : STEEP ***syn*** see HARD ***ant*** light, facile — **ar·du·ous·ly** *adv* — **ar·du·ous·ness** *n*

¹are [ME, fr. OE *earun;* akin to ON *eru, erum* are, OE *is* is] *pres 2d sing or pres pl of* BE

²are \ˈa(ə)r, ˈe(ə)r, ˈär\ *n* [F, fr. L *area*] — see METRIC SYSTEM table

ar·ea \ˈar-ē-ə, ˈer-\ *n* [L, piece of level ground, threshing floor, fr. *arēre* to be dry; akin to L *ardor*] **1** : a level piece of ground **2** : the surface included within a set of lines; *specif* : the number of unit squares equal in measure to the surface — see METRIC SYSTEM table, WEIGHT table **3** : AREAWAY ⟨went down the steps into the ~ of a house —James Joyce⟩ **4** : a particular extent of space or surface or one serving a special function **5** : the scope of a concept, operation, or activity : FIELD ⟨the whole ~ of foreign policy⟩ **6** : a part of the cerebral cortex having a particular function — **ar·e·al** \-ē-əl\ *adj* — **ar·e·al·ly** \-ə-lē\ *adv*

area code *n* : a 3-digit number that identifies each telephone service area in a country (as the U.S. or Canada)

area·way \ˈar-ē-ə-ˌwā, ˈer-\ *n* : a sunken space affording access, air, and light to a basement

are·ca \ə-ˈrē-kə, ˈar-i-kə\ *n* [NL, genus name, fr. Pg, fr. Malayalam *atekka*] : any of several tropical Asian palms (*Areca* or related genera); *esp* : BETEL PALM

arec·o·line \ə-ˈrek-ə-ˌlēn\ *n* [ISV *areca* + *-ol* + *-ine*] : a toxic alkaloid $C_8H_{13}NO_2$ that has parasympathomimetic effects, is used as a veterinary anthelmintic, and occurs naturally in betel nuts

are·na \ə-ˈrē-nə\ *n* [L *harena, arena* sand, sandy place] **1** : an area in a Roman amphitheater for gladiatorial combats **2 a** : an enclosed area used for public entertainment **b** : a building containing an arena **3** : a sphere of interest or activity : SCENE ⟨the political ~⟩

ar·e·na·ceous \ˌar-ə-ˈnā-shəs\ *adj* [L *arenaceus,* fr. *arena*] **1** : resembling, made of, or containing sand or sandy particles **2** : growing in sandy places

arena theater *n* : a theater in which the stage is located in the center of the auditorium — called also *theater-in-the-round*

ar·e·nic·o·lous \ˌar-ə-ˈnik-ə-ləs\ *adj* [L *arena* + E *-i-* + *-colous*] : living, burrowing, or growing in sand

aren't \(ˈ)ärnt, ˈär-ənt\ **1** : are not **2** : am not — used in questions

ar·eo·cen·tric \ˌar-ē-ō-ˈsen-trik\ *adj* [Gk *Areios* of Ares, fr. *Arēs*] : having or relating to the planet Mars as a center

are·o·la \ə-ˈrē-ə-lə\ *n, pl* **-lae** \-ˌlē\ *or* **-las** [NL, fr. L, small open space, dim. of *area*] : a small area between things or about something; *esp* : a colored ring (as about the nipple, a vesicle, or a pustule) — **are·o·lar** \-lər\ *adj* — **are·o·late** \-lət\ *adj* — **are·o·la·tion** \ə-ˌrē-ə-ˈlā-shən, ˌar-ē-ə-\ *n*

ar·e·ole \ˈar-ē-ˌōl\ *n* : a small pit or cavity

Ar·e·op·a·gite \ˌar-ē-ˈäp-ə-ˌjīt, -ˌgīt\ *n* : a member of the Areopagus — **Ar·e·op·a·git·ic** \-ˌäp-ə-ˈjit-ik\ *adj*

Ar·e·op·a·gus \-ˈäp-ə-gəs\ *n* [L, fr. Gk *Areios pagos,* fr. *Areios pagos* (lit., hill of Ares), a hill in Athens where the tribunal met] : the supreme tribunal of Athens

Ar·es \ˈa(ə)r-(ˌ)ēz, ˈe(ə)r-\ *n* [Gk *Arēs*] : the Greek god of war — compare MARS

arête \ə-ˈrāt\ *n* [F, lit., fish bone, fr. LL *arista,* fr. L, beard of grain] : a sharp-crested ridge in rugged mountains

ar·e·thu·sa \ˌar-ə-ˈth(y)ü-zə\ *n* [L, fr. Gk *Arethousa*] **1** *cap* : a wood nymph who fleeing the advances of the river god Alpheus was changed into a fountain **2** : any of a genus (*Arethusa*) of bog orchids with a single linear leaf and solitary purple flower

arg *abbr* **1** argent **2** argument

Arg *abbr* Argyll

ar·ga·li \ˈär-gə-lē\ *n* [Mongolian] : a large Asiatic wild sheep (*Ovis ammon*) noted for its large horns; *also* : any of several other large wild sheep (as the bighorn)

Ar·gand diagram \ˌär-ˌgän-, -ˌgan-\ *n* [John Robert *Argand* †1825 F mathematician] : a conventional diagram in which the complex number $x + iy$ is represented by the point whose rectangular coordinates are x and y

ar·gent \ˈär-jənt\ *n* [ME, fr. MF & L; MF, fr. L *argentum;* akin to L *arguere* to make clear, Gk *argyros* silver, *argos* white] **1** *archaic* : the metal silver; *also* : WHITENESS **2** : the heraldic color silver or white — **argent** *adj*

ar·gen·tic \är-ˈjent-ik\ *adj* : of, relating to, or containing silver esp. when bivalent

ar·gen·tif·er·ous \ˌär-jən-ˈtif-(ə-)rəs\ *adj* : producing or containing silver

¹ar·gen·tine \ˈär-jən-ˌtīn, -ˌtēn\ *adj* : SILVER, SILVERY

²argentine *n* : SILVER; *also* : any of various materials resembling it

ar·gen·tite \ˈär-jən-ˌtīt\ *n* : native silver sulfide Ag_2S having a metallic luster and dark lead-gray color and constituting a valuable ore of silver

ar·gen·tous \är-ˈjent-əs\ *adj* : of, relating to, or containing silver esp. when univalent

ar·gil \ˈär-jəl\ *n* [ME, fr. L *argilla,* fr. Gk *argillos;* akin to Gk *argos* white] : CLAY; *esp* : potter's clay

ar·gil·la·ceous \ˌär-jə-ˈlā-shəs\ *adj* : of, relating to, or containing clay or clay minerals : CLAYEY

ə abut	ᵊ kitten	ər further	a back	ā bake	ä cot, cart
au̇ out	ch chin	e less	ē easy	g gift	i trip	ī life
j joke	ŋ sing	ō flow	ȯ flaw	ȯi coin	th thin	t͟h this
ü loot	u̇ foot	y yet	yü few	yu̇ furious	zh vision

ar·gil·lite \'är-jə-ˌlīt\ *n* : a compact argillaceous rock differing from shale in being cemented by silica and from slate in having no slaty cleavage

ar·gi·nase \'är-jə-ˌnās, -ˌnāz\ *n* [ISV] : a crystalline enzyme that converts naturally occurring arginine into ornithine and urea

ar·gi·nine \'är-jə-ˌnēn\ *n* [G *arginin*] : a crystalline basic amino acid $C_6H_{14}N_4O_2$ derived from guanidine

Ar·give \'är-ˌjīv, -ˌgīv\ *adj* [L *Argivus*, fr. Gk *Argeios*, lit., of Argos, fr. *Argos* city-state of ancient Greece] : of or relating to the Greeks or Greece and esp. the Achaean city of Argos or the surrounding territory of Argolis — **Argive** *n*

Ar·go \'är-(ˌ)gō\ *n* [L (gen. *Argus*), fr. Gk *Argō*] : a large constellation in the southern hemisphere lying principally between Canis Major and the Southern Cross

ar·gol \'är-ˌgȯl\ *n* [ME *argoile*] : crude tartar deposited in wine casks during aging

ar·gon \'är-ˌgän\ *n* [Gk, neut. of *argos* idle, lazy, fr. *a-* + *ergon* work; fr. its relative inertness — more at WORK] : a colorless odorless gaseous element found in the air and in volcanic gases and used esp. as a filler for electric bulbs and electron tubes — see ELEMENT table

ar·go·naut \'är-gə-ˌnȯt, -ˌnät\ *n* [L *Argonautes*, fr. Gk *Argonautēs*, fr. *Argō*, ship in which the Argonauts sailed + *nautēs* sailor — more at NAUTICAL] **1 a** *cap* : one of a band of heroes sailing with Jason in quest of the Golden Fleece **b** : an adventurer engaged in a quest **2** : PAPER NAUTILUS

ar·go·sy \'är-gə-sē\ *n, pl* **-sies** [modif. of It *ragusea* Ragusan vessel, fr. *Ragusa*, Dalmatia (now Dubrovnik, Yugoslavia)] **1** : a large ship; *esp* : a large merchant ship ⟨three of your *argosies* are . . . come to harbor—Shak.⟩ **2** : a fleet of ships **3** : a rich supply ⟨an ~ of railway folklore —F.P. Donovan⟩

ar·got \'är-gət, -(ˌ)gō\ *n* [F] : an often more or less secret vocabulary and idiom peculiar to a particular group ⟨the American Negro has . . . developed his own ~, partly to put the white man off, partly to put him down —Daniel Stern⟩ ***syn*** see DIALECT

ar·gu·able \'är-gyə-wə-bəl\ *adj* : open to argument, dispute, or question — **ar·gu·ably** \-blē\ *adv*

ar·gue \'är-(ˌ)gyü, -gyə(-w)\ *vb* **ar·gued; ar·gu·ing** [ME *arguen*, fr. MF *arguer* to accuse, reason & L *arguere* to make clear; MF *arguer*, fr. L *argutare* to prate, fr. *argutus* clear, noisy, fr. pp. of *arguere*] *vi* **1** : to give reasons for or against something : REASON **2** : to contend or disagree in words : DISPUTE ~ *vt* **1** : to give evidence of : INDICATE **2** : to consider the pros and cons of : DISCUSS **3** : to prove or try to prove by giving reasons : MAINTAIN **4** : to persuade by giving reasons : INDUCE ***syn*** see DISCUSS — **ar·gu·er** \-gyə-wər\ *n*

ar·gu·fy \'är-gyə-ˌfī\ *vb* **-fied; -fy·ing** *vt* : DISPUTE, DEBATE ~ *vi* : WRANGLE — **ar·gu·fi·er** \-ˌfī(-ə)r\ *n*

ar·gu·ment \'är-gyə-mənt\ *n* [ME, fr. MF, fr. L *argumentum*, fr. *arguere*] **1** *obs* : an outward sign : INDICATION **2** : a reason given in proof or rebuttal **3 a** : the act or process of arguing : ARGUMENTATION **b** : a coherent series of reasons offered **c** : QUARREL, DISAGREEMENT **4** : an abstract or summary esp. of a literary work ⟨a later editor added an ~ to the poem⟩ **5** : the subject matter esp. of a literary work **6 a** : one of the independent variables upon whose value that of a function depends **b** : the angle that fixes the direction of a complex number ⟨if $a + bi$ is written as $re^{i\theta} = r(\cos\theta + i\sin\theta)$ then θ is the ~⟩

ar·gu·men·ta·tion \ˌär-gyə-mən-'tā-shən, -ˌmen-\ *n* **1** : the act or process of forming reasons and of drawing conclusions and applying them to a case in discussion **2** : DEBATE, DISCUSSION

ar·gu·men·ta·tive \ˌär-gyə-'ment-ət-iv\ *also* **ar·gu·men·tive** \-'ment-iv\ *adj* **1** : characterized by argument : CONTROVERSIAL **2** : given to argument : DISPUTATIOUS ⟨~ to the point of being cantankerous—J. S. Clarke⟩ — **ar·gu·men·ta·tive·ly** *adv*

ar·gu·men·tum \ˌär-gyə-'ment-əm\ *n, pl* **-men·ta** \-'ment-ə\ [L] : ARGUMENT 3b

Ar·gus \'är-gəs\ *n* [L, fr. Gk *Argos*] **1** : a hundred-eyed monster of Greek legend **2** : a watchful guardian

Ar·gus–eyed \ˌär-gə-'sīd\ *adj* : vigilantly observant

ar·gy–bar·gy \ˌär-gē-'bär-gē\ *n* [redupl. of Sc & E dial. *argy*, alter. of *argue*] *chiefly Brit* : a lively discussion : ARGUMENT, DISPUTE

ar·gyle *also* **ar·gyll** \'är-ˌgīl, är-'\ *n, often cap* [*Argyle, Argyll*, branch of the Scottish clan of Campbell, fr. whose tartan the design was adapted] : a geometric knitting pattern of varicolored diamonds in solid and outline shapes on a single background color; *also* : a sock knit in this pattern

Ar·gy·rol \'är-jə-ˌrȯl, -ˌrōl\ *trademark* — used for a silver-protein compound whose aqueous solution is used as a local antiseptic esp. for mucous membranes

ar·hat \'är-(ˌ)hət\ *n* [Skt, fr. prp. of *arhati* he deserves; akin to Gk *alphein* to gain] : a Buddhist who has reached the stage of enlightenment — **ar·hat·ship** \-ˌship\ *n*

aria \'är-ē-ə\ *n* [It, lit., atmospheric air, modif. of L *aer*] : AIR, MELODY, TUNE; *specif* : an accompanied elaborate melody sung (as in an opera) by a single voice

Ar·i·ad·ne \ˌar-ē-'ad-nē\ *n* [L, fr. Gk *Ariadnē*] : a daughter of Minos who gives Theseus the thread whereby he escapes from the labyrinth

Ar·i·an \'ar-ē-ən, 'er-\ *adj* : of or relating to Arius or his doctrines esp. that the Son is not of the same substance as the Father but was created as an agent for creating the world — **Arian** *n* — **Ar·i·an·ism** \-ə-ˌniz-əm\ *n*

-ar·i·an \'er-ē-ən, 'ar-\ *n suffix* [L *-arius* -ary] **1** : believer ⟨necessitarian⟩ : advocate ⟨latitudin*arian*⟩ **2** : producer ⟨disciplin*arian*⟩

ARIBA *abbr* Associate of the Royal Institute of British Architects

ari·bo·fla·vin·osis \ˌā-ˌrī-bə-ˌflā-və-'nō-səs\ *n* [NL] : a deficiency disease due to inadequate intake of riboflavin

ar·id \'ar-əd\ *adj* [F or L; F *aride*, fr. L *aridus* — more at ARDOR] **1** : excessively dry; *specif* : having insufficient rainfall to support agriculture **2** : lacking in interest and life : JEJUNE ***syn*** see DRY ***ant*** moist, verdant — **arid·i·ty** \ə-'rid-ət-ē, a-\ *n* — **ar·id·ness** \'ar-əd-nəs\ *n*

Ar·i·el \'ar-ē-əl, 'er-\ *n* **1** : a supernatural prankster in Shakespeare's *The Tempest* **2** : the inner satellite of Uranus

Ar·i·es \'ar-ē-ˌēz, 'er-\ *n* [L (gen. *Arietis*), lit., ram; akin to Gk *eriphos* kid, OIr *heirp* doe] **1** : a constellation between Pisces and Taurus pictured as a ram **2 a** : the 1st sign of the zodiac in astrology — see ZODIAC table **b** : one born under this sign

ari·et·ta \ˌär-ē-'et-ə, ˌar-\ *n* [It, dim. of *aria*] : a short aria

aright \ə-'rīt\ *adv* [ME, fr. OE *ariht*, fr. [1]*a-* + *riht* right] : RIGHTLY, CORRECTLY ⟨if I remember ~⟩

ar·il \'ar-əl\ *n* [prob. fr. NL *arillus*, fr. ML, raisin, grape seed] : an exterior covering or appendage of some seeds that develops after fertilization as an outgrowth from the ovule stalk — **ar·iled** \'ar-əld\ *adj* — **ar·il·late** \'ar-ə-ˌlāt\ *adj*

ari·o·so \ˌär-ē-'ō-(ˌ)sō, -(ˌ)zō\ *n, pl* **-sos** *also* **-si** \-(ˌ)sē, -(ˌ)zē\ [It, fr. *aria*] : a musical passage or composition having a mixture of free recitative and metrical song

arise \ə-'rīz\ *vi* **arose** \-'rōz\; **aris·en** \-'riz-ᵊn\; **aris·ing** \-'rī-ziŋ\ [ME *arisen*, fr. OE *ārīsan*, fr. *ā-*, perfective prefix + *rīsan* to rise — more at ABIDE] **1** : to get up : RISE **2 a** : to originate from a source **b** : to come into being or to attention **3** : ASCEND ***syn*** see SPRING

aris·ta \ə-'ris-tə\ *n, pl* **-tae** \-(ˌ)tē, -ˌtī\ *or* **-tas** [NL, fr. L, beard of grain] : a bristlelike structure or appendage — **aris·tate** \-ˌtāt\ *adj*

ar·is·toc·ra·cy \ˌar-ə-'stäk-rə-sē\ *n, pl* **-cies** [MF & LL; MF *aristocratie*, fr. LL *aristocratia*, fr. Gk *aristokratia*, fr. *aristos* best + *-kratia* -cracy] **1** : government by the best individuals or by a small privileged class **2 a** : a government in which power is vested in a minority consisting of those believed to be best qualified **b** : a state with such a government **3** : a governing body or upper class usu. made up of an hereditary nobility **4** : the aggregate of those believed to be superior

aris·to·crat \ə-'ris-tə-ˌkrat, a-; 'ar-ə-stə-\ *n* **1** : a member of an aristocracy; *esp* : NOBLE **2 a** : one who has the bearing and viewpoint typical of the aristocracy **b** : one who favors aristocracy

aris·to·crat·ic \ə-ˌris-tə-'krat-ik, (ˌ)a-ˌris-tə-, ˌar-ə-stə-\ *adj* [MF *aristocratique*, fr. ML *aristocraticus*, fr. Gk *aristokratikos*, fr. *aristos* + *-kratikos* -cratic] **1** : belonging to, having the qualities of, or favoring aristocracy **2 a** : socially exclusive ⟨an ~ neighborhood⟩ **b** : SNOBBISH — **aris·to·crat·i·cal·ly** \-i-k(ə-)lē\ *adv*

Ar·is·to·te·lian *or* **Ar·is·to·te·lean** \ˌar-ə-stə-'tēl-yən\ *adj* [L *Aristoteles* Aristotle, fr. Gk *Aristotelēs*] : of or relating to the Greek philosopher Aristotle or his philosophy — **Aristotelian** *n* — **Ar·is·to·te·lian·ism** \-yə-ˌniz-əm\ *n*

arith *abbr* arithmetic; arithmetical

arith·me·tic \ə-'rith-mə-ˌtik\ *n* [ME *arsmetrik*, fr. OF *arismetique*, fr. L *arithmetica*, fr. Gk *arithmētikē*, fr. fem. of *arithmētikos* arithmetical, fr. *arithmein* to count, fr. *arithmos* number; akin to Gk *arariskein* to fit] **1 a** : a branch of mathematics that deals with real numbers including sometimes the transfinite cardinals and computations with them **b** : a treatise on arithmetic **2** : COMPUTATION, CALCULATION — **ar·ith·met·ic** \ˌar-ith-'met-ik\ *or* **ar·ith·met·i·cal** \-i-kəl\ *adj* — **ar·ith·met·i·cal·ly** \-i-k(ə-)lē\ *adv* — **arith·me·ti·cian** \ə-ˌrith-mə-'tish-ən\ *n*

arithmetic mean *n* : a value that is computed by dividing the sum of a set of terms by the number of terms

arithmetic progression *n* : a progression (as 3, 5, 7, 9) in which the difference between any term and its predecessor is constant

-ar·i·um \'ar-ē-əm, 'er-\ *n suffix, pl* **-ariums** *or* **-ar·ia** \-ē-ə\ [L, fr. neut. of *-arius* -ary] : thing or place relating to or connected with ⟨planet*arium*⟩

Ariz *abbr* Arizona

ark \'ärk\ *n* [ME, fr. OE *arc*; akin to OHG *arahha* ark; both fr. a prehistoric Gmc word borrowed fr. L *arca* chest; akin to L *arcēre* to hold off, defend, Gk *arkein*] **1 a** : a boat or ship held to resemble that in which Noah and his family were preserved from the Deluge **b** : something that affords protection and safety **2 a** : the sacred chest representing to the Hebrews the presence of God among them **b** : a repository traditionally in or against the wall of a synagogue for the scrolls of the Torah

Ark *abbr* Arkansas

[1]arm \'ärm\ *n* [ME, fr. OE *earm*; akin to L *armus* shoulder, Gk *harmos* joint, L *arma* weapons, *ars* skill, Gk *arariskein* to fit] **1** : a human upper limb; *esp* : the part between the shoulder and the wrist **2** : something like or corresponding to an arm: as **a** : the forelimb of a vertebrate **b** : a limb of an invertebrate animal **c** : a branch or lateral shoot of a plant **d** : a slender part of a structure, machine, or an instrument projecting from a main part, axis, or fulcrum **e** : the end of a ship's yard; *also* : the part of an anchor from the crown to the fluke **3** : an inlet of water (as from the sea) **4** : POWER, MIGHT ⟨the long ~ of the law⟩ **5** : a support (as on a chair) for the elbow and forearm **6** : SLEEVE **7** : a functional division of a group or activity ⟨the logistical ~ of the air force⟩ — **armed** \'ärmd\ *adj* — **arm·less** \'ärm-ləs\ *adj* — **arm·like** \-ˌlīk\ *adj*

[2]arm *vb* [ME *armen*, fr. OF *armer*, fr. L *armare*, fr. *arma* weapons, tools] *vt* **1** : to furnish or equip with weapons **2** : to furnish with something that strengthens or protects **3** : to fortify morally **4** : to equip or ready for action or operation ⟨~ a bomb⟩ ~ *vi* : to prepare oneself for struggle or resistance ***syn*** see FURNISH

[3]arm *n* [ME *armes* (pl.) weapons, fr. OF, fr. L *arma*] **1 a** : a means of offense or defense; *esp* : FIREARM **b** : a combat branch (as of an army) **c** : an organized branch of national defense (as the navy) **2** *pl* **a** : the hereditary heraldic devices of a family **b** : heraldic devices adopted by a government **3** *pl* **a** : active hostilities : WARFARE **b** : military service

Arm *abbr* **1** Armagh **2** Armenian

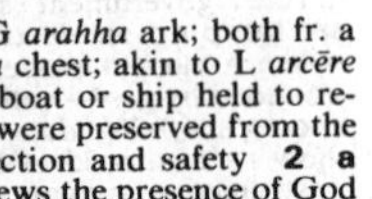
armadillo

ar·ma·da \är-'mäd-ə, -'mad-, -'mād-\ *n* [Sp, fr. ML *armata* army, fleet, fr. L, fem. of *armatus*, pp. of *armare*] **1** : a fleet of warships **2** : a large force of moving things ⟨an ~ of fishing boats⟩

ar·ma·dil·lo \ˌär-mə-'dil-(ˌ)ō\ *n, pl* **-los** [Sp, fr. dim. of *armado* armed one, fr. L *armatus*] : any of several burrowing chiefly nocturnal edentate mammals (family Dasypodidae) of warm parts of the Americas having body and head encased in an armor of small bony plates in which many of them can curl up into a ball when attacked

Ar·ma·ged·don \ˌär-mə-'ged-ᵊn\ n [Gk Armageddōn, Harmagedōn, scene of the battle foretold in Rev 16:14–16] **1 a :** a final and conclusive battle between the forces of good and evil **b :** the site or time of Armageddon **2 :** a vast decisive conflict

Ar·ma·gnac \'är-mən-ˌyak\ n [F, fr. Armagnac, region in southwest France] **:** a brown dry brandy produced in the Gers district of France

ar·ma·ment \'är-mə-mənt\ n [F armement, fr. L armamenta (pl.) utensils, military or naval equipment, fr. armare to arm, equip] **1 :** a military or naval force **2 a :** the aggregate of a nation's military strength **b :** arms and equipment (as of a combat unit) **c :** means of protection or defense : ARMOR **3 :** the process of preparing for war

ar·ma·men·tar·i·um \ˌär-mə-ˌmen-'ter-ē-əm, -mən-\ n, pl **-tar·ia** \-ē-ə\ [L, armory, fr. armamenta] **1 :** the equipment and methods used esp. in medicine **2 :** matter available or utilized for an undertaking or field of activity ⟨a whole ∼ of devices to create an illusion of real life —Kenneth Rexroth⟩

ar·ma·ture \'är-mə-ˌchú(ə)r, -chər, -ˌt(y)ú(ə)r\ n [L armatura armor, equipment, fr. armatus] **1 :** an organ or structure (as teeth or thorns) for offense or defense **2 a :** a piece of soft iron or steel that connects the poles of a magnet or of adjacent magnets **b :** a part which consists essentially of coils of wire around a metal core and in which electric current is induced in a generator or in which the input current interacts with a magnetic field to produce torque in a motor **c :** the movable part of an electromagnetic device (as a loudspeaker) **d :** a framework used by a sculptor to support a figure being modeled in a plastic material

¹arm·chair \'ärm-ˌche(ə)r, -ˌcha(ə)r, 'ärm-'\ n **:** a chair with armrests

²armchair adj **1 :** remote from direct dealing with problems ⟨∼ strategists⟩ **2 :** sharing vicariously in another's experiences ⟨an ∼ traveler⟩

armed forces n pl **:** the combined military, naval, and air forces of a nation

Ar·me·nian \är-'mē-nē-ən, -nyən\ n **1 :** a member of a people dwelling chiefly in Armenia **2 :** the Indo-European language of the Armenians — see INDO-EUROPEAN LANGUAGES table — **Armenian** adj

arm·ful \'ärm-ˌfúl\ n, pl **armfuls** \-ˌfúlz\ or **arms·ful** \'ärmz-ˌfúl\ **:** as much as the arm can hold

arm·hole \'ärm-ˌhōl\ n **:** an opening for the arm in a garment

ar·mi·ger \'är-mi-jər\ n [ML, fr. L, armor-bearer, fr. armiger bearing arms, fr. arma arms + -ger -gerous] **1 :** SQUIRE **2 :** one entitled to bear heraldic arms — **ar·mig·er·al** \är-'mij-ə-rəl\ adj

ar·mig·er·ous \är-'mij-ə-rəs\ adj **:** bearing heraldic arms

ar·mil·la·ry sphere \'är-mə-ˌler-ē-, är-ˌmil-ə-rē-\ n [F sphère armillaire, fr. ML armilla, fr. L, bracelet, iron ring, fr. armus arm, shoulder; akin to OE earm arm] **:** an old astronomical instrument composed of rings representing the positions of important circles of the celestial sphere

Ar·min·i·an \är-'min-ē-ən\ adj **:** of or relating to Arminius or his doctrines opposing the absolute predestination of strict Calvinism and maintaining the possibility of salvation for all — **Arminian** n — **Ar·min·i·an·ism** \-ē-ə-ˌniz-əm\ n

ar·mi·stice \'är-mə-stəs\ n [F or NL; F, fr. NL armistitium, fr. L arma + -stitium (as in solstitium solstice)] **:** temporary suspension of hostilities by agreement between the opponents : TRUCE

Armistice Day n [fr. the armistice terminating World War I on November 11, 1918] **:** VETERANS DAY — used before the official adoption of Veterans Day in 1954

arm·let \'ärm-lət\ n **1 :** a band (as of cloth or metal) worn around the upper arm **2 :** a small arm (as of the sea)

ar·moire \ärm-'wär, 'är-mər\ n [MF, fr. OF armaire, fr. L armarium, fr. arma] **:** a usu. large cupboard, wardrobe, or clothespress

ar·mor \'är-mər\ n [ME armure, fr. OF, fr. L armatura — more at ARMATURE] **1 :** defensive covering for the body; esp **:** covering (as of metal) used in combat **2 :** a quality or circumstance that affords protection ⟨the ∼ of prosperity⟩ **3 a :** a usu. metallic protective covering (as for a ship, fort, airplane, or automobile) **b :** a protective covering (as a diver's suit, the covering of a plant or animal, or a sheathing for wire, cordage, or hose) **4 :** armored forces and vehicles (as tanks) — **armor** vt — **ar·mored** \-mərd\ adj — **ar·mor·less** \-mər-ləs\ adj

¹ar·mor-clad \'är-mər-ˌklad\ adj **:** sheathed in or protected by armor

²armor-clad n **:** an armor-clad warship

armored scale n **:** any of numerous scales constituting a family (Diaspididae) and having a firm covering of wax best developed in the female

ar·mor·er \'är-mər-ər\ n **1 :** one that makes armor or arms **2 :** one that repairs, assembles, and tests firearms

ar·mo·ri·al \är-'mōr-ē-əl, -'mòr-\ adj [armory (heraldry)] **:** of, relating to, or bearing heraldic arms — **ar·mo·ri·al·ly** \-ē-ə-lē\ adv

Ar·mor·i·can \är-'mōr-i-kən, -'mär-\ or **Ar·mor·ic** \-ik\ n **:** a native or inhabitant of Armorica; esp **:** BRETON — **Armorican** or **Armoric** adj

ar·mory \'ärm-(ə-)rē\ n, pl **ar·mor·ies 1 a :** a supply of arms for defense or attack **b :** a collection of available resources **2 :** a place where arms and military equipment are stored; esp **:** one used for training military reserve personnel **3 :** a place where arms are manufactured

ar·mour \'är-mər\ chiefly Brit var of ARMOR

arm·pit \'ärm-ˌpit\ n **:** the hollow beneath the junction of the arm and shoulder

arm·rest \-ˌrest\ n **:** a support for the arm

arm-twist·ing \-ˌtwis-tiŋ\ n **:** the use of direct personal pressure in order to achieve a desired end ⟨for all the ∼, the . . . vote on the measure was unexpectedly tight —Newsweek⟩

arm wrestling n **:** a form of wrestling in which two opponents sit face to face gripping usu. their right hands and setting corresponding elbows firmly on a surface (as a tabletop) in an attempt to force each other's arm down — called also Indian wrestling

ar·my \'är-mē\ n, pl **armies** [ME armee, fr. MF, fr. ML armata — more at ARMADA] **1 a :** a large organized body of men armed and trained for war on land **b :** a unit capable of independent action and consisting usu. of a headquarters, two or more corps, and auxiliary troops **c** often cap **:** the complete military organization of a nation for land warfare **2 :** a great multitude ⟨an ∼ of bicycles —Norm Fruchter⟩ **3 :** a body of persons organized to advance a cause

army ant n **:** any of various nomadic social ants (subfamily Dorylinae)

ar·my·worm \'är-mē-ˌwərm\ n **:** any of numerous moths whose larvae travel in multitudes from field to field destroying grass, grain, and other crops; esp **:** the common armyworm (Pseudaletia unipuncta) of the northern U.S.

ar·ni·ca \'är-ni-kə\ n [NL, genus name] **1 :** any of many composite herbs (genus Arnica) including some with bright yellow ray flowers **2 :** the dried flower heads of an arnica (esp. Arnica montana) used esp. in the form of a tincture as a liniment (as for sprains or bruises); also **:** this tincture

ar·oid \'a(ə)r-ˌòid, 'e(ə)r-\ adj [NL Arum] **:** of or relating to the arum family — **aroid** n

aroint \ə-'ròint\ vb imper [origin unknown] archaic **:** BEGONE ⟨∼ thee, witch —Shak.⟩

aro·ma \ə-'rō-mə\ n [ME aromat spice, fr. OF, fr. L aromat-, aroma, fr. Gk arōmat-, arōma] **1 a :** a distinctive pervasive and usu. pleasant or savory smell; broadly **:** ODOR **b :** the bouquet of a wine **2 :** a distinctive quality or atmosphere : FLAVOR ⟨the ∼ of enjoyment —Stella D. Gibbons⟩ syn see SMELL

¹ar·o·mat·ic \ˌar-ə-'mat-ik\ adj **1 :** of, relating to, or having aroma: **a :** FRAGRANT **b :** having a strong smell **c :** having a distinctive quality **2 :** of, relating to, or characterized by the presence of at least one benzene ring — used of cyclic hydrocarbons and their derivatives — **ar·o·mat·i·cal·ly** \-i-k(ə-)lē\ adv — **aro·ma·tic·i·ty** \ˌar-ə-mə-'tis-ət-ē, ə-ˌrō-mə-\ n — **ar·o·mat·ic·ness** \ˌar-ə-'mat-ik-nəs\ n

²aromatic n **1 :** an aromatic plant, drug, or medicine **2 :** an aromatic organic compound

aro·ma·tize \ə-'rō-mə-ˌtīz\ vt **-tized; -tiz·ing 1 :** to make aromatic **:** FLAVOR **2 :** to convert into one or more aromatic compounds — **aro·ma·ti·za·tion** \-ˌrō-mət-ə-'zā-shən\ n

arose past of ARISE

¹around \ə-'raund\ adv [ME, fr. ¹a- + round] **1 a :** in circumference ⟨a tree five feet ∼⟩ **b :** in, along, or through a circuit ⟨the road goes ∼ by the lake⟩ **2 a :** on all or various sides ⟨papers lying ∼⟩ **b :** in close from all sides so as to surround **c :** NEARBY **3 a :** here and there in various places **b :** to a particular place **4 a :** in rotation or succession **b :** from beginning to end **:** THROUGH ⟨mild the year ∼⟩ **5 :** in or to an opposite direction or position **6 :** in the neighborhood of **:** APPROXIMATELY

²around prep **1 a :** on all sides of **b :** so as to encircle or enclose ⟨seated ∼ the table⟩ **c :** so as to avoid or get past **:** on or to another side of ⟨went ∼ the lake⟩ ⟨got ∼ his objections⟩ **d :** NEAR **2 :** in all directions outward from **3 :** here and there in or throughout ⟨barnstorming ∼ the country⟩ **4 :** so as to have a center or basis in ⟨a society organized ∼ kinship ties⟩

³around adj **1 :** ABOUT **1** ⟨has been up and ∼ for two days⟩ **2 :** being in existence, evidence, or circulation ⟨the most intelligent of the artists ∼ today —R. M. Coates⟩

around-the-clock adj **:** being in effect, continuing, or lasting 24 hours a day **:** CONSTANT

arouse \ə-'rauz\ vb **aroused; arous·ing** [a- (as in arise) + rouse] vt **1 :** to awaken from sleep **2 :** to rouse to action **:** EXCITE ⟨the book aroused debate⟩ ∼ vi **:** to awake from sleep **:** STIR — **arous·al** \-'rau-zəl\ n

ARP abbr air-raid precautions

ar·peg·gio \är-'pej-(ē-)ˌō\ n, pl **-gios** [It, fr. arpeggiare to play on the harp, fr. arpa harp, of Gmc origin; akin to OHG harpha harp] **1 :** production of the tones of a chord in succession and not simultaneously **2 :** a chord played in arpeggio

ar·pent \är-'pän, -'pä(n)z\ n, 'ä(n)z\ [MF] **1 :** any of various old French units of land area; esp **:** one used in French sections of Canada and the U.S. equal to about 0.85 acre **2 :** a unit of length equal to one side of a square arpent

arquebus \'är- var of HARQUEBUS

arr abbr **1** arranged **2** arrival; arrive

ar·rack \'är-ək, ə-'rak\ n [Ar 'araq sweet juice, liquor] **:** an alcoholic beverage of the Far East or Near East; esp **:** one distilled from the juice of the coconut palm or from a mash of rice and molasses

ar·raign \ə-'rān\ vt [ME arreinen, fr. MF araisner, fr. OF, fr. a- (fr. L ad-) + raisnier to speak, fr. (assumed) VL rationare, fr. L ration-, ratio reason — more at REASON] **1 :** to call (a prisoner) before a

armor 1: 1 helmet, 2 gorget, 3 shoulder piece, 4 pallette, 5 breastplate, 6 brassard, 7 elbow piece, 8 skirt of tasses, 9 tuille, 10 gauntlet, 11 cuisse, 12 knee piece, 13 jambeau, 14 solleret

court to answer to an indictment : CHARGE **2** : to accuse of wrong, inadequacy, or imperfection — **ar·raign·ment** \-mənt\ *n*

ar·range \ə-ˈrānj\ *vb* **-ranged; -rang·ing** [ME *arangen*, fr. MF *arangier*, fr. OF, fr. *a-* + *rengier* to set in a row, fr. *reng* row — more at RANK] *vt* **1** : to put into a proper order or into a correct or suitable sequence, relationship, or adjustment ⟨~ flowers in a vase⟩ ⟨~ cards alphabetically⟩ **2** : to make preparations for : PLAN ⟨*arranged* a reception for the visitor⟩ **3** : to bring about an agreement or understanding concerning : SETTLE ⟨~ an exchange of war prisoners⟩ **4 a** : to adapt (a musical composition) by scoring for voices or instruments other than those for which orig. written **b** : ORCHESTRATE ~ *vi* **1** : to bring about an agreement or understanding ⟨*arranged* to have a table at the restaurant⟩ **2** : to make preparations : PLAN ⟨*arranged* for a vacation with his family⟩ ***syn*** **1** see ORDER **2** see NEGOTIATE ***ant*** disarrange, derange — **ar·rang·er** *n*

ar·range·ment \ə-ˈrānj-mənt\ *n* **1 a** : the act of arranging ⟨the ~ of the details was quickly accomplished⟩ **b** : the state of being arranged : ORDER ⟨everything in neat ~⟩ **2** : something arranged: as **a** : a preliminary measure : PREPARATION ⟨travel ~*s*⟩ **b** : an adaptation of a musical composition by rescoring **c** : an informal agreement or settlement esp. on personal, social, or political matters ⟨~*s* under the new regime⟩ **3** : something made by arranging parts or things together ⟨a floral ~⟩

ar·rant \ˈar-ənt\ *adj* [alter. of *errant*] : being notoriously without moderation : EXTREME ⟨we are ~ knaves, all; believe none of us — Shak.⟩ ***syn*** see OUTRIGHT — **ar·rant·ly** *adv*

ar·ras \ˈar-əs\ *n, pl* **arras** [ME, fr. *Arras*, France] **1** : a tapestry of Flemish origin used esp. for wall hangings and curtains **2** : a wall hanging or screen of tapestry

[1]**ar·ray** \ə-ˈrā\ *vt* [ME *arrayen*, fr. OF *arayer*, fr. (assumed) VL *arredare*, fr. L *ad-* + a base of Gmc origin; akin to Goth *garaiths* arranged — more at READY] **1 a** : to set or place in order : draw up : MARSHAL **b** : to set or set forth in order (as a jury) for the trial of a cause **2** : to dress or decorate esp. in splendid or impressive attire : ADORN ***syn*** see LINE — **ar·ray·er** *n*

[2]**array** *n* **1 a** : a regular and imposing grouping or arrangement : ORDER **b** : military order ⟨forces in ~⟩ **c** : an orderly listing of jurors impaneled **d** : a group of individuals or kinds that has a definite modal point forming a center of variation **2 a** : CLOTHING, ATTIRE **b** : rich or beautiful apparel : FINERY **3** : a body of soldiers : MILITIA ⟨the baron and his feudal ~⟩ **4** : an imposing group : large number ⟨faced a whole ~ of problems⟩ **5 a** : a number of mathematical elements arranged in rows and columns **b** : a series of statistical data arranged in classes in order of magnitude **6** : an arrangement of computer memory elements (as magnetic cores) in a single plane

ar·rear \ə-ˈri(ə)r\ *n* [ME *arrere* behind, backward, fr. MF, fr. (assumed) VL *ad retro* backward, fr. L *ad* to + *retro* backward, behind — more at AT, RETRO-] **1** : the state of being behind in the discharge of obligations — usu. used in pl. ⟨in ~*s* with his payments⟩ **2 a** : an unfinished duty — usu. used in pl. ⟨~*s* of work that have piled up⟩ **b** : an unpaid and overdue debt — usu. used in pl. ⟨paying off the ~*s* of the past several months⟩

ar·rear·age \-ij\ *n* **1** : the condition of being in arrears **2** : something that is in arrears; *esp* : something unpaid and overdue

[1]**ar·rest** \ə-ˈrest\ *vt* [ME *aresten*, fr. MF *arester* to rest, arrest, fr. (assumed) VL *arrestare*, fr. L *ad-* + *restare* to remain, rest] **1 a** : to bring to a stop ⟨sickness ~*ed* his activities⟩ **b** : CHECK, SLOW **c** : to make inactive ⟨an ~*ed* tumor⟩ **2** : SEIZE, CAPTURE; *specif* : to take or keep in custody by authority of law **3** : to catch suddenly and engagingly — **ar·rest·er** *or* **ar·res·tor** \-ˈres-tər\ *n* — **ar·rest·ment** \-ˈres(t)-mənt\ *n*

[2]**arrest** *n* **1 a** : the act of stopping **b** : the condition of being stopped **2** : the taking or detaining in custody by authority of law **3** : a device for arresting motion — **under arrest** : in legal custody

ar·res·tant \ə-ˈres-tənt\ *n* : a substance that causes an insect to stop locomotion and begin to feed

arrest·ee \ə-ˌres-ˈtē\ *n* : one that is under arrest

ar·rest·ing \ə-ˈres-tiŋ\ *adj* : catching the attention : STRIKING, IMPRESSIVE — **ar·rest·ing·ly** \-tiŋ-lē\ *adv*

ar·rhyth·mia \ā-ˈrith-mē-ə\ *n* [NL, fr. Gk, lack of rhythm, fr. *arrhythmos* unrhythmical, fr. *a-* + *rhythmos* rhythm] : an alteration in rhythm of the heartbeat either in time or force

ar·rhyth·mic \-mik\ *adj* [Gk *arrhythmos*] : lacking rhythm or regularity ⟨~ locomotor activity⟩ — **ar·rhyth·mi·cal** \-mi-kəl\ *adj* — **ar·rhyth·mi·cal·ly** \-mi-k(ə-)lē\ *adv*

ar·ri·ère–ban \ˌar-ē-ˌe(ə)r-ˈbän, -ˈban\ *n* [F] : a proclamation of a king (as of France) calling his vassals to arms; *also* : the body of vassals summoned

ar·ri·ère–pen·sée \-päⁿ-ˈsā\ *n* [F, fr. *arrière* in back + *pensée* thought] : mental reservation

ar·ris \ˈar-əs\ *n, pl* **arris** *or* **ar·ris·es** [prob. modif. of MF *areste*, lit., fishbone, fr. LL *arista* — more at ARÊTE] : the sharp edge or salient angle formed by the meeting of two surfaces esp. in moldings

ar·riv·al \ə-ˈrī-vəl\ *n* **1** : the act of arriving **2** : the attainment of an end or state **3** : one that has recently reached a destination

[1]**ar·rive** \ə-ˈrīv\ *vi* **ar·rived; ar·riv·ing** [ME *ariven*, fr. OF *ariver*, fr. (assumed) VL *arripare* to come to shore, fr. L *ad-* + *ripa* shore — more at RIVE] **1 a** : to reach a destination **b** : to make an appearance ⟨all the guests have *arrived*⟩ **2 a** *archaic* : HAPPEN **b** : to be near in time : COME ⟨the moment has *arrived*⟩ **3** : to achieve success — **ar·riv·er** *n* — **arrive at** : to reach by effort or thought ⟨have *arrived at* a decision⟩

[2]**ar·ri·vé** \ˌar-i-ˈvā\ *n* [F, fr. pp. of *arriver* to arrive, fr. OF *ariver*] : one who has risen rapidly to success, power, or fame

ar·ri·viste \-ˈvēst\ *n* [F, fr. *arriver*] : one that is a new and uncertain arrival (as in social position or artistic endeavor)

ar·ro·ba \ə-ˈrō-bə\ *n* [Sp & Pg, fr. Ar *ar-rub'*, lit., the quarter] **1** : an old Spanish unit of weight equal to about 25 pounds used in some Spanish-American countries **2** : an old Portuguese unit of weight equal to about 32 pounds used in Brazil

ar·ro·gance \ˈar-ə-gən(t)s\ *n* : a feeling of superiority manifested in an overbearing manner or presumptuous claims

ar·ro·gant \-gənt\ *adj* [ME, fr. L *arrogant-*, *arrogans*, prp. of *arrogare*] **1** : exaggerating or disposed to exaggerate one's own worth or importance in an overbearing manner ⟨an ~ official⟩ **2** : proceeding from or characterized by arrogance ⟨~ manners⟩ ***syn*** see PROUD ***ant*** meek, unassuming — **ar·ro·gant·ly** *adv*

ar·ro·gate \-ˌgāt\ *vt* **-gat·ed; -gat·ing** [L *arrogatus*, pp. of *arrogare*, fr. *ad-* + *rogare* to ask — more at RIGHT] **1 a** : to claim or seize without justification **b** : to make undue claims to having : ASSUME **2** : to claim on behalf of another : ASCRIBE ***syn*** see APPROPRIATE — **ar·ro·ga·tion** \ˌar-ə-ˈgā-shən\ *n*

ar·ron·disse·ment \ə-ˈrän-də-smənt, ˈar-ˌōⁿ-(ˌ)dē-ˈsmäⁿ\ *n* [F] **1** : the largest division of a French department **2** : an administrative district of some large French cities

ar·row \ˈar-(ˌ)ō, -ə(-w)\ *n* [ME *arwe*, fr. OE; akin to Goth *arhwazna* arrow, L *arcus* bow, arch, arc] **1** : a missile weapon shot from a bow and usu. having a slender shaft, a pointed head, and feathers at the butt **2** : something shaped like an arrow; *esp* : a mark (as on a map or signboard) to indicate direction

ar·row·head \ˈar-ō-ˌhed, ˈar-ə-\ *n* **1** : the usu. separate wedge-shaped striking end of an arrow **2** : something resembling an arrowhead **3** : any of a genus (*Sagittaria*) of plants of the water-plantain family with leaves shaped like arrowheads

ar·row·root \-ˌrüt, -ˌrůt\ *n* **1 a** : any of a genus (*Maranta* of the family Marantaceae, the arrowroot family) of tropical American plants with tuberous roots; *esp* : one (*M. arundinacea*) whose roots yield a nutritive starch **b** : any of several plants (as coontie) that yield starch **2** : starch yielded by an arrowroot

ar·row·wood \-ˌwůd\ *n* : any of several shrubs (as several viburnums) having tough pliant shoots formerly used to make arrows

ar·row·worm \-ˌwərm\ *n* : CHAETOGNATH

ar·rowy \ˈar-ə-wē\ *adj* **1** : consisting of arrows **2** : resembling or suggesting an arrow; *esp* : swiftly moving

ar·royo \ə-ˈrȯi-ə, -(ˌ)ō\ *n, pl* **-royos** [Sp] **1** : a watercourse (as a creek or stream) in an arid region **2** : a water-carved gully or channel

ARS *abbr* Agricultural Research Service

arse *var of* ASS

ar·se·nal \ˈärs-nəl, -ᵊn-əl\ *n* [It *arsenale*, modif. of Ar *dār ṣināʽah* house of manufacture] **1 a** : an establishment for the manufacture or storage of arms and military equipment **b** : a collection of weapons **2** : STORE, REPERTORY ⟨the team's ~ of experienced players⟩

ar·se·nate \ˈärs-nət, -ᵊn-ət, -ᵊn-ˌāt\ *n* : a salt or ester of an arsenic acid

[1]**ar·se·nic** \ˈärs-nik, -ᵊn-ik\ *n* [ME, yellow orpiment, fr. MF & L; MF, fr. L *arsenicum*, fr. Gk *arsenikon*, *arrhenikon*, fr. Syr *zarnīg*, of Iranian origin; akin to Av *zaranya* gold, Skt *hari* yellowish — more at YELLOW] **1** : a trivalent and pentavalent solid poisonous element that is commonly metallic steel-gray, crystalline, and brittle — see ELEMENT table **2** : a poisonous trioxide As_2O_3 or As_4O_6 of arsenic used esp. as an insecticide or weed killer — called also *arsenic trioxide*

[2]**ar·sen·ic** \är-ˈsen-ik\ *adj* : of, relating to, or containing arsenic esp. with a valence of five

ar·sen·i·cal \är-ˈsen-i-kəl\ *adj* : of, relating to, or containing arsenic ⟨an ~ drug⟩ — **arsenical** *n*

ar·se·nic trisulfide \ˌärs-nik-, -ᵊn-ik-\ *n* : a yellow compound As_2S_3 occurring native as orpiment or prepared artificially and used in fireworks and as a pigment

ar·se·nide \ˈärs-ᵊn-ˌīd\ *n* : a binary compound of arsenic with a more positive element

ar·se·ni·ous \är-ˈsē-nē-əs\ *adj* : of, relating to, or containing arsenic esp. when trivalent

ar·se·nite \ˈärs-ᵊn-ˌīt\ *n* : a salt or ester of an arsenious acid

ar·se·no·py·rite \ˌärs-ᵊn-ō-ˈpī(ə)r-ˌīt\ *n* : a mineral FeAsS consisting of a combined sulfide and arsenide of iron occurring in prismatic orthorhombic crystals or in masses or grains

ar·sine \är-ˈsēn, ˈär-ˌ\ *n* [ISV, fr. *arsenic*] : a colorless flammable extremely poisonous gas AsH_3 with an odor like garlic; *also* : a derivative of arsine

ar·sis \ˈär-səs\ *n, pl* **ar·ses** \-ˌsēz\ [LL & Gk; LL, raising of the voice, accented part of foot, fr. Gk, upbeat, less important part of foot, lit., act of lifting, fr. *aeirein*, *airein* to lift] **1 a** : the lighter or shorter part of a poetic foot esp. in quantitative verse **b** : the accented or longer part of a poetic foot esp. in accentual verse **2** : the unaccented part of a musical measure — compare THESIS

ar·son \ˈärs-ᵊn\ *n* [obs. F, fr. OF, fr. *ars*, pp. of *ardre* to burn, fr. L *ardēre* — *more at* ARDOR] : the malicious or fraudulent burning of property (as a building) — **ar·son·ist** \-əst\ *n* — **ar·son·ous** \-əs\ *adj*

ars·phen·a·mine \ärs-ˈfen-ə-ˌmēn, -mən\ *n* [ISV *arsenic* + *phenamine*] : a light-yellow toxic hygroscopic powder $C_{12}Cl_2H_{14}As_2N_2O_2.2H_2O$ formerly used in the treatment of spirochetal diseases

[1]**art** \(ˈ)ärt, ərt\ [ME, fr. OE *eart*; akin to ON *est*, *ert* (thou) art, OE *is* is] *archaic pres 2d sing of* BE

[2]**art** \ˈärt\ *n* [ME, fr. OF, fr. L *art-*, *ars* — more at ARM] **1** : skill acquired by experience, study, or observation ⟨the ~ of making friends⟩ **2 a** : a branch of learning: (1) : one of the humanities (2) *pl* : LIBERAL ARTS **b** *archaic* : LEARNING, SCHOLARSHIP **3** : an occupation requiring knowledge or skill ⟨the ~ of organ building⟩ **4 a** : the conscious use of skill and creative imagination esp. in the production of aesthetic objects; *also* : works so produced **b** (1) : FINE ARTS (2) : one of the fine arts (3) : a graphic art **5 a** *archaic* : a skillful plan **b** : the quality or state of being artful **6** : decorative or illustrative elements in printed matter

syn ART, SKILL, CUNNING, ARTIFICE, CRAFT *shared meaning element* : the faculty of carrying out expertly what is planned or devised

[3]**art** *abbr* **1** article **2** artificial **3** artillery

-art — see -ARD

art de·co \ˌär(t)-dā-ˈkō, (ˈ)är(t)-ˈdā-(ˌ)-\ *n, often cap A&D* [F *Art Déco*, fr. *Exposition Internationale des Arts Décoratifs*, an exposition of decorative arts held in Paris, France, in 1925] : a pervasive deco-

rative style of the 1920s and 1930s characterized esp. by bold outlines, streamlined and rectilinear forms, and the use of new materials (as plastic)
artefact *var of* ARTIFACT
ar·tel \är-ˈtel(-yə)\ *n* [Russ *artel'*, fr. It *artieri*, pl. of *artiere* artisan, fr. *arte* art] : COLLECTIVE FARM
Ar·te·mis \ˈärt-ə-məs\ *n* [Gk] : a Greek goddess often portrayed as a virgin huntress and identified as a moon goddess — compare DIANA
ar·te·mi·sia \ˌärt-ə-ˈmizh-(ē-)ə, -ˈmiz-ē-ə\ *n* [NL, genus name, fr. L, artemisia, fr. Gk] : any of a genus (*Artemisia*) of composite herbs and shrubs with strong-smelling foliage
arteri- *or* **arterio-** *comb form* [MF, fr. LL, fr. Gk *artēri-*, *artērio-*, fr. *artēria* artery] **1** : artery ⟨*arteriology*⟩ **2** : arterial and ⟨*arteriovenous*⟩
¹ar·te·ri·al \är-ˈtir-ē-əl\ *adj* **1 a** : of or relating to an artery **b** : relating to or being the bright red blood present in most arteries that has been oxygenated in lungs or gills **2** : of, relating to, or constituting through-traffic facilities — **ar·te·ri·al·ly** \-ē-ə-lē\ *adv*
²arterial *n* : a through street or arterial highway
ar·te·ri·al·ize \är-ˈtir-ē-ə-ˌlīz\ *vt* **-ized; -iz·ing** : to transform (venous blood) into arterial blood by oxygenation — **ar·te·ri·al·iza·tion** \-ˌtir-ē-ə-lə-ˈzā-shən\ *n*
ar·te·rio·gram \är-ˈtir-ē-ə-ˌgram\ *n* [ISV] : a roentgenogram of an artery made by arteriography
ar·te·ri·og·ra·phy \är-ˌtir-ē-ˈäg-rə-fē\ *n, pl* **-phies** [ISV] : the roentgenographic visualization of an artery after injection of a special substance — **ar·te·rio·graph·ic** \-ē-ə-ˈgraf-ik\ *adj*
ar·te·ri·ole \är-ˈtir-ē-ˌōl\ *n* [F or NL; F *artériole*, prob. fr. NL *arteriola*, dim. of L *arteria*] : one of the small terminal twigs of an artery that ends in capillaries — **ar·te·ri·o·lar** \-ˌtir-ē-ˈō-ˌlär, -lər\ *adj*
ar·te·rio·scle·ro·sis \är-ˌtir-ē-ō-sklə-ˈrō-səs\ *n* [NL] : a chronic disease characterized by abnormal thickening and hardening of the arterial walls — **ar·te·rio·scle·rot·ic** \-ˈrät-ik\ *adj or n*
ar·te·rio·ve·nous \-ˈvē-nəs\ *adj* [ISV] : of, relating to, or connecting the arteries and veins
ar·ter·i·tis \ˌärt-ə-ˈrīt-əs\ *n* [NL] : arterial inflammation
ar·tery \ˈärt-ə-rē\ *n, pl* **-ter·ies** [ME *arterie*, fr. L *arteria*, fr. Gk *artēria*; akin to Gk *aortē* aorta] **1** : one of the tubular branching muscular- and elastic-walled vessels that carry blood from the heart through the body **2** : a channel (as a river or highway) of transportation or communication; *esp* : the principal channel in a branching system
ar·te·sian well \är-ˌtē-zhən-\ *n* [F *artésien*, lit., of Artois, fr. OF, fr. *Arteis* Artois, France] **1** : a well made by boring into the earth until water is reached which from internal pressure flows up like a fountain **2** : a deep-bored well
art film *n* : a motion picture produced as an artistic effort
art form *n* : a recognized form (as a symphony) or medium (as sculpture) of artistic expression
art·ful \ˈärt-fəl\ *adj* **1** : performed with or showing art or skill ⟨an ~ performance on the violin⟩ **2** : ARTIFICIAL ⟨trim walks and ~ bowers —William Wordsworth⟩ **3 a** : using or characterized by art and skill : DEXTEROUS ⟨an ~ prose stylist⟩ **b** : adroit in attaining an end often by insinuating or indirect means : WILY ⟨an ~ cross-examiner⟩ ***syn*** see SLY ***ant*** artless — **art·ful·ly** \-fə-lē\ *adv* — **art·ful·ness** *n*
art glass *n* : articles of glass designed primarily for decorative purposes; *esp* : novelty glassware
art–historical *adj* : of or relating to the history of art ⟨~ method⟩
art house *n* : ART THEATER
arthr- *or* **arthro-** *comb form* [L, fr. Gk, fr. *arthron*; akin to Gk *arariskein* to fit — more at ARM] : joint ⟨*arthralgia*⟩ ⟨*arthropathy*⟩
ar·thral·gia \är-ˈthral-j(ē-)ə\ *n* [NL] : neuralgic pain in one or more joints — **ar·thral·gic** \-jik\ *adj*
ar·thrit·ic \är-ˈthrit-ik\ *adj* **1** : of, relating to, or affected with arthritis **2** : being or showing effects associated with aging ⟨~ anxiety⟩ — **arthritic** *n* — **ar·thrit·i·cal·ly** \-i-k(ə-)lē\ *adv*
ar·thri·tis \är-ˈthrīt-əs\ *n, pl* **-thrit·i·des** \-ˈthrit-ə-ˌdēz\ [L, fr. Gk, fr. *arthron*] : inflammation of joints due to infectious, metabolic, or constitutional causes
ar·throd·e·sis \är-ˈthräd-ə-səs\ *n, pl* **-e·ses** \-ˌsēz\ [NL, fr. *arthr-* + Gk *desis* binding, fr. *dein* to bind] : the surgical immobilization of a joint so that the bones grow solidly together : artificial ankylosis
ar·throp·a·thy \är-ˈthräp-ə-thē\ *n, pl* **-thies** : a disease of a joint
ar·thro·pod \ˈär-thrə-ˌpäd\ *n* [NL *Arthropoda*, group name, fr. *arthr-* + Gk *pod-*, *pous* foot — more at FOOT] : any of a phylum (Arthropoda) of invertebrate animals (as insects, arachnids, and crustaceans) that have a jointed body and limbs, usu. a chitinous shell molted at intervals, and the brain dorsal to the alimentary canal and connected with a ventral chain of ganglia — **arthropod** *adj* — **ar·throp·o·dan** \-əd-ən\ *also* **ar·throp·o·dous** \-əd-əs\ *adj*
ar·thro·sis \är-ˈthrō-səs\ *n, pl* **-thro·ses** \-ˌsēz\ [NL, fr. Gk *arthrōsis* jointing, articulation, fr. *arthroun* to articulate, fr. *arthron*] : an articulation or line of juncture between bones
ar·thro·spore \ˈär-thrə-ˌspō(ə)r, -ˌspȯ(ə)r\ *n* **1** : a thick-walled vegetative resting cell formed by blue-green algae (as of the genus *Nostoc*) **2** : OIDIUM 1b — **ar·thro·spor·ic** \ˌär-thrə-ˈspōr-ik, -ˈspȯr-\ *or* **ar·thro·spo·rous** \-es; är-ˈthräs-pə-rəs\ *adj*
Ar·thur \ˈär-thər\ *n* : a possibly historical king of Britain
Ar·thu·ri·an \är-ˈth(y)u̇r-ē-ən\ *adj* : of or relating to King Arthur and his court
ar·ti·choke \ˈärt-ə-ˌchōk\ *n* [It dial. *articiocco*, fr. Ar *al-khurshūf* the artichoke] **1** : a tall composite herb (*Cynara scolymus*) like a thistle with coarse pinnately incised leaves; *also* : its edible flower head which is cooked as a vegetable **2** : JERUSALEM ARTICHOKE
¹ar·ti·cle \ˈärt-i-kəl\ *n* [ME, fr. OF, fr. L *articulus* joint, division, dim. of *artus* joint; akin to Gk *arariskein* to fit — more at ARM] **1 a** : a distinct often numbered section of a writing **b** : a separate clause **c** : a stipulation in a document (as a contract or a creed) **d** : a nonfictional prose composition usu. forming an independent part of a publication (as a magazine) **2** : an item of business : MATTER **3** : any of a small set of words or affixes (as *a*, *an*, and *the*) used with nouns to limit or give definiteness to the application **4** : a member of a class of things; *esp* : a piece of goods ⟨~*s* of value⟩ **5** : a thing of a particular and distinctive kind ⟨the genuine ~⟩
²article *vt* **ar·ti·cled; ar·ti·cling** \-k(ə-)liŋ\ : to bind by articles (as of apprenticeship)
ar·tic·u·la·ble \är-ˈtik-yə-lə-bəl\ *adj* : capable of being articulated
ar·tic·u·lar \är-ˈtik-yə-lər\ *adj* [ME *articuler*, fr. L *articularis*, fr. *articulus*] : of or relating to a joint ⟨~ cartilage⟩
¹ar·tic·u·late \är-ˈtik-yə-lət\ *adj* [NL *articulatus*, fr. L *articulus*] **1 a** : divided into syllables or words meaningfully arranged : INTELLIGIBLE **b** : able to speak **c** : expressing oneself readily, clearly, or effectively; *also* : expressed in this manner **2 a** : consisting of segments united by joints : JOINTED ⟨~ animals⟩ **b** : distinctly marked off — **ar·tic·u·late·ly** *adv* — **ar·tic·u·late·ness** *n*
²ar·tic·u·late \-ˌlāt\ *vb* **-lat·ed; -lat·ing** [L *articulatus*, pp. of *articulare*, fr. *articulus*] *vt* **1 a** : to utter distinctly ⟨*articulating* each note in the musical phrase⟩ **b** : to give clear and effective utterance to ⟨~ one's grievances⟩ **2 a** : to unite by means of a joint : JOINT **b** : to form or fit into a systematic whole ⟨*articulating* a program for all school grades⟩ ~ *vi* **1** : to utter articulate sounds **2** : to become united or connected by or as if by a joint — **ar·tic·u·la·tive** \-lət-iv, -ˌlāt-\ *adj* — **ar·tic·u·la·tor** \-ˌlāt-ər\ *n*
ar·tic·u·la·tion \(ˌ)är-ˌtik-yə-ˈlā-shən\ *n* **1 a** : the action or manner of jointing or interrelating **b** : the state of being jointed or interrelated **2 a** (1) : a joint or juncture between bones or cartilages in the skeleton of a vertebrate (2) : a movable joint between rigid parts of an animal **b** (1) : a joint between two separable plant parts (as the base of a leafstalk) (2) : a plant stem node or internode **3 a** : the act of giving utterance or expression **b** : the act or manner of articulating sounds **c** : an articulated utterance or sound; *specif* : CONSONANT **4** : OCCLUSION 1b
ar·tic·u·la·to·ry \är-ˈtik-yə-lə-ˌtōr-ē, -ˌtȯr-\ *adj* : of or relating to articulation
ar·ti·fact \ˈärt-ə-ˌfakt\ *n* [L *arte* by skill (abl. of *art-*, *ars* skill) + *factum*, neut. of *factus*, pp. of *facere* to do — more at ARM, DO] **1 a** : a usu. simple object (as a tool or ornament) showing human workmanship or modification **b** : a product of civilization ⟨an ~ of the jet age⟩ **c** : a product of artistic endeavor **2** : a product (as a structure on a prepared microscope slide) of artificial character due to extraneous (as human) agency — **ar·ti·fac·tu·al** \ˌärt-ə-ˈfak-chə(-wə)l, -ˈfaksh-wəl\ *adj*
ar·ti·fice \ˈärt-ə-fəs\ *n* [MF, fr. L *artificium*, fr. *artific-*, *artifex* artificer, fr. L *art-*, *ars* + *facere*] **1 a** : an artful stratagem : TRICK **b** : false or insincere behavior ⟨social ~⟩ **2 a** : an ingenious device or expedient **b** : clever or artful skill : INGENUITY ⟨not a show of ~ . . . but a genuine creative effort —Harry Hervey⟩ ***syn*** see ART, TRICK
ar·ti·fi·cer \är-ˈtif-ə-sər, ˈärt-ə-fə-sər\ *n* **1** : a skilled or artistic worker or craftsman **2** : one that makes or contrives : DEVISER ⟨had been the ~ of his own fortunes —*Times Lit. Supp.*⟩
ar·ti·fi·cial \ˌärt-ə-ˈfish-əl\ *adj* **1** : humanly contrived often on a natural model : MAN-MADE ⟨an ~ limb⟩ ⟨~ diamonds⟩ **2** : having existence in legal, economic, or political theory **3** *obs* : ARTFUL, CUNNING **4 a** : FEIGNED, ASSUMED **b** : lacking in natural quality : AFFECTED ⟨the ~ smile of one who is not really enjoying himself⟩ **c** : IMITATION, SHAM ⟨~ flavor⟩ **5** : based on differential morphological characters not necessarily indicative of natural relationships — **ar·ti·fi·cial·ly** \-ˈfish-(ə-)lē\ *adv* — **ar·ti·fi·cial·ness** \-ˈfish-əl-nəs\ *n*
syn ARTIFICIAL, FACTITIOUS, SYNTHETIC, ERSATZ *shared meaning element* : brought into being not by nature but by human art or effort ***ant*** natural
artificial horizon *n* **1** : HORIZON 1c **2** : an aeronautical instrument based on a gyroscope and designed to furnish a surface constantly perpendicular to the vertical and therefore parallel to the horizon

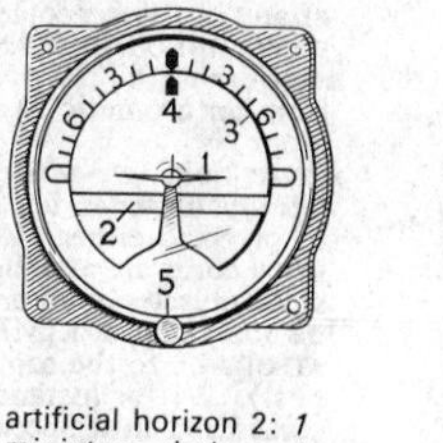

artificial horizon 2: *1* miniature airplane, *2* horizon bar, *3* degree of bank scale in 10s of degrees, *4* pointer, *5* inactivating knob

artificial insemination *n* : introduction of semen into the uterus or oviduct by other than natural means
ar·ti·fi·ci·al·i·ty \ˌärt-ə-ˌfish-ē-ˈal-ət-ē\ *n, pl* **-ties** **1** : the quality or state of being artificial **2** : something that is artificial ⟨the *artificialities* of social life⟩
artificial respiration *n* : the rhythmic forcing of air into and out of the lungs of a person whose breathing has stopped
ar·til·ler·ist \är-ˈtil-ə-rəst\ *n* : GUNNER, ARTILLERYMAN
ar·til·lery \är-ˈtil-(ə-)rē\ *n, pl* **-ler·ies** [ME *artillerie*, fr. MF] **1** : weapons (as bows, slings, and catapults) for discharging missiles **2** : large caliber crew-served mounted firearms (as guns, howitzers, and rockets) : ORDNANCE **3** : a branch of an army armed with artillery **4** : means of impressing, arguing, or persuading ⟨the ~ of satire⟩
ar·til·lery·man \-(ə-)rē-mən\ *n* : a soldier who is assigned to the artillery
ar·tio·dac·tyl \ˌärt-ē-ō-ˈdak-tᵊl\ *n* [deriv. of Gk *artios* fitting, even-numbered + *daktylos* finger, toe; akin to Gk *arariskein* to fit — more at ARM] : any of an order (Artiodactyla) of hoofed mammals (as the camel or ox) with an even number of functional toes on each foot — **artiodactyl** *or* **ar·tio·dac·ty·lous** \-tə-ləs\ *adj*
ar·ti·san \ˈärt-ə-zən, -sən, *chiefly Brit* ˌärt-ə-ˈzan\ *n* [MF, fr. OIt *artigiano*, fr. *arte* art, fr. L *art-*, *ars*] : one (as a carpenter, plumber, or tailor) trained to manual dexterity or skill in a trade

art·ist \'ärt-əst\ *n* **1 a :** one who professes and practices an imaginative art **b :** a person skilled in one of the fine arts **2 :** a skilled performer; *specif* **:** ARTISTE **3 a** *obs* **:** one skilled or versed in learned arts **b** *archaic* **:** PHYSICIAN **c** *archaic* **:** ARTISAN **4 :** one who is adept at deception

ar·tiste \är-'tēst\ *n* [F] **:** a skilled adept public performer; *specif* **:** a musical or theatrical entertainer

ar·tis·tic \är-'tis-tik\ *adj* **1 :** of, relating to, or characteristic of art or artists ⟨~ subjects⟩ **2 :** showing imaginative skill in arrangement or execution ⟨~ photography⟩ — **ar·tis·ti·cal·ly** \-ti-k(ə-)lē\ *adv*

art·ist·ry \'ärt-ə-strē\ *n* **1 :** artistic quality of effect or workmanship ⟨the ~ of his novel⟩ **2 :** artistic ability ⟨the ~ of the violinist⟩

art·less \'ärt-ləs\ *adj* **1 :** lacking art, knowledge, or skill **:** UNCULTURED **2 a :** made without skill **:** CRUDE **b :** free from artificiality **:** NATURAL ⟨~ grace⟩ **3 :** free from guile or craft **:** sincerely simple ***syn*** see NATURAL — **art·less·ly** *adv* — **art·less·ness** *n*

art·mo·bile \'ärt-mō-,bēl\ *n* [*art* + auto*mobile*] **:** a trailer that houses an art collection designed for exhibition on road tours

art nou·veau \,är(t)-nü-'vō\ *n, often cap A & N* [F, lit., new art] **:** a decorative style of late 19th century origin characterized esp. by sinuous lines and foliate forms

art song *n* **:** a usu. through-composed lyric song with melody and accompaniment

artsy–craftsy \,ärt-sē-'kraf(t)-sē\ *or* **arty–crafty** \ärt-ē-'kraf-tē\ *adj* [fr. the phrase *arts and crafts*] **:** ARTY

art theater *n* **:** a theater that specializes in the presentation of art films

art·work \'ärt-,wərk\ *n* **1 a :** an artistic production ⟨an 8-foot metal ~⟩ **b :** artistic work ⟨~ being sold on the sidewalk⟩ **2 :** ART 6

1arty \'ärt-ē\ *adj* **art·i·er; -est :** showily or pretentiously artistic ⟨~ lighting and photography⟩ — **art·i·ly** \'ärt-ᵊl-ē\ *adv* — **art·i·ness** \'ärt-ē-nəs\ *n*

2arty *abbr* artillery

ar·um \'ar-əm, 'er-\ *n* [NL, genus name, fr. L, arum, fr. Gk *aron*] **:** any of a genus (*Arum* of the family Araceae, the arum family) of Old World plants with flowers in a fleshy spathe subtended by a leafy bract; *broadly* **:** a plant of the arum family

ARV *abbr* American Revised Version

1-ary *US usu* ,er-ē *when an unstressed syllable precedes,* ə-rē *or* rē *when a stressed syllable precedes; Brit usu* ə-rē *or* rē *in all cases*\ *n suffix* [ME *-arie,* fr. OF & L; OF *-aire, -arie,* fr. L *-arius, -aria, -arium,* fr. *-arius,* adj. suffix] **1 :** thing belonging to or connected with; *esp* **:** place of ⟨ov*ary*⟩ **2 :** person belonging to, connected with, or engaged in ⟨function*ary*⟩

2-ary *adj suffix* [ME *-arie,* fr. MF & L; MF *-aire,* fr. L *-arius*] **:** of, relating to, or connected with ⟨budget*ary*⟩

1Ary·an \'ar-ē-ən, 'er-; 'är-yən\ *adj* [Skt *ārya* noble, belonging to the people speaking an Indo-European dialect who migrated into northern India] **1 :** of or relating to the Indo-European family of languages or to their hypothetical prototype **2 :** of or relating to speakers of Indo-European languages **3 a :** of or relating to a hypothetical ethnic type illustrated by or descended from early speakers of Indo-European languages **b :** NORDIC **4 :** of or relating to Indo-Iranian or its speakers

2Aryan *n* **1 :** a member of the Indo-European-speaking people early occupying the Iranian plateau or entering India and conquering and amalgamating with the earlier non-Indo-European inhabitants **2 a :** a member of the people speaking the language from which the Indo-European languages are derived **b :** an individual of any of those peoples speaking these languages since prehistoric times **:** INDO-EUROPEAN **c :** NORDIC **d :** GENTILE

ar·yl \'ar-əl\ *n* [ISV *ar*omatic + *-yl*] **:** a radical (as phenyl) derived from an aromatic hydrocarbon by the removal of one hydrogen atom

ar·y·te·noid \,ar-ə-'tē-,nȯid, ə-'rit-ᵊn-,ȯid\ *adj* [NL *arytaenoides,* fr. Gk *arytainoeidēs,* lit., ladle-shaped, fr. *arytaina* ladle] **1 :** relating to or being either of two small laryngeal cartilages to which the vocal cords are attached **2 :** relating to or being either of a pair of small muscles or an unpaired muscle of the larynx — **arytenoid** *n*

1as \əz, (,)az\ *adv* [ME, fr. OE *eallswā* likewise, just as — more at ALSO] **1 :** to the same degree or amount **:** EQUALLY ⟨~ deaf as a post⟩ **2 :** for instance ⟨various trees, ~ oak or pine⟩ **3 :** when considered in a specified form or relation — usu. used before a preposition or a participle ⟨my opinion ~ distinguished from his⟩

2as *conj* **1 :** as if ⟨looks ~ he had seen a ghost — S. T. Coleridge⟩ **2 :** in or to the same degree in which ⟨deaf ~ a post⟩ — usu. used as a correlative after an adjective or adverb modified by adverbial *as* or *so* ⟨as cool ~ a cucumber⟩ **3 :** in the way or manner that ⟨do ~ I do⟩ **4 :** in accordance with what or the way in which ⟨quite good ~ boys go⟩ **5 :** WHILE, WHEN ⟨spilled the milk ~ she got up⟩ **6 :** regardless of the degree to which **:** THOUGH ⟨improbable ~ it seems, it's true⟩ **7 :** for the reason that ⟨stayed home ~ she had no car⟩ **8 :** that the result is **:** THAT ⟨so clearly guilty ~ to leave no doubt⟩ — **as is :** in the presently existing condition without modification ⟨bought the clock at an auction *as is*⟩ — **as it were :** as if it were so **:** in a manner of speaking

3as *pron* **1 :** THAT, WHO, WHICH — used after *same* or *such* ⟨in the same building ~ my brother⟩ ⟨tears such ~ angels weep — John Milton⟩ and chiefly dial. after a substantive not modified by *same* or *such* ⟨that kind of fruit ~ maids call medlars — Shak.⟩ **2 :** a fact that ⟨is a foreigner, ~ is evident from his accent⟩

4as *prep* **1 a :** LIKE 2 ⟨all rose ~ one man⟩ **b :** LIKE 1a ⟨his face was ~ a mask — Max Beerbohm⟩ **2 :** in the capacity, character, condition, or role of ⟨works ~ an editor⟩

5as \'as\ *n, pl* **as·ses** \'as-,ēz, 'as-əz [L] **1 :** LIBRA 2a **2 a :** a bronze coin of the ancient Roman republic **b :** a unit of value equivalent to an as coin

1As *abbr* altostratus

2As *symbol* arsenic

AS *abbr* **1** after sight **2** airspeed **3** Anglo-Saxon **4** antisubmarine

as- — see AD-

ASA *abbr* **1** American Society of Appraisers **2** American Statistical Association

asa·fet·i·da *or* **asa·foe·ti·da** \,as-ə-'fit-əd-ē, -'fet-əd-ə\ *n* [ME *asafetida,* fr. ML *asafoetida,* fr. Per *azā* mastic + L *foetida,* fem. of *foetidus* fetid] **:** the fetid gum resin of various oriental plants (genus *Ferula*) of the carrot family formerly used in medicine as an antispasmodic and in folk medicine as a general prophylactic against disease

Asarh \'ä-,sär, ä-'sär\ *n* [Hindi *Asāṛh,* fr. Skt *Āṣāḍha*] **:** a month of the Hindu year — see MONTH table

asb *abbr* asbestos

as·bes·tos *also* **as·bes·tus** \as-'bes-təs, az-\ *n* [ME *albestron* mineral supposed to be inextinguishable when set on fire, prob. fr. MF, fr. ML *asbeston,* alter. of L *asbestos,* fr. Gk, unslaked lime, fr. *asbestos* inextinguishable, fr. *a-* + *sbennynai* to quench; akin to Lith *gesti* to be extinguished] **:** a mineral (as amphibole) that readily separates into long flexible fibers suitable for use as a noncombustible, nonconducting, or chemically resistant material

as·bes·to·sis \,as-,bes-'tō-səs, ,az-\ *n, pl* **-to·ses** \-,sēz\ **:** a pneumoconiosis due to asbestos particles

asc- *or* **asco-** *comb form* [NL, fr. *ascus*] **:** ascus ⟨*asco*carp⟩

ASCAP \'as-,kap\ *abbr* American Society of Composers, Authors and Publishers

as·ca·ri·a·sis \,as-kə-'rī-ə-səs\ *n, pl* **-a·ses** \-,sēz\ **:** infestation with or disease caused by ascarids

as·ca·rid \'as-kə-rəd\ *n* [deriv. of LL *ascarid-, ascaris* intestinal worm, fr. Gk *askarid-, askaris;* akin to Gk *skairein* to gambol — more at CARDINAL] **:** a nematode worm of a family (Ascaridae) including the common roundworm (*Ascaris lumbricoides*) parasitic in the human intestine

as·ca·ris \'as-kə-rəs\ *n, pl* **as·car·i·des** \as-'kar-ə-,dēz\ [LL] **:** ASCARID

ASCE *abbr* American Society of Civil Engineers

as·cend \ə-'send\ *vb* [ME *ascenden,* fr. L *ascendere,* fr. *ad-* + *scandere* to climb — more at SCAN] *vi* **1 a :** to move gradually upward **b :** to slope upward **2 a :** to rise from a lower level or degree **b :** to go back in time or in order of genealogical succession **~** *vt* **1 :** to go or move up or toward **2 :** to succeed to **:** OCCUPY — **as·cend·able** *or* **as·cend·ible** \-'sen-də-bəl\ *adj*

syn ASCEND, MOUNT, CLIMB, SCALE *shared meaning element* **:** to move upward to or toward a summit ***ant*** descend

as·cen·dance *also* **as·cen·dence** \ə-'sen-dən(t)s\ *n* **:** ASCENDANCY

as·cen·dan·cy *also* **as·cen·den·cy** \ə-'sen-dən-sē\ *n* **:** governing or controlling influence **:** DOMINATION ***syn*** see SUPREMACY

1as·cen·dant *also* **as·cen·dent** \ə-'sen-dənt\ *n* [ME *ascendent,* fr. ML *ascendent-, ascendens,* fr. L, prp. of *ascendere*] **1 :** the point of the ecliptic or degree of the zodiac that rises above the eastern horizon at any moment **2 :** a state or position of dominant power or importance ⟨his ideas are now in the ~⟩ **3 :** a lineal or collateral relative in the ascending line

2ascendant *also* **ascendent** *adj* **1 a :** moving upward **:** RISING **b :** directed upward ⟨an ~ stem⟩ **2 a :** SUPERIOR **b :** DOMINANT — **as·cen·dant·ly** *adv*

as·cend·er \ə-'sen-dər, 'a-\ *n* **:** the part of a lowercase letter (as b) that rises above the main body of the letter; *also* **:** a letter that has such a part

as·cend·ing \ə-'sen-diŋ\ *adj* **1 a :** mounting or sloping upward **b :** rising to a higher level or degree **2 :** rising upward usu. from a more or less prostrate base or point of attachment

ascending rhythm *n* **:** RISING RHYTHM

as·cen·sion \ə-'sen-chən\ *n* [ME, fr. L *ascension-, ascensio,* fr. *ascensus,* pp. of *ascendere*] **:** the act or process of ascending

as·cen·sion·al \ə-'sench-nəl, -ən-ᵊl\ *adj* **:** of or relating to ascension or ascent

Ascension Day *n* **:** the Thursday 40 days after Easter observed in commemoration of Christ's ascension into Heaven

as·cen·sive \ə-'sen(t)-siv\ *adj* **:** rising or tending to rise

as·cent \ə-'sent\ *n* [irreg. fr. *ascend*] **1 a :** the act of rising or mounting upward **:** CLIMB **b :** an upward slope or rising grade **:** ACCLIVITY **c :** the degree of elevation **:** INCLINATION, GRADIENT **2 :** an advance in social status or reputation **:** PROGRESS **3 :** a going back in time or upward in order of genealogical succession

as·cer·tain \,as-ər-'tān\ *vt* [ME *acertainen,* fr. MF *acertainer,* fr. *a-* (fr. L *ad-*) + *certain*] **1** *archaic* **:** to make certain, exact, or precise **2 :** to find out or learn with certainty ***syn*** see DISCOVER — **as·cer·tain·able** \-'tā-nə-bəl\ *adj* — **as·cer·tain·ment** \-'tān-mənt\ *n*

as·ce·sis \ə-'sē-səs\ *n, pl* **-ce·ses** \-'sē-(,)sēz\ [LL or Gk; LL, fr. Gk *askēsis,* lit., exercise, fr. *askein*] **:** SELF-DISCIPLINE, ASCETICISM

as·cet·ic \ə-'set-ik\ *also* **as·cet·i·cal** \-i-kəl\ *adj* [Gk *askētikos,* lit., laborious, fr. *askētēs* one that exercises, hermit, fr. *askein* to work, exercise] **1 :** practicing strict self-denial as a measure of personal and esp. spiritual discipline **2 :** austere in appearance, manner, or attitude ***syn*** see SEVERE ***ant*** luxurious, voluptuous — **ascetic** *n* — **as·cet·i·cal·ly** \-i-k(ə-)lē\ *adv* — **as·cet·i·cism** \-'set-ə-,siz-əm\ *n*

as·cid·i·an \ə-'sid-ē-ən\ *n* **:** any of an order (Ascidiacea) of simple or compound tunicates; *broadly* **:** TUNICATE

as·cid·i·um \ə-'sid-ē-əm\ *n, pl* **-cid·ia** \-ē-ə\ [NL, fr. Gk *askidion,* dim. of *askos* wineskin, bladder] **:** a pitcher-shaped or flask-shaped organ or appendage of a plant

as·ci·tes \ə-'sīt-ēz\ *n, pl* **ascites** [ME *aschytes,* fr. LL *ascites,* fr. Gk *askitēs,* fr. *askos*] **:** accumulation of serous fluid in the abdomen — **as·cit·ic** \-'sit-ik\ *adj*

as·cle·pi·ad \ə-'sklē-pē-əd, a-, -,ad\ *n* [deriv. of Gk *asklēpiad-, asklēpias* swallowwort] **:** MILKWEED

as·co·carp \'as-kə-,kärp\ *n* **:** the mature fruiting body of an ascomycetous fungus; *broadly* **:** such a body with its enclosed asci, spores, and paraphyses — **as·co·car·pous** \,as-kə-'kär-pəs\ *adj*

as·co·go·ni·um \,as-kə-'gō-nē-əm\ *n, pl* **-nia** \-nē-ə\ [NL, fr. *asc-* + Gk *gonos* procreation — more at GON-] **:** the fertile basal often one-celled portion of an archicarp; *broadly* **:** ARCHICARP

as·co·my·cete \,as-kō-'mī-,sēt, -,mī-'sēt\ *n* [deriv. of Gk *askos* + *mykēt-, mykēs* fungus; akin to L *mucus*] **:** any of a class (Ascomycetes) of higher fungi (as yeasts or molds) with septate hyphae and spores formed in asci — **as·co·my·ce·tous** \-,mī-'sēt-əs\ *adj*

ascor·bate \ə-'skȯr-,bāt, -bət\ *n* : a salt of ascorbic acid

ascor·bic acid \ə-,skȯr-bik-\ *n* [*a-* + NL *scorbutus* scurvy — more at SCORBUTIC] : VITAMIN C

as·co·spore \'as-kə-,spō(ə)r, -,spȯ(ə)r\ *n* : one of the spores contained in an ascus — **as·co·spo·ric** \,as-kə-'spȯr-ik, -'spȯr-\ *or* **as·co·spo·rous** \-'spȯr-əs, -'spȯr-; a-'skäs-pə-rəs\ *adj*

as·cot \'as-kət, -,kät\ *n* [*Ascot Heath,* racetrack near Ascot, England] : a broad neck scarf that is looped under the chin

as·cribe \ə-'skrīb\ *vt* **as·cribed; as·crib·ing** [ME *ascriven,* fr. MF *ascrivre,* fr. L *ascribere,* fr. *ad-* + *scribere* to write — more at SCRIBE] : to refer to a supposed cause, source, or author — **as·crib·able** \-'skrī-bə-bəl\ *adj*
syn ASCRIBE, ATTRIBUTE, ASSIGN, IMPUTE, REFER, CREDIT *shared meaning element* : to lay something to the account of a person or thing

as·crip·tion \ə-'skrip-shən\ *n* [LL *ascription-, ascriptio,* fr. L, written addition, fr. *ascriptus,* pp. of *ascribere*] : the act of ascribing : ATTRIBUTION

as·crip·tive \-'skrip-tiv\ *adj* : relating to or involving ascription

ASCU *abbr* Association of State Colleges and Universities

as·cus \'as-kəs\ *n, pl* **as·ci** \'as-,(k)ī, -,kē\ [NL, fr. Gk *askos* wineskin, bladder] : the membranous oval or tubular spore sac of an ascomycete

as·dic \'az-(,)dik\ *n* [*Anti-Submarine Detection Investigation Committee*] : SONAR

ASE *abbr* American Stock Exchange

-ase \,ās, -,āz\ *n suffix* [F, fr. *diastase*] : enzyme ⟨protease⟩

asep·sis \(')ā-'sep-səs, ə-\ *n* [NL] **1** : the condition of being aseptic **2** : the methods of making or keeping aseptic

asep·tic \-'sep-tik\ *adj* [ISV] **1 a** : preventing infection ⟨~ techniques⟩ **b** : free or freed from pathogenic microorganisms ⟨an ~ operating room⟩ **2 a** : lacking vitality, emotion, or warmth ⟨~ essays⟩ **b** : DETACHED, OBJECTIVE ⟨an ~ view of civilization⟩ **c** : having a cleansing or purifying effect — **asep·ti·cal·ly** \-ti-k(ə-)lē\ *adv*

asex·u·al \(')ā-'seksh-(ə-)wəl, -'sek-shəl\ *adj* **1** : lacking sex or functional sexual organs **2** : produced without sexual action or differentiation — **asex·u·al·ly** \-'seksh-(ə-)wə-lē, -(ə-)lē\ *adv*

asexual generation *n* : a generation that reproduces only by asexual processes — used of organisms exhibiting alternation of generations

asexual reproduction *n* : reproduction (as cell division, spore formation, fission, or budding) without union of individuals or germ cells

as for *prep* : with regard to : CONCERNING ⟨*as for* the others, they'll arrive later⟩

asg *abbr* assigned; assignment

As·gard \'as-,gärd, 'az-\ *n* [ON *āsgarthr*] : the home of the Norse gods

asgd *abbr* assigned

asgmt *abbr* assignment

¹ash \'ash\ *n* [ME *asshe,* fr. OE *æsc;* akin to OHG *ask* ash, L *ornus* wild mountain ash] **1** : any of a genus (*Fraxinus*) of trees of the olive family with pinnate leaves, thin furrowed bark, and gray branchlets **2** : the tough elastic wood of an ash **3** [OE *æsc,* name of the corresponding runic letter] : the ligature æ used in Old English to represent a low front vowel

²ash *n, often attrib* [ME *asshe,* fr. OE *asce;* akin to OHG *asca* ash, L *aridus* dry — more at ARDOR] **1 a** : the solid residue left when combustible material is thoroughly burned or is oxidized by chemical means **b** : fine particles of mineral matter from a volcanic vent **2** *pl* : RUINS **3** *pl* : the remains of the dead human body after cremation or disintegration **4** : something that symbolizes grief, repentance, or humiliation **5** *pl* : deathly pallor — **ash·less** \-ləs\ *adj*

³ash *vt* : to convert into ash

ashamed \ə-'shāmd\ *adj* [ME, fr. OE *āscamod,* pp. of *āscamian* to shame, fr. *ā-* (perfective prefix) + *scamian* to shame — more at ABIDE, SHAME] **1 a** : feeling shame, guilt, or disgrace **b** : feeling inferior or unworthy **2** : restrained by anticipation of shame ⟨was ~ to beg⟩ — **asham·ed·ly** \-'shā-məd-lē\ *adv*

Ashan·ti \ə-'shant-ē, -'shänt-\ *n, pl* **Ashanti** *or* **Ashantis** [*Ashanti A¹san³te¹*] **1** : a West African people of Ghana **2** : the dialect of Akan spoken by the Ashanti people

ash·can \'ash-,kan\ *adj, often cap* : of or relating to a group of 20th century American painters who depicted city life realistically ⟨~ school⟩

ash can *n* **1** : a metal receptacle for refuse **2** *slang* : DEPTH CHARGE

¹ash·en \'ash-ən\ *adj* : of, relating to, or made from the wood of the ash tree

²ashen *adj* **1** : consisting of or resembling ashes **2** : of the color of ashes **3** : deathly pale : BLANCHED ⟨his face was ~ with fear⟩

Ash·er \'ash-ər\ *n* [Heb *Āshēr*] : a son of Jacob and the traditional eponymous ancestor of one of the tribes of Israel

Ash·ke·nazi \,ash-kə-'naz-ē\ *n, pl* **-naz·im** \-'naz-əm\ [Heb *Ashkĕnāzī*] : a member of one of the two great divisions of Jews comprising the eastern European Yiddish-speaking Jews — **Ash·ke·naz·ic** \-'naz-ik\ *adj*

ash·lar \'ash-lər\ *n* [ME *asheler,* fr. MF *aisselier* traverse beam, fr. OF, fr. *ais* board, fr. L *axis,* alter. of *assis*] **1** : hewn or squared stone; *also* : masonry of such stone **2** : a thin squared and dressed stone for facing a wall of rubble or brick

ashore \ə-'shō(ə)r, -'shȯ(ə)r\ *adv* : on or to the shore

ash·ram \'äsh-rəm\ *n* [Skt *āśrama,* fr. *ā* toward + *śrama* religious exercise] **1 a** : a secluded dwelling of a Hindu sage **b** : the group of disciples instructed there **2** : a religious retreat

Ash·to·reth \'ash-tə-,reth\ *n* [Heb *Ashtōreth*] : ASTARTE

ash·tray \'ash-,trā\ *n* : a receptacle for tobacco ashes and for cigar and cigarette butts

Ashur \'ä-,shu̇(ə)r\ *n* [Assyrian *Ashūr*] : the chief deity of the Assyrian pantheon

Ash Wednesday *n* : the first day of Lent

ashy \'ash-ē\ *adj* **ash·i·er; -est 1** : of or relating to ashes **2** : deadly pale

ASI *abbr* airspeed indicator

Asian \'ā-zhən, -shən\ *adj* : of, relating to, or characteristic of the continent of Asia or its people — **Asian** *n*

Asian influenza *n* : influenza caused by a mutant strain of the influenza virus

Asi·at·ic \,ā-z(h)ē-'at-ik\ *adj* : ASIAN — sometimes taken to be offensive — **Asiatic** *n*

Asiatic cholera *n* : an acute infectious epidemic cholera of Asiatic origin caused by a bacterium (*Vibrio comma*)

¹aside \ə-'sīd\ *adv* **1** : to or toward the side ⟨stepped ~⟩ **2** : out of the way : AWAY **3** : set to one side ⟨jesting ~⟩

²aside *prep, obs* : BEYOND, PAST

³aside *n* **1** : an utterance meant to be inaudible to someone; *esp* : an actor's speech heard by the audience but supposedly not by other characters on stage **2** : a straying from the theme : DIGRESSION

aside from *prep* **1** : in addition to : BESIDES **2** : except for

as if *conj* **1** : as it would be if ⟨it was *as if* he had lost his last friend⟩ **2** : as one would do if ⟨he ran *as if* ghosts were chasing him⟩ **3** : THAT ⟨it seemed *as if* the day would never end⟩

Asin \'äs-(,)in\ *n* [Hindi *Āsin,* fr. Skt *Āśvina*] : a month of the Hindu year — see MONTH table

as·i·nine \'as-ᵊn-,īn\ *adj* [L *asininus,* fr. *asinus* ass] **1** : of, relating to, or resembling an ass **2** : marked by inexcusable failure to exercise intelligence or sound judgment ⟨an ~ excuse⟩ — *syn* see SIMPLE *ant* sensible, judicious — **as·i·nine·ly** *adv* — **as·i·nin·i·ty** \,as-ᵊn-'in-ət-ē\ *n*

ask \'ask, 'ȧsk\ *vb* **asked** \'as(k)t, 'ȧs(k)t\; **ask·ing** [ME *asken,* fr. OE *āscian;* akin to OHG *eiscōn* to ask, L *aeruscare* to beg] *vt* **1 a** : to call on for an answer **b** : to put a question about ⟨~ SPEAK, UTTER ⟨~ a question⟩ **2 a** : to make a request of ⟨she ~ed her teacher for help⟩ **b** : to make a request for ⟨she ~ed help from her teacher⟩ **3** : to call for : REQUIRE **4** : to set as a price ⟨~ed $3000 for the car⟩ **5** : INVITE ~ *vi* **1** : to seek information **2** : to make a request ⟨~ed for food⟩ **3** : LOOK — often used in the phrase *ask for trouble* — **ask·er** *n*
syn 1 ASK, QUESTION, INTERROGATE, QUERY, INQUIRE *shared meaning element* : to address a person in an attempt to elicit information
2 ASK, REQUEST, SOLICIT *shared meaning element* : to seek to obtain by making one's wants known

askance \ə-'skan(t)s\ *also* **askant** \-'skant\ *adv* [origin unknown] **1** : with a side glance : OBLIQUELY **2** : with disapproval or distrust : SCORNFULLY

as·ke·sis \ə-'skē-səs\ *var of* ASCESIS

askew \ə-'skyü\ *adv or adj* [prob. fr. *a-* + *skew*] : out of line : AWRY ⟨the picture hung ~⟩ — **askew·ness** *n*

ASLA *abbr* American Society of Landscape Architects

¹aslant \ə-'slant\ *adv or adj* : in a slanting direction : OBLIQUELY

²aslant *prep* : over or across in a slanting direction

¹asleep \ə-'slēp\ *adj* **1** : being in a state of sleep **2** : DEAD **3** : lacking sensation : NUMB **4 a** : INACTIVE, SLUGGISH **b** : not alert : INDIFFERENT

²asleep *adv* **1** : into a state of sleep **2** : into the sleep of death **3** : into a state of inactivity, sluggishness, or indifference

as long as *conj* **1** : provided that ⟨can do as they like *as long as* they have a B average⟩ **2** : inasmuch as : SINCE ⟨*as long as* you're going, I'll go too⟩

aslope \ə-'slōp\ *adj or adv* : being in a sloping or slanting position or direction

ASME *abbr* American Society of Mechanical Engineers

aso·cial \(')ā-'sō-shəl\ *adj* : not social: **a** : rejecting or lacking the capacity for social interaction ⟨an ~ or reclusive attitude — A. T. Weaver⟩ **b** : ANTISOCIAL *syn* see UNSOCIAL *ant* social

as of *prep* : ON, AT, FROM ⟨takes effect *as of* July 1⟩

¹asp \'asp\ *n* [ME] : ASPEN

²asp *n* [ME *aspis,* fr. L, fr. Gk] : a small venomous snake of Egypt variously identified as the cerastes or a small African cobra (*Naja haje*)

as·par·a·gine \ə-'spar-ə-jēn\ *n* [F, fr. L *asparagus*] : a white crystalline amino acid $C_4H_8N_2O_3$ that is an amide of aspartic acid and serves as a storage depot for amino groups in many plants

as·par·a·gus \ə-'spar-ə-gəs\ *n* [NL, genus name, fr. L, *asparagus* plant, fr. Gk *asparagos;* akin to Gk *spargan* to swell — more at SPARK] : any of a genus (*Asparagus*) of Old World perennial plants of the lily family having much-branched stems, minute scalelike leaves, and linear cladophylls; *esp* : one (*A. officinalis*) widely cultivated for its edible young shoots

as·par·tate \ə-'spär-,tāt\ *n* : a salt or ester of aspartic acid

as·par·tic acid \ə-,spärt-ik-\ *n* [ISV, irreg. fr. L *asparagus*] : a crystalline amino acid $C_4H_7NO_4$ found esp. in plants

as·par·to·ki·nase \ə-,spärt-ō-'kī-,nās, -,nāz\ *n* [*aspartic acid* + *-o-* + *kinase*] : an enzyme that catalyzes the phosphorylation of aspartic acid by ATP

as·pect \'as-,pekt\ *n* [ME, fr. L *aspectus,* fr. *aspectus,* pp. of *aspicere* to look at, fr. *ad-* + *specere* to look — more at SPY] **1 a** : the position of planets or stars with respect to one another held by astrologers to influence human affairs; *also* : the apparent position (as conjunction) of a body in the solar system with respect to the sun **b** : a position facing a particular direction : EXPOSURE **c** : the manner of presentation of a plane to a fluid through which it

ə abut	ᵊ kitten	ər further	a back	ā bake	ä cot, cart
au̇ out	ch chin	e less	ē easy	g gift	i trip	ī life
j joke	ŋ sing	ō flow	ȯ flaw	ȯi coin	th thin	th this
ü loot	u̇ foot	y yet	yü few	yu̇ furious	zh vision	

is moving or to a current **2 a** (1) : appearance to the eye or mind (2) : a particular appearance of countenance: MIEN ⟨a man surly in ~⟩ **b** : a particular status or phase in which something appears or may be regarded ⟨studied every ~ of the question⟩ **3** *archaic* : an act of looking : GAZE **4 a** : the nature of the action of a verb as to its beginning, duration, completion, or repetition and without reference to its position in time **b** : a set of inflected verb forms that indicate aspect ***syn*** see PHASE — **as·pec·tu·al** \a-ˈspek-chə(-wə)l\ *adj*

aspect ratio *n* : a ratio of one dimension to another: as **a** : the ratio or span to mean chord of an airfoil **b** : the ratio of the width of a television or motion-picture image to its height

as·pen \ˈas-pən\ *n* [alter of ME *asp*, fr. OE *æspe*; akin to OHG *aspa* aspen, Latvian *apsa*] : any of several poplars (esp. *Populus tremula* of Europe and *P. tremuloides* and *P. grandidentata* of No. America) with leaves that flutter in the lightest wind because of their flattened petioles — **aspen** *adj*

as·per·ges \ə-ˈspər-(ˌ)jēz\ *n* [L, thou wilt sprinkle, fr. *aspergere*] : a ceremony of sprinkling altar, clergy, and people with holy water

as·per·gil·lo·sis \ˌas-pər-(ˌ)jil-ˈō-səs\ *n, pl* **-lo·ses** \-ˌsēz\ : infection with or disease caused (as in poultry) by molds (genus *Aspergillus*)

as·per·gil·lum \ˌas-pər-ˈjil-əm\ *n, pl* **-la** \-ə\ *or* **-lums** [NL, fr. L *aspergere*] : a brush or small perforated container with a handle that is used for sprinkling holy water in a liturgical service

as·per·gil·lus \-ˈjil-əs\ *n, pl* **-gil·li** \-ˈjil-ˌī\ [NL, genus name, fr. *aspergillum*] : any of a genus (*Aspergillus*) of ascomycetous fungi with branched radiate sporophores including many common molds

as·per·i·ty \a-ˈsper-ət-ē, ə-\ *n, pl* **-ties** [ME *asprete*, fr. OF *aspreté*, fr. *aspre* rough, fr. L *asper*] **1** : RIGOR, SEVERITY **2 a** : roughness of surface : UNEVENNESS **b** : roughness of sound **3** : roughness of manner or of temper : HARSHNESS ***syn*** see ACRIMONY ***ant*** amenity

as·perse \ə-ˈspərs, a-\ *vt* **as·persed; as·pers·ing** [L *aspersus*, pp. of *aspergere*, fr. *ad-* + *spargere* to scatter — more at SPARK] **1** : SPRINKLE; *esp* : to sprinkle with holy water **2** : to attack with evil reports or false or injurious charges ***syn*** see MALIGN

as·per·sion \ə-ˈspər-zhən, -shən\ *n* **1** : a sprinkling with water esp. in religious ceremonies **2 a** : the act of calumniating : DEFAMATION **b** : a calumnious expression ⟨he cast ~*s* on her integrity⟩ ***syn*** see ANIMADVERSION

as·phalt \ˈas-ˌfȯlt\ *or* **as·phal·tum** \as-ˈfȯl-təm\ *n* [ME *aspalt*, fr. LL *aspaltus*, fr. Gk *asphaltos*] **1** : a brown to black bituminous substance that is found in natural beds and is also obtained as a residue in petroleum refining and that consists chiefly of hydrocarbons **2** : an asphaltic composition used for pavements and as a waterproof cement — **as·phal·tic** \as-ˈfȯl-tik\ *adj*

as·phalt·ite \ˈas-ˌfȯl-ˌtīt\ *n* : a native asphalt occurring in vein deposits below the surface of the ground

asphalt jungle *n* : a big city or a specified part of a big city

as·pher·ic \(ˈ)ā-ˈsfi(ə)r-ik, -ˈsfer-\ *or* **as·pher·i·cal** \-i-kəl\ *adj* **1** : departing slightly from the spherical form ⟨~ optical surface⟩ **2** : free from spherical aberration ⟨an ~ lens⟩

as·pho·del \ˈas-fə-ˌdel\ *n* [L *asphodelus*, fr. Gk *asphodelos*] : any of various Old World usu. perennial herbs (esp. genera *Asphodelus* and *Asphodeline*) of the lily family with flowers in long erect racemes

as·phyx·ia \as-ˈfik-sē-ə, əs-\ *n* [NL, fr. Gk, stopping of the pulse, fr. *a-* + *sphyzein* to throb] : a lack of oxygen or excess of carbon dioxide in the body that is usu. caused by interruption of breathing and that causes unconsciousness

as·phyx·i·ate \-sē-ˌāt\ *vb* **-at·ed; -at·ing** *vt* : to cause asphyxia in; *also* : to kill or make unconscious through want of adequate oxygen, presence of noxious agents, or other obstruction to normal breathing ~ *vi* : to become asphyxiated — **as·phyx·i·a·tion** \-ˌfik-sē-ˈā-shən\ *n* — **as·phyx·i·a·tor** \-ˈfik-sē-ˌāt-ər\ *n*

¹as·pic \ˈas-pik\ *n* [MF, alter. of *aspe*, fr. L *aspis*] *obs* : ²ASP

²aspic *n* [F, lit., asp] : a savory jelly (as of fish or meat stock) used cold to garnish meat or fish or to make a mold of meat, fish, or vegetables

as·pi·dis·tra \ˌas-pə-ˈdis-trə\ *n* [NL, irreg. fr. Gk *aspid-, aspis* shield] : an Asiatic plant (*Aspidistra lurida*) of the lily family that has large basal leaves and is often grown as a foliage plant

¹as·pi·rant \ˈas-p(ə-)rənt, ə-ˈspī-rənt\ *n* : one who aspires ⟨presidential ~*s*⟩

²aspirant *adj* : seeking to attain a desired position or status

¹as·pi·rate \ˈas-pə-ˌrāt\ *vt* **-rat·ed; -rat·ing** [L *aspiratus*, pp. of *aspirare*] **1** : to pronounce (a vowel, a consonant, or a word) with an accompanying *h*-sound **2 a** : to draw by suction **b** : to remove (as blood) by aspiration

²as·pi·rate \ˈas-p(ə-)rət\ *n* **1** : an independent sound \h\ or a character (as the letter *h*) representing it **2** : a consonant having aspiration as its final component ⟨in English the *p* of *pit* represents an ~⟩ **3** : material removed by aspiration

as·pi·ra·tion \ˌas-pə-ˈrā-shən\ *n* **1** : the pronunciation or addition of an aspirate; *also* : the aspirate or its symbol **2** : a drawing of something in, out, up, or through by or as if by suction: as **a** : the act of breathing and esp. of breathing in **b** : the withdrawal of fluid from the body **c** : the taking of foreign matter into the lungs with the respiratory current **3 a** : a strong desire to achieve something high or great **b** : an object of such desire ***syn*** see AMBITION

as·pi·ra·tor \ˈas-pə-ˌrāt-ər\ *n* : an apparatus for producing suction or moving or collecting materials by suction; *esp* : a hollow tubular instrument connected with a partial vacuum and used to remove fluid or tissue or foreign bodies from the body

as·pire \ə-ˈspī(ə)r\ *vi* **as·pired; as·pir·ing** [ME *aspiren*, fr. MF or L; MF *aspirer*, fr. L *aspirare*, lit., to breathe upon, fr. *ad-* + *spirare* to breathe — more at SPIRIT] **1** : to seek to attain or accomplish a particular goal ⟨*aspired* to a career in medicine⟩ **2** : ASCEND, SOAR — **as·pir·er** *n*

as·pi·rin \ˈas-p(ə-)rən\ *n, pl* **aspirin** *or* **aspirins** [ISV, fr. acetyl + *spir*aeic acid (former name of salicylic acid), fr. NL *Spiraea*, genus of shrubs — more at SPIREA] **1** : a white crystalline derivative $C_9H_8O_4$ of salicylic acid used for relief of pain and fever **2** : a tablet of aspirin

ASR *abbr* **1** airport surveillance radar **2** air-sea rescue

as regards *or* **as respects** *prep* : in regard to : with respect to

¹ass \ˈas\ *n* [ME, fr. OE *assa*, perh. fr. OIr *asan*, fr. L *asinus*] **1** : any of several hardy gregarious mammals (genus *Equus*) that are smaller than the horse, have long ears, and include the donkey **2** : a stupid, obstinate, or perverse person

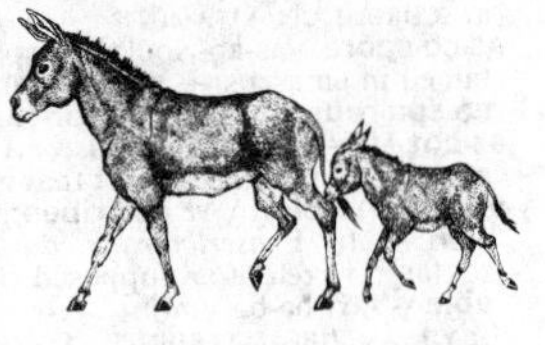

asses 1

²ass \ˈas\ *or* **arse** \ˈas, ˈärs\ *n* [ME *ars, ers*, fr. OE *ærs, ears*; akin to OHG & ON *ars* buttocks, Gk *orrhos*, Arm *oṙ*, Hitt *arraš*, OIr *err* tail] **1 a** : BUTTOCKS — often considered vulgar **b** : ANUS — often considered vulgar **2** : SEXUAL INTERCOURSE — usu. considered vulgar

as·sa·fet·i·da *or* **as·sa·foe·ti·da** *var of* ASAFETIDA

as·sai \ä-ˈsī\ *adv* [It, fr. (assumed) VL *ad satis* enough — more at ASSET] : VERY — used with tempo direction in music ⟨allegro ~⟩

as·sail \ə-ˈsā(ə)l\ *vt* [ME *assailen*, fr. OF *asaillir*, fr. (assumed) VL *assalire*, alter. of L *assilire* to leap upon, fr. *ad-* + *salire* to leap — more at SALLY] : to attack violently with blows or words ***syn*** see ATTACK — **as·sail·able** \-ˈsā-lə-bəl\ *adj* — **as·sail·ant** \-ˈsā-lənt\ *n*

As·sam·ese \ˌas-ə-ˈmēz, -ˈmēs\ *n, pl* **Assamese** **1** : a native or inhabitant of Assam, India **2** : the Indic language of Assam

as·sas·sin \ə-ˈsas-ᵊn\ *n* [ML *assassinus*, fr. Ar *ḥashshāshīn*, pl. of *ḥashshāsh* one who smokes or chews hashish] **1** *cap* : one of a secret order of Muslims that at the time of the Crusades terrorized Christians and other enemies by secret murder committed under the influence of hashish **2** : MURDERER; *esp* : one that murders a politically important person either for hire or from fanatical motives

as·sas·si·nate \ə-ˈsas-ᵊn-ˌāt\ *vt* **-nat·ed; -nat·ing** **1** : to murder by sudden or secret attack usu. for impersonal reasons ⟨~ a senator⟩ **2** : to injure or destroy unexpectedly and treacherously ***syn*** see KILL — **as·sas·si·na·tion** \-ˌsas-ᵊn-ˈā-shən\ *n* — **as·sas·si·na·tor** \-ˈsas-ᵊn-ˌāt-ər\ *n*

assassin bug *n* : any of a family (Reduviidae) of bugs that are usu. predatory on insects though some suck the blood of mammals : CONENOSE

¹as·sault \ə-ˈsȯlt\ *n* [ME *assaut*, fr. OF, fr. (assumed) VL *assaltus*, fr. *assaltus*, pp. of *assalire*] **1** : a violent physical or verbal attack **2 a** : an apparently violent attempt or a willful offer with force or violence to do hurt to another without the actual doing of the hurt threatened (as by lifting the fist in a threatening manner) — compare BATTERY 1b **b** : RAPE

²assault *vt* **1** : to make an assault on **2** : RAPE ~ *vi* : to make an assault ***syn*** see ATTACK — **as·sault·er** *n* — **as·saul·tive** \-ˈsȯl-tiv\ *adj* — **as·saul·tive·ly** *adv* — **as·saul·tive·ness** *n*

assault boat *n* : a small portable boat used in an amphibious military attack or in land warfare for crossing rivers or lakes

¹as·say \ˈas-ˌā, a-ˈsā\ *n* [ME, fr. OF *essai*, *assai* test, effort — more at ESSAY] **1** *archaic* : TRIAL, ATTEMPT **2** : examination and determination as to characteristics (as weight, measure, or quality) **3** : analysis (as of an ore or drug) to determine the presence, absence, or quantity of one or more components **4** : a substance to be assayed; *also* : the tabulated result of assaying

²as·say \a-ˈsā, ˈas-ˌā\ *vt* **1** : TRY, ATTEMPT **2 a** : to analyze (as an ore) for one or more valuable components **b** : to judge the worth of : ESTIMATE ~ *vi* : to prove up in an assay — **as·say·er** *n*

as·se·gai *or* **as·sa·gai** \ˈas-i-ˌgī\ *n* [deriv. of Ar *az-zaghāya* the assegai, fr. *al-* the + *zaghāya* assegai] : a slender hardwood spear or light javelin usu. tipped with iron and used in southern Africa

as·sem·blage \ə-ˈsem-blij, *for 3 also* ˌas-ˌäm-ˈbläzh\ *n* **1** : a collection of persons or things : GATHERING **2** : the act of assembling : the state of being assembled **3 a** : an artistic composition made from scraps, junk, and odds and ends (as of paper, cloth, wood, stone, or metal) **b** : the art of making assemblages

as·sem·blag·ist \-blij-əst, -ˈbläzh-əst\ *n* : an artist who specializes in assemblages

as·sem·ble \ə-ˈsem-bəl\ *vb* **as·sem·bled; as·sem·bling** \-b(ə-)liŋ\ [ME *assemblen*, fr. OF *assembler*, fr. (assumed) VL *assimulare*, fr. L *ad-* + *simul* together — more at SAME] *vt* **1** : to bring together (as in a particular place or for a particular purpose) **2** : to fit together the parts of ~ *vi* : to meet together : CONVENE ***syn*** see GATHER

as·sem·bler \-b(ə-)lər\ *n* **1** : one that assembles **2** : a computer program that automatically converts instructions written in a symbolic code into the equivalent machine code

as·sem·bly \ə-ˈsem-blē\ *n, pl* **-blies** [ME *assemblee*, fr. MF, fr. OF, fr. *assembler*] **1** : a company of persons gathered for deliberation and legislation, worship, or entertainment **2** *cap* : a legislative body; *specif* : the lower house of a legislature **3** : ASSEMBLAGE 1, 2 **4** : a signal given by drum, bugle, trumpet, or all field music for troops to assemble or fall in **5 a** : the fitting together of manufactured parts into a complete machine, structure, or unit of a machine **b** : a collection of parts so assembled **6** : the translation of symbolic code to machine code by an assembler

assembly language *n* : a symbolic language for programming a computer that is a close approximation of machine language

assembly line *n* **1** : an arrangement of machines, equipment, and workers in which work passes from operation to operation in direct line until the product is assembled **2** : a process for turning out a finished product in a mechanically efficient manner ⟨academic *assembly lines*⟩

as·sem·bly·man \ə-ˈsem-blē-mən\ *n* : a member of an assembly

Assembly of God : a congregation belonging to a Pentecostal body founded in the U.S. in 1914

as·sem·bly·wom·an \-ˌwu̇m-ən\ *n* : a female member of an assembly

1as·sent \ə-ˈsent\ *vi* [ME *assenten,* fr. OF *assenter,* fr. L *assentari,* fr. *assentire,* fr. *ad-* + *sentire* to feel — more at SENSE] : to agree to something esp. after thoughtful consideration : CONCUR — **as·sen·tor** *or* **as·sent·er** \-ˈsent-ər\ *n*
syn ASSENT, CONSENT, ACCEDE, ACQUIESCE, AGREE, SUBSCRIBE *shared meaning element* : to concur with what has been proposed ***ant*** dissent
2assent *n* : an act of assenting : ACQUIESCENCE, AGREEMENT
as·sen·ta·tion \ˌas-ᵊn-ˈtā-shən, ˌas-ˌen-\ *n* : ready assent esp. when insincere or obsequious
as·sert \ə-ˈsərt\ *vt* [L *assertus,* pp. of *asserere,* fr. *ad-* + *serere* to join — more at SERIES] **1** : to state or declare positively and often forcefully or aggressively **2 a** : to demonstrate the existence of ⟨~ his manhood —James Joyce⟩ **b** : POSIT, POSTULATE
syn* 1** ASSERT, DECLARE, AFFIRM, PROTEST, AVOW *shared meaning element* : to state or put forward positively usu. in anticipation of or in the face of denial or objection ***ant deny, controvert
2 see MAINTAIN
— **assert oneself** : to compel recognition esp. of one's rights
as·ser·tion \ə-ˈsər-shən\ *n* : the act of asserting; *also* : DECLARATION, AFFIRMATION
as·ser·tive \ə-ˈsərt-iv\ *adj* : disposed to or characterized by bold or confident assertion ***syn*** see AGGRESSIVE ***ant*** retiring, acquiescent — **as·ser·tive·ly** *adv* — **as·ser·tive·ness** *n*
asses *pl of* AS *or of* ASS
as·sess \ə-ˈses\ *vt* [ME *assessen,* prob. fr. ML *assessus,* pp. of *assidēre,* fr. L, to sit beside, assist in the office of a judge — more at ASSIZE] **1** : to determine the rate or amount of (as a tax) **2 a** : to impose (as a tax) according to an established rate **b** : to subject to a tax, charge, or levy **3** : to make an official valuation of (property) for the purposes of taxation **4** : to determine the importance, size, or value of ***syn*** see ESTIMATE — **as·sess·able** \-ˈses-ə-bəl\ *adj*
as·sess·ment \ə-ˈses-mənt\ *n* **1** : the act or an instance of assessing : APPRAISAL **2** : the amount assessed
as·ses·sor \ə-ˈses-ər\ *n* **1** : an official who assists a judge or magistrate **2** : an official who assesses property for taxation
as·set \ˈas-ˌet\ *n* [back-formation fr. *assets,* sing., sufficient property to pay debts and legacies, fr. AF *asetz,* fr. OF *assez* enough, fr. (assumed) VL *ad satis,* fr. L *ad* to + *satis* enough — more at SAD] **1** *pl* **a** : the property of a deceased person subject by law to the payment of his debts and legacies **b** : the entire property of all sorts of a person, association, corporation, or estate applicable or subject to the payment of his or its debts **2** : ADVANTAGE, RESOURCE ⟨his wit is his chief ~⟩ **3** *pl* : the items on a balance sheet showing the book value of property owned
as·sev·er·ate \ə-ˈsev-ə-ˌrāt\ *vt* **-at·ed; -at·ing** [L *asseveratus,* pp. of *asseverare,* fr. *ad-* + *severus* severe] : to affirm or aver positively or earnestly — **as·sev·er·a·tion** \-ˌsev-ə-ˈrā-shən\ *n* — **as·sev·er·a·tive** \-ˈsev-ə-ˌrāt-iv\ *adj*
as·si·du·ity \ˌas-ə-ˈd(y)ü-ət-ē\ *n, pl* **-ities 1** : the quality or state of being assiduous : DILIGENCE **2** : solicitous or obsequious attention to a person
as·sid·u·ous \ə-ˈsij-(ə-)wəs\ *adj* [L *assiduus,* fr. *assidēre*] : marked by careful unremitting attention or persistent application ⟨~ patrons of the opera⟩ ***syn*** see BUSY ***ant*** desultory — **as·sid·u·ous·ly** *adv* — **as·sid·u·ous·ness** *n*
1as·sign \ə-ˈsīn\ *vt* [ME *assignen,* fr. OF *assigner,* fr. L *assignare,* fr. *ad-* + *signare* to mark, fr. *signum* mark, sign] **1** : to transfer (property) to another esp. in trust or for the benefit of creditors **2 a** : to appoint to a post or duty **b** : PRESCRIBE ⟨~ the lesson⟩ **3** : to fix authoritatively : SPECIFY ⟨~ a limit⟩ **4** : to ascribe with assurance esp. as motive or reason ***syn*** see ALLOT, ASCRIBE — **as·sign·abil·i·ty** \-ˌsī-nə-ˈbil-ət-ē\ *n* — **as·sign·able** \-ˈsī-nə-bəl\ *adj* — **as·sign·er** \-ˈsī-nər\ *or* **as·sign·or** \ˌas-ə-ˈnȯ(ə)r, ˌas-ˌī-, ə-ˌsī-\ *n*
2assign *n* : ASSIGNEE
as·si·gnat \ˌas-(ˌ)ēn-ˈyä, ˈas-ig-ˌnat\ *n* [F, fr. L *assignatus,* pp. of *assignare*] : a bill issued as currency by the French Revolutionary government (1790–95) on the security of expropriated lands
as·sig·na·tion \ˌas-ig-ˈnā-shən\ *n* **1** : the act of assigning or the assignment made; *esp* : ALLOTMENT **2** : TRYST ⟨returned from an ~ with his mistress —W. B. Yeats⟩ — **as·sig·na·tion·al** \-shnəl, -shən-ᵊl\ *adj*
assigned risk *n* : a poor risk (as an accident-prone motorist) that insurance companies would normally reject but are forced to insure by state law
as·sign·ee \ˌas-ə-ˈnē, ˌas-ˌī-, ə-ˌsī-\ *n* **1** : a person to whom an assignment is made **2** : a person appointed to act for another **3** : a person to whom a right or property is legally transferred
as·sign·ment \ə-ˈsīn-mənt\ *n* **1** : the act of assigning **2 a** : a position, post, or office to which one is assigned **b** : a specified task or amount of work assigned or undertaken as if assigned by authority **3** : the transfer of property; *esp* : the transfer of property to be held in trust or to be used for the benefit of creditors ***syn*** see TASK
as·sim·i·la·ble \ə-ˈsim-ə-lə-bəl\ *adj* : capable of being assimilated — **as·sim·i·la·bil·i·ty** \-ˌsim-ə-lə-ˈbil-ət-ē\ *n*
1as·sim·i·late \ə-ˈsim-ə-ˌlāt\ *vb* **-lat·ed; -lat·ing** [ML *assimilatus,* pp. of *assimilare,* fr. L *assimulare* to make similar, fr. *ad-* + *simulare* to make similar, simulate] *vt* **1 a** : to take in and appropriate as nourishment : absorb into the system **b** : to take into the mind and thoroughly comprehend **2 a** : to make similar **b** : to alter by assimilation **c** : to absorb into the cultural tradition of a population or group ⟨the community *assimilated* many immigrants⟩ **3** : COMPARE, LIKEN ~ *vi* : to become assimilated ***syn*** see ABSORB — **as·sim·i·la·tor** \-ˌlāt-ər\ *n*
2as·sim·i·late \-lət, -ˌlāt\ *n* : something that is assimilated
as·sim·i·la·tion \ə-ˌsim-ə-ˈlā-shən\ *n* **1 a** : an act, process, or instance of assimilating **b** : the state of being assimilated **2** : the incorporation or conversion of nutrients into protoplasm that in animals follows digestion and absorption and in higher plants involves both photosynthesis and root absorption **3** : change of a sound in speech so that it becomes identical with or similar to a neighboring sound ⟨in the word *cupboard* the \p\ sound of the word *cup* has undergone complete ~⟩ ***syn*** see RECOGNITION
as·sim·i·la·tion·ism \-shə-ˌniz-əm\ *n* : a policy of assimilating differing racial or cultural groups — **as·sim·i·la·tion·ist** \-sh(ə-)nəst\ *n or adj*
as·sim·i·la·tive \ə-ˈsim-ə-ˌlāt-iv, -lət-\ *adj* : of, relating to, or causing assimilation
as·sim·i·la·to·ry \ə-ˈsim-ə-lə-ˌtōr-ē, -ˌtȯr-\ *adj* : ASSIMILATIVE
1as·sist \ə-ˈsist\ *vb* [MF or L; MF *assister* to help, stand by, fr. L *assistere,* fr. *ad-* + *sistere* to cause to stand; akin to L *stare* to stand — more at STAND] *vi* **1** : to give support or aid **2** : to be present as a spectator ~ *vt* : to give usu. supplementary support or aid to ⟨~ a lame man up the stairs⟩ ***syn*** see HELP ***ant*** hamper, impede
2assist *n* **1** : an act of assistance : AID **2** : the action of a player who by passing a ball or puck enables a teammate to make a putout or score a goal **3** : a mechanical device that provides assistance
as·sis·tance \ə-ˈsis-tən(t)s\ *n* : the act of assisting or the help supplied : AID ⟨financial and technical ~⟩
as·sis·tant \-tənt\ *n* : one who assists : HELPER; *also* : an auxiliary device or substance — **assistant** *adj*
assistant professor *n* : a member of a college or university faculty who ranks above an instructor and below an associate professor — **assistant professorship** *n*
as·sis·tant·ship \ə-ˈsis-tən(t)-ˌship\ *n* : an appointment awarded on an annual basis to a qualified graduate student that requires part-time teaching, research, or residence hall duties and carries a stipend
as·size \ə-ˈsīz\ *n* [ME *assise,* fr. OF, session, settlement, fr. *asseoir* to seat, fr. (assumed) VL *assedēre,* fr. L *assidēre* to sit beside, assist in the office of a judge, fr. *ad-* + *sedēre* to sit — more at SIT] **1** : an enactment made by a legislative assembly : ORDINANCE **2 a** : a statute regulating weights and measures of articles sold in the market **b** : the regulation of the price of bread or ale by the price of grain **3** : a fixed or customary standard **4 a** : a judicial inquest **b** : an action to be decided by such an inquest, the writ for instituting it, or the verdict or finding rendered by the jury **5 a** : the former periodical sessions of the superior courts in English counties for trial of civil and criminal cases — usu. used in pl. **b** : the time or place of holding such a court, the court itself, or a session of it — usu. used in pl.
assn *abbr* association
assoc *also* **asso** *abbr* **1** associate **2** association
as·so·cia·ble \ə-ˈsō-sh(ē-)ə-bəl, -sē-ə-\ *adj* : capable of being associated, joined, or connected in thought
1as·so·ci·ate \ə-ˈsō-s(h)ē-ˌāt\ *vb* **-at·ed; -at·ing** [ME *associat* associated, fr. L *associatus,* pp. of *associare* to unite, fr. *ad-* + *sociare* to join, fr. *socius* companion — more at SOCIAL] *vt* **1** : to join as a partner, friend, or companion **2** *obs* : to keep company with : ATTEND **3** : to join or connect together : COMBINE; *specif* : to subject to chemical association **4** : to bring together in any of various ways (as in memory or imagination) ~ *vi* **1** : to come together as partners, friends, or companions **2** : to combine or join with other parts : UNITE ***syn*** see JOIN
2as·so·ciate \ə-ˈsō-s(h)ē-ət, -shət, -s(h)ē-ˌāt\ *adj* **1** : closely connected (as in function or office) with another **2** : closely related esp. in the mind **3** : having secondary or subordinate status ⟨~ membership in a society⟩
3as·so·ciate *like* 2\ *n* **1** : a fellow worker : PARTNER, COLLEAGUE **2** : COMPANION, COMRADE **3** *often cap* : a degree conferred esp. by a junior college ⟨~ in arts⟩ — **as·so·ciate·ship** \-ˌship\ *n*
associate professor *n* : a member of a college or university faculty who ranks above an assistant professor and below a professor — **associate professorship** *n*
as·so·ci·a·tion \ə-ˌsō-sē-ˈā-shən, -shē-\ *n* **1 a** : the act of associating **b** : the state of being associated : PARTNERSHIP, COMBINATION **2** : an organization of persons having a common interest : SOCIETY **3** : something linked in memory or imagination with a thing or person **4** : the process of forming mental connections or bonds between sensations, ideas, or memories **5** : the formation of polymers by linkage through hydrogen bonds or of loosely bound chemical complexes **6** : a major unit in ecological community organization characterized by essential uniformity and usu. by two or more dominant species — **as·so·ci·a·tion·al** \-shnəl, -shən-ᵊl\ *adj*
association football *n* : SOCCER
as·so·cia·tive \ə-ˈsō-s(h)ē-ˌāt-iv, -shət-iv\ *adj* **1** : of or relating to association esp. of ideas or images **2** : dependent on or acquired by association or learning **3** : combining elements such that when the order of the elements is preserved the result is independent of the grouping ⟨addition is ~ since (a + b) + c = a + (b + c)⟩ — **as·so·cia·tive·ly** *adv* — **as·so·cia·tiv·i·ty** \-ˌsō-s(h)ē-ə-ˈtiv-ət-ē, -shə-ˈtiv-\ *n*
as·soil \ə-ˈsȯi(ə)l\ *vt* [ME *assoilen,* fr. OF *assoldre,* fr. L *absolvere* to absolve] **1** *archaic* : ABSOLVE, PARDON **2** *archaic* : ACQUIT, CLEAR **3** *archaic* : EXPIATE — **as·soil·ment** \-mənt\ *n, archaic*
as·so·nance \ˈas-ə-nən(t)s\ *n* [F, fr. L *assonare* to answer with the same sound, fr. *ad-* + *sonare* to sound — more at SOUND] **1** : resemblance of sound in words or syllables **2 a** : relatively close juxtaposition of similar sounds esp. of vowels **b** : repetition of vowels without repetition of consonants (as in *stony* and *holy*) used as an alternative to rhyme in verse — **as·so·nant** \-nənt\ *adj or n*
as soon as *conj* : immediately at or just after the time that
as·sort \ə-ˈsȯ(ə)rt\ *vb* [MF *assortir,* fr. *a-* (fr. L *ad-*) + *sorte* sort] *vt* **1** : to distribute into groups of a like kind : CLASSIFY **2** : to supply with an assortment or variety (as of goods) ~ *vi* **1** : to agree

ə abut ᵊ kitten ər further a back ā bake ä cot, cart
au̇ out ch chin e less ē easy g gift i trip ī life
j joke ŋ sing ō flow ȯ flaw ȯi coin th thin t͟h this
ü loot u̇ foot y yet yü few yu̇ furious zh vision

in kind : HARMONIZE **2** : to keep company : ASSOCIATE — **as·sor·ta·tive** \-'sȯrt-ət-iv\ *adj* — **as·sort·er** *n*

as·sort·ed \-'sȯrt-əd\ *adj* **1** : consisting of various kinds **2** : suited by nature, character, or design : MATCHED ⟨an ill-*assorted* pair⟩

as·sort·ment \-'sȯ(ə)rt-mənt\ *n* **1 a** : the act of assorting **b** : the state of being assorted **2** : a collection of assorted things or persons

ASSR *abbr* Autonomous Soviet Socialist Republic

asst *abbr* assistant

asstd *abbr* **1** assented **2** assorted

as·suage \ə-'swāj\ *vt* **as·suaged; as·suag·ing** [ME *aswagen,* fr. OF *assouagier,* fr. (assumed) VL *assuaviare,* fr. L *ad-* + *suavis* sweet — more at SWEET] **1** : to lessen the intensity of (something that pains or distresses) : EASE **2** : PACIFY, QUIET **3** : to put an end to by satisfying : APPEASE, QUENCH ⟨he *assuaged* his hunger with a sandwich⟩ ***syn*** see RELIEVE ***ant*** exacerbate, intensify — **as·suage·ment** \-'swāj-mənt\ *n*

as·sua·sive \ə-'swā-siv, -ziv\ *adj* : having a pleasantly soothing quality or effect : CALMING

as·sume \ə-'süm\ *vt* **as·sumed; as·sum·ing** [ME *assumen,* fr. L *assumere,* fr. *ad-* + *sumere* to take — more at CONSUME] **1 a** : to take up or in : RECEIVE **b** : to take into partnership, employment, or use **2 a** : to take to or upon oneself : UNDERTAKE **b** : to put on (clothing) : DON **3** : SEIZE, USURP **4** : to pretend to have or be : FEIGN ⟨*assumed* an air of confidence in spite of her dismay⟩ **5** : to take as granted or true : SUPPOSE **6** : to take over (the debts of another) as one's own — **as·sum·abil·i·ty** \-,sü-mə-'bil-ət-ē\ *n* — **as·sum·able** \-'sü-mə-bəl\ *adj* — **as·sum·ably** \-blē\ *adv*

syn ASSUME, AFFECT, PRETEND, SIMULATE, FEIGN, COUNTERFEIT, SHAM *shared meaning element* : to put on a false or deceptive appearance

as·sum·ing *adj* : PRETENTIOUS, PRESUMPTUOUS

as·sump·sit \ə-'səm(p)-sət\ *n* [NL, he undertook, fr. *assumere* to undertake, fr. L] **1 a** : a common-law action alleging damage from a breach of agreement **b** : an action to recover damages for breach of contract or promise **2** : a promise or contract not under seal on which an action of assumpsit may be brought

as·sump·tion \ə-'səm(p)-shən\ *n* [ME, fr. LL *assumption-, assumptio,* fr. L, taking up, fr. *assumptus,* pp. of *assumere*] **1 a** : the taking up of a person into heaven **b** *cap* : August 15 observed in commemoration of the Assumption of the Virgin Mary **2** : a taking to or upon oneself ⟨a delay in the ~ of his new position⟩ **3** : the act of laying claim to or taking possession of ⟨the ~ of power⟩ **4** : ARROGANCE, PRETENSION **5 a** : the supposition that something is true **b** : a fact or statement (as a proposition, axiom, postulate, or notion) taken for granted **6** : the taking over of another's debts

as·sump·tive \ə-'səm(p)-tiv\ *adj* **1** : taken as one's own **2** : taken for granted ⟨~ beliefs⟩ **3** : making undue claims : ASSUMING ⟨an ~ person⟩

as·sur·ance \ə-'shu̇r-ən(t)s\ *n* **1** : the act or action of assuring: as **a** : PLEDGE, GUARANTEE **b** : the act of conveying real property; *also* : the instrument by which it is conveyed **c** *chiefly Brit* : INSURANCE **2** : the state of being assured: as **a** : a being sure and safe : SECURITY **b** : a being certain in the mind : freedom from doubt ⟨the puritan's ~ of salvation⟩ **c** : confidence of mind or manner : easy freedom from self-doubt or uncertainty; *also* : excessive self-confidence : BRASHNESS, PRESUMPTION **3** : something that inspires or tends to inspire confidence ⟨gave repeated ~s of his goodwill⟩ ***syn* 1** see CERTAINTY ***ant*** mistrust, dubiousness **2** see CONFIDENCE ***ant*** diffidence

as·sure \ə-'shu̇(ə)r\ *vt* **as·sured; as·sur·ing** [ME *assuren,* fr. MF *assurer,* fr. ML *assecurare,* fr. L *ad-* + *securus* secure] **1** : to make safe (as from risks or against overthrow) : INSURE **2** : to give confidence to : REASSURE **3** : to make sure or certain : CONVINCE **4** : to inform positively ⟨*assured* her of his fidelity⟩ **5** : to make certain the coming or attainment of : GUARANTEE ⟨worked hard to ~ accuracy⟩ ***syn*** see ENSURE

[1]**as·sured** \ə-'shu̇(ə)rd\ *adj* **1** : characterized by certainty or security : GUARANTEED ⟨an ~ market⟩ **2 a** : characterized by self-confidence ⟨an ~ dancer⟩ **b** : characterized by smug self-satisfaction : COMPLACENT **3** : satisfied as to the certainty or truth of a matter : CONVINCED — **as·sured·ly** \-'shu̇r-əd-lē, -'shu̇(ə)rd-\ *adv* — **as·sured·ness** \-'shu̇r-əd-nəs, -'shu̇(ə)rd-\ *n*

[2]**assured** *n, pl* **assured** *or* **assureds** : INSURED

as·sur·er \ə-'shu̇r-ər\ *or* **as·sur·or** \ə-'shu̇r-ər, ə-,shu̇r-'ȯ(ə)r\ *n* : one that assures : INSURER

as·sur·gent \ə-'sər-jənt\ *adj* [L *assurgent-, assurgens,* prp. of *assurgere* to rise, fr. *ad-* + *surgere* to rise — more at SURGE] : moving upward : RISING; *esp* : ASCENDANT 1b

assy *abbr* assembly

Assyr *abbr* Assyrian

As·syr·i·an \ə-'sir-ē-ən\ *n* **1** : a member of an ancient Semitic race forming the Assyrian nation **2** : the Semitic language of the Assyrians — **Assyrian** *adj*

As·syr·i·ol·o·gist \ə-,sir-ē-'äl-ə-jəst\ *n* : a specialist in Assyriology

As·syr·i·ol·o·gy \-jē\ *n* : the science or study of the history, language, and antiquities of ancient Assyria and Babylonia — **As·syr·i·o·log·i·cal** \-,sir-ē-ə-'läj-i-kəl\ *adj*

-ast \,ast, əst\ *n suffix* [ME, fr. L *-astes,* fr. Gk *-astēs,* fr. verbs in *-azein*] : one connected with ⟨ecdysi*ast*⟩

astar·board \ə-'stär-bərd\ *adv* : toward or on the starboard side of a ship ⟨put the helm hard ~⟩

As·tar·te \ə-'stärt-ē\ *n* [L, fr. Gk *Astartē*] : the Phoenician goddess of fertility and of sexual love

astat·ic \(')ā-'stat-ik\ *adj* **1** : not static : not stable or steady **2** : having little or no tendency to take a fixed or definite position or direction — **astat·i·cal·ly** \-i-k(ə-)lē\ *adv* — **astat·i·cism** \-'stat-ə-,siz-əm\ *n*

as·ta·tine \'as-tə-,tēn\ *n* [Gk *astatos* unsteady, fr. *a-* + *statos* standing, fr. *histanai* to cause to stand — more at STAND] : a radioactive halogen element discovered by bombarding bismuth with helium nuclei and also formed by radioactive decay — see ELEMENT table

as·ter \'as-tər\ *n* **1** [NL, genus name, fr. L, aster, fr. Gk *aster-, astēr* star, aster — more at STAR] : any of various chiefly fall-blooming leafy-stemmed composite herbs (*Aster* and closely related genera) with often showy heads containing tubular flowers or both tubular and ray flowers — compare CHINA ASTER **2** [NL, fr. Gk *aster-, astēr*] : a system of gelated cytoplasmic rays typically arranged radially about a centrosome at either end of the mitotic spindle and sometimes persisting between mitoses

-as·ter \,as-tər, 'as-\ *n suffix* [ME, fr. L, suffix denoting partial resemblance] : one that is inferior, worthless, or not genuine ⟨criti*caster*⟩

as·te·ria \a-'stir-ē-ə\ *n* [L, a precious stone, fr. Gk, fem. of *asterios* starry, fr. *aster-, astēr*] : a gem stone cut to show asterism

as·te·ri·at·ed \-ē-,āt-əd\ *adj* [Gk *asterios*] : exhibiting asterism ⟨~ sapphire⟩

[1]**as·ter·isk** \'as-tə-,risk\ *n* [LL *asteriscus,* fr. Gk *asteriskos,* lit., little star, dim. of *aster-, astēr*] : the character * used in printing or writing as a reference mark, as an indication of the omission of letters or words, or to denote a hypothetical or nonoccurring linguistic form — **as·ter·isk·less** \-ləs\ *adj*

[2]**asterisk** *vt* : to mark with an asterisk : STAR

as·ter·ism \'as-tə-,riz-əm\ *n* [Gk *asterismos,* fr. *asterizein* to arrange in constellations, fr. *aster-, astēr*] **1 a** : CONSTELLATION **b** : a small group of stars **2** : a star-shaped figure exhibited by some crystals by reflected light (as in a star sapphire) or by transmitted light (as in some mica) **3** : three asterisks arranged in the form of a pyramid (as ⁎⁎⁎ or ⁂) esp. in order to direct attention to a following passage

astern \ə-'stərn\ *adv or adj* **1** : behind a ship **2** : at or toward the stern of a ship **3** : STERNFOREMOST, BACKWARD

[1]**as·ter·oid** \'as-tə-,rȯid\ *n* [Gk *asteroeidēs* starlike, fr. *aster-, astēr*] **1** : one of thousands of small planets between Mars and Jupiter with diameters from a fraction of a mile to nearly 500 miles **2** : STARFISH — **aster·oi·dal** \,as-tə-'rȯid-ᵊl\ *adj*

[2]**asteroid** *adj* **1** : resembling a star **2** : of or resembling a starfish

as·the·nia \as-'thē-nē-ə\ *n* [NL, fr. Gk *astheneia,* fr. *asthenēs* weak, fr. *a-* + *sthenos* strength] : lack or loss of strength : DEBILITY

as·then·ic \as-'then-ik\ *adj* **1** : of, relating to, or exhibiting asthenia : WEAK **2** : characterized by slender build and slight muscular development : ECTOMORPHIC

as·theno·sphere \as-'then-ə-,sfi(ə)r\ *n* [Gk *asthenēs* weak + E *-o-* + *sphere*] : a hypothetical zone of the earth which lies beneath the lithosphere and within which the material is believed to yield readily to persistent stresses

asth·ma \'az-mə\ *n* [ME *asma,* fr. ML, modif. of Gk *asthma*] : a condition often of allergic origin that is marked by continuous or paroxysmal labored breathing accompanied by wheezing, by a sense of constriction in the chest, and often by attacks of coughing or gasping — **asth·mat·ic** \az-'mat-ik\ *adj or n* — **asth·mat·i·cal·ly** \-i-k(ə-)lē\ *adv*

as though *conj* : as if

as·tig·mat·ic \,as-tig-'mat-ik\ *adj* [*a-* + Gk *stigmat-, stigma* mark — more at STIGMA] **1** : affected with, relating to, or correcting astigmatism **2** : showing incapacity for observation or discrimination ⟨an ~ fanaticism, a disregard for the facts—*N. Y. Herald Tribune*⟩ — **as·tig·mat·i·cal·ly** \-i-k(ə-)lē\ *adv*

astig·ma·tism \ə-'stig-mə-,tiz-əm\ *n* **1** : a defect of an optical system (as a lens) in consequence of which rays from a point fail to meet in a focal point resulting in a blurred and imperfect image **2** : a defect of vision due to astigmatism of the refractive system of the eye and esp. to corneal irregularity **3** : distorted understanding suggestive of the blurred vision of an astigmatic person

astir \ə-'stər\ *adj* **1** : exhibiting activity **2** : being out of bed : UP

ASTM *abbr* American Society for Testing and Materials

as to *prep* **1** : with regard or reference to : as for : ABOUT ⟨at a loss *as to* how to explain the mistake⟩ **2** : according to : BY ⟨graded *as to* size and color⟩

as·ton·ied \ə-'stän-ēd\ *adj* [ME, fr. pp. of *astonien*] **1** *archaic* : deprived briefly of the power to act : DAZED **2** *archaic* : filled with consternation or dismay

as·ton·ish \ə-'stän-ish\ *vt* [prob. fr. earlier *astony* (fr. ME *astonen, astonien,* fr. OF *estoner,* fr. — assumed — VL *extonare,* fr. L *ex-* + *tonare* to thunder) + *-ish* (as in *abolish*) — more at THUNDER] **1** *obs* : to strike with sudden fear **2** : to strike with sudden wonder or surprise ***syn*** see SURPRISE

as·ton·ish·ing \-iŋ\ *adj* : causing astonishment : SURPRISING — **as·ton·ish·ing·ly** \-iŋ-lē\ *adv*

as·ton·ish·ment \ə-'stän-ish-mənt\ *n* **1 a** : the state of being astonished **b** : CONSTERNATION **c** : AMAZEMENT **2** : a cause of amazement or wonder

[1]**as·tound** \ə-'stau̇nd\ *adj* [ME *astoned,* fr. pp. of *astonen*] *archaic* : overwhelmed with astonishment or amazement : ASTOUNDED

[2]**astound** *vt* : to fill with bewilderment and wonder ***syn*** see SURPRISE

as·tound·ing \ə-'stau̇n-diŋ\ *adj* : causing astonishment or amazement — **as·tound·ing·ly** \-diŋ-lē\ *adv*

ASTP *abbr* army specialized training program

astr- *or* **astro-** *comb form* [ME *astro-,* fr. OF, fr. L *astr-, astro-,* fr. Gk, fr. *astron* — more at STAR] **1** : star : heavens : outer space : astronomical ⟨*astro*physics⟩ **2** : aster of a cell ⟨*astro*sphere⟩

[1]**astrad·dle** \ə-'strad-ᵊl\ *adv* : on or above and extending onto both sides : ASTRIDE

[2]**astraddle** *prep* : with one leg on each side of : ASTRIDE

as·tra·gal \'as-tri-gəl\ *n* [L *astragalus,* fr. Gk *astragalos* anklebone, molding] **1** : a narrow half-round molding **2** : a projecting strip on the edge of a folding door

as·trag·a·lus \ə-'strag-ə-ləs\ *n, pl* **-li** \-,lī, -,lē\ [NL, fr. Gk *astragalos*] **1** : one of the proximal bones of the tarsus of the higher vertebrates — compare TALUS 1 **2** : ASTRAGAL

as·tra·khan *or* **as·tra·chan** \'as-trə-kən, -,kan\ *n, often cap* [*Astrakhan,* U.S.S.R.] **1** : karakul of Russian origin **2** : a cloth with a usu. wool, curled, and looped pile resembling karakul

as·tral \'as-trəl\ *adj* [LL *astralis*, fr. L *astrum* star, fr. Gk *astron* — more at STAR] **1 a :** of or relating to the stars **b :** consisting of stars : STARRY **2 :** of or relating to a mitotic aster **3 :** of or consisting of a supersensible substance held in theosophy to be held above the tangible world in refinement **4 a :** VISIONARY **b :** elevated in station or position : EXALTED — **as·tral·ly** \-trə-lē\ *adv*

astray \ə-'strā\ *adv or adj* [ME, fr. MF *estraié* wandering, fr. *estraier* to stray — more at STRAY] **1 :** off the right path or route : STRAYING **2 :** in error : away from a proper or desirable course or development

¹astride \ə-'strīd\ *adv* **1 :** with one leg on each side ⟨rode her horse ~⟩ **2 :** with the legs stretched wide apart ⟨standing ~ with arms folded⟩

²astride *prep* **1 :** on or above and with one leg on each side of **2 :** placed or lying on both sides of **3 :** extending over or across : SPANNING, BRIDGING

¹as·trin·gent \ə-'strin-jənt\ *adj* [prob. fr. MF, fr. L *astringent-, astringens*, prp. of *astringere* to bind fast, fr. *ad-* + *stringere* to bind tight — more at STRAIN] **1 :** able to draw together the soft organic tissues : STYPTIC, PUCKERY ⟨~ lotions⟩ ⟨an ~ fruit⟩ **2 :** suggestive of an astringent effect upon tissue : rigidly severe : AUSTERE ⟨dry ~ comments⟩; *also* : TONIC — **as·trin·gen·cy** \-jən-sē\ *n* — **as·trin·gent·ly** *adv*

²astringent *n* : an astringent agent or substance

as·tro·bi·ol·o·gy \ˌas-trō-(ˌ)bī-'äl-ə-jē\ *n* : EXOBIOLOGY — **as·tro·bi·o·log·i·cal** \-ˌbī-ə-'läj-i-kəl\ *adj* — **as·tro·bi·ol·o·gist** \-(ˌ)bī-'äl-ə-jəst\ *n*

as·tro·cyte \'as-trə-ˌsīt\ *n* [ISV] : a star-shaped cell (as of the neuroglia) — **as·tro·cyt·ic** \ˌas-trə-'sit-ik\ *adj*

as·tro·cy·to·ma \ˌas-trə-sī-'tō-mə\ *n, pl* **-mas** *or* **-ma·ta** \-mət-ə\ [NL] : a nerve-tissue tumor composed of astrocytes

as·tro·dome \'as-trə-ˌdōm\ *n* [ISV] : a transparent dome in the upper surface of an airplane from within which the navigator makes celestial observations

astrol *abbr* astrology

as·tro·labe \'as-trə-ˌlāb\ *n* [ME, fr. MF & ML; MF, fr. ML *astrolabium*, fr. LGk *astrolabion*, dim. of Gk *astrolabos*, fr. *astr-* + *lambanein* to take — more at LATCH] : a compact instrument used to observe the position of celestial bodies before the invention of the sextant

astrolabe

as·trol·o·ger \ə-'sträl-ə-jər\ *n* : one who practices astrology

as·trol·o·gy \ə-'sträl-ə-jē\ *n* [ME *astrologie*, fr. MF, fr. L *astrologia*, fr. Gk, fr. *astr-* + *-logia* -logy] **1** *obs* : ASTRONOMY **2** : the divination of the supposed influences of the stars and planets on human affairs and terrestrial events by their positions and aspects — **as·tro·log·i·cal** \ˌas-trə-'läj-i-kəl\ *adj* — **as·tro·log·i·cal·ly** \-k(ə-)lē\ *adv*

astron *abbr* astronomer; astronomy

as·tro·naut \'as-trə-ˌnȯt, -ˌnät\ *n* [*astr-* + *-naut* (as in *aeronaut*)] : a person who travels beyond the earth's atmosphere; *also* : a trainee for spaceflight

as·tro·nau·tics \ˌas-trə-'nȯt-iks\ *n pl but sing or pl in constr* **1** : the science of the construction and operation of vehicles for travel in space beyond the earth's atmosphere **2** : navigation in space beyond the earth's atmosphere — **as·tro·nau·tic** \-ik\ *or* **as·tro·nau·ti·cal** \-i-kəl\ *adj* — **as·tro·nau·ti·cal·ly** \-i-k(ə-)lē\ *adv*

as·tro·nav·i·ga·tion \ˌas-trō-ˌnav-ə-'gā-shən\ *n* : CELESTIAL NAVIGATION

as·tron·o·mer \ə-'strän-ə-mər\ *n* : one who is skilled in astronomy or who makes observations of celestial phenomena

as·tro·nom·i·cal \ˌas-trə-'näm-i-kəl\ *or* **as·tro·nom·ic** \-ik\ *adj* **1** : of or relating to astronomy **2** : enormously or inconceivably large ⟨~ numbers⟩ — **as·tro·nom·i·cal·ly** \-i-k(ə-)lē\ *adv*

astronomical unit *n* : a unit of length used in astronomy equal to the mean distance of the earth from the sun or about 93 million miles

as·tron·o·my \ə-'strän-ə-mē\ *n, pl* **-mies** [ME *astronomie*, fr. OF, fr. L *astronomia*, fr. Gk, fr. *astr-* + *-nomia* -nomy] **1** : the science of the celestial bodies and of their magnitudes, motions, and constitution **2** : a treatise on astronomy

as·tro·pho·tog·ra·phy \ˌas-(ˌ)trō-fə-'täg-rə-fē\ *n* [ISV] : photography as used in astronomical investigations

as·tro·phys·ics \ˌas-trə-'fiz-iks\ *n pl but sing or pl in constr* [ISV] : a branch of astronomy dealing with the physical and chemical constitution of the celestial bodies — **as·tro·phys·i·cal** \-i-kəl\ *adj* — **as·tro·phys·i·cist** \-'fiz-(ə-)səst\ *n*

as·tro·sphere \'as-trə-ˌsfi(ə)r\ *n* [ISV] : an aster exclusive of the centrosome

as·tute \ə-'st(y)üt, a-\ *adj* [L *astutus*, fr. *astus* craft] : exhibiting combined shrewdness and perspicacity often to the point of being artful or crafty ⟨an ~ observer⟩ ⟨an ~ appeal to the weakness of his victim⟩ *syn* see SHREWD *ant* gullible — **as·tute·ly** *adv* — **as·tute·ness** *n*

As·ty·a·nax \ə-'stī-ə-ˌnaks\ *n* [Gk] : a son of Hector and Andromache hurled by the Greeks from the walls of Troy

asun·der \ə-'sən-dər\ *adv or adj* **1** : into parts ⟨torn ~⟩ **2** : apart from each other in position ⟨wide ~⟩

ASV *abbr* American Standard Version

aswarm \ə-'swȯ(ə)rm\ *adj* : filled to overflowing : SWARMING ⟨streets ~ with people⟩

aswirl \ə-'swər(-ə)l\ *adj* : moving with a whirling motion

aswoon \ə-'swün\ *adj* : being in a swoon : DAZED

asy·lum \ə-'sī-ləm\ *n* [ME, fr. L, fr. Gk *asylon*, neut. of *asylos* inviolable, fr. *a-* + *sylon* right of seizure] **1** : an inviolable place of refuge and protection giving shelter to criminals and debtors : SANCTUARY **2** : a place of retreat and security : SHELTER **3 a** : the protection or inviolability afforded by an asylum : REFUGE **b** : protection from arrest and extradition given esp. to political refugees by a nation or by an embassy or other agency enjoying

diplomatic immunity **4** : an institution for the relief or care of the destitute or afflicted and esp. the insane

asym·met·ric \ˌā-sə-'me-trik\ *or* **asym·met·ri·cal** \-tri-kəl\ *adj* [Gk *asymmetria* lack of proportion, fr. *asymmetros* ill-proportioned, fr. *a-* + *symmetros* symmetrical — more at SYMMETRY] **1** : not symmetrical **2** : characterized by being bonded to different atoms or groups — **asym·met·ri·cal·ly** \-k(ə-)lē\ *adv* — **asym·me·try** \(')ā-'sim-ə-trē\ *n*

asymp·tom·at·ic \ˌā-ˌsim(p)-tə-'mat-ik\ *adj* : presenting no subjective evidence of disease — **asymp·tom·at·i·cal·ly** \-i-k(ə-)lē\ *adv*

as·ymp·tote \'as-əm(p)-ˌtōt\ *n* [prob. fr. (assumed) NL *asymptotus*, fr. Gk *asymptōtos*, fr. *asymptōtos* not meeting, fr. *a-* + *sympiptein* to meet — more at SYMPTOM] : a straight line associated with a curve such that as a point moves along an infinite branch of the curve the distance from the point to the line approaches zero and the slope of the curve at the point approaches the slope of the line — **as·ymp·tot·ic** \ˌas-əm(p)-'tät-ik\ *adj* — **as·ymp·tot·i·cal·ly** \-i-k(ə-)lē\ *adv*

asyn·ap·sis \ˌā-sə-'nap-səs\ *n, pl* **-ap·ses** \-ˌsēz\ [NL *²a-* + *synapsis*] : failure of pairing of homologous chromosomes in meiosis

asyn·chro·nous \-krə-nəs\ *adj* : not synchronous — **asyn·chro·nous·ly** *adv*

asyn·chro·ny \-krə-nē\ *or* **asyn·chro·nism** \(')ā-'siŋ-krə-ˌniz-əm, -'sin-\ *n* : the quality or state of being asynchronous : absence or lack of concurrence in time

as·yn·det·ic \ˌas-'n-'det-ik\ *adj* : marked by asyndeton — **as·yn·det·i·cal·ly** \-i-k(ə-)lē\ *adv*

asyn·de·ton \ə-'sin-də-ˌtän, (') ā-'sin-\ *n, pl* **-tons** *or* **-ta** \-dət-ə\ [LL, fr. Gk, fr. neut. of *asyndetos* unconnected, fr. *a-* + *syndetos* bound together, fr. *syndein* to bind together, fr. *syn-* + *dein* to bind — more at DIADEM] : omission of the conjunctions that ordinarily join coordinate words or clauses (as in "I came, I saw, I conquered")

¹at \ət, (')at\ *prep* [ME, fr. OE *æt*; akin to OHG *az* at, L *ad*] **1** — used as a function word to indicate presence or occurrence in, on, or near ⟨staying ~ a hotel⟩ ⟨~ a party⟩ ⟨sick ~ heart⟩ **2** — used as a function word to indicate the goal of an indicated or implied action or motion ⟨aim ~ the target⟩ ⟨laugh ~ him⟩ ⟨creditors are ~ him again⟩ **3** — used as a function word to indicate that with which one is occupied or employed ⟨~ work⟩ ⟨~ the controls⟩ ⟨an expert ~ chess⟩ **4** — used as a function word to indicate situation in an active or passive state or condition ⟨a criminal ~ liberty⟩ ⟨~ rest⟩ **5** — used as a function word to indicate the means, cause, or manner ⟨sold ~ auction⟩ ⟨laughed ~ his joke⟩ ⟨act ~ your own discretion⟩ **6 a** — used as a function word to indicate the rate, degree, or position in a scale or series ⟨the temperature ~ 90⟩ ⟨~ first⟩ **b** — used as a function word to indicate age or position in time ⟨will retire ~ 65⟩

²at \'ät\ *n, pl* **at** [Siamese] — see *kip* at MONEY table

³at *abbr* **1** airtight **2** atomic

At *symbol* astatine

AT *abbr* **1** air temperature **2** ampere-turn

at- — see AD-

At·a·brine \'at-ə-brən, -ˌbren\ *trademark* — used for quinacrine

At·a·lan·ta \ˌat-'l-'ant-ə\ *n* [L, fr. Gk *Atalantē*] : a Greek maiden of mythology who challenged each of her suitors to a footrace and was eventually married to Hippomenes who defeated her by dropping on the course three golden apples which she stopped to pick up

at all \ət-'ȯl, ə-'tȯl, at-'ȯl\ *adv* : in any way or respect : to the least extent or degree : under any circumstances ⟨doesn't smoke *at all*⟩

at·a·man \ˌat-ə-'man\ *n* [Russ] : HETMAN

at·a·mas·co lily \ˌat-ə-'mas-(ˌ)kō-\ *n* [*attamusco*, lit., it is red (in some Algonquian language of Virginia)] : any of a genus (*Zephyranthes*) of American bulbous herbs of the amaryllis family with pink, white, or yellowish flowers

at·a·rac·tic \ˌat-ə-'rak-tik\ *or* **at·a·rax·ic** \-'rak-sik\ *n* [ataractic fr. Gk *ataraktos* calm, fr. *a-* + *tarassein* to disturb; ataraxic fr. Gk *ataraxia* calmness, fr. *a-* + *tarassein* — more at DREG] : a tranquilizer drug — **ataractic** *or* **ataraxic** *adj*

at·a·vism \'at-ə-ˌviz-əm\ *n* [F *atavisme*, fr. L *atavus* ancestor] **1** : recurrence in an organism or in any of its parts of a form typical of ancestors more remote than the parents usu. due to genetic recombination **2** : an individual or character manifesting atavism : THROWBACK — **at·a·vist** \-vəst\ *n* — **at·a·vis·tic** \ˌat-ə-'vis-tik\ *adj* — **at·a·vis·ti·cal·ly** \-ti-k(ə-)lē\ *adv*

atax·ia \ə-'tak-sē-ə, (')ā-\ *n* [Gk, fr. *a-* + *tassein* to put in order — more at TACTICS] **1** : lack of order : CONFUSION **2** : an inability to coordinate voluntary muscular movements that is symptomatic of some nervous disorders — **atax·ic** \-sik\ *adj*

at bat \ət-'bat\ *n* : an official time at bat charged to a baseball batter except when he gets a base on balls or a sacrifice hit, is hit by a pitched ball, or is interfered with by the catcher ⟨three hits in five *at bats*⟩

¹ate *past of* EAT

²ate \'āt-ē, 'āt-, 'ä-ˌtā, 'ä-ˌtē\ *n* [Gk *atē*] : blind impulse, reckless ambition, or excessive folly that drives men to ruin

¹-ate \ət, ˌāt\ *n suffix* [ME *-at*, fr. OF, fr. L *-atus, -atum*, masc. & neut. of *-atus*, pp. ending] **1** : one acted upon (in a specified way) ⟨distill*ate*⟩ **2** [NL *-atum*, fr. L] : chemical compound or complex anion derived from a (specified) compound or element ⟨phenol*ate*⟩

asymptotes to the hyperbola

⟨ferr*ate*⟩; *esp* : salt or ester of an acid with a name ending in *-ic* and not beginning with *hydro-* ⟨bor*ate*⟩
[2]-ate *n suffix* [ME *-at*, fr. OF, fr. L *-atus*, fr. *-atus*, pp. ending] : office : function : rank : group of persons holding a (specified) office or rank or having a (specified) function ⟨vicar*ate*⟩
[3]-ate *adj suffix* [ME *-at*, fr. L *-atus*, fr. pp. ending of 1st conj. verbs, fr. *-a-*, stem vowel of 1st conj. + *-tus*, pp. suffix — more at -ED] : marked by having ⟨crani*ate*⟩
[4]-ate \ˌāt\ *vb suffix* [ME *-aten*, fr. L *-atus*, pp. ending] : act on (in a specified way) ⟨insul*ate*⟩ : cause to be modified or affected by ⟨camphor*ate*⟩ : cause to become ⟨activ*ate*⟩ : furnish with ⟨capacit*ate*⟩
At·e·brin \ˈat-ə-brən\ *trademark* — used for quinacrine
-at·ed \ˌāt-əd\ *adj suffix* : [3]-ATE ⟨locul*ated*⟩
at·el·ec·ta·sis \ˌat-ᵊl-ˈek-tə-səs\ *n, pl* **-ta·ses** \-ˌsēz\ [NL, fr. Gk *atelēs* incomplete, defective (fr. *a-* [2]a- + *telos* end) + *ektasis* extension, fr. *ekteinein* to stretch out, fr. *ex-* + *teinein* to stretch — more at WHEEL, THIN] : collapse of the expanded lung; *also* : defective expansion of the pulmonary alveoli at birth
ate·lier \ˌat-ᵊl-ˈyā\ *n* [F] **1** : an artist's or designer's studio or workroom **2** : WORKSHOP
a tem·po \ä-ˈtem-(ˌ)pō\ *adv or adj* [It] : in time — used as a direction in music to return to the original rate of speed
a ter·go \ä-ˈte(ə)r-(ˌ)gō\ *adv* [L] : from behind
Ate·ri·an \ə-ˈtir-ē-ən\ *adj* [F *atérien*, fr. Bir el-*Ater* (Constantine), Algeria] : of or relating to a Paleolithic culture of northern Africa characterized by Mousterian features, tanged arrow points, and leaf-shaped spearheads
Ath·a·na·sian \ˌath-ə-ˈnā-zhən, -ˈnā-shən\ *adj* : of or relating to Athanasius or his advocacy of the homoousian doctrine against Arianism
Athanasian Creed *n* : a Christian creed originating in Europe about A.D. 400 and relating esp. to the Trinity and Incarnation
Ath·a·pas·kan *or* **Ath·a·pas·can** \ˌath-ə-ˈpas-kən\ *or* **Ath·a·bas·can** *or* **Ath·a·bas·kan** \-ˈbas-\ *n* [Cree *Athap-askaw*, an Athapaskan people, lit., grass or reeds here and there] **1** : a language stock of the Na-dene group in No. America **2** : a member of a people speaking an Athapaskan language
athe·ism \ˈā-thē-ˌiz-əm\ *n* [MF *athéisme*, fr. *athée* atheist, fr. Gk *atheos* godless, fr. *a-* + *theos* god] **1 a** : a disbelief in the existence of deity **b** : the doctrine that there is no deity **2** : UNGODLINESS, WICKEDNESS
athe·ist \ˈā-thē-əst\ *n* : one who denies the existence of God — **athe·is·tic** \ˌā-thē-ˈis-tik\ *or* **athe·is·ti·cal** \ˌā-thē-ˈis-ti-kəl\ *adj* — **athe·is·ti·cal·ly** \-ti-k(ə-)lē\ *adv*
syn ATHEIST, AGNOSTIC, DEIST, FREETHINKER, UNBELIEVER, INFIDEL *shared meaning element* : one who does not take an orthodox religious position ***ant*** theist
ath·e·ling \ˈath-ə-liŋ, ˈath-\ *n* [ME, fr. OE *ætheling*, fr. *æthelu* nobility, akin to OHG *adal* nobility] : an Anglo-Saxon prince or nobleman; *esp* : the heir apparent or a prince of the royal family
ath·e·nae·um *or* **ath·e·ne·um** \ˌath-ə-ˈnē-əm\ *n* [L *Athenaeum*, a school in ancient Rome for the study of arts, fr. Gk *Athēnaion*, a temple of Athena, fr. *Athēnē*] **1** : a literary or scientific association **2** : a building or room in which books, periodicals, and newspapers are kept for use
Athe·ne \ə-ˈthē-nē\ *or* **Athe·na** \-nə\ *n* [Gk *Athēnē* & L *Athena*, fr. Gk *Athēnē*] : the Greek goddess of wisdom — compare MINERVA
ath·ero·gen·e·sis \ˌath-ə-rō-ˈjen-ə-səs\ *n* : the production of atheroma
ath·ero·gen·ic \-ˈjen-ik\ *adj* [*atheroma* + *-genic*] : relating to or producing degenerative changes in arterial walls ⟨~ diet⟩
ath·er·o·ma \ˌath-ə-ˈrō-mə\ *n* [NL *atheromat-*, *atheroma*, fr. L, a tumor containing matter resembling gruel, fr. Gk *atherōma*, fr. *athēra* gruel] : fatty degeneration of the inner coat of the arteries — **ath·er·o·ma·to·sis** \-ˌrō-mə-ˈtō-səs\ *n* — **ath·er·o·ma·tous** \-ˈrō-mət-əs\ *adj*
ath·ero·scle·ro·sis \ˌath-ə-rō-sklə-ˈrō-səs\ *n* [NL, fr. *atheroma* + *sclerosis*] : an arteriosclerosis characterized by the deposition of fatty substances in and fibrosis of the inner layer of the arteries — **ath·ero·scle·rot·ic** \-sklə-ˈrät-ik\ *adj* — **ath·ero·scle·rot·i·cal·ly** \-i-k(ə-)lē\ *adv*
athirst \ə-ˈthərst\ *adj* [ME, fr. OE *ofthyrst*, pp. of *ofthyrstan* to suffer from thirst, fr. *of* off, from + *thyrstan* to thirst — more at OF] **1** *archaic* : THIRSTY **2** : having a strong eager desire ⟨I that for ever feel ~ for glory —John Keats⟩ ***syn*** see EAGER
ath·lete \ˈath-ˌlēt\ *n* [ME, fr. L *athleta*, fr. Gk *athlētēs*, fr. *athlein* to contend for a prize, fr. *athlon* prize, contest] : one who is trained or skilled in exercises, sports, or games requiring physical strength, agility, or stamina
athlete's foot *n* : ringworm of the feet
ath·let·ic \ath-ˈlet-ik\ *adj* **1** : of or relating to athletes or athletics **2** : characteristic of an athlete; *esp* : VIGOROUS, ACTIVE **3** : characterized by heavy frame, large chest, and powerful muscular development : MESOMORPHIC **4** : used by athletes — **ath·let·i·cal·ly** \-i-k(ə-)lē\ *adv* — **ath·let·i·cism** \-ˈlet-ə-ˌsiz-əm\ *n*
ath·let·ics \ath-ˈlet-iks\ *n pl but sing or pl in constr* **1 a** : exercises, sports, or games engaged in by athletes **b** *Brit* : track-and-field sports **2** : the practice or principles of athletic activities
athletic supporter *n* : a supporter for the genitals worn by men participating in sports or strenuous activities
ath·o·dyd \ˈath-ə-ˌdid\ *n* [*aero-thermodynamic duct*] : a jet engine (as a ramjet engine) consisting essentially of a continuous duct of varying diameter which admits air at the forward end, adds heat to it by the combustion of fuel, and discharges it from the after end
at home \ət-ˈhōm\ *n* : a reception given at one's home
-athon \ə-ˌthän\ *n comb form* [*marathon*] : contest of endurance ⟨talk*athon*⟩
ath·ro·cyte \ˈath-rə-ˌsīt\ *n* [Gk *athroos* together, collected + ISV *-cyte*] : a cell capable of picking up foreign material and storing it in granular form in its cytoplasm — **ath·ro·cy·to·sis** \ˌath-rə-sī-ˈtō-səs\ *n*

[1]athwart \ə-ˈthwȯ(ə)rt, *naut often* -ˈthȯ(ə)rt\ *adv* **1** : across esp. in an oblique direction **2** : in opposition to the right or expected course ⟨and quite ~ goes all decorum —Shak.⟩
[2]athwart *prep* **1** : ACROSS ⟨a row of stepping-stones set ~ the creek —Eden Phillpotts⟩ **2** : in opposition to ⟨a procedure directly ~ the New England prejudices —R. G. Cole⟩
athwart·ship \-ˌship\ *adj* : being across the ship from side to side ⟨~ and longitudinal framing⟩
athwart·ships \-ˌships\ *adv* : across the ship from side to side
atilt \ə-ˈtilt\ *adv or adj* **1** : in a tilted position **2** : with lance in hand ⟨run ~ at death—Shak.⟩
atin·gle \ə-ˈtiŋ-gəl\ *adj* : tingling esp. with excitement or exhilaration
-a·tion \ˈā-shən\ *n suffix* [ME *-acioun*, fr. OF *-ation*, fr. L *-ation-*, *-atio*, fr. *-atus* -ate + *-ion-*, *-io* -ion] : action or process ⟨flirt*ation*⟩ : something connected with an action or process ⟨discolor*ation*⟩
-a·tive \ˌāt-iv, ət-\ *adj suffix* [ME, fr. MF *-atif*, fr. L *-ativus*, fr. *-atus* + *-ivus* -ive] : of, relating to, or connected with ⟨authorit*ative*⟩ : tending to ⟨talk*ative*⟩
At·ka mackerel \ˌat-kə-, ˌät-\ *n* [*Atka* Island, Alaska] : a greenling (*Pleurogrammus monopterygius*) of Alaska and adjacent regions valued as a food fish
Atl *abbr* Atlantic
[1]At·lan·te·an \ˌat-ˌlan-ˈtē-ən, ət-ˈlant-ē-\ *adj* : of, relating to, or resembling Atlas : STRONG
[2]Atlantean *adj* : of or relating to Atlantis
At·lan·tic \ət-ˈlant-ik, at-\ *adj* **1 a** : of, relating to, or found in, on, or near the Atlantic ocean **b** : of, relating to, or found on or near the east coast of the U.S. **2** : of or relating to the nations that border the Atlantic ocean ⟨the ~ community⟩
Atlantic croaker *n* : a small but important food fish (*Micropogan undulatus*) of the Gulf coast and the Atlantic coast south of Cape Cod — called also *hardhead*
At·lan·ti·cism \-ˈlant-ə-ˌsiz-əm\ *n* [*Atlantic (ocean)*] : a policy of military cooperation between European and No. American powers — **At·lan·ti·cist** \-səst\ *n*
Atlantic time *n* [*Atlantic (ocean)*] : the time of the 4th time zone west of Greenwich that includes the Canadian Maritime Provinces, Puerto Rico, and the Virgin Islands — called also *Atlantic standard time*
At·lan·tis \ət-ˈlant-əs, at-\ *n* : a fabled island that was traditionally placed west of the Strait of Gibraltar and that was swallowed up by the sea
at·las \ˈat-ləs\ *n* [L *Atlant-*, *Atlas*, fr. Gk] **1** *cap* : a Titan who for his part in the Titans' revolt against the gods was obliged to support the heavens with his head and hands **2** *cap* : one who bears a heavy burden **3 a** : a bound collection of maps **b** : a bound collection of tables, charts, or plates **4** : the first vertebra of the neck **5** *pl usu* **at·lan·tes** \ət-ˈlant-(ˌ)ēz, at-\ : a figure or half figure of a man used as a column to support an entablature
at·latl \ˈät-ˌlät-ᵊl\ *n* [of Uto-Aztecan origin; akin to Nahuatl *atlatl* atlatl] : a device for throwing a spear or dart that consists of a rod or board with a projection (as a hook or thong) at the rear end to hold the weapon in place until released
At·li \ˈät-lē\ *n* [ON] : a king of the Huns figuring in Germanic legend and corresponding to the historical Attila
atm *abbr* atmosphere; atmospheric
at·man \ˈät-mən\ *n, often cap* [Skt *ātman*, lit., breath, soul; akin to OHG *ātum* breath] **1** *Hinduism* : the innermost essence of each individual **2** *Hinduism* : the supreme universal self : BRAHMA 1
at·mom·e·ter \at-ˈmäm-ət-ər\ *n* [Gk *atmos* + E *-meter*] : an instrument for measuring the evaporating capacity of the air
at·mo·sphere \ˈat-mə-ˌsfi(ə)r\ *n* [NL *atmosphaera*, fr. Gk *atmos* vapor + L *sphaera* sphere; akin to Gk *aēnai* to blow — more at WIND] **1 a** : a gaseous mass enveloping a celestial body (as a planet) **b** : the whole mass of air surrounding the earth **2** : the air of a locality **3** : a surrounding influence or environment ⟨an ~ of mutual trust⟩ **4** : a unit of pressure equal to the pressure of the air at sea level or approximately 14.7 pounds to the square inch **5 a** : the overall aesthetic effect of a work of art **b** : a dominant aesthetic or emotional effect or appeal — **at·mo·sphered** \-ˌsfi(ə)rd\ *adj*
at·mo·spher·ic \ˌat-mə-ˈsfi(ə)r-ik, -ˈsfer-\ *adj* **1 a** : of or relating to the atmosphere **b** : resembling the atmosphere : AIRY **c** : occurring in or actuated by the atmosphere **2** : having, marked by, or contributing aesthetic or emotional atmosphere — **at·mo·spher·i·cal·ly** \-i-k(ə-)lē\ *adv*
at·mo·spher·ics \-iks\ *n pl* : audible disturbances produced in radio receiving apparatus by atmospheric electrical phenomena (as lightning); *also* : the electrical phenomena causing these disturbances
atmospheric tide *n* : TIDE 2a(5)
at·mo·sphe·ri·um \ˌat-mə-ˈsfir-ē-əm\ *n* [*atmosphere* + *-ium* (as in *planetarium*)] : an optical device for projecting images of meteorological phenomena (as clouds) on the inside of a dome; *also* : a room housing this device
at no *abbr* atomic number
atoll \ˈa-ˌtȯl, -ˌtäl, -ˌtōl, ˈā-\ *n* [*atolu*, native name in the Maldive islands] : a coral island consisting of a reef surrounding a lagoon

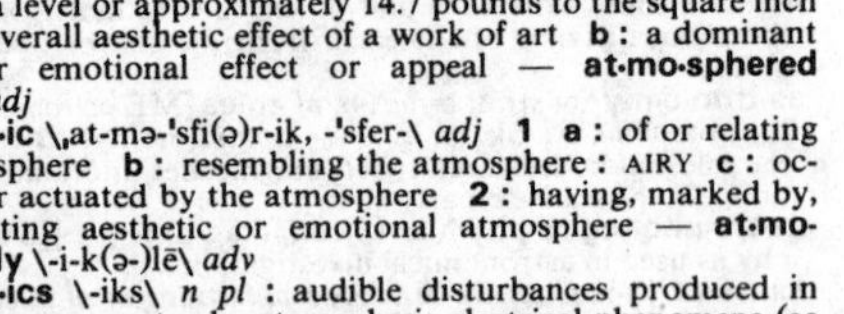

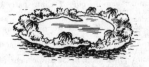

atoll

at·om \ˈat-əm\ *n* [ME, fr. L *atomus*, fr. Gk *atomos*, fr. *atomos* indivisible, fr. *a-* + *temnein* to cut — more at TOME] **1** : one of the minute indivisible particles of which according to ancient materialism the universe is composed **2 :** a tiny particle : BIT **3 a :** the smallest particle of an element that can exist either alone or in combination **b :** a group of such particles constituting the smallest quantity of a radical **4 :** the atom considered as a source of vast potential energy

atom bomb *n* **1 :** a bomb whose violent explosive power is due to the sudden release of atomic energy resulting from the splitting of nuclei of a heavy chemical element (as plutonium or uranium) by neutrons in a very rapid chain reaction — called also *atomic bomb, fission bomb* **2 :** a bomb whose explosive power is due to the release of atomic energy — **atom–bomb** *vt*

atom·ic \ə-ˈtäm-ik\ *adj* **1 :** of, relating to, or concerned with atoms, atomic energy, or atomic bombs **2 :** MINUTE **3** *of a chemical element* **:** existing in the state of separate atoms — **atom·i·cal·ly** \-i-k(ə-)lē\ *adv*

atomic clock *n* **:** a precision clock that depends for its operation on an electrical oscillator regulated by the natural vibration frequencies of an atomic system (as a beam of cesium atoms)

atomic cocktail *n* **:** a radioactive substance (as iodide of sodium) dissolved in water and administered orally to patients with cancer

atomic energy *n* **:** energy that can be liberated by changes in the nucleus of an atom (as by fission of a heavy nucleus or fusion of light nuclei into heavier ones with accompanying loss of mass)

at·o·mic·i·ty \ˌat-ə-ˈmis-ət-ē\ *n* **1 a :** VALENCE **b :** the number of atoms in the molecule of an element **c :** the number of replaceable atoms or groups in the molecule of a compound **2 :** the state of consisting of atoms

atomic mass *n* **:** the mass of any species of atom usu. expressed in atomic mass units

atomic mass unit *n* **:** a unit of mass for expressing masses of atoms, molecules, or nuclear particles equal to $^1/_{12}$ of the atomic mass of the most abundant carbon isotope $_6C^{12}$

atomic number *n* **:** an experimentally determined number characteristic of a chemical element that represents the number of protons in the nucleus which in a neutral atom equals the number of electrons outside the nucleus and that determines the place of the element in the periodic table — see ELEMENT table

atomic pile *n* **:** REACTOR 3b — called also *atomic reactor*

atom·ics \ə-ˈtäm-iks\ *n pl but sing in constr* **:** the science of atoms esp. when involving atomic energy

atomic theory *n* **1 :** a theory of the nature of matter: all material substances are composed of minute particles or atoms of a comparatively small number of kinds and all the atoms of the same kind are uniform in size, weight, and other properties — called also *atomic hypothesis* **2 :** any of several theories of the structure of the atom; *esp* **:** one based on experimentation and theoretical considerations holding that the atom is composed essentially of a small positively charged comparatively heavy nucleus surrounded by a comparatively large arrangement of electrons

atomic weight *n* **:** the average relative weight of an element referred to some element taken as a standard with oxygen of atomic weight 16 or usu. with carbon of atomic weight 12 being taken as a basis — see ELEMENT table

at·om·ism \ˈat-ə-ˌmiz-əm\ *n* **:** a doctrine that the universe is composed of simple indivisible minute particles — **at·om·ist** \-məst\ *n*

at·om·is·tic \ˌat-ə-ˈmis-tik\ *adj* **1 :** of or relating to atoms or atomism **2 :** composed of many simple elements; *also* **:** divided into unconnected or antagonistic fragments ⟨an ~ society⟩ — **at·om·is·ti·cal·ly** \-ti-k(ə-)lē\ *adv*

at·om·is·tics \-tiks\ *n pl but sing in constr* **:** a science dealing with the atom or with the use of atomic energy

at·om·ize \ˈat-ə-ˌmīz\ *vt* **-ized; -iz·ing 1 :** to reduce to minute particles or to a fine spray **2 :** to treat as made up of many discrete units **3 :** to subject to atomic bombing — **at·om·iza·tion** \ˌat-ə-mə-ˈzā-shən\ *n*

at·om·iz·er \ˈat-ə-ˌmī-zər\ *n* **:** an instrument for atomizing usu. a perfume, disinfectant, or medicament

atom smasher *n* **:** ACCELERATOR d

at·o·my \ˈat-ə-mē\ *n, pl* **-mies** [irreg. fr. L *atomi,* pl. of *atomus* atom] **:** a tiny particle : ATOM, MITE

aton·al \(ˈ)ā-ˈtōn-ᵊl, (ˈ)a-\ *adj* **:** marked by avoidance of traditional musical tonality; *esp* **:** organized without reference to key or tonal center and using the tones of the chromatic scale impartially — **aton·al·ism** \-ᵊl-ˌiz-əm\ *n* — **aton·al·ist** \-ᵊl-əst\ *n* — **aton·al·is·tic** \ˌā-ˌtōn-ᵊl-ˈis-tik, ˌa-\ *adj* — **ato·nal·i·ty** \ˌā-tō-ˈnal-ət-ē, ˌa-\ *n* — **aton·al·ly** \(ˈ)ā-ˈtōn-ᵊl-ē, (ˈ)a-\ *adv*

atone \ə-ˈtōn\ *vb* **atoned; aton·ing** [ME *atonen* to become reconciled, fr. *at on* in harmony, fr. *at* + *on* one] *vt* **1** *obs* **:** RECONCILE **2 :** to supply satisfaction for : EXPIATE ~ *vi* **:** to make amends

atone·ment \ə-ˈtōn-mənt\ *n* **1** *obs* **:** RECONCILIATION **2 :** the reconciliation of God and man through the sacrificial death of Jesus Christ **3 :** reparation for an offense or injury : SATISFACTION ⟨made ~ for his cruelty⟩ **4** *Christian Science* **:** the exemplifying of man's oneness with God

aton·ic \(ˈ)ā-ˈtän-ik, (ˈ)a-\ *adj* **1 :** characterized by atony **2 :** uttered without accent or stress — **ato·nic·i·ty** \ˌā-tō-ˈnis-ət-ē, ˌat-ə-ˈnis-\ *n*

at·o·ny \ˈat-ᵊn-ē\ *n* [LL *atonia,* fr. Gk, fr. *atonos* without tone, fr. *a-* + *tonos* tone] **:** lack of physiological tone esp. of a contractile organ

¹atop \ə-ˈtäp\ *prep* **:** on top of

²atop *adv or adj* **:** on, to, or at the top

at·o·py \ˈat-ə-pē\ *n* [Gk *atopia* uncommonness, fr. *atopos* out of the way, uncommon, fr. *a-* + *topos* place — more at TOPIC] **:** a probably hereditary allergy characterized by symptoms (as asthma, hay fever, or hives) produced upon exposure to the exciting antigen without inoculation — **atop·ic** \(ˈ)ā-ˈtäp-ik, -ˈtō-pik\ *adj*

-a·tor *n suffix* [ME *-atour,* fr. OF & L; OF, fr. L *-ator,* fr. *-atus* -ate + *-or*] **:** one that does ⟨totalizator⟩

ATP \ˌā-ˌtē-ˈpē, ā-ˈtē-ˌpē\ *n* [adenosine *tri*phosphate] **:** an adenosine ester derivative $C_{10}H_{16}N_5O_{13}P_3$ that supplies energy for many biochemical cellular processes by undergoing enzymatic hydrolysis esp. to ADP — called also *adenosine triphosphate*

ATPase \ˌā-ˌtē-ˈpē-ˌās, -ˌāz\ *n* **:** an enzyme that hydrolyzes ATP; *esp* **:** one that hydrolyzes ATP to ADP and inorganic phosphate

at·ra·bil·ious \ˌa-trə-ˈbil-yəs\ *adj* [L *atra bilis* black bile] **1 :** given to or marked by melancholy : GLOOMY **2 :** ILL-NATURED, PEEVISH — **at·ra·bil·ious·ness** *n*

at·ra·zine \ˈa-trə-ˌzēn\ *n* [ISV *atr-* (prob. fr. L *atr-, ater* black, dark) + *triazine*] **:** a photosynthesis-inhibiting persistent herbicide $C_8H_{14}ClN_5$ used esp. to kill annual weeds and quack grass

atrem·ble \ə-ˈtrem-bəl\ *adj* **:** shaking involuntarily : TREMBLING ⟨he was white as death and all ~ —Robert Coover⟩

atre·sia \ə-ˈtrē-zhə\ *n* [NL, fr. ²*a-* + Gk *trēsis* perforation, fr. *tetrainein* to pierce — more at THROW] **1 :** absence or closure of a natural passage of the body **2 :** involution of a part (as an ovarian follicle)

Atreus \ˈā-ˌtrüs, -trē-əs\ *n* [Gk] **:** a king of Mycenae who was the father of Agamemnon and Menelaus

atrio·ven·tric·u·lar \ˌā-trē-ō-ven-ˈtrik-yə-lər, -vən-\ *adj* [NL *atrium* + E *ventricular*] **:** of, relating to, or located between an atrium and ventricle of the heart

atrip \ə-ˈtrip\ *adj, of an anchor* **:** AWEIGH

atri·um \ˈā-trē-əm\ *n, pl* **atria** \-trē-ə\ *also* **atri·ums** [L] **1 :** the central hall of a Roman house **2** [NL, fr. L] **:** an anatomical cavity or passage; *esp* **:** the main chamber of an auricle of the heart or the entire auricle **3 :** a rectangularly shaped open patio around which a house is built — **atri·al** \-trē-əl\ *adj*

atro·cious \ə-ˈtrō-shəs\ *adj* [L *atroc-, atrox* gloomy, atrocious, fr. *atr-, ater* black + *-oc-, -ox* (akin to Gk *ōps* eye) — more at EYE] **1 :** extremely wicked, brutal, or cruel : BARBARIC **2 :** APPALLING, HORRIFYING ⟨the ~ weapons of modern war⟩ **3 a :** utterly revolting : ABOMINABLE ⟨~ working conditions⟩ **b :** of very poor quality ⟨~ handwriting⟩ ***syn*** see OUTRAGEOUS — **atro·cious·ly** *adv* — **atro·cious·ness** *n*

atroc·i·ty \ə-ˈträs-ət-ē\ *n, pl* **-ties 1 :** the quality or state of being atrocious **2 :** an atrocious act, object, or situation

¹at·ro·phy \ˈa-trə-fē\ *n, pl* **-phies** [LL *atrophia,* fr. Gk, fr. *atrophos* ill fed, fr. *a-* + *trephein* to nourish; akin to Gk *thrombos* clot, curd] **1 :** decrease in size or wasting away of a body part or tissue; *also* **:** arrested development or loss of a part or organ incidental to the normal development or life of an animal or plant **2 :** a wasting away or progressive decline : DEGENERATION ⟨the ~ of freedom⟩ — **atro·phic** \(ˈ)ā-ˈtrō-fik\ *adj*

²atrophy \ˈa-trə-fē, -ˌfī\ *vb* **-phied; -phy·ing** *vi* **:** to undergo atrophy ~ *vt* **:** to cause to undergo atrophy

at·ro·pine \ˈa-trə-ˌpēn\ *n* [G *atropin,* fr. NL *Atropa,* genus name of belladonna, fr. Gk *Atropos*] **:** a racemic mixture of hyoscyamine extracted from belladonna and related plants used esp. to relieve spasms and to dilate the pupil of the eye

att *abbr* **1** attached **2** attention **3** attorney

at·tach \ə-ˈtach\ *vb* [ME *attachen,* fr. MF *attacher,* fr. OF *estachier,* fr. *estache* stake, of Gmc origin; akin to OE *staca* stake] *vt* **1 :** to take by legal authority esp. under a writ ⟨the court's sheriffs ~*ed* his property⟩ **2 :** to bring (oneself) into an association **3 :** to bind by personal ties (as of affection or sympathy) ⟨was strongly ~*ed* to his family⟩ **4 :** to make fast (as by tying or gluing) ⟨~ a label to a package⟩ **5 :** ASCRIBE, ATTRIBUTE ⟨~*ed* great importance to public opinion polls⟩ ~ *vi* **:** to become attached : ADHERE ***syn*** see FASTEN ***ant*** detach — **at·tach·able** \-ˈtach-ə-bəl\ *adj*

at·ta·ché \ˌat-ə-ˈshā, ˌa-ˌta-, ə-ˌta-\ *n* [F, pp. of *attacher*] **1 :** a technical expert on the diplomatic staff of his country at a foreign capital ⟨a military ~⟩ **2 :** ATTACHÉ CASE

at·ta·ché case \ə-ˈtash-(ˌ)ā-, ; ˌat-ə-ˈshā-, , ˌa-ˌta-\ *n* **:** a small thin suitcase used esp. for carrying business papers

at·tached \ə-ˈtacht\ *adj* **:** permanently fixed when adult ⟨~ barnacles⟩

at·tach·ment \ə-ˈtach-mənt\ *n* **1 :** a seizure by legal process; *also* **:** the writ or precept commanding such seizure **2 a :** the state of being personally attached : FIDELITY ⟨~ to a cause⟩ **b :** affectionate regard ⟨a deep ~ to natural beauty⟩ **3 :** a device attached to a machine or implement **4 :** the physical connection by which one thing is attached to another **5 :** the process of physically attaching

¹at·tack \ə-ˈtak\ *vb* [MF *attaquer,* fr. (assumed) OIt *estaccare* to attach, fr. *stacca* stake, of Gmc origin; akin to OE *staca*] *vt* **1 :** to set upon forcefully **2 :** to threaten (a piece in chess) with immediate capture **3 :** to assail with unfriendly or bitter words **4 :** to begin to affect or to act on injuriously **5 :** to set to work on ~ *vi* **:** to make an attack

syn ATTACK, ASSAIL, ASSAULT, BOMBARD, STORM *shared meaning element* **:** to make an onslaught on

²attack *n* **1 :** the act of attacking : ASSAULT **2 :** a belligerent or antagonistic action **3 :** the beginning of destructive action (as by a chemical agent) **4 :** the setting to work on some undertaking ⟨made a new ~ on the problem⟩ **5 :** the act or manner of beginning a musical tone or phrase **6 :** a fit of sickness; *esp* **:** an active episode of a chronic or recurrent disease **7 a :** an offensive or scoring action ⟨won the game with an eight-hit ~⟩ **b :** offensive players or the positions taken up by them

at·tack·man \-ˌman\ *n* **:** a player (as in lacrosse) assigned to an offensive zone or position

at·tain \ə-ˈtān\ *vb* [ME *atteynen,* fr. OF *ataindre,* fr. (assumed) VL *attangere,* fr. L *attingere,* fr. *ad-* + *tangere* to touch — more at TANGENT] *vt* **1 :** to reach as an end : GAIN, ACHIEVE ⟨~ a goal⟩ ⟨struggled to ~ a natural effect⟩ **2 :** to come into possession of **:** OBTAIN ⟨he ~*ed* preferment over his fellows⟩ **3 :** to come to as

ə abut	ᵊ kitten	ər further	a back	ā bake	ä cot, cart
aù out	ch chin	e less	ē easy	g gift	i trip	ī life
j joke	ŋ sing	ō flow	ȯ flaw	ȯi coin	th thin	t͟h this
ü loot	ù foot	y yet	yü few	yù furious	zh vision

the end of a progression or course of movement ⟨they ~*ed* the top of the hill⟩ ⟨~ a ripe old age⟩ **~** *vi* **:** to come or arrive by motion, growth, or effort ***syn*** see REACH — **at·tain·abil·i·ty** \-ˌtā-nə-ˈbil-ət-ē\ *n* — **at·tain·able** \-ˈtā-nə-bəl\ *adj* — **at·tain·able·ness** *n*

at·tain·der \ə-ˈtān-dər\ *n* [ME *attaynder,* fr. MF *ataindre* to accuse, attain] **1 :** extinction of the civil rights and capacities of a person upon sentence of death or outlawry usu. after a conviction of treason **2** *obs* **:** DISHONOR

at·tain·ment \ə-ˈtān-mənt\ *n* **1 :** the act of attaining **:** the condition of being attained **2 :** something attained **:** ACCOMPLISHMENT ⟨scientific ~*s*⟩

1at·taint \ə-ˈtānt\ *vt* [ME *attaynten,* fr. MF *ataint,* pp. of *ataindre*] **1 :** to affect by attainder **2 a** *obs* **:** INFECT, CORRUPT **b** *archaic* **:** TAINT, SULLY **3** *archaic* **:** ACCUSE

2attaint *n, obs* **:** a stain upon honor or purity **:** DISGRACE

at·tar \ˈat-ər, ˈa-ˌtär\ *n* [Per *ʽatir* perfumed, fr. Ar, fr. *ʽitr* perfume] **:** a fragrant essential oil (as from rose petals); *also* **:** FRAGRANCE

1at·tempt \ə-ˈtem(p)t\ *vt* [L *attemptare,* fr. *ad-* + *temptare* to touch, try — more at TEMPT] **1 :** to make an effort to do, accomplish, solve, or effect ⟨~*ed* to swim the swollen river⟩ **2** *archaic* **:** TEMPT **3** *archaic* **:** to try to subdue **:** ATTACK — **at·tempt·able** \-ˈtem(p)-tə-bəl\ *adj*

syn ATTEMPT, TRY, ENDEAVOR, ESSAY, STRIVE, STRUGGLE *shared meaning element* **:** to make an effort to do or accomplish ***ant*** succeed

2attempt *n* **1 :** the act or an instance of attempting; *esp* **:** an unsuccessful effort **2** *archaic* **:** ATTACK, ASSAULT

at·tend \ə-ˈtend\ *vb* [ME *attenden,* fr. OF *atendre,* fr. L *attendere,* lit., to stretch to, fr. *ad-* + *tendere* to stretch — more at THIN] *vt* **1** *archaic* **:** to give heed to **2 :** to look after **:** take charge of **3** *archaic* **a :** to wait for **b :** to be in store for **4 a :** to go or stay with as a companion, nurse, or servant **b :** to visit professionally as a physician **5 :** to be present with **:** ACCOMPANY **6 :** to be present at **~** *vi* **1 :** to apply oneself ⟨~ to your work⟩ **2 :** to apply the mind or pay attention **:** HEED **3 :** to be ready for service ⟨ministers who ~ upon the king⟩ **4** *obs* **:** WAIT, STAY **5 :** to take charge **:** SEE ⟨I'll ~ to that⟩ ***syn*** see TEND, ACCOMPANY — **at·tend·er** *n*

at·ten·dance \ə-ˈten-dən(t)s\ *n* **1 :** the act or fact of attending ⟨a physician in ~⟩ **2 a :** the persons or number of persons attending ⟨daily ~ at the fair dwindled⟩ **b :** the number of times a person attends

1at·ten·dant \ə-ˈten-dənt\ *adj* **:** accompanying or following as a consequence ⟨problems ~ upon pollution⟩

2attendant *n* **1 :** one who attends another to perform a service; *esp* **:** an employee who waits on customers ⟨a parking-lot ~⟩ **2 :** something that accompanies **:** CONCOMITANT **3 :** ATTENDEE

at·tend·ee \ə-ˌten-ˈdē, ˌa-\ *n* **:** one who is present on a given occasion or at a given place **:** ATTENDER ⟨~*s* at a convention⟩

at·tend·ing \ə-ˈten-diŋ\ *adj* **:** serving as a physician on the staff of a teaching hospital ⟨~ surgeon⟩

at·ten·tion \ə-ˈten-chən\ *n* [ME *attencioun,* fr. L *attention-, attentio,* fr. *attentus,* pp. of *attendere*] **1 a :** the act or state of attending esp. through applying the mind to an object of sense or thought **b :** a condition of readiness for such attention involving esp. a selective narrowing or focusing of consciousness and receptivity **2 :** OBSERVATION, NOTICE; *esp* **:** consideration with a view to action ⟨a problem requiring prompt ~⟩ **3 a :** an act of civility or courtesy esp. in courtship **b :** sympathetic consideration of the needs and wants of others **:** ATTENTIVENESS **4 :** a position assumed by a soldier with heels together, body erect, arms at the sides, and eyes to the front — often used as a command — **at·ten·tion·al** \-ˈtench-nəl, -ˈten-chən-ᵊl\ *adj*

attention line *n* **:** a line usu. placed above the salutation in a business letter directing the letter to one specified

attention span *n* **:** the length of time during which an individual is able to concentrate

at·ten·tive \ə-ˈtent-iv\ *adj* **1 :** MINDFUL, OBSERVANT ⟨~ to what he is doing⟩ **2 :** heedful of the comfort of others **:** SOLICITOUS **3 :** offering attentions in or as if in the role of a suitor ***syn*** see THOUGHTFUL ***ant*** inattentive, neglectful — **at·ten·tive·ly** *adv* — **at·ten·tive·ness** *n*

1at·ten·u·ate \ə-ˈten-yə-ˌwāt\ *vb* **-at·ed; -at·ing** [L *attenuatus,* pp. of *attenuare* to make thin, fr. *ad-* + *tenuis* thin — more at THIN] *vt* **1 :** to make thin or slender **2 :** to lessen the amount, force, or value of **:** WEAKEN **3 :** to reduce the severity, virulence, or vitality of **4 :** to make thin in consistency **:** RAREFY **~** *vi* **:** to become thin, fine, or less — **at·ten·u·a·tion** \-ˌten-yə-ˈwā-shən\ *n*

2at·ten·u·ate \ə-ˈten-yə-wət\ *adj* **1 :** attenuated esp. in thickness, density, or force **2 :** tapering gradually usu. to a long slender point ⟨~ leaves⟩

at·ten·u·a·tor \-yə-ˌwāt-ər\ *n* **:** a device for attenuating; *esp* **:** one for reducing the amplitude of an electrical signal without appreciable distortion

at·test \ə-ˈtest\ *vb* [MF *attester,* fr. L *attestari,* fr. *ad-* + *testis* witness — more at TESTAMENT] *vt* **1 a :** to affirm to be true or genuine; *specif* **:** to authenticate by signing as a witness **b :** to authenticate officially **2 :** to establish or verify the usage of **3 :** to be proof of **:** MANIFEST ⟨the ruins of the city ~ its ancient magnificence⟩ **4 :** to put on oath **~** *vi* **:** to bear witness **:** TESTIFY ⟨~ to the truth of the statement⟩ — **at·tes·ta·tion** \ˌa-ˌtes-ˈtā-shən, ˌat-ə-ˈstā-\ *n* — **at·test·er** \ə-ˈtes-tər\ *n*

at·tic \ˈat-ik\ *n* [F *attique,* fr. *attique* of Attica, fr. L *Atticus*] **1 :** a low story or wall above the main order of a facade in the classical styles **2 :** a room behind an attic **3 :** a room or a space immediately below the roof of a building **:** GARRET

1At·tic \ˈat-ik\ *adj* [L *Atticus,* fr. Gk *Attikos,* fr. *Attikē* Attica, Greece] **1 :** Athenian **2 :** marked by simplicity, purity, and refinement ⟨an ~ prose style⟩

2Attic *n* **:** a dialect of ancient Greek orig. used in Attica and later the literary language of the Greek-speaking world

at·ti·cism \ˈat-ə-ˌsiz-əm\ *n, often cap* **1 :** a characteristic feature of Attic Greek occurring in another language or dialect **2 :** a witty or well-turned phrase

1at·tire \ə-ˈtī(ə)r\ *vt* **-tired; -tir·ing** [ME *attiren,* fr. OF *atirier,* fr. *a-* (fr. L *ad-*) + *tire* order, rank, of Gmc origin; akin to OE *tīr* glory; akin to L *deus* god — more at DEITY] **:** to put garments on **:** DRESS, ARRAY; *esp* **:** to clothe in fancy or rich garments

2attire *n* **1 :** DRESS, CLOTHES; *esp* **:** splendid or decorative clothing **2 :** the antlers or antlers and scalp of a stag or buck

at·ti·tude \ˈat-ə-ˌt(y)üd\ *n* [F, fr. It *attitudine,* fr. *attitudine* aptitude, fr. LL *aptitudin-, aptitudo* fitness — more at APTITUDE] **1 :** the arrangement of the parts of a body or figure **:** POSTURE **2 a :** a mental position with regard to a fact or state **b :** a feeling or emotion toward a fact or state **3 :** a position assumed for a specific purpose ⟨a threatening ~⟩ **4 :** a ballet position similar to the arabesque in which the raised leg is bent at the knee **5 :** the position of an aircraft or spacecraft determined by the relationship between its axes and a reference datum (as the horizon or a particular star) **6 :** an organismic state of readiness to respond in a characteristic way to a stimulus (as an object, concept, or situation) ***syn*** see POSITION

at·ti·tu·di·nal \ˌat-ə-ˈt(y)üd-nəl, -ᵊn-əl\ *adj* [*attitude* + *-inal* (as in *aptitudinal,* fr. L *aptitudin-, aptitudo*)] **:** relating to, based on, or expressive of personal attitudes or feelings ⟨~ judgment⟩

at·ti·tu·di·nize \ˌat-ə-ˈt(y)üd-ᵊn-ˌīz\ *vi* **-nized; -niz·ing :** to assume an affected mental attitude **:** POSE

attn *abbr* attention

at·to- \ˈat-(ˌ)ō\ *comb form* [ISV, fr. Dan or Norw *atten* eighteen, fr. ON *āttjān;* akin to OE *eahtatīene* eighteen] **:** one quintillionth (10^{-18}) part of ⟨*attogram*⟩

at·torn \ə-ˈtərn\ *vi* [ME *attournen,* fr. MF *atorner,* fr. OF, fr. *a-* (fr. L *ad-*) + *torner* to turn] **:** to agree to become tenant to a new owner or landlord of the same property — **at·torn·ment** \-mənt\ *n*

at·tor·ney \ə-ˈtər-nē\ *n, pl* **-neys** [ME *attourney,* fr. MF *atorné,* pp. of *atorner*] **:** one who is legally appointed by another to transact business for him; *specif* **:** a legal agent qualified to act for suitors and defendants in legal proceedings — **at·tor·ney·ship** \-ˌship\ *n*

attorney–at–law *n, pl* **attorneys–at–law :** a practitioner in a court of law who is legally qualified to prosecute and defend actions in such court on the retainer of clients

attorney general *n, pl* **attorneys general** *or* **attorney generals :** the chief law officer of a nation or state who represents the government in litigation and serves as its principal legal adviser

at·tract \ə-ˈtrakt\ *vb* [ME *attracten,* fr. L *attractus,* pp. of *attrahere,* fr. *ad-* + *trahere* to draw — more at DRAW] *vt* **:** to cause to approach or adhere: as **a :** to pull to or toward oneself or itself ⟨a magnet ~*s* iron⟩ **b :** to draw by appeal to natural or excited interest, emotion, or aesthetic sense **:** ENTICE ⟨~ attention⟩ **~** *vi* **:** to exercise attraction — **at·tract·able** \-ˈtrak-tə-bəl\ *adj* — **at·trac·tor** \-ˈtrak-tər\ *n*

syn ATTRACT, ALLURE, CHARM, CAPTIVATE, FASCINATE, BEWITCH, ENCHANT *shared meaning element* **:** to draw another by exerting a compelling influence ***ant*** repel

at·trac·tant \ə-ˈtrak-tənt\ *n* **:** something that attracts; *esp* **:** a substance (as a pheromone) that attracts insects or other animals

at·trac·tion \ə-ˈtrak-shən\ *n* **1 a :** the act, process, or power of attracting **b :** personal charm **2 :** the action or power of drawing forth a response **:** an attractive quality **3 :** a force acting mutually between particles of matter, tending to draw them together, and resisting their separation **4 :** something that attracts or is intended to attract people by appealing to their desires and tastes ⟨~*s* at the local theater⟩

syn ATTRACTION, AFFINITY, SYMPATHY *shared meaning element* **:** the relationship existing between persons or things that are naturally or involuntarily drawn together

at·trac·tive \ə-ˈtrak-tiv\ *adj* **1 :** having or relating to the power to attract ⟨~ forces between molecules⟩ ⟨an ~ offer⟩ **2 :** arousing interest or pleasure **:** CHARMING ⟨an ~ smile⟩ — **at·trac·tive·ly** *adv* — **at·trac·tive·ness** *n* — **at·trac·tiv·i·ty** \ə-ˌtrak-ˈtiv-ət-ē, ˌa-ˌtrak-\ *n*

attrib *abbr* attributive; attributively

1at·tri·bute \ˈa-trə-ˌbyüt\ *n* [ME, fr. L *attributus,* pp. of *attribuere* to attribute, fr. *ad-* + *tribuere* to bestow — more at TRIBUTE] **1 :** an inherent characteristic; *also* **:** an accidental quality **2 :** an object closely associated with or belonging to a specific person, thing, or office ⟨a scepter is the ~ of power⟩; *esp* **:** such an object used for identification in painting or sculpture **3 :** a word ascribing a quality; *esp* **:** ADJECTIVE

2at·trib·ute \ə-ˈtrib-yət\ *vt* **-ut·ed; -ut·ing 1 :** to explain by indicating a cause ⟨*attributed* his success to his coach⟩ **2 a :** to regard as a characteristic of a person or thing **b :** to reckon as made or originated in an indicated fashion ⟨*attributed* the invention to a Russian⟩ **c :** CLASSIFY, DESIGNATE ***syn*** see ASCRIBE — **at·trib·ut·able** \-yət-ə-bəl\ *adj* — **at·trib·ut·er** *n*

at·tri·bu·tion \ˌa-trə-ˈbyü-shən\ *n* **1 :** the act of attributing; *esp* **:** the ascribing of a work (as of literature or art) to a particular author or artist **2 :** an ascribed quality, character, or right — **at·tri·bu·tion·al** \-shnəl, -shən-ᵊl\ *adj*

at·trib·u·tive \ə-ˈtrib-yət-iv\ *adj* **1 :** relating to or of the nature of an attribute **:** ATTRIBUTING **2 :** joined directly to a modified noun without a linking verb ⟨*city* in *city streets* is an ~ noun⟩ — **attributive** *n* — **at·trib·u·tive·ly** *adv*

at·trit·ed \ə-ˈtrīt-əd\ *adj* **:** worn by attrition

at·tri·tion \ə-ˈtrish-ən\ *n* [L *attrition-, attritio,* fr. *attritus,* pp. of *atterere* to rub against, fr. *ad-* + *terere* to rub — more at THROW] **1** [ME *attricioun,* fr. (assumed) ML *attrition-, attritio,* fr. L] **:** sorrow for one's sins that arises from a motive other than that of the love of God **2 :** the act of rubbing together **:** FRICTION; *also* **:** the act of wearing or grinding down by friction **3 :** the act of weakening or exhausting by constant harassment or abuse **4 :** a reduction (as in personnel) chiefly as a result of resignation, retirement, or death — **at·tri·tion·al** \-ˈtrish-nəl, -ˈtrish-ən-ᵊl\ *adj*

at·tune \ə-ˈt(y)ün\ *vt* **:** to bring into harmony **:** TUNE — **at·tune·ment** \-mənt\ *n*

atty *abbr* attorney

atty gen *abbr* attorney general

at·wit·ter \ə-'twit-ər\ *adj* : nervously concerned : EXCITED ⟨gossips ~ with speculation —*Time*⟩

at wt *abbr* atomic weight

atyp·i·cal \(')ā-'tip-i-kəl\ *adj* : not typical : IRREGULAR, UNUSUAL — **atyp·i·cal·i·ty** \ā-,tip-ə-'kal-ət-ē\ *n* — **atyp·i·cal·ly** \(')ā-'tip-i-k(ə-)lē\ *adv*

Au *symbol* [L *aurum*] gold

AU *abbr* angstrom unit

au·bade \ō-'bäd\ *n* [F, fr. (assumed) OProv *aubada*, fr. OProv *alba*, *auba* dawn, fr. (assumed) VL *alba*, fr. L, fem. of *albus* white] **1** : a song or poem greeting the dawn **2 a** : a morning love song **b** : a song or poem of lovers parting at dawn **3** : morning music — compare NOCTURNE

¹au·burn \'ò-bərn\ *adj* [ME *auborne* blond, fr. MF, fr. ML *alburnus* whitish, fr. L *albus*] **1** : of the color auburn **2** : of a reddish brown color

²auburn *n* : a moderate brown

Au·bus·son \,ō-bə-'sōⁿ\ *n* [*Aubusson*, France] **1** : a figured scenic tapestry used for wall hangings and upholstery **2** : a rug woven to resemble Aubusson tapestry

AUC \ā-(,)yü-'sē\ *abbr* [L *ab urbe condita*] from the year of the founding of the city (of Rome)

au cou·rant \,ō-kü-'räⁿ\ *adj* [F, lit., in the current] **1** : fully informed : UP-TO-DATE **2** : fully familiar : CONVERSANT

¹auc·tion \'òk-shən\ *n* [L *auction-, auctio*, lit., increase, fr. *auctus*, pp. of *augēre* to increase — more at EKE] **1** : public sale of property to the highest bidder **2** : the act or process of bidding in some card games

²auction *vt* **auc·tioned; auc·tion·ing** \-sh(ə-)niŋ\ : to sell at auction ⟨~ed off his library⟩

auction bridge *n* : a bridge game differing from contract bridge in that tricks made in excess of the contract are scored toward game

auc·tion·eer \,òk-shə-'ni(ə)r\ *n* : an agent who sells goods at auction — **auctioneer** *vt*

auc·to·ri·al \òk-'tōr-ē-əl, -'tòr-\ *adj* [L *auctor* author — more at AUTHOR] : of or relating to an author

aud *abbr* audit; auditor

au·da·cious \ò-'dā-shəs\ *adj* [MF *audacieux*, fr. *audace* boldness, fr. L *audacia*, fr. *audac-, audax* bold, fr. *audēre* to dare, fr. *avidus* eager — more at AVID] **1 a** : intrepidly daring : ADVENTUROUS ⟨an ~ mountain climber⟩ **b** : recklessly bold : RASH **2** : contemptuous of law, religion, or decorum : INSOLENT **3** : marked by originality and verve ⟨a bright ~ comedy about love⟩ — **au·da·cious·ly** *adv* — **au·da·cious·ness** *n*

au·dac·i·ty \ò-'das-ət-ē\ *n, pl* **-ties** [ME *audacite*, fr. L *audac-, audax*] **1** : the quality or state of being audacious: **a** : intrepid boldness **b** : bold or arrogant disregard of normal restraints **2** : an audacious act — usu. used in pl. *syn* see TEMERITY *ant* circumspection

¹au·di·ble \'òd-ə-bəl\ *adj* [LL *audibilis*, fr. L *audire* to hear; akin to Gk *aisthanesthai* to perceive, Skt *āvis* evidently] : heard or capable of being heard — **au·di·bil·i·ty** \,òd-ə-'bil-ət-ē\ *n* — **au·di·bly** \'òd-ə-blē\ *adv*

²audible *n* : AUTOMATIC 2

au·di·ence \'òd-ē-ən(t)s, 'äd-\ *n* [ME, fr. MF, fr. L *audientia*, fr. *audient-, audiens*, prp. of *audire*] **1** : the act or state of hearing **2 a** : a formal hearing or interview ⟨an ~ with the pope⟩ **b** : an opportunity of being heard ⟨he would succeed if he were once given ~⟩ **3 a** : a group of listeners or spectators **b** : the reading public **4** : FOLLOWING

au·di·ent \-ənt\ *n* [L *audient-, audiens*, prp.] : one that hears

au·dile \'ò-,dīl\ *n* [L *audire* to hear] : a person whose mental imagery is auditory rather than visual or motor — **audile** *adj*

au·ding \'òd-iŋ\ *n* [L *audire* + E *-ing*] : the process of hearing, recognizing, and interpreting a spoken language

¹au·dio \'òd-ē-,ō\ *adj* [*audio-*] **1** : of or relating to acoustic, mechanical, or electrical frequencies corresponding to normally audible sound waves which are of frequencies approximately from 15 to 20,000 cycles per second **2 a** : of or relating to sound or its reproduction and esp. high-fidelity reproduction **b** : relating to or used in the transmission or reception of sound — compare VIDEO

²audio *n* **1** : the transmission, reception, or reproduction of sound **2** : the section of television or motion picture equipment that deals with sound **3** : an audio signal; *broadly* : SOUND

audio- *comb form* [L *audire* to hear] **1** : hearing ⟨*audio*meter⟩ **2** : sound ⟨*audio*phile⟩ **3** : auditory and ⟨*audio*visual⟩

au·dio·gen·ic \,òd-ē-ō-'jen-ik\ *adj* : produced by frequencies corresponding to sound waves — used esp. of epileptoid responses ⟨~ seizures⟩

au·dio–lin·gual \,òd-ē-ō-'liŋ-g(yə-)wəl\ *adj* : involving a drill routine of listening and speaking in language learning

au·di·ol·o·gy \,òd-ē-'äl-ə-jē\ *n* : a branch of science dealing with hearing; *specif* : therapy of individuals having impaired hearing — **au·di·o·log·i·cal** \-ē-ə-'läj-i-kəl\ *adj* — **au·di·ol·o·gist** \-ē-'äl-ə-jəst\ *n*

au·di·om·e·ter \,òd-ē-'äm-ət-ər\ *n* : an instrument used in measuring the acuity of hearing — **au·di·o·met·ric** \-ē-ə-'me-trik\ *adj* — **au·di·om·e·try** \-ē-'äm-ə-trē\ *n*

au·dio·phile \'òd-ē-ō-,fīl\ *n* : one who is enthusiastic about sound reproduction and esp. music from high-fidelity broadcasts or recordings

au·dio·tape \,òd-ē-ō-'tāp\ *n* : a tape recording of sound

au·dio·vi·su·al \,òd-ē-ō-(,)vizh-(ə-)wəl, -,vizh-əl\ *adj* **1** : of or relating to both hearing and sight **2** : designed to aid in learning or teaching by making use of both hearing and sight ⟨an extensive ~ department of films and recordings⟩

au·dio·vi·su·als \-wəlz, -əlz\ *n pl* : instructional materials (as filmstrips accompanied by recordings) that make use of both sight and sound

¹au·dit \'òd-ət\ *n* [ME, fr. L *auditus* act of hearing, fr. *auditus*, pp.] **1 a** : a formal or official examination and verification of an account book **b** : a methodical examination and review **2** : the final report of an examination of books of account by auditors — **au·dit·able** \-ə-bəl\ *adj*

²audit *vt* **1** : to examine with intent to verify ⟨~ the account books⟩ **2** : to attend (a course) without working for or expecting to receive formal credit

¹au·di·tion \ò-'dish-ən\ *n* [MF or L; MF, fr. L *audition-, auditio*, fr. *auditus*, pp. of *audire*] **1** : the power or sense of hearing **2** : the act of hearing; *esp* : a critical hearing ⟨an ~ of new recordings⟩ **3** : a trial performance to appraise an entertainer's merits

²audition *vb* **au·di·tioned; au·di·tion·ing** \-'dish-(ə-)niŋ\ *vt* : to test in an audition ~ *vi* : to give a trial performance

au·di·tive \'òd-ət-iv\ *adj* : AUDITORY

au·di·tor \'òd-ət-ər\ *n* **1** : one that hears or listens; *esp* : one that is a member of an audience **2** : one authorized to examine and verify accounts **3** : one that audits a course of study **4** : one that hears (as a court case) in the capacity of judge

au·di·to·ri·um \,òd-ə-'tōr-ē-əm, -'tòr-\ *n* **1** : the part of a public building where an audience sits **2** : a room, hall, or building used for public gatherings

¹au·di·to·ry \'òd-ə-,tōr-ē, -,tòr-\ *n* [ME *auditorie*, fr. L *auditorium* auditorium] **1** *archaic* : AUDIENCE **2** *archaic* : AUDITORIUM

²auditory *adj* [LL *auditorius*] : of, relating to, or experienced through hearing

auditory nerve *n* : either of the 8th pair of cranial nerves connecting the inner ear with the brain and transmitting impulses concerned with hearing and balance — see EAR illustration

au fait \ō-'fā\ *adj* [F, lit., to the point] **1** : fully competent : CAPABLE **2** : fully informed : FAMILIAR **3** : socially correct

Auf·klä·rung \'aúf-,klä-ren, -,kler-əŋ\ *n* [G] : ENLIGHTENMENT 2

au fond \ō-fōⁿ\ *adv* [F] : at bottom : FUNDAMENTALLY

auf Wie·der·seh·en \aúf-'vēd-ər-,zā-(ə-)n\ *interj* [G, lit., till seeing again] — used to express farewell

aug *abbr* augmentative

Aug *abbr* August

Au·ge·an \ò-'jē-ən\ *adj* [L *Augeas*, king of Elis, fr. Gk *Augeias*; fr. the legend that his stable, left neglected for 30 years, was finally cleaned by Hercules] : extremely formidable or difficult and occas. distasteful ⟨an ~ task⟩

Augean stable *n* : a condition or place marked by great accumulation of filth or corruption — usu. used in pl. ⟨every government should attend to cleaning its own *Augean stables*⟩

au·gend \'ò-,jend\ *n* [L *augendus*, gerundive of *augēre* to increase — more at EKE] : a quantity to which an addend is added

au·ger \'ò-gər\ *n* [ME, alter. (resulting from incorrect division of *a nauger*) of *nauger*, fr. OE *nafogār*; akin to OHG *nabugēr* auger; both fr. a prehistoric WGmc= NGmc compound whose constituents are represented by OE *nafu*, *nave* and *gār* spear — more at GORE] **1** : a tool for boring holes in wood consisting of a shank with a crosswise handle for turning, a central tapered screw, and a pair of cutting lips **2** : any of various instruments or devices made like an auger and used for boring (as in soil), forcing (as through a meat grinder), or for moving material (as in a snow thrower)

augers 1: 1, 2 screw, 3 tapering pod

¹aught \'òt, 'ät\ *pron* [ME, fr. OE *āwiht*, fr. *ā* ever + *wiht* creature, thing — more at AYE, WIGHT] **1** *archaic* : ANYTHING **2** : ALL ⟨for ~ I care⟩

²aught *adv, archaic* : at all

³aught *n* [alter. (resulting from incorrect division of *a naught*) of *naught*] **1** : ZERO, CIPHER **2** *archaic* : NONENTITY, NOTHING

au·gite \'ò-,jīt\ *n* [L *augites*, a precious stone, fr. Gk *augitēs*] **1** : a mineral consisting of an aluminous usu. black or dark green pyroxene that is found in igneous rocks **2** : PYROXENE — **au·git·ic** \ò-'jit-ik\ *adj*

¹aug·ment \òg-'ment\ *vb* [ME *augmenten*, fr. MF *augmenter*, fr. LL *augmentare*, fr. *augmentum* increase, fr. *augēre* to increase — more at EKE] *vi* : to become augmented ~ *vt* **1** : to make (something well or adequately developed) greater, more numerous, larger, or more intense **2** : to add an augment to *syn* see INCREASE *ant* abate — **aug·ment·able** \-ə-bəl\ *adj* — **aug·ment·er** *or* **aug·men·tor** \-'ment-ər\ *n*

²aug·ment \'òg-,ment\ *n* : a vowel prefixed or a lengthening of the initial vowel to mark past time esp. in Greek and Sanskrit verbs

aug·men·ta·tion \,òg-mən-'tā-shən, -,men-\ *n* **1** : the act or process of augmenting **b** : the state of being augmented **2** : something that augments : ADDITION

¹aug·men·ta·tive \òg-'ment-ət-iv\ *adj* **1** : able to augment **2** : indicating large size and sometimes awkwardness or unattractiveness — used of words and affixes; compare DIMINUTIVE

²augmentative *n* : an augmentative word or affix

aug·ment·ed \òg-'ment-əd\ *adj, of a musical interval* : made one half step greater than major or perfect ⟨an ~ fifth⟩

augmented matrix *n* : a matrix whose elements are the coefficients of a set of simultaneous linear equations with the constant terms of the equations entered in an added column

au gra·tin \ō-'grat-ⁿn, ò-, -'grät-\ *adj* [F, lit., with the burnt scrapings from the pan] : covered with bread crumbs, butter, and cheese and then browned

¹au·gur \'ò-gər\ *n* [L; prob. akin to L *augēre*] **1** : an official diviner of ancient Rome **2** : one held to foretell events by omens

²augur *vt* **1** : to foretell esp. from omens **2** : to give promise of : PRESAGE ⟨higher pay ~s a better future⟩ ~ *vi* : to predict the future esp. from omens

au·gu·ry \'ò-gyə-rē, -gə-\ *n, pl* **-ries** : divination from omens or portents or from chance events (as the fall of lots) **2** : OMEN, PORTENT

---

au·gust \ȯ-ˈgəst\ *adj* [L *augustus;* akin to L *augēre* to increase] : marked by majestic dignity or grandeur — **au·gust·ly** *adv* — **au·gust·ness** \-ˈgəs(t)-nəs\ *n*

Au·gust \ˈȯ-gəst\ *n* [ME, fr. OE, fr. L *Augustus,* fr. *Augustus* Caesar] : the 8th month of the Gregorian calendar

Au·gus·tan \ȯ-ˈgəs-tən, ə-\ *adj* **1** : of, relating to, or characteristic of Augustus Caesar or his age **2** : of, relating to, or characteristic of the neoclassical period in England — **Augustan** *n*

¹**Au·gus·tin·i·an** \ˌȯ-gə-ˈstin-ē-ən\ *adj* **1** : of or relating to St. Augustine or his doctrines **2** : of or relating to any of several orders under a rule ascribed to St. Augustine — **Au·gus·tin·i·an·ism** \-ē-ə-ˌniz-əm\ *n*

²**Augustinian** *n* **1** : a follower of St. Augustine **2** : a member of an Augustinian order; *specif* : a friar of the Hermits of St. Augustine founded in 1256 and devoted to educational, missionary, and parish work

au jus \ō-ˈzhü(s), -ˈjüs; ō-zhᵫ\ *adj* [F, lit., with juice] : served in the juice obtained from roasting

auk \ˈȯk\ *n* [Norw or Icel *alk, alka,* fr. ON *ālka;* akin to L *olor* swan] : any of several black and white short-necked diving seabirds (family Alcidae) that breed in colder parts of the northern hemisphere

great auk

auk·let \ˈȯ-klət\ *n* : any of several small auks of the No. Pacific coasts

auld \ˈȯl(d), ˈäl(d)\ *adj, chiefly Scot* : OLD

auld lang syne \ˌōl-ˌ(d)aŋ-ˈzīn, ˌōl-ˌ(d)laŋ-, ˌȯl-\ *n* [Sc, lit., old long ago] : the good old times

au na·tu·rel \ˌō-ˌnat-ə-ˈrel\ *adj* [F] **1 a** : being in natural style or condition **b** : NUDE **2** : cooked plainly

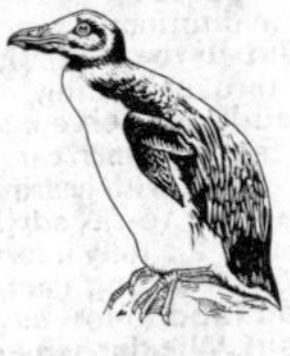

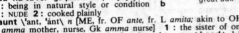

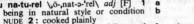

aunt \ˈant, ˈänt\ *n* [ME, fr. OF *ante,* fr. L *amita;* akin to OHG *amma* mother, nurse, Gk *amma* nurse] **1** : the sister of one's father or mother **2** : the wife of one's uncle — **aunt·hood** \-ˌhu̇d\ *n* — **aunt·like** \-ˌlīk\ *adj* — **aunt·ly** *adj*

Aunt Sal·ly \-ˈsal-ē\ *n, pl* **Aunt Sallies** [*Aunt Sally,* name given to an effigy of a woman smoking a pipe set up as an amusement attraction at English fairs for patrons to throw missiles at] **1** *Brit* : STRAW MAN 1 **2** *Brit* : one that is set up to invite attack or criticism : TARGET

au pair girl \ˈō-ˈpa(ə)r-, -ˈpe(ə)r-\ *n* [F *au pair,* on even terms] : a foreign girl living in England who does domestic work for a family in return for room and board and the opportunity to learn the English language — called also *au pair*

aur- *or* **auri-** *comb form* [L, fr. *auris* — more at EAR] **1** : ear ⟨*aur*al⟩ ⟨*auri*scope⟩ **2** : aural and ⟨*auri*nasal⟩

au·ra \ˈȯr-ə\ *n* [ME, fr. L, air, breeze, fr. Gk; akin to Gk *aēr* air] **1 a** : a subtle sensory stimulus (as an aroma) **b** : a distinctive atmosphere surrounding a given source ⟨the place had an ~ of mystery⟩ **2** : a luminous radiation : NIMBUS **3** : a subjective sensation (as of lights) experienced before an attack of some nervous disorders

au·ral \ˈȯr-əl\ *adj* : of or relating to the ear or to the sense of hearing — **au·ral·ly** \-ə-lē\ *adv*

aurar *pl of* EYRIR

au·re·ate \ˈȯr-ē-ət\ *adj* [ME *aureat,* fr. ML *aureatus* decorated with gold, fr. L *aureus* golden — more at ORIOLE] **1** : of a golden color or brilliance **2** : marked by grandiloquent and rhetorical style

au·re·ole \ˈȯr-ē-ˌōl\ *or* **au·re·o·la** \ȯ-ˈrē-ə-lə\ *n* [ME *aureole* heavenly crown worn by saints, fr. ML *aureola,* fr. L, fem. of *aureolus* golden — more at ORIOLE] **1** : a radiant light around the head or body of a representation of a sacred personage **2** : RADIANCE, AURA ⟨had about him an ~ of youth and health⟩ **3** : the luminous area surrounding the sun or other bright light when seen through thin cloud or mist : CORONA **4** : a ring-shaped zone around an igneous intrusion — **aureole** *vt*

Au·reo·my·cin \ˌȯr-ē-ō-ˈmīs-ᵊn\ *trademark* — used for chlortetracycline

au re·voir \ˌōr-əv-ˈwär, ˌȯr-\ *n* [F, lit., till seeing again] : GOOD-BYE — often used interjectionally

au·ric \ˈȯr-ik\ *adj* [L *aurum* gold — more at ORIOLE] : of, relating to, or derived from gold esp. when trivalent

au·ri·cle \ˈȯr-i-kəl\ *n* [L *auricula,* fr. dim. of *auris* ear] **1 a** : PINNA 2b **b** : the chamber or either of the chambers of the heart that receives blood from the veins and forces it into the ventricle or ventricles — see HEART illustration **2** : an angular or ear-shaped anatomic lobe or process

au·ric·u·la \ȯ-ˈrik-yə-lə\ *n* [NL, fr. L, external ear] **1** : a yellow-flowered Alpine primrose (*Primula auricula*) **2** : AURICLE

au·ric·u·lar \ȯ-ˈrik-yə-lər\ *adj* **1** : of, relating to, or using the ear or the sense of hearing **2** : told privately ⟨an ~ confession⟩ **3** : understood or recognized by the sense of hearing **4** : of or relating to an auricle or auricula

au·ric·u·late \ȯ-ˈrik-yə-lət\ *adj* : having ears or auricles

au·ric·u·lo·ven·tric·u·lar \ȯ-ˌrik-yə-(ˌ)lō-ven-ˈtrik-yə-lər, -vən-\ *adj* : ATRIOVENTRICULAR

au·rif·er·ous \ȯ-ˈrif-(ə-)rəs\ *adj* [L *aurifer,* fr. *aurum* + *-fer* -ferous] : gold-bearing

Au·ri·ga \ȯ-ˈrī-gə\ *n* [L (gen. *Aurigae*), lit., charioteer] : a constellation between Perseus and Gemini

Au·ri·gna·cian \ˌȯr-ēn-ˈyā-shən\ *adj* [F *aurignacien,* fr. *Aurignac,* France] : of or relating to an Upper Paleolithic culture marked by finely made artifacts of stone and bone, paintings, and engravings

au·rochs \ˈau̇(ə)r-ˌäks, ˈȯ(ə)r-\ *n, pl* **aurochs** [G, fr. OHG *ūrohso,* fr. *ūro* aurochs + *ohso* ox; akin to OE *ūr* aurochs — more at OX] **1** : URUS **2** : WISENT

au·ro·ra \ə-ˈrōr-ə, ȯ-, -ˈrȯr-\ *n, pl* **auroras** *or* **au·ro·rae** \-(ˌ)ē\ [L — more at EAST] **1** *cap* : the Roman goddess of dawn — compare EOS **2** : DAWN **3 a** : AURORA BOREALIS **b** : AURORA AUSTRALIS — **au·ro·ral** \-əl\ *adj* — **au·ro·re·an** \-ē-ən\ *adj*

aurora aus·tra·lis \-ȯ-ˈstrā-ləs, -ä-ˈstrā-\ *n* [NL, lit., southern aurora] : a phenomenon in the southern hemisphere corresponding to the aurora borealis in the northern hemisphere

aurora bo·re·al·is \-ˌbōr-ē-ˈal-əs, -ˌbȯr-\ *n* [NL, lit., northern dawn] : a luminous phenomenon that consists of streamers or arches of light in the sky at night, is held to be of electrical origin, and appears to best advantage in the arctic regions

au·rous \ˈȯr-əs\ *adj* [ISV, fr. L *aurum* gold — more at ORIOLE] : of, relating to, or containing gold esp. when univalent

AUS *abbr* Army of the United States

aus·cul·tate \ˈȯ-skəl-ˌtāt\ *vt* **-tat·ed; -tat·ing** [back-formation fr. *auscultation*] : to examine by auscultation — **aus·cul·ta·to·ry** \ȯ-ˈskəl-tə-ˌtōr-ē, -ˌtȯr-\ *adj*

aus·cul·ta·tion \ˌȯ-skəl-ˈtā-shən\ *n* [L *auscultation-, auscultatio* act of listening, fr. *auscultatus,* pp. of *auscultare* to listen; akin to L *auris* ear — more at EAR] : the act of listening to sounds arising within organs (as the lungs) as an aid to diagnosis and treatment

aus·land·er \ˈau̇-ˌslen-dər, -ˌslan-\ *n* [G *ausländer,* lit., outlander] : OUTSIDER, FOREIGNER

aus·pi·cate \ˈȯ-spə-ˌkāt\ *vt* **-cat·ed; -cat·ing** [L *auspicatus,* pp. of *auspicari* to take auspices, fr. *auspic-, auspex*] : to initiate or enter upon esp. under circumstances or with a procedure (as drinking a toast) calculated to ensure good luck

aus·pice \ˈȯ-spəs\ *n, pl* **aus·pic·es** \-spə-səz, -ˌsēz\ [L *auspicium,* fr. *auspic-, auspex* diviner by birds, fr. *avis* bird + *specere* to look, look at — more at AVIARY, SPY] **1** : observation by an augur esp. of the flight and feeding of birds to discover omens **2** : a prophetic sign; *esp* : a favorable sign **3** *pl* : kindly patronage and guidance

aus·pi·cious \ȯ-ˈspish-əs\ *adj* **1** : affording a favorable auspice : PROPITIOUS ⟨made an ~ beginning by getting an A⟩ **2** : attended by good auspices : PROSPEROUS ⟨an ~ year⟩ ***syn*** see FAVORABLE ***ant*** inauspicious, ill-omened — **aus·pi·cious·ly** *adv* — **aus·pi·cious·ness** *n*

Aus·sie \ˈȯ-sē, ˈäs-ē\ *n* [*Australian* + *-ie*] : a native or inhabitant of Australia

aus·ten·ite \ˈȯs-tə-ˌnīt, ˈäs-\ *n* [F, fr. Sir W. C. Roberts-*Austen*†1902 E metallurgist] : a solid solution in iron of carbon and sometimes other solutes that occurs as a constituent of steel under certain conditions — **aus·ten·it·ic** \ˌȯs-tə-ˈnit-ik, ˌäs-\ *adj*

aus·tere \ȯ-ˈsti(ə)r\ *adj* [ME, fr. MF, fr. L *austerus,* fr. Gk *austēros* harsh, severe; akin to Gk *hauos* dry — more at SERE] **1 a** : stern and forbidding in appearance and manner ⟨~ Puritan colonists⟩ **b** : SOMBER, GRAVE ⟨dressed all in ~ black for the funeral⟩ **2** : rigidly abstemious : ASCETIC ⟨an ~ old hermit living on berries and roots⟩ **3** : UNADORNED, SIMPLE ⟨an ~ chair with a straight back⟩ ***syn*** see SEVERE ***ant*** ardent (*as of persons*), exuberant (*as of style*) — **aus·tere·ly** *adv* — **aus·tere·ness** *n*

aus·ter·i·ty \ȯ-ˈster-ət-ē\ *n, pl* **-ties** **1** : the quality or state of being austere **2 a** : an austere act, manner, or attitude **b** : an ascetic practice **3** : enforced or extreme economy

¹**Austr-** *or* **Austro-** *comb form* [ME *austr-,* fr. L, fr. *Austr-, Auster* south wind; akin to L *aurora* dawn — more at EAST] **1** : south : southern ⟨*Austro*asiatic⟩ **2** : Australian and ⟨*Austro*-Malayan⟩

²**Austr-** *or* **Austro-** *comb form* [prob. fr. NL, fr. *Austria*] : Austrian and ⟨*Austro*-Hungarian⟩

aus·tral \ˈȯs-trəl, ˈäs-\ *adj* **1** : SOUTHERN **2** *cap* : AUSTRALIAN

Aus·tra·lia Day \ȯ-ˈstrāl-yə-, ä-\ *n* : a national holiday in Australia observed in commemoration of the landing of the British at Sydney Cove in 1788 and observed on Jan. 26 if a Monday and otherwise on the next Monday

¹**Aus·tra·lian** \ȯ-ˈstrāl-yən, ä-\ *n* **1** : a native or inhabitant of the Australian commonwealth **2** : the speech of the aboriginal inhabitants of Australia

²**Australian** *adj* **1** : of, relating to, or characteristic of the continent or commonwealth of Australia, its inhabitants, or the languages spoken there **2** : of, relating to, or being a biogeographic region that comprises Australia and the islands north of it from the Celebes eastward, Tasmania, New Zealand, and Polynesia

Australian ballot *n* : an official ballot printed at public expense on which the names of all the nominated candidates and proposals appear and which is distributed only at the polling place and marked in secret

Australian pine *n* : any of several casuarinas (esp. *Casuarina equisetifolia*) now widely grown as ornamentals in warm regions (as Florida)

Australian Rules football *n* : a game resembling rugby that is played between two teams of 18 players on a field 180–190 yards long that has four goalposts at each end

Australian terrier *n* : a small rather short-legged usu. grayish wirehaired terrier of Australian origin

Aus·tra·loid \ˈȯs-trə-ˌlȯid, ˈäs-\ *adj* [*Austral*ia + E *-oid*] : of or relating to an ethnic group including the Australian aborigines and other peoples of southern Asia and Pacific islands sometimes including the Ainu — **Australoid** *n*

aus·tra·lo·pith·e·cine \ȯ-ˌstrā-lō-ˈpith-ə-ˌsīn, ä-; ˌȯs-trə-, ˌäs-\ *adj* [deriv. of L *australis* southern (fr. *Austr-, Auster*) + Gk *pithēkos* ape — more at PITHECANTHROPUS] : of or relating to extinct southern African hominids (esp. genus *Australopithecus*) with near-human dentition and a relatively small brain — **australopithecine** *n*

Aus·tral·orp \ˈȯs-trə-ˌlȯ(ə)rp, ˈäs-\ *n* [*Austral*ian + *Orp*ington] : a usu. black domestic fowl developed in Australia and valued for egg production

Aus·tro·asi·at·ic \ˈȯs-(ˌ)trō-ˌā-z(h)ē-ˈat-ik, ˈäs- *also* -ˌā-shē-\ *adj* : of, relating to, or constituting a family of languages once widespread over northeastern India and Indochina

Aus·tro·ne·sian \ˌȯs-trə-ˈnē-zhən, ˌäs-, -shən\ *adj* [*Austronesia,* islands of the southern Pacific] : of, relating to, or constituting a family of agglutinative languages spoken in the area extending from Madagascar eastward through the Malay peninsula and archipelago to Hawaii and Easter Island and including practically all the native languages of the Pacific Islands with the exception of the Australian, Papuan, and Negrito languages

aut- *or* **auto-** *comb form* [Gk, fr. *autos* same, -self, self] **1** : self : same one ⟨*aut*ism⟩ ⟨*auto*biography⟩ **2** : automatic : self-acting : self-regulating ⟨*auto*dyne⟩

au·ta·coid \ˈȯt-ə-ˌkȯid\ *n* [*aut-* + Gk *akos* remedy; akin to OIr *hīcc* healing] : a specific organic substance (as a hormone) forming in one part of the body, moving in the body fluid or the sap, and modifying the activity of the cells of another part — **au·ta·coi·dal** \ˌȯt-ə-ˈkȯid-ᵊl\ *adj*

au·tar·chic \ȯ-ˈtär-kik\ *adj* : AUTARKIC — **au·tar·chi·cal** \-ki-kəl\ *adj*

¹au·tar·chy \ˈȯ-ˌtär-kē\ *n, pl* **-chies** [Gk *autarchia,* fr. *aut-* + *-archia* -archy] **1** : absolute sovereignty **2** : absolute or autocratic rule

²autarchy *n* [by alter.] : AUTARKY

au·tar·kic \ȯ-ˈtär-kik\ *adj* : of, relating to, or marked by autarky — **au·tar·ki·cal** \-ki-kəl\ *adj*

au·tar·ky \ˈȯ-ˌtär-kē\ *n* [G *autarkie,* fr. Gk *autarkeia,* fr. *autarkēs* self-sufficient, fr. *aut-* + *arkein* to defend, suffice — more at ARK] **1** : SELF-SUFFICIENCY, INDEPENDENCE; *specif* : national economic self-sufficiency and independence **2** : a policy of establishing a self-sufficient and independent national economy

aut·ecol·o·gy \ˌȯt-i-ˈkäl-ə-jē, ˌȯt-ē-\ *n* [ISV] : ecology dealing with individual organisms or individual kinds of organisms — **aut·eco·log·i·cal** \ˌȯt-ˌē-kə-ˈläj-i-kəl, -ˌek-ə-\ *adj*

au·teur theory \ō-ˈtər-\ *n* [part trans. of F *politique des auteurs,* fr. *auteur* author; fr. the view that directors are the true authors of a film] : a theory in motion-picture criticism that views the director as the primary creative force in a motion picture

auth *abbr* **1** authentic **2** author **3** authorized

au·then·tic \ə-ˈthent-ik, ȯ-\ *adj* [ME *autentik,* fr. MF *autentique,* fr. LL *authenticus,* fr. Gk *authentikos,* fr. *authentēs* perpetrator, master, fr. *aut-* + *-hentēs* (akin to Gk *anyein* to accomplish, Skt *sanoti* he gains)] **1** *obs* : AUTHORITATIVE **2** : worthy of acceptance or belief as conforming to fact or reality : TRUSTWORTHY **3 a** : not imaginary, false, or imitation ⟨one of the few remaining ~ colonial buildings⟩ **b** : conforming to an original so as to reproduce essential features ⟨an ~ reproduction of a colonial farmhouse⟩ **4 a** *of a church mode* : ranging upward from the keynote — compare PLAGAL 1 **b** *of a cadence* : progressing from the dominant chord to the tonic — compare PLAGAL 2 — **au·then·ti·cal·ly** \-i-k(ə-)lē\ *adv* — **au·then·tic·i·ty** \ˌȯ-ˌthen-ˈtis-ət-ē, -thən-\ *n*

syn AUTHENTIC, GENUINE, VERITABLE, BONA FIDE *shared meaning element* : being actually and precisely what is claimed. AUTHENTIC stresses fidelity to actuality and fact and may imply authority or trustworthiness in determining this relationship ⟨confirmed both by legend and *authentic* record —J. A. Froude⟩ GENUINE implies accordance with an original or type without counterfeiting, admixture, or adulteration ⟨*genuine* maple syrup⟩ or it may stress sincerity or the absence of factitiousness ⟨*genuine* piety⟩ VERITABLE implies a correspondence with truth and typically conveys a suggestion of affirmation ⟨though Christ be the *veritable* Son of God — A. T. Quiller-Couch⟩ or in figurative or hyperbolic contexts asserts the justice of the designation ⟨he is a *veritable* fool⟩ BONA FIDE, often interchangeable with *authentic* or *genuine,* can distinctively apply when good faith or sincerity is in question ⟨a *bona fide* sale of securities⟩ ***ant*** spurious

au·then·ti·cate \ə-ˈthent-i-ˌkāt, ȯ-\ *vt* **-cat·ed; -cat·ing** : to prove or serve to prove the authenticity of ***syn*** see CONFIRM ***ant*** impugn — **au·then·ti·ca·tion** \-ˌthent-i-ˈkā-shən\ *n* — **au·then·ti·ca·tor** \-ˈthent-i-ˌkāt-ər\ *n*

au·thor \ˈȯ-thər\ *n* [ME *auctour,* fr. ONF, fr. L *auctor* promoter, originator, author, fr. *auctus,* pp. of *augēre* to increase — more at EKE] **1** : the writer of a literary work (as a book) **2 a** : one that originates or gives existence : SOURCE ⟨trying to track down the ~ of the rumor⟩ ⟨the ~ of a theory⟩ **b** *cap* : GOD 1 ***syn*** see MAKER — **au·thor·ess** \ˈȯ-th(ə-)rəs\ *n* — **au·tho·ri·al** \ȯ-ˈthōr-ē-əl, -ˈthȯr-\ *adj*

au·thor·i·tar·i·an \ȯ-ˌthär-ə-ˈter-ē-ən, ə-, -ˌthȯr-\ *adj* **1** : of, relating to, or favoring blind submission to authority ⟨had ~ parents⟩ **2** : of, relating to, or favoring a concentration of power in a leader or an elite not constitutionally responsible to the people — **authoritarian** *n* — **au·thor·i·tar·i·an·ism** \-ē-ə-ˌniz-əm\ *n*

au·thor·i·ta·tive \ə-ˈthär-ə-ˌtāt-iv, ȯ-, -ˈthȯr-\ *adj* **1 a** : having or proceeding from authority : OFFICIAL ⟨~ church doctrine⟩ **b** : entitled to credit or acceptance : CONCLUSIVE ⟨a most ~ literary critique⟩ **2** : DICTATORIAL, PEREMPTORY — **au·thor·i·ta·tive·ly** *adv* — **au·thor·i·ta·tive·ness** *n*

au·thor·i·ty \ə-ˈthär-ət-ē, ȯ-, -ˈthȯr-\ *n, pl* **-ties** [ME *auctorite,* fr. OF *auctorité,* fr. L *auctoritat-, auctoritas* opinion, decision, power, fr. *auctor*] **1 a** (1) : a citation (as from a book or file) used in defense or support (2) : the source from which the citation is drawn **b** (1) : a conclusive statement or set of statements (as an official decision of a court) (2) : a decision taken as a precedent (3) : TESTIMONY **c** : an individual cited or appealed to as an expert **2 a** : power to influence or command thought, opinion, or behavior **b** : freedom granted by one in authority : RIGHT **3 a** : persons in command; *specif* : GOVERNMENT **b** : a governmental agency or corporation to administer a revenue-producing public enterprise ⟨the transit ~⟩ **4 a** : GROUNDS, WARRANT ⟨had excellent ~ for his strange actions⟩ **b** : convincing force : WEIGHT ⟨his strong tenor lent ~ to the performance⟩ ***syn*** see INFLUENCE

au·tho·ri·za·tion \ˌȯ-th(ə-)rə-ˈzā-shən\ *n* **1** : the act of authorizing **2** : an instrument that authorizes : SANCTION

au·tho·rize \ˈȯ-thə-ˌrīz\ *vt* **-rized; -riz·ing** **1** : to invest esp. with legal authority : EMPOWER ⟨*authorized* to act for her husband⟩ **2** : to establish by or as if by authority : SANCTION ⟨a custom *authorized* by time⟩ **3** *archaic* : to furnish a ground for : JUSTIFY — **au·tho·riz·er** *n*

Authorized Version *n* : a revision of the English Bishops' Bible carried out under James I, published in 1611, and widely used by Protestants

au·thor·ship \ˈȯ-thər-ˌship\ *n* **1** : the profession of writing **2 a** : the origin of a literary production **b** : the state or act of creating or causing

au·tism \ˈȯ-ˌtiz-əm\ *n* : absorption in self-centered subjective mental activity (as daydreams, fantasies, delusions, and hallucinations) esp. when accompanied by marked withdrawal from reality — **au·tis·tic** \ȯ-ˈtis-tik\ *adj*

¹au·to \ˈȯt-(ˌ)ō, ˈät-\ *n, pl* **autos** : AUTOMOBILE

²auto *abbr* automatic

¹auto- — see AUT-

²auto- *comb form* [¹*automobile*] : self-propelling : automotive ⟨*auto*truck⟩

au·to·an·ti·body \ˌȯt-(ˌ)ō-ˈant-i-ˌbäd-ē\ *n* : an antibody against one of the constituents of the tissues of the individual that produces it

au·to·bahn \ˈȯt-ō-ˌbän, ˈau̇t-\ *n* [G, fr. *auto* + *bahn* road] : a German expressway

au·to·bio·graph·i·cal \ˌȯt-ə-ˌbī-ə-ˈgraf-i-kəl\ *also* **au·to·bio·graph·ic** \-ik\ *adj* : of, relating to, or of the nature of an autobiography — **au·to·bio·graph·i·cal·ly** \-i-k(ə-)lē\ *adv*

au·to·bi·og·ra·phy \ˌȯt-ə-bī-ˈäg-rə-fē, -bē-\ *n* : the biography of a person narrated by himself — **au·to·bi·og·ra·pher** \-fər\ *n*

au·to·bus \ˈȯt-ō-ˌbəs\ *n* [*auto* + *bus*] : OMNIBUS 1

au·to·cade \ˈȯt-ō-ˌkād\ *n* : MOTORCADE

au·to·ca·tal·y·sis \ˌȯt-ō-kə-ˈtal-ə-səs\ *n, pl* **-y·ses** \-ˌsēz\ [NL] : catalysis of a reaction by one of its products — **au·to·cat·a·lyt·ic** \-ˌkat-ᵊl-ˈit-ik\ *adj*

au·to·ceph·a·lous \ˌȯt-ō-ˈsef-ə-ləs\ *adj* [LGk *autokephalos,* fr. Gk *aut-* + *kephalē* head — more at CEPHALIC] : being independent of external and esp. patriarchal authority — used esp. of Eastern national churches

au·toch·thon \ȯ-ˈtäk-thən\ *n, pl* **-thons** *or* **-tho·nes** \-thə-ˌnēz\ [Gk *autochthōn,* fr. *aut-* + *chthōn* earth — more at HUMBLE] **1 a** : one held to have sprung from the ground he inhabits **b** : ABORIGINE, NATIVE **2** : something that is autochthonous; *esp* : an indigenous plant or animal — **au·toch·tho·nism** \-thə-ˌniz-əm\ *n*

au·toch·tho·nous \ȯ-ˈtäk-thə-nəs\ *adj* : INDIGENOUS, NATIVE — **au·toch·tho·nous·ly** *adv* — **au·toch·tho·ny** \-nē\ *n*

¹au·to·clave \ˈȯt-ō-ˌklāv\ *n* [F, fr. *aut-* + L *clavis* key — more at CLAVICLE] : an apparatus (as for sterilizing) using superheated steam under pressure

²autoclave *vt* **-claved; -clav·ing** : to subject to the action of an autoclave

au·toc·ra·cy \ȯ-ˈtäk-rə-sē\ *n, pl* **-cies** **1** : government in which one person possesses unlimited power **2** : the authority or rule of an autocrat **3** : a community or state governed by autocracy

au·to·crat \ˈȯt-ə-ˌkrat\ *n* [F *autocrate,* fr. Gk *autokratēs* ruling by oneself, absolute, fr. *aut-* + *-kratēs* ruling — more at -CRAT] **1** : a person (as a monarch) ruling with unlimited authority **2** : one who has undisputed influence or power

au·to·crat·ic \ˌȯt-ə-ˈkrat-ik\ *adj* **1** : of, relating to, or being an autocracy : ABSOLUTE ⟨an ~ government⟩ **2** : characteristic of or resembling an autocrat : DESPOTIC ⟨an ~ ruler⟩ — **au·to·crat·i·cal** \-i-kəl\ *adj* — **au·to·crat·i·cal·ly** \-i-k(ə-)lē\ *adv*

au·to·cross \ˈȯt-ō-ˌkrȯs, ˈät-\ *n* [*auto*] : an automobile gymkhana

au·to–da–fé \ˌau̇t-ō-də-ˈfā, ˌȯt-\ *n, pl* **au·tos–da–fé** \-ōz-də-\ [Pg *auto da fé,* lit., act of the faith] : the ceremony accompanying the pronouncement of judgment by the Inquisition and followed by the execution of sentence by the secular authorities; *broadly* : the burning of a heretic

au·to·di·dact \ˌȯt-ō-ˈdī-ˌdakt, -dī-ˈ, -də-\ *n* [Gk *autodidaktos* self-taught, fr. *aut-* + *didaktos* taught, fr. *didaskein* to teach — more at DOCILE] : a self-taught person — **au·to·di·dac·tic** \-dī-ˈdak-tik, -də-\ *adj*

au·to·dyne \ˈȯt-ə-ˌdīn\ *n* [ISV *aut-* + hetero*dyne*] : a heterodyne in which the auxiliary current is generated in the device used for rectification

au·toe·cious \ȯ-ˈtē-shəs\ *adj* [*aut-* + Gk *oikia* house — more at VICINITY] : passing through all life stages on the same host ⟨~ rusts⟩ — **au·toe·cious·ly** *adv* — **au·toe·cism** \-ˈtē-ˌsiz-əm\ *n*

au·to·er·o·tism \ˌȯt-ō-ˈer-ə-ˌtiz-əm\ *or* **au·to·erot·i·cism** \-i-ˈrät-ə-ˌsiz-əm\ *n* **1** : sexual gratification obtained solely through one's own organism **2** : sexual feeling arising without known external stimulation — **au·to·erot·ic** \-i-ˈrät-ik\ *adj* — **au·to·erot·i·cal·ly** \-i-k(ə-)lē\ *adv*

au·tog·a·my \ȯ-ˈtäg-ə-mē\ *n* [ISV] : SELF-FERTILIZATION: as **a** : pollination of a flower by its own pollen **b** : conjugation of two sister cells or sister nuclei of protozoans or fungi — **au·tog·a·mous** \-məs\ *adj*

au·to·gen·e·sis \ˌȯt-ō-ˈjen-ə-səs\ *n* [NL] : ABIOGENESIS — **au·to·ge·net·ic** \-jə-ˈnet-ik\ *adj* — **au·to·ge·net·i·cal·ly** \-i-k(ə-)lē\ *adv*

au·tog·e·nous \ȯ-ˈtäj-ə-nəs\ *or* **au·to·gen·ic** \ˌȯt-ə-ˈjen-ik\ *adj* [Gk *autogenēs,* fr. *aut-* + *-genēs* born, produced — more at -GEN] **1** : produced independently of external influence or aid : ENDOGENOUS **2** : originating or derived from sources within the same individual ⟨an ~ graft⟩ ⟨~ vaccine⟩ **3** : not requiring a meal of blood to produce eggs ⟨~ mosquitoes⟩ — **au·tog·e·nous·ly** *adv*

au·to·gi·ro *also* **au·to·gy·ro** \ˌȯt-ō-ˈjī(ə)r-(ˌ)ō\ *n, pl* **-ros** [fr. *Autogiro,* a trademark] : a rotary-wing aircraft that employs a propeller for forward motion and a freely rotating rotor for lift

au·to·graft \ˈȯt-ō-ˌgraft\ *n* : a tissue or organ that is transplanted from one part to another part of the same body — **autograft** *vt*

¹au·to·graph \ˈȯt-ə-ˌgraf\ *n* [LL *autographum,* fr. L, neut. of *autographus* written with one's own hand, fr. Gk *autographos,* fr. *aut-* + *-graphos* written — more at -GRAPH] **1** : something written or made with one's own hand: **a** : an original manuscript or work of art **b** : a person's handwritten signature **2** : a representation or trace of an object produced in a photographic emulsion by the mechanical, electrical, chemical, or radiation effects of the object itself — **au·tog·ra·phy** \ȯ-ˈtäg-rə-fē\ *n*

²autograph *vt* **1** : to write with one's own hand **2** : to write one's signature in or on

au·to·graph·ic \ˌȯt-ə-ˈgraf-ik\ *adj* **1** : of, relating to, or constituting an autograph **2 a** *of an instrument* : SELF-RECORDING **b** *of a* *record* : recorded by a self-recording instrument — **au·to·graph·i·cal·ly** \-i-k(ə-)lē\ *adv*

Au·to·harp \ˈȯt-ō-ˌhärp\ *trademark* — used for a zither with button-controlled dampers for selected strings

au·to·hyp·no·sis \ˌȯt-ō-hip-ˈnō-səs\ *n* [NL] : self-induced and usu. automatic hypnosis — **au·to·hyp·not·ic** \-ˈnät-ik\ *adj*

au·to·im·mune \-im-ˈyün\ *adj* : of, relating to, or caused by autoantibodies ⟨~ diseases⟩ — **au·to·im·mu·ni·ty** \-ˈyü-nət-ē\ *n* — **au·to·im·mu·ni·za·tion** \-ˌim-yə-nə-ˈzā-shən *also* -im-ˌyü-\ *n*

au·to·in·fec·tion \-in-ˈfek-shən\ *n* [ISV] : reinfection with larvae produced by parasitic worms already in the body

au·to·in·oc·u·la·tion \ˌȯt-ō-in-ˌäk-yə-ˈlā-shən\ *n* [ISV] **1** : inoculation with vaccine prepared from material from one's own body **2** : spread of infection from one part to other parts of the same body

au·to·in·tox·i·ca·tion \-in-ˌtäk-sə-ˈkā-shən\ *n* [ISV] : a state of being poisoned by toxic substances produced within the body

au·to·load·ing \ˌȯt-ō-ˈlōd-iŋ\ *adj* : SEMIAUTOMATIC b

au·tol·o·gous \ȯ-ˈtäl-ə-gəs\ *adj* [*aut-* + *-ologous* (as in *homologous*)] : derived from the same individual

au·tol·y·sate \ȯ-ˈtäl-ə-ˌsāt, -ˌzāt\ *n* : a product of autolysis

au·tol·y·sin \-ə-sən\ *n* : a substance that produces autolysis

au·tol·y·sis \-ə-səs\ *n* [NL] : breakdown of all or part of a cell or tissue by self-produced enzymes — **au·to·lyt·ic** \ˌȯt-ᵊl-ˈit-ik\ *adj*

au·to·mak·er \ˈȯt-ō-ˌmā-kər, ˈät-\ *n* : a manufacturer of automobiles

au·to·ma·nip·u·la·tion \ˌȯt-ō-mə-ˌnip-yə-ˈlā-shən\ *n* : physical stimulation of the genital organs by oneself — **au·to·ma·nip·u·la·tive** \-ˈnip-yə-ˌlāt-iv\ *adj*

Au·to·mat \ˈȯt-ə-ˌmat\ *service mark* — used for a cafeteria in which food is obtained esp. from coin-operated compartments

au·to·mate \ˈȯt-ə-ˌmāt\ *vb* **-mat·ed; -mat·ing** [back-formation fr. *automation*] *vt* **1** : to operate by automation **2** : to convert to largely automatic operation : AUTOMATIZE ~ *vi* : to undergo automation — **au·to·mat·able** \-ˌmāt-ə-bəl\ *adj*

[1]au·to·mat·ic \ˌȯt-ə-ˈmat-ik\ *adj* [Gk *automatos* self-acting, fr. *aut-* + *-matos* (akin to L *ment-, mens* mind) — more at MIND] **1 a** : largely or wholly involuntary; *esp* : REFLEX 5 ⟨~ blinking of the eyelids⟩ **b** : acting or done spontaneously or unconsciously **c** : resembling an automaton : MECHANICAL ⟨knew the lesson so well that her answers were ~⟩ **2** : having a self-acting or self-regulating mechanism **3** *of a firearm* : using either gas pressure or force of recoil and mechanical spring action for repeatedly ejecting the empty cartridge shell, introducing a new cartridge, and firing it **syn** see SPONTANEOUS — **au·to·mat·i·cal·ly** \-i-k(ə-)lē\ *adv* — **au·to·ma·tic·i·ty** \-mə-ˈtis-ət-ē, -ma-\ *n*

[2]automatic *n* **1** : a machine or apparatus that operates automatically: as **a** : an automatic firearm **b** : an automatic gear-shifting mechanism **2** : a substitute offensive or defensive play called at the line of scrimmage in football — called also *audible*

automatic pilot *n* : a device for automatically steering ships, aircraft, and spacecraft — called also *autopilot*

automatic writing *n* : writing performed without conscious intention and sometimes without awareness as if of telepathic or spiritualistic origin

au·to·ma·tion \ˌȯt-ə-ˈmā-shən\ *n* [[1]*automatic*] **1** : the technique of making an apparatus, a process, or a system operate automatically **2** : the state of being operated automatically **3** : automatically controlled operation of an apparatus, process, or system by mechanical or electronic devices that take the place of human organs of observation, effort, and decision

au·tom·a·tism \ȯ-ˈtäm-ə-ˌtiz-əm\ *n* [F *automatisme,* fr. *automate* automaton, fr. L *automaton*] **1 a** : the quality or state of being automatic **b** : an automatic action **2** : a theory that views the body as a machine and consciousness as a noncontrolling adjunct of the body **3** : the power or fact of moving independently of external stimuli or under the influence of external stimuli but independent of conscious control **4** : suspension of the conscious mind to release subconscious images — **au·tom·a·tist** \-ˈtäm-ət-əst\ *n*

au·tom·a·ti·za·tion \ȯ-ˌtäm-ət-ə-ˈzā-shən\ *n* : AUTOMATION

au·tom·a·tize \ȯ-ˈtäm-ə-ˌtīz\ *vt* **-tized; -tiz·ing** [[1]*automatic*] : to make automatic

au·tom·a·ton \ȯ-ˈtäm-ət-ən, -ə-ˌtän\ *n, pl* **-atons** *or* **-a·ta** \-ət-ə, -ə-ˌtä\ [L, fr. Gk, neut. of *automatos*] **1** : a mechanism that is relatively self-operating; *esp* : ROBOT **2** : a machine or control mechanism designed to follow automatically a predetermined sequence of operations or respond to encoded instructions **3** : an individual who acts in a mechanical fashion

[1]au·to·mo·bile \ˌȯt-ə-mō-ˈbē(ə)l, ˈȯt-ə-mō-ˌbēl, ˌȯt-ə-ˈmō-ˌbēl\ *adj* [F, fr. *aut-* + *mobile*] : AUTOMOTIVE

[2]automobile *n* : a usu. four-wheeled automotive vehicle designed for passenger transportation and commonly propelled by an internal-combustion engine using a volatile fuel — **automobile** *vi* — **au·to·mo·bil·ist** \-ˈbē-ləst, -ˌbē-\ *n*

au·to·mor·phism \ˌȯt-ə-ˈmȯr-ˌfiz-əm\ *n* [*aut-* + isomorphism] : an isomorphism of a set (as a group) with itself

au·to·mo·tive \ˌȯt-ə-ˈmōt-iv\ *adj* **1** : SELF-PROPELLED **2** : of, relating to, or concerned with automotive vehicles or machines

au·to·nom·ic \ˌȯt-ə-ˈnäm-ik\ *adj* **1 a** : acting independently of volition ⟨~ reflexes⟩ **b** : relating to, affecting, or controlled by the autonomic nervous system **2** : due to internal causes or influences : SPONTANEOUS — **au·to·nom·i·cal·ly** \-i-k(ə-)lē\ *adv*

autonomic nervous system *n* : a part of the vertebrate nervous system that innervates smooth and cardiac muscle and glandular tissues and governs involuntary actions and that consists of the sympathetic nervous system and the parasympathetic nervous system

au·ton·o·mist \ȯ-ˈtän-ə-məst\ *n* : one who advocates autonomy

au·ton·o·mous \ȯ-ˈtän-ə-məs\ *adj* [Gk *autonomos* independent, fr. *aut-* + *nomos* law — more at NIMBLE] **1** : of, relating to, or marked by autonomy **2 a** : having the right or power of self-government **b** : undertaken or carried on without outside control : SELF-CONTAINED ⟨an ~ school system⟩ **3 a** : existing or capable of existing independently ⟨an ~ zooid⟩ **b** : responding, reacting, or developing independently of the whole ⟨an ~ growth⟩ **4** : controlled by the autonomic nervous system **syn** see FREE — **au·ton·o·mous·ly** *adv*

au·ton·o·my \-mē\ *n, pl* **-mies** **1** : the quality or state of being self-governing; *esp* : the right of self-government **2** : a self-governing state **3** : self-directing freedom and esp. moral independence

au·to·phyte \ˈȯt-ə-ˌfīt\ *n* : a plant capable of synthesizing its own food from simple inorganic substances — **au·to·phyt·ic** \ˌȯt-ə-ˈfit-ik\ *adj* — **au·to·phyt·i·cal·ly** \-i-k(ə-)lē\ *adv*

au·to·pi·lot \ˈȯt-ō-ˌpī-lət\ *n* : AUTOMATIC PILOT

au·to·plas·tic \ˌȯt-ō-ˈplas-tik\ *adj* : of, relating to, or involving repair of lesions with tissue from the same body — **au·to·plas·ti·cal·ly** \-ti-k(ə-)lē\ *adv* — **au·to·plas·ty** \ˈȯt-ō-ˌplas-tē\ *n*

au·top·sy \ˈȯ-ˌtäp-sē, ˈȯt-əp-\ *n, pl* **-sies** [Gk *autopsia* act of seeing with one's own eyes, fr. *aut-* + *opsis* sight, fr. *opsesthai* to be going to see — more at OPTIC] : POSTMORTEM EXAMINATION — **autopsy** *vt*

au·to·ra·dio·graph \ˌȯt-ō-ˈrād-ē-ə-ˌgraf\ *or* **au·to·ra·dio·gram** \-ˌgram\ *n* [ISV] : an image produced on a photographic film or plate by the radiations from a radioactive substance in an object which is in close contact with the emulsion — **au·to·ra·dio·graph·ic** \-ˌrād-ē-ə-ˈgraf-ik\ *adj* — **au·to·ra·di·og·ra·phy** \-ˌrād-ē-ˈäg-rə-fē\ *n*

au·to·ro·ta·tion \-rō-ˈtā-shən\ *n* : the turning of the rotor of an autogiro or a helicopter with the resulting lift caused solely by the aerodynamic forces induced by motion of the rotor along its flight path — **au·to·ro·tate** \-ˈrō-ˌtāt\ *vi* — **au·to·ro·ta·tion·al** \-rō-ˈtā-shnəl, -shən-ᵊl\ *adj*

autos–da–fé *pl of* AUTO-DA-FÉ

au·to·sex·ing \ˈȯt-ō-ˌsek-siŋ\ *adj* : showing different characters in the two sexes at birth or hatching

au·to·some \ˈȯt-ə-ˌsōm\ *n* : a chromosome other than a sex chromosome — **au·to·so·mal** \ˌȯt-ə-ˈsō-məl\ *adj* — **au·to·so·mal·ly** \-mə-lē\ *adv*

au·to·stra·da \ˌau̇t-ō-ˈsträd-ə, ˌȯt-ō-\ *n, pl* **-stradas** *or* **-stra·de** \-ˈsträd-(ˌ)ā\ [It, fr. *auto*mobile + *strada* street, fr. LL *strata* paved road — more at STREET] : a high-speed multilane highway first developed in Italy

au·to·sug·ges·tion \ˌȯt-ō-sə(g)-ˈjes(h)-chən\ *n* [ISV] : an influencing of one's own attitudes, behavior, or physical condition by mental processes other than conscious thought : SELF-HYPNOSIS — **au·to·sug·gest** \-sə(g)-ˈjest\ *vt*

au·to·tel·ic \ˌȯt-ō-ˈtel-ik, -ˈtē-lik\ *adj* [Gk *autotelēs,* fr. *aut-* + *telos* end — more at WHEEL] : having a purpose in itself

au·to·tet·ra·ploi·dy \ˌȯt-ō-ˈte-trə-ˌplȯid-ē\ *n* : the state of having four genomes due to doubling of the ancestral chromosome complement — **au·to·tet·ra·ploid** \-ˌplȯid\ *adj or n*

au·tot·o·mize \ȯ-ˈtät-ə-ˌmīz\ *vb* **-mized; -miz·ing** *vt* : to effect autotomy of ~ *vi* : to undergo autotomy

au·tot·o·my \-mē\ *n* [ISV] : reflex separation of a part from the body : division of the body into two or more pieces — **au·to·tom·ic** \ˌȯt-ə-ˈtäm-ik\ *or* **au·tot·o·mous** \ȯ-ˈtät-ə-məs\ *adj*

au·to·trans·form·er \-ˈtran(t)s-ˈfȯr-mər\ *n* : a transformer in which the primary and secondary coils have part or all of their turns in common

au·to·trans·plant \-ˈtran(t)s-ˌplant\ *n* : AUTOGRAFT — **au·to·trans·plant** \-tran(t)s-ˈ\ *vt*

au·to·trans·plan·ta·tion \-ˌtran(t)s-ˌplan-ˈtā-shən\ *n* : the action of autotransplanting : the condition of being autotransplanted

au·to·troph \ˈȯt-ə-ˌtrōf, -ˌträf\ *n* [G, fr. *autotroph,* adj.] : an autotrophic organism — **au·tot·ro·phy** \ȯ-ˈtä-trə-fē\ *n*

au·to·tro·phic \ˌȯt-ə-ˈtrō-fik\ *adj* [prob. fr. G *autotroph,* fr. Gk *autotrophos* supplying one's own food, fr. *aut-* + *trephein* to nourish — more at ATROPHY] **1** : needing only carbon dioxide or carbonates as a source of carbon and a simple inorganic nitrogen compound for metabolic synthesis **2** : not requiring a specified exogenous factor for normal metabolism — **au·to·tro·phi·cal·ly** \-fi-k(ə-)lē\ *adv*

au·tumn \ˈȯt-əm\ *n* [ME *autumpne,* fr. L *autumnus*] **1** : the season between summer and winter comprising in the northern hemisphere usu. the months of September, October, and November or as reckoned astronomically extending from the September equinox to the December solstice — called also *fall* **2** : a period of maturity or incipient decline ⟨in the ~ of her life⟩ — **au·tum·nal** \ȯ-ˈtəm-nəl\ *adj* — **au·tum·nal·ly** \-nə-lē\ *adv*

autumn crocus *n* : an autumn-blooming colchicum

au·tun·ite \ō-ˈtən-ˌīt, ˈȯt-ᵊn-\ *n* [*Autun,* France] : a radioactive lemon-yellow mineral $Ca(UO_2)(PO_4)_2.10–12H_2O$ occurring in tabular crystals with basal cleavage and in scales like mica

aux *or* **auxil** *abbr* auxiliary

aux·e·sis \ȯg-ˈzē-səs, ȯk-ˈsē-\ *n* [NL, fr. Gk *auxēsis* increase, growth, fr. *auxein* to increase — more at EKE] : GROWTH; *specif* : increase of cell size without cell division — **aux·et·ic** \-ˈzet-ik, -ˈset-\ *adj* — **aux·et·i·cal·ly** \-i-k(ə-)lē\ *adv*

[1]aux·il·ia·ry \ȯg-ˈzil-yə-rē, -ˈzil-(ə-)rē\ *adj* [L *auxiliaris,* fr. *auxilium* help; akin to Gk *auxein* to increase] **1 a** : offering or providing help **b** : functioning in a subsidiary capacity ⟨an ~ branch of the state university⟩ **2** *of a verb* : accompanying another verb and typically expressing person, number, mood, or tense **3 a** : SUPPLEMENTARY **b** : constituting a reserve ⟨an ~ power plant⟩ **4** : equipped with sails and a supplementary inboard engine

[2]auxiliary *n, pl* **-ries** **1 a** : an auxiliary person, group, or device; *specif* : a member of a foreign force serving a nation at war **b** : a Roman Catholic titular bishop assisting a diocesan bishop and not having the right of succession **2** : an auxiliary boat or ship **3** : an auxiliary verb

aux·in \ˈȯk-sən\ *n* [ISV, fr. Gk *auxein*] : an organic substance that is able in low concentrations to promote elongation of plant shoots and usu. to control other specific growth effects; *broadly* : PLANT HORMONE — **aux·in·ic** \ȯk-ˈsin-ik\ *adj* — **aux·in·i·cal·ly** \-i-k(ə-)lē\ *adv*

auxo·troph \ˈȯk-sə-ˌtrōf, -ˌträf\ *n* : an auxotrophic strain or individual

aux·o·tro·phic \ˌȯk-sə-ˈtrō-fik\ *adj* [Gk *auxein* to increase + *-o-* + E *-trophic*] : requiring a specific growth substance beyond the minimum required for normal metabolism and reproduction ⟨~ mutants of bacteria⟩ — **aux·ot·ro·phy** \ȯk-ˈsä-trə-fē\ *n*

av *abbr* **1** avenue **2** average **3** avoirdupois

AV *abbr* **1** ad valorem **2** audiovisual **3** Authorized Version

¹avail \ə-ˈvā(ə)l\ *vb* [ME *availen*, prob. fr. *a-* (as in *abaten* to abate) + *vailen* to avail, fr. OF *valoir* to be of worth, fr. L *valēre* — more at WIELD] *vi* : to be of use or advantage : SERVE ⟨our best efforts did not ~⟩ ~ *vt* **1** : to be of use or advantage to : PROFIT **2** : to result in : bring about ⟨his efforts ~*ed* him nothing⟩ — **avail oneself of** *also* **avail of** : to make use of : take advantage of

²avail *n* **1** : advantage toward attainment of a goal or purpose : USE ⟨effort was of little ~⟩ **2** *pl, archaic* : profits or proceeds esp. from a business or from the sale of property

avail·abil·i·ty \ə-ˌvā-lə-ˈbil-ət-ē\ *n, pl* **-ties** **1** : the quality or state of being available **2** : an available person or thing

avail·able \ə-ˈvā-lə-bəl\ *adj* **1** *archaic* : having a beneficial effect **2** : VALID — used of a legal plea or charge **3** : present or ready for immediate use **4** : ACCESSIBLE, OBTAINABLE ⟨articles ~ in any drugstore⟩ **5** : qualified or willing to do something or to assume a responsibility ⟨~ candidates⟩ **6** : present in such chemical or physical form as to be usable (as by a plant) ⟨~ nitrogen⟩ ⟨~ water⟩ — **avail·able·ness** *n* — **avail·ably** \-blē\ *adv*

¹av·a·lanche \ˈav-ə-ˌlanch\ *n* [F, fr. F dial. *lavantse, avalantse*] **1** : a large mass of snow, ice, earth, rock, or other material in swift motion down a mountainside or over a precipice **2** : a sudden great or overwhelming rush or accumulation of something ⟨office workers tied down with an ~ of paper work⟩ **3** : a cumulative process in which electrons or charge carriers accelerated by an electric field produce additional electrons or charge carriers through collisions (as with gas molecules)

²avalanche *vb* **-lanched; -lanch·ing** *vi* : to descend in an avalanche ~ *vt* : OVERWHELM, FLOOD

Av·a·lon \ˈav-ə-ˌlän\ *n* : a paradise in Arthurian legend to which Arthur is carried after his death

¹avant-garde \ˌäv-ˌän(t)-ˈgärd, ˌav-, ˌäv-; ə-ˈvänt-ˌ; ˌav-ˌōⁿ-ˈ, ˌav-ˌȯn(t)-ˈ\ *n* [F, vanguard] : an intelligentsia that develops new or experimental concepts esp. in the arts — **avant-gard·ism** \-ˈgärd-ˌiz-əm\ *n* — **avant-gard·ist** \-ˈgärd-əst\ *n*

²avant-garde *adj* : of or relating to an avant-garde ⟨~ writers⟩

av·a·rice \ˈav-(ə-)rəs\ *n* [ME, fr. OF, fr. L *avaritia*, fr. *avarus* avaricious, fr. *avēre* to covet — more at AVID] : excessive or insatiable desire for wealth or gain : GREEDINESS, CUPIDITY

av·a·ri·cious \ˌav-ə-ˈrish-əs\ *adj* : greedy of gain : excessively acquisitive esp. in seeking to hoard riches ***syn*** see COVETOUS ***ant*** generous — **av·a·ri·cious·ly** *adv* — **av·a·ri·cious·ness** *n*

avast \ə-ˈvast\ *vb imper* [perh. fr. D *houd vast* hold fast] — a nautical command to stop or cease

av·a·tar \ˈav-ə-ˌtär\ *n* [Skt *avatāra* descent, fr. *avatarati* he descends, fr. *ava-* away + *tarati* he crosses over — more at UKASE, THROUGH] **1** : the incarnation of a Hindu deity (as Vishnu) **2 a** : an incarnation in human form **b** : an embodiment (as of a concept or philosophy) usu. in a person **3** : a variant phase or version of a continuing basic entity

avaunt \ə-ˈvȯnt, -ˈvänt\ *adv* [ME, fr. MF *avant*, fr. L *abante* forward, before, fr. *ab* from + *ante* before — more at OF, ANTE-] : AWAY, HENCE

AVC *abbr* **1** American Veterans Committee **2** automatic volume control

avdp *abbr* avoirdupois

¹ave \ˈäv-(ˌ)ā\ *n* [ME, fr. L, hail] **1** : an expression of greeting or of leave-taking : HAIL, FAREWELL **2** *often cap* : AVE MARIA

²ave *abbr* avenue

avel·lan \ə-ˈvel-ən\ *or* **avel·lane** \ə-ˈvel-ˌān, ˈav-ə-ˌlān\ *adj* [L *abellana, avellana* filbert, fr. fem. of *Abellanus* of Abella, fr. *Abella*, ancient town in Italy] *of a heraldic cross* : having the four arms shaped like conventionalized filberts — see CROSS illustration

Ave Ma·ria \ˌäv-(ˌ)ā-mə-ˈrē-ə\ *n* [ME, fr. ML, hail, Mary] : HAIL MARY

avenge \ə-ˈvenj\ *vt* **avenged; aveng·ing** [ME *avengen*, prob. fr. *a-* (as in *abaten* to abate) + *vengen* to avenge, fr. OF *vengier* — more at VENGEANCE] **1** : to take vengeance for or on behalf of **2** : to exact satisfaction for (a wrong) by punishing the wrongdoer — **aveng·er** *n*

syn AVENGE, REVENGE *shared meaning element* : to punish one who has wronged oneself or another

av·ens \ˈav-ənz\ *n, pl* **avens** [ME *avence*, fr. OF] : any of a genus (*Geum*) of perennial herbs of the rose family with white, purple, or yellow flowers

av·en·tail \ˈav-ən-ˌtāl\ *n* [ME, modif. of OF *ventaille*] : VENTAIL

aven·tu·rine \ə-ˈven-chə-ˌrēn, -rən\ *n* [F, fr. *aventure* chance — more at ADVENTURE] **1** : glass containing opaque sparkling particles of foreign material usu. copper or chromic oxide **2** : a translucent quartz spangled throughout with scales of mica or other mineral

av·e·nue \ˈav-ə-ˌn(y)ü\ *n* [MF, fr. fem. of *avenu*, pp. of *avenir* to come to, fr. L *advenire* — more at ADVENTURE] **1** : a way of access : ROUTE **2** : a channel for pursuing a desired object ⟨~*s* of communication⟩ **3 a** *chiefly Brit* : the principal walk or driveway to a house situated off a main road **b** : a broad passageway bordered by trees **4** : an often broad street or road

aver \ə-ˈvər\ *vt* **averred; aver·ring** [ME *averren*, fr. MF *averer*, fr. ML *adverare* to confirm as authentic, fr. L *ad-* + *verus* true — more at VERY] **1 a** : to verify or prove to be true in pleading a cause **b** : to allege or assert in pleading **2** : to declare positively

¹av·er·age \ˈav-(ə-)rij\ *n* [modif. of MF *avarie* damage to ship or cargo, fr. OIt *avaria*, fr. Ar *ʽawārīyah* damaged merchandise] **1** : sundry petty charges regularly defrayed by the master of a ship and usu. included in the freight **2 a** : a less than total loss sustained by a ship or cargo **b** : a charge arising from damage caused by sea perils customarily distributed equitably and proportionately among all chargeable with it **3 a** : a single value (as a mean, mode, or median) that summarizes or represents the general significance of a set of unequal values **b** : MEAN 1b **4 a** : an estimation of or approximation to an arithmetic mean **b** : a level (as of intelligence) typical of a group, class, or series ⟨above the ~⟩ **5** : a ratio expressing the average performance esp. of an athletic team or an athlete computed according to the number of opportunities for successful performance

syn AVERAGE, MEAN, MEDIAN, NORM *shared meaning element* : something (as a quantity) that represents a middle point between extremes ***ant*** maximum, minimum

²average *adj* **1** : equaling an arithmetic mean **2 a** : being about midway between extremes ⟨a man of ~ height⟩ **b** : not out of the ordinary : COMMON ⟨the ~ person⟩ — **av·er·age·ly** *adv* — **av·er·age·ness** *n*

³average *vb* **av·er·aged; av·er·ag·ing** *vi* **1 a** : to be or come to an average ⟨the gain *averaged* out to 20 percent⟩ **b** : to have a medial value of ⟨a color *averaging* a pale purple⟩ **2** : to buy on a falling market or sell on a rising market additional shares or commodities so as to obtain a more favorable average price — usu. used with *down* or *up* ~ *vt* **1** : to do, get, or have on the average or as an average sum or quantity ⟨~*s* 12 hours of work a day⟩ **2** : to find the arithmetic mean of (a series of unequal quantities) **3 a** : to bring toward the average **b** : to divide among a number proportionately

aver·ment \ə-ˈvər-mənt\ *n* **1** : the act of averring **2** : something that is averred : AFFIRMATION

averse \ə-ˈvərs\ *adj* [L *aversus*, pp. of *avertere*] : having an active feeling of repugnance or distaste ⟨~ to strenuous exercise⟩ ***syn*** see DISINCLINED ***ant*** avid (*of* or *for*), athirst (*for*) — **averse·ly** *adv* — **averse·ness** *n*

aver·sion \ə-ˈvər-zhən, -shən\ *n* **1** *obs* : the act of turning away **2 a** : a feeling of repugnance toward something with a desire to avoid or turn from it ⟨regards drunkenness with ~⟩ **b** : a settled dislike : ANTIPATHY ⟨expressed an ~ to parties⟩ **3** *archaic* : one that is the object of aversion

aver·sive \ə-ˈvər-siv, -ziv\ *adj* : tending to avoid or causing avoidance of a noxious or punishing stimulus ⟨behavior modification by ~ stimulation⟩

avert \ə-ˈvərt\ *vt* [ME *averten*, fr. MF *avertir*, fr. L *avertere*, fr. *ab-* + *vertere* to turn — more at WORTH] **1** : to turn away or aside (as the eyes) in avoidance **2** : to see coming and ward off : AVOID ***syn*** see PREVENT

Aves·ta \ə-ˈves-tə\ *n* [MPer *Avastāk*, lit., original text] : the book of the sacred writings of Zoroastrianism

Aves·tan \-tən\ *n* : one of the two ancient languages of Old Iranian and that in which the sacred books of Zoroastrianism were written — see INDO-EUROPEAN LANGUAGES table — **Avestan** *adj*

avg *abbr* average

av·gas \ˈav-ˌgas\ *n* [*av*iation *gas*oline] : gasoline for airplanes

avi·an \ˈā-vē-ən\ *adj* [L *avis*] : of, relating to, or derived from birds

avi·an·ize \-vē-ə-ˌnīz\ *vt* **-ized; -iz·ing** : to modify or attenuate (as a virus) by repeated culture in the developing chick embryo

avi·a·rist \ˈā-vē-ə-rəst, -vē-ˌer-əst\ *n* : one who keeps an aviary

avi·ary \ˈā-vē-ˌer-ē\ *n, pl* **-ar·ies** [L *aviarium*, fr. *avis* bird; akin to Gk *aetos* eagle] : a place for keeping birds confined

avi·ate \ˈā-vē-ˌāt, ˈav-ē-\ *vi* **-at·ed; -at·ing** [back-formation fr. *aviation*] : to navigate the air (as in an airplane)

avi·a·tion \ˌā-vē-ˈā-shən, ˌav-ē-\ *n, often attrib* [F, fr. L *avis*] **1** : the operation of heavier-than-air aircraft **2** : military airplanes **3** : airplane manufacture, development, and design

aviation cadet *n* : one in training for a military or naval commission with an aeronautical rating

avi·a·tor \ˈā-vē-ˌāt-ər, ˈav-ē-\ *n* : the operator or pilot of an airplane

avi·a·tress \-ˌā-trəs\ *n* : AVIATRIX

avi·a·trix \ˌā-vē-ˈā-triks, ˌav-ē-\ *n, pl* **-trix·es** \-trik-səz\ *or* **-tri·ces** \-trə-ˌsēz\ : a woman aviator

avi·cul·ture \ˈā-və-ˌkəl-chər, ˈav-ə-\ *n* [L *avis* + E *culture*] : the raising and care of birds and esp. of wild birds in captivity — **avi·cul·tur·ist** \ˌā-və-ˈkəlch-(ə-)rəst, ˌav-ə-\ *n*

av·id \ˈav-əd\ *adj* [F or L; F *avide*, fr. L *avidus*, fr. *avēre* to covet; akin to Goth *awiliuth* thanks, Gk *enēēs* gentle] **1** : desirous to the point of greed : urgently eager : GREEDY ⟨~ fondness for publicity⟩ **2** : characterized by enthusiasm and vigorous pursuit ⟨~ readers⟩ ***syn*** see EAGER ***ant*** indifferent, averse — **av·id·ly** *adv* — **av·id·ness** *n*

av·i·din \ˈav-əd-ən\ *n* [fr. its avidity for biotin] : a protein found in white of egg that combines with biotin and makes it inactive

avid·i·ty \ə-ˈvid-ət-ē, a-\ *n, pl* **-ities** **1** : the quality or state of being avid: **a** : keen eagerness **b** : consuming greed **2 a** : the strength of an acid or base dependent on its degree of dissociation **b** : AFFINITY 2b

avi·fau·na \ˌā-və-ˈfȯn-ə, ˌav-ə-, -ˈfän-ə\ *n* [NL, fr. L *avis* + NL *fauna*] : the birds or the kinds of birds of a region, period, or environment — **avi·fau·nal** \-ᵊl\ *adj* — **avi·fau·nal·ly** \-ᵊl-ē\ *adv* — **avi·fau·nis·tic** \-fȯ-ˈnis-tik, -fä-\ *adj*

av·i·ga·tion \ˌav-ə-ˈgā-shən\ *n* [L *avis* + E *-gation* (as in *navigation*)] : the navigation of airplanes

avi·on·ics \ˌā-vē-ˈän-iks, ˌav-ē-\ *n pl* [*avi*ation electr*onics*] : the development and production of electrical and electronic devices for use in aviation, missilery, and astronautics; *also* : the devices and systems so developed — **avi·on·ic** \-ik\ *adj*

avir·u·lent \(ˈ)ā-ˈvir-(y)ə-lənt\ *adj* [ISV] : not virulent — compare NONPATHOGENIC

avi·ta·min·osis \ˌā-ˌvīt-ə-mə-ˈnō-səs\ *n, pl* **-o·ses** \-ˌsēz\ : disease (as pellagra) resulting from a deficiency of one or more vitamins — **avi·ta·min·ot·ic** \-mə-ˈnät-ik\ *adj*

avn *abbr* aviation

ə abut ᵊ kitten ər further a back ā bake ä cot, cart
aü out ch chin e less ē easy g gift i trip ī life
j joke ŋ sing ō flow ȯ flaw ȯi coin th thin t͟h this
ü loot u̇ foot y yet yü few yu̇ furious zh vision

avo \'av-(,)ü\ *n, pl* **avos** [Pg, fr. *avo* fractional part, fr. *-avo* ordinal suffix (as in *oitavo* eighth, fr. L *octavus*) — more at OCTAVE] — see *pataca* at MONEY table

av·o·ca·do \,av-ə-'käd-(,)ō, ,äv-\ *n, pl* **-dos** *also* **-does** [modif. of Sp *aguacate*, fr. Nahuatl *ahuacatl*] : the pulpy green or purple edible fruit of various tropical American trees (genus *Persea*) of the laurel family; *also* : a tree bearing avocados — called also *alligator pear, avocado pear*

av·o·ca·tion \,av-ə-'kā-shən\ *n* [L *avocation-, avocatio*, fr. *avocatus*, pp. of *avocare* to call away, fr. *ab-* + *vocare* to call, fr. *voc-, vox* voice — more at VOICE] **1** *archaic* : DIVERSION, DISTRACTION **2** : a subordinate occupation pursued in addition to one's vocation esp. for enjoyment : HOBBY **3** : customary employment : VOCATION — **av·o·ca·tion·al** \-shnəl, -shən-ᵊl\ *adj* — **av·o·ca·tion·al·ly** \-ē\ *adv*

av·o·cet \'av-ə-,set\ *n* [F & It; F *avocette*, fr. It *avocetta*] : any of several rather large long-legged shorebirds (genus *Recurvirostra*) with webbed feet and slender upward-curving bill

avoid \ə-'vȯid\ *vt* [ME *avoiden*, fr. OF *esvuidier*, fr. *es-* (fr. L *ex-*) + *vuidier* to empty — more at VOID] **1** *obs* : VOID, EXPEL **2** *archaic* : to depart or withdraw from : LEAVE **3** : to make legally void : ANNUL ⟨~ a plea⟩ **4** **a** : to keep away from : SHUN **b** : to prevent the occurrence or effectiveness of **c** : to refrain from ***syn*** see ESCAPE — **avoid·able** \-ə-bəl\ *adj* — **avoid·ably** \-blē\ *adv* — **avoid·er** *n*

avoid·ance \ə-'vȯid-ᵊn(t)s\ *n* **1** *obs* **a** : an action of emptying, vacating, or clearing away **b** : OUTLET **2** : ANNULMENT **3** : an act or practice of avoiding

av·oir·du·pois \,av-ərd-ə-'pȯiz, 'av-ərd-ə-,\ *n* [ME *avoir de pois* goods sold by weight, fr. OF, lit., goods of weight] **1** : AVOIRDUPOIS WEIGHT **2** : WEIGHT, HEAVINESS; *esp* : personal weight

avoirdupois weight *n* : the series of units of weight based on the pound of 16 ounces and the ounce of 16 drams — see WEIGHT table

avouch \ə-'vau̇ch\ *vt* [ME *avouchen* to cite as authority, fr. MF *avochier* to summon, fr. L *advocare* — more at ADVOCATE] **1** : to declare as a matter of fact or as a thing that can be proved : AFFIRM **2** : to vouch for : CORROBORATE **3** **a** : to acknowledge (as an act) as one's own **b** : CONFESS, AVOW

avouch·ment \-mənt\ *n* : an act of avouching : AVOWAL

avow \ə-'vau̇\ *vt* [ME *avowen*, fr. OF *avouer*, fr. L *advocare*] **1** : to declare assuredly **2** : to declare openly, bluntly, and without shame ⟨ever ready to ~ his reactionary outlook⟩ ***syn*** **1** see ASSERT **2** see ACKNOWLEDGE ***ant*** disavow — **avow·ed·ly** \-'vau̇-əd-lē\ *adv* — **avow·er** \-'vau̇(-ə)r\ *n*

avow·al \-'vau̇(-ə)l\ *n* : an open declaration or acknowledgment

avulse \ə-'vəls\ *vt* **avulsed; avuls·ing** [L *avulsus*, pp. of *avellere* to tear off, fr. *ab-* + *vellere* to pluck — more at VULNERABLE] : to separate by avulsion

avul·sion \ə-'vəl-shən\ *n* : a forcible separation or detachment: as **a** : a tearing away of a body part accidentally or surgically **b** : a sudden cutting off of land by flood, currents, or change in course of a body of water; *esp* : one separating land from one person's property and joining it to another's

avun·cu·lar \ə-'vəŋ-kyə-lər\ *adj* [L *avunculus* maternal uncle — more at UNCLE] **1** : of or relating to an uncle **2** : suggestive of an uncle esp. in kindliness or geniality ⟨~ indulgence⟩

aw \'ȯ\ *interj* — used to express mild sympathy, remonstrance, incredulity, or disgust

AW *abbr* **1** actual weight **2** aircraft warning **3** all water **4** articles of war **5** automatic weapon

await \ə-'wāt\ *vb* [ME *awaiten*, fr. ONF *awaitier*, fr. *a-* (fr. L *ad-*) + *waitier* to watch — more at WAIT] *vt* **1** *obs* : to lie in wait for **2** **a** : to wait for **b** : to remain in abeyance until ⟨a treaty ~*ing* ratification⟩ **3** : to be ready or waiting for ⟨wondered what ~*ed* him at the end of his journey⟩ ~ *vi* **1** *obs* : ATTEND **2** : to stay or be in waiting : WAIT **3** : to be in store ***syn*** see EXPECT ***ant*** despair

¹awake \ə-'wāk\ *vb* **awoke** \-'wōk\ *also* **awaked** \-'wākt\; **awaked** *also* **awoke** *or* **awo·ken** \-'wō-kən\; **awak·ing** *vi* **1** : to cease sleeping **2** : to become aroused or active again **3** : to become conscious or aware of something ⟨*awoke* to their danger⟩ ~ *vt* **1** : to arouse from sleep or a sleeplike state **2** : to make active : stir up ⟨*awoke* old memories⟩

²awake *adj* : roused from or as if from sleep ***syn*** see AWARE

awak·en \ə-'wā-kən\ *vb* **awak·ened; awak·en·ing** \-'wāk-(ə-)niŋ\ [ME *awakenen*, fr. OE *awæcnian*, fr. *a-* + *wæcnian* to waken] : AWAKE — **awak·en·er** \-'wāk-(ə-)nər\ *n*

¹award \ə-'wȯ(ə)rd\ *vt* [ME *awarden* to decide, fr. ONF *eswarder*, fr. *es-* (fr. L *ex-*) + *warder* to guard, of Gmc origin; akin to OHG *wartēn* to watch — more at WARD] **1** : to give by judicial decree or after careful weighing of evidence **2** : to confer or bestow as being deserved or merited or needed ⟨~ scholarships to ghetto students⟩ ***syn*** see GRANT — **award·able** \-'wȯrd-ə-bəl\ *adj* — **award·er** \-'wȯrd-ər\ *n*

²award *n* **1** **a** : a judgment or final decision; *esp* : the decision of arbitrators in a case submitted to them **b** : the document containing the decision of arbitrators **2** : something that is conferred or bestowed esp. on the basis of merit or need

award·ee \ə-,wȯr-'dē, -'wȯr-,\ *n* : one that receives an award

aware \ə-'wa(ə)r, -'we(ə)r\ *adj* [ME *iwar*, fr. OE *gewær*, fr. *ge-* (associative prefix) + *wær* wary — more at CO-, WARY] **1** *archaic* : WATCHFUL, WARY **2** : having or showing realization, perception, or knowledge — **aware·ness** *n*

syn AWARE, COGNIZANT, CONSCIOUS, SENSIBLE, ALIVE, AWAKE *shared meaning element* : having knowledge of something and esp. of something not generally known or apparent ***ant*** unaware

awash \ə-'wȯsh, -'wäsh\ *adj* **1** **a** : alternately covered and exposed by waves or tide **b** : washing about : AFLOAT **c** : covered with water : FLOODED **2** : marked by an abundance ⟨a post office ~ with holiday mail⟩

¹away \ə-'wā\ *adv* **1** : on the way : ALONG ⟨get ~ early⟩ **2** : from this or that place : HENCE, THENCE ⟨go ~⟩ **3** **a** : in a secure place or manner ⟨locked ~⟩ ⟨tucked ~⟩ **b** : in another direction **4** : out of existence : to an end ⟨echoes dying ~⟩ **5** : from one's possession ⟨gave ~ a fortune⟩ **6** **a** : ON, UNINTERRUPTEDLY ⟨clocks ticking ~⟩ **b** : without hesitation or delay **7** : by a long distance or interval : FAR ⟨~ back in 1910⟩

²away *adj* **1** : absent from a place : GONE ⟨~ for the weekend⟩ **2** : DISTANT ⟨a lake 10 miles ~⟩ **3** : played on an opponent's grounds ⟨home and ~ games⟩ **4** *baseball* : OUT ⟨two ~ in the 9th⟩ — **away·ness** *n*

¹awe \'ȯ\ *n* [ME, fr. ON *agi*; akin to OE *ege* awe, Gk *achos* pain] **1** *archaic* **a** : DREAD, TERROR **b** : the power to inspire dread **2** : emotion in which dread, veneration, and wonder are variously mingled: as **a** : profound and humbly fearful reverence inspired by deity or by something sacred or mysterious **b** : submissive and admiring fear inspired by authority or power ⟨they stood in ~ of the king⟩ **c** : wondering reverence tinged with fear inspired by the sublime ***syn*** see REVERENCE

²awe *vt* **awed; aw·ing** : to inspire with awe

awea·ry \ə-'wi(ə)r-ē\ *adj, archaic* : being weary

aweath·er \ə-'weth-ər\ *adv* : on or toward the weather or windward side — compare ALEE

awed \'ȯd\ *adj* : showing awe ⟨~ respect⟩

aweigh \ə-'wā\ *adj* : raised just clear of the ground — used of an anchor

awe·less *or* **aw·less** \'ȯ-ləs\ *adj* **1** : feeling no awe **2** *obs* : inspiring no awe

awe·some \'ȯ-səm\ *adj* **1** : expressive of awe ⟨~ tribute⟩ **2** : inspiring awe ⟨an ~ sight⟩ — **awe·some·ly** *adv* — **awe·some·ness** *n*

awe·struck \-,strək\ *also* **awe·strick·en** \-,strik-ən\ *adj* : filled with awe

¹aw·ful \'ȯ-fəl\ *adj* **1** : inspiring awe **2** : filled with awe: as **a** *obs* : AFRAID, TERRIFIED **b** : deeply respectful or reverential **3** : extremely disagreeable or objectionable **4** : exceedingly great — used as an intensive ⟨they took an ~ chance⟩ ***syn*** see FEARFUL — **aw·ful·ly** \'ȯ-fə-lē, *esp as adv of adj senses 3 & 4* -flē\ *adv* — **aw·ful·ness** \-fəl-nəs\ *n*

²awful *adv* : VERY, EXTREMELY ⟨~ tired⟩

awhile \ə-'hwī(ə)l, ə-'wī(ə)l\ *adv* : for a while

awhirl \ə-'hwər(-ə)l, -'wər(-ə)l\ *adj* : characterized by whirling

awk·ward \'ȯ-kwərd\ *adj* [ME *awkeward* in the wrong direction, fr. *awke* turned the wrong way, fr. ON *öfugr*; akin to OHG *abuh* turned the wrong way, L *opacus* obscure] **1** *obs* : PERVERSE **2** *archaic* : UNFAVORABLE, ADVERSE **3** : lacking dexterity or skill (as in the use of hands) ⟨~ with a needle and thread⟩ **b** : showing lack of expertness ⟨~ pictures⟩ **4** **a** : lacking ease or grace (as of movement or expression) **b** : lacking the right proportions, size, or harmony of parts : UNGAINLY **5** **a** : lacking social grace and assurance **b** : causing embarrassment ⟨an ~ moment⟩ **6** : poorly adapted for use or handling ⟨an ~ load⟩ **7** : requiring caution ⟨an ~ diplomatic situation⟩ — **awk·ward·ly** *adv* — **awk·ward·ness** *n*

syn AWKWARD, CLUMSY, MALADROIT, INEPT, GAUCHE *shared meaning element* : not marked by ease and smoothness (as in acting or functioning) ***ant*** handy, deft, graceful

awl \'ȯl\ *n* [ME *al*, fr. ON *alr*; akin to OHG *āla* awl, Skt *ārā*] : a pointed instrument for marking surfaces or piercing small holes (as in leather or wood)

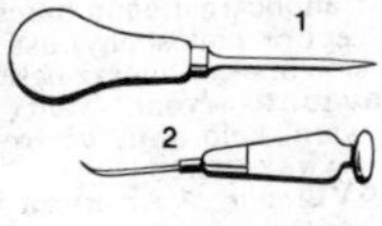

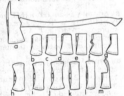

awls: *1* ordinary, *2* sewing

awl–shaped \-,shāpt\ *adj* : shaped like an awl; *specif* : being linear and tapering to a fine point

aw·mous \'ä-məs, 'ȯ-\ *n* [ME (northern dial.) *almous*, fr. ON *almusa*, fr. OS *almōsa* or OHG *alamuosan*] *Scot* : ALMS

awn \'ȯn\ *n* [ME, fr. OE *agen*, fr. ON *ögn*; akin to OHG *agana* awn, OE *ecg* edge — more at EDGE] : one of the slender bristles that terminate the glumes of the spikelet in some cereal and other grasses; *broadly* : a small pointed process — **awned** \'ȯnd\ *adj* — **awn·less** \'ȯn-ləs\ *adj*

aw·ning \'ȯn-iŋ, 'än-\ *n* [origin unknown] **1** : a rooflike cover extending over or before a place (as over the deck of a ship or before a window) as a shelter **2** : a shelter resembling an awning — **aw·ninged** \-iŋd\ *adj*

awoke *past of* AWAKE

awoken *past part of* AWAKE

¹AWOL \'ā-,wȯl, ,ā-,dəb-əl-yü-,ō-'el\ *adj, often not cap* [*a*bsent *w*ith*o*ut *l*eave] : absent without leave

²AWOL *n, often not cap* : one who is AWOL

awry \ə-'rī\ *adv or adj* **1** : in a turned or twisted position or direction : ASKEW **2** : out of the right or hoped-for course : AMISS

¹ax *or* **axe** \'aks\ *n* [ME, fr. OE *æcx*; akin to OHG *ackus* ax, L *ascia*, Gk *axinē*] **1** : a cutting tool that consists of a heavy edged head fixed to a handle with the edge parallel to the handle and that is used esp. for felling trees and chopping and splitting wood **2** : a hammer with a sharp edge for dressing or spalling stone **3** : abrupt removal (as from employment or from a budget) — **ax to grind** : an ulterior often selfish purpose to further

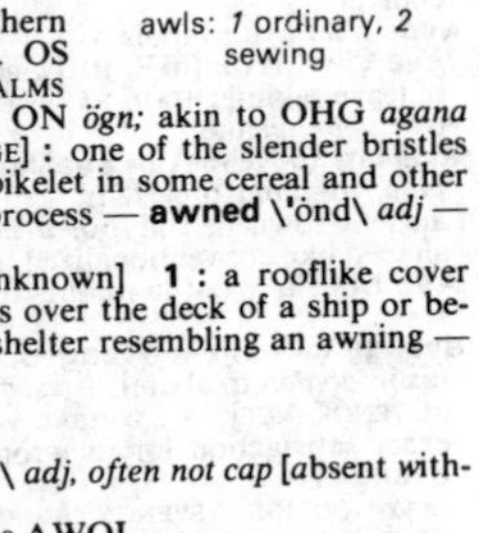

ax 1: *a* fireman's ax; *b-g* single-bit patterns: *b* Michigan, *c* Yankee, *d* Connecticut, *e* wedge, *f* rockaway, *g* Hudson Bay; *h-m* double-bit patterns: *h* crown, *i* Western, *j* peeling, *k* wedge, *l* Puget Sound falling, *m* forester's

²ax *or* **axe** *vt* **axed; ax·ing** **1** **a** : to shape, dress, or trim with an ax **b** : to chop, split, or sever with an ax **2** : to remove abruptly (as from employment or from a budget)

³ax *abbr* **1** axiom **2** axis

ax·el \'ak-səl, 'äk-\ *n* [*Axel* Paulsen *fl* 1890 Norw figure skater] : a jump in figure skating from the outer forward edge of one skate with $1\frac{1}{2}$ turns taken in the air and a return to the outer backward edge of the other skate

axe·nic \(ˈ)ā-ˈzen-ik, -ˈzēn-\ *adj* [*a-* + Gk *xenos* strange] : free from other living organisms — **axe·ni·cal·ly** \-i-k(ə-)lē\ *adv*

ax·i·al \ˈak-sē-əl\ *or* **ax·al** \-səl\ *adj* **1** : of, relating to, or having the characteristics of an axis **2 a** : situated around, in the direction of, on, or along an axis **b** : extending in a direction essentially perpendicular to the plane of a cyclic structure (as of cyclohexane) ⟨~ hydrogens⟩ — compare EQUATORIAL — **ax·i·al·i·ty** \ak-sē-ˈal-ət-ē\ *n* — **ax·i·al·ly** \ˈak-sē-ə-lē\ *adv*

axial skeleton *n* : the skeleton of the trunk and head

ax·il \ˈak-səl, -ˌsil\ *n* [NL *axilla*, fr. L] : the angle between a branch or leaf and the axis from which it arises

ax·ile \-ˌsīl\ *adj* : relating to or situated in an axis

ax·il·la \ag-ˈzil-ə, ak-ˈsil-\ *n, pl* **-lae** \-(ˌ)ē, -ˌī\ *or* **-las** [L] : ARMPIT

ax·il·lar \ag-ˈzil-ər, ak-ˈsil-, ˈag-zəl-, ˈak-səl-, -ˌär\ *n* : an axillary part (as a vein, nerve, or feather)

¹**ax·il·lary** \ˈak-sə-ˌler-ē\ *adj* **1** : of, relating to, or located near the axilla **2** : situated in or growing from an axil ⟨~ buds⟩

²**axillary** *n, pl* **-lar·ies** : AXILLAR; *esp* : one of the feathers arising from the axilla and closing the space between the flight feathers and body of a flying bird

axillary bud *n* : LATERAL BUD

ax·i·o·log·i·cal \ˌak-sē-ə-ˈläj-i-kəl\ *adj* : of or relating to axiology — **ax·i·o·log·i·cal·ly** \-i-k(ə-)lē\ *adv*

ax·i·ol·o·gy \ˌak-sē-ˈäl-ə-jē\ *n* [Gk *axios* + ISV *-logy*] : the study of the nature, types, and criteria of values and of value judgments esp. in ethics

ax·i·om \ˈak-sē-əm\ *n* [L *axioma*, fr. Gk *axiōma*, lit., honor, fr. *axioun* to think worthy, fr. *axios* worth, worthy; akin to Gk *agein* to drive — more at AGENT] **1** : a maxim widely accepted on its intrinsic merit **2 a** : a proposition regarded as a self-evident truth **b** : POSTULATE 1

ax·i·om·at·ic \ˌak-sē-ə-ˈmat-ik\ *adj* [MGk *axiōmatikos*, fr. Gk, honorable, fr. *axiōmat-, axiōma*] : of, relating to, or having the nature of an axiom : widely accepted as self-evident — **ax·i·om·at·i·cal·ly** \-i-k(ə-)lē\ *adv*

ax·is \ˈak-səs\ *n, pl* **ax·es** \-ˌsēz\ [L, axis, axle; akin to OE *eax* axis, axle, Gk *axōn*, L *axilla* armpit, *agere* to drive — more at AGENT] **1 a** : a straight line about which a body or a geometric figure rotates or may be supposed to rotate **b** : a straight line with respect to which a body or figure is symmetrical **c** : a straight line that bisects at right angles a system of parallel chords of a curve and divides the curve into two symmetrical parts **d** : a straight line about which a line, curve, or plane figure is conceived to revolve in generating a solid of revolution **e** : one of the reference lines of a coordinate system **2 a** : the second vertebra of the neck that serves as a pivot for the head to turn on **b** : any of various central, fundamental, or axial parts **3** : a plant stem **4** : one of several imaginary lines assumed in describing the positions of the planes by which a crystal is bounded and the positions of atoms in the structure of the crystal **5** : a main line of direction, motion, growth, or extension **6 a** : an implied line in painting or sculpture through a composition to which elements in the composition are referred **b** : a line actually drawn and used as the basis of measurements in an architectural or other working drawing **7** : any of three fixed lines of reference in an airplane which are usu. centroidal and mutually perpendicular and of which the first is the principal longitudinal line in the plane of symmetry, the second is perpendicular to the first in the plane of symmetry, and the third is perpendicular to the other two — called also respectively *longitudinal axis, normal axis, lateral axis* **8** : PARTNERSHIP, ALLIANCE

Axis *adj* : of or relating to the three powers Germany, Italy, and Japan engaged against the Allied nations in World War II

axi·sym·met·ric \ˌak-si-sə-ˈme-trik\ *also* **axi·sym·met·ri·cal** \-tri-kəl\ *adj* [*axis* + *symmetric*] : symmetric in respect to an axis — **axi·sym·met·ri·cal·ly** \-tri-k(ə-)lē\ *adv* — **axi·sym·me·try** \-ˈsim-ə-trē\ *n*

ax·le \ˈak-səl\ *n* [ME *axel-* (as in *axeltre*)] **1** *archaic* : AXIS **2 a** : a pin or shaft on or with which a wheel or pair of wheels revolves **b** (1) : the spindle of an axletree (2) : AXLETREE

axle·tree \-(ˌ)trē\ *n* [ME *axeltre*, fr. ON *öxultrē*, fr. *öxull* axle + *trē* tree] : a fixed bar or beam with bearings at its ends on which wheels (as of a cart) revolve

ax·man \ˈak-smən\ *n* : one who wields an ax

Ax·min·ster \ˈak-ˌsmin(t)-stər\ *n* [*Axminster*, England] : a machine-woven carpet with pile tufts inserted mechanically in a variety of textures and patterns

ax·o·lotl \ˈak-sə-ˌlät-ᵊl\ *n* [Nahuatl, lit., water doll] : any of several salamanders (genus *Ambystoma*) of mountain lakes of Mexico and the western U.S. that ordinarily live and breed without metamorphosing

ax·on \ˈak-ˌsän\ *also* **ax·one** \-ˌsōn\ *n* [NL *axon*, fr. Gk *axōn*] : a usu. long and single nerve-cell process that usu. conducts impulses away from the cell body — see NEURON illustration — **ax·o·nal** \ˈak-sən-ᵊl; ak-ˈsän-, -ˈsōn-\ *or* **ax·on·ic** \ak-ˈsän-ik, -ˈsōn-\ *adj*

ax·o·no·met·ric projection \ˌak-sə-nō-ˌme-trik-\ *n* [Gk *axōn* axis + E *-metric*] : a drawing projection in which an object is represented by means of its perpendicular projection on a surface in such a way that a rectangular solid appears as inclined and shows three faces

axo·plasm \ˈak-sə-ˌplaz-əm\ *n* [*axon* + *-plasm*] : the protoplasm of an axon — **axo·plas·mic** \ˌak-sə-ˈplaz-mik\ *adj*

ay \ˈī\ *interj* [MF *aymi* ay me] — usu. used with following *me* to express sorrow or regret

ayah \ˈī-ə, ˈä-yə, -(ˌ)yä\ *n* [Hindi *āyā*, fr. Pg *aia*, fr. L *avia* grandmother] : a nurse or maid native to India

AYC *abbr* American Youth Congress

AYD *abbr* American Youth for Democracy

¹**aye** *also* **ay** \ˈā\ *adv* [ME, fr. ON *ei*; akin to OE *ā* always, L *aevum* age, lifetime, Gk *aiōn* age] : EVER, ALWAYS, CONTINUALLY ⟨love that ~ endure —W. S. Gilbert⟩

²**aye** *also* **ay** \ˈī\ *adv* [perh. fr. ME *ye, yie* — more at YEA] : YES ⟨~, ~, sir⟩

³**aye** *also* **ay** \ˈī\ *n, pl* **ayes** : an affirmative vote or voter ⟨the ~s have it⟩

aye–aye \ˈī-ˌī\ *n* [F, fr. Malagasy *aiay*] : a nocturnal lemur (*Daubentonia madagascariensis*) of Madagascar

AYH *abbr* American Youth Hostels

ayin \ˈī-ən\ *n* [Heb *'ayin*, lit., eye] : the 16th letter of the Hebrew alphabet — see ALPHABET table

Ay·ma·ra \ˌī-mə-ˈrä\ *n, pl* **Aymara** *or* **Aymaras** [Sp *aymará*] **1** : a member of an Indian people of Bolivia and Peru **2 a** : the language of the Aymara people **b** : a language family of the Kechumaran stock comprising Aymara

Ayr *abbr* Ayrshire

Ayr·shire \ˈa(ə)r-ˌshi(ə)r, 'e(ə)r-, -shər; 'ash-ˌi(ə)r\ *n* [*Ayrshire*, Scotland] : any of a breed of hardy dairy cattle originated in Ayr that vary in color from white to red or brown

az *abbr* **1** azimuth **2** azure

AZ *abbr* Arizona

az- *or* **azo-** *comb form* [ISV, fr. *azote*] : containing nitrogen esp. as the bivalent group N = N ⟨*azine*⟩

aza- *or* **az-** *comb form* [ISV *az-* + *-a-*] : containing nitrogen in place of carbon and usu. the bivalent group NH for the group CH_2 or a single trivalent nitrogen atom for the group CH ⟨*azaguanine*⟩

aza·lea \ə-ˈzāl-yə\ *n* [NL, genus name, fr. Gk, fem. of *azaleos* dry; akin to L *aridus* dry — more at ARDOR] : any of a genus or subgenus (*Azalea*) of rhododendrons with funnel-shaped corollas and usu. deciduous leaves including many species and hybrid forms cultivated as ornamentals

aza·thi·o·prine \ˌaz-ə-ˈthī-ə-ˌprēn\ *n* [*aza-* + *thio-* + *purine*] : a purine antimetabolite $C_9H_7N_7O_2S$ that is used esp. to suppress antibody production

Aza·zel \ə-ˈzā-zəl, ˈaz-ə-ˌzel\ *n* [Heb *'ăzāzēl*] : an evil spirit of the wilderness to which a scapegoat was sent by the ancient Hebrews in a ritual of atonement

AZC *abbr* American Zionist Council

azide \ˈā-ˌzīd, ˈaz-ˌīd\ *n* : a compound containing the group N_3 combined with an element or radical — **az·i·do** \ˈaz-ə-ˌdō\ *adj*

az·i·muth \ˈaz-(ə-)məth\ *n* [ME, fr. (assumed) ML, fr. Ar *as-sumūt* the azimuth, pl. of *as-samt* the way] **1** : an arc of the horizon measured between a fixed point (as true north) and the vertical circle passing through the center of an object usu. in astronomy and navigation clockwise from the north point through 360 degrees **2** : horizontal direction expressed as the angular distance between the direction of a fixed point (as the observer's heading) and the direction of the object — **az·i·muth·al** \ˌaz-ə-ˈməth-əl\ *adj* — **az·i·muth·al·ly** \-ˈməth-ə-lē\ *adv*

azimuthal equidistant projection *n* : a map projection of the surface of the earth so centered at any given point that a straight line radiating from the center to any other point represents the shortest distance and can be measured to scale

azimuthal equidistant projection, centered on Washington, D.C.:
1 London, *2* Algiers, *3* Moscow, *4* Buenos Aires, *5* Tokyo, *6* Auckland

azine \ˈā-ˌzēn, ˈaz-ˌēn\ *n* **1** : any of numerous organic compounds with a nitrogenous 6-membered ring **2** : a compound of the general formula RCH = NN = CHR or $R_2C = NN = CR_2$ formed by the action of hydrazine on aldehydes or ketones

azin·phos·meth·yl \ˌaz-ᵊn-(ˌ)fäs-ˈmeth-əl, ˌaz-\ *n* [*azine* + *phosphorus* + *methyl*] : an organophosphorus pesticide used against insects and mites

azo \ˈā-(ˌ)zō, ˈaz-(ˌ)ō\ *adj* [*az-*] : relating to or containing the bivalent group N = N united at both ends to carbon

azo dye *n* : any of numerous versatile dyes containing azo groups

azo·ic \(ˈ)ā-ˈzō-ik\ *adj* [*a-* + Gk *zōē* life — more at QUICK] : having no life; *specif* : of or relating to the part of geologic time that antedates life — compare ARCHEAN

azole \ˈā-ˌzōl, ˈaz-ˌōl\ *n* : any of numerous compounds characterized by a 5-membered ring containing at least one atom of nitrogen

ə abut	ᵊ kitten	ər further	a back	ā bake	ä cot, cart
au̇ out	ch chin	e less	ē easy	g gift	i trip	ī life
j joke	ŋ sing	ō flow	ȯ flaw	oi coin	th thin	t͟h this
ü loot	u̇ foot	y yet	yü few	yu̇ furious	zh vision

azon·al \(')ā-'zōn-ºl\ *adj* : of, relating to, or being a soil or a major soil group marked by soils lacking well-developed horizons often because of immaturity — compare INTRAZONAL, ZONAL

azote \'ā-,zōt, 'az-,ōt\ *n* [F, irreg. fr. *a-* + Gk *zōē* life] : NITROGEN

azo·te·mia \,ā-zō-'tē-mē-ə, ,az-ō-\ *n* [ISV *azote* + NL *-emia*] : an excess of nitrogenous bodies in the blood as a result of kidney insufficiency — **azo·te·mic** \-mik\ *adj*

az·oth \'az-,ȯth\ *n* [Ar *az-zā'ūq* the mercury] **1** : mercury regarded by alchemists as the first principle of metals **2** : the universal remedy of Paracelsus

azo·to·bac·ter \ā-'zōt-ə-,bak-tər\ *n* [NL, genus name, fr. ISV *azote* + NL *bacterium*] : any of a genus (*Azotobacter*) of large rod-shaped or spherical bacteria occurring in soil and sewage and fixing atmospheric nitrogen

azo·tu·ria \,ā-zō-'t(y)ùr-ē-ə\ *n* [ISV *azote* + NL *-uria*] : an excess of urea or other nitrogenous substances in the urine

Az·tec \'az-,tek\ *n* [Sp *azteca*, fr. Nahuatl, pl. of *aztecatl*] **1 a** : a member of a Nahuatlan people that founded the Mexican empire conquered by Cortes in 1519 **b** : a member of any people under Aztec influence **2 a** : the language of the Aztec people **b** : NAHUATL — **Az·tec·an** \-ən\ *adj*

azure \'azh-ər\ *n* [ME *asur*, fr. OF *azur*, prob. fr. OSp, modif. of Ar *lāzaward*, fr. Per *lāzhuward*] **1** *archaic* : LAPIS LAZULI **2 a** : the blue color of the clear sky **b** : the heraldic color blue **3** : the unclouded sky — **azure** *adj*

azur·ite \'azh-ə-,rīt\ *n* [F, fr. *azur* azure] **1** : a mineral $Cu_3(OH)_2(CO_3)_2$ consisting of blue basic carbonate of copper, occurring in monoclinic crystals, in mass, and in earthy form, and constituting an ore of copper **2** : a semiprecious stone derived from azurite

azygo- *comb form* [ISV, fr. Gk *azygos*] : azygous

azygos *n* [NL, fr. Gk, unyoked, fr. *a-* + *zygon* yoke — more at YOKE] : an azygous anatomical part

azy·gous or **azy·gos** \(')ā-'zī-gəs\ *adj* [NL *azygos*] : not being one of a pair : SINGLE ⟨an ~ vein⟩

B

¹b \'bē\ *n, pl* **b's** or **bs** \'bēz\ *often cap, often attrib* **1 a** : the 2d letter of the English alphabet **b** : a graphic representation of this letter **c** : a speech counterpart of orthographic *b* **2** : the 7th tone of a C-major scale **3** : a graphic device for reproducing the letter *b* **4** : one designated *b* esp. as the 2d in order or class **5 a** : a grade rating a student's work as good but short of excellent **b** : one graded or rated with a B **6** : something shaped like the letter B

²b *abbr, often cap* **1** bachelor **2** bacillus **3** back **4** bag **5** bale **6** bass **7** basso **8** bat **9** Baumé **10** before **11** Bible **12** billion **13** bishop **14** black **15** blue **16** bolivar **17** book **18** born **19** brick **20** brightness **21** British **22** bulb **23** butut

B *symbol* **1** boron **2** magnetic induction

Ba *symbol* barium

BA *abbr* **1** bachelor of arts **2** batting average **3** Buenos Aires

baa or **ba** \'ba, 'bä\ *n* [imit.] : the bleat of a sheep — **baa** *vi*

BAA *abbr* bachelor of applied arts

BAAE *abbr* bachelor of aeronautical and astronautical engineering

baal \'bā(-ə)l\ *n, pl* **baals** or **baa·lim** \'bā-(ə-)ləm, 'bä-ə-,lim\ *often cap* [Heb *ba'al* lord] : any of numerous Canaanite and Phoenician local deities — **baal·ism** \'bā-(ə-),liz-əm\ *n, often cap*

ba·ba \'bäb-ə-,(,)ä, -ə\ *n* [F, fr. Pol, lit., old woman] : a rich cake soaked in a rum and sugar syrup

ba·bas·su \,bäb-ə-'sü\ *n* [Pg *babaçú*] : a tall pinnate-leaved palm (*Orbignya speciosa* or *O. martiana*) of northeastern Brazil with hard-shelled nuts yielding a valuable oil

¹bab·bitt \'bab-ət\ *n* : a babbitt-metal lining for a bearing

²babbitt *vt* : to line or furnish with babbitt metal

Bab·bitt \'bab-ət\ *n* [George F. *Babbitt*, character in the novel *Babbitt* (1922) by Sinclair Lewis] : a business or professional man who conforms unthinkingly to prevailing middle-class standards — **Bab·bitt·ry** \-ə-trē\ *n*

babbitt metal *n* [Isaac *Babbitt* †1862 Am inventor] : an alloy used for lining bearings; *esp* : one containing tin, copper, and antimony

bab·ble \'bab-əl\ *vb* **bab·bled**; **bab·bling** \-(ə-)liŋ\ [ME *babelen*, prob. of imit. origin] *vi* **1 a** : to utter meaningless or unintelligible sounds **b** : to talk foolishly : PRATTLE **c** : to talk excessively : CHATTER **2** : to make sounds as though babbling ~ *vt* **1** : to utter in an incoherently or meaninglessly repetitious manner **2** : to reveal by talk that is too free — **babble** *n* — **bab·ble·ment** \-əl-mənt\ *n* — **bab·bler** \-(ə-)lər\ *n*

Bab·cock test \,bab-,käk-\ *n* [Stephen M. *Babcock* †1931 Am agricultural chemist] : a test for determining the fat content of milk and milk products

babe \'bāb\ *n* [ME, prob. of imit. origin] **1 a** : INFANT, BABY **b** *slang* : GIRL, WOMAN **2** : a naive inexperienced person

Ba·bel \'bā-bəl, 'bab-əl\ *n* [Heb *Bābhel*, fr. Assyr-Bab *bāb-ilu* gate of god] **1** : a city in Shinar where the building of a tower is held in the Book of Genesis to have been interrupted by the confusion of tongues **2** *often not cap* **a** : a confusion of sounds or voices **b** : a scene of noise or confusion

ba·be·sia \bə-'bē-zh(ē-)ə\ *n* [NL, genus name, fr. Victor *Babeş* †1926 Rumanian bacteriologist] : any of a family (Babesiidae and esp. genus *Babesia*) of sporozoans parasitic in mammalian red blood cells (as in Texas fever) and transmitted by the bite of a tick — called also *piroplasm*

babe·si·a·sis \,bab-ə-'zī-ə-səs\ *n* [NL] : an infection with or disease caused by babesias

ba·boon \ba-'bün, *chiefly Brit* bə-\ *n* [ME *babewin*, fr. MF *babouin*, fr. *baboue* grimace] : any of several large African and Asiatic primates (*Papio* and related genera of the family Cercopithecidae) having doglike muzzles and usu. short tails — **ba·boon·ish** \-'bü-nish\ *adj*

ba·bu \'bäb-(,)ü\ *n* [Hindi *bābū*, lit., father] **1** : a Hindu gentleman — a form of address corresponding to *Mr.* **2 a** : an Indian clerk who writes English **b** : an Indian having some education in English — often used disparagingly

ba·bul \bə-'bül\ *n* [Per *babūl*] : an acacia tree (*Acacia arabica*) widespread in northern Africa and across Asia that yields gum arabic and tannins as well as fodder and timber

ba·bush·ka \bə-'bùsh-kə, -'büsh-\ *n* [Russ, grandmother, dim. of *baba* old woman] **1** : a usu. triangularly folded kerchief for the head **2** : a head covering resembling a babushka

¹ba·by \'bā-bē\ *n, pl* **babies** [ME, fr. *babe*] **1 a** (1) : an extremely young child; *esp* : INFANT (2) : an extremely young animal **b** : the youngest of a group **2** : an infantile person **3 a** *slang* : GIRL, WOMAN — often used in address **b** : PERSON, THING **c** *slang* : BOY, MAN — often used in address — **baby** *adj* — **ba·by·hood** \-hē-,hùd\ *n* — **ba·by·ish** \-ish\ *adj*

²baby *vt* **ba·bied**; **ba·by·ing** **1** : to tend or indulge with often excessive or inappropriate care and solicitude ⟨parents must resist the urge to ~ an only child⟩ **2** : to operate or treat with care ⟨~ a new motor⟩ *syn* see INDULGE

baby blue–eyes \-'blü-,īz\ *n pl but sing or pl in constr* : NEMOPHILA

baby carriage *n* : a four-wheeled push carriage usu. with a folding top — called also *baby buggy*

baby farm *n* : a place where care of babies is provided for a fee — **baby farming** *n*

baby grand *n* : a small grand piano five to six feet long

Bab·y·lon \'bab-ə-lən, -,län\ *n* [*Babylon*, ancient city of Babylonia] : a city devoted to materialism and the pursuit of sensual pleasure

¹Bab·y·lo·nian \,bab-ə-'lō-nyən, -nē-ən\ *n* **1** : a native or inhabitant of ancient Babylonia or Babylon **2** : the form of the Akkadian language used in ancient Babylonia

²Babylonian *adj* **1** : of, relating to, or characteristic of Babylonia or Babylon, the Babylonians, or Babylonian **2** : LUXURIOUS

baby's breath *n* **1** : GYPSOPHILA **2** : a bedstraw (*Galium sylvaticum*) with thin lanceolate leaves and white flowers

ba·by·sit \'bā-bē-,sit\ *vb* **-sat** \-,sat\; **-sit·ting** [back-formation fr. *baby-sitter*] *vi* : to care for children usu. during a short absence of the parents ~ *vt* : to baby-sit for — **ba·by–sit·ter** *n*

baby talk *n* **1** : the syntactically imperfect speech or phonetically modified forms used by small children learning to talk **2** : the consciously imperfect or mutilated speech or prattle often used by adults in speaking to small children

bac *abbr* [ML *baccalaureus*] bachelor

bac·ca \'bak-ə\ *n, pl* **bac·cae** \'bak-,sē, 'bak-,ī\ [NL, fr. L *baca, bacca* berry] : BERRY **1c** — **bac·cif·er·ous** \bak-'sif-(ə-)rəs\ *adj*

bac·ca·lau·re·ate \,bak-ə-'lȯr-ē-ət, -'lär-\ *n* [ML *baccalaureatus*, fr. *baccalaureus* bachelor, alter. of *baccalarius*] **1** : the degree of bachelor conferred by universities and colleges **2 a** : a sermon to a graduating class **b** : the service at which this sermon is delivered

bac·ca·rat \,bäk-ə-'rä, ,bak-\ *n* [F *baccara*] : a card game resembling chemin de fer in which three hands are dealt and players may bet either or both hands against the dealer's

bac·cate \'bak-,āt\ *adj* [L *bacca* berry] **1** : pulpy throughout like a berry **2** : bearing berries

Bac·chae \'bak-,ē, -,ī\ *n pl* [L, fr. Gk *Bakchai*, fr. *Bakchos* Bacchus] **1** : the female attendants or priestesses of Bacchus **2** : the women participating in the Bacchanalia

¹bac·cha·nal \'bak-ən-ºl\ *adj* [L *bacchanalis* of Bacchus] : of, relating to, or suggestive of the Bacchanalia : BACCHANALIAN

²bac·cha·nal \'bak-ən-ºl, ,bak-ə-'nal, ,bäk-ə-'näl\ *n* **1 a** : a devotee of Bacchus; *esp* : one who celebrates the Bacchanalia **b** : REVELER **2** : drunken revelry or carousal : ORGY

bac·cha·na·lia \,bak-ə-'nāl-yə\ *n, pl* **bacchanalia** [L, pl., fr. neut. pl. of *bacchanalis*] **1** *pl, cap* : a Roman festival of Bacchus celebrated with dancing, song, and revelry **2** : a drunken feast : ORGY — **bac·cha·na·lian** \-'nāl-yən\ *adj or n*

bac·chant \bə-'kant, 'bak-ənt\ *n, pl* **bacchants** or **bac·chantes** \bə-'kants, -'känts, -'kant-ēz, -'känt-ēz\ [L *bacchant-, bacchans*, fr. prp. of *bacchari* to take part in the orgies of Bacchus] : BACCHANAL — **bacchant** *adj* — **bac·chan·tic** \bə-'kant-ik, -'känt-\ *adj*

bac·chante \bə-'kant(-ē), -'känt(-ē)\ *n* [F, fr. L *bacchant-, bacchans*] : a priestess or female follower of Bacchus : MAENAD

bac·chic \'bak-ik\ *adj, often cap* **1** : of or relating to Bacchus **2** : of or relating to the Bacchanalia : BACCHANALIAN

Bac·chus \'bak-əs\ *n* [L, fr. Gk *Bakchos*] : the Greek god of wine — called also *Dionysus*

¹bach \'bach\ *vi* : to live as a bachelor — **bach** *n*

bach·e·lor \'bach-(ə-)lər\ *n* [ME *bacheler,* fr. OF, fr. ML *baccalarius* tenant farmer, squire, advanced student, of Celtic origin; akin to IrGael *bachlach* shepherd, peasant, fr. OIr *bachall* staff, fr. L *baculum* — more at BACTERIUM] **1** : a young knight who follows the banner of another : KNIGHT BACHELOR **2** : a person who has received what is usu. the lowest degree conferred by a four-year college, university, or professional school ⟨~ of arts⟩ **3 a** : an unmarried man **b** : a male animal (as a fur seal) without a mate during breeding time — **bach·e·lor·hood** \-,hud\ *n*

bachelor's button *n* : a European composite (*Centaurea cyanus*) having flower heads with blue, pink, or white rays that is often cultivated in No. America — called also *cornflower*

ba·cil·la·ry \'bas-ə-,ler-ē, bə-'sil-ə-rē\ *or* **ba·cil·lar** \bə-'sil-ər, 'bas-ə-lər\ *adj* [ML & NL *bacillus*] **1** : shaped like a rod; *also* : consisting of small rods **2** : of, relating to, or produced by bacilli

ba·cil·lus \bə-'sil-əs\ *n, pl* **-li** \-,ī *also* -ē\ [NL, fr. ML, small staff, rod, dim. of L *baculus* staff, alter. of *baculum* — more at BACTERIUM] **1** : any of a genus (*Bacillus*) of aerobic rod-shaped bacteria producing endospores that do not thicken the rod and including many saprophytes and some parasites (as *B. anthracis* of anthrax); *broadly* : a straight rod-shaped bacterium **2** : BACTERIUM: *esp* : a disease-producing bacterium

bac·i·tra·cin \,bas-ə-'trās-ᵊn\ *n* [NL *Bacillus subtilis* (species of bacillus producing the toxin) + Margaret *Tracy* b ab 1936 Am child in whose tissues it was found] : a toxic antibiotic isolated from a bacillus (*Bacillus subtilis*) and usu. used topically against cocci

¹back \'bak\ *n* [ME, fr. OE *bæc*; akin to OHG *bah* back] **1 a** : the rear part of the human body esp. from the neck to the end of the spine **b** : the corresponding part of a lower animal (as a quadruped) **c** : SPINAL COLUMN **d** : BACKBONE **4 2 a** : the side or surface opposite the front or face : the rear part; *also* : the farther or reverse side **b** : something at or on the back for support ⟨~ of a chair⟩ **3** : a position in some games (as football or soccer) behind the front line of players; *also* : a player in this position — **back·less** \'bak-ləs\ *adj*

²back *adv* **1 a** : to, toward, or at the rear **b** : in or into the past : AGO **c** : in or into a reclining position **d** (1) : under restraint (2) : in a delayed or retarded condition **2 a** : to, toward, or in a place from which a person or thing came **b** : to or toward a former state **c** : in return or reply — **back and forth** : backward and forward : from one place to another

³back *adj* **1 a** : being at or in the back ⟨~ door⟩ **b** : distant from a central or main area : REMOTE **c** : articulated at or toward the back of the oral passage **2** : being in arrears : OVERDUE **3** : moving or operating backward **4** : not current ⟨~ number of a magazine⟩ **5** : constituting the final nine holes of an 18-hole golf course

⁴back *vt* **1 a** : to support by material or moral assistance — often used with *up* **b** : SUBSTANTIATE **c** (1) : COUNTERSIGN, ENDORSE (2) : to assume financial responsibility for **2** : to cause to go back or in reverse **3 a** : to furnish with a back **b** : to be at the back of ~ *vi* **1** : to move backward **2** *of the wind* : to shift counterclockwise — compare VEER **3** : to have the back in the direction of something **syn** see SUPPORT, RECEDE — **back and fill 1** : to manage the sails of a ship so as to keep it clear of obstructions as it floats down with the current of a river or channel **2** : to take opposite positions alternately : SHILLY-SHALLY

⁵back *n* [D *bak*] : a shallow vat or tub used esp. by brewers or dyers

back·ache \'bak-,āk\ *n* : a pain in the lower back

back away *vi* : to move back (as from a theoretical position) : WITHDRAW

back–bench·er \'bak-'ben-chər\ *n* : a rank-and-file member of a British legislature

back·bite \-,bīt\ *vb* **-bit; -bitten; -biting** *vt* : to say mean or spiteful things about : SLANDER ~ *vi* : to backbite a person — **back·bit·er** *n*

back·board \-,bō(ə)rd, -,bȯ(ə)rd\ *n* : a board placed at or serving as the back of something; *specif* : a rounded or rectangular board that is behind the basket on a basketball court and that serves to keep missed shots from going out-of-bounds and as a surface from which the ball can be made to rebound into the basket

back·bone \-'bōn, -,bōn\ *n* **1** : SPINAL COLUMN, SPINE **2 a** : a chief mountain ridge, range, or system **b** : the foundation or most substantial or sturdiest part of something **3** : firm and resolute character **4** : the back of a book usu. lettered with the title and the author's and publisher's names **syn** see FORTITUDE **ant** spinelessness

back–check \-,chek\ *vi* : to skate back toward one's own goal while closely defending against the offensive rushes of an opposing player in ice hockey

back·coun·try \-,kən-trē\ *n* : a thinly settled rural area

back·court \-,kō(ə)rt, -,kȯ(ə)rt\ *n* **1** : the area near or nearest the back boundary lines or back wall of the playing area in a net or court game **2** : a basketball team's defensive half of the court; *also* : the part of the offensive half of the court farthest from the goal

back·court·man \-mən\ *n* : a guard on a basketball team

back·cross \'bak-,krȯs\ *vt* [²*back*] : to cross (a first-generation hybrid) with or as if with one parent — **backcross** *n*

back dive *n* : a dive from a position facing the diving board

back down *vi* : to withdraw from a commitment or position

back·drop \'bak-,dräp\ *n* **1** : a painted cloth hung across the rear of a stage **2** : BACKGROUND

back·er \'bak-ər\ *n* **1** : one that supports **2** : one who works with backs or backing

back·field \-,fēld\ *n* : the football players whose positions are behind the line of scrimmage; *also* : the positions themselves

¹back·fire \-,fī(ə)r\ *n* **1** : a fire started to check an advancing forest or prairie fire by clearing an area **2** : an improperly timed explosion of fuel mixture in the cylinder of an internal-combustion engine

²backfire *vi* **1** : to make or undergo a backfire **2** : to have the reverse of the desired or expected effect

back–formation *n* **1** : a word formed by subtraction of a real or supposed affix from an already existing longer word (as *burgle* from *burglar*) **2** : the formation of a back-formation

back·gam·mon \'bak-,gam-ən, bak-'\ *n* [perh. fr. ³*back* + ME *gamen, game* game] : a board game played with dice and counters in which each player tries to move his counters along the board and at the same time to block or capture his opponent's counters

backgammon board with men arranged as at the beginning of a game

¹back·ground \'bak-,graund\ *n* **1 a** : the scenery or ground behind something **b** : the part of a painting representing what lies behind objects in the foreground **2** : an inconspicuous position **3 a** : the conditions that form the setting within which something is experienced **b** (1) : the circumstances or events antecedent to a phenomenon or development (2) : information essential to understanding of a problem or situation **c** : the total of a person's experience, knowledge, and education **4** : intrusive sound that interferes with received or recorded electronic signals

²background *vt* : to provide with background ⟨~ a new employee⟩

background music *n* : music to accompany the dialogue or action of a motion picture or radio or television drama

¹back·hand \'bak-,hand\ *n* **1 a** : a stroke (as in tennis) made with the back of the hand turned in the direction of movement **b** : a catch (as in baseball) made to the side of the body opposite the hand being used **2** : handwriting whose strokes slant downward from left to right

²backhand *or* **back·hand·ed** \-'han-dəd\ *adv* : with a backhand

³backhand *vt* : to do, hit, or catch backhand

back·hand·ed \'bak-'han-dəd\ *adj* **1** : using or made with a backhand **2** : INDIRECT, DEVIOUS: *esp* : SARCASTIC — **back·hand·ed·ly** *adv*

back·hoe \-,hō\ *n* : an excavating machine whose bucket is rigidly attached to a hinged stick on the boom and is drawn toward the machine in operation

backhand 1

back·house \-,haus\ *n* : an outdoor toilet

back·ing \'bak-iŋ\ *n* **1** : something forming a back **2 a** : SUPPORT, AID **b** : endorsement esp. of a warrant by a magistrate

back judge *n* : a football official whose duties include keeping the game's official time and identifying eligible pass receivers

back·lash \'bak-,lash\ *n* **1** : a sudden violent backward movement or reaction **2** : a snarl in that part of a fishing line wound on the reel **3** : a strong adverse reaction (as to a recent political or social development) — **back·lash·er** *n*

¹back·log \-,lȯg, -,läg\ *n* **1** : a large log at the back of a hearth fire **2** : a reserve that promises continuing work and profit **3** : an accumulation of tasks unperformed or materials not processed

²backlog *vb* : ACCUMULATE

back matter *n* : matter following the main text of a book

back mutation *n* : mutation of a previously mutated gene to its former condition

back of *prep* : BEHIND

back off *vi* : to back down

back out *vi* : to withdraw esp. from a commitment or contest

¹back·pack \'bak-,pak\ *n* **1 a** : a load carried on the back **b** : a camping pack (as of canvas or nylon) supported by a usu. aluminum frame and carried on the back **2** : a piece of equipment designed for use while being carried on the back

²backpack *vt* : to carry (food or equipment) on the back esp. in hiking ~ *vi* : to hike with a backpack — **back·pack·er** *n*

back·ped·al \'bak-,ped-ᵊl\ *vi* : to retreat or move backward (as in boxing)

back·rest \-,rest\ *n* : a rest for the back

back room *n* **1** : a room situated in the rear **2** : the meeting place of a directing group that exercises its authority in an inconspicuous and indirect way

back·saw \'bak-,sȯ\ *n* : a saw with a metal rib along its back

back·scat·ter \-,skat-ər\ *or* **back·scat·ter·ing** \-ə-riŋ\ *n* : the scattering of radiation (as X rays) in a direction opposite to that of the incident radiation due to reflection from particles of the medium traversed; *also* : the radiation so reversed in direction

back·seat \-'sēt\ *n* **1** : a seat in the back (as of an automobile) **2** : an inferior position ⟨won't take a ~ to anyone⟩

back·set \'bak-,set\ *n* : SETBACK

back·side \-'sīd\ *n* : BUTTOCKS — often used in pl.

ə abut	ᵊ kitten	ər further	a back	ā bake	ä cot, cart
au̇ out	ch chin	e less	ē easy	g gift	i life
j joke	ŋ sing	ō flow	o̅ flaw	o̅i coin	th thin	th this
ü loot	u̇ foot	y yet	yü few	yu̇ furious	zh vision

back·slap \-ˌslap\ *vt* : to display excessive or effusive goodwill for ~ *vi* : to display excessive cordiality or good-fellowship — **back·slap·per** *n*

back·slide \-ˌslīd\ *vi* **-slid** \-ˌslid\; **-slid** *or* **-slid·den** \-ˌslid-ᵊn\; **-slid·ing** \-ˌslīd-iŋ\ : to lapse morally or in the practice of religion *syn* see LAPSE — **back·slid·er** \-ˌslīd-ər\ *n*

back·spin \-ˌspin\ *n* : a backward rotary motion of a ball

1**back·stage** \'bak-'stāj\ *adv* **1** : in or to a backstage area **2** : in private : SECRETLY

2**back·stage** \'bak-ˌstāj\ *adj* **1** : of, relating to, or occurring in the area behind the proscenium and esp. in the dressing rooms **2** : of or relating to the private lives of theater people **3** : of or relating to the inner working or operation (as of an organization)

back·stairs \-ˌsta(ə)rz, -ˌste(ə)rz\ *adj* **1** : SECRET, FURTIVE ⟨~ political deals⟩ **2** : SORDID, SCANDALOUS ⟨~ gossip⟩

back·stay \-ˌstā\ *n* **1** : a stay extending from the mastheads to the side of a ship and slanting aft **2** : a strengthening or supporting device at the back (as of a carriage or a shoe)

back·stitch \-ˌstich\ *n* : a hand stitch made by inserting the needle a stitch length to the right and bringing it up an equal distance to the left — **backstitch** *vb*

1**back·stop** \-ˌstäp\ *n* **1** : something at the back serving as a stop: as **a** : a screen or fence for keeping a ball from leaving the field of play **b** : a stop (as a pawl) that prevents a backward movement (as of a wheel) **2** : a player (as the catcher) whose position is behind the batter

2**backstop** *vt* **1** : to serve as a backstop to **2** : SUPPORT, BOLSTER

back·stretch \'bak-'strech\ *n* : the side opposite the homestretch on a racecourse

back·stroke \-ˌstrōk\ *n* : a swimming stroke executed on the back

back·swept \-ˌswept\ *adj* : swept or slanting backward

back swimmer *n* : a water bug (family Notonectidae) that swims on its back

back·swing \'bak-ˌswiŋ\ *n* : the movement of a club, racket, bat, or arm backward to a position from which the forward or downward swing is made

back·sword \-ˌsō(ə)rd, -ˌsȯ(ə)rd\ *n* **1** : a single-edged sword **2** : SINGLESTICK

back talk *n* : an impudent, insolent, or argumentative reply

back·track \'bak-ˌtrak\ *vi* **1** : to retrace one's course **2** : to reverse a position or stand

back·up \-ˌəp\ *n* : one that serves as a substitute or alternative ⟨a ~ for a rocket⟩

back up \-'əp\ *vi* : to accumulate in a congested state ⟨traffic *backed up* for miles⟩ ~ *vt* **1** : to hold back ⟨a dam *backing up* a huge lake⟩ **2** : to move into a position behind (a teammate) in order to assist on a play (as in stopping a missed ball)

1**back·ward** \'bak-wərd\ *or* **back·wards** \-wərdz\ *adv* **1 a** : toward the back **b** : with the back foremost **2 a** : in a reverse or contrary direction or way **b** : toward the past **c** : toward a worse state

2**backward** *adj* **1 a** : directed or turned backward **b** : done or executed backward **2** : DIFFIDENT, SHY **3** : retarded in development — **back·ward·ly** *adv* — **back·ward·ness** *n*

3**backward** *n* : the part behind or past

back·wash \'bak-ˌwȯsh, -ˌwäsh\ *n* **1** : backward movement (as of water or air) produced by a propelling force (as the motion of oars) **2** : a consequence or by-product of an event : AFTERMATH

back·wa·ter \-ˌwȯt-ər, -ˌwät-\ *n* **1 a** : water turned back in its course by an obstruction, an opposing current, or the tide **b** : a body of water turned back **2** : an isolated or backward place or condition

back·woods \-'wu̇dz\ *n pl but sing or pl in constr* **1** : wooded or partly cleared areas on the frontier **2** : a remote or culturally backward area — **back·woods·man** \-mən\ *n*

back·yard \-'yärd\ *n* **1** : an area at the rear of a house **2** : an area that is one's special domain

ba·con \'bā-kən\ *n* [ME, fr. MF, of Gmc origin; akin to OHG *bahho* side of bacon, *bah* back] : a side of a pig cured and smoked

Ba·co·ni·an \bā-'kō-nē-ən\ *adj* **1** : of, relating to, or characteristic of Francis Bacon or his doctrines **2** : of or relating to those who believe that Francis Bacon wrote the works usu. attributed to Shakespeare — **Baconian** *n*

bact *abbr* **1** bacterial **2** bacteriology **3** bacterium

bac·ter·emia \ˌbak-tə-'rē-mē-ə\ *n* [NL, alter. of *bacteriemia*, fr. *bacteri-* + *-emia*] : the usu. transient presence of bacteria or other microorganisms in the blood — **bac·ter·emic** \-mik\ *adj*

bacteri- *or* **bacterio-** *comb form* [NL *bacterium*] : bacteria ⟨*bacterial*⟩ ⟨*bacteriolysis*⟩

bacteria *pl of* BACTERIUM

bac·te·ri·al \bak-'tir-ē-əl\ *adj* : of, relating to, or caused by bacteria ⟨a ~ chromosome⟩ ⟨~ infection⟩ — **bac·te·ri·al·ly** \-ə-lē\ *adv*

bac·te·ri·cid·al \bak-ˌtir-ə-'sīd-ᵊl\ *adj* : destroying bacteria — **bac·te·ri·cid·al·ly** \-ᵊl-ē\ *adv* — **bac·te·ri·cide** \-'tir-ə-ˌsīd\ *n*

bac·ter·in \'bak-tə-rən\ *n* : a suspension of killed or attenuated bacteria for use as an antigen

bac·te·rio·chlo·ro·phyll \bak-ˌtir-ē-ō-'klōr-ə-ˌfil, -'klȯr-, -fəl\ *n* : a pyrrole derivative in photosynthetic bacteria related to the chlorophyll of higher plants

bac·te·rio·cin \bak-'tir-ē-ə-sən\ *n* [ISV *bacteri-* + *-cin* (as in *colicin*)] : an antibiotic (as colicin) produced by bacteria

bac·te·ri·ol·o·gy \(ˌ)bak-ˌtir-ē-'äl-ə-jē\ *n* [ISV] **1** : a science that deals with bacteria and their relations to medicine, industry, and agriculture **2** : bacterial life and phenomena — **bac·te·ri·o·log·ic** \bak-ˌtir-ē-ə-'läj-ik\ *or* **bac·te·ri·o·log·i·cal** \-'läj-i-kəl\ *adj* — **bac·te·ri·o·log·i·cal·ly** \-i-k(ə-)lē\ *adv* — **bac·te·ri·ol·o·gist** \(ˌ)bak-ˌtir-ē-'äl-ə-jəst\ *n*

bac·te·ri·ol·y·sis \(ˌ)bak-ˌtir-ē-'äl-ə-səs\ *n* [NL] : destruction or dissolution of bacterial cells — **bac·te·ri·o·lyt·ic** \bak-ˌtir-ē-ə-'lit-ik\ *adj*

bac·te·rio·phage \bak-'tir-ē-ə-ˌfāj, -ˌfäzh\ *n* [ISV] : any of various specific bacteriolytic viruses normally present in sewage and in body products — **bac·te·rio·phag·ic** \-ˌtir-ē-ə-'faj-ik\ *or* **bac·te·ri·oph·a·gous** \(ˌ)bak-ˌtir-ē-'äf-ə-gəs\ *adj* — **bac·te·ri·oph·a·gy** \(ˌ)bak-ˌtir-ē-'äf-ə-jē\ *n*

bac·te·rio·sta·sis \bak-ˌtir-ē-ō-'stā-səs\ *n* [NL] : inhibition of the growth of bacteria without destruction

bac·te·rio·stat \-'tir-ē-ō-ˌstat\ *n* : an agent that causes bacteriostasis — **bac·te·rio·stat·ic** \-ˌtir-ē-ō-'stat-ik\ *adj* — **bac·te·rio·stat·i·cal·ly** \-i-k(ə-)lē\ *adv*

bac·te·ri·um \bak-'tir-ē-əm\ *n, pl* **-ria** \-ē-ə\ [NL, fr. Gk *baktērion* staff; akin to L *baculum* staff] : any of a class (Schizomycetes) of microscopic plants having round, rodlike, spiral, or filamentous single-celled or noncellular bodies often aggregated into colonies or motile by means of flagella, living in soil, water, organic matter, or the bodies of plants and animals, and being autotrophic, saprophytic, or parasitic in nutrition and important to man because of their chemical effects and as pathogens

bac·te·ri·uria \bak-ˌtir-ē-'(y)u̇r-ē-ə\ *n* [NL] : the passage of bacteria in the urine

bac·te·rize \'bak-tə-ˌrīz\ *vt* **-rized; -riz·ing** : to subject to bacterial action — **bac·te·ri·za·tion** \ˌbak-tə-rə-'zā-shən\ *n*

bac·te·roid \'bak-tə-ˌrȯid\ *n* **1** : an irregularly shaped bacterium (as a rhizobium) found esp. in root nodules of legumes **2** : a microorganism like a bacterium found in cells of the fat body esp. of roaches

Bac·tri·an camel \ˌbak-trē-ən-\ *n* [fr. its habitat in ancient Bactria] : CAMEL 1b

1**bad** \'bad\ *adj* **worse** \'wərs\; **worst** \'wərst\ [ME] **1 a** : failing to reach an acceptable standard : POOR **b** : UNFAVORABLE ⟨make a ~ impression⟩ **c** : not fresh or sound : SPOILED, DILAPIDATED ⟨~ fish⟩ ⟨the house was in ~ condition⟩ **2 a** : morally objectionable **b** : MISCHIEVOUS, DISOBEDIENT **3** : inadequate or unsuited to a purpose ⟨a ~ plan⟩ ⟨~ lighting⟩ **4** : DISAGREEABLE, UNPLEASANT ⟨~ news⟩ **5 a** : INJURIOUS, HARMFUL **b** : SEVERE ⟨a ~ cold⟩ **6** : INCORRECT, FAULTY ⟨~ grammar⟩ **7 a** : suffering pain or distress ⟨felt generally ~⟩ **b** : UNHEALTHY, DISEASED ⟨~ teeth⟩ **8** : SORROWFUL, SORRY **9** : INVALID, VOID ⟨a ~ check⟩ — **bad** *adv* — **bad·ly** *adv* — **bad·ness** *n*

syn BAD, EVIL, ILL, WICKED, NAUGHTY *shared meaning element* : not ethically or morally acceptable. BAD, a very general term, is applicable to anyone or anything reprehensible for whatever reason and to whatever degree ⟨such a *bad* boy, he won't stay in the yard⟩ ⟨almost as *bad* . . . as kill a king, and marry with his brother —Shak.⟩ EVIL may add to *bad* a strong suggestion of the sinister or baleful ⟨watched silently with an *evil* glow in his eyes⟩ ⟨an *evil* deed⟩ ILL may suggest an active malevolence or vicious intent ⟨misled by *ill* counsel⟩ or it may merely attribute objectionableness or inferiority to someone or something ⟨a man held in *ill* repute⟩ WICKED usually implies serious moral reprehensibility ⟨the *wicked* sorcerers who have done people to death by their charms —J. G. Frazer⟩ or it may suggest malevolence and malice ⟨a brooding *wicked* spirit⟩ NAUGHTY, once a close synonym of *wicked*, is now usually restricted to trivial misdeeds (as of children) or used to suggest reprehensibility in a light or playful way ⟨a very *naughty* story⟩ *ant* good

2**bad** *n* **1** : something that is bad **2** : an evil or unhappy state

bad blood *n* : ill feeling : BITTERNESS

bad·der·locks \'bad-ər-ˌläks\ *n pl but sing in constr* [origin unknown] : a large blackish seaweed (*Alaria esculenta*) often eaten as a vegetable in Europe

bad·die *or* **bad·dy** \'bad-ē\ *n, pl* **baddies** : one that is bad; *esp* : an opponent of the hero (as in fiction or motion pictures)

bade *past of* BID

badge \'baj\ *n* [ME *bage, bagge*] **1** : a device or token esp. of membership in a society or group **2** : a characteristic mark **3** : an emblem awarded for a particular accomplishment — **badge** *vt*

1**bad·ger** \'baj-ər\ *n* [prob. fr. *badge*; fr. the white mark on its forehead] **1 a** : any of several sturdy burrowing mammals (genera *Meles* and *Taxidea* of the family Mustelidae) widely distributed in the northern hemisphere **b** : the pelt or fur of a badger **2** *cap* : a native or resident of Wisconsin — used as a nickname

2**badger** *vt* **bad·gered; bad·ger·ing** \'baj-(ə-)riŋ\ [fr. the sport of baiting badgers] : to harass or annoy persistently *syn* see BAIT

ba·di·nage \ˌbad-ᵊn-'äzh\ *n* [F] : playful repartee : BANTER

bad·land \'bad-ˌland\ *n* : a region marked by intricate erosional sculpturing, scanty vegetation, and fantastically formed hills — usu. used in pl.

bad·min·ton \'bad-ˌmint-ᵊn\ *n* [*Badminton*, residence of the Duke of Beaufort, England] : a court game played with light long-handled rackets and a shuttlecock volleyed over a net

bad–mouth \'bad-ˌmau̇th, -ˌmau̇t͟h\ *vt* : to criticize severely and persistently

BAE *abbr* **1** bachelor of aeronautical engineering **2** bachelor of agricultural engineering **3** bachelor of architectural engineering **4** bachelor of art education **5** bachelor of arts in education

BAEd *abbr* bachelor of arts in education

Bae·de·ker \'bād-i-kər\ *n* [Karl *Baedeker* †1859 G publisher of guidebooks] : GUIDEBOOK

BAeE *abbr* bachelor of aeronautical engineering

BAEE *abbr* bachelor of arts in elementary education

1**baf·fle** \'baf-əl\ *vt* **baf·fled; baf·fling** \-(ə-)liŋ\ [prob. alter. of ME (Sc) *bawchillen* to denounce, discredit publicly] **1** : to defeat or check (as a person or his plans) by confusing or puzzling : DISCONCERT **2 a** : to check or break the force or flow of by or as if by a baffle **b** : to prevent (sound waves) from interfering with each other (as by a baffle) *syn* see FRUSTRATE — **baf·fle·ment** \-əl-mənt\ *n* — **baf·fler** \-(ə-)lər\ *n* — **baf·fling·ly** \'baf-liŋ-lē\ *adv*

2**baffle** *n* : a device (as a plate, wall, or screen) to deflect, check, or regulate flow (as of a fluid or light) **2** : a partition or cabinet to impede the exchange of sound waves between the front and back of a loudspeaker

baffling wind *n* : a light wind that frequently shifts from one point to another

1**bag** \'bag\ *n* [ME *bagge*, fr. ON *baggi*] **1** : a usu. flexible container that may be closed for holding, storing, or carrying something: as **a** : PURSE; *esp* : HANDBAG **b** : a bag for game **c** : TRAVELING BAG **2** : something resembling a bag : **a** : a pouched or pendulous bodily part or organ; *esp* : UDDER **b** : a puffed-out sag or bulge in cloth **c** : a square white canvas container to mark a base in baseball **3** : the amount contained in a bag **4 a** (1) : a quantity of game taken (2) : the maximum quantity of game permitted by law **b** : SPOILS **c** : a group of persons or things **5** : a slovenly unattractive woman **6** : something one likes or does well **7 a** : a way of life **b** : a characteristic manner of expression — **in the bag** : SURE, CERTAIN

²bag *vb* **bagged; bag·ging** *vi* **1** : to swell out : BULGE **2** : to hang loosely ~ *vt* **1** : to cause to swell **2** : to put into a bag **3 a** : to take (animals) as game **b** : to get possession of esp. by strategy or stealth **c** : CAPTURE, SEIZE **d** : to shoot down : DESTROY *syn* see CATCH

BAg *abbr* bachelor of agriculture

ba·gasse \ba-'gas\ *n* [F] : plant residue (as of sugarcane or grapes) left after a product (as juice) has been extracted

bag·a·telle \ˌbag-ə-'tel\ *n* [F, fr. It *bagatella*] **1** : TRIFLE 1 **2** : a game played with a cue and balls on an oblong table having cups or cups and arches at one end

ba·gel \'bā-gəl\ *n* [Yiddish *beygel*, deriv. of OHG *boug* ring; akin to OE *bēag* ring — more at BEE] : a hard glazed doughnut-shaped roll

bag·ful \'bag-ˌful\ *n* **1** : as much or as many as a bag will hold **2** : a large number or amount (had a ~ of tricks)

bag·gage \'bag-ij\ *n* [ME *bagage*, fr. MF, fr. *bague* bundle] **1** : traveling bags and personal belongings of travelers : LUGGAGE **2** : transportable equipment esp. of a military force **3 a** : superfluous or intrusive things or circumstances **b** : outmoded theories or practices **4** [prob. modif. of MF *bagasse*, fr. OProv *bagassa*] **a** : a worthless or contemptible woman; *esp* : PROSTITUTE **b** : a young woman or girl

bag·ging \'bag-iŋ\ *n* : material (as cloth) for bags

bag·gy \'bag-ē\ *adj* **bag·gi·er; -est** : loose, puffed out, or hanging like a bag (~ trousers) — **bag·gi·ly** \'bag-ə-lē\ *adv* — **bag·gi·ness** \'bag-ē-nəs\ *n*

bag·man \'bag-mən\ *n* **1** *chiefly Brit* : TRAVELING SALESMAN **2** : a person who on behalf of another collects or distributes illicitly gained money

ba·gnio \'ban-(ˌ)yō\ *n, pl* **bagnios** [It *bagno*, lit., public baths (fr. the use of Roman baths at Constantinople for imprisonment of Christian prisoners by the Turks), fr. L *balneum*, fr. Gk *balaneion*; akin to OHG *quellan* to gush — more at DEVIL] **1** *obs* : PRISON **2** : BROTHEL

bag of waters : the double-walled fluid-filled sac that encloses and protects the fetus in the womb and that breaks releasing its fluid during the birth process

bag·pipe \'bag-ˌpīp\ *n* : a wind instrument consisting of a leather bag, a valve-stopped mouth tube, a reed melody pipe, and three or four drone pipes — often used in pl. — **bag·pip·er** \-ˌpī-pər\ *n*

ba·guette \ba-'get\ *n* [F, lit., rod] **1** : a small molding like but smaller than the astragal **2** : a gem having the shape of a long narrow rectangle; *also* : the shape itself

bag·wig \'bag-ˌwig\ *n* : an 18th century wig with the back hair enclosed in a small silk bag

bag·worm \-ˌwərm\ *n* : any of a family (Psychidae) of moths with wingless females and plant-feeding larvae that live in a silk case covered with plant debris; *esp* : one (*Thyridopteryx ephemeraeformis*) often destructive to deciduous and evergreen trees of the eastern U.S.

bagpipe

bah \'bä, 'ba\ *interj* — used to express disdain or contempt

Ba·ha·'i \bä-'hä-,ē, -'hī\ *n, pl* **Baha·'is** [Per *bahā'ī*, lit., of glory, fr. *bahā* glory] : an adherent of a religious movement originating among Shia Muslims in Iran in the 19th century and emphasizing the spiritual unity of mankind — **Baha·'i** *adj* — **Ba·ha·ism** \-'hä-ˌiz-əm, -'hī-ˌiz-\ *n* — **Ba·ha·ist** \-'hä-(ˌ)ist\ *n*

Ba·ha·sa In·do·ne·sia \bə-ˌhäs-ə-ˌin-də-'nē-zhə, -shə\ *n* [Indonesian *bahasa indonésia*, lit., Indonesian language] : INDONESIAN 2b

Ba·hia grass \bə-'hē-ə-\ *n* [*Bahia*, state in Brazil] : a perennial tropical American grass (*Paspalum notatum*) used in the southern U.S. as a pasture grass

baht \'bät\ *n, pl* **bahts** *or* **baht** [Thai *bāt*] — see MONEY table

¹bail \'bā(ə)l\ *n* [ME, custody, security for appearance, fr. MF, custody, fr. *baillier* to have in charge, deliver, fr. ML *bajulare* to control, fr. L, to carry a load, fr. *bajulus* porter] **1** : security given for the due appearance of a prisoner in order to obtain his release from imprisonment **2** : the temporary release of a prisoner on bail **3** : one who provides bail

²bail *vt* [In sense 1, fr. AF *baillier*, fr. F, to deliver; in other senses, fr. ¹*bail*] **1** : to deliver (property) in trust to another for a special purpose and for a limited period **2** : to release under bail **3** : to procure the release of by giving bail — often used with *out* **4** : to help from a predicament — used with *out* (~*ing* out impoverished countries)

³bail *n* [ME *baille* bailey, fr. OF] *chiefly Brit* : a device for confining or separating animals

⁴bail *n* [ME *baille*, fr. MF, bucket, fr. ML *bajula* water vessel, fr. fem. of L *bajulus*] : a container used to remove water from a boat

⁵bail *vt* **1** : to clear (water) from a boat by dipping and throwing over the side — usu. used with *out* **2** : to clear water from by dipping and throwing — usu. used with *out* ~ *vi* **1** : to parachute from an airplane — usu. used with *out* — **bail·er** *n*

⁶bail *n* [ME *beil, baile*, prob. of Scand origin; akin to Sw *bygel* bow, hoop; akin to OE *būgan* to bend — more at BOW] **1 a** : a supporting half hoop **b** : a hinged bar for holding paper against the platen of a typewriter **2** : the usu. arched handle of a kettle or pail

bail·able \'bā-lə-bəl\ *adj* **1** : entitled to bail **2** : allowing bail (a ~ offense)

bail·ee \bā-'lē\ *n* : the person to whom property is bailed

bai·ley \'bā-lē\ *n, pl* **baileys** [ME *bailli*, fr. OF *baille, balie* palisade, bailey] **1** : the outer wall of a castle or any of several walls surrounding the keep **2** : the space immediately within the external wall or between two outer walls of a castle

Bai·ley bridge \ˌbā-lē-\ *n* [Sir Donald *Bailey* b1901 E engineer] : a bridge designed for rapid construction from interchangeable latticed steel panels that are coupled with steel pins

bail·ie \'bā-lē\ *n* [ME] **1** *chiefly dial* : BAILIFF **2** : a Scottish municipal magistrate corresponding to an English alderman

bail·iff \'bā-ləf\ *n* [ME *baillif, bailie*, fr. OF *baillif*, fr. *bail* custody, jurisdiction — more at BAIL] **1 a** : an official employed by a British sheriff to serve writs and make arrests and executions **b** : a minor officer of some U.S. courts usu. serving as a messenger or usher **2** *chiefly Brit* : one who manages an estate or farm — **bail·iff·ship** \-ˌship\ *n*

bail·i·wick \'bā-li-ˌwik\ *n* [ME *bailliwik*, fr. *baillif* + *wik* dwelling place, village, fr. OE *wic*; akin to OHG *wich* dwelling place, town; both fr. a prehistoric WGmc word borrowed fr. L *vicus* village — more at VICINITY] **1** : the office or jurisdiction of a bailiff **2** : a special domain

bail·ment \'bā(ə)l-mənt\ *n* : the act of bailing a person or property

bail·or \bā-'lô(ə)r, 'bā-lər\ *or* **bail·er** \'bā-lər\ *n* : one who delivers goods or money to another in trust

bails·man \'bā(ə)lz-mən\ *n* : one who gives bail for another

bairn \'ba(ə)rn, 'be(ə)rn\ *n* [ME *bern, barn*, fr. OE *bearn* & ON *barn*; akin to OHG *barn* child] *chiefly Scot* : CHILD

Bai·sakh \'bī-ˌsäk\ *n* [Hindi, fr. Skt *Vaisākha*] : a month of the Hindu year — see MONTH table

¹bait \'bāt\ *vb* [ME *baiten*, fr. ON *beita*; akin to OE *bǣtan* to bait, *bitan* to bite] *vt* **1 a** : to persecute or exasperate with unjust, malicious, or persistent attacks **b** : to nag at **c** : TEASE **2 a** : to harass (as a chained animal) with dogs usu. for sport **b** : to attack by biting and tearing **3 a** : to furnish with bait **b** : ENTICE, LURE **4** : to give food and drink to (an animal) esp. on the road ~ *vi, archaic* : to stop for food and rest when traveling — **bait·er** *n*

syn BAIT, BADGER, HECKLE, HECTOR, CHIVY, HOUND *shared meaning element* : to harass persistently or annoyingly

²bait *n* [ON *beit* pasturage & *beita* food; akin to OE *bītan* to bite] **1 a** : something used in luring esp. to a hook or trap **b** : a poisonous material placed where it will be eaten by pests **2** : LURE, TEMPTATION

bai·za \'bī-(ˌ)zä\ *n* [colloq. Ar, fr. Hindi *paisā*] — see *rial* at MONEY table

baize \'bāz\ *n* [MF *baies*, pl. of *baie* baize, fr. fem. of *bai* bay-colored] : a coarse woolen or cotton fabric napped to imitate felt

¹bake \'bāk\ *vb* **baked; bak·ing** [ME *baken*, fr. OE *bacan*; akin to OHG *bahhan* to bake, Gk *phōgein* to roast] *vt* **1** : to prepare (as food) by dry heat esp. in an oven **2** : to dry or harden by subjecting to heat ~ *vi* **1** : to prepare food by baking it **2** : to become baked — **bak·er** *n*

²bake *n* **1** : the act or process of baking **2** : a social gathering at which a baked food is served

Ba·ke·lite \'bā-kə-ˌlīt, -ˌklīt\ *trademark* — used for any of various synthetic resins and plastics

baker's dozen *n* : THIRTEEN

bakers' yeast *n* : a yeast (as *Saccharomyces cerevisiae*) used or suitable for use as leaven

bak·ery \'bā-k(ə-)rē\ *n, pl* **-er·ies** : a place for baking or selling baked goods

bake·shop \'bāk-ˌshäp\ *n* : BAKERY

baking powder *n* : a powder used as a leavening agent in making baked goods (as quick breads) that consists of a carbonate, an acid substance, and starch or flour

baking soda *n* : SODIUM BICARBONATE

bak·sheesh \'bak-ˌshēsh, bak-'\ *n, pl* **baksheesh** [Per *bakhshīsh*, fr. *bakhshīdan* to give; akin to Gk *phagein* to eat, Skt *bhajati* he allots] : TIP, GRATUITY

bal *abbr* balance

¹BAL \ˌbē-ˌā-'el\ *n* [British Anti-*L*ewisite] : a compound $C_3H_8OS_2$ developed as an antidote against lewisite and used against other arsenicals and against mercurials

²BAL *n* [*b*asic *a*ssembly *l*anguage] : a generalized assembly language for programming a computer with a small memory

Ba·laam \'bā-ləm\ *n* [Gk, fr. Heb *Bil'ām*] : an Old Testament prophet who is reproached by the ass he is riding and rebuked by God's angel while on the way to meet with an enemy of Israel

bal·a·lai·ka \ˌbal-ə-'lī-kə\ *n* [Russ] : a stringed instrument with a triangular body used esp. in the U.S.S.R.

¹bal·ance \'bal-ən(t)s\ *n* [ME, fr. OF, fr. (assumed) VL *bilancia*, fr. LL *bilanc-, bilanx* having two scalepans, fr. L *bi-* + *lanc-, lanx* plate; akin to OE *eln* ell — more at ELL] **1** : an instrument for weighing: as **a** : a beam that is supported freely in the center and has two pans of equal weight suspended from its ends **b** : a device that uses the elasticity of a spiral spring for measuring weight or force **c** *cap* : LIBRA **2** : a means of judging or deciding **3** : a counterbalancing weight, force, or influence **4** : a vibrating wheel operating with a hairspring to regulate the movement of a timepiece **5 a** : stability produced by even distribution of weight on each side of the vertical axis **b** : equipoise between contrasting, opposing, or interacting elements **c** : equality between the totals of the two sides of an account **6 a** : an aesthetically pleasing integration of elements **b** : the juxtaposition in writing of syntactically parallel constructions containing similar or contrasting ideas **7 a :** physical equilibrium **b :** the ability to retain one's balance **8 a :** weight or force of one side in excess of another **b :** something left over : REMAINDER **c :** an amount in excess esp. on the credit side of an account **9 :** mental and emotional steadiness **10 :** the point on the trigger side of a rifle at which if the rifle is held the weight of the ends balance each other — **bal·anced** \-ən(t)st\ *adj* — **in the balance** *or* **in balance :** in an uncertain critical position : with the fate or outcome about to be determined — **on balance :** all things considered

²balance *vb* **bal·anced; bal·anc·ing** *vt* **1 a** (1) **:** to compute the difference between the debits and credits of (an account) (2) **:** to pay the amount due on : SETTLE **b** (1) **:** to arrange so that one set of elements exactly equals another ⟨~ a mathematical equation⟩ (2) **:** to complete (a chemical equation) so that the same number of atoms of each kind appears on each side **2 a :** COUNTERBALANCE, OFFSET **b :** to equal or equalize in weight, number, or proportion **3 a :** to compare the weight of in or as if in a balance **b :** to deliberate upon esp. by weighing opposing issues : PONDER **4 a :** to bring to a state or position of equipoise **b :** to poise in or as if in balance **c :** to bring into harmony or proportion **~** *vi* **1 :** to become balanced or established in balance **2 :** to be an equal counterpoise **3 :** FLUCTUATE, WAVER ⟨contempt for the mind that ~*s* and waits —P. E. More⟩ **4 :** to move with a swaying or swinging motion ***syn*** see COMPENSATE

balance beam *n* **1 :** a narrow wooden beam supported in a horizontal position approximately four feet above the floor and used for balancing feats in gymnastics **2 :** an event in gymnastics competition in which the balance beam is used

balance of payments : a summary of the international transactions of a country or region over a period of time including commodity and service transactions, capital transactions, and gold movements

balance of power : an equilibrium of power sufficient to discourage or prevent one nation or political party from imposing its will upon or interfering with the interests of another

balance of terror : an equilibrium of military power (as nuclear capability) between potentially opposing nations sufficient to deter one nation from waging war upon another

balance of trade : the difference in value over a period of time between a country's imports and exports

bal·anc·er \ˈbal-ən-sər\ *n* **:** one that balances; *specif* : HALTERE

balance sheet *n* **:** a statement of financial condition at a given date

balance wheel *n* **1 :** a wheel that regulates or stabilizes the motion of a mechanism **2 :** a balancing or stabilizing force ⟨serve as a vital *balance wheel* in this country's overall educational and cultural relations — F. A. Young⟩

Ba·lante \bə-ˈlänt\ *n, pl* **Balante** *or* **Balantes** [F, fr. Balante *Bulanda*] **1 :** a member of a Negro people of Senegal and Angola **2 :** the language of the Balante people

bal·as \ˈbal-əs\ *n* [ME, fr. MF *balais,* fr. Ar *balakhsh,* fr. *Balakhshān,* ancient region of Afghanistan] **:** a ruby spinel of a pale rose-red or orange

ba·la·ta \bə-ˈlät-ə\ *n* [Sp, of Cariban origin; akin to Galibi *balata*] **:** a substance like gutta-percha that is the dried juice of tropical American trees (esp. *Manilkara bidentata*) of the sapodilla family and is used esp. in belting and golf balls; *also* **:** a tree yielding balata

bal·boa \bal-ˈbō-ə\ *n* [Sp, fr. Vasco Núñez de *Balboa* †1517 Sp explorer] — see MONEY table

bal·brig·gan \bal-ˈbrig-ən\ *n* [*Balbriggan,* Ireland] **:** a knitted cotton fabric used esp. for underwear or hosiery

bal·co·ny \ˈbal-kə-nē\ *n, pl* **-nies** [It *balcone,* fr. OIt, scaffold, of Gmc origin; akin to OHG *balko* beam — more at BALK] **1 :** a platform that projects from the wall of a building and is enclosed by a parapet or railing **2 :** an interior projecting gallery in a public building (as a theater) — **bal·co·nied** \-nēd\ *adj*

¹bald \ˈbȯld\ *adj* [ME *balled;* akin to OE *bǣl* fire, pyre, Dan *bældet* bald, L *fulica* coot, Gk *phalios* having a white spot] **1 a :** lacking a natural or usual covering (as of hair, vegetation, or nap) **b :** having little or no tread ⟨~ tires⟩ **2 :** UNADORNED **3 :** UNDISGUISED, PALPABLE **4 :** marked with white ***syn*** see BARE — **bald·ish** \ˈbȯl-dish\ *adj* — **bald·ly** \ˈbȯl-(d)lē\ *adv* — **bald·ness** \ˈbȯl(d)nəs\ *n*

²bald *vi* **:** to become bald

bal·da·chin \ˈbȯl-də-kən, ˈbal-\ *or* **bal·da·chi·no** \ˌbal-də-ˈkē-(ˌ)nō, ˌbäl-\ *n, pl* **baldachins** *or* **baldachinos** [It *baldacchino,* fr. *Baldacco* Baghdad, Iraq] **1 :** a rich embroidered fabric of silk and gold **2 :** a cloth canopy fixed or carried over an important person or a sacred object **3 :** an ornamental structure resembling a canopy used esp. over an altar

bald cypress *n* **1 :** either of two large swamp trees (*Taxodium distichum* and *T. ascendens*) of the southern U.S. that are related to the sequoias **2 :** the hard red wood of bald cypress that is much used for shingles

bald eagle *n* **:** the common eagle (*Haliaeetus leucocephalus*) of No. America that is wholly brown when young but in full adult plummage has white head and neck feathers and a white tail

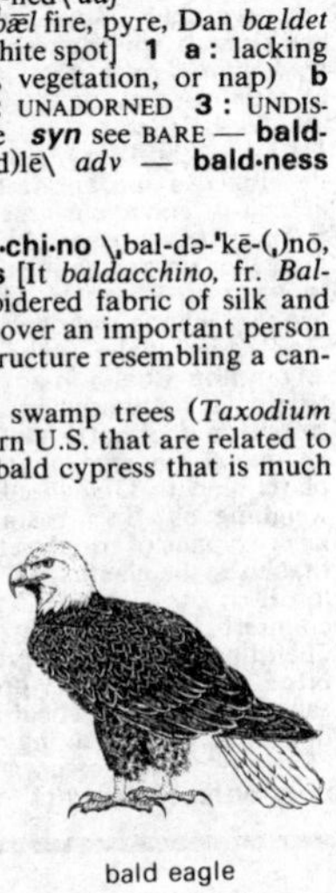
bald eagle

Bal·der \ˈbȯl-dər\ *n* [ON *Baldr*] **:** the son of Odin and Frigga and Norse god of light and peace slain through the trickery of Loki by a mistletoe sprig

bal·der·dash \ˈbȯl-dər-ˌdash\ *n* [origin unknown] **:** NONSENSE

bald-faced \ˈbȯl(d)-ˈfāst\ *adj* **:** BAREFACED

bald·head \ˈbȯld-ˌhed\ *n* **:** a baldheaded person

bald·pate \ˈbȯl(d)-ˌpāt\ *n* **1 :** BALDHEAD **2 :** a No. American widgeon (*Mareca americana*) with a white crown

bal·dric \ˈbȯl-drik\ *n* [ME *baudry, baudrik*] **:** an often ornamented belt worn over one shoulder to support a sword or bugle

¹bale \ˈbā(ə)l\ *n* [ME, fr. OE *bealu;* akin to OHG *balo* evil, OSlav *bolŭ* sick man] **1 :** great evil **2 :** WOE, SORROW

²bale *n* [ME, fr. OF, of Gmc origin; akin to OHG *balla* ball] **:** a large bundle of goods; *specif* **:** a large closely pressed package of merchandise bound and usu. wrapped ⟨a ~ of paper⟩ ⟨a ~ of hay⟩

³bale *vt* **baled; bal·ing :** to make up into a bale — **bal·er** *n*

ba·leen \bə-ˈlēn\ *n* [ME *baleine* whale, baleen, fr. L *balaena* whale, fr. Gk *phallaina;* akin to Gk *phallos* penis — more at BLOW] **:** WHALEBONE

bale·fire \ˈbā(ə)l-ˌfī(ə)r\ *n* [ME, fr. OE *bǣlfȳr* funeral fire, fr. *bǣl* pyre + *fȳr* fire — more at BALD] **:** an outdoor fire often used as a signal fire

bale·ful \-fəl\ *adj* **1 :** deadly or pernicious in influence **2 :** foreboding evil : OMINOUS ***syn*** see SINISTER — **bale·ful·ly** \-fə-lē\ *adv* — **bale·ful·ness** \-fəl-nəs\ *n*

¹balk \ˈbȯk\ *n* [ME *balke,* fr. OE *balca;* akin to OHG *balko* beam, L *fulcire* to prop, Gk *phalanx* log, phalanx] **1 :** a ridge of land left unplowed as a dividing line or through carelessness **2 :** BEAM, RAFTER **3 :** HINDRANCE, CHECK **4 a :** the space behind the balkline on a billiard table **b :** any of the outside divisions made by the balklines **5 :** failure of a player to complete a motion; *esp* **:** an illegal motion of the pitcher in baseball while in position

²balk *vt* **1** *archaic* **:** to pass over or by **2 :** to check or stop by or as if by an obstacle : BLOCK **~** *vi* **1 :** to stop short and refuse to proceed **2 :** to refuse abruptly — used with *at* **3 :** to commit a balk in sports ***syn*** see FRUSTRATE ***ant*** forward — **balk·er** *n*

bal·kan·ize \ˈbȯl-kə-ˌnīz\ *vt* **-ized; -iz·ing** *often cap* [*Balkan* peninsula] **:** to break up (as a region) into smaller and often hostile units — **bal·kan·iza·tion** \ˌbȯl-kə-nə-ˈzā-shən\ *n, often cap*

balk·line \ˈbȯ-ˌklīn\ *n* **1 :** a line across a billiard table near one end behind which the cue balls are placed in making opening shots **2 a :** one of four lines parallel to the cushions of a billiard table dividing it into nine compartments **b :** a carom billiards game that sets restrictions (as in scoring) determined by these lines

balky \ˈbȯ-kē\ *adj* **balk·i·er; -est :** refusing or likely to refuse to proceed or act as directed or expected ⟨a ~ mule⟩ ***syn*** see CONTRARY — **balk·i·ness** *n*

¹ball \ˈbȯl\ *n* [ME *bal,* fr. ON *böllr;* akin to OE *bealluc* testis, OHG *balla* ball, OE *bula* bull] **1 :** a round or roundish body or mass: as **a :** a spherical or ovoid body used in a game or sport **b :** EARTH, GLOBE **c :** a spherical or conical projectile; *also* **:** projectiles used in firearms **d :** a roundish protuberant anatomic structure; *esp* **:** the rounded eminence at the base of the thumb or great toe **2 a :** TESTIS — often considered vulgar **b** *pl* (1) **:** NONSENSE — often considered vulgar (2) **:** COURAGE — often considered vulgar **3 :** a game in which a ball is thrown, kicked, or struck; *esp* **:** BASEBALL **4 a :** the delivery of the ball ⟨a pitcher whose ~ curves⟩ **b :** a pitched baseball not struck at by the batter that fails to pass through the strike zone **c :** a hit or thrown ball in various games ⟨foul ~⟩ — **on the ball 1 :** marked by knowledgeableness and competence : ALERT ⟨the other introductory essay . . . is much more *on the ball* —*Times Lit. Supp.*⟩ ⟨keep *on the ball*⟩ **2 :** of ability or competence ⟨if the teacher has something *on the ball,* the pupils won't squirm much — *New Yorker*⟩

²ball *vi* **:** to form or gather into a ball **~** *vt* **1 :** to form or gather into a ball ⟨~*ed* the paper into a wad⟩ **2 :** to have sexual intercourse with — usu. considered vulgar

³ball *n* [F *bal,* fr. OF, fr. *baller* to dance, fr. LL *ballare,* fr. Gk *ballizein;* akin to Skt *balbalīti* he whirls] **1 :** a large formal gathering for social dancing **2 :** a very pleasant experience : a good time

bal·lad \ˈbal-əd\ *n* [ME *balade* song sung while dancing, song, fr. MF, fr. OProv *balada* dance, song sung while dancing, fr. *balar* to dance, fr. LL *ballare*] **1 :** a simple song : AIR **2 a :** a narrative composition in rhythmic verse suitable for singing **b :** an art song accompanying a traditional ballad **3 :** a popular song; *esp* **:** a slow romantic or sentimental song — **bal·lad·ic** \bə-ˈlad-ik, ba-\ *adj*

bal·lade \bə-ˈläd, ba-\ *n* [ME *balade,* fr. MF, ballad, ballade] **1 :** a fixed verse form consisting usu. of three stanzas with recurrent rhymes, an envoi, and an identical refrain for each part **2 a :** an elaborate musical setting of a ballad **b :** a musical composition usu. for piano suggesting the epic ballad

bal·lad·eer \ˌbal-ə-ˈdi(ə)r\ *n* **:** a singer of ballads

bal·lad·ist \ˈbal-əd-əst\ *n* **:** one who writes or sings ballads

bal·lad·ry \ˈbal-ə-drē\ *n* **:** BALLADS

ballad stanza *n* **:** a stanza consisting of four lines with the first and third lines unrhymed iambic tetrameters and the second and fourth lines rhymed iambic trimeters

ball-and-socket joint *n* **1 :** a joint in which a ball moves within a socket so as to allow rotary motion in every direction within certain limits **2 :** an articulation (as the hip joint) in which the rounded head of one bone fits into a cuplike cavity of the other and admits movement in any direction — called also *enarthrosis*

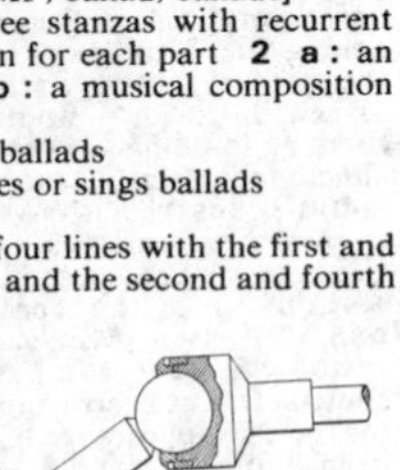
ball-and-socket joint 1

¹bal·last \ˈbal-əst\ *n* [prob. fr. LG, of Scand origin; akin to Dan & Sw *barlast* ballast; akin to OE *bær* bare & to OE *hlæst* load, *hladan* to load — more at LADE] **1 :** a heavy substance used to improve the stability and control the draft of a ship or the ascent of a balloon **2 :** something that gives stability esp. in character or conduct ⟨stated that his training had given him ~ and a sense of responsibility — *Current Biog.*⟩ **3 :** gravel or broken stone laid in a railroad bed or used in making concrete **4 :** a resistance used to stabilize the current in a circuit (as of a fluorescent lamp) — **in ballast** *of a ship* **:** having only ballast for a load

²ballast *vt* **1 :** to steady or equip with or as if with ballast **2 :** to fill in (as a railroad bed) with ballast

ball bearing *n* **:** a bearing in which the journal turns upon loose hardened steel balls that roll easily in a race; *also* **:** one of the balls in such a bearing

ball boy *n* : a tennis court attendant who retrieves balls for the players

ball·car·ri·er \'bȯl-ˌkar-ē-ər\ *n* : the football player carrying the ball on an offensive play

ball cock *n* : an automatic valve whose opening and closing are controlled by a spherical float at the end of a lever

ball control *n* : an offensive strategy (as in football or basketball) in which a team tries to maintain possession of the ball for extended periods of time

bal·le·ri·na \ˌbal-ə-'rē-nə\ *n* [It, fr. *ballare* to dance, fr. LL] : a female ballet dancer : DANSEUSE

bal·let \'ba-ˌlā, ba-'\ *n* [F, fr. It *balletto*, dim. of *ballo* dance, fr. *ballare*] **1 a** : dancing in which conventional poses and steps are combined with light flowing figures (as leaps and turns) **b** : a theatrical art form using ballet dancing, music, and scenery to convey a story, theme, or atmosphere **2** : music for a ballet **3** : a group that performs ballets — **bal·let·ic** \ba-'let-ik\ *adj*

ballet d'ac·tion \'ba-ˌlā-daks-'yōⁿ, ba-'lā-\ *n, pl* **ballets d'action** \-ˌlā(z)-, -'lā(z)-\ [F, ballet of action] : a ballet with a plot

bal·let·o·mane \ba-'let-ə-ˌmān\ *n* [*ballet* + *-o-* + *-mane* (fr. *mania*)] : a devotee of ballet

bal·let·o·ma·nia \-ˌlet-ə-'mā-nē-ə, -nyə\ *n* : enthusiasm for ballet

ball–flow·er \'bȯl-ˌflau̇(-ə)r\ *n* : an architectural ornament consisting of a ball placed in the flower-shaped hollow of a circular mold

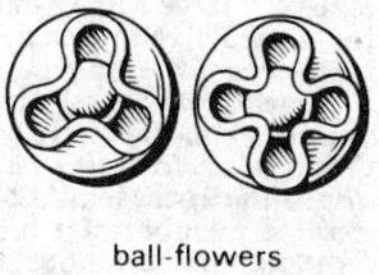

ball-flowers

ball hawk *n* **1** : one skillful in taking the ball away from opponents (as in football or basketball) **2** : a baseball outfielder skilled in catching fly balls

bal·lis·ta \bə-'lis-tə\ *n, pl* **-tae** \-ˌtē\ [L, fr. (assumed) Gk *ballistēs*, fr. *ballein* to throw — more at DEVIL] : an ancient military engine often in the form of a crossbow for hurling large missiles

bal·lis·tic \bə-'lis-tik\ *adj* [L *ballista*] : of or relating to ballistics or to a body in motion according to the laws of ballistics — **bal·lis·ti·cal·ly** \-ti-k(ə-)lē\ *adv*

ballistic missile *n* : a self-propelled missile guided in the ascent of a high-arch trajectory and freely falling in the descent

bal·lis·tics \bə-'lis-tiks\ *n pl but sing or pl in constr* **1 a** : the science of the motion of projectiles in flight **b** : the flight characteristics of a projectile **2 a** : the study of the processes within a firearm as it is fired **b** : the firing characteristics of a firearm or cartridge

bal·lis·to·car·dio·gram \bə-'lis-tō-'kärd-ē-ə-ˌgram\ *n* : the record made by a ballistocardiograph

bal·lis·to·car·dio·graph \-ˌgraf\ *n* [*ballistic* + *-o-* + *cardiograph*] : a device for measuring the amount of blood passing through the heart in a specified time by recording the recoil movements of the body that result from contraction of the heart muscle in ejecting blood from the ventricles — **bal·lis·to·car·dio·graph·ic** \-ˌkärd-ē-ə-'graf-ik\ *adj* — **bal·lis·to·car·di·og·ra·phy** \-ē-'äg-rə-fē\ *n*

ball lightning *n* : a rare form of lightning consisting of luminous balls that may move along solid objects or float in the air

ball of fire : a person of unusual energy, vitality, or drive

bal·lon \ba-'lōⁿ\ *n* [F, lit., balloon] : lightness of movement that exaggerates the duration of a ballet dancer's jump

bal·lo·net \ˌbal-ə-'nā\ *n* [F *ballonnet*, dim. of *ballon*] : a compartment of variable volume within the interior of a balloon or airship used to control ascent and descent

bal·lon·né \ˌbal-ə-'nā\ *n* [F, fr. *ballon*] : a wide circular jump in ballet usu. with a battement

¹bal·loon \bə-'lün\ *n* [F *ballon* large football, balloon, fr. It dial. *ballone* large football, aug. of *balla* ball, of Gmc origin] **1** : a nonporous bag of tough light material filled with heated air or a gas lighter than air so as to rise and float in the atmosphere **2** : a toy consisting of an inflatable rubber bag **3** : the outline enclosing words spoken or thought by a figure esp. in a cartoon

²balloon *vt* : INFLATE, DISTEND ~ *vi* **1** : to ascend or travel in a balloon **2** : to swell or puff out : EXPAND **3** : to increase rapidly

³balloon *adj* **1** : relating to, resembling, or suggesting a balloon ⟨a ~ sleeve⟩ **2** : having a final installment that is much larger than preceding ones in a term or installment note

bal·loon·ing \bə-'lü-niŋ\ *n* : the act or sport of riding in a balloon

bal·loon·ist \-nəst\ *n* : one who ascends in a balloon

balloon sail *n* : a large light sail set in addition to or in place of an ordinary light sail

balloon tire *n* : a pneumatic tire with a flexible carcass and large cross section designed to provide cushioning through low pressure

balloon vine *n* : a tropical American vine (*Cardiospermum halicacabum*) of the soapberry family bearing large ornamental pods

¹bal·lot \'bal-ət\ *n* [It *ballotta*, fr. It dial., dim. of *balla* ball] **1 a** : a small ball used in secret voting **b** : a sheet of paper used to cast a secret vote **2 a** : the action or system of secret voting **b** : the right to vote **c** : ¹VOTE 1a **3** : the number of votes cast

²ballot *vi* : to vote or decide by ballot — **bal·lot·er** *n*

bal·lotte·ment \bə-'lät-mənt\ *n* [F, lit., act of tossing, shaking, fr. *ballotter* to toss, fr. MF *baloter*, fr. *balotte* little ball, fr. It dial. *ballotta*] : a sharp upward pushing against the uterine wall with a finger for diagnosing pregnancy by feeling the return impact of the displaced fetus; *also* : a similar procedure for detecting a floating kidney

ball park *n* : a park in which ball games are played — **in the ball park** *slang* : approximately correct ⟨concede that the industry estimate . . . is "*in the ball park*" —Ronald Kessler⟩

ball–point pen *n* : a pen having as the writing point a small rotating metal ball that inks itself by contact with an inner magazine

ball·room \'bȯl-ˌrüm, -ˌru̇m\ *n* : a large room for dances

ball up *vt* : to make a mess of : CONFUSE, MUDDLE ⟨incompetents who *balled up* the whole program⟩ ~ *vi* : to become badly muddled or confused

ball valve *n* : a valve in which a ball regulates the aperture by its rise and fall due to fluid pressure, a spring, or its own weight

bal·ly·hoo \'bal-ē-ˌhü\ *n, pl* **-hoos** [origin unknown] **1** : a noisy attention-getting demonstration or talk **2** : flamboyant, exaggerated, or sensational advertising or propaganda — **ballyhoo** *vt*

bal·ly·rag \-ˌrag\ *var of* BULLYRAG

balm \'bäm, 'bälm\ *n* [ME *basme, baume*, fr. OF, fr. L *balsamum* balsam, fr. Gk *balsamon*] **1** : a balsamic resin; *esp* : one from small tropical evergreen trees (genus *Commiphora* of the family Burseraceae) **2** : an aromatic preparation (as a healing ointment) **3** : any of various aromatic plants (as of the genera *Melissa* or *Monarda*) **4** : a spicy aromatic odor **5** : a soothing restorative agency

bal·ma·caan \ˌbal-mə-'kan, -'kän\ *n* [*Balmacaan*, estate near Inverness, Scotland] : a loose single-breasted overcoat usu. made of rough woolens and having raglan sleeves, a short turnover collar, and a closing that may be buttoned up to the throat

balm of Gil·e·ad \-'gil-ē-əd\ [*Gilead*, region of ancient Palestine known for its balm (Jer 8:22)] **1** : a small evergreen African and Asian tree (*Commiphora meccanensis* of the family Burseraceae) with aromatic leaves; *also* : a fragant oleoresin from this tree **2** : an agency that soothes, relieves, or heals **3 a** : BALSAM FIR **b** : either of two poplars: (1) : a hybrid northern tree (*Populus gileadensis*) with broadly cordate leaves that are pubescent esp. on the underside (2) : BALSAM POPLAR

bal·mor·al \bal-'mȯr-əl, -'mär-\ *n* [*Balmoral* Castle, Scotland] **1** : a laced boot or shoe; *esp* : an oxford shoe with quarters meeting over a separate tongue **2** *often cap* : a round flat cap with a top projecting all around

balmy \'bäm-ē, 'bäl-mē\ *adj* **balm·i·er; -est** **1 a** : having the qualities of balm : SOOTHING **b** : MILD **2** : FOOLISH, INSANE — **balm·i·ly** \-ə-lē\ *adv* — **balm·i·ness** \-ē-nəs\ *n*

bal·ne·ol·o·gy \ˌbal-nē-'äl-ə-jē\ *n* [ISV, fr. L *balneum* bath — more at BAGNIO] : the science of the therapeutic use of baths

¹ba·lo·ney \bə-'lō-nē\ *var of* BOLOGNA

²baloney *n* [*bologna*] : pretentious nonsense : BUNKUM — often used as a generalized expression of disagreement ⟨it is a wish-gratifying intellectual toy. And a lot of ~ —H. D. Scott⟩

bal·sa \'bȯl-sə\ *n* [Sp] **1** : a tropical American tree (*Ochroma lagopus*) of the silk-cotton family with extremely light strong wood used esp. for floats; *also* : its wood **2** : RAFT; *specif* : one made of two cylinders of metal or wood joined by a framework and used for landing through surf

bal·sam \'bȯl-səm\ *n* [L *balsamum*] **1 a** : an aromatic and usu. oily and resinous substance flowing from various plants; *esp* : any of several resinous substances containing benzoic or cinnamic acid and used esp. in medicine **b** : a preparation containing resinous substances and having a balsamic odor **2 a** : a balsam-yielding tree; *esp* : BALSAM FIR **b** : IMPATIENS; *esp* : a common garden ornamental (*Impatiens balsamina*) **3** : BALM 5 — **bal·sam·ic** \bȯl-'sam-ik\ *adj*

balsam fir *n* : a resinous American evergreen tree (*Abies balsamea*) that is widely used for pulpwood and as a Christmas tree

balsam of Pe·ru \-pə-'rü\ : a leguminous balsam from a tropical American tree (*Myroxylon pereirae*) used in perfumery and medicine

balsam of To·lu \-tə-'lü\ [Santiago de *Tolú*, Colombia] : a balsam from a tropical American leguminous tree (*Myroxylon balsamum*) used esp. in cough syrups and perfumes

balsam poplar *n* : a No. American poplar (*Populus balsamifera*) that is often cultivated as a shade tree and has buds thickly coated with an aromatic resin — called also *balm of Gilead, hackmatack, tacamahac*

Bal·ti \'bəl-tē, 'bȯl-\ *n* : a Tibeto-Burman language of northern Kashmir

Bal·tic \'bȯl-tik\ *adj* [ML (*mare*) *balticum* Baltic sea] **1** : of or relating to the Baltic sea or to the states of Lithuania, Latvia, and Estonia **2** : of or relating to a branch of the Indo-European languages containing Latvian, Lithuanian, and Old Prussian — see INDO-EUROPEAN LANGUAGES table

Bal·ti·more chop \ˌbȯl-tə-ˌmō(ə)r-, -ˌmȯ(ə)r-, -mər-\ *n* [fr. its strategic use by the Baltimore team] : a batted baseball that usu. bounces too high for an infielder to have time to catch it and make a putout at first base

Baltimore oriole *n* [George Calvert, Lord *Baltimore*] : a common American oriole (*Icterus galbula*) in which the male is brightly colored with orange, black, and white and the female is primarily brown and greenish yellow

Bal·to–Slav·ic \ˌbȯl-(ˌ)tō-'slav-ik, -'släv-\ *n* : a subfamily of Indo-European languages consisting of the Baltic and the Slavic branches — see INDO-EUROPEAN LANGUAGES table

Ba·lu·chi \bə-'lü-chē\ *n, pl* **Baluchi** *or* **Baluchis** [Per *Balūchī*] **1 a** : an Indo-Iranian people of Baluchistan **b** : a member of this people **2** : the Iranian language of the Baluchi people

bal·us·ter \'bal-ə-stər\ *n* [F *balustre*, fr. It *balaustro*, fr. *balaustra* wild pomegranate flower, fr. L *balaustium*, fr. Gk *balaustion*; fr. its shape] **1** : an upright often vase-shaped support for a rail **2** : an object or vertical member (as the leg of a table, a round in the back of a chair, or the stem of a glass) having a vaselike or turned outline

bal·us·trade \-ə-ˌstrād\ *n* [F, fr. It *balaustrata*, fr. *balaustro*] : a row of balusters topped by a rail; *also* : a low parapet or barrier

BAM *abbr* **1** bachelor of applied mathematics **2** bachelor of arts in music

Bam·ba·ra \bam-'bär-ə\ *n, pl* **Bambara** *or* **Bambaras** **1** : a member of a Negroid people of the upper Niger **2** : a Mande language of the Bambara people

ə abut	ᵊ kitten	ər further	a back	ā bake	ä cot, cart
au̇ out	ch chin	e less	ē easy	g gift	i trip	ī life
j joke	ŋ sing	ō flow	ȯ flaw	ȯi coin	th thin	t͟h this
ü loot	u̇ foot	y yet	yü few	yu̇ furious	zh vision

bambino ● bang 86

bam·bi·no \bam-ˈbē-(ˌ)nō, bäm-\ *n, pl* **-nos** *or* **-ni** \-(ˌ)nē\ [It, dim. of *bambo* child] **1 :** CHILD, BABY **2** *pl usu bambini* **:** a representation of the infant Christ

bam·boo \(ˈ)bam-ˈbü\ *n, pl* **bamboos** [Malay *bambu*] **:** any of various chiefly tropical woody or arborescent grasses (as of the genera *Bambusa, Arundinaria,* and *Dendrocalamus*) including some with hollow stems used for building, furniture, or utensils and young shoots used for food — **bamboo** *adj*

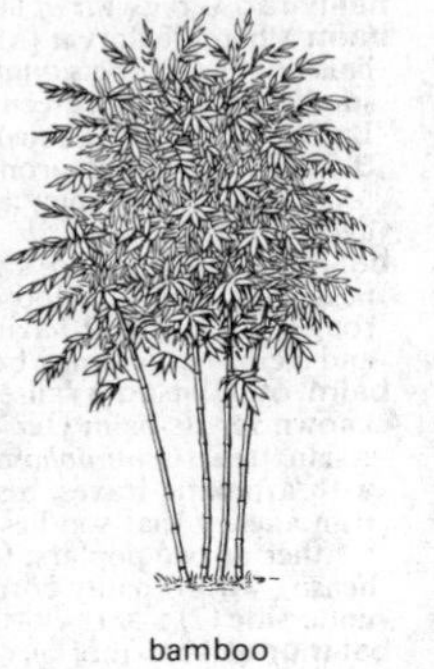
bamboo

bamboo curtain *n, often cap B&C* **:** a political, military, and ideological barrier in the Orient

bam·boo·zle \bam-ˈbü-zəl\ *vt* **bam·boo·zled; bam·boo·zling** \-ˈbüz-(ə-)liŋ\ [origin unknown] **:** to conceal one's true motives from esp. by elaborately feigning good intentions **:** HOODWINK — **bam·boo·zle·ment** \-ˈbü-zəl-mənt\ *n*

¹ban \ˈban\ *vb* **banned; ban·ning** [ME *bannen* to summon, curse, fr. OE *bannan* to summon; akin to OHG *bannan* to command, L *fari* to speak, Gk *phanai* to say, *phōnē* sound, voice] *vt* **1** *archaic* **:** CURSE **2 :** to prohibit esp. by legal means or social pressure **~** *vi* **:** to utter curses or maledictions ***syn*** see FORBID

²ban *n* [ME, partly fr. *bannen* & partly fr. OF *ban*, of Gmc origin; akin to OHG *bannan* to command] **1 :** the summoning in feudal times of the king's vassals for military service **2 :** ANATHEMA, EXCOMMUNICATION **3 :** MALEDICTION, CURSE **4 :** legal prohibition **5 :** censure or condemnation esp. through public opinion

³ban \ˈbän\ *n, pl* **ba·ni** \ˈbän-(ˌ)ē\ [Rum] — see *leu* at MONEY table

ba·nal \bə-ˈnäl, -ˈnal; bə-ˈnal, ba-ˈ, bā-ˈ; ˈbān-ᵊl\ *adj* [F, fr. MF, of compulsory feudal service, possessed in common, commonplace, fr. *ban*] **1 :** lacking originality, freshness, or novelty **:** TRITE **2 :** COMMON, ORDINARY ⟨a ~ inflammation⟩ ***syn*** see INSIPID ***ant*** original — **ba·nal·i·ty** \bə-ˈnal-ət-e *also* bā- *or* ba-\ *n* — **ba·nal·ly** \bə-ˈnäl-lē, -ˈnal; bə-ˈnal-lē, ba-, bā-; ˈbān-ᵊl-(l)ē\ *adv*

ba·nana \bə-ˈnan-ə, *esp Brit* -ˈnän-\ *n, often attrib* [Sp or Pg; Sp, fr. Pg, of African origin; akin to Wolof *banäna* banana] **1 :** an elongated usu. tapering tropical fruit with soft pulpy flesh enclosed in a soft usu. yellow rind **2 :** a widely cultivated perennial herb (genus *Musa* of the family Musaceae, the banana family) bearing bananas in compact pendent bunches

banana oil *n* **1 :** a colorless liquid acetate $C_7H_{14}O_2$ of amyl alcohol that has a pleasant fruity odor and is used as a solvent and in the manufacture of artificial fruit essences **2 :** a lacquer containing banana oil

banana seat *n* **:** an elongated bicycle saddle that often has an upward-curved back and a tapered front

banana split *n* **:** one or more scoops of ice cream served on a banana sliced in half lengthwise and usu. garnished with flavored syrups, fruits, nuts, and whipped cream

ba·nau·sic \bə-ˈnȯ-sik, -zik\ *adj* [Gk *banausikos* of an artisan, nonintellectual, vulgar, fr. *banausos* artisan] **1 a :** PRACTICAL, UTILITARIAN ⟨a ~ approach to literature⟩ **b :** DULL, PEDESTRIAN ⟨a ~ performance⟩ **2 a :** VOCATIONAL ⟨~ pursuits⟩ **b :** concerned with or tending to seek material things **:** MATERIALISTIC ⟨a ~ civilization⟩

¹band \ˈband\ *n* [in senses 1 & 2, fr. ME *band, bond* something that constricts, fr. ON *band;* akin to OE *bindan* to bind; in other senses, fr. ME *bande* strip, fr. MF, fr. (assumed) VL *binda*, of Gmc origin; akin to OHG *binta* fillet; akin to OE *bindan*] **1 :** something that confines or constricts while allowing a degree of movement **2 :** something that binds or restrains legally, morally, or spiritually: as **a :** a restraining obligation or tie affecting one's relations to others or to a tradition **b** *archaic* **:** a formal promise or guarantee **c** *archaic* **:** a pledge given **:** SECURITY **3 :** a strip serving to join or hold things together: as **a :** BELT 2 **b :** a cord or strip across the backbone of a book to which the sections are sewn **4 :** a thin flat encircling strip esp. for binding: as **a :** a close-fitting strip that confines material at the waist, neck, or cuff of clothing **b :** a strip of cloth used to protect a newborn baby's navel — called also *bellyband* **c :** a ring of elastic **5 :** an elongated surface or section with parallel or roughly parallel sides; *specif* **:** a more or less well-defined range of wavelengths, frequencies, or energies of optical, electric, or acoustic radiation **6 :** a narrow strip serving chiefly as decoration: as **a :** a narrow strip of material applied as trimming to an article of dress **b** *pl* **:** a pair of strips hanging at the front of the neck as part of a clerical, legal, or academic dress **c :** a ring without raised portions **7 :** a group of grooves on a phonograph record containing recorded sound

²band *vt* **1 :** to affix a band to or tie up with a band **2 :** to finish with a band **3 a :** to attach (oneself) to a group **b :** to gather together or summon for a purpose ⟨he ~*ed* all his resources together against the coming struggle⟩ **c :** to unite in a company or confederacy ⟨the farmers were ~*ed* against certain government controls⟩ **~** *vi* **:** to unite for a common purpose — often used with *together* ⟨fourteen of the largest cities have ~*ed* together in hopes of attacking the blight that is common to them all —J. B. Conant⟩ — **band·er** *n*

³band *n* [MF *bande* troop] **:** a group of persons, animals, or things; *esp* **:** a group of musicians organized for ensemble playing and using chiefly woodwinds, brass, and percussion instruments — compare ORCHESTRA

¹ban·dage \ˈban-dij\ *n* [MF, fr. *bande*] **1 :** a strip of fabric used esp. to dress and bind up wounds **2 :** a flexible strip or band used to cover, strengthen, or compress something

²bandage *vt* **ban·daged; ban·dag·ing :** to bind, dress, or cover with a bandage — **ban·dag·er** *n*

Band–Aid \ban-ˈdād\ *trademark* — used for a small adhesive strip with a gauze pad for covering minor wounds

ban·dan·na *or* **ban·dana** \ban-ˈdan-ə\ *n* [Hindi *bā̃dhnū* a dyeing process involving the tying of cloth in knots, cloth so dyed, fr. *bā̃dhnā* to tie, fr. Skt *badhnāti* he ties; akin to OE *bindan*] **:** a large figured handkerchief

band·box \ˈban(d)-ˌbäks\ *n* **1 :** a usu. cylindrical box of paperboard or thin wood for holding light articles of attire **2 :** a structure (as a theater or baseball park) having relatively small interior dimensions

ban·deau \ban-ˈdō\ *n, pl* **ban·deaux** \-ˈdōz\ [F, dim. of *bande*] **1 :** a fillet or band esp. for the hair **2 :** BRASSIERE

band·ed \ˈban-dəd\ *adj* **:** having or marked with bands ⟨a ~ pattern of clouds⟩

ban·de·ri·lla \ˌban-də-ˈrē(l)-yə\ *n* [Sp, dim. of *bandera* banner] **:** a decorated barbed dart that the banderillero thrusts into the neck or shoulders of the bull in a bullfight

ban·de·ri·lle·ro \ˌban-də-(ˌ)rē(l)-ˈye(ə)r-(ˌ)ō\ *n, pl* **-ros** [Sp, fr. *banderilla*] **:** one who thrusts in the banderillas in a bullfight

ban·de·role *or* **ban·de·rol** \ˈban-də-ˌrōl\ *n* [F *banderole*, fr. It *banderuola*, dim. of *bandiera* banner, of Gmc origin; akin to Goth *bandwo* sign — more at BANNER] **1 :** a long narrow forked flag or streamer **2 :** a long scroll bearing an inscription or a device

ban·di·coot \ˈban-di-ˌküt\ *n* [Telugu *pandikokku*] **1 :** any of several very large rats (*Nesokia* and related genera) of India and Ceylon destructive to rice fields and gardens **2 :** any of various small insectivorous and herbivorous marsupial mammals (family Peramelidae) of Australia, Tasmania, and New Guinea

ban·dit \ˈban-dət\ *n* [It *bandito*, fr. pp. of *bandire* to banish, of Gmc origin; akin to OHG *bannan* to command — more at BAN] **1** *pl also* **ban·dit·ti** \ban-ˈdit-ē\ **a :** an outlaw who lives by plunder; *esp* **:** a member of a band of marauders **b :** a political terrorist **:** GUERRILLA **2 :** ROBBER **3 :** one who takes unfair advantage of others ⟨the taxi ~*s* who tie up traffic —Bennett Cerf⟩ **4 :** an enemy plane — **ban·dit·ry** \ˈban-də-trē\ *n*

band·lead·er \ˈban-ˌdlēd-ər\ *n* **:** the director of a band

band·mas·ter \ˈban(d)-ˌmas-tər\ *n* **:** a conductor of a musical band

ban·dog \ˈban-ˌdȯg\ *n* [ME *bandogge*, fr. *band* + *dogge* dog] **:** a dog kept tied to serve as a watchdog or because of its ferocity

ban·do·lier *or* **ban·do·leer** \ˌban-də-ˈli(ə)r\ *n* [MF *bandouliere*, deriv. of OSp *bando* band, of Gmc origin; akin to Goth *bandwo*] **:** a belt worn over the shoulder and across the breast often for the suspending or supporting of some article (as cartridges) or as a part of an official or ceremonial dress

ban·dore \ˈban-ˌdō(ə)r, -ˌdȯ(ə)r\ *or* **ban·do·ra** \ban-ˈdōr-ə, -ˈdȯr-\ *n* [Sp *bandurria* or Pg *bandurra*, fr. LL *pandura* 3-stringed lute, fr. Gk *pandoura*] **:** a bass stringed instrument resembling a guitar

band razor *n* **:** a safety razor utilizing a cartridge that contains a narrow single-edged band of steel which may be advanced just enough to expose a new surface

band saw *n* **:** a saw in the form of an endless steel belt running over pulleys; *also* **:** a power sawing machine using this device

band shell *n* **:** a bandstand having at the rear a sounding board shaped like a huge concave seashell

bands·man \ˈban(d)z-mən\ *n* **:** a member of a musical band

band·stand \ˈban(d)-ˌstand\ *n* **:** a usu. roofed stand or raised platform on which a band or orchestra performs

b and w *abbr* black and white

band·wag·on \ˈban-ˌdwag-ən\ *n* **1 :** a usu. ornate and high wagon for a band of musicians esp. in a circus parade **2 :** a party, faction, or cause that attracts adherents or amasses power by its timeliness, showmanship, or momentum

band·width \ˈban-ˌdwidth\ *n* **:** the range within a band of wavelengths, frequencies, or energies

¹ban·dy \ˈban-dē\ *vb* **ban·died; ban·dy·ing** [prob. fr. MF *bander* to be tight, to bandy, fr. *bande* strip — more at BAND] *vt* **1 :** to bat (as a tennis ball) to and fro **2 a :** to toss from side to side or pass about from one to another often in a careless or inappropriate manner **b :** EXCHANGE; *esp* **:** to exchange (words) argumentatively **c :** to discuss lightly or banteringly **d :** to use in a glib or offhand manner — often used with *about* ⟨~ these statistics about with considerable bravado —Richard Pollak⟩ **3** *archaic* **:** to band together **~** *vi* **1** *obs* **:** CONTEND **2** *archaic* **:** UNITE

²bandy *n* [perh. fr. MF *bandé*, pp. of *bander*] **:** a game similar to hockey and believed to be its prototype

³bandy *adj* [prob. fr. *bandy* (hockey stick)] **1** *of legs* **:** BOWED **2 :** BOWLEGGED — **ban·dy–legged** \ˌban-dē-ˈleg(-ə)d, -ˈlāg(-ə)d\ *adj*

¹bane \ˈbān\ *n* [ME, fr. OE *bana;* akin to OHG *bano* death, Av *banta* ill] **1 a** *obs* **:** MURDERER, SLAYER **b :** POISON **c :** DEATH, DESTRUCTION ⟨money, thou ~ of bliss, and source of woe —George Herbert⟩ **d :** WOE **2 :** a source of harm or ruin **:** CURSE ⟨national frontiers have been more of a ~ than a boon for mankind —D. C. Thomson⟩

²bane *vt* **baned; ban·ing** *obs* **:** to kill esp. with poison

³bane *n* [ME (northern dial.) *ban*, fr. OE *bān*] *chiefly Scot* **:** BONE

bane·ber·ry \ˈbān-ˌber-ē\ *n* **:** the acrid poisonous berry of a plant (genus *Actaea*) of the buttercup family; *also* **:** the plant itself

bane·ful \ˈbān-fəl\ *adj* **1** *archaic* **:** POISONOUS **2 :** productive of destruction or woe **:** seriously harmful ⟨a ~ influence⟩ ***syn*** see PERNICIOUS ***ant*** beneficial — **bane·ful·ly** \-fə-lē\ *adv*

¹bang \ˈbaŋ\ *vb* [prob. of Scand origin; akin to Icel *banga* to hammer] *vt* **1 :** to strike sharply **:** BUMP ⟨fell and ~*ed* his knee⟩ **2 :** to knock, beat, or thrust vigorously often with a sharp noise **3 :** to have sexual intercourse with — often considered vulgar **~** *vi* **1 :** to strike with a sharp noise or thump ⟨the falling chair ~*ed* against the wall⟩ **2 :** to produce a sharp often metallic explosive or percussive noise or series of such noises

²bang *n* **1 :** a resounding blow **2 :** a sudden loud noise — often used interjectionally **3 a :** a sudden striking effect **b :** a quick burst of energy ⟨start off with a ~⟩ **c :** THRILL ⟨I get a ~ out of all this —W. H. Whyte⟩

³bang *adv* **:** RIGHT, DIRECTLY ⟨ran ~ up against more trouble⟩

⁴bang *n* [prob. short for *bangtail* (short tail)] **:** a fringe of banged hair — usu. used in pl.

⁵bang *vt* **:** to cut (as front hair) short and squarely across

ban·ga·lore torpedo \ˌbaŋ-gə-ˌlō(ə)r-, -ˌlȯ(ə)r-\ n [Bangalore, India] : a metal tube that contains explosives and a firing mechanism and is used to cut barbed wire and detonate buried mines

bang away vi 1 : to work with determined effort ⟨students *banging away* at their homework⟩ 2 : to attack persistently ⟨police are going to keep *banging away* at you —E. S. Gardner⟩

bang·er \ˈbaŋ-ər\ n, Brit : SAUSAGE

bang·kok \ˈbaŋ-ˌkäk, baŋ-ˈ\ n [earlier *bangkok*, a fine straw, fr. Bangkok, Thailand] : a hat woven of fine palm fiber in the Philippines

ban·gle \ˈbaŋ-gəl\ n [Hindi *baṅglī*] 1 : a stiff usu. ornamental bracelet or anklet slipped or clasped on 2 : an ornamental disk that hangs loosely (as on a bracelet or tambourine)

Bang's disease \ˈbaŋz-\ n [Bernhard L. F. *Bang* †1932 Dan veterinarian] : BRUCELLOSIS; specif : contagious abortion of cattle

bang·tail \ˈbaŋ-ˌtāl\ n [bangtail (short tail)] 1 : RACEHORSE 2 : a wild horse

bang-up \ˈbaŋ-ˌəp\ adj [³bang] : FIRST-RATE, EXCELLENT ⟨a ~ job⟩

bang up \-ˈəp\ vt [¹bang] : to cause extensive damage to

bani pl of BAN

ban·ish \ˈban-ish\ vt [ME *banishen*, fr. MF *baniss-*, stem of *banir*, of Gmc origin; akin to OHG *bannan* to command — more at BAN] 1 : to require by authority to leave a country 2 : to drive out or remove from a home or place of usual resort or continuance 3 : to clear away : DISPEL ⟨his discovery ~es anxiety —Stringfellow Barr⟩ — **ban·ish·er** n — **ban·ish·ment** \-ish-mənt\ n
syn BANISH, EXILE, DEPORT, TRANSPORT *shared meaning element* : to remove by authority or force from a country, state, or sovereignty

ban·is·ter also **ban·nis·ter** \ˈban-ə-stər\ n [alter. of *baluster*] 1 : one of the upright supports of a handrail alongside a staircase 2 a : a handrail with its supporting posts b : HANDRAIL

ban·jo \ˈban-(ˌ)jō\ n, pl banjos also banjoes [prob. of African origin; akin to Kimbundu *mbanza*, a similar instrument] : a musical instrument consisting of a drumlike body, a long fretted neck, and four or more strings that are strummed with the fingers — **ban·jo·ist** \-jō-əst\ n

¹bank \ˈbaŋk\ n [ME, prob. of Scand origin; akin to ON *bakki* bank; akin to OE *benc* bench — more at BENCH] 1 : a mound, pile, or ridge raised above the surrounding level: as a : a piled up mass of cloud or fog b : an undersea elevation rising esp. from the continental shelf 2 : the rising ground bordering a lake, river, or sea or forming the edge of a cut or hollow 3 a : a steep slope (as of a hill) b : the lateral inward tilt of a surface along a curve or of a vehicle (as an airplane) when taking a curve 4 : a protective or cushioning rim or piece

²bank vt 1 a : to raise a bank about b : to cover (as a fire) with fresh fuel and adjust the draft of air so as to keep in an inactive state c : to build (a curve) with the roadbed or track inclined laterally upward from the inside edge 2 : to heap or pile in a bank 3 : to drive (a ball in billiards) into a cushion 4 : to form or group in a tier ~ vi 1 : to rise in or form a bank — often used with up ⟨clouds would ~ up about midday, and showers fall —William Beebe⟩ 2 a : to incline an airplane laterally b (1) : to incline laterally (2) : to follow a curve or incline ⟨skiers ~ing around the turn⟩

³bank n [ME, fr. OF *banc* bench, of Gmc origin; akin to OE *benc*] 1 : a bench for the rowers of a galley 2 : a group or series of objects arranged near together in a row or a tier: as a : a row of keys on a typewriter b : a set of two or more elevators 3 : one of the horizontal and usu. secondary or lower divisions of a headline

⁴bank n [ME, fr. MF or OIt; MF *banque*, fr. OIt *banca*, lit., bench, of Gmc origin; akin to OE *benc*] 1 a obs : the table, counter, or place of business of a money changer b : an establishment for the custody, loan, exchange, or issue of money, for the extension of credit, and for facilitating the transmission of funds 2 : a person conducting a gambling house or game; specif : DEALER 3 : a supply of something held in reserve: as a : the fund of supplies (as money, chips, or pieces) held by the banker or dealer for use in a game b : a fund of pieces belonging to a game (as dominoes) from which the players draw 4 : a place where something is held available ⟨data ~⟩; esp : a depot for the collection and storage of a biological product of human origin for medical use

⁵bank vi 1 : to keep a bank 2 : to deposit money or have an account in a bank ~ vt : to deposit in a bank — **bank on** : to depend or rely on

bank·able \ˈbaŋ-kə-bəl\ adj : acceptable to or at a bank

bank acceptance n : a draft drawn on and accepted by a bank

bank annuities n pl : CONSOLS

bank·book \ˈbaŋk-ˌbuk\ n : the depositor's book in which a bank records his deposits and withdrawals — called also *passbook*

bank discount n : the interest discounted in advance on a note and computed on the face value of the note

¹bank·er \ˈbaŋ-kər\ n 1 : one that engages in the business of banking 2 : the player who keeps the bank in various games

²banker n : a man or boat employed in the cod fishery on the Newfoundland banks

³banker n : a sculptor's or mason's workbench

banker's bill n : a bill of exchange drawn by a bank on a foreign bank

bank holiday n 1 Brit : LEGAL HOLIDAY 2 : a period when banks in general are closed often by government fiat

bank·ing n : the business of a bank or a banker

bank line n [¹bank] : a fishing line attached to the shore and not constantly tended by a fisherman

bank money n : a medium of exchange consisting chiefly of checks and drafts

bank note n : a promissory note issued by a bank payable to bearer on demand without interest and acceptable as money

bank paper n 1 : circulating bank notes 2 : bankable commercial paper (as drafts or bills)

bank rate n : the discount rate fixed by a central bank

¹bank·roll \ˈbaŋ-ˌkrōl\ n : supply of money : FUNDS

²bankroll vt : to supply the capital for or pay the cost of (a business or project) — **bank·roll·er** n

¹bank·rupt \ˈbaŋ-(ˌ)krəpt\ n [modif. of MF & OIt; MF *banqueroute* bankruptcy, fr. OIt *bancarotta*, fr. *banca* bank + *rotta* broken, fr. L *rupta*, fem. of *ruptus*, pp. of *rumpere* to break — more at BANK, REAVE] 1 a : a person who has done any of the acts that by law entitle his creditors to have his estate administered for their benefit b : a person judicially declared subject to having his estate administered under the bankrupt laws for the benefit of his creditors c : a person who becomes insolvent 2 : one who is destitute of a particular thing ⟨a moral ~⟩

²bankrupt vt 1 : to reduce to bankruptcy 2 : IMPOVERISH ⟨war had ~ed the nation's natural resources⟩ *syn* see DEPLETE

³bankrupt adj 1 a : reduced to a state of financial ruin : IMPOVERISHED; specif : legally declared a bankrupt ⟨the company went ~⟩ b : of or relating to bankrupts or bankruptcy ⟨~ laws⟩ 2 a : BROKEN, RUINED ⟨a ~ professional career⟩ b : DEPLETED, STERILE ⟨a ~ old culture⟩ c : DESTITUTE — used with of or in ⟨~ of all merciful feelings⟩

bank·rupt·cy \ˈbaŋ-(ˌ)krəp-(t)sē\ n, pl -cies 1 : the quality or state of being bankrupt 2 : utter failure or impoverishment

bank shot n 1 : a shot in billiards and pool in which a player banks the cue ball or the object ball 2 : a shot in basketball played to rebound from the backboard into the basket

bank·sia \ˈbaŋ(k)-sē-ə\ n [NL, genus name, fr. Sir Joseph *Banks* †1820 E naturalist] : an Australian evergreen tree or shrub (genus *Banksia*) of the protea family with alternate leathery leaves and yellowish flowers in dense cylindrical heads

bank·side \ˈbaŋk-ˌsīd\ n 1 : the slope of a bank esp. of a stream 2 cap : the bank of the Thames at Southwark

¹ban·ner \ˈban-ər\ n [ME *banere*, fr. OF, of Gmc origin; akin to Goth *bandwo* sign, akin to ON *benda* to give a sign] 1 a : a piece of cloth attached by one edge to a staff and used by a monarch, feudal lord, or commander as his standard and as a rallying point in battle b : FLAG 1 c : an ensign displaying a distinctive or symbolic device or legend; esp : one presented as an award of honor or distinction 2 : a headline in large type running across a newspaper page 3 : a strip of cloth on which a sign is painted ⟨welcome ~s stretched across the street⟩ 4 : a name, slogan, or goal associated with a particular group or ideology ⟨the new ~ is "community control" —F. M. Hechinger⟩ — often used with *under* ⟨69th production under its own ~ —T. J. Smith⟩ ⟨every new administration arrives . . . under the ~ of change —John Cogley⟩

²banner adj 1 : distinguished from all others esp. in excellence ⟨a ~ year for business⟩ 2 : prominent in support of a political party ⟨a ~ Democratic county⟩

¹ban·ner·et \ˈban-ə-rət, ˌban-ə-ˈret\ n, often cap [ME *baneret*, fr. OF, fr. *banere*] : a knight leading his vassals into the field under his own banner and therefore ranking above a knight bachelor

²banneret also **ban·ner·ette** n : a small banner

ban·ne·rol also **ban·ner roll** \ˈban-ə-ˌrōl\ n : BANDEROLE

ban·nock \ˈban-ək\ n [ME *bannok*] 1 : an often unleavened bread of oat or barley flour baked in flat loaves 2 NewEng : CORN BREAD; esp : a thin cake baked on a griddle

banns \ˈbanz\ n pl [pl. of *bann*, fr. ME *bane*, *ban* proclamation, ban] : public announcement esp. in church of a proposed marriage

¹ban·quet \ˈban-kwət, ˈban- also -ˌkwet\ n [MF, fr. OIt *banchetto*, fr. dim. of *banca* bench, bank] : an elaborate and often ceremonious meal for numerous people often in honor of a person

²banquet vt : to treat with a banquet : FEAST ~ vi : to partake of a banquet — **ban·quet·er** n

banquet room n : a large room (as in a restaurant or hotel) suitable for banquets

ban·quette \ban-ˈket, ban-\ n [F, fr. Prov *banqueta*, dim. of *banc* bench, of Gmc origin; akin to OE *benc* bench] 1 a : a raised way along the inside of a parapet or trench for gunners or guns b South : SIDEWALK 2 a : a long upholstered seat b : a sofa having one roll-over arm c : a built-in upholstered bench along a wall

Ban·quo \ˈban-(ˌ)kwō, ˈban-\ n : a murdered Scottish thane in Shakespeare's *Macbeth* whose ghost appears to Macbeth

ban·shee \ˈban-(ˌ)shē, ban-\ n [ScGael *bean-sith*, fr. or akin to OIr *ben side* woman of fairyland] : a female spirit in Gaelic folklore whose appearance or wailing warns a family of the approaching death of a member

¹ban·tam \ˈbant-əm\ n [Bantam, former residency in Java] 1 : any of numerous small domestic fowls that are often miniatures of members of the standard breeds 2 : a person of diminutive stature and often combative disposition

²bantam adj 1 : SMALL, DIMINUTIVE 2 : pertly combative : SAUCY

ban·tam·weight \-ˌwāt\ n : a boxer who weighs more than 112 but not more than 118 pounds

¹ban·ter \ˈbant-ər\ vt [origin unknown] 1 : to speak to or address in a witty and teasing manner 2 archaic : DELUDE 3 chiefly South & Midland : CHALLENGE ~ vi : to speak or act playfully or wittily — **ban·ter·er** \-ər-ər\ n — **ban·ter·ing·ly** \ˈbant-ə-riŋ-lē\ adv

²banter n : good-natured and usu. witty and animated joking ⟨exchanged ~ with newsmen⟩

bant·ling \ˈbant-liŋ\ n [perh. modif. of G *bänkling* bastard, fr. *bank* bench, fr. OHG — more at BENCH] : a very young child

ə abut	ᵊ kitten	ər further	a back	ā bake	ä cot, cart
aů out	ch chin	e less	ē easy	g gift	i trip	ī life
j joke	ŋ sing	ō flow	ȯ flaw	ȯi coin	th thin	th this
ü loot	ů foot	y yet	yü few	yů furious	zh vision

Ban·tu \'ban-(,)tü, 'bän-\ *n, pl* **Bantu** *or* **Bantus** **1 a :** a family of Negroid peoples who occupy equatorial and southern Africa **b :** a member of any of these peoples **2 :** a group of African languages spoken generally south of a line from Cameroons to Kenya

Ban·tu·stan \,ban-tü-'stan, ,bän-tü-'stän\ *n* [*Bantu* + *-stan* land (as in *Hindustan*)] **:** an all-black enclave in the Republic of So. Africa with a limited degree of self-government

ban·yan \'ban-yən\ *n* [earlier *banyan* Hindu merchant, fr. Hindi *baniyā*; fr. a banyan pagoda erected under a tree of the species in Iran] **:** an East Indian tree (*Ficus bengalensis*) of the mulberry family with branches that send out shoots which grow down to the soil and root to form secondary trunks

ban·zai \(')bän-'zī\ *n* [Jap] **:** a Japanese cheer or battle cry — usu. used interjectionally

banzai attack *n* **:** a mass attack by Japanese soldiers

bao·bab \'baù-,bab, 'bā-ə-\ *n* [prob. native name in Africa] **:** a broad-trunked Old World tropical tree (*Adansonia digitata*) of the silk-cotton family with an edible acid fruit resembling a gourd and bark used in making paper, cloth, and rope

Bap *or* **Bapt** *abbr* Baptist

bap·ti·sia \bap-'tizh-(ē-)ə\ *n* [NL, genus name, fr. Gk *baptisis* a dipping, fr. *baptein*] **:** any of a genus (*Baptisia*) of No. American leguminous plants with showy papilionaceous flowers

bap·tism \'bap-,tiz-əm\ *n* **1 a :** a Christian sacrament marked by ritual use of water and admitting the recipient to the Christian community **b :** a non-Christian rite using water for ritual purification **c** *Christian Science* **:** purification by or submergence in Spirit **2 :** an act, experience, or ordeal by which one is purified, sanctified, initiated, or named — **bap·tis·mal** \bap-'tiz-məl\ *adj* — **bap·tis·mal·ly** \-mə-lē\ *adv*

baptismal name *n* **:** CHRISTIAN NAME 1

baptism of fire **1 :** a spiritual baptism by a gift of the Holy Spirit — often used in allusion to Acts 2:3-4; Mt. 3:11 (RSV) **2 :** an introductory or initial experience that is a severe ordeal; *specif* **:** a soldier's first exposure to enemy fire

bap·tist \'bap-təst\ *n* **1 :** one that baptizes **2** *cap* **:** a member or adherent of an evangelical Protestant denomination marked by congregational polity and baptism by immersion of believers only — **Baptist** *adj*

bap·tis·tery *or* **bap·tis·try** \'bap-tə-strē\ *n, pl* **-ter·ies** *or* **-tries :** a part of a church or formerly a separate building used for baptism

bap·tize \bap-'tīz, 'bap-,\ *vb* **bap·tized; bap·tiz·ing** [ME *baptizen*, fr. OF *baptiser*, fr. LL *baptizare*, fr. Gk *baptizein* to dip, baptize, fr. *baptos* dipped, fr. *baptein* to dip; akin to ON *kafa* to dive] *vt* **1 :** to administer baptism to **2 a :** to purify or cleanse spiritually esp. by a purging experience or ordeal **b :** INITIATE **3 :** to give a name to (as at baptism) **:** CHRISTEN ~ *vi* **:** to administer baptism — **bap·tiz·er** *n*

[1]**bar** \'bär\ *n, often attrib* [ME *barre*, fr. OF] **1 a :** a straight piece (as of wood or metal) that is longer than it is wide and has any of various uses (as for a lever, support, barrier, or fastening) **b :** a solid piece or block of material that is usu. rectangular and considerably longer than it is wide **c :** a usu. rigid piece (as of wood or metal) longer than it is wide that is used as a handle or support; *esp* **:** a handrail used by ballet dancers to maintain balance while exercising **2 :** something that obstructs or prevents passage, progress, or action: as **a :** the complete and permanent destruction of an action or claim in law; *also* **:** a plea or objection that effects such destruction **b :** an intangible or nonphysical impediment **c :** a submerged or partly submerged bank (as of sand) along a shore or in a river often obstructing navigation **3 a** (1) **:** the railing in a courtroom that encloses the place about the judge where prisoners are stationed or where the business of the court is transacted in civil cases (2) **:** COURT, TRIBUNAL (3) **:** a particular system of courts (4) **:** an authority or tribunal that hands down judgment **b** (1) **:** the barrier in the English Inns of Court that formerly separated the seats of the benchers or readers from the body of the hall occupied by the students (2) **:** the whole body of barristers or lawyers qualified to practice in any jurisdiction (3) **:** the profession of barrister or lawyer **4 :** a straight stripe, band, or line much longer than it is wide: as **a :** one of two or more horizontal stripes on a heraldic shield **b :** a metal or embroidered strip worn on a military uniform esp. to indicate rank or service **5 a :** a counter at which food or esp. alcoholic beverages are served **b :** BARROOM **6 a :** a vertical line across the musical staff before the initial measure accent **b :** MEASURE **7 :** a lace and embroidery joining covered with buttonhole stitch for connecting various parts of the pattern in needlepoint lace and cutwork

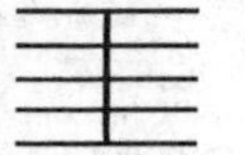

bar 6a

[2]**bar** *vt* **barred; bar·ring** **1 a :** to fasten with a bar **b :** to place bars across to prevent ingress or egress **2 :** to mark with bars **:** STRIPE **3 a :** to confine or shut in by or as if by bars **b :** to set aside **:** rule out **c :** to keep out **:** EXCLUDE **4 a :** to interpose legal objection to or to the claim of **b :** PREVENT, FORBID

[3]**bar** *prep* **:** EXCEPT

[4]**bar** *n* [G, fr. Gk *baros*] **1 :** a unit of pressure equal to one million dynes per square centimeter **2 :** the absolute cgs unit of pressure equal to one dyne per square centimeter

[5]**bar** *abbr* **1** barometer; barometric **2** barrel

Bar *abbr* Baruch

BAr *abbr* bachelor of architecture

BAR *abbr* Browning automatic rifle

bar- *or* **baro-** *comb form* [Gk *baros*; akin to Gk *barys* heavy — more at GRIEVE] **:** weight **:** pressure ⟨*barometer*⟩

Ba·rab·bas \bə-'rab-əs\ *n* [Gk, fr. Aram *Bar-abba*] **:** a Jewish prisoner according to Matthew, Mark, and John released in preference to Christ at the demand of the multitude

bar·a·thea \,bar-ə-'thē-ə\ *n* [fr. *Barathea*, a trademark] **:** a fabric that has a broken rib weave and a pebbly texture and that is made of silk, worsted, or synthetic fiber or a combination of these

[1]**barb** \'bärb\ *n* [ME *barbe* barb, beard, fr. MF, fr. L *barba* — more at BEARD] **1 a :** a sharp projection extending backward (as from the point of an arrow or fishhook) and preventing easy extraction; *also* **:** a sharp projection with its point similarly oblique to something else **b :** a biting or pointedly critical remark or comment **2 :** a medieval cloth headdress passing over or under the chin and covering the neck **3 :** [2]BARBEL **4 :** one of the side branches of the shaft of a feather **5 :** a plant hair or bristle ending in a hook

[2]**barb** *vt* **:** to furnish with a barb

[3]**barb** *n* [F *barbe*, fr. It *barbero*, fr. *barbero* of Barbary, fr. *Barberia* Barbary, coastal region in Africa] **1 :** any of a northern African breed of horses that are noted for speed and endurance and are related to Arabs **2 :** a pigeon of a domestic breed related to the carrier pigeons

bar·bar·ian \bär-'ber-ē-ən, -'bar-\ *adj* [L *barbarus*] **1 :** of or relating to a land, culture, or people alien and usu. believed to be inferior to one's own **2 :** lacking refinement, learning, or artistic or literary culture — **barbarian** *n* — **bar·bar·i·an·ism** \-ē-ə-,niz-əm\ *n*

syn BARBARIAN, BARBARIC, BARBAROUS, SAVAGE *shared meaning element* **:** characteristic of uncivilized man ***ant*** civilized

bar·bar·ic \bär-'bar-ik\ *adj* **1 a :** of, relating to, or characteristic of barbarians **b :** possessing or characteristic of a cultural level more complex than primitive savagery but less sophisticated than advanced civilization **2 a :** marked by a lack of restraint **:** WILD **b :** having a bizarre, primitive, or unsophisticated quality ***syn*** see BARBARIAN ***ant*** restrained, refined, subdued — **bar·bar·i·cal·ly** \-i-k(ə-)lē\ *adv*

bar·ba·rism \'bär-bə-,riz-əm\ *n* **1 :** an idea, act, or expression that in form or use offends against contemporary standards of good taste or acceptability **2 a :** a barbarian or barbarous social or intellectual condition **:** BACKWARDNESS **b :** the practice or display of barbarian acts, attitudes, or ideas

bar·bar·i·ty \bär-'bar-ət-ē\ *n, pl* **-ties** **1 :** BARBARISM **2 a :** barbarous cruelty **:** INHUMANITY **b :** an act or instance of barbarous cruelty

bar·ba·ri·za·tion \,bär-bə-rə-'zā-shən\ *n* **:** the act or process of barbarizing **:** the state of being barbarized

bar·ba·rize \'bär-bə-,rīz\ *vb* **-rized; -riz·ing** *vi* **:** to become barbarous ~ *vt* **:** to make barbarian or barbarous

bar·ba·rous \'bär-b(ə-)rəs\ *adj* [L *barbarus*, fr. Gk *barbaros* foreign, ignorant] **1 :** characterized by the occurrence of barbarisms **2 a :** UNCIVILIZED **b :** lacking culture or refinement **:** PHILISTINE **3 :** mercilessly harsh or cruel ***syn*** **1 see** BARBARIAN **2** see FIERCE ***ant*** clement — **bar·ba·rous·ly** *adv* — **bar·ba·rous·ness** *n*

Bar·ba·ry ape \,bär-b(ə-)rē-\ *n* [*Barbary*, Africa] **:** a tailless monkey (*Macaca sylvana*) of No. Africa and Gibraltar

Barbary Coast *n* **:** a district or section of a city noted as a center of gambling, prostitution, and riotous nightlife

bar·bate \'bär-,bāt\ *adj* [L *barbatus*, fr. *barba*] **:** bearded esp. with long stiff hairs

barbe \'bärb\ *n* [ME, fr. MF, lit., beard] **:** [1]BARB 2

[1]**bar·be·cue** \'bär-bi-,kyü\ *n* [AmerSp *barbacoa*, prob. fr. Taino] **1 :** an often portable fireplace over which meat and fish are roasted **2 :** a large animal (as a hog or steer) roasted or broiled whole or split over an open fire or barbecue pit **3 :** a social gathering esp. in the open air at which barbecued food is eaten

[2]**barbecue** *vt* **-cued; -cu·ing** **1 :** to roast or broil on a rack over hot coals or on a revolving spit before or over a source of cooking heat **2 :** to cook in a highly seasoned vinegar sauce — **bar·be·cu·er** *n*

barbed \'bärbd\ *adj* **1 :** having barbs **2 :** characterized by pointed and biting criticism ⟨~ witticisms⟩ — **barbed·ness** \'bär-bəd-nəs, 'barb(d)-nəs\ *n*

barbed wire \'bä(r)b-'(d)wī(ə)r\ *n* **:** twisted wires armed with barbs or sharp points — called also *barbwire*

[1]**bar·bel** \'bär-bəl\ *n* [ME, fr. MF, fr. (assumed) VL *barbellus*, dim. of L *barbus* barbel, fr. *barba* beard — more at BEARD] **:** a European freshwater cyprinid fish (*Barbus fluviatilis*) with four barbels on its upper jaw; *also* **:** any of various other fishes of this genus

[2]**bar·bel** *n* [obs. F, fr. MF, dim. of *barbe* barb, beard] **:** a slender tactile process on the lips of certain fishes (as catfishes)

bar·bell \'bär-,bel\ *n* **:** a bar with adjustable weighted disks attached to each end that is used for exercise and in weight lifting

bar·bel·late \'bär-bə-,lāt, bär-'bel-ət\ *adj* [NL *barbella* short stiff hair, dim. of L *barbula*, dim. of *barba*] **:** having short stiff hooked bristles or hairs ⟨a ~ fruit⟩

[1]**bar·ber** \'bär-bər\ *n* [ME, fr. MF *barbeor*, fr. *barbe* beard — more at BARB] **:** one whose business is cutting and dressing hair, shaving and trimming beards, and performing related services

[2]**barber** *vb* **bar·bered; bar·ber·ing** \-b(ə-)riŋ\ *vt* **:** to perform the services of a barber for ~ *vi* **:** to perform the services of a barber

bar·ber·ry \'bär-,ber-ē\ *n* [ME *barbere*, fr. MF *barbarin*, fr. Ar *barbāris*] **:** any of a genus (*Berberis* of the family Berberidaceae, the barberry family) of shrubs having spines, yellow flowers, and oblong red berries

[1]**bar·ber·shop** \'bär-bər-,shäp\ *n* **:** a barber's place of business

[2]**barbershop** *adj* [fr. the old custom of men in barbershops forming quartets for impromptu singing of sentimental songs] **:** having a style of impromptu unaccompanied vocal harmonizing of popular songs esp. by a male quartet and marked by chromatically altered tones

barber's itch *n* **:** ringworm of the face and neck

bar·bet \'bär-bət\ *n* [prob. fr. [1]*barb*] **:** any of numerous nonpasserine tropical birds (family Capitonidae) with a stout bill bearing bristles and usu. swollen at the base

bar·bette \bär-'bet\ *n* [F, dim. of *barbe* headdress] **1 :** a mound of earth or a protected platform from which guns fire over a parapet **2 :** a cylinder of armor protecting a gun turret on a warship

bar·bi·can \'bär-bi-kən\ *n* [ME, fr. OF *barbacane*, fr. ML *barbacana*] **:** an outer defensive work; *esp* **:** a tower at a gate or bridge

bar·bi·cel \'bär-bə-,sel\ *n* [NL *barbicella*, dim. of L *barba*] **:** one of the small hook-bearing processes on a barbule of a feather

bar·bi·tal \'bär-bə-,tȯl\ *n* [*barbituric* + *-al* (as in *Veronal*)] **:** a white crystalline addictive hypnotic $C_8H_{12}N_2O_3$ often administered in the form of its soluble sodium salt

bar·bi·tone \'bär-bə-ˌtōn\ n [barbituric + -one] Brit : BARBITAL
bar·bi·tu·rate \bär-'bich-ə-rət, -ˌrāt; ˌbär-bə-'t(y)ùr-ət, -'t(y)ù(ə)r-ˌāt\ n 1 : a salt or ester of barbituric acid 2 : any of various derivatives of barbituric acid used esp. as sedatives, hypnotics, and antispasmodics
bar·bi·tu·ric acid \ˌbär-bə-ˌt(y)ùr-ik-\ n [part trans. of G barbitursäure, irreg. fr. the name Barbara + ISV uric + G säure acid] : a synthetic crystalline acid $C_4H_4N_2O_3$ that is a derivative of pyrimidine
bar·bule \'bär-(ˌ)byü(ə)l\ n : a minute barb; esp : one of the processes that fringe the barbs of a feather
barb-wire n : BARBED WIRE
bar car n : a railroad car with facilities for preparing and serving refreshments and esp. drinks
bar·ca·role or **bar·ca·rolle** \'bär-kə-ˌrōl\ n [F barcarolle, fr. It barcarola, fr. barcarolo gondolier, fr. barca bark, fr. LL] 1 : a Venetian boat song usu. in ⁶⁄₈ or ¹²⁄₈ time characterized by the alternation of a strong and weak beat that suggests a rowing rhythm 2 : music imitating a barcarole
bar chart n : a graphic means of comparing quantities by rectangles with lengths proportional to the size of the quantities represented — called also bar graph
¹bard \'bärd\ n [ME, fr. ScGael & MIr] 1 a : a tribal poet-singer gifted in composing and reciting verses on heroes and their deeds b : a composer, singer, or declaimer of epic or heroic verse 2 : POET — **bard·ic** \-ik\ adj
²bard or **barde** \'bärd\ n [MF barde, fr. OSp barda, fr. Ar barda'ah] : a piece of armor or ornament for a horse's neck, breast, or flank
³bard vt : to furnish with bards
bard·ol·a·ter \bär-'däl-ət-ər\ n [Bard (of Avon), epithet of Shakespeare + idolater] : one who idolizes Shakespeare — **bard·ol·a·try** \-ə-trē\ n
¹bare \'ba(ə)r, 'be(ə)r\ adj **bar·er; bar·est** [ME, fr. OE bær; akin to OHG bar naked, Lith basas barefoot] 1 a : lacking a natural, usual, or appropriate covering b (1) : lacking clothing (2) obs : BAREHEADED c : UNARMED 2 : open to view : EXPOSED 3 a : unfurnished or scantily supplied b : DESTITUTE ⟨~ of all safeguards⟩ 4 a : having nothing left over or added : MERE b : devoid of amplification or adornment 5 obs : WORTHLESS — **bare·ness** n
  syn BARE, NAKED, NUDE, BALD, BARREN shared meaning element : deprived of naturally or conventionally appropriate covering ant covered
²bare vt **bared; bar·ing** : to make or lay bare : UNCOVER, REVEAL
³bare archaic past of BEAR
bare·back \-ˌbak\ or **bare·backed** \-'bakt\ adv or adj : on the bare back of a horse : without a saddle ⟨a young boy riding ~⟩ ⟨learned ~ riding among the Indians⟩
bare bones n pl : the barest essentials, facts, or elements ⟨stripped his proposition to its bare bones —A. H. Vandenberg †1951⟩
bare·faced \'ba(ə)r-ˈfāst, 'be(ə)r-\ adj 1 : having the face uncovered: a : BEARDLESS b : wearing no mask 2 a : OPEN, UNCONCEALED b : lacking scruples — **bare·faced·ly** \-'fā-səd-lē, -'fāst-lē\ adv — **bare·faced·ness** \-'fā-səd-nəs, -'fās(t)-nəs\ n
bare·foot \-ˌfùt\ or **bare·foot·ed** \-'fùt-əd\ adv or adj : with the feet bare : UNSHOD ⟨went ~ most of the summer⟩ ⟨~ boy, with cheek of tan —J. G. Whittier⟩
ba·rege \bə-'rezh\ n [F barège, fr. Barèges, town in the Pyrenees, France] : a sheer fabric of open weave for women's clothing usu. made of wool in combination with silk or cotton
bare–hand·ed \'ba(ə)r-'han-dəd, 'be(ə)r-\ adv or adj 1 : without gloves 2 : without tools or weapons ⟨fight an animal ~⟩
bare–head·ed \-'hed-əd\ adv or adj : without a hat or other covering for the head ⟨go ~ in the hot sun⟩ ⟨a ~ boy who had lost his cap⟩ — **bare–head·ed·ness** n
bare–knuck·le \-'nək-əl\ or **bare–knuck·led** \-əld\ adj or adv 1 : not using boxing gloves ⟨champion ~ prizefighter of England — Dennis Craig⟩ ⟨the days in which men fought ~⟩ 2 : having a fierce unrelenting character ⟨a . . . ~ polemic —Nat'l Review⟩ ⟨fighting ~ in congress for his beliefs⟩
bare·ly adv 1 : SCARCELY, HARDLY ⟨~ enough money to cover expenses⟩ 2 : in a meager manner : PLAINLY ⟨a ~ furnished room⟩
barf \'bärf\ vi [origin unknown] : VOMIT
bar·fly \'bär-ˌflī\ n : a drinker who frequents bars
¹bar·gain \'bär-gən\ n, often attrib 1 : an agreement between parties settling what each gives or receives in a transaction between them or what course of action or policy each pursues in respect to the other 2 : something acquired by or as if by bargaining; esp : an advantageous purchase 3 : a transaction, situation, or event regarded in the light of its results — **in the bargain** or **into the bargain** : BESIDES
²bargain vb [ME bargainen, fr. MF bargaignier, of Gmc origin; akin to OE borgian to borrow — more at BURY] vi 1 : to negotiate over the terms of a purchase, agreement, or contract : HAGGLE 2 : to come to terms : AGREE ~ vt : to sell or dispose of by bargaining : BARTER — **bar·gain·er** n — **bargain for** : EXPECT
bargain basement n : a section of a store (as the basement) where merchandise is sold at reduced prices
bargain counter n : a counter where merchandise is sold at bargain prices
¹barge \'bärj\ n [ME, fr. OF, fr. LL barca] : any of various boats: as a : a roomy usu. flat-bottomed boat used chiefly for the transport of goods on inland waterways and usu. propelled by towing b : a large motorboat supplied to the flag officer of a flagship c : a roomy pleasure boat; esp : a boat of state elegantly furnished and decorated
²barge vb **barged; barg·ing** vt : to carry by barge ~ vi 1 : to move ponderously or clumsily 2 : to thrust oneself heedlessly or unceremoniously
barge·board \'bärj-ˌbō(ə)rd, -ˌbò(ə)rd\ n [origin unknown] : an often ornamented board that conceals roof timbers projecting over gables
barg·ee \bär-'jē\ n, Brit : BARGEMAN

barge·man \'bärj-mən\ n : the master or a deckhand of a barge
bar graph n : BAR CHART
bar·hop \'bär-ˌhäp\ vi : to visit and drink at a series of bars in the course of an evening
bar·iat·rics \ˌbar-ē-'a-triks\ n pl but sing in constr [bar- + -iatrics] : a branch of medicine that deals with the treatment of obesity — **bar·ia·tri·cian** \ˌbar-ē-ə-'trish-ən\ n
bar·ic \'bar-ik\ adj : of or relating to barium
ba·ril·la \bə-'ril(l)-yə\ n [Sp barrilla] 1 : either of two European saltworts (Salsola kali and S. soda) or a related Algerian plant (Halogeton souda) 2 : an impure sodium carbonate made from barilla ashes and formerly used esp. in making soap and glass
bar·ite \'ba(ə)r-ˌīt, 'be(ə)r-\ n [Gk barytēs weight, fr. barys] : barium sulfate BaSO₄ occurring as a mineral
¹bari·tone \'bar-ə-ˌtōn\ n [F baryton or It baritono, fr. Gk barytonos deep sounding, fr. barys heavy + tonos tone — more at GRIEVE] 1 a : a male singing voice of medium compass between bass and tenor b : one having such a voice 2 : a saxhorn similar in range and tone to the euphonium — called also baritone horn — **bari·tonal** \ˌbar-ə-'tōn-ᵊl\ adj
²baritone adj : relating to or having the range or part of a baritone
bar·i·um \'bar-ē-əm, 'ber-\ n [NL, fr. bar-] : a silver-white malleable toxic bivalent metallic element of the alkaline-earth group that occurs only in combination — see ELEMENT table
barium sulfate n : a colorless crystalline insoluble compound BaSO₄ that occurs in nature as barite, is obtained artificially by precipitation, and is used as a pigment and extender, as a filler, and as a substance opaque to X rays in medical photography of the alimentary canal
¹bark \'bärk\ vb [ME berken, fr. OE beorcan; akin to ON berkja to bark, Lith burgéti to growl] vi 1 a : to make the characteristic short loud cry of a dog b : to make a noise resembling a bark 2 : to speak in a curt loud and usu. angry tone : SNAP ~ vt 1 : to utter in a curt loud usu. angry tone 2 : to advertise by persistent outcry ⟨newsboys ~ed their wares persistently⟩ — **bark up the wrong tree** : to proceed under a misapprehension
²bark n 1 a : the sound made by a barking dog b : a similar sound 2 : a short sharp peremptory tone of speech or utterance — **bark·less** \'bär-kləs\ adj
³bark n [ME, fr. ON bark-, börkr; akin to MD & MLG borke bark] 1 : the tough exterior covering of a woody root or stem 2 a : TANBARK b : CINCHONA 2 — **bark·less** \'bär-kləs\ adj
⁴bark vt 1 : to treat with an infusion of tanbark 2 a : to strip the bark from; specif : GIRDLE 3 b : to rub off or abrade the skin of
⁵bark n [ME, fr. MF barque, fr. OProv barca, fr. LL] 1 a : a small sailing ship b : a 3-masted ship with foremast and mainmast square-rigged and mizzenmast fore-and-aft rigged 2 : a craft propelled by sails or oars
bark beetle n : a beetle (family Scolytidae) that bores under the bark of trees both as larva and adult
bar·keep·er \'bär-ˌkē-pər\ or **bar·keep** \-ˌkēp\ n : BARTENDER
bar·ken·tine \'bär-kən-ˌtēn\ n [⁵bark + -entine, alter. of -antine (as in brigantine)] : a 3-masted ship having the foremast square-rigged and the mainmast and mizzenmast fore-and-aft rigged

bark 1b

¹bark·er \'bär-kər\ n : one that barks; esp : a person who advertises by hawking at an entrance to a show
²barker n : one that removes or prepares bark
barky \'bär-kē\ adj **bark·i·er; -est** : covered with or resembling bark
bar·ley \'bär-lē\ n [ME barly, fr. OE bærlic of barley; akin to OE bere barley, L far spelt] : a cereal grass (genus Hordeum, esp. H. vulgare) having the flowers in dense spikes with long awns and three spikelets at each joint of the rachis; also : its seed used in malt beverages and in breakfast foods and stock feeds
bar·ley–bree \-ˌbrē\ also **bar·ley–broo** \-ˌbrü\ n [barley + Sc bree or broo (bree)] 1 chiefly Scot : WHISKEY 2 chiefly Scot : BEER, ALE
bar·ley·corn \-ˌkó(ə)rn\ n 1 : a grain of barley 2 : an old unit of length equal to the third part of an inch
bar·low \'bär-ˌlō\ n [Russell Barlow 18th cent. E knife maker] : a sturdy inexpensive jackknife
barm \'bärm\ n [ME berme, fr. OE beorma; akin to L fermentum yeast, fervēre to boil — more at BURN] : yeast formed on fermenting malt liquors
bar·maid \'bär-ˌmād\ n : a female bartender
bar·man \-mən\ n : BARTENDER
Bar·me·cid·al \ˌbär-mə-'sid-ᵊl\ or **Bar·me·cide** \'bär-mə-ˌsīd\ adj [Barmecide, a wealthy Persian, who, in a tale of The Arabian Nights, invited a beggar to a feast of imaginary food] : providing only the illusion of plenty or abundance ⟨a ~ feast⟩
¹bar mitz·vah \bär-'mits-və\ n, often cap B&M [Heb bar miswāh, lit., son of the (divine) law] 1 : a Jewish boy who reaches his 13th birthday and attains the age of religious duty and responsibility 2 : the initiatory ceremony recognizing a boy as a bar mitzvah
²bar mitzvah vt **bar mitz·vahed; bar mitz·vah·ing** : to administer the ceremony of bar mitzvah to
barmy \'bär-mē\ adj **barm·i·er; -est** 1 : full of froth or ferment 2 : BALMY 2
barn \'bärn\ n [ME bern, fr. OE bereern, fr. bere barley + ærn place] 1 a : a usu. large building for the storage of farm prod-

ə abut	ᵊ kitten	ər further	a back	ā bake	ä cot, cart
aù out	ch chin	e less	ē easy	g gift	i trip	ī life
j joke	ŋ sing	ō flow	ò flaw	òi coin	th thin	th this
ü loot	ù foot	y yet	yü few	yù furious	zh vision

ucts, for feed, and usu. for the housing of farm animals or farm equipment **b** : an unusually large and usu. bare building ⟨a great ~ of a hotel —W. A. White⟩ **2** : a large building for the housing of a fleet of vehicles (as trolley cars or trucks) — **barny** \ˈbär-nē\ *adj*
Bar·na·bas \ˈbär-nə-bəs\ *n* [Gk, fr. Aram *Barnebhūʼāh*] : a companion of the apostle Paul on his first missionary journey
bar·na·cle \ˈbär-ni-kəl\ *n* [ME *barnakille,* alter. of *bernake,* of Celt origin; akin to Corn *brennyk* limpet] **1** : a European goose (*Branta leucopsis*) that breeds in the arctic and is larger than the related brant — called also *barnacle goose* **2** : any of numerous marine crustaceans (subclass Cirripedia) with feathery appendages for gathering food that are free-swimming as larvae but fixed to rocks or floating logs as adults — **bar·na·cled** \-kəld\ *adj*

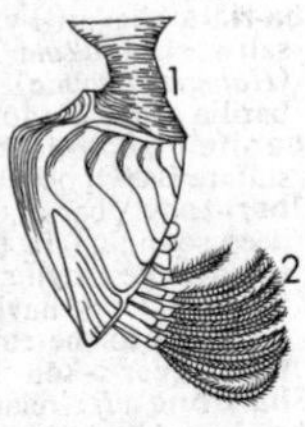

barnacle 2: *1* peduncle, *2* cirri

barn dance *n* : a rollicking American social dance orig. held in a barn with square dances, round dances, and traditional music and calls
barn lot *n, chiefly South & Midland* : BARNYARD
barn owl *n* : a widely distributed owl (*Tyto alba*) that has plumage mottled buff brown and gray above and chiefly white below, frequents barns and other buildings, and preys esp. on rodents
barn raising *n* : a gathering for the purpose of erecting a barn — compare [1]BEE 3
barn·storm \ˈbärn-ˌstȯrm\ *vi* **1** : to tour through rural districts staging theatrical performances usu. in one-night stands **2** : to travel from place to place making brief stops (as in a political campaign) **3** : to pilot one's airplane in sightseeing flights with passengers or in exhibition stunts in an unscheduled itinerant course esp. in rural districts ~ *vt* : to travel across while barnstorming — **barn·storm·er** *n*
[1]**barn·yard** \-ˌyärd\ *n* : a usu. fenced area adjoining a barn
[2]**barnyard** *adj* : EARTHY, SMUTTY, SCATOLOGICAL ⟨~ humor⟩
baro- — see BAR-
baro·gram \ˈbar-ə-ˌgram\ *n* [ISV] : a barographic tracing
baro·graph \-ˌgraf\ *n* [ISV] : a self-registering barometer — **baro·graph·ic** \ˌbar-ə-ˈgraf-ik\ *adj*
ba·rom·e·ter \bə-ˈräm-ət-ər\ *n* **1** : an instrument for determining the pressure of the atmosphere and hence for assisting in judgment as to probable weather changes and for determining the height of an ascent **2** : something that serves to register fluctuations (as in public opinion) — **baro·met·ric** \ˌbar-ə-ˈme-trik\ *or* **baro·met·ri·cal** \-tri-kəl\ *adj* — **baro·met·ri·cal·ly** \-tri-k(ə-)lē\ *adv* — **ba·rom·e·try** \bə-ˈräm-ə-trē\ *n*
barometric pressure *n* : the pressure of the atmosphere usu. expressed in terms of the height of a column of mercury
bar·on \ˈbar-ən\ *n* [ME, fr. OF, of Gmc origin; akin to OHG *baro* freeman] **1 a** : one of a class of tenants holding his rights and title by military or other honorable service directly from a feudal superior (as a king) **b** : a lord of the realm : NOBLE, PEER **2 a** : a member of the lowest grade of the peerage in Great Britain **b** : a nobleman on the continent of Europe of varying rank **c** : a member of the lowest order of nobility in Japan **3** : a man of great power or influence in some field of activity ⟨cattle ~⟩
bar·on·age \-ə-nij\ *n* : the whole body of barons or peers : NOBILITY 2
bar·on·ess \-ə-nəs\ *n* **1** : the wife or widow of a baron **2** : a woman who holds a baronial title in her own right
bar·on·et \ˈbar-ə-nət, *US also* ˌbar-ə-ˈnet\ *n* : the holder of a rank of honor below a baron and above a knight
bar·on·et·age \-ij\ *n* **1** : BARONETCY **2** : the whole body of baronets
bar·on·et·cy \-sē\ *n* : the rank of a baronet
ba·rong \bə-ˈrȯŋ, -ˈräŋ\ *n* [native name in the Philippines] : a thick-backed thin-edged knife or sword used by the Moro
ba·ro·ni·al \bə-ˈrō-nē-əl\ *adj* **1** : of or relating to a baron or the baronage **2** : STATELY, AMPLE ⟨a ~ room⟩
bar·ony \ˈbar-ə-nē\ *n, pl* **-on·ies** **1** : the domain, rank, or dignity of a baron **2** : a vast private landholding **3** : a field of activity under the sway of an individual or a special group
[1]**ba·roque** \bə-ˈrōk, ba-, -ˈräk\ *n* [F, fr. Pg *barrôco*] : an irregularly shaped pearl
[2]**ba·roque** \bə-ˈrōk, ba-, -ˈräk\ *adj* [F, fr. It *barocco*] : of, relating to, or having the characteristics of a style of artistic expression prevalent esp. in the 17th century that is marked generally by extravagant forms and elaborate and sometimes grotesque ornamentation and specifically also in architecture by dynamic opposition and the use of curved and plastic figures, in music by improvisation, contrasting effects, and powerful tensions, and in literature by complexity of form and bizarre, ingenious, and often ambiguous imagery — **ba·roque·ly** *adv*
baro·re·cep·tor \ˌbar-ō-ri-ˈsep-tər\ *n* [*bar-* + *receptor*] : a neural receptor (as of the arterial walls) sensitive to changes in pressure
ba·rouche \bə-ˈrüsh\ *n* [G *barutsche,* fr. It *biroccio,* deriv. of LL *birotus* two-wheeled, fr. L *bi-* + *rota* wheel — more at ROLL] : a four-wheeled carriage with a driver's seat high in front, two double seats inside facing each other, and a folding top over the back seat
bar pilot *n* : a pilot who navigates a ship from a pilot station over a bar and often into a harbor or to the harbor docks
barque \ˈbärk\, **bar·quen·tine** \ˈbär-kən-ˌtēn\ *var of* BARK, BARKENTINE
[1]**bar·rack** \ˈbar-ək, -ik\ *n* [F *baraque* hut, fr. Catal *barraca*] **1** : a building or set of buildings used esp. for lodging soldiers in garrison **2 a** : a structure resembling a shed or barn that provides temporary housing **b** : housing characterized by extreme plainness or dreary uniformity — usu. used in pl. in all senses
[2]**barrack** *vt* : to lodge in barracks
[3]**barrack** *vb* [origin unknown] *vi* **1** *chiefly Austral* : JEER, SCOFF **2** *chiefly Austral* : ROOT, CHEER — usu. used with *for* ~ *vt, chiefly Austral* : to shout at derisively or sarcastically — **bar·rack·er** *n*
barracks bag *n* : a fabric bag for carrying personal equipment
bar·ra·coon \ˌbar-ə-ˈkün\ *n* [Sp *barracón,* aug. of *barraca* hut, fr. Catal] : an enclosure or barracks formerly used for temporary confinement of slaves or convicts
bar·ra·cou·ta \ˌbar-ə-ˈküt-ə\ *n* [modif. of AmerSp *barracuda*] **1** : a large marine food fish (*Thyrsites atun*) **2** : BARRACUDA
bar·ra·cu·da \ˌbar-ə-ˈküd-ə\ *n, pl* **-da** *or* **-das** [AmerSp] : any of several predaceous marine fishes (genus *Sphyraena* of the family Sphyraenidae) of warm seas that include excellent food fishes as well as forms regarded as toxic
[1]**bar·rage** \ˈbär-ij\ *n* [F, fr. *barrer* to bar, fr. *barre* bar] : an artificial dam placed in a watercourse to increase the depth of water or to divert it into a channel for navigation or irrigation
[2]**bar·rage** \bə-ˈräzh, -ˈräj\ *n* [F (*tir de*) *barrage* barrier fire] **1** : a barrier of fire esp. of artillery laid on a line close to friendly troops to screen and protect them **2** : a rapid-fire massive or concentrated delivery or outpouring (as of speech or writing)
[3]**bar·rage** \bə-ˈräzh, -ˈräj\ *vt* **bar·raged; bar·rag·ing** : to deliver a barrage against
barrage balloon *n* : a small captive balloon used to support wires or nets as protection against air attacks
bar·ra·mun·da \ˌbar-ə-ˈmən-də\ *or* **bar·ra·mun·di** \-dē\ *n* [native name in Australia] : any of several Australian fishes: as **a** : a large red-fleshed lungfish (*Neoceratodus forsteri*) of Australian rivers used for food **b** : a river fish (*Scleropages leichhardtii*) that is used for food
bar·ran·ca \bə-ˈraŋ-kə\ *or* **bar·ran·co** \-(ˌ)kō\ *n, pl* **-cas** *or* **-cos** [Sp] **1** : a deep gulley or arroyo with steep sides **2** : a steep bank or bluff
bar·ra·tor *also* **bar·ra·ter** \ˈbar-ət-ər\ *n* : one who engages in barratry
bar·ra·try \ˈbar-ə-trē\ *n, pl* **-tries** [ME *barratrie,* fr. MF *baraterie* deception, fr. *barater* to deceive, exchange] **1** : the purchase or sale of office or preferment in church or state **2** : a fraudulent breach of duty on the part of a master of a ship or of the mariners to the injury of the owner of the ship or cargo **3** : the persistent incitement of litigation
barred \ˈbärd\ *adj* : marked by or divided off by bars; *specif* : having alternate bands of different color ⟨~ feather⟩
[1]**bar·rel** \ˈbar-əl\ *n* [ME *barel,* fr. MF *baril*] **1** : a round bulging vessel of greater length than breadth that is usu. made of staves bound with hoops and has flat ends of equal diameter **2 a** : the amount contained in a barrel; *esp* : the amount (as 31 gal. of fermented beverage or 42 gal. of petroleum) fixed for a certain commodity used as a unit of measure **b** : a great quantity **3** : a drum or cylindrical part: as **a** : the discharging tube of a gun **b** : the cylindrical metal box enclosing the mainspring of a timepiece **c** : the part of a fountain pen or of a pencil containing the ink or lead **d** : a cylindrical or tapering housing containing the optical components of a photographic-lens system and the iris diaphragm **e** : TUMBLING BARREL **f** : the fuel outlet from the carburetor on a gasoline engine **4** : the trunk of a quadruped — see COW illustration — **bar·reled** \-əld\ *adj* — **on the barrel** : asking for or granting no credit : in cash — **over a barrel** : at a disadvantage : in an awkward position
[2]**barrel** *vb* **-reled** *or* **-relled; -rel·ing** *or* **-rel·ling** *vt* : to put or pack in a barrel ~ *vi* : to move at a high speed
barrel chair *n* : an upholstered chair with a high solid rounded back
bar·rel·ful \ˈbar-əl-ˌfu̇l\ *n, pl* **barrelfuls** \-ˌfu̇lz\ *or* **bar·rels·ful** \-əlz-ˌfu̇l\ **1** : as much or as many as a barrel will hold **2** : a large number or amount
bar·rel·house \ˈbar-əl-ˌhau̇s\ *n* **1** : a cheap drinking and usu. dancing establishment **2** : a style of jazz characterized by a very heavy beat and simultaneous improvisation by each player
barrel organ *n* : an instrument for producing music by the action of a revolving cylinder studded with pegs on a series of valves that admit air from a bellows to a set of pipes
barrel roll *n* : an airplane maneuver in which a complete revolution about the longitudinal axis is made
[1]**bar·ren** \ˈbar-ən\ *adj* [ME *bareine,* fr. OF *baraine*] **1** : not reproducing: as **a** : incapable of producing offspring — used esp. of females or matings **b** : not yet or not recently pregnant **c** : habitually failing to fruit **2** : not productive: as **a** : lacking a normal or adequate cover of vegetation or crops : DESOLATE ⟨arid ~ soil⟩ **b** : unproductive of results or gain : FRUITLESS ⟨a ~ scheme⟩ **3** : DEVOID, LACKING — used with *of* ⟨~ of excitement⟩ **4** : lacking interest, information, or charm **5** : DULL, UNRESPONSIVE ***syn*** **1** see STERILE ***ant*** fecund **2** see BARE — **bar·ren·ly** *adv* — **bar·ren·ness** \-ən-nəs\ *n*
[2]**barren** *n* **1** : a tract of barren land **2** *pl* : an extent of usu. level land having an inferior growth of trees or little vegetation
bar·rette \bä-ˈret, bə-\ *n* [F, dim. of *barre* bar] : a clip or bar for holding a woman's hair in place
[1]**bar·ri·cade** \ˈbar-ə-ˌkād, ˌbar-ə-ˈ\ *vt* **-cad·ed; -cad·ing** **1** : to block off or stop up with a barricade **2** : to prevent access to by means of a barricade
[2]**barricade** *n* [F, fr. MF, fr. *barriquer* to barricade, fr. *barrique* barrel] **1** : an obstruction or rampart thrown up across a way or passage to check the advance of the enemy **2** : BARRIER, OBSTACLE **3** *pl* : a field of combat or dispute
bar·ri·ca·do \ˌbar-ə-ˈkād-(ˌ)ō\ *n, pl* **-does** [modif. of F *barricade*] *archaic* : BARRICADE — **barricado** *vt, archaic*
bar·ri·er \ˈbar-ē-ər\ *n* [ME *barrere,* fr. MF *barriere,* fr. *barre*] **1 a** : a material object or set of objects that separates, demarcates, or serves as a barricade **b** : an extension of the antarctic continental ice cap into the sea resting partly on the bottom **2** *pl, often cap* : a medieval war game in which combatants fight on foot with a fence or railing between them **3** : the movable gate or device at the starting line in a racetrack **4** : something immaterial that impedes or separates ⟨~*s* of reserve⟩ **5** : a factor that tends to restrict the

free movement, mingling, or interbreeding of individuals or populations ⟨behavioral and geographic ~s to hybridization⟩

barrier reef *n* : a coral reef roughly parallel to a shore and separated from it by a lagoon

bar·ring \ˈbär-iŋ\ *prep* : excluding by exception : EXCEPTING

bar·rio \ˈbär-ē-ˌō, ˈbar-\ *n, pl* **-ri·os** [Sp, fr. Ar *barrī* of the open country, fr. *barr* outside, open country] **1** : a ward, quarter, or district of a city or town in Spanish-speaking countries **2** : a Spanish-speaking quarter or neighborhood in a city or town in the U.S. esp. in the Southwest

bar·ris·ter \ˈbar-ə-stər\ *n* [[1]*bar* + *-i-* + *-ster*] : a counsel admitted to plead at the bar and undertake the public trial of causes in an English superior court — compare SOLICITOR

bar·room \ˈbär-ˌrüm, -ˌrüm\ *n* : a room or establishment whose main feature is a bar for the sale of liquor

[1]**bar·row** \ˈbar-(ˌ)ō, -ə(-w)\ *n* [ME *bergh*, fr. OE *beorg*; akin to OHG *berg* mountain, Skt *bṛhant* high] **1** : MOUNTAIN, MOUND — used only in the names of hills in England **2** : a large mound of earth or stones over the remains of the dead : TUMULUS

[2]**barrow** *n* [ME *barow*, fr. OE *bearg*; akin to OHG *barug* barrow, OE *borian* to bore] : a male hog castrated before sexual maturity

[3]**barrow** *n* [ME *barew*, fr. OE *bearwe*; akin to OE *beran* to carry — more at BEAR] **1 a** : HANDBARROW **b** : WHEELBARROW **2** : a cart with a shallow box body, two wheels, and shafts for pushing it : PUSHCART

barrow boy *n* : a boy who sells goods (as fruit or vegetables) from a barrow

bar sinister *n* **1** : a heraldic charge held to be a mark of bastardy **2** : the fact or condition of being of illegitimate birth

Bart *abbr* baronet

bar·tend·er \ˈbär-ˌten-dər\ *n* : one that serves liquor at a bar

[1]**bar·ter** \ˈbärt-ər\ *vb* [ME *bartren*, fr. MF *barater*] *vi* : to trade by exchanging one commodity for another ~ *vt* : to trade or exchange by or as if by bartering — **bar·ter·er** \-ər-ər\ *n*

[2]**barter** *n* **1** : the act or practice of carrying on trade by bartering **2** : the thing given in exchange in bartering

Bar·tho·lin's gland \ˌbärt-ᵊl-ənz-, ˌbär-thə-lənz-\ *n* [Kaspar *Bartholin* †1738 Dan physician] : either of two oval racemose glands lying one to each side of the lower part of the vagina and secreting a lubricating mucus — compare COWPER'S GLAND

bar·ti·zan \ˈbärt-ə-zən, ˌbärt-ə-ˈzan\ *n* [ME *bretasinge*, fr. *bretasce* parapet — more at BRATTICE] : a small structure (as a turret) projecting from a building and serving esp. for lookout or defense

Ba·ruch \bə-ˈrük, ˈbär-ˌük\ *n* [LL, fr. Gk *Barouch*, fr. Heb *Bārūkh*] : a homiletic book included in the Roman Catholic canon of the Old Testament and in the Protestant Apocrypha — see BIBLE table

bar·ware \ˈbär-ˌwa(ə)r, -ˌwe(ə)r\ *n* : equipment for outfitting a bar

bary·on \ˈbar-ē-ˌän\ *n* [ISV *bary-* (fr. Gk *barys* heavy) + [2]*-on* — more at GRIEVE] : any of a group of elementary particles with the same spin that have a mass equal to or greater than that of the proton — **bary·on·ic** \ˌbar-ē-ˈän-ik\ *adj*

ba·ry·ta \bə-ˈrīt-ə\ *n* [NL, modif. of Gk *barytēs* weight — more at BARITE] : any of several compounds of barium: as **a** : barium monoxide **b** : barium hydroxide **c** : BARIUM SULFATE — **ba·ryt·ic** \-ˈrit-ik\ *adj*

bar·yte \ˈba(ə)r-ˌīt, ˈbe(ə)r-\ *or* **ba·ry·tes** \bə-ˈrīt-ēz\ *var of* BARITE

bary·tone \ˈbar-ə-ˌtōn\ *var of* BARITONE

BAS *abbr* **1** bachelor of applied science **2** bachelor of arts and sciences

bas·al \ˈbā-səl, -zəl\ *adj* **1 a** : relating to, situated at, or forming the base **b** : arising from the base of a stem ⟨~ leaves⟩ **2 a** : of or relating to the foundation, base, or essence : FUNDAMENTAL **b** : of, relating to, or being essential for maintaining the fundamental vital activities of an organism : MINIMAL **c** : used for teaching beginners ⟨~ readers⟩ — **ba·sal·ly** \-ē\ *adv*

basal body *n* : a minute distinctively staining cell organelle found at the base of a flagellum or cilium and resembling a centriole in structure — called also *basal granule, kinetosome*

basal cell *n* : one of the innermost cells of the deeper epidermis of the skin

basal metabolic rate *n* : the rate at which heat is given off by an organism at complete rest

basal metabolism *n* : the turnover of energy in a fasting and resting organism using energy solely to maintain vital cellular activity, respiration, and circulation as measured by the basal metabolic rate

ba·salt \bə-ˈsölt, ˈbā-ˌ\ *n* [L *basaltes*, MS var. of *basanites* touchstone, fr. Gk *basanitēs* (*lithos*), fr. *basanos* touchstone, fr. Egypt *bḫnw*] : a dark gray to black dense to fine-grained igneous rock that consists of basic plagioclase, augite, and usu. magnetite — **ba·sal·tic** \bə-ˈsöl-tik\ *adj*

bas·cule \ˈbas-(ˌ)kyü(ə)l\ *n* [F, seesaw] : an apparatus or structure (as a bridge) in which one end is counterbalanced by the other on the principle of the seesaw or by weights

[1]**base** \ˈbās\ *n, pl* **bas·es** \ˈbā-səz\ [ME, fr. MF, fr. L *basis*, fr. Gk, step, base, fr. *bainein* to go — more at COME] **1 a** : the bottom of something considered as its support : FOUNDATION **b** (1) : the lower part of a wall, pier, or column considered as a separate architectural feature (2) : the lower part of a complete architectural design **c** : a side or face of a geometrical figure from which an altitude can be constructed; *esp* : one on which the figure stands **d** : that part of a bodily organ by which it is attached to another more central structure of the organism **2 a** : a main ingredient ⟨paint having a latex ~⟩ **b** : a supporting or carrying ingredient (as of a medicine) **3** : the fundamental part of something : GROUNDWORK **4** : the lower part of a heraldic field **5 a** : the point or line from which a start is made in an action or undertaking **b** : a line in a survey which serves as the origin for computations **c** : the locality or the installations on which a military force relies for supplies or from which it initiates operations **d** : the number with reference to which a number system or a mathematical table is constructed; *esp* : the number of units in a given digit's place that is required to give one in the next higher place **e** : ROOT 6 **6 a** : the starting place or goal in various games **b** : any one of the four stations at the corners of a baseball infield **7** : any of various typically water-soluble and acrid or brackish tasting compounds capable of reacting with an acid to form a salt that are molecules or ions able to take up a proton from an acid or substances able to give up an unshared pair of electrons to an acid **8** : a price level at which a security previously actively declining in price resists further price decline **9** : a sum of money in business which is multiplied by a rate (as of interest) or of which a percent is taken **10** : the part of a transformational grammar consisting of rules and a lexicon that generates the deep structures of a language — **based** \ˈbāst\ *adj* — **base·less** \ˈbā-sləs\ *adj*

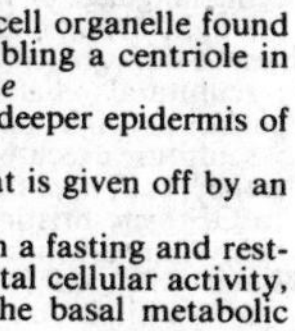

base of a column: *1* upper torus, *2* scotia, *3* lower torus, *4* plinth, *5* shaft, *6* fillets

syn BASE, BASIS, FOUNDATION, GROUND *shared meaning element* : something on which another thing is built up and by which it is supported ***ant*** top

— **off base 1** : completely or absurdly mistaken **2** : UNAWARES

[2]**base** *vt* **based; bas·ing 1** : to make, form, or serve as a base for **2** : to find a base or basis for — usu. used with *on* or *upon*

[3]**base** *adj* : constituting or serving as a base

[4]**base** *adj* [ME *bas*, fr. MF, fr. ML *bassus* short, low] **1** *archaic* : of little height **2** *obs* : low in place or position **3** *obs* : BASS **4** *archaic* : BASEBORN **5 a** : resembling a villein : SERVILE ⟨a ~ tenant⟩ **b** : held by villenage ⟨~ tenure⟩ **6 a** : being of comparatively low value and having relatively inferior properties (as resistance to corrosion) ⟨a ~ metal such as iron⟩ — compare NOBLE **b** : containing a larger than usual proportion of base metals ⟨~ silver denarii⟩ **7 a** : lacking or indicating the lack of higher qualities of mind or spirit : IGNOBLE ⟨a ~ betrayal⟩ **b** : lacking higher values : DEGRADING ⟨a drab ~ way of life⟩ **8** : of relatively little value — **base·ly** *adv* — **base·ness** *n*

syn BASE, LOW, VILE *shared meaning element* : contemptible because beneath what is expected of the average man. BASE stresses the ignoble and may suggest cruelty, treachery, greed, or grossness ⟨*base* self-centered indulgence and selfish ambition —W. R. Inge⟩ LOW may connote crafty cunning, vulgarity, or immorality and regularly implies an outraging of one's sense of decency or propriety ⟨refused to listen to such *low* talk⟩ VILE, the strongest of these words, tends to suggest disgusting depravity or filth ⟨a *vile* remark⟩ ⟨matricide, the *vilest* of crimes⟩ ***ant*** noble

base·ball \ˈbās-ˌböl\ *n, often attrib* : a game played with a bat and ball between two teams of nine players each on a large field centering on four bases that mark the course a runner must take to score; *also* : the ball used in this game

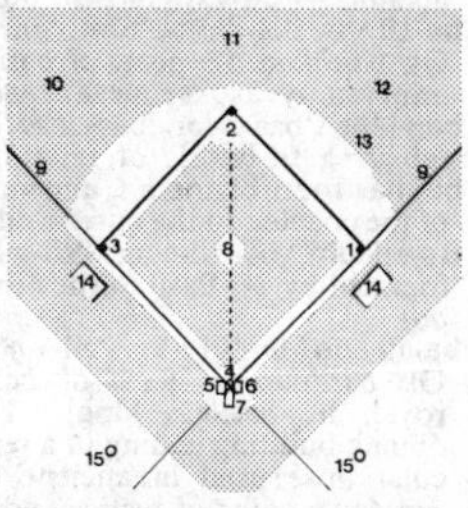

baseball field: *1* first base, *2* second base, *3* third base, *4* home base, *5* right-handed batter's box, *6* left-handed batter's box, *7* catcher's box, *8* pitcher's plate, *9* foul lines, *10* left field, *11* center field, *12* right field, *13* grass line, *14* coaches' boxes, *15* next batter's boxes

base·board \-ˌbō(ə)rd, -ˌbȯ(ə)rd\ *n* : a board situated at or forming the base of something; *specif* : a molding covering the joint of a wall and the adjoining floor

base·born \-ˈbȯ(ə)rn\ *adj* **1 a** : of humble birth : LOWLY **b** : of illegitimate birth : BASTARD **2** : MEAN, IGNOBLE

base burner *n* : a stove in which the fuel is fed from a hopper as the lower layer is consumed

base component *n* : BASE 10

base exchange *n* : a post exchange at a naval or air force base

base hit *n* : a hit in baseball that enables the batter to reach base safely without benefit of an error or fielder's choice

base·lev·el \ˈbā-ˌslev-əl\ *n* : the level below which a land surface cannot be reduced by running water

base·line \ˈbā-ˌslīn\ *n* **1** : a line serving as a base **2** : the area within which a baseball player must keep when running between bases **3** : the back line at each end of a court in various games (as tennis) **4** : FOUNDATION, BASIS 3

base·ment \ˈbā-smənt\ *n* [prob. fr. [1]*base*] **1** : the ground floor facade or interior in Renaissance architecture **2** : the part of a building that is wholly or partly below ground level **3** : the lowest or fundamental part of something **4** *chiefly New Eng* : TOILET, WASHROOM — **base·ment·less** \-ləs\ *adj*

basement membrane *n* : a usu. single-layered membrane of flat cells of connective tissue underlying the epithelial cells of many organs

ba·sen·ji \bə-ˈsen-jē, -ˈzen-\ *n* [of Bantu origin; akin to Lingala *basenji*, pl. of *mosenji* native] : any of an African breed of small compact curly-tailed chestnut-brown dogs that rarely bark

base on balls : an advance to first base given to a baseball player who during his turn at bat receives four pitches outside the strike zone that are not swung at

base path *n* : the area between the bases of a baseball field used by a base runner

base pay *n* : a rate or amount of pay for a standard work period, job, or position exclusive of additional payments or allowances

ə abut ᵊ kitten ər further a back ā bake ä cot, cart
aü out ch chin e less ē easy g gift i trip ī life
j joke ŋ sing ō flow ȯ flaw ȯi coin th thin t͟h this
ü loot u̇ foot y yet yü few yu̇ furious zh vision

base runner *n* : a baseball player of the team at bat who is on base or is attempting to reach a base — **base·run·ning** *n*

¹bash \'bash\ *vb* [origin unknown] *vt* 1 : to strike violently : HIT; *also* : to injure or damage by striking : SMASH — usu. used with *in* ~ *vi* : CRASH — **bash·er** *n*

²bash *n* 1 : a forceful blow 2 : a festive social gathering : PARTY 3 : an important sports contest 4 : TRY, ATTEMPT

ba·shaw \ba-'shȯ\ *var of* PASHA

bash·ful \'bash-fəl\ *adj* [obs. *bash* (to be abashed)] 1 : socially shy or timid; *esp* : exhibiting an immature lack of *savoir faire* 2 : characterized by, showing, or resulting from extreme sensitiveness, self-consciousness or shyness ⟨a ~ smile⟩ *syn* see SHY *ant* forward, brazen — **bash·ful·ly** \-fə-lē\ *adv* — **bash·ful·ness** \-fəl-nəs\ *n*

¹ba·sic \'bā-sik, -zik\ *adj* 1 : of, relating to, or forming the base or essence : FUNDAMENTAL 2 : constituting or serving as the basis or starting point 3 : of, relating to, containing, or having the character of a base **b** : having an alkaline reaction 4 *of rocks* : containing relatively little silica 5 : of, relating to, or made by a basic process — **ba·si·cal·ly** \-si-k(ə-)lē, -zi-\ *adv* — **ba·sic·i·ty** \bā-'sis-ət-ē\ *n*

²basic *n* 1 : something that is basic : FUNDAMENTAL ⟨the ~s of biology⟩ 2 : BASIC TRAINING

BA·SIC \'bā-sik, -zik\ *n* [*Beginner's All-purpose Symbolic Instruction Code*] : a standardized language for programming and interacting with a computer

basic process *n* : a process of making steel carried on in a furnace lined with basic material and under a slag that is dominantly basic

basic slag *n* : a slag low in silica and high in base-forming oxides that is used in the basic process of steelmaking and that is then useful as a fertilizer

basic training *n* : the initial period of training of a military recruit

ba·sid·io·my·cete \bə-ˌsid-ē-ō-'mī-ˌsēt, -ˌmī-'sēt\ *n* [deriv. of NL *basidium* + Gk *mykēt-, mykēs* fungus — more at MYC-] : any of a large class (Basidiomycetes) of higher fungi having septate hyphae, bearing spores on a basidium, and including rusts, smuts, mushrooms, and puffballs — **ba·sid·io·my·ce·tous** \-ē-ō-ˌmī-'sēt-əs\ *adj*

ba·sid·io·spore \bə-'sid-ē-ə-ˌspō(ə)r, -ˌspȯ(ə)r\ *n* [NL *basidium* + -*o-* + *spore*] : a spore produced by a basidium — **ba·sid·io·spo·rous** \-ˌsid-ē-ə-'spōr-əs, -'spȯr-; -ē-'äs-pə-rəs\ *adj*

ba·sid·i·um \bə-'sid-ē-əm\ *n, pl* -**ia** \-ē-ə\ [NL, fr. L *basis*] : a structure on a basidiomycete in which nuclear fusion occurs followed by meiosis and on which usu. four basidiospores are borne — **ba·sid·i·al** \-ē-əl\ *adj*

ba·si·fy \'bā-sə-ˌfī\ *vt* -**fied; -fy·ing** : to convert to a base or make alkaline — **ba·si·fi·ca·tion** \-ˌbā-sə-fə-'kā-shən\ *n*

ba·sil \'baz-əl, 'bas-, 'bas-, 'bāz-\ *n* [MF *basile*, fr. LL *basilicum*, fr. Gk *basilikon*, fr. neut. of *basilikos*] : any of several plants of the mint family: as **a** : SWEET BASIL **b** : BUSH BASIL

bas·i·lar \'baz-ə-lər, 'bas-\ *also* 'bāz- *or* 'bās-\ *also* **bas·i·lary** \-ˌler-ē\ *adj* [irreg. fr. *basis*] : of, relating to, or situated at the base

basilar membrane *n* : a membrane extending from the bony shelf of the cochlea to the outer wall and supporting the organ of Corti

Ba·sil·i·an \bə-'zil-ē-ən, -'sil-\ *n* : a member of the monastic order founded by St. Basil in the 4th century in Cappadocia — **Basilian** *adj*

ba·sil·i·ca \bə-'sil-i-kə, -'zil-\ *n* [L, fr. Gk *basilikē*, fr. fem. of *basilikos* royal, fr. *basileus* king] 1 : an oblong building ending in a semicircular apse used in ancient Rome esp. for a court of justice and place of public assembly 2 : an early Christian church building consisting of nave and aisles with clerestory and a large high transept from which an apse projects 3 : a Roman Catholic church given ceremonial privileges — **ba·sil·i·can** \-kən\ *adj*

bas·i·lisk \'bas-ə-ˌlisk, 'baz-\ *n* [ME, fr. L *basiliscus*, fr. Gk *basiliskos*, fr. dim. of *basileus*] 1 : a legendary reptile with fatal breath and glance 2 : any of several crested tropical American lizards (genus *Basiliscus*) related to the iguanas and noted for their ability to run on their hind legs — **basilisk** *adj*

basil thyme *n* : CALAMINT

ba·sin \'bās-ᵊn\ *n* [ME, fr. OF *bacin*, fr. LL *bacchinon*] 1 **a** : an open usu. circular vessel with sloping or curving sides used typically for holding water for washing **b** : the quantity contained in a basin 2 **a** : a dock built in a tidal river or harbor **b** : an enclosed or partly enclosed water area 3 **a** : a large or small depression in the surface of the land or in the ocean floor **b** : the entire tract of country drained by a river and its tributaries **c** : a great depression in the surface of the lithosphere occupied by an ocean 4 : a broad area of the earth beneath which the strata dip usu. from the sides toward the center — **ba·sin·al** \-ᵊn-əl\ *adj* — **ba·sined** \-ᵊnd\ *adj*

bas·i·net \ˌbas-ə-'net\ *n* [ME *bacinet*, fr. OF, dim. of *bacin*] : a light often pointed steel helmet

ba·sip·e·tal \bā-'sip-ət-ᵊl, -'zip-\ *adj* [L *basis* + *petere* to go toward — more at FEATHER] : proceeding from the apex toward the base or from above downward — **ba·sip·e·tal·ly** \-ᵊl-ē\ *adv*

ba·sis \'bā-səs\ *n, pl* **ba·ses** \-ˌsēz\ [L — more at BASE] 1 : FOUNDATION 2 : the principal component of something 3 : something on which something else is constructed or established 4 : the basic principle 5 : a set of linearly independent vectors in a vector space such that any vector in the vector space can be expressed as a linear combination of them with appropriately chosen coefficients *syn* see BASE

bask \'bask\ *vb* [ME *basken*, fr. ON *bathask*, refl. of *batha* to bathe; akin to OE *bæth* bath] *vi* 1 : to lie in or expose oneself to a pleasant warmth or atmosphere 2 : to take pleasure or derive enjoyment ~ *vt, obs* : to warm by continued exposure to heat

bas·ket \'bas-kət\ *n* [ME, prob. fr. (assumed) ONF *baskot;* akin to OF *baschoue* wooden vessel; both fr. L *bascauda* dishpan, of Celt origin; akin to MIr *basc* necklace — more at FASCIA] 1 **a** : a receptacle made of interwoven material (as osiers) **b** : any of various lightweight usu. wood containers **c** : the quantity contained in a basket 2 : something that resembles a basket esp. in shape or use 3 **a** : a net open at the bottom and suspended from a metal ring that constitutes the goal in basketball **b** : a field goal in basketball — **bas·ket·ful** \-ˌfu̇l\ *n* — **bas·ket·like** \-ˌlīk\ *adj* — **bas·ket·work** \-ˌwərk\ *n*

bas·ket·ball \-ˌbȯl\ *n, often attrib* : a usu. indoor court game between two teams of usu. five players each who score by tossing an inflated ball through a raised goal; *also* : the ball used in this game

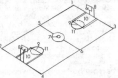

basketball court: *1-2, 3-4* sidelines, *1-3, 2-4* end lines, *5-6* division line, *7* center circle, *8* backboards and baskets, *9* free throw line, *10* lane, *11* free throw circle

basket case *n* 1 : one who has all four limbs amputated 2 : one that is totally incapacitated or inoperative

basket fern *n* 1 : MALE FERN 2 : a tropical American sword fern (*Nephrolepis pectinata*)

basket–handle arch *n* : a low-crowned elliptical arch drawn from three or more centers — see ARCH illustration

basket hilt *n* : a hilt with a basket-shaped guard to protect the hand — **bas·ket–hilt·ed** \ˌbas-kət-'hil-təd\ *adj*

Basket Maker *n* 1 : any of three stages of an ancient culture of the plateau area of southwestern U.S. that preceded and formed one cultural development with the Pueblo 2 : a member of the people who produced the Basket Maker culture

basket–of–gold *n* : a European perennial herb (*Alyssum saxatile*) widely cultivated for its grayish foliage and yellow flowers

bas·ket·ry \'bas-kə-trē\ *n, pl* -**ries** 1 : the art or craft of making baskets or objects woven like baskets 2 : objects produced by basketry

basket star *n* : an echinoderm (order Euryalida) resembling a starfish with slender complexly branched interlacing arms

basket weave *n* : a textile weave resembling the checkered pattern of a plaited basket

bas·ket·work \'bas-kət-ˌwərk\ *n* : BASKETRY 2

bas mitz·vah \ˌbä-'smits-və\ *n, often cap B&M* [Heb *bath miṣwāh,* lit., daughter of the (divine) law] 1 : a Jewish girl who at about 13 years of age assumes religious responsibilities 2 : the initiatory ceremony recognizing a girl as a bas mitzvah

ba·so·phil \'bā-sə-ˌfil, -zə-\ *or* **ba·so·phile** \-ˌfīl\ *n* : a basophilic substance or structure; *esp* : a white blood cell with basophilic granules

ba·so·phil·ia \ˌbā-sə-'fil-ē-ə, -zə-\ *n* [NL] 1 : tendency to stain with basic dyes 2 : an abnormality in which some tissue element has increased basophilia

ba·so·phil·ic \-'fil-ik\ *adj* [ISV *base* + -*o-* + -*philic*] : staining readily with basic stains

Basque \'bask\ *n* [F, fr. L *Vasco*] 1 : one of a people of obscure origin inhabiting the western Pyrenees on the Bay of Biscay 2 : the language of the Basques of unknown relationship 3 *not cap* : a tight-fitting bodice for women — **Basque** *adj*

bas–re·lief \ˌbä-ri-'lēf\ *n* [F, fr. *bas* low + *relief* raised work] 1 : sculptural relief in which the projection from the surrounding surface is slight and no part of the modeled form is undercut 2 : sculpture executed in bas-relief

¹bass \'bas\ *n, pl* **bass** *or* **bass·es** [ME *base,* alter. of OE *bærs;* akin to OE *byrst* bristle — more at BRISTLE] : any of numerous edible spiny-finned fishes (esp. families Centrarchidae and Serranidae)

²bass \'bās\ *adj* [ME *bas* base] 1 : deep or grave in tone 2 **a** : of low pitch **b** : relating to or having the range or part of a bass

³bass \'bās\ *n* 1 : a deep or grave tone : a low-pitched sound 2 **a** : the lowest part in 4-part tonal harmony **b** : the lower half of the whole vocal or instrumental tonal range — compare TREBLE **c** : the lowest adult male singing voice; *also* : a person having this voice **d** : a member of a family of instruments having the lowest range; *esp* : DOUBLE BASS

⁴bass \'bas\ *n* [alter. of *bast*] 1 : a coarse tough fiber from palms 2 : BASSWOOD l

bass clef *n* 1 : a clef placing the F below middle C on the fourth line of the staff 2 : the bass staff

bass drum *n* : a large drum having two heads and giving a booming sound of low indefinite pitch — see DRUM illustration

bass clef 1

bas·set hound \'bas-ət-\ *n* [F, *basset,* fr. MF, fr. *basset* short, fr. *bas* low — more at BASE] : any of an old French breed of short-legged slow-moving hunting dogs with very long ears and crooked front legs — called also *basset*

bass fiddle *n* : the double bass esp. as used in jazz orchestras

bass horn *n* : TUBA

bas·si·net \ˌbas-ə-'net\ *n* [prob. modif. of F *barcelonnette,* dim. of *berceau* cradle] 1 : a baby's basketlike bed (as of wickerwork or plastic) often with a hood over one end 2 : a perambulator that resembles a bassinet

bass·ist \'bā-səst\ *n* : a double bass player

bas·so \'bas-(ˌ)ō, 'bäs-\ *n, pl* **bassos** *or* **bas·si** \'bäs-ˌē\ [It, fr. ML *bassus,* fr. *bassus* short, low] : a bass singer; *esp* : an operatic bass

bas·soon \bə-'sün, ba-\ *n* [F *basson,* fr. It *bassone,* fr. *basso*] : a tenor or bass double-reed woodwind instrument having a long

U-shaped conical tube connected to the mouthpiece by a thin metal tube and a usual range two octaves lower than that of the oboe — **bas·soon·ist** \-'sü-nəst\ *n*

bas·so pro·fun·do \bas(,)ō-prə-'fən-(,)dō, ,bäs-, -'fün-\ *n, pl* **basso profun·dos** [It, lit., deep bass] **1** : a deep heavy bass voice with an exceptionally low range **2** : a person having a basso profundo voice

bas·so-re·lie·vo *also* **bas·so-ri·lie·vo** \bas-(,)ō-ri-'lē-(,)vō, ,bäs-(,)ō-rēl-'yā-(,)vō\ *n* [It *bassorilievo*, fr. *basso* low + *rilievo* relief] : BAS-RELIEF

bass viol *n* **1** : the largest member of the viol family : VIOLA DA GAMBA **2** : DOUBLE BASS

bassoon

bass·wood \'bas-,wůd\ *n* **1** : any of several New World lindens; *esp* : LINDEN 1b **2** : the straight-grained white wood of a bass-wood

bast \'bast\ *n* [ME, fr. OE *bæst*; akin to OHG & ON *bast*] **1** : PHLOEM **2** : a strong woody fiber obtained chiefly from the phloem of plants and used esp. in cordage, matting, and fabrics

¹bas·tard \'bas-tərd\ *n* [ME, fr. OF] **1** : an illegitimate child **2** : something that is spurious, irregular, inferior, or of questionable origin **3** a : an offensive or disagreeable person — used as a generalized term of abuse **b** : MAN, FELLOW — **bas·tard·ly** *adj*

²bastard *adj* **1** : ILLEGITIMATE **2** : of inferior breed or stock : MONGREL **3** : of abnormal shape or irregular size **4** : of a kind similar to but inferior to or less typical than some standard ⟨~ measles⟩ **5** : lacking genuineness or authority : FALSE

bas·tard·ize \'bas-tər-,dīz\ *vt* **-ized; -iz·ing 1** : to declare or prove to be a bastard **2** : to reduce from a higher to a lower state or condition : DEBASE — **bas·tard·iza·tion** \,bas-tərd-ə-'zā-shən\ *n*

bastard wing *n* : the process of a bird's wing corresponding to the thumb and bearing a few short quills — called also *alula*

bas·tar·dy \'bas-tərd-ē\ *n, pl* **-tard·ies 1** : the quality or state of being a bastard : ILLEGITIMACY **2** : the begetting of an illegitimate child

¹baste \'bāst\ *vt* **bast·ed; bast·ing** [ME *basten*, fr. MF *bastir*, of Gmc origin; akin to OHG *besten* to patch; akin to OE *bæst* bast] : to sew with long loose stitches in order to hold something in place temporarily — **bast·er** *n*

²baste *vt* **bast·ed; bast·ing** [origin unknown] : to moisten (as meat) at intervals with a liquid (as melted butter, fat, or pan drippings) esp. during cooking — **bast·er** *n*

³baste *vt* **bast·ed; bast·ing** [prob. fr. ON *beysta*; akin to OE *bēatan* to beat] **1** : to beat severely or soundly : THRASH **2** : to scold vigorously : BERATE

bas·tile *or* **bas·tile** \ba-'stē(ə)l\ *n* [F *bastille*, fr. the *Bastille*, tower in Paris used as a prison] : PRISON, JAIL

Bastille Day *n* : July 14 observed in France as a national holiday in commemoration of the fall of the Bastille in 1789

¹bas·ti·na·do \,bas-tə-'nād-(,)ō, -'näd-\ *or* **bas·ti·nade** \,bas-tə-'nād, -'näd\ *n, pl* **-na·does** *or* **-nades** [Sp *bastonada*, fr. *bastón* stick, fr. LL *bastum*] **1** : a blow with a stick or cudgel **2** a : a beating esp. with a stick **b** : a punishment consisting of beating the soles of the feet with a stick **3** : STICK, CUDGEL

²bastinado *vt* **-doed; -do·ing** : to subject to repeated blows

¹bast·ing \'bā-stiŋ\ *n* **1** : the action of a sewer who bastes **2** a : the thread used by a baster **b** : the stitching made by a baster

²basting *n* **1** : the action of one that bastes food **2** : the liquid used by a baster

³basting *n* : a severe beating

bas·tion \'bas-chən\ *n* [MF, fr. *bastille* fortress, modif. of OProv *bastida*, fr. *bastir* to build, of Gmc origin; akin to OHG *besten* to patch] **1** : a projecting part of a fortification **2** : a fortified area or position **3** : something that is considered a stronghold : BULWARK — **bas·tioned** \-chənd\ *adj*

bast ray *n* : PHLOEM RAY

Ba·su·to \bə-'süt-(,)ō\ *n, pl* **Basuto** *or* **Basutos** : one of the Bantu-speaking people of Basutoland

¹bat \'bat\ *n* [ME, fr. OE *batt*, prob. of Celt origin; akin to Gaulish *anda*bata, a gladiator — more at BATTLE] **1** : a stout solid stick : CLUB **2** : a sharp blow : STROKE **3** a : a wooden implement used for hitting the ball in various games **b** : a racket used in various games (as squash) **c** : the short whip used by a jockey **4** a : BATSMAN **b** : a turn at batting — usu. used in the phrase *at bat* **5** *or* **batt** : BATTING **6** *Brit* : rate of speed : GAIT **7** : BINGE — **off one's own bat** : through one's own efforts — **off the bat** : without delay : IMMEDIATELY

²bat *vb* **bat·ted; bat·ting** *vt* **1** : to strike or hit with or as if with a bat **2** a : to advance (a base runner) by batting **b** : to have a batting average of **3** : to compose esp. in a casual, careless, or hurried manner — usu. used with *out* **4** : to discuss at length : consider in detail ~ *vi* **1** a : to strike or hit a ball with a bat **b** : to take one's turn at bat **2** : to wander aimlessly — **bat the breeze** : CHAT 2

³bat *n* [alter. of ME *bakke*, prob. of Scand origin; akin to OSw *natt*bakka bat] : any of an order (Chiroptera) of nocturnal placental flying mammals with forelimbs modified to form wings

⁴bat *vt* **bat·ted; bat·ting** [prob. alter. of ²*bate*] : to wink esp. in surprise or emotion ⟨never *batted* an eye⟩

BAT *abbr* bachelor of arts in teaching

bat·boy \'bat-,bȯi\ *n* : a boy employed to look after the equipment (as bats) of a baseball team

¹batch \'bach\ *n* [ME *bache*; akin to OE *bacan* to bake] **1** : the quantity baked at one time : BAKING **2** a : the quantity of material prepared or required for one operation; *specif* : a mixture of raw materials ready for fusion into glass **b** : the quantity produced at one operation **c** : a group of jobs to be run on a computer at one time with the same program ⟨~ processing⟩ **3** : a group of persons or things : LOT

²batch *vt* : to bring together or process as a batch — **batch·er** *n*

³batch *var of* BACH

¹bate \'bāt\ *vb* **bat·ed; bat·ing** [ME *baten*, short for *abaten* to abate] *vt* **1** : to reduce the force or intensity of : RESTRAIN ⟨with *bated* breath⟩ **2** : to take away : DEDUCT **3** *archaic* : to lower esp. in amount or estimation **4** *archaic* : BLUNT ~ *vi, obs* : DIMINISH, DECREASE

²bate *vi* **bat·ed; bat·ing** [ME *baten*, fr. MF *batre* to beat — more at DEBATE] *of a falcon* : to beat the wings impatiently

ba·teau \ba-'tō\ *n, pl* **ba·teaux** \-'tō(z)\ [CanF, fr. F, fr. OF *batel*, fr. OE *bāt* boat — more at BOAT] : any of various small craft; *esp* : a flat-bottomed boat with raked bow and stern and flaring sides

Bates·ian mimicry \,bāt-sē-ən-\ *n* [Henry Walter *Bates* †1892 E naturalist] : resemblance of an innocuous species to another that is protected from predators by repellent qualities (as unpalatability)

bat·fish \'bat-,fish\ *n* : any of several fishes with winglike processes: as **a** : any of several flattened pediculate fishes (as a common West Indian form *Ogcocephalus vespertilio*) **b** : a flying gurnard (*Dactylopterus volitans*) of the Atlantic **c** : a California stingray (*Aetobatus californicus*)

bat·fowl \-,faůl\ *vi* : to catch birds at night by blinding them with a light and knocking them down with a stick or netting them

¹bath \'bath, 'båth\ *n, pl* **baths** \'bathz, 'bäthz, 'bäths, 'båths\ [ME, fr. OE *bæth*; akin to OHG *bad* bath, OE *bacan* to bake] **1** : a washing or soaking (as in water or steam) of all or part of the body **2** a : water used for bathing **b** (1) : a contained liquid for a special purpose (2) : a receptacle holding the liquid **c** (1) : a medium for regulating the temperature of something placed in or on it (2) : a vessel containing this medium **3** a : BATHROOM **b** : a building containing an apartment or a series of rooms designed for bathing **c** : SPA — usu. used in pl. **4** : the quality or state of being covered with a liquid **5** : BATHTUB

²bath *vt, Brit* : to give a bath to ~ *vi, Brit* : to take a bath

³bath *n* [Heb] : an ancient Hebrew liquid measure corresponding to the ephah of dry measure

bath- *or* **batho-** *comb form* [ISV, fr. Gk *bathos*, fr. *bathys* deep — more at BATHY-] : depth ⟨bathometer⟩

bath chair \'bath-, 'bäth-\ *n, often cap B* [*Bath*, England] : a hooded and sometimes glassed wheeled chair used esp. by invalids; *broadly* : WHEELCHAIR

¹bathe \'bāth\ *vb* **bathed; bath·ing** [ME *bathen*, fr. OE *bathian*; akin to OE *bæth* bath] *vt* **1** : to wash in a liquid (as water) **2** : MOISTEN, WET **3** : to apply water or a liquid medicament to **4** : to flow along the edge of : LAVE **5** : to suffuse with or as if with light ~ *vi* **1** : to take a bath **2** : to go swimming **3** : to become immersed or absorbed — **bath·er** \'bā-thər\ *n*

²bathe *n* **1** *Brit* : ¹BATH **2** *Brit* : SWIM, DIP

ba·thet·ic \bə-'thet-ik, bā-\ *adj* [*bathos* + *-etic* (as in *pathetic*)] : characterized by bathos — **ba·thet·i·cal·ly** \-i-k(ə-)lē\ *adv*

bath·house \'bath-,haůs, 'bäth-\ *n* **1** : a building equipped for bathing **2** : a building containing dressing rooms for bathers

Bath·i·nette \,bath-ə-'net, ,båth-\ *trademark* — used for a portable bathtub for babies

bathing beauty *n* : a woman in a bathing suit who is a contestant in a beauty contest

bathing suit *n* : SWIMSUIT

bath mat *n* : a usu. washable mat used in a bathroom

batho·lith \'bath-ə-,lith\ *n* [ISV] : a great mass of intruded igneous rock that for the most part stopped in its rise a considerable distance below the surface — **batho·lith·ic** \,bath-ə-'lith-ik\ *adj*

ba·thom·e·ter \bə-'thäm-ət-ər\ *n* : an instrument for measuring depths in water

ba·thos \'bā-,thäs\ *n* [Gk, lit., depth] **1** a : the sudden appearance of the commonplace in otherwise elevated matter or style **b** : ANTICLIMAX, LETDOWN **2** : exceptional commonplaceness : TRITENESS **3** : insincere or overdone pathos : SENTIMENTALISM **syn** see PATHOS

bath·robe \'bath-,rōb, 'bäth-\ *n* : a loose usu. absorbent robe worn before and after bathing or as a dressing gown

bath·room \-,rüm, -,rům\ *n* : a room containing a bathtub and shower and usu. a washbowl and toilet

bath salts *n* : a usu. colored crystalline compound for perfuming and softening bathwater

bath·tub \-,təb\ *n* : a usu. fixed tub for bathing — **bath·tub·ful** \-,fůl\ *n*

bathtub gin *n* : a usu. strong liquor often made illicitly under makeshift conditions from spirits flavored with essential oils

bath·wa·ter \'bath-,wȯt-ər, 'bäth-\ *n* : water for a bath

bathy- *comb form* [ISV, fr. Gk, fr. *bathys* deep; akin to Skt *gāhate* he dives into] **1** : deep : depth ⟨bathyal⟩ **2** : deep-sea ⟨bathysphere⟩

bathy·al \'bath-ē-əl\ *adj* : DEEP-SEA

bathy·met·ric \,bath-i-'me-trik\ *adj* : of or relating to bathymetry — **bathy·met·ri·cal** \-tri-kəl\ *adj* — **bathy·met·ri·cal·ly** \-tri-k(ə-)lē\ *adv*

ba·thym·e·try \bə-'thim-ə-trē\ *n, pl* **-tries** [ISV] : the measurement of depths of water in oceans, seas, and lakes

bathy·pe·lag·ic \,bath-i-pə-'laj-ik\ *adj* [*bathy-* + *pelagic*] : of, relating to, or living in the ocean depths esp. between 2000 and 12,000 feet

bathy·scaphe \'bath-i-,skaf, -,skäf\ *also* **bathy·scaph** \-,skaf\ *n* [ISV *bathy-* + Gk *skaphē* light boat] : a navigable submersible ship for deep-sea exploration having a spherical watertight cabin attached to its underside

bathy·sphere \-,sfi(ə)r\ *n* : a strongly built steel diving sphere for deep-sea observation

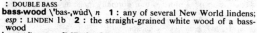

ə abut	ᵊ kitten	ər further	a back	ā bake	ä cot, cart
aů out	ch chin	e less	ē easy	g gift	i trip	ī life
j joke	ŋ sing	ō flow	ȯ flaw	ȯi coin	th thin	th this
ü loot	ů foot	y yet	yü few	yů furious	zh vision

ba·tik \bə-ˈtēk, ˈbat-ik\ *n* [Malay] **1 a :** an Indonesian method of hand-printing textiles by coating with wax the parts not to be dyed **b :** a design so executed **2 :** a fabric printed by batik
bat·ing \ˈbāt-iŋ\ *prep* **:** with the exception of **:** EXCEPTING
ba·tiste \bə-ˈtēst, ba-\ *n* [F] **:** a fine soft sheer fabric of plain weave made of various fibers
bat·man \ˈbat-mən\ *n* [deriv. of Gk *bastazein* to carry] **:** an orderly of a British military officer
bat mitz·vah \bät-ˈmits-və\ *often cap B&M, var of* BAS MITZVAH
ba·ton \bə-ˈtän, ba-, -ˈtōⁿ *also* ˈbat-ᵊn\ *n* [F *bâton,* fr. OF *baston,* fr. LL *bastum* stick] **1 :** CUDGEL, TRUNCHEON **2 :** a staff borne as a symbol of office **3 :** a narrow heraldic bend **4 :** a stick or wand with which a leader directs a band or orchestra **5 :** a hollow cylinder carried by each member of a relay team and passed to the succeeding runner **6 :** a hollow metal rod with a ball usu. at one end that is carried by a drum major or drum majorette
ba·tra·chi·an \bə-ˈtrā-kē-ən\ *n* [deriv. of Gk *batrachos* frog] **:** FROG, TOAD, SALIENTIAN; *broadly* **:** a vertebrate amphibian — **batrachian** *adj*
ba·tracho·tox·in \bə-ˌtrak-ə-ˈtäk-sən, ˌba-trə-kō-\ *n* [ISV *batracho-* (fr. Gk *batrachos* frog) + *toxin*] **:** a very powerful steroid venom ($C_{31}H_{42}N_2O_6$) extracted from the skin of a So. American frog (*Phyllobates aurotaenia*)
bats·man \ˈbat-smən\ *n* **:** a batter esp. in cricket
batt *var of* BAT
bat·tai·lous \ˈbat-ᵊl-əs\ *adj* [ME *bataillous,* fr. MF *bataillos,* fr. *bataille* battle] *archaic* **:** ready for battle **:** WARLIKE
bat·ta·lia \bə-ˈtāl-yə, -ˈtal-\ *n* [It *battaglia*] **1** *obs* **:** a large body of men in battle array **2** *archaic* **:** order of battle
bat·tal·ion \bə-ˈtal-yən\ *n* [MF *bataillon,* fr. OIt *battaglione,* aug. of *battaglia* company of soldiers, battle, fr. LL *battalia* combat — more at BATTLE] **1 :** a considerable body of troops organized to act together **:** ARMY **2 :** a military unit composed of a headquarters and two or more companies, batteries, or similar units **3 :** a large group ⟨a ~ of instructors teaching elementary composition —Douglas Bush⟩
batteau *var of* BATEAU
bat·te·ment \ˌbat-(ə-)ˈmäⁿ\ *n* [F, fr. *battre* to beat (fr. L *battuere*) + *-ment* — more at BATTLE] **:** a ballet movement in which the foot is extended in any direction usu. followed by a beat against the supporting foot
¹bat·ten \ˈbat-ᵊn\ *vb* **bat·tened; bat·ten·ing** \ˈbat-niŋ, -ᵊn-iŋ\ [prob. fr. ON *batna* to improve] *vi* **1 a :** to grow fat **b :** to feed gluttonously **2 :** to grow prosperous esp. at the expense of another ~ *vt* **:** FATTEN
²batten *n* [F *bâton*] **1 a** *Brit* **:** a piece of lumber used esp. for flooring **b :** a thin narrow strip of lumber used esp. to seal or reinforce a joint **2 :** a strip, bar, or support resembling or used similarly to a batten
³batten *vt* **bat·tened; bat·ten·ing** \ˈbat-niŋ, -ᵊn-iŋ\ **:** to furnish or fasten with battens — often used with *down*
¹bat·ter \ˈbat-ər\ *vb* [ME *bateren,* prob. freq. of *batten* to bat, fr. *bat*] *vt* **1 a :** to beat with successive blows so as to bruise, shatter, or demolish **b :** BOMBARD **2 :** to subject to strong, overwhelming, or repeated attack **3 :** to wear or damage by hard usage or blows ⟨a ~*ed* old hat⟩ ~ *vi* **:** to strike heavily and repeatedly **:** BEAT ***syn*** see MAIM
²batter *n* [ME *bater,* prob. fr. *bateren*] **1 :** a mixture that consists of flour, liquid, and other ingredients and is thin enough to pour or drop from a spoon **2 :** an instance of battering **3 :** a damaged area on a printing surface
³batter *vt* [origin unknown] **:** to give a receding upward slope to (as a wall)
⁴batter *n* **:** a receding upward slope of the outer face of a structure
⁵batter *n* **:** one that bats; *esp* **:** the player whose turn it is to bat
bat·te·rie \ˌbat-ə-ˈrē\ *n* [F, lit., beating — more at BATTERY] **:** a ballet movement consisting of beating together the feet or calves of the legs during a leap
battering ram *n* **1 :** a military siege engine consisting of a large wooden beam with a head of iron used in ancient times to beat down the walls of a besieged place **2 :** a heavy metal bar with handles used (as by firemen) to batter down doors and walls
bat·tery \ˈbat-ə-rē, ˈba-trē\ *n, pl* **-ter·ies** [MF *batterie,* fr. OF, fr. *battre* to beat, fr. L *battuere* — more at BATTLE] **1 a :** the act of battering or beating **b :** the unlawful beating or use of force on a person without his consent — compare ASSAULT 2a **2 a :** a grouping of artillery pieces for tactical purposes **b :** the guns of a warship **3 :** an artillery unit in the army equivalent to a company **4 a :** a combination of apparatus for producing a single electrical effect **b :** a group of two or more cells connected together to furnish electric current; *also* **:** a single cell that furnishes electric current ⟨a flashlight ~⟩ **5 a :** a number of similar articles, items, or devices arranged, connected, or used together **:** SET, SERIES **b :** an impressive or imposing group **:** ARRAY **6 :** the position of readiness of a gun for firing **7 :** the pitcher and catcher of a baseball team
bat·ting \ˈbat-iŋ\ *n* **1 a :** the act of one who bats **b :** the use of or ability with a bat **2 :** layers or sheets of raw cotton or wool used for lining quilts or for stuffing or packaging
batting average *n* **1 :** a ratio (as a rate per thousand) of base hits to official times at bat for a baseball player **2 :** a record of achievement or accomplishment ⟨an almost unbelievably high *batting average* in gaining and holding the friendship of the home folk —G. S. Perry⟩
¹bat·tle \ˈbat-ᵊl\ *n, often attrib* [ME *batel,* fr. OF *bataille* battle, fortifying tower, battalion, fr. LL *battalia* combat, alter. of *battualia* fencing exercises, fr. L *battuere* to beat, of Celt origin; akin to Gaulish anda*bata,* a gladiator; akin to L *fatuus* foolish, Russ *bat* cudgel] **1 :** a general encounter between armies, ships of war, or airplanes **2 :** a combat between two persons **3** *archaic* **:** BATTALION **4 :** an extended contest, struggle, or controversy
syn BATTLE, ENGAGEMENT, ACTION *shared meaning element* **:** a meeting between opposing forces
²battle *vb* **bat·tled; bat·tling** \ˈbat-liŋ, -ᵊl-iŋ\ *vi* **1 :** to engage in battle **:** FIGHT **2 :** to contend with full strength, vigor, craft, or resources **:** STRUGGLE ~ *vt* **1 :** to fight against **2 :** to force (as one's way) by battling — **bat·tler** \-lər, -ᵊl-ər\ *n*
³battle *vt* **bat·tled; bat·tling** [ME *batailen,* fr. MF *bataillier* to fortify, fr. OF, fr. *bataille*] *archaic* **:** to fortify with battlements
bat·tle–ax \ˈbat-ᵊl-ˌaks\ *n* **1 :** a broadax formerly used as a weapon of war **2 :** a quarrelsome domineering woman
battle cruiser *n* **:** a large heavily armed warship that is lighter, faster, and more maneuverable than a battleship
battle cry *n* **:** WAR CRY
battle fatigue *n* **:** COMBAT FATIGUE — **bat·tle–fa·tigued** *adj*
bat·tle·field \ˈbat-ᵊl-ˌfēld\ *n* **1 :** a place where a battle is fought **2 :** an area of conflict
bat·tle·front \-ˌfrənt\ *n* **:** the military sector in which actual combat takes place
bat·tle·ground \-ˌgrau̇nd\ *n* **:** BATTLEFIELD
battle group *n* **:** a military unit normally made up of five companies
bat·tle·ment \ˈbat-ᵊl-mənt\ *n* [ME *batelment,* fr. MF *bataille*] **:** a parapet with open spaces that surmounts a wall and is used for defense or decoration — **bat·tle·ment·ed** \-ˌment-əd\ *adj*

battlements: *1* crenels, *2* merlons, *3* machicolations

battle royal *n, pl* **battles royal** *or* **battle royals** **1 a :** a fight participated in by more than two combatants; *esp* **:** one in which the last man in the ring or on his feet is declared the winner **b :** a violent struggle **2 :** a heated dispute
bat·tle·ship \ˈbat-ᵊl-ˌship\ *n* [short for *line-of-battle ship*] **:** a warship of the largest and most heavily armed and armored class
bat·tle·wag·on \-ˌwag-ən\ *n* **:** BATTLESHIP
bat·tu \ba-ˈt(y)ü\ *adj* [F, fr. pp. of *battre* to beat] *of a ballet movement* **:** performed with a striking together of the legs
bat·tue \ba-ˈt(y)ü\ *n* [F, fr. *battre* to beat] **:** the beating of woods and bushes to flush game; *also* **:** a hunt in which this procedure is used
bat·ty \ˈbat-ē\ *adj* **bat·ti·er; -est** **1 :** of, relating to, or resembling a bat **2 :** mentally unstable **:** CRAZY — **bat·ti·ness** *n*
bau·ble \ˈbȯ-bəl, ˈbäb-əl\ *n* [ME *babel,* fr. MF] **1 :** TRINKET **2 :** a fool's scepter **3 :** TRIFLE
Bau·cis \ˈbȯ-səs\ *n* [L, fr. Gk *Baukis*] **:** the wife of Philemon who with him presided over a temple of Zeus
baud \ˈbȯd, ˈbōd\ *n, pl* **baud** *also* **bauds** [*baud* (telegraphic transmission speed unit), fr. J. M. E. *Baudot* †1903 F inventor] **:** a variable unit of data transmission speed usu. equal to one bit per second
bau·drons \ˈbȯd-rənz, ˈbȯth-\ *n* [ME] *Scot* **:** CAT
Bau·haus \ˈbau̇-ˌhau̇s\ *adj* [G *Bauhaus,* lit., architecture house, school founded by Gropius] **:** of, relating to, or influenced by a school of design noted esp. for a program that synthesized technology, craftsmanship, and design aesthetics
baulk *chiefly Brit var of* BALK
Bau·mé \bō-ˈmā\ *adj* [Antoine *Baumé*] **:** being, calibrated in accordance with, or according to either of two arbitrary hydrometer scales for liquids lighter than water or for liquids heavier than water that indicate specific gravity in degrees
baux·ite \ˈbȯk-ˌsīt, ˈbäk-\ *n* [F *bauxite,* fr. Les *Baux,* near Arles, France] **:** an impure mixture of earthy hydrous aluminum oxides and hydroxides that commonly contains similar compounds of iron and occas. of manganese, usu. has a concretionary or oolitic structure, and is the principal source of aluminum — **baux·it·ic** \bȯk-ˈsit-ik, bäk-\ *adj*
Bav *abbr* Bavaria; Bavarian
Ba·var·i·an \bə-ˈver-ē-ən, -ˈvar-\ *n* **1 :** a native or inhabitant of Bavaria **2 :** the High German dialect of Bavaria and Austria — **Bavarian** *adj*
baw·bee *or* **bau·bee** \ˈbȯ-(ˌ)bē, bȯ-ˈ\ *n* [prob. fr. Alexander Orrok, laird of Sille*bawbe fl* 1538 Sc master of the mint] **1 a :** any of various Scottish coins of small value **b :** an English halfpenny **2 :** TRIFLE
baw·cock \ˈbȯ-ˌkäk\ *n* [F *beau coq,* fr. *beau* fine + *coq* fellow, cock] *archaic* **:** a fine fellow
bawd \ˈbȯd\ *n* [ME *bawde*] **1** *obs* **:** PANDER **2 a :** one who keeps a house of prostitution **:** MADAM **b :** PROSTITUTE
bawd·ry \ˈbȯ-drē\ *n* [ME *bawderie,* fr. *bawde*] **1** *obs* **:** UNCHASTITY **2 :** suggestive, coarse, or obscene language
¹bawdy \ˈbȯd-ē\ *adj* **bawd·i·er; -est** [*bawd*] **1 :** OBSCENE, LEWD **2 :** boisterously or humorously indecent — **bawd·i·ly** \ˈbȯd-ᵊl-ē\ *adv* — **bawd·i·ness** \ˈbȯd-ē-nəs\ *n*
²bawdy *n* [prob. fr. ¹*bawdy*] **:** BAWDRY 2
¹bawl \ˈbȯl\ *vb* [ME *baulen,* prob. of Scand origin; akin to Icel *baula* to low] *vi* **1 :** to cry out loudly and unrestrainedly **:** YELL, BELLOW **2 :** to cry loudly **:** WAIL ~ *vt* **:** to cry out at the top of one's voice — **bawl·er** *n*
²bawl *n* **:** a loud prolonged cry **:** OUTCRY
bawl out *vt* **:** to reprimand loudly or severely
¹bay \ˈbā\ *adj* [ME, fr. MF *bai,* fr. L *badius;* akin to OIr *buide* yellow] **:** reddish brown ⟨a ~ mare⟩
²bay *n* **1 :** a bay-colored animal; *specif* **:** a horse with a bay-colored body and black mane, tail, and points — compare ¹CHESTNUT 4, ¹SORREL 1a **2 :** a reddish brown
³bay *n* [ME, berry, fr. MF *baie,* fr. L *baca*] **1 a :** LAUREL 1 **b :** any of several shrubs or trees (as of the genera *Magnolia, Myrica,* and *Gordonia*) resembling the laurel **2 a :** a garland or crown esp. of laurel given as a prize for victory or excellence **b :** HONOR, FAME — usu. used in pl.
⁴bay *n* [ME, fr. MF *baee* opening, fr. OF, fr. fem. of *baé,* pp. of *baer* to gape, yawn — more at ABEYANCE] **1 :** a principal compartment of the walls, roof, or other part of a building or of the whole building **2 :** a main division of a structure: as **a :** a compartment in a

barn **b** : BAY WINDOW **c** : the forward part of a ship on each side between decks often used as a ship's hospital **d** (1) : a longitudinal part of an elongated aircraft structure lying between two adjacent transverse members or walls (2) : any of several compartments in the fuselage of an airplane **e** : a compartment (as in a service station) for a car **3** : a vertical support on which various pieces of electronic apparatus are mounted

⁵bay *vb* [ME *baien, abaien,* fr. OF *abaiier,* of imit. origin] *vi* **1** : to bark with prolonged tones **2** : to cry out : SHOUT ~ *vt* **1** : to bark at **2** : to bring to bay **3** : to pursue with barking **4** : to utter in deep prolonged tones

⁶bay *n* **1** : the position of one unable to retreat and forced to face danger ⟨brought his quarry to ~⟩ **2** : the position of one checked ⟨police kept the rioters at ~⟩ **3** : a baying of dogs

⁷bay *n, often attrib* [ME *baye,* fr. MF *baie*] **1** : an inlet of the sea or other body of water usu. smaller than a gulf **2** : a small body of water set off from the main body **3** : any of various terrestrial formations resembling a bay of the sea

ba·ya·dere \ˈbī-ə-ˌdi(ə)r, -ˌde(ə)r\ *n* [F *bayadère* Hindu dancing girl] : a fabric with horizontal stripes in strongly contrasted colors

bay antler \ˈbā-\ *n* [earlier *bes antler,* fr. ME *bes-* secondary (fr. MF, fr. L *bis-* twice) + E *antler*] : the second tine from the base of a stag's antler — see ANTLER illustration

bay·ber·ry \ˈbā-ˌber-ē\ *n* **1** : a West Indian tree (*Pimenta racemosa*) of the myrtle family yielding a yellow aromatic oil **2 a** : a hardy shrub (*Myrica pensylvanica*) of coastal eastern No. America bearing dense clusters of small globular nuts covered with grayish white wax; *also* : WAX MYRTLE **b** : the fruit of a bayberry

Bayes·ian \ˈbā-zē-ən, -zhən\ *adj* [Thomas *Bayes* †1761 E mathematician] : being or relating to a theory (as of decision or statistical inference) in which probabilities are associated with individual events or statements and not merely with sequences of events (as in frequency theories)

bay leaf *n* : the dried leaf of the European laurel used in cooking

¹bay·o·net \ˈbā-ə-nət, -ˌnet, ˌbā-ə-ˈnet\ *n* [F *baïonnette,* fr. *Bayonne,* France] : a steel blade attached at the muzzle end of a shoulder arm and used in hand-to-hand combat

²bayonet *vb* **-net·ed** *also* **-net·ted; -net·ing** *also* **net·ting** *vt* **1** : to stab with a bayonet **2** : to compel or drive by or as if by the bayonet ~ *vi* : to use a bayonet

bay·ou \ˈbī-(ˌ)(y)ō, -(ˌ)(y)ü, -(y)ə\ *n* [LaF, fr. Choctaw *bayuk*] **1** : a creek, secondary watercourse, or minor river that is tributary to another body of water **2** : any of various usu. marshy or sluggish bodies of water

bay rum *n* : a fragrant cosmetic and medicinal liquid distilled from the leaves of the West Indian bayberry or usu. prepared from essential oils, alcohol, and water

Bay Stat·er \ˈbā-ˌstāt-ər\ *n* : a native or resident of Massachusetts — used as a nickname

bay window *n* **1** : a window or series of windows forming a bay or recess in a room and projecting outward from the wall **2** : POTBELLY

ba·zaar \bə-ˈzär\ *n* [Per *bāzār*] **1** : an Oriental market consisting of rows of shops or stalls selling miscellaneous goods **2 a** : a place for the sale of goods **b** : DEPARTMENT STORE **3** : a fair for the sale of articles esp. for charitable purposes

ba·zoo·ka \bə-ˈzü-kə\ *n* [*bazooka* (a crude musical instrument made of pipes and a funnel)] : a light portable shoulder weapon consisting of an open-breech smoothbore firing tube that launches armor-piercing rockets

¹BB \ˈbē-(ˌ)bē\ *n* **1** : a shot pellet 0.18 inch in diameter for use in a shotgun cartridge **2** : a shot pellet 0.175 inch in diameter for use in a gun that propels shot by compressed air produced by a plunger operated by a spring

²BB *abbr* **1** bachelor of business **2** ball bearing **3** base on balls **4** blue book **5** B'nai B'rith

BBA *abbr* bachelor of business administration

B battery *n* : an electric battery connected in the plate circuit of an electron tube to cause flow of electron current in the tube

BBB *abbr* Better Business Bureau

BBC *abbr* British Broadcasting Corporation

BBE *abbr* bachelor of business education

bbl *abbr* barrel; barrels

BC *abbr* **1** bachelor of commerce **2** before Christ — often printed in small capitals **3** British Columbia

BCD *abbr* binary-coded decimal

BCE *abbr* **1** bachelor of chemical engineering **2** bachelor of civil engineering

BCG vaccine \ˌbē-(ˌ)sē-ˈjē-\ *n* [bacillus, Calmette-Guérin (an attenuated strain of tubercle bacilli), fr. Albert *Calmette* †1933 and Camille *Guérin* †1961 F bacteriologists] : a vaccine prepared from a living attenuated strain of tubercle bacilli and used to vaccinate human beings against tuberculosis

BCh *abbr* bachelor of chemistry

BChE *abbr* bachelor of chemical engineering

BCL *abbr* **1** bachelor of canon law **2** bachelor of civil law

bcn *abbr* beacon

B complex *n* : VITAMIN B COMPLEX

BCS *abbr* **1** bachelor of chemical science **2** bachelor of commercial science

BCSE *abbr* Board of Civil Service Examiners

BC soil \ˈbē-ˈsē-\ *n* : a soil whose profile has only B-horizons and C-horizons

bd *abbr* **1** board **2** bound **3** boundary **4** bundle

BD *abbr* **1** bachelor of divinity **2** bank draft **3** barrels per day **4** bills discounted **5** bomb disposal **6** brought down

BDA *abbr* **1** bachelor of domestic arts **2** bachelor of dramatic art

bdel·li·um \ˈdel-ē-əm\ *n* [ME, fr. L, fr. Gk *bdellion*] : a gum resin similar to myrrh obtained from various trees (genus *Commiphora*) of the East Indies and Africa

bdel·lo·vi·brio \ˌdel-ō-ˈvib-rē-ˌō\ *n* [NL, genus name, fr. Gk *bdella* leech + NL *vibrio*] : a bacterium (genus *Bdellovibrio*) that is parasitic on other bacteria

bd ft *abbr* board foot

bdl *or* **bdle** *abbr* bundle

bdrm *abbr* bedroom

be \(ˈ)bē\ *vb, past 1st & 3d sing* **was** \(ˈ)wəz, ˈwäz\; *2d sing* **were** \(ˈ)wər\; *pl* **were**; *past subjunctive* **were**; *past part* **been** \(ˈ)bin, *chiefly Brit* (ˈ)bēn \; *pres part* **be·ing** \ˈbē-iŋ\; *pres 1st sing* **am** \əm, (ˈ)am\; *2d sing* **are** \ər, (ˈ)är\; *3d sing* **is** \(ˈ)iz, əz\; *pl* **are**; *pres subjunctive* **be** [ME *been,* fr. OE *bēon;* akin to OHG *bim* am, L *fui* I have been, *futurus* about to be, *fieri* to become, be done, Gk *phynai* to be born, be by nature, *phyein* to bring forth] *vi* **1 a** : to equal in meaning : have the same connotation as : SYMBOLIZE ⟨God *is* love⟩ ⟨January *is* the first month⟩ ⟨let *x* ~ 10⟩ **b** : to have identity with ⟨the first person I met *was* my brother⟩ **c** : to constitute the same class as **d** : to have a specified qualification or characterization ⟨the leaves *are* green⟩ **e** : to belong to the class of ⟨the fish *is* a trout⟩ — used regularly in senses 1a through 1e as the copula of simple predication **2 a** : to have an objective existence : have reality or actuality : LIVE ⟨ I think, therefore I *am*⟩ ⟨once upon a time there *was* a knight⟩ **b** : to have, maintain, or occupy a place, situation, or position ⟨the book *is* on the table⟩ **c** : to remain unmolested, undisturbed, or uninterrupted — used only in infinitive form ⟨let him ~⟩ **d** : to take place : OCCUR ⟨the concert *was* last night⟩ **e** *archaic* : BELONG, BEFALL ~ *verbal auxiliary* **1** — used with the past participle of transitive verbs as a passive-voice auxiliary ⟨the money *was* found⟩ ⟨the house is *being* built⟩ **2** — used as the auxiliary of the present participle in progressive tenses expressing continuous action ⟨he *is* reading⟩ ⟨I have *been* sleeping⟩ **3** — used with the past participle of some intransitive verbs as an auxiliary forming archaic perfect tenses ⟨Christ *is* risen from the dead — 1 Cor 15:20 (DV)⟩ **4** — used with the infinitive with *to* to express futurity, arrangement in advance, or obligation ⟨ I *am* to interview him today⟩ ⟨he *was* to become famous⟩

Be *symbol* beryllium

BE *abbr* **1** bachelor of education **2** bachelor of engineering **3** bill of exchange

be- *prefix* [ME, fr. OE *bi-, be-;* akin to OE *bī* by, near — more at BY] **1** : on : around : over ⟨*be*daub⟩ ⟨*be*smear⟩ **2** : to a great or greater degree : thoroughly ⟨*be*fuddle⟩ ⟨*be*rate⟩ **3** : excessively : ostentatiously — in intensive verbs formed from simple verbs ⟨*be*deck⟩ and in adjectives based on adjectives ending in *-ed* ⟨*be*ribboned⟩ **4** : about : to : at : upon : against : across ⟨*be*stride⟩ ⟨*be*speak⟩ **5** : make : cause to be : treat as ⟨*be*little⟩ ⟨*be*fool⟩ ⟨*be*friend⟩ **6** : call or dub esp. excessively ⟨*be*doctor⟩ **7** : affect, afflict, treat, provide, or cover with esp. excessively ⟨*be*devil⟩ ⟨*be*fog⟩

Bé *abbr* Baumé

¹beach \ˈbēch\ *n* [origin unknown] **1** : shore pebbles : SHINGLE **2 a** : a shore of an ocean, sea, or lake or the bank of a river covered by sand, gravel, or larger rock fragments **b** : a seashore area

²beach *vt* **1** : to run or drive ashore **2** : to make (a person) incapable or ineffective : DISABLE

beach ball *n* : a large inflated ball for use at the beach

beachboy *n* : a male beach attendant (as at a club or hotel)

beach break *n* : a wave that breaks close to the shore

beach buggy *n* : a motor vehicle with oversize tires for use on sand beaches

beach·comber \ˈbēch-ˌkō-mər\ *n* **1** : a white man living as a drifter or loafer esp. on the islands of the So. Pacific **2** : one who searches along a shore for useful or salable flotsam and refuse — **beach·comb** \-ˌkōm\ *vb*

beach flea *n* : any of numerous amphipod crustaceans (family Orchestiidae) living on ocean beaches and leaping like fleas

beach·front \ˈbēch-ˌfrənt\ *n* : a strip of land that fronts a beach — called also *shorefront*

beach grass *n* : any of several tough strongly rooted grasses that grow on exposed sandy shores; *esp* : a rhizomatous perennial (genus *Ammophila*) widely planted to bind sandy slopes

beach·head \ˈbēch-ˌhed\ *n* **1** : an area on a hostile shore occupied to secure further landing of troops and supplies **2** : FOOTHOLD

beach pea *n* : a wild pea (*Lathyrus maritimus*) with tough roots and purple flowers found along sandy seashores

beach plum *n* : a shrubby plum (*Prunus maritima*) having showy white flowers and growing along the northeastern coast of North America; *also* : its dark purple edible fruit that is often used in jams and jellies

beach·side \ˈbēch-ˌsīd\ *adj* : located on a beach

beach wagon *n* : STATION WAGON

beach·wear \ˈbēch-ˌwa(ə)r, -ˌwe(ə)r\ *n* : clothing for wear at a beach

beachy \ˈbē-chē\ *adj* : covered with pebbles or shingle

¹bea·con \ˈbē-kən\ *n* [ME *beken,* fr. OE *bēacen* sign; akin to OHG *bouhhan* sign] **1** : a signal fire commonly on a hill, tower, or pole **2 a** : a lighthouse or other signal for guidance **b** : a radio transmitter emitting signals for guidance of aircraft **3** : a source of light or inspiration

²beacon *vt* : to furnish with a beacon ~ *vi* : to shine as a beacon

¹bead \ˈbēd\ *n* [ME *bede* prayer, prayer bead, fr. OE *bed, gebed* prayer; akin to OE *biddan* to entreat, pray — more at BID] **1 a** *obs* : PRAYER — usu. used in pl. **b** *pl* : a series of prayers and meditations made with a rosary **2** : a small piece of material pierced for threading on a string or wire (as in a rosary) **3** *pl* **a** : ROSARY **b** : a necklace of beads or pearls **4** : a small ball-shaped body: as **a** : a drop of sweat or blood **b** : a bubble formed in or on a beverage **c** : a small metal knob on a firearm used as a front sight **d** : a blob or a line of weld metal **e** : a glassy drop of flux (as borax) used as a solvent and color test for several metallic oxides and salts **5** : a projecting rim, band, or molding

2bead *vt* **1** : to furnish, adorn or cover with beads or beading **2** : to string together like beads ~ *vi* : to form into a bead

bead·ing *n* **1** : material or a part or a piece consisting of a bead **2** : a beaded molding **3** : an openwork trimming **4** : BEADWORK

bea·dle \ˈbēd-ᵊl\ *n* [ME *bedel,* fr. OE *bydel;* akin to OHG *butil* bailiff, OE *bēodan* to command — more at BID] : a minor parish official whose duties include ushering and preserving order at services and sometimes civil functions

bead·roll \ˈbē-ˌdrōl\ *n* [fr. the reading in church of a list of names of persons for whom prayers are to be said] **1** : a list of names : CATALOG **2** : ROSARY

beads·man \ˈbēdz-mən\ *n, archaic* : one who prays for another

bead·work \ˈbē-ˌdwərk\ *n* **1** : ornamental work in beads **2** : joinery beading

beady \ˈbēd-ē\ *adj* **1 a** : resembling beads **b** : small, round, and shiny with interest or greed ⟨~ eyes⟩ **2** : marked by bubbles or beads ⟨a ~ liquor⟩

bea·gle \ˈbē-gəl\ *n* [ME *begle*] : a small short-legged smooth-coated hound

beak \ˈbēk\ *n* [ME *bec,* fr. OF, fr. L *beccus,* of Gaulish origin] **1 a** : the bill of a bird; *esp* : the bill of a bird of prey adapted for striking and tearing **b** (1) : any of various rigid projecting mouth structures (as of a turtle) (2) : the elongated sucking mouth of some insects (as the typical bugs) **c** : the human nose **2** : a pointed structure or formation: **a** : a metal-pointed beam projecting from the bow of an ancient galley for piercing an enemy ship **b** : the spout of a vessel **c** : a continuous slight architectural projection ending in an arris — see MOLDING illustration **d** : a process suggesting the beak of a bird **3** *chiefly Brit* **a** : MAGISTRATE **b** : HEADMASTER — **beaked** \ˈbēkt\ *adj*

bea·ker \ˈbē-kər\ *n* [ME *biker,* fr. ON *bikarr,* prob. fr. OS *bikeri;* akin to OHG *behhari* beaker; both fr. a prehistoric WGmc word borrowed fr. ML *bicarius* beaker, fr. Gk *bikos* earthen jug] **1** : a large drinking cup that has a wide mouth and is sometimes supported on a standard **2** : a deep widemouthed and often projecting-lipped thin vessel used esp. by chemists and pharmacists

be–all and end–all \ˈbē-ˌȯ-lən-ˈ(d)en-ˌdȯl\ *n* : prime cause : essential element

1beam \ˈbēm\ *n* [ME *beem,* fr. OE *bēam* tree, beam; akin to OHG *boum* tree] **1 a** : a long piece of heavy often squared timber suitable for use in construction **b** : a wood or metal cylinder in a loom on which the warp is wound **c** : the part of a plow to which handles, standard, and colter are attached **d** : the bar of a balance from which scales hang **e** : one of the principal horizontal supporting members of a building or ship ⟨a steel ~ supporting a floor⟩; *also* : BOOM, SPAR ⟨the ~ of a crane⟩ **f** : the extreme width of a ship at the widest part **g** : an oscillating lever on a central axis receiving motion at one end from an engine piston rod and transmitting it at the other **2 a** : a ray or shaft of light **b** : a collection of nearly parallel rays (as X rays) or particles (as electrons) **c** : a constant directional radio signal transmitted for the guidance of pilots; *also* : the course indicated by a radio beam **3** : the main stem of a deer's antler **4** : the width of the buttocks — **on the beam 1** : following a guiding beam **2** : proceeding or operating correctly

2beam *vt* **1** : to emit in beams or as a beam **2** : to support with beams **3 a** : to aim (a broadcast) by directional antennas **b** : to direct to a particular audience ~ *vi* **1** : to send out beams of light **2** : to smile with joy

beam–ends \ˈbē-ˈmen(d)z\ *n pl* : the ends of a ship's beams — **on her beam–ends** : inclined so much on one side that the beams approach a vertical position

beam·ish \ˈbē-mish\ *adj* : beaming and bright with optimism, promise, or achievement — **beam·ish·ly** *adv*

beamy \ˈbē-mē\ *adj* **1** : emitting beams of light : RADIANT **2** : broad in the beam ⟨a ~ cargo ship⟩

1bean \ˈbēn\ *n* [ME *bene,* fr. OE *bēan;* akin to OHG *bōna* bean] **1 a** : BROAD BEAN **b** : the seed of any of various erect or climbing leguminous plants (esp. genera *Phaseolus, Dolichos,* and *Vigna*) other than the broad bean **c** : a plant bearing beans **d** : a bean pod used when immature as a vegetable **2 a** : a valueless item **b** *pl* : a small amount ⟨didn't know ~s about it⟩ **3** : any of various seeds or fruits that resemble beans or bean pods ⟨catalpa ~⟩; *also* : a plant producing these **4** : a protuberance on the upper mandible of waterfowl **5** : HEAD, BRAIN **6** *pl* : EXUBERANCE — used in the phrase *full of beans*

2bean *vt* : to strike (a person) on the head with an object

bean·ball \ˈbēn-ˌbȯl\ *n* : a pitched baseball thrown at a batter's head

bean curd *n* : a soft vegetable cheese that is extensively eaten in the Orient and is prepared by treating soybean milk with coagulants (as magnesium chloride or dilute acids)

bean·ie \ˈbē-nē\ *n* : a small round tight-fitting skullcap worn esp. by schoolboys and college freshmen

beano \ˈbē-(ˌ)nō\ *n, pl* **beanos** [by alter.] : BINGO

bean sprouts *n pl* : the sprouts of bean seeds esp. of the mung bean

bean tree *n* : any of several trees having fruits resembling a bean pod: as **a** : a yellow-flowered Australian leguminous tree (*Castanospermum australe*) with large pods containing seeds like chestnuts **b** : CATALPA

1bear \ˈba(ə)r, ˈbe(ə)r\ *n, pl* **bears** *often attrib* [ME *bere,* fr. OE *bera;* akin to OHG *bero* bear, OE *brūn* brown] **1** *or pl* **bear** : any of a family (Ursidae of the order Carnivora) of large heavy mammals having long shaggy hair, rudimentary tail, and plantigrade feet and feeding largely on fruit and insects as well as on flesh **2** : a surly, uncouth, or shambling person **3** [prob. fr. the proverb about *selling the bearskin before catching the bear*] : one that sells securities or commodities in expectation of a price decline — compare BULL

2bear *vb* **bore** \ˈbō(ə)r, ˈbȯ(ə)r\; **borne** \ˈbō(ə)rn, ˈbȯ(ə)rn\ *also* **born** \ˈbȯ(ə)rn\; **bear·ing** [ME *beren,* fr. OE *beran;* akin to OHG *beran* to carry, L *ferre,* Gk *pherein*] *vt* **1 a** : to move while holding up and supporting **b** : to be equipped or furnished with **c** : to hold in the mind **d** : DISSEMINATE **e** : BEHAVE, CONDUCT ⟨~*ing* himself well⟩ **f** : to have as a feature or characteristic **g** : to give as testimony ⟨~ false witness⟩ **h** : to have as an identification ⟨*bore* the name of John⟩ **i** : LEAD, ESCORT **j** : RENDER, GIVE **2 a** : to give birth to **b** : to produce as yield **c** (1) : to permit growth of (2) : CONTAIN ⟨oil-*bearing* shale⟩ **3 a** : to support the weight of : SUSTAIN **b** : to put up with esp. without giving way ⟨couldn't ~ his wife's family⟩ **c** : ASSUME, ACCEPT **d** : to hold above, on top, or aloft **e** : to admit of : ALLOW **f** : to call for as suitable or essential ⟨his odd behavior ~s watching⟩ **4** : THRUST, PRESS ~ *vi* **1 a** : to force one's way **b** : to be situated : LIE **c** : to extend in a direction indicated or implied **d** : to become directed **e** : to go or incline in an indicated direction ⟨road ~s to the right⟩ **2 a** : APPLY, PERTAIN **b** : to exert influence or force **3** : to support a weight or strain — often used with *up* **4** : to produce fruit : YIELD

***syn* 1** see CARRY

2 BEAR, SUFFER, ENDURE, ABIDE, TOLERATE, STAND, BROOK *shared meaning element* : to put up with something trying or painful

— **bear a hand** : to join in and help out — **bear fruit** : to come to satisfying fruition, production, or development — **bear in mind** : to think of esp. as a warning : REMEMBER

bear·able \ˈbar-ə-bəl, ˈber-\ *adj* : capable of being borne — **bear·abil·i·ty** \ˌbar-ə-ˈbil-ət-ē, ˌber-\ *n* — **bear·ably** \-blē\ *adv*

bear·bait·ing \ˈba(ə)r-ˌbāt-iŋ, ˈbe(ə)r-\ *n* : the practice of setting dogs on a chained bear

bear·ber·ry \-ˌber-ē\ *n* **1** : a trailing evergreen plant (*Arctostaphylos uva-ursi*) of the heath family with astringent foliage and red berries **2** : the large cranberry (*Vaccinium macrocarpon*) **3** : CASCARA BUCKTHORN

1beard \ˈbi(ə)rd\ *n* [ME *berd,* fr. OE *beard;* akin to OHG *bart* beard, L *barba*] **1** : the hair that grows on a man's face often excluding the mustache **2** : a hairy or bristly appendage or tuft **3** : BEVEL 3; *also* : the bevel plus the shoulder — **beard·ed** \-əd\ *adj* — **beard·ed·ness** *n* — **beard·less** \-ləs\ *adj*

2beard *vt* **1** : to furnish with a beard **2** : to confront and oppose with boldness, resolution, and often effrontery : DEFY

bear down *vt* : OVERCOME, OVERWHELM ~ *vi* : to exert full strength and concentrated attention — **bear down on 1** : EMPHASIZE **2** : to weigh heavily on : BURDEN

beard·tongue \ˈbi(ə)rd-ˌtəŋ\ *n* : PENTSTEMON

bear·er \ˈbar-ər, ˈber-\ *n* : one that bears: as **a** : PORTER **b** : a plant yielding fruit **c** : PALLBEARER **d** : one holding a check, draft, or other order for payment esp. if marked payable to bearer

bear grass *n* : any of several plants (genera *Yucca, Nolina,* or *Xerophyllum*) of the lily family chiefly of the southern and western U.S. with foliage resembling coarse blades of grass

bear hug *n* : a rough tight embrace

bear·ing *n* **1** : the manner in which one bears or comports oneself ⟨a man of erect and soldierly ~⟩ **2 a** : the act, power, or time of bringing forth offspring or fruit **b** : a product of bearing : CROP **3** : PRESSURE, THRUST **4 a** : an object, surface, or point that supports **b** : a machine part in which another part (as a journal or pin) turns or slides **5** : a figure borne on a heraldic field **6 a** : the situation or horizontal direction of one point with respect to another or to the compass **b** : a determination of position **c** *pl* : comprehension of one's position, environment, or situation **d** : RELATION, CONNECTION; *also* : PURPORT **7** : the part of a structural member that rests upon its supports

syn BEARING, DEPORTMENT, DEMEANOR, MIEN, MANNER, CARRIAGE *shared meaning element* : the way in which a person outwardly manifests his personality or attitude

bearing rein *n* : CHECKREIN 1

bear·ish \ˈba(ə)r-ish, ˈbe(ə)r-\ *adj* **1** : resembling a bear in roughness, gruffness, or surliness **2 a** : marked by, tending to cause, or fearful of falling prices (as in a stock market) **b** : PESSIMISTIC — **bear·ish·ly** *adv* — **bear·ish·ness** *n*

bé·ar·naise sauce \ˌbā-är-ˌnāz-, -ər-\ *n* [F *béarnaise,* fem. of *béarnais* of Béarn, France] : hollandaise sauce flavored with wine, shallots, and herbs

bear out *vt* : CONFIRM, SUBSTANTIATE ⟨research *bore out* his theory⟩

bear·skin \ˈba(ə)r-ˌskin, ˈbe(ə)r-\ *n* : an article made of the skin of a bear; *esp* : a military hat made of the skin of a bear

bear up *vt* : SUPPORT, ENCOURAGE ~ *vi* : to summon up courage, resolution, or strength ⟨*bearing up* under the strain⟩

beast \ˈbēst\ *n* [ME *beste,* fr. OF, fr. L *bestia*] **1 a** : an animal as distinguished from a plant **b** : a lower animal as distinguished from man **c** : a four-footed mammal as distinguished from man, lower vertebrates, and invertebrates **d** : an animal under human control **2** : a contemptible person

beast epic *n* : a poem with epic conventions in which animals speak and act like human beings

beast fable *n* : a usu. didactic prose or verse fable in which animals speak and act like human beings

beas·tings \ˈbē-stiŋz\ *n pl but sing or pl in constr* [ME *bestynge,* fr. OE *bȳsting,* fr. *bēost* beastings] : the colostrum esp. of a cow

1beast·ly \ˈbēst-lē\ *adj* **beast·li·er; -est 1** : of, relating to, or resembling a beast : BESTIAL **2** : ABOMINABLE, DISAGREEABLE ⟨~ weather⟩ — **beast·li·ness** *n*

2beastly *adv* : VERY ⟨a ~ cold day⟩

beast of burden : an animal employed to carry heavy material or to perform other heavy work (as pulling a plow)

1beat \ˈbēt\ *vb* **beat; beat·en** \ˈbēt-ᵊn\ *or* **beat; beat·ing** [ME *beten,* fr. OE *bēatan;* akin to OHG *bōzan* to beat, L *-futare* to beat, *fustis* club] *vt* **1** : to strike repeatedly: **a** : to hit repeatedly so as to inflict pain — often used with *up* **b** : to walk on : TREAD **c** : to strike directly against forcefully and repeatedly : dash against **d** : to flap or thrash at vigorously **e** : to strike at in order to rouse game; *also* : to range over in or as if in quest of game **f** : to mix by stirring : WHIP — often used with *up* **g** : to strike repeatedly in order to produce music or a signal ⟨~ a drum⟩ **2 a** : to drive or force by blows **b** : to pound into a powder, paste, or pulp **c** : to make by repeated treading or driving over **d** (1) : to dislodge by

repeated hitting (2) : to lodge securely by repeated striking **e** : to shape by beating ⟨~ swords into plowshares⟩; *esp* : to flatten thin by blows **f** : to sound or express esp. by drumbeat **3** : to cause to strike or flap repeatedly **4 a** : OVERCOME, DEFEAT; *also* : SURPASS — often used with *out* **b** : to prevail despite ⟨~ the odds⟩ **c** : BEWILDER, BAFFLE **d** (1) : FATIGUE, EXHAUST (2) : to leave dispirited, irresolute, or hopeless **e** : CHEAT, SWINDLE **5 a** (1) : to act ahead of usu. so as to forestall (2) : to report a news item in advance of **b** : to come or arrive before **c** : CIRCUMVENT ⟨~ the system⟩ **6** : to indicate by beating ⟨~ the tempo⟩ ~ *vi* **1 a** : to become forcefully impelled : DASH **b** : to glare or strike with oppressive intensity **c** : to sustain distracting activity **d** : to beat a drum **2 a** (1) : PULSATE, THROB (2) : TICK **b** : to sound upon being struck **3 a** : to strike repeated blows **b** : to strike the air : FLAP **c** : to strike cover in order to rouse game; *also* : to range or scour for or as if for game **4** : to progress with much difficulty — **beat about the bush** *or* **beat around the bush** : to fail or refuse to come to the point in discourse — **beat it 1** : to hurry away : SCRAM **2** : HURRY, RUSH — **beat one's brains out** : to try intently to resolve something difficult by thinking — **beat the bushes** : to search thoroughly through all possible areas — **beat the rap** : to escape or evade the penalties connected with an accusation or charge
²beat *n* **1 a** : a single stroke or blow esp. in a series; *also* : PULSATION, TICK **b** : a sound produced by or as if by beating **c** : a driving impact or force **2** : one swing of the pendulum or balance of a timepiece **3** : each of the pulsations of amplitude produced by the union of sound or radio waves or electric currents having different frequencies **4** : an accented stroke (as of one leg or foot against the other) in dancing **5 a** : a metrical or rhythmic stress in poetry or music or the rhythmic effect of these stresses **b** : the tempo indicated (as by a conductor) to a musical performer **c** : the pronounced rhythm that is the characteristic driving force in jazz or rock music; *also* : ²ROCK 2 **6** : a regularly traversed round ⟨the cop on the ~⟩ **7 a** : something that excels ⟨I've never seen the ~ of it⟩ **b** : the reporting of a news story ahead of competitors **8** : DEADBEAT **9 a** : an act of beating to windward **b** : one of the reaches so traversed : TACK — **beat·less** \-ləs\ *adj*
³beat *adj* [ME *beten, bete,* fr. pp. of *beten*] **1 a** : being in a state of exhaustion : EXHAUSTED **b** : sapped of resolution or morale **2** : of, relating to, or being beatniks ⟨~ poets⟩
⁴beat *n* : BEATNIK
beat·en \'bēt-ᵊn\ *adj* **1** : hammered into a desired shape ⟨~ gold⟩ **2** : much trodden and worn smooth; *also* : FAMILIAR ⟨a ~ path⟩ **3** : being in a state of exhaustion : EXHAUSTED
beat·er \'bēt-ər\ *n* **1** : one that beats: as **a** : EGGBEATER **b** : a rotary blade attached to an electric mixer **c** : DRUMSTICK 1 **2** : one that strikes bushes or other cover to rouse game **3** : an advance publicity agent
be·atif·ic \,bē-ə-'tif-ik\ *adj* [L *beatificus* making happy, fr. *beatus* happy, fr. pp. of *beare* to bless; akin to L *bonus* good — more at BOUNTY] **1** : of, possessing, or imparting beatitude **2** : having a blissful or benign appearance : SAINTLY, ANGELIC ⟨a ~ smile⟩ — **be·atif·i·cal·ly** \-i-k(ə-)lē\ *adv*
beatific vision *n* : the direct knowledge of God enjoyed by the blessed in heaven
be·at·i·fy \bē-'at-ə-,fī\ *vt* **-fied; -fy·ing** [MF *beatifier,* fr. LL *beatificare,* fr. L *beatus*] **1** : to make supremely happy **2** : to declare to have attained the blessedness of heaven and authorize the title "Blessed" and limited public religious honor — **be·at·i·fi·ca·tion** \-,at-ə-fə-'kā-shən\ *n*
beat·ing \'bēt-iŋ\ *n* **1** : an act of striking with repeated blows so as to injure or damage; *also* : the injury or damage thus inflicted **2** : PULSATION **3** : SETBACK, DEFEAT
beating reed *n* : a reed in a musical instrument that vibrates against the edges of an air opening (as in a clarinet or organ pipe) to which it is attached — compare FREE REED
be·at·i·tude \bē-'at-ə-,t(y)üd\ *n* [L *beatitudo,* fr. *beatus*] **1 a** : a state of utmost bliss **b** — used as a title for a primate esp. of an Eastern church **2** : any of the declarations made in the Sermon on the Mount (Mt 5:3–12) beginning in the AV "Blessed are"
beat·nik \'bēt-nik\ *n* [³*beat* + Yiddish *-nik,* suffix denoting a person, fr. Russ & Pol] : a person who rejects the mores of established society (as by dressing and behaving unconventionally) and indulges in exotic philosophizing and self-expression
beat out *vt* **1** : to make or perform by or as if by beating **2** : to mark or accompany by beating **3** : to turn (a routine ground ball) into a hit in baseball by fast running to first base
Be·a·trice *n* [It] \,bā-ä-'trē-(,)chā, 'bē-ə-trəs\ : a Florentine woman immortalized in Dante's *Vita Nuova* and *Divina Commedia*
beau \'bō\ *n, pl* **beaux** \'bōz\ *or* **beaus** [F, fr. *beau* beautiful, fr. L *bellus* pretty] **1** : DANDY **2** : a man who is a frequent or steady escort of a woman : BOYFRIEND
Beau Brum·mell \bō-'brəm-əl\ *n* [nickname of G. B. *Brummell*] : DANDY
Beau·fort scale \,bō-fərt-\ *n* [Sir Francis *Beaufort*] : a scale in which the force of the wind is indicated by numbers from 0 to 12
beau geste \bō-'zhest\ *n, pl* **beaux gestes** *or* **beau gestes** \bō-'zhest\ [F, lit., beautiful gesture] **1** : a graceful or magnanimous gesture **2** : an ingratiating conciliatory gesture
beau ide·al \,bō-ī-'dē(-ə)l\ *n, pl* **beau ideals** [F *beau idéal* ideal beauty] : the perfect type or model
Beau·jo·lais \,bō-zhō-'lā\ *n* [F, fr. *Beaujolais,* region of central France] : a French red table wine
Beau·mé *var of* BAUMÉ
beau monde \bō-'mänd, -'mōⁿd\ *n, pl* **beau mondes** \-'män(d)z\ *or* **beaux mondes** \bō-'mōⁿd\ [F, lit., fine world] : the world of high society and fashion
beau·te·ous \'byüt-ē-əs\ *adj* [ME, fr. *beaute*] : BEAUTIFUL — **beau·te·ous·ly** *adv* — **beau·te·ous·ness** *n*
beau·ti·cian \byü-'tish-ən\ *n* [*beauty* + *-ician*] : COSMETOLOGIST
beau·ti·ful \'byüt-i-fəl\ *adj* **1** : having qualities of beauty : exciting aesthetic pleasure **2** : generally pleasing : EXCELLENT — **beau·ti·ful·ly** \-f(ə-)lē\ *adv* — **beau·ti·ful·ness** \-fəl-nəs\ *n*

BEAUFORT SCALE

BEAUFORT NUMBER	NAME	MILES PER HOUR	DESCRIPTION
0	calm	less than 1	calm; smoke rises vertically
1	light air	1–3	direction of wind shown by smoke but not by wind vanes
2	light breeze	4–7	wind felt on face; leaves rustle; ordinary vane moved by wind
3	gentle breeze	8–12	leaves and small twigs in constant motion; wind extends light flag
4	moderate breeze	13–18	raises dust and loose paper; small branches are moved
5	fresh breeze	19–24	small trees in leaf begin to sway; crested wavelets form on inland waters
6	strong breeze	25–31	large branches in motion; telegraph wires whistle; umbrellas used with difficulty
7	moderate gale (or near gale)	32–38	whole trees in motion; inconvenience in walking against wind
8	fresh gale (or gale)	39–46	breaks twigs off trees; generally impedes progress
9	strong gale	47–54	slight structural damage occurs; chimney pots and slates removed
10	whole gale (or storm)	55–63	trees uprooted; considerable structural damage occurs
11	storm (or violent storm)	64–72	very rarely experienced; accompanied by widespread damage
12	hurricane*	73–136	devastation occurs

*The U.S. uses 74 statute mph as the speed criterion for hurricane.

syn BEAUTIFUL, LOVELY, HANDSOME, PRETTY, COMELY, FAIR *shared meaning element* : pleasing to the mind, spirit, or senses **ant** ugly
beautiful people *n pl, often cap B & P* : people who are identified with international society
beau·ti·fy \'byüt-ə-,fī\ *vb* **-fied; -fy·ing** *vt* : to make beautiful or add beauty to : EMBELLISH ~ *vi* : to grow beautiful **syn** see ADORN — **beau·ti·fi·ca·tion** \byüt-ə-fə-'kā-shən\ *n* — **beau·ti·fi·er** \'byüt-ə-,fī(-ə)r\ *n*
beau·ty \'byüt-ē\ *n, pl* **beauties** [ME *beaute,* fr. OF *biauté,* fr. *bel, biau* beautiful, fr. L *bellus* pretty; akin to L *bonus* good — more at BOUNTY] **1** : the quality or aggregate of qualities in a person or thing that gives pleasure to the senses or pleasurably exalts the mind or spirit : LOVELINESS **2** : a beautiful person or thing; *esp* : a beautiful woman **3** : a brilliant, extreme, or egregious example or instance ⟨that mistake was a ~⟩ **4** : a particularly graceful, ornamental, or excellent quality
beauty bush *n* : a Chinese shrub (*Kolkwitzia amabilis*) of the honeysuckle family with pinkish flowers and bristly fruit
beauty shop *n* : an establishment or department where hairdressing, facials, and manicures are done — called also *beauty parlor, beauty salon*
beauty spot *n* **1** : ¹PATCH 2 **2 a** : NEVUS **b** : a minor blemish
beaux arts \bō-'zär\ *n pl* [F] : FINE ARTS
beaux esprits *pl of* BEL ESPRIT
¹bea·ver \'bē-vər\ *n, pl* **beavers** [ME *bever,* fr. OE *beofor;* akin to OHG *bibar* beaver, OE *brūn* brown] **1** *or pl* **beaver a** : either of two large semiaquatic rodents (genus *Castor*) having webbed hind feet and a broad flat tail, constructing dams and underwater lodges, and yielding valuable fur and castor **b** : the fur or pelt of the beaver **2 a** : a hat made of beaver fur or a fabric imitation **b** : SILK HAT **3** : a heavy fabric of felted wool or of cotton napped on both sides
²beaver *n* [ME *baviere,* fr. MF] **1** : a piece of armor protecting the lower part of the face **2** : a helmet visor
³beaver *vi* : to work energetically ⟨~ing away at the problem⟩
bea·ver·board \'bē-vər-,bō(ə)rd, -,bȯ(ə)rd\ *n* [fr. *Beaver Board,* a trademark] : a fiberboard used for partitions and ceilings
be·bop \'bē-,bäp\ *n* [imit.] : BOP — **be·bop·per** *n*
BEC *abbr* Bureau of Employees' Compensation
be·calm \bi-'käm, -'kälm\ *vt* **1** : to keep motionless by lack of wind **2** : to make calm : SOOTHE
be·cause \bi-'kȯz, -'(ˌ)kaz\ *conj* [ME *because that, because,* fr. *by cause that*] **1** : for the reason that : SINCE ⟨rested ~ he was tired⟩ **2** : the fact that : THAT ⟨the latter fact, we suggest, was because the world was . . . particularly attentive at that moment to the subject of violence —*Times Lit. Supp.*⟩

ə abut	ᵊ kitten	ər further	a back	ā bake	ä cot, cart
aů out	ch chin	e less	ē easy	g gift	i trip	ī life
j joke	ŋ sing	ō flow	ȯ flaw	ȯi coin	th thin	th this
ü loot	ů foot	y yet	yü few	yů furious	zh vision

because of *prep* : by reason of : on account of
bec·ca·fi·co \ˌbek-ə-ˈfē-(ˌ)kō\ *n, pl* **-cos** *or* **-coes** [It, fr. *beccare* to peck + *fico* fig, fr. L *ficus*] : any of various European songbirds that are sometimes served as a table delicacy
bé·cha·mel \ˌbā-shə-ˈmel\ *n* [F *sauce béchamelle,* fr. Louis de *Béchamel* †1703 F courtier] : a white sauce sometimes enriched with cream
be·chance \bi-ˈchan(t)s\ *vb, archaic* : BEFALL
bêche–de–mer \ˌbesh-də-ˈme(ə)r, ˌbāsh-\ *n* [F, lit., sea grub] **1** *pl* **bêche–de–mer** *or* **bêches–de–mer** \ˌbesh-(əz-)də-, ˌbāsh-\ : TREPANG **2** *cap B&M* : a lingua franca based on English and used esp. in New Guinea, the Bismarck archipelago, and the Solomon islands
[1]**beck** \ˈbek\ *n* [ME *bek,* fr. ON *bekkr;* akin to OE *bæc* brook, OHG *bah,* MIr *búal* flowing water] *Brit* : CREEK 2
[2]**beck** *vt* [ME *becken,* alter. of *beknen*] *archaic* : BECKON
[3]**beck** *n* **1** *chiefly Scot* : BOW, CURTSY **2 a** : a beckoning gesture **b** : SUMMONS, BIDDING — **at one's beck and call** : in obedient readiness to obey any command
beck·et \ˈbek-ət\ *n* [origin unknown] : a device for holding something in place: as **a** : a grommet or a loop of rope with a knot at one end to catch in an eye at the other **b** : a ring of rope or metal **c** : a loop of rope (as for a handle)
becket bend *n* : SHEET BEND
beck·on \ˈbek-ən\ *vb* **beck·oned; beck·on·ing** \ˈbek-(ə-)niŋ\ [ME *beknen,* fr. OE *biecnan,* fr. *bēacen* sign — more at BEACON] *vi* **1** : to summon or signal typically with a wave or nod **2** : to appear inviting : ATTRACT ~ *vt* : to beckon to — **beckon** *n*
be·cloud \bi-ˈklau̇d\ *vt* **1** : to obscure with or as if with a cloud **2** : to prevent clear perception or realization of : MUDDLE ⟨prejudices that ~ his judgment⟩
be·come \bi-ˈkəm\ *vb* **-came** \-ˈkām\; **-come; -com·ing** [ME *becomen* to come to, become, fr. OE *becuman,* fr. *be-* + *cuman* to come] *vi* **1 a** : to come into existence **b** : to come to be ⟨~ sick⟩ **2** : to undergo change or development ~ *vt* : to suit or be suitable to ⟨her clothes ~ her⟩ — **become of** : to happen to
be·com·ing \-ˈkəm-iŋ\ *adj* : SUITABLE, FITTING; *esp* : attractively suitable — **be·com·ing·ly** \-iŋ-lē\ *adv*
[1]**bed** \ˈbed\ *n* [ME, fr. OE *bedd;* akin to OHG *betti* bed, L *fodere* to dig] **1 a** : a piece of furniture on or in which one may lie and sleep **b** (1) : a place of marital sex relations (2) : marital relationship **c** : a place for sleeping **d** : SLEEP; *also* : a time for sleeping ⟨took a walk before ~⟩ **e** (1) : a mattress filled with soft material (2) : BEDSTEAD **f** : the equipment and services needed to care for one hospitalized patient or hotel guest **2** : a flat or level surface: as **a** : a plot of ground prepared for plants; *also* : the plants grown in such a plot **b** : the bottom of a body of water; *esp* : an area of sea bottom supporting a heavy growth of a particular organism ⟨an oyster ~⟩ **3** : a supporting surface or structure : FOUNDATION; *esp* : the earthwork that supports the ballast and track of a railroad **4** : LAYER, STRATUM **5 a** : the place or material in which a block or brick is laid **b** : the lower surface of a brick, slate, or tile **6** : a mass or heap resembling a bed ⟨a ~ of ashes⟩ — **in bed** : in the act of sexual intercourse
[2]**bed** *vb* **bed·ded; bed·ding** *vt* **1 a** : to furnish with a bed or bedding : settle in sleeping quarters — often used with *down* **b** : to put, take, or send to bed **2 a** : EMBED **b** : to plant or arrange in beds **c** : BASE, ESTABLISH **3 a** : to lay flat or in a layer **b** : to make a bed in or of ~ *vi* **1 a** : to find or make sleeping accommodations **b** : to go to bed **2** : to form a layer **3** : to lie flat or flush
BEd *abbr* bachelor of education
be·dab·ble \bi-ˈdab-əl\ *vt* : to wet or soil by dabbling
be·daub \bi-ˈdȯb, -ˈdäb\ *vt* **1** : to daub over : BESMEAR **2** : to ornament with vulgar excess
be·daz·zle \bi-ˈdaz-əl\ *vt* **1** : to confuse by a strong light : DAZZLE **2** : to impress forcefully : ENCHANT — **be·daz·zle·ment** \-mənt\ *n*
bed board *n* : a stiff thin wide board inserted usu. between bedspring and mattress esp. to give support to one's back or to protect a mattress from sagging springs
bed·bug \ˈbed-ˌbəg\ *n* : a wingless bloodsucking bug (*Cimex lectularius*) sometimes infesting houses and esp. beds and feeding on human blood
bed·cham·ber \-ˌchām-bər\ *n* : BEDROOM
bed check *n* : a night inspection to check the presence of persons (as soldiers) required by regulations to be in bed or in quarters
bed·clothes \ˈbed-ˌklō(th)z\ *n pl* : the covering (as sheets and blankets) used on a bed
bed·der \ˈbed-ər\ *n* **1** : one that makes up beds **2** : a bedding plant
[1]**bed·ding** \ˈbed-iŋ\ *n* [ME, fr. OE, fr. *bedd*] **1** : BEDCLOTHES **2** : a bottom layer : FOUNDATION **3** : material to provide a bed for livestock **4** : STRATIFICATION
[2]**bedding** *adj* [fr. gerund of [2]*bed*] : appropriate or adapted for culture in open-air beds
be·deck \bi-ˈdek\ *vt* : to clothe with finery : deck out
be·dev·il \bi-ˈdev-əl\ *vt* **1** : to possess with or as if with a devil **2** : to change for the worse : SPOIL **3** : to drive frantic : HARASS **4** : to confuse utterly : BEWILDER — **be·dev·il·ment** \-mənt\ *n*
be·dew \bi-ˈd(y)ü\ *vt* : to wet with or as if with dew
bed·fast \ˈbed-ˌfast\ *adj* : BEDRIDDEN
bed·fel·low \-ˌfel-(ˌ)ō, -ə(-w)\ *n* **1** : one who shares a bed with another **2** : a close associate : ALLY ⟨political ~s⟩
Bed·ford cord \ˌbed-fərd-\ *n* [perh. fr. New *Bedford,* Massachusetts] : a clothing fabric with lengthwise ribs that resembles corduroy; *also* : the weave used in making this fabric
be·dight \bi-ˈdīt\ *vt* **be·dight·ed** *or* **bedight; be·dight·ing** *archaic* : EQUIP, ARRAY
be·dim \bi-ˈdim\ *vt* **1** : to make less bright **2** : to make indistinct : OBSCURE
Bed·i·vere \ˈbed-ə-ˌvi(ə)r\ *n* : a knight of the Round Table
be·di·zen \bi-ˈdīz-ᵊn, -ˈdiz-\ *vt* : to dress or adorn with gaudy finery — **be·di·zen·ment** \-mənt\ *n*
bed·lam \ˈbed-ləm\ *n* [*Bedlam,* popular name for the Hospital of St. Mary of Bethlehem, London, an insane asylum, fr. ME *Bedlem* Bethlehem] **1** *obs* : MADMAN, LUNATIC **2** *archaic* : a lunatic asylum **3** : a place, scene, or state of uproar and confusion — **bedlam** *adj*
bed·lam·ite \-lə-ˌmīt\ *n* : MADMAN, LUNATIC — **bedlamite** *adj*
Bed·ling·ton terrier \ˌbed-liŋ-tən-\ *n* [*Bedlington,* England] : a swift rough-coated terrier of light build usu. groomed to resemble a lamb
bed·mate \ˈbed-ˌmāt\ *n* : one who shares one's bed; *esp* : a sexual partner
bed molding *n* : the molding of a cornice below the corona and above the frieze; *also* : a molding below a deep projection
bed of roses : a place or situation of agreeable ease
bed·ou·in *or* **bed·u·in** \ˈbed(-ə)-wən\ *n, pl* **bedouin** *or* **bedouins** *or* **beduin** *or* **beduins** *often cap* [F *bédouin,* fr. Ar *badāwi, bidwān,* pl. of *badawi* desert dweller] : a nomadic Arab of the Arabian, Syrian, or No. African deserts
bed·pan \ˈbed-ˌpan\ *n* : a shallow vessel used by a person in bed for urination or defecation
bed·plate \-ˌplāt\ *n* : a plate or framing used as a support
bed·post \-ˌpōst\ *n* : the usu. turned or carved post of a bed
be·drag·gle \bi-ˈdrag-əl\ *vt* : to wet thoroughly
be·drag·gled \bi-ˈdrag-əld\ *adj* **1** : left wet and limp by or as if by rain **2** : soiled and stained by or as if by trailing in mud **3** : DILAPIDATED ⟨~ buildings⟩
bed·rid·den \ˈbed-ˌrid-ᵊn\ *or* **bed·rid** \-ˌrid\ *adj* [alter. of ME *bedrede, bedreden,* fr. OE *bedreda* one confined to bed, fr. *bedd* bed + *-rida, -reda* rider, fr. *rīdan* to ride] : confined (as by illness) to bed
bed·rock \-ˈräk, -ˌräk\ *n* **1** : the solid rock underlying unconsolidated surface materials (as soil) **2 a** : lowest point : NADIR **b** : BASIS — **bedrock** *adj*
bed·roll \-ˌrōl\ *n* : bedding rolled up for carrying
[1]**bed·room** \-ˌrüm, -ˌru̇m\ *n* : a room furnished with a bed and intended primarily for sleeping
[2]**bed·room** *adj* **1** : dealing with, suggestive of, or inviting to sexual relations ⟨a ~ farce⟩ ⟨~ eyes⟩ **2** : inhabited or used by commuters ⟨~ suburbs⟩
Beds *abbr* Bedfordshire
[1]**bed·side** \ˈbed-ˌsīd\ *n* : the side of a bed : a place beside a bed
[2]**bedside** *adj* **1** : of, relating to, or conducted at the bedside ⟨a ~ diagnosis⟩ **2** : suitable for a bedridden person ⟨~ reading⟩
bedside manner *n* : the manner that a physician assumes toward his patients
bed–sit·ter \ˈbed-ˌsit-ər\ *n* [*bed*room + *sit*ting room + *-er*] *Brit* : a one-room apartment serving as both bedroom and sitting room — called also *bed-sit, bed-sitting-room*
bed·so·nia \bed-ˈsō-nē-ə\ *n* [NL, fr. Sir Samuel P. *Bedson* †1969 E bacteriologist] : any of a group of rickettsias (genus *Chlamydia*) including the causative agent of lymphogranuloma venereum
bed·sore \ˈbed-ˌsō(ə)r, -ˌsȯ(ə)r\ *n* : an ulceration of tissue deprived of nutrition by prolonged pressure
bed·spread \-ˌspred\ *n* : a usu. ornamental cloth cover for a bed
bed·spring \-ˌspriŋ\ *n* : a spring supporting a mattress
bed·stead \-ˌsted, -ˌstid\ *n* : the framework of a bed
bed·straw \-ˌstrȯ\ *n* [fr. its use for mattresses] : any of a genus (*Galium*) of herbs of the madder family having angled stems, opposite or whorled leaves, and small flowers
bed table *n* **1** : a small table used beside a bed **2** : an adjustable table used (as for eating or writing) by a person in bed
bed·time \-ˌtīm\ *n* : a time for going to bed
bedtime story *n* : a simple story for young children that often deals with animals
bed warmer *n* : a covered pan containing hot coals used to warm a bed
bed–wet·ting \-ˌwet-iŋ\ *n* : enuresis esp. when occurring in bed during sleep — **bed wetter** *n*
[1]**bee** \ˈbē\ *n* [ME, fr. OE *bēo;* akin to OHG *bīa* bee, Lith *bitis*] **1** : a social colonial hymenopterous insect (*Apis mellifera*) often kept in hives for the honey that it produces; *broadly* : any of numerous insects (superfamily Apoidea) that differ from the related wasps esp. in the heavier hairier body and in having sucking as well as chewing mouthparts, that feed on pollen and nectar, and that store both and often also honey **2** : an eccentric notion : FANCY **3** [perh. fr. E dial. *been* help given by neighbors, fr. ME *bene* prayer, boon, fr. OE *bēn* prayer — more at BOON] : a gathering of people for a specific purpose ⟨quilting ~⟩ — **bee·like** \-ˌlīk\ *adj* — **bee in one's bonnet** : [1]BEE 2
[2]**bee** *n* [ME *beghe* metal ring, fr. OE *bēag;* akin to OE *būgan* to bend — more at BOW] : a piece of hard wood at the side of a bowsprit to reeve fore-topmast stays through
[3]**bee** *n* : the letter *b*
BEE *abbr* bachelor of electrical engineering
bee balm *n* : any of several mints (as monarda) attractive to bees; *esp* : OSWEGO TEA
bee·bee *var of* BB
bee·bread \ˈbē-ˌbred\ *n* : bitter yellowish brown pollen stored up in honeycomb cells and used mixed with honey by bees as food
beech \ˈbēch\ *n, pl* **beech·es** *or* **beech** [ME *beche,* fr. OE *bēce;* akin to OE *bōc* beech, OHG *buohha,* L *fagus,* Gk *phēgos* oak] : any of a genus (*Fagus* of the family Fagaceae, the beech family) of hardwood trees with smooth gray bark and small edible nuts; *also* : its wood — **beech·en** \ˈbē-chən\ *adj*
beech·drops \ˈbēch-ˌdräps\ *n pl but sing or pl in constr* : a low wiry plant (*Epifagus virginiana*) of the broomrape family parasitic on the roots of beeches
beech·nut \-ˌnət\ *n* : the nut of the beech
bee eater *n* : any of a family (Meropidae) of brightly colored slender-billed insectivorous chiefly tropical Old World birds
[1]**beef** \ˈbēf\ *n, pl* **beefs** \ˈbēfs\ *or* **beeves** \ˈbēvz\ [ME, fr. OF *buef* ox, beef, fr. L *bov-, bos* head of cattle — more at COW] **1** : the flesh of an adult domestic bovine (as a steer or cow) when killed for food **2 a** : an ox, cow, or bull in a full-grown or nearly full-grown

state; *esp* : a steer or cow fattened for food ⟨quality Texas *beeves*⟩ ⟨a herd of good ∼⟩ **b** : a dressed carcass of a beef animal **3** : muscular flesh : BRAWN **4** *pl* **beefs** : COMPLAINT

2beef *vt* : to add weight, strength, or power to — usu. used with *up* ∼ *vi* : COMPLAIN

beef·cake \ˈbēf-ˌkāk\ *n* : a photographic display of muscular male physiques — compare CHEESECAKE

beef cattle *n pl* : cattle developed primarily for the efficient production of meat and marked by capacity for rapid growth, heavy well-fleshed body, and stocky build

beef·eat·er \ˈbē-ˌfēt-ər\ *n* : a yeoman of the guard of an English monarch

bee fly *n* : any of numerous two-winged flies (family Bombyliidae) many of which resemble bees

beef·steak \ˈbēf-ˌstāk\ *n* : a steak of beef usu. from the hindquarter

beefsteak fungus *n* : a bright red edible pore fungus (*Fistulina hepatica*) that grows on dead trees

beef Stro·ga·noff \-ˈstrō-gə-ˌnȯf, -ˈstrō-\ *n* [Count Paul *Stroganoff*, 19th cent. Russ diplomat] : beef sliced thin and cooked in a sour-cream sauce

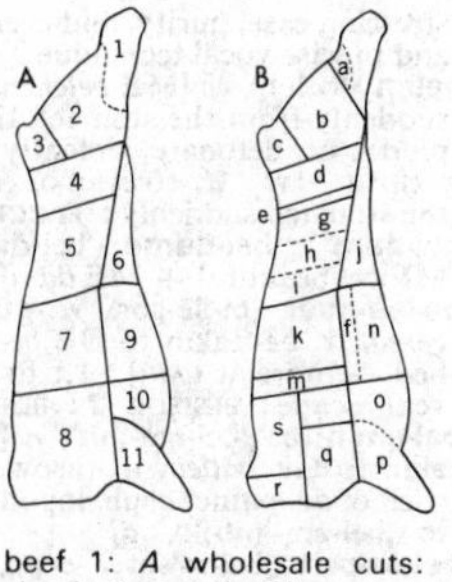

beef 1: *A* wholesale cuts: *1* shank, *2* round with rump and shank cut off, *3* rump, *4* sirloin, *5* short loin, *6* flank, *7* rib, *8* chuck, *9* plate, *10* brisket, *11* shank; *B* retail cuts: *a* heel pot roast, *b* round steak, *c* rump roast, *d* sirloin steak, *e* pinbone steak, *f* short ribs, *g* porterhouse steak, *h* T-bone steak, *i* club steak, *j* flank steak, *k* rib roast, *m* blade rib roast, *n* plate, *o* brisket, *p* crosscut shank, *q* arm pot roast, *r* boneless neck, *s* blade roast

beef·wood \ˈbēf-ˌwu̇d\ *n* : any of several hard heavy reddish chiefly tropical woods used esp. for cabinetwork; *also* : a tree (as a casuarina) yielding beefwood

beefy \ˈbē-fē\ *adj* **beef·i·er; -est** **1** : heavily and powerfully built **2** : full of beef

bee·hive \ˈbē-ˌhīv\ *n* **1** : HIVE 1 **2** : something resembling a hive for bees: as **a** : a scene of crowded activity **b** : a woman's hairdo that is conical in shape — **beehive** *adj*

bee·keep·er \-ˌkē-pər\ *n* : one who raises bees — **bee·keep·ing** *n*

bee·line \-ˌlīn\ *n* [fr. the belief that nectar-laden bees return to their hives in a direct line] : a straight direct course

Beel·ze·bub \bē-ˈel-zi-ˌbəb, ˈbēl-zi-, ˈbel-\ *n* [*Beelzebub*, prince of devils, fr. L, fr. Gk *Beelzeboub*, fr. Heb *Baʽal zĕbhūbh*, a Philistine god, lit., lord of flies] **1** : DEVIL **2** : a fallen angel in Milton's *Paradise Lost* ranking next to Satan

been *past part of* BE

1beep \ˈbēp\ *n* [imit.] : a sound (as from a horn or an electronic device) that serves as a signal or warning

2beep *vi* **1** : to sound a horn **2** : to make a beep ∼ *vt* : to cause (as a horn) to sound — **beep·er** *n*

beer \ˈbi(ə)r\ *n* [ME *ber*, fr. OE *bēor*; akin to OHG *bior* beer] **1** : a malted and hopped somewhat bitter alcoholic beverage; *specif* : such a beverage brewed by slow fermentation **2** : a carbonated nonalcoholic or a fermented slightly alcoholic beverage with flavoring from roots or other plant parts ⟨birch ∼⟩

beery \ˈbi(ə)r-ē\ *adj* **beer·i·er; -est** **1** : affected or caused by beer ⟨∼ voices⟩ **2** : smelling or tasting of beer ⟨∼ tavern⟩

bees·tings *var of* BEASTINGS

bees·wax \ˈbēz-ˌwaks\ *n* : WAX 1

beet \ˈbēt\ *n* [ME *bete*, fr. OE *bēte*, fr. L *beta*] : a biennial garden plant (genus *Beta*) of the goosefoot family with thick long-stalked edible leaves and swollen root used as a vegetable, as a source of sugar, or for forage; *also* : its root

beet armyworm *n* : an armyworm (*Spodoptera exigua*) that eats the foliage of beets, alfalfa, and vegetables

1bee·tle \ˈbēt-ᵊl\ *n* [ME *betylle*, fr. OE *bitula*, fr. *bītan* to bite] **1** : any of an order (Coleoptera) of insects having four wings of which the outer pair are modified into stiff elytra that protect the inner pair when at rest **2** : any of various insects resembling a beetle

2beetle *n* [ME *betel*, fr. OE *bietel*; akin to OE *bēatan* to beat] **1** : a heavy wooden hammering or ramming instrument **2** : a wooden pestle or bat for domestic tasks **3** : a machine for giving fabrics a lustrous finish

3beetle *adj* [ME *bitel-browed* having overhanging brows, prob. fr. *betylle*, *bitel* beetle] : being prominent and overhanging ⟨∼ brows⟩

4beetle *vi* **bee·tled; bee·tling** \ˈbēt-liŋ, -ᵊl-iŋ\ : PROJECT, JUT ⟨to scale the *beetling* crags —R. L. Stevenson⟩

beet leafhopper *n* : a leafhopper (*Eutettix tenellus*) that transmits a virus disease to sugar beets and other plants in the western U.S.

bee tree *n* : a hollow tree in which honeybees nest

beet·root \ˈbē-ˌtrüt\ *n*, *chiefly Brit* : the root of the beet

bef *abbr* before

BEF *abbr* British Expeditionary Force

be·fall \bi-ˈfȯl\ *vb* **-fell** \-ˈfel\; **-fall·en** \-ˈfȯ-lən\ *vi* : to happen esp. as if by fate ∼ *vt* : to happen to

be·fit \bi-ˈfit\ *vt* : to be proper or becoming to

be·fit·ting \-ˈfit-iŋ\ *adj* **1** : SUITABLE, APPROPRIATE **2** : PROPER, DECENT — **be·fit·ting·ly** \-iŋ-lē\ *adv*

be·fog \bi-ˈfȯg, -ˈfäg\ *vt* **1** : to make foggy : OBSCURE **2** : CONFUSE

be·fool \bi-ˈfül\ *vt* **1** : to make a fool of **2** : DELUDE, DECEIVE

1be·fore \bi-ˈfō(ə)r, -ˈfȯ(ə)r\ *adv* [ME, adv. & prep., fr. OE *beforan*, fr. *be-* + *foran* before, fr. *fore*] **1** : in advance : AHEAD **2** : at an earlier time : PREVIOUSLY

2before *prep* **1 a** (1) : in front of (2) : in the presence of ⟨stood ∼ the judge⟩ **b** : under the jurisdiction or consideration of ⟨the case ∼ the court⟩ **c** (1) : at the disposal of (2) : in store for **2** : preceding in time : earlier than **3** : in a higher or more important position than ⟨put quantity ∼ quality⟩

3before *conj* **1** : earlier than the time when **2** : sooner than

be·fore·hand \bi-ˈfō(ə)r-ˌhand, -ˈfȯ(ə)r-\ *adv or adj* **1 a** : in anticipation **b** : in advance **2** : ahead of time : EARLY — **be·fore·hand·ed·ness** \-ˌhan-dəd-nəs, -ˈhan-\ *n*

be·fore·time \-ˌtīm\ *adv*, *archaic* : FORMERLY

be·foul \bi-ˈfau̇(ə)l\ *vt* : to make foul with or as if with dirt or filth

be·friend \bi-ˈfrend\ *vt* : to act as a friend to

be·fud·dle \bi-ˈfəd-ᵊl\ *vt* **1** : to muddle or stupefy with or as if with drink **2** : CONFUSE, PERPLEX — **be·fud·dle·ment** \-mənt\ *n*

1beg \ˈbeg\ *vb* **begged; beg·ging** [ME *beggen*] *vt* **1** : to ask for as a charity **2** : to ask earnestly for : ENTREAT **3 a** : EVADE, SIDESTEP ⟨*begged* the real problems⟩ **b** : to assume as established or proved ⟨∼ the question⟩ ∼ *vi* **1** : to ask for alms **2** : to ask earnestly ⟨*begged* for mercy⟩

syn BEG, ENTREAT, BESEECH, IMPLORE, SUPPLICATE, ADJURE, IMPORTUNE *shared meaning element* : to ask or request urgently

— **beg off** : to ask to be released from something

2beg *abbr* begin; beginning

be·gat \bi-ˈgat\ *archaic past of* BEGET

be·get \bi-ˈget\ *vt* **-got** \-ˈgät\; **-got·ten** \-ˈgät-ᵊn\ *or* **-got; -get·ting** [ME *begeten*, alter. of *beyeten*, fr. OE *bigietan* — more at GET] **1** : to procreate as the father : SIRE **2** : to produce as an effect : CAUSE — **be·get·ter** *n*

1beg·gar \ˈbeg-ər\ *n* [ME *beggere*, *beggare*, fr. *beggen* to beg + *-ere*, *-are* -er] **1** : one that begs; *esp* : one that lives by asking for gifts **2** : PAUPER **3** : FELLOW

2beggar *vt* **beg·gared; beg·gar·ing** \ˈbeg-(ə-)riŋ\ **1** : to reduce to beggary **2** : to exceed the resources or abilities of ⟨∼*s* description⟩

beg·gar·ly \ˈbeg-ər-lē\ *adj* **1** : befitting or resembling a beggar; *esp* : marked by extreme poverty **2** : contemptibly mean, scant, petty, or paltry ***syn*** see CONTEMPTIBLE — **beg·gar·li·ness** *n*

beg·gar's-lice \ˈbeg-ərz-ˌlīs\ *or* **beg·gar-lice** \-ər-ˌlīs\ *n pl but sing or pl in constr* : any of several plants (as of the genera *Lappula*, *Hackelia*, and *Desmodium*) with prickly or adhesive fruits; *also* : one of these fruits

beg·gar-ticks *or* **beg·gar's-ticks** \-ˌtiks\ *n pl but sing or pl in constr* **1** : BUR MARIGOLD; *also* : its prickly achenes **2** : BEGGAR'S-LICE

beg·gar·weed \ˈbeg-ər-ˌwēd\ *n* **1** : any of various plants (as a knotgrass, spurrey, or dodder) that grow in waste ground **2** : any of several tick trefoils (genus *Desmodium*); *esp* : a West Indian forage plant (*D. tortuosum*) cultivated in the southern U.S.

beg·gary \ˈbeg-ə-rē\ *n*, *pl* **-gar·ies** **1** : POVERTY, PENURY **2** : the class or occupation of beggars **3** : the act of begging : MENDICANCY

be·gin \bi-ˈgin\ *vb* **be·gan** \-ˈgan\; **be·gun** \-ˈgən\; **be·gin·ning** [ME *beginnen*, fr. OE *beginnan*; akin to OHG *biginnan* to begin, OE *onginnan*] *vi* **1 a** : to do the first part of an action : START **b** : to undergo initial steps **2 a** : to come into existence : ARISE **b** : to have a starting point **3** : to do or succeed in the least degree ∼ *vt* **1** : to set about the activity of **2 a** : to call into being : FOUND **b** : ORIGINATE, INVENT **3** : to come first in

syn BEGIN, COMMENCE, START, INITIATE, INAUGURATE *shared meaning element* : to take the first step (as in a course, process, or operation) ***ant*** end

be·gin·ner \bi-ˈgin-ər\ *n* : one that begins something; *specif* : an inexperienced person

1be·gin·ning \bi-ˈgin-iŋ\ *n* **1** : the point at which something begins : START **2** : the first part **3** : ORIGIN, SOURCE **4 a** : a rudimentary stage or early period — usu. used in pl. **b** : something undeveloped or incomplete

2beginning *adj* **1** : just created or formed : INCIPIENT **2** : INTRODUCTORY, EARLY **3** : BASIC ⟨∼ chemistry⟩ **4** : just becoming familiar with the rudiments or practice ⟨a ∼ machinist⟩

beginning rhyme *n* **1** : rhyme at the beginning of successive lines of verse **2** : ALLITERATION

be·gird \bi-ˈgərd\ *vt* **1** : GIRD 1a **2** : SURROUND, ENCOMPASS

be·gone \bi-ˈgȯn *also* -ˈgän\ *vi* [ME, fr. *be gone* (imper.)] : to go away : DEPART — used esp. in the imperative

be·go·nia \bi-ˈgōn-yə\ *n* [NL, genus name, fr. Michel *Bégon* †1710 F governor of Santo Domingo] : any of a large genus (*Begonia* of the family Begoniaceae, the begonia family) of tropical herbs having asymmetrical leaves and being widely cultivated as ornamentals

be·gor·ra \bi-ˈgȯr-ə, -ˈgär-\ *interj* [euphemism for *by God*] *Irish* — used as a mild oath

be·grime \bi-ˈgrīm\ *vt* **be·grimed; be·grim·ing** **1** : to make dirty with grime **2** : SULLY, CORRUPT

be·grudge \bi-ˈgrəj\ *vt* **1** : to give or concede reluctantly **2 a** : to look upon with reluctance or disapproval **b** : to take little pleasure in : be annoyed by **3** : to envy the pleasure or enjoyment of — **be·grudg·er** *n* — **be·grudg·ing·ly** \-ˈgrəj-iŋ-lē\ *adv*

be·guile \bi-ˈgī(ə)l\ *vb* **be·guiled; be·guil·ing** *vt* **1** : to lead by deception **2 a** : HOODWINK **b** : to deprive by guile : CHEAT **3** : to while away esp. by some agreeable occupation **4** : to please or persuade by the use of wiles : CHARM ∼ *vi* : to deceive by wiles ***syn*** see DECEIVE, WHILE — **be·guile·ment** \-ˈgī(ə)l-mənt\ *n* — **be·guil·er** \-ˈgī-lər\ *n* — **be·guil·ing·ly** \-ˈgī-liŋ-lē\ *adv*

be·guine \bi-ˈgēn\ *n* [AmerF *béguine*, fr. F *béguin* flirtation] : a vigorous popular dance of the islands of Saint Lucia and Martinique that somewhat resembles the rumba

Be·guine \ˈbā-ˌgēn, ˌbā-ˈ\ *n* [MF] : a member of one of various ascetic and philanthropic communities of women not under vows founded chiefly in the Netherlands in the 13th century

be·gum \ˈbā-gəm, ˈbē-\ *n* [Hindi *begam*] : a Muslim woman of high rank

ə abut ᵊ kitten ər further a back ā bake ä cot, cart au̇ out ch chin e less ē easy g gift i trip ī life j joke ŋ sing ō flow ȯ flaw ȯi coin th thin t͟h this ü loot u̇ foot y yet yü few yu̇ furious zh vision

be·half \bi-'haf, -'hȧf\ *n* [ME, fr. *by* + *half* half, side] : INTEREST, BENEFIT; *also* : SUPPORT, DEFENSE ⟨argued in his ~⟩ — **in behalf of** *or* **on behalf of** : in the interest of : as a representative of
be·have \bi-'hāv\ *vb* **be·haved; be·hav·ing** [ME *behaven,* fr. *be-* + *haven* to have, hold] *vt* **1** : to bear or comport (oneself) in a particular way **2** : to conduct (oneself) in a proper manner ~ *vi* **1** : to act, function, or react in a particular way **2** : to conduct oneself properly — **be·hav·er** *n*
syn BEHAVE, CONDUCT, COMPORT, DEPORT, ACQUIT *shared meaning element* : to act or to cause or allow (oneself) to act in a particular way ***ant*** misbehave
be·hav·ior \bi-'hā-vyər\ *n* [alter. of ME *behavour,* fr. *behaven*] **1** : the manner of conducting oneself **2 a** : anything that an organism does involving action and response to stimulation **b** : the response of an individual, group, or species to its environment **3** : the way in which something (as a machine) behaves — **be·hav·ior·al** \-vyə-rəl\ *adj* — **be·hav·ior·al·ly** \-rə-lē\ *adv*
behavioral science *n* : a science (as psychology, sociology, or anthropology) dealing with human action and seeking generalizations of man's behavior in society — **behavioral scientist** *n*
be·hav·ior·ism \bi-'hā-vyə-,riz-əm\ *n* : a doctrine holding that the proper concern of psychology is the objective evidence of behavior and that consciousness and mind cannot be meaningfully defined or studied — **be·hav·ior·ist** \-vyə-rəst\ *adj or n* — **be·hav·ior·is·tic** \-,hā-vyə-'ris-tik\ *adj*
be·hav·iour *chiefly Brit var of* BEHAVIOR
be·head \bi-'hed\ *vt* : to cut off the head of : DECAPITATE
be·he·moth \bi-'hē-məth, 'bē-ə-,mäth\ *n* [ME, fr. L, fr. Heb *bĕhēmōth*] **1** *often cap* : an animal described in Job 40:15–24 that is prob. the hippopotamus **2** : something of oppressive or monstrous size or power — **be·he·moth·ic** \,bē-ə-'mäth-ik\ *adj*
be·hest \bi-'hest\ *n* [ME, promise, command, fr. OE *behǣs* promise, fr. *behātan* to promise, fr. *be-* + *hātan* to command, promise — more at HIGHT] **1** : an authoritative order : COMMAND **2** : an urgent prompting ⟨returned home at the ~ of his friends⟩
¹be·hind \bi-'hīnd\ *adv* [ME *behinde,* fr. OE *behindan,* fr. *be-* + *hindan* from behind; akin to OE *hinder* behind — more at HIND] **1 a** : in the place, situation, or time that is being or has been departed from ⟨stay ~⟩ **b** : in, to, or toward the back ⟨look ~⟩ **2 a** : in a secondary or inferior position **b** : in arrears ⟨~ in his payments⟩ **c** : SLOW **3** *archaic* : still to come
²behind *prep* **1 a** (1) : in or to a place or situation in back of or to the rear of ⟨look ~ you⟩ ⟨stayed ~ the troops⟩ (2) : beyond in past time ⟨left a great name ~ him⟩ **b** — used as a function word to indicate something that lies between one thing (as an observer) and another ⟨malice ~ the mask of friendship⟩ **2** — used as a function word to indicate backwardness ⟨~ his classmates in performance⟩, delay ⟨~ schedule⟩, or deficiency ⟨lagged ~ last year's sales⟩ **3 a** : in the background of ⟨the conditions ~ the strike⟩ **b** : in a supporting position at the back of ⟨solidly ~ their candidate⟩ — **behind the times** : OLD-FASHIONED, OUT-OF-DATE
³behind *n* [¹*behind*] : BUTTOCKS — sometimes considered vulgar
be·hind·hand \bi-'hīnd-,hand\ *adj* **1** : being in arrears **2 a** : lagging behind the times : BACKWARD **b** : being in an inferior position **c** : being behind schedule ***syn*** see TARDY ***ant*** beforehand
behind-the-scenes *adj* : kept, made, or held in secret
be·hold \bi-'hōld\ *vb* **-held** \-'held\; **-hold·ing** [ME *beholden* to keep, behold, fr. OE *behealdan,* fr. *be-* + *healdan* to hold] *vt* **1** : to perceive through sight or apprehension : SEE **2** : to gaze upon : OBSERVE ~ *vi* — used in the imperative esp. to call attention — **be·hold·er** *n*
be·hold·en \bi-'hōl-dən\ *adj* [ME, fr. pp. of *beholden*] : being under obligation for a favor or gift : INDEBTED
be·hoof \bi-'hüf\ *n* [ME *behof,* fr. OE *behōf;* akin to OE *hebban* to raise — more at HEAVE] : ADVANTAGE, PROFIT
be·hoove \bi-'hüv\ *or* **be·hove** \-'hōv\ *vb* **be·hooved** *or* **be·hoved; be·hoov·ing** *or* **be·hov·ing** [ME *behoven,* fr. OE *behōfian,* fr. *behōf*] *vt* : to be necessary, proper, or advantageous for ⟨it ~s us to fight⟩ ~ *vi* : to be necessary, fit, or proper
beige \'bāzh\ *n* [F] **1** : cloth made of natural undyed wool **2 a** : a variable color averaging light grayish yellowish brown **b** : a pale to grayish yellow — **beige** *adj* — **beigy** \'bā-zhē\ *adj*
¹be·ing \'bē-iŋ\ *n* **1 a** : the quality or state of having existence **b** (1) : something conceivable as existing (2) : something that actually exists (3) : the totality of existing things **c** : conscious existence : LIFE **2** : the qualities that constitute an existent thing : ESSENCE; *esp* : PERSONALITY **3** : a living thing; *esp* : PERSON
²being *adj* [prp. of *be*] : PRESENT — used in the phrase *for the time being*
Be·ja \'bā-jə\ *n, pl* **Beja 1 a** : a nomadic pastoral people living between the Nile and the Red sea **b** : a member of this people **2** : the Cushitic language of the Beja people
bel \'bel\ *n* [Alexander Graham *Bell*] : ten decibels
be·la·bor \bi-'lā-bər\ *vt* **1** : to work on or at to absurd lengths ⟨~ the obvious⟩ **2 a** : to beat soundly **b** : ASSAIL, ATTACK
be·la·bour *chiefly Brit var of* BELABOR
be·lat·ed \bi-'lāt-əd\ *adj* [pp. of *belate* (to make late)] **1** : delayed beyond the usual time **2** : existing or appearing past the normal or proper time — **be·lat·ed·ly** *adv* — **be·lat·ed·ness** *n*
be·laud \bi-'lȯd\ *vt* : to praise usu. to excess
¹be·lay \bi-'lā\ *vb* [ME *beleggen* to beset, fr. OE *belecgan,* fr. *be-* + *lecgan* to lay] *vt* **1 a** : to secure (as a rope) by turns around a cleat, pin, or bitt **b** : to make fast **2** : STOP **3 a** : to secure (a person) at the end of a rope **b** : to secure (a rope) to a person or object ~ *vi* **1** : to be made fast **2** : STOP, QUIT — used in the imperative ⟨~ there⟩ **3** : to make a line fast by turns around a cleat, pin, or bitt
²belay *n* **1** : the obtaining of a hold (as for a rope) during mountain climbing; *also* : a method of obtaining such a hold **2** : something (as a projection of rock) to which a mountain climber's rope is anchored
bel can·to \bel-'kän-(,)tō\ *n* [It, lit., beautiful singing] : operatic singing originating in 17th century and 18th century Italy and stressing ease, purity, and evenness of tone production and an agile and precise vocal technique
belch \'belch\ *vb* [ME *belchen,* fr. OE *bealcian*] *vi* **1** : to expel gas suddenly from the stomach through the mouth **2** : to erupt, explode, or detonate violently **3** : to issue forth spasmodically : GUSH ~ *vt* **1** : to eject or emit violently **2** : to expel (gas) from the stomach suddenly : ERUCT — **belch** *n*
bel·dam *or* **bel·dame** \'bel-dəm\ *n* [ME *beldam* grandmother, fr. MF *bel* beautiful + ME *dam*] : an old woman; *esp* : HAG
be·lea·guer \bi-'lē-gər\ *vt* **-guered; -guer·ing** \-g(ə-)riŋ\ [D *belegeren,* fr. *be-* (akin to OE *be-*) + *leger* camp; akin to OHG *legar* bed — more at LAIR] **1** : to surround with an army so as to prevent escape : BESIEGE **2** : BESET, HARASS ⟨~*ed* parents⟩
bel·em·nite \'bel-əm-,nīt\ *n* [F *bélemnite,* fr. Gk *belemnon* dart; akin to Gk *ballein* to throw — more at DEVIL] : a conical fossil shell of an extinct cephalopod (family Belemnitidae) — **bel·em·nit·ic** \,bel-əm-'nit-ik\ *adj*
bel es·prit \,bel-ə-'sprē, -e-\ *n, pl* **beaux es·prits** \,bō-,zes-'prē\ [F, lit., fine mind] : a person with a fine and gifted mind
bel·fry \'bel-frē\ *n, pl* **belfries** [ME *belfrey,* alter. of *berfrey,* fr. MF *berfrei,* deriv. of Gk *pyrgos phorētos* movable war tower] **1** : a bell tower; *esp* : one surmounting or attached to another structure **2** : a room in which a bell is hung in a tower **3** : a cupola, turret, or framework for enclosing a bell
Belg *abbr* Belgian; Belgium
bel·ga \'bel-gə\ *n* [F, fr. L *Belga* Belgian] : a former Belgian monetary unit for use in foreign exchange equal to five francs
Bel·gae \'bel-,gī, -,jē\ *n pl* [L, pl. of *Belga*] : a people occupying northern France, Belgium, and England in Caesar's time — **Bel·gic** \-jik\ *adj*
Bel·gian \'bel-jən\ *n* **1** : a native or inhabitant of Belgium **2** : any of a Belgian breed of heavy usu. roan or chestnut draft horses — **Belgian** *adj*
Belgian hare *n* : any of a breed of slender dark-red domestic rabbits
Belgian Ma·li·nois \-,mal-ən-'wä\ *n* : any of a breed of squarely built working dogs closely related to the Belgian sheepdog and having relatively short straight hair with a dense undercoat — called also *Malinois*
Belgian sheepdog *n* : any of a breed of hardy black or gray dogs developed in Belgium esp. for herding sheep
Belgian Ter·vu·ren \-(,)tər-'vyür-ən, -ter-\ *n* [*Tervuren,* commune in Brabant, Belgium] : any of a breed of working dogs closely related to the Belgian sheepdog but having abundant long straight fawn-colored hair with black tips
Bel·go- \'bel-(,)gō\ *comb form* [*Belgian*] : Belgian and ⟨*Belgo*-English⟩
Be·lial \'bē-lē-əl, 'bēl-yəl\ *n* [Gk, fr. Heb *bĕlīya'al* worthlessness] **1** — a biblical name of the devil or one of the fiends **2** : one of the fallen angels in Milton's *Paradise Lost*
be·lie \bi-'lī\ *vt* **-lied; -ly·ing 1 a** : to give a false impression of **b** : to contrast with **2 a** : to prove (something) false **b** : to run counter to : CONTRADICT ***syn*** see MISREPRESENT — **be·li·er** \-'lī(-ə)r\ *n*
be·lief \bə-'lēf\ *n* [ME *beleave,* prob. alter. of OE *geleāfa,* fr. *ge-,* associative prefix + *lēafa;* akin to OE *lȳfan*] **1** : a state or habit of mind in which trust or confidence is placed in some person or thing **2** : something believed; *specif* : a tenet or body of tenets held by a group **3** : conviction of the truth of some statement or the reality of some being or phenomenon esp. when based on examination of evidence
syn* 1** BELIEF, FAITH, CREDENCE, CREDIT *shared meaning element* : an assent or act of assenting to something offered for acceptance. BELIEF may suggest mental acceptance without directly implying certitude or certainty on the part of the believer ⟨had the strongest *belief* in his own capacity for success⟩ FAITH implies certitude and full trust and confidence in the source whether there be objective evidence or not ⟨*faith* is the substance of things hoped for, the evidence of things not seen —Heb. 11:1 (AV)⟩ CREDENCE implies intellectual acceptance but conveys nothing about the validity of the grounds for acceptance ⟨give *credence* to rumors⟩ CREDIT implies acceptance on grounds short of proof and especially on the past reputation of the source ⟨what *credit* can be attached to an anonymous report?⟩ ***ant unbelief, disbelief
2 see OPINION
be·liev·able \-'lē-və-bəl\ *adj* : capable of being believed esp. as within the range of known possibility or probability ***syn*** see PLAUSIBLE ***ant*** unbelievable — **be·liev·abil·i·ty** \-,lē-və-'bil-ət-ē\ *n* — **be·liev·ably** \-'lē-və-blē\ *adv*
be·lieve \bə-'lēv\ *vb* **be·lieved; be·liev·ing** [ME *beleven,* fr. OE *belēfan,* fr. *be-* + *lȳfan, lēfan* to allow, believe; akin to OHG *gilouben* to believe, OE *lēof* dear — more at LOVE] *vi* **1 a** : to have a firm religious faith **b** : to accept trustfully and on faith ⟨people who ~ in the natural goodness of man⟩ **2** : to have a firm conviction as to the reality or goodness of something ⟨~ in exercise⟩ **3** : to hold an opinion : THINK ~ *vt* **1** : to consider to be true or honest ⟨~ the reports⟩ **2** : to hold as an opinion : SUPPOSE ⟨I ~ it will rain soon⟩ ***syn*** see KNOW — **be·liev·er** *n*
be·like \bi-'līk\ *adv, archaic* : most likely : PROBABLY
be·lit·tle \bi-'lit-ᵊl\ *vt* **-lit·tled; -lit·tling** \-'lit-ᵊl-iŋ, -'lit-liŋ\ **1** : to cause (a person or thing) to seem little or less **2** : DISPARAGE 2 ⟨~*s* her efforts⟩ ***syn*** see DECRY ***ant*** aggrandize, magnify — **be·lit·tle·ment** \-'lit-ᵊl-mənt\ *n* — **be·lit·tler** \-'lit-ᵊl-ər, -'lit-lər\ *n*
be·live \bi-'līv\ *adv* [ME *bilive,* fr. *by* + *live,* dat. of *lif* life] *Scot* : in due time : by and by
¹bell \'bel\ *n* [ME *belle,* fr. OE; akin to OE *bellan* to roar — more at BELLOW] **1** : a hollow metallic device that vibrates and gives forth a ringing sound when struck **2** : the sounding of a bell as a signal **3 a** : a

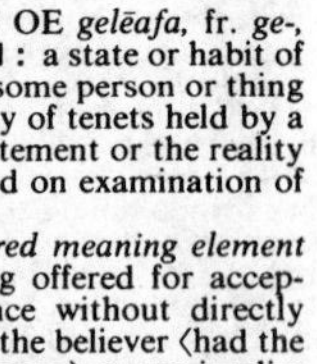

bell 1: *1* crown, *2* head, *3* shoulder, *4* waist, *5* bead lines, *6* sound bow, *7* lip, *8* mouth, *9* clapper

bell rung to tell the hour   **b** : a stroke of such a bell esp. on ship-board   **c** : the time so indicated   **d** : a half hour period of a watch on shipboard indicated by the strokes of a bell — see SHIP'S BELLS table below   **4** : something having the form of a bell: as   **a** : the corolla of a flower   **b** : the flared end of a wind instrument   **5 a** : a percussion instrument consisting of metal bars or tubes that when struck give out tones resembling bells — usu. used in pl.   **b** : GLOCKENSPIEL

²bell vt **1** : to provide with a bell   **2** : to make bell-mouthed ~ vi : to take the form of a bell : FLARE — **bell the cat** : to do a daring or risky deed

SHIP'S BELLS

NO. OF BELLS	HOUR (A.M. OR P.M.)		
1	12:30	4:30	8:30
2	1:00	5:00	9:00
3	1:30	5:30	9:30
4	2:00	6:00	10:00
5	2:30	6:30	10:30
6	3:00	7:00	11:00
7	3:30	7:30	11:30
8	4:00	8:00	12:00

³bell vi [ME bellen, fr. OE bellan] : to make a resonant bellowing or baying sound ⟨the wild buck ~s from ferny brake —Sir Walter Scott⟩

⁴bell n : BELLOW, ROAR

bel·la·don·na \,bel-ə-'dän-ə\ n [It., lit., beautiful lady]   **1** : a European poisonous plant (Atropa belladonna) of the nightshade family having reddish bell-shaped flowers, shining black berries, and root and leaves that yield atropine — called also deadly nightshade   **2** : a medicinal extract (as atropine) from the belladonna plant

belladonna lily n : an amaryllis (Amaryllis belladonna) often cultivated for its fragrant usu. white or rose flowers

bell-bird \'bel-,bərd\ n : any of several birds whose notes suggest the sound of a bell

bell–bot·toms \'bel-'bät-əmz\ n pl : pants with wide flaring bottoms — **bell–bottom** adj

bell-boy \'bel-,bȯi\ n : BELLHOP

bell buoy n : a buoy with a bell that rings by the action of the waves

bell captain n : CAPTAIN 1h(2)

belle \'bel\ n [F, fem. of beau beautiful — more at BEAU] : a popular and attractive girl or woman; esp : a girl or woman whose charm and beauty make her a favorite ⟨the ~ of the ball⟩

Bel·leek \bə-'lēk\ n [Belleek, town in Northern Ireland] : a very thin translucent porcelain with a lustrous pearly glaze first produced in Ireland in the mid-nineteenth century — called also Belleek china, Belleek ware

Bel·ler·o·phon \bə-'ler-ə-fən, -,fän\ n [L, fr. Gk Bellerophōn] : a legendary Greek hero noted for killing the Chimera

belles let·tres \bel-'letr\ n pl but sing in constr [F, lit., fine letters] : literature that is an end in itself and not practical or purely informative; specif : light, entertaining, and often sophisticated literature

bel·le·trist \bel-'le-trəst\ n [belles lettres] : a writer of belles lettres — **bel·le·tris·tic** \,bel-ə-'tris-tik\ adj

bell-flow·er \'bel-,flaů(-ə)r\ n : any of a genus (Campanula of the family Campanulaceae, the bellflower family) having an acrid juice, alternate leaves, and usu. showy bell-shaped flowers

bell-hop \-,häp\ n [short for bell-hopper] : a hotel or club employee who escorts guests to rooms, assists them with luggage, and runs errands

bel·li·cose \'bel-i-,kōs\ adj [ME, fr. L bellicosus, fr. bellicus of war, fr. bellum war] : favoring or inclined to start quarrels or wars   syn see BELLIGERENT   ant pacific, amicable — **bel·li·cose·ly** adv — **bel·li·cose·ness** n — **bel·li·cos·i·ty** \,bel-i-'käs-ət-ē\ n

-bel·lied \bel-ēd\ adj comb form : having (such) a belly ⟨a big-bellied man⟩

bel·lig·er·ence \bə-'lij-(ə-)rən(t)s\ n : an aggressive or truculent attitude, atmosphere, or disposition

bel·lig·er·en·cy \-rən-sē\ n   **1** : the state of being at war or in conflict; specif : the status of a legally recognized belligerent   **2** : BELLIGERENCE

bel·lig·er·ent \-rənt\ adj [modif. of L belligerant-, belligerans, prp. of belligerare to wage war, fr. belliger waging war, fr. bellum + gerere to wage — more at CAST]   **1** : waging war; specif : belonging to or recognized as a state at war and protected by and subject to the laws of war   **2** : inclined to or exhibiting assertiveness, hostility, or combativeness — **belligerent** n — **bel·lig·er·ent·ly** adv

syn BELLIGERENT, BELLICOSE, PUGNACIOUS, COMBATIVE, QUARRELSOME, CONTENTIOUS shared meaning element : having or taking an aggressive or truculent attitude   ant friendly

bell jar n : a bell-shaped usu. glass vessel designed to cover objects or to contain gases or a vacuum

bell–ly·ra \'bel-'lī-rə\ or **bell lyre** \-,lī(ə)r\ n [lyra fr. L, lyre] : a glockenspiel mounted in a portable lyre-shaped frame and used esp. in marching bands

bell·man \'bel-mən\ n   **1** : a man (as a town crier) who rings a bell   **2** : BELLHOP

bell metal n : bronze that consists usu. of three to four parts of copper to one of tin and that is used for making bells

Bel·lo·na \bə-'lō-nə\ n [L] : the Roman goddess of war

bel·low \'bel-(,)ō, -ə(-w)\ vb [ME belwen, fr. OE bylgian; akin to OE & OHG bellan to roar, Skt bhāsate he talks] vi   **1** : to make the loud deep hollow sound characteristic of a bull   **2** : to shout in a deep voice ~ vt : BAWL ⟨~ the orders⟩ — **bellow** n

bel·lows \'bel-(,)ōz, -əz\ n pl but sing or pl in constr [ME bely, below, belwes — more at BELLY]   **1** : an instrument or machine that by alternate expansion and contraction draws in air through a valve or orifice and expels it through a tube; also : any of various other blowers   **2** : LUNGS   **3** : the pleated expansible part in a camera

bell-pull \'bel-,půl\ n : a handle or knob attached to a cord by which one rings a bell; also : the cord itself

bell push n : a button that is pushed to ring a bell

bells \'belz\ n pl : BELL-BOTTOMS

bell tower n : a tower that supports or shelters a bell

bell-weth·er \'bel-'weth-ər, -,weth-\ n [ME, leading sheep of a flock, leader, fr. belle bell + wether; fr. the practice of belling the leader of a flock] : one that takes the lead or initiative : LEADER

bell-wort \'bel-,wərt, -,wȯ(ə)rt\ n : any of a small genus (Uvularia) of herbs of the lily family with yellow drooping bell-shaped flowers

¹bel·ly \'bel-ē\ n, pl **bellies** [ME bely bellows, belly, fr. OE belg bag, skin; akin to OHG balg bag, skin, OE blāwan to blow]   **1 a** : ABDOMEN 1   **b** : the undersurface of an animal's body; also : hide from this part   **c** : WOMB, UTERUS   **2** : the stomach and its adjuncts   **2** : an internal cavity : INTERIOR   **3** : appetite for food   **4** : a surface or object curved or rounded like a human belly   **5 a** : the part of a sail that swells out when filled with wind   **b** : the enlarged fleshy body of a muscle   **c** : the side of a piece of printer's type having the nick

²belly vb **bel·lied; bel·ly·ing** : SWELL, FILL

¹bel·ly·ache \'bel-ē-,āk\ n : pain in the abdomen and esp. in the bowels : COLIC

²bellyache vi : to complain whiningly or peevishly : find fault — **bel·ly·ach·er** n

bel·ly·band \'bel-ē-,band\ n : a band around or across the belly : as   **a** : GIRTH 1   **b** : BAND 4b

belly button n : NAVEL 1

belly dance n : a usu. solo dance emphasizing movements of the belly — **belly dance** vi — **belly dancer** n

belly flop n : a dive (as into water or in coasting prone on a sled) in which the front of the body strikes flat against another surface — called also belly flopper — **belly flop** vi

bel·ly·ful \'bel-ē-,fůl\ n : an excessive amount ⟨a ~ of advice⟩

bel·ly–land \-,land\ vi : to land an airplane on its undersurface without use of landing gear — **belly landing** n

belly laugh n : a deep hearty laugh

be·long \bi-'lȯŋ\ vb [ME belongen, fr. be- + longen to be suitable — more at LONG]   **1 a** : to be suitable, appropriate, or advantageous ⟨a telephone ~s in every home⟩   **b** : to be in a proper situation ⟨a man of his ability ~s in teaching⟩   **2 a** : to be the property of a person or thing — used with to   **b** : to be attached or bound by birth, allegiance, or dependency   **c** : to be a member of a club or organization   **3** : to be an attribute, part, adjunct, or function of a person or thing ⟨nuts and bolts ~ to a car⟩   **4** : to be properly classified

be·long·ing \-'lȯŋ-iŋ\ n   **1** : POSSESSION — usu. used in pl.   **2** : close or intimate relationship ⟨a sense of ~⟩

Belo·rus·sian \,bel-ō-'rəsh-ən\ n   **1** : a native or inhabitant of Belorussia, U.S.S.R.   **2** : the Slavic language of the Belorussians — **Belorussian** adj

be·loved \bi-'ləv(-ə)d\ adj [ME, fr. pp. of beloven to love, fr. be- + loven to love] : dearly loved — **beloved** n

¹be·low \bi-'lō\ adv [be- + low, adj.]   **1** : in or to a lower place   **2 a** : on earth   **b** : in or to Hades or hell   **3** : on or to a lower floor or deck   **4** : in, to, or at a lower rank or number   **5** : lower on the same page or on a following page   **6** : under the surface of the water

²below prep   **1** : in or to a lower place than : UNDER   **2** : inferior to (as in rank)   **3** : not suitable to the rank of : BENEATH

³below n : something that is below

⁴below adj : written or discussed lower on the same page or on a following page

Bel Pa·ese \,bel-pä-'ā-zə, -zē\ trademark — used for a mild soft creamy cheese in a firm rind

Bel·shaz·zar \bel-'shaz-ər\ n [Heb Bēlshaṣṣar] : a son of Nebuchadnezzar and king of Babylon

¹belt \'belt\ n [ME, fr. OE, akin to OHG balz belt; both fr. a prehistoric WGmc-NGmc word borrowed fr. L balteus belt]   **1 a** : a strip of flexible material worn esp. around the waist   **b** : a similar article worn as a corset or for protection or safety   **2** : a continuous band of tough flexible material for transmitting motion and power or conveying materials   **3** : an area characterized by some distinctive feature (as of culture, habitation, geology, or life forms); esp : one suited to a particular crop ⟨the corn ~⟩ — **belt·ed** \'bel-təd\ adj — **belt·less** \'belt-ləs\ adj — **below the belt** : UNFAIRLY — **under one's belt** : in one's possession : as part of one's experience

²belt vt **1 a** : to encircle or fasten with a belt   **b** : to strap on   **2 a** : to beat with or as if with a belt : THRASH   **b** : STRIKE, HIT   **3** : to mark with a band   **4** : to sing in a forceful manner or style ⟨~ing out popular songs⟩ ~ vi : to move or act in a vigorous or violent manner

³belt n   **1** : a jarring blow : WHACK   **2** : DRINK ⟨a ~ of brandy⟩

Bel·tane \'bel-tən\ n [ME, fr. ScGael bealltain]   **1** : the first day of May in the old Scottish calendar   **2** : the Celtic May Day festival

belt highway n : BELTWAY

belt·ing \'bel-tiŋ\ n   **1** : BELTS   **2** : material for belts

Belts·ville Small White \'belts-,vil-, -vəl-\ n [Beltsville, Md.] : a small white domestic turkey of a variety developed by the U.S. Department of Agriculture

belt tightening n : a reduction in spending

belt up vi, Brit : to shut up

belt·way \'belt-,wā\ n : a highway skirting an urban area

be·lu·ga \bə-'lü-gə\ n [Russ, fr. belyĭ white; akin to Gk phainein to show — more at FANCY]   **1** : a white sturgeon (Acipenser huso) of the Black sea, Caspian sea, and their tributaries   **2** [Russ belukha,

ə abut	ᵊ kitten	ər further	a back	ā bake	ä cot, cart
aů out	ch chin	e less	ē easy	g gift	i trip	ī life
j joke	ŋ sing	ō flow	ȯ flaw	ȯi coin	th thin	th this
ü loot	ů foot	y yet	yü few	yů furious	zh vision

fr. *belyĭ*] : a cetacean (*Delphinapterus leucas*) that is about 10 feet long and white when adult
bel·ve·dere \'bel-və-ˌdi(ə)r\ *n* [It, lit., beautiful view] : a structure (as a cupola or a summerhouse) designed to command a view
BEM *abbr* **1** bachelor of engineering of mines **2** British Empire Medal
be·ma \'bē-mə\ *n* [LL & LGk; LL, fr. LGk *bēma*, fr. Gk, step, tribunal, fr. *bainein* to go — more at COME] : the part of an Eastern church containing the altar — see BASILICA illustration
Bem·ba \'bem-bə\ *n, pl* **Bemba** *or* **Bembas** **1** : a member of a primarily agricultural Bantu-speaking people of northern Rhodesia **2** : a Bantu language of the Bemba people
be·med·aled *or* **be·med·alled** \bi-'med-ᵊld\ *adj* : wearing or decorated with medals
be·mire \bi-'mī(ə)r\ *vt* **1** : to soil with mud or dirt **2** : to drag through or sink in mire
be·moan \bi-'mōn\ *vt* **1** : to express deep grief or distress over ⟨implores their pity, and his pain ~*s* —John Dryden⟩ **2** : to regard with displeasure, disapproval, or regret ***syn*** see DEPLORE
be·mock \bi-'mäk, -'mȯk\ *vt, archaic* : MOCK
be·muse \bi-'myüz\ *vt* **1** : to make confused : BEWILDER **2** : to cause to become lost in thought — **be·mus·ed·ly** \-'myü-zəd-lē\ *adv* — **be·muse·ment** \-'myüz-mənt\ *n*
1ben \'ben\ *adv* [ME, fr. OE *binnan*, fr. *be-* + *innan* within, from within, fr. *in*] *Scot* : WITHIN
2ben \(ˈ)ben\ *prep, Scot* : WITHIN
3ben \'ben\ *n, Scot* : the inner room or parlor of a 2-room cottage
Bence–Jones protein \ˌben(t)s-ˌjōnz-\ *n* [Henry *Bence-Jones* †1873 E physician and chemist] : a globulin or a group of globulins found in the blood serum and urine in multiple myeloma and occas. in other bone diseases
1bench \'bench\ *n* [ME, fr. OE *benc*; akin to OHG *bank* bench] **1** **a** : a long seat for two or more persons **b** : a thwart in a boat **c** (1) : a seat on which the members of an athletic team await a turn or opportunity to play (2) : the reserve players on a team **2** **a** : the seat where a judge sits in court **b** : the office or dignity of a judge **c** : the place where justice is administered : COURT **d** : the persons who sit as judges **3** **a** : a seat for an official **b** : the office or dignity of such an official **c** : the officials occupying such a bench **4** **a** : a long worktable **b** : a table forming part of a machine **5** : TERRACE, SHELF; *esp* : a former wave-cut shore of a sea or lake or floodplain of a river **6** **a** : a platform on which a dog is placed at a dog show **b** : a dog show
2bench *vt* **1** : to furnish with benches **2** **a** : to seat on a bench **b** (1) : to remove from or keep out of a game (2) : to remove from the starting lineup **3** : to exhibit (dogs) on a bench ~ *vi* : to form a bench by natural processes
bench·er \'ben-chər\ *n* : one who sits on or presides at a bench
bench mark *n* **1** : a mark on a permanent object indicating elevation and serving as a reference in topographical surveys and tidal observations **2** *usu* **benchmark** **a** : a point of reference from which measurements may be made **b** : something that serves as a standard by which others may be measured
bench show *n* : an exhibition of small animals in competition for prizes on the basis of points of physical conformation and condition
bench warrant *n* : a warrant issued by a presiding judge or by a court against a person guilty of contempt or indicted for a crime
1bend \'bend\ *n* [ME, fr. MF *bende*, of Gmc origin; akin to OHG *binta, bant* band — more at BAND] **1** : a diagonal band that runs from the dexter chief to the sinister base on a heraldic shield **2** : the half of a butt or a hide trimmed of the thinner parts **3** [ME, band, fr. OE *bend* fetter — more at BAND] : a knot by which one rope is fastened to another or to some object
2bend *vb* **bent** \'bent\; **bend·ing** [ME *bendan*, fr. OE *bendan*; akin to OE *bend* fetter] *vt* **1** : to constrain or strain to tension ⟨~ a bow⟩ **2** **a** : to turn or force from straight or even to curved or angular **b** : to force back to an original straight or even condition **c** : to force from a proper shape **3** : FASTEN ⟨~ a sail to its yard⟩ **4** : to make submissive : SUBDUE **5** **a** : to cause to turn from a straight course : DEFLECT **b** : to guide or turn toward : DIRECT **c** : INCLINE, DISPOSE **6** : to direct strenuously or with interest : APPLY ~ *vi* **1** : to curve out of a straight line or position; *specif* : to incline the body in token of submission **2** : INCLINE, TEND **3** : to apply oneself vigorously ⟨~*ing* to their work⟩ **4** : to make concessions : COMPROMISE ***syn*** see CURVE — **bend over backwards** : to make extreme efforts at concession
3bend *n* **1** : the act or process of bending : the state of being bent **2** : something that is bent: as **a** : a curved part of a stream **b** : 1WALE 2 — usu. used in pl. **3** *pl but sing or pl in constr* : CAISSON DISEASE ⟨a case of the ~*s*⟩ — ***around the bend*** : MAD, CRAZY ⟨afraid his friend was going *around the bend*⟩
ben·day \'ben-'dā\ *adj, often cap* [Benjamin *Day* †1916 Am printer] : involving a process for adding shaded or tinted areas made up of dots for reproduction by line engraving — **benday** *vt*
bend·er \'ben-dər\ *n* **1** : one that bends **2** : SPREE
bend sinister *n* : a diagonal bend that runs from the sinister chief to the dexter base on a heraldic shield
1be·neath \bi-'nēth\ *adv* [ME *benethe*, fr. OE *beneothan*, fr. *be-* + *neothan* below; akin to OE *nithera* nether] **1** : in or to a lower position : BELOW **2** : directly under : UNDERNEATH
2beneath *prep* **1** **a** : in or to a lower position than : BELOW **b** : directly under **c** : at the foot of **2** : not suitable to the rank of : unworthy of **3** : under the control, pressure, or influence of
ben·e·dict \'ben-ə-ˌdikt\ *n* [alter. of *Benedick*, character in Shakespeare's *Much Ado about Nothing*] : a newly married man who has long been a bachelor
Ben·e·dic·tine \ˌben-ə-'dik-tən, -ˌtēn\ *n* : a monk or a nun of one of the congregations following the rule of St. Benedict and devoted esp. to scholarship and liturgical worship — **Benedictine** *adj*
bene·dic·tion \ˌben-ə-'dik-shən\ *n* [ME *benediccioun*, fr. LL *benediction-, benedictio*, fr. *benedictus*, pp. of *benedicere* to bless, fr. L, to speak well of, fr. *bene* well + *dicere* to say — more at BOUNTY, DICTION] **1** : an expression of good wishes **2** : the invocation of a blessing; *esp* : the short blessing with which public worship is concluded **3** *often cap* : a Roman Catholic or Anglo-Catholic devotion including the exposition of the eucharistic Host in the monstrance and the blessing of the people with it **4** : something that promotes goodness or well-being
bene·dic·to·ry \-'dik-t(ə-)rē\ *adj* : of or expressing benediction
Bene·dic·tus \-'dik-təs\ *n* [LL, blessed, fr. pp. of *benedicere*; fr. its first word] **1** : a canticle from Mt 21:9 beginning "Blessed is he that cometh in the name of the Lord" **2** : a canticle from Lk 1:68 beginning "Blessed be the Lord God of Israel"
bene·fac·tion \ˌben-ə-'fak-shən\ *n* [LL *benefaction-, benefactio*, fr. L *bene factus*, pp. of *bene facere* to do good to, fr. *bene* + *facere* to do — more at DO] **1** : the act of benefiting **2** : a benefit conferred; *esp* : a charitable donation
bene·fac·tor \'ben-ə-ˌfak-tər\ *n* : one that confers a benefit; *esp* : one that makes a gift or bequest — **bene·fac·tress** \-trəs\ *n*
be·nef·ic \bə-'nef-ik\ *adj* [L *beneficus*, fr. *bene* + *facere*] : BENEFICENT
ben·e·fice \'ben-ə-fəs\ *n* [ME, fr. MF, fr. ML *beneficium*, fr. L, favor, promotion, fr. *beneficus*] **1** : an ecclesiastical office to which the revenue from an endowment is attached **2** : a feudal estate in lands : FIEF — **benefice** *vt*
be·nef·i·cence \bə-'nef-ə-sən(t)s\ *n* [L *beneficentia*, fr. *beneficus*] **1** : the quality or state of being beneficent **2** : BENEFACTION
be·nef·i·cent \-sənt\ *adj* [back-formation fr. *beneficence*] **1** : doing or producing good; *esp* : performing acts of kindness and charity **2** : BENEFICIAL — **be·nef·i·cent·ly** *adv*
ben·e·fi·cial \ˌben-ə-'fish-əl\ *adj* [L *beneficium* favor, benefit] **1** : conferring benefits : conducive to personal or social well-being **2** : receiving or entitling one to receive advantage, use, or benefit ⟨the ~ owner of an estate⟩ ⟨a ~ legacy⟩ — **ben·e·fi·cial·ly** \-'fish-ə-lē\ *adv* — **ben·e·fi·cial·ness** *n*
syn BENEFICIAL, ADVANTAGEOUS, PROFITABLE *shared meaning element* : bringing good or gain ***ant*** harmful, detrimental
ben·e·fi·cia·ry \ˌben-ə-'fish-ē-ˌer-ē, -'fish-(ə-)rē\ *n, pl* **-ries** **1** : one that benefits from something ⟨*beneficiaries* of government programs⟩ **2** **a** : the person designated to receive the income of a trust estate **b** : the person named (as in an insurance policy) to receive proceeds or benefits — **beneficiary** *adj*
ben·e·fi·ci·ate \-'fish-ē-ˌāt\ *vt* **-at·ed; -at·ing** : to treat (a raw material) so as to improve properties; *esp* : to prepare (iron ore) for smelting — **ben·e·fi·ci·a·tion** \-ˌfish-ē-'ā-shən\ *n*
1ben·e·fit \'ben-ə-ˌfit\ *n* [ME, fr. AF *benfet*, fr. L *bene factum*, fr. neut. of *bene factus*] **1** *archaic* : an act of kindness : BENEFACTION **2** **a** : something that promotes well-being : ADVANTAGE **b** : useful aid : HELP **3** **a** : financial help in time of sickness, old age, or unemployment **b** : a payment or service provided for under an annuity, pension plan, or insurance policy **4** : an entertainment or social event to raise funds for a person or cause
2benefit *vb* **-fit·ed** \-ˌfit-əd\ *or* **-fit·ted; -fit·ing** *or* **-fit·ting** *vt* : to be useful or profitable to ⟨medicines that ~ mankind⟩ ~ *vi* : to receive benefit — **ben·e·fit·er** \-ˌfit-ər\ *n*
benefit of clergy **1** : clerical exemption from trial in a civil court **2** : the ministration or sanction of the church ⟨a couple living together without *benefit of clergy*⟩
be·nev·o·lence \bə-'nev(-ə)-lən(t)s\ *n* **1** : disposition to do good **2** **a** : an act of kindness **b** : a generous gift **3** : a compulsory levy by certain English kings with no other authority than the claim of prerogative
be·nev·o·lent \-lənt\ *adj* [ME, fr. L *benevolent-, benevolens*, fr. *bene* + *volent-, volens*, prp. of *velle* to wish — more at WILL] **1** **a** : marked by or disposed to doing good ⟨a ~ donor⟩ **b** : organized for the purpose of doing good ⟨a ~ society⟩ **2** : marked by or suggestive of goodwill ⟨~ smiles⟩ — **be·nev·o·lent·ly** *adv* — **be·nev·o·lent·ness** *n*
Ben·gal·ee \ben-'gȯl-ē, beŋ-\ *n* [Hindi *Baṅgālī* Bengali] : a native or resident of Bangladesh — **Bengalee** *adj*
Ben·gali \ben-'gȯ-lē, beŋ-\ *n* [Hindi *Baṅgālī*, fr. *Baṅgāl* Bengal] **1** : a native or resident of Bengal **2** : a native or inhabitant of Bangladesh **3** : the modern Indic language of Bengal — **Bengali** *adj*
ben·ga·line \'beŋ-gə-ˌlēn\ *n* [F, fr. *Bengal*] : a fabric with a crosswise rib made from textile fibers (as rayon, nylon, cotton, or wool) often in combination
Ben·gal light \ˌben-ˌgȯl-, ˌbeŋ-\ *n* **1** : a blue light used formerly for signaling and illumination **2** : any of various colored lights or flares
BEngr *abbr* bachelor of engineering
BEngS *abbr* bachelor of engineering science
be·night·ed \bi-'nīt-əd\ *adj* **1** : overtaken by darkness or night **2** : existing in a state of intellectual, moral, or social darkness : UNENLIGHTENED — **be·night·ed·ly** *adv* — **be·night·ed·ness** *n*
be·nign \bi-'nīn\ *adj* [ME *benigne*, fr. MF, fr. L *benignus*, fr. *bene* well + *gigni* to be born, pass. of *gignere* to beget — more at BOUNTY, KIN] **1** : of a gentle disposition : GRACIOUS ⟨a ~ teacher⟩ **2** **a** : showing kindness and gentleness ⟨~ faces⟩ **b** : FAVORABLE ⟨a ~ climate⟩ **3** : of a mild character ⟨~ tumor⟩ ***syn*** see KIND ***ant*** malign — **be·nig·ni·ty** \-'nig-nət-ē\ *n* — **be·nign·ly** \-'nīn-lē\ *adv*
be·nig·nan·cy \bi-'nig-nən-sē\ *n* : benignant quality
be·nig·nant \-nənt\ *adj* [*benign* + *-ant* (as in *malignant*)] **1** : serenely mild and kindly : BENIGN **2** : FAVORABLE, BENEFICIAL ⟨a ~ power⟩ ***syn*** see KIND ***ant*** malignant — **be·nig·nant·ly** *adv*
ben·i·son \'ben-ə-sən, -zən\ *n* [ME *beneson*, fr. OF *beneiçon*, fr. LL *benediction-, benedictio*] : BLESSING, BENEDICTION
Ben·ja·min \'benj-(ə-)mən\ *n* [Heb *Binyāmīn*] : a son of Jacob and the traditional eponymous ancestor of one of the tribes of Israel
ben·ne *or* **ben·ni** \'ben-ē\ *n* [of African origin; akin to Mandingo *bĕne* sesame] : SESAME 1
ben·ny \'ben-ē\ *n, pl* **bennies** [*Benzedrine* + *-ie*] *slang* : a tablet of amphetamine taken as a stimulant
1bent \'bent\ *n* [ME, grassy place, bent grass, fr. OE *beonot-*; akin to OHG *binuz* rush] **1** : unenclosed grassland **2** **a** (1) : a reedy grass (2) : a stalk of stiff coarse grass **b** : any of a genus

(*Agrostis*) including important chiefly perennial and rhizomatous pasture and lawn grasses with fine velvety or wiry herbage

²bent *adj* [ME, fr. pp. of *benden* to bend] **1** : changed by bending out of an original straight or even condition ⟨~ twigs⟩ **2** : strongly inclined : DETERMINED ⟨was ~ on winning⟩

³bent *n* [irreg. fr. ²*bend*] **1 a** : a strong inclination or interest : BIAS **b** : a special inclination or capacity : TALENT **2** : capacity of endurance **3** : a transverse framework (as in a bridge) to carry lateral as well as vertical loads *syn* see GIFT

Ben·tham·ism \'ben(t)-thə-ˌmiz-əm\ *n* : the utilitarian philosophy of Jeremy Bentham and his followers — **Ben·tham·ite** \-ˌmīt\ *n*

ben·thic \'ben(t)-thik\ *or* **ben·thal** \-thəl\ *adj* [*benthos*] **1** : of, relating to, or occurring at the bottom of a body of water **2** : of, relating to, or occurring in the depths of the ocean

ben·thon·ic \ben-'thän-ik\ *adj* [irreg. fr. *benthos*] : BENTHIC

ben·thos \'ben-ˌthäs\ *n* [NL, fr. Gk, depth, deep sea; akin to Gk *bathys* deep — more at BATHY-] : organisms that live on or in the bottom of bodies of water

ben·ton·ite \'bent-ᵊn-ˌīt\ *n* [*Fort Benton*, Montana] : an absorptive and colloidal clay used esp. as a filler (as in paper) or carrier (as of drugs) — **ben·ton·it·ic** \ˌbent-ᵊn-'it-ik\ *adj*

ben tro·va·to \ˌben-trō-'vät-(ˌ)ō\ *adj* [It, lit., well found] : characteristic or appropriate but not true

bent·wood \'bent-ˌwu̇d\ *adj* : made of wood that is bent and not cut into shape ⟨~ furniture⟩

be·numb \bi-'nəm\ *vt* [ME *benomen*, fr. *benomen, benome*, pp. of *benimen* to deprive, fr. OE *beniman*, fr. *be-* + *niman* to take — more at NIMBLE] **1** : to make inactive : DEADEN **2** : to make numb esp. by cold

benz- *or* **benzo-** *comb form* [ISV, fr. *benzoin*] : related to benzene or benzoic acid ⟨*benzophenone*⟩ ⟨*benzyl*⟩

benz·al·de·hyde \ben-'zal-də-ˌhīd\ *n* [G *benzaldehyd*, fr. *benz-* + *aldehyd* aldehyde] : a colorless nontoxic aromatic liquid C_6H_5CHO found in essential oils (as in peach kernels) and used in flavoring and perfumery, in pharmaceuticals, and in synthesis of dyes

benz·an·thra·cene \ben-'zan(t)-thrə-ˌsēn\ *n* [ISV] : a crystalline feebly carcinogenic cyclic hydrocarbon $C_{18}H_{12}$ that is found in small amounts in coal tar

Ben·ze·drine \'ben-zə-ˌdrēn\ *trademark* — used for amphetamine

ben·zene \'ben-ˌzēn, ben-'\ *n* [ISV *benz-* + *-ene*] : a colorless volatile flammable toxic liquid aromatic hydrocarbon C_6H_6 used in organic synthesis, as a solvent, and as a motor fuel — called also *benzol* — **ben·ze·noid** \'ben-zə-ˌnȯid\ *adj*

benzene ring *n* : a structural arrangement of atoms held to exist in benzene and other aromatic compounds and marked by six carbon atoms linked by alternate single and double bonds in a planar symmetrical hexagon with each carbon attached to hydrogen in benzene itself or to other atoms or groups in substituted benzenes — called also *benzene nucleus*; compare META- 4b, ORTH- 4b, PARA- 2b

formula for benzene ring

ben·zi·dine \'ben-zə-ˌdēn\ *n* [prob. fr. G *benzidin*, fr. *benzin* + *-idin* -idine] : a crystalline base $C_{12}H_{12}N_2$ prepared from nitrobenzene and used esp. in making dyes

benz·imid·azole \ˌben-zim-ə-'daz-ōl, ˌben-zə-'mid-ə-ˌzōl\ *n* [ISV *benz-* + *imidazole*] : a crystalline base $C_7H_6N_2$ that inhibits the growth of various organisms (as some viruses); *also* : one of its derivatives

ben·zine \'ben-ˌzēn, ben-'\ *n* [G *benzin*, fr. *benz-*] **1** : BENZENE **2** : any of various volatile flammable petroleum distillates used esp. as solvents or as motor fuels

ben·zo·ate \'ben-zə-ˌwāt\ *n* : a salt or ester of benzoic acid

benzoate of soda : SODIUM BENZOATE

ben·zo·caine \'ben-zə-ˌkān\ *n* [ISV] : a white crystalline ester $C_9H_{11}NO_2$ used as a local anesthetic

ben·zo·fu·ran \ˌben-zō-'fyu̇(ə)r-ˌan, -fyu̇-'ran\ *n* [*benz-* + *furan*] : COUMARONE

ben·zo·ic acid \ben-ˌzō-ik-\ *n* [ISV, fr. *benzoin*] : a white crystalline acid $C_7H_6O_2$ found naturally (as in benzoin or in cranberries) or made synthetically and used esp. as a preservative of foods, in medicine, and in organic synthesis

ben·zo·in \'ben-zə-wən, -ˌwēn; -ˌzȯin\ *n* [MF *benjoin*, fr. OCatal *benjuí*, fr. Ar *lubān jāwī*, lit., frankincense of Java] **1** : a hard fragrant yellowish balsamic resin from trees (genus *Styrax*) of southeastern Asia used esp. in medication, as a fixative in perfumes, and as incense **2** : a white crystalline hydroxy ketone $C_{14}H_{12}O_2$ made from benzaldehyde **3 a** : a tree yielding benzoin **b** : SPICEBUSH 1

ben·zol \'ben-ˌzȯl, -ˌzōl\ *n* [G, fr. *benz-* + *-ol*] : BENZENE; *also* : a mixture of benzene and other aromatic hydrocarbons

ben·zo·phe·none \ˌben-zō-fi-'nōn, -'fē-ˌnōn\ *n* [ISV] : a colorless crystalline ketone $C_{13}H_{10}O$ used chiefly in perfumery

ben·zo·py·rene \ˌben-zō-'pī(ə)r-ˌēn, ˌbenz-ō-pī-'rēn\ *or* **benz·py·rene** \benz-'pī(ə)r-ˌēn, ˌbenz-pī-'rēn\ *n* [ISV] : a yellow crystalline cancer-producing hydrocarbon $C_{20}H_{12}$ found in coal tar

ben·zo·yl \'ben-zə-ˌwil\ *n* [G, fr. *benzoësäure* benzoic acid + Gk *hylē* matter, lit., wood] : the radical C_6H_5CO of benzoic acid

ben·zyl \'ben-ˌzēl\ *n* [ISV] : a univalent radical $C_6H_5CH_2$ derived from toluene — **ben·zyl·ic** \ben-'zil-ik\ *adj*

Be·o·wulf \'bā-ə-ˌwu̇lf\ *n* : a legendary Geatish warrior and hero of the Old English poem *Beowulf*

be·paint \bi-'pānt\ *vt, archaic* : TINGE

be·queath \bi-'kwēth, -'kwēth\ *vt* [ME *bequethen*, fr. OE *becwethan*, fr. *be-* + *cwethan* to say — more at QUOTH] **1** : to give or leave by will — used esp. of personal property **2** : to hand down : TRANSMIT ⟨ideas ~ed to us by the 19th century⟩ — **be·queath·al** \-əl\ *n*

be·quest \bi-'kwest\ *n* [ME, irreg. fr. *bequethen*] **1** : the act of bequeathing **2** : something bequeathed : LEGACY

be·rate \bi-'rāt\ *vt* : to scold or condemn vehemently and at length *syn* see SCOLD

Ber·ber \'bər-bər\ *n* [Ar *Barbar*] **1** : a member of a Caucasoid people of northern Africa west of Tripoli **2 a** : a branch of the Afro-Asiatic language family comprising languages spoken by various tribal groups (as the Tuareg or the Kabyle) in northern Africa **b** : any one of these languages

ber·ber·ine \'bər-bə-ˌrēn\ *n* [G *berberin*, fr. NL *berberis* barberry root, fr. ML *barberis*, fr. Ar *barbāris*] : a bitter crystalline yellow alkaloid $C_{20}H_{19}NO_5$ obtained from the roots of various plants (as barberry) and used as a tonic and antiperiodic

ber·ceuse \be(ə)r-'sᵊz, -'sœz\ *n* [F] **1** : LULLABY **2** : a musical composition of a tranquil nature

be·reave \bi-'rēv\ *vt* **-reaved** *or* **-reft** \-'reft\; **-reav·ing** [ME *bereven*, fr. OE *berēafian*, fr. *be-* + *rēafian* to rob — more at REAVE] **1** *archaic* : to deprive of something — usu. used with *of* ⟨madam, you have *bereft* me of all words —Shak.⟩ **2** *archaic* : to take away (a valued or necessary possession) esp. by force

¹be·reaved *adj* : suffering the death of a loved one ⟨~ parents⟩

²bereaved *n, pl* **bereaved** : one who is bereaved

be·reave·ment \bi-'rēv-mənt\ *n* : the state or fact of being bereaved; *esp* : the loss of a loved one by death

be·reft \-'reft\ *adj* **1 a** : deprived or robbed of the possession or use of something — usu. used with *of* ⟨both players are instantly ~ of their poise —A. E. Wier⟩ **b** : lacking something needed, wanted, or expected — used with *of* ⟨the book is … completely ~ of an index —*Times Lit. Supp.*⟩ **2** : BEREAVED ⟨a ~ daughter mourning here on the heights —B. A. Williams⟩

Ber·e·ni·ce's Hair \ˌber-ə-ˌnī-sēz-\ *n* : COMA BERENICES

be·ret \bə-'rā\ *n* [F *berret*, fr. Prov — more at BIRETTA] : a visorless usu. woolen cap with a tight headband and a soft full flat top

berg \'bərg\ *n* : ICEBERG

ber·ga·mot \'bər-gə-ˌmät\ *n* [F *bergamote*, fr. It *bergamotta*, fr. Turkic origin; akin to Turk *bey-armudu* prince's pear] **1** : a pear-shaped orange (*Citrus bergamia*) whose rind yields an essential oil used in perfumery **2** : any of several mints (genus *Monarda*)

be·rib·boned \bi-'rib-ənd\ *adj* : adorned with ribbons

beri·beri \ˌber-ē-'ber-ē\ *n* [Sinhalese *bæribæri*] : a deficiency disease marked by inflammatory or degenerative changes of the nerves, digestive system, and heart and caused by a lack of or inability to assimilate thiamine

Be·ring time \ˌbi(ə)r-iŋ-, ˌbe(ə)r-\ *n* [*Bering* sea] : the time of the 11th time zone west of Greenwich that includes western Alaska and the Aleutian islands

Berke·le·ian *or* **Berke·ley·an** \'bär-klē-ən, 'bər-'; bär-', ˌbər-'\ *adj* : of, relating to, or suggestive of Bishop Berkeley or his system of philosophical idealism — **Berkeleian** *n* — **Berke·le·ian·ism** \-ə-ˌniz-əm\ *n*

berke·li·um \'bər-klē-əm\ *n* [NL, fr. *Berkeley*, Calif.] : a radioactive metallic element produced by bombarding americium 241 with helium ions — see ELEMENT table

Berks *abbr* Berkshire

Berk·shire \'bərk-ˌshi(ə)r, -shər\ *n* [*Berkshire*, England] : any of a breed of medium-sized black swine with white markings

ber·lin \(ˌ)bər-'lin\ *n* [F *berline*, fr. *Berlin*, Germany] : a four-wheeled two-seated covered carriage with a hooded rear seat

berm *or* **berme** \'bərm\ *n* [F *berme*, fr. D *berm* strip of ground along a dike; akin to ME *brimme* brim] : a narrow shelf, path, or ledge typically at the top or bottom of a slope

Ber·mu·da grass \(ˌ)bər-'myüd-ə-, *esp South* -'müd-\ *n* [*Bermuda* islands, No. Atlantic] : a trailing stoloniferous southern European grass (*Cynodon dactylon*)

Bermuda rig *n* : a fore-and-aft rig marked by a triangular sail and a mast with an extreme rake

Ber·mu·das \(ˌ)bər-'myüd-əz, *esp South* -'müd-\ *n pl* : BERMUDA SHORTS

Bermuda shorts *n pl* : knee-length walking shorts

Ber·nese mountain dog \bər-ˌnēz-, -ˌnēs-\ *n* [*Bern*, Switzerland] : any of a Swiss breed of large powerful long-coated black dogs with brown and white markings formerly used for draft

Ber·noul·li trial \bər-ˌnü-lē-, ˌber-ˌnü-ē-, ˌber-ˌnü-(y)ē-\ *n* [Jacques *Bernoulli* †1705 Swiss mathematician] : a statistical experiment that has two mutually exclusive outcomes each of which has a constant probability of occurrence

ber·ried \'ber-ēd\ *adj* **1** : furnished with berries : BACCATE **2** : bearing eggs ⟨a ~ lobster⟩

¹ber·ry \'ber-ē, *esp in compounds in which a stressed syllable immediately precedes, Brit often & US sometimes* b(ə-)rē\ *n, pl* **berries** [ME *berye*, fr. OE *berie*; akin to OHG *beri* berry] **1 a** : a pulpy and usu. edible fruit (as a strawberry, raspberry, or checkerberry) of small size irrespective of its structure **b** : a simple fruit (as a currant, grape, tomato, or banana) with a pulpy or fleshy pericarp **c** : the dry seed of some plants (as coffee) **2** : an egg of a fish or lobster

²berry \'ber-ē\ *vi* **ber·ried**; **ber·ry·ing** **1** : to bear or produce berries ⟨a ~*ing* shrub⟩ **2** : to gather or seek berries

ber·ry·like \'ber-ē-ˌlīk\ *adj* **1** : resembling a berry esp. in size or structure **2** : being small and rounded : COCCOID

ber·seem \(ˌ)bər-'sēm\ *n* [Ar *barsim*, fr. Copt *bersim*] : a succulent clover (*Trifolium alexandrinum*) cultivated as a forage plant and green-manure crop esp. in the alkaline soils of the Nile valley and in the southwestern U.S. — called also *Egyptian clover*

¹ber·serk \bə(r)-'sərk, -'zərk, 'bər-ˌserk, 'bər-ˌ\ *or* **ber·serk·er** \-ər\ *n* [ON *berserkr*, fr. *björn* bear + *serkr* shirt] **1** : an ancient Scandinavian warrior frenzied in battle and held to be invulnerable **2** : one whose actions are marked by reckless defiance

²berserk *adj* : FRENZIED, CRAZED — usu. used in the phrase *go berserk* — **berserk** *adv*

¹berth \'bərth\ *n* [prob. fr. ²*bear* + -*th*] **1 a** : sufficient distance for maneuvering a ship **b** : safe distance — used esp. with *wide* **2 a** : the place where a ship lies when at anchor or at a wharf **b** : a space for an automotive vehicle at rest ⟨a truck-loading ~⟩ **3** : a place to sit or sleep esp. on a ship or vehicle : ACCOMMODATION **4 a** : a billet on a ship **b** : JOB, POSITION

²berth *vt* **1** : to bring into a berth **2** : to allot a berth to ~ *vi* : to come into a berth

ber·tha \'bər-thə\ *n* [F *berthe*, fr. *Berthe* (Bertha) †783 queen of the Franks] : a wide round collar covering the shoulders

Ber·til·lon system \'bərt-ᵊl-,än-, 'bert-ē-,(y)ōⁿ-\ *n* [Alphonse *Bertillon* †1914 F criminologist] : a system of identification of persons by a description based on anthropometric measurements, standardized photographs, notation of markings, color, thumb line impressions, and other data

Berw *abbr* Berwick

ber·yl \'ber-əl\ *n* [ME, fr. OF *beril*, fr. L *beryllus*, fr. Gk *bēryllos*, of Indic origin; akin to Skt *vaiḍūrya* cat's-eye] : a mineral $Be_3Al_2Si_6O_{18}$ consisting of a silicate of beryllium and aluminum of great hardness and occurring in green, bluish green, yellow, pink, or white hexagonal prisms

be·ryl·li·um \bə-'ril-ē-əm\ *n* [NL, fr. Gk *bēryllion*, dim. of *bēryllos*] : a steel-gray light strong brittle toxic bivalent metallic element used chiefly as a hardening agent in alloys — see ELEMENT table

be·seech \bi-'sēch\ *vb* **-sought** \-'sȯt\ *or* **-seeched; -seech·ing** [ME *besechen*, fr. *be-* + *sechen* to seek] *vt* **1** : to beg for urgently or anxiously **2** : to request earnestly : IMPLORE ~ *vi* : to make supplication ***syn*** see BEG — **be·seech·ing·ly** \-'sē-chiŋ-lē\ *adv*

be·seem \bi-'sēm\ *vi, archaic* : to be fitting or becoming ~ *vt, archaic* : to be suitable to : BEFIT

be·set \bi-'set\ *vt* **1** : to set or stud with or as if with ornaments **2** : TROUBLE, HARASS ⟨inflation ~s the economy⟩ **3 a** : to set upon : ASSAIL ⟨the settlers were ~ by savages⟩ **b** : to hem in : SURROUND — **be·set·ment** \-mənt\ *n*

be·set·ting *adj* : constantly present or attacking : OBSESSIVE

be·shrew \bi-'shrü, *esp South* -'srü\ *vt, archaic* : CURSE

¹be·side \bi-'sīd\ *adv* [ME, adv. & prep., fr. OE *be sīdan* at or to the side, fr. *be* at (fr. *bī*) + *sīdan*, dat. & acc. of *sīde* side — more at BY] **1** *archaic* : NEARBY **2** *archaic* : BESIDES

²beside *prep* **1 a** : by the side of ⟨walk ~ me⟩ **b** : in comparison with **c** : on a par with **2** : BESIDES — **beside oneself** : in a state of extreme excitement

¹be·sides \bi-'sīdz\ *adv* **1** : over and above : ALSO **2** : MOREOVER, FURTHERMORE

²besides *prep* **1** : other than : EXCEPT **2** : in addition to

³besides *adj* : ELSE

be·siege \bi-'sēj\ *vt* **1** : to surround with armed forces **2 a** : to press with requests : IMPORTUNE **b** : to cause worry or distress to : BESET ⟨doubts that *besieged* him⟩ — **be·sieg·er** *n*

be·smear \bi-'smi(ə)r\ *vt* : SMEAR

be·smirch \bi-'smərch\ *vt* : SULLY, SOIL

be·som \'bē-zəm\ *n* [ME *beseme*, fr. OE *besma*; akin to OHG *besmo* broom] **1** : BROOM 2; *esp* : one made of twigs **2** : BROOM 1

be·sot \bi-'sät\ *vt* **be·sot·ted; be·sot·ting** [*be-* + *sot* (to stultify)] : to make dull or stupid; *esp* : to muddle with drunkenness or infatuation

be·spat·ter \bi-'spat-ər\ *vt* : SPATTER

be·speak \bi-'spēk\ *vt* **-spoke** \-'spōk\; **-spo·ken** \-'spō-kən\; **-speak·ing** **1** : to hire, engage, or claim beforehand **2** : to speak to esp. with formality : ADDRESS **3** : REQUEST ⟨~ a favor⟩ **4 a** : INDICATE, SIGNIFY ⟨her performance ~s considerable practice⟩ **b** : to show beforehand : FORETELL

be·spec·ta·cled \bi-'spek-ti-kəld, -,tik-əld\ *adj* : wearing spectacles

be·spoke \bi-'spōk\ *or* **be·spo·ken** \-'spō-kən\ *adj* [pp. of *bespeak*] **1** *Brit* **a** : CUSTOM-MADE **b** : dealing in or producing custom-made articles **2** *dial* : ENGAGED

be·sprent \bi-'sprent\ *adj* [ME *bespreynt*, fr. pp. of *besprengen* to besprinkle, fr. OE *besprengan*] *archaic* : sprinkled over

be·sprin·kle \bi-'spriŋ-kəl\ *vt* [ME *besprengeln*, freq. of *besprengen*] : SPRINKLE

Bes·se·mer converter \,bes-ə-mər-\ *n* : the furnace used in the Bessemer process

Bessemer process *n* [Sir Henry *Bessemer*] : a process of making steel from pig iron by burning out carbon and other impurities by means of a blast of air forced through the molten metal

¹best \'best\ *adj, superlative of* GOOD [ME, fr. OE *betst*; akin to OE *bōt* remedy — more at BETTER] **1** : excelling all others ⟨the ~ student⟩ **2** : most productive of good or of advantage, utility, or satisfaction ⟨what is the ~ thing to do⟩ **3** : MOST, LARGEST ⟨it rained for the ~ part of their vacation⟩

²best *adv, superlative of* WELL **1** : in the best way : to greatest advantage ⟨some things are ~ left unsaid⟩ **2** : MOST

³best *n* **1** : the best state or part **2** : one that is best ⟨the ~ falls short⟩ **3** : the greatest degree of good or excellence **4** : one's maximum effort ⟨do your ~⟩ **5** : best clothes ⟨Sunday ~⟩ — **at best** : under the most favorable circumstances

⁴best *vt* : to get the better of : OUTDO

best–ball \'bes(t)-'bȯl\ *adj* : relating to or being a golf match in which one player competes against the best individual score of two or more players for each hole — compare FOUR-BALL

¹be·stead *also* **be·sted** \bi-'sted\ *adj* [ME *bested*, fr. *be-* + *sted*, pp. of *steden* to place] **1** *archaic* : SITUATED **2** *archaic* : BESET

²bestead *vt* **be·stead·ed; be·stead; be·stead·ing** [*be-* + *stead*] **1** *archaic* : HELP **2** *archaic* : to be useful to : AVAIL

bes·tial \'bes(h)-chəl, 'bēs(h)-\ *adj* [ME, fr. MF, fr. L *bestialis*, fr. *bestia* beast] **1 a** : of or relating to beasts **b** : resembling a beast **2 a** : lacking intelligence or reason **b** : marked by base or inhuman instincts or desires : BRUTAL — **bes·tial·ize** \-chə-,līz\ *vt* — **bes·tial·ly** \-chə-lē\ *adv*

bes·ti·al·i·ty \,bes(h)-chē-'al-ət-ē, ,bēs(h)-\ *n, pl* **-ties** **1** : the condition or status of a lower animal **2** : display or gratification of bestial traits or impulses **3** : sexual relations between a human being and a lower animal

bes·ti·ary \'bes(h)-chē-,er-ē, 'bēs(h)-\ *n, pl* **-ar·ies** [ML *bestiarium*, fr. L, neut. of *bestiarius* of beasts, fr. *bestia*] : a medieval allegorical or moralizing work on the appearance and habits of real or imaginary animals

be·stir \bi-'stər\ *vt* : to stir up : rouse to action

best man *n* : the principal groomsman at a wedding

be·stow \bi-'stō\ *vt* [ME *bestowen*, fr. *be-* + *stowe* place — more at STOW] **1** : to put to use : APPLY ⟨~*ed* his spare time on study⟩ **2** : to put in a particular or appropriate place : STOW **3** : to provide with quarters : put up **4** : to convey as a gift — usu. used with *on* or *upon* ***syn*** see GIVE — **be·stow·al** \-'stō-əl\ *n*

be·strew \bi-'strü\ *vt* **-strewed; -strewed** *or* **-strewn** \-'strün\; **-strew·ing** **1** : STREW **2** : to lie scattered over

be·stride \bi-'strīd\ *vt* **-strode** \-'strōd\; **-strid·den** \-'strid-ᵊn\; **-strid·ing** \-'strīd-iŋ\ **1** : to ride, sit, or stand astride : STRADDLE **2** : to tower over : DOMINATE **3** *archaic* : to stride across

best–sell·er \'bes(t)-'sel-ər\ *n* : an article (as a book) whose sales are among the highest of its class — **best·sell·er·dom** \-dəm\ *n* — **best–sell·ing** \-'sel-iŋ\ *adj*

¹bet \'bet\ *n* [origin unknown] **1 a** : something that is laid, staked, or pledged typically between two parties on the outcome of a contest or a contingent issue : WAGER **b** : the act of giving such a pledge **2** : something to wager on

²bet *vb* **bet** *also* **bet·ted; bet·ting** *vt* **1 a** : to stake on the outcome of an issue **b** : to be able to be sure that — usu. used in the expression *you bet* ⟨you ~ I'll be there⟩ **2 a** : to maintain with or as if with a bet **b** : to make a bet with ~ *vi* : to lay a bet

³bet *abbr* between

¹be·ta \'bāt-ə, *chiefly Brit* 'bē-tə\ *n* [Gk *bēta*, of Sem origin; akin to Heb *bēth* beth] **1** : the 2d letter of the Greek alphabet — see ALPHABET table **2** : the second brightest star of a constellation **3 a** : BETA PARTICLE **b** : BETA RAY

²beta *or* *β*- *adj* : second in position in the structure of an organic molecule from a particular group or atom ⟨~ substitution⟩

be·ta–ad·ren·er·gic \-,ad-rə-'nər-jik\ *adj* : of, relating to, or being a beta-receptor ⟨~ blocking action⟩

beta globulin *n* [ISV] : any of several globulins of plasma or serum that have electrophoretic mobilities intermediate between those of the alpha globulins and gamma globulins

be·ta·ine \'bēt-ə-,ēn\ *n* [ISV, fr. L *beta* beet] : a sweet crystalline quaternary ammonium salt $C_6H_{12}NO_3$ occurring esp. in beet juice; *also* : its hydrate $C_5H_{13}NO_3$ or the chloride of this

be·take \bi-'tāk\ *vt* **-took** \-'tu̇k\; **-tak·en** \-'tā-kən\; **-tak·ing** **1** *archaic* : COMMIT **2** : to cause (oneself) to go

be·ta–ox·i·da·tion \'bāt-ə-,äk-sə-'dā-shən\ *n* : stepwise catabolism of fatty acids in which two-carbon fragments are successively removed from the carboxyl end of the chain

beta particle *n* : an electron or positron ejected from the nucleus of an atom during radioactive decay; *also* : a high-speed electron or positron

beta ray *n* **1** : BETA PARTICLE **2** : a stream of beta particles

be·ta–re·cep·tor \,bāt-ə-ri-'sep-tər\ *n* : a receptor that is associated with positive effects on heartbeat and muscular contractility, with vasodilation, and with inhibition of smooth muscle in the bronchi, intestine, and muscular layer of the wall of the uterus — called also *beta-adrenergic receptor*

be·ta·tron \'bāt-ə-,trän\ *n* [ISV] : an accelerator in which electrons are propelled by the inductive action of a rapidly varying magnetic field

be·tel \'bēt-ᵊl\ *n* [Pg, fr. Tamil *verrilai*] : a climbing pepper (*Piper betle*) whose leaves are chewed together with betel nut and lime as a stimulant masticatory esp. by southeastern Asians

Be·tel·geuse \'bēt-ᵊl-,jüs, 'bet-, -,jüz-, -,jə(r)z\ *n* [F *Bételgeuse*, fr. Ar *bayt al-jawzā'* Gemini, lit., the house of the twins (confused with Orion & Betelgeuse)] : a variable red giant star of the first magnitude near one shoulder of Orion

betel nut *n* [fr. its being chewed with betel leaves] : the astringent seed of the betel palm

betel palm *n* [*betel* nut] : an Asiatic pinnate-leaved palm (*Areca catechu*) that has an orange-colored drupe with an outer fibrous husk

bête noire \,bet-nə-'wär, ,bāt-\ *n, pl* **bêtes noires** \,bet-nə-'wär(z), ,bāt-\ [F, lit., black beast] : a person or thing strongly detested or avoided : BUGBEAR

beth \'bāt(h), 'bās\ *n* [Heb *bēth*, fr. *bayith* house] : the 2d letter of the Hebrew alphabet — see ALPHABET table

beth·el \'beth-əl\ *n* [Heb *bēth'ēl* house of God] **1** : a hallowed spot **2 a** : a chapel for Nonconformists **b** : a place of worship for seamen

be·think \bi-'thiŋk\ *vt* **-thought** \-'thȯt\; **-think·ing** **1 a** : REMEMBER, RECALL **b** : to cause (oneself) to be reminded **2** : to cause (oneself) to consider

be·tide \bi-'tīd\ *vt* : to happen to : BEFALL ~ *vi* : to happen esp. as if by fate

be·times \bi-'tīmz\ *adv* **1** : in good time : EARLY **2** *archaic* : in a short time : SPEEDILY **3** : at times : OCCASIONALLY

bê·tise \bā-'tēz\ *n, pl* **bê·tises** \-'tēz\ [F] **1** : lack of good sense : STUPIDITY **2** : an act of foolishness or stupidity

be·to·ken \bi-'tō-kən\ *vt* **be·to·kened; be·to·ken·ing** \-'tōk-(ə-)niŋ\ **1** : to give evidence of : SHOW **2** : to typify beforehand : PRESAGE

bet·o·ny \'bet-ᵊn-ē\ *n, pl* **-nies** [ME *betone*, fr. OF *betoine*, fr. L *vettonica, betonica*, fr. *Vettones*, an ancient people inhabiting the Iberian peninsula] : any of several woundworts (genus *Stachys*); *esp* : WOOD BETONY 1

be·tray \bi-'trā\ *vb* [ME *betrayen*, fr. *be-* + *trayen* to betray, fr. OF *traïr*, fr. L *tradere* — more at TRAITOR] *vt* **1** : to lead astray; *esp* : SEDUCE **2** : to deliver to an enemy by treachery **3** : to fail or desert esp. in time of need **4 a** : to reveal unintentionally **b** : SHOW, INDICATE **c** : to disclose in violation of confidence ~ *vi* : to prove false ***syn*** see REVEAL — **be·tray·al** \-'trā(-ə)l\ *n* — **be·tray·er** \-'trā-ər\ *n*

be·troth \bi-ˈträth, -ˈtrȯth, -ˈtrōth, *or with* t͟h\ *vt* [ME *betrouthen,* fr. *be-* + *trouthe* truth, troth] : to promise to marry or give in marriage
be·troth·al \-ˈtrōt͟h-əl, -ˈtrȯth-, -ˈtrōth-\ *n* **1** : the act of betrothing or fact of being betrothed **2** : a mutual promise or contract for a future marriage
be·trothed *n* : the person to whom one is betrothed
bet·ta \ˈbet-ə\ *n* [NL] : any of a genus (*Betta*) of small brilliantly colored long-finned freshwater fishes (as the Siamese fighting fish) of southeastern Asia
1bet·ter \ˈbet-ər\ *adj, comparative of* GOOD [ME *bettre,* fr. OE *betera;* akin to OE *bōt* remedy, Skt *bhadra* fortunate] **1** : more than half **2** : improved in health **3** : of higher quality
2better *adv, comparative of* WELL **1 a** : in a more excellent manner **b** : to greater advantage : PREFERABLY ⟨some things are ~ left unsaid⟩ **2 a** : to a higher or greater degree ⟨he knows the story ~ than you do⟩ **b** : MORE ⟨it is ~ than nine miles to the nearest gas station⟩
3better *n* **1 a** : something better **b** : a superior esp. in merit or rank **2** : ADVANTAGE, VICTORY ⟨get the ~ of him⟩
4better *vt* **1** : to make better: as **a** : to make more tolerable or acceptable ⟨trying to ~ the lot of slum dwellers⟩ **b** : to make more complete or perfect ⟨looked forward to ~*ing* her acquaintance with the new neighbors⟩ **2** : to surpass in excellence : EXCEL ~ *vi* : to become better ***syn*** see IMPROVE ***ant*** worsen
bet·ter·ment \ˈbet-ər-mənt\ *n* **1** : a making or becoming better **2** : an improvement that adds to the value of a property or facility
better–off \ˌbet-ə-ˈrȯf\ *adj* : being in comfortable economic circumstances ⟨the ~ people live in the older section of town⟩
betting shop *n, Brit* : a shop where bets are taken
bet·tor *or* **bet·ter** \ˈbet-ər\ *n* : one that bets
1be·tween \bi-ˈtwēn\ *prep* [ME *betwene,* prep. & adv., fr. OE *betwēonum,* fr. *be-* + *-twēonum* (dat. pl.) (akin to Goth *tweihnai* two each); akin to OE *twā* two] **1 a** : by the common action of : jointly engaging ⟨shared the work ~ the two of them⟩ ⟨talks ~ the three —*Time*⟩ **b** : in common to : shared by ⟨divided ~ his four grandchildren⟩ **2 a** : in the time, space, or interval that separates **b** : in intermediate relation to **3 a** : from one to the other of **b** : serving to join : CONNECTING ⟨air service ~ the two cities⟩ **c** : separating from ⟨the line ~ fact and fancy⟩ **4** : in point of comparison of ⟨not much to choose ~ the two coats⟩ — **between you and me** : in confidence
2between *adv* : in an intermediate space or interval
be·tween·brain \-ˌbrān\ *n* : DIENCEPHALON
be·tween·ness \bi-ˈtwēn-nəs\ *n* : the quality or state of being between two others in an ordered set
be·tween·times \bi-ˈtwēn-ˌtīmz\ *adv* : at or during intervals
be·tween·whiles \-ˌhwīlz, -ˌwīlz\ *adv* : BETWEENTIMES
be·twixt \bi-ˈtwikst\ *adv or prep* [ME, fr. OE *betwux,* fr. *be-* + *-twux* (akin to Goth *tweihnai*)] : BETWEEN
betwixt and between *adv or adj* : in a midway position : neither one thing nor the other
Beu·lah \ˈbyü-lə\ *n* : an idyllic land near the end of life's journey in Bunyan's *Pilgrim's Progress*
BeV *abbr* billion electron volts
1bev·el \ˈbev-əl\ *adj* : OBLIQUE, BEVELED
2bevel *n* [(assumed) MF, fr. OF *baïf* with open mouth, fr. *baer* to yawn — more at ABEYANCE] **1 a** : the angle that one surface or line makes with another when they are not at right angles **b** : the slant or inclination of such a surface or line **2** : an instrument consisting of two rules or arms jointed together and opening to any angle for drawing angles or adjusting surfaces to be given a bevel **3** : the part of printing type extending from face to shoulder — see TYPE illustration
3bevel *vb* **-eled** *or* **-elled; -el·ing** *or* **-el·ling** \ˈbev-(ə-)liŋ\ *vt* : to cut or shape to a bevel ~ *vi* : INCLINE, SLANT
bevel gear *n* : one of a pair of toothed wheels whose working surfaces are inclined to nonparallel axes

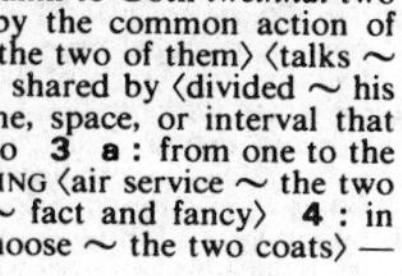

bevel gears

bev·er·age \ˈbev-(ə-)rij\ *n* [ME, fr. MF *bevrage,* fr. *beivre* to drink, fr. L *bibere* — more at POTABLE] : a liquid for drinking; *esp* : one that is not water
bevy \ˈbev-ē\ *n, pl* **bev·ies** [ME *bevey*] **1** : a large group or collection ⟨a ~ of girls⟩ **2** : a group of animals and esp. quail together
be·wail \bi-ˈwā(ə)l\ *vt* **1** : to wail over **2** : to express deep sorrow for usu. by wailing and lamentation ⟨wringing her hands and ~*ing* her fate⟩ ***syn*** see DEPLORE
be·ware \bi-ˈwa(ə)r, -ˈwe(ə)r\ *vb* [ME *been war,* fr. *been* to be + *war* careful — more at BE, WARE] *vi* : to be on one's guard ⟨~ of the dog⟩ ~ *vt* **1** : to take care of **2** : to be wary of
be·whis·kered \-ˈhwis-kərd, -ˈwis-\ *adj* : wearing whiskers
be·wigged \bi-ˈwigd\ *adj* : wearing a wig
be·wil·der \bi-ˈwil-dər\ *vt* **be·wil·dered; be·wil·der·ing** \-d(ə-)riŋ\ **1** : to cause to lose one's bearings **2** : to perplex or confuse esp. by a complexity, variety, or multitude of objects or considerations ***syn*** see PUZZLE — **be·wil·dered·ly** *adv* — **be·wil·dered·ness** *n* — **be·wil·der·ing·ly** \-d(ə-)riŋ-lē\ *adv*
be·wil·der·ment \-dər-mənt\ *n* **1** : the quality or state of being bewildered **2** : a bewildering tangle or confusion
be·witch \bi-ˈwich\ *vt* **1 a** : to influence or affect esp. injuriously by witchcraft **b** : to cast a spell over **2** : to attract as if by the power of witchcraft ⟨~*ed* by her beauty⟩ ~ *vi* : to bewitch someone or something ***syn*** see ATTRACT — **be·witch·ery** \-(ə-)rē\ *n* — **be·witch·ing·ly** \-iŋ-lē\ *adv*
be·witch·ment \-ˈwich-mənt\ *n* **1 a** : the act or power of bewitching **b** : a spell that bewitches **2** : the state of being bewitched
be·wray \bi-ˈrā\ *vt* [ME *bewreyen,* fr. *be-* + *wreyen* to accuse, fr. OE *wrēgan*] *archaic* : DIVULGE, BETRAY
bey \ˈbā\ *n* [Turk, gentleman, chief] **1 a** : a provincial governor in the Ottoman Empire **b** : the former native ruler of Tunis or Tunisia **2** — formerly used as a courtesy title in Turkey and Egypt
1be·yond \bē-ˈänd\ *adv* [ME, prep. & adv., fr. OE *begeondan,* fr. *be-* + *geondan* beyond, fr. *geond* yond — more at YOND] **1** : on or to the farther side : FARTHER **2** : in addition : BESIDES
2beyond *prep* **1** : on or to the farther side of : at a greater distance than **2 a** : out of the reach or sphere of **b** : in a degree or amount surpassing **c** : out of the comprehension of **3** : in addition to : over and above : BESIDES
3beyond *n* **1** : something that lies beyond **2** : something that lies outside the scope of ordinary experience; *specif* : 2HEREAFTER
be·zant \ˈbez-ᵊnt, bə-ˈzant\ *n* [ME *besant,* fr. MF, fr. ML *Byzantius* Byzantine, fr. *Byzantium,* ancient name of Istanbul] **1** : SOLIDUS 1 **2** : a flat disk used in architectural ornament
be·zel \ˈbē-zəl, ˈbez-əl\ *n* [prob. F dial., alter. of F *biseau*] **1** : a sloping edge or face esp. on a cutting tool **2** : the oblique side or face of a cut gem; *specif* : the upper faceted portion of a brilliant projecting from the setting — see BRILLIANT illustration **3** : a rim that holds a transparent covering (as on a watch, clock, or headlight) or that is rotatable and has special markings (as on a watch)
be·zique \bə-ˈzēk\ *n* [F *bésique*] : a card game similar to pinochle that is played with a pack of 64 cards
be·zoar \ˈbē-ˌzō(ə)r, -ˌzȯ(ə)r\ *n* [F *bézoard,* fr. Sp *bezoar,* fr. Ar *bāzahr,* fr. Per *pād-zahr,* fr. *pād* protecting (against) + *zahr* poison] : any of various concretions found chiefly in the alimentary organs of ruminants and formerly believed to possess magical properties
bf *abbr* boldface
BF *abbr* **1** bachelor of forestry **2** board foot **3** brought forward
BFA *abbr* bachelor of fine arts
bg *abbr* **1** background **2** bag **3** beige **4** being
BG *abbr* brigadier general
B Gen *abbr* brigadier general
B–girl *n* [prob. fr. *bar* + *girl*] : a woman who entertains bar patrons and encourages them to spend freely
BH *abbr* **1** bill of health **2** Brinell hardness
Bha·don \ˈbäd-ˌōn\ *n* [Hindi *bhādō,* fr. Skt *bhādrapada,* fr. *Bhadrapadā,* a constellation] : a month of the Hindu year — see MONTH table
Bha·ga·vad Gi·ta \ˌbäg-ə-ˌväd-ˈgēt-ə\ *n* [Skt *Bhagavadgītā,* lit., song of the blessed one (Krishna)] : a Hindu devotional work in poetic form
bhak·ti \ˈbək-tē\ *n* [Skt, lit., portion] : devotion to a deity constituting a way to salvation in Hinduism
bhang \ˈbaŋ\ *n* [Hindi *bhãg*] **1 a** : HEMP 1 **b** : the leaves and flowering tops of uncultivated hemp : CANNABIS — compare MARIJUANA **2** : an intoxicant product obtained from bhang — compare HASHISH
BHC \ˌbē-ˌāch-ˈsē\ *n* [*b*enzene *h*exa*c*hloride] : a compound $C_6H_6Cl_6$ that occurs in several stereoisomeric forms and is used as an insecticide — compare LINDANE
bhd *abbr* bulkhead
BHE *abbr* Bureau of Higher Education
BHL *abbr* **1** bachelor of Hebrew letters **2** bachelor of Hebrew literature
BHN *abbr* Brinell hardness number
Bhoj·puri \ˈbōj-ˌpu̇r-ē, ˈbäj-, pə-rē\ *n* [Hindi *Bhojpurī,* fr. *Bhojpur,* village in Bihar] : the dialect of Bihari spoken in Western Bihar and the eastern United Provinces, India
B–horizon *n* : a soil layer immediately beneath the A-horizon from which it obtains organic matter chiefly by illuviation and is usu. distinguished by less weathering
bhp *abbr* bishop
BHT *abbr* butylated hydroxytoluene
bi \ˈbī\ *n or adj* : BISEXUAL
Bi *symbol* bismuth
1bi- *prefix* [ME, fr. L; akin to OE *twi-*] **1 a** : two ⟨*bi*parous⟩ **b** : coming or occurring every two ⟨*bi*monthly⟩ ⟨*bi*weekly⟩ **c** : into two parts ⟨*bi*sect⟩ **2 a** : twice : doubly : on both sides ⟨*bi*convex⟩ ⟨*bi*serrate⟩ **b** : coming or occurring two times ⟨*bi*weekly⟩ — often disapproved in this sense because of the likelihood of confusion with sense 1b; compare SEMI- **3** : between, involving, or affecting two (specified) symmetrical parts ⟨*bi*aural⟩ **4 a** : containing one (specified) constituent in double the proportion of the other constituent or in double the ordinary proportion ⟨*bi*carbonate⟩ **b** : DI- 2 ⟨*bi*phenyl⟩
2bi- *or* **bio-** *comb form* [Gk, fr. *bios* mode of life — more at QUICK] : life : living organisms or tissue ⟨*bio*ecology⟩ ⟨*bio*luminescence⟩
BIA *abbr* **1** bachelor of industrial arts **2** Braille Institute of America **3** Bureau of Indian Affairs
Bi·a·fran \bē-ˈaf-rən, bī-, -ˈäf-\ *n* [*Biafra,* name adopted by Eastern Region of Nigeria during its secession, 1967–70] : a native or inhabitant of the secessionist Republic of Biafra — **Biafran** *adj*
bi·an·nu·al \(ˈ)bī-ˈan-yə(-wə)l\ *adj* : occurring twice a year — **bi·an·nu·al·ly** \-ē\ *adv*
1bi·as \ˈbī-əs\ *n* [MF *biais*] **1** : a line diagonal to the grain of a fabric; *esp* : a line at a 45° angle to the selvage often utilized in the cutting of garments for smoother fit **2 a** : an inclination of temperament or outlook; *esp* : a highly personal and unreasoned distortion of judgment : PREJUDICE ⟨a ~ in favor of jolly fat men⟩ **b** : BENT, TENDENCY ⟨a man of antiquarian ~⟩ **c** (1) : deviation of the expected value of a statistical estimate from the quantity it estimates (2) : systematic error introduced into sampling or testing by selecting or encouraging one outcome or answer over others **3 a** : a peculiarity in the shape of a bowl that causes it to swerve when rolled on the green **b** : the tendency of a bowl to swerve; *also* : the impulse causing this tendency **c** : the swerve of the

ə abut	ᵊ kitten	ər further	a back	ā bake	ä cot, cart	
au̇ out	ch chin	e less	ē easy	g gift	i trip	ī life
j joke	ŋ sing	ō flow	ȯ flaw	ȯi coin	th thin	t͟h this
ü loot	u̇ foot	y yet	yü few	yu̇ furious	zh vision	

bowl **4** : a voltage applied to a device (as the grid of an electron tube) to establish a reference level for operation **syn** see PREDILECTION — **on the bias** : ASKEW, OBLIQUELY

²**bias** *adj* : DIAGONAL, SLANTING — used chiefly of fabrics and their cut — **bi·as·ness** *n*

³**bias** *adv* **1** : in a slanting manner : DIAGONALLY ⟨cut cloth ∼⟩ **2** *obs* : AWRY

⁴**bias** *vt* **bi·ased** *or* **bi·assed; bi·as·ing** *or* **bi·as·sing 1** : to give a settled and often prejudiced outlook on ⟨his background ∼es him against foreigners⟩ **2** : to apply a slight negative or positive voltage to (as an electron-tube grid) **syn** see INCLINE

bi·ased *adj* **1** : exhibiting or characterized by bias **2** : tending to yield one outcome more frequently than others in a statistical experiment ⟨a ∼ coin⟩ **3** : having an expected value different from the quantity or parameter estimated ⟨a ∼ estimate⟩

bi·ath·lon \bī-'ath-lən, -,län\ *n* [¹*bi*- + Gk *athlon* contest — more at ATHLETE] : a composite athletic contest consisting of cross-country skiing and rifle sharpshooting

bi·ax·i·al \(')bī-'ak-sē-əl\ *adj* : having two axes ⟨a ∼ crystal⟩ — **bi·ax·i·al·ly** \-ə-lē\ *adv*

¹**bib** \'bib\ *vb* **bibbed; bib·bing** [ME *bibben*] : DRINK

²**bib** *n* **1** : a cloth or plastic shield tied under a child's chin to protect the clothes **2** : the part of an apron or of overalls extending above the waist — **bibbed** \'bibd\ *adj* — **bib·less** \'bib-ləs\ *adj*

³**bib** *abbr* Bible; biblical

bib and tucker *n* : an outfit of clothing — usu. used in the phrase *best bib and tucker*

bibb \'bib\ *n* [alter. of ²*bib*] : a side piece of timber bolted to the hounds of a ship's mast to support the trestletrees

bib·ber \'bib-ər\ *n* : one addicted to drinking : TIPPLER — **bib·bery** \'bib-ə-rē\ *n*

Bibb lettuce \'bib-\ *n* [Major John *Bibb*, 19th cent. Am grower] : lettuce of a variety that has a small head and dark green color

bib·cock \'bib-,käk\ *also* **bibb cock** *n* : a faucet having a bent-down nozzle

bi·be·lot \'bē-bə-,lō\ *n, pl* **bibelots** \-,lō(z)\ [F] **1** : a small household ornament or decorative object : TRINKET **2** : a miniature book esp. of elegant design or format

bi·ble \'bī-bəl\ *n* [ME, fr. OF, fr. ML *biblia*, fr. Gk, pl. of *biblion*

book, dim. of *byblos* papyrus, book, fr. *Byblos*, ancient Phoenician city from which papyrus was exported] **1** *cap* **a** : the sacred scriptures of Christians comprising the Old Testament and the New Testament **b** : the sacred scriptures of some other religion (as Judaism) **2** *obs* : BOOK **3** *cap* : a copy or an edition of the Bible **4** : a publication that is preeminent esp. in authoritativeness ⟨the fisherman's ∼⟩ **5** : something suggesting a book: as **a** : a small holystone **b** : OMASUM

Bible Belt *n* : an area chiefly in the southern U.S. believed to hold uncritical allegiance to the literal accuracy of the Bible; *broadly* : an area characterized by ardent religious fundamentalism

bib·li·cal \'bib-li-kəl\ *adj* [ML *biblicus*, fr. *biblia*] **1** : of, relating to, or being in accord with the Bible **2** : suggestive of the Bible or Bible times — **bib·li·cal·ly** \-k(ə-)lē\ *adv*

bib·li·cism \'bib-lə-,siz-əm\ *n, often cap* : adherence to the letter of the Bible — **bib·li·cist** \-lə-səst\ *n, often cap*

biblio- *comb form* [MF, fr. L, fr. Gk, fr. *biblion*] : book ⟨*bibliofilm*⟩

bib·li·og·ra·pher \,bib-lē-'äg-rə-fər\ *n* **1** : an expert in bibliography **2** : a compiler of bibliographies

bib·lio·graph·ic \,bib-lē-ə-'graf-ik\ *adj* : of or relating to bibliography — **bib·lio·graph·i·cal** \-i-kəl\ *adj* — **bib·lio·graph·i·cal·ly** \-k(ə-)lē\ *adv*

bib·li·og·ra·phy \,bib-lē-'äg-rə-fē\ *n, pl* **-phies** [prob. fr. NL *bibliographia*, fr. Gk, the copying of books, fr. *biblio-* + *-graphia* -graphy] **1** : the history, identification, or description of writings or publications **2 a** : a list often with descriptive or critical notes of writings relating to a particular subject, period, or author **b** : a list of works written by an author or printed by a publishing house **3** : the works or a list of the works referred to in a text or consulted by the author in its production

bib·li·o·la·ter \,bib-lē-'äl-ət-ər\ *n* **1** : one overly devoted to books **2** : one having excessive reverence for the letter of the Bible — **bib·li·ol·a·trous** \-'äl-ə-trəs\ *adj* — **bib·li·ol·a·try** \-trē\ *n*

bib·li·ol·o·gy \,bib-lē-'äl-ə-jē\ *n* **1** : the history and science of books as physical objects : bibliography in its broadest sense **2** *often cap* : the study of the theological doctrine of the Bible

bib·lio·ma·nia \,bib-lē-ə-'mā-nē-ə, -nyə\ *n* [F *bibliomanie*, fr. *biblio-* + *manie* mania, fr. LL *mania*] : extreme preoccupation with collecting books — **bib·lio·ma·ni·ac** \-nē-,ak\ *n* — **bib·lio·ma·ni·a·cal** \-lē-ō-mə-'nī-ə-kəl\ *adj*

bib·li·op·e·gy \,bib-lē-'äp-ə-jē\ *n* [deriv. of Gk *biblio-* + *pēgnynai* to fasten together — more at PACT] : the art of binding books — **bib·li·o·pe·gic** \,bib-lē-ə-'pej-ik, -'pēj-\ *adj* — **bib·li·o·pe·gist** \-i-k(ə-)lē\ *adv* — **bib·li·op·e·gist** \,bib-lē-'äp-ə-jəst\ *n* — **bib·li·op·e·gis·tic** \-,äp-ə-'jis-tik\ *adj*

bib·lio·phile \'bib-lē-ə-,fil\ *n* [F, fr. *biblio-* + *-phile*] : a lover of books esp. for qualities of format; *also* : a book collector — **bib·lio·phil·ic** \,bib-lē-ə-'fil-ik\ *adj* — **bib·li·oph·i·lism** \-äf-ə-,liz-əm\ *n* — **bib·li·oph·i·list** \-ləst\ *n* — **bib·li·oph·i·ly** \-lē\ *n*

bib·li·o·pole \'bib-lē-ə-,pōl\ *or* **bib·li·op·o·list** \,bib-lē-'äp-ə-ləst\ *n* [L *bibliopola* bookseller, fr. Gk *bibliopōlēs*, fr. *biblio-* + *pōlein* to sell] : a dealer esp. in rare or curious books — **bib·li·o·po·lic** \,bib-lē-ə-'pō-lik, -'päl-ik\ *adj*

bib·lio·the·ca \,bib-lē-ə-'thē-kə\ *n, pl* **-cas** *or* **-cae** \-,sē, -,kē\ [L, fr. Gk *bibliothēkē*, fr. *biblio-* + *thēkē* case; akin to Gk *tithenai* to put, place — more at DO] **1** : a collection of books **2** : a list of books — **bib·lio·the·cal** \-'thē-kəl\ *adj*

bib·li·ot·ics \,bib-lē-'ät-iks\ *n pl but sing in constr* [*biblio-* + connective *-t-* + *-ics*] : the study of handwriting, documents, and writing materials esp. for determining genuineness or authorship — **bib·li·ot·ic** \-ik\ *adj* — **bib·li·o·tist** \'bib-lē-ə-təst\ *n*

bib·u·lous \'bib-yə-ləs\ *adj* [L *bibulus*, fr. *bibere* to drink — more at POTABLE] **1** : highly absorbent **2 a** : inclined to drink **b** : of or relating to drink or drinking — **bib·u·lous·ly** *adv* — **bib·u·lous·ness** *n*

bi·cam·er·al \(')bī-'kam-(ə-)rəl\ *adj* : having, consisting of, or based on two legislative chambers ⟨a ∼ legislature⟩ — **bi·cam·er·al·ism** \-,iz-əm\ *n*

bi·cap·su·lar \(')bī-'kap-sə-lər\ *adj* [prob. fr. F *bicapsulaire*, fr. *bi-* + *capsulaire* capsular] : having two capsules or a 2-celled capsule

bi·car·bon·ate \(')bī-'kär-bə-,nāt, -nət\ *n* [ISV] : an acid carbonate

bicarbonate of soda : SODIUM BICARBONATE

bi·cen·te·na·ry \,bī-(,)sen-'ten-ə-rē, (')bī-'sent-²n-,er-ē, ,bī-(,)sen-'tē-nə-rē\ *n* : BICENTENNIAL — **bicentenary** *adj*

bi·cen·ten·ni·al \,bī-(,)sen-'ten-ē-əl\ *n* : a 200th anniversary or its celebration — **bicentennial** *adj*

bi·cen·tric \(')bī-'sen-trik\ *adj* : having or involving two centers — **bi·cen·tric·i·ty** \,bī-(,)sen-'tris-ət-ē\ *n*

bi·ceps \'bī-,seps\ *n* [NL *bicipit-, biceps*, fr. L, two-headed, fr. *bi-* + *capit-, caput* head — more at HEAD] : a muscle having two heads: as **a** : the large flexor muscle of the front of the upper arm **b** : the large flexor muscle of the back of the upper leg

bi·chlo·ride \(')bī-'klō(ə)r-,īd, -'klȯ(ə)r-\ *n* [ISV] **1** : DICHLORIDE **2** : MERCURIC CHLORIDE — called also *bichloride of mercury*

bi·chro·mate \(')bī-'krō-,māt, 'bī-krō-\ *n* : DICHROMATE; *esp* : one of sodium or potassium — **bi·chro·mat·ed** \-,māt-əd\ *adj*

bi·chrome \'bī-,krōm\ *adj* : two-colored

bi·cip·i·tal \bī-'sip-ət-²l\ *adj* : of, relating to, or being a biceps

¹**bick·er** \'bik-ər\ *n* [ME *biker*] **1** : petulant quarreling : ALTERCATION **2** : a sound of or as if of bickering

²**bicker** *vi* **bick·ered; bick·er·ing** \-(ə-)riŋ\ **1** : to contend in petulant or petty altercation **2 a** : to move quickly and unsteadily with a rapidly repeated noise **b** : QUIVER, FLICKER — **bick·er·er** \-ər-ər\ *n*

bi·col·or \'bī-,kəl-ər\ *adj* [L *bicolor*, fr. *bi-* + *color*] : two-colored — **bicolor** *or* **bi·col·ored** \-,kəl-ərd\ *adj*

bicolor lespedeza *n* : an Asiatic leguminous shrub (*Lespedeza bicolor*) with purple flowers in axillary racemes widely used as an ornamental, as a source of wild-bird food, and in erosion control

bi·col·our *chiefly Brit var of* BICOLOR

bi·con·cave \,bī-(,)kän-'kāv, (')bī-'kän-,\ *adj* [ISV] : concave on both sides — **bi·con·cav·i·ty** \,bī-(,)kän-'kav-ət-ē\ *n*

bi·con·di·tion·al \,bī-kən-'dish-nəl, -ən-²l\ *n* : a two-way implication

BOOKS OF THE OLD TESTAMENT

ROMAN CATHOLIC CANON	PROTESTANT CANON	ROMAN CATHOLIC CANON	PROTESTANT CANON
Genesis	Genesis	Wisdom	
Exodus	Exodus	Ecclesiasticus	
Leviticus	Leviticus	Isaias	Isaiah
Numbers	Numbers	Jeremias	Jeremiah
Deuteronomy	Deuteronomy	Lamentations	Lamentations
Josue	Joshua	Baruch	
Judges	Judges	Ezechiel	Ezekiel
Ruth	Ruth	Daniel	Daniel
1 & 2 Kings	1 & 2 Samuel	Osee	Hosea
3 & 4 Kings	1 & 2 Kings	Joel	Joel
1 & 2 Paralipom-enon	1 & 2 Chronicles	Amos	Amos
		Abdias	Obadiah
1 Esdras	Ezra	Jonas	Jonah
2 Esdras	Nehemiah	Micheas	Micah
Tobias		Nahum	Nahum
Judith		Habacuc	Habakkuk
Esther	Esther	Sophonias	Zephaniah
Job	Job	Aggeus	Haggai
Psalms	Psalms	Zacharias	Zechariah
Proverbs	Proverbs	Malachias	Malachi
Ecclesiastes	Ecclesiastes	1 & 2 Machabees	
Canticle of Canticles	Song of Solomon		

JEWISH SCRIPTURE

Law	1 & 2 Kings	Nahum	Song of Songs
Genesis	Isaiah	Habakkuk	Ruth
Exodus	Jeremiah	Zephaniah	Lamentations
Leviticus	Ezekiel	Haggai	Ecclesiastes
Numbers	Hosea	Zechariah	Esther
Deuteronomy	Joel	Malachi	Daniel
Prophets	Amos	*Hagiographa*	Ezra
Joshua	Obadiah	Psalms	Nehemiah
Judges	Jonah	Proverbs	1 & 2 Chronicles
1 & 2 Samuel	Micah	Job	

PROTESTANT APOCRYPHA

1 & 2 Esdras	Wisdom of Solomon	Baruch	Susanna
Tobit	Ecclesiasticus	Prayer of Azariah and the Song	Bel and the Dragon
Judith	or the Wisdom of Jesus Son	of the Three Holy Children	The Prayer of Manasses
Additions to Esther	of Sirach		1 & 2 Maccabees

BOOKS OF THE NEW TESTAMENT

Matthew	Romans	1 & 2 Thess-alonians	1 & 2 Peter
Mark	1 & 2 Corinthians		1, 2, 3 John
Luke	Galatians	1 & 2 Timothy	Jude
John	Ephesians	Titus	Revelation (Roman Catholic canon: Apocalypse)
Acts of the Apostles	Philippians	Philemon	
	Colossians	Hebrews	
		James	

bi·con·vex \ˌbī-(ˌ)kän-ˈveks, (ˈ)bī-ˈkän-ˌ, ˌbī-kən-ˈ\ *adj* [ISV] : convex on both sides — **bi·con·vex·i·ty** \ˌbī-kən-ˈvek-sət-ē, -(ˌ)kän-\ *n*
bi·corne \ˈbī-ˌkȯ(ə)rn\ *n* [F, fr. L *bicornis* two-horned, fr. *bi-* + *cornu* horn — more at HORN] : COCKED HAT 2
bi·cor·nu·ate \(ˈ)bī-ˈkȯr-nyə-wət\ *adj* [*bi-* + L *cornu*] : having two horns or horn-shaped processes
bi·cul·tur·al·ism \(ˈ)bī-ˈkəlch(-ə)-rə-ˌliz-əm\ *n* : the existence of two distinct cultures in one nation ⟨Canada's ~⟩ — **bi·cul·tur·al** \-rəl\ *adj*
1**bi·cus·pid** \(ˈ)bī-ˈkəs-pəd\ *also* **bi·cus·pi·date** \-pə-ˌdāt\ *adj* [NL *bicuspid-, bicuspis,* fr. *bi-* + L *cuspid-, cuspis* point] : having or ending in two points ⟨~ teeth⟩ ⟨~ leaves⟩
2**bicuspid** *n* : a human premolar tooth — see TOOTH illustration
bicuspid valve *n* : a cardiac valve that consists of two triangular flaps and guards the orifice between the left auricle and ventricle — called also *mitral valve*
1**bi·cy·cle** \ˈbī-ˌsik-əl *also* -ˌsī-k-\ *n* [F, fr. *bi-* + *-cycle* (as in *tricycle*)] : a vehicle with two wheels tandem, a steering handle, a saddle seat, and pedals by which it is propelled
2**bicycle** *vi* **bi·cy·cled; bi·cy·cling** \(-ə-)liŋ\ : to ride a bicycle — **bi·cy·cler** \-lər\ *n* — **bi·cy·clist** \-ləst\ *n*
bi·cy·clic \(ˈ)bī-ˈsī-klik, -ˈsik-lik\ *adj* [ISV] **1** : consisting of or arranged in two cycles **2** : containing two usu. fused rings in the structure of the molecule
1**bid** \ˈbid\ *vb* **bade** \ˈbad, ˈbād\ *or* **bid; bid·den** \ˈbid-ᵊn\ *or* **bid** *also* **bade; bid·ding** [partly fr. ME *bidden,* fr. OE *biddan;* akin to OHG *bitten* to entreat, Skt *bādhate* he harasses; partly fr. ME *beden* to offer, command, fr. OE *bēodan;* akin to OHG *biotan* to offer, Gk *pynthanesthai* to learn by inquiry] *vt* **1** **a** *obs* : BESEECH, ENTREAT **b** : to issue an order to : TELL **c** : to request to come : INVITE **2** : to give expression to ⟨*bade* a tearful farewell⟩ **3** **a** : OFFER — usu. used in the phrase *to bid defiance* **b** *past bid* (1) : to offer (a price) whether for payment or acceptance (2) : to make a bid of or in (a suit at cards) ~ *vi* : to make a bid ***syn*** see COMMAND ***ant*** forbid — **bid·der** *n* — **bid fair** : to seem likely
2**bid** *n* **1** **a** : the act of one who bids **b** : a statement of what one will give or take for something; *esp* : an offer of a price **c** : something offered as a bid **2** : an opportunity to bid **3** : INVITATION **4** **a** : an announcement of what a cardplayer proposes to undertake **b** : the amount of such a bid **c** : a biddable bridge hand **5** : an attempt or effort to win, achieve, or attract
BID *abbr* **1** bachelor of industrial design **2** [L *bis in die*] twice a day
bid·da·ble \ˈbid-ə-bəl\ *adj* **1** : easily led, taught, or controlled : DOCILE **2** : capable of being bid — **bid·da·bil·i·ty** \ˌbid-ə-ˈbil-ət-ē\ *n* — **bid·da·bly** \ˈbid-ə-blē\ *adv*
1**bid·dy** \ˈbid-ē\ *n, pl* **biddies** [perh. imit.] : HEN 1a; *also* : a young chicken
2**biddy** *n, pl* **biddies** [dim. of the name *Bridget*] **1** : a hired girl or cleaning woman **2** : WOMAN ⟨an eccentric old ~⟩
Bid·dy Basketball \ˌbit-ē-\ *n* [alter. of 2*bitty*] : basketball designed to be played by youngsters and marked by the use of a smaller ball, a shorter court, and baskets at a height of 8½ feet
bide \ˈbīd\ *vb* **bode** \ˈbōd\ *or* **bid·ed; bided; bid·ing** [ME *biden,* fr. OE *bīdan;* akin to OHG *bītan* to wait, L *fidere* to trust, Gk *peithesthai* to believe] *vi* **1** : to continue in a state or condition **2** : to wait awhile : TARRY **3** : to continue in a place : SOJOURN ~ *vt* **1** *past usu bided* : to wait for — used chiefly in the phrase *bide one's time* **2** *archaic* : to await confidently or defiantly : WITHSTAND ⟨two men . . . might ~ the winter storm — W. C. Bryant⟩ **3** *chiefly dial* : to put up with : TOLERATE — **bid·er** *n*
bi·det \bi-ˈdā\ *n* [F, small horse, bidet, fr. MF, fr. *bider* to trot] : a fixture about the height of the seat of a chair used esp. for bathing the external genitals and the posterior parts of the body
bi·di·a·lec·tal·ism \ˌbī-ˌdī-ə-ˈlek-tᵊl-ˌiz-əm\ *n* : the constant oral use of two dialects of the same language — **bi·di·a·lec·tal** *adj*
bi·don·ville \ˌbē-ˌdōⁿ-ˈvē(ə)l\ *n* [F, fr. *bidon* tin can + *ville* city] : a settlement of jerry-built dwellings on the outskirts of a city (as in France)
bid up *vt* : to raise the price of (as property at auction) by a succession of offers
BIE *abbr* bachelor of industrial engineering
bield \ˈbē(ə)ld\ *vt or n* [ME *belden* to encourage, protect, fr. OE *bieldan* to encourage; akin to OE *beald* bold] *chiefly Scot* : SHELTER
bi·en·ni·al \(ˈ)bī-ˈen-ē-əl\ *adj* **1** : occurring every two years **2** : continuing or lasting for two years; *specif* : growing vegetatively during the first year and fruiting and dying during the second — **biennial** *n* — **bi·en·ni·al·ly** \-ə-lē\ *adv*
bi·en·ni·um \bī-ˈen-ē-əm\ *n, pl* **-ni·ums** *or* **-nia** \-ē-ə\ [L, fr. *bi-* + *annus* year — more at ANNUAL] : a period of two years
bier \ˈbi(ə)r\ *n* [ME *bere,* fr. OE *bǣr;* akin to OE *beran* to carry — more at BEAR] **1** *archaic* : a framework for carrying **2** : a stand on which a corpse or coffin is placed; *also* : a coffin together with its stand
bi·fa·cial \(ˈ)bī-ˈfā-shəl\ *adj* **1** : having opposite surfaces alike ⟨~ leaves⟩ **2** : having two fronts or faces
biff \ˈbif\ *n* [prob. imit.] : WHACK, BLOW — **biff** *vt*
bi·fid \ˈbī-ˌfid, -fəd\ *adj* [L *bifidus,* fr. *bi-* + *-fidus* -fid] : divided into two equal lobes or parts by a median cleft ⟨a ~ leaf⟩ — **bi·fid·i·ty** \bī-ˈfid-ət-ē\ *n* — **bi·fid·ly** \ˈbī-ˌfid-lē, -fəd-\ *adv*
bi·fi·lar \(ˈ)bī-ˈfī-lər\ *adj* [ISV *bi-* + L *filum* thread — more at FILE] **1** : involving two threads or wires ⟨~ suspension of a pendulum⟩ **2** : involving a single thread or wire doubled back upon itself ⟨a ~ resistor⟩ — **bi·fi·lar·ly** *adv*
bi·fla·gel·late \(ˈ)bī-ˈflaj-ə-lət, -ˌlāt; ˌbī-flə-ˈjel-ət\ *adj* : having two flagella
1**bi·fo·cal** \(ˈ)bī-ˈfō-kəl\ *adj* [ISV] **1** : having two focal lengths **2** : having one part that corrects for near vision and one for distant vision ⟨a ~ eyeglass lens⟩
2**bifocal** *n* **1** : a bifocal glass or lens **2** *pl* : eyeglasses with bifocal lenses
bi·form \ˈbī-ˌfȯrm\ *adj* [L *biformis,* fr. *bi-* + *forma* form] : combining the qualities or forms of two distinct kinds of individuals
bi·fur·cate \ˈbī-(ˌ)fər-ˌkāt, bī-ˈfər-\ *vi* **-cat·ed; -cat·ing** [ML *bifurcatus,* pp. of *bifurcare,* fr. L *bifurcus* two-pronged, fr. *bi-* + *furca* fork] : to divide into two branches or parts — **bi·fur·cate** \(ˈ)bī-ˈfər-kət, -ˌkāt; ˈbī-(ˌ)fər-ˌkāt\ *adj* — **bi·fur·cate·ly** *adv*
bi·fur·ca·tion \ˌbī-(ˌ)fər-ˈkā-shən\ *n* **1** : the act of bifurcating : the state of being bifurcated **2** **a** : the point at which bifurcating occurs **b** : BRANCH
1**big** \ˈbig\ *adj* **big·ger; big·gest** [ME, prob. of Scand origin; akin to Norw dial. *bugge* important man; akin to OE *bȳl* boil, Skt *bhūri* abundant] **1** **a** *obs* : of great strength **b** : of great force ⟨a ~ storm⟩ **2** **a** : large in dimensions, bulk, or extent ⟨a ~ house⟩; *also* : large in quantity, number, or amount ⟨a ~ fleet⟩ **b** : conducted on a large scale ⟨~ government⟩ **3** **a** : PREGNANT; *esp* : nearly ready to give birth **b** : full to bursting : SWELLING ⟨~ with rage⟩ **c** *of the voice* : full and resonant **4** **a** : CHIEF, PREEMINENT ⟨the ~ issue of the campaign⟩ **b** : outstandingly worthy or able ⟨a truly ~ man⟩ **c** : of great importance or significance ⟨the ~ moment⟩ **d** : IMPOSING, PRETENTIOUS; *also* : marked by or given to boasting ⟨~ talk⟩ **e** : MAGNANIMOUS, GENEROUS ⟨a ~ heart⟩ **5** : POPULAR ⟨soft drinks are very ~ in Mexico — Russ Leadabrand⟩ ***syn*** see LARGE ***ant*** little — **big·ly** *adv* — **big·ness** *n*
2**big** *adv* **1** : to a large amount or extent ⟨eats ~ at noon⟩ **2** **a** : in an outstanding manner ⟨made it ~ in New York⟩ **b** : in a pretentious manner ⟨he talks ~⟩ **c** : in a magnanimous manner ⟨took his defeat ~⟩
big·a·mous \ˈbig-ə-məs\ *adj* **1** : guilty of bigamy **2** : involving bigamy — **big·a·mous·ly** *adv*
big·a·my \ˈbig-ə-mē\ *n* [ME *bigamie,* fr. ML *bigamia,* fr. L *bi-* + LL *-gamia* -gamy, fr. Gk, fr. *gamos* marriage; akin to L *gener* son-in-law] : the act of entering into a ceremonial marriage with one person while still legally married to another — **big·a·mist** \-məst\ *n*
Big·ar·reau \ˈbig-ə-ˌrō\ *n* [F] : any of several cultivated sweet cherries with rather firm often light-colored globular fruits
big bang theory *n* : a theory in astronomy: the universe originated billions of years ago from the explosion of a single mass of material so that the pieces are still flying apart — compare STEADY STATE THEORY
big beat *n, often cap both B's* : music (as rock 'n' roll) characterized by a heavy persistent beat
Big Ben \-ˈben\ *n* [after Sir *Benjamin* Hall †1867 E Chief Commissioner of Works] **1** : a large bell in the clock tower of the Houses of Parliament in London **2** : the tower that houses Big Ben; *also* : the clock in the tower
big brother *n* **1** : an older brother **2** : a man who befriends a delinquent or friendless boy **3** *cap both Bs* **a** : the leader of an authoritarian state or movement **b** : a seemingly benevolent but actually ruthless and all-powerful government ⟨proliferating data banks that tell *Big Brother* all about us —Herbert Brucker⟩
Big Broth·er·ism \-ˈbrət͟h-ə-ˌriz-əm\ *n* : authoritarian attempts at complete control (as of a person or a nation)
Big Dipper *n* : DIPPER 2a
bi·gem·i·ny \bī-ˈjem-ə-nē\ *n* [*bigeminal* (double, paired), fr. LL *bigeminus,* fr. *bi-* + *geminus* twin] : the state of having a pulse characterized by two beats close together with a pause following each pair of beats — **bi·gem·i·nal** \-ən-ᵊl\ *adj*
bi·ge·ner·ic \ˌbī-jə-ˈner-ik\ *adj* : of, relating to, or involving two genera ⟨a ~ hybrid⟩
big·eye \ˈbig-ˌī\ *n* : either of two small widely distributed reddish to silvery percoid fishes (*Priacanthus cruentatus* and *P. arenatus*) of tropical seas
big game *n* **1** : large animals sought or taken by hunting or fishing for sport **2** : an important objective esp. when involving risk
big·ge·ty *or* **big·gi·ty** \ˈbig-ət-ē\ *adj* [prob. irreg. fr. *big* + *-y*] **1** *South & Midland* : CONCEITED, VAIN **2** *South & Midland* : rudely self-important : IMPUDENT ⟨Mama never acted ~ in court, but she would bow her head only so low — Claude Brown⟩
1**big·gin** *or* **big·ging** \ˈbig-ən\ *n* [ME *bigging,* fr. *biggen* to dwell, fr. ON *byggja;* akin to OE *bēon* to be] *archaic* : BUILDING
2**biggin** *n* [MF *beguin*] *archaic* : CAP: **a** : a child's cap **b** : NIGHTCAP
big·gish \ˈbig-ish\ *adj* : somewhat big
big·head \ˈbig-ˌhed\ *n* **1** : any of several diseases of animals marked by swelling about the head **2** : an exaggerated opinion of one's importance : CONCEIT — **big·head·ed** \-ˈhed-əd\ *adj*
big·heart·ed \-ˈhärt-əd\ *adj* : being generous and kindly — **big·heart·ed·ly** *adv* — **big·heart·ed·ness** *n*
big·horn \ˈbig-ˌhȯ(ə)rn\ *n, pl* **bighorn** *or* **bighorns** : a usu. grayish brown wild sheep (*Ovis canadensis*) of mountainous western No. America
1**bight** \ˈbīt\ *n* [ME, fr. OE *byht;* akin to OE *būgan* to bend — more at BOW] **1** *obs* : a corner, bend, or angle esp. of a body part **2** **a** : the middle part of a slack rope **b** : a loop esp. in a rope **3** **a** : a bend esp. in a river or a mountain chain **b** : a bend in a coast forming an open bay; *also* : a bay formed by such a bend
2**bight** *vt* **1** : to lay or fasten (a rope) in bights **2** : to fasten with a bight
big league *n* **1** : MAJOR LEAGUE **2** : one that is outstanding of its kind — **big leagu·er** \-ˈlē-gər\ *n*
big·mouthed \ˈbig-ˈmau̇t͟hd, -ˈmau̇tht\ *adj*

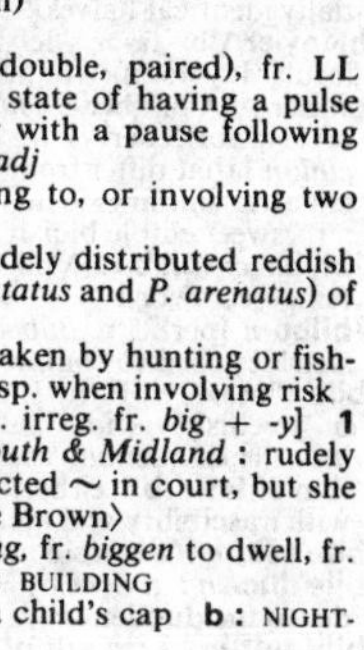

bighorn

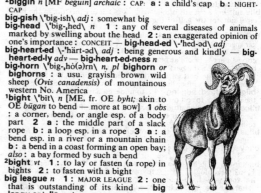

1 : having a large mouth 2 : LOUDMOUTHED
big–name \-'nām\ *adj* 1 : of top rank in popular recognition 2 : of or involving a big-name person, organization, or product
big name *n* : a big-name performer or personage
big·no·nia \big-'nō-nē-ə\ *n* [NL, genus name, fr. J. P. *Bignon* †1743 F royal librarian] : any of a genus (*Bignonia*) of American and Japanese woody vines of the trumpet-creeper family with compound leaves and tubular flowers
big·ot \'big-ət\ *n* [MF, hypocrite, bigot] : one obstinately or intolerantly devoted to his own church, party, belief, or opinion — **big·ot·ed** \-ət-əd\ *adj* — **big·ot·ed·ly** *adv*
big·ot·ry \'big-ə-trē\ *n, pl* **-ries** 1 : the state of mind of a bigot 2 : acts or beliefs characteristic of a bigot
big shot \'big-,shät\ *n* : a person of consequence or prominence
big stick *n* : threat esp. of military or political intervention
big–tick·et \'big-'tik-ət\ *adj* : high-priced
big time \-,tīm\ *n* 1 : a high-paying vaudeville circuit requiring only two performances a day 2 : the top rank — **big–tim·er** \-,tī-mər\ *n*
big toe *n* : the innermost and largest digit of the foot
big top *n* 1 : the main tent of a circus 2 : CIRCUS 2a, 2b, 2c
big tree *n* : a California evergreen (*Sequoiadendron giganteum*) of the pine family that sometimes exceeds 270 feet in height — called also *giant sequoia, sequoia*
big·wig \'big-,wig\ *n* : an important person
Bi·ha·ri \bi-'här-ē\ *n* : a group of Indic dialects spoken by the inhabitants of Bihar
bi·jou \'bē-,zhü\ *n, pl* **bijous** *or* **bijoux** \-,zhü(z)\ [F, fr. Bret *bizou* ring, fr. *biz* finger; akin to W *bys* finger] : a small dainty usu. ornamental piece of delicate workmanship : JEWEL — **bijou** *adj*
bi·jou·te·rie \bi-'zhüt-ə-(,)rē\ *n* [F, fr. *bijou*] : a collection of trinkets or ornaments : JEWELS; *also* : DECORATION
¹bike \'bīk\ *n* [ME] 1 *chiefly Scot* : a nest of wild bees, wasps, or hornets 2 *chiefly Scot* : a crowd or swarm of people
²bike *n* [by shortening & alter.] 1 : BICYCLE 2 : MOTORCYCLE 3 : MOTORBIKE — **bik·er** *n*
³bike *vi* **biked; bik·ing** : to ride a bike
bike·way \'bī-,kwā\ *n* : a thoroughfare esp. suitable for bicycles
bi·ki·ni \bə-'kē-nē\ *n* [F, fr. *Bikini*, atoll of the Marshall islands] : a woman's scanty two-piece bathing suit — **bi·ki·nied** \-nēd\ *adj*
¹bi·la·bi·al \(')bī-'lā-bē-əl\ *adj* [ISV] 1 *of a consonant* : produced with both lips 2 : of or relating to both lips
²bilabial *n* : a bilabial consonant
bi·la·bi·ate \-bē-ət\ *adj* : having two lips (a ~ corolla of a mint)
bi·lat·er·al \(')bī-'lat-ə-rəl, -'la-trəl\ *adj* 1 : having two sides 2 : affecting reciprocally two sides or parties (a ~ treaty) 3 : having bilateral symmetry — **bi·lat·er·al·ism** \-,iz-əm\ *n* — **bi·lat·er·al·ly** \-ē\ *adv* — **bi·lat·er·al·ness** *n*
bilateral symmetry *n* : a pattern of animal symmetry in which similar parts are arranged on opposite sides of a median axis so that one and only one plane can divide the individual into essentially identical halves
bi·lay·er \'bī-,lā-ər, -,le(-ə)r\ *n* : a film or membrane with two molecular layers (a ~ of phospholipid molecules)
bil·ber·ry \'bil-,ber-ē\ *n* [*bil-* (prob. of Scand origin; akin to Dan *bølle* whortleberry) + *berry*] : any of several plants (genus *Vaccinium*) that differ from the typical blueberries in having their flowers arise solitary or in very small clusters from axillary buds; *also* : its sweet edible bluish fruit
¹bil·bo *or* **bil·boa** \'bil-(,)bō\ *n* [*Bilboa, Bilbao*, Spain] : a finely tempered sword
²bilbo *n* [perh. fr. *Bilboa*, Spain] : a long bar of iron with sliding shackles used to confine the feet of prisoners esp. on shipboard
bile \'bī(ə)l\ *n* [F, fr. L *bilis*; akin to W *bustl* bile] 1 **a** : a yellow or greenish viscid alkaline fluid secreted by the liver and passed into the duodenum where it aids esp. in the digestion and absorption of fats **b** : either of two humors associated in old physiology with irascibility and melancholy 2 : inclination to anger : SPLEEN
bile acid *n* : a steroid acid (as cholic acid) of or derived from bile
bile duct *n* : a duct by which bile passes from the liver or gallbladder to the duodenum
bile salt *n* 1 : a salt of bile acid 2 *pl* : a dry mixture of the principal salts of the gall of the ox used as a liver stimulant and as a laxative
bi·lev·el \'bī-'lev-əl\ *adj* 1 : having two levels of freight or passenger space 2 : divided vertically into two ground-floor levels
¹bilge \'bilj\ *n* [prob. modif. of MF *boulge, bouge* leather bag, curved part — more at BUDGET] 1 : the bulging part of a cask or barrel 2 **a** : the part of the underwater body of a ship between the flat of the bottom and the vertical topsides **b** : the lowest point of a ship's inner hull 3 : stale or worthless remarks or ideas
²bilge *vi* **bilged; bilg·ing** 1 : to undergo damage (as a fracture) in the bilge 2 : to rest on the bilge
bilge keel *n* : a longitudinal projection like a fin secured for a distance along a ship near the turn of the bilge on either side to check rolling
bilge water *n* : water that collects by seepage or leakage in the bilge of a ship
bilgy \'bil-jē\ *adj* **bilg·i·er; -est** : resembling bilge water esp. in smell
bil·har·zia \bil-'här-zē-ə, -'härt-sē-\ *n* [NL, fr. Theodor *Bilharz* †1862 G zoologist] 1 : SCHISTOSOME 2 : SCHISTOSOMIASIS — **bil·har·zi·al** \-zē-əl\ *adj*
bil·har·zi·a·sis \bil-,här-'zī-ə-səs, -,härt-'sī-\ *n, pl* **-a·ses** \-,sēz\ [NL, fr. *bilharzia* + *-iasis*] : SCHISTOSOMIASIS
bil·i·ary \'bil-ē-,er-ē\ *adj* [F *biliaire*, fr. L *bilis*] : of, relating to, or conveying bile; *also* : affecting the bile-conveying structures (~ disorders)
bi·lin·ear \(')bī-'lin-ē-ər\ *adj* : linear with respect to each of two mathematical variables; *specif* : of or relating to an algebraic form each term of which involves one variable to the first degree from each of two sets of variables
bi·lin·gual \(')bī-'liŋ-g(yə-)wəl\ *adj* [L *bilinguis*, fr. *bi-* + *lingua* tongue — more at TONGUE] 1 : of, containing, or expressed in two

languages 2 : using or able to use two languages esp. with the fluency characteristic of a native speaker — **bilingual** *n* — **bi·lin·gual·ly** \-ē\ *adv*
bi·lin·gual·ism \-,iz-əm\ *n* : the constant oral use of two languages
bil·ious \'bil-yəs\ *adj* [MF *bilieux*, fr. L *biliosus*, fr. *bilis*] 1 **a** : of or relating to bile **b** : marked by or suffering from disordered liver function and esp. excessive secretion of bile **c** : appearing as though affected by a bilious disorder 2 : of a peevish ill-natured disposition — **bil·ious·ly** *adv* — **bil·ious·ness** *n*
bil·i·ru·bin \,bil-i-'rü-bən, 'bil-i-,\ *n* [L *bilis* + *ruber* red — more at RED] : a reddish yellow pigment $C_{33}H_{36}N_4O_6$ occurring in bile, blood, urine, and gallstones
bil·i·ver·din \-'vərd-ᵊn, -,vərd-\ *n* [Sw, fr. L *bilis* + obs. F *verd* green] : a green pigment $C_{33}H_{34}N_4O_6$ occurring in bile
¹bilk \'bilk\ *vt* [perh. alter. of *²balk*] 1 : to block the free development of : FRUSTRATE (fate ~s their hopes) 2 **a** : to cheat out of what is due **b** : to evade payment of (~s his creditors) 3 : to slip away from : ELUDE (~ his pursuers) — **bilk·er** *n*
²bilk *n* : an untrustworthy tricky person : CHEAT
¹bill \'bil\ *n* [ME *bile*, fr. OE; akin to OE *bill* (weapon)] 1 : the jaws of a bird together with their horny covering 2 : a mouthpart (as the beak of a turtle) that resembles a bird's bill 3 : a projection of land like a beak 4 : the end of an anchor fluke or of a sail yard 5 : the visor of a cap

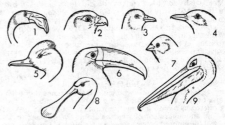

bills of birds: *1* flamingo, *2* hawk, *3* pigeon, *4* thrush, *5* duck (merganser), *6* toucan, *7* finch, *8* spoonbill, *9* pelican

²bill *vi* 1 : to touch and rub bill to bill 2 : to caress affectionately
³bill *n* [ME *bil*, fr. OE *bill*; akin to OHG *bill* pickax, Gk *phitros* log] 1 : a weapon in use up to the 18th century that consists of a long staff terminating in a hook-shaped blade 2 : BILLHOOK
⁴bill *n* [ME, fr. ML *billa*, alter. of *bulla*, fr. L, bubble, boss] 1 **a** : a written document **b** : MEMORANDUM **c** : LETTER 2 *obs* : a formal petition 3 : a draft of a law presented to a legislature for enactment 4 : a declaration in writing stating a wrong a complainant has suffered from a defendant or stating a breach of law by some person (a ~ of complaint) 5 : a paper carrying a statement of particulars (as a list of men and their duties as part of a ship's crew) 6 **a** : an itemized account of the separate cost of goods sold, services performed, or work done : INVOICE **b** : a statement in gross of a creditor's claim **c** : a statement of charges for food or drink : CHECK 7 **a** : a written or printed advertisement posted or otherwise distributed to announce an event of interest to the public; *esp* : an announcement of a theatrical entertainment **b** : a programmed presentation (as a motion picture, play, or concert) 8 **a** : a piece of paper money **b** : an individual or commercial note (~s receivable) **c** *slang* : one hundred dollars
⁵bill *vt* 1 **a** : to enter in a book of accounts : prepare a bill of (charges) **b** : to submit a bill of charges to **c** : to enter (as freight) in a waybill **d** : to issue a bill of lading to or for 2 **a** : to announce esp. by posters or placards **b** : to arrange for the presentation of : ADVERTISE (the book is ~ed as a "report" —P. G. Altbach)
bil·la·bong \'bil-ə-,bȯŋ, -,bäŋ\ *n* [native name in Australia] 1 *Austral* **a** : a blind channel leading out from a river **b** : a usu. dry stream bed that is filled seasonally 2 *Austral* : a backwater forming a stagnant pool
¹bill·board \'bil-,bō(ə)rd, -,bȯ(ə)rd\ *n* : a projection or ledge fixed on the bow of a vessel for the anchor to rest on
²billboard *n* [*⁴bill* + *board*] : a flat surface (as of a panel, wall, or fence) on which bills are posted; *specif* : a large panel designed to carry outdoor advertising
bill·bug \'bil-,bəg\ *n* [*¹bill* + *bug*] : a weevil (esp. genus *Calendra*) having larvae that eat the roots of cereal and other grasses
-billed \'bild\ *adj comb form* : having (such) a bill (hard-*billed*)
bill·er \'bil-ər\ *n* : one that bills: as **a** : a clerk who makes out bills **b** : a machine for making out bills
¹bil·let \'bil-ət\ *n* [ME *bylet*, fr. MF *billette*, dim. of *bulle* document, fr. ML *bulla*] 1 *archaic* : a brief letter : NOTE 2 **a** : an official order directing that a member of a military force be provided with board and lodging (as in a private home) **b** : quarters assigned by or as if by a billet 3 : POSITION, JOB (a lucrative ~)
²billet *vt* 1 : to assign lodging to (soldiers) by a billet : QUARTER 2 : to serve with a billet (~ a householder) ~ *vi* : to have quarters
³billet *n* [ME *bylet*, fr. MF *billete*, dim. of *bille* log, of Celt origin; akin to OIr *bile* sacred tree] 1 **a** : a chunky piece of wood (as for firewood) : BOLT 5 **b** *obs* : CUDGEL 2 **a** : a bar of metal **b** : a piece of semifinished iron or steel nearly square in section made by rolling an ingot or bloom **c** : a section of nonferrous metal ingot hot-worked by forging, rolling, or extrusion : a nonferrous casting suitable for rolling or extrusion
bil·let–doux \,bil-(,)ā-'dü\ *n, pl* **bil·lets–doux** \-(,)ā-'dü(z)\ [F *billet doux*, lit., sweet letter] : a love letter
bill·fish \'bil-,fish\ *n* : a fish (as a marlin or gar) with long slender jaws

bill·fold \-ˌfōld\ *n* [short for earlier *billfolder*] **1 :** a folding pocketbook for paper money **2 :** WALLET 2b
bill·head \-ˌhed\ *n* **:** a printed form usu. headed with a business address and used for billing charges
bill·hook \-ˌhu̇k\ *n* **:** a cutting tool consisting of a blade with a hooked point fitted with a handle and used esp. in pruning
bil·liard \ˈbil-yərd\ *n* [back-formation fr. *billiards*] **1 :** CAROM 1a **2 —** used as an attributive form of *billiards* ⟨~ ball⟩
bil·liards \-yərdz\ *n pl but sing in constr* [MF *billard* billiard cue, billiards, fr. *bille*] **:** any of several games played on an oblong table by driving small balls against one another or into pockets with a cue; *specif* **:** a game in which one scores by causing a cue ball to hit in succession two object balls — compare POOL
bill·ing \ˈbil-iŋ\ *n* [5*bill*] **1 :** ADVERTISING ⟨advance ~⟩ **2 :** total amount of business or investments (as of an advertising agency) within a given period **3 :** the relative prominence given a name (as of an actor) in advertising programs ⟨top ~⟩
bil·lings·gate \ˈbil-iŋz-ˌgāt, *Brit usu* -git\ *n* [*Billingsgate,* old gate and fish market, London, England] **:** coarsely abusive language *syn* see ABUSE
bil·lion \ˈbi(l)-yən\ *n* [F, fr. *bi-* + *-illion* (as in *million*)] **1 —** see NUMBER table **2 :** a very large number — **billion** *adj* — **bil·lionth** \-yən(t)th\ *adj or n*
bil·lion·aire \ˌbi(l)-yə-ˈna(ə)r, -ˈne(ə)r, ˈbi(l)-yə-ˌ\ *n* [*billion* + *-aire* (as in *millionaire*)] **:** one whose wealth is estimated at a billion or more (as of dollars or pounds)
bill of exchange : an unconditional written order from one person to another to pay a specified sum of money to a designated person
bill of fare **1 :** MENU **2 :** PROGRAM
bill of goods : a consignment of merchandise
bill of health **1 :** a certificate given to the ship's master at the time of leaving port that indicates the state of health of a ship's company and of a port with regard to infectious diseases **2 :** a report about a condition or situation ⟨gave the criticized textbook a clean *bill of health*⟩
bill of lading : a receipt listing goods shipped that is signed by the agent of the owner of a ship or issued by a common carrier
bill of rights *often cap B&R* **:** a summary of fundamental rights and privileges guaranteed to a people against violation by the state — used esp. of the first 10 amendments to the U.S. Constitution
bill of sale : a formal instrument for the conveyance or transfer of title to goods and chattels
bil·lon \ˈbil-ən\ *n* [F, fr. MF, fr. *bille* log — more at BILLET] **1 :** an alloy of silver containing more than 50 percent of copper by weight **2 :** gold or silver heavily alloyed with a less valuable metal
1**bil·low** \ˈbil-(ˌ)ō, -ə(-w)\ *n* [prob. fr. ON *bylgja;* akin to OHG *balg* bag — more at BELLY] **1 :** WAVE; *esp* **:** a great wave or surge of water **2 :** a rolling mass (as of flame or smoke) that resembles a high wave — **bil·lowy** \ˈbil-ə-wē\ *adj*
2**billow** *vi* **1 :** to rise or roll in waves or surges **2 :** to bulge or swell out (as through action of the wind) ~ *vt* **:** to cause to billow
bill·post·er \ˈbil-ˌpō-stər\ *n* **:** one that posts advertising bills — called also *billsticker* — **bill·post·ing** \-stiŋ\ *n*
1**bil·ly** \ˈbil-ē\ *n, pl* **billies** [prob. fr. the name *Billy*] **:** BILLY CLUB
2**billy** *n, pl* **billies** [prob. short for *billycan* (billy)] *chiefly Austral* **:** a can of metal or enamelware made with a lid and a wire bail and used for outdoor cooking or for carrying food or liquid
billy club *n* [1*billy*] **:** a heavy usu. wooden club; *specif* **:** a policeman's club
bil·ly·cock \ˈbil-ē-ˌkäk\ *n* [origin unknown] *Brit* **:** a stiff felt hat
bil·ly goat \ˈbil-ē-\ *n* [fr. the name *Billy*] **:** a male goat
bi·lobed \ˈbī-ˈlōbd\ *adj* **:** divided into two lobes
bi·loc·u·lar \(ˈ)bī-ˈläk-yə-lər\ *or* **bi·loc·u·late** \-lət\ *adj* [*bi-* + NL *loculus*] **:** divided into two cells or compartments ⟨~ ovary⟩
bil·tong \ˈbil-ˌtȯŋ, -ˌtäŋ\ *n* [Afrik, fr. *bil* buttock + *tong* tongue] *chiefly So Afr* **:** jerked meat
bi·man·u·al \(ˈ)bī-ˈman-yə(-wə)l\ *adj* **:** done with or requiring the use of both hands — **bi·man·u·al·ly** \-ē\ *adv*
bi·mes·ter \(ˈ)bī-ˈmes-tər, ˈbī-ˌ\ *n* [*bi-* + *-mester* (as in *semester*)] **:** a period of two months
bi·mes·tri·al \bī-ˈmes-trē-əl\ *adj* [L *bimestris,* fr. *bi-* + *mensis* month — more at MOON] **:** continuing for two months
bi·met·al \ˈbī-ˌmet-ᵊl\ *adj* **:** BIMETALLIC — **bimetal** *n*
bi·me·tal·lic \ˌbī-mə-ˈtal-ik\ *adj* **1 :** relating to, based on, or using bimetallism **2 :** composed of two different metals — often used of devices having a part in which two metals that expand differently are bonded together — **bimetallic** *n*
bi·met·al·lism \(ˈ)bī-ˈmet-ᵊl-ˌiz-əm\ *n* [F *bimétallisme,* fr. *bi-* + *métal* metal] **:** the use of two metals (as gold and silver) jointly as a monetary standard with both constituting legal tender at a predetermined ratio — **bi·met·al·list** \-ᵊl-əst\ *n* — **bi·met·al·lis·tic** \ˌbī-ˌmet-ᵊl-ˈis-tik\ *adj*
bi·mil·le·na·ry \(ˈ)bī-ˈmil-ə-ˌner-ē, ˌbī-mə-ˈlen-ə-rē\ *or* **bi·mil·len·ni·al** \ˌbī-mə-ˈlen-ē-əl\ *n* **1 :** a period of 2000 years **2 :** a 2000th anniversary — **bimillenary** *adj*
bi·mod·al \(ˈ)bī-ˈmōd-ᵊl\ *adj* **:** having two statistical modes — **bi·mo·dal·i·ty** \ˌbī-mō-ˈdal-ət-ē\ *n*
bi·mo·lec·u·lar \ˌbī-mə-ˈlek-yə-lər\ *adj* [ISV] **1 :** relating to or formed from two molecules **2 :** being two molecules thick — **bi·mo·lec·u·lar·ly** *adv*
1**bi·month·ly** \(ˈ)bī-ˈmən(t)th-lē\ *adj* **1 :** occurring every two months **2 :** occurring twice a month **:** SEMIMONTHLY
2**bimonthly** *n* **:** a bimonthly publication
3**bimonthly** *adv* **1 :** once every two months **2 :** twice a month
bi·mor·phe·mic \ˌbī-mȯr-ˈfē-mik\ *adj* **:** consisting of two morphemes
1**bin** \ˈbin\ *n* [ME *binn,* fr. OE] **:** a box, frame, crib, or enclosed place used for storage
2**bin** *vt* **binned; bin·ning :** to put into a bin
bin- *comb form* [ME, fr. LL, fr. L *bini* two by two; akin to OE *twīn* twine] **:** 1BI- ⟨*bin*aural⟩
1**bi·na·ry** \ˈbī-nə-rē\ *adj* [LL *binarius,* fr. L *bini*] **1 :** compounded or consisting of or marked by two things or parts **2 :** composed of two chemical elements, an element and a radical that acts as an element, or two such radicals **3 a :** relating to, being, or belonging to a system of numbers having 2 as its base ⟨the ~ digits 0 and 1⟩ **b :** involving a choice or condition of two alternatives (as on-off or yes-no) **4 :** relating two logical elements ⟨~ operation⟩ **5 a :** having two musical subjects or two complementary sections **b :** DUPLE — used of measure or rhythm
2**binary** *n, pl* **-ries :** something made of two things or parts
binary fission *n* **:** reproduction of a cell by division into two approximately equal parts ⟨the *binary fission* of protozoans⟩
binary star *n* **:** a system of two stars that revolve around each other under their mutual gravitation
bi·na·tion·al \(ˈ)bī-ˈnash-nəl, -ən-ᵊl\ *adj* **:** of or relating to two nations ⟨a ~ board of directors⟩
bin·au·ral \(ˈ)bī-ˈnȯr-əl, (ˈ)bin-ˈȯr-\ *adj* [ISV] **1 :** of, relating to, or used with two or both ears **2 :** of, relating to, or characterized by the placement of sound sources (as in sound transmission and recording) to achieve in sound reproduction an effect of hearing the sound sources in their original positions — **bin·au·ral·ly** \-ə-lē\ *adv*
1**bind** \ˈbīnd\ *vb* **bound** \ˈbau̇nd\; **bind·ing** [ME *binden,* fr. OE *bindan;* akin to OHG *bintan* to bind, Gk *peisma* cable] *vt* **1 a :** to make secure by tying **b :** to confine, restrain, or restrict as if with bonds **c :** to put under an obligation ⟨~*s* himself with an oath⟩ **d :** to constrain with legal authority **2 a :** to wrap around with something so as to enclose or cover **b :** BANDAGE **3 :** to fasten round about **4 :** to tie together (as stocks of wheat) **5 a :** to cause to stick together **b :** to take up and hold (as by chemical forces) **:** combine with **6 :** CONSTIPATE **7 :** to make firm or sure **:** SETTLE ⟨a deposit ~*s* the sale⟩ **8 :** to protect, strengthen, or decorate by a band or binding **9 :** to apply the parts of the cover to (a book) **10 :** to set at work as an apprentice **:** INDENTURE **11 :** to cause to be attached (as by gratitude) **12 :** to fasten together **13 :** to effect (an insurance policy) by an oral commitment or a written instrument ~ *vi* **1 :** to form a cohesive mass **2 :** to hamper free movement or natural action **3 :** to become hindered from free operation **4 :** to exert a restraining or compelling effect ⟨a promise that ~*s*⟩
2**bind** *n* **1 a :** something that binds **b :** the act of binding **:** the state of being bound **c :** a place where binding occurs **2 a :** TIE 3 **b :** SLUR 1a **3 :** a position that restricts an opponent's freedom of action (as in chess) — **in a bind :** in trouble
bind·er \ˈbīn-dər\ *n* **1 :** a person that binds something (as books) **2 a :** something used in binding **b :** a usu. detachable cover (as for holding sheets of paper) **c :** the sheet of tobacco that binds the filler in a cigar **3 :** something (as tar or cement) that produces or promotes cohesion in loosely assembled substances **4 :** a receipt for money paid to secure the right to purchase real estate on agreed terms; *also* **:** the money itself
bind·ery \ˈbīn-d(ə-)rē\ *n, pl* **-er·ies :** a place where books are bound
1**bind·ing** \ˈbīn-diŋ\ *n* **1 :** the action of one that binds **2 :** a material or device used to bind: as **a :** the cover and fastenings of a book **b :** a narrow fabric used to finish raw edges **c :** a set of ski fastenings for holding the boot firm on the ski
2**binding** *adj* **1 :** that binds **2 :** imposing an obligation — **bind·ing·ly** \-diŋ-lē\ *adv* — **bind·ing·ness** *n*
binding energy *n* **:** the energy required to break up a molecule, atom, or atomic nucleus completely into its constituent particles
bind off *vt* **:** to cast off in knitting
bind over *vt* **:** to put under bonds to do something (as to appear in court)
bind·weed \ˈbīn-ˌdwēd\ *n* **:** any of various twining plants (esp. genus *Convolvulus* of the morning-glory family) that mat or interlace with plants among which they grow
bine \ˈbīn\ *n* [alter. of 2*bind*] **:** a twining stem or flexible shoot (as of the hop); *also* **:** a plant (as woodbine) whose shoots are bines
Bi·net–Si·mon scale \bi-ˌnā-sē-ˈmōⁿ-\ *n* [Alfred *Binet* †1911 and Théodore *Simon* †1961 F psychologists] **:** an intelligence test consisting orig. of tasks graded from the level of the average 3-year-old to that of the average 12-year-old but later extended in range
binge \ˈbinj\ *n* [E dial. *binge* (to drink heavily)] **1 a :** a drunken revel **:** SPREE **b :** an unrestrained indulgence ⟨a buying ~⟩ **2 :** a social gathering **:** PARTY
bin·go \ˈbiŋ-(ˌ)gō\ *n, pl* **bingos** [earlier *bingo* (interj. used to announce an unexpected event)] **:** a game of chance played with cards having numbered squares corresponding to numbered balls drawn at random and won by covering five such squares in a row
bin·na·cle \ˈbin-i-kəl\ *n* [alter. of ME *bitakle,* fr. OPg or OSp; OPg *bitácola* & OSp *bitácula,* fr. L *habitaculum* dwelling place, fr. *habitare* to inhabit — more at HABITATION] **:** a case, box, or stand containing a ship's compass and a lamp
1**bin·oc·u·lar** \bī-ˈnäk-yə-lər, bə-\ *adj* **:** of, relating to, using, or adapted to the use of both eyes ⟨~ vision⟩ — **bin·oc·u·lar·i·ty** \(ˌ)bī-ˌnäk-yə-ˈlar-ət-ē, bə-\ *n* — **bin·oc·u·lar·ly** \bī-ˈnäk-yə-lər-lē, bə-\ *adv*
2**bin·oc·u·lar** \bə-ˈnäk-yə-lər, bī-\ *n* **1 :** a binocular optical instrument **2 :** FIELD GLASS — usu. used in pl.
bi·no·mi·al \bī-ˈnō-mē-əl\ *n* [NL *binomium,* fr. ML, neut. of *binomius* having two names, alter. of L *binominis,* fr. *bi-* + *nomin-, nomen* name — more at NAME] **1 :** a mathematical expression consisting of two terms connected by a plus sign or minus sign **2 :** a biological species name consisting of two terms — **binomial** *adj* — **bi·no·mi·al·ly** \-mē-ə-lē\ *adv*
binomial coefficient *n* **:** a coefficient of a term in the expansion of the binomial $(x + y)^n$ according to the binomial theorem
binomial distribution *n* **:** a probability function each of whose values gives the probability that an outcome with constant proba-

ə abut	ᵊ kitten	ər further	a back	ā bake	ä cot, cart
au̇ out	ch chin	e less	ē easy	g gift	i trip	ī life
j joke	ŋ sing	ō flow	ȯ flaw	ȯi coin	th thin	t͟h this
ü loot	u̇ foot	y yet	yü few	yu̇ furious	zh vision

bility of occurrence in a statistical experiment will occur a given number of times in a succession of repetitions of the experiment

binomial nomenclature *n* : a system of nomenclature in which each species of animal or plant receives a name of two terms of which the first identifies the genus to which it belongs and the second the species itself

binomial theorem *n* : a theorem that specifies the expansion of a binomial of the form $(x + y)^n$ in $n + 1$ terms of which the general term is of the form

$$\frac{n!}{k!(n-k)!}x^k y^{(n-k)}$$

bint \'bint\ *n* [Ar, girl, daughter] *slang Brit* : GIRL, WOMAN

bi·nu·cle·ate \(ˌ)bī-'n(y)ü-klē-ət\ *also* **bi·nu·cle·at·ed** \-klē-ˌāt-əd\ *adj* : having two nuclei

bio \'bī-(ˌ)ō\ *n, pl* **bi·os** : BIOGRAPHY

bio- — see BI-

bio·as·say \ˌbī-(ˌ)ō-'as-ˌā, -a-'sā\ *n* [*bio*logical *assay*] : determination of the relative strength of a substance (as a drug) by comparing its effect on a test organism with that of a standard preparation — **bio·as·say** \-a-'sā, -'as-ˌā\ *vt*

bio·as·tro·nau·tics \ˌbī-ō-ˌas-trə-'nȯt-iks, -'nät-\ *n pl but sing or pl in constr* : the medical and biological aspect of astronautics — **bio·as·tro·nau·ti·cal** \-i-kəl\ *adj*

bio·cat·a·lyst \ˌbī-ō-'kat-ᵊl-əst\ *n* : ENZYME

bio·ce·no·sis *or* **bio·coe·no·sis** \-sə-'nō-səs\ *n, pl* **-no·ses** \-ˌsēz\ [NL, fr. ²*bi-* + Gk *koinōsis* sharing, fr. *koinos* common — more at CO-] : an ecological community (as an oyster bed) esp. when forming a self-regulating unit — **bio·ce·not·ic** *or* **bio·coe·not·ic** \-'nät-ik\ *adj*

bio·chem·i·cal \ˌbī-ō-'kem-i-kəl\ *adj* [ISV] **1** : of or relating to biochemistry **2** : characterized by, produced by, or involving chemical reactions in living organisms — **biochemical** *n* — **bio·chem·i·cal·ly** \-k(ə-)lē\ *adv*

biochemical oxygen demand *n* : the oxygen used in meeting the metabolic needs of aerobic microorganisms in water rich in organic matter (as water polluted with sewage) — called also *biological oxygen demand*

bio·chem·is·try \ˌbī-ō-'kem-ə-strē\ *n* [ISV] : chemistry that deals with the chemical compounds and processes occurring in organisms — **bio·chem·ist** \-əst\ *n*

bio·cide \'bī-ə-ˌsīd\ *n* : a substance (as DDT) that is destructive to many different organisms — **bio·cid·al** \ˌbī-ə-'sīd-ᵊl\ *adj*

bio·clean \'bī-ō-ˌklēn\ *adj* : free or almost free of harmful or potentially harmful organisms (as bacteria) ⟨a ~ room⟩

bio·cli·mat·ic \ˌbī-ō-kli-'mat-ik\ *adj* : of or relating to the relations of climate and living matter

bio·de·grad·able \-di-'grād-ə-bəl\ *adj* [²*bi-* + *degrade* + *-able*] : capable of being broken down esp. into innocuous products by the action of living beings (as microorganisms) — **bio·de·grad·abil·i·ty** \-ˌgrād-ə-'bil-ət-ē\ *n* — **bio·deg·ra·da·tion** \-ˌdeg-rə-'dā-shən\ *n* — **bio·de·grade** \-di-'grād\ *vb*

bio·ecol·o·gy \ˌbī-ō-i-'käl-ə-jē\ *n* : ecology dealing with the interrelation of plants and animals with their common environment — **bio·eco·log·i·cal** \-ˌē-kə-'läj-i-kəl, -ˌek-ə-\ *adj* — **bio·ecol·o·gist** \-i-'käl-ə-jəst\ *n*

bio·elec·tric \-i-'lek-trik\ *or* **bio·elec·tri·cal** \-tri-kəl\ *adj* : of or relating to electric phenomena in animals and plants — **bio·elec·tric·i·ty** \-ˌlek-'tris-ət-ē, -'tris-tē\ *n*

bio·en·er·get·ics \-ˌen-ər-'jet-iks\ *n pl but sing in constr* : the biology of energy transformations and energy exchanges within and between living things and their environments — **bio·en·er·get·ic** \-'jet-ik\ *adj*

bio·en·gi·neer·ing \-ˌen-jə-'ni(ə)r-iŋ\ *n* : application to biological or medical science of engineering principles (as the theory of control systems in models of the nervous system) or engineering equipment (as in the construction of artificial organs)

bio·en·vi·ron·men·tal \-in-ˌvī-rən-'ment-ᵊl\ *adj* : concerned with the environment and esp. with deleterious factors in the environment of living beings

bio·feed·back \-'fēd-ˌbak\ *n* : the technique of making unconscious or involuntary bodily processes (as heartbeat or brain waves) perceptible to the senses (as by the use of an oscilloscope) in order to manipulate them by conscious mental control

bio·fla·vo·noid \-'flā-və-ˌnȯid\ *n* : a biologically active flavonoid — called also *vitamin P*

biog *abbr* biographer; biographical; biography

bio·gen·e·sis \ˌbī-ō-'jen-ə-səs\ *n* [NL] **1** : the development of life from preexisting life **2** : a supposed tendency for stages in the evolutionary history of a race to briefly recur during the development and differentiation of an individual of that race **3** : BIOSYNTHESIS — **bio·ge·net·ic** \-jə-'net-ik\ *adj*

bio·gen·ic \-'jen-ik\ *adj* : produced by living organisms

bio·geo·chem·is·try \-ˌjē-ō-'kem-ə-strē\ *n* [²*bi-* + *geochemistry*] : a science that deals with the relation of earth chemicals to plant and animal life in an area — **bio·geo·chem·i·cal** \-'kem-i-kəl\ *adj*

bio·ge·og·ra·phy \-jē-'äg-rə-fē\ *n* [ISV] : a branch of biology that deals with the geographical distribution of animals and plants — **bio·geo·graph·ic** \-ˌjē-ə-'graf-ik\ *or* **bio·geo·graph·i·cal** \-i-kəl\ *adj*

bi·og·ra·phee \bī-ˌäg-rə-'fē, bē-\ *n* : a person about whom a biography is written

bi·og·ra·pher \-'äg-rə-fər\ *n* : a writer of a biography

bio·graph·i·cal \ˌbī-ə-'graf-i-kəl\ *or* **bio·graph·ic** \-ik\ *adj* **1** : of, relating to, or constituting biography **2** : consisting of biographies ⟨a ~ dictionary⟩ **3** : relating to a list briefly identifying persons ⟨~ notes⟩ — **bio·graph·i·cal·ly** \-i-k(ə-)lē\ *adv*

bi·og·ra·phy \bī-'äg-rə-fē, bē-\ *n, pl* **-phies** [LGk *biographia*, fr. Gk *bi-* + *-graphia* -graphy] **1** : a usu. written history of a person's life **2** : biographical writings in general **3** : an account of the life of something (as an animal, a coin, or a building)

bio·in·stru·men·ta·tion \'bī-ō-ˌin-strə-mən-'tā-shən, -ˌmen-\ *n* : the development and use of instruments for recording and transmitting physiological data (as from astronauts in flight)

biol *abbr* biologic; biological; biologist; biology

¹**bi·o·log·ic** \ˌbī-ə-'läj-ik\ *adj* **1** : of or relating to biology or to life and living processes **2** : used in or produced by applied biology — **bi·o·log·i·cal** \-i-kəl\ *adj* — **bi·o·log·i·cal·ly** \-i-k(ə-)lē\ *adv*

²**biologic** *n* : a biological product used in medicine — **biological** *n*

biological clock *n* : an inherent timing mechanism responsible for various cyclical physiological and behavioral responses of living beings

biological control *n* : attack upon noxious organisms by interference with their ecological adjustment

biological oxygen demand *n* : BIOCHEMICAL OXYGEN DEMAND

biological warfare *n* : warfare involving the use of living organisms (as disease germs) or their toxic products against men, animals, or plants; *also* : warfare involving the use of synthetic chemicals harmful to plants

bi·ol·o·gism \bī-'äl-ə-ˌjiz-əm\ *n* : preoccupation with biological explanations in the analysis of social situations — **bi·ol·o·gis·tic** \-ˌäl-ə-'jis-tik\ *adj*

bi·ol·o·gy \bī-'äl-ə-jē\ *n* [G *biologie*, fr. *bi-* + *-logie* -logy] **1 a** : a branch of knowledge that deals with living organisms and vital processes **b** : ECOLOGY **2 a** : the plant and animal life of a region or environment **b** : the laws and phenomena relating to an organism or group — **bi·ol·o·gist** \-jəst\ *n*

bio·lu·mi·nes·cence \ˌbī-ō-ˌlü-mə-'nes-ᵊn(t)s\ *n* [ISV] : the emission of light from living organisms; *also* : the light so produced — **bio·lu·mi·nes·cent** \-ᵊnt\ *adj*

bio·mass \'bī-ō-ˌmas\ *n* : the amount of living matter (as in a unit area or volume of habitat)

bio·ma·te·ri·al \ˌbī-ō-mə-'tir-ē-əl\ *n* : material used for or suitable for use in prostheses that come in direct contact with living tissues

bi·ome \'bī-ˌōm\ *n* [²*bi-* + *-ome*] : a major ecological community type ⟨the grassland ~⟩

bio·med·i·cal \ˌbī-ō-'med-i-kəl\ *adj* **1** : of or relating to biomedicine **2** : of, relating to, or involving biological, medical, and physical science

bio·med·i·cine \-'med-ə-sən, *Brit usu* -'med-sən\ *n* : a branch of medical science concerned esp. with the capacity of human beings to survive and function in abnormally stressing environments and with the protective modification of such environments

bio·met·ric \-'me-trik\ *or* **bio·met·ri·cal** \-tri-kəl\ *adj* : of, relating to, or concerned with biometry

bio·met·rics \-'me-triks\ *n pl but sing or pl in constr* : BIOMETRY

bi·om·e·try \bī-'äm-ə-trē\ *n* [ISV] : the statistical analysis of biological observations and phenomena

bi·on·ics \bī-'än-iks\ *n pl but sing or pl in constr* [²*bi-* + *-onics* (as in *electronics*)] : a science concerned with the application of data about the functioning of biological systems to the solution of engineering problems — **bi·on·ic** \-ik\ *adj*

bi·o·nom·ics \ˌbī-ə-'näm-iks\ *n pl but sing or pl in constr* [*bionomic*, adj., prob. fr. F *bionomique*, fr. *bionomie* ecology, fr. *bi-* + *-nomie* -nomy] : ECOLOGY — **bi·o·nom·ic** \-ik\ *adj* — **bi·o·nom·i·cal** \-i-kəl\ *adj* — **bi·o·nom·i·cal·ly** \-i-k(ə-)lē\ *adv*

-bi·ont \'bī-ˌänt\ *comb form* [prob. fr. G, modif. of Gk *biount-*, *biōn*, prp. of *bioun* to live, fr. *bios* life] : one having a (specified) mode of life ⟨haplo*biont*⟩

bio·phys·ics \ˌbī-ō-'fiz-iks\ *n* : a branch of knowledge concerned with the application of physical principles and methods to biological problems — **bio·phys·i·cal** \-i-kəl\ *adj* — **bio·phys·i·cist** \-'fiz-(ə-)səst\ *n*

bio·poly·mer \ˌbī-ō-'päl-ə-mər\ *n* : a polymeric substance (as a protein or polysaccharide) formed in a biological system

bi·op·sy \'bī-ˌäp-sē\ *n, pl* **-sies** [ISV *bi-* + Gk *opsis* appearance — more at OPTIC] : the removal and examination of tissue, cells, or fluids from the living body

bio·sat·el·lite \ˌbī-ō-'sat-ᵊl-ˌīt\ *n* : an artificial satellite for carrying a living human being, animal, or plant

bio·sci·ence \-'sī-ən(t)s\ *n* : BIOLOGY 1a — **bio·sci·en·tif·ic** \-ˌsī-ən-'tif-ik\ *adj* — **bio·sci·en·tist** \-'sī-ənt-əst\ *n*

-bi·o·sis \(ˌ)bī-'ō-səs, bē-\ *n comb form, pl* **-bi·o·ses** \-ˌsēz\ [NL, fr. Gk *biōsis*, fr. *bioun* to live, fr. *bios*] : mode of life ⟨para*biosis*⟩

bio·sphere \'bī-ə-ˌsfi(ə)r\ *n* **1** : the part of the world in which life can exist **2** : living beings together with their environment

bio·syn·the·sis \ˌbī-ō-'sin(t)-thə-səs\ *n* [NL] : the production of a chemical compound by a living organism — **bio·syn·thet·ic** \-sin-'thet-ik\ *adj* — **bio·syn·thet·i·cal·ly** \-i-k(ə-)lē\ *adv*

bio·sys·tem·at·ic \-ˌsis-tə-'mat-ik\ *adj* : of or relating to experimental taxonomy esp. as based on cytogenetics — **bio·sys·tem·a·tist** \-'tem-ət-əst\ *n* — **bio·sys·tem·a·ty** \-sis-'tem-ət-ē\ *n*

bi·o·ta \bī-'ōt-ə\ *n* [NL, fr. Gk *biotē* life; akin to Gk *bios*] : the flora and fauna of a region

bio·tech·nol·o·gy \ˌbī-ō-tek-'näl-ə-jē\ *n* : the aspect of technology concerned with the application of biological and engineering data to problems relating to man and the machine — **bio·tech·no·log·i·cal** \-ˌtek-nə-'läj-i-kəl\ *adj*

bio·te·lem·e·try \-tə-'lem-ə-trē\ *n* : the remote detection and measurement of a condition, activity, or function relating to a man or animal — **bio·tel·e·met·ric** \-ˌtel-ə-'me-trik\ *adj*

bi·ot·ic \bī-'ät-ik\ *adj* [Gk *biōtikos*, fr. *bioun*] : of or relating to life; *esp* : caused or produced by living beings

-bi·ot·ic \(ˌ)bī-'ät-ik, bē-\ *adj comb form* [prob. fr. NL *-bioticus*, fr. Gk *biōtikos*] : having a (specified) mode of life ⟨endo*biotic*⟩

biotic potential *n* : the inherent capacity of an organism or species to reproduce and survive

bi·o·tin \'bī-ə-tən\ *n* [ISV, fr. Gk *biotos* life, sustenance; akin to Gk *bios*] : a colorless crystalline growth vitamin $C_{10}H_{16}N_2O_3S$ of the vitamin B complex found esp. in yeast, liver, and egg yolk

bi·o·tite \'bī-ə-ˌtīt\ *n* [G *biotit*, fr. Jean B. *Biot* †1862 F mathematician] : a generally black or dark green form of mica $K_2(Mg,Fe,Al)_6(Si,Al)_8O_{20}(OH)_4$ forming a constituent of crystalline rocks and consisting of a silicate of iron, magnesium, potassium, and aluminum — **bi·o·tit·ic** \ˌbī-ə-'tit-ik\ *adj*

bio·tope \'bī-ə-ˌtōp\ *n* [²*bi-* + Gk *topos* place — more at TOPIC] : a region uniform in environmental conditions and in its populations of animals and plants for which it is the habitat

bio·trans·for·ma·tion \ˈbī-ō-ˌtran(t)s-fər-ˈmā-shən, -ˌfor-\ n : the transformation of chemical compounds within a living system

bio·tron \ˈbī-ə-ˌträn\ n [²bi- + -tron (as in cyclotron)] : a climate control chamber used to study the effect of specific environmental factors on living organisms

bio·type \-ˌtīp\ n [ISV] : the organisms sharing a specified genotype; also : the genotype shared or its distinguishing peculiarity — **bio·typ·ic** \ˌbī-ə-ˈtip-ik\ adj

bi·ov·u·lar \(ˈ)bī-ˈäv-yə-lər, -ˈōv-\ adj, of fraternal twins : derived from two ova

bi·pack \ˈbī-ˌpak\ n : a pair of films each sensitive to a different color used by simultaneous exposure come through the other

bi·pa·ren·tal \ˌbī-pə-ˈrent-ᵊl\ adj : of, relating to, or derived from two parents — **bi·pa·ren·tal·ly** \-ᵊl-ē\ adv

bi·par·ti·san \(ˈ)bī-ˈpärt-ə-zən, -sən\ adj : of, relating to, or involving members of two parties ⟨a ~ commission⟩ — **bi·par·ti·san·ism** \-zə-ˌniz-əm, -sə-\ n — **bi·par·ti·san·ship** \-zən-ˌship, -sən-\ n

bi·par·tite \(ˈ)bī-ˈpär-ˌtīt\ adj [L bipartitus, pp. of bipartire to divide in two, fr. bi- + partire to divide, fr. part-, pars part] **1 a** : being in two parts **b** : having two correspondent parts one for each party ⟨a ~ contract⟩ **c** : shared by two ⟨a ~ treaty⟩ **2** : divided into two parts almost to the base ⟨a ~ leaf⟩ — **bi·par·tite·ly** adv — **bi·par·ti·tion** \ˌbī-(ˌ)pär-ˈtish-ən\ n

bi·ped \ˈbī-ˌped\ n [L biped-, bipes, fr. bi- + ped-, pes foot — more at FOOT] : a two-footed animal — **biped** or **bi·ped·al** \(ˈ)bī-ˈped-ᵊl\ adj

bi·phe·nyl \(ˈ)bī-ˈfen-ᵊl, -ˈfēn-\ n [ISV] : a white crystalline hydrocarbon $C_6H_5C_6H_5$ used esp. as a heat-transfer medium

bi·pin·nate \ˈbī-ˌpin-ˌāt\ adj : twice pinnate — **bi·pin·nate·ly** adv

bi·plane \ˈbī-ˌplān\ n : an airplane with two main supporting surfaces usu. placed one above the other

bi·pod \ˈbī-ˌpäd\ n [bi- + -pod (as in tripod)] : a two-legged support

bi·po·lar \(ˈ)bī-ˈpō-lər\ adj **1** : having or involving the use of two poles **2** : relating to or associated with the polar regions **3** : having or marked by two mutually repellent forces or diametrically opposed natures or views — **bi·po·lar·i·ty** \ˌbī-pō-ˈlar-ət-ē\ n — **bi·po·lar·ize** \(ˈ)bī-ˈpō-lə-ˌrīz\ vt

bi·pro·pel·lant \ˌbī-prə-ˈpel-ənt\ n : a rocket propellant consisting of separate fuel and oxidizer that come together only in a combustion chamber

bi·qua·drat·ic \ˌbī-kwä-ˈdrat-ik\ n : a fourth power or equation involving a fourth power in mathematics — **biquadratic** adj

bi·ra·cial \(ˈ)bī-ˈrā-shəl\ adj : of, relating to, or involving members of two races — **bi·ra·cial·ism** \-shə-ˌliz-əm\ n

bi·ra·di·al \(ˈ)bī-ˈrād-ē-əl\ adj : having both bilateral and radial symmetry

bi·ra·mous \(ˈ)bī-ˈrā-məs\ adj : having two branches

¹birch \ˈbərch\ n [ME, fr. OE beorc; akin to OHG birka birch, L fraxinus ash tree, OE beorht bright — more at BRIGHT] **1** : any of a genus (Betula of the family Betulaceae, the birch family) of monoecious deciduous usu. short-lived trees or shrubs having simple petioled leaves and typically a layered membranous outer bark that peels readily **2** : the hard pale close-grained wood of a birch **3** : a birch rod or bundle of twigs for flogging — **birch** or **birch·en** \ˈbər-chən\ adj

²birch vt : to beat with or as if with a birch — WHIP

birch·bark \ˈbərch-ˌbärk\ n : a canoe made of birch bark

Birch·er \ˈbər-chər\ n : a member or adherent of the John Birch Society — **Birch·ism** \ˈbər-ˌchiz-əm\ n — **Birch·ist** \-chəst\ or **Birch·ite** \-ˌchīt\ n

¹bird \ˈbərd\ n, often attrib [ME, fr. OE bridd] **1** archaic : the young of a feathered vertebrate **2** : any of a class (Aves) of warm-blooded vertebrates distinguished by having the body more or less completely covered with feathers and the forelimbs modified as wings **3** : a game bird **4** : CLAY PIGEON **5 a** : FELLOW; esp : a peculiar person **b** chiefly Brit : GIRL **6** : SHUTTLECOCK **7 a** : a hissing or jeering expressive of disapproval **b** : dismissal from employment **8** : GUIDED MISSILE — **bird·like** \-ˌlīk\ adj — **for the birds** : WORTHLESS, RIDICULOUS

²bird vi : to observe or identify wild birds in their natural environment

bird·bath \ˈbərd-ˌbath, -ˌbàth\ n : a usu. ornamental basin set up for birds to bathe in

bird·brain \-ˌbrān\ n **1** : a stupid person **2** : SCATTERBRAIN — **bird·brained** \-ˌbrānd\ adj

bird·call \-ˌkol\ n **1** : the note or cry of a bird; also : a sound imitative of it **2** : a device for imitating a birdcall

bird colonel n [fr. the eagle serving as his insignia] slang : COLONEL 1a

bird–dog \ˈbərd-ˌdóg\ vi : to watch closely ~ vt : to seek out : FOLLOW, DETECT

bird dog n **1** : a gundog trained to hunt or retrieve birds **2 a** : one (as a canvasser or talent scout) who seeks out something for another **b** : one who steals another's date

bird–dog·ging n **1** : the action of one that bird-dogs **2** : the stealing of another's date (as at a party)

bird·er \ˈbərd-ər\ n **1** : a catcher or hunter of birds esp. for market **2** : one that birds

bird·house \ˈbərd-ˌhaus\ n : an artificial nesting site for birds; also : AVIARY

¹bird·ie \ˈbərd-ē\ n **1** : a little bird **2** : a golf score of one stroke less than par on a hole — compare EAGLE

²birdie vt **bird·ied; bird·ie·ing** : to shoot in one stroke under par

bird·lime \ˈbərd-ˌlīm\ n **1** : a sticky substance usu. made from the bark of a holly (Ilex aquifolium) that is smeared on twigs to snare small birds **2** : something that ensnares — **birdlime** vt

bird louse n : any of numerous wingless insects (order Mallophaga) that are mostly parasitic on birds

bird·man \ˈbərd-mən, esp for 1 also -ˌman\ n **1** : one who deals with birds **2** : AVIATOR

bird of paradise : any of numerous brilliantly colored plumed oscine birds (family Paradiseidae) of the New Guinea area

bird of passage **1** : a migratory bird **2** : a person who leads a wandering or unsettled life

bird of prey : a carnivorous bird that feeds wholly or chiefly on meat taken by hunting

bird pepper n : a capsicum (Capsicum frutescens) having very small oblong extremely pungent red fruits

bird·seed \ˈbərd-ˌsēd\ n : a mixture of seeds (as of hemp, millet, and sunflowers) used for feeding caged and wild birds

¹bird's-eye \ˈbərd-ˌzī\ n **1** : any of numerous plants with small bright-colored flowers; esp : a speedwell (Veronica chamaedrys) **2 a** : an allover pattern for textiles consisting of a small diamond with a center dot **b** : a fabric woven with this pattern **3** : a small spot in wood surrounded with an ellipse of concentric fibers

²bird's-eye adj **1 a** : seen from above as if by a flying bird ⟨a ~ view⟩ **b** : CURSORY **2** : marked with spots resembling birds' eyes **3** : of or relating to wood (as maple) containing bird's-eyes

bird's-foot \ˈbərdz-ˌfüt\ n, pl **bird's-foots** : any of numerous plants with leaves or flowers resembling the foot of a bird; esp : any of several legumes (as of the genera Ornithopus, Lotus, and Trigonella) with bent and jointed pods

bird's-foot trefoil n : a European legume (Lotus corniculatus) having claw-shaped pods and widely used esp. in the U.S. as a forage and fodder plant

bird–watch \ˈbərd-ˌwäch\ vi [back-formation fr. bird-watcher] : BIRD

bird–watch·er \-ər\ n : BIRDER 2

birdy·back or **bird·ie·back** \ˈbərd-ē-ˌbak\ n [birdie + -back (as in piggyback)] : the movement of loaded truck trailers by airplane

bi·re·frin·gence \ˌbī-ri-ˈfrin-jən(t)s\ n [ISV] : the refraction of light in two slightly different directions to form two rays — **bi·re·frin·gent** \-jənt\ adj

bi·reme \ˈbī-ˌrēm\ n [L biremis, fr. bi- + remus oar — more at ROW] : a galley with two banks of oars common in the early classical period

bi·ret·ta \bə-ˈret-ə\ n [It berretta, fr. OProv berret cap, irreg. fr. LL birrus cloak with a hood, of Celt origin; akin to MIr berr short] : a square cap with three ridges on top worn by clergymen esp. of the Roman Catholic Church

biretta

birk \ˈbi(ə)rk\ n [ME birch, birk] chiefly Scot : BIRCH

birk·ie \ˈbi(ə)r-kē, ˈbər-\ n [origin unknown] **1** Scot : a lively smart assertive person **2** Scot : FELLOW, BOY

birl \ˈbər(-ə)l, Scot also ˈbir(ə)l\ vb [ME birlen, fr. OE byrelian; akin to OE beran to carry — more at BEAR] vt **1** chiefly Scot **a** : POUR **b** : to ply with drink **2 a** : to cause (a floating log) to rotate by treading **b** : SPIN ~ vi **1** chiefly Scot : CAROUSE **2** : to progress by whirling — **birl·er** \ˈbər-lər, ˈbi(ə)r-lər\ n

¹birr \ˈbər, ˈbi(ə)r\ n [ME, strong wind, attack, fr. OE byre strong wind & ON byrr favoring wind; both akin to OE beran] **1 a** : force or onward rush (as of the wind) **b** : VIGOR **2** : WHIR

²birr n, chiefly Scot : to make a whirring sound

³birr n, pl **birr** or **birrs** [Ar] — see MONEY table

birse \ˈbi(ə)rs, ˈbərs\ n [(assumed) ME birst, fr. OE byrst — more at BRISTLE] **1** chiefly Scot : a bristle or tuft of bristles **2** chiefly Scot : ANGER

¹birth \ˈbərth\ n, often attrib [ME, fr. ON byrth; akin to OE beran] **1 a** : the emergence of a new individual from the body of its parent **b** : the act or process of bringing forth young from the womb **2** : a state resulting from being born esp. at a particular time or place ⟨a Southerner by ~⟩ **3 a** : LINEAGE, EXTRACTION ⟨marriage between equals in ~⟩ **b** : high or noble birth **4 a** archaic : one that is born **b** : BEGINNING, START ⟨the ~ of an idea⟩

²birth vt **1** chiefly dial : to bring forth **2** : to give rise to : ORIGINATE ~ vi, dial : to bring forth a child or young

birth certificate n : a copy of an official record of a person's date and place of birth and parentage

birth control n : control of the number of children born esp. by preventing or lessening the frequency of conception

birth·day \ˈbərth-ˌdā\ n **1 a** : the day of a person's birth **b** : a day of origin **2** : an anniversary of a birth ⟨her 21st ~⟩

birthday suit n : unclothed skin : NAKEDNESS

birth·mark \ˈbərth-ˌmärk\ n : an unusual mark or blemish on the skin at birth : NEVUS — **birthmark** vt

birth pang n **1** : one of the regularly recurrent pains that are characteristic of childbirth — usu. used in pl. **2** pl : disorder and distress incident esp. to a major social change

bird 2 (waxwing): 1 bill, 2 forehead, 3 crown, 4 crest, 5 auricular region, 6 throat, 7 breast, 8 abdomen, 9 under-tail coverts, 10 tail, 11 primaries, 12 secondaries, 13 upper wing coverts, 14 scapulars

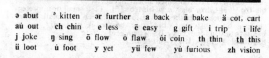

ə abut	ᵊ kitten	ər further	a back	ā bake	ä cot, cart
aù out	ch chin	e less	ē easy	g gift	i trip	ī life
j joke	ŋ sing	ō flow	o flaw	oi coin	th thin	th this
ü loot	ù foot	y yet	yü few	yù furious	zh vision

birth·place \'bərth-ˌplās\ *n* : place of birth or origin
birth·rate \'bər-ˌthrāt\ *n* : the ratio between births and individuals in a specified population and time often expressed as number of live births per hundred or per thousand population per year
birth·right \'bər-ˌthrīt\ *n* : a right, privilege, or possession to which a person is entitled by birth ***syn*** see HERITAGE
birth·root \'bər-ˌthrüt, -ˌthru̇t\ *n* : any of several trilliums with astringent roots used in folk medicine
birth·stone \'bərth-ˌstōn\ *n* : a gemstone associated symbolically with the month of one's birth
birth·wort \-ˌwərt, -ˌwȯ(ə)rt\ *n* : any of several plants (genus *Aristolochia* of the family Aristolochiaceae, the birthwort family) of herbs or woody vines with aromatic roots used in folk medicine to aid childbirth
bis \'bis\ *adv* [L, fr. OL *dvis;* akin to OHG *zwiro* twice, L *duo* two — more at TWO] **1** : AGAIN — used in music as a direction to repeat **2** : TWICE — used to point out the occurrence of an item twice (as in an account)
bis- \(ˌ)bis, 'bis\ *comb form* [L *bis*] : twice : doubled — esp. in complex chemical expressions ⟨*bis*-dithiocarbamate⟩
Bi·sa·yan \bə-'sī-ən\ *n* [Bisayan *Bisayâ*] **1** : a member of any of several peoples in the Visayan islands, Philippines **2** : the Austronesian language of the Bisayans
bis·cuit \'bis-kət\ *n* [ME *bisquite,* fr. MF *bescuit,* fr. *(pain) bescuit* twice-cooked bread] **1 a** : any of various hard or crisp dry baked products: (1) *Brit* : CRACKER 4 (2) *Brit* : COOKIE **b** : a small quick bread made from dough that has been rolled out and cut or dropped from a spoon **2** : earthenware or porcelain after the first firing and before glazing : BISQUE **3 a** : a light grayish yellowish brown **b** : a grayish yellow
bise \'bēz\ *n* [ME, fr. OF, of Gmc origin] : a cold dry north wind of southern France, Switzerland, and Italy
bi·sect \'bī-ˌsekt, bī-'\ *vt* : to divide into two usu. equal parts ~ *vi* : CROSS, INTERSECT — **bi·sec·tion** \'bī-ˌsek-shən, bī-'\ *n* — **bi·sec·tion·al** \-shnəl, -shən-ᵊl\ *adj* — **bi·sec·tion·al·ly** \-ē\ *adv*
bi·sec·tor \'bī-ˌsek-tər, bī-'\ *n* : one that bisects; *esp* : a straight line that bisects an angle or a line segment
bi·sex·u·al \(ˈ)bī-'seksh-(ə-)wəl, -'sek-shəl\ *adj* **1 a** : possessing characters of both sexes : HERMAPHRODITIC **b** : sexually oriented toward both sexes ⟨a ~ person who participates in both heterosexual and homosexual relationships⟩ **2** : of, relating to, or involving two sexes — **bisexual** *n* — **bi·sex·u·al·i·ty** \ˌbī-ˌsek-shə-'wal-ət-ē\ *n* — **bi·sex·u·al·ly** \(ˈ)bī-'seksh-(ə-)wə-lē, -(ə-)lē\ *adv*
bish·op \'bish-əp\ *n* [ME *bisshop,* fr. OE *bisceop,* fr. LL *episcopus,* fr. Gk *episkopos,* lit., overseer, fr. *epi-* + *skeptesthai* to look — more at SPY] **1** : one having spiritual or ecclesiastical supervision: as **a** : an Anglican, Eastern Orthodox, or Roman Catholic clergyman ranking above a priest, having authority to ordain and confirm, and typically governing a diocese **b** : any of various Protestant clerical officials who superintend other clergy **c** : a Mormon high priest presiding over a ward or over all other bishops and over the Aaronic priesthood **2** : either of two pieces of the same color in a set of chessmen having the power to move diagonally across any number of unoccupied squares **3** : a mulled beverage of port wine flavored with roasted orange and cloves
bish·op·ric \'bish-ə-(ˌ)prik\ *n* [ME *bisshopriche,* fr. OE *bisceoprīce,* fr. *bisceop* + *rīce* kingdom — more at RICH] **1** : DIOCESE **2** : the office of bishop **3** : a bishop's seat or residence **4** : the administrative body of a Mormon ward consisting of a bishop and two high priests as counselors
Bishops' Bible *n* [fr. its production by a number of bishops] : an officially commissioned English translation of the Bible published in 1568
bis·muth \'biz-məth\ *n* [obs. G *bismut* (now *wismut*), modif. of *wismut,* fr. *wise* meadow + *mut* claim to a mine] : a heavy brittle grayish white chiefly trivalent metallic element that is chemically like arsenic and antimony and that is used in alloys and pharmaceuticals — see ELEMENT table — **bis·mu·thic** \biz-'məth-ik, -'myü-thik\ *adj*
bi·son \'bīs-ᵊn, 'bīz-\ *n, pl* **bison** [L *bisont-, bison,* of Gmc origin; akin to OHG *wisant* aurochs; akin to OPruss *wissambrs* aurochs] : any of several large shaggy-maned usu. gregarious recent or extinct bovine mammals (genus *Bison*) having a large head with short horns and heavy forequarters surmounted by a large fleshy hump: as **a** : WISENT **b** : BUFFALO b — **bi·son·tine** \-ᵊn-ˌtīn\ *adj*

bison

[1]**bisque** \'bisk\ *n* [F] : odds allowed an inferior player: as **a** : a point taken when desired in a set of tennis **b** : an extra turn in croquet **c** : one or more strokes off a golf score
[2]**bisque** *n* [F] **1 a** : a thick cream soup made of shellfish or of the flesh of birds or rabbits **b** : a cream soup of pureed vegetables **2** : ice cream containing powdered nuts or macaroons
[3]**bisque** *n* [by shortening & alter.] : BISCUIT 2; *esp* : unglazed ceramic ware that is not to be glazed but is hard-fired and vitreous
bi·state \'bī-ˌstāt\ *adj* : of or relating to two states ⟨a ~ agency⟩
bis·ter *or* **bis·tre** \'bis-tər\ *n* [F *bistre*] **1** : a yellowish brown to dark brown pigment used in art **2** : a grayish to yellowish brown — **bis·tered** \-tərd\ *adj*
bis·tort \'bis-ˌtȯ(ə)rt, bis-'\ *n* [MF *bistorte,* fr. (assumed) ML *bistorta,* fr. L *bis-* + *torta,* fem. of *tortus,* pp. of *torquēre* to twist — more at TORTURE] : any of several polygonums; *esp* : a European herb (*Polygonum bistorta*) or a related American plant (*P. bistortoides*) with twisted roots used as astringents
bis·tro \'bēs-(ˌ)trō, 'bis-\ *n, pl* **bistros** [F] **1** : a small or unpretentious European wineshop or restaurant **2 a** : a small bar or tavern **b** : NIGHTCLUB — **bis·tro·ic** \bēs-'trō-ik, bis-\ *adj*
bi·sul·fate \(ˈ)bī-'səl-ˌfāt\ *n* [ISV] : an acid sulfate
bi·sul·fide \-ˌfīd\ *n* [ISV] : DISULFIDE
bi·sul·fite \-ˌfīt\ *n* [F, fr. *bi-* + *sulfite*] : an acid sulfite
[1]**bit** \'bit\ *n* [ME *bitt,* fr. OE *bite* act of biting; akin to OE *bītan*] **1** : something bitten or held with the teeth: **a** : the usu. steel part of a bridle inserted in the mouth of a horse **b** : the rimmed mouth end on the stem of a pipe or cigar holder **2 a** (1) : the biting or cutting edge or part of a tool (2) : a replaceable part of a compound tool that actually performs the function (as drilling or boring) for which the whole tool is designed **b** *pl* : the jaws or nippers of tongs or pincers **3** : something that curbs or restrains **4** : the part of a key that enters the lock and acts on the bolt and tumblers

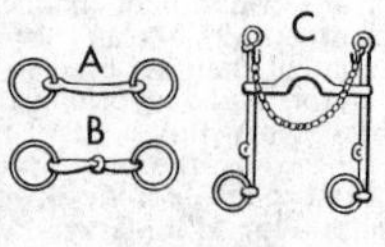

bits 1a: *A* bar bit, *B* snaffle, *C* curb

[2]**bit** *vt* **bit·ted; bit·ting** **1 a** : to put a bit in the mouth of (a horse) **b** : to control as if with a bit : CURB **2** : to form a bit on (a key)
[3]**bit** *n* [ME, fr. OE *bita;* akin to OE *bītan*] **1** : a small quantity of food; *esp* : a small delicacy **2 a** : a small piece or quantity of some material thing **b** (1) : a small coin (2) : a unit of value equal to 1/8 of a dollar ⟨four ~*s*⟩ **3** : something small or unimportant of its kind: as **a** : a brief period : WHILE **b** (1) : an indefinite usu. small degree, extent, or amount ⟨a ~ of a rascal⟩ ⟨every ~ as powerful⟩ (2) : the smallest or an insignificant amount or degree ⟨didn't feel a ~ sorry⟩ **c** (1) : a small part usu. with spoken lines in a theatrical performance (2) : a usu. short theatrical routine ⟨a corny comedy ~⟩ **4** : the aggregate of items, situations, or activities appropriate to a given style, genre, or role ⟨rejected the whole ~ about love-marriage-motherhood —Vance Packard⟩ — **a bit much** : a little more than one wants to endure — **bit by bit** : little by little : by degrees
[4]**bit** *n* [*binary digit*] **1** : a unit of computer information equivalent to the result of a choice between two alternatives (as *yes* or *no, on* or *off*) **2** : the physical representation (as in a computer tape or memory) of a bit by an electrical pulse, a magnetized spot, or a hole whose presence or absence indicates data
bi·tar·trate \(ˈ)bī-'tär-ˌtrāt\ *n* [ISV] : an acid tartrate
[1]**bitch** \'bich\ *n* [ME *bicche,* fr. OE *bicce;* akin to OE *bæc* back] **1** : the female of the dog or some other carnivorous mammals **2 a** : a lewd or immoral woman **b** : a malicious, spiteful, and domineering woman **3** : COMPLAINT **4** : something that is highly objectionable or unpleasant
[2]**bitch** *vt* **1** : SPOIL, BOTCH ⟨I must have ~*ed* up my life —Mavis Gallant⟩ **2** : to complain of or about ⟨was occasionally quite talkative about his wife . . . mostly he ~*ed* her, but not vehemently —Chandler Brossard⟩ **3** : CHEAT, DOUBLECROSS ~ *vi* : COMPLAIN ⟨wives ~ theatrically at their shrimpy husbands —Fred Powledge⟩
bitch·ery \'bich-ə-rē\ *n, pl* **-er·ies** : malicious, spiteful, or domineering behavior; *also* : an instance of such behavior
bitch goddess *n* : SUCCESS; *esp* : material or worldly success
bitchy \'bich-ē\ *adj* **bitch·i·er; -est** : characterized by malicious, spiteful, or arrogant behavior — **bitch·i·ly** \'bich-ə-lē\ *adv* — **bitch·i·ness** \'bich-ē-nəs\ *n*
[1]**bite** \'bīt\ *vb* **bit** \'bit\; **bit·ten** \'bit-ᵊn\ *also* **bit; bit·ing** \'bīt-iŋ\ [ME *biten,* fr. OE *bītan;* akin to OHG *bīzan* to bite, L *findere* to split] *vt* **1 a** : to seize esp. with teeth or jaws so as to enter, grip, or wound **b** : to wound, pierce, or sting esp. with a fang or a proboscis **2** : to cut or pierce with or as if with an edged weapon **3** : to cause sharp pain or stinging discomfort to **4** : to take hold of **5** : to eat into : CORRODE **6** *archaic* : to take in : CHEAT ~ *vi* **1** : to bite or have the habit of biting something **2** *of a weapon or tool* : to cut, pierce, or take hold **3** : to cause irritation or smarting **4** : CORRODE **5 a** *of fish* : to take a bait **b** : to respond so as to be caught (as by a trick) **6** : to take or maintain a firm hold — **bit·er** \'bīt-ər\ *n* — **bite off more than one can chew** : to undertake more than one can perform — **bite the dust** **1** : to fall dead esp. in battle **2** : to suffer humiliation or defeat — **bite the hand that feeds one** : to injure a benefactor maliciously
[2]**bite** *n* **1** : the act or manner of biting **2** : FOOD: **a** : the amount of food taken at a bite : MORSEL **b** : a small amount of food : SNACK **c** : a usu. impromptu meal **3** *archaic* **a** : CHEAT, TRICK **b** : SHARPER **4** : a wound made by biting **5** : the hold or grip by which friction is created or purchase is obtained **6** : a surface that creates friction or is brought into contact with another for the purpose of obtaining a hold **7 a** : a keen incisive quality ⟨the ~ of sharp analysis⟩ **b** : a sharp penetrating effect ⟨the ~ of raw whiskey⟩ **8** : the corroding of an etcher's plate by acid **9** : an amount taken usu. in one operation for one purpose : CUT ⟨the tax ~⟩
bite·wing \'bīt-ˌwiŋ\ *n* : a dental X-ray film designed to show the crowns of the upper and lower teeth simultaneously
bit·ing \'bīt-iŋ\ *adj* : having the power to bite ⟨a ~ wind⟩ ; *esp* : able to grip and impress deeply ⟨the report is ~ in its intolerance of deceit⟩ ***syn*** see INCISIVE — **bit·ing·ly** \-iŋ-lē\ *adv*
biting midge *n* : any of a family (Ceratopogonidae) of tiny biting two-winged flies of which some are vectors of filarial worms
bit·stock \'bit-ˌstäk\ *n* : a device for turning a bit by hand : BRACE
bit·sy \'bit-sē\ *adj* [*itsy-bitsy*] *dial* : TINY
[1]**bitt** \'bit\ *n* [perh. fr. ON *biti* beam; akin to OE *bōt* boat] **1** : a single or double post of metal or wood fixed on the deck of a ship for securing lines **2** : BOLLARD 1
[2]**bitt** *vt* : to make (a cable) fast about a bitt
[1]**bit·ter** \'bit-ər\ *adj* [ME, fr. OE *biter;* akin to OHG *bittar* bitter, OE *bītan*] **1 a** : having or being a peculiarly acrid, astringent, or disagreeable taste suggestive of an infusion of hops that is one of the four basic taste sensations — compare SALT, SOUR, SWEET **b** : distasteful or distressing to the mind : GALLING ⟨a ~ sense of shame⟩ **2** : marked by intensity or severity: **a** : accompanied by severe pain or suffering ⟨a ~ death⟩ **b** : being relentlessly determined : VEHEMENT ⟨a ~ partisan⟩ **c** : exhibiting intense animosity ⟨~ enemies⟩ **d** (1) : harshly reproachful ⟨~ complaints⟩ (2)

: marked by cynicism and rancor ⟨~ contempt⟩ **e** : intensely unpleasant esp. in coldness or rawness **3** : expressive of severe pain, grief, or regret ⟨~ tears⟩ — **bit·ter·ish** \'bit-ə-rish\ *adj* — **bit·ter·ly** *adv* — **bit·ter·ness** *n*

2bitter *adv* : in a bitter manner ⟨it's ~ cold⟩

3bitter *n* **1** : bitter quality **2 a** *pl* : a usu. alcoholic solution of bitter and often aromatic plant products used esp. in preparing mixed drinks or as a mild tonic **b** *Brit* : a very dry heavily hopped ale

4bitter *vt* : to make bitter ⟨~*ed* ale⟩

bit·ter·brush \'bit-ər-,brəsh\ *n* : a much-branched silvery shrub (*Purshia tridentata*) of arid western No. America that has 3-toothed leaves and yellow flowers and is valuable for forage

1bitt·er end \,bit-ə-'rend\ *n* [*bitter* (a turn of cable around the bitts)] : the inboard end of a ship's anchoring cable

2bit·ter end \,bit-ə-'rend\ *n* [prob. fr. *1bitter end*] : the last extremity however painful or calamitous — **bit·ter–end·er** \-'ren-dər\ *n*

1bit·tern \'bit-ərn\ *n* [ME *bitoure*, fr. MF *butor*] : any of various small or medium-sized nocturnal herons (*Botaurus* and related genera) with a characteristic booming cry

2bittern *n* [irreg. fr. *1bitter*] : the bitter mother liquor that remains in saltworks after the salt has crystallized out

bitter principle *n* : any of various neutral substances of strong bitter taste (as aloin) extracted from plants

bit·ter·root \'bit-ə(r)-,rüt, -,rů t\ *n* : a succulent Rocky mountain herb (*Lewisia rediviva*) of the purslane family with fleshy farinaceous roots and pink flowers

1bit·ter·sweet \'bit-ər-,swēt\ *n* **1** : something that is bittersweet; *esp* : pleasure alloyed with pain **2 a** : a sprawling poisonous weedy nightshade (*Solanum dulcamara*) with purple flowers and oval reddish orange berries **b** : a No. American woody climbing plant (*Celastrus scandens* of the family Celastraceae) having clusters of small greenish flowers succeeded by yellow capsules that open when ripe and disclose the scarlet aril

2bittersweet *adj* **1** : being at once bitter and sweet; *esp* : pleasant but including or marked by elements of suffering or regret ⟨a ~ ballad⟩ **2** : of or relating to a prepared chocolate containing little sugar — **bit·ter·sweet·ly** *adv* — **bit·ter·sweet·ness** *n*

bit·ter·weed \'bit-ər-,wēd\ *n* : any of several American plants containing a bitter principle: as **a** : HORSEWEED 1, 2 **b** : a sneezeweed (genus *Helenium*) **c** : an erect composite herb (*Actinea odorata*) of the southwestern U.S. having chiefly yellow terminal flowerheads and causing poisoning of livestock

bit·tock \'bit-ək\ *n, chiefly Scot* : a little bit

1bit·ty \'bit-ē\ *adj* : made up of or containing bits ⟨the contributors are given space to develop their thoughts, and it is not a ~ anthology —*Times Lit. Supp.*⟩

2bitty *adj, dial* : SMALL, TINY

bi·tu·men \bə-'t(y)ü-mən, bī-, *esp Brit also* 'bit-yə-\ *n* [ME *bithumen* mineral pitch, fr. L *bitumin-, bitumen*] **1** : an asphalt of Asia Minor used in ancient times as a cement and mortar **2** : any of various mixtures of hydrocarbons (as tar) often together with their nonmetallic derivatives that occur naturally or are obtained as residues after heat-refining naturally occurring substances (as petroleum); *specif* : such a mixture soluble in carbon disulfide — **bi·tu·mi·ni·za·tion** \bə-,t(y)ü-mə-nə-'zā-shən, bī-\ *n* — **bi·tu·mi·nize** \-t(y)ü-mə-,nīz\ *vt* — **bi·tu·mi·noid** \-,nȯid\ *adj*

bi·tu·mi·nous \bə-'t(y)ü-mə-nəs, bī-\ *adj* **1** : resembling, containing, or impregnated with bitumen **2** : of or relating to bituminous coal

bituminous coal *n* : a coal that when heated yields considerable volatile bituminous matter — called also *soft coal*

1bi·va·lent \(ˌ)bī-'vā-lənt\ *adj* **1** : having a valence of two **2** : associated in pairs in synapsis

2bivalent *n* : a pair of synaptic chromosomes

1bi·valve \'bī-,valv\ *also* **bi·valved** \-,valvd\ *adj* **1** : having a shell composed of two valves **2** : having or consisting of two corresponding movable pieces

2bivalve *n* : an animal (as a clam) with a 2-valved shell

bi·var·i·ate \(ˌ)bī-'ver-ē-ət, -'var-\ *adj* : of, relating to, or involving two variables ⟨a ~ frequency distribution⟩

1biv·ouac \'biv-(ə-)-,wak\ *n* [F, fr. LG *biwake*, fr. *bi* at + *wake* guard] **1** : a usu. temporary encampment under little or no shelter **2 a** : a camping out for a night **b** : a temporary shelter or settlement

2bivouac *vi* **-ouacked; -ouack·ing** : to make a bivouac : CAMP

1bi·week·ly \(ˌ)bī-'wē-klē\ *adj* **1** : occurring every two weeks : FORTNIGHTLY **2** : occurring twice a week — **biweekly** *adv*

2biweekly *n* **1** : a publication issued every two weeks **2** : SEMIWEEKLY

bi·year·ly \(ˌ)bī-'yi(ə)r-lē\ *adj* **1** : BIENNIAL **2** : BIANNUAL

1bi·zarre \bə-'zär\ *adj* [F, fr. It *bizzarro*] : strikingly out of the ordinary: as **a** : odd, extravagant, or eccentric in style or mode **b** : involving sensational contrasts or incongruities ***syn*** see FANTASTIC ***ant*** chaste, subdued — **bi·zarre·ly** *adv* — **bi·zarre·ness** *n*

2bizarre *n* : a flower with atypical striped marking

bi·zon·al \(ˌ)bī-'zōn-ᵊl\ *adj* : of or relating to the affairs of a zone governed or administered by two powers acting together — **bi·zone** \'bī-,zōn\ *n*

BJ *abbr* bachelor of journalism

bk *abbr* **1** bank **2** book **3** break **4** brook

Bk *symbol* berkelium

bkg *abbr* **1** banking **2** bookkeeping **3** breakage

bkgd *abbr* background

bks *abbr* barracks

bkt *abbr* **1** basket **2** bracket

bl *abbr* **1** bale **2** barrel **3** black **4** block **5** blue

BL *abbr* **1** bachelor of law **2** bachelor of letters **3** baseline **4** bats left **5** bill of lading **6** breath-length

1blab \'blab\ *n* [ME *blabbe;* akin to ME *blaberen*] **1** *archaic* : one that blabs : TATTLETALE **2** : idle or excessive talk : CHATTER — **blab·by** \'blab-ē\ *adj*

2blab *vb* **blabbed; blab·bing** *vt* : to reveal esp. by talking without reserve or discretion ~ *vi* **1** : to reveal a secret esp. by indiscreet chatter **2** : to talk idly or thoughtlessly : PRATTLE

1blab·ber \'blab-ər\ *vb* **blab·bered; blab·ber·ing** \-(ə-)riŋ\ [ME *blaberen*] *vi* : to talk foolishly or excessively : BABBLE ~ *vt* : to say indiscreetly

2blabber *n* : idle talk : BABBLE

3blabber *n* [*2blab*] : one that blabs

blab·ber·mouth \'blab-ər-,mau̇th\ *n* : one who talks too much; *esp* : TATTLETALE

1black \'blak\ *adj* [ME *blak*, fr. OE *blæc;* akin to OHG *blah* black, L *flagrare* to burn, Gk *phlegein*, OE *bǣl* fire — more at BALD] **1 a** : of the color black **b** (1) : very dark in color ⟨his face was ~ with rage⟩ (2) : having a very deep or low register ⟨a bass with a ~ voice⟩ (3) : HEAVY, SERIOUS ⟨the play was a ~ intrigue⟩ **2 a** : having dark skin, hair, and eyes : SWARTHY ⟨a ~ Irishman⟩ **b** (1) : of or relating to a group or race characterized by dark pigmentation; *esp* : of or relating to the Negro race ⟨~ Americans⟩ (2) : of or relating to the Afro-American people or culture ⟨~ literature⟩ ⟨~ theater⟩ ⟨~ pride⟩ **3** : dressed in black **4** : DIRTY, SOILED ⟨hands ~ with grime⟩ **5 a** : characterized by the absence of light ⟨a ~ night⟩ **b** : reflecting or transmitting little or no light ⟨~ water⟩ **c** : served without milk or cream ⟨~ coffee⟩ **6 a** : thoroughly sinister or evil : WICKED ⟨a ~ deed⟩ **b** : indicative of condemnation or discredit ⟨got a ~ mark for being late⟩ **7** : connected with or invoking the supernatural and esp. the devil ⟨a ~ curse⟩ **8 a** : very sad, gloomy, or calamitous ⟨~ despair⟩ **b** : marked by the occurrence of disaster ⟨~ Friday⟩ **9** : characterized by hostility or angry discontent : SULLEN ⟨~ resentment filled his heart⟩ **10** *chiefly Brit* : subject to boycott by trade-union members as employing or favoring nonunion workers or as operating under conditions considered unfair by the trade union ⟨declare a fish market ~⟩ **11** : showing a profit ⟨a ~ financial statement⟩ — compare RED **12 a** *of propaganda* : conducted so as to appear to originate within an enemy country and designed to weaken enemy morale — compare WHITE **b** : characterized by or connected with the use of black propaganda ⟨~ radio⟩ **13** : characterized by grim, distorted, or grotesque satire ⟨~ comedy⟩ ⟨~ humor⟩ — **black·ish** \'blak-ish\ *adj* — **black·ly** *adv* — **black·ness** *n*

2black *n* **1** : a black pigment or dye; *esp* : one consisting largely of carbon **2** : the achromatic object color of least lightness characteristically perceived to belong to objects that neither reflect nor transmit light **3** : something that is black: as **a** : black clothing ⟨looks good in ~⟩ **b** : a black animal (as a horse) **4 a** : a person belonging to a dark-skinned race or one stemming in part from such a race; *esp* : NEGRO **b** : AFRO-AMERICAN **5** : the pieces of a dark color in a two-handed board game (as chess) **6** : total or nearly total absence of light ⟨the ~ of night⟩ **7** : the condition of making a profit — usu. used with *the* ⟨operating in the ~⟩ — compare RED

3black *vi* : to become black ~ *vt* **1** : to make black **2** *chiefly Brit* : to declare (as a business or industry) subject to boycott by trade-union members

black·a·moor \'blak-ə-,mu̇(ə)r\ *n* [irreg. fr. *black* + *Moor*] : a dark-skinned person; *esp* : NEGRO

black–and–blue \,blak-ən-'blü\ *adj* : darkly discolored from blood effused by bruising

black–and–tan \-ən-'tan\ *adj* **1** : having a predominantly black color pattern with deep red or rusty tan on the feet, breeching, and cheek patches, above the eyes, and inside the ears **2** : favoring or practicing proportional representation of whites and blacks in politics — compare LILY-WHITE **3** : frequented by both blacks and whites ⟨a ~ bar⟩

black and tan *n* **1** : a member of a black-and-tan political organization (as in the southern U.S.) — compare LILY-WHITE **2** *cap B&T* [fr. the color of his uniform] : a recruit enlisted in England in 1920–21 for service in the Royal Irish Constabulary against the armed movement for Irish independence

black–and–tan coonhound *n* : any of an American breed of strong vigorous coonhounds that have black-and-tan markings

black–and–white \,blak-ən-'hwīt, -'wīt\ *adj* **1** : being in writing or print ⟨a ~ statement of the problem⟩ **2** : partly black and partly white in color ⟨a ~ cat⟩ **3** : executed in dark pigment on a light background or in light pigment on a dark ground ⟨a ~ drawing⟩ **4** : characterized by the reproduction or transmission of visual images in tones of gray rather than in colors ⟨~ film⟩ ⟨~ television⟩ **5 a** : sharply divided into good and evil groups, sides, or ideas **b** : evaluating or viewing things as either all good or all bad ⟨~ morality⟩ ⟨~ thinkers⟩

black and white *n* **1** : WRITING, PRINT **2** : a drawing or print done in black and white or in monochrome **3** : monochrome reproduction of visual images (as by photography or television)

black art *n* : magic practiced by or as if by conjurers and witches

black–a–vised \'blak-ə-,vīst\ *adj* [*black* + F *à vis* as to face] : dark-complexioned

1black·ball \'blak-,bȯl\ *n* **1** : a small black ball for use as a negative vote in a ballot box **2** : an adverse vote esp. against admitting someone to membership in an organization

2blackball *vt* **1** : to vote against; *esp* : to exclude from membership by casting a negative vote **2 a** : to exclude socially : OSTRACIZE **b** : BOYCOTT

black bass *n* : any of several highly prized freshwater sunfishes (genus *Micropterus*) native to eastern and central No. America

black beast *n* : BÊTE NOIRE

1black belt \'blak-,belt\ *n* **1** : an area characterized by rich black soil **2** *cap both Bs* : an area densely populated by blacks

ə abut	ᵊ kitten	ər further	a back	ā bake	ä cot, cart
au̇ out	ch chin	e less	ē easy	g gift	i trip	ī life
j joke	ŋ sing	ō flow	ȯ flaw	ȯi coin	th thin	t͟h this
ü loot	u̇ foot	y yet	yü few	yu̇ furious	zh vision

[2]**black belt** \-ˈbelt\ *n* **1** : a rating of expert in various arts of self-defense (as judo and karate) **2** : one who holds a black belt
black·ber·ry \ˈblak-ˌber-ē\ *n* **1** : the usu. black or dark purple juicy but seedy edible fruit of various brambles (genus *Rubus*) of the rose family **2** : a plant that bears blackberries
black bile *n* : a humor of medieval physiology believed to be secreted by the kidneys or spleen and to cause melancholy
[1]**black·bird** \ˈblak-ˌbərd\ *n* **1** : any of various birds of which the males are largely or entirely black: as **a** : a common and familiar British thrush *(Turdus merula)* that is black with orange bill and eye rim **b** : any of several American birds (family Icteridae) **2** : a Pacific islander kidnapped for use as a plantation laborer
[2]**blackbird** *vi* : to engage in the slave trade
black·bird·er *n* **1** : a person that blackbirds **2** : a ship used in blackbirding
black·board \ˈblak-ˌbō(ə)rd, -ˌbȯ(ə)rd\ *n* : a hard smooth usu. dark surface used esp. in a classroom for writing or drawing on with chalk
black·body \ˈblak-ˈbäd-ē\ *n* : an ideal body or surface that completely absorbs all radiant energy falling upon it with no reflection
black book *n* : a book containing a blacklist
black box *n* **1** : a usu. complicated electronic device that can be inserted in or removed as a unit from a larger assembly of parts (as those constituting a spacecraft) **2** : a usu. electronic device whose internal mechanism is hidden from or mysterious to the user
black·cap \ˈblak-ˌkap\ *n* **1** : BLACK RASPBERRY **2** : any of several birds with black heads or crowns: as **a** : a small European warbler (*Sylvia atricapilla*) with a black crown **b** : CHICKADEE
black–capped \-ˈkapt\ *adj, of a bird* : having the top of the head black
black·cock \-ˌkäk\ *n* : BLACK GROUSE; *specif* : the male black grouse
black cohosh *n* : a bugbane (*Cimicifuga racemosa*) of the eastern U.S.
black crappie *n* : a silvery black-mottled sunfish (*Pomoxis nigromaculatus*) of the Mississippi drainage and eastern U.S. having seven or eight protruding spines on the dorsal fins
black·damp \ˈblak-ˈdamp\ *n* : a carbon dioxide mixture occurring as a mine gas and incapable of supporting life or flame
black death *n, often cap B&D* [fr. the black patches formed on the skin of its victims] : a form of plague epidemic in Europe and Asia in the 14th century
black diamond *n* **1** *pl* : COAL 3a **2** : [3]CARBONADO **3** : dense black hematite
black·en \ˈblak-ən\ *vb* **black·ened; black·en·ing** \-(ə-)niŋ\ *vi* : to become dark or black ⟨the sky ~*s*⟩ ~ *vt* **1** : to make black **2** : DEFAME, SULLY — **black·en·er** \-(ə-)nər\ *n*
black·en·ing \-(ə-)niŋ\ *n* : BLACKING
black eye *n* **1** : a discoloration of the skin around the eye from bruising **2** : a bad reputation
black–eyed pea \ˌblak-ˌīd-\ *n* : COWPEA
black–eyed Su·san \-ˈsüz-ᵊn\ *n* : either of two No. American coneflowers (*Rudbeckia hirta* and *R. serotina*) having flower heads with deep yellow to orange rays and dark conical disks
black·face \ˈblak-ˌfās\ *n* **1** : makeup for a Negro role esp. in a minstrel show; *also* : an actor who plays this role **2** : BOLDFACE
black·fin \-ˌfin\ *n* : a whitefish (*Leucichthys nigripinnis*) of the Great Lakes used as a food fish
black·fish \-ˌfish\ *n* **1** : any of numerous dark-colored fishes: as **a** : TAUTOG **b** : a small food fish (*Dallia pectoralis*) of Alaska and Siberia that is remarkable for its ability to revive after being frozen for a long time **2** : any of several small toothed whales (genus *Globicephala*) related to the dolphins and found in the warmer seas
black–flag \-ˈflag\ *vt* : to signal (a race-car driver) to go immediately to the pits
black flag *n* : a pirate's flag usu. bearing a skull and crossbones
black·fly \ˈblak-ˌflī\ *n, pl* **-flies** *or* **-fly** : any of several small dark-colored insects; *esp* : a two-winged biting fly (*Simulium* or related genera) whose larvae usu. live in clear flowing streams
Black·foot \ˈblak-ˌfu̇t\ *n, pl* **Blackfeet** *or* **Blackfoot** **1 a** *pl* : an Amerindian confederacy of Montana, Alberta, and Saskatchewan **b** : a member of any of the Blackfoot peoples **2** : the Algonquian language of the Blackfeet
black–foot·ed albatross \ˌblak-ˌfu̇t-əd-\ *n* : an albatross (*Diomedea nigripes*) of the Pacific that is chiefly blackish with dusky bill and black feet and legs — called also *gooney, gooney bird*
black–footed ferret *n* : an American weasel (*Mustela nigripes*) that is related to the European polecat and resembles a yellow mink with dark feet, tail, and mask
black gold *n* : PETROLEUM
black grouse *n* : a large grouse (*Lyrurus tetrix*) of western Asia and Europe of which the male is black with white wing patches and the female is barred and mottled
[1]**black·guard** \ˈblag-ərd, -ˌärd; ˈblak-ˌgärd\ *n* **1** *obs* : the kitchen servants of a large household **2 a** : a rude or unscrupulous person : SCOUNDREL **b** : one who uses foul or abusive language — **black·guard·ism** \-ˌiz-əm\ *n* — **black·guard·ly** \-lē\ *adj or adv*
[2]**blackguard** *vt* : to talk about or address in abusive terms
black gum *n* : a tupelo (*Nyssa sylvatica*) of the eastern U.S. with light and soft but tough wood
black hand *n, often cap B&H* [*Black Hand,* a Sicilian and Italian-American society of the late 19th and 20th centuries] : a lawless secret society engaged in criminal activities (as terrorism or extortion) — **black·hand·er** \ˈblak-ˌhan-dər\ *n*
black·head \ˈblak-ˌhed\ *n* **1** : a small plug of sebum blocking the duct of a sebaceous gland esp. on the face **2** : a destructive disease of turkeys and related birds caused by a protozoan (*Histomonas meleagridis*) that invades the intestinal ceca and liver **3** : a larval clam or mussel attached to the skin or gills of a freshwater fish
black·heart \-ˌhärt\ *n* : a plant disease in which the central tissues blacken
black hole *n* : a hypothetical celestial body with a small diameter and intense gravitational field that is held to be a collapsed star

black·ing \ˈblak-iŋ\ *n* : a substance (as a paste or polish) that is applied to an object to make it black
[1]**black·jack** \-ˌjak\ *n* **1** [*black* + *jack* (vessel)] : a tankard for beer or ale usu. of tar-coated leather **2** : SPHALERITE **3** : a hand weapon typically consisting of a piece of leather-enclosed metal with a strap or springy shaft for a handle **4** : a common often scrubby oak (*Quercus marilandica*) of the southeastern and southern U.S. with black bark **5** : a card game the object of which is to be dealt cards having a higher count than those of the dealer up to but not exceeding 21 — called also *twenty-one, vingt-et-un*
[2]**blackjack** *vt* **1** : to strike with a blackjack **2** : to coerce with threats or pressure
black knot *n* : a destructive disease of plum and cherry trees characterized by black excrescences on the branches and caused by a fungus (*Dibotryon morbosa*)
black·land \ˈblak-ˌland\ *n* **1** : a heavy sticky black soil such as that covering large areas in Texas **2** *pl* : a region of blackland
black lead *n* : GRAPHITE
black·leg \ˈblak-ˌleg, -ˌlāg\ *n* **1** : an enzootic usu. fatal toxemia esp. of young cattle **2** : a cheating gamester : SWINDLER **3** *chiefly Brit* : a worker hostile to trade unionism or acting in opposition to union policies : SCAB
black letter *n* : a style of type or lettering with a heavy face and angular outlines used esp. by the earliest European printers — called also *Gothic, Old English*

Black Letter

black light *n* : invisible ultraviolet or infrared light
black–light trap \ˌblak-ˌlīt-\ *n* : a trap for insects that uses a form of black light perceptible to particular insects as an attractant
[1]**black·list** \ˈblak-ˌlist\ *n* : a list of persons who are disapproved of or are to be punished or boycotted
[2]**blacklist** *vt* : to put on a blacklist — **black·list·er** *n*
black locust *n* : a tall tree (*Robinia pseudoacacia*) of eastern No. America with pinnately compound leaves, drooping racemes of fragrant white flowers, and strong stiff wood
black lung *n* : a disease of the lungs caused by habitual inhalation of coal dust
black magic *n* : WITCHCRAFT
black·mail \ˈblak-ˌmāl\ *n* [*black* + [1]*mail*] **1** : a tribute anciently exacted on the Scottish border by freebooting chiefs for immunity from pillage **2 a** : extortion by threats esp. of public exposure or criminal prosecution **b** : the payment that is extorted — **blackmail** *vt* — **black·mail·er** *n*
Black Ma·ria \ˌblak-mə-ˈrī-ə\ *n* : PATROL WAGON
black–mar·ket *vi* : to buy or sell goods in the black market ~ *vt* : to sell in the black market — **black marketer** *or* **black marketeer** *n*
black market *n* : illicit trade in goods or commodities in violation of official regulations; *also* : a place where such trade is carried on
Black Mass *n* : a travesty of the Christian mass ascribed to the reputed worshipers of Satan
Black Muslim *n* : a member of an exclusively black group that professes Islamic religious belief and advocates a strictly separate black community
black nationalist *n, often cap B&N* : a member of a group of militant blacks who advocate separatism from the whites and the formation of self-governing black communities — **black nationalism** *n, often cap B&N*
black·out \ˈblak-ˌau̇t\ *n* **1 a** : a turning off of the stage lighting to separate scenes in a play, indicate that the play is over, or end a skit; *also* : a skit that ends with a blackout **b** : a period of darkness enforced as a precaution against air raids **c** : a period of darkness (as in a city) caused by a lack of illumination due to a failure of electrical power **2** : a transient dulling or loss of vision, consciousness, or memory ⟨an alcoholic ~⟩ **3 a** : a wiping out or erasure : OBLITERATION ⟨a sudden ~ of his policy by the insurance company⟩ **b** : a blotting out by censorship : SUPPRESSION ⟨a ~ of news about the invasion⟩ **4** : a usu. temporary loss of radio signal due to a magnetic storm or to a local effect at the transmitter of a spacecraft upon reentry
black out \(ˈ)blak-ˈau̇t\ *vi* **1** : to become enveloped in darkness **2** : to undergo a temporary loss of vision, consciousness, or memory **3** : to extinguish or screen all lights for protection esp. against air attack ~ *vt* **1** : to cause to black out ⟨*black out* the stage⟩ **2** : to make inoperative or temporarily nonexistent : DESTROY ⟨falling trees *blacked out* electric power lines⟩ **3 a** : to blot out or erase ⟨*blacked out* the event from his mind⟩ **b** : to suppress by censorship ⟨*black out* the news⟩
Black Panther *n* : a member of an organization of militant American Negroes
black pepper *n* : a pungent condiment that consists of the fruit of an East Indian plant (*Piper nigrum*) ground with the black husk still on
black perch *n* : any of various dark-colored fishes (as a bass)
black·poll \ˈblak-ˌpōl\ *n* : a No. American warbler (*Dendroica striata*) having the top of the head of the male bird black when in full plumage
black power *n* : the mobilization of the political and economic power of American Negroes esp. to further racial equality
black pudding *n, chiefly Brit* : BLOOD SAUSAGE
black racer *n* : an American blacksnake (*Coluber constrictor constrictor*) common in the eastern U.S.
black raspberry *n* : a raspberry (*Rubus occidentalis*) with a purplish black fruit that is native to eastern No. America and is the source of several cultivated varieties — called also *blackcap*
Black Rod *n* : the principal usher of the House of Lords
black rot *n* : a bacterial or fungous rot of plants marked by dark brown discoloration
black sheep *n* : a discreditable member of a respectable group
Black·shirt \ˈblak-ˌshərt\ *n* : a member of a fascist organization having a black shirt as a distinctive part of its uniform; *esp* : a member of the Italian Fascist party

black·smith \'blak-,smith\ *n* [fr. his working with iron, known as black metal] : a smith who forges iron — **black·smith·ing** \-iŋ\ *n*

black·snake \-,snāk\ *n* **1** : any of several snakes that are largely black or very dark in color; *esp* : either of two harmless snakes (*Coluber constrictor* and *Elaphe obsoleta*) of the U.S. **2** : a long tapering braided whip of rawhide or leather

black spot *n* : any of several plant diseases characterized by black spots or blotches

black studies *n pl* : studies (as history and literature) relating to American Negro culture

black·tail \'blak-,tāl\ *n* : BLACK-TAILED DEER

black–tailed deer \,blak-,tāl-'di(ə)r\ *n* : MULE DEER; *specif* : one of a subspecies (*Odocoileus hemionus columbianus*) esp. of British Columbia, Oregon, and Washington — see DEER illustration

black tea *n* : tea that is dark in color from complete fermentation of the leaf before firing

black·thorn \'blak-,thȯ(ə)rn\ *n* **1** : a European spiny plum (*Prunus spinosa*) with hard wood and small white flowers **2** : any of several American hawthorns

black–tie *adj* : characterized by or requiring the wearing of semiformal evening dress by men ⟨a ~ dinner⟩ — compare WHITE-TIE

black·top \'blak-,täp\ *n* : a bituminous material used esp. for surfacing roads; *also* : a surface paved with blacktop — **blacktop** *vt*

black vomit *n* **1** : vomitus consisting of dark-colored matter **2** : a condition characterized by black vomit; *esp* : YELLOW FEVER

Black·wall hitch \,blak-,wȯl-\ *n* [*Blackwall*, shipyard in London, England] : a hitch for securing a rope to a hook — see KNOT illustration

black walnut *n* : a walnut (*Juglans nigra*) of eastern No. America with hard strong heavy dark brown wood and oily edible nuts; *also* : its wood or nut

black·wash \'blak-,wȯsh, -,wäsh\ *vt* [*black* + *-wash* (as in *whitewash*)] : to uncover or bring to light : EXPOSE

black·wa·ter \'blak-,wȯt-ər, -,wät-\ *n* : any of several diseases of lower animals or man characterized by dark-colored urine

black widow *n* : a venomous New World spider (*Latrodectus mactans*) having the female black with an hourglass-shaped red mark on the underside of the abdomen

blad·der \'blad-ər\ *n* [ME, fr. OE *blǣdre;* akin to OHG *blātara* bladder, OE *blāwan* to blow] **1 a** : a membranous sac in animals that serves as the receptacle of a liquid or contains gas; *esp* : the urinary bladder **b** : VESICLE **2** : something (as the rubber bag inside a football) resembling a bladder — **blad·der·like** \-,līk\ *adj*

blad·der·nut \'blad-ər-,nət\ *n* : an ornamental shrub or small tree (genus *Staphylea* of the family Staphyleaceae, the bladdernut family) with panicles of small white flowers followed by inflated capsules; *also* : one of the capsules

bladder worm *n* : a bladderlike larval tapeworm (as a cysticercus)

blad·der·wort \'blad-ər-,wərt, -,wȯ(ə)rt\ *n* : any of a genus (*Utricularia* of the family Lentibulariaceae, the bladderwort family) of chiefly aquatic plants with vesicular floats or insect traps

bladder wrack *n* : a common black rockweed (*Fucus vesiculosus*) used in preparing kelp and as a manure

blade \'blād\ *n* [ME, fr. OE *blæd;* akin to OHG *blat* leaf, L *folium,* Gk *phyllon,* OE *blōwan* to blossom — more at BLOW] **1 a** : LEAF 1a(1); *esp* : the leaf of an herb or a grass **b** : the flat expanded part of a leaf as distinguished from the petiole **2** : something resembling the blade of a leaf: as **a** : the broad flattened part of an oar or paddle **b** : an arm of a screw propeller, electric fan, or steam turbine **c** : the broad flat or concave part of a machine (as a bulldozer or snowplow) that comes into contact with the material to be moved **d** : a broad flat body part; *specif* : SCAPULA — used chiefly in naming cuts of meat **e** : the flat portion of the tongue immediately behind the tip; *also* : this portion together with the tip **f** : the expanded rear portion of the comb of a single-comb fowl — see COCK illustration **3 a** : the cutting part of an implement **b** (1) : SWORD (2) : SWORDSMAN (3) : a dashing lively man **c** : the runner of an ice skate

blad·ed \'blād-əd\ *adj* : having blades — often used in combination ⟨broad-*bladed* leaves⟩

blae \'blā\ *adj* [ME *bla, blo,* fr. ON *blār;* akin to OHG *blāo* blue — more at BLUE] *chiefly Scot* : dark blue or bluish gray

[1]**blah** \'blä\ *also* **blah–blah** \-,blä\ *n* [imit.] **1** : silly or pretentious chatter or nonsense **2** *pl* [perh. influenced in meaning by *blasé*] : a feeling of boredom, discomfort, or general dissatisfaction

[2]**blah** *adj* : lacking interest : MEDIOCRE ⟨a ~ winter day⟩

blain \'blān\ *n* [ME, fr. OE *blegen;* akin to MLG *bleine* blain, OE *blāwan* to blow] : an inflammatory swelling or sore

blam·able \'blā-mə-bəl\ *adj* : deserving blame : REPREHENSIBLE *syn* see BLAMEWORTHY *ant* blameless — **blam·ably** \-blē\ *adv*

[1]**blame** \'blām\ *vt* **blamed; blam·ing** [ME *blamen,* fr. OF *blamer,* fr. LL *blasphemare* to blaspheme, fr. Gk *blasphēmein*] **1** : to find fault with : CENSURE ⟨the right to praise or ~ a literary work⟩ **2 a** : to hold responsible ⟨~ him for everything⟩ **b** : to place responsibility for ⟨~*s* it on me⟩ *syn* see CRITICIZE — **blam·er** *n* — **to blame** : at fault : RESPONSIBLE

[2]**blame** *n* **1** : an expression of disapproval or reproach : CENSURE **2 a** : a state of being blameworthy : CULPABILITY **b** *archaic* : FAULT, SIN **3** : responsibility for something believed to deserve censure ⟨they must share the ~ for the crime⟩ — **blame·less** \-ləs\ *adj* — **blame·less·ly** *adv* — **blame·less·ness** *n*

blame·ful \'blām-fəl\ *adj* : BLAMABLE — **blame·ful·ly** \-fə-lē\ *adv*

blame·wor·thy \-,wər-thē\ *adj* : being at fault : deserving blame — **blame·wor·thi·ness** *n*

syn BLAMEWORTHY, BLAMABLE, GUILTY, CULPABLE *shared meaning element* : deserving reproach or punishment for some act or course of action. BLAMEWORTHY and BLAMABLE acknowledge the fact of censurable quality in what is described but in themselves imply nothing about the degree of reprehensibility involved ⟨though not criminal, his behavior was certainly *blameworthy*⟩ ⟨a person is only *blamable* for his own faults⟩ GUILTY implies responsibility for or consciousness of crime, sin, or, at the least, grave error or misdoing ⟨found *guilty* of murder⟩ ⟨suspicion always haunts the *guilty* mind; the thief doth fear each bush an officer — Shak.⟩ CULPABLE is weaker than *guilty* and is likely to connote malfeasance or errors of ignorance, omission, or negligence ⟨avaricious victims, almost as *culpable* as the confidence man who tricked them⟩ ⟨*culpable* neglect⟩ *ant* blameless

blanc fixe \'blaŋk-'fiks\ *n* [F, lit., fixed white] : barium sulfate prepared as a heavy white powder and used esp. as a filler in paper, rubber, and linoleum or as a pigment

blanch \'blanch\ *vb* [ME *blaunchen,* fr. MF *blanchir,* fr. OF *blanche,* fem. of *blanc,* adj., white] *vt* **1** : to take the color out of: **a** : to bleach by excluding light ⟨~ celery⟩ **b** : to scald or parboil in water or steam in order to remove the skin from, whiten, or stop enzymatic action in (as food for freezing) **c** : to clean (a coin blank) in an acid solution **d** : to cover (sheet iron or steel) with a coating of tin **2** : to make ashen or pale ⟨fear ~*es* the cheek⟩ ~ *vi* : to become white or pale *syn* see WHITEN — **blanch·er** *n*

blanc·mange \blə-'mänj, -'mänzh\ *n* [ME *blancmanger,* fr. MF *blanc manger,* lit., white food] : a dessert made from gelatinous or starchy substances and milk usu. sweetened, flavored, and shaped in a mold

bland \'bland\ *adj* [L *blandus*] **1 a** : smooth and soothing in manner or quality ⟨a ~ smile⟩ **b** : exhibiting no personal concern or embarrassment : UNPERTURBED ⟨a ~ confession of guilt⟩ **2 a** : not irritating, stimulating, or invigorating : SOOTHING **b** : DULL, INSIPID ⟨~ stories with little plot or action⟩ *syn* **1** see SOFT *ant* piquant, savory **2** see SUAVE *ant* brusque — **bland·ly** \'blan-(d)lē\ *adv* — **bland·ness** \'blan(d)-nəs\ *n*

blan·dish \'blan-dish\ *vb* [ME *blandishen,* fr. MF *blandiss-,* stem of *blandir,* fr. L *blandiri,* fr. *blandus* mild, flattering] *vt* : to coax with flattery : CAJOLE ~ *vi* : to act or speak in a flattering or coaxing manner — **blan·dish·er** *n*

blan·dish·ment \-dish-mənt\ *n* : something that tends to coax or cajole : ALLUREMENT — often used in pl.

[1]**blank** \'blaŋk\ *adj* [ME, fr. MF *blanc,* of Gmc origin; akin to OHG *blanch* white; akin to L *flagrare* to burn — more at BLACK] **1** *archaic* : COLORLESS **2 a** : appearing or causing to appear dazed, confounded, or nonplussed ⟨stared in ~ dismay⟩ **b** : EXPRESSIONLESS ⟨a ~ stare⟩ **3 a** : lacking interest, variety, or change ⟨~ hours⟩ **b** : devoid of covering or content; *esp* : free from writing or marks ⟨~ paper⟩ **c** : having spaces to be filled in **d** : lacking any card : VOID ⟨a ~ suit at cards⟩ **4** : ABSOLUTE, UNQUALIFIED ⟨a ~ refusal⟩ **5** : UNFINISHED; *esp* : having a plain or unbroken surface where an opening is usual ⟨a ~ key⟩ ⟨a ~ arch⟩ *syn* see EMPTY — **blank·ly** *adv* — **blank·ness** *n*

[2]**blank** *n* **1 a** : an empty space (as on a paper) **b** : a paper with spaces for the entry of data ⟨a subscription ~⟩ **2 a** : an empty or featureless place or space ⟨my mind was a ~ during the test⟩ **b** : a vacant or uneventful period ⟨a long ~ in history⟩ **c** : something useless, valueless, or undesirable ⟨drew a ~⟩ **3** : the bull's-eye of a target **4** : a dash substituting for an omitted word **5 a** : a piece of material prepared to be made into something (as a key) by a further operation **b** : a cartridge loaded with powder but no bullet **6** : VOID 4

[3]**blank** *vt* **1 a** : OBSCURE, OBLITERATE ⟨~ out a line⟩ **b** : to stop access to : SEAL ⟨~ off a tunnel⟩ **2** : to keep (an opposing team) from scoring ⟨were ~*ed* for eight innings⟩ **3** : to cut with a die from a piece of stock ~ *vi* **1** : FADE — usu. used with *out* ⟨the music ~*ed* out⟩ **2** : to become confused or abstracted — often used with *out* ⟨his mind ~*ed* out momentarily⟩

blank check *n* **1** : a signed check with the amount unspecified **2** : complete freedom of action or control : CARTE BLANCHE

blank endorsement *n* : an endorsement of commercial paper without a qualifying phrase thus making the paper payable to the bearer

[1]**blan·ket** \'blaŋ-kət\ *n* [ME, fr. OF *blankete,* fr. *blanc*] **1 a** : a large usu. oblong piece of woven fabric used as a bed covering **b** : a similar piece of fabric used as a body covering (as for an animal) ⟨a horse ~⟩ **2** : something that resembles a blanket; *esp* : a covering or enclosing layer ⟨a ~ of fog⟩ ⟨a ~ of gloom⟩ — **blan·ket·like** \-,līk\ *adj*

[2]**blanket** *vt* **1** : to cover with a blanket ⟨new grass ~*s* the slope⟩ **2 a** : to cover so as to obscure, interrupt, suppress, or extinguish ⟨~ a fire with foam⟩ **b** : to apply or cause to apply to uniformly despite wide separation or diversity among the elements included ⟨freight rates that ~ a region⟩ **c** : to cause to be included ⟨automatically ~*ed* into the insurance program⟩ **3** *archaic* : to toss in a blanket (as by way of punishment)

[3]**blanket** *adj* **1** : covering all members of a group or class ⟨a ~ wage increase⟩ **2** : effective or applicable in all instances

blan·ket·flow·er \'blaŋ-kət-,flau̇(-ə)r\ *n* : GAILLARDIA

blanket stitch *n* : a buttonhole stitch with spaces of variable width used on materials too thick to hem — **blanket–stitch** *vt*

blank verse *n* : unrhymed verse; *specif* : unrhymed iambic pentameter verse

[1]**blare** \'bla(ə)r, 'ble(ə)r\ *vb* **blared; blar·ing** [ME *bleren;* akin to OE *blǣtan* to bleat] *vi* : to sound loud and strident ⟨radios *blaring*⟩ ~ *vt* **1** : to sound or utter raucously ⟨sat *blaring* the car horn⟩ **2** : to proclaim flamboyantly ⟨headlines *blared* his defeat⟩

[2]**blare** *n* **1** : a loud strident noise **2** : dazzling often garish brilliance **3** : FLAMBOYANCE

blar·ney \'blär-nē\ *n* [*Blarney stone,* a stone in Blarney Castle, near Cork, Ireland, held to bestow skill in flattery on those who kiss it] **1** : skillful flattery : BLANDISHMENT **2** : NONSENSE, HUMBUG ⟨gave her some ~ about why he was late⟩ — **blarney** *vb*

bla·sé \blä-'zā\ *adj* [F] **1** : apathetic to pleasure or excitement as a result of excessive indulgence or enjoyment : WORLD-WEARY **2** : SOPHISTICATED, WORLDLY-WISE

ə abut ᵊ kitten ər further a back ā bake ä cot, cart
au̇ out ch chin e less ē easy g gift i trip ī life
j joke ŋ sing ō flow ȯ flaw ȯi coin th thin th this
ü loot u̇ foot y yet yü few yu̇ furious zh vision

blas·pheme \blas-ˈfēm\ *vb* **blas·phemed; blas·phem·ing** [ME *blasfemen,* fr. LL *blasphemare* — more at BLAME] *vt* **1 :** to speak of or address with irreverence **2 :** REVILE, ABUSE ~ *vi* **:** to utter blasphemy — **blas·phem·er** *n*

blas·phe·mous \ˈblas-fə-məs\ *adj* **:** impiously irreverent **:** PROFANE — **blas·phe·mous·ly** *adv* — **blas·phe·mous·ness** *n*

blas·phe·my \ˈblas-fə-mē\ *n, pl* **-mies** **1 a :** the act of insulting or showing contempt or lack of reverence for God **b :** the act of claiming the attributes of deity **2 :** irreverence toward something considered sacred or inviolable

1blast \ˈblast\ *n* [ME, fr. OE *blǣst;* akin to OHG *blāst* blast, OE *blāwan* to blow] **1 a :** a violent gust of wind **b :** the effect or accompaniment (as sleet) of such a gust **2 :** the sound produced by an impulsion of air through a wind instrument or whistle **3 :** something resembling a gust of wind: as **a :** a stream of air or gas forced through a hole **b :** a violent outburst ⟨the speaker's ~ against special privileges⟩ **c :** the continuous blowing to which a charge of ore or metal is subjected in a blast furnace **4 a :** a sudden pernicious influence or effect ⟨the ~ of a huge epidemic⟩ **b :** a disease that suggests the effects of a noxious wind; *esp* **:** one of plants that causes the foliage or flowers to wither **5 a :** an explosion or violent detonation **b :** the explosive charge used esp. for shattering rock **c :** the violent effect produced in the vicinity of an explosion that consists of a wave of increased atmospheric pressure followed by a wave of decreased atmospheric pressure **6 :** SPEED, CAPACITY ⟨going full ~ down the road⟩ **7 :** OPERATION, ACTIVITY ⟨the furnace must be kept in continual ~⟩ **8 :** a riotous or exuberant occasion; *esp* **:** an enjoyable party **9 :** HOME RUN

2blast *vi* **1 :** to produce a strident sound ⟨music ~*ing* from the radio⟩ **2 a :** to use an explosive **b :** SHOOT **3 :** to make a vigorous attack **4 :** SHRIVEL, WITHER **5 :** to hit a golf ball out of a sand trap with explosive force ~ *vt* **1 a :** to injure by or as if by the action of wind **b :** to affect with a blighting influence **2 :** to shatter by or as if by an explosive **:** DEMOLISH **3 a :** to apply a forced draft to **b :** to strike with explosive force **4 :** to cause to blast off ⟨will ~ themselves from the moon's surface⟩ **5 :** to hit vigorously and effectively **6 :** to cause to emerge like a blast of wind ⟨the tenor ~*s* out the high C's⟩ — **blast·er** *n* — **blast·ing** *n or adj*

blast- *or* **blasto-** *comb form* [G, fr. Gk, fr. *blastos*] **:** bud **:** budding **:** germ ⟨*blasto*disc⟩ ⟨*blast*ula⟩

-blast \ˌblast\ *n comb form* [NL *-blastus,* fr. Gk *blastos* bud, shoot; akin to OE *molda* top of the head, Skt *mūrdhan* head] **:** formative unit esp. of living matter **:** germ **:** cell **:** cell layer ⟨epi*blast*⟩

blast·ed *adj* **1 a :** BLIGHTED, WITHERED **b :** damaged by or as if by an explosive, lightning, or the wind **:** BATTERED ⟨a ~ apple tree⟩ **2 :** CONFOUNDED, DETESTABLE ⟨this ~ weather⟩

blas·te·ma \bla-ˈstē-mə\ *n, pl* **-mas** *or* **-ma·ta** \-mət-ə\ [NL, fr. Gk *blastēma* offshoot, fr. *blastos*] **:** a mass of living substance capable of growth and differentiation — **blas·te·mat·ic** \ˌblas-tə-ˈmat-ik\ *or* **blas·te·mic** \bla-ˈstē-mik, -ˈstem-ik\ *adj*

blast furnace *n* **:** a furnace in which combustion is forced by a current of air under pressure; *esp* **:** one for the reduction of iron ore

-blas·tic \ˈblas-tik\ *adj comb form* [ISV, fr. *-blast*] **:** having (such or so many) buds, germs, cells, or cell layers ⟨diplo*blastic*⟩

blast·ie \ˈblas-tē\ *n* [Sc *blast* to wither, fr. 2*blast*] *Scot* **:** an ugly little creature

blast·ment \ˈblas(t)-mənt\ *n, archaic* **:** a blighting influence

blas·to·coel *or* **blas·to·coele** \ˈblas-tə-ˌsēl\ *n* [ISV] **:** the cavity of a blastula — see BLASTULA illustration — **blas·to·coe·lic** \ˌblas-tə-ˈsē-lik\ *adj*

blas·to·cyst \ˈblas-tə-ˌsist\ *n* **:** the modified blastula of a placental mammal

blas·to·derm \-ˌdərm\ *n* [G, fr. *blast-* + *-derm*] **:** a blastodisc after completion of cleavage and formation of the blastocoel — **blas·to·der·mat·ic** \ˌblas-tə-ˌdər-ˈmat-ik\ *or* **blas·to·der·mic** \-ˈdər-mik\ *adj*

blas·to·disc \ˈblas-tə-ˌdisk\ *n* **:** the embryo-forming portion of an egg with discoidal cleavage usu. appearing as a small disc on the upper surface of the yolk mass — see EGG illustration

blast–off \ˈblas-ˌtȯf\ *n* **:** a blasting off (as of a rocket)

blast off \(ˈ)blas-ˈtȯf\ *vi* **:** to take off — used esp. of rocket-propelled missiles and vehicles

blas·to·mere \ˈblas-tə-ˌmi(ə)r\ *n* [ISV] **:** a cell produced during cleavage of an egg — **blas·to·mer·ic** \ˌblas-tə-ˈmi(ə)r-ik, -ˈmer-\ *adj*

blas·to·my·cete \ˌblas-tə-ˈmī-ˌsēt, -ˌmī-ˈsēt\ *n* [deriv. of *blast-* + Gk *mykēt-, mykēs* fungus — more at MYC-] **:** any of a group (Blastomycetes) of pathogenic fungi growing typically like yeasts

blas·to·my·co·sis \-ˌmī-ˈkō-səs\ *n* **:** a disease caused by a blastomycete — **blas·to·my·cot·ic** \-ˈkät-ik\ *adj*

blas·to·pore \ˈblas-tə-ˌpō(ə)r, -ˌpȯ(ə)r\ *n* **:** the opening of the archenteron — **blas·to·por·al** \ˌblas-tə-ˈpōr-əl, -ˈpȯr-\ *or* **blas·to·por·ic** \-ˈpōr-ik, -ˈpȯr-\ *adj*

blas·to·sphere \ˈblas-tə-ˌsfi(ə)r\ *n* **:** BLASTULA — **blas·to·spher·ic** \ˌblas-tə-ˈsfi(ə)r-ik, -ˈsfer-\ *adj*

blas·tu·la \ˈblas-chə-lə\ *n, pl* **-las** *or* **-lae** \-ˌlē\ [NL, fr. Gk *blastos*] **:** an early metazoan embryo typically having the form of a hollow fluid-filled rounded cavity bounded by a single layer of cells — compare GASTRULA, MORULA — **blas·tu·lar** \-lər\ *adj* — **blas·tu·la·tion** \ˌblas-chə-ˈlā-shən\ *n*

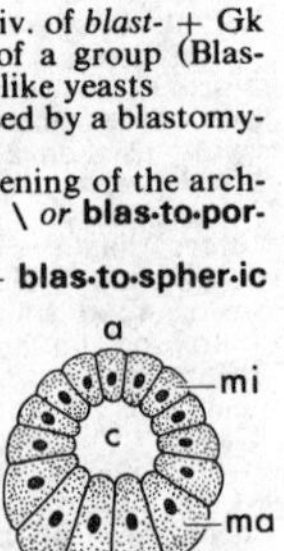

section of blastula: *c* blastocoel, *ma* macromere, *mi* micromere, *a* animal pole, *v* vegetal pole

blat \ˈblat\ *vb* **blat·ted; blat·ting** [imit.] *vi* **1 :** to cry like a calf or sheep **:** BLEAT **2 a :** to make a raucous noise **b :** BLAB ~ *vt* **:** to utter loudly or foolishly **:** BLURT — **blat** *n*

bla·tan·cy \ˈblāt-ᵊn-sē\ *n, pl* **-cies** **1 :** the quality or state of being blatant **2 :** something that is blatant

bla·tant \ˈblāt-ᵊnt\ *adj* [perh. fr. L *blatire* to chatter] **1 :** noisy esp. in a vulgar or offensive manner **:** CLAMOROUS **2 :** completely obvious, conspicuous, or obtrusive esp. in a crass or offensive manner **:** BRAZEN ***syn*** see VOCIFEROUS ***ant*** decorous, reserved — **bla·tant·ly** *adv*

blate \ˈblāt\ *adj* [ME] *chiefly Scot* **:** TIMID, SHEEPISH

1blath·er \ˈblat͟h-ər\ *vi* **blath·ered; blath·er·ing** \-(ə-)riŋ\ [ON *blathra;* akin to MHG *blōdern* to chatter] **:** to talk foolishly — **blath·er·er** \-ər-ər\ *n*

2blather *n* **1 :** voluble or nonsensical talk **2 :** STIR, COMMOTION

blath·er·skite \ˈblat͟h-ər-ˌskīt\ *n* [*blather* + Sc dial. *skate* a contemptible person] **1 :** a blustering talkative fellow **2 :** NONSENSE, BLATHER

blat·ter \ˈblat-ər\ *vi* [perh. fr. L *blaterare* to chatter — more at BLATANT] *dial* **:** to talk noisily and fast **:** PRATTLE

blaw \ˈblȯ\ *vb* **blawed; blawn** \ˈblȯn\; **blaw·ing** [ME (northern dial.) *blawen,* fr. OE *blāwan*] *chiefly Scot* **:** BLOW

1blaze \ˈblāz\ *n* [ME *blase,* fr. OE *blæse* torch; akin to OE *bǣl* fire — more at BALD] **1 a :** an intensely burning fire **b :** intense direct light often accompanied by heat ⟨the ~ of noon⟩ **c :** an active burning; *esp* **:** a sudden bursting forth of flame ⟨several ~*s* in the woods⟩ **2 :** something that resembles the blaze of a fire: as **a :** a dazzling display **b :** a sudden outburst ⟨a ~ of fury⟩ **c :** BRILLIANCE ⟨the ~ of autumn⟩
syn BLAZE, FLAME, FLARE, GLARE, GLOW *shared meaning element* **:** a brightly burning light or fire or something suggesting this

2blaze *vi* **blazed; blaz·ing** **1 a :** to burn brightly ⟨the sun *blazed* overhead⟩ **b :** to flare up **:** FLAME ⟨he suddenly *blazed* with anger⟩ **2 :** to be conspicuously brilliant or resplendent ⟨fields *blazing* with flowers⟩ **3 :** to shoot rapidly and repeatedly ⟨~ away at the target⟩ — **blaz·ing·ly** \ˈblā-ziŋ-lē\ *adv*

3blaze *vt* **blazed; blaz·ing** [ME *blasen,* fr. MD *blāsen* to blow; akin to OHG *blāst* blast] **:** to make public or conspicuous **:** PROCLAIM

4blaze *n* [G *blas,* fr. OHG *plas;* akin to OE *blæse*] **1 a :** a white mark on the face of an animal **b :** a white or gray streak in the hair of the head **2 :** a trail marker; *esp* **:** a mark made on a tree by chipping off a piece of the bark

5blaze *vt* **blazed; blaz·ing** **1 :** to mark (as a trail) with blazes **2 :** to lead or pioneer in some direction or activity — usu. used in the phrase *blaze the trail*

blaz·er \ˈblā-zər\ *n* **1 :** one that blazes **2 :** a sports jacket often with notched collar and patch pockets

blazing star *n* **1** *archaic* **:** COMET **2** *archaic* **:** a center of attraction **:** CYNOSURE **3 :** any of several plants having conspicuous flower clusters: as **a :** a plant (*Chamaelirium luteum*) of the bunchflower family **b :** BUTTON SNAKEROOT 1

1bla·zon \ˈblāz-ᵊn\ *n* [ME *blason,* fr. MF] **1 a :** armorial bearings **:** COAT OF ARMS **b :** the proper description or representation of heraldic or armorial bearings **2 :** DESCRIPTION, SHOW; *esp* **:** ostentatious display

2blazon *vt* **bla·zoned; bla·zon·ing** \ˈblāz-niŋ, -ᵊn-iŋ\ **1 :** to publish widely **:** PROCLAIM; *esp* **:** to boast of **2 a :** to describe (heraldic or armorial bearings) in technical terms **b :** to represent (armorial bearings) in drawing or engraving **3 a :** to depict or inscribe in colors **b :** DISPLAY **c :** DECK, ADORN ⟨forests ~*ed* with autumn colors⟩ — **bla·zon·er** \-nər, -ᵊn-ər\ *n* — **blazoning** *n*

bla·zon·ry \ˈblāz-ᵊn-rē\ *n, pl* **-ries** **1 a :** BLAZON 1b **b :** BLAZON 1a **2 :** a dazzling display

bld *abbr* **1** blond **2** blood

bldg *abbr* building

Bldg E *abbr* building engineer

bldr *abbr* builder

1bleach \ˈblēch\ *vb* [ME *blechen,* fr. OE *blǣcean;* akin to OE *blāc* pale, *bǣl* fire — more at BALD] *vt* **1 :** to remove color or stains from **2 :** to make whiter or lighter esp. by physical or chemical removal of color ~ *vi* **:** to grow white or lose color ***syn*** see WHITEN — **bleach·able** \ˈblē-chə-bəl\ *adj*

2bleach *n* **1 :** the act or process of bleaching **2 :** a preparation used in bleaching **3 :** the degree of whiteness obtained by bleaching

bleach·er \ˈblē-chər\ *n* **1 :** one that bleaches or is used in bleaching **2 :** a usu. uncovered stand of tiered planks providing seating space for spectators — usu. used in pl.

bleach·er·ite \ˈblē-chə-ˌrīt\ *n* **:** one who sits in the bleachers

bleaching powder *n* **:** a white powder consisting chiefly of calcium hydroxide, calcium chloride, and calcium hypochlorite used as a bleach, disinfectant, or deodorant

1bleak \ˈblēk\ *adj* [ME *bleke* pale; prob. akin to OE *blāc*] **1 :** exposed and barren and often windswept **2 :** COLD, RAW **3 a :** lacking in warmth or kindliness **b :** not hopeful or encouraging ⟨a ~ outlook⟩ **c :** severely simple or austere — **bleak·ish** \ˈblē-kish\ *adj* — **bleak·ly** *adv* — **bleak·ness** *n*

2bleak *n* [ME *bleke*] **:** a small European cyprinid river fish (*Alburnus lucidus*) with silvery scale pigment used in making artificial pearls

1blear \ˈbli(ə)r\ *vt* [ME *bleren*] **1 :** to make (the eyes) sore or watery **2 :** DIM, BLUR

2blear *adj* **1 :** dim with water or tears **2 :** obscure to the view or imagination ⟨clarifies the ~ side of things⟩ — **blear–eyed** \-ˈīd\ *adj*

bleary \ˈbli(ə)r-ē\ *adj* **1** *of the eyes or vision* **:** dull or dimmed esp. from fatigue or sleep **2 :** poorly outlined or defined **:** DIM **3 :** tired to the point of exhaustion — **blear·i·ly** \ˈblir-ə-lē\ *adv* — **blear·i·ness** \ˈblir-ē-nəs\ *n*

1bleat \ˈblēt\ *vb* [ME *bleten,* fr. OE *blǣtan;* akin to L *flēre* to weep, OE *bellan* to roar — more at BELLOW] *vi* **1 a :** to utter the natural cry of a sheep or goat **b :** to make a sound resembling this cry **c :** WHIMPER **2 a :** to talk complainingly or with a whine **b :** BLATHER ~ *vt* **:** to utter in a bleating manner — **bleat·er** *n*

2bleat *n* **1 a :** the cry of a sheep or goat **b :** a sound resembling this cry **2 :** whining or foolish talk **:** BLATHER

bleb \ˈbleb\ *n* [perh. alter. of *blob*] **1 :** a small blister **2 :** BUBBLE — **bleb·by** \ˈbleb-ē\ *adj*

1bleed \ˈblēd\ *vb* **bled** \ˈbled\; **bleed·ing** [ME *bleden,* fr. OE *blēdan,* fr. *blōd* blood] *vi* **1 a :** to emit or lose blood **b :** to sacrifice one's blood esp. in battle **2 :** to feel anguish, pain, or sympathy ⟨a heart that ~*s* at a friend's misfortune⟩ **3 :** to escape by oozing or flowing (as from a wound) **4 :** to give up some constituent (as sap or dye) by exuding or diffusing it **5 a :** to pay out or give money **b :** to have money extorted **6 :** to be printed so as to run off one or more edges of a printed page or sheet after trimming — often used with *off* **~** *vt* **1 :** to remove or draw blood from **2 :** to get or extort money from **3 :** to draw sap from (a tree) **4 a :** to extract or let out some or all of a contained substance from ⟨~ a tire⟩ **b :** to extract or cause to escape from a container **5 :** to cause (as a printed illustration) to bleed; *also* **:** to trim (as a page) so that some of the printing bleeds — **bleed white :** to drain of blood or resources

2bleed *n* **:** an illustration or a page that bleeds or is bled; *also* **:** the part trimmed off in bleeding or the corresponding area of the printing plate

bleed·er *n* **:** one that bleeds; *esp* **:** HEMOPHILIAC

bleeding heart *n* **1 :** a garden plant (*Dicentra spectabilis*) of the fumitory family with racemes of deep pink drooping heart-shaped flowers; *broadly* **:** any of several plants (genus *Dicentra*) **2 :** one who shows extravagant sympathy esp. for an object of alleged persecution

1bleep \'blēp\ *n* [imit.] **:** a short high-pitched sound (as from electronic equipment)

2bleep *vt* **:** BLIP

blel·lum \'blel-əm\ *n* [perh. blend of Sc *bleber* to babble and *skellum* rascal] *Scot* **:** a lazy talkative person

1blem·ish \'blem-ish\ *vt* [ME *blemisshen,* fr. MF *blesmiss-,* stem of *blesmir* to make pale, wound, of Gmc origin; akin to G *blass* pale; akin to OE *blæse* torch — more at BLAZE] **:** to spoil by a flaw

2blemish *n* **:** a noticeable imperfection; *esp* **:** one that seriously impairs appearance

syn BLEMISH, DEFECT, FLAW *shared meaning element* **:** an imperfection that mars or damages ***ant*** immaculateness

1blench \'blench\ *vi* [ME *blenchen* to deceive, blench, fr. OE *blencan* to deceive; akin to ON *blekkja* to impose on] **:** to draw back or turn aside from lack of courage **:** FLINCH ***syn*** see RECOIL

2blench *vb* [alter. of *blanch*] **:** BLEACH, WHITEN

1blend \'blend\ *vb* **blend·ed** *also* **blent** \'blent\; **blend·ing** [ME *blenden,* modif. of ON *blanda;* akin to OE *blandan* to mix, Lith *blandus* thick (of soup)] *vt* **1 :** MIX; *esp* **:** to combine or associate so that the separate constituents or the line of demarcation cannot be distinguished **2 :** to prepare by thoroughly intermingling different varieties or grades **3 :** to darken the tips of (a fur) with dye **~** *vi* **1 a :** to mingle intimately **b :** to combine into an integrated whole **2 :** to produce a harmonious effect ***syn*** see MIX

2blend *n* **:** something produced by blending: as **a :** a product prepared by blending **b :** a word (as *brunch*) produced by combining other words or parts of words

blende \'blend\ *n* [G, fr. *blenden* to blind, fr. OHG *blenten;* akin to OE *blind*] **1 :** SPHALERITE **2 :** any of several minerals (as metallic sulfides) with somewhat bright but nonmetallic luster

blended whiskey *n* **:** whiskey consisting of either a blend of two or more straight whiskeys or a blend of whiskey and neutral spirits

blend·er \'blen-dər\ *n* **:** one that blends; *esp* **:** an electric appliance for grinding or mixing ⟨a food ~⟩

blending inheritance *n* **:** inheritance by the progeny of characters intermediate between those of the parents

blen·ny \'blen-ē\ *n, pl* **blennies** [L *blennius,* a sea fish, fr. Gk *blennos*] **:** any of numerous usu. small and elongated and often scaleless fishes (Blenniidae and related families) living about rocky shores

blephar- *or* **blepharo-** *comb form* [NL, fr. Gk, fr. *blepharon*] **1 :** eyelid ⟨*blepharo*spasm⟩ **2 :** cilium **:** flagellum ⟨*blepharo*plast⟩

bleph·a·ro·plast \'blef-ə-rō-ˌplast\ n **:** a basal body esp. of a flagellated cell

bles·bok \'bles-ˌbäk\ *n* [Afrik, fr. *bles* blaze + *bok* male antelope] **:** a So. African antelope (*Damaliscus albifrons*) having a large white spot on the face

bless \'bles\ *vt* **blessed** \'blest\ *also* **blest** \'blest\; **bless·ing** [ME *blessen,* fr. OE *blētsian,* fr. *blōd* blood; fr. the use of blood in consecration] **1 :** to hallow or consecrate by religious rite or word **2 :** to hallow with the sign of the cross **3 :** to invoke divine care for **4 a :** PRAISE, GLORIFY ⟨~ his holy name⟩ **b :** to speak gratefully of ⟨~*ed* him for his kindness⟩ **5 :** to confer prosperity or happiness upon **6** *archaic* **:** PROTECT, PRESERVE

bless·ed \'bles-əd\ *also* **blest** \'blest\ *adj* **1 a :** held in reverence **:** VENERATED ⟨the ~ saints⟩ **b :** honored in worship **:** HALLOWED ⟨the ~ Trinity⟩ **c :** BEATIFIC ⟨a ~ visitation⟩ **2 :** of or enjoying happiness; *specif* **:** enjoying the bliss of heaven — used as a title for a beatified person **3 :** bringing pleasure or contentment **4** — used as an intensive ⟨no one gave us a ~ penny — *Saturday Rev.*⟩ — **bless·ed·ly** *adv* — **bless·ed·ness** *n*

Blessed Sacrament \ˌbles-əd-\ *n* **:** the Communion elements; *specif* **:** the consecrated Host

bless·ing *n* **1 a :** the act of one that blesses **b :** APPROVAL, ENCOURAGEMENT **2 :** a thing conducive to happiness or welfare **3 :** grace said at a meal

bleth·er \'bleth-ər\ *var of* BLATHER

blew *past of* BLOW

1blight \'blīt\ *n* [origin unknown] **1 a :** a disease or injury of plants resulting in withering, cessation of growth, and death of parts without rotting **b :** an organism that causes blight **2 :** something that frustrates plans or hopes **3 :** something that impairs or destroys **4 :** an impaired condition ⟨urban ~⟩

2blight *vt* **1 :** to affect (as a plant) with blight **2 :** to cause to deteriorate **~** *vi* **:** to suffer from or become affected with blight

blight·er \'blīt-ər\ *n* **1 :** one that blights **2** *chiefly Brit* **a :** one who is held in low esteem **b :** FELLOW, GUY

blimp \'blimp\ *n* [imit.; fr. the sound made by striking the gas bag with the thumb] **1 :** a nonrigid airship **2** *cap* **:** COLONEL BLIMP

blimp·ish \'blim-pish\ *adj, often cap* **:** of, relating to, or suggesting a Blimp ⟨a *Blimpish* colonel and his mousy, neglected wife —*Time*⟩ — **blimp·ish·ly** *adv* — **blimp·ish·ness** *n*

blin \'blin\ *n, pl* **bli·ni** \blə-'nē\ *or* **bli·nis** \blə-'nēz\ [Russ] **:** BLINTZE

1blind \'blīnd\ *adj* [ME, fr. OE; akin to OHG *blint* blind, OE *blandan* to mix — more at BLEND] **1 a** (1) **:** SIGHTLESS (2) **:** having less than $^1/_{10}$ of normal vision in the more efficient eye when refractive defects are fully corrected by lenses **b :** of or relating to sightless persons **2 a :** unable or unwilling to discern or judge **b :** unsupported by evidence or plausibility ⟨~ faith⟩ **3 a :** having no regard to rational discrimination, guidance, or restriction ⟨~ choice⟩ **b :** lacking a directing or controlling consciousness ⟨~ chance⟩ **c :** marked by complete insensibility **d :** DRUNK **4 :** made or done without sight of certain objects or knowledge of certain facts that could serve for guidance; *esp* **:** performed solely by the aid of instruments within an airplane ⟨a ~ landing⟩ **5 :** DEFECTIVE: as **a :** lacking a growing point or producing leaves instead of flowers **b :** lacking a complete or legible address ⟨~ mail⟩ **6 :** difficult to discern, make out, or discover: as **a :** ILLEGIBLE **b :** hidden from sight **:** COVERED ⟨~ seam⟩ **7 :** having but one opening or outlet ⟨~ sockets⟩ **8 :** having no opening for light or passage **:** BLANK ⟨~ wall⟩ — **blind·ly** \'blīn-(d)lē\ *adv* — **blind·ness** \'blīn(d)-nəs\ *n*

2blind *vt* **1 a :** to make blind **b :** DAZZLE **2 a :** to withhold light from **b :** HIDE, CONCEAL — **blind·ing·ly** \'blīn-diŋ-lē\ *adv*

3blind *n* **1 :** something to hinder sight or keep out light: as **a :** a window shutter **b :** a roller window shade **c :** VENETIAN BLIND **d :** BLINDER **2 :** a place of concealment; *esp* **:** a concealing enclosure from which one may shoot game or observe wildlife **3 a :** something put forward for the purpose of misleading **:** SUBTERFUGE **b** (1) **:** a person serving as an agent for another who keeps under cover (2) **:** one who acts as a decoy or distraction

4blind *adv* **:** BLINDLY: as **a :** to the point of insensibility ⟨~ drunk⟩ **b :** without seeing outside an airplane ⟨fly ~⟩

blind alley *n* **:** a fruitless or mistaken course or direction

blind date *n* **1 :** a date between two persons who have not previously met **2 :** either participant in a blind date

blind·er \'blīn-dər\ *n* **1 :** either of two flaps on a horse's bridle to prevent sight of objects at his sides **2** *pl* **:** an obstruction to sight or discernment

blind·fish \'blīn(d)-ˌfish\ *n* **:** any of several small fishes with vestigial functionless eyes found usu. in the waters of caves

1blind·fold \-ˌfōld\ *vt* [ME *blindfellen, blindfelden* to strike blind, blindfold, fr. *blind* + *fellen* to fell] **1 :** to cover the eyes of with or as if with a bandage **2 :** to hinder from seeing; *esp* **:** to keep from comprehension — **blindfold** *adj*

2blindfold *n* **1 :** a bandage for covering the eyes **2 :** something that obscures mental or physical vision

blind gut *n* **:** a digestive cavity open at only one end; *esp* **:** the cecum of the large intestine

blind·man's buff \ˌblīn(d)-ˌmanz-\ *n* **:** a group game in which a blindfolded player tries to catch and identify another player

blind pig *n* **:** BLIND TIGER

blind side *n* **1 :** the side on which one that is blind in one eye cannot see **2 :** the side away from which one is looking

blind spot *n* **1 a :** the point in the retina where the optic nerve enters that is not sensitive to light — see EYE illustration **b :** a portion of a field that cannot be seen or inspected with available equipment **2 :** an area in which one fails to exercise judgment or discrimination **3 :** a locality in which radio reception is markedly poorer than in the surrounding area

blind tiger *n* **:** a place that sells intoxicants illegally

blind·worm \'blīn-ˌdwərm\ n **:** a small burrowing limbless lizard with minute eyes; *esp* **:** a European lizard (*Anguis fragilis*) popularly believed to be blind — called also *slowworm*

1blink \'bliŋk\ *vb* [ME *blinken* to open one's eyes] *vi* **1 a** *obs* **:** to look glancingly **:** PEEP **b :** to look with half-shut eyes **c :** to close and open the eyes involuntarily (as when struggling against drowsiness or when dazzled) **2 :** to shine dimly or intermittently **3 a :** to look with too little concern **b :** to look with surprise or dismay **~** *vt* **1 a :** to cause to blink **b :** to remove (as tears) from the eye by blinking **2 :** to deny recognition to ***syn*** see WINK

2blink *n* **1** *chiefly Scot* **:** GLIMPSE, GLANCE **2 :** GLIMMER, SPARKLE **3 :** a usu. involuntary shutting and opening of the eye **4 a :** a whiteness about the horizon caused by the reflection of light from ice at sea **b :** a dark appearance of the sky about the horizon caused by the absence of reflected light due to open water — **on the blink :** in or into a disabled or useless condition

1blink·er \'bliŋ-kər\ *n* **1 :** one that blinks; *esp* **:** a light that flashes off and on (as for the directing of traffic or the coded signaling of messages) **2 a :** BLINDER 1 **b :** a cloth hood with shades projecting at the sides of the eye openings used on skittish racehorses — usu. used in pl. **3** *pl* **:** BLINDER 2

2blinker *vt* **:** to put blinders on

blin·tze \'blin(t)-sə\ *or* **blintz** \'blin(t)s\ *n* [Yiddish *blintse,* fr. Russ *blinets,* dim. of *blin* pancake] **:** a thin rolled pancake with a filling usu. of cheese

1blip \'blip\ *n* [imit.] **1 :** a short crisp sound **2 :** an image on a radar screen **3 :** an interruption of the sound received in a television program as a result of blipping

2blip *vt* **blipped; blip·ping :** to remove (recorded sound) from a videotape so that there is an interruption of the sound in the received television program ⟨a censor *blipped* the swearwords⟩

bliss \'blis\ *n* [ME *blisse,* fr. OE *bliss;* akin to OE *blithe* blithe] **1 :** complete happiness **2 :** PARADISE, HEAVEN

bliss·ful \'blis-fəl\ *adj* **:** full of, marked by, or causing bliss — **bliss·ful·ly** \-fə-lē\ *adv* — **bliss·ful·ness** *n*

1blis·ter \'blis-tər\ *n* [ME, modif. of OF or MD; OF *blostre* boil, fr. MD *bluyster* blister; akin to OE *blǣst* blast] **1 :** an elevation of the epidermis containing watery liquid **2 :** an enclosed raised

ə abut ᵊ kitten ər further a back ā bake ä cot, cart
au̇ out ch chin e less ē easy g gift i trip ī life
j joke ŋ sing ō flow ȯ flaw ȯi coin th thin t͟h this
ü loot u̇ foot y yet yü few yu̇ furious zh vision

spot (as in paint) resembling a blister **3** : an agent that causes blistering **4** : a disease of plants marked by large swollen patches on the leaves **5** : any of various structures (as a gunner's compartment on an airplane) that bulge out — **blis·tery** \-t(ə-)rē\ *adj*

[2]**blister** *vb* **blis·tered; blis·ter·ing** \-t(ə-)riŋ\ *vi* : to become affected with a blister ~ *vt* **1** : to raise a blister on **2** : to deal with severely ⟨~*ed* his opponent with charges of corruption⟩

blister beetle *n* : a beetle (as the Spanish fly) used medicinally dried and powdered to raise blisters on the skin; *broadly* : any of numerous soft-bodied beetles (family Meloidae)

blister copper *n* : metallic copper of a black blistered surface that is the product of converting copper matte and is about 98.5 to 99.5 percent pure

blis·ter·ing *adj* : extremely intense or severe — **blistering** *adv* — **blis·ter·ing·ly** \-t(ə-)riŋ-lē\ *adv*

blister rust *n* : any of several diseases of pines that are caused by rust fungi (genus *Cronartium*) in the aecial stage and that affect the sapwood and inner bark and produce blisters externally

blithe \'blīth, 'blīth\ *adj* **blith·er; blith·est** [ME, fr. OE *blīthe;* akin to OHG *blīdi* joyous, OE *bǣl* fire — more at BALD] **1** : of a happy lighthearted character or disposition ⟨hail to thee, ~ spirit — P. B. Shelley⟩ **2** : CASUAL, HEEDLESS ⟨~ unconcern⟩ ***syn*** see MERRY ***ant*** morose, atrabilious — **blithe·ly** *adv*

blith·er \'blith-ər\ *vi* : BLATHER

blithe·some \'blīth-səm, 'blīth-\ *adj* : GAY, MERRY — **blithe·some·ly** *adv*

BLitt *or* **BLit** *abbr* [ML *baccalaureus litterarum*] bachelor of letters; bachelor of literature

blitz \'blits\ *n* **1 a** : BLITZKRIEG 1 **b** (1) : an intensive aerial campaign (2) : AIR RAID **2 a** : an intensive nonmilitary campaign **b** : a rush of the passer by the defensive linebackers in football — **blitz** *vb*

blitz·krieg \-,krēg\ *n* [G, lit., lightning war, fr. *blitz* lightning + *krieg* war] **1** : war conducted with great speed and force; *specif* : a violent surprise offensive by massed air forces and mechanized ground forces in close coordination **2** : a sudden overpowering bombardment

bliz·zard \'bliz-ərd\ *n* [origin unknown] **1** : a long severe snowstorm **2** : an intensely strong cold wind filled with fine snow **3** : an overwhelming rush or deluge ⟨the ~ of mail at Christmas⟩ — **bliz·zardy** \-ē\ *adj*

blk *abbr* **1** black **2** block **3** bulk

[1]**bloat** \'blōt\ *adj* [alter. of ME *blout*] : BLOATED, PUFFY

[2]**bloat** *vt* **1** : to make turgid or swollen **2** : to fill to capacity or overflowing ~ *vi* : SWELL

[3]**bloat** *n* **1** : one that is bloated **2** : a flatulent digestive disturbance of domestic animals and esp. cattle marked by abdominal bloating

bloat·ed *adj* **1** : being much larger than what is warranted ⟨a ~ estimate⟩ **2** : obnoxiously vain

[1]**bloat·er** \'blōt-ər\ *n* [obs. *bloat* (to cure)] : a large fat herring or mackerel lightly salted and briefly smoked

[2]**bloater** *n* [[2]*bloat*] : a small but common cisco (*Coregonus hoyi*) of the Great Lakes

[1]**blob** \'bläb\ *n* [ME] **1 a** : a small drop or lump of something viscid or thick **b** : a daub or spot of color **2** : something ill-defined or amorphous

[2]**blob** *vt* **blobbed; blob·bing** : to mark with blobs : SPLOTCH

bloc \'bläk\ *n* [F, lit., block] **1 a** : a temporary combination of parties in a legislative assembly **b** : a group of legislators (as in a U.S. legislative assembly) who act together for some common purpose irrespective of party lines **2 a** : a combination of persons, groups, or nations forming a unit with a common interest or purpose **b** : a group of nations united by treaty or agreement for mutual support or joint action

[1]**block** \'bläk\ *n, often attrib* [ME *blok,* fr. MF *bloc,* fr. MD *blok;* akin to OHG *bloh* block, MIr *blog* fragment] **1** : a compact usu. solid piece of substantial material esp. when worked or altered from its natural state to serve a particular purpose: as **a** : the piece of wood on which a person condemned to be beheaded lays his neck for execution **b** : a mold or form on which articles are shaped or displayed **c** : a hollow rectangular building unit usu. of artificial material **d** : a light weight usu. cubical and solid wooden or plastic building toy that is usu. provided in sets **e** : the casting that contains the cylinders of an internal-combustion engine **2** *slang* : HEAD 1 **3 a** : OBSTACLE **b** : an obstruction of an opponent's play in sports; *esp* : a halting or impeding of the progress or movement of an opponent in football by use of the body **c** : interruption of normal physiological function of a tissue or organ; *esp* : HEART BLOCK **d** : an instance or the result of psychological blockage or blocking **4** : a wooden or metal case enclosing one or more pulleys and having a hook, eye, or strap by which it may be attached **5** : a platform from which property is sold at auction; *broadly* : sale at auction **6 a** : a quantity, number, or section of things dealt with as a unit **b** (1) : a large building divided into separate functional units (2) : a line of row houses (3) : a part of a building or integrated group of buildings distinctive in some respect **c** (1) : a usu. rectangular space (as in a city) enclosed by streets and occupied by or intended for buildings (2) : the distance along one of the sides of such a block **d** : a length of railroad track of defined limits the use of which is governed by block signals **7** : a piece of material (as wood or linoleum) having on its surface a hand-cut design from which impressions are to be printed

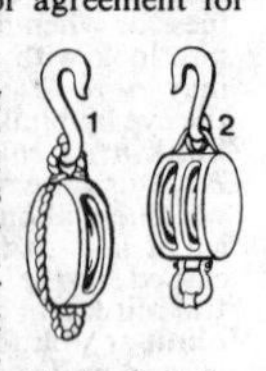

blocks 4: *1* single block, *2* double block

[2]**block** *vt* **1 a** : to make unsuitable for passage or progress by obstruction **b** *archaic* : BLOCKADE **c** : to hinder the passage, progress, or accomplishment of by or as if by interposing an obstruction ⟨~ a kick⟩ **d** : to shut off from view ⟨forest canopy ~*ing* the sun⟩ **e** : to interfere usu. legitimately with (as an opponent) in various games or sports **f** : to prevent normal functioning of **g** : to prohibit conversion of (foreign-held funds) into foreign exchange; *also* : to limit the use to be made of (such funds) within the country **2** : to mark or indicate the outline or chief lines of ⟨~ out a design⟩ ⟨~ in a sketched figure⟩ **3** : to shape on, with, or as if with a block ⟨~ a hat⟩ **4** : to make (two or more lines of writing or type) flush at the left or at both left and right **5** : to secure, support, or provide with a block **6** : to work out or chart the movements of stage performers or of mobile television equipment ~ *vi* : to block an opponent in sports ***syn*** see HINDER — **block·er** *n*

[1]**block·ade** \blä-'kād\ *n* **1** : the isolation by a warring nation of a particular enemy area (as a harbor) by means of troops or warships to prevent passage of persons or supplies; *broadly* : a restrictive measure designed to obstruct the commerce and communications of an unfriendly nation **2** : something that constitutes an obstacle **3** : interruption of normal physiological function (as transmission of nerve impulses) of a tissue or organ

[2]**blockade** *vt* **block·ad·ed; block·ad·ing** **1** : to subject to a blockade **2** : BLOCK, OBSTRUCT — **block·ad·er** *n*

block·ade–run·ner \-'kād-,rən-ər\ *n* : a ship or person that runs through a blockade — **block·ade–run·ning** \-,rən-iŋ\ *n*

block·age \'bläk-ij\ *n* : an act or instance of obstructing : the state of being blocked ⟨a ~ in the saltshaker⟩

block and tackle *n* : pulley blocks with associated rope or cable for hoisting or hauling

block·bust·er \'bläk-,bəs-tər\ *n* **1** : a huge high-explosive demolition bomb **2** : one that is notably effective or violent **3** : one who engages in blockbusting

block·bust·ing \-tiŋ\ *n* : profiteering by inducing property owners to sell hastily and often at a loss by appeals to fears of depressed values because of threatened minority encroachment and then reselling at inflated prices

block diagram *n* : a diagram (as of a system, process, or program) in which labeled figures (as rectangles) and interconnecting lines represent the relationship of parts

block·head \'bläk-,hed\ *n* : a stupid person

block·house \-,hau̇s\ *n* **1 a** : a structure of heavy timbers formerly used for military defense with sides loopholed and pierced for gunfire and often with a projecting upper story **b** : a small easily defended building for protection from enemy fire **2** : a building usu. of reinforced concrete serving as an observation point for an operation likely to be accompanied by heat, blast, or radiation hazard

block·ish \-ish\ *adj* : resembling a block — **block·ish·ly** *adv*

block letter *n* : an often hand-drawn bold simple capital letter composed of strokes of uniform thickness

block plane *n* : a small plane made with the blade set at a lower pitch than other planes and used chiefly on end grains of wood

block signal *n* : a fixed signal at the entrance of a block to govern railroad trains entering and using that block

block system *n* : a system by which a railroad track is divided into short sections and trains are run by guidance signals

blocky \'bläk-ē\ *adj* **block·i·er; -est** **1** : resembling a block in form or massiveness : CHUNKY **2** : filled with or made up of blocks or patches

bloke \'blōk\ *n* [origin unknown] *chiefly Brit* : MAN, FELLOW

[1]**blond** *or* **blonde** \'bländ\ *adj* [F *blond,* masc., *blonde,* fem.] **1 a** : of a flaxen, golden, light auburn, or pale yellowish brown color ⟨~ hair⟩ **b** : of a pale white or rosy white color ⟨~ skin⟩ **c** : being a blond ⟨a pretty ~ secretary⟩ **2 a** : of a light color **b** : of the color blond **c** : made light-colored by bleaching ⟨a table of ~ walnut⟩

[2]**blond** *or* **blonde** *n* **1** : a person having blond hair and usu. a light complexion and blue or gray eyes **2** : a light yellowish brown to dark grayish yellow

blond·ish \'blän-dish\ *adj* : somewhat blond

[1]**blood** \'bləd\ *n, often attrib* [ME, fr. OE *blōd;* akin to OHG *bluot* blood] **1 a** : the fluid that circulates in the heart, arteries, capillaries, and veins of a vertebrate animal carrying nourishment and oxygen to and bringing away waste products from all parts of the body **b** : a comparable fluid of an invertebrate **c** : a fluid resembling blood **2 a** : LIFEBLOOD; *broadly* : LIFE **b** : human stock or lineage; *esp* : royal lineage ⟨a prince of the ~⟩ **c** : relationship by descent from a common ancestor : KINSHIP **d** : persons related through common descent : KINDRED **e** (1) : honorable or high birth or descent (2) : descent from parents of recognized breed or pedigree **3** : the shedding of blood; *also* : the taking of life **4 a** : blood regarded as the seat of the emotions : TEMPER **b** *obs* : LUST **c** : a gay showy foppish man : RAKE **5** : PERSONNEL

[2]**blood** *vt* **1** : BLEED 1a **2** : to stain or wet with blood **3** : to expose (a hunting dog) to sight, scent, or taste of the blood of its prey

blood bank *n* : a place for storage of or an institution storing blood or plasma; *also* : blood so stored

blood·bath \'bləd-,bath, -,bȧth\ *n* : a great slaughter : MASSACRE

blood brother *n* **1** : a brother by birth **2** : one of two men pledged to mutual loyalty by a ceremonial use of each other's blood — **blood brotherhood** *n*

blood cell *n* : a cell normally present in blood

blood count *n* : the determination of the blood cells in a definite volume of blood; *also* : the number of cells so determined

blood·cur·dling \'bləd-,kərd-liŋ, -ᵊl-iŋ\ *adj* : arousing horror ⟨~ screams⟩ — **blood·cur·dling·ly** \-,kərd-liŋ-lē\ *adv*

blood·ed \'bləd-əd\ *adj* : being entirely or largely of superior breed ⟨a herd of ~ stock⟩

-blooded *adj comb form* : having (such) blood or temperament ⟨cold-*blooded*⟩ ⟨warm-*blooded*⟩

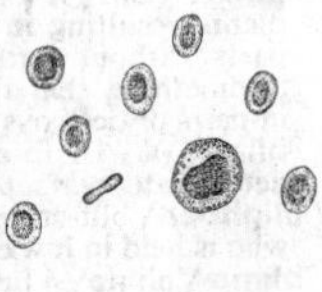
blood cells

blood feud *n* : a feud between different clans or families

blood·fin \'bləd-,fin\ *n* : a small silvery So. American fish (*Aphyocharax rubripinnis*) with deep-red fins

blood fluke *n* : SCHISTOSOME

blood group n : one of the classes into which human beings can be separated on the basis of the presence or absence in their blood of specific antigens — called also *blood type*

blood-guilt \'blɔd-ˌgilt\ n : guilt resulting from bloodshed — **blood-guilt·i·ness** \-ˌgil-tē-nəs\ n — **blood-guilty** \-tē\ adj

blood heat n : a temperature approximating that of the human body

blood-hound \'blɔd-ˌhau̇nd\ n 1 : a large powerful hound of a breed of European origin remarkable for acuteness of smell 2 : a person keen in pursuit

blood-less \'blɔd-ləs\ adj 1 : deficient in or free from blood 2 : not accompanied by loss or shedding of blood ⟨a ~ victory⟩ 3 : lacking in spirit or vitality ⟨~ young people with no spirit of fun⟩ 4 : lacking in human feeling ⟨~ statistics⟩ — **blood-less-ly** adv — **blood-less-ness** n

blood-let-ting \-ˌlet-iŋ\ n 1 : PHLEBOTOMY 2 : BLOODSHED 3 : attrition of personnel or resources

blood-line \-ˌlīn\ n : a sequence of direct ancestors esp. in a pedigree; also : FAMILY, STRAIN

blood-mo-bile \-mō-ˌbēl\ n [blood + automobile] : an automotive vehicle staffed and equipped for collecting blood from donors

blood money n 1 : money obtained at the cost of another's life 2 : money paid by a manslayer or members of his family, clan, or tribe to the next of kin of a person killed by him

blood platelet n : one of the minute protoplasmic disks of vertebrate blood that assist in blood clotting

blood poisoning n : SEPTICEMIA

blood pressure n : pressure exerted by the blood upon the walls of the blood vessels and esp. arteries varying with the muscular efficiency of the heart, the blood volume and viscosity, the age and health of the individual, and the state of the vascular wall

blood-red \'blɔd-'red\ adj : having the color of blood

blood-root \-ˌrüt, -ˌruṫ\ n : a plant (*Sanguinaria canadensis*) of the poppy family having a red root and sap and bearing a solitary lobed leaf and white flower in early spring

blood sausage n : very dark sausage containing a large proportion of blood — called also *blood pudding*

blood serum n : blood plasma from which the fibrin has been removed

blood-shed \'blɔd-ˌshed\ n 1 : the shedding of blood 2 : the taking of life : SLAUGHTER

blood-shot \-ˌshät\ adj, of an eye : inflamed to redness

blood-stain \-ˌstān\ n : a discoloration caused by blood

blood-stained \-ˌstānd\ adj : stained with blood 2 : involved with slaughter ⟨a ~ chronicle of war⟩

blood-stock \-ˌstäk\ n : horses of Thoroughbred breeding esp. when used for racing

blood-stone \-ˌstōn\ n : a green chalcedony sprinkled with red spots resembling blood

blood-stream \-ˌstrēm\ n 1 : ,the flowing blood in a circulatory system 2 : a mainstream of power or vitality ⟨introduce into the economic ~ a large amount of money — *Harper's*⟩

blood-suck-er \-ˌsək-ər\ n 1 : an animal that sucks blood; esp : LEECH 2 : a person who sponges or preys on another — **blood-suck-ing** \-iŋ\ adj

blood sugar n : the glucose in the blood; also : its concentration (as in milligrams per 100 milliliters)

blood test n : a test of the blood; esp : a serologic test for syphilis

blood-thirsty \'blɔd-ˌthər-stē\ adj : eager for or marked by the shedding of blood — **blood-thirst·i·ly** \-stə-lē\ adj — **blood-thirst·i·ness** \-stē-nəs\ n

blood-type \-ˌtīp\ vt : to determine the blood group of

blood vessel n : a vessel in which blood circulates in an animal

blood-worm \'blɔd-ˌwərm\ n 1 : any of various reddish annelid worms often used as bait 2 : the red aquatic larva of some midges

blood-wort \-ˌwərt, -ˌwȯ(ə)rt\ n : any of a family (Haemodoraceae, the bloodwort family) of perennial herbs with a deep red coloring matter in the roots

¹bloody \'blɔd-ē\ adj **blood·i·er; -est** 1 : containing or made up of blood 2 : of or contained in the blood 2 : smeared or stained with blood 3 : accompanied by or involving bloodshed; esp : marked by great slaughter 4 a : MURDEROUS b : MERCILESS, CRUEL 5 : BLOODRED 6 — used as an intensive; sometimes considered vulgar — **blood·i·ly** \'blɔd-ʹl-ē\ adv — **blood·i·ness** \'blɔd-ē-nəs\ n

²bloody vt **blood·ied; bloody·ing** : to make bloody or bloodred

³bloody adv — used as an intensive; sometimes considered vulgar

Bloody Mary, pl **Bloody Marys** [prob. fr. *Bloody Mary*, appellation of Mary I of England] : a cocktail consisting essentially of vodka and tomato juice

bloody–mind·ed·ness \ˌblɔd-ē-'mīn-dəd-nəs\ n 1 : willingness to accept violence or bloodshed 2 : CONTRARIETY, CANTANKEROUSNESS — **bloody-minded** adj

bloody shirt n : a means employed to stir up or revive party or sectional animosity

¹bloom \'blüm\ n [ME *blome* lump of metal, fr. OE *blōma*] 1 : a mass of wrought iron from the forge or puddling furnace 2 : a bar of iron or steel hammered or rolled from an ingot

²bloom n [ME *blome*, fr. ON *blōm*; akin to OE *blōwan* to blossom — more at BLOW] 1 a : FLOWER ⟨green leaves with large yellow ~s⟩ ⟨the apple trees had a very light ~ this spring⟩ b : the flowering state ⟨the roses in ~⟩ c : a period of flowering ⟨the spring ~⟩ d : an excessive growth of plankton 2 : a state or time of beauty, freshness, and vigor 3 : a surface coating or appearance: as a : a delicate powdery coating on some fruits and leaves b : a rosy appearance of the cheeks; broadly : an outward evidence of freshness or healthy vigor c : the grainy or powdery surface of a newly minted coin d : a cloudiness on a film of varnish or lacquer e : glare caused by an object reflecting too much light into a television camera 4 : BOUQUET 3a

³bloom vi 1 a : to produce or yield flowers b : to support abundant plant life ⟨make the desert ~⟩ 2 a : to flourish in youthful beauty, freshness or excellence b : to shine out : GLOW 3 : to appear or occur unexpectedly or in surprising quantity or

degree 4 : to become densely populated with microorganisms and esp. plankton — used of bodies of water ~ vt 1 obs : to cause to bloom 2 : to give bloom to

¹bloom·er \'blü-mər\ n 1 : a plant that blooms 2 : a person who reaches full competence or maturity 3 : a stupid blunder

²bloom·er \'blü-mər\ n [Amelia *Bloomer* †1894 Am pioneer in feminism] 1 : a costume for women consisting of a short skirt and long loose trousers gathered closely about the ankles 2 pl a : full loose trousers gathered at the knee formerly worn by women for athletics b : underpants of similar design worn chiefly by girls

bloom·ing \'blü-mən, -miŋ\ adj [prob. euphemism for *bloody*] chiefly Brit — used as a generalized intensive ⟨~ fool⟩

bloomy \'blü-mē\ adj 1 : full of bloom 2 : covered with bloom ⟨~ red plums —Elizabeth Bowen⟩ 3 : showing freshness or vitality ⟨all the ~ flush of life is fled —Oliver Goldsmith⟩

¹bloop \'blüp\ vt [prob. fr. *bloop* (an unpleasing sound)] : to hit (a fly ball) usu. just beyond the infield in baseball ⟨~ed a single to center field⟩

²bloop adj, of a baseball : hit in the air just beyond the infield

bloop·er \'blü-pər\ n [*bloop* (an unpleasing sound)] 1 : an embarrassing public blunder 2 a : a high baseball pitch lobbed to the batter b : a fly ball hit barely beyond a baseball infield

¹blos·som \'bläs-əm\ n [ME *blosme*, fr. OE *blōstm*; akin to OE *blōwan*] 1 a : the flower of a seed plant (apple ~s) b : the mass of bloom on a single plant; also : the state of bearing flowers 2 : a peak period or stage of development — **blos·somy** \-ə-mē\ adj

bloomer 1

²blossom vi 1 : BLOOM 2 a : to come into one's own : DEVELOP ⟨a ~ing talent⟩ b : to become evident : make an appearance

¹blot \'blät\ n [ME] 1 : a soiling or disfiguring mark : SPOT 2 : a mark of reproach : moral flaw

²blot vb **blot·ted; blot·ting** vt 1 : to spot, stain, or spatter with a discoloring substance 2 : to make obscure : ECLIPSE — usu. used with out 3 obs : MAR; esp : to stain with infamy 4 a : to dry with an absorbing agent (as blotting paper) b : to remove by blotting the surface ~ vi 1 : to make a blot 2 : to become marked with a blot — **blot one's copybook** : to do something that detracts from one's record or standing

³blot n [origin unknown] 1 : a backgammon man exposed to capture 2 archaic : a weak or exposed point

¹blotch \'bläch\ n [prob. alter. of *botch*] 1 : IMPERFECTION, BLEMISH 2 : a spot or mark (as of color or ink) esp. when large or irregular — **blotch·i·ly** \'bläch-ə-lē\ — **blotchy** \'bläch-ē\ adj

²blotch vt : to mark or mar with blotches

blot out vt 1 : to make insignificant or inconsequential ⟨this one good act blots out many bad ones⟩ 2 : to wipe out : DESTROY ⟨one such bomb can blot out a city⟩ syn see ERASE

blot·ter \'blät-ər\ n 1 : a piece of blotting paper 2 : a book in which entries (as of transactions or occurrences) are made temporarily pending their transfer to permanent record books ⟨police ~⟩

blotting paper n : a soft spongy unsized paper used to absorb ink

¹blouse \'blau̇s also 'blau̇z; many say 'blau̇z but 'blau̇-zəz\ n [F] 1 : a loose overgarment that resembles a shirt or smock, varies from hip-length to calf-length, and is worn esp. by workmen, artists, and peasants 2 : a usu. loose-fitting garment that covers the body from the neck to the waist and is worn esp. by women

²blouse vb **bloused; blous·ing** vi : to fall in a fold ⟨coats that ~ above the hip⟩ ~ vt : to cause to blouse ⟨trousers are *bloused* over the boots⟩

blou·son \'blau̇-ˌsän, 'blü-ˌzän\ n [F, fr. *blouse*] : a woman's garment (as a dress or blouse) having a close waistband with blousing of material over it

¹blow \'blō\ vb **blew** \'blü\; **blown** \'blōn\; **blow·ing** [ME *blowen*, fr. OE *blāwan*; akin to OHG *blāen* to blow, L *flare*, Gk *phallos* penis] vi 1 of air : to move with speed or force 2 : to send forth a current of air or other gas 3 a : to make a sound by or as if by blowing b of a wind instrument : SOUND 4 a : BOAST b : to talk windily 5 : PANT, GASP ⟨the horse blew heavily⟩ b of a cetacean : to eject moisture-laden air from the lungs through the blowhole 6 : to move or be carried by or as if by wind 7 of an electric fuse : to melt when overloaded — usu. used with out 8 of a tire : to release the contained air through a spontaneous rupture — usu. used with out ~ vt 1 a : to set (gas or vapor) in motion b : to act on with a current of gas or vapor 2 : to play or sound on (a wind instrument) 3 a : to spread by report b : DAMN, DISREGARD ⟨~ the expense⟩ 4 a : to drive with a current of gas or vapor b : to clear of contents by forcible passage of a current of air 5 a : to distend with or as if with gas b : to produce by the action of blown or injected air ⟨~ing bubbles⟩ ⟨~ glass⟩ 6 of insects : to deposit eggs or larvae on or in 7 a : to shatter, burst, or destroy by explosion 8 a : to put out of breath with exertion b : to let (as a horse) pause to catch the breath 9 a : to spend (money) recklessly b : to treat with unusual expenditure ⟨I'll ~ you to a steak⟩ 10 : to cause (a fuse) to blow 11 : to rupture by too much pressure ⟨*blew* a gasket⟩ 12 : to fail in using to an advantage : MUFF ⟨*blew* his chance⟩ 13 : to leave hurriedly ⟨*blew* town⟩ 14 : to propel with great force or ⟨*blew* a fast ball by the batter⟩ — **blow hot and cold** : to favorable at one moment and adverse the next — **blow in** : to appear or arrive at casually or unexpectedly ⟨*blew* into tow

— **blow one's cool** : to lose one's composure — **blow one's top** *or* **blow one's stack** 1 : to become violently angry 2 : to go crazy — **blow the mind of** : to overwhelm with wonder or bafflement — **blow the whistle on** 1 : to bring (something covert) into the open 2 : to inform against

²**blow** *n* 1 : a blowing of wind esp. when strong or violent 2 : BRAG, BOASTING 3 : an act or instance of blowing 4 a : the time during which air is forced through molten metal to refine it b : the quantity of metal refined during that time

³**blow** *vi* **blew** \'blü\; **blown** \'blōn\; **blow·ing** [ME *blowen,* fr. OE *blōwan;* akin to OHG *bluoen* to bloom, L *flōrēre* to bloom, *flor-, flos* flower] : FLOWER, BLOOM

⁴**blow** *n* 1 : ²BLOOM 1b ⟨lilacs in full ~⟩ 2 : BLOSSOMS ⟨peach ~⟩

⁵**blow** *n* [ME (northern dial.) *blaw*] 1 : a forcible stroke delivered with a part of the body or with an instrument 2 : a hostile act or state ⟨come to ~s⟩ 3 : a forcible or sudden act or effort : ASSAULT 4 : an unfortunate or calamitous happening ⟨failure to land the job came as a ~⟩

blow-by-blow \-,bī-, -bə-\ *adj* : minutely detailed ⟨a ~ account⟩

blow·er \'blō(-ə)r\ *n* 1 : one that blows 2 : BRAGGART 3 : a device for producing a current of air or gas ⟨snow ~⟩

blow·fish \-,fish\ *n* : PUFFER 2

blow·fly \-,flī\ *n* : any of various two-winged flies (family Calliphoridae) that deposit their eggs or maggots esp. on meat or in wounds; *esp* : a widely distributed bluebottle (*Calliphora vicina*)

blow·gun \-,gən\ *n* : a tube through which a projectile (as a dart) may be impelled by the force of the breath

blow·hard \-,härd\ *n* : BRAGGART

blow·hole \-,hōl\ *n* 1 : a hole in metal caused by a bubble of gas captured during solidification 2 : a nostril in the top of the head of a whale or other cetacean 3 : a hole in the ice to which aquatic mammals (as seals) come to breathe

blow in *vi* : to arrive casually or unexpectedly

blown \'blōn\ *adj* [ME *blowen,* fr. pp. of *blowen* to blow] 1 : SWOLLEN; *esp* : afflicted with bloat 2 : FLYBLOWN 3 : being out of breath

blow off *vt* : to relieve by vigorous speech or action — **blow off steam** : to release pent-up emotions

blow·out \'blō-,aút\ *n* 1 : a festive social affair 2 a : a bursting of a container (as a tire) by pressure of the contents on a weak spot b : a hole made in a container by such bursting 3 : an uncontrolled eruption of an oil or gas well

blow out \(')blō-'aút\ *vi* 1 : to become extinguished by a gust 2 : to erupt out of control — used of an oil or gas well ~ *vt* 1 : to extinguish by a gust 2 : to dissipate (itself) by blowing — used of storms

blow over *vi* : to pass away without effect

blow·pipe \'blō-,pīp\ *n* 1 : a small tubular instrument for directing a jet of air or other gas into a flame so as to concentrate and increase the heat 2 : a tubular instrument used for revealing or cleaning a bodily cavity by forcing air into it 3 : BLOWGUN 4 : a long metal tube on the end of which a glassmaker gathers a quantity of molten glass and through which he blows to expand and shape it

blow·sy *also* **blow·zy** \'blaú-zē\ *adj* [E dial. *blowse, blowze* (wench)] 1 : being coarse and ruddy of complexion 2 : having a sloppy appearance or aspect : FROWSY

blow·torch \'blō-,tórch\ *n* : a small burner having a device to intensify combustion by means of a blast of air or oxygen, usu. including a fuel tank pressurized by a hand pump, and used esp. in plumbing

blow·tube \-,t(y)üb\ *n* 1 : BLOWGUN 2 : BLOWPIPE 4

blow·up \'blō-,əp\ *n* 1 : a blowing up: as a : EXPLOSION b : an outburst of temper c : a photographic enlargement

blow up \(')blō-'əp\ *vt* 1 : to rend apart, shatter, or destroy by explosion 2 : to build up or tout to an unreasonable extent ⟨advertisers *blowing up* their products⟩ 3 : to bring into existence by blowing of wind ⟨it may *blow up* a storm⟩ 4 : to fill up with a gas and esp. air ⟨*blow up* a balloon⟩ 5 : to make a photographic enlargement of ~ *vi* 1 a : EXPLODE b : to be disrupted or destroyed (as by explosion) c : to lose self-control; *esp* : to become violently angry 2 a : to become filled with a gas and esp. air b : to become expanded to unreasonable proportions 3 : to become or come into being by or as if by blowing of wind

[blow]·ry \'blō-ē\ *adj* 1 : WINDY ⟨a ~ March day⟩ 2 : readily [bl]own about ⟨~ desert sand⟩

[ ]*br* 1 bachelor of liberal studies 2 bachelor of library science

[ ] Bureau of Labor Statistics

[ ]bacon, lettuce, and tomato sandwich

[blu]b \'bləb-ər\ *n* [ME *bluber* bubble, foam, prob. of imit. origin] 1 : the fat of whales and other large marine mammals 2 [ ] fat on the body 3 : the action of blubbering

[blub]·bered; blub·ber·ing \'bləb-(ə-)riŋ\ [ME *blubren*] bubbling sound, fr. *bluber*] *vi* 1 : to weep noisily ~ *vt* 1 [ ]distort, or wet with weeping 2 : to utter while weeping [ ] : puffed out : THICK ⟨~ lips⟩

[ ]bləb-(ə-)rē\ *adj* : ³BLUBBER

[ ] : having or characterized by blubber

[ ]-chər *also* -kər\ *n* [G. L. von *Blücher*] : a shoe having [ ]d vamp cut in one piece and the quarters lapped over [ ] laced together for closing

[ ]bləj-ən\ *n* [origin unknown] 1 : a short stick that [ ] thick or loaded end and is used as a weapon 2 [ ]sed to attack or bully ⟨the ~ of satire⟩

[ ]1 : to hit with heavy impact 2 : to overcome by [ ]ment

[ ] **blu·er; blu·est** [ME, fr. OF *blou,* of Gmc origin; [ ]*lāo* blue; akin to L *flavus* yellow, OE *bǣl* fire — [ ]**1** : of the color blue 2 a : BLUISH b : LIVID ⟨~ [ ]loluish gray ⟨~ cat⟩ 4 : low in spirits : MELANCHOLY; *also* : DEPRESSING ⟨a ~ funk⟩ ⟨things [ ]b :wearing blue 5 *of a woman* : LEARNED, INTELLECTUAL 7 a : PROFANE, INDECENT ⟨~ language⟩ [ ]QUÉ ⟨~ jokes⟩ 8 : of or relating to blues singing

⟨a ~ song⟩ — **blue in the face** : extremely exasperated — **blue·ly** *adv* — **blue·ness** *n*

²**blue** *n* 1 : a color whose hue is that of the clear sky or that of the portion of the color spectrum lying between green and violet 2 a : a pigment or dye that colors blue b : BLUING 3 a : blue clothing or cloth b *pl* : a blue costume or uniform 4 : one who wears a blue uniform: as a : a soldier in the Union army during the American Civil War b : the Union army 5 a (1) : SKY (2) : the far distance b : SEA 6 : a blue object 7 : BLUESTOCKING 8 : any of numerous small chiefly blue butterflies (family Lycaenidae) 9 : BLUEFISH — **out of the blue** : without advance notice : UNEXPECTEDLY ⟨a job offer that came *out of the blue*⟩

³**blue** *vb* **blued; blu·ing** *or* **blue·ing** *vt* : to make blue ~ *vi* : to turn blue

blue baby *n* : an infant with a bluish tint usu. from a congenital defect of the heart in which mingling of venous and arterial blood occurs

blue·beard \'blü-,bi(ə)rd\ *n* [*Bluebeard,* a fairy-tale character] : a man who marries and kills one wife after another

blue·bell \-,bel\ *n* 1 : any of various bellflowers; *esp* : HAREBELL 1 2 : any of various plants bearing blue bell-shaped flowers: as a : the European wood hyacinth or grape hyacinth b : a low tufted New Zealand plant (*Wahlenbergia gracilis,* family Campanulaceae) 3 : a blue-flowered columbine

blue·ber·ry \'blü-,ber-ē, -b(ə-)rē\ *n* : the edible blue or blackish berry of any of several plants (genus *Vaccinium*) of the heath family; *also* : a low or tall shrub producing these berries

blue·bird \-,bərd\ *n* : any of several small No. American songbirds (genus *Sialia*) related to the robin but more or less blue above

blue-black \-'blak\ *adj* : being of a dark bluish hue

blue blood *n* 1 \'blü-'bləd\ : membership in a noble or socially prominent family 2 \-,bləd\ : a member of a noble or socially prominent family — **blue-blood·ed** \-'bləd-əd\ *adj*

blue-bon·net \'blü-,bän-ət\ *n* 1 a : a wide flat round cap of blue wool formerly worn in Scotland b : one that wears such a cap; *specif* : SCOT 2 : a low-growing annual lupine of Texas with silky foliage and blue flowers usu. classified as a single variable species (*Lupinus subcarnosus*)

blue book *n* 1 : a book of specialized information often published under government auspices 2 : a register esp. of socially prominent persons 3 : a blue-covered booklet used for writing examinations

blue-bot·tle \'blü-,bät-²l\ *n* 1 a : BACHELOR'S BUTTON b : GRAPE HYACINTH 2 : any of several blowflies that have the abdomen or the whole body iridescent blue in color and that make a loud buzzing noise in flight

blue cat *n* : a large bluish catfish (*Ictalurus furcatus*) of the Mississippi valley that may exceed 100 pounds in weight

blue cheese *n* : cheese ripened by and marked with veins of greenish blue mold

blue chip *n* 1 a : a stock issue of high investment quality that usu. pertains to a substantial well-established company and enjoys public confidence in its worth and stability b : a consistently successful and profitable venture or enterprise 2 : an outstandingly worthwhile or valuable property or asset — **blue-chip** *adj*

blue·coat \'blü-,kōt\ *n* : one that wears a blue coat: as a : a Union soldier during the Civil War b : POLICEMAN

blue cohosh *n* : a perennial herb (*Caulophyllum thalictroides*) of the barberry family that has greenish yellow or purplish flowers and large blue fruits like berries

blue-col·lar \'blü-'käl-ər\ *adj* : of, relating to, or constituting the class of wage earners whose duties call for the wearing of work clothes or protective clothing — compare WHITE-COLLAR

blue crab *n* : any of several largely blue swimming crabs; *esp* : an edible crab (*Callinectes sapidus*) of the Atlantic and Gulf coasts

blue curls *n pl but sing or pl in constr* : a mint (genus *Trichostema*) with irregular blue flowers

blue devils *n pl* : low spirits : DESPONDENCY

blue-eyed grass \,blü-,īd-\ *n* : a plant (genus *Sisyrinchium*) of the iris family with grasslike foliage and delicate blue flowers

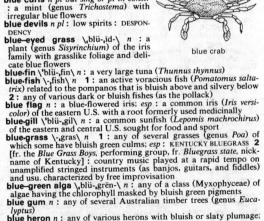

blue crab

blue-fin \'blü-,fin\ *n* : a very large tuna (*Thunnus thynnus*)

blue-fish \-,fish\ *n* 1 : an active voracious fish (*Pomatomus saltatrix*) related to the pompanos that is bluish above and silvery below 2 : any of various dark or bluish fishes (as the pollack)

blue flag *n* : a blue-flowered iris; *esp* : a common iris (*Iris versicolor*) of the eastern U.S. with a root formerly used medicinally

blue·gill \'blü-,gil\ *n* : a common sunfish (*Lepomis macrochirus*) of the eastern and central U.S. sought for food and sport

blue·grass \-,gras\ *n* 1 : any of several grasses (genus *Poa*) of which some have bluish green culms; *esp* : KENTUCKY BLUEGRASS 2 [fr. the *Blue Grass Boys,* performing group, fr. *Bluegrass state,* nickname of Kentucky] : country music played at a rapid tempo on unamplified stringed instruments (as banjos, guitars, and fiddles) and usu. characterized by free improvisation

blue-green alga \,blü-,grēn-\ *n* : any of a class (Myxophyceae) of algae having the chlorophyll masked by bluish green pigments

blue gum *n* : any of several Australian timber trees (genus *Eucalyptus*)

blue heron *n* : any of various herons with bluish or slaty plumage; *esp* : GREAT BLUE HERON

blue·jack \'blü-,jak\ *n* [*blue* + *jack* (as in *blackjack*)] : an oak (*Quercus cinerea*) of the southern U.S. with entire leaves and small acorns

blue·jack·et \-,jak-ət\ *n* : an enlisted man in the navy : SAILOR

blue jay \-,jā\ *n* : JAY 1b

blue jeans *n pl* : pants usu. made of blue denim

blue law n **1** : one of numerous extremely rigorous laws designed to regulate morals and conduct in colonial New England **2** : a statute regulating work, commerce, and amusements on Sundays

blue line n : either of two blue lines that divide an ice-hockey rink into three equal zones and that separate the offensive and defensive zones from the center-ice neutral zone

blue mold n **1** : a fungus (genus *Penicillium*) that produces blue or blue-green surface growths **2** : a disease of tobacco seedlings caused by a fungus (*Peronospora tabacina*) and characterized by yellowish spots and bluish gray mildew on the underside of the leaves

blue moon n : a very long period of time ⟨once in a *blue moon*⟩

blue·nose \'blü-,nōz\ n : one who advocates a rigorous moral code

blue note n [fr. its frequent use in blues music] : a flatted third or seventh note in a chord where a major interval would be expected

blue–pen·cil \-'pen(t)-səl\ vt : to edit by corrective change or deletion — **blue pen·cil·er** n

blue pe·ter \-'pēt-ər\ n : a blue signal flag with a white square in the center used to indicate that a merchant vessel is ready to sail

blue pike n : PIKE PERCH: *esp* : WALLEYE

blue plate adj : being a main course (as of a meat with vegetables) offered typically at a special price in a restaurant ⟨*blue plate* luncheon⟩

blue·point \'blü-,point\ n [*Blue Point*, Long Island] : a small oyster typically from the south shore of Long Island

blue point \-,point\ n : a Siamese cat having a bluish cream body and dark gray points

blue·print \-,print\ n **1** : a photographic print in white on a bright blue ground used esp. for copying maps, mechanical drawings, and architects' plans **2** : a program of action ⟨a ~ for victory⟩ — **blueprint** vt

blue racer n : a blacksnake of a bluish green subspecies (*Coluber constrictor flaviventris*) occurring from Ohio to Texas

blue–ribbon adj : selected for quality, reputation, or authority ⟨a ~ committee⟩

blue ribbon n **1** : a blue ribbon awarded the first-place winner in a competition **2** : an honor or award gained for preeminence

blue–ribbon jury n : SPECIAL JURY

blues \'blüz\ n pl but sing or pl in constr **1** : low spirits : MELANCHOLY **2** : a song often of lamentation characterized by usu. 12-bar phrases, 3-line stanzas in which the words of the second line usu. repeat those of the first, and continual occurrence of blue notes in melody and harmony

blue–sky \'blü-'skī\ adj **1** : having little or no value ⟨~ stock⟩ **2** : having no practical application ⟨~ thinking⟩

blue–sky law n : a law providing for the regulation of the sale of securities (as stock)

blues·man \'blüz-mən\ n : one who plays or sings the blues

blue·stem \'blü-,stem\ n **1** : an important hay and forage grass (*Andropogon furcatus*) of the western U.S. with smooth bluish leaf sheaths and slender spikes borne in pairs or clusters **2** : LITTLE BLUESTEM

blue·stock·ing \-,stäk-iŋ\ n [*Bluestocking* society, 18th cent. literary clubs] : a woman having intellectual or literary interests

blue·stone \-,stōn\ n : a building or paving stone of bluish gray color; *specif* : a sandstone quarried near the Hudson river

blue streak n **1** : something that moves very fast **2** : a constant stream of words ⟨talked a *blue streak*⟩

blu·esy \'blü-zē\ adj : characterized by the musical patterns of the blues

blu·et \'blü-ət\ n [prob. fr. ¹*blue*] : an American plant (*Houstonia caerulea*) of the madder family with bluish flowers and tufted stems

blue·tongue \'blü-,təŋ\ n : a serious virus disease esp. of sheep characterized by hyperemia, cyanosis, and punctate hemorrhages and by swelling and sloughing of the epithelium esp. about the mouth and tongue

blue vitriol n : a hydrated copper sulfate CuSO₄·5H₂O

blue·weed \'blü-,wēd\ n **1** : a coarse prickly blue-flowered European weed (*Echium vulgare*) of the borage family naturalized in the U.S. **2** : a small perennial (*Helianthus ciliaris*) of the southwestern U.S. with blue-green or gray-green foliage

bluey \'blü-ē\ n [fr. the blue blanket commonly used to wrap the bundle] *Austral* **a** : a swagman's bundle of personal effects; *broadly* : a bag of clothing carried in travel

¹bluff \'bləf\ adj [obs. D *blaf* flat; akin to MLG *blaff* smooth] **1 a** : having a broad flattened front **b** : rising steeply with a broad flat or rounded front **2** : good-naturedly frank and outspoken — **bluff·ly** adv — **bluff·ness** n

syn BLUFF, BLUNT, BRUSQUE, CURT, CRUSTY, GRUFF *shared meaning element* : abrupt and unceremonious in manner or speech *ant* smooth, suave

²bluff n : a high steep bank : CLIFF

³bluff vb [prob. fr. D *bluffen* to boast, play a kind of card game] vt **1** : to deceive (an opponent) in cards by a bold bet on an inferior hand with the result that the opponent withdraws a winning hand **2 a** : to deter or frighten by pretense or a mere show of strength **b** : DECEIVE **c** : FEIGN ~ vi : to bluff someone — **bluff·er** n

⁴bluff n **1 a** : an act or instance of bluffing **b** : the practice of bluffing **2** : one who bluffs

blu·ing or **blue·ing** \'blü-iŋ\ n : a preparation used in laundering to counteract yellowing of white fabrics

blu·ish \'blü-ish\ adj : somewhat blue : having a tinge of blue — **blu·ish·ness** n

¹blun·der \'blən-dər\ vb **blun·dered; blun·der·ing** \-d(ə-)riŋ\ [ME *blundren*] vi **1** : to move unsteadily or confusedly **2** : to make a mistake through stupidity, ignorance, or carelessness ~ vt **1** : to utter stupidly, confusedly, or thoughtlessly **2** : to make a stupid, careless, or thoughtless mistake in — **blun·der·er** \-dər-ər\ n — **blun·der·ing·ly** \-d(ə-)riŋ-lē\ adv

²blunder n : a gross error or mistake resulting usu. from stupidity, ignorance, or carelessness *syn* see ERROR

blun·der·buss \'blən-dər-,bəs\ n [by folk etymology fr. obs. D *donderbus*, fr. D *donder* thunder + obs. D *bus* gun] **1** : an obso-

lete short firearm having a large bore and usu. a flaring muzzle **2** : a blundering person

blunderbuss 1

¹blunt \'blənt\ adj [ME] **1 a** : slow or deficient in feeling : INSENSITIVE **b** : obtuse in understanding or discernment : DULL **2** : having an edge or point that is not sharp **3 a** : abrupt in speech or manner **b** : being straight to the point : DIRECT *syn* **1** see DULL *ant* keen, sharp **2** see BLUFF *ant* tactful, subtle — **blunt·ly** adv — **blunt·ness** n

²blunt vt : to make less sharp or definite ~ vi : to become blunt

¹blur \'blər\ n [perh. akin to ME *bleren* to blear] **1** : a smear or stain that obscures **2** : something that is vague or lacking definite outline or distinct character

²blur vb **blurred; blur·ring** vt **1** : to obscure or blemish by smearing **2** : SULLY **3** : to make dim, indistinct, or vague in outline or character **4** : to make cloudy or confused ~ vi **1** : to make blurs **2** : to become vague, indistinct, or indefinite — **blur·ring·ly** \'blər-iŋ-lē\ adv

blurb \'blərb\ n [coined by Gelett Burgess] : a short publicity notice (as on a book jacket)

blur·ry \'blər-ē\ adj **blur·ri·er; -est** : marked by blurring — **blur·ri·ly** \'blər-ə-lē\ adv — **blur·ri·ness** \'blər-e-nəs\ n

blurt \'blərt\ vt [prob. imit.] : to utter abruptly and impulsively — usu. used with *out* — **blurt·er** n

¹blush \'bləsh\ vi [ME *blusshen*, fr. OE *blyscan* to redden, fr. *blȳsa* flame; akin to OHG *bluhhen* to burn brightly] **1** : to become red in the face esp. from shame, modesty, or confusion **2** : to feel shame or embarrassment **3** : to have a rosy or fresh color : BLOOM — **blush·ing·ly** \-iŋ-lē\ adv

²blush n [ME, prob. fr. *blusshen*] **1** : APPEARANCE, VIEW ⟨at first ~⟩ **2** : a reddening of the face esp. from shame, modesty, or confusion **3** : a red or rosy tint — **blush·ful** \-fəl\ adj

blush·er \'bləsh-ər\ n **1** : one that blushes **2** : a cosmetic applied to the face to give a usu. pink color or to accent the cheekbones

¹blus·ter \'bləs-tər\ vb **blus·tered; blus·ter·ing** \-t(ə-)riŋ\ [ME *blustren*, prob. fr. MLG *blüsteren*] vi **1 a** : to blow in stormy noisy gusts **b** : to be windy and boisterous **2** : to talk or act with noisy swaggering threats ~ vt : to utter with noisy self-assertiveness **2** : to drive or force by blustering — **blus·ter·er** \-tər-ər\ n — **blus·ter·ing·ly** \-t(ə-)riŋ-lē\ adv

²bluster n **1** : a violent boisterous blowing **2** : violent commotion **3** : loudly boastful or threatening speech — **blus·ter·ous** \-t(ə-)rəs\ adj — **blus·tery** \-t(ə-)rē\ adj

blvd abbr boulevard

bm abbr beam

BM abbr **1** bachelor of medicine **2** bachelor of music **3** basal metabolism **4** bill of material **5** board measure **6** bowel movement **7** bronze medal

BME abbr **1** bachelor of mechanical engineering **2** bachelor of mining engineering **3** bachelor of music education

BMOC abbr big man on campus

BMR abbr basal metabolic rate

BMS abbr bachelor of marine science

BMT abbr bachelor of medical technology

bn abbr **1** baron **2** battalion **3** beacon **4** been

BN abbr **1** bachelor of nursing **2** bank note **3** Bureau of Narcotics

BNDD abbr Bureau of Narcotics and Dangerous Drugs

BNS abbr bachelor of naval sciences

BO abbr **1** bad order **2** body odor **3** box office **4** branch office **5** buyer's option

boa \'bō-ə\ n [L, a water snake] **1** : a large snake (as the boa constrictor, anaconda, or python) that crushes its prey **2** : a long fluffy scarf of fur, feathers, or delicate fabric

boa constrictor n : a tropical American boa (*Constrictor constrictor*) that is light brown barred or mottled with darker brown and reaches a length of 10 feet or more; *broadly* : BOA 1

boar \'bō(ə)r, 'bȯ(ə)r\ n [ME *bor*, fr. OE *bar*; akin to OHG & OS *bēr* boar] **1 a** : an uncastrated male swine **b** : the male of any of several mammals (as a guinea pig or raccoon) **2** : the Old World wild hog (*Sus scrofa*) from which most domestic swine derive — **boar·ish** \-ish\ adj

¹board \'bō(ə)rd, 'bȯ(ə)rd\ n [ME *bord* piece of sawed lumber, border, ship's side, fr. OE: akin to OHG *bort* ship's side, Skt *bardhaka* carpenter] **1** obs : BORDER, EDGE **2 a** : the side of a ship **b** : the stretch that a ship makes on one tack in beating to windward **3 a** : a piece of sawed lumber of little thickness and a length greatly exceeding its width **b** pl : STAGE 2a(2) **4 a** : archaic : TABLE 3a **b** : a table spread with a meal **c** : daily meals esp. when furnished for pay **d** : a table at which a council or magistrates sit **e** : a group of persons having managerial, supervisory, or investigatory powers ⟨~ of directors⟩ ⟨~ of examiners⟩ **f** : LEAGUE, ASSOCIATION **g** (1) : the exposed hands of all the players in a stud poker game (2) : an exposed dummy hand in bridge **5 a** : a flat usu. rectangular piece of material (as wood) designed for a special purpose: as (1) : BACKBOARD (2) : a diving board (3) : SURFBOARD **b** : a surface, frame, or device for posting notices or listing market quotations **c** : BLACKBOARD **d** : SWITCHBOARD **6 a** : any of various wood pulps or composition materials formed into stiff flat rectangular sheets **b** : PAPERBOARD **c** : the stiff foundation piece for the side of a book cover **7** : a securities or commodities exchange **8** pl : the low wooden wall enclosing a hockey rink — **board·like** \-,līk\ adj — **on board** : ABOARD

[2]board *vt* **1** *archaic* : to come up against or alongside (a ship) usu. to attack **2** : ACCOST, ADDRESS **3** : to go aboard (as a ship, train, airplane, or bus) **4** : to cover with boards ⟨~ up a window⟩ **5** : to provide with regular meals and often also lodging usu. for compensation **6** : to check (a player) against the rink boards in hockey ~ *vi* : to take one's meals usu. as a paying customer
board check *n* : a body check of an opposing player against the rink boards in ice hockey
board·er \ˈbōrd-ər, ˈbȯrd-\ *n* : one that boards; *esp* : one that is provided with regular meals or regular meals and lodging
board foot *n* : a unit of quantity for lumber equal to the volume of a board 12 x 12 x 1 inches — abbr. *bd ft*
board game *n* : a game of strategy (as checkers, chess, or backgammon) played by moving pieces on a board
board·ing·house \ˈbōrd-iŋ-ˌhau̇s, ˈbȯrd-\ *n* : a lodging house at which meals are provided
boarding school *n* : a school at which meals and lodging are provided
board·man \ˈbō(ə)rd-mən, ˈbȯ(ə)rd-, *esp for 2* -ˌman\ *n* **1** : one who works at a board **2** : a member of a board — **board·man·ship** *or* **boards·man·ship** \ˈbōrd(z)-mən-ˌship, ˈbȯrd(z)-\ *n*
board measure *n* : measurement in board feet
board of education : SCHOOL BOARD
board of trade **1** *cap B&T* : a British governmental department concerned with commerce and industry **2** : an organization of businessmen for the protection and promotion of business interests **3** : a commodities exchange
board·room \ˈbō(ə)rd-ˌrüm, ˈbȯ(ə)rd-, -ˌru̇m\ *n* **1** : a room that is designated for meetings of a board **2** : a room (as in a broker's office) containing a board for the listing of transactions or prices
board·walk \ˈbō(ə)rd-ˌwȯk, ˈbȯ(ə)rd-\ *n* **1** : a walk constructed of planking **2** : a walk constructed along a beach
boart \ˈbō(ə)rt, ˈbȯ(ə)rt\ *var of* BORT
[1]boast \ˈbōst\ *n* [ME *boost*] **1** : the act or an instance of boasting : BRAG **2** : a cause for pride — **boast·ful** \ˈbōst-fəl\ *adj* — **boast·ful·ly** \-fə-lē\ *adv* — **boast·ful·ness** *n*
[2]boast *vi* **1** : to puff oneself up in speech : speak vaingloriously **2** *archaic* : GLORY, EXULT ~ *vt* **1** : to speak of or assert with excessive pride **2** **a** : to possess and often call attention to (something that is a source of pride) ⟨their home ~*s* all the newest conveniences⟩ **b** : HAVE, CONTAIN ⟨a miserable room ~*ing* no more than a wobbly desk and a single chair⟩
syn BOAST, BRAG, VAUNT, CROW *shared meaning element* : to express pride in oneself or one's accomplishments. BOAST often suggests ostentation and exaggeration ⟨ready to *boast* of every trivial success⟩ but it may imply a claiming with proper and justifiable pride ⟨the town *boasts* one of the best hospitals in the area⟩ BRAG suggests crudity and artlessness in glorifying oneself ⟨boys *bragging* to each other⟩ VAUNT usually connotes more pomp and bombast than *boast* and less crudity or naiveté than *brag* ⟨charity *vaunteth* not itself, is not puffed up —1 Cor 13:4(AV)⟩ CROW usually implies exultant boasting or bragging ⟨loved to ~ about his ancestors⟩ ***ant*** depreciate (*as oneself*)
[3]boast *vt* [origin unknown] : to shape (stone) roughly with a broad chisel in sculpture and stonecutting as a preliminary to finer work
[1]boat \ˈbōt\ *n* [ME *boot*, fr. OE *bāt*; akin to ON *beit* boat] **1** : a small vessel propelled by oars or paddles or by sail or power **2** : SHIP **3** : a boat-shaped utensil or device ⟨a gravy ~⟩ — **in the same boat** : in the same situation or predicament
[2]boat *vt* : to place in or bring into a boat ⟨catch and ~ a fish⟩ ~ *vi* : to go by boat
boa·tel \bō-ˈtel\ *n* [blend of *boat* and *hotel*] : a waterside hotel having docks to accommodate persons traveling by boat
boat·er \ˈbōt-ər\ *n* **1** : one who travels in a boat **2** : a stiff straw hat
boat hook *n* : a pole-handled hook with a point or knob on the back used esp. to pull or push a boat, raft, or log into place
boat·man \ˈbōt-mən\ *n* : a man who works on, deals in, or operates boats — **boat·man·ship** \-ˌship\ *or* **boats·man·ship** \ˈbōts-\ *n*
boat·swain \ˈbōs-ᵊn\ *n* [ME *bootswein*, fr. *boot* boat + *swein* boy, servant] **1** : a petty officer on a merchant ship having charge of hull maintenance and related work **2** : a naval warrant officer in charge of the hull and all related equipment
boat train *n* : an express train for transporting passengers between a port and a city
[1]bob \ˈbäb\ *vb* **bobbed; bob·bing** [ME *boben*] *vt* **1** : to strike with a quick light blow : RAP **2** : to move up and down in a short quick movement ⟨~ the head⟩ **3** : to polish with a bob : BUFF ~ *vi* **1** **a** : to move up and down briefly or repeatedly ⟨a cork *bobbed* in the water⟩ **b** : to emerge, arise, or appear suddenly or unexpectedly ⟨the question *bobbed* up again⟩ **2** : to nod or curtsy briefly **3** : to try to seize a suspended or floating object with the teeth ⟨~ for apples⟩
[2]bob *n* **1** **a** : a short quick down-and-up motion **b** *Scot* : any of several folk dances **2** *obs* : a blow or tap esp. with the fist **3** **a** : a modification of the order in change ringing **b** : a method of change ringing using a bob **4** : a small polishing wheel of solid felt or leather with rounded edges
[3]bob *vt* **bobbed; bob·bing** [ME *bobben*, fr. MF *bober*] **1** *obs* : DECEIVE, CHEAT **2** *obs* : to take by fraud : FILCH
[4]bob *n* [ME *bobbe*] **1** **a** (1) : BUNCH, CLUSTER (2) *Scot* : NOSEGAY **b** : a knob, knot, twist, or curl esp. of ribbons, yarn, or hair **c** : a short haircut on a woman or child **2** : FLOAT 2a **3** : a hanging ball or weight (as on a plumb line or on the tail of a kite) **4** *archaic* : the refrain of a song; *specif* : a short and abrupt refrain often of two syllables **5** : a small insignificant piece : TRIFLE ⟨~*s* and trinkets⟩
[5]bob *vt* **bobbed; bob·bing** **1** : to cut shorter : CROP ⟨~ a horse's tail⟩ **2** : to cut (hair) in the style of a bob
[6]bob *n, pl* **bob** [perh. fr. the name *Bob*] *Brit* : SHILLING
[7]bob *n* **1** : BOBSLED **2** : SKIBOB
bob·ber \ˈbäb-ər\ *n* **1** : one that bobs **2** : one who rides or races on a bobsled
bob·bery \ˈbäb-ə-rē\ *n, pl* **-ber·ies** [Hindi *bāp re*, lit., oh father!] : HUBBUB
bob·bin \ˈbäb-ən\ *n* [origin unknown] **1** **a** : any of various small round devices on which threads are wound for working handmade lace **b** : a cylinder or spindle on which yarn or thread is wound (as in a sewing machine) **c** : a coil of insulated wire or the reel it is wound on **2** : a narrow cotton cord formerly used by dressmakers for piping
bob·bi·net \ˌbäb-ə-ˈnet\ *n* [blend of *bobbin* and *net*] : a machine-made net of cotton, silk, or nylon usu. with hexagonal mesh
[1]bob·ble \ˈbäb-əl\ *vb* **bob·bled; bob·bling** \-(ə-)liŋ\ [freq. of [1]*bob*] **1** : [1]BOB **2** : FUMBLE
[2]bobble *n* **1** : a repeated bobbing movement **2** : a small ball of fabric; *esp* : one in a series used on an edging ⟨curtains . . . with plush ~*s* —H. E. Bates⟩ **3** : ERROR, MISTAKE; *esp* : a fumble in baseball or football
bob·by \ˈbäb-ē\ *n, pl* **bobbies** [*Bobby*, nickname for *Robert*, after Sir *Robert* Peel, who organized the London police force] *Brit* : POLICEMAN
bob·by pin \ˈbäb-ē-\ *n* [[4]*bob*] : a flat wire hairpin with prongs that press close together
bob·by socks *or* **bobby sox** \ˈbäb-ē-\ *n pl* [fr. the name *Bobby*] : girls' socks reaching above the ankle
bob·by–sox·er \-ˌsäk-sər\ *n* : an adolescent girl
bob·cat \ˈbäb-ˌkat\ *n* [[4]*bob*; fr. the stubby tail] : a common No. American lynx (*Lynx rufus*) typically rusty or reddish in base color

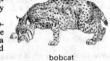

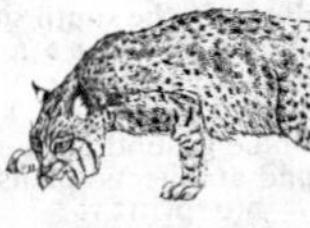
bobcat

bo·beche \bō-ˈbesh, -ˈbāsh\ *n* [F *bobèche*] : a usu. glass collar on a candle socket to catch drippings or on a candlestick or chandelier to hold suspended glass prisms
bob·o·link \ˈbäb-ə-ˌliŋk\ *n* [imit.] : an American migratory songbird (*Dolichonyx oryzivorus*)
bob·sled \ˈbäb-ˌsled\ *n* [perh. fr. [4]*bob*] **1** : a short sled usu. used as one of a pair joined by a coupling **2** : a large usu. metal sled used in racing and equipped with two pairs of runners in tandem, a long seat for two or more people, a steering wheel, and a hand brake — **bobsled** *vi* — **bob·sled·der** *n*
bob·sled·ding \-ˌsled-iŋ\ *n* : the act, skill, or sport of riding or racing on a bobsled
bob·stay \ˈbäb-ˌstā\ *n* [prob. fr. [2]*bob*] : a stay to hold a ship's bowsprit down
bob·tail \ˈbäb-ˌtāl\ *n* [[4]*bob*] **1** **a** : a bobbed tail **b** : a horse or dog with a bobbed tail; *esp* : OLD ENGLISH SHEEPDOG **2** : something curtailed or abbreviated — **bobtail** *or* **bob·tailed** \-ˌtāld\ *adj*
bob veal \ˈbäb-\ *n* [E dial. *bob* young calf] : the veal of a very young or unborn calf
bob·white \(ˈ)bäb-ˈ(h)wīt\ *n* [imit.] : any of a genus (*Colinus*) of quail; *esp* : a favorite game bird (*C. virginianus*) of the eastern and central U.S. — called also *partridge*
bo·cac·cio \bə-ˈkäch-(ē-ˌ)ō\ *n* [perh. deriv. of Sp *bocacha*, aug. of *boca* mouth] : a large rockfish (*Sebastes paucispinis*) of the Pacific coast locally important as a market fish
boc·cie *or* **boc·ci** *or* **boc·ce** \ˈbäch-ē\ *n* [It *bocce*, pl. of *boccia* ball, fr. (assumed) VL *bottia* boss] : a game of Italian origin similar to lawn bowling played on a long narrow usu. dirt court
bock \ˈbäk\ *n* [G, short for *bockbier*, by shortening & alter. fr. *Einbecker bier*, lit., beer from Einbeck, fr. *Einbeck*, Germany] : a heavy dark rich beer usu. sold in the early spring
bod \ˈbäd\ *n* : BODY
BOD *abbr* biochemical oxygen demand; biological oxygen demand
bo·da·cious \bō-ˈdā-shəs\ *adj* [back-formation fr. earlier *bodaciously* (thoroughly), alter. of earlier *bodyaciously*, perh. fr. *body* + *-aciously* (as in *graciously*)] **1** *South & Midland* : OUTRIGHT, UNMISTAKABLE **2** *South & Midland* : REMARKABLE, NOTEWORTHY ⟨I got some ~ gossip —Fred Lasswell⟩ — **bo·da·cious·ly** *adv*
[1]bode \ˈbōd\ *vt* **bod·ed; bod·ing** [ME *boden*, fr. OE *bodian*; akin to OE *bēodan* to proclaim — more at BID] **1** *archaic* : to announce beforehand : FORETELL **2** : to indicate by signs : PRESAGE ⟨this controversy . . . will ~ ill for both of us —A. H. Lowe⟩
[2]bode *past of* BIDE
bo·de·ga \bō-ˈdā-gə\ *n* [Sp, fr. L *apotheca* storehouse — more at APOTHECARY] **1** : a storehouse for wine **2** **a** : WINESHOP **b** : a combined wineshop and grocery store **c** : [1]BAR 5
bode·ment \ˈbōd-mənt\ *n* **1** : OMEN, FOREBODING **2** : PREDICTION, PROPHECY
bo·dhi·satt·va *or* **bod·dhi·satt·va** \ˌbōd-i-ˈsət-və\ *n* [Skt *bodhisattva* one whose essence is enlightenment, fr. *bodhi* enlightenment + *sattva* being] : a being that compassionately refrains from entering nirvana in order to save others and is worshiped as a deity in Mahayana Buddhism
bod·ice \ˈbäd-əs\ *n* [alter. of *bodies*, pl. of [1]*body*] **1** *archaic* : CORSET, STAYS **2** : the upper part of a woman's dress
-bodied \ˈbäd-ēd\ *adj comb form* : having a body of a specified nature ⟨full-*bodied*⟩ ⟨glass-*bodied*⟩
bodi·less \ˈbäd-i-ləs, ˈbäd-ᵊl-əs\ *adj* : having no body : INCORPOREAL
[1]bodi·ly \ˈbäd-ᵊl-ē\ *adj* **1** : having a body : PHYSICAL **2** : of or relating to the body ⟨~ comfort⟩ ⟨~ organs⟩
syn BODILY, PHYSICAL, CORPOREAL, CORPORAL, SOMATIC *shared meaning element* : of or relating to the human body
[2]bodily *adv* **1** : in the flesh **2** : as a whole : ALTOGETHER
bod·ing \ˈbōd-iŋ\ *n* : FOREBODING
bod·kin \ˈbäd-kən\ *n* [ME] **1** **a** : DAGGER, STILETTO **b** : a sharp slender instrument for making holes in cloth **c** : an ornamental hairpin shaped like a stiletto **2** : a blunt needle with a large eye for drawing tape or ribbon through a loop or hem
[1]body \ˈbäd-ē\ *n, pl* **bod·ies** [ME, fr. OE *bodig*; akin to OHG *botah* body] **1** **a** : the organized physical substance of an animal or plant either living or dead: as (1) : the material part or nature of man (2) : the dead organism : CORPSE (3) : the person of a human being before the law **b** : a human being : PERSON **2** **a** : the

main part of a plant or animal body esp. as distinguished from limbs and head : TRUNK **b** : the main, central, or principal part: as (1) : the nave of a church (2) : the bed or box of a vehicle on or in which the load is placed **3 a** : the part of a garment covering the body or trunk **b** : the main part of a literary or journalistic work : TEXT 2b **c** : the sound box or pipe of a musical instrument **4 a** : a mass of matter distinct from other masses ⟨a ~ of water⟩ **b** : one of the seven planets of the old astronomy **c** : something that embodies or gives concrete reality to a thing; *specif* : a sensible object in physical space **5** : a group of persons or things: as **a** : a fighting unit : FORCE **b** : a group of individuals organized for some purpose : CORPORATION ⟨a legislative ~⟩ **6 a** : VISCOSITY, CONSISTENCY — used esp. of oils and grease **b** : compactness or firmness of texture **c** : fullness or resonance of a musical tone **d** : richness of flavor — used of a beverage (as wine) **7** : the part of a printing type extending from foot to shoulder and underlying the bevel — see TYPE illustration

[2]body *vt* **bod·ied; body·ing 1 a** : to give form or shape to : EMBODY **b** : REPRESENT, SYMBOLIZE — usu. used with *forth* **2** : to increase the viscosity of (an oil)

body cavity *n* : a cavity within an animal body; *specif* : COELOM

body check *n* : a blocking of an opposing player with the body (as in ice hockey or lacrosse)

body corporate *n* : CORPORATION

body English *n* : the instinctive attempt of a person to influence the movement of a propelled object (as a ball or puck) by contorting his body in the desired direction

body·guard \ˈbäd-ē-ˌgärd\ *n* : a man or group of men whose duty is to protect a person from bodily harm

body louse *n* : a louse feeding primarily on the body; *esp* : a sucking louse (*Pediculus humanus*) feeding on the body and living in the clothing of man

body mechanics *n pl but sing or pl in constr* : systematic exercises (as for women) designed esp. to develop coordination, endurance, and poise

body politic *n* **1** *archaic* : CORPORATION 2 **2** : a group of persons politically organized under a single governmental authority **3** : a people considered as a collective unit

body shirt *n* **1** : a woman's close-fitting top made with a sewn-in or snapped crotch **2** : a close-fitting shirt or blouse

body shop *n* : a shop where automotive bodies are made or repaired

body snatcher *n* : one that without authority takes corpses from graves usu. for dissection

body stocking *n* : a sheer close-fitting one-piece garment for the torso that often has sleeves and legs

body·surf \ˈbäd-ē-ˌsərf\ *vi* : to ride on a wave without a surfboard by planing on the chest and stomach — **body·surf·er** *n*

body wall *n* : the external surface of the body in animals consisting of ectoderm and mesoderm and enclosing the body cavity

body·work \ˈbäd-ē-ˌwərk\ *n* **1** : a vehicle body **2** : the act or process of making or repairing vehicle bodies

boehm·ite \ˈbām-ˌīt, ˈbə(r)m-\ *n* [G *böhmit*, fr. J. *Böhm* (*Boehm*), 20th cent. G scientist] : a mineral consisting of an orthorhombic form of aluminum oxide and hydroxide AlO(OH) found in bauxite

Boer \ˈbō(ə)r, ˈbȯ(ə)r, ˈbu̇(ə)r\ *n* [D, lit., farmer — more at BOOR] : a South African of Dutch or Huguenot descent

boff \ˈbäf\ *or* **bof·fo** \ˈbäf-(ˌ)ō\ *n, pl* **boffs** *or* **boffos** [prob. fr. *box office*] **1** : a hearty laugh **2** : a gag or line that produces a hearty laugh **3** : something that is conspicuously successful : HIT

bof·fin \ˈbäf-ən\ *n* [origin unknown] *chiefly Brit* : a scientific expert

bof·fo \ˈbäf-(ˌ)ō\ *adj* : extraordinarily successful : SENSATIONAL

bof·fo·la \bä-ˈfō-lə\ *n* [irreg. fr. *boff*] : BOFF

Bo·fors gun \ˌbō-ˌfȯrz-, ˌbü-\ *n* [*Bofors*, munition works in Sweden] : a double-barreled automatic antiaircraft gun

[1]bog \ˈbäg, ˈbȯg\ *n* [prob. fr. IrGael *bogach* (fr. *bog* soft, fr. OIr *bocc*) & ScGael *boglach* (fr. *bog* soft); akin to OE *būgan* to bend — more at BOW] : wet spongy ground; *esp* : a poorly drained usu. acid area rich in plant residues, frequently surrounding a body of open water, and having a characteristic flora (as of sedges, heaths, and sphagnum) — **bog·gy** \ˈbäg-ē, ˈbȯg-\ *adj*

[2]bog *vb* **bogged; bog·ging** *vt* : to cause to sink into or as if into a bog : IMPEDE — usu. used with *down* ~ *vi* : to become impeded — usu. used with *down*

bog asphodel *n* : either of two bog herbs (*Narthecium ossifragum* of Europe and *N. americanum* of the U.S.) of the lily family

[1]bo·gey *also* **bo·gy** *or* **bo·gie** *n, pl* **bogeys** *also* **bogies** [prob. alter. of *bogle*] **1** \ˈbu̇g-ē, ˈbō-gē, ˈbü-gē\ : SPECTER, PHANTOM **2** \ˈbō-gē *also* ˈbu̇g-ē *or* ˈbü-gē\ : a source of fear, perplexity, or harassment **3** \ˈbō-gē\ **a** *chiefly Brit* : an average golfer's score used as a standard for a particular hole or course **b** : one stroke over par on a hole in golf **4** \ˈbō-gē\ : a numerical standard of performance set up as a mark to be aimed at in competition **5** \ˈbu̇g-ē, ˈbō-gē, ˈbü-gē\ *slang* : an unidentified flying object

[2]bo·gey \ˈbō-gē\ *vt* **bo·geyed; bo·gey·ing** : to shoot (a hole in golf) in one over par

bo·gey·man \ˈbu̇g-ē-ˌman, ˈbō-gē-, ˈbü-gē-, ˈbu̇g-ər-\ *n* : a monstrous imaginary figure used in threatening children; *broadly* : a terrifying person or thing : BUGBEAR

bog·gle \ˈbäg-əl\ *vb* **bog·gled; bog·gling** \-(ə-)liŋ\ [perh. fr. *bogle*] *vi* **1** : to start with fright or amazement : be overwhelmed ⟨the mind ~s at the amount of research yet to be done⟩ **2** : to hesitate because of doubt, fear, or scruples **3** : BUNGLE ~ *vt* : to overwhelm with wonder or bewilderment — **boggle** *n*

bo·gie *also* **bo·gey** *or* **bo·gy** \ˈbō-gē\ *n, pl* **bogies** *also* **bogeys** [origin unknown] **1** : a low strongly built cart **2 a** *chiefly Brit* : a swiveling railway truck **b** : the driving-wheel assembly consisting of the rear four wheels of a 6-wheel automotive truck **3** : one of the weight-carrying wheels on the inside perimeter of the tread of a tank serving to keep the treads in line

bo·gle \ˈbō-gəl\ *also* **bog·gle** \ˈbäg-əl\ *n* [E dial. (Sc & northern), terrifying apparition; akin to ME *bugge* scarecrow — more at BUG] *dial Brit* : GOBLIN, SPECTER; *also* : an object of fear or loathing

Bo·go·mil *also* **Bo·go·mile** \ˌbäg-ə-ˈmē(ə)l\ *n* [Russ *bogomil*, fr. OSlav *Bogomilŭ* Bogomil, 10th cent. Bulg priest, founder of the sect] : a member of a medieval Bulgarian sect holding that God is the father of two sons, the rebellious Satan and the obedient Jesus

bo·gus \ˈbō-gəs\ *adj* [*bogus* (a machine for making counterfeit money)] : not genuine : COUNTERFEIT, SHAM

bo·hea \bō-ˈhē\ *n, often cap* [Chin (Pek) *wu³-i²*, hills in China where it was grown] : a black tea

bo·he·mia \bō-ˈhē-mē-ə\ *n, often cap* [trans. of F *bohème*] : a community of bohemians : the world of bohemians

Bo·he·mi·an \-mē-ən\ *n* **1 a** : a native or inhabitant of Bohemia **b** : the group of Czech dialects used in Bohemia **2** *often not cap* **a** : VAGABOND, WANDERER; *esp* : GYPSY **b** : a person (as a writer or an artist) living an unconventional life usu. in a colony with others — **bohemian** *adj, often cap*

Bohemian Brethren *n pl* : a Christian body originating in Bohemia in 1467 and forming a parent body of the Moravian Brethren

bo·he·mi·an·ism \bō-ˈhē-mē-ə-ˌniz-əm\ *n, often cap* : the unconventional way of life of bohemians

Bohr theory \ˈbō(ə)r-, ˈbȯ(ə)r-\ *n* [Niels *Bohr*] : a theory in physical chemistry: an atom consists of a positively charged nucleus about which revolves one or more electrons

[1]boil \ˈbȯi(ə)l\ *n* [alter. of ME *bile*, fr. OE *bȳl* — more at BIG] : a localized swelling and inflammation of the skin resulting from infection in a skin gland, having a hard central core, and forming pus

[2]boil *vb* [ME *boilen*, fr. OF *boillir*, fr. L *bullire* to bubble, fr. *bulla* bubble] *vi* **1 a** : to generate bubbles of vapor when heated — used of a liquid **b** : to come to the boiling point **2** : to become agitated like boiling water : SEETHE **3** : to be moved, excited, or stirred up ⟨his blood ~s at the mention of it⟩ **4 a** : to rush headlong ⟨came ~*ing* through the door⟩ **b** : to burst forth : ERUPT ⟨water ~*ing* from a spring⟩ **5** : to undergo the action of a boiling liquid ~ *vt* **1** : to subject to the action of a boiling liquid ⟨~ eggs⟩ **2** : to heat to the boiling point ⟨~ water⟩ **3** : to form or separate (as sugar or salt) by boiling

[3]boil *n* **1** : the act or state of boiling **2** : a swirling upheaval (as of water)

boil down *vt* **1** : to reduce in bulk by boiling **2** : CONDENSE, SUMMARIZE ⟨*boil down* a report⟩ ~ *vi* **1** : to undergo reduction in bulk by boiling **2** : to be equivalent in summary : AMOUNT ⟨his speech *boiled down* to a plea for more money⟩

boiled oil *n* : a fatty oil (as linseed oil) whose drying properties have been improved by heating usu. with driers

boil·er \ˈbȯi-lər\ *n* **1** : one that boils **2 a** : a vessel used for boiling **b** : the part of a steam generator in which water is converted into steam and which consists usu. of metal shells and tubes **c** : a tank in which water is heated or hot water is stored

boil·er·mak·er \ˈbȯi-lər-ˌmā-kər\ *n* **1** : a workman who makes, assembles, or repairs boilers **2** : whiskey with a beer chaser

boiler suit *n* : COVERALL

[1]boil·ing \ˈbȯi-liŋ\ *adj* **1 a** : heated to the boiling point **b** : TORRID ⟨a ~ sun⟩ **2** : intensely agitated, excited, or stirred up ⟨a ~ sea⟩

[2]boiling *adv* : to an extreme degree : VERY ⟨~ mad⟩ ⟨~ hot⟩

boiling point *n* **1** : the temperature at which a liquid boils **2 a** : the point at which a person loses his temper **b** : the point at which decisive action becomes imperative : HEAD 18b ⟨matters had reached the *boiling point*⟩

boil over *vi* **1** : to overflow while boiling **2** : to become so incensed as to lose one's temper

bois d'arc \ˈbō-ˌdä(r)k\ *n, pl* **bois d'arcs** *or* **bois d'arc** [F, lit., bow wood] : OSAGE ORANGE

bois·ter·ous \ˈbȯi-st(ə-)rəs\ *adj* [ME *boistous* rough] **1** *obs* **a** : DURABLE, STRONG **b** : COARSE **c** : MASSIVE **2 a** : noisily turbulent : ROWDY **b** : marked by or expressive of exuberance and high spirits **3** : STORMY, TUMULTUOUS ***syn*** see VOCIFEROUS — **bois·ter·ous·ly** *adv* — **bois·ter·ous·ness** *n*

boîte \ˈbwät\ *n* [F, lit., box] : NIGHTCLUB

Bok·mål \ˈbu̇k-ˌmȯl, ˈbōk-\ *n* [Norw, lit., book language] : a literary form of Norwegian developed by the gradual reform of written Danish — compare NYNORSK

bo·la \ˈbō-lə\ *or* **bo·las** \-ləs\ *n, pl* **bolas** \-ləz\ *also* **bo·las·es** [AmerSp *bolas*, fr. Sp *bola* ball] : a weapon consisting of two or more stone or iron balls attached to the ends of a cord for hurling at and entangling an animal

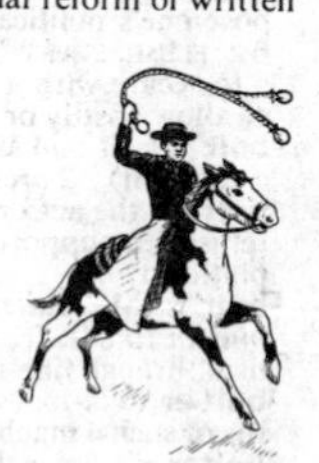

bola

bold \ˈbōld\ *adj* [ME, fr. OE *beald*; akin to OHG *bald* bold] **1 a** : fearless before danger : INTREPID **b** : showing or requiring a fearless daring spirit ⟨a ~ plan⟩ **2** : IMPUDENT, PRESUMPTUOUS **3** *obs* : ASSURED, CONFIDENT **4** : SHEER, STEEP ⟨~ cliffs⟩ **5** : ADVENTUROUS, DARING ⟨a ~ thinker⟩ **6** : standing out prominently : CONSPICUOUS **7** : being or set in boldface — **bold·ly** \ˈbōl-(d)lē\ *adv* — **bold·ness** \ˈbōl(d)-nəs\ *n*

bold·face \ˈbōl(d)-ˌfās\ *n* : a heavy-faced type; *also* : printing in boldface — **bold·faced** \-ˈfāst\ *adj*

bold–faced \ˈbōl(d)-ˈfāst\ *adj* : bold in manner or conduct : IMPUDENT ⟨a fine, gay, ~ ruffian —Sir Walter Scott⟩

bole \ˈbōl\ *n* [ME, fr. ON *bolr*] : the trunk of a tree

bo·le·ro \bə-ˈle(ə)r-(ˌ)ō\ *n, pl* **-ros** [Sp] **1** : a Spanish dance characterized by sharp turns, stamping of the feet, and sudden pauses in a position with one arm arched over the head; *also* : music in $^3/_4$ time

ə abut ᵊ kitten ər further a back ā bake ä cot, cart
au̇ out ch chin e less ē easy g gift i trip ī life
j joke ŋ sing ō flow ȯ flaw ȯi coin th thin t͟h this
ü loot u̇ foot y yet yü few yu̇ furious zh vision

for or suitable for a bolero **2 :** a loose waist-length jacket open at the front

bo·le·tus \bō-'lēt-əs\ *n, pl* **-tus·es** *or* **-ti** \-'lēt-,ī\ [NL, genus name, fr. L, a fungus, fr. Gk *bolitēs*] **:** any of a genus (*Boletus*) of soft pore fungi some of which are poisonous and others edible

bo·li·var \bə-'lē-,vär, 'bäl-ə-vər\ *n, pl* **-vars** *or* **-va·res** \,bäl-ə-'vär-,ās, ,bō-li-\ [AmerSp *bolívar,* fr. Simón *Bolívar*] — see MONEY table

bo·li·vi·a·no \bə-,liv-ē-'än-(,)ō\ *n, pl* **-nos** [Sp] **:** a former monetary unit of Bolivia replaced in 1963 by the peso

boll \'bōl\ *n* [ME] **:** the pod or capsule of a plant (as cotton)

bol·lard \'bäl-ərd\ *n* [perh. irreg. fr. *bole*] **1 :** a post of metal or wood on a wharf around which to fasten mooring lines **2 :** BITT 1

bol·lix \'bäl-iks\ *vt* [alter. of *ballocks,* pl. of *ballock* (testis), fr. ME, fr. OE *bealluc* — more at BALL] **:** to throw into disorder; *also* **:** BUNGLE — usu. used with *up* — **bollix** *n*

boll weevil *n* **:** a grayish weevil (*Anthonomus grandis*) about 1/4 inch long that infests the cotton plant and feeds on the squares and bolls both as a larva and an adult

boll·worm \'bōl-,wərm\ *n* **:** CORN EARWORM; *also* **:** any of several other moth larvae that feed on cotton bolls

bo·lo \'bō-(,)lō\ *n, pl* **bolos** [Sp] **:** a long heavy single-edged knife of Philippine origin

bo·lo·gna \bə-'lō-nē *also* -n(y)ə\ *n* [short for *Bologna sausage,* fr. *Bologna,* Italy] **:** a large smoked sausage of beef, veal, and pork

bo·lom·e·ter \bō-'läm-ət-ər\ *n* [Gk *bolē* + E *-o-* + *-meter*] **:** a very sensitive resistance thermometer used in the detection and measurement of feeble thermal radiation and esp. adapted to the study of infrared spectra — **bo·lo·met·ric** \,bō-lə-'me-trik\ *adj* — **bo·lo·met·ri·cal·ly** \-tri-k(ə-)lē\ *adv*

bo·lo·ney \bə-'lō-nē\ *var of* BALONEY

bo·lo tie \,bō-lō-\ *or* **bo·la tie** \-lə-\ *n* [prob. fr. *bola*] **:** a cord fastened around the neck with an ornamental clasp and worn as a necktie

Bol·she·vik \'bōl-shə-,vik, 'bȯl-, 'bäl-, -,vēk\ *n, pl* **Bolsheviks** *also* **Bol·she·vi·ki** \,bōl-shə-'vik-ē, ,bȯl-, ,bäl-, -'vē-kē\ [Russ *bol'shevik,* fr. *bol'she* larger] **1 :** a member of the extremist wing of the Russian Social Democratic party that seized supreme power in Russia by the Revolution of November 1917 **2 :** COMMUNIST 3 — **Bolshevik** *adj*

bol·she·vism \'bōl-shə-,viz-əm, 'bȯl-, 'bäl-\ *n, often cap* **1 :** the doctrine or program of the Bolsheviks advocating violent overthrow of capitalism **2 :** Russian communism

Bol·she·vist \-vəst\ *n or adj* **:** BOLSHEVIK

bol·she·vize \-,vīz\ *vt* **-vized; -viz·ing :** to make Bolshevist — **Bol·she·vi·za·tion** \,bōl-shə-və-'zā-shən, ,bȯl-, ,bäl-\ *n*

1bol·ster \'bōl-stər\ *n* [ME, fr. OE; akin to OE *belg* bag — more at BELLY] **1 :** a long pillow or cushion **2 :** a structural part designed to eliminate friction or provide support or bearing; *esp* **:** the horizontal connection between the volutes of an Ionic capital

2bolster *vt* **bol·stered; bol·ster·ing** \-st(ə-)riŋ\ **1 :** to support with or as if with a bolster **:** REINFORCE **2 :** to give a boost to ⟨news that ~*ed* his spirits⟩ — **bol·ster·er** \-stər-ər\ *n*

1bolt \'bōlt\ *n* [ME, fr. OE; akin to OHG *bolz* crossbow bolt, Lith *beldėti* to beat] **1 a :** a shaft or missile designed to be shot from a crossbow or catapult; *esp* **:** a short stout usu. blunt-headed arrow **b :** a lightning stroke **:** THUNDERBOLT **2 a :** a wood or metal bar or rod used to fasten a door **b :** the part of a lock that is shot or withdrawn by the key **3 a :** a roll of cloth of specified length **b :** a roll of wallpaper of specified length **4 :** a metal rod or pin for fastening objects together that usu. has a head at one end and a screw thread at the other and is secured by a nut **5 a :** a block of timber to be sawed or cut **b :** a short round section of a log **6 :** the breech closure of a breech-loading firearm

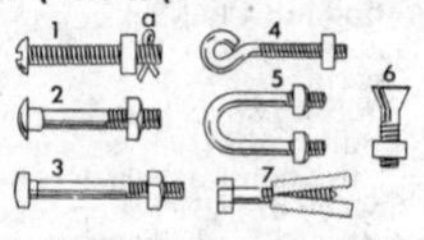

bolts 4: *1* stove bolt with cotter pin *a, 2* carriage bolt, *3* machine bolt, *4* eyebolt, *5* U bolt, *6* plow bolt, *7* expansion bolt

2bolt *vi* **1 :** to move suddenly or nervously **:** START **2 :** to move rapidly **:** DASH **3 a :** to dart off or away **:** FLEE **b :** to break away from control or a set course **4 :** to break away from or oppose one's political party ~ *vt* **1 a** *archaic* **:** SHOOT, DISCHARGE **b :** FLUSH, START ⟨~ rabbits⟩ **2 :** to say impulsively **:** BLURT **3 :** to secure with a bolt **4 :** to attach or fasten with bolts **5 :** to swallow hastily or without chewing **6 :** to break away from

3bolt *adv* **1 :** in an erect or straight-backed position **:** RIGIDLY ⟨sat ~ upright⟩ **2** *archaic* **:** DIRECTLY, STRAIGHT

4bolt *n* **:** the act or an instance of bolting: as **a :** DASH, RUN **b :** a refusal to support one's usual political party or its candidate or platform

5bolt *vt* [ME *bulten,* fr. OF *buleter,* of Gmc origin; akin to MHG *biuteln* to sift, fr. *biutel* bag, fr. OHG *būtil*] **1 :** to sift (as flour) usu. through fine-meshed cloth **2** *archaic* **:** SIFT 2

1bolt·er \'bōl-tər\ *n* **:** a machine for bolting flour; *also* **:** the operator of such a machine

2bolter *n* **1 :** a horse given to running away **2 :** a voter who bolts his party

bolt–operated *adj, of a firearm* **:** utilizing a sliding bolt to operate the action

bolt·rope \'bōlt-,rōp\ *n* **:** a strong rope stitched to the edges of a sail to strengthen it

bo·lus \'bō-ləs\ *n* [LL, fr. Gk *bōlos* lump] **:** a rounded mass: as **a :** a large pill **b :** a soft mass of chewed food

1bomb \'bäm\ *n* [F *bombe,* fr. It *bomba,* prob. fr. L *bombus* deep hollow sound, fr. Gk *bombos,* of imit. origin] **1 a :** an explosive device fused to detonate under specified conditions **b :** ATOM BOMB — usu. used with *the* **2 :** a vessel for compressed gases: as **a :** a pressure vessel for conducting chemical experiments **b :** a small dispenser for a substance (as paint or an insecticide) stored under pressure **3 :** a rounded mass of lava exploded from a volcano **4 :** a lead-lined container for radioactive material **5 :** a long pass in football **6 :** FAILURE, FLOP ⟨the play was awful — a complete ~⟩ **7** *slang Brit* **:** a large sum of money

2bomb *vt* **1 :** to attack with or as if with bombs **:** BOMBARD **2 a :** to score heavily against (an opponent) **b :** to defeat decisively ~ *vi* **:** to fall flat **:** FAIL

1bom·bard \'bäm-,bärd\ *n* [ME *bombarde,* fr. MF, prob. fr. L *bombus*] **:** a cannon used in late medieval times chiefly to hurl large stones

2bom·bard \bäm-'bärd *also* bəm-\ *vt* **1 :** to attack esp. with artillery or bombers **2 :** to assail vigorously or persistently (as with questions) **3 :** to subject to the impact of rapidly moving particles (as electrons or alpha rays) ***syn*** see ATTACK — **bom·bard·ment** \-mənt\ *n*

bom·bar·dier \,bäm-bə(r)-'di(ə)r\ *n* **1 a** *archaic* **:** ARTILLERYMAN **b :** a noncommissioned officer in the British artillery **2 :** a bomber-crew member who uses the bombsight and releases the bombs

bom·bar·don \'bäm-bər-,dōn, bäm-'bärd-ᵊn\ *n* [F, fr. It *bombardone*] **1 :** the bass member of the shawm family **2 :** a bass tuba

bom·bast \'bäm-,bast\ *n* [MF *bombace,* fr. ML *bombac-, bombax* cotton, alter. of L *bombyc-, bombyx* silkworm, silk, fr. Gk *bombyk-, bombyx*] **:** pretentious inflated speech or writing — **bombast** *adj* — **bom·bast·er** \-,bas-tər\ *n* — **bom·bas·tic** \bäm-'bas-tik\ *adj* — **bom·bas·ti·cal·ly** \-ti-k(ə-)lē\ *adv*

syn BOMBAST, RHAPSODY, RANT, FUSTIAN *shared meaning element* **:** speech or writing marked by high-flown pomposity or pretentiousness

bom·ba·zine \,bäm-bə-'zēn\ *n* [MF *bombasin,* fr. ML *bombacinum, bombycinum* silken texture, fr. L, neut. of *bombycinus* of silk, fr. *bombyc-, bombyx*] **1 :** a silk fabric in twill weave dyed black **2 :** a twilled fabric with silk warp and worsted filling

bomb bay *n* **:** a bomb-carrying compartment on the underside of a combat airplane

bombe \'bäm, 'bōⁿ(m)b\ *n* [F, lit., bomb] **:** a frozen dessert made by lining a round or melon-shaped mold with one mixture and filling it with another

bombed \'bämd\ *adj, slang* **:** affected by alcohol or drugs

bomb·er \'bäm-ər\ *n* **:** one that bombs; *specif* **:** an airplane designed for bombing

bom·bi·nate \'bäm-bə-,nāt\ *vi* **-nat·ed; -nat·ing** [NL *bombinatus,* pp. of *bombinare,* alter. of L *bombilare,* fr. *bombus*] **:** BUZZ, DRONE — **bom·bi·na·tion** \,bäm-bə-'nā-shən\ *n*

bomb·proof \'bäm-'prüf\ *adj* **:** safe from the force of bombs

bomb run *n* **:** the part of a bomber's attack during which the actual sighting for and release of bombs occurs

bomb·shell \'bäm-,shel\ *n* **1 :** BOMB 1a **2 :** one that stuns, amazes, or is devastatingly upsetting ⟨the book was a political ~⟩

bomb·sight \-,sīt\ *n* **:** a sighting device for aiming bombs

bona fide \'bō-nə-,fīd, 'bän-ə-; ,bō-nə-'fīd-ē, -'fīd-ə\ *adj* [L, in good faith] **1 :** made in good faith without fraud or deceit ⟨a *bona fide* offer to purchase a farm⟩ **2 :** made with earnest intent **:** SINCERE **3 :** neither specious nor counterfeit **:** GENUINE ⟨a *bona fide* antique⟩ ***syn*** see AUTHENTIC ***ant*** counterfeit, bogus

bo·na fi·des \,bō-nə-'fīd-,ēz\ *n* [L, good faith] **:** lack of fraud or deceit **:** SINCERITY ⟨a man on whom suspicion had never rested and whose *bona fides* was unshakeable —Victor Canning⟩

bo·nan·za \bə-'nan-zə\ *n* [Sp, lit., calm, fr. ML *bonacia,* alter. of L *malacia* calm at sea, fr. Gk *malakia,* lit., softness, fr. *malakos* soft] **1 :** an exceptionally large and rich ore shoot or pocket in veins carrying gold and silver **2 a :** something that is considered very valuable, profitable, or rewarding ⟨achieved a box-office ~⟩ **b :** an extremely large amount ⟨expected a ~ of sympathy⟩

Bo·na·part·ism \'bō-nə-,pärt-,iz-əm\ *n* **1 :** support of the French emperors Napoleon I, Napoleon III, or their dynasty **2 :** a political movement associated chiefly with authoritarian rule usu. by a military leader ostensibly supported by a popular mandate — **Bo·na·part·ist** \-,pärt-əst\ *n or adj*

bon·bon \'bän-,bän\ *n* [F, (baby talk), redupl. of *bon* good, fr. L *bonus* — more at BOUNTY] **:** a candy with chocolate or fondant coating and fondant center that sometimes contains fruits and nuts

1bond \'bänd\ *adj* [ME *bonde,* fr. *bonde* peasant, serf, fr. OE *bōnda* householder, fr. ON *bōndi*] *archaic* **:** bound in slavery

2bond *n* [ME *band, bond* — more at BAND] **1 :** something that binds or restrains **:** FETTER **2 :** a binding agreement **:** COVENANT **3 a :** a band or cord used to tie something **b :** a material or device for binding **c :** a mechanism by means of which atoms, ions, or groups of atoms are held together in a molecule or crystal — usu. represented in formulas by a line or dot **d :** an adhesive, cementing material, or fusible ingredient that combines, unites, or strengthens **4 :** a uniting or binding element or force ⟨the ~*s* of friendship⟩ **5 a :** an obligation made binding by a money forfeit; *also* **:** the amount of the money guarantee **b :** one who acts as bail or surety **c :** an interest-bearing certificate of public or private indebtedness ⟨a 20-year ~ issue to finance a new courthouse⟩ **d :** an insurance agreement pledging surety for financial loss caused to another by the act or default of a third person or by some contingency over which the third person may have no control **6 :** the systematic lapping of brick in a wall **7 :** the state of goods manufactured, stored, or transported under the care of bonded agencies until the duties or taxes on them are paid **8 :** a 100-proof straight whiskey that has been aged at least four years under government supervision before being bottled — called also *bonded whiskey*

3bond *vt* **1 :** to lap (as brick) for solidity of construction **2 a :** to secure payment of duties and taxes on (goods) by giving a bond **b :** to convert into a debt secured by bonds **c :** to provide a bond for or cause to provide such a bond ⟨~ an employee⟩ **3 a :** to cause to adhere firmly **b :** to embed in a matrix **c :** to hold together in a molecule or crystal by chemical bonds ~ *vi* **:** to hold together or solidify by or as if by means of a bond or binder **:** COHERE — **bond·able** \'bän-də-bəl\ *adj* — **bond·er** *n*

bond·age \'bän-dij\ *n* **1 :** the tenure or service of a villein, serf, or slave **2 :** a state of being bound usu. by compulsion (as of law or mastery): as **a :** CAPTIVITY, SERFDOM ⟨the ~ of the Israelites in Egypt⟩ **b :** servitude or subjugation to a controlling person or force ⟨young people in ~ to drugs⟩ ***syn*** see SERVITUDE

bond·ed \'bänd-əd\ *adj* : composed of two or more layers of the same or different fabrics held together by an adhesive : LAMINATED ⟨~ jersey⟩

bond·er·ize \'bän-də-ˌrīz\ *vt* **-ized; -iz·ing** [back-formation fr. *Bonderized*, a trademark] : to coat (steel) with a patented phosphate solution for protection against corrosion

bond·hold·er \'bänd-ˌhōl-dər\ *n* : one that holds a government or corporation bond

bond·maid \'bän(d)-ˌmād\ *n, archaic* : a female slave or bond servant

bond·man \'bän(d)-mən\ *n* : SLAVE, SERF

bond paper *n* : a strong durable paper orig. used for documents

bond servant *n* : one bound to service without wages; *also* : SLAVE

¹**bonds·man** \'bän(d)z-mən\ *n* : BONDMAN

²**bondsman** *n* : one who assumes the responsibility of a bond : SURETY

bond·stone \'bän(d)-ˌstōn\ *n* : a stone long enough to extend through the full thickness of a wall to bind it together

bond·wom·an \'bän-ˌdwùm-ən\ *n* : a female slave

¹**bone** \'bōn\ *n, often attrib* [ME *bon*, fr. OE *bān*; akin to OHG & ON *bein* bone] **1 a** : one of the hard parts of the skeleton of a vertebrate **b** : any of various hard animal substances or structures (as baleen or ivory) akin to or resembling bone **c** : the hard largely calcareous connective tissue of which the adult skeleton of most vertebrates is chiefly composed **2 a** : ESSENCE, CORE ⟨cut expenses to the ~⟩ ⟨a conservative to the ~⟩ **b** : the most deeply ingrained part : HEART — usu. used in pl. ⟨knew in his ~s that it was an evil deed⟩ **3** *pl* **a** (1) : SKELETON (2) : BODY ⟨ran as fast as his ~s would carry him⟩ (3) : CORPSE ⟨inter a person's ~s⟩ **b** : the basic design or framework (as of a play or novel) **4** : MATTER, SUBJECT ⟨a ~ of contention⟩ **5 a** *pl* : thin bars of bone, ivory, or wood held in pairs between the fingers and used to produce musical rhythms **b** : a strip of whalebone or steel used to stiffen a corset or dress **c** *pl* : DICE **6** : the bow wave of a ship when under way and esp. when traveling at a good speed — usu. used with the phrase *in her teeth* **7** *pl but sing or pl in constr, often cap* : an end man in a minstrel show who may perform on the bones **8** : something that is designed to placate : SOP ⟨throw a ~ to angry workers with a small pay increase⟩ **9** : a light beige — **boned** \'bōnd\ *adj* — **bone·less** \'bōn-ləs\ *adj* — **bone to pick** : a matter to argue or complain about

²**bone** *vb* **boned; bon·ing** *vt* **1** : to remove the bones from ⟨~ a fish⟩ **2** : to provide (a garment) with stays ~ *vi* **1** : to study hard : GRIND ⟨~ through medical school⟩ **2 a** : to try to master necessary information in a short time : CRAM — used with *up* ⟨better ~ up on those theories before the exam⟩ **b** : to renew one's skill or refresh one's memory — used with *up* ⟨~ up on the libretto before going to the opera⟩

³**bone** *adv* : ABSOLUTELY, UTTERLY ⟨~ tired⟩

bone ash *n* : the white porous residue chiefly of tribasic calcium phosphate from bones calcined in air used esp. in making pottery and glass and in cleaning jewelry

bone black *n* : the black residue chiefly of tribasic calcium phosphate and carbon from bones calcined in closed vessels used esp. as a pigment or as a decolorizing adsorbent in sugar manufacturing — called also *bone char*

bone china *n* : translucent white china made with bone ash or calcium phosphate and characterized by whiteness

bone-dry \'bōn-'drī\ *adj* **1** : very dry **2 a** : marked by the absence of intoxicating beverages ⟨the wedding reception was ~⟩ **b** : opposed to the sale of intoxicating beverages

bone·fish \'bōn-ˌfish\ *n* **1 a** : a slender silvery small-scaled fish (*Albula vulpes*) that is a notable sport and food fish of warm seas **b** : any of several fish of the same family (Albulidae) as the bonefish **2** : LADYFISH 2

bone·head \-ˌhed\ *n* : a stupid person : NUMSKULL — **bone·head·ed** \-'hed-əd\ *adj*

bone meal *n* : fertilizer or feed made of crushed or ground bone

bon·er \'bōn-ər\ *n* **1** : one that bones **2** : BLUNDER, HOWLER

bone·set \'bōn-ˌset\ *n* : any of several composite herbs (genus *Eupatorium*); *esp* : a perennial (*E. perfoliatum*) with opposite perfoliate leaves and white-rayed flower heads used in folk medicine

bone·set·ter \-ˌset-ər\ *n* : a person and usu. not a licensed physician who sets broken or dislocated bones

bone·yard \-ˌyärd\ *n* : a place where worn-out or irreparably damaged objects (as cars) are collected to await disposal

bon·fire \'bän-ˌfī(ə)r\ *n* [ME *bonefire* a fire of bones, fr. *bon* bone + *fire*] : a large fire built in the open air

¹**bong** \'bäŋ, 'bòŋ\ *n* [imit.] : the deep resonant sound esp. of a bell

²**bong** *vb* : RING

bon·go \'bäŋ-(ˌ)gō, 'bòŋ-\ *n, pl* **bongos** *also* **bongoes** [AmerSp *bongó*] : one of a pair of small tuned drums played with the hands — **bon·go·ist** \-gō-əst\ *n*

bon·ho·mie \ˌbän-ə-'mē, ˌbō-nə-\ *n* [F *bonhomie*, fr. *bonhomme* good-natured man, fr. *bon* good + *homme* man] : good-natured easy friendliness : GENIALITY

bon·i·face \'bän-ə-fəs, -ˌfäs\ *n* [*Boniface*, innkeeper in *The Beaux' Stratagem* (1707) by George Farquhar] : the proprietor of a hotel, nightclub, or restaurant

boning knife *n* : a short knife with a narrow blade and a sharp point for boning meat or fish

bo·ni·to \bə-'nēt-(ˌ)ō, -'nēt-ə\ *n, pl* **-tos** *or* **-to** [Sp, fr. *bonito* pretty, fr. L *bonus* good] : any of various medium-sized tunas (esp. genera *Sarda* and *Euthynnus*) intermediate between the smaller mackerels and the larger tunas

bon·kers \'bäŋ-kərz, 'bòŋ-\ *adj* [origin unknown] : CRAZY, MAD ⟨if I don't work, I go —Zoe Caldwell⟩

bon mot \bōⁿ-'mō\ *n, pl* **bons mots** \bōⁿ-'mō(z)\ *or* **bon mots** \-'mō(z)\ [F, lit., good word] : a clever remark : WITTICISM

bonne \'bòn\ *n* [F, fr. fem. of *bon*] : a French nursemaid or maidservant

¹**bon·net** \'bän-ət\ *n* [ME *bonet*, fr. MF, fr. ML *abonnis*] **1 a** (1) *chiefly Scot* : a man's or boy's cap (2) : a brimless Scotch cap of seamless woolen fabric — compare TAM-O'-SHANTER **2 b** : a cloth or straw hat tied under the chin and worn by women and small children **2 a** : an additional piece of canvas laced to the foot of a jib or foresail **b** *Brit* : an automobile hood **c** : a cover for an open fireplace or a cowl or hood to increase the draft of a chimney **d** : a metal covering for valve chambers, hydrants, or ventilators

²**bonnet** *vt* : to provide with or dress in a bonnet

bon·ny \'bän-ē\ *adj* **bon·ni·er; -est** [ME *bonie*, fr. OF *bon* good, fr. L *bonus* — more at BOUNTY] *chiefly Brit* : ATTRACTIVE, EXCELLENT — **bon·ni·ly** \-ə-lē\ *adv*

bon·ny·clab·ber \ˌbän-ē-'klab-ər\ *n* [IrGael *bainne clabair*, fr. *bainne* milk + *clabair*, gen. of *clabar* sour thick milk] *North & Midland* : ¹CLABBER

bon·sai \(ˌ)bōn-'sī, 'bōn-,\ *n, pl* **bonsai** [Jap] : a potted plant (as a tree) dwarfed by special methods of culture; *also* : the art of growing such a plant

bon·spiel \'bän-ˌspēl\ *n* [perh. fr. D *bond* league + *spel* game] : a match or tournament between curling clubs

bon ton \(ˈ)bän-'tän, 'bän-,\ *n* [F, lit., good tone] **1 a** : fashionable manner or style ⟨admired the worldliness and *bon ton* of the characters⟩ **b** : the fashionable or proper thing ⟨it was considered *bon ton* to go to the event⟩ **2** : high society

bo·nus \'bō-nəs\ *n* [L, good — more at BOUNTY] **1** : something given in addition to what is usual or strictly due **2 a** *Brit* : DIVIDEND 1b **b** : money or an equivalent given in addition to an employee's usual compensation **c** : a premium (as of stock) given by a corporation to a purchaser of its securities, to a promoter, or to an employee **d** (1) : a government subsidy to an industry (2) : a government payment to war veterans **e** : a sum in excess of salary given an athlete for signing with a professional team **3** : a sum of money in addition to interest or royalties charged for the granting of a loan or privilege to a company or for the lease or transfer of property

bon vi·vant \ˌbän-vē-'vänt, ˌbōⁿ-vē-'väⁿ\ *n, pl* **bons vivants** \ˌbän-vē-'vän(t)s, ˌbōⁿ-vē-'väⁿ(z)\ *or* **bon vivants** *same* \ [F, lit., good liver] : a person having cultivated, refined, and sociable tastes esp. in respect to pleasures of the table **syn** see EPICURE

bon voy·age \ˌbōⁿ-vwī-'äzh, ˌbän-vwä-'yäzh, ˌbōⁿ-ˌvòi-'äzh, ˌbän-\ *n* [F] : FAREWELL — often used interjectionally

bony *or* **bon·ey** \'bō-nē\ *adj* **bon·i·er; -est 1 a** : consisting of bone **b** : resembling bone **2 a** : full of bones ⟨a ~ piece of fish⟩ **b** : having prominent bones ⟨a rugged ~ face⟩ **3 a** : SKINNY, SCRAWNY **b** : BARREN, LEAN

bony fish *n* : TELEOST

bony labyrinth *n* : the cavity in the temporal bone that contains the membranous labyrinth of the ear

bonze \'bänz\ *n* [F, fr. Pg *bonzo*, fr. Jap *bonsō*] : a Buddhist monk

¹**boo** \'bü\ *interj* [ME *bo*] — used to express contempt or disapproval or to startle or frighten

²**boo** *n, pl* **boos 1** : a shout of disapproval or contempt **2** : any sound at all — usu. used in negative constructions ⟨never said ~⟩

³**boo** *vi* : to deride esp. by uttering *boo* ~ *vt* : to express disapproval of by booing ⟨the crowd ~ed the referee⟩

⁴**boo** *n* [origin unknown] : MARIJUANA

boob \'büb\ *n* [short for *booby*] **1** : a stupid awkward person : SIMPLETON **2** : BOOR, PHILISTINE **3** : BREAST — often considered vulgar

boob·oi·sie \ˌbüb-wä-'zē\ *n* [*boob* + *-oisie* (as in *bourgeoisie*)] : a class of the general public that is composed of boobs

boo-boo \'bü-(ˌ)bü\ *n, pl* **boo-boos** [prob. baby-talk alter. of *boohoo*, imitation of the sound of weeping] **1** : a usu. trivial physical injury (as a bruise or scratch) esp. on a child **2** : a foolish mistake : BLUNDER

boob tube *n* : TELEVISION; *specif* : a television set

¹**boo·by** \'bü-bē\ *n, pl* **boobies** [modif. of Sp *bobo*, fr. L *balbus* stammering, prob. of imit. origin] **1** : an awkward foolish person : DOPE **2** : any of several small gannets (genus *Sula*) of tropical seas **3** : the poorest performer or lowest scorer in a group

²**boo·by** \'büb-ē, 'büb-\ *n, pl* **boobies** [alter. of *bubby*, perh. imit. of the noise made by a sucking infant] : BREAST — often considered vulgar

booby hatch *n* **1** : an insane asylum **2** : a place thought to resemble a booby hatch

booby 2

booby prize *n* **1** : an award for the poorest performance in a game or competition **2** : an acknowledgment of notable inferiority

booby trap *n* **1** : a trap for the unwary or unsuspecting : PITFALL **2** : a concealed explosive device contrived to go off when some harmless-looking object is touched — **boo·by-trap** *vt*

boo·dle \'büd-ᵊl\ *n* [D *boedel* estate, lot, fr. MD; akin to ON *būth* booth] **1** : a collection or lot of persons : CABOODLE **2 a** : bribe money **b** : a large amount esp. of money

boog·er \'bùg-ər\ *n* [alter. of E dial. *buggard, boggart*, fr. ¹*bug* + *-ard*] : BOGEYMAN

boo·gey·man \'bùg-ē-ˌman, 'bü-gē-\ *or* **boog·er·man** \'bùg-ər-\ *n* [*boogey*, alter. of *booger* + *man*] : BOGEYMAN

boo·gie-woo·gie \ˌbùg-ē-'wùg-ē, ˌbü-gē-'wü-gē\ *n* [origin unknown] : a percussive style of playing blues on the piano characterized by a steady rhythmic ground bass of eighth notes in quadruple time and a simple often improvised melody — called also *boogie*

¹**book** \'bùk\ *n* [ME, fr. OE *bōc*; akin to OHG *buoh* book, OE *bōc* beech; prob. fr. the early Germanic practice of carving runic char-

acters on beech wood tablets — more at BEECH] **1 a :** a set of written sheets of skin or paper or tablets of wood or ivory **b :** a set of written, printed, or blank sheets bound together into a volume **c :** a long written or printed literary composition **d :** a major division of a treatise or literary work **e :** a volume of business records (as a ledger or journal) — often used in pl. ⟨their ~*s* show a profit⟩ **2** *cap* **:** BIBLE **3 :** something regarded as a source of enlightenment or instruction ⟨her face was an open ~⟩ **4 a :** the total available knowledge and experience that can be brought to bear on a task or problem ⟨tried every trick in the ~ to win the election⟩ **b :** the standards or authority relevant in a situation ⟨the factory is run according to the ~⟩ **5 a :** all the charges that can be made against an accused person ⟨they threw the ~ at him⟩ **b :** a position from which one must answer for certain acts **:** ACCOUNT ⟨the police try to bring criminals to ~⟩ **6 a :** LIBRETTO **b :** the script of a play **c :** the repertory of an orchestra or a musician **7 :** a packet of commodities bound together ⟨a ~ of matches⟩ **8 a** (1) **:** BOOKMAKER (2) **:** a bookmaker's business or base of operations **b :** the bets registered by a bookmaker **9 :** the number of tricks a card player or side must win before any trick can have scoring value — **book·ful** \-,fu̇l\ *n* — **in one's book :** in one's own opinion — **in one's good books :** in favor with one — **one for the book :** an act or occurrence worth noting — **on the books :** on the records

2book *vt* **1 a :** to enter, write, or register so as to engage transportation or reserve lodgings ⟨he is ~*ed* to sail Monday⟩ **b :** to schedule engagements for ⟨~ the band for a week⟩ **c :** to set aside time for **d :** to reserve in advance ⟨~ two seats at the theater⟩ **2 :** to enter charges against in a police register ~ *vi* **1 :** to reserve something in advance ⟨~ through your travel agent⟩ **2** *chiefly Brit* **:** to register in a hotel — **book·er** *n*

3book *adj* **1 :** derived from books and not from practical experience ⟨~ farming⟩ **2 :** shown by books of account

book·bind·ing \'bu̇k-,bīn-diŋ\ *n* **1 :** the binding of a book **2 :** the art or trade of binding books — **book·bind·er** \-,bīn-dər\ *n* — **book·bind·ery** \-d(ə-)rē\ *n*

book·case \-,kās\ *n* **:** a piece of furniture consisting of shelves to hold books

book·end \-,end\ *n* **:** a support placed at the end of a row of books

book·ie \'bu̇k-ē\ *n* [by shortening & alter.] **:** BOOKMAKER 2

book·ing \'bu̇k-iŋ\ *n* **1 :** the act of one that books **2 :** an engagement or scheduled performance ⟨she has ~*s* for several concerts⟩ **3 :** RESERVATION; *esp* **:** one for transportation, entertainment, or lodging

booking office *n, chiefly Brit* **:** a ticket office; *esp* **:** one in a railroad station

book·ish \'bu̇k-ish\ *adj* **1 a :** of or relating to books **b :** fond of books and reading **2 a :** inclined to rely on book knowledge rather than practical experience **b :** literary and formal as opposed to colloquial and informal ⟨many English words derived from Latin have a ~ flavor⟩ **c :** given to literary or scholarly pursuits; *also* **:** affectedly learned ***syn*** see PEDANTIC — **book·ish·ly** *adv* — **book·ish·ness** *n*

book·keep·er \'bu̇k-,kē-pər\ *n* **:** one who records the accounts or transactions of a business — **book·keep·ing** \-piŋ\ *n*

book·let \'bu̇k-lət\ *n* **:** a little book; *esp* **:** PAMPHLET

book louse *n* **:** a minute wingless insect (order Corrodentia); *esp* **:** an insect (as *Liposcelis divinatorius*) injurious esp. to books

book lung *n* **:** a saccular breathing organ in many arachnids containing numerous thin folds of membrane arranged like the leaves of a book

book·mak·er \'bu̇k-,mā-kər\ *n* **1 a :** a printer, binder, or designer of books **b :** one who compiles books from the writings of others **2 :** one who determines odds and receives and pays off bets — **book·mak·ing** \-kiŋ\ *n*

book·man \-mən\ *n* **1 :** one who is interested in books; *esp* **:** LITTERATEUR **2 :** one who sells books

book·mark \-,märk\ *or* **book·mark·er** \-,mär-kər\ *n* **:** a marker for finding a place in a book

book–match \-,mach\ *vt* **:** to match the grains of (as two sheets of veneer) so that one sheet seems to be the mirrored image of the other

book·mo·bile \'bu̇k-mō-,bēl\ *n* [*book* + auto*mobile*] **:** a truck that serves as a traveling library

book of account : a book of business records (as a ledger, journal, or register) that constitutes an integral part of a system of accounts

Book of Common Prayer : the service book of the Anglican Communion

book of original entry : that one of the books of account of an organization (as a cashbook or register of sales) in which transactions are first recorded

book·plate \'bu̇k-,plāt\ *n* **:** a book owner's identification label that is usu. pasted to the inside front cover of a book

book review *n* **:** a usu. written critical estimate of a book

book·sell·er \'bu̇k-,sel-ər\ *n* **:** one who sells books; *esp* **:** the proprietor of a bookstore — **book·sell·ing** \-,sel-iŋ\ *n*

book·shelf \-,shelf\ *n* **:** an open shelf for holding books

book·stall \-,stȯl\ *n* **1 :** a stall where books are sold **2** *chiefly Brit* **:** NEWSSTAND

book·store \-,stō(ə)r, -,stȯ(ə)r\ *n* **:** a place of business where books are the main item offered for sale — called also *bookshop*

book value *n* **:** the value of something as shown by the books of account of the business owning it; *esp* **:** a value of a share of capital stock consisting of its equity in corporate assets usu. exclusive of goodwill less its share in corporate liabilities

book·worm \'bu̇k-,wərm\ *n* **1 :** any of various insect larvae (as of a beetle) that feed on the binding and paste of books **2 :** a person unusually devoted to reading and study

Bool·ean \'bü-lē-ən\ *adj* [George *Boole* †1864 E mathematician] **:** of, relating to, or being a logical combinatorial system that represents symbolically relationships (as those implied by the linguistic operators AND, OR, and NOT) between entities (as sets, propositions, or on-off computer circuit elements) ⟨~ algebra⟩ ⟨~ expression⟩ ⟨~ search strategy for information retrieval⟩

1boom \'büm\ *n* [D, tree, beam; akin to OHG *boum* tree — more at BEAM] **1 :** a long spar used to extend the foot of a sail or facilitate handling of cargo or mooring **2 a :** a long beam projecting from the mast of a derrick to support or guide an object to be lifted or swung **b :** a long movable arm used to manipulate a microphone **3 :** a line of connected floating timbers across a river or enclosing an area of water to keep sawlogs together; *also* **:** the enclosed logs **4 :** a chain cable or line of spars extended across a river or the mouth of a harbor to defend it by obstructing navigation **5 :** a spar or outrigger connecting the tail surfaces and the main supporting structure of an airplane

2boom *vb* [imit.] *vi* **1 :** to make a deep hollow sound **2 a :** to increase in importance or esteem **b :** to experience a sudden rapid growth and expansion usu. with an increase in prices ⟨business was ~*ing*⟩ **c :** to develop rapidly in population and importance ⟨California ~*ed* when gold was discovered there⟩ ~ *vt* **1 :** to cause to resound — often used with *out* ⟨his voice ~*s* out the lyrics⟩ **2 :** to cause a rapid growth or increase of **:** BOOST

3boom *n* **1 :** a booming sound or cry **2 :** a rapid expansion or increase: as **a :** a general movement in support of a candidate for office **b :** rapid settlement and development of a town or district **c :** a rapid widespread expansion of economic activity

boom·er *n* **1 :** one that booms **2 :** one that joins a rush of settlers to a boom area **3 :** a transient worker (as a bridge builder)

boo·mer·ang \'bü-mə-,raŋ\ *n* [native name in Australia] **1 :** a bent or angular throwing club which can be thrown so as to return near the starting point **2 :** an act or utterance that backfires on its originator — **boomerang** *vi*

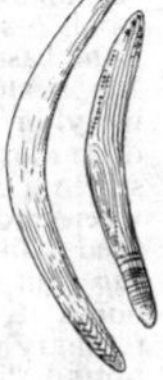

boomerangs 1

boom·let \'büm-lət\ *n* **:** a small boom; *specif* **:** a sudden often short-term increase or expansion ⟨a stock market ~⟩

boomy \'bü-mē\ *adj* **boom·i·er; -est 1 :** of, relating to, or characterized by an economic boom **2 :** having an excessive accentuation on the tones of lower pitch in reproduced sound

1boon \'bün\ *n* [ME, fr. ON *bōn* petition; akin to OE *bēn* prayer, *bannan* to summon — more at BAN] **1 :** BENEFIT, FAVOR; *esp* **:** one that is given in answer to a request **2 :** a timely benefit **:** BLESSING

2boon *adj* [ME *bon,* fr. MF, good — more at BONNY] **1** *archaic* **:** BOUNTEOUS, BENIGN **2 :** MERRY, CONVIVIAL ⟨a ~ companion⟩

boon·docks \'bün-,däks\ *n pl* [Tag *bundok* mountain] **1 :** rough country filled with dense brush **:** JUNGLE **2 :** a rural area **:** STICKS

boon·dog·gle \'bün-,däg-əl, -,dȯg-\ *n* [coined by Robert H. Link †1957 Am scoutmaster] **1 :** a handicraft article made of leather or wicker **2 :** a trivial, useless, or wasteful project or activity — **boondoggle** *vi* — **boon·dog·gler** \-(ə-)lər\ *n*

boon·ies \'bü-nēz\ *n pl, slang* **:** BOONDOCKS 2

boor \'bu̇(ə)r\ *n* [D *boer;* akin to OE *būan* to dwell — more at BOWER] **1 :** PEASANT **2 :** BOER **3 a :** YOKEL **b :** a rude or insensitive person

boor·ish \'bu̇(ə)r-ish\ *adj* **:** resembling or befitting a boor (as in crude insensitivity) — **boor·ish·ly** *adv* — **boor·ish·ness** *n* ***syn*** BOORISH, CHURLISH, LOUTISH, CLOWNISH *shared meaning element* **:** uncouth in manner or appearance ***ant*** gentlemanly

1boost \'büst\ *vb* [origin unknown] vt **1 :** to push or shove up from below **2 a :** INCREASE, RAISE ⟨plans to ~ production by 30 percent next year⟩ **b :** to aid or assist esp. towards progress or increase ⟨an extra holiday to ~ morale⟩ **3 :** to promote the cause or interests of **:** PLUG ⟨a campaign to ~ the new fashions⟩ **4 :** to increase in force, pressure, or amount; *esp* **:** to raise the voltage of or across (an electric circuit) **5** *slang* **:** STEAL, SHOPLIFT ~ *vi, slang* **:** SHOPLIFT ***syn*** see LIFT

2boost *n* **1 :** a push upwards **2 :** an increase in amount **3 :** an act that brings help or encouragement

boost·er \'bü-stər\ *n* **1 :** one that boosts **2 :** an enthusiastic supporter **3 :** an auxiliary device for increasing force, power, or pressure **4 :** a radio-frequency amplifier for a radio or television receiving set **5 :** the first stage of a multistage rocket providing thrust for the launching and the initial part of the flight **6 :** a substance that increases the effectiveness of a medicament; *esp* **:** a supplementary dose of an immunizing agent to increase immunity **7** *slang* **:** SHOPLIFTER

boost·er·ism \-ə-,riz-əm\ *n* **:** the activities and attitudes characteristic of boosters

1boot \'büt\ *n* [ME, fr. OE *bōt* remedy; akin to OE *betera* better] **1** *archaic* **:** DELIVERANCE **2** *chiefly dial* **:** something to equalize a trade **3** *obs* **:** AVAIL — **to boot :** BESIDES

2boot *vb, archaic* **:** AVAIL, PROFIT

3boot *n* [ME, fr. MF *bote*] **1 :** a covering of leather or rubber for the foot and leg **2 :** an instrument of torture used to crush the leg and foot **3 :** a sheath or casing resembling a boot that provides a protective covering for the foot or leg or for an object or part resembling a leg; *also* **:** a thick patch for the inside of a tire casing **4 :** a sheath enclosing the inflorescence **5** *Brit* **:** an automobile trunk **6 a :** a blow delivered by or as if by a booted foot **:** KICK; *also* **:** a rude discharge or dismissal **b :** pleasure or enjoyment esp. of a momentary kind **:** BANG ⟨got a big ~ out of the joke⟩ **7 :** a navy or marine recruit undergoing basic training

4boot *vt* **1 :** to put boots on **2 a :** KICK **b :** to eject or discharge summarily — often used with *out* ⟨was ~*ed* out of office⟩ **3 :** to make an error on (a grounder in baseball)

5boot *n* ['boot] *archaic* **:** BOOTY, PLUNDER

boot·black \'büt-,blak\ *n* **:** one who shines shoes

boot camp *n* **:** a navy or marine camp for basic training

boot·ed \'büt-əd\ *adj* **:** wearing boots

boo·tee *or* **boo·tie** \bü-'tē, *of infants' footwear* 'büt-ē\ *n* **:** a boot or sock with a short leg; *esp* **:** an infant's knitted or crocheted sock

Bo·ö·tes \bō-'ōt-ēz\ *n* [L (gen. *Boötis*), fr. Gk *Boōtēs,* lit., plowman, fr. *bous* head of cattle — more at COW] **:** a northern constellation containing the bright star Arcturus

[3]**bottom** *adj* **1** : of, relating to, or situated at the bottom ⟨~ rock⟩ **2** : frequenting the bottom ⟨~ fishes⟩
bot·tom·land \ˈbät-əm-ˌland\ *n* : BOTTOM 5
bot·tom·less \-ləs\ *adj* **1** : having no bottom ⟨a ~ chair⟩ **2 a** : extremely deep **b** : impossible to comprehend : UNFATHOMABLE ⟨a ~ mystery⟩ **c** : BOUNDLESS, UNLIMITED **3 a** [fr. the absence of lower as well as upper garments] : NUDE ⟨~ dancers⟩ **b** : featuring nude entertainers ⟨a ~ nightclub⟩ — **bot·tom·less·ly** *adv* — **bot·tom·less·ness** *n*
bot·tom·most \ˈbät-əm-ˌmōst\ *adj* **1 a** : situated at the very bottom : LOWEST, DEEPEST **b** : LAST ⟨the ~ part of the day —Alfred Kazin⟩ **2** : most basic ⟨the ~ problems facing the world⟩
bottom out *vi, of a security market* : to decline to a point where demand begins to exceed supply and a rise in prices is imminent
bottom round *n* : meat (as steak) from the outer part of a round of beef
bot·tom·ry \ˈbät-əm-rē\ *n, pl* **-ries** [modif. of D *bodmerij,* fr. *bodem* bottom, ship; akin to OHG *bodam*] : a contract by which a ship is hypothecated as security for repayment of a loan at the end of a successful voyage
bot·u·lin \ˈbäch-ə-lən\ *n* [prob. fr. NL *botulinus*] : a toxin that is formed by the botulinum and is the direct cause of botulism
bot·u·li·num \ˌbäch-ə-ˈlī-nəm\ *also* **bot·u·li·nus** \-nəs\ *n* [NL, fr. L *botulus* sausage] : a spore-forming bacterium (*Clostridium botulinum*) that secretes botulin — **bot·u·li·nal** \-ˈlīn-ᵊl\ *adj*
bot·u·lism \ˈbäch-ə-ˌliz-əm\ *n* : acute food poisoning caused by botulin in food
bou·clé *or* **bou·cle** \bü-ˈklā\ *n* [F *bouclé* curly, fr. pp. of *boucler* to curl, fr. *bocle* buckle, curl] **1** : an uneven yarn of three plies one of which forms loops at intervals **2** : a textile fabric of bouclé yarn
bou·doir \ˈbüd-ˌwär, ˈbu̇d-\ *n* [F, fr. *bouder* to pout] : a woman's dressing room, bedroom, or private sitting room
bouf·fant \bü-ˈfänt, ˈbü-ˌ\ *adj* [F, fr. MF, fr. prp. of *bouffer* to puff] : puffed out ⟨~ hairdos⟩ ⟨a ~ veil⟩
bou·gain·vil·lea *or* **bou·gain·vil·laea** \ˌbüg-ən-ˈvil-yə, ˌbōg-, ˌbu̇g-, -ˈvē-(y)ə\ *n* [NL, fr. Louis Antoine de *Bougainville*] : any of a genus (*Bougainvillaea*) of the four-o'clock family of ornamental tropical American woody vines with brilliant purple or red floral bracts
bough \ˈbau̇\ *n* [ME, shoulder, bough, fr. OE *bōg;* akin to OHG *buog* shoulder, Gk *pēchys* forearm] : a branch of a tree; *esp* : a main branch — **boughed** \ˈbau̇d\ *adj*
bought \ˈbȯt\ *adj* [pp. of *buy*] : READY-MADE ⟨~ clothes⟩
bought·en \-ᵊn\ *adj* [*bought* + *-en* (as in *forgotten*)] *chiefly dial* : BOUGHT ⟨the only ~ carpet in the region —H. W. Thompson⟩
bou·gie \ˈbü-ˌzhē, -ˌjē\ *n* [F, fr. *Bougie,* seaport in Algeria] **1** : a wax candle **2 a** : a tapering cylindrical instrument for introduction into a tubular passage of the body **b** : SUPPOSITORY
bouil·la·baisse \ˌbü-yə-ˈbās\ *n* [F] : a highly seasoned fish stew made of at least two kinds of fish
bouil·lon \ˈbu̇l-ˌyän, -yən; ˈbü-yän, ˈbu̇-\ *n* [F, fr. OF *boillon,* fr. *boillir* to boil] : a clear seasoned soup made usu. from lean beef
bouillon cube *n* : a cube of evaporated seasoned meat extract
boul·der \ˈbōl-dər\ *n* [short for *boulder stone,* fr. ME *bulder ston,* part trans. of a word of Scand origin; akin to Sw dial. *bullersten* large stone in a stream, fr. *buller* noise + *sten* stone] : a detached and rounded or much-worn mass of rock — **boul·dered** \-dərd\ *adj* — **boul·dery** \-d(ə-)rē\ *adj*
[1]**bou·le** \ˈbü-(ˌ)lē, bü-ˈlā\ *n* [Gk *boulē,* lit., will, fr. *boulesthai* to wish] : a legislative council of ancient Greece consisting first of an aristocratic advisory body and later of a representative senate
[2]**boule** \ˈbül\ *n* [F, ball — more at BOWL] : a pear-shaped mass (as of sapphire) formed synthetically in a special furnace with the atomic structure of a single crystal
bou·le·vard \ˈbu̇l-ə-ˌvärd, ˈbül-\ *n* [F, modif. of MD *bolwerc* bulwark] : a broad often landscaped thoroughfare
bou·le·vard·ier \ˌbu̇l-ə-ˌvär-ˈdyā, ˌbül-, -ˈdi(ə)r\ *n* [F, fr. *boulevard* + *-ier* -er] : a frequenter of the Parisian boulevards; *broadly* : MAN-ABOUT-TOWN
bou·le·ver·se·ment \bül-(ə-)ver-sə-mäⁿ\ *n* [F] **1** : REVERSAL **2** : a violent disturbance : DISORDER
boulle \ˈbül, ˈbyü(ə)l\ *n* [André Charles *Boulle* †1732 F cabinetmaker] : inlaid decoration of tortoiseshell, yellow metal, and white metal in cabinetwork
[1]**bounce** \ˈbau̇n(t)s\ *vb* **bounced; bounc·ing** [ME *bounsen*] *vt* **1** *obs* : BEAT, BUMP **2** : to cause to rebound ⟨~ a ball⟩ **3 a** : DISMISS, FIRE **b** : to expel precipitately from a place ~ *vi* **1** : to rebound after striking **2** : to recover from a blow or a defeat quickly — usu. used with *back* **3** : to be returned by a bank as no good ⟨his checks ~⟩ **4 a** : to leap suddenly : BOUND **b** : to walk with springing steps **5** : to hit a baseball so that it hits the ground before it reaches an infielder
[2]**bounce** *n* **1 a** : a sudden leap or bound **b** : REBOUND **2** : BLUSTER **3** : VERVE, LIVELINESS
bounc·er \ˈbau̇n(t)-sər\ *n* : one that bounces: as **a** : one employed to restrain or eject disorderly persons **b** : a batted baseball that bounces
bounc·ing \-siŋ\ *adj* **1** : enjoying good health : ROBUST **2** : LIVELY, ANIMATED — **bounc·ing·ly** \-siŋ-lē\ *adv*
bouncing bet \-ˈbet\ *n, often cap 2d B* [fr. *Bet,* nickname for *Elizabeth*] : a European perennial herb (*Saponaria officinalis*) of the pink family that is widely naturalized in the U.S. and has pink or white flowers and leaves which yield a detergent when bruised — called also *soapwort*
bouncy \ˈbau̇n(t)-sē\ *adj* **bounc·i·er; -est** **1** : BUOYANT, EXUBERANT **2** : RESILIENT **3** : marked by or producing bounces — **bounc·i·ly** \-sə-lē\ *adv*
[1]**bound** \ˈbau̇nd\ *adj* [ME *boun,* fr. ON *būinn,* pp. of *būa* to dwell, prepare; akin to OHG *būan* to dwell — more at BOWER] **1** *archaic* : READY **2** : intending to go : GOING ⟨~ for home⟩ ⟨college-*bound*⟩
[2]**bound** *n* [ME, fr. OF *bodne,* fr. ML *bodina*] **1 a** : a limiting line : BOUNDARY — usu. used in pl. **b** : something that limits or restrains ⟨beyond the ~s of decency⟩ **2** *usu pl* **a** : BORDERLAND **b** : the land within certain bounds
[3]**bound** *vt* **1** : to set limits to : CONFINE **2** : to form the boundary of : ENCLOSE **3** : to name the boundaries of
[4]**bound** *adj* [ME *bounden,* fr. pp. of *binden* to bind] **1 a** : fastened by or as if by a band : CONFINED ⟨desk-*bound*⟩ **b** : CERTAIN, SURE ⟨~ to rain soon⟩ **2** : placed under legal or moral restraint or obligation : OBLIGED ⟨duty-*bound*⟩ **3** : made costive : CONSTIPATED **4** *of a book* **a** : secured to the covers by cords or tapes **b** : cased in **5** : DETERMINED, RESOLVED **6** : held in chemical or physical combination ⟨~ water in a molecule⟩ **7** : always occurring in combination with another linguistic form ⟨*un-* in *unknown* and *-er* in *speaker* are ~ forms⟩ — compare FREE
[5]**bound** *n* [MF *bond,* fr. *bondir* to leap, fr. (assumed) VL *bombitire* to hum, fr. L *bombus* deep hollow sound — more at BOMB] **1** : LEAP, JUMP **2** : the action of rebounding : BOUNCE
[6]**bound** *vi* **1** : to move by leaping **2** : REBOUND, BOUNCE
bound·ary \ˈbau̇n-d(ə-)rē\ *n, pl* **-aries** : something that indicates or fixes a limit or extent; *specif* : a bounding or separating line
boundary layer *n* : a region of retarded fluid near the surface of a body which moves through a fluid or past which a fluid moves
bound·en \ˈbau̇n-dən\ *adj* [ME] **1** *archaic* : being under obligation : BEHOLDEN **2** : made obligatory : BINDING ⟨our ~ duty⟩
bound·er \-dər\ *n* **1** : one that bounds **2** : a man of objectionable social behavior : CAD
bound·er·ish \-də-rish\ *adj* : resembling or typical of a bounder — **bound·er·ish·ly** *adv*
bound·less \ˈbau̇n-dləs\ *adj* : having no boundaries : VAST — **bound·less·ly** *adv* — **bound·less·ness** *n*
bound up *adj* : closely involved or associated — usu. used with *with*
boun·te·ous \ˈbau̇nt-ē-əs\ *adj* [ME *bountevous,* fr. MF *bontif* kind, fr. OF, fr. *bonté*] **1** : giving or disposed to give freely **2** : liberally bestowed — **boun·te·ous·ly** *adv* — **boun·te·ous·ness** *n*
boun·tied \ˈbau̇nt-ēd\ *adj* **1** : having the benefit of a bounty **2** : rewarded or rewardable by a bounty
boun·ti·ful \ˈbau̇nt-i-fəl\ *adj* **1** : liberal in bestowing gifts or favors **2** : given or provided abundantly : PLENTIFUL ⟨a ~ harvest⟩ ***syn*** see LIBERAL ***ant*** niggardly — **boun·ti·ful·ly** \-f(ə-)lē\ *adv* — **boun·ti·ful·ness** \-fəl-nəs\ *n*
boun·ty \ˈbau̇nt-ē\ *n, pl* **bounties** [ME *bounte* goodness, fr. OF *bonté,* fr. L *bonitat-, bonitas,* fr. *bonus* good, fr. OL *duenos;* akin to MHG *zwīden* to grant, L *bene* well] **1** : liberality in giving : GENEROSITY **2** : something that is given generously **3** : yield esp. of a crop **4** : a reward, premium, or subsidy esp. when offered or given by a government: as **a** : an extra allowance to induce entry into the armed services **b** : a grant to encourage an industry **c** : a payment to encourage the destruction of noxious animals **d** : a payment for the capture of an outlaw
bounty hunter *n* **1** : one that hunts predatory animals for the reward offered **2** : one that tracks down and captures outlaws for whom a reward is offered
bou·quet \bō-ˈkā, bü-\ *n* [F, fr. MF, thicket, fr. ONF *bosquet,* fr. OF *bosc* forest — more at BOSCAGE] **1 a** : flowers picked and fastened together in a bunch : NOSEGAY **b** : a large flight of fireworks **2** : COMPLIMENT **3 a** : a distinctive and characteristic fragrance (as of wine) **b** : a subtle aroma or quality (as of an artistic performance or a piece of writing) ***syn*** see FRAGRANCE
bour·bon \ˈbu̇(ə)r-bən, ˈbō(ə)r-, ˈbȯ(ə)r-; *usu* ˈbər- *in sense 4*\ *n* [*Bourbon,* seigniory in France] **1** *cap* : a member of a French family founded in 1272 to which belong the rulers of France from 1589 to 1793 and from 1814 to 1830, of Spain from 1700 to 1808, from 1814 to 1868, from 1875 to 1931, and from 1975, of Naples from 1735 to 1805, and of the Two Sicilies from 1815 to 1860 **2** *often cap* : a person who clings obstinately to the social and political ideas of the old order of things; *specif* : an extremely conservative member of the U.S. Democratic party usu. from the South **3** [*Bourbon* (now Réunion), French island in the Indian ocean] : a rose (*Rosa borboniana*) of compact upright growth with shining leaves, prickly branches, and clustered flowers **4** [*Bourbon* county, Kentucky] : a whiskey distilled from a mash made up of not less than 51 percent corn plus malt and rye — compare CORN WHISKEY — **bour·bon·ism** \-bə-ˌniz-əm\ *n, often cap*
bour·don \ˈbu̇(ə)rd-ᵊn\ *n* [ME *burdoun,* fr. MF *bourdon* bass pipe, of imit. origin] : a drone bass (as in a bagpipe)
bourg \ˈbu̇(ə)r(g)\ *n* [ME, fr. MF, fr. OF *borc,* fr. L *burgus* fortified place, of Gmc origin; akin to OHG *burg* fortified place — more at BOROUGH] : TOWN, VILLAGE: as **a** : one neighboring a castle **b** : a market town
[1]**bour·geois** \ˈbu̇(ə)rzh-ˌwä, bu̇rzh-ˈ\ *n, pl* **bourgeois** \-ˌwä(z), -ˈwä(z)\ [MF, fr. OF *borjois,* fr. *borc*] **1 a** : BURGHER **b** : a middle-class person **2** : one with social behavior and political views held to be influenced by private-property interest : CAPITALIST **3** *pl* : BOURGEOISIE
[2]**bourgeois** *adj* **1** : of, relating to, or characteristic of the townsman or of the social middle class **2** : marked by a concern for material interests and respectability and a tendency toward mediocrity **3** : dominated by commercial and industrial interests : CAPITALISTIC — **bour·geois·ify** \bu̇rzh-ˈwäz-ə-ˌfī\ *vb*
bour·geoise \ˈbu̇(ə)rzh-ˌwäz, bu̇rzh-\ *n* [F, fem. of *bourgeois*] **1** : a woman of the middle class **2** : BOURGEOIS
bour·geoi·sie \ˌbu̇rzh-ˌwä-ˈzē\ *n* [F, fr. *bourgeois*] **1** : MIDDLE CLASS **2** : a social order dominated by bourgeois
bour·geon \ˈbər-jən\ *var of* BURGEON
[1]**bourn** *or* **bourne** \ˈbō(ə)rn, ˈbȯ(ə)rn, ˈbu̇(ə)rn\ *n* [ME *burn, bourne* — more at BURN] : STREAM, BROOK
[2]**bourn** *or* **bourne** *n* [MF *bourne,* fr, OF *bodne* — more at BOUND] **1** *archaic* : BOUNDARY, LIMIT **2** *archaic* : GOAL, DESTINATION

ə abut	ᵊ kitten	ər further	a back	ā bake	ä cot, cart
au̇ out	ch chin	e less	ē easy	g gift	i trip ī life
j joke	ŋ sing	ō flow	ȯ flaw	ȯi coin	th thin th this
ü loot	u̇ foot	y yet	yü few	yu̇ furious	zh vision

bour·rée \bü-'rā, 'bü-,\ *n* [F] **1 :** a 17th century French dance usu. in duple time beginning with an upbeat; *also* : a musical composition with the rhythm of this dance **2 :** PAS DE BOURRÉE

bourse \'bu̇(ə)rs\ *n* [F, lit., purse, fr. ML *bursa* — more at PURSE] **1 :** EXCHANGE 5a; *specif* : a European stock exchange **2 :** a sale of numismatic or philatelic items on tables (as at a convention)

bour·tree \'bu̇(ə)r-(,)trē\ *n* [ME *bourtre*] *Brit* : the common large black-fruited elder (*Sambucus nigra*) of Europe and Asia

bouse \'bau̇z\ *vb* **boused; bous·ing** [origin unknown] *vt* : to haul by means of a tackle ~ *vi* : to bouse something

bou·stro·phe·don \,bü-strə-'fēd-,än, -ᵊn\ *adj* [Gk *boustrophēdon,* adv., lit., turning like oxen in plowing, fr. *bous* ox, cow + *strephein* to turn — more at COW, STROPHE] : having alternate lines written in opposite directions (as from left to right and from right to left); *also* : of, relating to, or using boustrophedon writing

bout \'bau̇t\ *n* [E dial., a trip going and returning in plowing, fr. ME *bought* bend] : a spell of activity: as **a :** an athletic match (as of boxing) **b :** OUTBREAK, ATTACK **c :** SESSION

bou·tique \bü-'tēk\ *n* [F, shop] : a small fashionable specialty shop; *also* : a small shop within a large department store

bou·ton·niere \,büt-ᵊn-'i(ə)r, ,bü-tən-'ye(ə)r\ *n* [F *boutonnière* buttonhole, fr. MF, fr. *bouton* button] : a flower or bouquet worn in a buttonhole

Bou·vi·er des Flan·dres \,bü-vē-,ād-ə-'flan-dərz, -'flä̃ⁿdrᵊ\ *n* [F, lit., cowherd of Flanders] : any of a breed of large powerfully built rough-coated dogs originating in Belgium and used esp. for herding and in guard work

bou·zou·ki *also* **bou·sou·ki** \bu̇-'zü-kē\ *n* [NGk *mpouzouki;* prob. fr. Turk *büyük* large] : a long-necked stringed instrument of Greek origin that resembles a mandolin

[1]**bo·vine** \'bō-,vīn, -,vēn\ *adj* [LL *bovinus,* fr. L *bov-, bos* ox, cow — more at COW] **1 :** of, relating to, or resembling the ox or cow **2 :** having qualities (as sluggishness or patience) characteristic of oxen or cows — **bo·vine·ly** *adv* — **bo·vin·i·ty** \bō-'vin-ət-ē\ *n*

[2]**bovine** *n* : an ox (genus *Bos*) or a closely related animal

[1]**bow** \'bau̇\ *vb* [ME *bowen,* fr. OE *būgan;* akin to OHG *biogan* to bend, Skt *bhujati* he bends] *vi* **1 :** to suffer defeat in a contest : SUBMIT, YIELD **2 :** to bend the head, body, or knee in reverence, submission, or shame **3 :** to incline the head or body in salutation or assent or to acknowledge applause ~ *vt* **1 :** to cause to incline **2 :** to incline (as the head) esp. in respect or submission **3 :** to crush with a heavy burden **4 a :** to express by bowing **b :** to usher in or out with a bow

[2]**bow** *n* : a bending of the head or body in respect, submission, assent, or salutation

[3]**bow** \'bō\ *n* [ME *bowe,* fr. OE *boga;* akin to OE *būgan*] **1 a :** something bent into a simple curve : BEND, ARCH **b :** RAINBOW **2 :** a weapon that is made of a strip of flexible material (as wood) with a cord connecting the two ends and holding the strip bent and that is used to propel an arrow **3 :** ARCHER **4 a :** a metal ring or loop forming a handle (as of a key) **b :** a knot formed by doubling a ribbon or string into two or more loops **c :** BOW TIE **d :** a frame for the lenses of eyeglasses; *also* : the curved sidepiece of the frame passing over the ear **5 a :** a resilient wooden rod with horsehairs stretched from end to end used in playing an instrument of the viol or violin family **b :** a stroke of such a bow

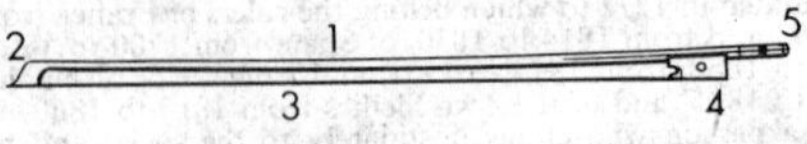

violin bow: *1* stick, *2* head, *3* hair, *4* frog, *5* screw

[4]**bow** \'bō\ *vi* **1 :** to bend into a curve **2 :** to play a stringed musical instrument with a bow ~ *vt* **1 :** to cause to bend into a curve **2 :** to play (a stringed instrument) with a bow

[5]**bow** \'bau̇\ *n* [prob. fr. Dan *bov* shoulder, bow, fr. ON *bōgr;* akin to OE *bōg* bough] **1 :** the forward part of a ship **2 :** [2]BOWMAN

Bow bells \'bō-\ *n pl* : the bells of the Church of St. Mary-le-Bow in London

bowd·ler·iza·tion \,bōd-lə-rə-'zā-shən, ,bau̇d-\ *n* : the act or result of bowdlerizing

bowd·ler·ize \'bōd-lə-,rīz, 'bau̇d-\ *vt* **-ized; -iz·ing** [Thomas *Bowdler* †1825 E editor] : to expurgate (as a book) by omitting or modifying parts considered vulgar — **bowd·ler·iz·er** *n*

[1]**bowed** \'bau̇d\ *adj* [pp. of [1]*bow*] **1 :** bent downward and forward ⟨listened with ~ heads⟩ **2 :** having the back and head inclined

[2]**bowed** \'bōd\ *adj* [partly fr. [3]*bow* + *-ed;* partly fr. pp. of [4]*bow*] : furnished with or shaped like a bow

bow·el \'bau̇(-ə)l\ *n* [ME, fr. OF *boel,* fr. ML *botellus,* fr. L, dim. of *botulus* sausage] **1 :** INTESTINE : one of the divisions of the intestines : GUT — usu. used in pl. except in medical use ⟨the large ~⟩ ⟨move your ~*s*⟩ **2** *archaic* : the seat of pity, tenderness, or courage — usu. used in pl. **3** *pl* : the interior parts; *esp* : the deep or remote parts ⟨~*s* of the earth⟩ — **bow·el·less** \'bau̇(-ə)l-ləs\ *adj*

[1]**bow·er** \'bau̇(-ə)r\ *n* [ME *bour* dwelling, fr. OE *būr;* akin to OE & OHG *būan* to dwell, OE *bēon* to be] **1 :** an attractive dwelling or retreat **2 :** a lady's private apartment in a medieval hall or castle **3 :** a shelter (as in a garden) made with tree boughs or vines twined together : ARBOR — **bow·ery** \-ē\ *adj*

[2]**bower** *vt* : EMBOWER, ENCLOSE

[3]**bower** *n* : an anchor carried at the bow of a ship

bow·er·bird \'bau̇(-ə)r-,bərd\ *n* : any of various passerine birds (family Paradisaeidae) of the Australian region in which the male builds a chamber or passage arched over with twigs and grasses, often adorned with bright-colored objects, and used esp. to attract the female

bow·ery \'bau̇(-ə-)rē\ *n, pl* **-er·ies** [D *bouwerij,* fr. *bouwer* farmer, fr. *bouwen* to till; akin to OHG *būan* to dwell] **1 :** a colonial Dutch plantation or farm **2** [*Bowery,* street in New York City] : a city district notorious for cheap bars and homeless derelicts

bow·fin \'bō-,fin\ *n* : a predaceous dull-green iridescent American freshwater ganoid fish (*Amia calva*) of little value for food or sport

bow·front \-,frənt\ *adj* **1 :** having an outward curving front ⟨~ furniture⟩ **2 :** having a bow window in front ⟨~ houses⟩

bow·head \-,hed\ *n* : the whalebone whale (*Balaena mysticetus*) of the Arctic

bow·ie knife \'bü-ē-, 'bō-\ *n* [James *Bowie* †1836 Am soldier] : a stout single-edged hunting knife with part of the back edge curved concavely to a point and sharpened

bow·ing \'bō-iŋ\ *n* : the technique of managing the bow in playing a stringed musical instrument

bow·knot \'bō-,nät, -'nät\ *n* : a knot with decorative loops

[1]**bowl** \'bōl\ *n* [ME *bolle,* fr. OE *bolla;* akin to OHG *bolla* blister, OE *blāwan* to blow] **1 :** a concave usu. hemispherical vessel used esp. for holding liquids; *specif* : a drinking vessel (as for wine) **2 :** the contents of a bowl **3 :** a bowl-shaped or concave part: as **a :** the hollow of a spoon or tobacco pipe **b :** the receptacle of a toilet **4 a :** a natural formation or geographical region shaped like a bowl **b :** a bowl-shaped structure; *esp* : an athletic stadium **5 :** a postseasonal football game between specially invited teams — **bowled** \'bōld\ *adj* — **bowl·ful** \-,fu̇l\ *n*

[2]**bowl** *n* [ME *boule,* fr. MF, fr. L *bulla* bubble] **1 a :** a ball (as of lignum vitae) weighted or shaped to give it a bias when rolled in lawn bowling **b** *pl but sing in constr* : LAWN BOWLING **2 :** a delivery of the ball in bowling **3 :** a cylindrical roller or drum (as for a mechanical device)

[3]**bowl** *vi* **1 a :** to participate in a game of bowling **b :** to roll a ball in bowling **2 :** to travel in a vehicle smoothly and rapidly ~ *vt* **1 a :** to roll (a ball) in bowling **b** (1) : to complete by bowling ⟨~ a string⟩ (2) : to score by bowling ⟨~*s* 150⟩ **2 :** to strike with a swiftly moving object **3 :** to overwhelm with surprise

bowlder *var of* BOULDER

bow·leg \'bō-,leg, -,lāg, 'bō-'\ *n* : a leg bowed outward at or below the knee — **bow·legged** \'bō-'leg(-ə)d, -'lāg(-ə)d\ *adj*

[1]**bowl·er** \'bō-lər\ *n* : one that bowls; *specif* : the player that delivers the ball to the batsman in cricket

[2]**bow·ler** \'bō-lər\ *n* [*Bowler,* 19th cent. family of E hatters] : a derby hat

bow·line \'bō-lən, -,līn\ *n* [ME *bouline,* perh. fr. *bowe* bow + *line*] **1 :** a rope used to keep the weather edge of a square sail taut forward **2 :** a knot used to form a loop that neither slips nor jams — see KNOT illustration

bowl·ing \'bō-liŋ\ *n* : any of several games in which balls are rolled on a green or down an alley at an object or group of objects

[1]**bow·man** \'bō-mən\ *n* : ARCHER

[2]**bow·man** \'bau̇-mən\ *n* : a boatman, oarsman, or paddler stationed in the front of a boat

Bow·man's capsule \,bō-mənz-\ *n* [Sir William *Bowman* †1892 E surgeon] : a thin membranous double-walled capsule surrounding the glomerulus of a vertebrate nephron

bow out \(')bau̇-\ *vi* : RETIRE, WITHDRAW

bow saw \'bō-\ *n* : a saw having a narrow blade held under tension by a light bow-shaped frame

bowse \'bau̇z\ *var of* BOUSE

bow·sprit \'bau̇-,sprit, 'bō-\ *n* [ME *bouspret,* prob. fr. MLG *bōchsprēt,* fr. *bōch* bow + *sprēt* pole] : a large spar projecting forward from the stem of a ship

bow·string \'bō-,striŋ\ *n* : a waxed or sized cord joining the ends of a shooting bow

bowstring hemp *n* : any of various Asiatic and African sansevierias; *also* : its soft tough leaf fiber used esp. in cordage

bow tie \'bō-\ *n* : a short necktie tied in a bowknot

bow window \'bō-\ *n* : a usu. curved bay window

bow·wow \'bau̇-,wau̇, bau̇-'\ *n* [imit.] **1 :** the bark of a dog; *also* : DOG **2 :** noisy clamor **3 :** arrogant dogmatic manner

bow·yer \'bō-yər\ *n* : one that makes shooting bows

[1]**box** \'bäks\ *n, pl* **box** *or* **box·es** [ME, fr. OE, fr. L *buxus,* fr. Gk *pyxos*] : an evergreen shrub or small tree (genus *Buxus* of the family Buxaceae, the box family) with opposite entire leaves and capsular fruits; *esp* : a widely cultivated shrub (*B. sempervirens*) used for hedges, borders, and topiary figures

[2]**box** *n* [ME, fr. OE, fr. LL *buxis,* fr. Gk *pyxis,* fr. *pyxos*] **1 a :** a rigid typically rectangular receptacle often with a cover **b :** something having a flat bottom and four upright sides **c :** the contents of a box as a measure of quantity **d :** the driver's seat on a carriage or coach **e** *slang* : GUITAR **f** *slang* : RECORD PLAYER **2** *Brit* : a gift in a box **3 a :** a small compartment (as for a group of spectators in a theater) **b :** PENALTY BOX **4 a :** a boxlike receptacle (as for a bearing) **b :** a signaling apparatus with its enclosing case ⟨a police ~⟩ **5 :** a square or oblong division or compartment **6 :** a square or oblong hollow space or recess **7 :** a small simple sheltering or enclosing structure **8 a :** printed matter enclosed by rules or white space **b :** FRAME 6b(1) **9 :** any of six spaces on a baseball diamond where the batter, coaches, pitcher, and catcher stand **10 :** PREDICAMENT, FIX — **box·ful** \-,fu̇l\ *n*

[3]**box** *vt* **1 :** to furnish (as a wheel hub) with a box **2 :** to enclose in or as if in a box **3 :** BOXHAUL **4 :** to enclose with boarding or lathing so as to bring to a required form **5 :** to mix (paint) by pouring back and forth between two containers **6 :** to hem in (as an opponent) — usu. used with *in, out,* or *up* ⟨~*ed* out the opposing tackle⟩ — **box the compass** **1 :** to name the 32 points of the compass in their order **2 :** to make a complete reversal

[4]**box** *n* [ME] : a punch or slap esp. on the ear

[5]**box** *vt* **1 :** to hit (as the ears) with the hand **2 :** to engage in boxing with ~ *vi* : to fight with the fists : engage in boxing

box calf *n* : calfskin that is tanned with chromium salts and has square markings on the grain

box camera *n* : a camera of simple box shape with a simple lens and rotary shutter

box·car \'bäk-,skär\ *n* : a roofed freight car usu. with sliding doors in the sides

box coat *n* **1 :** a heavy overcoat formerly worn for driving **2 :** a loose coat usu. fitted at the shoulders

box elder *n* : a No. American maple (*Acer negundo*) with compound leaves

¹box·er \'bäk-sər\ *n* : one that engages in the sport of boxing

²boxer *n* : one that makes boxes or packs things in boxes

³boxer *n* [G, fr. E ¹*boxer*] : a compact medium-sized short-haired usu. fawn or brindle dog of a breed originating in Germany

Box·er \'bäk-sər\ *n* (approx. trans. of Chin (Pek.) *i⁴ho²ch'üan²*, lit., righteous harmonious fist] : a member of a Chinese secret society that in 1900 attempted by violence to drive foreigners out of China and to force native converts to renounce Christianity

boxer shorts *n pl* : SHORT 4b

box·haul \'bäks-,hȯl\ *vt* : to put (a square-rigged ship) on the other tack by luffing and then veering short round on the heel

¹box·ing \'bäk-siŋ\ *n* **1** : an act of enclosing in a box **2** : a box-like enclosure : CASING **3** : material used for boxes and casings

²boxing *n* : the art of attack and defense with the fists practiced as a sport

Boxing Day *n* : the first weekday after Christmas observed as a legal holiday in parts of the British Commonwealth and marked by the giving of Christmas boxes to service workers (as postmen)

boxing glove *n* : one of a pair of leather mittens heavily padded on the back and worn in boxing

boxing ring

box kite *n* : a tailless kite consisting of two or more open-ended connected boxes

box·like \'bäk-,slīk\ *adj* : resembling a box esp. in shape

box lunch *n* : a lunch packed in a container (as a box)

box office *n* **1** : an office (as in a theater) where tickets of admission are sold **2** : success (as of a show) in attracting ticket buyers; *also* : something that enhances such success

box pleat *n* : a pleat made by forming two folded edges one facing right and the other left

box score *n* [fr. its arrangement in a newspaper box] : a printed score of a game (as baseball) giving the names and positions of the players and a record of the play arranged in tabular form; *broadly* : total count : SUMMARY

box seat *n* **1** : the driver's seat on a coach **2 a** : a seat in a box (as in a theater or grandstand) **b** : a position favorable for viewing something

box social *n* : a fund-raising affair at which box lunches or suppers are auctioned to the highest bidder

box spring *n* : a bedspring that consists of spiral springs attached to a foundation and enclosed in a cloth-covered frame

box stall *n* : an individual enclosure within a barn or stable in which an animal may move about freely without a restraining device (as a tether)

box·thorn \'bäks-,thȯ(ə)rn\ *n* : MATRIMONY VINE

box turtle *n* : any of several No. American land tortoises (genus *Terrapene*) capable of withdrawing entirely within the shell and closing it by hinged joints in the lower shell — called also *box tortoise*

box·wood \'bäk-,swud\ *n* **1** : the very close-grained heavy tough hard wood of the box (*Buxus*); *also* : a wood of similar properties **2** : a plant producing boxwood

boxy \'bäk-sē\ *adj* **box·i·er; -est** : resembling a box — **box·i·ness** *n*

boy \'bȯi\ *n, often attrib* [ME; akin to Fris *boi* boy] **1 a** : a male child from birth to puberty **b** : SON **c** : an immature male : YOUTH **d** : SWEETHEART, BEAU **2 a** : one native to a given place ⟨local ∼⟩ **b** : FELLOW, PERSON ⟨the ∼s at the office⟩ — often used interjectionally ⟨∼, what a game⟩ **3** : a male servant — sometimes taken to be offensive — **boy·hood** \-,hud\ *n* — **boy·ish** \-ish\ *adj* — **boy·ish·ly** *adv* — **boy·ish·ness** *n*

bo·yar *also* **bo·yard** \bō-'yär, 'bȯi-ər\ *n* [Russ *boyarin*, fr. OSlav *boljarinŭ*] : a member of a Russian aristocratic order next in rank below the ruling princes until its abolition by Peter the Great

¹boy·cott \'bȯi-,kät\ *vt* [Charles C. *Boycott* †1897 E land agent in Ireland who was ostracized for refusing to reduce rents] : to engage in a concerted refusal to have dealings with (as a person, store, or organization) usu. to express disapproval or to force acceptance of certain conditions — **boy·cot·ter** *n*

²boycott *n* : the process or an instance of boycotting

boy·friend \'bȯi-,frend\ *n* **1** : a male friend **2** : a frequent or regular male companion of a girl or woman **3** : a male lover

Boyg \'bȯig\ *n* [Norw *bøig* bugbear] : a formless or pervasive obstacle, problem, or enemy

boyo \'bȯi-(,)ō\ *n, pl* **boy·os** [*boy* + -*o*] *Irish* : BOY, LAD

boy scout *n* **1** : a member of the Boy Scouts of America **2** : one who performs a service for or gives assistance to others

boy·sen·ber·ry \'bȯiz-ⁿn-,ber-ē, 'bȯis-\ *n* [Rudolph *Boysen* †1950 Am horticulturist + E *berry*] : a large bramble fruit with a raspberry flavor; *also* : the trailing hybrid bramble yielding this fruit and developed by crossing several blackberries and raspberries

boy wonder *n* : a young man whose achievements arouse admiration

bo·zo \'bō-(,)zō\ *n, pl* **bozos** [origin unknown] *slang* : FELLOW, GUY

bp *abbr* **1** baptized **2** birthplace **3** bishop

BP *abbr* **1** before the present **2** blood pressure **3** blueprint **4** boiling point

BPD *abbr* barrels per day

BPE *abbr* **1** bachelor of petroleum engineering **2** bachelor of physical education

BPh *abbr* bachelor of philosophy

bpi *abbr* bits per inch; bytes per inch

bpl *abbr* birthplace

BPOE *abbr* Benevolent and Protective Order of Elks

BPW *abbr* **1** Board of Public Works **2** Business and Professional Women's Clubs

br *abbr* **1** branch **2** brass **3** brown

¹Br *abbr* British

²Br *symbol* bromine

BR *abbr* **1** bats right **2** bedroom **3** bills receivable

bra \'brä\ *n* : BRASSIERE

brab·ble \'brab-əl\ *vi* **brab·bled; brab·bling** \-(ə-)liŋ\ [MD *brabbelen*, of imit. origin] : SQUABBLE — **brabble** *n*

¹brace \'brās\ *n* [ME, pair, clasp, fr. MF, two arms, fr. L *bracchia*, pl. of *bracchium* arm, fr. Gk *brachiōn*, fr. compar. of *brachys* short — more at BRIEF] **1** *or pl* **brace** : two of a kind ⟨several ∼ of quail⟩ **2** : something (as a clasp) that connects or fastens **3** : a crank-shaped instrument for turning a bit **4** : something that transmits, directs, resists, or supports weight or pressure: as **a** : a diagonal piece of structural material that serves to strengthen something (as a framework) **b** : a rope rove through a block at the end of a ship's yard to swing it horizontally **c** *pl* : SUSPENDERS **d** : an appliance for supporting a body part **e** *pl* : dental appliances used to exert pressure to straighten misaligned teeth **5 a** : a mark { or } used to connect words or items to be considered together **b** (1) : this mark connecting two or more musical staffs the parts on which are to be performed simultaneously (2) : the staffs so connected — called also : BRACKET 3a **6** : an exaggerated position of rigidly erect bearing **7** : something that arouses energy or strengthens morale

²brace *vb* **braced; brac·ing** *vt* **1** *archaic* : to fasten tightly : BIND **2 a** : to prepare for use by making taut **b** : PREPARE, STEEL ⟨∼ yourself for the shock⟩ **c** : INVIGORATE, FRESHEN **3** : to turn (a sail yard) by means of a brace **4 a** : to furnish or support with a brace ⟨heavily *braced* because of polio⟩ **b** : to make stronger : REINFORCE **5** : to put or plant firmly ⟨∼s his foot in the stirrup⟩ **6** : to waylay esp. with demands or questions ∼ *vi* **1** : to take heart — used with *up* **2** : to get ready (as for an attack)

brace·let \'brā-slət\ *n* [ME, fr. MF, dim. of *bras* arm, fr. L *bracchium*] **1** : an ornamental band or chain worn around the wrist **2** : something (as handcuffs) resembling a bracelet

¹bra·cer \'brā-sər\ *n* [ME, fr. MF *braciere*, fr. OF, fr. *braz* arm, fr. L *bracchium*] : an arm or wrist protector esp. for use by an archer

²brac·er \'brā-sər\ *n* **1** : one that braces, binds, or makes firm **2** : a drink (as of liquor) taken as a stimulant

bra·ce·ro \brä-'se(ə)r-(,)ō\ *n, pl* **-ros** [Sp, laborer, fr. *brazo* arm, fr. L *brachium*] : a Mexican laborer admitted to the U.S. esp. for seasonal contract labor in agriculture — compare WETBACK

brace root *n* : PROP ROOT

bra·chi·ate \'brā-kē-,āt\ *vi* **-at·ed; -at·ing** [L *bracchium*] : to progress by swinging from one hold to another by the arms ⟨brachiating gibbon⟩ — **bra·chi·a·tion** \,brā-kē-'ā-shən\ *n*

bra·chio·pod \'brā-kē-ə-,päd\ *n* [deriv. of L *bracchium* + Gk *pod-, pous* foot — more at FOOT] : any of a phylum (Brachiopoda) of marine invertebrates with bivalve shells within which is a pair of arms bearing tentacles by which a current of water is made to bring microscopic food to the mouth — **brachiopod** *adj*

bra·chi·um \'brā-kē-əm\ *n, pl* **-chia** \-kē-ə\ [L *bracchium, brachium* arm] **1** : the upper part of the arm or forelimb from shoulder to elbow **2** : a process of an invertebrate comparable to an arm — **bra·chi·al** \-əl\ *adj*

brachy- *comb form* [Gk, fr. *brachys* — more at BRIEF] : short ⟨*brachydactylous*⟩

brachy·ce·phal·ic \,brak-i-sə-'fal-ik\ *adj* [NL *brachycephalus*, fr. Gk *brachy-* + *kephalē* head — more at CEPHALIC] : short-headed or broad-headed with a cephalic index of over 80 — **brachy·ceph·a·ly** \-'sef-ə-lē\ *n*

brachy·ceph·a·li·za·tion \-,sef-ə-lə-'zā-shən\ *n* : transition toward a more brachycephalic condition ⟨the increasing ∼ of Europe⟩

brachy·dac·ty·lous \,brak-i-'dak-tə-ləs\ *adj* : having abnormally short digits — **brachy·dac·ty·ly** \-lē\ *n*

bra·chyp·ter·ous \bra-'kip-tə-rəs\ *adj* [Gk *brachypteros*, fr. *brachy-* + *pteron* wing — more at FEATHER] : having rudimentary or abnormally small wings ⟨∼ insects⟩

brachy·uran \,brak-ē-'yur-ən\ *n* [deriv. of Gk *brachy-* + *oura* tail — more at SQUIRREL] : any of a tribe or suborder (Brachyura) of crustaceans (as the typical crabs) having the abdomen greatly reduced — **brachyuran** *adj* — **brachy·urous** \-'yur-əs\ *adj*

brac·ing \'brā-siŋ\ *adj* : giving strength, vigor, or freshness ⟨a ∼ breeze⟩

brack·en \'brak-ən\ *n* [ME *braken*, prob. of Scand origin; akin to OSw *brækne* fern] **1** : a large coarse fern; *esp* : a common brake (*Pteridium aquilinum*) **2** : a growth of brakes

¹brack·et \'brak-ət\ *n* [MF *braguette* codpiece, fr. dim. of *brague* breeches, fr. OProv *braga*, fr. L *braca*, fr. Gaulish *brāca*, of Gmc origin; akin to OHG *bruoh* breeches — more at BREECH] **1** : an overhanging member that projects from a structure (as a wall) and is usu. designed to support a vertical load or to strengthen an angle **2 a** : a short wall shelf **b** : a fixture (as for holding a lamp) projecting from a wall or column **3 a** : one of a pair of marks [ ] used in writing and printing to enclose matter or in mathematics and logic as signs of aggregation — called also *square bracket* **b** : one of the pair of marks ⟨ ⟩ used to enclose matter — called also *angle bracket* **c** : PARENTHESIS 3 **d** : BRACE 5b **4** : a pair of shots fired (as in front of and beyond a target) to aid in determining the exact distance from gun to target **5 a** : a section of a continuously numbered or graded series ⟨the 18 to 22 age ∼⟩ **b** : one of a graded series of income groups ⟨the $20,000 income ∼⟩

²bracket *vt* **1 a** : to place within or as if within brackets **b** : to eliminate from consideration ⟨his approach to moral questions ∼s off religion⟩ **2** : to furnish or fasten with brackets **3 a** : to put in the same category : ASSOCIATE **b** : to assign to a group : CLASSIFY **4 a** : to get the range on (a target) by firing over and short **b** : to establish a margin on either side of (as an estimation)

brack·et·ed *adj, of a serif* : joined to the stroke by a curved line

bracket fungus *n* : a basidiomycete that forms shelflike sporophores

brack·ish \'brak-ish\ *adj* [D *brac* salty; akin to MLG *brac* salty] **1** : somewhat salty **2 a** : not appealing to the taste ⟨~ tea⟩ **b** : REPULSIVE — **brack·ish·ness** *n*

bract \'brakt\ *n* [NL *bractea,* fr. L, thin metal plate] **1** : a leaf from the axil of which a flower or floral axis arises **2** : a leaf borne on a floral axis; *esp* : one subtending a flower or flower cluster — see COMPOSITE illustration — **brac·te·al** \'brak-tē-əl\ *adj* — **brac·te·ate** \-tē-ət, -ˌāt\ *adj* — **bract·ed** \-təd\ *adj*

brac·te·ole \'brak-tē-ˌōl\ *n* [NL *bracteola,* fr. L, dim. of *bractea*] : a small bract esp. on a floral axis — **brac·te·o·late** \ brak-'tē-ə-lət, 'brak-tē-ə-ˌlāt\ *adj*

¹brad \'brad\ *n* [ME, fr. ON *broddr* spike; akin to OE *byrst* bristle — more at BRISTLE] **1** : a thin nail of the same thickness throughout but tapering in width and having a slight projection at the top of one side instead of a head **2** : a slender wire nail with a small barrel-shaped head

²brad *vt* **brad·ded; brad·ding** : to fasten with brads

brad·awl \'brad-ˌȯl\ *n* : an awl with chisel edge used to make holes for brads or screws

bra·dy·car·dia \ˌbrad-i-'kärd-ē-ə *also* ˌbrad-\ *n* [NL, fr. Gk *bradys* slow + NL *-cardia*] : relatively slow heart action whether physiological or pathological — compare TACHYCARDIA

bra·dy·ki·nin \-'kī-nən\ *n* [Gk *bradys* slow] : a kinin that is formed in injured tissue, acts in vasodilation of small arterioles, is considered to play a part in inflammatory processes, and is composed of nine amino acids

brae \'brā\ *n* [ME *bra,* fr. ON *brā* eyelash; akin to OE *bregdan* to move quickly — more at BRAID] *chiefly Scot* : a hillside esp. along a river

¹brag \'brag\ *adj* **brag·ger; brag·gest** [ME] : FIRST-RATE

²brag *n* **1** : a pompous or boastful statement **2** : arrogant talk or manner : COCKINESS **3** : BRAGGART

³brag *vb* **bragged; brag·ging** *vi* : to talk boastfully : engage in self-glorification ~ *vt* : to assert boastfully **syn** see BOAST **ant** apologize — **brag·ger** \'brag-ər\ *n* — **brag·gy** \'brag-ē\ *adj*

brag·ga·do·cio \ˌbrag-ə-'dō-s(h)ē-ˌō, -(ˌ)shō\ *n, pl* **-cios** [*Braggadochio,* personification of boasting in *Faerie Queene* by Edmund Spenser] **1** : BRAGGART **2 a** : empty boasting **b** : arrogant pretension : COCKINESS

brag·gart \'brag-ərt\ *n* : a loud arrogant boaster — **braggart** *adj*

brah·ma \'bräm-ə, 'bram-, 'bram-\ *n* [*Brahmaputra* river, India] : any of an Asian breed of large domestic fowls with feathered legs

¹Brah·ma \'bräm-ə\ *n* [Skt *brahman*] **1** : the ultimate ground of all being in Hinduism **2** : the creator god of the Hindu sacred triad — compare SIVA, VISHNU

²Brah·ma \'brä-mə, 'bräm-ə\ *n* : BRAHMAN 2

Brah·man *or* **Brah·min** \'bräm-ən; *2 is* 'bräm-, 'bräm-, 'bram-\ *n* [Skt *brāhmana,* lit., having to do with prayer, fr. *brahman,* neut., prayer] **1** : a Hindu of the highest caste traditionally assigned to the priesthood **b** : ¹BRAHMA 1 **2** : any of an Indian breed of humped cattle : ZEBU; *esp* : a large vigorous heat-resistant and tick-resistant usu. silvery gray animal developed in the southern U.S. by interbreeding Indian cattle and used chiefly for crossbreeding — **Brah·man·ic** \brä-'man-ik\ *adj*

Brah·man·ism \'bräm-ə-ˌniz-əm\ *n* : orthodox Hinduism adhering to the pantheism of the Vedas and to the ancient sacrifices and family ceremonies

Brah·min \'bräm-ən\ *n* [var. of *Brahman*] : an intellectually and socially cultivated person regarded as aloof; *esp* : such a person from one of the older New England families ⟨Boston ~s⟩ — **Brahmin·i·cal** \brä-'min-i-kəl\ *adj* — **Brah·min·ism** \'bräm-ə-ˌniz-əm\ *n*

¹braid \'brād\ *vt* [ME *breyden,* lit., to move suddenly, fr. OE *bregdan;* akin to OHG *brettan* to draw (a sword), Gk *phorkon* something white or wrinkled] **1 a** : to form (three or more strands) into a braid **b** : to make by braiding **2** : to do up (the hair) by interweaving three or more strands **3** : INTERMINGLE, MIX ⟨~ fact with fiction⟩ **4** : to ornament esp. with ribbon or braid — **braid·er** *n*

²braid *n* **1 a** : a cord or ribbon having usu. three or more component strands forming a regular diagonal pattern down its length; *esp* : a narrow fabric of intertwined threads used esp. for trimming **b** : a length of braided hair **2** : high-ranking naval officers

braid·ed *adj* **1 a** : ornamented with braid **b** : made by intertwining three or more strands **2** : forming an interlacing network of channels ⟨a ~ river⟩

braid·ing \'brād-iŋ\ *n* : something made of braided material

¹brail \'brā(ə)l\ *n* [ME *brayle,* fr. AF *braiel,* fr. OF, strap] **1** : a rope fastened to the leech of a sail and used for hauling the sail up or in **2** : a dip net with which fish are hauled aboard a boat from a purse seine or trap

²brail *vt* **1** : to take in (a sail) by the brails **2** : to hoist (fish) by

braille \'brā(ə)l\ *n, often cap* [Louis *Braille*] : a system of writing for the blind that uses characters made up of raised dots — **braille** *vt*

braille·writ·er \-ˌrīt-ər\ *n, often cap* : a machine for writing braille

¹brain \'brān\ *n* [ME, fr. OE *brægen;* akin to MLG *bregen* brain, Gk *brechmos* front part of the head] **1 a** : the portion of the vertebrate central nervous system that constitutes the organ of thought and neural coordination, includes all the higher nervous centers receiving stimuli from the sense organs and interpreting and correlating them to formulate the motor impulses, is made up of neurons and supporting and nutritive structures, is enclosed within the skull, and is continuous with the spinal cord through the foramen magnum **b** : a nervous center in invertebrates comparable in position and function to the vertebrate brain **2 a** (1) : INTELLECT, MIND ⟨has a clever ~⟩ (2) : intellectual endowment : INTELLIGENCE — often used in pl. ⟨plenty of ~s in that family⟩ **b** (1) : a very intelligent or intellectual person (2) : the chief planner of an organization or enterprise — usu. used in pl. **3** : an automatic device (as a computer) that performs one or more of the functions of the human brain for control or computation

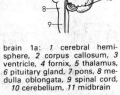

brain 1a: *1* cerebral hemisphere, *2* corpus callosum, *3* ventricle, *4* fornix, *5* thalamus, *6* pituitary gland, *7* pons, *8* medulla oblongata, *9* spinal cord, *10* cerebellum, *11* midbrain

²brain *vt* **1** : to kill by smashing the skull **2** : to hit on the head

brain·case \'brān-ˌkās\ *n* : the cranium enclosing the brain

brain·child \-ˌchīld\ *n* : a product of one's creative imagination

brain drain *n* : a migration of professional people (as scientists, professors, or physicians) from one country to another usu. for higher salaries or better living conditions

-brained \'brānd\ *adj comb form* : having (such) a brain ⟨big-brained⟩ ⟨featherbrained⟩

brain hormone *n* : a hormone that is secreted by neurosecretory cells of the insect brain and that stimulates the prothoracic glands to secrete ecdysone

brain·ish \'brā-nish\ *adj, archaic* : IMPETUOUS, HOTHEADED ⟨and in this ~ apprehension kills the unseen good old man —Shak.⟩

brain·less \'brān-ləs\ *adj* : devoid of intelligence : STUPID — **brainless·ly** *adv* — **brain·less·ness** *n*

brain·pan \'brān-ˌpan\ *n* : BRAINCASE

brain–pick·ing \-ˌpik-iŋ\ *n* : the act of picking information from another's mind — **brain–pick·er** *n*

brain–pow·er \-ˌpau̇(-ə)r\ *n* **1** : intellectual ability **2** : people with developed intellectual ability

brain·sick \-ˌsik\ *adj* **1** : mentally disordered **2** : arising from mental disorder ⟨a ~ frenzy⟩ — **brain·sick·ly** *adv*

brain stem *n* : the part of the brain composed of the mesencephalon, pons, and medulla oblongata and connecting the spinal cord with the forebrain and cerebrum

brain·storm \-ˌstȯ(ə)rm\ *n* **1** : a violent transient fit of insanity **2 a** : a sudden bright idea **b** : a harebrained idea

brain·storm·ing \-ˌstȯr-miŋ\ *n* : a group problem-solving technique that involves the spontaneous contribution of ideas from all members of the group — **brain·storm** *vt* — **brain·storm·er** *n*

brains trust *n, chiefly Brit* : BRAIN TRUST

brain·teas·er \-ˌtē-zər\ *n* : something (as a puzzle) that demands mental effort and acuity for its solution

brain trust *n* : expert advisers concerned esp. with planning and strategy who often lack official or acknowledged status — **brain trust·er** \-ˌtrəs-tər\ *n*

brain·wash·ing \'brān-ˌwȯsh-iŋ, -ˌwäsh-\ *n* [trans. of Chin (Pek) *hsi¹ nao³*] **1** : a forcible indoctrination to induce someone to give up basic political, social, or religious beliefs and attitudes and to accept contrasting regimented ideas **2** : persuasion by propaganda or salesmanship — **brain·wash** *vt* — **brainwash** *n* — **brain·wash·er** *n*

brain wave *n* **1 a** : rhythmic fluctuations of voltage between parts of the brain resulting in the flow of an electric current **b** : a current produced by brain waves **2** : BRAINSTORM 2a

brainy \'brā-nē\ *adj* **brain·i·er; -est** : having a well-developed intellect : INTELLIGENT ⟨he was ~ enough to outmaneuver the intransigents —W. V. Shannon⟩ — **brain·i·ness** *n*

braise \'brāz\ *vt* **braised; brais·ing** [F *braiser*] : to cook slowly in fat and little moisture in a closed pot

¹brake \'brāk\ *archaic past of* BREAK

²brake \'brāk\ *n* [ME, fern] : any of a genus (*Pteridium*) of tall ferns with ternately compound fronds

³brake *n* [ME, fr. MLG; akin to OE *brecan* to break] **1** : a toothed instrument or machine for separating out the fiber of flax or hemp by breaking up the woody parts **2** : a machine for bending, flanging, folding, and forming sheet metal

⁴brake *n* [ME] **1** : a device for arresting the motion of a mechanism usu. by means of friction **2** : something used to slow down or stop movement or activity ⟨interest rates acting as a ~ on expenditures⟩ — **brake·less** \'brā-kləs\ *adj*

⁵brake *vb* **braked; brak·ing** *vt* : to retard or stop by a brake ~ *vi* **1** : to operate or manage a brake; *esp* : to apply the brake on a vehicle **2** : to become checked by a brake

⁶brake *n* [ME *-brake*] : rough or marshy land overgrown usu. with one kind of plant — **braky** \'brā-kē\ *adj*

brake·man \'brāk-mən\ *n* **1** : a freight or passenger train crew member who inspects the train and assists the conductor **2** : the end man on a bobsled team who operates the brake

bram·ble \'bram-bəl\ *n* [ME *brembel,* fr. OE *brēmel;* akin to OE *brōm* broom] : any of a genus (*Rubus*) of usu. prickly shrubs of the

rose family including the raspberries and blackberries; *broadly* : a rough prickly shrub or vine — **bram·bly** \-b(ə-)lē\ *adj*
bran \'bran\ *n* [ME, fr. OF] : the broken coat of the seed of cereal grain separated from the flour or meal by sifting or bolting
¹branch \'branch\ *n, often attrib* [ME, fr. OF *branche,* fr. LL *branca* paw] **1** : a natural subdivision of a plant stem; *esp* : a secondary shoot or stem (as a bough) arising from a main axis (as of a tree) **2** : something that extends from or enters into a main body or source: as **a** (1) : a stream that flows into another usu. larger stream : TRIBUTARY (2) *South & Midland* : CREEK 2 **b** : a side road or way **c** : a slender projection (as the tine of an antler) **d** : a part of a mathematical curve separated from others **e** : a part of a computer program executed as a result of a program decision **3** : a part of a complex body: as **a** : a division of a family descending from a particular ancestor **b** : an area of knowledge that may be considered apart from related areas ⟨pathology is a ~ of medicine⟩ **c** (1) : a division of an organization (2) : a separate but dependent part of a central organization ⟨the neighborhood ~ of the city library⟩ **d** : a language group less inclusive than a family ⟨the Germanic ~ of the Indo-European language family⟩ — **branched** \'brancht\ *adj* — **branch·less** \'branch-ləs\ *adj* — **branchy** \'bran-chē\ *adj*
²branch *vi* **1** : to put forth branches : RAMIFY **2** : to spring out (as from a main stem) : DIVERGE **3** : to be an outgrowth — used with *from* ⟨poetry that ~*ed* from religious prose⟩ **4** : to extend activities — usu. used with *out* ⟨the business is ~*ing* out all over the state⟩ **5** : to follow one of two or more branches (as in a computer program) ~ *vt* **1** : to ornament with designs of branches **2** : to divide up : SECTION
bran·chia \'braŋ-kē-ə\ *n, pl* **-chi·ae** \-kē-ˌē, -ˌī\ [L, sing., fr. Gk, pl. of *branchion* gill; akin to Gk *bronchos* trachea — more at CRAW] : ²GILL — **bran·chi·al** \-kē-əl\ *adj* — **bran·chi·ate** \-kē-ət, -ˌāt\ *adj*
bran·chio·pod \'braŋ-kē-ə-ˌpäd\ *n* [deriv. of Gk *branchia* gills + *pod-, pous* foot — more at FOOT] : any of a group (Branchiopoda) of aquatic crustaceans typically having a long body, a carapace, and many pairs of leaflike appendages — **branchiopod** *adj* — **bran·chi·op·o·dan** \ˌbraŋ-kē-'äp-əd-ən\ *adj* — **bran·chi·op·o·dous** \-əd-əs\ *adj*
branch·let \'branch-lət\ *n* : a small usu. terminal branch
branch water *n* [¹*branch* (creek)] : plain water ⟨bourbon and *branch water*⟩
¹brand \'brand\ *n* [ME, torch, sword, fr. OE; akin to OE *bærnan* to burn] **1 a** : a charred piece of wood **b** : FIREBRAND 1 **c** : something (as lightning) that resembles a firebrand **2** : SWORD **3 a** (1) : a mark made by burning with a hot iron to attest manufacture or quality or to designate ownership (2) : a mark made with a stamp or stencil for similar purposes : TRADEMARK **b** (1) : a mark put on criminals with a hot iron (2) : a mark of disgrace : STIGMA ⟨the ~ of poverty⟩ **4 a** : a class of goods identified by name as the product of a single firm or manufacturer : MAKE **b** : a characteristic or distinctive kind : VARIETY ⟨a lively ~ of theater⟩ **5** : a tool used to produce a brand

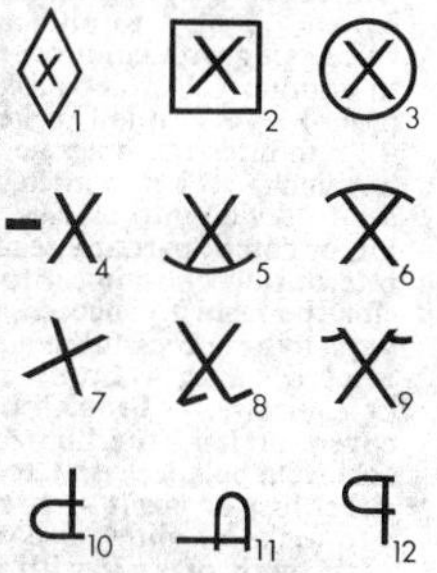

brands 3a(1) for cattle: *1* diamond X, *2* box X, *3* circle X, *4* bar X, *5* rocking X, *6* swinging X, *7* tumbling X, *8* walking X, *9* flying X, *10* crazy P, *11* lazy P, *12* reverse P

²brand *vt* **1** : to mark with a brand **2** : to mark with disapproval : STIGMATIZE **3** : to impress indelibly ⟨~ the lesson on his mind⟩ — **brand·er** *n*
¹bran·dish \'bran-dish\ *vt* [ME *braundisshen,* fr. MF *brandiss-,* stem of *brandir,* fr. OF, fr. *brand* sword, of Gmc origin; akin to OE *brand*] **1** : to shake or wave (as a weapon) menacingly **2** : to exhibit in an ostentatious or aggressive manner **syn** see SWING
²brandish *n* : an act or instance of brandishing
brand·ling \'bran-(d)liŋ\ *n* : a small yellowish earthworm (*Eisenia foetida*) with brownish purple rings that is found in dunghills
brand name *n* : TRADE NAME 1b
brand–new \'bran-'n(y)ü\ *adj* : conspicuously new and unused
¹bran·dy \'bran-dē\ *n, pl* **brandies** [short for *brandywine,* fr. D *brandewijn,* fr. MD *brantwijn,* fr. *brant* distilled + *wijn* wine] : an alcoholic liquor distilled from wine or fermented fruit juice (as of apples)
²brandy *vt* **bran·died; bran·dy·ing** : to flavor, blend, or preserve with brandy
brank \'braŋk\ *n* [origin unknown] : an instrument made of an iron frame surrounding the head and a sharp metal bit entering the mouth and formerly used to punish scolds — usu. used in pl.
bran·ni·gan \'bran-i-gən\ *n* [prob. fr. the name *Brannigan*] **1** : a drinking spree **2** : SQUABBLE
brant \'brant\ *n, pl* **brant** *or* **brants** [origin unknown] : a wild goose; *esp* : any of several small dark geese (genus *Branta*) that breed in the Arctic and migrate southward
¹brash \'brash\ *n* [obs. E *brash* to breach a wall] : a mass of fragments (as of ice)
²brash *adj* [origin unknown] **1** : BRITTLE ⟨~ wood⟩ **2 a** : tending to act in headlong fashion : IMPETUOUS ⟨the ~ young man darted into the traffic⟩ **b** : done in haste without regard for consequences : RASH ⟨~ acts⟩ **3** : uninhibitedly energetic or demonstrative : BUMPTIOUS ⟨a delightfully ~ comedian⟩ **4 a** : lacking restraint and discernment : TACTLESS ⟨made a ~ speech about his wife's bad habits⟩ **b** : aggressively self-assertive : IMPUDENT ⟨a man ~ to the point of arrogance⟩ **5** : piercingly sharp : HARSH ⟨a ~ squeal of brakes⟩ — **brash·ly** *adv* — **brash·ness** *n*
brass \'bras\ *n* [ME *bras,* fr. OE *bræs;* akin to MLG *bras* metal] **1** : an alloy consisting essentially of copper and zinc in variable proportions **2 a** : the brass instruments of an orchestra or band — often used in pl. **b** : a usu. brass memorial tablet **c** : bright metal fittings or utensils **d** : a brass, bronze, or gunmetal lining for a bearing **e** : empty fired cartridge shells **3** : brazen self-assurance : GALL **4** : BRASS HATS — **brass** *adj*
bras·sard \brə-'särd, 'bras-ˌärd\ *n* [F *brassard,* fr. MF *brassal,* fr. OIt *bracciale,* fr. *braccio* arm, fr. L *bracchium* — more at BRACE] **1** : armor for protecting the arm — see ARMOR illustration **2** : a cloth band worn around the upper arm usu. bearing an identifying mark
brass band *n* : a band consisting chiefly or solely of brass and percussion instruments
brass·bound \'bras-ˌbau̇nd, -'bau̇nd\ *adj* **1** : having trim made of brass or a metal resembling brass **2 a** (1) : tradition-bound and opinionated (2) : making no concessions : INFLEXIBLE **b** : BRAZEN, PRESUMPTUOUS
brass–collar \-'käl-ər\ *adj* : invariably voting the straight party ticket ⟨~ Democrats⟩
bras·se·rie \ˌbras-(ə-)'rē\ *n* [F, fr. MF *brasser* to brew, fr. OF *bracier,* fr. L *braces* spelt] : a restaurant that sells beer
brass hat *n* **1** : a high-ranking military officer **2** : a person in a high position in civilian life
bras·si·ca \'bras-i-kə\ *n* [NL, genus name, fr. L, cabbage] : any of a large genus (*Brassica*) of Old World temperate zone herbs (as cabbages) with beaked cylindrical pods
bras·siere \brə-'zi(ə)r *also* ˌbras-ē-'e(ə)r\ *n* [obs. F *brassière* bodice, fr. OF *braciere* arm protector, fr. *bras* arm — more at BRACELET] : a woman's close-fitting undergarment with cups for bust support
brass instrument *n* : one of a group of wind instruments (as a French horn, trombone, trumpet, or tuba) that is usu. characterized by a long cylindrical or conical metal tube commonly curved two or more times and ending in a flared bell, that produces tones by the vibrations of the player's lips against a usu. cup-shaped mouthpiece, and that usu. has valves or a slide by which the player may produce all the tones within the instrument's range
brass knuckles *n pl but sing or pl in constr* : KNUCKLE 4
brass tacks *n pl* : details of immediate practical importance — usu. used in the phrase *get down to brass tacks*
brassy \'bras-ē\ *adj* **brass·i·er; -est** **1 a** : being shamelessly bold **b** : OBSTREPEROUS **2** : resembling brass esp. in color **3** : resembling the sound of a brass instrument — **brass·i·ly** \'bras-ə-lē\ *adv* — **brass·i·ness** \'bras-ē-nəs\ *n*
brat \'brat\ *n* [perh. fr. E dial. *brat* (coarse garment)] : CHILD; *specif* : an ill-mannered annoying child — **brat·ti·ness** \'brat-ē-nəs\ *n* — **brat·tish** \'brat-ish\ *adj* — **brat·ty** \-ē\ *adj*
brat·tice \'brat-əs, 'brat-ish\ *n* [ME *bretais* parapet, fr. OF *bretesche,* fr. ML *breteschia*] : an often temporary partition of planks or cloth used esp. in a mine to control ventilation — **brattice** *vt*
¹brat·tle \'brat-ᵊl\ *n* [prob. imit.] *chiefly Scot* : CLATTER, SCAMPER
²brattle *vi* **brat·tled; brat·tling** *chiefly Scot* : to make a clattering or rattling sound
brat·wurst \'brät-(ˌ)wərst, -ˌvu̇(ə)rst, -ˌvu̇s(h)t\ *n* [G, fr. OHG *brātwurst,* fr. *brāt* meat without waste + *wurst* sausage] : fresh pork sausage for frying
braun·schweig·er \'brau̇n-ˌs(h)wī-gər\ *n* [G *Braunschweiger* (*wurst*), lit., Brunswick sausage] : smoked liverwurst
bra·va \'bräv-(ˌ)ä, brä-'vä\ *n* [It, fem. of *bravo*] : BRAVO — used interjectionally in applauding a woman
bra·va·do \brə-'väd-(ˌ)ō\ *n, pl* **-does** *or* **-dos** [MF *bravade* & OSp *bravata,* fr. OIt *bravata,* fr. *bravare* to challenge, show off, fr. *bravo*] **1 a** : blustering swaggering conduct **b** : a pretense of bravery **2** : the quality or state of being foolhardy
¹brave \'brāv\ *adj* **brav·er; brav·est** [MF, fr. OIt & OSp *bravo* courageous, wild, fr. L *barbarus* barbarous] **1** : having courage : DAUNTLESS **2** : making a fine show : COLORFUL ⟨~ banners flying in the wind⟩ **3** : EXCELLENT, SPLENDID ⟨the ~ fire I soon had going —J. F. Dobie⟩ — **brave·ly** *adv*
²brave *vb* **braved; brav·ing** *vt* **1** : to face or endure with courage **2** *obs* : to make showy ~ *vi, archaic* : to make a brave show — **brav·er** *n*
³brave *n* **1** *archaic* : BRAVADO **2** : one who is brave; *specif* : an American Indian warrior **3** *archaic* : BULLY, ASSASSIN
brav·ery \'brāv-(ə-)rē\ *n, pl* **-er·ies** **1 a** : fine clothes **b** : showy display **2** : the quality or state of being brave : COURAGE
¹bra·vo \'bräv-(ˌ)ō\ *n, pl* **bravos** *or* **bravoes** [It, fr. *bravo,* brave] : VILLAIN, DESPERADO; *esp* : a hired assassin
²bra·vo \'bräv-(ˌ)ō, brä-'vō\ *n, pl* **bravos** : a shout of approval — often used interjectionally in applauding a performance
³bra·vo \'bräv-(ˌ)ō, brä-'vō\ *vt* **bra·voed; bra·vo·ing** : to applaud by shouts of *bravo*
Bra·vo \'bräv-(ˌ)ō\ — a communications code word for the letter *b*
bra·vu·ra \brə-'v(y)u̇r-ə\ *n* [It, lit., bravery, fr. *bravare*] **1** : a florid brilliant style **2** : a musical passage requiring exceptional agility and technical skill in execution **3** : a show of daring or brilliance
braw \'brȯ, 'brä\ *adj* [modif. of MF *brave*] **1** *chiefly Scot* : GOOD, FINE **2** *chiefly Scot* : well dressed
¹brawl \'brȯl\ *vi* [ME *brawlen*] **1** : to quarrel or fight noisily : WRANGLE **2** : to make a loud confused noise ⟨the river ~*ing* by⟩ — **brawl·er** *n*
²brawl *n* **1** : a noisy quarrel or fight **2** : a loud tumultuous noise
brawly \'brȯ-lē\ *adj* **brawl·i·er; -est** **1** : inclined to brawl **2** : characterized by brawls or brawling
brawn \'brȯn\ *n* [ME, fr. MF *braon* muscle, of Gmc origin; akin to OE *bræd* flesh] **1 a** : full strong muscles esp. of the arm or leg **b** : muscular strength **2 a** *Brit* : the flesh of a boar **b** : HEADCHEESE

brawny \'brȯ-nē\ *adj* **brawn·i·er; -est** **1 :** MUSCULAR, STRONG **2 :** being swollen and hard ⟨a ~ infected foot⟩ — **brawn·i·ly** \-nə-lē\ *adv* — **brawn·i·ness** \-nē-nəs\ *n*

1bray \'brā\ *vb* [ME *brayen,* fr. OF *braire* to cry, fr. (assumed) VL *bragere,* of Celt origin; akin to MIr *braigid* he breaks wind; akin to L *frangere* to break — more at BREAK] *vi* **:** to utter the characteristic loud harsh cry of a donkey ~ *vt* **:** to utter or play loudly, harshly, or discordantly — **bray** *n*

2bray *vt* [ME *brayen,* fr. MF *broiier,* of Gmc origin; akin to OHG *brehhan* to break — more at BREAK] **1 :** to crush or grind fine ⟨~ seeds in a mortar⟩ **2 :** to spread thin ⟨~ printing ink⟩

bray·er \'brā-ər\ *n* **:** a printer's hand inking roller

Braz *abbr* Brazil; Brazilian

1braze \'brāz\ *vt* [irreg. fr. *brass*] *archaic* **:** HARDEN

2braze *vt* **brazed; braz·ing** [prob. fr. F *braser,* fr. OF, to burn, fr. *brese* live coals] **:** to solder with a nonferrous alloy that melts at a lower temperature than that of the metals being joined — **braz·er** *n*

1bra·zen \'brāz-ᵊn\ *adj* [ME *brasen,* fr. OE *bræsen,* fr. *bræs* brass] **1 :** made of brass **2 a :** sounding harsh and loud like struck brass **b :** of the color of polished brass **3 :** marked by contemptuous boldness — **bra·zen·ly** *adv* — **bra·zen·ness** \'brāz-ᵊn-(n)əs\ *n*

2brazen *vt* **bra·zened; bra·zen·ing** \'brāz-niŋ, -ᵊn-iŋ\ **:** to face with defiance or impudence — usu. used in the phrase *brazen it out*

bra·zen–faced \,brāz-ᵊn-'fāst\ *adj* **:** marked by insolence and bold disrespect ⟨~ assertions⟩

1bra·zier \'brā-zhər\ *n* [ME *brasier,* fr. *bras* brass] **:** one that works in brass

2brazier *n* [F *brasier,* fr. OF, fire of hot coals, fr. *brese*] **1 :** a pan for holding burning coals **2 :** a utensil in which food is exposed to heat through a wire grill

Bra·zil nut \brə-,zil-\ *n* [*Brazil,* So. America] **:** a tall So. American tree (*Bertholletia excelsa* of the family Lecythidaceae) that bears large globular capsules each containing several closely packed roughly triangular oily edible nuts; *also* **:** its nut

bra·zil·wood \brə-'zil-,wu̇d\ *n* [Sp *brasil,* fr. *brasa* live coals; fr. its color] **:** the heavy wood of any of various tropical leguminous trees (esp. genus *Caesalpinia*) that is used as red and purple dyewood and in cabinetwork

BRE *abbr* bachelor of religious education

1breach \'brēch\ *n* [ME *breche,* fr. OE *bryce;* akin to OE *brecan* to break] **1 :** infraction or violation of a law, obligation, tie, or standard **2 a :** a broken, ruptured, or torn condition or area **b :** a gap (as in a wall) made by battering **3 a :** a break in accustomed friendly relations **b :** a temporary gap in continuity **:** HIATUS **4 :** a leap esp. of a whale out of water

2breach *vt* **1 :** to make a breach in ⟨~ the city walls⟩ **2 :** BREAK, VIOLATE ⟨~ an agreement⟩ ~ *vi* **:** to leap out of water ⟨a whale ~*ing*⟩

breach of promise : violation of a promise esp. to marry

1bread \'bred\ *n* [ME *breed,* fr. OE *brēad;* akin to OHG *brōt* bread, OE *brēowan* to brew] **1 :** a usu. baked and leavened food made of a mixture whose basic constituent is flour or meal **2 :** FOOD, SUSTENANCE ⟨our daily ~⟩ **3 a :** LIVELIHOOD ⟨earns his ~ as a laborer⟩ **b** *slang* **:** MONEY — **bread upon the waters :** resources chanced or charitable deeds performed without expectation of return

2bread *vt* **:** to cover with bread crumbs ⟨a ~*ed* pork chop⟩

bread–and–butter *adj* **1 a :** being as basic as the earning of one's livelihood ⟨small paychecks, inadequate housing, and other ~ issues⟩ **b :** that can be depended upon ⟨a football team's ~ play⟩ ⟨the ~ repertoire of an orchestra⟩ **2 :** sent or given as thanks for hospitality ⟨a ~ letter⟩

bread and butter *n* **:** a means of sustenance or livelihood

bread and circuses *n pl* [trans. of L *panis et circenses*] **:** a palliative offered esp. to avert potential discontent

bread·bas·ket \'bred-,bas-kət\ *n* **1** *slang* **:** STOMACH **2 :** a major cereal-producing region

1bread·board \'bred-,bō(ə)rd, -,bȯ(ə)rd\ *n* **1 :** a board on which dough is kneaded or bread cut **2 :** a board on which electric or electronic circuit diagrams may be laid out

2breadboard *vt* **:** to make an experimental arrangement of (as an electronic circuit or a mechanical system) to test feasibility

bread·fruit \'bred-,früt\ *n* **:** a round usu. seedless fruit that resembles bread in color and texture when baked; *also* **:** a tall tropical tree (*Artocarpus altilis*) of the mulberry family that bears this fruit

bread·stuff \-,stəf\ *n* **1 :** a cereal product (as grain or flour) **2 :** BREAD

breadth \'bredth, 'bretth\ *n* [obs. E *brede* breadth (fr. ME, fr. OE *brǣdu,* fr. *brād* broad) + *-th* (as in *length*)] **1 :** distance from side to side **:** WIDTH **2 a :** something of full width **b :** a wide expanse ⟨~*s* of grass⟩ **3 a :** comprehensive quality **:** SCOPE ⟨the remarkable ~ of his learning⟩ **b :** liberality of views or taste

breadth·ways \-,wāz\ *adv or adj* **:** in the direction of the breadth ⟨a course of bricks laid ~⟩

breadth·wise \-,wīz\ *adv or adj* **:** BREADTHWAYS

bread·win·ner \'bred-,win-ər\ *n* **1 :** a member of a family whose wages supply its livelihood **2 :** a means of livelihood — **bread·win·ning** \-,win-iŋ\ *n*

1break \'brāk\ *vb* **broke** \'brōk\; **bro·ken** \'brō-kən\; **break·ing** [ME *breken,* fr. OE *brecan;* akin to OHG *brehhan* to break, L *frangere*] *vt* **1 a :** to separate into parts with suddenness or violence **b :** FRACTURE ⟨~ an arm⟩ **c :** MAIM, MUTILATE **d :** RUPTURE ⟨~ the skin⟩ **e :** to cut into and turn over the surface of **:** PLOW **2 a :** VIOLATE, TRANSGRESS ⟨~ the law⟩ **b :** to invalidate (a will) by action at law **3 a** *archaic* **:** to force entry into **b :** to burst and force a way through **c :** to escape by force from ⟨~ jail⟩ **d :** to make or effect by cutting, forcing, or pressing through ⟨~ a trail through the woods⟩ **4 :** to make ineffective as a binding force **:** SUNDER ⟨~*ing* his chains⟩ **5 a :** to disrupt the order or compactness of ⟨~ ranks⟩ **b :** to end, close, or destroy by dispersing ⟨~ up the partnership⟩ **6 a :** to defeat utterly and end as an effective force **:** DESTROY **b :** to crush the spirit of **c :** to make tractable or submissive: as (1) **:** to train (an animal) to adjust to the service or convenience of man (2) **:** INURE, ACCUSTOM **d :** to exhaust in health, strength, or capacity **7 a :** to ruin financially **b :** to reduce in rank **8 a :** to check the force or intensity of ⟨the bushes will ~ his fall⟩ **b :** to cause failure and discontinuance of (a strike) by measures outside bargaining processes **9 a :** EXCEED, SURPASS ⟨~ a speed record⟩ **b :** to score less than (a specified total) ⟨golfer trying to ~ 90⟩ **10 :** to ruin the prospects of ⟨could make or ~ her career⟩ **11 :** to demonstrate the falsity of ⟨~ an alibi⟩ **12 :** to cause a sharp reduction in the price of ⟨news likely to ~ the market sharply⟩ **13 a :** to stop or bring to an end suddenly **:** HALT ⟨~ a deadlock⟩ **b :** INTERRUPT, SUSPEND ⟨~ the silence with a cry⟩ **c :** to open and bring about suspension of operation ⟨~ an electric circuit⟩ **d :** to destroy unity or completeness of ⟨~ a dining room set by buying a chair⟩ **e :** to change the appearance of uniformity of ⟨a dormer ~*s* the level roof⟩ **f :** to split the surface of ⟨fish ~*ing* water⟩ **g :** to cause to discontinue a habit ⟨tried to ~ him of smoking⟩ **14 :** to make known **:** TELL ⟨~ the bad news gently⟩ **15 a :** to find an explanation or solution for **:** SOLVE ⟨the detective will ~ the case⟩ **b :** to discover the essentials of (a code or cipher system) **16 :** to split into smaller units, parts, or processes **:** DIVIDE ⟨~ a $5 bill⟩ — often used with *up* or *down* **17 :** to make (a propelled ball) curve, drop, or rise sharply **18 :** to open the action of (a gun) ~ *vi* **a :** to escape with sudden forceful effort — often used with *out* ⟨~ out of jail⟩ **b :** to come into being by or as if by bursting forth ⟨day was ~*ing*⟩ **c :** to give vent to expression with abruptness ⟨~*ing* into tears⟩ ⟨his face ~*s* out into a smile⟩ **d :** to effect a penetration ⟨~ through security lines⟩ **e :** to emerge through the surface of the water **f :** to come to pass **:** OCCUR ⟨report news stories as they ~⟩ **g :** to take a different course **:** DEPART ⟨~ away from tradition⟩ **h :** to make a sudden dash ⟨~ for cover⟩ **i :** to separate after a clinch in boxing **2 a :** to come apart or split into pieces **:** BURST, SHATTER **b :** to open spontaneously or by pressure from within ⟨his boil finally *broke*⟩ **c** *of a wave* **:** to curl over and fall apart in surf or foam **3 :** to become fair **:** CLEAR ⟨when the weather ~*s*⟩ **4 :** to give way in disorderly retreat **5 a :** to fail in health, strength, vitality, or control ⟨may ~ under questioning⟩ **b :** to become inoperative because of damage, wear, or strain **6 :** to undergo a sudden marked decrease in price or value ⟨rail stocks may ~ sharply⟩ **7 :** to end a relationship, connection, accord, or agreement — usu. used with *with* **8 a :** to swerve suddenly **b :** to curve, drop, or rise sharply ⟨a fastball that ~*s* away from the batter⟩ **9 a :** to alter sharply in tone, pitch, or intensity ⟨his voice ~*ing* with emotion ⟩ **b :** to shift abruptly from one register to another ⟨his voice *broke* from his new bass to his original soprano⟩ **10 :** to fail to keep a prescribed gait — used of a horse **11 :** to interrupt one's activity or occupation for a brief period ⟨~ for lunch⟩ **12 :** to make the opening shot of a game of pool **13 a :** to divide into classes, categories, or types **b :** to fold, bend, lift, or come apart at a seam, groove, or joint **c** *of cream* **:** to separate during churning into liquid and fat **14 :** HAPPEN, DEVELOP ⟨for the team to succeed, everything has to ~ right⟩ — **break a leg :** to be successful in a performance — used in the phrase *I hope you break a leg* — **break camp :** to pack up gear and leave a camp or campsite — **break cover** *or* **break covert :** to start from a covert or lair ⟨the hunted fox *broke cover*⟩ — **break even :** to achieve a balance; *esp* **:** to operate a business or enterprise without either loss or profit — **break ground 1 :** to begin excavating **2 :** to make or show discoveries **:** PIONEER — **break into 1 :** to begin with or as if with a sudden throwing off of restraint ⟨the horse *breaks into* a gallop⟩ **2 :** to make entry or entrance ⟨trying to *break into* show business⟩ **3 :** INTERRUPT ⟨*break into* a TV program with a news flash⟩ — **break one's heart :** to crush emotionally with sorrow — **break one's wrists :** to turn the wrists as part of the swing of a club or bat — **break service** *or* **break one's service :** to win a point against an opponent's service in a racket game — **break the back :** to subdue the main force ⟨*break the back* of inflation⟩ — **break the ice 1 :** to make a beginning **2 :** to get through the first difficulties in starting a conversation or discussion — **break through :** to make a penetration — **break wind :** to expel gas from the intestine

2break *n* **1 a :** an act or action of breaking **b :** the opening shot in a game of pool or billiards **c :** the process of opening a gap in an electrical circuit **2 a :** a condition produced by or as if by breaking **:** GAP ⟨a ~ in the clouds⟩ **b :** a gap in an otherwise continuous electric circuit **3 :** the action or act of breaking in, out, or forth ⟨convicts planning a jail ~⟩ **4 a :** DASH, RUSH ⟨a base runner making a ~ for home⟩ **b :** FAST BREAK **5 a :** the start of a race **b :** the act of separating after a clinch in boxing **6 :** an interruption in continuity ⟨a ~ in the weather⟩: as **a :** a notable change of subject matter, attitude, or treatment **b** (1) **:** an abrupt, significant, or noteworthy change or interruption in a continuous process, trend, or surface (2) **:** a respite from work or duty (3) **:** a planned interruption in a radio or television program ⟨a ~ for the commercial⟩ **c :** deviation of a pitched baseball from a straight line **d** *mining* **:** DISLOCATION, FAULT **e :** failure of a horse to maintain the prescribed gait **f :** an abrupt change in the quality or pitch of musical tone **g :** a notable variation in pitch, intensity, or tone in the voice **h :** the action or an instance of breaking service **7 a :** a rupture in previously agreeable relations ⟨a ~ between the two countries⟩ **b :** an abrupt split or difference with something previously adhered to or followed ⟨a sharp ~ with tradition⟩ **8 :** a sequence of successful shots in billiards **:** RUN **9 :** a place or situation at which a break occurs: **a :** the point where one musical register changes to another **b :** a short ornamental passage interpolated between phrases in jazz **c :** the place at which a word is divided esp. at the end of a line of print or writing **d :** a pause or interruption (as a caesura or diaeresis) within or at the end of a verse **e :** a failure to make a strike or a spare on a frame in bowling **10 :** a sudden and abrupt decline of prices or values **11 :** an awkward social blunder **12 :** a stroke of luck and esp. of good luck ⟨a bad ~⟩ ⟨got a ~⟩ **13 :** BREAKDOWN b ⟨suffered a mental ~⟩

break·able \ˈbrā-kə-bəl\ *adj* : capable of being broken — **break·able** *n*

break·age \ˈbrā-kij\ *n* **1 a** : the action of breaking **b** : a quantity broken **2** : allowance for things broken

¹break·away \ˈbrā-kə-ˌwā\ *n* **1 a** : one that breaks away **b** : an act or instance of breaking away (as from a group or tradition) **2** : an object made to shatter or collapse under pressure or impact

²breakaway *adj* **1** : favoring independence from an affiliation : SECEDING ⟨a ~ faction formed a new party⟩ **2** : made to break, shatter, or bend easily ⟨~ road signs for highway safety⟩

break ball *n* : a ball that must be pocketed before the cue ball breaks the rack in some forms of pool

break·bone fever \ˌbrāk-ˌbōn-\ *n* : DENGUE

break·down \ˈbrāk-ˌdau̇n\ *n* : the action or result of breaking down: as **a** : a failure to function **b** : a physical, mental, or nervous collapse **c** : failure to progress or have effect : DISINTEGRATION ⟨a ~ of negotiations⟩ **d** : the process of decomposing ⟨~ of food during digestion⟩ **e** : division into categories : CLASSIFICATION; *also* : an account analyzed into categories

break down \(ˈ)brāk-ˈdau̇n\ *vt* **1 a** : to cause to fall or collapse by breaking or shattering **b** : to make ineffective ⟨*break down* legal barriers⟩ **2 a** : to divide into parts or categories **b** : to separate (as a chemical compound) into simpler substances : DECOMPOSE **c** : to take apart esp. for storage or shipment and for later reassembling ~ *vi* **1 a** : to become inoperative through breakage or wear **b** : to become inapplicable or ineffective : DETERIORATE ⟨relations began to *break down*⟩ **2 a** : to be susceptible to analysis or subdivision ⟨the outline *breaks down* into three parts⟩ **b** : to undergo decomposition ***syn*** see ANALYZE

¹break·er \ˈbrā-kər\ *n* **1 a** : one that breaks **b** : a machine or plant for breaking rocks or coal **2** : a wave breaking into foam (as against the shore) **3** : a strip of fabric under the tread of a tire for extra protection of the carcass

²brea·ker \ˈbrā-kər\ *n* [by folk etymology fr. Sp *barrica*] : a small water cask

break–even \brā-ˈkē-vən\ *adj* : having equal loss and profit ⟨the ~ point in a business venture⟩

break·fast \ˈbrek-fəst\ *n* **1** : the first meal of the day esp. when taken in the morning **2** : the food prepared for a breakfast ⟨eat your ~⟩ — **breakfast** *vb* — **break·fast·er** *n*

break·front \ˈbrāk-ˌfrənt\ *n* : a large cabinet or bookcase whose center section projects beyond the flanking end sections

break–in \ˈbrā-ˌkin\ *n* **1** : the act or action of breaking in ⟨a rash of ~*s* at the new apartment house⟩ **2** : a performance or a series of performances serving as a trial run

break in \(ˈ)brā-ˈkin\ *vi* **1** : to enter a house or building by force **2 a** : to interrupt in a conversation **b** : INTRUDE ⟨*break in* upon his privacy⟩ **3** : to start in an activity or enterprise ⟨*breaking in* as a cub reporter⟩ ~ *vt* **1** : to accustom to a certain activity or occurrence ⟨*break in* the new quarterback⟩ **2** : to overcome the stiffness of (a new article)

breaking and entering *n* : HOUSEBREAKING

breaking point *n* **1** : the point at which a person gives way under stress **2** : the point at which a situation becomes crucial

break·neck \ˌbrāk-ˌnek\ *adj* : very fast or dangerous ⟨~ speed⟩

break off *vi* **1** : to become detached : SEPARATE **2** : to stop abruptly ⟨*break off* in the middle of a sentence⟩ ~ *vt* : DISCONTINUE ⟨*break off* diplomatic relations⟩

break·out \ˈbrā-ˌkau̇t\ *n* : a violent or forceful break from a restraining condition or situation; *esp* : a military attack to break from encirclement

break out \(ˈ)brā-ˈkau̇t\ *vi* **1** : to become affected with a skin eruption **2** : to develop or emerge with suddenness and force ⟨a riot *broke out*⟩ ~ *vt* **1 a** : to take from shipboard stowage preparatory to using **b** : to make ready for action or use ⟨*break out* the tents and make camp⟩ **c** : to produce for consumption ⟨*break out* a bottle⟩ **2 a** : to display flying and unfurled **b** : DISLODGE

break·point \ˈbrāk-ˌpȯint\ *n* : a point (as in a process) at which an interruption can be made

break·through \-ˌthrü\ *n* **1** : an act or point of breaking through an obstruction **2** : an offensive thrust that penetrates and carries beyond a defensive line in warfare **3** : a sudden advance esp. in knowledge or technique ⟨a medical ~⟩

break·up \ˈbrā-ˌkəp\ *n* **1** : DISSOLUTION, DISRUPTION ⟨the ~ of a marriage⟩ **2** : a division into smaller units ⟨the ~ of the large estates⟩

break up \(ˈ)brā-ˈkəp\ *vt* **1** : to disrupt the continuity or flow of ⟨too many footnotes can *break up* a text⟩ **2** : DECOMPOSE ⟨*break up* a chemical⟩ **3** : to bring to an end ⟨a fight *breaks up* the meeting⟩ **4 a** : to break into pieces in scrapping or salvaging : SCRAP **b** : CRUMBLE ⟨*break up* soil around growing plants⟩ **5** : to do away with : DESTROY ⟨the move to *break up* big school systems — F. H. Vaughn⟩ **6** : to cause to laugh heartily ⟨that joke *breaks* me *up*⟩ ~ *vi* **1 a** : to cease to exist as a unified whole ⟨their partnership *broke up*⟩ **b** : to end a romance **2** : to lose morale, composure, or resolution ⟨likely to *break up* under enemy attack⟩; *esp* : to become abandoned to laughter ⟨*breaks up* completely, laughing himself into a coughing fit —Gene Williams⟩

break·wa·ter \ˈbrā-ˌkwȯt-ər, -ˌkwät-\ *n* : an offshore structure (as a wall) used to protect a harbor or beach from the force of waves

¹bream \ˈbrim, ˈbrēm\ *n, pl* **bream** *or* **breams** [ME *breme*, fr. MF, of Gmc origin; akin to OHG *brahsima* bream, *brettan* to draw (a sword) — more at BRAID] **1** : a European freshwater cyprinid fish (*Abramis brama*); *broadly* : any of various related fishes **2 a** : a porgy or related fish (family Sparidae) **b** : any of various freshwater sunfishes (*Lepomis* and related genera); *esp* : BLUEGILL

²bream \ˈbrēm\ *vt* [prob. fr. D *brem* furze] : to clean (a ship's bottom) by heating and scraping

¹breast \ˈbrest\ *n* [ME *brest*, fr. OE *brēost*; akin to OHG *brust* breast, Russ *bryukho* belly] **1** : either of two protuberant milk-producing glandular organs situated on the front of the chest in the human female and some other mammals; *broadly* : a discrete mammary gland **2** : the fore or ventral part of the body between the neck and the abdomen **3** : the seat of emotion and thought : BOSOM ⟨caused little concern in official ~*s*⟩ **4 a** : something (as a front, swelling, or curving part) resembling a breast **b** : FACE 6

²breast *vt* **1** : to contend with resolutely : CONFRONT ⟨~ the rush traffic⟩ **2** *chiefly Brit* : CLIMB, ASCEND **3** : to thrust the chest against ⟨the sprinter ~*ed* the tape⟩

breast–beat·ing \ˈbrest-ˌbēt-iŋ\ *n* : noisy demonstrative protestation (as of grief, anger, or self-recrimination)

breast·bone \ˈbres(t)-ˈbōn, -ˌbōn\ *n* : STERNUM

breast drill *n* : a portable drill with a plate that is pressed by the breast in forcing the drill against the work

breast–feed \ˈbrest-ˌfēd\ *vt* : to feed (a baby) from a mother's breast rather than from a bottle

breast·plate \ˈbres(t)-ˌplāt\ *n* **1** : a metal plate worn as defensive armor for the breast — see ARMOR illustration **2** : a vestment worn in ancient times by a Jewish high priest and set with 12 gems bearing the names of the tribes of Israel **3** : a piece against which the workman presses his breast in operating a breast drill or similar tool **4** : PLASTRON 2

breast·stroke \ˈbres(t)-ˌstrōk\ *n* : a swimming stroke executed in a prone position by extending the arms in front of the head while drawing the knees forward and outward and then sweeping the arms back with palms out while kicking outward and backward — **breast·strok·er** \-ˌstrō-kər\ *n*

breast·work \ˈbres-ˌtwərk\ *n* : a temporary fortification

breath \ˈbreth\ *n* [ME *breth*, fr. OE *brǣth*; akin to OHG *brādam* breath, OE *beorma* yeast —more at BARM] **1 a** : air filled with a fragrance or odor **b** : a slight indication : SUGGESTION ⟨the faintest ~ of scandal⟩ **2 a** : the faculty of breathing ⟨recovering his ~ after the race⟩ **b** : an act of breathing ⟨fought to his last ~⟩ **c** : opportunity or time to breathe : RESPITE **3** : a slight breeze **4 a** : air inhaled and exhaled in breathing ⟨bad ~⟩ **b** : something (as moisture on a cold surface) produced by breath or breathing **5** : a spoken sound : UTTERANCE **6** : SPIRIT, ANIMATION **7** : expiration of air with the glottis wide open (as in the formation of \f\ and \s\ sounds) — **in one breath** *or* **in the same breath** : almost simultaneously — **out of breath** : breathing very rapidly (as from strenuous exercise)

breath·able \ˈbrē-t͟hə-bəl\ *adj* **1** : suitable for breathing ⟨~ air⟩ **2** : allowing air to pass through : POROUS ⟨a ~ synthetic fabric⟩ — **breath·abil·i·ty** \ˌbrē-t͟hə-ˈbil-ət-ē\ *n*

breathe \ˈbrēt͟h\ *vb* **breathed; breath·ing** [ME *brethen*, fr. *breth*] *vi* **1 a** *obs* : to emit a fragrance or aura **b** : to become perceptible **2 a** : to draw air into and expel it from the lungs : RESPIRE; *broadly* : to take in oxygen and give out carbon dioxide through natural processes **b** : to inhale and exhale freely **3** : LIVE **4** : to pause and rest before continuing **5** : to blow softly **6** *of an internal-combustion engine* : to use air to support combustion ~ *vt* **1 a** : to send out by exhaling **b** : to instill by or as if by breathing ⟨~ new life into the movement⟩ **2 a** : UTTER, EXPRESS ⟨don't ~ a word of it to anyone⟩ **b** : to make manifest : EVINCE ⟨the novel ~*s* despair⟩ **3** : to give rest from exertion to **4** : to take in in breathing ⟨~ the scent of pines⟩ — **breathe down one's neck 1** : to threaten esp. in attack or pursuit **2** : to keep one under close or constant surveillance ⟨parents always *breathing down his neck*⟩ — **breathe easily** *or* **breathe freely** : to enjoy relief (as from pressure or danger)

breathed \ˈbretht\ *adj* : VOICELESS 2

breath·er \ˈbrē-t͟hər\ *n* **1** : one that breathes **2** : a break in activity for rest or relief **3** : a small vent in an otherwise airtight enclosure

breath·ing \ˈbrē-t͟hiŋ\ *n* **1** : BREATHER 2 **2** : either of the marks ʽ and ʼ used in writing Greek to indicate aspiration or its absence

breathing space *n* : a period of inactivity esp. for rest and mustering up strength for subsequent efforts

breath·less \ˈbreth-ləs\ *adj* **1 a** : not breathing **b** : DEAD **2 a** : panting or gasping for breath **b** : leaving one breathless ⟨drove at a ~ speed⟩ **c** : holding one's breath from emotion ⟨~ in anticipation⟩ **d** : GRIPPING, INTENSE ⟨~ tension⟩ **3** : STALE, STUFFY ⟨~ air in the attic⟩ — **breath·less·ly** *adv* — **breath·less·ness** *n*

breath·tak·ing \ˈbreth-ˌtā-kiŋ\ *adj* **1** : making one out of breath **2 a** : EXCITING, THRILLING ⟨a ~ stock car race⟩ **b** : ASTONISHING ⟨his ~ ignorance⟩ — **breath·tak·ing·ly** \-kiŋ-lē\ *adv*

breathy \ˈbreth-ē\ *adj* **breath·i·er; -est** : characterized by or accompanied with the audible passage of breath

brec·cia \ˈbrech-(ē-)ə\ *n* [It] : a rock consisting of sharp fragments embedded in a fine-grained matrix (as sand or clay)

brec·ci·ate \ˈbrech-ē-ˌāt\ *vt* **-at·ed; -at·ing 1** : to break (rock) into fragments **2** : to form (rock) into breccia — **brec·ci·a·tion** \ˌbrech-ē-ˈā-shən\ *n*

Breck *abbr* Brecknockshire

brede \ˈbrēd\ *n* [alter. of *braid*] *archaic* : EMBROIDERY

bred–in–the–bone \ˌbred-ᵊn-t͟hə-ˈbōn\ *adj* **1** : very deeply inculcated ⟨~ honesty⟩ **2** : marked by an inveterate or lasting quality ⟨a ~ gambler⟩

bree \ˈbrē\ *n* [ME *bre*] *chiefly Scot* : BROTH, LIQUOR

breech \ˈbrēch; *"breeches" (garment) is usu* ˈbrich-əz\ *n* [ME, breeches, fr. OE *brēc*, pl. of *brōc* leg covering; akin to OHG *bruoh* breeches, OE *brecan* to break] **1** *pl* **a** : short trousers covering the hips and thighs and fitting snugly at the lower edges at or just below the knee **b** : TROUSERS **2** : the hind end of the body : BUTTOCKS **3 a** : the part of a firearm at the rear of the bore **b** : the bottom of a pulley block

breech·block \ˈbrēch-ˌbläk\ *n* : the block in breech-loading firearms that closes the rear of the bore against the force of the charge

breech·clout \ˈbrēch-ˌklau̇t, ˈbrich-\ *or* **breech·cloth** \-ˌklȯth\ *n* : LOINCLOTH

ə abut ᵊ kitten ər further a back ā bake ä cot, cart
au̇ out ch chin e less ē easy g gift i trip ī life
j joke ŋ sing ō flow ȯ flaw ȯi coin th thin t͟h this
ü loot u̇ foot y yet yü few yu̇ furious zh vision

breech·es buoy \'brē-chəz- *also* 'brich-əz-\ *n* : a canvas seat in the form of breeches hung from a life buoy running on a hawser and used to haul persons from one ship to another or from ship to shore esp. in rescue operations

breech·ing \'brē-chiŋ, 'brich-iŋ\ *n* **1** : the part of a harness that passes around the breech of a draft animal **2** : the short coarse wool on the breech and hind legs of a sheep or goat; *also* : the hair on the corresponding part of a dog

breech–load·er \'brēch-'lōd-ər\ *n* : a firearm that receives its ammunition at the breech — **breech–load·ing** \-'lōd-iŋ\ *adj*

¹breed \'brēd\ *vb* **bred** \'bred\; **breed·ing** [ME *breden*, fr. OE *brēdan*; akin to OE *brōd* brood] *vt* **1** : to produce (offspring) by hatching or gestation **2 a** : BEGET **1 b** : PRODUCE, ENGENDER ⟨despair often ∼s violence⟩ **3** : to propagate (plants or animals) sexually and usu. under controlled conditions ⟨*bred* several strains of corn together to produce a new high-lysine variety⟩ **4 a** : to bring up : NURTURE ⟨born and *bred* in the country⟩ **b** : to inculcate by training ⟨∼ good manners into one's children⟩ **5 a** : to mate with : INSEMINATE **b** : IMPREGNATE **6** : to produce (a fissionable element) by bombarding a nonfissionable element with neutrons from a radioactive element so that more fissionable material is produced than is used up ∼ *vi* **1** : to produce offspring by sexual union **2** : to propagate animals or plants

²breed *n* **1** : a group of animals or plants presumably related by descent from common ancestors and visibly similar in most characters; *esp* : such a group differentiated from the wild type under the influence of man **2** : a number of persons of the same stock **3** : CLASS, KIND ⟨a new ∼ of radicals⟩

breed·er *n* : one that breeds: as **a** : an animal or plant kept for propagation **b** : one engaged in the breeding of a specified organism

breed·ing *n* **1** : the action or process of bearing or generating **2** : ANCESTRY **3 a** *archaic* : EDUCATION ⟨she had her ∼ at my father's charge —Shak.⟩ **b** : training in or observance of the proprieties **4** : the sexual propagation of plants or animals

breeding ground *n* **1** : the place to which animals go to breed **2** : a place or set of circumstances considered favorable esp. to the propagation of certain ideas or conditions

breed of cat : TYPE, SORT — usu. used with *new* or *different*

breeks \'brēks, 'briks\ *n pl* [ME (northern dial.) *breke*, fr. OE *brēc*] *chiefly Scot* : BREECHES

¹breeze \'brēz\ *n* [ME *brise*] **1 a** : a light gentle wind **b** : a wind of from 4 to 31 miles an hour **2** : something easily done : CINCH — **breeze·less** \-ləs\ *adj* — **in a breeze** : EASILY ⟨won the talent contest *in a breeze*⟩

²breeze *vi* **breezed; breez·ing 1** : to move swiftly and airily ⟨she *breezed* in wearing chiffon⟩ **2** : to make progress quickly and easily ⟨∼ through the book⟩

³breeze *n* [prob. modif. of F *braise* cinders] : residue from the making of coke or charcoal

breeze·way \'brēz-,wā\ *n* : a roofed often open passage connecting two buildings (as a house and garage) or halves of a building

breezy \'brē-zē\ *adj* **breez·i·er; -est 1** : swept by breezes **2** : BRISK, LIVELY — **breez·i·ly** \-zə-lē\ *adv* — **breez·i·ness** \-zē-nəs\ *n*

breg·ma \'breg-mə\ *n, pl* **-ma·ta** \-mət-ə\ [NL *bregmat-, bregma,* fr. LL, front part of the head, fr. Gk; akin to Gk *brechmos* front part of the head — more at BRAIN] : the point of junction of the coronal and sagittal sutures of the skull — **breg·mat·ic** \breg-'mat-ik\ *adj*

brems·strah·lung \'brem(p)sh-,shträl-əŋ\ *n* [G, lit., decelerated radiation] : the electromagnetic radiation produced by the sudden retardation of an electrical particle in an intense electric field

brent \'brent\ *var of* BRANT

breth·ren \'breth-(ə-)rən, -ərn\ *pl of* BROTHER — used chiefly in formal or solemn address or in referring to the members of a profession, society, or sect

Brethren *n pl* : members of various sects originating chiefly in 18th century German Pietism; *esp* : DUNKERS

Bret·on \'bret-ⁿn\ *n* [F, fr. ML *Briton-, Brito,* fr. L, Briton] **1** : a native or inhabitant of Brittany **2** : the Celtic language of the Breton people — **Breton** *adj*

breve \'brēv, 'brev\ *n* [L, neut. of *brevis* brief — more at BRIEF] **1** : a curved mark ˘ used to indicate a short vowel or a short or unstressed syllable **2** : a note equivalent to four half notes

¹bre·vet \bri-'vet, *chiefly Brit* 'brev-it\ *n* [ME, an official message, fr. MF, fr. OF, dim. of *brief* letter — more at BRIEF] : a commission giving a military officer higher nominal rank than that for which he receives pay

breve 2

²brevet *vt* **bre·vet·ted** *or* **brev·et·ed; bre·vet·ting** *or* **brev·et·ing** : to confer rank upon by brevet

bre·via·ry \'brē-v(y)ə-rē, -vē-,er-ē\ *n, pl* **-ries** [L *breviarium,* fr. *brevis* — more at BRIEF] **1** : a brief summary : ABRIDGMENT **2** *often cap* [ML *breviarium,* fr. L] : a book containing the prayers, hymns, psalms, and readings for the canonical hours **b** : DIVINE OFFICE

brev·i·ty \'brev-ət-ē\ *n, pl* **-ties** [L *brevitas,* fr. *brevis*] **1** : shortness of duration **2** : expression in few words : CONCISENESS

¹brew \'brü\ *vb* [ME *brewen,* fr. OE *brēowan;* akin to L *fervēre* to boil — more at BURN] *vt* **1** : to prepare (as beer or ale) by steeping, boiling, and fermentation or by infusion and fermentation **2 a** : to bring about : FOMENT ⟨∼ trouble⟩ **b** : CONTRIVE, PLOT **3** : to prepare (as tea) by infusion in hot water ∼ *vi* **1** : to brew beer or ale **2** : to be in the process of formation ⟨a storm is ∼ing in the east⟩ — **brew·er** \'brü-ər, 'brü(-)ər\ *n*

²brew *n* **1 a** : a brewed beverage **b** (1) : a cup of coffee or tea (2) : a glass of beer **c** : a product of brewing **2** : the process of brewing

brew·age \'brü-ij\ *n* : BREW

brewer's yeast *n* : a yeast used or suitable for use in brewing; *specif* : the dried pulverized cells of such a yeast (*Saccharomyces cerevisiae*) used esp. as a source of B-complex vitamins

brew·ery \'brü-ə-rē, 'brú-(ə)r-ē\ *n, pl* **-er·ies** : a place where malt liquors are manufactured

brewis \'brüz, 'brü-əs\ *n* [ME *brewes,* fr. OF *broez,* nom. sing. acc. pl. of *broet,* dim. of *breu* broth, of Gmc origin] *dial* : BROTH

¹bri·ar \'brī-(ə)r\ *var of* BRIER

²briar *n* : a tobacco pipe made from the root of a brier

bri·ard \brē-'är(d)\ *n* [F, fr. *Brie,* district in France] : any of an old French breed of large strong usu. black dogs

¹bribe \'brīb\ *vb* **bribed; brib·ing** *vt* : to induce or influence by or as if by bribery ∼ *vi* : to practice bribery — **brib·able** \'brī-bə-bal\ *adj* — **brib·er** *n*

²bribe *n* [ME, something stolen, fr. MF, bread given to a beggar] **1** : money or favor given or promised to a person in a position of trust to influence his judgment or conduct **2** : something that serves to induce or influence

brib·ery \'brī-b(ə-)rē\ *n* : the act or practice of giving or taking a bribe

bric·a·brac \'brik-ə-,brak\ *n, pl* **bric·a·brac** [F *bric-à-brac*] **1** : a miscellaneous collection of small articles commonly of ornamental or sentimental value : CURIOS **2** : something suggesting bric-a-brac esp. in extraneous decorative quality

¹brick \'brik\ *n, often attrib* [ME *bryke,* fr. MF *brique,* fr. MD *bricke;* akin to OE *brecan* to break] **1** *pl* **bricks** *or* **brick** : a handy-sized unit of building or paving material typically being rectangular and about 2¼ x 3¾ x 8 inches and of moist clay hardened by heat **2** : a good-hearted person **3** : a rectangular compressed mass (as of ice cream) **4** : a semisoft cheese with numerous small holes, smooth texture, and usu. mild flavor

²brick *vt* : to close, face, or pave with bricks — usu. used with *up*

brick·bat \'brik-,bat\ *n* **1** : a fragment of a hard material (as a brick); *esp* : one used as a missile **2** : an uncomplimentary remark

brick·field \-,fēld\ *n, Brit* : BRICKYARD

brick·lay·er \'brik-,lā-ər, -,le(-ə)r\ *n* : one who lays brick — **brick·lay·ing** \-,lā-iŋ\ *n*

brick·le \'brik-əl\ *adj* [ME *brekyl*] *dial* : BRITTLE

brick red *n* : a variable color averaging a moderate reddish brown

brick·work \'brik-,wərk\ *n* : work of or with bricks and mortar

brick·yard \-,yärd\ *n* : a place where bricks are made

¹brid·al \'brid-ⁿl\ *n* [ME *bridale,* fr. OE *brȳdealu,* fr. *brȳd* + *ealu* ale — more at ALE] : a nuptial festival or ceremony : MARRIAGE

²bridal *adj* **1** : of or relating to a bride or a wedding : NUPTIAL **2** : intended for a newly married couple ⟨a ∼ suite⟩

bridal wreath *n* : a spirea (*Spiraea prunifolia*) widely grown for its umbels of small white flowers borne in spring

bride \'brīd\ *n* [ME, fr. OE *brȳd;* akin to OHG *brūt* bride] : a woman just married or about to be married

bride·groom \'brīd-,grüm, -,grüm\ *n* [ME *bridegome,* fr. OE *brȳdguma;* akin to OHG *brūtigomo* bridegroom; both fr. a prehistoric NGmc-WGmc compound whose constituents are represented by OE *brȳd* and by OE *guma* man — more at HOMAGE] : a man just married or about to be married

brides·maid \'brīdz-,mād\ *n* : a woman attendant of a bride

bride·well \'brī-,dwel, -dwəl\ *n* [*Bridewell,* London jail] : PRISON

¹bridge \'brij\ *n* [ME *brigge,* fr. OE *brycg;* akin to OHG *brucka* bridge, OSlav *brŭvŭno* beam] **1 a** : a structure carrying a pathway or roadway over a depression or obstacle **b** : a time, place, or means of connection or transition **2** : something resembling a bridge in form or function: as **a** : the upper bony part of the nose; *also* : the part of a pair of glasses that rests upon it **b** : an arch serving to raise the strings of a musical instrument **c** : a raised transverse platform on a ship from which it is conned **d** : GANTRY 2b **e** : the hand as a rest for a billiards or pool cue; *also* : a device used as a cue rest **f** : the position of a wrestler on his back with his body arched so that he is supported usu. by his head and feet **3 a** : something (as a partial denture anchored to adjacent teeth) that fills a gap **b** : a connection (as an atom or bond) that joins two different parts of a molecule (as opposite sides of a ring) **4** : an electrical instrument or network for measuring or comparing resistances, inductances, capacitances, or impedances by comparing the ratio of two opposing voltages to a known ratio — **bridge·less** \-ləs\ *adj*

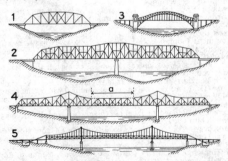

bridges 1a: *1* simple truss, *2* continuous truss, *3* steel arch, *4* cantilever, *a* suspended span, *5* suspension

²bridge *vt* **bridged; bridg·ing 1** : to make a bridge over or across; *also* : to traverse by a bridge **2** : to provide with a bridge — **bridge·able** \-ə-bəl\ *adj*

³bridge *n* [alter. of earlier *biritch,* of unknown origin] : any of various card games for usu. four players in two partnerships that bid for the right to name a trump suit, score points for tricks made in excess of six, and play with the hand of declarer's partner exposed and played by declarer; *esp* : CONTRACT BRIDGE

bridge·board \'brij-ˌbō(ə)rd, -ˌbȯ(ə)rd\ *n* : STRING 7a
bridge·head \-ˌhed\ *n* **1 a** : a fortification protecting the end of a bridge nearest an enemy **b** : a fortification protecting a bridge site, ford, or defile from attack from the other side **c** : an area around the end of a bridge **2** : an advanced position seized in hostile territory as a foothold for further advance
bridge·work \-ˌwərk\ *n* : a phase of prosthodontics concerned with the construction of dental bridges; *also* : the resulting structures
[1]**bri·dle** \'brīd-ᵊl\ *n* [ME *bridel,* fr. OE *bridel;* akin to OE *bregdan* to move quickly — more at BRAID] **1 a** : the headgear with which a horse is governed and which carries a bit and reins **b** : a strip of metal joining two parts of a machine esp. for limiting or restraining motion **2** : something resembling a bridle in shape or function: as **a** : a length of secured cable with a second cable attached to the bight to which force is applied **b** : CURB, RESTRAINT ⟨set a ~ on his power⟩ **c** : FRENUM
[2]**bridle** *vb* **bri·dled; bri·dling** \'brīd-liŋ, -ᵊl-iŋ\ *vt* **1** : to put a bridle on **2** : to restrain, check, or control with or as if with a bridle; *esp* : to get and keep under restraint ⟨you must learn to ~ your tongue⟩ ~ *vi* : to show hostility or resentment (as to an affront to one's pride or dignity) esp. by drawing back the head and chin ***syn*** **1** see RESTRAIN ***ant*** vent **2** see STRUT
bridle path *n* : a trail suitable for horseback riding
Brie \'brē\ *n* [F, fr. *Brie,* district in France] : a soft perishable surface-ripened cheese somewhat similar to Camembert
[1]**brief** \'brēf\ *adj* [ME *bref, breve,* fr. MF *brief,* fr. L *brevis;* akin to OHG *murg* short, Gk *brachys*] **1** : short in duration, extent, or length **2 a** : CONCISE ⟨a ~ report⟩ **b** : CURT, ABRUPT ⟨a cold and ~ welcome⟩ — **brief·ness** *n*
[2]**brief** *n* [ME *bref,* fr. MF, fr. ML *brevis,* fr. LL, summary, fr. L *brevis,* adj.] **1** : an official letter or mandate; *esp* : a papal letter less formal than a bull **2** : a brief written item or document: as **a** : a concise article **b** : SYNOPSIS, SUMMARY **c** : a concise statement of a client's case made out for the instruction of counsel in a trial at law **3** : an outline of an argument; *esp* : a formal outline esp. in law that sets forth the main contentions with supporting statements or evidence **4** *pl* : short snug underpants — **in brief** : in a few words : BRIEFLY
[3]**brief** *vt* **1** : to make an abstract or abridgment of **2** *Brit* : to retain as legal counsel **3 a** : to give final precise instructions to **b** : to coach thoroughly in advance **c** : to give essential information to — **brief·er** *n*
brief·case \'brēf-ˌkās\ *n* : a flat flexible case for carrying papers or books
brief·ing \'brē-fiŋ\ *n* **1** : an act or instance of giving precise instructions or essential information **2** : the instructions or information given at a briefing
brief·less \'brē-fləs\ *adj* : having no legal clients
brief·ly \'brē-flē\ *adv* **1 a** : in a brief way **b** : in brief **2** : for a short time
[1]**bri·er** \'brī(-ə)r\ *n* [ME *brere,* fr. OE *brēr*] : a plant (as of the genera *Rosa, Rubus,* and *Smilax*) with a woody thorny or prickly stem; *also* : a mass or twig of these — **bri·ery** \'brī(-ə)r-ē\ *adj*
[2]**brier** *n* [F *bruyère* heath, fr. (assumed) VL *brucaria,* fr. LL *brucus* heather, of Celt origin; akin to OIr *froech* heather; akin to Gk *ereikē* heather] : a heath (*Erica arborea*) of southern Europe with a root used for making pipes
bri·er·root \'brī(-ə)r-ˌrüt, -ˌru̇t\ *n* : a root (as of the brier *Erica arborea*) used for tobacco pipes
[1]**brig** \'brig\ *n* [short for *brigantine*] : a 2-masted square-rigged ship — compare HERMAPHRODITE BRIG
[2]**brig** *n* [prob. fr. [1]*brig*] **1** : a place (as on a ship) for temporary confinement of offenders in the U.S. Navy **2** : GUARDHOUSE, PRISON

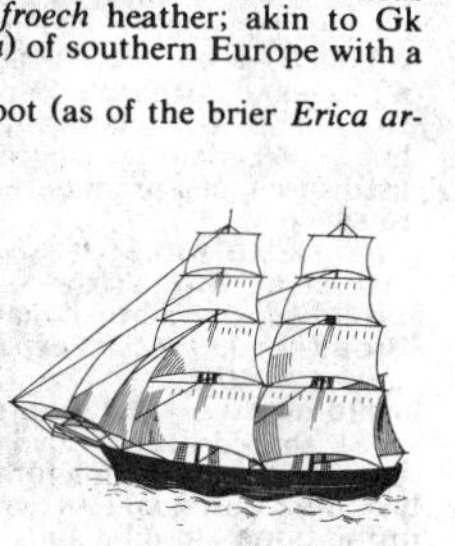

brig

[3]**brig** *abbr* brigade; brigadier
[1]**bri·gade** \brig-'ād\ *n* [F, fr. It *brigata,* fr. *brigare*] **1 a** : a large body of troops **b** : a tactical and administrative unit composed of a headquarters, one or more units of infantry or armor, and supporting units **2** : a group of people organized for special activity
[2]**brigade** *vt* **bri·gad·ed; bri·gad·ing** **1** : to form or unite into a brigade **2** : COMBINE ⟨an instance where speech and action are closely *brigaded* —W. O. Douglas⟩
brig·a·dier \ˌbrig-ə-'di(ə)r\ *n* [F, fr. *brigade*] **1** : BRIGADIER GENERAL **2** : an officer in the British army commanding a brigade and ranking immediately below a major general
brigadier general *n* : a commissioned officer in the army, air force, or marine corps who ranks above a colonel and whose insignia is one star
brig·and \'brig-ənd\ *n* [ME *brigaunt,* fr. MF *brigand,* fr. OIt *brigante,* fr. *brigare* to fight, fr. *briga* strife, of Celt origin; akin to OIr *brig* strength] : one who lives by plunder usu. as a member of a band : BANDIT — **brig·and·age** \-ən-dij\ *n* — **brig·and·ism** \-ˌdiz-əm\ *n*
brig·an·dine \'brig-ən-ˌdēn\ *n* [ME, fr. MF, fr. *brigand*] : medieval body armor of scales or plates
brig·an·tine \'brig-ən-ˌtēn\ *n* [MF *brigantin,* fr. OIt *brigantino,* fr. *brigante*] **1** : a 2-masted square-rigged ship differing from a brig in not carrying a square mainsail **2** : HERMAPHRODITE BRIG
Brig Gen *abbr* brigadier general
bright \'brīt\ *adj* [ME, fr. OE *beorht;* akin to OHG *beraht* bright Skt *bhrājate* it shines] **1 a** : radiating or reflecting light : SHINING **b** : radiant with happiness or good fortune ⟨~ faces⟩ **2** : ILLUSTRIOUS, GLORIOUS **3** : resplendent with charms **4** : of high saturation or brilliance ⟨~ colors⟩ **5 a** : INTELLIGENT, CLEVER ⟨a ~ idea⟩ **b** : LIVELY, CHEERFUL ⟨be ~ and jovial among your guests —Shak.⟩ — **bright** *adv* — **bright·ly** *adv*
syn BRIGHT, BRILLIANT, RADIANT, LUMINOUS, LUSTROUS *shared meaning element* : shining or glowing with light ***ant*** dull, dim

bright·en \'brīt-ᵊn\ *vb* **bright·ened; bright·en·ing** \'brīt-niŋ, -ᵊn-iŋ\ *vt* : to make bright or brighter ~ *vi* : to become bright or brighter — **bright·en·er** \-nər, -ᵊn-ər\ *n*
brightness *n* **1** : the quality or state of being bright; *also* : an instance of such a quality or state **2** : a psychological dimension in which visual stimuli are ordered continuously from light to dark and which is correlated with light intensity
Bright's disease \'brīts-\ *n* [Richard *Bright* †1858 E physician] : any of several kidney diseases marked by albumin in the urine
bright·work \'brīt-ˌwərk\ *n* : polished or plated metalwork
brill \'bril\ *n, pl* **brill** [perh. fr. Corn *brȳthel* mackerel] : a European flatfish (*Bothus rhombus*) related to the turbot; *broadly* : TURBOT
bril·liance \'bril-yən(t)s\ *n* : the quality or state of being brilliant
bril·lian·cy \-yən-sē\ *n, pl* **-cies** **1** : BRILLIANCE **2** : an instance of brilliance
[1]**bril·liant** \'bril-yənt\ *adj* [F *brillant,* prp. of *briller* to shine, fr. It *brillare,* fr. *brillo* beryl, fr. L *beryllus*] **1** : very bright : GLITTERING ⟨a ~ light⟩ **2 a** : STRIKING, DISTINCTIVE ⟨a ~ example⟩ **b** : distinguished by unusual mental keenness or alertness ***syn*** see BRIGHT ***ant*** subdued (*of light, color*) — **bril·liant·ly** *adv* — **bril·liant·ness** *n*
[2]**brilliant** *n* : a gem (as a diamond) cut in a particular form with numerous facets so as to have special brilliance
bril·lian·tine \'bril-yən-ˌtēn\ *n* **1** : a preparation for making hair glossy **2** : a light lustrous fabric that is similar to alpaca and is woven usu. with a cotton warp and mohair or worsted filling

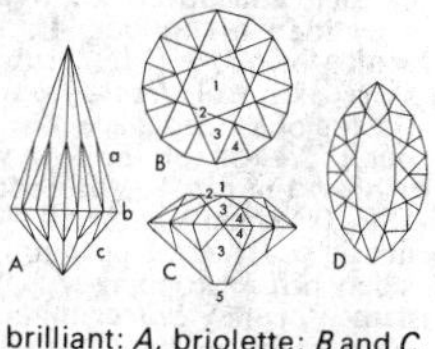

brilliant: *A,* briolette; *B* and *C,* American cut, top and side view; *D,* marquise; *a* bezel, *b* girdle, *c* pavilion: *1* table, *2* star facet, *3* main facet, *4* corner facet, *5* culet

Brill's disease \'brilz-\ *n* [Nathan E. *Brill* †1925 Am physician] : an acute infectious disease milder than epidemic typhus but caused by the same rickettsia
[1]**brim** \'brim\ *n* [ME *brimme;* akin to MHG *brem* edge] **1 a** (1) : an upper or outer margin : VERGE (2) *archaic* : the upper surface of a body of water **b** : the edge or rim of a hollow vessel, a natural depression, or a cavity **2** : the projecting rim of a hat ***syn*** see BORDER — **brim·less** \-ləs\ *adj*
[2]**brim** *vb* **brimmed; brim·ming** *vt* : to fill to the brim ~ *vi* **1** : to become full to the brim **2** : to reach or overflow a brim
brim·ful \'brim-'fu̇l\ *adj* : full to the brim : ready to overflow
-brimmed \'brimd\ *adj comb form* : having a brim of a specified nature ⟨a wide-*brimmed* hat⟩
brim·mer \'brim-ər\ *n* : a brimming cup or glass
brim·stone \'brim-ˌstōn\ *n* [ME *brinston,* prob. fr. *birnen* to burn + *ston* stone] : SULFUR
brind·ed \'brin-dəd\ *adj* [ME *brended*] *archaic* : BRINDLED
brin·dle \'brin-dᵊl\ *n* [*brindle,* adj.] **1** : a brindled color **2** : a brindled animal
brin·dled \-dᵊld\ *adj* [alter. of *brinded*] : having obscure dark streaks or flecks on a gray or tawny ground
[1]**brine** \'brīn\ *n* [ME, fr. OE *brȳne;* akin to MD *brine* brine, L *fricare* to rub — more at FRICTION] **1 a** : water saturated or strongly impregnated with common salt **b** : a strong saline solution (as of calcium chloride) **2** : the water of a sea or salt lake
[2]**brine** *vt* **brined; brin·ing** : to treat (as by steeping) with brine — **brin·er** *n*
Bri·nell hardness \brə-ˌnel-\ *n* [Johann A. *Brinell* †1925 Sw engineer] : the hardness of a metal or alloy measured by hydraulically pressing a hard ball under a standard load into the specimen
Brinell number *n* : a number expressing Brinell hardness and denoting the load applied in testing in kilograms divided by the spherical area of indentation produced in the specimen in square millimeters
brine shrimp *n* : any of a genus (*Artemia*) of branchiopod crustaceans
bring \'briŋ\ *vb* **brought** \'brȯt\; **bring·ing** \'briŋ-iŋ\ [ME *bringen,* fr. OE *bringan;* akin to OHG *bringan* to bring, W *hebrwng* to accompany] *vt* **1 a** : to convey, lead, carry, or cause to come along with one toward the place from which the action is being regarded **b** : to cause to be, act, or move in a special way: as (1) : ATTRACT ⟨her screams *brought* the neighbors⟩ (2) : PERSUADE, INDUCE (3) : FORCE, COMPEL (4) : to cause to come into a particular state or condition ⟨~ water to a boil⟩ **c** *dial* : ESCORT, ACCOMPANY **2** : to cause to exist or occur: as **a** : PRODUCE ⟨winter will ~ snow and ice⟩ **b** : to result in : EFFECT **c** : INSTITUTE ⟨~ legal action⟩ **d** : ADDUCE ⟨~ an argument⟩ **3** : PREFER ⟨~ a charge⟩ **4** : to procure in exchange : sell for ~ *vi, chiefly Midland* : YIELD, PRODUCE — **bring home** : to make unmistakably clear — **bring to account** **1** : to bring to book **2** : REPRIMAND — **bring to bear** **1** : to put to use ⟨*bring* knowledge *to bear* on the problem⟩ **2** : APPLY, EXERT ⟨*bring* pressure *to bear*⟩ — **bring to book** : to compel to give an account — **bring to light** : DISCLOSE, REVEAL — **bring to mind** : to cause to be recalled — **bring to terms** : to compel to agree, assent, or submit — **bring up the rear** : to come last or behind
bring about *vt* : to cause to take place : EFFECT
bring around *vt* **1** : to cause (someone) to adopt a particular opinion or course of action : PERSUADE **2** : to restore to consciousness : REVIVE
bring·down \'briŋ-ˌdau̇n\ *n* : something that is depressing or disappointing

ə abut ᵊ kitten ər further a back ā bake ä cot, cart
au̇ out ch chin e less ē easy g gift i trip ī life
j joke ŋ sing ō flow ȯ flaw ȯi coin th thin t͟h this
ü loot u̇ foot y yet yü few yu̇ furious zh vision

bring down \(ˈ)briŋ-ˈdau̇n\ *vt* **1 :** to cause to fall by or as if by shooting **2 :** to carry (a total) forward — **bring down the house :** to win the enthusiastic approval of the audience
bring forth *vt* **1 :** BEAR ⟨*brought forth* fruit⟩ **2 :** to give birth to : PRODUCE **3 :** ADDUCE ⟨*brought forth* arguments to persuade us⟩
bring forward *vt* **1 :** to produce to view : INTRODUCE **2 :** to carry (a total) forward
bring in *vt* **1 :** to produce as profit or return ⟨each sale *brought in* $5⟩ **2 :** INCLUDE, INTRODUCE **3 :** to enable (a man on base) to reach home plate by a hit **4 :** to report to a court ⟨jury *brought in* a verdict⟩ **5 a :** to cause (as an oil well) to be productive **b :** to win tricks with the long cards of (a suit) in bridge **6 :** EARN ⟨he *brings in* a good salary⟩
bring off *vt* **1 :** to cause to escape : RESCUE **2 :** to carry to a successful conclusion : ACHIEVE, ACCOMPLISH
bring on *vt* **:** to cause to appear or occur
bring out *vt* **1 :** to make clear **2 a :** to present to the public **b :** to introduce formally to society **3 :** UTTER
bring to *vt* **1 :** to cause (a boat) to lie to or come to a standstill **2 :** to restore to consciousness : REVIVE
bring up *vt* **1 :** to bring (a person) to maturity through nurturing care and education **2 :** to cause to stop suddenly **3 :** to bring to attention : INTRODUCE **4 :** VOMIT ~ *vi* **:** to stop suddenly
brink \ˈbriŋk\ *n* [ME, prob. of Scand origin; akin to ON *brekka* slope; akin to L *front-, frons* forehead] **1 :** EDGE; *esp* **:** the edge at the top of a steep place **2 :** a bank esp. of a river **3 :** the point of onset : VERGE ⟨on the ~ of war⟩ ***syn*** see BORDER
brink·man·ship \ˈbriŋk-mən-ˌship\ *also* **brinks·man·ship** \ˈbriŋ(k)-smən-\ *n* [*brink* + *-manship* (as in *horsemanship*)] **:** the art or practice of pushing a dangerous situation to the limit of safety before stopping
briny \ˈbrī-nē\ *adj* **brin·i·er; -est :** of, relating to, or resembling brine or the sea : SALTY — **brin·i·ness** *n*
brio \ˈbrē-(ˌ)ō\ *n* [It] **:** enthusiastic vigor : VIVACITY, VERVE
bri·oche \brē-ˈōsh, -ˈȯsh\ *n* [F, fr. MF dial., fr. *brier* to knead, of Gmc origin; akin to OHG *brehhan* to break — more at BREAK] **:** a roll baked from light yeast dough rich with eggs and butter
bri·o·lette \ˌbrē-ə-ˈlet\ *n* [F] **:** an oval or pear-shaped diamond cut in triangular facets — see BRILLIANT illustration
bri·quette *or* **bri·quet** \brik-ˈet\ *n* [F *briquette*, dim. of *brique* brick] **:** a compacted often brick-shaped mass of usu. fine material ⟨a charcoal ~⟩ — **briquette** *vt*
bri·sance \bri-ˈzän(t)s, -ˈzä^{n}s\ *n* [F, fr. *brisant*, prp. of *briser* to break, fr. OF *brisier*, of Celt origin; akin to OIr *brissim* I break; akin to L *fricare* to rub — more at FRICTION] **:** the shattering or crushing effect of an explosive — **bri·sant** \-ˈzänt, -ˈzä^{n}\ *adj*
Bri·se·is \brī-ˈsē-əs\ *n* [L, fr. Gk *Brisēis*] **:** a woman captive of Achilles taken away from him by Agamemnon
[1]**brisk** \ˈbrisk\ *adj* [prob. modif. of MF *brusque*] **1 :** keenly alert : LIVELY **2 a :** pleasingly tangy ⟨~ tea⟩ **b :** FRESH, INVIGORATING ⟨~ weather⟩ **3 :** sharp in tone or manner **4 :** ENERGETIC, QUICK ⟨a ~ pace⟩ ***syn*** see AGILE ***ant*** sluggish — **brisk·ly** *adv* — **brisk·ness** *n*
[2]**brisk** *vt* **:** to make brisk ~ *vi* **:** to become brisk — usu. used with *up* ⟨business ~*ed* up⟩
bris·ket \ˈbris-kət\ *n* [ME *brusket*; akin to OE *brēost* breast] **:** the breast or lower chest of a quadruped animal — see BEEF illustration
bris·ling *or* **bris·tling** \ˈbriz-liŋ, ˈbris-\ *n* [Norw *brisling*, fr. LG *bretling*, fr. *bret* broad; akin to OE *brād* broad] **:** a small herring (*Clupea sprattus*) that resembles and is processed like a sardine
[1]**bris·tle** \ˈbris-əl\ *n* [ME *bristil*, fr. *brust* bristle, fr. OE *byrst*; akin to OHG *burst* bristle, L *fastigium* top] **:** a short stiff coarse hair or filament — **bris·tle·like** \ˈbris-əl-ˌ(l)īk\ *adj*
[2]**bristle** *vb* **bris·tled; bris·tling** \ˈbris-(ə-)liŋ\ *vi* **1 a :** to rise and stand stiffly erect ⟨quills *bristling* in all directions⟩ **b :** to raise the bristles (as in anger) **2 :** to take on an aggressive attitude or appearance (as in response to a slight) **3 :** to be full of or covered with something suggestive of bristles ⟨roofs *bristled* with chimneys⟩ ~ *vt* **1 :** to furnish with bristles **2 :** to make bristly : RUFFLE ***syn*** see STRUT
bris·tle·cone pine \ˌbris-əl-ˌkōn-\ *n* **:** a pine (*Pinus aristata*) of the western U.S. that includes the oldest living trees
bris·tle·tail \ˈbris-əl-ˌtāl\ *n* **:** any of various wingless insects (orders Thysanura and Entotrophi) with two or three slender caudal bristles
bris·tly \ˈbris-(ə-)lē\ *adj* **bris·tli·er; -est** **1 a :** consisting of or resembling bristles **b :** thickly set with bristles **2 :** tending to bristle easily : BELLIGERENT
bris·tol \ˈbris-t^{ə}l\ *n* [*Bristol*, England] **:** cardboard with a smooth surface suitable for writing or printing — called also *bristol board*
Bristol fashion *adj* [*Bristol*, England, important seaport] **:** being in good order : SHIPSHAPE ⟨spick-and-span, shipshape and *Bristol fashion* —Jack Lusby⟩
brit *or* **britt** \ˈbrit\ *n* [Corn *brȳthel* mackerel] **1 :** young or small schooling fishes (as herring) **2 :** minute marine animals (as crustaceans and pteropods) upon which right whales feed
Brit *abbr* Britain; British
Bri·tan·nia metal \bri-ˌtan-yə-, -ˌtan-ē-ə-\ *n* [*Britannia*, poetic name for Great Britain, fr. L] **:** a silver-white alloy largely of tin, antimony, and copper that is similar to pewter
Bri·tan·nic \bri-ˈtan-ik\ *adj* **:** BRITISH
britch·es \ˈbrich-əz\ *n pl* [alter. of *breeches*] **:** BREECHES, TROUSERS
Brith Mi·lah \brit(h)-ˈmē-(ˌ)lä, bris-\ *n* [LHeb *bērīth mīlāh* covenant of circumcision] **:** the Jewish rite of circumcision
Brit·i·cism \ˈbrit-ə-ˌsiz-əm\ *n* [*Brit*ish + *-icism* (as in *gallicism*)] **:** a characteristic feature of British English
Brit·ish \ˈbrit-ish\ *n* [ME *Bruttische* of Britain, fr. OE *Brettisc*, of Celt origin; akin to W *Brython* Briton] **1 a :** the Celtic language of the ancient Britons **b :** BRITISH ENGLISH **2** *pl in constr* **:** the people of Great Britain or the British Commonwealth — **British** *adj* — **Brit·ish·ness** *n*
British English *n* **:** the native language of most inhabitants of England; *esp* **:** English characteristic of England and clearly distinguishable from that used elsewhere (as in the U.S. or Australia)
Brit·ish·er \ˈbrit-ish-ər\ *n* **:** BRITON 2
British thermal unit *n* **:** the quantity of heat required to raise the temperature of one pound of water one degree Fahrenheit at or near 39.2°F
Brit·on \ˈbrit-^{ə}n\ *n* [ME *Breton*, fr. MF & L; MF, fr. L *Briton-, Brito*, of Celt origin; akin to W *Brython*] **1 :** a member of one of the peoples inhabiting Britain prior to the Anglo-Saxon invasions **2 :** a native or subject of Great Britain; *esp* **:** ENGLISHMAN
Brit·ta·ny spaniel \ˌbrit-^{ə}n-ē-\ *n* [*Brittany*, region in France] **:** a large active spaniel of a French breed developed by interbreeding pointers with spaniels of Brittany
[1]**brit·tle** \ˈbrit-^{ə}l\ *adj* **brit·tler** \ˈbrit-lər, -^{ə}l-ər\; **brit·tlest** \-ləst, -^{ə}l-əst\ [ME *britil*; akin to OE *brēotan* to break, Skt *bhrūṇa* embryo] **1 a :** easily broken, cracked, or snapped ⟨~ clay⟩ ⟨~ glass⟩ **b :** easily disrupted, overthrown, or damaged : FRAIL ⟨a ~ friendship⟩ **2 :** easily hurt or offended : SENSITIVE ⟨a ~ personality⟩ **3 :** SHARP, TENSE ⟨~ staccato of snare drums⟩ **4 a :** PERISHABLE, MORTAL **b :** TRANSITORY, EVANESCENT **5 :** lacking warmth, depth, or generosity of spirit : COLD ⟨a ~ selfish person⟩ ***syn*** see FRAGILE ***ant*** supple — **brit·tle·ly** \ˈbrit-lē, -^{ə}l-(l)ē\ *adv* — **brit·tle·ness** \ˈbrit-^{ə}l-nəs\ *n*
[2]**brittle** *vi* **brit·tled; brit·tling** \ˈbrit-liŋ, -^{ə}liŋ\ **:** to become brittle : CRUMBLE, DETERIORATE
[3]**brittle** *n* **:** candy made by caramelizing sugar, adding nuts, and cooling in thin sheets ⟨peanut ~⟩
brittle star *n* **:** any of a subclass or class (Ophiuroidea) of echinoderms that have slender flexible arms
Brit·ton·ic \bri-ˈtän-ik\ *adj* [L *Britton-, Britto* Briton] **:** BRYTHONIC 2
Brix \ˈbriks\ *adj* **:** of or relating to a Brix scale
Brix scale *n* [Adolf F. *Brix* †1870 G scientist] **:** a hydrometer scale for sugar solutions so graduated that its readings at a specified temperature represent percentages by weight of sugar in the solution — called also *Brix*
brl *abbr* barrel
bro *abbr* brother; brothers
[1]**broach** \ˈbrōch\ *n* [ME *broche*, fr. MF, fr. (assumed) VL *brocca*, fr. L, fem. of *broccus* projecting] **1 :** any of various pointed or tapered tools, implements, or parts: as **a :** a spit for roasting meat **b :** a tool for tapping casks **c :** a cutting tool for removing material from metal or plastic to shape an outside surface or a hole **2 :** BROOCH
[2]**broach** *vt* **1 a :** to pierce (as a cask) in order to draw the contents : TAP **b :** to open up or break into (as a mine or stores) **2 :** to shape or enlarge (a hole) with a broach **3 a :** to make known for the first time **b :** to open up (a subject) for discussion ~ *vi* **:** to break the surface from below ***syn*** see EXPRESS — **broach·er** *n*
[3]**broach** *vb* [perh. fr. [2]*broach*] *vi* **:** to veer or yaw dangerously esp. in a following sea so as to lie broadside to the waves — used chiefly with *to* ~ *vt* **:** to cause (a boat) to broach
[1]**broad** \ˈbrȯd\ *adj* [ME *brood*, fr. OE *brād*; akin to OHG *breit* broad] **1 a :** having ample extent from side to side or between limits ⟨~ shoulders⟩ **b :** having a specified extension from side to side ⟨made the path 10 feet ~⟩ **2 :** extending far and wide : SPACIOUS ⟨the ~ plains⟩ **3 a :** OPEN, FULL ⟨~ daylight⟩ **b :** PLAIN, OBVIOUS ⟨a ~ hint⟩ **4 :** marked by lack of restraint, delicacy, or subtlety: **a** *obs* **:** OUTSPOKEN **b :** COARSE, RISQUÉ ⟨~ humor⟩ **5 a :** LIBERAL, TOLERANT ⟨~ views⟩ **b :** widely applicable or applied : GENERAL **6 :** relating to the main or essential points ⟨~ outlines⟩ **7 :** dialectal esp. in pronunciation **8** *of a vowel* **:** OPEN — used specif. of *a* pronounced as in *father* — **broad·ly** *adv* — **broad·ness** *n*
syn BROAD, WIDE, DEEP *shared meaning element* **:** having horizontal extent ***ant*** narrow
[2]**broad** *adv* **:** in a broad manner : FULLY
[3]**broad** *n* **1** *Brit* **:** an expansion of a river — often used in pl. **2** *slang* **:** WOMAN
broad arrow *n* **1 :** an arrow with a flat barbed head **2** *Brit* **:** a mark shaped like a broad arrow that identifies government property including clothing formerly worn by convicts
broad·ax \ˈbrȯ-ˌdaks\ *n* **:** a large ax with a broad blade
broad·band \ˈbrȯd-ˌband\ *adj* **:** of, having, or involving operation with uniform efficiency over a wide band of frequencies ⟨a ~ radio antenna⟩
broad bean *n* **:** the large flat edible seed of an Old World upright vetch (*Vicia faba*); *also* **:** this plant widely grown for its seeds and as fodder
[1]**broad·cast** \ˈbrȯd-ˌkast\ *adj* **1 :** cast or scattered in all directions **2 :** made public by means of radio or television **3 :** of or relating to radio or television broadcasting
[2]**broadcast** *n* **1 :** the act of transmitting sound or images by radio or television **2 :** a single radio or television program
[3]**broadcast** *vb* **broadcast** *also* **broad·cast·ed; broad·cast·ing** *vt* **1 :** to scatter or sow (seed) broadcast **2 :** to make widely known **3 :** to transmit as a broadcast ~ *vi* **1 :** to transmit a broadcast **2 :** to speak or perform on a broadcast program — **broad·cast·er** *n*
[4]**broadcast** *adv* **:** to or over a broad area
Broad Church *adj* **:** of or relating to a liberal party in the Anglican communion esp. in the later 19th century — **Broad Churchman** *n*
broad·cloth \ˈbrȯd-ˌklȯth\ *n* **1 :** a twilled napped woolen or worsted fabric with smooth lustrous face and dense texture **2 :** a fabric usu. of cotton, silk, or rayon made in plain and rib weaves with soft semigloss finish
broad·en \ˈbrȯd-^{ə}n\ *vb* **broad·ened; broad·en·ing** \ˈbrȯd-niŋ, -^{ə}n-iŋ\ *vi* **:** to become broad ~ *vt* **:** to make broader
broad gauge *n* **:** a railroad gauge wider than standard gauge — **broad–gauged** \ˈbrȯd-ˈgājd\ *adj*
broad jump *n* **:** LONG JUMP — **broad jumper** *n*
broad·leaf \ˈbrȯd-ˌlēf\ *adj* **:** BROAD-LEAVED
broad–leaved \-ˈlēvd\ *or* **broad–leafed** \-ˈlēft\ *adj* **:** having broad leaves; *specif* **:** having leaves that are not needles
[1]**broad·loom** \-ˌlüm\ *adj* **:** woven on a wide loom; *also* **:** so woven in solid color

[2]**broadloom** *n* : a broadloom carpet
broad–mind·ed \ˈbrȯd-ˈmīn-dəd\ *adj* **1 :** tolerant of varied views **2 :** inclined to condone minor departures from conventional behavior — **broad–mind·ed·ly** *adv* — **broad–mind·ed·ness** *n*
broad·sheet \-ˌshēt\ *n* : BROADSIDE 3b
[1]**broad·side** \-ˌsīd\ *n* **1 :** the side of a ship above the waterline **2 :** a broad or unbroken surface **3 a** *archaic* : a sheet of paper printed on one side **b :** a sheet printed on one or both sides and folded; *also* : something (as a ballad or an advertisement) printed on a broadside **4 a :** all the guns on one side of a ship; *also* : their simultaneous discharge **b :** a volley of verbal abuse or denunciation
[2]**broadside** *adj* : directed or placed broadside ⟨a ~ attack⟩
[3]**broadside** *adv* **1 :** with the broadside toward a given object or point **2 :** in one volley **3 :** at random
broad–spectrum *adj* : effective against various insects or microorganisms
broad·sword \ˈbrȯd-ˌsō(ə)rd, -ˌsȯ(ə)rd\ *n* : a sword with a broad blade for cutting rather than thrusting
broad·tail \-ˌtāl\ *n* **1 a :** KARAKUL 1 **b :** a fat-tailed sheep **2 :** the fur or skin of a very young or premature karakul lamb having a flat and wavy appearance resembling moiré silk
Broad·way \ˈbrȯd-ˌwā, -ˈwā\ *n* [*Broadway,* street in New York on or near which were once located the majority of the city's legitimate theaters] : the New York commercial theater and amusement world; *specif* : playhouses located in the area between Fifth Avenue and Ninth Avenue from 34th Street to 56th Street and between Fifth Avenue and the Hudson River from 56th Street to 72d Street — **Broadway** *adj* — **Broad·way·ite** \-ˌīt\ *n*
broad·wife \ˈbrȯd-ˌwīf\ *n* [*abroad* + *wife*] : the wife of a slave belonging to another master in the slaveholding states of the U.S.
Brob·ding·nag·ian \ˌbräb-diŋ-ˈnag-ē-ən, -dig-ˈnag-\ *n* : an inhabitant of a country in Swift's *Gulliver's Travels* where everything is on a giant scale — **Brobdingnagian** *adj*
bro·cade \brō-ˈkād\ *n* [Sp *brocado,* fr. Catal *brocat,* fr. It *broccato,* fr. *broccare* to spur, brocade, fr. *brocco* small nail, fr. L *broccus* projecting] **1 :** a rich oriental silk fabric with raised patterns in gold and silver **2 :** a fabric characterized by raised designs — **brocade** *vt* — **bro·cad·ed** *adj*
broc·a·telle \ˌbräk-ə-ˈtel\ *n* [F, fr. It *broccatello,* dim. of *broccato*] : a stiff decorating fabric with patterns in high relief
broc·co·li *or* **broc·o·li** \ˈbräk-(ə-)lē\ *n* [It, pl. of *broccolo* flowering top of a cabbage, dim. of *brocco* small nail, sprout] **1 :** a large hardy cauliflower **2 :** a branching cauliflower with a head of functional florets at the end of each branch that is cut for food while the florets are tight green or purplish buds — called also *sprouting broccoli*
bro·chette \brō-ˈshet\ *n* [F, fr. OF *brochete,* fr. *broche* pointed tool — more at BROACH] : SKEWER; *also* : food broiled on a skewer
bro·chure \brō-ˈshu̇(ə)r\ *n* [F, fr. *brocher* to sew, fr. MF, to prick, fr. OF *brochier,* fr. *broche*] : a small pamphlet : BOOKLET
brock \ˈbräk\ *n* [ME, fr. OE *broc,* of Celt origin; akin to W *broch* badger] : BADGER
brock·age \ˈbräk-ij\ *n* [E dial. *brock* rubbish + E *-age*] : an imperfectly minted coin
brock·et \ˈbräk-ət\ *n* [ME *broket*] **1 :** a male red deer two years old — compare PRICKET **2 :** any of several small So. American deer (genus *Mazama*) with unbranched horns
bro·gan \ˈbrō-gən, -ˌgan; brō-ˈgan\ *n* [IrGael *brōgan,* dim. of *brōg*] : a heavy shoe; *esp* : a coarse work shoe reaching to the ankle
[1]**brogue** \ˈbrōg\ *n* [IrGael & ScGael *brōg,* fr. MIr *brōc,* fr. ON *brōk* leg covering; akin to OE *brōc* leg covering — more at BREECH] **1 :** a stout coarse shoe worn formerly in Ireland and the Scottish Highlands **2 :** a heavy shoe often with a hobnailed sole : BROGAN **3 :** a stout oxford shoe with perforations and usu. a wing tip
[2]**brogue** *n* [perh. fr. IrGael *barrōg* wrestling hold; fr. the idea that unfamiliar features of pronunciation must be the result of a physical impediment of the tongue] : a dialect or regional pronunciation; *esp* : an Irish accent
broi·der \ˈbrȯid-ər\ *vt* [ME *broideren,* modif. of MF *broder* — more at EMBROIDER] : EMBROIDER — **broi·dery** \ˈbrȯid-(ə-)rē\ *n*
[1]**broil** \ˈbrȯi(ə)l\ *vb* [ME *broilen,* fr. MF *bruler* to burn, modif. of L *ustulare* to singe, fr. *ustus,* pp. of *urere* to burn] *vt* : to cook by direct exposure to radiant heat : GRILL ~ *vi* : to become broiled
[2]**broil** *n* **1 :** the act or state of broiling **2 :** something broiled
[3]**broil** *vb* [ME *broilen,* fr. MF *brouiller* to mix, broil, fr. OF *brooilier,* fr. *breu* broth — more at BREWIS] *vt* : EMBROIL ~ *vi* : BRAWL
[4]**broil** *n* : a noisy disturbance : TUMULT; *esp* : BRAWL
broil·er \ˈbrȯi-lər\ *n* **1 :** one that broils **2 :** a bird fit for broiling; *esp* : a young chicken of up to 2 1/2 pounds dressed weight
[1]**broke** \ˈbrōk\ *past of* BREAK
[2]**broke** *adj* [ME, alter. of *broken*] : PENNILESS
bro·ken \ˈbrō-kən\ *adj* [ME, fr. OE *brocen,* fr. pp. of *brecan* to break] **1 :** violently separated into parts : SHATTERED **2 :** damaged or altered by breaking: as **a :** having undergone or been subjected to fracture ⟨a ~ leg⟩ **b** *of land surfaces* : being irregular, interrupted, or full of obstacles **c :** violated by transgression ⟨a ~ promise⟩ **d :** DISCONTINUOUS, INTERRUPTED **e :** disrupted by change **f** *of a flower* : having an irregular, streaked, or blotched pattern esp. from virus infection **3 a :** made weak or infirm **b :** subdued completely : CRUSHED ⟨a ~ spirit⟩ **c :** BANKRUPT **d :** reduced in rank **4 a :** cut off : DISCONNECTED **b :** imperfectly spoken or written ⟨~ English⟩ **5 :** not complete or full — **bro·ken·ly** *adv* — **bro·ken·ness** \-kən-(n)əs\ *n*
bro·ken–down \ˌbrō-kən-ˈdau̇n\ *adj* : extremely infirm : WORN-OUT
bro·ken–field \ˌbrō-kən-ˌfēld\ *adj* : accomplished (as by a ballcarrier in football) against widely scattered opposition
bro·ken·heart·ed \ˌbrō-kən-ˈhärt-əd\ *adj* : overcome by grief or despair
broken home *n* : a family in which the parents are not living together
broken wind *n* : HEAVES — **bro·ken–wind·ed** \ˌbrō-kən-ˈwin-dəd\ *adj*
bro·ker \ˈbrō-kər\ *n* [ME, negotiator, fr. (assumed) AF *brocour;* akin to OF *broche* pointed tool, tap of a cask — more at BROACH] **1 :** one who acts as an intermediary: as **a :** an agent who arranges marriages **b :** an agent who negotiates contracts of purchase and sale (as of real estate, commodities, or securities) **2** *Brit* : a dealer in secondhand goods
bro·ker·age \ˈbrō-k(ə-)rij\ *n* **1 :** the business or establishment of a broker **2 :** the fee or commission for transacting business as a broker
brol·ly \ˈbräl-ē\ *n, pl* **brollies** [by shortening & alter.] *chiefly Brit* : UMBRELLA
brom- *or* **bromo-** *comb form* [prob. fr. F *brome,* fr. Gk *brōmos* bad smell] : bromine ⟨*brom*ide⟩
[1]**bro·mate** \ˈbrō-ˌmāt\ *n* : a salt of bromic acid
[2]**bromate** *vt* **bro·mat·ed; bro·mat·ing :** to treat with a bromate; *broadly* : BROMINATE
brome·grass \ˈbrōm-ˌgras\ *n* [NL *Bromus,* genus name, fr. L *bromos* oats, fr. Gk] : any of a large genus (*Bromus*) of tall grasses often having drooping spikelets
bro·me·lain \ˈbrō-mə-lən, -ˌlān\ *or* **bro·me·lin** \ˈbrō-mə-lən, brō-ˈmē-\ *n* [*bromelain* by alter. (influenced by *papain*) of *bromelin,* fr. NL *Bromelia,* genus name of the pineapple in some classifications + E *-in*] : a proteinase obtained from the juice of the pineapple
bro·me·li·ad \brō-ˈmē-lē-ˌad\ *n* [NL *Bromelia,* genus of tropical American plants, fr. Olaf *Bromelius* †1705 Sw botanist] : any of a family (Bromeliaceae) of chiefly tropical American and epiphytic herbaceous plants including the pineapple, Spanish moss, and various ornamentals
bro·mic \ˈbrō-mik\ *adj* : of, relating to, or containing bromine esp. with a valence of five
bromic acid *n* : an unstable strongly oxidizing acid $HBrO_3$ known only in solution or in the form of its salts
bro·mide \ˈbrō-ˌmīd\ *n* **1 :** a binary compound of bromine with another element or a radical including some (as potassium bromide) used as sedatives **2 a :** a commonplace or tiresome person : BORE **b :** a commonplace or hackneyed statement or notion
bro·mid·ic \brō-ˈmid-ik\ *adj* : lacking in originality : DULL, TRITE
bro·mi·nate \ˈbrō-mə-ˌnāt\ *vt* **-nat·ed; -nat·ing :** to treat or cause to combine with bromine or a compound of bromine — **bro·mi·na·tion** \ˌbrō-mə-ˈnā-shən\ *n*
bro·mine \ˈbrō-ˌmēn\ *n* [F *brome* bromine + E *-ine*] : a nonmetallic element normally a deep red corrosive toxic liquid giving off an irritating reddish brown vapor of disagreeable odor — see ELEMENT table
bro·mism \ˈbrō-ˌmiz-əm\ *n* : an abnormal state due to excessive or prolonged use of bromides
bro·mo \ˈbrō-(ˌ)mō\ *n, pl* **bromos** [*brom-*] : a proprietary effervescent mixture used as a headache remedy, sedative, and alkalinizing agent; *also* : a dose of such a mixture
bro·mo·ura·cil \ˌbrō-mō-ˈyu̇r-ə-ˌsil, -səl\ *n* [*bromo-* + *uracil*] : a mutagenic analogue of thymine and uracil derivative $C_4H_3N_2O_2Br$ that pairs readily with adenine and sometimes with guanine during bacterial or phage DNA synthesis
bronc \ˈbräŋk\ *n* : BRONCO
bronch- *or* **broncho-** *comb form* [prob. fr. F, throat, fr. LL, fr. Gk, fr. *bronchos* — more at CRAW] : bronchial tube : bronchial ⟨*bronch*itis⟩
bronchi- *or* **bronchio-** *comb form* [NL, fr. *bronchia,* pl., branches of the bronchi, fr. Gk, dim. of *bronchos* bronchus] : bronchial tubes ⟨*bronchi*ectasis⟩
bron·chi·al \ˈbräŋ-kē-əl\ *adj* : of or relating to the bronchi or their ramifications in the lungs — **bron·chi·al·ly** \-ə-lē\ *adv*
bronchial asthma *n* : asthma resulting from spasmodic contraction of bronchial muscles
bronchial pneumonia *n* : BRONCHOPNEUMONIA
bronchial tube *n* : a primary bronchus or any of its branches
bron·chi·ec·ta·sis \ˌbräŋ-kē-ˈek-tə-səs\ *n* [NL] : a chronic dilatation of bronchi or bronchioles
bron·chi·ole \ˈbräŋ-kē-ˌōl\ *n* [NL *bronchiolum,* dim. of *bronchia*] : a minute thin-walled branch of a bronchus — **bron·chi·o·lar** \ˌbräŋ-kē-ˈō-lər\ *adj*
bron·chi·tis \brän-ˈkīt-əs, bräŋ-\ *n* : acute or chronic inflammation of the bronchial tubes or a disease marked by this — **bron·chit·ic** \-ˈkit-ik\ *adj*
bron·cho·gen·ic \ˌbräŋ-kə-ˈjen-ik\ *adj* : of, relating to, or arising in or by way of the air passages of the lungs
bron·chog·ra·phy \brän-ˈkäg-rə-fē, bräŋ-\ *n* : the roentgenographic visualization of the bronchi and their branches after injection of a radiopaque substance — **bron·cho·graph·ic** \ˌbräŋ-kə-ˈgraf-ik\ *adj*
bron·cho·pneu·mo·nia \ˌbräŋ-(ˌ)kō-n(y)u̇-ˈmō-nyə\ *n* [NL] : pneumonia involving many relatively small areas of lung tissue
bron·cho·scope \ˈbräŋ-kə-ˌskōp\ *n* [ISV] : a tubular illuminated instrument used for inspecting or passing instruments into the bronchi — **bron·cho·scop·ic** \ˌbräŋ-kə-ˈskäp-ik\ *adj* — **bron·cho·scop·i·cal·ly** \-i-k(ə-)lē\ *adv* — **bron·chos·co·pist** \brän-ˈkäs-kə-pəst, bräŋ-\ *n* — **bron·chos·co·py** \-pē\ *n*
bron·chus \ˈbräŋ-kəs\ *n, pl* **bron·chi** \ˈbräŋ-ˌkī, -ˌkē\ [NL, fr. Gk *bronchos*] : either of the two primary divisions of the trachea that lead respectively into the right and the left lung; *broadly* : BRONCHIAL TUBE
bron·co \ˈbräŋ-(ˌ)kō\ *n, pl* **broncos** [MexSp, fr. Sp, rough, wild] : an unbroken or imperfectly broken range horse of western No. America; *broadly* : MUSTANG
bron·co·bust·er \-kō-ˌbəs-tər\ *n* : one who breaks wild horses to the saddle

ə abut ə kitten ər further a back ā bake ä cot, cart
au̇ out ch chin e less ē easy g gift i trip ī life
j joke ŋ sing ō flow ȯ flaw ȯi coin th thin t͟h this
ü loot u̇ foot y yet yü few yu̇ furious zh vision

bron·to·sau·rus \ˌbränt-ə-ˈsȯr-əs\ *also* **bron·to·saur** \ˈbränt-ə-ˌsȯ(ə)r\ *n* [deriv. of Gk *brontē* thunder + *sauros* lizard; akin to Gk *bremein* to roar — more at SAURIAN] : any of various large quadrupedal and prob. herbivorous dinosaurs (genus *Apatosaurus*)

Bronx cheer \ˈbräŋ(k)s-\ *n* [*Bronx*, borough of New York City] : RASPBERRY 2

1bronze \ˈbränz\ *vt* **bronzed; bronz·ing** : to give the appearance of bronze to — **bronz·er** *n*

2bronze *n, often attrib* [F, fr. It *bronzo*] **1 a** : an alloy of copper and tin and sometimes other elements **b** : any of various copper-base alloys with little or no tin **2** : a sculpture or artifact of bronze **3** : a moderate yellowish brown — **bronzy** \ˈbrän-zē\ *adj*

Bronze Age *n* : the period of human culture characterized by the use of bronze tools that began in Europe about 3500 B.C. and in western Asia and Egypt somewhat earlier

Bronze Star Medal *n* : a U.S. military decoration awarded for heroic or meritorious service not involving aerial flights

bronz·ing *n* : a bronze coloring or discoloration (as of leaves)

brooch \ˈbrōch, ˈbrüch\ *n* [ME *broche* pointed tool, brooch — more at BROACH] : an ornament that is held by a pin or clasp and is worn at or near the neck

1brood \ˈbrüd\ *n* [ME, fr. OE *brōd;* akin to OE *beorma* yeast — more at BARM] **1** : the young of an animal or a family of young; *esp* : the young (as of a bird or insect) hatched or cared for at one time **2** : a group having a common nature or origin

2brood *vt* **1 a** : to sit on or incubate (eggs) **b** : to produce by or as if by incubation : HATCH **2** *of a bird* : to cover (young) with the wings **3** : to think anxiously or gloomily about : PONDER ~ *vi* **1 a** *of a bird* : to brood eggs or young **b** : to sit quietly and thoughtfully : MEDITATE **2** : HOVER, LOOM **3 a** : to dwell gloomily on a subject : WORRY **b** : to be in a state of depression — **brood·ing·ly** \-iŋ-lē\ *adv*

3brood *adj* : kept for breeding ⟨a ~ mare⟩ ⟨a ~ flock⟩

brood·er \ˈbrüd-ər\ *n* **1** : one that broods **2** : a heated structure used for raising young fowl

broody \ˈbrüd-ē\ *adj* **1 a** : being in a state of readiness to brood eggs that is characterized by cessation of laying and by marked changes in behavior and physiology **b** : suitable for producing offspring ⟨a strong ~ mare⟩ **2** : given or conducive to introspection : CONTEMPLATIVE, MOODY — **brood·i·ness** *n*

1brook \ˈbru̇k\ *vt* [ME *brouken* to use, enjoy, fr. OE *brūcan;* akin to OHG *brūhhan* to use, L *frui* to enjoy] : to stand for : TOLERATE ⟨he would ~ no interference with his plans⟩ ***syn*** see BEAR

2brook *n* [ME, fr. OE *brōc;* akin to OHG *bruoh* marshy ground] : CREEK 2

brook·ite \ˈbru̇k-ˌīt\ *n* [Henry J. *Brooke* †1857 E mineralogist] : titanium dioxide TiO_2 occurring as a mineral in orthorhombic crystals commonly translucent brown or opaque brown to black

brook·let \ˈbru̇k-lət\ *n* : a small brook

brook trout *n* : the common speckled cold-water char (*Salvelinus fontinalis*) of eastern No. America

1broom \ˈbrüm, ˈbru̇m\ *n* [ME, fr. OE *brōm;* akin to OHG *brāmo* bramble, ME *brimme* brim] **1** : any of various leguminous shrubs (esp. genera *Cytisus* and *Genista*) with long slender branches, small leaves, and usu. showy yellow flowers **2** : a bundle of firm stiff twigs or fibers bound together on a long handle for sweeping and brushing

2broom *vt* **1** : to sweep with or as if with a broom **2** : to finish (as a concrete surface) by means of a broom

broom·ball \-ˌbȯl\ *n* : a variation of ice hockey played on ice without skates and with brooms and a soccer ball used instead of sticks and a puck — **broom·ball·er** \-ˌbȯ-lər\ *n*

broom·corn \-ˌkȯ(ə)rn\ *n* : any of several tall cultivated sorghums whose stiff-branched panicle is used in brooms and brushes

broom·rape \-ˌrāp\ *n* **1** : any of various leafless herbs (family Orobanchaceae, the broomrape family) growing as parasites on the roots of other plants **2** : INDIAN PIPE

broom·stick \-ˌstik\ *n* : the long thin handle of a broom

brose \ˈbrōz\ *n* [perh. alter. of Sc *bruis* broth, fr. ME *brewes* — more at BREWIS] : a chiefly Scottish dish made with a boiling liquid and meal

broth \ˈbrȯth\ *n, pl* **broths** \ˈbrȯths, ˈbrȯt͟hz\ [ME, fr. OE; akin to OHG *brod* broth, L *fervēre* to boil — more at BURN] **1** : liquid in which meat, fish, cereal grains, or vegetables have been cooked : STOCK **2** : a fluid culture medium

broth·el \ˈbräth-əl, ˈbrȯth-\ *n* [ME, worthless fellow, prostitute, fr. *brothen,* pp. of *brethen* to waste away, go to ruin, fr. OE *brēothan* to waste away; akin to OE *brēotan* to break — more at BRITTLE] : WHOREHOUSE

broth·er \ˈbrət͟h-ər\ *n, pl* **brothers** *also* **breth·ren** \ˈbret͟h-(ə-)rən, ˈbret͟h-ərn\ [ME, fr. OE *brōthor;* akin to OHG *bruodor* brother, L *frater,* Gk *phratēr* member of the same clan] **1** : a male who has the same parents as another or one parent in common with another **2 a** : KINSMAN **b** : one who shares with another a common national or racial origin **3** : a fellow member — used as a title for ministers in some evangelical denominations **4** : one related to another by common ties or interests **5 a** *cap* : a member of a congregation of men not in holy orders and usu. in hospital or school work **b** : a member of a men's religious order who is not preparing for or is not ready for holy orders ⟨a lay ~⟩

broth·er·hood \ˈbrət͟h-ər-ˌhu̇d\ *n* [ME *brotherhede, brotherhod,* alter. of *brotherrede,* fr. OE *brōthorrǣden,* fr. *brōthor* + *rǣden* condition — more at KINDRED] **1** : the quality or state of being brothers **2** : an association (as a labor union) for a particular purpose **3** : the whole body of persons engaged in business or profession

broth·er–in–law \ˈbrət͟h-(ə-)rən-ˌlȯ, ˈbrət͟h-ərn-ˌlȯ\ *n, pl* **brothers–in–law** \ˈbrət͟h-ər-zən-\ **1** : the brother of one's spouse **2 a** : the husband of one's sister **b** : the husband of one's spouse's sister

broth·er·ly \ˈbrət͟h-ər-lē\ *adj* **1** : of or relating to brothers **2** : natural or becoming to brothers : AFFECTIONATE ⟨~ love⟩ — **broth·er·li·ness** *n* — **brotherly** *adv*

brougham \ˈbrü(-ə)m, ˈbrō(-ə)m\ *n* [Henry Peter *Brougham,* Baron Brougham and Vaux †1868 Sc jurist] **1** : a light closed horse-drawn carriage with the driver outside in front **2** : a coupe automobile; *esp* : one driven electrically **3** : a sedan automobile having no roof over the driver's seat

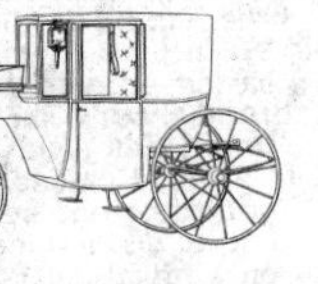

brougham 1

brought *past of* BRING

brou·ha·ha \ˈbrü-ˌhä-ˌhä, ˌbrü-ˈhä-ˈhä, brü-ˈhä-ˌhä\ *n* [F] : HUBBUB, UPROAR

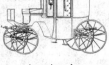

brow \ˈbrau̇\ *n* [ME, fr. OE *brū;* akin to ON *brūn* eyebrow, Gk *ophrys*] **1 a** : EYEBROW **b** : the ridge on which the eyebrow grows **c** : FOREHEAD **2** : the projecting upper part or margin of a steep place **3** : EXPRESSION, MIEN ⟨to cloak offenses with a cunning ~ —Shak.⟩

brow antler *n* : the first branch of a stag's antler — see ANTLER illustration

brow·beat \ˈbrau̇-ˌbēt\ *vt* **-beat; -beat·en** \-ˈbēt-ᵊn\ *or* **-beat; -beat·ing** : to intimidate or disconcert by a stern manner or arrogant speech : BULLY

-browed \ˈbrau̇d\ *adj comb form* : having brows of a specified nature ⟨smooth-*browed*⟩

1brown \ˈbrau̇n\ *adj* [ME *broun,* fr. OE *brūn;* akin to OHG *brūn* brown, Gk *phrynē* toad] : of the color brown; *esp* : of dark or tanned complexion

2brown *n* **1** : any of a group of colors between red and yellow in hue, of medium to low lightness, and of moderate to low saturation **2** : a brown-skinned person — **brown·ish** \ˈbrau̇-nish\ *adj* — **browny** \-nē\ *adj*

3brown *vi* : to become brown ~ *vt* : to make brown

brown alga *n* : any of a division (Phaeophyta) of variable mostly marine algae with chlorophyll masked by brown pigment

brown bag·ging \-ˈbag-iŋ\ *n* [fr. the brown paper bag in which the bottle is carried] **1** : the practice of carrying a bottle of liquor into a restaurant or club where setups are available **2** : the practice of carrying (as to work) one's lunch usu. in a brown paper bag — **brown bag·ger** \-ˈbag-ər\ *n*

brown Bet·ty \-ˈbet-ē\ *n* : a baked pudding of apples, bread crumbs, and spices

brown bread \-ˌbred\ *n* **1** : bread made of whole wheat flour **2** : a dark brown steamed bread made usu. of cornmeal, white or whole wheat flours, molasses, soda, and milk or water

brown coal *n* : LIGNITE

brown–eyed Su·san \ˌbrau̇-ˌnīd-ˈsüz-ᵊn\ *n* [*brown-eyed* + *Susan* (as in black-eyed *Susan*)] : a dark-centered coneflower (*Rudbeckia triloba*) of eastern No. America with tripartite lower leaves

brown fat *n* : a heat-producing tissue of hibernating mammals

Brown·ian movement \ˌbrau̇-nē-ən-\ *n* [Robert *Brown* †1858 Sc botanist] : a random movement of microscopic particles suspended in liquids or gases resulting from the impact of molecules of the fluid surrounding the particles — called also *Brownian motion*

brown·ie \ˈbrau̇-nē\ *n* [ˈ*brown*] **1** : a good-natured goblin believed to perform helpful services at night **2** *cap* : a member of the Girl Scouts from 7 through 9 years **3** : a small square or rectangle of rich usu. chocolate cake containing nuts

Brownie point *n* : a credit regarded as earned esp. by currying favor with a superior

Brow·ning automatic rifle \ˈbrau̇-niŋ-\ *n* [John M. *Browning* †1926 Am designer of firearms] : a .30 caliber gas-operated air-cooled magazine-fed automatic rifle often provided with a rest for the barrel and used by U.S. troops in World War II and the Korean war — abbr. *BAR*

Browning machine gun *n* : a .30 or .50 caliber recoil-operated air-or water-cooled machine gun fed by a cartridge belt and used by U.S. troops in World War II and the Korean war

brown·nose \ˈbrau̇n-ˌnōz\ *vt* [fr. the implication that servility is equivalent to kissing the hinder parts of the person from whom advancement is sought] *slang* : to ingratiate oneself with : curry favor with — **brownnose** *n* — **brown·nos·er** *n*

brown·out \ˈbrau̇-ˌnau̇t\ *n* [*brown* + *-out* (as in *blackout*)] : a curtailment of the use of electric power esp. in display lighting; *also* : a period of reduced illumination resulting from such curtailment

brown rat *n* : the common domestic rat (*Rattus norvegicus*)

brown recluse spider *n* : a venomous spider (*Loxosceles reclusa*) introduced into the southern U.S. that has a violin-shaped mark on the cephalothorax and produces a dangerous neurotoxin

brown·shirt \ˈbrau̇n-ˌshərt\ *n, often cap* : NAZI; *esp* : STORM TROOPER

brown·stone \-ˌstōn\ *n* **1** : a reddish brown sandstone used for building **2** : a dwelling faced with brownstone

brown study *n* : a state of serious absorption or abstraction

brown sugar *n* : soft sugar whose crystals are covered by a film of refined dark syrup

Brown Swiss *n* : any of a breed of large hardy brown dairy cattle originating in Switzerland

brown–tail moth \ˌbrau̇n-ˌtāl-\ *n* : a tussock moth (*Nygmia phaeorrhoea*) whose larvae feed on foliage and are irritating to the skin

brown trout *n* : a speckled European trout (*Salmo trutta*) widely introduced as a game fish

brows·abil·i·ty \ˌbrau̇-zə-ˈbil-ət-ē\ *n* : the property (as of an information retrieval system) of permitting users to browse

1browse \ˈbrau̇z\ *n* [prob. modif. of MF *brouts,* pl. of *brout* sprout, fr. OF *brost,* of Gmc origin; akin to OS *brustian* to sprout; akin to OE *brēost* breast] **1** : tender shoots, twigs, and leaves of trees and shrubs fit for food for cattle **2** : an act or instance of browsing

2browse *vb* **browsed; brows·ing** *vt* **1 a** : to consume as browse **b** : GRAZE **2** : to look over casually : SKIM ~ *vi* **1 a** : to feed on or as if on browse **b** : GRAZE **2 a** : to skim through a book reading at random passages that catch the eye **b** : to look over or through an aggregate of things casually esp. in search of something of interest — **brows·er** *n*

bru·cel·la \brü-'sel-ə\ *n, pl* **-cel·lae** \-'sel-(,)ē\ *or* **-cellas** [NL, genus name, fr. Sir David *Bruce* †1931 Brit bacteriologist] : any of a genus (*Brucella*) of nonmotile capsulated bacteria that cause disease in man and domestic animals

bru·cel·lo·sis \,brü-sə-'lō-səs\ *n, pl* **-lo·ses** \-,sēz\ : infection with or disease caused by brucellae esp. in man or cattle

bru·cine \'brü-,sēn\ *n* [prob. fr. F, fr. NL *Brucea* (genus name of *Brucea antidysenterica,* a shrub)] : a poisonous alkaloid $C_{23}H_{26}N_2O_4$ found with strychnine esp. in nux vomica

bru·in \'brü-ən\ *n* [D, name of the bear in *Reynard the Fox*] : BEAR

1**bruise** \'brüz\ *vb* **bruised; bruis·ing** [ME *brusen, brisen,* fr. MF & OE; MF *bruisier* to break, of Celt origin; akin to OIr *brūu* I shatter; OE *brȳsan* to bruise; akin to OIr *brūu,* L *frustum* piece] *vt* **1 a** *archaic* : DISABLE **b** : BATTER, DENT **2** : to inflict a bruise on : CONTUSE **3** : to break down (as leaves or berries) by pounding : CRUSH **4** : WOUND, INJURE; *esp* : to inflict psychological hurt on ~ *vi* **1** : to inflict a bruise **2** : to undergo bruising ⟨tomatoes ~ easily⟩

2**bruise** *n* **1 a** : an injury involving rupture of small blood vessels and discoloration without a break in the overlying skin : CONTUSION **b** : a similar injury to plant tissue **2** : ABRASION, SCRATCH **3** : an injury esp. to the feelings

bruis·er \'brü-zər\ *n* : a big husky man

1**bruit** *n* [ME, fr. MF, fr. OF, noise] **1** \'brüt\ *archaic* **a** : NOISE, DIN **b** : REPORT, RUMOR **2** \'brü-ē\ [F, lit., noise] : any of several generally abnormal sounds heard on auscultation

2**bruit** \'brüt\ *vt* : to noise abroad : REPORT

bru·mal \'brü-məl\ *adj, archaic* [L *brumalis,* fr. L *bruma* winter] : indicative of or occurring in the winter

brum·by \'brəm-bē\ *n, pl* **brumbies** [prob. native name in Queensland, Australia] *Austral* : a wild or unbroken horse

brume \'brüm\ *n* [F, mist, winter, fr. OProv *bruma,* fr. L, winter, fr. *brevis* short — more at BRIEF] : MIST, FOG — **bru·mous** \'brü-məs\ *adj*

1**brum·ma·gem** \'brəm-i-jəm\ *adj* [alter. of *Birmingham,* England, the source in the 17th cent. of counterfeit groats] : having a cheaply contrived and showy quality

2**brummagem** *n* : something cheap or inferior : TINSEL

brunch \'brənch\ *n* [*breakfast* + *lunch*] : a late breakfast, an early lunch, or a combination of the two

1**bru·net** *or* **bru·nette** \brü-'net\ *adj* [F *brunet,* masc., *brunette,* fem., brownish, fr. OF, fr. *brun* brown, fr. ML *brunus,* of Gmc. origin; akin to OHG *brūn,* brown] **1** : being a brunet ⟨his ~ wife⟩ **2** : of a dark-brown or black color ⟨~ hair⟩

2**brunet** *or* **brunette** *n* : a person having brown or black hair and usu. a relatively dark complexion

Brun·hild \'brün-,hilt\ *n* [G] : a queen in Germanic legend won by Siegfried for Gunther

bru·ni·zem \,brü-nə-'zem, -'zhōm\ *n* [*bruni-* (fr. ML *brunus* brown) + *-zem* earth (as in *chernozem*)] : any of a zonal group of deep dark prairie soils developed from loess

Bruns·wick stew \,brənz-(,)wik-\ *n* [*Brunswick* county, Va.] : a stew made of vegetables and usu. of two meats (as chicken and squirrel)

brunt \'brənt\ *n* [ME] **1** : the principal force, shock, or stress (as of an attack) **2** : the greater part : BURDEN

1**brush** \'brəsh\ *n* [ME *brusch,* fr. MF *broce*] **1** : BRUSHWOOD **2 a** : scrub vegetation **b** : land covered with scrub vegetation

2**brush** *n* [ME *brusshe,* fr. MF *broisse,* fr. OF *broce*] **1** : a device composed of bristles set into a handle and used esp. for sweeping, scrubbing, or painting **2** : something resembling a brush: as **a** : a bushy tail **b** : a feather tuft worn on a hat **3 a** : an electrical conductor (as of copper strips or carbon) that makes sliding contact between a stationary and a moving part of a generator or a motor **b** : BRUSH DISCHARGE **4 a** : an act of brushing **b** : a quick light touch or momentary contact in passing

3**brush** *vt* **1 a** : to apply a brush to **b** : to apply with a brush **2 a** : to remove with passing strokes (as of a brush) ⟨~*ed* the dirt off his coat⟩ **b** : to dispose of in an offhand way : DISMISS ⟨~*ed* him off⟩ **3** : to pass lightly over or across : touch gently against in passing — **brush·er** *n*

4**brush** *vi* [ME *bruschen* to rush, fr. MF *brosser* to dash through underbrush, fr. *broce*] : to move lightly or heedlessly ⟨~*ed* by the well-wishers in his path⟩

5**brush** *n* [ME *brusche* rush, hostile collision, fr. *bruschen*] : a brief encounter or skirmish

brush·abil·i·ty \,brəsh-ə-'bil-ət-ē\ *n* : ease of application with a brush ⟨~ of a paint⟩

brush·back \'brəsh-,bak\ *n* : a fastball thrown near the batter's head in baseball in an attempt to make him move back from home plate

brush border *n* : microvilli on the plasma membrane of an epithelial cell (as in a kidney tubule) that is specialized for absorption

brush discharge *n* : a faintly luminous relatively slow electrical discharge having no spark

brushed \'brəsht\ *adj* : finished with a nap ⟨a ~ fabric⟩

brush·fire \'brəsh-,fī(ə)r\ *adj* [*brush fire* (a fire involving brush but not full-sized trees)] : involving mobilization only on a small and local scale ⟨~ border wars⟩

brush·land \-,land\ *n* : an area covered with brush growth

brush–off \-,ȯf\ *n* : a quietly curt or disdainful dismissal

brush up \(')brəsh-'əp\ *vt* **1** : to polish by eliminating small imperfections **2** : to renew one's skill in ~ *vi* : to refresh one's memory : renew one's skill ⟨*brush up* on his math⟩ — **brush·up** \'brəsh-,əp\ *n*

brush·wood \'brəsh-,wu̇d\ *n* **1** : wood of small branches esp. when cut or broken **2** : a thicket of shrubs and small trees

brush·work \-,wərk\ *n* : work done with a brush (as in painting); *esp* : the characteristic work of an artist using a brush

1**brushy** \'brəsh-ē\ *adj* **brush·i·er; -est** : SHAGGY, ROUGH

2**brushy** *adj* **brush·i·er; -est** : covered with or abounding in brush or brushwood

brusque *also* **brusk** \'brəsk\ *adj* [F *brusque,* fr. It *brusco,* fr. ML *bruscus* butcher's-broom] **1** : markedly short and abrupt **2** : blunt in manner or speech often to the point of ungracious harshness **syn** see BLUFF **ant** unctuous, bland — **brusque·ly** *adv* — **brusque·ness** *n*

brus·que·rie \,brəs-kə-'rē\ *n* [F, fr. *brusque*] : abruptness of manner

Brus·sels carpet \,brəs-əlz-\ *n* [*Brussels,* Belgium] : a carpet made of colored worsted yarns first fixed in a foundation web of strong linen thread and then drawn up in loops to form the pattern

Brussels griffon *n* : any of a breed of short-faced compact rough- or smooth-coated toy dogs of Belgian origin — called also *griffon*

Brussels lace *n* **1** : any of various fine needlepoint or bobbin laces with floral designs made orig. in or near Brussels **2** : a machine-made net of hexagonal mesh

brussels sprout *n, often cap B* **1** : any of the edible small green heads borne on the stem of a plant (*Brassica oleracea gemmifera*) — usu. used in pl. **2** *pl* : the plant that bears brussels sprouts

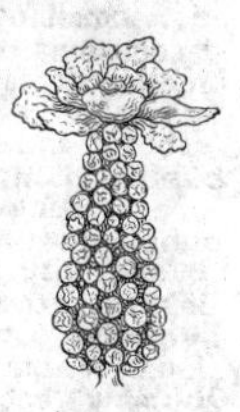
brussels sprouts

brut \'brüt, 'brūēt\ *adj* [F, lit., rough] *of champagne* : very dry; *specif* : containing less than 1.5 percent sugar by volume

bru·tal \'brüt-ᵊl\ *adj* **1** *archaic* : typical of beasts : ANIMAL **2** : befitting a brute: as **a** : grossly ruthless or unfeeling ⟨a ~ slander⟩ **b** : CRUEL, COLD-BLOODED ⟨a ~ attack⟩ **c** : HARSH, SEVERE ⟨~ weather⟩ **d** : unpleasantly accurate and incisive ⟨the ~ truth⟩ — **bru·tal·ly** \-ᵊl-ē\ *adv*

bru·tal·i·ty \brü-'tal-ət-ē\ *n, pl* **-ties** **1** : the quality or state of being brutal **2** : a brutal act or course of action

bru·tal·ize \'brüt-ᵊl-,īz\ *vt* **-ized; -iz·ing** **1** : to make brutal, unfeeling, or inhuman ⟨people *brutalized* by poverty and disease⟩ **2** : to treat brutally ⟨an accord not to ~ prisoners of war⟩ — **bru·tal·iza·tion** \,brüt-ᵊl-ə-'zā-shən\ *n*

1**brute** \'brüt\ *adj* [ME, fr. MF *brut* rough, fr. L *brutus* stupid, lit., heavy; akin to L *gravis* heavy — more at GRIEVE] **1** : of or relating to beasts ⟨the ways of the ~ world⟩ **2** : INANIMATE 1a **3** : characteristic of an animal in quality, action, or instinct: as **a** : CRUEL, SAVAGE ⟨~ force⟩ **b** : not working by reason ⟨~ instinct⟩ **4** : purely physical ⟨~ strength⟩ **5** : being of unrelieved severity ⟨~ necessity⟩

2**brute** *n* **1** : BEAST **2** : a brutal person

brut·ish \'brüt-ish\ *adj* **1** : befitting beasts ⟨lived a short and ~ life as a slave⟩ **2 a** : strongly and grossly sensual ⟨~ gluttony⟩ **b** : showing little intelligence or sensibility ⟨a ~ lack of understanding⟩ — **brut·ish·ly** *adv* — **brut·ish·ness** *n*

brux·ism \'brək-,siz-əm\ *n* [irreg. fr. Gk *brychein* to gnash the teeth + E *-ism*] : the habit of unconsciously gritting or grinding the teeth esp. in situations of stress or during sleep

Bryn·hild \'brin-,hild\ *n* [ON *Brynhildr*] : a Valkyrie waked from an enchanted sleep by Sigurd who later forgets her and is killed through her agency

bry·ol·o·gy \brī-'äl-ə-jē\ *n* [Gk *bryon* moss + ISV *-logy*] **1** : a branch of botany that deals with the bryophytes **2** : moss life or biology

bry·o·ny \'brī-ə-nē\ *n, pl* **-nies** [L *bryonia,* fr. Gk *bryōnia;* akin to Gk *bryon*] : any of a genus (*Bryonia*) of tendril-bearing vines of the gourd family with large leaves and red or black fruit

bryo·phyte \'brī-ə-,fīt\ *n* [deriv. of Gk *bryon* + *phyton* plant; akin to Gk *phyein* to bring forth — more at BE] : any of a division (Bryophyta) of nonflowering plants comprising the mosses and liverworts — **bryo·phyt·ic** \,brī-ə-'fit-ik\ *adj*

bryo·zo·an \,brī-ə-'zō-ən\ *n* [NL *Bryozoa,* class name, fr. Gk *bryon* + NL *-zoa*] : any of a phylum or class (Bryozoa) of aquatic mostly marine invertebrate animals that reproduce by budding and usu. form permanently attached branched or mossy colonies — **bryozoan** *adj*

Bryth·on \'brith-,än, -ən\ *n* **1** : a member of the British branch of Celts **2** : a speaker of a Brythonic language

1**Bry·thon·ic** \brith-'än-ik\ *adj* **1** : of, relating to, or characteristic of the Brythons **2** : of, relating to, or characteristic of the division of the Celtic languages that includes Welsh, Cornish, and Breton

2**Brythonic** *n* : the Brythonic branch of the Celtic languages — see INDO-EUROPEAN LANGUAGES table

BS *abbr* **1** bachelor of science **2** balance sheet **3** bill of sale **4** British standard

BSA *abbr* **1** bachelor of science in agriculture **2** Boy Scouts of America

BSAA *abbr* bachelor of science in applied arts

BSAE *abbr* **1** bachelor of science in aeronautical engineering **2** bachelor of science in agricultural engineering **3** bachelor of science in architectural engineering

BSAg *abbr* bachelor of science in agriculture

BSArch *abbr* bachelor of science in architecture

BSB *abbr* bachelor of science in business

BSc *abbr* bachelor of science

BSCh *abbr* bachelor of science in chemistry

BSEc *or* **BSEcon** *abbr* bachelor of science in economics

BSEd *or* **BSE** *abbr* bachelor of science in education

BSEE *abbr* bachelor of science in elementary education

BSFor *abbr* bachelor of science in forestry

BSFS *abbr* bachelor of science in foreign service

BSI *abbr* British Standards Institution

bskt *abbr* basket

BSL *abbr* **1** bachelor of sacred literature **2** bachelor of science in languages **3** bachelor of science in law **4** bachelor of science in linguistics

BSN *abbr* bachelor of science in nursing

ə abut ᵊ kitten ər further a back ā bake ä cot, cart
au̇ out ch chin e less ē easy g gift i trip ī life
j joke ŋ sing ō flow ȯ flaw ȯi coin th thin t͟h this
ü loot u̇ foot y yet yü few yu̇ furious zh vision

btry *abbr* battery
Btu *abbr* British thermal unit
bu *abbr* **1** bureau **2** bushel
[1]**bub·ble** \ˈbəb-əl\ *vb* **bub·bled; bub·bling** \ˈbəb-(ə-)liŋ\ [ME *bublen*] *vi* **1 :** to form or produce bubbles **2 :** to flow with a gurgling sound ⟨a brook *bubbling* over rocks⟩ **3 a :** to become lively or effervescent ⟨*bubbling* with good humor⟩ **b :** to speak in a lively and fluent manner ⟨*bubbled* excitedly about his prize⟩ ~ *vt* **1 :** to utter (as words) effervescently **2 :** to cause to bubble
[2]**bubble** *n, often attrib* **1 :** a small globule typically hollow and light: as **a :** a small body of gas within a liquid **b :** a thin film of liquid inflated with air or gas **c :** a globule in a transparent solid **d :** something that is hemispherical or semicylindrical **2 a :** something that lacks firmness, solidity, or reality **b :** a delusive scheme **3 :** a sound like that of bubbling
bubble and squeak *n, chiefly Brit* **:** a dish consisting of potatoes, cabbage, and sometimes meat fried together
bubble chamber *n* **:** a chamber of heated liquid in which the path of an ionizing particle is made visible by a string of vapor bubbles
bubble gum *n* **1 :** a chewing gum that can be blown into large bubbles **2 :** rock music characterized by simple repetitive phrasings and intended esp. for young teenagers
bub·bler \ˈbəb-(ə-)lər\ *n* **1 :** one that bubbles **2 :** a drinking fountain from which a stream of water bubbles upward
[1]**bub·bly** \ˈbəb-(ə-)lē\ *adj* **bub·bli·er; -est** **1 :** full of bubbles **:** EFFERVESCENT ⟨a ~ bottle of pop⟩ **2 :** showing lively good spirits ⟨a ~ group at the celebration⟩ **3 :** resembling a bubble ⟨a ~ dome⟩
[2]**bubbly** *n* **:** CHAMPAGNE
bubby *var of* BOOBY
bu·bo \ˈb(y)ü-(ˌ)bō\ *n, pl* **buboes** [ML *bubon-, bubo,* fr. Gk *boubōn*] **:** an inflammatory swelling of a lymph gland esp. in the groin — **bu·bon·ic** \b(y)ü-ˈbän-ik\ *adj*
bubonic plague *n* **:** plague in which the formation of buboes is a prominent feature
buc·cal \ˈbək-əl\ *adj* [L *bucca* cheek — more at POCK] **:** of, relating to, or involving the cheeks or the cavity of the mouth
buc·ca·neer \ˌbək-ə-ˈni(ə)r\ *n* [F *boucanier*] **1 :** one of the freebooters preying on Spanish ships and settlements esp. in the West Indies in the 17th century; *broadly* **:** PIRATE **2 :** an unscrupulous adventurer esp. in politics or business — **buccaneer** *vi* — **buc·ca·neer·ish** \-ish\ *adj*
Bu·ceph·a·lus \byü-ˈsef-ə-ləs\ *n* [L, fr. Gk *Boukephalos*] **:** the war-horse of Alexander the Great
[1]**buck** \ˈbək\ *n, pl* **bucks** [ME, fr. OE *bucca* stag, he-goat; akin to OHG *boc* he-goat, MIr *bocc*] **1** *or pl* **buck :** a male animal; *esp* **:** a male deer or antelope **2 a :** a male human being **:** MAN **b :** a dashing fellow **:** DANDY **3** *or pl* **buck :** ANTELOPE **4 a :** BUCKSKIN; *also* **:** an article (as a shoe) made of buckskin **b** *slang* **:** DOLLAR 3b **5** [short for *sawbuck*] **:** SAWHORSE **6 a :** a supporting rack or frame **b :** a short thick leather-covered block for gymnastic vaulting
[2]**buck** *vi* **1** *of a horse or mule* **:** to spring with a quick plunging leap **2 :** to charge against something (as an obstruction) **3 a :** to move or react jerkily **b :** to refuse assent **:** BALK **4 :** to strive for advancement sometimes without regard to ethical behavior ~ *vt* **1 :** to throw (as a rider) by bucking **2 a** *archaic* **:** [1]BUTT **b :** OPPOSE, RESIST ⟨~*ing* a trend⟩ **3 :** to charge into (as the opponent's line in football) **4 a :** to pass esp. from one person to another ⟨~*ed* the question on to someone else⟩ **b :** to move or load (as heavy objects) esp. with mechanical equipment — **buck·er** *n*
[3]**buck** *adj* [prob. fr. [1]*buck*] **:** of the lowest grade within a military category ⟨~ private⟩
[4]**buck** *n* [short for earlier *buckhorn knife*] **:** an object formerly used in poker to mark the next player to deal; *broadly* **:** a token used as a mark or reminder
[5]**buck** *adv* [origin unknown] *South & Midland* **:** STARK ⟨~ naked⟩
buck-and-wing \ˌbək-ən-ˈwiŋ\ *n* **:** a solo tap dance with sharp foot accents, springs, leg flings, and heel clicks
buck·a·roo *or* **buck·er·oo** \ˌbək-ə-ˈrü, ˈbək-ə-ˌ\ *n, pl* **-aroos** *or* **-eroos** [by folk etymology fr. Sp *vaquero,* fr. *vaca* cow, fr. L *vacca* — more at VACCINE] **1 :** COWBOY **2 :** BRONCOBUSTER
buck·bean \ˈbək-ˌbēn\ *n* **:** a plant (*Menyanthes trifoliata* of the family Menyanthaceae) growing in bogs and having racemes of white or purplish flowers
buck·board \-ˌbō(ə)rd, -ˌbȯ(ə)rd\ *n* [obs. E *buck* body of a wagon + E *board*] **:** a four-wheeled vehicle with a springy platform

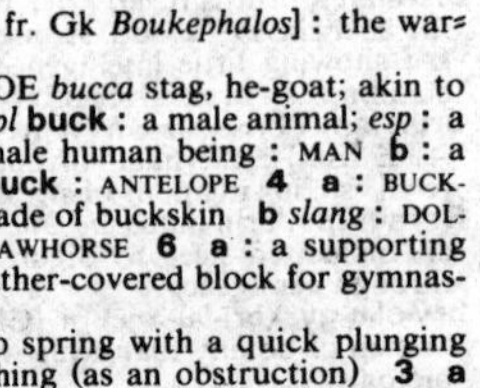
buckboard

[1]**buck·et** \ˈbək-ət\ *n* [ME, fr. AF *buket,* fr. OE *būc* pitcher, belly; akin to OHG *būh* belly, Skt *bhūri* abundant — more at BIG] **1 :** a typically round vessel for catching, holding, or carrying liquids or solids **2 :** something resembling a bucket: as **a :** the scoop of an excavating machine **b :** one of the receptacles on the rim of a waterwheel **c :** one of the cups of an endless-belt conveyor **d :** one of the vanes of a turbine rotor **3 :** a large quantity **4 :** BUCKET SEAT
[2]**bucket** *vt* **1 :** to draw or lift in buckets **2** *Brit* **a :** to ride (a horse) hard **b :** to drive hurriedly or roughly **3 :** to deal with in a bucket shop ~ *vi* **1 :** HUSTLE, HURRY **2 a :** to move about haphazardly or irresponsibly **b :** to move roughly or jerkily ⟨~*ing* over the rocky road⟩
bucket brigade *n* **:** a chain of persons acting to put out a fire by passing buckets of water from hand to hand
buck·et·ful \ˈbək-ət-ˌfu̇l\ *n, pl* **bucketfuls** \-ˌfu̇lz\ *or* **buck·ets·ful** \-əts-ˌfu̇l\ **:** as much as a bucket will hold
bucket seat *n* **:** a low separate seat for one person (as in automobiles and airplanes)
bucket shop *n* **1 :** a saloon in which liquor was formerly sold from or dispensed in open containers (as buckets or pitchers) **2 a :** an establishment in which security and commodity options and uncompleted purchases and sales at trivial margins are handled like bets **b :** a dishonest brokerage house; *esp* **:** one that fleeces customers by failing to execute orders on margin in anticipation of market fluctuations adverse to their interest
buck·eye \ˈbək-ˌī\ *n* **1 :** a shrub or tree (genus *Aesculus*) of the horse-chestnut family; *also* **:** its large nutlike seed **2** *cap* **:** a native or resident of Ohio — used as a nickname
buck fever *n* **:** nervous excitement of an inexperienced hunter at the sight of game
[1]**buck·le** \ˈbək-əl\ *n* [ME *bocle,* fr. MF, boss of a shield, buckle, fr. L *buccula,* dim. of *bucca* cheek — more at POCK] **1 :** a fastening for two loose ends that is attached to one and holds the other by a catch **2 :** an ornamental device that suggests a buckle **3** *archaic* **:** a crisp curl
[2]**buckle** *vb* **buck·led; buck·ling** \ˈbək-(ə-)liŋ\ *vt* **1 :** to fasten with a buckle **2 :** to prepare with vigor ⟨*buckled* himself to the task⟩ **3 :** to cause to bend, give way, or crumple ~ *vi* **1 :** to apply oneself with vigor ⟨~*s* down to the job⟩ **2 :** to bend, heave, warp, or kink usu. under the influence of some external agency ⟨cornstalk *buckling* in the high wind⟩ **3 :** COLLAPSE ⟨the supports *buckled* under the strain⟩ **4 :** to give way **:** YIELD ⟨one who does not ~ under pressure⟩
[3]**buckle** *n* **:** a product of buckling
[1]**buck·ler** \ˈbək-lər\ *n* [ME *bocler,* fr. OF, shield with a boss, fr. *bocle*] **1 a :** a small round shield held by a handle at arm's length **b :** a shield worn on the left arm **2 :** one that shields and protects
[2]**buckler** *vt* **:** to shield or defend with a buckler
bucko \ˈbək-(ˌ)ō\ *n, pl* **buck·oes** **1 :** one who is domineering and bullying **:** SWAGGERER **2** *chiefly Irish* **:** young fellow **:** LAD
buck passer *n* [[4]*buck*] **:** a person who habitually passes the buck — **buck-pass·ing** \ˈbək-ˌpas-iŋ\ *n*
[1]**buck·ram** \ˈbək-rəm\ *n* [ME *bukeram,* fr. OF *boquerant,* fr. OProv *bocaran,* fr. *Bokhara,* city of central Asia] **1 :** a stiff-finished heavily sized fabric of cotton or linen used for interlinings in garments, for stiffening in millinery, and in bookbinding **2** *archaic* **:** STIFFNESS, RIGIDITY
[2]**buckram** *adj* **:** suggesting buckram esp. in stiffness or formality
[3]**buckram** *vt* **1 :** to give strength or stiffness to (as with buckram) **2** *archaic* **:** to make pretentious
Bucks *abbr* Buckinghamshire
buck·saw \ˈbək-ˌsȯ\ *n* **:** a saw set in a usu. H-shaped frame that is used for sawing wood
buck·shee \ˈbək-(ˌ)shē\ *n* [Hindi *bakhśīś*] **1** *Brit* **:** something extra obtained free; *esp* **:** extra rations **2** *Brit* **:** WINDFALL, GRATUITY
buck·shot \ˈbək-ˌshät\ *n* **:** a coarse lead shot
buck·skin \-ˌskin\ *n* **1 a :** the skin of a buck **b :** a soft pliable usu. suede-finished leather **2 a** *pl* **:** buckskin breeches **b** *archaic* **:** a person dressed in buckskin; *esp* **:** an early American backwoodsman **3 :** a horse of a light yellowish dun color usu. with dark mane and tail — **buckskin** *adj*
buck·tail \-ˌtāl\ *n* **:** an angler's lure made typically of hairs from the tail of a deer
buck·thorn \-ˌthȯ(ə)rn\ *n* **1 :** any of a genus (*Rhamnus* of the family Rhamnaceae, the buckthorn family) of often thorny trees or shrubs some of which yield purgatives or pigments **2 :** a tree (*Bumelia lycioides*) of the sapodilla family of the southern U.S.
buck·tooth \-ˈtüth\ *n* **:** a large projecting front tooth — **buck·toothed** \-ˈtütht\ *adj*
buck up *vb* [[2]*buck*] *vi* **:** to become encouraged ~ *vt* **1 :** IMPROVE, SMARTEN **2 :** to raise the morale of
buck·wheat \ˈbək-ˌ(h)wēt\ *n* [D *boekweit,* fr. MD *boecweit,* fr. *boec-* (akin to OHG *buohha* beech tree) + *weit* wheat — more at BEECH] **1 :** any of a genus (*Fagopyrum* of the family Polygonaceae, the buckwheat family) of herbs with alternate leaves, clusters of apetalous pinkish white flowers and triangular seeds; *esp* **:** either of two plants (*F. esculentum* and *F. tartaricum*) cultivated for their edible seeds **2 :** the seed of a buckwheat used as a cereal grain
[1]**bu·col·ic** \byü-ˈkäl-ik\ *adj* [L *bucolicus,* fr. Gk *boukolikos,* fr. *boukolos* cowherd, fr. *bous* head of cattle + *-kolos* (akin to L *colere* to cultivate) — more at COW, WHEEL] **1 :** of or relating to shepherds or herdsmen **:** PASTORAL **2 :** relating to or typical of rural life ***syn*** see RURAL — **bu·col·i·cal·ly** \-i-k(ə-)lē\ *adv*
[2]**bucolic** *n* **:** a pastoral poem **:** ECLOGUE
[1]**bud** \ˈbəd\ *n* [ME *budde;* akin to OE *budda* beetle, Skt *bhūri* abundant — more at BIG] **1 :** a small lateral or terminal protuberance on the stem of a plant that may develop into a flower, leaf, or shoot **2 :** something not yet mature or at full development: as **a :** an incompletely opened flower **b :** CHILD, YOUTH **c :** an outgrowth of an organism that differentiates into a new individual **:** GEMMA; *also* **:** PRIMORDIUM — **in the bud :** in an early stage of development ⟨nipped the rebellion *in the bud*⟩
[2]**bud** *vb* **bud·ded; bud·ding** *vi* **1** *of a plant* **a :** to set or put forth buds **b :** to commence growth from buds **2 :** to develop by way of outgrowth **3 :** to reproduce asexually esp. by the pinching off of a small part of the parent ~ *vt* **1 :** to produce or develop from buds **2 :** to cause (as a plant) to bud **3 :** to insert a bud from a plant of one kind into an opening in the bark of (a plant of another kind) usu. in order to propagate a desired variety — **bud·der** *n*
Bud·dha \ˈbüd-ə, ˈbu̇d-\ *n* [Skt, enlightened] **1 :** a person who has attained Buddhahood **2 :** a representation of Gautama Buddha
Bud·dha·hood \-ˌhu̇d\ *n* **:** a state of perfect enlightenment sought in Buddhism
Bud·dhism \ˈbü-ˌdiz-əm, ˈbu̇d-ˌiz-\ *n* **:** a religion of eastern and central Asia growing out of the teaching of Gautama Buddha that suffering is inherent in life and that one can be liberated from it by mental and moral self-purification — **Bud·dhist** \ˈbüd-əst, ˈbu̇d-\ *n or adj* — **Bud·dhis·tic** \bü-ˈdis-tik, bu̇-\ *adj*
bud·ding \ˈbəd-iŋ\ *adj* **:** being in an early stage of development ⟨~ novelists⟩
bud·dle \ˈbəd-ᵊl\ *n* [origin unknown] **:** an apparatus on which crushed ore is washed
bud·dle·ia \ˈbəd-lē-ə, ˌbəd-ˈlē-\ *n* [NL, genus name, fr. Adam *Buddle* †1715 E botanist] **:** any of a genus (*Buddleia* of the family

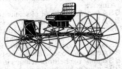

Loganiaceae) of shrubs or trees of warm regions with showy terminal clusters of usu. yellow or violet flowers

bud·dy \'bəd-ē\ *n, pl* **buddies** [prob. baby talk alter. of *brother*] **1** : COMPANION, PARTNER **2** : FELLOW — used esp. in informal address

buddy system *n* : an arrangement in which two individuals are paired (as for mutual safety in a hazardous situation)

1budge \'bəj\ *n* [ME *bugee*, fr. AF *bogee*] : a fur formerly prepared from lambskin dressed with the wool outward

2budge *vb* **budged; budg·ing** [MF *bouger*, fr. (assumed) VL *bullicare*, fr. L *bullire* to boil — more at BOIL] *vi* **1** : MOVE, SHIFT ⟨the mule wouldn't ~⟩ **2** : to give way : YIELD ⟨wouldn't ~ on the issue⟩ ~ *vt* : to cause to move

3budge *adj* [origin unknown] *archaic* : POMPOUS, SOLEMN

bud·ger·i·gar \'bəj-(ə-)rē-,gär, ,bəj-ə-'rē-\ *n* [native name in Australia] : a small Australian parrot (*Melopsittacus undulatus*) usu. light green with black and yellow markings in the wild but bred under domestication in many colors

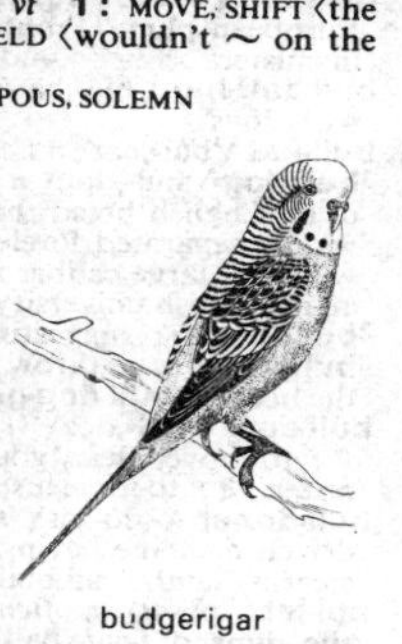
budgerigar

1bud·get \'bəj-ət\ *n* [ME *bowgette*, fr. MF *bougette*, dim. of *bouge* leather bag, fr. L *bulga*, of Gaulish origin; akin to MIr *bolg* bag; akin to OE *bælg* bag — more at BELLY] **1** *chiefly dial* : a usu. leather pouch, wallet, or pack; *also* : its contents **2** : STOCK, SUPPLY **3** **a** : a statement of the financial position of an administration for a definite period of time based on estimates of expenditures during the period and proposals for financing them **b** : a plan for the coordination of resources and expenditures **c** : the amount of money that is available for, required for, or assigned to a particular purpose — **bud·get·ary** \'bəj-ə-,ter-ē\ *adj*

2budget *vt* **1** **a** : to put or allow for in a budget **b** : to require to adhere to a budget ⟨~*ed* shoppers⟩ **2** **a** : to allocate funds for in a budget ⟨~*ing* a new hospital⟩ **b** : to plan or provide for the use of in detail ⟨~*ing* manpower in a tight labor market⟩ ~ *vi* : to put oneself on a budget ⟨~*ing* for a vacation⟩

bud·ge·teer \,bəj-ə-'ti(ə)r\ *or* **bud·get·er** \'bəj-ət-ər\ *n* **1** : one who prepares a budget **2** : one who is restricted to a budget

bud·gie \'bəj-ē\ *n* [by shortening and alter.] : BUDGERIGAR

bud scale *n* : one of the leaves resembling scales that form the sheath of a plant bud

bud sport *n* : a mutation arising in a plant bud

1buff \'bəf\ *n* [MF *buffle* wild ox, fr. OIt *bufalo*] **1** : a garment (as a uniform) made of buff leather **2** : the bare skin **3** **a** : a moderate orange yellow **b** : a light to moderate yellow **4** : a device (as a stick or block) having a soft absorbent surface (as of cloth) by which polishing material is applied **5** [earlier *buff* (an enthusiast about going to fires); fr. the buff overcoats worn by volunteer firemen in New York City *ab*1820] : FAN, ENTHUSIAST

2buff *adj* : of the color buff

3buff *vt* **1** : POLISH, SHINE ⟨waxed and ~*ed* the floor⟩ **2** : to give a buff or velvety surface to (leather)

1buf·fa·lo \'bəf-ə-,lō\ *n, pl* **-lo** *or* **-loes** *also* **-los** [It *bufalo* & Sp *búfalo*, fr. LL *bufalus*, alter. of L *bubalus*, fr. Gk *boubalos* African gazelle, irreg. fr. *bous* head of cattle — more at COW] **1** : any of several wild oxen: as **a** : WATER BUFFALO **b** : any of a genus (*Bison*); *esp* : a large shaggy-maned No. American wild ox (*B. bison*) with short horns and heavy forequarters with a large muscular hump **2** : any of several suckers (genus *Ictiobus*) found mostly in the Mississippi valley — called also *buffalofish*

2buffalo *vt* **-loed; -lo·ing** : BEWILDER, BAFFLE

buffalo berry *n* : either of two western U.S. shrubs (*Shepherdia argentea* and *S. canadensis*) of the oleaster family with silvery foliage; *also* : their edible scarlet berry

buffalo bug *n* : CARPET BEETLE

buffalofish *n* : BUFFALO 2

buffalo grass *n* : a low-growing grass (*Buchloë dactyloides*) of former feeding grounds of the American buffalo; *also* : GRAMA

buffalo robe *n* : the hide of an American buffalo lined on the skin side with fabric and used as a coverlet or rug

1buff·er \'bəf-ər\ *n* : one that buffs

2buffer *n* [*buff* (to react like a soft body when struck)] **1** : any of various devices or pieces of material for reducing shock due to contact **2** : a means or device used as a cushion against the shock of fluctuations in business or financial activity **3** : something that serves to separate two items: as **a** : BUFFER STATE **b** : a person who shields another esp. from annoying routine matters **4** : a substance capable in solution of neutralizing both acids and bases and thereby maintaining the original acidity or basicity of the solution; *also* : such a solution **5** : a temporary storage unit (as in a computer); *esp* : one that accepts information at one rate and delivers it at another

3buffer *vt* **1** : to lessen the shock of : CUSHION **2** : to treat (as a solution) with a buffer; *also* : to prepare (aspirin) with an antacid

buffer state *n* : a small neutral state lying between two larger potentially rival powers

buffer zone *n* : a neutral area separating conflicting forces; *broadly* : an area designed to separate

1buf·fet \'bəf-ət\ *n* [ME, fr. MF, fr. OF, dim. of *buffe*] **1** : a blow esp. with the hand **2** : something that strikes with telling force

2buffet *vt* **1** : to strike sharply esp. with the hand : CUFF **2** **a** : to strike repeatedly : BATTER ⟨the waves ~*ed* the shore⟩ **b** : to contend against ~ *vi* : to make one's way esp. under difficult conditions

3buf·fet \(,)bə-'fā, bü-', 'bü-,\ *n* [F] **1** : a sideboard often without a mirror **2** : a cupboard or set of shelves for the display of tableware **3** **a** : a counter for refreshments **b** *chiefly Brit* : a restaurant operated as a public convenience (as in a railway station) **c** : a meal set out on a buffet or table for ready access and informal service

4buffet *like*³\ *adj* : served informally (as from a buffet)

buffing wheel *n* : a wheel covered with material for polishing

buff leather *n* : a strong supple oil-tanned leather produced chiefly from cattle hides

buf·fle·head \'bəf-əl-,hed\ *n* [archaic E *buffle* buffalo + E *head*] : a small No. American diving duck (*Bucephala albeola*)

buf·fo \'bü-(,)fō\ *n, pl* **buf·fi** \-(,)fē\ *or* **buffos** [It, fr. *buffone*] : CLOWN, BUFFOON; *specif* : a male singer of comic roles in opera

buf·foon \(,)bə-'fün\ *n* [MF *bouffon*, fr. OIt *buffone*, fr. ML *bufon-*, *bufo*, fr. L, toad] **1** : a ludicrous figure : CLOWN **2** : a gross and usu. ill-educated or stupid person — **buf·foon·ish** \-ish\ *adj*

buf·foon·ery \-'fün-(ə-)rē\ *n, pl* **-er·ies** : coarse loutish behavior or practice

1bug \'bəg\ *n* [ME *bugge* scarecrow; akin to Norw dial. *bugge* important man — more at BIG] **1** *obs* : BOGEY, BUGBEAR **2** **a** : an insect or other creeping or crawling invertebrate **b** : any of several insects commonly considered esp. obnoxious: as (1) : BEDBUG (2) : COCKROACH (3) : HEAD LOUSE **c** : any of an order (Hemiptera and esp. its suborder Heteroptera) of insects that have sucking mouthparts, fore wings thickened at the base, and incomplete metamorphosis and are often economic pests — called also *true bug* **3** : an unexpected defect, fault, flaw, or imperfection **4** : a disease-producing germ; *also* : a disease caused by it **5** : a temporary enthusiasm **6** : ENTHUSIAST, HOBBYIST ⟨a camera ~⟩ **7** : a prominent person **8** : a concealed listening device **9** [fr. its designation by an asterisk on race programs] : a weight allowance given apprentice jockeys : HANDICAP

2bug *vt* **bugged; bug·ging** **1** : BOTHER, ANNOY ⟨don't ~ me with petty details⟩ **2** : to plant a concealed microphone in

bug·a·boo \'bəg-ə-,bü\ *n, pl* **-boos** [origin unknown] **1** : an imaginary object of fear : BUGBEAR, BOGEY **2** : a source of concern ⟨the national ~ of inflation⟩

bug·bane \'bəg-,bān\ *n* : any of several perennial herbs (esp. genus *Cimicifuga*) of the buttercup family that have two or three ternately divided serrate leaves and white flowers in long racemes; *esp* : BLACK COHOSH

bug·bear \-,ba(ə)r, -,be(ə)r\ *n* **1** : an imaginary goblin or specter used to excite fear **2** : an object or source of dread

bug-eye \-,ī\ *n* : a small boat with a flat bottom, a centerboard, and two raked masts

bug·ger \'bùg-ər, 'bəg-\ *n* [ME *bougre* heretic, sodomite, fr. MF, fr. ML *Bulgarus*, lit., Bulgarian] **1** : SODOMITE **2** **a** : a worthless person : RASCAL **b** : FELLOW, CHAP

bug·gery \-ə-rē\ *n* : SODOMY

1bug·gy \'bəg-ē\ *adj* : infested with bugs

2buggy *n, pl* **buggies** [origin unknown] **1** : a light one-horse carriage made with two wheels in England and with four wheels in the U.S. **2** : a small cart or truck for short transportations of heavy materials **3** : BABY CARRIAGE

1bug·house \'bəg-,haùs\ *n* : an insane asylum

2bughouse *adj* : mentally deranged : CRAZY

1bu·gle \'byü-gəl\ *n* [ME, fr. OF, fr. LL *bugula*] : any of a genus (*Ajuga*) of plants of the mint family; *esp* : a European annual (*A. reptans*) that has spikes of blue flowers and is naturalized in the U.S.

2bugle *n* [ME, buffalo, instrument made of buffalo horn, bugle, fr. OF, fr. L *buculus*, dim. of *bos* head of cattle — more at COW] : a valveless brass instrument that resembles a trumpet and is used esp. for military calls

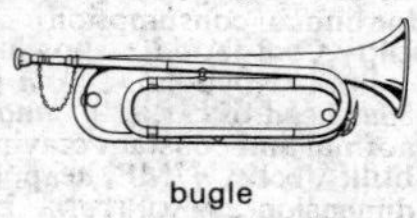
bugle

3bugle *vi* **bu·gled; bu·gling** \-g(ə-)liŋ\ **1** : to sound a bugle **2** : to utter a prolonged cry that is the characteristic rutting call of the bull elk

4bugle *n* [perh. fr. ²*bugle*] : a small cylindrical bead of glass or plastic used for trimming esp. on women's clothing — **bugle** *adj*

bu·gler \'byü-glər\ *n* : one who sounds a bugle

bu·gle·weed \'byü-gəl-,wēd\ *n* : any of a genus (*Lycopus*) of mints; *esp* : one (*L. virginicus*) that is mildly narcotic and astringent

bu·gloss \'byü-,gläs, -,glòs\ *n* [MF *buglosse*, fr. L *buglossa*, irreg. fr. Gk *bouglōssos*, fr. *bous* head of cattle + *glōssa* tongue — more at COW, GLOSS] : any of several coarse hairy plants (genera *Lycopsis* and *Anchusa*, esp. *A. officinalis*) of the borage family

bug·seed \'bəg-,sēd\ *n* : a fleshy annual herb (*Corispermum hyssopifolium*) of the goosefoot family with flat oval seeds

buhl \'bül, 'byü(ə)l\ *var of* BOULLE

buhr \'bər\ *n* : BUHRSTONE 2

buhr·stone \-,stōn\ *n* [prob. fr. *burr* + *stone*] **1** : a siliceous rock used for millstones **2** : a millstone cut from buhrstone

1build \'bild\ *vb* **built** \'bilt\; **build·ing** [ME *bilden*, fr. OE *byldan*; akin to OE *būan* to dwell — more at BOWER] *vt* **1** : to form by ordering and uniting materials by gradual means into a composite whole : CONSTRUCT **2** : to cause to be constructed **3** : to develop according to a systematic plan, by a definite process, or on a particular base **4** : INCREASE, ENLARGE ~ *vi* **1** : to engage in building **2** **a** : to increase in intensity ⟨~ to a climax⟩ **b** : to develop in extent ⟨a line of people ~*ing* along the avenue⟩

2build *n* : form or mode of structure : MAKE; *esp* : bodily conformation of a person or lower animal **syn** see PHYSIQUE

build·ed *archaic past of* BUILD

build·er \'bil-dər\ *n* **1** : one that builds; *esp* : one that contracts to build and supervises building operations **2** : a substance added to or used with detergents to increase their cleansing action

builder's knot *n* : CLOVE HITCH

build in *vt* : to construct or develop as an integral part of something

build·ing \'bil-diŋ\ n 1 : a usu. roofed and walled structure built for permanent use (as for a dwelling) 2 : the art or business of assembling materials into a structure

building block n : a unit of construction or composition

build-up \'bil-,dəp\ n 1 : the act or process of building up 2 : something produced by building up

build up \(')bil-'dəp\ vt 1 : to develop gradually by increments ⟨building up his endurance⟩ ⟨built up a library⟩ 2 : to promote the esteem of ⟨a salesman building up his product⟩ ~ vi 1 : to accumulate or develop appreciably ⟨clouds building up on the horizon⟩

built \'bilt\ adj : formed as to physique or bodily contours ⟨a slimly ~ girl⟩

built-in \'bil-'tin\ adj 1 : forming an integral part of a structure; esp : constructed as or in a recess in a wall 2 : INHERENT

built-up \'bil-'təp\ adj 1 : made of several sections or layers fastened together 2 : covered with buildings

buird·ly \'bu(ə)r(d)-lē\ adj [prob. alter. of burly] Scot : STURDY

bulb \'bəlb\ n [L bulbus, fr. Gk bolbos bulbous plant; akin to Arm bolk radish] 1 a : a resting stage of a plant (as the lily, onion, hyacinth, or tulip) that is usu. formed underground and consists of a short stem base bearing one or more buds enclosed in overlapping membranous or fleshy leaves b : a fleshy structure (as a tuber or corm) resembling a bulb in appearance c : a plant having or developing from a bulb 2 : a bulb-shaped part; specif : a rounded glass envelope enclosing the light source of an electric lamp or such an envelope together with the light source it encloses 3 : a rounded or swollen anatomical structure 4 : a camera setting that indicates that the shutter can be opened by pressing on the release and closed by ending the pressure — **bul·ba·ceous** \,bəl-'bā-shəs\ adj — **bulbed** \'bəlbd\ adj

bul·bar \'bəl-bər, -,bär\ adj : of or relating to a bulb; specif : involving the medulla oblongata

bul·bil \'bəl-bəl, -,bil\ n [F bulbille, dim. of bulbe bulb, fr. L bulbus] : a small or secondary bulb; esp : an aerial deciduous bud produced in a leaf axil or replacing the flowers

bul·bous \'bəl-bəs\ adj 1 : having a bulb : growing from or bearing bulbs 2 : resembling a bulb esp. in roundness ⟨a ~ nose⟩ — **bul·bous·ly** adv

bul·bul \'bul-,bul\ n [Per, fr. Ar] 1 : a Persian songbird frequently mentioned in poetry that is prob. a nightingale (Luscinia golzii) 2 : any of a group of gregarious passerine birds (family Pycnonotidae) of Asia and Africa

Bulg abbr Bulgaria; Bulgarian

Bul·gar \'bəl-,gär, 'bul-\ n [ML Bulgarus] : BULGARIAN

Bul·gar·i·an \,bəl-'gar-ē-ən, bul-, -'ger-\ n 1 : a native or inhabitant of Bulgaria 2 : the Slavic language of the Bulgarians — **Bulgarian** adj

¹**bulge** \'bəlj\ n [MF boulge, bouge leather bag, curved part — more at BUDGET] 1 : BILGE 1, 2 2 : a usu. localized swelling of a surface caused by pressure from within or below 3 : ADVANTAGE, UPPER HAND 4 : sudden expansion **syn** see PROJECTION

²**bulge** vb **bulged; bulg·ing** vi : to cause to bulge ~ vi 1 archaic : BILGE 1 2 a : to jut out : SWELL b : to bend outward c : to become swollen or protuberant

bul·gur \'bul-'gú(ə)r\ n [Turk] : parched crushed wheat prepared for human consumption

bulgy \'bəl-jē\ adj : showing a bulge : BULGING — **bulg·i·ness** n

bu·lim·ia \byü-'lim-ē-ə\ n [NL, fr. Gk boulimia great hunger, fr. bous head of cattle + limos hunger — more at COW, LESS] : an abnormal and constant craving for food

¹**bulk** \'bəlk\ n [ME, heap, bulk, fr. ON bulki cargo] 1 a : spatial dimension : MAGNITUDE b : material (as indigestible fibrous residues of food) that forms a mass in the intestine 2 a : BODY; esp : a large or corpulent human body b : an organized structure esp. when viewed primarily as a mass of material ⟨the shrouded ~s of snow-covered cars⟩ c : a ponderous shapeless mass of material ⟨on the living sea rolls an inanimate ~ —P. B. Shelley⟩ 3 : the main or greater part

syn BULK, MASS, VOLUME shared meaning element : the aggregate that forms a body or unit

— **in bulk** 1 : not divided into parts 2 : not packaged in separate units

²**bulk** vt 1 : to cause to swell or bulge : STUFF 2 : to gather into a mass or aggregate 3 : to have a bulk of ~ vi 1 : SWELL, EXPAND 2 : to appear as a factor : LOOM ⟨a consideration that ~s large in everyone's thinking⟩

³**bulk** adj 1 : being in bulk ⟨~ cement⟩ 2 : of or relating to materials in bulk

bulk·head \'bəlk-,hed, 'bəl-,ked\ n [bulk (structure projecting from a building) + head] 1 : an upright partition separating compartments 2 : a structure or partition to resist pressure or to shut off water, fire, or gas 3 : a retaining wall along a waterfront 4 : a projecting framework with a sloping door giving access to a cellar stairway or a shaft

bulky \'bəl-kē\ adj **bulk·i·er; -est** adj 1 a : having bulk b (1) : large of its kind (2) : CORPULENT 2 : having great volume in proportion to weight ⟨a ~ knit sweater⟩ — **bulk·i·ly** \-kə-lē\ adv — **bulk·i·ness** \-kē-nəs\ n

¹**bull** \'bul\ n [ME bule, fr. OE bula; akin to OE blāwan to blow] 1 a : an adult male bovine animal; also : a usu. adult male of various large animals b : ELEPHANT c : a draft ox 2 : one who buys securities or commodities in expectation of a price rise or who acts to effect such a rise — compare BEAR 3 : one that resembles a bull (as in brawny physique) 4 : BULLDOG 5 slang : POLICEMAN, DETECTIVE 6 cap : TAURUS

²**bull** adj 1 a : MALE b : of or relating to a bull 2 : suggestive of a bull 2 : large of its kind 3 : RISING ⟨a ~ market⟩

³**bull** vi : to advance forcefully ~ vt 1 : to try to raise the price of (as stocks) or in (a market) 2 a : to act on with violence b : FORCE ⟨~ed his way through the crowd⟩

⁴**bull** n [ME bulle, fr. ML bulla, fr. L, bubble, amulet] 1 : a solemn papal letter sealed with a bulla or with a red-ink imprint of the device on the bulla 2 : EDICT, DECREE

⁵**bull** n [perh. fr. obs. bull to mock] : a grotesque blunder in language

⁶**bull** n [short for bullshit] 1 slang : empty boastful talk 2 slang : NONSENSE

⁷**bull** vi, slang : to engage in idle and often boastful talk ~ vt, slang : to fool esp. by fast boastful talk

⁸**bull** abbr bulletin

bul·la \'bul-ə\ n, pl **bul·lae** \'bul-,ē, -,ī\ 1 [ML] : the round usu. lead seal attached to a papal bull 2 [NL, fr. L] : a hollow thin-walled rounded bony prominence 3 : a large vesicle or blister

bul·lace \'bul-əs\ n [ME bolace, fr. MF beloce, fr. ML bolluca] : a European plum (Prunus domestica insititia) with small ovoid fruit in clusters

bull-bait·ing \'bul-,bāt-iŋ\ n : the former practice of baiting bulls with dogs

bull-bat \'bul-,bat\ n : NIGHTHAWK 1a

¹**bull·dog** \'bul-,dóg\ n 1 : a compact muscular short-haired dog of an English breed that is marked by vigor and sagacity and has widely separated forelegs and an undershot lower jaw 2 : a revolver of large caliber and short barrel 3 : a proctor's attendant at an English university

²**bulldog** adj : suggestive of a bulldog ⟨~ tenacity⟩

³**bulldog** vt : to throw (a steer) by seizing the horns and twisting the neck — **bull·dog·ger** n

bull·doze \'bul-,dōz\ vt [perh. fr. ¹bull + alter. of dose] 1 : BULLY 2 : to move, clear, gouge out, or level off by pushing with a bulldozer 3 : to force insensitively or ruthlessly

bull·doz·er \-,dō-zər\ n 1 : one that bulldozes 2 : a tractor-driven machine having a broad blunt horizontal blade or ram for clearing land, road building, or comparable activities

bul·let \'bul-ət\ n [MF boulette small ball & boulet missile, dims. of boule ball — more at BOWL] 1 : a round or elongated missile (as of lead) designed to be fired from a firearm; broadly : CARTRIDGE 1a 2 : something resembling a bullet (as in curved form) 3 : a very fast and accurately thrown ball 4 : a ballot cast for a straight ticket — **bul·let-proof** \,bul-ət-'prüf\ adj

¹**bul·le·tin** \'bul-ət-ᵊn\ n [F, fr. It bulletino, dim. of bulla papal edict, fr. ML] 1 : a brief public notice issuing usu. from an authoritative source; specif : a brief news item intended for immediate publication 2 : PERIODICAL; esp : the organ of an institution or association

²**bulletin** vt : to make public by bulletin

bulletin board n : a board for posting notices (as at a school)

bull fiddle n : DOUBLE BASS — **bull fiddler** n

bull·fight \'bul-,fīt\ n : a spectacle in which men ceremonially excite, fight with, and in Hispanic tradition kill bulls in an arena for public amusement — **bull·fight·er** \-ər\ n

bull·fight·ing \-iŋ\ n : the action involved in a bullfight

bull·finch \'bul-,finch\ n : a European finch (Pyrrhula pyrrhula) having in the male rosy red underparts, blue-gray back, and black cap, chin, tail, and wings; also : any of several other finches

bull·frog \-,frog, -,fräg\ n : FROG; esp : a heavy-bodied deep-voiced frog (as of the genus Rana)

bull·head \-,hed\ n : any of various large-headed fishes (as a miller's-thumb or sculpin); esp : any of several common freshwater catfishes (genus Ictalurus) of the U.S.

bull·head·ed \'bul-'hed-əd\ adj : stupidly stubborn : HEADSTRONG — **bull·head·ed·ly** adv — **bull·head·ed·ness** n

bull·horn \'bul-,hó(ə)rn\ n 1 : a loudspeaker on a naval ship 2 : a hand-held combined microphone and loudspeaker

bul·lion \'bul-yən\ n [ME, fr. AF, mint] 1 a : gold or silver considered as so much metal; specif : uncoined gold or silver in bars or ingots b : metal in the mass ⟨lead ~⟩ 2 : lace, braid, or fringe of gold or silver threads

bull·ish \'bul-ish\ adj 1 : suggestive of a bull (as in brawniness) 2 a : marked by, tending to cause, or hopeful of rising prices (as in a stock market) b : OPTIMISTIC — **bull·ish·ly** adv — **bull·ish·ness** n

bull mastiff n : a large powerful dog of a breed developed by crossing bulldogs with mastiffs

Bull Moose n [bull moose, emblem of the Progressive party of 1912] : a follower of Theodore Roosevelt in the U.S. presidential campaign of 1912

Bull Moos·er \-'mü-sər\ n : BULL MOOSE

bull neck n : a thick short powerful neck — **bull-necked** \'bul-'nekt\ adj

bull·ock \'bul-ək\ n 1 : a young bull 2 : a castrated bull : STEER — **bull·ocky** \-ə-kē\ adj

bul·lous \'bul-əs\ adj : resembling or characterized by bullae : VESICULAR ⟨~ lesions⟩

bull pen n 1 : a large detention cell where prisoners are held until brought into court 2 a : a place on a baseball field where relief pitchers warm up during a game b : the relief pitchers of a baseball team

bull·pout \'bul-,paut\ n [bullhead + pout] : BULLHEAD; esp : the common dark bullhead (Ictalurus nebulosus)

bull·ring \'bul-,riŋ\ n : an arena for bullfights

bull session n [⁶bull] : an informal discursive group discussion

bull's-eye \'bul-,zī\ n, pl **bull's-eyes** 1 : a small thick disk of glass inserted (as in a deck) to let in light 2 : a very hard globular candy 3 a : the center of a target; also : something central or crucial b : a shot that hits the bull's-eye; broadly : something that precisely attains a desired end 4 : a simple lens of short focal distance; also : a lantern with such a lens — see LANTERN illustration 5 : a circular opening for air or light

bull's-eye window n : a circular window or one filling a bull's-eye

bull·shit \'bul-,shit\ n [¹bull + shit] : NONSENSE; esp : foolish insolent talk — usu. considered vulgar

bull snake n : any of several large harmless No. American snakes (genus Pituophis) that feed chiefly on rodents — called also gopher snake, pine snake

bull·ter·ri·er \'bul-'ter-ē-ər\ n [bulldog + terrier] : a short-haired terrier of a breed originated in England by crossing the bulldog with terriers

bull tongue *n* **:** a wide blade attached to a cultivator or plow to stir the soil, kill weeds, or mark furrows
bull·whip \'bu̇l-ˌhwip, -ˌwip\ *n* **:** a rawhide whip with plaited lash 15 to 25 feet long
1bul·ly \'bu̇l-ē\ *n, pl* **bullies** [prob. modif. of D *boel* lover, fr. MHG *buole*] **1** *archaic* **a :** SWEETHEART **b :** a fine chap **2 a :** a blustering browbeating fellow; *esp* **:** one habitually cruel to others weaker than himself **b :** the protector of a prostitute **:** PIMP **3 :** a hired ruffian
2bully *adj* **1 :** EXCELLENT, FIRST-RATE — often used in interjectional expressions ⟨~ for you⟩ **2 :** resembling or characteristic of a bully
3bully *vb* **bul·lied; bul·ly·ing** *vt* **:** to treat abusively **~** *vi* **:** to use browbeating language or behavior **:** BLUSTER
4bully *n* [prob. modif. of F (*bœuf*) *boulli* boiled beef] **:** pickled or canned usu. corned beef
bul·ly·boy \'bu̇l-ē-ˌbȯi\ *n* **:** a swaggering tough
bul·ly·rag \-ˌrag\ *vt* [origin unknown] **1 :** to intimidate by bullying **2 :** to vex by teasing **:** BADGER
bul·rush *also* **bull·rush** \'bu̇l-ˌrəsh\ *n* [ME *bulrysche*] **:** any of several large rushes or sedges growing in wetlands: as **a :** any of a genus of annual or perennial sedges (*Scirpus,* esp. *S. lacustris*) that bear solitary or much-clustered spikelets containing perfect flowers with a perianth of six bristles **b** *Brit* **:** either of two cattails (*Typha latifolia* and *T. angustifolia*) **c :** PAPYRUS
1bul·wark \'bu̇l-(ˌ)wərk, -ˌwȯrk; 'bəl-(ˌ)wərk\ *n* [ME *bulwerke,* fr. MD *bolwerc,* fr. MHG, fr. *bole* plank + *werc* work] **1 a :** a solid wall-like structure raised for defense **:** RAMPART **b :** BREAKWATER, SEAWALL **2 :** a strong support or protection **3 :** the side of a ship above the upper deck — usu. used in pl.
2bulwark *vt* **:** to fortify or safeguard with a bulwark
1bum \'bəm\ *n* [ME *bom*] *chiefly Brit* **:** BUTTOCKS — sometimes considered vulgar
2bum *vb* **bummed; bumming** [prob. back-formation fr. 1*bummer*] *vi* **1 :** LOAF **2 :** to spend time unemployed and often wandering **~** *vt* **:** to obtain by begging **:** CADGE
3bum *n* [prob. short for *bummer*] **1 a :** one who sponges off others and avoids work **b :** one who performs a function poorly ⟨called the umpire a ~⟩ **c :** one who devotes his time to a recreational activity ⟨a beach ~⟩ ⟨ski ~*s*⟩ **2 :** VAGRANT, TRAMP
4bum *adj* **1 a :** INFERIOR, WORTHLESS ⟨~ advice⟩ **b :** acutely disagreeable ⟨a ~ trip⟩ **2 :** not functioning because of damage or injury **:** DISABLED ⟨a ~ knee⟩
5bum *n* [prob. fr. 2*bum*] **:** a drinking spree **:** BENDER — **on the bum :** with no settled residence or means of support
bum·ber·shoot \'bəm-bər-ˌshüt\ *n* [*bumber-* (alter. of *umbr-* in *umbrella*) + *-shoot* (alter. of *-chute* in *parachute*)] **:** UMBRELLA
1bum·ble \'bəm-bəl\ *vi* **bum·bled; bum·bling** \-b(ə-)liŋ\ [ME *bomblen* to boom, of imit. origin] **1 :** BUZZ **2 :** DRONE, RUMBLE
2bumble *vb* **bumbled; bumbling** [prob. alter. of *bungle*] *vi* **1 :** BLUNDER; *specif* **:** to speak ineptly in a stuttering and faltering manner **2 :** to proceed unsteadily **:** STUMBLE **~** *vt* **:** BUNGLE — **bum·bler** \-b(ə-)lər\ *n* — **bum·bling·ly** \-b(ə-)liŋ-lē\ *adv*
bum·ble·bee \'bəm-bəl-ˌbē\ *n* **:** any of numerous large robust hairy social bees (genus *Bombus*)
bum·boat \'bəm-ˌbōt\ *n* [prob. fr. LG *bumboot,* fr. *bum* tree + *boot* boat] **:** a boat that brings provisions and commodities for sale to larger ships in port or offshore
bumf \'bəm(p)f\ *n* [Brit. slang *bumf* toilet paper, short for *bumfodder,* fr. 1*bum*] *Brit* **:** PAPERWORK
1bum·mer \'bəm-ər\ *n* [prob. modif. of G *bummler* loafer, fr. *bummel* to dangle, loaf] **:** one that bums
2bummer *n* [4*bum* + *-er*] *slang* **:** an unpleasant experience (as a bad reaction to a hallucinogenic drug)
1bump \'bəmp\ *vb* [imit.] *vt* **1 :** to strike or knock with force or violence **2 :** to collide with **3 a (1) :** to dislodge with a jolt **(2) :** to subject to a scalar change ⟨rates being ~*ed* up⟩ **b :** to oust usu. by virtue of seniority or priority ⟨was ~*ed* from the flight⟩ **4 :** to apply pressure to (as sheet metal) so as to make or remove a concavity or convexity **~** *vi* **1 :** to knock against something with a forceful jolt **2 :** to proceed in a series of bumps — **bump into :** to encounter esp. by chance
2bump *n* **1 a :** a sudden forceful blow, impact, or jolt **b :** DEMOTION **2 :** a relatively abrupt convexity or protuberance on a surface: as **a :** a swelling of tissue **b :** a cranial protuberance **3 :** an act of thrusting the hips forward in an erotic manner
1bum·per \'bəm-pər\ *n* [prob. fr. *bump* (to bulge)] **1 :** a brimming cup or glass **2 :** something unusually large
2bumper *adj* **:** unusually large ⟨a ~ crop⟩
3bump·er \'bəm-pər\ *n* **1 :** one that bumps **2 :** a device for absorbing shock or preventing damage (as in collision); *specif* **:** a metal bar at either end of an automobile
bumper-to-bumper *adj* **:** marked by long closed lines of cars ⟨~ traffic⟩
1bump·kin \'bəm(p)-kən\ *n* [perh. fr. Flem *bommekijn* small cask, fr. MD, fr. *bomme* cask] **:** an awkward and unsophisticated rustic — **bump·kin·ish** \-kə-nish\ *adj* — **bump·kin·ly** \-kən-lē\ *adj*
2bump·kin *or* **bum·kin** \'bəm(p)-kən\ *n* [prob. fr. Flem *boomken,* dim. of *boom* tree] **:** a spar projecting from the stern of a ship
bump off *vt* **:** to murder casually or cold-bloodedly
bump·tious \'bəm(p)-shəs\ *adj* [1*bump* + *-tious* (as in *fractious*)] **:** presumptuously, obtusely, and often noisily self-assertive **:** OBTRUSIVE — **bump·tious·ly** *adv* — **bump·tious·ness** *n*
bumpy \'bəm-pē\ *adj* **bump·i·er; -est 1 a :** having or covered with bumps ⟨a ~ road⟩ **b :** marked by ups and downs **:** UNEVEN **2 a :** marked by bumps or jolts ⟨a ~ ride⟩ **b :** rhythmically jerky ⟨~ dance music⟩ — **bump·i·ly** \-pə-lē\ *adv* — **bump·i·ness** \-pē-nəs\ *n*
1bun \'bən\ *n* [ME *bunne*] **1 :** any of various sweet or plain small breads; *esp* **:** a round roll **2 :** a knot of hair shaped like a bun
2bun *n* [perh. alter. of E dial. *bung* (intoxicated)] **:** LOAD 4
Bu·na \'b(y)ü-nə\ *trademark* — used for any of several rubbers made by polymerization or copolymerization of butadiene
1bunch \'bənch\ *n* [ME *bunche*] **1 :** PROTUBERANCE, SWELLING **2 a :** a number of things of the same kind **:** CLUSTER ⟨a ~ of grapes⟩ **b :** a homogeneous group ***syn*** see GROUP — **bunch·i·ly** \'bən-chə-lē\ *adv* — **bunchy** \-chē\ *adj*
2bunch *vi* **1 :** SWELL, PROTRUDE **2 :** to form a group or cluster — often used with *up* **~** *vt* **:** to form into a bunch
bunch·ber·ry \'bənch-ˌber-ē\ *n* **:** a creeping perennial herb (*Cornus canadensis*) that has whorled leaves and white floral bracts and bears red berries in capitate cymes
bunch·flow·er \'bənch-ˌflau̇(-ə)r\ *n* **:** a tall summer-blooming herb (*Melanthium virginicum*) of the lily family that is found in the eastern and southern U.S. and bears a panicle of small greenish flowers
bun·co *or* **bun·ko** \'bəŋ-(ˌ)kō\ *n, pl* **buncos** *or* **bunkos** [perh. alter. of Sp *banca* bench, bank, fr. It — more at BANK] **:** a swindling game or scheme — **bunco** *vt*
1bund \'bənd\ *n* [Hindi *band,* fr. Per; akin to OE *binden* to bind] **1 :** an embankment used esp. in India to control the flow of water **2 :** an embanked thoroughfare along a river or the sea esp. in the Far East
2bund \'bu̇nd, 'bənd\ *n, often cap* [G, fr. MHG *bunt;* akin to OE *byndel* bundle] **:** a political association; *specif* **:** a pro-Nazi German-American organization of the 1930s — **bund·ist** \-əst\ *n, often cap*
1bun·dle \'bən-dᵊl\ *n* [ME *bundel,* fr. MD; akin to OE *byndel* bundle, *bindan* to bind] **1 a :** a group of things fastened together for convenient handling **b :** PACKAGE, PARCEL **c :** a considerable number of things **:** LOT ⟨a ~ of contradictions⟩ **d :** a sizable sum of money **2 a :** a small band of mostly parallel fibers (as of nerve) **b :** VASCULAR BUNDLE
2bundle *vb* **bun·dled; bun·dling** \'bən-(d)liŋ, -dᵊl-iŋ\ *vt* **1 :** to make into a bundle or package **:** WRAP **2 :** to hustle or hurry unceremoniously ⟨*bundled* the children off to school⟩ **~** *vi* **1 :** HUSTLE, HURRY **2 :** to practice bundling — **bun·dler** \-dlər, -dᵊl-ər\ *n*
bundle of nerves : a very nervous person
bundle up *vi* **:** to dress warmly **~** *vt* **:** to dress (someone) warmly
bun·dling \'bən-(d)liŋ, -dᵊl-iŋ\ *n* **:** a former custom of an unmarried couple's occupying the same bed without undressing esp. during courtship
1bung \'bəŋ\ *n* [ME, fr. MD *bonne, bonghe,* fr. LL *puncta* puncture, fr. L, fem. of *punctus,* pp. of *pungere* to prick — more at PUNGENT] **1 :** the stopper in the bunghole of a cask; *also* **:** BUNGHOLE **2 :** the cecum or anus esp. of a slaughtered animal
2bung *vt* **:** to plug with or as if with a bung
bun·ga·low \'bəŋ-gə-ˌlō\ *n* [Hindi *baṅglā,* lit., (house) in the Bengal style] **:** a usu. one-storied house with a low-pitched roof
bung·hole \'bəŋ-ˌhōl\ *n* **:** a hole for emptying or filling a cask
bun·gle \'bəŋ-gəl\ *vb* **bun·gled; bun·gling** \-g(ə-)liŋ\ [perh. of Scand origin; akin to Icel *banga* to hammer] *vi* **:** to act or work clumsily and awkwardly **~** *vt* **:** MISHANDLE, BOTCH — **bun·gler** \-g(ə-)lər\ *n* — **bun·gling** *adj or n* — **bun·gling·ly** \-g(ə-)liŋ-lē\ *adv*
bun·gle·some \-gəl-səm\ *adj* **:** AWKWARD, CLUMSY
bung up *vt* **:** BATTER
bun·ion \'bən-yən\ *n* [prob. irreg. fr. *bunny* (swelling)] **:** an inflamed swelling of the small sac on the first joint of the big toe
1bunk \'bəŋk\ *n* [prob. short for *bunker*] **1 a :** a built-in bed (as on a ship) that is often one of a tier of berths **b :** a sleeping place **2 :** a feeding trough for cattle
2bunk *vi* **:** to occupy a bunk or bed **:** stay the night ⟨~*ed* with a friend for the night⟩ **~** *vt* **:** to provide with a bunk or bed
3bunk *n* **:** BUNKUM, NONSENSE
bunk bed *n* **:** one of two single beds usu. placed one above the other
1bun·ker \'bəŋ-kər\ *n* [Sc *bonker* chest, box] **1 :** a bin or compartment for storage; *esp* **:** one on shipboard for the ship's fuel **2 a :** a protective embankment or dugout; *esp* **:** a fortified chamber mostly below ground often built of reinforced concrete and provided with embrasures **b :** a sand trap or embankment constituting a hazard on a golf course
2bunker *vb* **bun·kered; bun·ker·ing** \-k(ə-)riŋ\ *vi* **:** to fill a ship's bunker with coal or oil **~** *vt* **:** to place or store in a bunker
bunk·house \'bəŋk-ˌhau̇s\ *n* **:** a rough simple building providing sleeping quarters
bun·kum *or* **bun·combe** \'bəŋ-kəm\ *n* [*Buncombe* county, N.C.; fr. the defense of a seemingly irrelevant speech made by its congressional representative that he was speaking to Buncombe] **:** insincere or foolish talk **:** NONSENSE
bun·ny \'bən-ē\ *n, pl* **bunnies** [E dial. *bun* (rabbit)] **:** RABBIT; *esp* **:** a young rabbit
Bun·ra·ku \bu̇n-'räk-(ˌ)ü\ *n* [Jap] **:** Japanese puppet theater featuring large costumed wooden puppets, puppeteers who are onstage, and a chanter who speaks all the lines
Bun·sen burner \ˌbən(t)-sən-\ *n* [Robert W. *Bunsen*] **:** a gas burner consisting typically of a straight tube with small holes at the bottom where air enters and mixes with the gas to produce an intensely hot blue flame
1bunt \'bənt\ *n* [perh. fr. LG, bundle, fr. MLG; akin to OE *byndel* bundle] **1 a :** the middle part of a square sail **b :** the part of a furled sail gathered up in a bunch at the center of the yard **2 :** the bagging part of a fishing net
2bunt *n* [origin unknown] **:** a destructive covered smut of wheat caused by a fungus (*Tilletia foetida* or *T. caries*)
3bunt *vb* [alter. of *butt*] *vt* **1 :** to strike or push with or as if with the head **:** BUTT **2 :** to push or tap (a baseball) lightly without swinging the bat **~** *vi* **:** to bunt a baseball — **bunt·er** *n*
4bunt *n* **1 :** an act or instance of bunting **2 :** a bunted ball

ə abut	ᵊ kitten	ər further	a back	ā bake	ä cot, cart
au̇ out	ch chin	e less	ē easy	g gift	i trip	ī life
j joke	ŋ sing	ō flow	ȯ flaw	ȯi coin	th thin	t͟h this
ü loot	u̇ foot	y yet	yü few	yu̇ furious	zh vision

[1]**bun·ting** \'bənt-iŋ\ *n* [ME] : any of various stout-billed birds (*Emberiza* and related genera) usu. included with the finches
[2]**bunting** *n* [perh. fr. E dial. *bunt* (to sift)] **1** : a lightweight loosely woven fabric used chiefly for flags and festive decorations **2 a** : FLAGS **b** : decorations esp. in the colors of the national flag
bunt·line \'bənt-,līn, -lən\ *n* : one of the ropes attached to the foot of a square sail to haul the sail up to the yard for furling
Bun·yan·esque \,bən-yə-'nesk\ *adj* **1** [John *Bunyan* †1688 E preacher & author] : of, relating to, or suggestive of the allegorical writings of John Bunyan **2** [Paul *Bunyan*, legendary giant lumberjack of U.S. & Canada] **a** : of, relating to, or suggestive of the tales of Paul Bunyan **b** : of fantastically large size ⟨enormous leaves . . . from some *Bunyanesque* species of maple tree —Bernard Malamud⟩
[1]**buoy** \'bü-ē, 'bói\ *n* [ME *boye*, fr. (assumed) MF *boie*, of Gmc origin; akin to OE *bēacen* sign — more at BEACON] **1** : FLOAT 2; *esp* : a floating object moored to the bottom to mark a channel or something (as a shoal) lying under the water **2** : LIFE BUOY
[2]**buoy** *vt* **1** : to mark by or as if by a buoy **2 a** : to keep afloat **b** : SUPPORT, SUSTAIN ⟨an economy ~*ed* by the dramatic postwar growth of industry—*Time*⟩ **3** : to raise the spirits of — usu. used with *up* ⟨hope ~*s* him up⟩ ~ *vi* : FLOAT
buoy·ance \-ən(t)s, -yən(t)s\ *n* : BUOYANCY
buoy·an·cy \'bói-ən-sē, 'bü-yən-\ *n* **1 a** : the tendency of a body to float or to rise when submerged in a fluid **b** : the power of a fluid to exert an upward force on a body placed in it **2** : the ability to recover quickly from depression or discouragement : RESILIENCE, VIVACITY
buoy·ant \'bói-ənt, 'bü-yənt\ *adj* : having buoyancy: as **a** : capable of floating **b** : CHEERFUL, GAY — **buoy·ant·ly** *adv*
buq·sha \'bük-shə\ *n* [Ar] — see *rial* at MONEY table
[1]**bur** *var of* BURR
[2]**bur** *abbr* bureau
Bur·ber·ry \'bər-bə-rē, 'bər-,ber-ē\ *trademark* — used for various fabrics used esp. for coats for outdoor wear
[1]**bur·ble** \'bər-bəl\ *vi* **bur·bled; bur·bling** \-b(ə-)liŋ\ [ME *burblen*] **1** : BUBBLE **2** : BABBLE, PRATTLE — **bur·bler** \-b(ə-)lər\ *n*
[2]**burble** *n* **1** : PRATTLE **2** : the breaking up of the streamline flow of air about the body (as an airplane wing) — **bur·bly** \-b(ə-)lē\ *adj*
bur·bot \'bər-bət\ *n, pl* **burbot** *also* **burbots** [ME *borbot*, fr. MF *bourbotte*, fr. *bourbeter* to burrow in the mud] : a freshwater fish (*Lota lota*) of the cod family having barbels on the nose and chin and existing in the northern parts of the New and the Old World
[1]**bur·den** \'bərd-ᵊn\ *n* [ME, fr. OE *byrthen;* akin to OE *beran* to carry — more at BEAR] **1 a** : something that is carried : LOAD **b** : DUTY, RESPONSIBILITY **2** : something oppressive or worrisome : ENCUMBRANCE **3 a** : the bearing of a load — usu. used in the phrase *beast of burden* **b** : capacity for carrying cargo ⟨a ship of a hundred tons ~⟩
[2]**burden** *vt* **bur·dened; bur·den·ing** \'bərd-niŋ, -ᵊn-iŋ\ : LOAD, OPPRESS ⟨the numerous petty things . . . which ~ the tables —Herbert Spencer⟩ ⟨I will not ~ you with a lengthy account⟩
[3]**burden** *n* [alter. of *bourdon*] **1** *archaic* : a bass or accompanying part **2 a** : CHORUS, REFRAIN **b** : a central topic : THEME
burden of proof : the duty of proving a disputed assertion or charge
bur·den·some \'bərd-ᵊn-səm\ *adj* : imposing or constituting a burden : OPPRESSIVE ⟨~ restrictions⟩ ***syn*** see ONEROUS — **bur·den·some·ly** *adv* — **bur·den·some·ness** *n*
bur·dock \'bər-,däk\ *n* : any of a genus (*Arctium*) of coarse composite herbs bearing globular flower heads with prickly bracts
bu·reau \'byu̇(ə)r-(,)ō\ *n, pl* **bureaus** *also* **bu·reaux** \-(,)ōz\ [F, desk, cloth covering for desks, fr. OF *burel* woolen cloth, fr. (assumed) OF *bure*, fr. LL *burra* shaggy cloth] **1 a** *Brit* : WRITING DESK; *esp* : one having drawers and a slant top **b** : a low chest of drawers for use in a bedroom **2 a** : a specialized administrative unit; *esp* : a subdivision of an executive department of a government **b** : a business establishment for exchanging information, making contacts, or coordinating activities **c** : a branch of a newspaper, newsmagazine, or wire service in an important news center
bu·reau·cra·cy \byu̇-'räk-rə-sē\ *n, pl* **-cies** [F *bureaucratie*, fr. *bureau* + *-cratie* -cracy] **1 a** : a body of nonelective government officials **b** : an administrative policy-making group **2** : government characterized by specialization of functions, adherence to fixed rules, and a hierarchy of authority **3** : a system of administration marked by officialism, red tape, and proliferation
bu·reau·crat \'byu̇r-ə-,krat\ *n* : a member of a bureaucracy; *esp* : a government official who follows a narrow rigid formal routine or who is established with great authority in his own department
bu·reau·crat·ic \,byu̇r-ə-'krat-ik\ *adj* : of, relating to, or having the characteristics of a bureaucracy or a bureaucrat ⟨~ government⟩ — **bu·reau·crat·i·cal·ly** \-i-k(ə-)lē\ *adv*
bu·reau·cra·tize \byu̇-'räk-rə-,tīz\ *vt* **-tized; -tiz·ing** : to make bureaucratic : subject to bureaucracy — **bu·reau·cra·ti·za·tion** \-,räk-rət-ə-'zā-shən\ *n*
bu·rette *or* **bu·ret** \byu̇-'ret\ *n* [F *burette*, fr. MF, cruet, fr. *buire* pitcher, alter. of OF *buie*, of Gmc origin; akin to OE *būc* pitcher — more at BUCKET] : a graduated glass tube with a small aperture and stopcock for delivering measured quantities of liquid or for measuring the liquid or gas received or discharged
burg \'bərg\ *n* [OE — more at BOROUGH] **1** : an ancient or medieval fortress or walled town **2** : CITY, TOWN
bur·gage \'bər-gij\ *n* [ME, property held by burgage tenure, fr. MF *bourgage*, lit., burgage, fr. OF, fr. *bourg, borc* town — more at BOURG] : a tenure by which real property in England and Scotland was held under the king or a lord for a yearly rent or for watching and warding
bur·gee \,bər-'jē, 'bər-,\ *n* [perh. fr. F dial. *bourgeais* shipowner] : a swallow-tailed flag used esp. by ships for signals or identification
bur·geon \'bər-jən\ *vi* [ME *burjonen*, fr. *burjon* bud, fr. OF, fr. (assumed) VL *burrion-, burrio*, fr. LL *burra* shaggy cloth] **1 a** : to send forth new growth (as buds or branches) : SPROUT **b** : BLOSSOM, BLOOM **2** : to grow and expand rapidly : FLOURISH ⟨one of Africa's great problems is to get well-educated people out of the ~*ing* cities . . . and into the backward rural areas —P. R. Gould⟩
-burg·er \-,bər-gər\ *n comb form* [*hamburger*] : a fried or grilled patty usu. served in a sandwich
bur·gess \'bər-jəs\ *n* [ME *burgeis*, fr. OF *borjois*, fr. *borc*] **1 a** : a citizen of a British borough **b** : a representative of a borough, corporate town, or university in the British Parliament **2** : a representative in the popular branch of the legislature of colonial Maryland and Virginia
burgh \'bər-(,)ō, 'bə-(,)rō, -ə(-w), -rə(-w)\ *n* [ME — more at BOROUGH] : BOROUGH; *specif* : an incorporated town in Scotland having local jurisdiction of certain services
bur·gher \'bər-gər\ *n* : an inhabitant of a borough or a town
bur·glar \'bər-glər\ *n* [AF *burgler*, fr. ML *burglator*, prob. alter. of *burgator*, fr. *burgatus*, pp. of *burgare* to commit burglary, fr. L *burgus* fortified place — more at BOURG] : one who commits burglary : THIEF
bur·glar·i·ous \,bər-'glar-ē-əs, -'gler-\ *adj* : of, relating to, or resembling burglary — **bur·glar·i·ous·ly** *adv*
bur·glar·ize \'bər-glə-,rīz\ *vb* **ized; -iz·ing** *vt* **1** : to break into and steal from **2** : to commit burglary against ~ *vi* : to commit burglary
bur·glar·proof \,bər-glər-'prüf\ *adj* : protected against or designed to afford protection against burglary
bur·glary \'bər-glə-rē\ *n, pl* **-glar·ies** : the act of breaking into a building esp. with intent to steal; *specif* : the act of breaking into and entering the dwelling house of another at night with intent to commit a felony
bur·gle \'bər-gəl\ *vt* **bur·gled; bur·gling** \-g(ə-)liŋ\ [back-formation fr. *burglar*] : BURGLARIZE
bur·go·mas·ter \'bər-gə-,mas-tər\ *n* [part modif., part trans. of D *burgemeester*, fr. *burg* town + *meester* master] : the chief magistrate of a town in certain European countries : MAYOR
bur·go·net \'bər-gə-nət, ,bər-gə-'net\ *n* [modif. of MF *bourguignotte*] : either of two 16th century helmets
bur·goo \'bər-,gü, (,)bər-'\ *n, pl* **burgoos** [origin unknown] **1** : oatmeal gruel **2** : hardtack and molasses cooked together **3 a** : a stew or thick soup of meat and vegetables orig. served at outdoor gatherings (as a political rally or barbecue) **b** : a picnic at which burgoo is served
Bur·gun·dy \'bər-gən-dē\ *n, pl* **-dies** [*Burgundy*, region in France] : a red or white table wine from the vineyards of Côte d'Or, Yonne, and Saône-et-Loire, France; *also* : a similar wine made elsewhere
buri·al \'ber-ē-əl\ *n, often attrib* [ME *beriel, berial*, back-formation fr. *beriels* (taken as a plural), fr. OE *byrgels;* akin to OS *burgisli* tomb, OE *byrgan* to bury — more at BURY] **1** : GRAVE, TOMB **2** : the act or process of burying
buri·er \'ber-ē-ər\ *n* : one that buries
bu·rin \'byu̇r-ən, 'bər-\ *n* [F] **1** : an engraver's steel cutting tool having the blade ground obliquely to a sharp point **2** : a prehistoric flint tool with a beveled point
burke \'bərk\ *vt* **burked; burking** [William *Burke* †1829 Ir criminal executed for this crime] **1** : to suffocate or strangle in order to obtain a body to be sold for dissection **2 a** : to suppress quietly or indirectly ⟨~ an inquiry⟩ **b** : BYPASS, AVOID ⟨~ an issue⟩
[1]**burl** \'bər(-ə)l\ *n* [ME *burle*, fr. (assumed) MF *bourle* tuft of wool, fr. (assumed) VL *burrula*, dim. of LL *burra* shaggy cloth] **1** : a knot or lump in thread or cloth **2 a** : a hard woody often flattened hemispherical outgrowth on a tree **b** : veneer made from burls
[2]**burl** *vt* : to finish (cloth) esp. by repairing loose threads and knots — **burl·er** *n*
bur·la·de·ro \,bu̇r-lə-'de(ə)r-(,)ō, ,bər-\ *n, pl* **-ros** [Sp, fr. *burlar* to make fun of, elude, fr. *burla* joke] : a wooden shield set parallel to the wall in a bullring and behind which bullfighters can take shelter if pursued
bur·lap \'bər-,lap\ *n* [alter. of earlier *borelapp*] **1** : a coarse heavy plain-woven fabric usu. of jute or hemp used for bagging and wrapping and in furniture and linoleum manufacture **2** : a lightweight material resembling burlap used in interior decoration or for clothing
burled \'bər(-ə)ld\ *adj* : having a distorted grain due to burls
[1]**bur·lesque** \(,)bər-'lesk\ *n* [*burlesque*, adj. (comic, droll), fr. F, fr. It *burlesco*, fr. *burla* joke, fr. Sp] **1** : a literary or dramatic work that seeks to ridicule by means of grotesque exaggeration or comic imitation **2** : mockery usu. by caricature **3** : theatrical entertainment of a broadly humorous often earthy character consisting of short turns, comic skits, and sometimes striptease acts ***syn*** see CARICATURE — **burlesque** *adj* — **bur·lesque·ly** *adv*
[2]**burlesque** *vb* **bur·lesqued; bur·lesqu·ing** *vt* : to imitate in a humorous or derisive manner : MOCK ~ *vi* : to employ burlesque — **bur·lesqu·er** *n*
bur·ley \'bər-lē\ *n* [prob. fr. the name *Burley*] : a thin-bodied air-cured tobacco grown mainly in Kentucky
bur·ly \'bər-lē\ *adj* **bur·li·er; -est** [ME] **1** : strongly and heavily built : HUSKY **2** : heartily direct and frank : BLUFF, FORTHRIGHT ⟨an evocative story less ~ than the real thing but entertaining—E. A. Weeks⟩ — **bur·li·ly** \-lə-lē\ *adv* — **bur·li·ness** \-lē-nəs\ *n*
bur marigold *n* : any of a genus (*Bidens*) of coarse composite herbs with prickly flattened achenes that adhere to clothing
Bur·mese \,bər-'mēz, -'mēs\ *n, pl* **Burmese** **1** : a native or inhabitant of Burma **2** : the Tibeto-Burman language of the Burmese people — **Burmese** *adj*
Burmese cat *n* : any of a breed of cats resembling the Siamese cat but of solid and darker color and with orange eyes
[1]**burn** \'bərn\ *n* [ME, fr. OE; akin to OHG *brunno* spring of water, L *fervēre* to boil] *Brit* : CREEK 2
[2]**burn** \'bərn\ *vb* **burned** \'bərnd, 'bərnt\ *or* **burnt** \'bərnt\; **burn·ing** [ME *birnan*, fr. OE *byrnan*, v.i., *bærnan*, v.t.; akin to OHG *brinnan* to burn, L *fervēre* to boil] *vi* **1 a** : to consume fuel and give off heat, light, and gases ⟨a small fire ~*s* on the hearth⟩ **b** : to undergo combustion; *also* : to undergo nuclear fission or

nuclear fusion **c** : to contain a fire ⟨little stove ~*ing* in the corner⟩ **d** : to give off light : SHINE, GLOW ⟨a light ~*ing* in the window⟩ **2 a** : to be hot ⟨the ~*ing* sand⟩ **b** : to produce or undergo discomfort or pain ⟨iodine ~*s* so⟩ ⟨ears ~*ing* from the cold⟩ **c** : to become emotionally excited or agitated: as (1) : to yearn ardently ⟨~*ing* to tell the story⟩ (2) : to be or become very angry or disgusted ⟨that remark really made him ~⟩ **3 a** : to undergo alteration or destruction by the action of fire or heat ⟨watched their house ~ down⟩ ⟨the potatoes ~*ed* to a crisp⟩ **b** : to die in the electric chair **4** : to force or make a way by or as if by burning ⟨her words ~*ed* into his heart⟩ **5** : to receive sunburn ⟨she ~*s* easily⟩ ~ *vt* **1 a** : to cause to undergo combustion; *esp* : to destroy by fire ⟨~*ed* the trash⟩ **b** : to use as fuel ⟨this furnace ~*s* gas⟩ **2 a** : to transform by exposure to heat or fire ⟨~ clay to bricks⟩ **b** : to produce by burning ⟨~*ed* a hole in his sleeve⟩ **3 a** : to injure or damage by exposure to fire, heat, or radiation : SCORCH ⟨~*ed* his hand⟩ **b** : to execute by burning ⟨heretics ~*ed* at the stake⟩ ; *also* : ELECTROCUTE **4 a** : IRRITATE, ANNOY — usu. used with *up* ⟨really ~*s* me up⟩ **b** : to take advantage of : DECEIVE, CHEAT — often used in passive **5** : to wear out : EXHAUST — **burn·able** \'bər-nə-bəl\ *adj* — **burn one's bridges** *also* **burn one's boats** : to cut off all means of retreat — **burn one's ears** : to rebuke strongly — **burn the candle at both ends** : to use one's resources or energies to excess — **burn the midnight oil** : to work or study far into the night

³burn *n* **1** : the act, process, or result of burning: as **a** : injury or damage resulting from exposure to fire, heat, caustics, electricity, or certain radiations **b** : a burned area ⟨a ~ on the table top⟩ **c** : an abrasion (as of the skin) having the appearance of a burn ⟨rope ~*s*⟩ **d** : a burning sensation ⟨the ~ of iodine on a cut⟩ **2** : the firing of a spacecraft rocket engine in flight **3** : ANGER; *esp* : increasing fury — used chiefly in the phrase *slow burn*

burned–out \'bərn-'daủt, 'bərnt-'aủt\ *or* **burnt–out** \'bərnt-'aủt\ *adj* : worn out by excessive or improper use ⟨~ bearings⟩; *also* : EXHAUSTED ⟨died a ~ man⟩

burn·er \'bər-nər\ *n* : one that burns; *esp* : the part of a fuel-burning device (as a stove or furnace) where the flame is produced

bur·net \(,)bər-'net, 'bər-nət\ *n* [ME, fr. OF *burnete,* fr. *brun* brown — more at BRUNET] : any of a genus (*Sanguisorba*) of herbs of the rose family with odd-pinnate stipulate leaves and spikes of apetalous flowers

burn in *vt* : to increase the density of (portions of a photographic print) during enlarging by giving extra exposure — compare DODGE

burn·ing \'bər-niŋ\ *adj* **1 a** : being on fire **b** : ARDENT, INTENSE ⟨~ enthusiasm⟩ **2 a** : affecting with or as if with heat ⟨a ~ fever⟩ **b** : resembling that produced by a burn ⟨a ~ sensation on the tongue⟩ **3** : of fundamental importance : URGENT ⟨one of the ~ issues of our time⟩ — **burn·ing·ly** \-niŋ-lē\ *adv*

burning bush *n* : any of several plants associated with fire (as by redness): as **a** : ²WAHOO **b** : SUMMER CYPRESS

burning ghat *n* : a level space at the head of a ghat for cremation

¹bur·nish \'bər-nish\ *vt* [ME *burnischen,* fr. MF *bruniss-,* stem of *brunir,* lit., to make brown, fr. *brun*] **1** : to make shiny or lustrous esp. by rubbing : POLISH **2** : to rub (a material) with a tool for compacting or smoothing or for turning an edge — **bur·nish·er** *n* — **bur·nish·ing** *adj or n*

²burnish *n* : LUSTER, GLOSS

bur·noose *or* **bur·nous** \(,)bər-'nüs\ *n* [F *burnous,* fr. Ar *burnus*] : a one-piece hooded cloak worn by Arabs and Moors

burn·out \'bər-,naủt\ *n* : the cessation of operation of a jet or rocket engine; *also* : the point at which burnout occurs

burn·sides \'bərn-,sīdz\ *n pl* [Ambrose E. *Burnside*] : SIDEWHISKERS; *esp* : full muttonchop whiskers

¹burp \'bərp\ *n* [imit.] : BELCH

²burp *vi* : BELCH ~ *vt* : to help (a baby) expel gas from the stomach esp. by patting or rubbing the back

burp gun *n* : a small submachine gun

¹burr \'bər\ *n* [ME *burre;* akin to OE *byrst* bristle — more at BRISTLE] **1** *usu* **bur a** : a rough or prickly envelope of a fruit **b** : a plant that bears burs **2 a** : something that sticks or clings ⟨a ~ in the throat⟩ **b** : HANGER-ON **3** [ME *burwhe* circle] : a small washer put on the end of a rivet before swaging it down **4** : an irregular rounded mass; *esp* : a tree burl **5** : a thin ridge or area of roughness produced in cutting or shaping metal **6 a** : a trilled uvular \r\ as used by some speakers of English esp. in northern England and in Scotland **b** : a tongue-point trill that is the usual Scottish \r\ **7 a** : a small rotary cutting tool **b** *usu* **bur** : a bit used on a dental drill **8** : a rough humming sound : WHIR — **burred** \'bərd\ *adj*

²burr *vi* **1** : to speak with a burr **2** : to make a whirring sound ~ *vt* **1** : to pronounce with a burr **2 a** : to form into a projecting edge **b** : to remove burrs from — **burr·er** *n*

³burr *n* [perh. fr. ¹*burr*] : BUHRSTONE

bur reed *n* : any of a genus (*Sparganium,* family Sparganiaceae) of plants with globose fruits resembling burs

bur·ro \'bər-(,)ō, 'bủr-, -ə(-w); 'bə-(,)rō, -rə(-w)\ *n, pl* **burros** [Sp, irreg. fr. *borrico,* fr. LL *burricus* small horse] : DONKEY; *esp* : a small one used as a pack animal

¹bur·row \'bər-(,)ō, 'bə-(,)rō, -ə(-w), -rə(-w)\ *n* [ME *borow*] : a hole or excavation in the ground made by an animal (as a rabbit) for shelter and habitation

²burrow *vt* **1** *archaic* : to hide in or as if in a burrow **2 a** : to construct by tunneling **b** : to penetrate by means of a burrow **3** : to make a motion suggestive of burrowing with : NESTLE ⟨she ~*s* her grubby hand into mine⟩ ~ *vi* **1** : to conceal oneself in or as if in a burrow **2 a** : to make a burrow **b** : to progress by or as if by digging **3** : to make a motion suggestive of burrowing : SNUGGLE, NESTLE ⟨~*ed* against his back for warmth⟩ — **bur·row·er** *n*

burrstone *var of* BUHRSTONE

bur·ry \'bər-ē\ *adj* **bur·ri·er; -est** **1** : containing burs **2** : PRICKLY **3** *of speech* : characterized by a burr

bur·sa \'bər-sə\ *n, pl* **bur·sas** \-səz\ *or* **bur·sae** \-,sē, -,sī\ [NL, fr. ML, bag, purse — more at PURSE] : a bodily pouch or sac; *esp* : a small serous sac between a tendon and a bone — **bur·sal** \-səl\ *adj*

bur·sar \'bər-sər, -,sär\ *n* [ML *bursarius,* fr. *bursa*] : an officer (as of a monastery or college) in charge of funds : TREASURER

bur·sa·ry \-s(ə-)rē\ *n, pl* **-ries** [ML *bursaria,* fr. *bursa*] **1** : the treasury of a college or monastery **2** : a monetary grant to a needy student : SCHOLARSHIP

burse \'bərs\ *n* [MF *bourse,* fr. ML *bursa*] **1** *obs* : EXCHANGE, BOURSE **2 a** : PURSE **b** : a square cloth case used to carry the corporal in a Communion service

bur·seed \'bər-,sēd\ *n* : STICKSEED

bur·si·tis \(,)bər-'sīt-əs\ *n* [NL, fr. *bursa*] : inflammation of a bursa esp. of the shoulder or elbow

¹burst \'bərst\ *vb* **burst** *or* **burst·ed; burst·ing** [ME *bersten,* fr. OE *berstan;* akin to OHG *brestan* to burst, MIr *brosc* noise] *vi* **1** : to break open, apart, or into pieces usu. from impact or from pressure from within **2 a** : to give way from an excess of emotion ⟨his heart will ~ with grief⟩ **b** : to give vent suddenly to a repressed emotion ⟨~ into tears⟩ ⟨~ out laughing⟩ **3 a** : to emerge or spring suddenly ⟨~ out of a house⟩ **b** : LAUNCH, PLUNGE ⟨~ into song⟩ **4** : to be filled to the breaking point ~ *vt* **1** : to cause to burst **2** : to force open (as a door) by strong or vigorous action **3** : to produce by or as if by bursting — **burst·er** *n* — **burst at the seams** : to be larger, fuller, or more crowded than could reasonably have been anticipated

²burst *n* **1 a** : a sudden outbreak; *esp* : a vehement outburst (as of emotion) **b** : EXPLOSION, ERUPTION **c** : a sudden intense effort ⟨a sudden ~ of speed⟩ **d** : a volley of shots **2** : an act of bursting **3** : a result of bursting; *specif* : a visible puff accompanying the explosion of a shell

bur·then \'bər-t͟hən\ *var of* BURDEN

bur·ton \'bərt-ᵊn\ *n* [origin unknown] : any of several arrangements of hoisting tackle; *esp* : one with a single and a double block

bur·weed \'bər-,wēd\ *n* : any of various plants (as a cocklebur or burdock) having burry fruit

bury \'ber-ē\ *vt* **bur·ied; bury·ing** [ME *burien,* fr. OE *byrgan;* akin to OHG *bergan* to shelter, Russ *berech'* to save] **1** : to dispose of by depositing in or as if in the earth; *esp* : to inter with funeral ceremonies **2 a** : to conceal by or as if by covering with earth ⟨~ a treasure⟩ ⟨the report was *buried* under miscellaneous papers⟩ **b** : to cover from view ⟨*buried* her face in her hands⟩ **3 a** : to put completely out of mind : have done with ⟨~*ing* their differences⟩ **b** : to conceal in obscurity ⟨*buried* the retraction among the classified ads⟩ **c** : SUBMERGE, ENGROSS — usu. used with *in* ⟨*buried* himself in his books⟩ **4** : to put (a playing card) out of play by placing it in or under the dealer's pack ***syn*** see HIDE — **bury the hatchet** : to settle a disagreement : become reconciled

¹bus \'bəs\ *n, pl* **bus·es** *or* **bus·ses** *often attrib* [short for *omnibus*] **1 a** : a large motor-driven passenger vehicle operating usu. according to a schedule along a fixed route **b** : AUTOMOBILE ⟨not a bad old ~ —A. J. Cronin⟩ **2** : a small hand truck **3** : a conductor or an assembly of conductors for collecting electric currents and distributing them to outgoing feeders — called also *bus bar*

²bus *vb* **bused** *or* **bussed; bus·ing** *or* **bus·sing** *vi* **1** : to travel by bus **2** : to work as a busboy ~ *vt* : to transport by bus

³bus *abbr* business

bus·boy \'bəs-,bȯi\ *n* [*omnibus* (busboy)] : a waiter's assistant; *specif* : one who removes dirty dishes and resets tables in a restaurant

bus·by \'bəz-bē\ *n, pl* **busbies** [prob. fr. the name *Busby*] **1** : a military full-dress fur hat with a pendent bag on one side usu. of the color of regimental facings **2** : the bearskin worn by British guardsmen

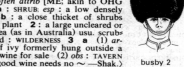

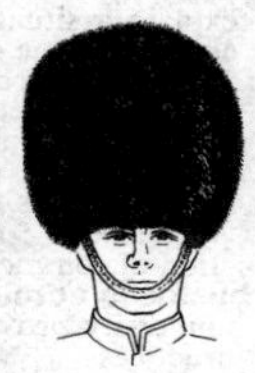
busby 2

¹bush \'bủsh\ *n, often attrib* [ME; akin to OHG *busc* forest] **1 a** : SHRUB; *esp* : a low densely branched shrub **b** : a close thicket of shrubs suggesting a single plant **2** : a large uncleared or sparsely settled area (as in Australia) usu. scrub-covered or forested : WILDERNESS **3 a** (1) *archaic* : a bunch of ivy formerly hung outside a tavern to indicate wine for sale (2) *obs* : TAVERN **b** : ADVERTISING ⟨good wine needs no ~ —Shak.⟩ **4** : a bushy tuft or mass ⟨a ~ of hair —Roger Senhouse⟩ ; *esp* : ²BRUSH 2a

²bush *vt* : to support, mark, or protect with bushes ~ *vi* : to extend like a bush : resemble a bush

³bush *n* [D *bus* bushing, box, fr. MD *busse* box, fr. LL *buxis* — more at BOX] **1** : BUSHING **2** : a threaded socket

⁴bush *vt* : to furnish with a bushing

bush baby *n* : GALAGO

bush basil *n* : a small cultivated annual herb (*Ocimum minimum*) with nearly entire leaves

bush bean *n* : any of a variety of the kidney bean with a low-growing compact bushy habit

bush·buck \'bủsh-,bək\ *n, pl* **bushbuck** *or* **bushbucks** [trans. of Afrik *bosbok*] : a small southern African striped antelope (*Strepsiceros scriptus* or *Tragelaphus scriptus*) having spirally twisted horns and frequenting forests; *also* : any of several related antelopes

bush clover *n* : any of several usu. shrubby lespedezas

bushed \'bủsht\ *adj* **1** : covered with or as if with a bushy growth **2** *chiefly Austral* **a** : lost esp. in the bush **b** : perplexed or confused esp. by a complexity or variety of considerations ⟨adapting

ə abut	ᵊ kitten	ər further	a back	ā bake	ä cot, cart	
aủ out	ch chin	e less	ē easy	g gift	i trip	ī life
j joke	ŋ sing	ō flow	ȯ flaw	ȯi coin	th thin	t͟h this
ü loot	ủ foot	y yet	yü few	yủ furious	zh vision	

his language to my ~ comprehension —Henry Lawson⟩ **3** : TIRED, EXHAUSTED

1**bush·el** \'bu̇sh-əl\ *n* [ME *busshel*, fr. OF *boissel*, fr. (assumed) OF *boisse* one sixth of a bushel, of Celt origin; akin to MIr *boss* palm of the hand] **1** : any of various units of dry capacity — see WEIGHT table **2** : a container holding a bushel **3** : a large quantity : LOTS ⟨always sends them a ~ of love⟩ — **bush·el·age** \-ə-lij\ *n*

2**bushel** *vb* **bush·eled; bush·el·ing** \-(ə-)liŋ\ [prob. fr. G *bosseln* to do poor work, to patch; akin to OE *bēatan* to beat] : REPAIR, RENOVATE — **bush·el·man** \-əl-mən\ *n*

bush·fire \'bu̇sh-,fī(ə)r\ *n, Austral* : an uncontrolled fire in a wooded area

Bu·shi·do \'bu̇sh-i-,dō, 'büsh-\ *n* [Jap *bushidō*] : a feudal-military Japanese code of chivalry valuing honor above life

bush·ing \'bu̇sh-iŋ\ *n* **1** : a usu. removable cylindrical lining for an opening (as of a mechanical part) used to limit the size of the opening, resist abrasion, or serve as a guide **2** : an electrically insulating lining for a hole to protect a through conductor

bush jacket *n* [fr. its use in rough country] : a long cotton jacket resembling a shirt and having four patch pockets, a belt, and a notched collar

bush–league *adj* : belonging to an inferior class or group of its kind : MEDIOCRE

bush league *n* : MINOR LEAGUE — **bush leaguer** *n*

bush lima *n* : a lima bean that resembles a bush bean in growth rather than a vine

bush·man \'bu̇sh-mən\ *n* **1** [modif. of obs. Afrik *boschjesman*, fr. *boschje* (dim. of *bosch* forest) + Afrik *man*] *cap* : a member of a race of nomadic hunters of southern Africa **2** : a Khoisan language of the Bushmen **3 a** : WOODSMAN **b** *chiefly Austral* : one that lives in the bush; *specif* : HICK

bush·mas·ter \-,mas-tər\ *n* : a tropical American pit viper (*Lachesis mutus*) that is the largest New World venomous snake

bush·rang·er \-,rān-jər\ *n* **1** : FRONTIERSMAN, WOODSMAN **2** *Austral* : an outlaw living in the bush — **bush·rang·ing** \-jiŋ\ *n*

bush shirt *n* [fr. its use in rough country] : a usu. loose fitting cotton shirt with patch pockets

bush·tit \-,tit\ *n* : any of several titmice (genus *Psaltriparus*) of western No. America

bush·whack \'bu̇sh-,hwak, -,wak\ *vb* [back-formation fr. *bushwhacker*] *vi* **1 a** : to clear a path through thick woods esp. by chopping down bushes and low branches **b** : to propel a boat by pulling on bushes along the bank **2 a** : to live or hide out in the woods **b** : to fight in or attack from the bush ~ *vt* : AMBUSH — **bush·whack·er** *n* — **bush·whack·ing** *n*

bushy \'bu̇sh-ē\ *adj* **bush·i·er; -est** **1** : full of or overgrown with bushes **2** : resembling a bush; *esp* : being thick and spreading — **bush·i·ly** \'bu̇sh-ə-lē\ *adv* — **bush·i·ness** \'bu̇sh-ē-nəs\ *n*

busi·ness \'biz-nəs, -nəz\ *n, often attrib* **1** *archaic* : purposeful activity : BUSYNESS **2 a** : ROLE, FUNCTION ⟨how the human mind went about its ~ of learning —H. A. Overstreet⟩ **b** : an immediate task or objective : MISSION ⟨what is your ~ here at this hour⟩ **c** : a particular field of endeavor ⟨the best in the ~⟩ **3 a** : a usu. commercial or mercantile activity engaged in as a means of livelihood : TRADE, LINE ⟨in the ~ of supplying emergency services to industry⟩ **b** : a commercial or sometimes an industrial enterprise ⟨sold his ~ and retired⟩; *also* : such enterprises ⟨~ seldom acts as a unit⟩ **c** : usu. economic dealings : PATRONAGE ⟨ready to take his ~ elsewhere unless service improved⟩ **4** : AFFAIR, MATTER ⟨a strange ~⟩ **5** : movement or action (as lighting a cigarette) by an actor intended esp. to establish atmosphere, reveal character, or explain a situation — called also *stage business* **6 a** : personal concern ⟨none of your ~⟩ **b** : RIGHT ⟨you have no ~ hitting her⟩ **7 a** : serious activity requiring time and effort and usu. the avoidance of distractions ⟨immediately got down to ~⟩ **b** : maximum effort **8 a** : a damaging assault **b** : a rebuke or tongue-lashing : a hard time **c** : DOUBLE CROSS

syn BUSINESS, COMMERCE, INDUSTRY, TRADE, TRAFFIC *shared meaning element* : activity concerned with the supplying and distribution of commodities

business administration *n* : a program of studies in a college or university providing general knowledge of business principles and practices

business card *n* : a small card that bears information (as name and address) about a business or a business representative — compare VISITING CARD

business cycle *n* : a recurring succession of fluctuations in economic activity

busi·ness·like \'biz-nə-,slīk, -nəz-,līk\ *adj* **1** : exhibiting qualities believed to be advantageous in business **2** : SERIOUS, PURPOSEFUL

busi·ness·man \'biz-nə-,sman\ *n* a man who transacts business; *esp* : a business executive

business reply mail *n* : printed postal matter (as a postcard) for use in replying, ordering, or subscribing and bearing a statement that postage for its use will be paid by the addressee

business size envelope *n* : an envelope measuring usu. $9^1/_2$ by $4^1/_8$ inches in size — called also *business envelope*

busi·ness·wom·an \'biz-nə-,swu̇m-ən\ *n* : a woman active in business; *esp* : a female business executive

bus·ing *or* **bus·sing** \'bəs-iŋ\ *n* : the act of transporting by bus; *specif* : the transporting of children to a school outside their residential area as a means of establishing racial balance in that school ⟨he opposes most ~ as a tool of desegregation —*Boston Sunday Herald Traveler*⟩

busk \'bəsk\ *vb* [ME *busken*, fr. ON *būask* to prepare oneself, refl. of *būa* to prepare, dwell] *chiefly Scot* : PREPARE

busk·er \'bəs-kər\ *n* [origin unknown] *chiefly Brit* : one who entertains esp. by singing or reciting on the street or in a pub

bus·kin \'bəs-kən\ *n* [perh. modif. of Sp *borcegui*] **1** : a laced boot reaching halfway or more to the knee **2 a** : COTHURNUS **b** : TRAGEDY; *esp* : tragedy resembling that of ancient Greek drama

bus·man's holiday \,bəs-mənz-\ *n* : a holiday spent in following or observing the practice of one's usual occupation

buss \'bəs\ *n* [prob. imit.] : KISS — **buss** *vt*

1**bust** \'bəst\ *n* [F *buste*, fr. It *busto*, fr. L *bustum* tomb] **1** : a sculptured representation of the upper part of the human figure including the head and neck and usu. part of the shoulders and breast **2** : the upper part of the human torso between neck and waist; *esp* : the breasts of a woman

2**bust** *vb* **bust·ed** *also* **bust; bust·ing** *vt* [alter. of *burst*] **1** : HIT, SLUG **2 a** : to break or smash esp. with force; *also* : to make inoperative ⟨~*ed* my watch this morning⟩ **b** : to bring an end to : break up ⟨helped ~ trusts —*Newsweek*⟩ ⟨reached second on a ~*ed* hit-and-run play —*Sporting News*⟩ — often used with *up* ⟨better not try to ~ up his happy marriage —*Forbes*⟩ **c** : to ruin financially **3** : DEMOTE **4** : TAME ⟨bronco ~*ing*⟩ **5** *slang* **a** : ARREST ⟨~*ed* for carrying guns — Saul Gottlieb⟩ **b** : RAID ⟨~*ed* the flat below . . . and found a sizable quantity of pot — Robert Courtney⟩ ~ *vi* **1 a** : BURST ⟨laughing fit to ~⟩ **b** : to break down **2** : to go broke **3 a** : to fail to complete a straight or flush in poker **b** : to lose at cards by exceeding a limit (as the count of 21 in blackjack)

3**bust** *n* **1** : PUNCH, SOCK **2 a** : a complete failure : FLOP **b** : a business depression **3 a** : a hearty drinking session ⟨a beer ~⟩ **b** : SPREE **4** *slang* : a police raid ⟨everyone knew of the . . . takeover of University Hall and the administration's decision to call the police, and the ~ in the stillness of the early hours — T.J. Cottle⟩

bus·tard \'bəs-tərd\ *n* [ME, modif. of MF *bistarde*, fr. OIt *bistarda*, fr. L *avis tarda*, lit., slow bird] : any of a family (Otididae) of Old World and Australian game birds

bust·er \'bəs-tər\ *n* **1 a** : an unusually sturdy child **b** *often cap* : FELLOW — usu. used as a noun of address ⟨hey ~, come here⟩ **2** : one that breaks or breaks up ⟨crime ~*s*⟩ : as **a** : PLOW **b** [short for *broncobuster*] : one who breaks horses **3** *Austral* : a sudden violent wind often coming from the south **4** : something having unusual destructive force: as **a** : a jarring fall **b** : BLOCKBUSTER

1**bus·tle** \'bəs-əl\ *vi* **bus·tled; bus·tling** \'bəs-(ə-)liŋ\ [prob. alter. of obs. *buskle* to prepare, freq. of *busk*] **1** : to move briskly and often ostentatiously **2** : to be busily astir : TEEM — **bustling** *adj* — **bus·tling·ly** \-(ə-)liŋ-lē\ *adv*

2**bustle** *n* : noisy, energetic, and often obtrusive activity ⟨the hustle and ~ of the big city⟩ ***syn*** see STIR

3**bustle** *n* [origin unknown] : a pad or framework expanding and supporting the fullness and drapery of the back of a woman's skirt

busty \'bəs-tē\ *adj* **bust·i·er, -est** : having a large bust

bu·sul·fan \byü-'səl-fən\ *n* [*butane* + *sulf*onyl] : an antineoplastic agent $C_6H_{14}O_6S_2$ used in the treatment of chronic myelogenous leukemia

1**busy** \'biz-ē\ *adj* **busi·er; -est** [ME *bisy*, fr. OE *bisig*; akin to MD & MLG *besich* busy] **1 a** : engaged in action : OCCUPIED **b** : being in use ⟨found the telephone ~⟩ **2** : full of activity : BUSTLING ⟨a ~ seaport⟩ **3** : foolishly or intrusively active : MEDDLING **4** : full of distracting detail ⟨a ~ design⟩ — **busi·ly** \'biz-ə-lē\ *adv* — **busy·ness** \'biz-ē-nəs\ *n*

syn BUSY, INDUSTRIOUS, DILIGENT, ASSIDUOUS, SEDULOUS *shared meaning element* : actively engaged or occupied (as in work or in accomplishing an end). BUSY stresses activity as opposed to idleness or leisure ⟨had plenty of work to keep him *busy*⟩ but does not in itself convey anything about the utility or effectiveness of the activity ⟨always too *busy* to get a job finished⟩ INDUSTRIOUS implies habitual or characteristic attentiveness and persistent earnest application (as to work or a business) ⟨an *industrious* boy, always ready to help his father⟩ DILIGENT suggests earnest application to a particular occupation ⟨a *diligent* student⟩ ASSIDUOUS stresses careful and unremitting application ⟨*assiduous* in his attentions to his bride⟩ SEDULOUS implies painstaking and persevering application ⟨taking *sedulous* care of her husband's needs⟩ ***ant*** idle, unoccupied

2**busy** *vb* **bus·ied; busy·ing** *vt* : to make busy : OCCUPY ~ *vi* : BUSTLE ⟨small boats *busied* to and fro —Quentin Crewe⟩

busy·body \'biz-ē-,bäd-ē\ *n* : an officious or inquistive person

busy·work \-,wərk\ *n* : work that usu. appears productive or of intrinsic value but actually only keeps one occupied

1**but** \(')bət\ *conj* [ME, fr. OE *būtan*, prep. & conj., outside, without, except, except that; akin to OHG *būzan* without, except; both fr. a prehistoric WGmc compound whose constituents are represented by OE *be* by and OE *ūtan* outside; akin to OE *ūt* out — more at BY, OUT] **1 a** : except for the fact ⟨would have protested ~ that he was afraid⟩ **b** : THAT — used after a negative ⟨there is no doubt ~ he won⟩ **c** : without the concomitant that ⟨it never rains ~ it pours⟩ **d** : if not : UNLESS **e** *substand* : THAN ⟨no sooner started ~ it stopped⟩ **2 a** : on the contrary : on the other hand : NOTWITHSTANDING — used to connect coordinate elements ⟨he was called ~ he did not answer⟩ ⟨not peace ~ a sword⟩ **b** : YET ⟨poor ~ proud⟩ **c** : with the exception of — used before a word often taken to be the subject of a clause ⟨none ~ the brave deserves the fair —John Dryden⟩ — **but what** : that . . . not ⟨I don't know *but what* I will go⟩

2**but** *prep* **1** *Scot* **a** : WITHOUT, LACKING **b** : OUTSIDE **2 a** : with the exception of : BARRING ⟨no one there ~ me⟩ — compare 1BUT 2c **b** : other than ⟨this letter is nothing ~ an insult⟩

3**but** *adv* **1** : ONLY, MERELY ⟨he is ~ a child⟩ **2** *Scot* : OUTSIDE **3** : to the contrary ⟨who knows ~ that he may succeed⟩ **4** : DEFINITELY, POSITIVELY ⟨get there ~ fast⟩

4**but** *pron* : that not : who not ⟨nobody ~ has his fault —Shak.⟩

5**but** \'bət\ *n* [Sc *but*, adj. (outer)] *Scot* : the kitchen or living quarters of a 2-room cottage

bu·ta·di·ene \,byüt-ə-'dī-,ēn, -,dī-'\ *n* [ISV *butane* + *di-* + *-ene*] : a flammable gaseous hydrocarbon C_4H_6 used in making synthetic rubbers

bu·tane \'byü-,tān\ *n* [ISV *butyric* + *-ane*] : either of two isomeric flammable gaseous paraffin hydrocarbons C_4H_{10} obtained usu. from petroleum or natural gas and used as a fuel

bu·ta·nol \'byüt-ᵊn-,ōl, -,ōl\ *n* : either of two butyl alcohols $C_4H_{10}O$ derived from normal butane

1**butch·er** \'bu̇ch-ər\ *n* [ME *bocher*, fr. OF *bouchier*, fr. *bouc* he-goat, prob. of Celt origin; akin to MIr *bocc* he-goat — more at

BUCK] **1 a :** one who slaughters animals or dresses their flesh **b :** a dealer in meat **2 :** one that kills ruthlessly or brutally **3 :** BOTCHER **4 :** a vendor esp. on trains or in theaters

[2]**butcher** *vt* **butch·ered; butch·er·ing** \-(ə-)riŋ\ **1 :** to slaughter and dress for market ⟨~ hogs⟩ **2 :** to kill in a barbarous manner **3 :** BOTCH ⟨~*ed* the play beyond recognition⟩ — **butch·er·er** \-ər-ər\ *n*

butch·er–bird \ˈbu̇ch-ər-ˌbərd\ *n* **:** any of various shrikes

butcher knife *n* **:** a heavy-duty knife usu. six to eight inches long having a broad blade that curves slightly at the tip

butch·er·ly \ˈbu̇ch-ər-lē\ *adj* **:** resembling a butcher **:** SAVAGE

butch·er's–broom \ˈbu̇ch-ərz-ˌbrüm, -ˌbru̇m\ *n* **:** a European leafless plant (*Ruscus aculeatus*) of the lily family with stiff-pointed leaflike twigs used for brooms

butch·ery \ˈbu̇ch-(ə-)rē\ *n, pl* **-er·ies** **1** *chiefly Brit* **:** SLAUGHTERHOUSE **2 :** the preparation of meat for sale **3 :** cruel and ruthless slaughter of human beings **4 :** BOTCH ***syn*** see MASSACRE

bu·tene \ˈbyü-ˌtēn\ *n* [ISV *butyl* + *-ene*] **:** a normal butylene

bu·teo \ˈbyüt-ē-ˌō\ *n, pl* **-te·os** [NL, genus name, fr. L, a hawk] **:** any of a genus (*Buteo*) of hawks with broad rounded wings and soaring flight; *broadly* **:** a hawk of similar appearance or habit of flight — **bu·te·o·nine** \byü-ˈtē-ə-ˌnīn, ˈbyüt-ē-\ *adj or n*

but·ler \ˈbət-lər\ *n* [ME *buteler*, fr. OF *bouteillier* bottle bearer, fr. *bouteille* bottle — more at BOTTLE] **1 :** a manservant having charge of the wines and liquors **2 :** the chief male servant of a household who has charge of other employees, receives guests, directs the serving of meals, and performs various personal services

butler's pantry *n* **:** a service room between kitchen and dining room

[1]**butt** \ˈbət\ *vb* [ME *butten*, fr. OF *boter*, of Gmc origin; akin to OHG *bōzan* to beat — more at BEAT] *vi* **:** to thrust or push head foremost **:** strike with the head or horns ~ *vt* **:** to strike or shove with the head or horns

[2]**butt** *n* **:** a blow or thrust usu. with the head or horns

[3]**butt** *n* [ME, partly fr. MF *but* target, end, of Gmc origin; akin to ON *būtr* log, LG *butt* blunt; partly fr. MF *bute* backstop, fr. *but* target] **1 a :** a backstop (as a mound or bank) for catching missiles shot at a target **b :** TARGET **c** *pl* **:** RANGE 5b **d :** a blind for shooting birds **2 a** *obs* **:** LIMIT, BOUND **b** *archaic* **:** GOAL ⟨here is my journey's end, here is my ~ —Shak.⟩ **3 :** an object of abuse or ridicule **:** VICTIM ⟨he was the ~ of all their jokes⟩

[4]**butt** *vb* [partly fr. [3]*butt*, partly fr. [5]*butt*] *vi* **:** ABUT — used with *on* or *against* ~ *vt* **1 :** to place end to end or side to side without overlapping **2 :** to trim or square off (as a log) at the end **3 :** to reduce (as a cigarette) to a butt by stubbing or stamping

[5]**butt** *n* [ME; prob. akin to ME *buttok* buttock, LG *butt* blunt, OHG *bōzan* to beat] **1 :** BUTTOCKS **2 :** the large or thicker end part of something: **a :** a lean upper cut of the pork shoulder **b :** the base of a plant from which the roots spring **c :** the thicker or handle end of a tool or weapon **3 :** an unused remainder **4 :** the part of a hide or skin corresponding to the animal's back and sides

[6]**butt** *n* [ME, fr. MF *botte*, fr. OProv *bota*, fr. LL *buttis*] **1 :** a large cask esp. for wine, beer, or water **2 :** any of various units of liquid capacity; *esp* **:** a measure equal to 108 imperial gallons

butte \ˈbyüt\ *n* [F, knoll, fr. MF *bute* mound of earth serving as a backstop] **:** an isolated hill or mountain with steep or precipitous sides usu. having a smaller summit area than a mesa

[1]**but·ter** \ˈbət-ər\ *n* [ME, fr. OE *butere*; akin to OHG *butera* butter; both fr. a prehistoric WGmc word borrowed fr. L *butyrum* butter, fr. Gk *boutyron*, fr. *bous* cow + *tyros* cheese; akin to Av *tūiri-* whey — more at COW] **1 :** a solid emulsion of fat globules, air, and water made by churning milk or cream and used as food **2 :** a buttery substance: as **a :** any of various fatty oils remaining nearly solid at ordinary temperatures **b :** a food spread made from fruit, nuts, or other food ⟨apple ~⟩ **3 :** FLATTERY — **but·ter·less** \-ləs\ *adj*

[2]**butter** *vt* **:** to spread with or as if with butter

but·ter–and–eggs \ˌbət-ə-rə-ˈnegz, -ˈnāgz\ *n pl but sing or pl in constr* **:** a common European perennial herb (*Linaria vulgaris*) of the snapdragon family that has showy yellow and orange flowers and is a naturalized weed in much of No. America — called also *toadflax*

but·ter·ball \ˈbət-ər-ˌbȯl\ *n* **1 :** a chubby person **2 :** BUFFLEHEAD

butter bean *n* **1 :** WAX BEAN **2 :** LIMA BEAN: as **a** *chiefly South & Midland* **:** a large dried lima bean **b :** SIEVA BEAN **3 :** a green shell bean esp. as opposed to a snap bean

butter clam *n* **:** either of two large delicately flavored clams (*Saxidomus nuttallii* and *S. giganteus*) of the Pacific coast of No. America

but·ter·cup \ˈbət-ər-ˌkəp\ *n* **:** any of numerous plants (genus *Ranunculus* of the family Ranunculaceae, the buttercup family) with yellow flowers and lobed leaves

but·ter·fat \-ˌfat\ *n* **:** the natural fat of milk and chief constituent of butter consisting essentially of a mixture of glycerides (as butyrin, olein, and palmitin)

but·ter·fin·gered \-ˌfiŋ-gərd\ *adj* **:** apt to let things fall or slip through the fingers **:** CARELESS — **but·ter·fin·gers** \-gərz\ *n pl but sing or pl in constr*

but·ter·fish \-ˌfish\ *n* **:** any of numerous mostly percoid fishes (esp. family Stromateidae) with a slippery coating of mucus

[1]**but·ter·fly** \-ˌflī\ *n, often attrib* **1 :** any of numerous slender-bodied diurnal insects (order Lepidoptera) with large broad often brightly colored wings **2 :** something that resembles or suggests a butterfly; *esp* **:** a person chiefly occupied with the pursuit of pleasure **3 :** a swimming stroke executed in a prone position by moving both arms in a circular motion while kicking the legs up and down simultaneously **4** *pl* **:** a feeling of hollowness or queasiness caused esp. by emotional or nervous tension or anxious anticipation

[2]**butterfly** *vt* **-flied; -fly·ing :** to split almost entirely and spread apart ⟨a *butterflied* steak⟩ ⟨*butterflied* shrimp⟩

butterfly bush *n* **:** BUDDLEIA

butterfly chair *n* **:** a chair for lounging consisting of a cloth sling supported by a frame of metal tubing or bars

but·ter·fly·er \ˈbət-ər-ˌflī(-ə)r\ *n* **:** a swimmer who specializes in the butterfly

butterfly fish *n* **:** a fish having variegated colors, broad expanded fins, or both: as **a :** a European blenny (*Blennius ocellaris*) **b :** FLYING GURNARD **c :** any of a family (Chaetodontidae) of small brilliantly colored spiny-finned fishes of tropical seas with a narrow deep body and fins partly covered with scales

butterfly valve *n* **1 :** a double clack valve **2 :** a damper or valve in a pipe consisting of a disk turning on a diametral axis

butterfly weed *n* **:** an orange-flowered showy milkweed (*Asclepias tuberosa*) of eastern No. America

but·ter·milk \ˈbət-ər-ˌmilk\ *n* **1 :** the liquid left after butter has been churned from milk or cream **2 :** cultured milk made by the addition of suitable bacteria to sweet milk

but·ter·nut \-ˌnət\ *n* **1 a :** the edible oily nut of an American tree (*Juglans cinerea*) of the walnut family **b :** a tree that bears butternuts **2 a :** a light yellowish brown **b** *pl* **:** homespun overalls dyed brown with a butternut extract **c :** a soldier or partisan of the Confederacy during the Civil War

but·ter·scotch \-ˌskäch\ *n* **1 :** a candy made from brown sugar, corn syrup, and water; *also* **:** the flavor of such candy **2 :** a moderate yellowish brown

butter up *vt* **:** to charm or beguile with lavish flattery or praise **:** CAJOLE

but·ter·weed \ˈbət-ər-ˌwēd\ *n* **:** any of several plants having yellow flowers or smooth soft foliage: as **a :** HORSEWEED 1 **b :** an American ragwort (*Senecio glabellus*)

but·ter·wort \-ˌwərt, -ˌwȯ(ə)rt\ *n* **:** any of a genus (*Pinguicula*) of herbs of the bladderwort family with fleshy greasy leaves that produce a viscid secretion serving to capture and digest insects

[1]**but·tery** \ˈbət-ə-rē, ˈbə-trē\ *n, pl* **-ter·ies** [ME *boterie*, fr. MF, fr. *botte* cask, butt — more at BUTT] **1 :** a storeroom for liquors **2 a** *chiefly dial* **:** PANTRY **b :** a room (as in an English college) stocking provisions for sale to students

[2]**but·tery** \ˈbət-ə-rē\ *adj* **1 a :** having the qualities, consistency, or appearance of butter **b :** containing or spread with butter **2 :** marked by flattery

butt hinge *n* **:** a hinge usu. mortised flush into the edge of a door

butt in *vi* **:** to meddle in the affairs of others **:** INTERFERE, INTRUDE

butt·in·sky *also* **butt·in·ski** \ˌbət-ˈin-skē\ *n, pl* **-skies** [*butt in* + *-sky, -ski* (last element in many Slavic names)] **:** one given to butting in **:** a troublesome meddler

butt joint *n* **:** a joint made by fastening the parts together end-to-end without overlap and often with reinforcement

but·tock \ˈbət-ək\ *n* [ME *buttok* — more at BUTT] **1 :** the back of a hip that forms one of the fleshy parts on which a person sits **2** *pl* **a :** the seat of the body **b :** RUMP

[1]**but·ton** \ˈbət-ᵊn\ *n, often attrib* [ME *boton*, fr. MF, fr. OF, fr. *boter* to thrust — more at BUTT] **1 a :** a small knob or disk secured to an article (as of clothing) and used as a fastener by passing it through a buttonhole or loop **b :** a usu. circular metal or plastic badge bearing a stamped design or printed slogan ⟨campaign ~⟩ **2 :** something that resembles a button: as **a :** any of various parts or growths of a plant or of an animal: as **(1) :** an immature whole mushroom **(2) :** the terminal segment of a rattlesnake's rattle **b :** a small globule of metal remaining after fusion in assaying **c :** a guard on the tip of a fencing foil **3 :** PUSH BUTTON **4 :** the point of the chin esp. as a target for a knockout blow — **on the button :** PRECISELY

[2]**but·ton** \ˈbət-ᵊn\ *vb* **but·toned; but·ton·ing** \ˈbət-niŋ, -ᵊn-iŋ\ *vt* **1 :** to furnish or decorate with buttons **2 :** to close or fasten with buttons — often used with *up* ⟨~ up your overcoat⟩ **3 :** to close (the lips) to prevent speech ⟨~ your lip⟩ ~ *vi* **:** to have buttons for fastening ⟨this dress ~s at the back⟩ — **but·ton·er** \-nər, -ᵊn-ər\ *n* — **but·ton·less** \ˈbət-ᵊn-ləs\ *adj*

but·ton·ball \ˈbət-ᵊn-ˌbȯl\ *n* **:** [2]PLANE

but·ton·bush \-ˌbu̇sh\ *n* **:** a No. American shrub (*Cephalanthus occidentalis*) of the madder family with globular flower heads

but·ton–down \-ˌdau̇n\ *adj* **1 a** *of a collar* **:** having the ends fastened to the garment with buttons **b** *of a garment* **:** having a button-down collar **2** *also* **but·toned–down** \-ᵊn-ˌdau̇n\ **:** lacking originality and imagination and adhering to conventional ideals esp. in dress and behavior

[1]**but·ton·hole** \ˈbət-ᵊn-ˌhōl\ *n* **:** a slit or loop through which a button is passed

[2]**buttonhole** *vt* **1 :** to furnish with buttonholes **2 :** to work with buttonhole stitch — **but·ton·hol·er** *n*

[3]**buttonhole** *vt* [alter. of *buttonhold*] **:** to detain in conversation by or as if by holding on to the outer garments of

buttonhole stitch *n* **:** a closely worked loop stitch used to make a firm edge (as on a buttonhole)

but·ton·hook \ˈbət-ᵊn-ˌhu̇k\ *n* **1 :** a hook for drawing small buttons through buttonholes **2 :** an offensive play in football in which the pass receiver runs straight downfield and then abruptly cuts back toward the line of scrimmage — **buttonhook** *vi*

button quail *n* **:** any of various small terrestrial Old World birds (family Turnicidae) that resemble quails, have only three toes on a foot with the hind toe being absent, and are related to the cranes and bustards

button snakeroot *n* **1 :** any of a genus (*Liatris*) of composite plants with spikes of rosy-purple rayless flower heads **2 :** any of several usu. prickly herbs (genus *Eryngium*) of the carrot family

but·ton·wood \ˈbət-ᵊn-ˌwu̇d\ *n* **:** [2]PLANE

but·tony \'bət-ᵊn-ē, 'bət-nē\ *adj* **1 :** ornamented with buttons **2 :** resembling a button ⟨~ eyes⟩
¹but·tress \'bə-trəs\ *n* [ME *butres,* fr. MF *bouterez,* fr. OF *boterez,* fr. *boter*] **1 :** a projecting structure of masonry or wood for supporting or giving stability to a wall or building **2 :** something that resembles a buttress: as **a :** a projecting part of a mountain or hill **b :** a horny protuberance on a horse's hoof at the heel — see HOOF illustration **c :** the broadened base of a tree trunk or a thickened vertical part of it **3 :** something that supports or strengthens ⟨a ~ of the cause of peace⟩ — **but·tressed** \-trəst\ *adj*

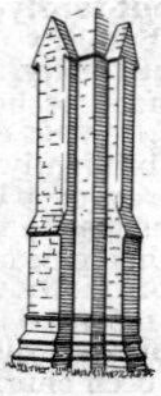
buttress 1

²buttress *vt* **:** to furnish or shore up with a buttress; *also* **:** SUPPORT, STRENGTHEN ⟨arguments ~*ed* by solid facts⟩
butt shaft *n* **:** a target arrow without a barb
butt·stock \'bət-ˌstäk\ *n* **:** the stock of a firearm in the rear of the breech mechanism
butt weld *n* **:** a butt joint made by welding — **butt-weld** *vt* — **butt welding** *n*
but·ty \'bət-ē\ *n, pl* **butties** [origin unknown] *chiefly Brit* **:** a fellow workman **:** CHUM, PARTNER
bu·tut \bu̇-'tüt\ *n* [native word in the Gambia] — see *dalasi* at MONEY table
bu·tyl \'byüt-ᵊl\ *n* [ISV *butyric* + *-yl*] **:** any of four isomeric univalent radicals C_4H_9 derived from butanes
Butyl *trademark* — used for any of various synthetic rubbers made by polymerizing isobutylene
butyl alcohol *n* **:** any of four flammable alcohols C_4H_9OH derived from butanes and used in organic synthesis and as solvents
bu·tyl·ate \'byüt-ᵊl-ˌāt\ *vt* **-at·ed; -at·ing :** to introduce the butyl group into (a compound) — **bu·tyl·ation** \ˌbyüt-ᵊl-'ā-shən\ *n*
butylated hy·droxy·tol·u·ene \-(ˌ)hī-ˌdräk-sē-'täl-yə-ˌwēn\ *n* **:** a crystalline phenolic antioxidant $C_{15}H_{24}O$ used esp. in dry cereals
bu·tyl·ene \'byüt-ᵊl-ˌēn\ *n* **:** any of three isomeric hydrocarbons C_4H_8 of the ethylene series obtained usu. by cracking petroleum
butyr- *or* **butyro-** *comb form* [ISV, fr. *butyric*] **:** butyric ⟨*butryal*⟩
bu·ty·ra·ceous \ˌbyüt-ə-'rā-shəs\ *adj* [L *butyrum* butter — more at BUTTER] **1 :** resembling or having the qualities of butter **2 :** yielding a buttery substance
bu·ty·ral \'byüt-ə-ˌral\ *n* **:** an acetal of butyraldehyde
bu·tyr·al·de·hyde \ˌbyüt-ə-'ral-də-ˌhīd\ *n* [ISV] **:** either of two aldehydes C_4H_8O used esp. in making polyvinyl butyral resins
bu·ty·rate \'byüt-ə-ˌrāt\ *n* **:** a salt or ester of butyric acid
bu·tyr·ic \byü-'tir-ik\ *adj* [F *butyrique,* fr. L *butyrum*] **:** relating to or producing butyric acid ⟨~ fermentation⟩
butyric acid *n* **:** either of two isomeric fatty acids $C_4H_8O_2$; *esp* **:** a normal acid of unpleasant odor found in rancid butter and in perspiration
bux·om \'bək-səm\ *adj* [ME *buxsum,* fr. (assumed) OE *būhsum,* fr. OE *būgan* to bend — more at BOW] **1** *obs* **a :** OBEDIENT, TRACTABLE **b :** offering little resistance **:** FLEXIBLE, PLIANT ⟨wing silently the ~ air —John Milton⟩ **2** *archaic* **:** full of gaiety **:** BLITHE **3 :** vigorously or healthily plump; *specif* **:** full-bosomed — **bux·om·ly** *adv* — **bux·om·ness** *n*
¹buy \'bī\ *vb* **bought** \'bȯt\; **buy·ing** [ME *byen,* fr. OE *bycgan;* akin to Goth *bugjan* to buy] *vt* **1 :** to acquire possession, ownership, or rights to the use or services of by payment esp. of money **:** PURCHASE **2 a :** to obtain in exchange for something often at a sacrifice ⟨they *bought* peace with their freedom⟩ **b :** REDEEM 6 **3 :** BRIBE, HIRE **4 :** to be the purchasing equivalent of ⟨the dollar ~s less today than it used to⟩ **5 :** ACCEPT, BELIEVE ⟨I don't ~ that hooey⟩ ~ *vi* **:** to make a purchase — **buy time :** to delay an imminent action or decision **:** STALL ⟨*buying time* against the day when air pollution . . . reaches critical and dangerous proportions —*Plainsman*⟩
²buy *n* **1 :** an act of buying **:** PURCHASE **2 :** something of value at a favorable price; *esp* **:** BARGAIN ⟨it's a real ~ at that price⟩
buy·er \'bī(-ə)r\ *n* **:** one that buys; *esp* **:** a department head of a retail store
buyer's market *n* **:** a market in which goods are plentiful, buyers have a wide range of choice, and prices tend to be low — compare SELLER'S MARKET
buy in *vt* **:** to obtain (a stock or supply of something) by purchase; *also* **:** to complete an outstanding securities transaction by purchase against the account of (a delaying or defaulting speculator or dealer) — **buy-in** *n*
buy off *vt* **1 :** to induce to refrain (as from prosecution) by a payment or other consideration **2 :** to free (as from military service) by payment
buy out *vt* **:** to purchase the share or interest of
buy up *vt* **1 :** to buy freely or extensively **2 :** to buy the entire available supply of
¹buzz \'bəz\ *vb* [ME *bussen,* of imit. origin] *vi* **1 :** to make a low continuous humming sound like that of a bee **2 a :** MURMUR, WHISPER **b :** to be filled with a confused murmur ⟨the room ~*ed* with excitement⟩ **3 :** to make a signal with a buzzer **4 :** to go quickly **:** HURRY; *also* **:** SCRAM — usu. used with *off* ~ *vt* **1 :** to utter covertly by or as if by whispering **2 :** to cause to buzz **3 :** to fly low and fast over ⟨planes ~ the crowd⟩ **4 :** to summon or signal with a buzzer **5** *dial Eng* **:** to drink to the last drop ⟨get some more port whilst I ~ this bottle —W. M. Thackeray⟩
²buzz *n* **1 :** a persistent vibratory sound **2 a :** a confused murmur or flurry of activity **b :** RUMOR, GOSSIP **3 :** a signal conveyed by buzzer; *specif* **:** a telephone call
buz·zard \'bəz-ərd\ *n* [ME *busard,* fr. OF, alter. of *buison,* fr. L *buteon-, buteo*] **1** *chiefly Brit* **:** BUTEO **2 :** any of various usu. large birds of prey (as the turkey buzzard) **3 :** a contemptible or rapacious person
buzz bomb *n* **:** ROBOT BOMB
buzz·er \'bəz-ər\ *n* **1 :** one that buzzes; *specif* **:** an electric signaling device that makes a buzzing sound **2 :** the sound of a buzzer ⟨sank a 20-foot jump shot at the ~⟩
buzz saw *n* **:** a circular saw having teeth on its periphery and revolving on a spindle
buzz·word \'bəz-ˌwərd\ *n* **:** an important-sounding usu. technical word or phrase often of little meaning used chiefly to impress laymen
BV *abbr* Blessed Virgin
B.V.D. \ˌbē-(ˌ)vē-'dē\ *trademark* — used for underwear
bvt *abbr* brevet
BW *abbr* **1** bacteriological warfare; biological warfare **2** black and white **3** bread and water
bwa·na \'bwän-ə\ *n* [Swahili, fr. Ar *abūna* our father] *chiefly East Africa* **:** MASTER, BOSS — often used as a noun of address
BWI *abbr* British West Indies
bx *abbr* box
BX *abbr* base exchange
¹by \(ˈ)bī, *esp before consonants* bə\ *prep* [ME, prep. & adv., fr. OE, prep., *be, bī;* akin to OHG *bī* by, near, L *ambi-* on both sides, around, Gk *amphi*] **1 :** in proximity to **:** NEAR ⟨standing ~ the window⟩ **2 a :** through or through the medium of **:** VIA ⟨enter ~ the door⟩ **b :** in the direction of **:** TOWARD ⟨north ~ east⟩ **c :** into the vicinity of and beyond **:** PAST ⟨went right ~ him⟩ **3 a :** during the course of ⟨studied ~ night⟩ **b :** not later than ⟨~ 2 p.m.⟩ **4 a :** through the agency or instrumentality of ⟨~ force⟩ **b :** sired by **5 :** with the witness or sanction of ⟨swear ~ all that is holy⟩ **6 a :** in conformity with ⟨acted ~ the rules⟩ **b :** in terms of ⟨always bought ~ brand⟩ ⟨called her ~ name⟩ **7 :** with respect to **8 a :** in or to the amount or extent of ⟨win ~ a nose⟩ **b** *chiefly Scot* **:** in comparison with **:** BESIDE **9 :** in successive units or increments ⟨succeeded little ~ little⟩ ⟨walk two ~ two⟩ **10 —** used as a function word in multiplication, in division, and in measurements ⟨divide *a* ~ *b*⟩ ⟨multiply 10 ~ 4⟩ ⟨a room 15 feet ~ 20 feet⟩
syn BY, THROUGH, WITH *shared meaning element* — used as a function word to qualify (a following word or phrase) as an agent, means, or instrument. BY is followed commonly by the agent or causative agency ⟨a wall built *by* the Romans⟩ ⟨destroyed *by* fire⟩ ⟨books *by* modern writers⟩ THROUGH implies intermediacy and is followed by the name of someone or something felt as the medium or means by which an end is gained or an effect produced ⟨he spoke *through* an interpreter⟩ ⟨gained his position *through* influence⟩ WITH is more often followed by the name of the instrument through which a causative agent or agency works ⟨ate *with* a fork⟩ ⟨struck a blow *with* his fist⟩ or it may take for its object something not consciously used as an instrument though serving as the instrumentality by which an effect is produced ⟨his speech impressed us *with* its brevity⟩ ⟨a face contorted *with* anger⟩
²by \'bī\ *adv* **1 a :** close at hand **:** NEAR **b :** at or to another's home ⟨stop ~ for a chat⟩ **2 :** PAST ⟨saw him go ~⟩ **3 :** ASIDE, AWAY
³by *or* **bye** \'bī\ *adj* **1 :** off the main route **:** SIDE **2 :** INCIDENTAL
⁴by *or* **bye** \'bī\ *n, pl* **byes** \'bīz\ **:** something of secondary importance **:** a side issue — **by the by :** by the way **:** INCIDENTALLY
⁵by *or* **bye** \'bī\ *interj* [short for *goodbye*] — used to express farewell; often used with following *now*
by-and-by \ˌbī-ən-'bī\ *n* **:** a future time or occasion
by and by \ˌbī-ən-'bī\ *adv* **:** before long **:** SOON
by and large \ˌbī-ən-'lärj\ *adv* **:** on the whole **:** in general
by-blow \'bī-ˌblō\ *n* **1 :** an indirect blow **2 :** an illegitimate child
bye \'bī\ *n* [alter. of ²*by*] **:** the position of a participant in a tournament who has no opponent after pairs are drawn and advances to the next round without playing
¹bye-bye *or* **by-by** \'bī-ˌbī, bī-'bī\ *interj* [baby-talk redupl. of *goodbye*] — used to express farewell
²bye-bye *or* **by-by** \'bī-ˌbī\ *adv* **:** out esp. for a walk or ride — used with the verb *go* ⟨if he wants to go ~ the baby may pat his head to indicate his desire for a hat —A.L. Gesell & Frances L. Ilg⟩
³bye-bye *or* **by-by** \'bī-ˌbī\ *n* **:** BED, SLEEP ⟨lie down . . . and go to ~ —Rudyard Kipling⟩
⁴bye-bye *or* **by-by** \'bī-ˌbī\ *adv* **:** to bed or sleep — used with the verb *go* ⟨I'll run in and read for just a second . . . and then perhaps I'll go ~ —Sinclair Lewis⟩
by-elec·tion *also* **bye-election** \'bī-ə-ˌlek-shən\ *n* **:** a special election held between regular elections in order to fill a vacancy
by·gone \'bī-ˌgȯn *also* -ˌgän\ *adj* **:** gone by **:** PAST; *esp* **:** OUTMODED — **bygone** *n*
by·law *or* **bye-law** \'bī-ˌlȯ\ *n* [ME *bilawe,* prob. fr. (assumed) ON *bȳlǫ̈g,* fr. ON *bȳr* town + *lǫ̈g* law] **:** a rule adopted by an organization chiefly for the government of its members and the regulation of its affairs
¹by-line \'bī-ˌlīn\ *n* **1 :** a secondary line **:** SIDELINE **2 :** a line at the head of a newspaper or magazine article giving the writer's name
²by-line *vt* **:** to write (an article) under a by-line — **by-lin·er** \-ˌlī-nər\ *n*
by·name \'bī-ˌnām\ *n* **1 :** a secondary name **2 :** NICKNAME
BYO *abbr* bring your own
BYOB *abbr* bring your own booze; bring your own bottle
byp *abbr* bypass
¹by·pass \'bī-ˌpas\ *n* **1 :** a passage to one side; *esp* **:** a deflected route usu. around a town **2 a :** a channel carrying a fluid around a part and back to the main stream **b :** SHUNT 1b
²bypass *vt* **1 a :** to avoid by means of a bypass **b :** to cause to follow a bypass **2 a :** to neglect or ignore usu. intentionally **b :** CIRCUMVENT
by·past \'bī-ˌpast\ *adj* **:** BYGONE
by·path \-ˌpath, -ˌpȧth\ *n* **:** BYWAY
by·play \-ˌplā\ *n* **:** action engaged in on the side while the main action proceeds (as during a dramatic production)
by-prod·uct \-ˌpräd-(ˌ)əkt\ *n* **1 :** something produced (as in manufacturing) in addition to the principal product **2 :** a secondary and sometimes unexpected or unintended result

byre \'bī(ə)r\ *n* [ME, fr. OE *bȳre*; akin to OE *bŭr* dwelling — more at BOWER] *chiefly Brit* : a cow barn
by-road \'bī-,rōd\ *n* : BYWAY
By-ron-ic \bī-'rän-ik\ *adj* : of, relating to, or having the characteristics of the poet Byron or his writings — **By-ron-i-cal-ly** \-i-k(ə-)lē\ *adv* — **By-ron-ism** \'bī-rə-,niz-əm\ *n*
bys-si-no-sis \,bis-ə-'nō-səs\ *n, pl* **-no-ses** \-,sēz\ [NL, fr. L *byssinus* of fine linen, fr. Gk *byssinos*, fr. *byssos* byssus] : a chronic industrial disease associated with the inhalation of cotton dust over a long period of time and characterized by chronic bronchitis sometimes complicated by emphysema or asthma
bys-sus \'bis-əs\ *n, pl* **bys-sus-es** *or* **bys-si** \-,ī, -(,)ē\ [L, fr. Gk *byssos* flax, of Sem origin; akin to Heb *būs* linen cloth] **1** : a fine prob. linen cloth of ancient times **2** [NL, fr. L] : a tuft of long tough filaments by which some bivalve mollusks (as mussels) make themselves fast
by-stand-er \'bī-,stan-dər\ *n* : one present but not taking part in a situation or event : a chance spectator
by-street \-,strēt\ *n* : a street off a main thoroughfare : side street
byte \'bīt\ *n* [perh. alter. of ²*bite*] : a group of adjacent binary digits often shorter than a word that a computer processes as a unit ⟨an 8-bit ~⟩

by the way *adv* : in passing : INCIDENTALLY
by virtue of *prep* : as a result of
by-way \'bī-,wā\ *n* **1** : a little traveled side road **2** : a secondary or little known aspect or field ⟨meandering more and more in the fascinating ~s of learning —*Times Lit. Supp.*⟩
by-word \-,wərd\ *n* **1** : a proverbial saying : PROVERB **2 a** : one that personifies a type **b** : one that is noteworthy or notorious **3** : EPITHET **4** : a frequently used word or phrase
¹**Byz-an-tine** \'biz-ᵊn-,tēn *also* -,tīn\ *n* : a native or inhabitant of Byzantium
²**Byzantine** *adj* **1** : of, relating to, or characteristic of the ancient city of Byzantium **2** : of, relating to, or having the characteristics of a style of architecture developed in the Byzantine Empire esp. in the 5th and 6th centuries featuring the dome carried on pendentives over a square and incrustation with marble veneering and with colored mosaics on grounds of gold **3** : of or relating to the churches using a traditional Greek rite and subject to Eastern canon law **4** : LABYRINTHINE ⟨searching in the ~ complexity of the record for leads, defenses, and, in the case of Government lawyers, evidence of perjured testimony —B. L. Collier⟩
By-zan-tin-ist \'biz-ᵊn-,tē-nəst, -,tī-\ *n* : a student of Byzantine culture

---

¹**c** \'sē\ *n, pl* **c's** *or* **cs** \'sēz\ **1 a** : the 3d letter of the English alphabet **b** : a graphic representation of this letter **c** : a speech counterpart of orthographic *c* **2 a** : one hundred — see NUMBER table **b** *slang* : a sum of $100 **3** : the keynote of a C-major scale **4** : a graphic device for reproducing the letter *c* **5** : one designated *c* esp. as the 3d in order or class **6 a** : a grade rating a student's work as fair or mediocre in quality **b** : one graded or rated with a C **7** : something shaped like the letter C
²**c** *abbr, often cap* **1** calm **2** calorie **3** Canadian **4** canceled **5** candle **6** carat **7** case **8** castle **9** catcher **10** Catholic **11** cedi **12** Celsius **13** cent **14** centavo **15** center **16** centi- **17** centigrade **18** centime **19** centimeter **20** centum **21** century **22** chairman **23** chapter **24** circa **25** circuit **26** circumference **27** clockwise **28** cloudy **29** cobalt **30** cocaine **31** codex **32** coefficient **33** college **34** colon **35** color **36** colt **37** [L *congius*] gallon **38** congress **39** conservative **40** contralto **41** copyright **42** cost **43** cubic
³**c** *symbol* speed of light
C *symbol* **1** capacitance **2** carbon
ca *abbr* **1** centare **2** circa
Ca *symbol* calcium
CA *abbr* **1** California **2** chartered accountant **3** chief accountant **4** chronological age **5** commercial agent **6** controller of accounts **7** current account
ca' \'kȯ, 'kä\ *Scot var of* CALL
¹**cab** \'kab\ *n* [Heb *qabh*] : an ancient Hebrew unit of capacity equal to about two quarts
²**cab** \'kab\ *n* [short for *cabriolet*] **1 a** (1) : CABRIOLET (2) : a similar light closed carriage (as a hansom) **b** : a carriage for hire **2** : TAXICAB **3** [short for *cabin*] **a** : the part of a locomotive that houses the engineer and operating controls **b** : a comparable shelter on a truck, tractor, or crane
CAB *abbr* Civil Aeronautics Board
¹**ca-bal** \kə-'bal\ *n* [F *cabale* cabala, intrigue, cabal, fr. ML *cabbala* cabala, fr. LHeb *qabbālāh*, lit., received (lore)] **1** : a number of persons secretly united to bring about an overturn or usurpation esp. in public affairs **2** : the artifices and intrigues of such a group
²**cabal** *vi* **ca-balled; ca-bal-ling** : to unite in or form a cabal
ca-ba-la *or* **cab-ba-la** *or* **cab-ba-lah** \'kab-ə-lə, kə-'bäl-ə\ *n, often cap* [ML *cabbala*] **1** : a medieval and modern system of Jewish theosophy, mysticism, and thaumaturgy marked by belief in creation through emanation and a cipher method of interpreting Scripture **2 a** : a traditional, esoteric, occult, or secret matter **b** : esoteric doctrine or mysterious art — **cab-a-lism** \'kab-ə-,liz-əm\ *n* — **cab-a-lis-tic** \,kab-ə-'lis-tik\ *adj*
ca-ba-let-ta \,kab-ə-'let-ə, ,käb-\ *n* [It] : an operatic song in simple popular style characterized by a uniform rhythm
¹**ca-ba-list** \'kab-ə-ləst, kə-'bäl-əst\ *n* **1** *often cap* : a student, interpreter, or devotee of the Jewish cabala **2** : one skilled in esoteric doctrine or mysterious art
²**cabalist** \-'bal-əst\ *n* : a member of a cabal
ca-bal-le-ro \,kab-əl-'e(ə)r-(,)ō, -ə(l)-'ye(ə)r-\ *n, pl* **-ros** [Sp, fr. LL *caballarius* hostler — more at CAVALIER] **1** : KNIGHT, CAVALIER **2** *chiefly Southwest* : HORSEMAN
ca-bana \kə-'ban-(y)ə\ *n* [Sp *cabaña*, lit., hut, fr. ML *capanna*] **1** : a shelter resembling a cabin usu. with an open side facing a beach or swimming pool **2** : a lightweight structure with living facilities
cabana set *n* : a two-piece beachwear ensemble for men consisting of loosely fitting shorts and a short-sleeved jacket
cab-a-ret \,kab-ə-'rā\ *n* [F, fr. ONF] **1** *archaic* : a shop selling

wines and liquors **2** : a restaurant serving liquor and providing entertainment (as by singers or dancers); *also* : the show provided
¹**cab-bage** \'kab-ij\ *n, often attrib* [ME *caboche*, fr. ONF, head] **1** : a leafy garden plant (*Brassica oleracea capitata*) of European origin that has a short stem and a dense globular head of usu. green leaves and is used as a vegetable **2** : a terminal bud of a palm tree that resembles a head of cabbage and is eaten as a vegetable **3** *slang* : paper money or bank notes
²**cabbage** *n* [perh. by folk etymology fr. MF *cabas* cheating, theft] *Brit* : pieces of cloth left in cutting out garments and traditionally kept by tailors as perquisites
³**cabbage** *vt* **cab-baged; cab-bag-ing** : to take surreptitiously : STEAL, FILCH
cabbage butterfly *n* : any of several largely white butterflies (family Pieridae) whose green larvae are cabbageworms; *esp* : a small cosmopolitan butterfly (*Pieris rapae*) that is a universal pest on cabbage
cabbage looper *n* : a moth (*Trichoplusia ni*) whose pale green white-striped larva is a measuring worm that feeds on cruciferous plants (as the cabbage)
cabbage palm *n* : a palm with terminal buds eaten as a vegetable
cabbage palmetto *n* : a fan-leaved cabbage palm (*Sabal palmetto*) native to coastal southern U.S. and the Bahamas
cab-bage-worm \'kab-ij-,wərm\ *n* : an insect larva (as of a cabbage butterfly) that feeds on cabbages
cab-by *or* **cab-bie** \'kab-ē\ *n, pl* **cabbies** : CABDRIVER
cab-driv-er \'kab-,drī-vər\ *n* : a driver of a cab
ca-ber \'käb-ər, 'kä-bər\ *n* [ScGael *cabar*] : POLE; *esp* : a young tree trunk used for tossing as a trial of strength in a Scottish sport
¹**cab-in** \'kab-ən\ *n* [ME *cabane*, fr. MF, fr. OProv *cabana* hut, fr. ML *capanna*] **1 a** : a private room on a ship for one or a few persons — compare CABIN CLASS **b** : a compartment below deck on a small boat for passengers or crew **c** : an airplane or airship compartment for cargo, crew, or passengers **2** : a small one-story dwelling usu. of simple construction **3** *chiefly Brit* : CAB 3 **b** : the part of a passenger trailer used for living quarters
²**cabin** *vi* : to live in or as if in a cabin ~ *vt* : CONFINE
cabin boy *n* : a boy acting as servant on a ship
cabin car *n* : CABOOSE
cabin class *n* : a class of accommodations on a passenger ship superior to tourist class and inferior to first class
cabin cruiser *n* : CRUISER 3
¹**cab-i-net** \'kab-(ə-)nət\ *n* [MF, small room, dim. of ONF *cabine* gambling house] **1 a** : a case or cupboard usu. having doors and shelves **b** : a collection of specimens esp. of mineralogical, biological, or numismatic interest **c** : an upright case housing a radio or television receiver : CONSOLE **d** : a chamber having temperature and humidity controls and used esp. for incubating biological samples **2** *archaic* : a small room providing seclusion **b** : a small exhibition room in a museum **3** *archaic* (1) : the private room serving as council chamber of the chief councillors or ministers of a sovereign (2) : the consultations and actions of these councillors **b** (1) *often cap* : a body of advisers of a head of state (as a sovereign or president) (2) : a similar advisory council of a governor of a state or a mayor **c** *Brit* : a meeting of a cabinet
²**cabinet** *adj* **1** : suitable by reason of size for a small room or by reason of attractiveness or perfection for preservation and display

---

in a cabinet **2 :** of or relating to a governmental cabinet **3 a :** used or adapted for cabinetmaking **b :** done or used by a cabinetmaker

cab·i·net·mak·er \-ˌmā-kər\ *n* **:** a skilled woodworker who makes fine furniture — **cab·i·net·mak·ing** \-ˌmā-kiŋ\ *n*

cab·i·net·work \-ˌwərk\ *n* **:** finished woodwork made by a cabinetmaker

cabin fever *n* **:** extreme irritability and restlessness resulting from the boredom of living in a remote region alone or with only a few companions; *also* **:** the same emotions resulting from living in a small enclosed space

[1]ca·ble \ˈkā-bəl\ *n, often attrib* [ME, fr. ONF, fr. ML *capulum* lasso, fr. L *capere* to take — more at HEAVE] **1 a :** a strong rope esp. of 10 or more inches in circumference **b :** a cable-laid rope **c :** a wire rope or metal chain of great tensile strength **d :** a wire or wire rope by which force is exerted to control or operate a mechanism **2 :** CABLE LENGTH **3 a :** an assembly of electrical conductors insulated from each other but laid up together usu. by being twisted around a central core **b :** CABLEGRAM **4 :** something resembling or fashioned like a cable

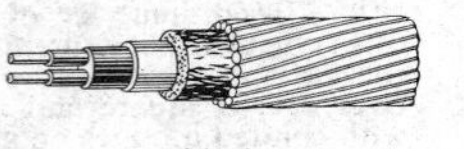

cable 3a

[2]cable *vb* **ca·bled; ca·bling** \ˈkā-b(ə-)liŋ\ *vt* **1 :** to fasten with or as if with a cable **2 :** to provide with cables **3 :** to telegraph by submarine cable **4 :** to make into a cable or into a form resembling a cable ~ *vi* **:** to communicate by a submarine cable

cable car *n* **:** a car made to be moved on a railway by an endless cable operated by a stationary motor or along an overhead cable

ca·ble·gram \ˈkā-bəl-ˌgram\ *n* **:** a message sent by a submarine telegraph cable

ca·ble–laid \ˌkā-bəl-ˈlād\ *adj* **:** composed of three ropes laid together left-handed with each containing three strands twisted together ⟨~ rope⟩

cable length *n* **:** a maritime unit of length variously reckoned as 100 fathoms, 120 fathoms, or 608 feet

ca·blet \ˈkā-blət\ *n* **:** a small cable; *specif* **:** a cable-laid rope less than 10 inches in circumference

cable TV *n* **:** COMMUNITY ANTENNA TELEVISION — called also *cable television*

ca·ble·way \ˈkā-bəl-ˌwā\ *n* **:** a suspended cable used as a track along which carriers can be pulled

cab·man \ˈkab-mən\ *n* **:** CABDRIVER

cab·o·chon \ˈkab-ə-ˌshän\ *n* [MF, aug. of ONF *caboche* head] **:** a gem or bead cut in convex form and highly polished but not faceted; *also* **:** this style of cutting — **cabochon** *adv*

ca·boo·dle \kə-ˈbüd-ᵊl\ *n* [prob. fr. *ca-* (intensive prefix, prob. of imit. origin) + *boodle*] **:** COLLECTION, LOT ⟨sell the whole ~⟩

ca·boose \kə-ˈbüs\ *n* [prob. fr. D *kabuis*, fr. MLG *kabūse*] **1 a :** a ship's galley **b :** an open-air cooking oven **2 :** a freight-train car attached usu. to the rear mainly for the use of the train crew **3 :** one that follows or brings up the rear

cab·o·tage \ˈkab-ə-ˌtäzh\ *n* [F, fr. *caboter* to sail along the coast] **1 :** trade or transport in coastal waters or between two points within a country **2 :** the right to engage in cabotage

ca·bret·ta \kə-ˈbret-ə\ *n* [modif. of Pg and Sp *cabra* goat] **:** a light soft leather from hair sheepskins

ca·bril·la \kə-ˈbrē-(y)ə, -ˈbril-ə\ *n* [Sp, fr. dim. of *cabra* goat, fr. L *capra* she-goat, fem. of *caper* he-goat — more at CAPRIOLE] **:** any of various sea basses of the Mediterranean, the California coast, and the warmer parts of the western Atlantic

cab·ri·ole \ˈkab-rē-ˌōl\ *n* [F, caper] **1 :** a curved furniture leg ending in an ornamental foot **2 :** a ballet leap in which one leg is extended in mid-air and the other struck against it

cab·ri·o·let \ˌkab-rē-ə-ˈlā\ *n* [F, fr. dim. of *cabriole* caper, alter. of MF *capriole*] **1 :** a light 2-wheeled one-horse carriage with a folding leather hood, a large apron, and upward-curving shafts **2 :** a convertible coupe

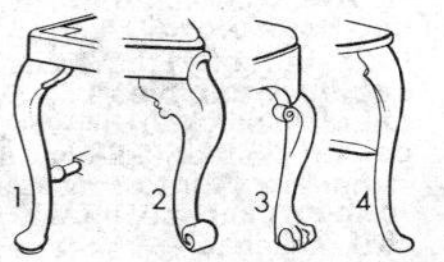

cabrioles 1: *1* early 18th century, *2* mid-18th century, *3* early Georgian, *4* second half of 18th century

cab·stand \ˈkab-ˌstand\ *n* **:** a place where cabs await hire

cac- *or* **caco-** *comb form* [NL, fr. Gk *kak-, kako-*, fr. *kakos* bad] **:** bad ⟨cacogenics⟩

ca' can·ny \kȯ-ˈkan-ē\ *n, Brit* **:** SLOWDOWN — **ca' canny** *vi, Brit*

ca·cao \kə-ˈkau̇, kə-ˈkā-(ˌ)ō\ *n, pl* **cacaos** [Sp, fr. Nahuatl *cacahuatl* cacao beans] **1 :** a So. American tree (*Theobroma cacao* of the family Sterculiaceae) with small yellowish flowers followed by fleshy yellow pods with many seeds — called also *chocolate tree* **2 :** the dried partly fermented fatty seeds of the cacao used in making cocoa, chocolate, and cocoa butter — called also *cacao bean, cocoa bean*

cacao butter *var of* COCOA BUTTER

cac·cia·to·re \ˌkäch-ə-ˈtōr-ē, -ˈtȯr-\ *adj* [It, fr. *cacciatore* hunter] **:** cooked with tomatoes and herbs and sometimes with wine ⟨veal ~⟩

cach·a·lot \ˈkash-ə-ˌlät, -ˌlō\ *n* [F] **:** SPERM WHALE

[1]cache \ˈkash\ *n* [F, fr. *cacher* to press, hide, fr. (assumed) VL *coacticare* to press together, fr. L *coactare* to compel, fr. *coactus*, pp. of *cogere* to compel — more at COGENT] **1 a :** a hiding place esp. for concealing and preserving provisions or implements **b :** a secure place of storage **2 :** something hidden or stored in a cache

[2]cache *vt* **cached; cach·ing :** to place, hide, or store in a cache

ca·chec·tic \kə-ˈkek-tik, ka-\ *adj* [F *cachectique*, fr. L *cachecticus*, fr. Gk *kachektikos*, fr. *kak-* + *echein*] **:** affected by cachexia

cache·pot \ˈkash-ˌpät, ˈkash-(ə-)ˌpō\ *n* [F, fr. *cacher* to hide + *pot* pot] **:** an ornamental receptacle to hold and usu. to conceal a flowerpot

ca·chet \ka-ˈshā\ *n* [MF, fr. *cacher* to press, hide] **1 a :** a seal used esp. as a mark of official approval **b :** an indication of approval carrying great prestige **2 a :** a characteristic feature or quality conferring prestige **b :** PRESTIGE **3 :** a flour-paste case in which an unpleasant medicine is swallowed **4 a :** a design or inscription on an envelope to commemorate a postal or philatelic event **b :** an advertisement forming part of a postal meter impression **c :** a motto or slogan included in a postal cancellation

ca·chex·ia \kə-ˈkek-sē-ə, ka-\ *also* **ca·chexy** \kə-ˈkek-sē, ka-; ˈkak-ˌek-\ *n* [LL *cachexia*, fr. Gk *kachexia* bad condition, fr. *kak-* cac- + *hexis* condition, fr. *echein* to have, be disposed — more at SCHEME] **:** general physical wasting and malnutrition usu. associated with chronic disease

cach·in·nate \ˈkak-ə-ˌnāt\ *vi* **-nat·ed; -nat·ing** [L *cachinnatus*, pp. of *cachinnare*, of imit. origin] **:** to laugh loudly or immoderately — **cach·in·na·tion** \ˌkak-ə-ˈnā-shən\ *n*

ca·chou \ka-ˈshü, ˈkash-(ˌ)ü\ *n* [F, fr. Pg *cachu*, fr. Malayalam *kāccu*] **1 :** CATECHU **2 :** a pill or pastille used to sweeten the breath

ca·chu·cha \kə-ˈchü-chə\ *n* [Sp, small boat, cachucha] **:** a gay Andalusian solo dance in triple time done with castanets

ca·cique \kə-ˈsēk\ *n* [Sp, of Arawakan origin; akin to Taino *cacique* chief] **1 a :** a native Indian chief in areas dominated primarily by a Spanish culture **b :** a local political boss in Spain and Latin America **2** [AmerSp, fr. Sp] **:** any of numerous tropical American orioles (as of the genus *Cacicus*) having the base of the bill expanded into a frontal shield — **ca·ciqu·ism** \-ˈsē-ˌkiz-əm\ *n*

cack·le \ˈkak-əl\ *vi* **cack·led; cack·ling** \-(ə-)liŋ\ [ME *cakelen*, of imit. origin] **1 :** to make the sharp broken noise or cry characteristic of a hen esp. after laying **2 :** to laugh in a way suggestive of a hen's cackle **3 :** CHATTER — **cackle** *n* — **cack·ler** \-(ə-)lər\ *n*

caco·de·mon \ˌkak-ə-ˈdē-mən\ *n* [Gk *kakodaimōn*, fr. *kak-* cac- + *daimōn* spirit] **:** DEMON — **caco·de·mon·ic** \-di-ˈmän-ik\ *adj*

cac·o·dyl \ˈkak-ə-ˌdil\ *n* [ISV, fr. Gk *kakōdēs* ill smelling, fr. *kak-* + *-ōdēs* (akin to Gk *ozein* to smell) — more at ODOR] **1 :** an arsenical radical $As(CH_3)_2$ whose compounds have a vile smell and are usu. poisonous **2 :** a colorless liquid $As_2(CH_3)_4$ consisting of two cacodyl radicals

cac·o·dyl·ic acid \ˌkak-ə-ˌdil-ik-\ *n* **:** a toxic crystalline compound of arsenic $C_2H_7AsO_2$ used esp. as an herbicide

caco·ë·thes \ˌkak-ə-ˈwē-(ˌ)thēz\ *n* [L, fr. Gk *kakoēthes* wickedness, fr. neut. of *kakoēthēs* malignant, fr. *kak-* cac- + *ēthos* character — more at ETHICAL] **:** an insatiable desire **:** MANIA

caco·gen·e·sis \ˌkak-ə-ˈjen-ə-səs\ *n* [NL] **:** racial deterioration esp. when due to the retention of inferior breeding stock — **caco·gen·ic** \-ˈjen-ik\ *adj*

caco·gen·ics \-ˈjen-iks\ *n pl but sing or pl in constr* [*cac-* + *-genics* (as in *eugenics*)] **1 :** DYSGENICS **2 :** CACOGENESIS

ca·cog·ra·phy \ka-ˈkäg-rə-fē\ *n* **1 :** bad handwriting — compare CALLIGRAPHY **2 :** bad spelling — compare ORTHOGRAPHY — **caco·graph·i·cal** \ˌkak-ə-ˈgraf-i-kəl\ *adj*

cac·o·mis·tle \ˈkak-ə-ˌmis-əl, ˌkak-ə-ˈmis(t)-lē\ *n* [MexSp, fr. Nahuatl *tlacomiztli*, fr. *tlaco* half + *miztli* mountain lion] **:** a carnivore (*Bassariscus astutus*) related to and resembling the raccoon; *also* **:** its fur or pelt

ca·coph·o·nous \ka-ˈkäf-ə-nəs\ *adj* [Gk *kakophōnos*, fr. *kak-* + *phōnē* voice, sound — more at BAN] **:** marked by cacophony **:** harsh-sounding — **ca·coph·o·nous·ly** *adv*

ca·coph·o·ny \-nē\ *n, pl* **-nies :** harsh or discordant sound **:** DISSONANCE; *specif* **:** harshness in the sound of words or phrases

cac·tus \ˈkak-təs\ *n, pl* **cac·ti** \-ˌtī, -(ˌ)tē\ *or* **cac·tus·es** [NL, genus name, fr. L, cardoon, fr. Gk *kaktos*] **:** any of a family (Cactaceae, the cactus family) of plants that have fleshy stems and branches with scales or spines instead of leaves and are found esp. in dry areas (as deserts)

ca·cu·mi·nal \ka-ˈkyü-mən-ᵊl, kə-\ *adj* [ISV, fr. L *cacumin-, cacumen* top, point] **:** RETROFLEX

cad \ˈkad\ *n* [E dial., unskilled assistant, short for Sc *caddie*] **1** *obs* **:** an omnibus conductor **2 :** a person without gentlemanly instincts

ca·das·tral \kə-ˈdas-trəl\ *adj* **1 :** of or relating to a cadastre **2 :** showing or recording property boundaries, subdivision lines, buildings, and related details — **ca·das·tral·ly** \-trə-lē\ *adv*

ca·das·tre \kə-ˈdas-tər\ *n* [F, fr. It *catastro*, fr. OIt *catastico*, fr. LGk *katastichon* notebook, fr. Gk *kata* by + *stichos* row, line — more at CATA-, DISTICH] **:** an official register of the quantity, value, and ownership of real estate used in apportioning taxes

ca·dav·er \kə-ˈdav-ər\ *n* [L, fr. *cadere* to fall] **:** a dead body usu. intended for dissection — **ca·dav·er·ic** \-(ə-)rik\ *adj*

ca·dav·er·ine \kə-ˈdav-ə-ˌrēn\ *n* **:** a syrupy colorless poisonous ptomaine $C_5H_{14}N_2$ formed by decarboxylation of lysine esp. in putrefaction of flesh

ca·dav·er·ous \kə-ˈdav-(ə-)rəs\ *adj* **1 a :** of or relating to a corpse **b :** suggestive of corpses or tombs **2 a :** PALLID, LIVID **b :** GAUNT, EMACIATED — **ca·dav·er·ous·ly** *adv*

cad·die *or* **cad·dy** \ˈkad-ē\ *n, pl* **caddies** [F *cadet* military cadet] **1** *Scot* **:** one that waits about for odd jobs **2 a :** one that assists a golfer esp. by carrying his clubs **b :** a wheeled device for conveying things not readily carried by hand — **caddie** *or* **caddy** *vi*

[1]cad·dis *also* **cad·dice** \ˈkad-əs\ *n* [ME *cadas* cotton wool, prob. fr. MF *cadaz*, fr. OProv *cadarz*] **:** worsted yarn; *specif* **:** a worsted ribbon or binding formerly used for garters and girdles

[2]caddis *or* **caddice** *n* **:** CADDISWORM

caddis fly *n* **:** any of an order (Trichoptera) of insects with four membranous wings, vestigial mouthparts, slender many-jointed antennae, and aquatic larvae — compare CADDISWORM

cad·dish \ˈkad-ish\ *adj* **:** resembling a cad — **cad·dish·ly** *adv* — **cad·dish·ness** *n*

cad·dis·worm \ˈkad-ə-ˌswərm\ *n* [prob. alter. of obs. *codworm*; fr. the case or tube in which it lives] **:** the larva of a caddis fly that lives in and carries around a silken case covered with bits of debris

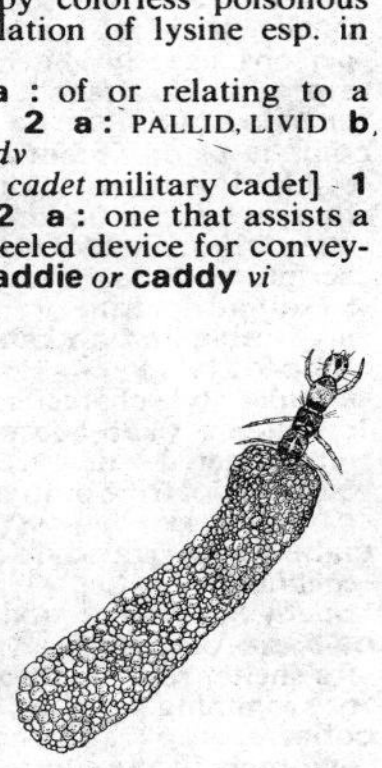

caddisworm

Cad·do \'kad-(,)ō\ *n, pl* **Caddo** *or* **Caddos** : a member of an Amerindian people ranging from No. Dakota south to Texas

cad·dy \'kad-ē\ *n, pl* **caddies** [Malay *kati* catty] **1** : a small box, can, or chest used esp. to keep tea in **2** : a container or device for storing or holding objects when they are not in use

¹cade \'kād\ *adj* [E dial. *cade* pet lamb, fr. ME *cad*] : left by its mother and reared by hand : PET ⟨a ~ lamb⟩ ⟨a ~ colt⟩

²cade \'kād\ *n* [MF, fr. OProv, fr. ML *catanus*] : a European juniper (*Juniperus oxycedrus*) whose wood yields by distillation a dark tarry liquid used locally in treating skin diseases

-cade \,kād, 'kād\ *n comb form* [cavalcade] : procession ⟨motorcade⟩

ca·delle \kə-'del\ *n* [F, fr. Prov *cadello*, fr. L *catella*, dim. of *catulus* young animal] : a small cosmopolitan black beetle (*Tenebroides mauritanicus*) destructive to stored grain

ca·dence \'kād-ᵊn(t)s\ *n* [ME, fr. OIt *cadenza*, fr. *cadere* to fall, fr. L — more at CHANCE] **1 a** : a rhythmic sequence or flow of sounds in language **b** : the beat, time, or measure of rhythmical motion or activity **2 a** : a falling inflection of the voice **b** : a concluding and usu. falling strain; *specif* : a musical chord sequence moving to a harmonic close or point of rest and giving the sense of harmonic completion **3** : the modulated and rhythmic recurrence of a sound esp. in nature — **ca·denced** \-ᵊn(t)st\ *adj* — **ca·den·tial** \kā-'den-chəl\ *adj*

ca·den·cy \'kād-ᵊn-sē\ *n* : CADENCE

ca·dent \'kād-ᵊnt\ *adj* [L *cadent-, cadens*, prp. of *cadere*] **1** *archaic* : being in the process of falling ⟨with ~ tears fret channels in her cheeks—Shak.⟩ **2** : having rhythmic fall

ca·den·za \kə-'den-zə\ *n* [It, cadence, cadenza] **1** : a parenthetic flourish in an aria or other solo piece commonly just before a final or other important cadence **2** : a technically brilliant sometimes improvised solo passage toward the close of a concerto

ca·det \kə-'det\ *n, often attrib* [F, fr. F dial. *capdet* chief, fr. LL *capitellum*, dim. of L *capit-, caput* head — more at HEAD] **1 a** : a younger brother or son **b** : youngest son **c** : a younger branch of a family or a member of it **2** : one in training for a military or naval commission; *esp* : a student in a service academy **3** : a junior in a business or occupation who is engaged principally in learning **4** *slang* : PIMP — **ca·det·ship** \-,ship\ *n*

Cadette scout \kə-,det-\ *n* [fr. *cadet*, after such pairs as F *brunet* male brunet: *brunette* female brunet] : a member of the Girl Scouts from 12 through 14 years of age

cadge \'kaj\ *vb* **cadged; cadg·ing** [back-formation fr. Sc *cadger* carrier, huckster, fr. ME *cadgear*, fr. *caggen* to tie] : BEG, SPONGE — **cadg·er** *n*

cad·mi·um \'kad-mē-əm\ *n* [NL, fr. L *cadmia* calamine; fr. the occurrence of its ores together with calamine — more at CALAMINE] : a bluish white malleable ductile toxic bivalent metallic element used esp. in protective platings and in bearing metals — see ELEMENT table

Cad·mus \'kad-məs\ *n* [L, fr. Gk *Kadmos*] : the legendary founder of Thebes

CADO *abbr* Central Air Documents Office

cad·re \'kad-rē, 'kä-drē\ *n* [F, fr. It *quadro*, fr. L *quadrum* square — more at QUARREL] **1** : FRAME, FRAMEWORK **2** : a nucleus esp. of trained personnel capable of assuming control and of training others

ca·du·ceus \kə-'d(y)ü-sē-əs, -shəs\ *n, pl* **-cei** \-sē-ī\ [L, modif. of Gk *karykeion*, fr. *karyx, kēryx* herald; akin to OE *hrēth* glory] **1** : the symbolic staff of a herald; *specif* : a representation of a staff with two entwined snakes and two wings at the top **2** : an insignia bearing a caduceus and symbolizing a physician — **ca·du·cean** \-sē-ən, -shən\ *adj*

ca·du·ci·ty \kə-'d(y)ü-sət-ē\ *n* [F *caducité*, fr. *caduc* transitory, fr. L *caducus*] **1** : the quality of being transitory or perishable **2** : SENILITY

ca·du·cous \kə-'d(y)ü-kəs\ *adj* [L *caducus* tending to fall, transitory, fr. *cadere* to fall — more at CHANCE] : falling off easily or before the usual time — used esp. of floral organs

cae·cal, cae·cum *var of* CECAL, CECUM

cae·ci·lian \si-'sil-yən, -'sēl-, -ē-ən\ *n* [deriv. of L *caecilia*, a lizard, fr. *caecus* blind] : any of an order (Gymnophiona) of chiefly tropical burrowing amphibians resembling worms — **caecilian** *adj*

caen- *or* **caeno-** *var of* CEN-

Caer·phil·ly \kär-'fil-ē\ *n* [*Caerphilly*, urban district in Wales] : a mild white whole-milk Welsh cheese

Cae·sar \'sē-zər\ *n* [Gaius Julius *Caesar*] **1** : any of the Roman emperors succeeding Augustus Caesar — used as a title **2 a** *often not cap* : a powerful ruler: (1) : EMPEROR (2) : AUTOCRAT, DICTATOR **b** [fr. the reference in Mt 22:21] : the civil power : a temporal ruler

caesarean *or* **caesarian** *often cap, var of* CESAREAN

Cae·sar·ism \'sē-zə-,riz-əm\ *n* : imperial authority or system : political absolutism : DICTATORSHIP — **Cae·sar·ist** \-zə-rəst\ *n*

Caesar salad \,sē-zər-\ *n* [*Caesar's*, restaurant in Tijuana, Mexico] : a tossed salad made typically with romaine, garlic, anchovies, and croutons and served with a dressing of olive oil, coddled egg, lemon juice, and grated cheese

cae·si·um *var of* CESIUM

caes·pi·tose \'ses-pə-,tōs\ *adj* [NL *caespitosus*, fr. L *caespit-, caespes* turf] **1** : forming a dense turf **2** : growing in clusters or tufts

cae·su·ra \si-'z(h)ür-ə\ *n, pl* **-suras** \-'z(h)úr(-ə)r-(,)ēᵊ\ [LL, fr. L, act of cutting, fr. *caedere* to cut — more at CONCISE] **1** *in Greek and Latin prosody* : a break in the flow of sound in a verse caused by the ending of a word within a foot **2** *in modern prosody* : a usu. rhetorical break in the flow of sound in the middle of a line of verse **3** : BREAK, INTERRUPTION **4** : a pause marking a rhythmic point of division in a melody — **cae·su·ral** \-'z(h)úr-əl\ *adj*

CAF *abbr* cost and freight

ca·fé *also* **ca·fe** \ka-'fā, kə-\ *n, often attrib* [F *café* coffee, café, fr. Turk *kahve* — more at COFFEE] **1** : COFFEE **2** : RESTAURANT **3** : BARROOM **4** : CABARET, NIGHTCLUB

ca·fé au lait \(,)ka-,fā-ō-'lā\ *n* [F, coffee with milk] **1** : coffee with usu. hot milk in about equal parts **2** : the color of coffee with milk

ca·fé noir \(,)ka-,fān-(ə-)'wär\ *n* [F, black coffee] : coffee without milk or cream; *also* : DEMITASSE

caf·e·te·ria \,kaf-ə-'tir-ē-ə\ *n* [AmerSp *cafetería* retail coffee store, fr. Sp *café* coffee] : a restaurant in which the customers serve themselves or are served at a counter and take the food to tables to eat

caf·e·to·ri·um \-'tōr-ē-əm, -'tór-\ *n* [blend of *cafeteria* and *auditorium*] : a large room (as in a school building) designed for use both as a cafeteria and an auditorium

caf·feine \ka-'fēn, 'ka-,\ *n* [G *kaffein*, fr. *kaffee* coffee, fr. F *café*] : a bitter compound $C_8H_{10}N_4O_2$ found esp. in coffee, tea, and kola nuts and used medicinally as a stimulant and diuretic — **caf·fein·ic** \ka-'fē-nik, ,kaf-ē-'in-ik\ *adj*

caf·tan \kaf-'tan, 'kaf-,\ *n* [Russ *kaftan*, fr. Turk, fr. Per *qaftān*] : a usu. cotton or silk ankle-length garment with long sleeves that is common throughout the Levant

¹cage \'kāj\ *n* [ME, fr. OF, fr. L *cavea* cavity, cage, fr. *cavus* hollow — more at CAVE] **1 a** : a box or enclosure having some openwork for confining or carrying animals (as birds) **2 a** : a barred cell for confining prisoners **b** : a fenced area for prisoners of war **3** : a framework serving as support ⟨the steel ~ of a skyscraper⟩ **4** : an enclosure resembling a cage in form or purpose **5 a** : a screen placed behind home plate to stop baseballs during batting practice **b** : a goal structure consisting of posts or a frame with a net attached (as in ice hockey) **c** : FIELD HOUSE 2; *also* : a basketball court **6** : a large building with unobstructed area for practicing outdoor sports and often adapted for indoor events **7** : a sheer one-piece dress that has no waistline, is often gathered at the neck, and is worn over a close-fitting underdress or slip

²cage *vt* **caged; cag·ing** **1** : to confine or keep in or as if in a cage **2** : to put (as a puck) into a cage and score a goal

cage bird *n* : a bird adaptable to being kept in a cage

cage·ling \'kāj-liŋ\ *n* : a caged bird

ca·gey *also* **ca·gy** \'kā-jē\ *adj* **ca·gi·er; -est** [origin unknown] **1** : hesitant about committing oneself **2** : wary of being trapped or deceived : SHREWD — **ca·gi·ly** \-jə-lē\ *adv* — **ca·gi·ness** *also* **ca·gey·ness** \-jē-nəs\ *n*

CAGS *abbr* Certificate of Advanced Graduate Study

ca·hier \kä-'yā, ki-'ā\ *n* [F, fr. MF *quaer, caier* quire — more at QUIRE] **1** : a report or memorial concerning policy esp. of a parliamentary body **2** : a number of sheets of paper put together for binding or bound loosely

ca·hoot \kə-'hüt\ *n* [perh. fr. F *cahute* cabin, hut] : PARTNERSHIP, LEAGUE — usu. used in pl. ⟨in ~s with the devil⟩

ca·how \kə-'haú\ *n* [imit.] : a brown-and-white earth-burrowing nocturnal bird (*Pterodroma cahow*) formerly abundant in Bermuda but now nearly extinct

CAI *abbr* computer-aided instruction; computer-assisted instruction

cai·man \'kā-mən; kā-'man, kī-\ *n* [Sp *caimán*, prob. fr. Carib *caymán*] : any of several Central and So. American crocodilians similar to alligators but often superficially resembling crocodiles

Cain \'kān\ *n* [Heb *Qayin*] : the brother and murderer of Abel

-caine \,kān, 'kān\ *n comb form* [G *-kain*, fr. *kokain* cocaine] : synthetic alkaloid anesthetic ⟨*procaine*⟩

ca·ique \kä-'ēk, 'kīk\ *n* [Turk *kayık*] **1** : a light skiff used on the Bosporus **2** : a Levantine sailing vessel

caird \'ke(ə)rd\ *n* [ScGael *ceard*; akin to Gk *kerdos* profit] *Scot* : a traveling tinker : TRAMP, GYPSY

cairn \'ka(ə)rn, 'ke(ə)rn\ *n* [ME *carne*, fr. ScGael *carn*; akin to OIr & W *carn* cairn] : a heap of stones piled up as a memorial or as a landmark — **cairned** \'ka(ə)rnd, 'ke(ə)rnd\ *adj*

cairn·gorm \'ka(ə)rn-,gó(ə)rm, 'ke(ə)rn-\ *n* [*Cairngorm*, mountain in Scotland] : a yellow or smoky-brown crystalline quartz

cairn terrier *n* [fr. its use in hunting among cairns] : a small compactly built hard-coated terrier of Scottish origin

cais·son \'kā-,sän, 'käs-ᵊn\ *n* [F, aug. of *caisse* box, fr. OProv *caissa*, fr. L *capsa* chest, case — more at CASE] **1 a** : a chest to hold ammunition **b** : a usu. 2-wheeled vehicle for artillery ammunition attachable to a horse-drawn limber **2 a** : a watertight chamber used in construction work under water or as a foundation **b** : a float for raising a sunken vessel **c** : a hollow floating box or a boat used as a floodgate for a dock or basin **3** : COFFER 4

caisson 1b

caisson disease *n* : a sometimes fatal disorder that is marked by neuralgic pains and paralysis, distress in breathing, and often collapse and that is caused by the release of gas bubbles in tissue upon too rapid decrease in air pressure after a stay in a compressed atmosphere — called also *bends*

Caith *abbr* Caithness

cai·tiff \'kāt-əf\ *adj* [ME *caitif*, fr. ONF, captive, vile, fr. L *captivus* captive] : being base, cowardly, or despicable — **caitiff** *n*

ca·jole \kə-'jōl\ *vt* **ca·joled; ca·jol·ing** [F *cajoler* to chatter like a jay in a cage, cajole, alter. of MF *gaioler*, fr. ONF *gaiole* birdcage, fr. LL *caveola*, dim. of L *cavea* cage — more at CAGE] **1 :** to persuade with deliberate flattery esp. in the face of reluctance ⟨the women ~ their husbands into giving them a vote —Kathleen Karr⟩ **2 :** to deceive with soothing words or false promises — **ca·jole·ment** \-'jōl-mənt\ *n* — **ca·jol·er** *n* — **ca·jol·ery** \-'jōl-(ə-)rē\ *n*

Ca·jun *also* **Ca·jan** \'kā-jən\ *n* [by alter. of *Acadian*] **1 :** ACADIAN 2a **2** *usu* *Cajan* **:** one of a people of mixed white, Indian, and Negro ancestry in southwest Alabama and southeast Mississippi

¹cake \'kāk\ *n* [ME, fr. ON *kaka;* akin to OHG *kuocho* cake] **1 a :** batter that may be fried or baked into a usu. small round flat shape **b :** sweet batter or dough usu. containing a leaven (as baking powder) that is first baked and then often coated with an icing **c :** a flattened usu. round mass of food that is baked or fried ⟨a codfish ~⟩ **2 a :** a block of compacted or congealed matter ⟨a ~ of ice⟩ **b :** a hard or brittle layer or deposit ⟨~ formed in a smoker's pipe⟩

²cake *vb* **caked; cak·ing** *vt* **1 :** ENCRUST ⟨*caked* with dust⟩ **2 :** to fill (a space) with a packed mass ~ *vi* **:** to form or harden into a mass

cake·walk \'kā-,kwȯk\ *n* **1 :** an American Negro entertainment having a cake as prize for the most accomplished steps and figures in walking **2 :** a stage dance developed from walking steps and figures typically involving a high prance with backward tilt **3 :** a one-sided contest — **cakewalk** *vi* — **cake·walk·er** *n*

cal *abbr* **1** calendar **2** caliber **3** calorie

Cal *abbr* **1** California **2** large calorie

Cal·a·bar bean \,kal-ə-,bär-\ *n* [*Calabar*, Nigeria] **:** the dark brown highly poisonous seed of a tropical African woody vine (*Physostigma venenosum*) that is used as a source of physostigmine and as an ordeal poison in native witchcraft trials

cal·a·bash \'kal-ə-,bash\ *n* [F & Sp; F *calebasse* gourd, fr. Sp *calabaza*, prob. fr. Ar *qar'ah yābisah* dry gourd] **1 :** GOURD; *esp* **:** one whose hard shell is used for a utensil (as a bottle) **2 :** a tropical American tree (*Crescentia cujete*) of the trumpet-creeper family; *also* **:** its hard globose fruit **3 :** a utensil made from the shell of a calabash

cal·a·boose \'kal-ə-,büs\ *n* [Sp *calabozo* dungeon] *dial* **:** JAIL; *esp* **:** a local jail

ca·la·di·um \kə-'lād-ē-əm\ *n* [NL, genus name, fr. Malay *kĕladi*, an aroid plant] **:** any of a genus (*Caladium*, esp. *C. bicolor*) of tropical American ornamental plants of the arum family with showy variously colored leaves

cal·a·man·der \'kal-ə-,man-dər, ,kal-ə-'\ *n* [prob. fr. D *kalamanderhout* calamander wood] **:** the hazel-brown black-striped wood of an East Indian tree (genus *Diospyros*, esp. *D. quaesita*) that is used in furniture manufacturing

cal·a·mary \'kal-ə-,mer-ē\ *or* **cal·a·mar** \-,mär\ *n, pl* **-maries** *or* **-mars** [L *calamarius* of a pen, fr. *calamus* reed; fr. the shape of its inner shell] **:** SQUID

cal·a·mine \'kal-ə-,mīn, -mən\ *n* [F, ore of zinc, fr. ML *calamina*, alter. of L *cadmia*, fr. Gk *kadmeia*, lit., Theban (earth), fr. fem. of *kadmeios* Theban, fr. *Kadmos* Cadmus, founder of Thebes] **:** a mixture of zinc oxide with a small amount of ferric oxide used in lotions, liniments, and ointments

cal·a·mint \'kal-ə-,mint\ *n* [ME *calament*, fr. OF, fr. ML *calamentum*, fr. Gk *kalaminthē*] **:** any of a genus (*Satureja*, esp. *S. calamintha*) of mints — called also *basil thyme*

cal·a·mite \'kal-ə-,mīt\ *n* [NL *Calamites*, genus of fossil plants, fr. L *calamus*] **:** a Paleozoic fossil plant (esp. genus *Calamites*) resembling a giant horsetail

ca·lam·i·tous \kə-'lam-ət-əs\ *adj* **:** causing or accompanied by calamity — **ca·lam·i·tous·ly** *adv* — **ca·lam·i·tous·ness** *n*

ca·lam·i·ty \kə-'lam-ət-ē\ *n, pl* **-ties** [MF *calamité*, fr. L *calamitat-*, *calamitas;* akin to L *clades* destruction — more at HALT] **1 :** a state of deep distress or misery caused by major misfortune or loss **2 :** an extraordinarily grave event marked by great loss and lasting distress and affliction ***syn*** see DISASTER

cal·a·mon·din \,kal-ə-'män-dən\ *n* [Tag *kalamundíng*] **:** a small spiny citrus tree (*Citrus mitis*) of the Philippines; *also* **:** its fruit

cal·a·mus \'kal-ə-məs\ *n, pl* **-mi** \-,mī, -,mē\ [L, reed, reed pen, fr. Gk *kalamos* — more at HAULM] **1 a :** SWEET FLAG **b :** the aromatic peeled and dried rhizome of the calamus that is the source of a carcinogenic essential oil **2 :** the barrel of a feather **:** QUILL

ca·lash \kə-'lash\ *n* [F *calèche*, fr. G *kalesche*, fr. Czech *kolesa* wheels, carriage; akin to Gk *kyklos* wheel — more at WHEEL] **1 a :** a light small-wheeled 4-passenger carriage with a folding top **b :** CALÈCHE 2 **2 a :** a large hood worn by women in the 18th century **b :** a folding carriage top

cal·a·thos \'kal-ə-,thäs\ *or* **cal·a·thus** \-thəs\ *n, pl* **-thi** \-,thī, -,thē\ [Gk *kalathos* basket] **:** a flared fruit basket borne on the head as a symbol of fruitfulness in Greek and Egyptian art

calc *abbr* calculate; calculated

calc- *or* **calci-** *or* **calco-** *comb form* [L *calc-*, *calx* lime — more at CHALK] **:** calcium **:** calcium salt ⟨calcic⟩ ⟨calcify⟩

cal·ca·ne·al \kal-'kā-nē-əl\ *adj* **:** relating to the heel or calcaneus

cal·ca·ne·um \-nē-əm\ *n, pl* **-nea** \-nē-ə\ [L, heel — more at CALK] **1 :** CALCANEUS **2 :** a process of the tarsometatarsus of a bird analogous to the calcaneus

cal·ca·ne·us \-nē-əs\ *n, pl* **-nei** \-nē-,ī\ [LL, heel, alter. of L *calcaneum*] **:** a tarsal bone that in man is the great bone of the heel

cal·car \'kal-,kär\ *n, pl* **cal·car·ia** \kal-'kar-ē-ə, -'ker-\ [L, fr. *calc-*, *calx* heel — more at CALK] **:** a spurred prominence (as of the calcaneum of a bat)

cal·car·e·ous \kal-'kar-ē-əs, -'ker-\ *adj* [L *calcarius* of lime, fr. *calc-*, *calx* lime] **1 a :** resembling calcite or calcium carbonate esp. in hardness **b :** consisting of or containing calcium carbonate; *also* **:** containing calcium **2 :** growing on limestone or in soil impregnated with lime — **cal·car·e·ous·ly** *adv* — **cal·car·e·ous·ness** *n*

cal·ce·o·lar·ia \,kal-sē-ə-'lar-ē-ə, -'ler-\ *n* [NL, genus name, fr. L *calceolus* small shoe, dim. of *calceus* shoe, fr. *calc-*, *calx* heel] **:** any of a genus (*Calceolaria*) of tropical American plants of the snapdragon family with showy pouch-shaped flowers

calces *pl of* CALX

cal·cic \'kal-sik\ *adj* **:** derived from or containing calcium or lime **:** rich in calcium

cal·ci·cole \'kal-sə-,kōl\ *n* [F, calcicolous, fr. *calc-* + *-cole* -colous] **:** a plant normally growing on calcareous soils — **cal·cic·o·lous** \kal-'sik-ə-ləs\ *adj*

cal·cif·er·ol \kal-'sif-ə-,rȯl, -,rōl\ *n* [blend of *calciferous* + *ergosterol*] **:** VITAMIN D_2

cal·cif·er·ous \kal-'sif-(ə-)rəs\ *adj* **:** producing or containing calcium carbonate

cal·cif·ic \kal-'sif-ik\ *adj* [*calcify*] **:** involving or caused by calcification ⟨~ lesions⟩

cal·ci·fi·ca·tion \,kal-sə-fə-'kā-shən\ *n* **1 :** the process of calcifying; *specif* **:** deposition of insoluble lime salts (as in tissue) **2 :** a calcified structure

cal·ci·fuge \'kal-sə-,fyüj\ *n* [F, calcifugous, fr. *calc-* + L *fugere* to flee — more at FUGITIVE] **:** a plant not normally growing on calcareous soils — **cal·cif·u·gous** \kal-'sif-yə-gəs\ *adj*

cal·ci·fy \'kal-sə-,fī\ *vb* **-fied; -fy·ing** *vt* **1 :** to make calcareous by deposit of calcium salts **2 :** to make inflexible or unchangeable ~ *vi* **1 :** to become calcareous **2 :** to become inflexible and changeless **:** HARDEN

cal·ci·mine \'kal-sə-,mīn\ *n* [alter. of *kalsomine*, of unknown origin] **:** a white or tinted wash that consists of glue, whiting or zinc white, and water and that is used esp. on plastered surfaces — **calcimine** *vt*

cal·ci·na·tion \,kal-sə-'nā-shən\ *n* **:** the act or process of calcining **:** the state of being calcined

¹cal·cine \kal-'sīn, 'kal-,\ *vb* **cal·cined; cal·cin·ing** [ME *calcenen*, fr. MF *calciner*, fr. L *calc-*, *calx* lime — more at CHALK] *vt* **:** to heat (as inorganic materials) to a high temperature but without fusing in order to drive off volatile matter or to effect changes (as oxidation or pulverization) ~ *vi* **:** to undergo calcination

²cal·cine \'kal-,sīn\ *n* **:** a product (as a metal oxide) of calcination or roasting

cal·ci·no·sis \,kal-sə-'nō-səs\ *n, pl* **-no·ses** \-,sēz\ [NL, irreg. (influenced by ISV *calcine*) fr. *calc-* + *-osis*] **:** the abnormal deposition of calcium salts in a part or tissue of the body

cal·ci·phy·lax·is \,kal-sə-fə-'lak-səs\ *n, pl* **-lax·es** \-,sēz\ [NL, fr. *calc-* + ana*phylaxis*] **:** an adaptive response that follows systemic sensitization by a calcifying factor (as a vitamin D) and a challenge (as with a metallic salt) and that involves local inflammation and sclerosis with calcium deposition — **cal·ci·phy·lac·tic** \-'lak-tik\ *adj* — **cal·ci·phy·lac·ti·cal·ly** \-ti-k(ə-)lē\ *adv*

cal·cite \'kal-,sīt\ *n* **:** a mineral $CaCO_3$ consisting of calcium carbonate crystallized in hexagonal form and including common limestone, chalk, and marble — **cal·cit·ic** \kal-'sit-ik\ *adj*

cal·ci·to·nin \,kal-sə-'tō-nən\ *n* [*calci-* + ¹*tonic* + *-in*] **:** THYROCALCITONIN

cal·ci·um \'kal-sē-əm\ *n, often attrib* [NL, fr. L *calc-*, *calx* lime] **:** a silver-white bivalent metallic element of the alkaline-earth group occurring only in combination — see ELEMENT table

calcium carbide *n* **:** a usu. dark gray crystalline compound CaC_2 used esp. for the generation of acetylene and for making calcium cyanamide

calcium carbonate *n* **:** a compound $CaCO_3$ found in nature as calcite and aragonite and in plant ashes, bones, and shells and used in making lime and portland cement

calcium chloride *n* **:** a white deliquescent salt $CaCl_2$ used in its anhydrous state as a drying and dehumidifying agent and in a hydrated state for controlling dust and ice on roads

calcium cyanamide *n* **:** a compound $CaCN_2$ used as a fertilizer and a weed killer and as a source of other nitrogen compounds

calcium hypochlorite *n* **:** a white powder $CaCl_2O_2$ used esp. as a bleaching agent and disinfectant

calcium light *n* **:** LIMELIGHT 1a, 1b

calcium phosphate *n* **:** any of various phosphates of calcium: as **a :** the phosphate $CaH_4P_2O_8$ used as a fertilizer and in baking powder **b :** the phosphate $CaHPO_4$ used in pharmaceutical preparations and animal feeds **c :** the phosphate $Ca_3P_2O_8$ used as a fertilizer **d :** a naturally occurring phosphate of calcium $Ca_5(F,Cl,OH,{}^1/_2CO_3)(PO_4)_3$ that contains other elements or radicals and is the chief constituent of phosphate rock, bones, and teeth

calcium silicate *n* **:** any of several silicates of calicum; *esp* **:** either of two Ca_3SiO_5 or Ca_2SiO_4 that are essential constituents of portland cement

calc·spar \'kalk-,spär\ *n* [part trans. of Sw *kalkspat*, fr. *kalk* lime + *spat* spar] **:** CALCITE

cal·cu·la·bil·i·ty \,kal-kyə-lə-'bil-ət-ē\ *n* **:** the quality of being calculable

cal·cu·la·ble \'kal-kyə-lə-bəl\ *adj* **1 :** subject to or ascertainable by calculation **2 :** that may be counted on **:** DEPENDABLE ⟨a systematic man, as ~ as the stars⟩ — **cal·cu·la·ble·ness** *n* — **cal·cu·la·bly** \-blē\ *adv*

cal·cu·late \'kal-kyə-,lāt\ *vb* **-lat·ed; -lat·ing** [L *calculatus*, pp. of *calculare*, fr. *calculus* pebble (used in reckoning), dim. of *calc-*, *calx* stone used in gaming, lime — more at CHALK] *vt* **1 a :** to determine by mathematical processes **b :** to reckon by exercise of practical judgment **:** ESTIMATE **c :** to solve or probe the meaning of **:** figure out ⟨trying to ~ his expression —Hugh MacLennan⟩ **2 :** to design or adapt for a purpose **3** *chiefly North* **a :** to judge to be true or probable **b :** INTEND ~ *vi* **1 a :** to make a calculation **b :** to forecast consequences **2 :** COUNT, RELY

cal·cu·lat·ed \-,lāt-əd\ *adj* **1 a :** worked out by mathematical calculation **b :** engaged in, undertaken, or displayed after reckoning or estimating the statistical probability of success or failure ⟨a ~ risk⟩ **2 :** planned or contrived to accomplish a purpose **3 :** brought about by deliberate intent **4 :** APT, LIKELY — **cal·cu·lat·ed·ly** *adv* — **cal·cu·lat·ed·ness** *n*

cal·cu·lat·ing \-,lāt-iŋ\ *adj* **1 :** making calculations ⟨~ machine⟩ **2 :** marked by prudent and deliberate analysis or by shrewd consideration of self-interest **:** SCHEMING — **cal·cu·lat·ing·ly** \-iŋ-lē\ *adv*

cal·cu·la·tion \,kal-kyə-'lā-shən\ *n* **1 a :** the process or an act of calculating **b :** the result of an act of calculating **2 a :** studied care in analyzing or planning **b :** cold heartless planning to promote self-interest ⟨by every effort of subterfuge and ~ —Hilaire Belloc⟩ — **cal·cu·lat·ive** \'kal-kyə-ˌlāt-iv\ *adj*

cal·cu·la·tor \'kal-kyə-ˌlāt-ər\ *n* **1 :** one that calculates: as **a :** a mechanical or electronic device for performing mathematical calculations automatically **b :** a person who operates a calculator **2 :** a set or book of tables for facilitating computations

cal·cu·lous \'kal-kyə-ləs\ *adj* **:** caused or characterized by a calculus or calculi

cal·cu·lus \-ləs\ *n, pl* **-li** \-ˌlī, -ˌlē\ *also* **-lus·es** [L, pebble, stone in the bladder or kidney, stone used in reckoning] **1 :** a concretion usu. of mineral salts around organic material found esp. in hollow organs or ducts **2** *archaic* **:** CALCULATION **3 a :** a method of computation or calculation in a special notation (as of logic or symbolic logic) **b :** the mathematical methods comprising differential and integral calculus

calculus of variations : a branch of mathematics dealing with maxima and minima of definite integrals which have an integrand that is a function of independent variables and of dependent variables and their derivatives

cal·de·ra \kal-'der-ə, kȯl-, -'dir-\ *n* [Sp, lit., caldron, fr. LL *caldaria*] **:** a crater with a diameter many times that of the volcanic vent formed by collapse of the central part of a volcano or by explosions of extraordinary violence

cal·dron \'kȯl-drən\ *n* [ME, alter. of *cauderon,* fr. ONF, dim. of *caudiere,* fr. LL *caldaria,* fr. L, warm bath, fr. fem. of *caldarius* suitable for warming, fr. *calidus* warm, fr. *calēre* to be warm — more at LEE] **1 :** a large kettle or boiler **2 :** something resembling a boiling caldron ⟨a ~ of intense emotions⟩

ca·lèche *or* **ca·leche** \kə-'lesh, -'lash\ *n* [F *calèche* — more at CALASH] **1 :** CALASH 1a **2 :** a 2-wheeled horse-drawn vehicle with a driver's seat on the splashboard used in Quebec **3 :** CALASH 2a

cal·e·fac·to·ry \ˌkal-ə-'fak-t(ə-)rē\ *n, pl* **-ries** [ML *calefactorium,* fr. L *calefactus,* pp. of *calefacere* to warm — more at CHAFE] **:** a monastery room warmed and used as a sitting room

¹cal·en·dar \'kal-ən-dər\ *n* [ME *calender,* fr. AF or ML; AF *calender,* fr. ML *kalendarium,* fr. L, moneylender's account book, fr. *kalendae* calends] **1 :** a system for fixing the beginning, length, and divisions of the civil year and arranging days and longer divisions of time (as weeks and months) in a definite order — see MONTH table **2 :** a tabular register of days according to a system usu. covering one year and referring the days of each month to the days of the week **3 :** an orderly list: as **a :** a list of cases to be tried in court **b :** a list of bills or other items reported out of committee for consideration by a legislative assembly **c :** a list of events giving dates and details **4** *Brit* **:** a university catalog

²calendar *vt* **-dared; -dar·ing** \-d(ə-)riŋ\ **:** to enter in a calendar

calendar year *n* **1 :** a period of a year beginning and ending with the dates that are conventionally accepted as marking the beginning and end of a numbered year (as January 1 and December 31 in the Gregorian calendar) **2 :** a period of time equal in length to that of the year in the calendar conventionally in use (as 365 days in the Gregorian calendar or when a Feb. 29 is included 366 days)

¹cal·en·der \'kal-ən-dər\ *vt* **-dered; -der·ing** \-d(ə-)riŋ\ [MF *calandrer,* fr. *calandre* machine for calendering, modif. of Gk *kylindros* cylinder — more at CYLINDER] **:** to press (as cloth, rubber, or paper) between rollers or plates in order to smooth and glaze or to thin into sheets — **cal·en·der·er** \-dər-ər\ *n*

²calender *n* **:** a machine for calendering something

³calender *n* [Per *qalandar,* fr. Ar, fr. Per *kalandar* uncouth man] **:** one of a Sufic order of wandering mendicant dervishes

ca·len·dri·cal \kə-'len-dri-kəl, ka-\ *also* **ca·len·dric** \-drik\ *adj* **:** of, relating to, characteristic of, or used in a calendar

cal·ends \'kal-ən(d)z, 'kāl-\ *n pl but sing or pl in constr* [ME *kalendes,* fr. L *kalendae, calendae*] **:** the 1st day of the ancient Roman month from which days were counted backward to the ides

ca·len·du·la \kə-'len-jə-lə\ *n* [NL, genus name, fr. ML, fr. L *calendae* calends] **:** any of a small genus (*Calendula*) of yellow-rayed composite herbs of temperate regions

cal·en·ture \'kal-ən-ˌchu̇(ə)r\ *n* [Sp *calentura,* fr. *calentar* to heat, fr. L *calent-, calens,* prp. of *calēre* to be warm — more at LEE] **:** a tropical fever caused by exposure to heat

¹calf \'kaf, 'ka̐f\ *n, pl* **calves** \'kavz, 'ka̐vz\ *also* **calfs** *often attrib* [ME, fr. OE *cealf;* akin to OHG *kalb* calf, ON *kālfi* calf of the leg, L *galla* gallnut] **1 a :** the young of the domestic cow; *also* **:** that of a closely related mammal (as a bison or water buffalo) **b :** the young of various large animals (as the elephant and whale) **2** *pl* *calfs* **:** the hide of the domestic calf; *esp* **:** CALFSKIN **3 :** an awkward or silly boy or youth **4 :** a small mass of ice set free from a coast glacier or from an iceberg or floe — **calf·like** \'kaf-ˌlīk, 'ka̐f-\ *adj* — **in calf :** PREGNANT — used of a cow

²calf *n, pl* **calves** \'kavz, 'ka̐vz\ [ME, fr. ON *kālfi*] **:** the fleshy hinder part of the leg below the knee

calf love *n* **:** PUPPY LOVE

calf's-foot jelly \ˌkavz-ˌfu̇t-, ˌkafs-, ˌka̐vz-, ˌka̐fs-\ *n* **:** jelly made from gelatin obtained by boiling calves' feet

calf·skin \'kaf-ˌskin, 'ka̐f-\ *n* **:** leather made of the skin of a calf

Cal·gon \'kal-ˌgän\ *trademark* — used for a water softener that is essentially a complex phosphate of sodium

Cal·i·ban \'kal-ə-ˌban\ *n* **:** a savage and deformed slave in Shakespeare's *The Tempest*

cal·i·ber *or* **cal·i·bre** \'kal-ə-bər, *Brit also* kə-'lē-\ *n* [MF *calibre,* fr. OIt *calibro,* fr. Ar *qālib* shoemaker's last] **1 a :** the diameter of a bullet or other projectile **b :** the diameter of a bore of a gun usu. expressed in modern U.S. and British usage in hundredths or thousandths of an inch and typically written as a decimal fraction ⟨.32 ~⟩ **2 :** the diameter of a round body; *esp* **:** the internal diameter of a hollow cylinder **3 a :** degree of mental capacity or moral quality **b :** degree of excellence or importance ***syn*** see QUALITY

cal·i·brate \'kal-ə-ˌbrāt\ *vt* **-brat·ed; -brat·ing 1 :** to ascertain the caliber of (as a thermometer tube) **2 :** to determine, rectify, or mark the graduations of (as a thermometer tube) **3 :** to standardize (as a measuring instrument) by determining the deviation from a standard so as to ascertain the proper correction factors — **cal·i·bra·tor** \-ˌbrāt-ər\ *n*

cal·i·bra·tion \ˌkal-ə-'brā-shən\ *n* **1 :** the act or process of calibrating **:** the state of being calibrated **2 :** a set of graduations to indicate values or positions — usu. used in pl. ⟨~*s* on a gauge⟩ ⟨~*s* on a radio dial⟩

ca·li·che \kə-'lē-chē\ *n* [AmerSp, fr. Sp, flake of lime, fr. *cal* lime, fr. L *calx* — more at CHALK] **1 :** the nitrate-bearing gravel or rock of the sodium nitrate deposits of Chile and Peru **2 :** a crust of calcium carbonate that forms on the stony soil of arid regions

cal·i·co \'kal-i-ˌkō\ *n, pl* **-coes** *or* **-cos** [*Calicut,* India] **1 a :** cotton cloth imported from India **b** *Brit* **:** a plain white cotton fabric that is heavier than muslin **c :** any of various cheap cotton fabrics with figured patterns **2 :** a blotched or spotted animal (as a piebald horse) — **calico** *adj*

calico bass *n* **1 :** BLACK CRAPPIE **2 :** KELP BASS

calico bush *n* **:** MOUNTAIN LAUREL

calico printing *n* **:** the process of making fast-color designs on cotton fabrics (as calico)

Calif *abbr* California

Cal·i·for·nia condor \ˌkal-ə-ˌfȯr-nyə-\ *n* [*California,* state of U.S.] **:** a large nearly extinct vulture (*Gymnogyps californianus*) that is related to the condor of So. America and is found in the mountains of southern California

California laurel *n* **:** a Pacific coast tree (*Umbellularia californica*) of the laurel family with evergreen foliage and small umbellate flowers

California poppy *n* **:** any of a genus (*Eschscholtzia*) of herbs of the poppy family; *esp* **:** one (*E. californica*) widely cultivated for its pale yellow to red flowers

California rosebay *n* **:** a usu. pink-flowered rhododendron (*Rhododendron macrophyllum*) of the Pacific coast

Cal·i·for·nio \ˌkal-ə-'fȯr-nē-ˌō\ *n, pl* **-nios** [Sp, fr. *California*] **:** one of the original Spanish colonists of California or their descendants

cal·i·for·ni·um \ˌkal-ə-'fȯr-nē-əm\ *n* [NL, fr. *California,* U.S.] **:** a radioactive element discovered by bombarding curium 242 with alpha particles — see ELEMENT table

ca·lig·i·nous \kə-'lij-ə-nəs\ *adj* [MF or L; MF *caligineux,* fr. L *caliginosus,* fr. *caligin-, caligo* darkness; akin to Gk *kelainos* black — more at COLUMBINE] **:** MISTY, DARK

Ca·li·na·go \ˌkal-ə-'nä-(ˌ)gō\ *n* **:** an Arawakan language of the Lesser Antilles and Central America

cal·i·pash \'kal-ə-ˌpash, ˌkal-ə-'\ *n* **:** a fatty gelatinous dull greenish edible substance next to the upper shell of a turtle

cal·i·pee \'kal-ə-ˌpē, ˌkal-ə-'\ *n* **:** a fatty gelatinous light yellow edible substance attached to the lower shell of a turtle

¹cal·i·per *or* **cal·li·per** \'kal-ə-pər\ *n* [alter. of *caliber*] **1 a :** a measuring instrument with two legs or jaws that can be adjusted to determine thickness, diameter, and distance between surfaces — usu. used in pl. ⟨a pair of ~*s*⟩ **b :** an instrument for measuring diameters (as of logs or trees) consisting of a graduated beam and at right angles to it a fixed arm and a movable arm **c :** a device consisting of two plates lined with a frictional material that press against the sides of a rotating wheel or disc in certain brake systems **2 :** thickness esp. of paper, paperboard, or a tree

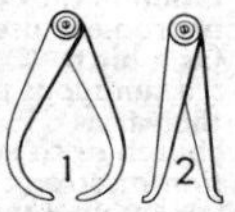

calipers 1a: *1* outside, *2* inside

²caliper *or* **calliper** *vt* **-pered; -per·ing** \-p(ə-)riŋ\ **:** to measure by or as if by calipers

ca·liph *or* **ca·lif** \'kā-ləf, 'kal-əf\ *n* [ME *caliphe,* fr. MF *calife,* fr. Ar *khalīfah* successor] **:** a successor of Muhammad as temporal and spiritual head of Islam — used as a title — **ca·liph·al** \-əl\ *adj*

ca·liph·ate \-ˌāt, -ət\ *n* **:** the office or dominion of a caliph

cal·is·then·ic \ˌkal-əs-'then-ik\ *adj* **:** of or relating to calisthenics

cal·is·then·ics \-iks\ *n pl but sing or pl in constr* [Gk *kalos* beautiful + *sthenos* strength — more at CALLIGRAPHY] **1 :** systematic rhythmic bodily exercises performed usu. without apparatus **2** *usu sing in constr* **:** the art or practice of calisthenics

ca·lix \'kā-liks, 'kal-iks\ *n, pl* **ca·li·ces** \'kā-lə-ˌsēz, 'kal-ə-\ [L *calic-, calix* — more at CHALICE] **:** CUP

¹calk \'kȯk\, **calk·er** \'kȯ-kər\ *var of* CAULK, CAULKER

²calk \'kȯk\ *n* [prob. alter. of *calkin,* fr. ME *kakun,* fr. MD or ONF; MD *calcoen* horse's hoof, fr. ONF *calcain* heel, fr. L *calcaneum,* fr. *calc-, calx* heel; akin to Gk *kōlon* limb, *skelos* leg] **:** a tapered piece projecting downward on the shoe of a horse to prevent slipping; *also* **:** a similar device worn on the sole of a shoe

³calk *vt* **1 :** to furnish with calks **2 :** to wound with a calk

¹call \'kȯl\ *vb* [ME *callen,* prob. fr. ON *kalla;* akin to OE hilde*calla* battle herald, OHG *kallōn* to talk loudly, OSlav *glasŭ* voice] *vi* **1 a :** to speak in a loud distinct voice so as to be heard at a distance **:** SHOUT ⟨~ for help⟩ **b :** to make a request or demand ⟨~ for an investigation⟩ **c** *of an animal* **:** to utter a characteristic note or cry **d :** to get or try to get into communication by telephone — often used with *up* **e :** to make a demand in card games (as for a particular card or for a show of hands) **f :** to give the calls for a square dance **2** *Scot* **:** DRIVE **3 :** to make a brief visit ⟨~*ed* to pay his respects⟩ ⟨~*ed* on a friend⟩ ~ *vt* **1 a (1) :** to utter in a loud distinct voice — often used with *out* ⟨~ out a number⟩ **(2) :** to announce or read loudly or authoritatively ⟨~ the roll⟩ ⟨~ off a row of figures⟩ **b (1) :** to command or request to come or be present ⟨~*ed* to testify⟩ **(2) :** to cause to come **:** BRING ⟨~*s* to mind an old saying⟩ **c :** to summon to a particular activity, employment, or office ⟨was ~*ed* to active duty⟩ **d :** to invite or command to meet **:** CONVOKE ⟨~ a meeting⟩ **e :** to rouse from sleep or summon to get up **f (1) :** to give the order for **:** bring into action

⟨~ a strike against the company⟩ (2) : to manage (as an offensive game) by giving the signals or orders ⟨that catcher ~*s* a good game⟩ **g** (1) : to make a demand in bridge for (a card or suit) (2) : to require (a player) to show the hand in poker by making an equal bet (3) : to challenge to make good on a statement (4) : to charge with or censure for an offense ⟨deserves to be ~*ed* on that⟩ **h** : to attract (as game) by imitating the characteristic cry **i** : to halt (as a baseball game) because of unsuitable conditions **j** : to rule on the status of (as a pitched ball or a player's action) ⟨~ balls and strikes⟩ ⟨~ a base runner safe⟩ **k** : to give the calls for (a square dance) — often used with *off* **l** (1) : to get or try to get in communication with by telephone (2) : to deliver (a message) by telephone (3) : to make a signal to in order to transmit a message ⟨~ the flagship⟩ **m** : SUSPEND ⟨time was ~*ed* while the field was cleared⟩ **n** (1) : to demand payment of esp. by formal notice ⟨~ a loan⟩ (2) : to demand presentation of (a bond issue) for redemption **2 a** : to speak of or address by a specified name : give a name to ⟨~ her Kitty⟩ **b** (1) : to regard or characterize as of a certain kind : CONSIDER ⟨can hardly be ~*ed* generous⟩ (2) : to estimate or consider for purposes of an estimate or for convenience ⟨~ it an even dollar⟩ **c** (1) : to describe correctly in advance of or without knowledge of the event : PREDICT (2) : to name or specify in advance ⟨~ the toss of a coin⟩ ***syn*** see SUMMON — **call a spade a spade** : to speak frankly — **call for 1** : to call (as at one's house) to get ⟨I'll *call for* you after dinner⟩ **2a** : to require as necessary or appropriate ⟨lifting the box *called for* all her strength⟩ **b** : to make necessary **3a** : to give an order for : DIRECT ⟨legislation *calling for* the establishment of new schools⟩ **b** : to provide for ⟨the design *calls for* three windows⟩ — **call forth** : to bring into being or action : ELICIT ⟨these events *call forth* great emotions⟩ — **call in question** : to cast doubt upon — **call it a day** : to stop at least for the present whatever one has been doing — **call it quits** : to call it a day — **call names** : to address or speak of a person or thing contemptuously or offensively — **call on 1** : to call upon **2** : to cause (as a student) to recite ⟨the teacher always *called on* her first⟩ — **call one's bluff** : to challenge and expose an empty pretense or threat — **call one's shot** : to predict the result of a shot in a game or sport — **call the shots** : to be in charge or control : determine the policy or procedure — **call the tune** : to call the shots — **call to account** : to hold responsible : REPRIMAND ⟨*called to account* for violation of the rules⟩ — **call to the colors** : to summon for active military duty — **call upon 1** : REQUIRE, OBLIGE ⟨may be *called upon* to do several jobs⟩ **2** : to make a demand on : depend on ⟨universities are *called upon* to produce trained men⟩

²call *n* **1 a** : an act of calling with the voice : SHOUT **b** : an imitation of the cry of a bird or other animal made to attract it **c** : an instrument used for calling ⟨a duck ~⟩ **d** : the cry of an animal (as a bird) **2 a** : a request or command to come or assemble **b** : a summons or signal on a drum, bugle, or pipe **c** : admission to the bar as a barrister **d** : an invitation to become the minister of a church or to accept a professional appointment **e** : a divine vocation or strong inner prompting to a particular course of action **f** : a summoning of actors to rehearsal ⟨the ~ is for 11 o'clock⟩ **g** : the attraction or appeal of a particular activity, condition, or place ⟨the ~ of the wild⟩ **h** : an order specifying the number of men to be inducted into the armed services during a specified period **i** : the selection of a play in football **3 a** : DEMAND, CLAIM **b** : NEED, JUSTIFICATION **c** : a demand for payment of money **d** : an option to buy a specified amount of a security (as stock) or commodity (as wheat) at a fixed price at or within a specified time — compare ²PUT 2 **e** : an instance of asking for something : REQUEST ⟨many ~*s* for Christmas stories⟩ **4** : ROLL CALL **5** : a short usu. formal visit **6** : the name or thing called ⟨the ~ was heads⟩ **7** : the act of calling in a card game **8** : the act of calling on the telephone **9** : the score at any given time in a tennis game **10** : a direction or a succession of directions for a square dance rhythmically called to the dancers **11** : a decision or ruling made by an official of a sports contest ***syn*** see VISIT — **at call** *or* **on call 1a** : available for use : at the service of ⟨thousands of men *at* his *call*⟩ **b** : ready to respond to a summons or command ⟨a doctor *on call*⟩ **2** : subject to demand for payment or return without previous notice ⟨money lent *at call*⟩ — **within call** : within hearing or reach of a summons : subject to summons

cal·la \ˈkal-ə\ *n* [NL, genus name, modif. of Gk *kallaia* rooster's wattles] **1** : a house or greenhouse plant (*Zantedeschia aethiopica*) of the arum family with a white showy spathe and yellow spadix — called also *calla lily* **2** : a plant resembling the calla

call·able \ˈkȯ-lə-bəl\ *adj* : capable of being called; *specif* : subject to a demand for presentation for payment ⟨~ bond⟩

cal·lant \ˈkal-ənt, ˈkäl-\ *or* **cal·lan** \-ən\ *n* [D or ONF; D *kalant* customer, fellow, fr. ONF *calland* customer, fr. L *calent-, calens,* prp. of *calēre* to be warm — more at LEE] *chiefly Scot* : BOY, LAD

call·back \ˈkȯl-ˌbak\ *n* : a recall by a manufacturer of a recently sold product (as an automobile) for correction of a defect

call–board \-ˌbō(ə)rd, -ˌbȯ(ə)rd\ *n* : a bulletin board

call box *n* **1** *Brit* : a public telephone booth **2** : a telephone usu. located on the side of a road for reporting emergencies (as fires or automobile breakdowns)

call·boy \ˈkȯl-ˌbȯi\ *n* **1** : BELLHOP, PAGE **2** : a boy who summons actors to go on stage

call down *vt* **1** : to cause or entreat to descend ⟨*call down* a blessing on the crops⟩ **2** : REPRIMAND ⟨*called* me *down* for being late⟩

called strike *n* : a pitched baseball not struck at by the batter that passes through the strike zone

¹cal·ler \ˈkal-ər\ *adj* [ME *callour*] **1** *Scot* : FRESH **2** *Scot* : COOL

²call·er \ˈkȯ-lər\ *n* : one that calls

cal·let \ˈkal-ət\ *n* [perh. fr. MF *caillette* frivolous person, fr. *Caillette fl* 1500 F court fool] *chiefly Scot* : PROSTITUTE

call girl *n* : a prostitute with whom an appointment may be made by telephone

call house *n* : a house or apartment where call girls may be procured

cal·lig·ra·pher \kə-ˈlig-rə-fər\ *n* **1** : one that writes a beautiful hand **2** : PENMAN ⟨a fair ~⟩ **3** : a professional copyist or engrosser

cal·lig·ra·phist \-fəst\ *n* : CALLIGRAPHER

cal·lig·ra·phy \-fē\ *n* [F or Gk; F *calligraphie,* fr. Gk *kalligraphia,* fr. *kalli-* beautiful (fr. *kallos* beauty) + *-graphia* -graphy; akin to Gk *kalos* beautiful, Skt *kalya* healthy] **1 a** : beautiful or elegant handwriting — compare CACOGRAPHY **b** : the art of producing such writing **2** : PENMANSHIP — **cal·li·graph·ic** \ˌkal-ə-ˈgraf-ik\ *adj* — **cal·li·graph·i·cal·ly** \-i-k(ə-)lē\ *adv*

call in *vt* **1** : to order to return or to be returned: as **a** : to withdraw from an advanced position ⟨*call in* the outposts⟩ **b** : to withdraw from circulation ⟨*call in* bank notes and issue new ones⟩ **2** : to summon to one's aid or for consultation ⟨*call in* a mediator to settle the dispute⟩ ~ *vi* : to communicate with a person by telephone — **call in sick** : to report by telephone that one will be absent because of illness

call·ing \ˈkȯ-liŋ\ *n* **1** : a strong inner impulse toward a particular course of action esp. when accompanied by conviction of divine influence **2** : the vocation or profession in which one customarily engages **3** : the characteristic cry of a female cat in heat; *also* : the period of heat

calling card *n* : VISITING CARD

cal·li·ope \kə-ˈlī-ə-(ˌ)pē, *in sense 2 also* ˈkal-ē-ˌōp\ *n* [L, fr. Gk *Kalliopē*] **1** *cap* : the Greek Muse of heroic poetry **2** : a keyboard musical instrument resembling an organ and consisting of a series of whistles sounded by steam or compressed air

cal·li·op·sis \ˌkal-ē-ˈäp-səs\ *n* [NL, fr. Gk *kalli-* + *opsis* appearance — more at OPTIC] : COREOPSIS — used esp. of annual forms

Cal·lis·to \kə-ˈlis-(ˌ)tō\ *n* [*Callisto,* Gk nymph] **1** : a nymph loved by Zeus, changed into a she-bear by Hera, and subsequently changed into the Great Bear constellation **2** : the so-called fourth but really fifth satellite of Jupiter

cal·li·thump \ˈkal-ə-ˌthəmp\ *n* [back-formation fr. *callithumpian,* adj., alter. of E dial. *gallithumpian* disturber of order at elections in 18th cent.] : a noisy boisterous parade — **cal·li·thump·ian** \ˌkal-ə-ˈthəm-pē-ən\ *adj*

call letters *n pl* : CALL SIGN

call loan *n* : a loan payable on demand of either party

call number *n* : a combination of characters assigned to a library book to indicate its place on a shelf

call off *vt* **1** : to draw away : DIVERT ⟨her attention was *called off* by a new arrival⟩ **2** : to give up : CANCEL ⟨*call* the trip *off*⟩

call of nature : the need to expel body wastes

cal·lose \ˈkal-ˌōs, -ˌōz\ *n* [L *callosus* callous] : a carbohydrate component of plant cell walls

cal·los·i·ty \ka-ˈläs-ət-ē, kə-\ *n, pl* **-ties 1** : the quality or state of being callous: as **a** : marked or abnormal hardness and thickness **b** : lack of feeling or capacity for emotion **2** : CALLUS 1

¹cal·lous \ˈkal-əs\ *adj* [MF *calleux,* fr. L *callosus,* fr. *callum, callus* callous skin; akin to Skt *kiṇa* callosity] **1 a** : being hardened and thickened **b** : having calluses **2 a** : feeling no emotion **b** : feeling no sympathy for others — **cal·lous·ly** *adv* — **cal·lous·ness** *n*

²callous *vt* : to make callous

call out *vt* **1** : to summon into action ⟨*call out* troops⟩ **2** : to challenge to a duel **3** : to order on strike ⟨*call out* the workers⟩

cal·low \ˈkal-(ˌ)ō, -ə(-w)\ *adj* [ME *calu* bald, fr. OE; akin to OHG *kalo* bald] **1** *of a bird* : not yet having enough feathers to fly **2** : lacking adult sophistication : IMMATURE ⟨~ youth⟩ ***syn*** see RUDE — **cal·low·ness** \ˈkal-ō-nəs, -ə-nəs\ *n*

call sign *n* : the combination of identifying letters or letters and numbers assigned to an operator, office, activity, or station for use in communication (as in the address of a message sent by radio)

call slip *n* : a form filled out by a library patron for a desired book

call to quarters : a bugle call usu. shortly before taps that summons soldiers to their quarters

call–up \ˈkȯ-ˌləp\ *n* : an order to report for military service

call up \(ˈ)kȯ-ˈləp\ *vt* **1** : to bring to mind : EVOKE **2** : to summon before an authority **3** : to summon together or collect (as for a united effort) ⟨*call up* all his forces for the attack⟩ **4** : to summon for active military duty **5** : to bring forward for consideration or action ⟨*call up* a bill for senate approval⟩

¹cal·lus \ˈkal-əs\ *n* [L] **1** : a thickening of or a hard thickened area on skin or bark **2** : a mass of exudate and connective tissue that forms around a break in a bone and is converted into bone in the healing of the break **3** : soft tissue that forms over a wounded or cut plant surface

²callus *vi* : to form callus ~ *vt* : to cause callus to form on

¹calm \ˈkäm, ˈkälm\ *n* [ME *calme,* fr. MF, fr. OIt *calma,* fr. LL *cauma* heat, fr. Gk *kauma,* fr. *kaiein* to burn — more at CAUSTIC] **1 a** : a period or condition of freedom from storms, high winds, or rough activity of water **b** : complete absence of wind or presence of wind having a speed no greater than one mile per hour **2** : a state of repose and freedom from turmoil or agitation

²calm *adj* **1** : marked by calm : STILL ⟨a ~ sea⟩ **2** : free from agitation, excitement, or disturbance ⟨a ~ manner⟩ — **calm·ly** *adv* — **calm·ness** *n*

syn CALM, TRANQUIL, SERENE, PLACID, PEACEFUL *shared meaning element* : quiet and free from whatever distrubs or hurts ***ant*** stormy, agitated

³calm *vi* : to become calm ~ *vt* : to make calm

calm·ative \ˈkäm-ət-iv, ˈkäl-mət-\ *n or adj* [³*calm* + *-ative* (as in *sedative*)] : SEDATIVE

cal·o·mel \ˈkal-ə-məl, -ˌmel\ *n* [prob. fr. (assumed) NL *calomelas,* fr. Gk *kalos* beautiful + *melas* black — more at CALLIGRAPHY, MULLET] : a white tasteless compound Hg_2Cl_2 used in medicine esp. as a purgative and fungicide — called also *mercurous chloride*

¹ca·lo·ric \kə-ˈlȯr-ik, -ˈlōr-, -ˈlär-; ˈkal-ə-rik\ *n* [F *calorique,* fr. L *calor*] **1** : a supposed form of matter formerly held responsible for the phenomena of heat and combustion **2** *archaic* : HEAT

²caloric *adj* **1** : of or relating to heat **2** : of or relating to calories — **ca·lo·ri·cal·ly** \kə-ˈlȯr-i-k(ə-)lē, -ˈlōr-, -ˈlär-\ *adv*

cal·o·rie also **cal·o·ry** \'kal-(ə-)rē\ n, pl **-ries** [F calorie, fr. L calor heat, fr. calēre to be warm — more at LEE] **1 a** : the amount of heat required at a pressure of one atmosphere to raise the temperature of one gram of water one degree centigrade — called also gram calorie, small calorie; abbr. cal **b** : the amount of heat required to raise the temperature of one kilogram of water one degree centigrade : 1000 gram calories or 3.968 Btu — called also kilogram calorie, large calorie; abbr. Cal **2 a** : a unit equivalent to the large calorie expressing heat-producing or energy-producing value in food when oxidized in the body **b** : an amount of food having an energy-producing value of one large calorie

cal·o·rif·ic \,kal-ə-'rif-ik\ adj [F or L; F calorifique, fr. L calorificus, fr. calor] **1** : CALORIC **2** : of or relating to the production of heat

cal·o·rim·e·ter \,kal-ə-'rim-ət-ər\ n [ISV, fr. L calor] : any of several apparatuses for measuring quantities of absorbed or evolved heat or for determining specific heats — **ca·lo·ri·met·ric** \kə-,lòr-ə-, -,lōr-, -,lär-\ adj — **ca·lo·ri·met·ri·cal·ly** \-tri-k(ə-)lē\ adv — **cal·o·rim·e·try** \,kal-ə-'rim-ə-trē\ n

ca·lotte \kə-'lät\ n [F] : SKULLCAP; esp : ZUCCHETTO

ca·loy·er \kə-'lòi(-ə)r, 'kal-ə-yər\ n [It & F; F caloyer, fr. obs. It caloiero, fr. MGk kalogeros venerable, fr. kalos beautiful + gēras old age] : a monk of the Eastern Church

cal·pac or **cal·pack** \'kal-,pak, kal-\ n [Turk kalpak] : a high-crowned cap worn in Turkey, Iran, and neighboring countries

calque \'kalk\ n [F, lit., copy, fr. calquer to trace, fr. It calcare to trample, trace, fr. L, to trample — more at CAULK] : LOAN TRANSLATION

cal·trop \'kal-trəp, 'kòl-\ also **cal·throp** \-thrəp\ n [ME calketrappe star thistle, fr. OE calcatrippe, fr. ML calcatrippa] **1 a** pl but sing or pl in constr : STAR THISTLE 1 **b** : PUNCTURE VINE; also : any of various related herbs (genera Tribulus and Kallstroemia) **c** : WATER CHESTNUT 1 **2** : a device with four metal points so arranged that when any three are on the ground the fourth projects upward as a hazard to the hoofs of horses or to pneumatic tires

caltrop 2

cal·u·met \'kal-yə-,met, -mət\ n [AmerF, fr. F dial., straw, fr. LL calamellus, dim. of L calamus reed — more at CALAMUS] : a highly ornamented ceremonial pipe of the American Indians

ca·lum·ni·ate \kə-'ləm-nē-,āt\ vt **-at·ed; -at·ing 1** : to utter maliciously false statements, charges, or imputations about **2** : to injure the reputation of by calumny syn see MALIGN ant eulogize, vindicate — **ca·lum·ni·a·tion** \-,ləm-nē-'ā-shən\ n — **ca·lum·ni·a·tor** \-'ləm-nē-,āt-ər\ n

ca·lum·ni·ous \kə-'ləm-nē-əs\ adj : constituting or marked by calumny : SLANDEROUS — **ca·lum·ni·ous·ly** adv

cal·um·ny \'kal-əm-nē also -yəm-\ n, pl **-nies** [MF & L; MF calomnie, fr. L calumnia, fr. calvi to deceive; akin to OE hōl calumny, Gk kēlein to beguile] **1** : the act of uttering false charges or misrepresentations maliciously calculated to damage another's reputation **2** : a misrepresentation intended to blacken another's reputation

cal·va·dos \,kal-və-'dōs\ n, often cap [F, fr. Calvados, Normandy, France] : a dry brown apple brandy

cal·var·i·um \kal-'var-ē-əm, -'ver-\ n, pl **-ia** \-ē-ə\ [NL, fr. L calvaria skull, fr. calvus bald; akin to Skt atikulva completely bald] : a skull lacking the lower jaw or lower jaw and facial portion

cal·va·ry \'kalv-(ə-)rē\ n, pl **-ries** [Calvary, the hill near Jerusalem where Jesus was crucified] **1** : an open-air representation of the crucifixion of Christ **2** : an experience of usu. intense mental suffering

Calvary cross n : a Latin cross usually mounted on three steps — see CROSS illustration

calve \'kav, 'kåv\ vb **calved; calv·ing** [ME calven, fr. OE cealfian, fr. cealf calf] vi **1** : to give birth to a calf; also : to produce offspring **2** of an ice mass : to separate or break so that a part becomes detached ~ vt **1** : to produce by birth **2** of an ice mass : to let become detached

calves pl of CALF

Cal·vin·ism \'kal-və-,niz-əm\ n [John Calvin] : the theological system of Calvin and his followers marked by strong emphasis on the sovereignty of God and esp. by the doctrine of predestination — **Cal·vin·ist** \-və-nəst\ n or adj — **Cal·vin·is·tic** \,kal-və-'nis-tik\ adj — **Cal·vin·is·ti·cal·ly** \-ti-k(ə-)lē\ adv

calx \'kalks\ n, pl **calx·es** or **cal·ces** \'kal-,sēz\ [ME cals, fr. L calx lime — more at CHALK] : the crumbly residue left when a metal or mineral has been subjected to calcination or combustion

ca·lyc·u·late \kə-'lik-yə-,lāt, -lət\ adj : having a calyculus

ca·lyc·u·lus \-ləs\ n, pl **-li** \-,lī, -,lē\ [NL, modif. of E caticle] : a small cup-shaped structure (as a taste bud)

1ca·lyp·so \kə-'lip-(,)sō\ n [L, fr. Gk Kalypsō] **1** cap : a sea nymph in Homer's Odyssey who kept Odysseus seven years on the island of Ogygia **2** pl calypsos [NL, genus name, prob. fr. L] : a bulbous bog orchid (genus Calypso) of northern regions bearing a single flower variegated with white, purple, pink, and yellow

2calypso n, pl **-sos** also **-soes** [prob. fr. Calypso] : an improvised ballad usu. satirizing current events in a style originating in the West Indies — **ca·lyp·so·ni·an** \kə-,lip-'sō-nē-ən, ,kal-(,)ip-\ n or adj

ca·lyp·tra \kə-'lip -trə\ n [NL, fr. Gk kalyptra veil, fr. kalyptein to cover — more at HELL] **1** : the archegonium of a liverwort or moss; esp : one forming a membranous hood over the capsule in a moss **2** : a covering (as the calyx of a California poppy) of a flower or fruit suggestive of a cap or hood **3** : ROOT CAP — **ca·lyp·trate** \kə-'lip-,trāt, 'kal-əp-\ adj

ca·lyx \'kā-liks, also 'kal-iks\ n, pl **ca·lyx·es** or **ca·ly·ces** \'kā-lə-,sēz also 'kal-ə-\ [L calyc-, calyx, fr. Gk kalyx — more at CHALICE] **1** : the external usu. green or leafy part of a flower consisting of sepals **2** : a cuplike animal structure — **ca·ly·ce·al** \,kā-lə-'sē-əl, ,kal-ə-\ adj

cam \'kam\ n [perh. fr. F came, fr. G kamm, lit., comb, fr. OHG kamb] : a rotating or sliding piece that imparts motion to a roller moving against its edge or to a pin free to move in a groove on its face or that receives motion from such a roller or pin

ca·ma·ra·de·rie \,käm-(ə-)'räd-ə-rē, ,kam-, -'rad-\ n [F, fr. camarade comrade] : a spirit of friendly good-fellowship existing among comrades

cam·a·ril·la \,kam-ə-'ril-ə, -'rē-(y)ə\ n [Sp, lit., small room] : a group of unofficial often secret and scheming advisers; also : CABAL

cam·as or **cam·ass** \'kam-əs\ n [Chinook Jargon kamass] : any of a genus (Camassia) of plants of the lily family of the western U.S. with edible bulbs — compare DEATH CAMAS

1cam·ber \'kam-bər\ vb **cam·bered; cam·ber·ing** \-b(ə-)riŋ\ [F cambrer, fr. MF cambre curved, fr. L camur — more at CHAMBER] vi : to curve upward in the middle ~ vt **1** : to arch slightly **2** : to impart camber to

2camber n **1** : a slight convexity, arching, or curvature (as of a beam, deck, or road) **2** : the convexity of the curve of an airfoil from the leading edge to the trailing edge **3** : a setting of the wheels of an automotive vehicle closer together at the bottom than at the top

cam·bi·um \'kam-bē-əm\ n, pl **-bi·ums** or **-bia** \-bē-ə\ [NL, fr. ML, exchange, fr. L cambiare to exchange — more at CHANGE] : a thin formative layer between the xylem and phloem of most vascular plants that gives rise to new cells and is responsible for secondary growth — **cam·bi·al** \-bē-əl\ adj

Cam·bo·di·an \kam-'bōd-ē-ən\ n **1** : a native or inhabitant of Cambodia **2** : KHMER 2 — **Cambodian** adj

Cam·bri·an \'kam-brē-ən\ adj [ML Cambria Wales, fr. MW Cymry Wales, Welshmen] **1** : WELSH **2** : of, relating to, or being the earliest geologic period of the Paleozoic era or the corresponding system of rocks marked by fossils of every great animal type except the vertebrate and by scarcely recognizable plant fossils — **Cambrian** n

cam·bric \'kām-brik\ n [obs. Flem Kameryk Cambrai, city of France] **1** : a fine thin white linen fabric **2** : a cotton fabric that resembles cambric

cambric tea n : a hot drink of water, milk, sugar, and often a small amount of tea

Cambs abbr Cambridgeshire

1came past of COME

2came \'kām\ n [origin unknown] : a slender grooved lead rod used to hold together panes of glass esp. in a stained-glass window

cam·el \'kam-əl\ n [ME, fr. OE & ONF, fr. L camelus, fr. Gk kamēlos, of Sem origin; akin to Heb & Phoenician gāmāl camel] **1** : either of two large ruminant mammals used as draft and saddle animals in desert regions esp. of Africa and Asia: **a** : the Arabian camel (Camelus dromedarius) with a single large hump on the back **b** : the camel (C. bactrianus) with two humps — called also Bactrian camel **2** : a watertight structure used esp. to lift submerged ships **3** : a variable color averaging a light yellowish brown

camels 1: 1 Arabian, 2 Bactrian

cam·el·back \'kam-əl-,bak\ n **1** : the back of a camel **2** : a steam locomotive with the cab astride the boiler **3** : an uncured compound chiefly of reclaimed or synthetic rubber used for retreading or recapping pneumatic tires

cam·el·eer \,kam-ə-'li(ə)r\ n : a camel driver

ca·mel·lia also **ca·me·lia** \kə-'mēl-yə\ n [NL Camellia, genus name, fr. Camellus (Georg Josef Kamel †1706 Moravian Jesuit missionary)] : any of several shrubs or trees (genus Camellia) of the tea family; esp : an ornamental greenhouse shrub (C. japonica) with glossy evergreen leaves and showy roselike flowers

ca·mel·o·pard \kə-'mel-ə-,pärd\ n [LL camelopardus, alter. of L camelopardalis, fr. Gk kamēlopardalis, fr. kamēlos + pardalis leopard] **1** : GIRAFFE **2** cap : CAMELOPARDALIS

Ca·mel·o·par·da·lis \kə-,mel-ə-'pärd-ʔl-əs\ n [L (gen. Camelopardalis), cameopard] : a northern constellation between Cassiopeia and Ursa Major

Cam·e·lot \'kam-ə-,lät\ n **1** : the site of King Arthur's palace and court in Arthurian legend **2** : a time, place, or atmosphere of idyllic happiness

camel's hair n **1** : the hair of the camel or a substitute for it (as hair from squirrels' tails) **2** : cloth made of camel's hair or a mixture of camel's hair and wool usu. light tan and of soft silky texture

Cam·em·bert \'kam-əm-,be(ə)r\ n [F, fr. Camembert, Normandy, France] : a soft surface-ripened cheese with a thin grayish white rind and a yellow interior

cam·eo \'kam-ē-,ō\ n, pl **-eos** [It] **1 a** : a gem carved in relief; esp : a small piece of sculpture on a stone or shell cut in relief in one layer with another contrasting layer serving as background **b** : a small medallion with a profiled head in relief **2** : a carving or sculpture made in the manner of a cameo **3** : a usu. brief literary or filmic piece that brings into delicate or sharp relief the character of a person, place, or event **4** : a small theatrical role (as in televi-

---

ə abut	ᵊ kitten	ər further	a back	ā bake ä cot, cart
aú out	ch chin	e less	ē easy	g gift i trip ī life
j joke	ŋ sing	ō flow	ò flaw	òi coin th thin th this
ü loot	ù foot	y yet	yü few	yù furious zh vision

sion) performed by a well-known actor and often limited to a single scene — **cameo** *adj* — **cameo** *vt*

cam·era \'kam(ə-)rə\ *n* [LL, room — more at CHAMBER] **1 :** the treasury department of the papal curia **2 a :** CAMERA OBSCURA **b :** a lightproof box fitted with a lens through the aperture of which the image of an object is recorded on a light-sensitive material **c :** the part of a television transmitting apparatus in which the image to be televised is formed for conversion into electrical impulses — **on camera :** before a live televising camera

cam·er·a·lism \'kam-(ə-)rə-,liz-əm\ *n* [G *kameralismus,* fr. ML *cameralis* of the royal treasury, fr. *camera* royal treasury, fr. LL, chamber] **:** the mercantilism of a group of 18th century German public administrators emphasizing economic policies designed to strengthen the power of the ruler — **cam·er·a·list** \-ləst\ *n*

camera lu·ci·da \,kam-(ə-)rə-'lü-səd-ə\ *n* [NL, lit., light chamber] **:** an instrument that by means of a prism or mirrors and often a microscope causes a virtual image of an object to appear as if projected upon a plane surface so that an outline may be traced

cam·era·man \'kam-(ə-)rə-,man, -mən\ *n* **1 :** one who operates a camera **2 :** one who sells photographic equipment

camera ob·scu·ra \,kam-(ə-)rə-əb-'skyůr-ə\ *n* [NL, lit., dark chamber] **:** a darkened enclosure having an aperture usu. provided with a lens through which light from external objects enters to form an image of the objects on the opposite surface

cam·er·len·go \,kam-ər-'leŋ-(,)gō\ *n, pl* **-gos** [It *camarlingo*] **:** a cardinal who heads the Apostolic Camera

ca·mion \kȧ-myōⁿ\ *n* [F] **:** MOTORTRUCK; *also* **:** BUS

cam·i·sa·do \,kam-ə-'säd-(,)ō, -'säd-\ *n, pl* **-does** [prob. fr. obs. Sp. *camisada*] *archaic* **:** an attack by night

ca·mise \kə-'mēz, -'mēs\ *n* [Ar *gamīṣ,* fr. LL *camisia*] **:** a light loose long-sleeved shirt, gown, or tunic

cam·i·sole \'kam-ə-,sōl\ *n* [F, prob. fr. OProv *camisolla,* dim. of *camisa* shirt, fr. LL *camisia*] **1 :** a short negligee jacket for women **2 :** a short sleeveless undergarment for women

cam·let \'kam-lət\ *n* [ME *cameloit,* fr. MF *camelot,* fr. Ar *hamlat* woolen plush] **1 a :** a medieval Asian fabric of camel's hair or angora wool **b :** a European fabric of silk and wool **c :** a fine lustrous woolen **2 :** a garment made of camlet

camomile *var of* CHAMOMILE

ca·mor·ra \kə-'mȯr-ə, -'mär-\ *n* [It] **:** a group of persons united for dishonest or dishonorable ends; *esp* **:** a secret organization formed about 1820 at Naples, Italy

ca·mor·ris·ta \,käm-ō-'rē-stə\ *n, pl* **-ti** \-(,)stē\ [It, fr. *camorra* + *-ista* -ist] **:** a member of a camorra

¹**cam·ou·flage** \'kam-ə-,fläzh, -,fläj\ *n* [F, fr. *camoufler* to disguise, fr. It *camuffare*] **1 :** the disguising esp. of military equipment or installations with paint, nets, or foilage; *also* **:** the disguise so applied **2 a :** concealment by means of disguise **b :** behavior or artifice designed to deceive or hide — **cam·ou·flag·ic** \,kam-ə-'fläzh-ik, -'fläj-\ *adj*

²**camouflage** *vb* **-flaged; -flag·ing** *vt* **:** to conceal or disguise by camouflage ~ *vi* **:** to practice camouflage — **cam·ou·flage·able** \'kam-ə-,fläzh-ə-bəl, -'fläj-\ *adj*

¹**camp** \'kamp\ *n, often attrib* [MF, prob. fr. ONF or OProv, fr. L *campus* plain, field; akin to OHG *hamf* crippled, Gk *kampē* bend] **1 a :** ground on which temporary shelters (as tents) are erected **b :** a group of shelters erected on such ground **c :** a temporary shelter (as a cabin or tent) **d :** an open-air location where one or more persons camp **e :** a settlement newly sprung up in a lumbering or mining region **2 a :** a body of persons encamped **b** (1) **:** a group or body of persons; *esp* **:** a group engaged in promoting or defending a theory, doctrine, or position ⟨liberal and conservative ~*s*⟩ (2) **:** an ideological position **3 :** military service or life

²**camp** *vi* **1 :** to pitch or occupy a camp **2 :** to live temporarily in a camp or outdoors — often used with *out* **3 :** to take up one's quarters **:** LODGE **4 :** to take up one's position **:** settle down ~ *vt* **:** to put into a camp; *also* **:** ACCOMMODATE

³**camp** *n* [origin unknown] **1 :** HOMOSEXUAL **2 :** exaggerated effeminate mannerisms exhibited esp. by homosexuals **3 :** something so outrageously artificial, affected, inappropriate, or out-of-date as to be considered amusing — **camp·i·ly** \-pə-lē\ *adv* — **camp·i·ness** \-pē-nəs\ *n* — **campy** \'kam-pē\ *adj*

⁴**camp** *adj* **1 :** of, relating to, or displaying camp ⟨~ send-ups of the songs of the fifties and sixties —John Elsom⟩ **2 :** of, relating to, or being a camp ⟨loose-limbed sensuality, which was sometimes macho and sometimes ~ —Jane Margold⟩

⁵**camp** *vi* **:** to engage in camp **:** exhibit the qualities of camp ⟨he . . . was ~*ing,* hands on hips, with a quick eye to notice every man who passed by —R. M. McAlmon⟩

¹**cam·paign** \(')kam-'pān\ *n* [F *campagne,* prob. fr. It *campagna* level country, campaign, fr. LL *campania* level country, fr. L, the level country around Naples] **1 :** a connected series of military operations forming a distinct phase of a war **2 :** a connected series of operations designed to bring about a particular result ⟨election ~⟩

²**campaign** *vi* **:** to go on, engage in, or conduct a campaign — **cam·paign·er** *n*

campaign ribbon *n* **:** a narrow ribbon-covered bar or a strip of ribbon whose distinctive coloring indicates a military campaign in which the wearer has taken part

cam·pa·nile \,kam-pə-'nē-lē, *esp of U.S. structures also* -'nē(ə)l\ *n, pl* **-ni·les** *or* **-ni·li** \-'nē-lē\ [It, fr. *campana* bell, fr. LL] **:** a usu. freestanding bell tower

cam·pa·nol·o·gist \,kam-pə-'näl-ə-jəst\ *n* **:** one that practices or is skilled in campanology

cam·pa·nol·o·gy \-jē\ *n* [NL *campanologia,* fr. LL *campana* + NL *-o-* + *-logia* -logy] **:** the art of bell ringing

cam·pan·u·la \kam-'pan-yə-lə\ *n* [NL, dim. of LL *campana*] **:** BELLFLOWER

cam·pan·u·late \-lət, -,lāt\ *adj* [NL *campanula* bell-shaped part, dim. of LL *campana*] **:** shaped like a bell

Camp·bell·ite \'kam-(b)ə-,līt\ *n* [Alexander *Campbell* †1866 Am preacher] **:** DISCIPLE 2 — often taken to be offensive

camp·craft \'kamp-,kraft\ *n* **:** skill and practice in the activities relating to camping

camp·er \'kam-pər\ *n* **1 :** one that camps **2 :** a portable dwelling (as a specially equipped trailer or automotive vehicle) for use during casual travel and camping

camp·er·ship \-,ship\ *n* [*camper* + *ship* (as in *scholarship*)] **:** a grant that enables a youngster to attend a summer camp

cam·pe·si·no \,kam-pə-'sē-(')nō\ *n, pl* **-nos** [Sp, fr. *campo* field, country, fr. L *campus* field — more at CAMP] **:** a native of a Latin-American rural area; *esp* **:** a Latin-American Indian farmer or farm laborer

cam·pes·tral \kam-'pes-trəl\ *adj* [L *campestr-, campester,* fr. *campus*] **:** of or relating to fields or open country **:** RURAL

camp fire girl *n* [fr. *Camp Fire Girls,* Inc.] **:** a member of a national organization of girls from 7 to 18

camp follower *n* **1 :** a civilian who follows a military unit to attend or exploit military personnel; *specif* **:** PROSTITUTE **2 :** a disciple or follower who is not of the main body of members or adherents; *esp* **:** a politician who joins the party or movement solely for personal gain

camp·ground \'kamp-,graůnd\ *n* **:** the area or place (as a field or grove) used for a camp, for camping, or for a camp meeting

cam·phene \'kam-,fēn\ *n* **:** any of several terpenes related to camphor; *esp* **:** a colorless crystalline terpene $C_{10}H_{16}$ used in insecticides

cam·phine *or* **cam·phene** \'kam-,fēn\ *n* [ISV, fr. *camphor*] **:** an explosive mixture of turpentine and alcohol formerly used as an illuminant

cam·phor \'kam(p)-fər\ *n* [ME *caumfre,* fr. AF, fr. ML *camphora,* fr. Ar *kāfūr,* fr. Malay *kāpūr*] **:** a tough gummy volatile fragrant crystalline compound $C_{10}H_{16}O$ obtained esp. from the wood and bark of the camphor tree and used as a carminative and stimulant in medicine, as a plasticizer, and as an insect repellent; *also* **:** any of several similar compounds (as some terpene alcohols and ketones) — **cam·pho·ra·ceous** \,kam(p)-fə-'rā-shəs\ *adj* — **cam·phor·ic** \kam-'fȯr-ik, -'fär-\ *adj*

cam·phor·ate \'kam(p)-fə-,rāt\ *vt* **-at·ed; -at·ing :** to impregnate or treat with camphor

camphor tree *n* **:** a large evergreen tree (*Cinnamomum camphora*) of the laurel family grown in most warm countries

cam·pi·on \'kam-pē-ən\ *n* [prob. fr. obs. *campion* (champion)] **:** any of various plants (genera *Lychnis* and *Silene*) of the pink family: as **a :** a European crimson-flowered plant (*L. coronaria*) **b :** an herb (*S. cucubalus*) with white flowers

camp meeting *n* **:** a series of evangelistic meetings usu. held outdoors or in a tent or wooden structure and attended by families who often camp nearby

cam·po \'kam-(,)pō, 'käm-\ *n, pl* **campos** [AmerSp, fr. Sp, field, fr. L *campus*] **:** a grassland plain in So. America with scattered perennial herbs

campong *var of* KAMPONG

camp·o·ree \,kam-pə-'rē\ *n* [*camp* + *jamboree*] **:** a gathering of boy scouts or girl scouts from a given geographic area

camp–out \'kam-,paůt\ *n* **:** an occasion on which a group camps out

camp·site \'kamp-,sīt\ *n* **:** a place suitable for or used as the site of a camp

camp·stool \-,stül\ *n* **:** a small portable backless folding stool

cam·pus \'kam-pəs\ *n* [L, plain — more at CAMP] **:** the grounds and buildings of a university, college, or school; *also* **:** the grassy area in the central part of the grounds

cam·py·lot·ro·pous \,kam-pi-'lä-trə-pəs\ *adj* [Gk *kampylos* bent + ISV *-tropous;* akin to Gk *kampē* bend — more at CAMP] **:** having the ovule curved

cam·shaft \'kam-,shaft\ *n* **:** a shaft to which a cam is fastened or of which a cam forms an integral part

cam wheel *n* **:** a wheel set or shaped to act as a cam

¹**can** \kən, (')kan *sometimes* kᵊŋ\ *vb, past* **could** \kəd, (')kůd\; *pres sing & pl* **can** [ME (1st & 3d sing. pres. indic.), fr. OE; akin to OHG *kan* (1st & 3d sing. pres. indic.) know, am able, OE *cnāwan* to know — more at KNOW] *vt* **1** *obs* **:** KNOW, UNDERSTAND **2 :** to be able to do, make, or accomplish ~ *vi, archaic* **:** to have knowledge or skill ~ *verbal auxiliary* **1 a :** know how to ⟨he ~ read⟩ **b :** be physically or mentally able to ⟨he ~ lift 200 pounds⟩ **c :** may perhaps ⟨do you think he ~ still be living⟩ **d :** be permitted by conscience or feeling to ⟨~ hardly blame him⟩ **e :** be made possible or probable by circumstances to ⟨he ~ hardly have meant that⟩ **f :** be inherently able or designed to ⟨everything that money ~ buy⟩ **g :** be logically or axiologically able to ⟨2 + 2 ~ also be written 3 + 1⟩ **h :** be enabled by law, agreement, or custom to **2 :** have permission to — used interchangeably with *may* ⟨you ~ go now if you like⟩

²**can** \'kan\ *n* [ME *canne,* fr. OE; akin to OHG *channa*] **1 :** a usu. cylindrical receptacle: **a :** a vessel for holding liquids; *specif* **:** a drinking vessel **b :** a typically cylindrical metal receptacle usu. with an open top, often with a removable cover, and sometimes with a spout or side handles (as for holding milk, oil, coffee, tobacco, ashes, or garbage) **c :** a container (as of tinplate) in which perishable foods or other products are hermetically sealed for preservation until use **d :** a jar for packing or preserving fruit or vegetables **2** *slang* **:** JAIL **3 :** TOILET **4 :** BUTTOCKS **5 :** DEPTH CHARGE **6 :** DESTROYER 2 **7** *slang* **:** an ounce of marijuana — **can·ful** \'kan-,fůl\ *adj* — **in the can** *of a film or videotape* **:** completed and ready for release

³**can** \'kan\ *vt* **canned; can·ning 1 a :** to put in a can **:** preserve by sealing in airtight cans or jars **b :** to hit (a golf ball) into the cup **2** *slang* **:** to expel from school **:** discharge from employment **3** *slang* **:** to put a stop or end to ⟨~ that racket —Nathaniel Burt⟩ **4 :** to record on discs or tape ⟨they *canned* the music for the broadcast⟩ — **can·ner** *n*

⁴**can** *abbr* **1** canceled; cancellation **2** cannon **3** canto

Can *or* **Canad** *abbr* Canada; Canadian

Ca·naan·ite \'kā-nə-ˌnīt\ *n* [Gk *Kananitēs*, fr. *Kanaan* Canaan] : a member of a Semitic people inhabiting ancient Palestine and Phoenicia from about 3000 B.C. — **Canaanite** *adj*

Can·a·da balsam \ˌkan-əd-ə-\ *n* [Canada, country in No. America] : a viscid yellowish to greenish oleoresin exudate of the balsam fir (*Abies balsmea*) that solidifies to a transparent mass and is used as a transparent cement esp. in microscopy

Canada goose *n* : the common wild goose (*Branta canadensis*) of No. America that is chiefly gray and brownish with black head and neck and a white patch running from the sides of the head under the throat

Canada lynx *n* : LYNX c

Canada thistle *n* : a European thistle (*Cirsium arvense*) that is a naturalized weed in No. America

Ca·na·di·an \kə-'nād-ē-ən\ *n* : a native or inhabitant of Canada — **Canadian** *adj*

Canada goose

Canadian bacon \kə-ˌnād-ē-ən-\ *n* : bacon cut from the loin of a pig

Canadian football *n* : a game resembling both American football and rugby that is played on a turfed field between two teams of 12 players each

Canadian French *n* : the language of the French Canadians

ca·naille \kə-'nī, -'nā(ə)l\ *n* [F, fr. It *canaglia*, fr. *cane* dog, fr. L *canis* — more at HOUND] **1** : RABBLE, RIFFRAFF **2** : PROLETARIAN

¹ca·nal \kə-'nal\ *n* [ME, fr. L *canalis* pipe, channel, fr. *canna* reed — more at CANE] **1** : CHANNEL, WATERCOURSE **2** : a tubular anatomical passage or channel : DUCT **3** : an artificial waterway for navigation or for draining or irrigating land **4** : any of various faint narrow markings on the planet Mars

²canal *vt* **-nalled** *or* **-naled; -nal·ling** *or* **-nal·ing** : to construct a canal through or across

ca·nal·boat \kə-'nal-,bōt\ *n* : a boat for use on a canal

can·a·lic·u·late \ˌkan-ᵊl-'ik-yə-lət, -ˌlāt\ *adj* : grooved or channeled longitudinally ⟨a ~ leafstalk⟩

can·a·lic·u·lus \-yə-ləs\ *n, pl* **-li** \-ˌlī, -ˌlē\ [L, dim. of *canalis*] : a minute canal in a bodily structure

can·a·li·za·tion \ˌkan-ᵊl-ə-'zā-shən\ *n* **1** : an act or instance of canalizing **2** : a system of channels

can·a·lize \'kan-ᵊl-,īz\ *vb* **-lized; -liz·ing** *vt* **1 a** : to provide with a canal or channel **b** : to make into or similar to a canal **2** : to provide with an outlet; *esp* : to direct into preferred channels ~ *vi* **1** : to flow in or into a channel **2** : to establish new channels

can·a·pé \'kan-ə-pē, -,pā\ *n* [F, lit., sofa, fr. ML *canopeum, canapeum* mosquito net — more at CANOPY] : an appetizer consisting of a piece of bread or toast or a cracker topped with a savory spread (as caviar or cheese) — compare HORS D'OEUVRE

ca·nard \kə-'närd *also* -'när\ *n* [F, lit., duck, fr. MF *vendre des canards à moitié* to cheat, lit., to half-sell ducks] : a false or unfounded report or story; *esp* : a fabricated report

ca·nary \kə-'ne(ə)r-ē\ *n, pl* **ca·nar·ies** [MF *canarie*, fr. OSp *canario*, fr. *Islas Canarias* Canary islands] **1** : a lively 16th century court dance **2** : a Canary islands usu. sweet wine similar to Madeira **3 a** : a small finch (*Serinus canarius*) of the Canary islands that is usu. greenish to yellow and is kept as a cage bird and singer **b** : any of various small birds largely yellow in color **4** [fr. his singing] *slang* : INFORMER 2

canary seed *n* **1** : seed of a Canary island grass (*Phalaris canariensis*) used as food for cage birds **2** : seed of a common plantain (*Plantago major*)

canary yellow *n* : a light to a moderate or vivid yellow

ca·nas·ta \kə-'nas-tə\ *n* [Sp, lit., basket] **1** : a form of rummy using two full decks in which players or partnerships try to meld groups of three or more cards of the same rank and score bonuses for 7-card melds **2** : a meld of seven cards of the same rank in canasta

canc *abbr* canceled

can·can \'kan-ˌkan\ *n* [F] : a woman's dance of French origin characterized by high kicking usu. while holding up the front of a full ruffled skirt

¹can·cel \'kan(t)-səl\ *vb* **-celed** *or* **-celled; -cel·ing** *or* **-cel·ling** \-s(ə-)liŋ\ [ME *cancellen*, fr. MF *canceller*, fr. LL *cancellare*, fr. L, to make like a lattice, fr. *cancelli* (pl.), dim. of *cancer* lattice, alter. of *carcer* prison] *vt* **1 a** : to mark or strike out for deletion **b** : OMIT, DELETE **2 a** : to destroy the force, effectiveness, or validity of : ANNUL ⟨~ a magazine subscription⟩ **b** : to bring to nothingness : DESTROY **c** : to match in force or effect : OFFSET — often used with *out* ⟨his irritability ~ed out his natural kindness — Osbert Sitwell⟩ **3** : to call off usu. without expectation of conducting or performing at a later time ⟨~ a football game⟩ **3 a** : to remove (a common divisor) from numerator and denominator **b** : to remove (equivalents) on opposite sides of an equation or account **4** : to deface (a postage or revenue stamp) esp. with a set of parallel lines so as to invalidate for reuse ~ *vi* : to neutralize each other's strength or effect : COUNTERBALANCE *syn* see ERASE — **can·cel·able** *or* **can·cel·la·ble** \-s(ə-)lə-bəl\ *adj* — **can·cel·er** *or* **can·cel·ler** \-s(ə)lər\ *n*

²cancel *n* **1** : CANCELLATION **2 a** : a deleted part or passage **b** : a passage or page from which something has been deleted **c** (1) : a leaf containing deleted matter (2) : a new leaf or slip substituted for matter already printed

can·cel·late \ˌkan-'sel-ət, 'kan(t)-sə-,lāt\ *adj* [L *cancellatus*, pp. of *cancellare*] : RETICULATE, CHAMBERED ⟨~ leaves⟩; *specif* : CANCELLOUS

can·cel·la·tion *also* **can·cel·ation** \ˌkan(t)-sə-'lā-shən\ *n* **1** : the act or an instance of canceling **2** : a released accommodation **3** : a mark used to cancel something (as a postage stamp)

can·cel·lous \ˌkan-'sel-əs, 'kan(t)-sə-ləs\ *adj* [NL *cancelli* intersecting osseous plates and bars in cancellous bone, fr. L, lattice] *of bone* : having a porous structure

can·cer \'kan(t)-sər\ *n* [ME, fr. L (gen. *Cancri*), lit., crab; akin to Gk *karkinos* crab, cancer] **1** *cap* **a** : a northern zodiacal constellation between Gemini and Leo **b** (1) : the 4th sign of the zodiac in astrology — see ZODIAC table (2) : one born under this sign **2** [L, crab, cancer] **a** : a malignant tumor of potentially unlimited growth that expands locally by invasion and systemically by metastasis **b** : an abnormal state marked by such tumors **3 a** : a source of evil or anguish ⟨the ~ of hidden resentment — *Irish Digest*⟩ **4 a** : an enlarged tumorlike growth **b** : a disease marked by such growths — **can·cer·ous** \'kan(t)s-(ə-)rəs\ *adj* — **can·cer·ous·ly** *adv*

can·cha \'kän-(ˌ)chä\ *n* [Sp, yard, court, fr. Quechua, yard] : a jai alai court

can·croid \'kaŋ-ˌkrȯid\ *adj* [L *cancr-, cancer* crab, cancer] **1** : resembling a crab **2** : resembling a cancer

can·de·la \kan-'dē-lə, -'del-ə\ *n* [L, candle] : CANDLE 3

can·de·la·bra \ˌkan-də-'läb-rə, -ˌlab-, -'lāb-\ *n* : CANDELABRUM

can·de·la·brum \-rəm\ *n, pl* **-bra** \-rə\ *also* **-brums** [L, fr. *candela*] : a branched candlestick or lamp with several lights

can·dent \'kan-dənt\ *adj* [L *candent-, candens*, prp. of *candēre*] : heated to whiteness : GLOWING

can·des·cence \kan-'des-ᵊn(t)s\ *n* : a candescent state : glowing whiteness

can·des·cent \-ᵊnt\ *adj* [L *candescent-, candescens*, prp. of *candescere* incho. of *candēre*] : glowing or dazzling esp. from great heat

C and F *abbr* cost and freight

can·did \'kan-dəd\ *adj* [F & L; F *candide*, fr. L *candidus* bright, white, fr. *candēre* to shine, glow; akin to LGk *kandaros* ember] **1** : WHITE ⟨~ flames⟩ **2** : free from bias, prejudice, or malice : FAIR ⟨a ~ observer⟩ **3 a** : marked by honest sincere expression **b** : indicating or suggesting sincere honesty and absence of deception **c** : disposed to criticize severely : BLUNT **4** : relating to photography of subjects acting naturally or spontaneously without being posed ⟨~ picture⟩ *syn* see FRANK *ant* evasive — **can·did·ly** *adv* — **can·did·ness** *n*

can·di·da \'kan-dəd-ə\ *n* [NL, genus name, fr. L, fem. of *candidus*, white] : any of a genus (*Candida*) of parasitic imperfect fungi that resemble yeasts, produce small amounts of mycelium, and include the causative agent of thrush

can·di·da·cy \'kan-(d)əd-ə-sē\ *n, pl* **-cies** : the state of being a candidate

can·di·date \'kan-(d)ə-ˌdāt, -(d)əd-ət\ *n* [L *candidatus*, fr. *candidatus* clothed in white, fr. *candidus* white; fr. the white toga worn by candidates for office in ancient Rome] : one that aspires to or is nominated or qualified for an office, membership, or award

can·di·da·ture \'kan-(d)əd-ə-ˌchu̇(ə)r, -chər\ *n, chiefly Brit* : CANDIDACY

candid camera *n* **1** : a usu. small camera equipped with a fast lens and used for taking informal photographs of unposed subjects often without their knowledge **2** : a miniature camera

can·di·di·a·sis \ˌkan-də-'dī-ə-səs\ *n, pl* **-a·ses** \-ˌsēz\ : infection with a disease caused by a candida

can·died \'kan-dēd\ *adj* **1** : encrusted or coated with sugar **2** : baked with sugar or syrup until translucent

¹can·dle \'kan-dᵊl\ *n* [ME *candel*, fr. OE, fr. L *candela*, fr. *candēre*] **1** : a usu. long slender cylindrical mass of tallow or wax containing a loosely twisted linen or cotton wick that is burned to give light **2** : something resembling a candle in shape or use ⟨a sulfur ~ for fumigating⟩ **3** : a unit of luminous intensity equal to one sixtieth of the luminous intensity of one square centimeter of a blackbody surface at the solidification temperature of platinum — called also *candela, new candle*

²candle *vt* **can·dled; can·dling** \'kan-(d)liŋ, -dᵊl-iŋ\ : to examine by holding between the eye and a light; *esp* : to test (eggs) in this way for staleness, blood clots, fertility, and growth — **can·dler** \-(d)lər, -dᵊl-ər\ *n*

can·dle·ber·ry \'kan-dᵊl-,ber-ē\ *n* **1 a** : CANDLENUT **b** : WAX MYRTLE **2** : the fruit of a candleberry

can·dle·fish \-,fish\ *n* **1** : EULACHON **2** : SABLEFISH

can·dle·foot \-'fu̇t\ *n* : FOOTCANDLE

can·dle·hold·er \-,hōl-dər\ *n* : CANDLESTICK

can·dle·light \'kan-dᵊl-(,)līt\ *n* **1 a** : the light of a candle **b** : a soft artificial light **2** : the time for lighting up : TWILIGHT

can·dle·light·er \-ər\ *n* **1** : a long-handled implement with a taper and a snuffer that is used for the ceremonial lighting and extinguishing of candles **2** : one who lights the candles for a ceremony (as a wedding)

Can·dle·mas \'kan-dᵊl-məs\ *n* [ME *candelmasse*, fr. OE *candelmæsse*, fr. *candel* + *mæsse* mass, feast; fr. the candles blessed and carried in celebration of the feast] : February 2 observed as a church festival in commemoration of the presentation of Christ in the temple and the purification of the Virgin Mary

can·dle·nut \-,nət\ *n* : the oily seed of a tropical tree (*Aleurites moluccana*) of the spurge family used locally to make candles and commercially as a source of oil; *also* : this tree

can·dle·pin \-,pin\ *n* **1** : a slender bowling pin tapering toward top and bottom **2** *pl but sing in constr* : a bowling game using candlepins and a smaller ball than that used in tenpins

can·dle·pow·er \-,pau̇(-ə)r\ *n* : luminous intensity expressed in candles

candelabrum

can·dle·snuff·er \-ˌsnəf-ər\ *n* **:** an implement for snuffing candles that consists of a small hollow cone attached to a handle
can·dle·stick \-ˌstik\ *n* **:** a holder with a socket for a candle
can·dle·wick \-ˌwik\ *n* **1 :** the wick of a candle **2 :** a soft cotton embroidery yarn; *also* **:** embroidery made with this yarn usu. in tufts
can·dle·wood \-ˌwu̇d\ *n* **1 :** any of several trees or shrubs (as ocotillo) chiefly of resinous character **2 :** slivers of resinous wood burned for light
can·dor \ˈkan-dər, -ˌdȯ(ə)r\ *n* [F&L; F *candeur,* fr. L *candor,* fr. *candēre* — more at CANDID] **1 a :** WHITENESS, BRILLIANCE **b** *obs* **:** unstained purity **2 :** freedom from prejudice or malice **:** FAIRNESS **3** *archaic* **:** KINDLINESS **4 :** unreserved, honest, or sincere expression **:** FORTHRIGHTNESS
can·dour \ˈkan-dər\ *chiefly Brit var of* CANDOR
C and W *abbr* country and western
[1]**can·dy** \ˈkan-dē\ *n, pl* **candies** [ME *sugre candy,* part trans. of MF *sucre candi,* part trans. of OIt *zucchero candi,* fr. *zucchero* sugar + Ar *qandi* candied, fr. *qand* cane sugar] **1 :** crystallized sugar formed by boiling down sugar syrup **2 a :** a confection made of sugar often with flavoring and filling **b :** a piece of such confection — **candy** *adj*
[2]**candy** *vb* **can·died; can·dy·ing** *vt* **1 :** to encrust in or coat with sugar often by cooking to a thicker consistency in a heavy syrup **2 :** to make attractive **:** SWEETEN **3 :** to crystallize into sugar ~ *vi* **:** to become coated or encrusted with sugar crystals **:** become crystallized into sugar
candy strip·er \-ˌstrī-pər\ *n* [fr. the striped uniform worn suggesting the stripes on some sticks of candy] **:** a teenage volunteer nurse's aide
can·dy·tuft \ˈkan-dē-ˌtəft\ *n* [*Candy* (now *Candia*) Crete, Greek island + E *tuft*] **:** any of a genus (*Iberis*) of plants of the mustard family cultivated for their white, pink, or purple flowers
[1]**cane** \ˈkān\ *n* [ME, fr. MF, fr. OProv *cana,* fr. L *canna,* fr. Gk *kanna,* of Sem origin; akin to Ar *qanāh* hollow stick, reed] **1 a** (1) **:** a hollow or pithy and usu. slender and flexible jointed stem (as of a reed) (2) **:** any of various slender woody stems; *esp* **:** an elongated flowering or fruiting stem (as of a rose) usu. arising directly from the ground **b :** any of various tall woody grasses or reeds; as (1) **:** any of a genus (*Arundinaria*) of coarse grasses (2) **:** SUGARCANE (3) **:** SORGHUM **2 :** cane dressed for use: as **a :** a cane walking stick; *broadly* **:** WALKING STICK **b :** a cane or rod for flogging **c :** RATTAN; *esp* **:** split rattan for wickerwork or basketry
[2]**cane** *vt* **caned; can·ing 1 :** to beat with a cane **2 :** to weave or furnish with cane ⟨~ the seat of a chair⟩
cane·brake \ˈkān-ˌbrāk\ *n* **:** a thicket of cane
can·er \ˈkā-nər\ *n* **:** one that weaves cane seats and backs of chairs
ca·nes·cent \kə-ˈnes-ᵊnt, ka-\ *adj* [L *canescent-, canescens,* prp. of *canescere,* incho. of *canēre* to be gray, be white, fr. *canus* white, hoary — more at HARE] **:** growing white, whitish, or hoary; *esp* **:** having a fine grayish white pubescence ⟨~ leaves⟩
cane sugar *n* **:** sugar from sugarcane
cane·ware \ˈkān-ˌwa(ə)r, -ˌwe(ə)r\ *n* [fr. its color] **:** a buff or yellowish stoneware
ca·nic·o·la fever \kə-ˌnik-ə-lə-\ *n* [NL *canicola* (specific epithet of *Leptospira canicola*) fr. L *canis* dog + *-cola* inhabitant — more at HOUND, -COLOUS] **:** an acute disease in man and dogs characterized by gastroenteritis and mild jaundice and caused by a spirochete (*Leptospira canicola*)
Ca·nic·u·la \kə-ˈnik-yə-lə\ *n* [L, dim. of *canis*] **:** SIRIUS
ca·nic·u·lar \kə-ˈnik-yə-lər\ *adj* **1 :** of or relating to the Dog Star or its rising **2 :** of or relating to the dog days
[1]**ca·nine** \ˈkā-ˌnīn\ *adj* [L *caninus,* fr. *canis* dog — more at HOUND] **1 :** of or relating to dogs or to the family (Canidae) including the dogs, wolves, jackals, and foxes **2 :** of, relating to, or resembling a dog
[2]**canine** *n* **1 :** a conical pointed tooth; *esp* **:** one situated between the lateral incisor and the first premolar — see TOOTH illustration **2 :** DOG
Ca·nis Ma·jor \ˌkā-nə-ˈsmā-jər, ˌkan-ə-\ *n* [L (gen. *Canis Majoris*), lit., greater dog] **:** a constellation to the southeast of Orion containing the Dog Star
Canis Mi·nor \-ˈsmī-nər\ *n* [L, (gen. *Canis Minoris*), lit., lesser dog] **:** a constellation to the east of Orion containing Procyon
can·is·ter *also* **can·nis·ter** \ˈkan-ə-stər\ *n* [L *canistrum* basket, fr. Gk *kanastron,* fr. *kanna* reed — more at CANE] **1 :** a small box or can for holding a dry product **2 :** encased shot for close-range artillery fire **3 :** a light perforated metal box for gas masks that contains material to adsorb, filter, or detoxify poisons and irritants in the air
[1]**can·ker** \ˈkaŋ-kər\ *n* [ME, fr. ONF *cancre,* fr. L *cancer* crab, cancer] **1 a** (1) **:** an erosive or spreading sore (2) *obs* **:** GANGRENE 1 (3) **:** an area of necrosis in a plant **b :** any of various disorders of animals marked by chronic inflammatory changes **2** *archaic* **:** a caterpillar destructive to plants **3** *chiefly dial* **a :** RUST **b :** VERDIGRIS 2 **4 :** a source of corruption or debasement **5** *chiefly dial* **:** a common European wild rose (*Rosa canina*) — **can·ker·ous** \-kaŋ-k(ə-)rəs\ *adj*
[2]**canker** *vb* **can·kered; can·ker·ing** \ˈkaŋ-k(ə-)riŋ\ *vt* **1** *obs* **:** to infect with a spreading sore **2 :** to corrupt with a malignancy of mind or spirit ⟨God help that country, ~*ed* deep by doubt —Archibald MacLeish⟩ ~ *vi* **1 :** to become infested with canker **2 :** to undergo corruption
canker sore *n* **:** a small painful ulcer esp. of the mouth
can·ker·worm \ˈkaŋ-kər-ˌwərm\ *n* **:** any of various insect larvae that injure plants esp. by feeding on buds and foliage
can·na \ˈkan-ə\ *n* [NL, genus name, fr. L, reed — more at CANE] **:** any of a genus (*Canna* of the family Cannaceae) of tropical herbs with simple stems, large leaves, and a terminal raceme of irregular flowers
can·na·bin \ˈkan-ə-bən\ *n* [L *cannabis*] **:** a dark resin from pistillate hemp plants that contains the physiologically active principles of cannabis
can·na·bis \-bəs\ *n* [L, hemp, fr. Gk *kannabis,* fr. the source of OE *hænep* hemp] **:** the dried flowering spikes of the pistillate plants of the hemp — compare HASHISH, MARIJUANA
canned \ˈkand\ *adj* **1 :** sealed in a can or jar **2 :** recorded for mechanical or electronic reproduction; *also* **:** prerecorded for addition to a sound track or a videotape ⟨~ laughter⟩ **3 a :** prepared in identical form for wide or repeated use **:** SYNDICATED ⟨~ editorials⟩ **b :** made trite by overuse **:** HACKNEYED ⟨~ phrases⟩ **4** *slang* **:** DRUNK
can·nel coal \ˌkan-ᵊl-\ *n* [prob. fr. E dial. *cannel* candle, fr. ME *candel*] **:** a bituminous coal containing much volatile matter that burns brightly
can·nery \ˈkan-(ə-)rē\ *n, pl* **-ner·ies :** a factory for the canning of foods
can·ni·bal \ˈkan-ə-bəl\ *n* [NL *Canibalis* Carib, fr. Sp *Caníbal,* fr. Arawakan *Caniba, Carib,* of Cariban origin; akin to Carib *Galibi* Caribs, lit., strong men] **1 :** a human being who eats human flesh **2 :** an animal that devours its own kind — **cannibal** *adj* — **can·ni·bal·ic** \ˌkan-ə-ˈbal-ik\ *adj* — **can·ni·bal·ism** \ˈkan-ə-bə-ˌliz-əm\ *n* — **can·ni·bal·is·tic** \ˌkan-ə-bə-ˈlis-tik\ *adj*
can·ni·bal·ize \ˈkan-ə-bə-ˌlīz\ *vb* **-ized; iz·ing** *vt* **1 :** to dismantle (a machine) for parts to be used as replacements in other machines **2 :** to deprive of parts or men in order to repair or strengthen another unit ~ *vi* **1 :** to practice cannibalism **2 :** to cannibalize one unit for the sake of another of the same kind — **can·ni·bal·iza·tion** \ˌkan-ə-bə-lə-ˈzā-shən\ *n*
can·ni·kin \ˈkan-i-kən\ *n* [prob. fr. obs. D *kanneken,* fr. MD *canneken,* dim. of *canne* can; akin to OE *canne* can] **:** a small can or drinking vessel
[1]**can·non** \ˈkan-ən\ *n, pl* **cannons** *or* **cannon** [MF *canon,* fr. It *cannone,* lit., large tube, aug. of *canna* reed, tube, fr. L, cane, reed — more at CANE] **1** *pl usu cannon* **a :** an artillery piece **:** big gun **b :** a heavy-caliber automatic aircraft gun firing explosive shells **2 :** a smooth round horse bit **3** *or* **can·on :** the projecting part of a bell by which it is hung **:** EAR **4 :** the part of the leg in which the cannon bone is found
[2]**cannon** *vi* **:** to discharge cannon ~ *vt* **:** CANNONADE
[3]**cannon** *n* [alter. of *carom*] *Brit* **:** a carom in billiards and bagatelle
[4]**cannon** *vi, Brit* **:** to carom in billiards ~ *vt, Brit* **:** to carom into
[1]**can·non·ade** \ˌkan-ə-ˈnād\ *n* **:** a heavy fire of artillery
[2]**cannonade** *vb* **-ad·ed; -ad·ing** *vt* **:** to attack with artillery ~ *vi* **:** to deliver artillery fire
[1]**can·non·ball** \ˈkan-ən-ˌbȯl\ *n* **1 a :** a round solid missile made for firing from a cannon **b :** a missile of a solid or hollow shape made for cannon **2 :** a jump into water made with the arms holding the knees tight against the chest **3 :** a hard straight tennis service **4 :** a fast train
[2]**cannonball** *vi* **:** to travel with great speed
cannon bone *n* [F *canon,* lit., cannon] **:** a bone in hoofed mammals that supports the leg from the hock joint to the fetlock
can·non·eer \ˌkan-ə-ˈni(ə)r\ *n* **:** an artillery gunner
cannon fodder *n* **:** soldiers subject to the risk of being wounded or killed by artillery fire
can·non·ry \ˈkan-ən-rē\ *n, pl* **-ries 1 :** CANNONADE **2 :** ARTILLERY
can·not \ˈkan-(ˌ)ät; kə-ˈnät, ka-ˈ\ **:** can not — **cannot but :** to be bound to **:** MUST
can·nu·la \ˈkan-yə-lə\ *n, pl* **-las** *or* **-lae** \-ˌlē, -ˌlī\ [NL, fr. L, dim. of *canna* reed — more at CANE] **:** a small tube for insertion into a body cavity or into a duct or vessel
can·nu·lar \ˈkan-yə-lər\ *adj* **:** TUBULAR
can·nu·la·tion \ˌkan-yə-ˈlā-shən\ *n* **:** the act or process of inserting a cannula — **can·nu·late** \ˈkan-yə-ˌlāt\ *vt*
[1]**can·ny** \ˈkan-ē\ *adj* **can·ni·er; -est** [[1]*can*] **1 :** being cautious and shrewd **:** CLEVER **2** *Scot* **a :** FORTUNATE, LUCKY **b :** free from unnatural powers or unfavorable aspects **c :** skilled in the supernatural or occult **3 a** *Scot* **:** CAREFUL, STEADY **b** *Scot* **:** QUIET, SNUG ⟨then ~, in some cozy place, they close the day — Robert Burns⟩ **c** *dial Brit* **:** agreeable to the eyes **:** PLEASANT — **can·ni·ly** \ˈkan-ᵊl-ē\ *adv* — **can·ni·ness** \ˈkan-ē-nəs\ *n*
[2]**canny** *adv, Scot* **:** in a canny manner
[1]**ca·noe** \kə-ˈnü\ *n* [F, fr. NL *canoa,* fr. Sp, fr. Arawakan, of Cariban origin; akin to Galibi *canaoua*] **:** a long light narrow boat with both ends sharp and sides curved that is usu. propelled by hand-driven paddles
[2]**canoe** *vb* **ca·noed; ca·noe·ing** *vi* **1 :** to paddle a canoe **2 :** to go or travel in a canoe ~ *vt* **:** to transport in a canoe — **ca·noe·ist** *n*
can of worms : PANDORA'S BOX
[1]**canon** \ˈkan-ən\ *n* [ME, fr. OE, fr. LL, fr. L, ruler, rule, model, standard, fr. Gk *kanōn;* akin to Gk *kanna* reed — more at CANE] **1 a :** a regulation or dogma decreed by a church council **b :** a provision of canon law **2** [ME, prob. fr. OF, fr. LL, fr. L, model] **:** the most solemn and unvarying part of the Mass including the consecration of the bread and wine **3** [ME, fr. LL, fr. L, standard] **a :** an authoritative list of books accepted as Holy Scripture **b :** the authentic works of a writer **4 a :** an accepted principle or rule **b :** a criterion or standard of judgment **c :** a body of principles, rules, standards, or norms **5** [LGk *kanōn,* fr. Gk, model] **:** a contrapuntal musical composition in two or more voice parts in which the melody is imitated exactly and completely by the successive voices though not always at the same pitch
[2]**canon** *n* [ME *canoun,* fr. AF *canunie,* fr. LL *canonicus* one living under a rule, fr. L, according to rule, fr. Gk *kanonikos,* fr. *kanōn*] **1 :** a clergyman belonging to the chapter or the staff of a cathedral or collegiate church **2 :** CANON REGULAR
ca·ñon \ˈkan-yən\ *var of* CANYON
can·on·ess \ˈkan-ə-nəs\ *n* **1 :** a woman living in community under a religious rule but not under a perpetual vow **2 :** a member of a Roman Catholic congregation of women corresponding to canons regular
ca·non·ic \kə-ˈnän-ik\ *adj* **1 :** CANONICAL **2 :** of or relating to musical canon
ca·non·i·cal \-i-kəl\ *adj* **1 :** of or relating to a canon **2 :** conforming to a general rule **:** ORTHODOX **3 :** accepted as forming the

canon of scripture **4** : of or relating to a clergyman who is a canon **5** : reduced to the simplest or clearest schema possible ⟨a ~ matrix⟩ — **ca·non·i·cal·ly** \-k(ə-)lē\ *adv*

canonical form *n* : the simplest form of a matrix; *specif* : the form of a square matrix that has zero elements everywhere except along the principal diagonal

canonical hour *n* **1** : a time of day canonically appointed for an office of devotion **2** : one of the daily offices of devotion that compose the Divine Office and include matins with lauds, prime, terce, sext, none, vespers, and compline

ca·non·i·cals \kə-ˈnän-i-kəlz\ *n pl* : the vestments prescribed by canon for an officiating clergyman

can·on·ic·i·ty \ˌkan-ə-ˈnis-ət-ē\ *n* : the quality or state of being canonical

can·on·ist \ˈkan-ə-nəst\ *n* : a specialist in canon law

can·on·ize \ˈkan-ə-ˌnīz\ *vt* **can·on·ized** \-ˌnīzd; *in "Hamlet", usu* kə-ˈnän-ˌīzd\; **can·on·iz·ing** [ME *canonizen*, fr. ML *canonizare*, fr. LL *canon* catalog of saints, fr. L, standard] **1** : to declare (a deceased person) an officially recognized saint **2** : to make canonical **3** : to sanction by ecclesiastical authority **4** : to attribute authoritative sanction or approval to — **can·on·iza·tion** \ˌkan-ə-nə-ˈzā-shən\ *n*

canon law *n* : the usu. codified law governing a church

canon lawyer *n* : CANONIST

canon regular *n, pl* **canons regular** : a member of one of several Roman Catholic religious institutes of regular priests living in community under a usu. Augustinian rule

can·on·ry \ˈkan-ən-rē\ *n, pl* **-ries** : the office of a canon; *also* : the endowment that financially supports a canon

ca·no·pic jar \kə-ˌnō-pik-, -ˌnäp-ik-\ *n, often cap C* [*Canopus*, Egypt] : a jar in which the ancient Egyptians preserved the viscera of a deceased person usu. for burial with the mummy

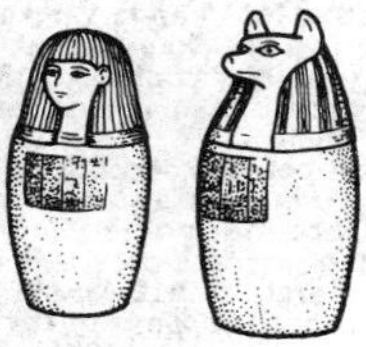

canopic jars

Ca·no·pus \kə-ˈnō-pəs\ *n* [L, fr. Gk *Kanōpos*] : a star of the first magnitude in the constellation Argo not visible north of 37° latitude

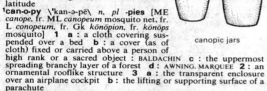

[1]**can·o·py** \ˈkan-ə-pē\ *n, pl* **-pies** [ME *canope*, fr. ML *canopeum* mosquito net, fr. L *conopeum*, fr. Gk *kōnōpion*, fr. *kōnōps* mosquito] **1 a** : a cloth covering suspended over a bed **b** : a cover (as of cloth) fixed or carried above a person of high rank or a sacred object : BALDACHIN **c** : the uppermost spreading branchy layer of a forest **d** : AWNING, MARQUEE **2** : an ornamental rooflike structure **3 a** : the transparent enclosure over an airplane cockpit **b** : the lifting or supporting surface of a parachute

[2]**canopy** *vt* **-pied; -py·ing** : to cover with or as if with a canopy

ca·no·rous \kə-ˈnōr-əs, -ˈnȯr-; ˈkan-ə-rəs\ *adj* [L *canorus*, fr. *canor* melody, fr. *canere* to sing — more at CHANT] : sounding pleasantly : MELODIOUS — **ca·no·rous·ly** *adv* — **ca·no·rous·ness** *n*

canst \kən(t)st, (ˈ)kan(t)st\ *archaic pres 2d sing of* CAN

[1]**cant** \ˈkant\ *adj* [ME, prob. fr. (assumed) MLG *kant*] *dial Eng* : LIVELY, LUSTY

[2]**cant** *n* [ME, prob. fr. MD or ONF; MD, edge, corner, fr. ONF, fr. L *canthus*, *cantus* iron tire, perh. of Celt origin; akin to W *cant* rim; akin to Gk *kanthos* corner of the eye] **1** *obs* : CORNER, NICHE **2** : an external angle (as of a building) **3** : a log slabbed on one or more sides **4 a** : a sudden thrust producing a bias **b** : the bias so caused **5** : an oblique or slanting surface **6** : an inclination from a given line : SLOPE

[3]**cant** *vt* **1** : to give a cant or oblique edge to : BEVEL **2** : to set at an angle : tip or tilt up or over **3** : to turn or throw off or out by tilting or rotating ⟨~ a rifle⟩ **4** *chiefly Brit* : to give a sudden turn or new direction to ~ *vi* **1** : to pitch to one side : LEAN **2** : SLOPE

[4]**cant** *adj* **1** : having canted corners or sides **2** : slanting with respect to a particular straight line

[5]**cant** *vi* [prob. fr. ONF *canter* to tell, lit., to sing, fr. L *cantare* — more at CHANT] **1** : BEG **2** : to speak in cant or technical terms **3** : to talk hypocritically

[6]**cant** *n* **1** : affected singsong speech **2 a** : the argot of the underworld **b** *obs* : the phraseology peculiar to a religious class or sect **c** : JARGON 2 **3** : a set or stock phrase **4** : the expression or repetition of conventional, trite, or unconsidered opinions or sentiments; *esp* : the insincere use of pious phraseology ***syn*** see DIALECT

Cant *abbr* **1** Canticle of Canticles **2** Cantonese

can't \(ˈ)kant, (ˈ)kánt, (ˈ)känt, *esp South* (ˈ)kānt\ : can not

Can·tab \ˈkan-ˌtab\ *n* [by shortening] : CANTABRIGIAN

can·ta·bi·le \kän-ˈtäb-ə-ˌlā, kan-ˈtab-ə-lē\ *adv or adj* [It, fr. LL *cantabilis* worthy to be sung, fr. L *cantare*] : in a singing manner — often used as a direction in music

Can·ta·bri·gian \ˌkant-ə-ˈbrij-(ē-)ən\ *n* [ML *Cantabrigia* Cambridge] **1** : a student or graduate of Cambridge University **2** : a native or resident of Cambridge, Mass. — **Cantabrigian** *adj*

can·ta·la \kan-ˈtäl-ə\ *n* [origin unknown] : a hard fiber produced from the leaves of an agave (*Agave cantala*)

can·ta·loupe \ˈkant-ᵊl-ˌōp\ *n* [*Cantalupo*, former papal villa near Rome, Italy] **1** : a muskmelon (*Cucumis melo cantalupensis*) with a hard ridged or warty rind and reddish orange flesh **2** : any of several muskmelons resembling the cantaloupe; *broadly* : MUSKMELON

can·tan·ker·ous \kan-ˈtaŋ-k(ə-)rəs, kən-\ *adj* [perh. irreg. fr. obs. *contack* (contention)] : ILL-NATURED, QUARRELSOME — **can·tan·ker·ous·ly** *adv* — **can·tan·ker·ous·ness** *n*

can·ta·ta \kən-ˈtät-ə\ *n* [It, fr. L, sung mass, ecclesiastical chant, fr. fem. of *cantatus*, pp. of *cantare*] : a usu. sacred choral composition comprising choruses, solos, recitatives, and interludes usu. accompanied by organ, piano, or orchestra

can·ta·trice \ˌkänt-ə-ˈtrē-(ˌ)chā, ˌkäⁿ-tə-ˈtrēs\ *n, pl* **can·ta·trices** \-ˈtrē-(ˌ)chāz, -ˈtrēs(-əz)\ *or* **can·ta·tri·ci** \ˌkänt-ə-ˈtrē-(ˌ)chē\ [It & F, fr. It, fr. LL *cantatric-*, *cantatrix*, fem. of L *cantator* singer, fr. *cantatus*, pp.] : a female singer; *esp* : an opera singer

cant dog *n* [[2]*cant*] : PEAVEY

can·teen \kan-ˈtēn\ *n* [F *cantine* bottle case, sutler's shop, fr. It *cantina* wine cellar, fr. *canto* corner, fr. L *canthus* iron tire — more at CANT] **1** : POST EXCHANGE **2** : a place of refreshment and recreation maintained by civilians for servicemen **3** : a temporary or mobile restaurant **4 a** : a partitioned chest or box for holding cutlery **b** : a soldier's mess kit **5** : a usu. cloth-jacketed flask for carrying liquids and esp. water

[1]**can·ter** \ˈkant-ər\ *n* : one that uses cant: as **a** : BEGGAR, VAGABOND **b** : a user of professional or religious cant

[2]**can·ter** \ˈkant-ər\ *vb* [short for obs. *canterbury*, fr. *canterbury*, n. (canter), fr. *Canterbury*, England; fr. the supposed gait of pilgrims to Canterbury] *vi* **1** : to move at or as if at a canter : LOPE **2** : to ride or go on a cantering horse ~ *vt* : to cause to go at a canter

[3]**can·ter** *n* **1** : a 3-beat gait resembling but smoother and slower than the gallop **2** : a ride at a canter

Can·ter·bury bell \ˌkant-ə(r)-ˌber-ē-\ *n* [*Canterbury*, England] : any of several bellflowers (as *Campanula medium*) cultivated for their showy flowers

can·tha·ris \ˈkan(t)-thə-rəs\ *n, pl* **can·thar·i·des** \kan-ˈthar-ə-ˌdēz\ [ME & L; ME *cantharide*, fr. L *cantharid-*, *cantharis*, fr. Gk *kantharid-*, *kantharis*] **1** : SPANISH FLY 1 **2** *pl but sing or pl in constr* : a preparation of dried beetles (as Spanish flies) used in medicine as a counterirritant and formerly as an aphrodisiac

cant hook *n* [[2]*cant*] : a stout wooden lever used esp. in handling logs that has a blunt usu. metal-clad end and a movable metal arm with a sharp spike

can·thus \ˈkan(t)-thəs\ *n, pl* **can·thi** \ˈkan-ˌthī, -ˌthē\ [LL, fr. Gk *kanthos* — more at CANT] : either of the angles formed by the meeting of the upper and lower eyelids

can·ti·cle \ˈkant-i-kəl\ *n* [ME, fr. L *canticulum*, dim. of *canticum* song, fr. *cantus*, pp. of *canere* to sing] : SONG; *specif* : one of several liturgical songs (as the Magnificat) taken from the Bible

Canticle of Canticles : SONG OF SOLOMON

Canticles *n pl but sing in constr* : SONG OF SOLOMON

can·ti·le·ver \ˈkant-ᵊl-ˌē-vər *also* -ˌev-ər\ *n* [perh. fr. [2]*cant* + -*i*- + *lever*] : a projecting beam or member supported at only one end: as **a** : a bracket-shaped member supporting a balcony or a cornice **b** : either of the two beams or trusses that project from piers toward each other and that when joined directly or by a suspended connecting member form a span of a cantilever bridge — see BRIDGE illustration

can·til·late \ˈkant-ᵊl-ˌāt\ *vt* **-lat·ed; -lat·ing** [L *cantillatus*, pp. of *cantillare* to sing low, fr. *cantare* to sing — more at CHANT] : to recite with usu. improvised musical tones — **can·til·la·tion** \ˌkant-ᵊl-ˈā-shən\ *n*

can·ti·na \kan-ˈtē-nə\ *n* [AmerSp, fr. Sp. canteen, fr. It, wine cellar — more at CANTEEN] **1** *Southwest* : a pouch or bag at the pommel of a saddle **2** *Southwest* : a small barroom : SALOON

cant·ing \ˈkant-iŋ\ *adj* [[5]*cant*] : affectedly pious or righteous ***syn*** see HYPOCRITICAL

can·tle \ˈkant-ᵊl\ *n* [ME *cantel*, fr. ONF, dim. of *cant* edge, corner — more at CANT] **1** : a segment cut off or out of something : PART, PORTION **2** : the upward projecting rear part of a saddle

can·to \ˈkan-(ˌ)tō\ *n, pl* **cantos** [It, fr. L *cantus* song, fr. *cantus*, pp. of *canere* to sing — more at CHANT] : one of the major divisions of a long poem

[1]**can·ton** \ˈkant-ᵊn, ˈkan-ˌtän\ *n* [MF, fr. OProv, fr. *cant* edge, corner, fr. L *canthus* iron tire — more at CANT] **1** *obs* : DIVISION, SECTION **2** [MF, fr. It *cantone*, fr. *canto* corner, fr. L *canthus*] : a small territorial division of a country: as **a** : one of the states of the Swiss confederation **b** : a division of a French arrondissement **3** : the top inner quarter of a flag **4** : the dexter chief region of a heraldic field — **can·ton·al** \ˈkant-ᵊn-əl, kan-ˈtän-ᵊl\ *adj*

[2]**can·ton** \ˈkant-ᵊn, ˈkan-ˌtän, *in sense 2 usu.* kan-ˈtōn *or* -ˈtän\ *vt* **1** : to divide into parts; *specif* : to divide into cantons **2** : to allot quarters to (as a body of troops)

can·ton crepe \ˌkan-ˌtän-\ *n, often cap 1st C* [*Canton*, China] : a soft thick crepe made in plain weave with fine crosswise ribs

Can·ton·ese \ˌkant-ᵊn-ˈēz, -ˈēs\ *n, pl* **Cantonese 1** : a native or inhabitant of Canton, China **2** : the dialect of Chinese spoken in and around Canton — **Cantonese** *adj*

can·ton flannel \ˌkan-ˌtän-\ *n, often cap C* [*Canton*, China] : FLANNEL 1c

can·ton·ment \kan-ˈtōn-mənt, -ˈtän-\ *n* **1** : the quartering of troops **2 a** : a group of more or less temporary structures for housing troops **b** : a permanent military station in India

Can·ton ware \ˈkan-ˌtän-\ *n* : ceramic ware exported from China esp. during the 18th and 19th centuries by way of Canton and including blue-and-white and enameled porcelain and various ornamented stonewares

can·tor \ˈkant-ər\ *n* [L, singer, fr. *cantus*, pp. of *canere* to sing] **1** : a choir leader : PRECENTOR **2** : a synagogue official who sings or chants liturgical music and leads the congregation in prayer

can·trip \ˈkan-trəp\ *n* [prob. alter. of *caltrop*] **1** *chiefly Brit* : a witch's trick : SPELL **2** *chiefly Brit* : a mischievous or whimsically eccentric act

can·tus \ˈkant-əs\ *n, pl* **can·tus** \ˈkant-əs, ˈkan-ˌtüs\ **1** : CANTUS FIRMUS **2** : the principal melody or voice

can·tus fir·mus \ˌkant-əs-ˈfi(ə)r-məs, -ˈfər-\ *n* [ML, lit., fixed song] **1** : the plainchant or simple Gregorian melody orig. sung in unison and prescribed as to form and use by ecclesiastical tradition **2** : a melodic theme or subject; *esp* : one for contrapuntal treatment

canty \ˈkant-ē\ *adj* [[1]*cant*] *dial Brit* : CHEERFUL, SPRIGHTLY

Ca·nuck \kə-ˈnək\ *n* [prob. alter. of *Canadian*] **1 :** CANADIAN **2** *chiefly Canad* **:** FRENCH CANADIAN **3 :** CANADIAN FRENCH — usu. used disparagingly

¹can·vas *also* **can·vass** \ˈkan-vəs\ *n, often attrib* [ME *canevas,* fr. ONF, fr. (assumed) VL *cannabaceus* hempen, fr. L *cannabis* hemp — more at CANNABIS] **1 :** a firm closely woven cloth usu. of linen, hemp, or cotton used for clothing and sails **2 :** a set of sails **:** SAIL **3 :** a piece of canvas used for a particular purpose **4 :** a military or camping tent; *also* **:** a group of such tents **5 a :** a cloth surface prepared to receive an oil painting; *also* **:** the painting on such a surface **b :** the background, setting, or scope of an historical or fictional account or narrative ⟨the crowded ~ of history⟩ **6 :** a coarse cloth so woven as to form regular meshes for working with the needle **7 :** the floor of a boxing or wrestling ring — **can·vas·like** \-və-ˌslīk\ *adj*

²canvas *vt* **-vased** *or* **-vassed; -vas·ing** *or* **-vass·ing :** to cover, line, or furnish with canvas

can·vas·back \ˈkan-vəs-ˌbak\ *n* **:** a No. American wild duck (*Aythya valisineria*) characterized esp. by the elongate sloping profile of the bill and head

¹can·vass *also* **can·vas** \ˈkan-vəs\ *vt* **1** *obs* **:** to toss in a canvas sheet in sport or punishment **2 a** *obs* **:** BEAT, TROUNCE **b** *archaic* **:** CASTIGATE **3 a :** to examine in detail; *specif* **:** to examine (votes) officially for authenticity **b :** DISCUSS, DEBATE **4 :** to go through (a district) or go to (persons) in order to solicit orders or political support or to determine opinions or sentiments ~ *vi* **:** to seek orders or votes **:** SOLICIT — **can·vass·er** *also* **can·vas·er** *n*

²canvass *n* **1 a :** a detailed examination or discussion **b :** a scrutiny esp. of votes **2 :** the act of canvassing ⟨a house-to-house ~⟩: as **a :** the personal solicitation of votes **b :** a survey to ascertain the probable vote before an election

can·yon \ˈkan-yən\ *n* [AmerSp *cañón,* prob. alter. of obs. Sp *callón,* aug. of *calle* street, fr. L *callis* footpath] **:** a deep narrow valley with precipitous sides often with a stream flowing through it

can·zo·ne \kan-ˈzō-nē, känt-ˈsō-(ˌ)nā\ *n, pl* **-nes** \-nēz, -(ˌ)nāz\ *or* **-ni** \-nē\ [It, fr. L *cantion-, cantio* song, fr. *cantus,* pp. of *canere* to sing — more at CHANT] **1 :** a medieval Italian or Provençal lyric poem **2 :** the melody of a canzone

can·zo·net \ˌkan-zə-ˈnet\ *n* [It *canzonetta,* dim. of *canzone*] **1 :** a part-song resembling but less elaborate than a madrigal **2 :** a light and graceful song

caou·tchouc \ˈkau̇-ˌchu̇k, -ˌchük, -ˌchü\ *n* [F, fr. obs. Sp *cauchuc* (now *caucho*), fr. Quechua] **:** ¹RUBBER 2a

¹cap \ˈkap\ *n, often attrib* [ME *cappe,* fr. OE *cæppe,* fr. LL *cappa* head covering, cloak] **1 :** a head covering; *esp* **:** one for men and boys that has a visor and no brim **2 :** a natural cover or top: as **a :** an overlying rock layer that is usu. hard to penetrate **b** (1) **:** PILEUS (2) **:** CALYPTRA **c :** the top of a bird's head or a patch of distinctively colored feathers in this area **3 a :** something that serves as a cover or protection esp. for a tip, knob, or end ⟨a bottle ~⟩ **b :** a fitting for closing the end of a tube (as a water pipe or electric conduit) **c :** a layer of new rubber fused onto the worn surface of a pneumatic tire **4 a :** a cardinal's biretta **b :** MORTARBOARD **5 :** an overlaying or covering structure ⟨the galleried ~ of the old water tower is open to visitors⟩ **6 :** a paper or metal container holding an explosive charge (as for a toy pistol)

²cap *vt* **capped; cap·ping 1 a :** to provide or protect with a cap **b :** to give a cap to as a symbol of honor or rank **2 :** to form a cap over **:** CROWN ⟨the mountains were *capped* with mist —John Buchan⟩ **3 a :** to follow with something more noticeable or more significant **:** OUTDO **b :** MATCH **c :** CLIMAX

³cap *abbr* **1** capacity **2** capital **3** capitalize; capitalized

CAP *abbr* Civil Air Patrol

ca·pa·bil·i·ty \ˌkā-pə-ˈbil-ət-ē\ *n, pl* **-ties 1 :** the quality or state of being capable **2 :** a feature or faculty capable of development **:** POTENTIALITY **3 :** the capacity for an indicated use or development ⟨the ~ of a metal to be fused⟩

ca·pa·ble \ˈkā-pə-bəl, ˈkāp-bəl\ *adj* [MF or LL; MF *capable,* fr. LL *capabilis,* irreg. fr. L *capere* to take — more at HEAVE] **1 :** SUSCEPTIBLE ⟨a remark ~ of being misunderstood⟩ **2** *obs* **:** COMPREHENSIVE **3 :** having attributes (as physical or mental power) required for performance or accomplishment ⟨a man ~ of intense concentration⟩ **4 :** having traits conducive to or admitting of ⟨this woman is ~ of murder by violence —Robert Graves⟩ **5 :** having general efficiency and ability **6** *obs* **:** having legal right to own, enjoy, or perform ***syn*** see ABLE ***ant*** incapable — **ca·pa·ble·ness** \ˈkā-pə-bəl-nəs\ *n* — **ca·pa·bly** \-pə-blē\ *adv*

ca·pa·cious \kə-ˈpā-shəs\ *adj* [L *capac-, capax* capacious, capable, fr. L *capere*] **:** able to contain a great deal ***syn*** see SPACIOUS — **ca·pa·cious·ly** *adv* — **ca·pa·cious·ness** *n*

ca·pac·i·tance \kə-ˈpas-ət-ən(t)s\ *n* [*capacity*] **1 a :** the property of an electric nonconductor that permits the storage of energy as a result of electric displacement when opposite surfaces of the nonconductor are maintained at a difference of potential **b :** the measure of this property equal to the ratio of the charge on either surface to the potential difference between the surfaces **2 :** a part of a circuit or network that possesses capacitance — **ca·pac·i·tive** \-ˈpas-ət-iv\ *adj* — **ca·pac·i·tive·ly** *adv*

ca·pac·i·tate \kə-ˈpas-ə-ˌtāt\ *vt* **-tat·ed; -tat·ing** *archaic* **:** to make capable **:** QUALIFY

ca·pac·i·tor \kə-ˈpas-ət-ər\ *n* **:** a device giving capacitance and usu. consisting of conducting plates or foils separated by thin layers of dielectric (as air or mica) with the plates on opposite sides of the dielectric layers oppositely charged by a source of voltage and the electrical energy of the charged system stored in the polarized dielectric

¹ca·pac·i·ty \kə-ˈpas-ət-ē, -ˈpas-tē\ *n, pl* **-ties** [ME *capacite,* fr. MF *capacité,* fr. L *capacitat-, capacitas,* fr. *capac-, capax*] **1 a :** the ability to hold, receive, store, or accommodate **b :** a measure of content **:** the measured ability to contain **:** VOLUME ⟨a jug with a ~ of one gallon⟩ — see METRIC SYSTEM table, WEIGHT table **c :** maximum production or output **d** (1) **:** CAPACITANCE (2) **:** the quantity of electricity that a battery can deliver under specified conditions **2 :** legal qualification, competency, power, or fitness **3 a :** ABILITY, CALIBER **b :** power to grasp and analyze ideas and cope with problems **c :** POTENTIALITY **4 :** a position or character assigned or assumed ⟨in his ~ as a judge⟩

²capacity *adj* **:** attaining to or equaling maximum capacity ⟨a ~ crowd⟩ ⟨~ production of electricity⟩

cap–a–pie *or* **cap–à–pie** \ˌkap-ə-ˈpē, -ˈpā\ *adv* [MF *(de) cap a pé* from head to foot] **:** from head to foot **:** at all points ⟨armed ~⟩

ca·par·i·son \kə-ˈpar-ə-sən\ *n* [MF *caparaçon,* fr. OSp *caparazón*] **1 a :** an ornamental covering for a horse **b :** decorative trappings and harness **2 :** rich clothing **:** ADORNMENT — **caparison** *vt*

¹cape \ˈkāp\ *n, often attrib* [ME *cap,* fr. MF, fr. OProv, fr. L *caput* head — more at HEAD] **:** a point or extension of land jutting out into water as a peninsula or as a projecting point

²cape *n* [prob. fr. Sp *capa* cloak, fr. LL *cappa* head covering, cloak] **1 :** a sleeveless outer garment or part of a garment that fits closely at the neck and hangs loosely from the shoulders **2 :** the short feathers covering the shoulders of a fowl below the hackle — see COCK illustration; see DUCK illustration

Cape buffalo \ˈkāp-\ *n* [*Cape* of Good Hope, Africa] **:** a large dangerous and often savage buffalo (*Syncerus caffer*) of southern Africa

Cape Cod cottage \(ˌ)kāp-ˌkäd-\ *n* [*Cape Cod,* Mass.] **:** a compact rectangular dwelling of one or one-and-a-half stories usu. with a central chimney and steep gable roof

Cape crawfish *n* [*Cape* of Good Hope] **:** the common edible spiny lobster (*Jasus lalandii*) of southern Africa

Cape Horn·er \kāp-ˈhȯr-nər\ *n* **:** a ship that voyages around Cape Horn

cape·let \ˈkāp-lət\ *n* **:** a small cape usu. covering the shoulders

cap·e·lin \ˈkap-(ə-)lən\ *n* [CanF *capelan,* fr. F, codfish, fr. OProv, chaplain, codfish, fr. ML *cappellanus* chaplain — more at CHAPLAIN] **:** a small northern sea fish (*Mallotus villosus*) related to the smelts

Ca·pel·la \kə-ˈpel-ə\ *n* [L, lit., she-goat, fr. *caper* he-goat — more at CAPRIOLE] **:** a star of the first magnitude in Auriga

Cape marigold *n* [*Cape* of Good Hope] **:** DIMORPHOTHECA

¹ca·per \ˈkā-pər\ *n* [back-formation fr. earlier *capers* (taken as a plural), fr. ME *caperis,* fr. L *capparis,* fr. Gk *kapparis*] **1 :** any of a genus (*Capparis* of the family Capparidaceae, the caper family) of low prickly shrubs of the Mediterranean region; *esp* **:** one (*C. spinosa*) cultivated for its buds **2 :** one of the greenish flower buds or young berries of the caper pickled for use as a relish

²caper *vi* **ca·pered; ca·per·ing** \-p(ə-)riŋ\ [prob. by shortening & alter. fr. *capriole*] **:** to leap about in a gay frolicsome way **:** PRANCE

³caper *n* **1 :** a gay bounding leap **2 :** a capricious escapade **:** PRANK **3 :** an illegal enterprise **:** CRIME

cap·er·cail·lie \ˌkap-ər-ˈkāl-(y)ē\ *or* **cap·er·cail·zie** \-ˈkāl-zē\ *n* [ScGael *capalcoille,* lit., horse of the woods] **:** the largest Old World grouse (*Tetrao urogallus*)

cape·skin \ˈkāp-ˌskin\ *n* [*Cape* of Good Hope] **:** a light flexible leather made from sheepskins with the natural grain retained and used esp. for gloves and garments

Ca·pe·tian \kə-ˈpē-shən\ *adj* [Hugh *Capet*] **:** of or relating to the French royal house that ruled from 987 to 1328 — **Capetian** *n*

cape·work \ˈkāp-ˌwərk\ *n* **:** the art of the bullfighter in working a bull with the cape

cap·ful \ˈkap-ˌfu̇l\ *n* **1 :** as much as a cap will hold ⟨a ~ of detergent⟩ **2 :** a light puff ⟨a ~ of wind⟩

cap gun *n* **:** CAP PISTOL

ca·pi·as \ˈkā-pē-əs\ *n* [ME, fr. L, you should seize, fr. *capere* to take — more at HEAVE] **:** a legal writ or process commanding the officer to arrest the person named in it

cap·il·lar·i·ty \ˌkap-ə-ˈlar-ət-ē\ *n, pl* **-ties 1 :** the property or state of being capillary **2 :** the action by which the surface of a liquid where it is in contact with a solid (as in a capillary tube) is elevated or depressed depending on the relative attraction of the molecules of the liquid for each other and for those of the solid

¹cap·il·lary \ˈkap-ə-ˌler-ē, *Brit usu* kə-ˈpil-ə-rē\ *adj* [F or L; F *capillaire,* fr. L *capillaris,* fr. *capillus* hair] **1 :** resembling a hair esp. in slender elongated form; *esp* **:** having a very small bore ⟨a ~ tube⟩ **2 :** involving, held by, or resulting from surface tension ⟨~ water in the soil⟩ **3 :** of or relating to capillaries or capillarity

²capillary *n, pl* **-lar·ies :** a capillary tube; *esp* **:** any of the smallest vessels of the blood-vascular system connecting arterioles with venules and forming networks throughout the body

capillary attraction *n* **:** the force of adhesion between a solid and a liquid in capillarity

¹cap·i·tal \ˈkap-ət-ᵊl, ˈkap-tᵊl\ *adj* [ME, fr. L *capitalis,* fr. *capit-, caput* head — more at HEAD] **1 a :** punishable by death ⟨a ~ crime⟩ **b :** involving execution ⟨~ punishment⟩ **c :** most serious ⟨ a ~ error⟩ **2** *of a letter* **:** of or conforming to the series A, B, C, etc. rather than a, b, c, etc. **3 a :** chief in importance or influence ⟨the ~ importance of criticism in the work of creation itself —T. S. Eliot⟩ **b :** being the seat of government **4 :** of or relating to capital **5 :** EXCELLENT ⟨a ~ book⟩

²capital *n* [F or It; F, fr. It *capitale,* fr. *capitale,* adj., chief, principal, fr. L *capitalis*] **1 a** (1) **:** a stock of accumulated goods esp. at a specified time and in contrast to income received during a specified period; *also* **:** the value of these accumulated goods (2) **:** accumulated goods devoted to the production of other goods (3) **:** accumulated possessions calculated to bring in income **b** (1) **:** net worth (2) **:** CAPITAL STOCK **c :** persons holding capital **d :** ADVANTAGE, GAIN **2** [¹*capital*] **a :** a capital letter; *esp* **:** an initial capital letter **b :** a letter belonging to a style of alphabet modeled on the style customarily used in inscriptions **3** [¹*capital*] **a :** a city serving as a seat of government **b :** a city preeminent in some special activity

³capital *n* [ME *capitale,* modif. of ONF *capitel,* fr. LL *capitellum* small head, top of column, dim. of L *capit-, caput*] **:** the uppermost member of a column or pilaster crowning the shaft and taking the weight of the entablature — see COLUMN illustration

capital assets *n pl* **:** tangible or intangible long-term assets

capital expenditure *n* **:** an expenditure for long-term additions or betterments properly chargeable to a capital assets account
capital gains distribution *n* **:** the part of a payment made by an investment company to its shareholders that consists of realized profits from the sale of securities and technically is not income
capital goods *n pl* **:** ²CAPITAL 1a(1), 1a(2)
cap·i·tal·ism \ˈkap-ət-ᵊl-ˌiz-əm, ˈkap-tᵊl-\ *n* **:** an economic system characterized by private or corporate ownership of capital goods, by investments that are determined by private decision rather than by state control, and by prices, production, and the distribution of goods that are determined mainly by competition in a free market
¹cap·i·tal·ist \-əst\ *n* **1 :** a person who has capital esp. invested in business; *broadly* **:** a person of wealth **:** PLUTOCRAT **2 :** a person who favors capitalism
²capitalist *or* **cap·i·tal·is·tic** \ˌkap-ət-ᵊl-ˈis-tik, ˌkap-tᵊl-\ *adj* **1 :** owning capital ⟨the ~ class⟩ **2 a :** practicing or advocating capitalism ⟨~ nations⟩ **b :** marked by capitalism ⟨the modern ~ period of history from 1815 to 1914 —Norman Thomas⟩ — **cap·i·tal·is·ti·cal·ly** \-ti-k(ə-)lē\ *adv*
cap·i·tal·iza·tion \ˌkap-ət-ᵊl-ə-ˈzā-shən, ˌkap-tᵊl-\ *n* **1 a :** the act or process of capitalizing **b :** a sum resulting from a process of capitalizing **c :** the total liabilities of a business including both ownership capital and borrowed capital **d :** the total par value or the stated value of no-par issues of authorized capital stock **2 :** the use of a capital letter in writing or printing
cap·i·tal·ize \ˈkap-ət-ᵊl-ˌīz, ˈkap-tᵊl-\ *vb* **-ized; -iz·ing** *vt* **1 :** to write or print with an initial capital or in capitals **2 :** to convert into capital ⟨~ the company's reserve fund⟩ **3 a :** to compute the present value of (an income extended over a period of time) **b :** to convert (a periodic payment) into an equivalent capital sum ⟨*capitalized* annuities⟩ **4 :** to supply capital for ~ *vi* **:** to gain by turning something to advantage **:** PROFIT ⟨~ on an opponent's mistake⟩
capital levy *n* **:** a levy on personal or industrial capital in addition to income tax and other taxes **:** a general property tax
cap·i·tal·ly \ˈkap-ət-ᵊl-ē, ˈkap-tᵊl-\ *adv* **1 :** in a manner involving capital punishment **2 :** in a capital manner **:** EXCELLENTLY, ADMIRABLY
capital ship *n* **:** a warship of the first rank in size and armament
capital sin *n* **:** DEADLY SIN
capital stock *n* **1 :** the outstanding shares of a joint-stock company considered as an aggregate **2 :** CAPITALIZATION 1d **3 :** the ownership element of a corporation divided into shares and represented by certificates
capital structure *n* **:** the makeup of the capitalization of a business in terms of the amounts and kinds of equity and debt securities **:** the equity and debt securities of a business together with its surplus and reserves
cap·i·tate \ˈkap-ə-ˌtāt\ *adj* [L *capitatus* headed, fr. *capit-, caput* head] **1 :** forming a head **2 :** abruptly enlarged and globose
cap·i·ta·tion \ˌkap-ə-ˈtā-shən\ *n* [LL *capitation-, capitatio* poll tax, fr. L *capit-, caput*] **1 :** a direct uniform tax imposed upon each head or person **:** POLL TAX **2 :** a uniform per capita payment or fee
cap·i·tol \ˈkap-ət-ᵊl, ˈkap-tᵊl\ *n* [L *Capitolium*, temple of Jupiter at Rome on the Capitoline hill] **1 a :** a building in which a state legislative body meets **b :** a group of buildings in which the functions of state government are carried out **2** *cap* **:** the building in which the U.S. Congress meets at Washington
Capitol Hill *n* [*Capitol Hill*, Washington, site of the U.S. Capitol] **:** the legislative branch of the U.S. government
Cap·i·to·line \ˈkap-ət-ᵊl-ˌīn, *Brit usu* kə-ˈpit-ə-ˌlīn\ *adj* [L *capitolinus*, fr. *Capitolium*] **:** of or relating to the smallest of the seven hills of ancient Rome, the temple on it, or the gods worshiped there
ca·pit·u·lar \kə-ˈpich-ə-lər\ *adj* [ML *capitularis*, fr. *capitulum* chapter] **:** of or relating to an ecclesiastical chapter
ca·pit·u·lary \-ˌler-ē\ *n, pl* **-lar·ies** [ML *capitulare*, lit., document divided into sections, fr. LL *capitulum* section, chapter — more at CHAPTER] **:** a civil or ecclesiastical ordinance; *also* **:** a collection of ordinances
ca·pit·u·late \kə-ˈpich-ə-ˌlāt\ *vi* **-lat·ed; -lat·ing** [ML *capitulatus*, pp. of *capitulare* to distinguish by heads or chapters, fr. LL *capitulum*] **1** *archaic* **:** PARLEY, NEGOTIATE **2 a :** to surrender often after negotiation of terms **b :** to cease resisting **:** ACQUIESCE ***syn*** see YIELD
ca·pit·u·la·tion \kə-ˌpich-ə-ˈlā-shən\ *n* **1 :** a set of terms or articles constituting an agreement between governments **2 :** the act or agreement of one that surrenders upon stipulated terms **3 :** a giving over of resistance usu. to something that presses or dominates ***syn*** see SURRENDER
ca·pit·u·lum \kə-ˈpich-ə-ləm\ *n, pl* **-la** \-lə\ [NL, fr. L, small head — more at CHAPTER] **1 :** a rounded protuberance of an anatomical part (as a bone) **2 :** a racemose inflorescence (as of the buttonbush) with the axis shortened and dilated to form a rounded or flattened cluster of sessile flowers — see INFLORESCENSE illustration
ca·po \ˈkā-(ˌ)pō\ *n, pl* **capos** [short for *capotasto*, fr. It, lit., head of fingerboard] **:** a movable bar attached to the fingerboard esp. of a guitar to uniformly raise the pitch of all the strings
ca·pon \ˈkā-ˌpän, -pən\ *n* [ME, fr. OE *capūn*, prob. fr. ONF *capon*, fr. L *capon-, capo*; akin to Gk *koptein* to cut] **:** a castrated male chicken — **ca·pon·ize** \-pə-ˌnīz\ *vt*
cap·o·ral \ˈkap-(ə-)rəl, ˌkap-ə-ˈral\ *n* [F, lit., corporal — more at CORPORAL] **:** a coarse tobacco
ca·pote \kə-ˈpōt\ *n* [F, fr. *cape* cloak, fr. LL *cappa*] **:** a usu. long and hooded cloak or overcoat
cap·per \ˈkap-ər\ *n* **1 :** one that caps; *esp* **:** an operator or a machine that applies the closure or cap **2 :** a lure or decoy esp. in an illicit or questionable activity **:** SHILL
cap·ping \ˈkap-iŋ\ *n* **:** something that caps
cap pistol *n* **:** a toy pistol that fires caps
cap·ric acid \ˌkap-rik-\ *n* [ISV, fr. L *capr-, caper* goat; fr. its odor — more at CAPRIOLE] **:** a fatty acid $C_{10}H_{20}O_2$ found in fats and oils and used in flavors and perfumes
ca·pric·cio \kə-ˈprē-ch(ē-ˌ)ō\ *n, pl* **-cios** [It] **1 :** WHIMSY, FANCY **2 :** CAPER, PRANK **3 :** an instrumental piece in free form usu. lively in tempo and brilliant in style
ca·price \kə-ˈprēs\ *n* [F, fr. It *capriccio*, lit., head with hair standing on end, shudder, fr. *capo* head (fr. L *caput*) + *riccio* hedgehog, fr. L *ericius* — more at HEAD, URCHIN] **1 a :** a sudden, impulsive, and seemingly unmotivated change of mind **b :** a sudden change or series of changes hard to explain or predict ⟨the ~s of the weather⟩ **2 :** a disposition to change one's mind impulsively **3 :** CAPRICCIO 3
syn CAPRICE, FREAK, WHIM, VAGARY, CROTCHET *shared meaning element* **:** an arbitrary and typically fanciful or impracticable notion. CAPRICE emphasizes lack of evident motivation and suggests willfulness ⟨my cousin's pet *caprice* is to affect a distaste for art, to which she is passionately devoted —G. B. Shaw⟩ FREAK suggests an impulsive causeless change of mind befitting a child or a lunatic ⟨chose to work or loaf as the *freak* took him⟩ WHIM often implies a quaint, fantastic, or humorous turn of mind that may lead to freakish or capricious acts or behavior ⟨had a *whim* to dress only in white⟩ ⟨a man subject to sudden *whims* and moods⟩ VAGARY stresses the erratic, irresponsible, or extravagant quality of a notion or impulse ⟨the *vagaries* of fashion⟩ ⟨straight they changed their minds, flew off, and into strange *vagaries* fell —John Milton⟩ CROTCHET implies a perversely heretical or eccentric opinion or preference, especially on some trivial matter ⟨she was eccentric . . . full of *crotchets*. She never drank water without some vinegar in it —to cleanse it, she said —Robert Henderson⟩
ca·pri·cious \kə-ˈprish-əs, -ˈprē-shəs\ *adj* **:** governed or characterized by caprice **:** apt to change suddenly or unpredictably ***syn*** see INCONSTANT ***ant*** steadfast — **ca·pri·cious·ly** *adv* — **ca·pri·cious·ness** *n*
Cap·ri·corn \ˈkap-ri-ˌkȯ(ə)rn\ *n* [ME *Capricorne*, fr. L *Capricornus* (gen. *Capricorni*), fr. *caper* goat + *cornu* horn — more at HORN] **1 :** a southern zodiacal constellation between Sagittarius and Aquarius **2 a :** the 10th sign of the zodiac in astrology — see ZODIAC table **b :** one born under this sign
cap·ri·fi·ca·tion \ˌkap-rə-fə-ˈkā-shən\ *n* [L *caprification-, caprificatio*, fr. *caprificatus*, pp. of *caprificare* to pollinate by caprification, fr. *caprificus*] **:** artificial pollination of figs that usu. bear only pistillate flowers by hanging male flowering branches of the caprifig in the trees to facilitate pollen transfer by a wasp to the edible figs
cap·ri·fig \ˈkap-rə-ˌfig\ *n* [ME *caprifige*, part trans. of L *caprificus*, fr. *capr-, caper* goat + *ficus* fig — more at FIG] **:** a wild fig (*Ficus carica sylvestris*) of southern Europe and Asia Minor used for caprification of the edible fig; *also* **:** its fruit
cap·rine \ˈkap-ˌrīn\ *adj* [L *caprinus*, fr. *capr-, caper*] **:** of, relating to, or being a goat
cap·ri·ole \ˈkap-rē-ˌōl\ *n* [MF or OIt; MF *capriole*, fr. OIt *capriola*, fr. *capriolo* roebuck, fr. L *capreolus* goat, roebuck, fr. *capr-, caper* he-goat; akin to OE *hæfer* goat, Gk *kapros* wild boar] **1 :** CAPER **2** *of a trained horse* **:** a vertical leap with a backward kick of the hind legs at the height of the leap — **capriole** *vi*
ca·pri pants \kə-ˌprē-\ *n pl, often cap C* [*Capri*, Italy] **:** close-fitting pants that have tapered legs with a slit on the outside of the leg bottom, extend almost to the ankle, and are used for informal wear esp. by women
ca·pro·ic acid \kə-ˌprō-ik-\ *n* [ISV, fr. L *capr-, caper*] **:** a liquid fatty acid $C_6H_{12}O_2$ that is found as a glycerol ester in fats and oils or made synthetically and used in pharmaceuticals and flavors
ca·pryl·ic acid \kə-ˌpril-ik-\ *n* [ISV *capryl*, a radical contained in it] **:** a fatty acid $C_8H_{16}O_2$ of rancid odor occurring in fats and oils and used in perfumes
caps *abbr* **1** capitals **2** capsule
cap·sa·icin \kap-ˈsā-ə-sən\ *n* [irreg. fr. NL *Capsicum*] **:** a colorless irritant phenolic amide $C_{18}H_{27}NO_3$ obtained from various capsicums
Cap·si·an \ˈkap-sē-ən\ *adj* [F *capsien*, fr. L *Capsa* Gafsa, Tunisia] **:** of or relating to a Paleolithic culture of northern Africa and southern Europe
cap·si·cum \ˈkap-si-kəm\ *n* [NL, genus name] **1 :** any of a genus (*Capsicum*) of tropical herbs and shrubs of the nightshade family widely cultivated for their many-seeded usu. fleshy-walled berries — called also *pepper* **2 :** the dried ripe fruit of some capsicums (as *C. frutescens*) used as a gastric and intestinal stimulant
cap·sid \ˈkap-səd\ *n* [L *capsa* case + E ²*-id* — more at CASE] **:** the outer protein shell of a virus particle — **cap·sid·al** \-səd-ᵊl\ *adj*
cap·size \ˈkap-ˌsīz, kap-ˈ\ *vb* **cap·sized; cap·siz·ing** [origin unknown] *vt* **:** to cause to overturn ⟨~ a canoe⟩ ~ *vi* **:** to turn over **:** UPSET ⟨the canoe *capsized*⟩
cap·stan \ˈkap-stən, -ˌstan\ *n* [ME] **1 :** a machine for moving or raising heavy weights by winding cable around a vertical spindle-mounted drum that is rotated manually or driven by steam or electric power **2 :** a rotating shaft that drives tape at a constant speed in a recorder
cap·stone \ˈkap-ˌstōn\ *n* [¹*cap*] **1 :** a coping stone **:** COPING **2 :** the crowning point **:** ACME
cap·su·lar \ˈkap-sə-lər\ *adj* **1 :** of, relating to, or resembling a capsule **2 :** CAPSULATE
cap·su·late \-ˌlāt, -lət\ *or* **cap·su·lat·ed** \-ˌlāt-əd\ *adj* **:** enclosed in a capsule

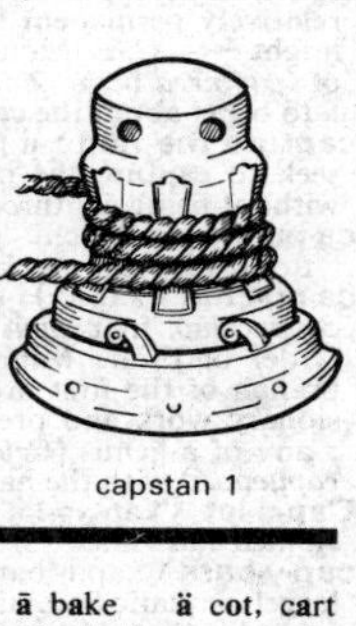
capstan 1

ə abut ᵊ kitten ər further a back ā bake ä cot, cart
au̇ out ch chin e less ē easy g gift i trip ī life
j joke ŋ sing ō flow ȯ flaw ȯi coin th thin t͟h this
ü loot u̇ foot y yet yü few yu̇ furious zh vision

1cap·sule \'kap-səl, -(,)sül\ *n* [F, fr. L *capsula,* dim. of *capsa* box — more at CASE] **1 a :** a membrane or sac enclosing a body part **b :** either of two layers of white matter in the cerebrum **2 :** a closed receptacle containing spores or seeds: as **a :** a dry dehiscent usu. many-seeded fruit composed of two or more carpels **b :** the spore sac of a moss **3 :** a gelatin shell enclosing medicine **4 :** an often polysaccharide envelope surrounding a microorganism **5 :** an extremely brief condensation : OUTLINE, SURVEY **6 :** a compact usu. detachable receptacle **7 :** a small pressurized compartment for an aviator or astronaut for flight or emergency escape; *specif* : SPACECRAFT

2capsule *vt* **cap·suled; cap·sul·ing 1 :** to equip with or enclose in a capsule **2 :** to condense into or formulate in a very brief compact form ⟨*capsuled* the news⟩

3capsule *adj* **1 :** extremely brief **2 :** small and very compact

cap·sul·ize \'kap-sə-,līz\ *vt* **-ized; -iz·ing :** CAPSULE

Capt *abbr* captain

1cap·tain \'kap-tən\ *n* [ME *capitane,* fr. MF *capitain,* fr. LL *capitaneus,* adj. & n., chief, fr. L *capit-, caput* head — more at HEAD] **1 a :** the commander of a body of troops or of a military establishment **b :** a commander under a sovereign or general **c** (1) **:** an officer in charge of a ship (2) **:** a commissioned officer in the navy or coast guard ranking above a commander and below a rear admiral **d :** a commissioned officer in the army, air force, or marine corps ranking above a first lieutenant and below a major **e :** a distinguished military leader **f :** a leader of a side or team in a sports contest **g :** a fire or police department officer usu. ranking between a lieutenant and a chief **h** (1) **:** a restaurant functionary in charge of waiters (2) **:** a hotel functionary in charge of bellboys — called also *bell captain* **2 :** a dominant figure ⟨∼*s* of commerce⟩ — **cap·tain·cy** \-sē\ *n* — **cap·tain·ship** \-,ship\ *n*

2captain *vt* **:** to be captain of : LEAD ⟨∼*ed* the football team⟩

captain of industry : the head of a great industrial enterprise : ENTREPRENEUR

captain's chair *n* **:** an armchair with a low curved back with vertical spindles and a saddle seat

captain's mast *n* **:** MAST 3

cap·tan \'kap-,tan\ *n* [origin unknown] **:** a fungicide $C_9H_8Cl_3NO_2S$ used on agricultural crops

1cap·tion \'kap-shən\ *n* [ME *capcioun,* fr. L *caption-, captio* act of taking, fr. *captus,* pp. of *capere* to take — more at HEAVE] **1 :** the part of a legal instrument that shows where, when, and by what authority it was taken, found, or executed **2 a :** the heading esp. of an article or document : TITLE **b :** the explanatory comment or designation accompanying a pictorial illustration **c :** a motion-picture subtitle — **cap·tion·less** \-ləs\ *adj*

2caption *vt* **cap·tioned; cap·tion·ing** \-sh(ə-)niŋ\ **:** to furnish with a caption : ENTITLE

cap·tious \'kap-shəs\ *adj* [ME *capcious,* fr. MF or L; MF *captieux* fr. L *captiosus,* fr. *captio* act of taking, deception] **1 :** calculated to confuse, entrap, or entangle in argument **2 :** marked by an often ill-natured inclination to stress faults and raise objections ***syn*** see CRITICAL ***ant*** appreciative — **cap·tious·ly** *adv* — **cap·tious·ness** *n*

cap·ti·vate \'kap-tə-,vāt\ *vt* **-vat·ed; -vat·ing 1** *archaic* **:** SEIZE, CAPTURE **2 :** to influence and dominate by some special charm, art, or trait and with an irresistible appeal ***syn*** see ATTRACT ***ant*** repulse — **cap·ti·va·tion** \,kap-tə-'vā-shən\ *n* — **cap·ti·va·tor** \'kap-tə-,vāt-ər\ *n*

cap·tive \'kap-tiv\ *adj* [ME, fr. L *captivus,* fr. *captus,* pp. of *capere*] **1 a :** taken and held as prisoner esp. by an enemy in war **b :** kept within bounds : CONFINED **c** (1) **:** held under control (2) **:** owned or controlled by another concern and operated for its needs rather than for an open market ⟨a ∼ mine⟩ **2 :** of or relating to captivity **3 :** extremely pleased or gratified : CAPTIVATED **4 :** being in a situation that makes departure or inattention difficult ⟨a ∼ audience⟩ — **captive** *n*

cap·tiv·i·ty \kap-'tiv-ət-ē\ *n* **1 :** the state of being captive ⟨some birds thrive in ∼⟩ **2** *obs* **:** a group of captives

cap·tor \'kap-tər, -,tȯ(ə)r\ *n* [LL, fr. L *captus*] **:** one that has captured a person or thing

1cap·ture \'kap-chər\ *n* [MF, fr. L *captura,* fr. *captus,* pp. of *capere*] **1 :** the act of catching or gaining control by force, stratagem, or guile **2 :** one that has been taken; *esp* **:** a prize ship **3 :** a move in various board games (as checkers or chess) that gains an opponent's man **4 :** the coalescence of an atomic nucleus with an elementary particle that may result in an emission from or fission of the nucleus

2capture *vt* **cap·tured; cap·tur·ing** \'kap-chə-riŋ, 'kap-shriŋ\ **1 a :** to take captive : WIN, GAIN ⟨∼ a city⟩ **b :** to preserve in a relatively permanent form ⟨at any such moment as a photograph might ∼ —C. E. Montague⟩ **c :** to captivate and hold the interest of ⟨*captured* her⟩ **2 :** to take according to the rules of a game **3 :** to bring about the capture of (an elementary particle)

capture the flag : a game in which players on each of two teams seek to capture the other team's flag and return it to their side without being captured and imprisoned

ca·puche \kə-'püch, -'püsh\ *n* [It *cappuccio,* fr. *cappa* cloak, fr. LL] **:** HOOD; *esp* **:** the cowl of a Capuchin friar

ca·pu·chin \'kap-(y)ə-shən, *esp for 3 also* kə-'p(y)ü-\ *n* [MF, fr. OIt *cappuccino,* fr. *cappuccio;* fr. his cowl] **1** *cap* **:** a member of the Order of Friars Minor Capuchin forming since 1529 an austere branch of the first order of St. Francis of Assisi engaged in missionary work and preaching **2 :** a hooded cloak for women **3 :** any of a genus (*Cebus*) of So. American monkeys; *esp* **:** one (*C. capucinus*) with the hair on its crown resembling a monk's cowl

Cap·u·let \'kap-yə-lət\ *n* **:** the family of Juliet in Shakespeare's *Romeo and Juliet*

cap·y·bara \,kap-i-'bar-ə, -'bär-\ *n* [Pg *capibara,* fr. Tupi] **:** a tailless largely aquatic So. American rodent (*Hydrochoerus capybara*) often exceeding four feet in length

car \'kär\ *n* [ME *carre,* fr. AF, fr. L *carra,* pl. of *carrum,* alter. of *carrus,* of Celt origin; akin to OIr & MW *carr* vehicle; akin to L *currere* to run] **1 :** a vehicle moving on wheels: **a** *archaic* **:** CARRIAGE, CART, WAGON **b :** a chariot of war or of triumph **c :** a vehicle adapted to the rails of a railroad or street railway **d :** AUTOMOBILE **2 :** the cage of an elevator **3 :** the part of an airship or balloon that carries the power plant, personnel, and cargo

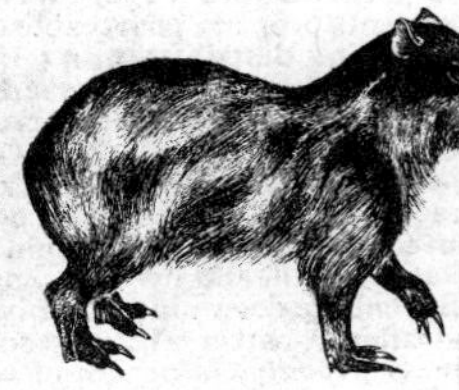

capybara

Car *abbr* Carlow

CAR *abbr* civil air regulations

ca·ra·bao \,kar-ə-'bau̇, ,kär-\ *n* [PhilSp, fr. Eastern Bisayan *karabáw*] **:** WATER BUFFALO

ca·ra·bid \'kar-ə-bəd, kə-'rab-əd\ *n* [deriv. of Gk *karabos* horned beetle] **:** any of a large family (Carabidae) of usu. carnivorous and often shining black or metallic beetles — **carabid** *adj*

car·a·bi·neer *or* **car·a·bi·nier** \,kar-ə-bə-'ni(ə)r\ *n* [F *carabinier,* fr. *carabine* carbine] **:** a soldier armed with a carbine

car·a·bi·ner \,kar-ə-'bē-nər\ *n* [G *karabiner*] **:** an oblong ring that snaps to the eye or link of a piton to hold a freely running rope

ca·ra·bi·ne·ro \,kar-ə-bə-'ne(ə)r-(,)ō, ,kär-\ *n, pl* **-ros** [Sp, fr. *carabina* carbine, fr. F *carabine*] **1 :** a member of a Spanish national police force serving esp. as frontier guards **2 :** a customs or coast guard officer in the Philippines

ca·ra·bi·nie·re \,kar-ə-bən-'ye(ə)r-(,)ā, ,kär-\ *n, pl* **-nie·ri** \-'ye(ə)r-ē\ [It, fr. F *carabinier*] **:** a member of the Italian national police force

ca·ra·ca·ra \,kar-ə-'kar-ə, -ə-kə-'rä\ *n* [Sp *caracara* & Pg *caracará,* fr. Tupi *caracará,* of imit. origin] **:** any of various large long-legged mostly So. American hawks resembling vultures in habits

car·a·cole \'kar-ə-,kōl\ *n* [F, fr. Sp *caracol* snail, spiral stair, caracole] **1 :** a half turn to right or left executed by a mounted horse **2 :** a turning or capering movement — **caracole** *vb*

car·a·cul \'kar-ə-kəl\ *n* [alter. of *karakul*] **:** the pelt of a karakul lamb after the curl begins to loosen

ca·rafe \kə-'raf, -'räf\ *n* [F, fr. It *caraffa,* fr. Ar *gharrāfah*] **:** a bottle with a flaring lip used to hold water or beverages

car·a·ga·na \,kar-ə-'gän-ə\ *n* [NL, genus name, of Turkic origin; akin to Kirghiz *karaghan* Siberian pea tree] **:** any of a genus (*Caragana*) of Asiatic leguminous shrubs or small trees extensively used in dry areas for hedges and in shelterbelts

car·a·geen *var of* CARRAGEEN

car·a·mel \'kar-ə-məl, -,mel; 'kär-məl\ *n* [F, fr. Sp *caramelo,* fr. Pg, icicle, caramel, fr. LL *calamellus* small reed — more at SHAWM] **1 :** an amorphous brittle brown and somewhat bitter substance obtained by heating sugar and used as a coloring and flavoring agent **2 :** a firm chewy usu. caramel-flavored candy

car·a·mel·ize \-mə-,līz\ *vb* **-ized; -iz·ing** *vt* **:** to change (sugar or the sugar content of a food) into caramel ∼ *vi* **:** to change to caramel

ca·ran·gid \kə-'ran-jəd, -'raŋ-gəd\ *adj* [deriv. of F *carangue* shad, horse mackerel, fr. Sp *caranga*] **:** of or relating to a large family (Carangidae) of marine spiny-finned fishes including important food fishes — **carangid** *n*

car·a·pace \'kar-ə-,pās\ *n* [F, fr. Sp *carapacho*] **1 :** a bony or chitinous case or shield covering the back or part of the back of an animal (as a turtle or crab) **2 :** a hard protective outer covering; *esp* **:** an attitude or state of mind (as indifference) serving to protect or isolate from external influence

1carat *var of* KARAT

2car·at \'kar-ət\ *n* [prob. fr. ML *carratus,* fr. Ar *qīrāt* bean pod, a small weight, fr. Gk *keration* carob bean, a small weight, fr. dim. of *kerat-, keras* horn — more at HORN] **:** a unit of weight for precious stones equal to 200 milligrams

1car·a·van \'kar-ə-,van\ *n* [It *caravana,* fr. Per *kārwān*] **1 a :** a company of travelers on a journey through desert or hostile regions; *also* **:** a train of pack animals **b :** a group of vehicles traveling together in a file **2 :** a covered vehicle: as **a :** a vehicle equipped as traveling living quarters **b** *Brit* **:** a nonautomotive vehicle designed to be hauled and to serve as a dwelling

2caravan *vi* **-vanned** *or* **-vaned** \-,vand\; **-van·ning** *or* **-van·ing :** to travel in a caravan

car·a·van·ner \-,van-ər\ *n* **1** *or* **car·a·van·er** \-,van-\ **:** one that travels in a caravan **2** *Brit* **:** one that goes camping with a trailer

car·a·van·sa·ry \,kar-ə-'van(t)-sə-rē\ *or* **car·a·van·se·rai** \-sə-,rī\ *n, pl* **-ries** *or* **-rais** *or* **-rai** [Per *kārwānsarāī,* fr. *kārwān* caravan + *sarāī* palace, inn] **1 :** a usu. large bare building surrounding a court in eastern countries where caravans rest at night **2 :** HOTEL, INN

car·a·vel \'kar-ə-,vel, -vəl\ *n* [MF *caravelle,* fr. OPg *caravela*] **:** any of several sailing ships; *specif* **:** a small 15th and 16th century ship with broad bows, high narrow poop, and lateen sails

car·a·way \'kar-ə-,wā\ *n* [ME, prob. fr. ML *carvi,* fr. Ar *karawyā,* fr. Gk *karon*] **:** a biennial usu. white-flowered aromatic herb (*Carum carvi*) of the carrot family with pungent fruits

carb- *or* **carbo-** *comb form* [F, fr. *carbone*] **:** carbon : carbonic : carbonyl : carboxyl ⟨*carb*ide⟩ ⟨*carbo*hydrate⟩

car·ba·chol \'kär-bə-,kȯl, -,kōl\ *n* [*carba*mic acid + *chol*ine] **:** a synthetic parasympathomimetic drug $C_6H_{15}ClN_2O_2$ that is used in veterinary medicine and topically in glaucoma

car·ba·mate \'kär-bə-,māt, kär-'bam-,āt\ *n* **:** a salt or ester of carbamic acid; *esp* **:** one that is a synthetic organic insecticide

car·bam·ic acid \(,)kär-,bam-ik-\ *n* [ISV *carb-* + *amide* + *-ic*] **:** an acid CH_3NO_2 known in the form of salts and esters that is a half amide of carbonic acid

carb·amide \'kär-bə-,mīd, kär-'bam-əd\ *n* [ISV *carb-* + *amide*] **:** UREA

carb·ami·no \,kär-bə-'mē-(,)nō\ *adj* **:** relating to any carbamic acid derivative formed by reaction of carbon dioxide with an amino acid or a protein (as hemoglobin)

car·ba·myl \'kär-bə-,mil\ *or* **car·bam·o·yl** \kär-'bam-ə-,wil\ *n* **:** the radical NH_2CO of carbamic acid

carb·an·ion \kär-'ban-,ī-ən, -,ī-,än\ *n* **:** an organic ion carrying a negative charge at a carbon position — compare CARBONIUM

car·barn \ˈkär-ˌbärn\ *n* : a building that houses the cars of a street railway or the buses of a bus system

car·ba·ryl \ˈkär-bə-ˌril\ *n* [*carb*amate + *ar*omatic + *-yl*] : a carbamate insecticide effective against numerous crop, forage, and forest pests

car·ba·zole \ˈkär-bə-ˌzōl\ *n* [ISV] : a crystalline slightly basic cyclic compound $C_{12}H_9N$ found in anthracene and used in making dyes

car bed *n* [fr. its use in carrying infants in cars] : a portable bed for an infant

car·bide \ˈkär-ˌbīd\ *n* [ISV] : a binary compound of carbon with a more electropositive element; *esp* : CALCIUM CARBIDE

car·bine \ˈkär-ˌbēn, -ˌbīn\ *n* [F *carabine,* fr. MF *carabin* carabineer] **1** : a short-barreled lightweight firearm orig. used by cavalry **2** : a .30 caliber gas-operated magazine fed semiautomatic or automatic rifle that is shorter and lighter and fires lighter ammunition than the M1 rifle and that was used by U.S. troops in World War II and the Korean war

car·bi·nol \ˈkär-bə-ˌnȯl, -ˌnōl\ *n* [ISV, fr. obs. G *karbin* methyl, fr. G *karb-* carb-] : METHANOL; *also* : an alcohol derived from it

car·bo·cy·clic \ˌkär-bō-ˈsī-klik, -ˈsik-lik\ *adj* [ISV] : being or having an organic ring composed of carbon atoms

car·bo·hy·drase \ˌkär-bō-ˈhī-ˌdrās, -bə-, -ˌdrāz\ *n* [ISV *carbohydr*ate + *-ase*] : any of a group of enzymes (as amylase) that promote hydrolysis or synthesis of a carbohydrate (as a disaccharide)

car·bo·hy·drate \-ˌdrāt, -drət\ *n* : any of various neutral compounds of carbon, hydrogen, and oxygen (as sugars, starches, and celluloses) most of which are formed by green plants and which constitute a major class of animal foods

car·bo·lat·ed \ˈkär-bə-ˌlāt-əd\ *adj* : impregnated with carbolic acid

car·bol·ic acid \(ˌ)kär-ˌbäl-ik-\ *n* [ISV *carb-* + L *oleum* oil — more at OIL] : PHENOL 1

car·bo·line \ˈkär-bə-ˌlēn\ *n* [*carb-* + ind*ole* + pyrid*ine*] : any of various isomers $C_{11}H_8N_2$ whose tricyclic structure is related to indole and pyridine and is found in many alkaloids

car·bon \ˈkär-bən\ *n, often attrib* [F *carbone,* fr. L *carbon-, carbo* ember, charcoal] **1** : a nonmetallic chiefly tetravalent element found native (as in the diamond and graphite) or as a constituent of coal, petroleum, and asphalt, of limestone and other carbonates, and of organic compounds or obtained artificially in varying degrees of purity esp. as carbon black, lampblack, activated carbon, charcoal, and coke — see ELEMENT table **2 a** : a sheet of carbon paper **b** : CARBON COPY **3 a** : a carbon rod used in an arc lamp **b** : a piece of carbon used as an element in a voltaic cell — **car·bon·less** \-ləs\ *adj*

car·bo·na·ceous \ˌkär-bə-ˈnā-shəs\ *adj* **1** : rich in carbon **2** : relating to, containing, or composed of carbon **3** : CARBONOUS 2

¹**car·bo·na·do** \ˌkär-bə-ˈnād-(ˌ)ō, -ˈnäd-\ *n, pl* **-dos** *or* **-does** [Sp *carbonada*] *archaic* : a broiled or grilled piece of meat scored before cooking

²**carbonado** *vt* **1** *archaic* : to make a carbonado of **2** *archaic* : CUT

³**carbonado** *n, pl* **-dos** [Pg, lit., carbonated] : an impure opaque dark-colored fine-grained aggregate of diamond particles valuable for its superior toughness

¹**car·bon·ate** \ˈkär-bə-ˌnāt, -nət\ *n* : a salt or ester of carbonic acid

²**car·bon·ate** \-ˌnāt\ *vt* **-at·ed; -at·ing 1** : to convert into a carbonate **2** : to impregnate with carbon dioxide ⟨*carbonated* beverage⟩ — **car·bon·ation** \ˌkär-bə-ˈnā-shən\ *n*

carbon black *n* : any of various colloidal black substances consisting wholly or principally of carbon obtained usu. as soot and used esp. as pigments

carbon copy *n* **1** : a copy made by carbon paper **2** : DUPLICATE

carbon cycle *n* **1** : a cycle of thermonuclear reactions in which four hydrogen atoms synthesize into a helium atom with the release of nuclear energy and which is held to be the source of most of the energy radiated by the sun and stars **2** : the cycle of carbon in living beings in which carbon dioxide is fixed by photosynthesis to form organic nutrients and is ultimately restored to the inorganic state by respiration and protoplasmic decay

carbon dating *n* : the determination of the age of old material (as an archaeological or paleontological specimen) by means of the content of carbon 14

carbon dioxide *n* : a heavy colorless gas CO_2 that does not support combustion, dissolves in water to form carbonic acid, is formed esp. by the combustion and decomposition of organic substances, is absorbed from the air by plants in photosynthesis, and is used in the carbonation of beverages

carbon disulfide *n* : a colorless flammable poisonous liquid CS_2 used as a solvent for rubber and as an insect fumigant — called also *carbon bisulfide*

carbon 14 \-(ˈ)fōr(t)-ˈtēn, -(ˈ)fȯr(t)-\ *n* : a heavy radioactive isotope of carbon of mass number 14 used esp. in tracer studies and in dating archaeological and geological materials

car·bon·ic \kär-ˈbän-ik\ *adj* : of, relating to, or derived from carbon, carbonic acid, or carbon dioxide

carbonic acid *n* : a weak dibasic acid H_2CO_3 known only in solution that reacts with bases to form carbonates

carbonic acid gas *n* : CARBON DIOXIDE

carbonic an·hy·drase \-an-ˈhī-ˌdrās, -ˌdrāz\ *n* [*carbonic* + *anhydr*ous + *-ase;* fr. its promotion of dehydration] : a zinc-containing enzyme that occurs in living tissues (as red blood cells) and aids carbon-dioxide transport from the tissues and its release from the blood in the lungs by catalyzing the reversible hydration of carbon dioxide to carbonic acid

car·bon·if·er·ous \ˌkär-bə-ˈnif-(ə-)rəs\ *adj* **1** : producing or containing carbon or coal **2** *cap* : of, relating to, or being the period of the Paleozoic era between the Devonian and the Permian or the corresponding system of rocks that includes coal beds — **Carboniferous** *n*

car·bo·ni·um \kär-ˈbō-nē-əm\ *n* [*carb-* + *-onium*] : an organic ion carrying a positive charge at a carbon position — compare CARBANION

car·bon·iza·tion \ˌkär-bə-nə-ˈzā-shən\ *n* : the process of carbonizing; *esp* : destructive distillation (as of coal)

car·bon·ize \ˈkär-bə-ˌnīz\ *vb* **-ized; -iz·ing** *vt* **1** : to convert into carbon or a carbonic residue **2** : CARBURIZE 1 ~ *vi* : to become carbonized : CHAR

carbon monoxide *n* : a colorless odorless very toxic gas CO that burns to carbon dioxide with a blue flame and is formed as a product of the incomplete combustion of carbon

car·bon·ous \ˈkär-bə-nəs\ *adj* **1** : derived from, containing, or resembling carbon **2** : brittle and dark in color

carbon paper *n* **1** : a thin paper faced with a waxy pigmented coating so that when placed between two sheets of paper the pressure of writing or typing on the top sheet causes transfer of pigment to the bottom sheet **2** : gelatin-coated paper used in the carbon process

carbon process *n* : a photographic printing process utilizing a sheet of paper coated with bichromated gelatin mixed with a pigment

carbon tetrachloride *n* : a colorless nonflammable toxic liquid CCl_4 that has an odor resembling that of chloroform and is used as a solvent (as in dry cleaning) and a fire extinguisher

car·bon·yl \ˈkär-bə-ˌnil, -ˌnēl\ *n* **1** : a bivalent radical CO occurring in aldehydes, ketones, carboxylic acids, esters, acid halides, and amides **2** : a compound of the carbonyl radical with a metal — **car·bon·yl·ic** \ˌkär-bə-ˈnil-ik\ *adj*

Car·bo·run·dum \ˌkär-bə-ˈrən-dəm\ *trademark* — used for various abrasives

carboxy- *or* **carbox-** *comb form* : carboxyl

car·box·yl \kär-ˈbäk-səl\ *n* [ISV] : a univalent radical COOH typical of organic acids — **car·box·yl·ic** \ˌkär-(ˌ)bäk-ˈsil-ik\ *adj*

car·box·yl·ase \kär-ˈbäk-sə-ˌlās, -lāz\ *n* [ISV] : an enzyme that catalyzes decarboxylation or carboxylation

¹**car·box·yl·ate** \-ˌlāt, -lət\ *n* : a salt or ester of a carboxylic acid

²**car·box·yl·ate** \-ˌlāt\ *vt* **-at·ed; -at·ing** : to introduce carboxyl or carbon dioxide into (a compound) with formation of a carboxylic acid — **car·box·yl·ation** \(ˌ)kär-ˌbäk-sə-ˈlā-shən\ *n*

carboxylic acid *n* : an organic acid (as acetic acid) containing one or more carboxyl groups

car·boxy·pep·ti·dase \kär-ˌbäk-sē-ˈpep-tə-ˌdās, -ˌdāz\ *n* : an enzyme that hydrolyzes peptides and esp. polypeptides by splitting off the amino acids containing free carboxyl groups

car·boy \ˈkär-ˌbȯi\ *n* [Per *qarāba,* fr. Ar *qarrābah* demijohn] : a bottle or rectangular container of about 5 to 15 gallons capacity for liquids that is made of glass, plastic, or metal and is often cushioned in a special container

car·bun·cle \ˈkär-ˌbəŋ-kəl\ *n* [ME, fr. MF, fr. L *carbunculus* small coal, carbuncle, dim. of *carbon-, carbo* charcoal, ember — more at CARBON] **1 a** *obs* : any of several red precious stones **b** : the garnet cut cabochon **2** : a painful local purulent inflammation of the skin and deeper tissues with multiple openings for the discharge of pus and usu. necrosis and sloughing of dead tissue — **car·bun·cled** \-kəld\ *adj* — **car·bun·cu·lar** \kär-ˈbəŋ-kyə-lər\ *adj*

car·bu·ret \ˈkär-b(y)ə-ˌrāt, *esp by chemists* -ˌret\ *vt* **-ret·ed,** *also* **-ret·ted; -ret·ing** *also* **-ret·ting** [obs. *carburet* (carbide)] **1** : to combine chemically with carbon **2** : to enrich (as gas) by mixing with volatile carbon compounds (as hydrocarbons) — **car·bu·re·tion** \ˌkär-b(y)ə-ˈrā-shən\ *n*

car·bu·re·tor \ˈkär-b(y)ə-ˌrāt-ər\ *n* : an apparatus for supplying an internal-combustion engine with atomized and vaporized fuel mixed with air in an explosive mixture

car·bu·rize \ˈkär-b(y)ə-ˌrīz\ *vt* **-rized; -riz·ing** [obs. *carburet* (carbide)] **1** : to combine or impregnate (as metal) with carbon **2** : CARBURET 2 — **car·bu·ri·za·tion** \ˌkär-b(y)ə-rə-ˈzā-shən\ *n*

car·ca·jou \ˈkär-kə-ˌjü, -ˌzhü\ *n* [CanF, of AmerInd origin] : WOLVERINE

car·ca·net \ˈkär-kə-nət\ *n* [MF *carcan*] *archaic* : an ornamental necklace or headband

car card *n* : a small cardboard placard for advertising esp. in or on streetcars and buses

car·case \ˈkär-kəs\ *Brit var of* CARCASS

car·cass \ˈkär-kəs\ *n* [MF *carcasse,* fr. OF *carcois*] **1** : a dead body : CORPSE; *esp* : the dressed body of a meat animal **2** : the living, material, or physical body **3** : the decaying or worthless remains of a structure ⟨the ~ of an abandoned automobile⟩ **4** : the foundation structure of something (as a tire)

carcin- *or* **carcino-** *comb form* [Gk *karkin-, karkino-,* fr. *karkinos* — more at CANCER] **1** : crab ⟨*carcinology*⟩ **2** : tumor : cancer ⟨*carcinogenic*⟩

car·cin·o·gen \kär-ˈsin-ə-jən, ˈkärs-ᵊn-ə-ˌjen\ *n* : a substance or agent producing or inciting cancer — **car·ci·no·gen·e·sis** \ˌkärs-ᵊn-ō-ˈjen-ə-səs\ *n* — **car·ci·no·gen·ic** \-ˈjen-ik\ *adj* — **car·ci·no·ge·nic·i·ty** \-jə-ˈnis-ət-ē\ *n*

car·ci·noid \ˈkärs-ᵊn-ˌȯid\ *n* : a usu. benign tumor arising esp. from the mucosa of the gastrointestinal tract (as in the stomach or appendix)

car·ci·no·ma \ˌkärs-ᵊn-ˈō-mə\ *n, pl* **-mas** *or* **-ma·ta** \-mət-ə\ [L, fr. Gk *karkinōma* cancer, fr. *karkinos*] : a malignant tumor of epithelial origin — **car·ci·no·ma·tous** \-ˈō-mət-əs\ *adj*

car·ci·no·ma·to·sis \-ˌō-mə-ˈtō-səs\ *n* [NL, fr. L *carcinomat-, carcinoma*] : a condition in which multiple carcinomas are developing simultaneously usu. after dissemination from a primary source

car·ci·no·sar·co·ma \ˈkärs-ᵊn-ō-(ˌ)sär-ˈkō-mə\ *n, pl* **-mas** *or* **-ma·ta** \-mət-ə\ : a malignant tumor combining elements of carcinoma and sarcoma

car coat *n* : a three-quarter-length overcoat

¹**card** \ˈkärd\ *vt* : to cleanse, disentangle, and collect together (as fibers) by the use of a card preparatory to spinning — **card·er** *n*

ə abut	ᵊ kitten	ər further	a back	ā bake	ä cot, cart
aù out	ch chin	e less	ē easy	g gift	i trip	ī life
j joke	ŋ sing	ō flow	ȯ flaw	ȯi coin	th thin	t͟h this
ü loot	ù foot	y yet	yü few	yù furious	zh vision

[2]**card** *n* [ME *carde,* fr. MF, fr. LL *cardus* thistle, fr. L *carduus* — more at CHARD] **1** : an implement for raising a nap on cloth **2** : an instrument or machine for carding fibers that consists usu. of bent wire teeth set closely in rows in a thick piece of leather fastened to a back

[3]**card** *n* [ME *carde,* modif. of MF *carte,* prob. fr. OIt *carta,* lit., leaf of paper, fr. L *charta* leaf of papyrus, fr. Gk *chartēs*] **1** : PLAYING CARD **2** *pl but sing or pl in constr* **a** : a game played with cards **b** : card playing **3** : something compared to a valuable playing card in one's hand **4** : a usu. clownishly amusing person : WAG **5** : COMPASS CARD **6 a** : a flat stiff usu. small and rectangular piece of paper or thin paperboard: as (1) : POSTCARD (2) : VISITING CARD **b** : PROGRAM; *esp* : a sports program **c** (1) : a wine list (2) : MENU **d** : GREETING CARD

[4]**card** *vt* **1** : to place or fasten on or by means of a card **2** : to provide with a card **3** : to list or record on a card **4** : SCORE

[5]**card** *abbr* cardinal

Card *abbr* Cardiganshire

car·da·mom \ˈkärd-ə-məm, -ˌmäm\ *n* [L *cardamomum,* fr. Gk *kardamōmon,* blend of *kardamon* peppergrass & *amōmon,* an Indian spice plant] : the aromatic capsular fruit of an East Indian herb (*Elettaria cardamomum*) of the ginger family with seeds used as a condiment and in medicine; *also* : this plant

[1]**card·board** \ˈkärd-ˌbō(ə)rd, -ˌbȯ(ə)rd\ *n* : a stiff moderately thick paperboard

[2]**cardboard** *adj* **1 a** : made of or as if of cardboard **b** : FLAT, TWO-DIMENSIONAL **2** : UNREAL, STEREOTYPED ⟨the story has too many ~ characters⟩

card–car·ry·ing \ˈkärd-ˌkar-ē-iŋ\ *adj* [fr. the assumption that such a person carries a card identifying him as a member] : being a regularly enrolled member of an organized group and esp. of the Communist party and not merely a sympathizer with its ideals and programs

card catalog *n* : a catalog (as of books) in which the entries are arranged systematically on cards

cardi- *or* **cardio-** *comb form* [Gk *kardi-, kardio-,* fr. *kardia* — more at HEART] : heart : cardiac : cardiac and ⟨*cardio*gram⟩ ⟨*cardio*vascular⟩

-car·dia \ˈkärd-ē-ə\ *n comb form* [NL, fr. Gk *kardia*] : heart action or location (of a specified type) ⟨dextro*cardia*⟩ ⟨tachy*cardia*⟩

[1]**car·di·ac** \ˈkärd-ē-ˌak\ *adj* [L *cardiacus,* fr. Gk *kardiakos,* fr. *kardia*] **1 a** : of, relating to, situated near, or acting on the heart **b** : of or relating to the part of the stomach into which the esophagus opens or to the stomach exclusive of the pyloric end **2** : of or relating to heart disease

[2]**cardiac** *n* : a person with heart disease

car·di·al·gia \ˌkärd-ē-ˈal-j(ē-)ə\ *n* [NL, fr. Gk *kardialgia,* fr. *kardia* + *-algia*] **1** : HEARTBURN **2** : pain in the heart

car·di·gan \ˈkärd-i-gən\ *n* [James Thomas Brudenell, 7th Earl of *Cardigan* †1868 E soldier] : a usu. collarless sweater or jacket that opens the full length of the center front

Cardigan *n* [*Cardigan* county, Wales] : a Welsh corgi with rounded ears, slightly bowed forelegs, and long tail — called also *Cardigan Welsh corgi*

[1]**car·di·nal** \ˈkärd-nəl, -ᵊn-əl\ *adj* [ME, fr. OF, fr. LL *cardinalis,* fr. L, of a hinge, fr. *cardin-, cardo* hinge; akin to OE *hratian* to rush, Gk *skairein* to gambol] : of basic importance : MAIN, CHIEF, PRIMARY ⟨the ~ virtue in the Shavian scale . . . is responsibility; every creed he has attacked Shaw has attacked on the grounds of irresponsibility —E. R. Bentley⟩ ***syn*** see ESSENTIAL — **car·di·nal·ly** \-ē\ *adv*

[2]**cardinal** *n* **1** : a high ecclesiastical official of the Roman Catholic Church who ranks next below the pope and is appointed by him to assist him as a member of the college of cardinals **2** : CARDINAL NUMBER — usu. used in pl. **3** : a woman's short hooded cloak orig. of scarlet cloth **4** [fr. its color, resembling that of the cardinal's robes] : any of several American finches (genus *Richmondena*) of the southern and middle U.S. of which the male is bright red with a black face and pointed crest — **car·di·nal·ship** \-ˌship\ *n*

car·di·nal·ate \-ət, -ˌāt\ *n* : the office, rank, or dignity of a cardinal

cardinal flower *n* : a No. American lobelia (*Lobelia cardinalis*) that bears a spike of brilliant red flowers

car·di·nal·i·ty \ˌkärd-ᵊn-ˈal-ət-ē\ *n, pl* **-ties** [[2]*cardinal* + *-ity*] : the number of elements in a given mathematical set

cardinal number *n* **1** : a number (as 1, 5, 15) that is used in simple counting and that indicates how many elements there are in an assemblage — see NUMBER table **2** : the property that a mathematical set has in common with all sets that can be put in one-to-one correspondence with it

cardinal point *n* : one of the four principal compass points north, south, east, and west

cardinal virtue *n* **1** : one of the four classically defined natural virtues prudence, justice, temperance, or fortitude **2** : a quality designated as a major virtue

car·dio·gram \ˈkärd-ē-ə-ˌgram\ *n* [ISV] : the curve or tracing made by a cardiograph

car·dio·graph \-ˌgraf\ *n* [ISV] : an instrument that registers graphically movements of the heart — **car·di·og·ra·pher** \ˌkärd-ē-ˈäg-rə-fər\ *n* — **car·dio·graph·ic** \ˌkärd-ē-ə-ˈgraf-ik\ *adj* — **car·di·og·ra·phy** \ˌkärd-ē-ˈäg-rə-fē\ *n*

car·di·oid \ˈkärd-ē-ˌȯid\ *n* : a heart-shaped curve that is traced by a point on the circumference of a circle rolling completely around an equal fixed circle and has the general equation $\rho = a(1 + \cos\theta)$ in polar coordinates

car·di·ol·o·gy \ˌkärd-ē-ˈäl-ə-jē\ *n* [ISV] : the study of the heart and its action and diseases — **car·di·o·log·i·cal** \-ē-ə-ˈläj-i-kəl\ *adj* — **car·di·ol·o·gist** \-ē-ˈäl-ə-jəst\ *n*

car·dio·my·op·a·thy \ˈkärd-ē-ō-(ˌ)mī-ˈäp-ə-thē\ *n, pl* **-thies** [*cardi-* + *my-* + *-pathy*] : a typically chronic disorder of heart muscle that may involve hypertrophy and obstructive damage to the heart

car·di·op·a·thy \ˌkärd-ē-ˈäp-ə-thē\ *n, pl* **-thies** : a disease of the heart

car·dio·pul·mo·nary \ˈkärd-ē-ō-ˈpu̇l-mə-ˌner-ē, -ˈpəl\ *adj* : of or relating to the heart and lungs

car·dio·re·spi·ra·to·ry \ˈkärd-ē-ō-ˈres-p(ə-)rə-ˌtōr-ē, -ri-ˈspī-rə-, -ˌtȯr-\ *adj* : of or relating to the heart and the respiratory system : CARDIOPULMONARY

car·dio·ton·ic \ˌkärd-ē-ō-ˈtän-ik\ *adj* : tending to increase the tonus of heart muscle — **cardiotonic** *n*

car·dio·vas·cu·lar \-ˈvas-kyə-lər\ *adj* [ISV] : of, relating to, or involving the heart and blood vessels

-car·di·um \ˈkärd-ē-əm\ *n comb form, pl* **car·dia** \-ē-ə\ [NL, fr. Gk *kardia*] : heart ⟨epi*cardium*⟩

car·doon \kär-ˈdün\ *n* [F *cardon,* fr. LL *cardon-, cardo* thistle, fr. *cardus,* fr. L *carduus* thistle, artichoke — more at CHARD] : a large perennial plant (*Cynara cardunculus*) related to the artichoke and cultivated for its edible root and leafstalks

card·play·er \ˈkärd-ˌplā-ər\ *n* : one that plays cards

card·sharp·er \-ˌshär-pər\ *or* **card·sharp** \-ˌshärp\ *n* : one who habitually cheats at cards

[1]**care** \ˈke(ə)r, ˈka(ə)r\ *n* [ME, fr. OE *caru;* akin to OHG *kara* lament, L *garrire* to chatter] **1** : suffering of mind : GRIEF **2 a** : a disquieted state of blended uncertainty, apprehension, and responsibility **b** : a cause for such anxiety **3** : painstaking or watchful attention **4** : regard coming from desire or esteem **5** : CHARGE, SUPERVISION ⟨under a doctor's ~⟩ **6** : a person or thing that is an object of attention, anxiety, or solicitude ⟨the flower garden was her special ~⟩

syn CARE, CONCERN, SOLICITUDE, ANXIETY, WORRY *shared meaning element* : a troubled or engrossed state of mind or the thing that causes this

[2]**care** *vb* **cared; car·ing** *vi* **1 a** : to feel trouble or anxiety **b** : to feel interest or concern ⟨~ about freedom⟩ **2** : to give care ⟨~ for the sick⟩ **3 a** : to have a liking, fondness, or taste ⟨don't ~ for her⟩ **b** : to have an inclination ⟨would you ~ for some pie⟩ ~ *vt* **1** : to be concerned about or to the extent of **2** : WISH — **car·er** *n*

CARE *abbr* Cooperative for American Relief to Everywhere

[1]**ca·reen** \kə-ˈrēn\ *n* [MF *carène* keel, fr. OIt *carena,* fr. L *carina* keel, lit., nutshell; akin to Gk *karyon* nut] *archaic* : the act or process of careening : the state of being careened

[2]**careen** *vt* **1 a** : to cause (a boat) to lean over on one side **b** : to clean, caulk, or repair (a boat) in this position **2** : to cause to heel over ~ *vi* **1 a** : to careen a boat **b** : to undergo this process **2** : to heel over **3** : to sway from side to side : LURCH ⟨a ~*ing* carriage being pulled wildly along a street by a team of runaway horses —J. P. Getty⟩

[1]**ca·reer** \kə-ˈri(ə)r\ *n* [MF *carrière,* fr. OProv *carriera* street, fr. ML *carraria* road for vehicles, fr. L *carrus* car] **1 a** : COURSE, PASSAGE **b** : full speed or exercise of activity ⟨he was now in the full ~ of conquest—T. B. Macaulay⟩ **2** : ENCOUNTER, CHARGE **3** : a field for or pursuit of consecutive progressive achievement esp. in public, professional, or business life ⟨Washington's ~ as a soldier⟩ **4** : a profession for which one trains and which is undertaken as a permanent calling ⟨a ~ diplomat⟩

[2]**career** *vi* : to go at top speed esp. in a headlong manner ⟨a car ~*ed* off the road⟩

ca·reer·ism \-ˌiz-əm\ *n* : the policy or practice of advancing one's career often at the cost of one's integrity — **ca·reer·ist** \-əst\ *n*

care·free \ˈke(ə)r-ˌfrē, ˈka(ə)r-\ *adj* : free from care : IRRESPONSIBLE ⟨is ~ with his money⟩ ⟨a ~ vacation⟩

care·ful \-fəl\ *adj* **care·ful·ler; care·ful·lest 1** *archaic* **a** : SOLICITOUS, ANXIOUS **b** : filling with care or solicitude **2** : exercising or taking care **3 a** : marked by attentive concern and solicitude **b** : marked by wary caution or prudence ⟨be very ~ with knives⟩ **c** : marked by painstaking effort to avoid errors or omissions — often used with *of* or an infinitive ⟨~ of money⟩ ⟨~ to adjust the machine⟩ — **care·ful·ly** \-f(ə-)lē\ *adv* — **care·ful·ness** \-fəl-nəs\ *n*

syn CAREFUL, METICULOUS, SCRUPULOUS, PUNCTILIOUS *shared meaning element* : showing close attention to detail (as of behavior or performance) ***ant*** careless

care·less \-ləs\ *adj* **1 a** : free from care : UNTROUBLED ⟨~ days⟩ **b** : INDIFFERENT, UNCONCERNED ⟨~ of the consequences⟩ **2** : not taking care **3** : not showing or receiving care: **a** : NEGLIGENT, SLOVENLY ⟨writing that is ~ and full of errors⟩ **b** : UNSTUDIED, SPONTANEOUS ⟨~ grace⟩ **c** *obs* : UNVALUED, DISREGARDED — **care·less·ly** *adv* — **care·less·ness** *n*

[1]**ca·ress** \kə-ˈres\ *n* [F *caresse,* fr. It *carezza,* fr. *caro* dear, fr. L *carus* — more at CHARITY] **1** : an act or expression of kindness or affection : ENDEARMENT **2 a** : a light stroking, rubbing, or patting **b** : KISS — **ca·res·sive** \-ˈres-iv\ *adj* — **ca·res·sive·ly** *adv*

[2]**caress** *vt* **1** : to treat with tokens of fondness, affection, or kindness : CHERISH **2 a** : to touch or stroke lightly in a loving or endearing manner **b** : to touch or affect as if with a caress ⟨echoes that ~ the ear⟩ — **ca·ress·er** *n* — **ca·ress·ing·ly** \-iŋ-lē\ *adv*

syn CARESS, FONDLE, PET, CUDDLE *shared meaning element* : to show affection by touching or handling

car·et \ˈkar-ət\ *n* [L, there is lacking, fr. *carēre* to lack, be without — more at CASTE] : a wedge-shaped mark made on written or printed matter to indicate the place where something is to be inserted

care·tak·er \ˈke(ə)r-ˌtā-kər, ˈka(ə)r-\ *n* **1** : one that takes care of the house or land of an owner who may be absent **2** : one temporarily fulfilling the function of office ⟨a ~ government⟩

care·worn \-ˌwō(ə)rn, -ˌwȯ(ə)rn\ *adj* : showing the effect of grief or anxiety ⟨a ~ face⟩

car·ex \ˈka(ə)r-ˌeks\ *n, pl* **car·i·ces** \ˈkar-ə-ˌsēz\ [NL, genus name, fr. L, sedge] : any of a genus (*Carex* of the family Cyperaceae) of perennial sedges that have seedlike achenes enclosed in a sac in the axil of a bract

car·fare \ˈkär-ˌfa(ə)r, -ˌfe(ə)r\ *n* : passenger fare (as on a bus)

car·ful \ˈkär-ˌfu̇l\ *n* : as much or as many as a car will hold

car·go \ˈkär-(ˌ)gō\ *n, pl* **cargoes** *or* **cargos** [Sp, load, charge, fr. *cargar* to load, fr. LL *carricare* — more at CHARGE] : the goods or merchandise conveyed in a ship, airplane, or vehicle : FREIGHT

car·hop \ˈkär-ˌhäp\ *n* [*car* + *-hop* (as in *bellhop*)] : one who serves customers at a drive-in restaurant

Car·ib \'kar-əb\ *n* [NL *Caribes* (pl.), fr. Sp *Caribe*, fr. Arawakan *Carib* — more at CANNIBAL] **1 :** a member of an American Indian people of northern So. America and the Lesser Antilles **2 :** the language of the Caribs

Ca·ri·ban \'kar-ə-bən, kə-'rē-bən\ *n* **1 :** a member of a group of American Indian peoples of northern So. America, the Lesser Antilles, and the Caribbean coast of Honduras, Guatemala, and British Honduras **2 :** the language family comprising the languages of the Cariban peoples

Ca·rib·be·an \,kar-ə-'bē-ən, kə-'rib-ē-\ *adj* [NL *Caribbaeus*, fr. *Caribes*] **:** of or relating to the Caribs, the eastern and southern West Indies, or the Caribbean sea

ca·ri·be \kə-'rē-bē\ *n* [AmerSp, fr. Sp, Carib, cannibal] **:** PIRANHA

car·i·bou \'kar-ə-,bü\ *n, pl* **caribou** *or* **caribous** [CanF, of Algonquian origin] **:** any of several large palmate-antlered deer (genus *Rangifer*) of northern No. America that are related to the reindeer

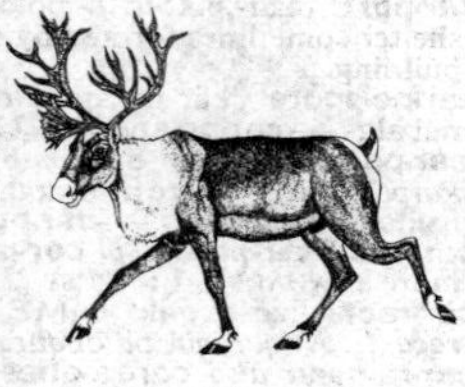
caribou

1car·i·ca·ture \'kar-i-kə-,chü(ə)r, -,t(y)ü(ə)r\ *n* [It *caricatura*, lit., act of loading, fr. *caricare* to load, fr. LL *carricare*] **1 :** exaggeration by means of often ludicrous distortion of parts or characteristics **2 :** a representation esp. in literature or art that has the qualities of caricature **3 :** a distortion so gross as to seem like caricature — **car·i·ca·tur·al** \,kar-i-kə-'chür-əl, -'t(y)ür-\ *adj* — **car·i·ca·tur·ist** \'kar-i-kə-,chür-əst, -,t(y)ür-\ *n*

syn CARICATURE, BURLESQUE, PARODY, TRAVESTY *shared meaning element* **:** a comic or grotesque imitation

2caricature *vt* **-tured; -tur·ing :** to make or draw a caricature of **:** represent in caricature ⟨his face has often been *caricatured* in the newspapers⟩

car·ies \'ka(ə)r-ēz, 'ke(ə)r-\ *n, pl* **caries** [L, decay; akin to Gk *kēr* death] **:** a progressive destruction of bone or tooth; *esp* **:** tooth decay

car·il·lon \'kar-ə-,län, -lən\ *n* [F, alter. of OF *quarregnon*, fr. LL *quaternion-, quaternio* set of four — more at QUATERNION] **1 a :** a set of fixed chromatically tuned bells sounded by hammers controlled from a keyboard **b :** an electronic instrument imitating a carillon **2 :** a composition for the carillon

car·il·lon·neur \,kar-ə-lə-'nər, ,kar-ē-ə-'nər\ *n* [F, fr. *carillon*] **:** a carillon player

ca·ri·na \kə-'rī-nə, -'rē-\ *n, pl* **-ri·nas** *or* **-ri·nae** \-'rī-,nē, -'rē-,nī\ [NL, fr. L, keel — more at CAREEN] **:** a keel-shaped anatomical part, ridge, or process; *esp* **:** the part of a papilionaceous flower that encloses the stamens and pistil — **ca·ri·nal** \-'rīn-ᵊl\ *adj*

car·i·nate \'kar-ə-,nāt, -nət\ *also* **car·i·nat·ed** \-,nāt-əd\ *adj* **:** shaped like the keel or prow of a ship **:** KEELED, RIDGED ⟨a ~ sepal⟩

ca·ri·o·ca \,kar-ē-'ō-kə\ *n* [Pg, fr. Tupi] **1** *cap* **:** a native or resident of Rio de Janeiro **2 a :** a variation of the samba **b :** the music for this dance

car·i·ole \'kar-ē-,ōl\ *n* [F *carriole*, fr. OProv *carriola*, deriv. of L *carrus* car] **1 :** a light one-horse carriage **2 :** a dog-drawn toboggan

car·i·ous \'kar-ē-əs, 'ker-\ *adj* [L *cariosus*, fr. *caries*] **:** affected with caries

1cark \'kärk\ *vb* [ME *carken*, lit., to load, burden, fr. ONF *carquier*, fr. LL *carricare*] *vt* **:** WORRY ~ *vi* **:** to be anxious

2cark *n* **:** TROUBLE, DISTRESS

carl *or* **carle** \'kär(ə)l\ *n* [ME, fr. OE *-carl*, fr. ON *karl* man, carl; akin to OE *ceorl* churl — more at CHURL] **1 :** a man of the common people **2** *chiefly dial* **:** CHURL, BOOR

car·line *or* **car·lin** \'kärlən\ *n* [ME *kerling*, fr. ON, fr. *karl* man] *chiefly Scot* **:** WOMAN; *esp* **:** an old woman

car·ling \'kär-liŋ, -lən\ *n* [F *carlingue*, fr. ONF *calingue*, fr. ON *kerling*, lit., old woman] **:** a fore-and-aft member supporting a deck of a ship or framing a deck opening

Car·list \'kär-ləst\ *n* [Sp *carlista*, fr. Don *Carlos* claimant to the Spanish throne under the Salic law] **:** a supporter of Don Carlos or his successors as having rightful title to the Spanish throne — **Carlist** *adj*

car·load \'kär-'lōd, -,lōd\ *n* **1 :** a load that fills a car **2 :** the minimum number of tons required for shipping at carload rates

carload rate *n* **:** a rate for large shipments lower than that quoted for less-than-carload lots of the same class

Car·lo·vin·gian \,kär-lə-'vin-j(ē-)ən\ *adj* [F *carlovingien*, prob. fr. ML *Carlus* Charles + F *-ovingien* (as in *mérovingien* Merovingian)] **:** CAROLINGIAN

Carm *abbr* Carmarthenshire

car·ma·gnole \'kär-mən-,yōl\ *n* [F] **1 :** a lively song popular at the time of the first French Revolution **2 :** a street dance in a meandering course to the tune of the carmagnole

car·mak·er \'kär-,mā-kər\ *n* **:** an automobile manufacturer

Car·mel·ite \'kär-mə-,līt\ *n* [ME, fr. ML *carmelita*, fr. *Carmel* Mount Carmel, Palestine] **:** a member of the Roman Catholic mendicant Order of Our Lady of Mount Carmel founded in the 12th century — **Carmelite** *adj*

car·mi·na·tive \kär-'min-ət-iv, 'kär-mə-,nāt-\ *adj* [F *carminatif*, fr. L *carminatus*, pp. of *carminare* to card, fr. *carmin-, carmen* card, fr. *carrere* to card — more at CHARD] **:** expelling gas from the alimentary canal so as to relieve colic or griping — **carminative** *n*

car·mine \'kär-mən, -,mīn\ *n* [F *carmin*, fr. ML *carminium*, irreg. fr. Ar *qirmiz* kermes + L *minium* — more at MINIUM] **1 :** a rich crimson or scarlet lake made from cochineal **2 :** a vivid red

Carn *abbr* Caernarvonshire

car·nage \'kär-nij\ *n* [MF, fr. ML *carnaticum* tribute consisting of animals or meat, fr. L *carn-, caro*] **1 :** the flesh of slain animals or men **2 :** great and bloody slaughter (as in battle) ***syn*** see MASSACRE

car·nal \'kärn-ᵊl\ *adj* [ME, fr. ONF or LL; ONF, fr. LL *carnalis*, fr. L *carn-, caro* flesh; akin to Gk *keirein* to cut — more at SHEAR] **1 :** BODILY, CORPOREAL **2 a :** marked by sexuality **b :** relating to or given to crude bodily pleasures and appetites **3 a :** TEMPORAL **b :** WORLDLY — **car·nal·i·ty** \kär-'nal-ət-ē\ *n* — **car·nal·ly** \'kärn-ᵊl-ē\ *adv*

syn CARNAL, FLESHLY, SENSUAL, ANIMAL *shared meaning element* **:** having or showing a physical rather than an intellectual or spiritual orientation or origin ***ant*** spiritual, intellectual

car·nall·ite \'kärn-ᵊl-,īt\ *n* [G *carnallit*, fr. Rudolf von *Carnall* †1874 G mining engineer] **:** a mineral $KMgCl_3.6H_2O$ consisting of hydrous potassium-magnesium chloride important as a source of potassium

car·nas·si·al \kär-'nas-ē-əl\ *adj* [F *carnassier* carnivorous, deriv. of L *carn-, caro*] **:** of, relating to, or being teeth of a carnivore larger and longer than adjacent teeth and adapted for cutting rather than tearing — **carnassial** *n*

car·na·tion \kär-'nā-shən\ *n* [MF, fr. OIt *carnagione*, fr. *carne* flesh, fr. L *carn-, caro*] **1 a** (1) **:** the variable color of human flesh (2) **:** a pale to grayish yellow **b :** a moderate red **2 :** any of numerous cultivated usu. double-flowered pinks derived from the common gillyflower

car·nau·ba \kär-'nō-bə, -'naù-; ,kär-nə-'ü-bə\ *n* [Pg] **:** a fan-leaved palm (*Copernicia cerifera*) of Brazil that has an edible root and yields a useful leaf fiber and carnauba wax

carnauba wax *n* **:** a hard brittle high-melting wax from the leaves of the carnauba palm used chiefly in polishes

Car·ne·gie unit \,kär-nə-gē-, (,)kär-,neg-ē-\ *n* [fr. its having been first defined by the Carnegie Foundation for the Advancement of Teaching] **:** the credit given for the successful completion of a year's study of one subject in a secondary school

car·ne·lian \kär-'nēl-yən\ *n* [alter. of *cornelian* fr. ME *corneline*, fr. MF, perh. fr. *cornelle* cornel] **:** a hard tough chalcedony that has a reddish color and is used in jewelry

car·ni·tine \'kär-nə-,tēn\ *n* [ISV, deriv. of L *carn-, caro* meat, flesh] **:** a white betaine that is an essential vitamin for some insect larvae (as a mealworm) and that occurs in vertebrate muscle

car·ni·val \'kär-nə-vəl\ *n* [It *carnevale*, alter. of earlier *carnelevare*, lit., removal of meat, fr. *carne* flesh (fr. L *carn-, caro*) + *levare* to remove, fr. L, to raise] **1 :** a season or festival of merrymaking before Lent **2 :** an instance of merrymaking, feasting, or masquerading **3 a :** a traveling enterprise offering amusements **b :** an organized program of entertainment or exhibition **:** FESTIVAL ⟨a winter ~⟩

car·ni·vore \'kär-nə-,vō(ə)r, -,vȯ(ə)r\ *n* [deriv. of L *carnivorus*] **1 :** a flesh-eating animal; *esp* **:** any of an order (Carnivora) of flesh-eating mammals **2 :** an insectivorous plant

car·niv·o·rous \kär-'niv-(ə-)rəs\ *adj* [L *carnivorus*, fr. *carn-, caro* flesh + *-vorus* -vorous — more at CARNAL] **1 :** subsisting or feeding on animal tissues **2** *of a plant* **:** subsisting on nutrients obtained from the breakdown of animal protoplasm **3 :** of or relating to the carnivores — **car·niv·o·rous·ly** *adv* — **car·niv·o·rous·ness** *n*

car·no·tite \'kär-nə-,tīt\ *n* [F, fr. M. A. *Carnot* †1920 F inspector general of mines] **:** a mineral $K_2(UO_2)_2(VO_4)_2.3H_2O$ consisting of a hydrous radioactive vanadate of uranium and potassium that is a source of radium and uranium

car·ny *or* **car·ney** *or* **car·nie** \'kär-nē\ *n, pl* **carnies** *or* **carneys 1 :** CARNIVAL 3a **2 :** one who works with a carnival — **carny** *adj*

car·ob \'kar-əb\ *n* [MF *carobe*, fr. ML *carrubium*, fr. Ar *kharrūbah*] **1 :** a Mediterranean evergreen leguminous tree (*Ceratonia siliqua*) with racemose red flowers **2 :** a carob pod; *also* **:** its sweet pulp

ca·roche \kə-'rōch, -'rōsh\ *n* [MF *carroche*, fr. OIt *carroccio*, aug. of *carro* car, fr. L *carrus*] **:** a luxurious or stately horse-drawn carriage

1car·ol \'kar-əl\ *n* [ME *carole*, fr. OF, modif. of LL *choraula* choral song, fr. L, choral accompanist, fr. Gk *choraulēs*, fr. *choros* chorus + *aulein* to play a reed instrument, fr. *aulos*, a reed instrument — more at ALVEOLUS] **1 :** an old round dance with singing **2 :** a song of joy or mirth ⟨the ~ of a bird —Lord Byron⟩ **3 :** a popular song or ballad of religious joy

2carol *vb* **-oled** *or* **-olled; -ol·ing** *or* **-ol·ling** *vi* **1 :** to sing esp. in a joyful manner **2 :** to sing carols; *specif* **:** to go about outdoors in a group singing Christmas carols ~ *vt* **1 :** to praise in or as if in song **2 :** to sing esp. in a cheerful manner **:** WARBLE

Car·o·line \'kar-ə-,lin, -lən\ *or* **Car·o·le·an** \,kar-ə-'lē-ən\ *adj* [NL *carolinus*, fr. ML *Carolus* Charles] **:** of or relating to Charles — used esp. with reference to Charles I and Charles II of England

Car·o·lin·gian \,kar-ə-'lin-j(ē-)ən\ *adj* [F *carolingien*, fr. ML *karolingi* French people, prob. fr. (assumed) OHG *karling* Frenchman, fr. *Karl* Charles] **:** of or relating to a Frankish dynasty dating from about A.D. 613 and including among its members the rulers of France from 751 to 987, of Germany from 752 to 911, and of Italy from 774 to 961 — **Carolingian** *n*

1car·om \'kar-əm\ *n* [by shortening & alter. fr. obs. *carambole*, fr. Sp *carambola*] **1 a :** a shot in billiards in which the cue ball strikes each of two object balls **b :** a shot in pool in which an object ball strikes another ball before falling into a pocket — compare COMBINATION SHOT **2 :** a rebounding esp. at an angle

2carom *vi* **1 :** to make a carom **2 :** to strike and rebound **:** GLANCE ⟨the car ~*ed* off several trees⟩

car·o·tene \'kar-ə-,tēn\ *n* [ISV, fr. LL *carota* carrot] **:** any of several orange or red crystalline hydrocarbon pigments (as $C_{40}H_{56}$) that occur in the chromoplasts of plants and in the fatty tissues of plant-eating animals and are convertible to vitamin A

ca·rot·enoid *also* **ca·rot·i·noid** \kə-'rät-ᵊn-,ȯid\ *n* **:** any of various usu. yellow to red pigments (as carotenes) found widely in plants

ə abut ᵊ kitten ər further a back ā bake ä cot, cart
aù out ch chin e less ē easy g gift i trip ī life
j joke ŋ sing ō flow ȯ flaw ȯi coin th thin t͟h this
ü loot ù foot y yet yü few yù furious zh vision

and animals and characterized chemically by a long aliphatic polyene chain composed of isoprene units — **carotenoid** *adj*

ca·rot·id \kə-ˈrät-əd\ *adj* [F or Gk; F *carotide*, fr. Gk *karōtides* carotid arteries, fr. *karoun* to stupefy; akin to Gk *kara* head — more at CEREBRAL] **:** of, relating to, or being the chief artery or pair of arteries that pass up the neck and supply the head — **carotid** *n*

carotid body *n* **:** a small body of vascular tissue that adjoins the carotid sinus, functions as a chemoreceptor sensitive to change in the oxygen tension of blood, and mediates reflex changes in respiratory activity

carotid sinus *n* **:** a small but richly innervated arterial enlargement that is located at the point in the neck where either carotid artery forms its main branches and that functions in the regulation of heart rate and blood pressure

ca·rous·al \kə-ˈrau̇-zəl\ *n* **:** CAROUSE 2

[1]**ca·rouse** \kə-ˈrau̇z\ *n* [MF *carrousse*, fr. *carous*, adv., all out (in *boire carous* to empty the cup), fr. G *garaus*] **1** *archaic* **:** a large draft of liquor **:** TOAST **2 :** a drunken revel

[2]**carouse** *vb* **ca·roused; carous·ing** *vi* **1 :** to drink liquor deeply or freely **2 :** to take part in a carouse ~ *vt, obs* **:** to drink up **:** QUAFF — **ca·rous·er** *n*

car·ou·sel \ˌkar-ə-ˈsel *also* -ˈzel; ˈkar-ə-ˌ\ *n* [F *carrousel*, fr. It *carosello*] **1 :** a tournament or exhibition in which horsemen execute evolutions **2 a :** MERRY-GO-ROUND **b :** a circular conveyer on which objects are placed ⟨the luggage ~ at the airport⟩

[1]**carp** \ˈkärp\ *vi* [ME *carpen*, of Scand origin; akin to Icel *karpa* to dispute] **:** to find fault or complain querulously — **carp·er** *n*

[2]**carp** *n, pl* **carp** *or* **carps** [ME *carpe*, fr. MF, fr. LL *carpa*, prob. of Gmc origin; akin to OHG *karpfo* carp] **1 :** a large variable Old World soft-finned freshwater fish (*Cyprinus carpio*) of sluggish waters often raised for food; *also* **:** any of various related cyprinid fishes **2 :** a fish (as the European sea bream) resembling a carp

carp- *or* **carpo-** *comb form* [F & NL, fr. Gk *karp-*, *karpo-*, fr. *karpos* — more at HARVEST] **:** fruit ⟨*carpology*⟩

-carp \ˌkärp\ *n comb form* [NL *-carpium*, fr. Gk *-karpion*, fr. *karpos*] **:** part of a fruit ⟨meso*carp*⟩ **:** fruit ⟨schizo*carp*⟩

[1]**car·pal** \ˈkär-pəl\ *adj* [NL *carpalis*, fr. *carpus*] **:** relating to the carpus

[2]**carpal** *n* **:** a carpal element **:** CARPALE

car·pa·le \kär-ˈpal-(ˌ)ē, -ˈpāl-, -ˈpäl-\ *n, pl* **-lia** \-ē-ə\ [NL, neut. of *carpalis*] **:** a carpal bone

car park *n, chiefly Brit* **:** an area set apart for the parking of motor vehicles **:** PARKING LOT

car·pe di·em \ˌkär-pe-ˈdē-ˌem, -ˈdī-, -əm\ *n* [L, enjoy the day] **:** the enjoyment of the pleasures of the moment without concern for the future ⟨the *carpe diem* theme in poetry⟩

car·pel \ˈkär-pəl\ *n* [NL *carpellum*, fr. Gk *karpos* fruit] **:** one of the structures in a seed plant comprising the innermost whorl of a flower, functioning as megasporophylls, and collectively constituting the gynoecium — **car·pel·lary** \-pə-ˌler-ē\ *adj* — **car·pel·late** \-ˌlāt, -lət\ *adj*

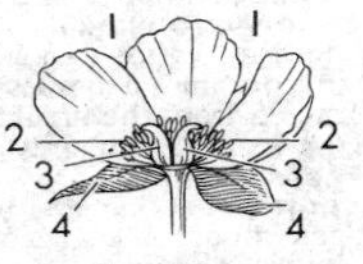

carpels: flower cut away: *1* petals; *2* stamens: *3* carpels: *4* sepals

[1]**car·pen·ter** \ˈkär-pən-tər, ˈkärp-ᵊm-tər\ *n* [ME, fr. ONF *carpentier*, fr. L *carpentarius* carriage maker, fr. *carpentum* carriage, of Celt origin; akin to OIr *carr* vehicle — more at CAR] **:** a workman who builds or repairs wooden structures or their structural parts

[2]**carpenter** *vb* **car·pen·tered; car·pen·ter·ing** \-t(ə-)riŋ\ *vi* **:** to follow the trade of a carpenter ⟨~*ed* when he was young⟩ ~ *vt* **1 :** to make by or as if by carpentry **2 :** to put together often in a mechanical manner ⟨~*ed* many television scripts⟩

carpenter ant *n* **:** an ant (esp. genus *Campanotus*) that gnaws galleries in dead or decayed wood

carpenter bee *n* **:** any of various solitary bees (*Xylocopa* and related genera) that gnaw galleries in sound timber

car·pen·try \-trē\ *n* **1 :** the art or trade of a carpenter; *specif* **:** the art of shaping and assembling structural woodwork **2 :** timberwork constructed by a carpenter **3 :** the form or manner of putting together the parts (as of a literary or musical composition) **:** STRUCTURE, ARRANGEMENT

car·pet \ˈkär-pət\ *n* [ME, fr. MF *carpite*, fr. OIt *carpita*, fr. *carpire* to pluck, modif. of L *carpere* to pluck — more at HARVEST] **1 :** a heavy woven or felted fabric used as a floor covering; *also* **:** a floor covering made of this fabric **2 :** a surface resembling or suggesting a carpet — **carpet** *vt* — **on the carpet :** before an authority for censure or reproof

[1]**car·pet·bag** \-ˌbag\ *n* **:** a traveling bag made of carpet and widely used in the U.S. in the 19th century

[2]**carpetbag** *adj* **:** of, relating to, or characteristic of carpetbaggers ⟨a ~ government⟩

car·pet·bag·ger \-ˌbag-ər\ *n* [fr. their carrying all their belongings in carpetbags] **1 :** a Northerner in the South after the American Civil War usu. seeking private gain under the reconstruction governments **2 :** a nonresident who meddles in politics — **car·pet·bag·gery** \-ˌbag-(ə-)rē\ *n*

carpet beetle *n* **:** a small beetle (*Bothynus gibbosus*) whose larva damages woolen goods; *broadly* **:** any beetle of similar habits

car·pet·ing \ˈkär-pət-iŋ\ *n* **:** material for carpets; *also* **:** CARPETS

carpet knight *n* [fr. the carpet's having been a symbol of luxury] **:** a knight devoted to idleness and luxury

car·pet·weed \ˈkär-pət-ˌwēd\ *n* **:** a No. American mat-forming weed (*Mollugo verticillata* of the family Aizoaceae, the carpetweed family)

-car·pic \ˈkär-pik\ *adj comb form* [prob. fr. NL *-carpicus*, fr. Gk *karpos* fruit] **:** -CARPOUS ⟨poly*carpic*⟩

carp·ing \ˈkär-piŋ\ *adj* **:** marked by or inclined to querulous and often perverse criticism ***syn*** see CRITICAL ***ant*** fulsome — **carp·ing·ly** \-piŋ-lē\ *adv*

car·po·go·ni·um \ˌkär-pə-ˈgō-nē-əm\ *n, pl* **-nia** \-nē-ə\ [NL] **1 :** the flask-shaped egg-bearing portion of the female reproductive branch in some thallophytes **2 :** ASCOGONIUM — **car·po·go·ni·al** \-nē-əl\ *adj*

car·pol·o·gy \kär-ˈpäl-ə-jē\ *n* [ISV] **:** a branch of plant morphology dealing with fruit and seeds

car pool *n* **:** a joint arrangement by a group of private automobile owners in which each in turn drives his own car and carries the other passengers; *also* **:** the group entering into such an agreement

car·poph·a·gous \kär-ˈpäf-ə-gəs\ *adj* [Gk *karpophagos*, fr. *karp-* carp- + *-phagos* -phagous] **:** feeding on fruits

car·po·phore \ˈkär-pə-ˌfō(ə)r, -ˌfȯ(ə)r\ *n* [prob. fr. NL *carpophorum*, fr. *carp-* + *-phorum* -phore] **1 :** the stalk of a fungal fruiting body; *also* **:** the entire fruiting body **2 :** a slender prolongation of a floral axis from which the carpels are suspended

car·port \ˈkär-ˌpō(ə)rt, -ˌpȯ(ə)rt\ *n* **:** an open-sided automobile shelter sometimes formed by extension of a roof from the side of a building

car·po·spore \ˈkär-pə-ˌspō(ə)r, -ˌspȯ(ə)r\ *n* **:** a diploid spore of a red alga — **car·po·spor·ic** \ˌkär-pə-ˈspōr-ik, -ˈspȯr-\ *adj*

-car·pous \ˈkär-pəs\ *adj comb form* [NL *-carpus*, fr. Gk *-karpos*, fr. *karpos* fruit — more at HARVEST] **:** having (such) fruit or (so many) fruits ⟨poly*carpous*⟩ — **-car·py** \ˌkär-pē\ *n comb form*

car·pus \ˈkär-pəs\ *n, pl* **car·pi** \-ˌpī, -(ˌ)pē\ [NL, fr. Gk *karpos* — more at WHARF] **1 :** WRIST **2 :** the bones of the wrist

car·rack \ˈkar-ək, -ik\ *n* [ME *carrake*, fr. MF *caraque*, fr. OSp *carraca*, fr. Ar *qarāqir*, pl. of *qurqūr* merchant ship] **:** a large galleon

car·ra·geen *also* **car·ra·gheen** \ˈkar-ə-ˌgēn\ *n* [*Carragheen*, near Waterford, Ireland] **1 :** a dark purple branching cartilaginous seaweed (*Chondrus crispus*) found on the coasts of northern Europe and No. America — called also *Irish moss* **2 :** CARRAGEENAN

car·ra·geen·an *or* **car·ra·geen·in** *also* **car·ra·gheen·in** \ˌkar-ə-ˈgē-nən\ *n* [*carrageen* + [3]*-an* or *-in*] **:** a colloid extracted esp. from carrageen and used esp. as a suspending agent (as in foods) and as a clarifying agent (as for beverages) and in controlling crystal growth in frozen confections

car·re·four \ˌkar-ə-ˈfu̇(ə)r\ *n* [MF, fr. LL *quadrifurcum*, neut. of *quadrifurcus* having four forks, fr. L *quadri-* + *furca* fork] **1 :** CROSSROADS **2 :** SQUARE, PLAZA ⟨the farmers . . . preferred the open ~ for their transactions —Thomas Hardy⟩

car·rel \ˈkar-əl\ *n* [alter. of ME *carole* round dance, ring — more at CAROL] **:** a table that is often partitioned or enclosed and is used for individual study esp. in a library

car·riage \ˈkar-ij\ *n* [ME *cariage*, fr. ONF, fr. *carier* to transport in a vehicle — more at CARRY] **1 :** the act of carrying **2 a** *archaic* **:** DEPORTMENT **b :** manner of bearing the body **:** POSTURE **3** *archaic* **:** MANAGEMENT **4 :** the price or expense of carrying **5** *obs* **:** BURDEN, LOAD **6** *obs* **:** IMPORT, SENSE **7 a :** a wheeled vehicle; *esp* **:** a horse-drawn vehicle designed for private use and comfort **b** *Brit* **:** a railway passenger coach **8 :** a wheeled support carrying a burden **9 :** a movable part of a machine for supporting some other movable object or part ⟨a typewriter ~⟩ **10** *obs* **:** a hanger for a sword ***syn*** see BEARING

carriage trade *n* **:** trade from well-to-do or upper-class people

car·riage·way \ˈkar-ij-ˌwā\ *n, Brit* **:** a road used by vehicular traffic **:** HIGHWAY; *specif* **:** LANE 2b

car·rick bend \ˌkar-ik-\ *n* [prob. fr. obs. E *carrick* carrack, fr. ME *carrake*, *carryk*] **:** a knot used to join the ends of two large ropes — see KNOT illustration

car·ri·er \ˈkar-ē-ər\ *n* **1 :** one that carries **:** BEARER, MESSENGER **2 a :** an individual or organization engaged in transporting passengers or goods for hire **b :** a transportation line carrying mail between post offices **c :** a postal employee who delivers or collects mail **d :** one that delivers newspapers **e :** an entity (as a hole or an electron) capable of carrying an electric charge **3 a :** a container for carrying **b :** a device or machine that carries **:** CONVEYER **4 :** AIRCRAFT CARRIER **5 :** a bearer and transmitter of a causative agent of disease; *esp* **:** one who carries in his system the causative agent of a disease (as typhoid fever) to which he is immune **6 a :** a usu. inactive accessory substance **:** VEHICLE ⟨a ~ for a drug or an insecticide⟩ **b :** a substance (as a catalyst) by whose agency some element or group is transferred from one compound to another **7 :** an electric wave or alternating current whose modulations are used as signals in radio, telephonic, or telegraphic transmission **8 :** an organization acting as an insurer

carrier pigeon *n* **1 :** a pigeon used to carry messages; *esp* **:** HOMING PIGEON **2 :** any of a breed of large long-bodied show pigeons

car·ri·ole *var of* CARIOLE

car·ri·on \ˈkar-ē-ən\ *n* [ME *caroine*, fr. AF, fr. (assumed) VL *caronia*, irreg. fr. L *carn-*, *caro* flesh — more at CARNAL] **:** dead and putrefying flesh; *also* **:** flesh unfit for food

carrion crow *n* **:** a common European black crow (*Corvus corone*)

car·ron·ade \ˌkar-ə-ˈnād\ *n* [*Carron*, Scotland] **:** an obsolete short light iron cannon

car·rot \ˈkar-ət\ *n* [MF *carotte*, fr. LL *carota*, fr. Gk *karōton*] **1 :** a biennial herb (*Daucus carota* of the family Umbelliferae, the carrot family) with a usu. orange spindle-shaped edible root; *also* **:** its root **2 :** a promised often illusory reward or advantage

car·roty \-ət-ē\ *adj* **1 :** resembling carrots in color **2 :** having hair the color of carrots

car·rou·sel *var of* CAROUSEL

[1]**car·ry** \ˈkar-ē\ *vb* **car·ried; car·ry·ing** [ME *carien*, fr. ONF *carier* to transport in a vehicle, fr. *car* vehicle, fr. L *carrus* — more at CAR] *vt* **1 :** to move while supporting (as a package) **:** TRANSPORT ⟨her legs refused to ~ her further —Ellen Glasgow⟩ **2 :** to convey by direct communication ⟨~ tales about a friend⟩ **3** *chiefly dial* **:** CONDUCT, ESCORT **4 :** to influence by mental or emotional appeal **:** SWAY **5 :** to get possession or control of **:** CAPTURE ⟨*carried* off the prize⟩ **6 :** to transfer from one place to another ⟨~ a number in adding⟩ **7 :** to contain and direct the course of ⟨the drain *carries* sewage⟩ **8 a :** to wear or have on one's person **b :** to bear upon or within one ⟨is ~*ing* an unborn child⟩ **9 a :** to have as a mark, attribute, or property ⟨~ a scar⟩ **b :** IMPLY, INVOLVE ⟨the crime *carried* a heavy penalty⟩ **10 :** to hold or comport (as one's person) in a specified manner **11 :** to sustain the weight or burden of ⟨pillars ~ an arch⟩ **12 :** to bear as a crop **13 :** to sing

with reasonable correctness of pitch ⟨~ a tune⟩ **14** **a :** to keep in stock for sale; *also* : to provide sustenance for ⟨land *~ing* 10 head of cattle⟩ **b :** to have or maintain on a list or record ⟨~ a person on a payroll⟩ **15 :** to maintain and cause to continue through financial support or personal effort ⟨he *carried* the magazine singlehandedly⟩ **16 :** to prolong in space, time, or degree ⟨~ a principle too far⟩ **17** **a :** to gain victory for; *esp* : to secure the adoption or passage of **b :** to win a majority of votes in (as a legislative body or a state) **18 :** PUBLISH ⟨newspapers ~ weather reports⟩ **19** **a :** to bear the charges of holding or having (as stocks or merchandise) from one time to another **b :** to keep on one's books as a debtor ⟨a merchant *carries* a customer⟩ **20 :** to hold to and follow after (as a scent) **21 :** to hoist and maintain (a sail) in use **22 :** to cover (a distance) or pass (an object) at a single stroke in golf **23 :** to allow (an opponent) to make a good showing by lessening one's opposition **~** *vi* **1 :** to act as a bearer **2** **a :** to reach or penetrate to a distance ⟨voices ~ well⟩ **b :** to convey itself to a reader or audience **3 :** to undergo or admit of carriage in a specified way **4** *of a hunting dog* : to keep and follow the scent **5 :** to win adoption ⟨the motion *carried* by a vote of 71-25⟩

syn CARRY, BEAR, CONVEY, TRANSPORT *shared meaning element* : to move something from one place to another

— **carry a torch** *or* **carry the torch** **1 :** CRUSADE **2 :** to be in love esp. without reciprocation : cherish a longing or devotion ⟨she still *carries a torch* for him even though their engagement is broken⟩ — **carry the ball :** to perform or assume the chief role : bear the major portion of work or responsibility — **carry the day :** WIN, PREVAIL

2carry *n* **1 :** carrying power; *esp* : the range of a gun or projectile or of a struck or thrown ball **2** **a :** the act or method of carrying ⟨fireman's ~⟩ **b :** PORTAGE **3 :** the position assumed by a color-bearer with the flag or guidon held in position for marching **4 :** a quantity that is transferred in addition from one number place to the adjacent one of higher place value

car·ry·all \ˈkar-ē-ˌȯl\ *n* **1** [by folk etymology fr. F *carriole* — more at CARIOLE] **a :** a light covered carriage for four or more persons **b :** a passenger automobile similar to a station wagon but with a higher body often on a truck chassis **2** [1*carry* + *all*] **:** a capacious bag or carrying case **3 :** a self-loading carrier esp. for hauling earth and crushed rock

carry away *vt* **1 :** CARRY OFF **2 :** to arouse to a high and often excessive degree of emotion or enthusiasm

carrying capacity *n* **:** the population (as of deer) that an area will support without undergoing deterioration

carrying charge *n* **1 :** expense incident to ownership or use of property **2 :** a charge added to the price of merchandise sold on the installment plan

car·ry·ing–on \ˌkar-ē-iŋ-ˈȯn, -ˈän\ *n, pl* **carryings–on :** foolish, excited, or improper behavior; *also* : an instance of such behavior ⟨scandalous *carryings-on*⟩

carry off *vt* **1 :** to cause the death of ⟨the plague *carried off* thousands⟩ **2 :** to perform easily or successfully ⟨the actress *carried off* her part brilliantly in spite of only a few rehearsals⟩ **3 :** to brave out

car·ry–on \ˈkar-ē-ˌȯn, -ˌän\ *n* **:** a piece of luggage suitable for being carried aboard an airplane by a passenger

carry on *vt* **:** CONDUCT, MANAGE ⟨*carried on* the business⟩ **~** *vi* **1 :** to behave in a foolish, excited, or improper manner ⟨embarrassed by the way he *carries on*⟩ **2 :** to continue one's course or activity in spite of hindrance or discouragement

car·ry·out \ˈkar-ē-ˌau̇t\ *n* **:** a food product packaged to be carried away from its place of sale rather than consumed on the premises — **carryout** *adj*

carry out \ˌkar-ē-ˈau̇t\ *vt* **1 :** to put into execution ⟨*carry out* a plan⟩ **2 :** to bring to a successful issue : COMPLETE, ACCOMPLISH ⟨you will be paid when you have *carried out* the assignment⟩ **3 :** to continue to an end or stopping point

car·ry–over \ˈkar-ē-ˌō-vər\ *n* **1 :** the act or process of carrying over **2 :** something carried over

carry over \ˌkar-ē-ˈō-vər\ *vt* **1** **a :** to hold over (as goods) for another season **b :** to transfer (an amount) to the succeeding column, page, or book relating to the same account **2 :** to deduct (a loss or an unused credit) for taxable income of a subsequent period **~** *vi* **:** to persist from one stage or sphere of activity to another

carry through *vt* **:** to carry out **~** *vi* **:** PERSIST, SURVIVE ⟨feelings that *carry through* to the present⟩

car·sick \ˈkär-ˌsik\ *adj* **:** affected with motion sickness esp. in an automobile — **car sickness** *n*

1cart \ˈkärt\ *n* [ME, prob. fr. ON *kartr;* akin to OE *cræt* cart, OE *cradol* cradle] **1 :** a heavy usu. horse-drawn 2-wheeled vehicle used for farming or transporting freight **2 :** a lightweight 2-wheeled vehicle drawn by a horse, pony, or dog **3 :** a small wheeled vehicle

2cart *vt* **1 :** to carry or convey in or as if in a cart ⟨buses to ~ the kids to and from school —L. S. Gannett⟩ **2 :** to take or drag away without ceremony or by force — usu. used with *off* ⟨they *~ed* him off to jail⟩ — **cart·er** *n*

cart·age \ˈkärt-ij\ *n* **:** the act of or rate charged for carting

carte blanche \ˈkärt-ˈblä^{n}sh, -ˈblänch\ *n, pl* **cartes blanches** \ˈkärt-ˈblä^{n}sh(-əz), -ˈblänch(-əz)\ [F, lit., blank document] **:** full discretionary power ⟨was given *carte blanche* to build, landscape, and furnish the house⟩

carte du jour \ˌkärt-də-ˈzhu̇(ə)r\ *n, pl* **cartes du jour** \ˌkärt(s)-\ [F, lit., card of the day] **:** MENU

car·tel \kär-ˈtel\ *n* [MF, letter of defiance, fr. OIt *cartello,* lit., placard, fr. *carta* leaf of paper — more at CARD] **1 :** a written agreement between belligerent nations **2 :** a combination of independent commercial enterprises designed to limit competition **3 :** a combination of political groups for common action

Car·te·sian \kär-ˈtē-zhən\ *adj* [NL *cartesianus,* fr. *Cartesius* Descartes] **:** of or relating to René Descartes or his philosophy — **Cartesian** *n* — **Car·te·sian·ism** \-zhə-ˌniz-əm\ *n*

Cartesian coordinate *n* **1 :** either of two coordinates that locate a point on a plane and measure its distance from either of two intersecting straight-line axes along a line parallel to the other axis **2 :** any of three coordinates that locate a point in space and measure its distance from any of three intersecting coordinate planes measured parallel to that one of three straight-line axes that is the intersection of the other two planes

Cartesian plane *n* **:** a plane whose points are labeled with Cartesian coordinates

Cartesian product *n* **:** a set that is constructed from two given sets and comprises all pairs of elements such that one element of the pair is from the first set and the other element is from the second set

Car·thu·sian \kär-ˈth(y)ü-zhən\ *n* [ML *cartusiensis,* irreg. fr. OF *Chartrouse,* motherhouse of the Carthusian order, near Grenoble, France] **:** a member of an austere contemplative religious order founded by St. Bruno in 1084 — **Carthusian** *adj*

car·ti·lage \ˈkärt-^{ə}l-ij, ˈkärt-lij\ *n* [L *cartilagin-, cartilago;* akin to L *cratis* wickerwork — more at HURDLE] **1 :** a translucent elastic tissue that composes most of the skeleton of the embryos and very young of vertebrates and becomes for the most part converted into bone in the higher vertebrates **2 :** a part or structure composed of cartilage

car·ti·lag·i·nous \ˌkärt-^{ə}l-ˈaj-ə-nəs\ *adj* **:** composed of, relating to, or resembling cartilage

cartilaginous fish *n* **:** any of the fishes (esp. class Chondrichthyes) having the skeleton wholly or largely composed of cartilage; *also* : CYCLOSTOME

cart·load \ˈkärt-ˈlōd, -ˌlōd\ *n* **1 :** as much as a cart will hold **2 :** one third of a cubic yard (as of dirt)

car·to·gram \ˈkärt-ə-ˌgram\ *n* [F *cartogramme,* fr. *carte* + *-gramme* -gram] **:** a map showing statistics geographically

car·tog·ra·pher \kär-ˈtäg-rə-fər\ *n* **:** one that makes maps

car·tog·ra·phy \-fē\ *n* [F *cartographie,* fr. *carte* card, map + *-graphie* -graphy — more at CARD] **:** the science or art of making maps — **car·to·graph·ic** \ˌkärt-ə-ˈgraf-ik\ *or* **car·to·graph·i·cal** \-i-kəl\ *adj*

car·to·man·cy \ˈkärt-ə-ˌman(t)-sē\ *n* [F *cartomancie,* fr. *carte* card + *-o-* + *-mancie* -mancy] **:** fortune-telling by the use of playing cards

1car·ton \ˈkärt-^{ə}n\ *n* [F, fr. It *cartone* pasteboard] **:** a cardboard box or container

2carton *vt* **:** to pack or enclose in a carton **~** *vi* **:** to shape cartons from cardboard sheets

car·toon \kär-ˈtün\ *n* [It *cartone* pasteboard, cartoon, aug. of *carta* leaf of paper — more at CARD] **1 :** a preparatory design, drawing, or painting (as for a fresco) **2** **a :** a satirical drawing commenting on public and usu. political matters **b :** COMIC STRIP **3 :** ANIMATED CARTOON — **cartoon** *vb* — **car·toon·ist** \-ˈtü-nəst\ *n*

car·top \ˈkär-ˌtäp\ *adj* **:** suitable in size and weight for carrying on top of an automobile ⟨a ~ fishing boat⟩

car·top·per \-ˌtäp-ər\ *n* **:** a small boat that may be transported on top of a car

car·touche *also* **car·touch** \kär-ˈtüsh\ *n* [F *cartouche,* fr. It *cartoccio,* fr. *carta*] **1 :** a gun cartridge with a paper case **2 :** an ornate or ornamental frame **3 :** an oval or oblong figure (as on ancient Egyptian monuments) enclosing a sovereign's name

car·tridge \ˈkär-trij, *dial or archaic* ˈka-trij\ *n* [alter. of earlier *cartage,* modif. of MF *cartouche*] **1** **a :** a tube of metal, paper, or both containing a complete charge for a firearm and usu. an initiating device (as a cap) **b :** a case containing an explosive charge for blasting **2 :** an often cylindrical container of material for insertion into a larger mechanism or apparatus **3 :** a small case in a phonograph pickup containing the needle and the mechanism for translating stylus motion into electrical voltage **4 :** a case containing a reel of magnetic tape arranged for insertion into a tape recorder

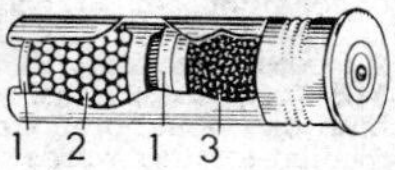

cartridge for shotgun: *1* wads, *2* shot, *3* powder

cartridge belt *n* **1 :** a belt having a series of loops for holding cartridges **2 :** a belt worn around the waist and designed for carrying various attachable equipment (as a cartridge case, canteen, or compass)

car·tu·lary \ˈkär-chə-ˌler-ē\ *n, pl* **-lar·ies** [ML *chartularium,* fr. *chartula* charter — more at CHARTER] **:** a collection of charters; *esp* : a book containing duplicates of the charters and title deeds of an estate

1cart·wheel \ˈkärt-ˌhwēl, -ˌwēl\ *n* **1 :** a large coin (as a silver dollar) **2 :** a lateral handspring with arms and legs extended

2cartwheel *vi* **:** to move like a turning wheel; *specif* : to perform cartwheels — **cart·wheel·er** *n*

ca·run·cle \ˈkar-ˌəŋ-kəl, kə-ˈrəŋ-\ *n* [obs. F *caruncule,* fr. L *caruncula* little piece of flesh, dim. of *caro* flesh — more at CARNAL] **1 :** a naked fleshy outgrowth (as a bird's wattle) **2 :** an outgrowth on a seed adjacent to the micropyle — **ca·run·cu·lar** \kə-ˈrəŋ-kyə-lər\ *adj* — **ca·run·cu·late** \-lət, -ˌlāt\ *or* **ca·run·cu·lat·ed** \-ˌlāt-əd\ *adj*

car·va·crol \ˈkär-və-ˌkrōl, -ˌkrōl\ *n* [ISV, fr. NL *carvi* (specific epithet of *Carum carvi* caraway) + L *acr-, acer* sharp — more at CARAWAY, EDGE] **:** a liquid phenol $C_{10}H_{14}O$ found in essential oils of various mints (as thyme) and used as an antiseptic

carve \ˈkärv\ *vb* **carved; carv·ing** [ME *kerven,* fr. OE *ceorfan;* akin to MHG *kerben* to notch, Gk *graphein* to scratch, write] *vt* **1 :** to cut with care or precision ⟨*carved* fretwork⟩ **2 :** to make or get by

or as if by cutting — often used with *out* ⟨~ out a fortune⟩ **3 :** to cut into pieces or slices ⟨*carved* the turkey⟩ ~ *vi* **1 :** to cut up and serve meat **2 :** to work as a sculptor or engraver — **carv·er** *n*
car·vel \'kär-vəl, -,vel\ *n* [ME *carvile,* fr. MF *caravelle, carvelle*] **:** CARAVEL
car·vel–built \-,bilt\ *adj* [prob. fr. D *karveel-,* fr. *karveel* caravel, fr. MF *carvelle*] **:** built with the planks meeting flush at the seams ⟨a ~ boat⟩
carv·en \'kär-vən\ *adj* **:** wrought or ornamented by carving **:** CARVED
carv·ing \'kär-viŋ\ *n* **1 :** the act or art of one who carves **2 :** a carved object, design, or figure
car wash *n* **:** an area or structure equipped with facilities for washing automobiles
cary- *or* **caryo-** — see KARY-
cary·at·id \,kar-ē-'at-əd\ *n, pl* **-ids** *or* **-i·des** \-ə-,dēz\ [L *caryatides,* pl., fr. Gk *karyatides* priestesses of Artemis at Caryae, caryatids, fr. *Karyai* Caryae in Laconia] **:** a draped female figure supporting an entablature
cary·op·sis \,kar-ē-'äp-səs\ *n, pl* **-op·ses** \-,sēz\ *or* **-si·des** \-sə-,dēz\ [NL] **:** a small one-seeded dry indehiscent fruit (as of Indian corn or wheat) in which the fruit and seed fuse in a single grain
CAS *abbr* certificate of advanced study
ca·sa \'käs-ə\ *n* [Sp & It, fr. L, cabin] *Southwest* **:** DWELLING
ca·sa·ba \kə-'säb-ə\ *n* [*Kasaba* (now Turgutlu), Turkey] **:** any of several winter melons with yellow rind and sweet flesh
Ca·sa·no·va \,kaz-ə-'nō-və, ,kas-\ *n* [Giacomo Girolamo *Casanova*] **:** LOVER; *esp* **:** a man who is a promiscuous and unscrupulous lover
Cas·bah \'kaz-,bä, 'käz-\ *n* [F, fr. Ar dial. *qaṣbah*] **1 :** a No. African castle or fortress **2 :** the native section of a No. African city
cas·ca·bel \'kas-kə-,bel\ *n* [Sp, lit., small bell like a sleigh bell] **1 :** a projection behind the breech of a muzzle-loading cannon **2 :** a small hollow perforated spherical bell enclosing a loose pellet
1cas·cade \(')kas-'kād\ *n* [F, fr. It *cascata,* fr. *cascare* to fall, fr. (assumed) VL *casicare,* fr. L *casus* pp. of *cadere* to fall] **1 :** a steep usu. small fall of water; *esp* **:** one of a series **2 a :** something arranged in a series or in a succession of stages so that each stage derives from or acts upon the product of the preceding **b :** a fall of material (as lace) that hangs in a zigzag line **3 :** something falling or rushing forth in quantity ⟨a ~ of sound⟩ ⟨a ~ of roses and daisies⟩
2cascade *vb* **cas·cad·ed; cas·cad·ing** *vi* **:** to fall or pour in or as if in a cascade ~ *vt* **1 :** to cause to fall like a cascade **2 :** to connect in a cascade arrangement
cas·cara \ka-'skar-ə\ *n* [Sp *cáscara* bark, fr. *cascar* to crack, break, fr. (assumed) VL *quassicare* to shake, break, fr. L *quassare* — more at QUASH] **1 :** CASCARA BUCKTHORN **2 :** CASCARA SAGRADA
cascara buckthorn *n* **:** a buckthorn (*Rhamnus purshiana*) of the Pacific coast of the U.S. yielding cascara sagrada
cascara sa·gra·da \-sə-'gräd-ə\ *n* [AmerSp *cáscara sagrada,* lit., sacred bark] **:** the dried bark of cascara buckthorn used as a mild laxative
cas·ca·ril·la \,kas-kə-'ril-ə, -'rē-(y)ə\ *n* [Sp, dim. of *cáscara*] **:** the aromatic bark of a West Indian shrub (*Croton eluteria*) of the spurge family used for making incense and as a tonic; *also* **:** this shrub
1case \'kās\ *n* [ME *cas,* fr. OF, fr. L *casus* fall, chance, fr. *casus,* pp. of *cadere* to fall — more at CHANCE] **1 a :** a set of circumstances or conditions **b** (1) **:** a situation requiring investigation or action (as by the police) (2) **:** the object of investigation or consideration **2 :** CONDITION; *specif* **:** condition of body or mind **3** [ME *cas,* fr. MF, fr. L *casus,* trans. of Gk *ptōsis,* lit., fall] **a :** an inflectional form of a noun, pronoun, or adjective indicating its grammatical relation to other words **b :** such a relation whether indicated by inflection or not **4 :** what actually exists or happens **:** FACT **5 a :** a suit or action in law or equity **b** (1) **:** the evidence supporting a conclusion or judgment (2) **:** ARGUMENT; *esp* **:** a convincing argument **6 a :** an instance of disease or injury; *also* **:** PATIENT **b :** an instance that directs attention to a situation or exhibits it in action **:** EXAMPLE **c :** a peculiar person **:** CHARACTER ***syn*** see INSTANCE — **in any case :** without regard to or in spite of other considerations **:** whatever else is done or is the case ⟨war is inevitable *in any case*⟩ ⟨*in any case* the seminar agreed that teachers of literature had to be concerned with . . . values —H. J. Muller⟩ — **in case 1 :** IF **2 :** as a precaution **3 :** as a precaution against the event that — **in case of :** in the event of ⟨*in case of* trouble, yell⟩
2case *n* [ME *cas,* fr. ONF *casse,* fr. L *capsa* chest, case, fr. *capere* to take — more at HEAVE] **1 a :** a box or receptacle for holding something **b :** a box together with its contents **c :** SET; *specif* **:** PAIR **2 :** an outer covering or housing **3 :** a shallow divided tray for holding printing type **4 :** the frame of a door or window **:** CASING
3case *vt* **cased; cas·ing 1 :** to enclose in or cover with a case **:** ENCASE **2 :** to line (as a well) with supporting material (as metal pipe) **3 :** to inspect or study esp. with intent to rob
ca·se·ate \'kā-sē-,āt\ *vi* **-at·ed; -at·ing** [L *caseus* cheese — more at CHEESE] **:** to undergo caseation
ca·se·ation \,kā-sē-'ā-shən\ *n* **:** necrosis with conversion of damaged tissue into a soft cheesy substance
case·bear·er \'kās-,bar-ər, -,ber-\ *n* **:** an insect larva that forms a protective case (as of silk)
case·book \-,bu̇k\ *n* **1 :** a book containing records of illustrative cases that is used for reference and instruction (as in law or medicine) **2 :** a compilation of primary and secondary documents relating to a central topic together with scholarly comment, exercises, and study aids that is designed to serve as a source book for short papers (as in a course in composition) or as a point of departure for a research paper
cased glass \'kāst-\ *n* **:** glass consisting of two or more fused layers of different colors often decorated by cutting so that the inner layers show through — called also *case glass*
case goods *n pl* **1 :** furniture (as bureaus or bookcases) that provides interior storage space; *also* **:** dining-room and bedroom furniture sold as sets **2 :** products (as liquor or canned milk) often sold by the case
case hard·en \'kās-,härd-ᵊn\ *vt* **1 :** to harden (a ferrous alloy) so that the surface layer is harder than the interior **2 :** to make callous — **case–hard·ened** *adj*
case history *n* **:** a record of history, environment, and relevant details (as of individual behavior or condition) esp. for use in analysis or illustration
ca·sein \kā-'sēn, 'kā-sē-ən\ *n* [prob. fr. F *caséine,* fr. L *caseus*] **:** a phosphoprotein of milk: as **a :** one that is precipitated from milk by heating with an acid or by the action of lactic acid in souring and is used in making paints and adhesives **b :** one that is produced when milk is curdled by rennet, is the chief constituent of cheese, and is used in making plastics
case knife *n* **1 :** SHEATH KNIFE **2 :** a table knife
case law *n* **:** law established by judicial decision in cases
case load *n* **:** the number of cases handled in a particular period (as by a court or clinic)
case·mate \'kā-,smāt\ *n* [MF, fr. OIt *casamatta*] **:** a fortified position or chamber or an armored enclosure on a warship from which guns are fired through embrasures
case·ment \'kā-smənt\ *n* [ME, hollow molding, prob. fr. ONF *encassement* frame, fr. *encasser* to enchase, frame, fr. *en-* + *casse*] **:** a window sash that opens on hinges at the side; *also* **:** a window with such a sash
ca·se·ous \'kā-sē-əs\ *adj* [L *caseus* cheese] **:** marked by caseation; *also* **:** CHEESY
ca·sern *or* **ca·serne** \kə-'zərn\ *n* [F *caserne*] **:** a military barracks in a garrison town
case shot *n* **:** an artillery projectile consisting of a number of balls or metal fragments enclosed in a case
case study *n* **1 :** an intensive analysis of an individual unit (as a person or community) stressing developmental factors in relation to environment **2 :** CASE HISTORY
case system *n* **:** a system of teaching law in which instruction is chiefly on the basis of leading or selected cases as primary authorities instead of from textbooks
case·work \'kā-,swərk\ *n* **:** social work involving direct consideration of the problems, needs, and adjustments of the individual case (as a person or family) — **case·work·er** \-,swər-kər\ *n*
1cash \'kash\ *n* [MF or OIt; MF *casse* money box, fr. OIt *cassa,* fr. L *capsa* chest — more at CASE] **1 :** ready money **2 :** money or its equivalent paid promptly after purchasing — **cash·less** \-ləs\ *adj*
2cash *vt* **1 :** to pay or obtain cash for ⟨~ a check⟩ **2 :** to lead and win a bridge trick with (a card that is the highest remaining card of its suit) — **cash·able** \-ə-bəl\ *adj*
3cash *n, pl* **cash** [Pg *caixa* fr. Tamil *kācu,* a small copper coin, fr. Skt *karsa,* a weight of gold or silver; akin to OPer *karsha-,* a weight] **1 :** any of various coins of small value in China and southern India; *esp* **:** a Chinese coin usu. of copper alloy that has a square hole in the center **2 :** a unit of value equivalent to one cash
1cash–and–car·ry \,kash-ən-'kar-ē\ *adj* **:** sold or provided for cash and usu. without delivery service
2cash–and–carry *n* **:** the policy of selling on a cash-and-carry basis
cash·book \'kash-,bu̇k\ *n* **:** a book in which record is kept of all cash receipts and disbursements
cash crop *n* **:** a readily salable crop (as cotton or tobacco) produced or gathered primarily for market
cash discount *n* **:** a discount granted in consideration of immediate payment or payment within a prescribed time
ca·shew \'kash-(,)ü, kə-'shü\ *n* [Pg *acajú, cajú,* fr. Tupi *acajú*] **:** a tropical American tree (*Anacardium occidentale*) of the sumac family grown for its edible kidney-shaped nut and receptacle and the gum it yields; *also* **:** its nut

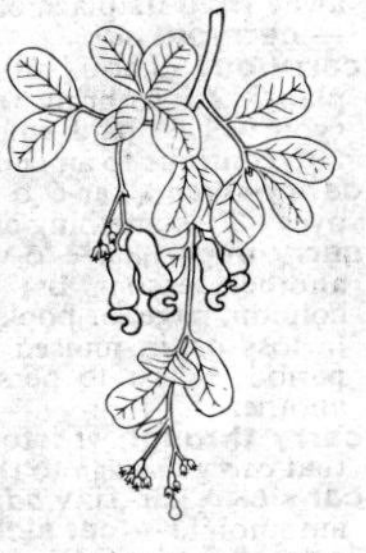

cashew

cash flow *n* **:** a measure of corporate worth that consists of net income after taxes plus certain noncash charges against income (as allowances for depreciation and depletion) and that is usu. figured in dollars per share of common stock outstanding
1ca·shier \ka-'shi(ə)r, kə-\ *vt* [D *casseren,* fr. MF *casser* to discharge, annul — more at QUASH] **1 :** to dismiss from service; *esp* **:** to dismiss dishonorably **2 :** REJECT, DISCARD
2cash·ier \ka-'shi(ə)r\ *n* [D or MF; D *kassier,* fr. MF *cassier,* fr. *casse* money box] **:** one that has charge of money: as **a :** a high officer in a bank or trust company responsible for moneys received and expended **b :** one who collects and records payments
cashier's check *n* **:** a check drawn by a bank on its own funds and signed by the cashier
cash in *vt* **:** to convert into cash ⟨*cashed in* all his bonds⟩ ~ *vi* **1 a :** to retire from a gambling game **b :** to settle accounts and withdraw from an involvement (as a business deal) **2 :** to obtain financial profit or advantage ⟨fly-by-night promoters trying to *cash in* — Tom McSloy⟩ — often used with *on* ⟨the chance of *cashing in* on a best-seller⟩
cash·mere \'kazh-,mi(ə)r, 'kash-\ *n* [*Cashmere* (Kashmir)] **1 :** fine wool from the undercoat of the Kashmir goat; *also* **:** a yarn of this wool **2 :** a soft twilled fabric made orig. from cashmere
cash register *n* **:** a business machine that usu. has a money drawer, indicates the amount of each sale, and records the amount of money received and often automatically makes change
cas·ing \'kā-siŋ\ *n* **1 :** something that encases **:** material for encasing: as **a :** an enclosing frame esp. around a door or window opening **b :** a metal pipe used to case a well **c :** TIRE 2b **d :** a membranous case for processed meat **2 :** a space formed between

two parallel lines of stitching through at least two layers of cloth into which something (as a rod or string) may be inserted

ca·si·no \kə-'sē-(,)nō\ *n, pl* **-nos** [It, fr. *casa* house, fr. L, cabin] **1** : a building or room used for social amusements; *specif* : one used for gambling **2** : SUMMERHOUSE **3** *also* **cas·si·no** : a card game in which each player wins cards by matching or combining cards in his hand with those exposed on the table

cask \'kask\ *n* [MF *casque* helmet, fr. Sp *casco* potsherd, skull, helmet, fr. *cascar* to break — more at CASCARA] **1** : a barrel-shaped vessel of staves, headings, and hoops usu. for liquids **2** : a cask and its contents; *also* : the quantity contained in a cask — **casky** \'kas-kē\ *adj*

cas·ket \'kas-kət\ *n* [ME, modif. of MF *cassette*] **1** : a small chest or box (as for jewels) **2** : a usu. fancy coffin — **casket** *vt*

casque \'kask\ *n* [MF — more at CASK] **1** : a piece of armor for the head : HELMET **2** : an anatomic structure suggestive of a helmet

cas·sa·ba *var of* CASABA

Cas·san·dra \kə-'san-drə\ *n* [L, fr. Gk *Kassandra*] **1** : a daughter of Priam endowed with the gift of prophecy but fated never to be believed **2** : one that predicts misfortune or disaster

cas·sa·va \kə-'säv-ə\ *n* [Sp *cazabe* cassava bread, fr. Taino *caçábi*] : any of several plants (genus *Manihot*) of the spurge family grown in the tropics for their fleshy edible rootstocks which yield a nutritious starch; *also* : the rootstock

cas·se·role \'kas-ə-,rōl *also* 'kaz-\ *n* [F, saucepan, fr. MF, irreg. fr. *casse* ladle, dripping pan, deriv. of Gk *kyathos* ladle] **1** : a deep round usu. porcelain dish with a handle used for heating substances in the laboratory **2** : a dish in which food may be baked and served **3** : the food cooked and served in a casserole ⟨a tuna ~⟩

cas·sette *or* **ca·sette** \kə-'set, ka-\ *n* [F, fr. MF, dim. of ONF *casse* case] **1** : CASKET 1 **2** : a lighttight magazine for holding film or plates for use in a camera **3** : a small plastic cartridge containing magnetic tape with the tape on one reel passing to the other

cas·sia \'kash-ə\ *n* [ME, fr. OE, fr. L, fr. Gk *kassia*, of Sem origin; akin to Heb *qĕṣī'āh* cassia] **1** : a coarse cinnamon bark (as from *Cinnamomum cassia*) **2** : any of a genus (*Cassia*) of leguminous herbs, shrubs, and trees of warm regions

cas·si·mere \'kaz-ə-,mi(ə)r, 'kas-\ *n* [obs. *Cassimere* (Kashmir)] : CASHMERE

Cas·si·o·pe·ia \,kas-ē-ə-'pē-(y)ə\ *n* [L, fr. Gk *Kassiopeia*] **1** : the wife of the Ethiopian King Cepheus who became mother of Andromeda by him and was later changed into a constellation **2** [L (gen. *Cassiopeiae*), fr. Gk *Kassiopeia*] : a northern constellation between Andromeda and Cepheus

Cassiopeia's Chair *n* : a group of stars in the constellation Cassiopeia resembling a chair

cas·sit·er·ite \kə-'sit-ə-,rīt\ *n* [F *cassitérite*, fr. Gk *kassiteros* tin] : a brown or black mineral that consists of tin dioxide SnO_2 and is the chief source of metallic tin

cas·sock \'kas-ək\ *n* [MF *casaque*, fr. Per *kazhāghand* padded jacket, fr. *kazh* raw silk + *āghand* stuffed] : an ankle-length garment with close-fitting sleeves worn esp. in Roman Catholic and Anglican churches by the clergy and by laymen assisting in services

cas·so·wary \'kas-ə-,wer-ē\ *n, pl* **-war·ies** [Malay *kĕsuari*] : any of several large ratite birds (genus *Casuarius*) esp. of New Guinea and Australia closely related to the emu

¹cast \'kast\ *vb* **cast; cast·ing** [ME *casten*, fr. ON *kasta*; akin to ON *kös* heap and perh. to L *gerere* to carry, wage] *vt* **1 a** : to cause to move by throwing ⟨~ a fishing lure⟩ **b** : DIRECT ⟨~ a glance⟩ **c** (1) : to put forth ⟨the fire ~s a warm glow⟩ (2) : to place as if by throwing ⟨~ doubt on their reliability⟩ **d** : to deposit (a ballot) formally **e** (1) : to throw off or away ⟨the horse ~ a shoe⟩ (2) : to get rid of : DISCARD ⟨~ off all restraint⟩ (3) : SHED, MOLT (4) : to bring forth; *esp* : to give birth to prematurely **f** : to throw to the ground esp. in wrestling **g** : to build by throwing up earth **2 a** (1) : to perform arithmetical operations on : ADD (2) : to calculate by means of astrology **b** *archaic* : DECIDE, INTEND **3 a** : to dispose or arrange into parts or into a suitable form or order **b** (1) : to assign the parts of (a dramatic production) to actors (2) : to assign (an actor) to a role or part **4 a** : to give a shape to (a substance) by pouring in liquid or plastic form into a mold and letting harden without pressure ⟨~ steel⟩ **b** : to form by this process ⟨~ machine parts⟩ **5** : TURN ⟨~ the scale slightly⟩ **6** : to make (a knot or stitch) by looping or catching up **7** : TWIST, WARP ⟨a beam ~ by age⟩ ~ *vi* **1** : to throw something; *specif* : to throw out a lure with a fishing rod **2** *dial Brit* : VOMIT **3** *dial Eng* : to bear fruit : YIELD **4 a** : to perform addition **b** *obs* : ESTIMATE, CONJECTURE **5** : WARP **6** : to range over land in search of a trail — used of hunting dogs or trackers **7 a** : VEER **b** : to wear ship **8** : to take form in a mold *syn* see THROW, DISCARD — **cast lots** : to draw lots to determine a matter by chance

²cast *n* **1 a** : an act of casting **b** : something that happens as a result of chance **c** : a throw of dice **d** : a throw of a line (as a fishing line) or net **2 a** : the form in which a thing is constructed **b** : the set of actors in a play or narrative **c** : the arrangement of draperies in a painting **3** : the distance to which a thing can be thrown; *specif* : the distance a bow can shoot **4 a** : a turning of the eye in a particular direction; *also* : EXPRESSION ⟨this freakish, elfish ~ came into the child's eye —Nathaniel Hawthorne⟩ **b** : a slight strabismus **5** : something that is thrown or the quantity thrown: as **a** : the number of hawks released by a falconer at one time **b** *Brit* : the leader of a fishing line **c** : the quantity of metal cast at a single operation **6 a** : something that is formed by casting in a mold or form: as (1) : a reproduction (as of a statue) in metal or plaster : CASTING (2) : a fossil reproduction of the details of a natural object by mineral infiltration **b** : an impression taken from an object with a liquid or plastic substance : MOLD **c** : a rigid dressing of gauze impregnated with plaster of paris for immobilizing a diseased or broken part **7** : FORECAST, CONJECTURE **8 a** : an overspread of a color or modification of the appearance of a substance by a trace of some added hue : SHADE ⟨gray with a greenish ~⟩ **b** : TINGE, SUGGESTION **9 a** : a ride on one's way in a vehicle : LIFT **b** *Scot* : HELP, ASSISTANCE **10 a** : SHAPE, APPEARANCE ⟨the delicate ~ of her features⟩ **b** : characteristic quality ⟨modern science . . . was in conflict with the humanist ~ of mind —T. F. O'Dea⟩ **11** : something that is shed, ejected, or thrown out or off: as **a** : the excrement of an earthworm **b** : a mass of plastic matter formed in cavities of diseased organs and discharged from the body **c** : the skin of an insect **12** : the ranging in search of a trail by a dog, hunting pack, or tracker

cast about *vt* : to lay plans concerning : CONTRIVE ⟨*cast about* how he was to go⟩ ~ *vi* : to look around : SEEK ⟨he *casts about* uncertainly for a place to sit⟩

cas·ta·net \,kas-tə-'net\ *n* [Sp *castañeta*, fr. *castaña* chestnut, fr. L *castanea* — more at CHESTNUT] : a rhythm instrument used esp. by dancers that consists of two small shells of ivory, hard wood, or plastic fastened to the thumb and clicked together by the other fingers — usu. used in pl.

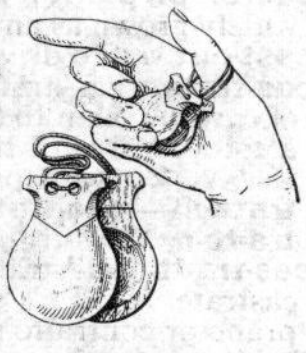

castanets

cast·away \'kas-tə-,wā\ *adj* **1** : thrown away : REJECTED **2 a** : cast adrift or ashore as a survivor of a shipwreck **b** : thrown out or left without friends or resources — **castaway** *n*

caste \'kast\ *n* [Pg *casta*, lit., race, lineage, fr. fem. of *casto* pure, chaste, fr. L *castus*; akin to L *carēre* to be without, Gk *keazein* to split, Skt *śasati* he cuts to pieces] **1** : one of the hereditary social classes in Hinduism that restrict the occupation of their members and their association with the members of other castes **2 a** : a division of society based on differences of wealth, inherited rank or privilege, profession, or occupation **b** : the position conferred by caste standing : PRESTIGE **3** : a system of rigid social stratification characterized by hereditary status, endogamy, and social barriers sanctioned by custom, law, or religion **4** : a specialized form (as the soldier or worker of an ant) of a polymorphic social insect that carries out a particular function in the colony — **caste·ism** \'kas-,tiz-əm\ *n*

cas·tel·lan \'kas-tə-lən\ *n* [ME *castelleyn*, fr. ONF *castelain*, fr. L *castellanus* occupant of a castle, fr. *castellanus* of a castle, fr. *castellum* castle] : a governor or warden of a castle or fort

cas·tel·lat·ed \'kas-tə-,lāt-əd\ *adj* [ML *castellatus*, pp. of *castellare* to fortify, fr. L *castellum*] **1** : having battlements like a castle **2** : having or supporting a castle

cast·er \'kas-tər\ *n* **1** : one that casts; *esp* : a machine that casts type **2** *or* **cas·tor** \-tər\ **a** : a usu. silver table vessel with a perforated top for sprinkling a seasoning (as sugar or spice) **b** : a usu. revolving metal stand bearing condiment containers (as cruets, mustard pot, and often shakers) for table use : a cruet stand **3** *or* **castor** : a wheel or set of wheels mounted in a swivel frame and used for supporting furniture, trucks, and portable machines

cas·ti·gate \'kas-tə-,gāt\ *vt* **-gat·ed; -gat·ing** [L *castigatus*, pp. of *castigare* — more at CHASTEN] : to subject to severe punishment, reproof, or criticism *syn* see PUNISH — **cas·ti·ga·tion** \,kas-tə-'gā-shən\ *n* — **cas·ti·ga·tor** \'kas-tə-,gāt-ər\ *n*

cas·tile soap \(,)kas-,tēl-\ *n, often cap C* [*Castile*, region of Spain] : a fine hard bland soap made from olive oil and sodium hydroxide; *also* : any of various similar soaps

Cas·til·ian \ka-'stil-yən\ *n* **1** : a native or inhabitant of Castile; *broadly* : SPANIARD **2 a** : the dialect of Castile **b** : the official and literary language of Spain based on this dialect — **Castilian** *adj*

cast·ing *n* **1** : the act of one that casts: as **a** : the throwing of a fishing line by means of a rod and reel **b** : the assignment of parts and duties to actors or performers **2** : something cast in a mold **3** : something that is cast out or off

casting director *n* : one who supervises the casting of dramatic productions (as films and plays)

casting vote *n* : a deciding vote cast by a presiding officer to break a tie

cast–iron *adj* **1** : made of cast iron **2** : resembling cast iron: as **a** : capable of withstanding great strain ⟨a ~ stomach⟩ **b** : not admitting change, adaptation, or exception : RIGID ⟨a man of ~ will⟩

cast iron *n* : a commercial alloy of iron, carbon, and silicon that is cast in a mold and is hard, brittle, nonmalleable, and incapable of being hammer-welded but more easily fusible than steel

¹cas·tle \'kas-əl\ *n* [ME *castel*, fr. OE, fr. ONF, fr. L *castellum* fortress, castle, dim. of *castrum* fortified place; akin to L *castrare* to castrate] **1 a** : a large fortified building or set of buildings **b** : a massive or imposing house **2** : a retreat safe against intrusion or invasion **3** : ³ROOK

²castle *vb* **cas·tled; cas·tling** \'kas-(ə-)liŋ\ *vt* **1** : to establish in a castle **2** : to move (the chess king) in castling ~ *vi* : to move a chess king two squares toward a rook and in the same move the rook to the square next past the king

cas·tled \'kas-əld\ *adj* : CASTELLATED

castle in the air : an impracticable project : DAYDREAM — called also *castle in Spain*

cast–off \'kas-,tȯf\ *adj* : thrown away or aside — **cast·off** *n*

cast off \(')kas-'tȯf\ *vt* **1** : LOOSE ⟨*cast off* a hunting dog⟩ **2** : UNFASTEN ⟨*cast off* a boat⟩ **3** : to remove (a stitch) from a knitting needle in such a way as to prevent unraveling ~ *vi* **1** : to unfasten or untie a boat or a line **2** : to turn one's partner in a square dance and pass around the outside of the set and back **3** : to finish a knitted fabric by casting off all stitches

cast on *vt* : to place (stitches) on a knitting needle for beginning or enlarging knitted work
cas·tor \'kas-tər\ *n* [ME, fr. L, fr. Gk *kastōr,* fr. *Kastōr* Castor] **1** : BEAVER 1a **2** : a bitter strong-smelling creamy orange-brown substance consisting of the dried perineal glands of the beaver and their secretion used esp. by perfumers **3** : a beaver hat
Cas·tor \'kas-tər\ *n* [L, fr. Gk *Kastōr*] **1** : one of the Dioscuri **2** : the more northern of the two bright stars in Gemini
castor bean *n* : the very poisonous seed of the castor-oil plant; *also* : CASTOR-OIL PLANT
castor oil *n* [prob. fr. its former use as a substitute for castor in medicine] : a pale viscous fatty oil from castor beans used esp. as a cathartic or lubricant
castor-oil plant *n* : a tropical Old World herb (*Ricinus communis*) widely grown as an ornamental or for its oil-rich castor beans
cast out *vt* : to drive out : EXPEL
cas·trate \'kas-,trāt\ *vt* **cas·trat·ed; cas·trat·ing** [L *castratus,* pp. of *castrare;* akin to Skt *śasati* he cuts to pieces — more at CASTE] **1 a** : to deprive of the testes : GELD **b** : to deprive of the ovaries : SPAY **2** : to deprive of vitality or effect : EMASCULATE — **cas·trate** *n* — **cas·trat·er** *n* — **cas·tra·tion** \ka-'strā-shən\ *n* — **cas·tra·to·ry** \'kas-trə-,tōr-ē, -,tȯr-\ *adj*
cas·tra·to \ka-'strät-(,)ō, kə-\ *n, pl* **-ti** \-ē\ [It, fr. pp. of *castrare* to castrate, fr. L] : a singer castrated in boyhood to preserve the soprano or contralto range of his voice
Cas·tro·ism \'kas-(,)trō-,iz-əm\ *n* : the political, economic, and social principles and policies of Fidel Castro — **Cas·tro·ite** \-,īt\ *n*
[1]**ca·su·al** \'kazh-(ə-)wəl, 'kazh-əl\ *adj* [ME, fr. MF & LL; MF *casuel,* fr. LL *casualis,* fr. L *casus* fall, chance — more at CASE] **1** : subject to, resulting from, or occurring by chance **2 a** : occurring without regularity : OCCASIONAL **b** : employed for irregular periods **3 a** : feeling or showing little concern : NONCHALANT **b** (1) : INFORMAL, NATURAL (2) : designed for informal use ***syn* 1** see ACCIDENTAL **2** see RANDOM ***ant*** deliberate — **ca·su·al·ly** \-ē\ *adv* — **ca·su·al·ness** *n*
[2]**casual** *n* **1** : a casual or migratory worker **2** : an officer or enlisted man awaiting assignment or transportation to his unit
ca·su·al·ty \'kazh-əl-tē, 'kazh-(ə-)wəl-\ *n, pl* **-ties 1** : serious or fatal accident : DISASTER **2 a** : a military person lost through death, wounds, injury, sickness, internment, or capture or through being missing in action **b** : a person or thing injured, lost, or destroyed ⟨the ex-senator was a ~ of the last election⟩
casual water *n* : a temporary accumulation of water not forming a regular hazard of a golf course
ca·su·a·ri·na \,kazh-ə-(wə-)'rē-nə\ *n* [NL, genus name, fr. Malay (*pohon*) *kĕsuari,* lit., cassowary tree; fr. the resemblance of its twigs to cassowary feathers] : any of a genus (*Casuarina* of the family Casuarinaceae) of dicotyledonous chiefly Australian trees which have whorls of scalelike leaves and jointed stems resembling horsetails and some of which yield a heavy hard wood
ca·su·ist \'kazh-(ə-)wəst\ *n* [prob. fr. Sp *casuista,* fr. L *casus* fall, chance — more at CASE] : one skilled in or given to casuistry — **ca·su·is·tic** \,kazh-ə-'wis-tik\ *or* **ca·su·is·ti·cal** \-ti-kəl\ *adj*
ca·su·ist·ry \'kazh-(ə-)wə-strē\ *n, pl* **-ries 1** : a method or doctrine dealing with cases of conscience and the resolution of questions of right or wrong in conduct **2** : false application of principles esp. with regard to morals or law ⟨no ~ will convince us that this serious loss is really a victory⟩
ca·sus bel·li \,käs-əs-'bel-,ē, ,kā-səs-'bel-,ī\ *n, pl* **ca·sus belli** \,käs-,üs-, ,kā-,süs-\ [NL, occasion of war] : an event or action that justifies or allegedly justifies war or conflict
[1]**cat** \'kat\ *n, often attrib* [ME, fr. OE *catt;* akin to OHG *kazza* cat; both fr. a prehistoric NGmc-WGmc word prob. borrowed fr. LL *cattus, catta* cat] **1 a** : a carnivorous mammal (*Felis catus*) long domesticated and kept by man as a pet or for catching rats and mice **b** : any of a family (Felidae) including the domestic cat, lion, tiger, leopard, jaguar, cougar, wildcat, lynx, and cheetah **c** : the fur or pelt of the domestic cat **2** : a malicious woman **3** : a strong tackle used to hoist an anchor to the cathead of a ship **4 a** : CATBOAT **b** : CATAMARAN **5** : CAT-O'-NINE-TAILS **6** : CATFISH **7** *slang* **a** : a player or devotee of hot jazz **b** : GUY **8** : a burglar who is esp. adept at entering and leaving the place he burglarizes without attracting notice
[2]**cat** *vb* **cat·ted; cat·ting** *vt* : to bring (an anchor) up to the cathead ~ *vi* : to search for a sexual mate — often used with *around;* often considered vulgar
[3]**cat** *abbr* **1** catalog **2** catalyst
Cat \'kat\ *trademark* — used for a Caterpillar tractor
CAT *abbr* **1** clear-air turbulence **2** college ability test
cata- *or* **cat-** *or* **cath-** *prefix* [Gk *kata-, kat-, kath-,* fr. *kata* down, in accordance with, by; akin to L *com-* with — more at CO-] : down ⟨*cata*clinal⟩
cat·a·bol·ic \,kat-ə-'bäl-ik\ *adj* : of or relating to catabolism — **cat·a·bol·i·cal·ly** \-i-k(ə-)lē\ *adv*
ca·tab·o·lism \kə-'tab-ə-,liz-əm\ *n* [Gk *katabolē* throwing down, fr. *kataballein* to throw down, fr. *kata-* + *ballein* to throw — more at DEVIL] : destructive metabolism involving the release of energy and resulting in the breakdown of complex materials within the organism
ca·tab·o·lite \-,līt\ *n* : a substance (as nectar or a waste product) produced in catabolism
ca·tab·o·lize \-,līz\ *vb* **-lized; -liz·ing** *vt* : to subject to catabolism ~ *vi* : to undergo catabolism
cat·a·chre·sis \,kat-ə-'krē-səs\ *n, pl* **-chre·ses** \-,sēz\ [L, fr. Gk *katachrēsis* misuse, fr. *katachrēsthai* to use up, misuse, fr. *kata-* + *chrēsthai* to use] **1** : use of the wrong word for the context **2** : use of a forced and esp. paradoxical figure of speech (as *blind mouths*) — **cat·a·chres·tic** \-'kres-tik\ *or* **cat·a·chres·ti·cal** \-ti-kəl\ *adj* — **cat·a·chres·ti·cal·ly** \-ti-k(ə-)lē\ *adv*
cat·a·clysm \'kat-ə-,kliz-əm\ *n* [F *cataclysme,* fr. L *cataclysmos,* fr. Gk *kataklysmos,* fr. *kataklyzein* to inundate, fr. *kata-* + *klyzein* to wash — more at CLYSTER] **1** : FLOOD, DELUGE **2** : a violent geologic change of the earth's surface **3** : a momentous and violent event marked by overwhelming upheaval and demolition ***syn*** see DISASTER — **cat·a·clys·mal** \,kat-ə-'kliz-məl\ *or* **cat·a·clys·mic** \-mik\ *adj*
cat·a·comb \'kat-ə-,kōm\ *n* [MF *catacombe,* prob. fr. OIt *catacomba,* fr. LL *catacumbae,* pl.] **1** : a subterranean cemetery of galleries with recesses for tombs — usu. used in pl. **2** : something resembling a catacomb: as **a** : an underground passageway or group of passageways ⟨the ~s of the Old Senate Office Building⟩ **b** : a complex set of interrelated things ⟨the endless ~s of formal education —Kingman Brewster, Jr.⟩ — **cat·a·comb·ic** \,kat-ə-'kō-mik\ *adj*
ca·tad·ro·mous \kə-'tad-rə-məs\ *adj* [prob. fr. NL *catadromus,* fr. *cata-* + *-dromus* -dromous] : living in fresh water and going to the sea to spawn ⟨~ eels⟩
cat·a·falque \'kat-ə-,falk, -,fȯ(l)k\ *n* [It *catafalco,* fr. (assumed) VL *catafalicum* scaffold, fr. *cata-* + L *fala* siege tower] **1** : an ornamental structure sometimes used in funerals for the lying in state of the body **2** : a pall-covered coffin-shaped structure used at requiem masses celebrated after burial
Cat·a·lan \'kat-ᵊl-ən, -,an\ *n* [Sp *Catalán*] **1** : a native or inhabitant of Catalonia **2** : the Romance language of Catalonia, Valencia, Andorra, and the Balearic islands — **Catalan** *adj*
cat·a·lase \'kat-ᵊl-,ās, -,āz\ *n* [*catalysis*] : a red crystalline enzyme that consists of a protein complex with hematin groups and catalyzes the decomposition of hydrogen peroxide into water and oxygen — **cat·a·lat·ic** \,kat-ᵊl-'at-ik\ *adj*
cat·a·lec·tic \,kat-ᵊl-'ek-tik\ *adj* [LL *catalecticus,* fr. Gk *katalēktikos,* fr. *katalēgein* to leave off, fr. *kata-* + *lēgein* to stop — more at SLACK] : lacking a syllable at the end or ending in an imperfect foot — **catalectic** *n*
cat·a·lep·sy \'kat-ᵊl-,ep-sē\ *n, pl* **-sies** [ME *catalempsi,* fr. ML *catalepsia,* fr. LL *catalepsis* fr. Gk *katalēpsis,* lit., act of seizing, fr. *katalambanein* to seize, fr. *kata-* + *lambanein* to take — more at LATCH] : a condition of suspended animation and loss of voluntary motion in which the limbs remain in whatever position they are placed — **cat·a·lep·tic** \,kat-ᵊl-'ep-tik\ *adj or n* — **cat·a·lep·ti·cal·ly** \-ti-k(ə-)lē\ *adv*
cat·a·lex·is \,kat-ᵊl-'ek-səs\ *n, pl* **-lex·es** \-,sēz\ [NL, fr. Gk *katalēxis* close, cadence, fr. *katalēgein*] : omission or incompleteness usu. in the last foot of a line in metrical verse
[1]**cat·a·log** *or* **cat·a·logue** \'kat-ᵊl-,ȯg, -,äg\ *n* [ME *cateloge,* fr. MF *catalogue,* fr. LL *catalogus,* fr. Gk *katalogos,* fr. *katalegein* to list, enumerate, fr. *kata-* + *legein* to gather, speak — more at LEGEND] **1** : LIST, REGISTER **2 a** : a complete enumeration of items arranged systematically with descriptive details **b** : a pamphlet or book that contains such a list **c** : material in such a list
[2]**catalog** *or* **catalogue** *vb* **-loged** *or* **-logued; -log·ing** *or* **-logu·ing** *vt* **1** : to make a catalog of **2** : to enter in a catalog; *esp* : to classify (books or information) descriptively ~ *vi* **1** : to make or work on a catalog **2** : to become listed in a catalog at a specified price ⟨this stamp ~s at two dollars⟩ — **cat·a·log·er** *or* **cat·a·logu·er** *n*
cat·a·logue rai·son·né \-,rāz-ᵊn-'ā\ *n, pl* **cat·a·logues rai·son·nés** \-,ȯg(z)-,rāz-ᵊn-'ā\ [F, lit., reasoned catalog] : a systematic annotated catalog; *esp* : a critical bibliography
ca·tal·pa \kə-'tal-pə, -'tȯl-\ *n* [Creek *kutuhlpa,* lit., head with wings] : any of a small genus (*Catalpa*) of American and Asiatic trees of the trumpet-creeper family with cordate leaves and pale showy flowers in terminal racemes
ca·tal·y·sis \kə-'tal-ə-səs\ *n, pl* **-y·ses** \-,sēz\ [Gk *katalysis* dissolution, fr. *katalyein* to dissolve, fr. *kata-* cata- + *lyein* to dissolve, release — more at LOSE] **1** : a modification and esp. increase in the rate of a chemical reaction induced by material unchanged chemically at the end of the reaction **2** : an action or reaction between two or more persons or forces precipitated by a separate agent and esp. by one that is essentially unaltered by the reaction ⟨a representative list of questions . . . valuable for the ~ of class discussions —B. S. Meyer & D. B. Anderson⟩
cat·a·lyst \'kat-ᵊl-əst\ *n* **1** : an agent that induces catalysis ⟨he was rumored to be the ~ in a native uprising —H. W. Wind⟩ ⟨the housing program is intended to become the ~ of the new French economy —Edmond Taylor⟩ **2** : a substance (as an enzyme) that initiates a chemical reaction and enables it to proceed under milder conditions (as at a lower temperature) than otherwise possible
cat·a·lyt·ic \,kat-ᵊl-'it-ik\ *adj* : causing, involving, or relating to catalysis ⟨a ~ reaction ⟩ ⟨a ~ personality⟩ — **cat·a·lyt·i·cal·ly** \-'it-i-k(ə-)lē\ *adv*
catalytic cracker *n* : the unit in a petroleum refinery in which cracking is carried out in the presence of a catalyst
cat·a·lyze \'kat-ᵊl-,īz\ *vt* **-lyzed; -lyz·ing 1** : to bring about the catalysis of (a chemical reaction) **2** : to bring about : INSPIRE **3** : to alter significantly by catalysis ⟨innovations in basic chemical theory that have *catalyzed* the field and its technology —*Newsweek*⟩ — **cat·a·lyz·er** *n*
cat·a·ma·ran \,kat-ə-mə-'ran, 'kat-ə-mə-,ran\ *n* [Tamil *kaṭṭumaram,* fr. *kaṭṭu* to tie + *maram* tree] **1** : a raft consisting of logs or pieces of wood lashed together and propelled by paddles or sails **2** : a boat with twin hulls or planing surfaces side by side
cata·me·nia \,kat-ə-'mē-nē-ə\ *n pl* [NL, fr. Gk *katamēnia,* fr. neut. pl. of *katamēnios* monthly, fr. *kata* by + *mēn* month — more at CATA-, MOON] : MENSES — **cata·me·ni·al** \-nē-əl\ *adj*
cat·a·mite \'kat-ə-,mīt\ *n* [L *catamitus,* fr. *Catamitus* Ganymede, fr. Etruscan *Catmite,* fr. Gk *Ganymēdēs*] : a boy kept by a pederast
cat·a·mount \'kat-ə-,maunt\ *n* [short for *cat-a-mountain*] : any of various wild cats: as **a** : COUGAR **b** : LYNX
cat–a–moun·tain \,kat-ə-'maunt-ᵊn\ *n* [ME *cat of the mountaine*] : any of various wild cats: as **a** : the European wildcat **b** : LEOPARD
cat–and–mouse \,kat-ᵊn-'maus\ *adj* : consisting of constant torment, continuous pursuit, near captures, repeated escapes, or watchful waiting for the best opportunity to attack ⟨the ~ technique of handling an opponent⟩
cat and mouse *n* : behavior like that of a cat with a mouse; *esp* : the act of toying with something before tormenting or destroying it

cat·a·pho·re·sis \,kat-ə-fə-'rē-səs\ *n, pl* **-re·ses** \-,sēz\ [NL] : ELECTROPHORESIS — **cat·a·pho·ret·ic** \-'ret-ik\ *adj* — **cat·a·pho·ret·i·cal·ly** \-i-k(ə-)lē\ *adv*

cat·a·pla·sia \,kat-ə-'plā-zh(ē-)ə\ *n* [NL] : reversion of cells or tissues to a more embryonic condition — **cat·a·plas·tic** \-'plas-tik\ *adj*

cat·a·plasm \'kat-ə-,plaz-əm\ *n* [MF *cataplasme,* fr. L *cataplasma,* fr. Gk *kataplasma,* fr. *kataplassein* to plaster over — more at PLASTER] : POULTICE

cat·a·plexy \'kat-ə-,plek-sē\ *n, pl* **-plex·ies** \-sēz\ [G *kataplexie,* fr. Gk *kataplēxis,* fr. *kataplēssein* to strike down, terrify, fr. *kata-* + *plēssein* to strike — more at PLAINT] : sudden loss of muscle power following a strong emotional stimulus

[1]**cat·a·pult** \'kat-ə-,pəlt, -,pu̇lt\ *n* [MF or L; MF *catapulte,* fr. L *catapulta,* fr. Gk *katapaltēs,* fr. *kata-* + *pallein* to hurl — more at POLEMIC] **1** : an ancient military device for hurling missiles **2** : a device for launching an airplane at flying speed (as from an aircraft carrier)

[2]**catapult** *vt* : to throw or launch by or as if by a catapult ~ *vi* : to become catapulted

cat·a·ract \'kat-ə-,rakt\ *n* [L *cataracta* waterfall, portcullis, fr. Gk *kataraktēs,* fr. *katarassein* to dash down, fr. *kata-* cata- + *arassein* to strike, dash] **1** [MF or ML; MF *cataracte,* fr. ML *cataracta,* fr. L, portcullis] : a clouding of the lens of the eye or of its capsule obstructing the passage of light **2 a** *obs* : WATERSPOUT **b** : WATERFALL; *esp* : a large one over a precipice **c** : steep rapids in a river **d** : DOWNPOUR, FLOOD — **cat·a·rac·tal** \,kat-ə-'rak-tᵊl\ *adj*

ca·tarrh \kə-'tär\ *n* [MF or LL; MF *catarrhe,* fr. LL *catarrhus,* fr. Gk *katarrhous,* fr. *katarrhein* to flow down, fr. *kata-* + *rhein* to flow — more at STREAM] : inflammation of a mucous membrane; *esp* : one chronically affecting the human nose and air passages — **ca·tarrh·al** \-əl\ *adj* — **ca·tarrh·al·ly** \-ə-lē\ *adv*

ca·tas·ta·sis \kə-'tas-tə-səs\ *n, pl* **-ta·ses** \-,sēz\ [Gk *katastasis* settlement, fr. *kathistanai* to set in order, fr. *kata-* + *histanai* to cause to stand — more at STAND] **1** : the complication immediately preceding the climax of a play **2** : the climax of a play

ca·tas·tro·phe \kə-'tas-trə-(,)fē\ *n* [Gk *katastrophē,* fr. *katastrephein* to overturn, fr. *kata-* + *strephein* to turn — more at STROPHE] **1** : the final event of the dramatic action esp. of a tragedy **2** : a momentous tragic event ranging from extreme misfortune to utter overthrow or ruin **3** : a violent and sudden change in a feature of the earth **4** : utter failure : FIASCO ***syn*** see DISASTER — **cat·a·stroph·ic** \,kat-ə-'sträf-ik\ *adj* — **cat·a·stroph·i·cal·ly** \-i-k(ə-)lē\ *adv*

cata·to·nia \,kat-ə-'tō-nē-ə\ *n* [NL, fr. G *katatonie,* fr. *kata-* cata- + NL *tonus*] **1** : CATALEPSY **2** : a disorder marked by catalepsy — **cata·ton·ic** \-'tän-ik\ *adj or n*

Ca·taw·ba \kə-'tö-bə\ *n* **1** *pl* **Catawba** *or* **Catawbas** : a member of an Amerindian people of No. Carolina and So. Carolina **2** : the language of the Catawba people **3** : a dry white wine produced from a native American grape; *also* : a sweet fortified wine made from this grape

cat·bird \'kat-,bərd\ *n* : an American songbird (*Dumetella carolinensis*) dark gray in color with black cap and reddish coverts under the tail

catbird seat *n* : a position of great prominence or advantage

cat·boat \'kat-,bōt\ *n* : a sailboat having a cat rig and usu. a centerboard and being of light draft and broad beam

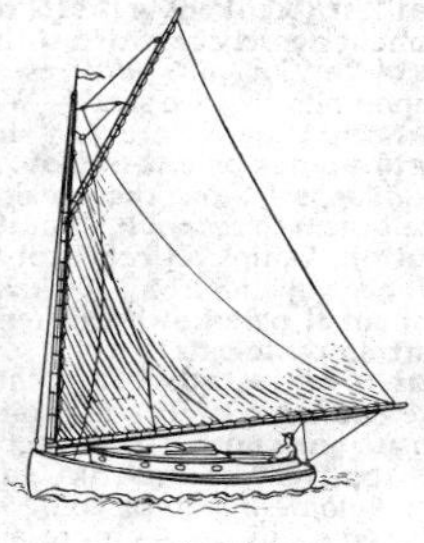
catboat

cat·bri·er \-,brī(-ə)r\ *n* : any of several prickly climbers (genus *Smilax*) of the lily family

cat·call \-,kȯl\ *n* : a loud or raucous cry made to express disapproval (as at a sports event) — **catcall** *vb*

[1]**catch** \'kach, 'kech\ *vb* **caught** \'kȯt\; **catch·ing** [ME *cacchen,* fr. ONF *cachier* to hunt, fr. (assumed) VL *captiare,* alter. of L *captare* to chase, fr. *captus,* pp. of *capere* to take — more at HEAVE] *vt* **1 a** : to capture or seize esp. after pursuit **b** : to take or entangle in or as if in a snare **c** : DECEIVE **d** : to discover unexpectedly : FIND ⟨*caught* in the act⟩ **e** : to check suddenly or momentarily **f** : to become suddenly aware of **2 a** : to take hold of : SEIZE **b** : to affect suddenly **c** : SNATCH, INTERCEPT **d** : to avail oneself of : TAKE **e** : to obtain through effort : GET **f** : to get entangled ⟨~ a sleeve on a nail⟩ **3** : to become affected by: as **a** : CONTRACT ⟨~ a cold⟩ **b** : to respond sympathetically to the point of being imbued with ⟨~ the spirit of an occasion⟩ **c** : to be struck by **4 a** : to seize and hold firmly **b** : FASTEN **5** : to take or get usu. momentarily or quickly ⟨~ a glimpse of a friend⟩ **6 a** : OVERTAKE **b** : to get aboard in time ⟨~ the bus⟩ **7** : ATTRACT, ARREST **8** : to make contact with **9** : to grasp by the senses or the mind : APPREHEND ~ *vi* **1** : to grasp hastily or try to grasp **2** : to become caught **3** *of a crop* : to come up and become established **4** : to play the position of catcher on a baseball team — **catch·able** \'kach-ə-bəl, 'kech-\ *adj*

syn **1** CATCH, TRAP, SNARE, ENTRAP, ENSNARE, BAG *shared meaning element* : to get into one's possession or under one's control by or as if by taking or seizing ***ant*** miss
2 see INCUR

— **catch fire** **1** : to become ignited **2** : to become fired with enthusiasm ⟨the poet *caught fire* from the philosopher's talk⟩ **3** : to increase greatly in scope, interest, or effectiveness ⟨this stock has not *caught fire* — yet —*Forbes*⟩ — **catch it** : to incur blame, reprimand, or punishment — **catch one's breath** : to rest long enough to restore normal breathing

[2]**catch** *n* **1** : something caught; *esp* : the total quantity caught at one time ⟨a large ~ of fish⟩ **2 a** : the act, action, or fact of catching **b** : a game in which a ball is thrown and caught **3** : something that checks or holds immovable ⟨the safety ~ of her pin broke⟩ **4** : one worth catching esp. as a spouse **5** : a round for three or more unaccompanied voices written out as one continuous melody with each succeeding singer taking up a part in turn **6** : FRAGMENT, SNATCH **7** : a concealed difficulty ⟨there must be a ~ to it somewhere⟩ **8** : the germination of a field crop to such an extent that replanting is unnecessary

catch·all \'kach-,ȯl, 'kech-\ *n* : something to hold various odds and ends

catch–as–catch–can \,kach-əz-,kach-'kan, ,kech-əz-,kech-\ *adj* : using any available means or method : UNPLANNED ⟨a ~ existence begging and running errands —*Time*⟩

catch·er \'kach-ər, 'kech-\ *n* : one that catches; *specif* : a baseball player stationed behind home plate

catch·fly \-,flī\ *n* : any of various plants (as of the genera *Lychnis* and *Silene*) with viscid stems to which small insects adhere

catch·ing *adj* **1** : INFECTIOUS, CONTAGIOUS **2** : CATCHY, ALLURING

catch·ment \'kach-mənt, 'kech-\ *n* **1** : the action of catching water **2** : something that catches water; *also* : the amount of water caught

catch on *vi* **1** : UNDERSTAND, LEARN ⟨the police *caught on* to what he was doing⟩ **2** : to become popular ⟨this movement has already *caught on* in other states — Bernard Smith⟩

catch out *vt* : to detect in error or wrongdoing : ENTRAP ⟨the Court . . . is now *caught out* by history — Ed Yoder⟩

catch·pen·ny \'kach-,pen-ē, 'kech-\ *adj* : designed esp. to appeal to the ignorant or unwary through sensationalism or cheapness ⟨a ~ newspaper with many lurid photographs⟩

catch·pole *or* **catch·poll** \-,pōl\ *n* [ME *cacchepol,* fr. OE *cæcepol,* fr. (assumed) ONF *cachepol,* lit., chicken chaser, fr. ONF *cachier* + *pol* chicken, fr. L *pullus* — more at CATCH, PULLET] : a sheriff's deputy; *esp* : one who makes arrests for debt

catch·up \'kech-əp, 'kach-; 'kat-səp\ *var of* CATSUP

catch up *vt* **1 a** : to pick up often abruptly ⟨the thief *caught* the purse *up* and ran⟩ **b** : ENSNARE, ENTANGLE ⟨education has been *caught up* in a stultifying mythology, largely of its own devising — N. M. Pusey⟩ **c** : ENTHRALL ⟨the . . . public was *caught up* in the car's magic — D. A. Jedlicka⟩ **2** : to provide with the latest information ⟨*catch* me *up* on the news⟩ ~ *vi* **1** : to travel fast enough to overtake an advance party ⟨*catch up* with the group ahead⟩ **2** : to bring about arrest for illicit activities ⟨the police *caught up* with the thieves⟩ **3 a** : to bring something to completion ⟨*catch up* on the bookkeeping⟩ **b** : to acquire belated information ⟨*catch up* on the news⟩

catch·word \'kach-,wərd, 'kech-\ *n* **1 a** : a word under the righthand side of the last line on a book page that repeats the first word on the following page **b** : GUIDE WORD **2** : a word or expression repeated until it becomes representative of a party, school, or point of view

catchy \-ē\ *adj* **catch·i·er; -est** **1** : tending to catch the interest or attention ⟨a ~ title⟩ **2** : TRICKY ⟨a ~ question⟩ **3** : FITFUL, IRREGULAR ⟨~ breathing⟩

cat distemper *n* : PANLEUCOPENIA

cate \'kāt\ *n* [ME, article of purchased food, short for *acate,* fr. ONF *acat* purchase, fr. *acater* to buy, fr. (assumed) VL *accaptare,* fr. L *acceptare* to accept] *archaic* : a dainty or choice food

cat·e·che·sis \,kat-ə-'kē-səs\ *n, pl* **-che·ses** \-,sēz\ [LL, fr. Gk *katēchēsis,* fr. *katēchein* to teach] : oral instruction of catechumens — **cat·e·chet·i·cal** \-'ket-i-kəl\ *adj*

cat·e·chin \'kat-ə-,kin\ *n* [ISV *catechu* + *-in*] : a crystalline compound $C_{15}H_{14}O_6$ that is related chemically to the flavones, is found in catechu, and is used in dyeing and tanning

cat·e·chism \'kat-ə-,kiz-əm\ *n* **1** : oral instruction **2** : a manual for catechizing; *specif* : a summary of religious doctrine often in the form of questions and answers **3** : a set of formal questions put as a test — **cat·e·chis·mal** \,kat-ə-'kiz-məl\ *adj* — **cat·e·chis·tic** \-'kis-tik\ *adj*

cat·e·chist \'kat-ə-,kist, 'kat-i-kəst\ *n* : one that catechizes: as **a** : a teacher of catechumens **b** : a native in a missionary district who does Christian teaching — **cat·e·chis·tic** \,kat-ə-'kis-tik\ *adj*

cat·e·chize \'kat-ə-,kīz\ *vt* **-chized; -chiz·ing** [LL *catechizare,* fr. Gk *katēchein* to teach, lit., to din into, fr. *kata-* cata- + *ēchein* to resound, fr. *ēchē* sound — more at ECHO] **1** : to instruct systematically esp. by questions, answers, and explanations and corrections; *specif* : to give religious instruction in such a manner **2** : to question systematically or searchingly — **cat·e·chi·za·tion** \,kat-i-kə-'zā-shən\ *n* — **cat·e·chiz·er** \'kat-ə-,kī-zər\ *n*

cat·e·chol \'kat-ə-,kȯl, -,kōl\ *n* **1** : CATECHIN **2** : PYROCATECHOL

cat·e·chol·amine \,kat-ə-'kō-lə-,mēn, -'kȯ-\ *n* : any of various amines (as epinephrine, norepinephrine, and dopamine) that function as hormones or neurotransmitters or both and are related to pyrocatechol

cat·e·chu \'kat-ə-,chü, -,shü\ *n* [prob. fr. Malay *kachu,* of Dravidian origin; akin to Tamil & Kannada *kācu* catechu] : any of several dry, earthy, or resinous astringent substances obtained from tropical Asiatic plants: as **a** : an extract of the heartwood of an East Indian acacia (*Acacia catechu*) **b** : GAMBIER

cat·e·chu·men \,kat-ə-'kyü-mən\ *n* [ME *cathecumyn,* fr. MF *cathecumine,* fr. LL *catechumenus,* fr. Gk *katēchoumenos,* pres. pass. part. of *katēchein* to teach] **1** : a convert to Christianity receiving training in doctrine and discipline before baptism **2** : one receiving instruction in the basic doctrines of Christianity before admission to communicant membership in a church

cat·e·gor·i·cal \,kat-ə-'gȯr-i-kəl, -'gär-\ *also* **cat·e·gor·ic** \-ik\ *adj* [LL *categoricus,* fr. Gk *katēgorikos,* fr. *katēgoria* affirmation, cate-

ə abut ᵊ kitten ər further a back ā bake ä cot, cart
au̇ out ch chin e less ē easy g gift i trip ī life
j joke ŋ sing ō flow ȯ flaw ȯi coin th thin th this
ü loot u̇ foot y yet yü few yu̇ furious zh vision

gory] **1 :** ABSOLUTE, UNQUALIFIED ⟨a ~ denial⟩ **2 :** of, relating to, or constituting a category — **cat·e·gor·i·cal·ly** \-i-k(ə-)lē\ *adv*

categorical imperative *n* **:** a moral obligation or command that is unconditionally and universally binding

cat·e·go·rize \ˈkat-i-gə-ˌrīz\ *vt* **-rized; -riz·ing :** to put into a category **:** CLASSIFY — **cat·e·go·ri·za·tion** \ˌkat-i-gə-rə-ˈzā-shən\ *n*

cat·e·go·ry \ˈkat-ə-ˌgōr-ē, -ˌgȯr-\ *n, pl* **-ries** [LL *categoria,* fr. Gk *katēgoria* predication, category, fr. *katēgorein* to accuse, affirm, predicate, fr. *kata-* + *agora* public assembly — more at GREGARIOUS] **1 a :** a general class to which a logical predicate or that which it predicates belongs **b :** one of the underlying forms to which any object of experience must conform **c :** one of the fundamental or ultimate classes of entities or of language **2 :** a division within a system of classification

ca·te·na \kə-ˈtē-nə\ *n, pl* **-nae** \-(ˌ)nē\ *or* **-nas** [ML, fr. L, chain — more at CHAIN] **:** a connected series of related things

cat·e·nary \ˈkat-ə-ˌner-ē, *esp Brit* kə-ˈtē-nə-rē\ *n, pl* **-nar·ies** [NL *catenaria,* fr. L, fem. of *catenarius* of a chain, fr. *catena*] **1 :** the curve assumed by a perfectly flexible inextensible cord of uniform density and cross section hanging freely from two fixed points **2 :** something in the form of a catenary — **catenary** *adj*

cat·e·nate \ˈkat-ə-ˌnāt\ *vt* **-nat·ed; -nat·ing** [L *catenatus,* pp. of *catenare,* fr. *catena*] **:** to connect in a series **:** LINK — **cat·e·na·tion** \ˌkat-ə-ˈnā-shən\ *n*

ca·ten·u·late \kə-ˈten-yə-lət\ *adj* [ISV, fr. LL *catenula,* dim. of L *catena*] **:** shaped like a chain ⟨~ colonies of bacteria⟩

ca·ter \ˈkāt-ər\ *vb* [obs. *cater* (buyer of provisions), fr. ME *catour,* short for *acatour,* fr. AF, fr. ONF *acater* to buy — more at CATE] *vi* **1 :** to provide a supply of food **2 :** to supply what is required or desired ⟨~*ed* to her whims all day long⟩ ~ *vt* **:** to provide food and service for ⟨~*ed* the banquet⟩ — **ca·ter·er** \-ər-ər\ *n* — **ca·ter·ess** \ˈkāt-ə-rəs\ *n*

cat·er·an \ˈkat-ə-rən\ *n* [ME *ketharan,* prob. fr. ScGael *ceathairneach* freebooter, robber] **:** a former military irregular or brigand of the Scottish Highlands

cat·er·cor·ner \ˌkat-ē-ˈkȯ(r)-nər, ˌkat-ə-, ˌkit-ē-\ *or* **cat·er–cor·nered** \-nərd\ *adv or adj* [obs. *cater* (four-spot) + E *corner*] **:** in a diagonal or oblique position **:** on a diagonal or oblique line ⟨the house stood ~ across the square⟩

ca·ter–cous·in \ˈkāt-ər-ˌkəz-ᵊn\ *n* [perh. fr. obs. *cater* (buyer of provisions)] **:** an intimate friend

cat·er·pil·lar \ˈkat-ə(r)-ˌpil-ər\ *n, often attrib* [ME *catyrpel,* fr. ONF *catepelose,* lit., hairy cat] **:** the elongated wormlike larva of a butterfly or moth; *also* **:** any of various similar larvae

Caterpillar *trademark* — used for a tractor made for use on rough or soft ground and moved on two endless metal belts

cat·er·waul \ˈkat-ər-ˌwȯl\ *vi* [ME *caterwawen*] **1 :** to make a harsh cry **2 :** to quarrel noisily — **caterwaul** *n*

cat·fac·ing \ˈkat-ˌfā-siŋ\ *n* **:** a disfigurement or malformation of fruit suggesting a cat's face in appearance

cat·fish \-ˌfish\ *n* **:** any of numerous usu. stout-bodied large-headed fishes (order Ostariophysi) with long tactile barbels

cat·gut \-ˌgət\ *n* **:** a tough cord made usu. from sheep intestines

cath *abbr* **1** cathedral **2** cathode

cath- — see CATA-

Cath·ar \ˈkath-ˌär\ *n, pl* **Cath·a·ri** \ˈkath-ə-ˌrī, -ˌrē\ *or* **Cathars** [LL *cathari* (pl.), fr. LGk *katharoi,* fr. Gk, pl. of *katharos,* adj.] **:** a member of one of various ascetic and dualistic Christian sects flourishing in the later Middle Ages teaching that matter is evil, and professing faith in an angelic Christ who did not really undergo human birth or death — **Cath·a·rism** \ˈkath-ə-ˌriz-əm\ *n* — **Cath·a·rist** \-rəst\ *or* **Cath·a·ris·tic** \ˌkath-ə-ˈris-tik\ *adj*

ca·thar·sis \kə-ˈthär-səs\ *n, pl* **ca·thar·ses** \-ˌsēz\ [NL, fr. Gk *katharsis,* fr. *kathairein* to cleanse, purge, fr. *katharos* pure] **1 :** PURGATION **2 a :** purification or purgation of the emotions (as pity and fear) primarily through art **b :** a purification or purgation that brings about spiritual renewal or release from tension **3 :** elimination of a complex by bringing it to consciousness and affording it expression

¹ca·thar·tic \kə-ˈthärt-ik\ *adj* [LL or Gk; LL *catharticus,* fr. Gk *kathartikos,* fr. *kathairein*] **:** of, relating to, or producing catharsis

²cathartic *n* **:** a cathartic medicine **:** PURGATIVE

cat·head \ˈkat-ˌhed\ *n* **:** a projecting piece of timber or iron near the bow of a ship to which the anchor is hoisted and secured

ca·thect \kə-ˈthekt, ka-\ *vt* [back-formation fr. *cathectic*] **:** to invest with mental or emotional energy

ca·thec·tic \kə-ˈthek-tik, ka-\ *adj* [NL *cathexis*] **:** of, relating to, or invested with mental or emotional energy

ca·the·dra \kə-ˈthē-drə\ *n* [L, chair — more at CHAIR] **:** a bishop's official throne

¹ca·the·dral \kə-ˈthē-drəl\ *adj* **1 :** of, relating to, or containing a cathedra **2 :** emanating from a chair of authority **3 :** suggestive of a cathedral

²cathedral *n* **1 :** a church that is the official seat of a diocesan bishop **2 :** something that resembles or suggests a cathedral ⟨higher education has been . . . the secular ~ of our time — David Riesman⟩

ca·thep·sin \kə-ˈthep-sən\ *n* [Gk *kathepsein* to digest (fr. *kata-* cata- + *hepsein* to boil) + E *-in*] **:** any of several intracellular proteinases of animal tissue that aid in autolysis in certain diseased conditions and after death

cath·er·ine wheel \ˌkath-(ə-)rən-\ *n, often cap C* [St. *Catherine* of Alexandria †*ab*307 Christian martyr] **1 :** a wheel with spikes projecting from the rim **2 :** PINWHEEL 2 **3 :** CARTWHEEL 2

cath·e·ter \ˈkath-ət-ər, ˈkath-tər\ *n* [LL, fr. Gk *kathetēr,* fr. *kathienai* to send down, fr. *kata-* cata- + *hienai* to send — more at JET] **:** a tubular medical device for insertion into canals, vessels, passageways, or body cavities usu. to permit injection or withdrawal of fluids or to keep a passage open

cath·e·ter·ize \ˈkath-ət-ə-ˌrīz, ˈkath-tə-\ *vt* **-ized; -iz·ing :** to introduce a catheter into — **cath·e·ter·iza·tion** \ˌkath-ət-ə-rə-ˈzā-shən, ˌkath-tə-rə-\ *n*

ca·thex·is \kə-ˈthek-səs, ka-\ *n, pl* **ca·thex·es** \-ˌsēz\ [NL (intended as trans. of G *besetzung*), fr. Gk *kathexis* holding, fr. *katechein* to hold fast, occupy, fr. *kata-* + *echein* to have, hold — more at SCHEME] **:** investment of mental or emotional energy in a person, object, or idea

cath·ode \ˈkath-ˌōd\ *n* [Gk *kathodos* way down, fr. *kata-* + *hodos* way — more at CEDE] **1 :** the negative terminal of an electrolytic cell — compare ANODE **2 :** the positive terminal of a primary cell or of a storage battery that is delivering current **3 :** the electron-emitting electrode of an electron tube — **ca·thod·ic** \ka-ˈthäd-ik\ *adj* — **ca·thod·i·cal·ly** \-i-k(ə-)lē\ *adv*

cathode ray *n* **1 :** one of the high-speed electrons projected in a stream from the heated cathode of a vacuum tube under the propulsion of a strong electric field **2 :** a stream of cathode-ray electrons

cathode–ray tube *n* **:** a vacuum tube in which cathode rays usu. in the form of a slender beam are projected on a fluorescent screen and produce a luminous spot

cath·o·lic \ˈkath-(ə-)lik\ *adj* [MF & LL; MF *catholique,* fr. LL *catholicus,* fr. Gk *katholikos* universal, general, fr. *katholou* in general, fr. *kata* by + *holos* whole — more at CATA-, SAFE] **1 :** COMPREHENSIVE, UNIVERSAL; *esp* **:** broad in sympathies, tastes, or interests **2** *cap* **a :** of, relating to, or forming the church universal **b :** of, relating to, or forming the ancient undivided Christian church or a church claiming historical continuity from it; *specif* **:** Roman Catholic — **ca·thol·i·cal·ly** \kə-ˈthäl-i-k(ə-)lē\ *adv* — **ca·thol·i·cize** \kə-ˈthäl-ə-ˌsīz\ *vb*

Cath·o·lic \ˈkath-(ə-)lik\ *n* **1 :** a person who belongs to the universal Christian church **2 :** a member of a Catholic church; *specif* **:** ROMAN CATHOLIC

Catholic Apostolic *adj* **:** of or relating to a Christian sect founded in 19th century England in anticipation of Christ's second coming

ca·thol·i·cate \kə-ˈthäl-ə-ˌkāt, -ˈthäl-i-kət\ *n* **:** the jurisdiction of a catholicos

Catholic Epistles *n pl* **:** the five New Testament letters including James, I and II Peter, I John, and Jude addressed to the early Christian churches at large

Ca·thol·i·cism \kə-ˈthäl-ə-ˌsiz-əm\ *n* **1 :** the faith, practice, or system of Catholic Christianity **2 :** ROMAN CATHOLICISM

cath·o·lic·i·ty \ˌkath-ə-ˈlis-ət-ē\ *n, pl* **-ties** **1** *cap* **:** the character of being in conformity with a Catholic church **2 a :** liberality of sentiments or views ⟨~ of viewpoint — W. V. O'Connor⟩ **b :** UNIVERSALITY **c :** comprehensive range ⟨the ~ of subjects represented by the press's trade list — *Current Biog.*⟩

ca·thol·i·con \kə-ˈthäl-ə-ˌkän\ *n* [F or ML; F, fr. ML, fr. Gk *katholikon,* neut. of *katholikos*] **:** CURE-ALL, PANACEA

ca·thol·i·cos \kə-ˈthäl-i-kəs\ *n, pl* **ca·thol·i·cos·es** \-kə-səz\ *or* **ca·thol·i·coi** \-ˈthäl-ə-ˌkȯi\ *often cap* [LGk *katholikos,* fr. Gk, general] **:** a primate of certain Eastern churches and esp. of the Armenian or of the Nestorian church

cat·house \ˈkat-ˌhau̇s\ *n* **:** a house of prostitution

cat·ion \ˈkat-ˌī-ən\ *n* [Gk *kation,* neut. of *katiōn,* prp. of *katienai* to go down, fr. *kata-* cata- + *ienai* to go — more at ISSUE] **:** the ion in an electrolyzed solution that migrates to the cathode; *broadly* **:** a positively charged ion

cat·ion·ic \ˌkat-(ˌ)ī-ˈän-ik\ *adj* **1 :** of or relating to cations **2 :** characterized by an active and esp. surface-active cation ⟨a ~ dye⟩ — **cat·ion·i·cal·ly** \-i-k(ə-)lē\ *adv*

cat·kin \ˈkat-kən\ *n* [fr. its resemblance to a cat's tail] **:** a usu. long ament densely crowded with bracts — **cat·kin·ate** \-kə-ˌnāt\ *adj*

cat·like \ˈkat-ˌlīk\ *adj* **:** resembling a cat **:** STEALTHY ⟨with ~ tread, upon our prey we steal —W. S. Gilbert⟩

cat·nap \-ˌnap\ *n* **:** a very short light nap — **catnap** *vi*

cat·nap·per *or* **cat·nap·er** \ˈkat-ˌnap-ər\ *n* [ˡ*cat* + *-napper* (as in *kidnapper*)] **:** one that steals cats; *esp* **:** one that does so in order to sell them to research laboratories

cat·nip \-ˌnip\ *n* [ˡ*cat* + obs. *nep* (catnip), fr. ME, fr. OE *nepte,* fr. L *nepeta*] **:** a strong-scented mint (*Nepeta cataria*) that has whorls of small pale flowers in terminal spikes and contains a substance attractive to cats

cat–o'–nine–tails \ˌkat-ə-ˈnīn-ˌtālz\ *n, pl* **cat–o'–nine–tails** [fr. the resemblance of its scars to the scratches of a cat] **:** a whip made of usu. nine knotted lines or cords fastened to a handle

ca·top·tric \kə-ˈtäp-trik\ *adj* [Gk *katoptrikos,* fr. *katoptron* mirror, fr. *katopsesthai* to be going to observe, fr. *kata-* cata- + *opsesthai* to be going to see — more at OPTIC] **:** of or relating to a mirror or reflected light; *also* **:** produced by reflection — **ca·top·tri·cal·ly** \-tri-k(ə-)lē\ *adv*

cat rig *n* **:** a rig consisting of a single mast far forward carrying a single large sail extended by a boom — **cat–rigged** \ˈkat-ˈrigd\ *adj*

cat's cradle *n* **1 :** a game in which a string looped in a pattern like a cradle on the fingers of one person's hands is transferred to the hands of another so as to form a different figure **2 :** INTRICACY ⟨the socioreligious *cat's cradle* of small Greek communities — *Times Lit. Supp.*⟩

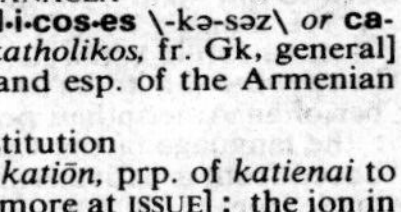

cat's cradle 1, first figure

cat's–eye \ˈkat-ˌsī\ *n, pl* **cat's–eyes** **1 :** any of various gems (as a chrysoberyl or a chalcedony) exhibiting opalescent reflections from within **2 :** a marble with eyelike concentric circles

cat's–foot \ˈkats-ˌfu̇t\ *n, pl* **cat's–feet** \-ˌfēt\ **1 :** GROUND IVY **2 :** any of several wooly composite plants (genus *Antennaria,* esp. *A. neodioica*) with small whitish discoid flower heads

cat's–paw \ˈkat-ˌspȯ\ *n, pl* **cat's–paws** **1 :** a light air that ruffles the surface of the water in irregular patches during a calm **2** [fr. the fable of the monkey that used a cat's paw to draw chestnuts from the fire] **:** one used by another as a tool **:** DUPE **3 :** a hitch in the bight of a rope so made as to form two eyes into which a tackle may be hooked — see KNOT illustration

cat·sup \ˈkech-əp, ˈkach-; ˈkat-səp\ *n* [Malay *kĕchap* spiced fish sauce] **:** a seasoned tomato puree

cat·tail \ˈkat-ˌtāl\ *n* **:** any of a genus (*Typha* of the family Typhaceae, the cattail family) of tall reedy marsh plants with brown furry fruiting spikes; *esp* : a plant (*Typha latifolia*) with long flat leaves used for making mats and chair seats

cat·ta·lo \ˈkat-ᵊl-ˌō\ *n, pl* **-loes** *or* **-los** [blend of *cattle* and *buffalo*] : a hybrid between the American buffalo and domestic cattle that is hardier than the latter

cat·tle \ˈkat-ᵊl\ *n pl* [ME, *catel,* fr. ONF, personal property, fr. ML *capitale,* fr. L, neut. of *capitalis* of the head — more at CAPITAL] **1** : domesticated quadrupeds held as property or raised for use; *specif* : bovine animals kept on a farm or ranch **2** : human beings esp. en masse

cattle grub *n* : any of several heel flies esp. in the larval stage; *esp* : COMMON CATTLE GRUB

cat·tle·man \-mən, -ˌman\ *n* : a man who tends or raises cattle

cattle tick *n* : a tick (*Boophilus annulatus*) that infests cattle in the southern U.S. and tropical America and transmits the causative agent of Texas fever

cat·tleya \ˈkat-lē-ə; kat-ˈlā-ə, -ˈlē-\ *n* [NL, fr. Wm. *Cattley* †1832 E patron of botany] : any of a genus (*Cattleya*) of tropical American epiphytic orchids with showy hooded flowers

¹cat·ty \ˈkat-ē\ *n, pl* **catties** [Malay *katī*] : any of various units of weight of China and southeast Asia varying around 1¹/₃ pounds; *also* : a standard Chinese unit equal to 1.1023 pounds

²catty *adj* **cat·ti·er; -est** **1 a** : resembling a cat: as (1) : STEALTHY (2) : AGILE **b** : slyly spiteful : MALICIOUS **2** : of or relating to a cat — **cat·ti·ly** \ˈkat-ᵊl-ē\ *adv* — **cat·ti·ness** \ˈkat-ē-nəs\ *n*

cat·ty–cor·ner *or* **cat·ty–cor·nered** *var of* CATERCORNER

CATV *abbr* community antenna television

cat·walk \ˈkat-ˌwȯk\ *n* : a narrow walkway (as along a bridge)

Cau·ca·sian \kȯ-ˈkā-zhən, -ˈkazh-ən\ *adj* **1** : of or relating to the Caucasus or its inhabitants **2 a** : of or relating to the white race of mankind as classified according to physical features **b** : of or relating to the white race as defined by law specif. as composed of persons of European, No. African, or southwest Asian ancestry — **Caucasian** *n* — **Cau·ca·soid** \ˈkȯ-kə-ˌsȯid\ *adj or n*

¹cau·cus \ˈkȯ-kəs\ *n* [prob. of Algonquian origin] : a closed meeting of a group of persons belonging to the same political party or faction usu. to select candidates or to decide on policy

²caucus *vi* : to hold or meet in a caucus

cau·dad \ˈkȯ-ˌdad\ *adv* [L *cauda*] : toward the tail or posterior end

cau·dal \ˈkȯd-ᵊl\ *adj* [NL *caudalis,* fr. L *cauda* tail — more at COWARD] **1** : of, relating to, or being a tail **2** : situated in or directed toward the hind part of the body — **cau·dal·ly** \-ᵊl-ē\ *adv*

cau·date \ˈkȯ-ˌdāt\ *also* **cau·dat·ed** \-ˌdāt-əd\ *adj* : having a tail or a taillike appendage : TAILED — **cau·da·tion** \kȯ-ˈdā-shən\ *n*

cau·dex \ˈkȯ-ˌdeks\ *n, pl* **cau·di·ces** \ˈkȯd-ə-ˌsēz\ *or* **cau·dex·es** [L, tree trunk or stem — more at CODE] **1** : the stem of a palm or tree fern **2** : the woody base of a perennial plant

cau·dil·lo \kau̇-ˈt͟hē-(ˌ)(y)ō, -ˈt͟hēl-(ˌ)yō\ *n, pl* **-llos** [Sp. fr. LL *capitellum* small head — more at CADET] : a Spanish or Latin-American military dictator

cau·dle \ˈkȯd-ᵊl\ *n* [ME *caudel,* fr. ONF, fr. *caut* warm, fr. L *calidus* — more at CALDRON] : a drink (as for invalids) usu. of warm ale or wine mixed with bread or gruel, eggs, sugar, and spices

¹caught \ˈkȯt\ *past of* CATCH

²caught *adj* : PREGNANT — often used in the phrase *get caught*

caul \ˈkȯl\ *n* [ME *calle,* fr. MF *cale*] **1** : the large fatty omentum covering the intestines **2** : the inner fetal membrane of higher vertebrates esp. when covering the head at birth

cauldron *var of* CALDRON

cau·les·cent \kȯ-ˈles-ᵊnt\ *adj* [ISV, fr. L *caulis*] : having a stem evident above ground

cau·li·cle \ˈkȯ-li-kəl\ *n* [L *cauliculus,* dim. of *caulis*] : a rudimentary stem (as of an embryo or seedling)

cau·li·flow·er \ˈkȯ-li-ˌflau̇(-ə)r, ˈkäl-i-\ *n, often attrib* [It *cavolfiore,* fr. *cavolo* cabbage (fr. LL *caulus,* fr. L *caulis* stem, cabbage) + *fiore* flower, fr. L *flor-, flos* — more at HOLE, BLOW] : a garden plant (*Brassica oleracea botrytis*) related to the cabbage and grown for its compact edible head of usu. white undeveloped flowers; *also* : its flower cluster

cauliflower ear *n* : an ear deformed from injury and excessive growth of reparative tissue

cau·line \ˈkȯ-ˌlīn\ *adj* [prob. fr. NL *caulinus,* fr. L *caulis*] : of, relating to, or growing on a stem; *specif* : growing on the upper part of a stem

¹caulk \ˈkȯk\ *vt* [ME *caulken,* fr. ONF *cauquer* to trample, fr. L *calcare,* fr. *calc-, calx* heel — more at CALK] **1** : to stop up and make watertight the seams of (as a boat) by filling with a waterproofing compound or material **2** : to stop up and make tight against leakage (as the seams of a boat, the cracks in a window frame, or the joints of a pipe) — **caulk·er** *n*

²caulk *var of* CALK

caus *abbr* causative

caus·al \ˈkȯ-zəl\ *adj* **1** : expressing or indicating cause : CAUSATIVE ⟨a ~ clause introduced by *since* or *because*⟩ **2** : of, relating to, or constituting a cause ⟨the ~ agent of a disease⟩ **3** : involving causation or a cause ⟨the relationship . . . was not one of ~ antecedence so much as one of analogous growth — H. O. Taylor⟩ **4** : arising from a cause ⟨a ~ development⟩ — **caus·al·ly** \-zə-lē\ *adv*

cau·sal·i·ty \kȯ-ˈzal-ət-ē\ *n, pl* **-ties** **1** : a causal quality or agency **2** : the relation between a cause and its effect or between regularly correlated events or phenomena

cau·sa·tion \kȯ-ˈzā-shən\ *n* **1 a** : the act or process of causing **b** : the act or agency by which an effect is produced **2** : CAUSALITY

caus·ative \ˈkȯ-zət-iv\ *adj* **1** : effective or operating as a cause or agent **2** : expressing causation — **causative** *n* — **caus·ative·ly** *adv*

¹cause \ˈkȯz\ *n* [ME, fr. OF, fr. L *causa*] **1 a** : something that brings about an effect or a result **b** : a person or thing that is the occasion of an action or state; *esp* : an agent that brings something about **c** : a reason for an action or condition : MOTIVE **2 a** : a ground of legal action **b** : CASE **3** : a matter or question to be decided **4** : a principle or movement militantly defended or supported — **cause·less** \-ləs\ *adj*

syn CAUSE, DETERMINANT, ANTECEDENT, REASON, OCCASION *shared meaning element* : something that precedes and usually induces an effect or result. CAUSE applies to anything (as an event, circumstance, or condition) that brings about or helps bring about an effect ⟨water and soil pollution are the root *causes* of mortality in the tropics — V. G. Heiser⟩ DETERMINANT applies to a cause that fixes the nature of what results ⟨the quality of education provided is a *determinant* of the quality of the child's later life⟩ ANTECEDENT stresses the fact of priority and usually suggests some degree of responsibility for what follows ⟨the *antecedents* and consequences of the war⟩ REASON applies to a traceable or explainable cause of a known effect ⟨trying to figure out the *reason* for her failure⟩ OCCASION applies to a precipitating cause and especially to a time or situation at which underlying causes become effective; thus, the *cause* of a war may be a longtime deep-rooted antipathy between peoples, its *occasion* some trivial incident

²cause *vt* **caused; caus·ing** **1** : to serve as a cause or occasion of **2** : to effect by command, authority, or force — **caus·er** *n*

ˈcause \(ˈ)kȯz, (ˈ)kəz\ *conj* : BECAUSE

cause cé·lè·bre \ˌkōz-sā-ˈlebrᵊ, ˌkȯz-\ *n, pl* **causes cé·lè·bres** *same*\ [F, lit., celebrated case] **1** : a legal case that excites widespread interest **2** : a notorious incident or episode

cau·se·rie \ˌkōz-(ə-)ˈrē\ *n* [F, fr. *causer* to chat, fr. L *causari* to plead, discuss, fr. *causa*] **1** : an informal conversation : CHAT **2** : a short informal composition

cause·way \ˈkȯz-ˌwā\ *n* [ME *cauciwey,* fr. *cauci* causey + *wey* way] **1** : a raised way across wet ground or water **2** : HIGHWAY; *esp* : one of ancient Roman construction in Britain — **causeway** *vt*

cau·sey \ˈkȯ-zē\ *n, pl* **causeys** [ME *cauci,* fr. ONF *caucie,* fr. ML *calciata* paved highway, fr. fem. of *calciatus* paved with limestone, fr. L *calc-, calx* limestone — more at CHALK] **1** : CAUSEWAY 1 **2** *obs* : CAUSEWAY 2

caus·tic \ˈkȯ-stik\ *adj* [L *causticus,* fr. Gk *kaustikos,* fr. *kaiein* to burn; akin to Lith *kūlė* smut of plants] **1** : capable of destroying or eating away by chemical action : CORROSIVE **2** : INCISIVE, BITING ⟨~ wit⟩ **3** : relating to or being the envelope of rays emanating from a point and reflected or refracted by a curved surface — **caustic** *n* — **caus·ti·cal·ly** \-sti-k(ə-)lē\ *adv* — **caus·tic·i·ty** \kȯ-ˈstis-ət-ē\ *n*

caustic lime *n* : ¹LIME 2a

caustic potash *n* : POTASSIUM HYDROXIDE

caustic soda *n* : SODIUM HYDROXIDE

cau·ter·i·za·tion \ˌkȯt-ə-rə-ˈzā-shən\ *n* : the act or effect of cauterizing

cau·ter·ize \ˈkȯt-ə-ˌrīz\ *vt* **-ized; -iz·ing** : to sear with a cautery or caustic

cau·tery \ˈkȯt-ə-rē\ *n, pl* **-ter·ies** [L *cauterium,* fr. Gk *kautērion* branding iron, fr. *kaiein*] **1** : CAUTERIZATION **2** : a hot iron, caustic, or other agent used to burn, sear, or destroy tissue

¹cau·tion \ˈkȯ-shən\ *n* [L *caution-, cautio* precaution, fr. *cautus,* pp. of *cavēre* to be on one's guard — more at HEAR] **1** : WARNING, ADMONISHMENT **2** : PRECAUTION **3** : prudent forethought to minimize risk **4** : one that arouses astonishment or commands attention ⟨some shoes you see . . . these days are a ~ — *Esquire*⟩ — **cau·tion·ary** \-shə-ˌner-ē\ *adj*

²caution *vt* **cau·tioned; cau·tion·ing** \ˈkȯ-sh(ə-)niŋ\ : to advise caution to ***syn*** see WARN

cau·tious \ˈkȯ-shəs\ *adj* : marked by or given to caution — **cau·tious·ly** *adv* — **cau·tious·ness** *n*

syn CAUTIOUS, CIRCUMSPECT, WARY, CHARY *shared meaning element* : prudently watchful and discreet in the face of danger or risk ***ant*** adventurous, temerarious

cav *abbr* **1** cavalry **2** cavity

cav·al·cade \ˌkav-əl-ˈkād, ˈkav-əl-ˌ\ *n* [MF, ride on horseback, fr. OIt *cavalcata,* fr. *cavalcare* to go on horseback, fr. LL *caballicare,* fr. L *caballus* horse; akin to Gk dial. *kaballeion* horse-drawn vehicle] **1 a** : a procession of riders or carriages **b** : a procession of vehicles or ships **2** : a dramatic sequence or procession : SERIES

¹cav·a·lier \ˌkav-ə-ˈli(ə)r\ *n* [MF, fr. OIt *cavaliere,* fr. OProv *cavalier,* fr. LL *caballarius* horseman, fr. L *caballus*] **1** : a gentleman trained in arms and horsemanship **2** : a mounted soldier : KNIGHT **3** *cap* : an adherent of Charles I of England **4** : GALLANT

²cavalier *adj* **1** : DEBONAIR **2** : given to offhand dismissal of important matters : DISDAINFUL **3 a** *cap* : of or relating to the party of Charles I of England in his struggles with the Puritans and Parliament **b** : ARISTOCRATIC **c** *cap* : of or relating to the English Cavalier poets of the mid-17th century — **ca·va·lier·ism** \-ˌiz-əm\ *n* — **cav·a·lier·ly** *adv*

ca·val·la \kə-ˈval-ə\ *n, pl* **-la** *or* **-las** [Sp *caballa,* a fish, fr. LL, mare, fem. of L *caballus*] **1** : CERO **2** *also* **ca·val·ly** \-ˈval-ē\ : any of various carangid fishes (esp. genus *Caranx*)

cav·al·ry \ˈkav-əl-rē\ *n, pl* **-ries** [It *cavalleria* cavalry, chivalry, fr. *cavaliere*] **1** : HORSEMEN ⟨a thousand ~ in flight⟩ **2** : an army component mounted on horseback or moving in motor vehicles and assigned to combat missions that require great mobility

cav·al·ry·man \-rē-mən, -ˌman\ *n* : a cavalry soldier

cav·a·ti·na \ˌkav-ə-ˈtē-nə, ˌkäv-\ *n* [It, fr. *cavata* production of sound from an instrument, fr. *cavare* to dig out, fr. L, to make hollow, fr. *cavus*] **1** : an operatic solo simpler and briefer than an aria **2** : a sustained melody

¹cave \ˈkāv\ *n* [ME, fr. OF, fr. L *cava,* fr. *cavus* hollow; akin to ON *hūnn* cub, Gk *kyein* to be pregnant, *koilos* hollow, Skt *śvayati* he swells] **1** : a natural underground chamber open to the surface **2**

[short for *cave of Adullam;* fr. the story in I Sam 22:1, 2 of David's being joined by malcontents in the cave of that name] *Brit* : a secession or a group of seceders from a political party

²**cave** *vt* **caved; cav·ing** : to form a cave in or under : HOLLOW, UNDERMINE — **cav·er** *n*

³**cave** \'kāv\ *vb* **caved; cav·ing** [prob. alter. of calve] *vi* **1** : to fall in or down esp. from being undermined **2** : to cease to resist : SUBMIT — usu. used with *in* ~ *vt* : to cause to fall or collapse — usu. used with *in*

ca·ve·at \'kav-ē-,ät, -,at; 'käv-ē-,ät\ *n* [L, let him beware, fr. *cavēre* — more at HEAR] **1 a** : a warning enjoining one from certain acts or practices **b** : an explanation to prevent misinterpretation **2** : a legal warning to a judicial officer to suspend a proceeding until the opposition has a hearing

caveat emp·tor \-'em(p)-tər, -,tȯ(ə)r\ *n* [NL, let the buyer beware] : a principle in commerce: without a warranty the buyer takes the risk of quality upon himself

cave dweller *n* **1** : one (as a prehistoric man) that dwells in a cave **2** : one that lives in a city apartment building

cave–in \'kā-,vin\ *n* **1** : the action of caving in **2** : a place where earth has caved in

cave·man \'kāv-,man\ *n* **1** : a cave dweller esp. of the Stone Age **2** : one who acts in a rough primitive manner esp. toward women

¹**cav·ern** \'kav-ərn\ *n* [ME *caverne,* fr. MF, fr. L *caverna,* fr. *cavus*] : an underground chamber often of large or indefinite extent : CAVE

²**cavern** *vt* **1** : to place in or as if in a cavern **2** : to form a cavern of : HOLLOW — used with *out*

cav·er·nic·o·lous \,kav-ər-'nik-ə-ləs\ *adj* : inhabiting caves ⟨a ~ fauna⟩

cav·ern·ous \'kav-ər-nəs\ *adj* **1** : having caverns or cavities **2** : constituting or suggesting a cavern **3** *of animal tissue* : composed largely of vascular sinuses and capable of dilating with blood to bring about the erection of a body part — **cav·ern·ous·ly** *adv*

ca·vet·to \kə-'vet-(,)ō, kä-\ *n, pl* **-ti** \-ē\ [It, fr. *cavo* hollow, fr. L *cavus*] : a concave molding having a curve that roughly approximates a quarter circle — see MOLDING illustration

cav·i·ar *or* **cav·i·are** \'kav-ē-,är *also* 'käv-\ *n* [earlier *cavery, caviarie,* fr. obs. It *caviari,* pl. of *caviaro,* fr. Turk *havyar*] **1** : processed salted roe of large fish (as sturgeon) prepared as an appetizer **2** : something considered too delicate or lofty for mass appreciation ⟨the play, I remember, pleased not the million; 'twas ~ to the general — Shak.⟩

cav·il \'kav-əl\ *vb* **-iled** *or* **-illed; -il·ing** *or* **-il·ling** \-(ə-)liŋ\ [L *cavillari* to jest, cavil, fr. *cavilla* raillery] *vi* : to raise trivial and frivolous objection ~ *vt* : to raise trivial objections to — **cavil** *n* — **cav·il·er** *or* **cav·il·ler** \-(ə-)lər\ *n*

cav·i·tary \'kav-ə-,ter-ē\ *adj* : of, relating to, or characterized by bodily cavitation ⟨~ tuberculosis⟩

cav·i·tate \'kav-ə-,tāt\ *vb* **-tat·ed; -tat·ing** *vi* : to form cavities or bubbles ~ *vt* : to cavitate in

cav·i·ta·tion \,kav-ə-'tā-shən\ *n* [*cavity* + *-ation*] : the process of cavitating: as **a** : the formation of partial vacuums in a liquid by a swiftly moving solid body (as a propeller) or by high-frequency sound waves; *also* : the pitting and wearing away of solid surfaces (as of metal or concrete) as a result of the collapse of these vacuums in surrounding liquid **b** : the formation of cavities in an organ or tissue esp. in disease

cav·i·ty \'kav-ət-ē\ *n, pl* **-ties** [MF *cavité,* fr. LL *cavitas,* fr. L *cavus* hollow] : an unfilled space within a mass; *esp* : a hollowed out space

ca·vort \kə-'vȯ(ə)rt\ *vi* [perh. alter. of *curvet*] **1** : PRANCE **2** : to engage in extravagant behavior

CAVU *abbr* ceiling and visibility unlimited

ca·vy \'kā-vē\ *n, pl* **cavies** [NL *Cavia,* genus name, fr. obs. Pg *çavía* (now *savía*), fr. Tupi *sawiya* rat] **1** : any of several short-tailed roughhaired So. American rodents (family Caviidae); *esp* : GUINEA PIG **2** : any of several rodents related to the cavies

caw \'kȯ\ *vi* [imit.] : to utter the harsh raucous natural call of the crow or a similar cry — **caw** *n*

cay \'kē, 'kā\ *n* [Sp *cayo* — more at KEY] : a low island or reef of sand or coral

cay·enne pepper \(,)kī-,en-, (,)kā-\ *n* [by folk etymology fr. earlier *cayan,* modif. of Tupi *kyinha*] **1** : a pungent condiment consisting of the ground dried fruits or seeds of hot peppers **2** : HOT PEPPER 2; *esp* : a cultivated pepper with very long twisted pungent red fruits **3** : the fruit of a cayenne pepper

cay·man *var of* CAIMAN

Ca·yu·ga \kā-'(y)ü-gə, ki-, kī-; 'kyü-\ *n, pl* **Cayuga** *or* **Cayugas** **1 a** : an Amerindian people of New York **b** : a member of this people **2** : the language of the Cayuga people

Cay·use \'kī-,(y)üs, kī-'\ *n, pl* **Cayuse** *or* **Cayuses** **1** : a member of an Amerindian people of Oregon and Washington **2** *pl cayuses, not cap, West* : a native range horse

¹**Cb** *abbr* cumulonimbus

²**Cb** *symbol* columbium

CB *abbr* **1** citizens band **2** confined to barracks

C battery *n* : a battery used to maintain the potential of a grid-controlled electron tube at a desired value constant except for signals superposed upon it

CBC *abbr* Canadian Broadcasting Corporation

CBD *abbr* cash before delivery

CBI *abbr* **1** computer-based instruction **2** Cumulative Book Index

CBS *abbr* Columbia Broadcasting System

CBW *abbr* chemical and biological warfare

cc *abbr* cubic centimeter

Cc *abbr* cirrocumulus

CC *abbr* **1** carbon copy **2** chief clerk **3** common carrier

CCAT *abbr* Cooperative College Ability Test

CCC *abbr* **1** Civilian Conservation Corps **2** Commodity Credit Corporation

CCCO *abbr* Central Committee for Conscientious Objectors

CCD *abbr* Confraternity of Christian Doctrine

CCF *abbr* **1** Chinese communist forces **2** Cooperative Commonwealth Federation (of Canada)

cckw *abbr* counterclockwise

C clef *n* : a movable clef indicating middle C by its placement on one of the lines of the staff

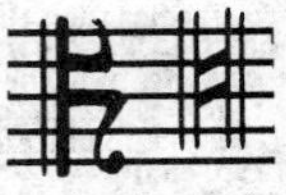

two forms of C clef

CCTV *abbr* closed-circuit television

ccw *abbr* counterclockwise

cd *abbr* **1** candle **2** cord

Cd *symbol* cadmium

CD *abbr* **1** carried down **2** certificate of deposit **3** civil defense **4** [F *corps diplomatique*] diplomatic corps **5** current density

CDD *abbr* certificate of disability for discharge

CDR *abbr* commander

CDT *abbr* central daylight time

Ce *symbol* cerium

CE *abbr* **1** chemical engineer **2** civil engineer **3** (International Society of) Christian Endeavor

CEA *abbr* **1** College English Association **2** Council of Economic Advisors

¹**cease** \'sēs\ *vb* **ceased; ceas·ing** [ME *cesen,* fr. OF *cesser,* fr. L *cessare* to delay, fr. *cessus,* pp. of *cedere*] *vt* : to bring to an end : TERMINATE ⟨the dying man soon *ceased* to breathe⟩ ~ *vi* **1 a** : to come to an end ⟨when will this quarreling ~?⟩ **b** : to bring an activity or action to an end : DISCONTINUE ⟨cried for hours without *ceasing*⟩ **2** *obs* : to die out : become extinct ***syn*** see STOP

²**cease** *n* : CESSATION — usu. used with *without*

cease and desist order *n* : an order from an administrative agency to refrain from a method of competition or a labor practice found by the agency to be unfair

cease–fire \'sēs-'fī(ə)r\ *n* **1** : a military order to cease firing **2** : a suspension of active hostilities

cease·less \'sē-sləs\ *adj* : continuing without cease : CONSTANT — **cease·less·ly** *adv* — **cease·less·ness** *n*

ce·cro·pia moth \si-,krō-pē-ə-\ *n* [NL *cecropia,* fr. L, fem. of *Cecropius* Athenian, fr. Gk *Kekropios,* fr. *Kekrops* Cecrops, legendary king of Athens] : a large silkworm moth (*Samia cecropia*) of the eastern U.S.

ce·cum \'sē-kəm\ *n, pl* **ce·ca** \-kə\ [NL, fr. L *intestinum caecum,* lit., blind intestine] : a cavity open at one end (as the blind end of a duct); *esp* : the blind pouch in which the large intestine begins and into which the ileum opens from one side — **ce·cal** \-kəl\ *adj* — **ce·cal·ly** \-kə-lē\ *adv*

CED *abbr* Committee for Economic Development

ce·dar \'sēd-ər\ *n* [ME *cedre,* fr. OF, fr. L *cedrus,* fr. Gk *kedros;* akin to Lith *kadagys* juniper] **1 a** : any of a genus (*Cedrus*) of usu. tall coniferous trees (as the cedar of Lebanon or the deodar) of the pine family noted for their fragrant durable wood **b** : any of numerous coniferous trees (as of the genera *Juniperus, Chamaecyparis,* or *Thuja*) that resemble the true cedars esp. in the fragrance and durability of their wood **2** : the wood of a cedar

ce·darn \'sēd-ərn\ *adj, archaic* : made or suggestive of cedar

cedar of Leb·a·non \-'leb(-ə)-nən\ : a long-lived evergreen tree (*Cedrus libani*) with short fascicled leaves and erect cones that is native to Asia Minor

cedar waxwing *n* : a long-crested brown waxwing (*Bombycilla cedrorum*) of temperate No. America with a yellow band on the tip of the tail — called also *cedarbird*

ce·dar·wood \'sēd-ər-,wu̇d\ *n* : the wood of a cedar that is esp. repellent to insects

cede \'sēd\ *vt* **ced·ed; ced·ing** [F or L; F *céder,* fr. L *cedere* to go, withdraw, yield; prob. akin to L *cis* on this side and to Gk *hodos* road, way, L *sedēre* to sit — more at HE, SIT] **1** : to yield or grant typically by treaty **2** : ASSIGN, TRANSFER — **ced·er** *n*

ce·di \'sād-ē\ *n* [Akan *sedie* cowry] — see MONEY table

ce·dil·la \si-'dil-ə\ *n* [Sp, the obs. letter *ç* (actually a medieval form of the letter *z*), cedilla, fr. dim. of *ceda, zeda* the letter *z,* fr. LL *zeta* — more at ZED] : the diacritical mark ¸ placed under a letter (as ç in French) to indicate an alteration or modification of its usual phonetic value (as in the French word *façade*)

cee \'sē\ *n* : the letter *c*

CEEB *abbr* College Entrance Examination Board

cei·ba \'sā-bə\ *n* [Sp] **1** : a massive tropical tree (*Ceiba pentandra*) of the silk-cotton family with large pods filled with seeds invested with a silky floss that yields the fiber kapok **2** : KAPOK

ceil \'sē(ə)l\ *vt* [ME *celen,* prob. fr. (assumed) MF *celer,* fr. L *caelare* to carve, fr. *caelum* chisel, fr. *caedere* to cut — more at CONCISE] **1** : to furnish (as a wooden ship) with a lining **2** : to furnish with a ceiling

ceil·ing \'sē-liŋ\ *n* **1 a** : the overhead inside lining of a room **b** : material used to ceil a wall or roof of a room **2** : something thought of as an overhanging shelter or a lofty canopy ⟨a ~ of stars⟩ **3 a** : the height above the ground from which prominent objects on the ground can be seen and identified **b** : the height above the ground of the base of the lowest layer of clouds when over half of the sky is obscured **4 a** : ABSOLUTE CEILING **b** : SERVICE CEILING **5** : an upper usu. prescribed limit ⟨a ~ on prices, rents, and wages⟩ — **ceil·inged** \-liŋd\ *adj*

ceil·om·e·ter \sē-'läm-ət-ər\ *n* [*ceiling* + *-o-* + *-meter*] : a photoelectric instrument for determining by triangulation the height of the cloud ceiling above the earth

cein·ture \saⁿ(n)-'t(y)u̇(ə)r, 'san-chər\ *n* [F, fr. L *cinctura* — more at CINCTURE] : a belt or sash for the waist

cel·an·dine \'sel-ən-,dīn, -,dēn\ *n* [ME *celidoine,* fr. MF, fr. L *chelidonia,* fr. fem. of *chelidonius* of the swallow, fr. Gk *chelidonios,* fr. *chelidon-, chelidōn* swallow] **1** : a yellow-flowered biennial herb (*Chelidonium majus*) of the poppy family **2** : a European perennial herb (*Ranunculus ficaria*) of the buttercup family that has been introduced locally into the U.S. — called also *lesser celandine*

-cele \,sēl\ *n comb form* [MF, fr. L, fr. Gk *kēlē;* akin to OE *hēala* hernia, OSlav *kyla*] : tumor : hernia ⟨varicocele⟩

cel·e·brant \'sel-ə-brənt\ *n* : one who celebrates; *specif* : the priest officiating at the Eucharist

cel·e·brate \'sel-ə-,brāt\ *vb* **-brat·ed; -brat·ing** [L *celebratus,* pp. of *celebrare* to frequent, celebrate, fr. *celebr-, celeber* much frequented, famous; akin to L *celer*] *vt* **1 :** to perform (a sacrament or solemn ceremony) publicly and with appropriate rites ⟨~ the mass⟩ **2 a :** to honor (as a holy day or feast day) by solemn ceremonies or by refraining from ordinary business **b :** to demonstrate satisfaction in (as an anniversary) by festivities or other deviation from routine **3 :** to hold up or play up for public acclaim : EXTOL ⟨his poetry ~s the glory of nature⟩ ⟨~ life⟩ ~ *vi* **1 :** to observe a holiday, perform a religious ceremony, or take part in a festival **2 :** to observe a notable occasion with festivities ***syn*** see KEEP — **cel·e·bra·tion** \,sel-ə-'brā-shən\ *n* — **cel·e·bra·tor** \'sel-ə-,brāt-ər\ *n* — **cel·e·bra·to·ry** \-brə-,tōr-ē, -,tȯr-\ *adj*

cel·e·brat·ed *adj* **:** widely known and often referred to ***syn*** see FAMOUS ***ant*** obscure — **cel·e·brat·ed·ness** *n*

ce·leb·ri·ty \sə-'leb-rət-ē\ *n, pl* **-ties 1 :** the state of being celebrated **2 :** a celebrated person

ce·le·ri·ac \sə-'ler-ē-,ak, -'lir-\ *n* [irreg. fr. *celery*] **:** a celery grown for its thickened edible root

ce·ler·i·ty \sə-'ler-ət-ē\ *n* [ME *celerite,* fr. MF *célérité,* fr. L *celeritat-, celeritas,* fr. *celer* swift — more at HOLD] **:** rapidity of motion or action

syn CELERITY, ALACRITY, LEGERITY *shared meaning element* **:** quickness in movement or action ***ant*** leisureliness

cel·ery \'sel-(ə-)rē\ *n, pl* **-er·ies** [prob. fr. It dial. *seleri,* pl. of *selero,* modif. of LL *selinon,* fr. Gk] **:** a European herb (*Apium graveolens*) of the carrot family; *specif* **:** one of a cultivated variety (*A. graveolens dulce*) with leafstalks eaten raw or cooked

ce·les·ta \sə-'les-tə\ *n* [F *célesta,* alter. of *céleste,* lit., heavenly, fr. L *caelestis*] **:** a keyboard instrument with hammers that strike steel plates producing a tone similar to that of a glockenspiel

[1]**ce·les·tial** \sə-'les(h)-chəl\ *adj* [ME, fr. MF, fr. L *caelestis* celestial, fr. *caelum* sky; akin to Skt *citra* bright] **1 :** of, relating to, or suggesting heaven or divinity **2 :** of or relating to the sky or visible heavens ⟨the sun, moon, and stars are ~ bodies⟩ **3 a :** ETHEREAL, OTHERWORLDLY **b :** OLYMPIAN, SUPREME **4** [*Celestial* Empire, old name for China] *cap* **:** of or relating to China or the Chinese — **ce·les·tial·ly** \-chə-lē\ *adv*

[2]**celestial** *n* **1 :** a heavenly or mythical being **2** *cap* **:** CHINESE 1a

celestial equator *n* **:** the great circle on the celestial sphere midway between the celestial poles

celestial globe *n* **:** a globe depicting the celestial bodies

celestial hierarchy *n* **:** a traditional hierarchy of angels ranked from lowest to highest into the following nine orders: angels, archangels, principalities, powers, virtues, dominions, thrones, cherubim, and seraphim

celestial marriage *n* **:** a special order of Mormon marriage solemnized in a Mormon temple and held to be binding for a future life as well as the present one

celestial navigation *n* **:** navigation by observation of the positions of celestial bodies

celestial pole *n* **:** one of the two points on the celestial sphere around which the diurnal rotation of the stars appears to take place

celestial sphere *n* **:** an imaginary sphere of infinite radius against which the celestial bodies appear to be projected and of which the apparent dome of the visible sky forms half

ce·les·tite \'sel-ə-,stīt, sə-'les-,tīt\ *n* [G *zölestin,* fr. L *caelestis*] **:** a usu. white mineral $SrSO_4$ consisting of the sulfate of strontium

ce·li·ac \'sē-lē-,ak\ *adj* [L *coeliacus,* fr. Gk *koiliakos,* fr. *koilia* cavity, fr. *koilos* hollow — more at CAVE] **:** of or relating to the abdominal cavity

celiac disease *n* **:** a chronic nutritional disturbance in young children characterized by defective digestion and utilization of fats and by abdominal distention, diarrhea, and fatty stools

cel·i·ba·cy \'sel-ə-bə-sē\ *n* **1 :** the state of not being married **2 a :** abstention from sexual intercourse **b :** abstention by vow from marriage

cel·i·bate \'sel-ə-bət\ *n* [L *caelibatus,* fr. *caelib-, caelebs* unmarried; akin to Skt *kevala* alone and to OE *libban* to live] **:** one who lives in celibacy — **celibate** *adj*

cell \'sel\ *n* [ME, fr. OE, religious house and OF *celle* hermit's cell, fr. L *cella* small room; akin to L *celare* to conceal — more at HELL] **1 :** a small religious house dependent on a monastery or convent **2 a :** a one-room dwelling occupied by a solitary person (as a hermit) **b :** a single room (as in a convent or prison) usu. for one person **3 :** a small compartment (as in a honeycomb), receptacle (as the calyculus of a polyp), cavity (as in a plant ovary), or bounded space (as in an insect wing) **4 :** a small usu. microscopic mass of protoplasm bounded externally by a semipermeable membrane, usu. including one or more nuclei and various nonliving products, capable alone or interacting with other cells of performing all the fundamental functions of life, and forming the least structural unit of living matter capable of functioning independently **5 a** (1) **:** a receptacle (as a cup or jar) containing electrodes and an electrolyte either for generating electricity by chemical action or for use in electrolysis (2) **:** FUEL CELL **b :** a single unit in a device for converting radiant energy into electrical energy or for varying the intensity of an electrical current in accordance with radiation **6 :** a set of points in one-to-one correspondence with a set in a euclidean space of any number of dimensions **7 :** the basic and usu. smallest unit of an organization or movement; *esp* **:** the primary unit of a Communist organization **8 :** a portion of the atmosphere that behaves as a unit **9 :** a basic subdivision of a computer memory that is addressable and can hold one unit of a computer's basic operating data unit (as a word)

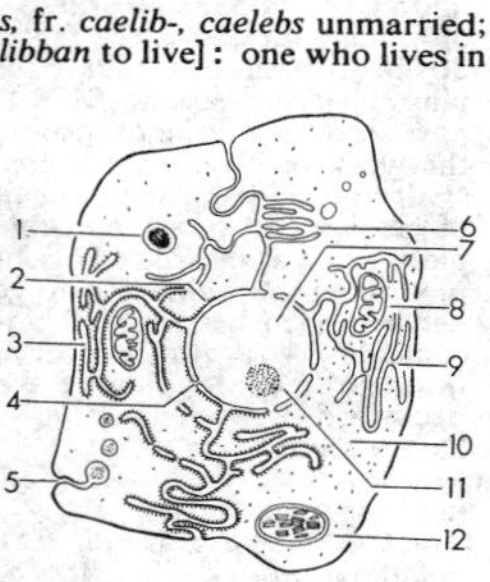

a schematic cell 4: *1* lysosome, *2* nuclear membrane, *3* endoplasmic reticulum with associated ribosomes, *4* nuclear pore, *5* intrusion of cell membrane, *6* Golgi apparatus, *7* nucleus, *8* mitochondrion, *9* endoplasmic reticulum, *10* cytoplasm and ribosomes, *11* nucleolus, *12* chloroplast

cel·lar \'sel-ər\ *n* [ME *celer,* fr. AF, fr. L *cellarium* storeroom, fr. *cella*] **1 a :** BASEMENT **b :** the lowest rank; *esp* **:** the lowest place in the standings (as of an athletic league) **2 :** a stock of wines

cel·lar·age \'sel-ə-rij\ *n* **1 :** cellar space esp. for storage **2 :** charge for storage in a cellar

cel·lar·er \'sel-ər-ər\ *n* [ME *celerer,* fr. OF, fr. LL *cellariarius,* fr. L *cellarium*] **:** an official (as in a monastery) in charge of provisions

cel·lar·ette *or* **cel·lar·et** \,sel-ə-'ret\ *n* **:** a case or sideboard for holding bottles of wine or liquor

cell body *n* **:** the nucleus-containing central part of a neuron exclusive of its axons and dendrites

cell division *n* **:** the process by which cells multiply involving both nuclear and cytoplasmic division — compare MEIOSIS, MITOSIS

-celled \'seld\ *adj comb form* **:** having (such or so many) cells ⟨single-*celled* organisms⟩

cell membrane *n* **1 :** PLASMA MEMBRANE **2 :** a cell wall

cel·lo \'chel-(,)ō\ *n, pl* **cellos** [short for *violoncello*] **:** the bass member of the violin family tuned an octave below the viola — **cel·list** \'chel-əst\ *n*

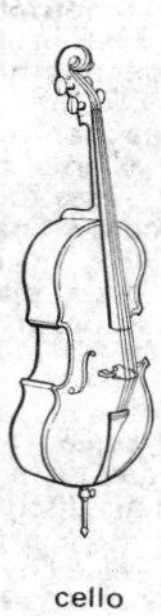

cello

cel·lo·bi·ose \,sel-ə-'bī-,ōs, -,ōz\ *n* [ISV *cellulose* + *-o-* + *biose* (disaccharide), fr. [1]*bi-* + *-ose*] **:** a faintly sweet disaccharide $C_{12}H_{22}O_{11}$ obtained by partial hydrolysis of cellulose

cel·loi·din \se-'lȯid-ᵊn\ *n* [*cell*ulose + *-oid* + *-in*] **:** a purified pyroxylin used chiefly in microscopy

cel·lo·phane \'sel-ə-,fān\ *n* [F, fr. *cellulose* + *-phane* (as in *diaphane* diaphanous, fr. ML *diaphanus*)] **:** regenerated cellulose in thin transparent sheets used esp. for packaging

cell plate *n* **:** a disk formed in the phragmoplast of a dividing plant cell that eventually forms the middle lamella of the wall between the daughter cells

cell sap *n* **1 :** the liquid contents of a plant cell vacuole **2 :** HYALOPLASM

cell theory *n* **:** a theory in biology that includes one or both of the statements that the cell is the fundamental structural and functional unit of living matter and that the organism is composed of autonomous cells with its properties being the sum of those of its cells

cel·lu·lar \'sel-yə-lər\ *adj* [NL *cellularis,* fr. *cellula* living cell, fr. L, dim. of *cella* small room] **1 :** of, relating to, or consisting of cells **2 :** containing cavities **:** having a porous texture ⟨~ rocks⟩ — **cel·lu·lar·i·ty** \,sel-yə-'lar-ət-ē\ *n* — **cel·lu·lar·ly** \'sel-yə-lər-lē\ *adv*

cel·lu·lase \'sel-yə-,lās, -,lāz\ *n* [ISV *cellulose* + *-ase*] **:** an enzyme that hydrolyzes cellulose

cel·lule \'sel-(,)yü(ə)l\ *n* [L *cellula*] **:** a small cell

cel·lu·li·tis \,sel-yə-'līt-əs\ *n* [NL, fr. *cellula*] **:** diffuse and esp. subcutaneous inflammation of connective tissue

cel·lu·loid \'sel-(y)ə-,lȯid\ *n* [fr. *Celluloid,* a trademark] **1 :** a tough flammable thermoplastic composed essentially of cellulose nitrate and camphor **2 :** a motion-picture film ⟨a work . . . now making its third appearance on ~ — John McCarten⟩ — **celluloid** *adj*

cel·lu·lo·lyt·ic \,sel-yə-lō-'lit-ik\ *adj* [*cellulose* + *-o-* + *-lytic*] **:** hydrolyzing or having the capacity to hydrolyze cellulose ⟨~ bacteria⟩ ⟨~ activity⟩

cel·lu·lose \'sel-yə-,lōs, -,lōz\ *n* [F, fr. *cellule* living cell, fr. NL *cellula*] **:** a polysaccharide $(C_6H_{10}O_5)_x$ of glucose units that constitutes the chief part of the cell walls of plants, occurs naturally in such fibrous products as cotton and kapok, and is the raw material of many manufactured goods (as paper, rayon, and cellophane)

cellulose acetate *n* **:** any of several compounds insoluble in water that are formed esp. by the action of acetic acid, anhydride of acetic acid, and sulfuric acid on cellulose and are used for making textile fibers, packaging sheets, photographic films, and varnishes

cellulose nitrate *n* **:** any of several esters of nitric acid formed by the action of nitric acid on cellulose (as paper, linen, or cotton) and used for making explosives, plastics, rayon, and varnishes

[1]**cel·lu·los·ic** \,sel-yə-'lō-sik, -zik\ *adj* **:** of, relating to, or made from cellulose ⟨~ fibers⟩

[2]**cellulosic** *n* **:** a substance made from cellulose or a derivative of cellulose

cell wall *n* **:** the firm nonliving and usu. chiefly cellulose wall that encloses and supports most plant cells

Cel·sius \'sel-sē-əs, -shəs\ *adj* [Anders *Celsius*] **:** CENTIGRADE ⟨10° ~⟩

celt \'selt\ *n* [LL *celtis* chisel] **:** a prehistoric stone or metal implement shaped like a chisel or ax head

Celt \'selt, 'kelt\ *n* [F *Celte,* sing. of *Celtes,* fr. L *Celtae*] **1 :** a member of a division of the early Indo-European peoples distributed from the British Isles and Spain to Asia Minor **2 :** a modern Gael, Highland Scot, Irishman, Welshman, Cornishman, or Breton

[1]**Celt·ic** \'sel-tik, 'kel-\ *adj* **:** of, relating to, or characteristic of the Celts or their languages

[2]**Celtic** *n* **:** a group of Indo-European languages usu. subdivided into Brythonic and Goidelic and confined to Brittany, Wales, western Ireland, and the Scottish Highlands — see INDO-EUROPEAN LANGUAGES table

ə abut	ᵊ kitten	ər further	a back	ā bake	ä cot, cart
aù out	ch chin	e less	ē easy	g gift	i trip ī life
j joke	ŋ sing	ō flow	ȯ flaw	ȯi coin	th thin t͟h this
ü loot	ù foot	y yet	yü few	yù furious	zh vision

Celtic cross *n* : a cross having essentially the form of a Latin cross with a ring about the intersection of the crossbar and upright shaft — see CROSS illustration

Celt·i·cist \'sel-tə-səst, 'kel-\ *n* : a specialist in Celtic languages or cultures

cem *abbr* cement

cem·ba·lo \'chem-bə-ˌlō\ *n, pl* **-ba·li** \-(ˌ)lē\ *or* **-balos** [It] : HARPSICHORD

1ce·ment \si-'ment\ *n* [ME *sement,* fr. OF *ciment,* fr. L *caementum* stone chips used in making mortar, fr. *caedere* to cut — more at CONCISE] **1** : a powder of alumina, silica, lime, iron oxide, and magnesia burned together in a kiln and finely pulverized and used as an ingredient of mortar and concrete **2** : a binding element or agency: as **a** : a substance to make objects adhere to each other **b** : something serving to unite firmly ⟨justice is the ~ that holds a political community together —R. M. Hutchins⟩ **3** : CEMENTUM **4** : a plastic composition usu. made of zinc, copper, or silica for filling dental cavities **5** : the fine-grained groundmass or glass of a porphyry

2cement *vt* **1** : to unite or make firm by or as if by cement **2** : to overlay with concrete **~** *vi* : to become cemented — **ce·ment·er** *n*

ce·men·ta·tion \ˌsē-ˌmen-'tā-shən\ *n* **1** : the act or process of cementing : the state of being cemented **2** : a process of surrounding a solid with a powder and heating the whole so that the solid is changed by chemical combination with the powder

ce·ment·ite \si-'ment-ˌīt\ *n* [1*cement*] : a hard brittle iron carbide Fe_3C in steel, cast iron, and iron-carbon alloys

ce·men·ti·tious \ˌsē-ˌmen-'tish-əs\ *adj* : having the properties of cement

ce·men·tum \si-'ment-əm\ *n* [NL, fr. L *caementum*] : a specialized external bony layer of the part of a tooth normally within the gum — see TOOTH illustration

cem·e·tery \'sem-ə-ˌter-ē\ *n, pl* **-ter·ies** [ME *cimitery,* fr. MF *cimitere,* fr. LL *coemeterium,* fr. Gk *koimētērion* sleeping chamber, burial place, fr. *koiman* to put to sleep; akin to L *cunae* cradle] : a burial ground

CEMF *abbr* counter electromotive force

cen *abbr* central

cen- *or* **ceno-** *or* **caen-** *or* **caeno-** *comb form* [Gk *kain-, kaino-,* fr. *kainos* — more at RECENT] : new : recent ⟨*Cenozoic*⟩

cen·a·cle \'sen-i-kəl\ *n* [LL *cenaculum,* the room where Christ and his disciples had the Last Supper, fr. L, dining room, fr. *cena* dinner] : a retreat house; *esp* : one for Roman Catholic women directed by nuns of the Society of Our Lady of the Cenacle

-cene \ˌsēn\ *adj comb form* [Gk *kainos*] : recent — in names of geologic periods ⟨Eocene⟩

cen·o·bite \'sen-ə-ˌbīt, *esp Brit* 'sēn-\ *n* [LL *coenobita,* fr. *coenobium* monastery, fr. LGk *koinobion,* deriv. of Gk *koin-* coen- + *bios* life — more at QUICK] : a member of a religious group living together in a monastic community — **cen·o·bit·ic** \ˌsen-ə-'bit-ik, ˌsēn-\ *or* **cen·o·bit·i·cal** \-i-kəl\ *adj*

ce·no·ge·net·ic \ˌsē-nə-jə-'net-ik, ˌsen-ə-\ *adj* [G *zänogenetisch,* fr. *zän-* cen- + *genetisch* genetic] : relating to or being a specialized adaptive character (as the amnion or chorion surrounding the embryo of higher vertebrates) that is not represented in primitive ancestral forms — **ce·no·ge·net·i·cal·ly** \-i-k(ə-)lē\ *adv*

ce·no·spe·cies \'sē-nə-ˌspē-(ˌ)shēz, 'sen-ə-, -(ˌ)sēz\ *n* [*coen-* + *species*] **1** : the sum of the possible expressions of a complex genotype **2** : a group of biological units capable by reason of closely related genotypes of essentially free gene interchange

ceno·taph \'sen-ə-ˌtaf\ *n* [F *cénotaphe,* fr. L *cenotaphium,* fr. Gk *kenotaphion,* fr. *kenos* empty + *taphos* tomb; akin to Arm *sin* empty — more at EPITAPH] : a tomb or a monument erected in honor of a person or group of persons whose remains are elsewhere

ce·no·te \si-'nōt-ē\ *n* [Sp, fr. Maya *tzonot*] : a deep sinkhole in limestone with a pool at the bottom that is found esp. in Yucatán

Ce·no·zo·ic \ˌsē-nə-'zō-ik, ˌsen-ə-\ *adj* : of, relating to, or being an era of geological history that extends from the beginning of the Tertiary period to the present time and is marked by a rapid evolution of mammals and birds and of grasses, shrubs, and higher flowering plants and by little change in the invertebrates; *also* : relating to the system of rocks formed in this era — see GEOLOGIC TIME table — **Cenozoic** *n*

cense \'sen(t)s\ *vt* **censed; cens·ing** [ME *censen,* prob. short for *encensen* to incense, fr. MF *encenser,* fr. LL *incensare,* fr. *incensum* incense] : to perfume esp. with a censer

cen·ser \'sen(t)-sər\ *n* : a vessel for burning incense; *esp* : a covered incense burner swung on chains in a religious ritual

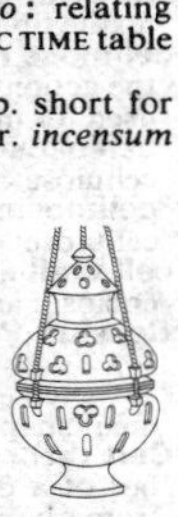

censer

1cen·sor \'sen(t)-sər\ *n* [L, fr. *censēre* to assess, tax; akin to Skt *śaṁsati* he recites] **1** : one of two magistrates of early Rome acting as census takers, assessors, and inspectors of morals and conduct **2** : one who supervises conduct and morals: as **a** : an official who examines publications or films for objectionable matter **b** : an official (as in time of war) who reads communications (as letters) and deletes material considered harmful to the interests of his organization **3** : a hypothetical psychic agency that represses unacceptable notions before they reach consciousness — **cen·so·ri·al** \sen-'sōr-ē-əl, -'sȯr-\ *adj*

2censor *vt* **cen·sored; cen·sor·ing** \'sen(t)s-(ə-)riŋ\ : to subject to censorship

cen·so·ri·ous \sen-'sōr-ē-əs, -'sȯr-\ *adj* [L *censorius* of a censor, fr. *censor*] : marked by or given to censure ***syn*** see CRITICAL ***ant*** eulogistic — **cen·so·ri·ous·ly** *adv* — **cen·so·ri·ous·ness** *n*

cen·sor·ship \'sen(t)-sər-ˌship\ *n* **1 a** : the institution, system, or practice of censoring **b** : the actions or practices of censors; *esp* : censorial control exercised repressively **2** : the office, power, or term of a Roman censor **3** : exclusion from consciousness by the psychic censor

cen·sur·able \'sench-(ə-)rə-bəl\ *adj* : deserving or open to censure

1cen·sure \'sen-chər\ *n* [L *censura,* fr. *censēre*] **1** : a judgment involving condemnation **2** *archaic* : OPINION, JUDGMENT **3** : the act of blaming or condemning sternly **4** : an official reprimand

2censure *vt* **cen·sured; cen·sur·ing** \'sench-(ə-)riŋ\ **1** *obs* : ESTIMATE, JUDGE **2** : to find fault with and criticize as blameworthy ***syn*** see CRITICIZE — **cen·sur·er** \'sen-chər-ər\ *n*

cen·sus \'sen(t)-səs\ *n* [L, fr. *censēre*] **1** : a count of the population and a property evaluation in early Rome **2** : a usu. complete enumeration of a population; *specif* : a periodic governmental enumeration of population **3** : COUNT, TALLY — **census** *vt*

1cent \'sent\ *n* [MF, hundred, fr. L *centum* — more at HUNDRED] **1** : a monetary unit equal to $\frac{1}{100}$ of a basic unit of value — see *dollar, gulden, leone, piaster, rand, rupee, shilling* at MONEY table **2** : a coin, token, or note representing one cent

2cent *abbr* **1** centigrade **2** central **3** centum **4** century

cen·tal \'sent-ᵊl\ *n* [L *centum* + E *-al* (as in *quintal*)] *chiefly Brit* : a short hundredweight

cent·are \'sen-ˌta(ə)r, -ˌte(ə)r, -ˌtär\ *or* **cen·ti·are** \'sent-ē-ˌa(ə)r, 'sänt-, -ˌe(ə)r, -ˌär\ *n* [F *centiare,* fr. *centi-* hundred + *are*] — see METRIC SYSTEM table

cen·taur \'sen-ˌtȯ(ə)r\ *n* [ME, fr. L *Centaurus,* fr. Gk *Kentauros*] : one of a race fabled to be half man and half horse and to live in the mountains of Thessaly

cen·tau·rea \sen-'tȯr-ē-ə\ *n* [NL, genus name, fr. ML] : any of a large genus (*Centaurea*) of composite herbs (as knapweed) including several cultivated for their showy heads of tubular florets

Cen·tau·rus \-'tȯr-əs\ *n* [L (gen. *Centauri*)] : a southern constellation between the Southern Cross and Hydra

cen·tau·ry \'sen-ˌtȯr-ē\ *n, pl* **-ries** [ME *centaure,* fr. MF *centaurée,* fr. ML *centaurea,* fr. L *centaureum,* fr. Gk *kentaureion,* fr. *Kentauros*] **1** : any of a genus (*Centaurium*) of low herbs of the gentian family; *esp* : an Old World herb (*C. umbellatum*) formerly used as a tonic **2** : an American plant (*Sabatia angularis*) closely related to centaury

1cen·ta·vo \sen-'täv-(ˌ)ō\ *n, pl* **-vos** [Sp, lit., hundredth, fr. L *centum* hundred] — see *colon, cordoba, lempira, peso, quetzal, sol, sucre* at MONEY table

2cen·ta·vo \-'täv-(ˌ)ü, -(ˌ)ō\ *n, pl* **-vos** [Pg, fr. Sp] — see *cruzeiro, escudo* at MONEY table

cen·te·nar·i·an \ˌsent-ᵊn-'er-ē-ən\ *n* : one that is 100 years old or older — **centenarian** *adj*

cen·te·na·ry \sen-'ten-ə-rē, 'sent-ᵊn-ˌer-ē, *esp Brit* sen-'tē-nə-rē\ *n, pl* **-ries** [LL *centenarium,* fr. L *centenarius* of a hundred, fr. *centeni* one hundred each, fr. *centum* hundred — more at HUNDRED] : CENTENNIAL — **centenary** *adj*

cen·ten·ni·al \sen-'ten-ē-əl\ *n* [L *centum* + E *-ennial* (as in *biennial*)] : a 100th anniversary or its celebration — **centennial** *adj* — **cen·ten·ni·al·ly** \-ə-lē\ *adv*

1cen·ter \'sent-ər\ *n* [ME *centre,* fr. MF, fr. L *centrum,* fr. Gk *kentron* sharp point, center of a circle, fr. *kentein* to prick; akin to OHG *hantag* pointed, Latvian *sīts* hunting spear] **1 a** : the point around which a circle or sphere is described; *broadly* : a point that is related to a geometrical figure in such a way that for any point on the figure there is another point on the figure such that a straight line joining the two points is bisected by the original point — called also *center of symmetry* **b** : the center of the circle inscribed in a regular polygon **2 a** : a point, area, person, or thing that is most important or pivotal in relation to an indicated activity, interest, or condition ⟨a railroad ~⟩ ⟨the ~ of the controversy⟩ **b** : a source from which something originates ⟨a propaganda ~⟩ **c** : a group of nerve cells having a common function ⟨respiratory ~⟩ **d** : a region of concentrated population ⟨an urban ~⟩ **3 a** : the middle part (as of the forehead or a stage) **b** *often cap* (1) : a grouping of political figures holding moderate views esp. between those of conservatives and liberals (2) : the views of such politicians (3) : the adherents of such views **4** : a player occupying a middle position on a team: as **a** : the football player in the middle of a line who passes the ball between his legs to a back to start a down **b** : the usu. tallest player on a basketball team who usu. plays near the basket **5 a** : one of two tapered rods which support work in a lathe or grinding machine and about or with which the work revolves **b** : a conical recess in the end of work (as a shaft) for receiving such a center

2center *vb* **cen·tered; cen·ter·ing** \'sent-ə-riŋ, 'sen-triŋ\ *vt* **1** : to place or fix at or around a center or central area or position ⟨~ the picture on the wall⟩ **2** : to gather to a center : CONCENTRATE ⟨~*s* her hopes on her son⟩ **3** : to adjust (as lenses) so that the axes coincide **4 a** : to pass (a ball or puck) from either side toward the middle of the playing area **b** : to hand or pass (a football) backward between one's legs to a back to start a down **~** *vi* : to have a center : FOCUS

cen·ter·board \'sent-ər-ˌbō(ə)rd, -ˌbȯ(ə)rd\ *n* : a retractable keel used esp. in sailboats

cen·tered \'sent-ərd\ *adj* **1** : having a center — often used in combination ⟨a dark-*centered* coneflower⟩ **2** : having a center of curvature — often used in combination ⟨a 3-*centered* arch⟩

center field *n* **1** : the part of the baseball outfield between right and left field **2** : the position of the player for defending center field — **center fielder** *n*

cen·ter·line \ˌsent-ər-'līn\ *n* : a real or imaginary line that is equidistant from the surface or sides of something (as a machine part or a roadway)

center of curvature : the center of the osculating circle at a given point of a curve

center of gravity **1** : CENTER OF MASS **2** : the point at which the entire weight of a body may be considered as concentrated so that if supported at this point the body would remain in equilibrium in any position **3** : CENTER 2a

center of mass : the point in a body or system of bodies at which the whole mass may be considered as concentrated

cen·ter·piece \'sent-ər-ˌpēs\ *n* : an object occupying a central position; *specif* : an adornment in the center of a table

center punch n : a hand punch consisting of a short steel bar with a hardened conical point at one end used for marking the centers of holes to be drilled

cen·tes·i·mal \sen-ˈtes-ə-məl\ adj [L centesimus hundredth, fr. centum] : marked by or relating to division into hundredths

¹**cen·tes·i·mo** \chen-ˈtez-ə-ˌmō\ n, pl -mi \-(ˌ)mē\ [It] — see lira at MONEY table

²**cen·tes·i·mo** \sen-ˈtes-ə-ˌmō\ n, pl -mos [Sp centésimo] — see balboa, escudo, peso at MONEY table

centi- comb form [F&L; F, hundredth, fr. L, hundred, fr. centum — more at HUNDRED] 1 : hundred ⟨centipede⟩ 2 : hundredth part ⟨centisecond⟩

cen·ti·grade \ˈsent-ə-ˌgrād, ˈsänt-\ adj [F, fr. L centi- hundred + F grade] relating to, conforming to, or having a thermometric scale on which the interval between the freezing point and the boiling point of water is divided into 100 degrees with 0° representing the freezing point and 100° the boiling point ⟨10° ∼⟩ — abbr. C

cen·ti·gram \-ˌgram\ n — see METRIC SYSTEM table

cen·ti·li·ter \ˈsent-i-ˌlēt-ər, ˈsänt-\ n — see METRIC SYSTEM table

cen·til·lion \sen-ˈtil-yən\ n, often attrib [L centum + E -illion (as in million)] — see NUMBER table

cen·time \ˈsän-ˌtēm, ˈsänt-\ n [F, fr. cent hundred, fr. L centum] — see dinar, franc, gourde at MONEY table

cen·ti·me·ter \ˈsent-ə-ˌmēt-ər, ˈsänt-\ n — see METRIC SYSTEM table

centimeter–gram–second adj : of, relating to, or being a system of units based on the centimeter as the unit of length, the gram as the unit of mass, and the mean solar second as the unit of time — abbr. cgs

cen·ti·mo \ˈsent-ə-ˌmō\ n, pl -mos [Sp céntimo] — see bolivar, colon, guarani, peseta at MONEY table

cen·ti·pede \ˈsent-ə-ˌpēd\ n [L centipeda, fr. centi- + ped-, pes foot — more at FOOT] : any of a class (Chilopoda) of long flattened many-segmented predaceous arthropods with each segment bearing one pair of legs of which the foremost pair is modified into poison fangs

cent·ner \ˈsent-nər\ n [prob. fr. LG] : a unit of weight used in Germany and Scandinavia usu. equal to 110.23 pounds; also : a unit used in the U.S.S.R. equal to 220.46 pounds

cen·to \ˈsen-(ˌ)tō\ n, pl cen·to·nes \sen-ˈtō-(ˌ)nēz\ [LL, fr. L, patchwork garment; akin to OHG hadara rag, Skt kanthā patched garment] : a literary work made up of parts from other works

CENTO abbr Central Treaty Organization

centr- or **centri-** or **centro-** comb form [Gk kentr-, kentro-, fr. kentron center — more at CENTER] : center ⟨centrifugal⟩ ⟨centroid⟩

¹**cen·tral** \ˈsen-trəl\ adj [L centralis, fr. centrum center — more at CENTER] 1 : containing or constituting a center 2 : of cardinal importance : ESSENTIAL, PRINCIPAL ⟨the ∼ character of the novel⟩ 3 a : situated at, in, or near the center ⟨the plains of ∼ North America⟩ b : easily accessible from outlying districts ⟨a ∼ location for the new theater⟩ 4 a : centrally placed and superseding separate scattered units ⟨∼ heating⟩ b : controlling or directing local or branch activities ⟨decided by the ∼ committee⟩ 5 : holding to a middle between extremes : MODERATE 6 : of, relating to, or comprising the brain and spinal cord; also : originating within the central nervous system ⟨∼ deafness⟩ — **cen·tral·ly** \-trə-lē\ adv

²**central** n 1 : a telephone exchange or operator 2 : a central office or bureau usu. controlling others ⟨weather ∼⟩

central angle n : an angle formed by two radii of a circle

central city n : a city that constitutes the densely populated center of a metropolitan area and is characterized by a concentration of cultural and commercial facilities serving the area and by a population disproportionately high in disadvantaged persons

cen·tral·ism \ˈsen-trə-ˌliz-əm\ n : the concentration of power and control in the central authority of an organization (as a political or educational system) — compare FEDERALISM — **cen·tral·ist** \-ləst\ n or adj — **cen·tral·is·tic** \ˌsen-trə-ˈlis-tik\ adj

cen·tral·i·ty \sen-ˈtral-ət-ē\ n, pl -ties 1 : the quality or state of being central 2 : central situation 3 : tendency to remain in or at the center

cen·tral·ize \ˈsen-trə-ˌlīz\ vb -ized; -iz·ing vi : to form a center : cluster around a center ∼ vt 1 : to bring to a center : CONSOLIDATE ⟨∼ all the data in one file⟩ 2 : to concentrate by placing power and authority in a center or central organization — **cen·tral·i·za·tion** \ˌsen-trə-lə-ˈzā-shən\ n — **cen·tral·iz·er** \ˈsen-trə-ˌlī-zər\ n

central limit theorem n : any of several fundamental theorems of probability and statistics that state the conditions under which the distribution of a sum of independent random variables is approximated by the normal distribution; esp : a special case of the central limit theorem which is much applied in sampling and which states that the distribution of a mean of a sample from a population with finite variance is approximated by the normal distribution as the number in the sample becomes large

central nervous system n : the part of the nervous system which in vertebrates consists of the brain and spinal cord, to which sensory impulses are transmitted and from which motor impulses pass out, and which supervises and coordinates the activity of the entire nervous system

central processing unit n : PROCESSOR 2a(2)

central tendency n : clustering of the values of a statistical distribution that is usu. measured by the arithmetic mean, mode, or median

central time n, often cap C : the time of the 6th time zone west of Greenwich that includes the central U.S. — see TIME ZONE illustration

cen·tre chiefly Brit var of CENTER

cen·tric \ˈsen-trik\ adj [Gk kentrikos of the center, fr. kentron] 1 : located in or at a center : CENTRAL ⟨a ∼ point⟩ 2 : concentrated about or directed to a center ⟨a ∼ activity⟩ 3 : of or relating to a nerve center 4 : of, relating to, or having a centromere 5 : of, relating to, or resembling an order (Centrales) of diatoms having the surface markings centrally arranged — **cen·tri·cal·ly** \-tri-k(ə-)lē\ adv — **cen·tric·i·ty** \sen-ˈtris-ət-ē\ n

-cen·tric \ˈsen-trik\ adj comb form [ML -centricus, fr. L centrum center] : having (such) a center or (such or so many) centers ⟨polycentric⟩ : having (something specified) as its center ⟨heliocentric⟩

¹**cen·trif·u·gal** \sen-ˈtrif-yə-gəl, -ˈtrif-i-gəl\ adj [NL centrifugus, fr. centr- + L fugere to flee — more at FUGITIVE] 1 : proceeding or acting in a direction away from a center or axis 2 : using or acting by centrifugal force ⟨a ∼ pump⟩ 3 : EFFERENT 4 : tending away from centralization : SEPARATIST ⟨∼ tendencies in modern society⟩ — **cen·trif·u·gal·ly** \-gə-lē\ adv

²**centrifugal** n : a centrifugal machine or a drum in such a machine

centrifugal force n 1 : the force that tends to impel a thing or parts of a thing outward from a center of rotation 2 : the force that an object moving along a circular path exerts on the body constraining the object and that acts outwardly away from the center of rotation ⟨a stone whirled about on the end of a string exerts centrifugal force on the string⟩

cen·trif·u·ga·tion \ˌsen-trə-fyü-ˈgā-shən\ n : the process of centrifuging

¹**cen·tri·fuge** \ˈsen-trə-ˌfyüj\ n [F, fr. centrifuge centrifugal, fr. NL centrifugus] : a machine using centrifugal force for separating substances of different densities, for removing moisture, or for simulating gravitational effects

²**centrifuge** vt -fuged; -fug·ing : to subject to centrifugal action esp. in a centrifuge

cen·tri·ole \ˈsen-trē-ˌol\ n [G zentriol, fr. zentrum center] : one of a pair of cellular organelles that are adjacent to the nucleus, function in the formation of the mitotic apparatus, and consist of a cylinder with nine microtubules arranged peripherally in a circle

cen·trip·e·tal \sen-ˈtrip-ət-³l\ adj [NL centripetus, fr. centr- + L petere to go to, seek — more at FEATHER] 1 : proceeding or acting in a direction toward a center or axis 2 : AFFERENT 3 : tending toward centralization : UNIFYING ⟨∼ tendencies in Western society⟩ — **cen·trip·e·tal·ly** \-³l-ē\ adv

centripetal force n : the force that is necessary to keep an object moving in a circular path and that is directed inward toward the center of rotation ⟨a string on the end of which a stone is whirled about exerts centripetal force on the stone⟩

cen·trist \ˈsen-trəst\ n 1 often cap : a member of a center party 2 : one who holds moderate views — **cen·trism** \-ˌtriz-əm\ n

cen·troid \ˈsen-ˌtrȯid\ n : CENTER OF MASS — **cen·troi·dal** \sen-ˈtrȯid-³l\ adj

cen·tro·mere \ˈsen-trə-ˌmi(ə)r\ n [ISV] : the point on a chromosome by which it appears to attach to the spindle in mitosis — **cen·tro·mer·ic** \ˌsen-trə-ˈmi(ə)r-ik, -ˈmer-\ adj

cen·tro·some \ˈsen-trə-ˌsōm\ n [G zentrosom, fr. zentr- centr- + -som -some] 1 : the centriole-containing region of clear cytoplasm adjacent to the cell nucleus 2 : CENTRIOLE — **cen·tro·so·mic** \ˌsen-trə-ˈsō-mik\ adj

cen·tro·sphere \ˈsen-trə-ˌsfi(ə)r\ n [ISV] 1 : the differentiated layer of cytoplasm surrounding the centriole within the centrosome 2 : the central part of the earth composed of very dense material

cen·trum \ˈsen-trəm\ n, pl centrums or cen·tra \-trə\ [L — more at CENTER] 1 : CENTER 2 : the body of a vertebra — see VERTEBRA illustration

cen·tum \ˈkent-əm, ˈken-ˌtùm\ adj [L, hundred; fr. the fact that its initial sound (a velar stop) is the representative of an IE palatal stop — more at HUNDRED] : of, relating to, or constituting an Indo-European language group characterized by the retention of the Proto-Indo-European stops k, g, and gh in certain environments — compare SATEM

cen·tu·ri·on \sen-ˈt(y)ùr-ē-ən\ n [ME, fr. MF & L; MF, fr. L centurion-, centurio, fr. centuria] : an officer commanding a Roman century

cen·tu·ry \ˈsench-(ə-)rē\ n, pl -ries [L centuria, irreg. fr. centum hundred] 1 : a subdivision of the Roman legion 2 : a group, sequence, or series of 100 like things 3 : a period of 100 years esp. of the Christian era or of the preceding period of human history 4 : a race over a hundred units (as yards or miles)

century plant n : a Mexican agave (Agave americana) maturing and flowering only once in many years and then dying

ceorl \ˈchā-ˌȯr(ə)l\ n [OE — more at CHURL] : a freeman of the lowest rank in Anglo-Saxon England

cephal- or **cephalo-** comb form [L, fr. Gk kephal-, kephalo-, fr. kephalē] : head ⟨cephalad⟩ ⟨Cephalopoda⟩

ceph·a·lad \ˈsef-ə-ˌlad\ adv : toward the head or anterior end of the body

ce·phal·ic \sə-ˈfal-ik\ adj [MF céphalique, fr. L cephalicus, fr. Gk kephalikos, fr. kephalē head; akin to OHG gebal skull, ON gafl gable, Toch A śpāl- head] 1 : of or relating to the head 2 : directed toward or situated on or in or near the head — **ce·phal·i·cal·ly** \-i-k(ə-)lē\ adv

cephalic index n : the ratio multiplied by 100 of the maximum breadth of the head to its maximum length

ceph·a·lin \ˈkef-ə-lən, ˈsef-\ n [ISV] : any of various acidic phosphatides of living tissues (as of the brain) with marked thromboplastic activity

ceph·a·li·za·tion \ˌsef-ə-lə-ˈzā-shən\ n : an evolutionary tendency to specialization of the body with concentration of sensory and neural organs in an anterior head

ceph·a·lom·e·try \ˌsef-ə-ˈläm-ə-trē\ n [ISV] : the science of measuring the head — **ceph·a·lo·met·ric** \-lō-ˈme-trik\ adj

cephalic index: dotted lines in the brachycephalic (right) and dolichocephalic (left) skulls above indicate measurements taken

ceph·a·lo·pod \'sef-ə-lə-,päd\ *n* [deriv. of *cephal-* + Gk *pod-, pous* foot — more at FOOT] : any of a class (Cephalopoda) of mollusks including the squids, cuttlefishes, and octopuses that have a tubular siphon under the head, a group of muscular arms around the front of the head which are usu. furnished with suckers, highly developed eyes, and usu. a bag of inky fluid which can be ejected for defense or concealment — **cephalopod** *adj* — **ceph·a·lop·o·dan** \,sef-ə-'läp-əd-ən\ *adj or n*
ceph·a·lor·i·dine \,sef-ə-'lȯr-ə-,dēn, -'lär-\ *n* [prob. fr. *cephalosporin* + *-idine*] : a broad-spectrum antibiotic $C_{19}H_{17}N_3O_4S_2$ derived from cephalosporin and used esp. in the treatment of gonorrhea
ceph·a·lo·spo·rin \,sef-ə-lə-'spōr-ən, -'spȯr-\ *n* [*Cephalosporium,* genus of fungi + *-in*] : any of several antibiotics produced by an imperfect fungus (genus *Cephalosporium*)
ceph·a·lo·tho·rax \,sef-ə-lə-'thō(ə)r-,aks, -,thȯ(ə)r-\ *n* [ISV] : the united head and thorax of an arachnid or higher crustacean
Ce·phe·id \'sē-fē-əd, 'sef-ē-\ *n* : one of a class of pulsating stars whose intrinsic light variations are very regular
Ce·pheus \'sē-,fyüs; 'sē-fē-əs, 'sef-ē-\ *n* [L (gen. *Cephei*), fr. Gk *Kēpheus*] : a constellation between Cygnus and the north pole
CER *abbr* conditioned emotional response
ce·ra·ceous \sə-'rā-shəs\ *adj* [L *cera* wax — more at CERUMEN] : resembling wax
ce·ra·mal \sə-'ram-əl, 'ser-ə-,mal\ *n* [*ceramic* + *alloy*] : CERMET
[1]**ce·ram·ic** \sə-'ram-ik, *esp Brit* kə-\ *adj* [Gk *keramikos,* fr. *keramos* potter's clay, pottery] : of or relating to the manufacture of any product (as earthenware, porcelain, brick, glass, vitreous enamels) made essentially from a nonmetallic mineral by firing at high temperatures; *also* : of or relating to such a product
[2]**ceramic** *n* **1** *pl but sing in constr* : the art or process of making ceramic articles **2** : a product of ceramic manufacture
ce·ra·mist \sə-'ram-əst, 'ser-ə-məst\ *or* **ce·ram·i·cist** \sə-'ram-ə-səst\ *n* : one who engages in ceramics
ce·ras·tes \sə-'ras-(,)tēz\ *n* [ME, fr. L, fr. Gk *kerastēs,* lit., horned, fr. *keras*] : a venomous viper (*Cerastes cornutus*) of the Near East having a horny process over each eye — called also *horned viper*
cerat- *or* **cerato-** *or* **kerat-** *or* **kerato-** *comb form* [NL, fr. Gk *kerat-, kerato-,* fr. *keras* horn — more at HORN] **1** : horn : horny ⟨*cerato*dus⟩ ⟨*kerat*in⟩ **2** *usu kerat- or kerato-* : cornea ⟨*kerat*itis⟩
ce·rate \'si(ə)r-,āt\ *n* [L *ceratum* wax salve, fr. *cera* wax — more at CERUMEN] : an unctuous preparation for external use consisting of wax or resin or spermaceti mixed with oil, lard, and medicinal ingredients
ce·rat·odus \sə-'rat-əd-əs\ *n* [NL, genus name, fr. *cerat-* + Gk *odous* tooth — more at TOOTH] : any of various recent or fossil dipnoan fishes (as of the genus *Ceratodus*); *esp* : BARRAMUNDA a
Cer·ber·us \'sər-b(ə-)rəs\ *n* [L, fr. Gk *Kerberos*] : a 3-headed dog that in Greek myth guards the entrance to Hades — **Cer·ber·e·an** \,sər-bə-'rē-ən\ *adj*
-cer·cal \'sər-kəl\ *adj comb form* [F *-cerque,* fr. Gk *kerkos* tail] : -tailed ⟨homo*cercal*⟩
cer·car·ia \(,)sər-'kar-ē-ə, -'ker-\ *n, pl* **-i·ae** \-ē-,ē\ [NL, fr. Gk *kerkos* tail] : a usu. tadpole-shaped larval trematode worm produced in a molluscan host by a redia — **cer·car·i·al** \-ē-əl\ *adj*
cer·cis \'sər-səs\ *n* [NL, genus name, fr. Gk *kerkis* Judas tree] : any of a small genus (*Cercis*) of leguminous shrubs or low trees (as a red bud)
cer·cus \'sər-kəs\ *n, pl* **cer·ci** \'sər-,sī, -,kī\ [NL, fr. Gk *kerkos* tail] : either of a pair of simple or segmented appendages at the posterior end of various arthropods
[1]**cere** \'si(ə)r\ *vt* **cered; cer·ing** [ME *ceren* to wax, fr. MF *cirer,* fr. L *cerare,* fr. *cera*] : to wrap in or as if in a cerecloth
[2]**cere** *n* [ME *sere,* fr. MF *cere,* fr. ML *cera,* fr. L, wax] : a usu. waxy protuberance or tumid area at the base of the bill of a bird
[1]**ce·re·al** \'sir-ē-əl\ *adj* [F or L; F *céréale,* fr. L *cerealis* of Ceres, of grain, fr. *Ceres*] : relating to grain or to the plants that produce it; *also* : made of grain
[2]**cereal** *n* **1** : a plant (as a grass) yielding farinaceous grain suitable for food; *also* : its grain **2** : a prepared foodstuff of grain
cereal leaf beetle *n* : a small reddish brown black-headed Old World chrysomelid beetle (*Oulema melanopa*) that feeds on cereal grasses and is a serious threat to U.S. grain crops
cer·e·bel·lum \,ser-ə-'bel-əm\ *n, pl* **-bellums** *or* **-bel·la** \-'bel-ə\ [ML, fr. L, dim. of *cerebrum*] : a large dorsally projecting part of the brain concerned esp. with the coordination of muscles and the maintenance of bodily equilibrium, situated anterior to and above the medulla which it partly overlaps, and formed in man of two lateral lobes and a median lobe — see BRAIN illustration — **cer·e·bel·lar** \-'bel-ər\ *adj*
cerebr- *or* **cerebro-** *comb form* [*cerebrum*] **1** : brain : cerebrum ⟨*cerebr*ation⟩ **2** : cerebral and ⟨*cerebro*spinal⟩
ce·re·bral \sə-'rē-brəl, 'ser-ə-\ *adj* [F *cérébral,* fr. L *cerebrum* brain; akin to Gk *kara* head, *keras* horn — more at HORN] **1 a** : of or relating to the brain or the intellect **b** : of, relating to, or being the cerebrum **2 a** : appealing to intellectual appreciation ⟨~ drama⟩ **b** : primarily intellectual in nature ⟨a ~ society⟩ — **ce·re·bral·ly** \-brə-lē\ *adv*
cerebral accident *n* : a sudden damaging occurrence (as of hemorrhage) within the cerebrum — compare APOPLEXY
cerebral cortex *n* : the surface layer of gray matter of the cerebral hemisphere that functions chiefly in coordination of higher nervous activity
cerebral hemisphere *n* : either of the two hollow convoluted lateral halves of the cerebrum — see BRAIN illustration
cerebral palsy *n* : a disability resulting from damage to the brain before or during birth and outwardly manifested by muscular incoordination and speech disturbances — **cerebral palsied** *adj*
cer·e·brate \'ser-ə-,brāt\ *vi* **-brat·ed; -brat·ing** [back-formation fr. *cerebration,* fr. *cerebrum*] : to use the mind : THINK — **cer·e·bra·tion** \,ser-ə-'brā-shən\ *n*
cer·e·bro·side \'ser-ə-brə-,sīd, sə-'rē-\ *n* [*cerebrose* (galactose)] : any of various lipids found esp. in nerve tissue
ce·re·bro·spi·nal \sə-,rē-brō-'spīn-ᵊl, ,ser-ə-brō-\ *adj* : of or relating to the brain and spinal cord or to these together with the cranial and spinal nerves that innervate voluntary muscles
cerebrospinal fluid *n* : a liquid that is comparable to serum and is secreted from the blood into the lateral ventricles of the brain
cerebrospinal meningitis *n* : inflammation of the meninges of both brain and spinal cord; *specif* : an infectious epidemic and often fatal meningitis caused by the meningococcus
ce·re·bro·vas·cu·lar \sə-,rē-brō-'vas-kyə-lər, ,ser-ə-brō-\ *adj* : of or involving the cerebrum and the blood vessels supplying it ⟨~ disease⟩
ce·re·brum \sə-'rē-brəm, 'ser-ə-brəm\ *n, pl* **-brums** *or* **-bra** \-brə\ [L] **1** : BRAIN 1a **2** : an enlarged anterior or upper part of the brain: **a** : the forebrain and midbrain with their derivatives **b** : FOREBRAIN 2a **c** : the expanded anterior portion of the brain that in higher mammals overlies the rest of the brain, consists of cerebral hemispheres and connecting structures, and is considered to be the seat of conscious mental processes : TELENCEPHALON
cere·cloth \'si(ə)r-,klȯth\ *n* [alter. of earlier *cered cloth* (waxed cloth)] : cloth treated with melted wax or gummy matter and formerly used esp. for wrapping a dead body
cere·ment \'ser-ə-mənt, 'si(ə)r-mənt\ *n* : a shroud for the dead; *esp* : CERECLOTH — usu. used in pl.
[1]**cer·e·mo·ni·al** \,ser-ə-'mō-nē-əl\ *adj* : marked by, involved in, or belonging to ceremony : stressing careful attention to form and detail — **cer·e·mo·ni·al·ism** \-ə-,liz-əm\ *n* — **cer·e·mo·ni·al·ist** \-ə-ləst\ *n* — **cer·e·mo·ni·al·ly** \-ə-lē\ *adv*
syn CEREMONIAL, CEREMONIOUS, FORMAL, CONVENTIONAL *shared meaning element* : marked by attention to or adhering strictly to prescribed forms, procedures, and details. CEREMONIAL and CEREMONIOUS both imply strict attention to what is prescribed (as by custom, code, or ritual) but CEREMONIAL more often applies to things that are or are pertinent to ceremonies ⟨read the service in a nasal *ceremonial* drawl⟩ and CEREMONIOUS to persons addicted to ceremony or to acts attended by ceremony ⟨an ever precise, utterly proper, and extremely *ceremonious* old gentleman⟩ FORMAL applies equally to things prescribed by and persons obedient to custom and often conveys a notion of stiff, restrained, or old-fashioned behavior ⟨paying *formal* attention to his hostess⟩ ⟨the committee made a *formal* report to the president⟩ CONVENTIONAL implies accord with general custom and usage and may suggest lack of originality or independence ⟨a *conventional* courtesy⟩ ⟨they are not moral; they are only *conventional*—G. B. Shaw⟩
[2]**ceremonial** *n* : a ceremonial act, action, or system
cer·e·mo·ni·ous \,ser-ə-'mō-nē-əs\ *adj* **1** : of, relating to, or constituting a ceremony **2** : devoted to forms and ceremony : PUNCTILIOUS **3** : according to formal usage or prescribed procedures **4** : marked by ceremony ***syn*** see CEREMONIAL ***ant*** unceremonious, informal — **cer·e·mo·ni·ous·ly** *adv* — **cer·e·mo·ni·ous·ness** *n*
cer·e·mo·ny \'ser-ə-,mō-nē\ *n, pl* **-nies** [ME *ceremonie,* fr. MF *cérémonie,* fr. L *caerimonia*] **1** : a formal act or series of acts prescribed by ritual, protocol, or convention ⟨the marriage ~⟩ **2 a** : a conventional act of politeness or etiquette ⟨the ~ of introduction⟩ **b** : an action performed only formally with no deep significance **c** : a routine action performed with elaborate pomp **3 a** : prescribed procedures : USAGES ⟨the ~ attending an inauguration⟩ **b** : observance of an established code of civility or politeness ⟨the door opened without ~ and the man strode in⟩
Ce·ren·kov radiation \chər-'(y)eŋ-kəf-\ *n* [P. A. *Cherenkov* b1904 Russ physicist] : light produced by charged particles (as electrons) traversing a transparent medium at a speed greater than that of light in the same medium
Ce·res \'si(ə)r-(,)ēz\ *n* [L] **1** : the Roman goddess of agriculture — compare DEMETER **2** : the largest asteroid and the one first discovered
ce·re·us \'sir-ē-əs\ *n* [NL, genus name, fr. L, wax candle, fr. *cera* wax — more at CERUMEN] : any of various cacti (as of the genus *Cereus*) of the western U.S. and tropical America
ce·ric \'si(ə)r-ik, 'ser-\ *adj* : of, relating to, or containing cerium esp. with a valence of four
ce·rise \sə-'rēs, -'rēz\ *n* [F, lit., cherry, fr. LL *ceresia* — more at CHERRY] : a moderate red
ce·ri·um \'sir-ē-əm\ *n* [NL, fr. *Ceres*] : a malleable ductile metallic element that is the most abundant of the rare-earth group — see ELEMENT table
cerium metal *n* : any of a group of related rare-earth metals comprising cerium, lanthanum, praseodymium, neodymium, promethium, samarium, and sometimes europium
cer·met \'sər-,met\ *n* [*ceramic* + *metal*] : a strong alloy of a heat-resistant compound (as titanium carbide) and a metal (as nickel) used esp. for turbine blades — called also *ceramal*
cer·nu·ous \'sər-nyə-wəs\ *adj* [L *cernuus* with the face turned earthward; akin to L *cerebrum*] : PENDULOUS, NODDING ⟨a ~ flower⟩
cero \'se(ə)r-(,)ō\ *n, pl* **cero** *or* **ceros** [modif. of Sp *sierra* saw, cero] : either of two large food and sport fishes (*Scomberomorus cavalla* and *S. regalis*) of the warmer parts of the western Atlantic ocean
ce·ro·tic acid \sə-,rōt-ik-, -,rät-\ *n* [L *cerotum,* a pomade, fr. Gk *kērōton,* fr. *kēros* wax — more at CERUMEN] : a solid fatty acid $C_{26}H_{52}O_2$ occurring in waxes (as beeswax) and some fats
ce·rous \'sir-əs\ *adj* : of, relating to, or containing cerium esp. with a valence of three
cert *abbr* certificate; certification; certified; certify
[1]**cer·tain** \'sərt-ᵊn\ *adj* [ME, fr. OF, fr. (assumed) VL *certanus,* fr. L *certus,* fr. pp. of *cernere* to sift, discern, decide; akin to Gk *krinein* to separate, decide, judge, *keirein* to cut — more at SHEAR] **1 a** : FIXED, SETTLED ⟨guaranteed a ~ percentage of the profit⟩ **b** : proved to be true **2** : of a specific but unspecified character, quantity, or degree : PARTICULAR ⟨the house has a ~ charm⟩ ⟨everyone has a ~ amount of success⟩ **3 a** : DEPENDABLE, RELIABLE ⟨a ~ remedy for the disease⟩ **b** : INDISPUTABLE ⟨it is ~ that we exist⟩ **4 a** : INEVITABLE ⟨the ~ advance of age and decay⟩ **b** : incapable of failing : DESTINED — used with a following infinitive ⟨she is ~ to do well⟩ **5** : assured in mind or action ***syn*** see SURE

181

ant uncertain — **cer·tain·ly** *adv* — **for certain** : as a certainty : ASSUREDLY

²certain *pron, pl in constr* : certain ones

cer·tain·ty \'sərt-ᵊn-tē\ *n, pl* **-ties** **1** : something that is certain **2** : the quality or state of being certain esp. on the basis of objective evidence

syn CERTAINTY, CERTITUDE, ASSURANCE, CONVICTION *shared meaning element* : a state of being free from doubt **ant** uncertainty

cer·tes \'sərt-ēz, 'sərts\ *adv* [ME, fr. OF, fr. cert certain, fr. L certus] *archaic* : in truth : CERTAINLY

¹cer·tif·i·cate \(,)sər-'tif-i-kət\ *n* [ME certificat, fr. MF, fr. ML certificatum, fr. LL, neut. of certificatus, pp. of certificare to certify] **1** : a document containing a certified statement esp. as to the truth of something; *specif* : a document certifying that one has fulfilled the requirements of and may practice in a field **2** : something serving the same end as a certificate **3** : a document evidencing ownership or debt (a ~ of deposit)

²cer·tif·i·cate \-'tif-ə-,kāt\ *vt* **-cat·ed; -cat·ing** : to testify to or authorize by a certificate — **cer·tif·i·ca·to·ry** \-'tif-i-kə-,tōr-ē, -,tȯr-\ *adj*

cer·tif·i·ca·tion \,sərt-ə-fə-'kā-shən\ *n* **1** : the act of certifying : the state of being certified **2** : a certified statement

certified check *n* : a check certified to be good by the bank on which it is drawn

certified mail *n* : first class mail for which proof of delivery is secured but no indemnity value is claimed

certified milk *n* : milk produced in dairies that operate under the rules and regulations of an authorized medical milk commission

certified public accountant *n* : an accountant who has met the requirements of a state law and has been granted a state certificate

cer·ti·fy \'sərt-ə-,fī\ *vt* **-fied; -fy·ing** [ME certifien, fr. MF certifier, fr. LL certificare, fr. L certus certain — more at CERTAIN] **1** : to attest authoritatively: as **a** : CONFIRM **b** : to present in formal communication **c** : to attest as being true or as represented or as meeting a standard **d** : to attest officially to the insanity of **2** : to inform with certainty : ASSURE **3** : to guarantee (a personal check) as to signature and amount by so indicating on the face **4** : CERTIFICATE, LICENSE **syn** see APPROVE — **cer·ti·fi·able** \-,fī-ə-bəl\ *adj* — **cer·ti·fi·ably** \-blē\ *adv* — **cer·ti·fi·er** \-,fī(-ə)r\ *n*

cer·tio·ra·ri \,sər-sh(ē-)ə-'ra(ə)r-ē, -'rär-ē\ *n* [ME, fr. L, to be informed; fr. the use of the word in the writ] : a writ of a superior court to call up the records of an inferior court or a body acting in a quasi-judicial capacity

cer·ti·tude \'sərt-ə-,t(y)üd\ *n* [ME, fr. LL certitudo, fr. L certus] **1** : the state of being or feeling certain **2** : unfailingness of act or event **syn** see CERTAINTY **ant** doubt

ce·ru·le·an \sə-'rü-lē-ən\ *adj* [L caeruleus dark blue] : resembling the blue of the sky

ce·ru·lo·plas·min \sə-,rü-lō-'plaz-mən\ *n* [ISV cerulo (fr. L caeruleus dark blue) + plasma + -in] : a plasma oxidase active in copper storage and transport

ce·ru·men \sə-'rü-mən\ *n* [NL, irreg. fr. L cera wax, prob. fr. Gk kēros; akin to Lith korys honeycomb] : the yellow waxy secretion from the glands of the external ear — called also earwax — **ce·ru·mi·nous** \-mə-nəs\ *adj*

ce·ruse \sə-'rüs, 'si(ə)r-,üs\ *n* [ME, fr. MF céruse, fr. L cerussa] **1** : white lead as a pigment **2** : a cosmetic containing white lead

ce·rus·site \sə-'rəs-,īt\ *n* [G zerussit, fr. L cerussa] : a mineral PbCO₃ consisting of lead carbonate occurring in colorless transparent crystals and also massive

cer·ve·lat \'sər-və-,lat, -,lä\ *n* [obs. F (now cervelas)] : smoked sausage made of varying proportions of pork and beef

cervic- *or* **cervici-** *or* **cervico-** *comb form* [L cervic-, cervex neck] : neck : cervix of an organ ⟨cervicitis⟩ : cervical and ⟨cervicothoracic⟩

cer·vi·cal \'sər-vi-kəl\ *adj* : of or relating to a neck or cervix

cer·vi·ci·tis \,sər-və-'sīt-əs\ *n* : inflammation of the uterine cervix

cer·vine \'sər-,vīn\ *adj* [L cervinus of a deer, fr. cervus stag, deer — more at HART] : of, relating to, or resembling deer

cer·vix \'sər-viks\ *n, pl* **cer·vi·ces** \'sər-və-,sēz, (,)sər-'vī-(,)sēz\ *or* **cer·vix·es** \'sər-vik-səz; cervix, cervix] **1** : NECK; *esp* : the back part of the neck **2** : a constricted portion of an organ or part; *esp* : the narrow outer end of the uterus

ce·sar·e·an *also* **ce·sar·i·an** \si-'zar-ē-ən, -'zer-\ *n* [fr. the belief that Julius Caesar was born this way] : surgical incision of the walls of the abdomen and uterus for delivery of offspring — **cesarean** *also* **cesarian** *adj*

ce·si·um \'sē-zē-əm\ *n* [NL, fr. L caesius bluish gray] : a silver-white soft ductile element of the alkali metal group that is the most electropositive element known and that is used esp. in photoelectric cells — see ELEMENT table

¹cess \'ses\ *n* [ME cessen to tax, short for assessen — more at ASSESS] : LEVY, TAX

²cess *n* [prob. fr. success] *chiefly Irish* : LUCK — usu. used in the phrase *bad cess to you*

ces·sa·tion \se-'sā-shən\ *n* [ME cessacioun, fr. MF cessation, fr. L cessation-, cessatio delay, idleness, fr. cessatus, pp. of cessare to delay, be idle — more at CEASE] : a temporary or final ceasing (as of action) : STOP

ces·sion \'sesh-ən\ *n* [ME, fr. MF, fr. L cession-, cessio, fr. cessus, pp. of cedere to withdraw — more at CEDE] : a yielding to another : CONCESSION

cess·pit \'ses-,pit\ *n* [cesspool + pit] : a pit for the disposal of refuse (as sewage)

cess·pool \'ses-,pül\ *n* [by folk etymology fr. ME suspiral vent, cesspool, fr. MF souspirail ventilator, fr. souspirer to sigh, fr. L suspirare, lit., to draw a long breath — more at SUSPIRE] : an underground catch basin for liquid waste (as household sewage)

ces·ta \'ses-tə\ *n* [Sp, lit., basket, fr. L cista box, basket] : a narrow curved wicker basket used to catch and propel the ball in jai alai

ces·tode \'ses-,tōd\ *n* [deriv. of Gk kestos girdle] : any of a subclass (Cestoda) of internally parasitic flatworms comprising the tapeworms — **cestode** *adj*

¹ces·tus \'ses-təs\ *n, pl* **ces·ti** \-,tī\ [L, girdle, belt, fr. Gk kestos, fr. kestos stitched; akin to Gk kentron sharp point — more at CENTER] : a woman's belt; *esp* : a symbolic one worn by a bride

²cestus *n* [L caestus, fr. caedere to strike — more at CONCISE] : a hand covering of leather bands often loaded with lead or iron and used by boxers in ancient Rome

ce·su·ra *var of* CAESURA

ce·ta·cean \si-'tā-shən\ *n* [deriv. of L cetus whale, fr. Gk kētos] : any of an order (Cetacea) of aquatic mostly marine mammals including the whales, dolphins, porpoises, and related forms with large head, fishlike nearly hairless body, and paddle-shaped forelimbs — **cetacean** *adj* — **ce·ta·ceous** \-shəs\ *adj*

ce·tane \'sē-,tān\ *n* [fr. cetyl (the radical C₁₆H₃₃)] : a colorless oily hydrocarbon C₁₆H₃₄ found in petroleum

cetane number *n* : a measure of the ignition value of a diesel fuel that represents the percentage by volume of cetane in a mixture of liquid methylnaphthalene that gives the same ignition lag as the oil being tested — called also *cetane rating* — compare OCTANE NUMBER

ce·te·ris pa·ri·bus \,kāt-ə-rə-'spar-ə-bəs\ *adv* [NL, other things being equal] : if all other relevant things, factors, or elements remain unaltered

Ce·tus \'sēt-əs\ *n* [L (gen. Ceti), lit., whale] : an equatorial constellation south of Pisces and Aries

cetyl alcohol \'sēt-ᵊl-\ *n* [ISV cet- (fr. L cetus whale) + -yl; fr. its occurrence in spermaceti] : a waxy crystalline alcohol C₁₆H₃₄O found in the form of its ester in spermaceti and used in pharmaceutical and cosmetic preparations and in making detergents

ce·vi·tam·ic acid \,sē-(,)vī-,tam-ik-\ *n* [cee + vitamin] : VITAMIN C

cf *abbr* **1** calf **2** [L confer, imper. of conferre to compare — more at CONFER] compare

Cf *symbol* californium

CF *abbr* **1** carried forward **2** centrifugal force **3** cost and freight **4** cystic fibrosis

CFI *abbr* **1** chief flying instructor **2** cost, freight, and insurance

CFM *abbr* cubic feet per minute

CFS *abbr* cubic feet per second

cg *or* **cgm** *abbr* centigram

CG *abbr* **1** center of gravity **2** coast guard **3** commanding general

cgs *abbr* centimeter-gram-second

CGT *abbr* [F Confédération Générale du Travail] General Confederation of Labor

ch *abbr* **1** chain **2** champion **3** chaplain **4** chapter **5** chief **6** child; children **7** church

CH *abbr* **1** clearinghouse **2** courthouse **3** customhouse

Cha·blis \'shab-(,)lē; sha-'blē, shä-\ *n, pl* **Cha·blis** \-(,)lēz, -'blēz\ [F, fr. Chablis, France] : a dry white Burgundy table wine

cha-cha \'chä-,chä\ *n* [AmerSp cha-cha-cha] : a fast rhythmic ballroom dance of Latin-American origin with a basic pattern of three steps and a shuffle

chac·ma \'chak-mə\ *n* [Hottentot] : a large dusky southern African baboon (Papio comatus)

cha·conne \shä-'kȯn, sha-, -'kän, -'kən\ *n* [F&Sp; F chaconne, fr. Sp chacona] **1** : an old Spanish dance tune resembling the passacaglia **2** : a musical composition in moderate ¾ time with stress on the second beat and typically consisting of variations on a repeated succession of chords

chad \'chad\ *n* [perh. fr. Sc. gravel] : small pieces of paper or cardboard produced in punching paper tape or data cards; *also* : a piece of chad — **chad·less** \-ləs\ *adj*

Chad \'chad\ *n* : a branch of the Afro-Asiatic language family comprising numerous languages of northern Nigeria and Cameroons

chae·ta \'kēt-ə\ *n, pl* **chae·tae** \'kē-,tē\ [NL, fr. Gk chaitē long flowing hair] : BRISTLE, SETA — **chae·tal** \'kēt-ᵊl\ *adj*

chae·to·gnath \'kēt-,äg-,nath, -ə(g)-\ *n* [deriv. of Gk chaitē + gnathos jaw — more at GNATH-] : any of a class or phylum (Chaetognatha) of small free-swimming marine worms with movable curved chaetae on either side of the mouth — **chaetognath** *adj* — **chae·tog·na·than** \kē-'täg-nə-thən\ *adj or n*

¹chafe \'chāf\ *vb* **chafed; chaf·ing** [ME chaufen to warm, fr. MF chaufer, fr. (assumed) VL calfare, alter. of L calefacere, fr. calēre to be warm + facere to make — more at LEE, DO] *vt* **1** : IRRITATE, VEX **2** : to warm by rubbing esp. with the hands **3 a** : to rub so as to wear away : ABRADE ⟨the boat chafed her sides against the dock⟩ **b** : to make sore by or as if by rubbing ~ *vi* **1** : to feel irritation or discontent : FRET ⟨~s at his restrictive desk job⟩ **2** : to rub and thereby cause wear or irritation

²chafe *n* **1** : a state of vexation : RAGE **2** : injury or wear caused by friction; *also* : FRICTION, RUBBING

cha·fer \'chā-fər\ *n* [ME cheaffer, fr. OE ceafor; akin to OE ceafl jowl — more at JOWL] : any of various large beetles (esp. family Scarabaeidae)

¹chaff \'chaf\ *n* [ME chaf, fr. OE ceaf; akin to OHG cheva husk] **1** : the seed coverings and other debris separated from the seed in threshing grain **2** : something comparatively worthless **3** : the scales borne on the receptacle among the florets in the heads of many composite plants **4** : material (as strips of foil or clusters of fine wires) ejected into the air for reflecting radar waves (as for confusing an enemy's radar detection or for tracking a descending spacecraft) — **chaffy** \-ē\ *adj*

²chaff *n* [prob. fr. ¹chaff] : light jesting talk : BANTER

³chaff *vt* : to tease good-naturedly ~ *vi* : JEST, BANTER

¹chaf·fer \'chaf-ər\ *n* [ME chaffare, fr. chep trade + fare journey — more at CHEAP, FARE] *archaic* : a haggling about price

2chaffer *vb* **chaf·fered; chaf·fer·ing** \'chaf-(ə-)riŋ\ *vi* **1** : HAGGLE **2** *Brit* : to exchange small talk : CHATTER ~ *vt* **1** : EXCHANGE, BARTER **2** : to bargain for — **chaf·fer·er** \-ər-ər\ *n*

chaf·finch \'chaf-(,)inch\ *n* [ME, fr. OE *ceaffinc,* fr. *ceaf* + *finc* finch] : a European finch (*Fringilla coelebs*) of which the male has a reddish breast plumage and a cheerful song

chaf·ing dish \'chā-fiŋ-\ *n* [ME *chafing,* prp. of *chaufen, chafen* to warm] : a utensil for cooking or keeping food warm esp. at the table

Cha·gas' disease \'shäg-əs-(əz-)\ *n* [Carlos *Chagas* †1934 Braz. physician] : a tropical American trypanosomiasis marked by prolonged high fever, edema, and enlargement of spleen, liver, and lymph nodes and caused by a flagellate (*Trypanosoma cruzi*)

1cha·grin \shə-'grin\ *n* [F, fr. *chagrin* sad] : disquietude or distress of mind caused by humiliation, disappointment, or failure

2chagrin *vt* **cha·grined** \-'grind\; **cha·grin·ing** \-'grin-iŋ\ : to vex acutely by disappointing or humiliating

Chai·ma \'chī-mə\ *n* **1** : a member of a Cariban people of the coast of Venezuela **2** : the language of the Chaima people

1chain \'chān\ *n, often attrib* [ME *cheyne,* fr. OF *chaeine,* fr. L *catena;* akin to L *cassis* net] **1 a** : a series of usu. metal links or rings connected to or fitted into one another and used for various purposes (as support, restraint, transmission of mechanical power, or measurement) **b** : a series of links used or worn as an ornament or insignia **c** (1) : a measuring instrument of 100 links used in surveying (2) : a unit of length equal to 66 feet **2** : something that confines, restrains or secures **3 a** : a series of things linked, connected, or associated together ⟨a ~ of events⟩ **b** : a number of atoms or chemical groups united like links in a chain

2chain *vt* **1** : to fasten, bind, or connect with or as if with a chain; *also* : FETTER **2** : to obstruct or protect by a chain

chaî·né \shā-'nā\ *n* [F, fr. pp. of *chaîner* to chain] : a series of short regular usu. fast turns by which a ballet dancer moves across the stage

chain gang *n* : a gang of convicts chained together esp. as an outside working party

chain letter *n* **1** : a social letter sent to a series of persons in succession and often added to by each **2** : a letter sent to several persons with a request that each send copies of the letter to an equal number of persons

chain mail *n* : flexible armor of interlinked metal rings

chain of command : a series of executive positions in order of authority ⟨a military *chain of command*⟩

chain·omat·ic \,chā-nə-'mat-ik\ *adj* [fr. *Chainomatic,* a trademark] *of a balance or scale* : having suspended from the beam an adjustable fine chain whose length is measured to determine minute weights

chain pickerel *n* [fr. the markings resembling chains on the sides] : a large greenish black pickerel (*Esox niger*) with dark markings along the sides that is common in quiet waters of eastern No. America

chain printer *n* : a line printer in which the printing element is a continuous chain

chain–reacting pile *n* : REACTOR 3b

chain reaction *n* **1** : a series of events so related to each other that each one initiates the next **2** : a self-sustaining chemical or nuclear reaction yielding energy or products that cause further reactions of the same kind — **chain–re·act** \,chān-rē-'akt\ *vt*

chain rule *n* : a mathematical rule concerning the differentiation of a function of a function (as $f[u(x)]$) by which under suitable conditions of continuity and differentiability one function is differentiated with respect to the second considered as an independent variable and then the second function is differentiated with respect to the independent variable ⟨if $v = u^2$ and $u = 3x^2 + 2$ the derivative of v by the *chain rule* is $2u(6x)$ or $12x(3x^2 + 2)$⟩

chain saw *n* : a portable power saw that has teeth linked together to form an endless chain

chain–smoke \'chān-'smōk\ *vi* : to smoke esp. cigarettes continually often by lighting each from the previous one ~ *vt* : to smoke (as cigarettes) almost without interruption

chain stitch *n* **1** : an ornamental stitch like the links of a chain **2** : a machine stitch forming a chain on the underside of the work

chain store *n* : one of numerous usu. retail stores having the same ownership and selling the same lines of goods

1chair \'che(ə)r, 'cha(ə)r\ *n* [ME *chaiere,* fr. OF, fr. L *cathedra,* fr. Gk *kathedra,* fr. *kata-* cata- + *hedra* seat — more at SIT] **1 a** : a seat typically having four legs and a back for one person **b** : ELECTRIC CHAIR **2 a** : an official seat or a seat of authority, state, or dignity **b** : an office or position of authority or dignity ⟨holds a university ~⟩ **c** : CHAIRMAN 1 **3** : a sedan chair **4** : a position of employment usu. of one occupying a chair or desk; *specif* : the position of a player in an orchestra or band **5** : any of various devices that hold up or support

2chair *vt* **1** : to install in office **2** *chiefly Brit* : to carry shoulder-high in acclaim ⟨the time you won your town the race we ~*ed* you through the market place —A. E. Housman⟩ **3** : to preside as chairman of

chair car *n* **1** : a railroad car having pairs of chairs with individually adjustable backs on each side of the aisle **2** : PARLOR CAR

chair lift *n* : a motor-driven conveyor consisting of a series of seats suspended from an overhead moving cable and used for transporting skiers or sightseers up or down a long slope or mountainside

1chair·man \'che(ə)r-mən, 'cha(ə)r-\ *n* **1 a** : the presiding officer of a meeting or an organization or committee **b** : the administrative officer of a department of instruction (as in a college) **2** : a carrier of a sedan chair — **chair·man·ship** \-,ship\ *n*

2chairman *vt* **-maned** *or* **-manned; -man·ing** *or* **-man·ning** : CHAIR 3

chair·per·son \-,pərs-ᵊn\ *n* : CHAIRMAN 1

chair·wom·an \-,wu̇m-ən\ *n* : a female chairman

chaise \'shāz\ *n* [F, chair, chaise, alter. of OF *chaiere*] **1 a** : a 2-wheeled carriage for one or two persons with a calash top and the body hung on leather straps and usu. drawn by one horse **b** : a similar 4-wheeled pleasure carriage **c** : POST CHAISE **2** : a light carriage or pleasure cart **3** : CHAISE LONGUE

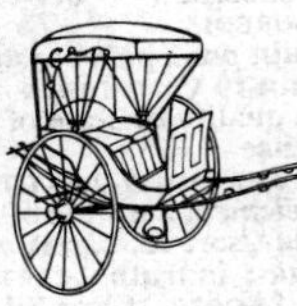

chaise 1a

chaise longue \'shāz-'lȯŋ\ *n, pl* **chaise longues** *also* **chaises longues** \'shāz-'lȯŋ(z)\ [F *chaise longue,* lit., long chair] : a long reclining chair

chaise lounge \'shāz-'lau̇nj, 'chās-\ *n* [by folk etymology fr. F *chaise longue*] : CHAISE LONGUE

Chait \'chīt\ *n* [Hindi *Cait,* fr. Skt *Caitra*] : a month of the Hindu year — see MONTH table

cha·la·za \kə-'lā-zə, -'laz-ə\ *n, pl* **-zae** \-,zē\ *or* **-zas** [NL, fr. Gk, hailstone; akin to Per *zhāla* hail] **1** : either of a pair of spiral bands in the white of a bird's egg that extend from the yolk and attach to opposite ends of the lining membrane — see EGG illustration **2** : the point at the base of a plant ovule where the seed stalk is attached — **cha·la·zal** \-'lā-zəl, -'laz-əl\ *adj*

Chal·ce·do·ni·an \,kal-sə-'dō-nē-ən\ *adj* : of or relating to Chalcedon or the ecumenical council held there in A.D. 451 declaring Monophysitism heretical — **Chalcedonian** *n*

chal·ced·o·ny \kal-'sed-ᵊn-ē\ *n, pl* **-nies** [ME *calcedonie,* a precious stone, fr. LL *chalcedonius,* fr. Gk *Chalkēdōn* Chalcedon] : a translucent quartz that is commonly pale blue or gray with nearly waxlike luster — **chal·ce·don·ic** \,kal-sə-'dän-ik\ *adj*

chal·cid \'kal-səd\ *n* [deriv. of Gk *chalkos* copper] : any of a large superfamily (Chalcidoidea) of mostly minute hymenopterous insects parasitic in the larval state on the larvae or pupae of other insects — **chalcid** *adj*

chal·co·gen \'kal-kə-jən\ *n* [prob. fr. G *chalkogen,* fr. *chalk-* bronze, ore (fr. Gk *chalkos* bronze) + *-gen*; fr. the occurrence of oxygen and sulfur in many ores] : any of the elements oxygen, sulfur, selenium, and tellurium

chal·co·gen·ide \-jə-,nīd\ *n* : a binary compound of a chalcogen with a more electropositive element or radical

chal·co·py·rite \,kal-kə-'pī-,rīt\ *n* [NL *chalcopyrites,* fr. Gk *chalkos* + L *pyrites*] : a yellow mineral $CuFeS_2$ consisting of copper-iron sulfide and constituting an important ore of copper

Chal·da·ic \kal-'dā-ik\ *adj or n* : CHALDEAN

Chal·de·an \kal-'dē-ən\ *n* [L *Chaldaeus* Chaldean, astrologer, fr. Gk *Chaldaios,* fr. *Chaldaia* Chaldea, region of ancient Babylonia] **1 a** : a member of an ancient Semitic people that became dominant in Babylonia **b** : the Semitic language of the Chaldeans **2** : a person versed in the occult arts — **Chaldean** *adj*

Chal·dee \'kal-,dē\ *n* [ME *Caldey,* prob. fr. MF *caldée,* fr. L *Chaldaeus*] **1** : the Aramaic vernacular that was the original language of some parts of the Bible **2** : CHALDEAN 1a

chal·dron \'chȯl-drən\ *n* [MF *chauderon,* fr. *chaudere* pot, fr. LL *caldaria* — more at CALDRON] : any of various old units of measure varying from 32 to 72 imperial bushels

cha·let \sha-'lā, 'shal-(,)ā\ *n* [F] **1** : a remote herdsman's hut in the Alps **2 a** : a Swiss dwelling with unconcealed structural members and a wide overhang at the front and sides **b** : a cottage or house in chalet style

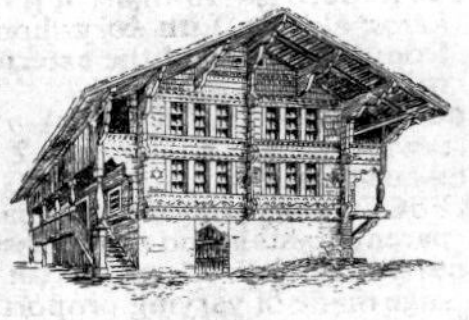

chalet 2a

chal·ice \'chal-əs\ *n* [ME, fr. AF, fr. L *calic-, calix;* akin to Gk *kalyx* calyx] **1** : a drinking cup : GOBLET; *esp* : the eucharistic cup **2** : the cup-shaped interior of a flower

1chalk \'chȯk\ *n* [ME, fr. OE *cealc;* akin to OHG & MLG *kalk* lime; all fr. a prehistoric WGmc word borrowed fr. L *calc-, calx* lime, fr. Gk *chalix* pebble; akin to Gk *skallein* to hoe — more at SHELL] **1 a** : a soft white, gray, or buff limestone composed chiefly of the shells of foraminifers **b** : chalk or a chalky material esp. when used in the form of a crayon **2 a** : a mark made with chalk **b** *Brit* : a point scored in a game — **chalky** \'chȯ-kē\ *adj*

2chalk *vt* **1** : to rub or mark with chalk **2** : to write or draw with chalk **3 a** : to delineate roughly : SKETCH ⟨~ out a plan of attack⟩ **b** : to set down or add up with or as if with chalk : TOT — usu. used with *up* ⟨~ up the casualties on the bulletin board⟩ ~ *vi* : to become chalky

chalk·board \'chȯk-,bō(ə)rd, -,bȯ(ə)rd\ *n* : BLACKBOARD

chalk up *vt* **1** : ASCRIBE, CREDIT **2** : ATTAIN, ACHIEVE ⟨*chalk up* a record score for the season⟩

1chal·lenge \'chal-ənj\ *vb* **chal·lenged; chal·leng·ing** [ME *chalengen* to accuse, fr. OF *chalengier,* fr. L *calumniari* to accuse falsely, fr. *calumnia* calumny] *vt* **1** : to demand as of right : REQUIRE ⟨an event that ~*s* explanation⟩ **2** : to order to halt and prove identity ⟨the sentry *challenged* the stranger at the gates⟩ **3** : to dispute esp. as being unjust, invalid, or outmoded : IMPUGN ⟨uncovered new data that ~*s* old assumptions⟩ **4** : to question formally the legality or legal qualifications of **5 a** : to defy boldly : DARE **b** : to call out to duel or combat **c** : to invite into competition **6** : STIMULATE, EXCITE ⟨math ~*s* him but English bores him⟩ **7** : to administer an immunologic challenge to (an organism) ~ *vi* **1** : to make or present a challenge **2** : to take legal exception — **chal·leng·er** *n*

2challenge *n* **1 a** : a calling to account or into question : PROTEST **b** : an exception taken to a juror before he is sworn **c** : a sentry's command to halt and prove identity **d** : a questioning of the right or validity of a vote or voter **2 a** : a summons that is often threatening, provocative, stimulating, or inciting; *specif* : a summons to a duel to answer an affront **b** : an invitation to compete in a sport **3** : a test of immunity by exposure to virulent infective material after specific immunization

chal·leng·ing \-ən-jiŋ\ *adj* **1** : arousing competitive interest, thought, or action ⟨the curriculum should have ~ intellectual content⟩ **2** : invitingly provocative : FASCINATING ⟨a ~ personality⟩ — **chal·leng·ing·ly** \-jiŋ-lē\ *adv*

chal·lis \'shal-ē\ n, pl **chal·lises** \-ēz\ [prob. fr. the name Challis] : a lightweight soft clothing fabric made of cotton, wool, or synthetic yarns

cha·lone \'kā-,lōn, 'kal-,ōn\ n [Gk chalōn, prp. of chalan to slacken] : an internal secretion that depresses activity — compare HORMONE

¹**cha·ly·be·ate** \kə-'lib-ē-ət, -'lē-bē-\ adj [prob. fr. NL chalybeatus, irreg. fr. L chalybs steel, fr. Gk chalyb-, chalyps, fr. Chalybes, ancient people in Asia Minor] : impregnated with salts of iron; also : having a taste due to iron ⟨~ springs⟩

²**chalybeate** n : a chalybeate liquid or medicine

cham \'kam\ var of KHAN

cham·ae·phyte \'kam-i-,fīt\ n [Gk chamai on the ground + E -phyte — more at HUMBLE] : a perennial plant that bears its overwintering buds just above the surface of the soil

¹**cham·ber** \'chām-bər\ n [ME chambre, fr. OF, fr. LL camera, fr. L, arched roof, fr. Gk kamara vault; akin to L camur curved] 1 : ROOM; esp : BEDROOM 2 : a natural or artificial enclosed space or cavity 3 a : a hall for the meetings of a deliberative, legislative, or judicial body ⟨the senate ~⟩ b : a room where a judge transacts business — usu. used in pl. c : the reception room of a person of rank or authority 4 a : a legislative or judicial body; esp : either of the houses of a bicameral legislature b : a voluntary board or council 5 a : the part of the bore of a gun that holds the charge b : a compartment in the cartridge cylinder of a revolver

²**chamber** vt **cham·bered; cham·ber·ing** \-b(ə-)riŋ\ 1 : to place in or as if in a chamber : HOUSE 2 : to serve as a chamber for; esp : to accommodate in the chamber of a firearm

³**chamber** adj : being, relating to, or performing chamber music

cham·bered \'chām-bərd\ adj : having a chamber ⟨the ~ nautilus⟩

¹**chamberer** n, obs : CHAMBERMAID

²**cham·ber·er** \'chām-bər-ər\ n [ME, chamberlain, fr. MF chamberier, fr. LL camerarius, fr. camera] archaic : GALLANT, LOVER

cham·ber·lain \'chām-bər-lən\ n [ME, fr. OF chamberlayn, of Gmc origin; akin to OHG chamarling chamberlain, fr. chamara chamber, fr. LL camera] 1 : an attendant on a sovereign or lord in his bedchamber 2 a : a chief officer in the household of a king or nobleman b : TREASURER 3 : an often honorary papal attendant; specif : a priest having a rank of honor below domestic prelate

cham·ber·maid \-,mād\ n : a maid who makes beds and does general cleaning of bedrooms (as in a hotel)

chamber music n : music and esp. instrumental ensemble music intended for performance in a private room or small auditorium and usu. having one performer for each part

chamber of commerce n : an association of businessmen to promote commercial and industrial interests in the community

chamber of horrors : a hall in which objects of macabre interest (as instruments of torture) are exhibited; also : a collection of such exhibits

chamber orchestra n : a small orchestra usu. with one player for each instrumental part

chamber pot n : a bedroom vessel for urine and feces

cham·bray \'sham-,brā, -brē\ n [irreg. fr. Cambrai, France] : a lightweight clothing fabric with colored warp and white filling yarns

cha·me·leon \kə-'mēl-yən\ n [ME camelion, fr. MF, fr. L chamaeleon, fr. Gk chamaileōn, fr. chamai on the ground + leōn lion — more at HUMBLE] 1 : any of a group (Rhiptoglossa) of Old World lizards with granular skin, prehensile tail, independently movable eyeballs, and unusual ability to change the color of the skin 2 : a fickle or changeable person or thing 3 : any of various American lizards (as of the genus Anolis) capable of changing their color; esp : AMERICAN CHAMELEON — **cha·me·le·on·ic** \-,mē-lē-'än-ik\ adj

¹**cham·fer** \'cham(p)-fər, 'cham-pər\ n [MF chanfreint, fr. pp. of chanfraindre to bevel, fr. chant edge (fr. L canthus iron tire) + fraindre to break, fr. L frangere — more at CANT, BREAK] : a beveled edge

²**chamfer** vt **cham·fered; cham·fer·ing** \-f(ə-)riŋ, -p(ə-)riŋ\ 1 : to cut a furrow in (as a column) : GROOVE 2 : to make a chamfer on : BEVEL

cham·fron \'sham-frən, 'cham-\ n [ME shamfron, fr. MF chanfrein] : the headpiece of a horse's armor

cham·ois \'sham-ē, in sense 1 also sham-'wä\ n, pl **cham·ois** also **cham·oix** \in sense 1 'sham-ē(z) or sham-'wä(z), in sense 2 'sham-ēz\ [MF, fr. LL camox] 1 : a small goatlike antelope (Rupicapra rupicapra) of Europe and the Caucasus 2 also **cham·my** or **sham·my** \'sham-ē\ : a soft pliant leather prepared from the skin of the chamois or from sheepskin

chamois 1

cham·o·mile \'kam-ə-,mīl, -,mēl\ n [ME camemille, fr. ML camomilla, modif. of L chamaemelon, fr. Gk chamaimēlon, fr. chamai + mēlon apple] : any of a genus (Anthemis, esp. the common European A. nobilis) of composite herbs with strong-scented foliage and flower heads that contain a bitter medicinal principle; also : a similar plant of a related genus (Matricaria)

¹**champ** \'champ, 'chämp, 'chomp\ vb [perh. imit.] vt 1 : CHOMP 2 : MASH, TRAMPLE ~ vi 1 : to make biting or gnashing movements 2 : to show impatience of delay or restraint — usu. used in the phrase champing at the bit ⟨the children were ~ing at the bit to get on board⟩

²**champ** \'champ\ n : CHAMPION

cham·pac or **cham·pak** \'cham-,pak, 'chəm-(,)pək\ n [Hindi & Skt; Hindi campak, fr. Skt campaka] : an East Indian tree (Michelia champaca) of the magnolia family with yellow flowers

cham·pagne \sham-'pān\ n [F, fr. Champagne, France] 1 : a white sparkling wine made in the old province of Champagne, France; also : a similar wine made elsewhere 2 : a pale orange yellow to light grayish yellowish brown

cham·paign \sham-'pān\ n [ME champaine, fr. MF champagne, fr. LL campania — more at CAMPAIGN] 1 : an expanse of level open country : PLAIN 2 archaic : BATTLEFIELD — **champaign** adj

cham·per·ty \'cham-pərt-ē\ n [ME champartie, fr. MF champartie field rent, fr. champ field (fr. L campus) + part portion — more at CAMP, PART] : a proceeding by which a person not a party in a suit bargains to aid in or carry on its prosecution or defense in consideration of a share of the matter in suit — **cham·per·tous** \-pərt-əs\ adj

cham·pi·gnon \sham-'pin-yən, cham-\ n [MF, fr. champagne] : an edible fungus; esp : the common meadow mushroom (Agaricus campestris)

¹**cham·pi·on** \'cham-pē-ən\ n [ME, fr. OF, fr. ML campion-, campio, of WGmc origin] 1 : WARRIOR, FIGHTER 2 : a militant advocate or defender ⟨an outspoken ~ of civil rights⟩ 3 : one that does battle for another's rights or honor ⟨God will raise me up a ~ —Sir Walter Scott⟩ 4 : a winner of first prize or first place in competition; also : one who shows marked superiority ⟨a ~ at telling stories⟩

²**champion** vt 1 archaic : CHALLENGE, DEFY 2 : to protect or fight for as a champion 3 : to act as militant supporter of : UPHOLD ⟨always ~s the cause of the underdog⟩ syn see SUPPORT

cham·pi·on·ship \-,ship\ n 1 : designation as champion 2 : the act of championing : DEFENSE ⟨his ~ of freedom of speech⟩ 3 : a contest held to determine a champion

champ·le·vé \,shäⁿl-ə-'vā\ adj [F] : of, relating to, or being a style of enamel decoration in which the enamel is applied and fired in cells depressed (as by incising) into a metal background — compare CLOISONNÉ — **champlevé** n

chan abbr channel

¹**chance** \'chan(t)s\ n [ME, fr. OF, fr. (assumed) VL cadentia fall, fr. L cadent-, cadens, prp. of cadere to fall; akin to Skt śad to fall] 1 a : something that happens unpredictably without discernible human intention or observable cause b : the assumed impersonal purposeless determiner of unaccountable happenings : LUCK c : the fortuitous or incalculable element in existence : CONTINGENCY 2 : a situation favoring some purpose : OPPORTUNITY ⟨the weekend gives him a ~ to relax⟩ 3 : a fielding opportunity in baseball 4 a : the possibility of an indicated or a favorable outcome in an uncertain situation; also : the degree of likelihood of such an outcome ⟨we have almost no ~ of winning⟩ b pl : the more likely indications ⟨~s are he's already heard the news⟩ 5 a : RISK ⟨took a ~ and guessed at the answer⟩ b : a ticket in a raffle — **chance** adj — **by chance** : in the haphazard course of events ⟨they met by chance but parted by design⟩

²**chance** vb **chanced; chanc·ing** vi 1 a : to take place or come about by chance : HAPPEN b : to be found by chance c : to have the good or bad luck 2 : to come or light by chance ~ vt 1 : to leave the outcome of to chance 2 : to accept the hazard of : RISK syn see HAPPEN

chance·ful \'chan(t)s-fəl\ adj 1 archaic : CASUAL 2 : EVENTFUL

chan·cel \'chan(t)-səl\ n [ME, fr. MF, fr. LL cancellus lattice, fr. L cancelli; fr. the latticework enclosing it] : the part of a church containing the altar and seats for the clergy and choir

chan·cel·lery or **chan·cel·lory** \'chan(t)-s(ə-)lə-rē, -səl-rē\ n, pl **-ler·ies** or **-lor·ies** 1 a : the position, court, or department of a chancellor b : the building or room where a chancellor has his office 2 : the office of secretary of the court of a person high in authority 3 : the office or staff of an embassy or consulate

chan·cel·lor \'chan(t)-s(ə-)lər\ n [ME chanceler, fr. OF chancelier, fr. LL cancellarius doorkeeper, secretary, fr. cancellus] 1 a : the secretary of a nobleman, prince, or king b : the lord chancellor of Great Britain c Brit : the chief secretary of an embassy d : a Roman Catholic priest heading the office in which diocesan business is transacted and recorded 2 a : the titular head of a British university b (1) : a university president (2) : the chief executive officer in some state systems of higher education 3 a : a lay legal officer or adviser of an Anglican diocese b : a judge in a court of chancery or equity in various states of the U.S. 4 : the chief minister of state in some European countries — **chan·cel·lor·ship** \-,ship\ n

chancellor of the exchequer often cap C&E : a member of the British cabinet in charge of the public income and expenditure

chance–med·ley \'chan(t)-'smed-lē\ n [AF chance medlée mingled chance] 1 : accidental homicide not entirely without fault of the killer but without evil intent 2 : haphazard action : CONFUSION

chance music n : music in which the elements of chance are introduced by the composer (as by selecting tempo, pitch, or dynamics by the throw of dice) or by the performer (as by choosing what parts to perform and the manner and order in which they are performed)

chan·cery \'chan(t)s-(ə-)rē\ n, pl **-cer·ies** [ME chancerie, alter. of chancellerie chancellery, fr. OF, fr. chancelier] 1 a : a high court of equity in England and Wales with common-law functions and jurisdiction over causes in equity b : a court of equity in the American judicial system c : the principles and practice of judicial equity 2 : a record office for public archives or those of ecclesiastical, legal, or diplomatic proceedings 3 a : a chancellor's court or office or the building in which he has his office b : the office in which the business of a Roman Catholic diocese is transacted and recorded c : the office of an embassy : CHANCELLERY 3 — **in chancery** 1 : in litigation in a court of chancery; also : under the superintendence of the lord chancellor ⟨a ward in chancery⟩ 2 : in a hopeless predicament

chan·cre \ˈshaŋ-kər\ *n* [F, fr. L *cancer*] **:** a primary sore or ulcer at the site of entry of a pathogen (as in tularemia); *esp* **:** the initial lesion of syphilis — **chan·crous** \-k(ə-)rəs\ *adj*
chan·croid \ˈshaŋ-ˌkrȯid\ *n* **:** a venereal disease caused by a hemophilic bacterium (*Hemophilus ducreyi*) and characterized by chancres that differ from those of syphilis in lacking firm indurated margins — called also *soft chancre* — **chan·croi·dal** \shaŋ-ˈkrȯid-ᵊl\ *adj*
chancy \ˈchan(t)-sē\ *adj* **chanc·i·er; -est** **1** *Scot* **:** bringing good luck **:** AUSPICIOUS **2 :** uncertain in outcome or prospect **:** RISKY **3 :** occurring by chance **:** HAPHAZARD — **chanc·i·ness** *n*
chan·de·lier \ˌshan-də-ˈli(ə)r\ *n* [F, lit., candlestick, modif. of L *candelabrum*] **:** a branched often ornate lighting fixture suspended from a ceiling
chan·delle \shan-ˈdel, shäⁿ-\ *n* [F, lit., candle] **:** an abrupt climbing turn of an airplane in which the momentum of the plane is used to attain a higher rate of climb — **chandelle** *vi*

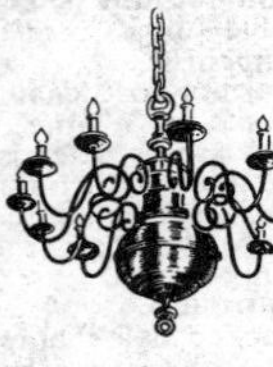
chandelier

chan·dler \ˈchan-(d)lər\ *n* [ME *chandeler*, fr. MF *chandelier*, fr. OF, fr. *chandelle* candle, fr. L *candela*] **1 :** a maker or seller of tallow or wax candles and usu. soap **2 :** a retail dealer in provisions and supplies or equipment of a specified kind ⟨a yacht ~⟩
chan·dlery \-(d)lə-rē\ *n, pl* **-dler·ies** **1 :** a place where candles are kept **2 :** the business of a chandler **3 :** the commodities sold by a chandler
¹change \ˈchānj\ *vb* **changed; chang·ing** [ME *changen*, fr. OF *changier*, fr. L *cambiare* to exchange, of Celt origin; akin to OIr *camm* crooked; akin to Gk *skambos* crooked] *vt* **1 a :** to make different in some particular ⟨never bothered to ~ his will⟩ **b :** to make radically different **:** TRANSFORM ⟨can't ~ human nature⟩ **c :** to give a different position, course, or direction to **d :** REVERSE ⟨~ one's vote⟩ **2 a :** to replace with another ⟨let's ~ the subject⟩ **b :** to make a shift from one to another **:** SWITCH ⟨always ~*s* sides in an argument⟩ **c :** to exchange for an equivalent sum or comparable item **d :** to undergo a loss or modification of ⟨foliage *changing* color⟩ **e :** to put fresh clothes or covering on ⟨~ a bed⟩ **~** *vi* **1 :** to become different ⟨her mood ~*s* every hour⟩ ⟨prices ~ overnight⟩ **2** *of the moon* **:** to pass from one phase to another **3 :** to shift one's means of conveyance **:** TRANSFER ⟨on the bus trip to New York he *changed* twice⟩ **4** *of the voice* **:** to shift to lower register **:** BREAK **5 :** to undergo transformation, transition, or substitution ⟨winter *changed* to spring⟩ **6 :** to put on different clothes **7 :** to engage in giving something and receiving something in return **:** EXCHANGE ⟨I need a sharper knife, so I'll ~ with you⟩
syn CHANGE, ALTER, VARY, MODIFY *shared meaning element* **:** to make or become different
— **change hands :** to pass from the possession of one person to that of another ⟨money *changes hands* many times⟩ — **change one's mind :** to reverse one's intention or opinion ⟨was going to drive but then *changed his mind* and took the bus⟩
²change *n* **1 :** the act, process, or result of changing: as **a :** ALTERATION ⟨there was little ~ in her daily routine⟩ **b :** TRANSFORMATION ⟨has undergone a great ~ since he was married⟩ **c :** SUBSTITUTION ⟨went to the country for a ~ of air⟩ **d :** the passage of the moon from one monthly revolution to another; *also* **:** the passage of the moon from one phase to another **2 :** a fresh set of clothes **3** *Brit* **:** EXCHANGE 5a **4 a :** money in small denominations received in exchange for an equivalent sum in larger denominations **b :** money returned when a payment exceeds the amount due **c :** coins of low denominations ⟨a pocketful of ~⟩ **5 :** an order in which a set of bells is struck in change ringing
syn CHANGE, MUTATION, PERMUTATION, VICISSITUDE *shared meaning element* **:** altered state
change·able \ˈchān-jə-bəl\ *adj* **:** capable of change: as **a :** able or apt to vary ⟨~ weather ⟩ **b :** subject to change **:** ALTERABLE ⟨a clause in the contract ~ at will⟩ **c :** FICKLE **d :** IRIDESCENT — **change·abil·i·ty** \ˌchān-jə-ˈbil-ət-ē\ *n* — **change·able·ness** \ˈchān-jə-bəl-nəs\ *n* — **change·ably** \-blē\ *adv*
change·ful \ˈchānj-fəl\ *adj* **:** notably variable **:** UNCERTAIN — **change·ful·ly** \-fə-lē\ *adv* — **change·ful·ness** *n*
change·less \ˈchānj-ləs\ *adj* **:** marked by the absence of change **:** CONSTANT — **change·less·ly** *adv* — **change·less·ness** *n*
change·ling \ˈchānj-liŋ\ *n* **1** *archaic* **:** TURNCOAT **2 :** a child secretly exchanged for another in infancy **3** *archaic* **:** IMBECILE — **changeling** *adj*
change off *vi* **1 :** to alternate with another at doing an act **2 :** to alternate between two different acts or instruments or between an action and a rest period
change of heart : a full reversal in position or attitude
change of life : ²CLIMACTERIC 2
change of pace **1 :** an interruption of continuity by a sudden shift (as for relief from monotony) to a different activity **2 :** CHANGE-UP
change·over \ˈchān-ˌjō-vər\ *n* **:** conversion to a different function or use of a different method
chang·er \ˈchān-jər\ *n* **1 :** one that changes **2** *obs* **:** MONEY CHANGER
change ringing *n* **:** the art or practice of ringing a set of tuned bells (as in the bell tower of a church) in continually varying order
change–up \ˈchān-ˌjəp\ *n* **:** a slow pitch in baseball thrown for deception with the same motion as a fastball
¹chan·nel \ˈchan-ᵊl\ *n* [ME *chanel*, fr. OF, fr. L *canalis* channel — more at CANAL] **1 a :** the bed where a natural stream of water runs **b :** the deeper part of a river, harbor, or strait **c :** a strait or narrow sea between two close land masses **d** (1) **:** a means of communication or expression ⟨the ~*s* between government and industry should be kept open⟩ (2) **:** a path along which data passes or along which data may be stored serially (as in a computer) **e** *pl* **:** a fixed or official course of communication ⟨went through established military ~*s* with his grievances⟩ **f :** a way, course, or direction of thought or action ⟨new ~*s* of exploration⟩ **g :** a band of frequencies of sufficient width for a single radio or television communication **2 :** a usu. tubular enclosed passage **:** CONDUIT **3 :** a long gutter, groove, or furrow **4 :** a metal bar of flattened U-shaped section
²channel *vt* **-neled** *or* **-nelled; -nel·ing** *or* **-nel·ling** **1 a :** to form, cut, or wear a channel in **b :** to make a groove in ⟨~ a chair leg⟩ **2 :** to convey into or through a channel ⟨~ his energy into constructive activities⟩
³channel *n* [alter. of *chainwale*, fr. *chain* + *wale*] **:** one of the flat ledges of heavy plank or metal bolted edgewise to the outside of a ship to increase the spread of the shrouds
channel bass *n* **:** a large coppery drum (*Sciaenops ocellatus*) with a black spot at the base of the tail that is an important game and food fish of the Atlantic coast of No. and So. America — called also *redfish*
chan·nel·ize \ˈchan-ᵊl-ˌīz\ *vt* **-ized; -iz·ing** **:** CHANNEL — **chan·nel·iza·tion** \ˌchan-ᵊl-ə-ˈzā-shən\ *n*
chan·son \shäⁿ-sōⁿ\ *n, pl* **chan·sons** \-sōⁿ(z)\ [F, fr. L *cantion-*, *cantio*, fr. *cantus*, pp.] **:** SONG; *specif* **:** a music-hall or cabaret song
chan·son de geste \-sōⁿ-də-zhest\ *n, pl* **chansons de geste** *same*\ [F, lit., song of heroic deeds] **:** any of several Old French epic poems of the 11th to the 13th centuries
chan·son·nier \ˌshäⁿ-sō-ˈnyā\ *n* [F, fr. *chanson*] **:** a writer or singer of chansons; *esp* **:** a cabaret singer
¹chant \ˈchant\ *vb* [ME *chaunten*, fr. MF *chanter*, fr. L *cantare*, fr. *cantus*, pp. of *canere*; akin to OE *hana* rooster, Gk *kanachē* ringing sound] *vi* **1 :** to make melodic sounds with the voice; *esp* **:** to sing a chant **2 :** to recite in a monotonous repetitive tone **~** *vt* **1 :** to utter as in chanting **2 :** to celebrate or praise in song or chant
²chant *n* **1 :** SONG **2 a :** a repetitive liturgical melody in which as many syllables are assigned to each tone as required **b :** a rhythmic monotonous utterance or song ⟨the ~ of an auctioneer⟩ **c :** a composition for chanting
chant·er \ˈchant-ər\ *n* **1 :** one that chants: **a :** CHORISTER **b :** CANTOR **2 :** the chief singer in a chantry **3 :** the reed pipe of a bagpipe with finger holes on which the melody is played — **chant·ress** \ˈchan-trəs\ *n*
chan·te·relle \ˌshant-ə-ˈrel, ˌshänt-\ *n* [F] **:** an edible mushroom (*Cantharellus cibarius*) of rich yellow color and pleasant aroma
chan·teuse \shäⁿ-ˈtə(r)z, shan-ˈtüz\ *n, pl* **chan·teuses** \-ˈtə(r)z(-əz), -ˈtüz(-əz)\ [F, fem. of *chanteur* singer, fr. *chanter*] **:** a female concert or nightclub singer
chan·tey *or* **chan·ty** \ˈshant-ē, ˈchant-\ *n, pl* **chanteys** *or* **chanties** [modif. of F *chanter*] **:** a song sung by sailors in rhythm with their work
chan·ti·cleer \ˌchant-ə-ˈkli(ə)r, ˌshant-\ *n* [ME *Chantecleer*, rooster in verse narratives, fr. OF *Chantecler*, rooster in the *Roman de Renart*] **:** ¹COCK 1
Chan·til·ly lace \shan-ˌtil-ē-\ *n* [trans. of F *dentelle de Chantilly*, fr. *Chantilly*, France] **:** a delicate silk, linen, or synthetic lace having a six-sided mesh ground and a floral or scrolled design — called also *Chantilly*
chan·try \ˈchan-trē\ *n, pl* **chantries** [ME *chanterie*, fr. MF, singing, fr. *chanter*] **1 :** an endowment for the chanting of masses commonly for the founder **2 :** a chapel endowed by a chantry
Cha·nu·kah \ˈkän-ə-kə, ˈhän-\ *var of* HANUKKAH
cha·os \ˈkā-ˌäs\ *n* [L, fr. Gk — more at GUM] **1** *obs* **:** CHASM, ABYSS **2 a** *often cap* **:** a state of things in which chance is supreme; *esp* **:** the confused unorganized state of primordial matter before the creation of distinct forms — compare COSMOS **b :** a state of utter confusion ⟨the citywide blackout caused ~⟩ **c :** a confused mass or heterogeneous agglomeration ⟨a ~ of television antennas⟩ — **cha·ot·ic** \kā-ˈät-ik\ *adj* — **cha·ot·i·cal·ly** \-i-k(ə-)lē\ *adv*
¹chap \ˈchap\ *n* [short for *chapman*] **1 :** FELLOW **2** *South & Midland* **:** BABY, CHILD
²chap *vb* **chapped; chap·ping** [ME *chappen*; akin to MD *cappen* to cut down] *vt* **:** to cause to open in slits or cracks ⟨*chapped* lips⟩ **~** *vi* **:** to open in slits or chinks **:** CRACK ⟨the hands and lips often ~ in winter⟩
³chap *n* **:** a crack in or a sore roughening of the skin caused by exposure to wind or cold
⁴chap \ˈchäp, ˈchap\ *n* [²*chap*] **1 a :** the fleshy covering of a jaw; *also* **:** JAW — usu. used in pl. ⟨the wolf's ~*s* were smeared with blood⟩ **2 :** the forepart of the face — usu. used in pl.
⁵chap *abbr* chapter
chap·a·ra·jos *or* **chap·a·re·jos** \ˌshap-ə-ˈrā-(ˌ)ōs, -əs\ *n pl* [MexSp *chaparreras*] **:** CHAPS
chap·ar·ral \ˌshap-ə-ˈral, -ˈrel\ *n* [Sp. fr. *chaparro* dwarf evergreen oak, fr. Basque *txapar*] **1 :** a thicket of dwarf evergreen oaks; *broadly* **:** a dense impenetrable thicket of shrubs or dwarf trees **2 :** an ecological community occurring widely in southern California and comprised of shrubby plants esp. adapted to dry summers and moist winters
chaparral bird *n* **:** ROADRUNNER — called also *chaparral cock*
chaparral pea *n* **1 :** a thorny California leguminous shrub (*Pickeringia montana*) forming dense thickets
chap·book \ˈchap-ˌbu̇k\ *n* [*chapman* + *book*] **:** a small book containing ballads, tales, or tracts
chape \ˈchāp, ˈchap\ *n* [ME, scabbard, fr. MF, cape, fr. LL *cappa*] **:** the metal mounting or trimming of a scabbard or sheath
cha·peau \sha-ˈpō, shə-\ *n, pl* **cha·peaus** \-ˈpōz\ *or* **cha·peaux** \-ˈpō(z)\ [MF, fr. OF *chapel* — more at CHAPLET] **:** HAT
cha·pel \ˈchap-əl\ *n* [ME, fr. OF *chapele*, fr. ML *cappella*, fr. dim. of LL *cappa* cloak; fr. the cloak of St. Martin of Tours preserved as a sacred relic in a chapel built for that purpose] **1 :** a subordinate or private place of worship: as **a :** a place of worship serving a residence or institution **b :** a small house of worship usu. related to a main church **c :** a room or recess in a church for meditation and prayer or small religious services **2 :** a choir of singers belonging to a chapel (as of a prince) **3 :** a chapel service or assembly at a school or college **4 :** an association of the employees in a printing office **5 :** a place of worship used by a Christian group

other than an established church ⟨a nonconformist ~⟩ **6 a :** FUNERAL HOME **b :** a room for funeral services in a funeral home

chapel of ease : a chapel or dependent church built to accommodate an expanding parish

¹chap·er·on *or* **chap·er·one** \'shap-ə-ˌrōn\ *n* [F *chaperon,* lit., hood, fr. MF, head covering, fr. *chape*] **1 :** a person (as a matron) who for propriety accompanies one or more young unmarried women in public or in mixed company **2 :** an older person who accompanies young people at a social gathering to ensure proper behavior; *broadly* **:** one delegated to ensure proper behavior

²chaperon *or* **chaperone** *vb* **-oned; -on·ing** *vt* **1 :** ESCORT **2 :** to act as chaperon to or for ~ *vi* **:** to act as a chaperon — **chap·er·on·age** \-ˌrō-nij\ *n*

chap·fall·en \'chap-ˌfȯ-lən, 'chäp-\ *adj* **1 :** having the lower jaw hanging loosely **2 :** cast down in spirit **:** DEPRESSED

chap·i·ter \'chap-ət-ər\ *n* [ME *chapitre,* fr. MF, alter. of OF *chapitle,* fr. L *capitulum,* lit., little head] **:** the capital of a column

chap·lain \'chap-lən\ *n* [ME *chapelain,* fr. OF, fr. ML *cappellanus,* fr. *cappella*] **1 :** a clergyman in charge of a chapel **2 :** a clergyman officially attached to a branch of the military, to an institution, or to a family or court **3 :** a person chosen to conduct religious exercises (as at a meeting of a club or society) **4 :** a clergyman appointed to assist a bishop (as at a liturgical function) — **chap·lain·cy** \-sē\ *n* — **chap·lain·ship** \-ˌship\ *n*

chap·let \'chap-lət\ *n* [ME *chapelet,* fr. MF, fr. OF, dim. of *chapel* hat, garland, fr. ML *cappellus* head covering, fr. LL *cappa*] **1 :** a wreath to be worn on the head **2 a :** a string of beads **b :** a part of a rosary comprising five decades **3 :** a small molding carved with small decorative forms — **chap·let·ed** \-lət-əd\ *adj*

Chap·lin·esque \ˌchap-lə-'nesk\ *adj* **:** resembling or suggesting the largely pantomime comedy of the motion-picture comedian Charles Chaplin

chap·man \'chap-mən\ *n* [ME, fr. OE *cēapman,* fr. *cēap* trade + *man*] **1** *archaic* **:** MERCHANT, TRADER **2** *Brit* **:** an itinerant dealer **:** PEDDLER

chaps \'shaps\ *n pl* [modif. of MexSp *chaparreras*] **:** leather leggings joined together by a belt or lacing, often having flared outer flaps, and worn over the trousers esp. by western ranch hands

chap·ter \'chap-tər\ *n* [ME *chapitre* division of a book, meeting of canons, fr. OF, fr. LL *capitulum* division of a book & ML, meeting place of canons, fr. L, dim. of *capit-, caput* head — more at HEAD] **1 a :** a main division of a book **b :** something resembling a chapter in being a significant specified unit ⟨with his death a ~ was closed in the history of the industry⟩ **2 a :** a regular meeting of the canons of a cathedral or collegiate church or of the members of a religious house **b :** the body of canons of a cathedral or collegiate church **3 :** a local branch of a society or fraternity

chapter house *n* **1 :** the building or rooms where a chapter meets **2 :** the residence of a local chapter of a fraternity or sorority

¹char \'chär\ *n, pl* **char** *or* **chars** [origin unknown] **:** any of a genus (*Salvelinus*) of small-scaled trouts

²char *vb* **charred; char·ring** [back-formation fr. *charcoal*] *vt* **1 :** to convert to charcoal or carbon usu. by heat **:** BURN **2 :** to burn slightly or partly **:** SCORCH ⟨the fire *charred* the beams⟩ ~ *vi* **:** to become charred **:** BURN

³char *n* **:** a charred substance **:** CHARCOAL; *specif* **:** a combustible residue remaining after the destructive distillation of coal

⁴char *vi* **charred; char·ring** [back-formation fr. *charwoman*] **:** to work as a cleaning woman

⁵char *n* [short for *charwoman*] *Brit* **:** CHARWOMAN

char·a·banc \'shar-ə-baŋ\ *n* [F *char à bancs,* lit., wagon with benches] *Brit* **:** a sightseeing motor coach

char·a·cin \'kar-ə-sən\ *n* [deriv. of Gk *charak-, charax* pointed stake, a fish] **:** any of a family (Characidae) of usu. small brightly colored tropical fishes — **characin** *adj*

¹char·ac·ter \'kar-ik-tər\ *n* [ME *caracter,* fr. MF *caractère,* fr. L *character* mark, distinctive quality, fr. Gk *charaktēr, fr. charassein* to scratch, engrave; akin to Lith *žerti* to scratch] **1 a :** a conventionalized graphic device placed on an object as an indication of ownership, origin, or relationship **b :** a graphic symbol (as a hieroglyph or alphabet letter) used in writing or printing **c :** a magical or astrological emblem **d :** ALPHABET **e (1) :** WRITING, PRINTING **(2) :** style of writing or printing **(3) :** CIPHER **f :** a symbol (as a letter or number) that represents information; *also* **:** a representation of such a character that may be accepted by a computer **2 a :** one of the attributes or features that make up and distinguish the individual **b (1) :** a feature used to separate distinguishable things into categories; *also* **:** a group or kind so separated ⟨people of this ~⟩ ⟨advertising of a very primitive ~⟩ **(2) :** the detectable expression of the action of a gene or group of genes **(3) :** the aggregate of distinctive qualities characteristic of a breed, strain, or type ⟨a wine of great ~⟩ **c :** the complex of mental and ethical traits marking and often individualizing a person, group, or nation ⟨assess a person's ~ by studying his handwriting⟩ **d :** main or essential nature esp. as strongly marked and serving to distinguish ⟨excess sewage gradually changed the ~ of the lake⟩ **3 :** POSITION, CAPACITY ⟨his ~ as a town official⟩ **4 :** a short literary sketch of the qualities of a social type **5 :** REFERENCE 4b **6 a :** a person marked by notable or conspicuous traits **:** PERSONAGE ⟨a notorious campus ~⟩ **b :** one of the persons of a drama or novel **c :** the personality or part which an actor recreates **d :** characterization esp. in drama or fiction **e :** PERSON, INDIVIDUAL ⟨some ~ just stole her purse⟩ **7 :** REPUTATION **8 :** moral excellence and firmness ⟨a man of sound ~⟩ ***syn*** see DISPOSITION, TYPE — **char·ac·ter·less** \-ləs\ *adj* — **in character :** in accord with a person's usual qualities or traits — **out of character :** not in accord with a person's usual qualities or traits

²character *vt* **1** *archaic* **:** ENGRAVE, INSCRIBE **2 a** *archaic* **:** REPRESENT, PORTRAY **b :** CHARACTERIZE

³character *adj* **1 :** capable of portraying an unusual or eccentric personality often markedly different (as in age) from the player ⟨a ~ actor⟩ **2 :** requiring the qualities of a character actor ⟨a ~ role⟩

character assassination *n* **:** the slandering of a person (as a public figure) with the intention of destroying public confidence in him

char·ac·ter·ful \'kar-ik-tər-fəl\ *adj* **1 :** markedly expressive of character ⟨a ~ face⟩ **2 :** marked by character ⟨a ~ decision⟩

¹char·ac·ter·is·tic \ˌkar-ik-tə-'ris-tik\ *adj* **:** serving to reveal and distinguish the individual character — **char·ac·ter·is·ti·cal·ly** \-ti-k(ə-)lē\ *adv*

syn CHARACTERISTIC, INDIVIDUAL, PECULIAR, DISTINCTIVE *shared meaning element* **:** revealing a special quality or identity

²characteristic *n* **1 :** a distinguishing trait, quality, or property **2 :** the integral part of a common logarithm **3 :** the smallest positive integer *n* which for an operation in a ring or field yields 0 when any element is used *n* times with the operation

characteristic equation *n* **:** an equation in which the characteristic polynomial of a matrix is set equal to 0

characteristic polynomial *n* **:** the determinant of a square matrix in which an arbitrary variable (as *x*) is subtracted from each of the elements along the principal diagonal

characteristic root *n* **:** a scalar such that for a linear transformation of a vector space there is some nonzero vector that when multiplied by the scalar is equal to the vector obtained by letting the transformation operate on the vector; *esp* **:** a root of the characteristic equation of a matrix — called also *characteristic value, eigenvalue*

characteristic vector *n* **:** a nonzero vector that is mapped by a linear transformation of a vector space onto a vector that is the product of a scalar multiplied by the original vector — called also *eigenvector*

char·ac·ter·iza·tion \ˌkar-ik-t(ə-)rə-'zā-shən\ *n* **:** the act of characterizing; *esp* **:** the artistic representation (as in fiction or drama) of human character or motives

char·ac·ter·ize \'kar-ik-tə-ˌrīz\ *vt* **-ized; -iz·ing 1 :** to describe the character or quality of **:** DELINEATE ⟨*characterized* him as soft-spoken yet ambitious⟩ **2 :** to be a characteristic of **:** DISTINGUISH ⟨a cool light fragrance ~s the cologne⟩

char·ac·ter·olog·i·cal \ˌkar-ik-t(ə-)rə-'läj-i-kəl\ *adj* [*characterology* (study of character)] **:** of, relating to, or based on character or the study of character including its development and its differences in different individuals — **char·ac·ter·olog·i·cal·ly** \-'läj-i-k(ə-)lē\ *adv*

character sketch *n* **:** a sketch dealing with a character usu. of marked individuality

character witness *n* **:** one that gives evidence concerning the reputation, conduct, and moral nature of a party to a legal action

char·ac·tery \'kar-ik-t(ə-)rē, kə-'rak-\ *n, pl* **-ter·ies :** a system of written letters or symbols used in the expression of thought

cha·rade \shə-'rād\ *n* [F] **1 :** a word represented in riddling verse or by picture, tableau, or dramatic action **2** *pl* **:** a game in which each syllable of a word or phrase is acted out by some of the persons playing the game while the others try to guess the word or phrase **3 :** an almost transparent pretense

cha·ras \'chär-əs\ *n* [Hindi *caras*] **:** HASHISH

char·coal \'chär-ˌkōl\ *n* [ME *charcole*] **1 :** a dark or black porous carbon prepared from vegetable or animal substances (as from wood by charring in a kiln from which air is excluded) **2 a :** a piece or pencil of fine charcoal used in drawing **b :** a charcoal drawing

chard \'chärd\ *n* [F *carde,* fr. OProv *cardo* edible cardoon, fr. L *carduus* thistle, artichoke; akin to MLG *harst* rake, L *carrere* to card] **:** a beet (*Beta vulgaris cicla*) whose large leaves and succulent stalks are often cooked as a vegetable — called also *Swiss chard*

chare \'cha(ə)r, 'che(ə)r\ *or* **char** \'chär\ *n* [ME *char* turn, piece of work, fr. OE *cierr;* akin to OE *cierran* to turn] **:** CHORE ⟨the peasant who does the humblest ~s — Thomas De Quincey⟩

¹charge \'chärj\ *vb* **charged; charg·ing** [ME *chargen,* fr. OF *chargier,* fr. LL *carricare,* fr. L *carrus* wheeled vehicle — more at CAR] *vt* **1 a** *archaic* **:** to lay or put a load on or in **:** LOAD **b (1) :** to place a charge (as of powder) in **(2) :** to load or fill to capacity **c (1) :** to restore the active materials in (a storage battery) by the passage of a direct current through in the opposite direction to that of discharge **(2) :** to give an electric charge to **d (1) :** to assume as a heraldic bearing **(2) :** to place a heraldic bearing on **e :** to fill or furnish fully ⟨a mind *charged* with fancies ⟩ ⟨the music is *charged* with excitement⟩ **2 a :** to impose a task or responsibility on ⟨~ him with the job of finding a new meeting place⟩ **b :** to command, instruct, or exhort with right or authority ⟨I ~ you not to accept the gift⟩ **c :** to give a charge to (a jury) — used of a judge **3 a :** BLAME ⟨~*s* him as the instigator⟩ **b :** to make an assertion against esp. by ascribing guilt for an offense **:** ACCUSE ⟨~*s* him with armed robbery⟩ ⟨~*s* them with hypocrisy⟩ **c :** to place the guilt or blame for ⟨~ her failure to negligence⟩ **d :** to assert as an accusation ⟨~*s* that he distorted the data⟩ **4 a :** to bring (a weapon) into position for attack **:** LEVEL ⟨~ a lance⟩ **b :** to rush against or bear down upon **:** ATTACK; *also* **:** to rush into (an opponent) usu. illegally in various games or sports **5 a (1) :** to impose a pecuniary burden on ⟨~ his estate with debts incurred⟩ **(2) :** to impose or record as pecuniary obligation ⟨~ debts to an estate⟩ **b (1) :** to fix or ask as fee or payment ⟨~*s* $10 for an office visit⟩ **(2) :** to ask payment of (a person) ⟨~ a client for expenses⟩ **c :** to record (an item) as an expense, debt, obligation, or liability ⟨~ a purchase to a customer⟩ ⟨~ a library book to a borrower⟩ ~ *vi* **1 :** to rush forward in or as if in assault **:** ATTACK; *also* **:** to charge an opponent in sports **2 :** to ask or set a price **3 :** to charge an item to an account ⟨~ now, pay later⟩ ***syn*** see COMMAND

[2]charge *n* **1 a** *obs* : a material load or weight **b** : a figure borne on a heraldic field **2 a** : the quantity that an apparatus is intended to receive and fitted to hold **b** : a store or accumulation of impelling force ⟨the deeply emotional ~ of the drama⟩ **c** : a definite quantity of electricity; *esp* : an excess or deficiency of electrons in a body **d** : THRILL, KICK ⟨got a ~ out of the game⟩ **3 a** : OBLIGATION, REQUIREMENT **b** : MANAGEMENT, SUPERVISION ⟨has ~ of the home office⟩ **c** : the ecclesiastical jurisdiction (as a parish) committed to a clergyman **d** : a person or thing committed to the care of another **4 a** : INSTRUCTION, COMMAND **b** : instruction in points of law given by a court to a jury **5 a** : EXPENSE, COST ⟨gave the banquet at his own ~⟩ **b** : the price demanded for something ⟨no admission ~⟩ **c** : a debit to an account ⟨the purchase was a ~⟩ **d** : the record of a loan (as of a book from a library) **6 a** : ACCUSATION, INDICTMENT ⟨a ~ of assault with intent to kill⟩ **b** : a statement of complaint or hostile criticism ⟨denied the ~*s* of nepotism that were leveled against him⟩ **7** : a violent rush forward (as to attack) — **in charge** : having control or custody of something ⟨he is *in charge* of the training program⟩

charge·able \'chär-jə-bəl\ *adj* **1** *archaic* : financially burdensome : EXPENSIVE **2 a** : liable to be accused or held responsible **b** : suitable to be charged to a particular account **c** : qualified to be made a charge on the county or parish — **charge·able·ness** *n*

charge account *n* : a customer's account with a creditor (as a merchant) to which the purchase of goods is charged

charge–a–plate \'chär-jə-ˌplāt\ *or* **charge plate** *n* [fr. *Charga-plate*, a trademark] : an embossed address plate used by a customer when buying on credit

charged \'chärjd\ *adj* **1** : possessing strong emotion or vigorous purpose ⟨attacked the author in an emotionally ~ review⟩ **2** : capable of arousing strong emotion ⟨a highly ~ political theme⟩

char·gé d'af·faires \(ˌ)shär-ˌzhād-ə-'fa(ə)r, -'fe(ə)r\ *n, pl* **chargés d'affaires** \-ˌzhād-ə-, -ˌzhāz-də-\ [F, lit., one charged with affairs] **1** : a subordinate diplomat who substitutes for an ambassador or minister in his absence **2** : a diplomat inferior in rank to an ambassador or minister and accredited by one government to the foreign minister of another

charge of quarters : an enlisted man designated to handle administrative matters in his unit esp. after duty hours

[1]char·ger \'chär-jər\ *n* [ME *chargeour;* akin to ME *chargen* to charge] *archaic* : a large flat platter for carrying meat

[2]charg·er *n* **1** : one that charges: as **a** : an appliance for holding or inserting a charge of powder or shot in a gun **b** : a cartridge clip **2** : a horse for battle or parade

char·i·ness \'char-ē-nəs, 'cher-\ *n* **1** : the quality or state of being chary : CAUTION **2** : carefully preserved state : INTEGRITY

[1]char·i·ot \'char-ē-ət\ *n* [ME, fr. MF, fr. OF, fr. *char* wheeled vehicle, fr. L *carrus*] **1** : a light 4-wheeled pleasure or state carriage **2** : a 2-wheeled horse-drawn battle car of ancient times used also in processions and races

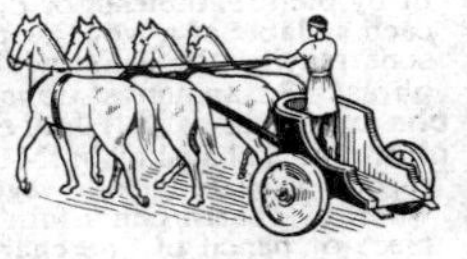
chariot 2

[2]chariot *vt* : to carry in or as if in a chariot ~ *vi* : to drive or ride in or as if in a chariot

char·i·o·teer \ˌchar-ē-ə-'ti(ə)r\ *n* **1** : one who drives a chariot **2** *cap* : the constellation Auriga

cha·ris·ma \kə-'riz-mə\ *also* **char·ism** \'ka(ə)r-ˌiz-əm\ *n, pl* **cha·ris·ma·ta** \kə-'riz-mət-ə\ *also* **charisms** [Gk *charisma* favor, gift, fr. *charizesthai* to favor, fr. *charis* grace; akin to Gk *chairein* to rejoice — more at YEARN] **1** : an extraordinary power (as of healing) given a Christian by the Holy Spirit for the good of the church **2 a** : a personal magic of leadership arousing special popular loyalty or enthusiasm for a public figure (as a political leader or military commander) **b** : a special magnetic charm or appeal ⟨the ~ of a popular actor⟩ — **char·is·mat·ic** \ˌkar-əz-'mat-ik\ *adj*

char·i·ta·ble \'char-ət-ə-bəl\ *adj* **1** : full of love for and goodwill toward others : BENEVOLENT **2 a** : liberal in benefactions to the poor : GENEROUS **b** : of or relating to charity ⟨~ institutions⟩ **3** : merciful or kind in judging others : LENIENT — **char·i·ta·ble·ness** *n* — **char·i·ta·bly** \-blē\ *adv*

char·i·ty \'char-ət-ē\ *n, pl* **-ties** [ME *charite*, fr. OF *charité*, fr. LL *caritat-, caritas* Christian love, fr. L, dearness, fr. *carus* dear; akin to Skt *kāma* love] **1** : benevolent goodwill toward or love of humanity **2 a** : kindly liberality and helpfulness esp. toward the needy or suffering; *also* : aid given to those in need **b** : an institution engaged in relief of the poor **c** : public provision for the relief of the needy **3 a** : a gift for public benevolent purposes **b** : an institution (as a hospital) founded by such a gift **4** : lenient judgment of others ***syn*** see MERCY ***ant*** malice, ill will

cha·ri·va·ri \ˌshiv-ə-'rē, 'shiv-ə-ˌ\ *n* [F, fr. LL *caribaria* headache, fr. Gk *karēbaria*, fr. *kara, karē* head + *barys* heavy — more at CEREBRAL, GRIEVE] : SHIVAREE

char·ka *or* **char·kha** \'chər-kə, 'chär-\ *n* [Hindi *carkha*] : a domestic spinning wheel used in India chiefly for spinning cotton

char·la·tan \'shär-lə-tən, -lət-ᵊn\ *n* [It *ciarlatano*, alter. of *cerretano*, lit., inhabitant of Cerreto, fr. *Cerreto*, village in Italy] **1** : QUACK 1 ⟨~*s* killing their patients with empirical procedures⟩ **2** : one making usu. noisy or showy pretenses to knowledge or ability : FRAUD, FAKER — **char·la·tan·ism** \-ˌiz-əm\ *n* — **char·la·tan·ry** \-rē\ *n*

Charles's Wain \ˌchärl-zəz-'wān, 'chärlz-'wān\ *n* [*Charlemagne*] : the Big Dipper

Charles·ton \'chärl-stən\ *n* [*Charleston*, S. C.] : a lively ballroom dance in which the knees are twisted in and out and the heels are swung sharply outward on each step

char·ley horse \'chär-lē-ˌhȯrs\ *n* [fr. *Charley*, nickname for *Charles*] : a muscular strain or bruise esp. of the quadriceps that is characterized by pain and stiffness

Char·lie \'chär-lē\ [fr. the name *Charlie*] — a communications code word for the letter *c*

char·lock \'chär-ˌläk, -lək\ *n* [ME *cherlok*, fr. OE *cerlic*] : a wild mustard (*Brassica kaber*) that is often troublesome in grainfields

char·lotte \'shär-lət\ *n* [F] : a dessert consisting of a filling (as of fruit, whipped cream, or custard) placed over cake, ladyfingers, or strips of bread

char·lotte russe \ˌshär-lət-'rüs\ *n* [F, lit., Russian charlotte] : a charlotte made with sponge cake or ladyfingers and a whipped-cream or custard-gelatin filling

[1]charm \'chärm\ *n* [ME *charme*, fr. OF, fr. L *carmen* song, fr. *canere* to sing — more at CHANT] **1 a** : the chanting or reciting of a magic spell : INCANTATION **b** : an act or expression believed to have magic power **2** : something worn about the person to ward off evil or ensure good fortune : AMULET **3 a** : a trait that fascinates, allures, or delights **b** : a physical grace or attraction — used in pl. **c** : compelling attractiveness ⟨the island possessed great ~⟩ **4** : a small ornament worn on a bracelet or chain ***syn*** see FETISH — **charm·less** \-ləs\ *adj*

[2]charm *vt* **1 a** : to affect by or as if by magic : COMPEL **b** : to please, soothe, or delight by compelling attraction ⟨~*s* women with his suave manner⟩ **2** : to endow with supernatural powers by means of charms; *also* : to protect by spells, charms, or supernatural influences **3** : to control (an animal) typically by charms (as the playing of music) ⟨~ a snake⟩ ~ *vi* **1** : to practice magic and enchantment **2** : to have the effect of a charm : FASCINATE ***syn*** see ATTRACT ***ant*** disgust

charm·er \'chär-mər\ *n* **1** : ENCHANTER, MAGICIAN **2** : one that pleases or fascinates; *esp* : an attractive woman

charm·ing \'chär-miŋ\ *adj* : extremely pleasing or delightful : ENTRANCING — **charm·ing·ly** \-miŋ-lē\ *adv*

charm school *n* : a school or course of instruction in which social graces are taught

char·nel \'chärn-ᵊl\ *n* [ME, fr. MF, fr. ML *carnale*, fr. LL, neut. of *carnalis* of the flesh — more at CARNAL] : a building or chamber in which bodies or bones are deposited — called also *charnel house* — **charnel** *adj*

Cha·ro·lais \ˌshar-ə-'lā\ *n* [*Charolais*, district in eastern France] : any of a French breed of large white cattle used primarily for beef and crossbreeding

Char·on \'kar-ən, 'ker-\ *n* [L, fr. Gk *Charōn*] : a son of Erebus who in Greek myth ferries the souls of the dead over the Styx

char·poy \'chär-ˌpȯi\ *n, pl* **charpoys** [Hindi *cārpāī*] : a bed consisting of a frame strung with tapes or light rope that is used esp. in India

char·qui \'chär-kē, 'shär-\ *n* [Sp, fr. Quechua *ch'arki* dried meat] : jerked beef

charr \'chär\ *var of* CHAR

[1]chart \'chärt\ *n* [MF *charte*, fr. L *charta* piece of papyrus, document — more at CARD] **1** : MAP: as **a** : an outline map exhibiting something (as climatic or magnetic variations) in its geographical aspects **b** : a map for the use of navigators **2 a** : a sheet giving information in tabular form **b** : GRAPH **c** : DIAGRAM **d** : a sheet of paper ruled and graduated for use in a recording instrument

[2]chart *vt* **1** : to make a map or chart of **2** : to lay out a plan for

char·ta·ceous \kär-'tā-shəs\ *adj* : resembling or made of paper ⟨a ~ plant part⟩

[1]char·ter \'chärt-ər\ *n* [ME *chartre*, fr. OF, fr. ML *chartula*, fr. L, dim. of *charta*] **1** : a written instrument or contract (as a deed) executed in due form **2 a** : a grant or guarantee of rights, franchises, or privileges from the sovereign power of a state or country **b** : an instrument in writing creating and defining the franchises of a city, educational institution, or corporation **c** : CONSTITUTION **3** : an instrument in writing from the authorities of a society creating a lodge or branch **4** : a special privilege, immunity, or exemption **5** : a mercantile lease of a ship or some principal part of it

[2]charter *vt* **1 a** : to establish, enable, or convey by charter **b** *Brit* : CERTIFY ⟨a ~*ed* mechanical engineer⟩ **2** : to hire, rent, or lease for usu. exclusive and temporary use ⟨~*ed* a boat for deep-sea fishing⟩ ***syn*** see HIRE — **char·ter·er** \-ər-ər\ *n*

[3]charter *adj* : of, relating to, or being a travel arrangement in which transportation (as a bus or plane) is hired by and for one specific group of people ⟨a ~ flight⟩

chartered accountant *n, Brit* : a member of a chartered institute of accountants

charter member *n* : an original member of a society or corporation — **charter membership** *n*

Char·tism \'chärt-ˌiz-əm\ *n* [ML *charta* charter, fr. L, document] : the principles and practices of a body of 19th century English political reformers advocating better social and industrial conditions for the working classes — **Char·tist** \'chärt-əst\ *n*

chart·ist \'chärt-əst\ *n* **1** : CARTOGRAPHER **2** : an analyst of market action whose predictions of market courses are based on study of graphic presentations of past market performance

char·treuse \shär-'trüz, -'trüs\ *n* [*Chartreuse*] : a variable color averaging a brilliant yellow green

Chartreuse *trademark* —used for a usu. green or yellow liqueur

char·tu·lary \'kär-chə-ˌler-ē\ *n, pl* **-lar·ies** [ML *chartularium*] : CARTULARY

char·wom·an \'chär-ˌwu̇m-ən\ *n* [*chare* + *woman*] **1** *Brit* : a woman hired to char **2** : a cleaning woman esp. in a large building

chary \'cha(ə)r-ē, 'che(ə)r-\ *adj* **chari·er; -est** [ME, sorrowful, dear, fr. OE *cearig* sorrowful, fr. *caru* sorrow — more at CARE] **1** *archaic* : DEAR, TREASURED **2** : discreetly cautious: as **a** : hesitant and vigilant about dangers and risks **b** : slow to grant, accept, or expend ⟨a man very ~ of compliments⟩ ***syn*** see CAUTIOUS — **cha·ri·ly** \'char-ə-lē, 'cher-\ *adv*

Cha·ryb·dis \kə-'rib-dəs\ *n* [L, fr. Gk] : a daughter of Poseidon and Gaea thrown into the sea off Sicily by Zeus where by swallowing and spewing water she created a whirlpool — compare SCYLLA

[1]chase \'chās\ *vb* **chased; chas·ing** [ME *chasen*, fr. MF *chasser*, fr. (assumed) VL *captiare* — more at CATCH] *vt* **1 a** : to follow rapidly : PURSUE **b** : HUNT **c** : to follow regularly or persistently with the intention of attracting or alluring ⟨he's too old to be *chasing* women⟩ **2** *obs* : HARASS **3** : to seek out — often used with down ⟨detectives *chasing* down clues⟩ **4** : to cause to depart or flee ⟨~ the dog out of the pantry⟩ **5** : to cause the removal of (a baseball pitcher) by a batting rally ~ *vi* **1** : to chase an animal, person, or thing ⟨~ after material possessions⟩ **2** : RUSH, HASTEN ⟨*chased* all over town looking for a place to stay⟩ **syn** see FOLLOW

²**chase** *n* **1 a** : the act of chasing : PURSUIT **b** : the hunting of wild animals — used with *the* **c** : an earnest or frenzied seeking after something desired **2** : something pursued : QUARRY **3 a** : a franchise to hunt within certain limits of land **b** : a tract of unenclosed land used as a game preserve **4** : a sequence (as in a movie) in which the characters pursue one another

³**chase** *vt* **chased; chas·ing** [ME *chassen*, modif. of MF *enchasser* to set] **1 a** : to ornament (metal) by indenting with a hammer and tools without a cutting edge **b** : to make by such indentation **c** : to set with gems **2 a** : GROOVE, INDENT **b** : to cut (a thread) with a chaser

⁴**chase** *n* [F *chas* eye of a needle, fr. L *capsus* enclosed space, fr. L, pen, alter. of *capsa* box — more at CASE] **1** : GROOVE, FURROW **2** : the bore of a cannon **3 a** : TRENCH **b** : a channel (as in a wall) for something to lie in or pass through

⁵**chase** *n* [prob. fr. F *châsse* frame, fr. L *capsa*] : a rectangular steel or iron frame into which letterpress matter is locked for printing or plating — compare FORM

¹**chas·er** \'chā-sər\ *n* **1** : one that chases **2** : a mild drink (as beer) taken after hard liquor

²**chaser** *n* : a skilled worker who produces ornamental chasing

³**chaser** *n* : a tool for cutting screw threads

Cha·sid \'has-əd, 'käs-\ *n, pl* **Cha·si·dim** \'has-əd-əm, kä-'sēd-\ *var of* HASID

chasm \'kaz-əm\ *n* [L *chasma*, fr. Gk; akin to L *hiare* to yawn — more at YAWN] **1** : a deep cleft in the earth : GORGE **2** : a marked division, separation, or difference ⟨a political ~ between the two countries⟩

¹**chas·sé** \sha-'sā\ *vi* **chas·séd; chas·sé·ing** [F, n., fr. pp. of *chasser* to chase] **1** : to make a chassé **2** : SASHAY

²**chassé** *n* : a sliding dance step resembling the galop

chasse·pot \'shas-(ə-)pō\ *n* [F, fr. Antoine A. *Chassepot* †1905 F inventor] : a bolt-action rifle firing a paper cartridge

chas·seur \sha-'sər\ *n* [F, fr. MF *chasser*] **1** : HUNTER, HUNTSMAN **2** : one of a body of light cavalry or infantry trained for rapid maneuvering **3** : a liveried attendant : FOOTMAN

chas·sis \'shas-ē, 'chas-ē also 'chas-əs\ *n, pl* **chas·sis** \-ēz\ [F *châssis*, fr. (assumed) VL *capsicum*, fr. L *capsa* box — more at CASE] **1** : the frame upon which is mounted the body (as of an automobile or airplane), the working parts (as of a radio), the recoiling parts (of a cannon), or the roof, walls, floors, and facing (as of a building) **2** : the frame and working parts as opposed to the body (as of an automobile) or cabinet (as of a radio or television set)

chaste \'chāst\ *adj* **chast·er; chast·est** [ME, fr. OF, fr. L *castus* pure — more at CASTE] **1** : innocent of unlawful sexual intercourse **2** : CELIBATE **3** : pure in thought and act : MODEST **4** : severely simple in design or execution : AUSTERE ⟨the ~ hospital corridor⟩ ⟨~ poetry⟩ — **chaste·ly** *adv* — **chaste·ness** \'chās(t)-nəs\ *n*

syn CHASTE, PURE, MODEST, DECENT *shared meaning element* : free from all taint of what is lewd or salacious **ant** lewd, wanton, immoral

chas·ten \'chās-ᵊn\ *vt* **chas·tened; chas·ten·ing** \-ᵊn-iŋ\ [alter. of obs. E *chaste* to chasten, fr. ME *chasten*, fr. OF *chastier*, fr. L *castigare*, fr. *castus* + *-igare* (fr. *agere* to drive) — more at ACT] **1** : to correct by punishment or suffering : DISCIPLINE; *also* : PURIFY **2** : to prune (as a work or style of art) of excess, pretense, or falsity : REFINE **ant** pamper, mollycoddle — **chas·ten·er** \'chās-nər, -ᵊn-ər\ *n*

chas·tise \(')chas-'tīz\ *vt* **chas·tised; chas·tis·ing** [ME *chastisen*, alter. of *chasten*] **1** : to inflict punishment on (as by whipping) **2** : to censure severely : CASTIGATE **3** *archaic* : CHASTEN 2 **syn** PUNISH — **chas·tise·ment** \(')chas-'tīz-mənt *also* 'chas-təz-\ *n* — **chas·tis·er** \(')chas-'tī-zər\ *n*

chas·ti·ty \'chas-tət-ē\ *n* **1** : the quality or state of being chaste: as **a** : abstention from unlawful sexual intercourse **b** : abstention from all sexual intercourse **c** : purity in conduct and intention **d** : restraint and simplicity in design or expression **2** : personal integrity

chastity belt *n* : a belt device (as of medieval times) designed to prevent sexual intercourse on the part of the woman wearing it

cha·su·ble \'chaz(h)-ə-bəl, 'chas-ə-\ *n* [F, fr. LL *casubla* hooded garment] : a sleeveless outer vestment worn by the officiating priest at mass

¹**chat** \'chat\ *vb* **chat·ted; chat·ting** [ME *chatten*, short for *chatteren*] *vi* **1** : CHATTER, PRATTLE **2** : to talk in an informal or familiar manner ~ *vt, Brit* : to talk to; *esp* : to talk lightly or glibly with — often used with *up*

²**chat** *n* **1** : idle small talk : CHATTER **2** : light familiar talk; *esp* : CONVERSATION **3** [imit.] : any of several songbirds (as of the genera *Saxicola* or *Icteria*)

châ·teau \sha-'tō\ *n, pl* **châ·teaus** \-'tōz\ *or* **châ·teaux** \-'tō(z)\ [F, fr. L *castellum* castle] **1** : a feudal castle or fortress in France **2** : a large country house : MANSION **3** : a French vineyard estate

cha·teau·bri·and \(,)sha-,tō-brē-'äⁿ\ *n, often cap* [François René de *Chateaubriand*] : a large tenderloin steak usu. grilled or broiled and served with a sauce (as béarnaise)

chat·e·lain \'shat-ᵊl-,än\ *n* [MF *châtelain*, fr. L *castellanus* occupant of a castle] : CASTELLAN

chasubles: *1* Gothic *2* fiddleback

chat·e·laine \'shat-ᵊl-,än\ *n* [F *châtelaine*, fem. of *châtelain*] **1 a** : the wife of a castellan **b** : the mistress of a château **2 a** : a clasp or hook for a watch, purse, or bunch of keys

cha·toy·ance \shə-'tȯi-ən(t)s\ *n* : CHATOYANCY

cha·toy·an·cy \-ən-sē\ *n* : the quality or state of being chatoyant

¹**cha·toy·ant** \shə-'tȯi-ənt\ *adj* [F, fr. prp. of *chatoyer* to shine like a cat's eyes] : having a changeable luster or color with an undulating narrow band of white light ⟨a ~ gem⟩

²**chatoyant** *n* : a chatoyant gem

chat·tel \'chat-ᵊl\ *n* [ME *chatel* property, fr. OF, fr. ML *capitale* — more at CATTLE] **1** : an item of tangible movable or immovable property except real estate, freehold, and the things which are parcel of it : a piece of personal property **2** : SLAVE, BONDSMAN

¹**chat·ter** \'chat-ər\ *vb* [ME *chatteren*, of imit. origin] *vi* **1** : to utter rapidly succeeding sounds suggestive of language but inarticulate and indistinct ⟨squirrels ~*ed* angrily⟩ ⟨a ~*ing* stream⟩ **2** : to talk idly, incessantly, or fast : JABBER **3 a** : to click repeatedly or uncontrollably ⟨teeth ~*ing* with cold⟩ ⟨machine guns ~*ing*⟩ **b** *of a tool* : to vibrate irregularly in cutting **c** : to operate with an irregularity that causes rapid intermittent noise or vibration ⟨~*ing* brakes⟩ ~ *vt* **1** : to utter rapidly, idly, or indistinctly **2** : to cut unevenly with a chattering tool

²**chatter** *n* **1** : the action or sound of chattering **2** : idle talk : PRATTLE

chat·ter·box \'chat-ər-,bäks\ *n* : one who engages in much idle talk

chat·ter·er \'chat-ər-ər\ *n* **1** : one that chatters **2** : any of various passerine birds (as a waxwing)

chatter mark *n* **1** : a fine undulation formed on the surface of work by a chattering tool **2** : one of a series of short curved cracks on a glaciated rock surface transverse to the glacial striae

chat·ty \'chat-ē\ *adj* **chat·ti·er; -est** **1** : fond of chatting : TALKATIVE ⟨a ~ neighbor⟩ **2** : having the style and manner of light familiar conversation ⟨a ~ letter⟩ — **chat·ti·ly** \'chat-ᵊl-ē\ *adv* — **chat·ti·ness** \'chat-ē-nəs\ *n*

¹**chauf·feur** \'shō-fər, shō-'\ *n* [F, lit., stoker, fr. *chauffer* to heat, fr. MF *chaufer* — more at CHAFE] **1** : a person employed to drive a motor vehicle **2** : one that transports others by operating a motor vehicle

²**chauffeur** *vb* **chauf·feured; chauf·feur·ing** \'shō-f(ə-)riŋ, shō-'fər-iŋ\ *vi* : to do the work of a chauffeur ~ *vt* **1** : to transport in the manner of a chauffeur ⟨~*s* the children to school⟩ **2** : to operate (as an automobile) as chauffeur

chaul·moo·gra \chȯl-'mü-grə\ *n* [Beng *cāulmugrā*] : any of several East Indian trees (family Flacourtiaceae) that yield an acrid oil used in treating leprosy and skin diseases

chaunt \'chȯnt, 'chänt\, **chaunter** *var of* CHANT, CHANTER

chaus·sure \shō-'sᵫr\ *n, pl* **chaussures** *same*\ [ME *chaucer*, fr. MF *chaussure*] **1** : FOOTGEAR **2** *pl* : SHOES

chau·tau·qua \shə-'tȯ-kwə\ *n* [*Chautauqua* lake] : an institution of the late 19th and early 20th centuries providing popular education combined with entertainment in the form of lectures, concerts, and plays often presented outdoors or in a tent

chau·vin·ism \'shō-və-,niz-əm\ *n* [F *chauvinisme*, fr. Nicolas *Chauvin fl* 1815 F soldier of excessive patriotism and devotion to Napoleon] **1** : excessive or blind patriotism — compare JINGOISM **2** : undue partiality or attachment to a group or place to which one belongs or has belonged ⟨male ~⟩ — **chau·vin·ist** \-və-nəst\ *n* — **chau·vin·is·tic** \,shō-və-'nis-tik\ *adj* — **chau·vin·is·ti·cal·ly** \-ti-k(ə-)lē\ *adv*

¹**chaw** \'chȯ\ *vb* [by alter.] *vt, dial* : to grind (as tobacco) with the teeth ~ *vi, dial* : CHEW

²**chaw** *n, dial* : a chew esp. of tobacco

¹**cheap** \'chēp\ *n* [ME *chep*, fr. OE *cēap* trade; akin to OHG *kouf* trade; both fr. a prehistoric Gmc stem borrowed fr. L *caupo* tradesman] *obs* : BARGAIN — **on the cheap** : at minimum expense : CHEAPLY ⟨schools that are run *on the cheap*⟩

²**cheap** *adj* **1 a** : purchasable below the going price or the real value **b** : charging a low price **c** : depreciated in value (as by currency inflation) ⟨~ dollars⟩ **2** : gained with little effort ⟨a ~ victory⟩ **3 a** : of inferior quality or worth : TAWDRY, SLEAZY **b** : contemptible because of lack of any fine, lofty, or redeeming qualities : STINGY **4 a** : yielding small satisfaction **b** : paying or able to pay less than going prices **5** *of money* : obtainable at a low rate of interest **6** *Brit* : specially reduced in price **syn** see CONTEMPTIBLE **ant** noble — **cheap** *adv* — **cheap·ish** \'chē-pish\ *adj* — **cheap·ish·ly** *adv* — **cheap·ly** \'chēp-lē\ *adv* — **cheap·ness** *n*

cheap·en \'chē-pən\ *vb* **cheap·ened; cheap·en·ing** \'chēp-(ə-)niŋ\ *vt* **1** [obs. E *cheap* to price, bid for)] *archaic* : to ask the price of **b** : to bid or bargain for **2 a** : to make cheap in price or value **b** : to lower in general esteem **c** : to make tawdry, vulgar, or inferior ~ *vi* : to become cheap

cheap·ie \'chē-pē\ *n* : one that is cheap ⟨$8 and $15 tires — the ~*s* — *Nat'l Observer*⟩ — **cheapie** *adj*

¹**cheap-jack** \'chēp-,jak\ *n* [*cheap* + the name *Jack*] **1** : a haggling huckster **2** : a dealer in cheap merchandise

²**cheap-jack** *adj* **1** : being inferior, cheap, or worthless ⟨~ movie companies⟩ **2** : unscrupulously opportunistic ⟨~ speculators⟩

cheap·skate \-,skāt\ *n* : a miserly or stingy person; *esp* : one who tries to avoid his share of costs or expenses

¹**cheat** \'chēt\ *n* [earlier *cheat* forfeited property, fr. ME *chet* escheat, short for *eschete* — more at ESCHEAT] **1** : the act or an instance of fraudulently deceiving : DECEPTION, FRAUD **2** : one that cheats : PRETENDER, DECEIVER **3** : any of several grasses; *esp* : the common chess (*Bromus secalinus*) **4** : the obtaining of property from another by an intentional active distortion of the truth

^{2}**cheat** *vt* **1 :** to deprive of something valuable by the use of deceit or fraud **2 :** to influence or lead by deceit, trick, or artifice **3 :** to defeat the purpose or blunt the effects of ⟨~ winter of its dreariness — Washington Irving⟩ ~ *vi* **1 a :** to practice fraud or trickery **b :** to violate rules dishonestly (as at cards or on an examination) **2 :** to be sexually unfaithful — often used with *on* — **cheat·er** *n*

syn CHEAT, COZEN, DEFRAUD, SWINDLE, OVERREACH *shared meaning element*: to get something by dishonest or deceitful means

^{1}**check** \'chek\ *n* [ME *chek,* fr. OF *eschec,* fr. Ar *shāh,* fr. Per, lit., king; akin to Gk *ktasthai* to acquire] **1 :** exposure of a chess king to an attack from which he must be protected or moved to safety **2 a :** a sudden stoppage of a forward course or progress : ARREST **b :** a checking of an opposing player (as in ice hockey) **3 :** a sudden pause or break in a progression **4** *archaic* **:** REPRIMAND, REBUKE **5 :** one that arrests, limits, or restrains : RESTRAINT ⟨against all ~*s,* rebukes, and manners, I must advance — Shak.⟩ **6 a :** a standard for testing and evaluation : CRITERION **b :** EXAMINATION **c :** INSPECTION, INVESTIGATION ⟨a loyalty ~ on government employees⟩ **d :** the act of testing or verifying; *also* **:** the sample or unit used for testing or verifying **7 :** a written order directing a bank to pay money as instructed : DRAFT **8 a :** a ticket or token showing ownership or identity or indicating payment made ⟨a baggage ~⟩ **b :** a counter in various games **c :** a slip indicating the amount due : BILL **9** [ME *chek,* short for *cheker* checker] **a :** a pattern in squares that resembles a checkerboard **b :** a fabric woven or printed with such a design **10 :** a mark typically ✓ placed beside an item to show it has been noted, examined, or verified **11 :** CRACK, BREAK **12 :** a rabbet-shaped cutting : RABBET — **check·less** \-ləs\ *adj* — **in check :** under restraint or control ⟨held the enemy *in check*⟩

^{2}**check** *vt* **1 :** to put (a chess king) in check **2** *chiefly dial* **:** REBUKE, REPRIMAND **3 a :** to slow or bring to a stop : BRAKE ⟨hastily ~*ed* the impulse⟩ **b :** to block the progress of (as a hockey player) **4 a :** to restrain or diminish the action or force of : CONTROL **b :** to slack or ease off and then belay again (as a rope) **5 a :** to compare with a source, original, or authority : VERIFY **b :** to inspect for satisfactory condition, accuracy, safety, or performance — usu. used with *out* **c :** to mark with a check as examined, verified, or satisfactory — often used with *off* ⟨~*ed* off each item⟩ **6 a :** to consign for shipment as a service to the holder of a passenger ticket ⟨~*ed* his bags before boarding⟩ **b :** to ship or accept for shipment under such a consignment **7 :** to mark into squares : CHECKER **8 :** to leave or accept for safekeeping in a checkroom **9 :** to make checks or chinks in : cause to crack ⟨the sun ~*s* timber⟩ ~ *vi* **1 a** *of a dog* **:** to stop in a chase esp. when scent is lost **b :** to halt through caution, uncertainty, or fear : STOP **2 a :** to investigate conditions ⟨~*ed* on the passengers' safety⟩ **b :** to correspond point for point : TALLY ⟨the description ~*s* with the photograph⟩ — often used with *out* ⟨his story ~*ed* out⟩ **3 :** to draw a check on a bank **4 :** to waive the right to initiate the betting in a round of poker **5 :** CRACK, SPLIT ***syn*** see RESTRAIN ***ant*** accelerate (*as speed*), advance (*as a plan*), release (*as feelings*) — **check·able** \'chek-ə-bəl\ *adj* — **check into 1 :** to check in at ⟨*check into* a hotel⟩ **2 :** INVESTIGATE ⟨*check into* a rumor⟩ — **check up on :** INVESTIGATE

check·book \'chek-,bu̇k\ *n* **:** a book containing blank checks to be drawn on a bank

^{1}**check·er** \'chek-ər\ *n* [ME *cheker,* fr. OF *eschequier,* fr. *eschec*] **1** *archaic* **:** CHESSBOARD **2 :** a square or spot resembling the markings of a checkerboard **3** [back-formation fr. *checkers*] **:** a man in checkers

^{2}**checker** *vt* **check·ered; check·er·ing** \'chek-(ə-)riŋ\ **1 a :** to variegate with different colors or shades **b :** to vary with contrasting elements or situations ⟨had a ~*ed* career as a racer⟩ **2 :** to mark into squares

^{3}**checker** *n* **:** one that checks; *esp* **:** an employee who checks out purchases in a self-service store (as a supermarket)

check·er·ber·ry \'chek-ə(r)-,ber-ē\ *n* [*checker* (wild service tree) + *berry*] **1 :** any of several reddish berries; *esp* **:** the spicy red berrylike fruit of an American wintergreen (*Gaultheria procumbens*) **2 :** a plant producing checkerberries

check·er·bloom \-ər-,blüm\ *n* [prob. fr. ^{1}*checker* + *bloom*] **:** a purple-flowered mallow (*Sidalcea malvaeflora*) of the western U.S.

check·er·board \-ə(r)-,bō(ə)rd, -,bȯ(ə)rd\ *n* **1 :** a board used in various games (as checkers) with usu. 64 squares in 2 alternating colors **2 :** something that has a pattern or arrangement like a checkerboard

check·ers \'chek-ərz\ *n pl but sing in constr* **:** a checkerboard game for 2 players each with 12 men

check in *vi* **1 :** to register at a hotel **2 :** to report one's presence or arrival by supplying requisite information ⟨*check in* at a convention⟩ ~ *vt* **:** to satisfy all requirements in returning ⟨*check in* the equipment after using⟩

checking account *n* **:** a bank account against which the depositor can draw checks

check·list \'chek-,list\ *n* **:** INVENTORY, CATALOG; *esp* **:** a complete list

check mark *n* **:** CHECK 10 — **check·mark** *vt*

^{1}**check·mate** \'chek-,māt\ *vt* [ME *chekmaten,* fr. *chekmate,* interj. used to announce checkmate, fr. MF *eschec mat,* fr. Ar *shāh māt,* fr. Per, lit., the king is left unable to escape] **1 :** to arrest, thwart, or counter completely **2 :** to check (a chess opponent's king) so that escape is impossible

^{2}**checkmate** *n* **1 a :** the act of checkmating **b :** the situation of a checkmated king **2 :** a complete check

check·off \'chek-,ȯf\ *n* **1 :** the deduction of union dues from a worker's paycheck by the employer **2 :** AUTOMATIC 2

check off \-'ȯf\ *vt* **1 :** to eliminate from further consideration ⟨robbery was *checked off* as a motive⟩ **2 :** to deduct (union dues) from a worker's paycheck ~ *vi* **:** to change a play at the line of scrimmage in football by calling an automatic

check·out \'chek-,au̇t\ *n* **1 :** the action or an instance of checking out **2 :** the time at which a lodger must vacate his room (as in a hotel) or be charged for retaining it **3 :** a counter at which checking out is done **4 a :** the action of examining and testing something for performance, suitability, or readiness **b :** the action of familiarizing oneself with the operation of a mechanical thing (as an airplane)

check out \-'au̇t\ *vi* **:** to vacate and pay for one's lodging (as at a hotel) ~ *vt* **1 :** to satisfy all requirements in taking away ⟨*checked out* a library book⟩ **2 a :** to itemize and reckon up the total cost of and receive payment for (outgoing merchandise) esp. in a self-service store **b :** to have the cost totaled and pay for (purchases) at a checkout counter

check over *vt* **:** EXAMINE, INVESTIGATE

check·point \'chek-,pȯint\ *n* **:** a point at which a check is performed ⟨vehicles were inspected at various ~*s*⟩

check·rein \-,rān\ *n* **1 :** a short rein looped over a hook on the saddle of a harness to prevent a horse from lowering his head **2 :** a branch rein connecting the driving rein of one horse of a span or pair with the bit of the other

check·room \-,rüm, -,ru̇m\ *n* **:** a room at which baggage, parcels, or clothing is checked

check·row \-,rō\ *vt* **:** to plant (as corn) at the points of intersection of right-angled rows to permit two-way cultivation

check·up \-,əp\ *n* **:** EXAMINATION; *esp* **:** a general physical examination

ched·dar \'ched-ər\ *n, often cap* [*Cheddar,* England] **:** a hard cheese of smooth texture and a flavor ranging from mild to sharp depending on the length of cure

che·der \'kād-ər, 'ked-\ *var of* HEDER

chee·cha·ko \chi-'chäk-(,)ō, -'chȯk-\ *n, pl* **-kos** [Chinook Jargon *chee chahco,* fr. Chinook *t'shi* new + Nootka *chako* to come] *chiefly Northwest* **:** TENDERFOOT 1

^{1}**cheek** \'chēk\ *n* [ME *cheke,* fr. OE *cēace;* akin to MLG *kāke* jawbone] **1 :** the fleshy side of the face below the eye and above and to the side of the mouth; *broadly* **:** the lateral aspect of the head **2 :** something suggestive of the human cheek in position or form; *esp* **:** one of two laterally paired parts **3 :** insolent boldness and flaunted self-assurance **4 :** BUTTOCK 1 ***syn*** see TEMERITY ***ant*** diffidence — **cheek·ful** \-,fu̇l\ *n* — **cheek by jowl :** in close proximity

^{2}**cheek** *vt* **:** to speak rudely or impudently to

cheek·bone \'chēk-'bōn, -,bōn\ *n* **:** the prominence below the eye that is formed by the zygomatic bone; *also* **:** ZYGOMATIC BONE

-cheeked \'chēkt\ *adj comb form* **:** having cheeks of a specified nature ⟨rosy-*cheeked*⟩

cheeky \'chē-kē\ *adj* **cheek·i·er; -est 1 :** having or showing cheek : IMPUDENT **2 :** having well-developed cheeks — used esp. of a bulldog — **cheek·i·ly** \-kə-lē\ *adv* — **cheek·i·ness** \-kē-nəs\ *n*

cheep \'chēp\ *vi* [imit.] **1 :** to utter faint shrill sounds : PEEP **2 :** to utter a single word or sound — **cheep** *n*

^{1}**cheer** \'chi(ə)r\ *n* [ME *chere* face, cheer, fr. OF, face] **1 a** *obs* **:** FACE **b** *archaic* **:** facial expression **2 :** state of mind or heart : SPIRIT ⟨be of good ~ — Mt 9:2(AV)⟩ **3 :** lightness of mind and feeling : ANIMATION, GAIETY **4 :** hospitable entertainment : WELCOME **5 :** food and drink for a feast : FARE **6 :** something that gladdens ⟨words of ~⟩ **7 :** a shout of applause or encouragement

^{2}**cheer** *vt* **1 a :** to instill with hope or courage : COMFORT — usu. used with *up* **b :** to make glad or happy — usu. used with *up* **2 :** to urge on or encourage esp. by shouts ⟨*cheered* the team on⟩ **3 :** to applaud with shouts ~ *vi* **1** *obs* **:** to be mentally or emotionally disposed **2 :** to grow or be cheerful : REJOICE — usu. used with *up* **3 :** to utter a shout of applause or triumph — **cheer·er** *n*

cheer·ful \'chir-fəl\ *adj* **1 a :** full of good spirits : MERRY **b :** UNGRUDGING ⟨~ obedience⟩ **2 :** conducive to cheer : likely to dispel gloom or worry ⟨sunny ~ room⟩ ***syn*** see GLAD ***ant*** glum, gloomy — **cheer·ful·ly** \-f(ə-)lē\ *adv* — **cheer·ful·ness** \-fəl-nəs\ *n*

cheer·io \,chi(ə)r-ē-'ō\ *interj* [*cheery* + *-o*] *chiefly Brit* — usu. used as a farewell and sometimes as a greeting or toast

cheer·lead·er \'chi(ə)r-,lēd-ər\ *n* **:** one that calls for and directs organized cheering (as at a football game) — **cheer·lead** \-,lēd\ *vt*

cheer·less \'chi(ə)r-ləs\ *adj* **:** lacking qualities that cheer : BLEAK, JOYLESS ⟨a ~ room⟩ — **cheer·less·ly** *adv* — **cheer·less·ness** *n*

cheers \'chi(ə)rz\ *interj* — used as a toast

cheery \'chi(ə)r-ē\ *adj* **cheer·i·er; -est 1 :** marked by cheerfulness or good spirits **2 :** causing or suggesting cheerfulness — **cheer·i·ly** \'chir-ə-lē\ *adv* — **cheer·i·ness** \'chir-ē-nəs\ *n*

^{1}**cheese** \'chēz\ *n, often attrib* [ME *chese,* fr. OE *cēse;* akin to OHG *kāsi* cheese; both fr. a prehistoric WGmc word borrowed fr. L *caseus* cheese; akin to OE *hwatherian* to foam, Skt *kvathati* he boils] **1 a :** curd separated from whey, consolidated by molding or pressure, and usu. ripened for use as food **b :** an often cylindrical cake of this food **2 :** something resembling cheese in shape or consistency

^{2}**cheese** *vt* **cheesed; chees·ing** [origin unknown] **:** to put an end to : STOP — **cheese it** — used in the imperative as a warning of danger ⟨*cheese it,* the cops⟩

^{3}**cheese** *n* [perh. fr. Urdu *chīz* thing] *slang* **:** someone important : BOSS ⟨the . . . big ~ who bought the program for his network — Neil Hickey⟩

cheese·burg·er \'chēz-,bər-gər\ *n* [*cheese* + ham*burger*] **:** a hamburger containing a slice of cheese

cheese·cake \-,kāk\ *n* **1 :** a cake made by baking a mixture of cream cheese or cottage cheese, eggs, and sugar or a filling of similar texture in a pastry shell or a mold lined with sweet crumbs **2 :** a photographic display of shapely and scantily clothed female figures — compare BEEFCAKE

cheese·cloth \-,klȯth\ *n* [fr. its use in cheesemaking] **:** a very lightweight unsized cotton gauze

cheese·mak·er \-,mā-kər\ *n* **:** one that makes cheese — **cheese·mak·ing** \-kiŋ\ *n*

cheese·par·ing \-,pa(ə)r-iŋ, -,pe(ə)r-\ *n* **1 :** something worthless or insignificant **2 :** miserly or petty economizing : STINGINESS — **cheeseparing** *adj*

cheesy \'chē-zē\ *adj* **chees·i·er; -est** **1 a :** resembling or suggesting cheese esp. in consistency or odor **b :** containing cheese **2** *slang* **:** SHABBY, CHEAP — **chees·i·ness** *n*

chee·tah \'chēt-ə\ *n* [Hindi *cītā*, fr. Skt *citrakāya* tiger, fr. *citra* bright + *kāya* body] **:** a long-legged spotted swift-moving African and formerly Asiatic cat (*Acinonyx jubatus*) about the size of a small leopard that has blunt nonretractile claws and is often trained to run down game

chef \'shef\ *n* [F, short for *chef de cuisine* head of the kitchen] **1 :** a skilled male cook who manages a kitchen **2 :** COOK — **chef·dom** \-dəm\ *n*

chef d'oeu·vre \shā-dœvrᵊ, (ˈ)shā-'də(r)v\ *n, pl* **chefs d'oeuvre** \-dœvrᵊ, -'də(r)v(z)\ [F *chef-d'oeuvre*, lit., leading work] **:** a masterpiece esp. in art or literature

che·la \'kē-lə\ *n, pl* **che·lae** \-(ˌ)lē\ [NL, fr. Gk *chēlē* claw] **:** a pincerlike organ or claw borne by a limb of a crustacean or arachnid

[1]**che·late** \'kē-ˌlāt\ *adj* **1 :** resembling or having chelae **2** [Gk *chēlē* claw, hoof] **:** of, relating to, or having a ring structure that usu. contains a metal ion held by coordination bonds — **chelate** *n*

[2]**chelate** *vb* **che·lat·ed; che·lat·ing** *vt* **:** to combine with (a metal) so as to form a chelate ring ~ *vi* **:** to react so as to form a chelate ring — **che·lat·able** \-ˌlāt-ə-bəl\ *adj* — **che·la·tion** \kē-'lā-shən\ *n* — **che·la·tor** \-ˌlāt-ər\ *n*

che·lic·era \ki-'lis-ə-rə\ *n, pl* **-er·ae** \-ˌrē\ [NL, fr. F *chélicère*, fr. Gk *chēlē* + *keras* horn — more at HORN] **:** one of the anterior pair of appendages of an arachnid often specialized as fangs — **che·lic·er·al** \-ə-rəl\ *adj*

Chel·le·an *or* **Chel·li·an** \'shel-ē-ən\ *adj* [F *chelléen*, fr. *Chelles*, France] **:** ABBEVILLIAN

che·lo·ni·an \ki-'lō-nē-ən\ *adj* [Gk *chelōnē* tortoise] **:** of, relating to, or being a tortoise or turtle — **chelonian** *n*

chem *abbr* chemical; chemist; chemistry

chem- *or* **chemo-** *also* **chemi-** *comb form* [NL, fr. LGk *chēmeia* alchemy — more at ALCHEMY] **1** chemical **:** chemistry ⟨*chemos*mosis⟩ ⟨*chemo*taxis⟩ **2 :** chemically ⟨*chemi*sorb⟩

Chem·a·ku·an \ˌchem-ə-'kü-ən\ *n* **:** a language stock of the Mosan phylum in the state of Washington

chem·ic \'kem-ik\ *adj* [NL *chimicus* alchemist, fr. ML *alchimicus*, fr. *alchymia* alchemy] **1** *archaic* **:** ALCHEMIC **2 :** CHEMICAL

[1]**chem·i·cal** \'kem-i-kəl\ *adj* **1 :** of, relating to, used in, or produced by chemistry **2 a :** acting or operated or produced by chemicals **b :** detectable by chemical means — **chem·i·cal·ly** \-i-k(ə-)lē\ *adv*

[2]**chemical** *n* **:** a substance (as an element or chemical compound) obtained by a chemical process or used for producing a chemical effect

chemical engineering *n* **:** engineering dealing with the industrial application of chemistry

chemical warfare *n* **:** tactical warfare using incendiary mixtures, smokes, or irritant, burning, poisonous, or asphyxiating gases

che·mi·lu·mi·nes·cence \ˌkem-i-ˌlü-mə-'nes-ᵊn(t)s, ˌkē-mi-\ *n* [ISV] **:** luminescence due to chemical reaction usu. at low temperatures; *esp* **:** BIOLUMINESCENCE — **che·mi·lu·mi·nes·cent** \-'nes-ᵊnt\ *adj*

che·min de fer \shə-ˌman-də-'fe(ə)r\ *n, pl* **che·mins de fer** \-ˌman-də-\ [F, lit., railroad] **:** a card game in which two hands are dealt, any number of players may bet against the dealer, and the winning hand is the one that comes closer to but does not exceed a count of nine on two or three cards

che·mise \shə-'mēz\ *n* [ME, fr. OF, shirt, fr. LL *camisia*] **1 :** a woman's one-piece undergarment **2 :** a loose straight-hanging dress

chem·i·sette \ˌshem-i-'zet\ *n* [F, dim. of *chemise*] **:** a woman's garment; *esp* **:** one (as of lace) to fill the open front of a dress

che·mism \'kem-ˌiz-əm, 'kē-ˌmiz-\ *n* **1 :** chemical activity or affinity **2 :** operation in obedience to chemical laws

che·mi·sorb \'kem-i-ˌsȯ(ə)rb, 'kēmi-, -ˌzȯ(ə)rb\ *or* **che·mo·sorb** \'kē-mə-, 'kem-ə-\ *vt* [*chem-* + *-sorb* (as in *adsorb*)] **:** to take up and hold usu. irreversibly by chemical forces — **che·mi·sorp·tion** \ˌkem-i-'sȯrp-shən, ˌkē-mi-, -'zȯrp-\ *n*

chem·ist \'kem-əst\ *n* [NL *chimista*, short for ML *alchimista*] **1 a** *obs* **:** ALCHEMIST **b :** one trained in chemistry **2** *Brit* **:** PHARMACIST

chem·is·try \'kem-ə-strē\ *n, pl* **-tries** **1 :** a science that deals with the composition, structure, and properties of substances and of the transformations that they undergo **2 a :** the composition and chemical properties of a substance ⟨the ~ of iron⟩ **b :** chemical processes and phenomena (as of an organism) ⟨blood ~⟩

che·mo·au·to·tro·phic \ˌkē-mō-ˌȯt-ə-'trō-fik *also* ˌkem-ō-\ *adj* **:** being autotrophic and oxidizing some inorganic compound as a source of energy — **chemo·au·to·tro·phi·cal·ly** \-fi-k(ə-)lē\ *adv* — **chemo·au·tot·ro·phy** \-ȯ-'tä-trə-fē\ *n*

che·mo·pro·phy·lax·is \-ˌprō-fə-'lak-səs *also* -ˌpräf-ə-\ *n* **:** the prevention of infectious disease by the use of chemical agents — **che·mo·pro·phy·lac·tic** \-'lak-tik\ *adj*

che·mo·re·cep·tion \-ri-'sep-shən\ *n* [ISV] **:** the physiological reception of chemical stimuli — **che·mo·re·cep·tive** \-'sep-tiv\ *adj* — **che·mo·re·cep·tiv·i·ty** \-ˌrē-ˌsep-'tiv-ət-ē, -ri-\ *n*

che·mo·re·cep·tor \-ri-'sep-tər\ *n* [ISV] **:** a sense organ (as a taste bud) responding to chemical stimuli

che·mo·sphere \'kē-mə-ˌsfi(ə)r, 'kem-ə-\ *n* **:** a stratum of the upper atmosphere in which photochemical reactions are prevalent and which begins about 20 miles above the earth's surface

che·mo·ster·il·ant \ˌkē-mō-'ster-ə-lənt *also* ˌkem-ō-\ *n* [*chemosteril*ize + *-ant*] **:** a substance that produces irreversible sterility (as of an insect) without marked alteration of mating habits or life expectancy

che·mo·sur·gery \-'sərj-(ə-)rē\ *n* **:** removal by chemical means of diseased or unwanted tissue — **che·mo·sur·gi·cal** \-'sər-ji-kəl\ *adj*

che·mo·syn·the·sis \-'sin(t)-thə-səs\ *n* [ISV] **:** synthesis of organic compounds (as in living cells) by energy derived from chemical reactions — **che·mo·syn·thet·ic** \-sin-'thet-ik\ *adj*

che·mo·tac·tic \-'tak-tik\ *adj* **:** involving or exhibiting chemotaxis — **che·mo·tac·ti·cal·ly** \-ti-k(ə-)lē\ *adv*

che·mo·tax·is \-'tak-səs\ *n* [NL] **:** orientation or movement of an organism in relation to chemical agents

che·mo·tax·on·o·my \-(ˌ)tak-'sän-ə-mē\ *n* **:** the classification of plants and animals based on similarities and differences in biochemical composition — **che·mo·tax·o·nom·ic** \-ˌtak-sə-'näm-ik\ *adj* — **che·mo·tax·o·nom·i·cal·ly** \-i-k(ə-)lē\ *adv* — **che·mo·tax·on·o·mist** \-(ˌ)tak-'sän-ə-məst\ *n*

che·mo·ther·a·peu·tic \-ˌther-ə-'pyüt-ik\ *or* **che·mo·ther·a·peu·ti·cal** \-i-kəl\ *adj* **:** of or relating to chemotherapy — **chemotherapeutic** *n* — **che·mo·ther·a·peu·ti·cal·ly** \-i-k(ə-)lē\ *adv*

che·mo·ther·a·py \-'ther-ə-pē\ *n* [ISV] **:** the use of chemical agents in the treatment or control of disease

che·mot·ro·pism \ki-'mä-trə-ˌpiz-əm, ke-\ *n* [ISV] **:** orientation of cells or organisms in relation to chemical stimuli

chem·ur·gy \'kem-(ˌ)ər-jē, kə-'mər-\ *n* **:** a branch of applied chemistry that deals with industrial utilization of organic raw materials esp. from farm products — **chem·ur·gic** \kə-'mər-jik, ke-\ *adj* — **chem·ur·gi·cal·ly** \-ji-k(ə-)lē\ *adv*

che·nille \shə-'nē(ə)l\ *n* [F, lit., caterpillar, fr. L *canicula*, dim. of *canis* dog; fr. its hairy appearance — more at HOUND] **1 :** a wool, cotton, silk, or rayon yarn with protruding pile; *also* **:** a pile-face fabric with a filling of this yarn **2 :** an imitation of chenille yarn or fabric

che·no·pod \'kē-nə-ˌpäd, 'ken-ə-\ *n* [deriv. of Gk *chēn* goose + *podion*, dim. of *pod-*, *pous* foot — more at FOOT] **:** a plant of the goosefoot family

cheong·sam \'chȯŋ-ˌsäm\ *n* [Chin (Cant) *ch'eūng shaam*, lit., long gown] **:** a dress with a slit skirt and a mandarin collar worn esp. by oriental women

cheque \'chek\ *chiefly Brit var of* [1]CHECK 7

che·quer \'chek-ər\ *chiefly Brit var of* CHECKER

cher·i·moya \ˌcher-ə-'mȯi-(y)ə, ˌchir-\ *n* [Sp *chirimoya*] **:** a small widely cultivated tropical American tree (*Annona cherimola*) of the custard-apple family with a round, oblong, or heart-shaped fruit that has a pitted rind

cher·ish \'cher-ish\ *vt* [ME *cherisshen*, fr. MF *cheriss-*, stem of *cherir* to cherish, fr. OF, fr. *chier* dear, fr. L *carus* — more at CHARITY] **1 a :** to hold dear **:** feel or show affection for **b :** to keep or cultivate with care and affection **:** NURTURE **2 :** to entertain or harbor in the mind deeply and resolutely ⟨still ~*es* that memory⟩ ***syn*** see APPRECIATE ***ant*** neglect — **cher·ish·able** \-ə-bəl\ *adj* — **cher·ish·er** *n*

cher·no·zem \ˌcher-nə-'zhȯm, -'zem\ *n* [Russ, lit., black earth] **:** a dark-colored zonal soil with a deep rich humus horizon found in temperate to cool climates of rather low humidity — **cher·no·zem·ic** \-'zhȯm-ik, -'zem-\ *adj*

Cher·o·kee \'cher-ə-(ˌ)kē\ *n, pl* **Cherokee** *or* **Cherokees** [prob. fr. Creek *tciloki* people of a different speech] **1 :** a member of an Amerindian people orig. of Tennessee and No. Carolina **2 :** the language of the Cherokee people

Cherokee rose *n* **:** a Chinese climbing rose (*Rosa laevigata*) with a fragrant white blossom

che·root \shə-'rüt, chə-\ *n* [Tamil *curuṭṭu*, lit., roll] **:** a cigar cut square at both ends

cher·ry \'cher-ē\ *n, pl* **cherries** [ME *chery*, fr. ONF *cherise* (taken as a plural), fr. LL *ceresia*, fr. L *cerasus* cherry tree, fr. Gk *kerasos* — more at CORNEL] **1 a :** any of numerous trees and shrubs (genus *Prunus*) of the rose family that bear pale yellow to deep red or blackish smooth-skinned drupes enclosing a smooth seed and that belong to any of several varieties including some cultivated for their fruits or ornamental flowers **b :** the fruit of a cherry **c :** the wood of a cherry **2 :** a variable color averaging a moderate red **3 a :** HYMEN **b :** VIRGINITY — **cher·ry·like** \-ē-ˌlīk\ *adj*

cherry bomb *n* **:** a powerful globular red firecracker

cherry picker *n* **:** a traveling crane equipped for holding a passenger at the end of the boom

cherry plum *n* **:** an Asiatic plum (*Prunus cerasifera*) used extensively in Europe as a stock on which to bud domestic varieties

cher·ry·stone \'cher-ē-ˌstōn\ *n* **:** a small quahog

cher·so·nese \'kər-sə-ˌnēz, -ˌnēs\ *n* [L *chersonesus*, fr. Gk *chersonēsos*, fr. *chersos* dry land + *nēsos* island] **:** PENINSULA

chert \'chərt, 'chat\ *n* [origin unknown] **:** a rock resembling flint and consisting essentially of cryptocrystalline quartz or fibrous chalcedony — **cherty** \-ē\ *adj*

cher·ub \'cher-əb\ *n*, [L, fr. Gk *cheroub*, fr. Heb *kĕrūbh*] **1** *pl* **cher·u·bim** \'cher-(y)ə-ˌbim, 'ker-\ **a :** a biblical attendant of God or of a holy place often represented as a being with large wings, a human head, and an animal body **1** *pl* **:** an order of angels — see CELESTIAL HIERARCHY **2** *pl* **cherubs** **a :** a beautiful usu. winged child in painting and sculpture **b :** an innocent-looking usu. chubby and rosy person — **che·ru·bic** \chə-'rü-bik\ *adj* — **che·ru·bi·cal·ly** \-bi-k(ə-)lē\ *adv* — **cher·ub·like** \'cher-əb-ˌlīk\ *adj*

cher·vil \'chər-vəl\ *n* [ME *cherville*, fr. OE *cerfille*; akin to OHG *kervila*] **:** an aromatic herb (*Anthriscus cerefolium*) of the carrot family with divided leaves that are often used in soups and salads; *also* **:** any of several related plants

Ches *abbr* Cheshire

Ches·a·peake Bay retriever \ˌches-(ə-)ˌpēk-ˌbā-\ *n* **:** a large powerful sporting dog developed in Maryland by crossing Newfoundlands with native retrievers

Chesh·ire cat \ˌchesh-ər-\ *n* [*Cheshire*, England] **:** a cat with a broad grin in Lewis Carroll's *Alice's Adventures in Wonderland*

Cheshire cheese *n* **:** a cheese similar to cheddar made chiefly in Cheshire, England

[1]**chess** \'ches\ *n* [ME *ches*, fr. OF *esches*, acc. pl. of *eschec* check at chess — more at CHECK] **:** a game for two players each of whom

ə abut ᵊ kitten ər further a back ā bake ä cot, cart
aủ out ch chin e less ē easy g gift i trip ī life
j joke ŋ sing ō flow ȯ flaw ȯi coin th thin th this
ü loot ủ foot y yet yü few yủ furious zh vision

moves his 16 pieces according to fixed rules across a checkerboard and tries to checkmate his opponent's king — **chess-board** \-,bō(ə)rd, -,bȯ(ə)rd\ *n* — **chess-man** \-,man, -mən\ *n*

²**chess** *n* [origin unknown] : a weedy annual bromegrass (*Bromus secalinus*) widely distributed as a weed esp. in grain; *broadly* : any of several weedy bromegrasses

chest \'chest\ *n* [ME, fr. OE *cest;* akin to OHG & ON *kista* chest] **1 a** : a container for storage or shipping; *esp* : a box with a lid used esp. for the safekeeping of belongings **b** : a cupboard used esp. for the storing of medicines or first-aid supplies **2** : the place where money of a public institution is kept : TREASURY; *also* : the fund so kept **3** : the part of the body enclosed by the ribs and breastbone — **chest-ful** \-,fùl\ *n*

-chest-ed \'ches-təd\ *adj comb form* : having (such) a chest ⟨flat-*chested*⟩ ⟨deep-*chested*⟩

ches-ter-field \'ches-tər-,fēld\ *n* [fr. a 19th cent. Earl of Chesterfield] **1** : a single-breasted or double-breasted semifitted overcoat with velvet collar **2** : a davenport usu. with upright armrests

Ches-ter White \,ches-tər-\ *n* [*Chester* County, Pa.] : any of a breed of large white swine

¹**chest-nut** \'ches-(,)nət\ *n* [ME *chasteine, chesten* chestnut tree, fr. MF *chastaigne,* fr. L *castanea,* fr. Gk *kastanea*] **1 a** : a tree or shrub (genus *Castanea*) of the beech family **b** : the edible nut of a chestnut **c** : the wood of a chestnut **2** : a grayish to reddish brown **3** : HORSE CHESTNUT **4** : a chestnut-colored animal; *specif* : a horse having a body color of any shade of pure or reddish brown with mane, tail, and points of the same or a lighter shade — compare ²BAY 1, ¹SORREL 1a **5** : a callosity on the inner side of the leg of the horse **6 a** : an old joke or story **b** : something (as a musical piece) repeated to the point of staleness

²**chestnut** *adj* **1** : of, relating to, or resembling a chestnut **2** : of the color chestnut

chestnut blight *n* : a destructive fungous disease of the American chestnut marked by cankers of bark and cambium

chest of drawers *n* : a piece of furniture designed to contain a set of drawers (as for holding clothing)

chesty *adj* **chest-i-er; -est 1** : marked by a large or well-developed chest **2** : proudly or arrogantly self-assertive

che-val-de-frise \shə-,val-də-'frēz\ *n, pl* **che-vaux-de-frise** \shə-,vōd-ə-\ [F, lit., horse from Friesland] **1** : a defense consisting of a timber or an iron barrel covered with projecting spikes and often strung with barbed wire **2** : a protecting line (as of spikes) on top of a wall — usu. used in pl.

che-val glass \shə-'val-\ *n* [F *cheval* horse, support] : a full-length mirror in a frame by which it may be tilted

che-va-lier \,shev-ə-'li(ə)r, *esp for 1b & 2 also* shə-'val-,yā\ *n* [ME, fr. MF, fr. LL *caballarius* horseman] **1 a** : CAVALIER 2 **b** : a member of any of various orders of knighthood or of merit (as the Legion of Honor) **2 a** : a member of the lowest rank of French nobility **b** : a cadet of the French nobility **3** : a chivalrous man

che-ve-lure \shə-'lùer\ *n* [F, fr. L *capillatura,* fr. *capillatus* having hair, fr. *capillus* hair] : a head of hair

chev-i-ot \'shev-ē-ət, *esp Brit* 'chev-\ *n, often cap* **1** : any of a breed of hardy hornless medium-wooled meat-type sheep that are a source of quality mutton and have their origin in the Cheviot hills **2 a** : a fabric of cheviot wool **b** : a heavy rough napped plain or twill fabric of coarse wool or worsted **c** : a sturdy soft-finished plain or twill cotton shirting

chev-ron \'shev-rən\ *n* [ME, fr. MF, rafter, chevron, fr. (assumed) VL *caprion-, caprio* rafter; akin to L *caper* goat] : a figure, pattern, or object having the shape of a V or an inverted V: as **a** *or* **chev-er-on** \-(ə-)rən\ : a heraldic charge consisting of two diagonal stripes meeting at an angle usu. with the point up **b** : a sleeve badge that usu. consists of one or more chevron-shaped stripes often with arcs or distinctive emblems and that indicates the wearer's rank and service (as in the armed forces) — **chev-roned** \-rənd\ *adj*

chevrons b: *1* marine staff sergeant, *2* air force staff sergeant, *3* army staff sergeant

chev-ro-tain \'shev-rə-,tān\ *n* [F, dim. of *chevrot* kid, fawn, fr. MF, dim. of *chèvre* goat, fr. L *capra* she-goat, fem. of *capr-, caper* he-goat] : any of several very small hornless ruminants (family Tragulidae) of tropical Asia and West Africa

¹**chew** \'chü\ *vb* [ME *chewen,* fr. OE *cēowan;* akin to OHG *kiuwan* to chew, OSlav *živati*] *vt* : to crush, grind, or gnaw (as food) with or as if with the teeth : MASTICATE ~ *vi* : to chew something; *specif* : to chew tobacco — **chew-able** \-ə-bəl\ *adj* — **chew-er** *n* — **chewy** \'chü-ē\ *adj* — **chew the rag** *or* **chew the fat** *slang* : to make friendly familiar conversation : CHAT

²**chew** *n* **1** : the act of chewing ⟨a ~ of tobacco⟩ **2** : something for chewing ⟨a ~ of tobacco⟩

chewing gum *n* : a sweetened and flavored insoluble plastic material (as a preparation of chicle) used for chewing

che-wink \chi-'wink\ *n* [imit.] : TOWHEE 1

chew out *vt* : to bawl out : REPRIMAND

chew over *vt* : to meditate on : think about reflectively

Chey-enne \shī-'an, -'en\ *n, pl* **Cheyenne** *or* **Cheyennes** [CanF, F, fr. Dakota *Shaiyena,* fr. *shaia* to speak unintelligibly] **1** : a member of an Amerindian people of the western plains of the U.S. **2** : the Algonquian language of the Cheyenne people

chg *abbr* **1** change **2** charge

chi \'kī\ *n* [Gk *chei*] : the 22d letter of the Greek alphabet — see ALPHABET table

Chi-an-ti \kē-'änt-ē, -'ant-\ *n* [It, fr. the *Chianti* mt. area, Italy] : a still dry usu. red table wine

Chi-an turpentine \'kī-ən-\ *n* [*Chios,* Greece] : TURPENTINE 1a

chiao \'tyaù\ *n, pl* **chiao** [Chin (Pek) *chiao³*] — see *yuan* at MONEY table

chiar-oscu-rist \kē-,är-ə-'sk(y)ùr-əst, kē-,ar-\ *n* : an artist in chiaroscuro

chiar-oscu-ro \-'sk(y)ù(ə)r-(,)ō\ *n, pl* **-ros** [It, fr. *chiaro* clear, light + *oscuro* obscure, dark] **1** : pictorial representation in terms of light and shade without regard to color **2** : the arrangement or treatment of light and dark parts in a pictorial work of art **3** : a 16th century woodcut technique involving the use of several blocks to print different tones of the same color; *also* : a print made by this technique

chi-asm \'kī-,az-əm\ *n* [NL *chiasma*] : CHIASMA 1

chi-as-ma \kī-'az-mə\ *n, pl* **-ma-ta** \-mət-ə\ [NL, X-shaped configuration, fr. Gk, crosspiece, fr. *chiazein* to mark with a chi, fr. *chi* (x)] **1** : an anatomical intersection or decussation — compare OPTIC CHIASMA **2** : a cross-shaped configuration of paired chromatids visible in the diplotene of meiotic prophase and considered the cytological equivalent of genetic crossing-over — **chi-as-mat-ic** \,kī-əz-'mat-ik\ *adj*

chi-as-mus \kī-'az-məs\ *n* [NL, fr. Gk *chiasmos,* fr. *chiazein* to mark with a chi] : an inverted relationship between the syntactic elements of parallel phrases (as in Goldsmith's *to stop too fearful, and too faint to go*)

chiaus \'chaús(h)\ *n* [Turk *çavuş,* fr. *çav* voice, news] : a Turkish messenger or courtier

Chib-cha \'chib-(,)chä\ *n, pl* **Chibcha** *or* **Chibchas** [Sp, of Amer-Ind origin] **1** : a member of an Amerindian people of central Colombia **2** : the extinct language of the Chibcha people

Chib-chan \-chən\ *adj* : of, relating to, or constituting a language stock of Colombia and Central America

chi-bouk *or* **chi-bouque** \chə-'bük, shə-\ *n* [F *chibouque,* fr. Turk *çubuk*] : a long-stemmed Turkish tobacco pipe with a clay bowl

¹**chic** \'shēk\ *n* [F] : smart elegance and sophistication esp. of dress or manner : STYLE ⟨wears her clothes with superb ~⟩

²**chic** *adj* **1** : cleverly stylish : SMART ⟨the woman who is ~ adapts fashion to her own personality —Elizabeth L. Post⟩ **2** : currently fashionable : MODISH ⟨a ~ restaurant⟩ — **chic-ly** *adv* — **chic-ness** *n*

chi-ca-lo-te \,chik-ə-'lōt-ē\ *n* [Sp, fr. Nahuatl *chicalotl*] : a white-flowered prickly poppy (*Argemone platyceras*) of Mexico and the southwestern U.S.

Chi-ca-na \chi-'kän-ə, shi-\ *n* [*Chicano* + *-a* (fr. Sp, fem. ending)] : a female Chicano — **Chicana** *adj*

¹**chi-cane** \shik-'ān, chik-\ *vb* **chi-caned; chi-can-ing** [F *chicaner,* fr. MF, to quibble, prevent justice] *vi* : to use chicanery ⟨a wretch he had taught to lie and ~ —George Meredith⟩ ~ *vt* : TRICK, CHEAT

²**chicane** *n* **1** : CHICANERY **2 a** : an obstacle on a racecourse **b** : a series of tight turns in opposite directions in an otherwise straight stretch of a road-racing course **3** : the absence of trumps in a hand of cards

chi-ca-nery \-'ān-(ə-)rē\ *n, pl* **-ner-ies 1** : deception by artful subterfuge or sophistry : TRICKERY **2** : a piece of sharp practice (as at law) : TRICK

Chi-ca-no \chi-'kän-(,)ō, shi-\ *n, pl* **-nos** [modif. of Sp *mejicano* Mexican] : an American of Mexican descent — **Chicano** *adj*

chi-chi \'shē-(,)shē, 'chē-(,)chē\ *adj* [F] **1** : elaborately ornamented : SHOWY, FRILLY ⟨a ~ dress⟩ **2** : ARTY, PRECIOUS ⟨~ poetry⟩ **3** : CHIC, FASHIONABLE ⟨a ~ nightclub⟩

²**chichi** *n* **1** : frilly or elaborate ornamentation **2** : AFFECTATION, PRECIOSITY **3** : CHIC

chick \'chik\ *n* **1 a** : CHICKEN; *esp* : one newly hatched **b** : the young of any bird **2** : CHILD **3** : a young woman

chick-a-dee \'chik-ə-(,)dē\ *n* [imit.] : any of several crestless American titmice (genus *Penthestes* or *Parus*) usu. with the crown of the head sharply demarked and darker than the body

chick-a-ree \'chik-ə-,rē\ *n* [imit.] : an American red squirrel (*Sciurus hudsonicus*); *also* : a related squirrel

Chick-a-saw \'chik-ə-,sȯ\ *n, pl* **Chickasaw** *or* **Chickasaws 1** : a member of an Amerindian people of Mississippi and Alabama **2** : a dialect of Choctaw spoken by the Chickasaw

¹**chick-en** \'chik-ən\ *n* [ME *chiken,* fr. OE *cicen* young chicken; akin to OE *cocc* cock] **1 a** : the common domestic fowl (*Gallus gallus*) esp. when young; *also* : its flesh used as food **b** : any of various birds or their young **2** : a young woman **3 a** : COWARD **b** : any of various contests in which the participants risk personal safety in order to see which one will give up first **4** *slang* : the petty details of duty or discipline

²**chicken** *adj* **1** *slang* : SCARED **2** *slang* : afraid to do something : insistent on petty esp. military discipline

³**chicken** *vi* **chick-ened; chick-en-ing** \'chik-(ə-)niŋ\ : to lose one's nerve — usu. used with *out* ⟨seemed to exhibit courage, manliness, and conviction when others ~*ed* out —J. R. Seeley⟩

chicken colonel *n* [fr. the eagle serving as his insignia] *slang* : COLONEL 1a

chicken feed *n, slang* : a paltry sum (as in profits or wages)

chicken hawk *n* : a hawk that preys or is believed to prey on chickens

chick-en-heart-ed \,chik-ən-'härt-əd\ *adj* : TIMID, COWARDLY

chick-en-liv-ered \-'liv-ərd\ *adj* : FAINTHEARTED, COWARDLY

chicken pox *n* : an acute contagious virus disease esp. of children that is marked by low-grade fever and formation of vesicles

chicken snake *n* : RAT SNAKE

chicken wire *n* [fr. its use for making enclosures for chickens] : a light galvanized wire netting of hexagonal mesh

chick-pea \'chik-,pē\ *n* [by folk etymology fr. ME *chiche,* fr. MF, fr. L *cicer*] : an Asiatic leguminous herb (*Cicer arietinum*) cultivated for its short pods with one or two seeds; *also* : its seed

chessboard with men arranged as at beginning of game

chick·weed \'chik-,wēd\ *n* **:** any of various low-growing small-leaved weedy plants of the pink family (esp. genera *Arenaria, Cerastium,* and *Stellaria*) several of which are relished by birds or used as potherbs

chi·cle \'chik-əl, -lē\ *n* [Sp, fr. Nahuatl *chictli*] **:** a gum from the latex of the sapodilla used as the chief ingredient of chewing gum

chi·co \'chē-(,)kō, 'chik-(,)ō\ *n, pl* **chicos** [modif. of Sp *chicalote*] **:** a common greasewood (*Sarcobatus vermiculatus*) of the western U.S.

chic·o·ry \'chik-(ə-)rē\ *n, pl* **-ries** [ME *cicoree,* fr. MF *cichorée, chicorée,* fr. L *cichoreum,* fr. Gk *kichoreia*] **1 :** a thick-rooted usu. blue-flowered European perennial composite herb (*Cichorium intybus*) widely grown for its roots and as a salad plant **2 :** the dried ground roasted root of chicory used to flavor or adulterate coffee

chide \'chīd\ *vb* **chid** \'chid\ *or* **chid·ed** \'chīd-əd\; **chid** *or* **chid·den** \'chid-ᵊn\ *or* **chided; chid·ing** \'chīd-iŋ\ [ME *chiden,* fr. OE *cīdan* to quarrel, chide, fr. *cīd* strife] *vi* **:** to speak out in angry or displeased rebuke ~ *vt* **:** to voice disapproval to **:** reproach in a usu. mild and constructive manner **:** SCOLD ***syn*** see REPROVE

¹chief \'chēf\ *n* [ME, fr. OF, head, chief, fr. L *caput* head — more at HEAD] **1 :** the upper part of a heraldic field **2 :** the head of a body of persons or an organization **:** LEADER ⟨~ of police⟩ **3 :** the principal or most valuable part — **chief·dom** \-dəm\ *n* — **chief·ship** \-,ship\ *n* — **in chief :** in the chief position or place — often used in titles ⟨commander *in chief*⟩

²chief *adj* **1 :** accorded highest rank or office ⟨~ librarian⟩ **2 :** of greatest importance, significance, or influence ⟨the ~ reasons⟩

³chief *adv, archaic* **:** CHIEFLY

chief executive *n* **:** a principal executive officer: as **a :** the president of a republic **b :** the governor of a state

chief justice *n* **:** the presiding or principal judge of a court of justice

¹chief·ly \'chē-flē\ *adv* **1 :** most importantly **:** PRINCIPALLY, ESPECIALLY **2 :** for the most part **:** MOSTLY, MAINLY

²chiefly *adj* **:** of or relating to a chief ⟨~ duties⟩

chief master sergeant *n* **:** a noncommissioned officer in the air force ranking above a senior master sergeant

chief master sergeant of the air force : the ranking noncommissioned officer in the air force serving as adviser to the chief of staff

chief of naval operations : the commanding officer of the navy and a member of the Joint Chiefs of Staff

chief of staff 1 : the ranking officer of a staff in the armed forces serving as principal adviser to a commander **2 :** the commanding officer of the army or air force and a member of the Joint Chiefs of Staff

chief of state : the formal head of a national state as distinguished from the head of the government

chief petty officer *n* **:** an enlisted man in the navy or coast guard ranking above a petty officer first class and below a senior chief petty officer

chief·tain \'chēf-tən\ *n* [ME *chieftaine,* fr. MF *chevetain,* fr. LL *capitaneus* chief — more at CAPTAIN] **:** a chief esp. of a band, tribe, or clan — **chief·tain·ship** \-,ship\ *n*

chief·tain·cy \-sē\ *n, pl* **-cies 1 :** the rank, dignity, office, or rule of a chieftain **2 :** a region or a people ruled by a chief **:** CHIEFDOM

chief warrant officer *n* **:** a warrant officer of senior rank in the armed forces; *also* **:** a commissioned officer in the navy or coast guard ranking below an ensign

chiel \'chē(ə)l\ *or* **chield** \'chē(ə)ld\ *n* [ME (Sc) *cheld,* alter. of ME *child* child] *chiefly Scot* **:** FELLOW, LAD

chiff·chaff \'chif-,chaf\ *n* [imit.] **:** a small grayish European warbler (*Phylloscopus collybita*)

¹chif·fon \shif-'än, 'shif-,\ *n* [F, lit., rag, fr. *chiffe* old rag, alter. of MF *chipe,* fr. ME *chip* chip] **1 :** an ornamental addition (as a knot of ribbons) to a woman's dress **2 :** a sheer fabric esp. of silk

²chiffon *adj* **1 :** resembling chiffon in sheerness or softness **2 :** having a light delicate texture achieved usu. by adding whipped egg whites or whipped gelatin ⟨lemon ~ pie⟩

chif·fo·nier \,shif-ə-'ni(ə)r\ *n* [F *chiffonnier,* fr. *chiffon*] **:** a high narrow chest of drawers

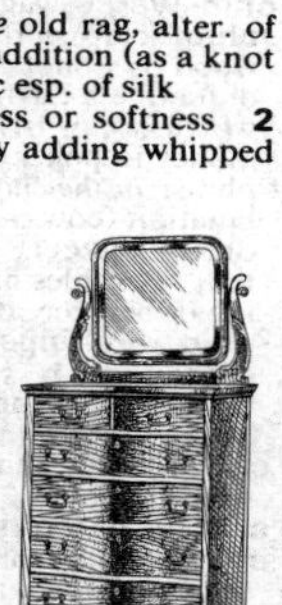
chiffonier

chif·fo·robe \'shif-ə-,rōb\ *n* [*chiffonier* + *wardrobe*] **:** a combination of wardrobe and chest of drawers

chig·ger \'chig-ər, 'jig-\ *n* **1 :** CHIGOE 1 **2** [of African origin; akin to Wolof *jiga* insect] **:** a 6-legged mite larva (family Trombiculidae) that sucks the blood of vertebrates and causes intense irritation

chi·gnon \'shēn-,yän\ *n* [F, fr. MF *chaignon* chain, collar, nape] **:** a knot of hair that is worn at the back of the head and esp. at the nape of the neck

chi·goe \'chig-(,)ō, 'chē-(,)gō\ *n* [of Cariban origin; akin to Galibi *chico* chigoe] **1 :** a tropical flea (*Tunga penetrans*) of which the fertile female causes great discomfort by burrowing under the skin— called also *chigger* **2 :** CHIGGER 2

Chi·hua·hua \chə-'wä-(,)wä, shə-, -wə\ *n* [MexSp, fr. *Chihuahua,* Mexico] **:** a very small round-headed large-eared short-coated dog believed to antedate Aztec civilization

chil·blain \'chil-,blān\ *n* [³*chill*] **:** an inflammatory swelling or sore caused by exposure (as of the feet or hands) to cold

child \'chī(ə)ld\ *n, pl* **chil·dren** \'chil-drən, -dərn\ *often attrib* [ME, fr. OE *cild;* akin to Goth *kilthei* womb, Skt *jathara* belly] **1 a :** an unborn or recently born person **b** *dial* **:** a female infant **2 a :** a young person esp. between infancy and youth **b :** a childlike or childish person **c :** a person not yet of age **3** *usu* **childe** \'chī(ə)ld\ *archaic* **:** a youth of noble birth **4 a :** a son or daughter of human parents **b :** DESCENDANT **5 :** one strongly influenced by another or by a place or state of affairs **6 :** PRODUCT, RESULT ⟨barbed wire . . . is truly a ~ of the plains — W. P. Webb⟩ — **child·less** \'chī(ə)l-(d)ləs\ *adj* — **child·less·ness** *n* — **with child :** PREGNANT

child·bear·ing \'chīl(d)-,bar-iŋ, -,ber-\ *n* **:** the act of bringing forth children **:** PARTURITION — **childbearing** *adj*

child·bed \-,bed\ *n* **:** the condition of a woman in childbirth

childbed fever *n* **:** PUERPERAL FEVER

childbirth \'chīl(d)-,bərth\ *n* **:** PARTURITION

child·hood \'chīld-,hu̇d\ *n* **1 :** the state or period of being a child **2 :** the early period in the development of something ⟨in the ~ of our culture —Michael Novak⟩

child·ish \'chīl-dish\ *adj* **1 :** of, relating to, or befitting a child or childhood ⟨a clear ~ voice⟩ ⟨calling back ~ memories⟩ **2 a :** marked by or suggestive of immaturity and lack of poise ⟨a ~ spiteful remark⟩ **b :** lacking complexity **:** SIMPLE ⟨it's a ~ device, but it works⟩ **c :** deteriorated with age esp. in mind **:** SENILE ⟨the old man was becoming ~⟩ — **child·ish·ly** *adv* — **child·ish·ness** *n*

syn CHILDISH, CHILDLIKE *shared meaning element* **:** having qualities natural or suitable to a child. CHILDISH tends to suggest unpleasing qualities (as fretful impatience or undeveloped taste and mentality) that are appropriate to children but deplorable in adults ⟨a *childish* determination to excel⟩ CHILDLIKE usu. suggests such attractive and admirable qualities of childhood as innocence, straightforwardness, or trust ⟨had a *childlike* faith⟩

child·like \'chī(ə)l-,(d)līk\ *adj* **:** of, relating to, or resembling a child or childhood; *esp* **:** marked by innocence, trust, and ingenuousness ***syn*** see CHILDISH — **child·like·ness** *n*

child·ly \'chī(ə)l-(d)lē\ *adj* **:** CHILDLIKE

child's play *n* **1 :** an extremely simple task or act **2 :** something that is insignificant ⟨his injury was *child's play* compared with the damage he inflicted⟩

Chile–bells \'chil-ē-,belz\ *n pl but sing or pl in constr* **:** COPIHUE

Chile saltpeter \'chil-ē-\ *n* [*Chile,* So. America] **:** sodium nitrate esp. occurring naturally (as in caliche) — called also *Chile niter*

chili *or* **chile** *or* **chil·li** \'chil-ē\ *n, pl* **chil·ies** *or* **chil·es** *or* **chil·lies** [Sp *chile,* fr. Nahuatl *chilli*] **1 a :** HOT PEPPER **b** *usu* *chilli, chiefly Brit* **:** a pepper whether hot or sweet **2 a :** a thick sauce of meat and chilies **b :** CHILI CON CARNE

chil·i·ad \'kil-ē-,ad, -əd\ *n* [LL *chiliad-, chilias,* fr. Gk, fr. *chilioi* thousand — more at MILE] **1 :** a group of 1000 **2 :** a period of 1000 years **:** MILLENNIUM

chil·i·asm \'kil-ē-,az-əm\ *n* [NL *chiliasmus,* fr. LL *chiliastes* one that believes in chiliasm, fr. *chilias*] **:** MILLENARIANISM — **chil·i·ast** \-ē-,ast, -ē-əst\ *n* — **chil·i·as·tic** \,kil-ē-'as-tik\ *adj*

chili con car·ne \,chil-ē-,kän-'kär-nē, -kən-\ *n* [Sp *chile con carne* chili with meat] **:** a spiced stew of ground beef and minced chilies or chili powder usu. with beans

chili sauce *n* **:** a spiced tomato sauce usu. made with red and green peppers

¹chill \'chil\ *vb* [ME *chillen,* fr. *chile* cold, frost, fr. OE *cele;* akin to OE *ceald* cold] *vi* **1 a :** to become cold **b :** to shiver or quake with or as if with cold **2 :** to become taken with a chill **3** *of a metal* **:** to become surface-hardened by sudden cooling ~ *vt* **1 a :** to make cold or chilly **b :** to make cool esp. without freezing **2 :** to affect as if with cold **:** DISPIRIT ⟨were ~*ed* by the drab austerity and the police-state atmosphere — William Attwood⟩ **3 :** to harden the surface of (metal) by sudden cooling — **chill·ing·ly** \-iŋ-lē\ *adv*

²chill *adj* **1 a :** moderately cold **b :** COLD, RAW **2 :** affected by cold ⟨~ travelers⟩ **3 :** DISTANT, FORMAL ⟨a ~ reception⟩ **4 :** DEPRESSING, DISPIRITING ⟨~ penury — Thomas Gray⟩ — **chill·ness** *n*

³chill *n* **1 a :** a sensation of cold accompanied by shivering **b :** a disagreeable sensation of coldness **2 :** a moderate but disagreeable degree of cold **3 :** a check to enthusiasm or warmth of feeling ⟨felt the ~ of his opponent's stare⟩

chill·er \'chil-ər\ *n* **1 :** one that chills **2 :** an eerie or frightening story of murder, violence, or the supernatural

chill factor *n* **:** WINDCHILL

chil·lum \'chil-əm\ *n* [Hindi *cilam,* fr. Per *chilam*] **1 :** the part of a water pipe that contains the substance (as tobacco or hashish) which is smoked; *also* **:** a quantity of a substance thus smoked **2 :** a funnel-shaped clay pipe for smoking

chilly \'chil-ē\ *adj* **chill·i·er; -est 1 :** noticeably cold **:** CHILLING **2 :** unpleasantly affected by cold **3 :** lacking warmth of feeling **4 :** tending to arouse fear or apprehension ⟨~ suspicions⟩ — **chill·i·ly** \'chil-ə-lē\ *adv* — **chill·i·ness** \'chil-ē-nəs\ *n*

chi·mae·ra \kī-'mir-ə, kə-\ *n* [NL, genus name, fr. L, chimera] **:** any of a family (Chimaeridae) of marine elasmobranch fishes with a tapering or threadlike tail and usu. no anal fin

¹chime \'chīm\ *n* [ME, cymbal, fr. OF *chimbe,* fr. L *cymbalum* cymbal] **1 :** an apparatus for chiming a bell or set of bells **2 a :** a musically tuned set of bells **b :** one of a set of objects giving a bell-like sound when struck **3 a :** the sound of a set of bells — usu. used in pl. **b :** a musical sound suggesting that of bells **4 :** ACCORD, HARMONY ⟨such happy ~ of fact and theory —Henry Maudsley⟩

²chime *vb* **chimed; chim·ing** *vi* **1 a :** to make a musical and esp. a harmonious sound **b :** to make the sounds of a chime **2 :** to be or act in accord ⟨the music and the mood *chimed* well together⟩ ~ *vt* **1 :** to cause to sound musically by striking **2 :** to produce by chiming **3 :** to call or indicate by chiming ⟨the clock *chimed* midnight⟩ **4 :** to utter repetitively **:** DIN 2 — **chim·er** *n*

³chime \'chīm\ *n* [ME *chimbe,* fr. OE *cimb-;* akin to OE *camb* comb] **:** the edge or rim of a cask

chime in *vi* **1 :** to break into a conversation or discussion esp. to express an opinion **2 :** to combine harmoniously ⟨the artist's illustrations *chime in* perfectly with the text —*Book Production*⟩ ~ *vt* **:** to remark while chiming in

ə abut ᵊ kitten ər further a back ā bake ä cot, cart
au̇ out ch chin e less ē easy g gift i trip ī life
j joke ŋ sing ō flow ȯ flaw ȯi coin th thin t͟h this
ü loot u̇ foot y yet yü few yu̇ furious zh vision

chi·me·ra *or* **chi·mae·ra** \kī-ˈmir-ə, kə-\ *n* [L *chimaera*, fr. Gk *chimaira* she-goat, chimera; akin to Gk *cheimōn* winter — more at HIBERNATE] **1 a** *cap* : a fire-breathing she-monster in Greek mythology having a lion's head, a goat's body, and a serpent's tail **b** : an imaginary monster compounded of incongruous parts **2** : an illusion or fabrication of the mind; *esp* : an unrealizable dream ⟨a fancy, a ~ in my brain, troubles me in my prayer —John Donne⟩ **3** : an individual, organ, or part consisting of tissues of diverse genetic constitution and occurring esp. in plants and most frequently at a graft union

chi·mere \shə-ˈmi(ə)r, chə-\ *n* [ME *chimmer, chemeyr*] : a loose sleeveless robe (as of black satin) worn by Anglican bishops over the rochet

chi·me·ri·cal \kī-ˈmer-i-kəl, kə-, -ˈmir-\ *or* **chi·me·ric** \-ik\ *adj* [*chimera*] **1** : existing only as the product of unrestrained imagination : fantastically visionary or improbable **2** : inclined to fantastic schemes or projects ***syn*** see IMAGINARY ***ant*** feasible — **chi·me·ri·cal·ly** \-i-k(ə-)lē\ *adv*

chi·me·rism \kī-ˈmi(ə)r-ˌiz-əm, kə-; ˈkī-mə-ˌriz-\ *n* : the state of being a genetic chimera

chim·ney \ˈchim-nē\ *n, pl* **chimneys** [ME, fr. MF *cheminée*, fr. LL *caminata*, fr. L *caminus* furnace, fireplace, fr. Gk *kaminos*; akin to Gk *kamara* vault] **1** *dial* : FIREPLACE, HEARTH **2** : a vertical structure incorporated into a building and enclosing a flue or flues that carry off smoke; *esp* : the part of such a structure extending above a roof **3** : SMOKESTACK **4** : a tube usu. of glass placed around a flame (as of a lamp) **5** : something (as a narrow cleft in rock) resembling a chimney

chim·ney·piece \ˈchim-nē-ˌpēs\ *n* : an ornamental construction over and around a fireplace that includes the mantel

chimney pot *n* : a usu. earthenware pipe placed at the top of a chimney

chimney sweep *n* : one whose occupation is cleaning soot from chimney flues — called also *chimney sweeper*

chimney swift *n* : a small sooty-gray bird (*Chaetura pelagica*) with long narrow wings that often builds its nest inside an unused chimney — called also *chimney swallow*

chimp \ˈchimp, ˈshimp\ *n* : CHIMPANZEE

chim·pan·zee \ˌchim-ˌpan-ˈzē, ˌshim-, -pən-; chim-ˈpan-zē, shim-\ *n* [Kongo dial. *chimpenzi*] : an anthropoid ape (*Pan troglodytes*) of equatorial Africa that is smaller, weaker, and more arboreal than the gorilla

¹chin \ˈchin\ *n* [ME, fr. OE *cinn*; akin to OHG *kinni* chin, L *gena* cheek, Gk *genys* jaw, cheek] **1** : the lower portion of the face lying below the lower lip and including the prominence of the lower jaw **2** : the surface beneath or between the branches of the lower jaw — **chin·less** \-ləs\ *adj*

²chin *vb* **chinned; chin·ning** *vt* **1** : to bring to or hold with the chin ⟨*chinned* his violin⟩ **2** : to raise (oneself) while hanging by the hands until the chin is level with the support ~ *vi, slang* : to talk idly : CHATTER

Chin *abbr* Chinese

chi·na \ˈchī-nə\ *n* [Per *chīnī* Chinese porcelain] **1** : PORCELAIN; *also* : vitreous porcelain wares (as dishes, vases, or ornaments) for domestic use **2** : earthenware or porcelain tableware ⟨set the table with the good ~⟩ **3** : CROCKERY

China aster *n* : a common annual garden aster (*Callistephus chinensis*) native to northern China that occurs in many shown forms

chi·na·ber·ry \ˈchī-nə-ˌber-ē, *South also* ˈchā-nē-ˌber-ē\ *n* **1** : a soapberry (*Sapindus saponaria*) of the southern U.S. and Mexico **2** : a small Asiatic tree (*Melia azedarach* of the mahogany family) naturalized in the southern U.S. where it is widely planted for shade or ornament

china clay *n* : KAOLIN

china closet *n* : a cabinet or cupboard for the storage or display of household china

Chi·na·man \ˈchī-nə-mən\ *n* : a native of China : CHINESE — often taken to be offensive

China rose *n* **1** : any of numerous garden roses derived from a shrubby Chinese rose (*Rosa chinensis*) **2** : a large showy-flowered Asiatic hibiscus (*Hibiscus rosa-sinensis*)

Chi·na·town \ˈchī-nə-ˌtaun\ *n* : the Chinese quarter of a city

China tree *n* : CHINABERRY

chi·na·ware \ˈchī-nə-ˌwa(ə)r, -ˌwe(ə)r\ *n* : tableware made of china

chin·bone \ˈchin-ˈbōn, -ˌbōn\ *n* : MANDIBLE; *esp* : the median anterior part of the human mandible

chinch \ˈchinch\ *n* [Sp *chinche*, fr. L *cimic-, cimex*] : BEDBUG

chinch bug *n* : a small black-and-white bug (*Blissus leucopterus*) very destructive to cereal grasses

chin·che·rin·chee \ˌchin-chə-ri(n)-ˈchē, ˌchiŋ-kə-\ *n, pl* **chincherinchee** *or* **chincherinchees** [origin unknown] : a southern African perennial bulbous herb (*Ornithogalum thyrsoides*) with long-lasting spikes of starry white blossoms

chin·chil·la \chin-ˈchil-ə\ *n* [Sp] **1** : a small rodent (*Chinchilla laniger*) that is the size of a large squirrel, has very soft fur of a pearly gray color, is native to the mountains of Peru and Chile, and is extensively bred in captivity; *also* : its fur **2** : a heavy twilled woolen coating

¹chine \ˈchīn\ *n* [ME, fr. MF *eschine*, of Gmc origin; akin to OHG *scina* shinbone, needle — more at SHIN] **1** : BACKBONE, SPINE; *also* : a cut of meat or fish including the backbone or part of it and the surrounding flesh **2** : RIDGE, CREST **3** : the intersection of the bottom and the sides of a flat or V-bottomed boat

²chine *vt* **chined; chin·ing** : to cut through the backbone of (as in butchering)

Chi·nese \chī-ˈnēz, -ˈnēs\ *n, pl* **Chinese 1 a** : a native or inhabitant of China **b** : a person of Chinese descent **2** : a group of related languages used by the people of China that are often mutually unintelligible in their spoken form but share a single system of writing and that constitute a branch of the Sino-Tibetan language family; *specif* : MANDARIN — **Chinese** *adj*

Chinese boxes *n pl* : a set of boxes graduated in size so that each fits into the next larger one

Chinese cabbage *n* : either of two Asiatic brassicas (*Brassica pekinensis* and *B. chinensis*) widely used as greens

Chinese checkers *n pl but sing or pl in constr* : a game in which each player seeks to be the first to transfer a set of marbles from a home point to the opposite point of a pitted 6-pointed star by single moves or jumps

Chinese chestnut *n* : an Asiatic chestnut (*Castanea mollissima*) that is resistant to chestnut blight

Chinese copy *n* : an exact imitation or duplicate that includes defects as well as desired qualities

Chinese date *n* : an Asiatic jujube (*Ziziphus jujuba*)

Chinese lacquer *n* : LACQUER 1b

Chinese lantern *n* : a collapsible lantern of thin colored paper

Chinese puzzle *n* **1** : an intricate or ingenious puzzle **2** : something intricate and obscure

Chinese wall *n* [*Chinese Wall*, a defensive wall built in the 3d cent. B.C. between China and Mongolia] : a strong barrier; *esp* : a serious obstacle to understanding

Ching *or* **Ch'ing** \ˈchiŋ\ *n* [Chin (Pek) *ch'ing*[1]] : a Manchu dynasty in China dated 1644–1912 and the last imperial dynasty

¹chink \ˈchiŋk\ *n* [prob. alter. of ME *chin* crack, fissure, fr. OE *cine*; akin to OE *cīnan* to gape, OHG *chīnan* to split open] **1** : a small cleft, slit, or fissure ⟨a ~ in the curtain⟩ **2** : a means of evasion or escape : LOOPHOLE ⟨a ~ in the law⟩ **3** : a narrow beam of light shining through a chink

²chink *vt* : to fill the chinks of (as by caulking) ⟨~ a log cabin⟩

³chink *n* [imit.] **1** : a short sharp sound **2** *archaic* : COIN, MONEY

⁴chink *vi* : to make a slight sharp metallic sound ~ *vt* : to cause to make a chink

chi·no \ˈchē-(ˌ)nō, ˈshē-\ *n, pl* **chinos** [AmerSp] **1** : a usu. khaki cotton twill of the type used for military uniforms **2** *pl* : an article of clothing made of chino

Chi·no- \ˌchī-(ˌ)nō\ *comb form* : Chinese and ⟨*Chino*-Japanese⟩

chi·noi·se·rie \ˌshēn-ˈwäz-(ə-)rē, ˌshēn-ˌwäz-(ə-)ˈrē\ *n* [F, fr. *chinois* Chinese, fr. *Chine* China] : a style in art (as in decoration) reflecting Chinese qualities or motifs; *also* : an object or decoration in this style

Chi·nook \shə-ˈnu̇k, chə-, -ˈnük\ *n, pl* **Chinook** *or* **Chinooks** [Chehalis *Tsinúk*] **1** : a member of an Amerindian people of Oregon **2** : a Chinookan language of the Chinook and other nearby peoples **3** *not cap* **a** : a warm moist southwest wind of the coast from Oregon northward **b** : a warm dry wind that descends the eastern slopes of the Rocky mountains

Chi·nook·an \-ən\ *n* : a language family of Washington and Oregon — **Chinookan** *adj*

Chinook Jargon *n* : a pidgin language based on Chinook and other Indian languages, French, and English and formerly used as a lingua franca in the northwestern U.S. and on the Pacific coast of Canada and Alaska

Chinook salmon *n* : a large commercially important salmon (*Oncorhynchus tshawytscha*) that occurs in the northern Pacific ocean and usu. has red flesh

chin·qua·pin \ˈchiŋ-ki-ˌpin\ *n* [alter. of earlier *chincomen*, of Algonquian origin] **1** : any of several trees (genera *Castanea* or *Castanopsis*); *esp* : a dwarf chestnut (*Castanea pumila*) of the U.S. **2** : the edible nut of a chinquapin

chintz \ˈchin(t)s\ *n* [earlier *chints*, pl. of *chint*, fr. Hindi *chīṭ*] **1** : a printed calico from India **2** : a usu. glazed printed cotton fabric

chintzy \ˈchin(t)-sē\ *adj* **chintz·i·er; -est 1** : decorated with or as if with chintz **2** : GAUDY, CHEAP ⟨~ toys⟩

chin–up \ˈchin-ˌəp\ *n* : the act or an instance of chinning oneself performed esp. as a conditioning exercise

chin–wag \-ˌwag\ *n, slang* : CONVERSATION, CHAT

¹chip \ˈchip\ *n* [ME] **1 a** : a small usu. thin and flat piece (as of wood or stone) cut, struck, or flaked off **b** (1) : a small thin slice of food; *esp* : POTATO CHIP (2) : FRENCH FRY **2** : something small, worthless, or trivial **3 a** : one of the counters used as a token for money in poker and other games **b** *pl* : MONEY — used esp. in the phrase *in the chips* **4** : a piece of dried dung — usu. used in combination ⟨cow ~⟩ **5** : a flaw left after a chip is removed **6** : INTEGRATED CIRCUIT **7** : CHIP SHOT — **chip off the old block** : a child that resembles his parent — **chip on one's shoulder** : a challenging or belligerent attitude

²chip *vb* **chipped; chip·ping** *vt* **1 a** : to cut or hew with an edged tool **b** (1) : to cut or break (a small piece) from something (2) : to cut or break a fragment from **2** *Brit* : CHAFF, BANTER ~ *vi* **1** : to break off in small pieces **2** : to play a chip shot

chip·board \ˈchip-ˌbō(ə)rd, -ˌbȯ(ə)rd\ *n* : a paperboard made from waste paper

chip in *vb* : CONTRIBUTE ⟨everyone *chipped in* for the gift⟩

chip·munk \ˈchip-ˌməŋk\ *n* [alter. of earlier *chitmunk*, of Algonquian origin; akin to Ojibwa *atchitamō* squirrel] : any of numerous small striped semiterrestrial American squirrels (genera *Tamias* and *Eutamias*)

chipped beef \ˈchip(t)-\ *n* : smoked dried beef sliced thin

Chip·pen·dale \ˈchip-ən-ˌdāl\ *adj* [Thomas *Chippendale*] : of or relating to an 18th century English furniture style characterized by graceful outline and often ornate rococo ornamentation

¹chip·per \ˈchip-ər\ *n* : one that chips

²chipper *adj* [perh. alter. of E dial. *kipper* (lively)] : GAY, SPRIGHTLY

Chip·pe·wa \ˈchip-ə-ˌwȯ, -ˌwä, -ˌwā, -wə\ *n, pl* **Chippewa** *or* **Chippewas** : OJIBWA

chip shot *n* : a short usu. low approach shot in golf that lofts the ball to the green and allows it to roll

chir- *or* **chiro-** *comb form* [L, fr. Gk *cheir-, cheiro-*, fr. *cheir*; akin to Hitt *kesar* hand] : hand ⟨*chiro*practic⟩

Chi–Rho \ˈkī-ˈrō, ˈkē-\ *n, pl* **Chi–Rhos** [*chi* + *rho*] : a Christian monogram and symbol formed from the first two letters X and P of the Greek word for *Christ* — called also *Christogram*

Chir·i·ca·hua \ˌchir-ə-ˈkä-wə\ *n, pl* **Chiricahua** *or* **Chiricahuas** : a member of an Apache people of Arizona

chirk \ˈchərk\ *vb* [ME *charken, chirken* to creak, chirp, fr. OE *cearcian* to creak; akin to OE *cracian* to crack] : CHEER ⟨play with her and ~ her up a little —Harriet B. Stowe⟩

chi·rog·ra·pher \kī-'räg-rə-fər\ *n* : one who studies or practices chirography

chi·rog·ra·phy \-fē\ *n* **1** : HANDWRITING, PENMANSHIP **2** : CALLIGRAPHY 1 — **chi·ro·graph·ic** \ˌkī-rə-'graf-ik\ *or* **chi·ro·graph·i·cal** \-i-kəl\ *adj*

chi·ro·man·cy \'kī-rə-ˌman(t)-sē\ *n* [prob. fr. MF *chiromancie*, fr. ML *chiromantia*, fr. Gk *cheir* chir- + *-manteia* -mancy — more at -MANCY] — **chi·ro·man·cer** \-ˌman(t)-sər\ *n*

chi·ron·o·mid \kī-'rän-ə-məd\ *n* [deriv. of Gk *cheironomos* one who gestures with his hands] : any of a family (Chironomidae) of midges that lack piercing mouthparts

chi·rop·o·dy \kə-'räp-əd-ē, shə- *also* kī-\ *n* [*chir-* + *pod-*, fr. its original concern with both hands and feet] : PODIATRY — **chi·rop·o·dist** \-əd-əst\ *n*

chi·ro·prac·tic \'kī-rə-ˌprak-tik\ *n* [*chir-* + Gk *praktikos* practical, operative — more at PRACTICAL] : a system of healing which holds that disease results from a lack of normal nerve function and which employs manipulation and specific adjustment of body structures (as the spinal column) — **chi·ro·prac·tor** \-tər\ *n*

chi·rop·ter \kī-'räp-tər, 'kī-ˌ\ *n* [deriv. of Gk *cheir* hand + *pteron* wing — more at FEATHER] : ³BAT — **chi·rop·ter·an** \kī-'räp-tə-rən\ *adj or n*

¹chirp \'chərp\ *n* [imit.] : the characteristic short sharp sound esp. of a small bird or insect — **chirp** *vi* — **chirp·i·ly** \'chər-pə-lē\ *adv* — **chirpy** \'chər-pē\ *adj*

chirr \'chər\ *n* [imit.] : the short vibrant or trilled sound characteristic of an insect (as a grasshopper or cicada) — **chirr** *vi*

¹chir·rup \'chər-əp, 'chir-\ *vi* [imit.] **1** : CHIRP **2** : to make a sound like a chirrup ~ *vt* : to utter by chirruping

²chirrup *n* : CHIRP

chi·rur·geon \kī-'rər-jən\ *n* [ME *cirurgian*, fr. OF *cirurgien*, fr. *cirurgie* surgery] *archaic* : SURGEON

¹chis·el \'chiz-əl\ *n* [ME, fr. ONF, prob. alter. of *chisoir* goldsmith's chisel, fr. (assumed) VL *caesorium* cutting instrument, fr. L *caesus*, pp. of *caedere* to cut — more at CONCISE] : a metal tool with a cutting edge at the end of a blade used in dressing, shaping, or working a solid material (as wood, stone, or metal)

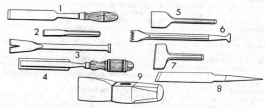

chisels: *1* socket paring chisel, *2* cold chisel, *3* box chisel, *4* beveled firmer chisel, *5* floor chisel, *6* stonecutter's chisel, *7* bricklayer's chisel, *8* turning chisel, *9* blacksmith's chisel

²chisel *vb* **-eled** *or* **-elled; -el·ing** *or* **-el·ling** \'chiz-(ə-)liŋ\ *vt* **1** : to cut or work with or as if with a chisel **2** : to employ shrewd or unfair practices in order to obtain one's end; *also* : to obtain by such practices (~ a job) ~ *vi* **1** : to work with a chisel **2 a** : to employ shrewd or unfair practices **b** : to thrust oneself : INTRUDE (~ in on a racket) — **chis·el·er** \-(ə-)lər\ *n*

chis·eled *or* **chis·elled** \'chiz-əld\ *adj* **1** : cut or wrought with a chisel **2** : appearing as if chiseled : CLEAR-CUT (sharply ~ features)

chi–square \'kī-ˌskwa(ə)r, -'skwe(ə)r\ *n* : a statistic that is a sum of terms each of which is a quotient obtained by dividing the square of the difference between the observed and theoretical values of a quantity by the theoretical value

chi–square distribution *n* : a probability density function that gives the distribution of the sum of the squares of a number of independent random variables each with a normal distribution with zero mean and unit variance, that has the property that the sum of two random variables with such a distribution also has one, and that is widely used in testing statistical hypotheses esp. about the theoretical and observed values of a quantity and about population variances and standard deviations

¹chit \'chit\ *n* [ME *chitte* kitten, cub] **1** : CHILD **2** : a pert young woman

²chit *n* [Hindi *citthī*] **1** : a short letter or note; *esp* : a signed voucher of a small debt (as for food) **2** : a small slip of paper with writing on it

chit·chat \'chit-ˌchat\ *n* [redupl. of *chat*] : SMALL TALK, GOSSIP — **chitchat** *vi*

chi·tin \'kī-tᵊn\ *n* [F *chitine*, fr. Gk *chitōn* chiton, tunic] : a horny polysaccharide that forms part of the hard outer integument esp. of insects and crustaceans — **chi·tin·ous** \'kīt-ᵊn-əs, 'kīt-nəs\ *adj*

chi·ton \'kīt-ᵊn, 'kī-ˌtän\ *n* [NL, genus name, fr. Gk *chitōn* tunic; of Sem origin; akin to Heb *kuttōneth* tunic] **1** : any of an order (Polyplacophora) of elongated bilaterally symmetrical marine mollusks with a dorsal shell of calcareous plates **2** [Gk *chitōn*] : the basic garment of ancient Greece worn usu. knee-length by men and full-length by women

chit·ter \'chit-ər\ *vi* [ME *chiteren*, prob. fr. imit. origin] : TWITTER, CHIRP; *also* : CHATTER

chit·ter·lings *or* **chit·lings** *or* **chit·lins** \'chit-lənz\ *n pl* [ME *chiterlinge*] : the intestines of hogs esp. when prepared as food

chi·val·ric \shə-'val-rik\ *adj* : relating to chivalry : CHIVALROUS

chiv·al·rous \'shiv-əl-rəs\ *adj* **1** : VALIANT **2** **a** : of, relating to, or characteristic of chivalry and knight-errantry **3 a** : marked by honor, generosity, and courtesy **b** : marked by gracious courtesy and high-minded consideration esp. to women *syn* see CIVIL *ant*

unchivalrous, churlish — **chiv·al·rous·ly** *adv* — **chiv·al·rous·ness** *n*

chiv·al·ry \'shiv-əl-rē\ *n, pl* **-ries** [ME *chivalrie*, fr. OF *chevalerie*, fr. *chevalier*] **1** : mounted men-at-arms **2** *archaic* **a** : martial valor **b** : knightly skill **3** : gallant or distinguished gentlemen **4** : the system, spirit, or customs of medieval knighthood **5** : the qualities (as bravery, honor, protection of the weak, and generous treatment of foes) of the ideal knight : chivalrous conduct

chive \'chīv\ *n* [ME, fr. ONF, fr. L *cepa* onion] : a perennial plant (*Allium schoenoprasum*) related to the onion

chivy *or* **chiv·vy** \'chiv-ē\ *vt* **chiv·ied** *or* **chiv·vied; chivy·ing** *or* **chiv·vy·ing** [*chivy*, n. (chase, hunt), prob. fr. E dial. *Chevy Chase* chase, confusion, fr. the name of a ballad describing the battle of Otterburn (1388)] **1** : to tease or annoy with persistent petty attacks : HARRY, HARASS **2** : MANEUVER, MANIPULATE *syn* see BAIT

chlam·y·do·mo·nas \ˌklam-əd-ə-'mō-nəs\ *n* [NL, genus name, fr. L *chlamyd-*, *chlamys* + NL *monas* monad] : any of a genus (*Chlamydomonas*) of single-celled photosynthetic flagellates or algae that have two flagella and are common in fresh water and damp soil

chla·my·do·spore \klə-'mid-ə-ˌspō(ə)r, -ˌspȯ(ə)r\ *n* [L *chlamyd-*, *chlamys* + ISV *spore*] : a thick-walled usu. resting spore — **chla·my·do·spor·ic** \kl ə-ˌmid-ə-'spōr-ik, -'spȯr-\ *adj*

chla·mys \'klam-əs, 'klām-əs\ *n, pl* **chla·mys·es** *or* **chla·my·des** \-ə-ˌdēz\ [L *chlamyd-*, *chlamys*, fr. Gk] : a short oblong mantle worn by young men of ancient Greece

Chloe \'klō-ē\ *n* [L, fr. Gk *Chloē*] : a lover of Daphnis in a Greek pastoral romance

chlor- *or* **chloro-** *comb form* [NL, fr. Gk, fr. *chlōros* greenish yellow — more at YELLOW] **1** : green (*chlorine*) (*chlorosis*) **2** : chlorine : containing chlorine (*chloric*) (*chloroprene*)

chlo·ral \'klōr-əl, 'klȯr-\ *n* [F, fr. *chlor-* + *alcool* alcohol] **1** : a pungent colorless oily aldehyde CCl_3CHO used in making DDT and chloral hydrate **2** : CHLORAL HYDRATE

chloral hydrate *n* : a bitter white crystalline drug $C_2H_3Cl_3O_2$ used as a hypnotic or in knockout drops

chlo·ral·ose \'klōr-ə-ˌlōs, 'klȯr-, -ˌlōz\ *n* : a bitter crystalline compound $C_8H_{11}Cl_3O_6$ used as a hypnotic — **chlo·ral·osed** \-ˌlōst, -ˌlōzd\ *adj*

chlor·am·bu·cil \klōr-'am-byə-ˌsil, klȯr-\ *n* [*chlor-* + *amin-* + *butyric* + *-cil* (of unknown origin)] : a nitrogen mustard derivative $C_{14}H_{19}Cl_2NO_2$ used esp. to treat leukemias and Hodgkin's disease

chlo·ra·mine \'klōr-ə-ˌmēn, 'klȯr-\ *n* [ISV] : any of various compounds containing nitrogen and chlorine

chlor·am·phen·i·col \ˌklōr-ˌam-'fen-i-ˌkȯl, ˌklȯr-, -ˌkȯl\ *n* [*chlor-* + *amid-* + *phen-* + *nitr-* + *glycol*] : a broad-spectrum antibiotic $C_{11}H_{12}Cl_2N_2O_5$ isolated from cultures of a soil microorganism (*Streptomyces venezuelae*) or prepared synthetically

chlo·rate \'klō(ə)r-ˌāt, 'klȯ(ə)r-\ *n* : a salt containing the radical ClO_3 (~ of potassium)

chlor·dane \'klō(ə)r-ˌdān\ *or* **chlor·dan** \-ˌdan\ *n* [*chlor-* + *indane*, indan (C₉H₁₀)] : a highly chlorinated viscous volatile liquid insecticide $C_{10}H_6Cl_8$

chlor·di·az·ep·ox·ide \ˌklōr-dī-ˌaz-ə-'päk-ˌsīd, ˌklȯr-\ *n* [*chlor-* + *di-* + *az-* + *epoxide*] : a compound $C_{16}H_{14}ClN_3O$ the hydrochloride of which is used as a tranquilizer in the treatment of various psychoneuroses and alcoholism

chlo·rel·la \klə-'rel-ə\ *n* [NL, genus name, fr. Gk *chlōros*] : any of a genus (*Chlorella*) of unicellular green algae potentially a cheap source of high-grade protein and B-complex vitamins

chlo·ric \'klōr-ik, 'klȯr-\ *adj* : relating to or obtained from chlorine esp. with a valence of five

chlo·ride \'klō(ə)r-ˌīd, 'klȯ(ə)r-\ *n* [G *chlorid*, fr. *chlor-* + *-id* -ide] : a compound of chlorine with another element or radical; *esp* : a salt or ester of hydrochloric acid

chloride of lime : BLEACHING POWDER

chlo·ri·nate \'klōr-ə-ˌnāt, 'klȯr-\ *vt* **-nat·ed; -nat·ing** : to treat or cause to combine with chlorine or a chlorine compound — **chlo·ri·na·tion** \ˌklōr-ə-'nā-shən, ˌklȯr-\ *n* — **chlo·ri·na·tor** \'klōr-ə-ˌnāt-ər, 'klȯr-\ *n*

chlorinated lime *n* : BLEACHING POWDER

chlo·rine \'klō(ə)r-ˌēn, 'klȯ(ə)r-, -ən\ *n* : a halogen element that is isolated as a heavy greenish yellow gas of pungent odor and is used esp. as a bleach, oxidizing agent, and disinfectant in water purification — see ELEMENT table

chlo·rin·i·ty \klōr-'in-ət-ē, klȯr-\ *n* [*chlorine* + *-ity*] : a measure of the amount of halides present in one kilogram of seawater

¹chlo·rite \'klō(ə)r-ˌīt, 'klȯ(ə)r-\ *n* [G *chlorit*, fr. L *chloritis*, a green stone, fr. Gk *chlōritis*, fr. *chlōros*] : any of a group of monoclinic usu. green minerals associated with and resembling the micas — **chlo·rit·ic** \klōr-'it-ik, klȯr-\ *adj*

²chlorite *n* [prob. fr. F, fr. *chlor-*] : a salt containing the group ClO_2 (~ of sodium)

chloro- — see CHLOR-

chlo·ro·ben·zene \ˌklōr-ō-'ben-ˌzēn, ˌklȯr-, -ˌben-\ *n* [ISV] : a colorless flammable volatile toxic liquid C_6H_5Cl used in organic synthesis (as of DDT) and as a solvent

¹chlo·ro·form \'klōr-ə-ˌfȯrm, 'klȯr-\ *n* [F *chloroforme*, fr. *chlor-* + *formyle* formyl; fr. its having been regarded as a trichloride of this radical] : a colorless volatile heavy toxic liquid $CHCl_3$ with an ether odor used esp. as a solvent or as a general anesthetic

²chloroform *vt* : to treat with chloroform esp. so as to produce anesthesia or death

chlo·ro·gen·ic acid \ˌklōr-ə-ˌjen-ik-, ˌklȯr-\ *n* : a crystalline acid $C_{16}H_{18}O_9$ occurring in various plant parts (as potatoes or coffee beans)

ə abut	⁹ kitten	ər further	a back	ā bake	ä cot, cart
aù out	ch chin	e less	ē easy	g gift	i trip	ī life
j joke	ŋ sing	ō flow	ȯ flaw	ȯi coin	th thin	th̲ this
ü loot	ù foot	y yet	yü few	yù furious	zh vision	

chlo·ro·hy·drin \,klōr-ə-'hī-drən, ,klȯr-\ n [ISV, fr. *chlor-* + *hydr-*] : any of various organic compounds derived from glycols or polyhydroxy alcohols by substitution of chlorine for part of the hydroxyl groups

Chlo·ro·my·ce·tin \,klōr-ō-mī-'sēt-ᵊn, ,klȯr-\ *trademark* — used for chloramphenicol

chlo·ro·phyll \'klōr-ə-,fil, 'klȯr-, -fəl\ n [F *chlorophylle*, fr. *chlor-* + Gk *phyllon* leaf — more at BLADE] 1 : the green photosynthetic coloring matter of plants found in chloroplasts and made up chiefly of a blue-black ester $C_{55}H_{72}MgN_4O_5$ and a dark green ester $C_{55}H_{70}MgN_4O_6$ — called also respectively *chlorophyll a, chlorophyll b* 2 : a waxy green chlorophyll-containing substance extracted from green plants and used as a coloring agent or deodorant — **chlo·ro·phyl·lose** \,klōr-ə-'fil-,ōs, ,klȯr-, -(,)fil-\ *adj* — **chlo·ro·phyl·lous** \-'fil-əs\ *adj*

chlo·ro·pic·rin \,klōr-ə-'pik-rən, ,klȯr-\ n [G *chlorpikrin*, fr. *chlor-* + Gk *pikros* bitter] : a heavy colorless liquid CCl_3NO_2 that causes tears and vomiting and is used esp. as a soil fumigant

chlo·ro·plast \'klōr-ə-,plast, 'klȯr-\ n [ISV] : a plastid that contains chlorophyll and is the site of photosynthesis and starch formation — see CELL illustration

chlo·ro·prene \-,prēn\ n [*chlor-* + *isoprene*] : a colorless liquid C_4H_5Cl used esp. in making neoprene by polymerization

chlo·ro·quine \,klōr-ə-,kwēn, 'klȯr-\ n [*chlor-* + *quinoline*] : an antimalarial drug $C_{18}H_{26}ClN_3$ administered as the bitter crystalline diphosphate

chlo·ro·sis \klə-'rō-səs\ n 1 : an iron-deficiency anemia in young girls characterized by a greenish color of the skin — called also *greensickness* 2 : a diseased condition in green plants marked by yellowing or blanching — **chlo·rot·ic** \-'rät-ik\ *adj* — **chlo·rot·i·cal·ly** \-i-k(ə-)lē\ *adv*

chlo·rous \'klōr-əs, 'klȯr-\ *adj* : relating to or obtained from chlorine esp. with a valence of three

chlor·prom·a·zine \klōr-'präm-ə-,zēn, klȯr-\ n [*chlor-* + *propyl* + *methyl* + *phenothiazine*] : a phenothiazine derivative $C_{17}H_{19}-ClN_2S$ used as a tranquilizer in the form of its hydrochloride

chlor·prop·amide \-'präp-ə-,mīd, -'prōp-\ n [*chlor-* + *propane* + *amide*] : a sulfonyl urea compound $C_{10}H_{13}ClN_2O_3S$ used to reduce blood sugar in the treatment of mild diabetes

chlor·tet·ra·cy·cline \,klōr-,te-trə-'sī-,klēn, ,klȯr-\ n : a yellow crystalline antibiotic $C_{22}H_{23}ClN_2O_8$ produced by a soil actinomycete (*Streptomyces aureofaciens*), used in the treatment of diseases, and added to animal feeds for stimulating growth

chm *abbr* 1 chairman 2 checkmate

cho·ano·cyte \kō-'an-ə-,sīt\ n [ISV *choan-* (funnel-shaped) (fr. Gk *choanē* funnel) + *-cyte*] : COLLAR CELL

¹chock \'chäk\ n [origin unknown] 1 : a wedge or block for steadying a body (as a cask) and holding it motionless, for filling in an unwanted space, or for blocking the movement of a wheel 2 : a heavy metal casting (as on the bow or stern of a ship) with two short horn-shaped arms curving inward between which ropes or hawsers may pass for mooring or towing

²chock *vt* 1 : to provide, stop, or make fast with or as if with chocks 2 : to raise or support on chocks

³chock *adv* : as close or as completely as possible

¹chock-a-block \'chäk-ə-,bläk\ *adj* 1 : brought close together 2 : very full : CROWDED

²chockablock *adv* : in a crowded manner or condition ⟨families living ~ ⟩

chock-full \'chək-'fúl, 'chäk-\ *adj* [ME *chokfull*, prob. fr. *choken* to choke + *full*] : full to the limit : CRAMMED

choc·o·late \'chäk-(ə-)lət, 'chȯk-\ n [Sp, fr. Nahuatl *xocoatl*] 1 : a food prepared from ground roasted cacao beans 2 : a beverage of chocolate in water or milk 3 : a small candy with a center (as a fondant) and a chocolate coating 4 : a variable color averaging a brownish gray — **chocolate** *adj*

chocolate-box *adj* [fr. the pictures formerly commonly seen on boxes of chocolates] : superficially pretty or sentimental ⟨his fiancée wanted him to paint her, and always in a ~ pose —L. S. Gannett⟩

chocolate tree n : CACAO 1

choc·o·laty *or* **choc·o·lat·ey** \'chäk-(ə-)lət-ē, 'chȯk-\ *adj* : made of or resembling chocolate

Choc·taw \'chäk-(,)tȯ\ n, pl **Choctaw** *or* **Choctaws** [Choctaw *Chahta*] 1 : a member of an Amerindian people of Mississippi, Alabama, and Louisiana 2 : the language of the Choctaw and Chickasaw people

¹choice \'chȯis\ n [ME *chois*, fr. OF, fr. *choisir* to choose, of Gmc origin; akin to OHG *kiosan* to choose — more at CHOOSE] 1 : the act of choosing : SELECTION 2 : power of choosing : OPTION 3 a : a person or thing chosen b : the best part : CREAM 4 : a sufficient number and variety to choose among 5 : care in selecting 6 : a grade of meat between prime and good

syn CHOICE, OPTION, ALTERNATIVE, PREFERENCE, SELECTION, ELECTION *shared meaning element* : the act or opportunity of choosing or the thing chosen

²choice *adj* **choic·er; choic·est** 1 : worthy of being chosen : SELECT 2 : selected with care : well chosen 3 a : of high quality b : of a grade between prime and good ⟨~ meat⟩ — **choice·ly** *adv* — **choice·ness** n

syn CHOICE, EXQUISITE, ELEGANT, RARE, DAINTY, DELICATE *shared meaning element* : having qualities that appeal to a cultivated taste **ant** indifferent

¹choir \'kwī(-ə)r\ n [ME *quer*, fr. OF *cuer*, fr. ML *chorus*, fr. L, chorus] 1 : an organized company of singers esp. in church service 2 : a group of instruments of the same class ⟨a brass ~ ⟩ 3 : an organized group of persons or things 4 : a division of angels 5 : the part of a church occupied by the singers or by the clergy; *specif* : the part of the chancel between sanctuary and nave 6 : a group organized for ensemble speaking

²choir *vi* : to sing or sound in chorus or concert

³choir *adj* : of the class in a religious order bound to recite the Divine Office and devoted chiefly to the order's special work

choir·boy \'kwī(-ə)r-,bȯi\ n : a boy member of a choir

choir loft n : a gallery occupied by a church choir

choir·mas·ter \-,mas-tər\ n : the director of a choir (as in a church)

¹choke \'chōk\ *vb* **choked; chok·ing** [ME *choken*, alter. of *achoken*, fr. OE *acēocian*] *vt* 1 : to check normal breathing of by compressing or obstructing the windpipe or by poisoning or adulterating available air 2 : to check or suppress expression of or by : SILENCE ⟨a cloture rule designed to ~ off discussion⟩ 3 a : to check the growth, development, or activity of ⟨the flowers were *choked* by the weeds⟩ b : to obstruct by filling up or clogging ⟨leaves *choked* the drain⟩ c : to fill completely : JAM ⟨dandelions *choked* the strips of lawn dividing the auto lanes —Herman Wouk⟩ 4 : to enrich the fuel mixture of (a motor) by partially shutting off the air intake of the carburetor 5 : to grip (as a baseball bat) some distance from the end of the handle ~ *vi* 1 : to become choked in breathing 2 a : to become obstructed or checked b : to become or feel constricted in the throat (as from strong emotion) — usu. used with *up* ⟨he *choked up* and couldn't finish his speech⟩ 3 : to shorten one's grip esp. on the handle of a bat — usu. used with *up* 4 : to lose one's composure and fail to perform effectively in a critical situation

²choke n 1 : the act of choking 2 : something that obstructs passage or flow: as a : a valve for choking a gasoline engine b : a constriction in an outlet (as of an oil well) that restricts flow c : REACTOR 2 d : a narrowing toward the muzzle in the bore of a gun e : an attachment that allows variation of muzzle constriction of a shotgun

choke·ber·ry \-,ber-ē\ n : a small berrylike astringent fruit; *also* : a shrub (genus *Aronia*) of the rose family bearing chokeberries

choke·cher·ry \-,cher-ē, -'cher-\ n : any of several American wild cherries with bitter or astringent fruit; *also* : this fruit

choke coil n : REACTOR 2

choke collar n : a collar that may be tightened as a noose and that is used esp. in training and controlling powerful or stubborn dogs

choke·damp \'chōk-,damp\ n : BLACKDAMP

chok·er \'chō-kər\ n 1 : one that chokes 2 : something worn closely about the throat or neck: as a : a wide ornamental cloth for the neck; *esp* : STOCK b : a high stiff collar c : a short necklace

chok·ing \'chō-kiŋ\ *adj* 1 : producing the feeling of strangulation ⟨a ~ cloud of smog⟩ 2 : indistinct in utterance — used esp. of a person's voice ⟨a low ~ laugh⟩ — **chok·ing·ly** \-kiŋ-lē\ *adv*

choky \'chō-kē\ *adj* : tending to cause choking or to become choked

chol- *or* **chole-** *or* **cholo-** *comb form* [Gk *chol-, cholē-, cholo-*, fr. *cholē, cholos* — more at GALL] : bile : gall ⟨*chol*ate⟩ ⟨*cholo*lith⟩

chol·an·gi·og·ra·phy \kō-,lan-jē-'äg-rə-fē, (,)kō-\ n [*chol-* + *angi-* + *-graphy*] : roentgenographic visualization of the bile ducts after ingestion or injection of a radiopaque substance — **chol·an·gio·graph·ic** \-jē-ə-'graf-ik\ *adj*

cho·late \'kō-,lāt\ n : a salt or ester of cholic acid

cho·le·cys·tec·to·my \,kō-lə-(,)sis-'tek-tə-mē\ n, pl **-mies** [NL *cholecystis* gallbladder (fr. *chol-* + Gk *kystis* bladder) + ISV *-ectomy* — more at CYST] : surgical excision of the gallbladder

cho·le·cys·ti·tis \-'tīt-əs\ n, pl **-tit·i·des** \-'tit-ə-,dēz\ [NL, fr. *cholecystis*] : inflammation of the gallbladder

cho·le·cys·to·ki·nin \-,sis-tə-'kī-nən\ n [NL *cholecystis* + E *-o-* + *kinin*] : a hormone secreted by the duodenal mucosa that regulates the emptying of the gallbladder and secretion of enzymes by the pancreas — called also *cholecystokinin-pancreozymin, pancreozymin*

cho·le·li·thi·a·sis \,kō-li-lith-'ī-ə-səs\ n [NL *chol-* + *lithiasis*] : production of gallstones; *also* : the resulting abnormal condition

cho·ler \'käl-ər, 'kō-lər\ n [ME *coler*, fr. MF *colere*, fr. L *cholera* bilious diesase, fr. Gk, fr. *cholē*] 1 a *archaic* : YELLOW BILE b *obs* : BILE 1a 2 *obs* : the quality or state of being bilious 3 : the quality or state of being irascible

chol·era \'käl-ə-rə\ n [ME *colera* bile, fr. L *cholera*] : any of several diseases of man and domestic animals usu. marked by severe gastrointestinal symptoms; *esp* : ASIATIC CHOLERA — **chol·e·ra·ic** \,käl-ə-'rā-ik\ *adj*

chol·era mor·bus \,käl-ə-rə-'mȯr-bəs\ n [NL, lit., the disease cholera] : a gastrointestinal disturbance characterized by griping, diarrhea, and sometimes vomiting — not used technically

cho·ler·ic \'käl-ə-rik, kə-'ler-ik\ *adj* 1 : easily moved to often unreasonable or excessive anger : hot-tempered 2 : ANGRY, IRATE

syn see IRASCIBLE **ant** placid, imperturbable

cho·les·ter·ol \kə-'les-tə-,rōl, -,rȯl\ n [F *cholestérine*, fr. *chol-* + Gk *stereos* solid] : a steroid alcohol $C_{27}H_{45}OH$ present in animal cells and body fluids, important in physiological processes, and implicated experimentally as a factor in arteriosclerosis

cho·lic acid \,kō-lik-\ n [Gk *cholikos*, fr. *cholē*] : a crystalline bile acid $C_{24}H_{40}O_5$

cho·line \'kō-,lēn\ n [ISV] : a base $C_5H_{15}NO_2$ that occurs in many animal and plant products and is a vitamin of the B complex essential to the liver function

cho·lin·er·gic \,kō-lə-'nər-jik\ *adj* [ISV *acetylcholine* + Gk *ergon* work — more at WORK] 1 *of autonomic nerve fibers* : liberating or activated by acetylcholine 2 : resembling acetylcholine esp. in physiologic action

cho·lin·es·ter·ase \,kō-lə-'nes-tə-,rās, -,rāz\ n 1 : ACETYLCHOLINESTERASE 2 : an enzyme that hydrolyzes choline esters and that is found esp. in blood plasma — called also *pseudocholinesterase*

cho·li·no·lyt·ic \,kō-lə-nō-'lit-ik\ *adj* [*choline* + *-o-* + *-lytic*] : interfering with the action of acetylcholine or cholinergic agents — **cholinolytic** n

chol·la \'chȯi-(y)ə\ n [MexSp, fr. Sp, head] : any of several arborescent very spiny cacti (genus *Opuntia*) of the southwestern U.S. and Mexico

chomp \'chämp, 'chȯmp\ *vb* [alter. of *champ*] *vt* : to chew or bite on ⟨he ~ed his cigar in anger —J. A. Michener⟩ ~ *vi* : to chew or bite on something

chon \'chän\ n, pl **chon** [Korean] — see *won* at MONEY table

chondr- *or* **chondri-** *or* **chondro-** *comb form* [NL, fr. Gk *chondr-, chondro-*, fr. *chondros* grain, cartilage] : cartilage ⟨*chondro*cranium⟩

chon·drio·some \'kän-drē-ə-‚sōm\ n [Gk chondrion, dim. of chon-dros, + ISV -some]: MITOCHONDRION

chon·drite \'kän-‚drīt\ n [ISV, fr. Gk chondros grain]: a meteoric stone characterized by the presence of chondrules — **chon·drit·ic** \kän-'drit-ik\ adj

chon·dro·cra·ni·um \‚kän-drō-'krā-nē-əm\ n : the embryonic cartilaginous cranium; also : the part of the adult skull derived therefrom

chon·droi·tin \kän-'dròit-ⁿn, -'drō-ət-ⁿn\ n [ISV chondroitic acid (an acid found in cartilage) (fr. chondr-) + -in]: a mucopolysaccharide occurring in sulfated form in various animal tissues (as cartilage and tendons)

chon·drule \'kän-(‚)drül\ n [Gk chondros grain]: a rounded granule of cosmic origin often found embedded in meteoric stones and sometimes free in marine sediments

choose \'chüz\ vb chose \'chōz\; cho·sen \'chōz-ⁿn\; choos·ing \'chü-zin\ [ME chosen, fr. OE cēosan; akin to OHG kiosan to choose, L gustare to taste] vt 1 a : to select freely and after consideration b : to decide on esp. by vote : ELECT ⟨chosen to serve as senator⟩ 2 a : to have a preference for b (1) : DECIDE ⟨chose to go by train⟩ (2) : PREFER ~ vi 1 : to make a selection 2 : to take an alternative — used after cannot and usu. followed by not ⟨when earth is so kind, men cannot ~ but be happy —J. A. Froude⟩ — **choos·er** \'chü-zər\ n

choose up vt : to form (sides) esp. for a game by having opposing captains choose their players ~ vi : to form sides for a game ⟨let's choose up and play ball⟩

choosy or **choos·ey** \'chü-zē\ adj choos·i·er; -est : fastidiously selective : PARTICULAR

¹chop \'chäp\ vb chopped; chop·ping [ME chappen, choppen — more at CHAP] vt 1 a : to cut into or sever usu. by repeated blows of a sharp instrument ⟨~ down a tree⟩ b : to cut into pieces : MINCE — often used with up ⟨~ up the vegetables⟩ c : to weed and thin out (young cotton) 2 : to strike (a ball) with a short downward stroke 3 : to subject to the action of a chopper ⟨~ a beam of light⟩ ~ vi 1 : to make a quick stroke or repeated strokes with or as if with a sharp instrument (as an ax) 2 archaic : to move or act suddenly or violently

²chop n 1 a : a forceful usu. slanting blow with or as if with an ax or cleaver b : a sharp downward blow or stroke 2 a : a small cut of meat often including part of a rib — see LAMB illustration b : a mark made by or as if by chopping 4 : material that has been chopped up 5 a : a short abrupt motion (as of a wave) b : a stretch of choppy sea — see CHOPPER 4

³chop vi chopped; chop·ping [ME chappen, choppen to barter, fr. OE cēapian] 1 : to change direction 2 : to veer with or as if with wind — **chop logic** : to argue with sophistical reasoning and minute distinctions

⁴chop n [Hindi chāp stamp] 1 a : a seal or official stamp or its impression b : a license validated by a seal 2 a : a mark on goods or coins to indicate nature or quality b : a kind, brand, or lot of goods bearing the same chop c : QUALITY, GRADE ⟨first-chop tea⟩

chop–chop \'chäp-‚chäp\ adv [Pidgin E, redupl. of chop fast — more at CHOPSTICK]: without delay : QUICKLY

chop·fall·en \'chäp-‚fò-lən\ var of CHAPFALLEN

chop·house \'chäp-‚haùs\ n : RESTAURANT

cho·pine \shä-'pēn, chä-\ n [MF chapin, fr. OSp] : a woman's shoe of the 16th and 17th centuries with a very high sole designed to increase stature and protect the feet from mud and dirt

¹chop·log·ic \'chäp-‚läj-ik\ n [obs. chop (to exchange, trade), fr. ME choppen to barter — more at CHOP] : involved and often specious argumentation

²choplogic adj : given to complex and often erroneous or absurd argumentation ⟨a ~ speech⟩

chop mark n : an indentation made on a coin to attest weight, silver content, or legality — **chop–marked** \'chäp-‚märkt\ adj

chop·per \'chäp-ər\ n 1 : one that chops 2 : HELICOPTER 3 : a device that interrupts an electric current or a beam of radiation (as light) at short regular intervals 4 : a high-bouncing batted baseball 5 : a customized motorcycle

chop·pi·ness \'chäp-ē-nəs\ n : the quality or state of being choppy

chopping block n : a wooden block on which material (as meat, wood, or vegetables) is cut, split, or diced

¹chop·py \'chäp-ē\ adj chop·pi·er; -est [²chop] : being roughened : CHAPPED

²choppy adj chop·pi·er; -est [³chop] of the wind : CHANGEABLE, VARIABLE

³choppy adj chop·pi·er; -est [¹chop] 1 : rough with small waves 2 : JERKY, DISCONNECTED ⟨criticized for his ~ novel⟩ — **chop·pi·ly** \'chäp-ə-lē\ adv

chops \'chäps\ n pl [alter. of ⁴chap] 1 : JAW 2 a : MOUTH b : the fleshy covering of the jaws ⟨the hungry dog licked his ~⟩

chop·stick \'chäp-‚stik\ n [Pidgin E, fr. chop fast (of Chinese origin; akin to Cant kap) + E stick] : one of a pair of slender sticks held between thumb and fingers and used chiefly in oriental countries to lift food to the mouth

chop su·ey \chäp-'sü-ē\ n, pl chop sueys [Chin (Cant) shap sui odds and ends, fr. shap miscellaneous + sui bits] : a dish prepared chiefly from bean sprouts, bamboo shoots, water chestnuts, onions, mushrooms, and meat or fish and served with rice and soy sauce

cho·ra·gus \kə-'rā-gəs\ or **cho·re·gus** \-'rē-, -'rä-\ n [L & Gk; fr. Gk choragos, chorēgos, fr. choros chorus + agein to lead — more at AGENT] 1 : the leader of a chorus or choir; broadly : the leader of any group or movement 2 : a leader of a dramatic chorus in ancient Greece — **cho·rag·ic** \-'raj-ik\ adj

chopsticks

cho·ral \'kōr-əl, 'kòr-\ adj [F or ML; F choral, fr. ML choralis, fr. L chorus] 1 a : of or relating to a chorus or choir ⟨a ~ group⟩ b : accompanied with song ⟨a ~ dance⟩ 2 : sung or designed for singing by a choir ⟨a ~ arrangement⟩ — **cho·ral·ly** \-ə-lē\ adv

cho·rale also **cho·ral** \kə-'ral, -'räl\ n [G choral, short for choralgesang choral song] 1 : a hymn or psalm sung to a traditional or composed melody in church; also : a hymn tune or a harmonization of a traditional melody ⟨a Bach ~⟩ 2 : CHORUS, CHOIR

chorale prelude n : a composition usu. for organ based on a chorale

choral speaking n : ensemble speaking of poetry or prose by a group often using various voice combinations and contrasts

¹chord \'kò(ə)rd\ n [alter. of ME cord, short for accord] : a combination of tones that blend harmoniously when sounded together

²chord vi 1 : ACCORD 2 : to play chords on a stringed instrument ~ vt 1 : to make chords on 2 : HARMONIZE

³chord n [alter. of ¹cord] 1 : CORD 3a 2 : a straight line joining two points on a curve; specif : the segment of a secant between its intersections with a curve 3 : an individual emotion or disposition 4 : either of the two outside members of a truss connected and braced by the web members 5 : the straight line joining the leading and trailing edges of an airfoil

chord·al \'kòrd-ⁿl\ adj 1 : of, relating to, or suggesting a chord 2 : relating to music characterized more by harmony than by counterpoint

chor·da·meso·derm \‚kòrd-ə-'mez-ə-‚dərm also -'mes-\ n [NL chorda cord + E mesoderm] : the portion of the embryonic mesoderm that forms notochord and related structures and serves as an inductor of neural structures — **chor·da·meso·der·mal** \-‚mez-ə-'dər-məl, -‚mes-\ adj

chor·date \'kòrd-ət, 'kò(ə)r-‚dāt\ n [deriv. of L chorda cord] : any of a phylum or subkingdom (Chordata) of animals having at least at some stage of development a notochord, dorsally situated central nervous system, and gill clefts and including the vertebrates, lancelets, and tunicates — **chordate** adj

chord organ n : an electronic or reed organ with buttons to produce simple chords

chore \'chō(ə)r, 'chò(ə)r\ n [alter. of chare] 1 pl : the regular or daily light work of a household or farm 2 : a routine task or job 3 : a difficult or disagreeable task syn see TASK

-chore \‚kō(ə)r, ‚kò(ə)r\ n comb form [Gk chōrein to withdraw, go; akin to Gk chēros bereaved — more at HEIR] : plant distributed by (such) an agency ⟨zoochore⟩ — **-cho·rous** \'kōr-əs, 'kòr-\ adj comb form — **-cho·ry** \‚kōr-ē, ‚kòr-\ n comb form

cho·rea \kə-'rē-ə\ n [NL, fr. L dance, fr. Gk choreia, fr. choros chorus] : a nervous disorder (as of man or dogs) marked by spasmodic movements of limbs and facial muscles and by incoordination

chore boy n : one who does chores; esp : a man who does the domestic maintenance tasks and helps the cook in a lumber camp 2 : a person who assumes responsibility for onerous detail in an undertaking

chore·man \'chō(ə)r-mən, 'chò(ə)r-\ n : a worker who performs menial jobs in a factory or camp (as a logging or construction camp)

cho·reo·dra·ma \‚kōr-ē-ō-'dräm-ə, -'dram-\ n [Gk choreia dance + E drama] : a dance drama for large groups

cho·reo·graph \'kōr-ē-ə-‚graf, 'kòr-\ vt : to compose the choreography of ~ vi : to engage in choreography — **cho·re·og·ra·pher** \‚kōr-ē-'äg-rə-fər, ‚kòr-\ n

cho·re·og·ra·phy \‚kōr-ē-'äg-rə-fē, ‚kòr-\ n, pl -phies [F chorégraphie, fr. Gk choreia + F -graphie -graphy] 1 : the art of symbolically representing dancing 2 : stage dancing as distinguished from social or ballroom dancing 3 a : the composition and arrangement of dances esp. for ballet b : a composition created by this art — **cho·reo·graph·ic** \‚kōr-ē-ə-'graf-ik, ‚kòr-\ adj — **cho·reo·graph·i·cal·ly** \-i-k(ə-)lē\ adv

chor·iamb \'kōr-ē-‚am(b), 'kòr-\ n, pl -iambs \-‚amz\ [LL choriambus, fr. Gk choriambos, fr. choreios of a chorus, (fr. choros) + iambos iambus] : a prosodic foot consisting of a trochee followed by an iamb — **chor·iam·bic** \‚kōr-ē-'am-bik, ‚kòr-\ adj

cho·ric \'kōr-ik, 'kòr-, 'kär-\ adj : of, relating to, or being in the style of a chorus and esp. a Greek chorus — **cho·ri·cal·ly** \-i-k(ə-)lē\ adv

cho·rine \'kō(ə)r-‚ēn, 'kò(ə)r-\ n [chorus + -ine] : CHORUS GIRL

cho·rio·al·lan·to·is \‚kōr-ē-ō-ə-'lant-ə-wəs, ‚kòr-\ n [NL, fr. Gk chorion + NL allantois] : a vascular fetal membrane composed of the fused chorion and adjacent wall of the allantois that in the hen's egg is used as a living culture medium for viruses and for tissues — **cho·rio·al·lan·to·ic** \-‚al-ən-'tō-ik\ adj

cho·rio·car·ci·no·ma \‚kōr-ē-ō-‚kärs-ⁿn-'ō-mə\ n [NL, fr. chorion + carcinoma] : a malignant tumor developing in the uterus from trophoblast and rarely in the testes from a neoplasm

cho·ri·on \'kōr-ē-‚än, 'kòr-\ n [NL, fr. Gk] : the highly vascular outer embryonic membrane of higher vertebrates that in placental mammals is associated with the allantois in the formation of the placenta — **cho·ri·on·ic** \‚kōr-ē-'än-ik, ‚kòr-\ adj

cho·ris·ter \'kōr-ə-stər, 'kòr-, 'kär-\ n [ME querister, fr. AF cueristre, fr. ML chorista, fr. L chorus] 1 : a singer in a choir; specif : CHOIRBOY 2 : the singer in a church choir who leads the singing and in the absence of instrumental accompaniment sets the pitch and tempo

cho·ri·zo \chə-'rē-(‚)zō, -(‚)sō\ n, pl -zos [Sp] : pork sausage that is highly seasoned with cayenne pepper, pimientos, garlic, and paprika

ə abut	⁹ kitten	ər further	a back	ā bake	ä cot, cart
aù out	ch chin	e less	ē easy	g gift	i trip	ī life
j joke	ŋ sing	ō flow	ò flaw	òi coin	th thin	th this
ü loot	ù foot	y yet	yü few	yù furious	zh vision

C–horizon *n* : the layer of a soil profile lying beneath the B-horizon and consisting essentially of more or less weathered parent rock
cho·rog·ra·phy \kə-'räg-rə-fē\ *n* [L *chorographia,* fr. Gk *chōrographia,* fr. *chōros* place + *-graphia* -graphy] **1** : the art of describing or mapping a region or district **2** : a description or map of a region; *also* : the physical conformation and features of such a region — **cho·ro·graph·ic** \ˌkȯr-ə-'graf-ik, ˌkär-\ *adj*
cho·roid \'kō(ə)r-ˌȯid, 'kȯ(ə)r-\ *also* **cho·ri·oid** \'kōr-ē-ˌȯid, 'kȯr-\ *n* [*choroid coat*] : a vascular membrane containing large branched pigment cells that lies between the retina and the sclerotic coat of the vertebrate eye — see EYE illustration — **choroid** *adj* — **cho·roi·dal** \kə-'rȯid-ᵊl\ *adj*
choroid coat *n* [NL *choroides* resembling the chorion, fr. Gk *chorioeidēs,* fr. *chorion*] : CHOROID
chor·tle \'chȯrt-ᵊl\ *vb* **chor·tled; chor·tling** \'chȯrt-liŋ, -ᵊl-iŋ\ [blend of *chuckle* and *snort*] *vi* **1** : to sing or chant exultantly ⟨he *chortled* in his joy —Lewis Carroll⟩ **2** : to laugh or chuckle esp. in satisfaction or exultation ~ *vt* : to express effervescently or with a chortling intonation — **chortle** *n* — **chor·tler** \'chȯrt-lər, -ᵊl-ər\ *n*
[1]**cho·rus** \'kōr-əs, 'kȯr-\ *n* [L, ring dance, chorus, fr. Gk *choros*] **1 a** : a company of singers and dancers in Athenian drama participating in or commenting on the action; *also* : a similar company in later plays **b** : a character in Elizabethan drama who speaks the prologue and epilogue and comments on the action **c** : an organized company of singers who sing in concert : CHOIR; *specif* : a body of singers who sing the choral parts of a work (as in opera) **d** : a group of dancers and singers supporting the featured players in a musical comedy or revue **2 a** : a part of a song or hymn recurring at intervals **b** : the part of a drama sung or spoken by the chorus **c** : a composition to be sung by a number of voices in concert **d** : the main part of a popular song **3** : something performed, sung, or uttered simultaneously by a number of persons or animals; *also* : sounds so uttered **4** : a unanimous utterance by members of a group ⟨a ~ of boos⟩ — **in chorus** : in unison
[2]**chorus** *vt* : to sing or utter in chorus
chorus boy *n* : a young man who sings or dances in the chorus of a theatrical production (as a musical comedy or revue)
chorus girl *n* : a young woman who sings or dances in the chorus of a theatrical production (as a musical comedy or revue) — called also *chorine*
[1]**chose** *past of* CHOOSE
[2]**chose** \'shōz\ *n* [F, fr. L *causa* cause, reason] : a piece of personal property : THING
[1]**cho·sen** \'chōz-ᵊn\ *adj* [ME, fr. pp. of *chosen* to choose] **1** : selected or marked for favor or special privilege ⟨an hour granted to a ~ few⟩ **2** : ELECT
[2]**chosen** *n, pl* **chosen** : one who is the object of choice or of divine favor : an elect person
chott \'shät\ *n* [F *chott,* fr. Ar *shaṭṭ*] : a shallow saline lake of northern Africa; *also* : the dried bed of such a lake
Chou \'jō\ *n* [Chin (Pek) *Chou*[1]] : a Chinese dynasty traditionally dated 1122 to about 256 B.C. and marked by the development of the philosophical schools of Confucius, Mencius, Lao-tzu, and Mo Ti
chough \'chəf\ *n* [ME] : a bird of an Old World genus (*Pyrrhocorax*) that is related to the crows and has red legs and glossy black plumage
[1]**chouse** \'chau̇s\ *vt* **choused; chous·ing** [Turk *çavuş* doorkeeper, messenger] : CHEAT, TRICK
[2]**chouse** *vt* **choused; chous·ing** [origin unknown] *West* : to drive or herd roughly
[1]**chow** \'chau̇\ *n* [perh. fr. Chin (Pek) *chiao*[3] meat dumpling] : FOOD, VICTUALS
[2]**chow** *vi* : EAT — often used with *down*
[3]**chow** *n* : CHOW CHOW
chow·chow \'chau̇-ˌchau̇\ *n* [Pidgin E] **1** : a Chinese preserve of ginger, fruits, and peels in heavy syrup **2** : a relish of chopped mixed pickles in mustard sauce
chow chow \'chau̇-ˌchau̇\ *n, often cap both Cs* [fr. a Chin dial. word akin to Cant *kaú* dog] : a heavy-coated blocky dog with a broad head and muzzle, a very full ruff of long hair, and a distinctive blue-black tongue and black-lined mouth — called also *chow*

chow chow

[1]**chow·der** \'chau̇d-ər\ *n* [F *chaudière* kettle, contents of a kettle, fr. LL *caldaria* — more at CALDRON] : a thick soup or stew of seafood (as clams or mussels) usu. made with milk, salt pork or bacon, onions and other vegetables (as potatoes); *also* : a soup resembling chowder ⟨corn ~⟩
[2]**chowder** *vt* : to make chowder of
chow·der·head \-ˌhed\ *n* : DOLT, BLOCKHEAD — **chow·der·head·ed** \ˌchau̇d-ər-'hed-əd\ *adj*
chow·hound \'chau̇-ˌhau̇nd\ *n* : one excessively fond of food : GLUTTON
chow line *n* : a line of people waiting to be served food (as in a military mess)
chow mein \'chau̇-'mān\ *n* [Chin (Pek) *ch'ao*[3] *mien*[4], fr. *ch'ao*[3] to fry + *mien*[4] dough] : a thick stew of shredded or diced meat, mushrooms, vegetables, and seasonings that is usu. served with fried noodles
chow·time \'chau̇-ˌtīm\ *n* : MEALTIME
chres·tom·a·thy \kre-'stäm-ə-thē\ *n, pl* **-thies** [NL *chrestomathia,* fr. Gk *chrēstomatheia,* fr. *chrēstos* useful + *manthanein* to learn; akin to Skt *hrasva* small — more at MATHEMATICAL] **1** : a selection of passages compiled as an aid to learning a language **2** : a volume of selections from an author
chrism \'kriz-əm\ *n* [ME *crisme,* fr. OE *crisma,* fr. LL *chrisma,* fr. Gk, ointment, fr. *chriein* to anoint; akin to OE *grēot* grit, sand] : consecrated oil used in Greek and Latin churches esp. in baptism, confirmation, and ordination
chris·mon \'kriz-ˌmän\ *n, pl* **chris·ma** \-mə\ *or* **chrismons** [ML, fr. L *Christus* Christ + LL *monogramma* monogram] : CHI-RHO
chris·om \'kriz-əm\ *n* [ME *crisom,* short for *crisom cloth,* fr. *crisom* chrism + *cloth*] : a white cloth or robe put on a person at baptism as a symbol of innocence
chrisom child *n* : a child that dies in its first month
Christ \'krīst\ *n* [ME *Crist,* fr. OE, fr. L *Christus,* fr. Gk *Christos,* lit., anointed, fr. *chriein* to anoint] **1** : MESSIAH **2** : JESUS **3** : an ideal type of humanity **4** *Christian Science* : the ideal truth that comes as a divine manifestation of God to destroy incarnate error
chris·ten \'kris-ᵊn\ *vt* **chris·tened; chris·ten·ing** \'kris-niŋ, -ᵊn-iŋ\ [ME *cristnen,* fr. OE *cristnian,* fr. *cristen* Christian, fr. L *christianus*] **1 a** : BAPTIZE **b** : to name at baptism **2** : to name or dedicate (as a ship) by a ceremony suggestive of baptism **3** : NAME **4** : to use for the first time
Chris·ten·dom \'kris-ᵊn-dəm\ *n* [ME *cristendom,* fr. OE *cristendōm,* fr. *cristen*] **1** : CHRISTIANITY **2** : the part of the world in which Christianity prevails
chris·ten·ing *n* : the ceremony of baptizing and naming a child
[1]**Chris·tian** \'kris(h)-chən\ *n* [L *christianus,* adj. & n., fr. Gk *christianos,* fr. *Christos*] **1 a** : one who professes belief in the teachings of Jesus Christ **b** (1) : DISCIPLE 2 (2) : a member of one of the Churches of Christ separating from the Disciples of Christ in 1906 (3) : a member of the Christian denomination having part in the union of the United Church of Christ concluded in 1961 **2** : the hero in Bunyan's *Pilgrim's Progress*
[2]**Christian** *adj* **1 a** : of or relating to Christianity ⟨~ scriptures⟩ **b** : based on or conforming with Christianity ⟨~ ethics⟩ **2 a** : of or relating to a Christian ⟨~ responsibilities⟩ **b** : professing Christianity ⟨a ~ affirmation⟩ **3** : commendably decent or generous ⟨has a very ~ concern for others⟩ — **Chris·tian·ly** *adv*
Christian Brother *n* : a member of the Roman Catholic institute of Brothers of the Christian Schools founded by St. John Baptist de la Salle in France in 1684 and dedicated to education
Christian era *n* : the period dating from the birth of Christ
chris·ti·ania \ˌkris(h)-chē-'an-ē-ə, ˌkris-tē-, -'än-\ *n* [*Christiania,* former name of Oslo, Norway] : CHRISTIE
Chris·tian·i·ty \ˌkris(h)-chē-'an-ət-ē, ˌkris-tē-'an-, kris(h)-'chan-\ *n* **1** : the religion derived from Jesus Christ, based on the Bible as sacred scripture, and professed by Eastern, Roman Catholic, and Protestant bodies **2** : conformity to the Christian religion
Chris·tian·ize \'kris(h)-chə-ˌnīz\ *vt* **-ized; -iz·ing** : to make Christian — **Chris·tian·iza·tion** \ˌkris(h)-chə-nə-'zā-shən\ *n* — **Chris·tian·iz·er** \'kris(h)-chə-ˌnī-zər\ *n*
Christian name *n* **1** : a name given at christening or confirmation **2** : a name that precedes one's surname; *esp* : FIRST NAME
Christian Science *n* : a religion discovered by Mary Baker Eddy in 1866 that was organized under the official name of the Church of Christ, Scientist, that derives its teachings from the Scriptures as understood by its adherents, and that includes a practice of spiritual healing based on the teaching that cause and effect are mental and that sin, sickness, and death will be destroyed by a full understanding of the divine principle of Jesus's teaching and healing — **Christian Scientist** *n*
chris·tie *or* **chris·ty** \'kris-tē\ *n, pl* **christies** [by shortening & alter. fr. *christiania*] : a skiing turn used for altering the direction of hill descent or for stopping and executed usu. at high speed by shifting the body weight forward and skidding into a turn with parallel skis — called also *christiania*
Christ·like \'krīst-ˌlīk\ *adj* : resembling Christ in character, spirit, or action — **Christ·like·ness** *n*
Christ·ly \'krīst-lē\ *adj* : of, relating to, or resembling Christ
Christ·mas \'kris-məs\ *n* [ME *Christemasse,* fr. OE *Cristes mæsse,* lit., Christ's mass] **1** : a Christian feast on December 25 or among the Eastern Orthodox on January 7 that commemorates the birth of Christ and is usu. observed as a legal holiday **2** : CHRISTMASTIDE — **Christ·mas·sy** \-mə-sē\ *adj*
Christmas cactus *n* [fr. its annual blooming around Christmastime] : a branching So. American cactus (*Zygocactus truncatus*) with flat stems, short joints, and showy red zygomorphic flowers — called also *crab cactus*
Christmas card *n* : an ornamental card with a greeting sent at Christmas
Christmas club *n* : a savings account in which regular deposits are made throughout the year to provide money for Christmas shopping
Christmas Eve *n* : the eve of Christmas
Christmas fern *n* : a No. American evergreen fern (*Polystichum acrostichoides*) used for decoration in winter — see FERN illustration
Christmas rose *n* : a European herb (*Helleborus niger*) of the buttercup family that has white or purplish flowers produced in winter
Christ·mas·tide \'kris-mə-ˌstīd\ *n* : the festival season from Christmas Eve till after New Year's Day or esp. in England till Epiphany
Christ·mas·time \-mə-ˌstīm\ *n* : the Christmas season
Christmas tree *n* **1** : a usu. evergreen tree decorated at Christmas **2** : an oil-well control device consisting of an assembly of fittings placed at the top of the well **3** : a set of flashing red, yellow, and green lights used to start drag races
Chris·to·cen·tric \ˌkris-tə-'sen-trik, ˌkrīs-\ *adj* [Gk *Christos* Christ + E *-centric*] : centering theologically on Christ
Chris·to·gram \'kris-tə-ˌgram, 'krīs-\ *n* [Gk *Christos* Christ + E *-gram*] : a graphic symbol of Christ; *esp* : CHI-RHO
Chris·tol·o·gy \kris-'täl-ə-jē, krīs-\ *n* [Gk *Christos* Christ + E *-logy*] : theological interpretation of the person and work of Christ — **Chris·to·log·i·cal** \ˌkris-tə-'läj-i-kəl, ˌkrīs-\ *adj*
Christ's–thorn \'krīs(ts)-ˌthȯ(ə)rn\ *n* : any of several prickly or thorny shrubs of Palestine (esp. the shrub *Paliurus spina-christi* or the jujube *Ziziphus jujuba*)
chrom- *or* **chromo-** *comb form* [F, fr. Gk *chrōma* color] **1** : chromium ⟨*chromize*⟩ **2 a** : color : colored ⟨*chromosphere*⟩ **b** : pigment ⟨*chromogen*⟩

chro·ma \ˈkrō-mə\ *n* [Gk *chrōma*] **1 :** SATURATION 4a **2 :** a quality of color combining hue and saturation

chro·maf·fin \ˈkrō-mə-fən\ *adj* [ISV *chrom-* + L *affinis* bordering on, related — more at AFFINITY] **:** staining deeply with chromium salts ⟨~ cells of the adrenal medulla⟩

chromat- *or* **chromato-** *comb form* [Gk *chrōmat-, chrōma*] **1 :** color ⟨*chromat*id⟩ **2 :** chromatin ⟨*chromato*lysis⟩

chro·mate \ˈkrō-ˌmāt\ *n* [F, fr. Gk *chrōma*] **:** a salt or ester of chromic acid

¹chro·mat·ic \krō-ˈmat-ik\ *adj* [Gk *chrōmatikos*, fr. *chrōmat-, chrōma* skin, color, modified tone; akin to OE *grēot* sand — more at GRIT] **1 a :** of or relating to color or color phenomena or sensations **b :** highly colored **2 :** of or relating to chroma **3 a :** of, relating to, or giving all the tones of the chromatic scale **b :** characterized by frequent use of nonharmonic tones or of harmonies based on nonharmonic tones — **chro·mat·i·cal·ly** \-i-k(ə-)lē\ *adv* — **chro·mat·i·cism** \-ˈmat-ə-ˌsiz-əm\ *n*

²chromatic *n* **:** ACCIDENTAL 2

chromatic aberration *n* **:** aberration caused by the differences in refraction of the colored rays of the spectrum

chro·ma·tic·i·ty \ˌkrō-mə-ˈtis-ət-ē\ *n* **1 :** the quality or state of being chromatic **2 :** the quality of color characterized by its dominant or complementary wavelength and purity taken together

chro·mat·ics \krō-ˈmat-iks\ *n pl but sing in constr* **:** the branch of colorimetry that deals with hue and saturation

chromatic scale *n* **:** a musical scale consisting entirely of half steps

chro·ma·tid \ˈkrō-mə-təd\ *n* **:** one of the paired complex constituent strands of a chromosome — compare CHROMONEMA

chro·ma·tin \ˈkrō-mət-ən\ *n* **:** the part of a cell nucleus that stains intensely with basic dyes; *specif* **:** a complex of a polymerized nucleic acid with basic proteins of protamine or histone type present in chromosomes and carrying the genes — **chro·ma·tin·ic** \ˌkrō-mə-ˈtin-ik\ *adj*

chro·mato·gram \krō-ˈmat-ə-ˌgram, krə-\ *n* **:** the pattern formed on the adsorbent medium by the layers of components separated by chromatography

chro·ma·tog·ra·phy \ˌkrō-mə-ˈtäg-rə-fē\ *n* **:** a process of separating esp. a solution of closely related compounds by allowing a solution to seep through an adsorbent (as clay or paper) so that each compound becomes adsorbed in a separate often colored layer — **chro·mato·graph** \krō-ˈmat-ə-ˌgraf, krə-\ *vt* — **chro·mato·graph·ic** \-ˌmat-ə-ˈgraf-ik\ *adj* — **chro·mato·graph·i·cal·ly** \-i-k(ə-)lē\ *adv*

chro·ma·tol·y·sis \ˌkrō-mə-ˈtäl-ə-səs\ *n* [NL] **:** the dissolution and breaking up of chromophil material (as chromatin) of a cell — **chro·mato·lyt·ic** \krō-ˌmat-ᵊl-ˈit-ik, krə-\ *adj*

chro·mato·phore \krō-ˈmat-ə-ˌfō(ə)r, krə-, -ˌfȯ(ə)r\ *n* [ISV] **1 :** a pigment-bearing cell; *esp* **:** one of the integumental cells of an animal capable of causing skin color changes by expanding or contracting **2 :** the organelle of photosynthesis in blue-green algae and photosynthetic bacteria; *broadly* **:** CHROMOPLAST, CHLOROPLAST

¹chrome \ˈkrōm\ *n* [F, fr. Gk *chrōma*] **1 a :** CHROMIUM **b :** a chromium pigment **2 :** something plated with an alloy of chromium

²chrome *vt* **chromed; chrom·ing 1 :** to treat with a compound of chromium (as in dyeing) **2 :** CHROMIZE

-chrome \ˌkrōm\ *n comb form or adj comb form* [ML *-chromat-, -chroma* colored thing, fr. Gk *chrōmat-, chrōma*] **1 :** colored thing ⟨helio*chrome*⟩ **:** colored ⟨hetero*chrome*⟩ **2 :** coloring matter ⟨uro*chrome*⟩

chrome alum *n* **:** an alum with trivalent chromium; *esp* **:** a dark violet salt $KCr(SO_4)_2.12H_2O$ used in tanning, in photography, and as a mordant in dyeing

chrome green *n* **:** any of various brilliant green pigments containing or consisting of chromium compounds

chrome red *n* **:** a red pigment consisting of basic lead chromate $PbCrO_4.PbO$

chrome yellow *n* **:** a yellow pigment consisting essentially of neutral lead chromate $PbCrO_4$

chro·mic \ˈkrō-mik\ *adj* **:** of, relating to, or derived from chromium esp. with a valence of three

chromic acid *n* **:** an acid H_2CrO_4 analogous to sulfuric acid but known only in solution and esp. in the form of its salts

chro·mide \ˈkrō-ˌmīd\ *n* [deriv. of Gk *chromis*, a sea fish] **:** any of several small brightly colored African fishes (family Cichlidae)

chro·mi·nance \ˈkrō-mən-ən(t)s\ *n* [*chrom-* + *luminance*] **:** the difference between a color and a chosen reference color of the same luminous intensity in color television

chro·mite \ˈkrō-ˌmīt\ *n* [G *chromit*, fr. *chrom-*] **1 :** a mineral $FeCr_2O_4$ that consists of an oxide of iron and chromium **2 :** an oxide of bivalent chromium

chro·mi·um \ˈkrō-mē-əm\ *n* [NL, fr. F *chrome*] **:** a blue-white metallic element found naturally only in combination and used esp. in alloys and in electroplating — see ELEMENT table

chro·mize \ˈkrō-ˌmīz\ *vt* **chro·mized; chro·miz·ing :** to treat (metal) with chromium in order to form a protective surface alloy

chro·mo \ˈkrō(ˌ)mō\ *n, pl* **chromos :** CHROMOLITHOGRAPH

chro·mo·gen \ˈkrō-mə-jən\ *n* [ISV] **1 a :** a precursor of a biochemical pigment **b :** a compound not itself a dye but containing a chromophore and so capable of becoming one **2 :** a pigment-producing microorganism — **chro·mo·gen·ic** \ˌkrō-mə-ˈjen-ik\ *adj*

chro·mo·litho·graph \ˌkrō-mə-ˈlith-ə-ˌgraf\ *n* **:** a picture printed in colors from a series of stones prepared by the lithographic process — **chro·mo·litho·graph·ic** \-ˌlith-ə-ˈgraf-ik\ *adj* — **chro·mo·li·thog·ra·phy** \-lith-ˈäg-rə-fē\ *n*

chro·mo·mere \ˈkrō-mə-ˌmi(ə)r\ *n* [ISV] **:** one of the small bead-shaped and heavily staining concentrations of chromatin that are linearly arranged along the chromosome — **chro·mo·mer·ic** \ˌkrō-mə-ˈmer-ik, -ˈmi(ə)r-\ *adj*

chro·mo·ne·ma \ˌkrō-mə-ˈnē-mə\ *n, pl* **-ne·ma·ta** \-ˈnē-mət-ə\ [NL, fr. *chrom-* + Gk *nēmat-, nēma* thread — more at NEMAT-] **:** the coiled filamentous core of a chromatid — **chro·mo·ne·mal** \-ˈnē-məl\ *or* **chro·mo·ne·ma·tal** \-ˈnē-mət-ᵊl, -ˈnem-ət-\ *or* **chro·mo·ne·mat·ic** \-ni-ˈmat-ik\ *adj*

chro·mo·phil \ˈkrō-mə-ˌfil\ *or* **chro·mat·o·phil** \krō-ˈmat-ə-ˌfil\ *adj* [ISV] **:** staining readily with dyes

chro·mo·phore \ˈkrō-mə-ˌfō(ə)r, -ˌfȯ(ə)r\ *n* [ISV] **:** a chemical group that gives rise to color in molecule — **chro·mo·phor·ic** \ˌkrō-mə-ˈfȯr-ik, -ˈfär-\ *adj*

chro·mo·plast \ˈkrō-mə-ˌplast\ *n* [ISV] **:** a colored plastid usu. containing red or yellow pigment (as carotene)

chro·mo·pro·tein \ˌkrō-mə-ˈprō-ˌtēn, -ˈprōt-ē-ən\ *n* **:** a compound (as hemoglobin) of a protein with a metal-containing pigment (as heme) or a carotenoid

chro·mo·some \ˈkrō-mə-ˌsōm, -ˌzōm\ *n* [ISV] **:** one of the usu. linear nucleoprotein-containing basophilic bodies of the cell nucleus made up of chromatids — **chro·mo·som·al** \ˌkrō-mə-ˈsō-məl, -ˈzō-\ *adj* — **chro·mo·som·al·ly** \-mə-lē\ *adv* — **chro·mo·so·mic** \-mik\ *adj*

chromosome number *n* **:** the usu. constant number of chromosomes characteristic of a particular kind of animal or plant

chro·mo·sphere \ˈkrō-mə-ˌsfi(ə)r\ *n* **:** the lower part of the atmosphere of the sun that is thousands of miles thick and is composed chiefly of hydrogen gas; *also* **:** a similar part of the atmosphere of any star — **chro·mo·spher·ic** \ˌkrō-mə-ˈsfi(ə)r-ik, -ˈsfer-\ *adj*

chro·mous \ˈkrō-məs\ *adj* **:** of, relating to, or derived from chromium esp. with a valence of two

chron *abbr* **1** chronicle **2** chronological; chronology

Chron *abbr* Chronicles

chron- *or* **chrono-** *comb form* [Gk, fr. *chronos*] **:** time ⟨*chrono*gram⟩

chron·ax·ie *or* **chron·axy** \ˈkrōn-ˌak-sē, ˈkrän-\ *n* [F *chronaxie*, fr. *chron-* + Gk *axia* value, fr. *axios* worthy] **:** the minimum time required for excitation of a structure (as a nerve cell) by a constant electric current of twice the threshold voltage

chron·ic \ˈkrän-ik\ *adj* [F *chronique*, fr. Gk *chronikos* of time, fr. *chronos*] **1 a :** marked by long duration or frequent recurrence **:** not acute ⟨~ indigestion⟩ ⟨~ experiments⟩ **b :** suffering from a chronic disease ⟨the special needs of ~ patients⟩ **2 a :** always present or encountered; *esp* **:** constantly vexing, weakening, or troubling ⟨~ petty warfare⟩ **b :** being such habitually ⟨a ~ grumbler⟩ ***syn*** see INVETERATE — **chronic** *n* — **chron·i·cal** \-i-kəl\ *adj* — **chron·i·cal·ly** \-i-k(ə-)lē\ *adv* — **chro·nic·i·ty** \krä-ˈnis-ət-ē, krō-\ *n*

¹chron·i·cle \ˈkrän-i-kəl\ *n* [ME *cronicle*, fr. AF, alter. of OF *chronique*, fr. L *chronica*, fr. Gk *chronika*, fr. neut. pl. of *chronikos*] **1 :** a usu. continuous and detailed historical account of events arranged in order of time without analysis or interpretation **2 :** NARRATIVE ***syn*** see HISTORY

²chronicle *vt* **-cled; -cling** \-k(ə-)liŋ\ **1 :** to record in or as if in a chronicle **2 :** LIST, DESCRIBE — **chron·i·cler** \-k(ə-)lər\ *n*

chronicle play *n* **:** a play with a theme from history consisting usu. of rather loosely connected episodes chronologically arranged

Chron·i·cles \ˈkrän-i-kəlz\ *n pl but sing in constr* **:** either of two historical books of canonical Jewish and Christian Scripture — see BIBLE table

chro·no·gram \ˈkrän-ə-ˌgram, ˈkrō-nə-\ *n* **1 :** an inscription, sentence, or phrase in which certain letters express a date or epoch **2 :** the record made by a chronograph — **chro·no·gram·mat·ic** \ˌkrän-ə-grə-ˈmat-ik, ˌkrō-nə-\ *or* **chro·no·gram·mat·i·cal** \-i-kəl\ *adj*

chro·no·graph \ˈkrän-ə-ˌgraf, ˈkrō-nə-\ *n* **:** an instrument for measuring and recording time intervals: as **a :** an instrument having a revolving drum on which a stylus makes marks **b :** a watch with a sweep-second hand **c :** an instrument for measuring the time of flight of projectiles — **chro·no·graph·ic** \ˌkrän-ə-ˈgraf-ik, ˌkrō-nə\ *adj* — **chro·nog·ra·phy** \krə-ˈnäg-rə-fē\ *n*

chro·nol·o·ger \krə-ˈnäl-ə-jər\ *n* **:** CHRONOLOGIST

chro·no·log·i·cal \ˌkrän-ᵊl-ˈäj-i-kəl, ˌkrōn-\ *also* **chro·no·log·ic** \-ik\ *adj* **:** of, relating to, or arranged in or according to the order of time ⟨~ tables of American history⟩ — **chro·no·log·i·cal·ly** \-i-k(ə-)lē\ *adv*

chro·nol·o·gist \krə-ˈnäl-ə-jəst\ *n* **:** an expert in chronology

chro·nol·o·gize \krə-ˈnäl-ə-ˌjīz\ *vt* **-gized; -giz·ing :** to arrange chronologically **:** establish the order in time of (as events or documents)

chro·nol·o·gy \-jē\ *n, pl* **-gies** [NL *chronologia*, fr. *chron-* + *-logia* -logy] **1 :** the science that deals with measuring time by regular divisions and that assigns to events their proper dates **2 :** a chronological table or list **3 :** an arrangement in order of occurrence

chro·nom·e·ter \krə-ˈnäm-ət-ər\ *n* **:** an instrument for measuring time **:** TIMEPIECE; *esp* **:** one designed to keep time with great accuracy

chro·no·met·ric \ˌkrän-ə-ˈme-trik, ˌkrō-nə-\ *or* **chro·no·met·ri·cal** \-tri-kəl\ *adj* **:** of or relating to a chronometer or chronometry — **chro·no·met·ri·cal·ly** \-tri-k(ə-)lē\ *adj*

chro·nom·e·try \-ə-trē\ *n* **1 :** the science of measuring time **2 :** the measuring of time by periods or divisions

chro·no·scope \ˈkrän-ə-ˌskōp, ˈkrō-nə-\ *n* **:** an instrument for precise measurement of small time intervals

chrys- *or* **chryso-** *comb form* [Gk, fr. *chrysos*] **:** gold **:** yellow ⟨*chrys*arobin⟩

chrys·a·lid \ˈkris-ə-ləd\ *n* **:** CHRYSALIS — **chrysalid** *adj*

chrys·a·lis \ˈkris-ə-ləs\ *n, pl* **chry·sal·i·des** \kris-ˈal-ə-ˌdēz\ *or* **chrys·a·lis·es** [L *chrysallid-, chrysallis* gold-colored pupa of butterflies, fr. Gk, fr. *chrysos* gold, of Sem origin] **1 :** a pupa of a butterfly; *broadly* **:** an insect pupa **2 :** a protecting covering **:** a sheltered state or stage of being or growth ⟨a budding writer could not emerge from his ~ too soon —William Du Bois⟩

chry·san·the·mum \kris-ˈan(t)-thə-məm *also* kriz-\ *n* [L, fr. Gk *chrysanthemon*, fr. *chrys-* + *anthemon* flower; akin to Gk *anthos*

ə abut	ᵊ kitten	ər further	a back	ā bake	ä cot, cart
au̇ out	ch chin	e less	ē easy	g gift	i trip
ī life	j joke	ŋ sing	ō flow	ȯ flaw	ȯi coin
th thin	t͟h this	ü loot	u̇ foot	y yet	yü few
yu̇ furious	zh vision				

flower] **1 :** any of various composite plants (genus *Chrysanthemum*) including weeds, ornamentals grown for their brightly colored often double flower heads, and others important as sources of medicinals and insecticides **2 :** a flower head of an ornamental chrysanthemum

chrys·a·ro·bin \ˌkris-ə-ˈrō-bən\ *n* [*chrys-* + araroba + *-in*] : a powder obtained from Goa powder and used to treat skin diseases

Chry·se·is \krī-ˈsē-əs\ *n* [L, fr. Gk *Chryseïs*] : a daughter of a priest of Apollo in the *Iliad* narrative taken at Troy by Agamemnon but later restored to her father

chryso·ber·yl \ˈkris-ə-ˌber-əl\ *n* [L *chrysoberyllus*, fr. Gk *chrysobēryllos*, fr. *chrys-* + *bēryllos* beryl] **1** *obs* : a yellowish beryl **2 :** a usu. yellow or pale green mineral $BeAl_2O_4$ consisting of beryllium aluminum oxide with a little iron and sometimes used as a gem

chrys·o·lite \ˈkris-ə-ˌlīt\ *n* [ME *crisolite*, fr. OF, fr. L *chrysolithos*, fr. Gk, fr. *chrys-* + *-lithos* -lite] : OLIVINE

chrys·o·me·lid \ˌkris-ə-ˈmel-əd, -ˈmēl-\ *n* [deriv. of Gk *chrysomēlonthē* golden cockchafer] : any of a large family (Chrysomelidae) of small, usu. oval and smooth, shining, and brightly colored beetles (as the Colorado potato beetle) — **chrysomelid** *adj*

chryso·phyte \ˈkris-ə-ˌfīt\ *n* [deriv. of Gk *chrysos* + *phyton* plant — more at PHYT-] : any of a major group (Chrysophyta) of algae (as diatoms) with yellowish green to golden brown pigments

chrys·o·prase \ˈkris-ə-ˌprāz\ *n* [ME *crisopace*, fr. OF, fr. L *chrysoprasus*, fr. Gk *chrysoprasos*, fr. *chrys-* + *prason* leek; akin to L *porrum* leek] : an apple-green chalcedony valued as a gem

chrys·o·tile \-ˌtil\ *n* [G *chrysotil*, fr. *chrys-* + *-til* fiber, fr. Gk *tillein* to pluck] : a mineral consisting of a fibrous silky serpentine and constituting a kind of asbestos

chthon·ic \ˈthän-ik\ *or* **chtho·ni·an** \ˈthō-nē-ən\ *adj* [Gk *chthon-*, *chthōn* earth — more at HUMBLE] : INFERNAL ⟨~ deities⟩

chub \ˈchəb\ *n, pl* **chub** *or* **chubs** [ME *chubbe*] **1 :** any of various freshwater cyprinid fishes (esp. of the genera *Gila, Hybopsis*, and *Nocomis*) **2 :** any of several marine or freshwater fishes not closely related to the true chub

chub·bi·ly \ˈchəb-ə-lē\ *adv* : in the manner of one that is chubby

chub·by \ˈchəb-ē\ *adj* **chub·bi·er; -est** [*chub*] : PLUMP ⟨a ~ boy⟩ — **chub·bi·ness** \ˈchəb-ē-nəs\ *n*

[1]**chuck** \ˈchək\ *vb* [ME *chukken*] : CLUCK

[2]**chuck** *n* — used as a term of endearment

[3]**chuck** *vt* [origin unknown] **1 :** PAT, TAP **2 a :** TOSS **b :** DISCARD ⟨~*ed* his old shirt⟩ **c :** DISMISS, OUST — used esp. with *out* ⟨was ~*ed* out of office⟩ **3 :** to have done with ⟨~*ed* up his job⟩ — **chuck it :** QUIT, YIELD

[4]**chuck** *n* **1 :** a pat or nudge under the chin **2 :** TOSS, JERK

[5]**chuck** *n* [E dial. *chuck* (lump)] **1 a :** a portion of a side of dressed beef including most of the neck, the parts about the shoulder blade, and those about the first three ribs — see BEEF illustration **b :** a similar cut of dressed veal or lamb **2** *chiefly West* : FOOD **3 :** an attachment for holding a workpiece or tool in a machine (as a drill press or lathe)

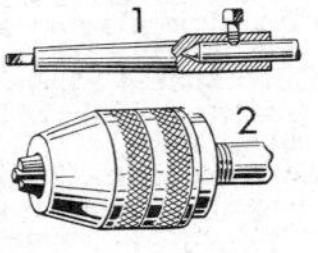

chucks 3: *1* with setscrew, *2* drill chuck

chuck·hole \ˈchək-ˌhōl, ˈchəg-\ *n* [[3]*chuck* + *hole*] : a hole or rut in a road

chuck·le \ˈchək-əl\ *vi* **chuck·led; chuck·ling** \-(ə-)liŋ\ [prob. freq. of [1]*chuck*] **1 :** to laugh inwardly or quietly **2 :** to make a continuous gentle sound resembling suppressed mirth ⟨the clear bright water *chuckled* over gravel—B. A. Williams⟩ — **chuckle** *n* — **chuck·le·some** \-əl-səm\ *adj* — **chuck·ling·ly** \-(ə-)liŋ-lē\ *adv*

chuck·le·head \ˈchək-əl-ˌhed\ *n* [*chuckle* (lumpish) + *head*] : BLOCKHEAD — **chuck·le·head·ed** \ˌchək-əl-ˈhed-əd\ *adj*

chuck wagon *n* [[5]*chuck*] : a wagon carrying a stove and provisions for cooking (as on a ranch)

chuck·wal·la \ˈchək-ˌwäl-ə\ *or* **chuck·a·wal·la** \ˈchək-ə-ˌwäl-ə\ *n* [MexSp *chacahuala*] : a large edible herbivorous lizard (*Sauromalus obesus* of the family Iguanidae) of desert regions of the southwestern U.S.

chuck–will's–wid·ow \ˌchək-ˌwilz-ˈwid-(ˌ)ō, -ˈwid-ə(-w)\ *n* [imit.] : a goatsucker (*Caprimulgus carolinensis*) of the southern U.S.

[1]**chuff** \ˈchəf\ *n* [ME *chuffe*] : BOOR, CHURL

[2]**chuff** *n* [imit.] : the sound of noisy exhaust or exhalations

[3]**chuff** *vi* : to produce noisy exhaust or exhalations : proceed or operate with chuffs ⟨the ~*ing* and snorting of switch engines —Paul Gallico⟩

chuf·fy \ˈchəf-ē\ *adj* **chuf·fi·er; -est** [perh. fr. E dial. *chuff* chubby] : FAT, CHUBBY

[1]**chug** \ˈchəg\ *n* [imit.] : a dull explosive sound made by or as if by a laboring engine

[2]**chug** *vi* **chugged; chug·ging :** to move or go with chugs ⟨a locomotive *chugging* along⟩ — **chug·ger** *n*

chug·a·lug \ˈchəg-ə-ˌləg\ *vb* **-lugged; -lug·ging** [imit.] *vt* : to drink a whole container of without pause ~ *vi* : to drink a whole container (as of beer) without pause

chu·kar \chə-ˈkär\ *n, pl* **chukar** *or* **chukars** [Hindi *cakor*] : a largely gray and black Indian partridge (*Alectoris graeca chukar*) introduced into dry parts of the western U.S.

chuk·ka \ˈchək-ə\ *n* [*chukka*, alter. of *chukker*; fr. a similar polo player's boot] : a usu. ankle-length leather boot with two pairs of eyelets or a buckle and strap

chuk·ker *or* **chuk·kar** \ˈchək-ər\ *or* **chuk·ka** \ˈchək-ə\ *n* [Hindi *cakkar* circular course, fr. Skt *cakra* wheel, circle — more at WHEEL] : a playing period of a polo game

[1]**chum** \ˈchəm\ *n* [perh. by shortening & alter. fr. *chamber fellow* (roommate)] : a close friend : PAL — **chum·ship** \-ˌship\ *n*

[2]**chum** *vi* **chummed; chum·ming 1 :** to room together **2 a :** to be a close friend **b :** to show affable friendliness

[3]**chum** *n* [origin unknown] : chopped fish or other matter thrown overboard to attract fish

[4]**chum** *vb* **chummed; chumming** *vi* : to throw chum overboard to attract fish ~ *vt* : to attract with chum ⟨*chumming* the fish with cut-up shrimp⟩

chum·my \ˈchəm-ē\ *adj* **chum·mi·er; -est :** INTIMATE, SOCIABLE — **chum·mi·ly** \ˈchəm-ə-lē\ *adv* — **chum·mi·ness** \ˈchəm-ē-nəs\ *n*

chump \ˈchəmp\ *n* [perh. blend of *chunk* and *lump*] : FOOL, DUPE

[1]**chunk** \ˈchəŋk\ *n* [perh. alter. of *chuck* (short piece of wood)] **1 :** a short thick piece or lump (as of wood or coal) **2 :** a large noteworthy quantity ⟨bet a sizable ~ of money on the race⟩ **3 :** a strong thickset horse usu. smaller than a draft horse

[2]**chunk** *vi* [imit.] : to make a dull plunging or explosive sound ⟨the rhythmic ~*ing* of thrown quoits —John Updike⟩

chunky \ˈchəŋ-kē\ *adj* **chunk·i·er; -est 1 :** STOCKY **2 :** filled with chunks ⟨breakfast . . . with toast and ~ marmalade —*The People*⟩ — **chunk·i·ly** \-kə-lē\ *adv*

chun·ter \ˈchənt-ər\ *vi* [prob. of imit. origin] *Brit* : to talk in a low inarticulate way : MUTTER

[1]**church** \ˈchərch\ *n* [ME *chirche*, fr. OE *cirice*; akin to OHG *kirihha* church; both fr. a prehistoric WGmc word derived fr. LGk *kyriakon*, fr. Gk, neut. of *kyriakos* of the lord, fr. *kyrios* lord, master, fr. *kyros* power; akin to L *cavus* hollow — more at CAVE] **1 :** a building for public and esp. Christian worship **2 :** the clergy or officialdom of a religious body **3 :** a body or organization of religious believers as: **a :** the whole body of Christians **b :** DENOMINATION **c :** CONGREGATION **4 :** a public divine worship ⟨goes to ~ every Sunday⟩ **5 :** the clerical profession ⟨considered the ~ as a possible career⟩

[2]**church** *vt* : to bring to church to receive one of its rites

[3]**church** *adj* **1 :** of or relating to a church ⟨~ government⟩ **2** *chiefly Brit* : of or relating to the established church

churched \ˈchərcht\ *adj* : affiliated with a church

church father *n* : FATHER 4

church·go·er \ˈchərch-ˌgō(-ə)r\ *n* : one who frequently attends church — **church·go·ing** \-ˌgō-iŋ, -ˌgȯ(-)iŋ\ *adj or n*

church·ian·i·ty \ˌchər-chē-ˈan-ət-ē\ *n* [*church* + *-ianity* (as in *Christianity*)] : the usu. excessive or sectarian attachment to the practices and interests of a particular church

church·ing *n* : the administration or reception of a rite of the church; *specif* : a ceremony in some churches by which women after childbirth are received in the church with prayers, blessings, and thanksgiving

church key *n* : an implement with a triangular pointed head for piercing the tops of cans (as of beer)

church·less \ˈchərch-ləs\ *adj* : not affiliated with a church

church·ly \ˈchərch-lē\ *adj* **1 :** of or relating to a church **2 :** suitable to or suggestive of a church **3 :** adhering to a church **4 :** CHURCHY 2 — **church·li·ness** *n*

church·man \ˈchərch-mən\ *n* **1 :** CLERGYMAN **2 :** a member of a church

church·man·ship \-mən-ˌship\ *n* : the attitude, belief, or practice of a churchman

church mode *n* : one of several usu. 8-tone scales prevalent in medieval music each utilizing a different pattern of intervals and each beginning on a different tone

Church of England : the established episcopal church of England

church register *n* : a parish register of baptisms, marriages, and deaths

church school *n* **1 :** a school providing a general education but supported by a particular church in contrast to a public school or a nondenominational private school **2 :** an organization of officers, teachers, and pupils for purposes of moral and religious education under the supervision of a local church

Church Slavic *n* : OLD CHURCH SLAVONIC

church·war·den \ˈchərch-ˌwȯrd-ᵊn\ *n* **1 :** one of two lay parish officers in Anglican churches with responsibility esp. for parish property and alms **2 :** a long-stemmed clay pipe

church·wom·an \-ˌwu̇m-ən\ *n* : a woman who is a member of a church

churchy \ˈchər-chē\ *adj* **1 :** of or suggesting a church **2 :** marked by strict conformity or zealous adherence to the forms or beliefs of a church

church·yard \-ˌyärd\ *n* : a yard that belongs to a church and is often used as a burial ground

churl \ˈchər(-ə)l\ *n* [ME, fr. OE *ceorl* man, ceorl; akin to Gk *gēras* old age — more at CORN] **1 :** CEORL **2 :** a medieval peasant **3 :** RUSTIC, COUNTRYMAN **4 a :** a rude ill-bred person **b :** a stingy morose person

churl·ish \ˈchər-lish\ *adj* **1 :** of or resembling a churl : VULGAR **2 :** resembling or befitting a churl (as in lack of refinement or delicacy of feelings) **3 :** difficult to work with or deal with : INTRACTABLE ⟨~ soil⟩ ***syn*** see BOORISH — **churl·ish·ly** *adv* — **churl·ish·ness** *n*

[1]**churn** \ˈchərn\ *n* [ME *chyrne*, fr. OE *cyrin*; akin to OE *corn* grain; fr. the granular appearance of cream as it is churned — more at CORN] : a vessel in which milk or cream is agitated to separate the oily globules from the other parts and thus to obtain butter

[2]**churn** *vt* **1 :** to agitate (milk or cream) in a churn in order to make butter **2 a :** to stir or agitate violently ⟨an old stern-wheeler ~*ing* the muddy river⟩ **b :** to make (as foam) by so doing **3 :** to make (the account of a client) excessively active by frequent purchases and sales primarily in order to generate commissions ~ *vi* **1 :** to work a churn **2 a :** to produce or be in violent motion **b :** to proceed by means of rotating members (as wheels)

churn out *vt* : to produce mechanically : grind out ⟨generators . . . able to *churn out* 2,100,000 kilowatts —Lawrence Mosher⟩

churr \ˈchər\ *vi* [imit.] : to make a vibrant or whirring noise like that made by some insects (as the cockchafer) or by some birds (as the partridge) — **churr** *n*

chur·ri·gue·resque \ˌchu̇r-i-gə-ˈresk\ *adj, often cap* [Sp *churrigueresco*, fr. José *Churriguera* †1725 Sp architect] : of or relating to a Spanish baroque architectural style characterized by elaborate surface decoration or its Latin-American adaptation

[1]**chute** \ˈshüt\ *n* [F, fr. OF, fr. *cheoir* to fall, fr. L *cadere* — more at CHANCE] **1 a :** FALL 6b **b :** a quick descent (as in a river) : RAPID **2 :** an inclined plane, sloping channel, or passage down or through which things may pass : SLIDE **3 :** PARACHUTE

²**chute** *vb* **chut·ed; chut·ing** *vt* : to convey by a chute ~ *vi* **1** : to go in or as if in a chute **2** : to utilize a chute (as by passing ore down it)

chut·ist \'shüt-əst\ *n* : PARACHUTIST

chut·ney \'chət-nē\ *n, pl* **chutneys** [Hindi *caṭnī*] : a condiment that is made of acid fruits with added raisins, dates, and onions and seasoned with spices

chutz·pah *or* **chutz·pa** \'hůt-spə, 'k̲ůt-, -(,)spä\ *n* [Yiddish, fr. L Heb *ḥuṣpāh*] : supreme self-confidence : NERVE, GALL

chyle \'kī(ə)l\ *n* [LL *chylus*, fr. Gk *chylos* juice, chyle, fr. *chein* to pour — more at FOUND] : lymph that is milky from emulsified fats, characteristically present in the lacteals, and most apparent during intestinal absorption of fats — **chy·lous** \'kī-ləs\ *adj*

chy·lo·mi·cron \,kī-lō-'mī-,krän\ *n* [Gk *chylos* + *mikron*, neut. of *mikros* small] : a microscopic lipid particle common in the blood during fat digestion and assimilation

chyme \'kīm\ *n* [NL *chymus*, fr. LL, chyle, fr. Gk *chymos* juice, fr. *chein*] : the semifluid mass of partly digested food expelled by the stomach into the duodenum — **chy·mous** \'kī-məs\ *adj*

chy·mo·tryp·sin \,kī-mō-'trip-sən\ *n* [*chyme* + *-o-* + *trypsin*] : a pancreatic proteinase acting on proteins by breaking internal peptide bonds

chy·mo·tryp·sin·o·gen \-,trip-'sin-ə-jən\ *n* : a zymogen that is converted by trypsin to chymotrypsin

Ci *abbr* **1** cirrus **2** curie

CI *abbr* **1** cast iron **2** certificate of insurance **3** cost and insurance

CIA *abbr* Central Intelligence Agency

cía *abbr* [Sp *compañía*] company

CIAA *abbr* Central Intercollegiate Athletic Association

ciao \'chaů\ *interj* [It, fr. It dial., alter. of *schiavo* (I am your) slave, fr. ML *sclavus*] — used conventionally as an utterance at meeting or parting

ci·bo·ri·um \sə-'bōr-ē-əm, -'bȯr-\ *n, pl* **-ria** \-ē-ə\ [ML, fr. L, cup, fr. Gk *kibōrion*] **1** : a goblet-shaped vessel for holding eucharistic bread **2** : BALDACHIN; *specif* : a freestanding vaulted canopy supported by four columns over a high altar

ci·ca·da \sə-'kād-ə, -'käd-; sī-'kād-\ *n* [NL, genus name, fr. L, cicada] : any of a family (Cicadidae) of homopterous insects with a stout body, wide blunt head, and large transparent wings

ci·ca·la \sə-'käl-ə\ *n* [It, fr. ML, alter. of L *cicada*] : CICADA

cic·a·tri·cial \,sik-ə-'trish-əl\ *adj* : of or relating to a cicatrix

cic·a·tri·cle \'sik-ə-,trik-əl\ *n* [L *cicatricula*] **1** : CICATRIX 2a **2** : BLASTODISC

ci·ca·trix \'sik-ə-,triks, sə-'kā-triks\ *n, pl* **ci·ca·tri·ces** \,sik-ə-'trī-(,)sēz, sə-'kā-trə-,sēz\ [L *cicatric-, cicatrix*] **1** : a scar resulting from formation and contraction of fibrous tissue in a flesh wound **2** : a mark resembling a scar esp. when caused by the previous attachment of a part or organ: as **a** : a mark left on a stem after the fall of a leaf or bract **b** : HILUM 1a

cic·a·trize \'sik-ə-,trīz\ *vb* **-trized; -triz·ing** *vt* **1** : to induce the formation of a scar in **2** : SCAR ~ *vi* : to heal by forming a scar — **cic·a·tri·za·tion** \,sik-ə-trə-'zā-shən\ *n*

ci·ce·ro·ne \,sis-ə-'rō-nē, ,chē-chə-\ *n, pl* **-ni** \-(,)nē\ [It, fr. *Cicerone* Cicero] : a guide who conducts sightseers

cich·lid \'sik-ləd\ *n* [deriv. of Gk *kichlē* thrush, a kind of wrasse; akin to Gk *chelidōn* swallow — more at CELANDINE] : any of a family (Cichlidae) of mostly tropical spiny-finned freshwater fishes including several kept in tropical aquariums — **cichlid** *adj*

ci·cis·beo \,chē-chəz-'bā-(,)ō\ *n, pl* **-bei** \-'bā-,ē\ [It] : LOVER, GALLANT — **ci·cis·be·ism** \-'bā-,iz-əm\ *n*

CID *abbr* **1** Criminal Investigation Department **2** cubic inch displacement

-cid·al \'sīd-ᵊl\ *adj comb form* [LL *-cidalis*, fr. L *-cida*] : killing : having power to kill ⟨filari*cidal*⟩

-cide \,sīd\ *n comb form* [MF, fr. L *-cida*, fr. *caedere* to cut, kill — more at CONCISE] **1** : killer ⟨insect*icide*⟩ **2** [MF, fr. L *-cidium*, fr. *caedere*] : killing ⟨sui*cide*⟩

ci·der \'sīd-ər\ *n* [ME *sidre*, fr. OF, fr. LL *sicera* strong drink, fr. Gk *sikera*, fr. Heb *shēkhār*] **1** : the expressed juice of fruit (as apples) used as a beverage or for making other products (as applejack) **2** *Brit* : fermented apple juice often made sparkling by carbonation or fermentation in a sealed container

cider vinegar *n* : vinegar made from fermented cider

ci–de·vant \,sēd-ə-'väⁿ\ *adj* [F, lit., formerly] : FORMER

cie *abbr* [F *compagnie*] company

CIF *abbr* **1** central information file **2** cost, insurance, and freight

ci·gar \sig-'är\ *n* [Sp *cigarro*] : a small roll of tobacco leaf for smoking

cig·a·rette *also* **cig·a·ret** \,sig-ə-'ret, 'sig-ə-,\ *n* [F *cigarette*, dim. of *cigare* cigar, fr. Sp *cigarro*] : a narrow tube of cut tobacco enclosed in paper and designed for smoking

cig·a·ril·lo \,sig-ə-'ril-(,)ō, -'rē-(,)(y)ō\ *n, pl* **-los** [Sp *cigarrillo* cigaret, dim. of *cigarro* cigar] **1** : a very small cigar **2** : a cigarette wrapped in tobacco rather than paper

cil·i·ary \'sil-ē-,er-ē\ *adj* **1** : of or relating to cilia **2** : of, relating to, or being the annular suspension of the lens of the eye

¹**cil·i·ate** \'sil-ē-ət, -ē-,āt\ *or* **cil·i·at·ed** \-,āt-əd\ *adj* : provided with cilia — **cil·i·ate·ly** *adv*

²**ciliate** *n* : any of a subphylum (Ciliophora) of ciliate protozoans

cil·i·um \'sil-ē-əm\ *n, pl* **-ia** \-ē-ə\ [NL, fr. L, eyelid] **1** : EYELASH **2** : a minute short hairlike process often forming part of a fringe; *esp* : one of a cell that is capable of lashing movement and serves esp. in free unicellular organisms to produce locomotion or in higher forms a current of fluid

ci·mex \'sī-,meks\ *n, pl* **ci·mi·ces** \'sī-mə-,sēz, 'sim-ə-\ [L *cimic-, cimex* — more at CHINCH] : BEDBUG

¹**Cim·me·ri·an** \sə-'mir-ē-ən\ *adj* : very dark or gloomy : STYGIAN ⟨there under ebon shades . . . in dark ~ desert ever dwell —John Milton⟩

²**Cimmerian** *n* [L *Cimmerii*, a mythical people, fr. Gk *Kimmerioi*] : one of a mythical people described by Homer as dwelling in a remote realm of mist and gloom

C in C *abbr* commander in chief

¹**cinch** \'sinch\ *n* [Sp *cincha*, fr. L *cingula* girdle, girth, fr. *cingere*] **1** : a strong girth for a pack or saddle **2** : a tight grip **3 a** : a thing done with ease **b** : a certainty to happen

²**cinch** *vt* **1** : to put a cinch on **2** : to make certain : ASSURE ~ *vi* : to perform the act of cinching : tighten the cinch — often used with *up*

cin·cho·na \siŋ-'kō-nə, sin-'chō-\ *n* [NL, genus name, fr. the countess of *Chinchón* †1641 wife of the Peruvian viceroy] **1** : any of a genus (*Cinchona*) of So. American trees and shrubs of the madder family **2** : the dried bark of a cinchona (as *C. ledgeriana*) containing alkaloids (as quinine) and used as a specific in malaria

cin·cho·nine \'siŋ-kə-,nēn, 'sin-chə-\ *n* : a bitter white crystalline alkaloid $C_{19}H_{22}N_2O$ found esp. in cinchona bark and used like quinine

cin·cho·nism \'siŋ-kə-,niz-əm, 'sin-chə-\ *n* : a disorder due to excessive or prolonged use of cinchona or its alkaloids and marked by temporary deafness, ringing in the ears, headache, dizziness, and rash

cinc·ture \'siŋ(k)-chər\ *n* [L *cinctura* girdle, fr. *cinctus*, pp. of *cingere* to gird; akin to Skt *kāñcī* girdle] **1** : the act of encircling **2 a** : an encircling area **b** : GIRDLE, BELT; *esp* : a cord or sash of cloth worn around an ecclesiastical vestment (as an alb) or the habit of a religious

cin·der \'sin-dər\ *n* [ME *sinder*, fr. OE; akin to OHG *sintar* dross, slag, OSlav *sędra* stalactite] **1** : the slag from a metal furnace : DROSS **2 a** *pl* : ASHES **b** : a fragment of ash **3 a** : a partly burned combustible in which fire is extinct **b** : a hot coal without flame **c** : a partly burned coal capable of further burning without flame **4** : a fragment of lava from an erupting volcano — **cinder** *vt* — **cin·dery** \-d(ə-)rē\ *adj*

cinder block *n* : a hollow rectangular building block made of cement and coal cinders

Cin·der·el·la \,sin-də-'rel-ə\ *n* **1** : a fairy-tale heroine who is used as a drudge by her stepmother but ends up happily married to a prince through the intervention of her fairy godmother **2** : one resembling the fairy-tale Cinderella: as **a** : one suffering undeserved neglect **b** : one suddenly lifted from obscurity to honor or significance

cine \'sin-ē\ *n* [short for *cinema*] : MOTION PICTURE

cine- *comb form* [*cinema*] : motion picture ⟨*cine*camera⟩ ⟨*cine*film⟩ ⟨*cine*-X ray⟩

cine·an·gio·car·di·og·ra·phy \,sin-ē-'an-jē-ō-,kärd-ē-'äg-rə-fē\ *n* [*cine-* + *angi-* + *cardi-* + *-graphy*] : motion-picture photography of a fluoroscopic screen recording passage of a contrasting medium through the chambers of the heart and large blood vessels — **cine·an·gio·car·dio·graph·ic** \-,kärd-ē-ə-'graf-ik\ *adj*

cine·an·gi·og·ra·phy \-,an-jē-'äg-rə-fē\ *n* [*cine-* + *angi-* + *-graphy*] : motion-picture photography of a fluorescent screen recording passage of a contrasting medium through the blood vessels — **cine·an·gio·graph·ic** \-jē-ə-'graf-ik\ *adj*

cine·ast \'sin-ē-,ast, -ē-əst\ *or* **ciné·aste** \'sin-ē-,ast\ *n* [F *cinéaste*, fr. *ciné* cine + *-aste* (as in *enthousiaste* enthusiast)] : a devotee of motion pictures

cin·e·ma \'sin-ə-mə\ *n* [short for *cinematograph*] **1** *chiefly Brit* **a** : MOTION PICTURE **b** : a motion-picture theater **2 a** : MOVIES; *esp* : the motion-picture industry **b** : the art or technique of making motion pictures

cin·e·ma·go·er \-,gō(-ə)r\ *n* : MOVIEGOER

cin·e·ma·theque \,sin-ə-mə-'tek\ *n* [F *cinémathèque* film library, fr. *cinéma* cinema + *-thèque* (as in *bibliothèque* library)] : a small movie house specializing in avant-garde films

cin·e·mat·ic \,sin-ə-'mat-ik\ *adj* **1** : filmed and presented as a motion picture ⟨~ fantasies⟩ **2** : of, relating to, or suitable for motion pictures or the filming of motion pictures ⟨~ principles and techniques⟩ — **cin·e·mat·i·cal·ly** \-'mat-i-k(ə-)lē\ *adv*

cin·e·ma·tize \'sin-ə-mə-,tīz\ *vt* **-tized; -tiz·ing** : to make a motion picture of (as a novel) : adapt for motion pictures

cin·e·mat·o·graph \,sin-ə-'mat-ə-,graf\ *n* [F *cinématographe*, fr. Gk *kinēmat-, kinēma* movement (fr. *kinein* to move) + *-o-* + *-graphe* -graph — more at HIGHT] **1** *chiefly Brit* : a motion-picture camera, projector, theater, or show **2** *chiefly Brit* : CINEMA 2b

cin·e·ma·tog·ra·pher \,sin-ə-mə-'täg-rə-fər\ *n* **1** : a motion-picture cameraman **2** : a motion-picture projectionist

cin·e·ma·tog·ra·phy \,sin-ə-mə-'täg-rə-fē\ *n* : the art or science of motion-picture photography — **cin·e·mat·o·graph·ic** \-,mat-ə-'graf-ik\ *also* **cin·e·mat·o·graph·i·cal** \-i-kəl\ *adj* — **cin·e·mat·o·graph·i·cal·ly** \-i-k(ə-)lē\ *adv*

ci·ne·ma ve·ri·té \'sin-ə-mə-,ver-ə-'tā\ *n* [F *cinéma-vérité*, lit., truth cinema] : the art or technique of filming a motion picture so as to convey candid realism

cin·e·ole \'sin-ē-,ōl\ *n* [ISV, by transposition fr. NL *oleum cinae* wormseed oil] : a liquid $C_{10}H_{18}O$ with a camphor odor contained in many essential oils (as of eucalyptus) and used esp. as an expectorant

cin·er·ar·ia \,sin-ə-'rer-ē-ə, -'rar-\ *n* [NL, fr. L, fem. of *cinerarius* of ashes, fr. *ciner-, cinis*] : any of several pot plants deriving from a perennial composite herb (*Senecio cruentus*) of the Canary islands and having heart-shaped leaves and clusters of bright flower heads

cin·er·ar·i·um \-ē-əm\ *n, pl* **-ia** \-ē-ə\ [L, fr. *ciner-, cinis*] : a place to receive the ashes of the cremated dead — **cin·er·ary** \'sin-ə-,rer-ē\ *adj*

ci·ne·re·ous \sə-'nir-ē-əs\ *adj* [L *cinereus*, fr. *ciner-, cinis* ashes] **1** : gray tinged with black **2** : resembling or consisting of ashes

cin·er·in \'sin-ə-rən\ *n* [L *ciner-, cinis* ashes] : either of two compounds $C_{20}H_{28}O_3$ and $C_{21}H_{28}O_5$ of high insecticidal properties

ə abut ᵊ kitten ər further a back ā bake ä cot, cart
aů out ch chin e less ē easy g gift i trip ī life
j joke ŋ sing ō flow ȯ flaw ȯi coin th thin t̲h̲ this
ü loot ů foot y yet yü few yů furious zh vision

cin·gu·lum \'siŋ-gyə-ləm\ *n, pl* **-la** \-lə\ [NL, fr. L, girdle, fr. *cingere* to gird — more at CINCTURE] : a differentiated band or a girdle (as of color) — **cin·gu·late** \-lət\ *adj*

cin·na·bar \'sin-ə-,bär\ *n* [ME *cynabare,* fr. MF & L; MF *cenobre,* fr. L *cinnabaris,* fr. Gk *kinnabari* of non-IE origin; akin to Ar *zinjafr* cinnabar] **1 :** native red mercuric sulfide HgS that is the only important ore of mercury **2 :** artificial red mercuric sulfide used esp. as a pigment **3 :** a European moth (*Tyria jacobeae*) with grayish black fore wings marked with red and clear reddish pink hind wings that has been introduced into the U.S. in attempts to control ragwort on the leaves of which its larvae feed — called also *cinnabar moth* — **cin·na·bar·ine** \-,bär-,īn, ,sin-ə-'bär-ən\ *adj*

cin·nam·ic \sə-'nam-ik\ *adj* [F *cinnamique,* fr. *cinname* cinnamon, fr. L *cinnamon*] : of, relating to, or obtained from cinnamon

cinnamic acid *n* : a white crystalline odorless acid $C_9H_8O_2$ found esp. in cinnamon oil and storax

cin·na·mon \'sin-ə-mən\ *n, often attrib* [ME *cynamone,* fr. L *cinnamomum, cinnamon,* fr. Gk *kinnamōmon, kinnamon,* of non-IE origin; akin to Heb *qinnāmōn* cinnamon] **1 a :** the highly aromatic bark of any of several trees (genus *Cinnamomum*) of the laurel family used as a spice **b :** a tree that yields cinnamon **2 :** a light yellowish brown

cinnamon fern *n* : a large No. American fern (*Osmunda cinnamomea*) with cinnamon-colored spore-bearing fronds shorter than and separate from the green foliage fronds

cinnamon stone *n* : ESSONITE

cin·quain \siŋ-'kān, 'saŋ-\ *n* [F, fr. *cinq* five, fr. L *quinque* — more at FIVE] : a five-line stanza

cin·que·cen·tist \,chiŋ-kwi-'chent-əst\ *n* : an Italian of the cinquecento; *esp* : a poet or artist of this period

cin·que·cen·to \,chiŋ-kwi-'chen-(,)tō\ *n* [It, lit., five hundred, fr. *cinque* five (fr. L *quinque*) + *cento* hundred, fr. L *centum* — more at HUNDRED] : the 16th century esp. in Italian art

cinque·foil \'siŋk-,fȯil, 'saŋk-\ *n* [ME *sink foil,* fr. MF *cincfoille,* fr. L *quinquefolium,* fr. *quinque* five + *folium* leaf — more at BLADE] **1 :** any of a genus (*Potentilla*) of plants of the rose family with 5-lobed leaves **2 :** a design enclosed by five joined foils

ci·on *var of* SCION

¹ci·pher \'sī-fər\ *n, often attrib* [ME, fr. MF *cifre,* fr. ML *cifra,* fr. Ar *ṣifr* empty, cipher, zero] **1 a :** ZERO 1a **b :** one that has no weight, worth, or influence : NONENTITY **2 a :** a method of transforming a text in order to conceal its meaning — compare CODE 3b **b :** a message in code **3 :** ARABIC NUMERAL **4 :** a combination of symbolic letters; *esp* : the interwoven initials of a name

²cipher *vb* **ci·phered; ci·pher·ing** \-f(ə-)riŋ\ *vi* : to use figures in a mathematical process ~ *vt* **1 :** ENCIPHER **2 :** to compute arithmetically

cipher alphabet *n* : a set of one-to-one equivalences between a sequence of plaintext letters and the sequence of their cipher substitutes used in cryptography

ci·pher·text \'sī-fər-,tekst\ *n* : the enciphered form of a text or of its elements — compare PLAINTEXT

ci·pho·ny \'sī-fə-nē\ *n* [*cipher* + *telephony*] : the electronic scrambling of voice transmissions

cir *abbr* circle, circular

circ *abbr* circular

cir·ca \'sər-kə, 'ki(ə)r-(,)kä\ *prep* [L, fr. *circum* around — more at CIRCUM-] : at, in, or of approximately — used esp. with dates ⟨born ~ 1600⟩

cir·ca·di·an \sər-'kad-ē-ən, -'kad-; sər-kə-'dē-ən, -'dī-\ *adj* [L *circa* about + *dies* day + E *-an* — more at DEITY] : being, having, characterized by, or occurring in approximately 24-hour periods or cycles (as of biological activity or function) ⟨~ oscillations⟩ ⟨~ periodicity⟩ ⟨~ rhythms in hatching⟩ ⟨~ leaf movements⟩ ***syn*** see DAILY

Cir·cas·sian \(,)sər-'kash-ən\ *n* [*Circassia,* Russia] **1 :** a member of a group of peoples of the Caucasus of Caucasian race but not of Indo-European speech **2 :** the language of the Circassian peoples — **Circassian** *adj*

Circassian walnut *n* : the light brown irregularly black-veined wood of the English walnut much used for veneer and cabinetwork

Cir·ce \'sər-(,)sē\ *n* [L, fr. Gk *Kirkē*] : a sorceress who changed Odysseus' men into swine but was forced by Odysseus to change them back

cir·ci·nate \'sərs-ᵊn-,āt\ *adj* [L *circinatus,* pp. of *circinare* to round, fr. *circinus* pair of compasses, fr. *circus*] : ROUNDED, COILED; *esp* : rolled up on the axis with the apex as a center ⟨~ fern fronds unfolding⟩ — **cir·ci·nate·ly** *adv*

¹cir·cle \'sər-kəl\ *n, often attrib* [ME *cercle,* fr. OF, fr. L *circulus,* dim. of *circus* circle, circus, fr. or akin to Gk *krikos, kirkos* ring] **1 a :** RING, HALO **b :** a closed plane curve every point of which is equidistant from a fixed point within the curve **c :** the plane surface bounded by such a curve **2 :** the orbit or period of revolution of a heavenly body **3 :** something in the form of a circle or section of a circle: as **a :** CIRCLET, DIADEM **b :** an instrument of astronomical observation the graduated limb of which consists of an entire circle **c :** a balcony or tier of seats in a theater **d :** a circle formed on the surface of a sphere by the intersection of a plane that passes through it ⟨~ of latitude⟩ **e :** ROTARY **4 :** an area of action or influence : REALM **5 a :** CYCLE, ROUND ⟨the wheel has come full ~⟩ **b :** fallacious reasoning in which something to be demonstrated is covertly assumed **6 :** a group of persons sharing a common interest or revolving about a common center ⟨ the sewing ~ of her church⟩ ⟨the gossip of court ~*s*⟩ **7 :** a territorial or administrative division or district ***syn*** see SET

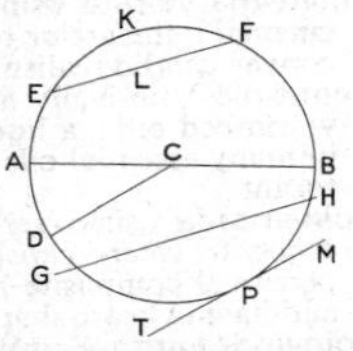

circle 1b: *AB* diameter: *C* center; *CD, CA, CB,* radii; *EKF* arc on chord *EF; EFKL* (area) segment on chord *EF; ACD* (area) sector; *GH* secant; *TPM* tangent at point *P; EKFBPDA* circumference

²circle *vb* **cir·cled; cir·cling** \-k(ə-)liŋ\ *vt* **1 :** to enclose in or as if in a circle **2 :** to move or revolve around ~ *vi* **1 a :** to move in or as if in a circle **b :** CIRCULATE **2 :** to describe or extend in a circle — **cir·cler** \-k(ə-)lər\ *n*

circle graph *n* : PIE CHART

cir·clet \'sər-klət\ *n* : a little circle; *esp* : a circular ornament

¹cir·cuit \'sər-kət\ *n, often attrib* [ME, fr. MF *circuite,* fr. L *circuitus,* fr. pp. of *circumire, circuire* to go around, fr. *circum-* + *ire* to go — more at ISSUE] **1 a :** a usu. circular line encompassing an area **b :** the space enclosed within such a line **2 a :** a course around a periphery **b :** a circuitous or indirect route **3 a :** a regular tour (as by a traveling judge or preacher) around an assigned district or territory **b :** the route traveled **c :** a group of church congregations ministered to by one pastor **4 a :** the complete path of an electric current including usu. the source of electric energy **b :** an assemblage of electronic elements : HOOKUP **c :** a two-way communication path between points (as in a computer) **5 a :** an association of similar groups : LEAGUE **b :** a group of establishments offering similar entertainment or presenting a series of contests; *esp* : a chain of theaters at which productions are successively presented — **cir·cuit·al** \-kət-ᵊl\ *adj*

²circuit *vt* : to make a circuit about ~ *vi* : to make a circuit

circuit breaker *n* : a switch that automatically interrupts an electric circuit under an infrequent abnormal condition

circuit court *n* : a court that sits at two or more places within one judicial district

circuit judge *n* : a judge who holds a circuit court

cir·cu·itous \(,)sər-'kyü-ət-əs\ *adj* **1 :** marked by a circular or winding course ⟨a ~ route⟩ **2 :** marked by roundabout or indirect procedure — **cir·cu·itous·ly** *adv* — **cir·cu·itous·ness** *n*

circuit rider *n* : a clergyman assigned to a circuit esp. in a rural area

cir·cuit·ry \'sər-kə-trē\ *n, pl* **-ries** **1 :** the detailed plan of an electric circuit **2 :** the components of an electric circuit

cir·cu·ity \(,)sər-'kyü-ət-ē\ *n, pl* **-ities** [irreg. fr. *circuit*] : lack of straightforwardness : INDIRECTION ⟨mired so deeply in its own complicated ~ of words —C. O. Gregory⟩

¹cir·cu·lar \'sər-kyə-lər\ *adj* [ME *circuler,* fr. MF, fr. LL *circularis,* fr. L *circulus* circle] **1 :** having the form of a circle : ROUND **2 :** moving in or describing a circle or spiral **3 :** CIRCUITOUS, INDIRECT ⟨a ~ explanation⟩ **4 :** characterized by reasoning in a circle ⟨~ arguments⟩ **5 :** marked by or moving in a cycle **6 :** intended for circulation — **cir·cu·lar·i·ty** \,sər-kyə-'lar-ət-ē\ *n* — **cir·cu·lar·ly** \'sər-kyə-lər-lē\ *adv* — **cir·cu·lar·ness** *n*

²circular *n* : a paper (as a leaflet) intended for wide distribution

circular file *n* : WASTEBASKET

circular function *n* : TRIGONOMETRIC FUNCTION

cir·cu·lar·ize \'sər-kyə-lə-,rīz\ *vt* **-ized; -iz·ing** **1 a :** to send circulars to **b :** to poll by questionnaire **2 :** PUBLICIZE — **cir·cu·lar·iza·tion** \,sər-kyə-lə-rə-'zā-shən\ *n*

circular measure *n* : the measure of an angle in radians

cir·cu·late \'sər-kyə-,lāt\ *vb* **-lat·ed; -lat·ing** [L *circulatus,* pp. of *circulare,* fr. *circulus* circle] *vi* **1 :** to move in a circle, circuit, or orbit; *esp* : to follow a course that returns to the starting point ⟨blood ~*s* through the body⟩ **2 :** to pass from person to person or place to place: as **a :** to flow without obstruction **b :** to become well known or widespread ⟨rumors *circulated* through the town⟩ **c :** to go from group to group at a social gathering **d :** to come into the hands of readers; *specif* : to become sold or distributed ~ *vt* : to cause to circulate — **cir·cu·lat·able** \-,lāt-ə-bəl\ *adj* — **cir·cu·la·tive** \-,lāt-iv\ *adj* — **cir·cu·la·tor** \-,lāt-ər\ *n* — **cir·cu·la·to·ry** \-lə-,tōr-ē, -,tȯr-\ *adj*

circulating decimal *n* : REPEATING DECIMAL

cir·cu·la·tion \,sər-kyə-'lā-shən\ *n* **1 :** FLOW **2 :** orderly movement through a circuit; *esp* : the movement of blood through the vessels of the body induced by the pumping action of the heart **3 a :** passage or transmission from person to person or place to place; *esp* : the interchange of currency ⟨coins in ~⟩ **b :** the extent of dissemination: as **(1) :** the average number of copies of a publication sold over a given period **(2) :** the total number of items taken by borrowers from a library

circulatory system *n* : the system of blood, blood vessels, lymphatics, and heart concerned with the circulation of the blood and lymph

circum- *prefix* [OF or L; OF, fr. L, fr. *circum,* fr. *circus* circle — more at CIRCLE] : around : about ⟨*circum*polar⟩

cir·cum·am·bi·ent \,sər-kə-'mam-bē-ənt\ *adj* [LL *circumambient-, circumambiens,* prp. of *circumambire* to surround in a circle, fr. L *circum-* + *ambire* to go around — more at AMBIENT] : being on all sides : ENCOMPASSING — **cir·cum·am·bi·ent·ly** *adv*

cir·cum·am·bu·late \-byə-,lāt\ *vt* **-lat·ed; -lat·ing** [LL *circumambulatus,* pp. of *circumambulare,* fr. L *circum-* + *ambulare* to walk] : to circle on foot esp. ritualistically

cir·cum·cise \'sər-kəm-,sīz\ *vt* **-cised; -cis·ing** [ME *circumcisen,* fr. L *circumcisus,* pp. of *circumcidere,* fr. *circum-* + *caedere* to cut — more at CONCISE] : to cut off the prepuce of (a male) or the clitoris of (a female) — **cir·cum·cis·er** *n*

cir·cum·ci·sion \,sər-kəm-'sizh-ən, 'sər-kəm-,\ *n* **1 a :** the act of circumcising; *specif* : a Jewish rite performed on male infants as a sign of inclusion in the Jewish religious community **b :** the condition of being circumcised **2** *cap* : January 1 observed as a church festival in commemoration of the circumcision of Jesus

cir·cum·fer·ence \sə(r)-'kəm(p)-fərn(t)s, -f(ə-)rən(t)s\ *n* [ME, fr. MF, fr. L *circumferentia,* fr. *circumferre* to carry around, fr. *circum-* + *ferre* to carry — more at BEAR] **1 :** the perimeter of a circle **2 :** the external boundary or surface of a figure or object : PERIPHERY — **cir·cum·fer·en·tial** \-,kəm(p)-fə-'ren-chəl\ *adj*

¹cir·cum·flex \'sər-kəm-,fleks\ *adj* [L *circumflexus,* pp. of *circumflectere* to bend around, mark with a circumflex, fr. *circum-* + *flectere* to bend] **1 a :** characterized by the pitch, quantity, or quality indicated by a circumflex **b :** marked with a circumflex **2 :** bending around ⟨a ~ artery⟩

²circumflex *n* : a mark ˆ, ˜, or ¯ orig. used in Greek over long vowels to indicate a rising-falling tone and in other languages to mark length, contraction, or a particular vowel quality
cir·cum·flu·ent \(ˌ)sər-ˈkəm-flə-wənt, ˌsər-kəm-ˈflü-ənt\ *adj* [fr. L *circumfluent-, circumfluens,* prp. of *circumfluere* to flow around, fr. *circum-* + *fluere* to flow] : flowing round or surrounding in the manner of a fluid — **cir·cum·flu·ous** \(ˌ)sər-ˈkəm-flə-wəs\ *adj*
cir·cum·fuse \ˌsər-kəm-ˈfyüz\ *vt* **-fused; -fus·ing** [L *circumfusus,* pp. of *circumfundere* to pour around, fr. *circum-* + *fundere* to pour — more at FOUND] : SURROUND, ENVELOP — **cir·cum·fu·sion** \-ˈfyü-zhən\ *n*
cir·cum·ja·cent \ˌsər-kəm-ˈjās-ᵊnt\ *adj* [L *circumjacent-, circumjacens,* prp. of *circumjacēre* to lie around, fr. *circum-* + *jacēre* to lie — more at ADJACENT] : lying adjacent on all sides : SURROUNDING
cir·cum·lo·cu·tion \ˌsər-kəm-lō-ˈkyü-shən\ *n* [L *circumlocution-, circumlocutio,* fr. *circum-* + *locutio* speech, fr. *locutus,* pp. of *loqui* to speak] **1** : the use of an unnecessarily large number of words to express an idea **2** : evasion in speech — **cir·cum·loc·u·to·ry** \-ˈläk-yə-ˌtōr-ē, -ˌtȯr-\ *adj*
cir·cum·lu·nar \ˌsər-kəm-ˈlü-nər\ *adj* : revolving about or surrounding the moon
cir·cum·nav·i·gate \-ˈnav-ə-ˌgāt\ *vt* [L *circumnavigatus,* pp. of *circumnavigare* to sail around, fr. *circum-* + *navigare* to navigate] : to go completely around (as the earth) esp. by water; *also* : to go around instead of through : BYPASS ⟨~ a congested area⟩ — **cir·cum·nav·i·ga·tion** \-ˌnav-ə-ˈgā-shən\ *n* — **cir·cum·nav·i·ga·tor** \-ˈnav-ə-ˌgāt-ər\ *n*
cir·cum·po·lar \ˌsər-kəm-ˈpō-lər\ *adj* **1** : continually visible above the horizon ⟨a ~ star⟩ **2** : surrounding or found in the vicinity of a terrestrial pole
cir·cum·scis·sile \-ˈsis-əl, -ˌīl\ *adj* [L *circumscissus,* pp. of *circumscindere* to tear around, fr. *circum-* + *scindere* to cut, split — more at SHED] : dehiscing by fissure around the circumference of the pyxidium
cir·cum·scribe \ˈsər-kəm-ˌskrīb\ *vt* [L *circumscribere,* fr. *circum-* + *scribere* to write, draw — more at SCRIBE] **1 a** : to draw a line around **b** : to surround by a boundary **2 a** : to constrict the range or activity of definitely and clearly **b** : to define or mark off carefully **3** : to encircle (a geometrical figure) so as to touch at as many points as possible ***syn*** see LIMIT ***ant*** expand, dilate
cir·cum·scrip·tion \ˌsər-kəm-ˈskrip-shən\ *n* [L *circumscription-, circumscriptio,* fr. *circumscriptus,* pp. of *circumscribere*] **1** : something that circumscribes: as **a** : LIMIT, BOUNDARY **b** : RESTRICTION **2** : the act of circumscribing : the state of being circumscribed: as **a** : DEFINITION, DELIMITATION **b** : LIMITATION **3** : a circumscribed area or district
cir·cum·spect \ˈsər-kəm-ˌspekt\ *adj* [ME, fr. MF or L; MF *circonspect,* fr. L *circumspectus,* fr. pp. of *circumspicere* to look around, be cautious, fr. *circum-* + *specere* to look — more at SPY] : careful to consider all circumstances and possible consequences : PRUDENT ***syn*** see CAUTIOUS ***ant*** audacious — **cir·cum·spec·tion** \ˌsər-kəm-ˈspek-shən\ *n* — **cir·cum·spect·ly** \ˈsər-kəm-ˌspek-tlē\ *adv*
cir·cum·stance \ˈsər-kəm-ˌstan(t)s, -stən(t)s\ *n* [ME, fr. MF, fr. L *circumstantia,* fr. *circumstant-, circumstans,* prp. of *circumstare* to stand around, fr. *circum-* + *stare* to stand — more at STAND] **1 a** : a condition, fact, or event accompanying, conditioning, or determining another : an essential or inevitable concomitant ⟨the weather is a ~ to be taken into consideration⟩ **b** : a subordinate or accessory fact or detail ⟨cost is a minor ~ in this case⟩ **c** : a piece of evidence that indicates the probability or improbability of an event (as a crime) ⟨the ~ of the missing weapon told against him⟩ ⟨the ~*s* suggest murder⟩ **2 a** : the sum of essential and environmental factors (as of an event or situation) ⟨constant and rapid change in economic ~ —G. M. Trevelyan⟩ **b** : state of affairs : EVENTUALITY ⟨open rebellion was a rare ~⟩ — often used in pl. ⟨a victim of ~*s*⟩ **c** *pl* : situation with regard to wealth ⟨he was in easy ~*s*⟩ **3** : attendant formalities and ceremonial ⟨pride, pomp, and ~ of glorious war —Shak.⟩ **4** : an event that constitutes a detail (as of a narrative or course of events) ⟨considering each ~ in turn⟩ ***syn*** see OCCURRENCE
cir·cum·stanced \-ˌstan(t)st, -stən(t)st\ *adj* : placed in particular circumstances esp. in regard to property or income
cir·cum·stan·tial \ˌsər-kəm-ˈstan-chəl\ *adj* **1** : belonging to, consisting in, or dependent on circumstances **2** : pertinent but not essential : INCIDENTAL **3** : marked by careful attention to detail : abounding in factual details ⟨a ~ account of the fight⟩ **4** : CEREMONIAL — **cir·cum·stan·ti·al·i·ty** \-ˌstan-chē-ˈal-ət-ē\ *n* — **cir·cum·stan·tial·ly** \-ˈstanch-(ə-)lē\ *adv*
syn CIRCUMSTANTIAL, MINUTE, PARTICULAR, DETAILED *shared meaning element* : dealing with a matter carefully and fully and usu. point by point ***ant*** abridged, summary
circumstantial evidence *n* : evidence that tends to prove a fact by proving other events or circumstances which afford a basis for a reasonable inference of the occurrence of the fact in issue
cir·cum·stan·ti·ate \ˌsər-kəm-ˈstan-chē-ˌāt\ *vt* **-at·ed; -at·ing** : to supply with circumstantial evidence or support
cir·cum·stel·lar \ˌsər-kəm-ˈstel-ər\ *adj* : surrounding or occurring in the vicinity of a star
¹cir·cum·val·late \-ˈval-ˌāt, -ˈval-ət\ *adj* : surrounded by or as if by a rampart; *esp* : enclosed by a ridge of tissue ⟨~ papilla⟩
²cir·cum·val·late \-ˈval-ˌāt\ *vt* **-lat·ed; -lat·ing** [L *circumvallatus,* pp. of *circumvallare,* fr. *circum-* + *vallum* rampart — more at WALL] : to surround by or as if by a rampart — **cir·cum·val·la·tion** \-ˌval-ˈā-shən\ *n*
cir·cum·vent \ˌsər-kəm-ˈvent\ *vt* [L *circumventus,* pp. of *circumvenire,* fr. *circum-* + *venire* to come — more at COME] **1 a** : to hem in **b** : to make a circuit around **2** : to check or defeat esp. by ingenuity or stratagem ***syn*** see FRUSTRATE ***ant*** conform (*as to laws*), cooperate (*with persons*) — **cir·cum·ven·tion** \-ˈven-chən\ *n*
cir·cum·vo·lu·tion \(ˌ)sər-ˌkəm-və-ˈlü-shən, ˌsər-kəm-vō-\ *n* [ME *circumvolucioun,* fr. ML *circumvolution-, circumvolutio,* fr. L *circumvolutus,* pp. of *circumvolvere* to revolve, fr. *circum-* + *volvere* to roll — more at VOLUBLE] : an act or instance of turning around an axis
cir·cus \ˈsər-kəs\ *n, often attrib* [L, circle, circus — more at CIRCLE] **1 a** : a large arena enclosed by tiers of seats on three or all four sides and used esp. for sports or spectacles (as athletic contests, exhibitions of horsemanship, or in ancient times chariot racing) **b** : a public spectacle **2 a** : an arena often covered by a tent and used for variety shows usu. including feats of physical skill and daring, wild animal acts, and performances by jugglers and clowns **b** : a circus performance **c** : the physical plant, livestock, and personnel of such a circus **d** : an activity suggesting a circus ⟨huge political clambakes, outsize chowder parties and other eating ~*es* —Thomas Mario⟩ **3 a** *obs* : CIRCLE, RING **b** *Brit* : a usu. circular area at an intersection of streets — **cir·cusy** \-kə-sē\ *adj*
cirque \ˈsərk\ *n* [F, fr. L *circus*] **1** *archaic* : CIRCUS **2** : CIRCLE, CIRCLET **3** : a deep steep-walled basin on a mountain shaped like half a bowl
cirr- *or* **cirri-** *or* **cirro-** *comb form* [NL *cirrus*] : cirrus ⟨*cirri*ped⟩ ⟨*cirr*ose⟩ ⟨*cirro*stratus⟩
cir·rho·sis \sə-ˈrō-səs\ *n, pl* **-rho·ses** \-ˌsēz\ [NL, fr. Gk *kirrhos* orange-colored] : fibrosis esp. of the liver with hardening caused by excessive formation of connective tissue followed by contraction — **cir·rhot·ic** \-ˈrät-ik\ *adj or n*
cir·ri·ped \ˈsir-ə-ˌped\ *or* **cir·ri·pede** \-ˌpēd\ *n* [deriv. of NL *cirr-* + L *ped-, pes* foot — more at FOOT] : any of a subclass (Cirripedia) of specialized marine crustaceans (as barnacles) free-swimming as larvae but permanently attached or parasitic as adults — **cirriped** *adj*
cir·ro·cu·mu·lus \ˌsir-ō-ˈkyü-myə-ləs\ *n* [NL] : a cloud form of small white rounded masses at a high altitude usu. in regular groupings forming a mackerel sky — see CLOUD illustration
cir·ro·stra·tus \ˌsir-ō-ˈstrāt-əs, -ˈstrat-\ *n* [NL] : a fairly uniform layer of high stratus darker than cirrus — see CLOUD illustration
cir·rous \ˈsir-əs\ *adj* : resembling cirrus clouds
cir·rus \ˈsir-əs\ *n, pl* **cir·ri** \ˈsi(ə)r-ˌī\ [NL, fr. L, curl] **1** : TENDRIL **2** : a slender usu. flexible animal appendage: as **a** : an arm of a barnacle — see BARNACLE illustration **b** : a filament of a crinoid **c** : a fused group of cilia functioning like a limb on some protozoans **d** : the male copulatory organ of various invertebrate animals **3** : a wispy white cloud usu. of minute ice crystals formed at altitudes of 20,000 to 40,000 feet — see CLOUD illustration
cis- *prefix* [L, fr. *cis* — more at HE] **1** : on this side ⟨*cis*-border⟩ ⟨*cis*atlantic⟩ **2** *usu ital* : characterized by having such atoms or groups on the same side of the molecule ⟨*cis*-dichloroethylene⟩
cis·al·pine \(ˈ)sis-ˈal-ˌpīn\ *adj* : situated on the south side of the Alps ⟨*Cisalpine* Gaul⟩ — compare TRANSALPINE
cis·co \ˈsis-(ˌ)kō\ *n, pl* **ciscoes** [short for CanF *ciscoette*] : any of various whitefishes (genus *Coregonus*) including important food fishes (esp. *C. artedii*) of the Great Lakes region
cis·lu·nar \(ˈ)sis-ˈlü-nər\ *adj* : lying between the earth and the moon or the moon's orbit ⟨~ space⟩
cist \ˈsist, ˈkist\ *n* [W, chest, fr. L *cista*] : a neolithic or Bronze Age burial chamber typically lined with stone
Cis·ter·cian \sis-ˈtər-shən\ *n* [ML *Cistercium* Cîteaux] : a member of a monastic order founded by St. Robert of Molesme in 1098 at Cîteaux, France, under an austere Benedictine rule — **Cistercian** *adj*
cis·tern \ˈsis-tərn\ *n* [ME, fr. OF *cisterne,* fr. L *cisterna,* fr. *cista* box, chest — more at CHEST] **1** : an artificial reservoir for storing liquids and esp. water; *specif* : an often underground tank for storing rainwater **2** : a large usu. silver vessel formerly used (as in cooling wine) at the dining table **3** : a fluid-containing sac or cavity in an organism
cis·ter·na \sis-ˈtər-nə\ *n, pl* **-nae** \-ˌnē\ [NL, fr. L, reservoir] : CISTERN 3: as **a** : one of the large spaces under the arachnoid membrane **b** : one of the interconnected vesicles or tubules comprising the endoplasmic reticulum
cis·tron \ˈsis-ˌträn\ *n* [*cis-* + *trans-* + ²*-on*] : a segment of DNA which specifies a single functional unit (as a protein or enzyme) and within which two heterozygous and closely linked recessive mutations are expressed in the phenotype when on different chromosomes but not when on the same chromosome — **cis·tron·ic** \sis-ˈträn-ik\ *adj*
cit *abbr* **1** citation; cited **2** citizen
cit·a·del \ˈsit-əd-ᵊl, -ə-ˌdel\ *n* [MF *citadelle,* fr. OIt *cittadella,* dim. of *cittade* city, fr. ML *civitat-, civitas* — more at CITY] **1** : a fortress that commands a city **2** : STRONGHOLD
ci·ta·tion \sī-ˈtā-shən\ *n* **1** : an official summons to appear (as before a court) **2 a** : an act of quoting; *esp* : the citing of a previously settled case at law **b** : EXCERPT, QUOTE **3** : MENTION: as **a** : a formal statement of the achievements of a person receiving an academic honor **b** : specific reference in a military dispatch to meritorious performance of duty ***syn*** see ENCOMIUM — **ci·ta·tion·al** \-shnəl, -shən-ᵊl\ *adj*
cite \ˈsīt\ *vt* **cit·ed; cit·ing** [MF *citer* to cite, summon, fr. L *citare* to put in motion, rouse, summon, fr. *citus,* pp. of *ciēre* to stir, move — more at HIGHT] **1** : to call upon officially or authoritatively to appear (as before a court) **2** : to quote by way of example, authority, or proof **3 a** : to refer to; *esp* : to mention formally in commendation or praise **b** : to name in a citation **4** : to bring forward or call to another's attention esp. as an example, proof, or precedent ***syn*** see SUMMON, QUOTE, ADDUCE — **cit·able** \ˈsīt-ə-bəl\ *adj*
cith·a·ra \ˈsith-ə-rə, ˈkith-\ *n* [L, fr. Gk *kithara*] : an ancient Greek stringed instrument of the lyre class
cith·er \ˈsith-ər, ˈsith-\ *n* [F *cithare,* fr. L *cithara*] : CITTERN
cit·ied \ˈsit-ēd\ *adj* : occupied by cities
citi·fy \ˈsit-i-ˌfī\ *vt* **-fied; -fy·ing** : URBANIZE

ə abut ᵊ kitten ər further a back ā bake ä cot, cart
aù out ch chin e less ē easy g gift i trip ī life
j joke ŋ sing ō flow ȯ flaw ȯi coin th thin t͟h this
ü loot ù foot y yet yü few yù furious zh vision

cit·i·zen \'sit-ə-zən\ *n* [ME *citizein,* fr. AF *citezein,* alter. of OF *citeien,* fr. *cité* city] **1 :** an inhabitant of a city or town; *esp* **:** one entitled to the rights and privileges of a freeman **2 a :** a member of a state **b :** a native or naturalized person who owes allegiance to a government and is entitled to protection from it **3 :** a civilian as distinguished from a specialized servant of the state — **cit·i·zen·ess** \-zə-nəs\ *n* — **cit·i·zen·ly** \-zən-lē\ *adj*
syn CITIZEN, SUBJECT, NATIONAL *shared meaning element* **:** a person owing allegiance to and entitled to the protection of a sovereign state

cit·i·zen·ry \-zən-rē\ *n, pl* **-ries :** a whole body of citizens

citizen's arrest *n* **:** an arrest made by a citizen who derives his authority from the fact that he is a citizen

citizens band *n* **:** one of the frequency bands that in the U.S. is allocated officially for private radio communications

cit·i·zen·ship \'sit-ə-zən-ˌship\ *n* **1 :** the status of being a citizen **2 :** the quality of an individual's response to membership in a community

citr- *or* **citri-** *or* **citro-** *comb form* [NL, fr. *Citrus,* genus name] **1 :** citrus ⟨*citri*culture⟩ **2 :** citric acid ⟨*citr*ate⟩

cit·ral \'si-ˌtral\ *n* [ISV] **:** an unsaturated liquid isomeric aldehyde $C_{10}H_{16}O$ of many essential oils that has a strong lemon and verbena odor and is used esp. in perfumery and as a flavoring

ci·trate \'si-ˌtrāt\ *n* [ISV] **:** a salt or ester of citric acid

cit·ric acid \ˌsi-trik-\ *n* [ISV] **:** a tricarboxylic acid $C_6H_8O_7$ occurring in cellular metabolism, obtained esp. from lemon and lime juices or by fermentation of sugars, and used as a flavoring

citric acid cycle *n* **:** KREBS CYCLE

cit·ri·cul·ture \'si-trə-ˌkəl-chər\ *n* **:** the cultivation of citrus fruits — **cit·ri·cul·tur·ist** \ˌsi-trə-'kəlch-(ə-)rəst\ *n*

[1]**cit·rine** \'si-ˌtrīn\ *adj* [ME, fr. MF *citrin,* fr. ML *citrinus,* fr. L *citrus* citron tree] **:** resembling a citron or lemon esp. in color

[2]**ci·trine** \si-'trēn\ *n* **:** a black quartz changed in color by heating into a semiprecious yellow stone resembling topaz

cit·ron \'si-trən\ *n* [ME, fr. MF, fr. OProv, modif. of L *citrus* citron tree] **1 a :** a fruit like the lemon in appearance and structure but larger **b :** a small shrubby citrus tree (*Citrus medica*) that produces citrons **c :** the preserved rind of the citron used esp. in cakes and puddings **2 :** a small hard-fleshed watermelon used esp. in pickles and preserves

cit·ro·nel·la \ˌsi-trə-'nel-ə\ *n* [NL, fr. F *citronnelle* lemon balm, fr. *citron*] **:** a fragrant grass (*Cymbopogon nardus*) of southern Asia that yields an oil used in perfumery and as an insect repellent; *also* **:** its oil

cit·ro·nel·lal \-'nel-ˌal\ *n* [ISV, fr. NL *citronella*] **:** a lemon-odored aldehyde $C_{10}H_{18}O$ found in many essential oils and used in perfumery

cit·rul·line \'si-trə-ˌlēn\ *n* [ISV, fr. NL *Citrullus,* genus name of the watermelon] **:** a crystalline amino acid $C_6H_{13}N_3O_3$ formed esp. as an intermediate in the conversion of ornithine to arginine in the living system

cit·rus \'si-trəs\ *n, pl* **citrus** *or* **cit·rus·es** *often attrib* [NL, genus name, fr. L, citron tree] **:** any of a genus (*Citrus*) of often thorny trees and shrubs of the rue family grown in warm regions for their edible fruit (as the orange) with firm usu. thick rind and pulpy flesh

citrus red mite *n* **:** a comparatively large mite (*Panonychus citri*) that is a destructive pest on the foliage of citrus — called also *citrus red spider*

cit·tern \'sit-ərn\ *or* **cith·ern** \'sith-ərn, 'sith-\ *or* **cith·ren** \'sith-rən\ *n* [blend of *cither* and *gittern*] **:** a guitar with a pear-shaped flat-backed body popular esp. in Renaissance England

city \'sit-ē\ *n, pl* **cit·ies** *often attrib* [ME *citie* large or small town, fr. OF *cité* capital city, fr. ML *civitat-, civitas,* fr. L, citizenship, state, city of Rome, fr. *civis* citizen — more at HOME] **1 a :** an inhabited place of greater size, population, or importance than a town or village **b :** an incorporated British town usu. of major size or importance having the status of an episcopal see **c :** a usu. large or important municipality in the U.S. governed under a charter granted by the state **d :** an incorporated municipal unit of the highest class in Canada **2 :** CITY-STATE **3 :** the people of a city

city council *n* **:** the legislative body of a city

city edition *n* **:** an edition of a usu. metropolitan newspaper that is designed for sale within the city

city editor *n* **:** a newspaper editor with varying functions but usu. in charge of local news and staff assignments

city father *n* **:** a member (as an alderman or councilman) of the governing body of a city

city hall *n* **1 :** the chief administrative building of a city **2 a :** a municipal government **b :** city officialdom or bureaucracy ⟨you can't fight *city hall*⟩

city manager *n* **:** an official employed by an elected council to direct the administration of a city government

city plan *n* **:** an organized arrangement (as of streets, parks, and business and residential areas) of a city with a view to convenience, appearance, healthful environment, and future growth — **city planning** *n*

city planner *n* **:** one that makes city plans; *esp* **:** a professional who participates in such activity

city room *n* **:** the department where local news is handled in a newspaper editorial office

city·scape \'sit-ē-ˌskāp\ *n* **1 :** a pictorial representation of a city **2 :** a city viewed as a scene ⟨the skyscrapers which now bedizen the American ~ —*Amer. Mercury*⟩ **3 :** a pictorial composition of urban elements

city slicker *n* **:** SLICKER 2b

city–state \'sit-ē-'stāt, -ˌstāt\ *n* **:** an autonomous state consisting of a city and surrounding territory

civ *abbr* civil; civilian

civ·et \'siv-ət\ *n* [MF *civette,* fr. OIt *zibetto,* fr. Ar *zabād* civet perfume] **:** a thick yellowish musky-odored substance found in a pouch near the sexual organs of the civet cat and used in perfume

civet cat *n* **1 a :** any of several carnivorous mammals (family Viverridae); *esp* **:** a long-bodied short-legged African animal (*Civettictis civetta*) that produces most of the civet of commerce **b :** CACOMISTLE **c :** any of the small spotted skunks (genus *Spilogale*) of western No. America **2 :** the fur of a civet cat

civet cat 1a

civ·ic \'siv-ik\ *adj* [L *civicus,* fr. *civis* citizen] **:** of or relating to a citizen, a city, citizenship, or civil affairs — **civ·i·cal·ly** \'siv-i-k(ə-)lē\ *adv*

civ·ic–mind·ed \ˌsiv-ik-'mīn-dəd\ *adj* **:** disposed to look after civic needs and interests — **civ·ic–mind·ed·ness** *n*

civ·ics \'siv-iks\ *n pl but sing or pl in constr* **:** a social science dealing with the rights and duties of citizens

civ·il \'siv-əl\ *adj* [ME, fr. MF, fr. L *civilis,* fr. *civis*] **1 a :** of or relating to citizens ⟨~ liberties⟩ **b :** of or relating to the state or its citizenry **2 a :** CIVILIZED ⟨~ society⟩ **b :** adequate in courtesy and politeness **:** MANNERLY **3 a :** of, relating to, or based on civil law **b :** relating to private rights and to remedies sought by action or suit distinct from criminal proceedings **c :** established by law **4** *of time* **:** based on the mean sun and legally recognized for use in ordinary affairs **5 :** of, relating to, or involving the general public, their activities, needs, or ways, or civic affairs as distinguished from special (as military or religious) affairs
syn CIVIL, POLITE, COURTEOUS, GALLANT, CHIVALROUS *shared meaning element* **:** observant of the forms required by good breeding. CIVIL is feeble in force, often suggesting little more than avoidance of overt rudeness. POLITE is more positive and commonly implies polish of manners and address more than warmth and cordiality ⟨the cultured, precise tone, *polite* but faintly superior —William Styron⟩ COURTEOUS implies an actively considerate and sometimes rather stately politeness ⟨listened with *courteous* attention⟩ *Gallant* and *chivalrous* imply courteous attentiveness esp. to women but GALLANT is likely to suggest dashing behavior and ornate expression ⟨ever ready with *gallant* remarks of admiration⟩ while CHIVALROUS tends to suggest high-minded and disinterested attentions ⟨felt at once *chivalrous* and paternal to the lost girl⟩ **ant** uncivil, rude

civil death *n* **:** the status of a living person equivalent in its legal consequences to natural death; *specif* **:** deprivation of civil rights

civil defense *n* **:** the complex of protective measures and emergency relief activities conducted by civilians in case of hostile attack, sabotage, or natural disaster

civil disobedience *n* **:** refusal to obey governmental demands or commands esp. as a nonviolent and usu. collective means of forcing concessions from the government

civil engineer *n* **:** an engineer whose training or occupation is in the designing and construction of public works (as roads or harbors) and of various private works — **civil engineering** *n*

ci·vil·ian \sə-'vil-yən\ *n* **1 :** a specialist in Roman or modern civil law **2 :** one not on active duty in a military, police, or firefighting force — **civilian** *adj*

ci·vil·ian·ize \-yə-ˌnīz\ *vt* **-ized; -iz·ing :** to convert from military to civilian status or control — **ci·vil·ian·iza·tion** \-ˌvil-yə-nə-'zā-shən\ *n*

civ·i·li·sa·tion, civ·i·lise *chiefly Brit var of* CIVILIZATION, CIVILIZE

ci·vil·i·ty \sə-'vil-ət-ē\ *n, pl* **-ties 1** *archaic* **:** training in the humanities **2 a :** COURTESY, POLITENESS **b :** a polite act or expression

civ·i·li·za·tion \ˌsiv-ə-lə-'zā-shən\ *n* **1 a :** a relatively high level of cultural and technological development; *specif* **:** the stage of cultural development at which writing and the keeping of written records is attained **b :** the culture characteristic of a particular time or place **2 :** the process of becoming civilized **3 a :** refinement of thought, manners, or taste **b :** a situation of urban comfort

civ·i·lize \'siv-ə-ˌlīz\ *vb* **-lized; -liz·ing** *vt* **1 :** to cause to develop out of a primitive state; *specif* **:** to bring to a technically advanced and rationally ordered stage of cultural development **2 a :** EDUCATE, REFINE **b :** SOCIALIZE 1 ~ *vi* **:** to acquire the customs and amenities of a civil community — **civ·i·liz·able** \-ˌlī-zə-bəl\ *adj* — **civ·i·liz·er** *n*

civ·i·lized *adj* **:** of or relating to peoples or nations in a state of civilization

civil law *n, often cap C&L* **1 :** Roman law esp. as set forth in the Justinian code **2 :** the body of private law developed from Roman law and used in Louisiana and in many countries outside the English-speaking world **3 :** the law established by a nation or state for its own jurisdiction **4 :** the law of civil or private rights

civil liberty *n* **:** freedom from arbitrary governmental interference (as with the right of free speech) specif. by denial of governmental power and in the U.S. esp. as guaranteed by the Bill of Rights — usu. used in pl. — **civil lib·er·tar·i·an** \-ˌlib-ər-'ter-ē-ən\ *n*

civ·il·ly \'siv-ə(l)-lē\ *adv* **1 :** in a civil manner **:** POLITELY **2 :** in terms of civil rights, law, or matters ⟨~ dead⟩

civil marriage *n* **:** a marriage performed by a magistrate

civil right·er \-'rīt-ər\ *n* **:** an advocate of civil rights; *esp* **:** one who works to gain civil rights for minority groups

civil right·ist \-'rīt-əst\ *n* **:** CIVIL RIGHTER

civil rights *n pl* **:** the nonpolitical rights of a citizen; *esp* **:** the rights of personal liberty guaranteed to U.S. citizens by the 13th and 14th amendments to the Constitution and by acts of Congress

civil servant *n* **1 :** a member of a civil service **2 :** a member of the administrative staff of an international agency (as the United Nations)

civil service *n* **:** the administrative service of a government or international agency exclusive of the armed forces; *esp* **:** one in which appointments are determined by competitive examination

civil war *n* **:** a war between opposing groups of citizens of the same country

Civ·i·tan \'siv-ə-ˌtan\ *n* [*Civitan (club)*] **:** a member of a major national and international service club

civ·vy *also* **civ·ie** \'siv-ē\ *n, pl* **civvies** *also* **civies 1** *pl* **:** civilian clothes as distinguished from a military uniform **2 :** CIVILIAN

CJ *abbr* chief justice
ck *abbr* **1** cask **2** check
cl *abbr* **1** centiliter **2** class **3** clause **4** close **5** closet **6** cloth
Cl *symbol* chlorine
CL *abbr* **1** carload **2** center line **3** civil law **4** common law
Cla *abbr* Clackmannanshire
CLA *abbr* College Language Association
¹clab·ber \ˈklab-ər\ *n* [short for *bonnyclabber*] *chiefly dial* : sour milk that has thickened or curdled
²clabber *vi, chiefly dial* : CURDLE
clach·an \ˈklak-ən\ *n* [ME, fr. ScGael] *Scot & Irish* : HAMLET
¹clack \ˈklak\ *vb* [ME *clacken*, of imit. origin] *vi* **1** : CHATTER, PRATTLE **2** : to make an abrupt striking sound or series of sounds **3** *of fowl* : CACKLE, CLUCK ~ *vt* **1** : to cause to make a clatter **2** : to produce with a chattering sound; *specif* : BLAB — **clack·er** *n*
²clack *n* **1 a** : rapid continuous talk : CHATTER **b** : TONGUE **2** *archaic* : an object (as a clack valve) that produces clapping or rattling noises usu. in regular rapid sequence **3** : a sound of clacking ⟨the ~ of a typewriter⟩
clack valve *n* : a valve usu. hinged at one edge that permits flow of fluid in one direction only and that closes with a clacking sound
Clac·to·ni·an \klak-ˈtō-nē-ən\ *adj* [*Clacton*-on-Sea, England] : of or relating to a Lower Paleolithic culture characterized by stone flakes with a half cone at the point of striking
¹clad \ˈklad\ *adj* [pp. of *clothe*] **1** : being covered or clothed ⟨ivy-*clad* buildings⟩ **2** *of a coin* : consisting of outer layers of one metal bonded to a core of a different metal
²clad *vt* **clad; clad·ding** : SHEATHE, FACE; *specif* : to cover (a metal) with another metal by bonding
³clad *n* **1** : a composite material formed by cladding; *specif* : a clad coin **2** : something that overlays : CLADDING; *specif* : the outer layer of a clad coin
clad·ding \ˈklad-iŋ\ *n* : something that covers or overlays ⟨stone ~ on a building wall⟩; *specif* : metal coating bonded to a metal core
clad·ode \ˈklad-ˌōd\ *n* [NL *cladodium*, fr. Gk *klados*] : CLADOPHYLL — **cla·do·di·al** \kla-ˈdōd-ē-əl\ *adj*
clado·gen·e·sis \ˌklad-ə-ˈjen-ə-səs\ *n* [NL, fr. Gk *klados* branch + L *genesis*] : evolutionary change characterized by treelike branching of taxa — **clado·ge·net·ic** \ˌklad-ō-jə-ˈnet-ik\ *adj* — **clado·ge·net·i·cal·ly** \-i-k(ə-)lē\ *adv*
clado·phyll \ˈklad-ə-ˌfil\ *n* [NL *cladophyllum*, fr. Gk *klados* branch + *phyllon* leaf —more at GLADIATOR, BLADE] : a branch assuming the form of and closely resembling an ordinary foliage leaf and often bearing leaves or flowers on its margins
¹claim \ˈklām\ *vt* [ME *claimen*, fr. OF *clamer*, fr. L *clamare* to cry out, shout; akin to L *calare* to call — more at LOW] **1 a** : to ask for esp. as a right ⟨~*ed* the inheritance⟩ **b** : to call for : REQUIRE ⟨this matter ~*s* our attention⟩ **2** : to take as the rightful owner ⟨went to ~ his bags at the station⟩ **3** : to assert in the face of possible contradiction : MAINTAIN ⟨~*ed* that he'd been cheated⟩ ***syn*** see DEMAND — **claim·able** \ˈklā-mə-bəl\ *adj* — **claim·er** *n*
²claim *n* **1** : a demand for something due or believed to be due ⟨insurance ~⟩ **2 a** : a right to something; *specif* : a title to a debt, privilege, or other thing in the possession of another **b** : an assertion open to challenge ⟨a ~ of authenticity⟩ **3** : something that is claimed; *esp* : a tract of land staked out
claim·ant \ˈklā-mənt\ *n* : one that asserts a right or title ⟨a ~ to an estate⟩
claiming race *n* : a horse race in which each entry is offered for sale for a specified price to a purchaser who pledges the selling price before the race
clair·au·di·ence \kla(ə)r-ˈȯd-ē-ən(t)s, kle(ə)r-, -ˈäd-\ *n* [*clair-* (as in *clairvoyance*) + *audience* (act of hearing)] : the power or faculty of hearing something not present to the ear but regarded as having objective reality
clair·au·di·ent \-ənt\ *adj* : of or relating to clairaudience — **clair·au·di·ent·ly** *adv*
clair·voy·ance \kla(ə)r-ˈvȯi-ən(t)s, kle(ə)r-\ *n* **1** : the power or faculty of discerning objects not present to the senses **2** : ability to perceive matters beyond the range of ordinary perception : PENETRATION
¹clair·voy·ant \-ənt\ *adj* [F, fr. *clair* clear (fr. L *clarus*) + *voyant*, prp. of *voir* to see, fr. L *vidēre*] **1** : unusually perceptive : DISCERNING **2** : of or relating to clairvoyance — **clair·voy·ant·ly** *adv*
²clairvoyant *n* : one having the power of clairvoyance
¹clam \ˈklam\ *n* [ME, fr. OE *clamm* bond, fetter; akin to OHG *klamma* constriction, L *glomus* ball] : CLAMP, CLASP
²clam *n, often attrib* [¹*clam*; fr. the clamping action of the shells] **1 a** : any of numerous edible marine bivalve mollusks living in sand or mud **b** : a freshwater mussel **2** : a stolid or closemouthed person **3** : CLAMSHELL
³clam *vi* **clammed; clam·ming** : to gather clams esp. by digging
cla·mant \ˈklā-mənt, ˈklam-ənt\ *adj* [L *clamant-, clamans*, prp. of *clamare* to cry out] **1** : CLAMOROUS, BLATANT **2** : demanding attention : URGENT — **cla·mant·ly** *adv*
clam·bake \ˈklam-ˌbāk\ *n* **1 a** : an outdoor party; *esp* : a seashore outing where food is cooked on heated rocks covered by seaweed **b** : the food served at a clambake **2** : a gathering characterized by noisy sociability; *esp* : a political rally

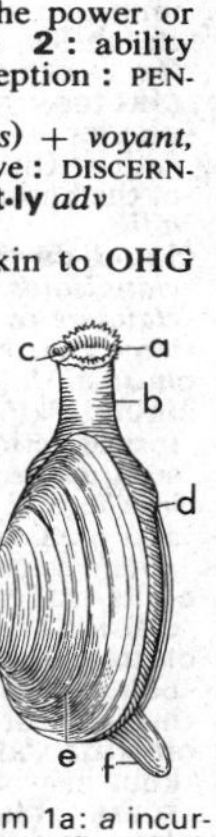

clam 1a: *a* incurrent orifice, *b* siphon, *c* excurrent orifice, *d* mantle, *e* shell, *f* foot

clam·ber \ˈklam-(b)ər\ *vi* **clam·bered; clam·ber·ing** \ˈklam-b(ə-)riŋ, ˈklam-(ə-)riŋ\ [ME *clambren*; akin to OE *climban* to climb] : to climb awkwardly (as by scrambling) ⟨~*ed* over the rocks⟩ — **clam·ber·er** \-(b)ər-ər\ *n*
clam·my \ˈklam-ē\ *adj* **clam·mi·er; -est** [ME, prob. fr. *clammen* to smear, stick, fr. OE *clǣman*; akin to OE *clǣg* clay] **1** : being damp, soft, sticky, and usu. cool ⟨a ~ and intensely cold mist —Charles Dickens⟩ **2 a** : lacking normal human warmth ⟨the ~ atmosphere of an institution⟩ **b** : ALOOF, REPELLENT — **clam·mi·ly** \ˈklam-ə-lē\ *adv* — **clam·mi·ness** \ˈklam-ē-nəs\ *n*
¹clam·or \ˈklam-ər\ *n* [ME, fr. MF *clamour*, fr. L *clamor*, fr. *clamare* to cry out — more at CLAIM] **1 a** : noisy shouting **b** : a loud continuous noise **2** : insistent public expression (as of support or protest) ⟨a ~ against increased taxes⟩
²clamor *vb* **clam·ored; clam·or·ing** \ˈklam-(ə-)riŋ\ *vi* **1** : to make a din **2** : to become loudly insistent ⟨~*ed* for his impeachment⟩ ~ *vt* **1** : to utter or proclaim insistently and noisily **2** : to influence by means of clamor
³clamor *vt* [origin unknown] *obs* : SILENCE
clam·or·ous \ˈklam-(ə-)rəs\ *adj* **1** : marked by confused din or outcry : TUMULTUOUS ⟨the busy ~ market⟩ **2** : noisily insistent ***syn*** see VOCIFEROUS ***ant*** taciturn — **clam·or·ous·ly** *adv* — **clam·or·ous·ness** *n*
clam·our \ˈklam-ər\ *chiefly Brit var of* CLAMOR
¹clamp \ˈklamp\ *n* [ME, prob. fr. (assumed) MD *klampe*; akin to OE *clamm* bond, fetter — more at CLAM] **1** : a device designed to bind or constrict or to press two or more parts together so as to hold them firmly **2** : any of various instruments or appliances having parts brought together for holding or compressing something
²clamp *vt* **1** : to fasten with or as if with a clamp **2 a** : to place by decree : IMPOSE — often used with *on* ⟨~*ed* on a curfew after the riots⟩ **b** : to hold tightly
clamp·down \ˈklamp-ˌdau̇n\ *n* : the act or action of making regulations and restrictions more stringent : CRACKDOWN ⟨a ~ on charge accounts, bank loans, and other inflationary influences —*Time*⟩
clamp down \(ˈ)klamp-ˈdau̇n\ *vi* : to impose restrictions : become repressive ⟨the police are *clamping down* on speeders⟩
clam·shell \ˈklam-ˌshel\ *n* **1** : a bucket or grapple (as on a dredge) having two hinged jaws **2** : an excavating machine having a clamshell
clam up *vi* : to become silent ⟨he *clammed up* when asked for details⟩
clam worm *n* : any of several large burrowing polychaete worms (as a nereis) often used as bait
clan \ˈklan\ *n* [ME, fr. ScGael *clann* offspring, clan, fr. OIr *cland* plant, offspring, fr. L *planta* plant] **1 a** : a Celtic group esp. in the Scottish Highlands comprising a number of households whose heads claim descent from a common ancestor **b** : SIB 3 **2** : a group united by a common interest or common characteristics
clan·des·tine \klan-ˈdes-tən *also* -ˌtīn *or* -ˌtēn *or* ˈklan-dəs-\ *adj* [MF or L; MF *clandestin*, fr. L *clandestinus*, irreg. fr. *clam* secretly; akin to L *celare* to hide — more at HELL] : held in or conducted with secrecy : SURREPTITIOUS ***syn*** see SECRET ***ant*** open — **clan·des·tine·ly** *adv* — **clan·des·tine·ness** *n*
¹clang \ˈklaŋ\ *vb* [L *clangere*; akin to Gk *klazein* to scream, bark, OE *hlōwan* to low] *vi* **1 a** : to make a loud metallic ringing sound ⟨anvils ~*ed*⟩ **b** : to go with a clang **2** : to utter the characteristic harsh cry of a bird ~ *vt* : to cause to clang ⟨~ a bell⟩
²clang *n* **1** : a loud ringing metallic sound ⟨the ~ of a fire alarm⟩ **2** : a harsh cry of a bird (as a crane or goose)
¹clan·gor \ˈklaŋ-ər *also* -gər\ *n* [L *clangor*, fr. *clangere*] : a resounding clang or medley of clangs ⟨the ~ of hammers⟩ — **clan·gor·ous** \-(g)ə-rəs\ *adj* — **clan·gor·ous·ly** *adv*
²clangor *vi* : to make a clangor
clan·gour \ˈklaŋ-ər, -gər\ *chiefly Brit var of* CLANGOR
¹clank \ˈklaŋk\ *vb* [prob. imit.] *vi* **1** : to make a clank or series of clanks ⟨the radiator hissed and ~*ed*⟩ **2** : to go with a clank ⟨tanks ~*ing* through the streets⟩ ~ *vt* : to cause to clank — **clank·ing·ly** \ˈklaŋ-kiŋ-lē\ *adv*
²clank *n* : a sharp brief metallic ringing sound
clan·nish \ˈklan-ish\ *adj* **1** : of or relating to a clan **2** : tending to associate only with a select group of similar background or status ⟨~ immigrants⟩ — **clan·nish·ly** *adv* — **clan·nish·ness** *n*
clans·man \ˈklanz-mən\ *n* : a member of a clan
¹clap \ˈklap\ *vb* **clapped** *also* **clapt; clap·ping** [ME *clappen*, fr. OE *clæppan*; akin to OHG *klaphōn* to beat, L *glēba* clod — more at CLIP] *vt* **1** : to strike (as two flat hard surfaces) together so as to produce a sharp percussive noise **2 a** : to strike (the hands) together repeatedly usu. in applause **b** : APPLAUD **3** : to strike with the flat of the hand in a friendly way ⟨*clapped* his friend on the shoulder⟩ **4** : to place, put, or set esp. energetically ⟨~ him into jail⟩ **5** : to improvise hastily ~ *vi* **1** : to produce a percussive sound; *esp* : SLAM **2** : to go abruptly or briskly **3** : APPLAUD
²clap *n* **1** : a device that makes a clapping noise **2** *obs* : a sudden stroke of fortune and esp. ill fortune **3** : a loud percussive noise; *specif* : a sudden crash of thunder **4 a** : a sudden blow **b** : a friendly slap ⟨a ~ on the shoulder⟩ **5** : the sound of clapping hands; *esp* : APPLAUSE
³clap *n* [MF *clapoir* bubo] : GONORRHEA
clap·board \ˈklab-ərd; ˈkla(p)-ˌbō(ə)rd, -ˌbȯ(ə)rd\ *n* [part trans. of D *klaphout* stave wood] **1** *archaic* : a size of board for making staves and wainscoting **2** : a narrow board usu. thicker at one edge than the other used for siding — **clapboard** *vt*
clap·per \ˈklap-ər\ *n* : one that makes a clapping sound: as **a** : the tongue of a bell — see BELL illustration **b** *slang* : the tongue of a talkative person **c** : a mechanical device that makes noise esp. by the banging of one part against another **d** : a person who applauds
clap·per·claw \ˈklap-ər-ˌklȯ\ *vt* [perh. fr. *clapper* + *claw* (v.)] **1** *dial Eng* : to claw with the nails **2** *dial Eng* : SCOLD, REVILE
¹clap·trap \ˈklap-ˌtrap\ *n* [²*clap*; fr. its attempt to win applause] : pretentious nonsense : TRASH

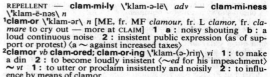

ə abut	ᵊ kitten	ər further	a back	ā bake	ä cot, cart	
au̇ out	ch chin	e less	ē easy	g gift	i trip	ī life
j joke	ŋ sing	ō flow	ȯ flaw	ȯi coin	th thin	th this
ü loot	u̇ foot	y yet	yü few	yu̇ furious	zh vision	

[2]claptrap *adj* : characterized by or suggestive of claptrap; *esp* : of a cheap showy nature ⟨~ sentiment⟩

claque \'klak\ *n* [F, fr. *claquer* to clap, of imit. origin] **1** : a group hired to applaud at a performance **2** : a group of sycophants

cla·queur \kla-'kər\ *n* [F, fr. *claquer* to clap] : a member of a claque

clar·ence \'klar-ən(t)s\ *n* [duke of *Clarence*, later William IV of England] : a closed four-wheeled four-passenger carriage

clar·et \'klar-ət\ *n* [ME, fr. MF (*vin*) *claret* clear wine, fr. *claret* clear, fr. *cler* clear] **1** : a dry red table wine from the Bordeaux district of France; *also* : a similar wine produced elsewhere **2** : a dark purplish red — **claret** *adj*

Cla·re·tian \klə-'rē-shən, kla-\ *n* [St. Anthony *Claret* †1870 Sp priest] : a member of the Congregation of the Missionary Sons of the Immaculate Heart of Mary founded by St. Anthony Claret in Vich, Spain, in 1849 — **Claretian** *adj*

clar·i·fy \'klar-ə-,fī\ *vb* **-fied; fy·ing** [ME *clarifien*, fr. MF *clarifier*, fr. LL *clarificare*, fr. L *clarus* clear — more at CLEAR] *vt* **1** : to make (as a liquid) clear or pure usu. by freeing from suspended matter **2** : to free of confusion **3** : to make understandable ~ *vi* : to become clear — **clar·i·fi·ca·tion** \,klar-ə-fə-'kā-shən\ *n* — **clar·i·fi·er** \'klar-ə-,fī(-ə)r\ *n*

clar·i·net \,klar-ə-'net, 'klar-ə-nət\ *n* [F *clarinette*, prob. deriv. of ML *clarion-*, *clario*] : a single-reed woodwind instrument having a cylindrical tube with a moderately flared bell and a usual range from D below middle C upward for 3½ octaves — **clar·i·net·ist** *or* **clar·i·net·tist** \,klar-ə-'net-əst\ *n*

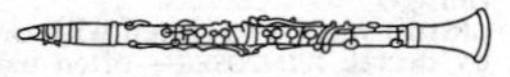
clarinet

[1]clar·i·on \'klar-ē-ən\ *n* [ME, fr. MF & ML; MF *clairon*, fr. ML *clarion-*, *clario*, fr. L *clarus* clear] **1** : a medieval trumpet with clear shrill tones **2** : the sound of or as if of a clarion

[2]clarion *adj* : brilliantly clear; *esp* : STENTORIAN ⟨a ~ call to action⟩

clar·i·ty \'klar-ət-ē\ *n* [ME *clarite*, fr. L *claritat-*, *claritas*, fr. *clarus*] : the quality or state of being clear : LUCIDITY ⟨the ~ of her voice⟩

clark·ia \'klär-kē-ə\ *n* [NL, fr. William *Clark* †1838 Am explorer] : a showy annual herb (genus *Clarkia*) of the evening-primrose family of the Pacific slope of No. America

cla·ro \'klär-(,)ō\ *n*, *pl* **claroes** [Sp, fr. *claro* light, fr. L *clarus*] : a light-colored generally mild cigar

clary \'kla(ə)r-ē, 'kle(ə)r-\ *n*, *pl* **clar·ies** [ME *clarie*, fr. MF *sclaree*, fr. ML *sclareia*] : an aromatic mint (*Salvia sclarea*) of southern Europe grown as a potherb and ornamental

[1]clash \'klash\ *vb* [imit] *vi* **1** : to make a clash ⟨cymbals ~*ed*⟩ **2** : to come into conflict ⟨where ignorant armies ~ by night —Matthew Arnold⟩ ~ *vt* : to cause to clash — **clash·er** *n*

[2]clash *n* **1** : a noisy usu. metallic sound of collision **2** **a** : a hostile encounter : SKIRMISH ⟨a ~ between the two armies⟩ **b** : a sharp conflict ⟨a ~ of opinions⟩

clas·mato·cyte \klaz-'mat-ə-,sīt\ *n* [ISV, fr. Gk *klasmat-*, *klasma* fragment (fr. *klan* to break) + ISV *-cyte* — more at HALT] : HISTIOCYTE — **clas·mato·cyt·ic** \(,)klaz-,mat-ə-'sit-ik\ *adj*

[1]clasp \'klasp\ *n* [ME *claspe*] **1** **a** : a device (as a hook) for holding objects or parts together **b** : a device (as a bar) attached to a military medal to indicate an additional award of the medal or the action or service for which it was awarded **2** : a holding or enveloping with or as if with the hands or arms ***syn*** see HOLD

[2]clasp *vt* **1** : to fasten with or as if with a clasp ⟨a robe ~*ed* with a brooch⟩ **2** : to enclose and hold with the arms; *specif* : EMBRACE **3** : to seize with or as if with the hand : GRASP

clasp·er \'klas-pər\ *n* : a male copulatory structure: **a** : one of a pair of external anal processes of an insect **b** : one of a pair of organs on the pelvic fins of elasmobranch fishes

clasp knife *n* : POCKETKNIFE; *esp* : a large one-bladed folding knife having a catch to hold the blade open

[1]class \'klas\ *n*, *often attrib* [F *classe*, fr. L *classis* group called to arms, class of citizens; akin to L *calare* to call — more at LOW] **1** **a** : a group sharing the same economic or social status ⟨the working ~⟩ **b** : social rank; *esp* : high social rank **c** : high quality : ELEGANCE **2** **a** : a course of instruction **b** : a body of students meeting regularly to study the same subject **c** : the period during which such a body meets **d** : a body of students or alumni whose year of graduation is the same **3** : a group, set, or kind sharing common attributes: as **a** : a major category in biological taxonomy ranking above the order and below the phylum or division **b** : a group of adjacent and discrete or continuous values of a random variable **c** : SET 19 **4** : a division or rating based on grade or quality

[2]class *vt* : CLASSIFY

class action *n* : a legal action undertaken by one or more plaintiffs on behalf of themselves and all other persons having an identical interest in the alleged wrong

class–con·scious *adj* **1** : actively aware of one's common status with others in a particular economic or social level of society **2** : believing in and actively aware of class struggle — **class con·scious·ness** *n*

[1]clas·sic \'klas-ik\ *adj* [F or L; F *classique*, fr. L *classicus* of the highest class of Roman citizens, of the first rank, fr. *classis*] **1** **a** : of recognized value : serving as a standard of excellence **b** : TRADITIONAL, ENDURING **c** : characterized by simple tailored lines in fashion year after year ⟨a ~ suit⟩ **2** : of or relating to the ancient Greeks and Romans or their culture : CLASSICAL **3** **a** : historically memorable **b** : noted because of special literary or historical associations ⟨Paris is the ~ refuge of expatriates⟩ **4** **a** : AUTHENTIC, AUTHORITATIVE **b** : TYPICAL ⟨a ~ example of guilt by association⟩

[2]classic *n* **1** : a literary work of ancient Greece or Rome **2** **a** : a work of enduring excellence; *also* : its author **b** : an authoritative source **3** : a typical example **4** : a traditional event ⟨a football ~⟩

clas·si·cal \'klas-i-kəl\ *adj* [L *classicus*] **1** : STANDARD, CLASSIC **2** **a** : of or relating to the ancient Greek and Roman world and esp. to its literature, art, architecture, or ideals **b** : versed in the classics **3** **a** : of or relating to music of the late 18th and early 19th centuries characterized by an emphasis on simplicity, objectivity, and proportion; *also* : of or relating to a composer of this music **b** : of, relating to, or being music in the educated European tradition that includes such forms as art song, chamber music, opera, and symphony as distinguished from folk or popular music or jazz **4** **a** : AUTHORITATIVE, TRADITIONAL **b** (1) : of or relating to a form or system considered of first significance in earlier times ⟨~ Mendelian genetics versus modern molecular genetics⟩ (2) : not involving relativity, wave mechanics, or quantum theory ⟨~ physics⟩ **c** : conforming to a pattern of usage sanctioned by a body of literature rather than by everyday speech **5** : concerned with or giving instruction in the humanities, the fine arts, and the broad aspects of science ⟨a ~ curriculum⟩

clas·si·cal·ism \'klas-i-kə-,liz-əm\ *n* : CLASSICISM — **clas·si·cal·ist** \-ləst\ *n*

clas·si·cal·i·ty \,klas-ə-'kal-ət-ē\ *n* **1** : the quality or state of being classic **2** : classical scholarship

clas·si·cal·ly \'klas-i-k(ə-)lē\ *adv* : in a classic or classical manner

clas·si·cism \'klas-ə-,siz-əm\ *n* **1** **a** : the principles or style embodied in the literature, art, or architecture of ancient Greece and Rome **b** : classical scholarship **c** : a classical idiom or expression **2** : adherence to traditional standards (as of simplicity, restraint, and proportion) that are universally and enduringly valid

clas·si·cist \-səst\ *n* **1** : an advocate or follower of classicism **2** : a classical scholar — **clas·si·cis·tic** \,klas-ə-'sis-tik\ *adj*

clas·si·cize \'klas-ə-,sīz\ *vb* **-cized; -ciz·ing** *vt* : to make classic or classical ~ *vi* : to follow classic style

clas·si·fi·ca·tion \,klas-(ə-)fə-'kā-shən\ *n* **1** : the act or process of classifying **2** **a** : systematic arrangement in groups or categories according to established criteria; *specif* : TAXONOMY **b** : CLASS, CATEGORY — **clas·si·fi·ca·to·ri·ly** \,klas-(ə-)fə-kə-'tōr-ə-lē, kla-,sif-ə-, -'tȯr-\ *adv* — **clas·si·fi·ca·to·ry** \'klas-(ə-)fə-kə-,tōr-ē, kla-'sif-ə-, -,tȯr-; 'klas-(ə-)fə-,kāt-ə-rē\ *adj*

clas·si·fied \'klas-ə-,fīd\ *adj* **1** : divided into classes or placed in a class ⟨~ ads⟩ **2** : withheld from general circulation for reasons of national security ⟨~ information⟩

clas·si·fi·er \'klas-ə-,fī(-ə)r\ *n* **1** : one that classifies; *specif* : a machine for sorting out the constituents of a substance (as ore) **2** : a word or morpheme used with numerals or with nouns designating countable or measurable objects

clas·si·fy \'klas-ə-,fī\ *vt* **-fied; -fy·ing** **1** : to arrange in classes ⟨~*ing* books according to subject matter⟩ **2** : to assign (as a document) to a category — **clas·si·fi·able** \-,fī-ə-bəl\ *adj*

class interval *n* : CLASS 3b; *also* : the width of a statistical class

clas·sis \'klas-əs\ *n*, *pl* **clas·ses** \'klas-,ēz\ [NL, fr. L, class] **1** : a governing body in some Reformed churches (as in the former Reformed Church in the U. S.) corresponding to a presbytery **2** : the district governed by a classis

class·less \'klas-ləs\ *adj* **1** : free from distinctions of social class ⟨a ~ society⟩ **2** : belonging to no particular social class — **class·less·ness** *n*

class·mate \-,māt\ *n* : a member of the same class in a school or college

class·room \-,rüm, -,ru̇m\ *n* : a place where classes meet

classy \'klas-ē\ *adj* **class·i·er; -est** : ELEGANT, STYLISH — **class·i·ness** *n*

clast \'klast\ *n* [Gk *klastos* broken] : a fragment of rock

clas·tic \'klas-tik\ *adj* [ISV, fr. Gk *klastos* broken, fr. *klan* to break — more at HALT] : made up of fragments of preexisting rocks ⟨a ~ sediment⟩ — **clastic** *n*

clath·rate \'klath-,rāt\ *adj* [L *clathratus*, fr. *clathri* (pl.) lattice, fr. Gk *klēithron* bar, fr. *kleiein* to close — more at CLOSE] **1** : resembling a lattice **2** : relating to or being a compound formed by the inclusion of molecules of one kind in cavities of the crystal lattice of another — **clathrate** *n*

[1]clat·ter \'klat-ər\ *vb* [ME *clatren*, fr. (assumed) OE *clatrian*; of imit. origin] *vi* **1** : to make a rattling sound ⟨the dishes ~*ed* on the shelf⟩ **2** : to move or go with a clatter ⟨~*ed* down the stairs⟩ **3** : PRATTLE ~ *vt* : to cause to clatter — **clat·ter·er** \-ər-ər\ *n* — **clat·ter·ing·ly** \'klat-ə-riŋ-lē\ *adv*

[2]clatter *n* **1** : a rattling sound (as of hard bodies striking together) ⟨the ~ of pots and pans⟩ **2** : COMMOTION ⟨the midday ~ of the business district⟩ **3** : noisy chatter — **clat·tery** \'klat-ə-rē\ *adj*

clau·di·ca·tion \,klȯd-ə-'kā-shən\ *n* [L *claudication-*, *claudicatio*, fr. *claudicatus*, pp. of *claudicare* to limp, fr. *claudus* lame; akin to L *claudere* to close — more at CLOSE] : the quality or state of being lame : LIMPING

claus·al \'klȯ-zəl\ *adj* : relating to or of the nature of a clause

clause \'klȯz\ *n* [ME, fr. OF, clause, fr. ML *clausa* close of a rhetorical period, fr. L, fem. of *clausus*, pp. of *claudere* to close] **1** : a separate section of a discourse or writing; *specif* : a distinct article in a formal document **2** : a group of words containing a subject and predicate and functioning as a member of a complex or compound sentence

claus·tral \'klȯ-strəl\ *adj* [ME, fr. ML *claustralis*, fr. *claustrum* cloister — more at CLOISTER] : CLOISTRAL

claus·tro·pho·bia \,klȯ-strə-'fō-bē-ə\ *n* [NL, fr. L *claustrum* bar, bolt + NL *phobia* — more at CLOISTER] : abnormal dread of being in closed or narrow spaces — **claus·tro·pho·bic** \-bik\ *adj*

cla·vate \'klā-,vāt\ *adj* [NL *clavatus*, fr. L *clava* club, fr. *clavus* nail, knot in wood] : gradually thickening near the distal end : CLAVIFORM — **cla·vate·ly** *adv* — **cla·va·tion** \klā-'vā-shən\ *n*

clave *past of* CLEAVE

cla·ver \'klā-vər\ *vi* [prob. of Celt origin; akin to ScGael *clabaire* babbler] *chiefly Scot* : PRATE, GOSSIP — **claver** *n*, *chiefly Scot*

clav·i·chord \'klav-ə-,kȯ(ə)rd\ *n* [ML *clavichordium*, fr. L *clavis* key + *chorda* string — more at CORD] : an early keyboard instrument having strings pressed by tangents attached directly to the key ends — **clav·i·chord·ist** \-əst\ *n*

clav·i·cle \'klav-i-kəl\ *n* [F *clavicule*, fr. NL *clavicula*, fr. L, dim. of L *clavis* key; akin to Gk *kleid-*, *kleis* key, L *claudere* to close — more at CLOSE] : a bone of the vertebrate shoulder girdle typically serving to link the scapula and sternum — **cla·vic·u·lar** \klə-ˈvik-yə-lər, klə-\ *adj*

cla·vier \klə-ˈvi(ə)r; ˈklāv-ē-ər, ˈklav-\ *n* [F, fr. OF, key bearer, fr. L *clavis* key] **1** : the keyboard of a musical instrument **2** [G *klavier*, fr. F *clavier*] : an early keyboard instrument — **cla·vier·ist** \klə-ˈvir-əst; ˈklāv-ē-ə-rəst, ˈklav-\ *n* — **cla·vier·is·tic** \klə-ˌvi(ə)r-ˈis-tik; ˌklāv-ē-ə-ˈris-tik, ˌklav-\ *adj*

clav·i·form \ˈklav-ə-ˌfȯrm\ *adj* [L *clava* club] : shaped like a club

[1]**claw** \ˈklȯ\ *n, often attrib* [ME *clawe*, fr. OE *clawu* hoof, claw; akin to ON *klō* claw, OE *cliewen* ball — more at CLEW] **1** : a sharp usu. slender and curved nail on the toe of an animal **2** : any of various similar sharp curved processes esp. if at the end of a limb (as of an insect); *also* : a limb ending in such a process **3** : one of the pincerlike organs terminating some limbs of various arthropods (as a lobster or scorpion) **4** : something that resembles a claw; *specif* : the forked end of a tool (as a hammer) **5** : a wound from or as if from a claw — **clawed** \ˈklȯd\ *adj*

[2]**claw** *vt* : to rake, seize, dig, or progress with or as if with claws ~ *vi* : to scrape, scratch, dig, or pull with or as if with claws

claw hammer *n* **1** : a hammer with one end of the head forked for pulling out nails **2** : TAILCOAT

[1]**clay** \ˈklā\ *n, often attrib* [ME, fr. OE *clæg*; akin to OHG *klīwa* bran, LL *glut-, glus* glue, MGk *glia*] **1** **a** : an earthy material that is plastic when moist but hard when fired, that is composed mainly of fine particles of hydrous aluminum silicates and other minerals, and that is used for brick, tile, and pottery; *specif* : soil composed chiefly of this material having particles less than a specified size **b** : EARTH, MUD **2** **a** : a substance that resembles clay in plasticity and is used for modeling **b** : the human body as distinguished from the spirit **3** : CLAY COURT — **clay·ey** \ˈklā-ē\ *adj* — **clay·ish** \ˈklā-ish\ *adj*

[2]**clay** *vt* : to treat or cover with clay; *also* : to filter through clay

clay·bank \ˈklā-ˌbaŋk\ *n* : a horse of yellowish color

clay court *n* : a tennis court with a clay surface

clay loam *n* : a loam containing from 20 to 30 percent clay

clay mineral *n* : any of a group of hydrous silicates of aluminum and sometimes other metals formed chiefly in weathering processes and occurring esp. in clay and shale

clay·more \ˈklā-ˌmō(ə)r, -ˌmȯ(ə)r\ *n* [ScGael *claidheamh mōr*, lit., great sword] : a large 2-edged sword formerly used by Scottish Highlanders; *also* : their basket-hilted broadsword

clay·pan \-ˌpan\ *n* : hardpan consisting mainly of clay

clay pigeon *n* : a saucer-shaped target usu. made of baked clay and pitch and thrown from a trap in skeet and trapshooting

clay·ware \ˈklā-ˌwa(ə)r, -ˌwe(ə)r\ *n* : articles made of fired clay

cld *abbr* **1** called **2** cleared

[1]**clean** \ˈklēn\ *adj* [ME *clene*, fr. OE *clǣne*; akin to OHG *kleini* delicate, dainty, Gk *glainoi* ornaments] **1** **a** : free from dirt or pollution ⟨changed to ~ clothes⟩ ⟨ship with a ~ bottom⟩ **b** : free from contamination or disease **c** : relatively free from radioactive fallout ⟨a ~ atomic explosion⟩ **2** **a** : UNADULTERATED, PURE ⟨the ~ thrill of one's first flight⟩ **b** *of a precious stone* : having no interior flaws visible **c** : free from growth that hinders tillage **3** **a** : free from moral corruption or sinister connections of any kind ⟨a candidate with a ~ record⟩ **b** : free from offensive treatment of sexual subjects and from the use of obscenity ⟨do you know a ~ joke⟩ **c** : observing the rules : FAIR ⟨a ~ fight⟩ **4** : ceremonially or spiritually pure ⟨and all who are ~ may eat flesh — Lev 7:19 (RSV)⟩ **5** **a** : THOROUGH, COMPLETE ⟨a ~ break with the past⟩ **b** : deftly executed : SKILLFUL ⟨~ ballet technique⟩ **6** **a** : relatively free from error or blemish : CLEAR; *specif* : LEGIBLE ⟨~ copy⟩ **b** : UNENCUMBERED ⟨~ bill of sale⟩ **7** **a** : characterized by clarity and precision : TRIM ⟨a ~ prose style⟩ ⟨architecture with ~ almost austere lines⟩ **b** : EVEN, SMOOTH ⟨a ~ edge⟩ ⟨a sharp blow causing a ~ break⟩ **8** **a** : EMPTY ⟨the whaling ship returned with a ~ hold⟩ **b** *slang* : carrying no concealed weapons **9** : habitually neat — **clean·ness** \ˈklēn-nəs\ *n*

[2]**clean** *adv* **1** **a** : so as to clean ⟨a new broom sweeps ~⟩ **b** : in a clean manner ⟨play the game ~⟩ **2** : all the way : COMPLETELY ⟨the bullet went ~ through his arm⟩

[3]**clean** *vt* **1** : to rid of dirt, impurities, or extraneous matter **2** **a** : STRIP, EMPTY ⟨the tree was ~*ed* of fruit by hurricane winds⟩ ⟨the hungry men quickly ~*ed* the platter⟩ **b** : to deprive of money or possessions — often used with *out* ⟨they ~*ed* him out completely⟩ ~ *vi* : to undergo or perform a process of cleaning ⟨~ up before dinner⟩ — **clean·able** \ˈklē-nə-bəl\ *adj* — **clean·er** *n* — **clean house** **1** : to clean a house and its furniture **2** : to eradicate whatever is obstructive, thwarting, or degrading

[4]**clean** *n* : an act of cleaning dirt esp. from the surface of something

clean and jerk *n* : a lift in weight lifting in which the weight is raised to shoulder height, held momentarily, and then quickly thrust overhead usu. with a lunge or a spring from the legs — compare PRESS, SNATCH

clean–cut \ˈklēn-ˈkət\ *adj* **1** : cut so that the surface or edge is smooth and even **2** : sharply defined **3** : of wholesome appearance

clean·er \ˈklē-nər\ *n* **1** : one whose work is cleaning **2** : a preparation for cleaning **3** : an implement or machine for cleaning — **to the cleaners** *slang* : to or through the experience of being deprived of all one's money

clean·hand·ed \ˈklēn-ˈhan-dəd\ *adj* : innocent of wrongdoing

cleaning woman *n* : a woman who hires herself out for housecleaning

clean–limbed \ˈklēn-ˈlimd\ *adj* : well proportioned : TRIM ⟨~ youths⟩

[1]**clean·ly** \ˈklen-lē\ *adj* **clean·li·er**; **-est** **1** : careful to keep clean : FASTIDIOUS **2** : habitually kept clean — **clean·li·ness** *n*

[2]**clean·ly** \ˈklēn-lē\ *adv* : in a clean manner

clean room \ˈklēn-ˌ\ *n* : a room for the manufacture or assembly of objects (as precision parts) that is maintained at a high level of cleanliness by special means

cleanse \ˈklenz\ *vb* **cleansed**; **cleans·ing** [ME *clensen*, fr. OE *clǣnsian* to purify, fr. *clǣne* clean] : CLEAN

cleans·er \ˈklen-zər\ *n* **1** : one that cleanses **2** : a preparation (as a scouring powder or a skin cream) used for cleaning

[1]**clean·up** \ˈklē-ˌnəp\ *n* **1** : an act or instance of cleaning **2** : an exceptionally large profit : KILLING

[2]**cleanup** *adj* : being in the fourth position in the batting order of a baseball team

clean up \(ˈ)klē-ˈnəp\ *vi* : to make a spectacular profit in a business enterprise or a killing in speculation or gambling

[1]**clear** \ˈkli(ə)r\ *adj* [ME *clere*, fr. OF *cler*, fr. L *clarus* clear, bright; akin to L *calare* to call — more at LOW] **1** **a** : BRIGHT, LUMINOUS **b** : CLOUDLESS; *specif* : less than one-tenth covered ⟨a ~ sky⟩ **c** : free from mist, haze, or dust ⟨a ~ day⟩ **d** : UNTROUBLED, SERENE ⟨a ~ gaze⟩ **2** : CLEAN, PURE: as **a** : free from blemishes **b** : easily seen through : TRANSPARENT **c** : free from abnormal sounds on auscultation **3** **a** : easily heard **b** : easily visible : PLAIN **c** : free from obscurity or ambiguity : easily understood : UNMISTAKABLE **4** **a** : capable of sharp discernment : KEEN **b** : free from doubt : SURE **5** : free from guile or guilt : INNOCENT **6** : unhampered by restriction or limitation: as **a** : unencumbered by debts or charges **b** : NET ⟨a ~ profit⟩ **c** : UNQUALIFIED, ABSOLUTE **d** : free from obstruction **e** : emptied of contents or cargo **f** : free from entanglement **g** : BARE, DENUDED — **clear·ly** *adv* — **clear·ness** *n*

syn **1** CLEAR, PERSPICUOUS, LUCID *shared meaning element* : quickly and easily understood ***ant*** unintelligible, abstruse **2** see EVIDENT

[2]**clear** *adv* **1** : in a clear manner ⟨to cry loud and ~⟩ **2** : all the way ⟨can see ~ to the mountains on a day like this⟩

[3]**clear** *vt* **1** **a** : to make clear or translucent **b** : to free from pollution or cloudiness **2** **a** : to free from accusation or blame : VINDICATE ⟨the opportunity to ~ himself⟩ **b** : to certify as trustworthy ⟨~ a man for top secret military work⟩ **3** **a** : to give insight to : ENLIGHTEN **b** : to make intelligible : EXPLAIN ⟨~ up the mystery⟩ **4** **a** : to free from obstruction: as (1) : OPEN (2) : DISENTANGLE ⟨~ a fishing line⟩ (3) : to rid or make a rasping noise as if ridding (the throat) of phlegm (4) : to erase accumulated totals or stored data from (as a business machine or computer memory) **b** (1) : to submit for approval (2) : AUTHORIZE ⟨the chairman ~*ed* the article for publication⟩ **5** **a** : to free from obligation or encumbrance **b** : SETTLE, DISCHARGE ⟨~ an account⟩ **c** (1) : to free (a ship or shipment) by payment of duties or harbor fees (2) : to pass through (customs) **d** : to gain without deduction : NET ⟨~ a profit⟩ **e** : to put through a clearinghouse **6** **a** : to get rid of : REMOVE ⟨~ the land of trees and brush⟩ **b** : TRANSMIT, DISPATCH **7** **a** : to go over, under, or by without touching **b** : PASS ⟨the bill ~*ed* the legislature⟩ ~ *vi* **1** **a** : to become clear ⟨it ~*ed* up quickly after the rain⟩ **b** : to go away : VANISH ⟨the symptoms ~*ed* gradually⟩ **c** : SELL **2** **a** : to obtain permission to discharge cargo **b** : to conform to regulations or pay requisite fees prior to leaving port **3** : to pass through a clearinghouse **4** : to go to an authority (as for approval) before becoming effective — **clear·able** \ˈklir-ə-bəl\ *adj* — **clear·er** \ˈklir-ər\ *n* — **clear the air** *also* **clear the atmosphere** : to remove elements of hostility, tension, confusion, or uncertainty from the mood or temper of the time

[4]**clear** *n* **1** : a clear space or part **2** : a high arcing shot over an opponent's head in badminton — **in the clear** **1** : in inside measurement **2** : free from guilt or suspicion **3** : in plaintext : not in code or cipher ⟨a message sent *in the clear*⟩

clear–air turbulence *n* : sudden severe turbulence occurring in cloudless regions that causes violent jarring or buffeting of aircraft — abbr. *CAT*

clear·ance \ˈklir-ən(t)s\ *n* **1** : an act or process of clearing: as **a** : the act of clearing a ship at the customhouse; *also* : the papers showing that a ship has cleared **b** : the offsetting of checks and other claims among banks through a clearinghouse **c** : certification as clear of objection : AUTHORIZATION **d** : a sale to clear out stock **2** : the distance by which one object clears another or the clear space between them

[1]**clear–cut** \ˈkli(ə)r-ˈkət\ *adj* **1** : sharply outlined : DISTINCT **2** : free from ambiguity or uncertainty : UNAMBIGUOUS ***syn*** see INCISIVE

[2]**clear–cut** *vt* **-cut**; **-cut·ting** : to cut all the trees in (a stand of timber)

clear–eyed \ˈkli(ə)r-ˈīd\ *adj* **1** : having clear eyes **2** : DISCERNING

clear·head·ed \-ˈhed-əd\ *adj* : having a clear understanding : PERCEPTIVE — **clear·head·ed·ly** *adv* — **clear·head·ed·ness** *n*

clear·ing \ˈkli(ə)r-iŋ\ *n* **1** : the act or process of making or becoming clear **2** : a tract of land cleared of wood and brush **3** **a** : a method of exchanging and offsetting commercial papers or accounts with cash settlement only of the balances due after the clearing **b** *pl* : the gross amount of balances so adjusted

clear·ing·house \-ˌhau̇s\ *n* **1** : an establishment maintained by banks for settling mutual claims and accounts **2** : a central agency for the collection, classification, and distribution esp. of information

clear–sight·ed \ˈkli(ə)r-ˈsīt-əd\ *adj* **1** : having clear vision **2** : DISCERNING — **clear–sight·ed·ly** *adv* — **clear–sight·ed·ness** *n*

clear·wing \-ˌwiŋ\ *n* : a moth (as of the families Aegeriidae or Sphingidae) having the wings largely transparent and devoid of scales

[1]**cleat** \ˈklēt\ *n* [ME *clete* wedge, fr. (assumed) OE *clēat*; akin to MHG *klōz* lump — more at CLOUT] **1** **a** : a wedge-shaped piece fastened to or projecting from something and serving as a support or check **b** : a wooden or metal fitting usu. with two projecting horns around which a rope may be made fast **2** **a** : a strip fas-

ə abut	ᵊ kitten	ər further	a back	ā bake	ä cot, cart
au̇ out	ch chin	e less	ē easy	g gift	i trip	ī life
j joke	ŋ sing	ō flow	ȯ flaw	ȯi coin	th thin	t͟h this
ü loot	u̇ foot	y yet	yü few	yu̇ furious	zh vision

tened across something to give strength or hold in position **b** (1) : a projecting piece (as on the bottom of a shoe) that furnishes a grip (2) *pl* : shoes equipped with cleats

²cleat *vt* **1** : to secure to or by a cleat **2** : to provide with a cleat

cleav·able \ˈklē-və-bəl\ *adj* : capable of being split

cleav·age \ˈklē-vij\ *n* **1 a** : the quality of a crystallized substance or rock of splitting along definite planes **b** : a fragment (as of a diamond) obtained by splitting **2** : the action of cleaving : the state of being cleft **3** : cell division; *esp* : the series of mitotic divisions of the egg that results in the formation of the blastomeres and changes the single-celled zygote into a multicellular embryo **4** : the splitting of a molecule into simpler molecules **5** : the depression between a woman's breasts esp. when made visible by the wearing of a low-cut dress

¹cleave \ˈklēv\ *vi* **cleaved** \ˈklēvd\ *or* **clove** \ˈklōv\ *also* **clave** \ˈklāv\; **cleav·ing** [ME *clevien,* fr. OE *clifian*] : to adhere firmly and closely or loyally and unwaveringly ***syn*** see STICK

²cleave *vb* **cleaved** \ˈklēvd\ *also* **cleft** \ˈkleft\ *or* **clove** \ˈklōv\; **cleaved** *also* **cleft** *or* **clo·ven** \ˈklō-vən\; **cleav·ing** [ME *cleven,* fr. OE *clēofan;* akin to ON *kljūfa* to split, L *glubere* to peel, Gk *glyphein* to carve] *vt* **1** : to divide by or as if by a cutting blow : SPLIT **2** : to separate into distinct parts and esp. into groups having divergent views ~ *vi* **1** : to split esp. along the grain **2** : to penetrate or pass through something by or as if by cutting ***syn*** see TEAR

cleav·er \ˈklē-vər\ *n* **1** : one that cleaves; *esp* : a butcher's implement for cutting animal carcasses into joints or pieces **2** : a rock ridge protruding from a glacier or snowfield

cleav·ers \ˈklē-vərz\ *n pl but sing or pl in constr* [ME *clivre,* alter. of OE *clife* burdock, cleavers; akin to OE *clifian* to cleave, adhere] **1** : an annual plant (*Galium aparine*) of the madder family that has numerous stalked white flowers, stems covered with curved prickles, and whorls of bristle-tipped leaves **2** : a plant related to cleavers

cleek \ˈklēk\ *n* [ME (northern) *cleke,* fr. *cleken* to clutch] *chiefly Scot* : a large hook (as for a pot over a fire)

clef \ˈklef\ *n* [F, lit., key, fr. L *clavis* — more at CLAVICLE] : a sign placed at the beginning of a musical staff to determine the position of the notes

¹cleft \ˈkleft\ *n* [ME *clift,* fr. OE *geclyft;* akin to OE *clēofan* to cleave] **1** : a space or opening made by splitting : FISSURE **2** : a usu. V-shaped indented formation : a hollow between ridges or protuberances ⟨the anal ~ of the human body⟩

²cleft *adj* [ME, fr. pp. of *cleven*] : partially split or divided; *specif* : divided about halfway to the midrib ⟨a ~ leaf⟩

cleft palate *n* : congenital fissure of the roof of the mouth

cleis·tog·a·my \klī-ˈstäg-ə-mē\ *n* [Gk *kleistos* closed (fr. *kleiein* to close) + ISV *-gamy* — more at CLOSE] : the production (as in violets) of small inconspicuous closed self-pollinating flowers additional to and often more fruitful than the showier type — **cleis·tog·a·mous** \-məs\ *or* **cleis·to·gam·ic** \ˌklī-stə-ˈgam-ik\ *adj* — **cleis·tog·a·mous·ly** *adv*

cle·ma·tis \ˈklem-ət-əs; kli-ˈmat-əs, -ˈmāt-, -ˈmät-\ *n* [NL, genus name, fr. L, fr. Gk *klēmatis* brushwood, clematis, fr. *klēmat-, klēma* twig, fr. Gk *klan* to break — more at HALT] : a vine or herb (genera *Clematis, Atragene,* or *Viorna*) of the buttercup family having three leaflets on each leaf and usu. white or purple flowers

clem·en·cy \ˈklem-ən-sē\ *n, pl* **-cies 1 a** : disposition to be merciful and esp. to moderate the severity of punishment due **b** : an act or instance of leniency **2** : pleasant mildness of weather ***syn*** see MERCY ***ant*** harshness

clem·ent \ˈklem-ənt\ *adj* [ME, fr. L *clement-, clemens*] **1** : inclined to be merciful : LENIENT ⟨a ~ judge⟩ **2** : MILD ⟨~ weather for November⟩ — **clem·ent·ly** *adv*

¹clench \ˈklench\ *vt* [ME *clenchen,* fr. OE *-clencan;* akin to OE *clingan* to cling] **1** : CLINCH 1 **2** : to hold fast : CLUTCH ⟨he ~*ed* the arms of his chair⟩ **3** : to set or close tightly ⟨~*ed* his teeth⟩ ⟨~*ed* his fists⟩

²clench *n* **1** : the end of a nail that is turned back in clinching it **2** : an act or instance of clenching

clepe \ˈklēp\ *vt* **cleped** \ˈklēpt, ˈklept\; **cleped** *or* **ycleped** \i-\ *or* **yclept** \i-ˈklept \; **clep·ing** \ˈklē-piŋ\ [ME *clepen,* fr. OE *clipian* to speak, call; akin to OFris *kleppa* to ring, knock] *archaic* : NAME, CALL

clep·sy·dra \ˈklep-sə-drə\ *n, pl* **-dras** *or* **-drae** \-ˌdrē, -ˌdrī\ [L, fr. Gk *klepsydra,* fr. *kleptein* to steal + *hydōr* water — more at KLEPT-, WATER] : WATER CLOCK

clere·sto·ry *or* **clear·sto·ry** \ˈkli(ə)r-ˌstōr-ē, -ˌstȯr-\ *n* [ME, fr. *clere* clear + *story*] **1** : an outside wall of a room or building that rises above an adjoining roof and contains windows **2** : GALLERY **3** : a ventilating section of a railroad car roof

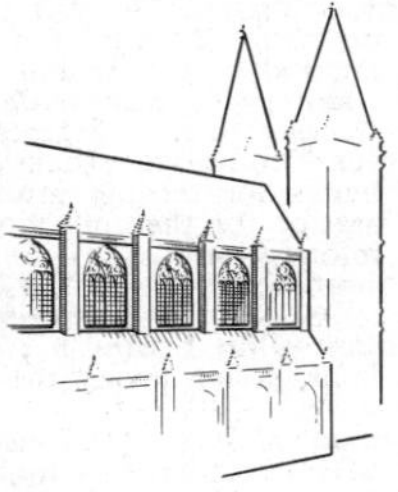

clerestory 1

cler·gy \ˈklər-jē\ *n* [ME *clergie,* fr. OF, knowledge, learning, fr. *clerc* clergyman] **1** : a group ordained to perform pastoral or sacerdotal functions in a Christian church **2** : the official or sacerdotal class of a non-Christian religion

cler·gy·man \-ji-mən\ *n* : a member of the clergy

cler·ic \ˈkler-ik\ *n* [LL *clericus*] : a member of the clergy; *specif* : one in orders below the grade of priest

¹cler·i·cal \ˈkler-i-kəl\ *adj* **1** : of, relating to, or characteristic of the clergy, a clergyman, or a cleric **2** : of or relating to a clerk or office worker — **cler·i·cal·ly** \-i-k(ə-)lē\ *adv*

²clerical *n* **1** : CLERGYMAN **2** : CLERICALIST **3** : CLERK

clerical collar *n* : a narrow stiffly upright white collar worn buttoned at the back of the neck by clergymen

cler·i·cal·ism \ˈkler-i-kə-ˌliz-əm\ *n* : a policy of maintaining or increasing the power of a religious hierarchy

cler·i·cal·ist \-ləst\ *n* : one that favors maintained or increased ecclesiastical power and influence

cler·i·hew \ˈkler-i-ˌhyü\ *n* [Edmund *Clerihew* Bentley †1956 E writer] : a light verse quatrain rhyming *aabb* and usu. dealing with a person named in the initial rhyme

cler·i·sy \ˈkler-ə-sē\ *n* [G *klerisei* clergy, fr. ML *clericia,* fr. LL *clericus* cleric] : INTELLIGENTSIA

¹clerk \ˈklərk, *Brit usu rhymes with "lark"*\ *n* [ME, fr. OF *clerc* & OE *cleric, clerc,* both fr. LL *clericus,* fr. LGk *klērikos,* fr. Gk *klēros* lot, inheritance (in allusion to Deut 18:2); akin to Gk *klan* to break — more at HALT] **1** : CLERIC **2** *archaic* : SCHOLAR **3 a** : an official responsible for correspondence, records, and accounts ⟨city ~⟩ **b** : one employed to keep records or accounts or to perform general office work **c** : one who works at a sales or service counter

²clerk *vi* : to act or work as a clerk ⟨~*ed* in his father's store⟩

clerk·ly \ˈklər-klē\ *adj* **1** : of, relating to, or characteristic of a clerk **2** *archaic* : SCHOLARLY — **clerkly** *adv*

clerk regular *n, pl* **clerks regular** : a Roman Catholic religious combining life in a monastic community with the ministry of a diocesan priest

clerk·ship \ˈklərk-ˌship\ *n* : the office or business of a clerk

clev·er \ˈklev-ər\ *adj* [ME *cliver,* prob. of Scand origin; akin to ON *kljūfa* to split — more at CLEAVE] **1 a** : skillful or adroit in using the hands or body : NIMBLE **b** : mentally quick and resourceful but often lacking in depth and soundness **2** : marked by wit or ingenuity **3** *dial* **a** : GOOD **b** : easy to use or handle — **clev·er·ish** \-(ə-)rish\ *adj* — **clev·er·ly** \-ər-lē\ *adv* — **clev·er·ness** \-ər-nəs\ *n*

syn* 1** see INTELLIGENT ***ant dull

2 CLEVER, ADROIT, CUNNING, INGENIOUS *shared meaning element* : having or showing practical wit or skill in contriving

clev·is \ˈklev-əs\ *n* [earlier *clevi,* prob. of Scand origin; akin to ON *kljūfa* to split] : a usu. U-shaped metal shackle that has the ends drilled to receive a pin or bolt and that is used for attaching or suspending parts

¹clew *or* **clue** \ˈklü\ *n* [ME *clewe,* fr. OE *cliewen;* akin to OHG *kliuwa* ball, Skt *glau* lump] **1** : a ball of thread, yarn, or cord **2** *usu clue* : something that guides through an intricate procedure or maze of difficulties; *specif* : a piece of evidence that leads one toward the solution of a problem **3 a** : a lower corner or only the after corner of a sail **b** : a metal loop attached to the lower corner of a sail **c** *pl* : a combination of lines by which a hammock is suspended

²clew *or* **clue** *vt* **clewed** *or* **clued; clew·ing** *or* **clue·ing** *or* **clu·ing 1** : to roll into a ball **2** *usu clue* **a** : to provide with a clue **b** : to give reliable information to ⟨~ me in on how it happened⟩ **3** : to haul (a sail) up or down by ropes through the clews

cli·ché \kli-ˈshā\ *n* [F, lit., stereotype, fr. pp. of *clicher* to stereotype, of imit. origin] **1** : a trite phrase or expression; *also* : the idea expressed by it **2** : a hackneyed theme or situation — **cliché** *adj*

cli·chéd \-ˈshād\ *adj* **1** : marked by or abounding in clichés **2** : HACKNEYED

¹click \ˈklik\ *n* [prob. imit.] **1 a** : a slight sharp noise **b** : a speech sound in some languages made by enclosing air between two stop articulations of the tongue, enlarging the enclosure to rarefy the air, and suddenly opening the enclosure **2** : DETENT

²click *vt* : to strike, move, or produce with a click ⟨~*ed* his heels together⟩ ~ *vi* **1** : to make a click ⟨the Geiger counter was ~*ing* furiously⟩ **2 a** : to fit or agree exactly **b** : to fit together : hit it off ⟨they did not ~ as friends⟩ **c** : to function smoothly **d** : SUCCEED ⟨a movie that ~*s*⟩

click beetle *n* : any of a family (Elateridae) of beetles able to right themselves with a click when inverted

click stop *n* : a turnable control device (as for a camera diaphragm opening) that engages with a definite click at specific setting positions

cli·ent \ˈklī-ənt\ *n* [ME, fr. MF & L; MF *client,* fr. L *client-, cliens;* akin to L *clinare* to lean — more at LEAN] **1** : a person under the protection of another : DEPENDENT **2 a** : a person who engages the professional advice or services of another ⟨a lawyer's ~*s*⟩ **b** : CUSTOMER ⟨hotel ~*s*⟩ **c** : a person served by or utilizing the services of a social agency ⟨a welfare ~⟩ — **cli·ent·age** \-ən-tij\ *n* — **cli·en·tal** \klī-ˈent-ᵊl,ˈklī-ənt-\ *adj*

cli·en·tele \ˌklī-ən-ˈtel, ˌklē-ən- *also* ˌklē-ˌän-\ *n* [F *clientèle,* fr. L *clientela,* fr. *client-, cliens*] : a body of clients ⟨a shop that caters to an exclusive ~⟩

cliff \ˈklif\ *n* [ME *clif,* fr. OE; akin to OE *clifian* to adhere to] : a very steep, vertical, or overhanging face of rock, earth, or ice : PRECIPICE — **cliffy** \ˈklif-ē\ *adj*

cliff dweller *n* **1** *often cap C&D* **a** : a member of a prehistoric Amerindian people of the southwestern U.S. who built their homes on rock ledges or in the natural recesses of canyon walls and cliffs **b** : a member of any cliff-dwelling people **2** : a person who lives in a large usu. metropolitan apartment building — **cliff dwelling** *n*

cliff–hang \ˈklif-ˌhaŋ\ *vi* [back-formation fr. *cliff-hanger*] : to end an installment of a cliff-hanger with a suspenseful melodramatic unresolved conflict; *also* : to await the outcome of a suspenseful situation

cliff–hang·er \-ˌhaŋ-ər\ *n* **1** : an adventure serial or melodrama; *esp* : one presented in installments each ending in suspense **2** : a contest whose outcome is in doubt up to the very end

¹cli·mac·ter·ic \klī-ˈmak-t(ə-)rik, ˌklī-ˌmak-ˈter-ik\ *adj* [L *climactericus,* fr. Gk *klimaktērikos,* fr. *klimaktēr* critical point, lit., rung of a ladder, fr. *klimak-, klimax* ladder] **1** : constituting or relating to a critical period (as of life) **2** : CRITICAL, CRUCIAL

²climacteric *n* **1** : a major turning point or critical stage **2** : MENOPAUSE; *also* : a corresponding period in the male during which sexual activity and competence are reduced **3** : the maximum to which the respiratory rate of fruit rises just prior to full ripening

cli·mac·tic \klī-'mak-tik\ *adj* : of, relating to, or constituting a climax — **cli·mac·ti·cal·ly** \-ti-k(ə-)lē\ *adv*
cli·mate \'klī-mət\ *n* [ME *climat*, fr. MF, fr. LL *climat-, clima*, fr. Gk *klimat-, klima* inclination, latitude, climate, fr. *klinein* to lean — more at LEAN] **1** : a region of the earth having specified climatic conditions **2** : the average course or condition of the weather at a place over a period of years as exhibited by temperature, wind velocity, and precipitation **3** : the prevailing temper or environmental conditions characterizing a group or period : MILIEU ⟨a ~ of fear⟩ — **cli·mat·ic** \klī-'mat-ik\ *adj* — **cli·mat·i·cal·ly** \-i-k(ə-)lē\ *adv*
cli·ma·tol·o·gy \,klī-mə-'täl-ə-jē\ *n* : the science that deals with climates and their phenomena — **cli·ma·to·log·i·cal** \,klī-mət-ᵊl-'äj-i-kəl\ *adj* — **cli·ma·to·log·i·cal·ly** \-k(ə-)lē\ *adv* — **cli·ma·tol·o·gist** \-mə-'täl-ə-jəst\ *n*
1**cli·max** \'klī-,maks\ *n* [L, fr. Gk *klimax* ladder, fr. *klinein* to lean] **1** : a figure of speech in which a series of phrases or sentences is arranged in ascending order of rhetorical forcefulness **2 a** : the highest point : CULMINATION **b** : the point of highest dramatic tension or a major turning point in the action (as of a play) **c** : ORGASM **d** : MENOPAUSE **3** : a relatively stable stage or community esp. of plants that is achieved through successful adjustment to an environment; *esp* : the final stage in ecological succession ***syn*** see SUMMIT
2**climax** *vi* : to come to a climax ⟨a riot ~*ing* in the destruction of several houses⟩ ~ *vt* : to bring to a climax ⟨~*ed* his boxing career with a knockout⟩
1**climb** \'klīm\ *vb* [ME *climben*, fr. OE *climban*; akin to OE *clamm* bond, fetter — more at CLAM] *vi* **1 a** : to go upward with gradual or continuous progress : RISE ⟨watching the smoke ~⟩ ⟨the airplane ~*ed* slowly⟩ **b** : to slope upward ⟨the road ~*s* steadily⟩ **2 a** : to go upward or raise oneself esp. by grasping or clutching with the hands ⟨~*ed* upon her father's knee⟩ **b** *of a plant* : to ascend in growth (as by twining) **3** : to go about or down usu. by grasping or holding with the hands ⟨~ down the ladder⟩ **4** : to get into or out of clothing usu. with some haste or effort ⟨the firemen ~*ed* into their clothes⟩ ~ *vt* **1** : to go upward on or along, to the top of, or over ⟨~ a hill⟩ **2** : to draw or pull oneself up, over, or to the top of by using hands and feet ⟨children ~*ing* the tree⟩ **3** : to grow up or over ***syn*** see ASCEND ***ant*** descend — **climb·able** \'klī-mə-bəl\ *adj*
2**climb** *n* **1** : a place where climbing is necessary to progress **2** : the act or an instance of climbing : ascent by climbing
climb·er \'klī-mər\ *n* : one that climbs or helps in climbing
climbing iron *n* : a steel framework with spikes attached that may be affixed to one's boots for climbing

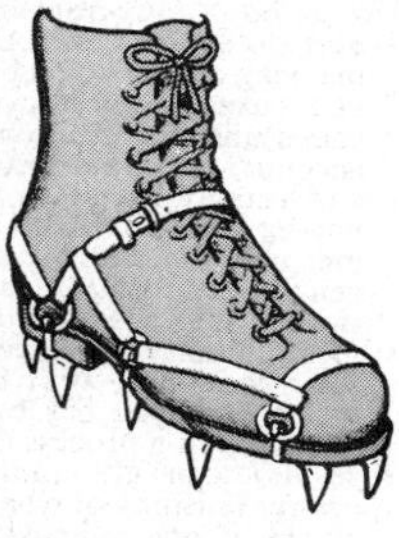
climbing iron

clime \'klīm\ *n* [LL *clima*] : CLIMATE ⟨traveled to warmer ~*s*⟩
clin *abbr* clinical
clin- *or* **clino-** *comb form* [NL, fr. Gk *klinein* to lean — more at LEAN] : lean : slant ⟨*clino*meter⟩
-cli·nal \'klīn-ᵊl\ *adj comb form* [ISV, fr. Gk *klinein*] : sloping ⟨mono*clinal*⟩
1**clinch** \'klinch\ *vb* [prob. alter. of 1*clench*] *vt* **1 a** : to turn over or flatten the protruding pointed end of (a driven nail); *also* : to treat (a screw, bolt, or rivet) in a similar way **b** : to fasten in this way **2** : CLENCH 3 **3** : to make final or irrefutable : SETTLE ⟨that ~*ed* the argument⟩ ~ *vi* **1** : to hold an opponent (as in boxing) at close quarters with one or both arms **2** : to hold fast or firmly — **clinch·ing·ly** \'klin-chiŋ-lē\ *adv*
2**clinch** *n* **1** : a fastening by means of a clinched nail, rivet, or bolt; *also* : the clinched part of a nail, rivet, or bolt **2** *archaic* : PUN **3** : an act or instance of clinching in boxing
clinch·er \'klin-chər\ *n* : one that clinches: as **a** : a decisive fact, argument, act, or remark ⟨the expense was the ~ that persuaded us to give up the enterprise⟩ **b** : an automobile tire with flanged beads fitting into the wheel rim
cline \'klīn\ *n* [Gk *klinein* to lean] : a graded series of morphological or physiological differences exhibited by a group of related organisms usu. along a line of environmental or geographic transition — **clin·al** \'klīn-ᵊl\ *adj* — **clin·al·ly** \-ᵊl-ē\ *adv*
-cline \,klīn\ *n comb form* [back-formation fr. *-clinal*] : slope ⟨mono*cline*⟩
1**cling** \'kliŋ\ *vi* **clung** \'kləŋ\; **cling·ing** [ME *clingen*, fr. OE *clingan*; akin to OHG *klunga* tangled ball of thread, MIr *glacc* hand] **1 a** : to hold together **b** : to adhere as if glued firmly **c** : to hold or hold on tightly or tenaciously **2 a** : to have a strong emotional attachment or dependence **b** : to remain or linger as if resisting complete dissipation or dispersal ⟨the odor *clung* to the room for hours⟩ ***syn*** see STICK — **clingy** \'kliŋ-ē\ *adj*
2**cling** *n* : an act or instance of clinging : ADHERENCE
cling·stone \'kliŋ-,stōn\ *n* : a fruit (as a peach) whose flesh adheres strongly to the pit
clin·ic \'klin-ik\ *n* [F *clinique*, fr. Gk *klinikē* medical practice at the sickbed, fr. fem. of *klinikos* of a bed, fr. *klinē* bed, fr. *klinein* to lean, recline — more at LEAN] **1** : a class of medical instruction in which patients are examined and discussed **2** : a group meeting devoted to the analysis and solution of concrete problems or to the acquiring of specific skills or knowledge in a particular field ⟨writing ~*s*⟩ ⟨golf ~*s*⟩ **3 a** : a facility (as of a hospital) for diagnosis and treatment of outpatients **b** : a group practice in which several physicians work cooperatively
-clin·ic \'klin-ik\ *adj comb form* [ISV, fr. Gk *klinein*] **1** : inclining : dipping ⟨iso*clinic*⟩ **2** : having (so many) oblique intersections of the axes ⟨mono*clinic*⟩ ⟨tri*clinic*⟩
clin·i·cal \'klin-i-kəl\ *adj* **1** : of, relating to, or conducted in or as if in a clinic: as **a** : involving direct observation of the patient **b** : apparent to or based on clinical observation **2** : analytical, detached, or coolly dispassionate ⟨a ~ attitude⟩ — **clin·i·cal·ly** \-k(ə-)lē\ *adv*
clinical thermometer *n* : a thermometer for measuring body temperature that has a constriction in the tube where the column of liquid breaks and continues to indicate the maximum temperature to which the thermometer was exposed until reset by shaking
cli·ni·cian \klin-'ish-ən\ *n* : one qualified in the clinical practice of medicine, psychiatry, or psychology as distinguished from one specializing in laboratory or research techniques
clinico- *comb form* : clinical and ⟨*clinico*pathological⟩ ⟨*clinico*statistical⟩
clin·i·co·path·o·log·ic \'klin-i-(,)kō-,path-ə-'läj-ik\ *or* **clin·i·co·path·o·log·i·cal** \-'läj-i-kəl\ *adj* : involving both clinical and pathologic factors, aspects, or approaches — **clin·i·co·path·o·log·i·cal·ly** \-i-k(ə-)lē\ *adv*
1**clink** \'kliŋk\ *vb* [ME *clinken*, of imit. origin] *vi* : to give out a slight sharp short metallic sound ~ *vt* : to cause to clink
2**clink** *n* : a clinking sound
3**clink** *n* [*Clink*, a prison in Southwark, London, England] *slang* : a prison cell : JAIL
1**clin·ker** \'kliŋ-kər\ *n* [alter. of earlier *klincard* (a hard yellowish Dutch brick)] **1** : a brick that has been burned too much in the kiln **2** : stony matter fused together : SLAG
2**clinker** *vb* **clin·kered; clin·ker·ing** \'kliŋ-k(ə-)riŋ\ *vt* **1** : to cause to form clinker **2** : to clear out the clinkers from ~ *vi* : to turn to clinker under heat
3**clink·er** \'kliŋ-kər\ *n* [1*clink*] **1** *Brit* : something first-rate **2 a** : a wrong note **b** : a serious mistake or error : BONER **c** : an utter failure : FLOP ⟨the play turned out to be a ~⟩
clink·er–built \-,bilt\ *adj* [*clinker*, n. (clinch)] : having the external planks or plates overlapping like the clapboards on a house ⟨a ~ boat⟩
clink·ety–clank \,kliŋ-kət-ē-'klaŋk\ *n* [imit.] : a repeated usu. rhythmic clanking sound ⟨the ~ of a loose tire chain⟩
cli·nom·e·ter \klī-'näm-ət-ər\ *n* : any of various instruments for measuring angles of elevation or inclination — **cli·no·met·ric** \,klī-nə-'me-trik\ *adj* — **cli·nom·e·try** \klī-'näm-ə-trē\ *n*
-cli·nous \'klī-nəs\ *adj comb form* [prob. fr. NL *-clinus*, fr. Gk *klinē* bed — more at CLINIC] : having the androecium and gynoecium in a (single or different) flower or (two separate) flowers ⟨di*clinous*⟩
1**clin·quant** \'kliŋ-kənt, klaⁿ-käⁿ\ *adj* [MF, fr. prp. of *clinquer* to glitter, lit., to clink, of imit. origin] : glittering with gold or tinsel
2**clinquant** *n* [F, fr. *clinquant*, adj.] : imitation gold leaf : TINSEL
clin·to·nia \klin-'tō-nē-ə\ *n* [NL, genus name, fr. DeWitt *Clinton*] : any of a genus (*Clintonia*) of herbs of the lily family with yellow or white flowers
Clio \'klī-(,)ō, 'klē-\ *n* [L, fr. Gk *Kleiō*] **1** : the Greek Muse of history **2** *pl* **Cli·os** : a statuette awarded annually by a professional organization for notable achievement in radio and television commercials
1**clip** \'klip\ *vb* **clipped; clip·ping** [ME *clippen*, fr. OE *clyppan*; akin to OHG *klāftra* fathom, L *gleba* clod, *globus* globe] *vt* **1** : ENCOMPASS **2 a** : to hold in a tight grip : CLUTCH **b** : to clasp or fasten with a clip
2**clip** *n* **1** : any of various devices that grip, clasp, or hook **2** : a device to hold cartridges for charging the magazines of some rifles; *also* : a magazine from which ammunition is fed into the chamber of a firearm **3** : a piece of jewelry held in position by a spring clip
3**clip** *vb* **clipped; clip·ping** [ME *clippen*, fr. ON *klippa*] *vt* **1 a** : to cut or cut off with or as if with shears ⟨~ a dog's hair⟩ ⟨~ an hour off traveling time⟩ **b** : to cut off the distal or outer part of **c** (1) : 3EXCISE (2) : to cut items out of (as a newspaper) **2 a** : CURTAIL, DIMINISH ⟨tried to ~ his influence⟩ **b** : to abbreviate in speech or writing **3** : HIT, PUNCH **4** : to illegally block (an opposing player) in football **5** : to take money from unfairly or dishonestly esp. by overcharging ⟨the nightclub *clipped* the tourist for $200⟩ ~ *vi* **1** : to clip something **2** : to travel or pass rapidly **3** : to clip an opposing player in football
4**clip** *n* **1 a** *pl*, *Scot* : SHEARS **b** : a 2-bladed instrument for cutting esp. the nails **2** : something that is clipped: as **a** : the product of a single shearing (as of sheep) **b** : a crop of wool of a sheep, a flock, or a region **c** : a section of filmed material **d** : a clipping esp. from a newspaper **3** : an act of clipping **4** : a sharp blow **5** : a rapid pace **6** : a single instance or occasion : TIME ⟨he charged $10 a ~⟩ — often used in the phrase *at a clip* ⟨trained 1000 workers at a *clip*⟩
clip·board \'klip-,bō(ə)rd, -,bò(ə)rd\ *n* : a small writing board with a spring clip at the top for holding papers
clip joint *n* **1** *slang* : a place of public entertainment (as a nightclub) that makes a practice of defrauding patrons (as by overcharging) **2** *slang* : a business that makes a practice of overcharging
clip–on \,klip-,òn, -,än\ *adj* : of or relating to something that clips on ⟨a ~ tie⟩ ⟨~ earrings⟩
clip on \(')klip-'òn, -'än\ *vi* : to be capable of being fastened by an attached clip ⟨the medal *clips on* to the coat lapel⟩
clip·per \'klip-ər\ *n* **1** : one that clips something **2** : an implement for clipping esp. hair, fingernails, or toenails — usu. used in pl. **3 a** : one that moves swiftly **b** : a fast sailing ship; *esp* : one with long slender lines, an overhanging bow, tall raking masts, and a large sail area
clip·ping \'klip-iŋ\ *n* : something that is clipped off or out of something; *esp* : an item clipped from a publication
clip·sheet \'klip-,shēt\ *n* : a sheet of newspaper material issued by an organization and usu. printed on only one side to facilitate clipping and reprinting

ə abut ᵊ kitten ər further a back ā bake ä cot, cart
aù out ch chin e less ē easy g gift i trip ī life
j joke ŋ sing ō flow ò flaw òi coin th thin th this
ü loot ù foot y yet yü few yù furious zh vision

clique \'klēk, 'klik\ *n* [F] **:** a narrow exclusive circle or group of persons; *esp* **:** one held together by a presumed identity of interests, views, or purposes ***syn*** see SET — **cliqu·ey** *or* **cliquy** \'klē-kē, 'klik-\ *adj* — **cliqu·ish** \-ish\ *adj* — **cliqu·ish·ly** *adv* — **cliqu·ish·ness** *n*

cli·tel·lum \klī-'tel-əm\ *n, pl* **-la** \-ə\ [NL, modif. of L *clitellae* packsaddle] **:** a thickened glandular section of the body wall of some annelids that secretes a viscid sac in which the eggs are deposited

cli·to·ris \'klit-ə-rəs, 'klīt-\ *n* [NL, fr. Gk *kleitoris*] **:** a small organ at the anterior or ventral part of the vulva homologous to the penis — **cli·to·ral** \'klit-ə-rəl, 'klīt-\ *or* **cli·tor·ic** \kli-'tȯr-ik, klī-, -'tär-\ *adj*

clk *abbr* clerk

clo *abbr* clothing

clo·aca \klō-'ā-kə\ *n, pl* **-acae** \-,kē, -,sē\ [L; akin to Gk *klyzein* to wash] **1 :** 3SEWER **2** [NL, fr. L] **:** the common chamber into which the intestinal, urinary, and generative canals discharge in birds, reptiles, amphibians, and many fishes; *also* **:** a comparable chamber of an invertebrate — **clo·acal** \-'ā-kəl\ *adj*

1**cloak** \'klōk\ *n* [ME *cloke*, fr. ONF *cloque* bell, cloak, fr. ML *clocca* bell; fr. its shape] **1 :** a loose outer garment **2 :** something that conceals **:** PRETENSE, DISGUISE

2**cloak** *vt* **:** to cover or hide with a cloak ***syn*** see DISGUISE

cloak-and-dag·ger *adj* **:** dealing in or suggestive of melodramatic intrigue and action usu. involving secret agents and espionage

cloak·room \'klō-,krüm, -,krům\ *n* **1 a :** a room in which outdoor clothing may be placed during one's stay **b :** a room or cubicle where garments, parcels, and luggage may be checked for temporary safekeeping (as in a theater) **2 :** an anteroom of a legislative chamber where members may keep their wraps, rest, and confer with colleagues

clob·ber \'kläb-ər\ *vt* **clob·bered; clob·ber·ing** \-(ə-)riŋ\ [origin unknown] **1 :** to pound mercilessly; *also* **:** to hit with force **:** SMASH **2 :** to defeat overwhelmingly

cloche \'klōsh\ *n* [F, lit., bell, fr. ML *clocca*] **:** a woman's small helmetlike hat usu. with deep rounded crown and very narrow brim

1**clock** \'kläk\ *n, often attrib* [ME *clok*, fr. MD *clocke* bell, clock, fr. ONF or ML; ONF *cloque* bell, fr. ML *clocca*, of Celt origin; akin to MIr *clocc* bell] **1 :** a device other than a watch for indicating or measuring time commonly by means of hands moving on a dial **2 :** a registering device with a dial and indicator attached to a mechanism to measure or gauge its functioning or to record its output; *specif* **:** SPEEDOMETER **3 :** TIME CLOCK **4 :** a synchronizing device (as in a computer) that produces pulses at regular intervals — **around the clock 1 :** continuously for 24 hours **:** day and night without cessation **2 :** without relaxation and heedless of time — **kill the clock** *or* **run out the clock :** to use up as much as possible of the playing time remaining in a game (as football) while retaining possession of the ball or puck esp. to protect a lead

2**clock** *vt* **1 :** to time with a stopwatch or by an electric timing device **2 :** to register on a mechanical recording device ⟨wind velocities were ~*ed* at 80 miles per hour⟩ ~ *vi* **:** to register on a time sheet or time clock **:** PUNCH — used with *in, out, on, off* ⟨he ~*ed* in late⟩ — **clock·er** *n*

3**clock** *n* [prob. fr. *clock* (bell); fr. its original bell-like shape] **:** an ornamental figure on the ankle or side of a stocking or sock

clock·like \'kläk-,līk\ *adj* **:** unusually regular, undeviating, and precise ⟨does his job with ~ efficiency⟩

clock-watcher \-,wäch-ər\ *n* **:** a person (as a worker or student) who displays lack of zeal or interest esp. by keeping close watch on the passage of time — **clock-watch·ing** \-iŋ\ *n*

clock·wise \'kläk-,wīz\ *adv* **:** in the direction in which the hands of a clock rotate as viewed from in front — **clockwise** *adj*

clock·work \-,wərk\ *n* **1 :** machinery containing a train of wheels of small size (as in a mechanical toy or a bomb-actuating device) **2 :** something that seems to perform in response to clockwork or to be controlled by clockwork

clod \'kläd\ *n* [ME, alter. of *clot*] **1 a :** a lump or mass esp. of earth or clay **b :** SOIL, EARTH **2 :** OAF, DOLT — **clod·dish** \'kläd-ish\ *adj* — **clod·dish·ness** *n* — **clod·dy** \'kläd-ē\ *adj*

clod·hop·per \'kläd-,häp-ər\ *n* **1 :** a clumsy and uncouth rustic **2 :** a large heavy shoe

clod·hop·ping \-,häp-iŋ\ *adj* **:** BOORISH, RUDE

clod·poll *or* **clod·pole** \'kläd-,pōl\ *n* **:** BLOCKHEAD

clo·fi·brate \klō-'fīb-,rāt, -'fib-\ *n* [perh. fr. *ch*lor- + *fibr-* + propio*nate*] **:** a compound $C_{12}H_{15}ClO_3$ used esp. in the treatment of hypercholesterolemia

1**clog** \'kläg\ *n* [ME *clogge* short thick piece of wood] **1 a :** a weight attached esp. to an animal to hinder motion **b :** something that shackles or impedes **:** ENCUMBRANCE 1 **2 :** a shoe, sandal, or overshoe having a thick typically wooden sole

2**clog** *vb* **clogged; clog·ging** *vt* **1 :** ENCUMBER **2 a :** to impede with a clog **:** HINDER **b :** to halt or retard the progress, operation, or growth of ⟨restraints that have been *clogging* the market —T. W. Arnold⟩ **3 :** to fill beyond capacity **:** OVERLOAD ⟨cars *clogged* the main street for hours⟩ ~ *vi* **1 :** to become filled with extraneous matter ⟨the heater *clogged* with dust⟩ **2 :** to unite in a mass **:** CLOT **3 :** to dance a clog dance ***syn*** see HAMPER ***ant*** expedite, facilitate

clog dance *n* **:** a dance in which the performer wears clogs and beats out a clattering rhythm on the floor — **clog dancer** *n* — **clog dancing** *n*

cloi·son·né \,klȯiz-ᵊn-'ā, klə-,wäz-\ *adj* [F, fr. pp. of *cloisonner* to partition] **:** of, relating to, or being a style of enamel decoration in which the enamel is applied and fired in raised cells (as of soldered wires) on a usu. metal background — compare CHAMPLEVÉ — **cloisonné** *n*

1**clois·ter** \'klȯi-stər\ *n* [ME *cloistre*, fr. OF, fr. ML *claustrum*, fr. L, bar, bolt, fr. *claudere* to close — more at CLOSE] **1 a :** an area within a monastery or convent to which the religious are normally restricted **b :** a monastic establishment **c :** monastic life **2 :** a covered passage on the side of a court usu. having one side walled and the other an open arcade or colonnade

2**cloister** *vt* **clois·tered; clois·ter·ing** \-st(ə-)riŋ\ **1 :** to seclude from the world in or as if in a cloister ⟨a scientist who ~*s* himself in a laboratory⟩ **2 :** to surround with a cloister ⟨~*ed* gardens⟩

clois·tral \'klȯi-strəl\ *adj* **:** of, relating to, or suggestive of a cloister

clois·tress \'klȯi-strəs\ *n, obs* **:** NUN

clo·mi·phene \'kläm-ə-,fēn, 'klōm-\ *n* [*ch*lor- + *amine* + *-phene* (fr. *phenyl*)] **:** an ovulation-inducing synthetic drug $C_{26}H_{28}ClNO$

1**clone** \'klōn\ *n* [Gk *klōn* twig, slip; akin to Gk *klan* to break] **:** the aggregate of the asexually produced progeny of an individual — **clon·al** \'klōn-ᵊl\ *adj* — **clon·al·ly** \-ᵊl-ē\ *adv*

2**clone** *vt* **cloned; clon·ing :** to cause to grow as a clone

1**clonk** \'kläŋk, 'klȯŋk\ *vi* [imit.] **:** to make a dull thumping sound as if from impact of a hard object on a hard but hollow surface ~ *vt* **:** to produce a clonk

2**clonk** *n* **:** a clonking sound

clo·nus \'klō-nəs\ *n* [NL, fr. Gk *klonos* agitation; akin to L *celer* swift] **:** a forced series of alternating contractions and partial relaxations of a muscle occurring in some nervous diseases — **clon·ic** \'klän-ik\ *adj* — **clo·nic·i·ty** \klō-'nis-ət-ē, klä-\ *n*

cloot \'klüt\ *n* [prob. of Scand origin; akin to ON *klō* claw] **1** *Scot* **:** a cloven hoof **2** *pl, cap, Scot* **:** CLOOTIE

Cloot·ie \'klüt-ē\ *n* [dim. of *cloot*] *chiefly Scot* — used as a name of the devil

clop \'kläp\ *n* [imit.] **:** a sound made by or as if by a hoof or wooden shoe against the pavement — **clop** *vi*

clop-clop \'kläp-,kläp\ *n* **:** a sound of rhythmically repeated clops — **clop-clop** *vi*

1**close** \'klōz\ *vb* **closed; clos·ing** [ME *closen*, fr. OF *clos-*, stem of *clore*, fr. L *claudere*] *vt* **1 a :** to move so as to bar passage through something ⟨~ the gate⟩ **b :** to block against entry or passage ⟨~ a street⟩ **c :** to deny access to ⟨because of drought the governor *closed* the woodlands⟩ **d :** SCREEN, EXCLUDE ⟨~ a view⟩ **e :** to suspend or stop the operations of ⟨~ school⟩ **2** *archaic* **:** ENCLOSE, CONTAIN **3 a :** to bring to an end or period ⟨~ a charge account⟩ **b :** to conclude discussion or negotiation about ⟨the question is *closed*⟩; *also* **:** to consummate by performing something previously agreed ⟨~ a transfer of real estate title⟩ **4 a :** to bring or bind together the parts or edges of ⟨a *closed* fist⟩ **b :** to fill up (as an opening) ⟨~ a crack with patching plaster⟩ ~ *vi* **1 a :** to contract, fold, swing, or slide so as to leave no opening ⟨the door *closed* quietly⟩ **b :** to cease operation ⟨the factory *closed* down⟩ ⟨the stores ~ at 9 p.m.⟩ **2 a :** to draw near ⟨the ship was *closing* with the island⟩ **b :** to engage in a struggle at close quarters **:** GRAPPLE ⟨~ with the enemy⟩ **3 :** to come together **:** MEET **4 :** to enter into or complete an agreement **5 :** to come to an end or period — **clos·able** *or* **close·able** \'klō-zə-bəl\ *adj* — **clos·er** *n*

syn CLOSE, END, CONCLUDE, FINISH, COMPLETE, TERMINATE *shared meaning element* **:** to bring or come to a stopping point or limit. CLOSE usually carries over from another sense the idea of action on something that is in some way open as well as unfinished ⟨*close* an account⟩ ⟨*close* a debate⟩ END conveys a stronger sense of finality and usually implies a progress or development which is felt as having been carried to a conclusion ⟨the harvest is past, the summer is *ended*, and we are not saved —Jer 8:20 (AV)⟩ CONCLUDE can imply a formal closing (as of a meeting) and often stresses less the fact than the form of that closing ⟨concluded his speech with a plea for unity⟩ or it can be very close to *close* or *end* ⟨*concluded* their game and went home⟩ FINISH implies that something proposed or begun has been done and may stress completion of a final step in a process ⟨*finished* the dress by carefully pressing the seams⟩ COMPLETE implies the removal of all deficiencies or a successful finishing of what has been undertaken ⟨[his] education was ended, if not *completed* —J. T. Farrell⟩ TERMINATE implies the setting of a limit in time or space ⟨the path *terminates* near the lake⟩

— **close one's doors 1 :** to refuse admission ⟨the nation *closed its doors* to immigrants⟩ **2 :** to go out of business ⟨after nearly 40 years he had to *close his doors* for lack of trade⟩ — **close one's eyes to :** to ignore deliberately — **close ranks :** to unite in a concerted stand esp. to meet a challenge — **close the door :** to be uncompromisingly obstructive ⟨his attitude *closed the door* to further negotiation⟩

2**close** \'klōz\ *n* **1 a :** a coming or bringing to a conclusion ⟨at the ~ of the party⟩ **b :** a conclusion or end in time or existence **:** CESSATION ⟨the decade drew to a ~⟩ **c :** the concluding passage (as of a speech or play) **2 :** the conclusion of a musical strain or period **:** CADENCE **3** *archaic* **:** a hostile encounter **4 :** the movement of the free foot in dancing toward or into contact with the supporting foot with or without a transfer of weight

3**close** \'klōs, *U.S. also* 'klōz\ *n* [ME *clos*, lit., enclosure, fr. OF *clos*, fr. L *clausum*, fr. neuter of *clausus*, pp.] **1 a :** an enclosed area **b** *Brit* **:** the precinct of a cathedral **2** *chiefly Brit* **a :** a narrow passage leading from a street to a court and the houses within or to the common stairway of tenements **b :** a road closed at one end

4**close** \'klōs\ *adj* **clos·er; clos·est** [ME *clos*, fr. MF, fr. L *clausus*, pp. of *claudere* to shut, close; akin to Gk *kleiein* to close, OHG *sliozan*] **1 :** having no openings **:** CLOSED **2 a :** confined or confining strictly ⟨five days of ~ arrest⟩ **b** (1) *of a vowel* **:** HIGH 12 (2) **:** formed with the tongue in a higher position than for the other vowel of a pair **3 :** restricted to a privileged class **4 a :** SECLUDED, SECRET **b :** SECRETIVE ⟨she could tell us something if she would . . . but she was as ~ as wax —A. Conan Doyle⟩ **5 :** STRICT, RIGOROUS ⟨keep ~ watch⟩ **6 :** hot and stuffy **7 :** reluctant to part with money or possessions **:** cautious and often stingy in expenditure **8 :** having little space between items or units **9 a :** fitting tightly or exactly **b :** very short or near to the surface ⟨the barber gave him a ~ shave⟩ **c :** matching or blending without gap **10 :** being near in time, space, effect, or degree **11 :** INTIMATE, FAMILIAR **12 a :** ACCURATE, PRECISE ⟨a ~ study⟩ **b :** marked by fidelity to an original ⟨a ~ copy of an old master⟩ **c :** TERSE, COMPACT **13 :** having an even or nearly even score ⟨a ~ baseball game⟩ **14 :** difficult to obtain ⟨money is ~⟩ **15** *of punctuation* **:** characterized by liberal use esp. of commas — **close·ly** *adv* — **close·ness** *n*

syn 1 CLOSE, DENSE, COMPACT, THICK *shared meaning element* : having constituent parts that are massed or gathered tightly together **ant** open
2 see STINGY **ant** liberal
— **close to home** : within one's personal interests so that one is strongly affected ⟨the audience felt that the speaker's remarks hit pretty *close to home*⟩
⁵close \'klōs\ *adv* : in a close position or manner : NEAR
close call \'klōs-\ *n* : a narrow escape
close corporation \'klōs-\ *n* : a corporation whose stock is held by a few persons who are often those active in the management
close–cropped \'klō-ˌskräpt\ *adj* **1** : clipped short **2** : having the hair clipped short
closed \'klōzd\ *adj* **1 a** : not open **b** : ENCLOSED ⟨a ~ porch⟩ **2 a** : forming a self-contained unit allowing no additions ⟨~ association⟩ **b** (1) : traced by a moving point that returns to an arbitrary starting point ⟨~ curve⟩; *also* : so formed that every plane section is a closed curve ⟨~ surface⟩ (2) : characterized by mathematical elements that when subjected to an operation produce only elements of the same set ⟨the set of whole numbers is ~ under addition and multiplication⟩ (3) : containing all the limit points of every possible subset ⟨a ~ set⟩ **c** : characterized by continuous return and reuse of the working substance ⟨a ~ cooling system⟩ **d** *of a racecourse* : having the same starting and finishing point **3 a** : confined to a few ⟨~ membership⟩ **b** : excluding participation of outsiders or witnesses : conducted in strict secrecy **c** : rigidly excluding outside influence ⟨~ economy⟩ ⟨a ~ mind⟩ **4** : ending in a consonant ⟨~ syllable⟩
closed chain *n* : RING 10
closed circuit *n* : a television installation in which the signal is transmitted by wire to a limited number of receivers
closed couplet *n* : a rhymed couplet in which the sense is complete
closed–door \ˌklōz-ˌdō(ə)r, -ˌdȯ(ə)r\ *adj* : done or carried on in a closed session barring public and press ⟨a ~ session of the investigating committee⟩
closed–end \ˌklōz-ˌdend\ *adj* : having a fixed capitalization of shares that are traded on the market at prices determined by the operation of the law of supply and demand ⟨a ~ investment company⟩ — compare OPEN-END
closed loop *n* : an automatic control system for an operation or process in which feedback in a closed path or group of paths acts to maintain output at a desired level
close down \(ˈ)klōz-\ *vi* : to settle or appear close around so as to block any outward view ⟨fog presently *closed down*⟩
closed shop *n* : an establishment in which the employer by agreement hires only union members in good standing
closed stance *n* : a preparatory position (as in baseball batting or golf) in which the forward foot (as the left foot of a right-handed person) is closer to the line of play than the back foot — compare OPEN STANCE
close·fist·ed \'klōs-'fis-təd\ *adj* : STINGY, TIGHTFISTED
close–grained \-'grānd\ *adj* : having a closely compacted smooth texture; *esp* : having narrow annual rings or small wood elements
close–hauled \-'hȯld\ *adj* : having the sails set for sailing as nearly against the wind as the ship will go
close in \(ˈ)klō-'zin\ *vi* **1** : to gather in close all around with an oppressing or isolating effect ⟨despair *closed in* on her⟩ **2** : to approach from various directions to close quarters esp. for an attack, raid, or arrest ⟨intelligence agents *closed in* on him⟩ **3** : to grow dark ⟨the short November day was already *closing in* —Ellen Glasgow⟩ ~ *vt* **1** : to encircle closely and isolate **2** : to enshroud to such an extent as to preclude entrance or exit ⟨the airport is *closed in*⟩
close–knit \'klō-'snit\ *adj* : bound together by intimate social or cultural ties or by close economic or political ties ⟨the immigrants had left their ~ little villages —Oscar Handlin⟩
close–lipped \'klō-'slipt\ *adj* : TIGHT-LIPPED
close·mouthed \'klō-'smau̇t͟hd, -'smau̇tht\ *adj* : cautious in speaking : UNCOMMUNICATIVE; *also* : SECRETIVE ⟨is ~ about her work⟩
close order *n* : an arrangement of troops for formations, drill, or marching according to an exact scheme prescribing fixed distances and intervals
close·out \'klō-ˌzau̇t\ *n* **1** : a clearing out by a sale usu. at reduced prices of the whole remaining stock (as of a business) **2** : an article offered or bought at a closeout
close out \(ˈ)klō-'zau̇t\ *vt* **1 a** : EXCLUDE **b** : PRECLUDE ⟨*close out* his chances⟩ **2 a** : to dispose of a whole stock of by sale **b** : to dispose of (a business) **c** : SELL ⟨*closed out* his share of the business⟩ **d** : to put (an account) in order for disposal or transfer **3 a** : TERMINATE **b** : to discontinue operation ~ *vi* **1** : to sell out a business **2** : to buy or sell securities or commodities in order to terminate an account (as when margin is exhausted)
close quarters \'klōs-\ *n pl* : immediate contact or close range ⟨fought at *close quarters*⟩
close shave \'klōs(h)-\ *n* : a narrow escape
close·stool \'klōs-ˌstül\ *n* : a stool holding a chamber pot
¹clos·et \'kläz-ət, 'klȯz-\ *n* [ME, fr. MF, dim. of *clos* enclosure] **1 a** : an apartment or small room for privacy **b** : a monarch's or official's private chamber for counsel or devotions **2** : a cabinet or recess for china, household utensils, or clothing : CUPBOARD **3** : a place of retreat or privacy **4** : WATER CLOSET **5** : a state or condition of secrecy, privacy, or obscurity — **clo·set·ful** \-ˌfu̇l\ *n*
²closet *adj* **1** : closely private **2** : working in or suited to the closet as the place of seclusion or study : THEORETICAL **3** : being so in private ⟨a ~ racist⟩
³closet *vt* **1** : to shut up in or as if in a closet **2** : to take into a closet for a secret interview
closet drama *n* : drama suited primarily for reading rather than production
closet queen *n* : one who secretly engages in homosexual activities while leading an ostensibly heterosexual life
close–up \'klō-ˌsəp *also* -ˌzəp\ *n* **1** : a photograph or movie shot taken at close range **2** : an intimate view or examination of something
clos·ing \'klō-ziŋ\ *n* **1** : a concluding part (as of a speech) **2** : a closable gap (as in an article of wear)
clos·trid·i·um \klä-'strid-ē-əm\ *n, pl* **-ia** \-ē-ə\ [NL, genus name, fr. Gk *klōstēr* spindle, fr. *klōthein* to spin] : any of various spore-forming mostly anaerobic soil or intestinal bacteria (esp. genus *Clostridium*) — compare BOTULISM — **clos·trid·i·al** \-ē-əl\ *adj*
¹clo·sure \'klō-zhər\ *n* [ME, fr. MF, fr. L *clausura*, fr. *clausus*, pp. of *claudere* to close — more at CLOSE] **1** *archaic* : means of enclosing : ENCLOSURE **2** : an act of closing : the condition of being closed ⟨~ of the eyelids⟩ **3** : something that closes ⟨pocket with zipper ~⟩ **4** [trans. of F *clôture*] : CLOTURE **5** : the property that a number system or a set has when it is mathematically closed under an operation **6** : a set that contains a given set together with all the limit points of the given set
²closure *vt* **clo·sured; clo·sur·ing** \'klōzh-(ə-)riŋ\ : CLOTURE
¹clot \'klät\ *n* [ME, fr. OE *clott*; akin to MHG *klōz* lump, ball — more at CLOUT] **1** : a portion of a substance cleaving together in a thick nondescript mass (as of clay or gum) **2 a** : a roundish viscous lump formed by coagulation of a portion of liquid or by melting **b** : the coagulum produced by clotting of blood **3** *Brit* : BLOCKHEAD **4** : CLUSTER
²clot *vb* **clot·ted; clot·ting** *vi* **1** : to become a clot : form clots **2** : to undergo a sequence of complex chemical and physical reactions that results in conversion of fluid blood into a coagulum : COAGULATE ~ *vt* **1** : to cause to clot **2** : to fill with clots
cloth \'klȯth\ *n, pl* **cloths** \'klȯt͟hz, 'klȯths*often attrib* [ME, fr. OE *clāth*; akin to OE *clīthan* to adhere to, LL *glut-, glus* glue] **1 a** : a pliable material made usu. by weaving, felting, or knitting natural or synthetic fibers and filaments **b** : a similar material (as of glass) **2** : a piece of cloth adapted for a particular purpose; *esp* : TABLECLOTH **3 a** : a distinctive dress of a profession or calling **b** : the dress of the clergy; *also* : CLERGY
clothe \'klōt͟h\ *vt* **clothed** *or* **clad** \'klad\; **cloth·ing** [ME *clothen*, fr. OE *clāthian*, fr. *clāth* cloth, garment] **1 a** : to cover with or as if with cloth or clothing : DRESS **b** : to provide with clothes **2** : to express or enhance by suitably significant language : COUCH ⟨treaties *clothed* in stately phraseology⟩ **3** : to endow esp. with power or a quality ⟨an act *clothing* Indians with United States citizenship⟩
clothes \'klō(t͟h)z\ *n pl, often attrib* [ME, fr. OE *clāthas*, pl. of *clāth* cloth, garment] **1** : CLOTHING **2** : BEDCLOTHES **3** : all the cloth articles of personal and household use that can be washed
clothes·horse \-ˌhȯ(ə)rs\ *n* **1** : a frame on which to hang clothes **2** : a conspicuously dressy person
¹clothes·line \-ˌlīn\ *n* **1** : a line (as of cord) on which clothes may be hung to dry **2** : a tackle in football in which a defensive player's outstretched arm catches the ballcarrier by the head and neck unawares
²clothesline *vt* : to hit (a football player) with an outstretched arm
clothes moth *n* : any of several small yellowish or buff-colored moths (esp. genera *Tinea* and *Tineola* of the family Tineidae) whose larvae eat wool, fur, or feathers
clothes·pin \'klō(t͟h)z-ˌpin\ *n* : a forked piece of wood or plastic or a small spring clamp used for fastening clothes on a clothesline
clothes·press \-ˌpres\ *n* : a receptacle for clothes
clothes tree *n* : an upright post-shaped stand with hooks or pegs around the top on which to hang clothes
cloth·ier \'klōt͟h-yər, 'klō-t͟hē-ər\ *n* [ME, alter. of *clother*, fr. *cloth*] : one who makes or sells cloth or clothing
cloth·ing \'klō-t͟hiŋ\ *n* : garments in general; *also* : COVERING
cloth yard *n* : a yard esp. for measuring cloth; *specif* : a unit of 37 inches equal to the Scotch ell and used also as a length for arrows
clotted cream *n* : a thick cream made chiefly in England by slowly heating whole milk on which the cream has been allowed to rise and then skimming the cooled cream from the top — called also *Cornish cream, Devonshire cream*
clo·ture \'klō-chər\ *n* [F *clôture*, lit., closure, alter. of MF *closure*] : the closing or limitation of debate in a legislative body esp. by calling for a vote ⟨attempted to end the filibuster by ~⟩ — **cloture** *vt*
¹cloud \'klau̇d\ *n, often attrib* [ME, rock, cloud, fr. OE *clūd*; akin to Gk *gloutos* buttock] **1 a** : a visible mass of particles of water or ice in the form of fog, mist, or haze suspended usu. at a considerable height in the air **b** : a light filmy, puffy, or billowy mass seeming to float in the air **2 a** : a usu. visible mass of minute particles suspended in the air or in a gas; *also* : one of the masses of obscuring matter in interstellar space **b** : an aggregate of charged particles (as electrons) **3** : a great crowd or multitude : SWARM ⟨~s of mosquitoes⟩ **4** : something that has a dark, lowering, or threatening aspect ⟨~s of another war began to loom over the horizon⟩ **5** : something that obscures or blemishes ⟨worked

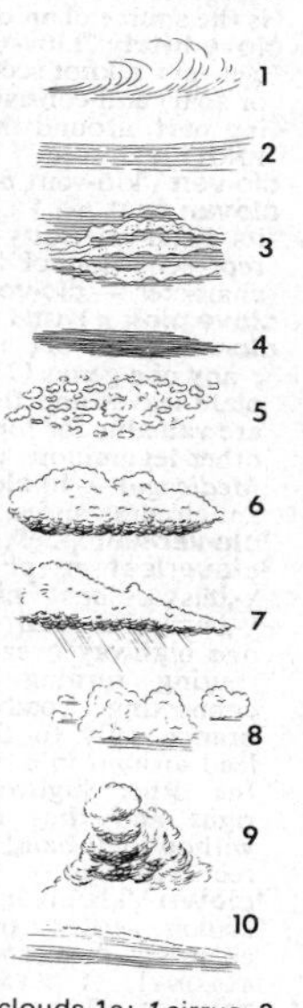

clouds 1a: *1* cirrus, *2* cirrostratus, *3* cirrocumulus, *4* altostratus, *5* altocumulus, *6* stratocumulus, *7* nimbostratus, *8* cumulus, *9* cumulonimbus, *10* stratus

ə abut ᵊ kitten ər further a back ā bake ä cot, cart
au̇ out ch chin e less ē easy g gift i trip ī life
j joke ŋ sing ō flow ȯ flaw ȯi coin th thin t͟h this
ü loot u̇ foot y yet yü few yu̇ furious zh vision

under ~s of secrecy⟩ 6 : a dark or opaque vein or spot (as in marble)

²**cloud** vi 1 : to grow cloudy — usu. used with over or up ⟨~ed over before the storm⟩ 2 a of facial features : to become troubled, apprehensive, or distressed in appearance b : to become blurry, dubious, or ominous 3 : to billow up in the form of a cloud ~ vt 1 a : to envelop or hide with or as if with a cloud ⟨smog ~ed our view⟩ b : to make opaque esp. by condensation of moisture c : to make murky esp. with smoke or mist 2 : to make unclear or confused 3 : TAINT, SULLY ⟨a ~ed reputation⟩ 4 : to cast gloom over

cloud·ber·ry \'klaüd-,ber-ē\ n : a creeping herbaceous raspberry (Rubus chamaemorus) of north temperate regions; also : its pale amber-colored edible fruit

cloud·burst \-,bərst\ n 1 : a sudden copious rainfall 2 : DELUGE 2

cloud chamber n : a vessel containing saturated water vapor whose sudden expansion reveals the passage of an ionizing particle by a trail of visible droplets

cloud·land \'klaüd-,land\ n 1 : the region of the clouds 2 : the realm of visionary speculation or poetic imagination

cloud·less \-ləs\ adj : free from clouds : CLEAR — **cloud·less·ly** adv — **cloud·less·ness** n

cloud·let \'klaüd-lət\ n : a small cloud

cloud nine n [perh. fr. the ninth and highest heaven of Dante's Paradise, whose inhabitants are most blissful because nearest to God] : a feeling of extreme well-being or elation — usu. used with on ⟨was on cloud nine after his victory⟩

cloudy \'klaüd-ē\ adj **cloud·i·er; -est** 1 : of, relating to, or resembling cloud 2 : darkened by gloom or anxiety 3 a : overcast with clouds; specif : six tenths to nine tenths covered with clouds b : having a cloudy sky 4 : obscure in meaning ⟨~ issues⟩ 5 : dimmed or dulled as if by clouds ⟨a ~ mirror⟩ 6 : uneven in color or texture 7 : having visible material in suspension : MURKY — **cloud·i·ly** \'klaüd-ᵊl-ē\ adv — **cloud·i·ness** \'klaüd-ē-nəs\ n

¹**clout** \'klaüt\ n [ME, fr. OE clūt; akin to MHG klōz lump, Russ gluda] 1 a dial chiefly Brit : a piece of cloth or leather : RAG b : a household cloth c : an article of clothing (as for infants) 2 : a blow esp. with the hand; also : a hit in baseball 3 : a white cloth on a stake or frame used as a target in archery 4 : PULL, INFLUENCE ⟨had a lot of ~ with the governor⟩

²**clout** vt 1 : to cover or patch with a clout 2 : to hit forcefully ⟨~ed the ball into the bleachers⟩ ⟨whose mother has just ~ed his head —G. B. Shaw⟩

¹**clove** \'klōv\ n [ME, fr. OE clufu; akin to OE clēofan to cleave] : one of the small bulbs (as in garlic) developed in the axils of the scales of a large bulb

²**clove** past of CLEAVE

³**clove** \'klōv\ n [alter. of ME clowe, fr. OF clou (de girofle), lit., nail of clove, fr. L clavus nail] : the dried flower bud of a tropical tree (Eugenia aromatica) of the myrtle family that is used as a spice and is the source of an oil; also : this tree

clove hitch \'klōv-\ n [ME cloven, clove divided, fr. pp. of clevien to cleave] : a knot securing a rope temporarily to an object (as a post or spar) and consisting of a turn around the object, over the standing part, around the object again, and under the last turn — see KNOT illustration

clo·ven \'klō-vən\ past part of CLEAVE

cloven foot n 1 : a foot (as of a sheep) divided into two parts at its distal extremity — called also cloven hoof 2 [fr. the traditional representation of Satan as cloven-footed] : the sign of devilish character — **clo·ven-foot·ed** \,klō-vən-'füt-əd\ adj

clove pink n : GILLYFLOWER 1

clo·ver \'klō-vər\ n [ME, fr. OE clǣfre; akin to OHG klēo clover] : any of a genus (Trifolium) of low leguminous herbs having trifoliolate leaves and flowers in dense heads and including many that are valuable for forage and attractive to bees; also : any of various other leguminous plants (as of the genera Melilotus, Lespedeza, or Medicago) — **in clover** or **in the clover** : in prosperity or in pleasant circumstances

¹**clo·ver·leaf** \-,lēf\ adj : resembling a clover leaf in shape

²**cloverleaf** n, pl **cloverleafs** \-,lēfs\ or **clo·ver·leaves** \-,lēvz\ : a road plan passing one highway over another and routing turning traffic onto connecting roadways which branch only to the right and lead around in a circle to enter the other highway from the right and thus merge traffic without left-hand turns or direct crossings

cloverleaf

¹**clown** \'klaün\ n [perh. fr. MF coulon settler, fr. L colonus colonist, farmer — more at COLONY] 1 : FARMER, COUNTRYMAN 2 : a rude ill-bred person : BOOR 3 a : a fool, jester, or comedian in an entertainment (as a play); specif : a grotesquely dressed comedy performer in a circus b : one who habitually plays the buffoon : JOKER

²**clown** vi : to act as a clown

clown·ery \'klaü-nə-rē\ n, pl **-er·ies** : clownish behavior or an instance of clownishness : BUFFOONERY

clown·ish \'klaü-nish\ adj : resembling or befitting a clown (as in ignorance and lack of sophistication) syn see BOORISH — **clown·ish·ly** adv — **clown·ish·ness** n

clox·a·cil·lin \,kläk-sə-'sil-ən\ n [chlor- + oxacillin] : a synthetic oral penicillin $C_{19}H_{17}ClN_3NaO_5S$ esp. effective against staphylococci

cloy \'klöi\ vb [ME acloien to lame, fr. MF encloer to drive in a nail, fr. ML inclavare, fr. L in + clavus, nail] vt : to surfeit with an excess usu. of something orig. pleasing ~ vi : to cause surfeit syn see SATIATE — **cloy·ing·ly** \-iŋ-lē\ adv

cloze \'klōz\ adj [by shortening and alter. fr. closure] : of, relating to, or being a test of reading comprehension that involves having the person being tested supply words which have been systematically deleted from a text

clr abbr clear; clearance

CLU abbr chartered life underwriter

¹**club** \'kləb\ n [ME clubbe, fr. ON klubba; akin to OHG kolbo club, OE clamm bond] 1 a : a heavy usu. tapering staff esp. of wood wielded as a weapon b : a stick or bat used to hit a ball in any of various games c : something resembling a club d : a light spar e : INDIAN CLUB 2 a : a figure that resembles a stylized clover leaf on each playing card of one of the four suits; also : a card marked with this figure b pl but sing or pl in constr : the suit comprising cards marked with a club 3 a : an association of persons for some common object usu. jointly supported and meeting periodically b : the meeting place of a club c : an association of persons participating in a plan by which they agree to make regular payments or purchases in order to secure some advantage d : NIGHTCLUB

²**club** vb **clubbed; club·bing** vt 1 a : to beat or strike with or as if with a club b : to gather into a club-shaped mass ⟨clubbed her hair⟩ c : to hold like a club 2 a : to unite or combine for a common cause b : to contribute to a common fund ~ vi 1 : to form a club : COMBINE 2 : to pay a share of a common expense : CONTRIBUTE

³**club** adj 1 : of or relating to a club 2 : consisting of foods in a fixed combination offered on a menu at a set price ⟨~ breakfast⟩

club·ba·ble or **club·able** \'kləb-ə-bəl\ adj : SOCIABLE

club bag n : a rectangular and usu. leather traveling bag that tapers to a narrow opening at the top and that is often zippered

clubbed \'kləbd\ adj : shaped like a club ⟨~ antennae⟩

club·ber \'kləb-ər\ n : a member of a club

club·by \'kləb-ē\ adj **club·bi·er; -est** : characteristic of a club or club members: as a : SOCIABLE b : open only to qualified or approved persons : SELECT — **club·bi·ness** n

club car n : LOUNGE CAR

club chair n : a deep low thickly upholstered easy chair often with rather low back and heavy sides and arms

club cheese n : a process cheese made by grinding cheddar and other cheeses usu. with added condiments and seasoning

club coupe n : an automobile resembling a coupe in having only two doors but with a full-width rear seat accessible by tilting the front-seat backs forward

club·foot \'kləb-'füt\ n : a misshapen foot twisted out of position from birth; also : this deformity — **club·foot·ed** \-'füt-əd\ adj

club fungus n : any of a family (Clavariaceae) of basidiomycetes with a simple or branched often club-shaped sporophore

club·house \'kləb-,haüs\ n 1 : a house occupied by a club or used for club activities 2 : locker rooms used by an athletic team

club moss n : any of an order (Lycopodiales) of primitive vascular plants (as ground pine) often with the sporangia borne in club-shaped strobiles

club·root \'kləb-,rüt, -,rüt\ n : a disease of cabbages and related plants caused by a slime mold (Plasmodiophora brassicae) producing swellings or distortions of the root

club sandwich n : a sandwich of three slices of bread with two layers of various meats (as chicken or turkey) and lettuce, tomato, and mayonnaise

club soda n : SODA WATER 2a

club steak n : a small steak cut from the end of the short loin — see BEEF illustration

club moss

¹**cluck** \'klək\ vb [imit.] vi 1 : to make a cluck 2 : to make a clicking sound with the tongue 3 : to express interest or concern ⟨critics ~ed over the new developments⟩ ~ vt 1 : to call with a cluck 2 : to express with interest or concern

²**cluck** n 1 : the characteristic sound made by a hen esp. in calling her chicks 2 : a broody fowl 3 : a stupid or naive person

clue var of CLEW

clum·ber spaniel \,kləm-bər-\ n, often cap C & S [Clumber, estate in Nottinghamshire, England] : a large massive heavyset spaniel with a dense silky leggy white coat

¹**clump** \'kləmp\ n [prob. fr. LG klump; akin to OE clamm] 1 : a group of things clustered together ⟨a ~ of bushes⟩ 2 : a compact mass 3 : a heavy tramping sound — **clumpy** \'kləm-pē\ adj

²**clump** vi 1 : to tread clumsily and noisily 2 : to form clumps ~ vt : to arrange in or cause to form clumps ⟨the serum ~s the bacteria⟩

clum·sy \'kləm-zē\ adj **clum·si·er; -est** [prob. fr. obs. E clumse (benumbed with cold)] 1 a : lacking dexterity, nimbleness, or grace ⟨~ fingers⟩ b : lacking tact or subtlety ⟨a ~ joke⟩ 2 : awkwardly or poorly made : UNWIELDY syn see AWKWARD ant adroit, facile — **clum·si·ly** \-zə-lē\ adv — **clum·si·ness** \-zē-nəs\ n

clung past of CLING

¹**clunk** \'kləŋk\ n [imit.] 1 : a blow or the sound of a blow : THUMP 2 : a dull or stupid person

²**clunk** vi 1 : to make a clunk 2 : to hit something with a clunk ~ vt : to strike or hit with a clunk

clunk·er \'kləŋ-kər\ n : a dilapidated rattling old machine; esp : JALOPY

clu·pe·id \'klü-pē-əd\ n [deriv. of L clupea, a small river fish] : any of a large family (Clupeidae) of soft-finned teleost fishes (as her-

211

rings) having a laterally compressed body and a forked tail — **clupeid** *adj*

¹clus·ter \'kləs-tər\ *n* [ME, fr. OE *clyster;* akin to OE *clott* clot] **1** : a number of similar things growing together or of things or persons collected or grouped closely together : BUNCH **2** : two or more consecutive consonants or vowels in a segment of speech **3** : a group of buildings and esp. houses built close together on a sizable tract in order to preserve open spaces larger than the individual yard for common recreation *syn* see GROUP — **clus·tery** \-t(ə-)rē\ *adj*

²cluster *vb* **clus·tered; clus·ter·ing** \-t(ə-)riŋ\ *vt* **1** : to collect into a cluster 〈~ the tents together〉 **2** : to furnish with clusters ~ *vi* : to grow or assemble in a cluster 〈men ~ed around the stove〉

cluster college *n* : a small residential college constituting a semiautonomous division of a university and usu. specializing in one area of knowledge (as history and the social sciences)

¹clutch \'kləch\ *vb* [ME *clucchen,* fr. OE *clyccan;* akin to MIr *glacc* hand — more at CLING] *vt* **1** : to grasp or hold with or as if with the hand or claws usu. strongly, tightly, or suddenly **2** *obs* : CLENCH ~ *vi* **1** : to seek to grasp and hold **2** : to operate an automobile clutch *syn* see TAKE

²clutch *n* **1 a** : the claws or a hand in the act of grasping or seizing firmly **b** : an often cruel or unrelenting control, power, or possession 〈the fell ~ of circumstance —W. E. Henley〉 **2** : the act of grasping, holding, or restraining **3 a** : a device for gripping an object (as at the end of a chain or tackle) **b** : a coupling used to connect and disconnect a driving and a driven part of a mechanism **b** : a lever operating such a clutch **4** : a tight or critical situation : PINCH 〈the batter came through with a hit in the ~〉 **5** : CLUTCH BAG *syn* see HOLD

³clutch *adj* **1** : made or done in a crucial situation 〈a ~ hit drove in the winning run〉 **2** : successful in a crucial situation 〈a ~ pitcher〉

⁴clutch *n* [alter. of dial. E *cletch* (hatching, brood)] **1** : a nest of eggs or a brood of chicks **2** : GROUP, BUNCH 〈a ~ of gossipy matrons〉

clutch bag *n* : a woman's small usu. strapless handbag — called also *clutch purse*

¹clut·ter \'klət-ər\ *vb* [ME *clotteren* to clot, fr. *clot*] *vt* **1** : to fill or cover with scattered or disordered things that impede movement or reduce effectiveness — often used with *up* 〈~ed up his room〉 ~ *vi,* *chiefly dial* : to run in disorder

²clutter *n* **1 a** : a crowded or confused mass or collection 〈a ~ of shops and tenements〉 **b** : LITTER, DISORDER 〈the ~ in her room〉 **2** : interfering echoes visible on a radar screen caused by reflection from objects other than the target **3** *chiefly dial* : DISTURBANCE, HUBBUB

Clydes·dale \'klīdz-ˌdāl\ *n* : a heavy feathered-legged draft horse of a breed orig. from Clydesdale, Scotland

Clydesdale terrier *n* : a small terrier of a breed distinguished by erect ears, long silky coat, and short legs

clyp·e·ate \'klip-ē-ət\ *or* **clyp·e·at·ed** \-ē-ˌāt-əd\ *adj* [L & NL *clypeus* + E *-ate*] **1** : shaped like a shield or buckler **2** : having a clypeus

clyp·e·us \'klip-ē-əs\ *n, pl* **clyp·ei** \-ē-ˌī, -ē-ˌē\ [NL, fr. L, round shield] : a plate on the anterior median aspect of an insect's head

clys·ter \'klis-tər\ *n* [ME, fr. MF or L; MF *clistere,* fr. L *clyster,* fr. Gk *klystēr,* fr. *klyzein* to wash out] : ENEMA

Cly·tem·nes·tra \ˌklīt-əm-'nes-trə\ *n* [L, fr. Gk *Klytaimnēstra*] : the wife and murderess of Agamemnon

cm *abbr* **1** centimeter **2** cumulative

Cm *symbol* curium

CM *abbr* **1** center matched **2** circular mil **3** common meter **4** Congregation of the Mission

cmd *abbr* command

cmdg *abbr* commanding

cmdr *abbr* commander

CMG *abbr* Companion of the Order of St. Michael and St. George

c–mitosis \ˌsē-\ *n* [colchicine + *mitosis*] : an artificially induced abortive nuclear division in which the chromosome number is doubled — **c–mitotic** *adj*

cml *abbr* commercial

CMSgt *abbr* chief master sergeant

CN *abbr* credit note

cni·do·blast \'nīd-ə-ˌblast\ *n* [NL *cnida* nematocyst, fr. Gk *knidē* nettle] : a cell that develops a nematocyst or develops into a nematocyst

CNO *abbr* chief of naval operations

CNS *abbr* central nervous system

co *abbr* **1** company **2** county

Co *symbol* cobalt

CO *abbr* **1** cash order **2** Colorado **3** commanding officer **4** conscientious objector

co– *prefix* [ME, fr. L, fr. *com-;* akin to OE *ge-,* perfective and collective prefix, Gk *koinos* common] **1** : with : together : joint : jointly 〈coexist〉 〈coheir〉 **2** : in or to the same degree 〈coextensive〉 **3 a** : one that is associated in an action with another : fellow : partner 〈coauthor〉 〈co-worker〉 **b** : having a usu. lesser share in duty or responsibility : alternate : deputy 〈copilot〉 **4** : of, relating to, or constituting the complement of an angle 〈cosine〉 〈codeclination〉

c/o *abbr* care of

co·ac·er·vate \kō-'as-ər-ˌvāt\ *n* [L *coacervatus,* pp. of *coacervare* to heap up, fr. *co-* + *acervus* heap] : an aggregate of colloidal droplets held together by electrostatic attractive forces — **co·acer·vate** \kō-'sər-vət\ *adj* — **co·ac·er·va·tion** \(ˌ)kō-ˌas-ər-'vā-shən\ *n*

¹coach \'kōch\ *n, often attrib* [ME *coche,* fr. MF, fr. G *kutsche*] **1 a** : a large usu. closed four-wheeled carriage having doors in the sides

coach 1a

and an elevated seat in front for the driver **b** : a railroad passenger car intended primarily for day travel **c** : BUS 1a **d** : a house trailer **e** : an automobile body esp. of a closed model **2** [fr. the concept that the tutor conveys the student through his examinations] **a** : a private tutor **b** : one who instructs or trains a performer or a team of performers; *specif* : one who instructs players in the fundamentals of a competitive sport and directs team strategy 〈football ~〉

²coach *vt* **1** : to train intensively by instruction, demonstration, and practice **2** : to act as coach to **3** : to direct the movements of (a player) ~ *vi* **1** : to go in a coach **2** : to instruct, direct, or prompt as a coach — **coach·er** *n*

coach dog *n* : DALMATIAN

coach·man \'kōch-mən\ *n* **1** : a man whose business is to drive a coach or carriage **2** : an artifical fishing fly with white wings, peacock feather body, brown hackle, and gold tag

co·act \kō-'akt\ *vi* : to act or work together — **co·ac·tive** \-'ak-tiv\ *adj*

co·ac·tion \-'ak-shən\ *n* **1** : joint action **2** : the interaction between individuals or kinds (as species) in an ecological community

co·adapt·ed \ˌkō-ə-'dap-təd\ *adj* : mutually adapted esp. by natural selection 〈~ gene complexes〉

co·ad·ju·tor \ˌkō-ə-'jüt-ər, kō-'aj-ət-ər\ *n* [ME *coadjutour,* fr. MF *coadjuteur,* fr. L *coadjutor,* fr. *co-* + *adjutor* aid, fr. *adjutus,* pp. of *adjuvare* to help — more at AID] **1** : one who works together with another : ASSISTANT **2** : a bishop assisting a diocesan bishop and often having the right of succession — **coadjutor** *adj*

co·ad·ju·trix \ˌkō-ə-'jü-triks, kō-'aj-ə-()triks\ *n, pl* **co·ad·ju·tri·ces** \ˌkō-ə-'jü-trə-ˌsēz, (ˌ)kō-ˌaj-ə-'trī-()sēz\ [NL, fem. of *coadjutor*] : a female coadjutor

co·ad·u·nate \kō-'aj-ə-nət, -ˌnāt\ *adj* [LL *coadunatus,* pp. of *coadunare* to combine, fr. L *co-* + *adunare* to unite, fr. *ad-* + *unus* one — more at ONE] : UNITED; *esp* : grown together — **co·ad·u·na·tion** \(ˌ)kō-ˌaj-ə-'nā-shən\ *n*

co·ag·u·lant \kō-'ag-yə-lənt\ *n* : something that produces coagulation

co·ag·u·lase \kō-'ag-yə-ˌlās, -ˌlāz\ *n* : an enzyme that causes coagulation

¹co·ag·u·late \-lət, -ˌlāt\ *adj, archaic* : being clotted or congealed

²co·ag·u·late \kō-'ag-yə-ˌlāt\ *vb* **-lat·ed; -lat·ing** [L *coagulatus,* pp. of *coagulare* to curdle, fr. *coagulum* curdling agent, fr. *cogere* to drive together — more at COGENT] *vt* **1** : to cause to become viscous or thickened into a coherent mass : CURDLE, CLOT **2** : to gather together or form into a mass or group ~ *vi* : to become coagulated — **co·ag·u·la·bil·i·ty** \kō-ˌag-yə-lə-'bil-ət-ē\ *n* — **co·ag·u·la·ble** \-'ag-yə-lə-bəl\ *adj* — **co·ag·u·la·tion** \-ˌag-yə-'lā-shən\ *n*

co·ag·u·lum \kō-'ag-yə-ləm\ *n, pl* **-u·la** \-lə\ *or* **-ulums** [L, coagulant] : a coagulated mass or substance : CLOT

¹coal \'kōl\ *n, often attrib* [ME *col,* fr. OE; akin to OHG & ON *kol* burning ember, IrGael *gual* coal] **1** : a piece of glowing carbon or charred wood : EMBER **2** : CHARCOAL 1 **3 a** : a black or brownish black solid combustible substance formed by the partial decomposition of vegetable matter without free access of air and under the influence of moisture and often increased pressure and temperature that is widely used as a natural fuel **b** *pl, Brit* : pieces or a quantity of this fuel broken up for burning

²coal *vt* **1** : to burn to charcoal : CHAR **2** : to supply with coal ~ *vi* : to take in coal

coal·er \'kō-lər\ *n* : something (as a ship) employed in transporting or supplying coal

co·alesce \ˌkō-ə-'les\ *vi* **co·alesced; co·alesc·ing** [L *coalescere,* fr. *co-* + *alescere* to grow — more at OLD] **1** : to grow together **2 a** : to unite into a whole : FUSE 〈allowing the new community to ~ ... into a major city —J. A. Michener〉 **b** : to unite for a common end : join forces 〈people with different points of view ~ into opposing factions —I. L. Horowitz〉 *syn* see MIX — **co·ales·cence** \-'les-ᵊn(t)s\ *n* — **co·ales·cent** \-ᵊnt\ *adj*

coal·field \'kōl-ˌfēld\ *n* : a region in which deposits of coal occur

coal·fish \-ˌfish\ *n* : any of several blackish or dark-backed fishes (as a pollack or sablefish)

coal gas *n* : gas made from coal: as **a** : the mixture of gases thrown off by burning coal **b** : gas made by carbonizing bituminous coal in retorts and used for heating and lighting

coal·hole \'kōl-ˌhōl\ *n* **1** : a hole for coal (as a trap or opening in a sidewalk leading to a coal bin) **2** *Brit* : a compartment for storing coal

coal·ifi·ca·tion \ˌkō-lə-fə-'kā-shən\ *n* : a process in which vegetable matter becomes converted into coal of increasingly higher rank with anthracite as the final product — **coal·ify** \'kō-lə-ˌfī\ *vt*

coaling station *n* : a port at which ships may coal

co·ali·tion \ˌkō-ə-'lish-ən\ *n* [MF, fr. L *coalitus,* pp. of *coalescere*] **1 a** : the act of coalescing : UNION **b** : a body formed by the coalescing of orig. distinct elements : COMBINATION **2** : a temporary alliance of distinct parties, persons, or states for joint action — **co·ali·tion·ist** \-'lish-(ə-)nəst\ *n*

coal measures *n pl* : beds of coal with the associated rocks

coal oil *n* **1** : petroleum or a refined oil prepared from it **2** : KEROSENE

Coal·sack \'kōl-ˌsak\ *n* : either of two dark nebulae in the Milky Way located one near the Northern Cross and the other near the Southern Cross

coal seam *n* : a bed of coal usu. thick enough to be mined with profit

coal tar *n* : tar obtained by distillation of bituminous coal and used esp. in making dyes and drugs

ə abut	ᵊ kitten	ər further	a back	ā bake	ä cot, cart
aù out	ch chin	e less	ē easy	g gift	i trip	ī life
j joke	ŋ sing	ō flow	ȯ flaw	ȯi coin	th thin	th this
ü loot	u̇ foot	y yet	yü few	yu̇ furious	zh vision	

coam·ing \ˈkō-miŋ\ *n* [prob. irreg. fr. *comb*] : a raised frame (as around a hatchway in the deck of a ship) to keep out water
co·apt \kō-ˈapt\ *vt* [LL *coaptare*, fr. L *co-* + *aptus* fastened, fit — more at APT] : to fit together and make fast — **co·ap·ta·tion** \(ˌ)kō-ˌap-ˈtā-shən\ *n*
co·arc·tate \kō-ˈärk-ˌtāt\ *adj* [L *coarctatus*, pp. of *coartare* to press together, fr. *co-* + *artus* narrow, confined; akin to L *artus* joint — more at ARTICLE] : CONSTRICTED; *specif* : enclosed in a rigid case ⟨~ insect pupae⟩ — **co·arc·ta·tion** \(ˌ)kō-ˌärk-ˈtā-shən\ *n*
coarse \ˈkō(ə)rs, ˈkȯ(ə)rs\ *adj* **coars·er; coars·est** [ME *cors*, fr. *course*, n.] **1** : of ordinary or inferior quality or value : COMMON **2 a** (1) : composed of relatively large parts or particles ⟨~ sand⟩ (2) : loose or rough in texture ⟨~ cloth⟩ **b** : adjusted or designed for heavy, fast, or less delicate work ⟨a ~ saw with large teeth⟩ **c** : not precise or detailed with respect to adjustment or discrimination **3** : crude or unrefined in taste, manners, or language **4** : harsh, raucous, or rough in tone — **coarse·ly** *adv* — **coarse·ness** *n*
syn COARSE, VULGAR, GROSS, OBSCENE, RIBALD *shared meaning element* : offensive to good taste or moral principles ***ant*** fine, refined
coarse–grained \ˈkō(ə)rs-ˈgrānd, ˈkȯ(ə)rs-\ *adj* **1** : having a coarse grain **2** : CRUDE
coars·en \ˈkōrs-ᵊn, ˈkȯrs-\ *vb* **coars·ened; coars·en·ing** \ˈkōrs-niŋ, ˈkȯrs-, -ᵊn-iŋ\ *vt* : to make coarse ~ *vi* : to become coarse
1**coast** \ˈkōst\ *n* [ME *cost*, fr. MF *coste*, fr. L *costa* rib, side; akin to OSlav *kostĭ* bone] **1** *obs* : BORDER, FRONTIER **2** : the land near a shore : SEASHORE **3 a** : a hill or slope suited to coasting **b** : a slide down a slope (as on a sled) **4** *often cap* : the Pacific coast of the U.S. — **coast·al** \ˈkōs-tᵊl\ *adj* — **coast·wise** \ˈkōs-ˌtwīz\ *adv or adj*
2**coast** *vt* **1** *obs* : to move along or past the side of : SKIRT **2** : to sail along the shore of ~ *vi* **1 a** *archaic* : to travel on land along a coast or along or past the side of something **b** : to sail along the shore **2 a** : to slide, run, or glide downhill by the force of gravity **b** : to move along without or as if without further application of propulsive power (as by momentum or gravity) **c** : to proceed easily without special application of effort or concern
coast artillery *n* : artillery for defending a coast
coast·er \ˈkō-stər\ *n* **1** : one that coasts: as **a** : a person engaged in coastal traffic or commerce **b** : a ship sailing along a coast or engaged in trade between ports of the same country **2** : a resident of a seacoast **3 a** : a tray or decanter stand usu. of silver and sometimes on wheels that is used for circulating a decanter after a meal **b** : a shallow container or a plate or mat to protect a surface **4 a** : a small vehicle (as a sled or wagon) used in coasting **b** : ROLLER COASTER
coaster brake *n* : a brake in the hub of the rear wheel of a bicycle operated by reverse pressure on the pedals
coaster wagon *n* : a child's toy wagon often used for coasting
coast guard *n* **1** : a military or naval force employed in guarding a coast or responsible for the safety, order, and operation of maritime traffic in neighboring waters **2** *usu* **coast·guard** *chiefly Brit* : COASTGUARDSMAN
coast·guards·man \ˈkōs(t)-ˌgärdz-mən\ *or* **coast·guard·man** \-ˌgärd-mən\ *n* : a member of a coast guard
coast·land \-ˌland\ *n* : land bordering the sea
coast·line \ˈkōst-ˌlīn\ *n* **1** : a line that forms the boundary between the land and the ocean or a lake **2** : the outline or shape of a coast
coast·ward \ˈkōs-twərd\ *or* **coast·wards** \-twərdz\ *adv* : toward the coast — **coastward** *adj*
1**coat** \ˈkōt\ *n, often attrib* [ME *cote*, fr. OF, of Gmc origin; akin to OHG *kozza* coarse mantle] **1 a** : an outer garment varying in length and style according to fashion and use **b** : something resembling a coat **2** : the external growth on an animal **3** : a layer of one substance covering another — **coat·ed** \-əd\ *adj*
2**coat** *vt* **1** : to cover with a coat **2** : to cover or spread with a finishing, protecting, or enclosing layer — **coat·er** *n*
coat·dress \ˈkōt-ˌdres\ *n* : a dress styled like a coat usu. with a front buttoning from neckline to hemline
coat hanger *n* : a slender arched device (as of wood, metal, or plastic) which is shaped typically somewhat like a person's shoulders and over which garments may be hung
co·ati \kə-ˈwät-ē, kwä-ˈtē\ *n* [Pg *coati*, fr. Tupi] : a tropical American mammal (genus *Nasua*) related to the raccoon but with a longer body and tail and a long flexible snout
co·ati·mun·di \kə-ˌwät-i-ˈmən-dē, ˌkwät-, -ˈmu̇n-\ *n* [Tupi] : COATI

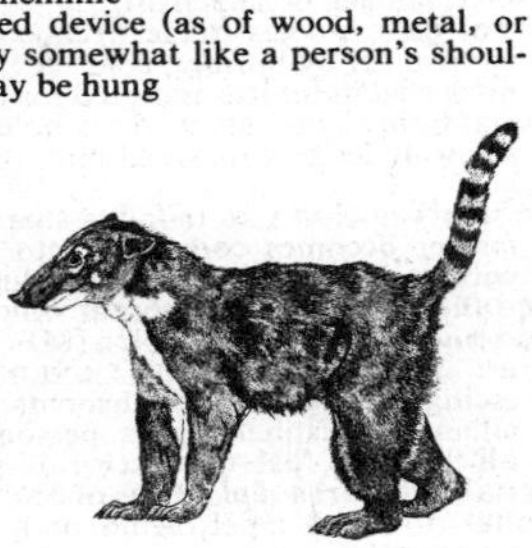
coati

coat·ing \ˈkōt-iŋ\ *n* **1** : COAT, COVERING **2** : cloth for coats
coat of arms [trans. of F *cotte d'armes*] **1** : a tabard or surcoat embroidered with armorial bearings **2 a** : the particular heraldic bearings (as of a person) usu. depicted on an escutcheon often with accompanying adjuncts (as a crest, motto, and supporters) **b** : a similar symbolic emblem
coat of mail : a garment of metal scales or chain mail worn as armor
coat·rack \ˈkōt-ˌrak\ *n* : a stand or rack fitted with pegs, hooks, or hangers and used for the temporary storage of garments
coat·room \-ˌrüm, -ˌru̇m\ *n* : CLOAKROOM
coat·tail \ˈkōt-ˌtāl\ *n* **1** : the rear flap of a man's coat **2** *pl* : the skirts of a dress coat, cutaway, or frock coat — **on one's coattails** : with the help of another; *esp* : with the benefit of another's political prestige ⟨congressmen riding into office *on the coattails* of the president⟩
coat tree *n* : CLOTHES TREE
1**co·au·thor** \(ˈ)kō-ˈȯ-thər\ *n* : a joint or associate author
2**coauthor** *vt* : to be coauthor of ⟨the two ~*ed* a novel⟩
coax \ˈkōks\ *vt* [earlier *cokes*, fr. *cokes*, n. (simpleton)] **1** *obs* : FONDLE, PET **2** : to influence or gently urge by caressing or flattering : WHEEDLE **3** : to draw, gain, or persuade by means of gentle urging or flattery ⟨~*ed* an answer out of her⟩ **4** : to manipulate with great perseverance and usu. with considerable effort toward a desired state or activity ⟨~ a fire to burn⟩
co·ax·i·al \(ˈ)kō-ˈak-sē-əl\ *adj* **1** : having coincident axes **2** : mounted on concentric shafts — **co·ax·i·al·ly** \-sē-ə-lē\ *adv*
coaxial cable *n* : a transmission line that consists of a tube of electrically conducting material surrounding a central conductor held in place by insulators and that is used to transmit telegraph, telephone, and television signals of high frequency — called also *coaxial line*
1**cob** \ˈkäb\ *n* [ME *cobbe* leader; akin to OE *cot* cottage — more at COT] **1** : a male swan **2** *dial Eng* : a rounded mass, lump, or heap **3** : CORNCOB 1 **4** : a short-legged stocky horse usu. with an artificially high stylish action — **cob·by** \ˈkäb-ē\ *adj*
2**cob** *n* [Sp *caba de barra*, lit., end of the bar] : a crudely struck old Spanish coin of irregular shape
3**cob** *n* [prob. fr. 1*cob*] : a mixture that consists of unburned clay usu. with straw as a binder and that is used for constructing walls of small buildings
co·bal·a·min \kō-ˈbal-ə-mən\ *also* **co·bal·a·mine** \-ˌmēn\ *n* [*cobalt* + *vitamin*] : a member of the vitamin B_{12} group; *broadly* : the vitamin B_{12} group
co·balt \ˈkō-ˌbȯlt\ *n* [G *kobalt*, alter. of *kobold*, lit., goblin, fr. MHG *kobolt*; fr. its occurrence in silver ore, believed to be due to goblins] : a tough lustrous silver-white magnetic metallic element that is related to and occurs with iron and nickel and is used esp. in alloys — see ELEMENT table
cobalt blue *n* : a greenish blue pigment consisting essentially of cobalt oxide and alumina
co·bal·tic \kō-ˈbȯl-tik\ *adj* : of, relating to, or containing cobalt esp. with a valence of three
co·balt·ite \ˈkō-ˌbȯl-ˌtīt, kō-ˈ\ *or* **co·balt·ine** \-ˌtēn\ *n* [*cobaltite*, alter. of *cobaltine*, fr. F, fr. *cobalt*] : a mineral consisting of a grayish to silver-white cobalt sulfarsenide CoAsS used in making smalt
co·bal·tous \kō-ˈbȯl-təs\ *adj* : of, relating to, or containing cobalt esp. with a valence of two
cobalt 60 *n* : a heavy radioactive isotope of cobalt of the mass number 60 produced in nuclear reactors and used as a source of gamma rays (as for radiotherapy)
cob·ber \ˈkäb-ər\ *n* [origin unknown] *Austral* : BUDDY
1**cob·ble** \ˈkäb-əl\ *vt* **cob·bled; cob·bling** \-(ə-)liŋ\ [ME *coblen*, perh. back-formation fr. *cobelere* cobbler] **1** *chiefly Brit* : to mend or patch coarsely **2** : REPAIR, MAKE ⟨*cobbled* shoes⟩ **3** : to make or put together roughly or hastily
2**cobble** *n* [back-formation fr. *cobblestone*] **1** : a naturally rounded stone larger than a pebble and smaller than a boulder; *esp* : such a stone used in paving a street or in construction **2** *pl, chiefly Brit* : lump coal about the size of small cobblestones
3**cobble** *vt* **cob·bled; cob·bling** \-(ə-)liŋ\ : to pave with cobblestones
cob·bler \ˈkäb-lər\ *n* [ME *cobelere*] **1** : a mender or maker of shoes and often of other leather goods **2** *archaic* : a clumsy workman **3** : a tall iced drink consisting usu. of wine, rum, or whiskey, and sugar garnished with mint or a slice of lemon or orange **4** : a deep-dish fruit pie with a thick top crust
cob·ble·stone \ˈkäb-əl-ˌstōn\ *n* [ME, fr. *cobble-* (prob. fr. *cob*) + *stone*] : 2COBBLE 1 — **cob·ble·stoned** \-ˌstōnd\ *adj*
co·bel·lig·er·ent \ˌkō-bə-ˈlij-(ə-)rənt\ *n* : a country fighting with another power against a common enemy — **cobelligerent** *adj*
co·bia \ˈkō-bē-ə\ *n* [origin unknown] : a large percoid fish (*Rachycentron canadum*) of warm seas that is a popular food and sport fish
co·ble \ˈkō-bəl\ *n* [ME] **1** *Scot* : a short flat-bottomed rowboat **2** : a flat-floored fishing boat with a rudder extending below the keel and a lugsail on a raking mast
cob·nut \ˈkäb-ˌnət\ *n* : the fruit of a European hazel (*Corylus avellana grandis*); *also* : the plant bearing this fruit
CO·BOL *or* **Co·bol** \ˈkō-ˌbȯl\ *n* [common business oriented language] : a standardized business language for programming a computer
co·bra \ˈkō-brə\ *n* [Pg *cobra* (*de capello*), lit., hooded snake, fr. L *colubra* snake] : any of several venomous Asiatic and African elapid snakes (genus *Naja*) that when excited expand the skin of the neck into a hood by movement of the anterior ribs; *also* : any of several related African snakes
cob·web \ˈkäb-ˌweb\ *n* [ME *coppeweb*, fr. *coppe* spider (fr. OE *ātorcoppe*) + *web*; akin to MD *coppe* spider] **1** : the network spread by a spider **2** : a single thread spun by a spider or insect larva **3** : something resembling a spider web ⟨filled with the ~*s* of bigotry, suspicion and restraint —Robert Smylie⟩ — **cob·webbed** \-ˌwebd\ *adj* — **cob·web·by** \-ˌweb-ē\ *adj*
co·ca \ˈkō-kə\ *n* [Sp, fr. Quechua *kúka*] **1** : any of several So. American shrubs (genus *Erythroxylon*, family Erythroxylaceae); *esp* : one (*E. coca*) with leaves resembling tea **2** : dried leaves of a coca (as *E. coca*) containing alkaloids including cocaine
co·caine \kō-ˈkān, ˈkō-ˌ\ *n* : a bitter crystalline alkaloid $C_{17}H_{21}NO_4$ that is obtained from coca leaves, is used as a local anesthetic, can result in psychological dependence, and in large doses produces intoxication like that from hemp
co·cain·ism \kō-ˈkā-ˌniz-əm\ *n* : habituation to cocaine
co·cain·ize \kō-ˈkā-ˌnīz\ *vt* **-ized; -iz·ing** : to treat or anesthetize with cocaine
co·car·box·yl·ase \ˌkō-kär-ˈbäk-sə-ˌlās, -ˌlāz\ *n* [*co-* + *carboxylase*] : a coenzyme $C_{12}H_{19}ClN_4O_7P_2S{\cdot}H_2O$ that is a pyrophosphate of thiamine and is important in metabolic reactions (as decarboxylation in the Krebs cycle)
coc·cid \ˈkäk-səd\ *n* [NL *Coccus*, genus of scales, fr. Gk *kokkos* grain, kermes] : SCALE INSECT, MEALYBUG

coc·cid·i·oi·do·my·co·sis \(ˌ)käk-ˌsid-ē-ˌȯid-ō-(ˌ)mī-ˈkō-səs\ *n* [NL, fr. *Coccidioides*, genus of fungi, (fr. *coccidium*) + *mycosis*] : a disease of man and lower animals caused by a fungus (*Coccidioides immitis*) and marked esp. by fever and localized pulmonary symptoms

coc·cid·i·o·sis \(ˌ)käk-ˌsid-ē-ˈō-səs\ *n, pl* **-oses** \-ˌsēz\ : infestation with or disease caused by coccidia

coc·cid·i·um \käk-ˈsid-ē-əm\ *n, pl* **-ia** \-ē-ə\ [NL, dim. of *coccus*] : any of an order (Coccidia) of protozoans usu. parasitic in the digestive epithelium of vertebrates

coc·coid \ˈkäk-ˌȯid\ *adj* : related to or resembling a coccus : GLOBOSE — **coccoid** *n*

coc·cus \ˈkäk-əs\ *n, pl* **coc·ci** \ˈkäk-ˌ(s)ī, ˈkäk-(ˌ)(s)ē\ [NL, fr. Gk *kokkos*] **1** : one of the separable carpels of a schizocarp **2** : a spherical bacterium — **coc·cal** \ˈkäk-əl\ *adj*

-coccus *n comb form, pl* **-cocci** [NL, fr. Gk *kokkos*] : berry-shaped organism ⟨Micro*coccus*⟩

coc·cy·geal \käk-ˈsij-(ē-)əl\ *adj* [ML *coccygeus* of the coccyx, fr. Gk *kokkyk-, kokkyx*] : of or relating to the coccyx

coc·cyx \ˈkäk-siks\ *n, pl* **coc·cy·ges** \ˈkäk-sə-ˌjēz\ *also* **coc·cyx·es** \ˈkäk-sik-səz\ [NL, fr. Gk *kokkyx* cuckoo, coccyx; fr. its resemblance to a cuckoo's beak] : the end of the vertebral column beyond the sacrum in man and tailless apes

co·chair \(ˈ)kō-ˈche(ə)r, -ˈcha(ə)r\ *vt* : to serve as cochairman of

co·chair·man \(ˈ)kō-ˈche(ə)r-mən, -ˈcha(ə)r-\ *n* : a joint chairman, vice-chairman, or assistant chairman

Co·chin Chi·na \ˌkō-chən-ˈchī-nə\ *n* [*Cochin China*, So. Vietnam] : any of an Asian breed of large domestic fowl with thick plumage, small wings and tail, and densely feathered legs and feet

co·chi·neal \ˈkäch-ə-ˌnēl, ˈkō-chə-\ *n* [MF & Sp; MF *cochenille*, fr. OSp *cochinilla* wood louse, cochineal] : a red dyestuff consisting of the dried bodies of female cochineal insects used esp. as a biological stain and as an indicator

cochineal insect *n* : a small bright red insect (*Dactylopius coccus*) that is related to and resembles the mealybug and feeds on cactus

co·chlea \ˈkō-klē-ə, ˈkäk-lē-\ *n pl* **co·chle·as** *or* **co·chle·ae** \-(k)lē-ˌē, -ˌī\ [NL, fr. L, snail, snail shell, fr. Gk *kochlias*, fr. *kochlos* land snail; akin to Gk *konchē* mussel] : a division of the labyrinth of the ear of higher vertebrates that is usu. coiled like a snail shell and is the seat of the hearing organ — see EAR illustration — **coch·le·ar** \-lē-ər\ *adj*

co·chle·ate \ˈkō-klē-ət, -ˌāt, ˈkäk-lē-\ *or* **co·chle·at·ed** \-ˌāt-əd\ *adj* : having the form of a snail shell

co·chro·ma·tog·ra·phy \ˌkō-ˌkrō-mə-ˈtäg-rə-fē\ *n* : chromatography of two or more samples together; *esp* : identification of an unknown substance by chromatographic comparison with a known substance

¹cock \ˈkäk\ *n* [ME *cok*, fr. OE *cocc*, of imit. origin] **1 a** : the adult male of the domestic fowl (*Gallus gallus*) **b** : the male of birds other than the domestic fowl **c** : WOODCOCK **d** *archaic* : the crowing of a cock; *also* : COCKCROW **e** : WEATHERCOCK **2** : a device (as a faucet or valve) for regulating the flow of a liquid **3 a** : a chief person : LEADER **b** : a person of spirit and often of a certain swagger or arrogance **4 a** : the hammer in the lock of a firearm **b** : the cocked position of the hammer **5** : PENIS — usu. considered vulgar — **cock of the walk** : one that dominates a group or situation esp. overbearingly

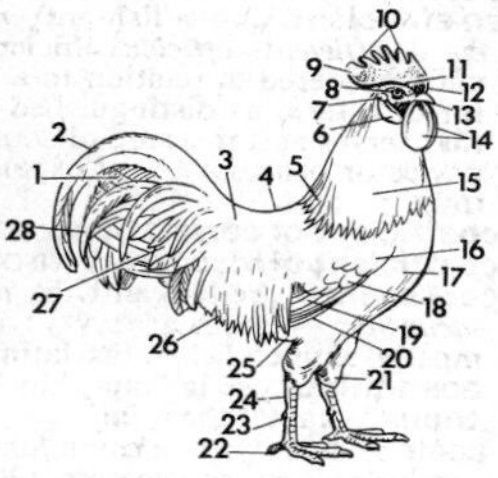

cock 1a: *1* main tail, *2* sickle feathers, *3* saddle, *4* back, *5* cape, *6* ear lobe, *7* ear, *8* eye, *9* blade, *10* points, *11* base, *12* comb, *13* beak, *14* wattles, *15* hackle, *16* wing bow, *17* breast, *18* wing bar, *19* secondaries, *20* primaries, *21* hock, *22* claw, *23* spur, *24* shank, *25* fluff, *26* saddle feathers, *27* tail coverts, *28* lesser sickle feathers

²cock *vi* **1** : STRUT, SWAGGER **2** : to turn, tip, or stick up **3** : to position the hammer of a firearm for firing ~ *vt* **1** : to draw the hammer of (a firearm) back and set for firing; *also* : to set (the trigger) for firing **b** : to draw or bend back in preparation for throwing or hitting **c** : to set a mechanism (as a camera shutter) for tripping **2 a** : to set erect **b** : to turn, tip, or tilt usu. to one side **c** : to lift and place high ⟨sat down and ~*ed* his feet up on the desk⟩ **3** : to turn up (as a hat brim) — **cock a snook** *or* **cock snooks** \-ˈsnu̇k(s), -ˈsnüks\ : to thumb the nose

³cock *n* : TILT, SLANT ⟨~ of the head⟩

⁴cock *n* [ME *cok*, of Scand origin] : a small pile (as of hay)

⁵cock *vt* : to put (as hay) into cocks

cock·ade \kä-ˈkād\ *n* [modif. of F *cocarde*, fr. fem. of *cocard* vain, fr. *coq* cock, fr. OF *coc*, of imit. origin] : a rosette or a similar ornament worn on the hat as a badge — **cock·ad·ed** \-ˈkād-əd\ *adj*

cock–a–hoop \ˌkäk-ə-ˈhüp, -ˈhu̇p\ *adj* [fr. the phrase *to set cock a hoop* to be festive] **1** : triumphantly boastful : EXULTING **2** : AWRY

Cock·aigne \kä-ˈkān\ *n* [ME *cokaygne*, fr. MF (*pais de*) *cocaigne* land of plenty] : an imaginary land of great luxury and ease

cock–a–leek·ie \ˌkäk-i-ˈlē-kē\ *n* [alter. of *cockie* (dim. of ¹*cock*) + *leekie*, dim. of *leek*] : a soup made of chicken boiled with leeks

cock·a·lo·rum \ˌkäk-ə-ˈlōr-əm, -ˈlȯr-\ *n, pl* **-rums** [prob. modif. of obs. Flem *kockeloeren* to crow, of imit. origin] **1** : a self-important little man **2** : the game of leapfrog **3** : boastful talk

cock·a·ma·my *or* **cock·a·ma·mie** \ˌkäk-ə-ˈmā-mē\ *adj* [E dial. *cockamamy* decal, alter. of E *decalcomania*] : RIDICULOUS, INCREDIBLE ⟨of all the ~ excuses I ever heard —Leo Rosten⟩

cock–and–bull story \ˌkäk-ən-ˈbu̇l-\ *n* : an incredible story told as true

cock·a·tiel \ˌkäk-ə-ˈtē(ə)l\ *n* [D *kaketielje*, deriv. of Malay *kakatua*] : a small crested gray Australian parrot (*Nymphicus hollandicus*) with a yellow head

cock·a·too \ˈkäk-ə-ˌtü\ *n, pl* **-toos** [D *kaketoe*, fr. Malay *kakatua*, fr. *kakak* elder sibling + *tua* old] : any of numerous large noisy usu. showy and crested chiefly Australasian parrots (esp. genus *Kakatoe*)

cock·a·trice \ˈkäk-ə-trəs, -ˌtrīs\ *n* [ME *cocatrice*, fr. MF *cocatris* ichneumon, cockatrice, fr. ML *cocatric-, cocatrix* ichneumon] : a legendary serpent that is hatched by a reptile from a cock's egg and that has a deadly glance

cock·boat \ˈkäk-ˌbōt\ *n* : a small boat; *esp* : one used as a tender to a larger boat

cock·cha·fer \ˈkäk-ˌchā-fər\ *n* [¹*cock* + *chafer*] : a large European beetle (*Melolontha melolontha*) destructive to vegetation as an adult and to roots as a larva; *also* : any of various related beetles

cock·crow \ˈkäk-ˌkrō\ *n* **1** : DAWN **2** : an utterance suggesting the triumphant crowing of a cock

cocked hat \ˈkäkt-\ *n* **1** : a hat with brim turned up to give a three-cornered appearance **2** : a hat with brim turned up on two sides and worn either front to back or sideways

¹cock·er \ˈkäk-ər\ *vt* [ME *cokeren*] : INDULGE, PAMPER

²cocker *n* : a keeper or handler of fighting cocks

cock·er·el \ˈkäk-(ə-)rəl\ *n* [ME *cokerelle*, fr. OF dial. *kokerel*, dim. of OF *coc*] : a young male domestic fowl

cock·er spaniel \ˌkäk-ər-\ *n* [*cocking* (woodcock hunting)] : a small spaniel with long ears, square muzzle, and silky coat

cock·eye \ˈkäk-ˈī, -ˌī\ *n* : a squinting eye

cock·eyed \ˈkäk-ˈīd\ *adj* **1** : having a cockeye **2 a** : ASKEW, AWRY **b** : slightly crazy : TOPSY-TURVY ⟨a ~ scheme⟩ **c** : DRUNK — **cock·eyed·ly** \(ˈ)käk-ˈī(-ə)d-lē\ *adv* — **cock·eyed·ness** \-ˈīd-nəs\ *n*

cock·fight \ˈkäk-ˌfīt\ *n* : a contest of gamecocks usu. fitted with metal spurs — **cock·fight·ing** \-ˌfīt-iŋ\ *adj or n*

cockfight chair *n* [fr. its use for viewing sports] : READING CHAIR

cock·horse \ˈkäk-ˌhȯ(ə)rs\ *n* [perh. fr. *cock*, adj., (male) + *horse*] : ROCKING HORSE

¹cock·le \ˈkäk-əl\ *n* [ME, fr. OE *coccel*] : any of several grainfield weeds; *esp* : CORN COCKLE

²cockle *n* [ME *cokille*, fr. MF *coquille* shell, modif. of L *conchylia*, pl. of *conchylium*, fr. Gk *konchylion*, fr. *konchē* conch] **1** : a bivalve mollusk (family Cardiidae) having a shell with convex radially ribbed valves; *esp* : a common edible European bivalve (*Cardium edule*) **2** : COCKLESHELL

³cockle *n* [MF *coquille*] : PUCKER, WRINKLE — **cockle** *vb*

cock·le·bur \ˈkäk-əl-ˌbər, ˈkək-\ *n* : any of a genus (*Xanthium*) of prickly-fruited composite plants; *also* : one of its stiff-spined fruits

cock·le·shell \ˈkäk-əl-ˌshel\ *n* **1 a** : the shell or one of the shell valves of a cockle **b** : a shell (as a scallop shell) suggesting a cockleshell **2** : a light flimsy boat

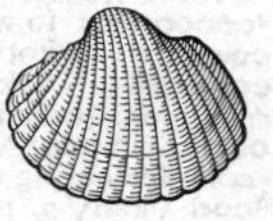

cockleshell 1a

cock·les of the heart \ˌkäk-əlz-\ [perh. fr. ²*cockle*] : the core of one's being — usu. used in the phrase *to warm the cockles of the heart*

cock·loft \ˈkäk-ˌlȯft\ *n* [prob. fr. ¹*cock*] : a small garret

cock·ney \ˈkäk-nē\ *n, pl* **cockneys** [ME *cokeney*, lit., cocks' egg, fr. *coken* (gen. pl. of *cok* cock) + *ey* egg, fr. OE *ǣg*] **1** *obs* **a** : a spoiled child **b** : a squeamish woman **2 a** : a native of London and esp. of the East End of London **b** : the dialect of London or of the East End of London — **cockney** *adj* — **cock·ney·ish** \-ish\ *adj* — **cock·ney·ism** \-ˌiz-əm\ *n*

cock·ney·fy \ˈkäk-ni-ˌfī\ *vt* **-fied; -fy·ing** : to make cockney or similar to a cockney

cock·pit \ˈkäk-ˌpit\ *n* **1 a** : a pit or enclosure for cockfights **b** : a place noted for esp. bloody, violent, or long-continued conflict ⟨in the ~ of Southeast Asia —James Morris⟩ **2** *obs* : the pit of a theater **3 a** : an apartment of an old sailing warship used as quarters for junior officers and for treatment of the wounded in an engagement **b** : an open space aft of a decked area from which a small ship is steered **c** : a space in the fuselage of an airplane for the pilot or the pilot and passengers or in large passenger planes the pilot and crew — see AIRPLANE illustration **d** : the driver's compartment in an automobile

cock·roach \ˈkäk-ˌrōch\ *n* [by folk etymology fr. Sp *cucaracha* cockroach, irreg. fr. *cuca* caterpillar] : any of an order (Blattaria) of chiefly nocturnal insects including some that are domestic pests

cocks·comb \ˈkäk-ˌskōm\ *n* **1** : COXCOMB **2** : a garden plant (genus *Celosia*) of the amaranth family grown for its flowers

cocks·foot \-ˌfu̇t\ *n* : a tall hay and pasture grass (*Dactylis glomerata*) that grows in tufts with loose open panicles

cock·shut \ˈkäk-ˌshət\ *n* [fr. the time poultry are shut in to rest] *dial Eng* : evening twilight

cock·shy \-ˌshī\ *n, pl* **cockshies** [¹*cock* + *shy*, n.] **1 a** : a throw at an object set up as a mark **b** : a mark or target so set up **2** : an object or person taken as a butt (as of constant criticism or ridicule)

cock·sure \ˈkäk-ˈshu̇(ə)r\ *adj* [prob. fr. ¹*cock* + *sure*] **1** : feeling perfect assurance sometimes on inadequate grounds **2** : marked by overconfidence or presumptuousness : COCKY ***syn*** see SURE ***ant*** dubious, doubtful — **cock·sure·ly** *adv* — **cock·sure·ness** *n*

¹cock·tail \ˈkäk-ˌtāl\ *n* [¹*cock* + *tail*] **1** : a horse with its tail docked **2** : a horse not of pure breed

²cocktail *n* [prob. fr. ¹*cock* + *tail*] **1 a** : an iced drink of distilled liquor mixed with flavoring ingredients **b** : something resembling or suggesting such a drink; *esp* : a mixture of diverse elements ⟨fog and smoke in equal parts — a city ~ familiar to all —*New Yorker*⟩ **2** : an appetizer (as tomato juice) served as a first course at a meal

ə abut	ᵊ kitten	ər further	a back	ā bake	ä cot, cart
au̇ out	ch chin	e less	ē easy	g gift	i trip	ī life
j joke	ŋ sing	ō flow	ȯ flaw	ȯi coin	th thin	t͟h this
ü loot	u̇ foot	y yet	yü few	yu̇ furious	zh vision

³cocktail *adj* **1 :** of, relating to, or set aside for cocktails ⟨a ~ hour⟩ **2 :** designed for semiformal wear ⟨~ dress⟩
cocktail glass *n* **:** a bell-shaped drinking glass usu. having a foot and stem and holding about three ounces
cocktail lounge *n* **:** a public room (as in a hotel, club, or restaurant) where cocktails and other drinks are served
cocktail party *n* **:** an informal or semiformal party or gathering at which cocktails are served
cocktail table *n* **:** COFFEE TABLE
cocky \ˈkäk-ē\ *adj* **cock·i·er; -est** **1 :** PERT, ARROGANT **2 :** JAUNTY — **cock·i·ly** \ˈkäk-ə-lē\ *adv* — **cock·i·ness** \ˈkäk-ē-nəs\ *n*
¹co·co \ˈkō-(ˌ)kō\ *n, pl* **cocos** [Sp & Pg; Sp, fr. Pg *côco,* lit., bogeyman] **:** the coconut palm; *also* **:** its fruit
²coco *adj* **:** made from the fibrous husk of the coconut ⟨~ matting⟩
co·coa \ˈkō-(ˌ)kō\ *n* [modif. of Sp *cacao*] **1 :** CACAO 1 **2 a :** chocolate deprived of a portion of its fat and pulverized **b :** a beverage prepared by heating powdered cocoa with water or milk
cocoa bean *n* **:** CACAO 2
cocoa butter *n* **:** a pale vegetable fat with a low melting point obtained from cacao beans
¹co·con·scious \(ˈ)kō-ˈkän-chəs\ *adj* **1 :** experiencing or aware of the same things ⟨a ~ people⟩ **2 :** of or relating to the coconscious
²coconscious *n* **:** mental processes outside the main stream of consciousness but sometimes available to it
co·con·scious·ness *n* **:** COCONSCIOUS
co·con·spir·a·tor \ˌkō-kən-ˈspir-ət-ər\ *n* **:** a fellow conspirator
co·co·nut \ˈkō-kə-(ˌ)nət\ *n* **1 :** the drupaceous fruit of the coconut palm whose outer fibrous husk yields coir and whose nut contains thick edible meat and coconut milk **2 :** the edible meat of the coconut
coconut crab *n* **:** PURSE CRAB
coconut oil *n* **:** a nearly colorless fatty oil or white semisolid fat extracted from fresh coconuts and used esp. in making soaps and food products
coconut palm *n* **:** a tall pinnate-leaved tropical palm (*Cocos nucifera*) prob. of American origin
¹co·coon \kə-ˈkün\ *n* [F *cocon,* fr. Prov *coucoun,* fr. *coco* shell, fr. L *coccum* excrescence on a tree, fr. Gk *kokkos* grain, seed, kermes] **1 a :** an envelope often largely of silk which an insect larva forms about itself and in which it passes the pupa stage — see SILKWORM illustration **b :** any of various other protective coverings produced by animals **2 a :** a covering suggesting a cocoon **b :** a protective covering placed or sprayed over military or naval equipment in storage
²cocoon *vt* **:** to wrap or envelop esp. tightly in or as if in a cocoon
co·cotte \kō-ˈkȯt\ *n, pl* **cocottes** \-ˈkȯt(s)\ [F] **:** PROSTITUTE
coc·o·zel·le \ˌkäk-ə-ˈzel-ē\ *n* [prob. deriv. of It *cocuzza* squash] **:** a summer squash resembling the zucchini
co·cur·ric·u·lar \ˌkō-kə-ˈrik-yə-lər\ *adj* **:** being outside of but usu. complementing the regular curriculum
¹cod \ˈkäd\ *n, pl* **cod** *also* **cods** [ME] **1 a :** a soft-finned fish (*Gadus morrhua*) of the colder parts of the No. Atlantic that is a major food fish **b :** a fish of the cod family (Gadidae); *esp* **:** a Pacific fish (*Gadus macrocephalus*) closely related to the Atlantic cod **2 :** any of various spiny-finned fishes resembling the true cods
²cod *abbr* codex
COD *abbr* **1** cash on delivery **2** collect on delivery
co·da \ˈkōd-ə\ *n* [It, lit., tail, fr. L *cauda*] **1 a :** a concluding musical section that is formally distinct from the main structure **b :** a concluding part of a literary or dramatic work **2 :** something that serves to round out, conclude, or summarize and that has an interest of its own
cod·dle \ˈkäd-ᵊl\ *vt* **cod·dled; cod·dling** \ˈkäd-liŋ, -ᵊl-iŋ\ [perh. fr. *caudle*] **1 :** to cook (as eggs) in liquid slowly and gently just below the boiling point **2 :** to treat with extreme care **:** PAMPER — **cod·dler** \ˈkäd-lər, -ᵊl-ər\ *n*
¹code \ˈkōd\ *n* [ME, fr. MF, fr. L *caudex, codex* trunk of a tree, tablet of wood covered with wax for writing on, book; akin to L *cudere* to beat — more at HEW] **1 :** a systematic statement of a body of law; *esp* **:** one given statutory force **2 :** a system of principles or rules ⟨moral ~⟩ **3 a :** a system of signals for communication **b :** a system of symbols (as letters, numbers, or words) used to represent assigned and often secret meanings **4 :** GENETIC CODE — **code·less** \-ləs\ *adj*
²code *vt* **cod·ed; cod·ing :** to put in or into the form or symbols of a code — **cod·able** \ˈkōd-ə-bəl\ *adj* — **cod·er** *n*
code book *n* **:** a book containing an alphabetical list of words or expressions with their code group equivalents for use in secret communications
co·dec·li·na·tion \(ˌ)kō-ˌdek-lə-ˈnā-shən\ *n* **:** the complement of the declination
co·de·fen·dant \ˌkō-di-ˈfen-dənt\ *n* **:** a joint defendant
code group *n* **:** one of the constituent groups of letters or numbers in an encoded text
co·deine \ˈkō-ˌdēn, ˈkōd-ē-ən\ *n* [F *codéine,* fr. Gk *kōdeia* poppyhead, fr. *kōos* cavity; akin to Gk *koilos* hollow] **:** a morphine derivative $C_{18}H_{21}NO_3.H_2O$ that is found in opium, is weaker in action than morphine, and is used esp. in cough remedies
co·den \ˈkō-ˌden\ *n* [irreg. fr. ¹*code*] **:** a code classification assigned to a library item (as a book, document, or periodical)
code name *n* **:** a word made to serve as a code designation
co·de·ter·mi·na·tion \ˌkō-di-ˌtər-mə-ˈnā-shən\ *n* **:** the participation of labor with management in the determination of business policy
code word *n* **1 :** CODE NAME **2 :** CODE GROUP
co·dex \ˈkō-ˌdeks\ *n, pl* **co·di·ces** \ˈkōd-ə-ˌsēz, ˈkäd-\ [L] **:** a manuscript book esp. of Scripture, classics, or ancient annals
cod·fish \ˈkäd-ˌfish\ *n* **:** COD; *also* **:** its flesh used as food
cod·ger \ˈkäj-ər\ *n* [prob. alter. of *cadger*] **:** a mildly eccentric or disreputable fellow
cod·i·cil \ˈkäd-ə-səl, -ˌsil\ *n* [MF *codicille,* fr. L *codicillus,* dim. of *codic-, codex* book] **1 :** a legal instrument made subsequently to a will and modifying it **2 :** APPENDIX, SUPPLEMENT — **cod·i·cil·la·ry** \ˌkäd-ə-ˈsil-ə-rē\ *adj*
cod·i·fy \ˈkäd-ə-ˌfī, ˈkōd-\ *vt* **-fied; -fy·ing** **1 :** to reduce to a code **2 a :** SYSTEMATIZE **b :** CLASSIFY — **cod·i·fi·abil·i·ty** \ˌkäd-ə-ˌfī-ə-ˈbil-ət-ē, ˌkōd-\ *n* — **cod·i·fi·ca·tion** \-fə-ˈkā-shən\ *n*
¹cod·ling \ˈkäd-liŋ\ *n* **1 :** a young cod **2 :** any of several hakes (esp. genus *Urophycis*)
²cod·ling \ˈkäd-liŋ\ *or* **cod·lin** \-lən\ *n* [alter. of ME *querdlyng*] **:** a small immature apple; *also* **:** any of several elongated greenish English cooking apples
codling moth *n* **:** a small moth (*Laspeyresia pomonella*) whose larva lives in apples, pears, quinces, and English walnuts
cod–liver oil *n* **:** an oil obtained from the liver of the cod and closely related fishes and used as a source of vitamins A and D
co·dom·i·nant \(ˈ)kō-ˈdäm-ə-nənt\ *adj* **1 a :** forming part of the main canopy of a forest ⟨~ trees⟩ **b :** sharing in the controlling influence of a biotic community **2 :** being fully expressed in the heterozygous condition ⟨two ~ alleles⟩ — **codominant** *n*
co·don \ˈkō-ˌdän\ *n* [¹*code* + ²-*on*] **:** a triplet of nucleotides that is part of the genetic code and that specifies a particular amino acid in a protein or starts or stops protein synthesis
cod·piece \ˈkäd-ˌpēs\ *n* [ME *codpese,* fr. *cod* bag, scrotum (fr. OE *codd*) + *pese* piece] **:** a flap or bag concealing an opening in the front of men's breeches esp. in the 15th and 16th centuries
cods·wal·lop \ˈkädz-ˌwäl-əp\ *n* [origin unknown] *Brit* **:** NONSENSE
¹co·ed \ˈkō-ˌed\ *n* [short for *coeducational student*] **:** a female student in a coeducational institution
²coed *adj* **1 :** COEDUCATIONAL **2 :** of or relating to a coed **3 :** open to both men and women
co–edi·tion \ˌkō-ə-ˈdish-ən\ *n* **:** an edition of a book published simultaneously by more than one publisher usu. in different countries and in different languages
co·ed·i·tor \(ˈ)kō-ˈed-ət-ər\ *n* **:** one who collaborates with another in editing a newspaper, magazine, or book

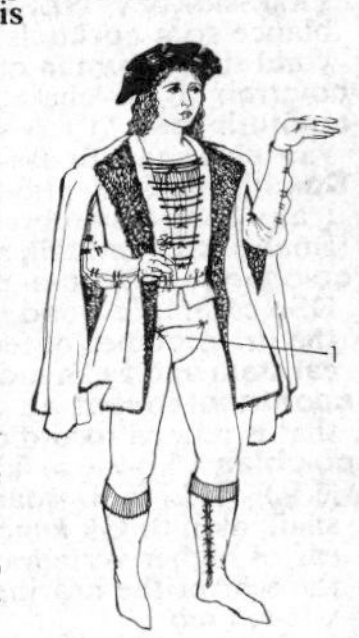
1 codpiece

co·ed·u·ca·tion \(ˌ)kō-ˌej-ə-ˈkā-shən\ *n* **:** the education of students of both sexes at the same institution
co·ed·u·ca·tion·al \-shnəl, -shən-ᵊl\ *adj* **:** of or relating to coeducation — **co·ed·u·ca·tion·al·ly** \-ē\ *adv*
coeff *or* **coef** *abbr* coefficient
co·ef·fi·cient \ˌkō-ə-ˈfish-ənt\ *n* [NL *coefficient-, coefficiens,* fr. L *co-* + *efficient-, efficiens* efficient] **1 :** any of the factors of a product considered in relation to a specific factor; *esp* **:** a constant factor of a term as distinguished from a variable **2 a :** a number that serves as a measure of some property or characteristic (as of a device or process) ⟨~ of expansion of a metal⟩ **b :** MEASURE, DEGREE
coefficient of correlation : CORRELATION COEFFICIENT
coefficient of viscosity : VISCOSITY 3
coel·acanth \ˈsē-lə-ˌkan(t)th\ *n* [deriv. of Gk *koilos* hollow + NL *-acanthus* — more at CAVE] **:** any of a family (Coelacanthidae) of mostly extinct fishes (as latimeria) — **coelacanth** *adj* — **coel·acan·thine** \ˌsē-lə-ˈkan-ˌthīn, -ˈkan(t)-thən\ *adj* — **coel·acan·thous** \-ˈkan(t)-thəs\ *adj*
-coele *or* **-coel** \ˌsēl\ *n comb form* [prob. fr. NL *-coela,* fr. neut. pl. of *-coelus* hollow, concave, fr. Gk *-koilos,* fr. *koilos*] **:** cavity **:** chamber **:** ventricle ⟨blasto*coel*⟩ ⟨entero*coele*⟩
coel·en·ter·ate \si-ˈlent-ə-ˌrāt, -rət\ *n* [deriv. of Gk *koilos* + *enteron* intestine — more at INTER-] **:** any of a phylum (Coelenterata) of basically radially symmetrical invertebrate animals including the corals, sea anemones, jellyfishes, and hydroids — **coelenterate** *adj*
coel·en·ter·on \-ˌrän, -rən\ *n, pl* **-tera** \-rə\ [NL, fr. Gk *koilos* + *enteron*] **:** the internal cavity of a coelenterate
coe·li·ac \ˈsē-lē-ˌak\ *var of* CELIAC
coe·lom \ˈsē-ləm\ *n, pl* **coeloms** *or* **coe·lo·ma·ta** \si-ˈlō-mət-ə\ [G, fr. Gk *koilōma* cavity, fr. *koilos*] **:** the usu. epithelium-lined space between the body wall and the digestive tract of metazoans above the lower worms — **coe·lo·mate** \ˈsē-lə-ˌmāt\ *adj or n* — **coe·lo·mic** \si-ˈläm-ik, -ˈlō-mik\ *adj*
coen- *or* **coeno-** *comb form* [NL, fr. Gk *koin-, koino-,* fr. *koinos* — more at CO-] **:** common **:** general ⟨*coeno*cyte⟩
coe·no·bite \ˈsē-nə-ˌbīt\ *var of* CENOBITE
coe·no·cyte \ˈsē-nə-ˌsīt\ *n* [ISV] **1 a :** a multinucleate mass of protoplasm resulting from repeated nuclear division unaccompanied by cell fission **b :** an organism consisting of such a structure **2 :** SYNCYTIUM 1 — **coe·no·cyt·ic** \ˌsē-nə-ˈsit-ik\ *adj*
coe·no·ge·net·ic \ˌsē-nə-jə-ˈnet-ik\ *var of* CENOGENETIC
coe·nu·rus \si-ˈn(y)ůr-əs\ *n, pl* **-nu·ri** \-ˈn(y)ů(ə)r-ˌī\ [NL, fr. *coen-* + Gk *oura* tail] **:** a complex tapeworm larva consisting of a sac from the inner wall of which numerous scolices develop
co·en·zyme \(ˈ)kō-ˈen-ˌzīm\ *n* **:** a thermostable nonprotein compound that forms the active portion of an enzyme system after combination with an apoenzyme — **co·en·zy·mat·ic** \(ˌ)kō-ˌen-zə-ˈmat-ik, -(ˌ)zī-\ *adj* — **co·en·zy·mat·i·cal·ly** \-i-k(ə-)lē\ *adv*
coenzyme A *n* **:** a coenzyme $C_{21}H_{36}N_7O_{16}P_3S$ that occurs in all living cells and is essential to the metabolism of carbohydrates, fats, and some amino acids — compare ACETYL COENZYME A
coenzyme Q *n* **:** UBIQUINONE
co·equal \(ˈ)kō-ˈē-kwəl\ *adj* **:** equal with one another — **co·equal·i·ty** \ˌkō-ē-ˈkwäl-ət-ē\ *n* — **co·equal·ly** \(ˈ)kō-ˈē-kwə-lē\ *adv*
co·erce \kō-ˈərs\ *vt* **co·erced; co·erc·ing** [L *coercēre,* fr. *co-* + *arcēre* to shut up, enclose — more at ARK] **1 :** to restrain or dominate by nullifying individual will **2 :** to compel to an act or choice ⟨they could ~ the citizens by threats but not persuade their agreement⟩ **3 :** to enforce or bring about by force or threat ***syn*** see FORCE — **co·erc·ible** \-ˈər-sə-bəl\ *adj*

co·er·cion \-'ər-zhən, -shən\ *n* : the act, process, or power of coercing

co·er·cive \-'ər-siv\ *adj* : serving or intended to coerce — **co·er·cive·ly** *adv* — **co·er·cive·ness** *n*

coercive force *n* : the opposing magnetic intensity that must be applied to a magnetized material to remove the residual magnetism

co·er·civ·i·ty \ˌkō-ˌər-'siv-ət-ē\ *n* : the property of a material determined by the value of the coercive force when the material has been magnetized to saturation

co·e·ta·ne·ous \ˌkō-ə-'tā-nē-əs\ *adj* [L *coaetaneus,* fr. *co-* + *aetas* age — more at AGE] : COEVAL

co·eter·nal \ˌkō-i-'tərn-ᵊl\ *adj* : equally or jointly eternal — **co·eter·nal·ly** \-ᵊl-ē\ *adv* — **co·eter·ni·ty** \-'tər-nət-ē\ *n*

co·eval \kō-'ē-vəl\ *adj* [L *coaevus,* fr. *co-* + *aevum* age, lifetime — more at AGE] : of the same or equal age, antiquity, or duration *syn* see CONTEMPORARY — **coeval** *n* — **co·eval·i·ty** \ˌkō-(ˌ)ē-'val-ət-ē\ *n*

co·ex·ist \ˌkō-ig-'zist\ *vi* **1** : to exist together or at the same time **2** : to live in peace with each other esp. as a matter of policy — **co·ex·is·tence** \-'zis-tən(t)s\ *n* — **co·ex·is·tent** \-tənt\ *adj*

co·ex·ten·sive \ˌkō-ik-'sten(t)-siv\ *adj* : having the same spatial or temporal scope or boundaries — **co·ex·ten·sive·ly** *adv*

co·fac·tor \'kō-ˌfak-tər\ *n* **1** : the signed minor of an element of a square matrix or of a determinant with the sign positive if the sum of the column number and row number of the element is even and with the sign negative if it is odd **2** : a substance that acts with another substance to bring about certain effects; *esp* : COENZYME

C of C *abbr* Chamber of Commerce

co·fea·ture \'kō-ˌfē-chər\ *n* : a feature (as in an entertainment) accompanying a main attraction

cof·fee \'kȯ-fē, 'käf-ē\ *n, often attrib* [It & Turk; It *caffè,* fr. Turk *kahve,* fr. Ar *qaḥwa*] **1 a** : a drink made by percolation, infusion, or decoction from the roasted and ground or pounded seeds of a coffee tree; *also* : these seeds either green or roasted **b** : COFFEE TREE 1 **2** : a cup of coffee ⟨two ~s⟩ **3** : COFFEE HOUR

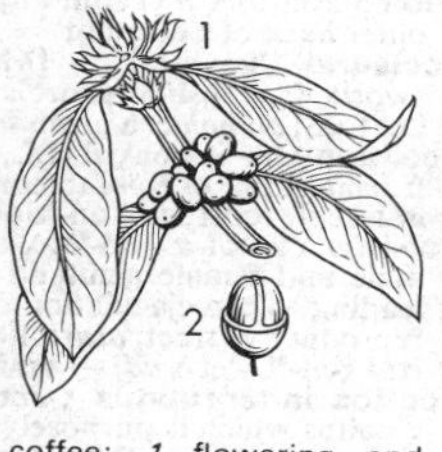

coffee break *n* : a short rest period (as in mid-morning or mid-afternoon) during which refreshments are often consumed

coffee cake *n* : a sweet rich bread often with added fruit, nuts, and spices that is sometimes glazed after baking

coffee hour *n* **1** : a usu. fixed occasion of informal meeting and chatting at which refreshments are served **2** : COFFEE BREAK

cof·fee·house \-ˌhau̇s\ *n* : an establishment that sells coffee and usu. other refreshments and that commonly serves as an informal club for its habitués

coffee klatch \-ˌklach\ *n* [part trans. of G *kaffeeklatsch*] : KAFFEEKLATSCH

coffee maker *n* : a utensil in which coffee is brewed

coffee mill *n* : a mill for grinding coffee beans

cof·fee·pot \-ˌpät\ *n* : a utensil for preparing or serving coffee

coffee ring *n* : coffee cake in the shape of a ring

coffee roll *n* : a roll made from sweet raised dough (as coffee cake dough)

coffee room *n* : a room where refreshments are served

coffee royal *n* : a drink of black coffee and a liquor (as brandy or rum) often sweetened with sugar

coffee service *n* : a usu. sterling silver or silverplate service consisting of coffeepot, sugar bowl, creamer, and tray

coffee set *n* **1** : COFFEE SERVICE **2** : a set of porcelain or pottery for the serving of coffee consisting typically of coffeepot, sugar bowl, cream pitcher, and matching cups and saucers

coffee shop *n* : a small restaurant

coffee table *n* : a low table customarily placed in front of a sofa — called also *cocktail table*

coffee–table book *n* : an expensive, lavishly illustrated, and oversize book suitable for display on a coffee table — called also *coffee-tabler*

coffee tree *n* **1 a** : a large evergreen shrub or small tree (*Coffea arabica*) of the madder family that is native to Africa but is now widely cultivated in warm regions for its seeds which form most of the coffee of commerce — called also *Arabian coffee* **b** : a tree (genus *Coffea*) related to the coffee tree **2** : KENTUCKY COFFEE TREE

¹cof·fer \'kȯ-fər, 'käf-ər\ *n* [ME *coffre,* fr. OF, fr. L *cophinus* basket, fr. Gk *kophinos*] **1** : CHEST, BOX; *esp* : STRONGBOX **2** : TREASURY, EXCHEQUER — usu. used in pl. **3** : the chamber of a canal lock **4** : a recessed panel in a vault, ceiling, or soffit

²coffer *vt* **1** : to store or hoard up in a coffer **2** : to form (as a ceiling) with recessed panels

cof·fer·dam \-ˌdam\ *n* **1** : a watertight enclosure from which water is pumped to expose the bottom of a body of water and permit construction (as of a pier) **2** : a watertight structure for making repairs below the waterline of a ship

¹cof·fin \'kȯ-fən\ *n* [ME, basket, receptacle, fr. MF *cofin,* fr. L *cophinus*] **1** : a box or chest for burying a corpse **2** : the horny body forming the hoof of a horse's foot

²coffin *vt* : to enclose in or as if in a coffin

coffin bone *n* : the bone enclosed within the hoof of the horse

coffin corner *n* : one of the corners formed by a goal line and a sideline on a football field into which a punt is often aimed so that it may go out of bounds close to the defender's goal line

coffin nail *n, slang* : CIGARETTE

cof·fle \'kȯ-fəl, 'käf-əl\ *n* [Ar *qāfila* caravan] : a train of slaves or animals fastened together

C of S *abbr* chief of staff

coffee: *1* flowering and fruiting branch with leaves, *2* fruit with pericarp partly removed to show seeds

co·func·tion \(')kō-'fən(k)-shən\ *n* : a trigonometric function whose value for the complement of an angle is equal to the value of a given trigonometric function for the angle itself (the sine is the ~ of the cosine)

¹cog \'käg\ *n* [ME *cogge,* of Scand origin; akin to Norw *kug* cog; akin to OE *cycgel* cudgel] **1 a** : a tooth on the rim of a wheel or gear **b** : a necessary but subordinate person or part — **cogged** \'kägd\ *adj*

²cog *vb* **cogged; cog·ging** [cog (a trick)] *vi* **1** *obs* : to cheat in throwing dice **2** *obs* : DECEIVE **3** *obs* : to use venal flattery ~ *vt* **1** : to direct the fall of (dice) fraudulently **2** *obs* : WHEEDLE

³cog *vt* **cogged; cog·ging** [prob. alter. of *cock* (cog)] : to connect (as timbers or joists) by means of tenons

⁴cog *n* : a tenon on a beam or timber received into a mortise in another beam to secure the two together

⁵cog *abbr* cognate

co·gen·cy \'kō-jən-sē\ *n* : the quality or state of being cogent

co·gent \'kō-jənt\ *adj* [L *cogent-, cogens,* prp. of *cogere* to drive together, collect, fr. *co-* + *agere* to drive — more at AGENT] **1** : having power to compel or constrain ⟨~ forces of nature⟩ **2 a** : appealing forcibly to the mind or reason : CONVINCING ⟨~ evidence⟩ **b** : presented in a way that brings out pertinent and fundamental points ⟨a ~ analysis of a problem⟩ *syn* see VALID — **co·gent·ly** *adv*

cog·i·ta·ble \'käj-ət-ə-bəl\ *adj* : capable of being brought before the mind as a thought or idea : THINKABLE

cog·i·tate \'käj-ə-ˌtāt\ *vb* **-tat·ed; -tat·ing** [L *cogitatus,* pp. of *cogitare* to think, think about, fr. *co-* + *agitare* to drive, agitate — more at AGITATE] *vt* **1** : to ponder or meditate on usu. with intentness and objectivity **2** : PLAN, PLOT ~ *vi* : to think deeply : PONDER *syn* see THINK

cog·i·ta·tion \ˌkäj-ə-'tā-shən\ *n* **1 a** : the act of cogitating : MEDITATION **b** : the capacity to think or reflect **2** : THOUGHT

cog·i·ta·tive \'käj-ə-ˌtāt-iv\ *adj* **1** : of or relating to cogitation **2** : capable of or given to cogitation

co·gi·to \'kō-gi-ˌtō\ *n* [NL *cogito, ergo sum* I think, therefore I am, principle stated by René Descartes] **1** : the philosophic principle that one's existence is demonstrated by the fact that one thinks **2** : the intellectual processes of the self or ego

co·gnac \'kōn-ˌyak\ *n* [F, fr. *Cognac, France*] **1** : a brandy from the departments of Charente and Charente-Maritime distilled from white wine **2** : a French brandy

¹cog·nate \'käg-ˌnāt\ *adj* [L *cognatus,* fr. *co-* + *gnatus, natus,* pp. of *nasci* to be born; akin to L *gignere* to beget — more at KIN] **1 a** : related by blood **b** : related on the mother's side **2 a** : related by descent from the same ancestral language **b** *of a word or morpheme* : related by derivation, borrowing, or descent **c** *of a substantive* : related usu. in derivation to the verb of which it is the object **3** : of the same or similar nature : generically alike *syn* see RELATED — **cog·nate·ly** *adv*

²cognate *n* : one that is cognate with another

cog·na·tion \käg-'nā-shən\ *n* : cognate relationship

cog·ni·tion \käg-'nish-ən\ *n* [ME *cognicioun,* fr. L *cognition-, cognitio,* fr. *cognitus,* pp. of *cognoscere* to become acquainted with, know, fr. *co-* + *gnoscere* to come to know — more at KNOW] : the act or process of knowing including both awareness and judgment; *also* : a product of this act — **cog·ni·tion·al** \-'nish-nəl, -'nish-ən-ᵊl\ *adj*

cog·ni·tive \'käg-nət-iv\ *adj* **1** : of, relating to, or involving cognition ⟨the ~ elements of perception —C. H. Hamburg⟩ **2** : based on or capable of being reduced to empirical factual knowledge — **cog·ni·tive·ly** *adv* — **cog·ni·tiv·i·ty** \ˌkäg-nə-'tiv-ət-ē\ *n*

cognitive dissonance *n* : psychological conflict resulting from incongruous beliefs and attitudes held simultaneously

cog·ni·za·ble \'käg-nə-zə-bəl, käg-'nī-\ *adj* **1** : capable of being known **2** : capable of being judicially heard and determined — **cog·ni·za·bly** \-blē\ *adv*

cog·ni·zance \'käg-nə-zən(t)s\ *n* [ME *conisaunce,* fr. OF *conoissance,* fr. *conoistre* to know, fr. L *cognoscere*] **1 a** : knowledge through voluntary effort and with responsibility as of one's own action; *also* : a distinguishing mark or emblem (as a heraldic bearing) **2 a** : SURVEILLANCE, CONTROL **b** : APPREHENSION, PERCEPTION **c** : range of apprehension **d** : NOTICE, OBSERVANCE **3 a** : the right and power to hear and decide controversies : JURISDICTION **b** : the judicial hearing of a matter

cog·ni·zant \-zənt\ *adj* : having cognizance; *esp* : having special or certain knowledge often from firsthand sources *syn* see AWARE *ant* ignorant

cog·nize \käg-'nīz\ *vt* **cog·nized; cog·niz·ing** [back-formation fr. *cognizance*] : KNOW — **cog·niz·er** *n*

cog·no·men \käg-'nō-mən\ *n, pl* **cognomens** *or* **cog·no·mi·na** \käg-'näm-ə-nə, -'nō-mə-\ [L, irreg. fr. *co-* + *nomen* name — more at NAME] **1** : SURNAME: *esp* : the third of usu. three names of a person among the ancient Romans **2** : NAME: *esp* : a distinguishing nickname or epithet — **cog·nom·i·nal** \käg-'näm-ən-ᵊl\ *adj*

co·gno·scen·te \ˌkän-(y)ə-'shent-ē, ˌkäg-nə-\ *n, pl* **-scen·ti** \-ē\ [obs. It (now *conoscente*), fr. *cognoscente,* adj., wise, fr. L *cognoscent-, cognoscens,* prp. of *cognoscere*] : a person having or claiming expert knowledge (as of fine arts or fashion) : CONNOISSEUR

cog·nos·ci·ble \käg-'näs-ə-bəl\ *adj* [LL *cognoscibilis,* fr. L *cognoscere*] : COGNIZABLE, KNOWABLE

co·gon \kō-'gōn\ *n* [Sp *cogón,* fr. Tag, Bisayan, & Bikol *kugon*] : any of several coarse tall grasses (genus *Imperata*) used esp. in the Philippines for thatching

cog railway *n* : a steep mountain railroad that has a rail with cogs which engages a cogwheel on the locomotive to ensure traction

ə abut	ᵊ kitten	ər further	a back	ā bake	ä cot, cart
au̇ out	ch chin	e less	ē easy	g gift	i trip	ī life
j joke	ŋ sing	ō flow	ȯ flaw	ȯi coin	th thin	th this
ü loot	u̇ foot	y yet	yü few	yu̇ furious	zh vision	

cogs·well chair \ˈkägz-ˌwel-, -wəl-\ *n, often cap 1st C* [fr. the name *Cogswell*] : an upholstered easy chair with inclined back, thin open arms, and cabriole legs

cog·wheel \ˈkäg-ˌhwēl, -ˌwēl\ *n* : a wheel with cogs or teeth

co·hab·it \kō-ˈhab-ət\ *vi* [LL *cohabitare,* fr. L *co-* + *habitare* to inhabit, fr. *habitus,* pp. of *habēre* to have] **1** : to live together as husband and wife **2 a** : to live together or in company ⟨buffaloes ~*ing* with crossbred cows —*Biol. Abstracts*⟩ **b** : to exist together ⟨two strains in his philosophy . . . ~ in each of his major works —Justus Buchler⟩ — **co·hab·i·tant** \-ət-ənt\ *n* — **co·hab·i·ta·tion** \(ˌ)kō-ˌhab-ə-ˈtā-shən\ *n*

co·heir \(ˈ)kō-ˈa(ə)r, -ˈe(ə)r\ *n* : a joint heir

co·heir·ess \-əs\ *n* : a joint heiress

co·here \kō-ˈhi(ə)r\ *vb* **co·hered; co·her·ing** [L *cohaerēre,* fr. *co-* + *haerēre* to stick — more at HESITATE] *vi* **1 a** : to hold together firmly as parts of the same mass; *broadly* : STICK, ADHERE **b** : to display cohesion of plant parts **2** : to consist of parts that cohere **3 a** : to become united in principles, relationships, or interests **b** : to be logically or aesthetically consistent ~ *vt* : to make (parts or components) fit or stick together in a suitable or orderly way ***syn*** see STICK

co·her·ence \-ən(t)s\ *n* **1** : the quality or state of cohering; *esp* : systematic connection esp. in logical discourse **2** : the property of being coherent

co·her·en·cy \kō-ˈhir-ən-sē, -ˈher-\ *n, pl* **-cies** : COHERENCE

co·her·ent \-ənt\ *adj* [MF or L; MF *cohérent,* fr. L *cohaerent-, cohaerens,* prp. of *cohaerēre*] **1** : having the quality of cohering **2** : logically consistent ⟨a ~ argument⟩ **3** : relating to electromagnetic waves that have a definite relationship to each other: as **a** : composed of wave trains in phase with each other ⟨~ light⟩ **b** : producing coherent light ⟨a ~ source⟩ — **co·her·ent·ly** *adv*

co·her·er \kō-ˈhir-ər\ *n* : a radio detector in which an imperfectly conducting contact between pieces of conductive material loosely resting against each other is materially improved in conductance by the passage of high-frequency current

co·he·sion \kō-ˈhē-zhən\ *n* [L *cohaesus,* pp. of *cohaerēre*] **1** : the act or process of sticking together tightly ⟨social and economic ~ . . . in a small city —J. B. Conant⟩ **2** : union between similar plant parts or organs **3** : molecular attraction by which the particles of a body are united throughout the mass — **co·he·sion·less** \-ləs\ *adj*

co·he·sive \kō-ˈhē-siv, -ziv\ *adj* : exhibiting or producing cohesion or coherence ⟨a ~ social unit⟩ ⟨~ soils⟩ — **co·he·sive·ly** *adv* — **co·he·sive·ness** *n*

co·ho \ˈkō-(ˌ)hō\ *n, pl* **cohos** *or* **coho** [origin unknown] : a rather small salmon (*Oncorhynchus kisutch*) with light-colored flesh that is native to both coasts of the No. Pacific and is stocked in the Great Lakes

co·hort \ˈkō-ˌhȯ(ə)rt\ *n* [MF & L; MF *cohorte,* fr. L *cohort-, cohors* — more at COURT] **1 a** : one of 10 divisions of an ancient Roman legion **b** : a group of warriors or soldiers **c** : BAND, GROUP **d** : a group of individuals having a statistical factor (as age or class membership) in common in a demographic study ⟨a ~ of premedical students⟩ **2 a** : COMPANION, ACCOMPLICE **b** : FOLLOWER, SUPPORTER

co·hosh \ˈkō-ˌhäsh\ *n* [of Algonquian origin; akin to Natick *kôshki* it is rough] : any of several American medicinal or poisonous plants: **a** : BLACK COHOSH **b** : BLUE COHOSH **c** : BANEBERRY

co·iden·ti·ty \ˌkō-ī-ˈden(t)-ət-ē, ˌkō-ə-ˈden(t)-\ *n* : identity between two or more things

[1]coif \ˈkȯif, *in sense 2 usu* ˈkwäf\ *n* [ME *coife,* fr. MF, fr. LL *cofea*] **1** : a close-fitting cap: as **a** : a hoodlike cap worn by nuns under a veil **b** : a protective usu. metal skullcap formerly worn under a hood of mail **c** : a white cap formerly worn by English lawyers and esp. by serjeants-at-law; *also* : the order or rank of a serjeant-at-law **2** : COIFFURE

[2]coif *vt* **coiffed; coif·fing** **1** : to cover or dress with or as if with a coif **2** : to arrange (hair) by brushing, combing, or curling

coif·feur \kwä-ˈfər\ *n* [F, fr. *coiffer*] : a male hairdresser

coif·feuse \kwä-ˈfə(r)z, -ˈf(y)üz\ *n* [F, fem. of *coiffeur*] : a female hairdresser

coif·fure \kwä-ˈfyu̇(ə)r\ *n* [F, fr. *coiffer* to cover with a coif, arrange (hair), fr. *coife*] : a style or manner of arranging the hair

coiffured *adj* **1** : being dressed ⟨beautifully ~ hair⟩ **2** : having the hair brushed, combed, and curled ⟨stylishly ~ women⟩

coign of van·tage \ˌkȯi-nə-ˈvant-ij\ [*coign,* earlier spelling of [1]*coin* (corner)] : an advantageous position

[1]coil \ˈkȯi(ə)l\ *n* [origin unknown] **1** : TURMOIL **2** : TROUBLE

[2]coil *vb* [MF *coillir, cuillir* to gather — more at CULL] *vt* **1** : to wind into rings or spirals **2** : to roll or twist into a shape resembling a coil ~ *vi* **1** : to move in a circular or spiral course **2** : to form or lie in a coil — **coil·abil·i·ty** \ˌkȯi-lə-ˈbil-ət-ē\ *n*

[3]coil *n* **1 a** (1) : a series of loops (2) : SPIRAL **b** : a single loop of such a coil **2** : a number of turns of wire esp. in spiral form usu. for electromagnetic effect or for providing electrical resistance **3** : a series of connected pipes in rows, layers, or windings **4** : a roll of postage stamps; *also* : a stamp from such a roll

[1]coin \ˈkȯin\ *n* [ME, fr. MF, wedge, corner, fr. L *cuneus* wedge] **1** *archaic* **a** : CORNER, CORNERSTONE **b** : WEDGE **2 a** : a usu. flat round piece of metal issued by governmental authority as money **b** : metal money **c** : something resembling a coin esp. in shape **3** : something accepted as having value or validity ⟨perhaps wisecracks . . . are respectable literary ~ in the U.S. —*Times Lit. Supp.*⟩ **4** : something having two different and usu. opposing sides **5** : MONEY ⟨I'm in it for the ~ —Sinclair Lewis⟩

[2]coin *vt* **1 a** : to make (a coin) esp. by stamping : MINT **b** : to convert (metal) into coins **c** : to shape (a piece of metal) in a mold or die **2** : CREATE, INVENT ⟨~ a phrase⟩ **3** : to make or earn (money) rapidly and in large quantity — **coin·er** *n*

[3]coin *adj* **1** : of or relating to coins ⟨a ~ show⟩ **2** : operated by coins ⟨a ~ laundry⟩

coin·age \ˈkȯi-nij\ *n* **1** : the act or process of coining **2 a** : COINS **b** : something (as a word) made up or invented

co·in·cide \ˌkō-ən-ˈsīd, ˈkō-ən-ˌ\ *vi* **-cid·ed; -cid·ing** [ML *coincidere,* fr. L *co-* + *incidere* to fall on, fr. *in-* + *cadere* to fall — more at CHANCE] **1 a** : to occupy the same place in space or time **b** : to occupy exactly corresponding or equivalent positions on a scale or in a series **2** : to correspond in nature, character, or function **3** : to be in accord or agreement : CONCUR ***syn*** see AGREE ***ant*** differ

co·in·ci·dence \kō-ˈin(t)-səd-ən(t)s, -sə-ˌden(t)s\ *n* **1** : the act or condition of coinciding : CORRESPONDENCE **2** : the occurrence of events that happen at the same time by accident but seem to have some connection; *also* : any of these happenings

co·in·ci·dent \-səd-ənt, -sə-ˌdent\ *adj* [F *coincident,* fr. ML *coincident-, coincidens,* prp. of *coincidere*] **1** : occupying the same space or time ⟨~ events⟩ **2** : of similar nature : HARMONIOUS ⟨a theory ~ with the facts⟩ ***syn*** see CONTEMPORARY — **co·in·ci·dent·ly** *adv*

co·in·ci·den·tal \(ˌ)kō-ˌin(t)-sə-ˈdent-ᵊl\ *adj* **1** : resulting from a coincidence ⟨similarity between the two texts is too consistent to be ~⟩ **2** : occurring or existing at the same time ⟨rebellion in Burma was ~ with . . . insurrection in Malaya —W. B. Hamilton⟩ — **co·in·ci·den·tal·ly** \-ˈdent-lē, -ᵊl-ē\ *adv*

coin lock *n* : a lock released by the insertion of a coin

coin machine *n* : SLOT MACHINE

coin–op \ˈkȯi-ˌnäp\ *n* : a self-service laundry where the machines are operated by coins

co·in·sur·ance \ˌkō-ən-ˈshu̇r-ən(t)s, *chiefly South* (ˈ)kō-ˈin-ˌ\ *n* **1** : joint assumption of risk (as by two underwriters) with another **2** : a system of insurance (as fire insurance) in which the insured is obligated to maintain coverage on a risk at a stipulated percentage of its total value or in the event of loss suffer a penalty in proportion to the deficiency

co·in·sure \ˌkō-ən-ˈshu̇(ə)r\ *vt* : to insure jointly — **co·in·sur·er** *n*

coir \ˈkȯi(-ə)r\ *n* [Tamil *kayiṟu* rope] : a stiff coarse fiber from the outer husk of a coconut

cois·trel \ˈkȯi-strəl\ *n* [MF *coustillier* soldier carrying a short sword, fr. *coustille* short sword, fr. L *cultellus* knife — more at CUTLASS] *archaic* : a mean fellow : VARLET

co·ition \kō-ˈish-ən\ *n* [LL, fr. L *coition-, coitio* a coming together, fr. *coitus,* pp. of *coire* to come together, fr. *co-* + *ire* to go — more at ISSUE] : COITUS — **co·ition·al** \-ˈish-nəl, -ən-ᵊl\ *adj*

co·itus \ˈkō-ət-əs, kō-ˈēt-\ *n* [L, fr. *coitus,* pp.] : physical union of male and female genitalia accompanied by rhythmic movements leading to the ejaculation of semen from the penis into the female reproductive tract; *also* : INTERCOURSE 3 — compare ORGASM — **co·ital** \-ət-ᵊl, -ˈēt-\ *adj* — **co·ital·ly** \-ᵊl-ē\ *adv*

coitus in·ter·rup·tus \-ˌint-ə-ˈrəp-təs\ *n* [NL, interrupted coitus] : coitus which is purposely interrupted in order to prevent ejaculation of sperm into the vagina

coitus re·ser·va·tus \-ˌrez-ər-ˈvāt-əs, -ˈvät-\ *n* [NL, reserved coitus] : COITUS INTERRUPTUS

[1]coke \ˈkōk\ *n* [ME; akin to Sw *kälk* pith, Gk *gelgis* bulb of garlic] : the residue of coal left after destructive distillation and used as fuel; *also* : a similar residue left by other materials (as petroleum) distilled to dryness

[2]coke *vb* **coked; cok·ing** *vt* : to change into coke ~ *vi* : to become coked

[3]coke *n* [by shortening & alter.] : COCAINE

[1]col \ˈkäl\ *n* [F, fr. MF, neck, fr. L *collum*] **1** : a pass in a mountain range **2** : a saddle-shaped depression in the crest of a ridge

[2]col *abbr* **1** colonial; colony **2** color; colored **3** column **4** counsel

[3]col *or* **coll** *abbr* **1** collateral **2** collect; collected; collection **3** college; collegiate

Col *abbr* **1** colonel **2** Colorado **3** Colossians

COL *abbr* cost of living

[1]col- — see COM-

[2]col- *or* **coli-** *or* **colo-** *comb form* [NL, fr. L *colon*] **1** : colon ⟨*colitis*⟩ ⟨*colostomy*⟩ **2** : colon bacillus ⟨*coliform*⟩

[1]cola *pl of* COLON

[2]co·la \ˈkō-lə\ *n* [fr. *Coca-Cola,* a trademark] : a carbonated soft drink flavored with extract from coca leaves, kola nut, sugar, caramel, and acid and aromatic substances

col·an·der \ˈkəl-ən-dər, ˈkäl-\ *n* [ME *colyndore,* prob. modif. of OProv *colador,* fr. ML *colatorium,* fr. L *colatus,* pp. of *colare* to sieve, fr. *colum* sieve] : a perforated utensil for washing or draining food

co·lat·i·tude \(ˈ)kō-ˈlat-ə-ˌt(y)üd\ *n* : the complement of the latitude

col·can·non \käl-ˈkan-ən\ *n* [IrGael *cāl ceannan,* lit., white-headed cabbage] : potatoes and cabbage boiled and mashed together with butter and seasoning

col·chi·cine \ˈkäl-chə-ˌsēn, ˈkäl-kə-\ *n* : a poisonous alkaloid $C_{22}H_{25}NO_6$ extracted from the corms or seeds of the meadow saffron (*Colchicum autumnale*) and used on mitotic cells to induce polyploidy and in the treatment of gout

col·chi·cum \ˈkäl-chi-kəm, ˈkäl-ki-\ *n* [NL, genus name, fr. L, a kind of plant with a poisonous root, fr. Gk *kolchikon,* lit., product of Colchis] **1** : any of a genus (*Colchicum*) of Old World corm-producing herbs of the lily family with flowers that resemble crocuses **2** : the dried corm or dried ripe seeds of autumn crocus containing colchicine, possessing emetic, diuretic, and cathartic action, and used for gout and rheumatism

col·co·thar \ˈkäl-kə-ˌthär\ *n* [ML, fr. MF or OSp; MF *colcotar,* fr. OSp *cólcotar,* fr. Ar dial. *qulquṭār*] : a reddish brown oxide of iron left as a residue when ferrous sulfate is heated and used as glass polish and as a pigment

[1]cold \ˈkōld\ *adj* [ME, fr. OE *ceald, cald;* akin to OHG *kalt* cold, L *gelu* frost, *gelare* to freeze] **1** : having a low temperature often below that compatible with human comfort **2 a** : marked by lack of warm feeling : UNEMOTIONAL **b** : marked by deliberation or calculation ⟨a ~ act of aggression⟩ **3 a** : previously cooked but served cold **b** : heated insufficiently ⟨the soup was ~⟩ **c** : not heated ⟨stored in a ~ cellar⟩ **d** : made cold ⟨~ drinks⟩ **e** : unheated while being worked ⟨~ conditioning of steel prior to rolling⟩ **4 a** : DEPRESSING, CHEERLESS **b** : producing a sensation of cold : CHILLING ⟨~ blank walls⟩ **c** : COOL 6a **5 a** : DEAD **b** : UNCONSCIOUS ⟨knocked out ~⟩ **c** : CERTAIN, SURE ⟨the actors had their lines ~ a week before opening night⟩ **6** : made uncomfortable by cold **7 a** : retaining only faint scents, traces, or clues ⟨a ~ trail⟩ **b** : STALE, UNINTERESTING ⟨~ news⟩ **8** : not illegal or suspect ⟨traded the hot car for a ~ one⟩ **9** : presented or regarded in a straightforward way : IMPERSONAL ⟨the ~ facts⟩ **10** : UNPREPARED **11** : intense and barely controlled ⟨a ~ fury⟩ — **cold·ish** *adj* — **cold·ly** \ˈkōl-(d)lē\ *adv* — **cold·ness** \ˈkōl(d)-nəs\ *n* — **in cold blood** : with premeditation : DELIBERATELY

[2]**cold** *n* **1 a** : a condition of low temperature **b** : cold weather **2** : bodily sensation produced by loss or lack of heat : CHILL **3** : a bodily disorder popularly associated with chilling; *specif* : COMMON COLD — **in the cold** : without heating — **out in the cold** : deprived of benefits given others : NEGLECTED ⟨the plan benefits management but leaves labor *out in the cold*⟩

[3]**cold** *adv* : with utter finality : TOTALLY, ABSOLUTELY ⟨he was turned down ~⟩

cold–blood·ed \ˈkōl(d)-ˈbləd-əd\ *adj* **1 a** : done or acting without consideration, compunction, or clemency ⟨~ murder⟩ **b** : MATTER-OF-FACT, EMOTIONLESS **2** : having cold blood; *specif* : having a body temperature not internally regulated but approximating that of the environment **3** *or* **cold·blood** \-ˈbləd\ : of mixed or inferior breeding **4** : noticeably sensitive to cold — **cold–blood·ed·ly** *adv* — **cold–blood·ed·ness** *n*

cold cash *n* : money in hand ⟨enough *cold cash* to close the deal⟩

cold chisel *n* : a chisel made of tool steel of a strength, shape, and temper suitable for chipping or cutting cold metal — see CHISEL illustration

cold comfort *n* : scant consolation : quite limited sympathy or encouragement

cold cream *n* : a soothing and cleansing cosmetic basically consisting of a perfumed emulsion of a bland vegetable oil or heavy mineral oil

cold cuts *n pl* : sliced assorted cold meats

cold duck *n* [trans. of G *kalte ente,* a drink made of a mixture of fine wines] : a beverage that consists of a blend of sparkling burgundy and champagne

cold feet *n pl* : apprehension or doubt strong enough to prevent a planned course of action

cold fish *n* : a cold aloof person

cold frame *n* : a usu. glass-covered frame without artificial heat used to protect plants and seedlings

cold front *n* : an advancing edge of a cold air mass

cold·heart·ed \ˈkōld-ˈhärt-əd\ *adj* : marked by lack of sympathy, interest, or sensitivity — **cold·heart·ed·ly** *adv* — **cold·heart·ed·ness** *n*

cold rubber *n* : a wear-resistant synthetic rubber made at a low temperature (as 41° F.) and used esp. for tire treads

cold shoulder *n* : intentionally cold or unsympathetic treatment — **cold–shoul·der** *vt*

cold sore *n* : the group of blisters appearing about or within the mouth in herpes simplex

cold storage *n* **1** : storage (as of food) in a cold place for preservation **2** : a condition of being held or continued without being acted on : ABEYANCE ⟨the second world war effectively put the question into *cold storage* —Leo Marquard⟩

cold store *n* : a building for cold storage

cold sweat *n* : concurrent perspiration and chill usu. associated with fear, pain, or shock

cold turkey *n* **1** : unrelieved blunt language or procedure ⟨I'm talking *cold turkey* to you . . . I think it wise if your relationship has ended —J. B. Clayton⟩ **2** : abrupt complete cessation of the use of an addictive drug either voluntarily or under medical supervision **3** : a cold aloof person

cold type *n* : composition or typesetting (as photocomposition) done without the casting of metal; *specif* : such composition produced directly on paper by a typewriter mechanism

cold war *n* **1** : a conflict carried on by methods short of sustained overt military action and usu. without breaking off diplomatic relations — compare HOT WAR **2** : a conflict short of violence esp. between power groups (as labor and management) — **cold warrior** *n*

cold–water *adj* **1** : of or relating to temperance groups **2 a** : provided only with running cold water **b** : not having all modern plumbing or heating facilities ⟨a ~ flat⟩

cold water *n* : depreciation of something as being ill-advised, unwarranted, or worthless ⟨throw *cold water* on our hopes⟩

cold wave *n* **1** : a period of unusually cold weather **2** : a permanent wave set by a chemical preparation without the use of curlers attached to a heating unit

cole \ˈkōl\ *n* [ME, fr. OE *cāl,* fr. L *caulis* stem, cabbage — more at HOLE] : any of a genus (*Brassica*) of herbaceous plants (as broccoli, Brussels sprouts, cabbage, cauliflower, kohlrabi, and rape)

cole·man·ite \ˈkōl-mə-ˌnīt\ *n* [William T. *Coleman* †1893 Am businessman and mine owner] : a mineral $Ca_2B_6O_{11}.5H_2O$ consisting of a hydrous calcium borate occurring in brilliant colorless or white massive monoclinic crystals

co·le·op·tera \ˌkō-lē-ˈäp-tə-rə\ *n pl* [NL, deriv. of Gk *koleon* sheath + *pteron* wing — more at FEATHER] : insects that are beetles — **co·le·op·ter·ist** \-tə-rəst\ *n* — **co·le·op·ter·ous** \-tə-rəs\ *adj*

co·le·op·ter·an \-tə-rən\ *n* : [1]BEETLE 1 — **coleopteran** *adj*

co·le·op·tile \-ˈäp-tᵊl\ *n* [NL *coleoptilum,* fr. Gk *koleon* + *ptilon* down; akin to Gk *pteron*] : the first leaf of a monocotyledon forming a protective sheath about the plumule

co·leo·rhi·za \ˌkō-lē-ə-ˈrī-zə\ *n, pl* **-zae** \-(ˌ)zē\ [NL, fr. Gk *koleon* + NL *-rhiza*] : the sheath investing the hypocotyl in some plants through which the roots burst

cole·slaw \ˈkōl-ˌslȯ\ *n* [D *koolsla,* fr. *kool* cabbage + *sla* salad] : a salad made of raw sliced or chopped cabbage

co·le·us \ˈkō-lē-əs\ *n* [NL, genus name, fr. Gk *koleos, koleon* sheath] : any of a large genus (*Coleus*) of herbs of the mint family

cole·wort \ˈkōl-ˌwərt, -ˌwȯ(ə)rt\ *n* : COLE; *esp* : one (as kale) that forms no head

coli- — see COL-

[1]**col·ic** \ˈkäl-ik\ *n* [ME, fr. MF *colique,* fr. L *colicus* colicky, fr. Gk *kōlikos,* fr. *kōlon,* alter. of *kolon* colon] : a paroxysm of acute abdominal pain localized in a hollow organ and caused by spasm, obstruction, or twisting

[2]**colic** *adj* : of or relating to colic : COLICKY ⟨~ crying⟩

[3]**co·lic** \ˈkō-lik, ˈkäl-ik\ *adj* : of or relating to the colon ⟨~ lymph glands⟩

co·li·cin \ˈkō-lə-sən\ *also* **co·li·cine** \-ˌsēn\ *n* [[3]*colic* + *-in* or *-ine*] : any of various antibacterial substances that are produced by some strains of intestinal bacteria and inhibit macromolecular synthesis (as of DNA or proteins)

col·icky \ˈkäl-ə-kē\ *adj* **1** : relating to or associated with colic ⟨~ pain⟩ **2** : suffering from colic ⟨~ babies⟩

col·ic·root \ˈkäl-ik-ˌrüt, -ˌru̇t\ *n* : any of several plants having roots used in folk medicine to treat colic: as **a** : either of two bitter herbs (*Aletris farinosa* and *A. aurea*) of the lily family **b** : a wild yam (*Dioscorea paniculata*)

col·ic·weed \-ˌwēd\ *n* : SQUIRREL CORN

co·li·form \ˈkō-lə-ˌfȯrm, ˈkäl-ə-\ *adj* [NL *Escherichia coli* colon bacillus + E *-form*] : relating to, resembling, or being the colon bacillus — **coliform** *n*

co·lin \kō-ˈlēn\ *n* [Sp *colín,* modif. of Nahuatl *çolin*] : BOBWHITE; *also* : a related New World game bird

co·lin·ear \(ˈ)kō-ˈlin-ē-ər\ *adj* **1** : COLLINEAR **2** : having corresponding parts arranged in the same linear order ⟨a gene and the protein it determines are ~⟩ — **co·lin·ear·i·ty** \(ˌ)kō-ˌlin-ē-ˈar-ət-ē\ *n*

co·li·phage \ˈkō-lə-ˌfāj, -ˌfäzh\ *n* [NL *Escherichia coli* colon bacillus + E *-phage*] : a bacteriophage active against the colon bacillus

col·i·se·um \ˌkäl-ə-ˈsē-əm\ *n* [ML *Colosseum, Colisseum*] **1** *cap* : COLOSSEUM 1 **2** : a large structure for public entertainments

co·lis·tin \kə-ˈlis-tən, kō-\ *n* [NL *colistinus,* specific epithet of the bacterium producing it] : a polymyxin produced by a bacterium (*Bacillus colistinus*) from Japanese soil

co·li·tis \kō-ˈlīt-əs, kə-\ *n* : inflammation of the colon

coll *abbr* — see COL

coll- *or* **collo-** *comb form* [NL, fr. Gk *koll-, kollo-,* fr. *kolla* — more at PROTOCOL] **1** : glue ⟨*coll*enchyma⟩ **2** : colloid ⟨*collo*type⟩

col·lab·o·rate \kə-ˈlab-ə-ˌrāt\ *vi* **-rat·ed; -rat·ing** [LL *collaboratus,* pp. of *collaborare* to labor together, fr. L *com-* + *laborare* to labor] **1** : to work jointly with others esp. in an intellectual endeavor **2** : to cooperate with or willingly assist an enemy of one's country and esp. an occupying force **3** : to cooperate with an agency or instrumentality with which one is not immediately connected — **col·lab·o·ra·tion** \-ˌlab-ə-ˈrā-shən\ *n* — **col·lab·o·ra·tive** \-ˈlab-ə-ˌrāt-iv, -(ə-)rət-\ *adj* — **col·lab·o·ra·tor** \-ˈlab-ə-ˌrāt-ər\ *n*

col·lab·o·ra·tion·ism \kə-ˌlab-ə-ˈrā-shə-ˌniz-əm\ *n* : the advocacy or practice of collaboration with an enemy — **col·lab·o·ra·tion·ist** \-sh(ə-)nəst\ *adj or n*

col·lage \kə-ˈläzh, kō-, kō-\ *n* [F, gluing, fr. *coller* to glue, fr. *colle* glue, fr. (assumed) VL *colla,* fr. Gk *kolla*] **1** : an artistic composition made of various materials (as paper, cloth, or wood) glued on a picture surface **2** : the art of making collages **3** : an assembly of diverse fragments ⟨a ~ of ideas⟩ **4** : a film showing disparate scenes in rapid succession without transitions — **col·lag·ist** \-ˈläzh-əst\ *n*

col·la·gen \ˈkäl-ə-jən\ *n* [Gk *kolla* + ISV *-gen*] : an insoluble fibrous protein that occurs in vertebrates as the chief constituent of connective tissue fibrils and in bones and yields gelatin and glue on prolonged heating with water — **col·la·gen·ic** \ˌkäl-ə-ˈjen-ik\ *adj* — **col·lag·e·nous** \kə-ˈlaj-ə-nəs\ *adj*

col·la·ge·nase \kə-ˈlaj-ə-ˌnās, ˈkäl-ə-jə-, -ˌnāz\ *n* : any of a group of proteolytic enzymes that decompose collagen and gelatin

[1]**col·lapse** \kə-ˈlaps\ *vb* **col·lapsed; col·laps·ing** [L *collapsus,* pp. of *collabi,* fr. *com-* + *labi* to fall, slide — more at SLEEP] *vi* **1** : to break down completely : DISINTEGRATE ⟨his case had *collapsed* in a mass of legal wreckage —Erle Stanley Gardner⟩ **2** : to fall or shrink together abruptly and completely : fall into a jumbled or flattened mass through the force of external pressure ⟨a blood vessel that *collapsed*⟩ **3** : to cave or fall in or give way **4** : to suddenly lose force, significance, effectiveness, or worth **5** : to break down in vital energy, stamina, or self-control through exhaustion or disease; *esp* : to fall helpless or unconscious **6** : to fold down into a more compact shape ⟨a telescope that ~*s*⟩ ~ *vt* : to cause to collapse — **col·laps·ibil·i·ty** \-ˌlap-sə-ˈbil-ət-ē\ *n* — **col·laps·ible** \-ˈlap-sə-bəl\ *adj*

[2]**collapse** *n* **1 a** : a breakdown in vital energy, strength, or stamina **b** : a state of extreme prostration and physical depression (as from circulatory failure or great loss of body fluids) **c** : an airless state of all or part of a lung originating spontaneously or induced surgically **2** : the act or action of collapsing ⟨the cutting of many tent ropes, the ~ of the canvas —Rudyard Kipling⟩ **3** : a sudden failure : BREAKDOWN, RUIN ⟨the tragedy inherent in the ~ of a society⟩ **4** : a sudden loss of force, value, or effect ⟨the ~ of respect for ancient law and custom —L. S. B. Leakey⟩ ⟨working to stave off ~ of the franc⟩

[1]**col·lar** \ˈkäl-ər\ *n* [ME *coler,* fr. OF, fr. L *collare,* fr. *collum* neck; akin to ON & OHG *hals* neck, OE *hwēol* wheel — more at WHEEL] **1** : a band, strip, or chain worn around the neck: as **a** : a band that serves to finish or decorate the neckline of a garment **b** : a short necklace **c** : a band about the neck of an animal **d** : a part of the harness of draft animals fitted over the shoulders and taking strain when a load is drawn **e** : an indication of control : a token of subservience ⟨refused to wear another man's ~⟩ **f** : a protective or supportive device (as a brace or cast) worn around the neck

2 : something resembling a collar in shape or use (as a ring or round flange to restrain motion or hold something in place) **3** : any of various animal structures or markings similar to a collar **4** : an act of collaring : ARREST, CAPTURE — **col·lared** \-ərd\ *adj* — **col·lar·less** \-ər-ləs\ *adj*

[2]**collar** *vt* **1 a** : to seize by the collar or neck **b** : APPREHEND, GRAB **c** : to get control of : PREEMPT ⟨with our machine . . . we can ~ nearly the whole of this market —Roald Dahl⟩ **d** : to stop and detain in unwilling conversation ⟨~*ed* the guest of honor⟩ **2** : to put a collar on

col·lar·bone \ˈkäl-ər-ˌbōn, ˌkäl-ər-ˈ\ *n* : CLAVICLE

collar cell *n* : a flagellated endodermal cell that lines the cavity of a sponge and has a contractile protoplasmic cup surrounding the flagellum — called also *choanocyte*

col·lard \ˈkäl-ərd\ *n* [alter. of *colewort*] : a stalked smooth-leaved kale — usu. used in pl.

collat *abbr* collateral

col·late \kə-ˈlāt, kä-, kō-; ˈkäl-ˌāt, ˈkōl-ˌ\ *vt* **col·lat·ed; col·lat·ing** [back-formation fr. *collation*] **1 a** : to compare critically **b** : to collect, compare carefully in order to verify, and often to integrate or arrange in order **2** [L *collatus*, pp.] : to institute (a cleric) to a benefice **3 a** : to verify the order of (printed sheets) **b** : to assemble in proper order; *esp* : to assemble (as printed sheets) in order for binding ***syn*** see COMPARE — **col·la·tor** \-ˈlāt-ər, -ˌāt-\ *n*

[1]**col·lat·er·al** \kə-ˈlat-ə-rəl, -ˈla-trəl\ *adj* [ME, prob. fr. MF, fr. ML *collateralis*, fr. L *com-* + *lateralis* lateral] **1 a** : accompanying as secondary or subordinate : CONCOMITANT ⟨digress into ~ matters⟩ **b** : INDIRECT **c** : serving to support or reinforce : ANCILLARY **2** : belonging to the same ancestral stock but not in a direct line of descent **3** : parallel, coordinate, or corresponding in position, order, time, or significance ⟨~ states like Athens and Sparta⟩ **4 a** : of, relating to, or being collateral used as security (as for payment of a debt or performance of a contract) **b** : secured by collateral — **col·lat·er·al·i·ty** \-ˌlat-ə-ˈral-ət-ē\ *n* — **col·lat·er·al·ly** \-ˈlat-ə-rə-lē, -ˈla-trə-\ *adv*

[2]**collateral** *n* **1** : a collateral relative **2** : property (as securities) pledged by a borrower to protect the interests of the lender **3** : a branch of a bodily part (as a vein)

col·lat·er·al·ize \kə-ˈlat-ə-rə-ˌlīz, -ˈla-trə-\ *vt* **-ized; -iz·ing** **1** : to make (a loan) secure with collateral **2** : to use (as securities) for collateral

col·la·tion \kə-ˈlā-shən, kä-, kō-\ *n* **1** [ME, fr. ML *collation-, collatio*, fr. LL, conference, fr. L, bringing together, comparison, fr. *collatus* (pp. of *conferre* to bring together, bestow upon), fr. *com-* + *latus*, pp. of *ferre* to carry] **a** : a light meal allowed on fast days in place of lunch or supper **b** : a light meal **2** [ME, fr. L *collation-, collatio*] : the act, process, or result of collating

col·league \ˈkäl-ˌēg *also* -ig\ *n* [MF *collegue*, fr. L *collega*, fr. *com-* + *legare* to appoint, depute — more at LEGATE] : an associate in a profession or in a civil or ecclesiastical office — **col·league·ship** \-ˌship\ *n*

col·leagues·man·ship \kə-ˈlēgz-mən-ˌship, kä-; ˈkäl-ˌēgz-, -igz-\ *n* : the theory or practice of attracting (as to a university) competent personnel by emphasizing the advantages to be gained by association with distinguished colleagues

[1]**col·lect** \ˈkäl-ikt *also* -ˌekt\ *n* [ME *collecte*, fr. OF, fr. ML *collecta*, short for *oratio ad collectam* prayer upon assembly] **1** : a short prayer comprising an invocation, petition, and conclusion; *specif*, *often cap* : one preceding the eucharistic Epistle and varying with the day **2** : COLLECTION

[2]**col·lect** \kə-ˈlekt\ *vb* [L *collectus*, pp. of *colligere* to collect, fr. *com-* + *legere* to gather] *vt* **1 a** : to bring together into one body or place **b** : to gather or exact from a number of persons or sources ⟨~ taxes⟩ **2** : INFER, DEDUCE **3** : to gain or regain control of ⟨~ his thoughts⟩ **4** : to claim as due and receive payment for **5** : to call for : pick up : ESCORT ⟨~ his girl and bring her in to the cinema —F. T. B. Macartney⟩ ~ *vi* **1** : to come together in a band, group, or mass : GATHER **2 a** : to collect objects **b** : to receive payment ⟨~*ing* on his insurance⟩ ***syn*** see GATHER — **col·lect·ible** *or* **col·lect·able** \-ˈlek-tə-bəl\ *adj*

[3]**col·lect** \kə-ˈlekt\ *adv or adj* : to be paid for by the receiver

col·lec·ta·nea \ˌkäl-ˌek-ˈtā-nē-ə\ *n pl* [L, neut. pl. of *collectaneus* collected, fr. *collectus*, pp.] : collected writings; *also* : literary items forming a collection

col·lect·ed \kə-ˈlek-təd\ *adj* **1** : gathered together ⟨the ~ works of Scott⟩ **2** : possessed of calmness and composure often through concentrated effort **3** *of a gait* : performed or performable by a horse from a state of collection ***syn*** see COOL ***ant*** distracted, distraught — **col·lect·ed·ly** *adv* — **col·lect·ed·ness** *n*

col·lect·ible \kə-ˈlek-tə-bəl\ *n* : a cultural object other than an antique or such traditionally collectible items as stamps, coins, or works of art that is the subject of fancier interest

col·lec·tion \kə-ˈlek-shən\ *n* **1** : the act or process of collecting **2** : something collected; *esp* : an accumulation of objects gathered for study, comparison, or exhibition **3** : a standard pose of a well-handled saddle horse in which it is responsive to the bit and has its head arched at the poll and the hocks well under the body so that the center of gravity is toward the rear quarters

[1]**col·lec·tive** \kə-ˈlek-tiv\ *adj* **1** : denoting a number of persons or things considered as one group or whole ⟨*flock* is a ~ word⟩ **2 a** : formed by collecting : AGGREGATED **b** *of a fruit* : MULTIPLE **3 a** : of, relating to, or being a group of individuals **4** : marked by similarity among or with the members of a group **5** : collectivized or characterized by collectivism **6** : shared or assumed by all members of the group — **col·lec·tive·ly** *adv*

[2]**collective** *n* **1** : a collective body : GROUP **2** : a cooperative unit or organization; *specif* : COLLECTIVE FARM

collective bargaining *n* : negotiation between an employer and union representatives usu. on wages, hours, and working conditions

collective farm *n* : a farm esp. in a communist country formed from many small holdings collected into a single unit for joint operation under governmental supervision

collective mark *n* : a trademark or a service mark of a group (as a cooperative association)

collective security *n* : the maintenance by common action of the security of all members of an association of nations

col·lec·tiv·isa·tion, col·lec·tiv·ise *chiefly Brit var of* COLLECTIVIZATION, COLLECTIVIZE

col·lec·tiv·ism \kə-ˈlek-ti-ˌviz-əm\ *n* : a political or economic theory advocating collective control esp. over production and distribution or a system marked by such control — **col·lec·tiv·ist** \-vəst\ *adj or n* — **col·lec·tiv·is·tic** \-ˌlek-ti-ˈvis-tik\ *adj* — **col·lec·tiv·is·ti·cal·ly** \-ti-k(ə-)lē\ *adv*

col·lec·tiv·i·ty \kə-ˌlek-ˈtiv-ət-ē, ˌkäl-ˌek-\ *n, pl* **-ties** **1** : the quality or state of being collective **2** : a collective whole; *esp* : the people as a body

col·lec·tiv·iza·tion \kə-ˌlek-ti-və-ˈzā-shən\ *n* : the act or process of collectivizing : the state of being collectivized

col·lec·tiv·ize \kə-ˈlek-ti-ˌvīz\ *vt* **-ized; -iz·ing** : to organize under collective control

col·lec·tor \kə-ˈlek-tər\ *n* **1** : an official who collects funds or moneys **2** : one that makes a collection ⟨stamp ~⟩ **3** : an object or device that collects ⟨the statuette was a dust ~⟩ **4** : a conductor maintaining contact between moving and stationary parts of an electric circuit — **col·lec·tor·ship** \-ˌship\ *n*

collector's item *n* : COLLECTIBLE

col·leen \kä-ˈlēn, ˈkäl-ˌēn\ *n* [IrGael *cailīn*] : an Irish girl

col·lege \ˈkäl-ij\ *n* [ME, fr. MF, fr. L *collegium* society, fr. *collega* colleague — more at COLLEAGUE] **1** : a body of clergy living together and supported by a foundation **2** : a building used for an educational or religious purpose **3 a** : a self-governing constituent body of a university offering living quarters and instruction but not granting degrees ⟨Balliol and Magdalen *Colleges* at Oxford⟩ **b** : a preparatory or high school **c** : an independent institution of higher learning offering a course of general studies leading to a bachelor's degree **d** : a part of a university offering a specialized group of courses **e** : an institution offering instruction usu. in a professional, vocational, or technical field ⟨war ~⟩ ⟨business ~⟩ ⟨barber ~⟩ **4** : COMPANY, GROUP; *specif* : an organized body of persons engaged in a common pursuit or having common interests or duties **5 a** : a group of persons considered by law to be a unit **b** : a body of electors — compare ELECTORAL COLLEGE **6** : the faculty, students, or administration of a college — **college** *adj*

college boards *n pl* : a set of examinations given by a college entrance examination board and required by some colleges of all candidates for admission and by others of all those whose academic records are below a certain standard

col·le·gial \kə-ˈlē-j(ē-)əl, *esp for 2a also* -ˈlē-gē-əl\ *adj* **1** : COLLEGIATE **2 a** : marked by power or authority vested equally in each of a number of colleagues **b** : characterized by equal sharing of authority esp. by Roman Catholic bishops — **col·le·gial·ly** \-ē\ *adv*

col·le·gi·al·i·ty \-ˌlē-jē-ˈal-ət-ē, -ˌlē-gē-\ *n* : the relationship of colleagues; *specif* : parity among bishops sharing collegial authority in the Roman Catholic Church

col·le·gian \kə-ˈlē-j(ē-)ən\ *n* : a student or recent graduate of a college

col·le·giate \kə-ˈlē-jət, -jē-ət\ *adj* [ML *collegiatus*, fr. L *collegium*] **1** : of or relating to a collegiate church **2** : of, relating to, or comprising a college **3** : COLLEGIAL 2 **4** : designed for or characteristic of college students — **col·le·giate·ly** *adv*

collegiate church *n* **1** : a church other than a cathedral that has a chapter of canons **2** : a church or corporate group of churches under the joint pastorate of two or more ministers

col·le·gi·um \kə-ˈleg-ē-əm, -ˈlāg-\ *n, pl* **-gia** \-ē-ə\ *or* **-gi·ums** [modif. of Russ *kollegya*, fr. L *collegium*] : a group in which each member has approximately equal power and authority; *esp* : one in a soviet organization

col·lem·bo·lan \kə-ˈlem-bə-lən\ *n* [deriv. of *coll-* + Gk *embolos* wedge, stopper — more at EMBOLUS] : any of an order (Collembola) of small primitive wingless arthropods related to or classed among the insects — called also *springtail* — **collembolan** *or* **col·lem·bo·lous** \-ləs\ *adj*

col·len·chy·ma \kə-ˈleŋ-kə-mə, kä-\ *n* [NL] : a plant tissue of living usu. elongated cells with walls variously thickened esp. at the angles but capable of further growth — compare SCLERENCHYMA — **col·len·chy·ma·tous** \ˌkäl-ən-ˈkim-ət-əs, -ˈkī-mət-\ *adj*

col·let \ˈkäl-ət\ *n* [MF, dim. of *col* collar, fr. L *collum* neck — more at COLLAR] : a metal band, collar, ferrule, or flange: as **a** : a small collar pierced to receive the inner end of a balance spring on a timepiece **b** : a circle or flange in which a gem is set

col·lide \kə-ˈlīd\ *vi* **col·lid·ed; col·lid·ing** [L *collidere*, fr. *com-* + *laedere* to injure by striking] **1** : to come together with solid impact **2** : CLASH

col·lie \ˈkäl-ē\ *n* [prob. fr. E dial. *colly* (black)] : a large dog of a breed developed in Scotland esp. for use in herding sheep

col·lier \ˈkäl-yər\ *n* [ME *colier*, fr. *col* coal] **1** : one that produces charcoal **2** : a coal miner **3** : a ship employed in transporting coal

col·liery \ˈkäl-yə-rē\ *n, pl* **-lier·ies** : a coal mine and its connected buildings

col·lie·shang·ie \ˈkäl-ē-ˌshaŋ-ē, ˈkəl-\ *n* [perh. fr. *collie* + *shang* (kind of meal)] *Scot* : SQUABBLE, BRAWL

col·li·gate \ˈkäl-ə-ˌgāt\ *vb* **-gat·ed; -gat·ing** [L *colligatus*, pp. of *colligare*, fr. *com-* + *ligare* to tie — more at LIGATURE] *vt* **1** : to bind, unite, or group together **2** : to subsume (isolated facts) under a general concept ~ *vi* : to be or become a member of a group or unit — **col·li·ga·tion** \ˌkäl-ə-ˈgā-shən\ *n*

col·li·ga·tive \ˈkäl-ə-ˌgāt-iv\ *adj* : depending on the number of particles (as molecules) and not on the nature of the particles ⟨pressure is a ~ property⟩

col·li·mate \ˈkäl-ə-ˌmāt\ *vt* **-mat·ed; -mat·ing** [L *collimatus*, pp. of *collimare*, MS var. of *collineare* to make straight, fr. *com-* + *linea* line] **1** : to make (as rays of light) parallel **2** : to adjust the line of sight of (a transit or level) — **col·li·ma·tion** \ˌkäl-ə-ˈmā-shən\ *n*

col·li·ma·tor \ˈkäl-ə-ˌmāt-ər\ *n* **1 :** a device for producing a beam of parallel rays of light or other radiation or for forming an infinitely distant virtual image that can be viewed without parallax **2 :** a device for obtaining a beam of molecules, atoms, or nuclear particles of limited cross section
col·lin·ear \kə-ˈlin-ē-ər, kä-\ *adj* [ISV] **1 :** lying on or passing through the same straight line **2 :** having axes lying end to end in a straight line ⟨~ antenna elements⟩ — **col·lin·ear·i·ty** \-ˌlin-ē-ˈar-ət-ē\ *n*
col·lins \ˈkäl-ənz\ *n* [prob. fr. the name *Collins*] **:** a tall iced drink that usu. has lemon juice added to a base of distilled liquor (as gin)
col·lin·sia \kə-ˈlin-zē-ə, kä-\ *n* [NL, genus name, fr. Zaccheus *Collins* †1831 Am botanist] **:** any of a genus (*Collinsia*) of U.S. biennial or annual herbs of the figwort family
col·li·sion \kə-ˈlizh-ən\ *n* [ME, fr. L *collision-, collisio,* fr. *collisus,* pp. of *collidere*] **1 :** an act or instance of colliding **:** CLASH **2 :** an encounter between particles (as atoms or molecules) resulting in exchange or transformation of energy — **col·li·sion·al** \-ˈlizh-nəl, -ən-ᵊl\ *adj*
collision course *n* **:** a course (as of moving bodies or antithetical philosophies) that will result in collision or conflict if continued unaltered ⟨Roosevelt's idealism was on a *collision course* with Stalin's spheres-of-interest realpolitik —E. M. Harrington⟩
collo- — see COLL-
col·lo·cate \ˈkäl-ə-ˌkāt\ *vb* **-cat·ed; -cat·ing** [L *collocatus,* pp. of *collocare,* fr. *com-* + *locare* to place, fr. *locus* place — more at STALL] *vt* **:** to set or arrange in a place or position; *esp* **:** to set side by side ~ *vi* **:** to occur in conjunction with something
col·lo·ca·tion \ˌkäl-ə-ˈkā-shən\ *n* **:** the act or result of placing or arranging together; *specif* **:** a noticeable arrangement or conjoining of linguistic elements (as words) — **col·lo·ca·tion·al** \-shnəl, -shən-ᵊl\ *adj*
col·lo·di·on \kə-ˈlōd-ē-ən\ *n* [modif. of NL *collodium,* fr. Gk *kollōdēs* glutinous, fr. *kolla* glue] **:** a viscous solution of pyroxylin used esp. as a coating for wounds or for photographic films
col·logue \kə-ˈlōg\ *vi* **col·logued; col·logu·ing** [origin unknown] **1** *dial* **:** INTRIGUE, CONSPIRE **2 :** to talk privately **:** CONFER
col·loid \ˈkäl-ˌȯid\ *n* [ISV *coll-* + *-oid*] **1 a :** a substance that is in a state of division preventing passage through a semipermeable membrane, consists of particles too small for resolution with an ordinary light microscope, and in suspension or solution fails to settle out and diffracts a beam of light **b :** a system consisting of a colloid together with the gaseous, liquid, or solid medium in which it is dispersed **2 :** a gelatinous or mucinous substance found in tissues in disease or normally (as in the thyroid) — **col·loi·dal** \kə-ˈlȯid-ᵊl, kä-\ *adj* — **col·loi·dal·ly** \-ᵊl-ē\ *adv*
col·lop \ˈkäl-əp\ *n* [ME] **1 :** a small piece or slice esp. of meat **2 :** a fold of fat flesh
colloq *abbr* colloquial
col·lo·qui·al \kə-ˈlō-kwē-əl\ *adj* **1 :** of or relating to conversation **:** CONVERSATIONAL **2 a :** used in or characteristic of familiar and informal conversation **b :** using conversational style — **colloquial** *n* — **col·lo·qui·al·i·ty** \-ˌlō-kwē-ˈal-ət-ē\ *n* — **col·lo·qui·al·ly** \-ˈlō-kwē-ə-lē\ *adv*
col·lo·qui·al·ism \-ˈlō-kwē-ə-ˌliz-əm\ *n* **1 a :** a colloquial expression **b :** a local or regional dialect expression **2 :** colloquial style
col·lo·quist \ˈkäl-ə-kwəst\ *n* **:** SPEAKER
col·lo·qui·um \kə-ˈlō-kwē-əm\ *n, pl* **-qui·ums** *or* **-quia** \-kwē-ə\ [L, colloquy] **:** a usu. academic meeting at which one or more specialists deliver addresses on a topic or on related topics and then answer questions relating thereto
col·lo·quy \ˈkäl-ə-kwē\ *n, pl* **-quies** [L *colloquium,* fr. *colloqui* to converse, fr. *com-* + *loqui* to speak] **1 :** CONVERSATION, DIALOGUE **2 :** a high-level serious discussion **:** CONFERENCE
col·lo·type \ˈkäl-ə-ˌtīp\ *n* [ISV] **1 :** a photomechanical process for making prints directly from a hardened film of gelatin or other colloid that has ink-receptive and ink-repellent parts **2 :** a print made by collotype
col·lude \kə-ˈlüd\ *vi* **col·lud·ed; col·lud·ing** [L *colludere,* fr. *com-* + *ludere* to play, fr. *ludus* game — more at LUDICROUS] **:** CONSPIRE, PLOT
col·lu·sion \kə-ˈlü-zhən\ *n* [ME, fr. MF, fr. L *collusion-, collusio,* fr. *collusus,* pp. of *colludere*] **:** secret agreement or cooperation for an illegal or deceitful purpose — **col·lu·sive** \-ˈlü-siv, -ziv\ *adj* — **col·lu·sive·ly** *adv*
col·lu·vi·um \kə-ˈlü-vē-əm\ *n, pl* **-via** \-vē-ə\ *or* **-vi·ums** [NL, fr. ML, offscourings, alter. of L *colluvies,* fr. *colluere* to wash, fr. *com-* + *lavere* to wash — more at LYE] **:** rock detritus and soil accumulated at the foot of a slope — **col·lu·vi·al** \-vē-əl\ *adj*
col·ly \ˈkäl-ē\ *vt* **col·lied; col·ly·ing** [alter. of ME *colwen,* fr. (assumed) OE *colgian,* fr. OE *col* coal] *dial chiefly Brit* **:** to blacken with or as if with soot
col·lyr·i·um \kə-ˈlir-ē-əm\ *n, pl* **-ia** \-ē-ə\ *or* **-i·ums** [L, fr. Gk *kollyrion* pessary, eye salve, fr. dim. of *kollyra* roll of bread] **:** an eye lotion **:** EYEWASH
col·ly·wob·bles \ˈkäl-ē-ˌwäb-əlz\ *n pl but sing or pl in constr* [prob. by folk etymology, fr. NL *cholera morbus,* lit., the disease cholera] **:** BELLYACHE
Colo *abbr* Colorado
colo- — see COL-
co·lo·cate \(ˈ)kō-ˈlō-ˌkāt, ˈkō-lō-\ *vt* **:** to place two or more units in close proximity so as to share common facilities
col·o·cynth \ˈkäl-ə-ˌsin(t)th\ *n* [L *colocynthis*] **:** a Mediterranean and African herbaceous vine (*Citrullus colocynthis*) related to the watermelon; *also* **:** its spongy fruit from which a powerful cathartic is prepared
colog *abbr* cologarithm
co·log·a·rithm \(ˈ)kō-ˈlȯg-ə-ˌrith-əm, -ˈläg-\ *n* **:** the logarithm of the reciprocal
co·logne \kə-ˈlōn\ *n* [*Cologne,* Germany] **1 :** a perfumed toilet water **2 :** a cream or paste of cologne sometimes formed into a semisolid stick — **co·logned** \-ˈlōnd\ *adj*

¹co·lon \ˈkō-lən\ *n, pl* **colons** *or* **co·la** \-lə\ [L, fr. Gk *kolon*] **:** the part of the large intestine that extends from the cecum to the rectum — **co·lon·ic** \kō-ˈlän-ik\ *adj*
²colon *n, pl* **colons** *or* **co·la** \-lə\ [L, part of a poem, fr. Gk *kōlon* limb, part of a strophe — more at CALK] **1** *pl* **cola :** a rhythmical unit of an utterance; *specif, in Greek or Latin verse* **:** a system or series of from two to not more than six feet having a principal accent and forming part of a line **2** *pl* **colons a :** a punctuation mark **:** used chiefly to direct attention to matter (as a list, explanation, or quotation) that follows **b :** the sign : used between the parts of a numerical expression of time in hours and minutes (as in 1:15) or in hours, minutes, and seconds (as in 8:25:30), in a bibliographical reference (as in *Nation* 130:20), in a ratio where it is usu. read as "to" (as in 4:1 read "four to one"), or in a proportion where it is usu. read as "is to" or when doubled as "as" (as in 2:1::8:4 read "two is to one as eight is to four")
³co·lon \kȯ-ˈlōn, kə-ˈlōn\ *n* [F, fr. L *colonus*] **:** a colonial farmer or plantation owner
⁴co·lon \kə-ˈlōn\ *n, pl* **co·lo·nes** \-ˈlō-ˌnās\ [Sp *colón*] — see MONEY table
colon bacillus *n* **:** any of various bacilli (esp. genera *Escherichia* and *Aerobacter*) that are normally commensal in vertebrate intestines; *esp* **:** one (*E. coli*) used extensively in genetic research
col·o·nel \ˈkərn-ᵊl\ *n* [alter. of *coronel,* fr. MF, modif. of OIt *colonnello* column of soldiers, colonel, dim. of *colonna* column, fr. L *columna*] **1 a :** a commissioned officer in the army, air force, or marine corps ranking above a lieutenant colonel and below a brigadier general **b :** LIEUTENANT COLONEL **2 :** a minor titular official of a state esp. in southern or midland U.S. — used as an honorific title — **col·o·nel·cy** \-ᵊl-sē\ *n*
Colonel Blimp \ˌkərn-ᵊl-ˈblimp\ *n* [*Colonel Blimp,* cartoon character created by David Low] **:** a pompous person with out-of-date or ultraconservative views; *broadly* **:** REACTIONARY — **Colonel Blimp·ism** \-ˈblim-ˌpiz-əm\ *n*
¹co·lo·nial \kə-ˈlō-nē-əl, -nyəl\ *adj* **1 :** of, relating to, or characteristic of a colony **2** *often cap* **:** of or relating to the original 13 colonies forming the United States: as **a :** made or prevailing in America during the colonial period ⟨~ architecture was a modification of English Georgian⟩ **b :** adapted from or reminiscent of an American colonial mode of design ⟨~ furniture⟩ **3 :** possessing or composed of colonies ⟨Britain's ~ empire⟩ — **co·lo·nial·ize** \-ˌīz\ *vt* — **co·lo·nial·ly** \-ē\ *adv* — **co·lo·nial·ness** *n*
²colonial *n* **1 :** a member or inhabitant of a colony **2 a :** a product made for use in a colony **b :** a product exhibiting colonial style
co·lo·nial·ism \-ˌiz-əm\ *n* **1 :** the quality or state of being colonial **2 :** something characteristic of a colony **3 a :** control by one power over a dependent area or people **b :** a policy advocating or based on such control — **co·lo·nial·ist** \-əst\ *n or adj* — **co·lo·nial·is·tic** \-ˌlō-nē-ə-ˈlis-tik, -nyə-ˈlis-\ *adj*
col·o·nist \ˈkäl-ə-nəst\ *n* **1 :** a member or inhabitant of a colony **2 :** one that colonizes or settles in a new country
col·o·ni·za·tion \ˌkäl-ə-nə-ˈzā-shən\ *n* **:** an act or instance of colonizing or of being colonized — **col·o·ni·za·tion·ist** \-sh(ə-)nəst\ *n*
col·o·nize \ˈkäl-ə-ˌnīz\ *vb* **-nized; -niz·ing** *vt* **1 a :** to establish a colony in or on or of **b :** to establish in a colony **2 :** to send illegal or irregularly qualified voters into ⟨the machine was *colonizing* doubtful districts⟩ **3 :** to infiltrate with usu. subversive militants for propaganda and strategy reasons ⟨~ industries⟩ ~ *vi* **:** to make or establish a colony **:** SETTLE — **col·o·niz·er** *n*
col·on·nade \ˌkäl-ə-ˈnād\ *n* [F, fr. It *colonnato,* fr. *colonna* column] **:** a series of columns set at regular intervals and usu. supporting the base of a roof structure — **col·on·nad·ed** \-ˈnād-əd\ *adj*
co·lo·nus \kə-ˈlō-nəs\ *n, pl* **-ni** \-ˌnī, -(ˌ)nē\ [L, lit., farmer] **:** a freeborn serf in the later Roman Empire who could sometimes own property but who was bound to the land and obliged to pay a rent usu. in produce
col·o·ny \ˈkäl-ə-nē\ *n, pl* **-nies** [ME *colonie,* fr. MF & L; MF, fr. L *colonia,* fr. *colonus* farmer, colonist, fr. *colere* to cultivate — more at WHEEL] **1 a :** a body of people living in a new territory but retaining ties with the parent state **b :** the territory inhabited by such a body **2 :** a distinguishable localized population within a species ⟨~ of termites⟩ **3 a :** a circumscribed mass of microorganisms usu. growing in or on a solid medium **b :** the aggregation of zooids of a compound animal **4 a :** a group of individuals or things with common characteristics or interests situated in close association ⟨an artist ~⟩ ⟨the growing ~ of off-Broadway satires —*Current Biog.*⟩ **b :** the section occupied by such a group **5 :** a group of persons institutionalized away from others (as for care or correction) ⟨a leper ~⟩ ⟨a penal ~⟩; *also* **:** the land or buildings occupied by such a group
col·o·phon \ˈkäl-ə-fən, -ˌfän\ *n* [L, fr. Gk *kolophōn* summit, finishing touch] **1 :** an inscription placed at the end of a book or manuscript usu. with facts relative to its production **2 :** an identifying device used by a printer or a publisher
co·loph·o·ny \kə-ˈläf-ə-nē, ˈkäl-ə-ˌfō-\ *n, pl* **-nies** [ME *colophonie,* deriv. of Gk *Kolophōn* Colophon, an Ionian city] **:** ROSIN

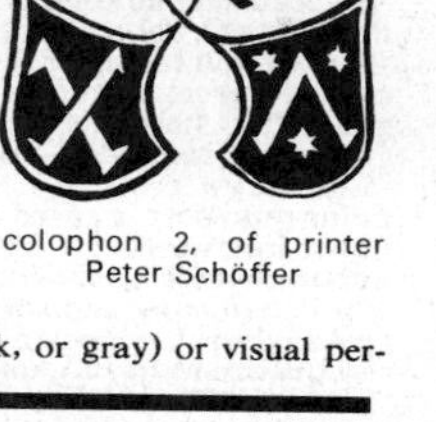

colophon 2, of printer Peter Schöffer

¹col·or \ˈkəl-ər\ *n, often attrib* [ME *colour,* fr. OF, fr. L *color;* akin to L *celare* to conceal — more at HELL] **1 a :** a phenomenon of light (as red, brown, pink, or gray) or visual per-

ə abut ᵊ kitten ər further a back ā bake ä cot, cart
au̇ out ch chin e less ē easy g gift i trip ī life
j joke ŋ sing ō flow ȯ flaw ȯi coin th thin th this
ü loot u̇ foot y yet yü few yu̇ furious zh vision

ception that enables one to differentiate otherwise identical objects **b** : the aspect of objects and light sources that may be described in terms of hue, lightness, and saturation for objects and hue, brightness, and saturation for light sources — used in this sense as the psychological basis for definitions of color in this dictionary **c** : a hue as contrasted with black, white, or gray **2 a** : an outward often deceptive show : APPEARANCE ⟨his story has the ~ of truth⟩ **b** : a legal claim to or appearance of a right, authority, or office **c** : a pretense offered as justification : PRETEXT ⟨she could have drawn from the Versailles treaty the ~ of legality for any action she chose —*Yale Rev.*⟩ **d** : an appearance of authenticity : PLAUSIBILITY ⟨lending ~ to this notion⟩ **3** : complexion tint: **a** : the tint characteristic of good health **b** : BLUSH **4 a** : vividness or variety of effects of language ⟨that ~ and force of style which were later to make him outstanding —Arthur Krock⟩ **b** : LOCAL COLOR **5 a** : an identifying badge, pennant, or flag — usu. used in pl. ⟨a ship sailing under Swedish ~*s*⟩ **b** : colored clothing distinguishing one as a member of a particular group or representative of a particular person or thing — usu. used in pl. ⟨a jockey riding under the ~*s* of his stable⟩ **6 a** *pl* : position as to a question or course of action : STAND ⟨the USSR changed neither its ~*s* nor its stripes during all of this —Norman Mailer⟩ **b** : CHARACTER, NATURE — usu. used in pl. ⟨showed himself in his true ~*s*⟩ **7** : the use or combination of colors **8** *pl* **a** : a naval or nautical salute to a flag being hoisted or lowered **b** : ARMED FORCES **9** : VITALITY, INTEREST ⟨the play had a good deal of ~ to it⟩ **10** : something used to give color : PIGMENT **11** : tonal quality in music ⟨the ~ and richness of the instrument⟩ **12** : skin pigmentation other than white characteristic of race **13** : a small particle of gold in a gold miner's pan after washing **14** : analysis of game action or strategy, statistics and background information on participants, and often anecdotes provided by a sportscaster to give variety and interest to the broadcast of a game or contest — **color** *adj* — **col·or·ism** \-ə-ˌriz-əm\ *n*

²**color** *vb* **col·ored; col·or·ing** \ˈkəl-(ə-)riŋ\ *vt* **1 a** : to give color to **b** : to change the color of (as by dyeing, staining, or painting) **2** : to change as if by dyeing or painting: as **a** : MISREPRESENT, DISTORT **b** : GLOSS, EXCUSE ⟨~ a lie⟩ **c** : INFLUENCE, AFFECT ⟨the lives of most of us have been ~*ed* by politics —Christine Weston⟩ **3** : CHARACTERIZE, LABEL ⟨call it progress; ~ it inevitable with shades of job security —C. E. Price⟩ ~ *vi* : to take on color; *specif* : BLUSH — **col·or·er** \ˈkəl-ər-ər\ *n*

col·or·able \ˈkəl-(ə-)rə-bəl\ *adj* **1** : seemingly valid or genuine **2** : intended to deceive : COUNTERFEIT ⟨~ piety⟩ ***syn*** see PLAUSIBLE — **col·or·ably** \-blē\ *adv*

Col·o·ra·do potato beetle \ˌkäl-ə-ˈrad-ō-, -ˈräd-\ *n* [*Colorado*, state of U.S.] : a black-and-yellow striped beetle (*Leptinotarsa decimlineata*) that feeds on the leaves of the potato — called also *potato beetle, potato bug*

col·or·ation \ˌkəl-ə-ˈrā-shən\ *n* **1 a** : the state of being colored ⟨the dark ~ of his skin⟩ **b** : use or choice of colors (as by an artist ⟨Millet's subdued ~⟩ **c** : arrangement of colors ⟨the brilliant ~ of a butterfly's wing⟩ **2 a** : characteristic quality ⟨the newspapers . . . took on the former ~ of the magazine —L. B. Seltzer⟩ **b** : aspect suggesting an attitude : PERSUASION ⟨the chameleon talent for taking on the intellectual ~ of whatever idea he happened to fasten onto —Budd Schulberg⟩ **3** : subtle variation of intensity or quality of tone ⟨a wide range of ~ from the orchestra⟩

col·or·a·tu·ra \ˌkəl-ə-rə-ˈt(y)u̇r-ə\ *n* [obs. It, lit., coloring, fr. LL, fr. L *coloratus*, pp. of *colorare* to color, fr. *color*] **1** : elaborate embellishment in vocal music; *broadly* : music with ornate figuration **2** : a soprano with a light, agile voice specializing in coloratura

color bar *n* : a barrier preventing colored persons from participating with whites in various activities — called also *color line*

col·or–bear·er \ˈkəl-ər-ˌbar-ər, -ˌber-\ *n* : one that carries a color or standard esp. in a military parade or drill

col·or–blind \-ˌblīnd\ *adj* **1** : affected with partial or total inability to distinguish one or more chromatic colors **2** : INSENSITIVE, OBLIVIOUS **3** : not recognizing differences of race ⟨tried to get the welfare establishment in Washington to abandon its ~ policy —D. P. Moynihan⟩; *esp* : free from racial prejudice ⟨a white man with an invisible black skin in a ~ community —James Farmer⟩ — **color blindness** *n*

col·or·breed \-ˌbrēd\ *vt* **-bred; -breed·ing** : to breed selectively for the development of particular colors ⟨~*ing* canaries for red⟩

col·or·cast \-ˌkast\ *n* [*color* + tele*cast*] : a television broadcast in color — **colorcast** *vb*

col·or·cast·er \-ˌkas-tər\ *n* [*color* + broad*caster*] : a broadcaster (as of a sports contest) who supplies vivid or picturesque details and often gives statistical or analytical information

¹**col·ored** \ˈkəl-ərd\ *adj* **1** : having color **2 a** : COLORFUL **b** : marked by exaggeration or bias **3 a** : of a race other than the white; *esp* : NEGRO **b** : of mixed race **4** : of or relating to colored persons

²**colored** *n, pl* **colored** *or* **coloreds** *often cap* : a colored person

col·or·fast \ˈkəl-ər-ˌfast\ *adj* : having color that retains its original hue without fading or running — **col·or·fast·ness** \-ˌfas(t)-nəs\ *n*

color filter *n* : FILTER 3b

col·or·ful \ˈkəl-ər-fəl\ *adj* **1** : having striking colors **2** : full of variety or interest — **col·or·ful·ly** \-f(ə-)lē\ *adv* — **col·or·ful·ness** \-fəl-nəs\ *n*

color guard *n* : a guard of honor for the colors of an organization

col·or·if·ic \ˌkəl-ə-ˈrif-ik\ *adj* : capable of communicating color

col·or·im·e·ter \ˌkəl-ə-ˈrim-ət-ər\ *n* [ISV] : an instrument or device for determining and specifying colors; *specif* : one used for chemical analysis by comparison of a liquid's color with standard colors — **col·or·i·met·ric** \ˌkəl-ə-rə-ˈme-trik\ *adj* — **col·or·i·met·ri·cal·ly** \-tri-k(ə-)lē\ *adv* — **col·or·im·e·try** \ˌkəl-ə-ˈrim-ə-trē\ *n*

col·or·ing \ˈkəl-(ə-)riŋ\ *n* **1 a** : the act of applying colors **b** : something that produces color or color effects **c** (1) : the effect produced by applying or combining colors (2) : natural color (3) : COMPLEXION, COLORATION **d** : change of appearance (as by adding color) **2** : INFLUENCE, BIAS **3** : COLOR 4 **4** : TIMBRE, QUALITY

col·or·ist \ˈkəl-ə-rəst\ *n* : one that colors or deals with color — **col·or·is·tic** \ˌkəl-ə-ˈris-tik\ *adj* — **col·or·is·ti·cal·ly** \-ti-k(ə-)lē\ *adv*

col·or·less \ˈkəl-ər-ləs\ *adj* : lacking color: as **a** : PALLID, BLANCHED **b** : DULL, UNINTERESTING — **col·or·less·ly** *adv* — **col·or·less·ness** *n*

color phase *n* **1 a** : a genetic variant manifested by the occurrence of a skin or pelage color unlike the wild type of the animal group in which it appears **b** : an individual marked by such a variant **2** : a seasonally variant pelage color

color photography *n* : photographic reproduction of images in nearly natural colors

color temperature *n* : the temperature at which a blackbody emits radiant energy competent to evoke a color the same as that evoked by radiant energy from a given source (as a lamp)

co·los·sal \kə-ˈläs-əl\ *adj* **1** : of, relating to, or resembling a colossus **2** : of a bulk, extent, power, or effect approaching or suggesting the stupendous or incredible **3** : of an exceptional or astonishing degree ***syn*** see HUGE — **co·los·sal·ly** \-ə-lē\ *adv*

col·os·se·um \ˌkäl-ə-ˈsē-əm\ *n* [ML, fr. L, neut. of *colosseus* colossal, fr. *colossus*] **1** *cap* : an amphitheater built in Rome in the first century A.D. **2** : COLISEUM 2

Co·los·sians \kə-ˈläsh-ənz *also* -ˈläs(h)-ē-ənz\ *n pl but sing in constr* : a letter written by St. Paul to the Christians of Colossae and included as a book in the New Testament — see BIBLE table

co·los·sus \kə-ˈläs-əs\ *n, pl* **co·los·sus·es** \-ˈläs-ə-səz\ *or* **co·los·si** \-ˈläs-ˌī\ [L, fr. Gk *kolossos*] **1** : a statue of gigantic size and proportions **2** : one that resembles a colossus in size or scope: **a** : a nation vastly larger and more powerful than those near it **b** : a huge industrial concern **c** : one remarkably outstanding and preeminent over others ⟨such an artistic ~ as Michelangelo —Hunter Mead⟩

co·los·to·my \kə-ˈläs-tə-mē\ *n, pl* **-mies** [ISV ²*col-* + *-stomy*] : surgical formation of an artificial anus

co·los·trum \kə-ˈläs-trəm\ *n* [L, beastings] : milk secreted for a few days after parturition and characterized by high protein and immune body content — **co·los·tral** \-trəl\ *adj*

col·our \ˈkəl-ər\ *chiefly Brit var of* COLOR

-c·o·lous \k-ə-ləs\ *adj comb form* [L *-cola* inhabitant; akin to L *colere* to inhabit — more at WHEEL] : living or growing in or on ⟨areni*colous*⟩

col·por·tage \ˈkäl-ˌpōrt-ij, -ˌpȯrt-; ˌkäl-pōr-ˈtäzh, -pȯr-\ *n* : a colporteur's work

col·por·teur \ˈkäl-ˌpōrt-ər, -ˌpȯrt-; ˌkäl-pōr-ˈtər, -pȯr-\ *n* [F, alter. of MF *comporteur*, fr. *comporter* to bear, peddle] : a peddler of religious books

colt \ˈkōlt\ *n* [ME, fr. OE; akin to OE *cild* child] **1 a** : FOAL **b** : a young male horse that is either sexually immature or has not attained an arbitrarily designated age **2** : a young untried person : NOVICE

colter *var of* COULTER

colt·ish \ˈkōl-tish\ *adj* **1 a** : not subjected to discipline **b** : FRISKY, PLAYFUL **2** : of, relating to, or resembling a colt — **colt·ish·ly** *adv* — **colt·ish·ness** *n*

colts·foot \ˈkōlts-ˌfu̇t\ *n, pl* **coltsfoots** : any of various plants with large rounded leaves resembling the foot of a colt; *esp* : a perennial composite herb (*Tussilago farfara*) with yellow flower heads appearing before the leaves

col·u·brid \ˈkäl-(y)ə-brəd\ *n* [deriv. of L *colubra* snake] : any of a large cosmopolitan family (Colubridae) of nonvenomous snakes — **colubrid** *adj*

col·u·brine \-ˌbrīn\ *adj* **1** : of, relating to, or resembling a snake **2** : COLUBRID

co·lu·go \kə-ˈlü-(ˌ)gō\ *n, pl* **-gos** [prob. native name in Malaya] : FLYING LEMUR

col·um·bar·i·um \ˌkäl-əm-ˈbar-ē-əm, -ˈber-\ *n, pl* **-ia** \-ē-ə\ [L, lit., dovecote, fr. *columba* dove] **1** : a structure of vaults lined with recesses for cinerary urns **2** : a recess in a columbarium

Co·lum·bia \kə-ˈləm-bē-ə\ *n* [NL, fr. Christopher *Columbus*] : the United States

Co·lum·bi·an \-bē-ən\ *adj* : of or relating to the United States or to Christopher Columbus

col·um·bine \ˈkäl-əm-ˌbīn\ *n* [ME, fr. ML *columbina*, fr. L, fem. of *columbinus* dovelike, fr. *columba* dove; akin to OHG *holuntar* elder tree, Gk *kolymbos* a bird, *kelainos* black] : any of a genus (*Aquilegia*) of plants of the buttercup family with irregular showy spurred flowers: as **a** : a red-flowered plant (*A. canadensis*) of eastern No. America **b** : a blue-flowered plant (*A. coerulea*) of the Rocky mountains

Col·um·bine \-ˌbīn, -ˌbēn\ *n* [It *Colombina*] : the saucy sweetheart of Harlequin in comedy and pantomime

co·lum·bite \kə-ˈləm-ˌbīt, ˈkäl-əm-\ *n* [NL *columbium*] : a black mineral $(Fe,Mn)(Cb,Ta)_2O_6$ consisting essentially of iron and columbium

co·lum·bi·um \kə-ˈləm-bē-əm\ *n* [NL, fr. *Columbia*] : NIOBIUM

Columbus Day *n* **1** : October 12 formerly observed as a legal holiday in many states of the U.S. in commemoration of the landing of Columbus in the Bahamas in 1492 **2** : the second Monday in October observed as a legal holiday in many states of the U.S.

col·u·mel·la \ˌkäl-(y)ə-ˈmel-ə\ *n, pl* **-mel·lae** \-ˈmel-(ˌ)ē, -ˌī\ [NL, fr. L, dim. of *columna*] **1 a** : the bony or partly cartilaginous rod connecting the tympanic membrane with the internal ear in birds and in many reptiles and amphibians **b** : the bony central axis of the cochlea **2** : the central column or axis of a spiral univalve shell **3** : the axis of the capsule in mosses and in some liverworts **4** : the central sterile portion of the sporangium in various fungi (*Mucor* and related genera) — **col·u·mel·lar** \-ˈmel-ər\ *adj* — **col·u·mel·late** \-ət, -ˌāt\ *adj*

col·umn \ˈkäl-əm\ *n* [ME *columne*, fr. MF *colomne*, fr. L *columna*, fr. *columen* top; akin to L *collis* hill — more at HILL] **1 a** : a vertical arrangement of items printed or written on a page **b** : one of two or more vertical sections of a printed page separated by a rule or blank space **c** : an accumulation arranged vertically : STACK **d** : a special department or feature in a newspaper or periodical **2** : a supporting pillar; *esp* : one consisting of a usu.

round shaft, a capital, and a base **3** : something resembling a column in form, position, or function ⟨a ~ of water⟩ **4** : a long row (as of soldiers) **5** : one of the vertical lines of elements of a determinant or matrix — **col·umned** \-əmd\ *adj*

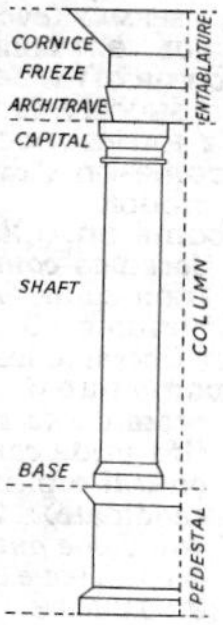
CORNICE
FRIEZE
ARCHITRAVE
ENTABLATURE
CAPITAL
SHAFT
COLUMN
BASE
PEDESTAL
column 2 with pedestal and entablature

co·lum·nar \kə-ˈləm-nər\ *adj* **1** : of, relating to, or characterized by columns **2** : of, relating to, being, or composed of tall narrow somewhat cylindrical or prismatic epithelial cells

co·lum·ni·a·tion \kə-ˌləm-nē-ˈā-shən\ *n* [modif. of L *columnation-, columnatio,* fr. *columna*] : the employment or the arrangement of columns in a structure

column inch *n* : a unit of measure for printed matter one column wide and one inch deep

col·um·nist \ˈkäl-əm-(n)əst *also* ˈkäl-yəm-\ *n* : one who writes a newspaper or magazine column — **col·um·nis·tic** \ˌkäl-əm-ˈnis-tik *also* -yəm-\ *adj*

col·za \ˈkäl-zə, ˈkōl-\ *n* [F, fr. D *koolzaad,* fr. MD *coolsaet,* fr. *coole* cabbage + *saet* seed] **1** : any of several coles; *esp* : one (as rape) producing seed used as a source of oil **2** : RAPESEED

¹com *abbr* **1** comedy; comic **2** comma

²com *or* **comm** *abbr* **1** command; commandant; commander; commanding **2** commentary **3** commerce; commercial **4** commission; commissioned; commissioner **5** committee **6** common; commoner **7** commonwealth **8** commune **9** communication **10** communist **11** community

COM *abbr* computer output microfilm; computer output microfilmer

com- *or* **col-** *or* **con-** *prefix* [ME, fr. OF, fr. L, with, together, thoroughly — more at CO-] : with : together : jointly — usu. *com-* before *b, p,* or *m* ⟨*com*mingle⟩, *col-* before *l* ⟨*col*linear⟩, and *con-* before other sounds ⟨*con*centrate⟩

¹co·ma \ˈkō-mə\ *n* [NL, fr. Gk *kōma* deep sleep] **1** : a state of profound unconsciousness caused by disease, injury, or poison **2** : a state of mental or physical sluggishness : TORPOR

²coma *n, pl* **co·mae** \-ˌmē, -ˌmī\ [L, hair, fr. Gk *komē*] **1** : a tufted bunch (as of branches, bracts, or seed hairs) **2** : the head of a comet usu. containing a nucleus **3** : an optical aberration in which the image of a point source is a comet-shaped blur — **co·mat·ic** \kō-ˈmat-ik\ *adj*

Co·ma Ber·e·ni·ces \ˈkō-mə-ˌber-ə-ˈnī-(ˌ)sēz\ *n* [L (gen. *Comae Berenices*), lit., Berenice's hair] : a constellation north of Virgo and between Boötes and Leo

co·mak·er \(ˈ)kō-ˈmā-kər\ *n* : one that participates in an agreement; *specif* : one who stands to meet a financial obligation in case of another's default

Co·man·che \kə-ˈman-chē\ *n, pl* **Comanche** *or* **Comanches** [Sp, of Shoshonean origin; perh. akin to Hopi *kománči* scalp lock] : a member of an Amerindian people ranging from Wyoming and Nebraska south into New Mexico and northwestern Texas

Co·man·che·an \-chē-ən\ *adj* [*Comanche,* Texas] : of, relating to, or being the period of the Mesozoic era between the Jurassic and the Cretaceous or the corresponding system of rocks — **Comanchean** *n*

co·mate \(ˈ)kō-ˈmāt, ˈkō-ˌ\ *n* : COMPANION

co·ma·tose \ˈkō-mə-ˌtōs, ˈkäm-ə-\ *adj* [F *comateux,* fr. Gk *kōmat-, kōma*] **1** : of, resembling, or affected with coma **2** : characterized by lethargic inertness : TORPID ⟨a ~ economy⟩ ***syn*** see LETHARGIC ***ant*** awake

co·mat·u·lid \kō-ˈmach-ə-ləd\ *n* [deriv. of LL *comatulus* having hair neatly curled, fr. L *comatus* hairy, fr. *coma*] : any of an order (Comatulida) of free-swimming stalkless crinoids — called also *feather star*

¹comb \ˈkōm\ *n* [ME, fr. OE *camb;* akin to OHG *kamb* comb, Gk *gomphos* tooth] **1 a** : a toothed instrument used esp. for adjusting, cleaning, or confining hair **b** : a structure resembling such a comb; *esp* : any of several toothed devices used in handling or ordering textile fibers **c** : CURRYCOMB **2 a** : a fleshy crest on the head of the domestic fowl and other gallinaceous birds — see COCK illustration **b** : something (as the ridge of a roof) resembling the comb of a cock **3** : HONEYCOMB — **combed** \ˈkōmd\ *adj* — **comb·like** \ˈkōm-ˌlīk\ *adj*

²comb *vt* **1** : to draw a comb through for the purpose of arranging or cleaning **2** : to pass across with a scraping or raking action **3 a** : to eliminate (as with a comb) by a thorough going over **b** : to search or examine systematically **4** : to use in a combing action ~ *vi* : to roll over or break into foam ⟨waves ~⟩

³comb *abbr* **1** combination; combined; combining **2** combustion

¹com·bat \kəm-ˈbat, ˈkäm-ˌ\ *vb* **-bat·ed** *or* **-bat·ted; -bat·ing** *or* **-bat·ting** [MF *combattre,* fr. (assumed) VL *combattere,* fr. L *com-* + *battuere* to beat — more at BATTLE] *vi* : to engage in combat : FIGHT ~ *vt* **1** : to fight with : BATTLE **2** : to struggle against; *esp* : to strive to reduce or eliminate ⟨~ inflation⟩ ***syn*** see OPPOSE

²com·bat \ˈkäm-ˌbat\ *n* **1** : a fight or contest between individuals or groups **2** : CONFLICT, CONTROVERSY **3** : active fighting in a war : ACTION ⟨casualties suffered in ~⟩

³com·bat \ˈkäm-ˌbat\ *adj* **1** : relating to combat ⟨~ missions⟩ **2** : designed or destined for combat ⟨~ troops⟩

com·bat·ant \kəm-ˈbat-ᵊnt *also* ˈkäm-bət-ənt\ *n* : one that is engaged in or ready to engage in combat — **combatant** *adj*

combat fatigue *n* : a traumatic psychoneurotic reaction or an acute psychotic reaction occurring under conditions (as wartime combat) that cause intense stress

com·bat·ive \kəm-ˈbat-iv\ *adj* : marked by eagerness to fight or contend ⟨the ~ element in human nature⟩ ***syn*** see BELLIGERENT ***ant*** pacifistic — **com·bat·ive·ly** *adv* — **com·bat·ive·ness** *n*

combe \ˈküm, ˈkōm\ *n* [of Celt origin; akin to W *cwm* valley] **1** *Brit* : a deep narrow valley **2** *Brit* : a valley or basin on the flank of a hill

comb·er \ˈkō-mər\ *n* **1** : one that combs **2** : a long curling wave of the sea

com·bin·abil·i·ty \kəm-ˌbī-nə-ˈbil-ət-ē\ *n* : ability to enter into combination — **com·bin·able** \-ˈbī-nə-bəl\ *adj*

com·bi·nate \ˈkäm-bə-ˌnāt\ *vt* **-nat·ed; -nat·ing** **1** [L *combinatus,* pp. of *combinare*] : COMBINE **2** [back-formation fr. *combination*] : to set up the combination of (a lock)

com·bi·na·tion \ˌkäm-bə-ˈnā-shən\ *n, often attrib* **1 a** : a result or product of combining; *esp* : an alliance of individuals, corporations, or states united to achieve a social, political, or economic end **b** : two or more persons working as a team ⟨a double-play ~⟩ **2** : an ordered sequence: as **a** : a sequence of letters or numbers chosen in setting a lock; *also* : the mechanism operating or moved by the sequence **b** : any of the different sets of *k* individuals (as letters) that can be chosen from a population of size *n* and are considered without regard to order within the set **3** : any of various one-piece undergarments for the upper and lower parts of the body **4** : an instrument designed to perform two or more tasks **5 a** : the act or process of combining; *esp* : that of uniting to form a chemical compound **b** : the quality or state of being combined — **com·bi·na·tion·al** \-shnəl, -shən-ᵊl\ *adj*

combination shot *n* : a shot in pool in which a ball is pocketed by an object ball

com·bi·na·tive \ˈkäm-bə-ˌnāt-iv, kəm-ˈbī-nət-\ *adj* **1** : tending or able to combine **2** : resulting from combination

com·bi·na·to·ri·al \ˌkäm-bə-nə-ˈtōr-ē-əl, kəm-ˌbī-nə-, -ˈtȯr-\ *adj* **1** : of, relating to, or involving combinations **2** : of or relating to the arrangement, operation, and selection of mathematical elements within finite sets and configurations ⟨~ mathematics⟩

combinatorial topology *n* : a study that deals with geometric forms based on their decomposition into combinations of the simplest geometric figures

com·bi·na·tor·ics \-ˈtȯr-iks, -ˈtär-\ *n pl but sing in constr* : combinatorial mathematics

com·bi·na·to·ry \kəm-ˈbī-nə-ˌtōr-ē, -ˌtȯr-\ *adj* : COMBINATIVE

¹com·bine \kəm-ˈbīn\ *vb* **com·bined; com·bin·ing** [ME *combinen,* fr. MF *combiner,* fr. LL *combinare,* fr. L *com-* + *bini* two by two — more at BIN-] *vt* **1 a** : to bring into such close relationship as to obscure individual characters : MERGE **b** : to cause to unite into a chemical compound **2** : INTERMIX, BLEND **3** : to possess in combination ~ *vi* **1 a** : to become one **b** : to unite to form a chemical compound **2** : to act together ***syn*** see JOIN ***ant*** separate — **com·bin·er** *n*

²com·bine \ˈkäm-ˌbīn\ *n* **1** : a combination esp. of industrial interests **2** : a harvesting machine that heads, threshes, and cleans grain while moving over a field

³com·bine \ˈkäm-ˌbīn\ *vt* **com·bined; com·bin·ing** : to harvest with a combine

comb·ing \ˈkō-miŋ\ *var of* COAMING

comb·ings \ˈkō-miŋz\ *n pl* : loose hair removed by a comb

combing wool *n* : long-staple strong-fibered wool found suitable for combing and used esp. in the manufacture of worsteds

com·bin·ing form \kəm-ˌbī-niŋ-\ *n* : a linguistic form that occurs only in compounds or derivatives and can be distinguished descriptively from an affix by its ability to occur as one immediate constituent of a form whose only other immediate constituent is an affix (as *cephal-* in *cephalic*) or by its being an allomorph of a morpheme having another allomorph that may occur alone or can be distinguished historically from an affix by the fact that it is borrowed from another language in which it is descriptively a word or a combining form

comb jelly *n* : CTENOPHORE

com·bo \ˈkäm-(ˌ)bō\ *n, pl* **combos** [*combination* + *-o*] **1** : COMBINATION **2** : a usu. small jazz or dance band

com·bust \kəm-ˈbəst\ *vb* [L *combustus,* pp. of *comburere* to burn up, irreg. fr. *com-* + *urere* to burn — more at EMBER] : BURN

com·bus·ti·ble \kəm-ˈbəs-tə-bəl\ *adj* **1** : capable of combustion **2** : easily excited — **com·bus·ti·bil·i·ty** \-ˌbəs-tə-ˈbil-ət-ē\ *n* — **combustible** *n* — **com·bus·ti·bly** \-ˈbəs-tə-blē\ *adv*

com·bus·tion \kəm-ˈbəs-chən\ *n* **1** : an act or instance of burning **2 a** : a chemical process (as an oxidation) accompanied by the evolution of light and heat **b** : a slower oxidation **3** : violent agitation : TUMULT ⟨he is seething with inner ~ —*Current Biog.*⟩ — **com·bus·tive** \-ˈbəs-tiv\ *adj*

com·bus·tor \-ˈbəs-tər\ *n* : a chamber (as in a gas turbine or a jet engine) in which combustion occurs

comd *abbr* command

comdg *abbr* commanding

comdr *abbr* commander

comdt *abbr* commandant

come \ˈkəm, *sometimes without stress when a stress follows*\ *vb* **came** \ˈkām\; **come; com·ing** \ˈkəm-iŋ\ [ME *comen,* fr. OE *cuman;* akin to OHG *queman* to come, L *venire,* Gk *bainein* to walk, go] *vi* **1 a** : to move toward something : APPROACH ⟨~ here⟩ **b** : to move or journey to a vicinity with a specified purpose ⟨he *came* to see us⟩ ⟨~ see us⟩ ⟨~ and see what's going on⟩ **c** (1) : to reach a particular station in a series ⟨now we ~ to the section on health⟩ (2) : to arrive in due course ⟨the time has ~⟩ **d** (1) : to approach in kind or quality ⟨this ~s near perfection⟩ (2) : to reach a condition ⟨*came* to regard him as a friend⟩ **e** (1) : to advance toward accomplishment ⟨learning new ways doesn't ~ easy⟩ ⟨the job is *coming* nicely⟩ (2) : to advance in a particular manner ⟨~ running when I call⟩ (3) : to advance, rise, or improve in rank or condition ⟨has ~ a long way⟩ **f** : to get along : FARE — often used with *along* **g** : EXTEND ⟨her dress *came* to her ankles⟩ **2 a** (1) : to arrive at a particular place, end, result, or conclusion ⟨*came* to his senses⟩ ⟨~ untied⟩ (2) : AMOUNT ⟨taxes ~ to more than it's worth⟩ **b** (1) : to appear to the mind ⟨the answer *came* to him⟩

(2) : to appear on a scene : make an appearance ⟨children ~ equipped to learn any language⟩ **c** : HAPPEN, OCCUR ⟨no harm will ~ to you⟩ **d** : ORIGINATE, ARISE ⟨wine ~s from grapes⟩ ⟨~ of sturdy stock⟩ ⟨the best play to ~ out of Europe this year⟩ **e** : to enter or assume a condition ⟨artillery *came* into action⟩ **f** : to fall within a field of view or a range of application ⟨this ~s within the terms of the treaty⟩ **g** : to issue forth ⟨a sob *came* from her throat⟩ **h** : to take form ⟨churn till the butter ~s⟩ **i** : to be available ⟨this model ~s in several sizes⟩ ⟨as good as they ~⟩ **j** : to experience orgasm **3** : to fall to a person in a division or inheritance of property **4** *obs* : to become moved favorably : RELENT **5** : to turn out to be ⟨good clothes ~ high⟩ ⟨*came* short of his goal⟩ **6** : BECOME ⟨a dream that *came* true⟩ ⟨things will ~ clear if we are patient⟩ ~ *vt* **1** : to approach or be near (an age) ⟨a child *coming* eight years old⟩ **2** : to take on the aspect of ⟨~ the stern parent⟩ — **come a cropper** : to fail completely — **come across** : to meet or find by chance ⟨*came across* a long lost friend today⟩ — **come alive** : to become animated or responsive — **come apart** : to disintegrate physically or mentally — **come at** : to accomplish an understanding or mastery of : ATTAIN ⟨art is not something to *come at* by dint of study —Clive Bell⟩ — **come between** : to cause to be estranged ⟨parents *came between* the lovers⟩ — **come by** : to get possession of : ACQUIRE ⟨a good job can be hard to *come by*⟩ — **come clean** : to tell the whole story : CONFESS — **come from** : to be or have been a native or resident of — **come into** : to acquire as a possession or achievement ⟨*come into* a fortune⟩ — **come into one's own** : to achieve one's potential; *also* : to gain recognition — **come off it** : to cease foolish or pretentious talk or behavior — **come over** : to seize suddenly and strangely ⟨what's *come over* you⟩ — **come to** : to be a question of ⟨when it *comes to* pitching horseshoes, he's the champ⟩ — **come to grips with** : to wrestle with : meet firmly ⟨*coming to grips with* the problem⟩ — **come to life** **1** : to regain consciousness or vitality **2** : to take on a real or lifelike quality ⟨a writer whose characters *come to life*⟩ — **come to oneself** : to get hold of oneself : regain self-control — **come to pass** : HAPPEN — **come upon** : to come across — **come with** : to be a concomitant of : accompany or follow upon as a matter of course ⟨the increase of traffic that *comes with* new roads⟩

come about *vi* **1** : to come to pass : HAPPEN **2** : to change direction ⟨the wind has *come about* into the north⟩ **3** : to shift to a new tack

come across *vi* **1** : to give over or furnish something demanded; *esp* : to pay over money **2** : to produce an impression ⟨*comes across* as a persuasive speaker⟩

come along *vi* **1** : to accompany someone who leads the way ⟨asked me to *come along* to keep him company⟩ **2** : to make progress : SUCCEED ⟨the work is *coming along* quite well⟩ **3** : to make an appearance ⟨wouldn't just marry the first man that *came along*⟩

come around *vi* **1** : to come round **2** : MENSTRUATE

come·back \ˈkəm-ˌbak\ *n* **1 a** : a sharp or witty reply : RETORT **b** : a cause for complaint **2** : RECOVERY

come back \(ˌ)kəm-ˈbak\ *vi* **1** : to return to life or vitality **2** : to return to memory ⟨it's all *coming back* to me now⟩ **3** : REPLY, RETORT **4** : to regain a former favorable condition or position

come by *vi* : to make a visit

co·me·di·an \kə-ˈmēd-ē-ən\ *n* **1** *archaic* **a** : a writer of comedies **b** : an actor who plays comic roles **2** : a comical individual; *specif* : a professional entertainer who uses any of various physical or verbal means to be amusing

co·me·dic \-ˈmēd-ik, -ˈmed-\ *adj* **1** : of or relating to comedy **2** : COMICAL 2

co·me·di·enne \-ˌmēd-ē-ˈen\ *n* [F *comédienne,* fem. of *comédien* comedian, fr. *comédie*] : a female comedian

com·e·do \ˈkäm-ə-ˌdō\ *n, pl* **com·e·do·nes** \ˌkäm-ə-ˈdō-(ˌ)nēz\ [NL, fr. L, glutton, fr. *comedere* to eat — more at COMESTIBLE] : BLACKHEAD 1

come·down \ˈkəm-ˌdau̇n\ *n* : a descent in rank or dignity

come down \(ˌ)kəm-ˈdau̇n\ *vi* **1** : to pass by tradition ⟨a story that has *come down* from medieval times⟩ **2 a** : to reduce itself : AMOUNT ⟨it *comes down* to this⟩ **b** : to deal directly with ⟨when you *come down* to it, we all depend on others⟩ **3** : to lose or fall in estate or condition ⟨he has *come down* in the world⟩ **4** : to place oneself in opposition ⟨the judge *came down* hard on gambling⟩ **5** : to become ill ⟨they *came down* with measles⟩ **6** : to recover from the effects of a stimulant drug

com·e·dy \ˈkäm-əd-ē\ *n, pl* **-dies** [ME, fr. MF *comedie,* fr. L *comoedia,* fr. Gk *kōmōidia,* fr. *kōmos* revel + *aeidein* to sing — more at ODE] **1 a** : a drama of light and amusing character and typically with a happy ending **b** : the genre of dramatic literature dealing with the comic or with the serious in a light or satirical manner — compare TRAGEDY **2 a** : a medieval narrative that ends happily ⟨Dante's Divine *Comedy*⟩ **b** : a literary work written in a comic style or treating a comic theme **3** : a ludicrous or farcical event or series of events **4** : the comic element ⟨the ~ of many life situations⟩

comedy drama *n* : serious drama that is interspersed with comedy

comedy of manners : comedy that satirically portrays the manners and fashions of a particular class or set

come–hith·er \(ˌ)kəm-ˈhith-ər, (ˌ)kə-ˈmith-\ *adj* : sexually provocative ⟨that ~ look in her eyes⟩

come in *vi* **1 a** : to arrive on a scene ⟨new models *coming in*⟩ **b** : to become available ⟨data began *coming in*⟩ **2** : to place among those finishing ⟨*came in* second⟩ **3 a** : to function in an indicated manner ⟨*come in* handy⟩ **b** : to make reply to a signal or call ⟨*came in* loud and clear⟩ **4** : to assume a role or function ⟨that's where you *come in*⟩ **5** : to attain maturity, fruitfulness, or production — **come in for** : to become subject to ⟨*coming in for* increasing criticism⟩

come·ly \ˈkəm-lē *also* ˈkōm- *or* ˈkäm-\ *adj* **come·li·er, -est** [ME *comly,* alter. of OE *cȳmlic* glorious, fr. *cȳme* lively, fine; akin to OHG *kūmig* weak, Gk *goan* to lament] **1** : having a generally pleasing appearance : not homely or plain **2** : pleasurably conforming to notions of good appearance, fitness, or proportion : SEEMLY ⟨everything in neat and ~ arrangement⟩ *syn* see BEAUTIFUL *ant* homely — **come·li·ness** *n*

come off *vi* **1** : to acquit oneself ⟨*came off* well in the contest⟩ **2** : SUCCEED ⟨a television series that never *came off* —*TV Guide*⟩ **3** : HAPPEN, OCCUR

come–on \ˈkəm-ˌȯn, -ˌän\ *n* : an attraction used esp. in sales promotion

come on \(ˌ)kəm-ˈȯn, -ˈän\ *vi* **1 a** : to advance by degrees ⟨as darkness *came on,* it got harder to see⟩ **b** : to begin by degrees ⟨rain *came on* toward noon⟩ **2** : PLEASE — used in cajoling or pleading **3** : to project an indicated personal image ⟨*comes on* as a liberal in his political speeches⟩

come out *vi* **1 a** : to come into public view : make a public appearance ⟨a new magazine has *come out*⟩ **b** : to become evident ⟨his pride *came out* in his refusal to accept help⟩ **2** : to declare oneself esp. in public utterance ⟨*came out* in favor of the popular candidate⟩ **3** : to turn out in an outcome : end up ⟨everything will *come out* all right⟩ **4** : to make a debut — **come out with** **1** : to give expression to ⟨he *came out with* an interesting proposal⟩ **2** : PUBLISH

come–out·er \(ˌ)kə-ˈmau̇t-ər\ *n* : RADICAL, REFORMER

come over *vi* **1 a** : to change from one side (as of a controversy) to the other **b** : to visit casually : drop in ⟨*come over* anytime; we're always in⟩ **2** *Brit* : BECOME

com·er \ˈkəm-ər\ *n* **1** : one that comes or arrives ⟨all ~s⟩ **2** : one making rapid progress or showing promise

come round *vi* **1** : to return to a former condition; *esp* : to come to **2** : to accede to a particular opinion or course of action ⟨the rest of the world has *come round* to his way of living —David Halberstam⟩ **3** : to change in direction ⟨the wind *came round* at dawn⟩

¹co·mes·ti·ble \kə-ˈmes-tə-bəl\ *adj* [MF, fr. ML *comestibilis,* fr. L *comestus,* pp. of *comedere* to eat, fr. *com-* + *edere* to eat — more at EAT] : EDIBLE

²comestible *n* : FOOD — usu. used in pl.

com·et \ˈkäm-ət\ *n* [ME *comete,* fr. OE *cometa,* fr. L, fr. Gk *komētēs,* lit., long-haired, fr. *koman* to wear long hair, fr. *komē* hair] : a celestial body that consists of a fuzzy head usu. surrounding a bright nucleus, that often when in the part of its orbit near the sun develops a long tail which points away from the sun, and that has an orbit varying in eccentricity between nearly round and parabolic — **com·e·tary** \-ə-ˌter-ē\ *adj* — **co·met·ic** \kə-ˈmet-ik, kä-\ *adj*

come through *vi* **1** : to do what is needed or expected **2** : to become communicated

come to *vi* **1** : to recover consciousness **2 a** : to bring a ship's head nearer the wind : LUFF **b** : to come to anchor or to a stop

come up *vi* **1** : to come near : make an approach ⟨*came up* and introduced himself⟩ **2** : to rise in rank or status ⟨an officer who *came up* from the ranks⟩ **3 a** : to come to attention or consideration ⟨the question never *came up* in discussion⟩ **b** : to occur in the course of time ⟨any problem that may *come up*⟩ **4** : to get up — used typically in a command to a horse **5** : RISE 6 — **come up with** : to produce esp. in dealing with a problem or challenge ⟨*came up with* a better solution⟩

come·up·pance \(ˌ)kə-ˈməp-ən(t)s\ *n* [*come up* + *-ance*] : a deserved rebuke or penalty : DESERTS

com·fit \ˈkəm(p)-fət, ˈkäm(p)-\ *n* [ME *confit,* fr. MF, fr. pp. of *confire* to prepare, fr. L *conficere,* fr. *com-* + *facere* to make — more at DO] : a confection consisting of a piece of fruit, a root, or a seed coated and preserved with sugar

¹com·fort \ˈkəm(p)-fərt\ *n* **1** : strengthening aid: **a** : ASSISTANCE, SUPPORT ⟨accused of giving aid and *comfort* to the enemy⟩ **b** : consolation in time of trouble or worry : SOLACE **2 a** : a feeling of relief or encouragement **b** : contented well-being **3** : a satisfying or enjoyable experience ⟨the ~ of a good meal after hard work⟩ **4** : one that gives or brings comfort ⟨the ~s of civilization⟩ — **com·fort·less** \-ləs\ *adj*

²comfort *vt* [ME *comforten,* fr. OF *conforter,* fr. LL *confortare* to strengthen greatly, fr. L *com-* + *fortis* strong] **1** : to give strength and hope to : CHEER **2** : to ease the grief or trouble of : CONSOLE — **com·fort·ing·ly** \-iŋ-lē\ *adv*

syn COMFORT, CONSOLE, SOLACE *shared meaning element* : to act to ease the griefs or sufferings of (another) *ant* afflict, bother

com·fort·able \ˈkəm(p)-fərt-ə-bəl, ˈkəm(p)(f)-tə(r)-bəl\ *adj* **1 a** : affording or enjoying contentment and security ⟨a ~ income⟩ **b** : affording or enjoying physical comfort ⟨a ~ chair⟩ ⟨was too ~ to move⟩ **2 a** : free from vexation or doubt ⟨~ assumptions that require no thought⟩ **b** : free from stress or tension ⟨a ~ routine⟩ — **com·fort·able·ness** *n* — **com·fort·ably** \-blē\ *adv*

syn COMFORTABLE, COZY, SNUG, EASY, RESTFUL *shared meaning element* : enjoying or providing circumstances that make for contentment and security *ant* uncomfortable, miserable

com·fort·er \ˈkəm(p)-fə(r)t-ər\ *n* **1 a** *cap* : HOLY SPIRIT **b** : one that gives comfort **2 a** : a long narrow usu. knitted neck scarf **b** : a warm bed covering : QUILT

comfort station *n* : REST ROOM

com·frey \ˈkəm(p)-frē\ *n, pl* **comfreys** [ME *cumfirie,* fr. OF, fr. L *conferva*] : any of a genus (*Symphytum*) of plants of the borage family with coarse hairy entire leaves and flowers in one-sided racemes

com·fy \ˈkəm(p)-fē\ *adj* **com·fi·er; -est** [by shortening & alter.] : COMFORTABLE

¹com·ic \ˈkäm-ik\ *adj* [L *comicus,* fr. Gk *kōmikos,* fr. *kōmos* revel] **1** : of, relating to, or marked by comedy **2** : causing laughter or amusement : FUNNY **3** : of or relating to comic strips *syn* see LAUGHABLE

²comic *n* **1** : COMEDIAN **2** : the comic element **3 a** : COMIC STRIP **b** (1) : COMIC BOOK (2) *pl* : the part of a newspaper devoted to comic strips

com·i·cal \ˈkäm-i-kəl\ *adj* **1** *obs* : of or relating to comedy **2** : being of a kind to excite laughter esp. because of a startlingly or

unexpectedly humorous impact **syn** see LAUGHABLE — **com·i·cal·i·ty** \ˌkäm-i-ˈkal-ət-ē\ n — **com·i·cal·ly** \ˈkäm-i-k(ə-)lē\ adv
comic book n : a magazine containing sequences of comic strips
comic-opera adj : not to be taken seriously ⟨a ～ regime⟩
comic opera n : opera having a usu. sentimental plot and characterized by spoken dialogue, humorous episodes, and usu. a happy ending
comic relief n : a relief from the emotional tension of a drama that is provided by the interposition of a comic episode
comic strip n : a group of cartoons in narrative sequence
¹com·ing \ˈkəm-iŋ\ n : an act or instance of arriving
²coming adj 1 : immediately due in sequence or development ⟨～ year⟩ 2 : gaining importance
Com·in·tern \ˈkäm-ən-ˌtərn\ n [Russ Komintern, fr. Kommunisticheskii Internatsional Communist International] : the Communist International established in 1919 in an attempt to supersede the Second International of Socialist organizations
co·mi·tia \kə-ˈmish-(ē-)ə\ n, pl **comitia** [L, pl. of comitium, fr. com- + itus, pp. of ire to go — more at ISSUE] : one of several public assemblies of the people in ancient Rome for the exercise of legislative, judicial, and electoral functions — **co·mi·tial** \-ˈmish-əl\ adj
co·mi·ty \ˈkäm-ət-ē, ˈkō-mət-\ n, pl **-ties** [L comitat-, comitas, fr. comis courteous, fr. OL cosmis, fr. com- + -smis (akin to Skt smayate he smiles) — more at SMILE] 1 a : friendly quality of social atmosphere : social harmony ⟨group activities promoting ～⟩ b : a loose widespread community based on common social institutions ⟨the ～ of civilization⟩ c : COMITY OF NATIONS d : the informal and voluntary recognition by courts of one jurisdiction of the laws and judicial decisions of another 2 : avoidance of proselytizing members of another religious denomination
comity of nations 1 : the courtesy and friendship of nations marked esp. by mutual recognition of executive, legislative, and judicial acts 2 : the group of nations practicing international comity
coml abbr commercial
comm abbr — see COM
com·ma \ˈkäm-ə\ n [LL, fr. L, part of a sentence, fr. Gk komma segment, clause, fr. koptein to cut — more at CAPON] 1 : a punctuation mark , used esp. as a mark of separation within the sentence 2 : PAUSE, INTERVAL 3 : any of several nymphalid butterflies (genus Polygonia) with a silvery comma-shaped mark on the underside of the hind wings
comma bacillus n : a bacterium (Vibrio comma) that causes Asiatic cholera
comma fault n : the careless or unjustified use of a comma between coordinate main clauses not connected by a conjunction
¹com·mand \kə-ˈmand\ vb [ME comanden, fr. OF comander, fr. (assumed) VL commandare, alter. of L commendare to commit to one's charge — more at COMMEND] vt 1 : to direct authoritatively : ORDER 2 : to exercise a dominating influence over: as a : to have at one's immediate disposal b : to demand as one's due : EXACT ⟨～s a high fee⟩ c : to overlook or dominate from a strategic position d : to have military command of as senior officer 3 obs : to order or request to be given ～ vi 1 : to have or exercise direct authority : GOVERN 2 : to give orders 3 : to be commander 4 : to have an overlook — **com·mand·able** \-ˈman-də-bəl\ adj
syn COMMAND, ORDER, BID, ENJOIN, DIRECT, INSTRUCT, CHARGE shared meaning element : to issue orders or issue an order to **ant** comply, obey
²command n 1 : the act of commanding 2 a : an order given b : an electrical signal that actuates a device (as a control mechanism in a spacecraft or one step in a computer); also : the activation of a device by means of such a signal 3 a : the ability to control : MASTERY b : the authority or right to command ⟨an air of ～⟩ ⟨the officer in ～⟩ c (1) : the power to dominate (2) : scope of vision d : facility in use ⟨a good ～ of French⟩ 4 : the personnel, area, or organization under a commander ⟨troops of the southern ～⟩; specif : a unit of the U.S. Air Force higher than an air force 5 : a position of highest usu. military authority
³command adj : done on command or request ⟨a ～ performance⟩
com·man·dant \ˈkäm-ən-ˌdant, -ˌdänt\ n : COMMANDING OFFICER
command car n : an open armored car designed esp. for military reconnaissance and capable of traveling over rough terrain
com·man·deer \ˌkäm-ən-ˈdi(ə)r\ vt [Afrik kommandeer, fr. F commander to command, fr. OF comander] 1 a : to compel to perform military service b : to seize for military purposes 2 : to take arbitrary or forcible possession of
com·mand·er \kə-ˈman-dər\ n 1 : one in an official position of command or control: as a : COMMANDING OFFICER b : the presiding officer of a society or organization 2 : a commissioned officer in the navy or coast guard ranking above a lieutenant commander and below a captain — **com·mand·er·ship** \-ˌship\ n
commander in chief : one who holds the supreme command of an armed force
com·mand·ery \kə-ˈman-d(ə-)rē\ n, pl **-er·ies** 1 : a district under the control of a commander of an order of knights 2 : an assembly or lodge in a secret order
com·mand·ing \kə-ˈman-diŋ\ adj : drawing attention or priority — **com·mand·ing·ly** \-diŋ-lē\ adv
commanding officer n : an officer in command; esp : an officer in the armed forces in command of an organization or installation
com·mand·ment \kə-ˈman(d)-mənt\ n 1 : the act or power of commanding 2 : something that is commanded; specif : one of the biblical Ten Commandments
command module n : a space vehicle module designed to carry the crew, the chief communication equipment, and the equipment for reentry
com·man·do \kə-ˈman-(ˈ)dō\ n, pl **-dos** or **-does** [Afrik kommando, fr. D commando command, fr. Sp comando, fr. comandar to command, fr. F commander] 1 So Afr : a military unit or command of the Boers b : a raiding expedition 2 a : a military unit trained and organized as shock troops esp. for hit-and-run raids

into enemy territory b : a member of such a specialized raiding unit
command post n : a post at which the commander of a unit in the field receives orders from his headquarters and exercises command over his unit
command sergeant major n : a noncommissioned officer in the army ranking above a first sergeant
comma splice n : COMMA FAULT
com·me·dia del·l'ar·te \kə-ˌmād-ē-ə-(ˌ)del-ˈärt-ē, -ˌmed-\ n [It, lit., comedy of art] : Italian comedy of the 16th to 18th centuries improvised from standardized situations and stock characters
comme il faut \ˌkəm-ē(l)-ˈfō\ adj [F, lit., as it should be] : conforming to accepted standards : PROPER
com·mem·o·rate \kə-ˈmem-ə-ˌrāt\ vt **-rat·ed; -rat·ing** [L commemoratus, pp. of commemorare, fr. com- + memorare to remind of, fr. memor mindful — more at MEMORY] 1 : to call to remembrance 2 : to mark by some ceremony or observation : OBSERVE 3 : to serve as a memorial of ⟨a plaque that ～s the battle⟩ **syn** see KEEP — **com·mem·o·ra·tor** \-ˌrāt-ər\ n
com·mem·o·ra·tion \kə-ˌmem-ə-ˈrā-shən\ n 1 : the act of commemorating 2 : something that commemorates
com·mem·o·ra·tive \kə-ˈmem-(ə-)rāt-iv, -ˈmem-ə-ˌrāt-iv\ adj : intended as a commemoration : COMMEMORATING — **commemorative** n — **com·mem·o·ra·tive·ly** adv
com·mence \kə-ˈmen(t)s\ vb **com·menced; com·menc·ing** [ME comencen, fr. MF comencer, fr. (assumed) VL cominitiare, fr. L com- + LL initiare to begin, fr. L to initiate] vt 1 : to enter upon : BEGIN 2 : to initiate formally by performing the first act of ⟨～ proceedings⟩ ～ vi 1 : to have or make a beginning : START 2 chiefly Brit : to begin to be or to act as 3 chiefly Brit : to take a degree at a university **syn** see BEGIN — **com·menc·er** n
com·mence·ment \kəm-ˈmen(t)-smənt\ n 1 : an act, instance, or time of commencing 2 a : the ceremonies or the day for conferring degrees or diplomas b : the period of activities at this time
com·mend \kə-ˈmend\ vb [ME commenden, fr. L commendare, fr. com- + mandare to entrust — more at MANDATE] vt 1 : to entrust for care or preservation 2 : to recommend as worthy of confidence or notice 3 : to mention with approbation : PRAISE ～ vi : to commend or serve as a commendation of something — **com·mend·able** \-ˈmen-də-bəl\ adj — **com·mend·ably** \-blē\ adv — **com·mend·er** n
com·men·da·tion \ˌkäm-ən-ˈdā-shən, -ˌen-\ n 1 a : an act of commending b : something (as a formal citation) that commends 2 archaic : COMPLIMENT
com·men·da·to·ry \kə-ˈmen-də-ˌtōr-ē, -ˌtōr-\ adj : serving to commend
com·men·sal \kə-ˈmen(t)s-əl\ adj [ME, fr. ML commensalis, fr. L com- + LL mensalis of the table, fr. L mensa table] 1 : of or relating to those who habitually eat together 2 : living in a state of commensalism — **commensal** n — **com·men·sal·ly** \-sə-lē\ adv
com·men·sal·ism \-sə-ˌliz-əm\ n : a relation between two kinds of organisms in which one obtains food or other benefits from the other without damaging or benefiting it
com·men·su·ra·ble \kə-ˈmen(t)s-(ə-)rə-bəl, -ˈmench-(ə-)\ adj 1 : having a common measure; specif : divisible by a common unit an integral number of times 2 : COMMENSURATE 2 — **com·men·su·ra·bil·i·ty** \-ˌmen(t)s-(ə-)rə-ˈbil-ət-ē, -ˈmench-(ə-)\ n — **com·men·su·ra·bly** \-ˈmen(t)s-(ə-)rə-blē, -ˈmench(ə-)\ adv
com·men·su·rate \kə-ˈmen(t)s-(ə-)rət, -ˈmench (ə-)\ adj [LL commensuratus, fr. L com- + LL mensuratus, pp. of mensurare to measure, fr. L mensura measure — more at MEASURE] 1 : equal in measure or extent : COEXTENSIVE ⟨lived a life ～ with the early years of the republic⟩ 2 : corresponding in size, extent, amount, or degree : PROPORTIONATE ⟨was given a job ～ with his abilities⟩ 3 : COMMENSURABLE 1 — **com·men·su·rate·ly** adv — **com·men·su·ra·tion** \-ˌmen(t)s-ə-ˈrā-shən, -ˌmen-chə-\ n
¹com·ment \ˈkäm-ˌent\ n [ME, fr. LL commentum, fr. L, invention, fr. neut. of commentus, pp. of comminisci to invent, fr. com- + -minisci (akin to ment-, mens mind) — more at MIND] 1 : COMMENTARY 2 : a note explaining, illustrating, or criticizing the meaning of a writing ⟨～s printed in the margin⟩ 3 a : an observation or remark expressing an opinion or attitude ⟨had no ～ for the press⟩ b : a judgment expressed indirectly ⟨this film is a ～ on current moral standards⟩
²comment vi : to explain or interpret something by comment ⟨～ing on recent developments⟩ ～ vt : to make a comment on ⟨the discovery … is hardly ～ed by the press —Nation⟩ **syn** see REMARK
com·men·tary \ˈkäm-ən-ˌter-ē\ n, pl **-tar·ies** 1 a : an explanatory treatise — usu. used in pl. b : a record of events usu. written by a participant — usu. used in pl. 2 a : a systematic series of explanations or interpretations (as of a writing) b : COMMENT 2 3 a : something that serves for illustration or explanation ⟨the dark, airless apartments and sunless factories … are a sad ～ upon our civilization —H. A. Overstreet⟩ b : an expression of opinion ⟨a scene that is a gem of satiric ～ on the world of art —Rose Feld⟩
com·men·tate \ˈkäm-ən-ˌtāt\ vb **-tat·ed; -tat·ing** [back-formation fr. commentator] vt : to give a commentary on ～ vi : to comment in a usu. expository or interpretive manner; also : to act as a commentator **syn** see REMARK
com·men·ta·tor \-ˌtāt-ər\ n : one who gives a commentary; specif : one who reports and discusses news on radio or television
¹com·merce \ˈkäm-(ˌ)ərs\ n [MF, fr. L commercium, fr. com- + merc-, merx merchandise] 1 : social intercourse : interchange of ideas, opinions, or sentiments 2 : the exchange or buying and

selling of commodities on a large scale involving transportation from place to place **3** : SEXUAL INTERCOURSE ***syn*** see BUSINESS

²**com·merce** \ˈkäm-(ˌ)ərs, kə-ˈmərs\ *vi* **com·merced; com·merc·ing** *archaic* : COMMUNE

¹**com·mer·cial** \kə-ˈmər-shəl\ *adj* **1 a** (1) : engaged in work designed for the market ⟨a ~ artist⟩ (2) : of or relating to commerce ⟨~ regulations⟩ (3) : characteristic of commerce ⟨~ weights⟩ (4) : suitable, adequate, or prepared for commerce ⟨found oil in ~ quantities⟩ **b** (1) : being of an average or inferior quality ⟨~ oxalic acid⟩ (2) : producing artistic work of low standards for quick market success **2 a** : viewed with regard to profit ⟨a ~ success⟩ **b** : designed for a large market **3** : emphasizing skills and subjects useful in business **4** : supported by advertisers ⟨~ TV⟩ — **com·mer·cial·ly** \-ˈmərsh-(ə-)lē\ *adv*

²**commercial** *n* : an advertisement broadcast on radio or television

commercial bank *n* : a bank including in its functions the acceptance of demand deposits subject to withdrawal by check

com·mer·cial·ism \kə-ˈmər-shə-ˌliz-əm\ *n* **1** : commercial spirit, institutions, or methods **2** : excessive emphasis on profit — **com·mer·cial·ist** \-ˈmərsh-(ə-)ləst\ *n* — **com·mer·cial·is·tic** \-ˌmər-shə-ˈlis-tik\ *adj*

com·mer·cial·ize \kə-ˈmər-shə-ˌlīz\ *vt* **-ized; -iz·ing 1 a** : to manage on a business basis for profit **b** : to develop commerce in **2** : to exploit for profit ⟨~ Christmas⟩ **3** : to debase in quality for more profit — **com·mer·cial·iza·tion** \-ˌmərsh-(ə-)lə-ˈzā-shən\ *n*

commercial paper *n* : short-term negotiable instruments arising out of commercial transactions

commercial traveler *n* : TRAVELING SALESMAN

com·mie \ˈkäm-ē\ *n, often cap* [by shortening and alter.] : COMMUNIST

com·mi·na·tion \ˌkäm-ə-ˈnā-shən\ *n* [ME, fr. MF or L; MF, fr. L *commination-, comminatio,* fr. *comminatus,* pp. of *comminari* to threaten, fr. *com-* + *minari* to threaten] : DENUNCIATION — **com·mi·na·to·ry** \ˈkäm-ə-nə-ˌtōr-ē, -ˌtȯr-; kə-ˈmin-ə-, -ˈmīn-\ *adj*

com·min·gle \kə-ˈmiŋ-gəl, kä-\ *vt* **1** : to blend thoroughly into a harmonious whole **2** : to combine (funds or properties) into a common fund or stock ⟨~ accounts⟩ ~ *vi* : to become commingled ***syn*** see MIX

com·mi·nute \ˈkäm-ə-ˌn(y)üt\ *vt* **-nut·ed; -nut·ing** [L *comminutus,* pp. of *comminuere,* fr. *com-* + *minuere* to lessen] : to reduce to minute particles : PULVERIZE — **com·mi·nu·tion** \ˌkäm-ə-ˈn(y)ü-shən\ *n*

com·mis·er·ate \kə-ˈmiz-ə-ˌrāt\ *vb* **-at·ed; -at·ing** [L *commiseratus,* pp. of *commiserari,* fr. *com-* + *miserari* to pity, fr. *miser* wretched] *vt* : to feel or express sorrow or compassion for ~ *vi* : to feel or express sympathy : CONDOLE ⟨~ over their hard luck⟩ — **com·mis·er·a·tive** \-ˈmiz-ə-ˌrāt-iv\ *adj*

com·mis·er·a·tion \-ˌmiz-ə-ˈrā-shən\ *n* : the act of commiserating

com·mis·sar \ˈkäm-ə-ˌsär\ *n* [Russ *komissar,* fr. G *kommissar,* fr. ML *commissarius*] **1 a** : a Communist party official assigned to a military unit to teach party principles and policies and to ensure party loyalty **b** : one that attempts to control public opinion or its expression **2** : the head of a government department in the U.S.S.R. until 1946

com·mis·sar·i·at \ˌkäm-ə-ˈser-ē-ət, -ˈsar-, *esp for 3* -ˈsär-\ *n* [NL *commissariatus,* fr. ML *commissarius*] **1** : a system for supplying an army with food **2** : food supplies **3** [Russ *komissariat,* fr. G *kommissariat,* fr. NL *commissariatus*] : a government department in the U.S.S.R. until 1946

com·mis·sary \ˈkäm-ə-ˌser-ē\ *n, pl* **-sar·ies** [ME *commissarie,* fr. ML *commissarius,* fr. L *commissus,* pp.] **1** : one delegated by a superior to execute a duty or an office **2 a** : a store for equipment and provisions; *specif* : a supermarket operated for military personnel **b** : food supplies **c** : a lunchroom esp. in a motion-picture studio

¹**com·mis·sion** \kə-ˈmish-ən\ *n* [ME, fr. MF, fr. L *commission-, commissio* act of bringing together, fr. *commissus,* pp. of *committere*] **1 a** : a formal written warrant granting the power to perform various acts or duties **b** : a certificate conferring military rank and authority; *also* : the rank and authority so conferred **2** : an authorization or command to act in a prescribed manner or to perform prescribed acts : CHARGE **3 a** : authority to act for, in behalf of, or in place of another **b** : a task or matter entrusted to one as an agent for another ⟨executed a ~ for me abroad⟩ **4 a** : a group of persons directed to perform some duty **b** : a government agency having administrative, legislative, or judicial powers **c** : a city council having legislative and executive functions **5** : an act of committing something ⟨charged with ~ of felonies⟩ **6** : a fee paid to an agent or employee for transacting a piece of business or performing a service; *esp* : a percentage of the money received from a total paid to the agent responsible for the business **7** : an act of entrusting or giving authority — **in commission** *or* **into commission 1** : under the authority of commissioners **2** *of a ship* : ready for active service **3** : in use or in condition for use — **on commission** : with commission serving as partial or full pay for work done — **out of commission 1** : out of active service or use **2** : out of working order

²**commission** *vt* **com·mis·sioned; com·mis·sion·ing** \-ˈmish-(ə-)niŋ\ **1** : to furnish with a commission: as **a** : to confer a formal commission on ⟨was ~*ed* lieutenant⟩ **b** : to appoint or assign to a task or function ⟨the writer who was ~*ed* to do the biography⟩ **2** : to order to be made ⟨wealthy persons who ~*ed* portraits of themselves⟩ **3** : to put (a ship) in commission

com·mis·sion·aire \kə-ˌmish-ə-ˈna(ə)r, -ˈne(ə)r\ *n* [F *commissionnaire,* fr. *commission*] *chiefly Brit* : a uniformed attendant

commissioned officer *n* : an officer of the armed forces holding by a commission a rank of second lieutenant or ensign or above

com·mis·sion·er \kə-ˈmish-(ə-)nər\ *n* : a person with a commission: as **a** : a member of a commission **b** : the representative of the governmental authority in a district, province, or other unit often having both judicial and administrative powers **c** : the officer in charge of a department or bureau of the public service **d** : the administrative head of a professional sport — **com·mis·sion·er·ship** \-ˌship\ *n*

commission merchant *n* : one who buys or sells another's goods for a commission

commission plan *n* : a method of municipal government under which a small elective commission exercises both executive and legislative powers and each commissioner directly administers one or more municipal departments

com·mis·sure \ˈkäm-ə-ˌshü(ə)r\ *n* [ME, fr. MF or L; MF, fr. L *commissura* a joining, fr. *commissus,* pp.] **1** : the place where two bodies or parts unite : CLOSURE **2** : a connecting band of nerve tissue in the brain or spinal cord — **com·mis·sur·al** \ˌkäm-ə-ˈshu̇r-əl\ *adj*

com·mit \kə-ˈmit\ *vb* **com·mit·ted; com·mit·ting** [ME *committen,* fr. L *committere* to connect, entrust, fr. *com-* + *mittere* to send] *vt* **1 a** : to put into charge or trust : ENTRUST **b** : to place in a prison or mental institution **c** : to consign or record for preservation ⟨~ it to memory⟩ **d** : to put into a place for disposal or safekeeping **e** : to refer (as a legislative bill) to a committee for consideration and report **2** : to carry into action deliberately ⟨~ a crime⟩ **3 a** : OBLIGATE, BIND **b** : to pledge or assign to some particular course or use ⟨all available troops were *committed* to the attack⟩ **c** : to reveal the views of ⟨refused to ~ himself on the issue⟩ ~ *vi, obs* : to perpetrate an offense — **com·mit·ta·ble** \-ˈmit-ə-bəl\ *adj*

syn COMMIT, ENTRUST, CONFIDE, CONSIGN, RELEGATE *shared meaning element* : to assign (as to a person or place) esp. for care or safekeeping

com·mit·ment \kə-ˈmit-mənt\ *n* **1 a** : an act of committing to a charge or trust: as (1) : a consignment to a penal or mental institution (2) : an act of referring a matter to a legislative committee **b** : MITTIMUS **2 a** : an agreement or pledge to do something in the future; *specif* : an engagement to assume a financial obligation at a future date **b** : something pledged **c** : the state of being obligated or emotionally impelled ⟨his ~ to unpopular causes⟩

com·mit·tal \kə-ˈmit-ᵊl\ *n* : COMMITMENT, CONSIGNMENT

com·mit·tee \kə-ˈmit-ē, *sense 1 also* ˌkäm-ə-ˈtē\ *n* **1** *archaic* : a person to whom a charge or trust is committed **2 a** : a body of persons delegated to consider, investigate, take action on, or report on some matter; *specif* : a group of fellow legislators chosen by a legislative body to give consideration to legislative matters **b** : a self-constituted organization for the promotion of a common object

com·mit·tee·man \kə-ˈmit-ē-mən, -ˌman\ *n* **1** : a member of a committee **2** : a party leader of a ward or precinct

committee of the whole : the whole membership of a legislative house sitting as a committee and operating under informal rules

com·mit·tee·woman \-ˌwu̇m-ən\ *n* : a female member of a committee

com·mix \kə-ˈmiks, kä-\ *vb* [back-formation fr. ME *comixt* blended, fr. L *commixtus,* pp. of *commiscēre* to mix together, fr. *com-* + *miscēre* to mix — more at MIX] *vt* : MINGLE, BLEND ~ *vi* : to become mingled or blended

com·mix·ture \-chər\ *n* [L *commixtura,* fr. *commixtus*] **1** : the act or process of mixing : the state of being mixed **2** : COMPOUND, MIXTURE

commo *abbr* commodore

com·mode \kə-ˈmōd\ *n* [F, fr. *commode,* adj., suitable, convenient, fr. L *commodus,* fr. *com-* + *modus* measure — more at METE] **1** : a woman's ornate cap popular in the late 17th and early 18th centuries **2 a** : a low chest of drawers **b** : a movable washstand with a cupboard underneath **c** : a boxlike structure holding a chamber pot under an open seat; *also* : CHAMBER POT **d** : TOILET 3b

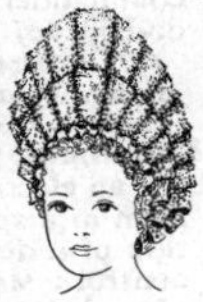

commode 1

com·mo·di·ous \kə-ˈmōd-ē-əs\ *adj* [ME, useful, fr. MF *commodieux,* fr. ML *commodiosus,* irreg. fr. L *commodum* convenience, fr. neut. of *commodus*] **1** *archaic* : HANDY, SERVICEABLE **2** : comfortably or conveniently spacious : ROOMY ⟨one ~ drawer held all his clothes⟩ ***syn*** see SPACIOUS — **com·mo·di·ous·ly** *adv* — **com·mo·di·ous·ness** *n*

com·mod·i·ty \kə-ˈmäd-ət-ē\ *n, pl* **-ties** [ME *commoditee,* fr. MF *commodité,* fr. L *commoditat-, commoditas,* fr. *commodus*] **1 a** : CONVENIENCE, ADVANTAGE **b** : something useful or valuable **2** : an economic good: as **a** : a product of agriculture or mining **b** : an article of commerce esp. when delivered for shipment **3** *obs* : QUANTITY, LOT

com·mo·dore \ˈkäm-ə-ˌdō(ə)r, -ˌdȯ(ə)r\ *n* [prob. modif. of D *commandeur* commander, fr. F, fr. OF *comandeor,* fr. *comander* to command] **1 a** : a former captain in the navy in command of a squadron **b** : a former commissioned officer in the navy ranking above captain and below rear admiral and having an insignia of one star **2** : the ranking officer commanding a body of merchant ships **3** : the chief officer of a yacht club or boating association

¹**com·mon** \ˈkäm-ən\ *adj* [ME *commun,* fr. OF, fr. L *communis* — more at MEAN] **1 a** : of or relating to a community at large : PUBLIC ⟨work for the ~ good⟩ **b** : known to the community ⟨~ nuisances⟩ **2 a** : belonging to or shared by two or more individuals or by all members of a group ⟨all destined to the ~ grave⟩ **b** : belonging equally to two or more quantities **c** : having two or more branches ⟨~ carotid artery⟩ **3 a** : occurring or appearing frequently : FAMILIAR ⟨a ~ sight⟩ **b** : of the best known kind ⟨~ salt⟩ **4 a** : WIDESPREAD, GENERAL ⟨being ~ knowledge⟩ **b** : characterized by a lack of privilege or special status ⟨~ people⟩ **c** : just satisfying accustomed criteria : ELEMENTARY ⟨~ decency⟩ **5 a** : falling below ordinary standards : SECOND-RATE **b** : lacking refinement ⟨~ manners⟩ **c** : completely unprincipled **6 a** : either masculine or feminine in gender **b** : denoting relations by a single case form that in a more highly inflected language might be denoted by two or more different case forms — **com·mon·ly** *adv* — **com·mon·ness** \-ən-nəs\ *n*

syn **1** see RECIPROCAL ***ant*** individual

2 COMMON, ORDINARY, PLAIN, FAMILIAR, POPULAR, VULGAR *shared meaning element* : being what is generally met with and not in any way special, strange, or unusual. COMMON implies usual everyday quality or frequency of occurrence ⟨a *common* error⟩ ⟨lacked *common* honesty⟩ and may additionally suggest inferiority or coarseness ⟨O hard is the bed . . . and *common* the blanket and cheap —A. E. Housman⟩ ORDINARY stresses conformance in quality or kind with the regular order of things ⟨an *ordinary* pleasant summer day⟩ ⟨a very *ordinary* sort of man⟩ PLAIN is likely to suggest homely simplicity ⟨the *plain* people everywhere . . . wish to live in peace — F. D. Roosevelt⟩ FAMILIAR stresses the fact of being generally known and easily recognized ⟨a *familiar* melody⟩ POPULAR applies to what is accepted by or prevalent among people in general sometimes in contrast to upper classes or special groups ⟨a *popular* tune⟩ VULGAR, otherwise similar to *popular,* is likely to carry derogatory connotations (as of inferiority or coarseness) ⟨goods designed to appeal to the *vulgar* taste⟩ ***ant*** uncommon, exceptional

[2]**common** *n* **1** *pl* **:** the common people **2** *pl but sing in constr* **:** a dining hall **3** *pl but sing or pl in constr, often cap* **a :** the political group or estate comprising the commoners **b :** the parliamentary representatives of the commoners **c :** HOUSE OF COMMONS **4 :** the legal right of taking a profit in another's land in common with the owner **5 :** a piece of land subject to common use: as **a :** undivided land used esp. for pasture **b :** a public open area in a municipality **6 a :** a religious service suitable for any of various festivals **b :** the ordinary of the Mass — **in common :** shared together

com·mon·age \ˈkäm-ə-nij\ *n* **1 :** community land **2 :** COMMONALTY 1a(2)

com·mon·al·i·ty \ˌkäm-ə-ˈnal-ət-ē\ *n, pl* **-ties** [ME *communalitie,* alter. of *communalte*] **1 a :** possession of common features or attributes **:** COMMONNESS **b :** a common feature or attribute ⟨can see *commonalities* as well as differences⟩ **2 :** the common people

com·mon·al·ty \ˈkäm-ən-ᵊl-tē\ *n, pl* **-ties** [ME *communalte,* fr. OF *comunalté,* fr. *comunal* communal] **1 a** (1) **:** the common people (2) **:** the political estate formed by the common people **b :** a usage or practice common to members of a group **2 :** a general group or body

common carrier *n* **:** an individual or corporation undertaking to transport for compensation persons, goods, or messages

common cattle grub *n* **:** a heel fly (*Hypoderma lineatum*) which is found throughout the U.S. and whose larva is particularly destructive to cattle

common chord *n* **:** TRIAD 2

common cold *n* **:** an acute virus disease of the upper respiratory tract marked by inflammation of mucous membranes

common denominator *n* **1 :** a common multiple of the denominators of a number of fractions **2 :** a common trait or theme

common divisor *n* **:** a number or expression that divides two or more numbers or expressions without remainder — called also *common factor*

com·mon·er \ˈkäm-ə-nər\ *n* **1 a :** one of the common people **b :** one who is not of noble rank **2 :** a student (as at Oxford) who pays for his own board

common fraction *n* **:** a fraction in which both the numerator and denominator are expressed as numbers and are separated by a horizontal or slanted line — compare DECIMAL

common informer *n* **:** INFORMER 2

common–law *adj* **1 :** of, relating to, or based on the common law **2 :** relating to or based on a common-law marriage ⟨his ~ wife⟩

common law *n* **:** the body of law developed in England primarily from judicial decisions based on custom and precedent, unwritten in statute or code, and constituting the basis of the English legal system and of the system in all of the U.S. except Louisiana

common–law marriage *n* **1 :** a marriage recognized in some jurisdictions and based on the parties' agreement to consider themselves married and sometimes also on their cohabitation **2 :** the cohabitation of a couple even when it does not constitute a legal marriage

common logarithm *n* **:** a logarithm whose base is 10

common market *n* **:** an economic unit formed to remove trade barriers among its members

common measure *n* **:** a meter consisting chiefly of iambic lines of 7 accents each arranged in alternately rhymed pairs usu. printed in 4-line stanzas — called also *common meter*

common multiple *n* **:** a multiple of each of two or more numbers or expressions

common noun *n* **:** a noun that may occur with limiting modifiers (as *a* or *an, some, every,* and *my*) and that designates any one of a class of beings or things

[1]**com·mon·place** \ˈkäm-ən-ˌplās\ *n* [trans. of L *locus communis* widely applicable argument, trans. of Gk *koinos topos*] **1** *archaic* **:** a striking passage entered in a commonplace book **2 a :** an obvious or trite observation **b :** something taken for granted

[2]**commonplace** *adj* **:** routinely found **:** ORDINARY, UNREMARKABLE — **com·mon·place·ness** *n*

commonplace book *n* **:** a book of memorabilia

common pleas *n* **1** *pl* **a :** actions over which the English crown did not claim exclusive jurisdiction **b :** civil actions between English subjects **2** *pl but sing in constr* **:** COURT OF COMMON PLEAS

common room *n* **1 :** a lounge available to all members of a residential community **2 :** a room in a college for the use of the faculty

common salt *n* **:** SALT 1a

common school *n* **:** a free public school

common sense *n* **1 :** sound and prudent but often unsophisticated judgment **2 :** the unreflective opinions of ordinary men ***syn*** see SENSE — **com·mon·sense** \ˌkäm-ən-ˌsen(t)s\ *adj* — **com·mon·sen·si·ble** \-ˈsen(t)-sə-bəl\ *adj* — **com·mon·sen·si·bly** \-blē\ *adv* — **com·mon·sen·si·cal** \- ˈsen(t)-si-kəl\ *adj*

common stock *n* **:** capital stock other than preferred stock

common time *n* **:** the musical tempo marked by four beats per measure

common touch *n* **:** the gift of appealing to or arousing sympathetic interest

com·mon·weal \ˈkäm-ən-ˌwēl\ *n* **1 :** the general welfare **2** *archaic* **:** COMMONWEALTH

com·mon·wealth \-ˌwelth\ *n* **1** *archaic* **:** COMMONWEAL 1 **2 :** a nation, state, or other political unit: as **a :** one founded on law and united by compact or tacit agreement of the people for the common good **b :** one in which supreme authority is vested in the people **c :** REPUBLIC **3** *cap* **a :** the English state from the death of Charles I in 1649 to the Restoration in 1660 **b :** PROTECTORATE 1b **4 :** a state of the U.S. — used officially of Kentucky, Massachusetts, Pennsylvania, and Virginia **5** *cap* **:** a federal union of constituent states — used officially of Australia **6** *often cap* **:** an association of self-governing autonomous states more or less loosely associated in a common allegiance (as to the British crown) **7** *often cap* **:** a political unit having local autonomy but voluntarily united with the U.S. — used officially of Puerto Rico

Commonwealth Day *n* **:** May 24 observed in parts of the British Commonwealth as the anniversary of Queen Victoria's birthday

common year *n* **:** a calendar year containing no intercalary period

com·mo·tion \kə-ˈmō-shən\ *n* [ME, fr. MF, fr. L *commotion-, commotio,* fr. *commotus,* pp. of *commovēre*] **1 :** a condition of civil unrest or insurrection **2 :** steady or recurrent motion **3 :** mental excitement or confusion **4 a :** a flurried disturbance **:** TO-DO ⟨a crowd raising a ~ in the street⟩ **b :** noisy confusion **:** AGITATION

com·move \kə-ˈmüv, kä-\ *vt* **com·moved; com·mov·ing** [ME *commoeven,* fr. MF *commuev-,* pres. stem of *commovoir,* fr. L *commovēre,* fr. *com-* + *movēre* to move] **1 :** to move violently **:** AGITATE **2 :** to rouse intense feeling in **:** excite to passion

com·mu·nal \kə-ˈmyün-ᵊl, ˈkäm-yən-ᵊl\ *adj* [F, fr. LL *communalis,* fr. L *communis*] **1 :** of or relating to one or more communes **2 :** of or relating to a community **3 a :** characterized by collective ownership and use of property **b :** participated in, shared, or used in common by members of a group or community **4 :** of, relating to, or based on racial or cultural groups

com·mu·nal·ism \-ᵊl-ˌiz-əm\ *n* **1 :** social organization on a communal basis **2 :** loyalty to a sociopolitical grouping based on religious affiliation — **com·mu·nal·ist** \-ᵊl-əst\ *n or adj*

com·mu·nal·i·ty \ˌkäm-yu̇-ˈnal-ət-ē\ *n, pl* **-ties 1 :** communal state or character **2 :** a feeling of group solidarity

com·mu·nal·ize \kə-ˈmyün-ᵊl-ˌīz, ˈkäm-yən-\ *vt* **-ized; -iz·ing :** to make communal

com·mu·nard \ˌkäm-yu̇-ˈnär(d)\ *n* [F] **1** *cap* **:** one who supported or participated in the Commune of Paris in 1871 **2 :** one that lives in a commune

[1]**com·mune** \kə-ˈmyün\ *vb* **com·muned; com·mun·ing** [ME *communen* to converse, administer Communion, fr. MF *comunier* to converse, administer or receive Communion, fr. LL *communicare,* fr. L] *vt, obs* **:** to talk over **:** DISCUSS ⟨have more to ~ — Shak.⟩ ~ *vi* **1 :** to receive Communion **2 :** to communicate intimately ⟨~ with nature⟩

[2]**com·mune** \ˈkäm-ˌyün; kə-ˈmyün, kä-\ *n* [F, alter. of MF *comugne,* fr. ML *communia,* fr. L, neut. pl. of *communis*] **1 :** the smallest administrative district of many countries esp. in Europe **2 :** COMMONALTY 1a **3 :** COMMUNITY: as **a :** a medieval usu. municipal corporation **b** (1) **:** MIR (2) **:** an often rural community organized on a communal basis

com·mu·ni·ca·ble \kə-ˈmyü-ni-kə-bəl\ *adj* **1 :** capable of being communicated **:** TRANSMITTABLE ⟨~ disease⟩ **2 :** COMMUNICATIVE — **com·mu·ni·ca·bil·i·ty** \-ˌmyü-ni-kə-ˈbil-ət-ē\ *n* — **com·mu·ni·ca·ble·ness** \-ˈmyü-ni-kə-bəl-nəs\ *n* — **com·mu·ni·ca·bly** \-blē\ *adv*

com·mu·ni·cant \-ˈmyü-ni-kənt\ *n* **1 :** a church member entitled to receive Communion; *broadly* **:** a member of a fellowship **2 :** one that communicates; *specif* **:** INFORMANT — **communicant** *adj*

com·mu·ni·cate \kə-ˈmyü-nə-ˌkāt\ *vb* **-cat·ed; -cat·ing** [L *communicatus,* pp. of *communicare* to impart, participate, fr. *communis* common — more at MEAN] *vt* **1** *archaic* **:** SHARE **2 a :** to convey knowledge of or information about **:** make known ⟨~ a story⟩ **b :** to reveal by clear signs ⟨his fear *communicated* itself to his friends⟩ **3 :** to cause to pass from one to another ⟨some diseases are easily *communicated*⟩ ~ *vi* **1 :** to receive Communion **2 :** to transmit information, thought, or feeling so that it is satisfactorily received or understood **3 :** to open into each other **:** CONNECT ⟨the rooms ~⟩

syn COMMUNICATE, IMPART *shared meaning element* **:** to convey or transmit something intangible (as information, feelings, or a flavor)

com·mu·ni·ca·tee \-ˌmyü-ni-kə-ˈtē\ *n* **:** one that receives a communication

com·mu·ni·ca·tion \kə-ˌmyü-nə-ˈkā-shən\ *n* **1 :** an act or instance of transmitting **2 a :** information communicated **b :** a verbal or written message **3 a :** a process by which information is exchanged between individuals through a common system of symbols, signs, or behavior ⟨the function of pheromones in insect ~⟩; *also* **:** exchange of information **b :** personal rapport ⟨a lack of ~ between old and young persons⟩ **4** *pl* **a :** a system (as of telephones) for communicating **b :** a system of routes for moving troops, supplies, and vehicles **c :** personnel engaged in communicating **5** *pl but sing or pl in constr* **a :** a technique for expressing ideas effectively (as in speech) **b :** the technology of the transmission of information (as by the printed word, telecommunication, or the computer) — **com·mu·ni·ca·tion·al** \-shnəl, -shən-ᵊl\ *adj*

com·mu·ni·ca·tive \kə-ˈmyü-nə-ˌkāt-iv, -ni-kət-iv\ *adj* **1 :** tending to communicate **:** TALKATIVE **2 :** of or relating to communication — **com·mu·ni·ca·tive·ly** *adv* — **com·mu·ni·ca·tive·ness** *n*

com·mu·ni·ca·tor \-ˌkāt-ər\ *n* **:** one that communicates

ə abut	ᵊ kitten	ər further	a back	ā bake	ä cot, cart
au̇ out	ch chin	e less	ē easy	g gift	i trip	ī life
j joke	ŋ sing	ō flow	ȯ flaw	ȯi coin	th thin	t͟h this
ü loot	u̇ foot	y yet	yü few	yu̇ furious	zh vision

com·mu·ni·ca·to·ry \kə-ˈmyü-ni-kə-ˌtōr-ē, -ˌtȯr-\ *adj* : designed to communicate information ⟨~ letters⟩

com·mu·nion \kə-ˈmyü-nyən\ *n* [ME, fr. L *communion-, communio* mutual participation, fr. *communis*] **1** : an act or instance of sharing **2 a** *cap* : a Christian sacrament in which bread and wine are partaken of as a commemoration of the death of Christ **b** : the act of receiving the sacrament **c** *cap* : the part of the Mass in which the sacrament is received **d** *cap* : a variable verse of scripture traditionally said or sung at mass during the people's communion — called also *Communion Verse* **3** : intimate fellowship or rapport : COMMUNICATION **4** : a body of Christians having a common faith and discipline

Communion Sunday *n* : a Sunday (as the first Sunday of the month) on which a Protestant church regularly holds a Communion service

com·mu·ni·qué \kə-ˈmyü-nə-ˌkā, -ˌmyü-nə-ˈ\ *n* [F, fr. pp. of *communiquer* to communicate, fr. L *communicare*] : BULLETIN 1

com·mu·nism \ˈkäm-yə-ˌniz-əm\ *n* [F *communisme,* fr. *commun* common] **1 a** : a theory advocating elimination of private property **b** : a system in which goods are owned in common and are available to all as needed **2** *cap* **a** : a doctrine based on revolutionary Marxian socialism and Marxism-Leninism that is the official ideology of the U.S.S.R. **b** : a totalitarian system of government in which a single authoritarian party controls state-owned means of production with the professed aim of establishing a stateless society **c** : a final stage of society in Marxist theory in which the state has withered away and economic goods are distributed equitably

com·mu·nist \ˈkäm-yə-nəst\ *n* **1** : an adherent or advocate of communism **2** *cap* : COMMUNARD **3 a** *cap* : a member of a Communist party or movement **b** *often cap* : an adherent or advocate of a Communist government, party, or movement **4** *often cap* : one held to engage in left-wing, subversive, or revolutionary activities — **communist** *adj, often cap* — **com·mu·nis·tic** \ˌkäm-yə-ˈnis-tik\ *adj, often cap* — **com·mu·nis·ti·cal·ly** \-ti-k(ə-)lē\ *adv*

com·mu·ni·tar·i·an \kə-ˌmyü-nə-ˈter-ē-ən\ *adj* : of or relating to social organization in small cooperative partially collectivist communities — **communitarian** *n* — **com·mu·ni·tar·i·an·ism** \-ē-ə-ˌniz-əm\ *n*

com·mu·ni·ty \kə-ˈmyü-nət-ē\ *n, pl* **-ties** [ME *comunete,* fr. MF *comuneté,* fr. L *communitat-, communitas,* fr. *communis*] **1** : a unified body of individuals: as **a** : STATE, COMMONWEALTH **b** : the people with common interests living in a particular area; *broadly* : the area itself ⟨the problems of a large ~⟩ **c** : an interacting population of various kinds of individuals (as species) in a common location **d** : a group of people with a common characteristic or interest living together within a larger society ⟨a ~ of retired persons⟩ **e** : a group linked by a common policy **f** : a body of persons or nations having a common history or common social, economic, and political interests ⟨the international ~⟩ **g** : a body of persons of common and esp. professional interests scattered through a larger society ⟨the academic ~⟩ **2** : society at large **3 a** : joint ownership or participation ⟨asserts that ~ of goods would be the ideal institution —G. L. Dickinson⟩ **b** : common character : LIKENESS ⟨bound by ~ of interests⟩ **c** : social activity : FELLOWSHIP **d** : a social state or condition

community antenna television *n* : a system of television reception in which signals from distant stations are picked up by a tall or elevated antenna and sent by cable to the individual receivers of paying subscribers

community center *n* : a building or group of buildings for a community's educational and recreational activities

community chest *n* : a general fund accumulated from individual subscriptions to defray demands on a community for charity and social welfare

community college *n* : a nonresidential junior college that is usu. government-supported

community property *n* : property held jointly by husband and wife

com·mu·ni·ty·wide \kə-ˌmyü-nət-ē-ˈwīd\ *adj* : operative or effective throughout a community

com·mu·nize \ˈkäm-yə-ˌnīz\ *vt* **-nized; -niz·ing** [back-formation fr. *communization*] **1 a** : to make common **b** : to make into state-owned property **2** : to subject to Communist principles of organization — **com·mu·ni·za·tion** \ˌkäm-yə-nə-ˈzā-shən\ *n*

com·mu·tate \ˈkäm-yə-ˌtāt\ *vt* **-tat·ed; -tat·ing** [back-formation fr. *commutation*] : to reverse every other half cycle of (an alternating current) so as to form a unidirectional current

com·mu·ta·tion \ˌkäm-yə-ˈtā-shən\ *n* [ME, fr. MF, fr. L *commutation-, commutatio,* fr. *commutatus,* pp. of *commutare*] **1** : EXCHANGE, TRADE **2** : REPLACEMENT; *specif* : a substitution of one form of payment or charge for another **3** : a change of a legal penalty or punishment to a lesser one **4** : an act or process of commuting **5** : the action of commutating

commutation ticket *n* : a transportation ticket sold for a fixed number of trips over the same route during a limited period

com·mu·ta·tive \ˈkäm-yə-ˌtāt-iv, kə-ˈmyüt-ət-\ *adj* **1** : of, relating to, or showing commutation **2** : combining elements or having elements that combine in such a manner that the result is independent of the order in which the elements are taken ⟨a ~ group⟩ ⟨addition of the positive integers is ~⟩

com·mu·ta·tiv·i·ty \kə-ˌmyüt-ə-ˈtiv-ət-ē, ˌkäm-yə-tə-\ *n* : the property of being commutative ⟨the ~ of a mathematical operation⟩

com·mu·ta·tor \ˈkäm-yə-ˌtāt-ər\ *n* **1** : a switch for reversing the direction of an electric current **2** : a series of bars or segments so connected to armature coils of a dynamo that rotation of the armature will in conjunction with fixed brushes result in unidirectional current output in the case of a generator and in the reversal of the current into the coils in the case of a motor **3** : an element of a mathematical group that when multiplied by the product of two given elements yields the product of the elements in reverse order

1com·mute \kə-ˈmyüt\ *vb* **com·mut·ed; com·mut·ing** [L *commutare* to change, exchange, fr. *com-* + *mutare* to change] *vt* **1 a** : to give in exchange for another : EXCHANGE **b** : CHANGE, ALTER **2** : to convert (as a payment) into another form **3** : to exchange (a penalty) for another less severe **4** : COMMUTATE ~ *vi* **1** : to make up : COMPENSATE **2** : to pay in gross **3** : to travel back and forth regularly (as between a suburb and a city) — **com·mut·able** \-ˈmyüt-ə-bəl\ *adj* — **com·mut·er** *n*

2commute *n* : a trip made in commuting

co·mo·no·mer \(ˈ)kō-ˈmän-ə-mər, -ˈmō-nə-\ *n* [*co-* + *monomer*] : one of the constituents of a copolymer

co·mose \ˈkō-ˌmōs\ *adj* [L *comosus* hairy, fr. *coma* hair — more at COMA] : bearing a tuft of soft hairs

1comp \ˈkəmp, ˈkämp\ *vi* [short for *accompany*] : to play an irregularly rhythmic jazz accompaniment

2comp *abbr* **1** comparative; compare **2** compensation **3** compiled; compiler **4** composition **5** compound **6** comprehensive **7** comptroller

1com·pact \kəm-ˈpakt, käm-ˈ, ˈkäm-ˌ\ *adj* [ME, firmly put together, fr. L *compactus,* fr. pp. of *compingere* to put together, fr. *com-* + *pangere* to fasten — more at PACT] **1** : COMPOSED, MADE **2 a** : having parts or units closely packed or joined ⟨a ~ woolen⟩ **b** : not diffuse or verbose ⟨a ~ statement⟩ **c** : occupying a small volume by reason of efficient use of space ⟨a ~ camera⟩ ⟨a ~ formation of troops⟩ ***syn*** see CLOSE — **com·pact·ly** *adv* — **com·pact·ness** *n*

2compact *vt* **1 a** : to knit or draw together : COMBINE, CONSOLIDATE **b** : to press together : COMPRESS **2** : to make up by connecting or combining : COMPOSE ~ *vi* : to become compacted — **com·pact·ible** \-ˈpak-tə-bəl, -ˌpak-\ *adj* — **com·pac·tor** *or* **com·pact·er** \-ˈpak-tər, -ˌpak-\ *n*

3com·pact \ˈkäm-ˌpakt\ *n* : something that is compact or compacted: **a** : a small cosmetic case (as for compressed powder) **b** : an automobile smaller than an intermediate but larger than a subcompact

4com·pact \ˈkäm-ˌpakt\ *n* [L *compactum,* fr. neut. of *compactus,* pp. of *compacisci* to make an agreement, fr. *com-* + *pacisci* to contract] : an agreement or covenant between two or more parties

com·pac·tion \kəm-ˈpak-shən, käm-\ *n* : the act or process of compacting : the state of being compacted

1com·pan·ion \kəm-ˈpan-yən\ *n* [ME *compainoun,* fr. OF *compagnon,* fr. LL *companion-, companio,* fr. L *com-* + *panis* bread, food] **1** : COMRADE, ASSOCIATE **2** *obs* : RASCAL **3 a** : one of a pair or set of matching things **b** : one employed to live with and serve another

2companion *vt* : ACCOMPANY ~ *vi* : to keep company : ASSOCIATE

3companion *n* [by folk etymology fr. D *kampanje* poop deck] **1** : a hood covering at the top of a companionway **2** : COMPANIONWAY

com·pan·ion·able \kəm-ˈpan-yə-nə-bəl\ *adj* : marked by, conducive to, or suggestive of companionship : SOCIABLE ⟨tells her story calmly in a quiet ~ voice —Edward Callan⟩ — **com·pan·ion·able·ness** *n* — **com·pan·ion·ably** \-blē\ *adv*

com·pan·ion·ate \kəm-ˈpan-yə-nət\ *adj* : relating to or in the manner of companions; *specif* : harmoniously or suitably accompanying

companionate marriage *n* : a proposed form of marriage in which legalized birth control would be practiced, the divorce of childless couples by mutual consent permitted, and neither party would have any financial or economic claim on the other

companion cell *n* : a living nucleated cell that is closely associated in origin, position, and probably function with a cell making up part of a sieve tube of a vascular plant

companion piece *n* : an object (as a literary work) that is associated with and complements another

com·pan·ion·ship \kəm-ˈpan-yən-ˌship\ *n* : the fellowship existing among companions

com·pan·ion·way \-yən-ˌwā\ *n* [3*companion*] : a ship's stairway from one deck to another

1com·pa·ny \ˈkəmp-(ə-)nē\ *n, pl* **-nies** *often attrib* [ME *companie,* fr. OF *compagnie,* fr. *compain* companion, fr. LL *companio*] **1 a** : association with another : FELLOWSHIP ⟨enjoy a person's ~⟩ **b** : COMPANIONS, ASSOCIATES ⟨know a person by the ~ he keeps⟩ **c** : VISITORS, GUESTS ⟨having ~ for dinner⟩ **2 a** : a group of persons or things ⟨a ~ of horsemen⟩ **b** : a body of soldiers; *specif* : a unit (as of infantry) consisting usu. of a headquarters and two or more platoons **c** : an organization of musical or dramatic performers ⟨an opera ~⟩ **d** : the officers and men of a ship **e** : a fire-fighting unit **3 a** : a chartered commercial organization or medieval trade guild **b** : an association of persons for carrying on a commercial or industrial enterprise **c** : those members of a partnership firm whose names do not appear in the firm name ⟨John Doe and *Company*⟩

2company *vt* **-nied; -ny·ing** : ACCOMPANY ⟨may . . . fair winds ~ your safe return —John Masefield⟩ ~ *vi* : ASSOCIATE

company officer *n* : a commissioned officer in the army, air force, or marine corps of the rank of captain, first lieutenant, or second lieutenant — called also *company grade officer;* compare FIELD OFFICER, GENERAL OFFICER

company town *n* : a community that is dependent on one firm for all or most of the necessary services or functions of town life (as employment, housing, and stores)

company union *n* : an unaffiliated labor union of the employees of a single firm; *esp* : one dominated by the employer

com·pa·ra·bil·i·ty \ˌkäm-p(ə-)rə-ˈbil-ət-ē\ *n* : the quality or state of being comparable

com·pa·ra·ble \ˈkäm-p(ə-)rə-bəl\ *adj* **1** : capable of or suitable for comparison **2** : EQUIVALENT, SIMILAR ⟨fabrics of ~ quality⟩ — **com·pa·ra·ble·ness** *n* — **com·pa·ra·bly** \-blē\ *adv*

com·par·a·tist \kəm-ˈpar-ət-əst\ *n* [*comparative* + *-ist*] : one that uses a comparative method (as in the study of literature)

1com·par·a·tive \kəm-ˈpar-ət-iv\ *adj* **1** : of, relating to, or constituting the degree of comparison in a language that denotes increase in the quality, quantity, or relation expressed by an adjective or adverb **2** : considered as if in comparison to something else as a standard not quite attained : RELATIVE ⟨~ stranger⟩ **3** : characterized by the systematic comparison of phenomena and esp. of likenesses and dissimilarities ⟨~ anatomy⟩ — **com·par·a·tive·ly** *adv* — **com·par·a·tive·ness** *n*

[2]**comparative** *n* **1 a :** one that compares with another esp. on equal footing : RIVAL **b :** one that makes witty or mocking comparisons **2 :** the comparative degree or form in a language

com·par·a·tiv·ist \kəm-ˈpar-ət-i-vəst\ *n* : COMPARATIST

com·par·a·tor \kəm-ˈpar-ət-ər\ *n* : a device for comparing something with a similar thing or with a standard measure

[1]**com·pare** \kəm-ˈpa(ə)r, -ˈpe(ə)r\ *vb* **com·pared; com·par·ing** [ME *comparen,* fr. MF *comparer,* fr. L *comparare* to couple, compare, fr. *compar* like, fr. *com-* + *par* equal] *vt* **1 :** to represent as similar : LIKEN **2 :** to examine the character or qualities of esp. in order to discover resemblances or differences **3 :** to inflect or modify (an adjective or adverb) according to the degrees of comparison ~ *vi* **1 :** to bear being compared **2 :** to make comparisons **3 :** to be equal or alike

syn COMPARE, CONTRAST, COLLATE *shared meaning element* : to set side by side in order to show likenesses and differences

[2]**compare** *n* : COMPARISON ⟨beauty beyond ~⟩

com·par·i·son \kəm-ˈpar-ə-sən\ *n* [ME, fr. MF *comparaison,* fr. L *comparation-, comparatio,* fr. *comparatus,* pp. of *comparare*] **1 :** the act or process of comparing: **a :** the representing of one thing or person as similar to or like another ⟨a ~ of man to monkey⟩ **b :** an examination of two or more items to establish similarities and dissimilarities **2 :** identity of features : SIMILARITY ⟨several points of ~ between two authors⟩ **3 :** the modification of an adjective or adverb to denote different levels of quality, quantity, or relation

com·part \kəm-ˈpärt\ *vt* [It *compartire,* fr. LL *compartiri* to share out, fr. L *com-* + *partiri* to share, fr. *part-, pars* part, share] : to mark out into parts; *specif* : to lay out in parts according to a plan

[1]**com·part·ment** \kəm-ˈpärt-mənt\ *n* [MF *compartiment,* fr. It *compartimento,* fr. *compartire*] **1 :** one of the parts into which an enclosed space is divided **2 :** a separate division or section — **com·part·men·tal** \kəm-ˌpärt-ˈment-ᵊl, ˌkäm-\ *adj*

[2]**com·part·ment** \-ˌment, -mənt\ *vt* : COMPARTMENTALIZE

com·part·men·tal·ize \kəm-ˌpärt-ˈment-ᵊl-ˌīz, ˌkäm-\ *vt* **-ized; -iz·ing :** to separate into isolated compartments or categories ⟨*compartmentalized* knowledge —H. M. McLuhan⟩ — **com·part·men·tal·iza·tion** \-ˌment-ᵊl-ə-ˈzā-shən\ *n*

com·part·men·ta·tion \kəm-ˌpärt-mən-ˈtā-shən, -ˌmen-\ *n* : division into separate sections or units

[1]**com·pass** \ˈkəm-pəs *also* ˈkäm-\ *vt* [ME *compassen,* fr. OF *compasser* to measure, fr. (assumed) VL *compassare* to pace off, fr. L *com-* + *passus* pace] **1 :** to devise or contrive often with craft or skill **2 a :** ENCOMPASS **b :** to travel entirely around ⟨~ the earth⟩ **3 a :** to bring about : ACHIEVE **b :** to get into one's possession or power : OBTAIN **4 :** COMPREHEND ***syn*** see REACH — **com·pass·able** \-pə-sə-bəl\ *adj*

[2]**compass** *n* **1 a :** BOUNDARY, CIRCUMFERENCE ⟨within the ~ of the city walls⟩ **b :** a circumscribed space ⟨within the narrow ~ of 21 pages —V. L. Parrington⟩ **c :** RANGE, SCOPE ⟨the ~ of a voice⟩ **2 :** a curved or roundabout course ⟨a ~ of seven days' journey —2 Kings 3:9 (AV)⟩ **3 a :** a device for determining directions by means of a magnetic needle or group of needles turning freely on a pivot and pointing to the magnetic north **b :** any of various nonmagnetic devices that serve the same purpose as the magnetic compass **c :** an instrument for describing circles or transferring measurements that consists of two pointed branches joined at the top by a pivot — usu. used in pl.; called also *pair of compasses*

[3]**compass** *adj* **1 :** forming a curve ⟨a ~ timber⟩ **2 :** semicircular in plan — used of a bow window

compass card *n* : the circular card attached to the needles of a mariner's compass on which are marked 32 points of the compass and the 360° of the circle

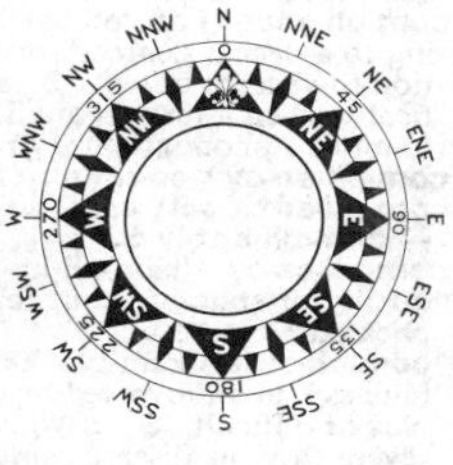

compass card

com·pas·sion \kəm-ˈpash-ən\ *n* [ME, fr. MF or LL; MF, fr. LL *compassion-, compassio,* fr *compassus,* pp. of *compati* to sympathize, fr. L *com-* + *pati* to bear, suffer — more at PATIENT] : sympathetic consciousness of others' distress together with a desire to alleviate it ***syn*** see SYMPATHY — **compas·sion·less** \-ləs\ *adj*

[1]**com·pas·sion·ate** \kəm-ˈpash-(ə-)nət\ *adj* **1 :** having or showing compassion : SYMPATHETIC **2 :** granted because of unusual distressing circumstances affecting an individual — used of leaves and other military privileges — **com·pas·sion·ate·ly** *adv* — **com·pas·sion·ate·ness** *n*

[2]**com·pas·sion·ate** \-ˈpash-ə-ˌnāt\ *vt* **-at·ed; -at·ing :** PITY

compass plant *n* : a coarse yellow-flowered composite plant (*Silphium laciniatum*) with large pinnatifid leaves—called also *rosinweed*

com·pat·i·ble \kəm-ˈpat-ə-bəl\ *adj* [MF, fr. ML *compatibilis,* lit., sympathetic, fr. LL *compati*] **1 :** capable of existing together in harmony **2 :** capable of cross-fertilizing freely or uniting vegetatively **3 :** being or relating to a system in which color television broadcasts may be received in black and white on receivers without special modification **4 :** capable of forming a homogeneous mixture that neither separates nor is altered by chemical interaction ***syn*** see CONSONANT ***ant*** incompatible — **com·pat·i·bil·i·ty** \-ˌpat-ə-ˈbil-ət-ē\ *n* — **com·pat·i·ble·ness** \-ˈpat-ə-bəl-nəs\ *n* — **com·pat·i·bly** \-blē\ *adv*

com·pa·tri·ot \kəm-ˈpā-trē-ət, käm-, -trē-ˌät, *chiefly Brit* -ˈpa-\ *n* [F *compatriote,* fr. LL *compatriota,* fr. L *com-* + LL *patriota* fellow countryman — more at PATRIOT] **1 :** a fellow countryman **2 :** COMPEER, COLLEAGUE — **com·pa·tri·ot·ic** \kəm-ˌpā-trē-ˈät-ik, ˌkäm-, *chiefly Brit* -ˌpa-\ *adj*

compd *abbr* compound

[1]**com·peer** \ˈkäm-ˌpi(ə)r, käm-ˈ, kəm-ˈ\ *n* **1** [ME, fr. OF *compere,* lit., godfather, fr. ML *compater,* fr. L *com-* + *pater* father — more at FATHER] : COMPANION **2** [modif. of L *compar,* fr. *compar,* adj., like — more at COMPARE] : EQUAL, PEER

[2]**compeer** *vt, obs* : EQUAL, MATCH

com·pel \kəm-ˈpel\ *vt* **com·pelled; com·pel·ling** [ME *compellen,* fr. MF *compellir,* fr. L *compellere,* fr. *com-* + *pellere* to drive — more at FELT] **1 :** to drive or urge forcefully or irresistibly ⟨poverty *compelled* him to work⟩ **2 :** to cause to do or occur by overwhelming pressure ⟨exhaustion of ammunition *compelled* their surrender⟩ **3** *archaic* : to drive together ***syn*** see FORCE — **com·pel·la·ble** \-ˈpel-ə-bəl\ *adj* — **com·pel·ler** *n*

com·pel·la·tion \ˌkäm-pə-ˈlā-shən, -ˌpel-ˈā-\ *n* [L *compellation-, compellatio,* fr. *compellatus,* pp. of *compellare* to address, fr. *com-* + *-pellare* (as in *appellare* to accost, appeal to)] **1 :** an act or action of addressing someone **2 :** APPELLATION 2

com·pend \ˈkäm-ˌpend\ *n* [ML *compendium*] : COMPENDIUM

com·pen·di·ous \kəm-ˈpen-dē-əs\ *adj* : marked by brief expression of a comprehensive matter ***syn*** see CONCISE — **com·pen·di·ous·ly** *adv* — **com·pen·di·ous·ness** *n*

com·pen·di·um \kəm-ˈpen-dē-əm\ *n, pl* **-di·ums** *or* **-dia** \-dē-ə\ [ML, fr. L, saving, shortcut, fr. *compendere* to weigh together, fr. *com-* + *pendere* to weigh — more at PENDANT] : a brief summary of a larger work or of a field of knowledge : ABSTRACT

com·pen·sa·ble \kəm-ˈpen(t)-sə-bəl\ *adj* : that is to be or can be compensated — **com·pen·sa·bil·i·ty** \kəm-ˌpen(t)-sə-ˈbil-ət-ē, ˌkäm-\ *n*

com·pen·sate \ˈkäm-pən-ˌsāt, -ˌpen-\ *vb* **-sat·ed; -sat·ing** [L *compensatus,* pp. of *compensare,* fr. *compensus,* pp. of *compendere*] *vt* **1 :** to be equivalent to : COUNTERBALANCE **2 :** to make an appropriate and usu. counterbalancing payment to ⟨~ a neighbor for damage to his property⟩ **3 a :** to provide with means of counteracting variation **b :** to neutralize the effect of (variations) ~ *vi* **1 :** to supply an equivalent — used with *for* **2 :** to offset an error, defect, or undesired effect — **com·pen·sa·tive** \ˈkäm-pən-ˌsāt-iv, -ˌpen-; kəm-ˈpen(t)-sət-\ *adj* — **com·pen·sa·tor** \ˈkäm-pən-ˌsāt-ər, -ˌpen-\ *n* — **com·pen·sa·to·ry** \kəm-ˈpen(t)-sə-ˌtōr-ē, -ˌtȯr-\ *adj*

syn **1** COMPENSATE, COUNTERVAIL, BALANCE, OFFSET *shared meaning element* : to make up for what is excessive or deficient or helpful or harmful
2 see PAY

com·pen·sa·tion \ˌkäm-pən-ˈsā-shən, -ˌpen-\ *n* **1 a (1) :** correction of an organic inferiority or loss by hypertrophy or by increased functioning of another organ or unimpaired parts of the same organ **(2) :** a psychological mechanism by which feelings of inferiority, frustration, or failure in one field are counterbalanced by achievement in another **b :** adjustment of the phase retardation of one light ray with respect to that of another **2 a :** something that constitutes an equivalent or recompense ⟨age has its ~*s*⟩; *specif* : payment to an unemployed or injured worker or his dependents **b :** PAYMENT, REMUNERATION — **com·pen·sa·tion·al** \-shnəl, -shən-ᵊl\ *adj*

[1]**com·pere** \ˈkäm-ˌpe(ə)r\ *n* [F *compère,* lit. godfather — more at COMPEER] *Brit* : the master of ceremonies of an entertainment (as a television program)

[2]**compere** *vb* **com·pered; com·per·ing** *vt, Brit* : to act as compere for ~ *vi, Brit* : to act as a compere

com·pete \kəm-ˈpēt\ *vi* **com·pet·ed; com·pet·ing** [LL *competere* to seek together, fr. L, to come together, agree, be suitable, fr. *com-* + *petere* to go to, seek — more at FEATHER] : to strive consciously or unconsciously for an objective (as position, profit, or a prize) : be in a state of rivalry ***syn*** see RIVAL

com·pe·tence \ˈkäm-pət-ən(t)s\ *n* **1 :** a sufficiency of means for the necessities and conveniences of life ⟨provided his family with a comfortable ~ —Rex Ingamells⟩ **2 :** the quality or state of being competent: as **a :** the properties of an embryonic field that enable it to respond in a characteristic manner to an inductor **b :** readiness of bacteria to undergo genetic transformation

com·pe·ten·cy \-pət-ən-sē\ *n, pl* **-cies :** COMPETENCE

com·pe·tent \ˈkäm-pət-ənt\ *adj* [ME, suitable, fr. MF & L; MF, fr. L *competent-, competens,* fr. prp. of *competere* to be suitable] **1 :** having requisite or adequate ability or qualities : FIT ⟨a ~ workman⟩ ⟨a ~ and well constructed novel —Elaine Bender⟩ **2 :** proper or rightly pertinent **3 :** legally qualified or adequate ⟨a ~ witness⟩ **4 :** having the capacity to function or develop in a particular way; *specif* : having the capacity to respond (as by producing an antibody) to an antigenic determinant ⟨immunologically ~ cells⟩ ***syn*** **1** see ABLE **2** see SUFFICIENT ***ant*** incompetent — **com·pe·tent·ly** *adv*

com·pe·ti·tion \ˌkäm-pə-ˈtish-ən\ *n* [LL *competition-, competitio,* fr. L *competitus,* pp. of *competere*] **1 :** the act or process of competing : RIVALRY **2 :** a contest between rivals ⟨a high-diving ~⟩; *also* : the person competing ⟨keep ahead of the ~⟩ **3 :** the effort of two or more parties acting independently to secure the business of a third party by offering the most favorable terms **4 :** active demand by two or more organisms or kinds of organisms for some environmental resource in short supply — **com·pet·i·to·ry** \kəm-ˈpet-ə-ˌtōr-ē, -ˌtȯr-\ *adj*

com·pet·i·tive \kəm-ˈpet-ət-iv\ *adj* **1 :** relating to, characterized by, or based on competition ⟨~ sports⟩ ⟨~ examinations⟩ **2 :** inclined, desiring, or suited to compete ⟨a ~ breed of men —Ken Purdy⟩ ⟨salary benefits must be ~ —M. S. Eisenhower⟩ **3 :** depending for effectiveness on the relative concentration of two or more substances ⟨~ inhibition of an enzyme⟩ — **com·pet·i·tive·ly** *adv* — **com·pet·i·tive·ness** *n*

com·pet·i·tor \kəm-ˈpet-ət-ər\ *n* **:** one that competes: as **a :** RIVAL **b :** one selling or buying goods or services in the same market as another **c :** an organism that lives in competition with another

com·pi·la·tion \ˌkäm-pə-ˈlā-shən *also* -ˌpī-\ *n* **1 :** the act or process of compiling **2 :** something compiled ⟨a ~ of statistics⟩

com·pile \kəm-ˈpī(ə)l\ *vt* **com·piled; com·pil·ing** [ME *compilen,* fr. MF *compiler,* fr. L *compilare* to plunder] **1 :** to collect into a volume **2 :** to compose out of materials from other documents

com·pil·er \kəm-ˈpī-lər\ *n* **1 :** one that compiles **2 :** a computer program that translates instructions written in a higher-level symbolic language (as COBOL) into machine language

com·pla·cence \kəm-ˈplās-ᵊn(t)s\ *n* **1 :** calm or secure satisfaction with one's self or lot **:** SELF-SATISFACTION **2** *obs* **:** COMPLAISANCE **3 :** UNCONCERN

com·pla·cen·cy \-ᵊn-sē\ *n, pl* **-cies 1 :** COMPLACENCE; *esp* **:** self-satisfaction accompanied by unawareness of actual dangers or deficiencies **2 :** an instance of complacency ⟨a book which broke up . . . theological *complacencies* — *Times Lit. Supp.*⟩

com·pla·cent \kəm-ˈplās-ᵊnt\ *adj* [L *complacent-, complacens,* prp. of *complacēre* to please greatly, fr. *com-* + *placēre* to please — more at PLEASE] **1 :** SELF-SATISFIED ⟨a ~ smile⟩ **2 :** COMPLAISANT 1 **3 :** UNCONCERNED ⟨~ about inflation —N. H. Jacoby⟩ — **com·pla·cent·ly** *adv*

com·plain \kəm-ˈplān\ *vi* [ME *compleynen,* fr. MF *complaindre,* fr. (assumed) VL *complangere,* fr. L *com-* + *plangere* to lament — more at PLAINT] **1 :** to express grief, pain, or discontent **2 :** to make a formal accusation or charge — **com·plain·er** *n* — **com·plain·ing·ly** \-ˈplā-niŋ-lē\ *adv*

com·plain·ant \kəm-ˈplā-nənt\ *n* **:** the party who makes the complaint in a legal action or proceeding

com·plaint \kəm-ˈplānt\ *n* [ME *compleynte,* fr. MF *complainte,* fr. OF, fr. *complaindre*] **1 :** expression of grief, pain, or resentment **2 a :** something that is the cause or subject of protest or outcry **b :** a bodily ailment or disease **3 :** a formal allegation against a party

com·plai·sance \kəm-ˈplās-ᵊn(t)s, -ˈplāz-; ˌkäm-plā-ˈzan(t)s, -plə-, -ˈzän(t)s\ *n* **:** disposition to please or comply **:** AFFABILITY

com·plai·sant \-ᵊnt, -ˈzant, -ˈzänt\ *adj* [F, fr. MF, fr. prp. of *complaire* to gratify, acquiesce, fr. L *complacēre* to please greatly] **1 :** marked by an inclination to please or oblige **2 :** tending to consent to others' wishes ***syn*** see AMIABLE ***ant*** contrary, perverse — **com·plai·sant·ly** *adv*

com·pleat \kəm-ˈplēt\ *adj* [archaic variant of *complete* in *The Compleat Angler* (1653) by Izaak Walton] **:** COMPLETE 3 ⟨the ~ conductor, experienced in opera as well as in the symphonic repertoire —Winthrop Sargeant⟩

com·plect·ed \kəm-ˈplek-təd\ *adj* [irreg. fr. *complexion*] **:** having a specified facial complexion ⟨a tall, thin man, fairly dark ~ —E. J. Kahn⟩

¹com·ple·ment \ˈkäm-plə-mənt\ *n* [ME, fr. L *complementum,* fr. *complēre*] **1 a :** something that fills up, completes, or makes perfect **b :** the quantity or number required to make a thing complete ⟨he had the usual ~ of eyes and ears —Francis Parkman⟩; *specif* **:** the whole force or personnel of a ship **c :** one of two mutually completing parts **:** COUNTERPART **2 a :** an angle or arc that when added to a given angle or arc equals a right angle **b :** the set of all elements that do not belong to a given set and are contained in a particular mathematical set containing the given set **c :** a number that when added to another number of the same sign yields zero if the significant digit farthest to the left is discarded **3 :** the interval in music required with a given interval to complete the octave **4 :** an added word or expression by which a predication is made complete ⟨*president* and *beautiful* in "they elected him president" and "he thought her beautiful" are ~*s*⟩ **5 :** the thermolabile substance in normal blood serum and plasma that in combination with antibodies causes the destruction of bacteria, foreign blood corpuscles, and other antigens

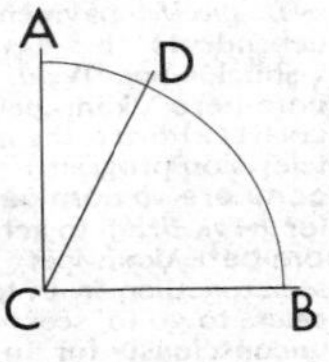

complement 2a: *ACB* right angle; *ACD* complement of *DCB* (and vice versa); *AD* complement of *DB* (and vice versa)

²com·ple·ment \-ˌment\ *vt* **1 :** to be complementary to **2** *obs* **:** COMPLIMENT ~ *vi, obs* **:** to exchange formal courtesies

com·ple·men·tal \ˌkäm-plə-ˈment-ᵊl\ *adj* **1 :** relating to or being a complement **2** *obs* **:** CEREMONIOUS, COMPLIMENTARY

com·ple·men·tar·i·ty \ˌkäm-plə-(ˌ)men-ˈtar-ət-ē, -mən-\ *n* **:** the quality or state of being complementary

com·ple·men·ta·ry \ˌkäm-plə-ˈment-ə-rē, -ˈmen-trē\ *adj* **1 :** serving to fill out or complete **2 :** mutually supplying each other's lack **3 :** relating to or constituting one of a pair of contrasting colors that produce a neutral color when combined in suitable proportions **4 :** of or relating to the precise pairing of purine and pyrimidine bases between strands of DNA and sometimes RNA such that the structure of one strand determines the other — **com·ple·men·ta·ri·ly** \-ˈmen-trə-lē, -(ˌ)men-ˈter-ə-lē, -ˈment-ə-rə-lē\ *adv* — **com·ple·men·ta·ri·ness** \-ˈment-ə-rē-nəs, -ˈmen-trē-\ *n* — **complementary** *n*

complementary angles *n pl* **:** two angles whose sum is 90 degrees

com·ple·men·ta·tion \ˌkäm-plə-(ˌ)men-ˈtā-shən, -mən-\ *n* **1 :** the determination of the complement of a given mathematical set **2 :** production of normal phenotype in an individual heterozygous for two closely related mutations with one on each homologous chromosome and at a slightly different position

complement fixation *n* **:** the absorption of complement to the product of the union of an antibody and the antigen for which it is specific when added to a mixture of such antibody and antigen

¹com·plete \kəm-ˈplēt\ *adj* **com·plet·er; -est** [ME *complet,* fr. MF, fr. L *completus* fr. pp. of *complēre* to fill up, complete, fr. *com-* + *plēre* to fill — more at FULL] **1 a :** having all necessary parts, elements, or steps ⟨~ diet⟩ ⟨~ analysis of a problem⟩ **b :** having all four sets of floral organs **:** MONOCLINOUS **c** *of a subject or predicate* **:** including modifiers, complements, or objects **2 :** brought to an end **:** CONCLUDED ⟨a ~ period of time⟩ **3 :** highly proficient ⟨a ~ artist⟩ **4 a :** fully carried out **:** THOROUGH ⟨a ~ renovation⟩ **b :** TOTAL, ABSOLUTE ⟨~ silence⟩ ***syn*** see FULL ***ant*** incomplete — **com·plete·ly** *adv* — **com·plete·ness** *n* — **com·ple·tive** \-ˈplēt-iv\ *adj*

²complete *vt* **com·plet·ed; com·plet·ing 1 :** to bring to an end and esp. into a perfected state ⟨~ a painting⟩ **2 a :** to make whole or perfect ⟨its song ~*s* the charm of this bird⟩ **b :** to mark the end of ⟨a rousing chorus ~*s* the show⟩ **c :** EXECUTE, FULFILL ⟨~ a contract⟩ **3 :** to carry out (a forward pass) successfully

complete fertilizer *n* **:** a fertilizer that contains the three chief plant nutrients nitrogen, phosphoric acid, and potash

com·ple·tion \kəm-ˈplē-shən\ *n* **1 :** the act or process of completing **2 :** the quality or state of being complete

¹com·plex \käm-ˈpleks, kəm-ˈ, ˈkäm-ˌ\ *adj* [L *complexus,* pp. of *complecti* to embrace, comprise (a multitude of objects), fr. *com-* + *plectere* to braid — more at PLY] **1 a :** composed of two or more parts **:** COMPOSITE **b (1)** *of a word* **:** having a bound form as one or both of its immediate constituents ⟨*unmanly* is a ~ word⟩ **(2)** *of a sentence* **:** consisting of a main clause and one or more subordinate clauses **2 :** hard to separate, analyze, or solve — **com·plex·ly** *adv* — **com·plex·ness** *n*

syn COMPLEX, COMPLICATED, INTRICATE, INVOLVED, KNOTTY *shared meaning element* **:** having confusingly interrelated parts ***ant*** simple

²com·plex \ˈkäm-ˌpleks\ *n* **1 :** a whole made up of complicated or interrelated parts ⟨a ~ of university buildings⟩ ⟨a ~ of welfare programs⟩ ⟨the military-industrial ~⟩ **2 a :** a group of culture traits relating to a single activity (as hunting), process (as use of flint), or culture unit **b (1) :** a group of repressed desires and memories that exerts a dominating influence upon the personality **(2) :** an exaggerated reaction to a subject or situation **c :** a group of obviously related units of which the degree and nature of the relationship is imperfectly known **3 :** a complex substance (as a coordination complex) in which the constituents are more intimately associated than in a simple mixture

³com·plex *like* ¹\ *vt* **1 :** to make complex or into a complex **2 :** CHELATE — **com·plex·ation** \ˌkäm-ˌplek-ˈsā-shən, kəm-\ *n*

complex fraction *n* **:** a fraction with a fraction or mixed number in the numerator or denominator or both — compare SIMPLE FRACTION

com·plex·ion \kəm-ˈplek-shən\ *n* [ME, fr. MF, fr. ML *complexion-, complexio,* fr. L, combination, fr. *complexus,* pp] **1 :** the combination of the hot, cold, moist, and dry qualities held in medieval physiology to determine the quality of a body **2 a :** an individual complex of ways of thinking or feeling **b :** a complex of attitudes and inclinations **3 :** the hue or appearance of the skin and esp. of the face ⟨a dark ~⟩ **4 :** overall aspect or impression ⟨by changing the ~ of the legislative branch —Travor Armbrister⟩ — **com·plex·ion·al** \-shnəl, -shən-ᵊl\ *adj* — **com·plex·ioned** \-shənd\ *adj*

com·plex·i·ty \kəm-ˈplek-sət-ē, käm-\ *n, pl* **-ties 1 :** the quality or state of being complex **2 :** something complex ⟨the *complexities* of today's society —John J. Gallagher⟩

complex number *n* **:** a number of the form $a + b\sqrt{-1}$ where *a* and *b* are real numbers

com·plex·om·e·try \ˌkäm-ˌplek-ˈsäm-ə-trē, kəm-\ *n* **:** a titrimetric technique involving the use of a complexing agent (as EDTA) as the titrant — **com·plex·o·met·ric** \(ˌ)käm-ˌplek-sə-ˈme-trik, kəm-\ *adj*

complex plane *n* **:** a plane whose points are identified by means of complex numbers

com·pli·ance \kəm-ˈplī-ən(t)s\ *n* **1 :** the act or process of complying to a desire, demand, or proposal or to coercion **2 :** a disposition to yield to others **3 a :** the ability of an object to yield elastically when a force is applied **:** FLEXIBILITY **b :** the force required to move a phonograph stylus a given distance

com·pli·an·cy \-ən-sē\ *n* **:** COMPLIANCE

com·pli·ant \-ənt\ *adj* **:** ready or disposed to comply **:** SUBMISSIVE — **com·pli·ant·ly** *adv*

com·pli·ca·cy \ˈkäm-pli-kə-sē\ *n, pl* **-cies** [²*complicate*] **1 :** the quality or state of being complicated **2 :** something that is complicated

¹com·pli·cate \ˈkäm-plə-ˌkāt\ *vb* **-cat·ed; -cat·ing** *vt* **1 :** to combine esp. in an involved or inextricable manner **2 :** to make complex or difficult **3 :** INVOLVE; *esp* **:** to cause to be more complex or severe ⟨a virus disease *complicated* by bacterial infection⟩ ~ *vi* **:** to become complicated

²com·pli·cate \-pli-kət\ *adj* [L *complicatus,* pp. of *complicare* to fold together, fr. *com-* + *plicare* to fold — more at PLY] **1 :** COMPLEX, INTRICATE **2 :** CONDUPLICATE

com·pli·cat·ed \ˈkäm-plə-ˌkāt-əd\ *adj* **1 :** consisting of parts intricately combined **2 :** difficult to analyze, understand, or explain ***syn*** see COMPLEX ***ant*** simple — **com·pli·cat·ed·ly** *adv* — **com·pli·cat·ed·ness** *n*

com·pli·ca·tion \ˌkäm-plə-ˈkā-shən\ *n* **1 a :** COMPLEXITY, INTRICACY; *specif* **:** a situation or a detail of character complicating the main thread of a plot **b :** a making difficult, involved, or intricate **c :** a complex or intricate feature or element **d :** a difficult factor or issue often appearing unexpectedly and changing existing plans, methods, or attitudes **2 :** a secondary disease or condition developing in the course of a primary disease

com·plice \ˈkäm-pləs, ˈkəm-\ *n* [ME, fr. MF, fr. LL *complic-, complex,* fr. L *com-* + *plicare* to fold] *archaic* **:** ASSOCIATE

com·plic·i·ty \kəm-ˈplis-ət-ē, -ˈplis-tē\ *n, pl* **-ties 1 :** association or participation in or as if in a wrongful act **2 :** an instance of complicity

com·pli·er \-ˈplī(-ə)r\ *n* **:** one that complies

¹com·pli·ment \ˈkäm-plə-mənt\ *n* [F, fr. It *complimento,* fr. Sp *cumplimiento,* fr. *cumplir* to be courteous — more at COMPLY] **1 a :** an expression of esteem, respect, affection, or admiration; *esp* **:** a flattering remark **b :** formal and respectful recognition

: HONOR ⟨a party in ~ of house guests⟩ 2 *pl* : best wishes : REGARDS ⟨accept my ~s⟩ ⟨~s of the season⟩

²com·pli·ment \-,ment\ *vt* 1 : to pay a compliment to 2 : to present with a token of esteem

com·pli·men·ta·ry \,käm-plə-'ment-ə-rē, -'men-trē\ *adj* 1 a : expressing or containing a compliment b : FAVORABLE ⟨the novel received ~ reviews⟩ 2 : given free as a courtesy or favor ⟨~ tickets⟩ — com·pli·men·ta·ri·ly \-'men-trə-lē, -(,)men-'ter-ə-lē, -'ment-ə-rə-lē\ *adv*

complimentary close *n* : the words (as *sincerely yours*) that conventionally come immediately before the signature of a letter and express the sender's regard for the receiver — called also *complimentary closing*

com·pline \'käm-plən, -,plīn\ *n, often cap* [ME *complie, compline*, fr. OF *complie*, modif. of LL *completa*, fr. L, fem. of *completus* complete] : the seventh and last of the canonical hours

¹com·plot \'käm-,plät\ *n* [MF *complot* crowd, plot] *archaic* : PLOT, CONSPIRACY

²com·plot \kəm-'plät, käm-\ *vb, archaic* : PLOT

com·ply \kəm-'plī\ *vi* com·plied; com·ply·ing [It *complire*, fr. Sp *cumplir* to complete, perform what is due, be courteous, fr. L *complēre* to complete] 1 *obs* : to be ceremoniously courteous 2 : to conform or adapt one's actions to another's wishes, to a rule, or to necessity *syn* see OBEY

com·po \'käm-(,)pō\ *n, pl* compos [short for *composition*] : any of various composition materials

¹com·po·nent \kəm-'pō-nənt, 'käm-,, käm-\ *n* [L *component-, componens*, prp. of *componere* to put together — more at COMPOUND] 1 : a constituent part : INGREDIENT 2 a : any one of the vector terms added to form a vector sum or resultant b : a coordinate of a vector ***ant*** composite, complex — com·po·nen·tial \,käm-pə-'nen-chəl\ *adj*

²component *adj* : serving or helping to constitute : CONSTITUENT

¹com·port \kəm-'pō(ə)rt, -'pó(ə)rt\ *vb* [MF *comporter* to bear, conduct, fr. L *comportare* to bring together, fr. *com-* + *portare* to carry — more at PORT] *vi* : to be fitting : ACCORD ⟨acts that ~ with ideals⟩ ~ *vt* : BEHAVE; *esp* : to behave in a manner conformable to what is right, proper, or expected ⟨~ed himself well in the emergency⟩ *syn* see AGREE, BEHAVE

²com·port \'käm-,pō(ə)rt, -,pó(ə)rt\ *n* : COMPOTE 2

com·port·ment \kəm-'pōrt-mənt, -'pórt-\ *n* : BEARING, DEMEANOR

com·pose \kəm-'pōz\ *vb* com·posed; com·pos·ing [MF *composer*, fr. L *componere* (perf. indic. *composui*) — more at COMPOUND] *vt* 1 a : to form by putting together : FASHION ⟨a committee *composed* of three representatives—*Current Biog.*⟩ b : to form the substance of : CONSTITUTE ⟨*composed* of many ingredients⟩ c : ARRANGE, SET, PHOTOCOMPOSE 2 a : to create by mental or artistic labor : PRODUCE ⟨~ a sonnet sequence⟩ b (1) : to formulate and write (a piece of music) (2) : to compose music for 3 : to deal with or act on so as to reduce to a minimum ⟨~ their differences⟩ 4 : to arrange in proper or orderly form ⟨~ her clothing⟩ 5 : to free from agitation : CALM, SETTLE ⟨~ a patient⟩ ~ *vi* : to practice composition

com·posed \-'pōzd\ *adj* : free from agitation : CALM; *esp* : SELF-POSSESSED *syn* see COOL ***ant*** discomposed, anxious — com·pos·ed·ly \-'pō-zəd-lē\ *adv* — com·pos·ed·ness \-'pō-zəd-nəs\ *n*

com·pos·er \kəm-'pō-zər\ *n* : one that composes; *esp* : a person who writes music

composing room *n* : the department in a printing office where typesetting and related operations are performed

composing stick *n* : a tray with an adjustable slide that is held in one hand by a compositor as he sets type into it with the other hand

¹com·pos·ite \käm-'päz-ət, kəm-', *esp Brit* 'käm-pə-zit\ *adj* [L *compositus*, pp. of *componere*] 1 : made up of distinct parts: as a *cap* : relating to or being a modification of the Corinthian order combining angular Ionic volutes with the acanthus-circled bell of the Corinthian b : of or relating to a very large family (Compositae) of dicotyledonous herbs, shrubs, and trees often considered to be the most highly evolved plants and characterized by florets arranged in dense heads that resemble single flowers c : factorable into two or more prime factors other than 1 and itself ⟨8 is a positive ~ integer⟩ 2 : combining the typical or essential characteristics of individuals making up a group ⟨the ~ man called the Poet—Richard Poirier⟩ 3 *of a statistical hypothesis* : specifying a range of values for one or more statistical parameters — compare SIMPLE 10 — com·pos·ite·ly *adv*

²composite *n* 1 : something composite 2 : COMPOUND 2 : a composite plant

³composite *vt* -it·ed; -it·ing : to make composite or into something composite ⟨*composited* four soil samples⟩

com·po·si·tion \,käm-pə-'zish-ən\ *n* [ME *composicioun*, fr. MF *composition*, fr. L *composition-, compositio*, fr. *compositus*] 1 a : the act or process of composing; *specif* : arrangement into proper proportion or relation esp. into artistic form b (1) : the arrangement of type for printing ⟨hand ~⟩ (2) : the production of type or typographic characters (as in photocomposition) arranged for printing 2 a : the manner in which something is composed b : general makeup ⟨the changing ethnic ~ of the city—Leonard Buder⟩ c : the qualitative and quantitative makeup of a chemical compound 3 : mutual settlement or agreement 4 : a product of mixing or combining various elements or ingredients 5 : an intellectual creation: as a : a piece of writing; *esp* : a school exercise in the form of a brief essay b : a written piece of music esp. of considerable size and complexity 6 : the quality or state of being compound — com·po·si·tion·al \-'zish-nəl, -ən-ᵊl\ *adj* — com·po·si·tion·al·ly \-ē\ *adv*

com·pos·i·tor \kəm-'päz-ət-ər\ *n* : one who sets type

com·pos men·tis \,käm-pə-'sment-əs\ *adj* [L, lit., having mastery of one's mind] : of sound mind, memory, and understanding

¹com·post \'käm-,pōst, *esp Brit* -,päst\ *n* [MF, fr. ML *compostum*, fr. L, neut. of *compositus, compostus*, pp. of *componere* to put together] 1 : a mixture that consists largely of decayed organic matter and is used for fertilizing and conditioning land 2 : MIXTURE, COMPOUND

²compost *vt* : to convert (as plant debris) to compost

com·po·sure \kəm-'pō-zhər\ *n* : a calmness or repose esp. of mind, bearing, or appearance : SELF-POSSESSION *syn* see EQUANIMITY ***ant*** discomposure, perturbation

com·pote \'käm-,pōt\ *n* [F, fr. OF *composte*, fr. L *composta*, fem. of *compostus*, pp.] 1 : whole fruits cooked in syrup 2 : a bowl of glass, porcelain, or metal usu. with a base and stem from which compotes, fruits, nuts, or sweets are served

¹com·pound \käm-'paúnd, kəm-', 'käm-,\ *vb* [ME *compounen*, fr. MF *compondre*, fr. L *componere*, fr. *com-* + *ponere* to put — more at POSITION] *vt* 1 : to put together (parts) so as to form a whole : COMBINE ⟨~ ingredients⟩ 2 : to form by combining parts ⟨~ a medicine⟩ 3 : to settle amicably : adjust by agreement ⟨~ a debt⟩ 4 : to pay (interest) on both the accrued interest and the principal 5 : to add to : AUGMENT ⟨~ed our error in later policy—Robert Lekachman⟩ 5 : to agree for a consideration not to prosecute (an offense) ⟨~ a felony⟩ ~ *vi* 1 : to become joined in a compound 2 : to come to terms of agreement — com·pound·able \-ə-bəl\ *adj* — com·pound·er *n*

²com·pound \'käm-,paúnd, käm-', kəm-'\ *adj* [ME *compouned*, pp. of *compounen*] 1 : composed of or resulting from union of separate elements, ingredients, or parts; *specif* : composed of united similar elements esp. of a kind usu. independent ⟨a ~ plant ovary⟩ 2 : involving or used in a combination 3 a *of a word* : constituting a compound b *of a sentence* : having two or more main clauses

³com·pound \'käm-,paúnd\ *n* 1 a : a word consisting of components that are words (as *rowboat, high school, devil-may-care*) b : a word consisting of any of various combinations of words, combining forms, or affixes (as *anthropology, kilocycle, builder*) 2 : something formed by a union of elements or parts; *specif* : a distinct substance formed by chemical union of two or more ingredients in definite proportion by weight

⁴com·pound \'käm-,paúnd\ *n* [by folk etymology fr. Malay *kampong* group of buildings, village] : a fenced or walled-in area containing a group of buildings and esp. residences

compound–complex *adj, of a sentence* : having two or more main clauses and one or more subordinate clauses

compound eye *n* : an eye (as of an insect) made up of many separate visual units

compound fracture *n* : a bone fracture produced in such a way as to form an open wound through which bone fragments usu. protrude

compound interest *n* : interest computed on the sum of an original principal and accrued interest

compound leaf *n* : a leaf in which the blade is divided to the midrib forming two or more leaflets on a common axis

compound microscope *n* : a microscope consisting of an objective and an eyepiece mounted in a drawtube

compound number *n* : a number (as 2 ft. 5 in.) involving different denominations or more than one unit

com·pra·dor \,käm-prə-'dó(ə)r\ *or* com·pra·dore \-'dō(ə)r, -'dó(ə)r\ *n* [Pg *comprador*, lit., buyer] : a Chinese agent engaged by a foreign establishment in China to have charge of its Chinese employees and to act as an intermediary in business affairs

com·pre·hend \,käm-pri-'hend\ *vt* [ME *comprehenden*, fr. L *comprehendere*, fr. *com-* + *prehendere* to grasp — more at PREHENSILE] 1 : to grasp the nature, significance, or meaning of 2 : to include as an integral part ⟨philosophy's scope ~s the truth of everything which man may understand —H. O. Taylor⟩ 3 : to include by construction or implication : COMPRISE *syn* see UNDERSTAND, INCLUDE — com·pre·hend·ible \-'hen-də-bəl\ *adj*

com·pre·hen·si·ble \-'hen(t)-sə-bəl\ *adj* : capable of being comprehended : INTELLIGIBLE ⟨~ examinations⟩ — com·pre·hen·si·bil·i·ty \-,hen(t)-sə-'bil-ət-ē\ *n* — com·pre·hen·si·ble·ness \-'hen(t)-sə-bəl-nəs\ *n* — com·pre·hen·si·bly \-blē\ *adv*

com·pre·hen·sion \,käm-pri-'hen-chən\ *n* [MF & L; MF, fr. L *comprehension-, comprehensio*, fr. *comprehensus*, pp. of *comprehendere* to understand, comprise] 1 a : the act or process of comprising b : the faculty or capability of including : COMPREHENSIVENESS 2 a : the act or action of grasping with the intellect : UNDERSTANDING b : knowledge gained by comprehending c : the capacity for understanding fully 3 : CONNOTATION 3

com·pre·hen·sive \-'hen(t)-siv\ *adj* 1 : covering completely or broadly : INCLUSIVE ⟨~ examinations⟩ ⟨~ insurance⟩ 2 : having or exhibiting wide mental grasp ⟨~ knowledge⟩ — com·pre·hen·sive·ly *adv* — com·pre·hen·sive·ness *n*

¹com·press \kəm-'pres\ *vb* [ME *compressen*, fr. LL *compressare* to press hard, fr. L *compressus*, pp. of *comprimere* to compress, fr. *com-* + *premere* to press] *vt* 1 : to press or squeeze together 2 : to reduce in size or volume as if by squeezing ~ *vi* : to undergo compression *syn* see CONTRACT ***ant*** stretch, spread

²com·press \'käm-,pres\ *n* [MF *compresse*, fr. *compresser* to compress, fr. LL *compressare*] 1 : a folded cloth or pad applied so as to press upon a body part 2 : a machine for compressing

com·pressed \kəm-'prest *also* 'käm-,\ *adj* 1 : pressed together : reduced in size or volume (as by pressure) 2 : flattened as though subjected to compression: a : flattened laterally ⟨petioles ~⟩ b : narrow from side to side and deep in a dorsoventral direction — com·pressed·ly \kəm-'prest-lē, -'pres-əd-lē\ *adv*

---

compressed air *n* : air under pressure greater than that of the atmosphere

com·press·ible \kəm-'pres-ə-bəl\ *adj* : capable of being compressed — **com·press·ibil·i·ty** \-,pres-ə-'bil-ət-ē\ *n*

com·pres·sion \kəm-'presh-ən\ *n* **1 a** : the act, process, or result of compressing **b** : the state of being compressed **2** : the process of compressing the fuel mixture in a cylinder of an internal-combustion engine (as in an automobile) **3** : a much compressed fossil plant — **com·pres·sion·al** \-'presh-nəl, -ən-ᵊl\ *adj*

compressional wave *n* : a longitudinal wave (as a sound wave) propagated by the elastic compression of the medium — called also *compression wave*

com·pres·sive \kəm-'pres-iv\ *adj* **1** : of or relating to compression **2** : tending to compress — **com·pres·sive·ly** *adv*

com·pres·sor \-'pres-ər\ *n* : one that compresses: as **a** : a muscle that compresses a part **b** : a machine that compresses gases

com·prise \kəm-'prīz\ *vt* **com·prised; com·pris·ing** [ME *comprisen*, fr. MF *compris*, pp. of *comprendre*, fr. L *comprehendere*] **1** : INCLUDE, CONTAIN **2** : to be made up of **3** : to make up : CONSTITUTE

¹com·pro·mise \'käm-prə-,mīz\ *n* [ME, mutual promise to abide by an arbiter's decision, fr. MF *compromis*, fr. L *compromissum*, fr. neut. of *compromissus*, pp. of *compromittere* to promise mutually, fr. *com-* + *promittere* to promise — more at PROMISE] **1 a** : settlement of differences by arbitration or by consent reached by mutual concessions **b** : something blending qualities of two different things **2** : a concession to something derogatory or prejudicial ⟨a ~ of principles⟩

²compromise *vb* **-mised; -mis·ing** *vt* **1** *obs* : to bind by mutual agreement **2** : to adjust or settle by mutual concessions **3** : to expose to discredit or mischief ~ *vi* **1** : to come to agreement by mutual concession **2** : to make a shameful or disreputable concession — **com·pro·mis·er** *n*

compt \'kaunt, 'käm(p)t\ *archaic var of* COUNT

comp·trol·ler \kən-'trō-lər, 'käm(p)-, ,käm(p)-'\ *n* [ME, alter. of *conterroller* controller] **1** : a royal-household official who examines and supervises expenditures **2** : a public official who audits government accounts and sometimes certifies expenditures **3** : CONTROLLER 1c — **comp·trol·ler·ship** \-,ship\ *n*

com·pul·sion \kəm-'pəl-shən\ *n* [ME, fr. MF or LL; MF, fr. LL *compulsion-, compulsio*, fr. L *compulsus*, pp. of *compellere* to compel] **1** : an act of compelling : the state of being compelled **b** : a force or agency that compels **2** : an irresistible impulse to perform an irrational act

com·pul·sive \-'pəl-siv\ *adj* **1** : having power to compel ⟨a strangely ~, resonant voice—L. C. Douglas⟩ **2** : of, relating to, caused by, or suggestive of psychological compulsion or obsession ⟨~ actions⟩ — **com·pul·sive·ly** *adv* — **com·pul·sive·ness** *n* — **com·pul·siv·i·ty** \,käm-,pəl-'siv-ət-ē\ *n*

com·pul·so·ry \kəm-'pəls-(ə-)rē\ *adj* **1** : MANDATORY, ENFORCED ⟨~ arbitration⟩ **2** : COERCIVE, COMPELLING — **com·pul·so·ri·ly** \-(ə-)rə-lē\ *adv*

com·punc·tion \kəm-'pəŋ(k)-shən\ *n* [ME *compunccioun*, fr. MF *componction*, fr. LL *compunction-, compunctio*, fr. L *compunctus*, pp. of *compungere* to prick hard, sting, fr. *com-* + *pungere* to prick — more at PUNGENT] **1 a** : anxiety arising from awareness of guilt ⟨~s of conscience⟩ **b** : distress of mind over an anticipated action or result ⟨he showed no ~ in planning devilish engines of . . . destruction—Havelock Ellis⟩ **2** : a twinge of misgiving : SCRUPLE ⟨cheated without ~⟩ *syn* see PENITENCE, QUALM — **com·punc·tious** \-shəs\ *adj*

com·pur·ga·tion \,käm-(,)pər-'gā-shən\ *n* [LL *compurgation-, compurgatio*, fr. L *compurgatus*, pp. of *compurgare* to clear completely, fr. *com-* + *purgare* to purge] : the clearing of an accused person by oaths of persons who swear to his veracity or innocence

com·pur·ga·tor \'käm-(,)pər-,gāt-ər\ *n* : one that under oath vouches for the character or conduct of an accused person

com·put·able \kəm-'pyüt-ə-bəl\ *adj* : capable of being computed — **com·put·abil·i·ty** \-,pyüt-ə-'bil-ət-ē\ *n*

com·pu·ta·tion \,käm-pyü-'tā-shən\ *n* **1 a** : the act or action of computing : CALCULATION **b** : the use or operation of a computer **2** : a system or reckoning **3** : an amount computed — **com·pu·ta·tion·al** \-shnəl, -shən-ᵊl\ *adj*

¹com·pute \kəm-'pyüt\ *n* : COMPUTATION ⟨numbers beyond ~⟩

²compute *vb* **com·put·ed; com·put·ing** [L *computare* — more at COUNT] *vt* **1** : to determine esp. by mathematical means ⟨~ your income tax⟩; *also* : to determine or calculate by means of a computer ~ *vi* **1** : to make calculation : RECKON **2** : to use a computer

com·put·er \kəm-'pyüt-ər\ *n* : one that computes; *specif* : a programmable electronic device that can store, retrieve, and process data — **com·put·er·like** \-,līk\ *adj*

com·put·er·ese \-,pyüt-ə-'rēz, -'rēs\ *n* **1** : MACHINE LANGUAGE **2** : jargon used by computer technologists

com·put·er·ise *chiefly Brit var of* COMPUTERIZE

com·put·er·ite \-'pyüt-ə-,rīt\ *n* : COMPUTERNIK

com·put·er·ize \kəm-'pyüt-ə-,rīz\ *vt* **-ized; -iz·ing** **1** : to carry out, control, or conduct by means of a computer **2** : to equip with computers — **com·put·er·iz·able** \-,rī-zə-bəl\ *adj* — **com·put·er·iza·tion** \-,pyüt-ə-rə-'zā-shən\ *n*

com·put·er·nik \kəm-'pyüt-ər-,nik\ *n* [*computer* + *-nik*] : a person who works with or has a deep interest in computers

comr *abbr* commissioner

com·rade \'käm-,rad, -rəd, *esp Brit* -,rād\ *n* [MF *camarade* group sleeping in one room, roommate, companion, fr. OSp *camarada*, fr. *cámara* room, fr. LL *camera, camara*] **1 a** : an intimate friend or associate : COMPANION **b** : a fellow soldier **2** [fr. its use as a form of address by communists] : COMMUNIST — **com·rade·ship** \-,ship\ *n*

com·rade·ly \-lē\ *adj* : of or resembling a comrade or partner — **com·rade·li·ness** *n*

com·rad·ery \'käm-,rad-(ə-)rē, -rəd-rē, -,rād-(ə-)rē\ *n* : CAMARADERIE

Comsat \'käm-,sat\ *service mark* — used for communications services involving an artificial satellite

Com·stock·ery \'käm-,stäk-ə-rē *also* 'kəm-\ *n* [Anthony *Comstock* + E *-ery*] **1** : strict censorship of materials (as books and plays) considered obscene **2** : censorious opposition to alleged immorality in art, literature, and the theater ⟨*Comstockery*, an idiotic and abominable thing —H.L. Mencken⟩

Com·stock·ian \käm-'stäk-ē-ən *also* ,kəm-\ *adj* : of or relating to Comstockery

Comt·ian *or* **Comt·ean** \'käm(p)-tē-ən, 'kōⁿ(t)-tē-\ *adj* : of or relating to Auguste Comte or his doctrines — **Comt·ism** \'käm(p)-,tiz-əm, 'kōⁿ(t)-,iz-\ *n* — **Comt·ist** \'käm(p)-təst, 'kōⁿ(t)-əst\ *adj or n*

¹con \'kän\ *vt* **conned; con·ning** [ME *connen* to know, learn, study, alter. of *cunnen* to know, infin. of *can* — more at CAN] **1** : to study or examine closely : PERUSE **2** : to commit to memory

²con *var of* CONN

³con *adv* [ME, short for *contra*] : on the negative side : in opposition ⟨so much has been written pro and ~⟩

⁴con *n* **1** : an argument or evidence in opposition **2** : the negative position or one holding it ⟨an appraisal of the pros and ~s⟩

⁵con *adj* : CONFIDENCE

⁶con *vt* **conned; con·ning** [⁵*con*] **1** : SWINDLE **2** : PERSUADE, CAJOLE

⁷con *n* : CONVICT

⁸con *n* [short for *consumption*] *slang* : a destructive disease of the lungs; *esp* : TUBERCULOSIS

⁹con *abbr* **1** [L *conjunx*] consort **2** consolidated **3** consul **4** continued

con- — see COM-

con amo·re \,kän-ə-'mōr-ē, ,kō-nə-'mōr-(,)ā, -'mȯr-\ *adv* [It] **1** : with love, devotion, or zest **2** : in a tender manner — used as a direction in music

con ani·ma \kän-ə-,mä, kō-'nän-i-\ *adv* [It, lit., with spirit] : in a spirited manner : with animation — used as a direction in music

co·na·tion \kō-'nā-shən\ *n* [L *conation-, conatio* act of attempting, fr. *conatus*, pp. of *conari* to attempt — more at DEACON] : an inclination (as an instinct, a drive, a wish, or a craving) to act purposefully : IMPULSE **3** — **co·na·tion·al** \-shnəl, -shən-ᵊl\ *adj* — **co·na·tive** \'kō-nət-iv, -,nāt-; 'kän-ət-\ *adj*

co·na·tus \kō-'nāt-əs, -'nāt-\ *n, pl* **co·na·tus** \-əs; -'nä-,tüs, -'nä-\ [NL, fr. L, attempt, effort, fr. *conatus*, pp.] : a natural tendency, impulse, or striving

con brio \kän-'brē-(,)ō, kōn-\ *adv* [It, lit., with vigor] : in a vigorous or brisk manner — used as a direction in music

conc *abbr* **1** concentrate; concentrated; concentration **2** concrete

con·ca·nav·a·lin \,kän-kə-'nav-ə-lən\ *n* [*com-* + *canavalin* (a noncrystalline globulin found in the jack bean), fr. NL *Canavalia*, genus name of the jack bean] : either of two crystalline globulins occurring in the jack bean; *esp* : one that is a potent hemagglutinin

¹con·cat·e·nate \kän-'kat-ə-nət, kən-\ *adj* [ME, fr. LL *concatenatus*, pp. of *concatenare* to link together, fr. L *com-* + *catena* chain — more at CHAIN] : linked together

²concatenate \-,nāt\ *vt* **-nat·ed; -nat·ing** : to link together in a series or chain — **con·cat·e·na·tion** \(,)kän-,kat-ə-'nā-shən, kən-\ *n*

¹con·cave \kän-'kāv, 'kän-,\ *adj* [MF, fr. L *concavus*, fr. *com-* + *cavus* hollow — more at CAVE] **1** : hollowed or rounded inward like the inside of a bowl **2** : arched in : curving in — used of the side of a curve or surface on which neighboring normals to the curve or surface converge and on which lies the chord joining two neighboring points of the curve or surface

²concave \'kän-,kāv\ *n* : a concave line or surface

con·cav·i·ty \kän-'kav-ət-ē\ *n, pl* **-ties** **1** : a concave line, surface, or space : HOLLOW **2** : the quality or state of being concave

con·ca·vo-con·cave \kän-,kā-(,)vō-\ *adj* : concave on both sides

concavo-convex *adj* **1** : concave on one side and convex on the other **2** : having the concave side curved more than the convex

con·ceal \kən-'sē(ə)l\ *vt* [ME *concelen*, fr. MF *conceler*, fr. L *concelare*, fr. *com-* + *celare* to hide — more at HELL] **1** : to prevent disclosure or recognition of **2** : to place out of sight *syn* see HIDE — **con·ceal·able** \-'sē-lə-bəl\ *adj* — **con·ceal·er** \-'sē-lər\ *n* — **con·ceal·ing·ly** \-'sē-liŋ-lē\ *adv* — **con·ceal·ment** \-'sē(ə)l-mənt\ *n*

con·cede \kən-'sēd\ *vb* **con·ced·ed; con·ced·ing** [F or L; F *concéder*, fr. L *concedere*, fr. *com-* + *cedere* to yield — more at CEDE] *vt* **1** : to grant as a right or privilege **2 a** : to accept as true, valid, or accurate ⟨the right of the state to tax is generally *conceded*⟩ **b** : to acknowledge grudgingly or hesitantly ~ *vi* **1** : to make concession : YIELD *syn* see GRANT *ant* deny — **con·ced·ed·ly** \-'sēd-əd-lē\ *adv* — **con·ced·er** *n*

¹con·ceit \kən-'sēt\ *n* [ME, fr. *conceiven*] **1 a** (1) : a result of mental activity : THOUGHT (2) : individual opinion **b** : favorable opinion; *esp* : excessive appreciation of one's own worth or virtue **2 a** : a fanciful idea **b** : an elaborate or strained metaphor **c** : use or presence of such conceits in poetry **3** : a fancy article

²conceit *vt* **1** *obs* : CONCEIVE, UNDERSTAND **2** *dial* : IMAGINE **3** *dial Brit* : to take a fancy to

con·ceit·ed \-'sēt-əd\ *adj* [¹*conceit*] **1** : ingeniously contrived : FANCIFUL **2** : having an excessively high opinion of oneself — **con·ceit·ed·ly** *adv* — **con·ceit·ed·ness** *n*

con·ceiv·able \kən-'sē-və-bəl\ *adj* : capable of being conceived : IMAGINABLE — **con·ceiv·abil·i·ty** \kən-,sē-və-'bil-ət-ē\ *n* — **con·ceiv·able·ness** \-'sē-və-bəl-nəs\ *n* — **con·ceiv·ably** \-blē\ *adv*

con·ceive \kən-'sēv\ *vb* **con·ceived; con·ceiv·ing** [ME *conceiven*, fr. OF *conceivre*, fr. L *concipere* to take in, conceive, fr. *com-* + *capere* to take — more at HEAVE] *vt* **1 a** : to become pregnant with (young) **b** : to cause to begin : ORIGINATE **2 a** : to take into one's mind ⟨a *prejudice* against him⟩ **b** : to form a conception of : IMAGINE, IMAGE **3** : to apprehend by reason or imagination : UNDERSTAND **4** : to be of the opinion ~ *vi* **1** : to become pregnant **2** : to have a conception — usu. used with *of* ⟨he ~s of death as emptiness⟩ *syn* see THINK — **con·ceiv·er** *n*

con·cel·e·brant \kən-ˈsel-ə-brənt, kän-\ *n* : one that concelebrates a Eucharist or Mass

con·cel·e·brate \kən-ˈsel-ə-ˌbrāt, kän-\ *vb* [L *concelebratus,* pp. of *concelebrare* to celebrate in great numbers, fr. *com-* + *celebrare* to celebrate] *vt* : to participate in (a Eucharist) as a joint celebrant who recites the canon in unison with other celebrants ~ *vi* : to participate as a celebrant in a concelebrated Eucharist — **con·cel·e·bra·tion** \(ˌ)kän-ˌsel-ə-ˈbrā-shən, kən-\ *n*

con·cent \kən-ˈsent\ *n* [L *concentus,* fr. *concentus,* pp. of *concinere* to sing together, fr. *com-* + *canere* to sing] *archaic* : HARMONY

con·cen·ter \kən-ˈsent-ər, kän-\ *vb* [MF *concentrer,* fr. *com-* + *centre* center] *vt* : to draw or direct to a common center : CONCENTRATE ~ *vi* : to come to a common center

[1]**con·cen·trate** \ˈkän(t)-sən-ˌtrāt, -ˌsen-\ *vb* **-trat·ed; -trat·ing** [*com-* + L *centrum* center] *vt* **1 a** : to bring or direct toward a common center or objective : FOCUS **b** : to gather into one body, mass, or force ⟨power was *concentrated* in a few able hands⟩ **2 a** : to make less dilute ⟨~ syrup⟩ **b** : to separate a valuable material from ⟨~ an ore⟩ **c** : to express or exhibit in condensed form ~ *vi* **1** : to draw toward or meet in a common center **2** : GATHER, COLLECT **3** : to concentrate one's powers, efforts, or attention ⟨~ on a problem⟩ — **con·cen·tra·tive** \-ˌtrāt-iv\ *adj* — **con·cen·tra·tor** \-ˌtrāt-ər\ *n*

[2]**concentrate** *n* : something concentrated

con·cen·tra·tion \ˌkän(t)-sən-ˈtrā-shən, -ˌsen-\ *n* **1** : the act or process of concentrating : the state of being concentrated; *specif* : direction of attention to a single object **2** : a concentrated mass or thing **3** : the relative content of a component : STRENGTH

concentration camp *n* : a camp where persons (as prisoners of war, political prisoners, or refugees) are detained or confined

con·cen·tric \kən-ˈsen-trik, (ˈ)kän-\ *adj* [ML *concentricus,* fr. L *com-* + *centrum* center] **1** : having a common center ⟨~ circles⟩ **2** : having a common axis : COAXIAL — **con·cen·tri·cal·ly** \-tri-k(ə-)lē\ *adv* — **con·cen·tric·i·ty** \ˌkän-ˌsen-ˈtris-ət-ē\ *n*

con·cept \ˈkän-ˌsept\ *n* [L *conceptum,* neut. of *conceptus,* pp. of *concipere* to conceive] **1** : something conceived in the mind : THOUGHT, NOTION **2** : an abstract or generic idea generalized from particular instances ***syn*** see IDEA

con·cep·ta·cle \kən-ˈsep-ti-kəl\ *n* [NL *conceptaculum,* fr. L, receptacle, fr. *conceptus,* pp. of *concipere* to take in] : an external cavity containing reproductive cells in algae (as of the genus *Fucus*)

con·cep·tion \kən-ˈsep-shən\ *n* [ME *concepcioun,* fr. OF *conception,* fr. L *conception-, conceptio,* fr. *conceptus,* pp. of *concipere* to take in, conceive] **1 a** (1) : the act of becoming pregnant : the state of being conceived (2) : EMBRYO, FETUS **b** *archaic* : BEGINNING ⟨joy had the like ~ in our eyes —Shak.⟩ **2 a** : the capacity, function, or process of forming or understanding ideas or abstractions or their symbols **b** : a general idea : CONCEPT **c** : a complex product of abstract or reflective thinking **d** : the sum of a person's ideas and beliefs concerning something **3** : the originating of something in the mind ***syn*** see IDEA — **con·cep·tion·al** \-shnəl, -shən-ᵊl\ *adj* — **con·cep·tive** \-ˈsep-tiv\ *adj*

con·cep·tu·al \kən-ˈsep-chə(-wə)l, kän-, -ˈsepsh-wəl\ *adj* [ML *conceptualis* of thought, fr. LL *conceptus* act of conceiving, thought, fr. L *conceptus,* pp.] : of, relating to, or consisting of concepts — **con·cep·tu·al·i·ty** \-ˌsep-chə-ˈwal-ət-ē, -shə-\ *n* — **con·cep·tu·al·ly** *adv*

con·cep·tu·al·ism \-ˈsep-chə(-wə)-ˌliz-əm, -ˈsepsh-wə-\ *n* : a theory intermediate between realism and nominalism that universals exist in the mind as concepts of discourse or as predicates which may be properly affirmed of reality — **con·cep·tu·al·ist** \-ləst\ *n* — **con·cep·tu·al·is·tic** \-ˌsep-chə(-wə) -lis-tik, -ˌsepsh-wə-\ *adj* — **con·cep·tu·al·is·ti·cal·ly** \-ti-k(ə-)lē\ *adv*

con·cep·tu·al·iza·tion \-ˌsep-chə(-wə)-lə-ˈzā-shən, -ˌsepsh-wə-\ *n* : the act or process of conceptualizing

con·cep·tu·al·ize \-ˈsep-chə(-wə)-ˌlīz, -ˈsepsh-wə-\ *vt* **-ized; -iz·ing** : to form a concept of; *esp* : to interpret conceptually — **con·cep·tu·al·iz·er** *n*

con·cep·tus \kən-ˈsep-təs\ *n* [L, one conceived, fr. pp. of *concipere* to conceive] : FETUS

[1]**con·cern** \kən-ˈsərn\ *vb* [ME *concernen,* fr. MF & ML; MF *concerner,* fr. ML *concernere,* fr. LL, to sift together, mingle, fr. L *com-* + *cernere* to sift — more at CERTAIN] *vt* **1 a** : to relate to : be about ⟨the novel ~*s* three soldiers⟩ **b** : to bear on **2** : to have an influence on : INVOLVE; *also* : to be the business or affair of ⟨the problem ~*s* us all⟩ **3** : to be a care, trouble, or distress to ⟨his ill health ~*s* me⟩ **4** : ENGAGE, OCCUPY ⟨he ~*s* himself with trivia⟩ ~ *vi, obs* : to be of importance : MATTER

[2]**concern** *n* **1** : something that relates or belongs to one : AFFAIR **2** : matter for consideration **3 a** : marked interest or regard usu. arising through a personal tie or relationship **b** : an uneasy state of blended interest, uncertainty, and apprehension **4** : an organization or establishment for business or manufacture **5** : CONTRIVANCE, GADGET ***syn*** see CARE ***ant*** unconcern

con·cerned *adj* **1** : DISTURBED, ANXIOUS ⟨~ for his safety⟩ **2 a** : interestedly engaged ⟨~ with books and music⟩ **b** : culpably involved : IMPLICATED ⟨arrested all ~⟩

con·cern·ing *prep* : relating to : REGARDING

con·cern·ment \kən-ˈsərn-mənt\ *n* **1** : something in which one is concerned **2** : IMPORTANCE, CONSEQUENCE **3** *archaic* : INVOLVEMENT, PARTICIPATION **4** : SOLICITUDE, ANXIETY

[1]**con·cert** \kən-ˈsərt\ *vb* [MF *concerter,* fr. OIt *concertare,* fr. LL, fr. L, to contend, fr. *com-* + *certare* to strive, fr. *certus* decided, determined — more at CERTAIN] *vt* **1** : to settle or adjust by conferring and reaching an agreement ⟨got together to ~ their differences⟩ **2** : to make a plan for ⟨~ measures for aiding the poor⟩ ~ *vi* : to act in harmony or conjunction ***syn*** see NEGOTIATE

[2]**con·cert** \ˈkän(t)-sərt, ˈkän-ˌsərt\ *n* [F, fr. It *concerto,* fr. *concertare*] **1 a** : agreement in design or plan : union formed by mutual communication of opinion and views **b** : a concerted action ⟨the sacrifice was hailed with a ~ of praise⟩ **2** : musical harmony : CONCORD **3** : a public performance of music or dancing; *esp* : a performance usu. by a group of musicians (as a chorus, band, or orchestra) that is made up of several individual compositions not joined in an integrated whole — compare BALLET, OPERA — **in concert** : TOGETHER ⟨he worked *in concert* with others⟩

con·cert·ed \kən-ˈsərt-əd\ *adj* **1 a** : mutually contrived or agreed on ⟨a ~ effort⟩ **b** : performed in unison ⟨~ artillery fire⟩ **2** : arranged in parts for several voices or instruments — **con·cert·ed·ly** *adv* — **con·cert·ed·ness** *n*

con·cert·go·er \ˈkän(t)-sərt-ˌgō(-ə)r, ˈkän-ˌsərt-\ *n* : one who frequently attends concerts

concert grand \ˌkän(t)-sərt-, ˌkän-ˌsərt-\ *n* : a grand piano of the largest size adapted in volume, timbre, and brilliance of tone to concert use

con·cer·ti·na \ˌkän(t)-sər-ˈtē-nə\ *n* **1** : a musical instrument of the accordion family **2** : a coiled barbed wire for use as an obstacle

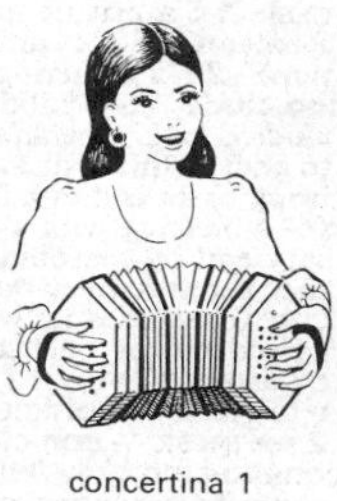
concertina 1

con·cer·ti·no \ˌkän-chər-ˈtē-(ˌ)nō\ *n, pl* **-nos** [It, dim. of *concerto*] **1** : the solo instruments in a concerto grosso **2** : a short concerto

con·cert·ize \ˈkän(t)-sər-ˌtīz\ *vi* **-ized; -iz·ing** : to perform professionally in concerts

con·cert·mas·ter \ˈkän(t)-sərt-ˌmas-tər\ *or* **con·cert·meis·ter** \-ˌmī-stər\ *n* [G *konzertmeister,* fr. *konzert* concert + *meister* master] : the leader of the first violins of an orchestra and by custom usu. the assistant to the conductor

con·cer·to \kən-ˈchert-(ˌ)ō\ *n, pl* **-ti** \-(ˌ)ē\ *or* **-tos** [It, fr. *concerto* concert] : a piece for one or more soloists and orchestra usu. in symphonic form with three contrasting movements

concerto gros·so \-ˈgrō-(ˌ)sō\ *n, pl* **concerti gros·si** \-(ˌ)sē\ [It, lit., big concerto] : a baroque orchestral composition featuring a small group of solo instruments contrasting with the full orchestra

concert pitch *n* **1** *archaic* : a tuning standard for use in a concert **2** : a high state of fitness, tension, or readiness

con·ces·sion \kən-ˈsesh-ən\ *n* [F or L; F, fr. L *concession-, concessio,* fr. *concessus,* pp. of *concedere* to concede] **1 a** : the act or an instance of conceding **b** : the admitting of a point claimed in argument **2** : something conceded: **a** : ACKNOWLEDGMENT, ADMISSION **b** : GRANT **c** (1) : a grant of land or property esp. by a government in return for services or for a particular use (2) : a right to undertake and profit by a specified activity (3) : a lease of a portion of premises for a particular purpose; *also* : the portion leased or the activities carried on — **con·ces·sion·al** \-ˈsesh-nəl, -ən-ᵊl\ *adj* — **con·ces·sion·ary** \-ˈsesh-ə-ˌner-ē\ *adj*

con·ces·sion·aire \kən-ˌsesh-ə-ˈna(ə)r, -ˈne(ə)r\ *n* [F *concessionnaire,* fr. *concession*] : the owner or operator of a concession; *esp* : one that operates a refreshment stand at a recreational center

con·ces·sion·er \kən-ˈsesh-(ə-)nər\ *n* : CONCESSIONAIRE

con·ces·sive \kən-ˈses-iv\ *adj* **1** : making for or being a concession **2** : denoting concession ⟨a ~ clause⟩ — **con·ces·sive·ly** *adv*

[1]**conch** \ˈkäŋk, ˈkänch, ˈkȯŋk\ *n, pl* **conchs** \ˈkäŋks, ˈkȯŋks\ *or* **conch·es** \ˈkän-chəz\ [L *concha* mussel, mussel shell, fr. Gk *konchē;* akin to Skt *śaṅkha* conch shell] **1** : any of various large spiral-shelled marine gastropod mollusks (as of the genera *Strombus* and *Cassis*); *also* : its shell used esp. for cameos **2** : CONCHA 2

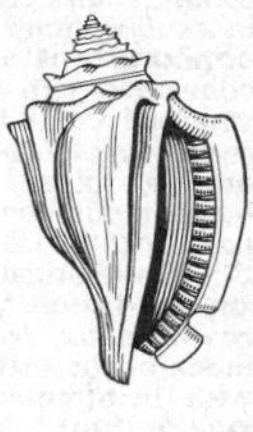
conch 1

[2]**conch** *or* **conchol** *abbr* conchology

conch- *or* **concho-** *comb form* [Gk *konch-, koncho-,* fr. *konchē*] : shell ⟨*conch*ology⟩ ⟨*conch*iolin⟩

con·cha \ˈkäŋ-kə\ *n, pl* **con·chae** \-ˌkē, -ˌkī\ [It & L; It *conca* semidome, apse, fr. LL *concha,* fr. L, shell] **1 a** : the plain semidome of an apse **b** : APSE **2** : something shaped like a shell; *esp* : the largest and deepest concavity of the external ear — **con·chal** \-kəl\ *adj*

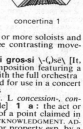

con·chi·o·lin \käŋ-ˈkī-ə-lən, kän-\ *n* [*conch-* + *-i-* + *-ol* + *-in*] : a scleroprotein forming the organic basis of mollusk shells

con·choi·dal \käŋ-ˈkȯid-ᵊl, kän-\ *adj* [Gk *konchoeidēs* like a mussel, fr. *konchē*] : having elevations or depressions shaped like the inside surface of a bivalve shell — **con·choi·dal·ly** \-ᵊl-ē\ *adv*

con·chol·o·gy \käŋ-ˈkäl-ə-jē\ *n* **1** : a branch of zoology that deals with shells **2** : a treatise on shells — **con·chol·o·gist** \-jəst\ *n*

con·cierge \kōⁿ-ˈsyerzh\ *n, pl* **con·cierges** \-ˈsyerzh(-əz)\ [F, modif. of L *conservus* fellow slave, fr. *com-* + *servus* slave] **1** : a resident in an apartment building esp. in France who serves as doorkeeper, landlord's representative, and janitor **2** : a usu. multilingual hotel staff member esp. in Europe who handles luggage and mail, makes reservations, and arranges tours for the guests

con·cil·i·ar \kən-ˈsil-ē-ər\ *adj* [L *concilium* council] : of, relating to, or issued by a council — **con·cil·i·ar·ly** *adv*

con·cil·i·ate \kən-ˈsil-ē-ˌāt\ *vb* **-at·ed; -at·ing** [L *conciliatus,* pp. of *conciliare* to assemble, unite, win over, fr. *concilium* assembly, council — more at COUNCIL] *vt* **1** : to gain (as goodwill) by pleasing acts **2** : to make compatible : RECONCILE **3** : APPEASE ~ *vi* : to become friendly or agreeable — **con·cil·i·a·tion** \-ˌsil-ē-ˈā-shən\ *n* — **con·cil·i·a·tive** \-ˈsil-ē-ˌāt-iv\ *adj* — **con·cil·i·a·tor** \-ˌāt-ər\ *n* — **con·cil·ia·to·ry** \-ˈsil-yə-ˌtōr-ē, -ˈsil-ē-ə-, -ˌtȯr-\ *adj*

con·cin·ni·ty \kən-ˈsin-ət-ē\ *n, pl* **-ties** [L *concinnitas,* fr. *concinnus* skillfully put together] : harmony and often elegance of design esp. of literary style in adaptation of parts to a whole or to each other

con·cise \kən-ˈsīs\ *adj* [L *concisus,* fr. pp. of *concidere* to cut up, fr. *com-* + *caedere* to cut, strike; akin to MHG *heie* mallet, Arm *xaitʻ* to prick] **1** : marked by brevity of expression or statement : free

from all elaboration and superfluous detail **2** : cut short : BRIEF — **con·cise·ly** *adv* — **con·cise·ness** *n*
syn CONCISE, TERSE, SUCCINCT, LACONIC, SUMMARY, PITHY, COMPENDIOUS *shared meaning element* : very brief in statement or expression ***ant*** redundant
con·ci·sion \kən-ˈsizh-ən\ *n* [ME, fr. L *concision-, concisio*, fr. *concisus*, pp.] **1** *archaic* : a cutting up or off **2** : the quality or state of being concise ⟨the commentary is exemplary in its ~ and lucidity⟩
con·clave \ˈkän-ˌklāv\ *n* [ME, fr. MF or ML; MF, fr. ML, fr. L, room that can be locked up, fr. *com-* + *clavis* key — more at CLAVICLE] **1** : a private meeting or secret assembly; *esp* : a meeting of Roman Catholic cardinals secluded continuously while choosing a pope **2** : a gathering of a group or association : CONVENTION
con·clude \kən-ˈklüd\ *vb* **con·clud·ed; con·clud·ing** [ME *concluden*, fr. L *concludere* to shut up, end, infer, fr. *com-* + *claudere* to shut — more at CLOSE] *vt* **1** *obs* : to shut up : ENCLOSE **2** : to bring to an end esp. in a particular way or with a particular action ⟨~ a meeting with a prayer⟩ **3 a** : to reach as a logically necessary end by reasoning : infer on the basis of evidence ⟨*concluded* that her argument was sound⟩ **b** : to make a decision about : DECIDE ⟨*concluded* he would wait a little longer⟩ **c** : to come to an agreement on : EFFECT ⟨~ a sale⟩ **4** : to bring about as a result : COMPLETE ~ *vi* **1** : END **2 a** : to form a final judgment **b** : to reach a decision or agreement ***syn* 1** see CLOSE ***ant*** open **2** see INFER — **con·clud·er** *n*
con·clu·sion \kən-ˈklü-zhən\ *n* [ME, fr. MF, fr. L *conclusion-, conclusio*, fr. *conclusus*, pp. of *concludere*] **1 a** : a reasoned judgment : INFERENCE **b** : the necessary consequence of two or more propositions taken as premises; *esp* : the inferred proposition of a syllogism **2** : the last part of something: as **a** : RESULT, OUTCOME **b** *pl* : trial of strength or skill — used in the phrase *try conclusions* **c** : a final summation **d** : the final decision in a law case **e** : the final part of a pleading in law **3** : an act or instance of concluding
con·clu·sive \-ˈklü-siv, -ziv\ *adj* **1** : of or relating to a conclusion **2** : putting an end to debate or question esp. by reason of irrefutability — **con·clu·sive·ly** *adv* — **con·clu·sive·ness** *n*
syn CONCLUSIVE, DECISIVE, DETERMINATIVE, DEFINITIVE *shared meaning element* : bringing to an end ***ant*** inconclusive
concn *abbr* concentration
con·coct \kən-ˈkäkt, kän-\ *vt* [L *concoctus*, pp. of *concoquere* to cook together, fr. *com-* + *coquere* to cook] **1** : to prepare by combining crude materials **2** : DEVISE, FABRICATE — **con·coct·er** *n* — **con·coc·tion** \-ˈkäk-shən\ *n* — **con·coc·tive** \-ˈkäk-tiv\ *adj*
con·com·i·tance \kən-ˈkäm-ət-ən(t)s, kän-\ *n* **1** : ACCOMPANIMENT; *esp* : a conjunction that is regular and is marked by correlative variation of accompanying elements ⟨there is a parallelism, or ~, between the mental and physical states: in this sense the body is the material expression of the soul —Frank Thilly⟩ **2** : CONCOMITANT
¹con·com·i·tant \-ət-ənt\ *adj* [L *concomitant-, concomitans*, prp. of *concomitari* to accompany, fr. *com-* + *comitari* to accompany, fr. *comit-, comes* companion — more at COUNT] : accompanying esp. in a subordinate or incidental way — **con·com·i·tant·ly** *adv*
²concomitant *n* : something that accompanies or is collaterally connected with something else : ACCOMPANIMENT
con·cord \ˈkän-ˌkȯ(ə)rd, ˈkäŋ-\ *n* [ME, fr. OF *concorde*, fr. L *concordia*, fr. *concord-, concors* agreeing, fr. *com-* + *cord-, cor* heart — more at HEART] **1 a** : a state of agreement : HARMONY **b** : a harmonious combination of simultaneously heard tones — compare DISCORD **2** : agreement by stipulation, compact, or covenant **3** : grammatical agreement
con·cor·dance \kən-ˈkȯrd-ᵊn(t)s, kän-\ *n* [ME, fr. MF, fr. ML *concordantia*, fr. L *concordant-, concordans*] **1** : an alphabetical index of the principal words in a book or the works of an author with their immediate contexts **2** : CONCORD, AGREEMENT
con·cor·dant \-ᵊnt\ *adj* [ME, fr. MF, fr. L *concordant-, concordans*, prp. of *concordare* to agree, fr. *concord-, concors*] : CONSONANT, AGREEING — **con·cor·dant·ly** *adv*
con·cor·dat \kən-ˈkȯr-ˌdat\ *n* [F, fr. ML *concordatum*, fr. L, neut. of *concordatus*, pp. of *concordare*] : COMPACT, COVENANT; *specif* : an agreement between a pope and a sovereign or government for the regulation of ecclesiastical matters
con·cours d'e·le·gance \(ˌ)kōⁿ-ˌkü(ə)r-ˌdā-lā-ˈgäⁿs\ *n* [F *concours d'élégance*, lit., competition of elegance] : a show or contest of vehicles and accessories in which the entries are judged chiefly on excellence of appearance and turnout
con·course \ˈkän-ˌkō(ə)rs, ˈkäŋ-, -ˌkȯ(ə)rs\ *n* [ME, fr. MF & L; MF *concours*, fr. L *concursus*, fr. *concursus*, pp. of *concurrere* to run together — more at CONCUR] **1** : an act or process of coming together and merging **2** : a meeting produced by voluntary or spontaneous coming together **3 a** : an open space where roads or paths meet **b** : an open space or hall (as in a railroad terminal) where crowds gather ***syn*** see JUNCTION
con·cres·cence \kən-ˈkres-ᵊn(t)s, kän-\ *n* [L *concrescentia*, fr. *concrescent-, concrescens*, prp. of *concrescere*] **1** : increase by the addition of particles **2** : a growing together : COALESCENCE; *esp* : convergence and fusion of the lateral lips of the blastopore to form the primordium of an embryo — **con·cres·cent** \-ᵊnt\ *adj*
¹con·crete \kän-ˈkrēt, ˈkän-ˌ\ *adj* [ME, fr. L *concretus*, fr. pp. of *concrescere* to grow together, fr. *com-* + *crescere* to grow — more at CRESCENT] **1** : formed by coalition of particles into one solid mass **2** : naming a real thing or class of things ⟨the word *poem* is ~, *poetry* is abstract⟩ **3 a** : characterized by or belonging to immediate experience of actual things or events **b** : SPECIFIC, PARTICULAR **c** : REAL, TANGIBLE **4** : relating to or made of concrete — **con·crete·ly** *adv* — **con·crete·ness** *n*
²con·crete \ˈkän-ˌkrēt, kän-ˈ\ *n* **1** : a mass formed by concretion or coalescence of separate particles of matter in one body **2** : a hard strong building material made by mixing a cementing material (as portland cement) and a mineral aggregate (as sand and gravel) with sufficient water to cause the cement to set and bind the entire mass **3** : a waxy essence of flowers prepared by extraction and evaporation and used in perfumery
³con·crete \ˈkän-ˌkrēt, kän-ˈ\ *vb* **con·cret·ed; con·cret·ing** *vt* **1 a** : to form into a solid mass : SOLIDIFY **b** : COMBINE, BLEND ⟨art *concreted* with nature to produce a gracious whole⟩ **2** : to make actual or real : cause to take on the qualities of reality **3** : to cover with, form of, or set in concrete ~ *vi* : to become concreted
concrete music *n* : MUSIQUE CONCRÈTE
concrete poetry *n* : poetry in which the poet's intent is conveyed by the graphic patterns of letters, words, or symbols rather than by the conventional arrangement of words
con·cre·tion \kän-ˈkrē-shən, kən-\ *n* **1** : the act or process of concreting : the state of being concreted ⟨~ of ideas in an hypothesis⟩ **2** : something concreted: as **a** : a hard usu. inorganic mass (as a bezoar or tophus) formed in a living body **b** : a mass of mineral matter found generally in rock of a composition different from its own and produced by deposition from aqueous solution in the rock — **con·cre·tion·ary** \-shə-ˌner-ē\ *adj*
con·cret·ism \kän-ˈkrēt-ˌiz-əm, ˈkän-ˌ\ *n* : representation of abstract things as concrete; *esp* : the theory or practice of emphasizing graphic rather than linguistic effects in poetry — **con·cret·ist** \-ˈkrēt-əst, -ˌkrēt-\ *n*
con·cret·ize \-ˌīz\ *vb* **-ized; -iz·ing** *vt* : to make concrete, specific, or definite ⟨tried to ~ his ideas⟩ ~ *vi* : to become concrete — **con·cret·i·za·tion** \(ˌ)kän-ˌkrēt-ə-ˈzā-shən\ *n*
con·cu·bi·nage \kän-ˈkyü-bə-nij, kən-\ *n* **1** : cohabitation of persons not legally married **2** : the state of being a concubine
con·cu·bine \ˈkäŋ-kyu̇-ˌbīn, ˈkän-\ *n* [ME, fr. OF, fr. L *concubina*, fr. *com-* + *cubare* to lie — more at HIP] **1** : a woman living in a socially recognized state of concubinage **2** : MISTRESS
con·cu·pis·cence \kän-ˈkyü-pə-sən(t)s, kən-\ *n* [ME, fr. MF, fr. LL *concupiscentia*, fr. L *concupiscent-, concupiscens*, prp. of *concupiscere* to desire ardently, fr. *com-* + *cupere* to desire — more at COVET] : strong desire; *esp* : sexual desire — **con·cu·pis·cent** \-sənt\ *adj*
con·cu·pis·ci·ble \-ˈkyü-pə-sə-bəl\ *adj* [ME, fr. MF or LL; MF, fr. LL *concupiscibilis*, fr. L *concupiscere*] : motivated by concupiscence : LUSTFUL
con·cur \kən-ˈkər, kän-\ *vi* **con·curred; con·cur·ring** [ME *concurren*, fr. L *concurrere*, fr. *com-* + *currere* to run] **1** *obs* : to come together : MEET **2** : to happen together : COINCIDE **3** : to act together to a common end or single effect **4 a** : APPROVE ⟨~ in a statement⟩ **b** : to express agreement ⟨~ with an opinion⟩ ***syn*** see AGREE ***ant*** contend, altercate
con·cur·rence \-ˈkər-ən(t)s, -ˈkə-rən(t)s\ *n* **1 a** : agreement or union in action : COOPERATION **b** (1) : agreement in opinion or design (2) : CONSENT **2** : a coming together : CONJUNCTION **3** : a coincidence of equal powers in law
con·cur·rent \-ˈkər-ənt, -ˈkə-rənt\ *adj* [ME, fr. MF & L; MF, fr. L *concurrent-, concurrens*, prp. of *concurrere*] **1 a** : CONVERGENT; *specif* : meeting or intersecting in a point **b** : running parallel **2** : operating or occurring at the same time **3** : acting in conjunction **4** : exercised over the same matter or area by two different authorities ⟨~ jurisdiction⟩ — **concurrent** *n* — **con·cur·rent·ly** *adv*
concurrent resolution *n* : a resolution passed by both houses of a legislative body that lacks the force of law
con·cuss \kən-ˈkəs\ *vt* [L *concussus*, pp.] : to affect with concussion
con·cus·sion \kən-ˈkəsh-ən\ *n* [MF or L; MF, fr. L *concussion-, concussio*, fr. *concussus*, pp. of *concutere* to shake violently, fr. *com-* + *quatere* to shake] **1** : AGITATION, SHAKING **2 a** : a hard blow or collision **b** : a stunning, damaging, or shattering effect from a hard blow; *esp* : a jarring injury of the brain resulting in disturbance of cerebral function — **con·cus·sive** \-ˈkəs-iv\ *adj* — **con·cus·sive·ly** *adv*
cond *abbr* conductivity
con·demn \kən-ˈdem\ *vt* [ME *condemnen*, fr. OF *condemner*, fr. L *condemnare*, fr. *com-* + *damnare* to condemn — more at DAMN] **1** : to declare to be reprehensible, wrong, or evil usu. after weighing evidence and without reservation **2 a** : to pronounce guilty : CONVICT **b** : SENTENCE, DOOM **3** : to adjudge unfit for use or consumption **4** : to declare convertible to public use under the right of eminent domain ***syn*** see CRITICIZE — **con·dem·nable** \-ˈdem-(n)ə-bəl\ *adj* — **con·dem·na·tory** \-nə-ˌtōr-ē, -ˌtȯr-\ *adj* — **con·demn·er** \-ˈdem-ər\ *or* **con·dem·nor** \kən-ˈdem-ər; kən-ˌdem-ˈnȯ(ə)r, ˌkän-\ *n*
con·dem·na·tion \ˌkän-ˌdem-ˈnā-shən, -dəm-\ *n* **1** : CENSURE, BLAME **2** : the act of judicially condemning **3** : the state of being condemned **4** : a reason for condemning
con·den·sate \ˈkän-dən-ˌsāt, -ˌden-; kən-ˈden-\ *n* : a product of condensation; *esp* : a liquid obtained by condensation of a gas or vapor ⟨steam ~⟩
con·den·sa·tion \ˌkän-ˌden-ˈsā-shən, -dən-\ *n* **1** : the act or process of condensing: as **a** : a chemical reaction involving union between molecules often with elimination of a simple molecule (as water) to form a new more complex compound of often greater molecular weight **b** : a reduction to a denser form (as from steam to water) **c** : compression of a written or spoken work into more concise form **2** : the quality or state of being condensed **3** : a product of condensing; *specif* : an abridgment of a literary work — **con·den·sa·tion·al** \-shnəl, -shən-ᵊl\ *adj*
con·dense \kən-ˈden(t)s\ *vb* **con·densed; con·dens·ing** [ME *condensen*, fr. MF *condenser*, fr. L *condensare*, fr. *com-* + *densare* to make dense, fr. *densus* dense] *vt* : to make denser or more compact; *esp* : to subject to condensation ~ *vi* : to undergo condensation ***syn*** see CONTRACT ***ant*** amplify *(as a speech)* — **con·dens·able** *also* **con·dens·ible** \-ˈden(t)-sə-bəl\ *adj*
con·densed *adj* : reduced to a more compact form; *specif* : having a face that is narrower than that of a typeface not so characterized
condensed milk *n* : evaporated milk with sugar added
con·dens·er \kən-ˈden(t)-sər\ *n* **1** : one that condenses: as **a** : a lens or mirror used to concentrate light on an object **b** : an apparatus in which gas or vapor is condensed **2** : CAPACITOR
con·de·scend \ˌkän-di-ˈsend\ *vi* [ME *condescenden*, fr. MF *condescendre*, fr. LL *condescendere*, fr. L *com-* + *descendere* to descend] **1 a** : to descend to a less formal or dignified level : UNBEND **b**

: to waive the privileges of rank **2** : to assume an air of superiority **syn** see STOOP
con·de·scen·dence \-'sen-dən(t)s\ *n* : CONDESCENSION
con·de·scend·ing *adj* : showing or characterized by condescension : PATRONIZING — **con·de·scend·ing·ly** \-'sen-diŋ-lē\ *adv*
con·de·scen·sion \ˌkän-di-'sen-chən\ *n* [LL *condescension-, condescensio*, fr. *condescensus*, pp. of *condescendere*] **1** : voluntary descent from one's rank or dignity in relations with an inferior **2** : a patronizing attitude
con·dign \kən-'dīn, 'kän-,\ *adj* [ME *condigne*, fr. MF, fr. L *condignus* very worthy, fr. *com-* + *dignus* worthy — more at DECENT] : DESERVED, APPROPRIATE ⟨∼ *punishment*⟩ — **con·dign·ly** *adv*
con·di·ment \'kän-də-mənt\ *n* [ME, fr. MF, fr. L *condimentum*, fr. *condire* to pickle, fr. *condere* to build, store up, fr. *com-* + *-dere* to put — more at DO] : something used to enhance the flavor of food; *esp* : a pungent seasoning — **con·di·men·tal** \ˌkän-də-'ment-ᵊl\ *adj*
¹con·di·tion \kən-'dish-ən\ *n* [ME *condicion*, fr. MF, fr. L *condicion-, condicio* terms of agreement, condition, fr. *condicere* to agree, fr. *com-* + *dicere* to say, determine — more at DICTION] **1 a** : a premise upon which the fulfillment of an agreement depends : STIPULATION **b** *obs* : COVENANT **c** : a provision making the effect of a legal instrument contingent upon an uncertain event; *also* : the event itself **2** : something essential to the appearance or occurrence of something else : PREREQUISITE: as **a** : an environmental requirement ⟨available oxygen is an essential ∼ for animal life⟩ **b** : the subordinate clause of a conditional sentence **3 a** : a restricting or modifying factor : QUALIFICATION **b** : a state of affairs that hampers or impedes or requires correction ⟨delayed by the ∼ of the road⟩ **c** : an unsatisfactory academic grade that may be raised by doing additional work **4 a** : a state of being **b** : social status : RANK **c** : a usu. defective state of health ⟨a serious heart ∼⟩ **d** : a state of physical fitness or readiness for use ⟨the car was in good ∼⟩ ⟨exercising to get into ∼⟩ **e** *pl* : attendant circumstances **5 a** *obs* : temper of mind **b** *obs* : TRAIT **c** *pl, archaic* : MANNERS, WAYS **syn** see STATE
²condition *vb* **con·di·tioned; con·di·tion·ing** \-'dish-(ə-)niŋ\ *vi, archaic* : to make stipulations ∼ *vt* **1** : to agree by stipulating **2** : to make conditional **3 a** : to put into a proper state for work or use **b** : AIR-CONDITION **4** : to give a grade of condition to **5 a** : to adapt, modify, or mold so as to conform to an environing culture **b** : to modify so that an act or response previously associated with one stimulus becomes associated with another **syn** see PREPARE — **con·di·tion·able** \-(ə-)nə-bəl\ *adj* — **con·di·tion·er** \-(ə-)nər\ *n*
con·di·tion·al \kən-'dish-nəl, -ən-ᵊl\ *adj* **1** : subject to, implying, or dependent upon a condition ⟨a ∼ promise⟩ **2** : expressing, containing, or implying a supposition ⟨the ∼ clause *if he speaks*⟩ **3 a** : true only for certain values of the variables or symbols involved ⟨∼ equations⟩ **b** : stating the case when one or more random variables are fixed or one or more events are known ⟨∼ frequency distribution⟩ **4 a** : CONDITIONED 3 ⟨∼ reflex⟩ **b** : response⟩ **b** : established by conditioning as the stimulus eliciting a conditional response — **conditional** *n* — **con·di·tion·al·i·ty** \-ˌdish-ə-'nal-ət-ē\ *n* — **con·di·tion·al·ly** \-'dish-nə-lē, -ən-ᵊl-ē\ *adv*
conditional probability *n* : the probability that a given event will occur if it is certain that another event has taken place or will take place
con·di·tioned *adj* **1** : CONDITIONAL **2** : brought or put into a specified state **3** : determined or established by conditioning
con·dole \kən-'dōl\ *vb* **con·doled; con·dol·ing** [LL *condolēre*, fr. L *com-* + *dolēre* to feel pain; akin to Gk *daidalos* ingeniously formed] *vi* **1** *obs* : GRIEVE **2** : to express sympathetic sorrow ⟨we ∼ with you in your misfortune⟩ ∼ *vt, archaic* : LAMENT, GRIEVE — **con·do·la·to·ry** \-'dō-lə-ˌtōr-ē, -ˌtór-\ *adj*
con·do·lence \kən-'dō-lən(t)s, 'kän-də-\ *n* **1** : sympathy with another in sorrow **2** : an expression of sympathy
con·dom \'kən-dəm, 'kän-\ *n* [origin unknown] : a sheath commonly of rubber worn over the penis (as to prevent conception or venereal infection during coitus)
con·do·min·i·um \ˌkän-də-'min-ē-əm\ *n, pl* **-ums** [NL, fr. L *com-* + *dominium* domain] **1 a** : joint dominion; *esp* : joint sovereignty by two or more nations **b** : a government operating under joint rule **2** : a politically dependent territory under condominium **3 a** : individual ownership of a unit in a multi-unit structure (as an apartment building); *also* : a unit so owned **b** : a building containing condominiums — **con·do·min·i·al** \-ē-əl\ *adj*
con·do·na·tion \ˌkän-də-'nā-shən, -dō-\ *n* : implied pardon of an offense by treating the offender as if it had not been committed
con·done \kən-'dōn\ *vt* **con·doned; con·don·ing** [L *condonare* to forgive, fr. *com-* + *donare* to give — more at DONATE] : to pardon or overlook voluntarily; *esp* : to treat as if trivial, harmless, or of no importance ⟨∼ corruption in politics⟩ **syn** see EXCUSE — **con·don·able** \-'dō-nə-bəl\ *adj* — **con·don·er** *n*
con·dor \'kän-dər, -ˌdò(ə)r\ *n* [Sp *cóndor*, fr. Quechua *kúntur*] **1** : a very large American vulture (*Vultur gryphus*) of the high Andes having the head and neck bare and the plumage dull black with a downy white neck ruff and white patches on the wings — compare CALIFORNIA CONDOR **2** *pl* **condors** *or* **con·do·res** \kän-'dōr-ˌās, -'dòr-\ : a coin (as the centesimo of Chile) bearing the picture of a condor
con·dot·tie·re \ˌkän-də-'tye(ə)r-ē, ˌkän-ˌdät-ē-'e(ə)r-\ *n, pl* **-tie·ri** \-ē\ [It *condottiere*] **1** : a leader of a band of mercenaries common in Europe between the 14th and 16th centuries; *also* : a member of such a band **2** : a mercenary soldier
con·duce \kən-'d(y)üs\ *vi* **con·duced; con·duc·ing** [ME *conducen* to conduct, fr. L *conducere* to conduct, conduce, fr. *com-* + *ducere* to lead — more at TOW] : to lead or tend to a particular and usu. desirable result : CONTRIBUTE
syn CONDUCE, CONTRIBUTE, REDOUND *shared meaning element* : to lead to an end **ant** ward off
con·du·cive \-'d(y)ü-siv\ *adj* : tending to promote or assist : CONTRIBUTIVE ⟨an atmosphere ∼ to education⟩ — **con·du·cive·ness** *n*
¹con·duct \'kän-(ˌ)dəkt\ *n* [alter. of ME *conduit*, fr. OF, act of leading, escort, fr. ML *conductus*, fr. L *conductus*, pp. of *conducere*] **1**

obs : ESCORT, GUIDE **2** : the act, manner, or process of carrying on : MANAGEMENT **3** : a mode or standard of personal behavior esp. as based on moral principles
²con·duct \kən-'dəkt\ *vt* **1** : to bring by or as if by leading : GUIDE ⟨∼ tourists through a museum⟩ **2** : to carry on or out usu. from a position of command or control ⟨∼ a siege⟩ ⟨∼ an experiment⟩ **3** : to convey in a channel **b** : to act as a medium for conveying **4** : to act or behave in a particular and esp. in a controlled or directed manner ∼ *vi* **1** *of a road or passage* : to show the way : LEAD **2 a** : to act as leader or director **b** : to have the quality of transmitting light, heat, sound, or electricity — **con·duct·ibil·i·ty** \kən-ˌdək-tə-'bil-ət-ē\ *n* — **con·duct·ible** \-'dək-tə-bəl\ *adj*
syn 1 CONDUCT, MANAGE, CONTROL, DIRECT *shared meaning element* : to use one's powers to lead, guide, or dominate **2** see BEHAVE
con·duc·tance \kən-'dək-tən(t)s\ *n* **1** : conducting power **2 a** : the readiness with which a conductor transmits an electric current **b** : the reciprocal of electrical resistance
con·duc·tion \kən-'dək-shən\ *n* **1** : the act of conducting or conveying **2** : transmission through or by means of a conductor; *also* : CONDUCTIVITY **3** : the transmission of excitation through living tissue and esp. nervous tissue
con·duc·tive \kən-'dək-tiv\ *adj* : having conductivity : relating to conduction (as of electricity)
con·duc·tiv·i·ty \ˌkän-ˌdək-'tiv-ət-ē, kən-\ *n, pl* **-ties** : the quality or power of conducting or transmitting: as **a** : the reciprocal of electrical resistivity **b** : the quality of living matter responsible for the transmission of and progressive reaction to stimuli
con·duc·to·met·ric *or* **con·duc·ti·met·ric** \kən-ˌdək-tə-'me-trik\ *adj* **1** : of or relating to the measurement of conductivity **2** : being or relating to titration based on determination of changes in the electrical conductivity of the solution
con·duc·tor \kən-'dək-tər\ *n* : one that conducts: as **a** : GUIDE **b** : a collector of fares in a public conveyance **c** : the leader of a musical ensemble **d** : a substance or body capable of transmitting electricity, heat, or sound — **con·duc·to·ri·al** \ˌkän-ˌdək-'tōr-ē-əl, kən-, -'tòr-\ *adj* — **con·duc·tress** \kən-'dək-trəs\ *n*
con·duit \'kän-ˌd(y)ü-ət *also* -d(w)ət\ *n* [ME, fr. MF, lit., act of leading] **1** : a natural or artificial channel through which something (as a fluid) is conveyed **2** *archaic* : FOUNTAIN **3** : a pipe, tube, or tile for protecting electric wires or cables
con·du·pli·cate \(')kän-'d(y)ü-pli-kət\ *adj* [L *conduplicatus*, pp. of *conduplicare* to double, fr. *com-* + *duplic-, duplex* double — more at DUPLEX] : folded lengthwise — used of leaves or petals in the bud — **con·du·pli·ca·tion** \ˌkän-ˌd(y)ü-pli-'kā-shən\ *n*
con·dy·lar \'kän-də-lər\ *adj* : of or relating to a condyle
con·dyle \'kän-ˌdil *also* -d°l\ *n* [F & L; F, fr. L, fr. Gk *kondylos* knuckle, fr. Gk *kondylos*] : an articular prominence of a bone; *esp* : one of a pair that resembles knuckles — **con·dy·loid** \-də-ˌlòid\ *adj*
con·dy·lo·ma \ˌkän-də-'lō-mə\ *n* [NL, fr. Gk *kondylōma*, fr. *kondylos*] : a warty growth on the skin or adjoining mucous membrane usu. near the anus and genital organs — **con·dy·lo·ma·tous** \-'mät-əs\ *adj*
¹cone \'kōn\ *n* [MF or L; MF, fr. L *conus*, fr. Gk *kōnos* — more at HONE] **1 a** : a mass of ovule-bearing or pollen-bearing scales or bracts in trees of the pine family or in cycads that are arranged usu. on a somewhat elongated axis **b** : any of several flower or fruit clusters suggesting a cone **2 a** : a solid generated by rotating a right triangle about one of its legs — called also *right circular cone* **b** : a solid bounded by a circular or other closed plane base and the surface formed by line segments joining every point of the boundary of the base to a common vertex — see VOLUME table **c** : a surface traced by a moving straight line passing through a fixed vertex **3** : something that resembles a cone in shape: as **a** : one of the short sensory end organs of the vertebrate retina that func-

condor 1

ə abut	ᵊ kitten	ər further	a back	ā bake	ä cot, cart
aú out	ch chin	e less	ē easy	g gift	i trip	ī life
j joke	ŋ sing	ō flow	ò flaw	òi coin	th thin	t̲h̲ this
ü loot	ú foot	y yet	yü few	yú furious	zh vision

tion in color vision **b :** any of numerous somewhat conical tropical gastropod mollusks (family Conidae) **c :** the apex of a volcano **d :** a crisp cone-shaped wafer for holding ice cream
[2]**cone** *vt* **coned; con·ing 1 :** to make cone-shaped **2 :** to bevel like the slanting surface of a cone ⟨~ a tire⟩
cone·flow·er \ˈkōn-ˌflau̇(-ə)r\ *n* **:** any of several composite plants having cone-shaped flower disks; *esp* **:** RUDBECKIA
cone·nose \ˈkōn-ˌnōz\ *n* **:** any of various large bloodsucking bugs (esp. genus *Triatoma*) including some capable of inflicting painful bites — called also *assassin bug, kissing bug*
con es·pres·sio·ne \ˌkän-ˌes-(ˌ)pres-ē-ˈō-nē, ˌkōn-, -ˈō-(ˌ)nā\ *adv* [It, lit., with expression] **:** with feeling — used as a direction in music

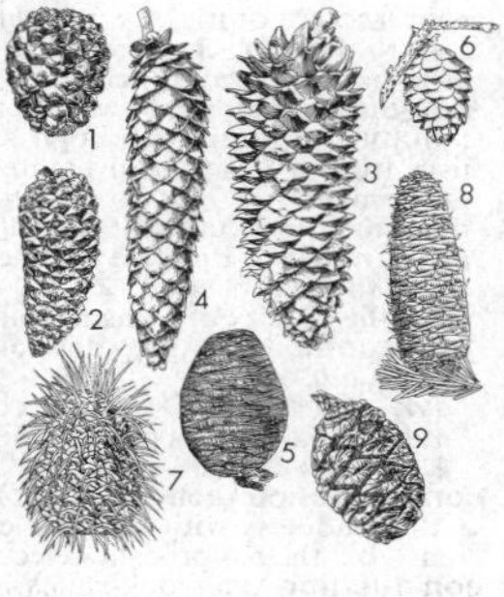

cones 1a: *1* stone pine, *2* cluster pine, *3* big-cone pine, *4* sugar pine, *5* deodar, *6* red spruce, *7* Santa Lucia fir, *8* Nordmann's fir, *9* giant sequoia

Con·es·to·ga \ˌkän-ə-ˈstō-gə\ *n* [*Conestoga,* Pa.] **:** a broad-wheeled covered wagon drawn usu. by six horses and used esp. for transporting freight across the prairies
co·ney \ˈkō-nē\ *n, pl* **coneys** [ME *conies,* pl., fr. OF *conis,* pl. of *conil,* fr. L *cuniculus*] **1 a** (1) **:** RABBIT; *esp* **:** the European rabbit (*Oryctolagus cuniculus*) (2) **:** PIKA **b :** HYRAX **c :** rabbit fur **2** *obs* **:** DUPE **3 :** any of several fishes; *esp* **:** a dusky black-spotted reddish-finned grouper (*Cephalopholis fulvus*) of the tropical Atlantic
conf *abbr* **1** conference **2** confidential
con·fab \kən-ˈfab, ˈkän-ˌ\ *vi* **con·fabbed; con·fab·bing :** CONFABULATE — **con·fab** \ˈkän-ˌfab, kən-ˈ\ *n*
con·fab·u·late \kən-ˈfab-yə-ˌlāt\ *vi* **-lat·ed; -lat·ing** [L *confabulatus,* pp. of *confabulari,* fr. *com-* + *fabulari* to talk, fr. *fabula* story — more at FABLE] **1 :** CHAT **2 :** to hold a discussion **:** CONFER — **con·fab·u·la·tion** \kən-ˌfab-yə-ˈlā-shən, ˌkän-\ *n* — **con·fab·u·la·tor** \kən-ˈfab-yə-ˌlāt-ər\ *n* — **con·fab·u·la·to·ry** \-lə-ˌtōr-ē, -ˌtȯr-\ *adj*
con·fect \kən-ˈfekt\ *vt* [L *confectus,* pp. of *conficere* to prepare — more at COMFIT] **1 :** to put together from varied material ⟨writers ~*ing* best sellers⟩ **2 a :** PREPARE **b :** PRESERVE — **con·fect** \ˈkän-ˌ\ *n*
con·fec·tion \kən-ˈfek-shən\ *n* **1 :** the act or process of confecting **2 :** something confected: as **a :** a fancy dish or sweetmeat **:** DELICACY; *esp* **:** a fruit or nut preserve **b :** a medicinal preparation usu. made with sugar, syrup, or honey **c :** a piece of fine craftsmanship
con·fec·tion·ary \-shə-ˌner-ē\ *n, pl* **-ar·ies 1** *archaic* **:** CONFECTIONER **2 :** CONFECTIONERY 3 **3 :** SWEETS — **confectionary** *adj*
con·fec·tion·er \-sh(ə-)nər\ *n* **:** a manufacturer of or dealer in confections
con·fec·tion·ery \-shə-ˌner-ē\ *n, pl* **-er·ies 1 :** sweet edibles (as candy or pastry) **2 :** the confectioner's art or business **3 :** a confectioner's shop
Confed *abbr* Confederate
con·fed·er·a·cy \kən-ˈfed-(ə-)rə-sē\ *n, pl* **-cies 1 :** a league or compact for mutual support or common action **:** ALLIANCE **2 :** a combination of persons for unlawful purposes **:** CONSPIRACY **3 :** the body formed by persons, states, or nations united by a league; *specif, cap* **:** the 11 southern states seceding from the U.S. in 1860 and 1861 — **con·fed·er·al** \-(ə-)rəl\ *adj* — **con·fed·er·al·ist** \-əst\ *n*
[1]**con·fed·er·ate** \kən-ˈfed-(ə-)rət\ *adj* [ME *confederat,* fr. LL *confoederatus,* pp. of *confoederare* to unite by a league, fr. L *com-* + *foeder-, foedus* compact — more at FEDERAL] **1 :** united in a league **:** ALLIED **2** *cap* **:** of or relating to the Confederate States of America
[2]**confederate** *n* **1 :** ALLY, ACCOMPLICE **2** *cap* **:** an adherent of the Confederate States of America or their cause
[3]**con·fed·er·ate** \-ˈfed-ə-ˌrāt\ *vb* **-at·ed; -at·ing** *vt* **:** to unite in a confederacy ~ *vi* **:** to band together — **con·fed·er·a·tive** \-ˈfed-(ə-)rət-iv, -ə-ˌrāt-\ *adj*
Confederate Memorial Day *n* **:** any of several days appointed for the commemoration of servicemen of the Confederacy: **a :** April 26 in Florida and Georgia **b :** the last Monday in April in Alabama and Mississippi **c :** May 10 in No. and So. Carolina **d :** the last Monday in May in Virginia **e :** June 3 in Kentucky, Louisiana, and Texas
confederate rose *n, often cap C* **:** a Chinese mallow (*Hibiscus mutabilis*) with white or pink flowers that become deep red at night
con·fed·er·a·tion \kən-ˌfed-ə-ˈrā-shən\ *n* **1 :** an act of confederating **:** a state of being confederated **:** ALLIANCE **2 :** LEAGUE
con·fer \kən-ˈfər\ *vb* **con·ferred; con·fer·ring** [L *conferre* to bring together, fr. *com-* + *ferre* to carry — more at BEAR] *vi* **1** *obs* **:** to call into comparison **2 :** to bestow from or as if from a position of superiority ⟨your trust ~*s* an honor on me⟩ ~ *vi* **:** to come together to compare views or take counsel **:** CONSULT ***syn*** see GIVE — **con·fer·ment** \-ˈfər-mənt\ *n* — **con·fer·ra·ble** \-ˈfər-ə-bəl\ *adj* — **con·fer·ral** \-ˈfər-əl\ *n* — **con·fer·rer** \-ˈfər-ər\ *n*
con·fer·ee \ˌkän-fə-ˈrē\ *n* **1 :** one conferred with **2 :** one on whom something (as a degree) is conferred
con·fer·ence \ˈkän-f(ə-)rən(t)s, -fərn(t)s, *for 2 usu* kən-ˈfər-ən(t)s\ *n* **1 a :** a usu. formal interchange of views **:** CONSULTATION **b :** a meeting of two or more persons for discussing matters of common concern **c :** a meeting of members of the two branches of a legislature to adjust differences **2** *also* **con·fer·rence** \kən-ˈfər-ən(t)s\ **:** BESTOWAL, CONFERMENT **3 a :** a representative assembly or administrative organization of a denomination **b :** a territorial division of a denomination **4 :** an association of athletic teams — **con·fer·en·tial** \ˌkän-fə-ˈren-chəl\ *adj*
con·fer·va \kən-ˈfər-və\ *n, pl* **-vae** \-(ˌ)vē, -ˌvī\ *also* **-vas** [L, a water plant, fr. *confervēre* to boil together, heal, fr. *com-* + *fervēre* to boil — more at BURN] **:** any of a genus (*Tribonema*) of filamentous freshwater yellow-green algae; *broadly* **:** any of various filamentous algae forming scums on still water — **con·fer·void** \-ˌvȯid\ *adj or n*
con·fess \kən-ˈfes\ *vb* [ME *confessen,* fr. MF *confesser,* fr. OF, fr. *confes* having confessed, fr. L *confessus,* pp. of *confitēri* to confess, fr. *com-* + *fatēri* to confess; akin to L *fari* to speak — more at BAN] *vt* **1 :** to tell or make known (as something wrong or damaging to oneself) **:** ADMIT **2 a :** to acknowledge (sin) to God or to a priest **b :** to receive the confession of (a penitent) **3 :** to declare faith in or adherence to **:** PROFESS **4 :** to give evidence of ~ *vi* **1 a :** to disclose one's faults; *specif* **:** to unburden one's sins or the state of one's conscience to God or to a priest **b :** to hear a confession **2 :** ADMIT, OWN ***syn*** see ACKNOWLEDGE — **con·fess·able** \-ə-bəl\ *adj*
con·fessed·ly \-ˈfes-əd-lē, -ˈfest-lē\ *adv* **:** by confession **:** ADMITTEDLY
con·fes·sion \kən-ˈfesh-ən\ *n* **1 :** an act of confessing; *specif* **:** a disclosure of one's sins in the sacrament of penance **2 :** a statement of what is confessed: as **a :** a written acknowledgment of guilt by a party accused of an offense **b :** a formal statement of religious beliefs **:** CREED **3 :** an organized religious body having a common creed — **con·fes·sion·al** \-ˈfesh-nəl, -ən-ᵊl\ *adj* — **con·fes·sion·al·ism** \-ˌiz-əm\ *n* — **con·fes·sion·al·ist** \-əst\ *n* — **con·fes·sion·al·ly** \-ē\ *adv*
confessional *n* **1 :** a place where a priest hears confessions **2 :** the practice of confessing to a priest
con·fes·sor \kən-ˈfes-ər *also (for 2 & 3)* ˈkän-ˌfes-ər *& (for 3)* ˈkän-fə-ˌsȯ(ə)r\ *n* **1 :** one that confesses **2 :** one who gives heroic evidence of faith but does not suffer martyrdom **3 a :** a priest who hears confessions **b :** a priest who is one's regular spiritual guide
con·fet·ti \kən-ˈfet-ē\ *n* [It, pl. of *confetto* sweetmeat, fr. ML *confectum,* fr. L, neut. of *confectus,* pp. of *conficere* to prepare] **:** small bits or streamers of brightly colored paper made for throwing (as at weddings)
con·fi·dant \ˈkän-fə-ˌdant, -ˌdänt, ˌkän-fə-ˈ\ *n* [F *confident,* fr. It *confidente,* fr. *confidente* confident, trustworthy, fr. L *confident-, confidens*] **:** one to whom secrets are entrusted; *esp* **:** INTIMATE
con·fi·dante *like* CONFIDANT\ *n* [F *confidente,* fem. of *confident*] **:** a female confidant
con·fide \kən-ˈfīd\ *vb* **con·fid·ed; con·fid·ing** [ME *confiden,* fr. MF or L; MF *confider,* fr. L *confidere,* fr. *com-* + *fidere* to trust — more at BIDE] *vi* **1 :** to have confidence **:** TRUST **2 :** to show confidence by imparting secrets ~ *vt* **1 :** to tell confidentially **2 :** ENTRUST ***syn*** see COMMIT — **con·fid·er** *n*
[1]**con·fi·dence** \ˈkän-fəd-ən(t)s, -fə-ˌden(t)s\ *n* **1 :** FAITH, TRUST ⟨their ~ in God's mercy⟩ **2 :** a feeling or consciousness of one's powers or of reliance on one's circumstances ⟨he had perfect ~ in his ability to succeed⟩ ⟨met the risk with brash ~⟩ **3 :** the quality or state of being certain **:** CERTITUDE ⟨they had every ~ of success⟩ **4 a :** a relation of trust or intimacy ⟨took his friend into his ~⟩ **b :** reliance on another's discretion ⟨their story was told in strictest ~⟩ **c :** legislative support ⟨vote of ~⟩ **5 :** a communication made in confidence **:** SECRET
syn CONFIDENCE, ASSURANCE, SELF-POSSESSION, APLOMB *shared meaning element* **:** a state of mind or a manner marked by easy coolness and freedom from uncertainty, diffidence, or embarrassment. CONFIDENCE stresses faith in oneself and one's powers without any suggestion of conceit or arrogance ⟨had the *confidence* that comes only from long experience⟩ ASSURANCE carries a stronger implication of certainty and may suggest arrogance or lack of objectivity in assessing one's own powers ⟨had a conceited *assurance* of his own worth⟩ SELF-POSSESSION implies an ease or coolness under stress that reflects perfect self-control and command of one's powers ⟨he answered the insolent question with complete *self-possession*⟩ APLOMB applies to the bearing or behavior under difficulties of a person with marked assurance or self-possession but usually carries none of the unpleasant connotations often felt in *assurance* ⟨meet a challenge with *aplomb*⟩ ***ant*** diffidence
[2]**confidence** *adj* **:** of or relating to swindling by false promises
confidence interval *n* **:** a group of continuous or discrete adjacent values that is used to estimate a statistical parameter (as a mean or variance) and that tends to include the true value of the parameter a predetermined proportion of the time if the process of finding the group of values is repeated a number of times
confidence limits *n pl* **:** the end points of a confidence interval
con·fi·dent \ˈkän-fəd-ənt, -fə-ˌdent\ *adj* [L *confident-, confidens,* fr. prp. of *confidere*] **1** *obs* **:** TRUSTFUL, CONFIDING **2 :** characterized by assurance; *esp* **:** SELF-RELIANT **3 a :** full of conviction **:** CERTAIN **b :** COCKSURE — **con·fi·dent·ly** *adv*
con·fi·den·tial \ˌkän-fə-ˈden-chəl\ *adj* **1 :** PRIVATE, SECRET **2 :** marked by intimacy or willingness to confide ⟨a ~ tone⟩ **3 :** entrusted with confidences ⟨~ clerk⟩ **4 :** containing information whose unauthorized disclosure could be prejudicial to the national interest — compare SECRET, TOP SECRET — **con·fi·den·ti·al·i·ty** \-ˌden-chē-ˈal-ət-ē\ *n* — **con·fi·den·tial·ly** \-ˈdench-(ə-)lē\ *adv* — **con·fi·den·tial·ness** \-ˈden-chəl-nəs\ *n*
con·fid·ing \kən-ˈfīd-iŋ\ *adj* **:** tending to confide **:** TRUSTFUL — **con·fid·ing·ly** \-iŋ-lē\ *adv* — **con·fid·ing·ness** *n*
con·fig·u·rat·ed \kən-ˈfig-(y)ə-ˌrāt-əd\ *adj* **:** having a patterned surface — used of glass or metal
con·fig·u·ra·tion \kən-ˌfig-(y)ə-ˈrā-shən, ˌkän-\ *n* [LL *configuration-, configuratio,* similar formation, fr. L *configuratus,* pp. of *configurare* to form from or after, fr. *com-* + *figurare* to form, fr. *figura* figure] **1 a :** relative arrangement of parts **b** (1) **:** something (as a figure, contour, pattern, or apparatus) produced by such arrangement (2) **:** a set of interconnected equipment forming a computer system **c :** the stable structural makeup of a chemical compound esp. with reference to the space relations of the

constituent atoms **2** : GESTALT ⟨personality ~⟩ ***syn*** see FORM — **con·fig·u·ra·tion·al** \-shnəl, -shən-ᵊl\ *adj* — **con·fig·u·ra·tion·al·ly** \-ē\ *adv* — **con·fig·u·ra·tive** \-ˈfig-(y)ə-rət-iv\ *adj*
con·fig·ure \kən-ˈfig-yər, *esp Brit* -ˈfig-ər\ *vt* **-ured; -ur·ing** : to give a configuration to : SHAPE ⟨a society *configured* by reliance on a few commodities —H. M. McLuhan⟩
¹con·fine \kən-ˈfīn\ *vb* **con·fined; con·fin·ing** *vi, archaic* : BORDER ~ *vt* **1** : to keep within limits : RESTRICT **2 a** : to shut up : IMPRISON **b** : to keep indoors ***syn*** see LIMIT — **con·fin·er** *n*
²con·fine \ˈkän-ˌfīn *also* kən-ˈ\ *n* [MF or L; MF *confines,* pl., fr. L *confine* border, fr. neut. of *confinis* adjacent, fr. *com-* + *finis* end] **1** *pl* **a** : BOUNDS, BORDERS ⟨in the ~*s* of the big city slums —J. B. Conant⟩ **b** : outlying parts : LIMITS ⟨feel more comfortable within the protective ~*s* of the system —Paul Potter⟩ **c** : TERRITORY ⟨the future of the city lies in the eastern corner of its ~*s* — *Springfield (Mass.) Daily News*⟩ **2 a** *archaic* : RESTRICTION **b** *obs* : PRISON
con·fined \kən-ˈfīnd\ *adj* **1** : kept within confines **2** : restricted to quarters; *esp* : undergoing childbirth
con·fine·ment \kən-ˈfīn-mənt\ *n* : an act of confining : the state of being confined; *esp* : LYING-IN
con·firm \kən-ˈfərm\ *vt* [ME *confirmen,* fr. OF *confirmer,* fr. L *confirmare,* fr. *com-* + *firmare* to make firm, fr. *firmus* firm] **1** : to make firm or firmer : STRENGTHEN **2** : to give approval to : RATIFY **3** : to administer the rite of confirmation to **4** : to give new assurance of the validity of : remove doubt about by authoritative act or indisputable fact **5** : ASSERT, MAINTAIN — **con·firm·abil·i·ty** \-ˌfər-mə-ˈbil-ət-ē\ *n* — **con·firm·able** \-ˈfər-mə-bəl\ *adj*
syn CONFIRM, CORROBORATE, SUBSTANTIATE, VERIFY, AUTHENTICATE, VALIDATE *shared meaning element* : to attest the truth or validity of something ***ant*** deny, contradict
con·fir·ma·tion \ˌkän-fər-ˈmā-shən\ *n* **1** : an act or process of confirming: as **a** (1) : a Christian rite conferring the gift of the Holy Spirit and among Protestants full church membership (2) : a ceremony confirming Jewish youths in their ancestral faith **b** : the ratification of an executive act by a legislative body **2 a** : confirming proof : CORROBORATION **b** : the process of supporting a statement by evidence — **con·fir·ma·tion·al** \-shnəl, -shən-ᵊl\ *adj*
con·fir·ma·to·ry \kən-ˈfər-mə-ˌtōr-ē, -ˌtȯr-\ *adj* : serving to confirm : CORROBORATIVE
con·firmed \kən-ˈfərmd\ *adj* **1 a** : made firm : STRENGTHENED **b** : being so fixed in habit as to be unlikely to change ⟨a ~ bachelor⟩ **c** : marked by long continuance and likely to persist ⟨a ~ habit⟩ **2** : having received the rite of confirmation ***syn*** see INVETERATE — **con·firm·ed·ly** \-ˈfər-məd-lē\ *adv* — **con·firmed·ness** \-ˈfər-məd-nəs, -ˈfərm(d)-nəs\ *n*
con·fis·ca·ble \kən-ˈfis-kə-bəl\ *adj* : liable to confiscation
con·fis·cat·able \ˈkän-fə-ˌskāt-ə-bəl\ *adj* : CONFISCABLE
¹con·fis·cate \ˈkän-fə-ˌskāt, kən-ˈfis-kət\ *adj* [L *confiscatus,* pp. of *confiscare* to confiscate, fr. *com-* + *fiscus* treasury — more at FISCAL] **1** : appropriated by the government : FORFEITED **2** : deprived of property by confiscation
²con·fis·cate \ˈkän-fə-ˌskāt\ *vt* **-cat·ed; -cat·ing** **1** : to seize as forfeited to the public treasury **2** : to seize by or as if by authority ***syn*** see APPROPRIATE — **con·fis·ca·tion** \ˌkän-fə-ˈskā-shən\ *n* — **con·fis·ca·tor** \ˈkän-fə-ˌskāt-ər\ *n* — **con·fis·ca·to·ry** \kən-ˈfis-kə-ˌtōr-ē, -ˌtȯr-\ *adj*
con·fi·te·or \kən-ˈfēt-ē-ər, -ē-ˌȯ(ə)r\ *n* [ME, fr. L, I confess, fr. *confitēri* to confess — more at CONFESS] : a liturgical form in which sinfulness is acknowledged and intercession for God's mercy requested
con·fi·ture \ˈkän-fə-ˌchu̇(ə)r, -ˌt(y)u̇(ə)r\ *n* [F, fr. MF, fr. *confit* comfit] : preserved or candied fruit : JAM
con·fla·grant \kən-ˈflā-grənt\ *adj* [L *conflagrant-, conflagrans,* prp. of *conflagrare* to burn, fr. *com-* + *flagrare* to burn — more at BLACK] : BURNING, BLAZING
con·fla·gra·tion \ˌkän-flə-ˈgrā-shən\ *n* [L *conflagration-, conflagratio,* fr. *conflagratus,* pp. of *conflagrare*] **1** : FIRE; *esp* : a large disastrous fire **2** : CONFLICT
con·flate \kən-ˈflāt\ *vt* **con·flat·ed; con·flat·ing** [L *conflare* to blow together, fuse, fr. *com-* + *flare* to blow — more at BLOW] **1 a** : to bring together : FUSE **b** : CONFUSE **2** : to combine (as two readings of a text) into a composite whole
con·fla·tion \-ˈflā-shən\ *n* : BLEND, FUSION; *esp* : a composite reading or text
¹con·flict \ˈkän-ˌflikt\ *n* [ME, fr. L *conflictus* act of striking together, fr. *conflictus* pp. of *confligere* to strike together, fr. *com-* + *fligere* to strike — more at PROFLIGATE] **1 a** : competitive or opposing action of incompatibles : antagonistic state or action (as of divergent ideas, interests, or persons) **b** : mental struggle resulting from incompatible or opposing needs, drives, wishes, or external or internal demands **2** : hostile encounter : FIGHT, BATTLE, WAR **3** : COLLISION **4** : the opposition of persons or forces that gives rise to the dramatic action in a drama or fiction ***syn*** see DISCORD ***ant*** harmony — **con·flict·ful** \ˈkän-ˌflikt-fəl\ *adj* — **con·flict·less** \-ˌflik-tləs\ *adj* — **con·flic·tu·al** \kän-ˈflik-ch(ə-w)əl, kən-\ *adj*
²con·flict \kən-ˈflikt, ˈkän-ˌ\ *vi* **1** *archaic* : to contend in warfare **2** : to show antagonism or irreconcilability — **con·flic·tion** \kən-ˈflik-shən, kän-\ *n* — **con·flic·tive** \kən-ˈflik-tiv, ˈkän-ˌ\ *adj*
con·flict·ing *adj* : being in conflict, collision, or opposition : INCOMPATIBLE — **con·flict·ing·ly** \-ˈflik-tiŋ-lē, -ˌflik-\ *adv*
conflict of interest : a conflict between the private interests and the official responsibilities of a person in a position of trust (as a government official)
con·flu·ence \ˈkän-ˌflü-ən(t)s, kən-ˈ\ *n* **1** : a coming or flowing together, meeting, or gathering at one point ⟨the ~ of scholarship that produced the atomic bomb⟩ **2 a** : the flowing together of two or more streams **b** : the place of meeting of two streams **c** : the combined stream formed by conjunction ***syn*** see JUNCTION
¹con·flu·ent \-ənt\ *adj* [L *confluent-, confluens,* prp. of *confluere* to flow together, fr. *com-* + *fluere* to flow — more at FLUID] **1** : flowing or coming together; *also* : run together ⟨~ pustules⟩ **2** : characterized by confluent lesions ⟨~ smallpox⟩
²confluent *n* : a confluent stream; *broadly* : TRIBUTARY
con·flux \ˈkän-ˌfləks\ *n* [ML *confluxus,* fr. L *confluxus,* pp. of *confluere*] : CONFLUENCE
con·fo·cal \(ˈ)kän-ˈfō-kəl\ *adj* : having the same foci ⟨~ ellipses⟩ ⟨~ lenses⟩ — **con·fo·cal·ly** \-kə-lē\ *adv*
¹con·form \kən-ˈfȯ(ə)rm\ *vb* [ME *conformen,* fr. MF *conformer,* fr. L *conformare,* fr. *com-* + *formare* to form, fr. *forma* form] *vt* : to give the same shape, outline, or contour to : bring into harmony or accord ⟨~ furrows to the slope of the land⟩ ~ *vi* **1** : to be similar or identical **2** : to be obedient or compliant; *esp* : to adapt oneself to prevailing standards or customs ***syn*** **1** see ADAPT **2** see AGREE ***ant*** diverge — **con·form·er** *n* — **con·form·ism** \-ˈfȯr-ˌmiz-əm\ *n* — **con·form·ist** \-məst\ *n*
²conform *adj* : CONFORMABLE
con·form·able \kən-ˈfȯr-mə-bəl\ *adj* **1** : corresponding in form or character : SIMILAR — usu. used with *to* ⟨decisions ~ to the will and desire of the people —David Fromkin⟩ **2** : SUBMISSIVE, COMPLIANT **3** : following in unbroken sequence — used of geologic strata formed under uniform conditions — **con·form·ably** \-blē\ *adv*
con·for·mal \kən-ˈfȯr-məl, (ˈ)kän-\ *adj* [LL *conformalis* having the same shape, fr. L *com-* + *formalis* formal, fr. *forma*] : leaving the size of the angle between corresponding curves unchanged ⟨~ transformation⟩; *esp, of a map* : representing small areas in their true shape
con·for·mance \kən-ˈfȯr-mən(t)s\ *n* : CONFORMITY
con·for·ma·tion \ˌkän-(ˌ)fȯr-ˈmā-shən, -fər-\ *n* **1** : the act of conforming or producing conformity : ADAPTATION **2** : formation of something by appropriate arrangement of parts or elements : an assembling into a whole ⟨the gradual ~ of the embryo⟩ **3 a** : correspondence esp. to a model or plan **b** : STRUCTURE **c** : the proportionate shape or contour esp. of an animal **d** : any of the spatial arrangements of a molecule that can be obtained by rotation of the atoms about a single bond ***syn*** see FORM — **con·for·ma·tion·al** \-shnəl, -shən-ᵊl\ *adj*
con·for·mi·ty \kən-ˈfȯr-mət-ē\ *n, pl* **-ties** **1** : correspondence in form, manner, or character : AGREEMENT ⟨behaved in ~ with his beliefs⟩ **2** : an act or instance of conforming **3** : action in accordance with some specified standard or authority : OBEDIENCE ⟨~ to social custom⟩
con·found \kən-ˈfau̇nd, kän-\ *vt* [ME *confounden,* fr. OF *confondre,* fr. L *confundere* to pour together, confuse, fr. *com-* + *fundere* to pour — more at FOUND] **1** *archaic* : to bring to ruin : DESTROY **2** *obs* : CONSUME, WASTE **3 a** : to put to shame : DISCOMFIT ⟨a performance that ~*ed* his critics⟩ **b** : REFUTE ⟨sought to ~ his arguments⟩ **4** : DAMN **5** : to throw (a person) into confusion or perplexity **6 a** : to fail to discern differences between : mix up **b** : to increase the confusion of ***syn*** **1** see PUZZLE **2** see MISTAKE ***ant*** distinguish, discriminate — **con·found·er** *n*
con·found·ed \kən-ˈfau̇n-dəd, (ˈ)kän-ˈ, ˈkän-ˌ\ *adj* **1** : CONFUSED, PERPLEXED **2** : DAMNED — **con·found·ed·ly** *adv*
con·fra·ter·ni·ty \ˌkän-frə-ˈtər-nət-ē\ *n* [ME *confraternite,* fr. MF *confraternité,* fr. ML *confraternitat-, confraternitas,* fr. *confrater* fellow, brother, fr. L *com-* + *frater* brother — more at BROTHER] **1** : a society devoted to a religious or charitable cause **2** : fraternal union
con·frere \ˈkän-ˌfre(ə)r, kōⁿ-ˌ, kän-ˈ, kōⁿ-ˈ, kən-ˈ\ *n* [ME, fr. MF, trans. of ML *confrater*] : COLLEAGUE, COMRADE
con·front \kən-ˈfrənt\ *vt* [MF *confronter* to border on, confront, fr. ML *confrontare* to bound, fr. L *com-* + *front-, frons* forehead, front — more at BRINK] **1** : to face esp. in challenge : OPPOSE ⟨scholars must ~ society, often in conflict —Paul Goodman⟩ **2 a** : to cause to meet : bring face to face ⟨~ a reader with statistics⟩ **b** : ENCOUNTER ⟨the problems that one ~*s* are enormous⟩ — **con·front·al** \-ˈfrənt-ᵊl\ *n* — **con·front·er** *n*
con·fron·ta·tion \ˌkän-(ˌ)frən-ˈtā-shən\ *n* : the act of confronting : the state of being confronted: as **a** : a face-to-face meeting **b** : the clashing of forces or ideas : CONFLICT **c** : COMPARISON ⟨the flashbacks bring into meaningful ~ present and past, near and far —R. J. Clements⟩ — **con·fron·ta·tion·al** \-shnəl, -shən-ᵊl\ *adj* — **con·fron·ta·tion·ism** \-shə-ˌniz-əm\ *n* — **con·fron·ta·tion·ist** \-sh(ə-)nəst\ *n*
Con·fu·cian \kən-ˈfyü-shən\ *adj* : of or relating to the Chinese philosopher Confucius or his teachings or followers — **Confucian** *n* — **Con·fu·cian·ism** \-shə-ˌniz-əm\ *n*
con·fuse \kən-ˈfyüz\ *vt* **con·fused; con·fus·ing** [back-formation fr. ME *confused* perplexed, fr. MF *confus,* fr. L *confusus,* pp. of *confundere*] **1** *archaic* : to bring to ruin **2 a** : to make embarrassed : ABASH **b** : to disturb in mind or purpose : throw off ⟨interrogators who do their best to frighten, ~ and bewilder him —Aldous Huxley⟩ **3 a** : to make indistinct : BLUR ⟨stop *confusing* the issue⟩ **b** : to mix indiscriminately : JUMBLE **c** : to fail to differentiate from an often similar or related other ⟨~ money with comfort⟩ ***syn*** see MISTAKE ***ant*** differentiate — **con·fus·ing** \-ˈfyü-ziŋ\ *adj* — **con·fus·ing·ly** \-ziŋ-lē\ *adv*
con·fused \-ˈfyüzd\ *adj* **1** : being perplexed or disconcerted ⟨the ~ students⟩ **2** : INDISTINGUISHABLE ⟨a zigzag, crisscross, ~ trail —Harry Hervey⟩ **3** : being disordered or mixed up ⟨a contradictory and often ~ philosophy⟩ — **con·fused·ly** \-ˈfyüz(-ə)d-lē\ *adv* — **con·fused·ness** \-ˈfyü-zəd-nəs, -ˈfyüz(d)-\ *n*
con·fu·sion \kən-ˈfyü-zhən\ *n* **1** : an act or instance of confusing **2** : the quality or state of being confused — **con·fu·sion·al** \-ˈfyüzh-nəl, -ˈfyü-zhən-ᵊl\ *adj*
con·fu·ta·tion \ˌkän-fyü-ˈtā-shən\ *n* **1** : the act or process of confuting : REFUTATION **2** : something (as an argument or statement) that confutes — **con·fu·ta·tive** \kən-ˈfyüt-ət-iv\ *adj*

ə abut ᵊ kitten ər further a back ā bake ä cot, cart
au̇ out ch chin e less ē easy g gift i trip ī life
j joke ŋ sing ō flow ȯ flaw ȯi coin th thin t͟h this
ü loot u̇ foot y yet yü few yu̇ furious zh vision

con·fute \kən-ˈfyüt\ *vt* **con·fut·ed; con·fut·ing** [L *confutare,* fr. *com-* + *-futare* to beat — more at BEAT] **1 :** to overwhelm in argument : refute conclusively ⟨Elijah . . . *confuted* the prophets of Baal . . . with . . . bitter mockery —G. B. Shaw⟩ **2** *obs* : CONFOUND ***syn*** see DISPROVE — **con·fut·er** *n*

cong *abbr* congress; congressional

con·ga \ˈkäŋ-gə\ *n* [AmerSp, fr. Sp, fem. of *congo* of the Congo, fr. *Congo,* region in Africa] **1 :** a Cuban dance of African origin involving three steps followed by a kick and performed by a group usu. in single file **2 :** a tall narrow bass drum beaten with the hands

con·gé \kōⁿ-ˈzhā, ˈkän-ˌjā\ *n* [F, fr. L *commeatus* going back and forth, leave, fr. *commeatus,* pp. of *commeare* to go back and forth, fr. *com-* + *meare* to go — more at PERMEATE] **1 a :** a formal permission to depart **b :** DISMISSAL **2 :** a ceremonious bow **3** : FAREWELL **4 :** an architectural molding of concave profile — see MOLDING illustration

con·geal \kən-ˈjē(ə)l\ *vb* [ME *congelen,* fr. MF *congeler,* fr. L *congelare,* fr. *com-* + *gelare* to freeze — more at COLD] *vt* **1 :** to change from a fluid to a solid state by or as if by cold **2 :** to make viscid or curdled : COAGULATE **3 :** to make rigid, inflexible, or immobile ~ *vi* : to become congealed — **con·geal·ment** \-mənt\ *n*

con·gee \ˈkän-(ˌ)jē\ *n* : CONGÉ

con·ge·la·tion \ˌkän-jə-ˈlā-shən\ *n* : the process or result of congealing

con·ge·ner \ˈkän-jə-nər, kən-ˈjē-\ *n* [L, of the same kind, fr. *com-* + *gener-, genus* kind — more at KIN] **1 :** a member of the same taxonomic genus as another plant or animal **2 :** a person or thing resembling another in nature or action ⟨the New England private schools and their ~*s* west of the Alleghenies —Oliver La Farge⟩ — **con·ge·ner·ic** \ˌkän-jə-ˈner-ik\ *adj* — **con·ge·ner·ous** \kən-ˈjē-nə-rəs, -ˈjen-ə-, (ˈ)kän-\ *adj*

con·ge·nial \kən-ˈjē-nyəl\ *adj* [*com-* + *genius*] **1 :** having the same nature, disposition, or tastes : KINDRED **2 a :** existing or associated together harmoniously **b :** PLEASANT; *esp* : agreeably suited to one's nature, tastes, or outlook **c :** SOCIABLE, GENIAL ***syn*** see CONSONANT ***ant*** uncongenial, antipathetic (*of persons*), abhorrent (*of tasks, duties*) — **con·ge·nial·i·ty** \-ˌjē-nē-ˈal-ət-ē, -ˌjēn-ˈyal-\ *n* — **con·ge·nial·ly** \-ˈjē-nyə-lē\ *adv*

con·gen·i·tal \kän-ˈjen-ə-tᵊl\ *adj* [L *congenitus,* fr. *com-* + *genitus* pp. of *gignere* to bring forth — more at KIN] **1 a :** existing at or dating from birth ⟨~ idiocy⟩ **b :** constituting an essential characteristic : INHERENT ⟨~ fear of snakes⟩ **c :** acquired during development in the uterus and not through heredity ⟨~ syphilis⟩ **2** : being such by nature ⟨~ liar⟩ ***syn*** see INNATE — **con·gen·i·tal·ly** \-tᵊl-ē\ *adv*

con·ger eel \ˌkäŋ-gər-\ *n* [ME *congre,* fr. OF, fr. L *congr-, conger,* fr. Gk *gongros;* akin to ON *kökkr* ball, L *gingiva* gum] : a large strictly marine scaleless eel (*Conger oceanicus*) important as a food fish; *broadly* : any of various related eels (family Congridae)

con·ge·ries \ˈkän-jə-(ˌ)rēz\ *n, pl* **congeries** *same*\ [L, fr. *congerere*] : AGGREGATION, COLLECTION ⟨the alternative was to turn linguistics into a ~ of meaningless guesses —C. A. Ladd⟩

con·gest \kən-ˈjest\ *vb* [L *congestus,* pp. of *congerere* to bring together, fr. *com-* + *gerere* to bear — more at CAST] *vt* **1 :** to cause an excessive fullness of the blood vessels of (as an organ) **2 :** CLOG ⟨traffic ~*ed* the highways⟩ **3 :** to concentrate in a small or narrow space ~ *vi* : to become congested — **con·ges·tion** \-ˈjes(h)-chən\ *n* — **con·ges·tive** \-ˈjes-tiv\ *adj*

con·glo·bate \kän-ˈglō-ˌbāt, kən-\ *vt* **-bat·ed; -bat·ing** [L *conglobatus,* pp. of *conglobare,* fr. *com-* + *globus* globe] : to form into a round compact mass — **con·glo·bate** \-bət, -ˌbāt\ *adj* — **con·glo·ba·tion** \ˌkän-(ˌ)glō-ˈbā-shən\ *n*

con·globe \kän-ˈglōb, kən-\ *vt* **con·globed; con·glob·ing** : CONGLOBATE

¹con·glom·er·ate \kən-ˈgläm-(ə-)rət\ *adj* [L *conglomeratus,* pp. of *conglomerare* to roll together, fr. *com-* + *glomerare* to wind into a ball, fr. *glomer-, glomus* ball — more at CLAM] : made up of parts from various sources or of various kinds ⟨an ethnically ~ culture⟩

²con·glom·er·ate \-ə-ˌrāt\ *vb* **-at·ed; -at·ing** *vt* : ACCUMULATE ~ *vi* : to gather into a mass or coherent whole ⟨numbers of dull people *conglomerated* round her —Virginia Woolf⟩ — **con·glom·er·a·tive** \-ˈgläm-(ə-)rət-iv, -ə-ˌrāt-\ *adj* — **con·glom·er·a·tor** \-ˈgläm-ə-ˌrāt-ər\ *n*

³con·glom·er·ate \-(ə-)rət\ *n* **1 :** a composite mass or mixture; *specif* : rock composed of rounded fragments varying from small pebbles to large boulders in a cement (as of hardened clay) **2 :** a widely diversified corporation — **con·glom·er·at·ic** \kən-ˌgläm-ə-ˈrat-ik, ˌkän-\ *adj*

con·glom·er·a·tion \kən-ˌgläm-ə-ˈrā-shən, ˌkän-\ *n* **1 :** the act of conglomerating : the state of being conglomerated **2 :** something conglomerated : a mixed coherent mass

con·glu·ti·nate \kən-ˈglüt-ᵊn-ˌāt, kän-\ *vb* **-nat·ed; -nat·ing** [L *conglutinatus,* pp. of *conglutinare* to glue together, fr. *com-* + *glutin-, gluten* glue] *vt* : to unite by or as if by a glutinous substance ~ *vi* : to become conglutinated ⟨blood platelets ~ in blood clotting⟩ — **con·glu·ti·na·tion** \kən-ˌglüt-ᵊn-ˈā-shən, kän-\ *n*

Con·go dye \ˌkäŋ-(ˌ)gō-\ *n* [*Congo,* territory in Africa] : any of various direct azo dyes mostly derived from benzidine

Congo red *n* : an azo dye $C_{32}H_{22}N_6Na_2O_6S_2$ that is red in alkaline and blue in acid solution and that is used esp. as an indicator and as a biological stain

congo snake *n* : an elongated bluish black amphibian (*Amphiuma means*) of the southeastern U.S. that has two pairs of very short limbs each with two or three toes — called also *congo eel*

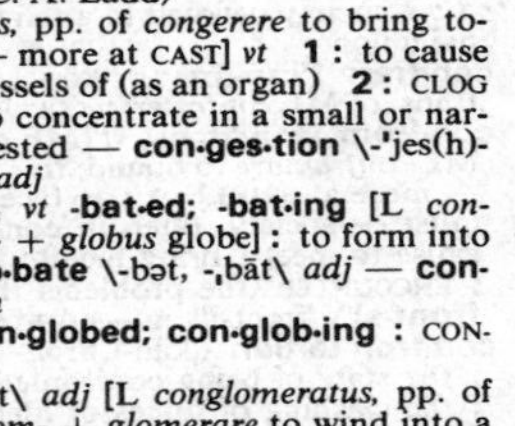

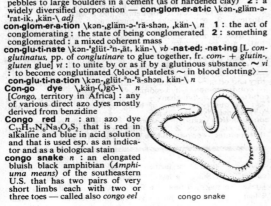

congo snake

con·gou \ˈkäŋ-(ˌ)gō, -(ˌ)gü\ *n* [prob. fr. Chin (Amoy) *kong-hu* pains taken] : a black tea from China

con·grat·u·late \kən-ˈgrach-ə-ˌlāt, *nonstand* -ˈgraj-\ *vt* **-lat·ed; -lat·ing** [L *congratulatus,* pp. of *congratulari* to wish joy, fr. *com-* + *gratulari* to wish joy, fr. *gratus* pleasing — more at GRACE] **1 :** to express pleasure to (a person) on account of success or good fortune **2** *archaic* : to express sympathetic pleasure at (an event) **3** *obs* : SALUTE, GREET — **con·grat·u·la·tor** \-ə-ˌlāt-ər\ *n* — **con·grat·u·la·to·ry** \-(ə-)lə-ˌtōr-ē, -ˌtȯr-\ *adj*

con·grat·u·la·tion \kən-ˌgrach-ə-ˈlā-shən, *nonstand* -ˌgraj-\ *n* **1** : the act of congratulating **2 :** a congratulatory expression — usu. used in pl.

con·gre·gant \-gənt\ *n* : one that congregates; *specif* : a member of a congregation

con·gre·gate \ˈkäŋ-gri-ˌgāt\ *vb* **-gat·ed; -gat·ing** [ME *congregaten,* fr. L *congregatus,* pp. of *congregare,* fr. *com-* + *greg-, grex* flock — more at GREGARIOUS] *vt* : to collect into a group or crowd : ASSEMBLE ~ *vi* : to come together into a group, crowd, or assembly ***syn*** see GATHER — **con·gre·ga·tor** \-ˌgāt-ər\ *n*

con·gre·ga·tion \ˌkäŋ-gri-ˈgā-shən\ *n* **1 a :** an assembly of persons : GATHERING; *esp* : an assembly of persons met for worship and religious instruction **b :** a religious community: as (1) : an organized body of believers in a particular locality (2) : a Roman Catholic religious institute with only simple vows (3) : a group of monasteries forming an independent subdivision of an order **2** : the act or an instance of congregating or bringing together : the state of being congregated **3 :** a body of cardinals and officials forming an administrative division of the papal curia

con·gre·ga·tion·al \-shnəl, -shən-ᵊl\ *adj* **1 :** of or relating to a congregation **2** *cap* : of or relating to a body of Protestant churches deriving from the English Independents of the 17th century and affirming the essential importance and the autonomy of the local congregation **3 :** of or relating to church government placing final authority in the assembly of the local congregation — **con·gre·ga·tion·al·ism** \-shnə-ˌliz-əm, -shən-ᵊl-ˌiz-\ *n, often cap* — **con·gre·ga·tion·al·ist** \-shnə-ləst, -shən-ᵊl-əst\ *n or adj, often cap*

con·gress \ˈkäŋ-grəs\ *n* [L *congressus,* fr. *congressus,* pp. of *congredi* to come together, fr. *com-* + *gradi* to go — more at GRADE] **1 a** : the act or action of coming together and meeting **b :** COITUS **2** : a formal meeting of delegates for discussion and usu. action on some question **3 :** the supreme legislative body of a nation and esp. of a republic **4 :** an association usu. made up of delegates from constituent organizations **5 :** a single meeting or session of a group — **con·gres·sio·nal** \kän-ˈgresh-nəl, -ən-ᵊl\ *adj* — **con·gres·sio·nal·ly** \-ē\ *adv*

congress gaiter *n, often cap C* [fr. its former popularity with U.S. congressmen] : an ankle-high shoe with elastic gussets in the sides

congressional district *n* : a territorial division of a state from which a member of the U.S. House of Representatives is elected

Congressional Medal *n* : MEDAL OF HONOR

con·gress·man \ˈkäŋ-grə-smən\ *n* : a member of a congress; *esp* : a member of the U.S. House of Representatives

con·gress·wom·an \-grə-ˌswu̇m-ən\ *n* : a female member of a congress; *esp* : a female member of the U.S. House of Representatives

con·gru·ence \kən-ˈgrü-ən(t)s, ˈkäŋ-grə-wən(t)s\ *n* **1 :** the quality or state of agreeing or coinciding **2 :** a statement that two numbers are congruent with respect to a modulus

con·gru·en·cy \-ən-sē, -wən-\ *n, pl* **-cies** : CONGRUENCE

con·gru·ent \kən-ˈgrü-ənt, ˈkäŋ-grə-wənt\ *adj* [L *congruent-, congruens,* prp. of *congruere*] **1 :** CONGRUOUS **2 :** superposable so as to be coincident throughout **3 :** having the difference divisible by a given modulus ⟨12 is ~ to 2 (modulo 5) since $12-2=2\cdot5$⟩ **4** : relating to the melting point at which there coexist for a compound both liquid and solid phases having the same composition — **con·gru·ent·ly** *adv*

con·gru·ity \kən-ˈgrü-ət-ē, kän-\ *n, pl* **-ities** **1 :** the quality or state of being congruent or congruous **2 :** a point of agreement

con·gru·ous \ˈkäŋ-grə-wəs\ *adj* [L *congruus,* fr. *congruere* to come together, agree, fr. *com-* + *-gruere* (akin to Gk *zachrēēs* attacking violently)] **1 a :** being in agreement, harmony, or correspondence **b :** conforming to the circumstances or requirements of a situation : APPROPRIATE ⟨a ~ room to work in —G. B. Shaw⟩ **2** : marked or enhanced by harmonious agreement among constituent elements ⟨a ~ theme in music⟩ ***syn*** see CONSONANT ***ant*** incongruous — **con·gru·ous·ly** *adv* — **con·gru·ous·ness** *n*

¹con·ic \ˈkän-ik\ *adj* **1 :** CONICAL **2 :** of or relating to a cone — **co·nic·i·ty** \kō-ˈnis-ət-ē\ *n*

²conic *n* : CONIC SECTION

con·i·cal \ˈkän-i-kəl\ *adj* : resembling a cone esp. in shape — **con·i·cal·ly** \-k(ə-)lē\ *adv* — **con·i·cal·ness** \-kəl-nəs\ *n*

conic section *n* **1 :** a plane curve, line, or point that is the intersection of or bounds the intersection of a plane and a cone with two nappes **2 :** a curve generated by a point which always moves so that the ratio of its distance from a fixed point to its distance from a fixed line is constant

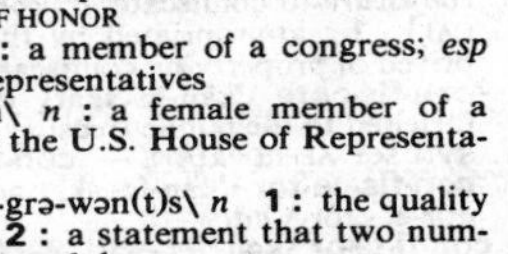

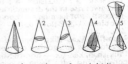

conic sections: *1* straight lines, *2* circle, *3* ellipse, *4* parabola, *5* hyperbola

co·nid·io·phore \kə-ˈnid-ē-ə-ˌfō(ə)r, -ˌfȯ(ə)r\ *n* [NL *conidium* + ISV *-phore*] : a structure that bears conidia; *specif* : a specialized hyphal branch that produces successive conidia usu. by abstriction — **co·nid·i·oph·o·rous** \-ˌnid-ē-ˈäf-(ə-)rəs\ *adj*

co·nid·i·um \kə-ˈnid-ē-əm\ *n, pl* **-ia** \-ē-ə\ [NL, fr. Gk *konis* dust — more at INCINERATE] : an asexual spore produced on a conidiophore — **co·nid·i·al** \-ē-əl\ *adj*

co·ni·fer \ˈkän-ə-fər *also* ˈkō-nə-\ *n* [deriv. of L *conifer* cone-bearing, fr. *conus* cone + *-fer*] : any of an order (Coniferales) of mostly evergreen trees and shrubs including forms (as pines) with true cones and others (as yews) with an arillate fruit — **co·nif·er·ous** \kō-ˈnif-(ə-)rəs, kə-\ *adj*

co·ni·ine \ˈkō-nē-ˌēn\ *n* [G *koniin*, fr. LL *conium*] : a poisonous alkaloid $C_8H_{17}N$ found in poison hemlock (*Conium maculatum*)

co·ni·um \kō-ˈnī-əm, ˈkō-nē-\ *n* [NL, genus name, fr. LL, hemlock, fr. Gk *kōneion*] : any of a genus (*Conium*) of poisonous herbs of the carrot family

conj *abbr* conjunction; conjunctive

con·jec·tur·al \kən-ˈjek-chə-rəl, -ˈjeksh-rəl\ *adj* **1** : of the nature of or involving or based on conjecture **2** : given to conjectures — **con·jec·tur·al·ly** \-ē\ *adv*

¹con·jec·ture \kən-ˈjek-chər\ *n* [ME, fr. MF or L; MF, fr. L *conjectura*, fr. *conjectus*, pp. of *conicere*, lit., to throw together, fr. *com-* + *jacere* to throw — more at JET] **1** *obs* **a** : interpretation of omens **b** : SUPPOSITION **2 a** : inference from defective or presumptive evidence **b** : a conclusion deduced by surmise or guesswork

²conjecture *vb* **-tured; -tur·ing** \-ˈjek-chə-riŋ, -ˈjek-shriŋ\ *vt* **1** : to arrive at by conjecture **2** : to make conjectures as to ~ *vi* : to form conjectures — **con·jec·tur·er** \-ˈjek-chər-ər\ *n*
syn CONJECTURE, SURMISE, GUESS *shared meaning element* : to draw an inference from slight evidence

con·join \kən-ˈjȯin, kän-\ *vb* [ME *conjoinen*, fr. MF *conjoindre*, fr. L *conjungere*, fr. *com-* + *jungere* to join — more at YOKE] *vt* : to join together (as separate entities) for a common purpose ~ *vi* : to join together for a common purpose

con·joined \-ˈjȯind\ *adj* : being, coming, or brought together so as to meet, touch, or overlap ⟨~ heads on a coin⟩

con·joint \-ˈjȯint\ *adj* [ME, fr. MF, pp. of *conjoindre*] **1** : UNITED, CONJOINED **2** : related to, made up of, or carried on by two or more in combination : JOINT — **con·joint·ly** *adv*

con·ju·gal \ˈkän-ji-gəl, kən-ˈjü-\ *adj* [MF or L; MF, fr. L *conjugalis*, fr. *conjug-*, *conjux* husband, wife, fr. *conjungere* to join, unite in marriage] : of or relating to the married state or to married persons and their relations : CONNUBIAL *syn* see MATRIMONIAL — **con·ju·gal·i·ty** \ˌkän-ji-ˈgal-ət-ē, -jü-\ *n* — **con·ju·gal·ly** \ˈkän-ji-gə-lē, kən-ˈjü-\ *adv*

conjugal rights *n pl* : the sexual rights or privileges implied by and involved in the marriage relationship : the right of sexual intercourse between husband and wife

con·ju·gant \ˈkän-ji-gənt\ *n* : either of a pair of conjugating gametes or organisms

¹con·ju·gate \ˈkän-ji-gət, -jə-ˌgāt\ *adj* [ME *conjugat*, fr. L *conjugatus*, pp. of *conjugare* to unite, fr. *com-* + *jugare* to join, fr. *jugum* yoke — more at YOKE] **1 a** : joined together esp. in pairs : COUPLED **b** : acting or operating as if joined **2** : having features in common but opposite or inverse in some particular **3** *of an acid or base* : related by the difference of a proton ⟨the acid NH_4 and the base NH_3 are ~ to each other⟩ **4** : having the same derivation and therefore usu. some likeness in meaning ⟨~ words⟩ **5** *of two leaves of a book* : forming a single piece — **con·ju·gate·ly** *adv* — **con·ju·gate·ness** *n*

²con·ju·gate \-jə-ˌgāt\ *vb* **-gat·ed; -gat·ing** *vt* **1** : to give in prescribed order the various inflectional forms of — used esp. of a verb **2** : to join together ~ *vi* **1** : to become joined together **2 a** : to pair and fuse in conjugation **b** : to pair in synapsis

³conjugate *like* ¹CONJUGATE\ *n* **1** : something conjugate : a product of conjugating **2** : CONJUGATE COMPLEX NUMBER **3** : an element of a mathematical group that is equal to a given element of the group multiplied on the right by another element and on the left by the inverse of the latter element

conjugate complex number *n* : one of two complex numbers (as $a + bi$ and $a - bi$) differing only in the sign of the imaginary part

con·ju·gat·ed *adj* **1** : formed by the union of two compounds or united with another compound ⟨~ bile acids⟩ **2** : relating to or containing a system of two double bonds separated by a single bond ⟨~ fatty acids⟩

conjugated protein *n* : a compound of a protein with a nonprotein ⟨hemoglobin is a *conjugated protein* of heme and globin⟩

con·ju·ga·tion \ˌkän-jə-ˈgā-shən\ *n* **1** : the act of conjugating : the state of being conjugated **2 a** : a schematic arrangement of the inflectional forms of a verb **b** : verb inflection **c** : a class of verbs having the same type of inflectional forms ⟨the weak ~⟩ **d** : a set of the simple or derivative inflectional forms of a verb esp. in Sanskrit or the Semitic languages ⟨the causative ~⟩ **3 a** : fusion of usu. similar gametes with ultimate union of their nuclei that among lower thallophytes replaces the typical fertilization of higher forms **b** : temporary cytoplasmic union with exchange of nuclear material that is the usual sexual process in ciliated protozoans **c** : the one-way transfer of DNA between bacteria in cellular contact — **con·ju·ga·tion·al** \-shnəl, -shən-ᵊl\ *adj* — **con·ju·ga·tion·al·ly** \-ē\ *adv* — **con·ju·ga·tive** \ˈkän-jə-ˌgāt-iv\ *adj*

¹con·junct \kən-ˈjəŋ(k)t, kän-\ *adj* [ME, fr. L *conjunctus*, pp. of *conjungere*] **1** : JOINED, UNITED **2** : JOINT **3** : relating to melodic progression by diatonic degrees — compare DISJUNCT

²con·junct \ˈkän-ˌjəŋ(k)t\ *n* : something joined or associated with another; *specif* : one of the components of a conjunction

con·junc·tion \kən-ˈjəŋ(k)-shən\ *n* **1** : the act or an instance of conjoining : the state of being conjoined **2** : occurrence together in time or space : CONCURRENCE **3 a** : the apparent meeting or passing of two or more celestial bodies in the same degree of the zodiac **b** : a configuration in which two celestial bodies have their least apparent separation **4** : an uninflected linguistic form that joins together sentences, clauses, phrases, or words : CONNECTIVE **5** : a complex sentence in logic true if and only if each of its components is true — **con·junc·tion·al** \-shnəl, -shən-ᵊl\ *adj* — **con·junc·tion·al·ly** \-ē\ *adv*

con·junc·ti·va \ˌkän-ˌjəŋ(k)-ˈtī-və, kən-\ *n, pl* **-vas** *or* **-vae** \-(ˌ)vē\ [NL, fr. LL, fem. of *conjunctivus* conjoining, fr. L *conjunctus*] : the mucous membrane that lines the inner surface of the eyelids and is continued over the forepart of the eyeball — see EYE illustration — **con·junc·ti·val** \-vəl\ *adj*

con·junc·tive \kən-ˈjəŋ(k)-tiv\ *adj* **1** : CONNECTIVE **2** : CONJUNCT, CONJOINED **3** : being or functioning like a conjunction **4** : COPULATIVE 1a — **conjunctive** *n* — **con·junc·tive·ly** *adv*

con·junc·ti·vi·tis \kən-ˌjəŋ(k)-ti-ˈvīt-əs\ *n* : inflammation of the conjunctiva

con·junc·ture \kən-ˈjəŋ(k)-chər\ *n* **1** : CONJUNCTION, UNION **2** : a combination of circumstances or events usu. producing a crisis : JUNCTURE

con·ju·ra·tion \ˌkän-jü-ˈrā-shən, ˌkən-\ *n* **1** : the act or process of conjuring : INCANTATION **2** : an expression or trick used in conjuring **3** : a solemn appeal : ADJURATION

con·jure *in vt 2 & vi senses* ˈkän-jər *also* ˈkən-; *in vt 1 sense* kən-ˈjü(ə)r\ *vb* **con·jured; con·jur·ing** \ˈkänj-(ə-)riŋ, ˈkənj-; kən-ˈjü(ə)r-iŋ\ [ME *conjuren*, fr. OF *conjurer*, fr. L *conjurare* to swear together, fr. *com-* + *jurare* to swear — more at JURY] *vt* **1** : to charge or entreat earnestly or solemnly **2 a** : to summon by invocation or incantation **b** (1) : to affect or effect by or as if by magic (2) : IMAGINE, CONTRIVE — often used with *up* ⟨we ~ up our own metaphors for our own needs —R. J. Kaufmann⟩ ~ *vi* **1 a** : to summon a devil or spirit by invocation or incantation **b** : to practice magical arts **2** : to use a conjurer's tricks : JUGGLE

con·jur·er *or* **con·ju·ror** \ˈkän-jər-ər, ˈkən-\ *n* **1** : one that practices magic arts : WIZARD **2** : one that performs feats of sleight of hand and illusion : MAGICIAN, JUGGLER

¹conk \ˈkäŋk, ˈkȯŋk\ *vt* [slang *conk* (head); prob. alter. of *conch*] : to hit esp. on the head : knock out

²conk *n* [prob. alter. of *conch*] : the visible fruiting body of a tree fungus; *also* : decay caused by such a fungus — **conky** \-ē\ *adj*

³conk *vi* [prob. imit.] **1** : to break down; *esp* : STALL — usu. used with *out* ⟨the motor suddenly ~*ed* out⟩ **2 a** : FAINT **b** : to go to sleep — usu. used with *off* or *out* ⟨~*ed* out for a while after lunch⟩ **c** : DIE ⟨I caught pneumonia. I almost ~*ed* —Truman Capote⟩

⁴conk *vt* [prob. by shortening & alter. fr. *congolene* (a hydrocarbon produced from Congo copal and used for straightening hair), fr. *Congolese* + *-ene*] : to straighten out (hair) usu. by the use of chemicals

⁵conk *n* : a hairstyle in which the hair is straightened out and flattened down or lightly waved — called also *process*

conk·er \ˈkäŋ-kər\ *n* [*conch* + *-er*, fr. the original use of a snail shell on a string in the game] **1** *pl* : a game popular in England in which each player swings a horse chestnut on a string to try to break one held by his opponent **2** : a horse chestnut esp. when used in conkers

con mo·to \kän-ˈmō-(ˌ)tō, kōn-\ *adv* [It] : with movement : in a spirited manner — used as a direction in music

¹conn \ˈkän\ *vt* [alter. of ME *condien* to conduct, fr. MF *conduire*, fr. L *conducere*] : to conduct or direct the steering of (as a ship)

²conn *n* : the control exercised by one who conns a ship

Conn *abbr* Connecticut

con·nate \kä-ˈnāt, ˈkän-ˌāt\ *adj* [LL *connatus*, pp. of *connasci* to be born together, fr. L *com-* + *nasci* to be born — more at NATION] **1** : INNATE, INBORN **2** : AKIN, CONGENIAL **3** : born or originated together **4** : congenitally or firmly united ⟨~ leaves⟩ **5** : entrapped in sediments at the time of their deposition ⟨~ water⟩ — **con·nate·ly** *adv*

con·nat·u·ral \kä-ˈnach-(ə-)rəl, kə-\ *adj* [ML *connaturalis*, fr. L *com-* + *naturalis* natural] **1** : connected by nature : INBORN **2** : of the same nature — **con·nat·u·ral·i·ty** \-ˌnach-ə-ˈral-ət-ē\ *n* — **con·nat·u·ral·ly** \-ˈnach-(ə-)rə-lē\ *adv*

con·nect \kə-ˈnekt\ *vb* [L *conectere*, *connectere*, fr. *com-* + *nectere* to bind] *vt* **1** : to join or fasten together usu. by something intervening **2** : to place or establish in relationship ~ *vi* **1** : to become joined ⟨the two rooms ~ by a hallway⟩ ⟨ideas that ~ easily to form a theory⟩ **2** : to make a successful hit, shot, or throw ⟨~*ed* for a home run⟩ ⟨~*ed* on 60 percent of his shots and on 10 of 11 free throws —*N.Y. Times*⟩ ⟨~*ed* with a right to the jaw⟩ *syn* see JOIN *ant* disconnect — **con·nect·able** *also* **con·nect·ible** \-ˈnek-tə-bəl\ *adj* — **con·nec·tor** *also* **con·nect·er** \-ˈnek-tər\ *n*

con·nect·ed *adj* **1** : joined or linked together **2** : having the parts or elements logically linked together ⟨presented a thoroughly ~ view of the problem⟩ **3** : related by blood or marriage **4** : having a social, professional, or commercial relationship ⟨for the well ~, there are elegantly overdone parties —John Griffin⟩ — **con·nect·ed·ly** *adv* — **con·nect·ed·ness** *n*

connecting rod *n* : a rod that transmits power from one rotating part of a machine to another in reciprocating motion

con·nec·tion \kə-ˈnek-shən\ *n* [L *connexion-*, *connexio*, fr. *conexus*, pp. of *conectere*] **1** : the act of connecting : the state of being connected: as **a** : causal or logical relation or sequence ⟨the ~ between two ideas⟩ **b** : contextual relations or associations ⟨in this ~ the word has a different meaning⟩ **c** : a relation of personal intimacy (as of family ties) **d** : COHERENCE, CONTINUITY **2 a** : something that connects : LINK ⟨a loose ~ in the wiring⟩ **b** : a means of communication or transport **3** : a person connected with others esp. by marriage, kinship, or common interest ⟨has powerful ~*s* in high places⟩ **4** : a social, professional, or commercial relationship: as **a** : POSITION, JOB **b** : an arrangement to execute orders or advance interests of another ⟨a firm's foreign ~*s*⟩ **c** : a source of contraband (as illegal drugs) **5** : a set of persons associated together: as **a** : DENOMINATION **b** : CLAN — **con·nec·tion·al** \-shnəl, -shən-ᵊl\ *adj*

¹con·nec·tive \kə-ˈnek-tiv\ *adj* : tending to connect — **con·nec·tive·ly** *adv* — **con·nec·tiv·i·ty** \(ˌ)kä-ˌnek-ˈtiv-ət-ē, kə-\ *n*

²connective *n* : something that connects: as **a** : the tissue connecting the pollen sacs of an anther **b** : a linguistic form that connects words or word groups

connective tissue *n* : a tissue of mesodermal origin rich in intercellular substance or interlacing processes with little tendency for the cells to come together in sheets or masses; *specif* : connective

ə abut	ᵊ kitten	ər further	a back	ā bake	ä cot, cart
aù out	ch chin	e less	ē easy	g gift	i trip	ī life
j joke	ŋ sing	ō flow	ȯ flaw	ȯi coin	th thin	th this
ü loot	ù foot	y yet	yü few	yù furious	zh vision

tissue of stellate or spindle-shaped cells with interlacing processes that pervades, supports, and binds together other tissues and forms ligaments, tendons, and aponeuroses

con·nex·ion \kə-'nek-shən\ *chiefly Brit var of* CONNECTION

conning tower *n* **1** : an armored pilothouse (as on a battleship) **2** : a raised structure on the deck of a submarine used as an observation post and often as an entrance to the vessel

conning tower 2

con·nip·tion \kə-'nip-shən\ *n* [origin unknown] : a fit of rage, hysteria, or alarm

con·niv·ance \kə-'nī-vən(t)s\ *n* : the act of conniving; *esp* : knowledge of and active or passive consent to wrongdoing

con·nive \kə-'nīv\ *vi* **con·nived; con·niv·ing** [F or L; F *conniver*, fr. L *conivēre, connivēre* to close the eyes, connive, fr. *com-* + *-nivēre* (akin to *nictare* to wink); akin to OE & OHG *hnigan* to bow, L *nicere* to beckon] **1** : to pretend ignorance of or fail to take action against something one ought to oppose **2 a** : to be indulgent or in secret sympathy : WINK **b** : to cooperate secretly or have a secret understanding **3** : CONSPIRE, INTRIGUE — **con·niv·er** *n*

con·ni·vent \-'nī-vənt\ *adj* [L *conivent-, conivens,* prp. of *conivēre*] : converging but not fused ⟨~ stamens⟩

con·niv·ery \-'nīv-(ə-)rē\ *n* : the practice of conniving

con·nois·seur \,kän-ə-'sər *also* -'sù(ə)r\ *n* [obs. F (now *connaisseur*), fr. OF *connoisseor,* fr. *connoistre* to know, fr. L *cognoscere* — more at COGNITION] **1** : EXPERT; *esp* : one who understands the details, technique, or principles of an art and is competent to act as a critical judge **2** : one who enjoys with discrimination and appreciation of subtleties ⟨a ~ of fine wines⟩ — **con·nois·seur·ship** \-,ship\ *n*

con·no·ta·tion \,kän-ə-'tā-shən\ *n* **1 a** : the suggesting of a meaning by a word apart from the thing it explicitly names or describes **b** : something suggested by a word or thing : IMPLICATION ⟨the ~s of comfort that surrounded that old chair⟩ **2** : the signification of something ⟨that abuse of logic which consists in moving counters about as if they were known entities with a fixed ~ —W. R. Inge⟩ **3** : the property or properties connoted by a term in logic — **con·no·ta·tion·al** \-shnəl, -shən-ʾl\ *adj*

con·no·ta·tive \'kän-ə-,tāt-iv, kə-'nōt-ət-iv\ *adj* **1** : connoting or tending to connote **2** : relating to connotation — **con·no·ta·tive·ly** *adv*

con·note \kə-'nōt, kä-\ *vt* **con·not·ed; con·not·ing** [ML *connotare,* fr. L *com-* + *notare* to note] **1** : to convey in addition to exact explicit meaning ⟨all the misery that poverty ~s⟩ **2** : to be associated with or inseparable from as a consequence or concomitant ⟨the remorse so often *connoted* by guilt⟩ **3** : to imply or indicate as a logically essential attribute of something denoted *syn see* DENOTE

con·nu·bi·al \kə-'n(y)ü-bē-əl\ *adj* [L *conubialis,* fr. *conubium, connubium* marriage, fr. *com-* + *nubere* to marry — more at NUPTIAL] : of or relating to the married state : CONJUGAL *syn see* MATRIMONIAL — **con·nu·bi·al·ism** \-bē-ə-,liz-əm\ *n* — **con·nu·bi·al·i·ty** \-,n(y)ü-bē-'al-ət-ē\ *n* — **con·nu·bi·al·ly** \-'n(y)ü-bē-ə-lē\ *adv*

con·odont \'kō-nə-,dänt\ *n* [ISV *con-* (fr. Gk *kōnos* cone) + *-odont*] : a Paleozoic fossil that may consist of the teeth of an extinct cyclostome or more probably the remains of an invertebrate

co·noid \'kō-,nöid\ *or* **co·noi·dal** \kō-'nöid-ʾl\ *adj* : shaped like or nearly like a cone — **conoid** *n*

con·quer \'käŋ-kər\ *vb* **con·quered; con·quer·ing** \-k(ə-)riŋ\ [ME *conqueren* to acquire, conquer, fr. OF *conquerre,* fr. (assumed) VL *conquaerere,* fr. L *conquirere* to search for, collect, fr. *com-* + *quaerere* to ask, search] *vt* **1** : to gain or acquire by force of arms : SUBJUGATE **2** : to overcome by force of arms : VANQUISH **3** : to gain mastery over or win by overcoming obstacles or opposition ⟨~ed the mountain⟩ ⟨after ~ing movies and television, he decided to write for the stage⟩ **4** : to overcome by mental or moral power : SURMOUNT ⟨~ed her fear⟩ ~ *vi* : to be victorious — **con·quer·or** \-kər-ər\ *n*

con·quest \'kän-,kwest, 'käŋ-; 'käŋ-kwəst\ *n* [ME, fr. OF, fr. (assumed) VL *conquaesitus,* alter. of L *conquisitus,* pp. of *conquirere*] **1** : the act or process of conquering **2 a** : something conquered; *esp* : territory appropriated in war **b** : a person whose favor or hand has been won *syn see* VICTORY

con·qui·an \'kän-kē-ən\ *n* [MexSp *con quien* — more at COONCAN] : a card game for two played with 40 cards from which all games of rummy developed

con·quis·ta·dor \kón-'kēs-tə-,dó(ə)r, kän-'k(w)is-, kən-\ *n, pl* **con·quis·ta·do·res** \(,)kón-,kēs-tə-'dór-ēz, -'dór-,ās, -'dór-, (,)kän-,k(w)is-, kən-\ *or* **con·quis·ta·dors** [Sp, deriv. of L *conquirere*] : one that conquers; *specif* : a leader in the Spanish conquest of America and esp. of Mexico and Peru in the 16th century

cons *abbr* **1** consecrated **2** conservative **3** consigned; consignment **4** consol; consolidated **5** consonant **6** constable **7** constitution **8** construction **9** consul **10** consulting

con·san·guine \kän-'saŋ-gwən, kən-\ *adj* : CONSANGUINEOUS

con·san·guin·e·ous \,kän-,san-'gwin-ē-əs, -,saŋ-\ *adj* [L *consanguineus,* fr. *com-* + *sanguin-, sanguis* blood — more at SANGUINE] : of the same blood or origin; *specif* : descended from the same ancestor — **con·san·guin·e·ous·ly** *adv*

con·san·guin·i·ty \-'gwin-ət-ē\ *n, pl* **-ties 1** : the quality or state of being consanguineous **2** : a close relation or connection : AFFINITY

con·science \'kän-chən(t)s\ *n* [ME, fr. OF, fr. L *conscientia,* fr. *conscient-, consciens,* prp. of *conscire* to be conscious, be conscious of guilt, fr. *com-* + *scire* to know — more at SCIENCE] **1 a** : the sense or consciousness of the moral goodness or blameworthiness of one's own conduct, intentions, or character together with a feeling of obligation to do right or be good **b** : a faculty, power, or principle enjoining good acts **c** : the part of the superego that transmits commands and admonitions to the ego **2** *archaic* : CONSCIOUSNESS **3** : conformity to the dictates of conscience : CONSCIENTIOUSNESS **4** : sensitive regard for fairness or justice : SCRUPLE — **con·science·less** \-ləs\ *adj* — **in all conscience** *or* **in conscience** : in all fairness

conscience money *n* : money paid usu. anonymously to relieve the conscience by restoring what has been wrongfully acquired

con·sci·en·tious \,kän-chē-'en-chəs\ *adj* **1** : governed by or conforming to the dictates of conscience : SCRUPULOUS ⟨a ~ public servant⟩ **2** : METICULOUS, CAREFUL ⟨a ~ listener⟩ *syn see* UPRIGHT *ant* unconscientious, unscrupulous — **con·sci·en·tious·ly** *adv* — **con·sci·en·tious·ness** *n*

conscientious objection *n* : objection on moral or religious grounds (as to service in the armed forces or to bearing arms)

conscientious objector *n* : one who refuses to serve in the armed forces or bear arms on the grounds of moral or religious principles

con·scio·na·ble \'känch-(ə-)nə-bəl\ *adj* [irreg. fr. *conscience*] : CONSCIENTIOUS

¹con·scious \'kän-chəs\ *adj* [L *conscius,* fr. *com-* + *scire* to know] **1** *archaic* : sharing another's knowledge or awareness of an inward state or outward fact **2** : perceiving, apprehending, or noticing with a degree of controlled thought or observation **3** : personally felt ⟨~ guilt⟩ **4** : capable of or marked by thought, will, design, or perception **5** : SELF-CONSCIOUS **6** : having mental faculties undulled by sleep, faintness, or stupor : AWAKE ⟨became ~ after the anesthesia wore off⟩ **7** : done or acting with critical awareness ⟨made a ~ effort to avoid the same mistakes⟩ **8 a** : likely to notice, consider, or appraise ⟨a bargain-*conscious* shopper⟩ **b** : being concerned or interested ⟨a budget-*conscious* businessman⟩ **c** : marked by strong feelings or notions ⟨a race-*conscious* society⟩ *syn see* AWARE *ant* unconscious — **con·scious·ly** *adv*

²conscious *n* : CONSCIOUSNESS 5

con·scious·ness \'kän-chə-snəs\ *n* **1 a** : the quality or state of being aware esp. of something within oneself **b** : the state or fact of being conscious of an external object, state, or fact **c** : CONCERN, AWARENESS ⟨race ~⟩ **2** : the state of being characterized by sensation, emotion, volition, and thought : MIND **3** : the totality of conscious states of an individual **4** : the normal state of conscious life **5** : the upper level of mental life of which the person is aware as contrasted with unconscious processes

con·scribe \kən-'skrīb\ *vt* **con·scribed; con·scrib·ing** [L *conscribere* to enroll] **1** : LIMIT, CIRCUMSCRIBE ⟨ill-health . . . *conscribed* the force of his intentions —*Times Lit. Supp.*⟩ **2** : to enlist forcibly : CONSCRIPT

¹con·script \'kän-,skript\ *adj* [MF, fr. L *conscriptus,* pp. of *conscribere* to enroll, fr. *com-* + *scribere* to write — more at SCRIBE] **1** : enrolled into service by compulsion : DRAFTED **2** : made up of conscripted persons

²conscript *n* : a conscripted person (as a military recruit)

³con·script \kən-'skript\ *vt* : to enroll into service by compulsion : DRAFT ⟨was ~ed into the army⟩

con·scrip·tion \kən-'skrip-shən\ *n* **1** : compulsory enrollment of persons esp. for military service : DRAFT **2** : a forced contribution (as of money) imposed by a government in time of emergency (as war)

¹con·se·crate \'kän(t)-sə-,krāt\ *adj* : dedicated to a sacred purpose : HALLOWED

²consecrate *vt* **-crat·ed; -crat·ing** [ME *consecraten,* fr. L *consecratus,* pp. of *consecrare,* fr. *com-* + *sacrare* to consecrate — more at SACRED] **1** : to induct (a person) into a permanent office with a religious rite; *specif* : to ordain to the office of bishop **2 a** : to make or declare sacred; *specif* : to devote irrevocably to the worship of God by a solemn ceremony **b** : to effect the liturgical transubstantiation of (eucharistic bread and wine) **c** : to devote to a purpose with deep solemnity or dedication **3** : to make inviolable or venerable ⟨principles *consecrated* by the weight of history⟩ *syn see* DEVOTE — **con·se·cra·tive** \-,krāt-iv\ *adj* — **con·se·cra·tor** \-,krāt-ər\ *n* — **con·se·cra·to·ry** \'kän(t)-si-krə-,tōr-ē, -,tór-\ *adj*

con·se·cra·tion \,kän(t)-sə-'krā-shən\ *n* **1** : the act or ceremony of consecrating **2** : the state of being consecrated **3** *cap* : the part of a Communion rite in which the bread and wine are consecrated

con·se·cu·tion \,kän(t)-si-'kyü-shən\ *n* [L *consecution-, consecutio,* fr. *consecutus,* pp. of *consequi* to follow along — more at CONSEQUENT] : SEQUENCE

con·sec·u·tive \kən-'sek-(y)ət-iv\ *adj* : following one after the other in order without gaps : CONTINUOUS — **con·sec·u·tive·ly** *adv* — **con·sec·u·tive·ness** *n* *syn* CONSECUTIVE, SUCCESSIVE *shared meaning element* : following one after the other *ant* inconsecutive

con·sen·su·al \kän-'sench-(ə-)wəl, -'sen-chəl\ *adj* [L *consensus* + E *-al*] **1** : existing or made by mutual consent without an act of writing ⟨a ~ contract⟩ **2** : relating to or being the constrictive pupillary response of an eye that is covered when the other eye is exposed to light — **con·sen·su·al·ly** \-ē\ *adv*

con·sen·sus \kən-'sen(t)-səs\ *n* [L, fr. *consensus,* pp. of *consentire*] **1** : group solidarity in sentiment and belief **2 a** : general agreement : UNANIMITY ⟨the ~ of their opinion, based on reports that had drifted back from the border —John Hersey⟩ **b** : the judgment arrived at by most of those concerned ⟨the ~ was to abandon the project⟩

1**con·sent** \kən-ˈsent\ *vi* [ME *consenten*, fr. L *consentire*, fr. *com-* + *sentire* to feel — more at SENSE] **1** *archaic* : to be in concord in opinion or sentiment **2** : to give assent or approval : AGREE ***syn*** see ASSENT ***ant*** dissent — **con·sent·ing·ly** \-iŋ-lē\ *adv*

2**consent** *n* **1** : compliance in or approval of what is done or proposed by another : ACQUIESCENCE ⟨he shall have power, by and with the advice and ~ of the Senate, to make treaties —*U.S. Constitution*⟩ **2** : agreement as to action or opinion; *specif* : voluntary agreement by a people to organize a civil society and give authority to the government — **con·sent·er** *n*

con·sen·ta·ne·ous \ˌkän(t)-sən-ˈtā-nē-əs, ˌkän-ˌsen-\ *adj* [L *consentaneus*, fr. *consentire* to agree] **1** : expressing agreement : SUITED **2** : done or made by the consent of all — **con·sen·ta·ne·ous·ly** *adv*

con·se·quence \ˈkän(t)-sə-ˌkwen(t)s, -si-kwən(t)s\ *n* **1** : something produced by a cause or necessarily following from a set of conditions **2** : a conclusion that results from reason or argument **3 a** : importance with respect to power to produce an effect : MOMENT **b** : social importance **4** : the appearance of importance; *esp* : SELF-IMPORTANCE ***syn* 1** see EFFECT ***ant*** antecedent **2** see IMPORTANCE — **in consequence** : as a result : CONSEQUENTLY

1**con·se·quent** \-kwənt, -ˌkwent\ *n* **1 a** : DEDUCTION 2b **b** : the conclusion of a conditional sentence **2** : the second term of a ratio

2**consequent** *adj* [MF, fr. L *consequent-*, *consequens*, prp. of *consequi* to follow along, fr. *com-* + *sequi* to follow — more at SUE] **1** : following as a result or effect ⟨removal of the trees and ~ exposure to sun, rain and wind . . . may cause serious degradation of the soil —C. J. Taylor⟩ **2** : observing logical sequence : RATIONAL

con·se·quen·tial \ˌkän(t)-sə-ˈkwen-chəl\ *adj* **1** : CONSEQUENT **2** : of the nature of a secondary result : INDIRECT **3** : having significant consequences : IMPORTANT ⟨a grave and ~ event⟩ **4** : SELF-IMPORTANT — **con·se·quen·ti·al·i·ty** \-ˌkwen-chē-ˈal-ət-ē\ *n* — **con·se·quen·tial·ly** \-ˈkwench-(ə-)lē\ *adv* — **con·se·quen·tial·ness** \-ˈkwen-chəl-nəs\ *n*

con·se·quent·ly \-ˌkwent-lē, -kwənt-\ *adv* : as a result : in view of the foregoing : ACCORDINGLY

con·ser·van·cy \kən-ˈsər-vən-sē\ *n, pl* **-cies** [alter. of obs. *conservacy* conservation, fr. AF *conservacie*, fr. ML *conservatia*, fr. L *conservatus*, pp.] **1** *Brit* : a board regulating fisheries and navigation in a river or port **2 a** : CONSERVATION **b** : an organization or area designated to conserve and protect natural resources

con·ser·va·tion \ˌkän(t)-sər-ˈvā-shən\ *n* [ME, fr. MF, fr. L *conservation-*, *conservatio*, fr. *conservatus*, pp. of *conservare*] **1** : a careful preservation and protection of something; *esp* : planned management of a natural resource to prevent exploitation, destruction, or neglect **2** : the process of conserving a quantity — **con·ser·va·tion·al** \-shnəl, -shən-ᵊl\ *adj*

con·ser·va·tion·ist \-sh(ə-)nəst\ *n* : one who advocates conservation esp. of natural resources

conservation of charge : a principle in physics: the total electric charge of an isolated system remains constant irrespective of whatever internal changes may take place

conservation of energy : a principle in physics: the total energy of an isolated system remains constant irrespective of whatever internal changes may take place with energy disappearing in one form reappearing in another

conservation of mass : a principle in classical physics: the total mass of any material system is neither increased nor diminished by reactions between the parts — called also *conservation of matter*

con·ser·va·tism \kən-ˈsər-və-ˌtiz-əm\ *n* **1 a** : disposition in politics to preserve what is established **b** : a political philosophy based on tradition and social stability, stressing established institutions, and preferring gradual development to abrupt change **2** *cap* **a** : the principles and policies of a Conservative party **b** : the Conservative party **3** : the tendency to prefer an existing situation to change

1**con·ser·va·tive** \kən-ˈsər-vət-iv\ *adj* **1** : PRESERVATIVE **2 a** : of or relating to a philosophy of conservatism **b** *cap* : of or constituting a political party professing the principles of conservatism: as (1) : of or constituting a party of the United Kingdom advocating support of established institutions (2) : Progressive Conservative **3 a** : tending or disposed to maintain existing views, conditions, or institutions : TRADITIONAL **b** : MODERATE, CAUTIOUS **c** : marked by or relating to traditional norms of taste, elegance, style, or manners ⟨a ~ suit⟩ **4** : of or relating to Conservative Judaism — **con·ser·va·tive·ly** *adv* — **con·ser·va·tive·ness** *n*

2**conservative** *n* **1 a** : an adherent or advocate of political conservatism **b** *cap* : a member or supporter of a conservative political party **2 a** : one who adheres to traditional methods or views **b** : a cautious or discreet person

Conservative Judaism *n* : Judaism as practiced esp. among some U.S. Jews with adherence to the Torah and Talmud but with allowance for some departures in keeping with differing times and circumstances — compare ORTHODOX JUDAISM

con·ser·va·tize \-ˌtīz\ *vb* **-tized; -tiz·ing** *vi* : to grow conservative ~ *vt* : to make conservative ⟨unions are being *conservatized* —Theodore Levitt⟩

con·ser·va·toire \kən-ˈsər-və-ˌtwär\ *n* [F, fr. It *conservatorio*] : CONSERVATORY 2

con·ser·va·tor \kən-ˈsər-vət-ər, -və-ˌtȯ(ə)r; ˈkän(t)-sər-ˌvāt-ər\ *n* **1 a** : one that preserves from injury or violation : PROTECTOR **b** : one that is responsible for the care, restoration, and repair of museum articles **2** : a person, official, or institution designated to take over and protect the interests of an incompetent **3** : an official charged with the protection of something affecting public welfare and interests — **con·ser·va·to·ri·al** \kən-ˌsər-və-ˈtōr-ē-əl, (ˌ)kän-, -ˈtȯr-\ *adj*

con·ser·va·to·ry \kən-ˈsər-və-ˌtōr-ē, -ˌtȯr-\ *n, pl* **-ries** **1** : a greenhouse for growing or displaying plants **2** [It *conservatorio* home for foundlings, music school, fr. L *conservatus*, pp.] : a school specializing in one of the fine arts ⟨a music ~⟩

1**con·serve** \kən-ˈsərv\ *vt* **con·served; con·serv·ing** [ME *conserven*, fr. MF *conserver*, fr. L *conservare*, fr. *com-* + *servare* to keep, guard, observe; akin to OE *searu* armor, Av *haurvaiti* he guards] **1** : to keep in a safe or sound state ⟨he *conserved* and enlarged the estate he inherited⟩; *esp* : to avoid wasteful or destructive use of ⟨~ natural resources⟩ **2** : to preserve with sugar **3** : to maintain (a quantity) constant during a process of chemical or physical change ***syn*** see SAVE — **con·serv·er** *n*

2**con·serve** \ˈkän-ˌsərv\ *n* **1** : SWEETMEAT; *esp* : a candied fruit **2** : PRESERVE; *specif* : one prepared from a mixture of fruits

con·sid·er \kən-ˈsid-ər\ *vb* **con·sid·ered; con·sid·er·ing** \-(ə-)riŋ\ [ME *consideren*, fr. MF *considerer*, fr. L *considerare*, lit., to observe the stars, fr. *com-* + *sider-*, *sidus* star — more at SIDEREAL] *vt* **1** : to think about with care or caution **2** : to regard or treat in an attentive, solicitous, or kindly way ⟨he ~*ed* her every wish⟩ **3** : to gaze on steadily or reflectively **4** : to come to judge or classify ⟨~ thrift essential⟩ **5** : REGARD ⟨his works are well ~*ed* abroad⟩ **6** : SUPPOSE ~ *vi* : REFLECT, DELIBERATE ⟨paused a moment to ~⟩
syn CONSIDER, STUDY, CONTEMPLATE, WEIGH *shared meaning element* : to apply one's mind to something in order to increase one's knowledge or understanding of it or to reach a decision about it

1**con·sid·er·able** \-ˈsid-ər(-ə)-bəl, -ˈsid-rə-bəl\ *adj* **1** : worth consideration : SIGNIFICANT **2** : large in extent or degree ⟨a ~ number⟩ — **con·sid·er·a·bly** \-blē\ *adv*

2**considerable** *n* : a considerable amount, degree, or extent

con·sid·er·ate \kən-ˈsid-(ə-)rət\ *adj* **1** : marked by or given to careful consideration : CIRCUMSPECT **2** : thoughtful of the rights and feelings of others ***syn*** see THOUGHTFUL ***ant*** inconsiderate — **con·sid·er·ate·ly** *adv* — **con·sid·er·ate·ness** *n*

con·sid·er·ation \kən-ˌsid-ə-ˈrā-shən\ *n* **1** : continuous and careful thought ⟨after long ~ he agreed to their requests⟩ **2 a** : something considered as a ground : REASON **b** : a taking into account **3** : thoughtful and sympathetic regard **4** : an opinion obtained by reflection **5** : ESTEEM, REGARD ⟨the family built themselves a large, ugly villa . . . and became people of ~ —V. S. Pritchett⟩ **6 a** : RECOMPENSE, PAYMENT **b** : the inducement to a contract or other legal transaction; *specif* : an act or forbearance or the promise thereof done or given by one party in return for the act or promise of another — **in consideration of** : as payment or recompense for ⟨a small fee *in consideration of* many kind services⟩

con·sid·ered \kən-ˈsid-ərd\ *adj* **1** : matured by extended deliberative thought ⟨his ~ opinion⟩ **2** : regarded with respect or esteem

1**con·sid·er·ing** \-(ə-)riŋ\ *prep* : in view of : taking into account ⟨he did well ~ his limitations⟩

2**considering** *conj* : inasmuch as ⟨~ he was new at the job, he did quite well⟩

con·sign \kən-ˈsīn\ *vb* [MF *consigner*, fr. L *consignare*, fr. *com-* + *signum* sign, mark, seal] *vt* **1** : to give over to another's care **2** : to give, transfer, or deliver into the hands or control of another; *also* : to assign as a destination or end ⟨~*ed* his books to the devil⟩ **3** : to send or address to an agent to be cared for or sold ~ *vi, obs* : AGREE, SUBMIT ***syn*** see COMMIT — **con·sign·able** \-ˈsī-nə-bəl\ *adj* — **con·sig·na·tion** \ˌkän-ˌsī-ˈnā-shən, ˌkän(t)-sig-\ *n* — **con·sign·or** \ˌkän(t)-sə-ˈnȯ(ə)r, ˌkän-ˌsī-, kən-ˌsī-\ *n*

con·sign·ee \ˌkän(t)-sə-ˈnē, ˌkän-ˌsī-, kən-ˌsī-\ *n* : one to whom something is consigned or shipped

1**con·sign·ment** \kən-ˈsīn-mənt\ *n* **1** : the act or process of consigning **2** : something consigned esp. in a single shipment — **on consignment** : shipped to a dealer who pays only for what he sells and who may return what is unsold ⟨goods shipped *on consignment*⟩

2**consignment** *adj* : of, relating to, or received as goods on consignment ⟨a ~ sale⟩

1**con·sist** \kən-ˈsist\ *vi* [MF & L; MF *consister*, fr. L *consistere*, lit., to stand together, fr. *com-* + *sistere* to take a stand; akin to L *stare* to stand — more at STAND] **1** : LIE, RESIDE — used with *in* ⟨liberty ~*s* in the absence of obstructions —A. E. Housman⟩ **2** *archaic* **a** : EXIST, BE **b** : to be capable of existing **3** : to become made up — used with *of* ⟨breakfast ~*ed* of cereal, milk, and fruit⟩ **4** : to be consistent ⟨it ~*s* with the facts⟩

2**con·sist** \ˈkän-ˌsist\ *n* : makeup or composition (as of coal sizes or a railroad train) by classes, types, or grades and arrangement

con·sis·tence \kən-ˈsis-tən(t)s\ *n* : CONSISTENCY

con·sis·ten·cy \kən-ˈsis-tən-sē\ *n, pl* **-cies** **1 a** *archaic* : condition of adhering together : firmness of material substance **b** : firmness of constitution or character : PERSISTENCY **2** : degree of firmness, density, viscosity, or resistance to movement or separation of constituent particles ⟨boil the juice to the ~ of a thick syrup⟩ **3 a** : agreement or harmony of parts or features to one another or a whole : CORRESPONDENCE; *specif* : ability to be asserted together without contradiction **b** : harmony of conduct or practice with profession ⟨followed his own advice with ~⟩

con·sis·tent \kən-ˈsis-tənt\ *adj* [L *consistent-*, *consistens*, prp. of *consistere*] **1** *archaic* : possessing firmness or coherence **2 a** : marked by harmonious regularity or steady continuity : free from irregularity, variation, or contradiction ⟨a ~ style in painting⟩ **b** : showing steady conformity to character, profession, belief, or custom ⟨a very ~ man, consistently bad-tempered⟩ **3** : tending to be arbitrarily close to the true value of the parameter estimated as the sample becomes large ⟨a ~ statistical estimator⟩ ***syn*** see CONSONANT ***ant*** inconsistent — **con·sis·tent·ly** *adv*

con·sis·to·ri·al \ˌkän-ˌsis-ˈtōr-ē-əl, -ˈtȯr-, kən-\ *adj* : of or relating to a consistory

con·sis·to·ry \kən-ˈsis-t(ə-)rē\ *n, pl* **-ries** [ME *consistorie*, fr. MF, fr. ML & LL; ML *consistorium* church tribunal, fr. LL, imperial council, fr. L *consistere* to stand together] **1 :** a solemn assembly : COUNCIL **2 :** a church tribunal or governing body: as **a :** a solemn meeting of Roman Catholic cardinals convoked and presided over by the pope **b :** a church session in some Reformed churches **3 :** the organization that confers the degrees of the Ancient and Accepted Scottish Rite of Freemasonry usu. from the 19th to the 32d inclusive; *also* : a meeting of such an organization

con·so·ci·ate \kən-ˈsō-s(h)ē-ˌāt\ *vb* **-at·ed; -at·ing** [L *consociatus,* pp. of *consociare,* fr. *com-* + *socius* companion — more at SOCIAL] *vt* : to bring into association ~ *vi* : to associate esp. in fellowship or partnership

con·so·ci·a·tion \-ˌsō-sē-ˈā-shən, -shē-\ *n* **1 :** association in fellowship or alliance **2 :** an association of churches or religious societies **3 :** an ecological community with a single dominant — **con·so·ci·a·tion·al** \-shnəl, -shən-ᵊl\ *adj*

¹con·sol \kən-ˈsäl, ˈkän-ˌ\ *n* [short for *Consolidated Annuities,* British government securities] : an interest-bearing government bond having no maturity date but redeemable on call; *specif* : one first issued by the British government in 1751 — usu. used in pl.

²consol *abbr* consolidated

con·so·la·tion \ˌkän(t)-sə-ˈlā-shən\ *n* **1 :** the act or an instance of consoling : the state of being consoled : COMFORT **2 :** something that consoles; *specif* : a contest held for those who have lost early in a tournament ⟨the losers met in a ~ game⟩ — **con·so·la·to·ry** \kən-ˈsō-lə-ˌtōr-ē, -ˈsäl-ə-, -ˌtȯr-\ *adj*

consolation prize *n* : a prize given to a runner-up or a loser in a contest

¹con·sole \kən-ˈsōl\ *vt* **con·soled; con·sol·ing** [F *consoler,* fr. L *consolari,* fr. *com-* + *solari* to console — more at SILLY] : to alleviate the grief or sense of loss of ⟨~ a widow⟩ ***syn*** see COMFORT — **con·sol·ing·ly** \-ˈsō-liŋ-lē\ *adv*

²con·sole \ˈkän-ˌsōl\ *n* [F, fr. MF, short for *consolateur* bracket in human shape, lit., consoler, fr. L *consolator,* fr. *consolatus,* pp. of *consolari*] **1 :** an architectural member projecting from a wall to form a bracket or from a keystone for ornament **2 a :** the desk from which an organ is played and which contains the keyboards, pedal board, and other controlling mechanisms **b :** a panel or cabinet on which are mounted dials, switches, and other apparatus used in centrally monitoring and controlling electrical or mechanical devices; *specif* : the part of a computer used for communication between the operator and the computer **3 a :** a cabinet (as for a radio or television set) designed to rest directly on the floor **b :** a small storage cabinet between bucket seats in an automobile

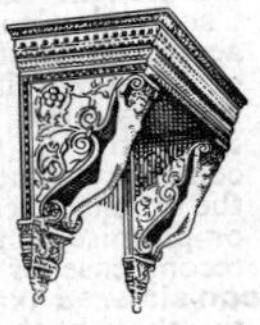

console 1

console table *n* : a table fixed to a wall with its top supported by consoles or front legs; *broadly* : a table designed to fit against a wall

con·so·lette \ˌkän(t)-sə-ˈlet\ *n* [²*console* + *-ette*] : a small cabinet containing a radio, television, or record player

con·sol·i·date \kən-ˈsäl-ə-ˌdāt\ *vb* **-dat·ed; -dat·ing** [L *consolidatus,* pp. of *consolidare* to make solid, fr. *com-* + *solidus* solid] *vt* **1 :** to join together into one whole : UNITE ⟨~ several small school districts⟩ **2 :** to make firm or secure : STRENGTHEN ⟨~ their hold on first place⟩ **3 :** to form into a compact mass ~ *vi* : to become consolidated; *specif* : MERGE ⟨the two companies *consolidated*⟩ — **con·sol·i·da·tor** \-ˌdāt-ər\ *n*

consolidated school *n* : a public school formed by merging other schools

con·sol·i·da·tion \kən-ˌsäl-ə-ˈdā-shən\ *n* **1 :** the act or process of consolidating : the state of being consolidated **2 :** the process of uniting : the quality or state of being united; *specif* : the unification of two or more corporations by dissolution of existing ones and creation of a single new corporation — compare MERGER **3 :** alteration of lung tissue from an aerated condition to one of solid consistency

con·som·mé \ˌkän(t)-sə-ˈmā\ *n* [F, fr. pp. of *consommer* to complete, boil down, fr. L *consummare* to complete — more at CONSUMMATE] : a clear soup made from well-seasoned meat broth

con·so·nance \ˈkän(t)-s(ə-)nən(t)s\ *n* **1 :** harmony or agreement among components **2 a :** correspondence or recurrence of sounds esp. in words; *specif* : recurrence or repetition of consonants esp. at the end of stressed syllables without the similar correspondence of vowels ⟨the final sounds of "stroke" and "luck" exhibit ~⟩ **b :** an agreeable combination of musical tones **c :** SYMPATHETIC VIBRATION, RESONANCE

con·so·nan·cy \-s(ə-)nən-sē\ *n, pl* **-cies** : CONSONANCE 1

¹con·so·nant \ˈkän(t)-s(ə-)nənt\ *n* [ME, fr. L *consonant-, consonans,* fr. prp. of *consonare*] **1 :** one of a class of speech sounds (as \p\, \g\, \n\, \l\, \s\, \r\) characterized by constriction or closure at one or more points in the breath channel **2 :** a letter representing a consonant; *esp* : any letter of the English alphabet except *a, e, i, o,* and *u*

²consonant *adj* [MF, fr. L *consonant-, consonans* prp. of *consonare* to sound together, agree, fr. *com-* + *sonare* to sound] **1 :** being in agreement or harmony : free from elements making for discord **2 :** marked by musical consonances **3 :** having similar sounds ⟨~ words⟩ **4 :** relating to or exhibiting consonance : RESONANT — **con·so·nant·ly** *adv*

syn CONSONANT, CONSISTENT, COMPATIBLE, CONGRUOUS, CONGENIAL, SYMPATHETIC *shared meaning element* : being in agreement one with another or agreeable one to another ***ant*** inconsonant

con·so·nan·tal \ˌkän(t)-sə-ˈnant-ᵊl\ *adj* : relating to, being, or marked by a consonant or group of consonants

consonant shift *n* : a set of regular changes in consonant articulation in the history of a language or dialect: **a :** such a set affecting the Indo-European stops and distinguishing the Germanic languages from the other Indo-European languages — called also *first consonant shift* **b :** such a set affecting the Germanic stops and distinguishing High German from the other Germanic languages — called also *second consonant shift*

¹con·sort \ˈkän-ˌsȯ(ə)rt\ *n* [ME, fr. MF, fr. L *consort-, consors,* lit., one who shares a common lot, fr. *com-* + *sort-, sors* lot, share] **1 :** ASSOCIATE **2 :** a ship accompanying another **3 :** SPOUSE — compare PRINCE CONSORT

²consort *n* [MF *consorte,* fr. *consort*] **1 :** GROUP, ASSEMBLY ⟨a ~ of specialists⟩ **2 :** CONJUNCTION, ASSOCIATION ⟨he ruled in ~ with his father⟩ **3 a :** a group of musicians entertaining by voice or instrument **b :** a set of musical instruments of the same family

³con·sort \kən-ˈsȯ(ə)rt, kän-ˈ, ˈkän-ˌ\ *vt* **1 :** UNITE, ASSOCIATE **2** *obs* : ESCORT ~ *vi* **1 :** to keep company ⟨~*ing* with criminals⟩ **2** *obs* : to make harmony : PLAY **3 :** ACCORD, HARMONIZE ⟨the illustrations ~ admirably with the text — *Times Lit. Supp.*⟩

con·sor·tium \kən-ˈsȯrt-ē-əm, -ˈsȯr-sh(ē-)əm\ *n, pl* **-sor·tia** \-ˈsȯrt-ē-ə, -ˈsȯr-sh(ē-)ə\ *also* **-sortiums** [L, fellowship, fr. *consort-, consors*] **1 :** an international business or banking agreement or combination **2 :** ASSOCIATION, SOCIETY **3 :** the legal right of one spouse to the company, affection, and service of the other

con·spe·cif·ic \ˌkän(t)-spi-ˈsif-ik\ *adj* : of the same species

con·spec·tus \kən-ˈspek-təs\ *n* [L, fr. *conspectus,* pp. of *conspicere*] **1 :** a usu. brief survey or summary often providing an overall view **2 :** OUTLINE, SYNOPSIS ***syn*** see ABRIDGMENT

con·spi·cu·i·ty \ˌkän(t)-spə-ˈkyü-ət-ē\ *n* : CONSPICUOUSNESS

con·spic·u·ous \kən-ˈspik-yə-wəs\ *adj* [L *conspicuus,* fr. *conspicere* to get sight of, fr. *com-* + *specere* to look — more at SPY] **1 :** obvious to the eye or mind **2 :** attracting attention : STRIKING **3 :** marked by a noticeable violation of good taste ***syn*** see NOTICEABLE ***ant*** inconspicuous — **con·spic·u·ous·ly** *adv*

conspicuous consumption *n* : lavish or wasteful spending thought to enhance social prestige

con·spic·u·ous·ness *n* : the quality or state of being conspicuous

con·spir·a·cy \kən-ˈspir-ə-sē\ *n, pl* **-cies** [ME *conspiracie,* fr. L *conspiratus,* pp. of *conspirare*] **1 :** the act of conspiring together **2 a :** an agreement among conspirators **b :** a group of conspirators

conspiracy of silence : a secret agreement to keep silent about an occurrence, situation, or subject esp. in order to promote or protect selfish interests

con·spi·ra·tion \ˌkän(t)-spə-ˈrā-shən, -(ˌ)spir-ˈā-\ *n* **1 :** the act or action of plotting or secretly combining **2 :** a joint effort toward a particular end — **con·spi·ra·tion·al** \-shnəl, -shən-ᵊl\ *adj*

con·spir·a·tor \kən-ˈspir-ət-ər\ *n* : one that conspires : PLOTTER

con·spir·a·to·ri·al \kən-ˌspir-ə-ˈtōr-ē-əl, -ˈtȯr-\ *adj* : of, relating to, or suggestive of a conspiracy — **con·spir·a·to·ri·al·ly** \-ē-ə-lē\ *adv*

con·spire \kən-ˈspī(ə)r\ *vb* **con·spired; con·spir·ing** [ME *conspiren,* fr. MF *conspirer,* fr. L *conspirare* to breathe together, agree, conspire, fr. *com-* + *spirare* to breathe — more at SPIRIT] *vt* : PLOT, CONTRIVE ~ *vi* **1 a :** to join in a secret agreement to do an unlawful or wrongful act or to use such means to accomplish a lawful end **b :** SCHEME **2 :** to act in harmony ⟨circumstances *conspired* to defeat his efforts⟩

con spi·ri·to \kän-ˈspir-ə-ˌtō, kōn-\ *adv* [It] : with spirit or animation — used as a direction in music

const *abbr* **1** constant **2** constitution; constitutional **3** construction

con·sta·ble \ˈkän(t)-stə-bəl, ˈkən(t)-\ *n* [ME *conestable,* fr. OF, fr. LL *comes stabuli,* lit., officer of the stable] **1 :** a high officer of a medieval royal or noble household **2 :** the warden or governor of a royal castle or a fortified town **3 a :** a public officer usually of a town or township responsible for keeping the peace and for minor judicial duties **b** *Brit* : POLICEMAN; *esp* : one ranking below sergeant

¹con·stab·u·lary \kən-ˈstab-yə-ˌler-ē\ *n, pl* **-lar·ies** **1 :** the organized body of constables of a particular district or country **2 :** an armed police force organized on military lines but distinct from the regular army

²constabulary *adj* : of or relating to a constable or constabulary

con·stan·cy \ˈkän(t)-stən-sē\ *n, pl* **-cies** **1 a :** steadfastness of mind under duress : FORTITUDE **b :** FIDELITY, LOYALTY **2 :** freedom from change

¹con·stant \ˈkän(t)-stənt\ *adj* [ME, fr. MF, fr. L *constant-, constans,* fr. prp. of *constare* to stand firm, be consistent, fr. *com-* + *stare* to stand — more at STAND] **1 :** marked by firm steadfast revolution or faithfulness : exhibiting constancy of mind or attachment **2 :** INVARIABLE, UNIFORM **3 :** continually occurring or recurring : REGULAR ***syn*** **1** see FAITHFUL ***ant*** inconstant, fickle **2** see CONTINUOUS ***ant*** fitful — **con·stant·ly** *adv*

²constant *n* : something invariable or unchanging: as **a :** a number that has a fixed value in a given situation or universally or that is characteristic of some substance or instrument **b :** a number that is assumed not to change value in a given mathematical discussion **c :** a term in logic with a fixed designation

con·stan·tan \ˈkän(t)-stən-ˌtan\ *n* [fr. the fact that its resistance remains constant under change of temperature] : an alloy of copper and nickel used for electrical resistors and in thermocouples

con·stel·late \ˈkän(t)-stə-ˌlāt\ *vb* **-lat·ed; -lat·ing** *vt* **1 :** to unite in a cluster **2 :** to set or adorn with or as if with constellations ~ *vi* : CLUSTER

con·stel·la·tion \ˌkän(t)-stə-ˈlā-shən\ *n* [ME *constellacioun,* fr. MF *constellation,* fr. LL *constellation-, constellatio,* fr. *constellatus* studded with stars, fr. L *com-* + *stella* star — more at STAR] **1 a :** the configuration of stars esp. at one's birth **b** *obs* : character or constitution as determined by the stars **2 :** any of 88 arbitrary configurations of stars or an area of the celestial sphere covering one of these configurations **3 :** an assemblage, collection, or gathering of usu. related persons, qualities, or things ⟨a ~ of . . . relatives, friends, and hangers-on —Brendan Gill⟩ **4 :** PATTERN, ARRANGEMENT ⟨taking advantage of the shifting ~ of power throughout the known world —H. D. Lasswell⟩ — **con·stel·la·to·ry** \kən-ˈstel-ə-ˌtōr-ē, -ˌtȯr-\ *adj*

con·ster·nate \ˈkän(t)-stər-ˌnāt\ *vt* **-nat·ed; -nat·ing** : to fill with consternation

con·ster·na·tion \ˌkän(t)-stər-ˈnā-shən\ *n* [F or L; F, fr. L *consternation-, consternatio,* fr. *consternatus,* pp. of *consternare* to bewilder, alarm, fr. *com-* + *-sternare* (akin to OE *starian* to stare)] : amazement or dismay that hinders or throws into confusion ⟨the two . . .

stared at each other in ~, and neither knew what to do —Pearl Buck⟩
con·sti·pate \ˈkän(t)-stə-ˌpāt\ *vt* **-pat·ed; -pat·ing** [ML *constipatus,* pp. of *constipare,* fr. L, to crowd together, fr. *com-* + *stipare* to press together — more at STIFF] **1 :** to make costive : cause constipation in **2 :** to make immobile, inactive, or dull : STULTIFY ⟨so much clutter . . . will tend to ~ the novel's working order —*Times Lit. Supp.*⟩
con·sti·pa·tion \ˌkän(t)-stə-ˈpā-shən\ *n* **1 :** abnormally delayed or infrequent passage of dry hardened feces **2 :** STULTIFICATION
con·stit·u·en·cy \kən-ˈstich-(ə-)wən-sē\ *n, pl* **-cies** **1 a :** a body of citizens entitled to elect a representative to a legislative or other public body **b :** the residents in an electoral district **c :** an electoral district **2 a :** a group or body that patronizes, supports, or offers representation ⟨there was no ~ of millionaires to back him⟩ **b :** the people involved in or served by an organization (as a business or institution) ⟨the big dailies and urban TV stations are not in touch with the special problems of their own *constituencies* —J. P. Lyford⟩
[1]**con·stit·u·ent** \kən-ˈstich-(ə-)wənt\ *n* [F *constituant,* fr. MF, fr. prp. of *constituer* to constitute, fr. L *constituere*] **1 :** one who authorizes another to act for him : PRINCIPAL **2 :** an essential part : COMPONENT, ELEMENT **3 :** one of two or more linguistic forms that enter into a construction or a compound and are either immediate (as *he* and *writes reviews* in the construction "he writes reviews") or ultimate (as *he, write, -s, review,* and *-s* in the same construction) **4 a :** one of a group who elects another to represent him in a public office **b :** a resident in a constituency ***syn*** see ELEMENT ***ant*** whole, aggregate
[2]**constituent** *adj* [L *constituent-, constituens,* prp. of *constituere*] **1 :** serving to form, compose, or make up a unit or whole : COMPONENT **2 :** having the power to create a government or frame or amend a constitution ⟨a ~ assembly⟩ — **con·stit·u·ent·ly** *adv*
con·sti·tute \ˈkän(t)-stə-ˌt(y)üt\ *vt* **-tut·ed; -tut·ing** [L *constitutus,* pp. of *constituere* to set up, constitute, fr. *com-* + *statuere* to set — more at STATUTE] **1 :** to appoint to an office, function, or dignity **2 :** to set up : ESTABLISH: as **a :** ENACT **b :** FOUND **c** (1) **:** to give due or lawful form to (2) **:** to legally process **3 :** to make up : FORM, COMPOSE ⟨twelve months ~ a year⟩ ⟨high school dropouts who ~ a major problem in large city slums —J. B. Conant⟩
con·sti·tu·tion \ˌkän(t)-stə-ˈt(y)ü-shən\ *n* **1 :** an established law or custom : ORDINANCE **2 :** the act of establishing, making, or setting up **3 a :** the physical makeup of the individual comprising inherited qualities modified by environment **b :** the structure, composition, physical makeup, or nature of something **4 :** the mode in which a state or society is organized; *esp* **:** the manner in which sovereign power is distributed **5 a :** the basic principles and laws of a nation, state, or social group that determine the powers and duties of the government and guarantee certain rights to the people in it **b :** a written instrument embodying the rules of a political or social organization ***syn*** see PHYSIQUE — **con·sti·tu·tion·less** \-ləs\ *adj*
[1]**con·sti·tu·tion·al** \-shnəl, -shən-ᵊl\ *adj* **1 :** relating to, inherent in, or affecting the constitution of body or mind **2 :** of, relating to, or entering into the fundamental makeup of something : ESSENTIAL **3 :** being in accordance with or authorized by the constitution of a state or society ⟨a ~ government⟩ **4 :** regulated by or ruling according to a constitution ⟨a ~ monarchy⟩ **5 :** of or relating to a constitution **6 :** loyal to or supporting an established constitution or form of government
[2]**constitutional** *n* **:** a walk taken for one's health
con·sti·tu·tion·al·ism \-ˌiz-əm\ *n* **:** adherence to or government according to constitutional principles; *also* **:** a constitutional system of government — **con·sti·tu·tion·al·ist** \-əst\ *n*
con·sti·tu·tion·al·i·ty \-ˌt(y)ü-shə-ˈnal-ət-ē\ *n* **:** the quality or state of being constitutional; *esp* **:** accordance with the provisions of a constitution ⟨questioned the ~ of the law⟩
con·sti·tu·tion·al·ize \-ˈt(y)ü-shnəl-ˌīz, -shən-ᵊl-\ *vt* **-ized; -iz·ing :** to provide with a constitution : organize along constitutional principles — **con·sti·tu·tion·al·iza·tion** \-ˌt(y)ü-shnəl-ə-ˈzā-shən, -shən-ᵊl-\ *n*
con·sti·tu·tion·al·ly \-ˈt(y)ü-shnə-lē, -shən-ᵊl-ē\ *adv* **1 a :** in accordance with one's constitution ⟨~ unable to grasp subtleties⟩ **b :** in structure, composition, or constitution ⟨despite repeated heatings the material remained ~ the same⟩ **2 :** in accordance with a political constitution ⟨was not ~ eligible to fill the office⟩
con·sti·tu·tive \ˈkän(t)-stə-ˌt(y)üt-iv, kən-ˈstich-ət-iv\ *adj* **1 :** having the power to enact or establish : CONSTRUCTIVE **2 :** CONSTITUENT, ESSENTIAL **3 :** relating to or dependent on constitution ⟨a ~ property of all electrolytes⟩ — **con·sti·tu·tive·ly** *adv*
constr *abbr* construction
con·strain \kən-ˈstrān\ *vt* [ME *constrainen,* fr. MF *constraindre,* fr. L *constringere* to constrict, constrain, fr. *com-* + *stringere* to draw tight — more at STRAIN] **1 a :** to force by imposed stricture, restriction, or limitation **b :** to restrict the motion of (a mechanical body) to a particular mode **2 :** to force or produce in an unnatural or strained manner ⟨a ~*ed* smile⟩ **3 :** to secure by or as if by bonds : CONFINE ⟨when winter frosts ~ the field with cold —John Dryden⟩ **4 :** to bring into narrow compass; *also* **:** to clasp tightly **5 :** to hold back by or as if by force ⟨~*ing* my mind not to wander from the task —Charles Dickens⟩ ***syn*** see FORCE — **con·strained·ly** \-ˈstrā-nəd-lē, -ˈstrān-dlē\ *adv*
con·straint \kən-ˈstrānt\ *n* [ME, fr. MF *constrainte,* fr. *constraindre*] **1 a :** the act of constraining **b :** the state of being checked, restricted, or compelled to avoid or perform some action ⟨the ~ and monotony of a monastic life —Matthew Arnold⟩ **c :** a constraining agency or force : CHECK ⟨put legal ~*s* on the board's activities⟩ **2 a :** repression of one's own feelings, behavior, or actions **b :** a sense of being constrained : EMBARRASSMENT
con·strict \kən-ˈstrikt\ *vb* [L *constrictus,* pp. of *constringere*] *vt* **1 a :** to make narrow by drawing together or squeezing **b :** COMPRESS, SQUEEZE ⟨~ a nerve⟩ **2 :** to stultify, stop, or cause to falter : INHIBIT ~ *vi* **:** to become constricted ***syn*** see CONTRACT — **con·stric·tive** \-ˈstrik-tiv\ *adj*
con·stric·tion \-ˈstrik-shən\ *n* **1 :** an act or product of constricting **2 :** the quality or state of being constricted **3 :** something that constricts
con·stric·tor \-ˈstrik-tər\ *n* **1 :** one that constricts **2 :** a muscle that contracts a cavity or orifice or compresses an organ **3 :** a snake (as a boa constrictor) that kills prey by compression in its coils
con·stringe \kən-ˈstrinj\ *vt* **con·stringed; con·string·ing** [L *constringere*] **1 :** CONSTRICT **2 :** to cause to shrink ⟨cold ~*s* the pores⟩ — **con·strin·gent** \-ˈstrin-jənt\ *adj*
con·stru·able \kən-ˈstrü-ə-bəl\ *adj* **:** that may be construed
[1]**con·struct** \kən-ˈstrəkt\ *vt* [L *constructus,* pp. of *construere,* fr. *com-* + *struere* to build — more at STRUCTURE] **1 :** to make or form by combining parts : BUILD **2 :** to set in logical order **3 :** to draw (a geometrical figure) with suitable instruments and under specified conditions — **con·struct·ible** \-ˈstrək-tə-bəl\ *adj* — **con·struc·tor** \-tər\ *n*
[2]**con·struct** \ˈkän-ˌstrəkt\ *n* **:** something constructed esp. by mental synthesis ⟨form a ~ of a physical object by mentally assembling and integrating sense-data⟩
con·struc·tion \kən-ˈstrək-shən\ *n* **1 :** the arrangement and connection of words or groups of words in a sentence : syntactical arrangement **2 :** the process, art, or manner of constructing; *also* **:** a thing constructed **3 :** the act or result of construing, interpreting, or explaining **4 :** a sculptural creation that is put together out of separate pieces of often disparate materials — **con·struc·tion·al** \-shnəl, -shən-ᵊl\ *adj* — **con·struc·tion·al·ly** \-ē\ *adv*
con·struc·tion·ist \-sh(ə-)nəst\ *n* **:** one who construes a legal document (as the U.S. Constitution) in a specific way ⟨a strict ~⟩
construction paper *n* **:** colored paper suitable for crayon or ink drawings and watercolors and for making cutouts
con·struc·tive \kən-ˈstrək-tiv\ *adj* **1 :** declared such by judicial construction or interpretation ⟨~ fraud⟩ **2 :** of or relating to construction **3 :** promoting improvement or development ⟨~ criticism⟩ — **con·struc·tive·ly** *adv* — **con·struc·tive·ness** *n*
con·struc·tiv·ism \kən-ˈstrək-ti-ˌviz-əm\ *n* **1 :** a nonobjective art movement originating in Russia and concerned with formal organization of planes and expression of volume in terms of modern industrial materials (as glass and plastic) **2 :** an abstract style of stage setting that employs skeletal structures instead of realistic props — **con·struc·tiv·ist** \-ti-vəst\ *adj or n*
[1]**con·strue** \kən-ˈstrü\ *vb* **con·strued; con·stru·ing** [ME *construen,* fr. LL *construere,* fr. L, to construct] *vt* **1 :** to analyze the arrangement and connection of words in (a sentence or sentence part) **2 :** to understand or explain the sense or intention of usu. in a particular way or with respect to a given set of circumstances ⟨*construed* my actions as hostile⟩ ~ *vi* **:** to construe a sentence or sentence part esp. in connection with translating
[2]**con·strue** \ˈkän-ˌstrü\ *n* **:** an act of construing esp. by piecemeal translation; *also* **:** the translated version resulting from such an act
con·sub·stan·tial \ˌkän(t)-səb-ˈstan-chəl\ *adj* [LL *consubstantialis,* fr. L *com-* + *substantia* substance] **:** of the same substance
con·sub·stan·ti·a·tion \ˌkän(t)-səb-ˌstan-chē-ˈā-shən\ *n* **:** the actual substantial presence and combination of the body of Christ with the eucharistic bread and wine according to a teaching associated with Martin Luther
con·sue·tude \ˈkän(t)-swi-ˌt(y)üd, kən-ˈsü-ə-\ *n* [ME, fr. L *consuetudo* — more at CUSTOM] **:** social usage : CUSTOM — **con·sue·tu·di·nary** \ˌkän(t)-swi-ˈt(y)üd-ᵊn-ˌer-ē, kən-ˌsü-ə-\ *adj*
con·sul \ˈkän(t)-səl\ *n* [ME, fr. L, fr. *consulere* to consult] **1 a :** either of two annually elected chief magistrates of the Roman republic **b :** one of three chief magistrates of the French republic from 1799 to 1804 **2 :** an official appointed by a government to reside in a foreign country to represent the commercial interests of citizens of the appointing country — **con·su·lar** \-s(ə-)lər\ *adj* — **con·sul·ship** \-səl-ˌship\ *n*
con·sul·ate \-s(ə-)lət\ *n* **1 :** a government by consuls **2 :** the office, term of office, or jurisdiction of a consul **3 :** the residence or official premises of a consul
consulate general *n, pl* **consulates general :** the residence, office, or jurisdiction of a consul general
consul general *n, pl* **consuls general :** a consul of the first rank stationed in an important place or having jurisdiction in several places or over several consuls
[1]**con·sult** \kən-ˈsəlt\ *vb* [MF or L; MF *consulter,* fr. L *consultare,* fr. *consultus,* pp. of *consulere* to deliberate, counsel, consult] *vt* **1 a :** to ask the advice or opinion of ⟨~ a doctor⟩ **b :** to refer to ⟨~ a dictionary⟩ **2 :** to have regard to : CONSIDER ~ *vi* **1 :** to consult an individual **2 :** to deliberate together : CONFER **3 :** to serve as a consultant — **con·sult·er** *n*
[2]**con·sult** \kən-ˈsəlt, ˈkän-ˌ\ *n* **:** CONSULTATION
con·sul·tan·cy \kən-ˈsəlt-ᵊn-sē\ *n, pl* **-cies** **1 :** an agency that provides consulting services **2 :** CONSULTATION
con·sul·tant \kən-ˈsəlt-ᵊnt\ *n* **1 :** one who consults another **2 :** one who gives professional advice or services : EXPERT — **con·sul·tant·ship** \-ˌship\ *n*
con·sul·ta·tion \ˌkän(t)-səl-ˈtā-shən\ *n* **1 :** COUNCIL, CONFERENCE; *specif* **:** a deliberation between physicians on a case or its treatment **2 :** the act of consulting or conferring
con·sul·ta·tive \kən-ˈsəl-tət-iv, ˈkän(t)-səl-ˌtāt-iv\ *adj* **:** of, relating to, or intended for consultation : ADVISORY ⟨~ committee⟩
con·sult·ing \kən-ˈsəl-tiŋ\ *adj* **1 :** providing professional or expert advice ⟨a ~ architect⟩ **2 :** of or relating to consultation or a consultant ⟨the ~ room of a psychiatrist⟩
con·sul·tive \kən-ˈsəl-tiv\ *adj* **:** CONSULTATIVE

ə abut	ᵊ kitten	ər further	a back	ā bake	ä cot, cart
au̇ out	ch chin	e less	ē easy	g gift	i trip	ī life
j joke	ŋ sing	ō flow	ȯ flaw	ȯi coin	th thin	t͟h this
ü loot	u̇ foot	y yet	yü few	yu̇ furious	zh vision

con·sul·tor \kən-ˈsəl-tər\ *n* : one that consults or advises; *esp* : an adviser to a Roman Catholic bishop, provincial, or sacred congregation

1con·sum·able \kən-ˈsü-mə-bəl\ *adj* : capable of being consumed

2consumable *n* : something that is consumable — usu. used in pl. ⟨the ~*s* on board their ship are adequate for the 14-day mission — R. C. Cowen⟩

con·sume \kən-ˈsüm\ *vb* **con·sumed; con·sum·ing** [ME *consumen,* fr. MF or L; MF *consumer,* fr. L *consumere,* fr. *com-* + *sumere* to take up, take, fr. *sub-* up + *emere* to take — more at SUB-, REDEEM] *vt* **1** : to do away with completely : DESTROY ⟨fire *consumed* several buildings⟩ **2 a** : to spend wastefully : SQUANDER **b** : to use up ⟨his correspondence *consumed* much of his time⟩ **3** : to eat or drink esp. in great quantity ⟨*consumed* several kegs of beer⟩ **4** : to engage fully : ENGROSS ⟨she was *consumed* with curiosity⟩ ~ *vi* : to waste or burn away : PERISH ***syn*** see WASTE, MONOPOLIZE — **con·sum·ing·ly** \-ˈsü-miŋ-lē\ *adv*

con·sum·ed·ly \-ˈsü-məd-lē\ *adv* : as if consumed : EXCESSIVELY

con·sum·er \kən-ˈsü-mər\ *n, often attrib* : one that consumes: as **a** : one that utilizes economic goods **b** : an organism requiring complex organic compounds for food which it obtains by preying on other organisms or by eating particles of organic matter — compare PRODUCER 4 — **con·sum·er·ship** \-ˌship\ *n*

consumer credit *n* : credit granted to an individual esp. to finance the purchase of consumer goods or to defray personal or family expenses

consumer goods *n pl* : goods that directly satisfy human wants

con·sum·er·ism \kən-ˈsü-mə-ˌriz-əm\ *n* **1** : the promotion of the consumer's interests **2** : the theory that an increasing consumption of goods is economically desirable — **con·sum·er·ist** \-rəst\ *n*

consumer price index *n* : an index measuring the change in the cost of typical wage-earner purchases of goods and services expressed as a percentage of the cost of these same goods and services in some base period — called also *cost-of-living index*

1con·sum·mate \kən-ˈsəm-ət, ˈkän(t)-sə-mət\ *adj* [ME, fr. L *consummatus,* pp. of *consummare* to sum up, finish, fr. *com-* + *summa* sum] **1** : complete in every detail : PERFECT **2** : extremely skilled and accomplished ⟨a ~ liar⟩ **3** : of the highest degree ⟨~ skill⟩ ⟨~ cruelty⟩ — **con·sum·mate·ly** *adv*

2con·sum·mate \ˈkän(t)-sə-ˌmāt\ *vb* **-mat·ed; -mat·ing** *vt* **1 a** : FINISH, COMPLETE ⟨~ a business deal⟩ **b** : to make perfect : ACHIEVE **2** : to make (marital union) complete by sexual intercourse ⟨~ a marriage⟩ ~ *vi* : to become perfected — **con·sum·ma·tive** \ˈkän(t)-sə-ˌmāt-iv, kən-ˈsəm-ət-iv\ *adj* — **con·sum·ma·tor** \ˈkän(t)-sə-ˌmāt-ər\ *n*

con·sum·ma·tion \ˌkän-sə-ˈmā-shən\ *n* **1** : the act of consummating ⟨the ~ of a contract by mutual signature⟩; *specif* : the consummating of a marriage **2** : the ultimate end : FINISH

con·sum·ma·to·ry \kən-ˈsəm-ə-ˌtōr-ē, -ˌtȯr-\ *adj* **1** : of or relating to consummation : CONCLUDING **2** : of, relating to, or being a response or act (as eating or copulating) that terminates a period of usu. goal-directed behavior

con·sump·tion \kən-ˈsəm(p)-shən\ *n* [ME *consumpcioun,* fr. L *consumption-, consumptio,* fr. *consumptus,* pp. of *consumere*] **1** : the act or process of consuming **2** : the utilization of economic goods in the satisfaction of wants or in the process of production resulting chiefly in their destruction, deterioration, or transformation **3 a** : a progressive wasting away of the body esp. from pulmonary tuberculosis **b** : TUBERCULOSIS

1con·sump·tive \-ˈsəm(p)-tiv\ *adj* **1** : tending to consume **2** : of, relating to, or affected with consumption — **con·sump·tive·ly** *adv*

2consumptive *n* : a person affected with consumption

cont *abbr* **1** containing **2** contents **3** continent; continental **4** continued **5** control

1con·tact \ˈkän-ˌtakt\ *n* [F or L; F, fr. L *contactus,* fr. *contactus,* pp. of *contingere* to have contact with — more at CONTINGENT] **1 a** : union or junction of surfaces **b** : the apparent touching or mutual tangency of the limbs of two celestial bodies or of the disk of one body with the shadow of another during an eclipse, transit, or occultation **c** (1) : the junction of two electrical conductors through which a current passes (2) : a special part made for such a junction **2 a** : ASSOCIATION, RELATIONSHIP **b** : CONNECTION, COMMUNICATION **c** : direct visual observation of the earth's surface made from an airplane esp. as an aid to navigation **d** : an establishing of communication with someone or an observing or receiving of a significant signal from a person or object ⟨radar ~ with Mars⟩ **3** : one serving as a carrier or source **4** : CONTACT LENS

2con·tact \ˈkän-ˌtakt, kən-ˈ\ *vt* **1** : to bring into contact **2 a** : to enter or be in contact with : JOIN **b** : to get in communication with ⟨~ your local dealer⟩ ~ *vi* : to make contact

3con·tact \ˈkän-ˌtakt\ *adj* : maintaining, involving, or activated or caused by contact ⟨~ poisons⟩

4con·tact \ˈkän-ˌtakt\ *adv* : by contact flying ⟨the ceiling was so low that the patrol was flown ~ —J. L. Foley⟩

contact flying \ˈkän-ˌtakt-\ *n* : navigation of an airplane by means of direct observation of landmarks

contact inhibition \ˈkän-ˌtakt\ *n* : cessation of cellular undulating movements upon contact with other cells with accompanying cessation of cell growth and division

contact lens \ˌkän-ˌtakt\ *n* : a thin lens designed to fit over the cornea

contact print \ˌkän-ˌtak(t)-\ *n* : a photographic print made with the negative in contact with the sensitized paper, plate, or film

con·ta·gion \kən-ˈtā-jən\ *n* [ME, fr. MF & L; MF, fr. L *contagion-, contagio,* fr. *contingere* to have contact with, pollute] **1 a** : the transmission of a disease by direct or indirect contact **b** : a contagious disease **c** : a disease-producing agent (as a virus) **2 a** : POISON **b** : contagious influence, quality, or nature **c** : corrupting influence or contact **3 a** : rapid communication of an influence (as a doctrine or emotional state) **b** : an influence that spreads rapidly

con·ta·gious \-jəs\ *adj* **1** : communicable by contact : CATCHING **2** : bearing contagion **3** : used for contagious diseases ⟨a ~ ward⟩ **4** : exciting similar emotions or conduct in others ⟨~ enthusiasm⟩ — **con·ta·gious·ly** *adv* — **con·ta·gious·ness** *n*

contagious abortion *n* : a contagious or infectious disease (as a brucellosis) of domestic animals characterized by abortion

con·ta·gium \kən-ˈtā-j(ē-)əm\ *n, pl* **-gia** \-j(ē-)ə\ [L, contagion, fr. *contingere*] : a virus or living organism capable of causing a communicable disease

con·tain \kən-ˈtān\ *vb* [ME *conteinen,* fr. OF *contenir,* fr. L *continēre* to hold together, hold in, contain, fr. *com-* + *tenēre* to hold — more at THIN] *vt* **1** : to keep within limits : hold back or hold down: as **a** : RESTRAIN, CONTROL **b** : CHECK, HALT **c** : to follow successfully a policy of containment toward **d** : to prevent (as an enemy or opponent) from advancing or from making a successful attack **2 a** : to have within : HOLD **b** : COMPRISE, INCLUDE **3 a** : to be divisible by usu. without a remainder **b** : ENCLOSE, BOUND ~ *vi* : to restrain oneself — **con·tain·able** \-ˈtā-nə-bəl\ *adj*

contained *adj* **1** : RESTRAINED, CONTROLLED **2** : COMPOSED, CALM

con·tain·er \kən-ˈtā-nər\ *n* : one that contains; *esp* : a receptacle or a flexible covering for the shipment of goods

con·tain·er·board \-ˌbō(ə)rd, -ˌbȯ(ə)rd\ *n* : a paperboard (as corrugated board or fiberboard) from which containers are made

con·tain·er·iza·tion \kən-ˌtā-nə-rə-ˈzā-shən\ *n* : a shipping method in which a large amount of material (as merchandise) is packaged together in one large container

con·tain·er·ize \kən-ˈtā-nə-ˌrīz\ *vt* **-ized; -iz·ing** : to ship by containerization

con·tain·er·ship \-nər-ˌship\ *n* : a ship esp. designed or equipped for carrying containerized cargo

con·tain·ment \kən-ˈtān-mənt\ *n* **1** : the act or process of containing **2** : the policy, process, or result of preventing the expansion of a hostile power or ideology

con·tam·i·nant \kən-ˈtam-ə-nənt\ *n* : something that contaminates

con·tam·i·nate \kən-ˈtam-ə-ˌnāt\ *vt* **-nat·ed; -nat·ing** [L *contaminatus,* pp. of *contaminare;* akin to L *contagio* contagion] **1 a** : to soil, stain, or infect by contact or association ⟨bacteria *contaminated* the wound⟩ **b** : to make inferior or impure by admixture ⟨iron *contaminated* with phosphorus⟩ **2** : to make unfit for use by the introduction of unwholesome or undesirable elements — **con·tam·i·na·tive** \-ˌnāt-iv\ *adj* — **con·tam·i·na·tor** \-ˌnāt-ər\ *n*

syn CONTAMINATE, TAINT, POLLUTE, DEFILE *shared meaning element* : to make impure or unclean. CONTAMINATE implies intrusion of or contact with dirt or foulness from an outside source ⟨water *contaminated* by industrial wastes⟩ ⟨filthy books that *contaminate* young minds⟩ TAINT stresses the loss of purity or cleanliness that follows contamination ⟨*tainted* meat⟩ ⟨his unkindness may defeat my life, but never *taint* my love —Shak.⟩ POLLUTE, sometimes interchangeable with *contaminate,* distinctively may imply that the process which begins with contamination is complete and that what was pure or clean has been made foul, poisoned, or filthy ⟨the *polluted* waters of Lake Erie, in parts no better than an open cesspool⟩ DEFILE implies befouling of what could or should have been kept clean and pure or held sacred and commonly suggests violation or desecration ⟨*defile* a hero's memory with slanderous innuendo⟩

con·tam·i·na·tion \kən-ˌtam-ə-ˈnā-shən\ *n* **1** : a process of contaminating : a state of being contaminated **2** : something that contaminates

contd *abbr* continued

conte \kōⁿt\ *n* [F] : a usu. short tale of adventure

con·temn \kən-ˈtem\ *vt* [ME *contempnen,* fr. MF *contempner,* fr. L *contemnere,* fr. *com-* + *temnere* to despise — more at STAMP] : to view or treat with contempt : SCORN ***syn*** see DESPISE — **con·tem·ner** *also* **con·tem·nor** \-ˈtem-(n)ər\ *n*

con·tem·plate \ˈkänt-əm-ˌplāt, ˈkän-ˌtem-\ *vb* **-plat·ed, -plat·ing** [L *contemplatus,* pp. of *contemplari,* fr. *com-* + *templum* space marked out for observation of auguries — more at TEMPLE] *vt* **1** : to view or consider with continued attention : meditate on **2** : to have in view as contingent or probable or as an end or intention ~ *vi* : PONDER, MEDITATE ***syn*** see CONSIDER — **con·tem·pla·tor** \-ˌplāt-ər\ *n*

con·tem·pla·tion \ˌkänt-əm-ˈplā-shən, ˌkän-ˌtem-\ *n* **1 a** : concentration on spiritual things as a form of private devotion **b** : a state of mystical awareness of God's being **2** : an act of considering with attention : STUDY **3** : the act of regarding steadily **4** : INTENTION, EXPECTATION

1con·tem·pla·tive \kən-ˈtem-plət-iv; ˈkänt-əm-ˌplāt-, ˈkän-ˌtem-\ *adj* : marked by or given to contemplation; *specif* : of or relating to a religious order devoted to prayer and penance — **con·tem·pla·tive·ly** *adv* — **con·tem·pla·tive·ness** *n*

2contemplative *n* : one who practices contemplation

con·tem·po·ra·ne·ity \kən-ˌtem-p(ə-)rə-ˈnē-ət-ē, -ˈnā-\ *n* : the quality or state of being contemporaneous

con·tem·po·ra·ne·ous \kən-ˌtem-pə-ˈrā-nē-əs\ *adj* [L *contemporaneus,* fr. *com-* + *tempor-, tempus* time — more at TEMPORAL] : existing, occurring, or originating during the same time ***syn*** see CONTEMPORARY — **con·tem·po·ra·ne·ous·ly** *adv* — **con·tem·po·ra·ne·ous·ness** *n*

1con·tem·po·rary \kən-ˈtem-pə-ˌrer-ē\ *adj* [*com-* + L *tempor-, tempus*] **1** : happening, existing, living, or coming into being during the same period of time **2 a** : SIMULTANEOUS **b** : marked by characteristics of the present period : MODERN — **con·tem·po·rar·i·ly** \-ˌtem-pə-ˈrer-ə-lē\ *adv*

syn CONTEMPORARY, CONTEMPORANEOUS, COEVAL, SYNCHRONOUS, SIMULTANEOUS, COINCIDENT *shared meaning element* : existing or occurring at the same time

2contemporary *n, pl* **-rar·ies** **1** : one that is contemporary with another **2** : one of the same or nearly the same age as another

con·tempt \kən-ˈtem(p)t\ *n* [ME, fr. L *contemptus,* fr. *contemptus,* pp. of *contemnere*] **1 a** : the act of despising : the state of mind of one who despises : DISDAIN ⟨had nothing but ~ for his weakness⟩ **b** : lack of respect or reverence for something **2** : the state of being despised **3** : willful disobedience to or open disrespect of a court, judge, or legislative body ⟨~ of court⟩

con·tempt·ible \kən-ˈtem(p)-tə-bəl\ *adj* **1 :** worthy of contempt **2** *obs* **:** SCORNFUL, CONTEMPTUOUS — **con·tempt·ible·ness** *n* — **con·tempt·ibly** \-blē\ *adv*
syn CONTEMPTIBLE, DESPICABLE, PITIABLE, SORRY, SCURVY, CHEAP, BEGGARLY *shared meaning element* **:** arousing or deserving scorn or contempt ***ant*** admirable, estimable, formidable

con·temp·tu·ous \-ˈtem(p)-chə(-wə)s, -ˈtem(p)sh-wəs\ *adj* [L *contemptus* contempt] **:** manifesting, feeling, or expressing contempt — **con·temp·tu·ous·ly** *adv* — **con·temp·tu·ous·ness** *n*

con·tend \kən-ˈtend\ *vb* [MF or L; MF *contendre,* fr. L *contendere,* fr. *com-* + *tendere* to stretch — more at TEND] *vi* **1 :** to strive or vie in contest or rivalry or against difficulties **2 :** to strive in debate **:** ARGUE ~ *vt* **1 :** MAINTAIN, ASSERT ⟨~*ed* that he was right⟩ **2 :** to struggle for — **con·tend·er** *n*

¹con·tent \kən-ˈtent\ *adj* [ME, fr. MF, fr. L *contentus,* fr. pp. of *continēre* to hold in, contain] **:** CONTENTED, SATISFIED ⟨~ to wait quietly⟩

²content *vt* **1 :** to appease the desires of **2 :** to limit (oneself) in requirements, desires, or actions

³content *n* **:** CONTENTMENT; *esp* **:** freedom from care or discomfort

⁴con·tent \ˈkän-ˌtent\ *n* [ME, fr. ML *contentum,* fr. L, neut. of *contentus,* pp. of *continēre* to contain] **1 a :** something contained — usu. used in pl. ⟨the jar's ~*s*⟩ ⟨the drawer's ~*s* ⟩ ⟨the bag's ~*s*⟩ **b :** the topics or matter treated in a written work ⟨table of ~*s*⟩ **2 a :** SUBSTANCE, GIST **b :** essential meaning **:** SIGNIFICANCE **c :** the events, physical detail, and information in a work of art — compare FORM 10c **3 a :** the matter dealt with in a field of study **b :** a part, element, or complex of parts **4 :** the amount of specified material contained **:** PROPORTION

content analysis *n* **:** analysis of the manifest and latent content of a body of communicated material (as a book or film) through a classification, tabulation, and evaluation of its key symbols and themes in order to ascertain its meaning and probable effect

con·tent·ed \kən-ˈtent-əd\ *adj* **:** manifesting satisfaction with one's possessions, status, or situation ⟨a ~ smile⟩ — **con·tent·ed·ly** *adv* — **con·tent·ed·ness** *n*

con·ten·tion \kən-ˈten-chən\ *n* [ME *contencioun,* fr. MF, fr. L *contention-, contentio,* fr. *contentus,* pp. of *contendere* to contend] **1 :** an act or instance of contending **2 :** a point advanced or maintained in a debate or argument **3 :** RIVALRY, COMPETITION ***syn*** see DISCORD

con·ten·tious \kən-ˈten-chəs\ *adj* **1 :** exhibiting an often perverse and wearisome tendency to quarrels and disputes ⟨a man of a most ~ nature⟩ **2 :** likely to cause contention ⟨a ~ argument⟩ ***syn*** see BELLIGERENT ***ant*** peaceable — **con·ten·tious·ly** *adv* — **con·ten·tious·ness** *n*

con·tent·ment \kən-ˈtent-mənt\ *n* **1 :** the quality or state of being contented **2 :** something that contents

content word \ˈkän-ˌtent-\ *n* **:** a word that primarily expresses lexical meaning — compare FUNCTION WORD

con·ter·mi·nous \kən-ˈtər-mə-nəs, kän-\ *adj* [L *conterminus,* fr. *com-* + *terminus* boundary — more at TERM] **1 :** having a common boundary **2 :** COTERMINOUS **3 :** enclosed within one common boundary ⟨the 48 ~ states of the United States⟩ ***syn*** see ADJACENT — **con·ter·mi·nous·ly** *adv*

¹con·test \kən-ˈtest, ˈkän-\ *vb* [MF *contester,* fr. L *contestari* (*litem*) to bring an action at law, fr. *contestari* to call to witness, fr. *com-* + *testis* witness — more at TESTAMENT] *vt* **:** to make the subject of dispute, contention, or litigation; *esp* **:** DISPUTE, CHALLENGE ~ *vi* **:** STRIVE, VIE — **con·test·able** \-ə-bəl\ *adj* — **con·test·er** *n*

²con·test \ˈkän-ˌtest\ *n* **1 :** a struggle for superiority or victory **2 :** a competition in which each contestant performs without direct contact with or interference from his competitors

con·tes·tant \kən-ˈtes-tənt, *also* ˈkän-ˌ\ *n* **1 :** one that participates in a contest **2 :** one that contests an award or decision

con·tes·ta·tion \ˌkän-ˌtes-ˈtā-shən\ *n* **:** CONTROVERSY

con·text \ˈkän-ˌtekst\ *n* [ME, weaving together of words, fr. L *contextus* connection of words, coherence, fr. *contextus,* pp. of *contexere* to weave together, fr. *com-* + *texere* to weave — more at TECHNICAL] **1 :** the parts of a discourse that surround a word or passage and can throw light on its meaning **2 :** the interrelated conditions in which something exists or occurs **:** ENVIRONMENT — **con·tex·tu·al** \kän-ˈteks-chə(-wə)l, kən-\ *adj* — **con·tex·tu·al·ly** \-ē\ *adv*

con·tex·ture \kən-ˈteks-chər, ˈkän-ˌ, kän-ˈ\ *n* [F, fr. L *contextus,* pp.] **1 :** the act, process, or manner of weaving parts into a whole; *also* **:** a structure so formed ⟨a ~ of lies⟩ **2 :** CONTEXT

contg *abbr* containing

con·ti·gu·ity \ˌkänt-ə-ˈgyü-ət-ē\ *n, pl* **-ities :** the quality or state of being contiguous **:** PROXIMITY

con·tig·u·ous \kən-ˈtig-yə-wəs\ *adj* [L *contiguus,* fr. *contingere* to have contact with — more at CONTINGENT] **1 :** being in actual contact **:** touching along a boundary or at a point **2** *of angles* **:** ADJACENT **3 :** next or near in time or sequence **4 :** CONTERMINOUS 3 ***syn*** see ADJACENT — **con·tig·u·ous·ly** *adv* — **con·tig·u·ous·ness** *n*

con·ti·nence \ˈkänt-ᵊn-ən(t)s\ *n* **1 :** self-restraint from yielding to impulse or desire **2 :** ability to refrain from a bodily activity

¹con·ti·nent \ˈkänt-ᵊn-ənt\ *adj* [ME, fr. MF, fr. L *continent-, continens,* fr. prp. of *continēre* to hold in — more at CONTAIN] **1 :** exercising continence **2** *obs* **:** RESTRICTIVE ***syn*** see SOBER ***ant*** incontinent — **con·ti·nent·ly** *adv*

²con·ti·nent \ˈkänt-ᵊn-ənt, ˈkänt-nənt\ *n* [in senses 1 & 2, fr. L *continent-, continens,* prp. of *continēre,* to hold together, contain; in senses 3 & 4, fr. L *continent-, continens* continuous mass of land, mainland, fr. *continent-, continens,* prp.] **1** *archaic* **:** CONTAINER, RECEPTACLE **2** *archaic* **:** a summary example **:** EPITOME **3 :** MAINLAND **4 a :** one of the usu. seven great divisions of land on the globe **b** *cap* **:** the continent of Europe — used with *the*

¹con·ti·nen·tal \ˌkänt-ᵊn-ˈent-ᵊl\ *adj* **1 :** of, relating to, or characteristic of a continent ⟨~ waters⟩; *specif* **:** of or relating to the continent of Europe as distinguished from the British Isles **2** *often cap* **:** of or relating to the colonies later forming the U.S. ⟨*Continental* Congress⟩ — **con·ti·nen·tal·ly** \-ᵊl-ē\ *adv*

²continental *n* **1 a** *often cap* **:** an American soldier of the Revolution in the Continental army **b :** a piece of Continental paper currency **c :** an inhabitant of a continent and esp. the continent of Europe **2 :** the least bit ⟨not worth a ~⟩

continental code *n* **:** the international Morse code

continental divide *n* **:** a divide separating streams that flow to opposite sides of a continent

continental drift *n* **:** a hypothetical slow movement of the continents on a deep-seated viscous zone within the earth

continental shelf *n* **:** a shallow submarine plain of varying width forming a border to a continent and typically ending in a steep slope to the oceanic abyss

con·tin·gence \kən-ˈtin-jən(t)s\ *n* **1 :** TANGENCY **2 :** CONTINGENCY

con·tin·gen·cy \kən-ˈtin-jən-sē\ *n, pl* **-cies 1 :** the quality or state of being contingent **2 :** a contingent event or condition: as **a :** an event (as an emergency) that is of possible but uncertain occurrence ⟨trying to provide for every ~⟩ **b :** something liable to happen as an adjunct to something else ***syn*** see JUNCTURE

contingency table *n* **:** a table that tabulates the frequency distribution of one variable in the rows and that of another variable in the columns and that is used esp. in the study of correlation between the variables

¹con·tin·gent \kən-ˈtin-jənt\ *adj* [ME, fr. MF, fr. L *contingent-, contingens,* prp. of *contingere* to have contact with, befall, fr. *com-* + *tangere* to touch — more at TANGENT] **1 :** likely but not certain to happen **:** POSSIBLE **2 a :** happening by chance or unforeseen causes **b :** intended for use in circumstances not completely foreseen **c :** UNPREDICTABLE **3 :** dependent on or conditioned by something else **4 :** not logically necessary; *esp* **:** EMPIRICAL, FACTUAL **5 :** not necessitated **:** FREE ***syn*** see ACCIDENTAL — **con·tin·gent·ly** *adv*

²contingent *n* **1 :** something contingent **:** CONTINGENCY **2 :** a quota or share esp. of persons supplied from or representative of an area or group

con·tin·u·al \kən-ˈtin-yə(-wə)l\ *adj* [ME, fr. MF, fr. L *continuus* continuous] **1 :** continuing indefinitely in time without interruption ⟨~ fear⟩ **2 :** recurring in steady rapid succession **3 :** forming a continuous series ***syn*** see CONTINUOUS ***ant*** intermittent — **con·tin·u·al·ly** \-ē\ *adv*

con·tin·u·ance \kən-ˈtin-yə-wən(t)s\ *n* **1 a :** the act or process of continuing in a state, condition, or course of action **b :** PROLONGATION, DURATION **2 :** CONTINUITY **3 :** SEQUEL **4 :** adjournment of court proceedings to a future day ***syn*** see CONTINUATION

con·tin·u·ant \-yə-wənt\ *n* **:** something that continues or serves as a continuation (as a consonant that may be prolonged without alteration during one emission of breath) — **continuant** *adj*

continuate *adj, obs* **:** CONTINUOUS

con·tin·u·a·tion \kən-ˌtin-yə-ˈwā-shən\ *n* **1 :** continuance in or prolongation of a state or activity **2 :** resumption after an interruption **3 :** something that continues, increases, or adds
syn CONTINUATION, CONTINUANCE, CONTINUITY *shared meaning element* **:** a persisting in being or continuing or an instance revealing such persistence

con·tin·u·a·tive \kən-ˈtin-yə-ˌwāt-iv, -wət-iv\ *adj* **:** relating to, causing, or being in the process of continuation

con·tin·u·a·tor \-ˌwāt-ər\ *n* **:** one that continues

con·tin·ue \kən-ˈtin-(ˌ)yü, -yə(-w)\ *vb* **-tin·ued; -tinu·ing** [ME *continuen,* fr. MF *continuer,* fr. L *continuare,* fr. *continuus*] *vi* **1 :** to maintain without interruption a condition, course, or action **2 :** to remain in existence **:** ENDURE **3 :** to remain in a place or condition **:** STAY **4 :** to resume an activity after interruption ~ *vt* **1 a :** to carry on or keep up **:** MAINTAIN ⟨~*s* walking⟩ **b :** PROLONG; *specif* **:** to resume after intermission **2 :** to cause to continue **3 :** to allow to remain in a place or condition **:** RETAIN **4 :** to postpone (a legal proceeding) by a continuance — **con·tinu·er** \-yə-wər\ *n*
syn CONTINUE, LAST, ENDURE, ABIDE, PERSIST *shared meaning element* **:** to exist over a period of time or indefinitely

con·tin·ued *adj* **1 :** lasting or extending without interruption **:** CONTINUOUS **2 :** resumed after interruption ⟨a ~ story⟩

continued fraction *n* **:** a fraction whose numerator is an integer and whose denominator is an integer plus a fraction whose numerator is an integer and whose denominator is an integer plus a fraction and so on

con·tinu·ing \kən-ˈtin-yə-wiŋ\ *adj* **1 :** CONTINUOUS, CONSTANT **2 :** needing no renewal **:** LASTING

continuing education *n* **:** an educational program designed to update the knowledge and skills of its participants

con·ti·nu·ity \ˌkänt-ᵊn-ˈ(y)ü-ət-ē\ *n, pl* **-ities 1 a :** uninterrupted connection, succession, or union **b :** persistence without essential change **c :** uninterrupted duration in time **2 :** something that has, exhibits, or provides continuity: as **a :** a script or scenario in the performing arts **b :** transitional spoken or musical matter esp. for a radio or television program **c :** the story and dialogue of a comic strip **3 :** the property characteristic of a continuous function; *also* **:** an example of this property ***syn*** see CONTINUATION

con·tin·uo \kən-ˈtin-(y)ə-ˌwō\ *n, pl* **-u·os** [It, fr. *continuo* continuous, fr. L *continuus*] **:** a bass part (as for a keyboard or stringed instrument) used esp. in baroque ensemble music and consisting of a succession of bass notes with figures that indicate the required chords — called also *figured bass, thoroughbass*

con·tin·u·ous \kən-ˈtin-yə-wəs\ *adj* [L *continuus,* fr. *continēre* to hold together — more at CONTAIN] **1 :** marked by uninterrupted extension in space, time, or sequence **2** *of a function* **:** having the numerical difference between the value at a point and the value at

ə abut ᵊ kitten ər further a back ā bake ä cot, cart
au̇ out ch chin e less ē easy g gift i trip ī life
j joke ŋ sing ō flow ȯ flaw ȯi coin th thin t͟h this
ü loot u̇ foot y yet yü few yu̇ furious zh vision

any point in a sufficiently small neighborhood of the point arbitrarily small — **con·tin·u·ous·ly** *adv* — **con·tin·u·ous·ness** *n*
syn CONTINUOUS, CONTINUAL, CONSTANT, INCESSANT, PERPETUAL, PERENNIAL *shared meaning element* : characterized by continued occurrence or recurrence ***ant*** interrupted

continuous waves *n pl* **1** : radio waves that continue with unchanging intensity or amplitude without modulation **2** : radio waves whose intensity continues unchanged except for modulation — abbr. *CW*

con·tin·u·um \kən-ˈtin-yə-wəm\ *n, pl* **-ua** \-yə-wə\ *also* **-ums** [L, neut. of *continuus*] **1** : something (as duration or extension) absolutely continuous and homogeneous of which no distinction of content can be affirmed except by reference to something else (as numbers) **2 a** : something in which a basic common character can be detected in a series of imperceptible variations ⟨the ~ of consciousness⟩ **b** (1) : an uninterrupted ordered sequence (2) : a series of ecological communities whose vegetation gradually changes along an environmental gradient **c** : an identity of substance uniting discrete parts; *broadly* : CONTINUITY **3** : a set with the same transfinite cardinal number as the set of real numbers

con·tort \kən-ˈtȯ(ə)rt\ *vb* [L *contortus,* pp. of *contorquēre,* fr. *com-* + *torquēre* to twist — more at TORTURE] *vt* : to twist in a violent manner ⟨features ~*ed* with fury⟩ ~ *vi* : to twist into a strained shape or expression ***syn*** see DEFORM — **con·tor·tion** \-ˈtȯr-shən\ *n* — **con·tor·tive** \-ˈtȯrt-iv\ *adj*

con·tor·tion·ist \kən-ˈtȯr-sh(ə-)nəst\ *n* : one who contorts; *specif* : an acrobat who specializes in unnatural body postures — **con·tor·tion·is·tic** \-ˌtȯr-shə-ˈnis-tik\ *adj*

[1]**con·tour** \ˈkän-ˌtu̇(ə)r\ *n* [F, fr. It *contorno,* fr. *contornare* to round off, sketch in outline, fr. L *com-* + *tornare* to turn in a lathe, fr. *tornus* lathe] : an outline esp. of a curving or irregular figure : SHAPE; *also* : the line representing this outline ***syn*** see OUTLINE

[2]**contour** *vt* **1 a** : to shape the contour of **b** : to shape so as to fit contours **2** : to construct (as a road) in conformity to a contour

[3]**contour** *adj* **1** : following contour lines or forming furrows or ridges along them ⟨~ flooding⟩ ⟨~ farming⟩ **2** : made to fit the contour of something ⟨a ~ couch⟩

contour feather *n* : one of the medium-sized feathers that form the general covering of a bird and determine the external contour

contour line *n* : a line (as on a map) connecting the points on a land surface that have the same elevation

contour map *n* : a map having contour lines

contr *abbr* **1** contract; contraction **2** contralto **3** contrary **4** control; controller

contra- *prefix* [ME, fr. L, fr. *contra* against, opposite — more at COUNTER] **1** : against : contrary : contrasting ⟨*contra*distinction⟩ **2** : pitched below normal bass ⟨*contra*octave⟩

con·tra·band \ˈkän-trə-ˌband\ *n* [It *contrabbando,* fr. ML *contrabannum,* fr. *contra-* + *bannus, bannum* decree, of Gmc origin — more at BAN] **1** : illegal or prohibited traffic **2** : goods or merchandise whose importation, exportation, or possession is forbidden; *also* : smuggled goods **3** : a Negro slave who during the Civil War escaped to or was brought within the Union lines — **contraband** *adj*

con·tra·band·ist \-ˌban-dəst\ *n* : SMUGGLER

con·tra·bass \ˈkän-trə-ˌbās\ *n* [It *contrabbasso,* fr. *contra-* + *basso* bass] : DOUBLE BASS — **con·tra·bass·ist** \-ˌbā-səst\ *n*

con·tra·bas·soon \ˌkän-trə-bə-ˈsün, -ba-\ *n* : a double-reed woodwind instrument having a range an octave lower than that of the bassoon

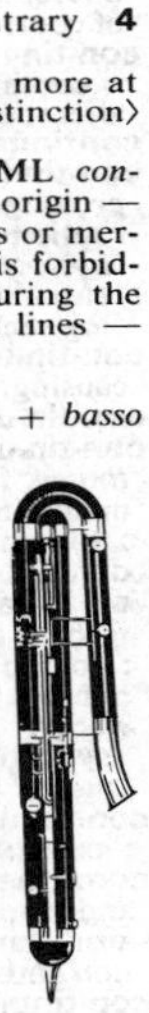
contrabassoon

con·tra·cep·tion \ˌkän-trə-ˈsep-shən\ *n* [*contra-* + *conception*] : voluntary prevention of conception or impregnation — **con·tra·cep·tive** \-ˈsep-tiv\ *adj or n*

[1]**con·tract** \ˈkän-ˌtrakt\ *n* [ME, fr. L *contractus,* fr. *contractus,* pp. of *contrahere* to draw together, make a contract, reduce in size, fr. *com-* + *trahere* to draw — more at DRAW] **1 a** : a binding agreement between two or more persons or parties : COVENANT **b** : BETROTHAL **2** : a writing made by the parties to evidence the terms and conditions of a contract **3** : the department or principles of law having to do with contracts **4** : an undertaking to win a specified number of tricks or points in bridge

[2]**con·tract** *vt 1a & vi 1 usu* ˈkän-ˌtrakt, *others usu* kən-ˈ\ *vb* [partly fr. MF *contracter* to agree upon, fr. L *contractus* n.; partly fr. L *contractus,* pp. of *contrahere* to draw together] *vt* **1 a** : to establish or undertake by contract **b** : BETROTH **2 a** : to acquire usu. involuntarily ⟨~ pneumonia⟩ **b** : to bring on oneself as an obligation : INCUR ⟨~ a debt⟩ **3 a** : LIMIT, RESTRICT **b** : KNIT, WRINKLE ⟨frown ~*ed* his brow⟩ **c** : to draw together : CONCENTRATE **4** : to reduce to smaller size by or as if by squeezing or forcing together **5** : to shorten (as a word) by omitting one or more sounds or letters ~ *vi* **1** : to make a contract **2** : to draw together so as to become diminished in size ⟨metal ~*s* on cooling⟩; *also* : to become less in compass, duration, or length ⟨muscle ~*s* in tetanus⟩ — **con·tract·ibil·i·ty** \kən-ˌtrak-tə-ˈbil-ət-ē, ˌkän-\ *n* — **con·tract·ible** \kən-ˈtrak-tə-bəl, ˈkän-ˌ\ *adj*
syn **1** see INCUR
2 CONTRACT, SHRINK, CONDENSE, COMPRESS, CONSTRICT, DEFLATE *shared meaning element* : to decrease in bulk or volume ***ant*** expand

contract bridge \ˌkän-ˌtrakt-\ *n* : a bridge game distinguished by the fact that overtricks do not count toward game or slam bonuses

con·trac·tile \kən-ˈtrak-tᵊl, -ˌtīl\ *adj* : having the power or property of contracting ⟨~ proteins of muscle fibrils⟩ — **con·trac·til·i·ty** \ˌkän-ˌtrak-ˈtil-ət-ē\ *n*

contractile vacuole *n* : a vacuole in a unicellular organism that contracts regularly to discharge fluid from the body and that probably has an excretory or hydrostatic function

con·trac·tion \kən-ˈtrak-shən\ *n* **1 a** : the action or process of contracting : the state of being contracted **b** : the shortening and thickening of a functioning muscle or muscle fiber **c** : a reduction in business activity **2** : a shortening of a word, syllable, or word group by omission of a sound or letter; *also* : a form produced by such shortening — **con·trac·tion·al** \-shnəl, -shən-ᵊl\ *adj* — **con·trac·tive** \kən-ˈtrak-tiv, ˈkän-ˌ\ *adj*

con·trac·tor \ˈkän-ˌtrak-tər (*usual for 1*), kən-ˈ\ *n* **1** : one that contracts or is party to a contract: as **a** : one that contracts to perform work or provide supplies on a large scale **b** : one that contracts to erect buildings **2** : something (as a muscle) that contracts or shortens

con·trac·tu·al \kən-ˈtrak-chə(-wə)l, kän-, -ˈtraksh-wəl\ *adj* [L *contractus* contract] : of, relating to, or constituting a contract — **con·trac·tu·al·ly** \-ē\ *adv*

con·trac·ture \kən-ˈtrak-chər\ *n* : a permanent shortening (as of muscle, tendon, or scar tissue) producing deformity or distortion

con·tra·dict \ˌkän-trə-ˈdikt\ *vt* [L *contradictus,* pp. of *contradicere,* fr. *contra-* + *dicere* to say, speak — more at DICTION] **1** : to resist or oppose in argument **2 a** : to assert the contrary of : GAINSAY **b** : to deny the truth of **3 a** : to be the contradictory of **b** : to go counter to **c** : to act in a manner contrary to ***syn*** see DENY ***ant*** corroborate — **con·tra·dict·able** \-ˈdik-tə-bəl\ *adj* — **con·tra·dic·tor** \-ˈdik-tər\ *n*

con·tra·dic·tion \ˌkän-trə-ˈdik-shən\ *n* **1** : the act of contradicting **2** : an expression or proposition containing contradictory parts **3 a** : logical incongruity **b** : opposition of factors inherent in a system or situation

con·tra·dic·tious \-shəs\ *adj* **1** : CONTRADICTORY, OPPOSITE **2** : given to or marked by contradiction : CONTRARY

[1]**con·tra·dic·to·ry** \ˌkän-trə-ˈdik-t(ə-)rē\ *n, pl* **-ries** **1 a** : something that contradicts **b** : OPPOSITE, CONTRARY **2** : a proposition so related to another that if either of the two is true the other is false and if either is false the other must be true — **con·tra·dic·to·ri·ly** \-t(ə-)rə-lē\ *adv* — **con·tra·dic·to·ri·ness** \-t(ə-)rē-nəs\ *n*

[2]**contradictory** *adj* **1** : CONTRADICTIOUS 2 ⟨an irritable ~ nature⟩ **2** : involving, causing, or constituting a contradiction ⟨ill-planned and often ~ proposals⟩ ***syn*** see OPPOSITE

con·tra·dis·tinc·tion \ˌkän-trə-dis-ˈtiŋ(k)-shən\ *n* : distinction by contrast ⟨painting in ~ to sculpture⟩ — **con·tra·dis·tinc·tive** \-ˈtiŋ(k)-tiv\ *adj* — **con·tra·dis·tinc·tive·ly** *adv*

con·tra·dis·tin·guish \-ˈtiŋ-gwish\ *vt* : to distinguish by contrast of qualities

con·trail \ˈkän-ˌtrāl\ *n* [*con*densation *trail*] : streaks of condensed water vapor created in the air by an airplane or rocket at high altitudes

con·tra·in·di·cate \ˌkän-trə-ˈin-də-ˌkāt\ *vt* : to make (a treatment or procedure) inadvisable — **con·tra·in·di·ca·tion** \-ˌin-də-ˈkā-shən\ *n* — **con·tra·in·dic·a·tive** \-in-ˈdik-ət-iv\ *adj*

con·tra·lat·er·al \-ˈlat-ə-rəl, -ˈla-trəl\ *adj* [ISV] : occurring on or acting in conjunction with similar parts on an opposite side

con·tral·to \kən-ˈtral-(ˌ)tō\ *n, pl* **-tos** [It, fr. *contra-* + *alto*] **1 a** : the lowest female singing voice **b** : a person having this voice **2** : the part sung by a contralto

con·tra·oc·tave \ˌkän-trə-ˈäk-tiv, -təv, -ˌtāv\ *n* : the musical octave that begins on the third C below middle C — see PITCH illustration

con·tra·po·si·tion \-pə-ˈzish-ən\ *n* [LL *contraposition-, contrapositio,* fr. L *contrapositus,* pp. of *contraponere* to place opposite, fr. *contra-* + *ponere* to place] **1** : OPPOSITION, ANTITHESIS **2** : the relationship between two propositions when the subject and predicate of one are respectively the negation of the predicate and the negation of the subject of the other

con·tra·pos·i·tive \-ˈpäz-ət-iv, -ˈpäz-tiv\ *n* : a proposition resulting from an operation of immediate inference in which the terms of a given proposition are permuted and negated ⟨"all not-*P* is not-*S*" is the ~ of "all *S* is *P*"⟩

con·trap·tion \kən-ˈtrap-shən\ *n* [perh. blend of *contrivance, trap,* and *invention*] : CONTRIVANCE, GADGET

con·tra·pun·tal \ˌkän-trə-ˈpənt-ᵊl\ *adj* [It *contrappunto* counterpoint, fr. ML *contrapunctus*] **1** : of or relating to counterpoint **2** : POLYPHONIC — **con·tra·pun·tal·ly** \-ᵊl-ē\ *adv*

con·tra·pun·tist \-ˈpənt-əst\ *n* : one who writes counterpoint

con·tra·ri·ety \ˌkän-trə-ˈrī-ət-ē\ *n, pl* **-eties** [ME *contrariete,* fr. MF *contrarieté,* fr. LL *contrarietat-, contrarietas,* fr. L *contrarius* contrary] **1** : the quality or state of being contrary **2** : something contrary

con·trar·i·ous \kən-ˈtrer-ē-əs, kän-\ *adj* : PERVERSE, ANTAGONISTIC

con·trari·wise \ˈkän-ˌtrer-ē-ˌwīz, kən-ˈ\ *adv* **1** : on the contrary **2** : vice versa : CONVERSELY **3** : in a contrary manner

[1]**con·trary** \ˈkän-ˌtrer-ē\ *n, pl* **-trar·ies** **1** : a fact or condition incompatible with another : OPPOSITE **2** : one of a pair of opposites **3 a** : a proposition so related to another that though both may be false they cannot both be true — compare SUBCONTRARY **b** : either of two terms (as black and white) that cannot both be affirmed of the same subject — **by contraries** : in a manner opposite to what is logical or expected — **on the contrary** : just the opposite : NO — **to the contrary** : NOTWITHSTANDING

[2]**con·trary** \ˈkän-ˌtrer-ē, *in sense 4 often* kən-ˈtre(ə)r-ē\ *adj* [ME *contrarie,* fr. MF *contraire,* fr. L *contrarius,* fr. *contra* opposite] **1 a** : diametrically different ⟨the result was ~ to our plan⟩ **b** : opposite in character : tending to an opposing course ⟨he remained firm in the ~ intention⟩ **c** : mutually opposed : ANTAGONISTIC ⟨they held ~ opinions⟩ **2** : opposite in position, direction, or nature **3** : UNFAVORABLE — used of wind or weather **4** : temperamentally unwilling to accept control or advice ⟨a ~ child⟩ — **con·trari·ly** \-ˌtrer-ə-lē, -ˈtrer-\ *adv* — **con·trari·ness** \-ˌtrer-ē-nəs, -ˈtrer-\ *n*
syn **1** see OPPOSITE
2 CONTRARY, PERVERSE, RESTIVE, BALKY, FROWARD, WAYWARD *shared meaning element* : unwilling or unable to conform to custom or submit to authority ***ant*** complaisant

[3]**con·trary** *like* [2]CONTRARY\ *adv* : CONTRARIWISE, CONTRARILY

contrary to *prep* : in opposition to ⟨*contrary to* orders, he set out alone⟩

[1]**con·trast** \ˈkän-ˌtrast\ *n* **1 a** : juxtaposition of dissimilar elements (as color, tone, or emotion) in a work of art **b** : degree of difference between the lightest and darkest parts of a picture **2**

: comparison of similar objects to set off their dissimilar qualities **3 :** a person or thing that exhibits differences when compared with another

²con·trast \kən-ˈtrast, ˈkän-ˌ\ *vb* [F *contraster,* fr. MF, to oppose, resist, alter. of *contrester,* fr. (assumed) VL *contrastare,* fr. L *contra-* + *stare* to stand — more at STAND] *vi* : to exhibit contrast **~** *vt* **1** : to put in contrast **2 :** to compare or appraise in respect to differences ⟨~ European and American manners⟩ ***syn*** see COMPARE — **con·trast·able** \-ə-bəl\ *adj*

con·tras·tive \kən-ˈtras-tiv, ˈkän-ˌ\ *adj* : forming or consisting of a contrast : CONTRASTING — **con·tras·tive·ly** *adv*

con·trasty \ˈkän-ˌtras-tē\ *adj* : having or producing in photography great contrast between highlights and shadows

con·tra·vene \ˌkän-trə-ˈvēn\ *vt* **-vened; -ven·ing** [MF or LL; MF *contrevenir,* fr. LL *contravenire,* fr. L *contra-* + *venire* to come — more at COME] **1 :** to go or act contrary to ⟨~ a law⟩ **2 :** to oppose in argument : CONTRADICT ⟨~ a proposition⟩ ***syn*** see DENY ***ant*** uphold (*as a law or principle*), allege (*as a right or claim*) — **con·tra·ven·er** *n*

con·tra·ven·tion \ˌkän-trə-ˈven-chən\ *n* [MF, fr. LL *contraventus,* pp. of *contravenire*] : the act of contravening : VIOLATION

con·tre·danse \ˈkän-trə-ˌdan(t)s, kōⁿ-trə-dãⁿs\ *or* **con·tra dance** \ˈkän-trə-ˌdan(t)s\ *n* [F *contredanse,* by folk etymology fr. E *country-dance*] **1 :** a folk dance in which couples face each other in two lines or in a square **2 :** a piece of music for a contredanse

con·tre·temps \ˈkän-trə-ˌtäⁿ, kōⁿ-trə-täⁿ\ *n, pl* **con·tre·temps** \-ˌ(ˌ)täⁿ(z)\ [F, fr. *contre-* counter- + *temps* time, fr. L *tempus* — more at TEMPORAL] : an inopportune and embarrassing occurrence

contrib *abbr* contribution; contributor

con·trib·ute \kən-ˈtrib-yət\ *vb* **-ut·ed; -ut·ing** [L *contributus,* pp. of *contribuere,* fr. *com-* + *tribuere* to grant — more at TRIBUTE] *vt* **1** : to give or supply in common with others **2 :** to supply (as an article) for a publication **~** *vi* **1 a :** to give a part to a common fund or store **b :** to play a significant part in bringing about an end or result **2 :** to submit articles to a publication ***syn*** see CONDUCE — **con·trib·u·tor** \-yət-ər\ *n*

con·tri·bu·tion \ˌkän-trə-ˈbyü-shən\ *n* **1 :** a payment (as a levy or tax) imposed by military, civil, or ecclesiastical authorities usu. for a special or extraordinary purpose **2 :** the act of contributing; *also* : the thing contributed **3 :** a writing for publication esp. in a periodical — **con·trib·u·tive** \kən-ˈtrib-yət-iv\ *adj* — **con·trib·u·tive·ly** *adv*

con·trib·u·to·ry \kən-ˈtrib-yə-ˌtōr-ē, -ˌtȯr-\ *adj* **1 a :** contributing to a common fund or enterprise **b :** subject to a levy of supplies, money, or men **2 :** of, relating to, or forming a contribution

con·trite \ˈkän-ˌtrīt, kən-ˈ\ *adj* [ME *contrit,* fr. MF, fr. ML, fr. L, pp. of *conterere* to grind, bruise, fr. *com-* + *terere* to rub — more at THROW] **1 :** grieving and penitent for sin or shortcoming **2** : proceeding from contrition ⟨~ sighs⟩ — **con·trite·ly** *adv* — **con·trite·ness** *n*

con·tri·tion \kən-ˈtrish-ən\ *n* : the state of being contrite : REPENTANCE ***syn*** see PENITENCE

con·triv·ance \kən-ˈtrī-vən(t)s\ *n* **1 :** the act or faculty of contriving : the state of being contrived **2 :** a thing contrived; *esp* : a mechanical device

con·trive \kən-ˈtrīv\ *vb* **con·trived; con·triv·ing** [ME *controven, contreven,* fr. MF *controver,* fr. LL *contropare* to compare] *vt* **1 a** : DEVISE, PLAN ⟨~ ways of handling the situation⟩ **b :** to form or create in an artistic or ingenious manner ⟨*contrived* household utensils from stone⟩ **2 :** to bring about by stratagem or with difficulty : MANAGE **~** *vi* : to make schemes — **con·triv·er** *n*

con·trived *adj* : ARTIFICIAL, LABORED

¹con·trol \kən-ˈtrōl\ *vt* **con·trolled; con·trol·ling** [ME *controllen,* fr. MF *contreroller,* fr. *contrerolle* copy of an account, audit, fr. *contre-* counter- + *rolle* roll, account] **1 :** to check, test, or verify by evidence or experiments **2 a :** to exercise restraining or directing influence over : REGULATE **b :** to have power over : RULE ***syn*** see CONDUCT — **con·trol·la·ble** \-ˈtrō-lə-bəl\ *adj* — **con·trol·ment** \-ˈtrōl-mənt\ *n*

²control *n* **1 a :** an act or instance of controlling; *also* : power or authority to guide or manage **b :** skill in the use of a tool, instrument, technique, or artistic medium **c :** direction, regulation, and coordination of business activities (as production and administration) **2 :** RESTRAINT, RESERVE **3 :** one that controls: as **a** (1) : an experiment in which the subjects are treated as in a parallel experiment except for omission of the procedure or agent under test and which is used as a standard of comparison in judging experimental effects — called also *control experiment* (2) : one (as an organism, culture, or group) that is part of a control **b :** a mechanism used to regulate or guide the operation of a machine, apparatus, or system **c :** an organization that directs a space flight ⟨mission ~⟩ **d :** a personality or spirit believed to actuate the utterances or performances of a spiritualist medium

control chart *n* : a chart that gives the results of periodic sampling for rejects of a manufactured product and that is used in making decisions concerning the maintenance of product quality

con·trolled \kən-ˈtrōld\ *adj* : RESTRAINED

con·trol·ler \kən-ˈtrō-lər, ˈkän-ˌ\ *n* [ME *conterroller,* fr. MF *contrerolleur,* fr. *contrerolle*] **1 a :** COMPTROLLER 1 **b :** COMPTROLLER 2 **c :** the chief accounting officer of a business enterprise or an institution (as a college) **2 :** one that controls or has power or authority to control — **con·trol·ler·ship** \-ˌship\ *n*

controlling interest *n* : sufficient stock ownership in a corporation to exert control over policy

control surface *n* : a movable airfoil designed to change the attitude of an aircraft

con·tro·ver·sial \ˌkän-trə-ˈvər-shəl, -ˈvər-sē-əl\ *adj* **1 :** of, relating to, or arousing controversy ⟨a ~ public figure⟩ **2 :** given to controversy : DISPUTATIOUS — **con·tro·ver·sial·ism** \-ˌiz-əm\ *n* — **con·tro·ver·sial·ist** \-əst\ *n* — **con·tro·ver·sial·ly** \-ē\ *adv*

con·tro·ver·sy \ˈkän-trə-ˌvər-sē\ *n, pl* **-sies** [ME *controversie,* fr. L *controversia,* fr. *controversus* disputable, lit., turned opposite, fr. *contro-* (akin to *contra-*) + *versus,* pp. of *vertere* to turn — more at WORTH] **1 :** a discussion marked esp. by the expression of opposing views : DISPUTE **2 :** QUARREL, STRIFE

con·tro·vert \ˈkän-trə-ˌvərt, ˌkän-trə-ˈ\ *vb* [*controversy*] *vt* : to dispute or oppose by reasoning ⟨~ a point in a discussion⟩ **~** *vi* : to engage in controversy ***syn*** see DISPROVE ***ant*** assert — **con·tro·vert·er** \-ər\ *n* — **con·tro·vert·ible** \-ə-bəl\ *adj*

con·tu·ma·cious \ˌkän-t(y)ə-ˈmā-shəs, ˌkän-chə-\ *adj* : stubbornly disobedient : REBELLIOUS — **con·tu·ma·cious·ly** *adv*

con·tu·ma·cy \kən-ˈt(y)ü-mə-sē; ˈkän-t(y)ə-, ˈkän-chə-\ *n* [ME *contumacie,* fr. L *contumacia,* fr. *contumac-, contumax* insubordinate, fr. *com-* + *tumēre* to swell, be proud — more at THUMB] : stubborn resistance to authority; *specif* : willful contempt of court

con·tu·me·li·ous \ˌkän-t(y)ə-ˈmē-lē-əs, ˌkän-chə-\ *adj* : insolently abusive and humiliating — **con·tu·me·li·ous·ly** *adv*

con·tume·ly \kən-ˈt(y)ü-mə-lē; ˈkän-t(y)ə-ˌmē-lē, ˈkän-chə-; ˈkän-təm-lē\ *n, pl* **-lies** [ME *contumelie,* fr. MF, fr. L *contumelia;* perh. akin to L *contumacia*] : rude language or treatment arising from haughtiness and contempt; *also* : an instance of such language or treatment

con·tuse \kən-ˈt(y)üz\ *vt* **con·tused; con·tus·ing** [MF *contuser,* fr. L *contusus,* pp. of *contundere* to crush, bruise, fr. *com-* + *tundere* to beat — more at STINT] : to injure (tissue) usu. without laceration : BRUISE — **con·tu·sion** \-ˈt(y)ü-zhən\ *n*

co·nun·drum \kə-ˈnən-drəm\ *n* [origin unknown] **1 :** a riddle whose answer is or involves a pun **2 a :** a question or problem having only a conjectural answer **b :** an intricate and difficult problem ***syn*** see MYSTERY

con·ur·ba·tion \ˌkän-(ˌ)ər-ˈbā-shən\ *n* [*com-* + L *urb-, urbs* city] : an aggregation or continuous network of urban communities

co·nus ar·te·ri·o·sus \ˈkō-nə-sär-ˌtir-ē-ˈō-səs\ *n, pl* **co·ni ar·te·ri·o·si** \-ˌnī-är-ˌtir-ē-ˈō-ˌsī\ [NL, lit., arterial cone] **1 :** a prolongation of the ventricle of amphibians and some fishes that has a spiral valve separating venous blood going to the respiratory arteries from blood going to the aorta and systemic arteries **2 :** a conical prolongation of the right ventricle in mammals from which the pulmonary arteries emerge — called also *conus*

conv *abbr* **1** convention; conventional **2** convertible **3** convocation

con·va·lesce \ˌkän-və-ˈles\ *vi* **-lesced; -lesc·ing** [L *convalescere,* fr. *com-* + *valescere* to grow strong, fr. *valēre* to be strong, be well — more at WIELD] : to recover health and strength gradually after sickness or weakness — **con·va·les·cence** \-ˈles-ᵊn(t)s\ *n* — **con·va·les·cent** \-ᵊnt\ *adj or n*

con·vect \kən-ˈvekt\ *vb* [back-formation fr. *convection*] *vi* : to transfer heat by convection **~** *vt* : to circulate (warm air) by convection

con·vec·tion \kən-ˈvek-shən\ *n* [LL *convection-, convectio,* fr. L *convectus,* pp. of *convehere* to bring together, fr. *com-* + *vehere* to carry — more at WAY] **1 :** the action or process of conveying **2** **a :** the circulatory motion that occurs in a fluid at a nonuniform temperature owing to the variation of its density and the action of gravity **b :** the transfer of heat by this automatic circulation of a fluid — **con·vec·tion·al** \-shnəl, -shən-ᵊl\ *adj* — **con·vec·tive** \-ˈvek-tiv\ *adj*

con·vec·tor \-ˈvek-tər\ *n* : a heating unit in which air heated by contact with a heating device (as a radiator or a tube with fins) in a casing circulates by convection

con·vene \kən-ˈvēn\ *vb* **con·vened; con·ven·ing** [ME *convenen,* fr. MF *convenir* to come together] *vi* : to come together in a body **~** *vt* **1 :** to summon before a tribunal **2 :** to cause to assemble ***syn*** see SUMMON — **con·ven·er** *n*

con·ve·nience \kən-ˈvē-nyən(t)s\ *n* **1 :** fitness or suitability for performing an action or fulfilling a requirement **2 :** an appliance, device, or service conducive to comfort **3 :** a suitable time : OPPORTUNITY **4 :** freedom from discomfort : EASE

con·ve·nien·cy \-nyən-sē\ *n, archaic* : CONVENIENCE

con·ve·nient \kən-ˈvē-nyənt\ *adj* [ME, fr. L *convenient-, conveniens,* fr. prp. of *convenire* to come together, be suitable] **1** *obs* : SUITABLE, PROPER **2 a :** suited to personal comfort or to easy performance **b :** suited to a particular situation **c :** affording accommodation or advantage **3 :** being near at hand : HANDY — **con·ve·nient·ly** *adv*

¹con·vent \ˈkän-vənt, -ˌvent\ *n* [ME *covent,* fr. OF, fr. ML *conventus,* fr. L, assembly, fr. *conventus,* pp. of *convenire*] : a local community or house of a religious order or congregation; *esp* : an establishment of nuns

²con·vent \kən-ˈvent\ *vb* [L *conventus,* pp.] *obs* : CONVENE

con·ven·ti·cle \kən-ˈvent-i-kəl\ *n* [ME, fr. L *conventiculum,* dim. of *conventus* assembly] **1 :** ASSEMBLY, MEETING **2 :** an assembly of an irregular or unlawful character **3 :** an assembly for religious worship; *esp* : a secret meeting for worship not sanctioned by law **4 :** MEETINGHOUSE — **con·ven·ti·cler** \-k(ə-)lər\ *n*

con·ven·tion \kən-ˈven-chən\ *n* [ME, fr. MF or L; MF, fr. L *convention-, conventio,* fr. *conventus,* pp. of *convenire* to come together, be suitable, fr. *com-* + *venire* to come — more at COME] **1 a** : AGREEMENT, CONTRACT **b :** an agreement between states for regulation of matters affecting all of them **c :** a compact between opposing commanders esp. concerning prisoner exchange or armistice **d :** a general agreement about basic principles; *also* : a principle that is true by convention **2 a :** the summoning or convening of an assembly **b :** an assembly of persons met for a common purpose; *esp* : a meeting of the delegates of a political party for the purpose of formulating a platform and selecting candidates for office **c :** the usu. state or national organization of a religious denomination **3 a :** usage or custom esp. in social matters **b** : a rule of conduct or behavior **c :** a practice in bidding or playing that conveys information between partners in a card game (as bridge) **d :** an established theatrical technique or practice (as a stage whisper or spotlighting)

con·ven·tion·al \kən-ˈvench-nəl, -ˈven-chən-ᵊl\ *adj* **1 :** formed by agreement or compact **2 a :** according with, sanctioned by, or based on convention **b :** lacking originality or individuality : TRITE **3 a :** according with a mode of artistic representation that simplifies or provides symbols or substitutes for natural forms **b :** of traditional design **4 :** of, resembling, or relating to a convention, assembly, or public meeting **5 :** not making use of nuclear powers ⟨~ warfare⟩ ***syn*** see CEREMONIAL ***ant*** unconventional — **con·ven·tion·al·ism** \-ˌiz-əm\ *n* — **con·ven·tion·al·ist** \-əst\ *n* — **con·ven·tion·al·ly** \-ē\ *adv*

con·ven·tion·al·i·ty \-ˌven-chə-ˈnal-ət-ē\ *n, pl* **-ties** **1 :** the quality or state of being conventional; *specif* **:** adherence to conventions **2 :** a conventional usage, practice, or thing

con·ven·tion·al·iza·tion \kən-ˌvench-nə-lə-ˈzā-shən, -ˌven-chən-ᵊl-ə-ˈzā-\ *n* **:** the act, practice, or product of conventionalizing

con·ven·tion·al·ize \kən-ˈvench-nə-ˌlīz, -ˈven-chən-ᵊl-ˌīz\ *vt* **-ized; -iz·ing :** to make conventional

con·ven·tion·eer \kən-ˌven-chə-ˈni(ə)r\ *n* **:** a person attending a convention

¹con·ven·tu·al \kən-ˈvench-(ə-)wəl, kän-\ *adj* [ME, fr. MF or ML; MF, fr. ML *conventualis,* fr. *conventus* convent] **1 :** of, relating to, or befitting a convent or monastic life : MONASTIC **2** *cap* **:** of or relating to the Conventuals — **con·ven·tu·al·ly** \-ē\ *adv*

²conventual *n* **1 :** a member of a conventual community **2** *cap* **:** a member of the Order of Friars Minor Conventual forming a branch of the first order of St. Francis of Assisi under a mitigated rule

con·verge \kən-ˈvərj\ *vb* **con·verged; con·verg·ing** [ML *convergere,* fr. L *com-* + *vergere* to bend, incline — more at WRENCH] *vi* **1 :** to tend or move toward one point or one another : come together : MEET **2 :** to come together and unite in a common interest or focus **3 :** to approach a limit as the number of terms increases without limit ~ *vt* **:** to cause to converge

con·ver·gence \kən-ˈvər-jən(t)s\ *n* **1 :** the act of converging and esp. moving toward union or uniformity; *esp* **:** coordinated movement of the two eyes resulting in impingement of the image of a point on corresponding retinal areas **2 :** the condition of converging; *esp* **:** independent development of similar characters (as of bodily structure or cultural traits) often associated with similarity of habits or environment

con·ver·gen·cy \-jən-sē\ *n* **:** CONVERGENCE

con·ver·gent \-jənt\ *adj* **1 :** tending to move toward one point or to approach each other : CONVERGING ⟨~ lines⟩ **2 :** exhibiting convergence in form, function, or development **3 a** *of an improper integral* **:** having a value that is a real number **b :** characterized by having the *n*th term or the sum of the first *n* terms approach a finite limit ⟨a ~ sequence⟩ ⟨a ~ series⟩

convergent lady beetle *n* [fr. the pattern of spots on its back] **:** a periodically migratory beneficial lady beetle (*Hippodamia convergens*) that feeds on various crop pests (as aphids) — called also *convergent*

con·vers·able \kən-ˈvər-sə-bəl\ *adj* **1 :** pleasant and easy to converse with **2** *archaic* **:** relating to or suitable for social interaction

con·ver·sance \kən-ˈvərs-ᵊn(t)s *also* ˈkän-vər-sən(t)s\ *n* **:** the quality or state of being conversant

con·ver·san·cy \-ᵊn-sē, -sən-sē\ *n* **:** CONVERSANCE

con·ver·sant \kən-ˈvərs-ᵊnt *also* ˈkän-vər-sənt\ *adj* **1** *archaic* **:** OCCUPIED, CONCERNED **2** *archaic* **:** having frequent, customary, or familiar association **3 :** having knowledge or experience — **con·ver·sant·ly** *adv*

con·ver·sa·tion \ˌkän-vər-ˈsā-shən\ *n* [ME *conversacioun,* fr. MF *conversation,* fr. L *conversation-, conversatio,* fr. *conversatus,* pp. of *conversari* to live, keep company with] **1** *obs* **:** CONDUCT, BEHAVIOR **2 a** (1) **:** oral exchange of sentiments, observations, opinions, or ideas (2) **:** an instance of such exchange : TALK **b :** an informal discussion of an issue by representatives of governments, institutions, or groups **c :** an exchange similar to conversation; *esp* **:** real-time interaction with a computer esp. through a keyboard — **con·ver·sa·tion·al** \-shnəl, -shən-ᵊl\ *adj* — **con·ver·sa·tion·al·ly** \-ē\ *adv*

con·ver·sa·tion·al·ist \-shnə-ləst, -shən-ᵊl-əst\ *n* **:** one who converses a great deal or who excels in conversation

conversation piece *n* **1 :** a painting of a group of persons in their customary surroundings **2 :** a novel or striking object that stimulates conversation

con·ver·sa·zi·o·ne \ˌkän-vər-ˌsät-sē-ˈō-nē, ˌkōn-\ *n, pl* **-ones** *or* **-o·ni** \-ˈō-(ˌ)nē\ [It, lit. conversation, fr. L *conversation-, conversatio*] **:** a meeting for conversation esp. about art, literature, or science

¹con·verse \kən-ˈvərs\ *vi* **con·versed; con·vers·ing** [ME *conversen,* fr. MF *converser,* fr. L *conversari* to live, keep company with, fr. *conversus,* pp. of *convertere* to turn around] **1** *archaic* **a :** to become occupied or engaged **b :** to have acquaintance or familiarity **2 a :** to exchange thoughts and opinions in speech : TALK **b :** to carry on an exchange similar to a conversation; *esp* **:** to interact with a computer ***syn*** see SPEAK — **con·vers·er** *n*

²con·verse \ˈkän-ˌvərs\ *n* **1** *obs* **:** social interaction **2 :** CONVERSATION

³con·verse \kən-ˈvərs, ˈkän-ˌ\ *adj* [L *conversus,* pp. of *convertere*] **:** reversed in order, relation, or action — **con·verse·ly** *adv*

⁴con·verse \ˈkän-ˌvərs\ *n* **:** something converse to another; *esp* **:** a proposition obtained by interchange of the subject and predicate of a logical proposition ⟨"no *P* is *S*" is the ~ of "no *S* is *P*"⟩

con·ver·sion \kən-ˈvər-zhən, -shən\ *n* [ME, fr. MF, fr. L *conversion-, conversio,* fr. *conversus,* pp. of *convertere*] **1 :** the act of converting : the process of being converted **2 :** an experience associated with a definite and decisive adoption of religion **3 a :** the operation of finding a converse in logic **b :** reduction of a mathematical expression by clearing of fractions **4 :** the making of a score on a try for point after touchdown in football or a free throw in basketball **5 :** something converted from one use to another — **con·ver·sion·al** \-ˈvərzh-nəl, -ˈvərsh-, -ən-ᵊl\ *adj*

conversion reaction *n* **:** a psychoneurosis in which bodily symptoms (as paralysis of the limbs) appear without physical basis — called also *conversion hysteria*

¹con·vert \kən-ˈvərt\ *vb* [ME *converten,* fr. OF *convertir,* fr. L *convertere,* to turn around, transform, convert, fr. *com-* + *vertere* to turn — more at WORTH] *vt* **1 a :** to bring over from one belief, view, or party to another **b :** to bring about a religious conversion in **2 a :** to alter the physical or chemical nature or properties of esp. in manufacturing **b** (1) **:** to change from one form or function to another (2) **:** to alter for more effective utilization (3) **:** to appropriate without right **c :** to exchange for an equivalent **3** *obs* **:** TURN **4 :** to subject to logical conversion **5 a :** to make a goal after receiving (a pass) from a teammate **b :** to make (a spare) in bowling ~ *vi* **1 :** to undergo conversion **2 :** to make good on a try for point after touchdown or on a free throw ***syn*** see TRANSFORM

²con·vert \ˈkän-ˌvərt\ *n* **:** one that is converted; *esp* **:** one who has experienced conversion

con·vert·er \kən-ˈvərt-ər\ *n* **:** one that converts: as **a :** the furnace used in the Bessemer process **b** *or* **con·ver·tor** \-ˈvərt-ər\ **:** a device employing mechanical rotation for changing electrical energy from one form to another; *also* **:** a radio device for converting one frequency to another **c :** a device for adapting a television receiver to receive channels for which it was not orig. designed **d :** a device that accepts data in one form and converts it to another ⟨analog-digital ~⟩

¹con·vert·ible \kən-ˈvərt-ə-bəl\ *adj* **1 :** capable of being converted **2 :** having a top that may be lowered or removed ⟨~ coupe⟩ **3 :** capable of being exchanged for a specified equivalent (as another currency or security) ⟨U.S. currency is no longer ~ to gold⟩ ⟨a bond ~ to 12 shares of common stock⟩ — **con·vert·ibil·i·ty** \-ˌvərt-ə-ˈbil-ət-ē\ *n* — **con·vert·ible·ness** \-ˈvərt-ə-bəl-nəs\ *n* — **con·vert·ibly** \-blē\ *adv*

²convertible *n* **:** something convertible; *esp* **:** a convertible automobile

con·verti·plane *or* **con·verta·plane** \kən-ˈvərt-ə-ˌplān\ *n* **:** an aircraft that takes off and lands like a helicopter and is convertible to a fixed-wing configuration for forward flight

con·vex \kän-ˈveks; ˈkän-ˌ, kən-ˈ\ *adj* [MF or L; MF *convexe,* fr. L *convexus* vaulted, concave, convex, fr. *com-* + *-vexus* (akin to OE *wōh* crooked, bent) — more at PREVARICATE] **1 :** curved or rounded like the exterior of a sphere or circle — used of a spherical surface or curved line viewed from without **2 :** arched up : bulging out — used of that side of a curve or surface on which the tangent line or plane lies or on which normals at neighboring points diverge

con·vex·i·ty \kən-ˈvek-sət-ē, kän-\ *n, pl* **-ties** **1 :** the quality or state of being convex **2 :** a convex surface or part

con·vexo–con·cave \-ˌvek-(ˌ)sō-\ *adj* **1 :** CONCAVO-CONVEX **2 :** having the convex side of greater curvature than the concave

con·vey \kən-ˈvā\ *vt* [ME *conveyen,* fr. OF *conveier* to accompany, escort, fr. (assumed) VL *conviare,* fr. L *com-* + *via* way — more at VIA] **1** *obs* **:** LEAD, CONDUCT **2 a :** to bear from one place to another; *esp* **:** to move in a continuous stream or mass **b :** to impart or communicate by statement, suggestion, gesture, or appearance **c** (1) *archaic* **:** STEAL (2) *obs* **:** to carry away secretly **d :** to transfer or deliver to another; *specif* **:** to transfer by a sealed writing **e :** to cause to pass from one place or person to another : TRANSMIT ***syn*** see CARRY, TRANSFER

con·vey·ance \kən-ˈvā-ən(t)s\ *n* **1 :** the action of conveying **2 :** a means or way of conveying: as **a :** an instrument by which title to property is conveyed **b :** a means of transport : VEHICLE

con·vey·anc·er \-ən-sər\ *n* **:** one whose business is conveyancing

con·vey·anc·ing \-ən-siŋ\ *n* **:** the act or business of drawing deeds, leases, or other writings for transferring the title to property

con·vey·er *or* **con·vey·or** \kən-ˈvā-ər\ *n* **:** one that conveys: as **a :** a person who transfers property **b** *usu conveyor* **:** a mechanical apparatus for carrying packages or bulk material from place to place (as by an endless moving belt or a chain of receptacles)

con·vey·or·ize \-ə-ˌrīz\ *vt* **-ized; -iz·ing :** to equip with a conveyor — **con·vey·or·iza·tion** \-ˌvā-ə-rə-ˈzā-shən\ *n*

¹con·vict \kən-ˈvikt\ *adj, archaic* **:** CONVICTED

²con·vict \kən-ˈvikt\ *vt* [ME *convicten,* fr. L *convictus,* pp. of *convincere* to refute, convict] **1 :** to find or prove to be guilty **2 :** to convince of error or sinfulness

³con·vict \ˈkän-ˌvikt\ *n* **1 :** a person convicted of and under sentence for a crime **2 :** a person serving a prison sentence usu. for a long term

con·vic·tion \kən-ˈvik-shən\ *n* **1 :** the act or process of convicting of a crime esp. in a court of law **2 a :** the act of convincing a person of error or of compelling the admission of a truth **b :** the state of being convinced of error or compelled to admit the truth **3 a :** a strong persuasion or belief **b :** the state of being convinced ***syn*** see CERTAINTY, OPINION

con·vince \kən-ˈvin(t)s\ *vt* **con·vinced; con·vinc·ing** [L *convincere* to refute, convict, prove, fr. *com-* + *vincere* to conquer — more at VICTOR] **1 a** *obs* **:** to overcome by argument **b** *obs* **:** OVERPOWER, OVERCOME **2** *obs* **:** DEMONSTRATE, PROVE **3 :** to bring by argument to belief, consent, or a course of action : PERSUADE ⟨*convinced* them to leave the country⟩ ⟨they were *convinced* that he had drowned⟩ — **con·vinc·er** *n*

con·vinc·ing \kən-ˈvin(t)-siŋ\ *adj* **1 :** satisfying or assuring by argument or proof ⟨a ~ test of a new product⟩ **2 :** having power to convince of the truth, rightness, or reality of something : PLAUSIBLE ⟨told a ~ story⟩ ***syn*** see VALID ***ant*** unconvincing — **con·vinc·ing·ly** \-siŋ-lē\ *adv* — **con·vinc·ing·ness** *n*

con·viv·ial \kən-ˈviv-yəl, -ˈviv-ē-əl\ *adj* [LL *convivialis,* fr. L *convivium* banquet, fr. *com-* + *vivere* to live — more at QUICK] **:** relating to, occupied with, or fond of feasting, drinking, and good company — **con·viv·i·al·i·ty** \-ˌviv-ē-ˈal-ət-ē\ *n* — **con·viv·ial·ly** \-ˈviv-yə-lē, -ˈviv-ē-ə-lē\ *adv*

con·vo·ca·tion \ˌkän-və-ˈkā-shən\ *n* [ME, fr. MF, fr. L *convocation-, convocatio,* fr. *convocatus,* pp. of *convocare*] **1 a :** an assembly of persons convoked **b** (1) **:** an assembly of bishops and

representative clergy of the Church of England (2) : a consultative assembly of clergy and lay delegates from one part of an Episcopal diocese; *also* : a territorial division of an Episcopal diocese **c** : a ceremonial assembly of members of a college or university **2** : the act or process of convoking — **con·vo·ca·tion·al** \-shnəl, -shən-ᵊl\ *adj*
con·voke \kən-ˈvōk\ *vt* **con·voked; con·vok·ing** [MF *convoquer,* fr. L *convocare,* fr. *com-* + *vocare* to call — more at VOICE] : to call together to a meeting ***syn*** see SUMMON ***ant*** prorogue, dissolve
[1]**con·vo·lute** \ˈkän-və-ˌlüt\ *vb* **-lut·ed; -lut·ing** [L *convolutus,* pp. of *convolvere*] : TWIST, COIL
[2]**convolute** *adj* : rolled or wound together with one part upon another : COILED ⟨a ~ shell⟩ — **con·vo·lute·ly** *adv*
con·vo·lut·ed *adj* **1** : folded in curved or tortuous windings; *specif* : having convolutions **2** : INVOLVED, INTRICATE
convoluted tubule *n* **1** : PROXIMAL CONVOLUTED TUBULE **2** : DISTAL CONVOLUTED TUBULE
con·vo·lu·tion \ˌkän-və-ˈlü-shən\ *n* **1** : one of the irregular ridges on the surface of the brain and esp. of the cerebrum of higher mammals **2** : a convoluted form or structure — **con·vo·lu·tion·al** \-shnəl, -shən-ᵊl\ *adj*
con·volve \kən-ˈvälv, -ˈvȯlv\ *vb* **con·volved; con·volv·ing** [L *convolvere,* fr. *com-* + *volvere* to roll — more at VOLUBLE] *vt* : to roll together : WRITHE ~ *vi* : to roll together or circulate involvedly
con·vol·vu·lus \kən-ˈväl-vyə-ləs, -ˈvȯl-\ *n, pl* **-lus·es** *or* **-li** \-ˌlī, -ˌlē\ [NL, fr. L *convolvere* to roll together, roll up] : any of a genus (*Convolvulus*) of erect, trailing, or twining herbs and shrubs of the morning-glory family
[1]**con·voy** \ˈkän-ˌvȯi, kən-ˈ\ *vt* [ME *convoyen,* fr. MF *conveier, convoier* — more at CONVEY] : ACCOMPANY, GUIDE; *esp* : to escort for protection
[2]**con·voy** \ˈkän-ˌvȯi\ *n* **1** : one that convoys; *esp* : a protective escort (as for ships) **2** : the act of convoying **3** : a group convoyed or organized for convenience or protection in moving
con·vul·sant \kən-ˈvəl-sənt\ *adj* : causing convulsions : CONVULSIVE 1 — **convulsant** *n*
con·vulse \kən-ˈvəls\ *vt* **con·vulsed; con·vuls·ing** [L *convulsus,* pp. of *convellere* to pluck up, convulse, fr. *com-* + *vellere* to pluck — more at VULNERABLE] : to shake or agitate violently; *esp* : to shake with or as if with irregular spasms ***syn*** see SHAKE
con·vul·sion \kən-ˈvəl-shən\ *n* **1** : an abnormal violent and involuntary contraction or series of contractions of the muscles **2 a** : a violent disturbance **b** : an uncontrolled fit : PAROXYSM — **con·vul·sion·ary** \-shə-ˌner-ē\ *adj*
con·vul·sive \kən-ˈvəl-siv\ *adj* **1** : constituting or producing a convulsion **2** : attended or affected with convulsions ***syn*** see FITFUL — **con·vul·sive·ly** *adv* — **con·vul·sive·ness** *n*
cony *var of* CONEY
coo \ˈkü\ *vi* [imit.] **1** : to make the low soft cry of a dove or pigeon or a similar sound **2** : to talk fondly, amorously, or appreciatively ⟨an album that will be ~*ed* over by condescending classical music critics —Ellen Sander⟩ — **coo** *n*
[1]**cook** \ˈku̇k\ *n* [ME, fr. OE *cōc;* akin to OHG *koch;* both fr. a prehistoric WGmc word borrowed fr. L *coquus,* fr. *coquere* to cook; akin to OE *āfigen* fried, Gk *pessein* to cook] **1** : one who prepares food for eating **2** : a technical or industrial process comparable to cooking food; *also* : a substance so processed
[2]**cook** *vi* **1** : to prepare food for eating by means of heat **2** : to undergo the action of being cooked ⟨the rice is ~*ing* now⟩ **3** : OCCUR, HAPPEN ⟨find out what was ~*ing* in the committee⟩ ~ *vt* **1** : CONCOCT, IMPROVISE — usu. used with *up* ⟨~*ed* up a scheme⟩ **2** : to prepare for eating by a heating process **3** : FALSIFY, DOCTOR ⟨an old hand at company manipulation, he prepares to ~ the books —*Punch*⟩ **4** : to subject to the action of heat or fire — **cook one's goose** : to ruin (one) irretrievably
cook·book \-ˌbu̇k\ *n* : a book of cooking directions and recipes; *broadly* : a book of detailed instructions
cook cheese *n* : a soft unripened cheese made from curd that has been heated to the consistency of honey and poured into containers
cooked cheese \ˈku̇k-ˈchēz\ *n* : COOK CHEESE
cook·er \ˈku̇k-ər\ *n* : one that cooks: as **a** : a utensil, device, or apparatus for cooking **b** : one who tends a cooking process : COOK **c** *Brit* : STOVE
cook·ery \ˈku̇k-(ə-)rē\ *n, pl* **-er·ies** **1** : the art or practice of cooking **2** : an establishment for cooking
cookery book *n, chiefly Brit* : COOKBOOK
cook·ie *or* **cooky** \ˈku̇k-ē\ *n, pl* **cook·ies** [D *koekje,* dim. of *koek* cake] **1** : any of various small sweet flat or slightly raised cakes **2 a** : an attractive woman ⟨a buxom French ~ who haunts the . . . colony's one night spot —*Newsweek*⟩ **b** : PERSON, GUY ⟨a very tough ~ indeed, who can break a man's wrist without a quiver of distaste —John Crosby⟩
cookie sheet *n* : a flat rectangle of metal with at least one rolled edge used esp. for the baking of cookies or biscuits
cook·ing *adj* : suitable for or used in cooking ⟨~ apples⟩ ⟨~ sherry⟩ ⟨~ utensils⟩
cooking top *n* : a built-in cabinet-top cooking apparatus consisting usu. of four heating units for gas or electricity
cook off *vi, of a cartridge* : to fire as a result of being allowed to rest in the chamber of an overheated weapon
cook·out \ˈku̇k-ˌau̇t\ *n* : an outing at which a meal is cooked and served in the open; *also* : the meal cooked
cook·shack \-ˌshak\ *n* : a shack used for cooking
cook·shop \-ˌshäp\ *n* : a shop supplying or serving cooked food
Cook's tour \ˈku̇ks-\ *n* [Thomas *Cook* & Son, E travel agency] : a quick tour in which attractions are viewed briefly and cursorily
cook·ware \ˈku̇k-ˌwa(ə)r, -ˌwe(ə)r\ *n* : utensils used in cooking
[1]**cool** \ˈkül\ *adj* [ME *col,* fr. OE *cōl;* akin to OHG *kuoli* cool, OE *ceald* cold] **1** : moderately cold : lacking in warmth ⟨warm days and ~ nights⟩ **2 a** : marked by steady dispassionate calmness and self-control ⟨a ~ and calculating administrator —*Current Biog.*⟩ **b** : lacking ardor or friendliness ⟨the ~, impersonal manner of some of the bright young men . . . who administer the antipoverty programs —J. C. Cort⟩ **c** (1) : marked by restrained emotion or excitement ⟨~ jazz⟩ (2) : free from racial tensions or violence ⟨meeting with minority groups in an attempt to keep the city ~⟩ **3** — used as an intensive ⟨a ~ million dollars⟩ **4** : marked by deliberate effrontery or lack of due respect or discretion ⟨a ~ reply⟩ **5** : facilitating or suggesting relief from heat ⟨a ~ dress⟩ **6 a** *of a color* : producing an impression of being cool; *specif* : of a hue in the range violet through blue to green **b** *of a musical tone* : relatively lacking in timbre or resonance **7** *slang* : very good : EXCELLENT **8** : employing understatement and a minimum of detail to convey information and usu. requiring the listener, viewer, or reader to complete the message ⟨another indication of the very ~ . . . character of this medium —H. M. McLuhan⟩ — **cool·ish** \ˈkü-lish\ *adj* — **cool·ly** *also* **cooly** \-ˈkül-(l)ē\ *adv* — **cool·ness** \ˈkül-nəs\ *n*
syn COOL, COMPOSED, COLLECTED, UNRUFFLED, IMPERTURBABLE, NONCHALANT *shared meaning element* : actually or apparently free from agitation or excitement ***ant*** ardent, agitated
[2]**cool** *vi* **1** : to become cool : lose heat or warmth ⟨placed the pie in the window to ~⟩ — sometimes used with *off* or *down* **2** : to lose ardor or passion ⟨his anger ~*ed*⟩ ~ *vt* **1** : to make cool : impart a feeling of coolness to ⟨~*ed* the room with a fan⟩ — often used with *off* or *down* ⟨a swim ~*ed* us off a little⟩ **2 a** : to moderate the heat, excitement, or force of : CALM ⟨~*ed* her growing anger⟩ **b** : to slow or lessen the growth or activity of — usu. used with *off* or *down* ⟨wants to ~ off the economy without freezing it —*Newsweek*⟩ — **cool it** : to calm down : go easy ⟨the word went out to the young to *cool it* —W. M. Young⟩ — **cool one's heels** : to wait or be kept waiting for a long time esp. from or as if from disdain or discourtesy
[3]**cool** *n* **1** : a cool time, place, or situation ⟨the ~ of the evening⟩ **2 a** : a lack of excitement or enthusiasm : INDIFFERENCE ⟨wears her ~ like perfume, without a . . . single expression to disturb her aristocratic unconcern —Hubert Saal⟩ **b** : SELF-ASSURANCE, SOPHISTICATION ⟨girls, from 9 to 12, who are only beginning to awaken to the world around and have not yet developed any ~ about themselves —J. K. Sale & Ben Apfelbaum⟩ **3** : POISE, COMPOSURE ⟨press questions . . . seemed to rattle him and he lost his ~ —*New Republic*⟩
[4]**cool** *adv* : in a casual and nonchalant manner ⟨they learn to play it ~, not really involve themselves —Marilyn B. Noble⟩
cool·ant \ˈkü-lənt\ *n* : a usu. fluid cooling agent
cool·er \ˈkü-lər\ *n* **1** : one that cools: as **a** : a container for cooling liquids **b** : REFRIGERATOR **2** : LOCKUP, JAIL; *esp* : a cell for violent or unmanageable prisoners **3** : an iced drink usu. with an alcoholic beverage as base
Coo·ley's anemia \ˌkü-lēz-\ *n* [Thomas B. *Cooley* †1945 Amer pediatrician] : THALASSEMIA
cool·head·ed \ˈkül-ˈhed-əd\ *adj* : not easily excited
coo·lie \ˈkü-lē\ *n* [Hindi *kulī*] : an unskilled laborer or porter usu. in or from the Far East hired for low or subsistence wages
coolie hat *n* : a conical-shaped usu. straw hat worn esp. to protect the head from the heat of the sun
cool·ing–off \ˌkü-liŋ-ˈȯf\ *adj* : designed to allow passions to cool or to permit negotiation between parties ⟨a ~ period⟩
coombe *or* **coomb** \ˈküm\ *var of* COMBE
coon \ˈkün\ *n* : RACCOON
coon·can \ˈkün-ˌkan\ *n* [by folk etymology fr. MexSp *conquián* conquian, fr. Sp *¿con quién?* with whom?] : a game of rummy played with two packs including two jokers
coon cat *n, chiefly NewEng* : ANGORA CAT
coon cheese \ˈkün-\ *n* [prob. fr. *coon* (Negro), fr. *coon* (raccoon)] : a sharp cheddar cheese that has been cured at higher than usual temperature and humidity and that is usu. coated with black wax
coon·hound \ˈkün-ˌhau̇nd\ *n* : a sporting dog trained to hunt raccoons; *esp* : BLACK AND TAN COONHOUND
coon's age *n* : a long while ⟨best fried chicken I've tasted for a *coon's age* —Sinclair Lewis⟩
coon·skin \ˈkün-ˌskin\ *n* **1** : the skin or pelt of the raccoon **2** : an article (as a cap or coat) made of coonskin
coon·tie \ˈkünt-ē\ *n* [Seminole *kunti* coontie flour] : any of several tropical American woody plants (genus *Zamia*) of the cycad family whose roots and stems yield a starchy foodstuff — called also *arrowroot*
[1]**coop** \ˈküp, ˈku̇p\ *n* [ME *cupe;* akin to OE *cȳpe* basket, *cot* cot] **1** : a cage or small enclosure (as for poultry); *also* : a small building for housing poultry **2 a** : a confined area **b** : JAIL
[2]**coop** *vt* **1** : to confine in a restricted and often crowded area — usu. used with *up* **2** : to place or keep in a coop : PEN — often used with *up*
co–op \ˈkō-ˌäp, kō-ˈ; ˈküp\ *n* : COOPERATIVE
[1]**coo·per** \ˈkü-pər, ˈku̇p-ər\ *n* [ME *couper, cowper,* fr. MD *cūper* (fr. *cūpe* cask) or MLG *kūper,* fr. *kūpe* cask; MD *cūpe* & MLG *kūpe,* fr. L *cupa;* akin to Gk *kypellon* cup — more at HIVE] : one that makes or repairs wooden casks or tubs
[2]**cooper** *vb* **coo·pered; coo·per·ing** \ˈkü-p(ə-)riŋ, ˈku̇p-(ə-)riŋ\ *vt* : to work as a cooper on ~ *vi* : to work at or do coopering
coo·per·age \ˈkü-p(ə-)rij, ˈku̇p-(ə-)\ *n* **1** : a cooper's place of business **2** : a cooper's work or products
co·op·er·ate \kō-ˈäp-(ə-)ˌrāt\ *vi* [LL *cooperatus,* pp. of *cooperari,* fr. L *co-* + *operari* to work — more at OPERATE] **1** : to act or work with another or others : act together **2** : to associate with another or others for mutual benefit — **co·op·er·a·tor** \-ˌrāt-ər\ *n*
co·op·er·a·tion \(ˌ)kō-ˌäp-ə-ˈrā-shən\ *n* **1** : the action of cooperating : common effort **2** : association of persons for common benefit **3** : a dynamic social process in ecological aggregations (as communities or colonies) in which mutual benefits outweigh the

disadvantages (as competition) of crowding — **co·op·er·a·tion·ist** \-sh(ə-)nəst\ *n*

1co·op·er·a·tive \kō-'äp-(ə-)rət-iv, -'äp-ə-ˌrāt-\ *adj* **1 a :** marked by cooperation ⟨~ efforts⟩ **b :** marked by a willingness and ability to work with others ⟨~ neighbors⟩ **2 :** of, relating to, or organized as a cooperative **3 :** relating to or comprising a program of combined liberal arts and technical studies at different schools — **co·op·er·a·tive·ly** *adv* — **co·op·er·a·tive·ness** *n*

2cooperative *n* **:** an enterprise or organization owned by and operated for the benefit of those using its services

Coo·per's hawk \'kü-pərz-\ *n* [William *Cooper* †1864 Amer. naturalist] **:** an American hawk (*Accipiter cooperii*) that is larger than the similarly colored sharp-shinned hawk and has a more rounded tail

co–opt \kō-'äpt\ *vt* [L *cooptare,* fr. *co-* + *optare* to choose] **1 a :** to choose or elect as a member **b :** to appoint as a colleague or assistant **2 a :** to take into a group (as a faction, movement, or culture) **:** ABSORB, ASSIMILATE ⟨the students are ~*ed* by a system they serve even in their struggle against it —A. C. Danto⟩ **b :** to take over **:** APPROPRIATE — **co–op·ta·tion** \ˌkō-ˌäp-'tā-shən\ *n* — **co–op·ta·tive** \kō-'äp-tət-iv\ *adj* — **co–op·tion** \-'äp-shən\ *n* — **co–op·tive** \-'äp-tiv\ *adj*

1co·or·di·nate \kō-'ȯrd-nət, -ᵊn-ət, -ᵊn-ˌāt\ *adj* [back-formation fr. *coordination*] **1 a :** equal in rank, quality, or significance **b :** being of equal rank in a sentence ⟨~ clauses⟩ **2 :** relating to or marked by coordination **3 a :** being a university that awards degrees to men and women taught usu. by the same faculty but attending separate classes often on separate campuses **b :** being one of the colleges and esp. the women's branch of a coordinate university **4 :** of, relating to, or being a system of indexing by two or more terms so that documents may be retrieved through the intersection of index terms — **co·or·di·nate·ly** *adv* — **co·or·di·nate·ness** *n*

2coordinate *n* **1 :** one who is of equal rank, authority, or importance with another **2 a :** any of a set of numbers used in specifying the location of a point on a line, on a surface, or in space **b :** any one of a set of variables used in specifying the state of a substance or the motion of a particle or momentum **3** *pl* **:** articles (as of clothing) designed to be used together and to attain their effect through pleasing contrast (as of color, material, or texture)

3co·or·di·nate \kō-'ȯrd-ᵊn-ˌāt\ *vb* **-nat·ed; -nat·ing** [back-formation fr. *coordination*] *vt* **1 :** to put in the same order or rank **2 :** to bring into a common action, movement, or condition **:** HARMONIZE **3 :** to attach so as to form a coordination complex ~ *vi* **1 :** to be or become coordinate esp. so as to act together in a smooth concerted way **2 :** to combine by means of a coordinate bond — **co·or·di·na·tive** \kō-'ȯrd-nət-iv, -ᵊn-ət-, -ᵊn-ˌāt-\ *adj* — **co·or·di·na·tor** \-ᵊn-ˌāt-ər\ *n*

coordinate bond *n* **:** a covalent bond held to consist of a pair of electrons supplied by only one of the two atoms it joins

co·or·di·nat·ed \-ᵊn-ˌāt-əd\ *adj* **:** able to use more than one set of muscle movements to a single end ⟨a well-*coordinated* athlete⟩

coordinate geometry *n* **:** ANALYTIC GEOMETRY

coordinating conjunction *n* **:** a conjunction that joins together words or word groups of equal grammatical rank

co·or·di·na·tion \(ˌ)kō-ˌȯrd-ᵊn-'ā-shən\ *n* [F or LL; F, fr. LL *coordination-, coordinatio,* fr. L *co-* + *ordination-, ordinatio* arrangement] **1 :** the act or action of coordinating **2 :** the state of being coordinate or coordinated

coordination complex *n* **:** a compound or ion with a central usu. metallic atom or ion combined by coordinate bonds with a definite number of surrounding ions, groups, or molecules

coot \'küt\ *n* [ME *coote;* akin to D *koet* coot] **1 :** any of various sluggish slow-flying slaty-black birds (genus *Fulica*) of the rail family that somewhat resemble ducks and have lobed toes and the upper mandible prolonged on the forehead as a horny frontal shield **2 :** any of several No. American scoters **3 :** a harmless simple person; *broadly* **:** FELLOW

coo·tie \'küt-ē\ *n* [perh. modif. of Malay *kutu*] **:** BODY LOUSE

1cop \'käp\ *n* [ME, fr. OE *copp*] **1** *dial chiefly Eng* **:** TOP, CREST **2 :** a cylindrical or conical mass of thread, yarn, or roving wound on a quill or tube; *also* **:** a quill or tube upon which it is wound

2cop *vt* **copped; cop·ping** [perh. fr. D *kapen* to steal, fr. Fris *kāpia* to take away; akin to OHG *kouf* trade — more at CHEAP] **1** *slang* **:** to get hold of **:** CATCH, CAPTURE; *also* **:** PURCHASE **2** *slang* **:** STEAL, SWIPE — **cop a plea :** to plead guilty to a lesser charge in order to avoid standing trial for a more serious one; *broadly* **:** to admit fault and plead for mercy

3cop *n* [short for *3copper*] **:** POLICEMAN

4cop *abbr* **1** copper **2** copulative **3** copy **4** copyright

Cop *abbr* Coptic

co·pa·ce·tic *or* **co·pe·se·tic** \ˌkō-pə-'set-ik, -'sēt-\ *adj* [origin unknown] **:** very satisfactory

co·pai·ba \kō-'pī-bə, -'pā-; ˌkō-pə-'ē-bə\ *n* [Sp & Pg; Sp, fr. Pg *copaíba,* of Tupian origin; akin to Guarani *cupaiba* copaiba] **:** a stimulant oleoresin obtained from several pinnate-leaved So. American leguminous trees (genus *Copaifera*); *also* **:** one of these trees

co·pal \'kō-pəl, -ˌpal; kō-'pal\ *n* [Sp, fr. Nahuatl *copalli* resin] **:** a recent or fossil resin from various tropical trees

co·par·ce·nary \kō-'pärs-ᵊn-ˌer-ē\ *n, pl* **-nar·ies 1 :** joint heirship **2 :** joint ownership

co·par·ce·ner \-'pärs-nər, -ᵊn-ər\ *n* **:** a joint heir

co·part·ner \(')kō-'pärt-nər\ *n* **:** PARTNER — **co·part·ner·ship** \-ˌship\ *n*

1cope \'kōp\ *n* [ME, fr. OE *-cāp,* fr. LL *cappa* head covering] **1 :** a long enveloping ecclesiastical vestment **2 a :** something resembling a cope (as by concealing or covering) ⟨the dark sky's starry ~ —P. B. Shelley⟩ **b :** COPING

2cope *vt* **coped; cop·ing :** to cover or furnish with a cope or coping

3cope *vb* **coped; cop·ing** [ME *copen,* fr. MF *couper* to strike, cut, fr. OF, fr. *coup* blow, fr. LL *colpus,* alter. of L *colaphus,* fr. Gk *kolaphos* buffet] *vi* **1** *obs* **:** STRIKE, FIGHT **2 a :** to maintain a contest or combat usu. on even terms or with success — used with *with* **b :** to deal with and attempt to overcome problems and difficulties — usu. used with *with* **3** *archaic* **:** MEET, ENCOUNTER ~ *vt* **1** *obs* **:** to meet in combat **2** *obs* **:** to come in contact with **3** *obs* **:** MATCH

4cope *vt* **coped; cop·ing** [prob. fr. F *couper* to cut] **1 :** NOTCH **2 :** to shape (a structural member) to fit a coping or conform to the shape of another member

copeck *var of* KOPECK

copemate *or* **copesmate** *n* [*3cope* + *mate*] **1** *obs* **:** ANTAGONIST **2** *obs* **:** PARTNER, COMRADE

co·pen \'kō-pən\ *n* [short for *copenhagen blue,* fr. *Copenhagen,* Denmark] **:** a variable color averaging a moderate blue — called also *copen blue*

co·pe·pod \'kō-pə-ˌpäd\ *n* [deriv. of Gk *kōpē* oar + *pod-, pous* foot] **:** any of a large subclass (Copepoda) of usu. minute freshwater and marine crustaceans — **copepod** *adj*

cop·er \'kō-pər\ *n* [E dial. *cope* (to trade)] *Brit* **:** a horse dealer; *esp* **:** a dishonest one

Co·per·ni·can \kō-'pər-ni-kən\ *adj* **1 :** of or relating to Copernicus or the belief that the earth rotates daily on its axis and the planets revolve in orbits around the sun **2 :** of radical or major importance or degree ⟨effected a ~ revolution in philosophy —*Times Lit. Supp.*⟩ — **Copernican** *n* — **Co·per·ni·can·ism** \-kə-ˌniz-əm\ *n*

cope·stone \'kōp-ˌstōn\ *n* **1 :** a stone forming a coping **2 :** a finishing touch **:** CROWN

copi·er \'käp-ē-ər\ *n* **:** one that copies; *specif* **:** a machine for making copies of graphic matter (as printing, drawings, or pictures)

co·pi·hue \kō-'pē-(ˌ)wā\ *n* [AmerSp, fr. Araucan *copiu*] **:** a showy climbing vine (*Lapageria rosea*) with deep rosy red trumpet-shaped flowers and oval edible yellowish fruits that is the national flower of Chile — called also *Chile-bells*

co·pi·lot \'kō-ˌpī-lət\ *n* **:** a qualified pilot who assists or relieves the pilot but is not in command

cop·ing \'kō-piŋ\ *n* **:** the covering course of a wall usu. with a sloping top

cop·ing saw \'kō-piŋ-\ *n* [fr. prp. of *4cope*] **:** a handsaw with a very narrow blade held under tension in a U-shaped frame and used esp. for cutting curves in wood

cop·ing·stone \'kō-piŋ-ˌstōn\ *n, chiefly Brit* **:** COPESTONE

co·pi·ous \'kō-pē-əs\ *adj* [ME, fr. L *copiosus,* fr. *copia* abundance, fr. *co-* + *ops* wealth — more at OPULENT] **1 :** yielding something abundantly ⟨a ~ harvest⟩ ⟨~ springs⟩ **2 a :** full of thought, information, or matter **b :** profuse or exuberant in words, expression, or style ⟨she was evidently a ~ talker, and now poured forth a breathless stream of anecdote —W. S. Maugham⟩ **3 :** present in large quantity **:** taking place on a large scale ⟨~ rainfall⟩ ⟨~ eating and still more ~ drinking —Aldous Huxley⟩ ***syn*** see PLENTIFUL ***ant*** meager — **co·pi·ous·ly** *adv* — **co·pi·ous·ness** *n*

co·pla·nar \(')kō-'plā-nər, -ˌnär\ *adj* **:** lying or acting in the same plane — **co·pla·nar·i·ty** \ˌkō-plā-'nar-ət-ē\ *n*

co·pol·y·mer \(')kō-'päl-ə-mər\ *n* **:** a product of copolymerization — **co·pol·y·mer·ic** \ˌkō-ˌpäl-ə-'mer-ik\ *adj*

co·po·ly·mer·ize \ˌkō-pə-'lim-ə-ˌrīz, (')kō-'päl-ə-mə-\ *vb* **:** to polymerize (as two different monomers) together — **co·po·ly·mer·iza·tion** \ˌkō-pə-ˌlim-ə-rə-'zā-shən, ˌkō-ˌpäl-ə-mə-\ *n*

cop–out \'käp-ˌau̇t\ *n* **1 :** an excuse for copping out **:** PRETEXT **2 :** the means for copping out **3 :** one who cops out **4 :** the act or an instance of copping out

cop out \(')käp-'au̇t\ *vi* **:** to back out (as of an unwanted responsibility) — often used with *on* or *of* ⟨young Americans who *cop out* on society —*Christian Science Monitor*⟩ ⟨*copping out* of jury duty through a variety of machinations —H. F. Waters⟩

1cop·per \'käp-ər\ *n, often attrib* [ME *coper,* fr. OE; akin to OHG *kupfar* copper; both fr. a prehistoric WGmc-NGmc word borrowed fr. LL *cuprum* copper, fr. L (*aes*) *Cyprium,* lit., Cyprian metal] **1 :** a common reddish metallic element that is ductile and malleable and one of the best conductors of heat and electricity — see ELEMENT table **2 :** a coin or token made of copper or bronze **3** *chiefly Brit* **:** a large boiler (as for cooking) **4 :** any of various small butterflies (family Lycaenidae) with usu. copper-colored wings — **cop·pery** \'käp-(ə-)rē\ *adj*

2copper *vt* **cop·pered; cop·per·ing** \'käp-(ə-)riŋ\ **1 :** to coat or sheathe with or as if with copper **2 a :** to bet against (as in faro) **b :** HEDGE

3copper *n* [*2cop*] **:** POLICEMAN

cop·per·as \'käp-(ə-)rəs\ *n* [alter. of ME *coperose,* fr. MF, fr. (assumed) VL *cuprirosa,* fr. LL *cuprum* + L *rosa* rose] **:** a green hydrated ferrous sulfate $FeSO_4 \cdot 7H_2O$ used esp. in making inks and pigments

cop·per·head \'käp-ər-ˌhed\ *n* **1 :** a common pit viper usu. having a copper-colored head and markings that is found esp. in uplands of the eastern U.S. **2 :** a person in the northern states who sympathized with the South during the Civil War

cop·per·plate \ˌkäp-ər-'plāt\ *n* **:** an engraved or etched copper printing plate; *also* **:** a print made from such a plate

copper pyrites *n* **:** CHALCOPYRITE

cop·per·smith \'käp-ər-ˌsmith\ *n* **:** a worker in copper

copper sulfate *n* **:** a sulfate of copper; *esp* **:** the normal sulfate that is white in the anhydrous form but blue in the crystalline hydrous form $CuSO_4 \cdot 5H_2O$ and that is often used as an algicide and fungicide

cop·pice \'käp-əs\ *n* [MF *copeiz,* fr. *couper* to cut — more at COPE] **1 :** a thicket, grove, or growth of small trees **2 :** forest originating mainly from shoots or root suckers rather than seed

copr- *or* **copro-** *comb form* [NL, fr. Gk *kopr-, kopro-,* fr. *kopros* akin to Skt *śakṛt* dung] **:** dung **:** feces ⟨coprolite⟩

co·pra \'kō-prə *also* 'käp-rə\ *n* [Pg, fr. Malayalam *koppara*] **:** dried coconut meat yielding coconut oil

co·pro·duce \ˌkō-prə-'d(y)üs\ *vt* **:** to produce in cooperation with another — **co·pro·duc·er** *n* — **co·pro·duc·tion** \-'dək-shən\ *n*

co·prod·uct \(')kō-'präd-(ˌ)əkt\ *n* **:** BY-PRODUCT 1

cop·ro·lite \'käp-rə-ˌlīt\ *n* **:** fossil excrement — **cop·ro·lit·ic** \ˌkäp-rə-'lit-ik\ *adj*

co·proph·a·gous \kä-'präf-ə-gəs\ *adj* [Gk *koprophagos*, fr. *kopr-* + *-phagos* -phagous] : feeding on dung — **co·proph·a·gy** \-jē\ *n*
cop·ro·phil·ia \,käp-rə-'fil-ē-ə\ *n* [NL] : marked interest in excrement; *esp* : the use of feces or filth for sexual excitement — **cop·ro·phil·i·ac** \-ē-,ak\ *n*
cop·roph·i·lous \kä-'präf-ə-ləs\ *adj* : growing or living on dung ⟨~ fungi⟩
copse \'käps\ *n* [by alter.] : COPPICE 1
¹Copt \'käpt\ *n* [Ar *qubt* Copts, fr. Coptic *gyptios* Egyptian, fr. Gk *aigyptios*] **1** : a member of a people descended from the ancient Egyptians **2** : a member of the traditional Monophysite Christian church originating and centering in Egypt
²Copt *abbr* Coptic
cop·ter \'käp-tər\ *n* : HELICOPTER
¹Cop·tic \'käp-tik\ *adj* : of or relating to the Copts, their liturgical language, or their church
²Coptic *n* : an Afro-Asiatic language descended from ancient Egyptian and used as the liturgical language of the Coptic church
co·pub·lish \(')kō-'pəb-lish\ *vt* : to publish in cooperation with another publisher — **co·pub·lish·er** *n*
cop·u·la \'käp-yə-lə\ *n* [L, bond] : something that connects: as **a** : the connecting link between subject and predicate of a proposition **b** : a word or expression (as a form of *be, become, feel,* or *seem*) that links a subject with its predicate
cop·u·late \'käp-yə-,lāt\ *vi* **-lat·ed; -lat·ing** [L *copulatus,* pp. of *copulare* to join, fr. *copula*] **1** : to engage in sexual intercourse **2** *of gametes* : to fuse permanently — **cop·u·la·tion** \,käp-yə-'lā-shən\ *n* — **cop·u·la·to·ry** \'käp-yə-lə-,tōr-ē, -,tȯr-\ *adj*
¹cop·u·la·tive \'käp-yə-,lāt-iv\ *adj* **1 a** : joining together coordinate words or word groups and expressing addition of their meanings ⟨a ~ conjunction⟩ **b** : functioning as a copula **2** : relating to or serving for copulation **3** : of or relating to coupling of chemical compounds or radicals — **cop·u·la·tive·ly** *adv*
²copulative *n* : a copulative word
¹copy \'käp-ē\ *n, pl* **cop·ies** [ME *copie,* fr. MF, fr. ML *copia,* fr. L, abundance — more at COPIOUS] **1** : an imitation, transcript, or reproduction of an original work (as a letter, a painting, a piece of furniture, or a dress) **2** : one of a series of esp. mechanical reproductions of an original impression; *also* : an individual example of such a reproduction ⟨a presentation ~⟩ **3** *archaic* : something to be imitated : MODEL **4 a** : matter to be set up for printing or photoengraving **b** : something considered printable or newsworthy — used in the singular and without an article ⟨at the mercy of newsmen ... who found anything she did to be good ~ —*Current Biog.*⟩
²copy *vb* **cop·ied; copy·ing** *vt* **1** : to make a copy of **2** : to model oneself on ~ *vi* **1** : to make a copy **2** : to undergo copying ⟨the document did not ~ well⟩
  syn COPY, IMITATE, MIMIC, APE, MOCK *shared meaning element* : to make something so that it resembles an existing thing **ant** originate
copy·book \'käp-ē-,bůk\ *n* : a book formerly used in teaching penmanship and containing models for imitation
copy·boy \-,bȯi\ *n* : one who carries copy and runs errands
¹copy·cat \-,kat\ *n* : one who slavishly imitates or adopts the behavior or practices of another
²copycat *vb* **copy·cat·ted; copy·cat·ting** *vi* : to act as a copycat ~ *vt* : IMITATE
copy·desk \-,desk\ *n* : the desk at which newspaper copy is edited
copy editor *n* **1** : COPYREADER **2 a** : an editor who prepares copy for the printer **b** : an editor in charge of a copydesk and the copyreaders on a newspaper
copy·hold \'käp-ē-,hōld\ *n* **1** : a former tenure of land in England and Ireland by right of being recorded in the court of the manor **2** : an estate held by copyhold
copy·hold·er \-,hōl-dər\ *n* **1** : a device for holding copy esp. for a typesetter **2** : one who reads copy for a proofreader
copy·ist \'käp-ē-əst\ *n* **1** : one who makes copies **2** : IMITATOR
copy·read·er \-,rēd-ər\ *n* : a publishing-house editor who reads and corrects manuscript copy; *also* : one who edits and headlines newspaper copy
¹copy·right \-,rīt\ *n* : the exclusive legal right to reproduce, publish, and sell the matter and form of a literary, musical, or artistic work — **copyright** *adj*
²copyright *vt* : to secure a copyright on
copy·writ·er \'käp-ē-,rīt-ər\ *n* : a writer of advertising or publicity copy
coq au vin \,kȯk-ō-'vaⁿ, ,käk-ō-\ *n* [F, cock with wine] : chicken cooked in usu. red wine
¹co·quet *n* [F, dim. of *coq* cock] **1** \kō-'ket, -'kā\ *obs* : a man who indulges in coquetry **2** \-'ket\ : COQUETTE
²co·quet \kō-'ket\ *adj* : COQUETTISH
³co·quet *or* **co·quette** \-'ket\ *vi* **co·quet·ted; co·quet·ting 1** : to play the coquette : FLIRT **2** : to deal with something playfully rather than seriously *syn* see TRIFLE
co·que·try \'kō-kə-trē, kō-'ke-trē\ *n, pl* **-tries** : a flirtatious act or attitude
co·quette \kō-'ket\ *n* [F, fem. of *coquet*] : a woman who endeavors without sincere affection to gain the attention and admiration of men
co·quett·ish \kō-'ket-ish\ *adj* : having the air or nature of a coquette or of coquetry — **co·quett·ish·ly** *adv* — **co·quett·ish·ness** *n*
co·qui·lla nut \kō-,kē-(y)ə-, -,kēl-yə-\ *n* [Pg *coquilho,* dim. of *côco* coconut] : the nut of a piassava palm (*Attalea funifera*) of Brazil having a hard brown shell much used by turners
co·qui·na \kō-'kē-nə\ *n* [Sp, prob. irreg. dim. of *concha* shell] **1 a** : a small marine clam (genus *Donax*) used for broth or chowder **2 a** : a soft whitish limestone formed of broken shells and corals cemented together and used for building
¹cor *abbr* **1** corner **2** coroner **3** corpus
²cor *or* **corr** *abbr* **1** correct; corrected; correction **2** correspondence; correspondent; corresponding **3** corrupt; corruption
Cor *abbr* Corinthians

co·rac·ii·form \kə-'ras-ē-ə-,fȯrm\ *adj* [deriv. of Gk *korak-, korax* raven + L *forma* form — more at RAVEN] : of or relating to an order (Coraciiformes) of arboreal nonpasserine birds including the rollers, kingfishers, and hornbills
cor·a·cle \'kȯr-ə-kəl, 'kär-\ *n* [W *corwgl*] **1** : a small boat made by covering a wicker frame with hide or leather and used by the ancient Britons **2** : a boat made of broad hoops covered with horsehide or tarpaulin and used in parts of the British Isles
cor·a·coid \'kȯr-ə-,kȯid, 'kär-\ *adj* [NL *coracoides,* fr. Gk *korakoeidēs,* lit., like a raven, fr. *korak-, korax*] : of, relating to, or being a process or cartilage bone of many vertebrates that extends from the scapula to or toward the sternum — **coracoid** *n*
cor·al \'kȯr-əl, 'kär-\ *n* [ME, fr. MF, fr. L *corallium,* fr. Gk *korallion*] **1 a** : the calcareous or horny skeletal deposit produced by anthozoan or rarely hydrozoan polyps; *esp* : a richly red precious coral secreted by a gorgonian (*Corallium nobile*) **b** : a polyp or polyp colony together with its membranes and skeleton **2** : a piece of coral and esp. of red coral **3 a** : a bright reddish ovary (as of a lobster or scallop) **b** : a variable color averaging a deep pink — **coral** *adj* — **cor·al·loid** \-ə-,lȯid\ *or* **cor·al·loi·dal** \,kȯr-ə-'lȯid-ᵊl, ,kär-\ *adj*

coral 1b

cor·al·bells \'kȯr-əl-,belz, 'kär-\ *n pl but sing or pl in constr* (*Heuchera sanguinea*) : a perennial alumroot widely cultivated for its feathery spikes of tiny coral flowers
cor·al·ber·ry \-,ber-ē\ *n* : an American dwarf shrub (*Symphoricarpos orbiculatus*) that bears clusters of small flowers succeeded by red berries
¹cor·al·line \'kȯr-ə-,līn, 'kär-\ *adj* [F *corallin,* fr. LL *corallinus,* fr. L *corallium*] : of, relating to, or resembling coral or a coralline
²coralline *n* **1** : any of a family (Corallinaceae) of calcareous red algae **2** : a bryozoan or hydroid that resembles a coral
coral pink *n* : a moderate yellowish pink
coral snake *n* : any of several venomous chiefly tropical New World elapid snakes (genus *Micrurus*) brilliantly banded in red, black, and yellow or white that include two (*M. fulvius* and *M. euryxanthus*) ranging northward into the southern U.S. **2** : any of several harmless snakes resembling the coral snakes
co·ran·to \kə-'rant-(,)ō\ *n, pl* **-tos** *or* **-toes** [modif. of F *courante*] : COURANTE
cor·ban \'kȯ(ə)r-,ban\ *n* [Heb *qorbān* offering] : a sacrifice or offering to God among the ancient Hebrews
cor·beil *or* **cor·beille** \'kȯr-bəl, kȯr-'bā\ *n* [F *corbeille,* lit., basket, fr. LL *corbicula,* dim. of *corbis* basket] : a sculptured basket of flowers or fruit as an architectural decoration
¹cor·bel \'kȯr-bəl\ *n* [ME, fr. MF, fr. dim. of *corp* raven, fr. L *corvus* — more at RAVEN] : an architectural member that projects from within a wall and supports a weight; *esp* : one that is stepped upward and outward from a vertical upthrust
²corbel *vt* **-beled** *or* **-belled; -bel·ing** *or* **-bel·ling** : to furnish with or make into a corbel
corbeling *n* **1** : corbel work **2** : the construction of a corbel
cor·bic·u·la \kȯr-'bik-yə-lə\ *n, pl* **-lae** \-(,)lē, -,lī\ [LL, basket] : POLLEN BASKET
cor·bie \'kȯr-bē\ *n* [ME, modif. of OF *corbin,* fr. L *corvinus* of a raven] *chiefly Scot* : a carrion crow; *also* : RAVEN
corbie gable *n* : a gable having corbiesteps
cor·bie·step \-,step\ *n* : one of a series of steps terminating the upper part of a gable wall
cor·bi·na \kȯr-'bē-nə\ *n* [MexSp, fr. Sp *corvina,* an acanthopterygian fish, fr. fem. of *corvino* of a raven, fr. L *corvinus*] : any of several American marine fishes; *esp* : a spotted whiting (*Menticirrhus undulatus*) favored by surf casters along the California coast
¹cord \'kȯ(ə)rd\ *n* [ME, fr. OF *corde,* fr. L *chorda* string, fr. Gk *chordē* — more at YARN] **1 a** : a long slender flexible material usu. consisting of several strands (as of thread or yarn) woven or twisted together **b** : the hangman's rope **2** : a moral, spiritual, or emotional bond **3 a** : an anatomical structure (as a nerve) resembling a cord **b** : a small flexible insulated electrical cable having a plug at one or both ends used to connect a lamp or other appliance with a receptacle **4** : a unit of wood cut for fuel equal to a stack 4x4x8 feet or 128 cubic feet **5 a** : a rib like a cord on a textile **b** (1) : a fabric made with such ribs or a garment made of such a fabric (2) *pl* : trousers made of such a fabric
²cord *vt* **1** : to furnish, bind, or connect with a cord **2** : to pile up (wood) in cords — **cord·er** *n*
cord·age \'kȯrd-ij\ *n* **1** : ropes or cords; *esp* : the ropes in the rigging of a ship **2** : the number of cords (as of wood) on a given area
cor·date \'kȯ(ə)r-,dāt\ *adj* [NL *cordatus,* fr. L *cord-, cor*] : shaped like a heart ⟨a ~ leaf⟩ — **cor·date·ly** *adv*
cord·ed \'kȯrd-əd\ *adj* **1 a** : made of or provided with cords or ridges; *specif* : muscled in ridges **b** *of a muscle* : TENSE, TAUT **2** : bound, fastened, or wound about with cords **3** : striped or ribbed with or as if with cord : TWILLED
¹cor·dial \'kȯr-jəl\ *adj* [ME, fr. ML *cordialis,* fr. L *cord-, cor* heart — more at HEART] **1** *obs* : of or relating to the heart : VITAL **2** : tending to revive, cheer, or invigorate **3** : warmly and genially affable : HEARTFELT ⟨she received a most ~ welcome⟩ *syn* see GRACIOUS **ant** uncordial — **cor·dial·ly** \'kȯrj-(ə)-lē\ *adv* — **cor·dial·ness** \'kȯr-jəl-nəs\ *n*
²cordial *n* **1** : a stimulating medicine or drink **2** : LIQUEUR

cor·dial·i·ty \ˌkȯr-jē-ˈal-ət-ē, kȯr-ˈjal- *also* kȯrd-ˈyal-\ *n* : sincere affection and kindness : cordial regard
cordia pulmonalia *pl of* COR PULMONALE
cor·di·er·ite \ˈkȯrd-ē-ə-ˌrīt\ *n* [F, fr. Pierre L. A. *Cordier* †1861 F geologist] : a blue mineral $(Mg,Fe)_2Al_4Si_5O_{18}$ with vitreous luster and strong dichroism consisting of a silicate of aluminum, iron, and magnesium
cor·di·form \ˈkȯrd-ə-ˌfȯrm\ *adj* [F *cordiforme,* fr. L *cord-, cor* + F *-iforme* -iform] : shaped like a heart
cor·dil·le·ra \ˌkȯrd-ᵊl-ˈ(y)er-ə, kȯr-ˈdil-ə-rə\ *n* [Sp] : a system of mountain ranges often consisting of a number of more or less parallel chains — **cor·dil·le·ran** \-ˈ(y)er-ən, -ə-rən\ *adj*
cord·ite \ˈkȯ(ə)r-ˌdīt\ *n* : a smokeless powder composed of nitroglycerin, guncotton, and a petroleum substance usu. gelatinized by addition of acetone and pressed into cords resembling brown twine
cord·less \ˈkȯrd-ləs\ *adj* : having no cord; *esp* : powered by a battery ⟨~ tools⟩
cor·do·ba \ˈkȯrd-ə-bə, -ə-və\ *n* [Sp *córdoba,* fr. Francisco Fernández de *Córdoba* †1526 Sp explorer] — see MONEY table
1cor·don \ˈkȯrd-ᵊn, ˈkȯ(ə)r-ˌdän\ *n* [F, dim. of *corde* cord] **1 a** : an ornamental cord used esp. on costumes **b** : a cord or ribbon worn as a badge of honor or as a decoration **c** : STRINGCOURSE **2 a** : a line of troops or of military posts enclosing an area to prevent passage **b** : a line of persons or objects around a person or place ⟨a ~ of police⟩
2cordon *vt* **1** : to ornament with a cordon **2** : to form a protective or restrictive cordon around — often used with *off*
1cor·do·van \ˈkȯrd-ə-vən\ *adj* [OSp *cordovano,* fr. *Córdova* (now *Córdoba*), Spain] **1** *cap* : of or relating to Córdoba and esp. Córdoba, Spain **2** : made of cordovan leather
2cordovan *n* **1** : a soft fine-grained colored leather **2** : leather tanned from the inner layer of horsehide and characterized by nonporosity and density
1cor·du·roy \ˈkȯrd-ə-ˌrȯi\ *n, pl* **-roys** [perh. alter. of the name *Corderoy*] **1 a** : a durable usu. cotton pile fabric with vertical ribs or wales **b** *pl* : trousers of corduroy **2** : a road built of logs laid side by side transversely
2corduroy *vt* **-royed; -roy·ing** : to build (a road) of logs laid side by side transversely
cord·wain \ˈkȯ(ə)r-ˌdwān\ *n* [ME *cordwane,* fr. MF *cordoan,* fr. OSp *cordovano, cordován*] *archaic* : cordovan leather
cord·wain·er \-ˌdwā-nər\ *n* **1** *archaic* : a worker in cordovan leather **2** : SHOEMAKER — **cord·wain·ery** \-ˌdwā-nə-rē\ *n*
cord·wood \ˈkȯ(ə)r-ˌdwu̇d\ *n* : wood piled or sold in cords; *also* : standing timber suitable for use as fuel
1core \ˈkȯ(ə)r, ˈkȯ(ə)r\ *n* [ME] **1** : a central and often foundational part usu. distinct from the enveloping part by a difference in nature ⟨~ of the city⟩: as **a** : the usu. inedible central part of some fruits (as a pineapple); *esp* : the papery or leathery carpels composing the ripened ovary in a pome fruit **b** : the portion of a foundry mold that shapes the interior of a hollow casting **c** : a part removed from the interior of a mass esp. to determine the interior composition or a hidden condition **d** : the central strand around which other strands twist in some ropes **e** (1) : a mass of iron serving to concentrate and intensify the magnetic field resulting from a current in a surrounding coil (2) : a tiny doughnut-shaped piece of magnetic material (as ferrite) used in computer memories — called also *magnetic core* (3) : a computer memory consisting of an array of cores strung on fine wires; *broadly* : the internal memory of a computer — called also *core memory, core storage* **f** : the central part of the earth having a radius of about 2100 miles and physical properties different from those of the surrounding parts **g** : a nodule of stone (as flint or obsidian) from which flakes have been struck for making implements **h** : the conducting wire with its insulation in an electric cable **i** : a layer of wood on which veneers are glued (as in making plywood) **j** : an arrangement of a course of studies that combines under certain basic topics material from subjects conventionally separated and aims to provide a common background for all students **k** : the place in a nuclear reactor where fission occurs **2 a** : a basic, essential, or enduring part (as of an individual, a class, or an entity) **b** : the essential meaning : GIST ⟨the ~ of the book is thus an attempt to comprehend the nature of total war — *Times Lit. Supp.*⟩ **c** : the inmost or most intimate part ⟨honest to the ~⟩
2core *vt* **cored; cor·ing** : to remove a core from — **cor·er** *n*
3core *n* [ME *chore* chorus, company, fr. L *chorus*] *chiefly Scot* : a group of people
CORE \ˈkō(ə)r, ˈkȯ(ə)r\ *abbr* Congress of Racial Equality
co·re·cip·i·ent \ˌkō-ri-ˈsip-ē-ənt\ *n* : a joint recipient (as of an honor or a prize)
core city *n* : INNER CITY
co·re·late \ˌkō-ri-ˈlāt\ *vt* **-lat·ed; -lat·ing** [back-formation fr. *correlation*] *chiefly Brit* : CORRELATE — **co·re·la·tion** \-ˈlā-shən\ *n* — **co·rel·a·tive** \kō-ˈrel-ət-iv, kə-\ *adj* — **co·rel·a·tive·ly** *adv*
co·re·li·gion·ist \ˌkō-ri-ˈlij-(ə-)nəst\ *n* : one of the same religion
co·re·mi·um \kə-ˈrē-mē-əm\ *n, pl* **-mia** \-mē-ə\ [NL, fr. Gk *korēma* broom, fr. *korein* to sweep] : a fruiting body characteristic of certain imperfect fungi (as the Stilbellaceae) that consists of a sterile stalk of parallel or fascicled hyphae and a terminal head of fertile or spore-bearing branches
co·re·op·sis \ˌkōr-ē-ˈäp-səs, ˌkȯr-\ *n* [NL, genus name, fr. Gk *koris* bedbug + NL *-opsis;* akin to Gk *keirein* to cut — more at SHEAR] : any of a genus (*Coreopsis*) of composite herbs widely grown for their showy flower heads
co·re·pres·sor \ˌkō-ri-ˈpres-ər\ *n* : a substance that activates a particular genetic repressor by combining with it
co·req·ui·site \kō-ˈrek-wə-zət\ *n* : a formal course of study required to be taken simultaneously with another
co·re·spon·dent \ˌkō-ri-ˈspän-dənt\ *n* : a person named as guilty of adultery with the defendant in a divorce suit
corf \ˈkȯ(ə)rf\ *n, pl* **corves** \ˈkȯ(ə)rvz\ [ME, basket, fr. MD *corf* or MLG *korf*] *Brit* : a basket, tub, or truck used in a mine
cor·gi \ˈkȯr-gē\ *n, pl* **corgis** [W, fr. *cor* dwarf + *ci* dog; akin to OIr *cū* dog, OE *hund* — more at HOUND] : WELSH CORGI
co·ri·a·ceous \ˌkōr-ē-ˈā-shəs, ˌkȯr-\ *adj* [LL *coriaceus* — more at CUIRASS] : resembling leather
co·ri·an·der \ˈkōr-ē-ˌan-dər, ˌkōr-ē-ˈ, ˈkȯr-, ˌkȯr-\ *n* [ME *coriandre,* fr. OF, fr. L *coriandrum,* fr. Gk *koriandron*] **1** : an Old World herb (*Coriandrum sativum*) of the carrot family with aromatic fruits **2** : the ripened dried fruit of coriander used as a flavoring — called also *coriander seed*
1Co·rin·thi·an \kə-ˈrin(t)-thē-ən\ *n* **1** : a native or resident of Corinth, Greece **2 a** : a gay profligate man **b** : a fashionable man-about-town; *esp* : SPORTSMAN **c** : an amateur yachtsman
2Corinthian *adj* **1** : of, relating to, or characteristic of Corinth or Corinthians **2** : of or relating to the lightest and most ornate of the three Greek orders of architecture characterized esp. by its bell-shaped capital enveloped with acanthuses
Co·rin·thi·ans \-thē-ənz\ *n pl but sing in constr* : either of two letters written by St. Paul to the Christians of Corinth and included as books in the New Testament — see BIBLE table
Co·ri·o·lis force \ˌkōr-ē-ˌō-ləs-, ˌkȯr-, -ē-ə-ˌlēs-\ *n* [Gaspard G. *Coriolis* †1843 F civil engineer] : an apparent force that as a result of the earth's rotation deflects moving objects (as projectiles or air currents) to the right in the northern hemisphere and to the left in the southern hemisphere
co·ri·um \ˈkōr-ē-əm, ˈkȯr-\ *n, pl* **co·ria** \-ē-ə\ [NL, fr. L, leather — more at CUIRASS] : DERMIS
1cork \ˈkȯ(ə)rk\ *n* [ME, cork, bark, prob. fr. Ar *qurq,* fr. L *cortic-, cortex*] **1 a** : the elastic tough outer tissue of the cork oak that is used esp. for stoppers and insulation **b** : PHELLEM **2** : a usu. cork stopper for a bottle or jug **3** : an angling float
2cork *vt* **1** : to furnish or fit with cork or a cork **2** : to stop up with a cork **3** : to blacken with burnt cork
cork·board \ˈkȯ(ə)rk-ˌbō(ə)rd, -ˌbȯ(ə)rd\ *n* : a heat-insulating material made of compressed granulated cork
cork cambium *n* : PHELLOGEN
cork·er \ˈkȯr-kər\ *n* **1** : one that corks containers (as bottles) **2** : one that is excellent or remarkable
cork·ing \ˈkȯr-kiŋ\ *adj or adv* : extremely fine — often used as an intensive esp. before *good* ⟨had a ~ good time⟩
cork oak *n* : an oak (*Quercus suber*) of southern Europe and northern Africa that is the source of the cork of commerce
1cork·screw \ˈkȯrk-ˌskrü\ *n* : a pointed spiral piece of metal with a handle used for drawing corks from bottles
2corkscrew *vt* **1** : WIND **2** : to draw out with difficulty **3** : to twist into a spiral ~ *vi* : to move in a winding course
3corkscrew *adj* : resembling a corkscrew : SPIRAL ⟨the single ~ staircase that connected the two floors —G. K. Chesterton⟩
cork·wood \ˈkȯr-ˌkwu̇d\ *n* : any of several trees having light or corky wood; *esp* : a small or shrubby tree (*Leitneria floridana*) of the southeastern U.S. that has extremely light soft wood
corky \ˈkȯr-kē\ *adj* **cork·i·er; -est** : resembling cork
corm \ˈkȯ(ə)rm\ *n* [NL *cormus,* fr. Gk *kormos* tree trunk, fr. *keirein* to cut — more at SHEAR] : a rounded thick modified underground stem base bearing membranous or scaly leaves and buds and acting as a vegetative reproductive structure — compare BULB, TUBER
corm·el \ˈkȯr-məl, kȯr-ˈmel\ *n* [dim. of *corm*] : a small or secondary corm produced by a larger corm
cor·mo·rant \ˈkȯrm-(ə-)rənt, ˈkȯr-mə-ˌrant\ *n* [ME *cormeraunt,* fr. MF *cormorant,* fr. OF *cormareng,* fr. *corp* raven + *marenc* of the sea, fr. L *marinus*] **1** : any of various dark-colored web-footed seabirds (family Phalacrocoracidae) that have a long neck, wedge-shaped tail, hooked bill, and a patch of bare often brightly colored distensible skin under the mouth and are used in eastern Asia for catching fish **2** : a gluttonous, greedy, or rapacious person
1corn \ˈkȯ(ə)rn\ *n, often attrib* [ME, fr. OE; akin to OHG & ON *korn* grain, L *granum,* Gk *gēras* old age] **1** *chiefly dial* : a small hard particle : GRAIN **2** : a small hard seed **3 a** : the seeds of a cereal grass and esp. of the important cereal crop of a particular region (as wheat in Britain, oats in Scotland and Ireland, and Indian corn in the New World and Australia) **b** : the kernels of sweet corn served as a vegetable while still soft and milky **4** : a plant that produces corn **5** : CORN WHISKEY **6** : something (as writing, music, or acting) that is corny
2corn *vt* **1** : to form into grains : GRANULATE **2 a** : to preserve or season with salt in grains **b** : to cure or preserve in brine containing preservatives and often seasonings ⟨~*ed* beef⟩ **3** : to feed with corn ⟨~ the horses⟩
3corn *n* [ME *corne,* fr. MF, horn, corner, fr. L *cornu* horn, point] : a local hardening and thickening of epidermis (as on a toe)
Corn *abbr* **1** Cornish **2** Cornwall
1corn·ball \ˈkȯ(ə)rn-ˌbȯl\ *n* [*corn ball* (ball of popcorn and molasses); influenced in meaning by 1*corn* 5] : an unsophisticated person : HICK
2cornball *adj* : CORNY ⟨terrible ~ clichés —Bosley Crowther⟩
corn borer *n* : any of several insects that bore in maize: as **a** : EUROPEAN CORN BORER **b** : SOUTHWESTERN CORN BORER
corn bread *n* : bread made with cornmeal
corn chip *n* : a piece of a dry crisp snack food prepared from a seasoned cornmeal batter
corn·cob \ˈkȯ(ə)rn-ˌkäb\ *n* **1** : the axis on which the kernels of Indian corn are arranged **2** : an ear of Indian corn
corncob pipe *n* : a tobacco pipe with a bowl made from a corncob
corn cockle *n* : an annual hairy weed (*Agrostemma githago*) with purplish red flowers that is found in grainfields
corn·crake \ˈkȯ(ə)rn-ˌkrāk\ *n* : a common Eurasian short-billed rail (*Crex crex*) that frequents grainfields — called also *land rail*
corn·crib \-ˌkrib\ *n* : a crib for storing ears of Indian corn
corn dodger *n, chiefly South & Midland* : a cake of corn bread that is fried, baked, or boiled as a dumpling
cor·nea \ˈkȯr-nē-ə\ *n* [ML, fr. L, fem. of *corneus* horny, fr. *cornu*] : the transparent part of the coat of the eyeball that covers the iris and pupil and admits light to the interior — see EYE illustration — **cor·ne·al** \-əl\ *adj*
corn earworm *n* : a noctuid moth (*Heliothis zea*) whose large striped yellow-headed larva is esp. destructive to Indian corn

cor·nel \'kȯrn-ᵊl, 'kȯr-ˌnel\ *n* [deriv. of L *cornus* cornel cherry tree; akin to Gk *kerasos* cherry tree] : any of various shrubs or trees (*Cornus* and related genera) with very hard wood and perfect flowers; *specif* : DOGWOOD

cor·ne·lian \kȯr-'nēl-yən\ *n* : CARNELIAN

cor·ne·ous \'kȯr-nē-əs\ *adj* [L *corneus*] : HORNY

¹**cor·ner** \'kȯ(r)-nər\ *n* [ME, fr. OF *cornere,* fr. *corne* horn, corner] **1 a** : the point where converging lines, edges, or sides meet : ANGLE **b** : the place of intersection of two streets or roads **c** : a piece (as a leather or metal cap for the corner of a book) designed to form, mark, or protect a corner **2** : the angular part or space between meeting lines, edges, or borders near the vertex of the angle ⟨the southwest ~ of the state is hilly⟩ ⟨lift up the ~*s* of the tablecloth⟩: as **a** : the area of a playing field or court near the intersection of the sideline and the goal line or baseline ⟨hit four for six from the ~⟩ **b** (1) : either of the four angles of a boxing ring; *esp* : the angle in which a boxer rests or is worked on by his seconds during periods between rounds (2) : a group of supporters, well-wishers, or adherents associated esp. with a contestant **c** : the side of home plate nearest to or farthest from a batter ⟨a fast ball over the outside ~⟩ **d** : CORNER KICK **e** : the outside of a football formation **3 a** : a private, secret, or remote place ⟨a quiet ~ of a small New England town⟩ ⟨to every ~ of the earth⟩ **b** : a difficult or embarrassing situation : a position from which escape or retreat is difficult or impossible ⟨talked himself into a ~⟩ **4** : control or ownership of enough of the available supply of a commodity or security esp. to permit manipulation of the price **5** : a point at which significant change occurs — often used in the phrase *turn a corner* — **cor·nered** \-nərd\ *adj* — **around the corner** : at hand : IMMINENT ⟨promised that good times were just *around the corner*⟩

²**corner** *vb* **cor·nered; cor·ner·ing** \'kȯ(r)n-(ə-)riŋ\ *vt* **1 a** : to drive into a corner ⟨the animal is dangerous when ~*ed*⟩ ⟨the prosecutor ~*ed* the witness and forced out the truth⟩ **b** : to catch and hold the attention of esp. so as to force an interview ⟨he ~*s* the secretary on his way to lunch . . . and says what he has to say right in his ear —Clarence Woodbury⟩ **2** : to get a corner on ⟨~ the wheat market⟩ ~ *vi* **1** : to meet or converge at a corner or angle **2** : to turn a corner ⟨a car that ~*s* well⟩

³**corner** *adj* **1** : situated at a corner ⟨the ~ drugstore⟩ **2** : used or fitted for use in or on a corner ⟨a ~ table⟩ **3** : of or relating to the corners of a playing area

cor·ner·back \'kȯ(r)-nər-ˌbak\ *n* : a defensive halfback in football who defends the flank and whose duties include covering a pass receiver

corner kick *n* : a free kick in soccer from close to the point of intersection of the goal line and touchline allowed to the attacking team when a member of the defending team has sent the ball behind his own goal line

cor·ner·man \'kȯ(r)-nər-ˌman\ *n* : one who plays in or near the corner: as **a** : CORNERBACK **b** : a basketball forward

cor·ner·stone \'kȯ(r)-nər-ˌstōn\ *n* **1** : a stone forming a part of a corner or angle in a wall; *specif* : such a stone laid at a formal ceremony **2** : the most basic element : FOUNDATION ⟨a ~ of foreign policy⟩

cor·ner·ways \-ˌwāz\ *adv* : DIAGONALLY

cor·ner·wise \-ˌwīz\ *adv* : DIAGONALLY

cor·net \kȯr-'net, *Brit usu* 'kȯr-nit\ *n* [ME, fr. MF, fr. dim. of *corn* horn, fr. L *cornu*] **1** : a valved brass instrument resembling a trumpet in design and range but having a shorter tube and less brilliant tone **2** : something shaped like a cone: as **a** : a piece of paper twisted for use as a container **b** : a cone-shaped pastry shell that is often filled with whipped cream **c** *Brit* : an ice-cream cone — **cor·net·ist** *or* **cor·net·tist** \-'net-əst, -ni-tist\ *n*

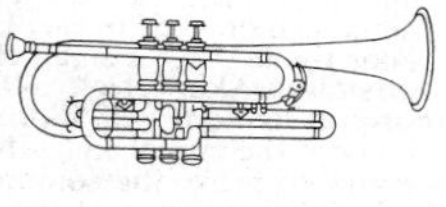

cornet 1

corn–fed \'kȯ(ə)rn-ˌfed\ *adj* **1** : fed or fattened on grain (as corn) ⟨~ hogs⟩ **2** : PLUMP ⟨she was gorgeous. A little ~, but gorgeous —Albert Morgan⟩

corn·field \-ˌfēld\ *n* : a field in which corn is grown

corn·flakes \-ˌflāks\ *n pl* : toasted flakes made from the coarse meal of hulled corn for use as a breakfast cereal

corn flour *n, Brit* : CORNSTARCH

corn·flow·er \'kȯ(ə)rn-ˌflau̇(-ə)r\ *n* **1** : CORN COCKLE **2** : BACHELOR'S BUTTON

cornflower blue *n* : a variable color averaging a moderate purplish blue

corn·husk·ing \'kȯrn-ˌhəs-kiŋ\ *n* : the husking of corn; *specif* : HUSKING

¹**cor·nice** \'kȯr-nəs, -nish\ *n* [MF, fr. It] **1 a** : the molded and projecting horizontal member that crowns an architectural composition **b** : a top course that crowns a wall **2** : a decorative band of metal or wood used to conceal curtain fixtures **3** : an overhanging mass of snow, ice, or rock usu. on a ridge

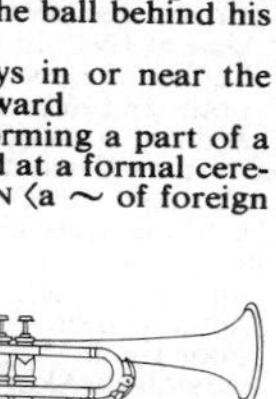

1, cornice 1a

²**cornice** *vt* **cor·niced; cor·nic·ing** : to furnish or crown with a cornice

cor·niche \kȯr-'nēsh\ *n* [F *cornice, corniche,* lit., cornice] : a road built along a coast and esp. along the face of a cliff

cor·nic·u·late cartilage \kȯr-ˌnik-yə-lət-\ *n* [L *corniculatus* horned, fr. *corniculum,* dim. of *cornu* horn] : a small nodule of yellow elastic cartilage articulating with the apex of the arytenoid

cor·ni·fi·ca·tion \ˌkȯr-nə-fə-'kā-shən\ *n* [L *cornu* horn + E *-i-* + *-fication*] **1** : conversion into horn or a horny substance or tissue **2** : the conversion of the vaginal epithelium from the columnar to the squamous type

¹**Cor·nish** \'kȯr-nish\ *adj* [*Cornwall,* England + E *-ish*] : of, relating to, or characteristic of Cornwall, Cornishmen, or Cornish

²**Cornish** *n* **1** : a Celtic language of Cornwall extinct since the late 18th century **2** : any of an English breed of domestic fowls much used in crossbreeding for meat production

Cor·nish·man \-mən\ *n* : a native or resident of Cornwall, England

Corn Law *n* : one of a series of laws in force in Great Britain before 1846 prohibiting or discouraging the importation of foreign grain

corn leaf aphid *n* : a dusky greenish or brownish aphid (*Rhopalosiphum maidis*) that feeds on the flowers and foliage of various commercially important grasses (as Indian corn)

corn·meal \'kȯ(ə)rn-'mē(ə)l, -ˌmēl\ *n* : meal ground from corn

corn pone *n, South & Midland* : corn bread often made without milk or eggs and baked or fried

corn poppy *n* : an annual red-flowered poppy (*Papaver rhoeas*) common in European grainfields and cultivated in several varieties

corn rootworm *n* : any of several beetles (genus *Diabrotica* of the family Galerucidae) whose root-eating larvae are pests esp. of Indian corn

corn silk *n* : the silky styles on an ear of Indian corn

corn snow *n* : granular snow formed by alternate thawing and freezing

corn·stalk \'kȯ(ə)rn-ˌstȯk\ *n* : a stalk of Indian corn

corn·starch \-ˌstärch\ *n* : starch made from corn and used in foods as a thickening agent, in making corn syrup and sugars, and in the manufacture of adhesives and sizes for paper and textiles

corn sugar *n* : DEXTROSE; *esp* : that made by hydrolysis of cornstarch

corn syrup *n* : a syrup containing dextrins, maltose, and dextrose that is obtained by partial hydrolysis of cornstarch

cor·nu \'kȯr-(ˌ)n(y)ü\ *n, pl* **cor·nua** \-n(y)ə-wə\ [L] : HORN; *esp* : a horn-shaped anatomical structure — **cor·nu·al** \-n(y)ə-wəl\ *adj*

cor·nu·co·pia \ˌkȯr-n(y)ə-'kō-pē-ə\ *n* [LL, fr. L *cornu copiae* horn of plenty] **1** : a curved goat's horn overflowing with fruit and ears of grain that is used as a decorative motif emblematic of abundance **2** : an inexhaustible store : ABUNDANCE ⟨a pair of books that . . . add up to a 550-page ~ of humor —Bernard Kalb⟩ **3** : a receptacle shaped like a horn or cone — **cor·nu·co·pi·an** \-pē-ən\ *adj*

cor·nu·to \kȯr-'n(y)üt-(ˌ)ō\ *n, pl* **-tos** [It, fr. L *cornutus* having horns, fr. *cornu*] : CUCKOLD

corn whiskey *n* : whiskey distilled from a mash made up of not less than 80 percent corn — compare BOURBON

¹**corny** \'kȯr-nē\ *adj* **corn·i·er; -est** **1** *archaic* : tasting strongly of malt **2** : of or relating to corn **3** : mawkishly old-fashioned : tiresomely simple and sentimental : TRITE — **corn·i·ly** \'kȯrn-ᵊl-ē\ *adv* — **corn·i·ness** \'kȯr-nē-nəs\ *n*

²**corny** *adj* **corn·i·er; -est** : relating to or having corns on the feet

cor·o·dy \'kȯr-əd-ē, 'kär-\ *n, pl* **-dies** [ME *corrodie,* fr. ML *corrodium*] : an allowance of provisions for maintenance dispensed as a charity

co·rol·la \kə-'räl-ə\ *n* [NL, fr. L, dim. of *corona*] : the petals of a flower constituting the inner floral envelope surrounding the sporophylls — **co·rol·late** \kə-'räl-ət; 'kȯr-ə-ˌlāt, 'kär-\ *adj*

cor·ol·lary \'kȯr-ə-ˌler-ē, 'kär-, *Brit* kə-'räl-ə-rē\ *n, pl* **-lar·ies** [ME *corolarie,* fr. LL *corollarium,* fr. L, money paid for a garland, gratuity, fr. *corolla*] **1** : an immediate inference from a proved proposition **2 a** : something that naturally follows : RESULT **b** : something that incidentally or naturally accompanies or parallels — **corollary** *adj*

cor·o·man·del \ˌkȯr-ə-'man-dᵊl, ˌkär-\ *n* [*Coromandel* coast region, India] : an East Indian timber tree (*Diospyros melanoxylon*) with a hard dark-colored wood — called also *coromandel ebony*

co·ro·na \kə-'rō-nə\ *n* [L, garland, crown, cornice — more at CROWN] **1** : the projecting part of a classic cornice **2 a** : a usu. colored circle often seen around and close to a luminous body (as the sun or moon) caused by diffraction produced by suspended droplets or occas. particles of dust **b** : the tenuous outermost part of the atmosphere of the sun appearing as a halo around the moon's black disk during a total eclipse of the sun; *also* : a similar portion of the atmosphere of a star **c** : a circle of light made by the apparent convergence of the streamers of the aurora borealis **d** : the upper portion of a bodily part (as a tooth or the skull) **e** : an appendage on the inner side of the corolla in some flowers (as the daffodil, jonquil, or milkweed) **f** : a faint glow adjacent to the surface of an electrical conductor at high voltage **3** [fr. *La Corona,* a trademark] : a long cigar having the sides straight to the unsealed end and being roundly blunt at the sealed end

Corona Aus·tra·lis \-ȯ-'strā-ləs, -ä-\ *n* [L (gen. *Coronae Australis*), lit., southern crown] : a southern constellation adjoining Sagittarius on the south

Corona Bo·re·al·is \-ˌbōr-ē-'al-əs, -ˌbȯr-\ *n* [L (gen. *Coronae Borealis*), lit., northern crown] : a northern constellation between Hercules and Boötes

cor·o·nach \'kȯr-ə-nə͟k, 'kär-\ *n* [ScGael *corranach* & IrGael *corānach*] : a funeral dirge sung or played on the bagpipes in Scotland and Ireland

co·ro·na·graph *also* **co·ro·no·graph** \kə-'rō-nə-ˌgraf\ *n* : a telescope for observation of the sun's corona

¹**cor·o·nal** *also* **cor·o·nel** \'kȯr-ən-ᵊl, 'kär-\ *n* [ME *coronal,* fr. AF, fr. L *coronalis* of a crown, fr. *corona*] : a circlet for the head usu. implying rank or dignity

²**co·ro·nal** \'kȯr-ən-ᵊl, 'kär-; kə-'rōn-\ *adj* **1** : of or relating to a corona or crown **2 a** : lying in the direction of the coronal suture **b** : of or relating to the frontal plane that passes through the long axis of the body

coronal suture *n* : a suture extending across the skull between the parietal and frontal bones

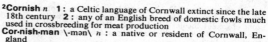

ə abut ᵊ kitten ər further a back ā bake ä cot, cart
au̇ out ch chin e less ē easy g gift i trip ī life
j joke ŋ sing ō flow ȯ flaw ȯi coin th thin t͟h this
ü loot u̇ foot y yet yü few yu̇ furious zh vision

co·ro·na ra·di·a·ta \kə-ˈrō-nə-ˌrād-ē-ˈāt-ə, -ˈät-\ *n, pl* **co·ro·nae ra·di·a·tae** \-(ˌ)nē-ˌrād-ē-ˈāt-(ˌ)ē, -ˈät-\ [NL, lit., crown with rays] : the zone of small follicular cells immediately surrounding the ovum in the Graafian follicle and accompanying the ovum on its discharge from the follicle

[1]**cor·o·nary** \ˈkȯr-ə-ˌner-ē, ˈkär-\ *adj* **1** : of, relating to, resembling, or being a crown or coronal **2** : relating to or being the coronary arteries or veins of the heart; *broadly* : of or relating to the heart

[2]**coronary** *n, pl* **-nar·ies** **1 a** : CORONARY ARTERY **b** : CORONARY VEIN **2** : CORONARY THROMBOSIS

coronary artery *n* : either of two arteries, one on the right and one on the left, that arise from the aorta immediately above the semilunar valves and supply the tissues of the heart itself

coronary occlusion *n* : the partial or complete blocking (as by a thrombus, by spasm, or by sclerosis) of a coronary artery

coronary sinus *n* : a venous channel that is derived from the sinus venosus, is continuous with the largest of the cardiac veins, receives most of the blood from the walls of the heart, and empties into the right atrium

coronary thrombosis *n* : the blocking of a coronary artery of the heart by a thrombus

coronary vein *n* : any of several veins that drain the tissues of the heart and empty into the coronary sinus

cor·o·na·tion \ˌkȯr-ə-ˈnā-shən, ˌkär-\ *n* [ME *coronacion*, fr. MF *coronation*, fr. *coroner* to crown] : the act or ceremony of investing a sovereign or his consort with the royal crown

cor·o·ner \ˈkȯr-ə-nər, ˈkär-\ *n* [ME, an officer of the crown, fr. AF, fr. OF *corone* crown, fr. L *corona*] : a public officer whose principal duty is to inquire by an inquest into the cause of any death which there is reason to suppose is not due to natural causes

cor·o·net \ˌkȯr-ə-ˈnet, ˌkär-\ *n* [MF *coronette*, fr. OF *coronete*, fr. *corone*] **1** : a small or lesser crown usu. signifying a rank below that of a sovereign **2** : an ornamental wreath or band for the head usu. for wear by women on formal occasions **3** : the lower part of a horse's pastern where the horn terminates in skin — see HORSE illustration

co·ro·tate \(ˈ)kō-ˈrō-ˌtāt\ *vi* : to rotate in conjunction with or at the same rate as another rotating body — **co·ro·ta·tion** \ˌkō-rō-ˈtā-shən\ *n*

corp *abbr* **1** corporal **2** corporation

corpora *pl of* CORPUS

[1]**cor·po·ral** \ˈkȯr-p(ə-)rəl\ *n* [ME, fr. MF, fr. ML *corporale*, fr. L, neut. of *corporalis*; fr. the doctrine that the bread of the Eucharist becomes or represents the body of Christ] : a linen cloth on which the eucharistic elements are placed

[2]**corporal** *adj* [ME, fr. MF, fr. L *corporalis*, fr. *corpor-, corpus* body] **1** : of, relating to, or affecting the body ⟨~ punishment⟩ **2** *obs* : CORPOREAL, PHYSICAL **syn** see BODILY — **cor·po·ral·ly** \-p(ə-)rə-lē\ *adv*

[3]**corporal** *n* [MF, lowest noncommissioned officer, alter. of *caporal*, fr. OIt *caporale*, fr. *capo* head, fr. L *caput* — more at HEAD] : a noncommissioned officer ranking in the army above a private first class and below a sergeant and in the marine corps above a lance corporal and below a sergeant

cor·po·ral·i·ty \ˌkȯr-pə-ˈral-ət-ē\ *n, pl* **-ties** : the quality or state of being or having a body or a material or physical existence

corporal's guard *n* **1** : the small detachment commanded by a corporal **2** : a small group

cor·po·rate \ˈkȯr-p(ə-)rət\ *adj* [L *corporatus*, pp. of *corporare* to make into a body, fr. *corpor-, corpus*] **1 a** : formed into an association and endowed by law with the rights and liabilities of an individual : INCORPORATED **b** : of or relating to a corporation ⟨a plan to reorganize the ~ structure⟩ **2** : of, relating to, or formed into a unified body of individuals ⟨human law arises by the ~ action of a people —G. H. Sabine⟩ ⟨the yeomen . . . were a ~ society like the country gentry —Adrian Bell⟩ **3** : CORPORATIVE 2 — **cor·po·rate·ly** *adv*

cor·po·ra·tion \ˌkȯr-pə-ˈrā-shən\ *n* **1 a** *obs* : a group of merchants or traders united in a trade guild **b** : the municipal authorities of a town or city **2** : a body formed and authorized by law to act as a single person although constituted by one or more persons and legally endowed with various rights and duties including the capacity of succession **3** : an association of employers and employees in a basic industry or of members of a profession organized as an organ of political representation in a corporative state **4** : POTBELLY 1

cor·po·rat·ism \ˈkȯr-p(ə-)rət-ˌiz-əm\ *n* : the organization of a society into industrial and professional corporations serving as organs of political representation and exercising some control over persons and activities within their jurisdiction — **cor·po·rat·ist** \-p(ə-)rət-əst\ *adj*

cor·po·ra·tive \ˈkȯr-pə-ˌrāt-iv, -p(ə-)rət-\ *adj* **1** : of or relating to a corporation **2** : of or relating to corporatism ⟨a ~ state⟩

cor·po·ra·tiv·ism \ˈkȯr-pə-ˌrāt-i-ˌviz-əm, -p(ə-)rət-\ *n* : CORPORATISM

cor·po·ra·tor \ˈkȯr-pə-ˌrāt-ər\ *n* : a corporation organizer, member, or stockholder

cor·po·re·al \kȯr-ˈpōr-ē-əl, -ˈpȯr-\ *adj* [L *corporeus* of the body, fr. *corpor-, corpus*] **1** : having, consisting of, or relating to a physical material body: as **a** : not spiritual **b** : not immaterial or intangible : SUBSTANTIAL **2** *archaic* : CORPORAL **syn 1** see MATERIAL **ant** incorporeal **2** see BODILY — **cor·po·re·al·ly** \-ē-ə-lē\ *adv* — **cor·po·re·al·ness** *n*

cor·po·re·al·i·ty \(ˌ)kȯr-ˌpōr-ē-ˈal-ət-ē, -ˌpȯr-\ *n, pl* **-ties** : corporeal existence

cor·po·re·ity \ˌkȯr-pə-ˈrē-ət-ē, -ˈrā-\ *n, pl* **-ities** : the quality or state of having or being a body : MATERIALITY

cor·po·sant \ˈkȯr-pə-ˌsant, -ˌzant\ *n* [Pg *corpo-santo*, lit., holy body] : SAINT ELMO'S FIRE

corps \ˈkō(ə)r, ˈkȯ(ə)r\ *n, pl* **corps** \ˈkō(ə)rz, ˈkȯ(ə)rz\ [F, fr. L *corpus* body] **1 a** : an organized subdivision of the military establishment ⟨Marine *Corps*⟩ ⟨Signal *Corps*⟩ **b** : a tactical unit usu. consisting of two or more divisions and auxiliary arms and services **2 a** : a group of persons associated together or acting under common direction; *esp* : a body of persons having a common activity or occupation ⟨the press ~⟩ **b** : an association of German university students **3** : CORPS DE BALLET

corps area *n* : a former territorial division of the U. S. for purposes of military administration and training

corps de bal·let \ˌkōrd-ə-(ˌ)ba-ˈlā, ˌkȯrd-\ *n, pl* **corps de ballet** *same, or* ˌkōrz-də-, ˌkȯrz-\ [F] : the ensemble of a ballet company

corps d'elite \ˌkōr-dā-ˈlēt, ˌkȯr-\ *n, pl* **corps d'elite** *same, or* ˌkōrz-dā-, ˌkȯrz-\ [F *corps d'élite*] **1** : a body of picked troops **2** : a group of the best people in a category ⟨thirteen reporters — the *corps d'elite* of a great newspaper —*N.Y. Herald Tribune*⟩

corpse \ˈkȯ(ə)rps\ *n* [ME *corps*, fr. MF, fr. L *corpus* — more at MIDRIFF] **1** *obs* : a human or animal body whether living or dead **2 a** : a dead body esp. of a human being **b** : something discarded or defunct ⟨it was an awful thing to look at the ~ of a city —*Nat'l Geographic*⟩

corps·man \ˈkō(ə)r(z)-mən, ˈkȯ(ə)r(z)-\ *n* **1** : an enlisted man trained to give first aid and minor medical treatment **2** : a member of a government-sponsored service corps

cor·pu·lence \ˈkȯr-pyə-lən(t)s\ *n* : the state of being excessively fat

cor·pu·len·cy \-lən-sē\ *n, pl* **-cies** : CORPULENCE

cor·pu·lent \-lənt\ *adj* [ME, fr. L *corpulentus*, fr. *corpus*] : having a large bulky body : OBESE — **cor·pu·lent·ly** *adv*

cor pul·mo·na·le \ˌkȯr-ˌpu̇l-mə-ˈnäl-ē, -ˌpəl-, -ˈnal-\ *n, pl* **cor·dia pul·mo·na·lia** \ˈkȯrd-ē-ə- . . . -ˈnäl-ē-ə, -ˈnal-\ [NL, lit., pulmonary heart] : disease of the heart characterized by hypertrophy and dilatation of the right ventricle and secondary to disease of the lungs or their blood vessels

cor·pus \ˈkȯr-pəs\ *n, pl* **cor·po·ra** \-p(ə-)rə\ [ME, fr. L] **1** : the body of a man or animal esp. when dead **2 a** : the main part or body of a bodily structure or organ ⟨the ~ of the uterus⟩ **b** : the main body or corporeal substance of a thing; *specif* : the principal of a fund or estate as distinct from income or interest **3 a** : all the writings of a particular kind or on a particular subject; *esp* : the complete works of an author **b** : a collection or body of knowledge or evidence; *esp* : a collection of recorded utterances used as a basis for the descriptive analysis of a language

corpus al·la·tum \-ə-ˈlāt-əm, -ˈlät-\ *n, pl* **corpora al·la·ta** \-ˈlāt-ə, -ˈlät-ə\ [NL, lit., applied body] : one of a pair of separate or fused bodies in many insects that are sometimes closely associated with the corpora cardiaca and that secrete hormones (as juvenile hormone)

corpus cal·lo·sum \-ka-ˈlō-səm\ *n, pl* **corpora cal·lo·sa** \-sə\ [NL, lit., callous body] : the great band of commissural fibers uniting the cerebral hemispheres in man and in the higher mammals — see BRAIN illustration

corpus car·di·a·cum \-kär-ˈdī-ə-kəm\ *n, pl* **corpora car·di·a·ca** \-ə-kə\ [NL, lit., cardiac body] : one of a pair of separate or fused bodies of nervous tissue in many insects that lie posterior to the brain and dorsal to the esophagus and that function in the storage and secretion of brain hormone

Cor·pus Chris·ti \ˌkȯr-pə-ˈskris-tē\ *n* [ME, fr. ML, lit., body of Christ] : the Thursday after Trinity Sunday observed as a Roman Catholic festival in honor of the Eucharist

cor·pus·cle \ˈkȯr-(ˌ)pəs-əl\ *n* [L *corpusculum*, dim. of *corpus*] **1** : a minute particle **2 a** : a living cell; *esp* : one (as a red or white blood cell or a cell in cartilage or bone) not aggregated into continuous tissues **b** : a small circumscribed multicellular body — **cor·pus·cu·lar** \kȯr-ˈpəs-kyə-lər\ *adj*

cor·pus de·lic·ti \-di-ˈlik-ˌtī, -(ˌ)tē\ *n, pl* **corpora delicti** [NL, lit., body of the crime] **1** : the substantial and fundamental fact necessary to prove the commission of a crime **2** : the material substance (as the body of the victim of a murder) upon which a crime has been committed

corpus lu·te·um \-ˈlüt-ē-əm\ *n, pl* **corpora lu·tea** \-ē-ə\ [NL, lit., yellowish body] : a reddish yellow mass of endocrine tissue that forms from a ruptured Graafian follicle in the mammalian ovary

corr *abbr* — see COR

cor·rade \kə-ˈrād\ *vb* **cor·rad·ed; cor·rad·ing** [L *corradere* to scrape together, fr. *com-* + *radere* to scrape — more at RAT] *vt* : to wear away by abrasion ~ *vi* : to crumble away through abrasion — **cor·ra·sion** \-ˈrā-zhən\ *n* — **cor·ra·sive** \-ˈrā-siv, -ziv\ *adj*

[1]**cor·ral** \kə-ˈral, -ˈrel\ *n* [Sp, fr. (assumed) VL *currale* enclosure for vehicles, fr. L *currus* cart, fr. *currere* to run — more at CURRENT] **1** : a pen or enclosure for confining or capturing livestock **2** : an enclosure made with wagons for defense of an encampment

[2]**corral** *vt* **cor·ralled; cor·ral·ling** **1** : to enclose in a corral **2** : to arrange (wagons) so as to form a corral **3** : COLLECT, GATHER ⟨helped elect certain municipal council members by *corralling* the necessary votes —R. L. Maullin⟩

[1]**cor·rect** \kə-ˈrekt\ *vt* [ME *correcten*, fr. L *correctus*, pp. of *corrigere*, fr. *com-* + *regere* to lead straight — more at RIGHT] **1 a** : to make or set right : AMEND **b** : COUNTERACT, NEUTRALIZE **c** : to alter or adjust so as to bring to some standard or required condition ⟨~ a lens for spherical aberration⟩ **2 a** : to punish (as a child) with a view to reforming or improving **b** : to point out for amendment the errors or faults of ⟨spent the whole day *~ing* examination papers⟩ — **cor·rect·able** \-ˈrek-tə-bəl\ *adj* — **cor·rec·tor** \-ˈrek-tər\ *n*

syn 1 CORRECT, RECTIFY, EMEND, REMEDY, REDRESS, AMEND, REFORM, REVISE *shared meaning element* : to make right what is wrong
2 see PUNISH

[2]**correct** *adj* [ME, corrected, fr. L *correctus*, fr. pp. of *corrigere*] **1** : conforming to an approved or conventional standard ⟨relations . . . were ~ but not very friendly —W. L. Shirer⟩ ⟨find him a courteous, ~, if not always candid, subject —Robert Neville⟩ **2** : conforming to or agreeing with fact, logic, or known truth **3** : conforming to a set figure ⟨enclosed the ~ return postage⟩ — **cor·rect·ly** \kə-ˈrek-(t)lē\ *adv* — **cor·rect·ness** \-ˈrek(t)-nəs\ *n*

syn CORRECT, ACCURATE, EXACT, PRECISE, NICE, RIGHT *shared meaning element* : conforming to fact, truth, or a standard **ant** incorrect

corrected time *n* **:** a boat's elapsed time less her time allowance in yacht racing

cor·rec·tion \kə-ˈrek-shən\ *n* **1 :** the action or an instance of correcting: as **a :** AMENDMENT, RECTIFICATION **b :** REBUKE, PUNISHMENT **c :** a bringing into conformity with a standard **d :** NEUTRALIZATION, COUNTERACTION ⟨~ of acidity⟩ **2 :** a decline in market price or business activity following and counteracting a rise **3 a :** something substituted in place of what is wrong ⟨marking ~s on the students' papers⟩ **b :** a quantity applied by way of correcting (as for adjustment or inaccuracy of an instrument) **4 :** the treatment and rehabilitation of offenders through a program involving penal custody, parole, and probation; *also* **:** the administration of such treatment as a matter of public policy — usu. used in pl. — **cor·rec·tion·al** \-shnəl, -shən-ᵊl\ *adj*

cor·rec·ti·tude \kə-ˈrek-tə-ˌt(y)üd\ *n* [blend of *correct* and *rectitude*] **:** correctness or propriety of conduct

cor·rec·tive \kə-ˈrek-tiv\ *adj* **:** tending to correct ⟨~ lenses⟩ ⟨~ punishment⟩ — **corrective** *n* — **cor·rec·tive·ly** *adv* — **cor·rec·tive·ness** *n*

¹cor·re·late \ˈkȯr-ə-lət, ˈkär-, -ˌlāt\ *n* [back-formation fr. *correlation*] **1 :** either of two things so related that one directly implies or is complementary to the other (as husband and wife) **2 :** a phenomenon (as brain activity) that accompanies another phenomenon (as behavior), is usu. parallel to it (as in form, type, development, or distribution), and is related in some way to it ***syn*** see PARALLEL — **correlate** *adj*

²cor·re·late \-ˌlāt\ *vb* **-lat·ed; -lat·ing** *vi* **:** to bear reciprocal or mutual relations ~ *vt* **1 a :** to establish a mutual or reciprocal relation of **b :** to show a causal relationship between **2 :** to relate so that to each member of one set or series a corresponding member of another is assigned **3 :** to present or set forth so as to show relationship ⟨he ~s the findings of the scientists, the psychologists, and the mystics —Eugene Exman⟩ — **cor·re·lat·able** \-ˌlāt-ə-bəl\ *adj*

cor·re·la·tion \ˌkȯr-ə-ˈlā-shən, ˌkär-\ *n* [ML *correlation-, correlatio,* fr. L *com-* + *relation-, relatio* relation] **1 a :** the act of correlating **b :** the state of being correlated; *specif* **:** a relation of phenomena as invariable accompaniments of each other ⟨the assumption that there is a positive ~ between performance and pay —Kermit Eby⟩ **2 :** reciprocal relation in the occurrence of different structures, characteristics, or processes in organisms **3 :** an interdependence between mathematical variables esp. in statistics — **cor·re·la·tion·al** \-shnəl, -shən-ᵊl\ *adj*

correlation coefficient *n* **:** a number or function that indicates the degree of correlation between two sets of data or between two random variables and that is equal to their covariance divided by the product of their standard deviations

cor·rel·a·tive \kə-ˈrel-ət-iv\ *adj* **1 :** naturally related **:** CORRESPONDING **2 :** reciprocally related **3 :** regularly used together but typically not adjacent ⟨the ~ conjunctions *either . . . or*⟩ — **correlative** *n* — **cor·rel·a·tive·ly** *adv*

cor·re·spond \ˌkȯr-ə-ˈspänd, ˌkär-\ *vi* [MF or ML; MF *correspondre,* fr. ML *correspondēre,* fr. L *com-* + *respondēre* to respond] **1 a :** to be in conformity or agreement **:** SUIT ⟨fulfillment seldom ~s to anticipation⟩ **b :** to compare closely **:** MATCH — usu. used with *to* or *with* **c :** to be equivalent or parallel **2 :** to communicate with a person by exchange of letters ⟨frequently ~s with his cousin⟩ ***syn*** see AGREE

cor·re·spon·dence \-ˈspän-dən(t)s\ *n* **1 a :** the agreement of things with one another **b :** a particular similarity **c :** association of one or more members of one set with each member of a second set **:** FUNCTION, MAPPING **2 a :** communication by letters; *also* **:** the letters exchanged **b :** the news, information, or opinion contributed by a correspondent to a newspaper or periodical

correspondence school *n* **:** a school that teaches nonresident students by mailing them lessons and exercises which upon completion are returned to the school for grading

cor·re·spon·den·cy \ˌkȯr-ə-ˈspän-dən-sē, ˌkär-\ *n, pl* **-cies :** CORRESPONDENCE

¹cor·re·spon·dent \ˌkȯr-ə-ˈspän-dənt, ˌkär-\ *adj* [ME, fr. MF or ML; MF, fr. ML *correspondent-, correspondens,* prp. of *correspondēre*] **1 :** CORRESPONDING ⟨each advantage having ~ disadvantages⟩ **2 :** FITTING, CONFORMING — used with *with* or *to* ⟨the outcome was entirely ~ with my wishes⟩

²correspondent *n* **1 :** something that corresponds **2 a :** one who communicates with another by letter **b :** one who has regular commercial relations with another **c :** one who contributes news or comment to a publication (as a newspaper) or a radio or television network often from a distant place ⟨a war ~⟩

cor·re·spond·ing *adj* **1 a :** agreeing in some respect (as kind, degree, position, or function) ⟨the figures are large but the ~ totals next year will be larger⟩ **b :** RELATED, ACCOMPANYING ⟨all rights carry with them ~ responsibilites —W. P. Paepcke⟩ **2 a :** charged with the duty of writing letters ⟨~ secretary⟩ **b :** participating or serving at a distance and by mail ⟨a ~ member of the society⟩ — **cor·re·spond·ing·ly** \-ˈspän-diŋ-lē\ *adv*

cor·re·spon·sive \ˌkȯr-ə-ˈspän(t)-siv, ˌkär-\ *adj* **:** mutually responsive

cor·ri·da \kō-ˈrē-t͟hə\ *n* [Sp, lit., act of running] **:** BULLFIGHT

cor·ri·dor \ˈkȯr-əd-ər, ˈkär-, -ə-ˌdȯ(ə)r\ *n* [MF, fr. OIt *corridore,* fr. *correre* to run, fr. L *currere* — more at CURRENT] **1 :** a passageway (as in a hotel) into which compartments or rooms open **2 :** a usu. narrow passageway or route: as **a :** a narrow strip of land through foreign-held territory **b** (1) **:** a restricted lane for air traffic (2) **:** a restricted path a spacecraft must follow to accomplish its mission **:** WINDOW 3 **3 :** a densely populated strip of land including two or more major cities ⟨the Northeast ~ stretching from Washington into New England —S. D. Browne⟩

cor·rie \ˈkȯr-ē, ˈkär-ē\ *n* [ScGael *coire,* lit., kettle] **:** CIRQUE 3

Cor·rie·dale \-ˌdāl\ *n* [*Corriedale,* ranch in New Zealand] **:** any of a dual-purpose breed of rather large usu. hornless sheep developed in New Zealand

cor·ri·gen·dum \ˌkȯr-ə-ˈjen-dəm, ˌkär-\ *n, pl* **-da** \-də\ [L, neut. of *corrigendus,* gerundive of *corrigere* to correct] **:** an error in a printed work discovered after printing and shown with its correction on a separate sheet bound with the original

cor·ri·gi·ble \ˈkȯr-ə-jə-bəl, ˈkär-\ *adj* [ME, fr. MF, fr. ML *corrigibilis,* fr. L *corrigere*] **:** capable of being set right **:** REPARABLE ⟨a ~ defect⟩ — **cor·ri·gi·bil·i·ty** \ˌkȯr-ə-jə-ˈbil-ət-ē, ˌkär-\ *n* — **cor·ri·gi·bly** \ˈkȯr-ə-jə-blē, ˈkär-\ *adv*

cor·ri·val \kə-ˈrī-vəl, kō-, kō-\ *n* [MF, fr. L *corrivalis,* fr. *com-* + *rivalis* rival] **:** RIVAL, COMPETITOR — **corrival** *adj*

cor·rob·o·rant \kə-ˈräb-ə-rənt\ *adj, archaic* **:** having an invigorating effect — used of a medicine

cor·rob·o·rate \kə-ˈräb-ə-ˌrāt\ *vt* **-rat·ed; -rat·ing** [L *corroboratus,* pp. of *corroborare,* fr. *com-* + *robor-, robur* strength] **:** to support with evidence or authority **:** make more certain ***syn*** see CONFIRM ***ant*** contradict — **cor·rob·o·ra·tion** \-ˌräb-ə-ˈrā-shən\ *n* — **cor·rob·o·ra·tive** \-ˈräb-ə-ˌrāt-iv, -ˈräb-(ə-)rət-\ *adj* — **cor·rob·o·ra·tor** \-ˈräb-ə-ˌrāt-ər\ *n* — **cor·rob·o·ra·to·ry** \-ˈräb-(ə-)rə-ˌtōr-ē, -ˌtȯr-\ *adj*

cor·rob·o·ree \kə-ˈräb-ə-rē\ *n* [fr. native name in New South Wales, Australia] **1 :** a nocturnal festivity with songs and symbolic dances by which the Australian aborigines celebrate events of importance **2** *Austral* **a :** a noisy festivity **b :** TUMULT

cor·rode \kə-ˈrōd\ *vb* **cor·rod·ed; cor·rod·ing** [ME *corroden,* fr. L *corrodere* to gnaw to pieces, fr. *com-* + *rodere* to gnaw — more at RAT] *vt* **1 :** to eat away by degrees as if by gnawing; *esp* **:** to wear away gradually usu. by chemical action ⟨the metal was *corroded* beyond repair⟩ **2 :** to weaken or destroy gradually ⟨manners and miserliness that ~ the human spirit —Bernard DeVoto⟩ ~ *vi* **:** to undergo corrosion ⟨the bare metal will ~ after a few weeks of exposure to the weather⟩ — **cor·rod·ible** \-ˈrōd-ə-bəl\ *adj*

cor·ro·dy *var of* CORODY

cor·ro·sion \kə-ˈrō-zhən\ *n* [ME, fr. LL *corrosion-, corrosio* act of gnawing, fr. L *corrosus,* pp. of *corrodere*] **1 :** the action, process, or effect of corroding **2 :** a product of corroding

cor·ro·sive \-ˈrō-siv, -ziv\ *adj* **1 :** tending or having the power to corrode ⟨~ acids⟩ ⟨~ action⟩ **2 a :** weakening or destroying by a gradual process ⟨the ~ influence of industrialization —Louise C. Hunter⟩ **b :** bitingly sarcastic ⟨~ satire⟩ — **corrosive** *n* — **cor·ro·sive·ly** *adv* — **cor·ro·sive·ness** *n*

corrosive sublimate *n* **:** MERCURIC CHLORIDE

cor·ru·gate \ˈkȯr-ə-ˌgāt, ˈkär-\ *vb* **-gat·ed; -gat·ing** [L *corrugatus,* pp. of *corrugare,* fr. *com-* + *ruga* wrinkle — more at ROUGH] *vt* **:** to form or shape into wrinkles or folds or into alternating ridges and grooves **:** FURROW ⟨*corrugated* his brows in thought —John Buchan⟩ ~ *vi* **:** to become corrugated

corrugated iron *n* **:** usu. galvanized sheet iron or sheet steel shaped into straight parallel regular and equally curved ridges and hollows

cor·ru·ga·tion \ˌkȯr-ə-ˈgā-shən, ˌkär-\ *n* **1 :** the act of corrugating **2 :** a ridge or groove of a corrugated surface

¹cor·rupt \kə-ˈrəpt\ *vb* [ME *corrupten,* fr. L *corruptus,* pp. of *corrumpere,* fr. *com-* + *rumpere* to break — more at REAVE] *vt* **1 a :** to change from good to bad in morals, manners, or actions; *also* **:** BRIBE **b :** to degrade with unsound principles or moral values **2 :** ROT, SPOIL **3 :** to subject (a person) to corruption of blood **4 :** to alter from the original or correct form or version ~ *vi* **1 a :** to become tainted or rotten **b :** to become morally debased **2 :** to cause disintegration or ruin ***syn*** see DEBASE — **cor·rupt·er** *or* **cor·rup·tor** \-ˈrəp-tər\ *n* — **cor·rupt·ibil·i·ty** \-ˌrəp-tə-ˈbil-ət-ē\ *n* — **cor·rupt·ible** \-ˈrəp-tə-bəl\ *adj* — **cor·rupt·ibly** \-blē\ *adv*

²corrupt *adj* [ME, fr. MF or L; MF, fr. L *corruptus,* fr. pp. of *corrumpere*] **1 a :** morally degenerate and perverted **:** DEPRAVED **b :** characterized by bribery, the selling of political favors, or other improper conduct ⟨~ judges⟩ **2** *archaic* **:** PUTRID, TAINTED ***syn*** see VICIOUS — **cor·rupt·ly** \-ˈrəp-(t)lē\ *adv* — **cor·rupt·ness** \-ˈrəp(t)-nəs\ *n*

cor·rup·tion \kə-ˈrəp-shən\ *n* **1 a :** impairment of integrity, virtue, or moral principle **:** DEPRAVITY **b :** DECAY, DECOMPOSITION **c :** inducement to wrong by bribery or other unlawful or improper means **d :** a departure from what is pure or correct **2** *archaic* **:** an agency or influence that corrupts **3** *chiefly dial* **:** PUS

cor·rup·tion·ist \-sh(ə-)nəst\ *n* **:** one who practices or defends corruption esp. in politics

corruption of blood : the effect of an attainder upon a person which bars him from inheriting, retaining, or transmitting any estate, rank, or title

cor·rup·tive \kə-ˈrəp-tiv\ *adj* **:** producing or tending to produce corruption — **cor·rup·tive·ly** *adv*

cor·sage \kȯr-ˈsäzh, -ˈsäj, ˈkȯr-ˌ\ *n* [F, bust, bodice, fr. OF, bust, fr. *cors* body, fr. L *corpus*] **1 :** the waist or bodice of a woman's dress **2 :** an arrangement of flowers to be worn by a woman

cor·sair \ˈkȯr-ˌsa(ə)r, -ˌse(ə)r\ *n* [MF & OIt; MF *corsaire* pirate, fr. OProv *corsari,* fr. OIt *corsaro,* fr. ML *cursarius,* fr. L *cursus* course — more at COURSE] **:** PIRATE; *esp* **:** a privateer of the Barbary coast

corse \ˈkȯ(ə)rs\ *n* [ME *cors,* fr. OF, body] *archaic* **:** CORPSE

corse·let *for 1* ˈkȯr-slət, *for 2* ˌkȯr-sə-ˈlet\ *n* **1** *or* **cors·let** [MF, dim. of *cors* body, bodice] **a :** a piece of armor covering the trunk but usu. not the arms or legs **b :** a pikeman's armor including helmet **2** *or* **cor·se·lette** [fr. *Corselette,* a trademark] **:** an undergarment combining girdle and brassiere

¹cor·set \ˈkȯr-sət\ *n* [ME, fr. OF, dim. of *cors*] **1 :** a usu. close-fitting and often laced medieval jacket **2 :** a woman's close-fitting boned supporting undergarment that is often hooked and laced and that extends from above or beneath the bust or from the waist to below the hips and has garters attached

²corset *vt* **1 :** to dress in or fit with a corset **2 :** to restrict closely **:** control rigidly

corset cover *n* : a woman's undergarment worn over a corset
cor·se·tiere \ˌkȯr-sə-ˈti(ə)r, -ˈtye(ə)r\ *n* [F *corsetière,* fem. of *corsetier,* fr. *corset*] : one who makes, fits, or sells corsets, girdles, or brassieres
cor·tege *also* **cor·tège** \kȯr-ˈtezh, ˈkȯr-ˌ\ *n* [F *cortège,* fr. It *corteggio,* fr. *corteggiare* to court, fr. *corte* court, fr. L *cohort-, cohors* throng — more at COURT] **1** : a train of attendants : RETINUE **2** : PROCESSION; *esp* : a funeral procession
cor·tex \ˈkȯr-ˌteks\ *n, pl* **cor·ti·ces** \ˈkȯrt-ə-ˌsēz\ *or* **cor·tex·es** [L *cortic-, cortex* bark — more at CUIRASS] **1** : a plant bark or rind (as cinchona) used medicinally **2 a** : the outer or superficial part of an organ or body structure (as the kidney, adrenal gland, or a hair); *esp* : the outer layer of gray matter of the cerebrum and cerebellum **b** : the outer part of some organisms (as paramecia) **3 a** : the typically parenchymatous layer of tissue external to the vascular tissue and internal to the corky or epidermal tissues of a green plant; *broadly* : all tissues external to the xylem **b** : an outer or investing layer of various algae, lichens, or fungi
cor·ti·cal \ˈkȯrt-i-kəl\ *adj* **1** : of, relating to, or consisting of cortex **2** : involving or resulting from the action or condition of the cerebral cortex — **cor·ti·cal·ly** \-k(ə-)lē\ *adv*
cor·ti·cate \ˈkȯrt-ə-ˌkāt\ *adj* : having a cortex
cortico- *comb form* **1** : cortex ⟨*cortico*adrenal⟩ **2** : cortical and ⟨*cortico*spinal⟩
cor·ti·coid \ˈkȯrt-i-ˌkȯid\ *n* : any of various adrenal-cortex steroids
cor·ti·co·ste·roid \ˌkȯrt-i-kō-ˈsti(ə)r-ˌȯid *also* -ˈste(ə)r-\ *n* : CORTICOID
cor·ti·co·ste·rone \ˌkȯrt-ə-ˈkäs-tə-ˌrōn, -i-kō-stə-ˈ\ *n* : a colorless crystalline steroid hormone $C_{21}H_{30}O_4$ of the adrenal cortex that is important in protein and carbohydrate metabolism
cor·ti·co·tro·pin \-ˈtrō-pən\ *or* **cor·ti·co·tro·phin** \-fən\ *n* [*corticotropic* + *-in*] : ADRENOCORTICOTROPHIC HORMONE; *also* : a preparation of ACTH that is used esp. in the treatment of rheumatoid arthritis and rheumatic fever
cor·tin \ˈkȯrt-ᵊn\ *n* : the active principle of the adrenal cortex
cor·ti·sol \ˈkȯrt-ə-ˌsȯl, -ˌzȯl, -ˌsōl, -ˌzōl\ *n* [*cortisone* + *-ol*] : a crystalline hormone $C_{21}H_{30}O_5$ of the adrenal cortex that is a dihydro derivative of cortisone and is used in the treatment of rheumatoid arthritis — called also *hydrocortisone*
cor·ti·sone \-ˌsōn, -ˌzōn\ *n* [alter. of *corticosterone*] : a steroid hormone $C_{21}H_{28}O_5$ of the adrenal cortex used esp. in the treatment of rheumatoid arthritis
co·run·dum \kə-ˈrən-dəm\ *n* [Tamil *kuruntam,* fr. Skt *kuruvinda* ruby] : a very hard mineral Al_2O_3 that consists of aluminum oxide occurring in massive form and as variously colored crystals which include the ruby and sapphire, that can be synthesized, and that is used as an abrasive (hardness 9, sp. gr. 3.95–4.10)
co·rus·cant \kə-ˈrəs-kənt\ *adj* : SHINING, GLITTERING
cor·us·cate \ˈkȯr-ə-ˌskāt, ˈkär-\ *vi* **-cat·ed; -cat·ing** [L *coruscatus,* pp. of *coruscare*] **1** : to give off or reflect light in bright beams or flashes : SPARKLE **2** : to be brilliant or showy in technique or style
syn see FLASH
cor·us·ca·tion \ˌkȯr-ə-ˈskā-shən, ˌkär-\ *n* **1** : GLITTER, SPARKLE **2** : a flash of wit
cor·vée \ˈkȯr-ˌvā, kȯr-ˈ\ *n* [ME *corvee,* fr. MF, fr. ML *corrogata,* fr. L, fem. of *corrogatus,* pp. of *corrogare* to collect, requisition, fr. *com-* + *rogare* to ask — more at RIGHT] **1** : unpaid labor (as on roads) due from a feudal vassal to his lord **2** : labor exacted in lieu of taxes by public authorities esp. for highway construction or repair
corves *pl of* CORF
cor·vette \kȯr-ˈvet\ *n* [F] **1** : a warship ranking in the old sailing navies next below a frigate **2** : a highly maneuverable armed escort ship that is smaller than a destroyer
cor·vi·na \kȯr-ˈvē-nə\ *var of* CORBINA
cor·vine \ˈkȯr-ˌvīn\ *adj* [L *corvinus,* fr. *corvus* raven — more at RAVEN] : of or relating to the crows : resembling a crow
Cor·vus \ˈkȯr-vəs\ *n* [L (gen. *Corvi*), lit., raven] : a small constellation adjoining Virgo on the south
Cor·y·bant \ˈkȯr-ə-bant, ˈkär-\ *n, pl* **Cor·y·bants** \-ˌban(t)s\ *or* **Cor·y·ban·tes** \ˌkȯr-ə-ˈbant-ēz, ˌkär-\ [F *Corybante,* fr. L *Corybas,* fr. Gk *Korybas*] : one of the attendants or priests of Cybele noted for orgiastic processions and rites — **cor·y·ban·tic** \ˌkȯr-ə-ˈbant-ik, ˌkär-\ *adj*
co·ryd·a·lis \kə-ˈrid-ᵊl-əs\ *n* [NL, genus name, fr. Gk *korydallis* crested lark; akin to L *cornu* horn — more at HORN] : any of a large genus (*Corydalis*) of herbs of the fumitory family with racemose irregular flowers
cor·ymb \ˈkȯr-ˌim(b), ˈkär-, -əm(b)\ *n, pl* **cor·ymbs** \-ˌimz, -əmz\ [F *corymbe,* fr. L *corymbus* cluster of fruit or flowers, fr. Gk *korymbos*] : a flat-topped inflorescence; *specif* : one in which the flower stalks arise at different levels on the main axis and reach about the same height and in which the outer flowers open first and the inflorescence is indeterminate — **cor·ymbed** \-ˌimd, -əmd\ *adj* — **cor·ym·bose** \-əm-ˌbōs\ *adj* — **cor·ym·bose·ly** *adv*

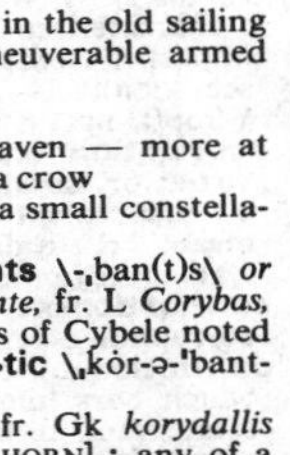

corymb of cherry: *1* peduncle, *2* pedicels, *3* bracts

co·ry·ne·bac·te·ri·um \ˌkȯr-ə-(ˌ)nē-bak-ˈtir-ē-əm, kə-ˌrin-ə-\ *n* [NL, genus name, fr. Gk *korynē* club; akin to L *cornu* horn] : any of a large genus (*Corynebacterium*) of usu. gram-positive nonmotile bacteria that occur as irregular or branching rods and include numerous important parasites of man, lower animals, and plants — **co·ry·ne·bac·te·ri·al** \-ē-əl\ *adj*
co·ryne·form \kə-ˈrin-ə-ˌfȯrm\ *adj* : being or resembling corynebacteria
cor·y·phae·us \ˌkȯr-ə-ˈfē-əs, ˌkär-\ *n, pl* **-phaei** \-ˈfē-ˌī\ [L, leader, fr. Gk *koryphaios,* fr. *koryphē* summit; akin to L *cornu*] **1** : the leader of a chorus **2** : the leader of a party or school of thought
co·ry·phée \ˌkȯr-i-ˈfā\ *n* [F, fr. L *coryphaeus*] : a ballet dancer who dances in a small group instead of in the corps de ballet or as a soloist
co·ry·za \kə-ˈrī-zə\ *n* [LL, fr. Gk *koryza* nasal mucus; akin to OHG *hroz* nasal mucus, Skt *kardama* mud] : an acute inflammatory contagious disease involving the upper respiratory tract; *esp* : COMMON COLD — **co·ry·zal** \-zəl\ *adj*
[1]**cos** *abbr* consul; consulship
[2]**cos** *symbol* cosine
COS *abbr* **1** cash on shipment **2** chief of staff
cosec *abbr* cosecant
co·se·cant \(ˈ)kō-ˈsē-ˌkant, -kənt\ *n* [NL *cosecant-, cosecans,* fr. *co-* + *secant-, secans* secant] : the trigonometric function that for an acute angle is the ratio between the hypotenuse of a right triangle of which the angle is considered part and the side opposite the angle
co·set \ˈkō-ˌset\ *n* : a subset of a mathematical group that consists of all the products obtained by multiplying either on the right or the left a fixed element of the group by each of the elements of a given subgroup
[1]**cosh** \ˈkäsh\ *n* [perh. fr. Romany *kosh* stick] *chiefly Brit* : a weighted weapon similar to a blackjack; *also* : an attack with a cosh
[2]**cosh** *vt, chiefly Brit* : to strike or assault with or as if with a cosh
co·sig·na·to·ry \(ˈ)kō-ˈsig-nə-ˌtōr-ē, -ˌtȯr-\ *n* : a joint signer
co·sign·er \ˈkō-ˌsī-nər\ *n* : COSIGNATORY; *esp* : a joint signer of a promissory note
co·sine \ˈkō-ˌsīn\ *n* [NL *cosinus,* fr. *co-* + ML *sinus* sine] : the trigonometric function that for an acute angle is the ratio between the side adjacent to the angle when it is considered part of a right triangle and the hypotenuse
cos lettuce \ˈkäs-, ˈkōs-\ *n* [*Kos, Cos,* Gk island] : a lettuce (*Lactuca sativa longifolia*) with long crisp leaves and columnar heads
[1]**cos·met·ic** \käz-ˈmet-ik\ *n* : a cosmetic preparation for external use
[2]**cosmetic** *adj* [Gk *kosmētikos* skilled in adornment, fr. *kosmein* to arrange, adorn, fr. *kosmos* order] **1** : of, relating to, or making for beauty esp. of the complexion : BEAUTIFYING ⟨~ salves⟩ **2** : correcting defects esp. of the face ⟨~ surgery⟩
cosmetic case *n* : a small piece of luggage esp. for cosmetics
cos·me·ti·cian \ˌkäz-mə-ˈtish-ən\ *n* : one who is professionally trained in the use of cosmetics
cos·me·tol·o·gist \-ˈtäl-ə-jəst\ *n* : one who gives beauty treatments (as to skin and hair) — called also *beautician*
cos·me·tol·o·gy \-jē\ *n* [F *cosmétologie,* fr. *cosmétique* cosmetic (fr. E *cosmetic*) + *-logie* -logy] : the cosmetic treatment of the skin, hair, and nails
cos·mic \ˈkäz-mik\ *also* **cos·mi·cal** \-mi-kəl\ *adj* [Gk *kosmikos,* fr. *kosmos* order, universe] **1** : of or relating to the cosmos, the extraterrestrial vastness, or the universe in contrast to the earth alone **2** : characterized by greatness esp. in extent, intensity, or comprehensiveness ⟨an abiding illness of the 20th century . . . — a ~ boredom —Albert Hubbell⟩ — **cos·mi·cal·ly** \-mi-k(ə-)lē\ *adv*
cosmic dust *n* : very fine particles of solid matter in any part of the universe
cosmic noise *n* : GALACTIC NOISE
cosmic ray *n* : a stream of atomic nuclei of heterogeneous extremely penetrating character that enter the earth's atmosphere from outer space at speeds approaching that of light and bombard atmospheric atoms to produce mesons as well as secondary particles possessing some of the original energy
cos·mo·chem·is·try \ˌkäz-mō-ˈkem-ə-strē\ *n* [Gk *kosmos* universe] : a branch of chemistry that deals with the chemical composition and changes in the universe — **cos·mo·chem·i·cal** \-ˈkem-i-kəl\ *adj*
cos·mo·gen·ic \ˌkäz-mə-ˈjen-ik\ *adj* [*cosm*ic ray + *-o-* + *-genic*] : produced by the action of cosmic rays ⟨~ carbon 14⟩
cos·mog·o·ny \käz-ˈmäg-ə-nē\ *n, pl* **-nies** [NL *cosmogonia,* fr. Gk *kosmogonia,* fr. *kosmos* + *gonos* offspring] **1** : the creation or origin of the world or universe **2** : a theory of the origin of the universe — **cos·mo·gon·ic** \ˌkäz-mə-ˈgän-ik\ *or* **cos·mo·gon·i·cal** \-i-kəl\ *adj* — **cos·mog·o·nist** \käz-ˈmäg-ə-nəst\ *n*
cos·mog·ra·phy \käz-ˈmäg-rə-fē\ *n, pl* **-phies** [ME *cosmographie,* fr. LL *cosmographia,* fr. Gk *kosmographia,* fr. *kosmos* + *-graphia* -graphy] **1** : a general description of the world or of the universe **2** : the science that deals with the constitution of the whole order of nature — **cos·mog·ra·pher** \-fər\ *n* — **cos·mo·graph·ic** \ˌkäz-mə-ˈgraf-ik\ *or* **cos·mo·graph·i·cal** \-i-kəl\ *adj* — **cos·mo·graph·i·cal·ly** \-i-k(ə-)lē\ *adv*
Cosmoline \ˈkäz-mə-ˌlēn\ *trademark* — used for petrolatum
cos·mol·o·gy \käz-ˈmäl-ə-jē\ *n, pl* **-gies** [NL *cosmologia,* fr. Gk *kosmos* + NL *-logia* -logy] **1** : a branch of metaphysics that deals with the universe as an orderly system **2** : a branch of astronomy that deals with the origin, structure, and space-time relationships of the universe — **cos·mo·log·ic** \ˌkäz-mə-ˈläj-ik\ *or* **cos·mo·log·i·cal** \-i-kəl\ *adj* — **cos·mo·log·i·cal·ly** \-i-k(ə-)lē\ *adv* — **cos·mol·o·gist** \käz-ˈmäl-ə-jəst\ *n*
cos·mo·naut \ˈkäz-mə-ˌnȯt, -ˌnät\ *n* [part trans. of Russ *kosmonavt,* fr. Gk *kosmos* + Russ *-navt* (as in *aeronavt* aeronaut)] : a Soviet traveler beyond the earth's atmosphere : ASTRONAUT
cos·mop·o·lis \käz-ˈmäp-ə-ləs\ *n* [NL, back-formation fr. *cosmopolites*] : cosmopolitan city
[1]**cos·mo·pol·i·tan** \ˌkäz-mə-ˈpäl-ət-ᵊn\ *adj* **1** : having worldwide rather than limited or provincial scope or bearing **2** : having wide international sophistication **3** : composed of persons, constituents, or elements from all or many parts of the world **4** : found in most parts of the world and under varied ecological conditions ⟨a ~ herb⟩ — **cos·mo·pol·i·tan·ism** \-ᵊn-ˌiz-əm\ *n*
[2]**cosmopolitan** *n* : COSMOPOLITE
cos·mop·o·lite \käz-ˈmäp-ə-ˌlīt\ *n* [NL *cosmopolites,* fr. Gk *kosmopolitēs,* fr. *kosmos* + *politēs* citizen] : a cosmopolitan person or organism — **cos·mop·o·lit·ism** \käz-ˈmäp-ə-ˌlīt-ˌiz-əm, -lə-ˌtiz-; ˌkäz-mə-ˈpäl-ə-ˌtiz-\ *n*
cos·mos \ˈkäz-məs, *1 & 2 also* -ˌmōs, -ˌmäs\ *n* [G *kosmos,* fr. Gk] **1 a** : an orderly harmonious systematic universe — compare CHAOS **b** : ORDER, HARMONY **2** : a complex orderly self-inclusive system **3** *pl* **cosmos** \-məs, -məz\ *also* **cos·mos·es** \-mə-səz\ [NL, genus

name, fr. Gk *kosmos*] : any of a genus (*Cosmos*) of tropical American composite herbs; *esp* : a widely cultivated tall fall-blooming annual (*C. bipinnatus*) with yellow or red disks and showy ray flowers

co·spon·sor \'kō-,spän(t)-sər, -'spän(t)-\ *n* : a joint sponsor — **cosponsor** *vt* — **co·spon·sor·ship** \-,ship\ *n*

cos·sack \'käs-,ak, -ək\ *n* [Russ *kazak* & Ukrainian *kozak*, fr. Turk *kazak* free person] : a member of a group of frontiersmen of southern Russia organized as cavalry in the czarist army

¹**cos·set** \'käs-ət\ *n* [origin unknown] : a pet lamb; *broadly* : PET
²**cosset** *vt* : to treat as a pet : PAMPER

¹**cost** \'kȯst\ *n* **1 a** : the amount or equivalent paid or charged for something : PRICE **b** : the outlay or expenditure (as of effort or sacrifice) made to achieve an object **2** : loss or penalty incurred in gaining something **3** *pl* : expenses incurred in litigation; *esp* : those given by the law or the court to the prevailing party against the losing party — **cost·less** \-ləs\ *adj* — **cost·less·ly** *adv*
²**cost** *vb* **cost; cost·ing** [ME *costen*, fr. MF *coster*, fr. L *constare* to stand firm, to cost — more at CONSTANT] *vi* **1** : to require expenditure or payment ⟨the best goods ~ more⟩ **2** : to require effort, suffering, or loss ~ *vt* **1** : to have a price of **2** : to cause (someone) to pay, suffer, or lose something ⟨frequent absences ~ him his job⟩ **3** : to estimate or set the cost of

cos·ta \'käs-tə\ *n, pl* **cos·tae** \-(,)tē, -,tī\ [L — more at COAST] **1** : ¹RIB 1a **2** : a part (as the midrib of a leaf or the anterior vein of an insect wing) that resembles a rib — **cos·tal** \-t³l\ *adj* — **cos·tate** \-,tāt\ *adj*

cost accountant *n* : a specialist in cost accounting

cost accounting *n* : the systematic recording and analysis of the costs of material, labor, and overhead incident to production

¹**co-star** \'kō-,stär\ *n* : a star whose role in a motion picture or play is equal in importance to that of another leading player
²**co-star** *vi* : to appear as a co-star in a motion picture or play ~ *vt* : to feature (a player) as a co-star

cos·tard \'käs-tərd\ *n* [ME] **1** : any of several large English cooking apples **2** *archaic* : NODDLE, PATE

cost–ef·fec·tive \,kȯs-tə-'fek-tiv\ *adj* : economical in terms of tangible benefits produced by money spent ⟨~ measures to combat poverty⟩ — **cost–ef·fec·tive·ness** *n*

cos·ter \'käs-tər\ *n, Brit* : COSTERMONGER

cos·ter·mon·ger \-,mən-gər, -,män-\ *n* [*costard* + *monger*] *Brit* : a hawker of fruit or vegetables

cos·tive \'käs-tiv\ *adj* [ME, fr. MF *costivé*, pp. of *costiver* to constipate, fr. L *constipare*] **1 a** : affected with constipation **b** : causing constipation **2** : slow in action or expression **3** : NIGGARDLY — **cos·tive·ly** *adv* — **cos·tive·ness** *n*

cost·ly \'kȯs(t)-lē\ *adj* **cost·li·er; -est 1** : commanding a high price usu. because of intrinsic worth ⟨~ gems⟩ **2** : GORGEOUS, SPLENDID **3** : made at heavy expense or sacrifice — **cost·li·ness** *n*
syn COSTLY, EXPENSIVE, DEAR, VALUABLE, PRECIOUS, INVALUABLE, PRICELESS *shared meaning element* : having a high value or valuation esp. in terms of money *ant* cheap

cost·mary \'kȯst-,mer-ē, 'käst-\ *n, pl* **-mar·ies** [ME *costmarie*, fr. *coste* costmary (fr. OE *cost*, fr. L *costum*, fr. Gk *kostos*, a fragrant root) + *Marie* the Virgin Mary] : a tansy-scented composite herb (*Chrysanthemum majus*) used as a potherb and in flavoring

cost of living : the cost of purchasing those goods and services which are included in an accepted standard level of consumption

cost–of–living index *n* : CONSUMER PRICE INDEX

cost–plus \'kȯs(t)-'pləs\ *adj* : paid on the basis of a fixed fee or a percentage added to actual cost ⟨a ~ contract⟩

cost–push \'kȯs(t)-,push\ *n* : an increase or upward trend in production costs (as wages) that tends to result in increased consumer prices irrespective of the level of demand — compare DEMAND–PULL — **cost–push** *adj*

cos·trel \'käs-trəl\ *n* [ME, fr. MF *costerel*, fr. *costier* at the side, fr. *coste* rib, side — more at COAST] : a flat usu. earthenware container for liquids with loops through which a belt or cord may be passed for easy carrying — called also *pilgrim bottle*

¹**cos·tume** \'käs-,t(y)üm *also* -təm *or* -,chüm\ *n* [F, fr. It, custom, dress, fr. L *consuetudin-, consuetudo* custom — more at CUSTOM] **1** : the prevailing fashion in coiffure, jewelry, and apparel of a period, country, or class **2** : a suit or dress characteristic of a period, country, or class **3** : a person's ensemble of outer garments; *esp* : a woman's ensemble of dress with coat or jacket — **cos·tum·ey** *adj*
²**cos·tume** \käs-'t(y)üm *also* -'chüm; *or like* ¹\ *vt* **cos·tumed; cos·tum·ing 1** : to provide with a costume **2** : to design costumes for ⟨~ a play⟩
³**costume** *like* ¹\ *adj* **1** : characterized by the use of costumes ⟨a ~ ball⟩ ⟨a ~ drama⟩ **2** : suitable for or enhancing the effect of a particular costume ⟨a ~ handbag⟩

costume jewelry *n* : inexpensive jewelry designed for wear with current fashions

cos·tum·er \'käs-,t(y)ü-mər *also* -,chü-; käs-'\ *n* **1** : one that deals in or makes costumes **2** : CLOTHES TREE

cos·tum·ery \-mə-rē\ *n* **1** : articles of costume **2** : the art of costuming

cos·tu·mi·er \käs-'t(y)ü-mē-,ā, -mē-ər\ *n* [F] : COSTUMER 1

co·sy \'kō-zē\ *var of* COZY

¹**cot** \'kät\ *n* [ME, fr. OE; akin to ON *kot* small hut, L *guttur* throat] **1** : a small house **2** : COVER, SHEATH; *esp* : STALL 4
²**cot** *n* [Hindi *khāṭ* bedstead, fr. Skt *khatvā*, of Dravidian origin; akin to Tamil *kaṭṭil* bedstead] : a small usu. collapsible bed of fabric stretched on a frame
³**cot** *symbol* cotangent

co·tan·gent \(')kō-'tan-jənt\ *n* [NL *cotangent-, cotangens*, fr. *co-* + *tangent-, tangens* tangent] : the trigonometric function that for an acute angle is the ratio between the side adjacent to the angle and the side opposite

¹**cote** \'kōt, 'kät\ *n* [ME, fr. OE] **1** *dial Eng* : ¹COT 1 **2** : a shed or coop for small domestic animals and esp. pigeons
²**cote** \'kōt\ *vt* [prob. fr. MF *cotoyer*] *obs* : to pass by

co·te·rie \'kōt-ə-(,)rē, ,kōt-ə-'\ *n* [F, fr. MF, tenants, fr. (assumed) MF *cotier* cotter, fr. ML *cotarius*] : an intimate and often exclusive group of persons with a unifying common interest or purpose *syn* see SET

co·ter·mi·nous \(')kō-'tər-mə-nəs\ *adj* [alter. of *conterminous*] **1** : having the same or coincident boundaries ⟨~ states⟩ **2** : coextensive in scope or duration ⟨~ interests⟩ — **co·ter·mi·nous·ly** *adv*

co·thur·nus \kō-'thər-nəs\ *n, pl* **-ni** \-,nī, -(,)nē\ [L, fr. Gk *kothornos*] **1** : a high thick-soled laced boot worn by actors in Greek and Roman tragic drama — called also *cothurn* **2** : the dignified somewhat stylized spirit of ancient tragedy

co·tid·al \(')kō-'tīd-³l\ *adj* : indicating equality in the tides or a coincidence in the time of high or low tide

co·til·lion \kō-'til-yən\ *also* **co·til·lon** \kō-'til-yən, kȯ-tē-(y)ōⁿ\ *n* [F *cotillon*, lit., petticoat, fr. OF, fr. *cote* coat] **1** : a ballroom dance for couples that resembles the quadrille **2** : an elaborate dance with frequent changing of partners carried out under the leadership of one couple at formal balls **3** : a formal ball

co·to·neas·ter \kə-'tō-nē-,as-tər, 'kät-³n-,ēs-\ *n* [NL, genus name, fr. L *cydonia, cotoneum* quince + NL *-aster*] : any of a genus (*Cotoneaster*) of Old World flowering shrubs of the rose family

cot·quean \'kät-,kwēn\ *n* **1** *archaic* : a coarse masculine woman **2** *archaic* : a man who busies himself with women's work or affairs

Cots·wold \'kät-,swōld\ *n* [*Cotswold* hills, England] : a sheep of an English breed of large long-wooled sheep

cot·ta \'kät-ə\ *n* [ML, of Gmc origin; akin to OHG *kozza* coarse mantle — more at COAT] : a waist-length surplice

cot·tage \'kät-ij\ *n* [ME *cotage*, fr. (assumed) AF, fr. ME *cot*] **1** : the dwelling of a farm laborer or small farmer **2** : a small usu. frame one-family house **3** : a small detached dwelling unit at an institution **4** : a small house for vacation use — **cot·tag·ey** \-ij-ē\ *adj*

cottage cheese *n* : a soft uncured cheese made from soured skim milk — called also *Dutch cheese, pot cheese, smearcase*

cottage curtains *n pl* : a double set of upper and lower straight-hanging window curtains

cottage industry *n* : an industry whose labor force consists of family units working at home with their own equipment

cottage pudding *n* : plain cake covered with a hot sweet sauce

cot·tag·er \'kät-ij-ər\ *n* : one who lives in a cottage (as at a vacation resort)

cottage tulip *n* : any of various tall-growing tulips that flower in the middle of the tulip-flowering season

¹**cot·ter** *or* **cot·tar** \'kät-ər\ *n* [ME *cottar*, fr. ML *cotarius*, fr. ME *cot*] : a peasant or farm laborer who occupies a cottage and sometimes a small holding of land usu. in return for services
²**cotter** *n* [origin unknown] **1** : a wedge-shaped or tapered piece used to fasten together parts of a structure **2** : COTTER PIN

cotter pin *n* : a half-round metal strip bent into a pin whose ends can be flared after insertion through a slot or hole

¹**cot·ton** \'kät-³n\ *n, often attrib* [ME *coton*, fr. MF, fr. Ar *quṭn*] **1 a** : a soft usu. white fibrous substance composed of the hairs surrounding the seeds of various erect freely branching tropical plants (genus *Gossypium*) of the mallow family **b** : a plant producing cotton; *esp* : one grown for its cotton **c** : a crop of cotton **2 a** : fabric made of cotton **b** : yarn spun from cotton **3** : a downy cottony substance produced by various plants (as the cottonwood)
²**cotton** *vi* **cot·toned; cot·ton·ing** \'kät-niŋ, -³n-iŋ\ **1** : to take a liking ⟨~s to people easily⟩ **2** : to come to understand : catch on : TUMBLE ⟨~ed on to the fact that our children work furiously —H. M. McLuhan⟩

cotton candy *n* : a candy made of spun sugar

cotton gin *n* : a machine that separates the seeds, hulls, and foreign material from cotton

cotton: *1* flowering branch, *2* fruit, unopened, *3* fruit, partly opened

cotton grass *n* : any of a genus (*Eriophorum*) of sedges with tufted spikes

cot·ton·mouth \'kät-³n-,mau̇th\ *n* : WATER MOCCASIN

cottonmouth moccasin *n* : WATER MOCCASIN

cot·ton–pick·ing \,kät-³n-,pik-iŋ, -,pik-ən\ *adj* **1** : DAMNED — used as a generalized expression of disapproval ⟨a ~ hypocrite⟩ **2** : DAMNED — used as an intensive ⟨out of his ~ mind —Irving Kristol⟩

cot·ton·seed \'kät-³n-,sēd\ *n* : the seed of the cotton plant

cottonseed oil *n* : a pale yellow semidrying fatty oil that is obtained from the cottonseed and is used chiefly in salad and cooking oils and after hydrogenation in shortenings and margarine

cotton stainer *n* : any of several red and black or dark brown bugs (genus *Dysdercus*) that damage and stain the lint of developing cotton; *specif* : a red and brown bug (*D. suturellus*) that attacks cotton in the southern U.S.

cot·ton·tail \'kät-³n-,tāl\ *n* : any of several rather small No. American rabbits (genus *Sylvilagus*) sandy brown in color with a white-tufted underside of the tail

cot·ton·weed \-,wēd\ *n* : any of various weedy plants (as cudweed) with hoary pubescence or cottony seeds

cot·ton·wood \-ˌwu̇d\ *n* : a poplar with a tuft of cottony hairs on the seed; *esp* : one (*Populus deltoides*) of the eastern and central U.S. often cultivated for its rapid growth and luxuriant foliage

cotton wool *n* : raw cotton; *esp* : cotton batting

cot·tony \ˈkät-nē, -ᵊn-ē\ *adj* : resembling cotton in appearance or character: as **a** : covered with hairs or pubescence **b** : SOFT

cotyl- *or* **cotyli-** *or* **cotylo-** *comb form* [Gk *kotyl-*, *kotylo-*, fr. *kotylē*] : cup : organ or part like a cup ⟨*cotyl*oid⟩ ⟨*cotyli*form⟩

-cot·yl \ˌkät-ᵊl\ *n comb form* [*cotyledon*] : cotyledon ⟨*dicotyl*⟩

cot·y·le·don \ˌkät-ᵊl-ˈēd-ᵊn\ *n* [NL, fr. Gk *kotylēdōn* cup-shaped hollow, fr. *kotylē* cup] **1** : a placental lobule **2** : the first leaf or one of the first pair or whorl of leaves developed by the embryo of a seed plant or of some lower plants (as ferns) — see PLUMULE illustration — **cot·y·le·don·al** \-ˈēd-nəl, -ᵊn-əl\ *adj* — **cot·y·le·don·ary** \-ˈēd-ᵊn-ˌer-ē\ *or* **cot·y·le·don·ous** \-ˈēd-nəs, -ᵊn-əs\ *adj*

co·ty·lo·saur \ˈkät-ᵊl-ō-ˌsȯ(ə)r, kə-ˈtil-ə-\ *n* [NL *Cotylosauria*, group name, deriv. of Gk *kotylē* cup & *sauros* lizard] : any of an order (Cotylosauria) of extinct ancient primitive reptiles with short legs and massive bodies that were prob. the earliest truly terrestrial vertebrate animals

co·type \ˈkō-ˌtīp\ *n* : any of several secondary taxonomic types

[1]**couch** \ˈkau̇ch\ *vb* [ME *couchen*, fr. MF *coucher*, fr. L *collocare* to set in place — more at COLLOCATE] *vt* **1** : to lay (oneself) down for rest or sleep **2** : to embroider (a design) by laid threads fastened by small stitches at regular intervals **3** : to place or hold level and pointed forward ready for use **4** : to phrase in a specified manner ⟨the memorandum was ~*ed* in strong language —W. L. Shirer⟩ **5** : to treat (a cataract) by displacing the lens of the eye into the vitreous humor ~ *vi* **1** : to lie down or recline for sleep or rest **2** : to lie in ambush

[2]**couch** *n* **1 a** : an article of furniture (as a bed or sofa) for sitting or reclining **b** : a couch on which a patient reclines when undergoing psychoanalysis **2** : the den of an animal (as an otter) — **on the couch** : receiving psychiatric treatment

couch·ant \ˈkau̇-chənt\ *adj* [ME, fr. MF, fr. prp. of *coucher*] : lying down esp. with the head up ⟨a heraldic lion ~⟩

couch grass \ˈkau̇ch-, ˈküch-\ *n* [alter. of *quitch grass*] **1** : QUACK GRASS **2** : any of several grasses that resemble quack grass in spreading by creeping rhizomes

cou·dé \kü-ˈdā\ *adj* [F *coudé* bent like an elbow, fr. *coude* elbow, fr. L *cubitum* — more at HIP] **1** *of a telescope* : constructed so that the light is reflected along the polar axis to come to a focus at a fixed place where the holder for a photographic plate or a spectrograph may be mounted **2** : of or relating to a coudé telescope

cou·gar \ˈkü-gər, -ˌgär\ *n, pl* **cougars** *also* **cougar** [F *couguar*, fr. NL *cuguacuarana*, modif. of Tupi *suasuarana*, lit., false deer, fr. *suasú* deer + *rana* false] : a large powerful tawny brown cat (*Felis concolor*) formerly widespread in the Americas but now extinct in many areas — called also *catamount*, *mountain lion*, *panther*, *puma*

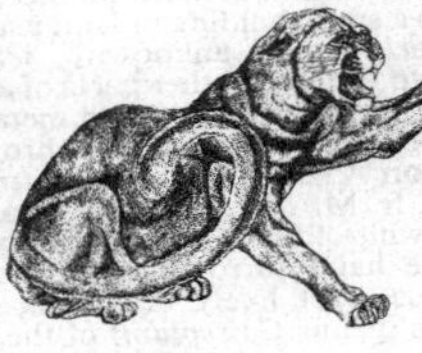
cougar

[1]**cough** \ˈkȯf\ *vb* [ME *coughen*, fr. (assumed) OE *cohhian*; akin to MHG *küchen* to breathe heavily] *vi* **1** : to expel air from the lungs suddenly with an explosive noise **2** : to make a noise like that of coughing ~ *vt* : to expel by coughing — often used with *up* ⟨~ up mucus⟩

[2]**cough** *n* **1** : a condition marked by repeated or frequent coughing **2** : an act or sound of coughing

cough drop *n* : a lozenge or troche used to relieve coughing

cough syrup *n* : any of various sweet usu. medicated liquids used to relieve coughing

cough up *vt* : to hand over : DELIVER, PAY ⟨*cough up* the money⟩

could \kəd, (ˈ)ku̇d\ [ME *couthe*, *coude*, fr. OE *cūthe*; akin to OHG *konda* could] *past of* CAN — used in auxiliary function in the past ⟨he found he ~ go⟩, in the past conditional ⟨he said he would go if he ~⟩, and as an alternative to *can* suggesting less force or certainty or as a polite form in the present ⟨~ you do this for me⟩ ⟨if you ~ come we would be pleased⟩

could·est \ˈku̇d-əst\ *archaic past 2d sing of* CAN

couldn't \ˈku̇d-ᵊnt\ : could not

couldst \kədst, (ˈ)ku̇dst, kətst, (ˈ)ku̇tst\ *archaic past 2d sing of* CAN

cou·lee \ˈkü-lē\ *n* [CanF *coulée*, fr. F, flowing, flow of lava, fr. *couler* to flow, fr. L *colare* to strain, fr. *colum* sieve] **1 a** : a small stream **b** : a dry stream bed **c** : a usu. small or shallow ravine : GULLY **2** : a thick sheet or stream of lava

cou·lisse \kü-ˈlēs, -ˈlis\ *n* [F] **1 a** : a side scene of a theater stage; *also* : the space between the side scenes **b** : a backstage area **c** : HALLWAY **2** : a piece of timber having a groove in which something glides

cou·loir \kül-ˈwär\ *n* [F, lit., strainer, fr. LL *colatorium*, fr. L *colatus*, pp. of *colare*] : a mountainside gorge esp. in the Swiss Alps

[1]**cou·lomb** \ˈkü-ˌläm, -ˌlōm, kü-ˈ\ *n* [Charles A. de *Coulomb*] : the practical mks unit of electric charge equal to the quantity of electricity transferred by a current of one ampere in one second

[2]**coulomb** *or* **cou·lom·bic** \kü-ˈläm-(b)ik, -ˈlōm-\ *adj* : of, relating to, or being the electrostatic force of attraction or repulsion between charged particles

cou·lom·e·try \kü-ˈläm-ə-trē\ *n* [alter. of earlier *coulombmeter*] : chemical analysis performed by determining the amount of a substance released in an electrolysis by measuring the number of coulombs used — **cou·lo·met·ric** \ˌkü-lə-ˈme-trik\ *adj* — **cou·lo·met·ri·cal·ly** \-tri-kə-lē\ *adv*

coul·ter \ˈkōl-tər\ *n* [ME *colter*, fr. OE *culter* & OF *coltre*, both fr. L *culter* plowshare] : a cutting tool (as a knife or sharp disc) that is attached to the beam of a plow, makes a vertical cut in the surface, and permits clean separation and effective covering of the soil and materials being turned under

cou·ma·phos \ˈkü-mə-ˌfäs\ *n* [*coumarin* + *phosphorus*] : an organophosphorus systemic insecticide $C_{14}H_{16}ClO_5PS$ used esp. on cattle and poultry

cou·ma·rin \ˈkü-mə-rən\ *n* [F *coumarine*, fr. *coumarou* tonka bean tree, fr. Sp or Pg; Sp *coumarú*, fr. Pg, fr. Tupi] : a toxic white crystalline lactone $C_9H_6O_2$ with an odor of new-mown hay found in plants or made synthetically and used esp. in perfumery

cou·ma·rone \-ˌrōn\ *n* [ISV *coumarin* + *-one*] : a compound C_8H_6O found in coal tar and polymerized with indene to form thermoplastic resins used esp. in coatings and printing inks — called also *benzofuran*

[1]**coun·cil** \ˈkau̇n(t)-səl\ *n* [ME *counceil*, fr. OF *concile*, fr. L *concilium*, fr. *com-* + *calare* to call — more at LOW] **1** : an assembly or meeting for consultation, advice, or discussion **2** : a group elected or appointed as an advisory or legislative body **3 a** : a usu. administrative body **b** : an executive body whose members are equal in power and authority **c** : a governing body of delegates from local units of a federation **4** : deliberation in a council **5 a** : a federation of or a central body uniting a group of organizations **b** : a local chapter of an organization **c** : CLUB, SOCIETY

[2]**council** *adj* **1** : used for councils esp. by or with No. American Indians ⟨a ~ ground⟩ **2** *Brit* : built, maintained, or operated by a local governing agency ⟨a ~ house⟩ ⟨~ flats⟩

coun·cil·lor *or* **coun·cil·or** \ˈkau̇n(t)-s(ə-)lər\ *n* : a member of a council — **coun·cil·lor·ship** \-ˌship\ *n*

coun·cil·man \ˈkau̇n(t)-səl-mən\ *n* : a member of a council (as of a town or city) — **coun·cil·man·ic** \ˌkau̇n(t)-səl-ˈman-ik\ *adj*

council of ministers *often cap C&M* : CABINET 3b

coun·cil·wom·an \ˈkau̇n(t)-səl-ˌwu̇m-ən\ *n* : a female member of a council

[1]**coun·sel** \ˈkau̇n(t)-səl\ *n* [ME *conseil*, fr. OF, fr. L *consilium*, fr. *consulere* to consult] **1 a** : advice given esp. as a result of consultation **b** : a policy or plan of action or behavior **2** : DELIBERATION, CONSULTATION **3 a** *archaic* : PURPOSE **b** : guarded thoughts or intentions **4 a** *pl* **counsel** (1) : a lawyer engaged in the trial or management of a case in court (2) : a lawyer appointed to advise and represent in legal matters an individual client or a corporate and esp. a public body **b** : CONSULTANT 2

[2]**counsel** *vb* **-seled** *or* **-selled; -sel·ing** *or* **-sel·ling** \-s(ə-)liŋ\ *vt* : ADVISE ⟨~*ed* them to avoid rash actions —George Orwell⟩ ~ *vi* : CONSULT ⟨~*ed* with her husband⟩

coun·sel·ee \ˌkau̇n(t)-sə-ˈlē\ *n* : one who is being counseled

coun·sel·ing *n* : professional guidance of the individual by utilizing psychological methods esp. in collecting case history data, using various techniques of the personal interview, and testing interests and aptitudes

coun·sel·or *or* **coun·sel·lor** \ˈkau̇n(t)-s(ə-)lər\ *n* **1** : ADVISER **2** : LAWYER; *specif* : one that gives advice in law and manages cases for clients in court **3** : one who has supervisory duties at a summer camp — **coun·sel·or·ship** \-ˌship\ *n*

counselor–at–law *n, pl* **counselors–at–law** : COUNSELOR 2

[1]**count** \ˈkau̇nt\ *vb* [ME *counten*, fr. MF *compter*, fr. L *computare*, fr. *com-* + *putare* to consider — more at PAVE] *vt* **1 a** : to indicate or name by units or groups so as to find the total number of units involved : NUMBER **b** : to name the numbers in order up to and including ⟨~ ten⟩ **c** : to include in a tallying and reckoning ⟨about 100 present, ~*ing* children⟩ **d** : to call aloud (beats or time units) ⟨~ cadence ⟩ ⟨~ eighth notes⟩ **2 a** : CONSIDER, ACCOUNT ⟨~ oneself lucky⟩ **b** : ESTIMATE, ESTEEM **c** : to record as of an opinion or persuasion ⟨~ me as uncommitted⟩ **3** : to include or exclude by or as if by counting ⟨~ me in⟩ ~ *vi* **1 a** : to recite or indicate the numbers in order by units or groups ⟨~ by fives⟩ **b** : to count the units in a group **2** : to rely or depend on someone or something ⟨~*ed* on his brother to help with the expenses⟩ **3** : ADD, TOTAL ⟨it ~*s* up to a sizable amount⟩ **4** : to have value or significance ⟨these are the men who really ~⟩ ***syn*** see RELY — **count heads** *or* **count noses** : to count the number present — **count on** : to look forward to as certain : ANTICIPATE ⟨*counted on* winning⟩

[2]**count** *n* **1 a** : the action or process of counting **b** : a total obtained by counting : TALLY **2** *archaic* **a** : RECKONING, ACCOUNT **b** : CONSIDERATION, ESTIMATION **3 a** : ALLEGATION, CHARGE; *specif* : one separately stating the cause of action or prosecution in a legal declaration or indictment ⟨guilty on all ~*s*⟩ **b** : a specific point under consideration : ISSUE **4** : the total number of individual things in a given unit or sample ⟨blood ~⟩ **5 a** : the calling off of the seconds from one to ten when a boxer has been knocked down **b** : the number of balls and strikes charged to a baseball batter during one turn ⟨the ~ stood at 3 and 2⟩ **c** : SCORE ⟨tied the ~ with a minute to play⟩

[3]**count** *n* [MF *comte*, fr. LL *comit-*, *comes*, fr. L, companion, one of the imperial court, fr. *com-* + *ire* to go — more at ISSUE] : a European nobleman whose rank corresponds to that of a British earl

count·able \ˈkau̇nt-ə-bəl\ *adj* : capable of being counted; *esp* : DENUMERABLE ⟨a ~ set⟩ — **count·abil·i·ty** \ˌkau̇nt-ə-ˈbil-ət-ē\ *n* — **count·ably** \ˈkau̇nt-ə-blē\ *adv*

count·down \ˈkau̇nt-ˌdau̇n\ *n* : an audible backward counting in fixed units (as seconds) from an arbitrary starting number to mark the time remaining before an event; *also* : preparations carried on during such a count — **count down** \-ˈdau̇n\ *vi*

[1]**coun·te·nance** \ˈkau̇nt-ᵊn-ən(t)s, ˈkau̇nt-nən(t)s\ *n* [ME *contenance*, fr. MF, fr. ML *continentia*, fr. L, restraint, fr. *continent-*, *continens*, prp. of *continēre* to hold together — more at CONTAIN] **1** *obs* : BEARING, DEMEANOR **2 a** : calm expression **b** : mental composure **c** : LOOK, EXPRESSION **3** *archaic* **a** : ASPECT, SEMBLANCE **b** : PRETENSE **4** : FACE, VISAGE; *esp* : the face as an indication of mood, emotion, or character **5** : bearing or expression that offers approval or sanction : moral support ***syn*** see FAVOR

[2]**countenance** *vt* **-nanced; -nanc·ing** : to extend approval or toleration to : SANCTION ⟨he never *countenanced* violence⟩ — **coun·te·nanc·er** *n*

[1]**count·er** \ˈkau̇nt-ər\ *n* [ME *countour*, fr. MF *comptouer*, fr. ML *computatorium* computing place, fr. L *computatus*, pp. of *computare*] **1** : a piece (as of metal or ivory) used in reckoning or in

games **2** : something of value in bargaining : ASSET **3** : a level surface (as a table) over which transactions are conducted or food is served or on which goods are displayed or work is conducted ⟨a lunch ~⟩ — **over the counter** **1** : in or through a broker's office rather than through a stock exchange ⟨stock bought *over the counter*⟩ **2** : without a prescription ⟨drugs available *over the counter*⟩ — **under the counter** : by surreptitious means : in an illicit and private manner

[2]**count·er** *n* [ME, fr. MF *conteor,* fr. *compter* to count] : one that counts; *esp* : a device for indicating a number or amount

[3]**coun·ter** \ˈkau̇nt-ər\ *vb* [ME *countren,* fr. MF *contre*] *vt* **1 a** : to act in opposition to : OPPOSE **b** : OFFSET, NULLIFY ⟨tried to ~ the trend toward depersonalization⟩ **2** : to adduce in answer ⟨he ~*ed* that his warnings had been ignored⟩ ~ *vi* : to meet attacks or arguments with defensive or retaliatory steps

[4]**coun·ter** *adv* [ME *contre,* fr. MF, fr. L *contra* against, opposite; akin to L *com-* with, together — more at CO-] **1** : in an opposite or wrong direction **2** : to or toward a different or opposite direction, result, or effect ⟨values that run ~ to those of established society⟩

[5]**coun·ter** *n* **1** : CONTRARY, OPPOSITE **2** : the after portion of a boat from the waterline to the extreme outward swell or stern overhang **3 a** : the act of making an attack while parrying one (as in boxing or fencing); *also* : a blow thus given in boxing **b** : an agency or force that offsets : CHECK **4** : a stiffener to give permanent form to a boot or shoe upper around the heel **5** : an area in the face of a letter that is less than type-high and enclosed by the strokes — see TYPE illustration **6** : a football play in which the ballcarrier goes in a direction opposite to the movement of the play

[6]**coun·ter** *adj* **1** : marked by or tending toward or in an opposite direction or effect **2** : given to or marked by opposition, hostility, or antipathy **3** : situated or lying opposite ⟨the ~ side⟩ **4** : recalling or ordering back by a superseding contrary order : COUNTERMANDING ⟨~ orders from the colonel⟩ ***syn*** see ADVERSE

coun·ter- *prefix* [ME *contre-,* fr. MF, fr. *contre*] **1 a** : contrary : opposite ⟨*counter*clockwise⟩ ⟨*counter*march⟩ **b** : opposing : retaliatory ⟨*counter*irritant⟩ ⟨*counter*offensive⟩ **2** : complementary : corresponding ⟨*counter*weight⟩ ⟨*counter*part⟩ **3** : duplicate : substitute ⟨*counter*foil⟩

coun·ter·act \ˌkau̇nt-ə-ˈrakt\ *vt* : to make ineffective or restrain or neutralize the usu. ill effects of by an opposite force — **coun·ter·ac·tion** \-ˈrak-shən\ *n*

coun·ter·ac·tive \-ˈrak-tiv\ *adj* : tending to counteract ***syn*** see ADVERSE

[1]**coun·ter·at·tack** \ˈkau̇nt-ə-rə-ˌtak\ *n* : an attack made to counter an enemy's attack

[2]**counterattack** *vi* : to make a counterattack ~ *vt* : to make a counterattack against — **coun·ter·at·tack·er** *n*

[1]**coun·ter·bal·ance** \ˈkau̇nt-ər-ˌbal-ən(t)s, ˌkau̇nt-ər-ˈ\ *n* **1** : a weight that balances another **2** : a force or influence that offsets or checks an opposing force

[2]**counterbalance** \ˌkau̇nt-ər-ˈ, ˈkau̇nt-ər-ˌ\ *vt* **1** : to oppose or balance with an equal weight or force **2** : to equip with counterbalances

coun·ter·blow \ˈkau̇nt-ər-ˌblō\ *n* : a retaliatory blow

coun·ter·change \-ˌchānj\ *vt* **1** : INTERCHANGE, TRANSPOSE **2** : CHECKER 1a

[1]**coun·ter·check** \-ˌchek\ *n* : a check or restraint often operating against something that is itself a check

[2]**countercheck** *vt* **1** : CHECK, COUNTERACT **2** : to check a second time for verification

counter check *n* : a check obtainable at a bank usu. to be cashed only at the bank by the drawer

[1]**coun·ter·claim** \ˈkau̇nt-ər-ˌklām\ *n* : an opposing claim esp. in law

[2]**counterclaim** *vi* : to enter or plead a counterclaim ~ *vt* : to ask in a counterclaim

coun·ter·clock·wise \ˌkau̇nt-ər-ˈkläk-ˌwīz\ *adv* : in a direction opposite to that in which the hands of a clock rotate as viewed from in front — **counterclockwise** *adj*

coun·ter·con·di·tion·ing \-kən-ˈdish-(ə-)niŋ\ *n* : conditioning in order to replace an undesirable response (as fear) to a stimulus (as an engagement in public speaking) by a favorable one

coun·ter·coup \ˈkau̇nt-ər-ˌkü\ *n* : a coup directed toward overthrowing a government which seized power by a coup

coun·ter·cul·ture \-ˌkəl-chər\ *n* : a culture esp. of the young with values and mores that run counter to those of established society — **coun·ter·cul·tur·al** \ˌkau̇nt-ər-ˈkəlch-(ə-)rəl\ *adj* — **coun·ter·cul·tur·ist** \-(ə-)rəst\ *n*

[1]**coun·ter·cur·rent** \ˈkau̇nt-ər-ˌkər-ənt, -ˌkə-rənt\ *n* : a current flowing in a direction opposite that of another current

[2]**countercurrent** \ˌkau̇nt-ər-ˈ\ *adj* **1** : flowing in an opposite direction **2** : involving flow of materials in opposite directions ⟨~ dialysis⟩ — **coun·ter·cur·rent·ly** *adv*

coun·ter·dem·on·stra·tion \ˈkau̇nt-ər-ˌdem-ən-ˈstrā-shən\ *n* : a demonstration opposing another demonstration — **coun·ter·dem·on·strate** \ˌkau̇nt-ər-ˈdem-ən-ˌstrāt\ *vi* — **coun·ter·dem·on·stra·tor** \-ˌstrāt-ər\ *n*

coun·ter·es·pi·o·nage \ˌkau̇nt-ə-ˈres-pē-ə-ˌnäzh, -nij, -ˌnäj; -rə-ˈspē-ə-nij\ *n* : espionage directed toward detecting and thwarting enemy espionage

coun·ter·ex·am·ple \ˈkau̇nt-ə-rig-ˌzam-pəl\ *n* : an example that disproves a theorem or proposition

[1]**coun·ter·feit** \ˈkau̇nt-ər-ˌfit\ *vt* : to imitate or copy closely esp. with intent to deceive ⟨~*ed* interest that she did not feel⟩ ~ *vi* **1** : to try to deceive by pretense or dissembling **2** : to engage in counterfeiting something of value ***syn*** see ASSUME — **coun·ter·feit·er** *n*

[2]**counterfeit** *adj* [ME *countrefet,* fr. MF *contrefait,* fr. pp. of *contrefaire* to imitate, fr. *contre-* + *faire* to make, fr. L *facere* — more at DO] **1** : made in imitation of something else with intent to deceive : FORGED ⟨~ money⟩ **2 a** : INSINCERE, FEIGNED ⟨~ sympathy⟩ **b** : marked by false pretense : SHAM, PRETENDED

[3]**counterfeit** *n* **1** : something counterfeit : FORGERY **2** : something likely to be mistaken for something of higher value ⟨pity was a ~ of love —Harry Hervey⟩ ***syn*** see IMPOSTURE

coun·ter·foil \ˈkau̇nt-ər-ˌfȯil\ *n* : a detachable stub (as on a check or ticket) usu. serving as a record or receipt

coun·ter·force \-ˌfōrs, -ˌfȯrs\ *n* : a force or trend that runs counter to another force or trend

coun·ter·guer·ril·la *also* **coun·ter·gue·ril·la** \ˌkau̇nt-ər-gə-ˈril-ə, -g(y)i-, -ge-\ *n* : a guerrilla who is trained to thwart enemy guerrilla operations

coun·ter·in·sur·gen·cy \ˌkau̇nt-ə-rin-ˈsər-jən-sē\ *n* : organized military activity designed to counter insurgency — **coun·ter·in·sur·gent** \-jənt\ *n*

coun·ter·in·tel·li·gence \ˌkau̇nt-ə-rin-ˈtel-ə-jən(t)s\ *n* : organized activity of an intelligence service designed to block an enemy's sources of information, to deceive the enemy, to prevent sabotage, and to gather political and military information

coun·ter·ir·ri·tant \-ˈrir-ə-tənt\ *n* **1** : an agent applied locally to produce superficial inflammation with the object of reducing inflammation in deeper adjacent structures **2** : an irritation or discomfort that diverts attention from another — **counterirritant** *adj*

count·er·man \ˈkau̇nt-ər-ˌman, -mən\ *n* : one who tends a counter

[1]**coun·ter·mand** \ˈkau̇nt-ər-ˌmand, ˌkau̇nt-ər-ˈ\ *vt* [ME *countermaunden,* fr. MF *contremander,* fr. *contre-* counter- + *mander* to command, fr. L *mandare*] **1** : to revoke (a command) by a contrary order **2** : to recall or order back by a superseding contrary order ⟨~ reinforcements⟩

[2]**coun·ter·mand** \ˈkau̇nt-ər-ˌmand\ *n* **1** : a contrary order **2** : the revocation of an order or command

coun·ter·march \ˈkau̇nt-ər-ˌmärch\ *n* **1** : a marching back; *specif* : a movement in marching by which a unit of troops reverses direction while marching but keeps the same order **2** : a march (as of political demonstrators) designed to counter the effect of another march — **countermarch** *vi*

coun·ter·mea·sure \-ˌmezh-ər, -ˌmā-zhər\ *n* : a measure designed to counter another measure

[1]**coun·ter·mine** \-ˌmīn\ *n* **1** : a tunnel for intercepting an enemy mine **2** : a stratagem for defeating an attack : COUNTERPLOT

[2]**countermine** *vt* **1** : to thwart by secret measures **2** : to oppose or intercept with a countermine ~ *vi* : to make or lay down countermines

coun·ter·move \ˈkau̇nt-ər-ˌmüv\ *n* : a move designed to counter another move

coun·ter·move·ment \-mənt\ *n* : a movement in an opposite direction

coun·ter·of·fen·sive \ˈkau̇nt-ə-rə-ˌfen(t)-siv\ *n* : a large-scale military offensive undertaken by a force previously on the defensive

coun·ter·of·fer \-ˌrȯf-ər, -ˌräf-\ *n* : a return offer made by one who has rejected an offer

coun·ter·pane \ˈkau̇nt-ər-ˌpān\ *n* [alter. of ME *countrepointe,* modif. of MF *coute pointe,* lit., embroidered quilt] : BEDSPREAD

coun·ter·part \-ˌpärt\ *n* **1** : one of two corresponding copies of a legal instrument : DUPLICATE **2 a** : a thing that fits another perfectly **b** : something that completes : COMPLEMENT **3 a** : one remarkably similar to another **b** : one having the same function or characteristics as another : EQUIVALENT ⟨college presidents and their ~*s* in business⟩ ***syn*** see PARALLEL

coun·ter·plan \ˈkau̇nt-ər-ˌplan\ *n* **1** : a plan designed to counter another plan **2** : an alternate or substitute plan

coun·ter·plea \-ˌplē\ *n* : a replication to a legal plea : an answering plea

[1]**coun·ter·plot** \-ˌplät\ *vt* : to intrigue against : foil with a plot

[2]**counterplot** *n* : a plot designed to thwart an opponent's plot

[1]**coun·ter·point** \ˈkau̇nt-ər-ˌpȯint\ *n* [MF *contrepoint,* fr. ML *contrapunctus,* fr. L *contra-* counter- + ML *punctus* musical note, melody, fr. L, act of pricking, fr. *punctus,* pp. of *pungere* to prick — more at POINT] **1 a** : one or more independent melodies added above or below a given melody **b** : the combination of two or more independent melodies into a single harmonic texture in which each retains its linear character : POLYPHONY **2 a** : a complementing or contrasting item : OPPOSITE **b** : use of contrast or interplay of elements in a work of art (as a drama)

[2]**counterpoint** *vt* **1** : to compose or arrange in counterpoint **2** : to set off or emphasize by contrast or juxtaposition : set in contrast ⟨~*s* opposing themes . . . hope and apathy —Curt Leviant⟩

[1]**coun·ter·poise** \-ˌpȯiz\ *vt* [ME *countrepesen,* fr. MF *contrepeser,* fr. *contre-* + *peser* to weigh — more at POISE] : COUNTERBALANCE

[2]**counterpoise** *n* **1** : COUNTERBALANCE **2** : an equivalent power or force acting in opposition **3** : a state of balance

coun·ter·pose \ˌkau̇nt-ər-ˈpōz\ *vt* [*counter-* + *-pose* (as in *compose*)] : to place in opposition, contrast, or equilibrium ⟨*counterposed* an alternative solution to the problem⟩

coun·ter·pro·duc·tive \-prə-ˈdək-tiv\ *adj* : tending to hinder the attainment of a desired goal ⟨violence as a means to achieve an end is ~ —W. E. Brock *b*1930⟩

coun·ter·pro·gram·ming \ˌkau̇nt-ər-ˈprō-ˌgram-iŋ, -grəm-\ *n* : the scheduling of programs by television networks so as to attract audiences away from simultaneously telecast programs of competitors

coun·ter·pro·pa·gan·da \-ˌpräp-ə-ˈgan-də, -ˌprō-pə-\ *n* : propaganda designed to counter enemy propaganda

coun·ter·pro·pos·al \ˈkau̇nt-ər-prə-ˌpō-zəl\ *n* : a return proposal made by one who has rejected a proposal

coun·ter·punch \ˈkau̇nt-ər-ˌpənch\ *n* : a counter in boxing; *also* : a countering blow or attack — **coun·ter·punch·er** \-ˌpən-chər\ *n*

ə abut   ᵊ kitten   ər further   a back   ā bake   ä cot, cart
au̇ out   ch chin   e less   ē easy   g gift   i trip   ī life
j joke   ŋ sing   ō flow   ȯ flaw   ȯi coin   th thin   t͟h this
ü loot   u̇ foot   y yet   yü few   yu̇ furious   zh vision

coun·ter·ref·or·ma·tion \ˌkaůnt-ə(r)-ˌref-ər-ˈmā-shən\ *n* **1** : a reformation designed to counter the effects of a previous reformation **2** *usu* **Counter-Reformation** : the reform movement in the Roman Catholic Church following the Reformation

coun·ter·rev·o·lu·tion \-ˌrev-ə-ˈlü-shən\ *n* : a revolution directed toward overthrowing a government or social system established by a previous revolution — **coun·ter·rev·o·lu·tion·ary** \-shə-ˌner-ē\ *adj or n* — **coun·ter·rev·o·lu·tion·ist** \-sh(ə-)nəst\ *n*

coun·ter·shaft \ˈkaůnt-ər-ˌshaft\ *n* : a shaft that receives motion from a main shaft and transmits it to a working part

[1]**coun·ter·sign** \-ˌsīn\ *n* **1** : a signature attesting the authenticity of a document already signed by another **2** : a sign given in reply to another; *specif* : a military secret signal that must be given by one wishing to pass a guard

[2]**countersign** *vt* **1** : to add one's signature to (a document) after another's so as to attest authenticity **2** : CONFIRM, CORROBORATE — **coun·ter·sig·na·ture** \ˌkaůnt-ər-ˈsig-nə-ˌchů(ə)r, -chər, -ˌt(y)ů(ə)r\ *n*

[1]**coun·ter·sink** \ˈkaůnt-ər-ˌsiŋk\ *vt* **-sunk** \-ˌsəŋk\; **-sink·ing** **1** : to make a countersink on **2** : to set the head of (as a screw) at or below the surface

[2]**countersink** *n* **1** : a funnel-shaped enlargement at the outer end of a drilled hole **2** : a bit or drill for making a countersink

coun·ter·spy \ˈkaůnt-ər-ˌspī\ *n* : a spy engaged in counterespionage

coun·ter·state·ment \-ˌstāt-mənt\ *n* : a statement opposing or denying another statement : REJOINDER

coun·ter·ten·or \-ˌten-ər\ *n* [ME *countretenour*, fr. MF *contreteneur*, fr. *contre-* + *teneur* tenor] : a tenor with an unusually high range and tessitura

coun·ter·ter·ror·ism \ˌkaůnt-ər-ˈter-ər-ˌiz-əm\ *n* : retaliatory terrorism — **coun·ter·ter·ror·ist** \-ər-əst\ *adj*

coun·ter·trend \ˈkaůnt-ər-ˌtrend\ *n* : a trend that runs counter to another trend

coun·ter·vail \ˌkaůnt-ər-ˈvā(ə)l\ *vb* [ME *countrevailen*, fr. MF *contrevaloir*, fr. *contre-* counter- + *valoir* to be worth, fr. L *valēre* — more at WIELD] *vt* **1** : to compensate for **2** *archaic* : EQUAL, MATCH **3** : to exert force against : COUNTERACT ~ *vi* : to exert force against an opposing and often bad or harmful force or influence ***syn*** see COMPENSATE

coun·ter·view \ˈkaůnt-ər-ˌvyü\ *n* **1** *archaic* : CONFRONTATION **2** : an opposite point of view

coun·ter·weight \-ˌwāt\ *n* : an equivalent weight : COUNTERBALANCE — **counterweight** *vt*

count·ess \ˈkaůnt-əs\ *n* **1** : the wife or widow of an earl or count **2** : a woman who holds in her own right the rank of earl or count

coun·ti·an \ˈkaůnt-ē-ən\ *n* : a native or resident of a usu. specified county

count·ing·house \ˈkaůnt-iŋ-ˌhaůs\ *n* : a building, room, or office used for keeping books and transacting business

counting room *n* : COUNTINGHOUSE

counting tube *n* : an ionization chamber designed to respond to passage through it of fast-moving ionizing particles and usu. connected to some device for counting the particles — called also *counter tube*

count·less \ˈkaůnt-ləs\ *adj* : too numerous to be counted : MYRIAD — **count·less·ly** *adv*

count noun *n* : a noun (as *bean* or *sheet*) that forms a plural and is used with a numeral, with words such as *many* or *few*, or with the indefinite article *a* or *an* — compare MASS NOUN

count palatine *n* **1** **a** : a high judicial official in the Holy Roman Empire **b** : a count of the Holy Roman Empire having imperial powers in his own domain **2** : the proprietor of a county palatine in England or Ireland

coun·tri·fied *also* **coun·try·fied** \ˈkən-tri-ˌfīd\ *adj* [*country* + *-fied* (as in *glorified*)] **1** : RURAL, RUSTIC **2** : UNSOPHISTICATED

[1]**coun·try** \ˈkən-trē\ *n, pl* **countries** [ME *contree*, fr. OF *contrée*, fr. ML *contrata*, fr. L *contra* against, on the opposite side] **1** : an indefinite usu. extended expanse of land : REGION **2** **a** : the land of a person's birth, residence, or citizenship **b** : a political state or nation or its territory **3** **a** : the people of a state or district : POPULACE **b** : JURY **c** : ELECTORATE **4** : rural as distinguished from urban areas **5** : COUNTRY MUSIC — **coun·try·ish** \-trē-ish\ *adj*

[2]**country** *adj* **1** : of, relating to, or characteristic of the country **2** : prepared or processed with farm supplies and procedures **3** : of or relating to country music ⟨~ singers⟩

country and western *n* : COUNTRY MUSIC

country club *n* : a suburban club for social life and recreation

coun·try–dance \ˈkən-trē-ˌdan(t)s\ *n* : any of various native English dances in which partners face each other esp. in rows

country gentleman *n* **1** : a well-to-do country resident : an owner of a country estate **2** : one of the English landed gentry

country house *n* : a house in the country; *specif* : COUNTRYSEAT

coun·try·man \ˈkən-trē-mən, *3 often* -ˌman\ *n* **1** : an inhabitant or native of a specified country **2** : COMPATRIOT **3** : one living in the country or marked by country ways : RUSTIC

country music *n* : music derived from or imitating the folk style of the southern U.S. or of the Western cowboy

coun·try·seat \ˌkən-trē-ˈsēt\ *n* : a mansion or estate in the country

coun·try·side \ˈkən-trē-ˌsīd\ *n* **1** : a rural area **2** : the inhabitants of a countryside

country singer *n* : one who sings country music or in the style of country music

coun·try·wom·an \ˈkən-trē-ˌwům-ən\ *n* **1** : a woman compatriot **2** : a woman resident of the country

[1]**coun·ty** \ˈkaůnt-ē\ *n, pl* **counties** [ME *counte*, fr. OF *conté*, fr. ML *comitatus*, fr. LL, office of a count, fr. *comit-*, *comes* count — more at COUNT] **1** : the domain of a count **2** **a** : one of the territorial divisions of Great Britain and Ireland constituting the chief units for administrative, judicial, and political purposes **b** (1) : the people of a county (2) *Brit* : the gentry of a county **3** : the largest territorial division for local government within a state of the U.S. **4** : the largest local administrative unit in various countries — **county** *adj*

[2]**county** *n, pl* **counties** [modif. of MF *comte*] *obs* : [3]COUNT

county agent *n* : a consultant employed jointly by federal and state governments to provide information about agriculture and home economics by means of lectures, demonstrations, and discussions in rural areas

county court *n* : a court in some states that has a designated jurisdiction usu. both civil and criminal within the limits of a county

county fair *n* : a fair usu. held annually at a set location in a county esp. to exhibit local agricultural products and livestock

county palatine *n* : the territory of a count palatine

county seat *n* : a town that is the seat of county administration

county town *n, chiefly Brit* : COUNTY SEAT

[1]**coup** \ˈkōp\ *vb* [ME *coupen* to strike, fr. MF *couper* — more at COPE] *chiefly Scot* : OVERTURN, UPSET

[2]**coup** \ˈkü\ *n, pl* **coups** \ˈküz\ [F, blow, stroke — more at COPE] **1** : a brilliant, sudden, and usu. highly successful stroke or act **2** : COUP D'ETAT

coup de grace \ˌküd-ə-ˈgräs\ *n, pl* **coups de grace** \ˌküd-ə-\ [F *coup de grâce*, lit., stroke of mercy] **1** : a death blow or shot administered to end the suffering of one mortally wounded **2** : a decisive finishing blow, act, or event

coup de main \-ˈmaⁿ\ *n, pl* **coups de main** \ˌküd-ə-\ [F, lit., hand stroke] : a sudden attack in force

coup d'etat \ˌküd-ə-ˈtä, ˌküd-(ˌ)ā-\ *n, pl* **coups d'etat** \ˌküd-ə-ˈtä(z), ˌküd-(ˌ)ā-\ [F *coup d'état*, lit., stroke of state] : a sudden decisive exercise of force in politics; *esp* : the violent overthrow or alteration of an existing government by a small group

coup de the·atre \ˌküd-ə-tā-ˈätrᵊ\ *n, pl* **coups de theatre** \ˌküd-ə-\ [F *coup de théâtre*, lit., stroke of theater] **1** : a sudden sensational turn in a play; *also* : a sudden dramatic turn of events **2** : a theatrical success

coup d'oeil \kü-ˈdə(r), -ˈdəi\ *n, pl* **coups d'oeil** *same*\ [F, lit., stroke of the eye] : a brief survey : GLANCE

cou·pé *or* **coupe** \kü-ˈpā, *2 often* ˈküp\ *n* [F *coupé*, fr. pp. of *couper* to cut] **1** : a four-wheeled closed horse-drawn carriage for two persons inside with an outside seat for the driver in front **2** *usu coupe* **a** : a closed 2-door automobile for usu. two persons **b** : a usu. closed 2-door automobile with a full-width rear seat

[1]**cou·ple** \ˈkəp-əl\ *vb* **cou·pled; cou·pling** \-(ə-)liŋ\ *vt* **1** : to connect for consideration together ⟨*coupled* his praise with a request⟩ **2** **a** : to fasten together : LINK **b** : to bring (two electric circuits) into such close proximity as to permit mutual influence **3** : to join in marriage or sexual union ~ *vi* **1** : to unite in sexual union **2** : JOIN **3** : to unite chemically usu. with elimination of a simple molecule

[2]**couple** \ˈkəp-əl; *"couple of" is often* ˌkəp-lə(v)\ *n* [ME, pair, bond, fr. OF *cople*, fr. L *copula* bond, fr. *co-* + *apere* to fasten — more at APT] **1** **a** : a man and woman married, engaged, or otherwise paired **b** : two persons paired together **2** : PAIR, BRACE **3** : something that joins or links two things together: as **a** : two equal and opposite forces that act along parallel lines **b** : GALVANIC COUPLE **4** : an indefinite small number : FEW ⟨a ~ of days ago⟩

[3]**couple** *adj* : TWO — used with *a* ⟨a ~ more drinks⟩

cou·ple·ment \ˈkəp-əl-mənt\ *n* [MF, fr. *coupler* to join, fr. L *copulare*, fr. *copula*] *archaic* : the act or result of coupling

cou·pler \ˈkəp-(ə-)lər\ *n* **1** : one that couples **2** : a contrivance on a keyboard instrument by which keyboards or keys are connected to play together

cou·plet \ˈkəp-lət\ *n* [MF, dim. of *cople*] **1** : two successive lines of verse forming a unit marked usu. by rhythmic correspondence, rhyme, or the inclusion of a self-contained utterance : DISTICH **2** : COUPLE **3** : one of the musical episodes alternating with the main theme (as in a rondo)

cou·pling \ˈkəp-liŋ (*usual for 2*), -ə-liŋ\ *n* **1** : the act of bringing or coming together : PAIRING; *specif* : sexual union **2** : a device that serves to connect the ends of adjacent parts or objects **3** : the joining of or the part of the body that joins the hindquarters to the forequarters of a quadruped **4** : means of electric connection of two electric circuits by having a part common to both

cou·pon \ˈk(y)ü-ˌpän\ *n* [F, fr. OF, piece, fr. *couper* to cut — more at COPE] **1** : a statement of due interest to be cut from a bearer bond when payable and presented for payment **2** : a form surrendered in order to obtain an article, service, or accommodation: as **a** : one of a series of attached tickets or certificates often to be detached and presented as needed **b** : a ticket or form authorizing purchases of rationed commodities **c** : a certificate or similar evidence of a purchase redeemable in premiums **d** : a part of a printed advertisement to be cut off for use as an order blank or inquiry form

cour·age \ˈkər-ij, ˈkə-rij\ *n* [ME *corage*, fr. OF, fr. *cuer* heart, fr. L *cor* — more at HEART] : mental or moral strength to venture, persevere, and withstand danger, fear, or difficulty

syn COURAGE, METTLE, SPIRIT, RESOLUTION, TENACITY *shared meaning element* : mental or moral strength to resist opposition, danger, or hardship. COURAGE implies firmness of mind and will in the face of danger or extreme difficulty ⟨but screw your *courage* to the sticking place, and we'll not fail —Shak.⟩ METTLE suggests an ingrained capacity for meeting strain or stress with fortitude and resilience ⟨a situation to try the *mettle* of the most resolute man⟩ SPIRIT suggests a quality of temperament that enables one to hold one's own against opposition, interference, or temptation ⟨constant unremitting drudgery had slowly broken his *spirit*⟩ RESOLUTION stresses firmness of character and determination to achieve one's ends ⟨approach an unpleasant task with *resolution*⟩ TENACITY adds an implication of stubborn persistence and unwillingness to acknowledge defeat ⟨the *tenacity* of the bulldog breed⟩ ***ant*** cowardice

cou·ra·geous \kə-ˈrā-jəs\ *adj* : having or characterized by courage : BRAVE — **cou·ra·geous·ly** *adv* — **cou·ra·geous·ness** *n*

cou·rante \kü-'ränt, -'rant\ *n* [MF, fr. *courir* to run, fr. L *currere*] **1 :** a dance of Italian origin marked by quick running steps **2 :** music in quick triple time or in a mixture of 3/2 and 6/4 time

cou·reur de bois \kü-ˌrərd-əb-'wä\ *n, pl* **coureurs de bois** *same*\ [CanF, lit., woods runner] **:** a French or half-breed trapper of No. America and esp. of Canada

cour·gette \kůr-'zhet\ *n* [F dial., dim. of *courge* gourd, fr. L *cucurbita*] *chiefly Brit* **:** ZUCCHINI

cou·ri·er \'kůr-ē-ər, 'kər-ē-, 'kə-rē-\ *n* [MF *courrier,* fr. OIt *corriere,* fr. *correre* to run, fr. L *currere*] **1 :** MESSENGER: as **a :** a member of a diplomatic service entrusted with bearing messages **b** (1) **:** an espionage agent transferring secret information (2) **:** a runner of contraband **c :** a member of the armed services whose duties include carrying mail, information, or supplies **2 :** a traveler's paid attendant; *esp* **:** a tourists' guide employed by a travel agency

cour·lan \'kůr(ə)r-lən\ *n* [F, modif. of Galibi *kurliri*] **:** a long-billed bird (*Aramus guarana*) that is intermediate in some respects between the cranes and rails and occurs in So. and Central America

1**course** \'kō(ə)rs, 'kȯ(ə)rs\ *n* [ME, fr OF, fr. L *cursus,* fr. *cursus,* pp. of *currere* to run — more at CAR] **1 a :** the act or action of moving in a path from point to point **b :** LIFE HISTORY, CAREER **2 :** the path over which something moves: as **a :** RACECOURSE **b** (1) **:** the direction of flight of an airplane usu. measured as a clockwise angle from north (2) **:** a point of the compass **c :** WATERCOURSE **d :** GOLF COURSE **3 a :** accustomed procedure or normal action ⟨the law taking its ~⟩ **b :** a chosen manner of conducting oneself **:** BEHAVIOR ⟨our wisest ~ is to retreat⟩ **c :** progression through a series of acts or events or a development or period **4 :** an ordered process or succession: as **a :** a series of lectures or other matter dealing with a subject; *also* **:** a series of such courses constituting a curriculum **b :** a series of doses or medicaments administered over a designated period **5 a :** a part of a meal served at one time **b :** ROW, LAYER; *esp* **:** a continuous level range of brick or masonry throughout a wall **c :** the lowest sail on a square-rigged mast — **in due course :** after a normal passage of time **:** in the expected or allotted time — **of course 1 :** following the ordinary way or procedure **2 :** as might be expected

2**course** *vb* **coursed; cours·ing** *vt* **1 a :** to hunt or pursue (game) with hounds **b :** to cause (dogs) to run (as after game) **2 :** to follow close upon **:** PURSUE **3 :** to run or move swiftly through or over **:** TRAVERSE ⟨jets *coursed* the area daily⟩ ~ *vi* **:** to run or pass rapidly along or as if along an indicated path ⟨blood *coursing* through his veins⟩

course of study 1 : the total number of courses offered by a school **:** CURRICULUM **2 :** COURSE 4a

1**cours·er** \'kōr-sər, 'kȯr-\ *n* [ME, fr. OF *coursier,* fr. *course* course, run] **:** a swift or spirited horse **:** CHARGER

2**courser** *n* **1 :** a dog for coursing **2 :** one that courses **:** HUNTSMAN **3 :** any of various birds (subfamily Cursoriinae of the family Glareolidae) of Africa and southern Asia related to the plovers and noted for their speed in running

cours·ing *n* **1 :** the act of one that courses **2 :** the pursuit of running game with dogs that follow by sight instead of by scent

1**court** \'kō(ə)rt, 'kȯ(ə)rt\ *n, often attrib* [ME, fr. OF, fr. L *cohort-, cohors* enclosure, throng, cohort, fr. *co-* + *-hort-, -hors* (akin to *hortus* garden) — more at YARD] **1 a :** the residence or establishment of a sovereign or similar dignitary **b :** a sovereign's formal assembly of his councillors and officers **c :** the sovereign and his officers and advisers who are the governing power **d :** the family and retinue of a sovereign **e :** a reception held by a sovereign **2 a** (1) **:** a manor house or large building surrounded by usu. enclosed grounds (2) **:** MOTEL **b :** an open space enclosed wholly or partly by buildings or circumscribed by a single building **c :** a quadrangular space walled or marked off for playing one of various games with a ball (as lawn tennis, racquets, handball, or basketball) or a division of such a court **d :** a wide alley with only one opening onto a street **3 a :** an official assembly for the transaction of judicial business **b :** a session of such a court ⟨~ is now adjourned⟩ **c :** a place (as a chamber) for the administration of justice **d :** a judge or judges in session **e :** a faculty or agency of judgment or evaluation ⟨rest our case in the ~ of world opinion — L. H. Marks⟩ **4 a :** an assembly or board with legislative or administrative powers **b :** PARLIAMENT, LEGISLATURE **5 :** conduct or attention intended to win favor or dispel hostility **:** HOMAGE ⟨pay ~ to the king⟩

2**court** *vt* **1 a :** to seek to gain or achieve **b** (1) **:** ALLURE, TEMPT (2) **:** to act so as to invite or provoke ⟨~*s* disaster⟩ **2 a :** to seek the affections of **b** *of an animal* **:** to perform actions in order to attract for mating **3 :** to seek to attract by attentions and flatteries ~ *vi* **1 :** to engage in social activities leading to engagement and marriage **2** *of an animal* **:** to engage in activity leading to mating ***syn*** see INVITE

cour·te·ous \'kərt-ē-əs, *esp Brit* 'kȯrt-\ *adj* [ME *corteis,* fr. OF, fr. *court*] **1 :** marked by polished manners, gallantry, or ceremonial usage of a court **2 :** marked by respect for and consideration of others ***syn*** see CIVIL ***ant*** discourteous — **cour·te·ous·ly** *adv* — **cour·te·ous·ness** *n*

cour·te·san \'kōrt-ə-zən, 'kȯrt-, -ˌzan *also* 'kərt-\ *n* [MF *courtisane,* fr. OIt *cortigiana* woman courtier, fem. of *cortigiano* courtier, fr. *corte* court, fr. L *cohort-, cohors*] **:** a prostitute with a courtly, wealthy, or upper-class clientele

1**cour·te·sy** \'kərt-ə-sē, *esp Brit* 'kȯrt-\ *n, pl* **-sies** [ME *corteisie,* fr. OF, fr. *corteis*] **1 a :** courteous behavior **b :** a courteous act or expression **2 a :** general allowance despite facts **:** INDULGENCE ⟨hills called mountains by ~ only⟩ **b :** consideration, cooperation, and generosity in providing; *also* **:** AGENCY, MEANS

2**courtesy** *adj* **:** granted, provided, or performed as a courtesy or by way of courtesy ⟨made a ~ call on the ambassador⟩

courtesy card *n* **:** a card entitling its holder to some special privilege

courtesy title *n* **1 :** a title (as "Lord" added to the Christian name of a peer's younger son) used in addressing certain lineal relatives of British peers **2 :** a title (as "Professor" for any teacher) taken by the user and commonly accepted without consideration of official right

court game *n* **:** an athletic game (as tennis, handball, or basketball) played on a court

court·house \'kō(ə)rt-ˌhau̇s, 'kȯ(ə)rt-\ *n* **1 a :** a building in which courts of law are regularly held **b :** the principal building in which county offices are housed **2 :** COUNTY SEAT

court·ier \'kōrt-ē-ər, 'kōrt-yər, 'kȯrt-; 'kōr-chər, 'kȯr-\ *n* **1 :** one in attendance at a royal court **2 :** one who practices flattery

1**court·ly** \'kō(ə)rt-lē, 'kȯ(ə)rt-\ *adj* **court·li·er; -est 1 a :** of a quality befitting the court **:** ELEGANT **b :** insincerely flattering **2 :** favoring the policy or party of the court — **court·li·ness** *n*

2**courtly** *adv* **:** in a courtly manner **:** POLITELY

courtly love *n* **:** a late medieval conventionalized code prescribing conduct and emotions of ladies and their lovers

1**court–mar·tial** \'kōrt-ˌmär-shəl, 'kȯrt-, -'mär-\ *n, pl* **courts–martial** *also* **court–martials 1 :** a court consisting of commissioned officers and in some instances enlisted personnel for the trial of members of the armed forces or others within its jurisdiction **2 :** a trial by court-martial

2**court–martial** *vt* **–mar·tialed** *also* **–mar·tialled; –mar·tial·ing** *also* **–mar·tial·ling** \-ˌmärsh-(ə-)liŋ, -'märsh-\ **:** to subject to trial by court-martial

court of appeal : a court hearing appeals from the decisions of lower courts — called also *court of appeals*

court of claims : a court that has jurisdiction over claims (as against a government)

court of common pleas 1 : a former English superior court having civil jurisdiction **2 :** an intermediate court in some American states that usu. has civil and criminal jurisdiction

court of domestic relations : a court that has jurisdiction and often special advisory powers over family disputes involving the rights and duties of husband, wife, parent, or child esp. in matters affecting the support, custody, and welfare of children

court of honor : a tribunal (as a military court) for investigating questions of personal honor

court of inquiry : a military court that inquires into and reports on some military matter (as an officer's questionable conduct)

court of law : a court that hears cases and decides them on the basis of statutes or the common law

court of record : a court whose acts and proceedings are kept on permanent record

Court of St. James's \-sānt-'jāmz, -sənt-\ [fr. *St. James's* Palace, London, former seat of the British court] **:** the British court

court of sessions : any of various state criminal courts of record

court order *n* **:** an order issuing from a competent court that requires a person to do or abstain from doing a specified act

court plaster *n* [fr. its use for beauty spots by ladies at royal courts] **:** an adhesive plaster esp. of silk coated with isinglass and glycerin

court reporter *n* **:** a stenographer who records and transcribes a verbatim report of all proceedings in a court of law

court·room \'kō(ə)rt-ˌrüm, 'kȯ(ə)rt-, -ˌru̇m\ *n* **:** a room in which a court of law is held

court·ship \-ˌship\ *n* **:** the act, process, or period of courting

court·side \-ˌsīd\ *n* **:** the area at the edge of a court (as for tennis or basketball)

court tennis *n* **:** a game played with a ball and racket in an enclosed court divided by a net

court·yard \'kō(ə)rt-ˌyärd, 'kȯ(ə)rt-\ *n* **:** a court or enclosure adjacent to a building (as a house or palace)

cous·in \'kəz-ᵊn\ *n* [ME *cosin,* fr. OF, fr. L *consobrinus,* fr. *com-* + *sobrinus* cousin on the mother's side, fr. *soror* sister — more at SISTER] **1 a :** a child of one's uncle or aunt **b :** a relative descended from one's grandparent or more remote ancestor in a different line **c :** KINSMAN, RELATIVE ⟨a distant ~⟩ **2 :** one associated with another **:** EQUIVALENT **3** — used as a title by a sovereign in addressing a nobleman **4 :** a person of a race or people ethnically or culturally related ⟨our English ~*s*⟩ — **cous·in·hood** \-ˌhu̇d\ *n* — **cous·in·ship** \-ˌship\ *n*

cous·in·age \'kəz-ᵊn-ij\ *n* **1 :** relationship of cousins **:** KINSHIP **2 :** a collection of cousins **:** KINFOLK

cous·in–ger·man \ˌkəz-ᵊn-'jər-mən\ *n, pl* **cous·ins–ger·man** \-ᵊnz-\ [ME *cosin germain,* fr. MF, fr. OF, fr. *cosin* + *germain* german] **:** COUSIN 1a

Cousin Jack \ˌkəz-ᵊn-'jak\ *n* **:** CORNISHMAN; *esp* **:** a Cornish miner

1**couth** \'küth\ *adj* [back-formation fr. *uncouth*] **:** SOPHISTICATED, POLISHED

2**couth** *n* **:** POLISH, REFINEMENT ⟨lacks ~ but has ample energy and acting talent —*Newsweek*⟩

couth·ie \'kü-thē\ *adj* [ME *couth*] *chiefly Scot* **:** PLEASANT, KINDLY

cou·ture \kü-'tu̇(ə)r, -'tu̇er\ *n* [F, fr. OF *cousture* sewing, fr. (assumed) VL *consutura,* fr. L *consutus,* pp. of *consuere* to sew together, fr. *com-* + *suere* to sew — more at SEW] **:** the business of designing, making, and selling fashionable custom-made women's clothing; *also* **:** the designers and establishments engaged in this business

cou·tu·ri·er \kü-'tu̇r-ē-ər, -ē-ˌā\ *n* [F, dressmaker, fr. OF *cousturier* tailor's assistant, fr. *cousture*] **:** an establishment engaged in couture; *also* **:** the proprietor of or designer for such an establishment

cou·tu·ri·ere \kü-'tu̇r-ē-ər, -ē-ˌe(ə)r\ *n* [F *couturière,* fr. OF *cousturiere,* fem. of *cousturier*] **:** a female couturier

cou·vade \kü-'väd\ *n* [F, fr. MF, cowardly inactivity, fr. *cover* to sit on, brood over — more at COVEY] **:** a custom among some primitive peoples in accordance with which when a child is born the father takes to bed as if bearing the child, cares for it, and submits himself to fasting, purification, or taboos

co·va·lence \(')kō-'vā-lən(t)s\ *n* : valence characterized by the sharing of electrons; *also* : the number of pairs of electrons an atom can share with its neighbors — compare ELECTROVALENCE — **co·va·lent** \-lənt\ *adj* — **co·va·lent·ly** *adv*

co·va·len·cy \-lən-sē\ *n* : COVALENCE

covalent bond *n* : a nonionic chemical bond formed by shared electrons

co·var·i·ance \(')kō-'ver-ē-ən(t)s, -'var-\ *n* **1** : the expected value of the product of the deviations of two random variables from their respective means **2** : the arithmetic mean of the products of the deviations of corresponding values of two quantitative variables from their respective means

co·var·i·ant \-ənt\ *adj* [ISV] : varying with something else so as to preserve certain mathematical interrelations

¹cove \'kōv\ *n* [ME, den, fr. OE *cofa*; akin to OE *cot*] **1** : a recessed place : CONCAVITY: as **a** : an architectural member with a concave cross section **b** : a trough for concealed lighting at the upper part of a wall **2** : a small sheltered inlet or bay **3 a** : a deep recess or small valley in the side of a mountain **b** : a level area sheltered by hills or mountains

²cove *vt* **coved; cov·ing** : to make in a hollow concave form

³cove *n* [Romany *kova* thing, person] *Brit* : MAN, FELLOW

co·ven \'kəv-ən, 'kō-vən\ *n* [ME *covin* band, fr. MF, fr. ML *convenium* agreement, fr. L *convenire* to agree — more at CONVENTION] : an assembly or band of usu. 13 witches

¹cov·e·nant \'kəv-(ə-)nənt\ *n* [ME, fr. OF, fr. prp. of *covenir* to agree, fr. L *convenire*] **1** : a usu. formal, solemn, and binding agreement : COMPACT **2 a** : a written agreement or promise usu. under seal between two or more parties esp. for the performance of some action **b** : the common-law action to recover damages for breach of such a contract — **cov·e·nan·tal** \,kəv-ə-'nant-ᵊl\ *adj*

²cov·e·nant \'kəv-(ə-)nənt, -ə-,nant\ *vi* : to promise by a covenant : PLEDGE ~ *vt* : to enter into a covenant : CONTRACT

cov·e·nan·tee \,kəv-ə-nan-'tē, -nən-\ *n* : the person to whom a promise in the form of a covenant is made

cov·e·nant·er \'kəv-ə-,nant-ər, 2 also ,kəv-ə-'\ *n* **1** : one that makes a covenant **2** *cap* : a signer or adherent of the Scottish National Covenant of 1638

cov·e·nan·tor \'kəv-ə-,nant-ər; ,kəv-ə-nan-'tȯ(ə)r, -nən-\ *n* : the party to a covenant bound to perform the obligation expressed in it

Cov·en·try \'kəv-ən-trē, 'käv-\ *n* [*Coventry*, England] : a state of ostracism or exclusion (sent to ~)

¹cov·er \'kəv-ər\ *vb* **cov·ered; cov·er·ing** \'kəv-(ə-)riŋ\ [ME *coveren*, fr. OF *covrir*, fr. L *cooperire*, fr. co- + *operire* to close, cover — more at WEIR] *vt* **1 a** : to guard from attack **b** (1) : to have within the range of one's guns : COMMAND (2) : to hold within range of an aimed firearm **c** (1) : to afford protection or security to : INSURE (2) : to afford protection against or compensation for **d** (1) : to guard (an opponent) in order to obstruct a play (2) : to be in position to receive a throw to (a base in baseball) **e** (1) : to make provision for (a demand or charge) by means of a reserve or deposit (his balance was insufficient to ~ his check) (2) : to maintain a check on esp. by patrolling (3) : to protect by contrivance or expedient **2 a** : to hide from sight or knowledge : CONCEAL (~ up a scandal) **b** : to lie over : ENVELOP **3** : to lay or spread something over : OVERLAY **4 a** : to spread over **b** : to appear here and there on the surface of **5** : to place or set a cover or covering over **6 a** : to copulate with (a female animal) (a horse ~s a mare) **b** : to sit on and incubate (eggs) **7** : to invest with a large or excessive amount of something (~s himself with glory) **8** : to play a higher-ranking card on (a previously played card) **9** : to have sufficient scope to include or take into account **10** : to deal with : TREAT **11 a** : to have as one's territory or field of activity (one salesman ~s the whole state) **b** : to report news about **12** : to pass over : TRAVERSE **13** : to place one's stake in equal jeopardy with in a bet **14** : to buy securities or commodities for delivery against (an earlier short sale) ~ *vi* **1** : to conceal something illicit, blameworthy, or embarrassing from notice (~ up for a friend) **2** : to act as a substitute or replacement during an absence — **cov·er·able** \'kəv-(ə-)rə-bəl\ *adj*

cov·er·er \-ər-ər\ *n* — **cover one's tracks** : to conceal traces in order to elude pursuers — **cover the ground** *or* **cover ground 1** : to traverse a course or distance with satisfying speed **2** : to handle an assignment thoroughly and efficiently

²cover *n*, *often attrib* **1** : something that protects, shelters, or guards: as **a** : natural shelter for an animal; *also* : the factors that provide such shelter **b** (1) : a position or situation affording protection from enemy fire (2) : the protection offered by airplanes in tactical support of a military operation **2** : something that is placed over or about another thing: **a** : LID, TOP **b** : a binding or case for a book; *also* : the front or back of such a binding **c** : an overlay or outer layer esp. for protection (a mattress ~) **d** : a tablecloth and the other table fittings **e** : COVER CHARGE **f** : ROOF **g** : a cloth used on a bed **h** : something (as vegetation or snow) that covers the ground **i** : the extent to which clouds obscure the sky **3 a** : something that conceals or obscures (under ~ of darkness) **b** : a masking device : PRETEXT (the project was a ~ for intelligence operations) **4** : an envelope or wrapper for mail **5** : one who substitutes for another during an absence — **cov·er·less** \-ər-ləs\ *adj* — **under cover 1** : in an envelope or wrapper **2** : under concealment : in secret

cov·er·age \'kəv-(ə-)rij\ *n* **1** : the act or fact of covering: **a** : something that covers: as **a** : inclusion within the scope of an insurance policy or protective plan : INSURANCE **b** : the amount available to meet liabilities **c** : inclusion within the scope of discussion or reporting (the news ~ of the trial) **3** : the total group covered : SCOPE: as **a** : all the risks covered by the terms of an insurance contract **b** : the number or percentage of persons reached by a communications medium

cov·er·all \'kəv-ər-,rȯl\ *n* : a one-piece outer garment worn to protect other garments — usu. used in pl. — **cov·er·alled** \-,rȯld\ *adj*

cover·all \'kəv-ər-,rȯl\ *adj* : COMPREHENSIVE (~ provisions)

cover charge *n* : a charge made by a restaurant or nightclub in addition to the charge for food and drink

cover crop *n* : a crop planted to prevent soil erosion and to provide humus

covered bridge *n* : a bridge that has its roadway protected by a roof and enclosing sides

covered smut *n* : a smut disease of grains in which the spore masses are held together by the persistent grain membrane and glumes

covered wagon *n* : a wagon with a canvas top supported by bowed strips of wood or metal

cover girl *n* : an attractive girl whose picture appears on a magazine cover

cover glass *n* **1** : a piece of very thin glass used to cover material on a glass microscope slide **2** : a sheet of plain glass applied to a transparency for protection

¹cov·er·ing \'kəv-(ə-)riŋ\ *n* : something that covers or conceals

²covering *adj* : containing explanation of or additional information about an accompanying communication (a ~ letter)

cov·er·let \'kəv-ər-lət, -(,)lid\ *n* [ME, alter. of *coverlite*, fr. AF *coverelyth*, fr. OF *covrir* + *lit* bed, fr. L *lectus* — more at LIE] : BEDSPREAD

cover shot *n* : a wide-angle photographic shot that includes a whole scene

cov·er·slip \'kəv-ər-,slip\ *n* : COVER GLASS 1

cover story *n* : a story accompanying a magazine-cover illustration

¹co·vert \'kō-(,)vərt, kō-'; 'kəv-ərt\ *adj* [ME, fr. OF, pp. of *covrir* to cover] **1** : not openly shown, engaged in, or avowed : VEILED (a ~ alliance) (~ dislike concealed under apparent goodwill) **2** : covered over : SHELTERED **3** : being married and under the authority or protection of one's husband *syn* see SECRET *ant* overt — **co·vert·ly** *adv* — **co·vert·ness** *n*

²co·vert \'kəv-ərt, 'kō-vərt\ *n* **1 a** : hiding place : SHELTER **b** : a thicket affording cover for game **c** : a masking or concealing device **2** : a feather covering the bases of the quills of the wings and tail of a bird — see BIRD illustration **3** : a firm durable twilled sometimes waterproofed cloth usu. of mixed-color yarns

cover text *n* : a text in plain language within which a ciphertext is concealed

cov·er·ture \'kəv-ər-,chù(ə)r, -chər, -,t(y)ù(ə)r\ *n* **1 a** : COVERING **b** : SHELTER **2** : the status a woman acquires upon marriage under common law

cov·er·up \'kəv-ər-,əp\ *n* : a device or stratagem for masking or concealing (indifference to others ... is a ~ for a lack of easy sociability —Marguerite Barze)

cov·et \'kəv-ət\ *vb* [ME *coveiten*, fr. OF *coveitier*, fr. *coveitié* desire, modif. of L *cupiditat-, cupiditas*, fr. *cupidus* desirous, fr. *cupere* to desire; akin to L *vapor* steam, vapor, Gk *kapnos* smoke] *vt* **1** : to wish for enviously **2** : to desire (what belongs to another) inordinately or culpably ~ *vi* : to feel inordinate desire for what belongs to another *syn* see DESIRE — **cov·et·able** \-ə-bəl\ *adj* — **cov·et·er** \-ər\ *n* — **cov·et·ing·ly** \-iŋ-lē\ *adv*

cov·et·ous \-əs\ *adj* **1** : marked by inordinate desire for wealth or possessions or for another's possessions **2** : having a craving for possession (~ of power) — **cov·et·ous·ly** *adv* — **cov·et·ous·ness** *n*

syn COVETOUS, GREEDY, ACQUISITIVE, GRASPING, AVARICIOUS *shared meaning element* : having or showing a strong desire for possessions and esp. material possessions

cov·ey \'kəv-ē\ *n, pl* **coveys** [ME, fr. MF *covee*, fr. OF, fr. *cover* to sit on, brood over, fr. L *cubare* to lie — more at HIP] **1** : a mature bird or pair of birds with a brood of young; *also* : a small flock **2** : COMPANY, GROUP

¹cow \'kaù\ *n* [ME *cou*, fr. OE *cū*; akin to OHG *kuo* cow, L *bos* head of cattle, Gk *bous*, Skt *go*] **1** : the mature female of cattle (genus *Bos*) or of any animal the male of which is called *bull* (as the moose) **2** : a domestic bovine animal regardless of sex or age — **cowy** \-ē\ *adj*

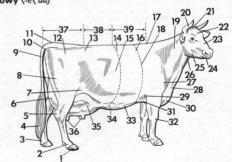

cow: 1 hoof, 2 pastern, 3 dewclaw, 4 switch, 5 hock, 6 rear udder, 7 flank, 8 thigh, 9 tail, 10 pinbone, 11 tail head, 12 thurl, 13 hip, 14 barrel, 15 ribs, 16 crops, 17 withers, 18 heart girth, 19 neck, 20 horn, 21 poll, 22 forehead, 23 bridge of nose, 24 muzzle, 25 jaw, 26 throat, 27 point of shoulder, 28 dewlap, 29 point of elbow, 30 brisket, 31 chest floor, 32 knee, 33 milk well, 34 milk vein, 35 fore udder, 36 teats, 37 rump, 38 loin, 39 chine

²cow *vt* [alter. of *coll* (to poll)] *chiefly Scot* : to cut short : POLL

³cow *vt* [prob. of Scand origin; akin to Dan *kue* to subdue] : to intimidate with threats or show of strength : DAUNT (~ed them with his hard, intelligent eyes —Arthur Morrison) — **cowed·ly** \'kaù-(ə)d-lē\ *adv*

cow·age *or* **cow·hage** \'kaù-ij\ *n* [Hindi *kavāc*] : a tropical leguminous woody vine (*Mucuna pruritum*) with crooked pods covered with barbed hairs that cause severe itching; *also* : these hairs sometimes used as a vermifuge

cow·ard \\'kaú-(ə)rd\\ *n* [ME, fr. OF *coart*, fr. *coe* tail, fr. L *cauda*] : one who shows disgraceful fear or timidity — **coward** *adj*

cow·ard·ice \\-əs\\ *n* [ME *cowardise*, fr. OF *coardise*, fr. *coart*] : lack of courage or resolution

¹cow·ard·ly \\-lē\\ *adv* : in a cowardly manner

²cowardly *adj* : resembling or befitting a coward ⟨a ~ retreat⟩ — **cow·ard·li·ness** *n*

cow·bane \\'kaú-ˌbān\\ *n* : any of several poisonous plants (as a water hemlock) of the carrot family

cow·bell \\-ˌbel\\ *n* : a bell hung around the neck of a cow to make a sound by which it can be located

cow·ber·ry \\-ˌber-ē\\ *n* : any of several pasture shrubs (as mountain cranberry); *also* : the fruit of a cowberry

cow·bird \\-ˌbərd\\ *n* : a small No. American blackbird (*Molothrus ater*) that lays its eggs in the nests of other birds

cow·boy \\-ˌbói\\ *n* : one who tends or drives cattle; *esp* : a usu. mounted cattle ranch hand

cowboy boot *n* : a boot made with a high arch, a high Cuban heel, and usu. fancy stitching

cowboy hat *n* : a wide-brimmed hat with a large soft crown — called also *ten-gallon hat*

cow·catch·er \\'kaú-ˌkach-ər, -ˌkech-\\ *n* : an inclined frame on the front of a railroad locomotive for throwing obstacles off the track

cow college *n* **1** : a college that specializes in agriculture **2** : a provincial college or university that lacks culture, sophistication, and tradition

cow·er \\'kaú-(ə)r\\ *vi* [ME *couren*, of Scand origin; akin to Norw *kura* to cower; akin to Gk *gyros* circle, OE *cot*] : to shrink away or crouch quivering (as in abject fear or grave distress) from something that menaces, domineers, or dismays ⟨~*ing* in their huts . . . listening in fear —Charles Kingsley⟩

cow·fish \\'kaú-ˌfish\\ *n* **1 a** : any of various small cetaceans **b** : SIRENIAN **2** : any of various small bright-colored fishes (family Ostraciidae) with projections resembling horns over the eyes

cow·girl \\-ˌgər(-ə)l\\ *n* : a female cowboy

cow·hand \\-ˌhand\\ *n* : COWBOY

cow·herd \\-ˌhərd\\ *n* : one who tends cows

¹cow·hide \\-ˌhīd\\ *n* **1** : the hide of a cow; *also* : leather made from this hide **2** : a coarse whip of rawhide or braided leather

²cowhide *vt* **cow·hid·ed; cow·hid·ing** : to flog with a cowhide whip

cow horse *n* : COW PONY

¹cowl \\'kaú(ə)l\\ *n* [ME *cowle*, fr. OE *cugele*, fr. LL *cuculla* monk's hood, fr. L *cucullus* hood] **1** : a hood or long hooded cloak esp. of a monk **2 a** : a chimney covering designed to improve the draft **b** : the top portion of the front part of an automobile body forward of the two front doors to which are attached the windshield and instrument board **c** : COWLING

²cowl *vt* : to cover with or as if with a cowl

cowled \\'kaú(ə)ld\\ *adj* : shaped like a hood ⟨HOODED ⟨a ~ flower⟩

cow·lick \\'kaú-ˌlik\\ *n* [fr. its appearance of having been licked by a cow] : a lock or tuft of hair growing in a different direction from the rest of the hair

cowl·ing \\'kaú-liŋ\\ *n* : a removable metal covering that houses the engine and sometimes a part of the fuselage or nacelle of an airplane; *also* : a metallic cover for an engine

cowl·staff \\'kōl-ˌstaf, 'kaú(ə)l-\\ *n* [ME *cuvelstaff*, fr. *cuvel* vessel (fr. OE *cȳfel*, fr. ONF *cuvele* small vat) + *staff*] *archaic* : a staff from which a vessel is suspended and carried between two persons

cow·man \\'kaú-mən, -ˌman\\ *n* **1** : COWHERD, COWBOY **2** : a cattle owner or rancher

co·work·er \\'kō-ˌwər-kər\\ *n* : a fellow worker

cow parsnip *n* : a tall perennial No. American plant (*Heracleum maximum*) of the carrot family with large compound leaves and broad umbels of white or purplish flowers; *also* : a related plant (*H. sphondylium*) naturalized in the U.S. from the Old World

cow·pat \\'kaú-ˌpat\\ *n* : a dropping of cow dung

cow·pea \\'kaú-ˌpē\\ *n* : a sprawling leguminous herb (*Vigna sinensis*) related to the bean and widely cultivated in southern U.S. esp. for forage and green manure; *also* : its edible seed — called also *black-eyed pea*

Cow·per's gland \\ˌkaú-pərz-, ˌkü-pərz-, ˌkúp-ərz-\\ *n* [William *Cowper* †1709 E surgeon] : either of two small glands discharging into the male urethra

cow·poke \\'kaú-ˌpōk\\ *n* : COWBOY

cow pony *n* : a light saddle horse trained for herding cattle

cow·pox \\'kaú-ˌpäks\\ *n* : a mild eruptive disease of the cow that when communicated to man protects against smallpox

cow·punch·er \\-ˌpən-chər\\ *n* : COWBOY

cow·rie *or* **cow·ry** \\'kaú(ə)r-ē\\ *n, pl* **cowries** [Hindi *kaurī*] : any of numerous marine gastropods (family Cypraeidae) widely distributed in warm seas with glossy and often brightly colored shells

cow·slip \\'kaú-ˌslip\\ *n* [ME *cowslyppe*, fr. OE *cūslyppe*, lit., cow dung, fr. *cū* cow + *slypa, slyppe* paste] **1** : a common British primrose (*Primula veris*) with fragrant yellow or purplish flowers **2** : MARSH MARIGOLD **3** : SHOOTING STAR **4** : VIRGINIA COWSLIP

cow·shed \\'kaú-ˌshed\\ *n* : a shed for the housing of cows

cow town *n* **1** : a town or city that serves as a market center or shipping point for cattle **2** : a small unsophisticated town within a cattle-raising area

¹cox \\'käks\\ *n* : COXSWAIN

²cox *vb* : COXSWAIN

coxa \\'käk-sə\\ *n, pl* **cox·ae** \\-ˌsē, -ˌsī\\ [L, hip; akin to OHG *hāhsina* hock, Skt *kakṣa* armpit] : the basal segment of a limb of various arthropods (as an insect) — **cox·al** \\-səl\\ *adj*

cox·comb \\'käk-ˌkōm\\ *n* [ME *cokkes comb*, lit., cock's comb] **1 a** *obs* : a jester's cap adorned with a strip of red **b** *archaic* : PATE, HEAD **2 a** *obs* : FOOL **b** : a conceited foolish person : FOP — **cox·comb·i·cal** \\käk-'skō-mi-kəl, -'skäm-i-\\ *adj*

cox·comb·ry \\'käk-ˌskōm-rē, -ˌskäm-\\ *n, pl* **-ries** : behavior that is characteristic of a coxcomb : FOPPERY

Cox·sack·ie virus \\(ˌ)kúk-ˌsäk-ē-, -ˌsak-; -(ˌ)käk-ˌsak-ē-\\ *n* [*Coxsackie*, N.Y.] : any of several viruses related to that of poliomyelitis and associated with human diseases

¹cox·swain \\'käk-sən, -ˌswān\\ *n* [ME *cokswayne*, fr. *cok* cockboat + *swain* servant] **1** : a sailor who has charge of a ship's boat and its crew and who usu. steers **2** : a steersman of a racing shell who usu. directs the crew

²coxswain *vt* : to direct as coxswain ~ *vi* : to act as coxswain

¹coy \\'kói\\ *adj* [ME, quiet, shy, fr. MF *coi* calm, fr. L *quietus* quiet] **1 a** : shrinking from contact or familiarity **b** : marked by cute, coquettish, or artful playfulness **2** : showing reluctance to make a definite commitment *syn* see SHY *ant* pert — **coy·ly** *adv* — **coy·ness** *n*

²coy *vt, obs* : CARESS ~ *vi, archaic* : to act coyly

coy·ote \\'kī-ˌōt, kī-'ōt-ē\\ *n, pl* **coyotes** *or* **coyote** [MexSp, fr. Nahuatl *coyotl*] : a small wolf (*Canis latrans*) native to western No. America

coy·o·til·lo \\ˌkí-ə-'til-(ˌ)ō, ˌkói-ə-, -'tē-(ˌ)y)ō\\ *n* [MexSp, dim. of *coyote*] : a low poisonous shrub (*Karwinskia humboldtiana*) of the buckthorn family of the southwestern U.S. and Mexico

coyote

coy·pu \\'kói-(ˌ)pü, kói-\\ *n* [AmerSp *coipú*, fr. Araucan *coypu*] **1** : a So. American aquatic rodent (*Myocastor coypus*) with webbed feet and dorsal mammae that has been introduced into the U.S. on the Gulf coast and in the Pacific Northwest **2** : NUTRIA 2

coz \\'kəz\\ *n* [by shortening & alter.] : COUSIN

coz·en \\'kəz-ᵊn\\ *vt* **coz·ened; coz·en·ing** \\'kəz-niŋ, -ᵊn-iŋ\\ [obs. It *cozzonare*, fr. It *cozzone* horse trader, fr. L *cocion-, cocio* trader] **1** : to deceive, win over, or induce to do something by artful coaxing and wheedling or shrewd trickery ⟨tried to ~ his opponent's supporters⟩ **2** : to gain by cozening someone ⟨~*ed* his supper out of the old woman⟩ *syn* see CHEAT — **coz·en·er** \\'kəz-nər, -ᵊn-ər\\ *n*

coz·en·age \\'kəz-nij, -ᵊn-ij\\ *n* **1** : the art or practice of cozening : FRAUD **2** : an act or an instance of cozening

¹co·zy \\'kō-zē\\ *adj* **co·zi·er; -est** [prob. of Scand origin; akin to Norw *koselig* cozy] **1** : enjoying or affording warmth and ease : SNUG **2 a** : marked by the intimacy of the family or a close group **b** : suggesting close association or connivance ⟨a ~ agreement⟩ **3** : marked by a discreet and cautious attitude or procedure *syn* see COMFORTABLE — **co·zi·ly** \\-zə-lē\\ *adv* — **co·zi·ness** \\-zē-nəs\\ *n*

²cozy *adv* : in a cautious manner ⟨play it ~ and wait for the other team to make a mistake —Bobby Dodd⟩

³cozy *n, pl* **cozies** : a padded covering esp. for a teapot to keep the contents hot

cozy up *vi* : to attain or try to attain familiarity, friendship, or intimacy : ingratiate onself ⟨*cozying up* to the party leaders⟩

cp *abbr* **1** compare **2** coupon

CP *abbr* **1** candlepower **2** Cape Province **3** center of pressure **4** charter party **5** chemically pure **6** command post **7** communist party **8** Congregation of the Passion **9** custom of port

CPA *abbr* **1** Catholic Press Association **2** certified public accountant

cpd *abbr* compound

CPFF *abbr* cost plus fixed fee

CPI *abbr* consumer price index

cpl *abbr* **1** complete **2** compline

Cpl *abbr* corporal

CPM *abbr* **1** cost per thousand **2** cycles per minute

CPO *abbr* chief petty officer

CPOM *abbr* master chief petty officer

CPOS *abbr* senior chief petty officer

CPS *abbr* **1** cards per second **2** certified professional secretary **3** characters per second **4** Civilian Public Service **5** cycles per second

CPT *abbr* captain

cpu *abbr* central processing unit

¹CQ \\ˌsē-'kyü\\ [abbr. for *call to quarters*] — communication code letters used at the beginning of radiograms of general information or safety notices or by shortwave amateurs as an invitation to talk to other shortwave amateurs

²CQ *abbr* **1** call to quarters **2** charge of quarters **3** commercial quality

CQT *abbr* College Qualification Test

cr *abbr* **1** center **2** circular **3** commander **4** cream **5** creased **6** credit; creditor **7** crescendo **8** cruzeiro

Cr *symbol* chromium

CR *abbr* **1** carrier's risk **2** cathode ray **3** class rate **4** conditioned reflex; conditioned response **5** current rate

¹crab \\'krab\\ *n, often attrib* [ME *crabbe*, fr. OE *crabba*; akin to OHG *krebiz* crab, OE *ceorfan* to carve] **1** : any of numerous chiefly marine broadly built crustaceans: **a** : any of a tribe (Brachyura) with a short broad usu. flattened carapace, a small abdomen that curls forward beneath the body, short antennae, and the anterior pair of limbs modified as grasping pincers **b** : any of various crustaceans (tribe Anomura) resembling true crabs in the more or less reduced condition of the abdomen **2** *cap* : CANCER 1 **3** : any of various machines for raising or hauling heavy weights **4** : failure to raise an oar clear of the water on recovery of a stroke or missing the water altogether when attempting a stroke ⟨catch a

~⟩ **5** *pl* : infestation with crab lice **6** : apparent sideways motion of an airplane headed into a crosswind

²crab *vb* **crabbed; crab·bing** *vt* **1** : to cause to move sideways or in an indirect or diagonal manner; *specif* : to head (an airplane) by means of the rudder into a crosswind to counteract drift **2** : to subject to crabbing ~ *vi* **1 a** (1) : to move sideways indirectly or diagonally (2) : to crab an airplane **b** : to scuttle or scurry sideways **2** : to fish for crabs — **crab·ber** *n*

³crab *n* [ME *crabbe*, perh. fr. *crabbe* ¹crab] : CRAB APPLE

⁴crab *vb* **crabbed; crab·bing** [ME *crabben*, prob. back-formation fr. *crabbed*] *vt* **1** : to make sullen : SOUR ⟨old age has *crabbed* his nature⟩ **2** : to complain about peevishly **3** : SPOIL, RUIN ~ *vi* : CARP, GROUSE ⟨always ~*s* about the weather⟩ — **crab·ber** *n*

⁵crab *n* : an ill-tempered person : CROSSPATCH

crab apple *n* [³*crab*] **1** : a small wild sour apple **2** : a cultivated apple with small usu. highly colored acid fruit

crab·bed \ˈkrab-əd\ *adj* [ME, partly fr. *crabbe* ¹crab, partly fr. *crabbe* ³crab] **1** : MOROSE, PEEVISH **2** : difficult to read or understand ⟨~ handwriting⟩ — **crab·bed·ly** *adv* — **crab·bed·ness** *n*

crab·by \ˈkrab-ē\ *adj* **crab·bi·er; -est** [³*crab*] : CROSS, ILL-NATURED

crab cactus *n* : CHRISTMAS CACTUS

crab·grass \ˈkrab-ˌgras\ *n* : a grass (esp. *Digitaria sanguinalis*) that has creeping or decumbent stems which root freely at the nodes and that is often a pest in turf or cultivated lands

crab louse *n* : a louse (*Phthirus pubis*) infesting the pubic region of the human body

crab·stick \ˈkrab-ˌstik\ *n* **1** : a stick, cane, or cudgel of crab apple tree wood **2** : a crabbed ill-natured person

crab·wise \-ˌwīz\ *adv* **1** : SIDEWAYS **2** : in a sidling or cautiously indirect manner

¹crack \ˈkrak\ *vb* [ME *crakken*, fr. OE *cracian*; akin to Skt *jarate* it crackles — more at CRANE] *vi* **1** : to make a very sharp explosive sound ⟨the whip ~*s* through the air⟩ **2** : to break, split, or snap apart ⟨the friendly atmosphere began to ~⟩ **3** : FAIL: as **a** : to lose control or effectiveness under pressure — often used with *up* **b** : to fail in tone ⟨his voice ~*ed*⟩ **4** : to go at good speed; *specif* : to proceed under full sail or steam **5** : to break up into simpler chemical compounds usu. as a result of heating ~ *vt* **1 a** : to break so that fissures appear on the surface ⟨~ a mirror⟩ **b** : to break with a sudden sharp sound ⟨~ nuts⟩ **2** : to utter esp. suddenly or strikingly ⟨~ a joke⟩ **3** : to strike with a sharp noise : RAP ⟨then ~*s* him over the head⟩ ⟨~*ed* a two-run homer in the fifth —*N. Y. Times*⟩ **4 a** (1) : to open (as a bottle) for drinking (2) : to open (a book) for studying **b** : to puzzle out and expose, solve, or reveal the mystery of ⟨~ a code⟩ **c** : to break into ⟨~ a safe⟩ **d** : to open slightly ⟨~ the throttle⟩ **e** : to break through (as a barrier) so as to gain acceptance or recognition **5 a** : to impair seriously or irreparably : WRECK ⟨~ a car up⟩ **b** : to destroy the tone of (a voice) **c** : DISORDER, CRAZE **d** : to interrupt sharply or abruptly ⟨the criticism ~*ed* our complacency⟩ **6** : to cause to make a sharp noise ⟨~ one's knuckles⟩ **7 a** (1) : to subject (hydrocarbons) to cracking (2) : to produce by cracking ⟨~*ed* gasoline⟩ **b** : to break up (chemical compounds) into simpler compounds by means of heat

²crack *n* **1 a** : a loud roll or peal ⟨a ~ of thunder⟩ **b** : a sudden sharp noise ⟨the ~ of rifle fire⟩ **2** : a sharp witty remark : QUIP **3 a** : a narrow break : FISSURE ⟨a ~ in the ice⟩ **b** : a narrow opening ⟨leave the door open a ~⟩ **4 a** : a weakness or flaw caused by decay, age, or deficiency : UNSOUNDNESS **b** : a broken tone of the voice **c** : CRACKPOT **5** : MOMENT, INSTANT ⟨the ~ of dawn⟩ ⟨the ~ of doom⟩ **6** : HOUSEBREAKING, BURGLARY **7** : a sharp resounding blow ⟨gave him a ~ on the head⟩ **8** : ATTEMPT, TRY ⟨her first ~ at writing a novel⟩

³crack *adj* : of superior excellence or ability ⟨a ~ marksman⟩

crack·back \ˈkrak-ˌbak\ *n* : a blind-side block on a defensive back in football by a pass receiver who starts downfield and then cuts back to the middle of the line

crack·brain \-ˌbrān\ *n* : an erratic person : CRACKPOT — **crack-brained** \-ˈbrānd\ *adj*

crack·down \-ˌdau̇n\ *n* : an act or instance of cracking down

crack down \-ˈdau̇n\ *vi* : to take positive regulatory or disciplinary action

cracked \ˈkrakt\ *adj* **1 a** : broken (as by a sharp blow) so that the surface is fissured ⟨~ china⟩ **b** : broken into coarse particles ⟨~ wheat⟩ **c** : marked by harshness, dissonance, or failure to sustain a tone ⟨a ~ voice⟩ **2** : mentally disturbed : CRAZY

crack·er \ˈkrak-ər\ *n* **1** *chiefly dial* : a bragging liar : BOASTER **2** : something that makes a cracking or snapping noise: as **a** : FIRECRACKER **b** : the snapping end of a whiplash : SNAPPER **c** : a paper holder for a party favor that pops when the ends are pulled sharply **3** *pl* : NUTCRACKER **4** : a dry thin crisp bakery product that may be leavened or unleavened and that is made in various shapes **5 a** : a poor usu. Southern white — usu. used disparagingly **b** *cap* : a native or resident of Florida or Georgia — used as a nickname **6** : the equipment in which cracking (as of petroleum) is carried out

crack·er–bar·rel \-ˌbar-əl\ *adj* [*cracker barrel*, a barrel in which crackers were kept in country stores and around which customers lounged for informal conversation] : suggestive of the friendly homespun character of a country store ⟨a ~ philosopher⟩

crack·er·jack \ˈkrak-ər-ˌjak\ *also* **crack·a·jack** \-ə-ˌjak\ *n* [¹*crack* + *-er* + *jack*] : a person or thing of marked excellence — **crackerjack** *adj*

Cracker Jack *trademark* — used for a candied popcorn confection

crack·ers \ˈkrak-ərz\ *adj* [prob. alter. of *cracked*] *chiefly Brit* : CRAZY

¹crack·ing \ˈkrak-iŋ\ *adj* : very impressive or effective : GREAT

²cracking *adv* : VERY, EXTREMELY ⟨a ~ good book⟩

³cracking *n* : a process in which relatively heavy hydrocarbons are broken up by heat into lighter products (as gasoline)

¹crack·le \ˈkrak-əl\ *vb* **crack·led; crack·ling** \-(ə-)liŋ\ [freq. of ¹*crack*] *vi* **1 a** : to make small sharp sudden repeated noises ⟨the fire ~*s* on the hearth⟩ **b** : to show animation : SPARKLE ⟨the essays ~ with wit⟩ **2** : to develop a surface network of fine cracks ~ *vt* : to crush or crack with snapping noises

²crackle *n* **1 a** : the noise of repeated small cracks or reports **b** : SPARKLE, EFFERVESCENCE **2** : a network of fine cracks on an otherwise smooth surface

crack·le·ware \ˈkrak-əl-ˌwa(ə)r, -ˌwe(ə)r\ *n* : ceramic ware with a designedly crackled glaze

crack·ling *n* **1** \ˈkrak-(ə-)liŋ\ : a series of small sharp cracks or reports ⟨the ~ of frozen snow as we walk⟩ **2** \ˈkrak-lən, -liŋ\ : the crisp residue left after the rendering of lard from meat or the frying or roasting of the skin (as of pork or goose) — usu. used in pl.

crack·ly \ˈkrak-(ə-)lē\ *adj* : inclined to crackle : CRISP

crack·nel \ˈkrak-nᵊl\ *n* [ME *krakenelle*] **1** : a hard brittle biscuit **2** : CRACKLING 2 — usu. used in pl.

crack·pot \ˈkrak-ˌpät\ *n* : one given to eccentric or lunatic notions — **crackpot** *adj*

cracks·man \ˈkrak-smən\ *n* : BURGLAR; *also* : SAFECRACKER

crack–up \ˈkrak-ˌəp\ *n* **1 a** : a mental collapse : NERVOUS BREAKDOWN ⟨his wife's death brought on his ~⟩ **b** : COLLAPSE, BREAKDOWN **2** : CRASH, WRECK ⟨an automobile ~⟩

crack up \-ˈəp\ *vi* : to smash up a vehicle (as by losing control) ⟨*cracked up* on a curve⟩ ~ *vt* **1** : EXTOL, PRAISE ⟨wasn't all that it was *cracked up* to be⟩ **2** : to cause much amusement to ⟨that joke really *cracks* him *up*⟩

-c·ra·cy \k-rə-sē\ *n comb form* [MF & LL; MF *-cratie*, fr. LL *-cratia*, fr. Gk *-kratia*, fr. *kratos* strength, power — more at HARD] **1** : form of government; *also* : state having such a form ⟨mono*cracy*⟩ **2** : social or political class (as of powerful persons) ⟨mob*ocracy*⟩ **3** : theory of social organization ⟨techno*cracy*⟩

¹cra·dle \ˈkrād-ᵊl\ *n* [ME *cradel*, fr. OE *cradol*; akin to OHG *kratto* basket, Skt *grantha* knot] **1 a** : a bed or cot for a baby usu. on rockers or pivots **b** : a framework or support suggestive of a baby's cradle: as (1) : a framework of bars and rods (2) : the support for a telephone receiver or handset **c** (1) : an implement with rods like fingers attached to a scythe and used formerly for harvesting grain (2) : a low frame on casters on which mechanics lie while working under an automobile **d** : a frame to keep the bedclothes from contact with an injured part of the body **2 a** : the earliest period of life : INFANCY ⟨from the ~ to the grave⟩ **b** : a place of origin ⟨believed that the Nile valley was the ~ of civilization⟩ **3** : a rocking device used in panning for gold

²cradle *vb* **cra·dled; cra·dling** \ˈkrād-liŋ, -ᵊl-iŋ\ *vt* **1 a** : to place or keep in or as if in a cradle **b** : SHELTER, REAR **c** : to support protectively or intimately ⟨*cradling* the injured man's head in her arms⟩ **2** : to cut (grain) with a cradle scythe **3** : to place, raise, support, or transport on a cradle **4** : to wash in a miner's cradle ~ *vi*, *obs* : to rest in or as if in a cradle

cra·dle·song \ˈkrād-ᵊl-ˌsȯŋ\ *n* : LULLABY, BERCEUSE

¹craft \ˈkraft\ *n* [ME, strength, skill, fr. OE *cræft*; akin to OHG *kraft* strength] **1** : skill in planning, making, or executing : DEXTERITY — often used in combination ⟨wine*craft*⟩ **2** : an occupation or trade requiring manual dexterity or artistic skill ⟨the carpenter's ~⟩ **3** : skill in deceiving to gain an end ⟨used ~ and guile to close the deal⟩ **4** : the members of a trade or trade association **5** *pl usu* **craft a** : a boat esp. of small size **b** : AIRCRAFT **c** : SPACECRAFT ***syn*** see ART

²craft *vt* : to make by or as if by hand ⟨is ~*ing* a new sculpture⟩ ⟨a carefully ~*ed* story⟩

crafts·man \ˈkraf(t)-smən\ *n* **1** : a workman who practices a trade or handicraft : ARTISAN **2** : one who creates or performs with skill or dexterity esp. in the manual arts ⟨jewelry made by European *craftsmen*⟩ — **crafts·man·like** \-ˌlīk\ *adj* — **crafts·man·ship** \-ˌship\ *n*

crafts·wom·an \ˈkraf(t)-ˌswu̇m-ən\ *n* : a female craftsman

craft union *n* : a labor union with membership limited to workmen of the same craft — compare INDUSTRIAL UNION

crafty \ˈkraf-tē\ *adj* **craft·i·er; -est** **1** *dial chiefly Brit* : SKILLFUL, CLEVER **2 a** : adept in the use of subtlety and cunning **b** : marked by subtlety and guile ⟨a ~ scheme⟩ ***syn*** see SLY — **craft·i·ly** \ˈkraf-tə-lē\ *adv* — **craft·i·ness** \-tē-nəs\ *n*

¹crag \ˈkrag\ *n* [ME, of Celt origin; akin to OIr *crec* crag] **1** : a steep rugged rock or cliff **2** *archaic* : a sharp detached fragment of rock — **crag·ged** \ˈkrag-əd\ *adj*

²crag *n* [ME, fr. MD *crāghe*] *chiefly Scot* : NECK, THROAT

crag·gy \ˈkrag-ē\ *adj* **crag·gi·er; -est** **1** : full of crags ⟨~ slopes⟩ **2** : ROUGH, RUGGED ⟨a ~ face⟩ — **crag·gi·ly** \ˈkrag-ə-lē\ *adv* — **crag·gi·ness** \ˈkrag-ē-nəs\ *n*

crags·man \ˈkragz-mən\ *n* : one that is expert in climbing crags or cliffs

crake \ˈkrāk\ *n* [ME, prob. fr. ON *krāka* crow or *krākr* raven; akin to OE *crāwan* to crow] **1** : any of various rails; *esp* : a short-billed rail (as the corncrake) **2** : the corncrake's cry

¹cram \ˈkram\ *vb* **crammed; cram·ming** [ME *crammen*, fr. OE *crammian*; akin to Gk *ageirein* to collect] *vt* **1** : to pack tight : JAM ⟨~ a suitcase with clothes⟩ **2 a** : to fill (as poultry) with food to satiety : STUFF **b** : to eat voraciously : BOLT ⟨the child ~*s* his food⟩ **3** : to thrust in or as if in a rough or forceful manner ⟨*crammed* the letters angrily into his pocket⟩ **4** : to prepare hastily for an examination ⟨~ the students for the test⟩ ~ *vi* **1** : to eat greedily or to satiety : STUFF **2** : to study hastily for an imminent examination — **cram·mer** *n*

²cram *n* **1** : a compressed multitude or crowd : CRUSH **2** : last-minute study for an examination

cram·be \ˈkram-(ˌ)bē\ *n* [NL, genus name, fr. L, cabbage, fr. Gk *krambē*] : an annual Mediterranean crucifer (*Crambe abyssinica*) cultivated as an oilseed crop

cram·bo \ˈkram-(ˌ)bō\ *n*, *pl* **cramboes** [alter. of earlier *crambe*, fr. L, cabbage] **1** : a game in which one player gives a word or line of verse to be matched in rhyme by other players **2** : sloppy rhyme

cram·oi·sie *or* **cram·oi·sy** \ˈkram-ˌȯi-zē, ˈkram-ə-zē\ *n*, *pl* **-sies** [ME *crammassy*, fr. MF *cramoisi*, fr. *cramoisi* crimson] : crimson cloth

¹cramp \ˈkramp\ *n* [ME *crampe*, fr. MF, of Gmc origin; akin to LG *krampe* hook] **1** : a painful involuntary spasmodic contraction of a muscle **2** : a temporary paralysis of muscles from overuse — compare WRITER'S CRAMP **3** : sharp abdominal pain — usu. used in pl.

[2]cramp *n* [LG or obs. D *krampe* hook; akin to OE *cradol* cradle] **1 a** : a usu. iron device bent at the ends and used to hold timbers or blocks of stone together **b** : [1]CLAMP **2 a** : something that confines : SHACKLE **b** : the state of being confined — **cramp** *adj*

[3]cramp *vt* **1** : to affect with or as if with cramp **2 a** : CONFINE, RESTRAIN ⟨felt ~*ed* in the tiny apartment⟩ **b** : to restrain from free expression — used esp. in the phrase *cramp one's style* **3** : to turn (the front wheels of a vehicle) to right or left **4** : to fasten or hold with a cramp ~ *vi* : to suffer from cramps

cramp·fish \ˈkramp-ˌfish\ *n* : ELECTRIC RAY

cram·pit \ˈkram-pət\ *n* [alter. of *crampette* (chape), fr. ME, fr. MD *crampe* hook] : a sheet of iron on which a player stands to deliver his stone in curling

cram·pon \ˈkram-ˌpän\ *n* [MF *crampon*, of Gmc origin; akin to LG *krampe*] **1** : a hooked clutch or dog for raising heavy objects — usu. used in pl. **2** : CLIMBING IRON — usu. used in pl.

cran·ber·ry \ˈkran-ˌber-ē, -b(ə-)rē\ *n* [part trans. of LG *kraanbere*, fr. *kraan* crane + *bere* berry] **1** : the red acid berry produced by some plants (as *Vaccinium oxycoccos* and *V. macrocarpon*) of the heath family; *also* : a plant producing these **2** : any of various plants with a fruit that resembles a cranberry

cranberry bush *n* : a shrubby or arborescent viburnum (*Viburnum trilobum*) of No. America and Europe with prominently 3-lobed leaves and red fruit

cranch \ˈkränch\ *var of* CRAUNCH

[1]crane \ˈkrān\ *n* [ME *cran*, fr. OE; akin to OHG *krano* crane, Gk *geranos*, L *grus*, Skt *jarate* it crackles] **1** : any of a family (Gruidae of the order Gruiformes) of tall wading birds superficially resembling the herons but structurally more nearly related to the rails **2** : any of several herons **3** : an often horizontal projection swinging about a vertical axis: as **a** : a machine for raising, shifting, and lowering heavy weights by means of a projecting swinging arm or with the hoisting apparatus supported on an overhead track **b** : an iron arm in a fireplace for supporting kettles **c** : a boom for holding a motion-picture or television camera

[2]crane *vb* **craned; cran·ing** *vt* **1** : to raise or lift by or as if by a crane **2** : to stretch (as the neck) toward an object of attention ⟨*craning* her neck to get a better view⟩ ~ *vi* **1** : to stretch one's neck toward an object of attention ⟨I *craned* out of the window of my compartment —Webb Waldron⟩ **2** : HESITATE

crane fly *n* : any of numerous long-legged slender two-winged flies (family Tipulidae) that resemble large mosquitoes but do not bite

cranes·bill \ˈkrānz-ˌbil\ *n* : GERANIUM 1

crani- *or* **cranio-** *comb form* [ML *cranium*] : cranium ⟨*crani*ate⟩ : cranial and ⟨*cranio*sacral⟩

cra·ni·al \ˈkrā-nē-əl\ *adj* **1** : of or relating to the skull or cranium **2** : CEPHALIC — **cra·ni·al·ly** \-ə-lē\ *adv*

cranial index *n* : the ratio of the maximum breadth of the skull to its maximum height multiplied by 100

cranial nerve *n* : any of the paired nerves that arise from the lower surface of the brain and pass through openings in the skull to the periphery of the body and that comprise 12 pairs in reptiles, birds, and mammals and usu. 10 in fishes and amphibians

cra·ni·ate \ˈkrā-nē-ət, -ˌāt\ *adj* : having a cranium — **craniate** *n*

cra·nio·ce·re·bral \ˌkrā-nē-ō-sə-ˈrē-brəl, -ˈser-ə-\ *adj* : involving both cranium and brain ⟨~ injury⟩

cra·nio·fa·cial \-ˈfā-shəl\ *adj* : of, relating to, or involving both the cranium and the face

cra·ni·ol·o·gy \ˌkrā-nē-ˈäl-ə-jē\ *n* [prob. fr. G *kraniologie*, fr. *kranio-* crani- + *-logie* -logy] : a science dealing with variations in size, shape, and proportions of skulls among the races of men

cra·ni·om·e·try \-ˈäm-ə-trē\ *n* [ISV] : a science dealing with cranial measurement

cra·nio·sa·cral \-ˈsak-rəl, -ˈsā-krəl\ *adj* **1** : of or relating to the cranium and the sacrum **2** : PARASYMPATHETIC

cra·ni·um \ˈkrā-nē-əm\ *n, pl* **-ni·ums** *or* **-nia** \-nē-ə\ [ML, fr. Gk *kranion*; akin to Gk *kara* head — more at CEREBRAL] : SKULL; *specif* : the part that encloses the brain

[1]crank \ˈkraŋk\ *n* [ME *cranke*, fr. OE *cranc-* (as in *crancstæf*, a weaving instrument); akin to OE *cradol* cradle] **1** : a bent part of an axle or shaft or an arm keyed at right angles to the end of a shaft by which circular motion is imparted to or received from the shaft or by which reciprocating motion is changed into circular motion or vice versa **2 a** *archaic* : BEND **b** : a twist or turn of speech : CONCEIT — used esp. in the phrase *quips and cranks* **c** (1) : CAPRICE, CROTCHET (2) : an eccentric person; *also* : one that is overly enthusiastic about a particular subject or activity **d** : a bad-tempered person : GROUCH

[2]crank *vi* **1** : to move with a winding course : ZIGZAG **2 a** : to turn a crank (as in starting an automobile engine) **b** : to come into being or get started by or as if by the turning of a crank ⟨as the political season ~*s* up, with barbecues ... in the offing —*Newsweek*⟩ ~ *vt* **1** : to bend into the shape of a crank **2** : to furnish or fasten with a crank **3 a** : to move or operate by or as if by a crank ⟨~ the window down⟩ **b** : to start by use of a crank — often used with *up*

[3]crank *adj* [Sc, bent, distorted, prob. fr. [1]*crank*] : out of kilter : LOOSE ⟨~ machinery⟩

[4]crank *adj* [ME *cranke*, of unknown origin] **1** *chiefly dial* : MERRY, HIGH-SPIRITED **2** *chiefly dial* : COCKY, CONFIDENT

[5]crank *adj* [short for *crank-sided* (easily tipped)] *of a boat* : easily tipped by an external force

crank·case \ˈkraŋk-ˌkās\ *n* : the housing of a crankshaft

[1]cran·kle \ˈkraŋ-kəl\ *vb* **cran·kled; cran·kling** \-k(ə-)liŋ\ [freq. of [2]*crank*] *vt, obs* : to break into turns, bends, or angles : CRINKLE ~ *vi, archaic* : WIND, ZIGZAG

[2]crankle *n* : BEND, CRINKLE

crank out *vt* : to produce esp. in a mechanical manner ⟨*cranks out* two novels a year⟩

crank·pin \ˈkraŋk-ˌpin\ *n* : the cylindrical piece which forms the handle of a crank or to which the connecting rod is attached

crank·shaft \ˈkraŋk-ˌshaft\ *n* : a shaft driven by or driving a crank

[1]cranky \ˈkraŋ-kē\ *adj* **crank·i·er; -est** [[1]*crank* & [3]*crank*] **1** *dial* : IMBECILE, CRAZY **2** : working erratically : UNPREDICTABLE ⟨a ~ old tractor⟩ **3 a** : marked by eccentricity **b** : given to fretful fussiness : readily angered when opposed : CROTCHETY **4** : full of twists and turns : TORTUOUS ⟨a ~ road⟩ ***syn*** see IRASCIBLE — **crank·i·ly** \-kə-lē\ *adv* — **crank·i·ness** \-kē-nəs\ *n*

[2]cranky *adj* [[5]*crank*] *of a boat* : liable to heel or tip

cran·nog \ˈkran-ˌóg, kra-ˈnōg\ *n* [ScGael *crannag* & IrGael *crannōg*] : an artificial fortified island constructed in a lake or marsh orig. in prehistoric Ireland and Scotland

cran·ny \ˈkran-ē\ *n, pl* **crannies** [ME *crany*, fr. MF *cren, cran* notch] **1** : a small break or slit : CREVICE **2** : an obscure nook or corner — **cran·nied** \-ēd\ *adj*

cran·reuch \ˈkran-ˌrük\ *n* [prob. modif. of ScGael *crannreotha*] *Scot* : HOARFROST, RIME

[1]crap \ˈkrap\ *n* [ME *crappe* chaff, residue from rendered fat, fr. MD, piece torn off, fr. *crappen* to break off] **1 a** : EXCREMENT — usu. considered vulgar **b** : DEFECATION — usu. considered vulgar **2** : NONSENSE, RUBBISH — sometimes considered vulgar

[2]crap *vi* **crapped; crap·ping** : DEFECATE — usu. considered vulgar

[3]crap *n* [back-formation fr. *craps*] **1** : a throw of 2, 3, or 12 in the game of craps losing the shooter his bet unless he has a point — called also *craps*; compare NATURAL **2** — used as an attributive form of *craps* ⟨~ game⟩ ⟨~ table⟩

[4]crap *vi* **crapped; crap·ping** **1** : to throw a crap **2** : to throw a seven while trying to make a point — usu. used with *out*

[1]crape \ˈkrāp\ *n* [alter. of F *crêpe*, fr. MF *crespe*, fr. *crespe* curly, fr. L *crispus* — more at CRISP] **1** : CREPE **2** : a band of crepe worn on a hat or sleeve as a sign of mourning

[2]crape *vt* **craped; crap·ing** : to cover or shroud with or as if with crape

[3]crape *vt* **craped; crap·ing** [F *crêper*, fr. L *crispare*, fr. *crispus*] : to make (the hair) curly

crape myrtle *n* : an East Indian shrub (*Lagerstroemia indica*) of the loosestrife family widely grown in warm regions for its flowers

crap·per \ˈkrap-ər\ *n* [[2]*crap*] : TOILET — usu. considered vulgar

crap·pie \ˈkräp-ē\ *n* [CanF *crapet*] **1** : BLACK CRAPPIE **2** : WHITE CRAPPIE

crap·py \ˈkrap-ē\ *adj* **crap·pi·er; -est** [[1]*crap*] *slang* : markedly inferior in quality : LOUSY

craps \ˈkraps\ *n pl but sing or pl in constr* [LaF, fr. F *crabs, craps*, fr. E *crabs* lowest throw at hazard, fr. pl. of [1]*crab*] **1** : a gambling game played with two dice **2** : [3]CRAP 1

crap·shoot·er \ˈkrap-ˌshüt-ər\ *n* : one who plays craps

crap·u·lous \ˈkrap-yə-ləs\ *adj* [LL *crapulosus*, fr. L *crapula* intoxication, fr. Gk *kraipalē*] **1** : marked by intemperance esp. in eating or drinking **2** : sick from excessive indulgence in liquor

[1]crash \ˈkrash\ *vb* [ME *crasschen*] *vt* **1 a** : to break violently and noisily : SMASH **b** : to damage (an airplane) in landing **2 a** : to cause to make a loud noise ⟨~ the cymbals together⟩ **b** : to force (as one's way) through with loud crashing noises **3** : to enter or attend without invitation or without paying ⟨~ the party⟩ ~ *vi* **1 a** : to break or go to pieces with or as if with violence and noise **b** : to crash an airplane **2** : to make a smashing noise ⟨thunder ~*ing* overhead⟩ **3** : to move or force one's way with or as if with a crash ⟨~*es* into the room⟩ **4** *slang* : to spend the night in a particular place : SLEEP ⟨hippies who had ... been up all night because they couldn't find a place to ~ —Nicholas Von Hoffman⟩ **5** *slang* : to return to a normal state after a drug-induced experience

[2]crash *n* **1** : a loud sound (as of things smashing) ⟨a ~ of thunder⟩ **2** : a breaking to pieces by or as if by collision; *also* : an instance of crashing ⟨a plane ~⟩ **3** : a sudden decline or failure (as of a business) ⟨a stockmarket ~⟩

[3]crash *adj* : marked by a concerted effort and effected in the shortest possible time ⟨a ~ program to teach dropouts how to read⟩

[4]crash *n* [prob. fr. Russ *krashenina* colored linen] : a coarse fabric used for draperies, toweling, and clothing

crash dive *n* : a dive made by a submarine in the least possible time — **crash–dive** *vi*

crash helmet *n* : a usu. plastic or leather helmet that is worn (as by motorcyclists) as protection for the head in the event of an accident

crash·ing \ˈkrash-iŋ\ *adj* **1** : UTTER, ABSOLUTE ⟨a ~ bore⟩ **2** : SUPERLATIVE ⟨a ~ effect⟩

crash–land \ˈkrash-ˈland\ *vt* : to land (an airplane) under emergency conditions usu. with damage to the craft ~ *vi* : to crash-land an airplane — **crash landing** *n*

crash pad *n* **1** : protective padding (as on the inside of an automobile or a military tank) **2** : a place where free temporary lodging is available ⟨a hippie *crash pad*⟩

crash·wor·thy \ˈkrash-ˌwər-thē\ *adj* : resistant to the effects of collision ⟨~ cars⟩ — **crash·wor·thi·ness** *n*

crass \ˈkras\ *adj* [L *crassus* thick, gross] : having such grossness of mind as precludes delicacy and discrimination : INSENSITIVE ***syn*** see STUPID ***ant*** brilliant — **crass·ly** *adv* — **crass·ness** *n*

cras·si·tude \ˈkras-ə-ˌt(y)üd\ *n* : the quality or state of being crass : GROSSNESS; *also* : an instance of grossness

-crat \ˌkrat\ *n comb form* [F *-crate*, back-formation fr. *-cratie* -cracy] **1** : advocate or partisan of a (specified) theory of government ⟨theo*crat*⟩ **2** : member of a (specified) dominant class ⟨pluto*crat*⟩ — **-crat·ic** \ˈkrat-ik\ *adj comb form*

cratch \ˈkrach\ *n* [ME *cracche*, fr. OF *creche* manger — more at CRÈCHE] **1** *dial Brit* : a crib or rack esp. for fodder; *also* : FRAME **2** *archaic* : MANGER

ə abut	ᵊ kitten	ər further	a back	ā bake	ä cot, cart	
au̇ out	ch chin	e less	ē easy	g gift	i trip	ī life
j joke	ŋ sing	ō flow	ȯ flaw	ȯi coin	th thin	t͟h this
ü loot	u̇ foot	y yet	yü few	yu̇ furious	zh vision	

1crate \'krāt\ *n* [L *cratis* wickerwork — more at HURDLE] **1 :** an open box of wooden slats or a usu. wooden protective case or framework for shipping **2 :** JALOPY

2crate *vt* **crated; crat·ing :** to pack in a crate

1cra·ter *n* [L, mixing bowl, crater, fr. Gk *kratēr,* fr. *kerannynai* to mix; akin to Skt *āśirta* mixed] **1** \'krāt-ər\ **a :** the bowl-shaped depression around the orifice of a volcano **b :** a depression formed by the impact of a meteorite **c :** a hole in the ground made by the explosion of a bomb or shell **d :** an eroded lesion **e :** a dimple in a painted surface **2** \'krāt-ər, krä-'te(ə)r\ **:** KRATER

2cra·ter \'krāt-ər\ *vi* **:** to exhibit or form craters ~ *vt* **:** to form craters in

cra·ter·let \'krāt-ər-lət\ *n* **:** a small crater

C ration *n* **:** a canned field ration of the U. S. Army

cra·ton \'krā-,tän, 'kra-\ *n* [G *kraton,* modif. of Gk *kratos* strength — more at HARD] **:** a stable relatively immobile area of the earth's crust that forms the nuclear mass of a continent or the central basis of an ocean — **cra·ton·ic** \krə-'tän-ik, krā-, kra-\ *adj*

craunch \'krȯnch, 'kränch\ *vb* [prob. imit.] **:** CRUNCH — **craunch** *n*

cra·vat \krə-'vat\ *n* [F *cravate,* fr. *Cravate* Croatian] **1 :** a band or scarf formerly worn around the neck **2 :** NECKTIE

crave \'krāv\ *vb* **craved; crav·ing** [ME *craven,* fr. OE *crafian;* akin to OHG *krāpfo* hook, OE *cradol* cradle] *vt* **1 :** to ask for earnestly **:** BEG, DEMAND ⟨~ a pardon for neglect⟩ **2 a :** to want greatly **:** NEED ⟨~*s* drugs⟩ **b :** to yearn for ⟨she ~*s* her vanished youth⟩ ~ *vi* **:** to have a strong or inward desire ⟨~*s* after affection⟩ ***syn*** see DESIRE — **crav·er** *n*

cra·ven \'krā-vən\ *adj* [ME *cravant*] **1** *archaic* **:** DEFEATED, VANQUISHED **2 :** lacking any courage **:** contemptibly fainthearted — **craven** *n* — **cra·ven·ly** *adv* — **cra·ven·ness** \-vən-nəs\ *n*

crav·ing \'krā-viŋ\ *n* **:** a great desire or longing; *esp* **:** an abnormal desire (as for a habit-forming drug)

craw \'krȯ\ *n* [ME *crawe,* fr. (assumed) OE *crawa;* akin to Gk *bronchos* trachea, throat, L *vorare* to devour — more at VORACIOUS] **1 :** the crop of a bird or insect **2 :** the stomach esp. of a lower animal

1craw·fish \'krȯ-,fish\ *n* [by folk etymology fr. ME *crevis, kraveys*] **1 :** CRAYFISH **2 :** SPINY LOBSTER

2crawfish *vi* **:** to retreat from a position **:** back out

1crawl \'krȯl\ *vb* [ME *crawlen,* fr. ON *krafla;* akin to OE *crabba* crab] *vi* **1 :** to move slowly in a prone position without or as if without the use of limbs ⟨the snake ~*ed* into its hole⟩ **2 :** to move or progress slowly or laboriously ⟨traffic ~*s* along at 10 miles an hour⟩ **3 :** to advance by guile or servility ⟨~*ing* into favor by toadying to his boss⟩ **4 :** to spread by extending stems or tendrils **5 a :** to be alive or swarming with or as if with creeping things ⟨a kitchen ~*ing* with ants⟩ **b :** to have the sensation of insects creeping over one ⟨the story made her flesh ~⟩ **6 :** to fail to stay evenly spread — used of paint, varnish, or glaze ~ *vt* **1 :** to move upon in or as if in a creeping manner ⟨the meanest man who ever ~*ed* the earth⟩ **2** *slang* **:** to reprove harshly ⟨they got no good right to ~ me for what I wrote —Marjorie K. Rawlings⟩ ***syn*** see CREEP

2crawl *n* **1 a :** the act or action of crawling **b :** slow or laborious progress **c** *chiefly Brit* **:** a going from one pub to another **2 :** a prone speed swimming stroke consisting of alternating overarm strokes and a flutter kick

3crawl *n* [Afrik *kraal* pen —more at KRAAL] **:** an enclosure in shallow waters (as for confining lobsters)

crawl·er *n* **1 :** one that crawls **2 a :** a Caterpillar tractor **b :** a vehicle (as a crane) that travels on endless chain belts like those of such a tractor

crawl·way \'krȯl-,wā\ *n* **:** a low passageway (as in a cave) that can be traversed only by crawling

crawly \'krȯ-lē\ *adj* **:** CREEPY

cray·fish \'krā-,fish\ *n* [by folk etymology fr. ME *crevis,* fr. MF *crevice,* of Gmc origin; akin to OHG *krebiz* crab — more at CRAB] **1 :** any of numerous freshwater crustaceans (tribe Astacura) resembling the lobster but usu. much smaller **2 :** SPINY LOBSTER

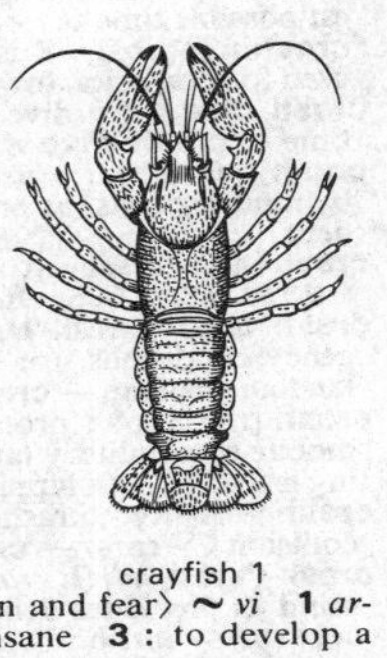
crayfish 1

1cray·on \'krā-,än, -ən; 'kran\ *n* [F, crayon, pencil, fr. dim. of *craie* chalk, fr. L *creta*] **1 :** a stick of white or colored chalk or of colored wax used for writing or drawing **2 :** a crayon drawing

2crayon *vt* **:** to draw with a crayon — **cray·on·ist** \'krā-ə-nəst\ *n*

1craze \'krāz\ *vb* **crazed; craz·ing** [ME *crasen* to crush, craze, of Scand origin; akin to OSw *krasa* to crush] *vt* **1** *obs* **:** BREAK, SHATTER **2 :** to produce minute cracks on the surface or glaze of **3 :** to make insane or as if insane ⟨*crazed* by pain and fear⟩ ~ *vi* **1** *archaic* **:** SHATTER, BREAK **2 :** to become insane **3 :** to develop a mesh of fine cracks

2craze *n* **1** *obs* **a :** BREAK, FLAW **b :** physical weakness **:** INFIRMITY **2 :** an exaggerated and often transient enthusiasm **:** MANIA **3 :** a crack in a surface or coating (as of glaze or enamel) ***syn*** see FASHION

1cra·zy \'krā-zē\ *adj* **cra·zi·er; -est 1 a :** full of cracks or flaws **:** UNSOUND **b :** CROOKED, ASKEW **2 a :** MAD, INSANE **b** (1) **:** IMPRACTICAL (2) **:** ERRATIC **c :** being out of the ordinary **:** UNUSUAL ⟨a taste for ~ hats⟩ **3 a :** distracted with desire or excitement ⟨a thrill-*crazy* mob⟩ **b :** absurdly fond **:** INFATUATED ⟨he's ~ about the girl⟩ **c :** passionately preoccupied **:** OBSESSED ⟨~ about boats⟩ — **cra·zi·ly** \-zə-lē\ *adv* — **cra·zi·ness** \-zē-nəs\ *n* — **like crazy :** to an extreme degree ⟨everyone dancing *like crazy*⟩

2crazy *n, pl* **cra·zies :** one who is or acts crazy

crazy bone *n* **:** FUNNY BONE

crazy quilt *n* **1 :** a patchwork quilt without a design **2 :** JUMBLE, HODGEPODGE

cra·zy·weed \'krā-zē-,wēd\ *n* **:** LOCOWEED

CRC *abbr* Civil Rights Commission

C-re·ac·tive protein \,sē-rē-,ak-tiv-\ *n* [*C-polysaccharide* (a polysaccharide found in the cell wall of pneumococci and precipitated by this protein), fr. *carbohydrate*] **:** a protein present in blood serum in various abnormal states (as inflammation or neoplasia)

1creak \'krēk\ *vi* [ME *creken* to croak, of imit. origin] **:** to make a prolonged grating or squeaking sound

2creak *n* **:** a rasping or grating noise

creaky \'krē-kē\ *adj* **creak·i·er; -est 1 :** marked by creaking **:** SQUEAKY ⟨~ shoes⟩ **2 :** DILAPIDATED, DECREPIT ⟨a ~ old house⟩ — **creak·i·ly** \-kə-lē\ *adv*

1cream \'krēm\ *n, often attrib* [ME *creime, creme,* fr. MF *craime, cresme,* fr. LL *cramum,* of Celt origin; akin to W *cramen* scab] **1 :** the yellowish part of milk containing from 18 to about 40 percent butterfat **2 a :** a food prepared with cream **b :** something having the consistency of cream; *esp* **:** a usu. emulsified medicinal or cosmetic preparation **3 :** the choicest part ⟨the ~ of the crop⟩ **4 :** CREAMER 2 **5 a :** a pale yellow **b :** a cream-colored animal — **cream·i·ly** \'krē-mə-lē\ *adv* — **cream·i·ness** \-mē-nəs\ *n* — **creamy** \-mē\ *adj*

2cream *vi* **1 :** to form cream or a surface layer like the cream on standing milk **2 :** to break into or cause something to break into a creamy froth; *also* **:** to move like froth ~ *vt* **1 a :** SKIM 1c **b** (1) **:** to take the choicest part of ⟨got in first with a new blade and ~*ed* the market⟩ (2) **:** to take off the choicest part of ⟨exporters ~*ed* consumer goods from the market⟩ **2 :** to furnish, prepare, or treat with cream; *also* **:** to dress with a cream sauce **3 a :** to beat into a creamy froth **b :** to work or blend to the consistency of cream ⟨~ butter and sugar together⟩ **c** (1) **:** to drub thoroughly ⟨was ~*ed* in the first round⟩ (2) **:** WRECK ⟨~*ed* the car on the turnpike⟩ **4 :** to cause to form a surface layer of or like cream

cream cheese *n* **:** a mild soft unripened cheese made from whole sweet milk enriched with cream

cream·cups \'krēm-,kəps\ *n pl but sing or pl in constr* **:** any of several California annuals (esp. *Platystemon californicus*) of the poppy family

cream·er \'krē-mər\ *n* **1 :** a device for separating cream from milk **2 :** a small vessel for serving cream

cream·ery \'krēm-(ə-)rē\ *n, pl* **-er·ies :** an establishment where butter and cheese are made or where milk and cream are prepared or sold

cream of tartar : a white crystalline salt $C_4H_5KO_6$ used esp. in baking powder and in certain treatments of metals

cream puff *n* **1 :** a round shell of light pastry filled with whipped cream or a cream filling **2 :** an ineffectual person **3 :** something of little or no consequence

cream soda *n* **:** a carbonated soft drink flavored with vanilla and sweetened with sugar

1crease \'krēs\ *n* [prob. alter. of earlier *creaste,* fr. ME *creste* crest] **1 :** a line or mark made by or as if by folding a pliable substance **2 :** a specially marked area in various sports; *esp* **:** an area surrounding or in front of a goal (as in lacrosse or hockey) forbidden to attacking players unless the ball or puck is in it — **crease·less** \-ləs\ *adj*

2crease *vb* **creased; creas·ing** *vt* **1 :** to make a crease in or on **:** WRINKLE ⟨old age had *creased* her face⟩ **2 :** to wound slightly esp. by grazing ~ *vi* **:** to become creased — **creas·er** *n*

1cre·ate \krē-'āt, 'krē-,\ *adj, archaic* **:** CREATED

2create *vt* **cre·at·ed; cre·at·ing** [ME *createn,* fr. L *creatus,* pp. of *creare*] **1 :** to bring into existence ⟨God *created* the heaven and the earth —Gen 1:1 (AV)⟩ **2 a :** to invest with a new form, office, or rank ⟨was *created* a lieutenant⟩ **b :** to produce or bring about by a course of action or behavior ⟨her arrival *created* a terrible fuss⟩ ⟨~ new jobs for the unemployed⟩ **3 :** CAUSE, OCCASION ⟨famine ~*s* high food prices⟩ **4 a :** to produce through imaginative skill ⟨~ a painting⟩ **b :** DESIGN ⟨~*s* dresses⟩ ***syn*** see INVENT

cre·atine \'krē-ə-,tēn, -ət-ᵊn\ *n* [ISV, fr. Gk *kreat-, kreas* flesh — more at RAW] **:** a white crystalline nitrogenous substance $C_4H_9N_3O_2$ found esp. in the muscles of vertebrates free or as phosphocreatine

creatine phosphate *n* **:** PHOSPHOCREATINE

cre·at·i·nine \krē-'at-ᵊn-,ēn, -ᵊn-ən\ *n* [G *kreatinin,* fr. *kreatin* creatine] **:** a white crystalline strongly basic compound $C_4H_7N_3O$ formed from creatine and found esp. in muscle, blood, and urine

cre·ation \krē-'ā-shən\ *n* **1 :** the act of creating; *esp* **:** the act of bringing the world into ordered existence **2 :** the act of making, inventing, or producing: as **a :** the act of investing with a new rank or office **b :** the first representation of a dramatic role **3 :** something that is created: as **a :** WORLD **b :** creatures singly or in aggregate **c :** an original work of art **d :** a new usu. striking article of clothing

cre·ative \krē-'āt-iv\ *adj* **1 :** marked by the ability or power to create **:** given to creating ⟨the ~ impulse⟩ ⟨nature is a ~ agent⟩ **2 :** PRODUCTIVE — used with *of* ⟨news ~ of alarm⟩ **3 :** having the quality of something created rather than imitated **:** IMAGINATIVE ⟨the ~ arts⟩ — **cre·ative·ly** *adv* — **cre·ative·ness** *n*

creative evolution *n* [trans. of F *évolution créatrice*] **:** evolution that is a creative product of a vital force rather than a naturalistically explicable process

cre·ativ·i·ty \,krē-(,)ā-'tiv-ət-ē, ,krē-ə-\ *n* **1 :** the quality of being creative **2 :** the ability to create

cre·ator \krē-'āt-ər\ *n* **:** one that creates usu. by bringing something new or original into being; *esp, cap* **:** GOD 1 ***syn*** see MAKER

crea·ture \'krē-chər\ *n* **1 :** something created: as **a :** a lower animal; *esp* **:** a farm animal **b :** a human being **:** PERSON **c :** a being of anomalous or uncertain aspect or nature ⟨~*s* of fantasy⟩ **2 :** one who is the servile dependent or tool of another — **crea·tur·al** \'krēch-(ə-)rəl\ *adj* — **crea·ture·hood** \'krē-chər-,hu̇d\ *n* — **crea·ture·li·ness** \-chər-lē-nəs\ *n* — **crea·ture·ly** \-chər-lē\ *adj*

creature comfort *n* **:** something (as food or warmth) that gives bodily comfort

crèche \'kresh, 'krāsh\ *n* [F, fr. OF *creche* manger, crib, of Gmc origin; akin to OHG *krippa* manger — more at CRIB] **1 :** DAY

NURSERY **2** : a foundling hospital **3** : a representation of the Nativity scene

cre·dence \ˈkrēd-ᵊn(t)s\ *n* [ME, fr. MF or ML; MF, fr. ML *credentia,* fr. L *credent-, credens,* prp. of *credere* to believe, trust — more at CREED] **1** : mental acceptance as true or real ⟨give ~ to gossip⟩ **2** : CREDENTIALS — used in the phrase *letters of credence* **3** [MF, fr. OIt *credenza*] : a Renaissance sideboard used chiefly for valuable plate **4** : a small table where the bread and wine rest before consecration ***syn*** see BELIEF

credence 3

cre·dent \ˈkrēd-ᵊnt\ *adj* [L *credent-, credens,* prp.] **1** *archaic* : giving credence : CONFIDING **2** *obs* : CREDIBLE

¹cre·den·tial \kri-ˈden-chəl\ *adj* : warranting credit or confidence — used chiefly in the phrase *credential letters*

²credential *n* **1** : something that gives a title to credit or confidence **2** *pl* : testimonials showing that a person is entitled to credit or has a right to exercise official power **3** : CERTIFICATE, DIPLOMA

cre·den·za \kri-ˈden-zə\ *n* [It, lit., belief, confidence, fr. ML *credentia*] **1** : CREDENCE 3 **2** : a sideboard, buffet, or bookcase patterned after a Renaissance credence; *esp* : one without legs

credibility gap *n* **1 a** : lack of trust ⟨a special *credibility gap* is likely to open between the generations —Kenneth Keniston⟩ **b** : lack of believability ⟨a *credibility gap* created by contradictory official statements —Samuel Ellenport⟩ **2** : DISCREPANCY ⟨the *credibility gap* between the professed ideals . . . and their actual practices —Jeanne L. Noble⟩

cred·i·ble \ˈkred-ə-bəl\ *adj* [ME, fr. L *credibilis,* fr. *credere*] : offering reasonable grounds for being believed ⟨a ~ account of an accident⟩ ⟨~ witnesses⟩ ***syn*** see PLAUSIBLE ***ant*** incredible — **cred·i·bil·i·ty** \ˌkred-ə-ˈbil-ət-ē\ *n* — **cred·i·bly** \ˈkred-ə-blē\ *adv*

¹cred·it \ˈkred-ət\ *n* [MF, fr. OIt *credito,* fr. L *creditum* something entrusted to another, loan, fr. neut. of *creditus,* pp. of *credere* to believe, entrust — more at CREED] **1 a** : the balance in a person's favor in an account **b** : an amount or sum placed at a person's disposal by a bank **c** : time given for payment for goods or services sold on trust ⟨long-term ~⟩ **d** (1) : an entry on the right-hand side of an account constituting an addition to a revenue, net worth, or liability account (2) : a deduction from an expense or asset account **e** : any one of or the sum of the items entered on the right-hand side of an account **f** : a deduction from an amount otherwise due **2** : reliance on the truth or reality of something ⟨too ready to give ~ to idle rumors⟩ **3 a** : influence or power derived from enjoying the confidence of another or others **b** : good name : ESTEEM; *also* : financial or commercial trustworthiness **4** *archaic* : CREDIBILITY **5** : a source of honor ⟨he was a ~ to his upbringing⟩ **6 a** : something that gains or adds to reputation or esteem : HONOR ⟨took no ~ for his kindly act⟩ **b** : RECOGNITION, ACKNOWLEDGMENT ⟨quite willing to accept undeserved ~⟩ **7** : recognition by name of a person contributing to a performance (as a film or telecast) **8 a** : recognition by a school or college that a student has fulfilled a requirement leading to a degree **b** : CREDIT HOUR ***syn* 1** see BELIEF **2** see INFLUENCE ***ant*** discredit

²credit *vt* [partly fr. ¹*credit;* partly fr. L *creditus,* pp.] **1** : to supply goods on credit to **2** : to trust in the truth of : BELIEVE **3** *archaic* : to bring credit or honor upon **4** : to enter upon the credit side of an account **5 a** : to consider usu. favorably as the source, agent, or performer of an action or the possessor of a trait ⟨~*s* him with an excellent sense of humor⟩ **b** : to attribute to some person ⟨they ~ the invention to him⟩ ***syn*** see ASCRIBE

cred·it·able \ˈkred-ət-ə-bəl\ *adj* **1** : worthy of belief **2** : worthy of esteem or praise **3** : worthy of commercial credit **4** : capable of being assigned ⟨victory was directly ~ to his efforts⟩ — **cred·it·abil·i·ty** \ˌkred-ət-ə-ˈbil-ət-ē\ *n* — **cred·it·able·ness** \ˈkred-ət-ə-bəl-nəs\ *n* —**cred·it·ably** \-blē\ *adv*

credit card *n* : a card authorizing purchases on credit

credit hour *n* : the unit of measuring educational credit based on a given number of classroom periods per week throughout a semester ⟨received three *credit hours* for freshman composition⟩

credit line *n* **1** : a line, note, or name that acknowledges the source of an item (as a news dispatch or television program) **2** : the maximum credit allowed a buyer or borrower

cred·i·tor \ˈkred-ət-ər\ *n* : one to whom a debt is owed; *esp* : a person to whom money or goods are due

credit union *n* : a cooperative association that makes small loans to its members at low interest rates

cre·do \ˈkrēd-(ˌ)ō, ˈkrād-\ *n, pl* **credos** [ME, fr. L, I believe] : CREED

cre·du·li·ty \kri-ˈd(y)ü-lət-ē\ *n* : undue readiness of belief : GULLIBILITY

cred·u·lous \ˈkrej-ə-ləs\ *adj* [L *credulus,* fr. *credere*] **1** : ready to believe esp. on slight or uncertain evidence **2** : proceeding from credulity — **cred·u·lous·ly** *adv* — **cred·u·lous·ness** *n*

Cree \ˈkrē\ *n, pl* **Cree** *or* **Crees** [short for earlier *Christeno,* fr. CanF *Christino,* prob. modif. of Ojibwa *Kenistenoag*] **1** : a member of an Amerindian people of Manitoba and Saskatchewan **2** : the Algonquian language of the Cree Indians

creed \ˈkrēd\ *n* [ME *crede,* fr. OE *crēda,* fr. L *credo* (first word of the Apostles' and Nicene Creeds), fr. *credere* to believe, trust, entrust; akin to OIr *cretim* I believe, Skt *śrad-dadhāti* he believes] **1** : a brief authoritative formula of religious belief **2** : a set of fundamental beliefs — **creed·al** *or* **cre·dal** \ˈkrēd-ᵊl\ *adj*

creek \ˈkrēk, ˈkrik\ *n* [ME *crike, creke,* fr. ON *-kriki* bend; akin to ON *krōkr* hook — more at CROOK] **1** *chiefly Brit* : a small inlet or bay narrower and extending farther inland than a cove **2** : a natural stream of water normally smaller than and often tributary to a river **3** *archaic* : a narrow or winding passage — **up the creek** : in a difficult or perplexing situation

Creek \ˈkrēk\ *n* **1** : an Amerindian confederacy of peoples chiefly of Muskogean stock of Alabama, Georgia, and Florida **2** : a member of any of the Creek peoples **3** : the Muskogean language of the Creek Indians

creel \ˈkrē(ə)l\ *n* [ME *creille, crele,* prob. fr. (assumed) MF *creille* grill, fr. L *craticula* — more at GRILL] **1** : a wickerwork receptacle (as for newly caught fish) **2** : a bar with skewers for holding bobbins in a spinning machine

¹creep \ˈkrēp\ *vi* **crept** \ˈkrept\; **creep·ing** [ME *crepen,* fr. OE *crēopan;* akin to Gk *grypos* curved, bent] **1 a** : to move along with the body prone and close to the ground **b** : to move slowly on hands and knees **2 a** : to go very slowly ⟨the hours *crept* by⟩ **b** : to go timidly or cautiously so as to escape notice ⟨she *crept* away from the festive scene⟩ **c** : to enter or advance stealthily ⟨age ~*s* upon us⟩ ⟨a note of irritation *crept* into her voice⟩ **3 a** : to move or stir slightly by swelling or shrinking ⟨the thought makes his flesh ~⟩ **b** *of a plant* : to spread or grow over a surface rooting at intervals or clinging with tendrils, stems, or aerial roots **4 a** : to slip or gradually shift position **b** : to change shape permanently from prolonged stress or exposure to high temperatures

syn CREEP, CRAWL *shared meaning element* : to move along a surface in a prone or crouching position

²creep *n* **1** : a movement of or like creeping ⟨traffic moving at a ~⟩ **2** : a distressing sensation like that caused by the creeping of insects over one's flesh; *esp* : a feeling of apprehension or horror — usu. used in pl. **3** : an enclosure that young animals can enter while adults are excluded **4** : the slow change of dimensions of an object from prolonged exposure to high temperature or stress **5** : an obnoxious or insignificant person

creep·age \ˈkrē-pij\ *n* : gradual movement : CREEP

creep·er \ˈkrē-pər\ *n* **1** : one that creeps: as **a** : a creeping plant **b** : a bird (as of the family Certhiidae) that creeps about on trees or bushes searching for insects **c** : a creeping insect or reptile **2** : any of various tools or implements: as **a** : a fixture with iron points worn on the shoe to prevent slipping **b** : CLIMBING IRON **c** : a strip (as of sealskin) attachable to the bottom of a ski to prevent sliding backward in uphill climbing **d** : GRAPNEL **3** : a device for supplying or moving material in a steady flow

creep·ing \ˈkrē-piŋ\ *adj* : developing or advancing by slow imperceptible degrees ⟨a period of ~ inflation⟩

creeping eruption *n* : a skin disorder marked by a spreading red line of eruption and caused esp. by larvae (as of hookworms not normally parasitic in man) burrowing beneath the human skin

creepy \ˈkrē-pē\ *adj* **creep·i·er; -est** : producing a nervous shivery apprehension ⟨~ things were crawling over us⟩ ⟨a ~ horror story⟩ — **creep·i·ness** *n*

creese *var of* KRIS

cre·mains \kri-ˈmānz\ *n pl* [blend of *cremated* and *remains*] : the ashes of a cremated human body

cre·mate \ˈkrē-ˌmāt, kri-ˈ\ *vt* **cre·mat·ed; cre·mat·ing** [L *crematus,* pp. of *cremare* to burn up, cremate] : to reduce (as a dead body) to ashes by burning — **cre·ma·tion** \kri-ˈmā-shən\ *n*

cre·ma·to·ri·um \ˌkrē-mə-ˈtōr-ē-əm, ˌkrem-ə-, -ˈtȯr-\ *n, pl* **-ri·ums** *or* **-ria** \-ē-ə\ : CREMATORY

cre·ma·to·ry \ˈkrē-mə-ˌtōr-ē, ˈkrem-ə-, -ˌtȯr-\ *n, pl* **-ries** : a furnace for cremating; *also* : an establishment containing such a furnace — **crematory** *adj*

crème \ˈkrem, ˈkrēm\ *n, pl* **crèmes** \ˈkrem(z), ˈkrēmz\ [F, fr. OF *cresme* — more at CREAM] **1** : cream or cream sauce as used in cookery **2** : a sweet liqueur **3** : CREAM 2b

crème de ca·cao \ˌkrēm-də-ˈkō-(ˌ)kō; ˌkrem-də-kə-ˈkau̇, -kə-ˈkā-(ˌ)ō\ *n* [F, lit., cream of cacao] : a sweet liqueur flavored with cacao beans and vanilla

crème de la crème \ˌkrem-də-lä-ˈkrem, -lə-\ *n* [F, lit., cream of the cream] : the very best

crème de menthe \ˌkrēm-də-ˈmint, -ˈmen(t)th; ˌkrem-də-ˈmänt\ *n* [F, lit., cream of mint] : a sweet green or white mint-flavored liqueur

cre·nate \ˈkrē-ˌnāt\ *or* **cre·nat·ed** \-ˌnāt-əd\ *adj* [NL *crenatus,* fr. ML *crena* notch] : having the margin cut into rounded scallops ⟨a ~ leaf⟩ — **cre·nate·ly** *adv*

cre·na·tion \kri-ˈnā-shən\ *n* **1 a** : a crenate formation; *esp* : one of the rounded projections on an edge (as of a coin) **b** : the quality or state of being crenate **2** : shrinkage of red blood cells in hypertonic solution resulting in crenate margins

¹cren·el \ˈkren-ᵊl\ *or* **cre·nelle** \krə-ˈnel\ *n* [MF *crenel,* fr. OF, dim. of *cren* notch, fr. *crener* to notch; akin to ML *crena* notch] : one of the embrasures alternating with merlons in a battlement — see BATTLEMENT illustration

²cren·el *vt* **-eled** *or* **-elled; -el·ing** *or* **-el·ling** : CRENELLATE

cren·el·late *or* **cren·el·ate** \ˈkren-ᵊl-ˌāt\ *vt* **-lat·ed** *or* **-at·ed; -lat·ing** *or* **-at·ing** : to furnish with battlements — **cren·el·late** \-ˌāt, -ət\ *adj* — **cren·el·la·tion** \ˌkren-ᵊl-ˈā-shən\ *n*

cren·el·lat·ed \ˈkren-ᵊl-ˌāt-əd\ *adj* : having battlements

cren·u·late \ˈkren-yə-lət, -ˌlāt\ *also* **cren·u·lat·ed** \-ˌlāt-əd\ *adj* [NL *crenulatus,* fr. *crenula,* dim. of ML *crena*] : having an irregularly wavy or serrate outline ⟨a ~ shoreline⟩

cren·u·la·tion \ˌkren-yə-ˈlā-shən\ *n* **1** : a minute crenation **2** : the state of being crenulate

cre·ole \ˈkrē-ˌōl\ *adj* **1** *often cap* : of or relating to Creoles or their language **2** : of, relating to, or being a domestic animal of a native breed or strain esp. in Latin America **3** : prepared with rice, okra, tomatoes, peppers, and high seasoning ⟨shrimp ~⟩

Cre·ole \ˈkrē-ˌōl\ *n* [F *créole,* fr. Sp *criollo,* fr. Pg *crioulo* white person born in the colonies] **1** : a person of European descent born esp. in the West Indies or Spanish America **2** : a white person descended from early French or Spanish settlers of the U.S. Gulf states and preserving their speech and culture **3** : a person of mixed French or Spanish and Negro descent speaking a dialect of French or Spanish **4 a** : the French dialect spoken by many Negroes in southern Louisiana **b** : HAITIAN **c** *not cap* : a language based on two or more languages that serves as the native language of its speakers

cre·o·sol \ˈkrē-ə-ˌsȯl, -ˌsōl\ *n* [ISV *creosote* + *-ol*] : a colorless aromatic phenol $C_8H_{10}O_2$ obtained from guaiacum resin and the tar made from beech

¹cre·o·sote \ˈkrē-ə-ˌsōt\ *n* [G *kreosot,* fr. Gk *kreas* flesh + *sōtēr* preserver, fr. *sōzein* to preserve, fr. *sōs* safe; fr. its antiseptic properties — more at RAW, THUMB] **1** : a clear or yellowish oily liquid mixture of phenolic compounds obtained by the distillation of wood tar esp. from beech wood **2** : a brownish oily liquid consisting chiefly of aromatic hydrocarbons obtained by distillation of coal tar and used esp. as a wood preservative

²creosote *vt* **-sot·ed; -sot·ing** : to impregnate with creosote

creosote bush *n* : a resinous desert shrub (*Covillea mexicana* of the family Zygophyllaceae) found in the southwestern U.S. and Mexico

crepe *or* **crêpe** \ˈkrāp\ *n* [F *crêpe*] **1** : a light crinkled fabric woven of any of various fibers **2** : CRAPE 2 **3** : a small very thin pancake — **crepe** *adj* — **crep·ey** *or* **crepy** \ˈkrā-pē\ *adj*

crepe de chine \ˌkrāp-də-ˈshēn\ *n, often cap 2d C* [F *crêpe de Chine,* lit., China crepe] : a soft fine clothing crepe

crepe myrtle *or* **crêpe myrtle** *n* : CRAPE MYRTLE

crepe paper *n* : paper with a crinkled or puckered texture

crepe rubber *n* : crude rubber in the form of nearly white to brown crinkled sheets used esp. for shoe soles

crepe su·zette \ˌkrāp-sü-ˈzet\ *n, pl* **crepes suzette** \ˌkrāp(s)-sü-ˈzet\ *or* **crepe suzettes** \ˌkrāp-sü-ˈzets\ [F *crêpe Suzette,* fr. *crêpe* pancake + *Suzette* Susy] : a thin folded or rolled pancake in a hot orange-butter sauce that is sprinkled with a liqueur (as cognac or curaçao) and set ablaze for serving

crep·i·tant \ˈkrep-ət-ənt\ *adj* : having or making a crackling sound

crep·i·tate \ˈkrep-ə-ˌtāt\ *vi* **-tat·ed; -tat·ing** [L *crepitatus,* pp. of *crepitare* to crackle, fr. *crepitus,* pp. of *crepare* to rattle, crack — more at RAVEN] : to make a crackling sound : CRACKLE — **crep·i·ta·tion** \ˌkrep-ə-ˈtā-shən\ *n*

crept *past of* CREEP

cre·pus·cu·lar \kri-ˈpəs-kyə-lər\ *adj* **1** : of, relating to, or resembling twilight : DIM **2** : active in the twilight ⟨~ insects⟩

cre·pus·cule \kri-ˈpəs-(ˌ)kyü(ə)l\ *or* **cre·pus·cle** \-ˈpəs-əl\ *n* [L *crepusculum,* fr. *creper* dusky] : TWILIGHT

cresc *abbr* crescendo

¹cre·scen·do \krə-ˈshen-(ˌ)dō\ *n, pl* **-dos** *or* **-does** **1 a** : a gradual increase; *esp* : a gradual increase in volume of a musical passage **b** : the peak of a gradual increase : CLIMAX ⟨complaints about stifling smog conditions reach a ~ — *Down Beat*⟩ **2** : a crescendo musical passage — **crescendo** *vi*

mark indicating crescendo 2

²crescendo *adv or adj* : with an increase in volume — used as a direction in music

¹cres·cent \ˈkres-ᵊnt\ *n* [ME *cressant,* fr. MF *creissant,* fr. prp. of *creistre* to grow, increase, fr. L *crescere;* akin to OHG *hirsi* millet, L *creare* to create, Gk *koros* boy] **1 a** : the moon at any stage between new moon and first quarter and between last quarter and the succeeding new moon when less than half of the illuminated hemisphere is visible **b** : the figure of the moon at such a stage defined by a convex and a concave edge **2** : something shaped like a crescent — **cres·cen·tic** \kre-ˈsent-ik, krə-\ *adj*

²crescent *adj* [L *crescent-, crescens,* prp. of *crescere*] : marked by an increase

cres·cive \ˈkres-iv\ *adj* [L *crescere* to grow] : capable of growth : INCREASING — **cres·cive·ly** *adv*

cre·sol \ˈkrē-ˌsȯl, -ˌsōl\ *n* [ISV, irreg. fr. *creosote*] : any of three poisonous colorless crystalline or liquid isomeric phenols C_7H_8O

cress \ˈkres\ *n* [ME *cresse,* fr. OE *cærse, cressa;* akin to OHG *kressa* cress] : any of numerous crucifers (esp. genera *Rorippa, Arabis,* and *Barbarea*) with moderately pungent leaves used in salads and garnishes

cres·set \ˈkres-ət\ *n* [ME, fr. MF, fr. OF *craisset,* fr. *craisse* grease — more at GREASE] : an iron vessel or basket used for holding an illuminant (as burning oil) and mounted as a torch or suspended as a lantern

Cres·si·da \ˈkres-əd-ə\ *n* : a Trojan woman of medieval legend who pledges herself to Troilus but while a captive of the Greeks gives herself to Diomedes

¹crest \ˈkrest\ *n* [ME *creste,* fr. MF, fr. L *crista;* akin to OE *hrisian* to shake, L *curvus* curved — more at CROWN] **1 a** : a showy tuft or process on the head of an animal and esp. a bird — see BIRD illustration **b** : the plume or identifying emblem worn on a knight's helmet **c** (1) : a heraldic representation of the crest (2) : a heraldic device depicted above the escutcheon but not upon a helmet (3) : COAT OF ARMS 2a **2** : something suggesting a crest esp. in being an upper prominence, edge, or limit: as **a** : PEAK; *esp* : the top line of a mountain or hill **b** : the ridge or top of a wave or roof **3 a** : a high point of an action or process **b** : CLIMAX, CULMINATION ⟨at the ~ of his fame⟩ — **crest·al** \ˈkres-tᵊl\ *adj*

²crest *vt* **1** : to furnish with a crest : CROWN **2** : to reach the crest of ⟨~*ed* the hill and looked about him⟩ ~ *vi* : to rise to a crest ⟨waves ~*ing* in the storm⟩

crest·ed \ˈkres-təd\ *adj* : having a crest ⟨a ~ bird⟩

crested wheatgrass *n* : either of two grasses (*Agropyron cristatum* or *A. desertorum*) that were introduced from Russia and are grown in the U.S. for forage and for erosion control

crest·fall·en \ˈkrest-ˌfȯ-lən\ *adj* **1** : having a drooping crest or hanging head **2** : feeling shame or humiliation : DEJECTED — **crest·fall·en·ly** *adv* — **crest·fall·en·ness** \-lən-nəs\ *n*

crest·less \ˈkrest-ləs\ *adj* : lacking a crest; *specif* : LOWBORN

cre·syl \ˈkres-əl, ˈkrē-ˌsil\ *n* [ISV *cresol* + *-yl*] : TOLYL

cre·syl·ic \kri-ˈsil-ik\ *adj* [ISV *cresyl* + *-ic*] : of or relating to cresol or creosote

cre·ta·ceous \kri-ˈtā-shəs\ *adj* [L *cretaceus,* fr. *creta* chalk] **1** : having the characteristics of or abounding in chalk **2** *cap* : of, relating to, or being the last period of the Mesozoic era or the corresponding system of rocks — **cretaceous** *n* — **cre·ta·ceous·ly** *adv*

cre·tin \ˈkrēt-ᵊn\ *n* [F *crétin,* fr. F dial. *cretin* Christian, human being, kind of idiot found in the Alps, fr. L *christianus* Christian] : one afflicted with cretinism; *broadly* : a person with marked mental deficiency — **cre·tin·ous** \-ᵊn-əs\ *adj*

cre·tin·ism \-ᵊn-ˌiz-əm\ *n* : a usu. congenital abnormal condition marked by physical stunting and mental deficiency and caused by severe thyroid deficiency

cre·tonne \ˈkrē-ˌtän, kri-ˈ\ *n* [F, fr *Creton,* Normandy] : a strong unglazed cotton or linen cloth used esp. for curtains and upholstery

cre·val·le \kri-ˈval-ē\ *n* [by alter.] : CAVALLA 2; *esp* : JACK CREVALLE

cre·vasse \kri-ˈvas\ *n* [F, fr. OF *crevace*] **1** : a deep crevice or fissure (as in a glacier or the earth) **2** : a breach in a levee

crev·ice \ˈkrev-əs\ *n* [ME, fr. MF *crevace,* fr. OF, fr. *crever* to break, fr. L *crepare* to crack — more at RAVEN] : a narrow opening resulting from a split or crack : FISSURE

¹crew \ˈkrü\ *chiefly Brit past of* CROW

²crew \ˈkrü\ *n* [ME *crue,* lit., reinforcement, fr. MF *creue* increase, fr. *creistre* to grow — more at CRESCENT] **1** *archaic* : a band or force of armed men **2** : a company of people temporarily associated together : ASSEMBLAGE **3 a** : a group of people held together by common traits or interests ⟨a wily politician and his ~ of henchmen⟩ **b** : a company of men working on one job or under one foreman or operating a machine **4 a** : the whole company belonging to a ship sometimes including the officers and master **b** : the persons who man an aircraft in flight **c** : the body of men manning a racing shell; *also* : ROWING — **crew·less** \-ləs\ *adj* — **crew·man** \-mən\ *n*

³crew *vi* : to act as a member of a crew ⟨~*ed* on the winning sailboat⟩ ~ *vt* : to serve as a crew member on (as a ship or aircraft)

crew cut *n* : a very short haircut in which the hair resembles the bristle surface of a brush

crew·el \ˈkrü-əl\ *n* [ME *crule*] : slackly twisted worsted yarn used for embroidery

crew·el·work \-ˌwərk\ *n* : embroidery worked with crewel

¹crib \ˈkrib\ *n* [ME, fr. OE *cribb;* akin to OHG *krippa* manger, Gk *griphos* reed basket, OE *cradol* cradle] **1** : a manger for feeding animals **2** : an enclosure esp. of framework: as **a** : a stall for a stabled animal **b** : a small child's bedstead with high enclosing usu. slatted sides **c** : any of various devices resembling a crate or framework in structure **d** : a building for storage : BIN **3** : a small narrow room or dwelling : HUT, SHACK **4** : the cards discarded in cribbage for the dealer to use in scoring **5 a** : a small theft **b** : PLAGIARISM **c** : a literal translation; *esp* : PONY 3 **d** : something used for cheating in an examination **6** : CRÈCHE 3

²crib *vb* **cribbed; crib·bing** *vt* **1** : CONFINE, CRAMP **2** : to provide with or put into a crib; *esp* : to line or support with a framework of timber **3** : PILFER, STEAL; *esp* : PLAGIARIZE ~ *vi* **1 a** : STEAL, PLAGIARIZE **b** : to use a crib : CHEAT **2** : to have the vice of crib biting — **crib·ber** *n*

crib·bage \ˈkrib-ij\ *n* [¹*crib*] : a card game for two players in which each player attempts to form various counting combinations of cards

crib·bing \ˈkrib-iŋ\ *n* : material for use in a crib

crib biting *n* : a vice of horses in which they gnaw (as at the manger) while slobbering and salivating

crib·ri·form \ˈkrib-rə-ˌfȯrm\ *adj* [L *cribrum* sieve; akin to L *cernere* to sift — more at CERTAIN] : pierced with small holes

cri·ce·tid \krī-ˈsēt-əd, -ˈset-\ *n* [deriv. of NL *Cricetus,* genus name, of Slav origin; akin to Czech *křeček* hamster] : any of a family (Cricetidae) of small rodents including the hamsters — **cricetid** *adj*

¹crick \ˈkrik\ *n* [ME *cryk*] : a painful spasmodic condition of muscles (as of the neck or back)

²crick *vt* **1** : to cause a crick in (as the neck) **2** : to turn or twist (as the head) esp. into a strained position

¹crick·et \ˈkrik-ət\ *n* [ME *criket,* fr. MF *criquet,* of imit. origin] **1** : a leaping orthopteran insect (family Gryllidae) noted for the chirping notes produced by the male by rubbing together specially modified parts of the fore wings **2** : a low wooden footstool **3** : a small metal toy or signaling device that makes a sharp click or snap when pressed

²cricket *n* [MF *criquet* goal stake in a bowling game] **1** : a game played with a ball and bat by two sides of usu. 11 players each on a large field centering upon two wickets each defended by a batsman **2** : fair and honorable behavior

³cricket *vi* : to play the game of cricket — **crick·et·er** *n*

cri·coid \ˈkrī-ˌkȯid\ *adj* [NL *cricoides,* fr. Gk *krikoeidēs* ring-shaped, fr. *krikos* ring — more at CIRCLE] : of, relating to, or being a cartilage of the larynx with which arytenoid cartilages articulate

cri·er \ˈkrī(-ə)r\ *n* : one that cries: **a** : an officer who proclaims the orders of a court **b** : TOWN CRIER

crim con *abbr* criminal conversation

crime \ˈkrīm\ *n* [ME, fr. L *crimen* accusation, fault, crime] **1** : an act or the commission of an act that is forbidden or the omission of a duty that is commanded by a public law and that makes the offender liable to punishment by that law; *esp* : a gross violation of law **2** : a grave offense esp. against morality **3** : criminal activity **4** : something reprehensible, foolish, or disgraceful ⟨it's a ~ to waste good food⟩ *syn* see OFFENSE

crime against humanity : atrocity (as extermination or enslavement) that is directed esp. against an entire population or part of a population on specious grounds and without regard to individual guilt or responsibility even on such grounds

crime against nature : SODOMY

[1]**crim·i·nal** \'krim-ən-ᵊl, 'krim-nəl\ *adj* [ME, fr. MF or LL; MF *criminel,* fr. LL *criminalis,* fr. L *crimin- crimen* crime] **1 :** involving or being a crime **2 :** relating to crime or its punishment **3 :** guilty of crime **4 :** DISGRACEFUL — **crim·i·nal·ly** \-ē\ *adv*
[2]**criminal** *n* **1 :** one that has committed a crime : MALEFACTOR **2 :** a person who has been convicted of a crime
criminal conversation *n* **:** adultery considered as a tort
criminal court *n* **:** a court that has jurisdiction to try and punish offenders against criminal law
crim·i·nal·i·ty \,krim-ə-'nal-ət-ē\ *n* **:** the quality or state of being criminal
criminal law *n* **:** the law of crimes and their punishments
crim·i·nate \'krim-ə-,nāt\ *vt* **-nat·ed; -nat·ing** [L *criminatus,* pp. of *criminari,* fr. *crimin-, crimen* accusation] **1 a :** to accuse of a crime **b :** INCRIMINATE **2 :** to represent as criminal : CONDEMN — **crim·i·na·tion** \,krim-ə-'nā-shən\ *n*
criminol *abbr* criminologist; criminology
crim·i·nol·o·gy \,krim-ə-'näl-ə-jē\ *n* [It *criminologia,* fr. L *crimin-, crimen* + It *-o-* + *-logia* -logy] **:** the scientific study of crime as a social phenomenon, of criminals, and of penal treatment — **crim·i·no·log·i·cal** \-ən-ᵊl-'äj-i-kəl\ *adj* — **crim·i·no·log·i·cal·ly** \-k(ə-)lē\ *adv* — **crim·i·nol·o·gist** \,krim-ə-'näl-ə-jəst\ *n*
crim·i·nous \'krim-ə-nəs\ *adj* **:** CRIMINAL
[1]**crimp** \'krimp\ *vt* [D or LG *krimpen* to shrivel; akin to LG *krampe* hook — more at CRAMP] **1 :** to cause to become wavy, bent, or warped: as **a :** to form (leather) into a desired shape **b :** to draw or pinch in or together in glass manufacturing ⟨~ the neck of a vase⟩ **c :** to roll the edge of **d :** to pinch or press together (as the margins of a pie crust) in order to seal **2 :** to put a crimp in : INHIBIT ⟨dealers whose sales had been ~*ed* by credit controls — *Time*⟩
[2]**crimp** *n* **1 :** something produced by or as if by crimping: as **a :** a section of hair artificially waved or curled **b :** a succession of waves (as in wool fiber) **2 :** something that cramps or inhibits
[3]**crimp** *n* [perh. fr. [1]*crimp*] **:** a person who entraps or forces men into shipping as sailors or into enlisting in an army or navy
[4]**crimp** *vt* **:** to trap into military or sea service : IMPRESS
crimpy \'krim-pē\ *adj* **crimp·i·er; -est :** having a crimped appearance : FRIZZY
[1]**crim·son** \'krim-zən\ *n* [ME *crimisin,* fr. OSp *cremesín,* fr. Ar *qirmizī,* fr. *qirmiz* kermes] **:** any of several deep purplish reds
[2]**crimson** *adj* **:** of the color crimson
[3]**crimson** *vt* **:** to make crimson ~ *vi* **:** to become crimson
[1]**cringe** \'krinj\ *vi* **cringed; cring·ing** [ME *crengen;* akin to OE *cringan* to yield, *cradol* cradle] **1 :** to draw in or contract one's muscles involuntarily **2 :** to shrink in fear or servility **3 :** to approach someone with fawning and self-abasement ***syn*** see FAWN — **cring·er** *n*
[2]**cringe** *n* **:** a cringing act; *specif* **:** a servile bow
crin·gle \'kriŋ-gəl\ *n* [LG *kringel,* dim. of *kring* ring; akin to OE *cradol* cradle] **:** a thimble, grommet, eyelet, or rope loop worked into or attached to the edge of a sail and used for making rope and lines fast
[1]**crin·kle** \'kriŋ-kəl\ *vb* **crin·kled; crin·kling** \-k(ə-)liŋ\ [ME *crynkelen;* akin to OE *cringan* to yield] *vi* **1 a :** to form many short bends or turns **b :** WRINKLE, RIPPLE **2 :** to give forth a thin crackling sound : RUSTLE ⟨*crinkling* silks⟩ ~ *vt* **:** to cause to crinkle
[2]**crinkle** *n* **1 :** WINDING, WRINKLE **2 :** any of several plant diseases marked by crinkling of leaves — **crin·kly** \-k(ə-)lē\ *adj*
cri·noid \'krī-,nȯid\ *n* [deriv. of Gk *krinon* lily] **:** any of a large class (Crinoidea) of echinoderms usu. having a somewhat cup-shaped body with five or more feathery arms — **crinoid** *adj*
crin·o·line \'krin-ᵊl-ən\ *n* [F, fr. It *crinolino,* fr. *crino* horsehair (fr. L *crinis* hair; akin to L *crista* crest) + *lino* flax, linen, fr. L *linum*] **1 :** an open-weave fabric of horsehair or cotton that is usu. stiffened and used esp. for interlinings and millinery **2 a :** HOOPSKIRT **b :** a full stiff skirt or underskirt — **crinoline** *adj*
cri·num \'krī-nəm\ *n* [NL, genus name, fr. L, lily, fr. Gk *krinon*] **:** any of a large genus (*Crinum*) of chiefly tropical bulbous herbs of the amaryllis family (family Amaryllidaceae) grown for their umbels of often fragrant white red-marked flowers
cri·o·llo \krē-'ō(l)-(,)yō\ *n, pl* **-llos** [Sp] **1 a :** a person of pure Spanish descent born in Spanish America **b :** a person born and usu. raised in a Spanish-American country **2 :** a domestic animal of a breed or strain developed in Latin America — **criollo** *adj*
[1]**crip·ple** \'krip-əl\ *n* [ME *cripel,* fr. OE *crypel;* akin to OE *crēopan* to creep — more at CREEP] **1 :** a lame or partly disabled person or animal **2 :** something flawed or imperfect
[2]**cripple** *adj* **1 :** beaing a cripple : LAME **2 :** worn out : INFERIOR
[3]**cripple** *vt* **crip·pled; crip·pling** \-(ə-)liŋ\ **1 :** to deprive of the use of a limb and esp. a leg **2 :** to deprive of strength, efficiency, wholeness, or capability for service ***syn*** see MAIM, WEAKEN — **crip·pler** \-(ə-)lər\ *n*
cri·sis \'krī-səs\ *n, pl* **cri·ses** \'krī-,sēz\ [L, fr. Gk *krisis,* lit., decision, fr. *krinein* to decide — more at CERTAIN] **1 a :** the turning point for better or worse in an acute disease or fever **b :** a paroxysmal attack of pain, distress, or disordered function **c :** an emotionally significant event or radical change of status in a person's life **2 :** the decisive moment (as in a literary plot) **3 a :** an unstable or crucial time or state of affairs whose outcome will make a decisive difference for better or worse **b :** the period of strain following the culmination of a period of business prosperity when forced liquidation occurs ***syn*** see JUNCTURE
[1]**crisp** \'krisp\ *adj* [ME, fr. OE, fr. L *crispus;* akin to L *curvus* curved — more at CROWN] **1 a :** CURLY, WAVY; *also* **:** having close stiff or wiry curls or waves **b :** having the surface roughened into small folds or curling wrinkles **2 a :** easily crumbled : BRITTLE **b** *of pastry* **:** SHORT **c :** being desirably firm and fresh ⟨~ lettuce⟩ **3 a :** being sharp, clean-cut, and clear ⟨a ~ illustration⟩ **b :** noticeably neat **c :** SPRIGHTLY, LIVELY ⟨~ banter between the debating opponents⟩ **d :** FROSTY, SNAPPY ⟨~ winter weather⟩; *also* **:** FRESH, INVIGORATING ⟨~ autumn air⟩ ***syn*** see FRAGILE, INCISIVE — **crisp·ly** *adv* — **crisp·ness** *n*
[2]**crisp** *vt* **1 :** CURL, CRIMP **2 :** to cause to ripple : WRINKLE **3 :** to make or keep crisp ~ *vi* **1 :** CURL **2 :** RIPPLE **3 :** to become crisp — **crisp·er** *n*
[3]**crisp** *n* **1 :** something crisp or brittle **2** *chiefly Brit* **:** POTATO CHIP
cris·pa·tion \kris-'pā-shən\ *n* **1 :** the act or process of curling : the state of being curled **2 :** a slight spasmodic contraction
crisp·en \'kris-pən\ *vt* **:** to make crisp ⟨celery ~*ed* by refrigeration⟩ ~ *vi* **:** to become crisp ⟨a pastry shell ~*ing* in the oven⟩
crispy \'kris-pē\ *adj* **crisp·i·er; -est :** CRISP — **crisp·i·ness** *n*
[1]**criss·cross** \'kris-,krȯs\ *n* [obs. *christcross, crisscross* (mark of a cross)] **1 :** a crisscross pattern : NETWORK **2 :** a confused state ⟨there was a ~ of comment in the room, all of it impatient — Eric Goldman⟩
[2]**crisscross** *vt* **1 :** to mark with intersecting lines **2 :** to pass back and forth through or over ~ *vi* **:** to go or pass back and forth
[3]**crisscross** *adj* **:** marked or characterized by crisscrossing
[4]**crisscross** *adv* **1 :** in a way to cross something else **2 :** AWRY
cris·ta \'kris-tə\ *n, pl* **cris·tae** \-,tē, -,tī\ [NL, fr. L, crest] **:** any of the inwardly projecting folds of the inner membrane of a mitochondrion
crit *abbr* critical; criticism; criticized
cri·te·ri·on \krī-'tir-ē-ən *also* krə-\ *n, pl* **-ria** \-ē-ə\ *also* **-rions** [Gk *kritērion,* fr. *krinein* to judge, decide — more at CERTAIN] **1 :** a characterizing mark or trait **2 :** a standard on which a judgment or decision may be based ***syn*** see STANDARD
[1]**crit·ic** \'krit-ik\ *n* [L *criticus,* fr. Gk *kritikos,* fr. *kritikos* able to discern or judge, fr. *krinein* to judge] **1 a :** one who expresses a reasoned opinion on any matter involving a judgment of its value, truth, or righteousness, an appreciation of its beauty or technique, or an interpretation **b :** one who engages often professionally in the analysis, evaluation, or appreciation of works of art **2 :** one given to harsh or captious judgment : CARPER
[2]**critic** *adj* **:** CRITICAL ⟨felt that the world was looking at him with a ~ eye —Thomas Wolfe⟩
[3]**critic** *n* [Gk *kritikē* art of the critic, fr. fem. of *kritikos* able to discern] **1** *archaic* **:** CRITICISM **2** *archaic* **:** CRITIQUE
crit·i·cal \'krit-i-kəl\ *adj* **1 a :** inclined to criticize severely and unfavorably **b :** consisting of or involving criticism ⟨~ writings⟩; *also* **:** of or relating to the judgment of critics ⟨the play was a ~ success⟩ **c :** exercising or involving careful judgment or judicious evaluation **d :** including variant readings and scholarly emendations ⟨a ~ edition⟩ **2 a :** of, relating to, or being a turning point or specially important juncture ⟨~ phase⟩ **b :** relating to or being a state in which or a measurement or point at which some quality, property, or phenomenon suffers a definite change ⟨~ temperature⟩ **c :** CRUCIAL, DECISIVE ⟨~ test⟩ **d :** indispensable for the weathering, solution, or overcoming of a crisis ⟨the stockpiling of strategic and ~ materials —T. P. Neill⟩ **e :** being in or approaching a state of crisis esp. through economic disorders or by virtue of a disaster ⟨remedy a situation made ~ by the increase of the tax burden —Broadus Mitchell⟩ **3 :** characterized by risk or uncertainty **4 a :** of sufficient size to sustain a chain reaction — used of a mass of fissionable material **b :** sustaining a chain reaction — used of a nuclear reactor — **crit·i·cal·i·ty** \,krit-ə-'kal-ət-ē\ *n* — **crit·i·cal·ly** \'krit-i-k(ə-)lē\ *adv* — **crit·i·cal·ness** \-kəl-nəs\ *n*
syn **1** CRITICAL, HYPERCRITICAL, FAULTFINDING, CAPTIOUS, CARPING, CENSORIOUS *shared meaning element* **:** exhibiting the spirit of one who looks for and points out faults and defects ***ant*** uncritical
2 see ACUTE ***ant*** noncritical
critical angle *n* **1 :** the least angle of incidence at which total reflection takes place **2 :** the angle of attack at which the flow about an airfoil changes abruptly with corresponding abrupt changes in the lift and drag
critical point *n* **:** a point on the graph of a function where the derivative is zero or infinite
critical region *n* **:** the set of outcomes of a statistical test for which the null hypothesis is to be rejected
critical value *n* **:** the value of an independent variable corresponding to a critical point of a function
crit·ic·as·ter \'krit-i-,kas-tər\ *n* **:** an inferior or petty critic
crit·i·cism \'krit-ə-,siz-əm\ *n* **1 a :** the act of criticizing usu. unfavorably **b :** a critical observation or remark **c :** CRITIQUE **2 :** the art of evaluating or analyzing with knowledge and propriety works of art or literature **3 :** the scientific investigation of literary documents (as the Bible) in regard to such matters as origin, text, composition, character, or history
crit·i·cize \'krit-ə-,sīz\ *vb* **-cized; -ciz·ing** *vi* **:** to act as a critic ~ *vt* **1 :** to consider the merits and demerits of and judge accordingly : EVALUATE **2 :** to stress the faults of : cavil at — **crit·i·ciz·able** \-,sī-zə-bəl\ *adj* — **crit·i·ciz·er** *n*
syn CRITICIZE, REPREHEND, BLAME, CENSURE, REPROBATE, CONDEMN, DENOUNCE *shared meaning element* **:** to find fault with openly
[1]**cri·tique** \krə-'tēk, kri-\ *n* [alter. of [3]*critic*] **:** an act of criticizing; *esp* **:** a critical estimate or discussion
[2]**critique** *vt* **cri·tiqued; cri·tiqu·ing :** CRITICIZE, REVIEW
crit·ter \'krit-ər\ *n* [by alter.] *dial* **:** CREATURE
[1]**croak** \'krōk\ *vb* [ME *croken,* of imit. origin] *vi* **1 a :** to make a deep harsh sound **b :** to speak in a hoarse throaty voice **2 :** to grumble dourly : COMPLAIN **3** *slang* **:** DIE ~ *vt* **1 :** to forebode or utter in a hoarse raucous voice **2** *slang* **:** KILL
[2]**croak** *n* **:** a hoarse harsh cry (as of a frog) — **croaky** \'krō-kē\ *adj*
croak·er \'krō-kər\ *n* **1 :** an animal that croaks **2 :** any of various fishes (esp. family Sciaenidae) that produce croaking or grunting noises **3 :** one that habitually forbodes evil : GRUMBLER

Croat \'krōt, 'krō-,at\ *n* [NL *Croata*, fr. Serbo-Croatian *Hrvat*] : CROATIAN

Cro·a·tian \krō-'ā-shən\ *n* **1** : a native or inhabitant of Croatia **2** : a south Slavic language spoken by the Croatian people and distinct from Serbian chiefly in its use of the Latin alphabet — **Cro·a·tian** *adj*

¹cro·chet \krō-'shā\ *n* [F, hook, crochet, fr. MF *croche*, hook, of Scand origin; akin to ON *krōkr* hook — more at CROOK] : needlework consisting of the interlocking of looped stitches formed with a single thread and a hooked needle

²crochet *vt* : to make of crochet ⟨~ed a doily⟩ ~ *vi* : to work with crochet — **cro·chet·er** \-'shā-ər\ *n*

cro·cid·o·lite \krō-'sid-ᵊl-,īt\ *n* [G *krokydolith*, fr. Gk *krokyd-, krokys* nap on cloth + G *-lith* -lite] : a lavender-blue or leek-green mineral of the amphibole group that occurs in silky fibers and massively — compare TIGEREYE

¹crock \'kräk\ *n* [ME, fr. OE *crocc*; akin to MHG *krūche* crock] **1** : a thick earthenware pot or jar **2** [fr. its formation on cooking pots] *dial* : SOOT, SMUT **3** : coloring matter that rubs off from cloth or dyed leather

²crock *vt, dial* : to soil with crock : SMUDGE ~ *vi* : to transfer color under rubbing ⟨a suede that will not ~⟩

³crock *n* [ME *crok*, prob. of Scand origin; akin to Norw dial. *krokje* crock] **1** : one that is broken down, disabled, or impaired **2** : a complaining medical patient whose illness is largely imaginary or psychosomatic

⁴crock *vt* : to cause to become disabled ~ *vi* : to break down

crock·ery \'kräk-(ə-)rē\ *n* : EARTHENWARE

crock·et \'kräk-ət\ *n* [ME *croket*, fr. ONF *croquet* crook, dim. of *croc* hook, of Scand origin; akin to ON *krōkr* hook] : an ornament usu. in the form of curved and bent foliage used on the edge of a gable or spire — **crock·et·ed** \-ət-əd\ *adj*

croc·o·dile \'kräk-ə-,dīl\ *n* [ME & L; ME *cocodrille*, fr. OF, fr. ML *cocodrillus*, alter. of L *crocodilus*, fr. Gk *krokodilos* lizard, crocodile, fr. *krokē* pebble + *drilos* worm; akin to Skt *śarkara* pebble — more at SUGAR] **1 a** : any of several large voracious thick-skinned long-bodied aquatic reptiles (as of the genus *Crocodylus*) of tropical and subtropical waters; *broadly* : CROCODILIAN **b** : the skin or hide of a crocodile **2** *archaic* : one who hypocritically affects sorrow

crocodile 1a

crocodile bird *n* : an African plover (*Pluvianus aegyptius*) that lights on the crocodile and eats its insect parasites

crocodile tears *n pl* : false or affected tears : hypocritical sorrow

croc·o·dil·i·an \,kräk-ə-'dil-ē-ən, -'dil-yən\ *n* : any of an order (Loricata) of reptiles including the crocodiles, alligators, and related extinct forms — **crocodilian** *adj*

croc·o·ite \'kräk-ə-,wīt\ *or* **croc·oi·site** \'kräk-ə-,zīt\ *n* [G *krokoisit, krokoit*, fr. F *crocoise*, fr. Gk *krokoeis* saffron-colored, fr. *krokos*] : a mineral PbCrO₄ consisting of lead chromate

cro·cus \'krō-kəs\ *n, pl* **cro·cus·es** [NL, genus name, fr. L, saffron, fr. Gk *krokos*, of Sem origin] **1** *pl also* **cro·ci** \-,kī, -,kē, -,sī\ : any of a large genus (*Crocus*) of herbs of the iris family having solitary long-tubed flowers and slender linear leaves **2 a** : a dark red ferric oxide used for polishing metals **b** : SAFFRON 2

croft \'krȯft\ *n* [ME, fr. OE; akin to OE *crēopan* to creep — more at CREEP] **1** *chiefly Brit* : a small enclosed field usu. adjoining a house **2** *chiefly Brit* : a small farm worked by a tenant — **croft·er** \'krȯf-tər\ *n*

crois·sant \k(rə-,)wä-'sän\ *n, pl* **croissants** \-'sän(z)\ [F, lit., crescent, fr. MF *creissant*] : a rich crescent-shaped roll

Croix de Guerre \k(rə-,)wäd-i-'ge(ə)r\ *n* [F, lit., war cross] : a French military decoration awarded for gallant action in war

Cro-Ma·gnon \krō-'mag-nən, -'man-yən\ *n* [*Cro-Magnon*, a cave near Les Eyzies, France] : a tall erect race of men known from skeletal remains found chiefly in southern France and classified as the same species (*Homo sapiens*) as recent man

crom·lech \'kräm-,lek\ *n* [W, lit., bent stone] **1** : DOLMEN **2** : a circle of monoliths usu. enclosing a dolmen or mound

crone \'krōn\ *n* [ME, fr. ONF *carogne*, lit., carrion, fr. (assumed) VL *caronia* — more at CARRION] : a withered old woman

Cro·nus \'krō-nəs, 'krän-əs\ *n* [L, fr. Gk *Kronos*] : a Titan dethroned by his son Zeus

cro·ny \'krō-nē\ *n, pl* **cronies** [perh. fr. Gk *chronios* long-lasting, fr. *chronos* time] : a close friend esp. of long standing : CHUM

cro·ny·ism \-nē-,iz-əm\ *n* : partiality to cronies esp. as evidenced in the appointment of political hangers-on to office without regard to their qualifications

¹crook \'krúk\ *n* [ME *crok*, fr. ON *krōkr* hook; akin to OE *cradol* cradle] **1** : an implement having a bent or hooked form: as **a** : POTHOOK **b** (1) : a shepherd's staff (2) : CROSIER **2** : a person given to fraudulent practices : THIEF **3** : BEND, CURVE **4** : a part of something that is hook-shaped, curved, or bent ⟨the ~ of an umbrella handle⟩

²crook *vt* **1** : BEND ⟨~ed my neck so I could see⟩ **2** *slang* **a** : CHEAT **b** : STEAL ~ *vi* : CURVE, WIND ⟨a river ~ing through a valley⟩

crook·back \'krúk-,bak\ *n* **1** *obs* : a crooked back **2** *obs* : HUNCHBACK — **crook·backed** \-'bakt\ *adj*

crook·ed \'krúk-əd\ *adj* **1** : having or marked by a crook or curve : BENT **2** : deviating from rectitude ⟨~ dealings⟩; *also* : DISHONEST ⟨a ~ politician⟩ ⟨~ profits⟩ — **crook·ed·ly** *adv* — **crook·ed·ness** *n*

syn CROOKED, DEVIOUS, OBLIQUE *shared meaning element* : not straight or straightforward ***ant*** straight

Crookes tube \'krúks-\ *n* [Sir William *Crookes*] : a vacuum tube evacuated to a high degree for demonstrating the properties of cathode rays

crook·neck \'krúk-,nek\ *n* : a squash with a long recurved neck

croon \'krün\ *vb* [ME *croynen*, fr. MD *cronen*; akin to OE *cran* crane] *vi* **1** *chiefly Scot* **a** : BELLOW, BOOM **b** : WAIL, LAMENT **2 a** : to make a continued moaning sound **b** : to sing in a gentle murmuring manner **c** : to sing in half voice ~ *vt* : to sing in a crooning manner ⟨~ a lullaby⟩ — **croon** *n*

croon·er \'krü-nər\ *n* : one that croons; *esp* : a singer of popular songs who uses a soft-voice method adapted to amplifying systems

¹crop \'kräp\ *n* [ME, craw, head of a plant, yield of a field, fr. OE *cropp* craw, head of a plant; akin to OHG *kropf* goiter, craw, OE *crēopan* to creep — more at CREEP] **1** : the stock or handle of a whip; *also* : a riding whip with a short straight stock and a loop **2** : a pouched enlargement of the gullet of many birds that serves as a receptacle for food and for its preliminary maceration; *also* : an enlargement of the gullet of another animal (as an insect) **3** [²crop] **a** : an earmark on an animal; *esp* : one made by a straight cut squarely removing the upper part of the ear **b** : a close cut of the hair **4 a** : a plant or animal or plant or animal product that can be grown and harvested extensively for profit or subsistence ⟨an apple ~⟩ ⟨a ~ of wool⟩ **b** : the product or yield of something formed together ⟨the ice ~⟩ **c** : a batch or lot of something produced during a particular cycle ⟨a whole new ~ of college freshmen⟩ **d** : COLLECTION ⟨a ~ of lies⟩ **5** : the total yearly production from a specified area ⟨the county's cotton ~ had never been better⟩

²crop *vb* **cropped; crop·ping** *vt* **1 a** : to remove the upper or outer parts of ⟨~ a hedge⟩ **b** : HARVEST ⟨~ trout⟩ **c** : to cut off short : TRIM ⟨~ a photograph⟩ **2** : to cause (land) to bear a crop ⟨planned to ~ another 40 acres⟩; *also* : to grow as a crop ~ *vi* **1** : to feed by cropping something **2** : to yield or make a crop **3** : to appear unexpectedly or casually ⟨problems ~ up daily⟩

crop-eared \'kräp-'i(ə)rd\ *adj* **1** : having the ears cropped **2** : having the hair cropped so that the ears are conspicuous

crop·land \-,land\ *n* : land that is suited to or used for crops

¹crop·per \'kräp-ər\ *n* **1** : one that crops **2** : one that raises crops; *specif* : SHARECROPPER

²cropper *n* [prob. fr. E dial. *crop* neck, fr. ¹crop] **1** : a severe fall **2** : a sudden or violent failure or collapse

crop rotation *n* : the practice of growing different crops in succession on the same land chiefly to preserve the productive capacity of the soil

cro·quet \krō-'kā\ *n* [F dial., hockey stick, fr. ONF, crook — more at CROCKET] **1** : a game in which players drive wooden balls with mallets through a series of wickets set out on a lawn **2** : the act of driving away an opponent's croquet ball by striking one's own ball placed against it — **croquet** *vt*

cro·quette \krō-'ket\ *n* [F, fr. *croquer* to crunch, of imit. origin] : a small cone-shaped or rounded mass consisting usu. of minced fowl, meat, or vegetable coated with egg and bread crumbs and fried in deep fat

cro·qui·gnole \'krō-kən-,(y)ōl\ *n* [F, a kind of biscuit, fr. *croquer*] : a method used in waving the hair by winding it on curlers from the ends of the hair toward the scalp

cro·quis \krō-'kē\ *n, pl* **cro·quis** \-'kē(z)\ [F, fr. *croquer* to crunch, sketch] : a rough draft : SKETCH

crore \'krō(ə)r, 'krȯ(ə)r\ *n, pl* **crores** *also* **crore** [Hindi *karoṛ*] : ten million; *specif* : a unit of value equal to ten million rupees or 100 lakhs

cro·sier \'krō-zhər\ *n* [ME *croser* crosier bearer, fr. MF *crossier*, fr. OF *crosse* crosier, of Gmc origin; akin to OE *crycc* crutch — more at CRUTCH] **1** : a staff resembling a shepherd's crook carried by bishops and abbots as a symbol of office — see VESTMENT illustration **2** : a plant structure with a coiled end

¹cross \'krȯs\ *n* [ME, fr. OE, fr. ON *or* OIr; ON *kross*, fr. (assumed) OIr *cross*, fr. L *cruc-, crux* — more at RIDGE] **1 a** : a structure consisting of an upright with a transverse beam used esp. by the ancient Romans for execution **b** *often cap* : the cross on

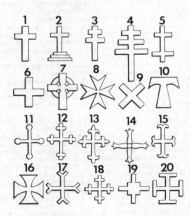

crosses 4a: *1* Latin, *2* Calvary, *3* patriarchal, *4* papal, *5* Lorraine, *6* Greek, *7* Celtic, *8* Maltese, *9* Saint Andrew's, *10* tau, *11* pommée, *12* botonée, *13* fleury, *14* avellan, *15* moline, *16* formée, *17* fourchée, *18* crosslet, *19* quadrate, *20* potent

which Jesus was crucified **2 a :** CRUCIFIXION **b :** an affliction that tries one's virtue, steadfastness, or patience **3 :** a cruciform sign made to invoke the blessing of Christ esp. by touching the forehead, breast, and shoulders **4 a :** a device composed of an upright bar traversed by a horizontal one; *specif* : one used as a Christian emblem **b** *cap* : the Christian religion **5 :** a structure (as a monument) shaped like or surmounted by a cross **6 :** a figure or mark formed by two intersecting lines crossing at their midpoints; *specif* : such a mark used as a signature **7 :** a cruciform badge, emblem, or decoration **8 :** the intersection of two ways or lines : CROSSING **9 :** ANNOYANCE, THWARTING ⟨a ~ in love⟩ **10 a :** an act of crossing dissimilar individuals **10 b :** a crossbred individual or kind **c :** one that combines characteristics of two different types or individuals **11 a :** a fraudulent or dishonest contest **b :** dishonest or illegal practices — used esp. in the phrase *on the cross* **12 :** a movement from one part of a theater stage to another **13 :** a hook thrown over the opponent's lead in boxing **14** *cap* **a :** NORTHERN CROSS **b :** SOUTHERN CROSS **15 :** a security transaction in which a broker acts for both buyer and seller (as in the placing of a large lot of common stock) — called also *cross-trade*

[2]**cross** *vt* **1 a :** to lie or be situated across **1 b :** INTERSECT **2 :** to make the sign of the cross upon or over **3 :** to cancel by marking a cross on or drawing a line through : strike out ⟨~ names off a list⟩ **4 :** to place or fold crosswise one over the other ⟨~ the arms⟩ **5 a** (1) : to run counter to : OPPOSE (2) : to deny the validity of : CONTRADICT **b :** to confront in a troublesome manner : OBSTRUCT **c** (1) : to spoil completely : DISRUPT — used with *up* ⟨his failure to appear ~*ed* up the whole program⟩ (2) : to turn against : BETRAY ⟨~*ed* me up on the deal⟩ **6 a :** to extend across : TRAVERSE ⟨a highway ~*ing* the entire state⟩ **b :** REACH, ATTAIN ⟨only two ~*ed* the finish line⟩ **c :** to go from one side of to the other ⟨~ a street⟩ **7 a :** to draw a line across **b :** to mark or figure with lines : STREAK **8 :** to cause (an animal or plant) to interbreed with one of a different kind : HYBRIDIZE **9 :** to meet and pass on the way ⟨our letters must have ~*ed* each other⟩ **10 :** to occur to ⟨it never ~*ed* my mind⟩ **11 :** to carry or take across something ⟨~*ed* the children at the intersection⟩ ~ *vi* **1 :** to move, pass, or extend across something; *specif* : to pass from one side of the theater stage to another — used with *over* **2 :** to lie or be athwart each other **3 :** to meet in passing esp. from opposite directions **4 :** INTERBREED, HYBRIDIZE — **cross·er** *n* — **cross swords :** to come to grips

[3]**cross** *adj* **1 a :** lying across or athwart **b :** moving across ⟨~ traffic⟩ **2 a :** running counter : OPPOSITE ⟨~ winds⟩ **b :** mutually opposed ⟨~ purposes⟩ **3 :** involving mutual interchange : RECIPROCAL **4 :** marked by typically transitory bad temper : GRUMPY **5 :** extending over or treating several groups or classes ⟨a ~ sample from 25 colleges⟩ **6 :** CROSSBRED, HYBRID ***syn*** see IRASCIBLE — **cross·ly** *adv* — **cross·ness** *n*

[4]**cross** *prep* : ACROSS

[5]**cross** *adv* : not parallel : CRISSCROSS, CROSSWISE

cross·abil·i·ty \ˌkrȯ-sə-ˈbil-ət-ē\ *n* : the ability of different species or varieties to cross with each other

cross·able \ˈkrȯ-sə-bəl\ *adj* : capable of being crossed

cross action *n* : a legal action brought by a defendant in a suit against the person who has sued him and on the same subject matter

cross·bar \ˈkrȯs-ˌbär\ *n* : a transverse bar or stripe

cross·bear·er \ˈkrȯs-ˌbar-ər, -ˌber-\ *n* : CRUCIFER 1

cross·bill \-ˌbil\ *n* : any of a genus (*Loxia*) of finches with strongly curved mandibles that cross each other

cross·bones \-ˌbōnz\ *n pl* : two leg or arm bones placed or depicted crosswise — compare SKULL AND CROSSBONES

cross·bow \-ˌbō\ *n* : a weapon for discharging quarrels and stones that consists chiefly of a short bow mounted crosswise near the end of a wooden stock

cross·bow·man \-mən\ *n* : one (as a soldier or a hunter) whose weapon is a crossbow

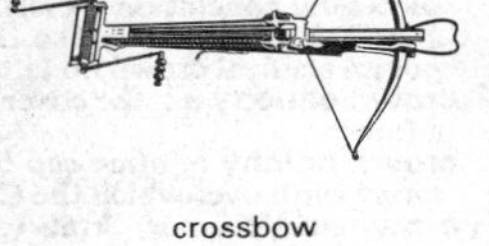

crossbow

cross·bred \ˈkrȯs-ˈbred\ *adj* : HYBRID: *specif* : produced by interbreeding two pure but different breeds, strains, or varieties — **cross·bred** \-ˌbred\ *n*

[1]**cross·breed** \ˈkrȯs-ˌbrēd, -ˈbrēd\ *vb* **-bred** \-ˈbred\; **-breed·ing** *vt* : HYBRIDIZE, CROSS: *esp* : to interbreed (two varieties or breeds) within the same species ~ *vi* : to engage in or undergo interbreeding

[2]**cross·breed** \-ˌbrēd\ *n* : HYBRID

[1]**cross–check** \-ˈchek\ *vt* **1 :** to obstruct in ice hockey or lacrosse by thrusting one's stick held in both hands across an opponent's face or body **2 :** to check (as data or reports) from various angles or sources to determine validity or accuracy

[2]**cross–check** *n* : an act or instance of cross-checking

[1]**cross–coun·try** \ˈkrȯ-ˈskən-trē\ *adj* **1 :** extending or moving across a country ⟨a ~ concert tour⟩ **2 :** proceeding over countryside (as across fields and through woods) and not by roads **3 :** of or relating to racing over the countryside instead of over a track or run ⟨~ skiers⟩ — **cross–country** *adv*

[2]**cross–country** *n* : cross-country sports; *specif* : distance running over the countryside instead of on an oval track

cross·court \ˈkrȯ-ˈskō(ə)rt, -ˈskȯ(ə)rt\ *adv or adj* : to or toward the opposite side of a court (as in tennis or basketball)

cross–cul·tur·al \ˈkrȯ-ˈskəlch-(ə-)rəl\ *adj* : dealing with or offering comparison between two or more different cultures or cultural areas

cross·cur·rent \ˈkrȯ-ˈskər-ənt, -ˈskə-rənt\ *n* **1 :** a current running counter to the general forward direction **2 :** a conflicting tendency — usu. used in pl. ⟨political ~*s*⟩

[1]**cross·cut** \ˈkrȯ-ˌskət, -ˈskət\ *vt* **1 :** to cut with a crosscut saw **2 :** to cut, go, or move across or through : INTERSECT

[2]**crosscut** *adj* **1 :** made or used for cutting transversely ⟨a saw with ~ teeth⟩ **2 :** cut across or transversely ⟨a ~ incision⟩

[3]**cross·cut** \ˈkrȯ-ˌskət\ *n* **1 :** something that cuts across or through; *specif* : a mine working driven horizontally and at right angles to an adit, drift, or level **2 :** CROSS SECTION

crosscut saw *n* : a saw designed chiefly to cut across the grain of wood — compare RIPSAW

crosse \ˈkrȯs\ *n* [F, lit., crosier — more at CROSIER] : the stick used in lacrosse

crosse–check \-ˌchek\ *vi* : to hit an opponent's stick in lacrosse with one's own stick in order to knock the ball loose or to prevent the opponent from picking up the ball

cross–ex·am·i·na·tion \ˌkrȯ-sig-ˌzam-ə-ˈnā-shən\ *n* : the act or process of cross-examining

cross–ex·am·ine \-ˈzam-ən\ *vt* : to examine by a series of questions designed to check or discredit the answers to previous questions — **cross–ex·am·in·er** \-ˈzam-(ə-)nər\ *n*

cross–eye \ˈkrȯ-ˌsī\ *n* **1 :** strabismus in which the eye turns inward toward the nose **2** *pl* \-ˈsīz\ : eyes affected with cross-eye — **cross–eyed** \-ˈsīd\ *adj*

cross–fer·tile \ˈkrȯs-ˈfərt-ᵊl\ *adj* : fertile in a cross or capable of cross-fertilization

cross–fer·til·iza·tion \-ˌfərt-ᵊl-ə-ˈzā-shən\ *n* **1 a :** fertilization in which the gametes are produced by separate individuals or sometimes by individuals of different kinds **b :** CROSS-POLLINATION **2 :** interchange or interaction (as between different ideas, cultures, or categories) esp. of a broadening or productive nature ⟨~ of practical expertise with theoretical learning⟩

cross–fer·til·ize \-ˈfərt-ᵊl-ˌīz\ *vt* : to accomplish cross-fertilization of ~ *vi* : to undergo cross-fertilization

cross–file \-ˈfī(ə)l\ *vi* : to register as a candidate in the primary elections of more than one political party ~ *vt* : to register (a person) as a candidate for more than one party

cross fire *n* **1 :** firing (as in combat) from two or more points so that the lines of fire cross; *also* : a situation wherein the forces of opposing factions meet or cross **2 :** rapid or heated interchange

cross–grained \ˈkrȯs-ˈgrānd\ *adj* **1 :** having the grain or fibers running diagonally, transversely, or irregularly **2 :** difficult to deal with — **cross–grained·ness** \-ˈgrā-nəd-nəs, -ˈgrān(d)-nəs\ *n*

cross hair *n* : one of the fine wires or threads in the focus of the eyepiece of an optical instrument used as a reference line in the field or for marking the instrumental axis

cross·hatch \ˈkrȯs-ˌhach\ *vt* : to mark with two series of parallel lines that intersect — **crosshatch** *n* — **cross–hatch·ing** *n*

cross·head \-ˌhed\ *n* : a metal block to which one end of a piston rod is secured, which slides on parallel guides, and which has a pin for attachment of the connecting rod

cross–in·dex \ˈkrȯ-ˈsin-ˌdeks\ *vt* **1 .** to refer by means of a note at one place to matter at another place **2 :** to refer from (as a variant) to a main entry — **cross–index** *n*

cross·ing \ˈkrȯ-siŋ\ *n* **1 :** the act or action of crossing: as **a :** a traversing or traveling across **b :** an opposing, blocking, or thwarting esp. in an unfair or dishonest manner **2 a :** a place or structure (as on a street or over a river) where pedestrians or vehicles cross; *esp* : CROSSWALK **b :** a place where a railroad track crosses a highway or street

cross·ing–over \ˌkrȯ-siŋ-ˈō-vər\ *n* : an interchange of genes or segments between homologous chromosomes

cross–legged \ˈkrȯ-ˈsleg(-ə)d, -ˈslāg(-ə)d\ *adv or adj* **1 :** with legs crossed and knees spread wide apart **2 :** with one leg placed over and across the other

cross·let \ˈkrȯ-slət\ *n* : a small cross; *esp* : one used as a heraldic bearing — see CROSS illustration

cross–link \ˈkrȯ-ˌsliŋk\ *n* : a crosswise connecting part (as an atom or group) that connects parallel chains in a complex chemical molecule (as a polymer) — **cross–link** *vb*

cross multiply *vi* : to find the two products obtained by multiplying the numerator of each of two fractions by the denominator of the other — **cross multiplication** *n*

cross–na·tion·al \ˈkrȯ-ˈsnash-nəl, -ən-ᵊl\ *adj* : of or relating to two or more nations ⟨~ survey of the aged in the United Kingdom, Denmark, and the U.S.A. —Lenore E. Bixby⟩

cross of Lor·raine \-lə-ˈrān, -lȯ-\ [*Lorraine,* France] : a cross with two crossbars having the upper one intersecting the upright above its middle and the lower one which is longer than the upper one intersecting the upright below its middle — see CROSS illustration

cross·over \ˈkrȯ-ˌsō-vər\ *n* **1 :** CROSSING 2a **2 :** an instance or product of genetic crossing-over **3 :** interchange of the control group and the experimental group during the course of an experiment **4 :** one who votes in an election for a political party which is not the one he has usu. voted for in past elections

cross·patch \ˈkrȯ-ˌspach\ *n* [[3]*cross* + *patch* (fool)] : GROUCH 2

cross·piece \ˈkrȯ-ˌspēs\ *n* : a horizontal member (as of a structure)

cross–pol·li·nate \ˈkrȯ-ˈspäl-ə-ˌnāt\ *vt* : to subject to cross-pollination

cross–pol·li·na·tion \ˌkrȯ-ˌspäl-ə-ˈnā-shən\ *n* : the transfer of pollen from one flower to the stigma of another

cross–pol·li·nize \ˈkrȯ-ˈspäl-ə-ˌnīz\ *vt* : CROSS-POLLINATE

cross product *n* : VECTOR PRODUCT

cross–pur·pose \ˈkrȯ-ˈspər-pəs\ *n* : a purpose usu. unintentionally contrary to another purpose of oneself or of someone else ⟨the two men were always working at ~*s*⟩

cross–ques·tion \ˈkrȯ-ˈskwes(h)-chən\ *n* : a question asked in cross-examination — **cross–question** *vt*

cross–re·ac·tion \ˌkrȯs-rē-ˈak-shən\ *n* : reaction of one antigen with antibodies developed against another antigen

ə abut	ᵊ kitten	ər further	a back	ā bake	ä cot, cart
au̇ out	ch chin	e less	ē easy	g gift	i trip	ī life
j joke	ŋ sing	ō flow	ȯ flaw	ȯi coin	th thin	t͟h this
ü loot	u̇ foot	y yet	yü few	yu̇ furious	zh vision

cross-re·fer \ˌkrȯs-ri-ˈfər\ *vt* : to refer (a reader) by a notation or direction from one place to another (as in a book, list, or catalog) ~ *vi* : to make a cross-reference

1cross-ref·er·ence \ˈkrȯs-ˈref-ərn(t)s, -ˈref-(ə-)rən(t)s\ *n* : a notation or direction at one place (as in a book or filing system) to pertinent information at another place

2cross-reference *vb* : CROSS-REFER

cross-re·sis·tance \ˌkrȯs-ri-ˈzis-tən(t)s\ *n* : tolerance (as of an insect population) to a normally toxic substance (as an insecticide) that is acquired not as a result of direct exposure but by exposure to a related substance

cross·road \ˈkrȯs-ˌrōd, -ˈrōd\ *n* **1** : a road that crosses a main road or runs cross-country between main roads **2** *usu pl but sing or pl in constr* **a** : the place of intersection of two or more roads **b** (1) : a small community located at such a crossroads (2) : a central meeting place **c** : a crucial point esp. where a decision must be made

cross·ruff \ˈkrȯs-ˌrəf, -ˈrəf\ *n* : a series of plays in a card game in which partners alternately trump different suits and lead to each other for that purpose — **crossruff** *vb*

cross section *n* **1** : a cutting or piece of something cut off at right angles to an axis; *also* : a representation of such a cutting **2** : a measure of the probability of an encounter between particles such as will result in a specified effect (as ionization or capture) **3** : a composite representation typifying the constituents of a thing in their relations — **cross-sec·tion·al** *adj*

cross-ster·ile \ˈkrȯs-ˈ(s)ter-əl\ *adj* : mutually sterile — **cross-ste·ril·i·ty** \ˌkrȯs-(s)tə-ˈril-ət-ē\ *n*

cross-stitch \ˈkrȯs-ˌ(s)tich\ *n* **1** : a needlework stitch that forms an X **2** : work having cross-stitch — **cross-stitch** *vb*

cross talk *n* : unwanted signals in a communication channel that come from another channel or in one track of a tape recording that come from another track

cross·town \ˈkrȯ-ˈstau̇n\ *adj* **1** : situated at opposite points of a town **2** : extending or running across a town ⟨a ~ street⟩ ⟨a ~ bus⟩

cross-trade \ˈkrȯ-ˌstrād\ *n* : CROSS 15

cross-trees \ˈkrȯ-(ˌ)strēz\ *n* : two horizontal crosspieces of timber or metal supported by trestletrees at a masthead that spread the upper shrouds in order to support the mast

cross vault *n* : a vault formed by the intersection of two or more simple vaults — called also *cross vaulting*

cross·walk \ˈkrȯ-ˌswȯk\ *n* : a specially paved or marked path for pedestrians crossing a street or road

cross·way \ˈkrȯ-ˌswā\ *n* : CROSSROAD — often used in pl.

cross·ways \-ˌswāz\ *adv* : CROSSWISE, DIAGONALLY

cross·wind \ˈkrȯ-ˌswind\ *n* : a wind blowing in a direction not parallel to a course (as of an airplane)

1cross·wise \ˈkrȯ-ˌswīz\ *adv* **1** *archaic* : in the form of a cross **2** : so as to cross something : ACROSS ⟨logs laid ~⟩

2crosswise *adj* : TRANSVERSE, CROSSING

cross·word puzzle \ˌkrȯ-ˌswərd-\ *n* : a puzzle in which words are filled into a pattern of numbered squares in answer to correspondingly numbered clues and in such a way that the words read across and down

crotch \ˈkräch\ *n* [prob. alter. of *1crutch*] **1** : a pole with a forked end used esp. as a prop **2** : an angle formed by the parting of two legs, branches, or members — **crotched** \ˈkrächt\ *adj*

crotch·et \ˈkräch-ət\ *n* [ME *crochet,* fr. MF — more at CROCHET] **1** *obs* **a** : a small hook or hooked instrument **b** : BROOCH **2 a** : a highly individual and usu. eccentric opinion or preference **b** : a peculiar trick, dodge, or device **3** : QUARTER NOTE ***syn*** see CAPRICE

crotch·ety \ˈkräch-ət-ē\ *adj* **1** : given to crotchets : subject to whims, crankiness, or ill temper ⟨a ~ old man⟩ **2** : full of or arising from crotchets — **crotch·et·i·ness** *n*

cro·ton \ˈkrōt-ᵊn\ *n* [NL, genus name, fr. Gk *krotōn* castor-oil plant] **1** : any of a genus (*Croton*) of herbs and shrubs of the spurge family: as **a** : one (*C. eluteria*) of the Bahamas yielding cascarilla bark **b** : an East Indian plant (*C. tiglium*) yielding a viscid acrid fixed oil used as a drastic cathartic, a vesicant, or a pustulant **2** : any of a genus (*Codiaeum*) of shrubs related to the crotons

Cro·ton bug \ˈkrōt-ᵊn-\ *n* [*Croton* river, N.Y., used as a water supply for New York City] : GERMAN COCKROACH

crouch \ˈkrau̇ch\ *vb* [ME *crouchen*] *vi* **1 a** : to lower the body stance esp. by bending the legs ⟨a sprinter ~*ed* and waited for the gun⟩ **b** : to lie close to the ground with the legs bent ⟨a pair of cats, ~*ing* on the brink of a fight —Aldous Huxley⟩ **2** : to bend or bow servilely : CRINGE ~ *vt* : to bow esp. in humility or fear : BEND — **crouch** *n*

1croup \ˈkrüp\ *n* [ME *croupe,* fr. OF, of Gmc origin; akin to OHG *kropf* craw — more at CROP] : the rump of a quadruped

2croup *n* [E dial. *croup* to cry hoarsely, cough, prob. of imit. origin] : a spasmodic laryngitis esp. of infants marked by episodes of difficult breathing and hoarse metallic cough — **croup·ous** \ˈkrü-pəs\ *adj* — **croupy** \-pē\ *adj*

crou·pi·er \ˈkrü-pē-ər, -pē-ˌā\ *n* [F, lit., rider on the croup of a horse, fr. *croupe* croup] : an employee of a gambling casino who collects and pays bets and assists at the gaming tables

crouse \ˈkrüs\ *adj* [ME] *chiefly Scot* : BRISK, LIVELY

crou·ton \ˈkrü-ˌtän, krü-ˈ\ *n* [F *croûton,* dim. of *croûte* crust, fr. MF *crouste*] : a small cube of toasted or crisply fried bread

1crow \ˈkrō\ *n* [ME *crowe,* fr. OE *crāwe;* akin to OHG *krāwa* crow, OE *crāwan* to crow] **1** : any of various large usu. entirely glossy black oscine birds (family Corvidae and esp. genus *Corvus*) **2** : CROWBAR **3** *cap* **a** : a member of an Amerindian people of the region between the Platte and Yellowstone rivers **b** : the language of the Crow people **4** *cap* : CORVUS — **as the crow flies** : in a straight line

2crow *vi* **crowed** \ˈkrōd\ *also in sense 1 chiefly Brit* **crew** \ˈkrü\; **crow·ing** [ME *crowen,* fr. OE *crāwan*] **1** : to make the loud shrill sound characteristic of a cock **2** : to utter a sound expressive of pleasure **3 a** : to exult gloatingly esp. over the distress of another **b** : to brag exultantly or blatantly ***syn*** see BOAST

3crow *n* **1** : the cry of the cock **2** : a triumphant cry

crow·bar \ˈkrō-ˌbär\ *n* : an iron or steel bar that is usu. wedge-shaped at the working end for use as a pry or lever

crow·ber·ry \ˈkrō-ˌber-ē\ *n* **1** : any of several low shrubby evergreen plants (family Empetraceae); *esp* : an undershrub (*Empetrum nigrum*) of arctic and alpine regions with an insipid black berry **2** : the fruit of a crowberry

1crowd \ˈkrau̇d\ *vb* [ME *crouden,* fr. OE *crūdan;* akin to MHG *kroten* to crowd, OE *crod* multitude, MIr *gruth* curds] *vi* **1 a** : to press on : HURRY **b** : to press close **2** : to collect in numbers ~ *vt* **1 a** : to fill by pressing or thronging together **b** : to press, force, or thrust into a small space **2** : PUSH, FORCE ⟨~*ed* us off the sidewalk⟩ **3 a** : to urge on **b** : to put on (sail) in excess of the usual for greater speed **4** : to put pressure on **5** : THRONG, JOSTLE **6** : to press close to

2crowd *n* **1** : a large number of persons esp. when collected into a somewhat compact body without order : THRONG **2** : the great body of the people : POPULACE **3** : a large number of things close together **4** : a group of people having something (as a habit, interest, or occupation) in common ⟨in with the wrong ~⟩ ***syn*** CROWD, THRONG, CRUSH, MOB, HORDE *shared meaning element* : an assembled multitude usu. of persons

3crowd \ˈkrau̇d, ˈkrüd\ *n* [ME *crowde,* fr. MW *crwth*] **1** : an ancient Celtic stringed instrument played by plucking or with a short bow — called also *crwth* **2** *dial Eng* : FIDDLE

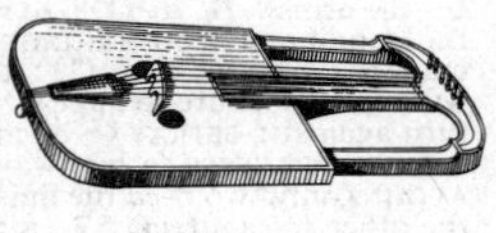

crowd

crowd·ed·ness \ˈkrau̇d-əd-nəs\ *n* : the quality or state of being crowded

crow·foot \ˈkrō-ˌfu̇t\ *n, pl* **crow·feet** \-ˌfēt\ **1** *pl usu* **crowfoots** : any of numerous plants having leaves with cleft lobes; *esp* : any of a genus (*Ranunculus*) of plants of the buttercup family that are mostly yellow-flowered herbs **2** : CROW'S-FOOT 1 — usu. used in pl. **3** : a number of small lines of a boat rove through a long block

crow·keep·er \ˈkrō-ˌkē-pər\ *n, Brit* : a person employed to scare off crows

1crown \ˈkrau̇n\ *n, often attrib* [ME *coroune, crowne,* fr. OF *corone,* fr. L *corona* wreath, crown, fr. Gk *korōnē;* akin to Gk *korōnos* curved, L *curvus,* MIr *cruind* round] **1** : a reward of victory or mark of honor; *esp* : the title representing the championship in a sport **2** : a royal or imperial headdress or cap of sovereignty : DIADEM **3** : the highest part: as **a** : the topmost part of the skull or head **b** : the summit of a mountain **c** : the head of foliage of a tree or shrub **d** : the part of a hat or other headgear covering the crown of the head **e** : the part of a tooth external to the gum or an artificial substitute for this — see TOOTH illustration **4** : a wreath, band, or circular ornament for the head **5** : something resembling a wreath or crown **6** *often cap* **a** (1) : imperial or regal power : SOVEREIGNTY (2) : the government under a constitutional monarchy **b** : MONARCH **7** : something that imparts splendor, honor, or finish : CULMINATION **8 a** (1) : any of several old gold coins with a crown as part of the device (2) : a former usu. silver British coin worth five shillings **b** : a size of paper usu. 15 x 20 in. **9 a** : KORUNA **b** : KRONA **c** : KRONE **10 a** : the region of a seed plant at which stem and root merge **b** : the thick arching end of the shank of an anchor where the arms join it — **crowned** \ˈkrau̇nd\ *adj*

2crown *vt* [ME *corounen,* fr. OF *coroner,* fr. L *coronare,* fr. *corona*] **1 a** : to place a crown or wreath on the head of; *specif* : to invest with regal dignity and power **b** : to recognize officially as ⟨they ~*ed* him athlete of the year⟩ **2** : to bestow something on as a mark of honor or recompense : ADORN **3** : SURMOUNT, TOP; *esp* : to top (a checker) with a checker to make a king **4** : to bring to a successful conclusion : CLIMAX **5** : to provide with something like a crown: as **a** : to fill so that the surface forms a crown **b** : to put an artifical crown on (a tooth) **6** : to hit on the head

crown canopy *n* : the cover formed by the top branches of trees in a forest

crown colony *n, often cap both Cs* : a colony of the British Commonwealth over which the Crown retains some control

crow·ner \ˈkrü-nər, ˈkrau̇-\ *n* [ME, alter. of *coroner*] *chiefly dial* : CORONER

crown·et \ˈkrau̇-nət\ *n, archaic* : CORONET

crown gall *n* : a plant disease that is esp. destructive to stone and pome fruits and that is caused by a bacterium (*Agrobacterium tumefaciens*) which forms tumorous enlargements just below the ground on the stem

crown glass *n* **1** : a glass blown and whirled into the form of a disk with a center lump left by the worker's rod **2** : alkali-lime silicate optical glass having relatively low index of refraction and low dispersion value

crown jewels *n pl* : the jewels (as crown and scepter) belonging to a sovereign's regalia

crown land *n* **1** : land belonging to the crown and yielding revenues that the reigning sovereign is entitled to **2** : public land in some British dominions or colonies

crown lens *n* : the crown glass component of an achromatic lens

crown of thorns : a starfish (*Acanthaster planci*) of the Pacific region that is covered with long spines and is destructive to the coral of coral reefs

crown prince *n* : an heir apparent to a crown or throne

crown princess *n* **1** : the wife of a crown prince **2** : a female heir apparent or heir presumptive to a crown or throne

crown rust *n* : a leaf rust of oats and other grasses that is caused by a fungus (*Puccinia coronata*) and is characterized by rounded light-orange uredinia and buried telia

crown saw *n* : a saw having teeth at the edge of a hollow cylinder

crown vetch *n* : a European herb (*Coronilla varia*) that is naturalized in the eastern U.S. and has umbels of pink-and-white flowers and sharp-angled pods

crow's–foot \ˈkrōz-ˌfu̇t\ *n, pl* **crow's–feet** \-ˌfēt\ **1** : any of the wrinkles around the outer corners of the eyes — usu. used in pl. **2** : CROWFOOT 1

crow's nest *n* : a partly enclosed platform high on a ship's mast for use as a lookout; *also* : a similar lookout (as on a traffic-control tower)

cro·zier *var of* CROSIER

CRT *abbr* cathode-ray tube

cruces *pl of* CRUX

cru·cial \ˈkrü-shəl\ *adj* [F, fr. L *cruc-, crux* cross — more at RIDGE] **1** *archaic* : CRUCIFORM **2 a** : important or essential as resolving a crisis : DECISIVE **b** : marked by final determination of a doubtful issue : TRYING **c** : marked by or possessing importance or significance ⟨what use we make of them will be the ~ question —Stanley Kubrick⟩ ***syn*** see ACUTE — **cru·cial·ly** \ˈkrüsh-(ə-)lē\ *adv*

cru·cian carp \ˌkrü-shən-\ *n* [modif. of LG *karuse,* fr. MHG *karusse,* fr. Lith *karušis*] : a European carp (*Carassius carassius*) — called also *crucian*

cru·ci·ate \ˈkrü-shē-ˌāt\ *adj* [NL *cruciatus,* fr. L *cruc-, crux*] : cross-shaped : CRUCIFORM — **cru·ci·ate·ly** *adv*

cru·ci·ble \ˈkrü-sə-bəl\ *n* [ME *corusible,* fr. ML *crucibulum,* modif. of OF *croiseul*] **1** : a vessel of a very refractory material (as porcelain) used for melting and calcining a substance that requires a high degree of heat **2** : a severe test

crucible steel *n* : hard cast steel made in pots that are lifted from the furnace before the metal is poured into molds

cru·ci·fer \ˈkrü-sə-fər\ *n* [deriv. of L *cruc-, crux* + *-fer*] **1** : one who carries a cross esp. at the head of an ecclesiastical procession **2** : any of a family (Cruciferae) of plants including the cabbage and mustard — **cru·cif·er·ous** \krü-ˈsif-(ə-)rəs\ *adj*

cru·ci·fix \ˈkrü-sə-ˌfiks\ *n* [ME, fr. LL *crucifixus* the crucified Christ, fr. *crucifixus,* pp. of *crucifigere* to crucify, fr. L *cruc-, crux* + *figere* to fasten — more at DIKE] : a representation of Christ on the cross

cru·ci·fix·ion \ˌkrü-sə-ˈfik-shən\ *n* **1 a** : the act of crucifying **b** *cap* : the crucifying of Christ **2** : extreme and painful punishment, affliction, or suffering

cru·ci·form \ˈkrü-sə-ˌfȯrm\ *adj* [L *cruc-, crux* + E *-form*] : forming or arranged in a cross — **cruciform** *n* — **cru·ci·form·ly** *adv*

cru·ci·fy \ˈkrü-sə-ˌfī\ *vt* **-fied; -fy·ing** [ME *crucifien,* fr. OF *crucifier,* fr. LL *crucifigere*] **1** : to put to death by nailing or binding the hands and feet to a cross **2** : to destroy the power of : MORTIFY ⟨~ the flesh⟩ **3** : to treat cruelly : TORTURE, PERSECUTE

1crud \ˈkrəd\ *n* [ME *curd, crudd*] **1** *dial* : 1CURD **2 a** : a deposit or incrustation of filth, grease, or refuse **b** *slang* : something disagreeable or contemptible : RUBBISH, CRAP **3** : a usu. ill-defined or imperfectly identified bodily disorder — **crud·dy** \ˈkrəd-ē\ *adj*

2crud *vb* **crud·ded; crud·ding** *dial* : 2CURD

1crude \ˈkrüd\ *adj* **crud·er; crud·est** [ME, fr. L *crudus* raw — more at RAW] **1** : existing in a natural state and unaltered by cooking or processing ⟨~ rubber⟩ **2** *archaic* : UNRIPE, IMMATURE **3** : marked by the primitive, gross, or elemental or by uncultivated simplicity or vulgarity **4** : rough or inexpert in plan or execution ⟨a ~ shelter⟩ **5** : lacking a covering, glossing, or concealing element : OBVIOUS ⟨~ facts⟩ **6** : tabulated without being broken down into classes ⟨~ death rate⟩ ***syn*** see RUDE ***ant*** finished — **crude·ly** *adv* — **crude·ness** *n*

2crude *n* : a substance in its natural unprocessed state; *esp* : unrefined petroleum

cru·di·ty \ˈkrüd-ət-ē\ *n, pl* **-ties** **1** : the quality or state of being crude **2** : something that is crude

cru·el \ˈkrü-əl\ *adj* **cru·el·er** *or* **cru·el·ler; cru·el·est** *or* **cru·el·lest** [ME, fr. OF, fr. L *crudelis,* irreg. fr. *crudus*] **1** : disposed to inflict pain or suffering : devoid of humane feelings **2 a** : causing or conducive to injury, grief, or pain **b** : unrelieved by leniency ***syn*** see FIERCE ***ant*** pitiful — **cru·el·ly** \ˈkrü-ə-lē\ *adv* — **cru·el·ness** *n*

cru·el·ty \ˈkrü-əl-tē\ *n, pl* **-ties** [ME *cruelte,* fr. OF *cruelté,* fr. L *crudelitat-, crudelitas,* fr. *crudelis*] **1** : the quality or state of being cruel **2 a** : a cruel action **b** : inhuman treatment **3** : marital conduct held (as in a divorce action) to endanger life or health or to cause mental suffering or fear

cru·et \ˈkrü-ət\ *n* [ME, fr. AF, dim. of OF *crue,* of Gmc origin; akin to OE *crocc* crock] **1** : a vessel to hold wine or water for the Eucharist **2** : a usu. glass bottle used to hold a condiment (as oil or vinegar) for use at the table

1cruise \ˈkrüz\ *vb* **cruised; cruis·ing** [D *kruisen* to make a cross, cruise, fr. MD *crucen,* fr. *crūce* cross, fr. L *cruc-, crux* — more at RIDGE] *vi* **1** : to sail about touching at a series of ports **2** : to be on one's way : GO ⟨I'll ~ over to her house to see if she's home⟩ **3** : to travel for the sake of traveling **4 a** : to go about the streets at random but on the lookout for possible developments ⟨the cabdriver *cruised* for an hour before being hailed⟩ **b** : to search (as in public places) for a sexual partner **5 a** *of an airplane* : to fly at the most efficient operating speed **b** *of an automobile* : to travel at a speed suitable for being maintained for a long distance ~ *vt* **1** : to cruise over or about **2** : to inspect (as land) with reference to possible lumber yield

2cruise *n* : an act or an instance of cruising; *esp* : a tour by ship

cruise missile *n* : a guided missile that has a terrain-seeking radar system and that flies at moderate speed and low altitude

cruis·er \ˈkrü-zər\ *n* **1** : a boat or vehicle that cruises; *specif* : SQUAD CAR **2** : a large fast moderately armored and gunned warship usu. of 6000 to 15,000 tons displacement **3** : a motorboat with cabin, plumbing, and other arrangements necessary for living aboard — called also *cabin cruiser* **4** : a person who cruises; *specif* : one who estimates the volume and value of marketable timber on a tract of land and maps it out for logging

crul·ler \ˈkrəl-ər\ *n* [D *krulle,* a twisted cake, fr. *krul* curly, fr. MD *crul*] **1** : a small sweet cake in the form of a twisted strip fried in deep fat **2** *North & Midland* : an unraised doughnut

1crumb \ˈkrəm\ *n* [ME *crumme,* fr. OE *cruma;* akin to MHG *krume* crumb] **1** : a small fragment esp. of bread **2** : BIT **3** : the soft part of bread **4** *slang* : a worthless person

2crumb *vt* **1** : to break into crumbs **2** : to cover or thicken with crumbs **3** : to remove crumbs from ⟨~ a table⟩

crum·ble \ˈkrəm-bəl\ *vb* **crum·bled; crum·bling** \-b(ə-)liŋ\ [alter. of ME *kremelen,* freq. of OE *gecrymian* to crumble, fr. *cruma*] *vt* : to break into small pieces ~ *vi* : to fall into small pieces : DISINTEGRATE — **crumble** *n*

crum·blings \ˈkrəm-b(ə-)liŋz\ *n pl* : crumbled particles : CRUMBS

crum·bly \-b(ə-)lē\ *adj* **crum·bli·er; -est** : easily crumbled : FRIABLE ⟨~ soil⟩ — **crum·bli·ness** *n*

crum·mie *or* **crum·my** \ˈkrəm-ē\ *n, pl* **crummies** [Sc *crumb* crooked, fr. ME, fr. OE] *chiefly Scot* : COW; *esp* : one with crumpled horns

crum·my *or* **crumby** \ˈkrəm-ē\ *adj* **crum·mi·er** *or* **crumb·i·er; -est** [ME *crumme*] **1** *obs* : CRUMBLY **2 a** : MISERABLE, FILTHY **b** : CHEAP, WORTHLESS

1crump \ˈkrəmp\ *vi* [imit.] **1** : CRUNCH **2** : to explode heavily

2crump *n* **1** : a crunching sound **2** : SHELL, BOMB

3crump *adj* [perh. alter. of *crimp* (friable)] *chiefly Scot* : BRITTLE

crum·pet \ˈkrəm-pət\ *n* [perh. fr. ME *crompid (cake)* wafer, lit., curled-up cake, fr. *crumped,* pp. of *crumpen* to curl up, fr. *crump, crumb* crooked] : a small round cake of rich unsweetened batter cooked on a griddle and usu. split and toasted before serving

1crum·ple \ˈkrəm-pəl\ *vb* **crum·pled; crum·pling** \-p(ə-)liŋ\ [(assumed) ME *crumplen,* freq. of ME *crumpen*] *vt* **1** : to press, bend, or crush out of shape : RUMPLE **2** : to cause to collapse ~ *vi* **1** : to become crumpled **2** : COLLAPSE

2crumple *n* : a wrinkle or crease made by crumpling

1crunch \ˈkrənch\ *vb* [alter. of *craunch*] *vi* **1** : to chew or press with a crushing noise **2** : to make one's way with a crushing noise ~ *vt* : to chew, press, or grind with a crunching sound

2crunch *n* **1** : an act of crunching **2** : a sound made by crunching **3** : a tight or critical situation: as **a** : a critical point in the buildup of pressure between opposing elements **b** : a severe economic squeeze (as on credit)

crunch·er \ˈkrən-chər\ *n* **1** : one that crunches **2** : a finishing blow

crunchy \ˈkrən-chē\ *adj* **crunch·i·er; -est** : CRISP — **crunch·i·ness** *n*

crup·per \ˈkrəp-ər, ˈkru̇p-\ *n* [ME *cruper,* fr. OF *crupiere,* fr. *croupe* hindquarters] **1** : a leather loop passing under a horse's tail and buckled to the saddle **2** : 1CROUP; *broadly* : BUTTOCKS

cru·ral \ˈkru̇(ə)r-əl\ *adj* [L *crur-, crus* leg] : of or relating to the thigh or leg; *specif* : FEMORAL

crus \ˈkrüs, ˈkrəs\ *n, pl* **cru·ra** \ˈkru̇(ə)r-ə\ [L *crur-, crus;* akin to Arm *srunk* shinbones] **1** : the part of the hind limb between the femur or thigh and the tarsus or ankle : SHANK **2** : any of various parts that resemble a leg or a pair of legs

1cru·sade \krü-ˈsād\ *n* [blend of MF *croisade* & Sp *cruzada;* both derivs. of L *cruc-, crux* cross] **1** *cap* : any of the military expeditions undertaken by Christian powers in the 11th, 12th, and 13th centuries to win the Holy Land from the Muslims **2** : a remedial enterprise undertaken with zeal and enthusiasm

2crusade *vi* **cru·sad·ed; cru·sad·ing** : to engage in a crusade — **cru·sad·er** *n*

cru·sa·do \krü-ˈsād-(ˌ)ō\ *also* **cru·za·do** \-ˈzäd-(ˌ)ō, -(ˌ)ü\ *n, pl* **-does** *or* **-dos** [Pg *cruzado,* lit., marked with a cross] : an old gold or silver coin of Portugal having a cross on the reverse

cruse \ˈkrüz, ˈkrüs\ *n* [ME; akin to OE *crūse* pitcher] : a small vessel (as a jar or pot) for holding a liquid (as water or oil)

1crush \ˈkrəsh\ *vb* [ME *crusshen,* fr. MF *cruisir,* of Gmc origin; akin to MLG *krossen* to crush] *vt* **1 a** : to squeeze or force by pressure so as to alter or destroy structure **b** : to squeeze together into a mass **2** : HUG, EMBRACE **3** : to reduce to particles by pounding or grinding **4 a** : to suppress or overwhelm as if by pressure or weight **b** : to oppress or burden grievously **c** : to subdue completely **5** : CROWD, PUSH **6** *archaic* : DRINK ~ *vi* **1** *obs* : CRASH **2** : to become crushed **3** : to advance with or as if with crushing — **crush·able** \-ə-bəl\ *adj* — **crush·er** *n*

syn CRUSH, QUELL, EXTINGUISH, SUPPRESS, QUENCH, QUASH *shared meaning element* : to bring to an end by destroying or defeating

2crush *n* **1** : an act of crushing **2** : a crowding together esp. of many people **3** : an intense and usu. passing infatuation; *also* : the object of infatuation ***syn*** see CROWD

crust \ˈkrəst\ *n* [ME, fr. L *crusta;* akin to OE *hrūse* earth, Gk *kryos* icy cold, *krystallos* ice, crystal] **1 a** : the hardened exterior or surface part of bread **b** : a piece of this or of bread grown dry or hard **2** : the pastry cover of a pie **3** : a hard or brittle external coat or covering: as **a** : a hard surface layer (as of soil or snow) **b** : the outer part of the earth composed essentially of crystalline rocks **c** : a deposit built up on the interior surface of a wine bottle during long aging **d** : an encrusting deposit of dried secretions or exudate; *esp* : SCAB **4** : IMPUDENCE, NERVE — **crust** *vb*

crus·ta·cea \ˌkrəs-ˈtā-sh(ē-)ə\ *n pl* [NL, group name, fr. neut. pl. of *crustaceus*] : arthropods that are crustaceans

crus·ta·cean \ˌkrəs-ˈtā-shən\ *n* : any of a large class (Crustacea) of mostly aquatic arthropods that have a chitinous or calcareous and chitinous exoskeleton, a pair of often much modified appendages on each segment, and two pairs of antennae and that include the lobsters, shrimps, crabs, wood lice, water fleas, and barnacles — **crustacean** *adj*

crus·ta·ceous \-shəs\ *adj* [NL *crustaceus,* fr. L *crusta* crust, shell] : of, relating to, having, or forming a crust or shell; *esp* : CRUSTOSE

crust·al \ˈkrəs-tᵊl\ *adj* : relating to a crust (as of the earth)

ə abut	ᵊ kitten	ər further	a back	ā bake	ä cot, cart
au̇ out	ch chin	e less	ē easy	g gift	i trip ī life
j joke	ŋ sing	ō flow	ȯ flaw	ȯi coin	th thin t͟h this
ü loot	u̇ foot	y yet	yü few	yu̇ furious	zh vision

crust·ifi·ca·tion \ˌkrəs-tə-fə-ˈkā-shən\ *n* : INCRUSTATION

crus·tose \ˈkrəs-ˌtōs\ *adj* [L *crustosus* crusted] : having a thin thallus adhering closely to the substratum of rock, bark, or soil ⟨~ lichens⟩ — compare FOLIOSE, FRUTICOSE

crusty \ˈkrəs-tē\ *adj* **crust·i·er; -est** **1** : having or being a crust **2** : giving an effect of surly incivility in address or disposition ***syn*** see BLUFF — **crust·i·ly** \-tə-lē\ *adv* — **crust·i·ness** \-tē-nəs\ *n*

[1]**crutch** \ˈkrəch\ *n* [ME *crucche,* fr. OE *crycc;* akin to OHG *krucka* crutch, OE *cradol* cradle] **1** **a** : a support typically fitting under the armpit for use by the disabled in walking **b** : PROP, STAY **2** : a forked leg rest constituting the pommel of a sidesaddle **3** : the crotch of a human being or an animal **4** : a forked support

[2]**crutch** *vt* : to support on crutches : prop up

crux \ˈkrəks, ˈkru̇ks\ *n, pl* **crux·es** *also* **cru·ces** \ˈkrü-ˌsēz\ [L *cruc-, crux* cross, torture — more at RIDGE] **1** : a puzzling or difficult problem : an unsolved question **2** : an essential point requiring resolution or resolving an outcome ⟨the ~ of the problem⟩ **3** : a main or central feature (as of an argument)

Cru·zan \krü-ˈzan\ *n* [(assumed) AmerSp *cruzano,* fr. *Santa Cruz* St. Croix] : a native or inhabitant of St. Croix — **Cruzan** *adj*

cru·zei·ro \krü-ˈze(ə)r-(ˌ)ō, -(ˌ)ü\ *n, pl* **-ros** [Pg] — see MONEY table

crwth \ˈkrüth\ *n* [W] : [3]CROWD 1

[1]**cry** \ˈkrī\ *vb* **cried; cry·ing** [ME *crien,* fr. OF *crier,* fr. L *quiritare* to cry out for help (from a citizen), to scream, fr. *Quirit-, Quiris* Roman citizen] *vi* **1** : to call loudly : SHOUT **2** : WEEP, SOB **3** : to utter a characteristic sound or call **4** : to require or suggest strongly a remedy or a disposition ⟨a hundred things which ~ out for planning —Roger Burlingame⟩ ~ *vt* **1** : BEG, BESEECH **2** : to utter loudly : SHOUT **3** : to proclaim publicly : ADVERTISE ⟨~ their wares⟩ — **cry havoc** : to sound an alarm — **cry over spilled milk** : to express vain regrets for what cannot be recovered or undone — **cry wolf** : to give alarm unnecessarily

[2]**cry** *n, pl* **cries** **1** : an instance of crying: as **a** : an inarticulate utterance of distress, rage, or pain **b** *obs* : OUTCRY, CLAMOR **2** **a** *obs* : PROCLAMATION **b** *pl, Scot* : BANNS **3** : ENTREATY, APPEAL **4** : a loud shout **5** : WATCHWORD, SLOGAN ⟨"death to the invader" was the ~⟩ **6** **a** : common report **b** : a general opinion **7** : the public voice raised in protest or approval **8** **a** : a pack of hounds **b** : PURSUIT — used in the phrase *in full cry* **9** : DISTANCE — usu. used in the phrase *a far cry* ⟨but simple trading is a far ~ from running modern corporations —George Melloan⟩

cry- *or* **cryo-** *comb form* [G *kryo-,* fr. Gk, fr. *kryos* — more at CRUST] : cold : freezing ⟨*cry*anesthesia⟩ ⟨*cryo*gen⟩

cry·ba·by \ˈkrī-ˌbā-bē\ *n* : one who cries or complains easily or often

cry down *vt* : DISPARAGE, DEPRECIATE

cry·ing \ˈkrī-iŋ\ *adj* **1** : calling for notice ⟨a ~ need⟩ **2** : NOTORIOUS, HEINOUS ⟨a ~ shame⟩

cry·mo·ther·a·py \ˌkrī-mō-ˈther-ə-pē\ *n* [Gk *krymos, kryos* icy cold + ISV *therapy*] : CRYOTHERAPY

cryo·bi·ol·o·gy \ˌkrī-ō-bī-ˈäl-ə-jē\ *n* : the study of the effects of extremely low temperature on biological systems — **cryo·bi·o·log·i·cal** \-ˌbī-ə-ˈläj-i-kəl\ *adj* — **cryo·bi·o·log·i·cal·ly** \-k(ə-)lē\ *adv* — **cryo·bi·ol·o·gist** \-bī-ˈäl-ə-jəst\ *n*

cry off *vt* : to call off (as an agreement) ~ *vi, chiefly Brit* : to beg off

cryo·gen \ˈkrī-ə-jən\ *n* : a substance for obtaining low temperatures : REFRIGERANT — called also *cryogenic*

cryo·gen·ic \ˌkrī-ə-ˈjen-ik\ *adj* **1** **a** : of or relating to the production of very low temperatures **b** : being or relating to very low temperatures **2** **a** : requiring or involving the use of a cryogenic temperature **b** : requiring cryogenic storage **c** : suitable for storage of a cryogenic substance — **cryo·gen·i·cal·ly** \-i-k(ə-)lē\ *adv*

cryo·gen·ics \-iks\ *n pl but sing or pl in constr* : a branch of physics that deals with the production and effects of very low temperatures

cry·og·e·ny \krī-ˈäj-ə-nē\ *n* : CRYOGENICS

cryo·lite \ˈkrī-ə-ˌlīt\ *n* [ISV] : a mineral Na_3AlF_6 consisting of sodium-aluminum fluoride found in Greenland usu. in white cleavable masses and used in making soda and aluminum

cry·on·ics \krī-ˈän-iks\ *n pl but usu sing in constr* [*cry-* + *-onics* (as in *electronics*)] : the practice of freezing a dead diseased human being in hopes of bringing him back to life at some future time when a cure for his disease has been developed — **cry·on·ic** \-ik\ *adj*

cryo·phil·ic \ˌkrī-ə-ˈfil-ik\ *adj* : thriving at low temperatures

cryo·probe \ˈkrī-ə-ˌprōb\ *n* : a blunt instrument used to apply cold to tissues in cryosurgery

cryo·pro·tec·tive \ˌkrī-ō-prə-ˈtek-tiv\ *adj* : serving to protect from freezing ⟨an extracellular ~ agent⟩

cryo·scope \ˈkrī-ə-ˌskōp\ *n* : an instrument for determining freezing points

cry·os·co·py \krī-ˈäs-kə-pē\ *n* [ISV] : the determination of the lowered freezing points produced in liquid by dissolved substances to determine molecular weights of solutes and various properties of solutions — **cryo·scop·ic** \ˌkrī-ə-ˈskäp-ik\ *adj*

cryo·stat \ˈkrī-ə-ˌstat\ *n* [ISV] : an apparatus for maintaining a constant low temperature

cryo·sur·gery \ˌkrī-ō-ˈsərj-(ə-)rē\ *n* : surgery in which extreme cold chilling (as by use of liquid nitrogen) produces the desired dissection — **cryo·sur·geon** \-ˈsər-jən\ *n* — **cryo·sur·gi·cal** \-ji-kəl\ *adj*

cryo·ther·a·py \-ˈther-ə-pē\ *n* : the therapeutic use of cold

cryo·tron \ˈkrī-ə-ˌträn\ *n* [*cry-* + *-tron*] : a device performing some of the functions of an electron tube and utilizing the fact that a changing magnetic field can cause a superconductive element to oscillate between a state of low and high resistance

crypt \ˈkript\ *n* [L *crypta,* fr. Gk *kryptē,* fr. fem. of *kryptos* hidden, fr. *kryptein* to hide; akin to ON *hreysar* heap of stones, Lith *krauti* to pile up] **1** : a chamber (as a vault) wholly or partly underground; *esp* : a vault under the main floor of a church **2** : a simple gland, glandular cavity, or tube : FOLLICLE — **crypt·al** \ˈkrip-tᵊl\ *adj*

crypt- *or* **crypto-** *comb form* [NL, fr. Gk *kryptos*] **1** : hidden : covered ⟨*crypto*genic⟩ **2** : unavowed ⟨*crypto*fascist⟩ **3** : CRYPTOGRAPHIC ⟨*crypto*system⟩ ⟨*crypto*security⟩

crypt·anal·y·sis \ˌkrip-tə-ˈnal-ə-səs\ *n* [*crypto*gram + *analysis*] **1** : the solving of cryptograms or cryptographic systems **2** : the theory of solving cryptograms or cryptographic systems : the art of devising methods for this — called also *cryptanalytics* — **crypt·an·a·lyt·ic** \ˌkrip-ˌtan-ᵊl-ˈit-ik\ *also* **crypt·an·a·lyt·i·cal** \-ˈit-i-kəl\ *adj* — **crypt·an·a·lyze** \krip-ˈtan-ᵊl-ˌīz\ *vt*

crypt·an·a·lyst \krip-ˈtan-ᵊl-əst\ *n* : a specialist in cryptanalysis

cryp·tic \ˈkrip-tik\ *adj* [LL *crypticus,* fr. Gk *kryptikos,* fr. *kryptos*] **1** : SECRET, OCCULT **2** : intended to be obscure or mysterious ⟨a ~ policy⟩ **3** : serving to conceal ⟨~ coloration in animals⟩ **4** : UNRECOGNIZED **5** : employing cipher or code ***syn*** see OBSCURE — **cryp·ti·cal** \-ti-kəl\ *adj* — **cryp·ti·cal·ly** \-ti-k(ə-)lē\ *adv*

[1]**cryp·to** \ˈkrip-(ˌ)tō\ *n, pl* **cryptos** [*crypt-*] : one who adheres or belongs secretly to a party, sect, or other group

[2]**crypto** *adj* : CRYPTOGRAPHIC

cryp·to·coc·co·sis \ˌkrip-tə-(ˌ)kä-ˈkō-səs\ *n, pl* **-co·ses** \-(ˌ)sēz\ : an infectious disease that is caused by a fungus (*Cryptococcus neoformans*) and is characterized by the production of nodular lesions or abscesses in the lungs, subcutaneous tissues, joints, and esp. the brain and meninges

cryp·to·coc·cus \-ˈkäk-əs\ *n, pl* **-coc·ci** \-ˈkäk-ˌ(s)ī, -(ˌ)(s)ē\ [NL, genus name, fr. *crypt-* + *-coccus*] : any of a genus (*Cryptococcus*) of budding imperfect fungi that resemble yeasts and include a number of saprophytes and a few serious pathogens — **cryp·to·coc·cal** \-ˈkäk-əl\ *adj*

cryp·to·crys·tal·line \ˌkrip-tō-ˈkris-tə-lən\ *adj* [ISV] : having a crystalline structure so fine that no distinct particles are recognizable under the microscope

cryp·to·gam \ˈkrip-tə-ˌgam\ *n* [deriv. of Gk *kryptos* + *-gamia* -gamy] : a plant (as a fern, moss, alga, or fungus) reproducing by spores and not producing flowers or seed — **cryp·to·gam·ic** \ˌkrip-tə-ˈgam-ik\ *or* **cryp·tog·a·mous** \krip-ˈtäg-ə-məs\ *adj*

cryp·to·gen·ic \ˌkrip-tə-ˈjen-ik\ *adj* : of obscure or unknown origin ⟨a ~ disease⟩

cryp·to·gram \ˈkrip-tə-ˌgram\ *n* [F *cryptogramme,* fr. *crypt-* + *-gramme* -gram] **1** : a communication in cipher or code **2** : a figure or representation having a hidden significance — **cryp·to·gram·mic** \ˌkrip-tə-ˈgram-ik\ *adj*

[1]**cryp·to·graph** \ˈkrip-tə-ˌgraf\ *n* **1** : CRYPTOGRAM **2** : a device for enciphering and deciphering

[2]**cryptograph** *vt* : ENCRYPT

cryp·tog·ra·pher \-fər\ *n* : a specialist in cryptography : as **a** : a clerk who enciphers and deciphers messages **b** : one who devises cryptographic methods or systems **c** : CRYPTANALYST

cryp·to·graph·ic \ˌkrip-tə-ˈgraf-ik\ *adj* : of, relating to, or using cryptography — **cryp·to·graph·i·cal·ly** \-i-k(ə-)lē\ *adv*

cryp·tog·ra·phy \krip-ˈtäg-rə-fē\ *n* [NL *cryptographia,* fr. *crypt-* + *-graphia* -graphy] **1** : secret writing : cryptic symbolization **2** : the enciphering and deciphering of messages in secret code **3** : CRYPTANALYSIS

cryp·tol·o·gy \krip-ˈtäl-ə-jē\ *n* : the scientific study of cryptography and cryptanalysis — **cryp·to·log·ic** \ˌkrip-tə-ˈläj-ik\ *or* **cryp·to·log·i·cal** \-i-kəl\ *adj* — **cryp·tol·o·gist** \krip-ˈtäl-ə-jəst\ *n*

cryp·to·me·ria \ˌkrip-tə-ˈmir-ē-ə\ *n* [NL, genus name, fr. *crypt-* + Gk *meros* part] : an evergreen tree (*Cryptomeria japonica*) of the pine family that is a valuable timber tree of Japan

crypt·or·chid \krip-ˈtȯr-kəd\ *n* [NL *cryptorchid-, cryptorchis,* fr. *crypt-* + *orchid-, orchis* testicle, fr. Gk *orchis* — more at ORCHIS] : one affected with cryptorchidism — **cryptorchid** *adj*

crypt·or·chi·dism \-kə-ˌdiz-əm\ *also* **crypt·or·chism** \-ˌkiz-əm\ *n* : a condition in which one or both testes fail to descend normally

cryp·to·zo·ite \ˌkrip-tə-ˈzō-ˌīt\ *n* [*crypt-* + *-zoite* (as in *sporozoite*)] : a malaria parasite that develops in tissue cells and gives rise to the forms that invade blood cells

cryst *abbr* crystalline; crystallized

[1]**crys·tal** \ˈkris-tᵊl\ *n* [ME *cristal,* fr. OF, fr. L *crystallum,* fr. Gk *krystallos* — more at CRUST] **1** : quartz that is transparent or nearly so and that is either colorless or only slightly tinged **2** : something resembling crystal in transparency and colorlessness **3** : a body that is formed by the solidification of a chemical element, a compound, or a mixture and has a regularly repeating internal arrangement of its atoms and often external plane faces **4** : a clear colorless glass of superior quality; *also* : objects or ware of such glass **5** : the glass or transparent plastic cover over a watch or clock dial **6** : a crystalline material used in electronics as a frequency-determining element or for rectification **7** : powdered methamphetamine

[2]**crystal** *adj* **1** : consisting of or resembling crystal : CLEAR, LUCID **2** : relating to or using a crystal ⟨a ~ radio receiver⟩

crystal ball *n* **1** : a sphere esp. of quartz crystal traditionally used by fortune-tellers **2** : a means or method of predicting future events

crystal detector *n* : a detector that depends for its operation on the rectifying action of the surface of contact between various crystals (as of galena) and a metallic electrode

crystal gazing *n* **1** : the art or practice of concentrating on a glass or crystal globe with the aim of inducing a psychic state in which divination can be performed **2** : the attempt to predict future events or make difficult judgments esp. without adequate data — **crystal gazer** *n*

crystall- *or* **crystallo-** *comb form* [Gk *krystallos*] : crystal ⟨*crystal*liferous⟩

crys·tal·lif·er·ous \ˌkris-tə-ˈlif-(ə-)rəs\ *adj* [ISV] : producing or bearing crystals

crys·tal·line \ˈkris-tə-lən *also* -ˌlīn, -ˌlēn\ *adj* [ME *cristallin,* fr. MF & L; MF, fr. L *crystallinus,* fr. Gk *krystallinos,* fr. *krystallos*] **1** : made of crystal : composed of crystals **2** : resembling crystal: as **a** : TRANSPARENT **b** : CLEAR-CUT **3** : constituting or relating to a crystal — **crys·tal·lin·i·ty** \ˌkris-tə-ˈlin-ət-ē\ *n*

crystalline lens *n* : the lens of the eye in vertebrates

crys·tal·lite \ˈkris-tə-ˌlīt\ *n* [G *kristallit,* fr. Gk *krystallos*] **1 a :** a minute mineral form like those common in glassy volcanic rocks usu. not referable to any mineral species but marking the first step in crystallization **b :** a single grain in a medium composed of many crystals **2 :** MICELLE — **crys·tal·lit·ic** \ˌkris-tə-ˈlit-ik\ *adj*

crys·tal·li·za·tion \ˌkris-tə-lə-ˈzā-shən\ *n* **:** the process of crystallizing; *also* **:** a form resulting from this

crys·tal·lize *also* **crys·tal·ize** \ˈkris-tə-ˌlīz\ *vt* **-lized; -liz·ing 1 :** to cause to form crystals or assume crystalline form **2 :** to cause to take a definite form ⟨tried to ~ his thoughts⟩ **3 :** to coat with crystals esp. of sugar ⟨~ grapes⟩ ~ *vi* **:** to become crystallized — **crys·tal·liz·able** \-ˌlī-zə-bəl\ *adj* — **crys·tal·liz·er** *n*

crys·tal·lized *adj* **1 :** formed into crystals **2 :** coated with crystals esp. of sugar **:** CANDIED **3 :** definite in form ⟨failure to distinguish between ~ and uncrystallized opinion — *Psychological Abstracts*⟩

crys·tal·log·ra·phy \ˌkris-tə-ˈläg-rə-fē\ *n* **:** the science dealing with the system of forms among crystals, their structure, and their forms of aggregation — **crys·tal·log·ra·pher** \-fər\ *n* — **crys·tal·lo·graph·ic** \-lə-ˈgraf-ik\ *or* **crys·tal·lo·graph·i·cal** \-i-kəl\ *adj* — **crys·tal·lo·graph·i·cal·ly** \-i-k(ə-)lē\ *adv*

crys·tal·loid \ˈkris-tə-ˌlȯid\ *n* **1 :** a substance that forms a true solution and is capable of being crystallized **2 :** a particle of protein that has the properties of crystal and is found esp. in oily seeds — **crystalloid** *adj* — **crys·tal·loi·dal** \ˌkris-tə-ˈlȯid-ᵊl\ *adj*

crystal violet *n* **:** a triphenylmethane dye found in gentian violet

cry up *vt* **:** to enhance in value or repute by public praise **:** EXTOL

cs *abbr* **1** case; cases **2** census **3** consciousness **4** consul

1Cs *abbr* cirrostratus

2Cs *symbol* cesium

CS *abbr* **1** capital stock **2** Christian Science practitioner **3** civil service **4** conditioned stimulus **5** county seat

C/S *abbr* cycles per second

CSA *abbr* Confederate States of America

csc *symbol* cosecant

CSC *abbr* **1** Civil Service Commission **2** [L *Congregatio a Sancta Cruce*] Congregation of Holy Cross

CSF *abbr* cerebrospinal fluid

CSM *abbr* command sergeant major

CSS *abbr* College Scholarship Service

CSsR *abbr* [L *Congregatio Sanctissimi Redemptoris*] Congregation of the Most Holy Redeemer

CST *abbr* **1** central standard time **2** convulsive shock therapy

ct *abbr* **1** carat **2** cent **3** count **4** county **5** court

CT *abbr* **1** central time **2** certificated teacher; certified teacher **3** code telegram **4** Connecticut

CTC *abbr* centralized traffic control

cte·noid \ˈten-ˌȯid, ˈtē-ˌnȯid\ *adj* [ISV, fr. Gk *ktenoeidēs,* fr. *kten-, kteis* comb — more at PECTINATE] **:** having the margin toothed ⟨~ scale⟩; *also* **:** having or consisting of ctenoid scales ⟨~ fishes⟩

cte·noph·o·ran \ti-ˈnäf-ə-rən\ *adj* **:** of or relating to a ctenophore — **ctenophoran** *n*

cteno·phore \ˈten-ə-ˌfō(ə)r, -ˌfȯ(ə)r\ *n* [deriv. of Gk *kten-, kteis* + *pherein* to carry — more at BEAR] **:** any of a phylum (Ctenophora) of marine animals superficially resembling jellyfishes but having decided biradial symmetry and swimming by means of eight meridional bands of transverse ciliated plates — called also *comb jelly*

ctf *abbr* certificate

ctg *or* **ctge** *abbr* cartage

ctn *abbr* **1** carton **2** cotangent

cto *abbr* concerto

c to c *abbr* center to center

ctr *abbr* **1** center **2** counter

cu *abbr* **1** cubic **2** cumulative

1Cu *abbr* cumulus

2Cu *symbol* [L *cuprum*] copper

CU *abbr* close-up

cua·dri·lla \kwä-ˈdrē(l)-yə\ *n* [Sp, dim. of *cuadra* square, fr. L *quadra*] **:** the team assisting the matador in the bullring

cub \ˈkəb\ *n* [origin unknown] **1 a :** a young carnivorous mammal (as a bear or lion) **b :** a young shark **2 :** a young person **3 :** APPRENTICE; *esp* **:** an inexperienced newspaper reporter

cub·age \ˈkyü-bij\ *n* **:** cubic content, volume, or displacement

Cu·ban heel \ˌkyü-bən-\ *n* [*Cuba,* West Indies] **:** a broad medium-high heel with a moderately curved back

cu·ba·ture \ˈkyü-bə-ˌchü(ə)r, -chər, -ˌt(y)ů(ə)r\ *n* [*cube* + *-ature* (as in *quadrature*)] **1 :** determination of cubic contents **2 :** cubic content

cub·by \ˈkəb-ē\ *n, pl* **cubbies** [obs. E *cub* pen, fr. D *kub* thatched roof; akin to OE *cofa* den — more at COVE] **:** a snug place **:** a cramped space

cub·by·hole \ˈkəb-ē-ˌhōl\ *n* **1 :** CUBBY **2 :** PIGEONHOLE 2

1cube \ˈkyüb\ *n* [ME, fr. L *cubus,* fr. Gk *kybos* cube, vertebra — more at HIP] **1 :** the regular solid of six equal square sides — see VOLUME table **2 :** the product got by taking a number three times as a factor **3** *pl* **:** cubic inches — used of the displacement of an automobile engine

2cube *vt* **cubed; cub·ing 1 :** to raise to the third power **2 :** to form into a cube **3 :** to cut partly through (a steak) in a checkered pattern to increase tenderness by breaking the fibers — **cub·er** *n*

3cube *adj* **:** raised to the third power

4cu·be \ˈkyü-ˌbā, kyü-ˈ\ *n* [AmerSp *cubé*] **:** any of several tropical American plants (genus *Lonchocarpus*) furnishing rotenone

cu·beb \ˈkyü-ˌbeb\ *n* [MF *cubebe,* fr. OF, fr. ML *cubeba,* fr. Ar *kubābah*] **:** the dried unripe berry of a tropical shrub (*Piper cubeba*) of the pepper family that is crushed and smoked in cigarettes for catarrh

cube root *n* **:** a number whose cube is a given number

cube steak *n* **:** a thin slice of beef that has been cubed

1cu·bic \ˈkyü-bik\ *adj* **1 :** having the form of a cube **:** CUBICAL **2 a :** relating to the cube considered as a crystal form **b :** ISOMETRIC 1b **3 a :** THREE-DIMENSIONAL **b :** being the volume of a cube whose edge is a specified unit ⟨~ inch⟩ **4 :** of third degree, order, or power ⟨a ~ polynomial⟩ — **cu·bic·ly** *adv*

2cubic *n* **:** a cubic curve, equation, or polynomial

cu·bi·cal \ˈkyü-bi-kəl\ *adj* **1 :** CUBIC; *esp* **:** shaped like a cube **2 :** relating to volume — **cu·bi·cal·ly** \-k(ə-)lē\ *adv*

cubic equation *n* **:** a polynomial equation in which the highest sum of exponents of variables in any term is three

cu·bi·cle \ˈkyü-bi-kəl\ *n* [L *cubiculum,* fr. *cubare* to lie, recline — more at HIP] **1 :** a sleeping compartment partitioned off from a large room **2 :** a small partitioned space; *esp* **:** CARREL

cubic measure *n* **:** a unit (as cubic inch or cubic centimeter) for measuring volume — see METRIC SYSTEM table, WEIGHT table

cu·bi·form \ˈkyü-bə-ˌfȯrm\ *adj* [L *cubus* + E *-form*] **:** having the shape of a cube

cub·ism \ˈkyü-ˌbiz-əm\ *n* **:** a style of art that stresses abstract structure at the expense of other pictorial elements esp. by displaying several aspects of the same object simultaneously and by fragmenting the form of depicted objects — **cub·ist** \-bəst\ *n* — **cubist** *or* **cu·bis·tic** \kyü-ˈbis-tik\ *adj*

cu·bit \ˈkyü-bət\ *n* [ME, fr. L *cubitum* elbow, cubit — more at HIP] **:** any of various ancient units of length based on the length of the forearm from the elbow to the tip of the middle finger and usu. equal to about 18 inches but sometimes to 21 or more

cu·boid \ˈkyü-ˌbȯid\ *adj* **:** approximately cubic in shape; *specif* **:** being the outermost of the distal row of tarsal bones of many higher vertebrates

cu·boi·dal \kyü-ˈbȯid-ᵊl\ *adj* **1 :** somewhat cubical **2 :** composed of nearly cubical elements ⟨~ epithelium⟩

cub scout *n* **:** a member of the scouting program of the Boy Scouts of America for boys of the age range 8–10

cuck·ing stool \ˈkək-iŋ-\ *n* [ME *cucking stol,* lit., defecating chair] **:** a chair formerly used for punishing offenders (as dishonest tradesmen) by public exposure or ducking in water

1cuck·old \ˈkək-əld, ˈkůk-\ *n* [ME *cokewold*] **:** a man whose wife is unfaithful

2cuckold *vt* **:** to make a cuckold of

cuck·old·ry \-əl-drē\ *n* **1 :** the practice of making cuckolds **2 :** the state of being a cuckold

1cuck·oo \ˈkük-(ˌ)ü, ˈkůk-\ *n, pl* **cuckoos** [ME *cuccu,* of imit. origin] **1 :** a largely grayish brown European bird (*Cuculus canorus*) that is a parasite given to laying its eggs in the nests of other birds which hatch them and rear the offspring; *broadly* **:** any of a large family (Cuculidae of the order Cuculiformes) to which this bird belongs **2 :** the call of the cuckoo **3 :** a silly or slightly crackbrained person

2cuckoo *vt* **:** to repeat monotonously as a cuckoo does its call

3cuckoo *adj* **1 :** of, relating to, or resembling the cuckoo **2 :** deficient in sense or intelligence **:** SILLY

cuckoo clock *n* **:** a wall or shelf clock that announces the hours by sounds resembling a cuckoo's call

cuck·oo·flow·er \ˈkük-(ˌ)ü-ˌflaů(-ə)r, ˈkůk-\ *n* **1 :** a bitter cress (*Cardamine pratensis*) of Europe and America **2 :** RAGGED ROBIN **3 :** WOOD SORREL 1

cuck·oo·pint \-ˌpint\ *n* [ME *cuccupintel,* fr. *cuccu* + *pintel* pintle] **:** a European arum (*Arum maculatum*) with erect spathe and short purple spadix

cuckoo spit *n* **1 :** a frothy secretion exuded on plants by the nymphs of spittle insects **2 :** SPITTLE INSECT

cu·cul·late \ˈkyü-kə-ˌlāt, kyü-ˈkəl-ət\ *also* **cu·cul·lat·ed** \ˈkyü-kə-ˌlāt-əd\ *adj* [ML *cucullatus,* fr. L *cucullus* hood] **:** having the shape of a hood **:** HOODED ⟨a ~ leaf⟩

cu·cum·ber \ˈkyü-(ˌ)kəm-bər\ *n* [ME, fr. MF *cocombre,* fr. L *cucumer-, cucumis*] **:** the fruit of a vine (*Cucumis sativus*) of the gourd family cultivated as a garden vegetable; *also* **:** this vine

cucumber mosaic *n* **:** a virus disease esp. of cucumbers that is transmitted by an aphid and produces mottled foliage and often pale warty fruits

cucumber tree *n* **:** any of several American magnolias (esp. *Magnolia acuminata*) having fruit resembling a small cucumber

cu·cur·bit \kyü-ˈkər-bət\ *n* [ME *cucurbite,* fr. MF, fr. L *cucurbita* gourd] **1 :** a vessel or flask for distillation used with or forming part of an alembic — see ALEMBIC illustration **2 :** a plant of the gourd family

cud \ˈkəd, ˈkůd\ *n* [ME *cudde,* fr. OE *cwudu;* akin to OHG *kuti* glue, Skt *jatu* gum] **1 :** food brought up into the mouth by a ruminating animal from its first stomach to be chewed again **2 :** 2QUID

cud·bear \ˈkəd-ˌba(ə)r, -ˌbe(ə)r\ *n* [irreg. fr. Dr. *Cuthbert* Gordon, 18th cent. Sc chemist] **:** a reddish coloring matter from lichens

1cud·dle \ˈkəd-ᵊl\ *vb* **cud·dled; cud·dling** \ˈkəd-liŋ, -ᵊl-iŋ\ [origin unknown] *vt* **:** to hold close for warmth or comfort or in affection ~ *vi* **:** to lie close or snug **:** NESTLE, SNUGGLE ***syn*** see CARESS

2cuddle *n* **:** a close embrace

cud·dle·some \ˈkəd-ᵊl-səm\ *adj* **:** CUDDLY

cud·dly \ˈkəd-lē, -ᵊl-ē\ *adj* **cud·dli·er; -est :** fit for or inviting cuddling

1cud·dy \ˈkəd-ē\ *n, pl* **cuddies** [origin unknown] **1 a :** a small cabin formerly under the poop deck **b :** the galley or pantry of a small ship **2 :** a small room or cupboard

2cud·dy *or* **cud·die** \ˈkůd-ē, ˈkəd-\ *n, pl* **cuddies** [perh. fr. *Cuddy,* nickname for *Cuthbert*] **1** *dial Brit* **:** DONKEY **2** *dial Brit* **:** BLOCKHEAD

1cud·gel \ˈkəj-əl\ *n* [ME *kuggel,* fr. OE *cycgel;* akin to MHG *kugele* ball, OE *cot* hut — more at COT] **:** a short heavy club

2cudgel *vt* **-geled** *or* **-gelled; -gel·ing** *or* **-gel·ling** \-(ə-)liŋ\ **:** to beat with or as if with a cudgel — **cudgel one's brains :** to think hard (as for a solution to a problem)

ə abut ᵊ kitten ər further a back ā bake ä cot, cart
aů out ch chin e less ē easy g gift i trip ī life
j joke ŋ sing ō flow ȯ flaw ȯi coin th thin t̲h̲ this
ü loot ů foot y yet yü few yů furious zh vision

cud·weed \ˈkəd-ˌwēd, ˈku̇d-\ *n* : any of several composite plants (as of the genus *Gnaphalium*) with silky or woolly foliage

[1]**cue** \ˈkyü\ *n* [ME *cu*] : the letter *q*

[2]**cue** *n* [prob. fr. *qu*, abbr. (used as a direction in actors' copies of plays) of L *quando* when] **1 a** : a signal (as a word, phrase, or bit of stage business) to a performer to begin a specific speech or action **b** : something serving a comparable purpose : HINT **2** : a feature indicating the nature of something perceived **3** : the part one has to perform in or as if in a play **4** *archaic* : MOOD, HUMOR

[3]**cue** *vt* **cued; cu·ing** *or* **cue·ing 1** : to give a cue to : PROMPT **2** : to insert into a continuous performance ⟨~ in sound effects⟩

[4]**cue** *n* [F *queue*, lit., tail, fr. L *cauda*] **1** : QUEUE 2 **2 a** : a leather-tipped tapering rod for striking the cue ball (as in billiards and pool) **b** : a long-handled instrument with a concave head for shoving disks in shuffleboard

[5]**cue** *vb* **cued; cu·ing** *or* **cue·ing** *vt* **1** : QUEUE **2** : to strike with a cue ~ *vi* **1** : QUEUE **2** : to use a cue

cue ball *n* : the ball a player strikes with his cue in billiards and pool

cue bid *n* [[2]*cue*] : a bid in contract bridge that usu. indicates an ace or a void in the suit bid — **cue–bid** *vt*

cues·ta \ˈkwes-tə\ *n* [Sp, fr. L *costa* side, rib — more at COAST] : a hill or ridge with a steep face on one side and a gentle slope on the other

[1]**cuff** \ˈkəf\ *n* [ME] **1** : something (as a part of a sleeve or glove) encircling the wrist **2** : the turned-back hem of a trouser leg **3** : HANDCUFF — usu. used in pl. **4** : an inflatable band that is wrapped around an extremity to control the flow of blood through the part when recording blood pressure with a sphygmomanometer — **cuff·less** \-ləs\ *adj* — **off the cuff** : SPONTANEOUS, INFORMAL — **on the cuff** : on credit

[2]**cuff** *vt* **1** : to furnish with a cuff **2** : HANDCUFF

[3]**cuff** *vb* [perh. fr. obs. E, glove, fr. ME] *vt* : to strike esp. with or as if with the palm of the hand : BUFFET ~ *vi* : FIGHT, SCUFFLE

[4]**cuff** *n* : a blow with the hand esp. when open : SLAP

cuff link *n* : a usu. ornamental device consisting of two parts joined by a shank, chain, or bar for passing through buttonholes to fasten shirt cuffs — usu. used in pl.

cui bo·no \(ˈ)kwē-ˈbō-(ˌ)nō\ *n* [L, to whose advantage?] **1** : a principle that probable responsibility for an act or event lies with one having something to gain **2** : usefulness or utility as a principle in estimating the value of an act or policy

[1]**cui·rass** \kwi-ˈras, kyu̇-\ *n* [ME *curas*, fr. MF *curasse*, fr. LL *coreacea*, fem. of *coreaceus* leathern, fr. L *corium* skin, leather; akin to OE *heortha* deerskin, L *cortex* bark, Gk *keirein* to cut — more at SHEAR] **1** : a piece of armor covering the body from neck to waist; *also* : the breastplate of such a piece **2** : something (as bony plates covering an animal) resembling a cuirass

[2]**cuirass** *vt* : to cover or armor with a cuirass

cui·ras·sier \ˌkwir-ə-ˈsi(ə)r, ˌkyu̇r-\ *n* : a mounted soldier wearing a cuirass

cui·sine \kwi-ˈzēn\ *n* [F, lit., kitchen, fr. LL *coquina* — more at KITCHEN] : manner of preparing food : style of cooking; *also* : the food prepared

cuisse \ˈkwis\ *also* **cuish** \ˈkwish\ *n* [ME *cusseis*, pl., fr. MF *cuissaux*, pl. of *cuissel*, fr. *cuisse* thigh, fr. L *coxa* hip — more at COXA] : a piece of plate armor for the front of the thigh — see ARMOR illustration

cuit·tle \ˈküt-ᵊl\ *vt* **cuit·tled; cuit·tling** \ˈküt-liŋ, -ᵊl-iŋ\ [origin unknown] *Scot* : COAX, WHEEDLE

cuke \ˈkyük\ *n* : CUCUMBER

cul–de–sac \ˌkəl-di-ˈsak, ˌku̇l-\ *n, pl* **culs–de–sac** \ˌkəl(z)-, ˌku̇l(z)-\ *also* **cul–de–sacs** \ˌkəl-də-ˈsaks, ˌku̇l-\ [F, lit., bottom of the bag] **1** : a blind diverticulum or pouch **2** : a street closed at one end

cu·let \ˈkyü-lət, ˈkəl-ət\ *n* [F, fr. dim. of *cul* backside, fr. L *culus;* akin to OE *hȳdan* to hide] **1** : the small flat facet at the bottom of a brilliant parallel to the table — see BRILLIANT illustration **2** : plate armor covering the buttocks

cu·lex \ˈkyü-ˌleks\ *n* [NL, genus name, fr. L, gnat; akin to OIr *cuil* gnat] : any of a large cosmopolitan genus (*Culex*) of mosquitoes that includes the common house mosquito (*C. pipiens*) of Europe and No. America — see MOSQUITO illustration — **cu·li·cine** \ˈkyü-lə-ˌsīn\ *adj or n*

cu·li·nary \ˈkəl-ə-ˌner-ē, ˈkyü-lə-\ *adj* [L *culinarius*, fr. *culina* kitchen — more at KILN] : of or relating to the kitchen or cookery

[1]**cull** \ˈkəl\ *vt* [ME *cullen*, fr. MF *cuillir*, fr. L *colligere* to bind together — more at COLLECT] **1** : to select from a group : CHOOSE ⟨~*ed* the best passages from the poet's work⟩ **2** : to identify and remove the culls from — **cull·er** *n*

[2]**cull** *n* : something rejected esp. as being inferior or worthless ⟨how to separate good-looking pecans from ~*s* —*Washington Post*⟩

cul·len·der *var of* COLANDER

cul·let \ˈkəl-ət\ *n* [perh. fr. F *cueillette* act of gathering, fr. L *collecta*, fr. fem. of *collectus*, pp. of *colligere*] : broken or refuse glass usu. added to new material to facilitate melting in making glass

cul·lion \ˈkəl-yən\ *n* [ME *coillon* testicle, fr. MF, fr. (assumed) VL *coleon-, coleo*, fr. L *coleus* scrotum] *archaic* : a mean or base fellow

[1]**cul·ly** \ˈkəl-ē\ *n, pl* **cullies** [perh. alter. of *cullion*] : one easily tricked or imposed on : DUPE

[2]**cully** *vt* **cul·lied; cul·ly·ing** *archaic* : CHEAT, DECEIVE

[1]**culm** \ˈkəlm\ *n* [ME] **1** : refuse coal screenings : SLACK **2** : a Lower Carboniferous formation in which marine fossil-bearing beds alternate with those containing plant remains

[2]**culm** *n* [L *culmus* stalk — more at HAULM] : a monocotyledonous stem

cul·mi·nant \ˈkəl-mə-nənt\ *adj* **1** : being at greatest altitude or on the meridian **2** : fully developed

cul·mi·nate \ˈkəl-mə-ˌnāt\ *vb* **-nat·ed; -nat·ing** [ML *culminatus*, pp. of *culminare*, fr. LL, to crown, fr. L *culmin-, culmen* top — more at HILL] *vi* **1** *of a celestial body* : to reach its highest altitude; *also* : to be directly overhead **2 a** : to rise to or form a summit **b** : to reach the highest or a climactic or decisive point ~ *vt* : to bring to a head or to the highest point

cul·mi·na·tion \ˌkəl-mə-ˈnā-shən\ *n* **1** : the action of culminating **2** : culminating position : CLIMAX *syn* see SUMMIT

cu·lotte \ˈkü-ˌlät, ˈkyü-; k(y)ü-ˈlät\ *n* [F, breeches, fr. dim. of *cul* backside — more at CULET] : a divided skirt; *also* : a garment having a divided skirt — often used in pl.

culotte

cul·pa·ble \ˈkəl-pə-bəl\ *adj* [ME *coupable*, fr. MF, fr. L *culpabilis*, fr. *culpare* to blame, fr. *culpa* guilt] **1** *archaic* : GUILTY, CRIMINAL **2** : meriting condemnation or blame esp. as wrong or harmful ⟨~ negligence⟩ *syn* see BLAMEWORTHY — **cul·pa·bil·i·ty** \ˌkəl-pə-ˈbil-ət-ē\ *n* — **cul·pa·ble·ness** \ˈkəl-pə-bəl-nəs\ *n* — **cul·pa·bly** \-blē\ *adv*

cul·prit \ˈkəl-prət, -ˌprit\ *n* [AF *cul.* (abbr. of *culpable* guilty) + *prest, prit* ready (i.e. to prove it), fr. L *praestus* — more at PRESTO] **1** : one accused of or charged with a crime **2** : one guilty of a crime or a fault

cult \ˈkəlt\ *n* [F & L; F *culte*, fr. L *cultus* care, adoration, fr. *cultus*, pp. of *colere* to cultivate — more at WHEEL] **1** : formal religious veneration : WORSHIP **2** : a system of religious beliefs and ritual; *also* : its body of adherents **3** : a religion regarded as unorthodox or spurious; *also* : its body of adherents **4** : a system for the cure of disease based on dogma set forth by its promulgator **5 a** : great devotion to a person, idea, or thing; *esp* : such devotion regarded as a literary or intellectual fad **b** : a usu. small circle of persons united by devotion or allegiance to an artistic or intellectual movement or figure — **cul·tic** \ˈkəl-tik\ *adj* — **cult·ism** \ˈkəl-ˌtiz-əm\ *n* — **cult·ist** \ˈkəl-təst\ *n*

cultch *or* **culch** \ˈkəlch\ *n* [perh. fr. a F dial. form of F *couche* couch] **1** : material (as oyster shells) laid down on oyster grounds to furnish points of attachment for the spat **2** *chiefly NewEng* : CLUTTER, TRASH

cul·ti·gen \ˈkəl-tə-jən\ *n* [*culti*vated + *-gen*] **1** : a cultivated organism (as Indian corn) of a variety or species for which a wild ancestor is unknown **2** : CULTIVAR

cul·ti·va·ble \ˈkəl-tə-və-bəl\ *adj* : capable of being cultivated — **cul·ti·va·bil·i·ty** \ˌkəl-tə-və-ˈbil-ət-ē\ *n*

cul·ti·var \ˈkəl-tə-ˌvär, -ˌve(ə)r, -ˌva(ə)r\ *n* [*culti*vated + *var*iety] : an organism of a kind originating and persistent under cultivation

cul·ti·vate \ˈkəl-tə-ˌvāt\ *vt* **-vat·ed; -vat·ing** [ML *cultivatus*, pp. of *cultivare*, fr. *cultivus* cultivable, fr. L *cultus*, pp.] **1** : to prepare or prepare and use for the raising of crops; *specif* : to loosen or break up the soil about (growing plants) **2 a** : to foster the growth of ⟨~ vegetables⟩ **b** : CULTURE 2a **c** : to improve by labor, care, or study : REFINE ⟨~ the mind⟩ **3** : FURTHER, ENCOURAGE ⟨~ the arts⟩ **4** : to seek the society of : make friends with — **cul·ti·vat·able** \-ˌvāt-ə-bəl\ *adj*

cul·ti·vat·ed *adj* : REFINED, EDUCATED ⟨~ speech⟩ ⟨~ tastes⟩

cul·ti·va·tion \ˌkəl-tə-ˈvā-shən\ *n* **1** : the act or art of cultivating; *specif* : TILLAGE **2** : CULTURE, REFINEMENT ⟨a man of charm and ~⟩

cul·ti·va·tor \ˈkəl-tə-ˌvāt-ər\ *n* : one that cultivates; *esp* : an implement to loosen the soil while crops are growing

cul·tur·al \ˈkəlch(-ə)-rəl\ *adj* **1** : of or relating to culture or culturing **2** : concerned with the fostering of plant or animal growth — **cul·tur·al·ly** \-rə-lē\ *adv*

cultural anthropology *n* : anthropology that deals with the study of culture and that uses the methods, concepts, and data of archaeology, ethnology, and ethnography, folklore and linguistics, and sometimes those of sociology and psychology — compare PHYSICAL ANTHROPOLOGY — **cultural anthropologist** *n*

[1]**cul·ture** \ˈkəl-chər\ *n* [ME, fr. MF, fr. L *cultura*, fr. *cultus*, pp.] **1** : CULTIVATION, TILLAGE **2** : the act of developing the intellectual and moral faculties esp. by education **3** : expert care and training ⟨beauty ~⟩ **4 a** : enlightenment and excellence of taste acquired by intellectual and aesthetic training **b** : acquaintance with and taste in fine arts, humanities, and broad aspects of science as distinguished from vocational and technical skills **5 a** : the integrated pattern of human behavior that includes thought, speech, action, and artifacts and depends upon man's capacity for learning and transmitting knowledge to succeeding generations **b** : the customary beliefs, social forms, and material traits of a racial, religious, or social group **6** : cultivation of living material in prepared nutrient media; *also* : a product of such cultivation

[2]**culture** *vt* **cul·tured; cul·tur·ing** \ˈkəlch-(ə-)riŋ\ **1** : CULTIVATE **2 a** : to grow in a prepared medium **b** : to start a culture from

cul·tured \ˈkəl-chərd\ *adj* **1** : CULTIVATED **2** : produced under artificial conditions ⟨~ viruses⟩ ⟨~ pearls⟩

cul·tus \ˈkəl-təs\ *n* [L, adoration] : CULT

cul·ver \ˈkəl-vər, ˈku̇l-\ *n* [ME, fr. OE *culfer*, fr. (assumed) VL *columbra*, fr. L *columbula*, dim. of L *columba* dove — more at COLUMBINE] : PIGEON

cul·ver·in \ˈkəl-və-rən\ *n* [ME, fr. MF *couleuvrine*, fr. *couleuvre* snake, fr. L *colubra*] : an early firearm: **a** : a rude musket **b** : a long cannon (as an 18-pounder) of the 16th and 17th centuries

cul·vert \ˈkəl-vərt\ *n* [origin unknown] **1** : a transverse drain **2** : a conduit for a culvert **3** : a bridge over a culvert

[1]**cum** \(ˌ)ku̇m, (ˌ)kəm\ *prep* [L; akin to L *com-* — more at CO-] : WITH : combined with : along with ⟨served as an office-*cum*-den⟩

[2]**cum** *abbr* cumulative

Cu·ma·na·go·to \(ˌ)kü-ˌmän-ə-ˈgōt-(ˌ)ō\ *n, pl* **Cumanagoto** *or* **Cumanagotos** [Sp, of AmerInd origin] **1** : a member of a Cariban people of Venezuela **2** : the language of the Cumanagoto people

Cumb *abbr* Cumberland

[1]cum·ber \'kəm-bər\ *vt* **cum·bered; cum·ber·ing** \-b(ə-)riŋ\ [ME *cumbren*] **1** *archaic* : TROUBLE, HARASS **2 a** : to hinder by being in the way ⟨~*ed* with heavy clothing⟩ **b** : to clutter up ⟨rocks ~*ing* the yard⟩ **c** : to burden needlessly ⟨~ the memory with trival facts⟩

[2]cumber *n* : something that cumbers; *esp* : HINDRANCE

cum·ber·some \'kəm-bər-səm\ *adj* **1** *dial* : BURDENSOME, TROUBLESOME **2** : unwieldy because of heaviness and bulk ⟨trying to move a ~ old Victorian sideboard⟩ **3** : slow-moving : PONDEROUS ***syn*** see HEAVY — **cum·ber·some·ly** *adv* — **cum·ber·some·ness** *n*

cum·brous \'kəm-b(ə-)rəs\ *adj* : CUMBERSOME ***syn*** see HEAVY — **cum·brous·ly** *adv* — **cum·brous·ness** *n*

cum·in \'kəm-ən\ *n* [ME, fr. OE *cymen;* akin to OHG *kumīn* cumin; both fr. a prehistoric WGmc word borrowed fr. L *cuminum,*fr. Gk *kyminon,* of Sem origin] : a low plant (*Cuminum cyminum*) of the carrot family long cultivated for its aromatic seeds

cum lau·de \ku̇m-'lau̇d-ə, -ē; ˌkəm-'lȯd-ē\ *adv or adj* [NL, with praise] : with distinction ⟨graduated *cum laude*⟩ — compare MAGNA CUM LAUDE, SUMMA CUM LAUDE

cum·mer·bund \'kəm-ər-ˌbənd\ *n* [Hindi *kamarband,* fr. Per, fr. *kamar* waist + *band* band] : a broad waistband usu. worn in place of a vest with men's dress clothes and adapted in various styles of women's clothes

cumquat *var of* KUMQUAT

cum·shaw \'kəm-ˌshȯ\ *n* [Chin (Amoy) *kam sia* grateful thanks (a phrase used by beggars)] : PRESENT, GRATUITY

cumul- *or* **cumuli-** *or* **cumulo-** *comb form* [NL, fr. L *cumulus*] : cumulus and ⟨*cumulo*cirrus⟩

cu·mu·late \'kyü-myə-ˌlāt\ *vb* **-lat·ed, -lat·ing** [L *cumulatus,* pp. of *cumulare,* fr. *cumulus* mass] *vt* **1** : to gather or pile in a heap **2** : to combine into one **3** : to build up by addition of new material ~ *vi* : to become massed — **cu·mu·late** \-lət, -ˌlāt\ *adj* — **cu·mu·la·tion** \ˌkyü-myə-'lā-shən\ *n*

cu·mu·la·tive \'kyü-myə-lət-iv, -ˌlāt-\ *adj* **1 a** : made up of accumulated parts **b** : increasing by successive additions **2 a** : tending to prove the same point ⟨~ evidence⟩ **b** : additional rather than repeated ⟨~ legacy⟩ **3 a** : taking effect upon completion of another sentence ⟨~ sentence⟩ **b** : increasing in severity with repetition of the offense ⟨~ penalty⟩ **4** : to be added if not paid when due to the next or a future payment ⟨~ dividends⟩ **5** : formed by the addition of new material of the same kind ⟨~ book index⟩ **6** : summing or integrating overall data or values of a random variable less than or less than or equal to a specified value ⟨~ normal distribution⟩ ⟨~ frequency distribution⟩ — **cu·mu·la·tive·ly** *adv* — **cu·mu·la·tive·ness** *n*

cumulative distribution function *n* : DISTRIBUTION FUNCTION

cumulative voting *n* : a system of voting for corporate directors in which each shareholder is entitled to a number of votes equal to the number of shares he holds multiplied by the number of directors to be elected and has the right to divide his votes among candidates in any way he chooses

cu·mu·lo·cir·rus \ˌkyü-myə-lō-'sir-əs\ *n* [NL] : a small cumulus cloud at a high altitude having the white delicacy of the cirrus

cu·mu·lo·nim·bus \-'nim-bəs\ *n* [NL] : cumulus cloud often spread out in the shape of an anvil extending to great heights — see CLOUD illustration

cu·mu·lo·stra·tus \-'strāt-əs, -'strat-\ *n* [NL] : a cumulus whose base extends horizontally as a stratus cloud

cu·mu·lous \'kyü-myə-ləs\ *adj* : resembling cumulus

cu·mu·lus \-ləs\ *n, pl* **-li** \-ˌlī, -ˌlē\ [L] **1** : HEAP, ACCUMULATION **2** [NL, fr. L] : a massy cloud form having a flat base and rounded outlines often piled up like a mountain — see CLOUD illustration

cunc·ta·tion \ˌkəŋ(k)-'tā-shən\ *n* [L *cunctation-, cunctatio,* fr. *cunctatus,* pp. of *cunctari* to hesitate; akin to Skt *śaṅkate* he wavers] : DELAY — **cunc·ta·tive** \'keŋ(k)-ˌtāt-iv, -tət-\ *adj*

cu·ne·ate \'kyü-nē-ˌāt, -ət\ *adj* [L *cuneatus,* fr. *cuneus* wedge; akin to Skt *śūla* spear] : narrowly triangular with the acute angle toward the base ⟨a ~ leaf⟩ — **cu·ne·ate·ly** *adv*

[1]cu·ne·i·form \kyu̇-'nē-ə-ˌfȯrm, 'kyü-n(ē-)ə-\ *adj* [prob. fr. F *cunéiforme,* fr. MF, fr. L *cuneus* + MF *-iforme* -iform] **1** : having the shape of a wedge **2** : composed of or written in wedge-shaped characters ⟨~ alphabet⟩

[2]cuneiform *n* **1** : cuneiform writing **2** : a cuneiform part; *specif* : a cuneiform bone or cartilage

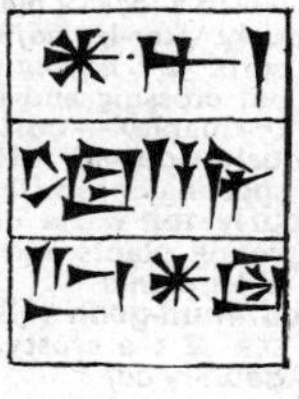
cuneiform 1

cun·ner \'kən-ər\ *n* [origin unknown] : either of two wrasses: **a** : an English wrasse (*Crenilabrus melops*) **b** : a wrasse (*Tautogolabrus adspersus*) abundant on the New England shore

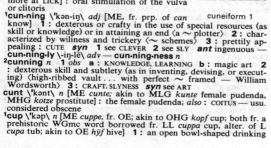

cun·ni·lin·gus \ˌkən-i-'liŋ-gəs\ *or* **cun·ni·linc·tus** \-'liŋ(k)-təs\ *n* [*cunnilingus,* NL, fr. L, one who licks the vulva, fr. *cunnus* vulva + *lingere* to lick; *cunnilinctus,* NL, fr. L *cunnus* + *linctus,* act of licking, fr. *linctus,* pp. of *lingere* — more at LICK] : oral stimulation of the vulva or clitoris

[1]cun·ning \'kən-iŋ\ *adj* [ME, fr. prp. of *can* know] **1** : dexterous or crafty in the use of special resources (as skill or knowledge) or in attaining an end ⟨a ~ plotter⟩ **2** : characterized by wiliness and trickery ⟨~ schemes⟩ **3** : prettily appealing : CUTE ***syn*** **1** see CLEVER **2** see SLY ***ant*** ingenuous — **cun·ning·ly** \-iŋ-lē\ *adv* — **cun·ning·ness** *n*

[2]cunning *n* **1** *obs* **a** : KNOWLEDGE, LEARNING **b** : magic art **2** : dexterous skill and subtlety (as in inventing, devising, or executing) ⟨high-ribbed vault . . . with perfect ~ framed — William Wordsworth⟩ **3** : CRAFT, SLYNESS ***syn*** see ART

cunt \'kənt\ *n* [ME *cunte;* akin to MLG *kunte* female pudenda, MHG *kotze* prostitute] : the female pudenda; *also* : COITUS — usu. considered obscene

[1]cup \'kəp\ *n* [ME *cuppe,* fr. OE; akin to OHG *kopf* cup; both fr. a prehistoric WGmc word borrowed fr. LL *cuppa* cup, alter. of L *cupa* tub; akin to OE *hȳf* hive] **1** : an open bowl-shaped drinking vessel **2 a** : a drinking vessel and its contents **b** : the consecrated wine of the Communion **3** : something that falls to one's lot **4** : an ornamental cup offered as a prize (as in a championship) **5 a** : something resembling a cup **b** : a cup-shaped plant organ **c** : an athletic supporter reinforced usu. with plastic to provide extra protection to the wearer **d** : either of two parts of a brassiere that are shaped like and fit over the breasts **e** : the metal case inside a hole in golf; *also* : the hole itself **6** : a usu. iced beverage resembling punch but served from a pitcher rather than a bowl **7** : a half pint : eight ounces **8** : a food served in a cup-shaped usu. footed vessel ⟨fruit ~⟩ **9** : the symbol ∪ indicating the union of two sets — **cup·like** \-ˌlīk\ *adj* — **in one's cups** : DRUNK

[2]cup *vt* **cupped; cup·ping** **1** : to treat by cupping **2 a** : to curve into the shape of a cup ⟨*cupped* his hands around his mouth⟩ **b** : to place in a cup

cup·bear·er \'kəp-ˌbar-ər, -ˌber-\ *n* : one who has the duty of filling and handing around the cups in which wine is served

cup·board \'kəb-ərd\ *n* : a closet with shelves where dishes, utensils, or food is kept; *also* : a small closet

cup·cake \'kəp-ˌkāk\ *n* : a small cake baked in a cuplike mold

[1]cu·pel \kyü-'pel, 'kyü-pəl\ *n* [F *coupelle,* dim. of *coupe* cup, fr. LL *cuppa*] : a small shallow porous cup esp. of bone ash used in assaying to separate precious metals from lead

[2]cupel *vt* **-pelled** *or* **-peled; -pel·ling** *or* **-pel·ing** : to refine by means of a cupel — **cu·pel·ler** *n*

cu·pel·la·tion \ˌkyü-pə-'lā-shən, -ˌpe-\ *n* : refinement (as of gold or silver) in a cupel by exposure to high temperature in a blast of air by which the lead, copper, tin, and other unwanted metals are oxidized and partly sink into the porous cupel

cup·ful \'kəp-ˌfu̇l\ *n, pl* **cup·fuls** \-ˌfu̇lz\ *also* **cups·ful** \'kəps-ˌfu̇l\ **1** : as much as a cup will hold **2** : CUP 7

cup fungus *n* : any of an order (Pezizales) of epigeal mostly saprophytic fungi with a fleshy or horny apothecium that is often colored and is typically shaped like a cup, saucer, or disk

Cu·pid \'kyü-pəd\ *n* [L *Cupido*] **1** : the Roman god of erotic love — compare EROS **2** *not cap* : a figure that represents Cupid as a naked usu. winged boy often holding a bow and arrow

cu·pid·i·ty \kyu̇-'pid-ət-ē\ *n, pl* **-ties** [ME *cupidite,* fr. MF *cupidité,* fr. L *cupiditat-, cupiditas* — more at COVET] **1** : strong desire : LUST **2** : inordinate desire for wealth : AVARICE, GREED

Cupid's bow *n* : a bow that consists of two convex curves usu. with recurved ends

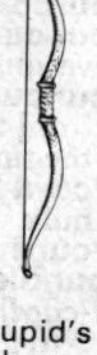
Cupid's bow

cup of tea **1** : something one likes or excels in ⟨as for me, I see already that storytelling isn't my *cup of tea* — John Barth⟩ **2** : a thing to be reckoned with : MATTER ⟨poltergeists are a different *cup of tea* — D. B. W. Lewis⟩

cu·po·la \'kyü-pə-lə, -ˌlō\ *n* [It, fr. L *cupula,* dim. of *cupa* tub] **1 a** : a rounded vault resting on a circular or other base and forming a roof or a ceiling **b** : a small structure built on top of a roof **2** : a vertical cylindrical furnace for melting iron in the foundry that has tuyeres and tapping spouts near the bottom

cup·pa \'kəp-ə\ *n* [short for *cuppa tea,* pronunciation spelling of *cup of tea*] *chiefly Brit* : a cup of tea

cup·ping *n* : an operation of drawing blood to the surface of the body by use of a glass vessel evacuated by heat

cup·py \'kəp-ē\ *adj* **cup·pi·er; -est** **1** : resembling a cup **2** : full of small depressions ⟨a ~ racetrack⟩

cupr- *or* **cupri-** *or* **cupro-** *comb form* [LL *cuprum* — more at COPPER] **1** : copper ⟨*cupri*ferous⟩ **2** : copper and ⟨*cupro*nickel⟩

cu·pram·mo·nium rayon \ˌk(y)ü-prə-'mō-nē-əm-, -nyəm-\ *n* : a rayon made from cellulose dissolved in an ammoniacal copper solution

cu·pre·ous \'k(y)ü-prē-əs\ *adj* [LL *cupreus,* fr. *cuprum*] : containing or resembling copper : COPPERY

cu·pric \-prik\ *adj* : of, relating to, or containing copper with a valence of two

cu·prif·er·ous \k(y)ü-'prif-(ə-)rəs\ *adj* : containing copper

cu·prite \'k(y)ü-ˌprīt\ *n* [G *kuprit,* fr. LL *cuprum*] : a mineral Cu_2O consisting of copper oxide and constituting an ore of copper

cu·pro·nick·el \ˌk(y)ü-prō-'nik-əl\ *n* : an alloy of copper and nickel; *esp* : one containing about 70 percent copper and 30 percent nickel

cu·prous \'k(y)ü-prəs\ *adj* : of, relating to, or containing copper with a valence of one

cu·pu·late \'kyü-pyə-ˌlāt, -lət\ *also* **cu·pu·lar** \-lər\ *adj* : shaped like, having, or bearing a cupule

cu·pule \'kyü-(ˌ)pyü(ə)l\ *n* [NL *cupula,* fr. LL, dim. of L *cupa* tub — more at CUP] : a cup-shaped anatomical structure: as **a** : an involucre characteristic of the oak in which the bracts are indurated and coherent **b** : an outer integument partially enclosing the seed of some seed ferns

[1]cur \'kər\ *n* [ME, short for *curdogge,* fr. (assumed) ME *curren* to growl + ME *dogge* dog; akin to OE *cran* crane] **1** : a mongrel or inferior dog **2** : a surly or cowardly fellow

[2]cur *abbr* **1** currency **2** current

cur·able \'kyu̇r-ə-bəl\ *adj* : capable of being cured — **cur·abil·i·ty** \ˌkyu̇r-ə-'bil-ət-ē\ *n* — **cur·able·ness** \'kyu̇r-ə-bəl-nəs\ *n* — **cur·ably** \-blē\ *adv*

cu·ra·çao \'k(y)u̇r-ə-ˌsō, -ˌsau̇, ˌk(y)u̇r-ə-'\ *also* **cu·ra·çoa** *same, or* ˌk(y)u̇r-ə-'sō-ə\ *n* [D *curaçao,* fr. *Curaçao,* Netherlands Antilles] : a liqueur flavored with the dried peel of the sour orange

cu·ra·cy \'kyu̇r-ə-sē\ *n, pl* **-cies** : the office or term of office of a curate

ə abut ᵊ kitten ər further a back ā bake ä cot, cart
au̇ out ch chin e less ē easy g gift i trip ī life
j joke ŋ sing ō flow ȯ flaw ȯi coin th thin t͟h this
ü loot u̇ foot y yet yü few yu̇ furious zh vision

cu·ra·re *or* **cu·ra·ri** \k(y)u̇-ˈrär-ē\ *n* [Pg & Sp *curare,* fr. Carib *kurari*] **:** a dried aqueous extract esp. of a vine (as *Strychnos toxifera* of the family Loganiaceae or *Chondodendron tomentosum* of the family Menispermaceae) used in arrow poisons by So. American Indians and in medicine to produce muscular relaxation

cu·ra·rine \-ˈrär-ən, -ˌēn\ *n* **:** any of several alkaloids from curare

cu·ra·rize \-ˈrär-ˌīz\ *vt* **-rized; -riz·ing :** to treat with curare — **cu·ra·ri·za·tion** \-ˌrär-ə-ˈzā-shən\ *n*

cu·ras·sow \ˈk(y)u̇r-ə-ˌsō\ *n* [alter. of *Curaçao*] **:** any of several large arboreal game birds (esp. genus *Crax*) of So. and Central America related to the domestic fowls

cu·rate \ˈkyu̇r-ət *also* ˈkyu̇(ə)r-ˌāt\ *n* [ME, fr. ML *curatus,* fr. *cura* cure of souls, fr. L, care] **1 :** a clergyman in charge of a parish **2 :** a clergyman serving as assistant (as to a rector) in a parish

cu·ra·tive \ˈkyu̇r-ət-iv\ *adj* **:** relating to or used in the cure of diseases — **curative** *n* — **cu·ra·tive·ly** *adv*

cu·ra·tor \kyu̇-ˈrāt-ər, ˈkyu̇r-ət-\ *n* [L, fr. *curatus,* pp. of *curare* to care, fr. *cura* care] **:** one that has the care and superintendence of something; *esp* **:** one in charge of a museum, zoo, or other place of exhibit — **cu·ra·to·ri·al** \ˌkyu̇r-ə-ˈtōr-ē-əl, -ˈtȯr-\ *adj* — **cu·ra·tor·ship** \kyu̇-ˈrāt-ər-ˌship, ˈkyu̇r-ət-\ *n*

[1]curb \ˈkərb\ *n* [MF *courbe* curve, curved piece of wood or iron, fr. *courbe* curved, fr. L *curvus*] **1 :** a chain or strap on the upper part of the branches of a bit used to restrain a horse — see BIT illustration **2 :** an enclosing frame, border, or edging **3 :** CHECK, RESTRAINT ⟨a price ~⟩ **4 :** a raised edge or margin to strengthen or confine **5 :** an edging (as of concrete) built along a street to form part of a gutter **6** [fr. the fact that it orig. transacted its business on the street] **:** a market for trading in securities not listed on a stock exchange

[2]curb *vt* **1 :** to furnish with a curb **2 :** to check or control with or as if with a curb ⟨trying to ~ her curiosity⟩ **3 :** to lead (a dog) to a suitable place (as a gutter) for defecation ***syn*** see RESTRAIN ***ant*** spur

curb·ing \ˈkər-biŋ\ *n* **1 :** the material for a curb **2 :** CURB

curb roof *n* **:** a roof with a ridge at the center and a double slope on each of its two sides

curb service *n* **:** service extended (as by a restaurant) to persons sitting in parked automobiles

[1]curb·stone \ˈkərb-ˌstōn\ *n* **:** a stone or edging of concrete forming a curb

[2]curbstone *adj* **1 :** operating on the street without maintaining an office ⟨a ~ broker⟩ **2 :** not having the benefit of training or experience ⟨a ~ critic⟩

curch \ˈkərch\ *n* [ME] *Scot* **:** KERCHIEF 1

cur·cu·lio \(ˌ)kər-ˈkyü-lē-ˌō\ *n, pl* **-li·os** [L, grain weevil] **:** any of various weevils; *esp* **:** one that injures fruit

cur·cu·ma \ˈkər-kyə-mə\ *n* [NL, genus name, fr. Ar *kurkum* saffron] **:** any of a genus (*Curcuma*) of Old World tropical herbs (as the turmeric) of the ginger family with tuberous roots

[1]curd \ˈkərd\ *n* [ME] **1 :** the thick casein-rich part of coagulated milk **2 :** something suggesting the curd of milk — **curdy** \-ē\ *adj*

[2]curd *vb* **:** COAGULATE, CURDLE

cur·dle \ˈkərd-ᵊl\ *vb* **cur·dled; cur·dling** \ˈkərd-liŋ, -ᵊl-iŋ\ [freq. of [2]*curd*] *vt* **1 :** to cause curds to form in **2 :** SPOIL, SOUR ~ *vi* **1 :** to form curds **:** COAGULATE **2 :** to go bad or wrong **:** SPOIL

[1]cure \ˈkyu̇(ə)r\ *n* [ME, fr. OF, fr. ML & L; ML *cura,* cure of souls, fr. L, care] **1 a :** spiritual charge **:** CARE **b :** pastoral charge of a parish **2 a :** recovery or relief from a disease **b :** something (as a drug or treatment) that cures a disease **c :** a course or period of treatment ⟨take the ~ for alcoholism⟩ **d :** SPA **3 :** something that corrects, heals, or permanently alleviates a harmful or troublesome situation ⟨more money is not a certain ~ for the problem⟩ **4 :** a process or method of curing — **cure·less** \-ləs\ *adj*

[2]cure *vb* **cured; cur·ing** *vt* **1 a :** to restore to health, soundness, or normality **b :** to bring about recovery from **2 a :** to deal with in a way that eliminates or rectifies ⟨nothing would ~ the unpleasant odor⟩ **b :** to free from something objectionable or harmful **3 :** to prepare by chemical or physical processing for keeping or use ~ *vi* **1 :** to undergo a curing process **2 :** to effect a cure — **cur·er** *n*

syn CURE, HEAL, REMEDY *shared meaning element* **:** to rectify an unhealthy or undesirable condition

cu·ré \kyu̇-ˈrā, ˈkyu̇(ə)r-ˌā\ *n* [OF, fr. ML *curatus* — more at CURATE] **:** a parish priest

cure–all \ˈkyu̇(ə)r-ˌȯl\ *n* **:** a remedy for all ills **:** PANACEA

cu·ret·tage \ˌkyu̇r-ə-ˈtäzh\ *n* **:** a surgical scraping or cleaning by means of a curette

[1]cu·rette *or* **cu·ret** \kyu̇-ˈret\ *n* [F *curette,* fr. *curer* to cure, fr. L *curare,* fr. *cura*] **:** a scoop, loop, or ring used in performing curettage

[2]curette *or* **curet** *vt* **cu·rett·ed; cu·rett·ing :** to perform curettage on — **cu·rette·ment** \kyu̇-ˈret-mənt\ *n*

cur·few \ˈkər-(ˌ)fyü\ *n* [ME, fr. MF *covrefeu,* signal given to bank the hearth fire, curfew, fr. *covrir* to cover + *feu* fire, fr. L *focus* hearth] **1 :** a regulation enjoining the withdrawal of usu. specified persons (as juveniles or military personnel) from the streets or the closing of business establishments or places of assembly at a stated hour **2 a :** the sounding of a bell or other signal to announce the beginning of a time of curfew **b :** the signal used **3 a :** the hour at which a curfew becomes effective **b :** the period during which a curfew is in effect

cu·ria \ˈk(y)u̇r-ē-ə\ *n, pl* **cu·ri·ae** \ˈkyu̇r-ē-ˌē, ˈku̇r-ē-ˌī\ [L, fr. *co-* + *vir* man — more at VIRILE] **1 a :** a division of the ancient Roman people comprising several gentes of a tribe **b :** the place of assembly of one of these divisions **2 a :** the court of a medieval king **b :** a court of justice **3** *often cap* **:** the body of congregations, tribunals, and offices through which the pope governs the Roman Catholic Church — **cu·ri·al** \ˈkyu̇r-ē-əl\ *adj*

cu·rie \ˈkyu̇(ə)r-(ˌ)ē, kyu̇-ˈrē\ *n* [Mme. Marie *Curie*] **1 :** a unit quantity of any radioactive nuclide in which 3.7×10^{10} disintegrations occur per second **2 :** a unit of radioactivity equal to 3.7×10^{10} disintegrations per second

Curie point *n* [Pierre *Curie*] **1 :** the temperature at which there is a transition between the ferromagnetic and paramagnetic phases **2 :** a temperature at which the anomalies that characterize a ferroelectric substance disappear — called also *Curie temperature*

cu·rio \ˈkyu̇r-ē-ˌō\ *n, pl* **cu·ri·os** [short for *curiosity*] **:** something considered novel, rare, or bizarre **:** CURIOSITY

cu·ri·o·sa \ˌkyu̇r-ē-ˈō-sə, -ˈō-zə\ *n pl* [NL, fr. L, neut. pl. of *curiosus*] **:** CURIOSITIES, RARITIES; *esp* **:** strange or unusual books

cu·ri·os·i·ty \ˌkyu̇r-ē-ˈäs-ət-ē, -ˈäs-tē\ *n, pl* **-ties 1 :** desire to know: **a :** inquisitive interest in others' concerns **:** NOSINESS **b :** interest leading to inquiry ⟨intellectual ~⟩ **2** *archaic* **:** undue nicety or fastidiousness **3 a :** one that arouses interest esp. for uncommon or exotic characteristics **b :** an unusual knickknack **:** CURIO **c :** a curious trait or aspect

cu·ri·ous \ˈkyu̇r-ē-əs\ *adj* [ME, fr. MF *curios,* fr. L *curiosus* careful, inquisitive, fr. *cura* cure] **1 a** *archaic* **:** made carefully **b** *obs* **:** ABSTRUSE **c** *archaic* **:** precisely accurate **2 a :** marked by desire to investigate and learn **b :** marked by inquisitive interest in others' concerns **:** NOSY **3 :** exciting attention as strange or novel **:** ODD — **cu·ri·ous·ly** *adv* — **cu·ri·ous·ness** *n*

syn CURIOUS, INQUISITIVE, PRYING *shared meaning element* **:** interested in what is not one's personal or proper concern. CURIOUS, the most general and the only neutral one of these words, basically implies a lively desire to learn or to know ⟨children are *curious* about everything⟩ ⟨*curious* onlookers got in the way of the firemen⟩ INQUISITIVE applies to impertinent and habitual curiosity and usually suggests quizzing and peering after information ⟨*inquisitive* old women watching from behind drawn curtains⟩ PRYING adds to *inquisitive* the implication of busy meddling and officiousness ⟨I will not bare my soul to their shallow *prying* eyes — Oscar Wilde⟩ ***ant*** incurious, uninterested

cu·rite \ˈkyu̇(ə)r-ˌīt\ *n* [F, fr. Pierre *Curie*] **:** a radioactive mineral $2PbO.5UO_3.4H_2O$ found in orange acicular crystals

cu·ri·um \ˈkyu̇r-ē-əm\ *n* [NL, fr. Marie & Pierre *Curie*] **:** a metallic radioactive trivalent element artificially produced — see ELEMENT table

[1]curl \ˈkər(-ə)l\ *vb* [ME *curlen,* fr. *crul* curly, prob. fr. MD; akin to OHG *krol* curly, OE *cradol* cradle] *vt* **1 :** to form into coils or ringlets ⟨~ one's hair⟩ **2 :** to form into a curved shape **:** TWIST ⟨~*ed* his lip in a sneer⟩ **3 :** to furnish with curls ~ *vi* **1 a :** to grow in coils or spirals **b :** to form ripples or crinkles ⟨bacon ~*ing* in a pan⟩ **2 :** to move or progress in curves or spirals **:** WIND ⟨the path ~*ed* along the mountainside⟩ **3 :** TWIST, CONTORT **4 :** to play the game of curling

[2]curl *n* **1 :** a lock of hair that coils **:** RINGLET **2 :** something having a spiral or winding form **:** COIL **3 :** the action of curling **:** the state of being curled **4 :** an abnormal rolling or curling of leaves **5 :** a curved or spiral marking in the grain of wood **6 :** TENDRIL **7 :** a hollow arch of water formed when the crest of a breaking wave spills forward

curl·er \ˈkər-lər\ *n* **1 :** one that curls; *esp* **:** a device on which hair is wound for curling **2 :** a player of curling

cur·lew \ˈkərl-(ˌ)(y)ü\ *n, pl* **curlews** *or* **curlew** [ME, fr. MF *corlieu,* of imit. origin] **:** any of various largely brownish chiefly migratory birds (esp. genus *Numenius*) related to the woodcocks but distinguished by long legs and a long slender down-curved bill

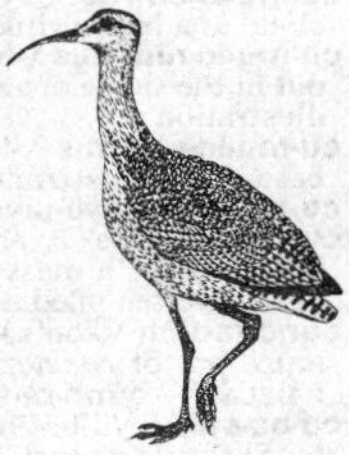

curlew

[1]curli·cue *also* **curly·cue** \ˈkər-li-ˌkyü\ *n* [*curly* + *cue* (a braid of hair)] **:** a fancifully curved or spiral figure (as a flourish in handwriting)

[2]curlicue *vb* **-cued; -cu·ing** *vi* **:** to form curlicues ~ *vt* **:** to decorate with curlicues

curl·ing \ˈkər-liŋ\ *n* **:** a game in which two teams of four men each slide curling stones over a stretch of ice toward a target circle

curling iron *n* **:** a rod-shaped usu. metal instrument which is heated and around which a lock of hair to be curled or waved is wound

curling stone *n* **:** an ellipsoid stone or occas. piece of iron with a gooseneck handle used in the game of curling

curl·pa·per \ˈkər(-ə)l-ˌpā-pər\ *n* **:** a strip or piece of paper around which a lock of hair is wound for curling

curly \ˈkər-lē\ *adj* **curl·i·er; -est 1 :** tending to curl; *also* **:** having curls **2 :** having the grain composed of fibers that undulate without crossing and that often form alternating light and dark lines ⟨~ maple⟩ — **curl·i·ness** *n*

curly–coat·ed retriever \ˌkər-lē-ˌkōt-əd-\ *n* **:** any of a breed of sporting dogs with a short curly coat

curly top *n* **:** a destructive virus disease esp. of beets that kills young plants and causes curling and puckering of the leaves in older plants

cur·mud·geon \(ˌ)kər-ˈməj-ən\ *n* [origin unknown] **1** *archaic* **:** MISER **2 :** a crusty, ill-tempered, and usu. old man — **cur·mud·geon·ly** *adj*

curn \ˈkərn\ *or* **cur·ran** \ˈkə-rən\ *n* [ME *curn;* akin to ME *corn*] **1** *Scot* **:** GRAIN **2** *Scot* **:** a small number **:** FEW

curr \ˈkər\ *vi* [imit.] **:** to make a murmuring sound (as of doves)

cur·ragh *or* **cur·rach** \ˈkə-rə(k)\ *n* [ScGael *curach* & IrGael *currach;* akin to MIr *curach* coracle] **1** *Irish* **:** marshy wasteland **2** *Irish & Scot* **:** CORACLE

cur·rant \ˈkər-ənt, ˈkə-rənt\ *n* [ME *raison of Coraunte,* lit., raisin of Corinth] **1 :** a small seedless raisin grown chiefly in the Levant **2 :** the acid edible fruit of several shrubs (genus *Ribes*) of the saxifrage family; *also* **:** a plant bearing currants

cur·ren·cy \ˈkər-ən-sē, ˈkə-rən-\ *n, pl* **-cies 1 a :** circulation as a medium of exchange **b :** general use, acceptance, or prevalence **2 a :** something (as coins, government notes, and bank notes) that is in circulation as a medium of exchange **b :** paper money in circulation **c :** a common article for bartering

[1]cur·rent \ˈkər-ənt, ˈkə-rənt\ *adj* [ME *curraunt,* fr. OF *curant,* prp. of *courre* to run, fr. L *currere* — more at CAR] **1 a** *archaic* **:** RUN-

NING, FLOWING **b** (1) : presently elapsing (2) : occurring in or belonging to the present time (3) : most recent ⟨~ issue⟩ **2** : used as a medium of exchange **3** : generally accepted, used, practiced, or prevalent at the moment ***syn*** see PREVAILING — **cur·rent·ly** *adv* — **cur·rent·ness** *n*

[2]**current** *n* **1 a** : the part of a fluid body moving continuously in a certain direction **b** : the swiftest part of a stream **c** : a tidal or nontidal movement of lake or ocean water **d** : flow marked by force or strength **2** : a tendency or course of events that is usu. the resultant of an interplay of forces ⟨~s of public opinion that alter with the economic situation⟩ ⟨an increasing ~ of radicalism⟩ **3** : a flow of electric charge; *also* : the rate of such flow ***syn*** see TENDENCY

current assets *n pl* : assets of a short-term nature

cur·ri·cle \ˈkər-i-kəl, ˈkə-ri-\ *n* [L *curriculum* running, chariot] : a 2-wheeled chaise usu. drawn by two horses

cur·ric·u·lar \kə-ˈrik-yə-lər\ *adj* : of or relating to a curriculum

cur·ric·u·lum \-ləm\ *n, pl* **-la** \-lə\ *also* **-lums** [NL, fr. L, running, fr. *currere*] **1** : the courses offered by an educational institution or one of its branches **2** : a set of courses constituting an area of specialization

cur·ric·u·lum vi·tae \kə-ˌrik-ə-ləm-ˈwē-ˌtī, -yə-ləm-ˈvīt-ē\ *n, pl* **cur·ric·u·la vitae** \-lə-\ [L, course of (one's) life] : a short account of one's career and qualifications prepared typically by an applicant for a position

cur·ri·ery \ˈkər-ē-ə-rē, ˈkə-rē-\ *n, pl* **-er·ies** **1** : the trade of a currier of leather **2** : a place where currying is done

cur·rish \ˈkər-ish\ *adj* **1** : resembling a cur : MONGREL **2** : IGNOBLE — **cur·rish·ly** *adv*

[1]**cur·ry** \ˈkər-ē, ˈkə-rē\ *vt* **cur·ried; cur·ry·ing** [ME *currayen*, fr. OF *correer* to prepare, curry, fr. (assumed) VL *conredare*, fr. L *com-* + a base of Gmc origin; akin to Goth *garaiths* arrayed — more at READY] **1** : to dress the coat of (as a horse) with a currycomb **2** : to treat (tanned leather) esp. by incorporating oil or grease **3** : BEAT, THRASH — **cur·ri·er** *n* — **curry fa·vor** \-fā-vər\ [ME *currayen favel* to curry a chestnut horse] : to seek to gain favor by flattery or attention

[2]**cur·ry** *also* **cur·rie** \ˈkər-ē, ˈkə-rē\ *n, pl* **curries** [Tamil-Malayalam *kaṟi*] **1** : CURRY POWDER **2** : a food or dish seasoned with curry powder ⟨shrimp ~⟩

[3]**curry** *vt* **cur·ried; cur·ry·ing** : to flavor or cook with curry powder

cur·ry·comb \-ˌkōm\ *n* : a comb made of rows of metallic teeth or serrated ridges and used esp. to curry horses — **currycomb** *vt*

curry powder *n* : a condiment consisting of several pungent ground spices (as cayenne pepper, fenugreek, and turmeric)

[1]**curse** \ˈkərs\ *n* [ME *curs*, fr. OE] **1** : a prayer or invocation for harm or injury to come upon one : IMPRECATION **2** : something that is cursed or accursed **3** : evil or misfortune that comes as if in response to imprecation or as retribution **4** : a cause of great harm or misfortune : TORMENT **5** : MENSTRUATION — used with *the*

[2]**curse** *vb* **cursed; curs·ing** *vt* **1 a** : to call upon divine or supernatural power to send injury upon **b** : to execrate in fervent and often profane terms **2** : to use profanely insolent language against : BLASPHEME **3** : to bring great evil upon : AFFLICT ~ *vi* : to utter imprecations : SWEAR ***syn*** see EXECRATE ***ant*** bless

cursed \ˈkər-səd, ˈkərst\ *also* **curst** \ˈkərst\ *adj* : being under or deserving a curse — **cursed·ly** *adv* — **cursed·ness** *n*

[1]**cur·sive** \ˈkər-siv\ *adj* [F or ML; F *cursif*, fr. ML *cursivus*, lit., running, fr. L *cursus*, pp. of *currere* to run] : RUNNING, COURSING: as **a** *of writing* : flowing often with the strokes of successive characters joined and the angles rounded **b** : having a flowing, easy, impromptu character — **cur·sive·ly** *adv* — **cur·sive·ness** *n*

[2]**cursive** *n* **1** : a manuscript written in cursive writing **2** : a style of printed letter resembling handwriting

cur·so·ri·al \ˌkər-ˈsōr-ē-əl, -ˈsȯr-\ *adj* : adapted to running

cur·so·ry \ˈkərs-(ə-)rē\ *adj* [LL *cursorius* of running, fr. L *cursus* running, fr. *cursus*, pp.] : rapidly and often superficially performed : HASTY ⟨a ~ glance⟩ ***syn*** see SUPERFICIAL ***ant*** painstaking — **cur·so·ri·ly** \-rə-lē\ *adv* — **cur·so·ri·ness** \-rē-nəs\ *n*

curt \ˈkərt\ *adj* [L *curtus* shortened — more at SHEAR] **1 a** : sparing of words : TERSE **b** : marked by rude or peremptory shortness : BRUSQUE **2** : shortened in linear dimension ***syn*** see BLUFF ***ant*** voluble — **curt·ly** *adv* — **curt·ness** *n*

cur·tail \(ˌ)kər-ˈtā(ə)l\ *vt* [alter. of *curtal* to make a curtal of, fr. *curtal*, n.] : to make less by or as if by cutting off or away some part ⟨~ the power of the executive branch⟩ ⟨~ inflation⟩ ***syn*** see SHORTEN ***ant*** prolong, enlarge — **cur·tail·er** \-ˈtā-lər\ *n*

cur·tail·ment \-ˈtā(ə)l-mənt\ *n* : the act of curtailing : the state of being curtailed

[1]**cur·tain** \ˈkərt-ᵊn\ *n* [ME *curtine*, fr. OF, fr. LL *cortina*, fr. L *cohort-*, *cohors* enclosure, court — more at COURT] **1** : a hanging screen usu. capable of being drawn back or up; *esp* : window drapery **2** : a device or agency that conceals or acts as a barrier — compare IRON CURTAIN **3 a** : the part of a bastioned front that connects two neighboring bastions **b** (1) : a similar stretch of plain wall (2) : a nonbearing exterior wall **4 a** : the movable screen separating the stage from the auditorium of a theater **b** : the ascent or opening (as at the beginning of a play) of a stage curtain; *also* : its descent or closing (as at the end of an act) **c** : the final situation, line, or scene of an act or play **d** : the time at which a theatrical performance begins **e** *pl* : END; *esp* : DEATH ⟨it was ~s for him when his treason was discovered⟩

[2]**curtain** *vt* **cur·tained; cur·tain·ing** \ˈkərt-niŋ, -ᵊn-iŋ\ **1** : to furnish with or as if with curtains **2** : to veil or shut off with or as if with a curtain

curtain call *n* : an appearance by a performer (as after the final curtain of a play) in response to the applause of the audience

curtain lecture *n* [fr. its orig. being given behind the curtains of a bed] : a private lecture by a wife to her husband

curtain raiser *n* **1** : a short play usu. of one scene that is presented before the main full-length drama **2** : a usu. short preliminary to a main event

[1]**cur·tal** \ˈkərt-ᵊl\ *n, obs* : an animal with a docked tail

[2]**curtal** *adj* [MF *courtault*, fr. *court* short, fr. L *curtus*] **1** *obs* : having a docked tail **2** *obs* : BRIEF, CURTAILED **3** *archaic* : wearing a short frock

cur·tal ax *or* **cur·tle ax** \ˈkərt-ᵊl-\ *n* [modif. of MF *coutelas*] : CUTLASS

cur·te·sy \ˈkərt-ə-sē\ *n, pl* **-sies** [ME *corteisie* courtesy] : the future potential interest that a husband has in the real property of his wife arising upon the birth to them of a child alive and capable for at least an instant of inheriting from her — compare DOWER

cur·ti·lage \ˈkərt-ᵊl-ij\ *n* [ME, fr. OF *cortillage*, fr. *cortil* courtyard, fr. *cort* court] : a piece of ground (as a yard or courtyard) within the fence surrounding a house

[1]**curt·sy** *or* **curt·sey** \ˈkərt-sē\ *n, pl* **curtsies** *or* **curtseys** [alter. of *courtesy*] : an act of civility, respect, or reverence made mainly by women and consisting of a slight lowering of the body with bending of the knees

[2]**curtsy** *or* **curtsey** *vi* **curt·sied** *or* **curt·seyed; curt·sy·ing** *or* **curt·sey·ing** : to make a curtsy

cu·rule \ˈkyu̇(ə)r-ˌül\ *adj* [L *curulis* alter. of *currulis* of a chariot, fr. *currus* chariot, fr. *currere* to run] **1** : of or relating to a seat reserved in ancient Rome for the use of the highest dignitaries and usu. made like a campstool with curved legs **2** : privileged to sit in a curule chair

cur·va·ceous *also* **cur·va·cious** \ˌkər-ˈvā-shəs\ *adj* : having a well-proportioned feminine figure marked by pronounced curves

cur·va·ture \ˈkər-və-ˌchu̇(ə)r, -chər, -ˌt(y)u̇(ə)r\ *n* **1** : the act of curving : the state of being curved **2** : a measure or amount of curving; *specif* : the rate of change of the angle through which the tangent to a curve turns in moving along the curve and which for a circle is equal to the reciprocal of the radius **3 a** : an abnormal curving (as of the spine) **b** : a curved surface of an organ

[1]**curve** \ˈkərv\ *adj* [L *curvus* curved] *archaic* : bent or formed into a curve

[2]**curve** *vb* **curved; curv·ing** [L *curvare*, fr. *curvus*] *vi* : to have or take a turn, change, or deviation from a straight line without sharp breaks or angularity ~ *vt* **1** : to cause to curve **2** : to throw a curveball to (a batter) **3** : to grade (as an examination) on a curve ***syn*** CURVE, BEND, TURN, TWIST *shared meaning element* : to swerve or cause to swerve from a straight line or course

[3]**curve** *n* **1** : a curving line or surface : BEND **2** : something curved: as **a** : a curving line of the human body **b** *pl* : PARENTHESIS **3 a** : CURVEBALL **b** : TRICK, DECEPTION **4** : a graphical representation of a variable (as one measuring development of progress) affected by conditions **5 a** : a line that may be precisely defined by an equation in such a way that the coordinates of its points are functions of a single independent variable or parameter **b** (1) : the intersection of two geometrical surfaces (2) : the path of a moving point **6** : a distribution indicating the relative performance of individuals measured against each other that is used esp. in assigning good, medium, or poor grades to usu. predetermined proportions of students rather than in assigning grades based on predetermined standards of achievement — **curvy** \ˈkər-vē\ *adj*

curve·ball \ˈkərv-ˌbȯl\ *n* : a baseball pitch thrown so that it swerves from a normal or expected course; *esp* : one that curves to the left when thrown from the right hand or to the right when thrown from the left hand — **curveball** *vb*

[1]**cur·vet** \(ˌ)kər-ˈvet\ *n* [It *corvetta*, fr. MF *courbette*, fr. *courber* to curve, fr. L *curvare*] : a prancing leap of a horse in which first the forelegs and then the hind are raised so that for an instant all the legs are in the air

[2]**curvet** *vi* **-vet·ted** *or* **-vet·ed; -vet·ting** *or* **-vet·ing** : to make a curvet; *also* : PRANCE, CAPER

cur·vi·lin·eal \ˌkər-və-ˈlin-ē-əl\ *adj* : CURVILINEAR

cur·vi·lin·ear \ˌkər-və-ˈlin-ē-ər\ *adj* [L *curvus* + *linea* line] **1** : consisting of or bounded by curved lines : represented by a curved line **2** : marked by flowing tracery ⟨~ Gothic⟩ — **cur·vi·lin·ear·i·ty** \-ˌlin-ē-ˈar-ət-ē\ *n* — **cur·vi·lin·ear·ly** \-ˈlin-ē-ər-lē\ *adv*

cu·sec \ˈkyü-ˌsek\ *n* [cubic foot per second] : a volumetric unit of flow equal to a cubic foot per second

cush·at \ˈkəsh-ət\ *n* [ME *cowschote*, fr. OE *cūscote*] *chiefly Scot* : RINGDOVE 1

cu·shaw \ku̇-ˈshȯ, ˈkü-ˌ\ *n* [perh. of Algonquian origin; akin to *escushaw* it is green (in some Algonquian language of Virginia)] : WINTER CROOKNECK

Cush·ing's disease \ˈku̇sh-iŋz-\ *n* [Harvey *Cushing*] : a disease characterized by obesity and muscular weakness associated with adrenal or pituitary dysfunction — called also *Cushing's syndrome*

[1]**cush·ion** \ˈku̇sh-ən\ *n* [ME *cusshin*, fr. MF *coissin*, fr. (assumed) VL *coxinus*, fr. L *coxa* hip — more at COXA] **1** : a soft pillow or pad usu. used for sitting, reclining, or kneeling **2** : a bodily part resembling a pad **3** : something resembling a cushion: as **a** : PILLOW 3 **b** : RAT 3 **c** : a pad of springy rubber along the inside of the rim of a billiard table **d** : the head of a drill brace **e** : a padded insert in a shoe **f** : a strip of soft resilient rubber between the breaker and carcass of a pneumatic tire **g** : an artificial pool provided to absorb the kinetic energy of falling water and so prevent erosion **h** : an elastic body for reducing shock **i** : a mat laid under a large rug to ease the effect of wear **4** : something serving to mitigate the effects of disturbances or disorders: as **a** : a factor that lessens adverse developments in the economy **b** : a medical procedure or drug that eases a patient's discomfort — **cush·ion·less** \-ləs\ *adj* — **cush·iony** \-ə-nē\ *adj*

[2]**cushion** *vt* **cush·ioned; cush·ion·ing** \-(ə-)niŋ\ **1** : to seat or place on a cushion **2** : to suppress by ignoring **3** : to furnish

with a cushion **4** **a** : to mitigate the effects of **b** : to protect against force or shock **5** : to check gradually so as to minimize shock of moving parts

Cush·it·ic \ˌkəsh-ˈit-ik, ku̇sh-\ *n* [*Cush* (Kush), Africa] : a subfamily of the Afro-Asiatic language family comprising various languages spoken in East Africa and esp. in Ethiopia and Somaliland — **Cushitic** *adj*

cushy \ˈku̇sh-ē\ *adj* **cushi·er; cushi·est** [Hindi *khush* pleasant, fr. Per *khūsh*] : entailing little hardship or difficulty : EASY ⟨a ~ job with a high salary⟩ — **cushi·ly** \ˈku̇sh-ə-lē\ *adv*

cusk \ˈkəsk\ *n, pl* **cusk** *or* **cusks** [prob. alter. of *tusk* (a kind of codfish)] **1** : a large edible marine fish (*Brosme brosme*) related to the cod **2** : the New World burbot (*Lota lota maculosa*)

cusp \ˈkəsp\ *n* [L *cuspis* point] : POINT, APEX: as **a** : either horn of a crescent moon **b** : a fixed point on a mathematical curve at which a point tracing the curve would exactly reverse its direction of motion **c** : a pointed projection formed by or arising from the intersection of two arcs or foils **d** (1) : a point on the grinding surface of a tooth (2) : a fold or flap of a cardiac valve — **cus·pate** \ˈkəs-ˌpāt, -pət\ *also* **cus·pat·ed** \-ˌpāt-əd\ *adj*

cus·pid \ˈkəs-pəd\ *n* [back-formation fr. *bicuspid*] : a canine tooth

cus·pi·date \ˈkəs-pə-ˌdāt\ *or* **cus·pi·dat·ed** \-ˌdāt-əd\ *adj* [L *cuspidatus*, pp. of *cuspidare* to make pointed, fr. *cuspid-, cuspis* point] : having a cusp : terminating in a point ⟨a ~ leaf⟩

cus·pi·da·tion \ˌkəs-pə-ˈdā-shən\ *n* : decoration with cusps ⟨the ~ of an arch⟩

cus·pi·dor \ˈkəs-pə-ˌdo̊(ə)r, -ˌdō(ə)r\ *n* [Pg *cuspidouro* place for spitting, fr. *cuspir* to spit, fr. L *conspuere*, fr. *com-* + *spuere* to spit — more at SPEW] : SPITTOON

[1]**cuss** \ˈkəs\ *n* [alter. of *curse*] **1** : CURSE **2** : FELLOW ⟨an ornery old ~⟩

[2]**cuss** *vb* : CURSE ⟨~*ed* and decried the generally poor quality of TV newscasting —W. R. Williams⟩ — **cuss·er** *n*

cuss·ed \ˈkəs-əd\ *adj* **1** : CURSED **2** : OBSTINATE, CANTANKEROUS — **cuss·ed·ly** *adv*

cuss·ed·ness *n* : disposition to willful perversity : OBSTINACY

cuss·word \ˈkəs-ˌwərd\ *n* **1** : SWEARWORD **2** : a term of abuse : a derogatory term

cus·tard \ˈkəs-tərd\ *n* [ME, a kind of pie] : a pudding-like usu. sweetened mixture made of eggs and milk

custard apple *n* **1** **a** : any of several chiefly tropical American soft-fleshed edible fruits **b** : any of a genus (*Annona* of the family Annonaceae, the custard-apple family) of trees or shrubs bearing this fruit; *esp* : a small West Indian tree (*A. reticulata*) **2** : PAPAW 2

cus·to·di·al \ˌkəs-ˈtōd-ē-əl\ *adj* : relating to guardianship; *specif* : marked by or given to watching and protecting rather than seeking to cure ⟨~ care⟩

cus·to·di·an \ˌkəs-ˈtōd-ē-ən\ *n* : one that guards and protects or maintains; *esp* : one entrusted with guarding and keeping property or records or with custody or guardianship of prisoners or inmates — **cus·to·di·an·ship** \-ˌship\ *n*

cus·to·dy \ˈkəs-təd-ē\ *n, pl* **-dies** [ME *custodie*, fr. L *custodia* guarding, fr. *custod-, custos* guardian] : immediate charge and control exercised by a person or an authority (as over a ward or a suspect) : SAFEKEEPING

[1]**cus·tom** \ˈkəs-təm\ *n* [ME *custume*, fr. OF, fr. L *consuetudin-, consuetudo*, fr. *consuetus*, pp. of *consuescere* to accustom, fr. *com-* + *suescere* to accustom; akin to *suus* one's own — more at SUICIDE] **1** **a** : a usage or practice common to many or to a particular place or class or habitual with an individual **b** : long-established practice considered as unwritten law **c** : repeated practice **d** : the whole body of usages, practices, or conventions that regulate social life **2** *pl* **a** : duties, tolls, or imposts imposed by the sovereign law of a country on imports or exports **b** *usu sing in constr* : the agency, establishment, or procedure for collecting such customs **3** **a** : business patronage **b** : usu. habitual patrons : CUSTOMERS ***syn*** see HABIT

[2]**custom** *adj* **1** : made or performed according to personal order **2** : specializing in custom work or operation ⟨a ~ tailor⟩

cus·tom·ary \ˈkəs-tə-ˌmer-ē\ *adj* **1** : based on or established by custom **2** : commonly practiced, used, or observed ***syn*** see USUAL ***ant*** occasional — **cus·tom·ari·ly** \ˌkəs-tə-ˈmer-ə-lē\ *adv* — **cus·tom·ari·ness** \ˈkəs-tə-ˌmer-ē-nəs\ *n*

cus·tom–built \ˌkəs-təm-ˈbilt\ *adj* : built to individual specifications

cus·tom·er \ˈkəs-tə-mər\ *n* [ME *custumer*, fr. *custume*] **1** **a** : one that purchases usu. systematically or frequently a commodity or service **b** : one that is a patron (as of a restaurant) or that uses the services (as of a store) **2** : an individual usu. having some specified distinctive trait ⟨a real tough ~⟩

cus·tom·house \ˈkəs-təm-ˌhau̇s\ *also* **cus·toms·house** \-təmz-\ *n* : a building where customs and duties are paid or collected and where vessels are entered and cleared

cus·tom·ize \ˈkəs-tə-ˌmīz\ *vt* **-ized; -iz·ing** : to build, fit, or alter according to individual specifications ⟨~ a car⟩ — **cus·tom·iz·er** *n*

cus·tom–made \ˌkəs-təm-ˈ(m)ād\ *adj* : made to individual specifications

cus·tom–tai·lor \-ˈtā-lər\ *vt* : to alter, plan, or build according to individual specifications or needs

[1]**cut** \ˈkət\ *vb* **cut; cut·ting** [ME *cutten*] *vt* **1** **a** : to penetrate with or as if with an edged instrument **b** : to hurt the feelings of **c** : to strike sharply with a cutting effect **d** : to strike (a ball) with a glancing blow that imparts a reverse spin **e** : to experience the growth of (a tooth) through the gum **2** **a** : TRIM, PARE ⟨~ one's nails⟩ **b** : to shorten by omissions **c** : DISSOLVE, DILUTE, ADULTERATE **d** : to reduce in amount ⟨~ costs⟩ **3** **a** : MOW, REAP ⟨~ hay⟩ **b** (1) : to divide into parts with an edged tool ⟨~ bread⟩ (2) : FELL, HEW ⟨~ timber⟩ **c** : to separate from an organization : DETACH **d** : to change the direction of sharply **e** : to go or pass around or about **4** **a** : to divide into segments **b** : INTERSECT, CROSS **c** : BREAK, INTERRUPT ⟨~ our supply lines⟩ **d** (1) : to divide (a deck of cards) into two portions (2) : to draw (a card) from the deck **e** : to divide into shares : SPLIT **5** **a** : STOP, CEASE ⟨~ the nonsense⟩ **b** : to refuse to recognize (an acquaintance) : OSTRACIZE **c** : to absent oneself from (as a class) **d** : to stop (a motor) by opening a switch **e** : to terminate the filming of (a motion-picture scene) **6** **a** : to make by or as if by cutting: as (1) : CARVE ⟨~ stone⟩ (2) : to shape by grinding ⟨~ a diamond⟩ (3) : ENGRAVE (4) : to shear or hollow out **b** : to record sounds (as speech or music) on (a phonograph record) **c** : to type on a stencil **7** **a** : to engage in (a frolicsome or mischievous action) ⟨on summer nights strange capers are ~ under the thin guise of a Christian festival —D. C. Peattie⟩ ⟨in his sixty-seventh year with a heart that ~ didoes —H. R. Warfel⟩ **b** : to give the appearance or impression of ⟨~ a fine figure⟩ **8** : to be able to manage or handle a situation — usu. used in negative constructions ⟨can't ~ that kind of work anymore⟩ **~** *vi* **1** **a** : to function as or as if as an edged tool **b** : to undergo incision or severance ⟨cheese ~*s* easily⟩ **c** : to perform the operation of dividing, severing, incising, or intersecting **d** : to make a stroke with a whip, sword, or other weapon **e** : to wound feelings or sensibilities **f** : to cause constriction or chafing **g** : to be of effect, influence, or significance ⟨an analysis that ~*s* deep⟩ **2** **a** (1) : to divide a pack of cards esp. in order to decide the deal or settle a bet (2) : to draw a card from the pack **b** : to divide spoils : SPLIT **3** **a** : to proceed obliquely from a straight course ⟨~ across the yard⟩ **b** : to move swiftly ⟨a yacht *cutting* through the water⟩ **c** : to describe an oblique or diagonal line **d** : to change sharply in direction : SWERVE **e** : to make an abrupt transition from one sound or image to another in motion pictures, radio, or television **4** : to stop photographing motion pictures — **cut corners** : to perform some action in the quickest, easiest, or cheapest way — **cut ice** : to be of importance — usu. used in negative constructions ⟨his opinion *cuts* no *ice* with them⟩ — **cut one's teeth on** : to learn, do, or perform as a beginning or at the start of one's career — **cut short** **1** : to check abruptly : INTERRUPT **2** : to terminate usu. in a premature manner : END — **cut the mustard** : to achieve the standard of performance necessary for success

[2]**cut** *n* **1** : something that is cut or cut off: as **a** : a length of cloth varying from 40 to 100 yards in length **b** : the yield of products cut esp. during one harvest **c** : a segment or section of a meat carcass or a part of one **d** : a group of animals selected from a herd **e** : SHARE ⟨took his ~ of the profits⟩ **2** : a product of cutting: as **a** : a creek, channel, or inlet made by excavation or worn by natural action **b** (1) : an opening made with an edged instrument (2) : a wound made by something sharp : GASH **c** : a surface or outline left by cutting **d** : a passage cut as a roadway **e** : a grade or step esp. in a social scale ⟨a ~ above the ordinary person⟩ **f** : a subset of a set such that when it is subtracted from the set the remainder is not connected **g** : a pictorial illustration **3** : the act or an instance of cutting: as **a** : a gesture or expression that hurts the feelings ⟨made an unkind ~⟩ **b** : a straight passage or course **c** : a stroke or blow with the edge of a knife or other edged tool **d** : a lash with or as if with a whip **e** : the act of reducing or removing a part ⟨a ~ in pay⟩ **f** : an act or turn of cutting cards; *also* : the result of cutting **4** : a voluntary absence from a class **5** **a** : a stroke that cuts a ball; *also* : the spin imparted by such a stroke **b** : a swing by a batter at a pitched baseball **c** : an exchange of captures in checkers **6** : an abrupt transition from one sound or image to another in motion pictures, radio, or television **7** **a** : the shape and style in which a thing is cut, formed, or made ⟨clothes of the latest ~⟩ **b** : PATTERN, TYPE **c** : HAIRCUT **8** : BAND 7 — **cut of one's jib** : the appearance of one's face

cut·abil·i·ty \ˌkət-ə-ˈbil-ət-ē\ *n* : the proportion of lean salable meat yielded by a carcass

cut–and–dried \ˌkət-ᵊn-ˈdrīd\ *also* **cut–and–dry** \-ˈdrī\ *adj* : being or done according to a plan, set procedure, or formula : ROUTINE

cut–and–try \-ᵊn-ˈtrī\ *adj* : marked by experimental procedure : EMPIRICAL ⟨early development of ships and yachts was achieved by the ~ method —D. F. Hora⟩

cu·ta·ne·ous \kyu̇-ˈtā-nē-əs\ *adj* [NL *cutaneus*, fr. L *cutis* skin — more at HIDE] : of, relating to, or affecting the skin — **cu·ta·ne·ous·ly** *adv*

[1]**cut·away** \ˈkət-ə-ˌwā\ *adj* : having or showing parts cut away

[2]**cutaway** *n* **1** : a coat with skirts tapering from the front waistline to form tails at the back **2** **a** : a cutaway picture or representation **b** : a shot that interrupts the main action of a film or television program to take up a related subject or to depict action supposed to be going on at the same time as the main action **3** : a back dive in which the head is lowered toward the board after the takeoff

cut·back \ˈkət-ˌbak\ *n* **1** : something cut back **2** : REDUCTION

cut back \ˈkət-ˈbak\ *vt* **1** : to shorten by cutting : PRUNE **2** : REDUCE, DECREASE ⟨*cut back* expenditures⟩ **~** *vi* : to interrupt the sequence of a plot (as of a movie) by introducing events prior to those last presented

cutch \ˈkəch\ *n* [modif. of Malay *kachu*] : CATECHU a

cut down *vt* **1** **a** : to remodel by removing extras or unwanted furnishings and fittings **b** : to remake in a smaller size **2** **a** : to strike down and kill or incapacitate **b** : to knock down **3** : REDUCE, CURTAIL ⟨*cut down* expenses⟩ **~** *vi* : to reduce or curtail volume or activity ⟨*cut down* on his smoking⟩ — **cut down to size** : to reduce from an inflated or exaggerated importance to true or suitable stature

cute \ˈkyüt\ *adj* **cut·er; cut·est** [short for *acute*] **1** : CLEVER, SHREWD **2** : attractive or pretty esp. in a dainty or delicate way **3** : obviously straining for effect — **cute·ly** *adv* — **cute·ness** *n*

cute·sy \ˈkyüt-sē\ *adj* **cute·si·er; -est** [*cute* + *-sy* (as in *folksy*)] : self-consciously cute : MANNERED ⟨here and there the script is ~, trying for a few mild laughs —H. C. Schonberg⟩

cut glass *n* : glass ornamented with patterns cut into its surface by an abrasive wheel and polished

cut–grass \ˈkət-ˌgras\ *n* : a grass (esp. genus *Leersia*) with minute hooked bristles along the edges of the leaf blade

cu·ti·cle \ˈkyüt-i-kəl\ *n* [L *cuticula*, dim. of *cutis* skin — more at HIDE] **1** : SKIN, PELLICLE: as **a** : an external investment secreted usu. by epidermal cells **b** : the outermost layer of animal integument (as in man) when composed of epidermis **c** : a thin continuous fatty film on the external surface of many higher plants **2** : dead or horny epidermis — **cu·tic·u·lar** \kyü-'tik-yə-lər\ adj

cut·ie or **cut·ey** \'kyüt-ē\ n, pl **cuties** or **cuteys** [cute + -ie] : an attractive person; esp : a pretty girl

cu·tin \'kyüt-ᵊn\ n [ISV, fr. L cutis] : an insoluble mixture containing waxes, fatty acids, soaps, and resinous material that forms a continuous layer on the outer epidermal wall of a plant

cut-in \'kət-,in\ n : something cut in — **cut-in** adj

cut in \'kət-'in\ vi **1** : to thrust oneself into a position between others or belonging to another **2** : to join in something suddenly 〈cut in on the conversation〉 **3** : to interrupt a dancing couple and take one as one's partner **4** : to become automatically connected or started in operation ~ vt **1** : to mix with cutting motions 〈after sifting the flour into a mixing bowl, cut the lard in〉 **2** : to introduce into a number, group, or sequence **3** : to connect into an electrical circuit to a mechanical apparatus so as to permit operation **4** : to include esp. among those benefiting or favored 〈cut them in on the profits〉

cu·tin·ized \'kyüt-ᵊn-,īzd\ adj : infiltrated with cutin 〈~ epidermal cells〉

cu·tis \'kyüt-əs\ n, pl **cu·tes** \'kyü-,tēz\ or **cu·tis·es** [L] : DERMIS

cut·lass also **cut·las** \'kət-ləs\ n [MF coutelas, aug. of coutel knife, fr. L cultellus, dim. of culter knife, plowshare] **1** : a short curving sword formerly used by sailors on warships **2** : MACHETE

cutlass 1

cut·ler \'kət-lər\ n [ME, fr. MF coutelier, fr. LL cultellarius, fr. L cultellus] : one who makes, deals in, or repairs cutlery

cut·lery \'kət-lə-rē\ n **1** : edged or cutting tools; specif : implements for cutting and eating food **2** : the business of a cutler

cut·let \'kət-lət\ n [F côtelette, fr. OF costelette, dim. of coste rib, side, fr. L costa — more at COAST] **1** : a small slice of meat for broiling or frying 〈a veal ~〉 **2** : a flat croquette of chopped meat or fish

cut·line \'kət-,līn\ n : CAPTION, LEGEND

cut·off \'kət-,ȯf\ n **1** : the act or action of cutting off **2** **a** : the new and relatively short channel formed when a stream cuts through the neck of an oxbow **b** : SHORTCUT **3** **c** : a channel made to straighten a stream **4** : a device for cutting off **5** : the point, date, or period for a cutoff — **cutoff** adj

cut off \'kət-'ȯf\ vt **1** : to strike off : SEVER **2** : to bring to an untimely end **3** : to stop the passage of **4** : to shut off : BAR **5** : to break off : TERMINATE **6** : SEPARATE, ISOLATE **7** : DISINHERIT **8** **a** : to stop the operation of : turn off **b** : to stop or interrupt while in communication 〈the operator cut me off〉 ~ vi : to cease operating

cut·out \'kət-,aȯt\ n **1** : something cut out or off from something else **2** : one that cuts out — **cutout** adj

¹**cut out** \'kət-'aȯt\ vt **1** : to form by erosion **2** : to form or shape by cutting **3** : to determine or assign through necessity 〈his work is cut out for him〉 **4** : to take the place of : SUPPLANT **5** : to put an end to : desist from 〈wasteful expenditures that must be cut out〉 **6** : DEPRIVE, DEFRAUD **7** : to remove from a series or circuit : DISCONNECT **b** : to make inoperative ~ vi **1** : to depart in haste **2** : to cease operating **3** : to swerve out of a traffic line

²**cut out** adj : naturally fitted or suited 〈not cut out to be a lawyer〉

cut·over \,kət-,ō-vər\ adj : having most of the salable timber cut 〈~ land〉

cut·purse \'kət-,pərs\ n : PICKPOCKET

cut-rate \'kət-'rāt\ adj **1** : marked by, offering, or making use of a reduced rate or price 〈~ stores〉 **2** : SECOND-RATE, CHEAP

cut·ta·ble \'kət-ə-bəl\ adj : capable of being cut : ready for cutting

cut·ter \'kət-ər\ n **1** : one that cuts: **a** : one whose work is cutting or involves cutting **b** (1) : an instrument, machine, machine part, or tool that cuts (2) : a device for vibrating a cutting stylus in disc recording (3) : the cutting stylus or its point **2** **a** : a ship's boat for carrying stores or passengers **b** : a fore-and-aft rigged sailing boat with a jib, forestaysail, mainsail, and single mast **c** : a small armed boat in government service **3** : a light sleigh

¹**cut·throat** \'kət-,thrōt\ n **1** : one likely to cut throats **2** : a cruel unprincipled person

²**cutthroat** adj **1** : MURDEROUS, CRUEL **2** : marked by unprincipled practices : RUTHLESS 〈~ competition〉 **3** : characterized by each player playing for himself rather than having a permanent partner — used esp. of partnership games adapted for three players 〈~ bridge〉

cutthroat contract n : contract bridge in which partnerships are determined by the bidding

cutthroat trout n : a large trout (Salmo clarki) native to cold lakes and rivers from northern California to southern Alaska — called also **cutthroat**

cut time n : duple or quadruple time with the beat represented by a half note

¹**cut·ting** n **1** : something cut or cut off, out, or over: as **a** : a plant section originating from stem, leaf, or root and capable of developing into a new plant **b** : HARVEST **2** : something made by cutting; esp : RECORDING

²**cutting** adj **1** : given to or designed for cutting; esp : SHARP, EDGED **2** : marked by sharp piercing cold **3** : inclined or likely to wound the feelings of others esp. because of a ruthlessly incisive quality 〈a ~ remark〉 **4** : INTENSE, PIERCING 〈a ~ pain〉 syn see INCISIVE — **cut·ting·ly** \-in-lē\ adv

cutting board n : a board on which something (as food or cloth) is placed for cutting

cutting horse n : a quick light saddle horse trained for use in separating cattle from a herd

cut·tle·bone \'kət-ᵊl-,bōn\ n [ME cotul cuttlefish (fr. OE cudele) + E bone] : the shell of cuttlefishes used for polishing powder or for supplying cage birds with lime and salts

cut·tle·fish \-,fish\ n [ME cotul + E fish] : a 10-armed marine cephalopod mollusk (family Sepiidae) differing from the related squid in having a calcified internal shell

cut·ty sark \'kət-ē-,särk\ n [E dial. cutty (short) + sark] **1** chiefly Scot : a short garment; esp : a woman's short undergarment **2** chiefly Scot : WOMAN, HUSSY

cutty stool n **1** chiefly Scot : a low stool **2** : a seat in a Scottish church where offenders formerly sat for public rebuke

cut-up \'kət-,əp\ n : one that clowns or acts boisterously

cut up \,kət-'əp\ vt **1** **a** : to cut into parts or pieces **b** : to injure or damage by or as if by cutting : GASH, SLASH **2** : to subject to hostile criticism : CENSURE ~ vi **1** : to undergo being cut up **2** : to behave in a comic, boisterous, or unruly manner : CLOWN

cuttlefish

cut·wa·ter \'kət-,wȯt-ər, -,wät-\ n : the forepart of a ship's stem

cut·work \-,wərk\ n : embroidery usu. on linen in which a design is outlined in buttonhole stitch and the intervening material then cut away

cut·worm \-,wərm\ n : any of various smooth-bodied chiefly nocturnal caterpillars (family Noctuidae) many of which feed on plant stems near ground level

cu·vette \kyü-'vet\ n [F, dim. of cuve tub, fr. L cupa — more at HIVE] : a small often transparent laboratory vessel (as a tube)

cv or **cvt** abbr convertible

CV abbr **1** cardiovascular **2** chief value

CVA abbr Columbia Valley Authority

cw abbr clockwise

CW abbr **1** chemical warfare **2** chief warrant officer **3** continuous waves

cwm \'küm\ n [W, valley] : CIRQUE 3

CWO abbr **1** cash with order **2** chief warrant officer

CWS abbr Chemical Warfare Service

cwt abbr hundredweight

CY abbr calendar year

-cy \sē\ n suffix [ME -cie, fr. OF, fr. L -tia, partly fr. -t- (final stem consonant) + -ia -y, partly fr. Gk -tia, -teia, fr. -t- (final stem consonant) + -ia, -eia -y] : action : practice 〈mendicancy〉 : rank : office 〈baronetcy〉 〈chaplaincy〉 : body : class 〈magistracy〉 : state : quality 〈accuracy〉 〈bankruptcy〉 〈normalcy〉 — often replacing a final -t or -te of the base word

cy·an \'sī-,an, -ən\ n [Gk kyanos] : a greenish blue color — used in photography of one of the primary colors

cyan- or **cyano-** comb form [G, fr. Gk kyan-, kyano-, fr. kyanos dark blue enamel] **1** : dark blue : blue 〈cyanotype〉 **2** : cyanogen 〈cyanide〉 **3** : cyanide 〈cyanogenetic〉

cy·an·a·mide \sī-'an-ə-məd\ n [ISV] **1** : a caustic acidic compound CH_2N_2 **2** : CALCIUM CYANAMIDE

cy·a·nate \'sī-ə-,nāt, -nət\ n [ISV] : a salt (as ammonium cyanate) or ester of cyanic acid

cy·an·ic \sī-'an-ik\ adj [ISV] **1** : relating to or containing cyanogen **2** : of a blue or bluish color

cyanic acid n : a strong acid HOCN used to prepare cyanates

¹**cy·a·nide** \'sī-ə-,nīd, -nəd\ n [ISV] : a compound (as potassium cyanide) of cyanogen usu. with a more electropositive element or radical

²**cy·a·nide** \-,nīd\ vt **-nid·ed; -nid·ing** : to treat with a cyanide; specif : to treat (iron or steel) with molten cyanide to produce a hard surface

cyanide process n : a method of extracting gold and silver from ores by treatment with a sodium cyanide or calcium cyanide solution

cy·a·nine \'sī-ə-,nēn, -nən\ n [ISV] : any of various dyes that sensitize photographic film to light from the green, yellow, red, and infrared regions of the spectrum

cy·a·nite \'sī-ə-,nīt\ var of KYANITE

cy·a·no \'sī-ə-(,)nō, sī-'an-(,)ō\ adj [cyan-] : relating to or containing the cyanogen group

cy·a·no·ac·ry·late \,sī-ə-nō-'ak-rə-,lāt, sī-,an-ō-\ n : any of several liquid acrylate monomers that readily polymerize anionically and are used as adhesives in industry and on living tissue in medicine to close wounds as an adjunct to surgery

cy·a·no·co·bal·a·min \,sī-ə-nō-'bal-ə-mən\ also **cy·a·no·co·bal·a·mine** \-,mēn\ n [cyan- + cobalt + vitamin] : VITAMIN B_{12}

cy·a·no·eth·yl·ate \,sī-ə-nō-'eth-ə-,lāt\ vt : to introduce a cyano-ethyl group CNC_2H_4 into (a compound) usu. by means of acrylonitrile 〈~ cotton〉 — **cy·a·no·eth·yl·a·tion** \-,eth-ə-'lā-shən\ n

cy·a·no·gen \sī-'an-ə-jən\ n [F cyanogène, fr. cyan- + gène -gen] **1** : a univalent radical CN present in simple and complex cyanides **2** : a colorless flammable poisonous gas $(CN)_2$

cy·a·no·gen·e·sis \,sī-ə-nō-'jen-ə-səs, sī-,an-ō-\ n : production of cyanide (as by plants) — **cy·a·no·ge·net·ic** \-jə-'net-ik\ adj — **cy·a·no·gen·ic** \-'jen-ik\ adj

cy·a·no·hy·drin \-'hī-drən\ n [ISV] : any of various compounds containing both cyano and alcoholic hydroxyl groups

cy·a·nosed \'sī-ə-,nōst, -,nōzd\ adj : affected with cyanosis

cy·a·no·sis \,sī-ə-'nō-səs\ n [NL, fr. Gk kyanōsis dark blue color, fr. kyan- cyan-] : a bluish or purplish discoloration (as of skin) due to deficient oxygenation of the blood — **cy·a·not·ic** \-'nät-ik\ adj

cy·an·urate \ˌsī-ə-ˈn(y)u̇(ə)r-ˌāt, -ˈn(y)u̇r-ət\ *n* : a salt or ester of cyanuric acid

cy·an·uric acid \ˌsī-ə-ˌn(y)u̇r-ik-\ *n* [*cyan-* + *urea*] : a crystalline weak acid $C_3N_3(OH)_3$ yielding cyanic acid when heated

Cyb·e·le \ˈsib-ə-(ˌ)lē\ *n* [L, fr. Gk *Kybelē*] : a nature goddess of the ancient peoples of Asia Minor

cy·ber·nat·ed \ˈsī-bər-ˌnāt-əd\ *adj* : characterized by or involving cybernation ⟨a ~ bakery⟩ ⟨a ~ society⟩

cy·ber·na·tion \ˌsī-bər-ˈnā-shən\ *n* [*cybernetics* + *-ation*] : the automatic control of a process or operation (as in manufacturing) by means of computers

cy·ber·net·ic \ˌsī-bər-ˈnet-ik\ *also* **cy·ber·net·i·cal** \-i-kəl\ *adj* : of, relating to, or involving cybernetics — **cy·ber·net·i·cal·ly** \-i-k(ə-)lē\ *adv*

cy·ber·ne·ti·cian \ˌsī-(ˌ)bər-nə-ˈtish-ən\ *n* : a specialist in cybernetics

cy·ber·net·i·cist \ˌsī-bər-ˈnet-ə-səst\ *n* : CYBERNETICIAN

cy·ber·net·ics \ˌsī-bər-ˈnet-iks\ *n pl but sing or pl in constr* [Gk *kybernētēs* pilot, governor (fr. *kybernan* to steer, govern) + E *-ics*] : the science of communication and control theory that is concerned esp. with the comparative study of automatic control systems (as the nervous system and brain and mechanical-electrical communication systems)

cy·borg \ˈsī-ˌbȯ(ə)rg\ *n* [*cybernetic* + *organism*] : a human being who is linked (as for temporary adaptation to a hostile space environment) to one or more mechanical devices upon which some of his vital physiological functions depend

cyc *or* **cycl** *abbr* cyclopedia

cy·cad \ˈsī-kəd\ *n* [NL *Cycad-, Cycas*] : any of an order (Cycadales) of gymnosperms that are represented by a single surviving family (Cycadaceae) of tropical plants resembling palms but reproducing by means of spermatozoids

cy·cad·e·oid \sī-ˈkad-ē-ˌȯid\ *n* [NL *Cycadeoidales*, group name, deriv. of *Cycad-, Cycas*] : any of an extinct order (Cycadeoidales or Bennettitales) of cycadophytes that differ from the cycads chiefly in having the reproductive organs on the trunk embedded in a thick external covering of persistent leaf bases

cy·cado·phyte \sī-ˈkad-ə-ˌfīt\ *n* [NL *Cycadophytae*, group name, irreg. fr. *Cycad-, Cycas* + *phyton* plant — more at -PHYTE] : any of a subclass (Cycadophytae) of unbranched gymnosperms with pinnate leaves, large pith, little xylem, and a thick cortex that includes the cycads, cycadeoids, and seed ferns

cy·cas \ˈsī-kəs\ *n* [NL *Cycad-, Cycas* genus name] : any of a genus (*Cycas*) of cycads between tree ferns and palms in appearance

cy·ca·sin \ˈsī-kə-sən\ *n* [*cycas* + *-in*] : a glucoside $C_8H_{16}N_2O_7$ that occurs in cycads and results in toxic and carcinogenic effects when introduced into mammals

cycl- *or* **cyclo-** *comb form* [NL, fr. Gk *kykl-, kyklo-*, fr. *kyklos*] **1** : circle ⟨*cyclo*meter⟩ **2** : cyclic ⟨*cyclo*hexane⟩

cy·cla·mate \ˈsī-klə-ˌmāt, -mət\ *n* [*cyclo*hexyl-sulf*amate*] : an artificially prepared salt of sodium or calcium used esp. formerly as a sweetener — compare CYCLOHEXYLAMINE

cy·cla·men \ˈsī-klə-mən, ˈsik-lə-\ *n* [NL, genus name, fr. Gk *kyklaminos*] : any of a genus (*Cyclamen*) of plants of the primrose family having showy nodding flowers

cy·clase \ˈsī-ˌklās, -ˌklāz\ *n* [*cycl-* + *-ase*] : an enzyme (as adenyl cyclase) that catalyzes cyclization of a compound

cy·claz·o·cine \sī-ˈklaz-ə-ˌsēn, -sən\ *n* [*cycl-* + *azocine* (C_7H_7N), of unknown origin] : an analgesic $C_{18}H_{25}NO$ that inhibits the effect of morphine and related addictive drugs and is used in the treatment of drug addiction

¹cy·cle \ˈsī-kəl, *6 is also* ˈsik-əl\ *n* [F or LL; F, fr. LL *cyclus*, fr. Gk *kyklos* circle, wheel, cycle — more at WHEEL] **1** : an interval of time during which a sequence of a recurring succession of events or phenomena is completed **2 a** : a course or series of events or operations that recur regularly and usu. lead back to the starting point **b** : one complete performance of a vibration, electric oscillation, current alternation, or other periodic process **c** : a permutation of a set of ordered elements in which each element takes the place of the next and the last becomes first **3** : a circular or spiral arrangement: as **a** : an imaginary circle or orbit in the heavens **b** : WHORL **c** : RING 10 **4** : a long period of time : AGE **5 a** : a group of poems, plays, novels, or songs treating the same theme **b** : a series of narratives dealing typically with the exploits of a legendary hero **6 a** : BICYCLE **b** : TRICYCLE **c** : MOTORCYCLE **7** : the series of a single, double, triple, and home run hit by one player during one baseball game ⟨hit for the ~⟩ — **cy·clic** \ˈsī-klik *also* ˈsik-lik\ *or* **cy·cli·cal** \ˈsī-kli-kəl, ˈsik-li-\ *adj* — **cy·cli·cal·ly** \-k(ə-)lē\ *or* **cy·clic·ly** \ˈsī-kli-klē, ˈsik-li-\ *adv*

²cy·cle \ˈsī-kəl, *2 is also* ˈsik-əl\ *vb* **cy·cled; cy·cling** \ˈsī-k(ə-)liŋ, ˈsik(-ə-)\ *vi* **1 a** : to pass through a cycle **b** : to recur in cycles **2** : to ride a cycle; *specif* : BICYCLE ~ *vt* : to cause to go through a cycle — **cy·cler** \ˈsī-k(ə-)lər, ˈsik(-ə-)\ *n*

cyclic AMP *n* : a cyclic mononucleotide of adenosine that has been implicated in control mechanisms regulating metabolism and function in the nervous system — called also *adenosine monophosphate;* compare ACRASIN

cyclic group *n* : a mathematical group that has an element such that every element of the group can be expressed as one of its powers

cyclic poets *n pl* [*Epic Cycle*, the series of epics dealing with the causes, events, and aftermath of the Trojan War] : the poets after Homer who composed epics on the Trojan War and its heroes

cy·clist \ˈsī-k(ə-)ləst, ˈsik(-ə-)\ *n* : one who rides a cycle

cy·cli·tol \ˈsī-klə-ˌtȯl, ˈsik-lə-ˌtōl\ *n* [*cycl-* + *-itol* (as in *inositol*)] : an alicyclic polyhydroxy compound (as inositol)

cy·cli·za·tion \ˌsīk-(ə-)lə-ˈzā-shən, ˌsik-\ *n* : formation of one or more rings in a chemical compound

cy·clize \ˈsīk-(ə-)ˌlīz, ˈsik-\ *vb* **cy·clized; cy·cliz·ing** *vt* : to subject to cyclization ~ *vi* : to undergo cyclization

cy·clo \ˈsē-(ˌ)klō, ˈsik-(ˌ)lō\ *n, pl* **cyclos** [prob. fr. F, short for (assumed) *cyclotaxi*, fr. motocyclette motorcycle + *-o-* + *taxi*] : a 3-wheeled motor-driven taxi

cy·clo·ad·di·tion \-ə-ˈdish-ən\ *n* : a chemical reaction leading to ring formation in a compound

cy·clo·al·i·phat·ic \ˌsī-klō-ˌal-ə-ˈfat-ik\ *adj* : ALICYCLIC

cy·clo·di·ene \-ˈdī-ˌēn, -dī-ˈ\ *n* [*cycl-* + *diene*] : an organic insecticide (as aldrin, dieldrin, chlordane, or endosulfan) with a chlorinated methylene group forming a bridge across a 6-membered carbon ring

cy·clo·gen·e·sis \-ˈjen-ə-səs\ *n* [*cyclone* + *genesis*] : the development or intensification of a cyclone

cy·clo·hex·ane \ˌsī-klō-ˈhek-ˌsān\ *n* [ISV] : a pungent saturated cyclic hydrocarbon C_6H_{12} found in petroleum or made synthetically and used chiefly as a solvent and in organic synthesis

cy·clo·hex·a·none \-ˈhek-sə-ˌnōn\ *n* [*cyclohexane* + *-one*] : a liquid ketone $C_6H_{10}O$ used esp. as a solvent and in organic synthesis

cy·clo·hex·i·mide \-ˈhek-sə-ˌmīd, -məd\ *n* [*cyclohexane* + *imide*] : an agricultural fungicide $C_{15}H_{23}NO_4$ that is obtained from a soil bacterium (*Streptomyces griseus*)

cy·clo·hex·yl·a·mine \-hek-ˈsil-ə-ˌmēn\ *n* [*cyclohexane* + *-yl* + *amine*] : an amine ($C_6H_{11}NH_2$) of cyclohexane that is a probably harmful metabolic breakdown product of cyclamate

¹cy·cloid \ˈsī-ˌklȯid\ *n* [F *cycloïde*, fr. Gk *kykloeidēs* circular, fr. *kyklos*] **1 a** : a curve that is generated by a point on the circumference of a circle as it rolls along a straight line **b** : something having a curved or circular form ⟨a cloud ~⟩ **2** : CYCLOTHYME — **cy·cloi·dal** \sī-ˈklȯid-ᵊl\ *adj*

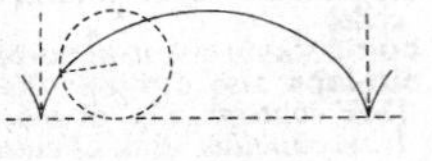

cycloid 1a

²cycloid *adj* **1** : CIRCULAR; *esp* : arranged or progressing in circles **2** : smooth with concentric lines of growth ⟨~ scales⟩; *also* : having or consisting of cycloid scales **3** : CYCLOTHYMIC

cy·clom·e·ter \sī-ˈkläm-ət-ər\ *n* : a device made for recording the revolutions of a wheel and often used for registering distance traversed by a wheeled vehicle

cy·clone \ˈsī-ˌklōn\ *n* [modif. of Gk *kyklōma* wheel, coil, fr. *kykloun* to go around, fr. *kyklos* circle] **1 a** : a storm or system of winds that rotates about a center of low atmospheric pressure clockwise in the southern hemisphere and counterclockwise in the northern, advances at a speed of 20 to 30 miles an hour, and often brings abundant rain **b** : TORNADO **c** : LOW 1b **2** : any of various centrifugal devices for separating materials (as solid particles from gases or liquids) — **cy·clon·ic** \sī-ˈklän-ik\ *adj* — **cy·clon·i·cal·ly** \-i-k(ə-)lē\ *adv*

cyclone cellar *n* : a cellar or covered excavation designed for protection from dangerous windstorms (as tornadoes)

cy·clo·ole·fin \ˌsī-klō-ˈō-lə-fən\ *n* [ISV] : a hydrocarbon (as of the formula C_nH_{2n-2}) containing an unsaturated ring — **cy·clo·ole·fin·ic** \-ˌō-lə-ˈfin-ik\ *adj*

cy·clo·par·af·fin \-ˈpar-ə-fən\ *n* : a saturated cyclic hydrocarbon of the formula C_nH_{2n}

cy·clo·pe·an \ˌsī-klə-ˈpē-ən, sī-ˈklō-pē-\ *adj* **1** *often cap* : of, relating to, or characteristic of a Cyclops **2** : HUGE, MASSIVE **3** : of or relating to a style of stone construction marked typically by the use of large irregular blocks without mortar

cy·clo·pe·dia *or* **cy·clo·pae·dia** \ˌsī-klə-ˈpēd-ē-ə\ *n* : ENCYCLOPEDIA — **cy·clo·pe·dic** \-ˈpēd-ik\ *adj*

cy·clo·phos·pha·mide \ˌsī-klō-ˈfäs-fə-ˌmīd\ *n* : an immunosuppressive and antineoplastic agent $C_7H_{15}Cl_2N_2O_2P$ used esp. against lymphomas and some leukemias

cy·clo·pro·pane \ˌsī-klə-ˈprō-ˌpān\ *n* [ISV] : a saturated cyclic gaseous hydrocarbon C_3H_6 used esp. as an anesthetic

cy·clops \ˈsī-ˌkläps\ *n* [L, fr. Gk *Kyklōps*, fr. *kykl-* cycl- + *ōps* eye] **1** *pl* **cy·clo·pes** \sī-ˈklō-(ˌ)pēz\ *cap* : one of a race of giants in Greek mythology with a single eye in the middle of the forehead **2** *pl* **cyclops** [NL, genus name, fr. L] : WATER FLEA

cy·clo·ra·ma \ˌsī-klə-ˈram-ə, -ˈräm-\ *n* [*cycl-* + *-orama* (as in *panorama*)] **1** : a large pictorial representation encircling the spectator and often having real objects as a foreground **2** : a curved curtain or wall used as a background of a stage set to suggest unlimited space — **cy·clo·ram·ic** \-ˈram-ik\ *adj*

cy·clo·ser·ine \ˌsī-klō-ˈse(ə)r-ˌēn\ *n* : an amino antibiotic $C_3H_6N_2O_2$ produced by an actinomycete (*Streptomyces orchidaceus*)

cy·clo·sis \sī-ˈklō-səs\ *n* [NL, fr. Gk *kyklōsis* encirclement, fr. *kykloun* to go around] : the streaming of protoplasm within a cell

cy·clos·to·mate \sī-ˈkläs-tə-mət\ *also* **cy·clo·sto·ma·tous** \ˌsī-klə-ˈstäm-ət-əs, -ˈstōm-\ *adj* [*cycl-* + Gk *stomat-, stoma* mouth] **1** : having a circular mouth **2** : CYCLOSTOME

cy·clo·stome \ˈsī-klə-ˌstōm\ *n* [deriv. of Gk *kykl-* + *stoma* mouth — more at STOMACH] : any of a class (Cyclostomi or Cyclostomata) of lowly craniate vertebrates having a large sucking mouth with no jaws and comprising the hagfishes and lampreys — **cyclostome** *adj*

¹cy·clo·style \-ˌstīl\ *n* [fr. *Cyclostyle*, a trademark] : a machine for making multiple copies that utilizes a stencil cut by a graver whose tip is a small rowel

²cyclostyle *vt* : to make multiple copies of by cyclostyle

cy·clo·thyme \ˈsī-klə-ˌthīm\ *n* [back-formation fr. *cyclothymia*] : a cyclothymic individual

cy·clo·thy·mia \ˌsī-klə-ˈthī-mē-ə\ *n* [NL, fr. G *zyklothymie*, fr. *zykl-* cycl- + *-thymie* -thymia] : a temperament marked by alternate lively and depressed moods — **cy·clo·thy·mic** \-ˈthī-mik\ *adj*

cy·clo·tom·ic \-ˈtäm-ik\ *adj* [*cyclotomy* (mathematical theory of the division of the circle into equal parts), fr. *cycl-* + *-tomy*] : relating to, being, or containing a polynomial of the form $x^{p-1} + x^{p-2} + \ldots + x + 1$ where p is a prime number

cy·clo·tron \ˈsī-klə-ˌträn\ *n* [*cycl-* + *-tron;* fr. the circular movement of the particles] : an accelerator in which particles (as protons, deuterons, or ions) are propelled by an alternating electric field in a constant magnetic field

cy·der *Brit var of* CIDER

cyg·net \ˈsig-nət\ *n* [ME *sygnett*, fr. MF *cygne* swan, fr. L *cycnus, cygnus*, fr. Gk *kyknos*] : a young swan

Cyg·nus \ˈsig-nəs\ *n* [L (gen. *Cygni*), lit., swan] : a northern constellation between Lyra and Pegasus in the Milky Way
cyl *abbr* cylinder
cyl·in·der \ˈsil-ən-dər\ *n* [MF or L; MF *cylindre,* fr. L *cylindrus,* fr. Gk *kylindros,* fr. *kylindein* to roll; akin to OE *sceol* squinting, L *scelus* crime, Gk *skelos* leg, *skolios* crooked] **1 a :** the surface traced by a straight line moving parallel to a fixed straight line and intersecting a fixed curve **b :** the space bounded by a cylinder and two parallel planes cutting all its elements — see VOLUME table **2 :** a cylindrical body: as **a :** the turning chambered breech of a revolver **b** (1) **:** the piston chamber in an engine (2) **:** a chamber in a pump from which the piston expels the fluid **c :** any of various rotating members in printing presses; *esp* **:** one that impresses paper on an inked form **d :** a cylindrical clay object inscribed with cuneiform inscriptions — **cyl·in·dered** \-dərd\ *adj*
cylinder seal *n* **:** a cylinder (as of stone) engraved in intaglio and used esp. in ancient Mesopotamia to roll an impression on wet clay
cy·lin·dri·cal \sə-ˈlin-dri-kəl\ *or* **cy·lin·dric** \-drik\ *adj* **:** relating to or having the form or properties of a cylinder — **cy·lin·dri·cal·ly** \-dri-k(ə-)lē\ *adv*
cylindrical coordinate *n* **:** any of the coordinates in space obtained by constructing in a plane a polar coordinate system and on a line perpendicular to the plane a linear coordinate system
cy·ma \ˈsī-mə\ *n* [Gk *kyma,* lit., wave] **1 :** a projecting molding whose profile is a double curve **2 :** a double curve formed by the union of a concave line and a convex line
cy·ma·tium \sī-ˈmā-sh(ē-)əm\ *n, pl* **-tia** \-sh(ē-)ə\ [L, fr. Gk *kymation,* dim. of *kymat-, kyma*] **:** a crowning molding in classic architecture; *esp* **:** CYMA
cym·bal \ˈsim-bəl\ *n* [ME, fr. OE *cymbal* & MF *cymbale,* fr. L *cymbalum,* fr. Gk *kymbalon,* fr. *kymbē* bowl — more at HUMP] **:** a concave brass plate that produces a brilliant clashing tone and that is struck with a drumstick or is used in pairs struck glancingly together — **cym·bal·ist** \-bə-ləst\ *n*
cym·bid·i·um \sim-ˈbid-ē-əm\ *n* [NL, genus name, fr. L *cymba* boat, fr. Gk *kymbē* bowl, boat] **:** any of a genus (*Cymbidium*) of tropical Old World orchids with showy boat-shaped flowers
cyme \ˈsīm\ *n* [NL *cyma,* fr. L, cabbage sprout, fr. Gk *kyma* swell, wave, cabbage sprout, fr. *kyein* to be pregnant] **:** an inflorescence in which all floral axes terminate in a single flower; *esp* **:** a determinate inflorescence of this type containing several flowers with the first-opening central flower terminating the main axis and subsequent flowers developing from lateral buds — see INFLORESCENCE illustrated
cy·mene \ˈsī-ˌmēn\ *n* [F *cymène,* fr. Gk *kyminon* cumin + F *-ène* -ene — more at CUMIN] **:** any of three liquid isomeric hydrocarbons $C_{10}H_{14}$; *esp* **:** a colorless liquid of pleasant odor from essential oils
cym·ling \ˈsim-lən, -liŋ\ *n* [prob. alter. of *simnel*] **:** a summer squash having a scalloped edge
cy·mo·gene \ˈsī-mə-ˌjēn\ *n* [ISV *cymene* + *-o-* + *-gen*] **:** a flammable gaseous petroleum product consisting chiefly of butane
cy·mo·phane \-ˌfān\ *n* [F, fr. Gk *kyma* wave + F *-phane*] **:** CHRYSOBERYL; *esp* **:** an opalescent chrysoberyl
cy·mose \ˈsī-ˌmōs\ *adj* **:** of, relating to, being, or bearing a cyme — **cy·mose·ly** *adv*
¹Cym·ric \ˈkim-rik, ˈkəm-\ *adj* **:** of, relating to, or characteristic of the non-Gaelic Celtic people of Britain or their language; *specif* **:** WELSH
²Cymric *n* **:** BRYTHONIC; *specif* **:** the Welsh language
Cym·ry \-rē\ *n pl* [W] **:** the Brythonic Celts; *specif* **:** WELSH
cyn·ic \ˈsin-ik\ *n* [MF or L, MF *cynique,* fr. L *cynicus,* fr. Gk *kynikos,* lit., like a dog, fr. *kyn-, kyōn* dog — more at HOUND] **1** *cap* **:** an adherent of an ancient Greek school of philosophers who held the view that virtue is the only good and that its essence lies in self-control and independence **2 :** a faultfinding captious critic; *esp* **:** one who believes that human conduct is motivated wholly by self-interest — **cynic** *adj*
cyn·i·cal \ˈsin-i-kəl\ *adj* **1 :** CAPTIOUS, PEEVISH **2 :** having the attitude or temper of a cynic; *esp* **:** contemptuously distrustful of human nature and motives ⟨provide a smashing answer for those ~ men who say that democracy cannot be honest and efficient—F.D. Roosevelt⟩ — **cyn·i·cal·ly** \-k(ə-)lē\ *adv*
syn CYNICAL, MISANTHROPIC, PESSIMISTIC, MISOGYNIC *shared meaning element* **:** deeply distrustful
cyn·i·cism \ˈsin-ə-ˌsiz-əm\ *n* **1** *cap* **:** the doctrine of the Cynics **2 a :** cynical character or quality **b :** an expression of such quality
cy·no·mol·gus \ˌsī-nə-ˈmäl-gəs\ *n, pl* **-gi** \-ˌgī, -ˌjī\ [NL, alter. of *cynamolgus,* fr. L, member of an ancient tribe in Africa, fr. Gk *Kynamolgoi,* lit., dog milkers] **:** MACAQUE; *esp* **:** one (*Macaca irus*) of southeastern Asia, Borneo, and the Philippines that is used esp. in medical research
cy·no·sure \ˈsī-nə-ˌshu̇(ə)r, ˈsin-ə-\ *n* [MF & L; MF, Ursa Minor, guide, fr. L *cynosura* Ursa Minor, fr. Gk *kynosoura,* fr. *kynos oura* dog's tail] **1** *cap* **:** the northern constellation Ursa Minor; *also* **:** NORTH STAR **2 :** a center of attraction or attention
Cyn·thia \ˈsin(t)-thē-ə\ *n* [L, fr. fem. of *Cynthius* of Cynthus, fr. *Cynthus,* mountain on Delos where she was born] **1 :** ARTEMIS **2 :** MOON
CYO *abbr* Catholic Youth Organization
cy·pher *chiefly Brit var of* CIPHER
¹cy pres \(ˈ)sī-ˈprā, (ˈ)sē-\ *adv* **:** in accordance with the rule of cy pres
²cy pres *n* [AF, so near, as near (as may be)] **:** a rule providing for the interpretation of instruments in equity as nearly as possible in conformity to the intention of the testator when literal construction is illegal, impracticable, or impossible — called also *cy pres doctrine*
¹cy·press \ˈsī-prəs\ *n* [ME, fr. OF *ciprès,* fr. L *cyparissus,* fr. Gk *kyparissos*] **1 a** (1) **:** any of a genus (*Cupressus*) of symmetrical mostly evergreen trees of the pine family with overlapping leaves resembling scales (2) **:** any of several coniferous trees other than the cypresses; *esp* **:** BALD CYPRESS 1 **b :** the wood of a cypress tree **2 :** branches of cypress used as a symbol of mourning
²cypress *n* [ME *ciprus, cipres,* fr. *Cyprus,* Mediterranean island] **:** a silk or cotton usu. black gauze formerly used for mourning
cypress vine *n* **:** a tropical American vine (*Quamoclit pennata*) of the morning-glory family with red or white tubular flowers and finely dissected leaves
cyp·ri·an \ˈsip-rē-ən\ *n, often cap* [L *cyprius* of Cyprus, fr. Gk *kyprios,* fr. *Kypros* Cyprus, birthplace of Aphrodite] **:** PROSTITUTE
cyp·ri·nid \ˈsip-rə-nəd\ *n* [deriv. of L *cyprinus* carp, fr. Gk *kyprinos*] **:** any of a family (Cyprinidae) of soft-finned freshwater fishes including the carps and minnows — **cyprinid** *adj*
cy·prin·odont \sə-ˈprin-ə-ˌdänt\ *n* [deriv. of L *cyprinus* + Gk *odont-, odous* tooth — more at TOOTH] **:** any of an order (Microcyprini) of soft-finned fishes including the topminnows and killifishes — **cyprinodont** *adj*
cyp·ri·pe·di·um \ˌsip-rə-ˈpēd-ē-əm\ *n* [NL, genus name, fr. LL *Cypris,* a name for Venus + Gk *pedilon* sandal] **:** any of a genus (*Cypripedium* or *Paphiopedalum*) of leafy-stemmed terrestrial orchids having large usu. showy drooping flowers with the lip inflated or pouched
cy·pro·hep·ta·dine \ˌsī-prō-ˈhep-tə-ˌdēn\ *n* [*cyclic* + *propyl* + *hepta-* + *piperidine*] **:** a drug $C_{21}H_{21}N$ that acts antagonistically to histamine and serotonin and is used esp. in the treatment of asthma
cy·prot·er·one \sī-ˈprät-ə-ˌrōn\ *n* [prob. fr. *cycl-* + *progesterone*] **:** a synthetic steroid that inhibits androgenic secretions (as testosterone)
cyp·se·la \ˈsip-sə-lə\ *n, pl* **-lae** \-ˌlē\ [NL, fr. Gk *kypselē* vessel, box] **:** an achene with two carpels and adherent calyx tube
Cy·re·na·ic \ˌsir-ə-ˈnā-ik, ˌsī-rə-\ *n* [L *cyrenaicus,* fr. Gk *kyrēnaikos,* fr. *Kyrēnē* Cyrene, Africa, home of Aristippus, author of the doctrine] **:** an adherent or advocate of the doctrine that pleasure is the chief end of life — **Cyrenaic** *adj* — **Cy·re·na·icism** \-ˈnā-ə-ˌsiz-əm\ *n*
Cy·ril·lic \sə-ˈril-ik\ *adj* [St. *Cyril* †869, apostle of the Slavs, reputed inventor of the Cyrillic alphabet] **:** of, relating to, or constituting an alphabet used for writing Old Church Slavonic and for Russian and various other Slavic languages
cyst \ˈsist\ *n* [NL *cystis,* fr. Gk *kystis* bladder, pouch] **1 :** a closed sac having a distinct membrane and developing abnormally in a cavity or structure of the body **2 :** a body resembling a cyst: as **a :** a resting spore of many algae **b :** an air vesicle (as of a rockweed) **c :** a capsule formed about a minute organism going into a resting or spore stage; *also* **:** this capsule with its contents **d :** a resistant cover about a parasite produced by the parasite or the host
cyst- *or* **cysti-** *or* **cysto-** *comb form* [F, fr. Gk *kyst-, kysto-,* fr. *kystis*] **:** bladder ⟨*cystitis*⟩ **:** sac ⟨*cystocarp*⟩
-cyst \ˌsist\ *n comb form* [NL *-cystis,* fr. Gk *kystis*] **:** bladder **:** sac ⟨blasto*cyst*⟩
cys·ta·mine \ˈsis-tə-ˌmēn\ *n* [*cystine* + *amine*] **:** a cystine derivative $C_4H_{12}N_2S_2$ used in the prevention of radiation sickness (as of cancer patients)
cys·ta·thi·o·nine \ˌsis-tə-ˈthī-ə-ˌnēn\ *n* [irreg. fr. *cysteine* + *methionine*] **:** a sulfur-containing amino acid $C_7H_{14}N_2O_4S$ formed as an intermediate in the conversion of methionine to cysteine in animal organisms
cys·te·amine \sis-ˈtē-ə-mən\ *n* [*cysteine* + *amine*] **:** a cysteine derivative C_2H_7NS used in the prevention of radiation sickness (as of cancer patients)
cys·te·ine \ˈsis-tə-ˌēn\ *n* [ISV, fr. *cystine* + *-ein*] **:** a crystalline sulfur-containing amino acid $C_3H_7NO_2S$ readily oxidizable to cystine
cys·tic \ˈsis-tik\ *adj* **1 :** relating to, composed of, or containing cysts **2 :** of or relating to the urinary bladder or the gallbladder **3 :** enclosed in a cyst
cys·ti·cer·coid \ˌsis-tə-ˈsər-ˌkȯid\ *n* **:** a tapeworm larva having an invaginated scolex and solid tailpiece
cys·ti·cer·co·sis \ˌsis-tə-(ˌ)sər-ˈkō-səs\ *n, pl* **-co·ses** \-ˈkō-ˌsēz\ [NL] **:** infestation with or disease caused by cysticerci
cys·ti·cer·cus \-ˈsər-kəs\ *n, pl* **-cer·ci** \-ˈsər-ˌsī, -ˌkī\ [NL, fr. *cyst-* + Gk *kerkos* tail] **:** a tapeworm larva consisting of a scolex invaginated in a fluid-filled sac in tissues of an intermediate host
cystic fibrosis *n* **:** a common hereditary disease esp. in Caucasian populations that appears usu. in early childhood, involves generalized disorder of exocrine glands, and is marked esp. by deficiency of pancreatic enzymes, respiratory symptoms, and excessive loss of salt in the sweat
cys·tine \ˈsis-ˌtēn\ *n* [fr. its discovery in bladder stones] **:** a crystalline amino acid $C_6H_{12}N_2O_4S_2$ that is widespread in proteins (as keratins) and is a major metabolic sulfur source
cys·tin·uria \ˌsis-tə-ˈn(y)u̇r-ē-ə\ *n* [NL] **:** a familial metabolic defect characterized by excretion of excessive amounts of cystine in the urine
cys·ti·tis \sis-ˈtīt-əs\ *n* [NL] **:** inflammation of the urinary bladder
cys·to·carp \ˈsis-tə-ˌkärp\ *n* [ISV] **:** the fruiting structure produced in the red algae after fertilization
¹cys·toid \ˈsis-ˌtȯid\ *adj* [ISV] **:** resembling a bladder
²cystoid *n* **:** a cystoid structure; *specif* **:** a mass resembling a cyst but lacking a membrane
cys·to·lith \ˈsis-tə-ˌlith\ *n* [G *zystolith,* fr. *zyst-* cyst- + *-lith*] **1 :** a calcium carbonate concretion arising from the cellulose wall of cells of higher plants **2 :** a urinary calculus
cys·to·scope \ˈsis-tə-ˌskōp\ *n* [ISV] **:** an instrument for the visual examination of the bladder and the passage of instruments under visual control — **cys·to·scop·ic** \ˌsis-tə-ˈskäp-ik\ *adj*
cyt- *or* **cyto-** *comb form* [G *zyt-, zyto-,* fr. Gk *kytos* hollow vessel — more at HIDE] **1 :** cell ⟨*cytology*⟩ **2 :** cytoplasm ⟨*cytokinesis*⟩
cyt·as·ter \ˈsīt-ˌas-tər\ *n* [ISV] **:** ASTER 2

ə abut ᵊ kitten ər further a back ā bake ä cot, cart
au̇ out ch chin e less ē easy g gift i trip ī life
j joke ŋ sing ō flow ȯ flaw ȯi coin th thin t͟h this
ü loot u̇ foot y yet yü few yu̇ furious zh vision

-cyte \sīt\ *n comb form* [NL *-cyta*, fr. Gk *kytos* hollow vessel] : cell ⟨leuko*cyte*⟩

Cyth·er·ea \,sith-ə-'rē-ə\ *n* : [L, fr. Gk *Kythereia*, fr. *Kythēra* Cythera, island associated with Aphrodite] : APHRODITE

Cyth·er·e·an \-'rē-ən\ *adj* : of or relating to the planet Venus

cy·ti·dine \'sit-ə-,dēn, 'sīt-\ *n* [*cytosine* + *-idine*] : a nucleoside containing cytosine

cy·ti·dyl·ic acid \,sit-ə-,dil-ik-, ,sīt-\ *n* [*cytidine* + *-yl* + *-ic*] : a nucleotide containing cytosine

cy·to·ar·chi·tec·ture \,sīt-ō-'är-kə-,tek-chər\ *n* : the cellular makeup of a bodily tissue or structure

cy·to·chem·is·try \-'kem-ə-strē\ *n* **1** : microscopical biochemistry **2** : the chemistry of cells — **cy·to·chem·i·cal** \-'kem-i-kəl\ *adj*

cy·to·chrome \'sit-ə-,krōm\ *n* : any of several intracellular hemoprotein respiratory pigments that are enzymes functioning as transporters of electrons to molecular oxygen by undergoing alternate oxidation and reduction

cytochrome c *n, often ital 2d c* : the most abundant and stable of the cytochromes

cytochrome oxidase *n* : an iron-porphyrin enzyme important in cell respiration because of its ability to catalyze the oxidation of reduced cytochrome c in the presence of oxygen

cy·to·dif·fer·en·ti·a·tion \'sit-ō-,dif-ə-,ren-chē-'ā-shən\ *n* : the development of specialized cells (as muscle, blood, or nerve cells) from undifferentiated precursors

cy·to·ge·net·ic \,sit-ō-jə-'net-ik\ *adj* [ISV] : of or relating to cytogenetics — **cy·to·ge·net·i·cal** \-i-kəl\ *adj* — **cy·to·ge·net·i·cal·ly** \-i-k(ə-)lē\ *adv* — **cy·to·ge·net·i·cist** \-'net-ə-səst\ *n*

cy·to·ge·net·ics \-jə-'net-iks\ *n pl but sing or pl in constr* [ISV] : a branch of biology that deals with the study of heredity and variation by the methods of both cytology and genetics

cy·to·ki·ne·sis \,sit-ō-kə-'nē-səs, -ki-\ *n* [NL, fr. *cyt-* + Gk *kinēsis* motion] **1** : cytoplasmic changes accompanying karyokinesis **2** : cleavage of the cytoplasm into daughter cells following nuclear division — **cy·to·ki·net·ic** \-'net-ik\ *adj*

cy·to·ki·nin \,sit-ə-'ki-nən\ *n* [*cyt-* + *kinin*] : any of various plant growth substances that are usu. derivatives of adenine

cytol *abbr* cytological; cytology

cy·tol·o·gy \sī-'täl-ə-jē\ *n* [ISV] **1** : a branch of biology dealing with the structure, function, multiplication, pathology, and life history of cells **2** : the cytological aspects of a process or structure — **cy·to·log·i·cal** \,sit-ᵊl-'äj-i-kəl\ *or* **cy·to·log·ic** \-'äj-ik\ *adj* — **cy·to·log·i·cal·ly** \-i-k(ə-)lē\ *adv* — **cy·tol·o·gist** \sī-'täl-ə-jəst\ *n*

cy·to·ly·sin \,sit-ᵊl-'īs-ᵊn\ *n* [ISV] : a substance (as an antibody that lyses bacteria) producing cytolysis

cy·tol·y·sis \sī-'täl-ə-səs\ *n* [NL] : the usu. pathologic dissolution or disintegration of cells — **cy·to·lyt·ic** \,sit-ᵊl-'it-ik\ *adj*

cy·to·me·gal·ic \,sit-ō-mi-'gal-ik\ *adj* [NL *cytomegalia* condition of having enlarged cells (fr. *cyt-* + *megal-* + *-ia*) + E *-ic*] : characterized by or causing the formation of enlarged cells

cy·to·meg·a·lo·vi·rus \,sit-ə-,meg-ə-lō-'vi-rəs\ *n* [NL, fr. *cytomegalia* + *-o-* + *virus*] : any of several viruses that cause cellular enlargement and formation of eosinophilic inclusion bodies esp. in the nucleus and include the causative agent of a severe disease esp. of newborns that usu. affects the salivary glands, brain, kidneys, liver, and lungs

cy·to·mor·phol·o·gy \,sit-ə-mȯr-'fäl-ə-jē\ *n* : the morphology of cells — **cy·to·mor·pho·log·i·cal** \-,mȯr-fə-'läj-i-kəl\ *adj*

cy·to·path·ic \,sīt-ə-'path-ik\ *adj* : of, relating to, characterized by, or producing pathological changes in cells

cy·to·patho·gen·ic \-,path-ə-'jen-ik\ *adj* [*cyt-* + *pathogenic*] : pathologic for or destructive to cells — **cy·to·patho·ge·nic·i·ty** \-jə-'nis-ət-ē\ *n*

cy·to·phil·ic \,sīt-ə-'fil-ik\ *adj* : having an affinity for cells ⟨~ antibodies⟩

cy·to·pho·tom·e·try \-fō-'täm-ə-trē\ *n* : photometry applied to the study of the cell or its constituents — **cy·to·pho·to·met·ric** \-,fōt-ə-'me-trik\ *adj*

cy·to·plasm \'sīt-ə-,plaz-əm\ *n* [ISV] : the protoplasm of a cell external to the nuclear membrane — see CELL illustration — **cy·to·plas·mic** \,sit-ə-'plaz-mik\ *adj* — **cy·to·plas·mi·cal·ly** \-mi-k(ə-)lē\ *adv*

cy·to·sine \'sit-ə-,sēn\ *n* [ISV *cyt-* + *-ose* + *-ine*] : a pyrimidine base $C_4H_5N_3O$ that codes genetic information in the polynucleotide chain of DNA or RNA — compare ADENINE, GUANINE, THYMINE, URACIL

cy·to·sol \'sit-ə-,säl, -,sȯl\ *n* : the fluid portion of the cytoplasm exclusive of organelles and membranes that is usu. obtained as the supernatant fraction from high-speed centrifugation of a tissue homogenate

cy·to·stat·ic \,sit-ə-'stat-ik\ *adj* : tending to retard cellular activity and multiplication ⟨~ treatment of tumor cells⟩ — **cytostatic** *n* — **cy·to·stat·i·cal·ly** \-i-k(ə-)lē\ *adv*

cy·to·tax·on·o·my \,sit-ō-(,)tak-'sän-ə-mē\ *n* **1** : study of the relationships and classification of organisms using both classical systematic techniques and comparative studies of chromosomes **2** : the nuclear cytologic makeup of a kind of organism — **cy·to·tax·o·nom·ic** \-,tak-sə-'näm-ik\ *adj* — **cy·to·tax·o·nom·i·cal·ly** \-i-k(ə-)lē\ *adv*

cy·to·tech·nol·o·gist \,sit-ə-tek-'näl-ə-jəst\ *n* : a medical technician trained in the identification of cells and cellular abnormalities (as in cancer)

cy·to·tox·ic \,sit-ə-'täk-sik\ *adj* **1** : of or relating to a cytotoxin **2** : toxic to cells ⟨~ properties of platinum⟩ — **cy·to·tox·ic·i·ty** \-(,)täk-'sis-ət-ē\ *n*

cy·to·tox·in \-'täk-sən\ *n* : a substance (as a toxin or antibody) having a toxic effect on cells

cy·to·tro·pic \,sit-ə-'trō-pik, -'träp-ik\ *adj* : attracted to cells ⟨a ~ virus⟩

CZ *abbr* Canal Zone

czar \'zär\ *n* [NL *czar*, fr. Russ *tsar'*, fr. Goth *kaisar*, fr. Gk or L; Gk, fr. L *Caesar* — more at CAESAR] **1** : EMPEROR: *specif* : the ruler of Russia until the 1917 revolution **2** : one having great power or authority ⟨retained the title of undisputed ~ over taxation —Marjorie Hunter⟩ — **czar·dom** \'zärd-əm\ *n*

czar·das \'chär-,dash, -,däsh\ *n, pl* **czardas** *same*\ [Hung *csárdás*] : a Hungarian dance to music in duple time in which the dancers start slowly and finish with a rapid whirl

czar·e·vitch \'zär-ə-,vich\ *n* [Russ *tsarevich*, fr. *tsar'* + *-evich*, patronymic suffix] : an heir apparent of a Russian czar

cza·ri·na \zä-'rē-nə\ *n* [prob. modif of G *zarin*, fr. *zar* czar, fr. Russ *tsar'*] : the wife of a czar

czar·ism \'zär-,iz-əm\ *n* **1** : the government of Russia under the czars **2** : autocratic rule — **czar·ist** \'zär-əst\ *n or adj*

cza·ri·tza \zä-'rit-sə, -'rēt-\ *n* [Russ *tsaritsa*, fem. of *tsar'*] : CZARINA

Czech \'chek\ *n* [Czech *Cech*] **1** : a native or inhabitant of Czechoslovakia; *esp* : a native or inhabitant of Bohemia, Moravia, or Silesia provinces **2** : the Slavic language of the Czechs — **Czech** *adj* — **Czech·ish** \-ish\ *adj*

D

¹d \ˈdē\ *n, pl* **d's** *or* **ds** \ˈdēz\ *often cap, often attrib* **1 a :** the 4th letter of the English alphabet **b :** a graphic representation of this letter **c :** a speech counterpart of orthographic *d* **2 :** 500 — see NUMBER table **3 :** the 2d tone of a C-major scale **4 :** a graphic device for reproducing the letter *d* **5 :** one designated *d* esp. as the 4th in order or class **6 a :** a grade rating a student's work as poor in quality **b :** one graded or rated with a D **7 :** something shaped like the letter D; *specif* **:** a semicircle on a pool table about 22 inches in diameter for use esp. in snooker
²d *abbr, often cap* **1** date **2** daughter **3** day **4** dead **5** deceased **6** deci- **7** degree **8** [L *denarius, denarii*] penny; pence **9** depart; departure **10** diameter **11** dimensional **12** distance **13** dorsal **14** drive; driving **15** Dutch
³d *symbol* differential
D *symbol* **1** derivative **2** deuterium
d- \ˌdē, ˈdē\ *prefix* [ISV, fr. *dextr-*] **1 :** dextrorotatory ⟨*d-* tartaric acid⟩ **2 :** having a similar configuration at a selected carbon atom to the configuration of dextrorotatory glyceraldehyde — usu. printed as a small capital ⟨D-fructose⟩
-d *symbol* — used after the figure 2 or 3 to indicate the ordinal number second or third ⟨2*d*⟩ ⟨53*d*⟩
'd \d, əd\ *vb* **1 :** HAD **2 :** WOULD **3 :** DID
DA *abbr* **1** days after acceptance **2** delayed action **3** deposit account **4** Dictionary of Americanisms **5** district attorney **6** doctor of arts **7** documents against acceptance **8** documents for acceptance **9** don't answer
¹dab \ˈdab\ *n* [ME *dabbe*] **1 :** a sudden blow or thrust **:** POKE **2 :** a gentle touch or stroke **:** PAT
²dab *vb* **dabbed; dab·bing** *vt* **1 :** to strike or touch lightly **:** PAT **2 :** to apply lightly or irregularly **:** DAUB **~** *vi* **:** to make a dab
³dab *n* **1 :** DAUB **2 :** a small amount
⁴dab *n* [AF *dabbe*] **:** FLATFISH; *esp* **:** any of several flounders (genus *Limanda*)
⁵dab *n* [perh. alter. of *adept*] *chiefly Brit* **:** a skillful person **:** EXPERT
DAB *abbr* Dictionary of American Biography
dab·ber \ˈdab-ər\ *n* **1 :** one that dabs **2 :** a pad, brush, or ball used to ink type or engraving plates
dab·ble \ˈdab-əl\ *vb* **dab·bled; dab·bling** \-(ə-)liŋ\ [perh. freq. of *dab*] *vt* **:** to wet by splashing or by little dips or strokes **:** SPATTER **~** *vi* **1 a :** to paddle, splash, or play in or as if in water **b :** to reach with the bill to the bottom of shallow water in order to obtain food **2 :** to work or concern oneself superficially ⟨~*s* in art⟩
dab·bler \-(ə-)lər\ *n* **:** one that dabbles: as **a :** one not deeply engaged in or concerned with something **b :** a duck (as a mallard or shoveler) that feeds by dabbling — called also *dabbling duck, puddle duck, river duck, surface feeder* **syn** see AMATEUR
dab·bling \-(ə-)liŋ\ *n* **:** a superficial or intermittent interest, investigation, or experiment ⟨his ~*s* in philosophy and art⟩
dab·chick \ˈdab-ˌchik\ *n* [prob. irreg. fr. obs. E *dop* (to dive) + E *chick*] **:** any of several small grebes
da ca·po \dä-ˈkäp-(ˌ)ō, də-\ *adv or adj* [It] **:** from the beginning — used as a direction in music to repeat
dace \ˈdās\ *n, pl* **dace** [ME, fr. MF *dars,* fr. ML *darsus*] **1 :** a small freshwater European cyprinid fish (*Leuciscus leuciscus*) **2 :** any of various small No. American freshwater cyprinid fishes
da·cha \ˈdäch-ə\ *n* [Russ, lit., gift; fr. its frequently being the gift of a ruler] **:** a Russian country cottage used esp. in the summer
dachs·hund \ˈdäks-ˌhu̇nt, ˈdäk-sənt\ *n, pl* **dachshunds** *or* **dachs·hun·de** \ˈdäks-ˌhu̇n-də\ [G, fr. *dachs* badger + *hund* dog] **:** a small dog of a breed of German origin with a long body, short legs, and long drooping ears

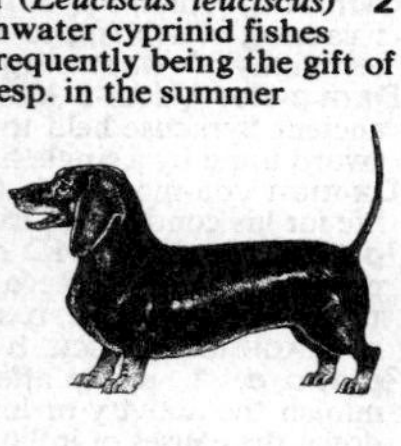
dachshund

Da·cron \ˈdā-ˌkrän, ˈdak-ˌrän\ *trademark* — used for a synthetic polyester textile fiber
dac·tyl \ˈdak-tᵊl\ *n* [ME *dactile,* fr. L *dactylus,* fr. Gk *daktylos,* lit., finger; fr. the fact that the three syllables have the first one longest like the joints of the finger] **:** a metrical foot consisting of one long and two short syllables or of one stressed and two unstressed syllables (as in *tenderly*) — **dac·tyl·ic** \dak-ˈtil-ik\ *adj or n*
dactyl- *or* **dactylo-** *comb form* [Gk *daktyl-, daktylo-,* fr. *daktylos*] **:** finger **:** toe **:** digit ⟨*dactylitis*⟩
dac·ty·lol·o·gy \ˌdak-tə-ˈläl-ə-jē\ *n* **:** the art of communicating ideas by signs made with the fingers
-dac·ty·lous \ˈdak-tə-ləs\ *adj comb form* [Gk *-daktylos,* fr. *daktylos*] **:** having (such or so many) fingers or toes ⟨*didactylous*⟩
dac·ty·lus \ˈdak-tə-ləs\ *n, pl* **-li** \-ˌlī, -ˌlē\ [NL, fr. Gk *daktylos* finger, toe] **:** one or more joints of the tarsus of some insects following the enlarged and modified first joint
dad \ˈdad\ *n* [prob. baby talk] **:** FATHER
da·da \ˈdäd-(ˌ)ä\ *n, often cap* [F] **:** a movement in art and literature based on deliberate irrationality and negation of traditional artistic values; *also* **:** the art and literature produced by this movement
da·da·ism \-ˌiz-əm\ *n, often cap* **:** DADA — **da·da·ist** \-ˌist\ *n, often cap* — **da·da·is·tic** \ˌdäd-ä-ˈis-tik\ *adj, often cap*
dad·dy \ˈdad-ē\ *n, pl* **daddies :** FATHER
dad·dy long·legs \ˌdad-ē-ˈlȯŋ-ˌlegz, -ˌlägz\ *n pl but sing or pl in constr* **:** any of various animals with long slender legs: as **a :** CRANE FLY **b :** HARVESTMAN
¹da·do \ˈdād-(ˌ)ō\ *n, pl* **dadoes** [It, die, plinth] **1 a :** the part of a pedestal of a column between the base and the surbase **b :** the lower part of an interior wall when specially decorated or faced; *also* **:** the decoration adorning this part of a wall **2 :** a groove made by dadoing **3 :** a tool (as a plane) for dadoing

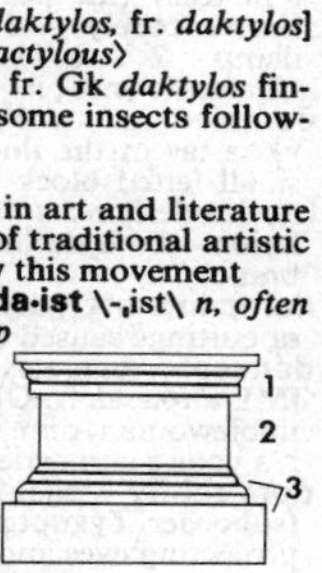

dado 1a: *1* surbase, *2* dado, *3* base

²dado *vt* **da·doed; da·do·ing 1 :** to provide with a dado **2 a :** to set into a groove **b :** to cut a rectangular groove in (as a plank)
DAE *abbr* Dictionary of American English
dae·dal \ˈdēd-ᵊl\ *adj* [L *daedalus,* fr. Gk *daidalos*] **1 a :** INTRICATE ⟨the computer's ~ circuitry⟩ **b :** SKILLFUL, ARTISTIC ⟨words made accessible in a novel and ~ way —*Publisher's Weekly*⟩ **2 :** adorned with many things ⟨visions of cloud and light and ~ earth are the airman's daily scene —Laurence Binyon⟩
Dae·da·lus \ˈded-ᵊl-əs, ˈdēd-\ *n* [L, fr. Gk *Daidalos*] **:** the legendary builder of the Cretan labyrinth and the inventor of wings whereby he flew to escape imprisonment — **Dae·da·lian** \di-ˈdāl-yən\ *or* **Dae·da·lean** \di-ˈdāl-yən; ˌded-ᵊl-ˈē-ən, ˌdēd-\ *adj*
dae·mon *var of* DEMON
daff \ˈdaf\ *vt* [alter. of *doff*] **1** *archaic* **:** to thrust aside **2** *obs* **:** to put off (as with an excuse)
daf·fo·dil \ˈdaf-ə-ˌdil\ *n* [prob. fr. D *de affodil* the asphodel, fr. *de* the (fr. MD) + *affodil* asphodel, fr. MF *afrodille,* fr. L *asphodelus;* akin to OHG *thaz* the — more at THAT, ASPHODEL] **:** any of various bulbous herbs (genus *Narcissus*); *esp* **:** a plant whose flowers have a large corona elongated into a trumpet — compare JONQUIL
daf·fy \ˈdaf-ē\ *adj* **daf·fi·er; -est** [obs. E *daff,* n. (fool)] **:** CRAZY, FOOLISH ⟨the story is slight, but it has a ~ kind of logic —*N.Y. Times Bk. Rev.*⟩
daft \ˈdaft\ *adj* [ME *dafte* gentle, stupid; akin to OE *gedæfte* mild, gentle, ME *defte* deft, L *faber* smith] **1 a :** SILLY, FOOLISH **b :** MAD, INSANE **2** *Scot* **:** frivolously gay — **daft·ly** *adv* — **daft·ness** \ˈdaf(t)-nəs\ *n*
¹dag \ˈdag\ *n* [ME *dagge*] **1 :** a hanging end or shred **2 :** matted or manure-coated wool
²dag *abbr* dekagram
dag·ger \ˈdag-ər\ *n* [ME] **1 :** a short weapon for stabbing **2 a :** something that resembles a dagger **b :** a character † used as a reference mark or to indicate a death date
da·go \ˈdā-(ˌ)gō\ *n, pl* **dagos** *or* **dagoes** [alter. of earlier *diego,* fr. *Diego,* a common Sp given name] **:** a person of Italian or Spanish birth or descent — usu. used disparagingly
da·guerre·o·type \də-ˈger-(ē-)ə-ˌtīp\ *n* [F *daguerréotype,* fr. L. J. M. *Daguerre* †1851 F painter + F *-o-* + *type*] **:** an early photograph produced on a silver or a silver-covered copper plate; *also* **:** the process of producing such photographs — **daguerreotype** *vt* — **da·guerre·o·typy** \-ˌtī-pē\ *n*
dah \ˈdä\ *n* [imit.] **:** a dash in radio or telegraphic code
DAH *abbr* Dictionary of American History
dahl·ia \ˈdal-yə, ˈdäl-, *U.S. also & Brit usu* ˈdāl-\ *n* [NL, genus name, fr. Anders *Dahl* †1789 Sw botanist] **:** any of a genus (*Dahlia*) of American tuberous-rooted composite herbs having opposite pinnate leaves and rayed flower heads and including many that are cultivated as ornamentals
¹dai·ly \ˈdā-lē\ *adj* **1 a :** occurring, made, or acted upon every day **b :** issued every day or every weekday **c :** of or providing for every day **2 a :** reckoned by the day ⟨average ~ wage⟩ **b :** covering the period of or based on a day ⟨~ statistics⟩ — **dai·li·ness** *n*
syn DAILY, DIURNAL, QUOTIDIAN, CIRCADIAN *shared meaning element* **:** of each or every day. DAILY is used with reference to the ordinary concerns of the day or daytime ⟨*daily* food⟩ ⟨a *daily* duty⟩ Distinctively, it may refer to weekdays as contrasted with holidays and Sundays and sometimes also Saturdays, and it may imply an opposition to *nightly* ⟨the *daily* anodyne, the nightly draught —Alexander Pope⟩ DIURNAL is used in contrast to *nocturnal* and occurs chiefly in poetic or technical contexts ⟨rolled round in earth's *diurnal* course —William Wordsworth⟩ ⟨*diurnal* mammals, active only by day⟩ QUOTIDIAN emphasizes the quality of daily recurrence ⟨a *quotidian* fever⟩ and may attribute a commonplace, routine, or everyday quality to what it describes ⟨*quotidian* routine⟩ CIRCADIAN, a chiefly technical word of recent coinage, differs from *daily* or *quotidian* in implying only approximate equation with the twenty-four hour day ⟨*circadian* rhythms in insect behavior⟩
²daily *adv* **:** every day **:** every weekday
³daily *n, pl* **dailies 1 :** a newspaper published every weekday **2** *Brit* **:** a servant who works on a daily basis
daily double *n* **:** a system of betting (as on horse races) in which the bettor must pick the winners of two stipulated races in order to win
daily dozen *n* **1 :** a series of physical exercises to be performed daily **:** WORKOUT **2 :** a set of routine duties or tasks
dai·mon \ˈdī-ˌmōn\ *n, pl* **dai·mo·nes** \ˈdī-mə-ˌnēz\ *or* **daimons** [Gk *daimōn*] **:** DEMON 1, 3 — **dai·mon·ic** \dī-ˈmän-ik\ *adj*
dai·myo *or* **dai·mio** \ˈdī-mē-ˌō, (ˈ)dī-ˈmyō\ *n, pl* **-myos** *or* **-mios** [Jap *daimyō*] **:** a Japanese feudal baron
¹dain·ty \ˈdānt-ē\ *n, pl* **dainties** [ME *deinte,* fr. OF *deintié,* fr. L *dignitat-, dignitas* dignity, worth] **1 a :** something delicious to the taste **b :** something choice or pleasing **2** *obs* **:** FASTIDIOUSNESS
²dainty *adj* **dain·ti·er; -est 1 a :** tasting good **:** TASTY **b :** attractively prepared and served **2 :** of a kind to appeal to a fastidious taste esp. because of fragile beauty or diminutive charm and grace **3** *obs* **:** CHARY, RELUCTANT **4 a :** marked by fastidious discrimination or finical taste **b :** showing avoidance of anything rough **syn 1** see CHOICE **ant** gross **2** see NICE — **dain·ti·ly** \ˈdānt-ᵊl-ē\ *adv* — **dain·ti·ness** \ˈdānt-ē-nəs\ *n*
dai·qui·ri \ˈdī-kə-rē, ˈdak-ə-\ *n* [*Daiquirí,* Cuba] **:** a cocktail made of rum, lime juice, and sugar

dairy \'de(ə)r-ē, 'da(ə)r-\ *n, pl* **dair·ies** [ME *deyerie,* fr. *deye* dairymaid, fr. OE *dǣge* kneader of bread; akin to OE *dāg* dough — more at DOUGH] **1** : a room, building, or establishment where milk is kept and butter or cheese is made **2 a** : the department of farming or of a farm that is concerned with the production of milk, butter, and cheese **b** : a farm devoted to such production **3** : an establishment for the sale or distribution chiefly of milk and milk products
dairy breed *n* : a cattle breed developed chiefly for milk production
dairy cattle *n pl* : cattle of one of the dairy breeds
dairy·ing \'der-ē-iŋ\ *n* : the business of operating a dairy
dairy·maid \-ē-,mād\ *n* : a woman employed in a dairy
dairy·man \-ē-mən, -,man\ *n* : one who operates a dairy farm or works in a dairy
da·is \'dā-əs, 'dī-\ *n* [ME *deis,* fr. OF, fr. L *discus* dish, quoit — more at DISH] : a raised platform in a hall or large room
dai·shi·ki \dī-'shē-kē\ *var of* DASHIKI
dai·sy \'dā-zē\ *n, pl* **daisies** [ME *dayeseye,* fr. OE *dægesēage,* fr. *dæg* day + *ēage* eye] **1** : a composite plant (as of the genera *Bellis* or *Chrysanthemum*) having a flower head with well-developed ray flowers usu. arranged in one or a few whorls: as **a** : a low European herb (*Bellis perennis*) with white or pink ray flowers — called also *English daisy* **b** : a leafy-stemmed perennial herb (*Chrysanthemum leucanthemum*) that has long white ray flowers and a yellow disk and is often a troublesome weed in parts of the U.S. — called also *oxeye daisy* **2** : the flower head of a daisy **3** : a first-rate person or thing
daisy ham *n* : a boned and smoked piece of pork from the shoulder
Da·ko·ta \də-'kōt-ə\ *n, pl* **Dakotas** *also* **Dakota** **1** : a member of an Amerindian people of the northern Mississippi valley **2** : the language of the Dakota people
dal *abbr* dekaliter
Da·lai La·ma \,däl-,ī-'läm-ə, ,däl-,ā-, ,dal-\ *n* [Mongolian *dalai* ocean] : the spiritual head of Lamaism
dal·a·pon \'dal-ə-,pän\ *n* [perh. fr. *di-* + *alpha* + *propionic* acid] : an herbicide that kills monocotyledonous plants selectively and is used esp. on unwanted grasses
da·la·si \dä-'läs-ē\ *n, pl* **dalasi** [native name in The Gambia] — see MONEY table
dale \'dā(ə)l\ *n* [ME, fr. OE *dæl;* akin to OHG *tal* valley, Gk *tholos* rotunda] : VALE, VALLEY ⟨went riding over hill and ∼⟩
dales·man \'dā(ə)lz-mən\ *n, Brit* : one living or born in a dale
da·leth \'däl-,eth, -,et\ *n* [Heb *dāleth,* fr. *deleth* door] : the 4th letter of the Hebrew alphabet — see ALPHABET table
dal·li·ance \'dal-ē-ən(t)s\ *n* : an act of dallying: as **a** : FOREPLAY **b** : frivolous action : TRIFLING
Dal·lis grass \'dal-əs-\ *n* [perh. alter. of *Dallas,* Texas] : a tall tufted tropical perennial grass (*Paspalum dilatatum*) introduced as a pasture and forage grass in the southern U.S.
Dall sheep \'dȯl-\ *or* **Dall's sheep** \'dȯlz-\ *n* [William H. *Dall* †1927 Am naturalist] : a large white wild sheep (*Ovis montana dalli* or *O. dalli*) of northwestern No. America
dal·ly \'dal-ē\ *vi* **dal·lied; dal·ly·ing** [ME *dalyen,* fr. AF *dalier*] **1 a** : to act playfully; *esp* : to play amorously **b** : to deal lightly : TOY ⟨accused him of ∼*ing* with a serious problem⟩ **2 a** : to waste time **b** : LINGER, DAWDLE ***syn*** see TRIFLE — **dal·li·er** *n*
dal·ma·tian \dal-'mā-shən\ *n, often cap* [fr. the supposed origin of the breed in Dalmatia] : any of a breed of large dogs having a white short-haired coat with black or brown spots
dal·mat·ic \dal-'mat-ik\ *n* [LL *dalmatica,* fr. L, fem. of *dalmaticus* Dalmatian, fr. *Dalmatia*] : a wide-sleeved overgarment with slit sides worn by a deacon or prelate; *also* : a similar robe worn by a British sovereign at his coronation

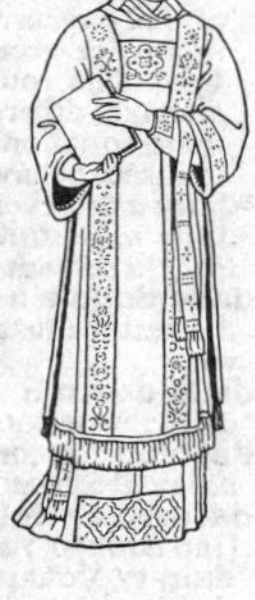
dalmatic

dal se·gno \däl-'sān-(,)yō\ *adv* [It, from the sign] — used as a direction in music to return to the sign that marks the beginning of a repeat
1dam \'dam\ *n* [ME *dam, dame* lady, dam — more at DAME] : a female parent — used esp. of a domestic animal
2dam *n* [ME] **1 a** : a barrier preventing the flow of water or of loose solid materials (as soil or snow); *esp* : a barrier built across a watercourse for impounding water **b** : a barrier to check the flow of liquid, gas, or air **2** : a body of water confined by a dam
3dam *vt* **dammed; dam·ming** **1** : to provide or restrain with a dam **2** : to stop up : BLOCK
4dam *abbr* dekameter
1dam·age \'dam-ij\ *n* [ME, fr. OF, fr. *dam* damage, fr. L *damnum*] **1** : loss or harm resulting from injury to person, property, or reputation **2** *pl* : compensation in money imposed by law for loss or injury **3** : EXPENSE, COST ⟨"What's the ∼?" he said, asking how much his bill was⟩
2damage *vt* **dam·aged; dam·ag·ing** : to cause damage to ***syn*** see INJURE — **dam·ag·er** *n*
dam·ag·ing *adj* : causing or able to cause damage : INJURIOUS ⟨has a ∼ effect on wildlife⟩ — **dam·ag·ing·ly** \'dam-ij-iŋ-lē\ *adv*
1dam·a·scene \'dam-ə-,sēn, ,dam-ə-'\ *n* **1** *cap* : a native or inhabitant of Damascus **2** : DAMASK 2b
2damascene *adj* **1** *cap* : of, relating to, or characteristic of Damascus or the Damascenes **2** : of or relating to damask or the art of damascening
3damascene *vt* **-scened; -scen·ing** [MF *damasquiner,* fr. *damasquin* of Damascus] : to ornament (as iron or steel) with wavy patterns like those of watered silk or with inlaid work of precious metals
Da·mas·cus steel \də-,mas-kə(s)-\ *n* : hard elastic steel ornamented with wavy patterns and used esp. for sword blades
1dam·ask \'dam-əsk\ *n* [ME *damaske,* fr. ML *damascus,* fr. *Damascus*] **1** : a firm lustrous fabric (as of linen, cotton, silk, or rayon) made with flat patterns in a satin weave on a plain-woven ground on jacquard looms **2 a** : DAMASCUS STEEL **b** : the characteristic markings of this steel **3** : a grayish red
2damask *adj* **1** : made of or resembling damask **2** : of the color damask
damask rose *n* [obs. *Damask* of Damascus, fr. obs. *Damask* Damascus] : a large hardy fragrant pink rose (*Rosa damascena*) that is cultivated in Asia Minor as a source of attar of roses and is a parent of many hybrid perpetual roses
dame \'dām\ *n* [ME, fr. OF, fr. L *domina,* fem. of *dominus* master; akin to L *domus* house — more at TIMBER] **1** : a woman of rank, station, or authority: as **a** *archaic* : the mistress of a household **b** : the wife or daughter of a lord **c** : a female member of an order of knighthood — used as a title prefixed to the given name **2 a** : an elderly woman **b** : WOMAN
dame school *n* : a school in which the rudiments of reading and writing were taught by a woman in her own home
dame's violet *n* : a Eurasian perennial plant (*Hesperis matronalis*) widely cultivated for its spikes of showy, single or double, and fragrant white or purple flowers — called also *dame's rocket*
dam·mar *or* **dam·ar** *also* **dam·mer** \'dam-ər\ *n* [Malay *damar*] **1** : any of various hard resins derived esp. from evergreen trees (genus *Agathis*) of the pine family **2** : a clear to yellow resin obtained in Malaya from several timber trees (family Dipterocarpaceae) and used in varnishes and inks
dam·mit \'dam-ət\ : damn it
1damn \'dam\ *vb* **damned; damn·ing** \'dam-iŋ\ [ME *dampnen,* fr. OF *dampner,* fr. L *damnare,* fr. *damnum* damage, loss, fine] *vt* **1** : to condemn to a punishment or fate; *esp* : to condemn to hell **2 a** : to condemn vigorously and often irascibly for some real or fancied fault or defect ⟨∼*ed* the storm for their delay⟩ **b** : to condemn as a failure by public criticism **3** : to bring ruin on **4** : to swear at : CURSE ∼ *vi* : CURSE, SWEAR ***syn*** see EXECRATE
2damn *n* **1** : the utterance of the word *damn* as a curse **2** : a minimum amount or degree (as of care or consideration) : the least bit
3damn *adj or adv* : DAMNED ⟨a ∼ nuisance⟩ ⟨ran ∼ fast⟩ — **damn well** : beyond doubt or question : CERTAINLY ⟨knew *damn well* what would happen⟩
dam·na·ble \'dam-nə-bəl\ *adj* **1** : liable to or deserving condemnation **2** : very bad : DETESTABLE ⟨∼ weather⟩ — **dam·na·ble·ness** *n* — **dam·na·bly** \-blē\ *adv*
dam·na·tion \dam-'nā-shən\ *n* : the act of damning : the state of being damned
dam·na·to·ry \'dam-nə-,tōr-ē, -,tȯr-\ *adj* : expressing, imposing, or causing condemnation : CONDEMNATORY
1damned \'dam(d)\ *adj* **damned·er** \'dam-dər\; **damned·est** *or* **damnd·est** \-dəst\ **1** : DAMNABLE ⟨hoping to get away from this ∼ smog⟩ **2** : COMPLETE, UTTER **3** : EXTRAORDINARY — used in the superlative ⟨the ∼*est* contraption he ever saw⟩
2damned \'dam(d)\ *adv* : EXTREMELY, VERY ⟨a ∼ good job⟩
damned·est *or* **damnd·est** \'dam-dəst\ *n* : UTMOST, BEST — used chiefly in the phrase *do one's damnedest* ⟨doing his ∼ to succeed⟩
dam·ni·fy \'dam-nə-,fī\ *vt* **-fied; -fy·ing** [MF *damnifier,* fr. OF, fr. LL *damnificare,* fr. L *damnificus* injurious, fr. *damnum* damage] : to cause loss or damage to ⟨intimidation — the freedom to ∼ another person with impunity —Henry Hazlitt⟩
damn·ing \'dam-iŋ\ *adj* **1** : bringing damnation ⟨a ∼ sin⟩ **2** : causing or leading to condemnation or ruin ⟨presented some ∼ testimony⟩ — **damn·ing·ly** \-iŋ-lē\ *adv*
Dam·o·cles \'dam-ə-,klēz\ *n* [L, fr. Gk *Damoklēs*] : a courtier of ancient Syracuse held to have been seated at a banquet beneath a sword hung by a single hair — **Dam·o·cle·an** \,dam-ə-'klē-ən\ *adj*
Da·mon \'dā-mən\ *n* [L, fr. Gk *Damōn*] : a Sicilian who pledges his life for his condemned friend Pythias
1damp \'damp\ *n* [MD or MLG, vapor; akin to OHG *damph* vapor, OE *dim* dim] **1** : a noxious gas esp. in a coal mine **2** : MOISTURE: **a** : HUMIDITY, DAMPNESS **b** *archaic* : FOG, MIST **3 a** : DISCOURAGEMENT, CHECK **b** *archaic* : DEPRESSION, DEJECTION
2damp *vt* **1 a** : to affect with a noxious gas : CHOKE **b** : to diminish the activity or intensity of — often used with *down* ⟨∼*ing* down the causes of inflation⟩ **c** : to check the vibration or oscillation of (as a string or voltage) **2** : DAMPEN ∼ *vi* : to diminish progressively in vibration or oscillation
3damp *adj* **1 a** *archaic* : being confused, bewildered, or shocked : STUPEFIED **b** : DEPRESSED, DULL **2** : slightly or moderately wet ***syn*** see WET — **damp·ish** \'dam-pish\ *adj* — **damp·ly** *adv* — **damp·ness** *n*
damp·en \'dam-pən\ *vb* **damp·ened; damp·en·ing** \'damp-(ə-)niŋ\ *vt* **1** : to check or diminish the activity or vigor of : DEADEN ⟨the heat ∼*ed* our spirits⟩ **2** : to make damp ⟨the shower barely ∼*ed* the ground⟩ **3** : DAMP 1c ∼ *vi* **1** : to become damp **2** : to become deadened or depressed — **damp·en·er** \'damp-(ə-)nər\ *n*
damp·er \'dam-pər\ *n* **1** : a device that damps: as **a** : a valve or plate (as in the flue of a furnace) for regulating the draft **b** : a small felted block to stop the vibration of a piano string **c** : a device designed to bring a mechanism to rest with minimum oscillation **2** : a dulling or deadening influence ⟨put a ∼ on the celebration⟩
damp·ing–off \,dam-piŋ-'ȯf\ *n* : a diseased condition of seedlings or cuttings caused by fungi and marked by wilting or rotting
dam·sel \'dam-zəl\ *also* **dam·o·sel** *or* **dam·o·zel** \'dam-ə-,zel\ *n* [ME *damesel,* fr. OF *dameisele,* fr. (assumed) VL *domnicella* young noblewoman, dim. of L *domina* lady] : a young woman: **a** *archaic* : a young unmarried woman of noble birth **b** : GIRL
dam·sel·fly \'dam-zəl-,flī\ *n* : any of numerous odonate insects (suborder Zygoptera) distinguished from dragonflies by laterally projecting eyes and petiolate wings folded above the body when at rest
dam·son \'dam-zən\ *n* [ME, fr. L *prunum damascenum,* lit., plum of Damascus] : an Asiatic plum (*Prunus insititia* or *P. domestica insititia*) cultivated for its small acid purple fruit; *also* : its fruit

[1]Dan \ˈdan\ *n* [Heb *Dān*] : a son of Jacob and the traditional eponymous ancestor of one of the tribes of Israel
[2]Dan \(ˈ)dan\ *n* [ME, title of members of religious orders, fr. MF, fr. ML *domnus*, fr. L *dominus* master] *archaic* : MASTER, SIR
[3]Dan *abbr* **1** Daniel **2** Danish
Dan·aë \ˈdan-ə-ˌē\ *n* [L, fr. Gk *Danaē*] : a princess of Argos visited by Zeus in the form of a shower of gold and by him the mother of Perseus
[1]dance \ˈdan(t)s\ *vb* **danced; danc·ing** [ME *dauncen*, fr. OF *dancier*] *vi* **1** : to engage in or perform a dance **2** : to move quickly up and down or about ~ *vt* **1** : to perform or take part in as a dancer **2** : to cause to dance **3** : to bring into a specified condition by dancing — **dance·able** \ˈdan(t)-sə-bəl\ *adj* — **danc·er** *n*
[2]dance *n, often attrib* **1** : an act or instance of dancing **2** : a series of rhythmic and patterned bodily movements usu. performed to music **3** : a social gathering for dancing **4** : a piece of music by which dancing may be guided **5** : the art of dancing
D & C *abbr* dilatation and curettage
dan·de·li·on \ˈdan-dᵊl-ˌī-ən\ *n* [MF *dent de lion*, lit., lion's tooth] : any of a genus (*Taraxacum*) of yellow-flowered composite plants; *esp* : an herb (*T. officinale*) sometimes grown as a potherb and nearly cosmopolitan as a weed
dan·der \ˈdan-dər\ *n* [alter. of *dandruff*] **1** : minute scales from hair, feathers, or skin that may be allergenic **2** : ANGER, TEMPER ⟨got his ~ up and shouted at his wife⟩
dan·di·a·cal \dan-ˈdī-ə-kəl\ *adj* [[1]*dandy* + *-acal* (as in *demoniacal*)] : of, relating to, or suggestive of a dandy — **dan·di·a·cal·ly** \-k(ə-)lē\ *adv*
Dan·die Din·mont terrier \ˌdan-dē-ˈdin-ˌmänt-\ *n* [*Dandie Dinmont*, character owning 2 such dogs in the novel *Guy Mannering* by Sir Walter Scott] : a terrier of a breed characterized by short legs, a long body, pendulous ears, a rough coat, and a full silky topknot
dan·di·fy \ˈdan-di-ˌfī\ *vt* **-fied; -fy·ing** : to cause to resemble a dandy — **dan·di·fi·ca·tion** \ˌdan-di-fə-ˈkā-shən\ *n*
dan·dle \ˈdan-dᵊl\ *vt* **dan·dled; dan·dling** \-(d)liŋ, -dᵊl-iŋ\ [origin unknown] **1** : to move (as a baby) up and down in one's arms or on one's knee in affectionate play **2** : PAMPER, PET
dan·druff \ˈdan-drəf\ *n* [prob. fr. *dand-* (origin unknown) + *-ruff*, of Scand origin; akin to ON *hrūfa* scab; akin to OHG *hruf* scurf, Lith *kraupus* rough] : a scurf that forms on the scalp and comes off in small white or grayish scales — **dan·druffy** \-ē\ *adj*
[1]dan·dy \ˈdan-dē\ *n, pl* **dandies** [prob. short for *jack-a-dandy*, fr. [1]*jack* + *a* (of) + *dandy* (origin unknown)] **1** : a man who gives exaggerated attention to dress **2** : something excellent in its class **3** : a small 2-masted sailboat with a modified ketch rig — **dan·dy·ish** \-dē-ish\ *adj* — **dan·dy·ish·ly** *adv*
[2]dandy *adj* **dan·di·er; -est** **1** : of, relating to, or suggestive of a dandy : FOPPISH **2** : very good : FIRST-RATE ⟨a ~ place to stay⟩
dan·dy·ism \ˈdan-dē-ˌiz-əm\ *n* **1** : the style or conduct of a dandy **2** : a literary and artistic style of the latter part of the 19th century marked by artificiality and excessive refinement
Dane \ˈdān\ *n* [ME *Dan*, fr. ON *Danr*] **1** : a native or inhabitant of Denmark **2** : a person of Danish descent
dane·geld \ˈdān-ˌgeld\ *n, often cap* : an annual tax believed to have been imposed orig. to buy off Danish invaders in England or to maintain forces to oppose them but continued as a land tax
Dane·law \ˈdān-ˌlȯ\ *n* **1** : the law in force in the part of England held by the Danes before the Norman Conquest **2** : the part of England under the Danelaw
[1]dan·ger \ˈdān-jər\ *n* [ME *daunger*, fr. OF *dangier*, alter. of *dongier*, fr. (assumed) VL *dominiarium*, fr. L *dominium* ownership] **1 a** *archaic* : JURISDICTION **b** *obs* : REACH, RANGE **2** *obs* : HARM, DAMAGE **3** : exposure or liability to injury, pain, or loss ⟨a place where children could play without ~⟩ **4** : a case or cause of danger ⟨the ~s of mining⟩
[2]danger *vt, archaic* : ENDANGER
dan·ger·ous \ˈdānj-(ə-)rəs\ *adj* **1** : exposing to or involving danger **2** : able or likely to inflict injury — **dan·ger·ous·ly** *adv* — **dan·ger·ous·ness** *n*
syn DANGEROUS, HAZARDOUS, PRECARIOUS, PERILOUS, RISKY *shared meaning element* : bringing or involving the chance of loss or injury ***ant*** safe, secure
[1]dan·gle \ˈdaŋ-gəl\ *vb* **dan·gled; dan·gling** \-g(ə-)liŋ\ [prob. of Scand origin; akin to Dan *dangle* to dangle] *vi* **1** : to hang loosely and usu. so as to be able to swing freely **2** : to be a hanger-on or a dependent **3** : to occur in a sentence without having a normally expected syntactic relation to the rest of the sentence ⟨the word *climbing* in "Climbing the mountain the cabin came into view" is *dangling*⟩ ~ *vt* **1** : to cause to dangle : SWING **2** : to keep hanging uncertainly — **dan·gler** \-g(ə-)lər\ *n* — **dan·gling·ly** \-g(ə-)liŋ-lē\ *adv*
[2]dangle *n* **1** : the action of dangling **2** : something that dangles
Dan·iel \ˈdan-yəl *also* ˈdan-ᵊl\ *n* [Heb *Dānīʼēl*] **1** : the Jewish hero of the Book of Daniel who as an exile in Babylon interprets dreams, gives accounts of apocalyptic visions, and is divinely delivered from a den of lions **2** : a book of narratives, visions, and prophecies in canonical Jewish and Christian Scripture — see BIBLE table
da·nio \ˈdā-nē-ˌō\ *n, pl* **da·ni·os** [NL, genus name] : any of several small brightly colored Asiatic cyprinid fishes
[1]Dan·ish \ˈdā-nish\ *adj* : of, relating to, or characteristic of Denmark, the Danes, or the Danish language
[2]Danish *n* **1** : the Germanic language of the Danes **2** *pl* **Danish** : a piece of Danish pastry
Danish pastry *n* : a pastry made of a rich yeast-raised dough
dank \ˈdaŋk\ *adj* [ME *danke*] : unpleasantly moist or wet ***syn*** see WET — **dank·ly** *adv* — **dank·ness** *n*
dan·seur \dänⁿ-ˈsər, dän-\ *n* [F, fr. *danser* to dance] : a male ballet dancer
dan·seuse \dänⁿ-ˈsə(r)z, dän-ˈsüz\ *n* [F, fem. of *danseur*] : a female ballet dancer
Dan·te·an \ˈdant-ē-ən\ *n* : a student or admirer of Dante
daph·ne \ˈdaf-nē\ *n* [NL, genus name, fr. L, laurel, fr. Gk *daphnē*] : any of a genus (*Daphne*) of Eurasian shrubs of the mezereon family with apetalous flowers whose colored calyx resembles a corolla
Daph·ne \ˈdaf-nē\ *n* [L, fr. Gk *Daphnē*] : a nymph transformed into a laurel tree and thus enabled to escape the pursuing Apollo
daph·nia \ˈdaf-nē-ə\ *n* [NL, genus name] : any of a genus (*Daphnia*) of minute freshwater branchiopod crustaceans with biramous antennae used as locomotor organs — compare WATER FLEA
Daph·nis \ˈdaf-nəs\ *n* [L, fr. Gk] : a son of Hermes who gained renown as a musician and a reputation for being the father of pastoral poetry
dap·per \ˈdap-ər\ *adj* [ME *dapyr*, fr. MD *dapper* quick, strong; akin to OHG *tapfar* heavy, OSlav *debelŭ* thick] **1 a** : neat and trim in appearance **b** : excessively spruce and stylish **2** : alert and lively in movement and manners — **dap·per·ly** *adv* — **dap·per·ness** *n*
[1]dap·ple \ˈdap-əl\ *n* [ME *dappel-gray*, adj., gray variegated with spots of a different color] **1** : any of numerous usu. cloudy and rounded spots or patches of a color or shade different from their background **2** : the quality or state of being dappled ⟨the ~ of the leaf-filtered light —Anthony West⟩ **3** : a dappled animal
[2]dapple *vb* **dap·pled; dap·pling** \-(ə-)liŋ\ *vt* : to mark with dapples ~ *vi* : to become marked with dapples
DAR *abbr* Daughters of the American Revolution
darb \ˈdärb\ *n* [perh. alter. of [5]*dab*] : one that is extremely attractive or desirable
Dar·by and Joan \ˌdär-bē-ən-ˈjō(-ə)n, -jō-ˈan\ *n* [prob. fr. *Darby & Joan*, couple in an 18th cent. song] : a happily married usu. elderly couple
Dard \ˈdärd\ *n* : a complex of Indic languages spoken in the upper valley of the Indus — see INDO-EUROPEAN LANGUAGES table
Dar·dan \ˈdärd-ᵊn\ *adj or n* [L *Dardanus*, fr. Gk *Dardanos*] *archaic* : TROJAN
Dar·da·ni·an \där-ˈdā-nē-ən\ *adj* : TROJAN
Dar·dic \ˈdärd-ik\ *n* : DARD
[1]dare \ˈda(ə)r, ˈde(ə)r\ *vb* **dared; dar·ing** [ME *dar* (1st & 3d sing. pres. indic.), fr. OE *dear*; akin to OHG *gitar* (1st & 3d sing. pres. indic.) dare, L *infestus* hostile] *verbal auxiliary* : to be sufficiently courageous to ⟨no one *dared* say a word⟩ ~ *vi* : to have sufficient courage ⟨try it if you ~⟩ ~ *vt* **1 a** : to challenge to perform an action esp. as a proof of courage ⟨*dared* him to jump⟩ **b** : to confront boldly : DEFY ⟨*dared* the anger of his family⟩ **2** : to have the courage to contend against, venture, or try ⟨the actress *dared* a new interpretation of this classic role⟩ — **dar·er** \ˈdar-ər, ˈder-\ *n*
[2]dare *n* **1** : an act or instance of daring : CHALLENGE ⟨foolishly took a ~⟩ **2** : imaginative or vivacious boldness : DARING
[1]dare·dev·il \ˈda(ə)r-ˌdev-əl, ˈde(ə)r-\ *n* : a recklessly bold person — **dare·dev·il·ry** \-əl-rē\ *n* — **dare·dev·il·try** \-əl-trē\ *n*
[2]daredevil *adj* : recklessly and often ostentatiously daring ***syn*** see ADVENTUROUS
dareful *adj, obs* : DARING
dare·say \(ˈ)da(ə)r-ˈsā, (ˈ)de(ə)r-\ *vt* : venture to say : think probable — used in pres. 1st sing. ~ *vi* : SUPPOSE, AGREE — used in pres. 1st sing.
[1]dar·ing *adj* : venturesomely bold in action or thought ***syn*** see ADVENTUROUS — **dar·ing·ly** \-iŋ-lē\ *adv* — **dar·ing·ness** *n*
[2]daring *n* : venturesome boldness
Dar·jee·ling \där-ˈjē-liŋ\ *n* [*Darjeeling*, India] : a tea of high quality grown esp. in the mountainous districts of northern India
[1]dark \ˈdärk\ *adj* [ME *derk*, fr. OE *deorc*; akin to OHG *tarchannen* to hide, Gk *thrassein* to trouble] **1 a** : devoid or partially devoid of light : not receiving, reflecting, transmitting, or radiating light **b** : transmitting only a portion of light **2 a** : wholly or partially black **b** *of a color* : of low or very low lightness **3 a** : arising from or showing evil traits or desires : EVIL ⟨the ~ powers that lead to war⟩ **b** : DISMAL, SAD ⟨had a ~ view of the future⟩ **c** : lacking knowledge or culture **4** : not clear to the understanding **5** : not fair : SWARTHY ⟨her ~ good looks⟩ **6** : SECRET ⟨kept his plans ~⟩ **7** : possessing depth and richness ⟨the ~, voluminous abundance of his voice —Irving Kolodin⟩ **8** : closed to the public ⟨the theater is ~ in the summer⟩ — **dark·ish** \ˈdär-kish\ *adj* — **dark·ly** *adv* — **dark·ness** *n*
syn **1** DARK, DIM, DUSKY, MURKY, GLOOMY *shared meaning element* : more or less destitute of light ***ant*** light
2 see OBSCURE ***ant*** lucid
[2]dark *n* **1 a** : absence of light : DARKNESS **b** : a place or time of little or no light : NIGHT, NIGHTFALL **2** : a dark or deep color — **in the dark** **1** : in secrecy ⟨most of his dealings were done *in the dark*⟩ **2** : in ignorance ⟨kept the public *in the dark* about the agreement⟩
[3]dark *vi, obs* : to grow dark ~ *vt* : to make dark
dark adaptation *n* : the phenomena including dilatation of the pupil, increase in retinal sensitivity, shift of the region of maximum luminosity toward the blue, and regeneration of visual purple by which the eye adapts to conditions of reduced illumination — **dark–adapt·ed** \ˌdär-kə-ˈdap-təd\ *adj*
Dark Ages *n pl* : the period from about A.D. 476 to about 1000; *broadly* : MIDDLE AGES
dark·en \ˈdär-kən\ *vb* **dark·ened; dark·en·ing** \ˈdärk-(ə-)niŋ\ *vi* : to grow dark : become obscured ~ *vt* **1** : to make dark **2** : to make less clear : OBSCURE ⟨the financial crisis ~*ed* the future of the company⟩ **3** : TAINT, TARNISH **4** : to cast a gloom over **5** : to make of darker color — **dark·en·er** \ˈdärk-(ə-)nər\ *n*
dark field *n* : the dark area that serves as the background for objects viewed in an ultramicroscope
dark–field microscope *n* : ULTRAMICROSCOPE

ə abut ᵊ kitten ər further a back ā bake ä cot, cart
aù out ch chin e less ē easy g gift i trip ī life
j joke ŋ sing ō flow ȯ flaw ȯi coin th thin t͟h this
ü loot ù foot y yet yü few yù furious zh vision

dark horse *n* **1 :** a usu. little known contestant (as a racehorse) that makes an unexpectedly good showing **2 :** a political candidate unexpectedly nominated usu. as a compromise between factions
dark lantern *n* **:** a lantern that can be closed to conceal the light
dar·kle \'där-kəl\ *vi* **dar·kled; dar·kling** \-k(ə-)liŋ\ [back-formation fr. *darkling*] **1 :** to become concealed in the dark **2 a :** to grow dark **b :** to become clouded or gloomy
¹dark·ling \'där-kliŋ\ *adv* [ME *derkelyng,* fr. *derk* dark + *-lyng* -ling] **:** in the dark
²dark·ling *adj* **1 :** DARK **2 :** done or taking place in the dark
darkling beetle *n* **:** a usu. hard-bodied black sluggish terrestrial plant-eating beetle (family Tenebrionidae)
dark reaction *n* **:** the synthetic phase of photosynthesis that does not require the presence of light and that involves the reduction of carbon dioxide to form carbohydrate
dark·room \'där-,krüm, -,krům\ *n* **:** a room with no light or with a safelight for handling and processing light-sensitive photographic materials
dark·some \'därk-səm\ *adj* **:** gloomily somber **:** DARK
¹dar·ling \'där-liŋ\ *n* [ME *derling,* fr. OE *dēorling,* fr. *dēore* dear] **1 :** a dearly loved person **2 :** FAVORITE
²darling *adj* **1 :** dearly loved **:** FAVORITE **2 :** very pleasing **:** CHARMING — **dar·ling·ly** \-liŋ-lē\ *adv* — **dar·ling·ness** *n*
¹darn \'därn\ *vb* [prob. fr. F dial. *darner*] *vt* **1 :** to mend with interlacing stitches **2 :** to embroider by filling in with long running or interlacing stitches **~** *vi* **:** to do darning — **darn·er** *n*
²darn *n* **:** a place that has been darned ⟨a sweater full of **~***s*⟩
³darn *vb* [euphemism] **:** DAMN — **darned** \'därn(d)\ *adj or adv*
⁴darn *adj or adv* **:** DAMNED
⁵darn *n* **:** DAMN
dar·nel \'därn-ᵊl\ *n* [ME] **:** any of several usu. weedy grasses (genus *Lolium*)
darning needle *n* **1 :** a long needle with a large eye for use in darning **2 :** DRAGONFLY, DAMSELFLY
¹dart \'därt\ *n* [ME, fr. MF, of Gmc origin; akin to OHG *tart* dart] **1 a** *archaic* **:** a light spear **b (1) :** a small missile usu. with a pointed shaft at one end and feathers at the other **(2)** *pl but sing in constr* **:** a game in which darts are thrown at a target **2 a :** something projected with sudden speed; *esp* **:** a sharp glance **b :** something causing sudden pain or distress ⟨**~***s* of sarcasm⟩ **3 :** something with a slender pointed shaft or outline; *specif* **:** a stitched tapering fold in a garment **4 :** a quick movement ⟨made a **~** for the door⟩
²dart *vt* **1 :** to throw with a sudden movement **2 :** to thrust or move with sudden speed **~** *vi* **:** to move suddenly or rapidly ⟨**~***ed* across the street⟩
dart board *n* **:** a usu. circular board (as of cork) used as a target in the game of darts
dart·er \'därt-ər\ *n* **1 :** SNAKEBIRD **2 :** any of numerous small American freshwater percoid fishes (esp. genera *Ammocrypta, Etheostoma,* and *Percina* of the family Percidae)
Dar·win·ian \där-'win-ē-ən\ *adj* **:** of or relating to Charles Darwin, his theories, or his followers — **Darwinian** *n*
Dar·win·ism \'där-wə-,niz-əm\ *n* **:** a theory of the origin and perpetuation of new species of animals and plants that offspring of a given organism vary, that natural selection favors the survival of some of these variations over others, that new species have arisen and may continue to arise by these processes, and that widely divergent groups of plants and animals have arisen from the same ancestors; *broadly* **:** biological evolutionism — **Dar·win·ist** \-wə-nəst\ *n* — **darwinist** *or* **dar·win·is·tic** \,där-wə-'nis-tik\ *adj, often cap*
Dar·win's finches \,där-wənz-\ *n pl* [Charles *Darwin*] **:** finches of a subfamily (Geospizinae) having great variation in bill shape and confined mostly to the Galapagos islands
Dar·win tulip \,där-wən-\ *n* **:** a tall late-flowering tulip with the flowers single and of one color
das *abbr* dekastere
¹dash \'dash\ *vb* [ME *dasshen*] *vt* **1 :** to knock, hurl, or thrust violently **2 :** to break by striking or knocking **3 :** SPLASH, SPATTER **4 a :** DESTROY, RUIN ⟨the news **~***ed* his hopes⟩ **b :** DEPRESS, SADDEN **c :** to make ashamed **5 :** to affect by mixing in something different ⟨milk **~***ed* with brandy⟩ ⟨his delight was **~***ed* with bitterness over the delay⟩ **6 :** to complete, execute, or finish off hastily — used with *down* or *off* ⟨**~***ed* down a drink⟩ ⟨**~** off a letter⟩ **7** [euphemism]**:** ¹DAMN 4 **~** *vi* **1 :** to move with sudden speed ⟨**~***ed* through the rain⟩ **2 :** SMASH
²dash *n* **1 a** *archaic* **:** BLOW **b (1) :** a sudden burst or splash **(2) :** the sound produced by such a burst **2 a :** a stroke of a pen **b :** a punctuation mark — used esp. to indicate a break in the thought or structure of a sentence **3 :** a small usu. distinctive addition ⟨a **~** of salt⟩ **4 :** flashy display **5 :** animation in style and action **6 a :** a sudden onset, rush, or attempt **b :** a short fast race **7 :** a long click or buzz forming a letter or part of a letter (as in Morse code) **8 :** DASHBOARD 2
dash·board \'dash-,bō(ə)rd, -,bȯ(ə)rd\ *n* **1 :** a screen on the front of a vehicle to intercept water, mud, or snow **2 :** a panel extending across an automobile, airplane, or motorboat below the windshield and usu. containing dials and controls
dash·er \'dash-ər\ *n* **1 :** a dashing person **2 :** one that dashes; *specif* **:** a device having blades for agitating a liquid or semisolid
da·shi·ki \də-'shē-kē\ *n* [alter. of Yoruba *danshiki*] **:** a usu. brightly colored loose-fitting pullover garment
dash·ing *adj* **1 :** marked by vigorous action **:** SPIRITED ⟨a **~** young horse⟩ **2 :** marked by smartness esp. in dress and manners — **dash·ing·ly** \-iŋ-lē\ *adv*
dash·pot \'dash-,pät\ *n* **:** a device for cushioning or damping a movement (as of a mechanical part) to avoid shock
das·sie \'däs-ē\ *n* [Afrik] **:** a hyrax (genus *Procavia*) of southern Africa
das·tard \'das-tərd\ *n* [ME] **:** COWARD; *esp* **:** one who commits malicious acts
das·tard·ly \-lē\ *adj* **:** despicably mean or cowardly — **das·tard·li·ness** *n*
dasy·ure \'das-ē-,(y)ů(ə)r\ *n* [deriv. of Gk *dasys* thick with hair + *oura* tail] **:** any of a genus (*Dasyurus*) of arboreal carnivorous marsupial mammals of Australia and Tasmania resembling martens
dat *abbr* dative
DAT *abbr* differential aptitude test
da·ta \'dāt-ə, 'dat-, 'dät-\ *n pl but sing or pl in constr* [pl. of *datum*] **:** factual information (as measurements or statistics) used as a basis for reasoning, discussion, or calculation ⟨the **~** is plentiful and easily available —H. A. Gleason, Jr.⟩ ⟨comprehensive **~** on economic growth have been published —N. H. Jacoby⟩
data bank *n* **1 :** a collection of data organized esp. for rapid search and retrieval (as by computer) **2 :** an institution whose chief concern is building and maintaining a data bank
data base *n* **:** DATA BANK 1
data processing *n* **:** the converting of raw data to machine-readable form and its subsequent processing (as storing, updating, combining, rearranging, or printing out) by a computer — **data processor** *n*
¹date \'dāt\ *n* [ME, fr. OF, deriv. of L *dactylus,* fr. Gk *daktylos,* lit., finger] **1 :** the oblong edible fruit of a palm (*Phoenix dactylifera*) **2 :** the tall palm with pinnate leaves that yields the date
²date *n* [ME, fr. MF, fr. LL *data,* fr. *data* (as in *data Romae* given at Rome), fem. of L *datus,* pp. of *dare* to give; akin to Gk *didonai* to give] **1 a :** the time at which an event occurs ⟨the **~** of his birth⟩ **b :** a statement of the time of execution or making ⟨the **~** on the letter⟩ **2 :** DURATION **3 :** the period of time to which something belongs **4 a :** an appointment for a specified time; *esp* **:** a social engagement between two persons of opposite sex **b :** a person of the opposite sex with whom one has a social engagement **5 :** an engagement for a professional performance (as of a dance band) — **to date :** up to the present moment
³date *vb* **dat·ed; dat·ing** *vt* **1 :** to determine the date of ⟨**~** an antique⟩ **2 :** to record the date of **3 a :** to mark with characteristics typical of a particular period **b :** to show up plainly the age of **4 :** to make or have a date with **~** *vi* **1 :** to reckon chronologically **2 :** to become dated and written **3 a :** ORIGINATE **b :** EXTEND ⟨a friendship *dating* from college days⟩ — **dat·able** *or* **date·able** \'dāt-ə-bəl\ *adj* — **dat·er** \'dāt-ər\ *n*
dat·ed *adj* **1 :** provided with a date ⟨a **~** document⟩ **2 :** OUT-OF-DATE, OLD-FASHIONED ⟨**~** formalities⟩ — **dat·ed·ly** *adv* — **dat·ed·ness** *n*
date·less \'dāt-ləs\ *adj* **1 :** ENDLESS **2 :** having no date **3 :** too ancient to be dated **4 :** TIMELESS ⟨the play's **~** theme⟩
date·line \'dāt-,līn\ *n* **1 :** a line in a written document or a printed publication giving the date and place of composition or issue **2** *usu* **date line :** a hypothetical line approximately along the 180th meridian designated as the place where each calendar day begins — **dateline** *vt*
dating bar *n* **:** a bar that caters esp. to young unmarried men and women
¹da·tive \'dāt-iv\ *adj* [ME *datif,* fr. L *dativus,* lit., relating to giving, fr. *datus*] **:** of, relating to, or being the grammatical case that marks typically the indirect object of a verb, the object of some prepositions, or a possessor
²dative *n* **:** a dative case or form
dative bond *n* [fr. the donation of electrons by one of the atoms] **:** COORDINATE BOND
da·tum \'dāt-əm, 'dat-, 'dät-\ *n* [L, fr. neut. of *datus*] **1** *pl* **da·ta** \-ə\ **:** something given or admitted esp. as a basis for reasoning or inference **2** *pl* **datums :** something used as a basis for calculating or measuring
da·tu·ra \də-'t(y)ůr-ə\ *n* [NL, genus name, fr. Hindi *dhatūrā* jimsonweed] **:** any of a genus (*Datura*) of widely distributed strong-scented herbs, shrubs, or trees of the nightshade family
¹daub \'dȯb, 'däb\ *vb* [ME *dauben,* fr. OF *dauber*] *vt* **1 :** to cover or coat with soft adhesive matter **:** PLASTER **2 :** to coat with a dirty substance **3 a :** to apply coloring material crudely to **b :** to apply (as paint) crudely **~** *vi* **1** *archaic* **:** to put on a false exterior **2 :** to apply colors crudely — **daub·er** *n*
²daub *n* **1 :** material used to daub walls **2 :** an act or instance of daubing **3 :** something daubed on **:** SMEAR **4 :** a crude picture
¹daugh·ter \'dȯt-ər\ *n* [ME *doughter,* fr. OE *dohtor;* akin to OHG *tohter* daughter, Gk *thygatēr*] **1 a (1) :** a human female having the relation of child to parent **(2) :** a female offspring of a lower animal **b :** a human female having a specified ancestor or belonging to a group of common ancestry **2 :** something considered as a daughter ⟨the United States is a **~** of Great Britain⟩ **3 :** an atomic species that is the immediate product of the radioactive decay of a given element — **daugh·ter·less** \-ləs\ *adj*
²daughter *adj* **1 :** having the characteristics or relationship of a daughter **2 :** belonging to the first generation of offspring, organelles, or molecules produced by reproduction, division, or replication ⟨**~** cell⟩ ⟨**~** DNA molecules⟩
daugh·ter-in-law \'dȯt-ə-rən-,lȯ, -ərn-,lȯ\ *n, pl* **daugh·ters-in-law** \-ər-zən-\ **:** the wife of one's son
dau·no·my·cin \,dȯ-nə-'mīs-ᵊn, ,daů-\ *n* [(assumed) It *daunomicina,* fr. *Daunia,* ancient region of Apulia, Italy + It *-o-* + *-micina* (as in *streptomicina* streptomycin)] **:** an antibiotic $C_{27}H_{29}NO_{10}$ that is a nitrogenous glycoside and is used experimentally as an antineoplastic agent
daunt \'dȯnt, 'dänt\ *vt* [ME *daunten,* fr. OF *danter,* alter. of *donter,* fr. L *domitare* to tame, fr. *domitus,* pp. of *domare* — more at TAME] **:** to lessen the courage of **:** COW, SUBDUE ***syn*** see DISMAY
daunt·less \-ləs\ *adj* **:** FEARLESS, UNDAUNTED ⟨a **~** hero⟩ — **daunt·less·ly** *adv* — **daunt·less·ness** *n*
dau·phin \'dȯ-fən\ *n, often cap* [MF *dalfin,* fr. OF, title of lords of the Dauphiné, fr. *Dalfin,* a surname] **:** the eldest son of a king of France
dau·phine \dȯ-'fēn\ *n, often cap* [F] **:** the wife of the dauphin
DAV *abbr* Disabled American Veterans
da·ven \'däv-ən\ *vi* [Yiddish *davnen*] **:** to utter Jewish prayers esp. of a ritual character

dav·en·port \'dav-ən-ˌpō(ə)rt, 'dav-ᵊm-, -ˌpô(ə)rt\ n [prob. fr. the name *Davenport*] **1 :** a small compact writing desk **2 :** a large upholstered sofa often convertible into a bed

Da·vid \'dā-vəd\ n [Heb *Dāwidh*] : a Hebrew shepherd who became the second king of Israel in succession to Saul according to Biblical accounts — **Da·vid·ic** \də-'vid-ik, dā-\ *adj*

da·vit \'dā-vət, 'dav-ət\ n [prob. fr. the name *David*] : a crane that projects over the side of a ship or a hatchway and is used esp. for boats, anchors, or cargo

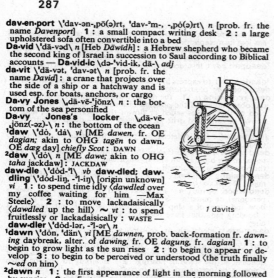

1 davits

Da·vy Jones \ˌdā-vē-'jōnz\ n : the bottom of the sea personified

Da·vy Jones's locker \-də-vē-ˌjōnz(-əz)-\ n : the bottom of the ocean

¹daw \'dô, 'dä\ vi [ME *dawen*, fr. OE *dagian*; akin to OHG *tagēn* to dawn, OE *dæg* day] *chiefly Scot* : DAWN

²daw \'dô\ n [ME *dawe*; akin to OHG *taha* jackdaw] : JACKDAW

daw·dle \'dôd-ᵊl\ vb **daw·dled; daw·dling** \'dôd-liŋ, -ᵊl-iŋ\ [origin unknown] vi **1 :** to spend time idly ⟨*dawdled* over my coffee waiting for him —Max Steele⟩ **2 :** to move lackadaisically ⟨*dawdled* up the hill⟩ ~ vt : to spend fruitlessly or lackadaisically • WASTE — **daw·dler** \'dôd-lər, -ᵊl-ər\ n

¹dawn \'dôn, 'dän\ vi [ME *dawnen*, prob. back-formation fr. *dawning* daybreak, alter. of *dawing*, fr. OE *dagung*, fr. *dagian*] **1 :** to begin to grow light as the sun rises **2 :** to begin to appear or develop **3 :** to begin to be perceived or understood ⟨the truth finally ~ed on him⟩

²dawn n **1 :** the first appearance of light in the morning followed by sunrise **2 :** a first appearance : BEGINNING ⟨the ~ of the space age⟩

day \'dā\ n [ME, fr. OE *dæg*; akin to OHG *tag* day] **1 a :** the time of light between one night and the next **b :** DAYLIGHT **2 a :** the period of the earth's rotation on its axis **b :** the time required by a celestial body to turn once on its axis **3 :** the mean solar day of 24 hours beginning at mean midnight **4 :** a specified day or date **5 :** a specified time or period : AGE ⟨in grandfather's ~⟩ **6 :** the conflict or contention of the day ⟨played hard and won the ~⟩ **7 :** the time established by usage or law for work, school, or business **8 :** a period of existence or prominence of a person or thing ⟨a new ~ for black people⟩ — **day after day :** for an indefinite or seemingly endless number of days — **day in, day out :** for an indefinite number of successive days

Day·ak \'dī-ˌak\ n [Malay, up-country] **1 :** a member of any of several Indonesian peoples of the interior of Borneo **2 :** the language of the Dayak peoples

day-bed \'dā-ˌbed\ n **1 :** a chaise longue of a type made 1680–1780 **2 :** a couch that can be converted into a bed

day·book \-ˌbůk\ n **1 :** DIARY, JOURNAL **2 :** a book formerly used in accounting for recording the transactions of the day

day·break \-ˌbrāk\ n : DAWN

day-care \'dā-ˌke(ə)r, -ˌka(ə)r\ adj : of, relating to, or providing supervision and facilities for preschool children during the day ⟨~ centers⟩

¹day·dream \'dā-ˌdrēm\ n : a pleasant visionary usu. wishful creation of the imagination — **day-dream·like** \-ˌlīk\ adj

²daydream vi : to have a daydream — **day-dream·er** n

day·glow \'dā-ˌglō\ n : airglow seen during the day

day in court 1 : a day or opportunity for appearance in a lawsuit **2 :** an opportunity to present one's point of view

day laborer n : one who works for daily wages esp. as an unskilled laborer

day letter n : a telegram sent during the day that has a lower priority than a regular telegram

¹day·light \'dā-ˌlīt\ n **1 :** the light of day **2 :** DAWN **3 a :** knowledge or understanding of something that has been obscure ⟨began to see ~ on the problem⟩ **b :** the quality or state of being open : OPENNESS **4** *pl* **a :** CONSCIOUSNESS **b :** mental soundness or stability : WITS ⟨scared the ~s out of him⟩

²daylight vt **1 :** to provide with daylight **2 :** to remove obstructions (as trees and brush) from in order to provide greater visibility ⟨~ an intersection⟩ ~ vi : to supply daylight

daylight saving time n : time usu. one hour ahead of standard time — called also *daylight time*

day lily n **1 :** any of various Eurasian plants (genus *Hemerocallis*) of the lily family that have short-lived flowers resembling lilies and are widespread in cultivation and as escapes **2 :** PLANTAIN LILY

day·long \'dā-ˌlôŋ\ adj : lasting all day ⟨a ~ tour⟩

day·mare \'dā-ˌma(ə)r, -ˌme(ə)r\ n [*day* + *-mare* (as in *nightmare*)] : a nightmarish fantasy experienced while awake

day-neutral adj : developing and maturing regardless of relative length of alternating exposures to light and dark periods — compare LONG-DAY, SHORT-DAY

day nursery n : a public center for the care and training of young children; *specif* : NURSERY SCHOOL

Day of Atonement n : YOM KIPPUR

day of reckoning n : a time when the consequences of a course of mistakes or misdeeds are felt

day·room \'dā-ˌrüm, -ˌrům\ n : a room (as in a military barracks) equipped for reading, writing, and recreation

days \'dāz\ adv : in the daytime repeatedly : on any day

day school n **1 :** an elementary or secondary school held on weekdays; *specif* : a private school without boarding facilities

days of grace : the days allowed for payment of a note or an insurance premium after it becomes due

day·star \'dā-ˌstär\ n **1 :** MORNING STAR **2 :** SUN 1a

day student n : a student who attends regular classes at a college or preparatory school but does not live at the institution

¹day·time \'dā-ˌtīm\ n : the time during which there is daylight

²daytime adj : taking place, existing, or presented during the daytime ⟨~ flights⟩ ⟨~ soap operas⟩

day-to-day \ˌdāt-ə-ˌdā\ adj **1 :** taking place, made, or done in the course of successive days ⟨~ problems⟩ **2 :** providing for a day at a time with little thought for the future ⟨lived an aimless ~ existence⟩

day-trip·per \'dā-ˌtrip-ər\ n : one who takes a trip that does not last overnight

daze \'dāz\ vt **dazed; daz·ing** [ME *dasen*, fr. ON *dasa* (in *dasask* to become exhausted)] **1 :** to stupefy esp. by a blow : STUN **2 :** to dazzle with light — **dazed·ness** \'dā-zəd-nəs, 'dāz(d)-\ n

daz·zle \'daz-əl\ vb **daz·zled; daz·zling** \-(ə-)liŋ\ [freq. of *daze*] vi **1 :** to lose clear vision esp. from looking at bright light **2 a :** to shine brilliantly **b :** to arouse admiration by an impressive display ~ vt **1 :** to overpower with light **2 :** to impress deeply, overpower, or confound with brilliance ⟨*dazzled* the crowd with his oratory⟩ — **dazzle** n — **daz·zler** \-(ə-)lər\ n — **daz·zling·ly** \-(ə-)liŋ-lē\ adv

db abbr **1** debenture **2** decibel

DB abbr daybook

DBA abbr **1** doctor of business administration **2** doing business as

DBE abbr Dame Commander of the Order of the British Empire

DBH abbr diameter at breast height

dbl abbr double

DC abbr **1** [It *da capo*] from the beginning **2** decimal classification **3** direct current **4** District of Columbia **5** doctor of chiropractic **6** double crochet

DChE abbr doctor of chemical engineering

DCL abbr **1** doctor of canon law **2** doctor of civil law

dd abbr **1** dated **2** delivered

DD abbr **1** days after date **2** demand draft **3** dishonorable discharge **4** doctor of divinity **5** due date

D day n [*D*, abbr. for *day*] : a day set for launching an operation; *specif* : June 6, 1944, on which the Allies began the invasion of France in World War II

DDC abbr Dewey Decimal Classification

DDD \ˌdēd-(ˌ)ē-'dē\ n [*dichloro-diphenyl-dichloro-ethane*] : an insecticide $(ClC_6H_4)_2CHCHCl_2$ closely related chemically and similar in properties to DDT

DDS abbr **1** doctor of dental science **2** doctor of dental surgery

DDT \ˌdēd-(ˌ)ē-'tē\ n [*dichloro-diphenyl-trichloro-ethane*] : a colorless odorless water-insoluble crystalline insecticide $C_{14}H_9Cl_5$ that tends to accumulate in ecosystems and has toxic effects on many vertebrates

DDVP \ˌdēd-(ˌ)ē-ˌvē-'pē\ n [*d*imethyl + *d*ichlor- + *v*inyl + *p*hosphate] : DICHLORVOS

DE abbr **1** defensive end **2** Delaware **3** doctor of engineering

de- *prefix* [ME *de-, des-*, partly fr. L *de-* from, down, away (fr. *de*) and partly fr. L *dis-*; L *de* akin to OIr *di* from, OE *tō* to — more at TO, DIS-] **1 a :** do the opposite of ⟨*devitalize*⟩ ⟨*deactivate*⟩ **b :** reverse of ⟨*de-emphasis*⟩ **2 a :** remove (a specified thing) from ⟨*delouse*⟩ ⟨*dehydrogenate*⟩ **b :** remove from (a specified thing) ⟨*dethrone*⟩ **3 :** reduce ⟨*devalue*⟩ **4 :** something derived from (a specified thing) ⟨*decompound*⟩ : derived from something (of a specified nature) ⟨*denominative*⟩ **5 :** get off of (a specified thing) ⟨*detrain*⟩ **6 :** having a molecule characterized by the removal of one or more atoms (of a specified element) ⟨*deoxy-*⟩

de·acid·i·fy \ˌdē-ə-'sid-ə-ˌfī\ vt : to remove acid from : reduce the acidity of (as by neutralization) — **de·acid·i·fi·ca·tion** \-ˌsid-ə-fə-'kā-shən\ n

dea·con \'dē-kən\ n [ME *dekene*, fr. OE *dēacon*, fr. LL *diaconus*, fr. Gk *diakonos*, lit., servant, fr. *dia-* + *-konos* (akin to *enkonein* to be active); akin to L *conari* to attempt] : a subordinate officer in a Christian church: as **a :** a Roman Catholic cleric ranking below a priest and above a subdeacon **b :** one of the laymen elected by a church with congregational polity to serve in worship, in pastoral care, and on administrative committees **c :** a Mormon in the lowest grade of the Aaronic priesthood

dea·con·ess \'dē-kə-nəs\ n : a woman chosen to assist in the church ministry; *specif* : one in a Protestant order

deacon's bench n : a bench with usu. spindled arms and back

de·ac·ti·vate \(ˈ)dē-'ak-tə-ˌvāt\ vt : to make inactive or ineffective — **de·ac·ti·va·tion** \(ˌ)dē-ˌak-tə-'vā-shən\ n — **de·ac·ti·va·tor** \(ˈ)dē-'ak-tə-ˌvāt-ər\ n

¹dead \'ded\ adj [ME *ded*, fr. OE *dēad*; akin to ON *dauthr* dead, *deyja* to die — more at DIE] **1 :** deprived of life : having died **2 a** (1) **:** having the appearance of death : DEATHLY ⟨~ faint⟩ (2) **:** lacking power to move, feel, or respond : NUMB **b :** very tired **c** (1) **:** incapable of being stirred emotionally or intellectually : UNRESPONSIVE ⟨~ to pity⟩ (2) **:** grown cold : EXTINGUISHED ⟨~ coals⟩ **3 a :** INANIMATE, INERT ⟨~ matter⟩ **b :** BARREN, INFERTILE ⟨~ soil⟩ **c :** no longer producing or functioning : EXHAUSTED ⟨a ~ battery⟩ **4 a** (1) **:** lacking power or effect ⟨a ~ law⟩ (2) **:** no longer having interest, relevance, or significance ⟨a ~ issue⟩ **b :** no longer in use : OBSOLETE ⟨a ~ language⟩ **c :** no longer active : EXTINCT ⟨a ~ volcano⟩ **d :** lacking in gaiety or animation ⟨a ~ party⟩ **e** (1) **:** lacking in commercial activity : QUIET (2) **:** commercially idle or unproductive ⟨~ capital⟩ **f :** lacking elasticity ⟨a ~ tennis ball⟩ **g :** being out of action or out of use; *specif* : free from any connection to a source of voltage and free from electric charges **h** (1) **:** being out of play ⟨a ~ ball⟩ (2) *croquet* : temporarily forbidden to play or to make a certain play **5 a :** not running or circulating : STAGNANT ⟨~ water⟩ **b :** not turning ⟨a ~ lathe center⟩ **c :** not imparting

motion or power although otherwise functioning ⟨a ~ rear axle⟩ **d** : lacking warmth, vigor, or taste **6 a** : absolutely uniform ⟨a ~ level⟩ **b** (1) : UNERRING (2) : EXACT ⟨~ center of the target⟩ (3) : DOOMED ⟨a ~ duck⟩ (4) : IRREVOCABLE ⟨a ~ loss⟩ **c** : ABRUPT ⟨brought to a ~ stop⟩ **d** : COMPLETE, ABSOLUTE ⟨a ~ silence⟩ **7** : DESERTED ⟨~ villages⟩ — **dead·ness** *n*
syn DEAD, DEFUNCT, DECEASED, DEPARTED, LATE *shared meaning element* : devoid of life ***ant*** alive

2dead *n, pl* **dead 1** : one that is dead — usu. used collectively **2** : the state of being dead ⟨raised him from the ~ —Col 2:12(RSV)⟩ **3** : the time of greatest quiet ⟨the ~ of night⟩

3dead *adv* **1** : ABSOLUTELY, UTTERLY ⟨~ certain⟩ **2** : suddenly and completely ⟨stopped ~⟩ **3** : DIRECTLY ⟨~ ahead⟩

dead air *n* : a period of silence esp. during a radio or television broadcast

dead–air space *n* : a sealed or unventilated air space

1dead·beat \ˈded-ˌbēt\ *adj* : having a pointer that gives a reading with little or no oscillation

2deadbeat *n* **1** : one who persistently fails to pay his debts or his way **2** : LOAFER

dead center *n* : either of the two positions at the ends of a stroke in a crank and connecting rod when the crank and rod are in the same straight line — called also *dead point*

dead·en \ˈded-ᵊn\ *vb* **dead·ened; dead·en·ing** \ˈded-niŋ, -ᵊn-iŋ\ *vt* **1** : to impair in vigor or sensation : BLUNT ⟨~*ed* his enthusiasm⟩ **2 a** : to deprive of brilliance **b** : to make vapid or spiritless **c** : to make (as a wall) impervious to sound **3** : to deprive of life : KILL **~** *vi* : to become dead : lose life or vigor — **dead·en·er** \ˈded-nər, -ᵊn-ər\ *n* — **dead·en·ing·ly** \-niŋ-lē, -ᵊn-iŋ-\ *adv*

1dead–end \ˌded-ˌend\ *adj* **1 a** : lacking opportunities for advancement ⟨a ~ job⟩ **b** : lacking an exit ⟨a ~ street⟩ **2** : TOUGH ⟨~ kids⟩ — **dead–end·ed·ness** \(ˈ)ded-ˈen-dəd-nəs\ *n*

2dead–end \ˈded-ˈend\ *vi* : to come to a dead end : TERMINATE

dead end \ˈded-ˈend\ *n* **1** : an end (as of a street) without an exit **2** : a position, situation, or course of action that leads to nothing further

dead·en·ing *n* : material used to soundproof walls or floors

dead·eye \ˈded-ˌī\ *n* **1** : a rounded wood block that is encircled by a rope or an iron band and pierced with holes to receive the lanyard and that is used esp. to set up shrouds and stays **2** : an unerring marksman

deadeyes 1

dead·fall \-ˌfȯl\ *n* : a trap so constructed that a weight (as a heavy log) falls on an animal and kills or disables it

dead hand *n* **1** : MORTMAIN 2 **2** : the oppressive influence of the past

1dead·head \ˈded-ˌhed\ *n* **1** : one who has not paid for a ticket **2** : a dull or stupid person

2deadhead *vi* : to make a return trip without a load — used esp. of a truck

dead heat *n* : a tie with no single winner of a race

dead horse *n* [fr. the proverbial futility of flogging a dead horse to make him go] : an exhausted or profitless topic or issue

dead letter *n* **1** : something that has lost its force or authority without being formally abolished **2** : a letter that is undeliverable and unreturnable by the post office

dead·light \ˈded-ˌlīt\ *n* **1 a** : a metal cover or shutter fitted to a port to keep out light and water **b** : a heavy glass set in a ship's deck or hull to admit light **2** : a skylight made so as not to open

dead·line \-ˌlīn\ *n* **1** : a line drawn within or around a prison that a prisoner passes at the risk of being shot **2** : a date or time before which something must be done; *specif* : the time after which copy is not accepted for a particular issue of a publication

dead load *n* : a constant load that in structures (as a bridge, building, or machine) is due to the weight of the members, the supported structure, and permanent attachments or accessories

dead·lock \ˈded-ˌläk\ *n* **1** : a state of inaction or neutralization resulting from the opposition of equally powerful uncompromising persons or factions : STANDSTILL **2** : a tie score — **deadlock** *vt*

1dead·ly \ˈded-lē\ *adj* **dead·li·er; -est 1** : likely to cause or capable of producing death ⟨a ~ disease⟩ ⟨a ~ instrument⟩ **2 a** : aiming to kill or destroy : IMPLACABLE ⟨a ~ enemy⟩ **b** : highly effective ⟨a ~ exposé⟩ **c** : UNERRING ⟨a ~ marksman⟩ **d** : marked by determination or extreme seriousness **3 a** : tending to deprive of force or vitality ⟨a ~ habit⟩ **b** : suggestive of death esp. in dullness or lack of animation ⟨~ bores⟩ ⟨a ~ conversation⟩ **4** : very great : EXTREME — **dead·li·ness** *n*
syn DEADLY, MORTAL, FATAL, LETHAL *shared meaning element* : causing or capable of causing death. DEADLY applies to whatever is certain or extremely likely to cause death ⟨a *deadly* poison⟩ ⟨*deadly* weapons⟩ MORTAL applies distinctively to what has caused or is about to cause death ⟨a *mortal* wound⟩ FATAL, which stresses the inevitability of eventual death, may be preferred when considerable time intervenes between the causative event and death ⟨his injuries were ultimately *fatal*⟩ and is regularly used in predictions ⟨there is little doubt that his injuries will prove *fatal*⟩ LETHAL applies to something that by its very nature is bound to cause death or which exists for the purpose of destroying life ⟨took a *lethal* dose of poison⟩ ⟨a *lethal* weapon⟩ All these terms are capable of extension in which they are less weighty and typically imply a disconcerting, oppressing, or disturbing that may cause fear, dread, or distress rather than physical or spiritual death; thus, a *deadly* shaft of irony causes complete discomfiture; *mortal* terror is the most extreme terror; a *fatal* error is one that leads to the destruction of one's plans or hopes; a *lethal* verbal attack is utterly devastating to one's composure or position

2deadly *adv* **1** *archaic* : in a manner to cause death : MORTALLY **2** : suggesting death **3** : EXTREMELY ⟨~ serious⟩

deadly nightshade *n* : BELLADONNA 1

deadly sin *n* : one of seven sins of pride, covetousness, lust, anger, gluttony, envy, and sloth held to be fatal to spiritual progress — called also *capital sin*

dead man's float *n* : a prone floating position with the arms extended forward

dead march *n* : a solemn march for a funeral

dead metaphor *n* : a word or phrase (as *time is running out*) that has lost its metaphoric force through common usage

1dead·pan \ˈded-ˌpan\ *adj* : marked by an impassive matter-of-fact manner, style, or expression ⟨a ~ commentary⟩

2deadpan *adv* : in a deadpan manner ⟨played the role completely ~⟩

3deadpan *vt* : to express in a deadpan manner — **dead·pan·ner** *n*

dead point *n* : DEAD CENTER

dead reckoning *n* **1** : the determination without the aid of celestial observations of the position of a ship or aircraft from the record of the courses sailed or flown, the distance made, and the known or estimated drift **2** : GUESSWORK — **dead reckon** *vb* — **dead reckoner** *n*

dead set *adj* : firmly determined : RESOLUTE ⟨*dead set* on winning⟩ ⟨*dead set* against it⟩

dead space *n* : the portion of the respiratory system which is external to the bronchioles and through which air must pass to reach the bronchioles and alveoli

dead·weight \ˈded-ˈwāt\ *n* **1** : the unrelieved weight of an inert mass **2** : DEAD LOAD

dead·wood \-ˌwu̇d\ *n* **1** : wood dead on the tree **2** : useless personnel or material **3** : solid timbers built in at the extreme bow and stern of a ship when too narrow to permit framing **4** : bowling pins that have been knocked down but remain on the alley

de·aer·ate \(ˈ)dē-ˈa(-ə)r-ˌāt, -ˈe(-ə)r-\ *vt* : to remove air or gas from — **de·aer·a·tion** \ˌdē-ˌa(-ə)r-ˈā-shən, -ˌe(-ə)r-\ *n*

deaf \ˈdef\ *adj* [ME *deef*, fr. OE *dēaf*; akin to Gk *typhlos* blind, *typhein* to smoke, L *fumus* smoke — more at FUME] **1** : lacking or deficient in the sense of hearing **2** : unwilling to hear or listen : not to be persuaded ⟨was overwrought and ~ to reason⟩ — **deaf·ish** \ˈdef-ish\ *adj* — **deaf·ly** *adv* — **deaf·ness** *n*

deaf·en \ˈdef-ən\ *vb* **deaf·ened; deaf·en·ing** \-(ə-)niŋ\ *vt* **1** : to make deaf **2** : to make (as a wall) soundproof **~** *vi* : to cause deafness or stun one with noise — **deaf·en·ing·ly** \-(ə-)niŋ-lē\ *adv*

deaf–mute \ˈdef-ˌmyüt\ *n* : a deaf person who cannot speak — **deaf–mute** *adj*

1deal \ˈdē(ə)l\ *n* [ME *deel*, fr. OE *dǣl*; akin to OE *dāl* division, portion, OHG *teil* part] **1** *obs* : PART, PORTION **2** : a usu. large or indefinite quantity or degree ⟨the search was thorough . . . and a ~ of money was spent —J. F. Dobie⟩ ⟨a great ~ of support⟩ ⟨a good ~ faster⟩ **3 a** : the act or right of distributing cards to players in a card game **b** : HAND 9b **4 a** : an extensive governmental program — compare NEW DEAL **b** : the period of such a program

2deal *vb* **dealt** \ˈdelt\; **deal·ing** \ˈdē-liŋ\ *vt* **1 a** : to give as one's portion : APPORTION ⟨tried to ~ justice to all men⟩ ⟨*dealt* out three sandwiches apiece⟩ **b** : to distribute (playing cards) to players in a game **2** : ADMINISTER, BESTOW ⟨*dealt* him a blow⟩ **3** : SELL ⟨~*s* marijuana⟩ **~** *vi* **1** : to distribute the cards in a card game **2** : to concern oneself or itself ⟨the book ~*s* with education⟩ **3 a** : to engage in bargaining : TRADE **b** : to sell or distribute something as a business ⟨~ in insurance⟩ **4** : to take action with regard to someone or something ⟨~ with an offender⟩ ***syn*** see DISTRIBUTE, TREAT — **deal·er** \ˈdē-lər\ *n*

3deal *n* **1** : an act of dealing : TRANSACTION **2** : PACKAGE DEAL **3** : treatment received ⟨a dirty ~⟩ **4** : an arrangement for mutual advantage

4deal *n* [MD or MLG *dele* plank; akin to OHG *dili* plank — more at THILL] **1 a** *Brit* : a board of fir or pine **b** : sawed yellow-pine lumber nine inches or wider and three, four, or five inches thick **2** : pine or fir wood — **deal** *adj*

de·alate \(ˈ)dē-ˈā-ˌlāt\ *n* : a dealated insect

de·alat·ed \-ˌlāt-əd\ *adj* : divested of the wings — used of postnuptial adults of insects (as ants) that drop their wings after a nuptial flight — **de·ala·tion** \ˌdē-(ˌ)ā-ˈlā-shən\ *n*

deal·er·ship \ˈdē-lər-ˌship\ *n* : an authorized sales agency ⟨an automobile ~⟩

deal·fish \ˈdē(ə)l-ˌfish\ *n* [*4deal*] : any of several long thin fishes (genus *Trachipterus* of the family Trachipteridae) inhabiting the deep sea

deal·ing *n* **1** *pl* : friendly or business interactions **2** : method of business : manner of conduct

dealing box *n* : a case that holds a deck of playing cards so that they may be dealt one by one

de·am·i·nase \(ˈ)dē-ˈam-ə-ˌnās, -ˌnāz\ *n* [*de-* + *amino* + *-ase*] : an enzyme that hydrolyzes amino compounds (as amino acids) with removal of the amino group

de·am·i·nate \-ˌnāt\ *vt* **-nat·ed; -nat·ing** : to remove the amino group from (a compound) — **de·am·i·na·tion** \(ˌ)dē-ˌam-ə-ˈnā-shən\ *n*

de·am·i·nize \(ˈ)dē-ˈam-ə-ˌnīz\ *vt* **-nized; -niz·ing** : DEAMINATE

dean \ˈdēn\ *n* [ME *deen*, fr. MF *deien*, fr. LL *decanus*, lit., chief of ten, fr. L *decem* ten — more at TEN] **1 a** : the head of the chapter of a collegiate or cathedral church **b** : a Roman Catholic priest who supervises one district of a diocese **2 a** : the head of a division, faculty, college, or school of a university **b** : a college or secondary school administrator in charge of counseling and disciplining students ⟨~ of men⟩ **3** : DOYEN 1 — **dean** *vi* — **dean·ship** \-ˌship\ *n*

dean·ery \ˈdēn-(ə-)rē\ *n, pl* **-er·ies** : the office, jurisdiction, or official residence of a clerical dean

dean's list *n* : a list of students receiving special recognition from the dean of a college because of superior scholarship

1dear \ˈdi(ə)r\ *adj* [ME *dere*, fr. OE *dēor*] : SEVERE, SORE ⟨in our ~ peril —Shak.⟩

2dear *adj* [ME *dere*, fr. OE *dēore*] **1** *obs* : NOBLE **2** : highly valued : PRECIOUS ⟨a ~ friend⟩ **3** : AFFECTIONATE, FOND **4** : high or exorbitant in price : exceedingly expensive ⟨eggs are very ~ just now⟩ **5** : HEARTFELT ***syn*** see COSTLY ***ant*** cheap — **dear** *adv* — **dear·ly** *adv* — **dear·ness** *n*

3dear *n* **1** : a loved one : SWEETHEART **2** : a lovable person

Dear John \-'jän\ *n* : a letter (as to a soldier) in which a wife asks for a divorce or a girl friend breaks off an engagement or a friendship

dearth \'dərth\ *n* [ME *derthe*, fr. *dere* dear, costly] **1** : scarcity that makes dear; *specif* : FAMINE **2** : an inadequate supply : LACK

dea·sil \'dē-zəl\ *adv* [ScGael *deiseil*; akin to L *dexter*] : CLOCKWISE — compare WIDDERSHINS

death \'deth\ *n* [ME *deeth*, fr. OE *dēath*; akin to ON *dauthi* death, *deyja* to die — more at DIE] **1** : a permanent cessation of all vital functions : the end of life **2** : the cause or occasion of loss of life ⟨drinking was the ~ of him⟩ **3** *cap* : the destroyer of life represented usu. as a skeleton with a scythe **4** : the state of being dead **5 a** : the passing or destruction of something inanimate ⟨the ~ of vaudeville⟩ **b** : EXTINCTION **6** : CIVIL DEATH **7** : SLAUGHTER **8** *Christian Science* : the lie of life in matter : that which is unreal and untrue : ILLUSION — **to death** : beyond endurance : EXCESSIVELY

death·bed \'deth-'bed\ *n* **1** : the bed in which a person dies **2** : the last hours of life — **on one's deathbed** : near the point of death

death benefit *n* : money payable to the beneficiary of a deceased

death-blow \'deth-'blō\ *n* : a destructive or killing stroke or event

death camas *n* : any of several plants (genus *Zigadenus*) of the lily family that cause poisoning of livestock in the western U. S.

death camp *n* : a camp where large numbers of persons (as prisoners) are put to death

death cup *n* : a destroying angel (*Amanita phalloides*)

death duty *n, chiefly Brit* : DEATH TAX

death instinct *n* : an innate and unconscious tendency toward self-destruction postulated in psychoanalytic theory to explain aggressive and destructive behavior not satisfactorily explained by the pleasure principle

death·less \'deth-ləs\ *adj* : IMMORTAL, IMPERISHABLE ⟨~ fame⟩ — **death·less·ly** *adv* — **death·less·ness** *n*

death·ly \'deth-lē\ *adj* **1** : FATAL **2** : of, relating to, or suggestive of death ⟨a ~ pallor⟩ — **deathly** *adv*

death mask *n* : a cast taken from the face of a dead person

death point *n* : a limit (as of degree of heat or cold) beyond which an organism or living protoplasm cannot survive

death rattle *n* : a rattling or gurgling sound produced by air passing through mucus in the lungs and air passages of a dying person

death's–head \'deths-,hed\ *n* : a human skull emblematic of death

deaths·man \'deth-smən\ *n, archaic* : EXECUTIONER

death tax *n* : a tax arising on the transmission of property after the owner's death; *esp* : ESTATE TAX

death trap *n* : a structure or situation that is potentially very dangerous to life ⟨the risk of going on in a boat that was a *death trap* —Ken Gardner⟩

death warrant *n* **1** : a warrant for the execution of a death sentence **2** : DEATHBLOW

¹death·watch \'deth-,wäch\ *n* [*death* + *watch* (timepiece); fr. the superstition that its ticking presages death] : a small insect that makes a ticking sound: as **a** : any of various small beetles (family Anobiidae) that are common in old houses where they bore in woodwork and furniture — called also *deathwatch beetle* **b** : BOOK LOUSE

²deathwatch *n* [*death* + *watch* (vigil)] **1** : a vigil kept with the dead or dying **2** : the guard set over a criminal before his execution

death wish *n* : the conscious or unconscious desire for the death of another or of oneself

deb *abbr* debenture

de·ba·cle \di-'bäk-əl, -'bak-; dā-'bäk(l²), 'dä-, ; *also* 'deb-i-kəl\ *n* [F *débâcle*, fr. *débâcler* to unbar, fr. MF *desbacler*, fr. *des-* de- + *bacler* to bar, fr. OProv *baclar*, fr. (assumed) VL *bacculare*, fr. L *baculum* staff — more at BACTERIUM] **1** : a tumultuous breakup of ice in a river **2** : a violent disruption (as of an army) : ROUT **3 a** : a great disaster **b** : a complete failure : FIASCO

de·bar \di-'bär\ *vt* [ME *debarren*, fr. MF *desbarrer* to unbar, fr. *des-* de- + *barrer* to bar] : to bar from having or doing something : PRECLUDE *syn* see EXCLUDE — **de·bar·ment** \-mənt\ *n*

de·bark \di-'bärk\ *vb* [F *débarquer*, fr. *de-* + *barque* bark] : DISEMBARK — **de·bar·ka·tion** \dē-,bär-'kā-shən\ *n*

de·base \di-'bās\ *vt* **1** : to lower in status, esteem, quality, or character **2 a** : to reduce the intrinsic value of (a coin) by increasing the base-metal content **b** : to reduce the exchange value of (a monetary unit) — **de·base·ment** \-'bā-smənt\ *n* — **de·bas·er** \-'bā-sər\ *n*

syn **1** DEBASE, VITIATE, DEPRAVE, CORRUPT, DEBAUCH, PERVERT *shared meaning element* : to cause to become lowered or impaired in quality or character *ant* elevate (*as taste*), amend (*as morals*) **2** see ABASE

de·bat·able \di-'bāt-ə-bəl\ *adj* **1** : claimed by more than one country ⟨~ border territory⟩ **2 a** : open to dispute : QUESTIONABLE ⟨a ~ conclusion⟩ **b** : open to debate **3** : capable of being debated

¹de·bate \di-'bāt\ *n* : a contention by words or arguments: as **a** : the formal discussion of a motion before a deliberative body according to the rules of parliamentary procedure **b** : a regulated discussion of a proposition between two matched sides

²debate *vb* **de·bat·ed; de·bat·ing** [ME *debaten*, fr. MF *debatre*, fr. OF, fr. *de-* + *batre* to beat, fr. L *battuere* — more at BATTLE] *vi* **1** *obs* : FIGHT, CONTEND **2** : to contend in words : to discuss a question by considering opposed arguments **3** : to participate in a debate ~ *vt* **1 a** : to argue about **b** : to engage (an opponent) in debate **2** : to turn over in one's mind *syn* see DISCUSS — **de·bate·ment** \-'bāt-mənt\ *n* — **de·bat·er** *n*

¹de·bauch \di-'bòch, -'bäch\ *vt* [MF *debaucher*, fr. OF *desbauchier* to scatter, rough-hew (timber), fr. *des-* de- + *bauch* beam, of Gmc origin; akin to OHG *balko* beam — more at BALK] **1 a** *archaic* : to make disloyal **b** : to seduce from chastity **c** : to lead away from virtue or excellence **d** : to corrupt by intemperance or sensuality *syn* see DEBASE — **de·bauch·er** *n*

²debauch *n* **1** : an act or occasion of debauchery **2** : ORGY

de·bauch·ee \di-,bòch-'ē, -,bäch-; ,deb-ə-'shē, -'shä\ *n* [F *débauché*, fr. pp. of *débaucher*] : one given to debauchery

de·bauch·ery \di-'bòch-(ə-)rē, -'bäch-\ *n, pl* **-er·ies 1 a** : extreme indulgence in sensuality **b** *pl* : ORGIES **2** *archaic* : seduction from virtue or duty

de·ben·ture \di-'ben-chər\ *n* [ME *debentur*, fr. L, they are due, 3d pl. pres. pass. of *debēre* to owe] **1** : a writing or certificate signed by a public officer as evidence of a debt or of a right to demand a sum of money **2 a** *Brit* : a corporate security other than an equity security : BOND **b** : a bond backed by the general credit of a corporation rather than a specific lien on particular assets

de·bil·i·tate \di-'bil-ə-,tāt\ *vt* **-tat·ed; -tat·ing** [L *debilitatus*, pp. of *debilitare* to weaken, fr. *debilis*] : to impair the strength of : ENFEEBLE *syn* see WEAKEN *ant* invigorate — **de·bil·i·ta·tion** \-,bil-ə-'tā-shən\ *n*

de·bil·i·ty \di-'bil-ət-ē\ *n, pl* **-ties** [MF *debilité*, fr. L *debiltat-, debilitas*, fr. *debilis* weak] : WEAKNESS, INFIRMITY

¹deb·it \'deb-ət\ *n* [L *debitum* debt] **1** : a record of an indebtedness; *specif* : an entry on the left-hand side of an account constituting an addition to an expense or asset account or a deduction from a revenue, net worth, or liability account **2** : the sum of the items so entered **3** : a charge against a bank deposit account **4** : DRAWBACK, SHORTCOMING ⟨a film of almost equally divided merits and ~s —Richard Corliss⟩

²debit *vt* : to enter on the left-hand side of an account : charge with a debit

deb·o·nair \,deb-ə-'na(ə)r, -'ne(ə)r\ *adj* [ME *debonere*, fr. OF *debonaire*, fr. *de bonne aire* of good family or nature] **1** *archaic* : GENTLE, COURTEOUS **2 a** : SUAVE, URBANE **b** : LIGHTHEARTED, NONCHALANT — **deb·o·nair·ly** *adv* — **deb·o·nair·ness** *n*

de·bone \(')dē-'bōn\ *vt* : BONE ⟨*deboned* the meat⟩ — **de·bon·er** *n*

Deb·o·rah \'deb-(ə-)rə\ *n* [Heb *Dēbhōrāh*] : a Hebrew prophetess who rallied the Israelites in their early struggles against the Canaanites

de·bouch \di-'bauch, -'büsh\ *vb* [F *déboucher*, fr. *dé-* de- + *bouche* mouth, fr. L *bucca* cheek — more at POCK] *vi* **1** : to march out (as from a defile) into open ground **2** : EMERGE, ISSUE ~ *vt* : to cause to emerge : let out

de·bouch·ment \-mənt\ *n* **1** : the act or process of debouching **2** : a mouth or outlet esp. of a river

de·bou·chure \di-,bü-'shù(ə)r\ *n* : DEBOUCHMENT 2

de·bride·ment \di-'brēd-mənt, dā-, -,mänt, -,mäⁿ\ *n* [F *débridement*, fr. *débrider* to remove unhealthy tissue, lit., to unbridle, fr. MF *desbrider*, fr. *des-* de- + *bride* bridle, fr. MHG *bridel* — more at BRIDLE] : the surgical removal of lacerated, devitalized, or contaminated tissue

de·brief \di-'brēf, 'dē-\ *vt* **1** : to interrogate (as a pilot) in order to obtain useful information **2** : to instruct not to reveal any classified information after release from a sensitive position

de·bris \də-'brē, dā-', 'dā-, *Brit usu* 'deb-(,)rē\ *n, pl* **de·bris** \-'brēz, -,brēz, -(,)rēz\ [F *débris*, fr. MF, fr. *debriser* to break to pieces, fr. OF *debrisier*, fr. *de-* + *brisier* to break — more at BRISANCE] **1** : the remains of something broken down or destroyed : RUINS **2** : an accumulation of fragments of rock

debt \'det\ *n* [ME *dette, debte*, fr. OF *dette* something owed, fr. (assumed) VL *debita*, fr. L, pl. of *debitum* debt, fr. neut. of *debitus*, pp. of *debēre* to owe, fr. *de-* + *habēre* to have — more at HABIT] **1** : SIN, TRESPASS **2** : a state of owing **3** : something owed : OBLIGATION **4** : the common-law action for the recovery of money held to be due — **debt·less** \-ləs\ *adj*

debt·or \'det-ər\ *n* **1** : one guilty of neglect or violation of duty **2** : one who owes a debt

de·bug \(')dē-'bəg\ *vt* **1** : to eliminate errors in or malfunctions of ⟨~ a computer program⟩ **2** : to remove a concealed microphone or wiretapping device from

de·bunk \(')dē-'bəŋk\ *vt* : to expose the sham or falseness of ⟨~ a hero legend⟩ — **de·bunk·er** *n*

de·but \'dā-,byü, dā-'\ *n* [F *début*, fr. *debuter* to begin, fr. MF *desbuter* to play first, fr. *des-* de- + *but* starting point, goal — more at BUTT] **1** : a first public appearance **2** : a formal entrance into society — **debut** *vi*

deb·u·tant \'deb-yù-,tänt\ *n* [F *débutant*, fr. prp. of *débuter*] : one making a debut

deb·u·tante \'deb-yù-,tänt\ *n* [F *débutante*, fem. of *débutant*] : a young woman making her formal entrance into society

dec *abbr* **1** deceased **2** declaration **3** declared **4** declination **5** decorated **6** decorative **7** decrease **8** decrescendo

Dec *abbr* December

deca- *or* **dec-** *or* **deka-** *comb form* [ME, fr. L, fr. Gk *deka-, dek-*, fr. *deka* — more at TEN] : ten ⟨*decamerous*⟩ ⟨*dekavolt*⟩

de·cade \'dek-,ād, -əd; de-'kād; *3 is usually* 'dek-əd\ *n* [ME, fr. MF *décade*, fr. LL *decad-, decas*, fr. Gk *dekad-, dekas*, fr. *deka*] **1** : a group or set of 10 **2** : a period of 10 years **3** : a division of the rosary that consists primarily of 10 Hail Marys

dec·a·dence \'dek-əd-ən(t)s *also* di-'kād-²n(t)s\ *n* [MF, fr. ML *decadentia*, fr. LL *decadent-, decadens*, prp. of *decadere* to fall, sink — more at DECAY] **1** : the process of becoming decadent : the quality or state of being decadent **2** : a period of decline *syn* see DETERIORATION *ant* rise, flourishing

dec·a·den·cy \-ən-sē, -²n-sē\ *n* : DECADENCE 1

¹dec·a·dent \'dek-əd-ənt *also* di-'kād-²nt\ *adj* [back-formation fr. *decadence*] **1** : marked by decay or decline **2** : of, relating to, or having the characteristics of the decadents — **dec·a·dent·ly** *adv*

²decadent *n* **1** : one that is decadent **2** : one of a group of late 19th century French and English writers tending toward artificial and unconventional subjects and subtilized style

ə abut	² kitten	ər further	a back	ā bake	ä cot, cart
aù out	ch chin	e less	ē easy	g gift	i trip	ī life
j joke	ŋ sing	ō flow	ò flaw	òi coin	th thin	th this
ü loot	ù foot	y yet	yü few	yù furious	zh vision	

de·caf·fein·ate \(ˈ)dē-ˈkaf-(ē-)ə-ˌnāt\ *vt* **-at·ed; -at·ing** : to remove caffeine from ⟨*decaffeinated* coffee⟩

deca·gon \ˈdek-ə-ˌgän\ *n* [NL *decagonum,* fr. Gk *dekagōnon,* fr. *deka-* deca- + *-gōnon* -gon] : a plane polygon of 10 angles and 10 sides

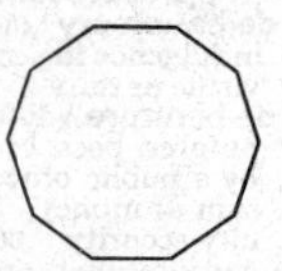

decagon

deca·gram \-ˌgram\ *n* [F *décagramme,* fr. *déca-* deca- + *gramme* gram] : DEKAGRAM

deca·he·dron \ˌdek-ə-ˈhē-drən\ *n* [ISV] : a polyhedron of 10 faces

de·cal \ˈdē-ˌkal, di-ˈkal, ˈdek-əl\ *n* [short for *decalcomania*] : a picture, design, or label made to be transferred (as to glass) from specially prepared paper

de·cal·ci·fi·ca·tion \(ˌ)dē-ˌkal-sə-fə-ˈkā-shən\ *n* : the removal or loss of calcium or calcium compounds (as from bones or soil)

de·cal·ci·fy \(ˈ)dē-ˈkal-sə-ˌfī\ *vt* [ISV] : to remove calcium or calcium compounds from

de·cal·co·ma·nia \di-ˌkal-kə-ˈmā-nē-ə\ *n* [F *décalcomanie,* fr. *décalquer* to copy by tracing (fr. *dé-* de- + *calquer* to trace, fr. It *calcare,* lit., to trample, fr. L) + *manie* mania, fr. LL *mania* — more at CAULK] **1** : the art or process of transferring pictures and designs from specially prepared paper (as to glass) **2** : DECAL

de·ca·les·cence \ˌdē-kə-ˈles-ᵊn(t)s, ˌdek-ə-\ *n* [ISV *de-* + *-calescence* (as in *recalescence*)] : a decrease in temperature that occurs while heating metal through a range in which change in structure occurs

deca·li·ter \ˈdek-ə-ˌlēt-ər\ *n* [F *décalitre,* fr. *déca-* + *litre* liter] : DEKALITER

deca·logue \ˈdek-ə-ˌlȯg, -ˌläg\ *n* [ME *decaloge,* fr. LL *decalogus,* fr. Gk *dekalogos,* fr. *deka-* + *logos* word — more at LEGEND] **1** *cap* : TEN COMMANDMENTS **2** : a basic set of rules carrying binding authority

¹de·cam·e·ter \de-ˈkam-ət-ər, də-\ *n* [Gk *dekametron,* fr. *deka-* + *metron* measure, meter] : a line of verse consisting of 10 metrical feet

²deca·me·ter \ˈdek-ə-ˌmēt-ər\ *n* [F *décamètre,* fr. *déca-* + *mètre* meter] : DEKAMETER

deca·me·tho·ni·um \ˌdek-ə-mə-ˈthō-nē-əm\ *n* [*decamethonium* (an ammonium ion), fr. *deca-* + *methylene* + *-onium*] : any of several halogen salts of a synthetic ion whose curarizing effect produces relaxation of skeletal muscles

deca·met·ric \ˌdek-ə-ˈme-trik\ *adj* [*decameter* + *-ic;* fr. the wavelength range being between 1 and 10 dekameters] : of, relating to, or being a radio wave of high frequency

de·camp \di-ˈkamp\ *vi* [F *décamper,* fr. MF *descamper,* fr. *des-* de- + *camper* to camp] **1** : to break up a camp **2** : to depart suddenly : ABSCOND — **de·camp·ment** \-mənt\ *n*

dec·ane \ˈdek-ˌān\ *n* [ISV *deca-*] : any of several isomeric liquid hydrocarbons $C_{10}H_{22}$ of the methane series

dec·a·no·ic acid \ˌdek-ə-ˌnō-ik-\ *n* [ISV, fr. *decane*] : CAPRIC ACID

de·cant \di-ˈkant\ *vt* [NL *decantare,* fr. L *de-* + ML *cantus* side, fr. L, iron ring round a carriage wheel — more at CANT] **1** : to pour from one vessel into another **2** : to draw off without disturbing the sediment or the lower liquid layers — **de·can·ta·tion** \ˌdē-ˌkan-ˈtā-shən\ *n*

de·cant·er \di-ˈkant-ər\ *n* : a vessel used to decant or to receive decanted liquids; *esp* : an ornamental glass bottle used for serving wine

de·cap·i·tate \di-ˈkap-ə-ˌtāt\ *vt* **-tat·ed; -tat·ing** [LL *decapitatus,* pp. of *decapitare,* fr. L *de-* + *capit-, caput* head — more at HEAD] : to cut off the head of : BEHEAD — **de·cap·i·ta·tion** \-ˌkap-ə-ˈtā-shən\ *n* — **de·cap·i·ta·tor** \-ˈkap-ə-ˌtāt-ər\ *n*

deca·pod \ˈdek-ə-ˌpäd\ *n* [NL *Decapoda,* order name] **1** : any of an order (Decapoda) of highly organized crustaceans (as shrimps, lobsters, and crabs) with five pairs of thoracic appendages one or more of which are modified into pincers, stalked eyes, and the head and thorax fused into a cephalothorax and covered by a carapace **2** : any of an order (Decapoda) of cephalopod mollusks including the cuttlefishes, squids, and related forms that have 10 arms — **decapod** *adj* — **de·cap·o·dal** \di-ˈkap-əd-ᵊl\ *adj* — **de·cap·o·dan** \-əd-ən\ *adj or n* — **de·cap·o·dous** \-əd-əs\ *adj*

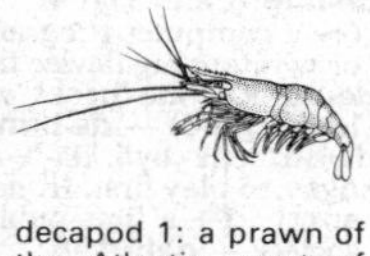

decapod 1: a prawn of the Atlantic coast of America

de·car·bon·ate \(ˈ)dē-ˈkär-bə-ˌnāt\ *vt* : to remove carbon dioxide or carbonic acid from — **de·car·bon·ation** \(ˌ)dē-ˌkär-bə-ˈnā-shən\ *n* — **de·car·bon·ator** \(ˈ)dē-ˈkär-bə-ˌnāt-ər\ *n*

de·car·bon·ize \(ˈ)dē-ˈkär-bə-ˌnīz\ *vt* [ISV] : to remove carbon from — **de·car·bon·iz·er** *n*

de·car·box·yl·ase \ˌdē-kär-ˈbäk-sə-ˌlās, -ˌlāz\ *n* : any of a group of enzymes that accelerate decarboxylation esp. of amino acids

de·car·box·yl·ate \-sə-ˌlāt\ *vt* : to remove carboxyl from — **de·car·box·yl·ation** \-ˌbäk-sə-ˈlā-shən\ *n*

de·car·bu·rize \(ˈ)dē-ˈkär-b(y)ə-ˌrīz\ *vt* : DECARBONIZE — **de·car·bu·ri·za·tion** \(ˌ)dē-ˌkär-b(y)ə-rə-ˈzā-shən\ *n*

dec·are \ˈdek-ˌa(ə)r, -ˌe(ə)r, -ˌär\ *n* [F *décare,* fr. *déca-* deca- + *are*] : a metric unit of area equal to 10 ares or 0.2471 acre

deca·stere \ˈdek-ə-ˌsti(ə)r, -ˌste(ə)r\ *n* [F *décastère,* fr. *déca-* + *stère* stere] : DEKASTERE

de·ca·su·al·iza·tion \(ˌ)dē-ˌkazh-(ə-)wə-lə-ˈzā-shən, -ˌkazh-ə-lə-\ *n* : the process of eliminating the employment of casual workers in order to stabilize the work force

deca·syl·lab·ic \ˌdek-ə-sə-ˈlab-ik\ *adj* [prob. fr. F *décasyllabique,* fr. Gk *dekasyllabos* decasyllabic, fr. *deka-* deca- + *syllabē* syllable] : consisting of 10 syllables or composed of verses of 10 syllables — **decasyllabic** *n* — **deca·syl·la·ble** \ˈdek-ə-ˌsil-ə-bəl, ˌdek-ə-\ *n*

de·cath·lon \di-ˈkath-lən, -ˌlän\ *n* [F *décathlon,* fr. *déca-* deca- + Gk *athlon* contest — more at ATHLETE] : a 10-event composite athletic contest consisting of the 100-meter, 400-meter, and 1500-meter runs, the 110-meter high hurdles, the javelin and discus throws, shot put, pole vault, high jump, and long jump

¹de·cay \di-ˈkā\ *vb* [ME *decayen,* fr. ONF *decaïr,* fr. LL *decadere* to fall, sink, fr. L *de-* + *cadere* to fall — more at CHANCE] *vi* **1** : to decline from a sound or prosperous condition **2** : to decrease gradually in quantity, activity, or force **3** : to fall into ruin **4** : to decline in health, strength, or vigor **5** : to undergo decomposition ~ *vt* **1** *obs* : to cause to decay : IMPAIR ⟨infirmity that ~s the wise —Shak.⟩ **2** : to destroy by decomposition — **de·cay·er** *n*
syn DECAY, DECOMPOSE, ROT, PUTREFY, SPOIL *shared meaning element* : to undergo destructive changes

²decay *n* **1** : gradual decline in strength, soundness, or prosperity or in degree of excellence or perfection **2** : a wasting or wearing away : RUIN **3** *obs* : DESTRUCTION, DEATH **4 a** : ROT; *specif* : aerobic decomposition of proteins chiefly by bacteria **b** : the product of decay **5** : a decline in health or vigor **6** : decrease in quantity, activity, or force: as **a** : spontaneous decrease in the number of radioactive atoms in radioactive material **b** : spontaneous disintegration (as of an atom or a meson)

Dec·ca \ˈdek-ə\ *n* [*Decca* Co., British firm which developed it] : a system of long-range navigation utilizing the phase differences of continuous-wave signals from synchronized ground transmitters

decd *abbr* deceased

de·cease \di-ˈsēs\ *n* [ME *deces,* fr. MF, fr. L *decessus* departure, death, fr. *decessus,* pp. of *decedere* to depart, die, fr. *de-* + *cedere* to go — more at CEDE] : departure from life : DEATH — **decease** *vi*

¹de·ceased \-ˈsēst\ *adj* : no longer living; *esp* : recently dead — used of persons ***syn*** see DEAD

²deceased *n, pl* **deceased** : a dead person ⟨the will of the ~⟩

de·ce·dent \di-ˈsēd-ᵊnt\ *n* [L *decedent-, decedens,* prp. of *decedere*] : a deceased person — used chiefly in law

de·ceit \di-ˈsēt\ *n* [ME *deceite,* fr. OF, fr. L *decepta,* fem. of *deceptus,* pp. of *decipere*] **1** : the act or practice of deceiving : DECEPTION **2** : an attempt or device to deceive : TRICK **3** : the quality of being deceitful : DECEITFULNESS

de·ceit·ful \-fəl\ *adj* : having a tendency or disposition to deceive: **a** : not honest ⟨a ~ child⟩ **b** : DECEPTIVE, MISLEADING ***syn*** see DISHONEST ***ant*** trustworthy — **de·ceit·ful·ly** \-fə-lē\ *adv* — **de·ceit·ful·ness** *n*

de·ceiv·able \di-ˈsē-və-bəl\ *adj* **1** *archaic* : DECEITFUL, DECEPTIVE **2** *archaic* : capable of being deceived — **de·ceiv·able·ness** *n, archaic*

de·ceive \di-ˈsēv\ *vb* **de·ceived; de·ceiv·ing** [ME *deceiven,* fr. OF *deceivre,* fr. L *decipere,* fr. *de-* + *capere* to take — more at HEAVE] *vt* **1** *archaic* : ENSNARE **2 a** *obs* : to be false to **b** *archaic* : to fail to fulfill **3** *obs* : CHEAT **4** : to cause to accept as true or valid what is false or invalid **5** *archaic* : to while away ~ *vi* : to practice deceit — **de·ceiv·er** *n* — **de·ceiv·ing·ly** \-ˈsē-viŋ-lē\ *adv*
syn DECEIVE, MISLEAD, DELUDE, BEGUILE *shared meaning element* : to lead astray ***ant*** undeceive, enlighten

de·cel·er·ate \(ˈ)dē-ˈsel-ə-ˌrāt\ *vb* **-at·ed; -at·ing** [*de-* + *accelerate*] *vt* **1** : to reduce the speed of : slow down **2** : to decrease the rate of progress of ~ *vi* : to move at decreasing speed — **de·cel·er·a·tion** \(ˌ)dē-ˌsel-ə-ˈrā-shən\ *n* — **de·cel·er·a·tor** \(ˈ)dē-ˈsel-ə-ˌrāt-ər\ *n*

De·cem·ber \di-ˈsem-bər\ *n* [ME *Decembre,* fr. OF, fr. L *December* (tenth month), fr. *decem* ten — more at TEN] : the 12th month of the Gregorian calendar

De·cem·brist \-brəst\ *n* : one taking part in the unsuccessful uprising against the Russian emperor Nicholas I in December 1825

de·cem·vir \di-ˈsem-vər\ *n* [L, back-formation fr. *decemviri,* pl., fr. *decem* + *viri,* pl. of *vir* man — more at VIRILE] : one of a ruling body of 10; *specif* : one of a body of 10 magistrates in ancient Rome — **de·cem·vi·ral** \-və-rəl\ *adj* — **de·cem·vi·rate** \-rət\ *n*

de·cen·cy \ˈdēs-ᵊn-sē\ *n, pl* **-cies** **1** *archaic* **a** : FITNESS **b** : ORDERLINESS **2 a** : the quality or state of being decent : PROPRIETY **b** : conformity to standards of taste, propriety, or quality **3** : standard of propriety — usu. used in pl. **4** *pl* : conditions or services considered essential for a proper standard of living **5** : literary decorum

de·cen·ni·al \di-ˈsen-ē-əl\ *adj* **1** : consisting of or lasting for 10 years **2** : occurring or being done every 10 years — **decennial** *n* — **de·cen·ni·al·ly** \-ē-ə-lē\ *adv*

de·cen·ni·um \-ē-əm\ *n, pl* **-ni·ums** *or* **-nia** \-ē-ə\ [L, fr. *decem* + *annus* year — more at ANNUAL] : a period of 10 years : DECADE

de·cent \ˈdēs-ᵊnt\ *adj* [MF or L; MF, fr. L *decent-, decens,* prp. of *decēre* to be fitting; akin to L *decus* honor, *dignus* worthy, Gk *dokein* to seem, seem good] **1** *archaic* **a** : APPROPRIATE **b** : well-formed : HANDSOME **2 a** : conforming to standards of propriety, good taste, or morality **b** : modestly clothed **3** : free from immodesty or obscenity **4** : conforming to current standards of living ⟨~ wages⟩ ⟨~ housing⟩ **5** : having praiseworthy qualities ***syn*** see CHASTE ***ant*** indecent, obscene — **de·cent·ly** *adv*

de·cen·tral·iza·tion \(ˌ)dē-ˌsen-trə-lə-ˈzā-shən\ *n* **1** : the dispersion or distribution of functions and powers from a central authority to regional and local authorities **2** : the redistribution of population and industry from urban centers to outlying areas — **de·cen·tral·iza·tion·ist** \(ˌ)dē-ˌsen-trə-lə-ˈzā-sh(ə-)nəst\ *n*

de·cen·tral·ize \(ˈ)dē-ˈsen-trə-ˌlīz\ *vt* : to bring about the decentralization of ~ *vi* : to undergo decentralization

de·cep·tion \di-ˈsep-shən\ *n* [ME *decepcioun,* fr. MF *deception,* fr. LL *deception-, deceptio,* fr. L *deceptus,* pp. of *decipere* to deceive] **1 a** : the act of deceiving **b** : the fact or condition of being deceived **2** : something that deceives : TRICK — **de·cep·tion·al** \-shnəl, -shən-ᵊl\ *adj*

de·cep·tive \di-ˈsep-tiv\ *adj* : tending or having power to deceive : MISLEADING — **de·cep·tive·ly** *adv* — **de·cep·tive·ness** *n*

¹de·cer·e·brate \(ˈ)dē-ˈser-ə-ˌbrāt\ *vt* : to remove the cerebrum from; *also* : to make incapable of cerebral activity — **de·cer·e·bra·tion** \(ˌ)dē-ˌser-ə-ˈbrā-shən\ *n*

²de·cer·e·brate \(ˈ)dē-ˈser-ə-brət, -ˌbrāt; ˌdē-sə-ˈrē-brət\ *adj* **1** : having the cerebrum removed or made inactive **2** : characteristic of decerebration ⟨~ rigidity⟩

de·cer·ti·fy \(ˈ)dē-ˈsərt-ə-ˌfī\ *vt* : to withdraw or revoke the certification of — **de·cer·ti·fi·ca·tion** \(ˌ)dē-ˌsərt-ə-fə-ˈkā-shən\ *n*

de·chlo·ri·nate \(ˈ)dē-ˈklōr-ə-ˌnāt, -ˈklȯr-\ *vt* : to remove chlorine from ⟨~ water⟩ — **de·chlo·ri·na·tion** \(ˌ)dē-ˌklōr-ə-ˈnā-shən, -ˌklȯr-\ *n*

deci- *comb form* [F *déci-*, fr. L *decimus* tenth, fr. *decem* ten — more at TEN] : tenth part ⟨*deci*normal⟩

deci·are \ˈdes-ē-ˌa(ə)r, -ˌe(ə)r, -ˌär\ *n* [F *déciare*, fr. *déci-* + *are*] : a metric unit of area equal to 10 square meters or 11.96 square yards

deci·bel \ˈdes-ə-ˌbel, -bəl\ *n* [ISV *deci-* + *bel*] **1 a** : a unit for expressing the ratio of two amounts of electric or acoustic signal power equal to 10 times the common logarithm of this ratio **b** : a unit for expressing the ratio of the magnitudes of two electric voltages or currents or analogous acoustic quantities equal to 20 times the common logarithm of the voltage or current ratio **2** : a unit for expressing the relative intensity of sounds on a scale from zero for the average least perceptible sound to about 130 for the average pain level

de·cide \di-ˈsīd\ *vb* **de·cid·ed; de·cid·ing** [ME *deciden*, fr. MF *decider*, fr. L *decidere*, lit., to cut off, fr. *de-* + *caedere* to cut — more at CONCISE] *vt* **1** : to arrive at a solution that ends uncertainty or dispute about ⟨important . . . that we ~ borderline cases in favor of individual freedom —Milton Friedman⟩ **2** : to bring to a definitive end ⟨one blow *decided* the fight⟩ **3** : to induce to come to a choice ⟨her pleas *decided* him to help⟩ ~ *vi* : to make a choice or judgment — **de·cid·abil·i·ty** \-ˌsīd-ə-ˈbil-ət-ē\ *n* — **de·cid·able** \-ˈsīd-ə-bəl\ *adj* — **de·cid·er** *n*

syn DECIDE, DETERMINE, SETTLE, RULE, RESOLVE *shared meaning element* : to come or cause to come to a conclusion

de·cid·ed *adj* **1** : UNQUESTIONABLE ⟨a ~ advantage⟩ **2** : free from doubt or wavering — **de·cid·ed·ly** *adv* — **de·cid·ed·ness** *n*

de·cid·ing *adj* : that decides : DECISIVE ⟨drove in the ~ run⟩

de·cid·ua \di-ˈsij-ə-wə\ *n, pl* **-u·ae** \-ə-ˌwē\ [NL, fr. L, fem. of *deciduus*] **1** : the part of the mucous membrane lining the uterus that in higher placental mammals undergoes special modifications in preparation for and during pregnancy and is cast off at parturition **2** : the part of the mucous membrane of the uterus cast off in the process of menstruation — **de·cid·u·al** \-wəl\ *adj*

de·cid·u·ate \-wət\ *adj* : having the fetal and maternal tissues firmly interlocked so that a layer of maternal tissue is torn away at parturition and forms a part of the afterbirth

de·cid·u·ous \di-ˈsij-ə-wəs\ *adj* [L *deciduus*, fr. *decidere* to fall off, fr. *de-* + *cadere* to fall — more at CHANCE] **1** : falling off or shed seasonally or at a certain stage of development in the life cycle ⟨~ leaves⟩ ⟨~ teeth⟩ **2** : having deciduous parts ⟨~ trees⟩ **3** : EPHEMERAL — **de·cid·u·ous·ly** *adv* — **de·cid·u·ous·ness** *n*

deci·gram \ˈdes-ə-ˌgram\ *n* [F *décigramme*, fr. *déci-* + *gramme* gram] — see METRIC SYSTEM table

dec·ile \ˈdes-ˌīl, -əl\ *n* [L *decem* ten — more at TEN] : any one of nine numbers in a series dividing the distribution of the individuals in the series into 10 groups of equal frequency; *also* : any one of these 10 groups — **decile** *adj*

deci·li·ter \ˈdes-ə-ˌlēt-ər\ *n* [F *décilitre*, fr. *déci-* + *litre* liter] — see METRIC SYSTEM table

de·cil·lion \di-ˈsil-yən\ *n, often attrib* [L *decem* + E *-illion* (as in *million*)] — see NUMBER table

¹dec·i·mal \ˈdes(-ə)-məl\ *adj* [(assumed) NL *decimalis*, fr. ML, of a tithe, fr. L *decima* tithe — more at DIME] : numbered or proceeding by tens: **a** : based on the number 10 **b** : subdivided into 10th or 100th units **c** : expressed in a decimal fraction — **dec·i·mal·ly** \-mə-lē\ *adv*

²decimal *n* : a proper fraction in which the denominator is a power of 10 usu. not expressed but signified by a point placed at the left of the numerator (as $.2=2/10$, $.25=25/100$, $.025=25/1000$) — called also *decimal fraction*

dec·i·mal·ize \ˈdes(-ə)-mə-ˌlīz\ *vt* **-ized; -iz·ing** : to convert to a decimal system ⟨~ currency⟩ — **dec·i·mal·iza·tion** \ˌdes(-ə)-mə-lə-ˈzā-shən\ *n*

decimal point *n* : the dot at the left of a decimal fraction

dec·i·mate \ˈdes-ə-ˌmāt\ *vt* **-mat·ed; -mat·ing** [L *decimatus*, pp. of *decimare*, fr. *decimus* tenth, fr. *decem* ten] **1** : to select by lot and kill every tenth man of **2** : to take a tenth from : TITHE **3** : to destroy a large part of — **dec·i·ma·tion** \ˌdes-ə-ˈmā-shən\ *n*

deci·me·ter \ˈdes-ə-ˌmēt-ər\ *n* [F *décimètre*, fr. *déci-* deci- + *mètre* meter] — see METRIC SYSTEM table

de·ci·pher \di-ˈsī-fər\ *vt* **1 a** : to convert into intelligible form **b** : DECODE **2** *obs* : DEPICT **3** : to make out the meaning of despite indistinctness or obscurity — **de·ci·pher·able** \-f(ə-)rə-bəl\ *adj* — **de·ci·pher·er** \-fər-ər\ *n* — **de·ci·pher·ment** \-fər-mənt\ *n*

de·ci·sion \di-ˈsizh-ən\ *n* [MF, fr. L *decision-, decisio*, fr. *decisus*, pp. of *decidere* to decide] **1 a** : the act or process of deciding **b** : a determination arrived at after consideration : CONCLUSION **2** : a report of a conclusion **3** : promptness and firmness in deciding : DETERMINATION ⟨a man of courage and ~⟩ — **de·ci·sion·al** \-ˈsizh-nəl, -ən-ᵊl\ *adj*

de·ci·sive \di-ˈsī-siv\ *adj* **1** : having the power or quality of deciding **2** : marked by or indicative of determination or firmness : RESOLUTE **3** : UNMISTAKABLE, UNQUESTIONABLE ⟨a ~ superiority⟩ ***syn*** see CONCLUSIVE ***ant*** indecisive — **de·ci·sive·ly** *adv* — **de·ci·sive·ness** *n*

deci·stere \ˈdes-ə-ˌsti(ə)r, -ˌste(ə)r\ *n* [F *décistère*, fr. *déci-* + *stère* stere] — see METRIC SYSTEM table

¹deck \ˈdek\ *n* [prob. modif. of (assumed) LG *verdeck* (whence G *verdeck*), fr. (assumed) MLG *vordeck*, fr. MLG *vordecken* to cover, fr. *vor-* (akin to OHG *fur-* for-) + *decken* to cover; akin to OHG *decken* to cover — more at THATCH] **1** : a platform in a ship serving usu. as a structural element and forming the floor for its compartments **2** : something resembling the deck of a ship: as **a** : a story or tier of a building **b** : the roadway of a bridge **c** : a flat floored roofless area adjoining a house **d** : the lid of the compartment at the rear of the body of an automobile; *also* : the compartment **e** : a layer of clouds **f** : TAPE DECK 1b **3 a** : a pack of playing cards **b** : a packet of narcotics **c** : a group of usu. punched data processing cards — **on deck 1** : ready for duty **2** : next in line

²deck *vt* [D *dekken* to cover; akin to OHG *decken*] **1** *obs* : COVER **2 a** : to clothe elegantly : ARRAY ⟨~*ed* out in furs⟩ **b** : DECORATE ⟨~ the halls with boughs of holly —*English carol*⟩ **3** [ˈ*deck*] : to furnish with or as if with a deck **4** [ˈ*deck*] : to knock down forcibly : FLOOR ⟨~*ed* his opponent with a left hook⟩ ***syn*** see ADORN

deck chair *n* : a folding chair often having an adjustable leg rest

deck·er \ˈdek-ər\ *n* : something having a deck or a specified number of levels, floors, or layers — often used in combination ⟨many of the city's buses are double-*deckers*⟩

deck·hand \ˈdek-ˌhand\ *n* : a seaman who performs manual duties

deck·house \-ˌhau̇s\ *n* : a superstructure on a ship's upper deck

deck·ing \ˈdek-iŋ\ *n* : DECK; *also* : material for a deck

deck·le \ˈdek-əl\ *n* [G *deckel*, lit., cover, fr. *decken* to cover, fr. OHG] **1** : a detachable wooden frame around the outside edges of a hand mold used in making paper **2** : either of the bands that run longitudinally on the edges of the wire of a paper machine and determine the width of the web

deckle edge *n* : the rough untrimmed edge of paper left by a deckle or produced artificially — **deck·le–edged** \ˌdek-ə-ˈlejd\ *adj*

deck tennis *n* [fr. its being played chiefly on the decks of ocean liners] : a game in which players toss a ring or quoit back and forth over a net stretched across a small court

de·claim \di-ˈklām\ *vb* [ME *declamen*, fr. L *declamare*, fr. *de-* + *clamare* to cry out; akin to L *calare* to call — more at LOW] *vi* **1** : to speak rhetorically; *specif* : to recite something as an exercise in elocution **2** : to speak pompously or bombastically : HARANGUE ~ *vt* : to deliver rhetorically; *specif* : to recite in elocution — **de·claim·er** *n* — **dec·la·ma·tion** \ˌdek-lə-ˈmā-shən\ *n*

de·clam·a·to·ry \di-ˈklam-ə-ˌtōr-ē, -ˌtȯr-\ *adj* : of, relating to, or marked by declamation or rhetorical display

de·clar·ant \di-ˈklar-ənt, -ˈkler-\ *n* : one that makes a declaration; *specif* : an alien who has declared his intention of becoming a citizen of the U.S. by signing his first papers

dec·la·ra·tion \ˌdek-lə-ˈrā-shən\ *n* **1** : the act of declaring : ANNOUNCEMENT **2 a** : the first pleading in a common-law action **b** : a statement made by a party to a legal transaction usu. not under oath **3 a** : something that is declared **b** : the document containing such a declaration

de·clar·a·tive \di-ˈklar-ət-iv, -ˈkler-\ *adj* : making a declaration : DECLARATORY ⟨~ sentence⟩ — **de·clar·a·tive·ly** *adv*

de·clar·a·to·ry \-ə-ˌtōr-ē, -ˌtȯr-\ *adj* **1** : serving to declare, set forth, or explain **2 a** : declaring what is the existing law ⟨~ statute⟩ **b** : declaring a legal right or interpretation ⟨a ~ judgment⟩

de·clare \di-ˈkla(ə)r, -ˈkle(ə)r\ *vb* **de·clared; de·clar·ing** [ME *declaren*, fr. MF *declarer*, fr. L *declarare*, fr. *de-* + *clarare* to make clear, fr. *clarus* clear — more at CLEAR] *vt* **1** *obs* : to make clear **2** : to make known formally or explicitly **3** : to make evident : SHOW **4** : to state emphatically : AFFIRM ⟨~*s* his innocence⟩ **5** : to make a full statement of (one's taxable or dutiable property) **6 a** : to announce (as a trump suit) in a card game **b** : MELD **7** : to make payable ~ *vi* **1** : to make a declaration **2** : to avow one's support — **de·clar·able** \-ˈklar-ə-bəl, -ˈkler-\ *adj*

***syn* 1** DECLARE, ANNOUNCE, PUBLISH, ADVERTISE, PROCLAIM, PROMULGATE *shared meaning element* : to make known publicly **2** see ASSERT

de·clar·er \di-ˈklar-ər, -ˈkler-\ *n* : one that declares; *specif* : the bridge player who names the trump and plays both his own hand and that of the dummy

de·class \(ˈ)dē-ˈklas\ *vt* : to remove from a class; *esp* : to assign to a lower social status ***syn*** see DEGRADE

dé·clas·sé \ˌdā-ˌklas-ˈā, -ˌkläs-\ *adj* [F, fr. pp. of *déclasser* to declass] **1** : fallen or lowered in class, rank, or social position **2** : of inferior status

de·clas·si·fy \(ˈ)dē-ˈklas-ə-ˌfī\ *vt* : to remove or reduce the security classification of ⟨~ a secret document⟩

de·clen·sion \di-ˈklen-chən\ *n* [prob. alter. of earlier *declenson*, modif. of MF *declinaison*, fr. LL *declination-, declinatio*, fr. L, grammatical inflection, turning aside, fr. *declinatus*, pp. of *declinare* to inflect, turn aside] **1 a** : noun, adjective, or pronoun inflection esp. in some prescribed order of the forms **b** : a class of nouns or adjectives having the same type of inflectional forms **2** : a falling off or away : DETERIORATION **3** : DESCENT, SLOPE — **de·clen·sion·al** \-ˈklench-nəl, -ˈklen-chən-ᵊl\ *adj*

dec·li·nate \ˈdek-lə-ˌnāt, -nət\ *adj* : bent or curved down or aside

dec·li·na·tion \ˌdek-lə-ˈnā-shən\ *n* [ME *declinacioun*, fr. MF *declination*, fr. L *declination-, declinatio* turning aside, altitude of the pole] **1** : angular distance north or south from the celestial equator measured along a great circle passing through the celestial poles **2** : a turning aside or swerving **3** : DETERIORATION ⟨moral ~⟩ **4** : a bending downward : INCLINATION **5** : a formal refusal **6** : the angle formed between a magnetic needle and the geographical meridian — **dec·li·na·tion·al** \-shnəl, -shən-ᵊl\ *adj*

¹de·cline \di-ˈklīn\ *vb* **de·clined; de·clin·ing** [ME *declinen*, fr. MF *decliner*, fr. L *declinare* to turn aside, inflect, fr. *de-* + *clinare* to incline — more at LEAN] *vi* **1** : to turn from a straight course : STRAY **2 a** : to slope downward : DESCEND **b** : to bend down : DROOP **c** : to stoop to what is unworthy **3 a** *of a celestial body* : to sink toward setting **b** : to draw toward a close : WANE **4** : to withhold consent ~ *vt* **1** : to give in prescribed order the grammatical forms of (a noun, pronoun, or adjective) **2** *obs* **a** : AVERT **b** : AVOID **3** : to cause to bend or bow downward **4 a** : to refuse to undertake, engage in, or comply with **b** : to refuse courteously ⟨~ an invitation⟩ — **de·clin·able** \-ˈklī-nə-bəl\ *adj*

ə abut ᵊ kitten ər further a back ā bake ä cot, cart
au̇ out ch chin e less ē easy g gift i trip ī life
j joke ŋ sing ō flow ȯ flaw ȯi coin th thin t͟h this
ü loot u̇ foot y yet yü few yu̇ furious zh vision

syn DECLINE, REFUSE, REJECT, REPUDIATE, SPURN *shared meaning element* : to turn away by not accepting, receiving, or considering ***ant*** accept

[2]**decline** *n* **1 :** the process of declining: **a :** a gradual physical or mental sinking and wasting away **b :** a change to a lower state or level **2 :** the period during which something is approaching its end **3 :** a downward slope : DECLIVITY **4 :** a wasting disease; *esp* : pulmonary tuberculosis ***syn*** see DETERIORATION

de·cliv·i·tous \di-ˈkliv-ət-əs\ *adj* : moderately steep

de·cliv·i·ty \-ət-ē\ *n, pl* **-ties** [L *declivitat-, declivitas,* fr. *declivis* sloping down, fr. *de-* + *clivus* slope, hill; akin to L *clinare*] **1** : downward inclination **2 :** a descending slope

de·coct \di-ˈkäkt\ *vt* [L *decoctus,* pp. of *decoquere,* fr. *de-* + *coquere* to cook — more at COOK] **1 :** to extract the flavor of by boiling **2 :** to boil down : CONCENTRATE

de·coc·tion \di-ˈkäk-shən\ *n* **1 :** the act or process of decocting **2 :** an extract obtained by decocting

de·code \(ˌ)dē-ˈkōd\ *vt* : to convert (a coded message) into intelligible language — **de·cod·er** *n*

de·col·late \di-ˈkäl-ˌāt\ *vt* **-lat·ed; -lat·ing** [L *decollatus,* pp. of *decollare,* fr. *de-* + *collum* neck — more at COLLAR] : BEHEAD — **de·col·la·tion** \ˌdē-ˌkä-ˈlā-shən\ *n*

dé·col·le·tage \(ˌ)dā-ˌkäl-ə-ˈtäzh, ˌdek-(ə-)lə-\ *n* [F, action of cutting or wearing a low neckline, fr. *décolleter*] **1** : the low-cut neckline of a dress **2** : a décolleté dress

décolletage 1

dé·col·le·té \-ˈtā\ *adj* [F, fr. pp. of *décolleter* to give a low neckline to, fr. *dé-* de- + *collet* collar, fr. OF *colet,* fr. *col* collar, neck, fr. L *collum* neck] **1** : wearing a strapless or low-necked dress **2 :** having a low-cut neckline

de·col·o·nize \(ˈ)dē-ˈkäl-ə-ˌnīz\ *vt* : to free from colonial status — **de·col·o·ni·za·tion** \(ˌ)dē-ˌkäl-ə-nə-ˈzā-shən\ *n*

de·col·or·ize \(ˈ)dē-ˈkəl-ə-ˌrīz\ *vt* **-ized; -iz·ing :** to remove color from ⟨~ vinegar by adsorption of impurities on activated charcoal⟩ — **de·col·or·iza·tion** \(ˌ)dē-ˌkəl-ə-rə-ˈzā-shən\ *n* — **de·col·or·iz·er** \(ˈ)dē-ˈkəl-ə-ˌrī-zər\ *n*

de·com·mis·sion \ˌdē-kə-ˈmish-ən\ *vt* : to remove (as a ship) from service

de·com·pen·sate \(ˈ)dē-ˈkäm-pən-ˌsāt, -ˌpen-\ *vi* [prob. back-formation fr. *decompensation*] : to undergo decompensation — **de·com·pen·sa·to·ry** \ˌdē-kəm-ˈpen(t)-sə-ˌtōr-ē, -ˌtȯr-\ *adj*

de·com·pen·sa·tion \(ˌ)dē-ˌkäm-pən-ˈsā-shən, -ˌpen-\ *n* [ISV] : loss of compensation; *esp* : inability of the heart to maintain adequate circulation

de·com·pose \ˌdē-kəm-ˈpōz\ *vb* [F *décomposer,* fr. *dé-* de + *composer* to compose] *vt* **1 :** to separate into constituent parts or elements or into simpler compounds ⟨~ water by electrolysis⟩ **2** : ROT ~ *vi* : to undergo chemical breakdown : DECAY, ROT ⟨fruit ~s⟩ ***syn*** see DECAY — **de·com·pos·abil·i·ty** \-ˌpō-zə-ˈbil-ət-ē\ *n* — **de·com·pos·able** \-ˈpō-zə-bəl\ *adj* — **de·com·po·si·tion** \(ˌ)dē-ˌkäm-pə-ˈzish-ən\ *n* — **de·com·po·si·tion·al** \-ˈzish-nəl, -ˈzish-ən-ᵊl\ *adj*

de·com·pos·er \ˌdē-kəm-ˈpō-zər\ *n* : any of various organisms (as many bacteria and fungi) that return constituents of organic substances to ecological cycles by feeding on and breaking down dead protoplasm

de·com·pound \ˈdē-ˈkäm-ˌpau̇nd; ˌdē-ˌkäm-ˈ, -kəm-ˈ\ *adj, of a leaf* : having divisions that are themselves compound

de·com·press \ˌdē-kəm-ˈpres\ *vt* : to release from pressure or compression — **de·com·pres·sion** \-ˈpresh-ən\ *n*

de·con·cen·trate \(ˈ)dē-ˈkän(t)-sən-ˌtrāt, -ˌsen-\ *vt* : DECENTRALIZE

de·con·di·tion \ˌdē-kən-ˈdish-ən\ *vt* **1 :** to cause to lose physical fitness ⟨inactivity ~s a bedridden person⟩ **2 :** to cause extinction of (a conditioned response)

de·con·gest \ˌdē-kən-ˈjest\ *vt* : to relieve the congestion of — **de·con·ges·tion** \-ˈjes(h)-chən\ *n* — **de·con·ges·tive** \-ˈjes-tiv\ *adj*

de·con·ges·tant \ˌdē-kən-ˈjes-tənt\ *n* : an agent that relieves congestion (as of mucous membranes)

de·con·se·crate \(ˈ)dē-ˈkän(t)-sə-ˌkrāt\ *vt* : to remove the sacred character of ⟨~ a church⟩ — **de·con·se·cra·tion** \(ˌ)dē-ˌkän(t)-sə-ˈkrā-shən\ *n*

de·con·tam·i·nate \ˌdē-kən-ˈtam-ə-ˌnāt\ *vt* : to rid of contamination — **de·con·tam·i·na·tion** \-ˌtam-ə-ˈnā-shən\ *n* — **de·con·tam·i·na·tor** \-ˈtam-ə-ˌnāt-ər\ *n*

de·con·trol \ˌdē-kən-ˈtrōl\ *vt* : to end control of — **decontrol** *n*

de·cor *or* **dé·cor** \dā-ˈkȯ(ə)r, di-ˈ; ˈdek-ˌȯ(ə)r, ˈdāk-ˌ\ *n* [F *décor,* fr. *décorer* to decorate, fr. L *decorare*] **1 a :** DECORATION **b :** the style and layout of interior furnishings **2 :** a stage setting

dec·o·rate \ˈdek-ə-ˌrāt\ *vt* **-rat·ed; -rat·ing** [L *decoratus,* pp. of *decorare,* fr. *decor-, decus* ornament — more at DECENT] **1 :** to add honor to **2 :** to furnish with something ornamental **3 :** to award a mark of honor to ***syn*** see ADORN

dec·o·ra·tion \ˌdek-ə-ˈrā-shən\ *n* **1 :** the act or process of decorating **2 :** ORNAMENT **3 :** a badge of honor (as a U.S. military award)

Decoration Day *n* [fr. the custom of decorating graves on this day] : MEMORIAL DAY

dec·o·ra·tive \ˈdek-(ə-)rət-iv, ˈdek-ə-ˌrāt-\ *adj* : serving to decorate; *esp* : purely ornamental — **dec·o·ra·tive·ly** *adv* — **dec·o·ra·tive·ness** *n*

[1]**dec·o·ra·tor** \ˈdek-ə-ˌrāt-ər\ *n* : one that decorates; *esp* : one that designs or executes interiors and their furnishings

[2]**decorator** *adj* : suitable for interior decoration ⟨~ fabrics⟩

dec·o·rous \ˈdek-ə-rəs *also* di-ˈkōr-əs *or* -ˈkȯr-\ *adj* [L *decorus,* fr. *decor* beauty, grace; akin to L *decēre* to be fitting — more at DECENT] : marked by propriety and good taste : CORRECT ⟨~ conduct⟩ — **dec·o·rous·ly** *adv* — **dec·o·rous·ness** *n*

de·cor·ti·cate \(ˈ)dē-ˈkȯrt-ə-ˌkāt\ *vt* **-cat·ed; -cat·ing** [L *decorticatus,* pp. of *decorticare* to remove the bark from, fr. *de-* + *cortic-, cortex* bark — more at CORTEX] **1 :** to peel the outer covering from **2 :** to remove all or part of the cortex from (as the brain) — **de·cor·ti·ca·tion** \(ˌ)dē-ˌkȯrt-ə-ˈkā-shən\ *n* — **de·cor·ti·ca·tor** \(ˈ)dē-ˈkȯrt-ə-ˌkāt-ər\ *n*

de·co·rum \di-ˈkōr-əm, -ˈkȯr-\ *n* [L, fr. neut. of *decorus*] **1 :** literary and dramatic propriety : FITNESS **2 :** propriety and good taste in conduct or appearance **3 :** ORDERLINESS **4** *pl* : the conventions of polite behavior

de·cou·page *or* **dé·cou·page** \ˌdā-(ˌ)kü-ˈpäzh\ *n* [F *découpage,* lit., act of cutting out, fr. MF, fr. *decouper* to cut out, fr. *de-* + *couper* to cut — more at COPE] **1 :** the art of decorating surfaces by applying cutouts (as of paper) and then coating with usu. several layers of finish (as lacquer or varnish) **2 :** work produced by decoupage

[1]**de·coy** \ˈdē-ˌkȯi, di-ˈ\ *n* [prob. fr. D *de kooi,* lit., the cage, fr. *de,* masc. def. art. (akin to OE *thæt,* neut. def. article) + *kooi* cage, fr. L *cavea* — more at THAT, CAGE] **1 :** a pond into which wildfowl are lured for capture **2 :** one that is used to lure or lead another into a trap; *esp* : an artificial bird used to attract live birds within shot

[2]**de·coy** \di-ˈkȯi, ˈdē-ˌ\ *vt* : to lure by or as if by a decoy : ENTICE ***syn*** see LURE

[1]**de·crease** \di-ˈkrēs, ˈdē-ˌ\ *vb* **de·creased; de·creas·ing** [ME *decreessen,* fr. (assumed) AF *decreistre,* fr. L *decrescere,* fr. *de-* + *crescere* to grow — more at CRESCENT] *vi* : to grow progressively less (as in size, amount, number, or intensity) ~ *vt* : to cause to decrease — **de·creas·ing·ly** \di-ˈkrē-siŋ-lē\ *adv*

syn DECREASE, LESSEN, DIMINISH, REDUCE, ABATE, DWINDLE *shared meaning element* : to grow or make less ***ant*** increase

[2]**de·crease** \ˈdē-ˌkrēs, di-ˈ\ *n* **1 :** the process of decreasing **2 :** an amount of diminution : REDUCTION

[1]**de·cree** \di-ˈkrē\ *n* [ME, fr. MF *decré,* fr. L *decretum,* fr. neut. of *decretus,* pp. of *decernere* to decide, fr. *de-* + *cernere* to sift, decide — more at CERTAIN] **1 :** an order usu. having the force of law **2 a :** a religious ordinance enacted by council or titular head **b :** a foreordaining will **3 a :** a judicial decision of the Roman emperor **b :** a judicial decision esp. in an equity or probate court

[2]**decree** *vb* **de·creed; de·cree·ing** *vt* **1 :** to command or enjoin by decree ⟨~ an amnesty⟩ **2 :** to determine or order judicially ⟨~ a punishment⟩ ~ *vi* : ORDAIN — **de·cre·er** \-ˈkrē-ər\ *n*

de·cree–law \di-ˈkrē-ˌlȯ\ *n* : a decree of a ruler or ministry having the force of a law enacted by the legislature

dec·re·ment \ˈdek-rə-mənt\ *n* [L *decrementum,* fr. *decrescere*] **1** : a gradual decrease in quality or quantity **2 a :** the quantity lost by diminution or waste **b :** a negative mathematical increment — **dec·re·men·tal** \ˌdek-rə-ˈment-ᵊl\ *adj*

de·crep·it \di-ˈkrep-ət\ *adj* [ME, fr. MF, fr. L *decrepitus*] **1** : wasted and weakened by or as if by the infirmities of old age **2 a :** impaired by use or wear : WORN-OUT **b :** fallen into ruin or disrepair **3 :** DILAPIDATED, RUN-DOWN ***syn*** see WEAK ***ant*** sturdy — **de·crep·it·ly** *adv*

de·crep·i·tate \di-ˈkrep-ə-ˌtāt\ *vb* [prob. fr. (assumed) NL *decrepitatus,* pp. of *decrepitare,* fr. L *de-* + *crepitare* to crackle — more at CREPITATE] *vt* : to roast or calcine (as salt) so as to cause crackling or until crackling stops ~ *vi* : to become decrepitated — **de·crep·i·ta·tion** \-ˌkrep-ə-ˈtā-shən\ *n*

de·crep·i·tude \di-ˈkrep-ə-ˌt(y)üd\ *n* : the quality or state of being decrepit

[1]**de·cre·scen·do** \ˌdā-krə-ˈshen-(ˌ)dō\ *adv or adj* [It, lit., decreasing, fr. L *decrescendum,* gerund of *decrescere*] : with a decrease in volume — used as a direction in music

[2]**decrescendo** *n, pl* **-dos 1 :** a gradual decrease in volume of a musical passage **2 :** a decrescendo musical passage

mark indicating decrescendo 2

de·cres·cent \di-ˈkres-ᵊnt\ *adj* [alter. of earlier *decressant,* prob. fr. AF, prp. of (assumed) AF *decreistre* to decrease] : becoming less by gradual diminution : DECREASING, WANING

de·cre·tal \di-ˈkrēt-ᵊl\ *n* [ME *decretale,* fr. MF, fr. LL *decretalis* of a decree, fr. L *decretum* decree] : DECREE; *esp* : a papal letter giving an authoritative decision on a point of canon law

de·cre·tive \-ˈkrēt-iv\ *adj* : having the force of a decree : DECRETORY

dec·re·to·ry \ˈdek-rə-ˌtōr-ē, -ˌtȯr-; di-ˈkrēt-ə-rē\ *adj* : relating to or fixed by a decree or decision

de·cry \di-ˈkrī\ *vt* [F *décrier,* fr. OF *descrier,* fr. *des-* de- + *crier* to cry] **1 :** to depreciate (as a coin) officially or publicly **2 :** to express strong disapproval of ⟨~ the emphasis on sex⟩ — **de·cri·er** \-ˈkrī(-ə)r\ *n*

syn DECRY, DEPRECIATE, DISPARAGE, BELITTLE, MINIMIZE *shared meaning element* : to give expression to one's low opinion of something ***ant*** extol

de·crypt \(ˈ)dē-ˈkript\ *vt* [ISV *de-* + *crypto*gram, *crypto*graph] **1** : DECIPHER **2 :** DECODE — **de·cryp·tion** \-ˈkrip-shən\ *n*

de·cryp·to·graph \-ˈkrip-tə-ˌgraf\ *vt* : DECRYPT

de·cum·bent \di-ˈkəm-bənt\ *adj* [L *decumbent-, decumbens,* prp. of *decumbere* to lie down, fr. *de-* + *-cumbere* to lie down — more at SUCCUMB] **1 :** lying down **2** *of a plant* : reclining on the ground but with ascending apex or extremity

dec·u·ple \ˈdek-yə-pəl\ *adj* [F *décuple,* fr. MF, fr. LL *decuplus,* fr. L *decem* ten + *-plus* multiplied by — more at TEN, DOUBLE] **1 :** TENFOLD **2 :** taken in groups of 10

de·cu·ri·on \di-ˈkyu̇r-ē-ən\ *n* [ME *decurioun,* fr. L *decurion-, decurio,* fr. *decuria* division of ten, fr. *decem*] **1 :** a Roman cavalry officer in command of 10 men **2 :** a member of a Roman senate

de·curved \(ˈ)dē-ˈkərvd\ *adj* [part trans. of LL *decurvatus,* fr. L *de-* + *curvatus* curved] : curved downward : bent down

[1]**de·cus·sate** \ˈdek-ə-ˌsāt, di-ˈkəs-ˌāt\ *vb* **-sat·ed; -sat·ing** [L *decussatus,* pp. of *decussare,* fr. *decussis* the number ten, numeral X, intersection, fr. *decem* + *ass-, as* unit — more at ACE] : INTERSECT

293

²de·cus·sate \'dek-ə-ˌsāt, di-'kəs-ət\ *adj* 1 : shaped like an X 2 : arranged in pairs each at right angles to the next pair above or below ⟨~ leaves⟩ — **de·cus·sate·ly** *adv*

de·cus·sa·tion \ˌdek-ə-'sā-shən, ˌdē-kə-\ *n* 1 : an intersection in the form of an X 2 : a band of nerve fibers that connects unlike centers of opposite sides of the central nervous system

de-dans \də-'däⁿ\ *n, pl* dedans \-'däⁿ(z)\ [F, lit., interior] 1 : an open gallery at the service end of the court in court tennis 2 : the spectators at a court-tennis match

¹ded·i·cate \'ded-i-kət\ *adj* [ME, fr. L *dedicatus*, pp. of *dedicare* to dedicate, fr. *de-* + *dicare* to proclaim, dedicate — more at DICTION] : DEDICATED

²ded·i·cate \'ded-i-ˌkāt\ *vt* -cat·ed; -cat·ing 1 : to devote to the worship of a divine being; *specif* : to set apart (a church) to sacred uses with solemn rites 2 a : to set apart to a definite use ⟨money *dedicated* to their vacation fund⟩ b : to become committed to as a goal or way of life ⟨ready to ~ his life to public service⟩ 3 : to inscribe or address by way of compliment ⟨~ a book to a friend⟩ 4 : to open to public use *syn see* DEVOTE — **ded·i·ca·tor** \-ˌkāt-ər\ *n*

ded·i·cat·ed *adj* 1 : devoted to a cause, ideal, or purpose : ZEALOUS ⟨a ~ scholar⟩ 2 : given over to a particular purpose ⟨a ~ process control computer⟩ — **ded·i·cat·ed·ly** *adv*

ded·i·ca·tion \ˌded-i-'kā-shən\ *n* 1 : an act or rite of dedicating to a divine being or to a sacred use 2 : a devoting or setting aside for a particular purpose 3 : a name and often a message prefixed to a literary, musical, or artistic production in tribute to a person or cause 4 : self-sacrificing devotion — **ded·i·ca·tive** \'ded-i-ˌkāt-iv, -ˌkət-\ *adj* — **ded·i·ca·to·ry** \'ded-i-kə-ˌtōr-ē, -ˌtȯr-\ *adj*

de·dif·fer·en·ti·a·tion \(ˌ)dē-ˌdif-ə-ˌren-chē-'ā-shən\ *n* : reversion of specialized structures (as cells) to a more generalized or primitive condition often as a preliminary to major change

de·duce \di-'d(y)üs\ *vt* de·duced; de·duc·ing [L *deducere*, lit., to lead away, fr. *de-* + *ducere* to lead — more at TOW] 1 : to trace the course of 2 : to determine by deduction; *specif* : to infer from a general principle — compare INDUCE *syn see* INFER — **de·duc·ible** \-'d(y)ü-sə-bəl\ *adj*

de·duct \di-'dəkt\ *vt* [L *deductus*, pp. of *deducere*] 1 : to take away (an amount) from a total : SUBTRACT 2 : DEDUCE, INFER

¹de·duct·ible \di-'dək-tə-bəl\ *adj* : capable of being deducted — **de·duct·ibil·i·ty** \-ˌdək-tə-'bil-ət-ē\ *n*

²deductible *n* : a clause in an insurance policy that relieves the insurer of responsibility for an initial specified loss of the kind insured against

de·duc·tion \di-'dək-shən\ *n* 1 a : an act of taking away ⟨~ of legitimate business expenses⟩ b : something that is or may be subtracted ⟨~s from his taxable income⟩ 2 a : the deriving of a conclusion by reasoning; *specif* : inference in which the conclusion follows necessarily from the premises b : a conclusion reached by logical deduction

de·duc·tive \di-'dək-tiv\ *adj* 1 a : of or relating to deduction b : employing deduction in reasoning 2 : capable of being deduced from premises : INFERENTIAL — **de·duc·tive·ly** *adv*

dee \'dē\ *n* : the letter d

¹deed \'dēd\ *n* [ME *dede*, fr. OE *dǣd*; akin to OE *dōn* to do] 1 : something that is done ⟨evil ~s⟩ 2 : a usu. illustrious act or action : FEAT, EXPLOIT 3 : the act of performing ⟨a righteous man who never mistook the word for the ~⟩ 4 : a signed and usu. sealed instrument containing some legal transfer, bargain, or contract *syn see* ACTION — **deed·less** \-ləs\ *adj*

²deed *vt* : to convey or transfer by deed *syn see* TRANSFER

deed poll \-'pōl\ *n, pl* deeds poll [¹deed + poll, adj. (having the edges cut even rather than indented), fr. ²poll] : a deed made and executed by only one party

deedy \'dēd-ē\ *adj* deed·i·er; -est *dial chiefly Eng* : INDUSTRIOUS

dee·jay \'dē-ˌjā\ *n* [disc jockey] : DISC JOCKEY

deem \'dēm\ *vb* [ME *demen*, fr. OE *dēman*; akin to OHG *tuomen* to judge, OE *dōm* doom] *vt* 1 : to come to think or judge : HOLD ⟨~ed it wise to go slow⟩ ~ *vi* : to have an opinion : BELIEVE

de-em·pha·size \(')dē-'em(p)-fə-ˌsīz\ *vt* : to play down — **de-em·pha·sis** \-fə-səs\ *n*

¹deep \'dēp\ *adj* [ME, fr. OE *dēop*; akin to OHG *tiof* deep, OE *dyppan* to dip — more at DIP] 1 : extending far from some surface or area: as a : extending far downward ⟨a ~ well⟩ b (1) : extending well inward from an outer surface ⟨a ~ gash⟩ ⟨a *deep*-chested animal⟩ (2) : not located superficially within the body ⟨~ pressure receptors in muscles⟩ c : extending well back from a front surface ⟨a ~ closet⟩ d : extending far laterally from the center ⟨~ borders of lace⟩ e : occurring or located near the outer limits of the playing area ⟨hit to ~ right field⟩ 2 : having a specified extension in an implied direction usu. downward or backward ⟨shelf 20 inches ~⟩ ⟨cars parked three-*deep*⟩ 3 a : difficult to penetrate or comprehend : RECONDITE ⟨~ mathematical problems⟩ b : MYSTERIOUS, OBSCURE ⟨a ~ dark secret⟩ c : grave in nature or effect : GRIEVOUS ⟨in ~est disgrace⟩ d : of penetrating intellect : WISE ⟨a ~ thinker⟩ e : ENGROSSED, INVOLVED ⟨a man ~ in debt⟩ f : characterized by profundity of feeling or quality ⟨a ~ sleep⟩; *also* : DEEP-SEATED ⟨~ religious beliefs⟩ 4 a : of color : high in saturation and low in lightness b : having a low musical pitch or pitch range ⟨a ~ voice⟩ 5 a : situated well within the boundaries ⟨a house ~ in the woods⟩ b : remote in time or space ⟨had its roots ~ in the Middle Ages —Roy Lewis & Angus Maude⟩ c : being below the level of the conscious ⟨~ neuroses⟩ d : covered, enclosed, or filled to a specified degree — usu. used in combination ⟨she was ankle-*deep* in mud⟩ — **deep·ly** *adv* — **deep·ness** *n*

syn 1 DEEP, PROFOUND, ABYSMAL *shared meaning element* : having great extension downward or inward

2 *see* BROAD *ant* shallow

in deep water : in difficulty or distress

²deep *adv* 1 : to a great depth : DEEPLY ⟨still waters run ~⟩ 2 : far on : LATE ⟨danced ~ into the night⟩ 3 : near the outer limits of the playing area ⟨the shortstop was playing ~⟩

³deep *n* 1 : any of the fathom points on a sounding line that is not a mark 2 a : a vast or immeasurable extent : ABYSS b (1) : the

extent of surrounding space or time (2) : OCEAN 3 : the middle or most intense part ⟨the ~ of winter⟩ 4 : one of the deep portions of any body of water; *specif* : a generally long and narrow area in the ocean where the depth exceeds 3000 fathoms

deep–dish pie *n* : a pie usu. with a fruit filling and no bottom crust that is baked in a deep dish

deep·en \'dē-pən, 'dēp-ᵊm\ *vb* deep·ened; deep·en·ing \'dēp-(ə-)niŋ\ *vt* : to make deep or deeper ~ *vi* : to become deeper or more profound

deep fat *n* : hot fat or oil deep enough in a cooking utensil to cover the food to be fried

deep–freeze \'dēp-'frēz\ *vt* -froze \-'frōz\; -fro·zen \-'frōz-ᵊn\ 1 : QUICK-FREEZE 2 : CHILL, REFRIGERATE

deep–go·ing \'dēp-'gō-iŋ, -ˌgȯ(-)iŋ\ *adj* : FUNDAMENTAL ⟨a ~ theory⟩

deep kiss *n* : FRENCH KISS

deep–root·ed \'dēp-'prüt-əd, -'prüt-\ *adj* : deeply implanted or established ⟨a ~ loyalty⟩ *syn see* INVETERATE

deep–sea \ˌdēp-'sē\ *adj* : of, relating to, or occurring in the deeper parts of the sea ⟨~ fishing⟩

deep–seat·ed \'dēp-'sēt-əd\ *adj* 1 : situated far below the surface ⟨a ~ inflammation⟩ 2 : firmly established ⟨a ~ tradition⟩ *syn see* INVETERATE

deep–six \ -vt 1 *slang* : to throw overboard 2 *slang* : to throw away : DISCARD

deep six *n* [naval slang for "burial at sea"; perh. fr. the tradition of burying bodies six feet under ground] *slang* : a place of disposal or abandonment — used esp. in the phrase *give it the deep six*

deep space *n* : space well beyond the limits of the earth's atmosphere including space outside the solar system

deep structure *n* : a formal representation of the underlying semantic content of a sentence; *also* : the structure which such a representation specifies

deer \'di(ə)r\ *n, pl* deer *also* deers [ME, deer, animal, fr. OE *dēor* beast; akin to OHG *tior* wild animal, Skt *dhvaṃsati* he perishes] 1 *archaic* : ANIMAL; *esp* : a small mammal 2 : a ruminant mammal (family Cervidae, the deer family) having two large and two small hoofs on each foot and antlers borne by the males of nearly all and by the females of a few forms

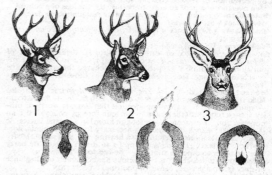

deer 2: *1* blacktailed deer, *2* whitetail, *3* mule deer

deer·ber·ry \-ˌber-ē\ *n* 1 : either of two shrubs (*Vaccinium stamineum* or *V. caesium*) of dry woods and scrub of the eastern U.S. 2 : the edible fruit of a deerberry

deer·fly \'di(ə)r-ˌflī\ *n* : any of numerous small horseflies (as of the genus *Chrysops*) that include important vectors of tularemia

deer·hound \-ˌhaünd\ *n* : SCOTTISH DEERHOUND

deer mouse *n* [fr. its agility] : WHITE-FOOTED MOUSE

deer·skin \'di(ə)r-ˌskin\ *n* : leather made from the skin of a deer; *also* : a garment of this leather

deer·stalk·er hat \-ˌstȯ-kər-\ *n* : a close-fitting hat with a visor at the front and the back and with earflaps that may be worn up or down — called also *deerstalker*

deer·yard \'di(ə)r-ˌyärd\ *n* : a place where deer herd in winter

de-es·ca·late \(')dē-'es-kə-ˌlāt, *nonstand* -kyə-\ *vi* : to decrease in extent, volume, or scope ~ *vt* : LIMIT 2 — **de-es·ca·la·tion** \(ˌ)ēs-kə-'lā-shən, *nonstand* -kyə-\ *n* — **de-es·ca·la·to·ry** \(')dē-'es-kə-lə-ˌtōr-ē, -ˌtȯr-, *nonstand* -kyə-\ *adj*

def *abbr* 1 defendant 2 defense 3 deferred 4 defined 5 definite 6 definition

de·face \di-'fās\ *vt* [ME *defacen*, fr. MF *desfacier*, fr. OF, fr. *des-* + *face* ¹face] 1 : to mar the external appearance of : injure by effacing significant details ⟨~ an inscription⟩ 2 : IMPAIR 3 *obs* : DESTROY — **de·face·ment** \-'fā-smənt\ *n* — **de·fac·er** *n*

syn DEFACE, DISFEATURE, DISFIGURE *shared meaning element* : to mar the appearance of

¹de fac·to \di-'fak-(ˌ)tō, dā-\ *adv* [NL] : in reality : ACTUALLY

²de facto *adj* 1 : exercising power as if legally constituted ⟨a *de facto* government⟩ 2 : ACTUAL ⟨a *de facto* state of war⟩ — compare DE JURE

de·fal·cate \di-'fal-ˌkāt, di-'fȯl-; 'def-əl-\ *vb* -cat·ed; -cat·ing [ML *defalcatus*, pp. of *defalcare*, fr. L *de-* + *falc-, falx* sickle] *vt, archaic*

: DEDUCT, CURTAIL ~ *vi* : to engage in embezzlement — **de·fal·ca·tor** \-ˌkāt-ər\ *n*

de·fal·ca·tion \ˌdē-ˌfal-ˈkā-shən, ˌdē-ˌfȯl-, di-; ˌdef-əl-\ *n* **1** *archaic* : DEDUCTION **2** : the act or an instance of embezzling **3** : a failure to meet a promise or an expectation

def·a·ma·tion \ˌdef-ə-ˈmā-shən\ *n* : the act of defaming another : CALUMNY — **de·fam·a·to·ry** \di-ˈfam-ə-ˌtōr-ē, -ˌtȯr-\ *adj*

de·fame \di-ˈfām\ *vt* **de·famed; de·fam·ing** [ME *diffamen, defamen,* fr. MF & L; ME *diffamen* fr. MF *diffamer,* fr. L *diffamare,* fr. *dis-* + *fama* fame; ME *defamen* fr. MF *defamer,* fr. ML *defamare,* fr. L *de-* + *fama*] **1** *archaic* : DISGRACE **2** : to harm the reputation of by libel or slander **3** *archaic* : ACCUSE ***syn*** see MALIGN — **de·fam·er** *n*

de·fat \(ˈ)dē-ˈfat\ *vt* : to remove fat from

1de·fault \di-ˈfȯlt\ *n* [ME *defaute, defaulte,* fr. OF *defaute,* fr. (assumed) VL *defallita,* fr. fem. of *defallitus,* pp. of *defallere* to be lacking, fail, fr. L *de-* + *fallere* to deceive] **1** : failure to do something required by duty or law : NEGLECT **2** *archaic* : FAULT **3** : a failure to pay financial debts **4** **a** : failure to appear at the required time in a legal proceeding **b** : failure to compete in or to finish an appointed contest — **in default of** : in the absence of

2default *vi* : to fail to fulfill a contract, agreement, or duty: as **a** : to fail to meet a financial obligation **b** : to fail to appear in court **c** : to fail to compete in or to finish an appointed contest; *also* : to forfeit a contest by such failure ~ *vt* **1** : to fail to perform, pay, or make good **2** : FORFEIT — **de·fault·er** *n*

de·fea·sance \di-ˈfēz-ᵊn(t)s\ *n* [ME *defesance,* fr. AF, fr. OF *deffesant,* prp. of *deffaire*] **1** **a** : a rendering null or void **b** (1) : the termination of a property interest in accordance with stipulated conditions (as in a deed) (2) : an instrument stating such conditions of limitation **2** : DEFEAT, OVERTHROW

de·fea·si·ble \di-ˈfē-zə-bəl\ *adj* : capable of being annulled or made void ⟨a ~ claim to an estate⟩ — **de·fea·si·bil·i·ty** \-ˌfē-zə-ˈbil-ət-ē\ *n*

1de·feat \di-ˈfēt\ *vt* [ME *deffeten,* fr. MF *deffait,* pp. of *deffaire* to destroy, fr. ML *disfacere,* fr. L *dis-* + *facere* to do — more at DO] **1** *obs* : DESTROY **2** **a** : NULLIFY ⟨~ an estate⟩ **b** : FRUSTRATE ⟨~ a hope⟩ **3** : to win victory over : BEAT ⟨~ the opposing team⟩

2defeat *n* **1** *obs* : DESTRUCTION **2** : frustration by nullification or by prevention of success ⟨the bill suffered ~ in the Senate⟩ **3** **a** : an overthrow esp. of an army in battle **b** : the loss of a contest

de·feat·ism \-ˌiz-əm\ *n* : acceptance of or resignation to defeat — **de·feat·ist** \-əst\ *n or adj*

1de·fea·ture \di-ˈfē-chər\ *n* [prob. fr. *de-* + *feature*] *archaic* : DISFIGUREMENT

2defeature *n* [1*defeat*] *archaic* : DEFEAT

def·e·cate \ˈdef-i-ˌkāt\ *vb* **-cat·ed; -cat·ing** [L *defaecatus,* pp. of *defaecare,* fr. *de-* + *faec-, faex* dregs, lees] *vt* **1** : to free from impurity or corruption : REFINE **2** : to discharge through the anus ~ *vi* : to discharge feces from the bowels — **def·e·ca·tion** \ˌdef-i-ˈkā-shən\ *n*

1de·fect \ˈdē-ˌfekt, di-ˈ\ *n* [ME *defaicte,* fr. MF *defect,* fr. L *defectus* lack, fr. *defectus,* pp. of *deficere* to desert, fail, fr. *de-* + *facere* to do — more at DO] **1** **a** : an imperfection that impairs worth or utility : SHORTCOMING ⟨the grave ~s in our foreign policy⟩ **b** : an imperfection (as a vacancy or a foreign atom) in a crystal lattice **2** [L *defectus*] : a lack of something necessary for completeness, adequacy, or perfection : DEFICIENCY ⟨a hearing ~⟩ ***syn*** see BLEMISH

2de·fect \di-ˈfekt\ *vi* [L *defectus,* pp.] : to desert a cause or party often in order to espouse another — **de·fec·tor** \-ˈfek-tər\ *n*

de·fec·tion \di-ˈfek-shən\ *n* : conscious abandonment of allegiance or duty (as to a person, cause, or doctrine) : DESERTION

1de·fec·tive \di-ˈfek-tiv\ *adj* **1** : lacking something essential : FAULTY ⟨a ~ pane of glass⟩ ⟨~ eyesight⟩ **2** : lacking one or more of the usual forms of grammatical inflection ⟨*must* is a ~ verb⟩ **3** : markedly subnormal mentally or physically — **de·fec·tive·ly** *adv* — **de·fec·tive·ness** *n*

2defective *n* : a person who is subnormal physically or mentally

defective year *n* : a common year of 353 days or a leap year of 383 days in the Jewish calendar

de·fem·i·nize \(ˈ)dē-ˈfem-ə-ˌnīz\ *vt* : to divest of feminine qualities or characteristics : MASCULINIZE

de·fend \di-ˈfend\ *vb* [ME *defenden,* fr. OF *defendre,* fr. L *defendere,* fr. *de-* + *-fendere* to strike; akin to OE *gūth* battle, war, Gk *theinein* to strike] *vt* **1** *archaic* : PREVENT, FORBID **2** **a** : to drive danger or attack away from **b** : to maintain in the face of argument or hostile criticism **c** : to attempt to prevent an opponent from scoring at ⟨elects to ~ the south goal⟩ **3** : to act as attorney for **4** : to deny or oppose the right of a plaintiff in regard to (a suit or a wrong charged) : CONTEST ~ *vi* **1** : to take action against attack or challenge ⟨couldn't fight back, could only ~⟩ **2** : to play or be on defense ⟨playing deep to ~ against a pass⟩ **3** : to play against the high bidder in a card game

syn **1** DEFEND, PROTECT, SHIELD, GUARD, SAFEGUARD *shared meaning element* : to keep secure (as from danger or against attack) ***ant*** combat, attack

2 see MAINTAIN

de·fend·able \di-ˈfen-də-bəl\ *adj* : DEFENSIBLE

1de·fen·dant \di-ˈfen-dənt\ *n* : a person required to make answer in a legal action or suit — compare PLAINTIFF

2defendant *adj* : being on the defensive : DEFENDING

de·fend·er \di-ˈfen-dər\ *n* **1** : one that defends **2** : a player in a sport (as football) assigned to a defensive position

de·fen·es·tra·tion \(ˌ)dē-ˌfen-ə-ˈstrā-shən\ *n* [*de-* + L *fenestra* window] : a throwing of a person or thing out of a window — **de·fen·es·trate** \(ˈ)dē-ˈfen-ə-ˌstrāt\ *vt*

1de·fense *or* **de·fence** \di-ˈfen(t)s; *as antonym of "offense," often* ˈdē-ˌ\ *n* [ME, fr. OF, fr. (assumed) VL *defensa,* fr. L, fem. of *defensus,* pp. of *defendere*] **1** **a** : the act or action of defending ⟨the ~ of one's country⟩ ⟨to speak out in ~ of justice⟩ **b** : a defendant's denial, answer, or plea **2** : capability of resisting attack **3** **a** : means or method of defending or protecting oneself or another; *also* : a defensive structure **b** : an argument in support or justification **c** : the collected facts and method adopted by a defendant to protect himself against a plaintiff's action **d** : a sequence of moves available in chess to the second player in the opening **4** **a** : a defending party or group (as in a court of law) ⟨the ~ rested its case⟩ **b** : a defensive team **5** : the military, governmental, and industrial aggregate esp. in its capacity of authorizing and supervising arms production ⟨~ budget⟩ ⟨~ contract⟩ — **de·fense·less** \-ləs\ *adj* — **de·fense·less·ly** *adv* — **de·fense·less·ness** *n*

2defense *vt* **de·fensed; de·fens·ing** : to take specific defensive action against (an opposing team or player)

de·fense·man \-mən, -ˌman\ *n* : a player in a sport (as hockey) assigned to a defensive zone or position

defense mechanism *n* **1** : a defensive reaction by an organism **2** : an often unconscious mental process (as repression, projection, or sublimation) that enables the ego to reach compromise solutions to problems

de·fen·si·ble \di-ˈfen(t)-sə-bəl\ *adj* : capable of being defended — **de·fen·si·bil·i·ty** \di-ˌfen(t)-sə-ˈbil-ət-ē, ˌdē-\ *n* — **de·fen·si·bly** \-blē\ *adv*

1de·fen·sive \di-ˈfen(t)-siv, ˈdē-ˌ\ *adj* **1** : serving to defend or protect **2** **a** : devoted to resisting or preventing aggression or attack **b** : of or relating to the attempt to keep an opponent from scoring in a game or contest **3** **a** : valuable in defensive play ⟨a ~ card in bridge⟩ **b** : designed to keep an opponent from being the highest bidder ⟨a ~ bid⟩ — **de·fen·sive·ly** *adv* — **de·fen·sive·ness** *n*

2defensive *n* : a defensive position — **on the defensive** : in the state or condition of being prepared for an expected aggression or attack

1de·fer \di-ˈfər\ *vt* **de·ferred; de·fer·ring** [ME *deferren, differren,* fr. MF *differer,* fr. L *differre* to postpone, be different — more at DIFFER] : to put off : DELAY ⟨forced to ~ college because of financial problems⟩ — **de·fer·rer** *n*

syn DEFER, POSTPONE, INTERMIT, SUSPEND, STAY *shared meaning element* : to delay an action or proceeding

2defer *vb* **deferred; deferring** [ME *deferren, differren,* fr. MF *deferer, defferer,* fr. LL *deferre,* fr. L, to bring down, bring, fr. *de-* + *ferre* to carry — more at BEAR] *vt* : to delegate to another ⟨he could ~ his job to no one —J. A. Michener⟩ ~ *vi* : to submit to another's wishes, opinion, or governance usu. through deference or respect ⟨a man who *deferred* only to God⟩ ***syn*** see YIELD

def·er·ence \ˈdef-(ə-)rən(t)s\ *n* : respect and esteem due a superior or an elder; *also* : affected or ingratiating regard for another's wishes ***syn*** see HONOR ***ant*** disrespect — **in deference to** : in consideration of

1def·er·ent \ˈdef-ə-rənt, -ˌer-ənt\ *adj* [L *deferent-, deferens,* prp. of *deferre*] : serving to carry down or out ⟨a ~ conduit⟩

2def·er·ent \ˈdef-(ə-)rənt\ *adj* [back-formation fr. *deference*] : DEFERENTIAL

def·er·en·tial \ˌdef-ə-ˈren-chəl\ *adj* : showing or expressing deference ⟨~ attention⟩ — **def·er·en·tial·ly** \-ˈrench-(ə-)lē\ *adv*

de·fer·ment \di-ˈfər-mənt\ *n* : the act of delaying or postponing; *specif* : official postponement of military service

de·fer·ra·ble \di-ˈfər-ə-bəl\ *adj* : capable of or suitable or eligible for being deferred — **deferrable** *n*

de·fer·ral \di-ˈfər-əl\ *n* : DEFERMENT

de·ferred *adj* **1** : withheld for or until a stated time ⟨a ~ payment⟩ **2** : charged in cases of delayed handling ⟨a ~ rate⟩

de·fer·ves·cence \ˌdē-(ˌ)fər-ˈves-ᵊn(t)s, ˌdef-ər-\ *n* [G *deferveszenz,* fr. L *defervescent-, defervescens,* prp. of *defervescere* to stop boiling, fr. *de-* + *fervescere* to begin to boil — more at EFFERVESCE] : the subsidence of a fever

de·fi·ance \di-ˈfī-ən(t)s\ *n* **1** : the act or an instance of defying : CHALLENGE **2** : disposition to resist or contempt of opposition — **in defiance of** : contrary to : DESPITE ⟨worked *in defiance of* doctor's orders⟩

de·fi·ant \-ənt\ *adj* [F *défiant,* fr. OF, prp. of *defier* to defy] : full of defiance : BOLD — **de·fi·ant·ly** *adv*

de·fi·bril·late \(ˈ)dē-ˈfib-rə-ˌlāt, -ˈfīb-\ *vt* : to restore the rhythm of (a fibrillating heart) — **de·fi·bril·la·tion** \(ˌ)dē-ˌfib-rə-ˈlā-shən, -ˌfīb-\ *n* — **de·fi·bril·la·tive** \(ˈ)dē-ˈfib-rə-ˌlāt-iv, -ˈfīb-\ *adj* — **de·fi·bril·la·tor** \-ˌlāt-ər\ *n* — **de·fi·bril·la·to·ry** \(ˈ)dē-ˈfib-rə-lə-ˌtōr-ē, -ˈfīb-; ˌdē-fī-ˈbril-ə-\ *adj*

de·fi·brin·ate \(ˈ)dē-ˈfib-rə-ˌnāt, -ˈfīb-\ *vt* **-at·ed -at·ing** : to remove fibrin from (blood) — **de·fi·brin·ation** \(ˌ)dē-ˌfib-rə-ˈnā-shən, -ˌfīb-\ *n*

de·fi·cien·cy \di-ˈfish-ən-sē\ *n, pl* **-cies** **1** : the quality or state of being deficient : INADEQUACY **2** **a** : a shortage of substances necessary to health **b** : absence of one or more genes from a chromosome

deficiency disease *n* : a disease (as scurvy) caused by a lack of essential dietary elements and esp. a vitamin or mineral

1de·fi·cient \di-ˈfish-ənt\ *adj* [L *deficient-, deficiens,* prp. of *deficere* to be wanting — more at DEFECT] **1** : lacking in some necessary quality or element ⟨~ in judgment⟩ **2** : not up to a normal standard or complement : DEFECTIVE ⟨~ strength⟩ — **de·fi·cient·ly** *adv*

2deficient *n* : one that is deficient ⟨a mental ~⟩

def·i·cit \ˈdef-ə-sət *also, esp Brit,* di-ˈfis-ət *or* ˈdē-fə-sət\ *n* [F *déficit,* fr. L *deficit* it is wanting, 3d sing. pres. indic. of *deficere*] **1** **a** : deficiency in amount or quality ⟨a ~ in rainfall⟩ **b** : DISADVANTAGE ⟨a two-run homer in the sixth that overcame a 2-1 ~⟩ **2** **a** : an excess of expenditure over revenue **b** : a loss in business operations

deficit spending *n* : the spending of public funds raised by borrowing rather than by taxation

de·fi·er \di-ˈfī(-ə)r\ *n* : one that defies

1def·i·lade \ˈdef-ə-ˌlād, -ˌläd\ *vt* **-lad·ed; -lad·ing** [prob. fr. *de-* + *-filade* (as in *enfilade*)] : to arrange (fortifications) so as to protect the lines from frontal or enfilading fire and the interior of the works from plunging or reverse fire

2defilade *n* : the act or process of defilading

1de·file \di-ˈfī(ə)l\ *vt* **de·filed; de·fil·ing** [ME *defilen,* alter. of *defoulen* to trample, defile, fr. OF *defouler* to trample, fr. *de-* + *fouler* to trample, lit., to full — more at FULL] : to make unclean or impure : BEFOUL, BESMIRCH: as **a** : to corrupt the purity or perfection of : DEBASE ⟨the countryside *defiled* by billboards⟩ **b** : to denude of chastity : DEFLOWER **c** : to make physically unclean esp. with something unpleasant or contaminating ⟨boots *defiled* with blood⟩ **d** : to make ceremonially unclean ⟨~ a sanctuary⟩ **e** : SULLY, DISHONOR ***syn*** see CONTAMINATE — **de·file·ment** \-ˈfī(ə)l-mənt\ *n* — **de·fil·er** \-ˈfī-lər\ *n*

²de·file \di-ˈfī(ə)l, ˈdē-ˌfīl\ *vi* **de·filed; de·fil·ing** [F *défiler*, fr. *dé-* de- + *filer* to move in a column — more at FILE] : to march off in a line

³de·file \di-ˈfī(ə)l, ˈdē-ˌfīl\ *n* [F *défilé*, fr. pp. of *défiler*] : a narrow passage or gorge

de·fin·able \di-ˈfī-nə-bəl\ *adj* : capable of being defined, limited, or explained — **de·fin·ably** \-blē\ *adv*

de·fine \di-ˈfīn\ *vb* **de·fined; de·fin·ing** [ME *definen*, fr. MF & L; MF *definer*, fr. L *definire*, fr. *de-* + *finire* to limit, end, fr. *finis* boundary, end — more at FINAL] *vt* **1 a** : to fix or mark the limits of : DEMARCATE ⟨rigidly *defined* property lines⟩ **b** : to make distinct, clear, or detailed in outline ⟨the issues aren't too well *defined*⟩ **2 a** : to determine or identify the essential qualities or meaning of ⟨~ a powerful position by salary and prestige⟩ ⟨whatever ~*s* us as human⟩ **b** : to discover and set forth the meaning of (as a word) **3** : CHARACTERIZE, DISTINGUISH ⟨good manners ~ the gentleman⟩ ~ *vi* : to make a definition — **de·fine·ment** \-ˈfīn-mənt\ *n* — **de·fin·er** \-ˈfī-nər\ *n*

de·fin·i·en·dum \di-ˌfin-ē-ˈen-dəm\ *n, pl* **-da** \-də\ [L, something to be defined, neut. of *definiendus*, gerundive of *definire*] : an expression that is being defined

de·fin·i·ens \di-ˈfin-ē-ˌenz\ *n, pl* **de·fin·i·en·tia** \di-ˌfin-ēz'en-ch(ē-)ə\ [L, prp. of *definire*] : an expression that defines : DEFINITION

def·i·nite \ˈdef-(ə-)nət\ *adj* [L *definitus*, pp. of *definire*] **1** : having distinct or certain limits ⟨set ~ standards for pupils to meet⟩ **2 a** : free of all ambiguity, uncertainty, or obscurity ⟨demanded a ~ answer⟩ **b** : UNQUESTIONABLE, DECIDED ⟨the quarterback was a ~ hero today⟩ **3** : typically designating an identified or immediately identifiable person or thing ⟨the ~ article *the*⟩ **4 a** : being constant in number, usu. less than 20, and occurring in multiples of the petal number ⟨stamens ~⟩ **b** : CYMOSE ***syn*** see EXPLICIT ***ant*** indefinite, equivocal — **def·i·nite·ly** *adv* — **def·i·nite·ness** *n*

definite integral *n* : a number that is the difference between the values of the indefinite integral of a given function for two values of the independent variable

def·i·ni·tion \ˌdef-ə-ˈnish-ən\ *n* **1** : an act of determining; *specif* : the formal proclamation of a Roman Catholic dogma **2** : a word or phrase expressing the essential nature of a person or thing : MEANING ⟨the confinement of God within our human ~⟩ **3 a** : a statement of the meaning of a word or word group or a sign or symbol ⟨dictionary ~*s*⟩ **b** : the action or process of stating such a meaning **4 a** : the action or the power of describing, explaining, or making definite and clear ⟨the ~ of a telescope⟩ ⟨her comic genius is beyond ~⟩ **b** (1) : distinctness of outline or detail (as in a photograph) (2) : clarity esp. of musical sound in reproduction **c** : sharp demarcation of outlines or limits ⟨a jacket with definite waist ~⟩ — **def·i·ni·tion·al** \-ˈnish-nəl, -ˈnish-ən-ᵊl\ *adj*

¹de·fin·i·tive \di-ˈfin-ət-iv\ *adj* **1** : serving to provide a final solution ⟨a ~ victory⟩ **2** : authoritative and apparently exhaustive ⟨a ~ biography⟩ **3** : serving to define or specify precisely ⟨~ laws⟩ **4** : fully differentiated or developed **5** *of a postage stamp* : issued as a regular stamp for the country or territory in which it is to be used ***syn*** see CONCLUSIVE ***ant*** tentative, provisional — **de·fin·i·tive·ly** *adv* — **de·fin·i·tive·ness** *n*

²definitive *n* : a definitive postage stamp — compare PROVISIONAL

definitive host *n* : the host in which the sexual reproduction of a parasite takes place

de·fi·ni·tize \ˈdef-(ə-)nə-ˌtīz, di-ˈfin-ə-\ *vt* **-tized; -tiz·ing** : to make definite

de·fin·i·tude \di-ˈfin-ə-ˌt(y)üd, -ˈfī-nə-\ *n* [irreg. fr. *definite*] : PRECISION, DEFINITENESS

def·la·grate \ˈdef-lə-ˌgrāt\ *vb* **-grat·ed; -grat·ing** [L *deflagratus*, pp. of *deflagrare* to burn down, fr. *de-* + *flagrare* to burn — more at BLACK] *vi* : to burn rapidly with intense heat and sparks being given off ~ *vt* : to cause to deflagrate — compare DETONATE — **def·la·gra·tion** \ˌdef-lə-ˈgrā-shən\ *n*

de·flate \di-ˈflāt, ˈdē-\ *vb* **de·flat·ed; de·flat·ing** [*de-* + *-flate* (as in *inflate*)] *vt* **1** : to release air or gas from **2** : to reduce in size or importance ⟨~ his ego with cutting remarks⟩ **3** : to reduce (a price level) or cause (a volume of credit) to contract ~ *vi* : to lose firmness through or as if through the escape of contained gas ***syn*** see CONTRACT ***ant*** inflate — **de·fla·tor** \-ˈflāt-ər\ *n*

de·fla·tion \di-ˈflā-shən, ˈdē-\ *n* **1** : an act or instance of deflating : the state of being deflated **2** : a contraction in the volume of available money or credit that results in a decline of the general price level **3** : the erosion of soil by the wind — **de·fla·tion·ary** \-shə-ˌner-ē\ *adj*

de·flect \di-ˈflekt\ *vb* [L *deflectere* to bend down, turn aside, fr. *de-* + *flectere* to bend] *vt* : to turn from a straight course or fixed direction : BEND ~ *vi* : to turn aside : DEVIATE — **de·flec·tive** \-ˈflek-tiv\ *adj* — **de·flec·tor** \-tər\ *n*

de·flec·tion \di-ˈflek-shən\ *n* **1** : a turning aside or off course : DEVIATION **2** : the departure of an indicator or pointer from the zero reading on the scale of an instrument

de·flexed \ˈdē-ˌflekst, di-ˈ\ *adj* [L *deflexus*, pp. of *deflectere*] : turned abruptly downward ⟨a ~ leaf⟩

de·flo·ra·tion \ˌdef-lə-ˈrā-shən, ˌdē-flə-\ *n* [ME *defloracioun*, fr. LL *defloration-, defloratio*, fr. *defloratus*, pp. of *deflorare*] : rupture of the hymen

de·flow·er \(ˈ)dē-ˈflau̇(-ə)r\ *vt* [ME *deflouren*, fr. MF or LL; MF *deflorer*, fr. LL *deflorare*, fr. L *de-* + *flor-, flos* flower — more at BLOW] **1** : to deprive of virginity : RAVISH **2** : to take away the prime beauty of — **de·flow·er·er** *n*

de·foam \(ˈ)dē-ˈfōm\ *vt* : to remove foam from : prevent the formation of foam in — **de·foam·er** *n*

de·fog \(ˈ)dē-ˈfȯg, -ˈfäg\ *vt* : to remove fog or condensed moisture from — **de·fog·ger** *n*

de·fo·li·ant \(ˈ)dē-ˈfō-lē-ənt\ *n* : a chemical spray or dust applied to plants in order to cause the leaves to drop off prematurely

de·fo·li·ate \-lē-ˌāt\ *vt* [LL *defoliatus*, pp. of *defoliare*, fr. L *de-* + *folium* leaf — more at BLADE] : to deprive of leaves esp. prematurely — **de·fo·li·ate** \-lē-ət\ *adj* — **de·fo·li·a·tion** \(ˌ)dē-ˌfō-lē-ˈā-shən\ *n* — **de·fo·li·a·tor** \(ˈ)dē-ˈfō-lē-ˌāt-ər\ *n*

de·force \(ˈ)dē-ˈfō(ə)rs, -ˈfȯ(ə)rs\ *vt* [ME *deforcen*, fr. OF *deforcier*, fr. *de-* + *forcier* to force] **1** : to keep (as lands) by force from the rightful owner **2** : to eject (a person) from possession by force — **de·force·ment** \-ˈfōr-smənt, -ˈfȯr-\ *n*

de·for·ciant \di-ˈfōr-shənt, -ˈfȯr-\ *n* [AF, fr. OF, prp. of *deforcier*] : one who deforces the rightful owner

de·for·est \(ˈ)dē-ˈfȯr-əst, -ˈfär-\ *vt* : to clear of forests — **de·for·es·ta·tion** \(ˌ)dē-ˌfȯr-ə-ˈstā-shən, -ˌfär-\ *n* — **de·for·est·er** \(ˈ)dē-ˈfȯr-ə-stər, -ˈfär-\ *n*

de·form \di-ˈfȯ(ə)rm, ˈdē-\ *vb* [ME *deformen*, fr. MF or L; MF *deformer*, fr. L *deformare*, fr. *de-* + *formare* to form, fr. *forma* form] *vt* **1** : to spoil the form of **2 a** : to spoil the looks of : DISFIGURE ⟨a face ~*ed* by bitterness⟩ **b** : to make hideous or monstrous **3** : to alter the shape of by stress ~ *vi* : to become misshapen or changed in shape

syn DEFORM, DISTORT, CONTORT, WARP *shared meaning element* : to mar or spoil by or as if by twisting

de·for·mal·ize \(ˈ)dē-ˈfȯr-mə-ˌlīz\ *vt* : to make less formal ⟨~ a group learning situation⟩

de·for·ma·tion \ˌdē-ˌfȯr-ˈmā-shən, ˌdef-ər-\ *n* **1** : the action of deforming : the state of being deformed **2** : change for the worse ⟨a most extensive ecclesiastical reformation (or ~, as it may turn out) —Richard Whately⟩ **3** : alteration of form or shape; *also* : the product of such alteration — **de·for·ma·tion·al** \-shnəl, -shən-ᵊl\ *adj*

de·for·ma·tive \di-ˈfȯr-mət-iv\ *adj* : tending to deform

deformed *adj* : distorted or unshapely in form : MISSHAPEN

de·for·mi·ty \di-ˈfȯr-mət-ē\ *n, pl* **-ties** [ME *deformite*, fr. MF *deformité*, fr. L *deformitat-, deformitas*, fr. *deformis* deformed, fr. *de-* + *forma*] **1** : the state of being deformed **2** : a physical blemish or distortion : DISFIGUREMENT **3** : a moral or esthetic flaw or defect

de·fraud \di-ˈfrȯd\ *vt* [ME *defrauden*, fr. MF *defrauder*, fr. L *defraudare*, fr. *de-* + *fraudare* to cheat, fr. *fraud-, fraus* fraud] : to deprive of something by deception or fraud ***syn*** see CHEAT — **de·frau·da·tion** \ˌdē-ˌfrȯ-ˈdā-shən\ *n* — **de·fraud·er** \di-ˈfrȯd-ər\ *n*

de·fray \di-ˈfrā\ *vt* [MF *deffrayer*, fr. *des-* de- + *frayer* to expend, fr. OF, fr. (assumed) OF *frai* expenditure, lit., damage by breaking, fr. L *fractum*, neut. of *fractus*, pp. of *frangere* to break — more at BREAK] **1** : to provide for the payment of : PAY **2** *archaic* : to bear the expenses of — **de·fray·able** \-ə-bəl\ *adj* — **de·fray·al** \-ˈfrā(-ə)l\ *n*

de·frock \(ˈ)dē-ˈfräk\ *vt* : UNFROCK

de·frost \di-ˈfrȯst, ˈdē-\ *vt* **1** : to release from a frozen state ⟨~ meat⟩ **2** : to free from ice ⟨~ the refrigerator⟩ ~ *vi* : to thaw out esp. from a deep-frozen state — **de·frost·er** *n*

deft \ˈdeft\ *adj* [ME *defte*] : marked by facility and skill ***syn*** see DEXTEROUS ***ant*** awkward — **deft·ly** *adv* — **deft·ness** \ˈdef(t)-nəs\ *n*

de·funct \di-ˈfəŋ(k)t\ *adj* [L *defunctus*, fr. pp. of *defungi* to finish, die, fr. *de-* + *fungi* to perform — more at FUNCTION] : having finished the course of life or existence ⟨her ~ aunt's will⟩ ⟨a ~ philosophy⟩ ***syn*** see DEAD ***ant*** alive, live

de·fuse \(ˈ)dē-ˈfyüz\ *vt* **1** : to remove the fuse from (as a mine or bomb) **2** : to make less harmful, potent, or tense : CALM ⟨~ the crisis⟩

¹de·fy \di-ˈfī\ *vt* **de·fied; de·fy·ing** [ME *defyen* to renounce faith in, challenge, fr. OF *defier*, fr. *de-* + *fier* to entrust, fr. (assumed) VL *fidare*, alter. of L *fidere* to trust — more at BIDE] **1** *archaic* : to challenge to combat **2** : to challenge to do something considered impossible : DARE **3** : to confront with assured power of resistance : DISREGARD ⟨~ public opinion⟩ **4** : to resist attempts at : WITHSTAND ⟨the paintings ~ classification⟩

²de·fy \di-ˈfī, ˈdē-ˌ\ *n, pl* **defies** : CHALLENGE, DEFIANCE

deg *abbr* degree

dé·ga·gé \ˌdā-ˌgä-ˈzhā\ *adj* [F, fr. pp. of *dégager* to redeem a pledge, free, fr. OF *desgagier*, fr. *des-* de- + *gage* pledge — more at GAGE] **1** : free of constraint : NONCHALANT **2** : being free and easy ⟨clothes with a ~ look⟩ **3** : extended with toe pointed in preparation for a ballet step

de·gas \(ˈ)dē-ˈgas\ *vt* : to remove gas from ⟨~ an electron tube⟩

de Gaull·ism \di-ˈgō-ˌliz-əm, -ˈgȯ-\ *n* : GAULLISM — **de Gaull·ist** \-ləst\ *n*

de·gauss \(ˈ)dē-ˈgau̇s\ *vt* **1** : DEMAGNETIZE **2** : to make (a steel ship) effectively nonmagnetic by means of electrical coils carrying currents that neutralize the magnetism of the ship — **de·gauss·er** *n*

de·gen·er·a·cy \di-ˈjen-(ə-)rə-sē\ *n, pl* **-cies** **1** : the state of being degenerate **2** : the process of becoming degenerate **3** : sexual perversion **4** : the coding of an amino acid by more than one codon of the genetic code

¹de·gen·er·ate \di-ˈjen-(ə-)rət\ *adj* [ME *degenerat*, fr. L *degeneratus*, pp. of *degenerare* to degenerate, fr. *de-* + *gener-, genus* race, kind — more at KIN] **1 a** : having declined (as in nature, character, structure, or function) from an ancestral or former state **b** : having sunk to a condition below that which is normal to a type; *esp* : having sunk to a lower and usu. peculiarly corrupt and vicious state **c** : DEGRADED **2** : being mathematically simpler (as by having a factor or constant equal to zero) than the typical case

ə abut ᵊ kitten ər further a back ā bake ä cot, cart au̇ out ch chin e less ē easy g gift i trip ī life j joke ŋ sing ō flow ȯ flaw ȯi coin th thin t͟h this ü loot u̇ foot y yet yü few yu̇ furious zh vision

⟨the graph of a second degree equation yielding two intersecting lines is a ~ hyperbola⟩ **3** : characterized by atoms stripped of their electrons and by very great density ⟨~ matter⟩; *also* : consisting of degenerate matter ⟨a ~ star⟩ **4** : having two or more states or subdivisions ⟨~ energy level⟩ **5** : having more than one codon representing an amino acid; *also* : being such a codon ***syn*** see VICIOUS — **de·gen·er·ate·ly** *adv* — **de·gen·er·ate·ness** *n*

[2]**degenerate** *n* : one that is degenerate: as **a** : one degraded from the normal moral standard **b** : one debased by a psychopathic tendency **c** : a sexual pervert **d** : one showing signs of reversion to an earlier culture stage

[3]**de·gen·er·ate** \di-ˈjen-ə-ˌrāt\ *vi* **1** : to pass from a higher to a lower type or condition : DETERIORATE ⟨the road *degenerated* into a bumpy brush-filled path⟩ **2** : to sink into a low intellectual or moral state **3** : to decline in quality ⟨his poetry gradually *degenerated* into jingles⟩ **4** : to decline from a condition or from standards proper to a species, race, or breed **5** : to evolve or develop into a less autonomous or less functionally active form ⟨*degenerated* into dependent parasites⟩ ⟨the digestive system *degenerated*⟩ ~ *vt* : to cause to degenerate

de·gen·er·a·tion \di-ˌjen-ə-ˈrā-shən, ˌdē-\ *n* **1** : a lowering of effective power, vitality, or essential quality to an enfeebled and worsened kind or state **2 a** : intellectual or moral decline **b** : degenerate condition **3 a** : progressive deterioration of physical characters from a level representing the norm of earlier generations or forms **b** : deterioration of a tissue or an organ in which its function is diminished or its structure is impaired **4** : marked decline in excellence (as of workmanship or originality) ***syn*** see DETERIORATION

de·gen·er·a·tive \di-ˈjen-ə-ˌrāt-iv, -ˈjen-(ə-)rət-\ *adj* : of, relating to, or tending to cause degeneration ⟨a ~ disease⟩

de·glu·ti·tion \ˌdē-glü-ˈtish-ən, ˌdeg-lü-\ *n* [F *déglutition*, fr. L *deglutitus*, pp. of *deglutire* to swallow down, fr. *de-* + *glutire, gluttire* to swallow — more at GLUTTON] : the act or process of swallowing

de·grad·able \di-ˈgrād-ə-bəl\ *adj* : capable of being chemically degraded ⟨~ detergents⟩ — compare BIODEGRADABLE

deg·ra·da·tion \ˌdeg-rə-ˈdā-shən\ *n* **1** : the act or process of degrading **2 a** : decline to a low, destitute, or demoralized state **b** : moral or intellectual decadence : DEGENERATION

de·grade \di-ˈgrād\ *vb* [ME *degraden*, fr. MF *degrader*, fr. LL *degradare*, fr. L *de-* + *gradus* step, grade] *vt* **1 a** : to lower in grade, rank, or status : DEMOTE **b** : to strip of rank or honors **c** : to deprive of standing or true function : PERVERT **d** : to scale down in desirability or salability **2 a** : to bring to low esteem or into disrepute **b** : to drag down in moral or intellectual character : CORRUPT ⟨*degraded* his office as president⟩ **3** : to impair in respect to some physical property **4** : to wear down by erosion **5** : to reduce the complexity of (a chemical compound) : DECOMPOSE ~ *vi* **1** : to pass from a higher grade or class to a lower **2** *of a chemical compound* : to become reduced in complexity — **de·grad·er** *n*

syn* 1** DEGRADE, DEMOTE, DECLASS, DISRATE *shared meaning element* : to lower in station, rank, or grade ***ant elevate

2 see ABASE ***ant*** uplift

de·grad·ed *adj* **1** : reduced far below ordinary standards of civilized life and conduct **2** : characterized by degeneration of structure or function — **de·grad·ed·ly** *adv* — **de·grad·ed·ness** *n*

de·grad·ing *adj* : that degrades : DEBASING — **de·grad·ing·ly** \-ˈgrād-iŋ-lē\ *adv*

de·gran·u·la·tion \(ˌ)dē-ˌgran-yə-ˈlā-shən\ *n* : the process of losing granules ⟨~ of leukocytes⟩

de·gree \di-ˈgrē\ *n* [ME, fr. OF *degré*, fr. (assumed) VL *degradus*, fr. L *de-* + *gradus*] **1 a** *obs* : STEP, STAIR **b** *archaic* : a member of a series arranged in steps **2** : a step or stage in a process, course, or order of classification ⟨advanced by ~*s*⟩ **3** : a measure of damage to tissue caused esp. by disease **4 a** : the extent, measure, or scope of an action, condition, or relation ⟨the company's ~ of expansion was small⟩ **b** : relative intensity **c** : one of the forms or sets of forms used in the comparison of an adjective or adverb **d** : a legal measure of guilt or negligence ⟨found guilty of robbery in the first ~⟩ **5 a** : a rank or grade of official, ecclesiastical, or social position ⟨people of low ~⟩ **b** *archaic* : a particular standing esp. as to dignity or worth **c** : the civil condition or status of a person **6** : a step in a direct line of descent or in the line of ascent to a common ancestor **7 a** : a grade of membership attained in a ritualistic order or society **b** : the formal ceremonies observed in the conferral of such a distinction **c** : a title conferred on students by a college, university, or professional school on completion of a unified program of study **d** : an academic title conferred honorarily **8** *archaic* : a position or space on the earth or in the heavens as measured by degrees of latitude **9** : one of the divisions or intervals marked on a scale of a measuring instrument; *specif* : any of various units for measuring temperature **10** : a 360th part of the circumference of a circle **11 a** : the sum of the exponents of the variable factors of a monomial **b** : the sum of the exponents of the variable factors of the term of highest degree in a polynomial **c** : the greatest power of the derivative of highest order in a differential equation after the equation has been rationalized and cleared of fractions with respect to the derivative **12 a** : a line or space of the musical staff **b** : a step, note, or tone of a musical scale — **de·greed** \-ˈgrēd\ *adj* — **to a degree 1** : to a remarkable extent **2** : in a small way

de·gree–day \di-ˈgrē-ˈdā\ *n* : a unit that represents one degree of declination from a given point (as 65°) in the mean daily outdoor temperature and that is used to measure heat requirements

degree of freedom 1 : any of a limited number of ways in which a body may move or in which a dynamic system may change **2** : one of the capabilities of a statistic for variation of which there are as many as the number of unrestricted and independent variables determining its value

de·gres·sive \di-ˈgres-iv, ˈdē-\ *adj* [*degression* (downward motion), (fr. ME, fr. ML *degression-, degressio*, fr. L *degressus*, pp. of *degredi* to step down, fr. *de-* + *gradi* to step) + *-ive* — more at GRADE] : tending to descend or decrease — **de·gres·sive·ly** *adv*

dé·grin·go·lade \ˌdā-ˌgra^{n}(n)-gə-ˈläd\ *n* [F, fr. *dégringoler* to tumble down, fr. *dé-* de- + *gringoler* to tumble] : a rapid decline or deterioration (as in strength, position, or condition) : DOWNFALL

de·gum \(ˈ)dē-ˈgəm\ *vt* : to free from gum, a gummy substance, or sericin

de·gust \di-ˈgəst\ *vt* [L *degustare*, fr. *de-* + *gustare* to taste — more at CHOOSE] : TASTE, SAVOR

de·gus·ta·tion \ˌdē-ˌgəs-ˈtā-shən, di-\ *n* : the action or an instance of degusting

de haut en bas \də-ō-tä^{n}-bä\ *adj or adv* [F, lit., from top to bottom] : having a superior or condescending manner ⟨there is a *de haut en bas* tone about such a judgment —*Times Lit. Supp.*⟩ ⟨the landlady looked at him *de haut en bas* —D. H. Lawrence⟩

de·hisce \di-ˈhis\ *vi* **de·hisced; de·hisc·ing** [L *dehiscere* to split open, fr. *de-* + *hiscere* to gape; akin to L *hiare* to yawn — more at YAWN] : to split along a natural line; *also* : to discharge contents by so splitting ⟨seedpods *dehiscing* at maturity⟩

de·his·cence \di-ˈhis-^{ə}n(t)s\ *n* [NL *dehiscentia*, fr. L *dehiscent-, dehiscens*, prp. of *dehiscere*] : an act or instance of dehiscing ⟨pollen freed by ~ of the anther⟩ — **de·his·cent** \-^{ə}nt\ *adj*

de·horn \(ˈ)dē-ˈhȯ(ə)rn\ *vt* **1** : to deprive of horns **2** : to prevent the growth of the horns of — **de·horn·er** *n*

de·hu·man·iza·tion \(ˌ)dē-ˌhyü-mə-nə-ˈzā-shən, (ˌ)dē-ˌyü-\ *n* : the act or process or an instance of dehumanizing

de·hu·man·ize \(ˈ)dē-ˈhyü-mə-ˌnīz, (ˈ)dē-ˈyü-\ *vt* : to divest of human qualities or personality ⟨fear that the machines will ~ education —J. G. Miller⟩

de·hu·mid·i·fy \ˌdē-hyü-ˈmid-ə-ˌfī, ˌdē-yü-\ *vt* : to remove moisture from (as air) — **de·hu·mid·i·fi·ca·tion** \-ˌmid-ə-fə-ˈkā-shən\ *n* — **de·hu·mid·i·fi·er** \-ˈmid-ə-ˌfī(-ə)r\ *n*

dehydr- *or* **dehydro-** *comb form* **1** : dehydrated **2** : dehydrogenated

de·hy·drase \(ˈ)dē-ˈhī-ˌdrās, -ˌdrāz\ *n* **1** : DEHYDRATASE **2** : DEHYDROGENASE

de·hy·dra·tase \-drə-ˌtās, -ˌtāz\ *n* : an enzyme that catalyzes the removal of oxygen and hydrogen from metabolites in the proportion in which they form water

de·hy·drate \(ˈ)dē-ˈhī-ˌdrāt\ *vt* **1 a** : to remove bound water or hydrogen and oxygen from (a chemical compound) in the proportion in which they form water **b** : to remove water from (as foods) **2** : to deprive of vitality or savor ~ *vi* : to lose water or body fluids — **de·hy·dra·tor** \-ˌdrāt -ər\ *n*

de·hy·dra·tion \ˌdē-hī-ˈdrā-shən\ *n* : the process of dehydrating; *esp* : an abnormal depletion of body fluids

de·hy·dro·chlo·ri·nase \(ˌ)dē-ˌhī-drə-ˈklōr-ə-ˌnās, -ˈklȯr-, -ˌnāz\ *n* : an enzyme that dehydrochlorinates a chlorinated hydrocarbon (as DDT) and is found esp. in some DDT resistant insects

de·hy·dro·chlo·ri·nate \-ˌnāt\ *vt* [*de-* + *hydr-* + *chlorine*] : to remove hydrogen and chlorine or hydrogen chloride from (a compound) — **de·hy·dro·chlo·ri·na·tion** \-ˌklōr-ə-ˈnā-shən, -ˌklȯr-\ *n*

de·hy·dro·ge·nase \ˌdē-(ˌ)hī-ˈdräj-ə-ˌnās, (ˈ)dē-ˈhī-drə-jə-, -ˌnāz\ *n* [ISV] : an enzyme that accelerates the removal of hydrogen from metabolites and its transfer to other substances ⟨succinic ~⟩

de·hy·dro·ge·nate \ˌdē-(ˌ)hī-ˈdräj-ə-ˌnāt, (ˈ)dē-ˈhī-drə-jə-\ *vt* : to remove hydrogen from — **de·hy·dro·ge·na·tion** \ˌdē-(ˌ)hī-ˌdräj-ə-ˈnā-shən, (ˌ)dē-ˌhī-drə-jə-\ *n*

de·hyp·no·tize \(ˈ)dē-ˈhip-nə-ˌtīz\ *vt* : to remove from hypnosis

de·ice \(ˈ)dē-ˈīs\ *vt* : to keep free or rid of ice — **de·ic·er** *n*

de·i·cide \ˈdē-ə-ˌsīd, ˈdā-ə-\ *n* [deriv. of L *deus* god & *-cidium, -cida* -cide] **1** : the act of killing a divine being or a symbolic substitute of such a being **2** : the killer or destroyer of a god

deic·tic \ˈdīk-tik, ˈdāk-; dē-ˈik-\ *adj* [Gk *deiktikos*, fr. *deiktos*, verbal of *deiknynai* to show] : showing or pointing out directly ⟨the words *this, that,* and *those* have a ~ function⟩

de·i·fi·ca·tion \ˌdē-ə-fə-ˈkā-shən, ˌdā-\ *n* **1** : the act or an instance of deifying **2** : absorption of the soul into deity

de·i·fy \ˈdē-ə-ˌfī, ˈdā-\ *vt* **-fied; -fy·ing** [ME *deifyen*, fr. MF *deifier*, fr. LL *deificare*, fr. L *deus* god] **1 a** : to make a god of **b** : to take as an object of worship **2** : to glorify as of supreme worth

deign \ˈdān\ *vb* [ME *deignen*, fr. OF *deignier*, fr. L *dignare, dignari*, fr. *dignus* worthy — more at DECENT] *vi* : to condescend reluctantly and with a strong sense of the affront to one's superiority that is involved ⟨he barely ~*ed* to acknowledge their greeting⟩ ~ *vt* : to condescend to give or offer ***syn*** see STOOP

deil \ˈdē(ə)l\ *n* [ME *devel, del*] *Scot* : DEVIL

de·in·dus·tri·al·iza·tion \ˌdē-in-ˌdəs-trē-ə-lə-ˈzā-shən\ *n* : the act or process of reducing or destroying the industrial organization and potential esp. of a defeated nation

de–in·sti·tu·tion·al·ize \(ˌ)dē-ˌin(t)-stə-ˈt(y)üsh-nə-ˌlīz, -ˈt(y)ü-shən-^{ə}l-ˌīz\ *vt* : to remove the status or character of an institution from — **de–in·sti·tu·tion·al·iza·tion** \-ˌt(y)üsh-nə-lə-ˈzā-shən, -ˌt(y)ü-shən-^{ə}l-ə-ˈzā-\ *n*

de·ion·ize \(ˈ)dē-ˈī-ə-ˌnīz\ *vt* : to remove ions from ⟨~ water by ion exchange⟩ — **de·ion·iza·tion** \(ˌ)dē-ˌī-ə-nə-ˈzā-shən\ *n*

de·ism \ˈdē-ˌiz-əm, ˈdā-\ *n, often cap* : a movement or system of thought advocating natural religion based on human reason rather than revelation, emphasizing morality, and in the 18th century denying the interference of the Creator with the laws of the universe

de·ist \ˈdē-əst, ˈdā-\ *n, often cap* : an adherent of deism ***syn*** see ATHEIST — **de·is·tic** \dē-ˈis-tik, dā-\ *adj* — **de·is·ti·cal** \-ti-kəl\ *adj* — **de·is·ti·cal·ly** \-ti-k(ə-)lē\ *adv*

de·i·ty \ˈdē-ət-ē, ˈdā-\ *n, pl* **-ties** [ME *deitee*, fr. MF *deité*, fr. LL *deitat-, deitas*, fr. L *deus* god; akin to OE *Tīw*, god of war, L *divus* god, *dies* day, Gk *dios* heavenly] **1 a** : the rank or essential nature of a god : DIVINITY **b** *cap* : SUPREME BEING, GOD 1 **2** : a god or goddess ⟨the *deities* of ancient Greece⟩ **3** : one exalted or revered as supremely good or powerful

dé·jà vu \ˌdā-ˌzhä-ˈv(y)ü, dā-zhá-vüē\ *n* [F *déjà vu*, adj., already seen] **1** : PARAMNESIA b **2** : something overly or unpleasantly familiar ⟨the appointment seems like a case of *déjà vu* —E. B. Fiske⟩

1de·ject \di-ˈjekt\ *vt* [ME *dejecten* to throw down, fr. L *dejectus,* pp. of *deicere,* fr. *de-* + *jacere* to throw — more at JET] **:** to make gloomy

2deject *adj, archaic* **:** DEJECTED

de·jec·ta \di-ˈjek-tə\ *n pl* [NL, fr. L, neut. pl. of *dejectus*] **:** EXCREMENTS

de·ject·ed *adj* **1 :** cast down in spirits **:** DEPRESSED **2 a** *obs, of the eyes* **:** DOWNCAST **b** *archaic* **:** thrown down **3** *obs* **:** lowered in rank or condition — **de·ject·ed·ly** *adv* — **de·ject·ed·ness** *n*

de·jec·tion \di-ˈjek-shən\ *n* **:** lowness of spirits

de ju·re \(ˈ)dē-ˈju̇(ə)r-ē, (ˈ)dā-ˈyu̇(ə)r-\ *adv or adj* [NL] **:** by right **:** of right ⟨recognition extended *de jure* to the new government⟩

deka- *or* **dek-** — see DECA-

deka·gram \ˈdek-ə-ˌgram\ *n* — see METRIC SYSTEM table

deka·li·ter \-ˌlēt-ər\ *n* — see METRIC SYSTEM table

deka·me·ter \-ˌmēt-ər\ *n* — see METRIC SYSTEM table

deka·stere \-ˌsti(ə)r, -ˌste(ə)r\ *n* — see METRIC SYSTEM table

del *abbr* **1** delegate; delegation **2** delete

Del *abbr* Delaware

de·lam·i·nate \(ˈ)dē-ˈlam-ə-ˌnāt\ *vi* **:** to undergo delamination

de·lam·i·na·tion \(ˌ)dē-ˌlam-ə-ˈnā-shən\ *n* **1 :** separation into constituent layers **2 :** gastrula formation in which the endoderm is split off as a layer from the inner surface of the blastoderm and the archenteron is represented by the space between this endoderm and the yolk mass

de·late \di-ˈlāt\ *vt* **de·lat·ed; de·lat·ing** [L *delatus* (pp. of *deferre* to bring down, report, accuse), fr. *de-* + *latus,* pp. of *ferre* to bear — more at TOLERATE, BEAR] **1** *Scot* **:** ACCUSE, DENOUNCE **2** *archaic* **:** REPORT, RELATE **3** *archaic* **:** REFER — **de·la·tion** \-ˈlā-shən\ *n* — **de·la·tor** \-ˈlāt-ər\ *n*

Del·a·ware \ˈdel-ə-ˌwa(ə)r, -ˌwe(ə)r, -wər\ *n, pl* **Delaware** *or* **Delawares** [*Delaware* river] **1 :** a member of an Amerindian people orig. of the Delaware valley **2 :** the Algonquian language of the Delaware

1de·lay \di-ˈlā\ *n* **1 a :** the act of delaying **:** the state of being delayed **b :** an instance of being delayed **2 :** the time during which something is delayed **3 :** a football play in which an offensive back delays momentarily as if to block and then runs his prescribed pattern

2delay *vb* [ME *delayen,* fr. OF *delaier,* fr. *de-* + *laier* to leave, alter. of *laissier,* fr. L *laxare* to slacken — more at RELAX] *vt* **1 :** to put off **:** POSTPONE ⟨decided to ~ our vacation until next month⟩ **2 :** to stop, detain, or hinder for a time ~ *vi* **1 :** to move or act slowly **2 :** to pause momentarily — **de·lay·er** *n* — **de·lay·ing** *adj*
syn DELAY, RETARD, SLOW, SLACKEN, DETAIN *shared meaning element* **:** to cause to be late or behind in movement or progress ***ant*** expedite, hasten

1de·le \ˈdē-(ˌ)lē\ *vt* **de·led; de·le·ing** [L, imper. sing. of *delēre*] **1 :** to remove (as a word or character) from typeset matter **2 :** to mark with a dele

2dele *n* **:** a mark indicating that something is to be deled

1de·lec·ta·ble \di-ˈlek-tə-bəl\ *adj* [ME, fr. MF, fr. L *delectabilis,* fr. *delectare* to delight — more at DELIGHT] **1 :** highly pleasing **:** DELIGHTFUL **2 :** DELICIOUS — **de·lec·ta·bil·i·ty** \-ˌlek-tə-ˈbil-ət-ē\ *n* — **de·lec·ta·ble·ness** \-ˈlek-tə-bəl-nəs\ *n* — **de·lec·ta·bly** \-blē\ *adv*

2delectable *n* **:** something that is delectable ⟨~*s* from the bakery⟩

de·lec·ta·tion \ˌdē-ˌlek-ˈtā-shən, di-; ˌdel-ək-\ *n* **1 :** DELIGHT **2 :** ENJOYMENT

del·e·ga·ble \ˈdel-i-gə-bəl\ *adj* **:** capable of being delegated

del·e·ga·cy \-gə-sē\ *n, pl* **-cies 1 a :** the act of delegating **b :** appointment as delegate **2 :** a body of delegates **:** BOARD

1del·e·gate \ˈdel-i-gət, -ˌgāt\ *n* [ME *delegat,* fr. ML *delegatus,* fr. L, pp. of *delegare* to delegate, fr. *de-* + *legare* to send — more at LEGATE] **:** a person acting for another**:** as **a :** a representative to a convention or conference **b :** a representative of a U.S. territory in the House of Representatives **c :** a member of the lower house of the legislature of Maryland, Virginia, or West Virginia

2del·e·gate \-ˌgāt\ *vb* **-gat·ed; -gat·ing** *vt* **1 :** to entrust to another ⟨~ one's authority⟩ **2 :** to appoint as one's representative **:** DEPUTIZE ~ *vi* **:** to assign responsibility or authority

del·e·ga·tion \ˌdel-i-ˈgā-shən\ *n* **1 :** the act of empowering to act for another **2 :** a group of persons chosen to represent others

de·lete \di-ˈlēt\ *vt* **de·let·ed; de·let·ing** [L *deletus,* pp. of *delēre* to wipe out, destroy, fr. *de-* + *-lēre* (akin to L *linere* to smear) — more at LIME] **:** to eliminate esp. by blotting out, cutting out, or erasing ⟨*deleted* his name from the list⟩ ***syn*** see ERASE

del·e·te·ri·ous \ˌdel-ə-ˈtir-ē-əs\ *adj* [Gk *dēlētērios,* fr. *dēleisthai* to hurt — more at CONDOLE] **:** having an often concealed or unexpected harmful effect ⟨whether prolonged weightlessness has ~ effects —*The Sciences*⟩ ***syn*** see PERNICIOUS ***ant*** salutary — **del·e·te·ri·ous·ly** *adv* — **del·e·te·ri·ous·ness** *n*

de·le·tion \di-ˈlē-shən\ *n* [L *deletion-, deletio* destruction, fr. *deletus*] **1 :** an act of deleting **2 a :** something deleted **b :** DEFICIENCY 2b; *esp* **:** a large deficiency not including either end of a chromosome

delft \ˈdelft\ *n* [*Delft,* Netherlands] **1 :** tin-glazed Dutch earthenware with blue and white or polychrome decoration **2 :** a ceramic ware resembling or imitative of Dutch delft

delft·ware \ˈdelf-ˌtwa(ə)r, -ˌtwe(ə)r\ *n* **:** DELFT

deli \ˈdel-ē\ *n, pl* **del·is :** DELICATESSEN

1de·lib·er·ate \di-ˈlib-(ə-)rət\ *adj* [L *deliberatus,* pp. of *deliberare* to weigh in mind, ponder, irreg. fr. *de-* + *libra* scale, pound] **1 :** characterized by or resulting from careful and thorough consideration **2 :** characterized by awareness of the consequences **:** WILLFUL **3 :** slow, unhurried, and steady as though allowing time for decision on each individual action involved ⟨walked with a ~ step⟩ ***syn*** see VOLUNTARY ***ant*** impulsive — **de·lib·er·ate·ly** *adv* — **de·lib·er·ate·ness** *n*

2de·lib·er·ate \di-ˈlib-ə-ˌrāt\ *vb* **-at·ed; -at·ing** *vt* **:** to think about deliberately and often with formal discussion before reaching a decision ~ *vi* **:** to ponder issues and decisions carefully ***syn*** see THINK

de·lib·er·a·tion \di-ˌlib-ə-ˈrā-shən\ *n* **1 :** the act of deliberating **2 :** a discussion and consideration by a group of persons of the reasons for and against a measure **3 :** the quality or state of being deliberate — **de·lib·er·a·tive** \-ˈlib-ə-ˌrāt-iv, -ˈlib-(ə-)rət-\ *adj* — **de·lib·er·a·tive·ly** *adv* — **de·lib·er·a·tive·ness** *n*

del·i·ca·cy \ˈdel-i-kə-sē\ *n, pl* **-cies 1** *obs* **a :** the quality or state of being luxurious **b :** INDULGENCE **2 :** something pleasing to eat that is considered rare or luxurious ⟨considered caviar a ~⟩ **3 a :** the quality or state of being dainty **:** FINENESS ⟨lace of great ~⟩ **b :** FRAILTY **4 :** fineness or subtle expressiveness of touch (as in painting or music) **5 a :** precise and refined perception and discrimination **b :** extreme sensitivity **:** PRECISION ⟨an electronic instrument of great ~⟩ **6 a :** refined sensibility in feeling or conduct **b :** the quality or state of being squeamish **7 :** the quality or state of requiring delicate treatment

1del·i·cate \ˈdel-i-kət\ *adj* [ME *delicat,* fr. L *delicatus* delicate, addicted to pleasure; akin to L *delicere* to allure] **1 :** pleasing to the senses: **a :** generally pleasant **b :** pleasing to the sense of taste or smell esp. in a mild or subtle way **c :** marked by daintiness or charm of color, lines, or proportions **2 a :** marked by keen sensitivity or fine discrimination **b :** FASTIDIOUS, SQUEAMISH **c :** SCRUPULOUS **3 a :** marked by minute precision **b :** exhibiting extreme sensitivity ⟨a ~ instrument⟩ **4 :** calling for or involving meticulously careful treatment ⟨the ~ balance of power⟩ **5 a :** marked by meticulous technique or operation or by execution with adroit finesse ⟨a ~ pirouette⟩ **b :** marked by fineness of structure, workmanship, or texture ⟨~ handwriting⟩ **c (1) :** easily torn or hurt ⟨a ~ butterfly wing⟩ **(2) :** WEAK, SICKLY **d :** marked by fine subtlety ⟨~ irony⟩ **e :** marked by tact; *also* **:** requiring tact ***syn*** see CHOICE ***ant*** gross — **del·i·cate·ly** *adv* — **del·i·cate·ness** *n*

2delicate *n* **1** *obs* **:** DELIGHT, LUXURY **2** *archaic* **:** a table delicacy

del·i·ca·tes·sen \ˌdel-i-kə-ˈtes-ᵊn\ *n pl* [obs. G (now *delikatessen*), pl. of *delicatesse* delicacy, fr. F *délicatesse,* prob. fr. OIt *delicatezza,* fr. *delicato* delicate, fr. L *delicatus*] **1 :** ready-to-eat food products (as cooked meats and prepared salads) **2** *sing, pl* **delicatessens** [*delicatessen* (*store*)] **:** a store where delicatessen are sold

1de·li·cious \di-ˈlish-əs\ *adj* [ME, fr. OF, fr. LL *deliciosus,* fr. L *deliciae* delight, fr. *delicere* to allure] **1 :** affording great pleasure **:** DELIGHTFUL **2 :** appealing to one of the bodily senses esp. of taste or smell — **de·li·cious·ly** *adv* — **de·li·cious·ness** *n*

2delicious *n, pl* **de·li·cious·es** *or* **delicious** *often cap* **:** an important red or yellow market apple of American origin that has a crown of five rounded prominences at the blossom end

de·lict \di-ˈlikt\ *n* [L *delictum* fault, fr. neut. of *delictus,* pp. of *delinquere*] **:** an offense against the law

1de·light \di-ˈlīt\ *n* **1 :** a high degree of gratification **:** JOY; *also* **:** extreme satisfaction **2 :** something that gives great pleasure ⟨the new puppy was a ~⟩ **3** *archaic* **:** the power of affording pleasurable emotion

2delight *vb* [ME *deliten,* fr. OF *delitier,* fr. L *delectare,* fr. *delectus,* pp. of *delicere* to allure, fr. *de-* + *lacere* to allure; akin to OE *lǣl* switch] *vi* **1 :** to take great pleasure ⟨he ~*ed* in playing his guitar⟩ **2 :** to give keen enjoyment ⟨a book certain to ~⟩ ~ *vt* **:** to give joy or satisfaction to ⟨~*ed* the audience with his performance⟩ — **de·light·er** *n*

de·light·ed *adj* **1** *obs* **:** DELIGHTFUL **2 :** highly pleased — **de·light·ed·ly** *adv* — **de·light·ed·ness** *n*

de·light·ful \di-ˈlīt-fəl\ *adj* **:** highly pleasing — **de·light·ful·ly** \-fə-lē\ *adv* — **de·light·ful·ness** *n*

de·light·some \-ˈlīt-səm\ *adj* **:** very pleasing **:** DELIGHTFUL — **de·light·some·ly** *adv*

De·li·lah \di-ˈlī-lə\ *n* [Heb *Dĕlīlāh*] **:** the mistress and betrayer of Samson in the book of Judges

de·lim·it \di-ˈlim-ət\ *vt* [F *délimiter,* fr. L *delimitare,* fr. *de-* + *limitare* to limit, fr. *limit-, limes* boundary, limit — more at LIMB] **1 :** to fix the limits of ⟨~ a boundary⟩ **2 :** to spell out **:** DELINEATE ⟨the problems can be defined and the solutions to the problems explicitly ~*ed* as to generality —Eugene Wall⟩

de·lim·i·tate \di-ˈlim-ə-ˌtāt\ *vt* **-tat·ed; -tat·ing :** DELIMIT — **de·lim·i·ta·tion** \di-ˌlim-ə-ˈtā-shən, ˌdē-\ *n* — **de·lim·i·ta·tive** \di-ˈlim-ə-ˌtāt-iv\ *adj*

de·lim·it·er \di-ˈlim-ət-ər\ *n* **:** a character that marks the beginning or end of a unit of data (as on a magnetic tape)

de·lin·eate \di-ˈlin-ē-ˌāt\ *vt* **-eat·ed; -eat·ing** [L *delineatus,* pp. of *delineare,* fr. *de-* + *linea* line] **1 a :** to indicate by lines drawn in the form or figure of **:** PORTRAY **b :** to represent accurately **2 :** to describe in usu. sharp or vivid detail ⟨~*s* the complexity of the large urban university —J. M. Hester⟩ — **de·lin·ea·tor** \-ē-ˌāt-ər\ *n*

de·lin·ea·tion \di-ˌlin-ē-ˈā-shən\ *n* **1 :** the act of representing, portraying, or describing graphically or verbally **2 :** something made by delineating — **de·lin·ea·tive** \-ˈlin-ē-ˌāt-iv\ *adj*

de·lin·quen·cy \di-ˈliŋ-kwən-sē, -ˈlin-\ *n, pl* **-cies 1 :** the quality or state of being delinquent **2 :** conduct that is out of accord with accepted behavior or the law; *also* **:** a tendency to engage or the practice of engaging in such conduct — used esp. when emphasis is placed on social or psychological maladjustment rather than criminal intent **3 :** a debt on which payment is overdue

1de·lin·quent \-kwənt\ *n* **:** a delinquent person

2delinquent *adj* [L *delinquent-, delinquens,* prp. of *delinquere* to fail, offend, fr. *de-* + *linquere* to leave — more at LOAN] **1 :** offending by neglect or violation of duty or of law **2 :** being overdue in payment ⟨a ~ charge account⟩ **3 :** of, relating to, or characteristic of delinquents **:** marked by delinquency — **de·lin·quent·ly** *adv*

del·i·quesce \ˌdel-i-ˈkwes\ *vi* **-quesced; -quesc·ing** [L *deliquescere,* fr. *de-* + *liquescere,* incho. of *liquēre* to be fluid — more at LIQUID] **1 :** to melt away: **a :** to dissolve gradually and become liquid by attracting and absorbing moisture from the air **b :** to become soft

or liquid with age — used of plant structures (as mushrooms) **2** : to divide repeatedly and so end in fine divisions — used esp. of the veins of a leaf — **del·i·ques·cence** \-ˈkwes-ᵊn(t)s\ *n* — **del·i·ques·cent** \-ᵊnt\ *adj*
de·lir·i·ous \di-ˈlir-ē-əs\ *adj* **1** : of, relating to, or characteristic of delirium **2** : affected with or marked by delirium — **de·lir·i·ous·ly** *adv* — **de·lir·i·ous·ness** *n*
de·lir·i·um \di-ˈlir-ē-əm\ *n* [L, fr. *delirare* to be crazy, fr. *de-* + *lira* furrow — more at LEARN] **1** : a mental disturbance characterized by confusion, disordered speech, and hallucinations **2** : frenzied excitement ⟨he would stride about his room in a ~ of joy — Thomas Wolfe⟩
delirium tre·mens \-ˈtrē-mənz, -ˈtrem-ənz\ *n* [NL, lit., trembling delirium] : a violent delirium with tremors that is induced by excessive and prolonged use of alcoholic liquors — called also *D.T.'s*
de·list \(ˈ)dē-ˈlist\ *vt* : to remove from a list; *esp* : to remove (a security) from the list of securities that may be dealt in on a particular exchange
de·liv·er \di-ˈliv-ər\ *vb* **de·liv·ered; de·liv·er·ing** \-(ə-)riŋ\ [ME *deliveren*, fr. OF *delivrer*, fr. LL *deliberare*, fr. L *de-* + *liberare* to liberate] *vt* **1** : to set free ⟨and lead us not into temptation, but ~ us from evil —Mt 6:13 (AV)⟩ **2** : to hand over : CONVEY ⟨~*ed* the stolen goods to the police⟩ **3 a** : to assist in giving birth **b** : to aid in the birth of **4** : UTTER, RELATE ⟨~*ed* his speech effectively⟩ **5** : to send (something aimed or guided) to an intended target or destination ⟨~*ed* a left hook to the jaw⟩ **6** : to bring (as votes) to the support of a candidate or cause ~ *vi* : to produce the promised, desired, or expected results : come through ⟨make sure he ~*s* on his promise⟩ ***syn*** see RESCUE — **de·liv·er·abil·i·ty** \-ˌliv-(ə-)rə-ˈbil-ət-ē\ *n* — **de·liv·er·able** \-ˈliv-(ə-)rə-bəl\ *adj* — **de·liv·er·er** \-ˈliv-ər-ər\ *n*
de·liv·er·ance \di-ˈliv-(ə-)rən(t)s\ *n* **1** : the act of delivering : the state of being delivered: as **a** : LIBERATION, RESCUE **b** *archaic* : the act of speaking **2** : something delivered or communicated; *esp* : an opinion or decision (as the verdict of a jury) expressed publicly
de·liv·ery \di-ˈliv-(ə-)rē\ *n, pl* **-er·ies** **1** : a delivering from restraint **2 a** : the act of handing over **b** : the physical and legal transfer of a shipment from consignor to consignee ⟨every ~ of perishables was insured against loss⟩ **c** : the act of putting into the legal possession of another **d** : something delivered at one time or in one unit ⟨got my morning ~ of milk⟩ **3** : the act of giving birth **4** : a delivering esp. of a speech; *also* : manner or style of uttering in speech or song **5** : the act or manner of sending forth or throwing ⟨a hitch in the pitcher's ~⟩
delivery boy *n* : a person employed by a retail store to deliver small orders to customers on call
de·liv·ery·man \-(ə-)rē-mən, -ˌman\ *n* : a person who delivers wholesale or retail goods to customers usu. over a regular local route
dell \ˈdel\ *n* [ME *delle*; akin to MHG *telle* ravine, OE *dæl* valley — more at DALE] : a secluded hollow or small valley usu. covered with trees or turf
delly *var of* DELI
de·lo·cal·ize \(ˈ)dē-ˈlō-kə-ˌlīz\ *vt* : to free from the limitations of locality; *specif* : to remove (electrons) from a particular position — **de·lo·cal·iza·tion** \(ˌ)dē-ˌlō-kə-lə-ˈzā-shən\ *n*
de·louse \(ˈ)dē-ˈlau̇s, -ˈlau̇z\ *vt* : to remove lice from
Del·phi·an \ˈdel-fē-ən\ *adj* : DELPHIC
Del·phic \ˈdel-fik\ *adj* **1** : of or relating to ancient Delphi or its oracle **2** : AMBIGUOUS, OBSCURE — **del·phi·cal·ly** \-fi-k(ə-)lē\ *adv*
del·phin·i·um \del-ˈfin-ē-əm\ *n* [NL, genus name, fr. Gk *delphinion* larkspur, dim. of *delphin-, delphis* dolphin — more at DOLPHIN] : any of a large genus (*Delphinium*) of the buttercup family that comprises chiefly perennial erect branching herbs with palmately divided leaves and irregular flowers in showy spikes and includes several that are poisonous

delphinium

Del·phi·nus \del-ˈfī-nəs, -ˈfē-\ *n* [L (gen. *Delphini*), lit., dolphin — more at DOLPHIN] : a northern constellation nearly west of Pegasus
¹del·ta \ˈdel-tə\ *n* [ME *deltha*, fr. Gk *delta*, of Sem origin; akin to Heb *dāleth* daleth] **1** : the 4th letter of the Greek alphabet — see ALPHABET table **2** : something shaped like a capital Greek delta; *esp* : the alluvial deposit at the mouth of a river **3** : an increment of a variable — symbol Δ— **del·ta·ic** \del-ˈtā-ik\ *adj*
²delta *or* δ- *adj* : fourth in position in the structure of an organic molecule from a particular group or atom
Delta — a communications code word for the letter *d*
delta ray *n* : an electron ejected by an ionizing particle in its passage through matter
delta wing *n* [¹*delta*; fr. its shape] : a triangular swept-back airplane wing with straight trailing edge
¹del·toid \ˈdel-ˌtȯid\ *n* [NL *deltoides*, fr. Gk *deltoeidēs* shaped like a delta, fr. *delta*] : a large triangular muscle that covers the shoulder joint and serves to raise the arm laterally
²deltoid *adj* : shaped like a capital delta : TRIANGULAR ⟨a ~ leaf⟩
del·toi·de·us \del-ˈtȯid-ē-əs\ *n, pl* **del·toi·dei** \-ē-ˌī\ [NL, alter. of *deltoides*] : DELTOID
de·lude \di-ˈlüd\ *vt* **de·lud·ed; de·lud·ing** [ME *deluden*, fr. L *deludere*, fr. *de-* + *ludere* to play — more at LUDICROUS] **1** : to mislead the mind or judgment of : impose on : DECEIVE, TRICK **2** *obs* **a** : FRUSTRATE, DISAPPOINT **b** : EVADE, ELUDE ***syn*** see DECEIVE ***ant*** enlighten — **de·lud·er** *n* — **de·lud·ing·ly** \-ˈlüd-iŋ-lē\ *adv*
¹del·uge \ˈdel-(ˌ)yüj\ *n* [ME, fr. MF, fr. L *diluvium*, fr. *diluere* to wash away, fr. *dis-* + *lavere* to wash — more at LYE] **1 a** : an overflowing of the land by water **b** : a drenching rain **2** : an overwhelming amount or number ⟨a ~ of criticism⟩ ⟨a ~ of letters⟩
²deluge *vt* **del·uged; del·ug·ing** **1** : to overflow with water : INUNDATE **2** : OVERWHELM, SWAMP
de·lu·sion \di-ˈlü-zhən\ *n* [ME, fr. L *delusion-, delusio*, fr. *delusus* pp. of *deludere*] **1 a** : the act of deluding : the state of being deluded **b** : an abnormal mental state characterized by the occurrence of delusions **2 a** : something that is falsely or delusively believed or propagated **b** : a false belief regarding the self or persons or objects outside the self that persists despite the facts and is common in some psychotic states — **de·lu·sion·al** \-ˈlüzh-nəl, -ˈlü-zhən-ᵊl\ *adj* — **de·lu·sion·ary** \-zhə-ˌner-ē\ *adj*
syn DELUSION, ILLUSION, HALLUCINATION, MIRAGE *shared meaning element* : something accepted as true that is actually false or unreal
de·lu·sive \-ˈlü-siv, -ˈlü-ziv\ *adj* **1** : likely to delude **2** : constituting a delusion — **de·lu·sive·ly** *adv* — **de·lu·sive·ness** *n*
de·lu·so·ry \-sə-rē, -zə-\ *adj* : DECEPTIVE, DELUSIVE
de·lus·ter \(ˈ)dē-ˈləs-tər\ *vt* : to reduce the sheen of (as yarn or fabric)
de·luxe \di-ˈlu̇ks, -ˈləks, -ˈlüks\ *adj* [F *de luxe*, lit., of luxury] : notably luxurious or elegant ⟨a ~ edition⟩ ⟨~ hotels⟩
¹delve \ˈdelv\ *vb* **delved; delv·ing** [ME *delven*, fr. OE *delfan*; akin to OHG *telban* to dig] *vt, archaic* : EXCAVATE ~ *vi* **1** : to dig or labor with a spade **2** : to make a careful or detailed search for information ⟨*delved* into the past⟩ — **delv·er** *n*
²delve *n, archaic* : CAVE, HOLLOW
dely *abbr* delivery
dem *abbr* **1** demonstrative **2** demurrage
Dem *abbr* Democrat; Democratic
de·mag·ne·tize \(ˈ)dē-ˈmag-nə-ˌtīz\ *vt* : to deprive of magnetic properties — **de·mag·ne·ti·za·tion** \(ˌ)dē-ˌmag-nət-ə-ˈzā-shən\ *n* — **de·mag·ne·tiz·er** \(ˈ)dē-ˈmag-nə-ˌtī-zər\ *n*
dem·a·gog·ic \ˌdem-ə-ˈgäg-ik *also* -ˈgäj- *or* -ˈgōj-\ *adj* : of, relating to, or characteristic of a demagogue : employing demagoguery — **dem·a·gog·i·cal** \-i-kəl\ *adj* — **dem·a·gog·i·cal·ly** \-i-k(ə-)lē\ *adv*
dem·a·gog·ism \ˈdem-ə-ˌgäg-ˌiz-əm\ *n* : DEMAGOGUERY
dem·a·gogue *or* **dem·a·gog** \ˈdem-ə-ˌgäg\ *n* [Gk *dēmagōgos*, fr. *dēmos* people (akin to Gk *daiesthai* to divide) + *agōgos* leading, fr. *agein* to lead — more at TIDE, AGENT] **1** : a leader championing the cause of the common people in ancient times **2** : a leader who makes use of popular prejudices and false claims and promises in order to gain power
dem·a·gogu·ery \-ˌgäg-(ə-)rē\ *n* : the principles or practices of a demagogue
dem·a·gogy \-ˌgäg-ē, -ˌgäj-ē, -ˌgō-jē\ *n* : DEMAGOGUERY
¹de·mand \di-ˈmand\ *n* **1 a** : an act of demanding or asking esp. with authority **b** : something claimed as due **2** *archaic* : QUESTION **3 a** : an expressed desire for ownership or use **b** : willingness and ability to purchase a commodity or service **c** : the quantity of a commodity or service wanted at a specified price and time **4 a** : a seeking or state of being sought after ⟨gold is in great ~⟩ **b** : urgent need **5** : the requirement of work or of the expenditure of a resource — **on demand** : upon presentation and request for payment
²demand *vb* [ME *demaunden*, fr. MF *demander*, fr. ML *demandare*, fr. L *de-* + *mandare* to enjoin — more at MANDATE] *vi* : to make a demand : ASK ~ *vt* **1** : to ask or call for with authority : claim as due or just ⟨~ payment of a debt⟩ **2** : to call for urgently, peremptorily, or insistently ⟨~*ed* that the rioters disperse⟩ **3 a** : to ask authoritatively or earnestly to be informed of **b** : to require to come : SUMMON **4** : to call for as useful or necessary — **de·mand·able** \-ˈman-də-bəl\ *adj* — **de·mand·er** *n*
syn DEMAND, CLAIM, REQUIRE, EXACT *shared meaning element* : to ask or call for something as or as if one's right or due
de·man·dant \di-ˈman-dənt\ *n* **1** : the plaintiff in a real action **2** : one who makes a demand or claim
demand deposit *n* : a bank deposit that can be withdrawn without advance notice
de·mand·ing *adj* : EXACTING — **de·mand·ing·ly** \-ˈman-diŋ-lē\ *adv*
demand loan *n* : CALL LOAN
demand note *n* : a note payable on demand
de·mand–pull \di-ˈman(d)-ˌpu̇l\ *n* : an increase or upward trend in spendable money that tends to result in increased competition for available goods and services and a corresponding increase in consumer prices — compare COST-PUSH — **demand–pull** *adj*
dem·an·toid \ˈdem-ən-ˌtȯid\ *n* [G, fr. obs. G *demant* diamond, fr. MHG *diemant*, fr. OF *diamant*] : a green andradite used as a gem
de·mar·cate \di-ˈmär-ˌkāt, ˈdē-ˌ\ *vt* **-cat·ed; -cat·ing** [back-formation fr. *demarcation*, fr. Sp *demarcación* & Pg *demarcação*, fr. *demarcar* to delimit, fr. *de-* + *marcar* to mark, fr. It *marcare*, of Gmc origin; akin to OHG *marha* boundary — more at MARCH] **1** : to mark the limits of **2** : to set apart : SEPARATE — **de·mar·ca·tion** *also* **de·mar·ka·tion** \ˌdē-ˌmär-ˈkā-shən\ *n*
de·marche \dā-ˈmärsh, di-ˈ, ˈdā-ˌ\ *n* [F *démarche*, lit., gait, fr. MF, fr. *demarcher* to march, fr. OF *demarchier*, fr. *de-* + *marchier* to march] **1 a** : a course of action : MANEUVER **b** : a diplomatic move or maneuver **2 a** : a diplomatic representation **b** : a representation of views to a public official
de·mark \di-ˈmärk\ *vt* : DEMARCATE
deme \ˈdēm\ *n* [Gk *dēmos*, lit., people] **1** : a unit of local government in ancient Attica **2** : a local population of closely related organisms; *esp* : GAMODEME
¹de·mean \di-ˈmēn\ *vt* **de·meaned; de·mean·ing** [ME *demenen*, fr. OF *demener* to conduct, fr. *de-* + *mener* to drive, fr. L *minare*, fr. *minari* to threaten — more at MOUNT] : to conduct or behave (oneself) usu. in a proper manner
²demean *vt* **de·meaned; de·mean·ing** [*de-* + *mean*] : DEGRADE, DEBASE ***syn*** see ABASE
de·mean·or \di-ˈmē-nər\ *n* : behavior toward others : outward manner ***syn*** see BEARING
de·ment·ed \di-ˈment-əd\ *adj* : MAD, INSANE — **de·ment·ed·ly** *adv* — **de·ment·ed·ness** *n*
de·men·tia \di-ˈmen-chə\ *n* [L, fr. *dement-, demens* mad, fr. *de-* + *ment-, mens* mind — more at MIND] **1** : a condition of deteriorated mentality **2** : MADNESS, INSANITY — **de·men·tial** \-chəl\ *adj*

dementia prae·cox \-'prē-ˌkäks\ n [NL, lit., premature dementia] : SCHIZOPHRENIA

de·mer·it \di-'mer-ət\ n [ME, fr. MF demerite, fr. de- + merite merit] **1** obs : OFFENSE **2 a** : a quality that deserves blame or lacks merit : FAULT, DEFECT **b** : lack of merit **3** : a mark usu. entailing a loss of privilege given to an offender

de·mesne \di-'mān, -'mēn\ n [ME, alter. of demeyne, fr. OF demaine — more at DOMAIN] **1** : legal possession of land as one's own **2** : manorial land actually possessed by the lord and not held by tenants **3 a** : the land attached to a mansion **b** : landed property : ESTATE **c** : REGION, TERRITORY **4** : REALM, DOMAIN

De·me·ter \di-'mēt-ər\ n [L, fr. Gk Dēmētēr] : the Greek goddess of agriculture — compare CERES

demi- prefix [ME, fr. demi, fr. MF, fr. L dimidius, prob. back-formation fr. dimidiare to halve, fr. dis- + medius mid — more at MID] **1** : half ⟨demibastion⟩ **2** : one that partly belongs to (a specified type or class) ⟨demigod⟩

demi·god \'dem-i-ˌgäd\ n **1** : a mythological being with more power than a mortal but less than a god **2** : a person so outstanding that he seems to approach the divine — **demi·god·dess** \-ˌgäd-əs\ n

demi·john \'dem-i-ˌjän\ n [by folk etymology fr. F dame-jeanne, lit., Lady Jane] : a narrow-necked bottle of glass or stoneware enclosed in wickerwork and holding from 1 to 10 gallons

de·mil·i·ta·rize \(')dē-'mil-ə-tə-ˌrīz, di-\ vt **1 a** : to do away with the military organization and potential of **b** : to prohibit (as a zone or frontier area) from being used for military purposes **2** : to deprive of military characteristics or purposes — **de·mil·i·tar·i·za·tion** \(ˌ)dē-ˌmil-ə-t(ə-)rə-'zā-shən, di-\ n

demi·mon·daine \ˌdem-i-ˌmän-'dān, -'män-\ n [F demi-mondaine, fr. fem. of demi-mondain, fr. demi-monde] : a woman of the demimonde

demi·monde \'dem-i-ˌmänd\ n [F demi-monde, fr. demi- + monde world, fr. L mundus — more at MUNDANE] **1 a** : a class of women on the fringes of respectable society supported by wealthy lovers **b** : PROSTITUTES **2** : DEMIMONDAINE **3** : a group engaged in activity of doubtful legality or propriety

de·min·er·al·ize \(')dē-'min-(ə-)rə-ˌlīz\ vt : to remove the mineral matter from : DESALT — **de·min·er·al·iza·tion** \(ˌ)dē-ˌmin-(ə-)rə-lə-'zā-shən\ n — **de·min·er·al·iz·er** \(')dē-'min-(ə-)rə-ˌlī-zər\ n

demi·rep \'dem-i-ˌrep\ n [demi- + rep (reprobate)] : DEMIMONDAINE

¹de·mise \di-'mīz\ vb **de·mised**; **de·mis·ing** vt **1** : to convey (as an estate) by will or lease **2** obs : CONVEY, GIVE **3** : to transmit by succession or inheritance ~ vi **1** : DIE, DECEASE **2** : to pass by descent or bequest ⟨the property demised to the king⟩

²demise n [MF, fem. of demis, pp. of demettre to dismiss, fr. L demittere to send down, fr. de- + mittere to send — more at SMITE] **1** : the conveyance of an estate **2** : transfer of the sovereignty to a successor **3 a** : DEATH **b** : a cessation of existence or activity

demi·semi·qua·ver \ˌdem-i-'sem-i-ˌkwā-vər\ n : THIRTY-SECOND NOTE

de·mis·sion \di-'mish-ən\ n [MF, fr. L demission-, demissio lowering, fr. demissus, pp. of demittere] : RESIGNATION, ABDICATION

de·mit \di-'mit\ vb **de·mit·ted**; **de·mit·ting** [MF demettre] vt **1** archaic : DISMISS **2** : RESIGN ~ vi : to withdraw from office or membership

demi·tasse \'dem-i-ˌtas, -ˌtäs\ n [F demi-tasse, fr. demi- + tasse cup, fr. MF, fr. Ar tass, fr. Per tašt] : a small cup of black coffee; also : the cup used to serve it

demi·urge \'dem-ē-ˌərj\ n [LL demiurgus, fr. Gk dēmiourgos, lit., one who works for the people, fr. dēmios of the people (fr. dēmos people) + -ourgos worker (fr. ergon work) — more at DEMAGOGUE, WORK] **1** cap **a** : a Platonic subordinate deity who fashions the sensible world in the light of eternal ideas **b** : a Gnostic subordinate deity who is the creator of the material world **2** : something that is an autonomous creative force or decisive power — **demi·ur·geous** \ˌdem-ē-'ər-jəs\ adj — **demi·ur·gic** \-jik\ or **demi·ur·gi·cal** \-ji-kəl\ adj — **demi·ur·gi·cal·ly** \-ji-k(ə-)lē\ adv

demi·world \'dem-i-ˌwərld\ n [part trans. of F demimonde] : DEMIMONDE 3

demo \'dem-(ˌ)ō\ n, pl **dem·os** **1** cap : DEMOCRAT 2 **2** : DEMONSTRATION 2

¹de·mob \(')dē-'mäb, di-\ vt, chiefly Brit : DEMOBILIZE

²demob n, chiefly Brit : the act or process of demobilizing : DEMOBILIZATION

de·mo·bi·lize \di-'mō-bə-ˌlīz, (')dē-\ vt **1** : DISBAND **2** : to discharge from military service — **de·mo·bi·li·za·tion** \di-ˌmō-bə-lə-'zā-shən, (ˌ)dē-\ n

de·moc·ra·cy \di-'mäk-rə-sē\ n, pl **-cies** [MF democratie, fr. LL democratia, fr. Gk dēmokratia, fr. dēmos + -kratia -cracy] **1 a** : government by the people; esp : rule of the majority **b** : a government in which the supreme power is vested in the people and exercised by them directly or indirectly through a system of representation usu. involving periodically held free elections **2** : a political unit that has a democratic government **3** cap : the principles and policies of the Democratic party in the U.S. **4** : the common people esp. when constituting the source of political authority **5** : the absence of hereditary or arbitrary class distinctions or privileges

dem·o·crat \'dem-ə-ˌkrat\ n **1 a** : an adherent of democracy **b** : one who practices social equality **2** cap : a member of the Democratic party of the U.S.

dem·o·crat·ic \ˌdem-ə-'krat-ik\ adj **1** : of, relating to, or favoring democracy **2** often cap : of or relating to one of the two major political parties in the U.S. evolving in the early 19th century from the anti-Federalists and the Democratic-Republican party and associated in modern times with policies of broad social reform and internationalism **3** : of, relating to, or appealing to the broad masses of the people ⟨~ art⟩ **4** : favoring social equality : not snobbish — **dem·o·crat·i·cal·ly** \-i-k(ə-)lē\ adv

democratic centralism n : participation of Communist party members in discussion of policy and election of higher party organizations and strict obedience of members and lower party bodies to decisions of the higher units

Democratic–Republican adj : of or relating to a major American political party of the early 19th century favoring a strict interpretation of the constitution to restrict the powers of the federal government and emphasizing states' rights

de·moc·ra·tize \di-'mäk-rə-ˌtīz\ vt **-tized; -tiz·ing** : to make democratic — **de·moc·ra·ti·za·tion** \-ˌmäk-rət-ə-'zā-shən\ n — **de·moc·ra·tiz·er** \-'mäk-rə-ˌtī-zər\ n

dé·mo·dé \ˌdā-mō-'dā\ adj [F, fr. dé- de- + mode] : no longer fashionable : OUT-OF-DATE

de·mod·ed \(')dē-'mōd-əd\ adj : DÉMODÉ

de·mod·u·late \(')dē-'mäj-ə-ˌlāt\ vt : to extract the intelligence from (a modulated radio, laser, or computer signal) — **de·mod·u·la·tor** \-ˌlāt-ər\ n

de·mod·u·la·tion \(ˌ)dē-ˌmäj-ə-'lā-shən\ n : the process of demodulating

De·mo·gor·gon \ˌdē-mə-'gȯr-gən, 'dē-mə-\ n [LL] : a mysterious spirit or deity often explained as a primeval creator god who antedates the gods of Greek mythology

de·mo·graph·ic \ˌdē-mə-'graf-ik, ˌdem-ə-\ adj **1** : of or relating to demography **2** : of or relating to the dynamic balance of a population esp. with regard to density and capacity for expansion or decline — **de·mo·graph·i·cal·ly** \-i-k(ə-)lē\ adv

de·mog·ra·phy \di-'mäg-rə-fē\ n [F démographie, fr. Gk dēmos people + F -graphie -graphy] : the statistical study of human populations esp. with reference to size and density, distribution, and vital statistics — **de·mog·ra·pher** \-fər\ n

dem·oi·selle \ˌdem-(w)ə-'zel\ n [F, fr. OF dameisele — more at DAMSEL] **1 a** : a young lady **2** : a small Old World crane (Anthropoides virgo) with long secondaries and breast feathers **3** : DAMSELFLY

De·Moi·vre's theorem \di-'mȯi-vərz-, -'mwäv-(rə)z-\ n [Abraham De Moivre †1754 F mathematician] : a theorem of complex numbers: the nth power of a complex number has for its absolute value and its argument respectively the nth power of the absolute value and n times the argument of the complex number

demoiselle 2

de·mol·ish \di-'mäl-ish\ vt [MF demoliss-, stem of demolir, fr. L demoliri, fr. de- + moliri to construct, fr. moles mass — more at MOLE] **1 a** : to tear down : RAZE **b** : to break to pieces : SMASH **2 a** : to do away with : DESTROY **b** : to put into a very weak position : DISCREDIT — **de·mol·ish·er** n — **de·mol·ish·ment** \-ish-mənt\ n

de·mo·li·tion \ˌdem-ə-'lish-ən, ˌdē-mə-\ n **1** : the act of demolishing; esp : destruction in war by means of explosives **2** pl : explosives for destruction in war — **de·mo·li·tion·ist** \-'lish-(ə-)nəst\ n

demolition derby n : a contest in which skilled drivers ram old cars into one another until only one car remains running

de·mon or **dae·mon** \'dē-mən\ n [ME demon, fr. LL & L; LL daemon evil spirit, fr. L, divinity, spirit, fr. Gk daimōn] **1** usu daemon : an attendant power or spirit : GENIUS **2 a** : an evil spirit **b** : an evil or undesirable emotion, trait, or state **3** usu daemon : a supernatural being of Greek mythology intermediate between gods and men **4** : one that has unusual drive or effectiveness ⟨a ~ for work⟩ — **de·mon·ess** \-mə-nəs\ n — **de·mo·ni·an** \di-'mō-nē-ən\ adj — **de·mon·iza·tion** \ˌdē-mə-nə-'zā-shən, -ˌnī-\ n — **de·mon·ize** \'dē-mə-ˌnīz\ vt

de·mon·e·tize \(')dē-'män-ə-ˌtīz, -'mən-\ vt [F démonétiser, fr. dé- de- + L moneta coin — more at MINT] **1** : to stop using (a metal) as a monetary standard **2** : to deprive of value for official payment — **de·mon·e·ti·za·tion** \(ˌ)dē-ˌmän-ət-ə-'zā-shən, -ˌmən-\ n

¹de·mo·ni·ac \di-'mō-nē-ˌak\ also **de·mo·ni·a·cal** \ˌdē-mə-'nī-ə-kəl\ adj [ME demoniak, fr. LL daemoniacus, fr. Gk daimoniakos, fr. daimon-, daimōn] **1** : possessed or influenced by a demon **2** : of, relating to, or suggestive of a demon : FIENDISH ⟨~ cruelty⟩ — **de·mo·ni·a·cal·ly** \ˌdē-mə-'nī-ə-k(ə-)lē\ adv

²demoniac n : one regarded as possessed by a demon

de·mon·ic \di-'män-ik\ also **de·mon·i·cal** \-i-kəl\ adj : DEMONIAC 2 — **de·mon·i·cal·ly** \-i-k(ə-)lē\ adv

de·mon·ol·o·gy \ˌdē-mə-'näl-ə-jē\ n **1** : the study of demons or evil spirits **2** : belief in demons : a doctrine of evil spirits **3** : a catalog of enemies ⟨the liberal creed at that time put Big Business in a central place in its ~ —Carl Kaysen⟩

de·mon·stra·ble \di-'män(t)-strə-bəl\ adj **1** : capable of being demonstrated **2** : APPARENT, EVIDENT — **de·mon·stra·bil·i·ty** \-ˌmän(t)-strə-'bil-ət-ē\ n — **de·mon·stra·ble·ness** \-'män(t)-strə-bəl-nəs\ n — **de·mon·stra·bly** \-blē\ adv

dem·on·strate \'dem-ən-ˌstrāt\ vb **-strat·ed; -strat·ing** [L demonstratus, pp. of demonstrare, fr. de- + monstrare to show — more at MUSTER] vt **1** : to show clearly **2 a** : to prove or make clear by reasoning or evidence **b** : to illustrate and explain esp. with many examples **3** : to show or prove the value or efficiency of to a prospective buyer ~ vi : to make a demonstration **syn** see SHOW

dem·on·stra·tion \ˌdem-ən-'strā-shən\ n **1** : an outward expression or display **2 a** : an act, process, or means of demonstrating to the intelligence: as **a** (1) : conclusive evidence : PROOF (2) : a proof in which the conclusion is the immediate sequence of reasoning from premises **b** : a showing to a prospective buyer of the merits of a product **3** : a show of armed force **4** : a public display of group feelings toward a person or cause — **dem·on·stra-**

tion·al \-shnəl, -shən-ᵊl\ *adj* — **dem·on·stra·tion·ist** \-sh(ə-)nəst\ *n*

¹**de·mon·stra·tive** \di-'män(t)-strət-iv\ *adj* **1 a** : demonstrating as real or true **b** : characterized or established by demonstration **2** : pointing out the one referred to and distinguishing it from others of the same class ⟨~ pronouns⟩ **3 a** : marked by display of feeling **b** : inclined to display feelings openly — **de·mon·stra·tive·ly** *adv* — **de·mon·stra·tive·ness** *n*

²**demonstrative** *n* : a demonstrative word or morpheme

dem·on·stra·tor \'dem-ən-‚strāt-ər\ *n* **1** : one that demonstrates **2** : a product (as an automobile) used to demonstrate performance or merits to prospective buyers

de·mor·al·ize \di-'mȯr-ə-‚līz, dē-, -'mär-\ *vt* **1** : to corrupt the morals of **2 a** : to weaken the morale of : DISCOURAGE, DISPIRIT **b** : to upset or destroy the normal functioning of **c** : to throw into disorder — **de·mor·al·iza·tion** \di-‚mȯr-ə-lə-'zā-shən, ‚dē-, -‚mär-\ *n* — **de·mor·al·iz·er** \di-'mȯr-ə-‚lī-zər, 'dē-, -'mär-\ *n* — **de·mor·al·iz·ing·ly** \-‚zin-lē\ *adv*

de·mos \'dē-‚mäs\ *n* [Gk *dēmos* — more at DEMAGOGUE] **1** : the common people of an ancient Greek state **2** : POPULACE

de·mote \di-'mōt, 'dē-\ *vt* **de·mot·ed; de·mot·ing** [*de-* + *-mote* (as in *promote*)] : to reduce to a lower grade or rank **syn** see DEGRADE — **de·mo·tion** \-'mō-shən\ *n*

de·mot·ic \di-'mät-ik\ *adj* [Gk *dēmotikos*, fr. *dēmotēs* commoner, fr. *dēmos*] **1** : POPULAR 1 **2** : of, relating to, or written in a simplified form of the ancient Egyptian hieratic writing **3** : of or relating to the form of Modern Greek that is based on colloquial use

de·mount \(')dē-'maunt\ *vt* **1** : to remove from a mounted position **2** : DISASSEMBLE — **de·mount·able** \-ə-bəl\ *adj*

¹**de·mul·cent** \di-'məl-sənt\ *adj* [L *demulcent-, demulcens,* prp. of *demulcēre* to soothe, fr. *de-* + *mulcēre* to soothe] : SOOTHING

²**demulcent** *n* : a usu. mucilaginous or oily substance (as tragacanth) capable of soothing or protecting an abraded mucous membrane

¹**de·mur** \di-'mər\ *vi* **de·murred; de·mur·ring** [ME *demeoren* to linger, fr. OF *demorer,* fr. L *demorari,* fr. *de-* + *morari* to linger, fr. *mora* delay — more at MEMORY] **1** : to file a demurrer **2** : to take exception : OBJECT ⟨he demurred at the horseplay⟩ **3** *archaic* : DELAY, HESITATE

²**demur** *n* **1** : hesitation (as in doing or accepting) usu. based on doubt of the acceptability of something offered or proposed ⟨women who follow fashion without ~⟩ **2** : OBJECTION, PROTEST **syn** see QUALM

de·mure \di-'myu̇(ə)r\ *adj* [ME] **1** : RESERVED, MODEST **2** : affectedly modest, reserved, or serious : COY — **de·mure·ly** *adv* — **de·mure·ness** *n*

de·mur·rage \di-'mər-ij, -'mə-rij\ *n* **1** : the detention of a ship by the freighter beyond the time allowed for loading, unloading, or sailing **2** : a charge for detaining a ship, freight car, or truck

de·mur·ral \di-'mər-əl, -'mə-rəl\ *n* : an act or instance of demurring

¹**de·mur·rer** \di-'mər-ər, -'mə-rər\ *n* [MF *demorer,* v.] **1** : a pleading by a party to a legal action that assumes the truth of the matter alleged by the opposite party and sets up that it is insufficient in law to sustain his claim or that there is some other defect on the face of the pleadings constituting a legal reason why the opposing party should not be allowed to proceed further **2** : OBJECTION

²**de·mur·rer** \-'mər-ər\ *n* [¹*demur*] : one that demurs

de·my \di-'mī\ *n* [ME *demi* half — more at DEMI-] : a size of paper typically 16 x 21 inches

de·my·elin·ate \(')dē-'mī-ə-lə-‚nāt\ *vt* **-at·ed; -at·ing** : to remove or destroy the myelin of — **de·my·elin·ation** \(‚)dē-‚mī-ə-lə-'nā-shən\ *n*

de·mys·ti·fy \(')dē-'mis-tə-‚fī\ *vt* **1** : to remove the mystery from : EXPLICATE — **de·mys·ti·fi·ca·tion** \(‚)dē-‚mis-tə-fə-'kā-shən\ *n*

de·my·thol·o·gize \‚dē-mith-'äl-ə-‚jīz\ *vt* **1** : to divest of mythological forms in order to uncover the meaning underlying them ⟨~ the Gospels⟩ **2** : to divest of mythical elements or associations — **de·my·thol·o·gi·za·tion** \-‚äl-ə-jə-'zā-shən\ *n* — **de·my·thol·o·giz·er** \-'äl-ə-‚jī-zər\ *n*

¹**den** \'den\ *n* [ME, fr. OE *denn;* akin to OE *denu* valley, OHG *tenni* threshing floor, Gk *thenar* palm of the hand] **1** : the lair of a wild usu. predatory animal **2 a** (1) : a hollow or cavern used esp. as a hideout (2) : a center of secret activity **b** : a small usu. squalid dwelling **3** : a comfortable usu. secluded room **4** : a subdivision of a cub-scout pack made up of two or more boys

²**den** *vb* **denned; den·ning** *vi* : to live in or retire to a den ~ *vt* : to drive into a den

¹**Den** *abbr* Denmark

²**Den** *or* **Denb** *abbr* Denbighshire

de·nar·i·us \di-'nar-ē-əs, -'ner-\ *n, pl* **de·nar·ii** \-ē-‚ī, -ē-‚ē\ [ME, fr. L — more at DENIER] **1** : a small silver coin of ancient Rome **2** : a gold coin of the Roman Empire equivalent to 25 denarii

de·na·tion·al·ize \(')dē-'nash-nə-‚līz, -'nash-ən-ᵊl-‚īz\ *vt* **1** : to divest of national character or rights **2** : to remove from ownership or control by the national government — **de·na·tion·al·iza·tion** \(‚)dē-‚nash-nə-lə-'zā-shən, -‚nash-ən-ᵊl-ə-'zā-\ *n*

de·nat·u·ral·ize \(')dē-'nach-(ə-)rə-‚līz\ *vt* **1** : to make unnatural **2** : to deprive of the rights and duties of a citizen — **de·nat·u·ral·iza·tion** \(‚)dē-‚nach-(ə-)rə-lə-'zā-shən\ *n*

de·na·tur·ant \(')dē-'nāch-(ə-)rənt\ *n* : a denaturing agent

de·na·tur·ation \dē-‚nā-chə-'rā-shən\ *n* : the process of denaturing — **de·na·tur·ation·al** \-shnəl, -shən-ᵊl\ *adj*

de·na·ture \(')dē-'nā-chər\ *vt* **de·na·tured; de·na·tur·ing** \-(ə-)riŋ\ **1** : to deprive of natural qualities: as **a** : to make (alcohol) unfit for drinking (as by adding an obnoxious substance) without impairing usefulness for other purposes **b** : to modify the molecular structure of (a protein) esp. by heat, acid, alkali, or ultraviolet radiation so as to destroy or diminish some of the original properties and esp. the specific biological activity **c** : to add nonfissionable material to (fissionable material) so as to make unsuitable for use in an atomic bomb **2** : DEHUMANIZE

de·na·zi·fy \(')dē-'nät-si-‚fī, -'nat-\ *vt* **-fied; -fying** : to rid of Nazism and its influence — **de·na·zi·fi·ca·tion** \(‚)dē-‚nät-si-fə-'kā-shən, -‚nat-\ *n*

dendr- *or* **dendro-** *comb form* [Gk, fr. *dendron;* akin to Gk *drys* tree — more at TREE] : tree ⟨dendrophilous⟩ : resembling a tree ⟨dendrite⟩

den·dri·form \'den-drə-‚fȯrm\ *adj* : resembling a tree in structure

den·drite \'den-‚drīt\ *n* **1** : a branching treelike figure produced on or in a mineral by a foreign mineral; *also* : the mineral so marked **2** : a crystallized arborescent form **3** : any of the usu. branching protoplasmic processes that conduct impulses toward the body of a nerve cell — see NEURON illustration — **den·drit·ic** \den-'drit-ik\ *also* **den·drit·i·cal** \-i-kəl\ *adj* — **den·drit·i·cal·ly** \-i-k(ə-)lē\ *adv*

den·dro·chro·nol·o·gy \‚den-(‚)drō-krə-'näl-ə-jē\ *n* : the science of dating events and variations in environment in former periods by comparative study of growth rings in trees and aged wood — **den·dro·chro·no·log·i·cal** \-‚krän-ᵊl-'äj-i-kəl, -‚krōn-\ *adj* — **den·dro·chro·no·log·i·cal·ly** \-i-k(ə-)lē\ *adv*

den·droid \'den-‚drȯid\ *adj* [Gk *dendroeidēs,* fr. *dendron*] : resembling a tree in form : ARBORESCENT

den·drol·o·gy \den-'dräl-ə-jē\ *n* : the study of trees — **den·dro·log·ic** \‚den-drə-'läj-ik\ *or* **den·dro·log·i·cal** \-i-kəl\ *adj* — **den·drol·o·gist** \den-'dräl-ə-jəst\ *n*

dene \'dēn\ *n* [ME, fr. OE *denu*] *Brit* : VALLEY

Dé·né \'den-ē\ *n, pl* **Déné** *or* **Dénés** \-‚ēz\ [F, fr. Déné] **1** : a member of an Athapaskan people of the interior of Alaska and northwestern Canada **2** : the language of the Déné people

Den·eb \'den-‚eb, -əb\ *n* [Ar *dhanab al-dajāja,* lit., the tail of the hen] : a star of the first magnitude in Cygnus

den·e·ga·tion \‚den-i-'gā-shən\ *n* [ME *denegacioun,* fr. MF or L; MF *denegation,* fr. L *denegation-, denegatio,* fr. *denegatus,* pp. of *denegare* to deny — more at DENY] : DENIAL

de·ner·vate \'dē-(‚)nər-‚vāt\ *vt* **-vat·ed; -vat·ing** : to deprive of a nerve supply (as by cutting a nerve) — **de·ner·va·tion** \‚dē-(‚)nər-'vā-shən\ *n*

den·gue \'deŋ-gē, -‚gā\ *n* [Sp] : an acute infectious viral disease characterized by headache, severe joint pain, and a rash

de·ni·able \di-'nī-ə-bəl\ *adj* : capable of being denied

de·ni·al \di-'nī(-ə)l\ *n* **1** : refusal to satisfy a request or desire **2 a** (1) : refusal to admit the truth or reality (as of a statement or charge) (2) : assertion that an allegation is false **b** : refusal to acknowledge a person or a thing : DISAVOWAL **3** : the denying by the defendant of an allegation of the opposite party in a lawsuit **4** : SELF-DENIAL **5** : negation in logic

de·nic·o·tin·ize \(')dē-'nik-ə-‚tē-‚nīz\ *vt* **-ized; -iz·ing** : to remove part of the nicotine from (tobacco)

¹**de·ni·er** \di-'nī(-ə)r\ *n* : one that denies

²**de·nier** *n* [ME *denere,* fr. MF *denier,* fr. L *denarius,* coin worth ten asses, fr. *denarius* containing ten, fr. *deni* ten each, fr. *decem* ten — more at TEN] **1** \də-'ni(ə)r, dən-'yā\ : a small orig. silver coin of France and western Europe from the 8th to the 19th century **2** \'den-yər\ : a unit of fineness for silk, rayon, or nylon yarn equal to the fineness of a yarn weighing one gram for each 9000 meters

den·i·grate \'den-i-‚grāt\ *vt* **-grat·ed; -grat·ing** [L *denigratus,* pp. of *denigrare,* fr. *de-* + *nigrare* to blacken, fr. *nigr-, niger* black] **1** : to cast aspersions on : DEFAME ⟨expatriates whom we are in the habit of denigrating — Henry Miller⟩ **2** : to deny the importance or validity of : BELITTLE ⟨he was a philosopher and inclined to ~ ideas in literature — W. C. DeVane⟩ — **den·i·gra·tion** \‚den-i-'grā-shən\ *n* — **den·i·gra·tive** \'den-i-‚grāt-iv\ *adj* — **den·i·gra·tor** \'den-i-‚grāt-ər\ *n* — **den·i·gra·to·ry** \'den-i-grə-‚tōr-ē, -‚tȯr-\ *adj*

den·im \'den-əm\ *n* [F *serge de Nîmes* serge of Nîmes, France] **1 a** : a firm durable twilled usu. cotton fabric woven with colored warp and white filling threads **b** : a similar fabric woven in colored stripes **2** *pl* : overalls or trousers usu. of blue denim

de·ni·tri·fi·ca·tion \(‚)dē-‚nī-trə-fə-'kā-shən\ *n* : an act or process of denitrifying; *specif* : reduction of nitrates or nitrites commonly by bacteria and usu. resulting in the escape of nitrogen into the air

de·ni·tri·fy \(')dē-'nī-trə-‚fī\ *vt* **1** : to remove nitrogen or its compound from **2** : to convert (a nitrate or a nitrite) into a compound of a lower state of oxidation

den·i·zen \'den-ə-zən\ *n* [ME *denysen,* fr. MF *denzein,* fr. OF, inner, fr. *denz* within, fr. LL *deintus,* fr. L *de-* + *intus* within — more at ENT-] **1** : INHABITANT **2** : one admitted to residence in a foreign country; *esp* : an alien admitted to rights of citizenship **3 a** : a naturalized plant or animal **b** : one that frequents a place

den mother *n* : a female adult leader of a cub-scout den

de·nom·i·nate \di-'näm-ə-‚nāt\ *vt* [L *denominatus,* pp. of *denominare,* fr. *de-* + *nominare* to name — more at NOMINATE] : to give a name to : DESIGNATE

de·nom·i·nate number \di-‚näm-ə-nət-\ *n* [L *denominatus*] : a number (as 7 in 7 *feet*) that specifies a quantity in terms of a unit of measurement

de·nom·i·na·tion \di-‚näm-ə-'nā-shən\ *n* **1** : an act of denominating **2** : NAME, DESIGNATION; *esp* : a general name for a category **3** : a religious organization uniting in a single legal and administrative body a number of local congregations **4** : a value or size of a series of values or sizes (as of money) — **de·nom·i·na·tion·al** \-shnəl, -shən-ᵊl\ *adj* — **de·nom·i·na·tion·al·ly** \-ē\ *adv*

de·nom·i·na·tion·al·ism \-shnəl-‚iz-əm, -shən-ᵊl-\ *n* **1** : devotion to denominational principles or interests **2** : the emphasizing of denominational differences to the point of being narrowly exclusive : SECTARIANISM — **de·nom·i·na·tion·al·ist** \-shnə-ləst, -shən-ᵊl-əst\ *n*

de·nom·i·na·tive \di-'näm-(ə-)nət-iv\ *adj* [L *de* from + *nomin-, nomen* name] : derived from a noun or adjective — **denominative** *n*

de·nom·i·na·tor \di-'näm-ə-‚nāt-ər\ *n* **1** : the part of a fraction that is below the line signifying division and that in fractions with 1 as the numerator indicates into how many parts the unit is divided : DIVISOR **2 a** : a common trait **b** : the average level (as of taste or opinion) : STANDARD

de·no·ta·tion \‚dē-nō-'tā-shən\ *n* **1** : an act or process of denoting **2** : MEANING; *esp* : a direct specific meaning as distinct from connotations **3 a** : a denoting term : NAME **b** : SIGN, INDICATION

⟨visible ~*s* of divine wrath⟩ **4 :** the totality of things to which a term is applicable esp. in logic

de·no·ta·tive \'dē-nō-ˌtāt-iv, di-'nōt-ət-iv\ *adj* **1 :** denoting or tending to denote **2 :** relating to denotation

de·note \di-'nōt\ *vt* [MF *denoter,* fr. L *denotare,* fr. *de-* + *notare* to note] **1 :** to serve as an indication of : BETOKEN ⟨the swollen bellies that ~ starvation⟩ **2 :** to serve as an arbitrary mark for ⟨red flares *denoting* danger⟩ **3 :** to make known : ANNOUNCE ⟨his crestfallen look *denoted* his distress⟩ **4 a :** to serve as a linguistic expression of the notion of : MEAN **b :** to stand for : signify by way of logical denotation — **de·note·ment** \-'nōt-mənt\ *n* — **de·no·tive** \-'nōt-iv\ *adj*

syn DENOTE, CONNOTE *shared meaning element* : to mean. In spite of this shared element of meaning, these terms are complementary rather than strictly synonymous and cannot be interchanged without significant loss of precision. DENOTE applies to the definitive meaning content of a term: in a noun, the thing or the definable class of things or ideas which it names; in a verb, the act or state which is affirmed. CONNOTE applies to the ideas or associations that are added to a term and cling to it, often as a result of personal experience but sometimes as a result of something extraneous (as a widely known context or connection with a widely known event). "Home", for example, *denotes* the place where one lives, but to one person it may *connote* comforts, intimacy, and affection and to another misery, estrangement, and abuse

de·noue·ment \ˌdā-ˌnü-'mäⁿ, dā-'nü-ˌ\ *n* [F *dénouement,* lit., untying, fr. MF *desnouement,* fr. *desnouer* to untie, fr. OF *desnoer,* fr. *des-* de- + *noer* to tie, fr. L *nodare,* fr. *nodus* knot — more at NET] **1 :** the final outcome of the main dramatic complication in a literary work **2 :** the outcome of a complex sequence of events

de·nounce \di-'naůn(t)s\ *vt* **de·nounced; de·nounc·ing** [ME *denouncen,* fr. OF *denoncier* to proclaim, fr. L *denuntiare,* fr. *de-* + *nuntiare* to report — more at ANNOUNCE] **1 :** to pronounce esp. publicly to be blameworthy or evil **2** *archaic* **a :** PROCLAIM **b :** to announce threateningly **3 :** to inform against : ACCUSE **4** *obs* : PORTEND **5 :** to announce formally the termination of (as a treaty) ***syn*** see CRITICIZE ***ant*** eulogize — **de·nounce·ment** \-'naůn(t)-smənt\ *n* — **de·nounc·er** *n*

de no·vo \di-'nō-(ˌ)vō, dā-\ *adv* [L] : over again : ANEW ⟨a case tried *de novo*⟩

dense \'den(t)s\ *adj* **dens·er; dens·est** [L *densus;* akin to Gk *dasys* thick with hair or leaves] **1 :** marked by compactness or crowding together of parts **2 a :** marked by a stupid imperviousness to ideas or impressions : THICKHEADED **b :** EXTREME ⟨~ ignorance⟩ **3 :** having between any two elements at least one element ⟨the rational numbers are ~⟩ **4 :** demanding concentration to follow or comprehend ⟨~ prose⟩ **5 :** possessing relatively great retarding power upon light waves and consequently relatively high density ⟨a ~ glass⟩ **6 :** having high or relatively high opacity ⟨a ~ fog⟩ ⟨a ~ photographic negative⟩

syn* 1** see CLOSE ***ant sparse (*as of forests, population*), tenuous (*as of clouds*) **2** see STUPID ***ant*** subtle, bright — **dense·ly** *adv* — **dense·ness** \'den(t)-snəs\ *n*

den·si·fy \'den(t)-sə-ˌfī\ *vt* **-fied; -fy·ing :** to make denser; *specif* : to increase the density of (wood) by pressure usu. with impregnation of a resin — **den·si·fi·ca·tion** \ˌden(t)-sə-fə-'kā-shən\ *n*

den·sim·e·ter \den-'sim-ət-ər\ *n* [L *densus* + ISV *-meter*] : an instrument for determining density or specific gravity — **den·si·met·ric** \ˌden(t)-sə-'me-trik\ *adj*

den·si·tom·e·ter \ˌden(t)-sə-'täm-ət-ər\ *n* **:** an instrument for determining optical or photographic density — **den·si·to·met·ric** \ˌden(t)-sət-ə-'me-trik\ *adj* — **den·si·tom·e·try** \ˌden(t)-sə-'täm-ə-trē\ *n*

den·si·ty \'den(t)-sət-ē, -stē\ *n, pl* **-ties 1 :** the quality or state of being dense **2 :** the quantity per unit volume, unit area, or unit length: as **a :** the mass of a substance per unit volume **b :** the distribution of a quantity (as mass, electricity, or energy) per unit usu. of space **c :** the average number of individuals or units per space unit ⟨a population ~ of 500 persons per square mile⟩ ⟨a housing ~ of 10 houses per acre⟩ **3 :** STUPIDITY **4 a :** the degree of opacity of a translucent medium **b :** the common logarithm of the opacity

[1]**dent** \'dent\ *n* [ME, blow, alter. of *dint*] **1 :** a depression or hollow made by a blow or by pressure **2 a :** an impression or effect often made against resistance and usu. having a weakening effect **b :** initial progress : HEADWAY

[2]**dent** *vt* **1 :** to make a dent in **2 :** to have a weakening effect on ~ *vi* **:** to form a dent by sinking inward : become dented

[3]**dent** *n* [F, lit., tooth, fr. L *dent-, dens*] : TOOTH 3a

[4]**dent** *abbr* dental; dentist; dentistry

dent- *or* **denti-** *or* **dento-** *comb form* [ME *denti-,* fr. L, fr. *dent-, dens* tooth — more at TOOTH] **1 :** tooth : teeth ⟨*dent*algia⟩ ⟨*denti*form⟩ **2 :** dental and ⟨*dento*surgical⟩

[1]**den·tal** \'dent-ᵊl\ *adj* [L *dentalis,* fr. *dent-, dens*] **1 :** of or relating to the teeth or dentistry **2 :** articulated with the tip or blade of the tongue against or near the upper front teeth — **den·tal·ly** \-ē\ *adv*

[2]**dental** *n* **:** a dental consonant

dental floss *n* **:** a waxed thread used to clean between the teeth

dental hygienist *n* **:** one who assists a dentist esp. in cleaning teeth

den·ta·li·um \den-'tā-lē-əm\ *n, pl* **-lia** \-lē-ə\ [NL, genus name, fr. L *dentalis*] : any of a genus (*Dentalium*) of widely distributed tooth shells; *broadly* : TOOTH SHELL

dental technician *n* **:** a technician who makes dental appliances

den·tate \'den-ˌtāt\ *or* **den·tat·ed** \-ˌtāt-əd\ *adj* [L *dentatus,* fr. *dent-, dens*] : having teeth or pointed conical projections ⟨multi*dentate*⟩ ⟨~ leaves⟩ — **den·tate·ly** *adv* — **den·ta·tion** \den-'tā-shən\ *n*

dent corn *n* **:** an Indian corn having kernels that contain both hard and soft starch and that become indented at maturity

den·ti·cle \'dent-i-kəl\ *n* [ME, fr. L *denticulus,* dim. of *dent-, dens*] : a small tooth or other conical pointed projection

den·tic·u·late \den-'tik-yə-lət\ *or* **den·tic·u·lat·ed** \-ˌlāt-əd\ *adj* **1 a :** covered with small pointed projections ⟨a ~ shell⟩; *esp* : SERRATE **b :** finely dentate **2 :** cut into dentils — **den·tic·u·late·ly** *adv* — **den·tic·u·la·tion** \(ˌ)den-ˌtik-yə-'lā-shən\ *n*

den·ti·form \'dent-ə-ˌfȯrm\ *adj* **1 :** shaped like a tooth **2 :** divided into dentate processes

den·ti·frice \'dent-ə-frəs\ *n* [MF, fr. L *dentifricium,* fr. *denti-* + *fricare* to rub — more at FRICTION] : a powder, paste, or liquid for cleaning the teeth

den·tig·er·ous \den-'tij-ə-rəs\ *adj* **:** bearing dentate structures

den·til \'dent-ᵊl, 'den-ˌtil\ *n* [obs. F *dentille,* fr. MF, dim. of *dent*] : one of a series of small projecting rectangular blocks esp. under a cornice

den·tin \'dent-ᵊn\ *or* **den·tine** \'den-ˌtēn, den-'\ *n* **:** a calcareous material similar to but harder and denser than bone that composes the principal mass of a tooth — **den·tin·al** \den-'tēn-ᵊl, 'dent-ᵊn-əl\ *adj*

den·tist \'dent-əst\ *n* [F *dentiste,* fr. *dent*] : one who is skilled in and licensed to practice the prevention, diagnosis, and treatment of diseases, injuries, and malformations of the teeth, jaws, and mouth and who makes and inserts false teeth

den·tist·ry \'dent-ə-strē\ *n* **:** the art or profession of a dentist

den·ti·tion \den-'tish-ən\ *n* [L *dentition-, dentitio,* fr. *dentitus,* pp. of *dentire* to cut teeth, fr. *dent-, dens*] **1 :** the development and cutting of teeth **2 :** the number, kind, and arrangement of teeth see TOOTH illustration **3 :** the character of the teeth as determined by their form and arrangement

den·tu·lous \'den-chə-ləs\ *adj* [back-formation fr. *edentulous*] : having teeth

den·ture \'den-chər\ *n* [F, fr. MF, fr. *dent*] **1 :** a set of teeth **2 :** an artificial replacement for one or more teeth; *esp* : a set of false teeth

de·nu·cle·ar·ize \(')dē-'n(y)ü-klē-ə-ˌrīz\ *vt* **-ized; -iz·ing :** to remove nuclear arms from : prohibit the use of nuclear arms in — **de·nu·cle·ar·iza·tion** \(ˌ)dē-ˌn(y)ü-klē-ə-rə-'zā-shən\ *n*

de·nu·da·tion \ˌdē-(ˌ)n(y)ü-'dā-shən, ˌden-yů-\ *n* **:** an act or process of denuding — **de·nu·da·tion·al** \-shnəl, -shən-ᵊl\ *adj*

de·nude \di-'n(y)üd\ *vt* **de·nud·ed; de·nud·ing** [L *denudare,* fr. *de-* + *nudus* bare — more at NAKED] **1 a :** to strip of all covering **b :** to lay bare by erosion **c :** to strip (land) of forests **2 :** to divest of something important — **de·nude·ment** \-'n(y)üd-mənt\ *n* — **de·nud·er** *n*

de·nu·mer·a·ble \di-'n(y)üm-(ə-)rə-bəl\ *adj* **:** capable of being put into one-to-one correspondence with the positive integers — **de·nu·mer·a·bil·i·ty** \-ˌn(y)üm-(ə-)rə-'bil-ət-ē\ *n* — **de·nu·mer·a·bly** \-'n(y)üm-(ə-)rə-blē\ *adv*

de·nun·ci·a·tion \di-ˌnən(t)-sē-'ā-shən\ *n* **:** an act of denouncing; *esp* : a public condemnation — **de·nun·ci·a·tive** \-'nən(t)-sē-ˌāt-iv\ *adj* — **de·nun·ci·a·to·ry** \-sē-ə-ˌtōr-ē, -ˌtȯr-\ *adj*

de·ny \di-'nī\ *vt* **de·nied; de·ny·ing** [ME *denyen,* fr. OF *denier,* fr. L *denegare,* fr. *de-* + *negare* to deny — more at NEGATE] **1 :** to declare untrue **2 :** to disclaim connection with or responsibility for : DISAVOW **3 a :** to give a negative answer to **b :** to refuse to grant **c :** to restrain (oneself) from gratification of desires **4** *archaic* : DECLINE **5 :** to refuse to accept the existence, truth, or validity of — **de·ny·ing·ly** \-'nī-iŋ-lē\ *adv*

syn DENY, GAINSAY, CONTRADICT, NEGATIVE, IMPUGN, CONTRAVENE *shared meaning element* : to refuse to accept as true, valid, or worthy of consideration ***ant*** confirm, concede

de·o·dar \'dē-ə-ˌdär\ *or* **de·o·da·ra** \ˌdē-ə-'där-ə\ *n* [Hindi *deodār,* fr. Skt *devadāru,* lit., timber of the gods, fr. *deva* god + *dāru* wood] : an East Indian cedar (*Cedrus deodara*)

de·odor·ant \dē-'ōd-ə-rənt\ *n* **:** a preparation that destroys or masks unpleasant odors — **deodorant** *adj*

de·odor·ize \dē-'ōd-ə-ˌrīz\ *vt* **1 :** to eliminate or prevent the offensive odor of **2 :** to make (something unpleasant) more acceptable ⟨their buccaneering was *deodorized* by the fact that their victims were Madagascar pirates —*N.Y. Herald Tribune Bk. Rev.*⟩ — **de·odor·iza·tion** \-ˌōd-ə-rə-'zā-shən\ *n* — **de·odor·iz·er** *n*

de·on·tol·o·gy \ˌdē-ˌän-'täl-ə-jē\ *n* [Gk *deont-, deon* that which is obligatory, fr. neut. of prp. of *dein* to lack, be needful — more at DEUTER-] : the theory or study of moral obligation — **de·on·to·log·i·cal** \ˌdē-ˌänt-ᵊl-'äj-i-kəl\ *adj* — **de·on·tol·o·gist** \ˌdē-ˌän-'täl-ə-jəst\ *n*

Deo vo·len·te \ˌdā-(ˌ)ō-və-'lent-ē, ˌdē-\ [L] : God being willing

de·ox·i·dize \(')dē-'äk-sə-ˌdīz\ *vt* **:** to remove oxygen from — **de·ox·i·da·tion** \(ˌ)dē-ˌäk-sə-'dā-shən\ *n* — **de·ox·i·diz·er** \(')dē-'äk-sə-ˌdī-zər\ *n*

deoxy- *or* **desoxy-** *comb form* [ISV] : containing less oxygen in the molecule than the compound to which it is closely related ⟨*deoxy*ribonucleic acid⟩

de·oxy·cor·ti·co·ste·rone \dē-ˌäk-si-ˌkȯrt-i-'käs-tə-ˌrōn, -i-kō-stə-'rōn\ *n* [ISV] : a steroid hormone $C_{21}H_{30}O_3$ of the adrenal cortex

de·ox·y·gen·ate \(')dē-'äk-si-jə-ˌnāt, ˌdē-äk-'sij-ə-\ *vt* **:** to remove oxygen from — **de·ox·y·gen·ation** \(ˌ)dē-ˌäk-si-jə-'nā-shən, ˌdē-äk-ˌsij-ə-\ *n*

de·ox·y·gen·at·ed *adj* **:** having the hemoglobin in the reduced state

de·oxy·ri·bo·nu·cle·ase \(')dē-'äk-si-ˌrī-bō-'n(y)ü-klē-ˌās, -ˌāz\ *n* [*deoxyribonucle*ic acid + *-ase*] : an enzyme that hydrolyzes DNA to nucleotides — called also *DNase*

de·oxy·ri·bo·nu·cle·ic acid \(')dē-'äk-si-ˌrī-bō-n(y)ů-ˌklē-ik-, -ˌklā-\ *n* [*deoxyribose* + *nucleic acid*] : DNA

de·oxy·ri·bo·nu·cle·o·tide \-'n(y)ü-klē-ə-ˌtīd\ *n* **:** a nucleotide that contains deoxyribose and is a constituent of DNA

de·oxy·ri·bose \(ˌ)dē-ˌäk-si-'rī-ˌbōs, -ˌbōz\ *n* [ISV *deoxy-* + *ribose*] : a pentose sugar $C_5H_{10}O_4$ that is a structural element of DNA

dep *abbr* **1** depart **2** department **3** departure **4** deponent **5** deposed **6** deposit **7** depot **8** deputy

ə abut	ᵊ kitten	ər further	a back	ā bake	ä cot, cart
aů out	ch chin	e less	ē easy	g gift	i trip
j joke	ŋ sing	ō flow	ȯ flaw	ȯi coin	th thin
ü loot	ů foot	y yet	yü few	yů furious	zh vision

ī life; th this

de·part \di-ˈpärt\ *vb* [ME *departen* to divide, go away, fr. OF *departir*, fr. *de-* + *partir* to divide, fr. L *partire*, fr. *part-*, *pars* part] *vi* **1 a** : to go away : LEAVE **b** : DIE **2** : to turn aside : DEVIATE ~ *vt* : to go away from : LEAVE **syn 1** see GO **ant** arrive, remain, abide **2** see SWERVE

de·part·ed *adj* **1** : BYGONE **2** : having died, esp. recently ⟨mourning our ~ friend⟩ **syn** see DEAD

de·part·ment \di-ˈpärt-mənt\ *n* [F *département*; fr. MF, fr. *departir*] **1** : a distinct sphere : PROVINCE **2** : a functional or territorial division: as **a** : a major administrative division of a government **b** : a major territorial administrative subdivision **c** : a division of a college or school giving instruction in a particular subject **d** : a major division of a business **e** : a section of a department store **f** : a territorial subdivision made for the administration and training of military units — **de·part·men·tal** \di-ˌpärt-ˈment-ᵊl, ˌdē-\ *adj* — **de·part·men·tal·ly** \-ᵊl-ē\ *adv*

de·part·men·tal·ize \di-ˌpärt-ˈment-ᵊl-ˌīz, ˌdē-\ *vt* **-ized; -iz·ing** : to divide into departments — **de·part·men·tal·iza·tion** \-ˌment-ᵊl-ə-ˈzā-shən\ *n*

department store *n* : a store selling a wide variety of goods arranged in several departments

de·par·ture \di-ˈpär-chər\ *n* **1 a** (1) : the act of going away (2) *archaic* : DEATH **b** : a ship's position in latitude and longitude at the beginning of a voyage as a point from which to begin dead reckoning **c** : a setting out (as on a new course) **2** : the distance due east or west made by a ship in its course **3** : DIVERGENCE

de·pau·per·ate \di-ˈpȯ-pə-rət\ *adj* [ME *depauperat*, fr. ML *depauperatus*, pp. of *depauperare* to impoverish, fr. L *de-* + *pauperare* to impoverish, fr. *pauper* poor — more at POOR] : falling short of natural development or size — **de·pau·per·ation** \-ˌpȯ-pə-ˈrā-shən\ *n*

de·pend \di-ˈpend\ *vi* [ME *dependen*, fr. MF *dependre*, modif. of L *dependēre*, fr. *de-* + *pendēre* to hang — more at PENDANT] **1 a** : to be contingent **b** : to exist by virtue of a necessary relation **2** : to be pending or undecided **3 a** : to place reliance or trust **b** : to be dependent esp. for financial support **4** : to hang down **syn** see RELY

de·pend·able \di-ˈpen-də-bəl\ *adj* : capable of being depended on : RELIABLE — **de·pend·abil·i·ty** \-ˌpen-də-ˈbil-ət-ē\ *n* — **de·pend·able·ness** *n* — **de·pend·ably** \-blē\ *adv*

de·pen·dence *also* **de·pen·dance** \di-ˈpen-dən(t)s\ *n* **1** : the quality or state of being dependent; *esp* : the quality or state of being influenced by or subject to another **2** : RELIANCE, TRUST **3** : one that is relied on ⟨he was her sole ~⟩ **4 a** : drug addiction **b** : HABITUATION 2b

de·pen·den·cy \-dən-sē\ *n*, *pl* **-cies 1** : DEPENDENCE 1 **2** : something that is dependent on something else; *specif* : a territorial unit under the jurisdiction of a nation but not formally annexed by it

¹de·pen·dent \di-ˈpen-dənt\ *adj* [ME *dependant*, fr. MF, prp. of *dependre*] **1** : hanging down **2 a** : determined or conditioned by another : CONTINGENT **b** : relying on another for support **c** : subject to another's jurisdiction **d** : SUBORDINATE 3a — **de·pen·dent·ly** *adv*

²dependent *also* **de·pen·dant** \-dənt\ *n* **1** *archaic* : DEPENDENCY **2** : one that is dependent; *esp* : a person who relies on another for support

dependent variable *n* : a mathematical variable whose value is determined by that of one or more other variables in a function ⟨in $z = x^2 + 3xy + y^2$, *z* is the *dependent variable*⟩

de·perm \(ˈ)dē-ˈpərm\ *vt* [*de-* + *permanent magnetism*] : to reduce the magnetism of (a ship's steel hull) as a precaution against magnetically operated mines

de·per·son·al·iza·tion \(ˌ)dē-ˌpər-snə-lə-ˈzā-shən, -ˌpərs-ᵊn-ə-lə-\ *n* **1 a** : an act or process of depersonalizing **b** : the quality or state of being depersonalized **2** : loss of the sense of personal identity

de·per·son·al·ize \(ˈ)dē-ˈpər-snə-ˌlīz, -ˈpərs-ᵊn-ə-\ *vt* **1** : to deprive of personality ⟨schools that ~ students⟩ **2** : to make impersonal

de·pict \di-ˈpikt\ *vt* [L *depictus*, pp. of *depingere*, fr. *de-* + *pingere* to paint — more at PAINT] **1** : to represent by a picture **2** : DESCRIBE — **de·pic·ter** \-ˈpik-tər\ *n* — **de·pic·tion** \-ˈpik-shən\ *n*

de·pig·men·ta·tion \(ˌ)dē-ˌpig-mən-ˈtā-shən, -ˌmen-\ *n* : loss of normal pigmentation

dep·i·late \ˈdep-ə-ˌlāt\ *vt* **-lat·ed; -lat·ing** [L *depilatus*, pp. of *depilare*, fr. *de-* + *pilus* hair — more at PILE] : to remove hair from — **dep·i·la·tion** \ˌdep-ə-ˈlā-shən\ *n*

de·pil·a·to·ry \di-ˈpil-ə-ˌtōr-ē, -ˌtȯr-\ *n*, *pl* **-ries** : an agent for removing hair, wool, or bristles — **depilatory** *adj*

de·plane \(ˈ)dē-ˈplān\ *vi* : to get off an airplane

de·plete \di-ˈplēt\ *vt* **de·plet·ed; de·plet·ing** [L *depletus*, pp. of *deplēre*, fr. *de-* + *plēre* to fill — more at FULL] **1** : to empty of a principal substance **2** : to lessen markedly in quantity, content, power, or value — **de·plet·able** \-ˈplēt-ə-bəl\ *adj* — **de·ple·tion** \-ˈplē-shən\ *n* — **de·ple·tive** \-ˈplēt-iv\ *adj*

syn DEPLETE, DRAIN, EXHAUST, IMPOVERISH, BANKRUPT *shared meaning element* : to deprive of something essential to existence or potency

de·plor·able \di-ˈplōr-ə-bəl, -ˈplȯr-\ *adj* **1** : LAMENTABLE **2** : BAD, WRETCHED — **de·plor·able·ness** *n* — **de·plor·ably** \-blē\ *adv*

de·plore \di-ˈplō(ə)r, -ˈplȯ(ə)r\ *vt* **de·plored; de·plor·ing** [MF or L; MF *deplorer*, fr. L *deplorare*, fr. *de-* + *plorare* to wail] **1 a** : to feel or express grief for **b** : to regret strongly **2** : to consider unfortunate or deserving of deprecation — **de·plor·er** \-ˈplōr-ər\ *n* — **de·plor·ing·ly** \-iŋ-lē\ *adv*

syn DEPLORE, LAMENT, BEWAIL, BEMOAN *shared meaning element* : to manifest grief or sorrow for something

de·ploy \di-ˈplȯi\ *vb* [F *déployer*, fr. L *displicare* to scatter — more at DISPLAY] *vt* **1 a** : to extend (a military unit) esp. in width **b** : to place in battle formation or appropriate positions **2** : to spread out, utilize, or arrange esp. strategically ~ *vi* : to move in being deployed — **de·ploy·able** \-ə-bəl\ *adj* — **de·ploy·ment** \-mənt\ *n*

de·plume \(ˈ)dē-ˈplüm\ *vt* [ME *deplumen*, fr. MF *deplumer*, fr. ML *deplumare*, fr. L *de-* + *pluma* feather — more at FLEECE] **1** : to pluck off the feathers of **2** : to strip of possessions, honors, or attributes

de·po·lar·ize \(ˈ)dē-ˈpō-lə-ˌrīz\ *vt* **1** : to cause to become partially or wholly unpolarized **2** : to prevent or remove polarization of (as a dry cell or cell membrane) **3** : DEMAGNETIZE — **de·po·lar·iza·tion** \(ˌ)dē-ˌpō-lə-rə-ˈzā-shən\ *n* — **de·po·lar·iz·er** \(ˈ)dē-ˈpō-lə-ˌrī-zər\ *n*

de·po·lit·i·cize \ˌdē-pə-ˈlit-ə-ˌsīz\ *vt* : to remove the political character of : take out of the realm of politics ⟨~ our foreign aid program⟩

de·pone \di-ˈpōn\ *vb* **de·poned; de·pon·ing** [ML *deponere*, fr. L, to put down, fr. *de-* + *ponere* to put — more at POSITION] : TESTIFY

¹de·po·nent \di-ˈpō-nənt\ *adj* [LL *deponent-*, *deponens*, fr. L, prp. of *deponere*] : occurring with passive or middle voice forms but with active voice meaning ⟨the ~ verbs in Latin and Greek⟩

²deponent *n* **1** : a deponent verb **2** : one who gives evidence

de·pop·u·late \(ˈ)dē-ˈpäp-yə-ˌlāt\ *vt* [L *depopulatus*, pp. of *depopulari*, fr. *de-* + *populari* to ravage] **1** *obs* : RAVAGE **2** : to reduce greatly the population of — **de·pop·u·la·tion** \(ˌ)dē-ˌpäp-yə-ˈlā-shən\ *n* — **de·pop·u·la·tor** \(ˈ)dē-ˈpäp-yə-ˌlāt-ər\ *n*

de·port \di-ˈpō(ə)rt, -ˈpȯ(ə)rt\ *vt* [MF *deporter*, fr. L *deportare* to carry away, fr. *de-* + *portare* to carry — more at FARE] **1** : to behave or comport (oneself) esp. in accord with a code **2** [L *deportare*] **a** : to carry away **b** : to send out of the country by legal deportation **syn** see BANISH, BEHAVE

de·port·able \di-ˈpōrt-ə-bəl, -ˈpȯrt-\ *adj* **1** : subject to deportation ⟨~ aliens⟩ **2** : punishable by deportation ⟨~ offenses⟩

de·por·ta·tion \ˌdē-ˌpōr-ˈtā-shən, -ˌpȯr-, -pər-\ *n* **1** : an act or instance of deporting **2** : the removal from a country of an alien whose presence is unlawful or prejudicial

de·por·tee \ˌdē-ˌpōr-ˈtē, di-, -ˌpȯr-\ *n* : one who has been deported or is under sentence of deportation

de·port·ment \di-ˈpōrt-mənt, -ˈpȯrt-\ *n* : the manner in which one conducts oneself : BEHAVIOR **syn** see BEARING

de·pos·al \di-ˈpō-zəl\ *n* : an act of deposing from office

de·pose \di-ˈpōz\ *vb* **de·posed; de·pos·ing** [ME *deposen*, fr. OF *deposer*, fr. LL *deponere* (perf. indic. *deposui*), fr. L, to put down] *vt* **1** : to remove from a throne or other high position **2** : to put down : DEPOSIT **3 a** [ME *deposen*, fr. ML *deponere*, fr. LL] : to testify to under oath or by affidavit **b** : AFFIRM, ASSERT ~ *vi* : to bear witness

¹de·pos·it \di-ˈpäz-ət\ *vb* **de·pos·it·ed** \-ˈpäz-ət-əd, -ˈpäz-təd\; **de·pos·it·ing** \-ˈpäz-ət-iŋ, -ˈpäz-tiŋ\ [L *depositus*, pp. of *deponere*] *vt* **1** : to place esp. for safekeeping or as a pledge; *esp* : to put in a bank **2 a** : to lay down : PLACE **b** : to let fall (as sediment) ~ *vi* : to become deposited : SETTLE — **de·pos·i·tor** \-ˈpäz-ət-ər, -ˈpäz-tər\ *n*

²deposit *n* **1** : the state of being deposited **2** : something placed for safekeeping: as **a** : money deposited in a bank **b** : money given as a pledge or down payment **3** : a place of deposit : DEPOSITORY **4** : an act of depositing **5 a** : something laid down; *esp* : matter deposited by a natural process **b** : a natural accumulation (as of iron ore, coal, or gas)

de·pos·i·tary \di-ˈpäz-ə-ˌter-ē\ *n*, *pl* **-tar·ies 1** : a person to whom something is entrusted **2** : DEPOSITORY 2

de·po·si·tion \ˌdep-ə-ˈzish-ən, ˌdē-pə-\ *n* **1** : an act of removing from a position of authority **2 a** : a testifying esp. before a court **b** : DECLARATION; *specif* : testimony taken down in writing under oath **3** : an act or process of depositing **4** : something deposited : DEPOSIT — **de·po·si·tion·al** \-ˈzish-nəl, -ən-ᵊl\ *adj*

de·pos·i·to·ry \di-ˈpäz-ə-ˌtōr-ē, -ˌtȯr-\ *n*, *pl* **-ries 1** : DEPOSITARY 1 **2** : a place where something is deposited esp. for safekeeping

depository library *n* : a library designated to receive U.S. government publications

deposit slip *n* : a slip listing and accompanying bank deposits

de·pot *1 & 2 are* ˈdep-(ˌ)ō *also* ˈdēp-, *3 is* ˈdē-pō *sometimes* ˈdep-\ *n* [F *dépôt*, fr. ML *depositum*, fr. L, neut. of *depositus*] **1 a** : a place for the storage of military supplies **b** : a place for the reception and forwarding of military replacements **2 a** : a place for storing goods or motor vehicles **b** : STORE, DEPOSIT, COLLECTION, CACHE **3** : a building for railroad or bus passengers or freight : STATION

depr *abbr* **1** depreciation **2** depression

de·prave \di-ˈprāv\ *vt* **de·praved; de·prav·ing** [ME *depraven*, fr. MF *depraver*, fr. L *depravare* to pervert, fr. *de-* + *pravus* crooked, bad — more at PRAIRIE] **1** *archaic* : to speak ill of : MALIGN **2** : to make bad : CORRUPT; *esp* : to corrupt morally **syn** see DEBASE — **de·pra·va·tion** \ˌdep-rə-ˈvā-shən, ˌdē-ˌprā-\ *n* — **de·prave·ment** \di-ˈprāv-mənt\ *n* — **de·prav·er** \di-ˈprā-vər\ *n*

de·praved \di-ˈprāvd\ *adj* : marked by corruption or evil; *esp* : PERVERTED — **de·praved·ly** \-ˈprā-vəd-lē, -ˈprāv-dlē\ *adv* — **de·praved·ness** \-ˈprā-vəd-nəs, -ˈprāv(d)-nəs\ *n*

de·prav·i·ty \di-ˈprav-ət-ē *also* -ˈprāv-\ *n*, *pl* **-ties 1** : the quality or state of being depraved **2** : a corrupt act or practice

dep·re·cate \ˈdep-ri-ˌkāt\ *vt* **-cat·ed; -cat·ing** [L *deprecatus*, pp. of *deprecari* to avert by prayer, fr. *de-* + *precari* to pray — more at PRAY] **1** : to express mild or regretful disapproval of **2** : DEPRECIATE **syn** see DISAPPROVE **ant** endorse — **dep·re·cat·ing·ly** \-ˌkāt-iŋ-lē\ *adv* — **dep·re·ca·tion** \ˌdep-ri-ˈkā-shən\ *n*

dep·re·ca·to·ry \ˈdep-ri-kə-ˌtōr-ē, -ˌtȯr-\ *adj* **1** : seeking to avert disapproval : APOLOGETIC **2** : serving to deprecate : DISAPPROVING — **dep·re·ca·to·ri·ly** \ˌdep-ri-kə-ˈtōr-ə-lē, -ˈtȯr-\ *adv*

de·pre·ci·ate \di-ˈprē-shē-ˌāt\ *vb* **-at·ed; -at·ing** [LL *depretiatus*, pp. of *depretiare*, fr. L *de-* + *pretium* price — more at PRICE] *vt* **1** : to lower the price or estimated value of **2** : to represent as of little value and esp. as of less value than usu. assigned : DISPARAGE ~ *vi* : to fall in value **syn** see DECRY **ant** appreciate — **de·pre·cia·ble** \-shə-bəl\ *adj* — **de·pre·ci·at·ing·ly** \-shē-ˌāt-iŋ-lē\ *adv* — **de·pre·ci·a·tion** \-ˌprē-shē-ˈā-shən\ *n* — **de·pre·ci·a·tive** \-ˈprē-shət-iv, -shē-ˌāt-iv\ *adj* — **de·pre·ci·a·tor** \-shē-ˌāt-ər\ *n* — **de·pre·cia·to·ry** \-shə-ˌtōr-ē, -ˌtȯr-\ *adj*

dep·re·date \ˈdep-rə-ˌdāt\ *vb* **-dat·ed; -dat·ing** [LL *depraedatus*, pp. of *depraedari*, fr. L *de-* + *praedari* to plunder — more at PREY] *vt* : to lay waste : PLUNDER, RAVAGE ~ *vi* : to engage in plunder — **dep·re·da·tion** \ˌdep-rə-ˈdā-shən\ *n* — **dep·re·da·tor** \ˈdep-rə-ˌdāt-ər, di-ˈpred-ət-\ *n* — **de·pre·da·to·ry** \di-ˈpred-ə-ˌtōr-ē, ˈdep-ri-də-, -ˌtȯr-\ *adj*

de·press \di-ˈpres\ *vt* [ME *depressen,* fr. MF *depresser,* fr. L *depressus,* pp. of *deprimere* to press down, fr. *de-* + *premere* to press — more at PRESS] **1** *obs* : REPRESS, SUBJUGATE **2 a** : to press down ⟨~ a typewriter key⟩ **b** : to cause to sink to a lower position **3** : to lessen the activity or strength of **4** : SADDEN, DISCOURAGE **5** : to decrease the market value or marketability of — **de·press·ible** \-ə-bəl\ *adj* — **de·press·ing·ly** \-iŋ-lē\ *adv*

de·pres·sant \di-ˈpres-ᵊnt\ *n* : one that depresses; *specif* : an agent that reduces bodily functional activity — **depressant** *adj*

de·pressed *adj* **1** : low in spirits : SAD **2 a** : vertically flattened ⟨a ~ cactus⟩ **b** : having the central part lower than the margin **c** : lying flat or prostrate **d** : dorsoventrally flattened **3** : suffering from economic depression; *esp* : UNDERPRIVILEGED **4** : being below the standard ⟨his reading achievement is ~⟩

de·press·ing *adj* : that depresses; *esp* : causing emotional depression ⟨a ~ story⟩ — **de·press·ing·ly** \-iŋ-lē\ *adv*

de·pres·sion \di-ˈpresh-ən\ *n* **1 a** : the angular distance of a celestial object below the horizon **b** : the size of an angle of depression **2** : an act of depressing or a state of being depressed: as **a** : a pressing down : LOWERING **b** (1) : a state of feeling sad : DEJECTION (2) : a psychoneurotic or psychotic disorder marked by sadness, inactivity, difficulty in thinking and concentration, and feelings of dejection **c** (1) : a reduction in activity, amount, quality, or force (2) : a lowering of vitality or functional activity **3** : a depressed place or part : HOLLOW **4** : LOW 1b **5** : a period of low general economic activity marked esp. by rising levels of unemployment

¹de·pres·sive \di-ˈpres-iv\ *adj* **1** : tending to depress **2** : of or relating to psychological depression — **de·pres·sive·ly** *adv*

²depressive *n* : one who is psychologically depressed

de·pres·sor \di-ˈpres-ər\ *n* [LL, fr. L *depressus*] : one that depresses: as **a** : a muscle that draws down a part — compare LEVATOR **b** : a device for pressing a part down or aside **c** : a nerve or nerve fiber that decreases the activity or the tone of the organ or part it innervates

de·pri·va·tion \ˌdep-rə-ˈvā-shən, ˌdē-ˌprī-\ *n* **1** : an act or instance of depriving : LOSS **2** : the state of being deprived : PRIVATION; *specif* : removal from an office, dignity, or benefice

de·prive \di-ˈprīv\ *vt* **de·prived; de·priv·ing** [ME *depriven,* fr. ML *deprivare,* fr. L *de-* + *privare* to deprive — more at PRIVATE] **1** *obs* : REMOVE **2** : to take something away from ⟨a reorganization of the school . . . *deprived* him of his professorship —J. M. Phalen⟩ **3** : to remove from office **4** : to withhold something from ⟨a citizen *deprived* by accident of birth of one of his . . . rights —L. M. Chamberlain⟩

de·prived *adj* : marked by deprivation esp. of the necessities of life or of healthful environmental influences ⟨culturally ~ children⟩

dept *abbr* department

depth \ˈdepth\ *n, pl* **depths** \ˈdep(t)s, ˈdepths\ [ME, prob. fr. *dep* deep] **1 a** (1) : a deep place in a body of water (2) : a part that is far from the outside or surface ⟨the ~*s* of the woods⟩ (3) : ABYSS **b** (1) : a profound or intense state (as of thought or feeling) ⟨the ~*s* of reflection⟩; *also* : a reprehensibly low condition ⟨hadn't realized that standards had fallen to such ~*s*⟩ (2) : the middle of a time (as winter) (3) : an extreme state (as of misery) (4) : the worst part **2 a** : the perpendicular measurement downward from a surface **b** : the direct linear measurement from the point of viewing usu. from front to back **3** : the quality of being deep **4** : the degree of intensity ⟨~ of a color⟩; *also* : the quality of being profound (as in insight) or full (as of knowledge) **5** : the quality or state of being complete or thorough : THOROUGHNESS ⟨~ of indexing⟩ — **depth·less** \ˈdepth-ləs\ *adj* — **beyond one's depth** *or* **out of one's depth 1** : in water that is deeper than one's height **2** : beyond one's ability to understand — **in depth 1** : extending over a considerable distance ⟨these fortifications are built *in depth* —Max Werner⟩ **2** : with great thoroughness ⟨a study *in depth* of the poems⟩

depth charge *n* : an explosive projectile for use underwater esp. against submarines — called also *depth bomb*

depth interview *n* : an interview designed to probe attitudes, feelings, or motives not usu. tapped by the asking of standard questions

depth perception *n* : the ability to judge the distance of objects and the spatial relationship of objects at different distances

depth psychology *n* : PSYCHOANALYSIS

dep·u·ta·tion \ˌdep-yə-ˈtā-shən\ *n* **1** : the act of appointing a deputy **2** : a group of people appointed to represent others

de·pute \di-ˈpyüt\ *vt* **de·put·ed; de·put·ing** [ME *deputen* to appoint, fr. MF *deputer,* fr. LL *deputare* to assign, fr. L, to consider (as), fr. *de-* + *putare* to consider — more at PAVE] : DELEGATE, ASSIGN

dep·u·tize \ˈdep-yə-ˌtīz\ *vb* **-tized; -tiz·ing** *vt* : to appoint as deputy ~ *vi* : to act as deputy — **dep·u·ti·za·tion** \ˌdep-yət-ə-ˈzā-shən\ *n*

dep·u·ty \ˈdep-yət-ē\ *n, pl* **-ties** [ME, fr. MF *deputé,* pp. of *deputer*] **1 a** : a person appointed as a substitute with power to act **b** : a second-in-command or assistant who usu. takes charge when his superior is absent **2** : a member of the lower house of some legislative assemblies

der *or* **deriv** *abbr* derivation; derivative

de·rac·i·nate \(ˈ)dē-ˈras-ᵊn-ˌāt\ *vt* **-nat·ed; -nat·ing** [F *déraciner,* fr. MF *desraciner,* fr. *des-* de- + *racine* root, fr. LL *radicina,* fr. L *radic-, radix* — more at ROOT] : UPROOT — **de·rac·i·na·tion** \(ˌ)dē-ˌras-ᵊn-ˈā-shən\ *n*

de·rail \di-ˈrā(ə)l\ *vb* [F *dérailler,* fr. *dé-* de- + *rail,* fr. E] *vt* **1** : to cause to run off the rails **2** : to throw off course ~ *vi* : to leave the rails — **de·rail·ment** \-mənt\ *n*

de·rail·leur \di-ˈrā-lər\ *n* [F *dérailleur,* fr. *dérailler* to throw off the track, fr. *dé-* de- + *rail* rail, fr. E] : a mechanism for shifting gears on a bicycle that operates by moving the chain from one set of exposed gears to another; *also* : a bicycle having such a mechanism

de·range \di-ˈrānj\ *vt* **de·ranged; de·rang·ing** [F *déranger,* fr. OF *desrengier,* fr. *de-* + *reng* place — more at RANK] **1** : DISARRANGE ⟨hatless, with tie *deranged* —G. W. Stonier⟩ **2** : to disturb the operation or functions of **3** : to make insane — **de·range·ment** \-mənt\ *n*

derby 3

der·by \ˈdər-bē, *esp Brit* ˈdär-\ *n, pl* **derbies** [Edward Stanley †1834, 12th earl of *Derby*] **1** : any of several horse races held annually and usu. restricted to three-year-olds **2** : a race or contest open to all comers or to a specified category of contestants ⟨bicycle ~⟩ **3** : a man's stiff felt hat with dome-shaped crown and narrow brim

Derbys *abbr* Derbyshire

de·re·al·iza·tion \(ˌ)dē-ˌrē-ə-lə-ˈzā-shən, -ˌri-ə-\ *n* : a feeling of altered reality that occurs often in schizophrenia and in some drug reactions

de·reg·u·la·tion \(ˌ)dē-ˌreg-yə-ˈlā-shən\ *n* : the act or process of removing restrictions and regulations (as on the taxi industry) — **de·reg·u·late** \(ˈ)dē-ˈreg-yə-ˌlāt\ *vt*

¹der·e·lict \ˈder-ə-ˌlikt\ *adj* [L *derelictus,* pp. of *derelinquere* to abandon, fr. *de-* + *relinquere* to leave — more at RELINQUISH] **1** : abandoned esp. by the owner or occupant : RUN-DOWN **2** : lacking a sense of duty : NEGLIGENT

²derelict *n* **1 a** : something voluntarily abandoned; *specif* : a ship abandoned on the high seas **b** : a tract of land left dry by receding water **2** : a person no longer able to support himself : BUM

der·e·lic·tion \ˌder-ə-ˈlik-shən\ *n* **1 a** : an intentional abandonment **b** : the state of being abandoned **2** : a recession of water leaving permanently dry land **3 a** : intentional or conscious neglect : DELINQUENCY ⟨~ of duty⟩ **b** : FAULT, SHORTCOMING

de·re·press \ˌdē-ri-ˈpres\ *vt* : to activate (a gene) by releasing from a blocked state — **de·re·pres·sion** \-ˈpresh-ən\ *n*

de·ride \di-ˈrīd\ *vt* **de·rid·ed; de·rid·ing** [L *deridēre,* fr. *de-* + *ridēre* to laugh — more at RIDICULOUS] **1** : to laugh at contemptuously **2** : to subject to usu. bitter or contemptuous ridicule ***syn*** see RIDICULE — **de·rid·er** *n* — **de·rid·ing·ly** \-ˈrīd-iŋ-lē\ *adv*

de ri·gueur \də-(ˌ)rē-ˈgər\ *adj* [F] : prescribed or required by fashion, etiquette, or custom : PROPER ⟨instructions as to when and where a tuxedo is *de rigueur*⟩

de·ri·sion \di-ˈrizh-ən\ *n* [ME, fr. MF, fr. LL *derision-, derisio,* fr. L *derisus,* pp. of *deridēre*] **1 a** : an act of deriding **b** : a state of being derided **2** : an object of ridicule or scorn : LAUGHINGSTOCK

de·ri·sive \di-ˈrī-siv, -ziv; -ˈriz-iv, -ˈris-\ *adj* : expressing or causing derision — **de·ri·sive·ly** *adv* — **de·ri·sive·ness** *n*

de·ri·so·ry \di-ˈrī-sə-rē, -zə-\ *adj* **1** : expressing derision : DERISIVE ⟨scornful ~ smiles —Katherine A. Porter⟩ **2** : worthy of derision : RIDICULOUS

de·riv·able \di-ˈrī-və-bəl\ *adj* : capable of being derived

der·i·vate \ˈder-ə-ˌvāt\ *n* : DERIVATIVE

der·i·va·tion \ˌder-ə-ˈvā-shən\ *n* **1 a** (1) : the formation of a word from another word or base (as by the addition of a usu. noninflectional affix) (2) : an act of ascertaining or stating the derivation of a word (3) : ETYMOLOGY 1 **b** : the relation of a word to its base **2 a** : SOURCE, ORIGIN **b** : DESCENT, ORIGINATION **3** : something derived : DERIVATIVE **4** : an act or process of deriving **5** : a sequence of statements (as in logic or mathematics) showing that a result (as a formula) is a necessary consequence of previously accepted statements — **der·i·va·tion·al** \-shnəl, -shən-ᵊl\ *adj*

¹de·riv·a·tive \di-ˈriv-ət-iv\ *adj* **1** : formed by derivation **2** : made up of or marked by derived elements — **de·riv·a·tive·ly** *adv* — **de·riv·a·tive·ness** *n*

²derivative *n* **1** : a word formed by derivation **2** : something derived **3** : the limit of the ratio of the change in a function to the corresponding change in its independent variable as the latter change approaches zero **4 a** : a chemical substance related structurally to another substance and theoretically derivable from it **b** : a substance that can be made from another substance in one or more steps

de·rive \di-ˈrīv\ *vb* **de·rived; de·riv·ing** [ME *deriven,* fr. MF *deriver,* fr. L *derivare,* fr. *de-* + *rivus* stream — more at RISE] *vt* **1 a** : to take or receive esp. from a specified source **b** : to obtain from a specified source; *specif* : to obtain (a chemical substance) actually or theoretically from a parent substance **2** : INFER, DEDUCE **3** *archaic* : BRING **4** : to trace the derivation of ~ *vi* : to have or take origin : come as a derivative ***syn*** see SPRING — **de·riv·er** *n*

¹derm \ˈdərm\ *n* [NL *derma & dermis*] **1** : DERMIS **2** : SKIN 2a **3** : CUTICLE 1a

²derm *abbr* dermatologist; dermatology

derm- *or* **derma-** *or* **dermo-** *comb form* [NL, fr. Gk *derm-, dermo-,* fr. *derma,* fr. *derein* to skin — more at TEAR] : skin ⟨*derm*al⟩ ⟨*dermo*tropic⟩

-derm \ˌdərm\ *n comb form* [prob. fr. F *-derme,* fr. Gk *derma*] : skin : covering ⟨ecto*derm*⟩

der·ma \ˈdər-mə\ *n* [NL, fr. Gk] : DERMIS

-der·ma \ˈdər-mə\ *n comb form, pl* **-dermas** *or* **-der·ma·ta** \-mət-ə\ [NL, fr. Gk *dermat-, derma* skin] : skin or skin ailment of a (specified) type ⟨sclero*derma*⟩

der·mal \ˈdər-məl\ *adj* **1** : of or relating to skin and esp. to the dermis : CUTANEOUS **2** : EPIDERMAL

der·map·ter·an \(ˌ)dər-ˈmap-tə-rən\ *n* [NL *Dermaptera,* order name, fr. *derm-* + Gk *pteron* wing — more at FEATHER] : any of an order (Dermaptera) of insects consisting of the earwigs and usu. a few related forms — **dermapteran** *adj* — **der·map·ter·ous** \-tə-rəs\ *adj*

ə abut	ᵊ kitten	ər further	a back	ā bake	ä cot, cart
au̇ out	ch chin	e less	ē easy	g gift	i trip	ī life
j joke	ŋ sing	ō flow	ȯ flaw	ȯi coin	th thin	t͟h this
ü loot	u̇ foot	y yet	yü few	yu̇ furious	zh vision

der·mat- *or* **dermato-** *comb form* [Gk, fr. *dermat-, derma*] : skin ⟨*dermat*itis⟩ ⟨*dermato*logy⟩
der·ma·ti·tis \ˌdər-mə-ˈtīt-əs\ *n* : inflammation of the skin
der·mat·o·gen \(ˌ)dər-ˈmat-ə-jən\ *n* [ISV] : the outer primary meristem of a plant or plant part
der·ma·to·glyph·ics \ˌdər-mət-ə-ˈglif-iks\ *n pl but sing or pl in constr* [*dermat-* + Gk *glyphein* to carve + E *-ics* — more at CLEAVE] **1** : skin patterns; *esp* : patterns of the specialized skin of the inferior surfaces of the hands and feet **2** : the science of the study of skin patterns — **der·ma·to·glyph·ic** \-ik\ *adj*
der·ma·toid \ˈdər-mə-ˌtȯid\ *adj* : resembling skin
der·ma·tol·o·gy \ˌdər-mə-ˈtäl-ə-jē\ *n* : a branch of science dealing with the skin, its structure, functions, and diseases — **der·ma·to·log·ic** \-mət-ᵊl-ˈäj-ik\ *or* **der·ma·to·log·i·cal** \-i-kəl\ *adj* — **der·ma·tol·o·gist** \-mə-ˈtäl-ə-jəst\ *n*
der·ma·tome \ˈdər-mə-ˌtōm\ *n* [ISV *dermat-* + *-ome*] : the lateral wall of a somite from which the dermis is produced — **der·ma·to·mic** \ˌdər-mə-ˈtō-mik, -ˈtäm-ik\ *adj*
der·ma·to·phyte \(ˌ)dər-ˈmat-ə-ˌfīt, ˈdər-mət-\ *n* [ISV] : a fungus parasitic on the skin or skin derivatives (as hair or nails) — **der·ma·to·phyt·ic** \(ˌ)dər-ˌmat-ə-ˈfit-ik, ˌdər-mət-\ *adj*
der·ma·to·sis \ˌdər-mə-ˈtō-səs\ *n, pl* **-to·ses** \-ˌsēz\ : a disease of the skin
-der·ma·tous \ˈdər-mət-əs\ *adj comb form* [Gk *dermat-, derma* skin] : having a (specified) type of skin ⟨sclero*dermatous*⟩
der·mes·tid \(ˌ)dər-ˈmes-təd\ *n* [deriv. of Gk *dermēstēs*, a leather-eating worm, lit., skin eater, fr. *derm-* + *edmenai* to eat — more at EAT] : any of a family (Dermestidae) of beetles with clubbed antennae that are very destructive to dried meat, fur, wool, and insect collections — **dermestid** *adj*
der·mis \ˈdər-məs\ *n* [NL, fr. LL *-dermis*] : the sensitive vascular inner mesodermic layer of the skin — called also *corium, cutis*
-der·mis \ˈdər-məs\ *n comb form* [LL, fr. Gk, fr. *derma*] : layer of skin or tissue ⟨endo*dermis*⟩
der·moid \ˈdər-ˌmȯid\ *also* **der·moi·dal** \(ˌ)dər-ˈmȯid-ᵊl\ *adj* **1** : made up of cutaneous elements and esp. ectodermal derivatives ⟨a ~ tumor⟩ **2** : resembling skin
der·mop·ter·an \(ˌ)dər-ˈmäp-tə-rən\ *n* [NL *Dermoptera*, order of mammals, fr. *derm-* + Gk *pteron*] : FLYING LEMUR — **dermopteran** *adj* — **der·mop·ter·ous** \-tə-rəs\ *adj*
der·mo·tro·pic \ˌdər-mə-ˈtrō-pik, -ˈträp-ik\ *adj* : attracted to, localizing in, or entering by way of the skin ⟨~ viruses⟩
der·nier cri \ˌdern-ˌyā-ˈkrē\ *n* [F, lit., last cry] : the newest fashion
der·o·gate \ˈder-ə-ˌgāt\ *vb* **-gat·ed; -gat·ing** [LL *derogatus*, pp. of *derogare*, fr. L, to annul (a law), detract, fr. *de-* + *rogare* to ask, propose (a law) — more at RIGHT] *vt* : to cause to seem inferior : DISPARAGE ~ *vi* **1** : to take away a part so as to impair : DETRACT **2** : to act beneath one's position or character — **der·o·ga·tion** \ˌder-ə-ˈgā-shən\ *n* — **de·rog·a·tive** \di-ˈräg-ət-iv, ˈder-ə-ˌgāt-\ *adj*
de·rog·a·to·ry \di-ˈräg-ə-ˌtōr-ē, -ˌtȯr-\ *adj* **1** : DEGRADING, DETRACTING **2** : expressive of a low opinion : DISPARAGING — **de·rog·a·to·ri·ly** \-ˌräg-ə-ˈtōr-ə-lē, -ˈtȯr-\ *adv*
der·rick \ˈder-ik\ *n* [obs. *derrick* hangman, gallows, fr. *Derick*, name of 17th cent. E hangman] **1** : a hoisting apparatus employing a tackle rigged at the end of a beam **2** : a framework or tower over a deep drill hole (as of an oil well) for supporting boring tackle or for hoisting and lowering
der·ri·ere *or* **der·ri·ère** \ˌder-ē-ˈe(ə)r\ *n* [F *derrière*, fr. *derrière*, adj., hinder, fr. OF *deriere* adv., behind, fr. L *de retro*, fr. *de* from + *retro* back — more at DE-, RETRO-] : BUTTOCKS
der·ring–do \ˌder-iŋ-ˈdü\ *n* [ME *dorring don* daring to do, fr. *dorring* (gerund of *dorren* to dare) + *don* to do] : daring action : DARING ⟨deeds of ~⟩
der·rin·ger \ˈder-ən-jər\ *n* [Henry *Deringer*, 19th cent. Am inventor] : a short-barreled pocket pistol
der·ris \ˈder-əs\ *n* [NL, genus name, fr. Gk, skin, fr. *derein* to skin — more at TEAR] **1** : any of a large genus (*Derris*) of leguminous tropical Old World shrubs and woody vines including sources of poisons and esp. commercial sources of rotenone **2** : a preparation of derris roots and stems used as an insecticide
der·vish \ˈdər-vish\ *n* [Turk *derviş*, lit., beggar, fr. Per *darvēsh*] **1** : a member of a Muslim religious order noted for devotional exercises (as bodily movements leading to a trance) **2** : one that whirls or dances with or as if with the abandonment of a dervish
des- *prefix* [F *dés-*, fr. OF *des-* — more at DE-] : DE- 6 — esp. before vowels ⟨*des*oxy-⟩
de·sa·cral·ize \(ˈ)dē-ˈsā-krə-ˌlīz, -ˈsak-rə-\ *vt* **-ized; -iz·ing** : to divest ceremonial of supernatural qualities
de·sa·li·nate \(ˈ)dē-ˈsal-ə-ˌnāt *also* -ˈsā-lə-\ *vt* **-nat·ed; -nat·ing** : DESALT — **de·sa·li·na·tion** \(ˌ)dē-ˌsal-ə-ˈnā-shən *also* -ˌsā-lə-\ *n* — **de·sa·li·na·tor** \(ˈ)dē-ˈsal-ə-ˌnāt-ər *also* -ˈsā-lə-\ *n*
de·sa·li·nize \(ˈ)dē-ˈsal-ə-ˌnīz *also* -ˈsā-lə-\ *vt* **-nized; -niz·ing** : DESALT — **de·sa·li·ni·za·tion** \(ˌ)dē-ˌsal-ə-nə-ˈzā-shən *also* -ˌsā-lə-\ *n*
de·salt \(ˈ)dē-ˈsȯlt\ *vt* : to remove salt from — **de·salt·er** *n*
1**des·cant** \ˈdes-ˌkant\ *n* [ME *dyscant*, fr. ONF & ML; ONF *descant*, fr. ML *discantus*, fr. L *dis-* + *cantus* song — more at CHANT] **1 a** : a melody or counterpoint sung above the plainsong of the tenor **b** : the art of composing or improvising contrapuntal part music; *also* : the music so composed or improvised **c** : SOPRANO, TREBLE **d** : a superimposed counterpoint to a simple melody sung typically by some or all of the sopranos **2 a** : a song or strain of melody **b** : a musical prelude in which a theme is varied **3** : discourse or comment on a theme
2**des·cant** \ˈdes-ˌkant, des-ˈ, dis-ˈ\ *vi* **1 a** : to sing or play a descant **b** : SING, WARBLE **2** : to talk or write at considerable length : DILATE ⟨he ~*ed* to his heart's content on his favorite topic —G. B. Shaw⟩
de·scend \di-ˈsend\ *vb* [ME *descenden*, fr. OF *descendre*, fr. L *descendere*, fr. *de-* + *scandere* to climb — more at SCAN] *vi* **1** : to pass from a higher place or level to a lower one ⟨~*ed* from the platform⟩ **2** : to pass in discussion from what is logically prior or more comprehensive **3 a** : to come down from a stock or source : DERIVE — usu. used in passive ⟨was ~*ed* from an ancient family⟩ **b** : to pass by inheritance ⟨an heirloom that has ~*ed* in the family⟩ **c** : to pass by transmission ⟨songs ~*ed* from early ballads⟩ **4** : to incline, lead, or extend downward ⟨the road ~*s* to the river⟩ **5** : to swoop or pounce down or make a sudden attack ⟨the plague ~*ed* upon them⟩ **6** : to proceed in a sequence or gradation from higher to lower or from more remote to nearer or more recent **7 a** : to sink in status or dignity : STOOP **b** : to worsen and sink in condition or estimation ~ *vt* **1** : to pass, move, or climb down or down along **2** : to extend down along — **de·scend·ible** \-ˈsen-də-bəl\ *adj*
1**de·scen·dant** *or* **de·scen·dent** \di-ˈsen-dənt\ *adj* [MF & L; MF *descendant*, fr. L *descendent-, descendens*, prp. of *descendere*] **1** : moving or directed downward **2** : proceeding from an ancestor or source
2**descendant** *or* **descendent** *n* [F & L; F *descendant*, fr. LL *descendent-, descendens*, fr. L, prp. of *descendere*] **1** : one descended from another or from a common stock **2** : one deriving directly from a precursor or prototype
de·scend·er \di-ˈsen-dər, ˈdē-ˌ\ *n* : the part of a lowercase letter (as p) that descends below the main body of the letter; *also* : a letter that has such a part
descending rhythm *n* : FALLING RHYTHM
de·scen·sion \di-ˈsen-chən\ *n, archaic* : DESCENT 1
de·scent \di-ˈsent\ *n* [ME, fr. MF *descente*, fr. *descendre*] **1** : the act or process of descending from a higher to a lower level or state **2** : a downward step (as in station or value) : DECLINE ⟨~ of the family to actual poverty⟩ **3 a** : derivation from an ancestor : BIRTH, LINEAGE ⟨of French ~⟩ **b** : transmission or devolution of an estate by inheritance usu. in the descending line **c** : the fact or process of originating from an ancestral stock **d** : the shaping or development in nature and character by transmission from a source : DERIVATION **4 a** : an inclination downward : SLOPE **b** : a descending way (as a downgrade or stairway) **c** *obs* : the lowest part **5 a** : a sudden disconcerting appearance **b** : a hostile raid or predatory assault **6** : a step downward in a scale of gradation; *specif* : one generation in an ancestral line or genealogical scale
de·scribe \di-ˈskrīb\ *vt* **de·scribed; de·scrib·ing** [L *describere*, fr. *de-* + *scribere* to write — more at SCRIBE] **1** : to represent or give an account of in words ⟨~ a picture⟩ **2** : to represent by a figure, model, or picture : DELINEATE **3** : to trace or traverse the outline of ⟨~ a circle⟩ **4** *obs* : DISTRIBUTE **5** *archaic* : OBSERVE, PERCEIVE — **de·scrib·able** \-ˈskrī-bə-bəl\ *adj* — **de·scrib·er** *n*
de·scrip·tion \di-ˈskrip-shən\ *n* [ME *descripcioun*, fr. MF & L; MF *description*, fr. L *description-, descriptio*, fr. *descriptus*, pp. of *describere*] **1 a** : an act of describing; *specif* : discourse intended to give a mental image of something experienced (as a scene, person, or sensation) **b** : a descriptive statement or account ⟨a fascinating ~ of his adventures⟩ **2** : kind or character esp. as determined by salient features ⟨opposed to any tax of so radical a ~⟩ ***syn*** see TYPE
de·scrip·tive \di-ˈskrip-tiv\ *adj* **1** : serving to describe ⟨a ~ account⟩ **2** : referring to, constituting, or grounded in matters of observation or experience ⟨the ~ basis of science⟩ **3** *of a modifier* **a** : expressing the quality, kind, or condition of what is denoted by the modified term ⟨*hot* in "hot water" is a ~ adjective⟩ **b** : NONRESTRICTIVE **4** : of, relating to, or dealing with the structure of a language at a particular time usu. with exclusion of historical and comparative data ⟨~ linguistics⟩ — **de·scrip·tive·ly** *adv* — **de·scrip·tive·ness** *n*
de·scrip·tor \di-ˈskrip-tər\ *n* : a word or phrase (as an index term) used to identify an item (as a subject or document) esp. in an information retrieval system; *also* : an alphanumeric symbol used similarly
1**de·scry** \di-ˈskrī\ *vt* **de·scried; de·scry·ing** [ME *descrien*, fr. OF *descrier* to proclaim, decry] **1 a** : to catch sight of **b** : to find out : DISCOVER **2** *obs* : to make known : REVEAL
2**descry** *n, obs* : discovery or view from afar
Des·de·mo·na \ˌdez-də-ˈmō-nə\ *n* : the wife of Othello in Shakespeare's *Othello*
des·e·crate \ˈdes-i-ˌkrāt\ *vt* **-crat·ed; -crat·ing** [*de-* + *-secrate* (as in *consecrate*)] **1** : to violate the sanctity of : PROFANE **2** : to treat irreverently or contemptuously often in a way that provokes outrage on the part of others ⟨the kind of shore development . . . that has *desecrated* so many waterfronts — John Fischer⟩ — **des·e·crat·er** *or* **des·e·cra·tor** \-ˌkrāt-ər\ *n*
des·e·cra·tion \ˌdes-i-ˈkrā-shən\ *n* : an act or instance of desecrating : the state of being desecrated ***syn*** see PROFANATION
de·seg·re·gate \(ˈ)dē-ˈseg-ri-ˌgāt\ *vt* : to eliminate segregation in; *specif* : to free of any law, provision, or practice requiring isolation of the members of a particular race in separate units ~ *vi* : to bring about desegregation
de·seg·re·ga·tion \(ˌ)dē-ˌseg-ri-ˈgā-shən\ *n* **1** : the act or process or an instance of desegregating **2** : the state of being desegregated
de·se·lect \ˌdē-sə-ˈlekt\ *vt* : to dismiss (a trainee) from a training program
de·sen·si·tize \(ˈ)dē-ˈsen(t)-sə-ˌtīz\ *vt* **1** : to make (a sensitized or hypersensitive individual) insensitive or nonreactive to a sensitizing agent **2** : to make (a photographic material) less sensitive or completely insensitive to radiation **3** : to make emotionally insensitive or callous — **de·sen·si·ti·za·tion** \(ˌ)dē-ˌsen-sət-ə-ˈzā-shən, -ˌsen-stə-ˈzā-\ *n* — **de·sen·si·tiz·er** \(ˈ)de-ˈsen-sə-ˌtī-zər\ *n*
1**des·ert** \ˈdez-ərt\ *n* [ME, fr. OF, fr. LL *desertum*, fr. L, neut. of *desertus*, pp. of *deserere* to desert, fr. *de-* + *serere* to join together — more at SERIES] **1** *archaic* : a wild uninhabited and uncultivated tract **2 a** : an arid barren tract incapable of supporting any considerable population without an artificial water supply **b** : an area of ocean apparently devoid of marine life **3** : a desolate or forbidding area ⟨lost in a ~ of doubt⟩ ⟨tiny figures lost in an immense ~ of darkness —Beverley Nichols⟩ — **de·ser·tic** \de-ˈzərt-ik\ *adj*
2**des·ert** \ˈdez-ərt\ *adj* **1** *archaic* : FORSAKEN **2** : desolate and sparsely occupied or unoccupied ⟨a ~ island⟩ **3** : of or relating to a desert

³de·sert \di-ˈzərt\ *n* [ME *deserte*, fr. OF, fr. fem. of *desert*, pp. of *deservir* to deserve] **1 :** the quality or fact of deserving reward or punishment **2 :** deserved reward or punishment — usu. used in plural ⟨got his just ~*s*⟩ **3 :** EXCELLENCE, WORTH

⁴de·sert \di-ˈzərt\ *vb* [F *déserter*, fr. LL *desertare*, fr. *desertus*] *vt* **1 :** to withdraw from or leave usu. without intent to return **2 a :** to leave in the lurch ⟨~ a friend in trouble⟩ **b :** to abandon (military service) without leave ~ *vi* **:** to quit one's post, allegiance, or service without leave or justification; *esp* **:** to absent oneself from military duty without leave and without intent to return ***syn*** see ABANDON ***ant*** stick (*to*), cleave (*to*) — **de·sert·er** *n*

de·ser·tion \di-ˈzər-shən\ *n* **1 :** an act of deserting; *esp* **:** the abandonment without consent or legal justification of a person, post, or relationship and the duties and obligations connected therewith ⟨sued for divorce on grounds of ~⟩ **2 :** a state of being deserted or forsaken **:** DESOLATION

desert locust *n* **:** a destructive migratory locust (*Schistocerca gregaria*) of southwestern Asia and parts of northern Africa

desert soil *n* **:** a soil that develops under sparse shrub vegetation in warm to cool arid climates with a light-colored surface soil usu. underlain by calcareous material and a hardpan layer

de·serve \di-ˈzərv\ *vb* **de·served; de·serv·ing** [ME *deserven*, fr. OF *deservir*, fr. L *deservire* to serve zealously, fr. *de-* + *servire* to serve] *vt* **:** to be worthy of **:** MERIT ⟨~*s* another chance⟩ ~ *vi* **:** to be worthy, fit, or suitable for some reward or requital ⟨have become recognized as they ~ —T. S. Eliot⟩ — **de·serv·er** *n*

de·served \-ˈzərvd\ *adj* **:** of, relating to, or being that which one deserves ⟨a ~ reputation⟩ — **de·served·ly** \-ˈzər-vəd-lē, -ˈzərv-dlē\ *adv* — **de·served·ness** \-ˈzər-vəd-nəs, -ˈzərv(d)-nəs\ *n*

¹de·serv·ing \-ˈzər-viŋ\ *n* **:** DESERT, MERIT ⟨reward the proud according to their ~*s* —Charles Kingsley⟩

²deserving *adj* **:** MERITORIOUS, WORTHY; *specif* **:** meriting financial aid ⟨scholarships for ~ students⟩

de·sex \(ˈ)dē-ˈseks\ *vt* **:** DESEXUALIZE 1

de·sex·u·al·ize \(ˈ)dē-ˈseksh-(ə-)wə-ˌlīz, -ˈsek-shə-ˌlīz\ *vt* **1 :** to deprive of sexual characters or power **2 :** to divest of sexual quality — **de·sex·u·al·iza·tion** \(ˌ)dē-ˌseksh-(ə-)wə-lə-ˈzā-shən, -ˌsek-shə-lə-\ *n*

des·ha·bille \ˌdes-ə-ˈbē(ə)l, -ˈbil, -ˈbē\ *var of* DISHABILLE

des·ic·cant \ˈdes-i-kənt\ *n* **:** a drying agent (as calcium chloride)

des·ic·cate \ˈdes-i-ˌkāt\ *vb* **-cat·ed; -cat·ing** [L *desiccatus*, pp. of *desiccare* to dry up, fr. *de-* + *siccare* to dry, fr. *siccus* dry — more at SACK] *vt* **1 :** to dry up **2 :** to preserve (a food) by drying **:** DEHYDRATE **3 :** to drain of emotional or intellectual vitality ~ *vi* **:** to become dried up — **des·ic·ca·tion** \ˌdes-i-ˈkā-shən\ *n* — **de·sic·ca·tive** \ˈdes-i-ˌkāt-iv, di-ˈsik-ət-\ *adj* — **des·ic·ca·tor** \ˈdes-i-ˌkāt-ər\ *n*

de·sid·er·ate \di-ˈsid-ə-ˌrāt, -ˈzid-\ *vt* **-at·ed; -at·ing** [L *desideratus*, pp. of *desiderare* to desire] **:** to entertain or express a wish to have or attain — **de·sid·er·a·tion** \-ˌsid-ə-ˈrā-shən, -ˌzid-\ *n* — **de·sid·er·a·tive** \-ˈsid-ə-ˌrāt-iv, -ˈsid-(ə-)rət-, -ˈzid-\ *adj*

de·sid·er·a·tum \-ˌsid-ə-ˈrät-əm, -ˌzid-, -ˈrāt-\ *n, pl* **-ta** \-ə\ [L, neut. of *desideratus*] **:** something desired as essential

¹de·sign \di-ˈzīn\ *vb* [MF *designer*, fr. L *designare*, fr. *de-* + *signare* to mark, mark out — more at SIGN] *vt* **1 a :** to conceive and plan out in the mind ⟨he ~*ed* the perfect crime⟩ **b :** to have as a purpose **:** INTEND ⟨he ~*ed* to excel in his studies⟩ **c :** to devise for a specific function or end ⟨a book ~*ed* primarily as a college textbook⟩ **2** *archaic* **:** to indicate with a distinctive mark, sign, or name **3 a :** to make a drawing, pattern, or sketch of **b :** to draw the plans for **c :** to create, fashion, execute, or construct according to plan **:** DEVISE, CONTRIVE ~ *vi* **1 :** to conceive or execute a plan **2 :** to draw, lay out, or prepare a design — **de·sign·ed·ly** \-ˈzī-nəd-lē\ *adv* — **de·sign·er** \-ˈzī-nər\ *n*

²design *n* **1 :** a mental project or scheme in which means to an end are laid down **2 a :** a particular purpose held in view by an individual or group ⟨he has ambitious ~*s* for his son⟩ **b :** deliberate purposive planning ⟨battle was joined . . . more by accident than ~ —John Buchan⟩ **3 a :** a deliberate undercover project or scheme **:** PLOT **b** *pl* **:** aggressive or evil intent — used with *on* or *against* ⟨he has ~*s* on the money⟩ **4 :** a preliminary sketch or outline showing the main features of something to be executed **:** DELINEATION **5 :** an underlying scheme that governs functioning, developing, or unfolding **:** PATTERN, MOTIF ⟨the general ~ of the epic⟩ **6 :** the arrangement of elements that go into human productions (as of art or machinery) **7 :** a decorative pattern ***syn*** see PLAN, INTENTION

¹des·ig·nate \ˈdez-ig-ˌnāt, -nət\ *adj* [L *designatus*, pp. of *designare*] **:** chosen for an office but not yet installed ⟨ambassador ~⟩

²des·ig·nate \-ˌnāt\ *vt* **-nat·ed; -nat·ing 1 a :** to point out the location of ⟨a marker *designating* the crest of the flood waters⟩ **b :** INDICATE ⟨any task *designated* by the employer⟩ **c :** to distinguish as to class ⟨the area we ~ as that of spiritual values —J. B. Conant⟩ **d :** SPECIFY, STIPULATE **2 :** to call by a distinctive title, term, or expression **3 :** to indicate and set apart for a specific purpose, office, or duty **4 :** DENOTE — **des·ig·na·tive** \-ˌnāt-iv\ *adj* — **des·ig·na·tor** \-ˌnāt-ər\ *n* — **des·ig·na·to·ry** \-nə-ˌtōr-ē, -ˌtȯr-\ *adj*

designated hitter *n* **:** a baseball player designated at the start of the game to bat in place of the pitcher without causing the pitcher to be removed from the game

des·ig·na·tion \ˌdez-ig-ˈnā-shən\ *n* **1 :** the act of indicating or identifying **2 :** a distinguishing name, sign, or title **3 :** appointment to or selection for an office, post, or service **4 :** the relation between a sign and the thing signified

des·ig·nee \ˌdez-ig-ˈnē\ *n* **:** one who is designated

de·sign·ing \di-ˈzī-niŋ\ *adj* **1 :** practicing forethought **2 :** CRAFTY, SCHEMING ⟨~ widows⟩

de·sign·ment \di-ˈzīn-mənt\ *n, obs* **:** PLAN, PURPOSE

de·si·pra·mine \ˌdez-ə-ˈpram-ən, də-ˈzip-rə-ˌmēn\ *n* [*des*methyl + *imipramine*] **:** a tricyclic drug $C_{18}H_{22}N_2$ used as a psychic stimulant

de·sir·abil·i·ty \di-ˌzī-rə-ˈbil-ət-ē\ *n, pl* **-ties 1 :** the quality, fact, or degree of being desirable **2** *pl* **:** desirable conditions ⟨had understood and studied certain *desirabilities* —D. D. Eisenhower⟩

¹de·sir·able \di-ˈzī-rə-bəl\ *adj* **1 :** having pleasing qualities or properties **:** ATTRACTIVE ⟨a ~ woman⟩ **2 :** worth seeking or doing as advantageous, beneficial, or wise **:** ADVISABLE ⟨~ legislation⟩ — **de·sir·able·ness** *n* — **de·sir·ably** \-blē\ *adv*

²desirable *n* **:** one that is desirable

¹de·sire \di-ˈzī(ə)r\ *vb* **de·sired; de·sir·ing** [ME *desiren*, fr. OF *desirer*, fr. L *desiderare*, fr. *de-* + *sider-*, *sidus* star] *vt* **1 :** to long or hope for **2 a :** to express a wish for **:** REQUEST **b :** to express a wish to **:** ASK **3** *obs* **:** INVITE **4** *archaic* **:** to feel the loss of ~ *vi* **:** to have or feel desire

syn DESIRE, WISH, WANT, CRAVE, COVET *shared meaning element* **:** to have a longing for something

²desire *n* **1 :** conscious impulse toward an object or experience that promises enjoyment or satisfaction in its attainment **2 a :** LONGING, CRAVING **b :** sexual attraction or appetite **3 :** a usu. formal request or petition for some action **4 :** something desired

de·sir·ous \di-ˈzī(ə)r-əs\ *adj* **:** impelled or governed by desire ⟨~ of fame⟩ — **de·sir·ous·ly** *adv* — **de·sir·ous·ness** *n*

de·sist \di-ˈzist, -ˈsist\ *vi* [MF *desister*, fr. L *desistere*, fr. *de-* + *sistere* to stand, stop; akin to L *stare* to stand — more at STAND] **:** to cease to proceed or act ***syn*** see STOP ***ant*** persist — **de·sis·tance** \-ˈzis-tən(t)s, -ˈsis-\ *n*

desk \ˈdesk\ *n* [ME *deske*, fr. ML *desca*, modif. of OIt *desco* table, fr. L *discus* dish, disc — more at DISH] **1 a :** a table, frame, or case with a sloping or horizontal surface esp. for writing and reading and often with drawers, compartments, and pigeonholes **b :** a reading table or lectern to support the book from which the liturgical service is read **c :** a table, counter, stand, or booth at which a person performs his duties **d :** a music stand **2 :** a division of an organization specializing in a particular phase of activity ⟨the Russian ~ in the Department of State⟩

desk·man \ˈdesk-ˌman, -mən\ *n* **:** one that works at a desk; *specif* **:** a newspaperman who processes news and prepares copy

desm- *or* **desmo-** *comb form* [NL, fr. Gk, fr. *desmos*, fr. *dein* to bind — more at DIADEM] **:** bond **:** ligament ⟨*desmo*cyte⟩

des·man \ˈdez-mən\ *n, pl* **desmans** [short for Sw *desmansråtta*, fr. *desman* musk + *råtta* rat] **:** an aquatic insectivorous mammal (*Desmana moschata*) of Russia that resembles a mole

des·mid \ˈdez-məd\ *n* [deriv. of Gk *desmos*] **:** any of numerous unicellular or colonial green algae (order Zygnematales)

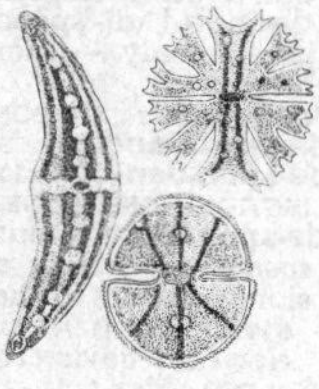

desmids

des·mo·some \ˈdez-mə-ˌsōm\ *n* [*desm-* + *-some*] **:** a specialized local thickening of the cell membrane of an epithelial cell that serves to anchor contiguous cells together

¹des·o·late \ˈdes-ə-lət, ˈdez-\ *adj* [ME *desolat*, fr. L *desolatus*, pp. of *desolare* to abandon, fr. *de-* + *solus* alone — more at SOLE] **1 :** devoid of inhabitants and visitors **:** DESERTED **2 :** joyless, disconsolate, and sorrowful through or as if through separation from a loved one **3 a :** showing the effects of abandonment and neglect **:** DILAPIDATED **b :** BARREN, LIFELESS ⟨a ~ landscape⟩ **c :** devoid of warmth, comfort, or hope **:** GLOOMY ⟨~ memories⟩ ***syn*** see ALONE — **des·o·late·ly** *adv* — **des·o·late·ness** *n*

²des·o·late \-ˌlāt\ *vt* **-lat·ed; -lat·ing :** to make desolate**: a :** to deprive of inhabitants **b :** to lay waste **c :** FORSAKE **d :** to make wretched — **des·o·lat·er** *or* **des·o·la·tor** \-ˌlāt-ər\ *n* — **des·o·lat·ing·ly** \-ˌlāt-iŋ-lē\ *adv*

des·o·la·tion \ˌdes-ə-ˈlā-shən, ˌdez-\ *n* **1 :** the action of desolating **2 :** the condition of being desolated **:** DEVASTATION, RUIN ⟨the flood left ~ in its wake⟩ **3 :** barren wasteland **4 a :** GRIEF, SADNESS **b :** LONELINESS

de·sorb \(ˈ)dē-ˈsȯ(ə)rb, -ˈzȯ(ə)rb\ *vt* **:** to remove (a sorbed substance) by the reverse of adsorption or absorption

de·sorp·tion \-ˈsȯrp-shən, -ˈzȯrp-\ *n* **:** the process of desorbing

desoxy- — see DEOXY-

des·oxy·cor·ti·co·ste·rone \de-ˌzäk-sē-ˌkȯrt-i-ˈkäs-tə-ˌrōn, de-ˌsäk-, -i-kō-stə-ˈrōn\ *n* **:** DEOXYCORTICOSTERONE

des·oxy·ri·bo·nu·cle·ic acid \-ˈrī-bō-n(y)u̇-ˌklē-ik-, -ˌklā-\ *n* **:** DNA

¹de·spair \di-ˈspa(ə)r, -ˈspe(ə)r\ *vb* [ME *despeiren*, fr. MF *desperer*, fr. L *desperare*, fr. *de-* + *sperare* to hope; akin to L *spes* hope — more at SPEED] *vi* **:** to lose all hope or confidence ⟨~ of winning⟩ ~ *vt, obs* **:** to lose hope for — **de·spair·er** *n*

²despair *n* **1 :** utter loss of hope ⟨~, which may find expression in . . . suicide —Rudyard Kipling⟩ **2 :** a cause of hopelessness ⟨an incorrigible child is the ~ of his parents⟩

de·spair·ing *adj* **:** given to, arising from, or marked by despair **:** devoid of hope ***syn*** see DESPONDENT ***ant*** hopeful — **de·spair·ing·ly** \-iŋ-lē\ *adv*

des·patch \dis-ˈpach\ *var of* DISPATCH

des·per·a·do \ˌdes-pə-ˈräd-(ˌ)ō, -ˈrād-\ *n, pl* **-does** *or* **-dos** [prob. alter. of obs. *desperate* desperado, fr. *desperate*, adj.] **:** a bold or violent criminal; *esp* **:** a bandit of the western U.S. in the 19th century

des·per·ate \ˈdes-p(ə-)rət, -pərt\ *adj* [L *desperatus*, pp. of *desperare*] **1 a :** having lost hope ⟨a ~ spirit crying for relief⟩ **b :** giving no ground for hope ⟨his situation was ~⟩ **2 a :** moved by despair ⟨men made ~ by abuse⟩ **b :** involving or employing extreme measures in an attempt to escape defeat or frustration ⟨the bitter, ~ striving unto death of the oppressed race —Rose Macaulay⟩ **3 :** suffering extreme need or anxiety ⟨~ for money⟩ ⟨~ for something to do⟩ **4 :** of extreme intensity **:** OVERPOWERING **5 :** SHOCK-

ING, OUTRAGEOUS **syn** see DESPONDENT — **des·per·ate·ly** *adv* — **des·per·ate·ness** *n*

des·per·a·tion \ˌdes-pə-ˈrā-shən\ *n* **1 :** loss of hope and surrender to despair **2 :** a state of hopelessness leading to rashness

de·spi·ca·ble \di-ˈspik-ə-bəl, ˈdes-(ˌ)pik-\ *adj* [LL *despicabilis*, fr. L *despicari* to despise] **:** deserving to be despised **:** so worthless or obnoxious as to rouse moral indignation ⟨a ~ excuse of a father⟩ **syn** see CONTEMPTIBLE **ant** praiseworthy, laudable — **de·spi·ca·ble·ness** *n* — **de·spi·ca·bly** \-blē\ *adv*

de·spir·i·tu·al·ize \(ˈ)dē-ˈspir-ich-(ə-)wə-ˌlīz, -ich-ə-ˌlīz\ *vt* **:** to deprive of spiritual character or influence ⟨~ education and you devitalize life —W. L. Sullivan⟩

de·spise \di-ˈspīz\ *vt* **de·spised; de·spis·ing** [ME *despisen*, fr. OF *despis-*, stem of *despire*, fr. L *despicere*, fr. *de-* + *specere* to look — more at SPY] **1 :** to look down on with contempt or aversion ⟨*despised* the weak⟩ **2 :** to regard as negligible, worthless, or distasteful — **de·spise·ment** \-ˈspīz-mənt\ *n* — **de·spis·er** \-ˈspī-zər\ *n*

syn DESPISE, CONTEMN, SCORN, DISDAIN, SCOUT *shared meaning element* **:** to regard as beneath one's notice and unworthy of consideration or interest **ant** appreciate

1**de·spite** \di-ˈspīt\ *n* [ME, fr. OF *despit*, fr. L *despectus*, fr. *despectus*, pp. of *despicere*] **1 :** the feeling or attitude of despising **:** CONTEMPT **2 :** MALICE, SPITE **3 a :** an act showing contempt or defiance **b :** HARM, INJURY ⟨I know of no government which stands to its obligations, even in its own ~, more solidly —Sir Winston Churchill⟩ — **in despite of :** in spite of

2**despite** *vt* **de·spit·ed; de·spit·ing** **1** *archaic* **:** to treat with contempt **2** *obs* **:** to provoke to anger **:** VEX

3**despite** *prep* **:** in spite of **:** NOTWITHSTANDING ⟨ran ~ his injury⟩

de·spite·ful \di-ˈspīt-fəl\ *adj* **:** expressing malice or hate — **de·spite·ful·ly** \-fə-lē\ *adv* — **de·spite·ful·ness** *n*

de·spit·eous \dis-ˈpit-ē-əs\ *adj*, *archaic* **:** feeling or showing despite **:** MALICIOUS — **de·spit·eous·ly** *adv*, *archaic*

de·spoil \di-ˈspȯi(ə)l\ *vt* [ME *despoylen*, fr. OF *despoillier*, fr. L *despoliare*, fr. *de-* + *spoliare* to strip, rob — more at SPOIL] **:** to strip of belongings, possessions, or value **:** PILLAGE — **de·spoil·er** *n* — **de·spoil·ment** \-ˈspȯi(ə)l-mənt\ *n*

de·spo·li·a·tion \di-ˌspō-lē-ˈā-shən\ *n* [LL *despoliation-*, *despoliatio*, fr. *despoliatus*, pp. of *despoliare*] **:** the act of plundering **:** the condition of being despoiled **:** SPOLIATION

1**de·spond** \di-ˈspänd\ *vi* [L *despondēre*, fr. *de-* + *spondēre* to promise solemnly — more at SPOUSE] **:** to become discouraged or disheartened

2**despond** *n* **:** DESPONDENCY

de·spon·dence \di-ˈspän-dən(t)s\ *n* **:** DESPONDENCY

de·spon·den·cy \-dən-sē\ *n* **:** the state of being despondent **:** DEJECTION, HOPELESSNESS

de·spon·dent \-dənt\ *adj* [L *despondent-*, *despondens*, prp. of *despondēre*] **:** feeling extreme discouragement, dejection, or depression ⟨~ about his health⟩ — **de·spon·dent·ly** *adv*

syn DESPONDENT, DESPAIRING, DESPERATE, HOPELESS *shared meaning element* **:** having lost all or nearly all hope **ant** lighthearted

des·pot \ˈdes-pət, -ˌpät\ *n* [MF *despote*, fr. Gk *despotēs*; akin to Skt *dampati* lord of the house; both fr. a prehistoric IE compound whose constituents are akin to L *domus* house and to L *potis* able — more at TIMBER, POTENT] **1 a :** a Byzantine emperor or prince **b :** a bishop or patriarch of the Eastern Orthodox Church **c :** an Italian hereditary prince or military leader during the Renaissance **2 a :** a ruler with absolute power and authority **:** AUTOCRAT **b :** a person exercising power abusively, oppressively, or tyrannically

des·pot·ic \des-ˈpät-ik, dis-\ *adj* **:** of, relating to, or having the characteristics of a despot — **des·pot·i·cal·ly** \-i-k(ə-)lē\ *adv*

des·po·tism \ˈdes-pə-ˌtiz-əm\ *n* **1 a :** rule by a despot **b :** despotic exercise of power **2 a :** a system of government in which the ruler has unlimited power **:** ABSOLUTISM **b :** a despotic state

des·qua·mate \ˈdes-kwə-ˌmāt\ *vi* **-mat·ed; -mat·ing** [L *desquamatus*, pp. of *desquamare*, fr. *de-* + *squama* scale — more at SQUALOR] **:** to peel off in scales — **des·qua·ma·tion** \ˌdes-kwə-ˈmā-shən\ *n*

des·sert \di-ˈzərt\ *n* [MF, fr. *desservir* to clear the table, fr. *des-* de- + *servir* to serve, fr. L *servire*] **1 :** a course of fruit, pastry, pudding, ice cream, or cheese served at the close of a meal **2** *Brit* **:** a fresh fruit served after a sweet course

des·sert·spoon \-ˌspün\ *n* **:** a spoon intermediate in size between a teaspoon and a tablespoon for use in eating dessert

des·sert·spoon·ful \di-ˌzərt-ˈspün-ˌfu̇l, -ˈzərt-ˌ\ *n* **1 :** as much as a dessertspoon will hold **2 :** a unit of measure equal to about 2½ fluidrams

dessert wine *n* **:** a usu. sweet wine containing over 14 percent alcohol by volume and often served with dessert or between meals

de·sta·bi·lize \(ˈ)dē-ˈstā-bə-ˌlīz\ *vt* **:** to make unstable — **de·sta·bi·li·za·tion** \(ˌ)dē-ˌstā-bə-lə-ˈzā-shən\ *n*

de·stain \(ˈ)dē-ˈstān\ *vt* **:** to selectively remove stain from (a specimen for microscopic study)

de·sta·lin·iza·tion \(ˌ)dē-ˌstäl-ə-nə-ˈzā-shən, -ˌstal-\ *n* **:** the deflation of Stalin and his policies

de·ster·il·ize \(ˈ)dē-ˈster-ə-ˌlīz\ *vt* **:** to release (gold) from an insulated condition in the treasury to useful service

de Stijl \də-ˈstī(ə)l, -ˈstā(ə)l\ *n* [D *De Stijl*, lit., the style, magazine published by members of the school] **:** an influential school of art founded in Holland in 1917 typically using rectangular forms and the primary colors plus black and white and asymmetric balance

des·ti·na·tion \ˌdes-tə-ˈnā-shən\ *n* **1 :** an act of appointing, setting aside for a purpose, or predetermining **2 :** the purpose for which something is destined ⟨a ~ above the objects . . . of this world —J. B. Mozley⟩ **3 :** a place which is set for the end of a journey or to which something is sent ⟨the couple kept their ~ secret⟩

des·tine \ˈdes-tən\ *vt* **des·tined; des·tin·ing** [ME *destinen*, fr. OF *destiner*, fr. L *destinare*, fr. *de-* + *-stinare* (akin to L *stare* to stand) — more at STAND] **1 :** to decree beforehand **:** PREDETERMINE **2 a :** to designate, assign, or dedicate in advance ⟨the younger son was *destined* for the church⟩ **b :** to direct, devise, or set apart for a specific purpose or end ⟨freight *destined* for English ports⟩

des·ti·ny \ˈdes-tə-nē\ *n*, *pl* **-nies** [ME *destinee*, fr. MF, fr. fem. of *destiné*, pp. of *destiner*] **1 :** something to which a person or thing is destined **:** FORTUNE **2 :** a predetermined course of events often held to be a resistless power or agency **syn** see FATE

des·ti·tute \ˈdes-tə-ˌt(y)üt\ *adj* [ME, fr. L *destitutus*, pp. of *destituere* to abandon, deprive, fr. *de-* + *statuere* to set up — more at STATUTE] **1 :** lacking something needed or desirable ⟨a lake ~ of fish⟩ **2 :** lacking possessions and resources; *esp* **:** suffering extreme want ⟨a ~ old man⟩ — **des·ti·tute·ness** *n*

des·ti·tu·tion \ˌdes-tə-ˈt(y)ü-shən\ *n* **:** the state of being destitute; *esp* **:** such extreme want as threatens life unless relieved **syn** see POVERTY

des·trier \ˈdes-trē-ər, də-ˈstri(ə)r\ *n* [ME, fr. OF, fr. *destre* right hand, fr. L *dextra*, fr. fem. of *dexter*] *archaic* **:** WAR-HORSE; *also* **:** a charger used esp. in medieval tournaments

de·stroy \di-ˈstrȯi\ *vb* [ME *destroyen*, fr. OF *destruire*, fr. (assumed) VL *destrugere*, alter. of L *destruere*, fr. *de-* + *struere* to build — more at STRUCTURE] *vt* **1 :** to ruin the structure, organic existence, or condition of **:** DEMOLISH ⟨priceless art ~*ed* by water⟩ **2 a :** to put out of existence **:** KILL **b :** NEUTRALIZE ⟨the moon ~*s* the light of the stars⟩ **c :** to subject to a crushing defeat **:** ANNIHILATE ⟨armies had been crippled but not ~*ed* —W. L. Shirer⟩ ~ *vi* **:** to cause destruction

de·stroy·er \di-ˈstrȯi(-ə)r\ *n* **1 :** one that destroys **2 :** a small fast warship usu. armed with 5-inch guns, depth charges, torpedoes, mines, and sometimes guided missiles

destroyer escort *n* **:** a warship similar to but smaller than a destroyer

destroying angel *n* **:** a very poisonous mushroom (*Amanita phalloides*) varying in color from pure white to olive or yellow and having a prominent volva at the base; *also* **:** a related poisonous mushroom (*A. verna*)

1**de·struct** \di-ˈstrəkt\ *vt* [back-formation fr. *destruction*] **:** DESTROY

2**de·struct** \di-ˈstrəkt, ˈdē-ˌ\ *n* **:** the deliberate destruction of a rocket after launching esp. during a test; *also* **:** the deliberate destruction of a device or material (as to prevent its falling into enemy hands)

de·struc·ti·ble \di-ˈstrək-tə-bəl\ *adj* **:** capable of being destroyed — **de·struc·ti·bil·i·ty** \di-ˌstrək-tə-ˈbil-ət-ē\ *n*

de·struc·tion \di-ˈstrək-shən\ *n* [ME *destruccioun*, fr. MF *destruction*, fr. L *destruction-*, *destructio*, fr. *destructus*, pp. of *destruere*] **1 :** the action or process of destroying something **2 :** the state or fact of being destroyed **:** RUIN **3 :** a destroying agency **syn** see RUIN

de·struc·tion·ist \-sh(ə-)nəst\ *n* **:** one who delights in or advocates destruction

de·struc·tive \di-ˈstrək-tiv\ *adj* **1 :** causing destruction **:** RUINOUS ⟨~ storm⟩ **2 :** designed or tending to destroy ⟨~ criticism⟩ — **de·struc·tive·ly** *adv* — **de·struc·tive·ness** *n*

destructive distillation *n* **:** decomposition of a substance (as wood, coal, or oil) by heat in a closed container and collection of the volatile products produced

de·struc·tiv·i·ty \di-ˌstrək-ˈtiv-ət-ē, ˌdē-\ *n* **:** capacity for destruction

de·struc·tor \di-ˈstrək-tər\ *n* **1 :** a furnace for burning refuse **:** INCINERATOR **2 :** a device for destroying a missile in flight

de·sue·tude \ˈdes-wi-ˌt(y)üd, di-ˈsü-ə-ˌt(y)üd\ *n* [F or L; F *désuétude*, fr. L *desuetudo*, fr. *desuetus*, pp. of *desuescere* to become unaccustomed, fr. *de-* + *suescere* to become accustomed; akin to L *sui* of oneself — more at SUICIDE] **:** discontinuance from use or exercise **:** DISUSE ⟨after . . . twenty years of innocuous ~ these laws are brought forth —Grover Cleveland⟩

de·sul·fur·ize \(ˈ)dē-ˈsəl-fə-ˌrīz\ *vt* **:** to remove sulfur or sulfur compounds from — **de·sul·fur·iza·tion** \(ˈ)dē-ˌsəl-fə-rə-ˈzā-shən\ *n*

des·ul·to·ry \ˈdes-əl-ˌtōr-ē, -ˌtȯr- *also* ˈdez-\ *adj* [L *desultorius*, fr. *desultus*, pp. of *desilire* to leap down, fr. *de-* + *salire* to leap — more at SALLY] **1 :** marked by lack of definite plan, regularity, or purpose ⟨a dragged-out ordeal of . . . ~ shopping —Herman Wouk⟩ **2 :** not connected with the main subject **syn** see RANDOM **ant** assiduous (*as study*), methodical — **des·ul·to·ri·ly** \ˌdes-əl-ˈtōr-ə-lē, ˌdez-, -ˈtȯr-\ *adv* — **des·ul·to·ri·ness** \ˈdes-əl-ˌtōr-ē-nəs, ˈdez-, -ˌtȯr-\ *n*

det *abbr* **1** detached; detachment **2** detail **3** determine

de·tach \di-ˈtach\ *vt* [F *détacher*, fr. OF *destachier*, fr. *des-* de- + *-tachier* (as in *atachier* to attach)] **1 :** to separate esp. from a larger mass and usu. without violence or damage **2 :** DISENGAGE, WITHDRAW — **de·tach·abil·i·ty** \-ˌtach-ə-ˈbil-ət-ē\ *n* — **de·tach·able** \-ˈtach-ə-bəl\ *adj* — **de·tach·ably** \-blē\ *adv*

de·tached \di-ˈtacht\ *adj* **1 :** standing by itself **:** SEPARATE, UNCONNECTED; *specif* **:** not sharing any wall with another building ⟨~ house⟩ **2 :** exhibiting an aloof objectivity usu. free from prejudice or self-interest ⟨a ~ observer⟩ **syn** see INDIFFERENT **ant** interested — **de·tached·ly** \-ˈtach-əd-lē, -ˈtach-tlē\ *adv* — **de·tached·ness** \-ˈtach-əd-nəs, -ˈtach(t)-nəs\ *n*

detached service *n* **:** military service away from one's assigned organization

de·tach·ment \di-ˈtach-mənt\ *n* **1 :** the action or process of detaching **:** SEPARATION **2 a :** the dispatch of a body of troops or part of a fleet from the main body for a special mission or service **b :** the part so dispatched **c :** a permanently organized separate unit usu. smaller than a platoon and different in composition from normal units **3 a :** indifference to worldly concerns **:** ALOOFNESS **b :** freedom from bias or prejudice

1**de·tail** \di-ˈtā(ə)l, ˈdē-ˌtāl\ *n* [F *détail*, fr. OF *detail* slice, piece, fr. *detaillier* to cut in pieces, fr. *de-* + *taillier* to cut — more at TAILOR] **1 :** extended treatment of or attention to particular items **2 :** a part of a whole: as **a :** a small and subordinate part **:** PARTICULAR; *also* **:** a reproduction of such a part of a work of art **b :** a part considered or requiring to be considered separately from the whole **c :** the small elements that collectively constitute a work of art **d :** the small elements of a photographic image corresponding to those of the subject **3 a :** selection for a particular task (as in military service) of a person or a body of persons **b** (1) **:** the person or body selected (2) : the task to be performed ***syn*** see ITEM

²detail *vt* **1** : to report minutely and distinctly : SPECIFY ⟨~*ed* his petty grievances⟩ **2** : to assign to a particular task **3** : to furnish with the smaller elements of design and finish ⟨trimmings that ~ slips and petticoats⟩ ~ *vi* : to make detail drawings — **de·tail·er** *n*

de·tailed \di-ˈtā(ə)ld, ˈdē-ˌtāld\ *adj* : marked by abundant detail or by thoroughness in treating small items or parts ⟨the ~ study of history⟩ ***syn*** see CIRCUMSTANTIAL — **de·tailed·ly** \di-ˈtāl(-ə)d-lē, ˈdē-ˌ\ *adv* — **de·tailed·ness** \di-ˈtā-ləd-nəs, -ˈtāl(d)-, ˈdē-ˌ\ *n*

detail man *n* : a representative of a drug manufacturer who introduces new drugs esp. to pharmacists and physicians

de·tain \di-ˈtān\ *vt* [ME *deteynen*, fr. MF *detenir*, fr. L *detinēre*, fr. *de-* + *tenēre* to hold — more at THIN] **1** : to hold or keep in or as if in custody **2** *obs* : to keep back (as something due) : WITHHOLD **3** : to restrain esp. from proceeding : STOP ***syn*** see KEEP, DELAY — **de·tain·ment** \-mənt\ *n*

de·tain·ee \di-ˌtā-ˈnē, ˌdē-\ *n* : a person held in custody esp. for political reasons

de·tain·er \di-ˈtā-nər\ *n* [AF *detener*, fr. *detener* to detain, fr. L *detinēre*] **1** : the act of keeping something in one's possession; *specif* : the withholding from the rightful owner of something which has lawfully come into the possession of the holder **2** : detention in custody **3** : a writ authorizing the keeper of a prison to continue to hold a person in custody

detd *abbr* determined

de·tect \di-ˈtekt\ *vt* [ME *detecten*, fr. L *detectus*, pp. of *detegere* to uncover, detect, fr. *de-* + *tegere* to cover — more at THATCH] **1** : to discover the true character of **2** : to discover or determine the existence, presence, or fact of ⟨~ alcohol in the blood⟩ **3** : DEMODULATE — **de·tect·abil·i·ty** \-ˌtek-tə-ˈbil-ət-ē\ *n* — **de·tect·able** \-ˈtek-tə-bəl\ *adj*

de·tect·a·phone \-ˈtek-tə-ˌfōn\ *n* : a telephonic apparatus with an attached microphone transmitter used esp. for secret listening

de·tec·tion \di-ˈtek-shən\ *n* **1** : the act of detecting : the state or fact of being detected **2** : DEMODULATION

¹de·tec·tive \di-ˈtek-tiv\ *adj* **1** : fitted for or used in detecting something ⟨a ~ device for coal gas⟩ **2** : of or relating to detectives or their work ⟨a ~ novel⟩

²detective *n* : one employed or engaged in detecting lawbreakers or in getting information that is not readily or publicly accessible

de·tec·tor \di-ˈtek-tər\ *n* : one that detects: as **a** : a device for detecting the presence of electric waves or of radioactivity **b** : a rectifier of high-frequency current used esp. for extracting the intelligence from a radio signal

de·tent \ˈdē-ˌtent, di-ˈ\ *n* [F *détente*, fr. MF *destente*, fr. *destendre* to slacken, fr. OF, fr. *des-* de- + *tendre* to stretch, fr. L *tendere* — more at THIN] : a device (as a catch, dog, or spring-operated ball) for positioning and holding one mechanical part in relation to another so that the device can be released by force applied to one of the parts

dé·tente \dā-täⁿ(n)t\ *n* [F] : a relaxation of strained relations or tensions (as between nations)

de·ten·tion \di-ˈten-chən\ *n* [MF or LL; MF, fr. LL *detention-*, *detentio*, fr. L *detentus*, pp. of *detinēre* to detain] **1** : the act or fact of detaining or holding back; *esp* : a holding in custody **2** : the state of being detained; *esp* : a period of temporary custody prior to disposition by a court

detention home *n* : a house of detention for juvenile delinquents usu. under the supervision of a juvenile court

de·ter \di-ˈtər\ *vt* **de·terred; de·ter·ring** [L *deterrēre*, fr. *de-* + *terrēre* to frighten — more at TERROR] **1** : to turn aside, discourage, or prevent from acting (as by fear) **2** : INHIBIT — **de·ter·ment** \-ˈtər-mənt\ *n* — **de·ter·rer** \-ˈtər-ər\ *n*

de·terge \di-ˈtərj\ *vt* **de·terged; de·terg·ing** [F or L; F *déterger*, fr. L *detergēre*, fr. *de-* + *tergēre* to wipe — more at TERSE] : to wash off : CLEANSE — **de·terg·er** *n*

de·ter·gen·cy \di-ˈtər-jən-sē\ *n* : cleansing quality or power

¹de·ter·gent \-jənt\ *adj* : that cleanses : CLEANSING

²detergent *n* : a cleansing agent: as **a** : SOAP **b** : any of numerous synthetic water-soluble or liquid organic preparations that are chemically different from soaps but are able to emulsify oils, hold dirt in suspension, and act as wetting agents **c** : an oil-soluble substance that holds insoluble foreign matter in suspension and is used in lubricating oils and dry-cleaning solvents

de·te·ri·o·rate \di-ˈtir-ē-ə-ˌrāt\ *vb* **-rat·ed; -rat·ing** [LL *deterioratus*, pp. of *deteriorare*, fr. L *deterior* worse, fr. *de-* + *-ter* (suffix as in L *uter* which of two) + *-ior* (compar. suffix) — more at WHETHER, -ER] *vt* **1** : to make inferior in quality or value : IMPAIR **2** : DISINTEGRATE ~ *vi* **1** : to grow worse in quality or state ⟨allowed a tradition of academic excellence to ~⟩ **2** : DEGENERATE

de·te·ri·o·ra·tion \di-ˌtir-ē-ə-ˈrā-shən\ *n* : the action or process of deteriorating : the state of having deteriorated

syn DETERIORATION, DEGENERATION, DECADENCE, DECLINE *shared meaning element* : a falling from a higher to a lower level (as of quality, character, or vitality) ***ant*** improvement, amelioration

de·te·ri·o·ra·tive \di-ˈtir-ē-ə-ˌrāt-iv\ *adj* : tending to deteriorate

de·ter·min·able \-ˈtərm-(ə)-nə-bəl\ *adj* **1** : capable of being determined, definitely ascertained, or decided upon **2** : liable to be terminated : TERMINABLE — **de·ter·min·able·ness** *n* — **de·ter·min·ably** \-blē\ *adv*

de·ter·mi·na·cy \di-ˈtər-mə-nə-sē\ *n, pl* **-cies** **1** : the quality or state of being determinate **2 a** : the state of being definitely and unequivocally characterized : EXACTNESS **b** : the state of being determined or necessitated

de·ter·mi·nant \di-ˈtərm-(ə-)nənt\ *n* **1** : an element that identifies or determines the nature of something or that fixes or conditions an outcome **2** : a square array of numbers bordered on either side by a straight line with a value that is the algebraic sum of all the products that can be formed by taking as factors one element in succession from each row and column and giving to each product a positive or negative sign depending upon whether the number of permutations necessary to place the indices representing each factor's position in its row or column in the order of the natural numbers is odd or even **3** : GENE; *broadly* : a comparable subordinate agent (as a plasmagene) ***syn*** see CAUSE — **de·ter·mi·nan·tal** \-ˌtər-mə-ˈnant-ᵊl\ *adj*

de·ter·mi·nate \di-ˈtərm-(ə-)nət\ *adj* [ME, fr. L *determinatus*, pp. of *determinare*] **1** : having defined limits : ESTABLISHED **2** : definitely settled : ARBITRARY **3** : conclusively determined : DEFINITIVE **4** : CYMOSE **5** *of an egg* : undergoing determinate cleavage — **de·ter·mi·nate·ly** *adv* — **de·ter·mi·nate·ness** *n*

determinate cleavage *n* : cleavage of an egg in which each division irreversibly separates portions of the zygote with specific potencies for further development

de·ter·mi·na·tion \di-ˌtər-mə-ˈnā-shən\ *n* **1 a** : a judicial decision settling and ending a controversy **b** : the resolving of a question by argument or reasoning **2** *archaic* : TERMINATION **3 a** : the act of deciding definitely and firmly; *also* : the result of such an act of decision **b** : the power or habit of deciding definitely and firmly **4** : a fixing of the position, magnitude, or character of something: as **a** : the act, process, or result of an accurate measurement **b** : an identification of the taxonomic position of a plant or animal **5 a** : the definition of a concept in logic by its essential constituents **b** : the addition of a differentia to a concept to limit its denotation **6** : direction or tendency to a certain end : IMPULSION **7** : the fixation of the destiny of undifferentiated embryonic tissue

¹de·ter·mi·na·tive \-ˈtər-mə-ˌnāt-iv, -ˈtərm-(ə-)nət-\ *adj* : having power or tendency to determine : tending to fix, settle, or define something ⟨regard experiments as ~ of the principles from which deductions could be made —S. F. Mason⟩ ***syn*** see CONCLUSIVE — **de·ter·mi·na·tive·ly** *adv* — **de·ter·mi·na·tive·ness** *n*

²determinative *n* : one that serves to determine

de·ter·mi·na·tor \di-ˈtər-mə-ˌnāt-ər\ *n* : DETERMINER

de·ter·mine \di-ˈtər-mən\ *vb* **de·ter·mined; de·ter·min·ing** \-ˈtərm-(ə-)niŋ\ [ME *determinen*, fr. MF *determiner*, fr. L *determinare*, fr. *de-* + *terminare* to limit, fr. *terminus* boundary, limit — more at TERM] *vt* **1 a** : to fix conclusively or authoritatively **b** : to decide by judicial sentence **c** : to settle or decide by choice of alternatives or possibilities **d** : RESOLVE **2 a** : to fix the form or character of beforehand : ORDAIN ⟨two points ~ a straight line⟩ **b** : to bring about as a result : REGULATE ⟨demand ~*s* the price⟩ **3 a** : to fix the boundaries of **b** : to limit in extent or scope **c** : to put or set an end to : TERMINATE ⟨~ an estate⟩ **4 a** : to obtain definite and firsthand knowledge of ⟨~ a position at sea⟩ **b** : to discover the taxonomic position or the generic and specific names of **5** : to bring about the determination of ⟨~ the fate of a cell⟩ ~ *vi* **1** : to come to a decision **2** : to come to an end or become void ***syn*** see DECIDE, DISCOVER

de·ter·mined \-ˈtər-mənd\ *adj* **1** : DECIDED, RESOLVED **2** : FIRM, RESOLUTE — **de·ter·mined·ly** \-mən-dlē, -mə-nəd-lē\ *adv* — **de·ter·mined·ness** \-mən(d)-nəs\ *n*

de·ter·min·er \-ˈtərm-(ə-)nər\ *n* : one that determines: as **a** : GENE, DETERMINANT **b** : a word (as *his* in "his new car") belonging to a group of limiting noun modifiers characterized by occurrence before descriptive adjectives modifying the same noun

de·ter·min·ism \di-ˈtər-mə-ˌniz-əm\ *n* **1 a** : a doctrine that acts of the will, occurrences in nature, or social or psychological phenomena are determined by antecedent causes **b** : a belief in predestination **2** : the quality or state of being determined — **de·ter·min·ist** \-(ə-)nəst\ *n or adj* — **de·ter·min·is·tic** \-ˌtər-mə-ˈnis-tik\ *adj* — **de·ter·min·is·ti·cal·ly** \-ti-k(ə-)lē\ *adv*

de·ter·ra·ble \di-ˈtər-ə-bəl\ *adj* : capable of being deterred — **de·ter·ra·bil·i·ty** \-ˌtər-ə-ˈbil-ət-ē\ *n*

de·ter·rence \di-ˈtər-ən(t)s, -ˈter-; -ˈtə-rən(t)s\ *n* **1** : the act or process of deterring ⟨the penalty for the crime of perjury is often no ~ to lying under oath —*New Republic*⟩ **2** : the maintaining of vast military power and weaponry in order to discourage war

de·ter·rent \-ənt, -rənt\ *adj* [L *deterrent-*, *deterrens*, prp. of *deterrēre* to deter] **1** : serving to deter **2** : relating to deterrence — **deterrent** *n* — **de·ter·rent·ly** *adv*

de·ter·sive \di-ˈtər-siv, -ziv\ *adj* [MF *detersif*, fr. L *detersus*, pp. of *detergēre* to deterge] : DETERGENT, CLEANSING — **detersive** *n*

de·test \di-ˈtest\ *vt* [ME *detesten*, fr. L *detestari*, lit., to curse while calling a deity to witness, fr. *de-* + *testari* to call to witness — more at TESTAMENT] **1** : to feel intense and often violent antipathy toward : LOATHE **2** *obs* : CURSE, DENOUNCE ***syn*** see HATE ***ant*** adore — **de·test·er** *n*

de·test·able \di-ˈtes-tə-bəl\ *adj* : arousing or meriting intense dislike : ABOMINABLE — **de·test·able·ness** *n* — **de·test·ably** \-blē\ *adv*

de·tes·ta·tion \ˌdē-ˌtes-ˈtā-shən, di-\ *n* **1** : extreme hatred or dislike : ABHORRENCE, LOATHING ⟨had a ~ of hypocrites⟩ **2** : an object of hatred or contempt

de·throne \di-ˈthrōn\ *vt* : to remove from a throne or place of power or prominence : DEPOSE — **de·throne·ment** \-mənt\ *n* — **de·thron·er** *n*

de·tick \(ˈ)dē-ˈtik\ *vt* : to remove ticks from ⟨dogs should be ~*ed* and sprayed⟩ — **de·tick·er** *n*

det·i·nue \ˈdet-ᵊn-ˌ(y)ü\ *n* [ME *detenewe*, fr. MF *detenue* detention, fr. fem. of *detenu*, pp. of *detenir* to detain] **1** : detention of something due; *esp* : the unlawful detention of a personal chattel from another **2** : a common-law action for the recovery of a personal chattel wrongfully detained or of its value

detn *abbr* **1** detention **2** determination

det·o·na·ble \ˈdet-ᵊn-ə-bəl, -ə-nə-\ *adj* : capable of being detonated — **det·o·na·bil·i·ty** \ˌdet-ᵊn-ə-ˈbil-ət-ē, ˌdet-ə-nə-\ *n*

det·o·nate \ˈdet-ᵊn-ˌāt, ˈdet-ə-ˌnāt\ *vb* **-nat·ed; -nat·ing** [L *detonatus*, pp. of *detonare* to thunder down, fr. *de-* + *tonare* to thunder —

more at THUNDER] *vi* : to explode with sudden violence ~ *vt* **1** : to cause to detonate ⟨~ an atom bomb⟩ — compare DEFLAGRATE **2** : to set off in a burst of activity : ACTIVATE ⟨has *detonated* a . . . Puerto Rican tourist boom —Horace Sutton⟩ — **det·o·nat·able** \-ˌāt-ə-bəl, -ˌnāt-\ *adj* — **det·o·na·tive** \ˈdet-ᵊn-ˌāt-iv, ˈdet-ə-ˌnāt- \ *adj*

det·o·na·tion \ˌdet-ᵊn-ˈā-shən, ˌdet-ə-ˈnā-\ *n* **1** : the action or process of detonating **2** : rapid combustion in an internal-combustion engine that results in knocking — **det·o·na·tion·al** \-shnəl, -shən-ᵊl\ *adj*

det·o·na·tor \ˈdet-ᵊn-ˌāt-ər, -ə-ˌnāt-\ *n* : a device or small quantity of explosive used for detonating a high explosive

[1]de·tour \ˈdē-ˌtu̇(ə)r *also* di-ˈ\ *n* [F *détour*, fr. OF *destor*, fr. *destorner* to divert, fr. *des-* de- + *torner* to turn — more at TURN] : a deviation from a direct course or the usual procedure; *specif* : a roundabout way temporarily replacing part of a route

[2]detour *vi* : to proceed by a detour ⟨~ around road construction⟩ ~ *vt* **1** : to send by a circuitous route **2** : to avoid by going around : BYPASS

de·tox·i·cate \(ˈ)dē-ˈtäk-sə-ˌkāt\ *vt* **-cat·ed; -cat·ing** [*de-* + L *toxicum* poison — more at TOXIC] : DETOXIFY — **de·tox·i·cant** \-si-kənt\ *n* — **de·tox·i·ca·tion** \(ˌ)dē-ˌtäk-sə-ˈkā-shən\ *n*

de·tox·i·fy \(ˈ)dē-ˈtäk-sə-ˌfī\ *vt* **-fied; -fy·ing** : to remove a poison or toxin or the effect of such from — **de·tox·i·fi·ca·tion** \(ˌ)dē-ˌtäk-sə-fə-ˈkā-shən\ *n*

de·tract \di-ˈtrakt\ *vb* [ME *detracten*, fr. L *detractus*, pp. of *detrahere* to withdraw, disparage, fr. *de-* + *trahere* to draw — more at DRAW] *vt* **1** *archaic* : to speak ill of **2** *archaic* : to take away **3** : DIVERT ⟨~ attention⟩ ~ *vi* : to take away something — **de·trac·tor** \-ˈtrak-tər\ *n*

de·trac·tion \di-ˈtrak-shən\ *n* **1** : a lessening of reputation or esteem esp. by envious, malicious, or petty criticism : BELITTLING, DISPARAGEMENT **2** : a taking away ⟨it is no ~ from its dignity or prestige —J. F. Golay⟩ — **de·trac·tive** \-ˈtrak-tiv\ *adj* — **de·trac·tive·ly** *adv*

de·train \(ˈ)dē-ˈtrān\ *vi* : to get off a railroad train ~ *vt* : to remove from a railroad train — **de·train·ment** \-mənt\ *n*

de·trib·al·ize \(ˈ)dē-ˈtrī-bə-ˌlīz\ *vt* **-ized; -iz·ing** : to cause to relinquish tribal customs : ACCULTURATE — **de·trib·al·iza·tion** \(ˌ)dē-ˌtrī-bə-lə-ˈzā-shən\ *n*

det·ri·ment \ˈde-trə-mənt\ *n* [ME, fr. MF or L; MF, fr. L *detrimentum*, fr. *deterere* to wear away, impair, fr. *de-* + *terere* to rub — more at THROW] **1** : INJURY, DAMAGE ⟨did hard work without ~ to his health⟩ **2** : a cause of injury or damage ⟨the long strike was a ~ to the industry⟩

[1]det·ri·men·tal \ˌde-trə-ˈment-ᵊl\ *adj* : obviously harmful : DAMAGING ⟨the ~ effects of heroin⟩ ***syn*** see PERNICIOUS ***ant*** beneficial — **det·ri·men·tal·ly** \-ᵊl-ē\ *adv*

[2]detrimental *n* : an undesirable or harmful person or thing

de·tri·tion \di-ˈtrish-ən\ *n* : a wearing off or away

de·tri·tus \di-ˈtrīt-əs\ *n, pl* **de·tri·tus** \-ˈtrīt-əs, -ˈtrī-ˌtüs\ [F *détritus*, fr. L *detritus*, pp. of *deterere*] **1** : loose material (as rock fragments or organic particles) that results directly from disintegration **2** : a product of disintegration or wearing away — **de·tri·tal** \-ˈtrīt-ᵊl\ *adj*

de trop \də-ˈtrō\ *adj* [F] : too much or too many : SUPERFLUOUS ⟨a topcoat was *de trop* with the thermometer standing at 72 degrees —Irving Kolodin⟩

de·tu·mes·cence \ˌde-t(y)ü-ˈmes-ᵊn(t)s\ *n* : subsidence or diminution of swelling — **de·tu·mes·cent** \-ᵊnt\ *adj*

Deu·ca·lion \d(y)ü-ˈkāl-yən\ *n* [L, fr. Gk *Deukaliōn*] : a survivor with his wife Pyrrha of a great flood by which according to Greek mythology Zeus destroyed the rest of the human race

[1]deuce \ˈd(y)üs\ *n* [MF *deus* two, fr. L *duos*, acc. masc. of *duo* two — more at TWO] **1 a** (1) : the face of a die that bears two spots (2) : a playing card bearing an index number two **b** : a throw of the dice yielding two points **2** : a tie in tennis after each side has scored 40 and requiring two consecutive points by one side to win **3** [obs. E *deuce* bad luck] **a** : DEVIL, DICKENS — used chiefly as a mild oath ⟨what the ~ is he up to now⟩ **b** : something notable of its kind ⟨a ~ of a mess⟩

[2]deuce *vt* **deuced; deuc·ing** : to bring the score of (a tennis game or set) to deuce

deuc·ed \ˈd(y)ü-səd\ *adj* : DAMNED, CONFOUNDED ⟨in a ~ fix⟩ — **deuc·ed** *or* **deuc·ed·ly** *adv*

deuces wild *n* : a card game (as poker) in which each deuce may represent any card designated by its holder

de·us ex ma·chi·na \ˌdā-ə-ˌsek-ˈsmäk-i-nə, -ˌnä; -ˈsmak-ə-nə\ *n* [NL, a god from a machine, trans. of Gk *theos ek mēchanēs*] **1** : a god introduced by means of a crane in ancient Greek and Roman drama to decide the final outcome **2** : a person or thing (as in fiction or drama) that appears or is introduced suddenly and unexpectedly and provides a contrived solution to an apparently insoluble difficulty

Deut *abbr* Deuteronomy

deut- *or* **deuto-** *comb form* [ISV, fr. *deuter-*] : second : secondary ⟨*deuto*nymph⟩

[1]deuter- *or* **deutero-** *comb form* [alter. of ME *deutro-*, modif. of LL *deutero-*, fr. Gk *deuter-*, *deutero-*, fr. *deuteros*; prob. akin to L *dudum* formerly, Gk *dein* to lack] : second : secondary ⟨*deutero*genesis⟩

[2]deuter- *or* **deutero-** *comb form* [ISV] : deuterium : containing deuterium ⟨*deuter*ated⟩ ⟨*deutero*alkanes⟩

deu·ter·ag·o·nist \ˌd(y)üt-ə-ˈrag-ə-nəst\ *n* [Gk *deuteragōnistēs*, fr. *deuter-* + *agōnistēs* combatant, actor — more at PROTAGONIST] **1** : the actor taking the part of second importance in a classical Greek drama **2** : a person who serves as a foil to another

deu·ter·an·ope \ˈd(y)üt-ə-rə-ˌnōp\ *n* : an individual affected with deuteranopia

deu·ter·an·opia \ˌd(y)üt-ə-rə-ˈnō-pē-ə\ *n* [NL, fr. [1]*deuter-* + [2]*a-* + *-opia*; fr. the blindness to green, regarded as the second primary color] : color blindness marked by confusion of purplish red and green — **deu·ter·an·opic** \-ˈnō-pik, -ˈnäp-ik\ *adj*

deu·ter·ate \ˈd(y)üt-ə-ˌrāt\ *vt* **-at·ed; -at·ing** : to introduce deuterium into (a compound) — **deu·ter·a·tion** \ˌd(y)üt-ə-ˈrā-shən\ *n*

deu·te·ri·um \d(y)ü-ˈtir-ē-əm\ *n* [NL, fr. Gk *deuteros* second] : the hydrogen isotope that is of twice the mass of ordinary hydrogen and that occurs in water — called also *heavy hydrogen*

deuterium oxide *n* : heavy water D_2O composed of deuterium and oxygen

deu·tero·ca·non·i·cal \ˌd(y)üt-ə-rō-kə-ˈnän-i-kəl\ *adj* [NL *deuterocanonicus*, fr. [1]*deuter-* + LL *canonicus* canonical] : of, relating to, or constituting the books of Scripture contained in the Septuagint but not in the Hebrew canon

deu·ter·og·a·my \ˌd(y)üt-ə-ˈräg-ə-mē\ *n* [LGk *deuterogamia*, fr. Gk *deuter-* + *-gamia* -gamy] : DIGAMY

deu·tero·gen·e·sis \ˌd(y)üt-ə-rō-ˈjen-ə-səs\ *n* : the appearance of a new adaptive character late in life

deu·ter·on \ˈd(y)üt-ə-ˌrän\ *n* [*deuterium*] : the nucleus of the deuterium atom consisting of one proton and one neutron

Deu·ter·o·nom·ic \ˌd(y)üt-ə-rə-ˈnäm-ik\ *adj* **1** : of or relating to the book of Deuteronomy **2** : marked by the literary style or theological content of Deuteronomy

Deu·ter·on·o·mist \ˌd(y)üt-ə-ˈrän-ə-məst\ *n* : one of the writers or editors of a Deuteronomic body of source material often distinguished in the earlier books of the Old Testament — **Deu·ter·on·o·mis·tic** \-ˌrän-ə-ˈmis-tik\ *adj*

Deu·ter·on·o·my \ˌd(y)üt-ə-ˈrän-ə-mē\ *n* [ME *Deutronomie*, fr. LL *Deuteronomium*, fr. Gk *Deuteronomion*, fr. *deuter-* + *nomos* law — more at NIMBLE] : the fifth book of canonical Jewish and Christian Scripture containing Mosaic laws and narrative material — see BIBLE table

deu·tero·stome \ˈd(y)üt-ə-rə-ˌstōm\ *n* [NL *Deuterostomia*, group name, fr. *deuter-* + Gk *stoma* mouth — more at STOMACH] : any of a major division (Deuterostomia) of the animal kingdom that includes the bilaterally symmetrical animals (as the chordates) with indeterminate cleavage and a mouth that does not arise from the blastopore

deu·to·plasm \ˈd(y)üt-ə-ˌplaz-əm\ *n* [ISV] : the nutritive inclusions of protoplasm; *esp* : the yolk reserves of an egg — **deu·to·plas·mic** \ˌd(y)üt-ə-ˈplaz-mik\ *adj*

deut·sche mark \ˌdȯi-chə-ˈmärk\ *n* [G, German mark] — see MONEY table

deut·zia \ˈd(y)üt-sē-ə\ *n* [NL, fr. Jean Deutz †1784? D patron of botanical research] : any of a genus (*Deutzia*) of the saxifrage family of ornamental shrubs with white or pink flowers

dev *abbr* deviation

de·val·u·ate \(ˈ)dē-ˈval-yə-ˌwāt\ *vb* : DEVALUE

de·val·u·a·tion \(ˌ)dē-ˌval-yə-ˈwā-shən\ *n* **1** : an official reduction in the exchange value of a currency by a lowering of its gold equivalency **2** : a lessening esp. of status or stature : DECLINE

de·val·ue \(ˈ)dē-ˈval-(ˌ)yü, -yə(-w)\ *vt* **1** : to institute the devaluation of (money) **2** : to cause or be responsible for a devaluation of (as a person or a literary work) ~ *vi* : to institute devaluation

De·va·na·ga·ri \ˌdā-və-ˈnäg-ə-rē\ *n* [Skt *devanāgarī*, fr. *deva* divine + *nāgarī* script of the city; akin to L *divus* divine — more at DEITY] : an alphabet usu. employed for Sanskrit and also used as a literary hand for various modern languages of India — see ALPHABET table

dev·as·tate \ˈdev-ə-ˌstāt\ *vt* **-tat·ed; -tat·ing** [L *devastatus*, pp. of *devastare*, fr. *de-* + *vastare* to lay waste — more at WASTE] **1** : to bring to ruin or desolation by violent action **2** : to reduce to chaos or disorder : OVERWHELM ⟨her answer *devastated* the class⟩ ***syn*** see RAVAGE — **dev·as·tat·ing·ly** \-ˌstāt-iŋ-lē\ *adv* — **dev·as·ta·tive** \-ˌstāt-iv\ *adj* — **dev·as·ta·tor** \-ˌstāt-ər\ *n*

dev·as·ta·tion \ˌdev-ə-ˈstā-shən\ *n* : the action of devastating : the state of being devastated : DESOLATION ***syn*** see RUIN

de·vel·op \di-ˈvel-əp\ *vb* [F *développer*, fr. OF *desvoloper*, fr. *des-* de- + *voloper* to wrap] *vt* **1 a** : to set forth or make clear by degrees or in detail : EXPOUND **b** : to make visible or manifest **c** : to treat (as in dyeing) with an agent to cause the appearance of color **d** : to subject (exposed photograph material) esp. to chemicals in order to produce a visible image; *also* : to make visible by such a method **e** : to elaborate by the unfolding of a musical idea and by the working out of rhythmic and harmonic changes in the theme **2** : to evolve the possibilities of **3 a** (1) : to make active (2) : to promote the growth of ⟨~*ed* his muscles⟩ **b** : to make available or usable ⟨~ its resources⟩ **c** : to move (a chess piece) from the original position to one providing more opportunity for effective use **4 a** : to cause to unfold gradually ⟨~*ed* his argument⟩ **b** : to expand by a process of growth ⟨~*ed* mature breasts in her early teens⟩ **c** : to cause to grow and differentiate along lines natural to its kind ⟨rain and sun ~ the grain⟩ **5** : to acquire gradually ⟨~ an appreciation for ballet⟩ **6** : to superimpose (a three-dimensional surface) on a plane without stretching ~ *vi* **1 a** : to go through a process of natural growth, differentiation, or evolution by successive changes ⟨a blossom ~*s* from a bud⟩ **b** : to acquire secondary sex characters **c** : EVOLVE, DIFFERENTIATE; *broadly* : GROW **2 a** : to become gradually manifest **b** : to become apparent **3** : to develop one's pieces in chess — **de·vel·op·able** \-ˈvel-ə-pə-bəl\ *adj*

de·vel·op·er \-ə-pər\ *n* : one that develops: as **a** : a chemical used to develop exposed photographic materials **b** : a person who develops real estate; *esp* : one that improves and subdivides land and builds and sells houses thereon

de·vel·op·ment \di-ˈvel-əp-mənt\ *n* **1** : the act, process, or result of developing **2** : the state of being developed **3** : a developed tract of land; *esp* : one that has houses built thereon — **de·vel·op·men·tal** \-ˌvel-əp-ˈment-ᵊl\ *adj* — **de·vel·op·men·tal·ly** \-ᵊl-ē\ *adv*

de·verb·a·tive \(ˈ)dē-ˈvər-bət-iv\ *adj* **1** : derived from a verb ⟨the ~ noun *developer* is derived from *develop*⟩ **2** : used in derivation from a verb ⟨the ~ suffix *-er* in *developer*⟩ — **deverbative** *n*

de·vest \di-ˈvest\ *vt* [MF *desvestir*, fr. ML *disvestire*, fr. L *dis-* + *vestire* to clothe — more at VEST] : DIVEST

de·vi·ance \ˈdē-vē-ən(t)s\ *n* : deviant quality, state, or behavior

de·vi·an·cy \-ən-sē\ *n, pl* **-cies** : DEVIANCE

de·vi·ant \-ənt\ *adj* **1 :** deviating esp. from an accepted norm ⟨~ behavior⟩ **2 :** characterized by deviation ⟨a ~ child⟩ — **deviant** *n*

¹de·vi·ate \'dē-vē-,āt\ *vb* **-at·ed; -at·ing** [LL *deviatus,* pp. of *deviare,* fr. L *de-* + *via* way — more at VIA] *vi* **1 :** to turn aside esp. from a norm **2 :** to stray esp. from a standard, principle, or topic ~ *vt* **:** to cause to turn out of a previous course ***syn*** see SWERVE — **de·vi·a·tor** \-,āt-ər\ *n* — **de·vi·a·to·ry** \-ə-,tōr-ē, -,tȯr-\ *adj*

²de·vi·ate \-vē-ət, -vē-,āt\ *adj* **:** characterized by or given to significant departure from the behavioral norms of a particular society

³de·vi·ate \-vē-ət, -vē-,āt\ *n* **1 :** one that deviates from a norm; *esp* **:** a person who differs markedly from his group norm **2 :** a statistical variable that gives the deviation of another variable from a fixed value (as the mean)

de·vi·a·tion \,dē-vē-'ā-shən\ *n* **:** an act or instance of deviating: as **a :** deflection of the needle of a compass caused by local magnetic influences (as in a ship) **b :** the difference between a value in a frequency distribution and a fixed number **c :** evolutionary differentiation involving interpolation of new stages in the ancestral pattern of morphogenesis **d :** departure from an established ideology or party line **e :** noticeable or marked departure from accepted norms of behavior — **de·vi·a·tion·ism** \-shə-,niz-əm\ *n* — **de·vi·a·tion·ist** \-sh(ə-)nəst\ *n*

de·vice \di-'vīs\ *n* [ME *devis, devise,* fr. OF, division, intention, fr. *deviser* to divide, regulate, tell — more at DEVISE] **1 :** something devised or contrived: as **a :** a scheme to deceive **:** STRATEGEM **b :** something fanciful, elaborate, or intricate in design **c :** something (as a figure of speech) in a literary work designed to achieve a particular artistic effect **d** *archaic* **:** MASQUE, SPECTACLE **e :** a conventional stage practice or means (as a stage whisper) used to achieve a particular dramatic effect **f :** a piece of equipment or a mechanism designed to serve a special purpose or perform a special function **2 :** DESIRE, WILL ⟨left to his own ~s⟩ **3 :** an emblematic design used esp. as a heraldic bearing

¹dev·il \'dev-əl\ *n* [ME *devel,* fr. OE *dēofol,* fr. LL *diabolus,* fr. Gk *diabolos,* lit., slanderer, fr. *diaballein* to throw across, slander, fr. *dia-* + *ballein* to throw; akin to OHG *quellan* to well, gush] **1** *often cap* **:** the personal supreme spirit of evil often represented in Jewish and Christian belief as the tempter of mankind, the leader of all apostate angels, and the ruler of hell — often used as an interjection, an intensive, or a generalized term of abuse **2 :** a malignant spirit **:** DEMON **3 a :** an extremely and malignantly wicked person **:** FIEND **b** *archaic* **:** a great evil **4 :** a person of notable energy, recklessness, and dashing spirit ⟨a ~ with the ladies⟩ **5 a :** FELLOW, MAN — usu. used in the phrase *poor devil* **b :** PRINTER'S DEVIL **6 :** any of various machines or devices (as a paper shredder) **7** *Christian Science* **:** the opposite of Truth **:** a belief in sin, sickness, and death **:** EVIL, ERROR

²devil *vb* **-iled** *or* **-illed; -il·ing** *or* **-il·ling** \'dev-(ə-)liŋ\ *vt* **1 :** TEASE, ANNOY **2 :** to season highly ⟨~ed eggs⟩ **3 :** to tear to pieces in a devil ⟨~ rags⟩ ~ *vi* **:** to serve or function as a devil

dev·il·fish \'dev-əl-,fish\ *n* **1 :** any of several extremely large rays (genera *Manta* and *Mobula*) widely distributed in warm seas **2 :** OCTOPUS; *broadly* **:** any large cephalopod

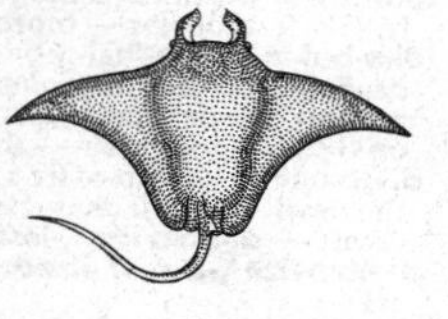

devilfish 1

dev·il·ish \'dev-(ə-)lish\ *adj* **1 :** of, relating to, or characteristic of the devil ⟨~ tricks⟩ **2 :** EXTREME, EXCESSIVE ⟨in a ~ hurry⟩ — **devilish** *adv* — **dev·il·ish·ly** *adv* — **dev·il·ish·ness** *n*

dev·il·kin \'dev-əl-kən\ *n* **:** a little devil **:** IMP

dev·il–may–care \,dev-əl-(,)mā-'ke(ə)r, -'ka(ə)r\ *adj* **1 :** heedless of authority **:** RECKLESS **2 :** ²RAKISH, INFORMAL

dev·il·ment \'dev-əl-mənt, -,ment\ *n* **1 :** devilish conduct **2 :** reckless mischief

dev·il·ry \'dev-əl-rē\ *or* **dev·il·try** \-əl-trē\ *n, pl* **-il·ries** *or* **-il·tries** **1 a :** action performed with the help of the devil **:** WITCHCRAFT **b :** gross or malignant cruelty **:** WICKEDNESS **c :** reckless unrestrained conduct **:** MISCHIEF **2 :** an act of devilry

devil's advocate *n* [trans. of NL *advocatus diaboli*] **1 :** a Roman Catholic official whose duty is to examine critically the evidence on which a demand for beatification or canonization rests **2 :** a person who champions the less accepted or approved cause for the sake of argument

devil's darning needle *n* **1 :** DRAGONFLY **2 :** DAMSELFLY

dev·il's food cake \'dev-əlz-,füd-,kāk\ *n* **:** a rich chocolate cake

devil's paintbrush *n* **:** ORANGE HAWKWEED; *broadly* **:** any of various hawkweeds that are naturalized weeds in the eastern U.S.

dev·il·wood \'dev-əl-,wu̇d\ *n* **:** a small tree (*Osmanthus americanus*) of the southern U.S. that is related to the olive

de·vi·ous \'dē-vē-əs\ *adj* [L *devius,* fr. *de* from + *via* way — more at DE-, VIA] **1 :** OUT-OF-THE-WAY, REMOTE **2 a :** deviating from a straight line **:** ROUNDABOUT **b :** moving without a fixed course **:** ERRANT ⟨~ breezes⟩ **3 a :** deviating from a right, accepted, or common course **:** ERRING **b :** not straightforward **c :** TRICKY ***syn*** see CROOKED ***ant*** straightforward — **de·vi·ous·ly** *adv* — **de·vi·ous·ness** *n*

de·vis·al \di-'vī-zəl\ *n* **:** the act of devising

¹de·vise \di-'vīz\ *vt* **de·vised; de·vis·ing** [ME *devisen,* fr. OF *deviser* to divide, regulate, tell, modif. of (assumed) VL *divisare,* fr. L *divisus,* pp. of *dividere* to divide] **1 a :** to form in the mind by new combinations or applications of ideas or principles **:** INVENT **b** *archaic* **:** SUPPOSE **c :** to plan to obtain or bring about **:** PLOT **2 :** to give (real estate) by will — compare BEQUEATH — **de·vis·able** \-'vī-zə-bəl\ *adj* — **de·vis·er** *n*

²devise *n* **1 :** the act of giving or disposing of real property by will **2 :** a will or clause of a will disposing of real property **3 :** property devised by will

de·vi·see \,dev-ə-'zē, di-,vī-'zē\ *n* **:** one to whom a devise of property is made

de·vi·sor \,dev-ə-'zȯ(ə)r; di-'vī-zər, -,vī-'zȯ(ə)r\ *n* **:** one who devises property in a will

de·vi·tal·ize \(')dē-'vīt-ᵊl-,īz\ *vt* **:** to deprive of life, vigor, or effectiveness ⟨malaria seizes and ~s many more people than it actually kills —R. S. Shiwalkar⟩

de·vit·ri·fy \(')dē-'vi-trə-,fī\ *vt* [F *dévitrifier,* fr. *dé-* de- + *vitrifier* to vitrify] **:** to deprive of glassy luster and transparency; *esp* **:** to change (as a glass) from a vitreous to a crystalline condition — **de·vit·ri·fi·able** \-,fī-ə-bəl\ *adj* — **de·vit·ri·fi·ca·tion** \(,)dē-,vi-trə-fə-'kā-shən\ *n*

de·vo·cal·ize \(')dē-'vō-kə-,līz\ *vt* **:** DEVOICE

de·voice \(')dē-'vȯis\ *vt* **:** to pronounce (as a sometimes or formerly voiced sound) without vibration of the vocal cords

de·void \di-'vȯid\ *adj* [ME, prob. short for *devoided,* pp. of *devoiden* to vacate, fr. MF *desvuidier* to empty, fr. OF, fr. *des-* dis- + *vuidier* to empty — more at VOID] **:** not having or using **:** DESTITUTE ⟨a poem totally ~ of real quality⟩

de·voir \dəv-'wär, 'dev-,\ *n* [ME, alter. of *dever,* fr. OF *deveir,* fr. *devoir, deveir* to owe, be obliged, fr. L *debēre* — more at DEBT] **1 :** DUTY, RESPONSIBILITY **2 :** a formal act of civility or respect

de·vo·lu·tion \,dev-ə-'lü-shən *also* ,dē-və-\ *n* [ML *devolution-, devolutio,* fr. L *devolutus,* pp. of *devolvere*] **1 :** transference from one individual to another: as **a :** a passing or devolving (as of rights) upon a successor **b :** delegation or conferral to a subordinate **c :** the surrender of powers to local authorities by a central government **2 :** retrograde evolution **:** DEGENERATION — **de·vo·lu·tion·ary** \-shə-,ner-ē\ *adj* — **de·vo·lu·tion·ist** \-sh(ə-)nəst\ *n*

de·volve \di-'välv, -'vȯlv\ *vb* **de·volved; de·volv·ing** [ME *devolven,* fr. L *devolvere,* fr. *de-* + *volvere* to roll — more at VOLUBLE] *vt* **1** *archaic* **:** to cause to roll onward or downward **2 :** to transfer from one person to another **:** hand down ~ *vi* **1 :** to pass by transmission or succession **2 :** to flow or roll onward or downward

dev·on \'dev-ən\ *n, often cap* [*Devon,* England] **:** any of a breed of vigorous red dual-purpose cattle of English origin

Devon *abbr* Devonshire

De·vo·ni·an \di-'vō-nē-ən\ *adj* [*Devon,* England] **1 :** of or relating to Devonshire, England **2 :** of, relating to, or being the period of the Paleozoic era between the Silurian and the Mississippian or the corresponding system of rocks — **Devonian** *n*

Dev·on·shire cream \,dev-ən-,shi(ə)r-, -shər-\ *n* **:** CLOTTED CREAM

de·vote \di-'vōt\ *vt* **de·vot·ed; de·vot·ing** [L *devotus,* pp. of *devovēre,* fr. *de-* + *vovēre* to vow] **1 :** to dedicate by a solemn act ⟨Christians are by their baptism *devoted* to God —William Law⟩ **2 a :** to give over (as to a cause, use, or end) wholly or purposefully ⟨land *devoted* to agriculture⟩ **b :** to center the attention or activities of (oneself) ⟨*devoting* herself to the care of her family⟩ — **de·vote·ment** \-'vōt-mənt\ *n*

syn DEVOTE, DEDICATE, CONSECRATE, HALLOW *shared meaning element* **:** to set apart for a particular and often a better or higher use or end. DEVOTE is likely to imply compelling motives and often attachment to an objective ⟨*devoted* his evenings to study⟩ ⟨*devote* money to charity⟩ DEDICATE implies solemn and exclusive devotion to a sacred or serious use or purpose ⟨we Americans are *dedicated* to improvement —Louis Kronenberger⟩ CONSECRATE stresses investment with a solemn or sacred quality ⟨*consecrate* a church to the worship of God⟩ and even in general use carries a strong connotation of intense devotion ⟨rules . . . *consecrated* by time —Edmund Burke⟩ HALLOW, often differing little from *dedicate* or *consecrate,* may distinctively imply an attribution of intrinsic sanctity ⟨the Lord blessed the sabbath day, and *hallowed* it —Exod 20:11 (AV)⟩

de·vot·ed *adj* **1 :** ARDENT, DEVOUT **2 :** AFFECTIONATE — **de·vot·ed·ly** *adv* — **de·vot·ed·ness** *n*

dev·o·tee \,dev-ə-'tē, -'tā; di-,vō-'tē\ *n* **1 :** a person preoccupied with religious duties and ceremonies **2 :** an ardent follower, supporter, or enthusiast ⟨a ~ of opera⟩

de·vo·tion \di-'vō-shən\ *n* **1 a :** religious fervor **:** PIETY **b :** an act of prayer or supplication — usu. used in pl. **c :** a religious exercise or practice other than the regular corporate worship of a congregation; *specif* **:** one directed in Roman Catholic piety to a particular object of faith **2 a :** the act of devoting or quality of being devoted **b :** ardent love or affection ***syn*** see FIDELITY

¹de·vo·tion·al \-shnəl, -shən-ᵊl\ *adj* **:** of, relating to, or characterized by devotion — **de·vo·tion·al·ly** \-ē\ *adv*

²devotional *n* **:** a short worship service

de·vour \di-'vau̇(ə)r\ *vt* [ME *devouren,* fr. MF *devourer,* fr. L *devorare,* fr. *de-* + *vorare* to devour — more at VORACIOUS] **1 :** to eat up greedily or ravenously **2 :** to seize upon and destroy **:** CONSUME ⟨~*ed* by fire⟩ **3 :** to prey upon ⟨a man ~*ed* by guilt⟩ **4 :** to enjoy avidly ⟨~*s* books⟩ — **de·vour·er** *n*

de·vout \di-'vau̇t\ *adj* [ME *devot,* fr. OF, fr. LL *devotus,* fr. L, pp. of *devovēre*] **1 :** devoted to religion or to religious duties or exercises **2 :** expressing devotion or piety **3 :** warmly devoted **:** SINCERE — **de·vout·ly** *adv* — **de·vout·ness** *n*

syn DEVOUT, RELIGIOUS, PIOUS, PIETISTIC, SANCTIMONIOUS *shared meaning element* **:** showing fervor in the practice of religion

dew \'d(y)ü\ *n* [ME, fr. OE *dēaw;* akin to OHG *tou* dew, Gk *thein* to run] **1 :** moisture condensed upon the surfaces of cool bodies esp. at night **2 :** something resembling dew in purity, freshness, or power to refresh **3 :** moisture esp. when appearing in minute droplets: as **a :** TEARS **b :** SWEAT **c :** droplets of water produced by a plant in transpiration — **dew** *vt* — **dew·less** \-ləs\ *adj*

DEW *abbr* distant early warning

de·wan \di-'wän\ *n* [Hindi *dīwān,* fr. Per, account book] **:** an Indian official; *esp* **:** the prime minister of an Indian state

ə abut ᵊ kitten ər further a back ā bake ä cot, cart
au̇ out ch chin e less ē easy g gift i trip ī life
j joke ŋ sing ō flow ȯ flaw ȯi coin th thin t͟h this
ü loot u̇ foot y yet yü few yu̇ furious zh vision

Dew·ar flask \ˌd(y)ü-ər-\ *n* [Sir James *Dewar*] : a glass or metal container that has an evacuated space between the walls, is often silvered on the innermost surface to prevent heat transfer, and is used esp. for storing liquefied gases — compare VACUUM BOTTLE

de·wa·ter \(ˈ)dē-ˈwȯt-ər, -ˈwät-\ *vt* : to remove water from — **de·wa·ter·er** *n*

dew·ber·ry \ˈd(y)ü-ˌber-ē\ *n* **1** : any of several sweet edible berries related to and resembling blackberries **2** : a trailing or decumbent bramble (genus *Rubus*) that bears dewberries

dew·claw \ˈd(y)ü-ˌklȯ\ *n* : a vestigial digit not reaching to the ground on the foot of a mammal; *also* : a claw or hoof terminating such a digit — see COW illustration — **dew·clawed** \-ˌklȯd\ *adj*

dew·drop \ˈd(y)ü-ˌdräp\ *n* : a drop of dew

Dew·ey decimal classification \ˌd(y)ü-ē-\ *n* [Melvil *Dewey*] : a system of classifying books and other publications whereby main classes are designated by a three-digit number and subdivisions are shown by numbers after a decimal point

dew·fall \ˈd(y)ü-ˌfȯl\ *n* : formation of dew; *also* : the time when dew begins to deposit

dew·lap \ˈd(y)ü-ˌlap\ *n* : a hanging fold of skin under the neck esp. of a bovine animal — see COW illustration — **dew·lapped** \-ˌlapt\ *adj*

de·worm \(ˈ)dē-ˈwərm\ *vt* : to rid (as a dog) of worms : WORM 1

dew point *n* : the temperature at which a vapor begins to condense

dew worm *n* : NIGHT CRAWLER

dewy \ˈd(y)ü-ē\ *adj* **dew·i·er; -est** : moist with, affected by, or suggestive of dew — **dew·i·ly** \ˈd(y)ü-ə-lē\ *adv* — **dew·i·ness** \ˈd(y)ü-ē-nəs\ *n*

dewy-eyed \ˌd(y)ü-ē-ˈīd\ *adj* : naively credulous

dex \ˈdeks\ *n* : the sulfate of dextroamphetamine

dexa·meth·a·sone \ˌdek-sə-ˈmeth-ə-ˌsōn, -ˌzōn\ *n* [perh. fr. *Dexa*myl, a trademark + *meth*yl + *-sone* (as in *cortisone*)] : a synthetic adrenocortical steroid $C_{22}H_{29}FO_5$ used esp. as an anti-inflammatory agent

Dex·e·drine \ˈdek-sə-ˌdrēn, -drən\ *trademark* — used for a preparation of the sulfate of dextroamphetamine

dex·ies \ˈdek-sēz\ *n pl* [*dex* + *-ie* + *-s*] : tablets or capsules of the sulfate of dextroamphetamine

dex·io·tro·pic \ˌdek-sē-ə-ˈtrō-pik, -ˈträp-ik\ *or* **dex·i·ot·ro·pous** \-sē-ˈä-trə-pəs\ *adj* [Gk *dexios* situated on the right + E *-tropic* or *-tropous*] : turning to the right : DEXTRAL

dex·ter \ˈdek-stər\ *adj* [L; akin to Gk *dexios* situated on the right, L *decēre* to be fitting — more at DECENT] **1** : relating to or situated on the right **2** : being or relating to the side of a heraldic shield at the right of the person bearing it **3** : appearing or facing toward the right and considered of good omen — **dexter** *adv*

dex·ter·i·ty \dek-ˈster-ət-ē\ *n, pl* **-ties** [MF or L; MF *dexterité*, fr. L *dexteritat-, dexteritas*, fr. *dexter*] **1** : readiness and grace in physical activity; *esp* : skill and ease in using the hands **2** : mental skill or quickness : ADROITNESS

dex·ter·ous *or* **dex·trous** \ˈdek-st(ə-)rəs\ *adj* [L *dextr-, dexter* dextral, skillful] **1** : skillful and competent with the hands **2** : mentally adroit and skillful : EXPERT **3** : done with dexterity : ARTFUL — **dex·ter·ous·ly** *adv* — **dex·ter·ous·ness** *n*

syn DEXTEROUS, ADROIT, DEFT *shared meaning element* : ready and skilled in physical movements or, sometimes, mental activity ***ant*** clumsy

dextr- *or* **dextro-** *comb form* [LL, fr. L *dextr-, dexter*] **1** : right : on or toward the right ⟨*dextro*rotatory⟩ **2** *usu* *dextro-* : dextrorotatory ⟨*dextro*-tartaric acid⟩

dex·tral \ˈdek-strəl\ *adj* : of or relating to the right : inclined to the right: as **a** : RIGHT-HANDED **b** *of a flatfish* : having the right side uppermost **c** *of a gastropod shell* : having the whorls turning from the left toward the right as viewed with the apex toward the observer or having the aperture open toward the observer to the right of the axis when held with the spire uppermost — **dex·tral·i·ty** \dek-ˈstral-ət-ē\ *n* — **dex·tral·ly** \ˈdek-strə-lē\ *adv*

dex·tran \ˈdek-stran, -strən\ *n* [*dextr*ose + *-an*] : any of numerous polysaccharides $(C_6H_{10}O_5)_n$ that yield only glucose on hydrolysis: as **a** : any such compound of high molecular weight obtained by fermentation of sugar **b** : any such compound of reduced molecular weight obtained by acid hydrolysis of native dextran and used as a plasma substitute

dex·tran·ase \-strə-ˌnās, -ˌnāz\ *n* : a hydrolase that breaks down dextran and is effective in attacking dental plaque

dex·trin \ˈdek-strən\ *also* **dex·trine** \-ˌstrēn, -strən\ *n* [F *dextrine*, fr. *dextr-*] : any of various soluble gummy polysaccharides $(C_6H_{10}O_5)_n$ obtained from starch by the action of heat, acids, or enzymes and used as adhesives, as sizes for paper and textiles, and in syrups and beer

dex·tro \ˈdek-(ˌ)strō\ *adj* [*dextr-*] : DEXTROROTATORY

dex·tro·am·phet·amine \ˈdek-(ˌ)strō-am-ˈfet-ə-ˌmēn, -mən\ *n* : AMPHETAMINE 2b

dex·tro-glu·cose \ˌdek-strə-ˈglü-ˌkōs, -ˌkōz\ *n* : DEXTROSE

dex·tro·ro·ta·tion \ˌdek-strə-rō-ˈtā-shən\ *n* : right-handed or clockwise rotation — used of the plane of polarization of light

dex·tro·ro·ta·to·ry \-ˈrōt-ə-ˌtōr-ē, -ˌtȯr-\ *also* **dex·tro·ro·ta·ry** \-ˈrōt-ə-rē\ *adj* : turning clockwise or toward the right; *esp* : rotating the plane of polarization of light toward the right ⟨~ crystals⟩ — compare LEVOROTATORY

dex·trorse \ˈdek-ˌstrȯ(ə)rs\ *adj* [NL *dextrorsus*, fr. L, toward the right, fr. *dextr-* + *versus*, pp. of *vertere* to turn — more at WORTH] **1** *of a plant or its parts* : twining spirally upward around an axis from left to right — compare SINISTRORSE **2** : DEXTRAL c — **dex·trorse·ly** *adv*

dex·trose \ˈdek-ˌstrōs, -ˌstrōz\ *n* : dextrorotatory glucose

dey \ˈdā\ *n* [F, fr. Turk *dayı*, lit., maternal uncle] : a ruling official of the Ottoman empire in northern Africa

DF *abbr* **1** damage free **2** direction finder; direction finding **3** doctor of forestry

DFA *abbr* doctor of fine arts

DFC *abbr* Distinguished Flying Cross

DFM *abbr* Distinguished Flying Medal

dft *abbr* **1** defendant **2** draft

dg *abbr* decigram

DG *abbr* **1** [LL *Dei gratia*] by the grace of God **2** director general

DH *abbr* **1** designated hitter **2** doctor of humanities

dhar·ma \ˈdər-mə\ *n* [Skt, fr. *dhārayati* he holds; akin to L *firmus* firm] **1** *Hinduism* : an individual's duty fulfilled by observance of custom or law **2** *Hinduism & Buddhism* **a** : the basic principles of cosmic or individual existence : NATURE **b** : conformity to one's duty and nature — **dhar·mic** \-mik\ *adj*

DHL *abbr* doctor of Hebrew letters; doctor of Hebrew literature

dhole \ˈdōl\ *n* [perh. fr. Kanarese *tōla* wolf] : a fierce wild dog (*Cuon dukhunensis*) of India that hunts in packs

dho·ti \ˈdōt-ē\ *or* **dhoo·tie** \ˈdüt-ē\ *n* [Hindi *dhotī*] **1** : a loincloth worn by Hindu men **2** : a fabric used for dhotis

dhow \ˈdau̇\ *n* [Ar *dāwa*] : an Arab lateen-rigged boat usu. having a long overhang forward, a high poop, and an open waist

Dhu'l–Hij·ja \ˌdül-(ə)l-ˈhij-(ˌ)ä\ *n* [Ar *Dhū-l-ḥijjah*, lit., the one of the pilgrimage] : the 12th month of the Muhammadan year — see MONTH table

Dhu'l–Qa'·dah \-ˈkäd-(ˌ)ä\ *n* [Ar *Dhū-l-qa'dah*, lit., the one of the sitting] : the 11th month of the Muhammadan year — see MONTH table

di- *comb form* [ME, fr. MF, fr. L, fr. Gk; akin to OE *twi-*] **1** : twice : twofold : double ⟨*di*chromatic⟩ **2** : containing two atoms, radicals, or groups ⟨*di*chloride⟩

dia *abbr* diameter

dia- *also* **di-** *prefix* [ME, fr. OF, fr. L, fr. Gk, through, apart, fr. *dia*; akin to L *dis-*] : through ⟨*dia*positive⟩ : across ⟨*dia*dromous⟩

di·a·base \ˈdī-ə-ˌbās\ *n* [F, fr. Gk *diabasis* act of crossing over, fr. *diabainein* to cross over, fr. *dia-* + *bainein* to go — more at COME] **1** *archaic* : DIORITE **2** *chiefly Brit* : an altered basalt **3** : a fine-grained rock of the composition of gabbro but with an ophitic texture — **di·a·ba·sic** \ˌdī-ə-ˈbā-sik\ *adj*

di·a·be·tes \ˌdī-ə-ˈbēt-ēz, -ˈbēt-əs\ *n* [L, fr. Gk *diabētēs*, fr. *diabainein*] : any of various abnormal conditions characterized by the secretion and excretion of excessive amounts of urine

diabetes in·sip·i·dus \-in-ˈsip-əd-əs\ *n* [NL, lit., insipid diabetes] : a disorder of the pituitary gland characterized by intense thirst and by the excretion of large amounts of urine

diabetes mel·li·tus \-ˈmel-ət-əs\ *n* [NL, lit., honey-sweet diabetes] : a familial constitutional disorder of carbohydrate metabolism characterized by inadequate secretion or utilization of insulin, by polyuria and excessive amounts of sugar in the blood and urine, and by thirst, hunger, and loss of weight

¹di·a·bet·ic \ˌdī-ə-ˈbet-ik\ *adj* **1** : of or relating to diabetes or diabetics **2** : affected with diabetes

²diabetic *n* : a person affected with diabetes

di·a·ble·rie \dē-ˈäb-lə-(ˌ)rē, -ˈab-\ *n* [F, fr. OF, fr. *diable* devil, fr. LL *diabolus* — more at DEVIL] **1** : black magic : SORCERY **2 a** : a representation in words or pictures of black magic or of dealings with the devil **b** : demon lore **3 a** : mischievous conduct or manner **b** : the quality or state of being wicked

diabol- *or* **diabolo-** *comb form* [ME *deabol-*, fr. MF *diabol-*, fr. LL, fr. Gk, fr. *diabolos* — more at DEVIL] : devil ⟨*diabol*ism⟩

di·a·bol·ic \ˌdī-ə-ˈbäl-ik\ *or* **di·a·bol·i·cal** \-ˈbäl-i-kəl\ *adj* [ME *deabolik*, fr. MF *diabolique*, fr. LL *diabolicus*, fr. *diabolus*] : of, relating to, or characteristic of the devil : FIENDISH — **di·a·bol·i·cal·ly** \-i-k(ə-)lē\ *adv* — **di·a·bol·i·cal·ness** \-i-kəl-nəs\ *n*

di·ab·o·lism \dī-ˈab-ə-ˌliz-əm\ *n* **1** : dealings with or possession by the devil **2** : evil character or conduct **3** : belief in or worship of devils — **di·ab·o·list** \-ləst\ *n*

di·ab·o·lize \-ˌlīz\ *vt* **-lized; -liz·ing** : to represent as or make diabolical

dia·chron·ic \ˌdī-ə-ˈkrän-ik\ *adj* : of, relating to, or dealing with phenomena esp. of language as they occur or change over a period of time — **dia·chron·i·cal·ly** \-ˈkrän-i-k(ə-)lē\ *adv* — **dia·chron·ic·ness** \-ik-nəs\ *n*

di·ach·ro·ny \dī-ˈak-rə-nē\ *n* [ISV *dia-* + *-chrony* (as in *synchrony*)] **1** : diachronic analysis **2** : change extending through time

¹di·ac·id \(ˈ)dī-ˈas-əd\ *or* **di·acid·ic** \ˌdī-ə-ˈsid-ik\ *adj* **1** : able to react with two molecules of a monobasic acid or one of a dibasic acid to form a salt or ester — used esp. of bases **2** : containing two replaceable hydrogen atoms — used esp. of acid salts

²diacid *n* [ISV] : an acid with two acid hydrogen atoms

di·ac·o·nal \dī-ˈak-ən-ᵊl, dē-\ *adj* [LL *diaconalis*, fr. *diaconus* deacon — more at DEACON] : of or relating to a deacon or deaconess

di·ac·o·nate \-ˈak-ə-nət, -ˌnāt\ *n* **1** : the office or period of office of a deacon or deaconess **2** : an official body of deacons

di·a·crit·ic \ˌdī-ə-ˈkrit-ik\ *n* : a modifying mark near or through an orthographic or phonetic character or combination of characters indicating a phonetic value different from that given the unmarked or otherwise marked element

DIACRITICS

´	(é)	acute accent	˘	(ŭ)	breve
`	(è)	grave accent	ˇ	(č)	haček
^	(ô) *or* ⌢ *or* ~	circumflex	¨	(oö)	diaeresis
~	(ñ)	tilde	¸	(ç)	cedilla
¯	(ō)	macron			

di·a·crit·i·cal \ˌdī-ə-ˈkrit-i-kəl\ *also* **di·a·crit·ic** \-ˈkrit-ik\ *adj* [Gk *diakritikos* separative, fr. *diakrinein* to distinguish, fr. *dia-* + *krinein* to separate — more at CERTAIN] **1** : serving as a diacritic **2 a** : serving to distinguish : DISTINCTIVE ⟨the ~ elements in culture — S. F. Nadel⟩ **b** : capable of distinguishing ⟨students of superior ~ powers⟩

di·adel·phous \ˌdī-ə-ˈdel-fəs\ *adj* [*di-* + *-adelphous*] : united by filaments into two fascicles — used of stamens

di·a·dem \ˈdī-ə-ˌdem, -əd-əm\ *n* [ME *diademe*, fr. OF, fr. L *diadema*, fr. Gk *diadēma*, fr. *diadein* to bind around, fr. *dia-* +

dein to bind; akin to Alb *duai* sheaf, Skt *dāman* rope] **1 :** CROWN; *specif* **:** a headband worn as a badge of royalty **2 :** regal power or dignity

di·ad·ro·mous \dī-ˈad-rə-məs\ *adj, of a fish* **:** migratory between salt and fresh waters

di·aer·e·sis \dī-ˈer-ə-səs\ *n, pl* **-e·ses** \-ˌsēz\ [LL *diaeresis,* fr. Gk *diairesis,* fr. *diairein* to divide, fr. *dia-* + *hairein* to take] **1 :** a mark ¨ placed over a vowel to indicate that the vowel is pronounced in a separate syllable (as in *naïve* or *Brontë*) **2 :** the break in a verse caused by the coincidence of the end of a foot with the end of a word — **di·ae·ret·ic** \ˌdī-ə-ˈret-ik\ *adj*

diag *abbr* **1** diagonal **2** diagram

dia·gen·e·sis \ˌdī-ə-ˈjen-ə-səs\ *n* [NL] **1 :** recombination or rearrangement of constituents (as of a chemical or mineral) resulting in a new product **2 :** the conversion (as by compaction or chemical reaction) of sediment into rock — **dia·ge·net·ic** \ˌdī-ə-jə-ˈnet-ik\ *adj* — **dia·ge·net·i·cal·ly** \-ˈnet-i-k(ə-)lē\ *adv*

dia·ge·ot·ro·pism \ˌdī-ə-jē-ˈä-trə-ˌpiz-əm\ *or* **dia·ge·ot·ro·py** \-pē\ *n* **:** the tendency of growing organs (as branches or roots) to extend the axis at right angles to the line of gravity — **dia·geo·tro·pic** \-jē-ə-ˈtrō-pik, -ˈträp-ik\ *adj*

di·ag·nose \ˈdī-ig-ˌnōs, -ˌnōz, ˌdī-ig-ˈ, -əg-\ *vb* **-nosed; -nos·ing** [back-formation fr. *diagnosis*] *vt* **:** to recognize (as a disease) by signs and symptoms ~ *vi* **:** to make a diagnosis — **di·ag·nos·able** *or* **di·ag·nose·able** \ˌdī-ig-ˈnō-sə-bəl, -əg-, -zə- \ *adj*

di·ag·no·sis \ˌdī-ig-ˈnō-səs, -əg-\ *n, pl* **-no·ses** \-ˌsēz\ [NL, fr. Gk *diagnōsis,* fr. *diagignōskein* to distinguish, fr. *dia-* + *gignōskein* to know — more at KNOW] **1 :** the art or act of identifying a disease from its signs and symptoms **2 :** a concise technical description of a taxon **3 a :** investigation or analysis of the cause or nature of a condition, situation, or problem ⟨~ of engine trouble⟩ **b :** a statement or conclusion concerning the nature or cause of some phenomenon

1**di·ag·nos·tic** \-ˈnäs-tik\ *also* **di·ag·nos·ti·cal** \-ti-kəl\ *adj* **:** of or relating to diagnosis — **di·ag·nos·ti·cal·ly** \-ti-k(ə-)lē\ *adv*

2**diagnostic** *n* **1 :** the art or practice of diagnosis — often used in pl. **2 :** a distinguishing mark — **di·ag·nos·ti·cian** \-(ˌ)näs-ˈtish-ən\ *n*

1**di·ag·o·nal** \dī-ˈag-ən-əl, -ˈag-nəl\ *adj* [L *diagonalis,* fr. Gk *diagōnios* from angle to angle, fr. *dia-* + *gōnia* angle; akin to Gk *gony* knee — more at KNEE] **1 a :** joining two nonadjacent vertices of a rectilinear or polyhedral figure **b :** passing through two nonadjacent edges of a polyhedron **2 a :** inclined obliquely from a reference line (as the vertical) ⟨wood with a ~ grain⟩ **b :** having diagonal markings or parts ⟨a ~ weave⟩

2**diagonal** *n* **1 :** a diagonal straight line or plane **2 a** (1) **:** a diagonal direction (2) **:** a diagonal row, arrangement, or pattern **b :** a twilled fabric esp. of wool **c :** something placed diagonally **3 :** a mark / used typically to denote "or" (as in *and/or*), "and or" (as in *straggler/deserter*), or "per" (as in *feet/second*) — called also *solidus, virgule*

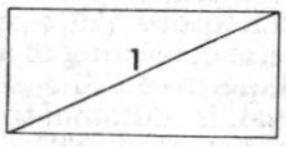

1, diagonal 1

di·ag·o·nal·ize \-ˌīz\ *vt* **-ized; -iz·ing :** to put (a matrix) in a form with all the nonzero elements along the diagonal from upper left to lower right — **di·ag·o·nal·iz·able** \-ˌī-zə-bəl\ *adj* — **di·ag·o·nal·iza·tion** \-ˌag-ən-əl-ə-ˈzā-shən, -ˌag-nə-lə-ˈzā-\ *n*

di·ag·o·nal·ly \dī-ˈag-ən-əl-ē, -ˈag-nə-lē\ *adv* **:** in a diagonal manner

diagonal matrix *n* **:** a matrix that has all the nonzero elements located along the diagonal from upper left to lower right

1**di·a·gram** \ˈdī-ə-ˌgram\ *n* [Gk *diagramma,* fr. *diagraphein* to mark out by lines, fr. *dia-* + *graphein* to write — more at CARVE] **1 :** a line drawing made for mathematical or scientific purposes **2 a :** a graphic design that explains rather than represents **b :** a drawing that shows arrangement and relations (as of parts) **:** CHART — **di·a·gram·ma·ble** \-ˌgram-ə-bəl\ *adj* — **di·a·gram·mat·ic** \ˌdī-ə-grə-ˈmat-ik\ *also* **di·a·gram·mat·i·cal** \-ˈmat-i-kəl\ *adj* — **di·a·gram·mat·i·cal·ly** \-i-k(ə-)lē\ *adv*

2**diagram** *vt* **-gramed** \-ˌgramd\ *or* **-grammed; -gram·ing** \-ˌgram-iŋ\ *or* **-gram·ming :** to represent by or put into the form of a diagram

dia·ki·ne·sis \ˌdī-ə-kə-ˈnē-səs, -(ˌ)kī-\ *n, pl* **-ne·ses** \-ˌsēz\ [NL, fr. *dia-* + Gk *kinēsis* motion, fr. *kinein* to move; akin to L *ciēre* to move — more at HIGHT] **:** the final stage of the meiotic prophase marked by contraction of the bivalents — **dia·ki·net·ic** \-ˈnet-ik\ *adj*

1**di·al** \ˈdī(-ə)l\ *n* [ME, fr. L *dies* day — more at DEITY] **1 :** the face of a sundial **2** *obs* **:** TIMEPIECE **3 :** the graduated face of a timepiece **4 a :** a face upon which some measurement is registered usu. by means of graduations and a pointer ⟨the thermometer ~ reads 70°F⟩ **b :** a device (as a disk) that may be operated to make electrical connections or to regulate the operation of a machine and that usu. has guiding marks around its border ⟨a radio ~⟩ ⟨a telephone ~⟩

2**dial** *vb* **di·aled** *or* **di·alled; di·al·ing** *or* **di·al·ling** *vt* **1 :** to measure with a dial **2 :** to manipulate a device (as a dial) so as to operate, regulate, or select ⟨~ your favorite program⟩ ⟨he ~*ed* the wrong number⟩ ~ *vi* **1 :** to manipulate a dial **2 :** to make a call on a dial telephone — **di·al·er** *n*

3**dial** *abbr* **1** dialect **2** dialectical

di·a·lect \ˈdī-ə-ˌlekt\ *n, often attrib* [MF *dialecte,* fr. L *dialectus,* fr. Gk *dialektos* conversation, dialect, fr. *dialegesthai* to converse — more at DIALOGUE] **1 a :** a regional variety of language distinguished by features of vocabulary, grammar, and pronunciation from other regional varieties and constituting together with them a single language of which no one variety is construed as standard ⟨the Doric ~ of ancient Greek⟩ **b :** one of two or more cognate languages ⟨French and Italian are Romance ~*s*⟩ **c :** a regional variety of a language usu. transmitted orally and differing distinctively from the standard language ⟨the Lancashire ~ of English⟩ **d :** a variety of a language used by the members of an occupational group ⟨the ~ of the atomic physicist⟩ **e :** a variety of language whose identity is fixed by a factor (as social class or educational level of its habitual users) other than geography ⟨spoke a rough peasant ~⟩ **2 :** manner or means of expressing oneself **:** PHRASEOLOGY — **di·a·lec·tal** \ˌdī-ə-ˈlek-təl\ *adj* — **di·a·lec·tal·ly** \-təl-ē\ *adv*

syn DIALECT, VERNACULAR, LINGO, JARGON, CANT, ARGOT, SLANG *shared meaning element* **:** a form of language that is not recognized as standard

dialect atlas *n* **:** LINGUISTIC ATLAS

dialect geography *n* **:** LINGUISTIC GEOGRAPHY

di·a·lec·tic \ˌdī-ə-ˈlek-tik\ *n* [ME *dialetik,* fr. MF *dialetique,* fr. L *dialectica,* fr. Gk *dialektikē,* fr. fem. of *dialektikos* of conversation, fr. *dialektos*] **1 a :** discussion and reasoning by dialogue as a method of intellectual investigation; *specif* **:** the Socratic techniques of exposing false beliefs and eliciting truth **b :** the Platonic investigation of the eternal ideas **2 :** LOGIC 1a(1) **3 :** the logic of fallacy **4 a :** the Hegelian process of change in which a concept or its realization passes over into and is preserved and fulfilled by its opposite; *also* **:** the critical investigation of this process **b** (1) *usu pl but sing or pl in constr* **:** development through the stages of thesis, antithesis, and synthesis in accordance with the laws of dialectical materialism (2) **:** the investigation of this process (3) **:** the theoretical application of this process esp. in the social sciences **5** *usu pl but sing or pl in constr* **a :** any systematic reasoning, exposition, or argument that juxtaposes opposed or contradictory ideas and usu. seeks to resolve their conflict **b :** an intellectual exchange of ideas **6 :** the dialectical tension or opposition between two interacting forces or elements

di·a·lec·ti·cal \ˌdī-ə-ˈlek-ti-kəl\ *also* **di·a·lec·tic** \-tik\ *adj* **1 a :** of, relating to, or in accordance with dialectic ⟨~ method⟩ **b :** practicing, devoted to, or employing dialectic ⟨a ~ philosopher⟩ **2 :** of, relating to, or characteristic of a dialect — **di·a·lec·ti·cal·ly** \-ti-k(ə-)lē\ *adv*

dialectical materialism *n* **:** the Marxian theory that maintains the material basis of a reality constantly changing in a dialectical process and the priority of matter over mind — compare HISTORICAL MATERIALISM

di·a·lec·ti·cian \ˌdī-ə-ˌlek-ˈtish-ən\ *n* **1 :** one who is skilled in or practices dialectic **2 :** a student of dialects

di·a·lec·tol·o·gist \-ˈtäl-ə-jəst\ *n* **:** a specialist in dialectology

di·a·lec·tol·o·gy \-jē\ *n* [ISV] **1 :** the systematic study of dialect **2 :** the body of data available for study of a dialect — **di·a·lec·to·log·i·cal** \-ˌlek-tə-ˈläj-i-kəl\ *adj* — **di·a·lec·to·log·i·cal·ly** \-k(ə-)lē\ *adv*

di·al·lel \ˈdī-ə-ˌlel\ *adj* [Gk *diallēlos* reciprocating, confused, fr. *di' allēlōn* through or across one another] **:** relating to or being the crossing of each of several individuals with two or more others in order to determine the relative genetic contribution of each parent to certain characters in the offspring

di·a·log·ic \ˌdī-ə-ˈläj-ik\ *adj* **:** of, relating to, or characterized by dialogue ⟨~ writing⟩ — **di·a·log·i·cal** \-ˈläj-i-kəl\ *adj* — **di·a·log·i·cal·ly** \-i-k(ə-)lē\ *adv*

di·a·lo·gist \dī-ˈal-ə-jəst; ˈdī-ə-ˌlȯg-əst, -ˌläg-\ *n* **1 :** one who participates in a dialogue **2 :** a writer of dialogues — **di·a·lo·gis·tic** \(ˌ)dī-ˌal-ə-ˈjis-tik; ˌdī-ə-ˌlȯ-ˈgis-, -ˌlä-ˈgis-\ *adj*

1**di·a·logue** *or* **di·a·log** \ˈdī-ə-ˌlȯg, -ˌläg\ *n* [MF, fr. OF, fr. L *dialogus,* fr. Gk *dialogos,* fr. *dialegesthai* to converse, fr. *dia-* + *legein* to speak] **1 :** a written composition in which two or more characters are represented as conversing **2 a :** a conversation between two or more persons; *also* **:** a similar exchange between a person and something else (as a computer) **b :** an exchange of ideas and opinions **3 :** the conversational element of literary or dramatic composition **4 :** a musical composition for two or more parts suggestive of a conversation

2**dialogue** *vb* **-logued; -logu·ing** *vi* **:** to take part in a dialogue ~ *vt* **:** to express in dialogue

dial tone *n* **:** a tone emitted by a telephone as a signal that the system is ready for dialing

di·al·y·sate \dī-ˈal-ə-ˌzāt, -ˌsāt\ *or* **di·al·y·zate** \-ˌzāt\ *n* [*dialysis* or *dialyze* + *-ate*] **:** the material that passes through the membrane in dialysis; *also* **:** the liquid into which this material passes

di·al·y·sis \dī-ˈal-ə-səs\ *n, pl* **-y·ses** \-ˌsēz\ [NL, fr. Gk, separation, fr. *dialyein* to dissolve, fr. *dia-* + *lyein* to loosen — more at LOSE] **:** the separation of substances in solution by means of their unequal diffusion through semipermeable membranes; *esp* **:** such a separation of colloids from soluble substances — **di·a·lyt·ic** \ˌdī-ə-ˈlit-ik\ *adj*

di·a·lyze \ˈdī-ə-ˌlīz\ *vb* **-lyzed; -lyz·ing** *vt* **:** to subject to dialysis ~ *vi* **:** to undergo dialysis — **di·a·lyz·abil·i·ty** \ˌdī-ə-ˌlī-zə-ˈbil-ət-ē\ *n* — **di·a·lyz·able** \ˈdī-ə-ˌlī-zə-bəl\ *adj* — **di·a·lyz·er** \-ˌlī-zər\ *n*

diam *abbr* diameter

dia·mag·net \ˈdī-ə-ˌmag-nət\ *or* **dia·mag·net·ic** \ˌdī-ə-mag-ˈnet-ik\ *n* [*diamagnet* back-formation fr. *diamagnetic,* adj.] **:** a diamagnetic substance

diamagnetic *adj* **:** having a magnetic permeability less than that of a vacuum **:** slightly repelled by a magnet — **dia·mag·ne·tism** \-ˈmag-nə-ˌtiz-əm\ *n*

di·am·e·ter \dī-ˈam-ət-ər\ *n* [ME *diametre,* fr. MF, fr. L *diametros,* fr. Gk, fr. *dia-* + *metron* measure — more at MEASURE] **1 :** a chord passing through the center of a figure or body **2 :** the length of a straight line through the center of an object **3 :** a unit of magnification of observations with a magnifying device equal to the number of times the linear dimensions of the object are increased ⟨a microscope magnifying 60 ~*s*⟩ — **di·am·e·tral** \-ˈam-ə-trəl\ *adj*

di·a·met·ric \ˌdī-ə-ˈme-trik\ *or* **di·a·met·ri·cal** \-tri-kəl\ *adj* **1 :** of, relating to, or constituting a diameter **:** located at the diameter **2**

ə abut	ə kitten	ər further	a back	ā bake	ä cot, cart
au̇ out	ch chin	e less	ē easy	g gift	i trip	ī life
j joke	ŋ sing	ō flow	ȯ flaw	ȯi coin	th thin	th this
ü loot	u̇ foot	y yet	yü few	yu̇ furious	zh vision

: completely opposed or opposite ⟨in ~ contradiction to his claims⟩ — **di·a·met·ri·cal·ly** \-tri-k(ə-)lē\ *adv*

di·amide \ˈdī-ə-ˌmīd, dī-ˈam-əd\ *n* : a compound containing two amido groups

di·amine \ˈdī-ə-ˌmēn, dī-ˈam-ən\ *n* [ISV] : a compound containing two amino groups

di·am·mo·ni·um phosphate \-ə-ˌmō-nē-əm-, -nyəm-\ *n* : an ammonium phosphate $(NH_4)_2HPO_4$

¹di·a·mond \ˈdī-(ə-)mənd\ *n, often attrib* [ME *diamaunde,* fr. MF *diamant,* fr. LL *diamant-, diamas,* alter. of L *adamant-, adamas,* hardest metal, diamond, fr. Gk] **1 a** : a native crystalline carbon that is usu. nearly colorless, that when transparent and free from flaws is highly valued as a precious stone, and that is used industrially as an abrasive powder and in rock drills because of its great hardness; *also* : a piece of this substance **b** : crystallized carbon produced artificially **2** : something that resembles a diamond **3** : a square or rhombus-shaped configuration usu. having a distinctive orientation **4 a** : a red diamond-shaped mark impressed on a playing card; *also* : a card so marked **b** *pl but sing or pl in constr* : the suit comprising cards so marked **5 a** : INFIELD 2a **b** : the entire playing field in baseball

²diamond *vt* : to adorn with or as if with diamonds

¹di·a·mond·back \ˈdī-(ə-)mən(d)-ˌbak\ *also* **di·a·mond–backed** \ˌdī-(ə-)mən(d)-ˈbakt\ *adj* : having marks like diamonds or lozenges on the back

²diamondback *n* : a large and deadly rattlesnake (*Crotalus adamanteus*) of the southern U.S.

diamondback terrapin *n* : any of several edible terrapins (genus *Malaclemys*) formerly widely distributed in salt marshes along the Atlantic and Gulf coasts but now much restricted

di·a·mond·if·er·ous \ˌdī-(ə-)mən-ˈdif-(ə-)rəs\ *adj* : yielding diamonds ⟨~ earth⟩

Di·ana \dī-ˈan-ə\ *n* [L] : an ancient Italian goddess of the forest and of childbirth who was identified with Artemis by the Romans

di·an·drous \(ˈ)dī-ˈan-drəs\ *adj* : having two stamens

di·an·thus \dī-ˈan(t)-thəs\ *n* [NL, genus name, fr. Gk *dios* heavenly + *anthos* flower — more at DEITY, ANTHOLOGY] : ³PINK 1

di·a·pa·son \ˌdī-ə-ˈpāz-ᵊn, -ˈpās-\ *n* [ME, fr. L, fr. Gk (*hē*) *dia pasōn* (*chordōn symphōnia*) the concord through all the notes, fr. *dia* through + *pasōn,* gen. fem. pl. of *pas* all — more at DIA-, PAN-] **1 a** (1) : a burst of harmonious sound (2) : a full deep outburst of sound **b** : the principal foundation stop in the organ extending through the complete range of the instrument **c** (1) : the entire compass of musical tones (2) : RANGE, SCOPE ⟨the vast ~ of his poetic talent⟩ **2 a** : TUNING FORK **b** : a standard of pitch

dia·pause \ˈdī-ə-ˌpȯz\ *n* [Gk *diapausis* pause, fr. *diapauein* to pause, fr. *dia-* + *pauein* to stop — more at PAUSE] : a period of physiologically enforced dormancy (as developmental arrest in an insect) between periods of activity

dia·paus·ing \-ˌpȯ-ziŋ\ *adj* : undergoing diapause

di·a·pe·de·sis \ˌdī-ə-pə-ˈdē-səs\ *n, pl* **-de·ses** \-ˌsēz\ [NL, fr. Gk *diapēdēsis* act of oozing through, fr. *diapēdan* to ooze through, fr. *dia-* + *pēdan* to leap] : the passage of blood cells through capillary walls into the tissues — **di·a·pe·det·ic** \-ˈdet-ik\ *adj*

¹di·a·per \ˈdī(-ə)-pər\ *n* [ME *diapre,* fr. MF, fr. ML *diasprum*] **1** : a fabric with a distinctive pattern: **a** : a rich silk fabric **b** : a soft usu. white linen or cotton fabric used for tablecloths or towels **2** : a basic garment for infants consisting of a folded cloth or other absorbent material drawn up between the legs and fastened about the waist **3** : an allover pattern consisting of one or more small repeated units of design (as geometric figures) connecting with one another or growing out of one another with continuously flowing or straight lines

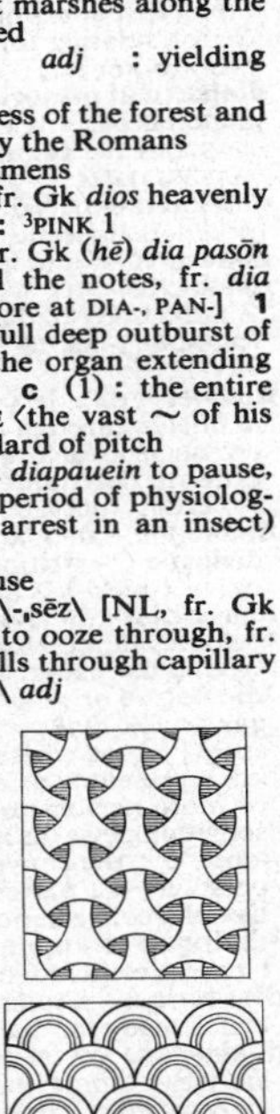
diaper 3

²diaper *vt* **di·a·pered; di·a·per·ing** \-p(ə-)riŋ\ **1** : to ornament with diaper designs **2** : to put on or change the diaper of (an infant)

di·a·pha·ne·ity \(ˌ)dī-ˌaf-ə-ˈnē-ət-ē, ˌdī-ə-fə-, -ˈnā-\ *n* : the quality or state of being diaphanous

di·aph·a·nous \dī-ˈaf-ə-nəs\ *adj* [ML *diaphanus,* fr. Gk *diaphanēs,* fr. *diaphainein* to show through, fr. *dia-* + *phainein* to show — more at FANCY] **1** : characterized by such fineness of texture as to permit seeing through **2** : characterized by extreme delicacy of form : ETHEREAL ⟨painted ~ landscapes⟩ **3** : INSUBSTANTIAL, VAGUE ⟨had only a ~ hope of success⟩ — **di·aph·a·nous·ly** *adv* — **di·aph·a·nous·ness** *n*

dia·phone \ˈdī-ə-ˌfōn\ *n* : a fog signal similar to a siren but producing a blast of two tones

di·aph·o·rase \dī-ˈaf-ə-ˌrās, -ˌrāz\ *n* [Gk *diaphoros* different + E *-ase*] : a flavoprotein enzyme capable of oxidizing the reduced form of NAD

di·a·pho·re·sis \ˌdī-ə-fə-ˈrē-səs, (ˌ)dī-ˌaf-ə-\ *n, pl* **-re·ses** \-ˌsēz\ [LL, fr. Gk *diaphorēsis,* fr. *diaphorein* to dissipate by perspiration, fr. *dia-* + *pherein* to carry — more at BEAR] : PERSPIRATION; *esp* : profuse perspiration artificially induced

di·a·pho·ret·ic \-ˈret-ik\ *adj* : having the power to increase perspiration — **diaphoretic** *n*

¹di·a·phragm \ˈdī-ə-ˌfram\ *n* [ME *diafragma,* fr. LL *diaphragma,* fr. Gk, fr. *diaphrassein* to barricade, fr. *dia-* + *phrassein* to enclose — more at FARCE] **1** : a body partition of muscle and connective tissue; *specif* : the partition separating the chest and abdominal cavities in mammals **2** : a dividing membrane or thin partition esp. in a tube **3 a** : a more or less rigid partition in the body or shell of an invertebrate **b** : a transverse septum in a plant stem **4** : a device that limits the aperture of a lens or optical system — compare IRIS DIAPHRAGM **5** : a thin flexible disk that vibrates (as in a microphone) **6** : a molded cap usu. of thin rubber fitted over the uterine cervix to act as a mechanical contraceptive barrier — **di·a·phrag·mat·ic** \ˌdī-ə-frə(g)-ˈmat-ik, -ˌfrag-\ *adj* — **di·a·phrag·mat·i·cal·ly** \-ˈmat-i-k(ə-)lē\ *adv*

²diaphragm *vt* **1** : to equip with a diaphragm **2** : to cut down the aperture of (as a lens) by a diaphragm

di·aph·y·sis \dī-ˈaf-ə-səs\ *n, pl* **-y·ses** \-ˌsēz\ [NL, fr. Gk, spinous process of the tibia, fr. *diaphyesthai* to grow between, fr. *dia-* + *phyein* to bring forth — more at BE] : the shaft of a long bone — **di·aph·y·se·al** \(ˌ)dī-ˌaf-ə-ˈsē-əl\ *or* **di·a·phys·i·al** \ˌdī-ə-ˈfiz-ē-əl\ *adj*

di·a·pir \ˈdī-ə-ˌpi(ə)r\ *n* [Gk *diapeirein* to drive through, fr. *dia-* + *peirein* to pierce; akin to Gk *poros* passage — more at FARE] : an anticlinal fold in which a mobile core has broken through brittle overlying rocks — **di·a·pir·ic** \ˌdī-ə-ˈpir-ik\ *adj*

di·apoph·y·sis \ˌdī-ə-ˈpäf-ə-səs\ *n, pl* **-y·ses** \-ˌsēz\ [NL, fr. *dia-* + *apophysis*] : a transverse process of a vertebra that is an outgrowth of the neural arch on the dorsal side; *esp* : one of the dorsal pair of such processes when two or more pairs are present

dia·pos·i·tive \ˌdī-ə-ˈpäz-ət-iv, -ˈpäz-tiv\ *n* : a transparent photographic positive (as a transparency)

di·ap·sid \dī-ˈap-səd\ *adj* [deriv. of Gk *di-* + *hapsid-, hapsis* arch — more at APSIS] : of, relating to, or including reptiles (as the crocodiles) with two pairs of temporal openings in the skull

di·ar·chy *var of* DYARCHY

di·a·rist \ˈdī-ə-rəst\ *n* : one who keeps a diary

di·ar·rhea *or* **di·ar·rhoea** \ˌdī-ə-ˈrē-ə\ *n* [ME *diaria,* fr. LL *diarrhoea,* fr. Gk *diarrhoia,* fr. *diarrhein* to flow through, fr. *dia-* + *rhein* to flow — more at STREAM] : abnormally frequent intestinal evacuations with more or less fluid stools — **di·ar·rhe·al** \-ˈrē-əl\ *or* **di·ar·rhe·ic** \-ˈrē-ik\ *also* **di·ar·rhet·ic** \-ˈret-ik\ *adj*

di·ar·thro·sis \ˌdī-är-ˈthrō-səs\ *n, pl* **-thro·ses** \-ˌsēz\ [NL, fr. Gk *diarthrōsis,* fr. *diarthroun* to joint, fr. *dia-* + *arthroun* to fasten by a joint, fr. *arthron* joint — more at ARTHR-] **1** : articulation that permits free movement **2** : a freely movable joint

di·a·ry \ˈdī-(ə-)rē\ *n, pl* **-ries** [L *diarium,* fr. *dies* day — more at DEITY] **1** : a record of events, transactions, or observations kept daily or at frequent intervals : JOURNAL; *esp* : a daily record of personal activities, reflections, or feelings **2** : a book intended or used for a diary

di·as·po·ra \dī-ˈas-p(ə-)rə\ *n* [Gk, dispersion, fr. *diaspeirein* to scatter, fr. *dia-* + *speirein* to sow — more at SPROUT] **1** *cap* **a** : the settling of scattered colonies of Jews outside Palestine after the Babylonian exile **b** : the area outside Palestine settled by Jews **c** : the Jews living outside Palestine or modern Israel **2** : MIGRATION ⟨the great black ~ to the cities of the North and West in the 1940s and 1950s —*Newsweek*⟩

di·a·spore \ˈdī-ə-ˌspō(ə)r, -ˌspȯ(ə)r\ *n* [F, fr. Gk *diaspora*] : a mineral consisting of aluminum hydrogen oxide $HAlO_2$

di·a·stase \ˈdī-ə-ˌstās, -ˌstāz\ *n* [F, fr. Gk *diastasis* separation, interval, fr. *diistanai* to separate, fr. *dia-* + *histanai* to cause to stand — more at STAND] **1** : AMYLASE; *esp* : a mixture of amylases from malt **2** : ENZYME

di·as·ta·sis \dī-ˈas-tə-səs\ *n, pl* **-ta·ses** \-ˌsēz\ [NL, fr. Gk, interval] : the rest phase of cardiac diastole occurring between the filling of the ventricle and the start of auricular contraction

di·a·stat·ic \ˌdī-ə-ˈstat-ik\ *adj* : relating to or having the properties of diastase; *esp* : converting starch into sugar

di·a·ste·ma \ˌdī-ə-ˈstē-mə\ *n, pl* **-ma·ta** \-mət-ə\ [NL, fr. LL, interval, fr. Gk *diastēma,* fr. *diistanai*] : a space between teeth in a jaw — **di·a·ste·mat·ic** \-sti-ˈmat-ik\ *adj*

di·a·ste·reo·iso·mer \ˌdī-ə-ˌster-ē-ō-ˈī-sə-mər, -ˌstir-\ *or* **di·a·ste·reo·mer** \-ˈster-ē-ō-(ˌ)mər, -ˈstir-\ *n* : a stereoisomer that does not have a mirror image — compare ENANTIOMORPH — **di·a·ste·reo·iso·mer·ic** \-ˈster-ē-ō-ˌī-sə-ˈmer-ik, -ˈstir-\ *adj* — **di·a·ste·reo·isom·er·ism** \-ī-ˈsäm-ə-ˌriz-əm\ *n*

di·as·to·le \dī-ˈas-tə-(ˌ)lē\ *n* [Gk *diastolē* dilatation, fr. *diastellein* to expand, fr. *dia-* + *stellein* to send — more at STALL] : a rhythmically recurrent expansion; *esp* : the dilatation of the cavities of the heart during which they fill with blood — **di·a·stol·ic** \ˌdī-ə-ˈstäl-ik\ *adj*

di·as·tro·phism \dī-ˈas-trə-ˌfiz-əm\ *n* [Gk *diastrophē* twisting, fr. *diastrephein* to distort, fr. *dia-* + *strephein* to twist — more at STROPHE] : the process of deformation that produces in the earth's crust its continents and ocean basins, plateaus and mountains, folds of strata, and faults — **di·a·stroph·ic** \ˌdī-ə-ˈsträf-ik\ *adj* — **di·a·stroph·i·cal·ly** \-i-k(ə-)lē\ *adv*

di·a·tes·sa·ron \ˌdī-ə-ˈtes-ə-rən\ *n* [ME, fr. L, fr. Gk (*hē*) *dia tessarōn* (*chordōn symphōnia*) the concord through four notes, fr. *dia* through + *tessarōn,* gen. of *tessares* four — more at DIA-, FOUR] : a harmony of the four Gospels edited and arranged into a single connected narrative

dia·ther·ma·nous \ˌdī-ə-ˈthər-mə-nəs\ *adj* [Gk *diatherman-,* stem of *diathermainein* to heat through] : DIATHERMIC 1

dia·ther·mic \ˌdī-ə-ˈthər-mik\ *adj* **1** : transmitting infrared radiation **2** : of or relating to diathermy ⟨~ treatment⟩

dia·ther·my \ˈdī-ə-ˌthər-mē\ *n* [ISV] : the generation of heat in tissue by electric currents for medical or surgical purposes

di·ath·e·sis \dī-ˈath-ə-səs\ *n, pl* **-e·ses** \-ˌsēz\ [NL, fr. Gk, lit., arrangement, fr. *diatithenai* to arrange, fr. *dia-* + *tithenai* to set — more at DO] **1** : a constitutional predisposition toward an abnormality or disease **2** : a disposition toward or aptitude for a particular mental development — **di·a·thet·ic** \ˌdī-ə-ˈthet-ik\ *adj*

di·a·tom \ˈdī-ə-ˌtäm\ *n* [deriv. of Gk *diatomos* cut in half, fr. *diatemnein* to cut through, fr. *dia-* + *temnein* to cut — more at TOME] : any of a class (Bacillariophyceae) of minute planktonic unicellular or colonial algae with silicified skeletons that form diatomite

di·a·to·ma·ceous \ˌdī-ət-ə-ˈmā-shəs, (ˌ)dī-ˌat-\ *adj* : consisting of or abounding in diatoms or their siliceous remains ⟨~ silica⟩

diatomaceous earth *n* : DIATOMITE

di·atom·ic \ˌdī-ə-ˈtäm-ik\ *adj* [ISV] **1** : consist-

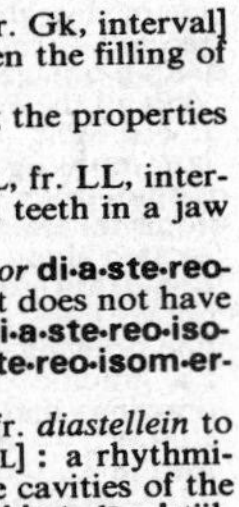
diatoms

ing two atoms in the molecule **2 :** having two replaceable atoms or radicals

di·at·o·mite \dī-ˈat-ə-ˌmīt\ *n* **:** a light friable siliceous material derived chiefly from diatom remains and used esp. as a filter

dia·ton·ic \ˌdī-ə-ˈtän-ik\ *adj* [LL *diatonicus,* fr. Gk *diatonikos,* fr. *diatonos* stretching, fr. *diateinein* to stretch out, fr. *dia-* + *teinein* to stretch — more at THIN] **:** relating to a musical scale having eight tones to the octave and using a fixed pattern of intervals without chromatic deviation — **dia·ton·i·cal·ly** \-ˈtän-i-k(ə-)lē\ *adv*

di·a·tribe \ˈdī-ə-ˌtrīb\ *n* [L *diatriba,* fr. Gk *diatribē* pastime, discourse, fr. *diatribein* to spend (time), wear away, fr. *dia-* + *tribein* to rub — more at THROW] **1** *archaic* **:** a prolonged discourse **2 :** a bitter and abusive speech or writing **3 :** ironical or satirical criticism

di·at·ro·pism \dī-ˈa-trə-ˌpiz-əm\ *n* [ISV] **:** the tropistic tendency of plant organs to place themselves transversely to the line of action of a stimulus — **dia·tro·pic** \ˌdī-ə-ˈtrō-pik, -ˈträp-ik\ *adj*

di·az·e·pam \dī-ˈaz-ə-ˌpam\ *n* [*di-* + *az-* + *e*poxide + *-am* (of unknown origin)] **:** a tranquilizer $C_{16}H_{13}ClN_2O$ used esp. to relieve anxiety and tension and as a muscle relaxant

di·a·zine \ˈdī-ə-ˌzēn, dī-ˈaz-ᵊn\ *n* [ISV *di-* + *az-* + *-ine*] **:** any of three compounds $C_4H_4N_2$ containing a ring that is composed of four carbon atoms and two nitrogen atoms

di·azo \dī-ˈaz-(ˌ)ō\ *adj* [ISV *diaz-, diazo-,* fr. *di-* + *az-*] **1 :** relating to or containing the group N_2 composed of two nitrogen atoms united to a single carbon atom of an organic radical **2 :** relating to or containing diazonium **3 :** of or relating to a photograph or photocopy whose production involves the use of a coating of a diazo compound that is decomposed by exposure to light

di·a·zo·ni·um \ˌdī-ə-ˈzō-nē-əm\ *n* [ISV *di-* + *az-* + *-onium*] **:** the univalent cation N_2^+ that is composed of two nitrogen atoms united to carbon in an organic radical and that usu. exists in salts used in the manufacture of azo dyes

di·az·o·tize \dī-ˈaz-ə-ˌtīz\ *vt* **-tized; -tiz·ing** [*di-* + *azote* + *-ize*] **:** to convert (a compound) into a diazo compound (as a diazonium salt) — **di·az·o·ti·za·tion** \-ˌaz-ət-ə-ˈzā-shən\ *n*

di·ba·sic \(ˈ)dī-ˈbā-sik\ *adj* **1 :** having two replaceable hydrogen atoms — used of acids **2 :** containing two atoms of a univalent metal ⟨~ sodium phosphate Na_2HPO_4⟩ **3 :** having two hydroxyl groups — used of bases and basic salts

dib·ber \ˈdib-ər\ *n* **:** DIBBLE

¹dib·ble \ˈdib-əl\ *n* [ME *debylle*] **:** a small hand implement used to make holes in the ground for plants, seeds, or bulbs

²dibble *vt* **dib·bled; dib·bling** \ˈdib-(ə-)liŋ\ **1 :** to plant with a dibble **2 :** to make holes in (soil) with or as if with a dibble

di·bran·chi·ate \(ˈ)dī-ˈbraŋ-kē-ət\ *adj* [deriv. of Gk *di-* + *branchia*] **:** of or relating to a group (Dibranchia) of cephalopod mollusks including the squids and octopuses and having 2 gills, 2 auricles, 2 nephridia, an apparatus for emitting an inky fluid, and either 8 or 10 cephalic arms bearing suckers or hooks

dibs \ˈdibz\ *n pl* [short for *dibstones* (jacks), fr. obs. *dib* (to dab)] **1** *slang* **:** money esp. in small amounts **2 :** CLAIM, RIGHTS ⟨I have ~ on that piece of cake⟩

di·bu·tyl phthal·ate \ˌdī-ˌbyüt-ᵊl-ˈthal-ˌāt\ *n* [*di-* + *butyl* + *phthalic* acid + *-ate*] **:** a colorless oily ester $C_{16}H_{22}O_4$ used chiefly as a solvent and plasticizer

di·car·box·yl·ic \ˌdī-ˌkär-ˌbäk-ˈsil-ik\ *adj* **:** containing two carboxyl groups in the molecule

di·cast \ˈdī-ˌkast, ˈdik-ˌast\ *n* [Gk *dikastēs,* fr. *dikazein* to judge, fr. *dikē* judgment — more at DICTION] **:** an ancient Athenian performing the functions of both judge and juror at a trial

¹dice \ˈdīs\ *n, pl* **dice** [ME *dyce,* fr. *dees, dyce,* pl. of *dee* die — more at DIE] **1 a :** DIE 1 **b :** a gambling game played with dice **2** *pl also* **dices :** a small cubical piece (as of food) **3 :** a close contest between two racing-car drivers for position during a race — **no dice :** of no avail **:** no use **:** FUTILE

²dice *vb* **diced; dic·ing** [ME *dycen,* fr. *dyce*] *vt* **1 a :** to cut into small cubes **b :** to ornament with square markings ⟨*diced* leather⟩ **2 a :** to bring by playing dice ⟨~ himself into debt⟩ **b :** to lose by dicing ⟨~ his money away⟩ ~ *vi* **1 :** to play games with dice ⟨~ for drinks in the bar —Malcolm Lowry⟩ **2 :** to take a chance ⟨the temptation to ~ with death —*Newsweek*⟩ — **dic·er** *n*

di·cen·tra \dī-ˈsen-trə\ *n* [NL *Dicentra,* genus name, fr. *di-* + Gk *kentron* sharp point — more at CENTER] **:** any of a genus (*Dicentra*) of herbs of the fumitory family with dissected leaves and irregular flowers

dic·ey \ˈdī-sē\ *adj* **dic·i·er; -est** [¹*dice* + *-y*] **:** RISKY, UNPREDICTABLE

dich- *or* **dicho-** *comb form* [LL, fr. Gk, fr. *dicha;* akin to Gk *di-*] **:** in two **:** apart ⟨*dicho*gamous⟩

di·cha·sium \dī-ˈkā-z(h)ē-əm, -zhəm\ *n, pl* **-sia** \-z(h)ē-ə, -zhə\ [NL, fr. Gk *dichasis* halving, fr. *dichazein* to halve, fr. *dicha*] **:** a cymose inflorescence that produces two main axes — **di·cha·sial** \-z(h)ē-əl, -zhəl\ *adj*

di·chla·myd·e·ous \ˌdī-klə-ˈmid-ē-əs\ *adj* [*di-* + Gk *chlamyd-, chlamys* mantle] **:** having both calyx and corolla

dichlor- *or* **dichloro-** *comb form* **:** containing two atoms of chlorine ⟨*dichloro*ethylene⟩

di·chlo·ride \(ˈ)dī-ˈklō(ə)r-ˌīd, -ˈklȯ(ə)r-\ *n* **:** a binary compound containing two atoms of chlorine combined with an element or radical

di·chlo·ro·ben·zene \(ˌ)dī-ˌklōr-ə-ˈben-ˌzēn, -ˌklȯr-, -(ˌ)ben-ˈ\ *n* **:** any of three isomeric compounds $C_6H_4Cl_2$; *esp* **:** PARADICHLOROBENZENE

di·chlo·ro·di·flu·o·ro·meth·ane \-ˌflu̇r-ə-ˈmeth-ˌān\ *n* [*dichlor-* + *di-* + *fluor-* + *methane*] **:** a nontoxic nonflammable easily liquefiable gas CCl_2F_2 used as a refrigerant and as a propellant **:** a Freon gas

di·chlor·vos \(ˈ)dī-ˈklō(ə)r-ˌväs, -ˈklȯ(ə)r-, -vəs\ *n* [*dichlor-* + vinyl + phosphate] **:** a nonpersistent organophosphorus pesticide $C_4H_7Cl_2O_4P$ that is used esp. against insects and is of low toxicity to man

di·chog·a·mous \dī-ˈkäg-ə-məs\ *or* **di·cho·gam·ic** \ˌdī-kə-ˈgam-ik\ *adj, of a hermaphroditic organism* **:** characterized by production at different times of male and female reproductive elements that ensures cross-fertilization — **di·chog·a·my** \dī-ˈkäg-ə-mē\ *n*

di·chon·dra \dī-ˈkän-drə\ *n* [NL, genus name, fr. *di-* + Gk *chondros* grain] **:** any of a genus (*Dichondra*) of chiefly tropical perennial herbs of the morning glory family that includes some (esp. *D. repens* or its varieties) used as a ground cover and a substitute for lawn grasses in warmer parts of the U.S.

dich·otic \(ˈ)dī-ˈkōt-ik\ *adj* [*dich-* + ²*-otic*] **:** affecting or relating to the two ears differently in regard to a conscious aspect (as pitch or loudness) or a physical aspect (as frequency or energy) of sound — **dich·oti·cal·ly** \-i-k(ə-)lē\ *adv*

di·chot·o·mist \dī-ˈkät-ə-məst *also* də-\ *n* **:** one that dichotomizes

di·chot·o·mize \-ˌmīz\ *vb* **-mized; -miz·ing** [LL *dichotomos*] *vt* **:** to divide into two parts, classes, or groups ~ *vi* **:** to exhibit dichotomy — **di·chot·o·mi·za·tion** \-ˌkät-ə-mə-ˈzā-shən\ *n*

di·chot·o·mous \dī-ˈkät-ə-məs *also* də-\ *adj* [LL *dichotomos,* fr. Gk, fr. *dich-* + *temnein* to cut — more at TOME] **1 :** dividing into two parts **2 :** relating to, involving, or proceeding from dichotomy — **di·chot·o·mous·ly** *adv* — **di·chot·o·mous·ness** *n*

di·chot·o·my \dī-ˈkät-ə-mē *also* də-\ *n, pl* **-mies** [Gk *dichotomia,* fr. *dichotomos*] **1 :** a division or the process of dividing into two esp. mutually exclusive or contradictory groups **2 :** the phase of the moon or an inferior planet in which half its disk appears illuminated **3 a :** FORKING; *esp* **:** repeated bifurcation **b :** a system of branching in which the main axis forks repeatedly into two branches **c :** branching of an ancestral line into two equal diverging branches

di·chro·ic \dī-ˈkrō-ik\ *also* **di·chro·it·ic** \ˌdī-(ˌ)krō-ˈit-ik\ *adj* [Gk *dichroos* two-colored, fr. *di-* + *chrōs* color — more at CHROMATIC] **1 :** having the property of dichroism ⟨a ~ crystal⟩ ⟨a ~ mirror⟩ **2 :** DICHROMATIC

di·chro·ism \ˈdī-(ˌ)krō-ˌiz-əm\ *n* **1 :** the property according to which the colors are unlike when a crystal is viewed in the direction of two different axes **2 a :** the property of a solid of differing in color with the thickness of the transmitting layer or of a liquid with the degree of concentration of the solution **b :** the property of a surface of reflecting light of one color and transmitting light of other colors **3 :** DICHROMATISM

di·chro·mat \ˈdī-krō-ˌmat, (ˈ)dī-ˈ\ *n* [back-formation fr. *dichromatic*] **:** one affected with dichromatism

di·chro·mate \(ˈ)dī-ˈkrō-ˌmāt, ˈdī-krō-\ *n* [ISV] **:** a usu. orange to red chromium salt containing the radical Cr_2O_7 ⟨~ of potassium⟩ — called also *bichromate*

di·chro·mat·ic \ˌdī-krō-ˈmat-ik\ *adj* [*di-* + *chromatic*] **1 :** having or exhibiting two colors **2 :** having two color varieties or color phases independently of age or sex ⟨a ~ bird⟩ **3 :** of, relating to, or exhibiting dichromatism

di·chro·ma·tism \dī-ˈkrō-mə-ˌtiz-əm\ *n* **1 :** the state or condition of being dichromatic **2 :** partial color blindness in which only two colors are perceptible

di·chro·scope \ˈdī-krə-ˌskōp\ *n* **:** an instrument for examining crystals for dichroism

dick \ˈdik\ *n* [*Dick,* nickname for *Richard*] **1** *chiefly Brit* **:** FELLOW, CHAP **2 :** PENIS — usu. considered vulgar **3** [by shortening & alter.] **:** DETECTIVE

dick·cis·sel \dik-ˈsis-əl, ˈdik-ˌ\ *n* [imit.] **:** a common migratory black-throated finch (*Spiza americana*) of the central U.S.

dick·ens \ˈdik-ənz\ *n* [euphemism] **:** DEVIL, DEUCE

¹dick·er \ˈdik-ər\ *n* [ME *dyker;* akin to MHG *techer;* both fr. a prehistoric WGmc word borrowed fr. L *decuria* quantity of ten, fr. *decem* ten — more at TEN] **:** the number or quantity of 10 esp. of hides or skins

²dicker *vi* **dick·ered; dick·er·ing** \ˈdik-(ə-)riŋ\ [origin unknown] **:** BARGAIN

³dicker *n* **1 :** BARTER **2 :** an act or session of haggling or bargaining

dick·ey *or* **dicky** *also* **dick·ie** \ˈdik-ē\ *n, pl* **dickeys** *or* **dick·ies** [*Dicky,* nickname for *Richard*] **1 :** any of various articles of clothing: as **a :** a man's separate or detachable shirtfront **b :** a small fabric insert worn to fill in the neckline **2 :** a small bird **3** *chiefly Brit* **a :** the driver's seat in a carriage **b :** a seat at the back of a carriage or automobile

Dick test \ˈdik-\ *n* [George F. *Dick* †1967 and Gladys H. *Dick* †1963 Am physicians] **:** a test to determine susceptibility or immunity to scarlet fever by an injection of scarlet fever toxin

di·cli·nous \(ˈ)dī-ˈklī-nəs\ *adj* **:** having the stamens and pistils in separate flowers — **di·cli·ny** \ˈdī-ˌklī-nē\ *n*

di·cot \ˈdī-ˌkät\ *also* **di·cot·yl** \-ˌkät-ᵊl\ *n* **:** DICOTYLEDON

di·cot·y·le·don \dī-ˌkät-ᵊl-ˈēd-ᵊn\ *n* [deriv. of NL *di-* + *cotyledon*] **:** a plant with two seed leaves **:** a member of the one (Dicotyledones) of the two subclasses of angiospermous plants that comprises those with two cotyledons — **di·cot·y·le·don·ous** \-ᵊn-əs\ *adj*

di·cou·ma·rin \(ˈ)dī-ˈkü-mə-rən\ *n* [fr. *di-* + *coumarin*] **:** a crystalline compound $C_{19}H_{12}O_6$ orig. obtained from spoiled sweet clover hay and used to delay clotting of blood

di·crot·ic \dī-ˈkrät-ik\ *adj* [Gk *dikrotos* having a double beat] **:** being or relating to the second expansion of the artery that occurs during the diastole of the heart — **di·cro·tism** \ˈdī-krə-ˌtiz-əm\ *n*

dict *abbr* dictionary

Dic·ta·phone \ˈdik-tə-ˌfōn\ *trademark* — used for a dictating machine

¹dic·tate \ˈdik-ˌtāt, dik-ˈ\ *vb* **dic·tat·ed; dic·tat·ing** [L *dictatus,* pp. of *dictare* to assert, dictate, fr. *dictus,* pp. of *dicere* to say — more at DICTION] *vi* **1 :** to give dictation **2 :** to speak or act domineeringly **:** PRESCRIBE ~ *vt* **1 :** to speak or read for a person to tran-

scribe or for a machine to record **2 a** : to issue as an order **b** : to impose, pronounce, or specify authoritatively
²dic·tate \'dik-ˌtāt\ *n* **1 a** : an authoritative rule, prescription, or injunction **b** : a ruling principle ⟨according to the ~*s* of his conscience⟩ **2** : a command by one in authority
dictating machine *n* : a machine used esp. for the recording of dictated matter
dic·ta·tion \dik-'tā-shən\ *n* **1 a** : PRESCRIPTION **b** : arbitrary command **2 a** (1) : the act or manner of uttering words to be transcribed (2) : material that is dictated or transcribed **b** (1) : the performing of music to be reproduced by a student (2) : music so reproduced
dic·ta·tor \'dik-ˌtāt-ər, dik-'\ *n* [L, fr. *dictatus*] **1 a** : a person granted absolute emergency power; *esp* : one appointed by the senate of ancient Rome **b** : one holding complete autocratic control **c** : one ruling absolutely and often oppressively **2** : one that dictates — **dic·ta·tress** \'dik-ˌtā-trəs, dik-'\ *n*
dic·ta·to·ri·al \ˌdik-tə-'tōr-ē-əl, -'tȯr-\ *adj* **1 a** : of, relating to, or befitting a dictator ⟨~ power⟩ **b** : ruled by a dictator **2** : oppressive to or contemptuously overbearing toward others : arrogantly domineering — **dic·ta·to·ri·al·ly** \-ē-ə-lē\ *adv* — **dic·ta·to·ri·al·ness** *n*
syn DICTATORIAL, MAGISTERIAL, DOGMATIC, DOCTRINAIRE, ORACULAR *shared meaning element* : imposing one's will or opinions on others
dic·ta·tor·ship \dik-'tāt-ər-ˌship, 'dik-ˌ\ *n* **1** : the office of dictator **2** : autocratic rule, control, or leadership **3 a** : a form of government in which absolute power is concentrated in a dictator or a small clique **b** : a government organization or group in which absolute power is so concentrated **c** : a despotic state
dictatorship of the proletariat : the assumption of political power by the proletariat held in Marxism to be an essential part of the transition from capitalism to communism
dic·tion \'dik-shən\ *n* [L *diction-, dictio* speaking, style, fr. *dictus,* pp. of *dicere* to say; akin to OE *tēon* to accuse, L *dicare* to proclaim, dedicate, Gk *deiknynai* to show, *dikē* judgment, right] **1** *obs* : verbal description **2** : choice of words esp. with regard to correctness, clearness, or effectiveness **3 a** : vocal expression : ENUNCIATION **b** : pronunciation and enunciation of words in singing — **dic·tion·al** \-shnəl, -shən-ᵊl\ *adj* — **dic·tion·al·ly** \-ē\ *adv*
dic·tio·nary \'dik-shə-ˌner-ē\ *n, pl* **-nar·ies** [ML *dictionarium,* fr. LL *diction-, dictio* word, fr. L, speaking] **1** : a reference book containing words usu. alphabetically arranged along with information about their forms, pronunciations, functions, etymologies, meanings, and syntactical and idiomatic uses **2** : a reference book listing alphabetically terms or names important to a particular subject or activity along with discussion of their meanings and applications **3** : a reference book giving for words of one language equivalents in another **4** : a list (as of phrases, synonyms, or hyphenation instructions) stored in machine-readable form (as on a disk) for reference by an automatic system (as for information retrieval or computerized typesetting)
Dic·to·graph \'dik-tə-ˌgraf\ *trademark* — used for a telephonic device for recording sounds or for picking them up in one room and transmitting them to another
dic·tum \'dik-təm\ *n, pl* **dic·ta** \-tə\ *also* **dictums** [L, fr. neut. of *dictus*] **1** : a formal authoritative pronouncement of a principle, proposition, or opinion **2** : a judicial opinion on a point other than the precise issue involved in determining a case
dicty- *or* **dictyo-** *comb form* [NL, fr. Gk *dikty-, diktyo-,* fr. *diktyon,* fr. *dikein* to throw] : net ⟨*dictyo*stele⟩ ⟨*dictyo*some⟩
dic·tyo·some \'dik-tē-ə-ˌsōm\ *n* : GOLGI BODY
dic·tyo·stele \'dik-tē-ə-ˌstēl, ˌdik-tē-ə-'stē-lē\ *n* : a stele in which the vascular cylinder is broken up into a longitudinal series or network of vascular strands around a central pith (as in many ferns)
di·cy·clic \(ˈ)dī-'sī-klik, -'sik-lik\ *adj* **1** : BICYCLIC 2 **2** : having two maxima of population each year — **di·cy·cly** \'dī-ˌsī-klē\ *n*
did *past of* DO
di·dact \'dī-ˌdakt\ *n* [back-formation fr. *didactic*] : a didactic person
di·dac·tic \dī-'dak-tik, də-\ *adj* [Gk *didaktikos,* fr. *didaskein* to teach] **1 a** : designed or intended to teach **b** : intended to convey instruction and information as well as pleasure and entertainment **2** : making moral observations — **di·dac·ti·cal** \-ti-kəl\ *adj* — **di·dac·ti·cal·ly** \-ti-k(ə-)lē\ *adv* — **di·dac·ti·cism** \-tə-ˌsiz-əm\ *n*
di·dac·tics \-tiks\ *n pl but sing or pl in constr* : systematic instruction : PEDAGOGY, TEACHINGS
di·dap·per \'dī-ˌdap-ər\ *n* [ME *dydoppar*] : a dabchick or other small grebe
did·dle \'did-ᵊl\ *vb* **did·dled; did·dling** \'did-liŋ, -ᵊl-iŋ\ [origin unknown] *vi* : DAWDLE, FOOL ~ *vt* **1** *chiefly dial* : to move with short rapid motions **2** : to waste (as time) in trifling **3** : HOAX, SWINDLE — **did·dler** \'did-lər, -ᵊl-ər\ *n*
di·del·phic \(ˈ)dī-'del-fik\ *adj* [*di-* + Gk *delphys* womb — more at DOLPHIN] **1 a** : having or relating to a double uterus **b** : having the female genital tract doubled — used esp. of some worms **2** [NL *Didelphia,* genus name, fr. Gk *di-* + *delphys*] : MARSUPIAL
didn't \'did-ᵊnt\ : did not
di·do \'dīd-(ˌ)ō\ *n, pl* **didoes** *or* **didos** [origin unknown] **1** : a mischievous or unconventional act : PRANK, ANTIC — often used in the phrase *cut didoes* **2** : something that is frivolous or showy
Di·do \'dīd-(ˌ)ō\ *n* [L, fr. Gk *Deidō*] : a queen of Carthage in Vergil's *Aeneid* who entertains Aeneas, falls in love with him, and on his departure stabs herself
didst \(ˈ)didst, (ˈ)ditst\ *archaic past 2d sing of* DO
di·dym·i·um \dī-'dim-ē-əm\ *n* [NL, fr. Gk *didymos*] : a mixture of rare-earth elements made up chiefly of neodymium and praseodymium and used esp. for coloring glass for optical filters
did·y·mous \'did-ə-məs\ *adj* [Gk *didymos* double, twin (adj. & n.), testicle, fr. *dyo* two — more at TWO] : growing in pairs : TWIN
di·dy·na·mous \(ˈ)dī-'din-ə-məs\ *adj* [deriv. of Gk *di-* + *dynamis* power — more at DYNAMIC] : having four stamens disposed in pairs of unequal length — **di·dy·na·my** \-mē\ *n*
¹die \'dī\ *vi* **died; dy·ing** \'dī-iŋ\ [ME *dien,* fr. or akin to ON *deyja* to die; akin to OHG *touwen* to die, OIr *duine* human being] **1** : to pass from physical life : EXPIRE **2** : to pass out of existence : CEASE ⟨their anger *died* at these words⟩ **3 a** : to suffer or face the pains of death **b** : SINK, LANGUISH ⟨*dying* from fatigue⟩ **c** : to long keenly or desperately ⟨*dying* to go⟩ **4** : to cease to be subject ⟨let them ~ to sin⟩ **5 a** : to pass into an inferior state or situation ⟨they have developed competence which we . . . must utilize lest it wither and ~ —Ruth G. Strickland⟩ **b** : STOP ⟨the motor *died*⟩
²die \'dī\ *n, pl* **dice** \'dīs\ *or* **dies** \'dīz\ [ME *dee,* fr. MF *dé*] **1** *pl* **dice** : a small cube marked on each face with from one to six spots and used usu. in pairs in various games and in gambling by being shaken and thrown to come to rest at random on a flat surface **2** *pl usu* **dice** : something determined by or as if by a cast of dice : CHANCE **3** *pl* **dies** : DADO 1a **4** *pl* **dies** : any of various tools or devices for imparting a desired shape, form, or finish to a material or for impressing an object or material: as **a** (1) : the larger of a pair of cutting or shaping tools that when moved toward each other produce a desired form in or impress a desired device on an object by pressure or by a blow (2) : a device composed of a pair of such tools **b** : a hollow internally threaded screw-cutting tool used for forming screw threads **c** : a cutter to cut out blanks **d** : a mold into which molten metal or other material is forced **e** : a perforated block through which metal or plastic is drawn or extruded for shaping

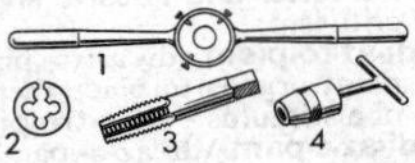

die 4b: four pieces of a tap-and-die set: *1* diestock, *2* adjustable round split die, *3* tap, *4* tap wrench

³die *vt* **died; die·ing** : to cut or shape with a die
die·back \'dī-ˌbak\ *n* : a condition in woody plants in which peripheral parts are killed esp. by parasites
di·ecious *var of* DIOECIOUS
die down *vi* **1** : to undergo death of the aboveground portions **2** : DIMINISH, SUBSIDE ⟨the storm *died down*⟩
die·hard \'dī-ˌhärd\ *n* : an irreconcilable opponent of change ⟨party ~*s* who insisted that no concession of any kind be made⟩
die–hard \'dī-ˌhärd\ *adj* : strongly resisting change : completely and determinedly fixed ⟨a ~ conservative⟩ — **die–hard·ism** \-ˌiz-əm\ *n*
di·el \'dī-əl, -ˌel\ *adj* [irreg. fr. L *dies* day + E *-al*] : involving a 24-hour period that usu. includes a day and the adjoining night ⟨~ fluctuations in temperature⟩
diel·drin \'dē(ə)l-drən\ *n* [*Diels*-Alder reaction, after Otto *Diels* & Kurt *Alder*] : a white crystalline persistent chlorinated hydrocarbon insecticide $C_{12}H_8Cl_6O$
di·elec·tric \ˌdī-ə-'lek-trik\ *n* [*dia-* + *electric*] : a nonconductor of direct electric current — **dielectric** *adj*
dielectric heating *n* : the rapid and uniform heating throughout a nonconducting material by means of a high-frequency electromagnetic field
di·en·ceph·a·lon \ˌdī-ən-'sef-ə-ˌlän, ˌdī-(ˌ)en-, -lən\ *n* [NL, fr. *dia-* + *encephalon*] : the posterior subdivision of the forebrain — **di·en·ce·phal·ic** \-sə-'fal-ik\ *adj*
di·ene \'dī-ˌēn\ *n* [*di-* + *-ene*] : a compound containing two double bonds; *esp* : DIOLEFIN
die–off \'dī-ˌȯf\ *n* : a sudden sharp decline of a population (as rabbits) that is not caused directly by human activity (as hunting)
die out *vi* : to become extinct
di·er·e·sis *var of* DIAERESIS
die·sel \'dē-zəl, -səl\ *n* [Rudolf *Diesel*] **1** : DIESEL ENGINE **2** : a vehicle driven by a diesel engine
diesel–electric *adj* : of, relating to, or employing the combination of a diesel engine driving an electric generator ⟨a ~ locomotive⟩
diesel engine *n* : an internal-combustion engine in which air is compressed to a temperature sufficiently high to ignite fuel injected into the cylinder where the combustion actuates a piston
die·sel·ize \'dē-zə-ˌlīz, 'dē-sə-\ *vt* **-ized; -iz·ing** : to equip with a diesel engine or with electric locomotives having electric generators powered by diesel engines
die·sink·er \'dī-ˌsiŋ-kər\ *n* : one that makes cutting and shaping dies — **die·sink·ing** *n*
Di·es Irae \ˌdē-(ˌ)ā-'sē-ˌrā\ *n* [ML, day of wrath; fr. the first words of the hymn] : a medieval Latin hymn on the Day of Judgment sung in requiem masses
di·esis \'dī-ə-səs\ *n, pl* **di·eses** \-ˌsēz\ [NL, sharp (in music), fr. L, small interval, fr. Gk, fr. *diienai* to send through, fr. *dia-* + *hienai* to send — more at JET] : DOUBLE DAGGER
di·es·ter \'dī-ˌes-tər\ *n* : a compound containing two ester groupings
die·stock \'dī-ˌstäk\ *n* : a stock to hold dies used for cutting threads
di·es·trous \(ˈ)dī-'es-trəs\ *or* **di·es·tru·al** \-trə-wəl\ *adj* [NL *diestrus* period of sexual quiescence, fr. *dia-* + *estrus*] : of, relating to, or having a period of sexual quiescence that intervenes between two periods of estrus — **di·es·trus** \-trəs\ *n*
¹di·et \'dī-ət\ *n* [ME *diete,* fr. OF, fr. L *diaeta* prescribed diet, fr. Gk *diaita,* lit., manner of living, fr. *dia-* + *-aita* (akin to Gk *aisa* share)] **1 a** : food and drink regularly provided or consumed **b** : habitual nourishment **c** : the kind and amount of food prescribed for a person or animal for a special reason **2** : something provided esp. habitually (as for use or enjoyment) ⟨a ~ of Broadway shows and nightclubs —Frederick Wyatt⟩
²diet *vt* **1** : to cause to take food : FEED **2** : to cause to eat and drink sparingly or according to prescribed rules ~ *vi* : to eat sparingly or according to prescribed rules — **di·et·er** *n*
³diet *n* [ML *dieta,* day's journey, assembly, fr. L *dies* day — more at DEITY] **1** : a formal deliberative assembly of princes or estates **2** : any of various national or provincial legislatures

[1]**di·etary** \'dī-ə-,ter-ē\ *n, pl* **di·etar·ies** : the kinds and amounts of food available to or eaten by an individual, group, or population

[2]**dietary** *adj* : of or relating to a diet or to the rules of a diet — **di·etari·ly** \,dī-ə-'ter-ə-lē\ *adv*

dietary law *n* : one of the laws observed by Orthodox Jews that permit or prohibit certain foods

di·etet·ic \,dī-ə-'tet-ik\ *adj* **1** : of or relating to diet **2** : adapted for use in special diets — **di·etet·i·cal·ly** \-i-k(ə-)lē\ *adv*

di·etet·ics \-'tet-iks\ *n pl but sing or pl in constr* : the science or art of applying the principles of nutrition to feeding

di·eth·yl ether \(,)dī-,eth-əl-\ *n* : ETHER 3a

di·eth·yl·stil·bes·trol \-stil-'bes-,trōl, -,trȯl\ *n* [ISV] : a colorless crystalline synthetic compound $C_{18}H_{20}O_2$ used as a potent estrogen — called also *stilbestrol*

di·eti·tian *or* **di·eti·cian** \,dī-ə-'tish-ən\ *n* [*dietitian* irreg. fr. [1]*diet*] : a specialist in dietetics

dif *or* **diff** *abbr* difference

dif·fer \'dif-ər\ *vi* **dif·fered; dif·fer·ing** \-(ə-)riŋ\ [ME *differen,* fr. MF or L; MF *differer* to postpone, be different, fr. L *differre,* fr. *dis-* + *ferre* to carry — more at BEAR] **1 a** : to be unlike or distinct in nature, form, or characteristics ⟨the law of one state ~s from that of another⟩ **b** : to change from time to time or from one instance to another : VARY **2** : to be of unlike or opposite opinion : DISAGREE ⟨men who ~ on religious matters⟩

[1]**dif·fer·ence** \'dif-ərn(t)s, 'dif-(ə-)rən(t)s\ *n* **1 a** : the quality or state of being different **b** : an instance of differing in nature, form, or quality **c** *archaic* : a characteristic that distinguishes one from another or from the average **d** : the element or factor that separates or distinguishes contrasting situations **2** : distinction or discrimination in preference **3 a** : disagreement in opinion : DISSENSION **b** : an instance or cause of disagreement **4** : the degree or amount by which things differ in quantity or measure; *specif* : REMAINDER b(1) **5** : a significant change in or effect on a situation *syn* see DISCORD

[2]**difference** *vt* **-enced; -enc·ing** **1** : DIFFERENTIATE, DISTINGUISH **2** : to compute the difference between

dif·fer·ent \'dif-ərnt, 'dif-(ə-)rənt\ *adj* [MF, fr. L *different-, differens,* prp. of *differre*] **1** : partly or totally unlike in nature, form, or quality : DISSIMILAR ⟨could hardly be more ~⟩ — often followed by *from, than,* or chiefly Brit. *to* ⟨small, neat hand, very ~ from the captain's tottery characters —R. L. Stevenson⟩ ⟨vastly ~ in size than it was twenty-five years ago —N. M. Pusey⟩ ⟨a very ~ situation to the . . . one under which we live —Sir Winston Churchill⟩ **2** : not the same: as **a** : DISTINCT ⟨~ age groups⟩ **b** : VARIOUS ⟨~ members of the class⟩ **c** : ANOTHER ⟨did not like the TV program so switched to a ~ channel⟩ **3** : UNUSUAL, SPECIAL ⟨she was ~ and superior⟩ — **dif·fer·ent·ness** *n*

syn DIFFERENT, DIVERSE, DIVERGENT, DISPARATE, VARIOUS *shared meaning element* : unlike in kind or character *ant* identical, alike, same

dif·fer·en·tia \,dif-ə-'ren-ch(ē-)ə\ *n, pl* **-ti·ae** \-chē-,ē, -chē-,ī\ [L, difference, fr. *different-, differens*] : the element, feature, or factor that distinguishes one entity, state, or class from another; *esp* : a characteristic trait distinguishing a species from other species of the same genus

[1]**dif·fer·en·tial** \,dif-ə-'ren-chəl\ *adj* **1 a** : of, relating to, or constituting a difference : DISTINGUISHING **b** : making a distinction between individuals or classes **c** : based on or resulting from a differential **d** : functioning or proceeding differently or at a different rate **2** : relating to or involving a differential or differentiation **3 a** : relating to quantitative differences **b** : producing effects by reason of quantitative differences — **dif·fer·en·tial·ly** \-'rench-(ə-)lē\ *adv*

[2]**differential** *n* **1 a** : the product of the derivative of a function of one variable by the increment of the independent variable **b** : the sum of the products of each partial derivative of a function of several variables by the arbitrary increments of the corresponding variables **2** : a difference between comparable individuals or classes ⟨the price ~ between nationally advertised and private brands of staple food items⟩; *also* : the amount of such a difference ⟨the ~ between regular and high-test gasoline may exceed five cents a gallon⟩ **3 a** : DIFFERENTIAL GEAR **b** : a case covering a differential gear

differential calculus *n* : a branch of mathematics dealing chiefly with the rate of change of functions with respect to their variables

differential equation *n* : an equation containing differentials or derivatives of functions

differential gear *n* : an arrangement of gears forming an epicyclic train for connecting two shafts or axles in the same line, dividing the driving force equally between them, and permitting one shaft to revolve faster than the other — called also *differential gearing*

dif·fer·en·ti·ate \,dif-ə-'ren-chē-,āt\ *vb* **-at·ed; -at·ing** *vt* **1** : to obtain the mathematical derivative of **2** : to mark or show a difference in **3** : to develop differential characteristics in **4** : to cause differentiation of in the course of development **5** : to express the specific difference of : DISCRIMINATE ~ *vi* **1** : to recognize a difference **2** : to become distinct or different in character **3** : to undergo differentiation — **dif·fer·en·tia·bil·i·ty** \-,ren-ch(ē-)ə-'bil-ət-ē\ *n* — **dif·fer·en·tia·ble** \-'ren-ch(ē-)ə-bəl\ *adj*

dif·fer·en·ti·a·tion \-,ren-chē-'ā-shən\ *n* **1** : the act or process of differentiating **2** : development from the one to the many, the simple to the complex, or the homogeneous to the heterogeneous **3 a** : modification of body parts for performance of particular functions **b** : the sum of the processes whereby apparently indifferent cells, tissues, and structures attain their adult form and function **4** : the processes by which various rock types are produced from a common magma

dif·fer·ent·ly \'dif-ərnt-lē, 'dif-(ə-)rənt-\ *adv* **1** : in a different manner **2** : OTHERWISE

dif·fi·cile *adj* [MF, fr. L *difficilis,* fr. *dis-* + *facilis* easy — more at FACILE] **1** \də-'fis-əl\ *obs* : DIFFICULT **2** \,dē-fi-'sē(ə)l\ [F, lit., difficult] : STUBBORN, UNREASONABLE

dif·fi·cult \'dif-i-(,)kəlt\ *adj* [back-formation fr. *difficulty*] **1** : hard to do, make, or carry out : ARDUOUS ⟨a ~ climb⟩ **2 a** : hard to deal with, manage, or overcome ⟨a ~ child⟩ **b** : hard to understand : PUZZLING ⟨~ reading⟩ *syn* see HARD *ant* simple — **dif·fi·cult·ly** *adv*

dif·fi·cul·ty \-,kəl-tē, -kəl-\ *n, pl* **-ties** [ME *difficulte,* fr. L *difficultas,* irreg. fr. *difficilis*] **1** : the quality or state of being difficult **2** : something difficult : IMPEDIMENT **3** : OBJECTION **4** : EMBARRASSMENT, TROUBLE — usu. used in pl. **5** : CONTROVERSY, DISAGREEMENT

syn DIFFICULTY, HARDSHIP, RIGOR, VICISSITUDE *shared meaning element* : something obstructing one's course and demanding effort and endurance if one's end is to be attained

dif·fi·dence \'dif-əd-ən(t)s, -ə-,den(t)s\ *n* : the quality or state of being diffident

dif·fi·dent \-əd-ənt, -ə-,dent\ *adj* [L *diffident-, diffidens,* prp. of *diffidere* to distrust, fr. *dis-* + *fidere* to trust — more at BIDE] **1** *archaic* : DISTRUSTFUL **2** : hesitant in acting or speaking through lack of self-confidence **3** : RESERVED, UNASSERTIVE *syn* see SHY *ant* confident — **dif·fi·dent·ly** *adv*

dif·fract \dif-'rakt\ *vt* [back-formation fr. *diffraction*] : to cause to undergo diffraction

dif·frac·tion \dif-'rak-shən\ *n* [NL *diffraction-, diffractio,* fr. L *diffractus,* pp. of *diffringere* to break apart, fr. *dis-* + *frangere* to break — more at BREAK] : a modification which light undergoes in passing by the edges of opaque bodies or through narrow slits or in being reflected from ruled surfaces and in which the rays appear to be deflected and to produce fringes of parallel light and dark or colored bands; *also* : a similar modification of other waves (as sound waves)

diffraction grating *n* : GRATING 3

[1]**dif·fuse** \dif-'yüs\ *adj* [L *diffusus,* pp. of *diffundere* to spread out, fr. *dis-* + *fundere* to pour — more at FOUND] **1** : not concentrated or localized : SCATTERED **2** : being at once verbose and ill-organized *syn* see WORDY *ant* succinct — **dif·fuse·ly** *adv* — **dif·fuse·ness** *n*

[2]**dif·fuse** \dif-'yüz\ *vb* **dif·fused; dif·fus·ing** [MF or L; MF *diffuser,* fr. L *diffusus,* pp.] *vt* **1 a** : to pour out and permit or cause to spread freely **b** : EXTEND, SCATTER **c** : to spread thinly or wastefully **2** : to subject to diffusion; *esp* : to break up and distribute (incident light) by reflection ~ *vi* **1** : to spread out or become transmitted esp. by contact **2** : to undergo diffusion

dif·fuse–po·rous \dif-,yüs-'pōr-əs, -'pȯr-\ *adj* [[1]*diffuse*] : having vessels more or less evenly distributed throughout an annual ring and not varying greatly in size — compare RING-POROUS

dif·fus·er \dif-'yü-zər\ *n* **1** : one that diffuses: as **a** : a device (as a reflector) for distributing the light of a lamp evenly **b** : a screen (as of cloth or frosted glass) for softening lighting (as in photography) **c** : a device (as slats at different angles) for deflecting air from an outlet in various directions **2** : a device for reducing the velocity and increasing the static pressure of a fluid passing through a system

dif·fus·ible \dif-'yü-zə-bəl\ *adj* : capable of diffusing or of being diffused

dif·fu·sion \dif-'yü-zhən\ *n* **1** : the action of diffusing : the state of being diffused **2** : PROLIXITY, DIFFUSENESS **3 a** : the process whereby particles of liquids, gases, or solids intermingle as the result of their spontaneous movement caused by thermal agitation and in dissolved substances move from a region of higher to one of lower concentration **b (1)** : reflection of light by a rough reflecting surface **(2)** : transmission of light through a translucent material : SCATTERING **4** : the softening of sharp outlines in a photographic image — **dif·fu·sion·al** \-'yüzh-nəl, -ən-ᵊl\ *adj*

dif·fu·sive \dif-'yü-siv, -ziv\ *adj* : tending to diffuse : characterized by diffusion ⟨~ motion of atoms⟩ — **dif·fu·sive·ly** *adv* — **dif·fu·sive·ness** *n*

di·func·tion·al \(')dī-'fəŋ(k)-shnəl, -shən-ᵊl\ *adj* : of, relating to, or being a compound with two sites in the molecule that are highly reactive

[1]**dig** \'dig\ *vb* **dug** \'dəg\; **dig·ging** [ME *diggen*] *vi* **1** : to turn up, loosen, or remove earth : DELVE **2** : to work hard or laboriously **3** : to advance by or as if by removing or pushing aside material ~ *vt* **1 a** : to break up, turn, or loosen (earth) with an implement **b** : to prepare the soil of ⟨~ a garden⟩ **2** : to bring to the surface by digging : UNEARTH **3** : to hollow out or form by removing earth : EXCAVATE **4** : to drive down so as to penetrate : THRUST **5** : POKE, PROD **6 a** : to pay attention to : NOTICE ⟨~ that fancy hat⟩ **b** : UNDERSTAND, APPRECIATE ⟨if you . . . do something subtle . . . only one tenth of the audience will ~ it —Nat Hentoff⟩ **c** : LIKE, ADMIRE ⟨high school students ~ short poetry —David Burmester⟩

[2]**dig** *n* **1 a** : THRUST, POKE **b** : a cutting remark **2** *pl, chiefly Brit* : DIGGINGS 3 **3** : an archaeological excavation site; *also* : the excavation itself

[3]**dig** *abbr* digest

di·ga·met·ic \,dī-gə-'met-ik\ *adj* : forming two kinds of germ cells

dig·a·my \'dig-ə-mē\ *n, pl* **-mies** [LL *digamia,* fr. LGk, fr. Gk *digamos* married to two people, fr. *di-* + *-gamos* -gamous] : a second marriage after the termination of the first

di·gas·tric \(')dī-'gas-trik\ *adj* [NL *digastricus,* fr. *di-* + *gastricus* gastric] : of, relating to, or being a muscle with two bellies separated by a median tendon

di·gen·e·sis \(')dī-'jen-ə-səs\ *n* [NL] : successive reproduction by sexual and asexual methods

di·ge·net·ic \,dī-jə-'net-ik\ *adj* **1** : of or relating to digenesis **2** : of or relating to a subclass (Digenea) of trematode worms in which sexual reproduction as an internal parasite of a vertebrate alternates with asexual reproduction in a mollusk

ə abut ᵊ kitten ər further a back ā bake ä cot, cart
aù out ch chin e less ē easy g gift i trip ī life
j joke ŋ sing ō flow ȯ flaw ȯi coin th thin th this
ü loot ù foot y yet yü few yù furious zh vision

¹di·gest \'dī-,jest\ *n* [ME *Digest* compilation of Roman laws ordered by Justinian, fr. LL *Digesta*, pl., fr. L, collection of writings arranged under headings, fr. neut. pl. of *digestus*, pp. of *digerere* to arrange, distribute, digest, fr. *dis-* + *gerere* to carry — more at CAST] **1** : a summation or condensation of a body of information: as **a** : a systematic compilation of legal rules, statutes, or decisions **b** : a literary abridgment **2** : a product of digestion
²di·gest \dī-'jest, də-\ *vb* [ME *digesten*, fr. L *digestus*] *vt* **1** : to distribute or arrange systematically : CLASSIFY **2** : to convert (food) into absorbable form **3** : to take into the mind or memory; *esp* : to assimilate mentally **4 a** : to soften or decompose by heat and moisture or chemicals **b** : to extract soluble ingredients from by warming with a liquid **5** : to compress into a short summary ~ *vi* **1** : to digest food **2** : to become digested
di·gest·er \-'jes-tər\ *n* **1** : one that digests or makes a digest **2** : a vessel for digesting esp. plant or animal materials
di·gest·ibil·i·ty \-,jes-tə-'bil-ət-ē\ *n, pl* **-ties** **1** : the fitness of something for digestion **2** : the percentage of a foodstuff taken into the digestive tract that is absorbed into the body
di·gest·ible \-'jes-tə-bəl\ *adj* : capable of being digested
di·ges·tion \dī-'jes(h)-chən, də-\ *n* : the action, process, or power of digesting: as **a** : the process of making food absorbable by dissolving it and breaking it down into simpler chemical compounds that occurs in the living body chiefly through the action of enzymes secreted into the alimentary canal **b** : the process in sewage treatment by which organic matter in sludge is decomposed by anaerobic bacteria with the release of a burnable mixture of gases
¹di·ges·tive \-'jes-tiv\ *n* : something that aids digestion
²digestive *adj* **1** : relating to digestion **2** : having the power to cause or promote digestion ⟨~ enzymes⟩ — **di·ges·tive·ly** *adv* — **di·ges·tive·ness** *n*
digestive gland *n* : a gland secreting digestive enzymes
dig·ger \'dig-ər\ *n* **1 a** : one that digs **b** : a tool or machine for digging **2** *cap* : a No. American Indian (as a Paiute) who digs roots for food **3** *Austral* : SOLDIER **4** : a theater ticket speculator
digger wasp *n* : a burrowing wasp; *esp* : a usu. solitary wasp (superfamily Sphecoidea) that digs nest burrows in the soil and provisions them with insects or spiders paralyzed by stinging
dig·gings *n pl* **1** : material dug out **2** : a place of excavating esp. for ore, metals, or precious stones **3 a** : PREMISES, QUARTERS **b** *chiefly Brit* : lodgings for a student
dight \'dīt\ *vt* **dight·ed** *or* **dight; dight·ing** [ME *dighten*, fr. OE *dihtan* to arrange, compose, fr. a prehistoric WGmc word borrowed fr. L *dictare* to dictate, compose] *archaic* : DRESS, ADORN
dig in *vt* : to cover or incorporate by burying ⟨*dig in* compost⟩ ~ *vi* **1** : to dig defensive trenches **2** : to hold stubbornly to a position **3 a** : to go resolutely to work **b** : to begin eating **4** : to run hard **5** : to make and stand in small depressions in the ground for added stability and leverage while batting (as in baseball)
dig·it \'dij-ət\ *n* [ME, fr. L *digitus* finger, toe — more at TOE] **1 a** : any of the Arabic numerals 1 to 9 and usu. the symbol 0 **b** : one of the elements that combine to form numbers in a system other than the decimal system **2** : a unit of length based on the breadth of a finger and equal in English measure to ¾ inch **3** : one of the divisions in which the limbs of amphibians and all higher vertebrates terminate, which are typically five in number but may be reduced (as in the horse), and which typically have a series of phalanges bearing a nail, claw, or hoof at the tip : FINGER, TOE
¹dig·i·tal \'dij-ət-ᵊl\ *adj* **1** : of or relating to the fingers or toes : DIGITATE **2** : done with a finger **3** : of or relating to calculation by numerical methods or by discrete units **4** : of or relating to data in the form of numerical digits **5** : providing a readout in numerical digits ⟨a ~ voltmeter⟩ — **dig·i·tal·ly** \-ᵊl-ē\ *adv*
²digital *n* : a part (as a key of an organ) that is depressed with a finger to produce a mechanical effect (as the moving of a lever or the closing of a circuit)
digital computer *n* : a computer that operates with numbers expressed directly as digits — compare ANALOG COMPUTER, HYBRID COMPUTER
dig·i·tal·in \,dij-ə-'tal-ən *also* -'tāl-\ *n* [NL *Digitalis*] **1** : a white crystalline steroid glycoside $C_{36}H_{56}O_{14}$ obtained from seeds of the common foxglove **2** : a mixture of the glycosides of digitalis leaves or seeds
dig·i·tal·is \-'tal-əs *also* -'tāl-\ *n* [NL, genus name, fr. L, of a finger, fr. *digitus*; fr. its finger-shaped corolla] **1** : FOXGLOVE **2** : the dried leaf of the common foxglove containing important glycosides and serving as a powerful cardiac stimulant and a diuretic
¹dig·i·ta·lize \'dij-ət-ᵊl-,īz\ *vt* **-lized; -liz·ing** [*digitalis*] : to subject to the administration of digitalis until the desired physiologic adjustment is obtained — **dig·i·ta·li·za·tion** \,dij-ət-ᵊl-ə-'zā-shən\ *n*
²dig·i·tal·ize \'dij-ət-ᵊl-,īz\ *vt* **-ized; -iz·ing** [¹*digital*] : DIGITIZE
dig·i·tate \'dij-ə-,tāt\ *adj* **1** : having digits **2** : resembling a finger; *specif* : having divisions arranged like the fingers of a hand ⟨~ leaf⟩ — **dig·i·tate·ly** *adv* — **dig·i·ta·tion** \,dij-ə-'tā-shən\ *n*
digiti- *comb form* [F, fr. L *digitus*] : digit : finger ⟨*digiti*form⟩
dig·i·ti·grade \'dij-ət-ə-,grād\ *adj* [F, fr. *digiti-* + *-grade*] : walking on the digits with the posterior of the foot more or less raised
dig·i·tize \'dij-ə-,tīz\ *vt* **-tized; -tiz·ing** : to put (as data) into digital notation — **dig·i·ti·za·tion** \,dij-ət-ə-'zā-shən\ *n* — **dig·i·tiz·er** \'dij-ə-,tī-zər\ *n*
dig·i·to·nin \,dij-ə-'tō-nən\ *n* [ISV *digit-* (fr. NL *Digitalis*) + *saponin*] : a steroid saponin $C_{56}H_{92}O_{29}$ occurring in the leaves and seeds of foxglove
digi·toxi·gen·in \,dij-ə-,täk-sə-'jen-ən\ *n* [ISV, blend of *digitoxin* and *-gen*] : a steroid lactone $C_{23}H_{34}O_4$ obtained esp. by hydrolysis of digitoxin
digi·tox·in \,dij-ə-'täk-sən\ *n* [ISV, blend of NL *Digitalis* and ISV *toxin*] : a poisonous glycoside $C_{41}H_{64}O_{13}$ occurring as the most active principle of digitalis; *also* : a mixture of digitalis glycosides consisting chiefly of digitoxin
dig·ni·fied \'dig-nə-,fīd\ *adj* : showing or expressing dignity
dig·ni·fy \'dig-nə-,fī\ *vt* **-fied; -fy·ing** [MF *dignifier*, fr. LL *dignificare*, fr. L *dignus* worthy — more at DECENT] **1** : to give distinction to : ENNOBLE **2** : to confer dignity upon by changing name, appearance, or character
dig·ni·tary \'dig-nə-,ter-ē\ *n, pl* **-tar·ies** : one who possesses exalted rank or holds a position of dignity or honor — **dignitary** *adj*
dig·ni·ty \'dig-nət-ē\ *n, pl* **-ties** [ME *dignete*, fr. OF *digneté*, fr. L *dignitat-, dignitas*, fr. *dignus*] **1** : the quality or state of being worthy, honored, or esteemed **2 a** : high rank, office, or position **b** : a legal title of nobility or honor **3** *archaic* : DIGNITARY **4** : formal reserve of manner or language
dig out *vt* **1** : to make hollow by digging **2** : FIND, UNEARTH
di·gox·in \dij-'äk-sən, dig-\ *n* [ISV *dig-* (fr. NL *Digitalis*) + *toxin*] : a poisonous cardiotonic steroid $C_{41}H_{64}O_{14}$ obtained from a foxglove (*Digitalis lanata*) and used similarly to digitalis
di·graph \'dī-,graf\ *n* **1** : a group of two successive letters whose phonetic value is a single sound (as *ea* in *bread* or *ng* in *sing*) or whose value is not the sum of a value borne by each in other occurrences (as *ch* in *chin* where the value is /t/ + /sh/) **2** : a group of two successive letters **3** : LIGATURE 4 — **di·graph·ic** \dī-'graf-ik\ *adj* — **di·graph·i·cal·ly** \-i-k(ə-)lē\ *adv*
di·gress \dī-'gres, də-\ *vi* [L *digressus*, pp. of *digredi*, fr. *dis-* + *gradi* to step — more at GRADE] : to turn aside esp. from the main subject of attention or course of argument in writing or speaking ***syn*** see SWERVE
di·gres·sion \-'gresh-ən\ *n* **1** *archaic* : a going aside **2** : the act or an instance of digressing in a discourse or other usu. organized literary work — **di·gres·sion·al** \-'gresh-nəl, -ən-ᵊl\ *adj* — **di·gres·sion·ary** \-'gresh-ə-,ner-ē\ *adj*
di·gres·sive \-'gres-iv\ *adj* : characterized by digressions ⟨a ~ book⟩ — **di·gres·sive·ly** *adv* — **di·gres·sive·ness** *n*
dihal- *or* **dihalo-** *comb form* : containing two atoms of a halogen
¹di·he·dral \(ˈ)dī-'hē-drəl\ *adj* **1** *of an airplane* : having wings that make with one another a dihedral angle esp. when the angle between the upper sides is less than 180° **2** *of airplane wing pairs* : inclined at a dihedral angle to each other
²dihedral *n* **1** : DIHEDRAL ANGLE **2** : the angle between an aircraft supporting surface and a horizontal transverse line; *esp* : the angle between either an upwardly inclined wing or a downwardly inclined wing and such a line
dihedral angle *n* [*di-* + *-hedral*] : a figure formed by two intersecting planes
di·hy·brid \(,)dī-'hī-brəd\ *adj* [ISV] : of, relating to, or being an individual or strain that is heterozygous at two genetic loci — **dihybrid** *n*
dihydr- *or* **dihydro-** *comb form* : combined with two atoms of hydrogen
di·hy·dro·er·got·a·mine \(,)dī-,hī-drō-,ər-'gät-ə-,mēn\ *n* : a hydrogenated derivative $C_{33}H_{37}N_5O_5$ of ergotamine that is used in the treatment of migraine
di·hy·dro·strep·to·my·cin \-,strep-tə-'mīs-ᵊn\ *n* : an antibiotic $C_{21}H_{41}N_7O_{12}$ used esp. in the treatment of tuberculosis and tularemia
dihydroxy- *comb form* : containing two hydroxyl groups
di·hy·droxy·ac·e·tone \,dī-hī-,dräk-sē-'as-ə-,tōn\ *n* : a triose $C_3H_6O_3$ that is used esp. to produce artificial tanning of the skin
dik–dik \'dik-,dik\ *n* [native name in East Africa] : any of several small East African antelopes (genera *Madoqua, Rhynchotragus*)
¹dike \'dīk\ *n* [ME, fr. OE *dīc* ditch, dike; akin to MHG *tīch* pond, dike, L *figere* to fasten, pierce] **1** : an artificial watercourse : DITCH **2 a** *dial Brit* : a wall or fence of turf or stone **b** : a bank usu. of earth constructed to control or confine water : LEVEE **c** : a barrier preventing passage esp. of something undesirable **3 a** : a raised causeway **b** : a tabular body of igneous rock that has been injected while molten into a fissure
²dike *vt* **diked; dik·ing** **1** : to surround or protect with a dike **2** : to drain by a dike — **dik·er** *n*
³dike \'dīk\ *n* [origin unknown] : LESBIAN
dik·tat \dik-'tät\ *n* [G, lit., something dictated, fr. NL *dictatum*, fr. L, neut. of *dictatus*, pp. of *dictare* to dictate] : a harsh settlement unilaterally imposed (as on a defeated nation)
dil *abbr* dilute
Di·lan·tin \dī-'lant-ᵊn, də-\ *trademark* — used for diphenylhydantoin
di·lap·i·date \də-'lap-ə-,dāt\ *vb* **-dat·ed; -dat·ing** [L *dilapidatus*, pp. of *dilapidare* to squander, destroy, fr. *dis-* + *lapidare* to throw stones, fr. *lapid-, lapis* stone — more at LAPIDARY] *vt* **1** : to bring into a condition of decay or partial ruin ⟨furniture is *dilapidated* by use —Janet Flanner⟩ **2** *archaic* : SQUANDER ~ *vi* : to become dilapidated ***syn*** see RUIN — **di·lap·i·da·tion** \-,lap-ə-'dā-shən\ *n* — **di·lap·i·da·tor** \-'lap-ə-,dāt-ər\ *n*
di·lap·i·dat·ed *adj* : decayed, deteriorated, or fallen into partial ruin esp. through neglect or misuse ⟨a junkyard filled with ~ autos⟩
di·lat·an·cy \dī-'lāt-ᵊn-sē\ *n* : the property of being dilatant
di·lat·ant \-ᵊnt\ *adj* : increasing in viscosity and setting to a solid as a result of deformation by expansion, pressure, or agitation
di·la·ta·tion \,dil-ə-'tā-shən, ,dī-lə-\ *n* **1** : amplification in writing or speech **2 a** : the condition of being stretched beyond normal dimensions esp. as a result of overwork or disease or of abnormal relaxation ⟨~ of the heart⟩ ⟨~ of the stomach⟩ **b** : DILATION 2 **3** : the action of expanding : the state of being expanded **4** : a dilated part or formation — **di·la·ta·tion·al** \-shnəl, -shən-ᵊl\ *adj*
di·late \dī-'lāt, 'dī-,\ *vb* **di·lat·ed; di·lat·ing** [ME *dilaten*, fr. MF *dilater*, fr. L *dilatare*, lit., to spread wide, fr. *dis-* + *latus* wide — more at LATITUDE] *vt* **1** *archaic* : to describe or set forth at length or in detail **2** : to enlarge or expand in bulk or extent : DISTEND ~ *vi* **1** : to comment at length : DISCOURSE ⟨~ on a topic⟩ **2** : to become wide : SWELL ***syn*** see EXPAND ***ant*** constrict, circumscribe, attentuate — **di·lat·abil·i·ty** \(,)dī-,lāt-ə-'bil-ət-ē\ *n* — **di·lat·able** \dī-'lāt-ə-bəl, 'dī-,\ *adj* — **di·la·tor** \dī-'lāt-ər, 'dī-,\ *n*
di·lat·ed *adj* **1** : expanded laterally **2** *of an insect part* : having a broad expanded border **3** : expanded normally or abnormally in all dimensions — **di·lat·ed·ly** *adv* — **di·lat·ed·ness** *n*

di·la·tion \dī-ˈlā-shən\ *n* **1** : the act or action of dilating : the state of being dilated : EXPANSION, DILATATION **2** : the action of stretching or enlarging an organ or part of the body

di·la·tive \dī-ˈlāt-iv, ˈdī-ˌ\ *adj* : causing dilation : tending to dilate

di·la·tom·e·ter \ˌdil-ə-ˈtäm-ət-ər, ˌdī-lə-\ *n* [ISV] : an instrument for measuring expansion — **di·la·to·met·ric** \-tō-ˈme-trik\ *adj* — **di·la·tom·e·try** \-ˈtäm-ə-trē\ *n*

dil·a·to·ry \ˈdil-ə-ˌtōr-ē, -ˌtȯr-\ *adj* [LL *dilatorius,* fr. L *dilatus* (pp. of *differre* to postpone, differ), fr. *dis-* + *latus,* pp. of *ferre* to carry — more at DIFFER, TOLERATE] **1** : tending or intended to cause delay ⟨~ tactics⟩ **2** : characterized by procrastination : TARDY ⟨~ in answering letters⟩ — **dil·a·to·ri·ly** \ˌdil-ə-ˈtōr-ə-lē, -ˈtȯr-\ *adv* — **dil·a·to·ri·ness** \ˈdil-ə-ˌtōr-ē-nəs, -ˌtȯr-\ *n*

dil·do \ˈdil-(ˌ)dō\ *n, pl* **dildos** [origin unknown] : an object serving as a penis substitute for vaginal insertion

di·lem·ma \də-ˈlem-ə *also* dī-\ *n* [LL, fr. LGk *dilēmmat-, dilēmma,* prob. back-formation fr. Gk *dilēmmatos* involving two assumptions, fr. *di-* + *lēmmat-, lēmma* assumption — more at LEMMA] **1** : an argument presenting two or more equally conclusive alternatives against an opponent **2 a** : a choice or a situation involving choice between equally unsatisfactory alternatives **b** : a problem seemingly incapable of a satisfactory solution ⟨unemployment . . . the great central ~ of our advancing technology —August Heckscher⟩ — **dil·em·mat·ic** \ˌdil-ə-ˈmat-ik *also* ˌdī-lə-\ *adj*

dil·et·tante \ˈdil-ə-ˌtänt, -ˌtant; ˌdil-ə-ˈtänt(-ē), -ˈtant(-ē)\ *n, pl* **-tantes** *or* **-tan·ti** \-ˈtänt-ē, -ˈtant-ē\ [It, fr. prp. of *dilettare* to delight, fr. L *dilectare* — more at DELIGHT] **1** : an admirer or lover of the arts **2** : a person having a superficial interest in an art or a branch of knowledge : DABBLER ***syn*** see AMATEUR — **dilettante** *adj*

dil·et·tant·ish \-ˌtänt-ish, -ˌtant-, ˌdil-ə-ˈ\ *adj* : of, relating to, or characteristic of a dilettante

dil·et·tan·tism \-ˌtän-ˌtiz-əm, -ˌtan-, ˌdil-ə-ˈ\ *n* : dilettantish quality or procedure — **dil·et·tan·tist** \-ˌtänt-əst, -ˌtant-, ˌdil-ə-ˈ\ *adj*

[1]**dil·i·gence** \ˈdil-ə-jən(t)s\ *n* [MF, fr. L *diligentia,* fr. *diligent-, diligens*] **1 a** : persevering application : ASSIDUITY **b** *obs* : SPEED, HASTE **2** : the attention and care legally expected or required of a person

[2]**di·li·gence** \ˈdil-ə-ˌzhäⁿs, ˈdil-ə-jən(t)s\ *n* [F, lit., haste, fr. MF, persevering application] : STAGECOACH

dil·i·gent \ˈdil-ə-jənt\ *adj* [ME, fr. MF, fr. L *diligent-, diligens,* fr. prp. of *diligere* to esteem, love, fr. *di-* (fr. *dis-* apart) + *legere* to select — more at LEGEND] : characterized by steady, earnest, and energetic application and effort : PAINSTAKING ***syn*** see BUSY ***ant*** dilatory — **dil·i·gent·ly** *adv*

dill \ˈdil\ *n* [ME *dile,* fr. OE; akin to OHG *tilli* dill] **1** : any of several plants of the carrot family; *esp* : a European herb (*Anethum graveolens*) with aromatic foliage and seeds both of which are used in flavoring foods and esp. pickles **2** : DILL PICKLE

dill pickle *n* : a pickle seasoned with fresh dill or dill juice

dil·ly \ˈdil-ē\ *n, pl* **dillies** [obs. slang *dilly,* adj. (delightful), irreg. fr. E *delightful*] : one that is remarkable or outstanding ⟨comes up with some *dillies* in his newspaper column —R. M. Rennick⟩

dil·ly bag \ˈdil-ē-\ *n* [Australian *dhilla* hair] : an Australian mesh bag made of native fibers

dil·ly·dal·ly \ˈdil-ē-ˌdal-ē\ *vi* [redupl. of *dally*] : to waste time by loitering : DAWDLE

[1]**dil·u·ent** \ˈdil-yə-wənt\ *n* [L *diluent-, diluens,* prp. of *diluere*] : a diluting agent

[2]**diluent** *adj* [L *diluent-, diluens*] : making thinner or less concentrated by admixture : DILUTING

[1]**di·lute** \dī-ˈlüt, də-\ *vt* **di·lut·ed; di·lut·ing** [L *dilutus,* pp. of *diluere* to wash away, dilute, fr. *di-* + *lavere* to wash — more at LYE] **1** : to make thinner or more liquid by admixture **2** : to diminish the strength, flavor, or brilliance of by admixture **3** : ATTENUATE — **di·lut·er** *or* **di·lu·tor** \-ˈlüt-ər\ *n* — **di·lu·tive** \-ˈlüt-iv\ *adj*

[2]**dilute** *adj* : WEAK, DILUTED — **di·lute·ness** *n*

di·lu·tion \dī-ˈlü-shən, də-\ *n* **1** : the action of diluting : the state of being diluted **2** : something (as a solution) that is diluted **3** : a lessening of real value (as of equity) by a decrease in relative worth through attrition ⟨~ of savings by inflation⟩

di·lu·vi·al \də-ˈlü-vē-əl, dī-\ *or* **di·lu·vi·an** \-vē-ən\ *adj* [LL *diluvialis,* fr. L *diluvium* deluge — more at DELUGE] : of, relating to, or effected by a flood

[1]**dim** \ˈdim\ *adj* **dim·mer; dim·mest** [ME, fr. OE; akin to OHG *timber* dark, Skt *dhamati* he blows] **1 a** : emitting a limited or insufficient amount of light **b** : DULL, LUSTERLESS **c** : lacking pronounced, clear-cut, or vigorous quality or character **2 a** : seen indistinctly or without clear outlines or details **b** : perceived by the senses or mind indistinctly or weakly : FAINT ⟨had only a ~ notion of what was going on⟩ **c** : having little prospect of favorable result or outcome ⟨a ~ future⟩ **d** : characterized by an unfavorable, skeptical, or pessimistic attitude — usu. used in the phrase *take a dim view of* **3** : not perceiving clearly and distinctly ⟨peered at her with ~ eyes —Louis Bromfield⟩ ***syn*** see DARK ***ant*** bright, distinct — **dim·ly** *adv* — **dim·ma·ble** \ˈdim-ə-bəl\ *adj*

[2]**dim** *vb* **dimmed; dim·ming** *vt* **1** : to make dim or lusterless **2** : to reduce the light from (headlights) by switching to the low beam ~ *vi* : to become dim

[3]**dim** *n* **1** *archaic* : DUSK, DIMNESS **2 a** : a small light on an automobile for use in parking **b** : LOW BEAM

[4]**dim** *abbr* **1** dimension **2** diminished **3** diminuendo **4** diminutive

dime \ˈdīm\ *n* [ME, tenth part, tithe, fr. MF, fr. L *decima,* fr. fem. of *decimus* tenth, fr. *decem* ten — more at TEN] **1 a** : a coin of the U.S. worth 1/10 dollar **b** : a petty sum of money **2** : a Canadian 10-cent piece — **a dime a dozen** : so plentiful or commonplace as to be of little esteem or slight value — **on a dime** : in a very small area ⟨these cars can turn *on a dime*⟩

di·men·hy·dri·nate \ˌdī-ˌmen-ˈhī-drə-ˌnāt\ *n* [*di-* + methyl + amine + *hydr-* + amine + *-ate*] : a crystalline compound $C_{24}H_{28}ClN_5O_3$ used esp. as an antihistaminic and to prevent nausea

dime novel *n* : a usu. paperback melodramatic novel — **dime novelist** *n*

[1]**di·men·sion** \də-ˈmen-chən *also* dī-\ *n* [ME, fr. MF, fr. L *dimension-, dimensio,* fr. *dimensus,* pp. of *dimetiri* to measure out, fr. *dis-* + *metiri* to measure — more at MEASURE] **1 a** (1) : measure in one direction; *specif* : one of three or four coordinates determining a position in space or space and time (2) : one of a group of properties whose number is necessary and sufficient to determine uniquely each element of a system of usu. mathematical entities (as an aggregate of points in real or abstract space) ⟨the surface of a sphere has two ~*s*⟩; *also* : a parameter or coordinate variable assigned to such a property ⟨the three ~*s* of momentum⟩ (3) : the number of elements in a basis of a vector space **b** : the quality of spatial extension : MAGNITUDE, SIZE **c** : the range over which or the degree to which something extends : SCOPE **d** : one of the elements or factors making up a complete personality or entity : ASPECT **2** *obs* : bodily form or proportions **3** : wood or stone cut to pieces of specified size — **di·men·sion·al** \-ˈmench-nəl, -ˈmen-chən-ᵊl\ *adj* — **di·men·sion·al·i·ty** \-ˌmen-chə-ˈnal-ət-ē\ *n* — **di·men·sion·al·ly** \ˈmench-nə-lē, -ˈmen-chen-ᵊl-ē\ *adv*

[2]**dimension** *vt* **di·men·sioned; di·men·sion·ing** \-ˈmench-(ə-)niŋ\ **1** : to form to the required dimensions **2** : to indicate the dimensions on (a drawing)

di·men·sion·less \-ˈmen-chən-ləs\ *adj* : having no dimensions ⟨a ratio of two lengths is a ~ quantity⟩

di·mer \ˈdī-mər\ *n* [ISV *di-* + *-mer* (as in *polymer*)] : a compound formed by the union of two radicals or two molecules of a simpler compound; *specif* : a polymer formed from two molecules of a monomer — **di·mer·iza·tion** \ˌdī-mə-rə-ˈzā-shən\ *n* — **di·mer·ize** \ˈdī-mə-ˌrīz\ *vt*

di·mer·ic \(ˈ)dī-ˈmer-ik\ *adj* [NL *dimerus*] **1** : consisting of two parts ⟨a ~ chromosome⟩ **2** : of or relating to a dimer

dim·er·ous \ˈdim-ə-rəs\ *adj* [NL *dimerus,* fr. L *di-* + NL *-merus* -merous] : consisting of two parts: as **a** *of an insect* : having the tarsi two-jointed **b** *of a flower* : having two members in each whorl — **dim·er·ism** \-ə-ˌriz-əm\ *n*

dime store *n* : FIVE-AND-TEN

dim·e·ter \ˈdim-ət-ər\ *n* [LL, fr. Gk *dimetros,* adj., being a dimeter, fr. *di-* + *metron* measure — more at MEASURE] : a line of verse consisting of two metrical feet or of two dipodies

di·meth·o·ate \dī-ˈmeth-ə-ˌwāt\ *n* [*dimethyl-* + *thio* acid + [1]*-ate*] : an insecticide $C_5H_{12}NO_3PS_2$ used on livestock and various crops

dimethyl- *comb form* : containing two methyl groups

di·meth·yl·hy·dra·zine \ˌdī-ˌmeth-əl-ˈhī-drə-ˌzēn\ *n* : either of two flammable corrosive isomeric liquids $C_2H_8N_2$ which are methylated derivatives of hydrazine and of which one is used in rocket fuels

di·meth·yl·sulf·ox·ide \-ˌsəl-ˈfäk-ˌsīd\ *n* [*dimethyl-* + *sulf-* + *oxide*] : a compound $(CH_3)_2SO$ obtained as a by-product in wood-pulp manufacture and used as a solvent and in experimental medicine — called also *DMSO*

di·meth·yl·tryp·ta·mine \-ˈtrip-tə-ˌmēn\ *n* [*dimethyl-* + *tryptophan* + *amine*] : an easily synthesized hallucinogenic drug $C_{12}H_{16}N_2$ that is chemically similar to but shorter acting than psilocybin

dimin *abbr* diminuendo

di·min·ish \də-ˈmin-ish\ *vb* [ME *deminishen,* alter. of *diminuen,* fr. MF *diminuer,* fr. LL *diminuere,* alter. of L *deminuere,* fr. *de-* + *minuere* to lessen — more at MINOR] *vt* **1** : to make less or cause to appear less **2** : to lessen the authority, dignity, or reputation of : BELITTLE **3** : to cause to taper ~ *vi* **1** : to become gradually less (as in size or importance) : DWINDLE **2** : TAPER ***syn*** see DECREASE — **di·min·ish·able** \-ə-bəl\ *adj* — **di·min·ish·ment** \-mənt\ *n*

di·min·ished *adj, of a musical interval* : made one half step less than perfect or minor ⟨a ~ fifth⟩

diminishing returns *n pl* : a rate of yield that beyond a certain point fails to increase in proportion to additional investments of labor or capital

di·min·u·en·do \də-ˌmin-(y)ə-ˈwen-(ˌ)dō\ *adv or adj* [It, lit., diminishing, fr. LL *diminuendum,* gerund of *diminuere*] : DECRESCENDO — **diminuendo** *n*

dim·i·nu·tion \ˌdim-ə-ˈn(y)ü-shən\ *n* [ME *diminucioun,* fr. MF *diminution,* fr. ML *diminution-, diminutio,* alter. of L *deminution-, deminutio,* fr. *deminutus,* pp. of *deminuere*] : the act, process, or an instance of diminishing : DECREASE — **dim·i·nu·tion·al** \-shnəl, -shən-ᵊl\ *adj*

[1]**di·min·u·tive** \də-ˈmin-yət-iv\ *n* [ME *diminutif,* fr. ML *diminutivum,* alter. of LL *deminutivum,* fr. neut. of *deminutivus*] **1** : a diminutive word, affix, or name **2** : a diminutive individual

[2]**diminutive** *adj* **1** : indicating small size and sometimes the state or quality of being familiarly known, lovable, pitiable, or contemptible — used of affixes (as *-ette, -kin, -ling*) and of words formed with them (as *kitchenette, manikin, duckling*), of clipped forms (as *Jim*), and of altered forms (as *Peggy*); compare AUGMENTATIVE **2** : exceptionally or abnormally small : MINUTE ***syn*** see SMALL — **di·min·u·tive·ly** *adv* — **di·min·u·tive·ness** *n*

dim·i·ty \ˈdim-ət-ē\ *n, pl* **-ties** [alter. of ME *demyt,* prob. fr. MGk *dimitos* of double thread, fr. Gk *di-* + *mitos* warp thread] : a sheer usu. corded cotton fabric of plain weave in checks or stripes

dim·mer \ˈdim-ər\ *n* **1** : a device for regulating the intensity of an electric lighting unit **2** *pl* **a** : small lights on an automobile for use in parking **b** : headlights on low beam

dimness *n* **1** : the quality or state of being dim **2** : something dim

di·mor·phic \(ˈ)dī-ˈmȯr-fik\ *adj* **1 a :** DIMORPHOUS 1 **b :** occurring in two distinct forms ⟨~ leaves of emergent plants⟩ ⟨a sexually ~ butterfly⟩ **2 :** combining qualities of two kinds of individuals in one
di·mor·phism \-ˌfiz-əm\ *n* [ISV] **:** the condition or property of being dimorphic or dimorphous: as **a** (1) **:** the existence of two different forms (as of color or size) of a species esp. in the same population **a** (2) **:** the existence of an organ (as the leaves of a plant) in two different forms **b :** crystallization of a chemical compound in two different forms
di·mor·pho·the·ca \(ˌ)dī-ˌmȯr-fə-ˈthē-kə\ *n* [NL *Dimorphotheca,* genus name, fr. Gk *dimorphos* + NL *theca*] **:** any of a genus (*Dimorphotheca*) of southern African composite herbs or subshrubs with showy terminal solitary flower heads and conspicuously toothed leaves
di·mor·phous \(ˈ)dī-ˈmȯr-fəs\ *adj* [Gk *dimorphos* having two forms, fr. *di-* + *-morphos* -morphous] **1 :** crystallizing in two different forms **2 :** DIMORPHIC 1b
dim·out \ˈdim-ˌau̇t\ *n* **:** a restriction limiting the use or showing of lights at night esp. during the threat of an air raid; *also* **:** a condition of partial darkness produced by this restriction
¹dim·ple \ˈdim-pəl\ *n* [ME *dympull;* akin to OHG *tumphilo* whirlpool, OE *dyppan* to dip — more at DIP] **1 :** a slight natural indentation in the surface of some part of the human body **2 :** a depression or indentation on a surface (as of a golf ball) — **dim·ply** \-p(ə-)lē\ *adj*
²dimple *vb* **dim·pled; dim·pling** \-p(ə-)liŋ\ *vt* **:** to mark with dimples ~ *vi* **:** to exhibit or form dimples
dim·wit \ˈdim-ˌwit\ *n* **:** a stupid or mentally slow person
dim–wit·ted \-ˈwit-əd\ *adj* **:** not mentally bright **:** STUPID — **dim–wit·ted·ly** *adv* — **dim–wit·ted·ness** *n*
¹din \ˈdin\ *n* [ME, fr. OE *dyne;* akin to ON *dynr* din, Skt *dhvanati* it roars] **:** a loud continued noise; *esp* **:** a welter of discordant sounds ⟨a world of savage violence and incessant ~ —Thomas Wolfe⟩
²din *vb* **dinned; din·ning** *vt* **1 :** to assail or deafen with loud continued noise **2 :** to impress by insistent repetition ~ *vi* **:** to make a loud noise
³din *abbr* dinar
di·nar \di-ˈnär, ˈdē-ˌ\ *n* [Ar *dīnār,* fr. Gk *dēnarion* denarius, fr. L *denarius*] **1 :** a gold coin formerly used in Muslim countries **2 a** —see MONEY table **b** —see *rial* at MONEY table
¹dine \ˈdīn\ *vb* **dined; din·ing** [ME *dinen,* fr. OF *diner,* fr. (assumed) VL *disjejunare* to break one's fast, fr. L *dis-* + LL *jejunare* to fast, fr. L *jejunus* fasting] *vi* **:** to take dinner ~ *vt* **:** to give a dinner to **:** FEED ⟨wined and *dined* his friends⟩
²dine *n, Scot* **:** DINNER
din·er \ˈdī-nər\ *n* **1 :** one that dines **2 a :** DINING CAR **b :** a restaurant usu. resembling a dining car in shape
din·er–out \ˌdī-nə-ˈrau̇t\ *n, pl* **diners–out :** one who dines away from home esp. in the course of an active social life
di·nette \dī-ˈnet\ *n* **:** a small space usu. off a kitchen used for informal dining; *also* **:** furniture for such a space
¹ding \ˈdiŋ\ *vb* [prob. imit.] *vt* **:** to dwell on with tiresome repetition ⟨keeps ~*ing* it into him that the less he smokes the better —Samuel Butler †1902⟩ ~ *vi* **1 :** to make a ringing sound **:** CLANG **2 :** to speak with tiresome reiteration
²ding *n* [*ding* (to strike), fr. ME *dingen*] **:** a damaged area esp. on the surface of a surfboard
ding–a–ling *n* [prob. euphemism for *damn fool*] **:** NITWIT, KOOK
ding·bat \ˈdiŋ-ˌbat\ *n* [origin unknown] **:** a typographical ornament (as an asterisk) used typically to call attention to an opening sentence or to make a break between two paragraphs
¹ding·dong \ˈdiŋ-ˌdȯŋ, -ˌdäŋ\ *n* [imit.] **:** the ringing sound produced by repeated strokes esp. on a bell
²dingdong *vi* **1 :** to make a dingdong sound **2 :** to repeat a sound or action tediously or insistently
³dingdong *adj* **1 :** of, relating to, or resembling the ringing sound made by a bell **2 :** marked by a rapid exchange or alternation (as of blows or words)
din·ghy \ˈdiŋ-(k)ē, -gē\ *n, pl* **dinghies** [Bengali *ḍiṅgi* & Hindi *ḍiṅgī*] **1 :** an East Indian rowboat or sailboat **2 :** a small boat propelled by oars, sails, or motor that is often carried on a larger boat as a tender or a lifeboat **3 :** a rubber life raft
din·gle \ˈdiŋ-gəl\ *n* [ME, abyss] **:** a small wooded valley **:** DELL
din·gle·ber·ry \ˈdiŋ-gəl-ˌber-ē\ *n* [origin unknown] **:** a shrub (*Vaccinium erythrocarpus*) of the southeastern U.S.; *also* **:** its globose dark red edible berry
din·go \ˈdiŋ-(ˌ)gō\ *n, pl* **dingoes** [native name in Australia] **:** a reddish brown wild dog (*Canis dingo*) of Australia
din·gus \ˈdiŋ-(g)əs\ *n* [D or G; D *dinges,* prob. fr. G *dings,* fr. gen. of *ding* thing, fr. OHG — more at THING] **:** something (as a gadget) whose common name is unknown or forgotten
din·gy \ˈdin-jē\ *adj* **din·gi·er; -est** [origin unknown] **1 :** DIRTY, DISCOLORED **2 :** SHABBY, SQUALID — **din·gi·ly** \-jə-lē\ *adv* — **din·gi·ness** \-jē-nəs\ *n*

dingo

dining car *n* **:** a railroad car in which meals are served
dining room *n* **:** a room used for the taking of meals
dinitro- *comb form* **:** containing two nitro groups
di·ni·tro·ben·zene \(ˌ)dī-ˌnī-trō-ˈben-ˌzēn, -(ˌ)ben-ˈ\ *n* [ISV] **:** any of three isomeric toxic compounds $C_6H_4(NO_2)_2$; *esp* **:** the yellow meta-isomer used chiefly as a dye intermediate
di·ni·tro·phe·nol \-ˈfē-ˌnōl, -fi-ˈ\ *n* **:** any of six isomeric crystalline compounds $C_6H_4N_2O_5$ some of whose derivatives are pesticides; *esp* **:** a highly toxic compound that increases fat metabolism and was formerly used in weight control
¹dink \ˈdiŋk\ *n* [*dink* (to hit with a drop shot), prob. of imit. origin] **:** DROP SHOT
²dink *n* [prob. alter. of *dick*] **:** PENIS — usu. considered vulgar
din·key *or* **din·ky** \ˈdiŋ-kē\ *n, pl* **dinkeys** *or* **dinkies** [prob. fr. *dinky*] **:** a small locomotive used esp. for hauling freight, logging, and shunting
¹din·kum \ˈdiŋ-kəm\ *adj* [prob. fr. E dial. *dinkum,* n., work] *Austral* **:** AUTHENTIC, GENUINE
²dinkum *adv, Austral* **:** TRULY, HONESTLY
din·ky \ˈdiŋ-kē\ *adj* **din·ki·er; -est** [Sc *dink* neat] **:** SMALL, INSIGNIFICANT
din·ner \ˈdin-ər\ *n, often attrib* [ME *diner,* fr. OF, fr. *diner* to dine] **1 a :** the principal meal of the day **b :** a formal feast or banquet **2 :** TABLE D'HÔTE 2 **3 :** the food prepared for a dinner ⟨eat your ~⟩ **4 :** a packaged meal usu. for quick preparation ⟨warmed up a frozen Chinese ~⟩ — **din·ner·less** \-ləs\ *adj*
dinner jacket *n* **:** a jacket for formal evening wear
din·ner·ware \ˈdin-ər-ˌwa(ə)r, -ˌwe(ə)r\ *n* **:** tableware other than flatware
di·no·fla·gel·late \ˌdī-nō-ˈflaj-ə-lət, -ˌlāt; -flə-ˈjel-ət\ *n* [deriv. of Gk *dinos* rotation, eddy + NL *flagellum*] **:** any of an order (Dinoflagellata) of chiefly marine planktonic usu. solitary plantlike flagellates that include luminescent forms, forms important in marine food chains, and forms causing red tide
di·no·saur \ˈdī-nə-ˌsȯ(ə)r\ *n* [deriv. of Gk *deinos* terrible + *sauros* lizard — more at DIRE, SAURIAN] **1 :** any of a group (Dinosauria) of extinct chiefly terrestrial carnivorous or herbivorous reptiles **2 :** any of various large extinct reptiles — **di·no·sau·ri·an** \ˌdī-nə-ˈsȯr-ē-ən\ *adj or n* — **di·no·sau·ric** \-ˈsȯr-ik\ *adj*
di·no·there \ˈdī-nə-ˌthi(ə)r\ *n* [NL *Deinotherium,* genus name, fr. Gk *deinos* + NL *-therium*] **:** any of a genus (*Deinotherium*) of extinct proboscidean mammals with a pair of downward-directed tusks
¹dint \ˈdint\ *n* [ME, fr. OE *dynt*] **1** *archaic* **:** BLOW, STROKE **2 :** FORCE, POWER **3 :** ¹DENT — **by dint of :** by force of **:** because of
²dint *vt* **1 :** to make a dint in **2 :** to impress or drive in with force
di·nu·cle·o·tide \(ˌ)dī-ˈn(y)ü-klē-ə-ˌtīd\ *n* **:** a nucleotide consisting of two units each composed of a phosphate, a pentose, and a nitrogen base
di·oc·e·san \dī-ˈäs-ə-sən *also* ˌdī-ə-ˈsēz-ᵊn\ *n* **:** a bishop having jurisdiction over a diocese
di·o·cese \ˈdī-ə-səs, -ˌsēz, -ˌsēs\ *n, pl* **-ces·es** \-sə-səz, -ˌsē-zəz, -ˌsē-səz, -ə-ˌsēz\ [ME *diocise,* fr. MF, fr. LL *diocesis,* alter. of *dioecesis,* fr. L, administrative division, fr. Gk *dioikēsis* administration, administrative division, fr. *dioikein* to keep house, govern, fr. *dia-* + *oikein* to dwell, manage, fr. *oikos* house — more at VICINITY] **:** the territorial jurisdiction of a bishop — **di·oc·e·san** \dī-ˈäs-ə-sən *also* ˌdī-ə-ˈsēz-ᵊn\ *adj*
di·ode \ˈdī-ˌōd\ *n* [ISV] **1 :** a 2-electrode electron tube having a cathode and an anode **2 :** a rectifier that consists of a semiconducting crystal with two terminals and that is analogous in use to an electron tube diode
di·oe·cious \(ˈ)dī-ˈē-shəs\ *adj* [deriv. of Gk *di-* + *oikos* house] **1 :** having male reproductive organs in one individual and female in another **2 :** having staminate and pistillate flowers borne on different individuals — **di·oe·cious·ly** *adv* — **di·oe·cism** \-ˈē-ˌsiz-əm\ *n*
di·oi·cous \-ˈȯi-kəs\ *adj* [NL *dioicus,* fr. *di-* + Gk *oikos*] **:** having archegonia and antheridia on separate plants
di·ol \ˈdī-ˌōl, -ˌȯl\ *n* [ISV *di-* + ¹*-ol*] **:** a compound (as glycol) containing two hydroxyl groups
di·ole·fin \dī-ˈō-lə-fən\ *n* [ISV *di-* + *olefin*] **:** any of a series of aliphatic hydrocarbons containing two double bonds — called also *diene*
Di·o·me·des \ˌdī-ə-ˈmēd-ēz\ *n* [L, fr. Gk *Diomēdēs*] **:** one of the Greek heroes of the Trojan War
Di·o·ny·sia \ˌdī-ə-ˈniz(h)-ē-ə, -ˈnis(h)-; -ˈnizh-ə, -ˈnish-; -ˈnī-sē-ə, -ˈnē-, -zē-\ *n pl* [L, fr. Gk, fr. neut. pl. of *dionysios* of Dionysus fr. *Dionysos*] **:** ancient Greek festival observances held in seasonal cycles in honor of Dionysus; *esp* **:** such observances marked by dramatic performances
Di·o·ny·si·ac \-ˈniz(h)-ē-ˌak, -ˈnis(h)-; -ˈnī-zē-, -ˈnē-, -sē-\ *adj* [L *dionysiacus,* fr. Gk *dionysiakos,* fr. *Dionysos*] **:** DIONYSIAN 2 — **Dionysiac** *n*
Di·o·ny·sian \-ˈniz(h)-ē-ən, -ˈnis(h)-; -ˈnizh-ən, -ˈnish-; -ˈnī-sē-ən, -ˈnē-, -zē-\ *adj* **1 a :** of or relating to Dionysius **b :** of or related to the theological writings once mistakenly attributed to Dionysius the Areopagite **2 a :** devoted to the worship of Dionysus **b :** being of a frenzied or orgiastic character
Di·o·ny·sus \ˌdī-ə-ˈnī-səs, -ˈnē-\ *n* [L, fr. Gk *Dionysos*] **:** the Greek god of wine **:** BACCHUS
Di·o·phan·tine equation \ˌdī-ə-ˈfan-ˌtīn-, -ˈfant-ᵊn-\ *n* [*Diophantus,* 3d cent. A.D. Gk mathematician] **:** an indeterminate polynomial equation with integral coefficients for which it is required to find all integral solutions
di·op·side \dī-ˈäp-ˌsīd\ *n* [F, fr. *di-* + Gk *opsis* appearance — more at OPTIC] **:** a green to white mineral that consists of pyroxene containing little or no aluminum — **diopsidic** *adj*
di·op·ter *also* **di·op·tre** \dī-ˈäp-tər\ *n* [*diopter* (an optical instrument), fr. MF *dioptre,* fr. L *dioptra,* fr. Gk, fr. *dia-* + *opsesthai* to be going to see] **:** a unit of measurement of the refractive power of lenses equal to the reciprocal of the focal length in meters
di·op·tom·e·ter \(ˌ)dī-ˌäp-ˈtäm-ət-ər\ *n* **:** an instrument used in measuring the accommodation and refraction of the eye — **di·op·tom·e·try** \-ˈtäm-ə-trē\ *n*
di·op·tric \dī-ˈäp-trik\ *adj* [Gk *dioptrikos* of a diopter (instrument), fr. *dioptra*] **1 :** that effects or serves in refraction of a beam of light **:** REFRACTIVE; *specif* **:** that assists vision by refracting and focalizing light **2 :** produced by means of refraction
di·o·ra·ma \ˌdī-ə-ˈram-ə, -ˈräm-\ *n* [F, fr. *dia-* + *-orama* (as in *panorama,* fr. E)] **1 :** a scenic representation in which a partly trans-

lucent painting is seen from a distance through an opening **2 a** : a scenic representation in which sculptured figures and lifelike details are displayed usu. in miniature so as to blend indistinguishably with a realistic painted background **b** : a life-size exhibit of a wildlife specimen or scene with realistic natural surroundings and a painted background — **di·oram·ic** \-ˈram-ik\ *adj*

di·o·rite \ˈdī-ə-ˌrīt\ *n* [F, irreg. fr. Gk *diorizein* to distinguish, fr. *dia-* + *horizein* to define — more at HORIZON] : a granular crystalline igneous rock commonly of acid plagioclase and hornblende, pyroxene, or biotite — **di·o·rit·ic** \ˌdī-ə-ˈrit-ik\ *adj*

Di·os·cu·ri \ˌdī-əs-ˈkyu̇(ə)r-ˌī, dī-ˈäs-kyə-ˌrī\ *n pl* [NL, fr. Gk *Dioskouroi*, lit., sons of Zeus, fr. *Dios* (gen. of *Zeus;* akin to L *divus* divine) + *kouroi*, pl. of *koros, koaros* boy — more at DEITY, CRESCENT] : the twins Castor and Pollux reunited as stars in the sky by Zeus after Castor's death and regarded as patrons of athletes, soldiers, and mariners

di·ox·ane \dī-ˈäk-ˌsān\ *n* [ISV *di-* + *ox-* + *-ane*] : a flammable toxic liquid diether $C_4H_8O_2$ used esp. as a solvent

di·ox·ide \(ˈ)dī-ˈäk-ˌsīd\ *n* [ISV] : an oxide (as carbon dioxide) containing two atoms of oxygen in the molecule

¹dip \ˈdip\ *vb* **dipped; dip·ping** [ME *dippen*, fr. OE *dyppan;* akin to OHG *tupfen* to wash, Lith *dubus* deep] *vt* **1 a** : to plunge or immerse momentarily or partially under the surface (as of a liquid) so as to moisten, cool, or coat ⟨~ candles⟩ **b** : to thrust in a way to suggest immersion **c** : to immerse (as a hog) in an antiseptic or parasiticidal solution **2** : to lift a portion of by reaching below the surface with something shaped to hold liquid : LADLE **3 a** *archaic* : INVOLVE **b** : MORTGAGE **4** : to lower and then raise again ⟨~ a flag in salute⟩ ~ *vi* **1 a** : to plunge into a liquid and quickly emerge **b** : to immerse something into a processing liquid or finishing material **2 a** : to suddenly drop down or out of sight **b** *of an airplane* : to drop suddenly before climbing **c** : to decline or decrease moderately and usu. temporarily ⟨prices *dipped*⟩ **3 a** : to reach down inside or below a surface esp. to withdraw a part of the contents **b** : to make inroads for funds — used with *into* ⟨*dipped* into the family's savings⟩ **4** : to examine something casually or tentatively; *specif* : to read superficially **5** : to incline downward from the plane of the horizon — **dip·pa·ble** \ˈdip-ə-bəl\ *adj*

²dip *n* **1** : an act of dipping; *esp* : a brief plunge into the water for sport or exercise **2** : inclination downward: **a** : PITCH **b** : a sharp downward course : DROP **c** : the angle that a stratum or similar geological feature makes with a horizontal plane **3** : the angle formed with the horizon by a magnetic needle free to rotate in the vertical plane **4** : HOLLOW, DEPRESSION **5** : something obtained by or used in dipping **6 a** : a sauce or soft mixture into which food may be dipped **b** : a liquid preparation into which an object may be dipped (as for cleansing or coloring) **7** *slang* : PICKPOCKET

di·pep·ti·dase \dī-ˈpep-tə-ˌdās, -ˌdāz\ *n* : any of various enzymes that hydrolyze dipeptides but not polypeptides

di·pep·tide \(ˈ)dī-ˈpep-ˌtīd\ *n* : a peptide that yields two molecules of amino acid on hydrolysis

di·phase \ˈdī-ˌfāz\ *or* **di·pha·sic** \(ˈ)dī-ˈfā-zik\ *adj* : having two phases

di·phe·nyl \(ˈ)dī-ˈfen-ᵊl, -ˈfēn-\ *n* : BIPHENYL

di·phe·nyl·amine \(ˌ)dī-ˌfen-ᵊl-ə-ˈmēn, -ˌfēn-, -ᵊl-ˈam-ən\ *n* [ISV] : a crystalline pleasant-smelling compound $(C_6H_5)_2NH$ used chiefly in the manufacture of dyes and in stabilizing explosives

di·phe·nyl·hy·dan·to·in \-hī-ˈdant-ə-wən\ *n* [*diphenyl* + *hydrogen* + *allantoin* (a chemical found in the allantoic liquid of cows)] : a crystalline compound $C_{15}H_{12}N_2O_2$ used in the form of its sodium salt in the treatment of epilepsy

di·phos·gene \(ˈ)dī-ˈfäz-ˌjēn\ *n* [ISV] : a liquid compound $C_2Cl_4O_2$ used as a poison gas in World War I

di·phos·phate \(ˈ)dī-ˈfäs-ˌfāt\ *n* : a phosphate containing two phosphate groups

di·phos·pho·glyc·er·ic acid \(ˈ)dī-ˈfäs-fō-glis-ˌer-ik-\ *n* : a diphosphate of glyceric acid that is an important intermediate in photosynthesis and in glycolysis and fermentation

di·phos·pho·pyr·i·dine nucleotide \-ˌpir-ə-ˌdēn-\ *n* [*di-* + *phosph-* + *pyridine*] : NAD

diph·the·ria \dif-ˈthir-ē-ə, dip-\ *n* [NL, fr. F *diphthérie*, fr. Gk *diphthera* leather; fr. the toughness of the false membrane] : an acute febrile contagious disease marked by the formation of a false membrane esp. in the throat and caused by a bacterium which produces a toxin causing inflammation of the heart and nervous system — **diph·the·ri·al** \-ē-əl\ *or* **diph·the·ri·an** \-ē-ən\ *adj* — **diph·the·rit·ic** \ˌdif-thə-ˈrit-ik, ˌdip-\ *adj*

¹diph·the·roid \ˈdif-thə-ˌrȯid\ *adj* : resembling diphtheria

²diphtheroid *n* : a bacterium that resembles the bacterium of diphtheria but does not produce diphtheria toxin

diph·thong \ˈdif-ˌthȯŋ, ˈdip-\ *n* [ME *diptonge*, fr. MF *diptongue*, fr. LL *dipthongus*, fr. Gk *diphthongos*, fr. *di-* + *phthongos* voice, sound] **1** : a gliding monosyllabic speech sound (as the vowel combination that forms the last part of *toy*) that starts at or near the articulatory position for one vowel and moves to or toward the position of another **2** : DIGRAPH **3** : a form of the ligature æ or œ — **diph·thon·gal** \dif-ˈthȯŋ-(g)əl, dip-\ *adj*

diph·thong·iza·tion \(ˌ)dif-ˌthȯŋ-ə-ˈzā-shən, (ˌ)dip-\ *n* : the act of diphthongizing : the state of being diphthongized

diph·thong·ize \ˈdif-ˌthȯŋ-ˌīz, ˈdip-\ *vb* **-ized; -iz·ing** *vi, of a simple vowel* : to change into a diphthong ~ *vt* : to pronounce as a diphthong

diphy- *or* **diphyo-** *comb form* [NL, fr. Gk *diphy-*, fr. *diphyēs*, fr. *di-* + *phyein* to bring forth — more at BE] : double : bipartite ⟨*diphy*odont⟩

diphy·cer·cal \ˌdif-i-ˈsər-kəl\ *adj* [*diphy-* + *-cercal*] **1** *of a tail fin* : having the upper and lower portions alike or nearly so and the vertebral column extending to the tip **2** : having a diphycercal tail fin — **diphy·cer·cy** \ˈdif-i-ˌsər-sē, -ˌsər-kē\ *n*

di·phy·let·ic \ˌdī-fī-ˈlet-ik\ *adj* [*di-* + *phyletic*] : derived from two lines of evolutionary descent ⟨~ dinosaurs⟩

di·phyl·lous \(ˈ)dī-ˈfil-əs\ *adj* [NL *diphyllus*, fr. *di-* + *-phyllus* -phyllous] : having two leaves

di·phy·odont \(ˈ)dī-ˈfī-ə-ˌdänt\ *adj* [ISV] : marked by the successive development of deciduous and permanent sets of teeth

dipl- *or* **diplo-** *comb form* [Gk, fr. *diploos* — more at DOUBLE] **1** : double : twofold ⟨*dipl*opia⟩ **2** : diploid ⟨*diplo*phase⟩

di·ple·gia \dī-ˈplē-j(ē-)ə\ *n* [NL] : paralysis of corresponding parts on both sides of the body

di·plex \ˈdī-ˌpleks\ *adj* [alter. of *duplex*] : relating to or being simultaneous transmission or reception of two radio signals

dip·lo·ba·cil·lus \ˌdip-lō-bə-ˈsil-əs\ *n* [NL] : any of various small aerobic gram-negative bacilli parasitic on mucous membranes

dip·lo·blas·tic \-ˈblas-tik\ *adj* : having two germ layers — used of an embryo or lower invertebrate that lacks a true mesoderm

dip·lo·coc·cus \-ˈkäk-əs\ *n* [NL, genus name] : any of a genus (*Diplococcus*) of gram-positive encapsulated bacteria that occur usu. in pairs, are parasitic, and include serious pathogens — **dip·lo·coc·cal** \-ˈkäk-əl\ *or* **dip·lo·coc·cic** \-ˈkäk-(s)ik\ *adj*

di·plod·o·cus \də-ˈpläd-ə-kəs, dī-\ *n* [NL, genus name, fr. *dipl-* + Gk *dokos* beam, fr. *dekesthai, dechesthai* to receive; akin to L *decēre* to be fitting — more at DECENT] : any of a genus (*Diplodocus*) of very large herbivorous dinosaurs from Colorado and Wyoming

dip·loe \ˈdip-lə-ˌwē\ *n* [NL, fr. Gk *diploē*, fr. *diploos* double] : cancellous bony tissue between the external and internal layers of the skull — **di·plo·ic** \də-ˈplō-ik, dī-\ *adj*

¹dip·loid \ˈdip-ˌlȯid\ *adj* : having the basic chromosome number doubled — **dip·loi·dy** \-ˌlȯid-ē\ *n*

²diploid *n* **1** : a diploid cell **2** : an individual or generation characterized by the diploid chromosome number

di·plo·ma \də-ˈplō-mə\ *n, pl* **diplomas** [L, passport, diploma, fr. Gk *diplōma* folded paper, passport, fr. *diploun* to double, fr. *diploos*] **1** *pl also* **di·plo·ma·ta** \-mət-ə\ : an official or state document : CHARTER **2** : a writing usu. under seal conferring some honor or privilege **3** : a document bearing record of graduation from or of a degree conferred by an educational institution

di·plo·ma·cy \də-ˈplō-mə-sē\ *n* **1** : the art and practice of conducting negotiations between nations **2** : skill in handling affairs without arousing hostility : TACT

diploma mill *n* **1** : an institution of higher education operating without supervision of a state or professional agency and granting diplomas without the usual required courses and attendance **2** : an institution of higher education whose academic demands are minimal

dip·lo·mat \ˈdip-lə-ˌmat\ *n* [F *diplomate*, back-formation fr. *diplomatique*] : one employed or skilled in diplomacy

dip·lo·mate \ˈdip-lə-ˌmāt\ *n* [*diploma* + ¹*-ate*] : one who holds a diploma; *esp* : a physician qualified to practice in a medical specialty by advanced training and experience in the specialty followed by passing an intensive examination by a national board of senior specialists

dip·lo·mat·ic \ˌdip-lə-ˈmat-ik\ *adj* [in sense 1, fr. NL *diplomaticus*, fr. L *diplomat-, diploma;* in other senses, fr. F *diplomatique* connected with documents regulating international relations, fr. NL *diplomaticus*] **1 a** : PALEOGRAPHIC **b** : exactly reproducing the original ⟨a ~ edition⟩ **2 a** : concerned with or skilled in international relations **b** : of or relating to those conducting international relations ⟨~ immunity⟩ **3** : employing tact and conciliation esp. in situations of stress **syn** see SUAVE — **dip·lo·mat·i·cal·ly** \-i-k(ə-)lē\ *adv*

di·plo·ma·tist \də-ˈplō-mət-əst\ *n* : DIPLOMAT

dip·lont \ˈdip-ˌlänt\ *n* [ISV] : an organism with somatic cells having the diploid chromosome number — compare HAPLONT — **dip·lon·tic** \dip-ˈlänt-ik\ *adj*

dip·lo·phase \ˈdip-lə-ˌfāz\ *n* : a diploid phase in a life cycle

dip·lo·pia \dip-ˈlō-pē-ə\ *n* [NL] : a disorder of vision in which two images of a single object are seen because of unequal action of the eye muscles — **dip·lo·pic** \-ˈlō-pik, -ˈläp-ik\ *adj*

dip·lo·pod \ˈdip-lə-ˌpäd\ *n* [deriv. of Gk *dipl-* + *pod-, pous* foot — more at FOOT] : MILLIPEDE — **dip·lop·o·dous** \dip-ˈläp-əd-əs\ *adj*

dip·lo·sis \dip-ˈlō-səs\ *n* [NL, fr. Gk *diplōsis* action of doubling, fr. *diploun*] : restoration of the somatic chromosome number by fusion of two gametes in fertilization

dip·lo·tene \ˈdip-lə-ˌtēn\ *n* [ISV] : a stage of meiotic prophase which follows the pachytene and during which the paired homologous chromosomes begin to separate and chiasmata become visible — **diplotene** *adj*

dip net *n* : a small bag net with a handle that is used esp. to scoop small fish from the water

dip·no·an \ˈdip-nə-wən\ *adj* [deriv. of Gk *dipnoos*, fr. *di-* + *pnoē* breath, fr. *pnein* to breathe — more at SNEEZE] : of or relating to a group (Dipnoi) of fishes with pulmonary circulation, gills, and lungs — **dipnoan** *n*

dip·o·dy \ˈdip-əd-ē\ *n, pl* **-dies** [LL *dipodia*, fr. Gk, fr. *dipod-, dipous* having two feet, fr. *di-* + *pod-, pous*] : a prosodic unit or measure of two feet — **di·pod·ic** \dī-ˈpäd-ik\ *adj*

di·po·lar \ˈdī-ˌpō-lər, -ˈpō-\ *adj* : of, relating to, or having a dipole

di·pole \ˈdī-ˌpōl\ *n* [ISV] **1 a** : a pair of equal and opposite electric charges or magnetic poles of opposite sign separated by a small distance **b** : a body or system (as a molecule) having such charges **2** : a radio antenna consisting of two horizontal rods in line with each other with their ends slightly separated

dip·per \ˈdip-ər\ *n* **1** : one that dips: as **a** : a worker who dips articles **b** : something (as a long-handled cup) used for dipping **2** *cap* **a** : the seven principal stars in the constellation of Ursa Major arranged in a form resembling a dipper — called also *Big Dipper* **b** : the seven principal stars in Ursa Minor similarly arranged with the North Star forming the outer end of the handle — called also *Little Dipper* **3** : any of several birds (as a bufflehead or water ouzel) skilled in diving — **dip·per·ful** \-ˌfu̇l\ *n*

di·pro·pel·lant \ˌdī-prə-ˈpel-ənt\ *n* : BIPROPELLANT

dip·so·ma·nia \ˌdip-sə-ˈmā-nē-ə, -nyə\ *n* [NL, fr. Gk *dipsa* thirst + LL *mania*] : an uncontrollable craving for alcoholic liquors — **dip·so·ma·ni·ac** \-nē-ˌak\ *n* — **dip·so·ma·ni·a·cal** \ˌdip-sō-mə-ˈnī-ə-kəl\ *adj*

dip·stick \ˈdip-ˌstik\ *n* : a graduated rod for indicating depth (as of oil in a crankcase)

dip·ter·an \ˈdip-tə-rən\ *adj* [deriv. of Gk *dipteros*] : of, relating to, or being a two-winged fly — **dipteran** *n*

dip·tero·carp \ˈdip-tə-rō-ˌkärp\ *n* [NL *Dipterocarpaceae*, group name, fr. *Dipterocarpus*, genus name, fr. *dipterus* dipterous + *-carpus* -carpous] : any of a family (Dipterocarpaceae) of tall trees of tropical Asia, Indonesia, and the Philippines that have a 2-winged fruit and are the source of valuable timber, aromatic oils, and resins; *esp* : a member of the type genus (*Dipterocarpus*)

dip·ter·on \ˈdip-tə-ˌrän\ *n, pl* **-tera** \-rə\ [Gk, neut. of *dipteros*] : TWO-WINGED FLY

dip·ter·ous \ˈdip-tə-rəs\ *adj* [NL *dipterus*, fr. Gk *dipteros*, fr. *di-* + *pteron* wing — more at FEATHER] **1** : having two wings or winglike appendages **2** : of or relating to the two-winged flies

dip·tych \ˈdip-(ˌ)tik\ *n* [LL *diptycha*, pl., fr. Gk, fr. neut. pl. of *diptychos* folded in two, fr. *di-* + *ptychē* fold] **1** : a 2-leaved hinged tablet folding together to protect writing on its waxed surfaces **2** : a picture or series of pictures (as an altarpiece) painted or carved on two hinged tablets **3** : a work made up of two matching parts

diptych 2

di·quat \ˈdī-ˌkwät\ *n* [*di-* + *quat*ernary] : a powerful nonpersistent herbicide $C_{12}H_{12}Br_2N_2$ that has been used to control water weeds (as the water hyacinth)

dir *abbr* director

dir·dum \ˈdi(ə)rd-əm, ˈdərd-\ *n* [ME (northern dial.) *durdan*, fr. ScGael, grumbling, hum, dim. of *durd* hum] *Scot* : BLAME

dire \ˈdī(ə)r\ *adj* **dir·er; dir·est** [L *dirus*; akin to Gk *deinos* terrible, Skt *dvesti* he hates] **1 a** : exciting horror ⟨~ suffering⟩ **b** : DISMAL, OPPRESSIVE ⟨~ days⟩ **2** : warning of disaster ⟨a ~ forecast⟩ **3 a** : desperately urgent ⟨~ need⟩ **b** : EXTREME ⟨~ poverty⟩ — **dire·ly** *adv* — **dire·ness** *n*

¹di·rect \də-ˈrekt, dī-\ *vb* [ME *directen*, fr. L *directus*, pp. of *dirigere* to set straight, direct — more at DRESS] *vt* **1 a** *obs* : to write (a letter) to a person **b** : to mark with the name and address of the intended recipient **c** : to impart orally **d** : to adapt in expression so as to have particular applicability ⟨a lawyer who ~*s* his appeals to intelligence and character⟩ **2** : to cause to turn, move, or point undeviatingly or to follow a straight course ⟨X rays are ~*ed* through the body⟩ **3** : to point, extend, or project in a specified line or course **4** : to show or point out the way for **5 a** : to regulate the activities or course of **b** : to carry out the organizing, energizing, and supervising of **c** : to dominate and determine the course of **d** : to train and lead performances of **6** : to request or enjoin with authority ~ *vi* **1** : to point out, prescribe, or determine a course or procedure **2** : to act as director **syn** see CONDUCT, COMMAND

²direct *adj* [ME, fr. L *directus*, fr. pp. of *dirigere*] **1 a** : proceeding from one point to another in time or space without deviation or interruption : STRAIGHT **b** : proceeding by the shortest way ⟨the ~ route⟩ **2 a** : stemming immediately from a source ⟨~ result⟩ **b** : being or passing in a straight line or descent from parent to offspring : LINEAL ⟨~ ancestor⟩ **c** : having no compromising or impairing element ⟨~ insult⟩ **3** : characterized by close logical, causal, or consequential relationship ⟨~ evidence⟩ **4** : NATURAL, STRAIGHTFORWARD ⟨~ manner⟩ **5 a** : marked by absence of an intervening agency, instrumentality, or influence **b** : effected by the action of the people or the electorate and not by representatives **c** : consisting of or reproducing the exact words of a speaker or writer **6** : capable of dyeing without the aid of a mordant : SUBSTANTIVE **7** *of a celestial body* : moving in the general planetary direction from west to east : not retrograde — **di·rect·ness** \-ˈrek(t)-nəs\ *n*

³direct *adv* : in a direct way: as **a** : from point to point without deviation : by the shortest way ⟨suggesting I write to her ~ —John Willett⟩ **b** : from the source without interruption or diversion ⟨the writer must take his material ~ from life —Douglas Stewart⟩ **c** : without an intervening agency or step ⟨those who did go ~ to the people . . . rallied a considerable majority of the voters —H. S. Ashmore⟩

direct action *n* : action that seeks to achieve an end directly and by the most immediately effective means (as boycott or strike)

direct current *n* : an electric current flowing in one direction only and substantially constant in value — abbr. *DC*

di·rect·ed *adj* **1** : having a positive or negative sense ⟨~ line segment⟩ **2** : subject to supervision or regulation ⟨a ~ reading program for students⟩

di·rec·tion \də-ˈrek-shən, dī-\ *n* **1** : guidance or supervision of action or conduct : MANAGEMENT **2 a** : the art and technique of directing an orchestra or theatrical production **b** : a word, phrase, or sign indicating the appropriate tempo, mood, or intensity of a passage or movement in music **3** *archaic* : SUPERSCRIPTION **4 a** : something imposed as authoritative instruction or bidding : ORDER **b** : an explicit instruction **5** : the line or course on which something is moving or is aimed to move or along which something is pointing or facing **6 a** : a channel or direct course of thought or action **b** : TENDENCY, TREND **c** : a guiding, governing, or motivating purpose **7** *archaic* : DIRECTORATE 1 — **di·rec·tion·less** \-ləs\ *adj*

di·rec·tion·al \-shnəl, -shən-ᵊl\ *adj* **1** : of, relating to, or indicating direction in space: **a** : suitable for detecting the direction from which radio signals come or for sending out radio signals in one direction only **b** : operating most effectively in a particular direction **2** : relating to direction or guidance esp. of thought or effort — **di·rec·tion·al·i·ty** \-ˌrek-shə-ˈnal-ət-ē\ *n*

direction angle *n* : an angle made by a given line with an axis of reference; *specif* : one of these angles made by a straight line with the three axes of a rectangular Cartesian coordinate system — usu. used in pl.

direction cosine *n* : one of the cosines of the three angles between a directed line in space and the positive direction of the axes of a rectangular Cartesian coordinate system — usu. used in pl.

direction finder *n* : a radio receiving device for determining the direction of incoming radio waves that typically consists of a coil antenna rotating freely on a vertical axis

¹di·rec·tive \də-ˈrek-tiv, dī-\ *adj* **1** : serving or intended to guide, govern, or influence **2** : serving to point direction; *specif* : DIRECTIONAL 1b **3** : of or relating to psychotherapy or counseling in which the counselor introduces information, content, or attitudes not previously expressed by the client

²directive *n* : something that serves to direct, guide, and usu. impel toward an action or goal; *esp* : an authoritative instrument issued by a high-level body or official

di·rec·tiv·i·ty \də-ˌrek-ˈtiv-ət-ē, (ˌ)dī-\ *n* : the property of being directional

direct lighting *n* : lighting in which the greater part of the light goes directly from the source to the area lit

¹di·rect·ly \də-ˈrek-(t)lē, dī-, *in sense 2* də-ˈrek-lē *or* ˈdrek-lē\ *adv* **1** : in a direct manner ⟨~ relevant⟩ ⟨the road runs ~ east and west⟩ **2 a** : without delay : IMMEDIATELY **b** : in a little while : SHORTLY **syn** see PRESENTLY

²di·rect·ly \də-ˈrek-(t)lē, dī-; ˈdrek-lē\ *conj, chiefly Brit* : immediately after : as soon as ⟨~ I received it I rang up the shipping company —F. W. Crofts⟩

di·rect·ness \də-ˈrek(t)-nəs, dī-\ *n* **1** : the character of being accurate in course or aim **2** : strict pertinence : STRAIGHTFORWARDNESS

direct object *n* : a grammatical object representing the primary goal or the result of the action of a verb ⟨*me* in "he hit me" and *house* in "we built a house" are *direct objects*⟩

di·rec·tor \də-ˈrek-tər, dī-\ *n* : one that directs: as **a** : the head of an organized group or administrative unit (as a bureau or school) **b** : one of a group of persons entrusted with the overall direction of a corporate enterprise **c** : one that supervises the production of a show (as for stage or screen) with responsibility for action, lighting, music, and rehearsals **d** : CONDUCTOR c — **di·rec·tor·ship** \-ˌship\ *n*

di·rec·tor·ate \də-ˈrek-t(ə-)rət, dī-\ *n* **1** : the office of director **2 a** : a board of directors (as of a corporation) **b** : membership on a board of directors **3** : an executive staff (as of a program, bureau, or department)

di·rec·to·ri·al \də-ˌrek-ˈtōr-ē-əl, (ˌ)dī-, -ˈtȯr-\ *adj* **1** : serving to direct **2** : of or relating to a director or to theatrical direction **3** : of, relating to, or administered by a directory

director's chair *n* [fr. its use by motion picture directors on the set] : a lightweight folding armchair with a back and seat usu. of cotton duck

¹di·rec·to·ry \də-ˈrek-t(ə-)rē, dī-\ *adj* : serving to direct; *specif* : providing advisory but not compulsory guidance

²directory *n, pl* **-ries** [ML *directorium*, fr. neut. of LL *directorius* directorial, fr. L *directus*, pp.] **1 a** : a book or collection of directions, rules, or ordinances **b** : an alphabetical or classified list (as of names and addresses) **2** : a body of directors

direct primary *n* : a primary in which nominations of candidates for office are made by direct vote

di·rec·tress \də-ˈrek-trəs, dī-\ *n* : a female director

di·rec·trix \-triks\ *n, pl* **-trix·es** \-trik-səz\ *also* **-tri·ces** \-trə-ˌsēz\ [ML, fem. of LL *director*, fr. L *directus*, pp.] **1** *archaic* : DIRECTRESS **2** : a fixed curve with which a generatrix maintains a given relationship in generating a geometric figure; *specif* : a straight line the distance to which from any point of a conic section is in fixed ratio to the distance from the same point to a focus

direct tax *n* : a tax exacted directly from the person on whom the ultimate burden of the tax is expected to fall

dire·ful \ˈdī(ə)r-fəl\ *adj* **1** : DREADFUL **2** : OMINOUS — **dire·ful·ly** \-fə-lē\ *adv*

dire wolf *n* : a large lupine mammal (*Canis dirus* or *Aenocyon dirus*) found in Pleistocene deposits of No. America

dirge \ˈdərj\ *n* [ME *dirige*, the Office of the Dead, fr. the first word of a LL antiphon, fr. L, imper. of *dirigere*] **1** : a song or hymn of grief or lamentation; *esp* : one intended to accompany funeral or memorial rites **2** : a slow, solemn, and mournful piece of music

dir·ham \də-ˈram\ *n* [Ar, fr. L *drachma* drachma] **1** — see MONEY table **2** — see *dinar* at MONEY table

¹di·ri·gi·ble \ˈdir-ə-jə-bəl, də-ˈrij-ə-\ *adj* [L *dirigere*] : capable of being steered

²dirigible *n* [*dirigible (balloon)*] : AIRSHIP

¹dirk \ˈdərk\ *n* [Sc *durk*] : a long straight-bladed dagger

²dirk *vt* : to stab with a dirk

dirl \ˈdir(ə)l, ˈdərl\ *vi* [prob. alter. of *thirl*] *Scot* : TREMBLE, QUIVER

dirndl \ˈdərn-dᵊl\ *n* [short for G *dirndlkleid*, fr. G dial. *dirndl* girl + G *kleid* dress] **1** : a dress style with tight bodice, short sleeves, low neck, and gathered skirt **2** : a full skirt with a tight waistband

dirt \ˈdərt\ *n* [ME *drit*, fr. ON; akin to OE *drītan* to defecate, L *foria* diarrhea] **1 a** : EXCREMENT **b** : a filthy or soiling substance (as mud, dust, or grime) **c** *archaic* : something worthless **d** : a contemptible person **2 a** : loose or packed soil or sand : EARTH **b** (1) : alluvial earth in placer mining (2) : slate and waste in coal mines **3 a** : an abject or filthy state : SQUALOR **b** : CORRUPTION, CHICANERY **c** : licentiousness of language or theme **d** : scandalous or malicious gossip

dirt farmer *n* : a farmer who earns his living by farming his own land; *esp* : one who farms without the help of hired hands or tenants
dirt road *n* : an unpaved road
[1]**dirty** \ˈdərt-ē\ *adj* **dirt·i·er; -est** **1** **a** : not clean or pure ⟨~ clothes⟩ **b** : likely to befoul or defile with dirt ⟨~ jobs⟩ **c** : tedious, disagreeable, and unrecognized or thankless ⟨undertook the ~ tasks that no one else wanted to bother with⟩ **d** : contaminated with infecting organisms ⟨~ wounds⟩ **2** **a** : BASE, SORDID ⟨war is a ~ business⟩ **b** : UNSPORTSMANLIKE ⟨a ~ trick⟩ ⟨~ players⟩ **c** : highly regrettable : GRIEVOUS ⟨a ~ shame⟩ **3** : INDECENT, SMUTTY ⟨~ language⟩ **4** : FOGGY, STORMY **5** **a** *of color* : not clear and bright : DULLISH ⟨drab *dirty*-pink walls⟩ **b** : characterized by a husky, rasping, or raw tonal quality — used esp. of jazz **6** : conveying ill-natured resentment ⟨gave him a ~ look⟩ **7** : having considerable fallout ⟨~ bombs⟩ — **dirt·i·ly** \ˈdərt-ᵊl-ē\ *adv* — **dirt·i·ness** \ˈdərt-ē-nəs\ *n*
syn DIRTY, FILTHY, FOUL, NASTY, SQUALID *shared meaning element* : conspicuously unclean or impure. DIRTY emphasizes the fact of the presence of dirt more than an emotional reaction to it ⟨children *dirty* from play⟩ ⟨a *dirty* littered street⟩ FILTHY carries a strong suggestion of offensiveness and typically of gradually accumulated dirt that begrimes and besmears ⟨a stained greasy floor, utterly *filthy*⟩ FOUL implies extreme offensiveness and an accumulation of what is rotten or stinking ⟨the *foul* oil-and-garbage whiffs from the river —Herman Wouk⟩ NASTY applies to what is actually foul or is repugnant to one used to or expecting freshness, cleanliness, or sweetness ⟨it's a *nasty* job to clean up after a sick cat⟩ In practice, *nasty* is often weakened to the point of being no more than a synonym of *unpleasant* or *disagreeable* ⟨had a *nasty* fall⟩ ⟨his answer gave her a *nasty* shock⟩ SQUALID adds to the idea of dirtiness and filth that of slovenly neglect ⟨living in *squalid* poverty⟩ ⟨*squalid* slums⟩
All these terms are applicable to moral uncleanness or baseness or obscenity. DIRTY then stresses meanness or despicableness ⟨the creature's at his *dirty* work again —Alexander Pope⟩ while FILTHY and FOUL describe disgusting obscenity or loathsome behavior ⟨*filthy* language⟩ ⟨a *foul* story⟩ and NASTY implies a peculiarly offensive unpleasantness ⟨a cheap and *nasty* imitation of the real thing —Robert Wilkes⟩ Distinctively, SQUALID implies sordidness as well as baseness and dirtiness ⟨her life was a series of *squalid* affairs⟩ ***ant*** clean
[2]**dirty** *vb* **dirt·ied; dirty·ing** *vt* **1** : to make dirty **2** **a** : to stain with dishonor : SULLY **b** : to debase by distorting the real nature of ~ *vi* : to become soiled
dirty linen *n* : private matters whose public exposure brings distress and embarrassment
dirty old man *n* : a lecherous mature man
dirty pool *n* : underhanded or unsportsmanlike conduct
dirty word *n* : a word or expression that is inappropriate, opprobrious, or derogatory in a particular frame of reference
dirty work *n* : behavior or an act that is mean, treacherous, or unfair ⟨the *dirty work* in general elections is often pale by contrast with the primaries —B. L. Felknor⟩
dis *abbr* **1** discharge **2** discount **3** distance
Dis \ˈdis\ *n* [L] : the Roman god of the underworld — compare PLUTO
dis- *prefix* [ME *dis-, des-*, fr. OF & L; OF *des-, dis-*, fr. L *dis-*, lit., apart; akin to OE *te-* apart, L *duo* two — more at TWO] **1** **a** : do the opposite of ⟨*dis*establish⟩ **b** : deprive of (a specified quality, rank, or object) ⟨*dis*able⟩ ⟨*dis*prince⟩ ⟨*dis*frock⟩ **c** : exclude or expel from ⟨*dis*bar⟩ **2** : opposite or absence of ⟨*dis*union⟩ ⟨*dis*affection⟩ **3** : not ⟨*dis*agreeable⟩ **4** : completely ⟨*dis*annul⟩ **5** [by folk etymology] : DYS- ⟨*dis*function⟩
dis·abil·i·ty \ˌdis-ə-ˈbil-ət-ē\ *n* **1** **a** : the condition of being disabled **b** : inability to pursue an occupation because of physical or mental impairment **2** **a** : lack of legal qualification to do something **b** : a nonlegal disqualification, restriction, or disadvantage
dis·able \dis-ˈā-bəl, diz-\ *vt* **dis·abled; dis·abling** \-b(ə-)liŋ\ **1** : to deprive of legal right, qualification, or capacity **2** : to make incapable or ineffective; *esp* : to deprive of physical, moral, or intellectual strength : CRIPPLE ***syn*** see WEAKEN ***ant*** rehabilitate — **dis·able·ment** \-bəl-mənt\ *n*
dis·abuse \ˌdis-ə-ˈbyüz\ *vt* [F *désabuser*, fr. *dés-* dis- + *abuser* to abuse] : to free from error or fallacy
di·sac·cha·ri·dase \(ˈ)dī-ˈsak-ə-rə-ˌdās, -ˌdāz\ *n* : an enzyme (as maltase or lactase) that hydrolyzes disaccharides
di·sac·cha·ride \(ˈ)dī-ˈsak-ə-ˌrīd\ *n* : any of a class of sugars (as sucrose) that yields on hydrolysis two monosaccharide molecules
[1]**dis·ac·cord** \ˌdis-ə-ˈkȯ(ə)rd\ *vi* [ME *disacorden*, fr. MF *desacorder*, fr. *desacort* disagreement, fr. *des-* dis- + *acort* accord] : CLASH, DISAGREE
[2]**disaccord** *n* : lack of harmony : DISAGREEMENT
dis·ac·cus·tom \ˌdis-ə-ˈkəs-təm\ *vt* [MF *desaccoustumer*, fr. OF *desacostumer*, fr. *des-* + *acostumer* to accustom] : to free from a habit
[1]**dis·ad·van·tage** \ˌdis-əd-ˈvant-ij\ *n* [ME *disavauntage*, fr. MF *desavantage*, fr. OF, fr. *des-* + *avantage* advantage] **1** : loss or damage esp. to reputation, credit, or finances : DETRIMENT **2** **a** : an unfavorable, inferior, or prejudicial condition ⟨we were at a ~⟩ **b** : HANDICAP ⟨it put us under a serious ~⟩
[2]**disadvantage** *vt* : to place at a disadvantage : HARM
[1]**dis·ad·van·taged** *adj* : lacking in the basic resources or conditions (as standard housing, medical and educational facilities, and civil rights) believed to be necessary for an equal position in society — **dis·ad·van·taged·ness** \-ij(d)-nəs\ *n*
[2]**disadvantaged** *n, pl* **disadvantaged** : one that is deprived and underprivileged (as in cultural, economic, and social matters)
dis·ad·van·ta·geous \(ˌ)dis-ˌad-ˌvan-ˈtā-jəs, -vən-\ *adj* **1** : constituting a disadvantage **2** : DEROGATORY, DISPARAGING — **dis·ad·van·ta·geous·ly** *adv* — **dis·ad·van·ta·geous·ness** *n*
dis·af·fect \ˌdis-ə-ˈfekt\ *vt* : to alienate the affection or loyalty of ***syn*** see ESTRANGE ***ant*** win (*as to a cause*) — **dis·af·fec·tion** \-ˈfek-shən\ *n*
dis·af·fect·ed *adj* : discontented and resentful esp. against authority : REBELLIOUS
dis·af·fil·i·ate \ˌdis-ə-ˈfil-ē-ˌāt\ *vt* : DISASSOCIATE ~ *vi* : to terminate an affiliation — **dis·af·fil·i·a·tion** \-ˌfil-ē-ˈā-shən\ *n*
dis·af·firm \ˌdis-ə-ˈfərm\ *vt* **1** : CONTRADICT **2** : to refuse to confirm : ANNUL, REPUDIATE — **dis·af·fir·mance** \-ˈfər-mən(t)s\ *n* — **dis·af·fir·ma·tion** \(ˌ)dis-ˌaf-ər-ˈmā-shən\ *n*
dis·ag·gre·gate \(ˈ)dis-ˈag-ri-ˌgāt\ *vt* : to separate into component parts ⟨~ sandstone⟩ ⟨~ demographic data⟩ ~ *vi* : to break up or apart ⟨the molecules of a gel ~ to form a sol⟩ — **dis·ag·gre·ga·tion** \(ˌ)dis-ˌag-ri-ˈgā-shən\ *n* — **dis·ag·gre·ga·tive** \(ˈ)dis-ˈag-ri-ˌgāt-iv\ *adj*
dis·agree \ˌdis-ə-ˈgrē\ *vi* [ME *disagreen*, fr. MF *desagreer*, fr. *des-* + *agreer* to agree] **1** : to fail to agree ⟨the two accounts ~⟩ **2** : to differ in opinion ⟨he *disagreed* with me on every topic⟩ **3** : to be unsuitable ⟨fried foods ~ with me⟩
dis·agree·able \-ə-bəl\ *adj* **1** : causing discomfort : UNPLEASANT, OFFENSIVE **2** : marked by ill temper : PEEVISH — **dis·agree·abil·i·ty** \-ˌgrē-ə-ˈbil-ət-ē\ *n* — **dis·agree·able·ness** *n* — **dis·agree·ably** \-blē\ *adv*
dis·agree·ment \ˌdis-ə-ˈgrē-mənt\ *n* **1** : the act of disagreeing **2** **a** : the state of being at variance : DISPARITY **b** : QUARREL
dis·al·low \ˌdis-ə-ˈlau̇\ *vt* **1** : to deny the force, truth, or validity of **2** : to refuse to allow — **dis·al·low·ance** \-ən(t)s\ *n*
dis·am·big·u·ate \ˌdis-am-ˈbig-yə-ˌwāt\ *vt* **-ated; -at·ing** : to establish a single semantic or grammatical interpretation for — **dis·am·big·u·a·tion** \-ˌbig-yə-ˈwā-shən\ *n*
dis·an·nul \ˌdis-ə-ˈnəl\ *vt* : ANNUL, CANCEL
dis·ap·pear \ˌdis-ə-ˈpi(ə)r\ *vi* **1** : to pass from view suddenly or gradually **2** : to cease to be — **dis·ap·pear·ance** \-ˈpir-ən(t)s\ *n*
dis·ap·point \ˌdis-ə-ˈpȯint\ *vb* [MF *desapointier*, fr. *des-* dis- + *apointier* to arrange — more at APPOINT] *vt* : to fail to meet the expectation or hope of : FRUSTRATE ~ *vi* : to cause disappointment ⟨where the show ~*s* most is in the work of the younger generation —John Ashbery⟩
dis·ap·point·ed *adj* **1** : defeated in expectation or hope : THWARTED **2** *obs* : not adequately equipped — **dis·ap·point·ed·ly** *adv*
dis·ap·point·ing *adj* : failing to meet expectations — **dis·ap·point·ing·ly** \-iŋ-lē\ *adv*
dis·ap·point·ment \ˌdis-ə-ˈpȯint-mənt\ *n* **1** : the act or an instance of disappointing : the state or emotion of being disappointed **2** : one that disappoints
dis·ap·pro·ba·tion \(ˌ)dis-ˌap-rə-ˈbā-shən\ *n* : the act or state of disapproving : the state of being disapproved : CONDEMNATION
dis·ap·prov·al \ˌdis-ə-ˈprü-vəl\ *n* : DISAPPROBATION, CENSURE
dis·ap·prove \-ˈprüv\ *vt* **1** : to pass unfavorable judgment on : CONDEMN **2** : to refuse approval to : REJECT ~ *vi* : to feel or express disapproval — **dis·ap·prov·er** *n* — **dis·ap·prov·ing·ly** \-ˈprü-viŋ-lē\ *adv*
syn DISAPPROVE, DEPRECATE *shared meaning element* : to feel or express an objection ***ant*** approve
dis·arm \(ˈ)dis-ˈärm, diz-\ *vb* [ME *desarmen*, fr. MF *desarmer*, fr. OF, fr. *des-* + *armer* to arm] *vt* **1** **a** : to divest of arms **b** : to deprive of a means of attack or defense **c** : to make harmless **2** **a** : to deprive of means, reason, or disposition to be hostile **b** : to win over ~ *vi* **1** : to lay aside arms **2** : to give up or reduce armed forces — **dis·ar·ma·ment** \-ˈär-mə-mənt\ *n* — **dis·arm·er** *n*
dis·arm·ing *adj* : allaying criticism or hostility : INGRATIATING — **dis·arm·ing·ly** \-ˈär-miŋ-lē\ *adv*
dis·ar·range \ˌdis-ə-ˈrānj\ *vt* : to disturb the arrangement or order of — **dis·ar·range·ment** \-mənt\ *n*
[1]**dis·ar·ray** \ˌdis-ə-ˈrā\ *n* **1** : a lack of order or sequence : CONFUSION, DISORDER **2** : disorderly dress : DISHABILLE
[2]**disarray** *vt* [ME *disarayen*, fr. MF *desarroyer*, fr. OF *desareer*, fr. *des-* + *areer* to array] **1** : to throw into disorder **2** : UNDRESS
dis·ar·tic·u·late \ˌdis-är-ˈtik-yə-ˌlāt\ *vi* : to become disjointed ~ *vt* : DISJOINT — **dis·ar·tic·u·la·tion** \-ˌtik-yə-ˈlā-shən\ *n*
dis·as·sem·ble \ˌdis-ə-ˈsem-bəl\ *vt* : to take apart ⟨~ a watch⟩ ~ *vi* **1** : to come apart ⟨the automobile parts ~ into sections⟩ **2** : DISPERSE, SCATTER ⟨the crowd began to ~⟩ — **dis·as·sem·bla·ble** \-b(ə-)lə-bəl\ *adj* — **dis·as·sem·bly** \-blē\ *n*
dis·as·so·ci·ate \ˌdis-ə-ˈsō-s(h)ē-ˌāt\ *vt* : to detach from association : DISSOCIATE — **dis·as·so·ci·a·tion** \-ˌsō-sē-ˈā-shən, -shē-\ *n*
di·sas·ter \diz-ˈas-tər, dis-\ *n* [MF & OIt; MF *desastre*, fr. OIt *disastro*, fr. *dis-* (fr. L) + *astro* star, fr. L *astrum* — more at ASTRAL] **1** *obs* : an unfavorable aspect of a planet or star **2** : a sudden calamitous event bringing great damage, loss, or destruction; *broadly* : a sudden or great misfortune
syn DISASTER, CALAMITY, CATASTROPHE, CATACLYSM *shared meaning element* : an event or situation that is regarded as a terrible misfortune
disaster area *n* : an area officially declared to be the scene of an emergency created by a disaster and therefore qualified to receive certain types of governmental aid (as emergency loans and relief supplies)
di·sas·trous \diz-ˈas-trəs *also* dis-\ *adj* : attended by or causing suffering or disaster : CALAMITOUS — **di·sas·trous·ly** *adv*
dis·avow \ˌdis-ə-ˈvau̇\ *vt* [ME *desavowen*, fr. MF *desavouer*, fr. OF, fr. *des-* dis- + *avouer* to avow] **1** : to refuse to acknowledge : DISCLAIM **2** : to deny responsibility for : REPUDIATE — **dis·avow·able** \-ə-bəl\ *adj* — **dis·avow·al** \-ˈvau̇(-ə)l\ *n*
dis·band \dis-ˈband\ *vb* [MF *desbander*, fr. *des-* + *bande* band] *vt* : to break up the organization of : DISSOLVE ~ *vi* : to break up as an organization : DISPERSE — **dis·band·ment** \-ˈban(d)-mənt\ *n*

ə abut   ᵊ kitten   ər further   a back   ā bake   ä cot, cart
au̇ out   ch chin   e less   ē easy   g gift   i trip   ī life
j joke   ŋ sing   ō flow   ȯ flaw   ȯi coin   th thin   th this
ü loot   u̇ foot   y yet   yü few   yu̇ furious   zh vision

dis·bar \dis-ˈbär\ *vt* **:** to expel from the bar or the legal profession **:** deprive (an attorney) of legal status and privileges — **dis·bar·ment** \-mənt\ *n*

dis·be·lief \ˌdis-bə-ˈlēf\ *n* **:** the act of disbelieving **:** mental rejection of something as untrue ***syn*** see UNBELIEF ***ant*** belief

dis·be·lieve \-ˈlēv\ *vt* **:** to hold not to be true or real **~** *vi* **:** to withhold or reject belief ⟨~*s* in the sanctity of the status quo —W. C. Brownell⟩ — **dis·be·liev·er** *n*

dis·bound \dis-ˈbau̇nd\ *adj* **:** no longer having a binding ⟨a ~ pamphlet⟩

dis·branch \(ˌ)dis-ˈbranch\ *vt* [MF *desbrancher,* fr. *des-* + *branche* branch] **:** to tear off (as a branch)

dis·bud \(ˌ)dis-ˈbəd\ *vt* **1 :** to thin out flower buds in order to improve the quality of bloom of **2 :** to dehorn (cattle) by destroying the undeveloped horn bud

dis·bur·den \(ˌ)dis-ˈbərd-ᵊn\ *vt* **1 a :** to rid of a burden ⟨~ a pack animal⟩ **b :** UNBURDEN ⟨~ your conscience⟩ **2 :** UNLOAD ⟨~*ed* their merchandise in the town square⟩ **~** *vi* **:** DISCHARGE ⟨the vessels ~*ed* at the dock⟩ — **dis·bur·den·ment** \-mənt\ *n*

dis·burse \dis-ˈbərs\ *vt* **dis·bursed; dis·burs·ing** [MF *desbourser,* fr. OF *desborser,* fr. *des-* + *borser* to get money, fr. *borse* purse, fr. ML *bursa* — more at PURSE] **1 a :** to pay out **:** expend esp. from a fund **b :** to make a payment in settlement of **:** DEFRAY **2 :** DISTRIBUTE ⟨~ property by will⟩ — **dis·burs·er** *n*

dis·burse·ment \-ˈbər-smənt\ *n* **:** the act of disbursing; *also* **:** funds paid out

[1]**disc** *var of* DISK

[2]**disc** *abbr* discount

disc- *or* **disci-** *or* **disco-** *comb form* [L, fr. Gk *disk-, disko-,* fr. *diskos*] **1 :** disk ⟨*disc*igerous⟩ **2 :** phonograph record ⟨*disco*phile⟩

dis·calced \(ˌ)dis-ˈkalst\ *adj* [part trans. of L *discalceatus,* fr. *dis-* + *calceatus,* pp. of *calceare* to put on shoes, fr. *calceus* shoe, fr. *calc-, calx* heel — more at CALK] **:** UNSHOD, BAREFOOT ⟨~ friars⟩

dis·cant \ˈdis-ˌkant\ *var of* DESCANT

[1]**dis·card** \dis-ˈkärd, ˈdis-ˌ\ *vt* **1 a :** to remove (a playing card) from one's hand **b :** to play (any card except a trump) from a suit different from the one led **2 :** to get rid of as useless or unpleasant **~** *vi* **:** to discard a playing card — **dis·card·able** \-ə-bəl\ *adj* — **dis·card·er** *n*

syn DISCARD, CAST, SHED, SLOUGH, SCRAP, JUNK *shared meaning element* **:** to get rid of as of no further use, value, or service

[2]**dis·card** \ˈdis-ˌkärd\ *n* **1 a :** the act of discarding in a card game **b :** a card discarded **2 :** one that is cast off or rejected

disc brake *n* **:** a brake that operates by the friction of a caliper pressing against the sides of a rotating disc

dis·cern \dis-ˈərn, diz-\ *vb* [ME *discernen,* fr. MF *discerner,* fr. L *discernere* to separate, distinguish between, fr. *dis-* apart + *cernere* to sift — more at DIS-, CERTAIN] *vt* **1 a :** to detect with the eyes **b :** to detect with other senses than vision **2 :** to come to know or recognize mentally **3 :** to recognize or identify as separate and distinct **:** DISCRIMINATE **~** *vi* **:** to see or understand the difference — **dis·cern·er** *n* — **dis·cern·ible** *also* **dis·cern·able** \-ˈər-nə-bəl\ *adj* — **dis·cern·ibly** \-blē\ *adv*

dis·cern·ing *adj* **:** revealing insight and understanding **:** DISCRIMINATING ⟨a ~ critic⟩ — **dis·cern·ing·ly** \-ˈər-niŋ-lē\ *adv*

dis·cern·ment \dis-ˈərn-mənt, diz-\ *n* **1 :** an act of discerning **2 :** the quality of being able to grasp and comprehend what is obscure **:** skill in discerning

syn DISCERNMENT, DISCRIMINATION, PERCEPTION, PENETRATION, INSIGHT, ACUMEN *shared meaning element* **:** keen intellectual vision. DISCERNMENT stresses skill and accuracy (as in reading character or appreciating art) ⟨a man of great intelligence and *discernment*⟩ ⟨the *discernment* revealed in her novels⟩ DISCRIMINATION emphasizes a capacity for distinguishing and selecting the excellent, the appropriate, or the true ⟨nobody should reproach them for reading indiscriminately . . . only by so doing can they learn *discrimination —Times Lit. Supp.*⟩ PERCEPTION implies quick acute discernment and delicacy of feeling ⟨persecutors were ordinary, reasonably well-intentioned people lacking in keen *perception* —C. H. Sykes⟩ PENETRATION implies a searching mind that goes beyond the obvious or superficial ⟨analyzed the underlying causes of the discontent with great *penetration*⟩ INSIGHT emphasizes depth of discernment coupled with understanding sympathy ⟨the ecstasy of imaginative vision, the sudden *insight* into the nature of things —Edmund Wilson⟩ ACUMEN suggests consistent penetration accompanied by shrewd soundness of judgment ⟨it is clear and bold, reflecting astute scholarship and logical *acumen* —L. L. Gerson⟩

[1]**dis·charge** \dis(h)-ˈchärj, ˈdis(h)-ˌ\ *vb* [ME *dischargen,* fr. MF *descharger,* fr. LL *discarricare,* fr. L *dis-* + LL *carricare* to load — more at CHARGE] *vt* **1 :** to relieve of a charge, load, or burden: **a :** UNLOAD **b :** to release from an obligation **2 a :** to let go **:** clear out **b :** SHOOT ⟨~ an arrow⟩ **c :** to release from confinement, custody, or care ⟨~ a prisoner⟩ **d :** to give outlet or vent to **:** EMIT **3 a** (1) **:** to dismiss from employment (2) **:** to release from service or duty ⟨~ a soldier⟩ **b :** to get rid of (as a debt or obligation) by performing an appropriate action (as payment) **:** FULFILL **c :** to set aside **:** ANNUL **d :** to order (a legislative committee) to end consideration of a bill in order to bring it before the house for action **4 :** to bear and distribute (as the weight of a wall above an opening) **5 :** to bleach out or remove (color or dye) in dyeing and printing textiles **6 :** to cancel the record of the loan of (a library book) upon return **~** *vi* **1 :** to throw off or deliver a load, charge, or burden **2 a :** to go off **:** FIRE — used of a gun **b :** RUN ⟨some dyes ~⟩ **c :** to pour forth fluid or other contents ***syn*** see FREE, PERFORM — **dis·charge·able** \-ə-bəl\ *adj* — **dis·charg·ee** \(ˌ)dis(h)-ˌchär-ˈjē\ *n* — **dis·charg·er** \dis(h)-ˈchär-jər, ˈdis(h)-ˌ\ *n*

[2]**dis·charge** \ˈdis(h)-ˌchärj, dis(h)-ˈ\ *n* **1 a :** the act of relieving of something that oppresses **:** RELEASE **b :** something that discharges or releases; *esp* **:** a certification of release or payment **2 :** the state of being discharged or relieved **3 :** the act of discharging or unloading **4 :** legal release from confinement **5 :** a firing off **6 a :** a flowing or issuing out ⟨a ~ of spores⟩; *also* **:** a rate of flow **b :** something that is emitted ⟨a purulent ~⟩ **7 :** the act of removing an obligation or liability **8 a :** release or dismissal esp. from an office or employment **b :** complete separation from military service **9 a :** the equalization of a difference of electric potential between two points **b :** the conversion of the chemical energy of a battery into electrical energy

discharge lamp *n* **:** an electric lamp in which discharge of electricity between electrodes causes luminosity of the enclosed vapor or gas or in which the luminosity of the enclosed gas is enhanced by phosphors

discharge tube *n* **:** an electron tube which contains gas or vapor at low pressure and through which conduction takes place when a high voltage is applied

dis·ci·flo·ral \ˌdis-(k)i-ˈflōr-əl, -ˈflȯr-\ *adj* **:** having flowers with the receptacle enlarged into a conspicuous disc

dis·ci·form \ˈdis-(k)ə-ˌfȯrm\ *adj* **:** round or oval in shape

dis·ci·ple \dis-ˈī-pəl\ *n* [ME, fr. OE *discipul* & OF *desciple,* fr. LL and L; LL *discipulus* follower of Jesus Christ in his lifetime, fr. L, pupil] **1 :** one who accepts and assists in spreading the doctrines of another: as **a :** one of the twelve in the inner circle of Christ's followers according to the Gospel accounts **b :** a convinced adherent of a school or individual **2** *cap* **:** a member of the Disciples of Christ founded in the U.S. in 1809 that holds the Bible alone to be the rule of faith and practice, baptizes by immersion, and has a congregational polity ***syn*** see FOLLOWER — **dis·ci·ple·ship** \-ˌship\ *n*

dis·ci·plin·able \ˌdis-ə-ˈplin-ə-bəl; ˈdis-ə-plən-\ *adj* **1 :** DOCILE, TEACHABLE **2 :** subject to or deserving discipline ⟨a ~ offense⟩

dis·ci·pli·nar·i·an \ˌdis-ə-plə-ˈner-ē-ən\ *n* **:** one who disciplines or enforces order — **disciplinarian** *adj*

dis·ci·plin·ary \ˈdis-ə-plə-ˌner-ē, *esp Brit* ˌdis-ə-ˈplin-ə-rē\ *adj* **1 a :** of or relating to discipline **b :** designed to correct or punish breaches of discipline ⟨took ~ action⟩ **2 :** of or relating to a particular field of study — **dis·ci·plin·ar·i·ly** \ˌdis-ə-plə-ˈner-ə-lē\ *adv* — **dis·ci·plin·ar·i·ty** \-ˈnar-ət-ē\ *n*

[1]**dis·ci·pline** \ˈdis-ə-plən\ *n* [ME, fr. MF & L; MF, fr. L *disciplina* teaching, learning, fr. *discipulus* pupil] **1** *obs* **:** INSTRUCTION **2 :** a subject that is taught **:** a field of study **3 :** training that corrects, molds, or perfects the mental faculties or moral character **4 :** PUNISHMENT **5 a :** control gained by enforcing obedience or order **b :** orderly or prescribed conduct or pattern of behavior **c :** SELF-CONTROL **6 :** a rule or system of rules governing conduct or activity — **dis·ci·plin·al** \-plən-ᵊl\ *adj*

[2]**discipline** *vt* **-plined; plin·ing** **1 :** to punish or penalize for the sake of discipline **2 :** to train or develop by instruction and exercise esp. in self-control **3 a :** to bring (a group) under control ⟨~ troops⟩ **b :** to impose order upon ⟨the writer ~*s* and refines his style⟩ ***syn*** see TEACH, PUNISH — **dis·ci·plin·er** *n*

dis·ci·plined *adj* **:** marked by or possessing discipline ⟨a ~ mind⟩

disc jockey *n* **:** an announcer of a radio or TV show of popular recorded music who often intersperses comments not related to the music

dis·claim \dis-ˈklām\ *vb* [AF *disclaimer,* fr. *dis-* + *claimer* to claim, fr. OF *clamer*] *vi* **1 :** to make a disclaimer **2 a** *obs* **:** to disavow all part or share **b :** to utter denial **~** *vt* **1 :** to renounce a legal claim to **2 :** DENY, DISAVOW

dis·claim·er \-ˈklā-mər\ *n* [AF, fr. *disclaimer,* v.] **1 a :** a denial or disavowal of legal claim **:** relinquishment of or formal refusal to accept an interest or estate **b :** a writing that embodies a legal disclaimer **2 a :** DENIAL, DISAVOWAL **b :** REPUDIATION

dis·cla·ma·tion \ˌdis-klə-ˈmā-shən\ *n* **:** RENUNCIATION, DISAVOWAL

disc·like *var of* DISKLIKE

dis·cli·max \(ˌ)dis-ˈklī-ˌmaks\ *n* **:** a relatively stable ecological community often including kinds of organisms foreign to the region and displacing the climax because of disturbance esp. by man

[1]**dis·close** \dis-ˈklōz\ *vt* [ME *disclosen,* fr. MF *desclos-,* stem of *desclore* to disclose, fr. ML *disclaudere* to open, fr. L *dis-* + *claudere* to close — more at CLOSE] **1** *obs* **:** to open up **2 a :** to expose to view **b** *archaic* **:** HATCH **c :** to make known or public (something previously held close or secret) ⟨demands that politicians ~ the sources of their income⟩ ***syn*** see REVEAL — **dis·clos·er** *n*

[2]**disclose** *n, obs* **:** DISCLOSURE

dis·clo·sure \dis-ˈklō-zhər\ *n* **1 :** the act or an instance of disclosing **:** EXPOSURE **2 :** something disclosed **:** REVELATION

dis·co \ˈdis-(ˌ)kō\ *n, pl* **discos** **:** DISCOTHEQUE

disco- — see DISC-

dis·cog·ra·pher \dis-ˈkäg-rə-fər\ *n* **:** one that compiles discographies

dis·cog·ra·phy \-fē\ *n, pl* **-phies** [F *discographie,* fr. *disc-* + *-graphie* -graphy] **1 :** a descriptive list of phonograph records by category, composer, performer, or date of release **2 :** the history of recorded music — **dis·co·graph·i·cal** \ˌdis-kə-ˈgraf-i-kəl\ *also* **dis·co·graph·ic** \-ik\ *adj* — **dis·co·graph·i·cal·ly** \-i-k(ə-)lē\ *adv*

dis·coid \ˈdis-ˌkȯid\ *adj* [LL *discoides* quoit-shaped, fr. Gk *diskoeidēs,* fr. *diskos* disk] **1 :** resembling a disk or discus **:** being flat and circular **2 :** relating to or having a disk: as **a** *of a composite floret* **:** situated in the floral disk **b** *of a composite flower head* **:** having only tubular florets

dis·coi·dal \dis-ˈkȯid-ᵊl\ *adj* **:** of, resembling, or producing a disk: as **a** *of a gastropod shell* **:** having the whorls form a flat coil **b :** having the villi restricted to one or more disklike areas

dis·col·or \(ˌ)dis-ˈkəl-ər\ *vb* [ME *discolouren,* fr. MF *descolourer,* fr. LL *discolorari,* fr. L *discolor* of another color, fr. *dis-* + *color*] *vt* **:** to alter or change the hue or color of **~** *vi* **:** to change color **:** STAIN, FADE

dis·col·or·ation \(ˌ)dis-ˌkəl-ə-ˈrā-shən\ *n* **1 :** the act of discoloring **:** the state of being discolored **2 :** a discolored spot or formation **:** STAIN

dis·com·bob·u·late \ˌdis-kəm-ˈbäb-(y)ə-ˌlāt\ *vt* **-lat·ed; -lat·ing** [prob. alter. of *discompose*] **:** UPSET, CONFUSE ⟨the offensive had *discombobulated* all the German defensive arrangements —A. J. Liebling⟩ — **dis·com·bob·u·la·tion** \-ˌbäb-(y)ə-ˈlā-shən\ *n*

1dis·com·fit \dis-ˈkəm(p)-fət, *esp South* ˌdis-kəm-ˈfit\ *vt* [ME *discomfiten,* fr. OF *desconfit,* pp. of *desconfire,* fr. *des-* + *confire* to prepare — more at COMFIT] **1 a** *archaic* : to defeat in battle **b** : to frustrate the plans of : THWART **2** : to put into a state of perplexity and embarrassment : DISCONCERT ***syn*** see EMBARRASS

2discomfit *n* : DISCOMFITURE

dis·com·fi·ture \dis-ˈkəm(p)-fə-ˌchu̇(ə)r, -chər, -ˌt(y)u̇(ə)r\ *n* : the act of discomfiting : the state of being discomfited

1dis·com·fort \dis-ˈkəm(p)-fərt\ *vt* [ME *discomforten,* fr. MF *desconforter,* fr. OF, fr. *des-* + *conforter* to comfort] **1** *archaic* : DISMAY **2** : to make uncomfortable or uneasy — **dis·com·fort·able** \-ˈkəm(p)-fərt-ə-bəl, -ˈkəm(p)(f)-tə(r)-bəl\ *adj* — **dis·com·fort·er** \-ˈkəm(p)-fərt-ər\ *n*

2discomfort *n* **1** *archaic* : DISTRESS, GRIEF **2** : mental or physical uneasiness : ANNOYANCE ⟨he gave every sign of intense ~⟩

dis·com·mend \ˌdis-kə-ˈmend\ *vt* **1** : DISAPPROVE, DISPARAGE **2** : to cause to be viewed unfavorably — **dis·com·mend·able** \-ˈmen-də-bəl\ *adj* — **dis·com·men·da·tion** \(ˌ)dis-ˌkäm-ən-ˈdā-shən, -ˌkäm-ˌen-\ *n*

dis·com·mode \ˌdis-kə-ˈmōd\ *vt* **-mod·ed; -mod·ing** [MF *discommoder,* fr. *dis-* + *commode* convenient — more at COMMODE] : to cause inconvenience to : TROUBLE

dis·com·pose \ˌdis-kəm-ˈpōz\ *vt* **1** : to destroy the composure or serenity of **2** : to disturb the order of — **dis·com·po·sure** \-ˈpō-zhər\ *n*

syn DISCOMPOSE, DISQUIET, DISTURB, PERTURB, AGITATE, UPSET, FLUSTER, FLURRY *shared meaning element* : to destroy or impair one's capacity for collected thought or decisive action ***ant*** compose

dis·con·cert \ˌdis-kən-ˈsərt\ *vt* [obs. F *disconcerter,* alter. of MF *desconcerter,* fr. *des-* + *concerter* to concert] **1** : to throw into confusion **2** : to disturb the composure of ***syn*** see EMBARRASS — **dis·con·cert·ing** *adj* — **dis·con·cert·ing·ly** \-iŋ-lē\ *adv*

dis·con·firm \ˌdis-kən-ˈfərm\ *vt* : to establish as invalid : DISPROVE

dis·con·form·able \ˌdis-kən-ˈfȯr-mə-bəl\ *adj* : of or relating to a disconformity in rocks — **dis·con·form·ably** \-blē\ *adv*

dis·con·for·mi·ty \ˌdis-kən-ˈfȯr-mət-ē\ *n* **1** *archaic* : NONCONFORMITY **2** : a break in a sequence of sedimentary rocks all of which have approximately the same dip

dis·con·nect \ˌdis-kə-ˈnekt\ *vt* : to sever the connection of or between ~ *vi* **1** : to terminate a connection **2** : to become detached or withdrawn ⟨he has periods when he ~s into silences — *Current Biog.*⟩

dis·con·nect·ed *adj* : not connected : INCOHERENT — **dis·con·nect·ed·ly** *adv* — **dis·con·nect·ed·ness** *n*

dis·con·so·late \dis-ˈkän(t)-s(ə-)lət\ *adj* [ME, fr. ML *disconsolatus,* fr. L *dis-* + *consolatus,* pp. of *consolari* to console] **1** : DEJECTED, DOWNCAST ⟨the team returned ~ from three losses⟩ **2** : CHEERLESS ⟨a clutch of ~ houses —D. H. Lawrence⟩ — **dis·con·so·late·ly** *adv* — **dis·con·so·late·ness** *n* — **dis·con·so·la·tion** \(ˌ)dis-ˌkän(t)-sə-ˈlā-shən\ *n*

1dis·con·tent \ˌdis-kən-ˈtent\ *adj* : DISCONTENTED

2discontent *n* : one who is discontented : MALCONTENT

3discontent *vt* : to make discontented — **dis·con·tent·ment** \-mənt\ *n*

4discontent *n* : lack of contentment: **a** : a sense of grievance : DISSATISFACTION ⟨the winter of our ~ —Shak.⟩ **b** : restless aspiration for improvement

dis·con·tent·ed *adj* : DISSATISFIED, MALCONTENT — **dis·con·tent·ed·ly** *adv* — **dis·con·tent·ed·ness** *n*

dis·con·tin·u·ance \ˌdis-kən-ˈtin-yə-wən(t)s\ *n* **1** : the act or an instance of discontinuing **2** : the interruption or termination of a legal action by failure to continue or by the plaintiff's entry of a discontinuing order

dis·con·tin·ue \ˌdis-kən-ˈtin-(ˌ)yü, -yə(-w)\ *vb* [ME *discontinuen,* fr. MF *discontinuer,* fr. ML *discontinuare,* fr. L *dis-* + *continuare* to continue] *vt* **1** : to break the continuity of : cease to operate, administer, use, or take **2** : to abandon or terminate by a legal discontinuance ~ *vi* : to come to an end; *specif* : to cease publication ***syn*** see STOP ***ant*** continue

dis·con·ti·nu·i·ty \(ˌ)dis-ˌkänt-ᵊn-ˈ(y)ü-ət-ē\ *n* **1** : lack of continuity or cohesion **2** : GAP 5 **3** : a value of an argument at which a function is not continuous

dis·con·tin·u·ous \ˌdis-kən-ˈtin-yə-wəs\ *adj* **1 a** (1) : not continuous ⟨a ~ series of events⟩ (2) : not continued : DISCRETE ⟨~ features of terrain⟩ **b** : lacking sequence or coherence ⟨this ~ style⟩ **2** : having one or more discontinuities — used of a variable or a function — **dis·con·tin·u·ous·ly** *adv*

dis·co·phile \ˈdis-kə-ˌfīl\ *n* : one who studies and collects phonograph records

1dis·cord \ˈdis-ˌkȯ(ə)rd\ *n* **1 a** : lack of agreement or harmony (as between persons, things, or ideas) **b** : active quarreling or conflict resulting from discord among persons or factions : STRIFE **2 a** (1) : a combination of musical sounds that strike the ear harshly (2) : DISSONANCE **b** : a harsh or unpleasant sound

syn DISCORD, STRIFE, CONFLICT, CONTENTION, DISSENSION, DIFFERENCE, VARIANCE *shared meaning element* : the state of those who disagree and lack harmony or the acts and circumstances marking such a state

2dis·cord \ˈdis-ˌkȯ(ə)rd, dis-ˈ\ *vi* [ME *discorden,* fr. OF *discorder,* fr. L *discordare,* fr. *discord-, discors* discordant, fr. *dis-* + *cord-, cor* heart — more at HEART] : DISAGREE, CLASH

dis·cor·dance \dis-ˈkȯrd-ᵊn(t)s\ *n* **1** : the state or an instance of being discordant **2** : DISSONANCE

dis·cor·dan·cy \-ᵊn-sē\ *n, pl* **-cies** : DISCORDANCE

dis·cor·dant \-ᵊnt\ *adj* **1 a** : being at variance : DISAGREEING **b** : QUARRELSOME **2** : relating to a discord — **dis·cor·dant·ly** *adv*

dis·co·theque \ˈdis-kə-ˌtek, ˌdis-kə-ˈ\ *n* [F *discothèque,* fr. *disque* disk, record + *-o-* + *-thèque* (as in *bibliothèque* library)] : a small intimate nightclub for dancing to live or recorded music; *broadly* : a nightclub often featuring psychedelic and mixed-media attractions (as slides, movies, special lighting effects, and kinetic sound)

1dis·count \ˈdis-ˌkau̇nt\ *n* **1** : a reduction made from the gross amount or value of something: as **a** (1) : a reduction made from a regular or list price (2) : a proportionate deduction from a debt account usu. made for cash or prompt payment **b** : a deduction made for interest in advancing money upon or purchasing a bill or note not due **2** : the act or practice of discounting **3** : a deduction taken or allowance made

2dis·count \ˈdis-ˌkau̇nt, dis-ˈ\ *vb* [modif. of F *décompter,* fr. OF *desconter,* fr. ML *discomputare,* fr. L *dis-* + *computare* to count — more at COUNT] *vt* **1 a** : to make a deduction from usu. for cash or prompt payment **b** : to sell or offer for sale at a discount **2** : to lend money on after deducting the discount **3 a** : to leave out of account : DISREGARD **b** : to underestimate the importance of : MINIMIZE **c** (1) : to make allowance for bias or exaggeration in (2) : to view with doubt : DISBELIEVE **d** : to take into account (as a future event) in present calculations ~ *vi* : to give or make discounts

dis·count·able \dis-ˈkau̇nt-ə-bəl, ˈdis-ˌ\ *adj* **1** : capable of being discounted ⟨a ~ note⟩ **2** : set apart for discounting ⟨within the ~ period⟩

1dis·coun·te·nance \dis-ˈkau̇nt-ᵊn-ən(t)s, -ˈkau̇nt-nən(t)s\ *vt* **1** : ABASH, DISCONCERT **2** : to look with disfavor on : discourage by evidence of disapproval

2discountenance *n* : DISFAVOR, DISAPPROVAL

dis·count·er \ˈdis-ˌkau̇nt-ər, dis-ˈ\ *n* : one that discounts; *specif* : DISCOUNT STORE

discount house *n* : DISCOUNT STORE

discount rate *n* **1** : the interest on an annual basis deducted in advance on a bank or other loan **2** : the charge levied by a central bank for advances and rediscounts

discount store *n* : a store where merchandise (as consumer durable goods) is sold at a discount from suggested list price

dis·cour·age \dis-ˈkər-ij, -ˈkə-rij\ *vt* **-aged; -ag·ing** [MF *descorager,* fr. OF *descoragier,* fr. *des-* dis- + *corage* courage] **1** : to deprive of courage or confidence : DISHEARTEN **2 a** : to hinder by disfavoring : DETER **b** : to attempt to dissuade — **dis·cour·age·able** \-ə-bəl\ *adj* — **dis·cour·ag·er** *n*

dis·cour·age·ment \-mənt\ *n* **1** : the act of discouraging : the state of being discouraged **2** : something that discourages : DETERRENT

dis·cour·ag·ing *adj* : lessening courage : DISHEARTENING — **dis·cour·ag·ing·ly** \-ij-iŋ-lē\ *adv*

1dis·course \ˈdis-ˌkō(ə)rs, -ˌkȯ(ə)rs, dis-ˈ\ *n* [ME *discours,* fr. ML & LL *discursus;* ML, argument, fr. LL, conversation, fr. L, act of running about, fr. *discursus,* pp. of *discurrere* to run about, fr. *dis-* + *currere* to run — more at CAR] **1** *archaic* : the capacity of orderly thought or procedure : RATIONALITY **2** : verbal interchange of ideas; *esp* : CONVERSATION **3 a** : formal and orderly and usu. extended expression of thought on a subject **b** : connected speech or writing **4** *obs* : social familiarity

2dis·course \dis-ˈkō(ə)rs, -ˈkȯ(ə)rs, ˈdis-ˌ\ *vb* **dis·coursed; dis·cours·ing** *vi* **1** : to express oneself esp. in oral discourse **2** : TALK, CONVERSE ~ *vt, archaic* : to give forth : UTTER — **dis·cours·er** *n*

dis·cour·te·ous \(ˈ)dis-ˈkərt-ē-əs\ *adj* : lacking courtesy : RUDE — **dis·cour·te·ous·ly** *adv* — **dis·cour·te·ous·ness** *n*

dis·cour·te·sy \-ˈkərt-ə-sē\ *n* **1** : RUDENESS **2** : a rude act

dis·cov·er \dis-ˈkəv-ər\ *vb* **dis·cov·ered; dis·cov·er·ing** \-ˈkəv-(ə-)riŋ\ [ME *discoveren,* fr. OF *descovrir,* fr. LL *discooperire,* fr. L *dis-* + *cooperire* to cover — more at COVER] *vt* **1 a** : to make known or visible : EXPOSE **b** *archaic* : DISPLAY **2** : to obtain sight or knowledge of for the first time : FIND ⟨~ the solution of a puzzle⟩ ~ *vi* : to make a discovery — **dis·cov·er·able** \-ˈkəv-(ə-)rə-bəl\ *adj* — **dis·cov·er·er** \-ər-ər\ *n*

syn **1** see REVEAL

2 DISCOVER, ASCERTAIN, DETERMINE, UNEARTH, LEARN *shared meaning element* : to find out something not previously known to one

3 see INVENT

dis·cov·ery \dis-ˈkəv-(ə-)rē\ *n, pl* **-er·ies** **1 a** : the act or process of discovering **b** (1) *archaic* : DISCLOSURE (2) *obs* : DISPLAY **c** *obs* : EXPLORATION **2** : something discovered

Discovery Day *n* : COLUMBUS DAY

1dis·cred·it \(ˈ)dis-ˈkred-ət\ *vt* **1** : to refuse to accept as true or accurate : DISBELIEVE **2** : to cause disbelief in the accuracy or authority of **3** : to deprive of good repute : DISGRACE

2discredit *n* **1** : loss of credit or reputation ⟨I knew stories to the ~ of England —W. B. Yeats⟩ **2** : lack or loss of belief or confidence : DOUBT ⟨contradictions cast ~ on his testimony⟩

dis·cred·it·able \-ə-bəl\ *adj* : injurious to reputation — **dis·cred·it·ably** \-blē\ *adv*

dis·creet \dis-ˈkrēt\ *adj* [ME, fr. MF *discret,* fr. ML *discretus,* fr. L, pp. of *discernere* to separate, distinguish between — more at DISCERN] **1** : having or showing discernment or good judgment in conduct and esp. in speech : PRUDENT; *esp* : capable of preserving prudent silence **2** : UNPRETENTIOUS, MODEST ⟨the warmth and ~ elegance of a civilized home —Joseph Wechsberg⟩ — **dis·creet·ly** *adv* — **dis·creet·ness** *n*

dis·crep·an·cy \dis-ˈkrep-ən-sē\ *n, pl* **-cies** **1** : the quality or state of being discrepant : DIFFERENCE **2** : an instance of being discrepant

dis·crep·ant \-ənt\ *adj* [L *discrepant-, discrepans,* prp. of *discrepare* to sound discordantly, fr. *dis-* + *crepare* to rattle, creak — more at RAVEN] : being at variance : DISAGREEING ⟨widely ~ conclusions⟩ — **dis·crep·ant·ly** *adv*

dis·crete \dis-ˈkrēt, ˈdis-ˌ\ *adj* [ME, fr. L *discretus*] **1** : constituting a separate entity : individually distinct **2 a** : consisting of distinct or unconnected elements : NONCONTINUOUS **b** : taking on or having a finite or countably infinite number of values : not mathematically continuous ⟨a ~ random variable⟩ ***syn*** see DISTINCT — **dis·crete·ly** *adv* — **dis·crete·ness** *n*

dis·cre·tion \dis-ˈkresh-ən\ *n* **1** : the quality of being discreet : CIRCUMSPECTION; *esp* : cautious reserve in speech **2** : ability to make responsible decisions **3 a** : individual choice or judgment ⟨left the decision to his ~⟩ **b** : power of free decision or latitude of choice within certain legal bounds ⟨reached the age of ~⟩ **4** : the result of separating or distinguishing ⟨breaking down every operation into discrete parts, and then making verbal the ~s that are made —Elinor Langer⟩

dis·cre·tion·ary \-ˈkresh-ə-ˌner-ē\ *adj* **1** : left to discretion : exercised at one's own discretion **2** : available for discretionary use ⟨~ purchasing power⟩

discretionary account *n* : a security or commodity market account in which an agent (as a broker) is given power of attorney allowing him to make independent decisions and buy and sell for the account of his principal

dis·crim·i·na·bil·i·ty \-ˌkrim-(ə-)nə-ˈbil-ət-ē\ *n, pl* **-ties 1** : the quality of being discriminable ⟨the ~ of the various senses of a word⟩ **2** : the ability to discriminate

dis·crim·i·na·ble \dis-ˈkrim-(ə-)nə-bəl\ *adj* : capable of being discriminated — **dis·crim·i·na·bly** \-blē\ *adv*

dis·crim·i·nant \-ˈkrim-(ə-)nənt\ *n* : a mathematical expression providing a criterion for the behavior of another more complicated expression, relation, or set of relations

dis·crim·i·nate \dis-ˈkrim-ə-ˌnāt\ *vb* **-nat·ed; -nat·ing** [L *discriminatus*, pp. of *discriminare*, fr. *discrimin-*, *discrimen* distinction, fr. *discernere* to distinguish between — more at DISCERN] *vt* **1 a** : to mark or perceive the distinguishing or peculiar features of **b** : DISTINGUISH, DIFFERENTIATE ⟨~ hundreds of colors⟩ **2** : to distinguish by discerning or exposing differences; *esp* : to distinguish (one like object) from another ~ *vi* **1 a** : to make a distinction ⟨~ among the methods which should be used⟩ **b** : to use good judgment **2** : to make a difference in treatment or favor on a basis other than individual merit ⟨~ in favor of your friends⟩ ⟨~ against a certain nationality⟩

dis·crim·i·nat·ing *adj* **1** : making a distinction : DISTINGUISHING **2** : marked by discrimination: **a** : DISCERNING, JUDICIOUS **b** : DISCRIMINATORY — **dis·crim·i·nat·ing·ly** \-ˌnāt-iŋ-lē\ *adv*

dis·crim·i·na·tion \dis-ˌkrim-ə-ˈnā-shən\ *n* **1 a** : the act of discriminating **b** : the process by which two stimuli differing in some aspect are responded to differently : DIFFERENTIATION **2** : the quality or power of finely distinguishing **3 a** : the act, practice, or an instance of discriminating categorically rather than individually **b** : prejudiced or prejudicial outlook, action, or treatment ⟨provided major opportunities for Negro advancement on purely equal terms involving neither ~ nor preference —D. P. Moynihan⟩ ***syn*** see DISCERNMENT — **dis·crim·i·na·tion·al** \-shnəl, -shən-ᵊl\ *adj*

dis·crim·i·na·tive \dis-ˈkrim-ə-ˌnāt-iv, ˈkrim-(ə-)nət-\ *adj* **1** : making distinctions **2** : DISCRIMINATORY 1 ⟨permitted tariffs which were grossly ~ —Mabel R. Gillis⟩

dis·crim·i·na·tor \dis-ˈkrim-ə-ˌnāt-ər\ *n* : one that discriminates; *specif* : a circuit that can be adjusted to accept or reject signals of different characteristics (as amplitude or frequency)

dis·crim·i·na·to·ry \dis-ˈkrim-(ə-)nə-ˌtōr-ē, -ˌtȯr-\ *adj* **1** : applying or favoring discrimination in treatment **2** : DISCRIMINATIVE 1 — **dis·crim·i·na·to·ri·ly** \-ˌkrim-(ə-)nə-ˈtōr-ə-lē, -ˈtȯr-\ *adv*

dis·cur·sive \dis-ˈkər-siv\ *adj* [ML *discursivus*, fr. L *discursus*, pp. of *discurrere* to run about — more at DISCOURSE] **1** : passing from one topic to another : DIGRESSIVE **2** : marked by analytical reasoning — **dis·cur·sive·ly** *adv* — **dis·cur·sive·ness** *n*

dis·cus \ˈdis-kəs\ *n, pl* **dis·cus·es** [L — more at DISH] **1 a** : a disk (as of wood, rubber, or metal) that is thicker in the center than at the perimeter and that is hurled for distance **b** : a field event in which a discus of about 4½ pounds is hurled **2** : DISK 2, 3

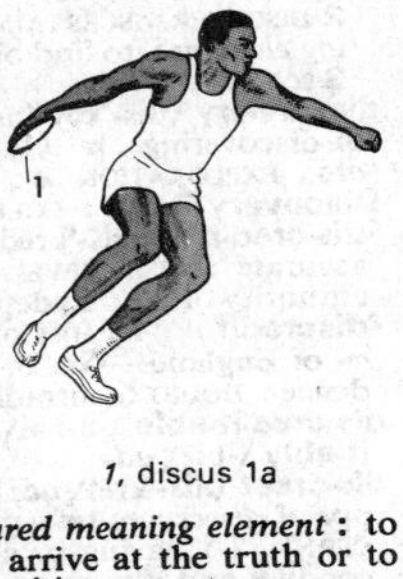

1, discus 1a

dis·cuss \dis-ˈkəs\ *vt* [ME *discussen*, fr. L *discussus*, pp. of *discutere*, fr. *dis-* apart + *quatere* to shake — more at DIS-, QUASH] **1** *obs* : DISPEL **2 a** : to investigate by reasoning or argument **b** : to present in detail for examination or consideration ⟨~*ed* plans for the party⟩ **c** : to talk about **3** *obs* : DECLARE — **dis·cuss·able** *or* **dis·cuss·ible** \-ə-bəl\ *adj* — **dis·cuss·er** *n*

syn DISCUSS, ARGUE, DEBATE, DISPUTE ***shared meaning element*** : to discourse about something in order to arrive at the truth or to convince others of the validity of one's position

dis·cus·sant \dis-ˈkəs-ᵊnt\ *n* : one who takes part in a formal discussion or symposium

dis·cus·sion \dis-ˈkəsh-ən\ *n* **1** : consideration of a question in open and usu. informal debate **2** : a formal treatment of a topic

¹dis·dain \dis-ˈdān\ *n* [ME *desdeyne*, fr. OF *desdeign*, fr. *desdeignier*] : a feeling of contempt for what is beneath one : SCORN

²disdain *vt* [ME *desdeynen*, fr. MF *desdeignier*, fr. (assumed) VL *disdignare*, fr. L *dis-* + *dignare* to deign — more at DEIGN] **1** : to look with scorn on **2** : to refuse or abstain from because of disdain **3** : to treat disdainfully ***syn*** see DESPISE ***ant*** favor

dis·dain·ful \-fəl\ *adj* : full of or expressing disdain ***syn*** see PROUD — **dis·dain·ful·ly** \-fə-lē\ *adv* — **dis·dain·ful·ness** *n*

dis·ease \diz-ˈēz\ *n* [ME *disese*, fr. MF *desaise*, fr. *des-* dis- + *aise* ease] **1** *obs* : TROUBLE **2** : a condition of the living animal or plant body or of one of its parts that impairs the performance of a vital function : SICKNESS, MALADY **3** : a harmful development (as in a social institution) ⟨the various ~s of civilization⟩ — **dis·eased** \-ˈēzd\ *adj*

dis·econ·o·my \ˌdis-i-ˈkän-ə-mē\ *n* **1** : a lack of economy **2** : a factor responsible for an increase in cost

dis·em·bark \ˌdis-əm-ˈbärk\ *vb* [MF *desembarquer*, fr. *des-* + *embarquer* to embark] *vt* : to put ashore from a ship ~ *vi* **1** : to go ashore out of a ship **2** : to get out of a vehicle — **dis·em·bar·ka·tion** \(ˌ)dis-ˌem-ˌbär-ˈkā-shən, -bər-\ *n*

dis·em·bar·rass \ˌdis-əm-ˈbar-əs\ *vt* : to free from something troublesome or superfluous ***syn*** see EXTRICATE

dis·em·body \ˌdis-əm-ˈbäd-ē\ *vt* : to divest of a body, of corporeal existence, or of reality

dis·em·bogue \ˌdis-əm-ˈbōg\ *vb* **-bogued; -bogu·ing** [modif. of Sp *desembocar*, fr. *des-* dis- (fr. L *dis-*) + *embocar* to put into the mouth, fr. *en* in (fr. L *in*) + *boca* mouth, fr. L *bucca* — more at POCK] *vi* : to flow or come forth from or as if from a channel ~ *vt* : to pour out : EMPTY

dis·em·bow·el \ˌdis-əm-ˈbau̇(-ə)l\ *vt* **1** : to take out the bowels of : EVISCERATE **2** : to remove the substance of — **dis·em·bow·el·ment** \-mənt\ *n*

dis·en·chant \ˌdis-ᵊn-ˈchant\ *vt* [MF *desenchanter*, fr. *des-* + *enchanter* to enchant] : to free from illusion — **dis·en·chant·er** *n* — **dis·en·chant·ing** *adj* — **dis·en·chant·ing·ly** \-iŋ-lē\ *adv* — **dis·en·chant·ment** \-mənt\ *n*

dis·en·cum·ber \ˌdis-ᵊn-ˈkəm-bər\ *vt* [MF *desencombrer*, fr. *des-* + *encombrer* to encumber] : to free from encumbrance : DISBURDEN ***syn*** see EXTRICATE

dis·en·dow \ˌdis-ᵊn-ˈdau̇\ *vt* : to strip of endowment — **dis·en·dow·er** \-ˈdau̇(-ə)r\ *n* — **dis·en·dow·ment** \-ˈdau̇-mənt\ *n*

dis·en·fran·chise \ˌdis-ᵊn-ˈfran-ˌchīz\ *vt* : DISFRANCHISE — **dis·en·fran·chise·ment** \-ˌchīz-mənt, -chəz-\ *n*

dis·en·gage \ˌdis-ᵊn-ˈgāj\ *vb* [F *désengager*, fr. MF, fr. *des-* + *engager* to engage] *vt* : to release from something that engages ~ *vi* : to release or detach oneself : WITHDRAW — **dis·en·gage·ment** \-mənt\ *n*

dis·en·tail \ˌdis-ᵊn-ˈtā(ə)l\ *vt* : to free from entail

dis·en·tan·gle \ˌdis-ᵊn-ˈtaŋ-gəl\ *vt* : to free from entanglement : UNRAVEL ~ *vi* : to become disentangled ***syn*** see EXTRICATE ***ant*** entangle — **dis·en·tan·gle·ment** \-mənt\ *n*

dis·en·thrall *also* **dis·en·thral** \ˌdis-ᵊn-ˈthrȯl\ *vt* : to free from bondage : LIBERATE

dis·equil·i·brate \ˌdis-i-ˈkwil-ə-ˌbrāt\ *vt* : to put out of balance — **dis·equil·i·bra·tion** \-ˌkwil-ə-ˈbrā-shən\ *n*

dis·equi·lib·ri·um \(ˌ)dis-ˌē-kwə-ˈlib-rē-əm, -ˌek-wə-\ *n* : loss or lack of equilibrium

dis·es·tab·lish \ˌdis-ə-ˈstab-lish\ *vt* : to deprive of an established status; *esp* : to deprive of the status and privileges of an established church — **dis·es·tab·lish·ment** \-mənt\ *n*

dis·es·tab·lish·men·tar·i·an \-ˌstab-lish-ˌmen-ˈter-ē-ən, -mən-\ *n, often cap* [*disestablishment*] : one who opposes an established order — **disestablishmentarian** *adj, often cap*

¹dis·es·teem \ˌdis-ə-ˈstēm\ *vt* : to regard with disfavor

²disesteem *n* : DISFAVOR, DISREPUTE

di·seuse \dē-ˈzə(r)z, -ˈzüz\ *n, pl* **di·seuses** \-ˈzə(r)z(-əz), -ˈzüz(-əz)\ [F, fem. of *diseur*, fr. OF, fr. *dire* to say, fr. L *dicere* — more at DICTION] : a skilled and usu. professional woman reciter

¹dis·fa·vor \(ˈ)dis-ˈfā-vər\ *n* [prob. fr. MF *desfaveur*, fr. *des-* dis- + *faveur* favor, fr. OF *favor*] **1** : DISAPPROVAL, DISLIKE ⟨practices looked upon with ~⟩ **2** : the state or fact of being deprived of favor ⟨fell into ~⟩ **3** : DISADVANTAGE

²disfavor *vt* : to withhold or withdraw favor from

dis·fea·ture \(ˈ)dis-ˈfē-chər\ *vt* : to mar the features of ***syn*** see DEFACE — **dis·fea·ture·ment** \-mənt\ *n*

dis·fig·ure \dis-ˈfig-yər, *esp Brit* -ˈfig-ər\ *vt* [ME *disfiguren*, fr. MF *desfigurer*, fr. *des-* + *figure*] **1** : to impair (as in beauty) by deep and persistent injuries ⟨a girl *disfigured* by smallpox⟩ **2** *obs* : DISGUISE ***syn*** see DEFACE — **dis·fig·ure·ment** \-mənt\ *n*

dis·fran·chise \(ˈ)dis-ˈfran-ˌchīz\ *vt* : to deprive of a franchise, of a legal right, or of some privilege or immunity; *esp* : to deprive of the right to vote — **dis·fran·chise·ment** \-ˌchīz-mənt, -chəz-\ *n*

dis·frock \(ˈ)dis-ˈfräk\ *vt* : UNFROCK

dis·func·tion *var of* DYSFUNCTION

dis·fur·nish \(ˈ)dis-ˈfər-nish\ *vt* [MF *desfourniss-*, stem of *desfournir*, fr. *des-* + *fournir* to furnish — more at FURNISH] : to make destitute of possessions : DIVEST — **dis·fur·nish·ment** \-mənt\ *n*

dis·gorge \(ˈ)dis-ˈgȯ(ə)rj\ *vb* [MF *desgorger*, fr. *des-* + *gorge*] *vt* **1 a** : to discharge by the throat and mouth : VOMIT **b** : to discharge violently, confusedly, or as a result of force **c** : to give up on request or under pressure ⟨refused to ~ his ill-gotten gains⟩ **2** : to discharge the contents of (as the stomach) ~ *vi* : to discharge contents ⟨where the river ~s into the sea⟩

¹dis·grace \dis-ˈgrās\ *vt* **1** *archaic* : to humiliate by a superior showing **2** : to bring reproach or shame to ⟨*disgraced* his family⟩ **3** : to cause to lose favor or standing ⟨was *disgraced* by the hint of scandal⟩ — **dis·grac·er** *n*

²disgrace *n* [MF, fr. OIt *disgrazia*, fr. *dis-* (fr. L) + *grazia* grace, fr. L *gratia* — more at GRACE] **1 a** : loss of grace, favor, or honor **b** : the condition of one fallen from grace or honor **2** : something that disgraces ⟨that boy's manners are a ~⟩

syn DISGRACE, DISHONOR, DISREPUTE, SHAME, INFAMY, IGNOMINY, OPPROBRIUM ***shared meaning element*** : loss of esteem and good repute and the resulting denigration and contempt ***ant*** respect, esteem

dis·grace·ful \dis-ˈgrās-fəl\ *adj* : bringing or involving disgrace — **dis·grace·ful·ly** \-fə-lē\ *adv* — **dis·grace·ful·ness** *n*

dis·grun·tle \dis-ˈgrənt-ᵊl\ *vt* **dis·grun·tled; dis·grun·tling** \-ˈgrənt-liŋ, -ᵊl-iŋ\ [*dis-* + *gruntle* (to grumble), fr. ME *gruntlen*, freq. of *grunten* to grunt] : to make ill-humored or discontented ⟨the workers are *disgruntled* with their wages⟩ — **dis·grun·tle·ment** \-ᵊl-mənt\ *n*

¹dis·guise \dis-ˈgīz\ *vt* **dis·guised; dis·guis·ing** [ME *disgisen*, fr. MF *desguiser*, fr. OF, fr. *des-* + *guise*] **1 a** : to change the customary dress or appearance of **b** : to furnish with a false appearance or an assumed identity **2** *obs* : DISFIGURE **3** : to obscure the existence or true state or character of : CONCEAL — **dis·guised·ly** \-ˈgīz(-ə)d-lē\ *adv* — **dis·guise·ment** \-ˈgīz-mənt\ *n* — **dis·guis·er** *n*

syn DISGUISE, CLOAK, MASK, DISSEMBLE ***shared meaning element*** : to alter so as to hide the true appearance, identity, intention, meaning, or feelings

2disguise *n* **1 :** apparel assumed to conceal one's identity or counterfeit another's **2 a :** form misrepresenting the true nature of something ⟨blessings in ~⟩ **b :** an artificial manner : PRETENSE ⟨threw off all ~⟩ **3 :** the act of disguising
1dis·gust \dis-ˈgəst\ *n* **:** marked aversion aroused by something highly distasteful : REPUGNANCE
2disgust *vb* [MF *desgouster,* fr. *des-* dis- + *goust* taste, fr. L *gustus;* akin to L *gustare* to taste — more at CHOOSE] *vt* **1 :** to provoke to loathing, repugnance, or aversion : be offensive to **2 :** to cause (one) to lose an interest or intention ⟨his failures ~*ed* him to the point that he stopped trying⟩ ~ *vi* **:** to cause disgust — **dis·gust·ed** *adj* — **dis·gust·ed·ly** *adv*
dis·gust·ful \-ˈgəst-fəl\ *adj* **1 :** provoking disgust **2 :** full of or accompanied by disgust — **dis·gust·ful·ly** \-fə-lē\ *adv*
dis·gust·ing *adj* **:** exciting disgust — **dis·gust·ing·ly** \-ˈgəs-tiŋ-lē\ *adv*
1dish \ˈdish\ *n* [ME, fr. OE *disc* plate; akin to OHG *tisc* plate, table; both fr. a prehistoric WGmc word borrowed fr. L *discus* quoit, disk, dish, fr. Gk *diskos,* fr. *dikein* to throw] **1 a :** a more or less concave vessel from which food is served **b :** the contents of a dish ⟨a ~ of strawberries⟩ **2 :** food prepared in a particular way **3 a** (1) **:** any of various shallow concave vessels; *broadly* **:** something shallowly concave (2) **:** a directional microwave antenna having a concave usu. parabolic reflector **b :** the state of being concave or the degree of concavity **4 a :** something that is favored ⟨entertainment that is just his ~⟩ **b :** an attractive woman
2dish *vt* **1 :** to put (as food for serving) into a dish — often used with *up* **2 :** PRESENT — usu. used with *up* **3 :** to make concave like a dish
dis·ha·bille \ˌdis-ə-ˈbē(ə)l, -ˈbil, -ˈbē\ *n* [F *déshabillé,* fr. pp. of *déshabiller* to undress, fr. *dés-* dis- + *habiller* to dress — more at HABILIMENT] **1 a** *archaic* **:** NEGLIGEE **b :** the state of being dressed in a casual or careless style **2 :** a deliberately careless or casual manner
dis·har·mon·ic \ˌdis-(ˌ)här-ˈmän-ik\ *adj* **1 :** having a combination of bodily characters that results in an unusual form or appearance **2 :** exhibiting or marked by allometry
dis·har·mo·ni·ous \-ˈmō-nē-əs\ *adj* **1 :** lacking in harmony **2 :** DISHARMONIC
dis·har·mo·nize \(ˈ)dis-ˈhär-mə-ˌnīz\ *vt* **:** to make disharmonious
dis·har·mo·ny \-nē\ *n* **:** lack of harmony : DISCORD
dish·cloth \ˈdish-ˌklȯth\ *n* **:** a cloth for washing dishes
dishcloth gourd *n* **:** the fruit of any of several gourds (genus *Luffa*) having a fibrous interior that is dried and used like a sponge
dish·clout \ˈdish-ˌklau̇t\ *n, Brit* **:** DISHCLOTH
dis·heart·en \(ˈ)dis-ˈhärt-ᵊn\ *vt* **:** to cause to lose spirit or morale — **dis·heart·en·ing·ly** \-ˈhärt-niŋ-lē, -ᵊn-iŋ-\ *adv* — **dis·heart·en·ment** \-ˈhärt-ᵊn-mənt\ *n*
dished \ˈdisht\ *adj* **1 :** CONCAVE **2** *of a pair of vehicle wheels* **:** nearer together at the bottom than at the top
di·shev·el \dish-ˈev-əl\ *vt* **di·shev·eled** *or* **di·shev·elled; di·shev·el·ing** *or* **di·shev·el·ling** \-ˈev-(ə-)liŋ\ [back-formation fr. *disheveled*] **:** to throw into disorder or disarray
di·shev·eled *or* **di·shev·elled** *adj* [ME *discheveled,* part trans. of MF *deschevelé,* fr. pp. of *descheveler* to disarrange the hair, fr. *des-* + *chevel* hair, fr. L *capillus*] **:** marked by disorder or disarray
dis·hon·est \(ˈ)dis-ˈän-əst\ *adj* [ME, fr. MF *deshoneste,* fr. *des-* + *honeste* honest] **1** *obs* **:** SHAMEFUL, UNCHASTE **2 :** characterized by lack of truth, honesty, or trustworthiness — **dis·hon·est·ly** *adv*
syn DISHONEST, DECEITFUL, LYING, MENDACIOUS, UNTRUTHFUL *shared meaning element* **:** unworthy of trust or belief *ant* honest
dis·hon·es·ty \-ə-stē\ *n* **1 :** lack of honesty or integrity : disposition to defraud or deceive **2 :** a dishonest act : FRAUD
1dis·hon·or \(ˈ)dis-ˈän-ər\ *n* [ME *dishonour,* fr. OF *deshonor,* fr. *des-* + *honor*] **1 :** lack or loss of honor or reputation **2 :** the state of one who has lost honor or prestige : SHAME ⟨would rather die than live in ~⟩ **3 :** a cause of disgrace ⟨became a ~ to his family⟩ **4 :** the nonpayment or nonacceptance of commercial paper by the party on whom it is drawn *syn* see DISGRACE *ant* honor — **dis·hon·or·er** \-ˈän-ər-ər\ *n*
2dishonor *vt* **1 a :** to treat in a degrading manner **b :** to bring shame on **2 :** to refuse to accept or pay (as a draft, bill, check, or note)
dis·hon·or·able \(ˈ)dis-ˈän-(ə-)rə-bəl, -ˈän-ər-bəl\ *adj* **1 :** lacking honor : SHAMEFUL ⟨~ conduct⟩ **2** *archaic* **:** not honored — **dis·hon·or·able·ness** *n* — **dis·hon·or·ably** \-blē\ *adv*
dish out *vt* **1 :** to serve (food) from a dish **2 :** to give freely ⟨the blatant picturing of crime and disorder *dished out* by the cinema — R. T. Flewelling⟩
dish·pan \ˈdish-ˌpan\ *n* **:** a large flat-bottomed pan used for washing dishes
dishpan hands *n pl but sing or pl in constr* **:** a condition of dryness, redness, and scaling of the hands that results typically from repeated exposure to, sensitivity to, or overuse of cleaning materials (as detergents) used in housework
dish·rag \ˈdish-ˌrag\ *n* **:** DISHCLOTH
dish towel *n* **:** a cloth for drying dishes
dish·ware \ˈdish-ˌwa(ə)r, -ˌwe(ə)r\ *n* **:** tableware (as of china) used in serving food
dish·wash·er \-ˌwȯsh-ər, -ˌwäsh-\ *n* **1 :** a worker employed to wash dishes **2 :** a machine for washing dishes
dish·wa·ter \-ˌwȯt-ər, -ˌwät-\ *n* **:** water in which dishes have been or are to be washed
dishy \ˈdish-ē\ *adj, chiefly Brit* **:** ATTRACTIVE
1dis·il·lu·sion \ˌdis-ə-ˈlü-zhən\ *n* **:** the condition of being disenchanted
2disillusion *vt* **dis·il·lu·sioned; dis·il·lu·sion·ing** \-ˈlüzh-(ə-)niŋ\ **:** to leave without illusion — **dis·il·lu·sion·ment** \-ˈlü-zhən-mənt\ *n*
dis·in·cen·tive \ˌdis-ᵊn-ˈsent-iv\ *n* **:** DETERRENT
dis·in·cli·na·tion \(ˌ)dis-ˌin-klə-ˈnā-shən, -ˌiŋ-\ *n* **:** a preference for avoiding something : slight aversion
dis·in·cline \ˌdis-ᵊn-ˈklīn\ *vt* **:** to make unwilling
dis·in·clined *adj* **:** unwilling because of mild dislike or disapproval
syn DISINCLINED, HESITANT, RELUCTANT, LOATH, AVERSE *shared meaning element* **:** lacking the will or desire to do something indicated
dis·in·fect \ˌdis-ᵊn-ˈfekt\ *vt* [MF *desinfecter,* fr. *des-* + *infecter* to infect] **:** to free from infection esp. by destroying harmful microorganisms; *broadly* **:** CLEANSE — **dis·in·fec·tion** \-ˈfek-shən\ *n*
dis·in·fec·tant \-ˈfek-tənt\ *n* **:** an agent that frees from infection; *esp* **:** a chemical that destroys vegetative forms of harmful microorganisms but not ordinarily bacterial spores
dis·in·fest \ˌdis-ᵊn-ˈfest\ *vt* **:** to rid of small animal pests (as insects or rodents) — **dis·in·fes·ta·tion** \(ˌ)dis-ˌin-ˌfes-ˈtā-shən\ *n*
dis·in·fes·tant \ˌdis-ᵊn-ˈfes-tənt\ *n* **:** a disinfesting agent
dis·in·fla·tion \ˌdis-ᵊn-ˈflā-shən\ *n* **:** a reversal of inflationary pressures — **dis·in·fla·tion·ary** \-shə-ˌner-ē\ *adj*
dis·in·gen·u·ous \ˌdis-ᵊn-ˈjen-yə-wəs\ *adj* **:** lacking in candor; *also* **:** giving a false appearance of simple frankness : CALCULATING — **dis·in·gen·u·ous·ly** *adv* — **dis·in·gen·u·ous·ness** *n*
dis·in·her·it \ˌdis-ᵊn-ˈher-ət\ *vt* **1 :** to prevent deliberately (as by making a will) from inheriting **2 :** to deprive of natural or human rights or of previously held special privileges — **dis·in·her·i·tance** \-ˈher-ət-ən(t)s\ *n*
dis·in·hi·bi·tion \(ˌ)dis-ˌin-(h)ə-ˈbish-ən\ *n* **:** loss of a conditioned reflex (as by the action of interfering stimuli)
dis·in·sec·tion \ˌdis-ᵊn-ˈsek-shən\ *n* [*dis-* + *insect* + *-ion*] **:** DISINSECTIZATION
dis·in·sect·iza·tion \-ˌsek-tə-ˈzā-shən\ *n* **:** removal of insects (as from an aircraft)
dis·in·te·grate \(ˈ)dis-ˈint-ə-ˌgrāt\ *vt* **1 :** to break or decompose into constituent elements, parts, or small particles **2 :** to destroy the unity or integrity of ~ *vi* **1 :** to break or separate into constituent elements or parts **2 :** to lose unity or integrity by or as if by breaking into parts **3 :** to undergo a change in composition ⟨an atomic nucleus that ~*s* because of radioactivity⟩ — **dis·in·te·gra·tion** \(ˌ)dis-ˌint-ə-ˈgrā-shən\ *n* — **dis·in·te·gra·tive** \(ˈ)dis-ˈint-ə-ˌgrāt-iv\ *adj* — **dis·in·te·gra·tor** \-ˌgrāt-ər\ *n*
dis·in·ter \ˌdis-ᵊn-ˈtər\ *vt* **1 :** to take out of the grave or tomb **2 :** to bring to light : UNEARTH — **dis·in·ter·ment** \-mənt\ *n*
1dis·in·ter·est \(ˈ)dis-ˈin-trəst; -ˈint-ə-rəst, -ə-ˌrest, -ərst; -ˈin-ˌtrest\ *vt* **:** to divest of interest
2disinterest *n* **1 :** DISADVANTAGE **2 :** lack of self-interest : DISINTERESTEDNESS **3 :** lack of interest : APATHY
dis·in·ter·est·ed *adj* **1 :** not having the mind or feelings engaged : UNINTERESTED ⟨is supremely ~ in all efforts to find a peaceful solution —C. L. Sulzberger⟩ **2 :** free from selfish motive or interest : UNBIASED ⟨a ~ decision⟩ ⟨~ intellectual curiosity is the lifeblood of real civilization —G. M. Trevelyan⟩ *syn* see INDIFFERENT *ant* interested — **dis·in·ter·est·ed·ly** *adv* — **dis·in·ter·est·ed·ness** *n*
dis·in·tox·i·cate \ˌdis-ᵊn-ˈtäk-sə-ˌkāt\ *vt* **:** to free (as a drug user or an alcoholic) from an intoxicating agent in the body or from dependence on such an agent — **dis·in·tox·i·ca·tion** \-ˌtäk-sə-ˈkā-shən\ *n*
dis·in·vest·ment \ˌdis-ᵊn-ˈves(t)-mənt\ *n* **:** consumption of capital
dis·join \(ˈ)dis-ˈjȯin\ *vb* [MF *desjoindre,* fr. L *disjungere,* fr. *dis-* + *jungere* to join — more at YOKE] *vt* **:** to end the joining of ~ *vi* **:** to become detached
1dis·joint \-ˈjȯint\ *adj* [ME *disjoynt,* fr. MF *desjoint,* pp. of *desjoindre*] **1** *obs* **:** DISJOINTED 2a **2 :** having no elements in common ⟨~ mathematical sets⟩
2disjoint *vt* **1 :** to disturb the orderly structure or arrangement of **2 :** to take apart at the joints ~ *vi* **:** to come apart at the joints
dis·joint·ed *adj* **1 :** separated at or as if at the joint **2 a :** being thrown out of orderly function ⟨a ~ society⟩ **b :** lacking coherence or orderly sequence ⟨an incomplete and ~ history⟩ — **dis·joint·ed·ly** *adv* — **dis·joint·ed·ness** *n*
1dis·junct \dis-ˈjəŋ(k)t\ *adj* [L *disjunctus,* pp. of *disjungere* to disjoin] **:** marked by separation of or from usu. contiguous parts or individuals: as **a :** DISCONTINUOUS **b :** relating to melodic progression by intervals larger than a major second — compare CONJUNCT **c** *of an insect* **:** having head, thorax, and abdomen separated by deep constrictions
2dis·junct \ˈdis-ˌjəŋ(k)t, dis-ˈ\ *n* **:** any of the alternatives comprising a logical disjunction
dis·junc·tion \dis-ˈjəŋ(k)-shən\ *n* **1 :** a sharp cleavage : DISUNION, SEPARATION ⟨the ~ between theory and practice⟩ **2 a :** a complex sentence in logic that is true when either one or both of its constituent sentences are true — compare INCLUSIVE DISJUNCTION **b :** a complex sentence in logic that is true when one and only one of its constituent sentences is true — compare EXCLUSIVE DISJUNCTION
1dis·junc·tive \-ˈjəŋ(k)-tiv\ *n* **:** a disjunctive conjunction
2disjunctive *adj* **1 :** marked by breaks or disunity ⟨a ~ narrative sequence⟩ **2 a :** being or belonging to a complex proposition one or both of whose terms are true **b :** expressing an alternative or opposition between the meanings of the words connected ⟨the ~ conjunction *or*⟩ **c :** expressed by mutually exclusive alternatives joined by *or* ⟨~ pleading⟩ **3** *of a pronoun form* **:** stressed and not attached to the verb as an enclitic or proclitic — **dis·junc·tive·ly** *adv*
dis·junc·ture \-ˈjəŋ(k)-chər\ *n* **:** DISJUNCTION
1disk *or* **disc** \ˈdisk\ *n, often attrib* [L *discus* — more at DISH] **1 a** *archaic* **:** DISCUS 1 **b :** the seemingly flat figure of a celestial body ⟨the solar ~⟩ **2 a :** the central part of the flower head of a typical composite made up of closely packed tubular flowers **b** *usu disc* **:** an enlargement of the torus around, beneath, or above the pistil of a flower **3 :** any of various rounded and flattened animal

anatomical structures **4 a** : a thin circular object **b** *usu disc* : a phonograph record **c** : a round flat plate coated with a magnetic substance on which data for a computer is stored **5** *usu disc* : one of the concave circular steel tools with sharpened edge making up the working part of a disc harrow or plow; *also* : an implement employing such tools — **disk·like** \-ˌlīk\ *adj*

[2]**disk** *or* **disc** *vt* **1** : to cultivate with an implement (as a harrow or plow) that turns and loosens the soil with a series of disks **2** *usu disc* : to record on a phonograph disc

disk flower *n* : one of the tubular flowers in the disk of a composite plant — called also *disk floret*

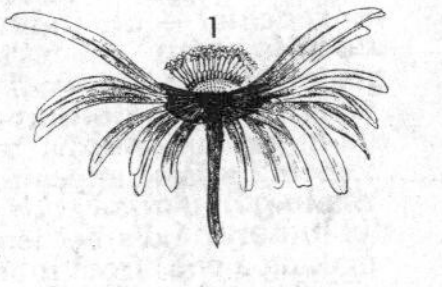

1 disk flowers

disk wheel *n* : a wheel presenting a solid surface from hub to rim

dis·lik·able *also* **dis·like·able** \(ˈ)dis-ˈlī-kə-bəl\ *adj* : easy to dislike

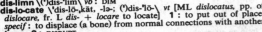

[1]**dis·like** \(ˈ)dis-ˈlīk\ *vt* **1** *archaic* : DISPLEASE **2** : to regard with dislike : DISAPPROVE **3** *obs* : to show aversion to — **dis·lik·er** *n*

[2]**dislike** *n* **1** : a feeling of aversion or disapproval **2** *obs* : DISCORD

dis·limn \(ˈ)dis-ˈlim\ *vb* : DIM

dis·lo·cate \ˈdis-lō-ˌkāt, -lə-; (ˈ)dis-ˈlō-\ *vt* [ML *dislocatus*, pp. of *dislocare*, fr. L *dis-* + *locare* to locate] **1** : to put out of place; *specif* : to displace (a bone) from normal connections with another bone **2** : DISRUPT

dis·lo·ca·tion \ˌdis-(ˌ)lō-ˈkā-shən, -lə-\ *n* : the act of dislocating : the state of being dislocated: as **a** : displacement of one or more bones at a joint **b** : a discontinuity in the otherwise normal lattice structure of a crystal **c** : disruption of an established order

dis·lodge \(ˈ)dis-ˈläj\ *vb* [ME *disloggen*, fr. MF *desloger*, fr. *des-* + *loger* to lodge, fr. *loge* lodge] *vt* **1** : to force out of a secure or settled position ⟨*dislodged* the rock with a shovel⟩ **2** : to drive from a position of hiding, defense, or advantage ~ *vi* : to leave a lodging place

dis·loy·al \(ˈ)dis-ˈlȯi(-ə)l\ *adj* [MF *desloial*, fr. OF, fr. *des-* + *loial* loyal] : lacking in loyalty : untrue to personal obligations or allegiance ⟨his ~ refusal to help his friend⟩ **syn** see FAITHLESS **ant** loyal — **dis·loy·al·ly** \-ˈlȯi-ə-lē\ *adv*

dis·loy·al·ty \-ˈlȯi(-ə)l-tē\ *n* : lack of loyalty

dis·mal \ˈdiz-məl\ *adj* [ME, fr. *dismal*, n., days marked as unlucky in medieval calendars, fr. AF, fr. ML *dies mali*, lit., evil days] **1** *obs* : DISASTROUS, DREADFUL **2** : showing or causing gloom or depression **3** : lacking interest or merit — **dis·mal·ly** \-mə-lē\ *adv* — **dis·mal·ness** *n*

dis·man·tle \(ˈ)dis-ˈmant-ᵊl\ *vt* **dis·man·tled; dis·man·tling** \-ˈmant-liŋ, -ᵊl-iŋ\ [MF *desmanteler*, fr. *des-* + *mantel* mantle] **1** : to strip of dress or covering : DIVEST **2** : to strip of furniture and equipment **3** : to take to pieces — **dis·man·tle·ment** \-ˈmant-ᵊl-mənt\ *n*

dis·mast \(ˈ)dis-ˈmast\ *vt* : to remove or break off the mast of

[1]**dis·may** \dis-ˈmā, diz-\ *vt* [ME *dismayen*, fr. (assumed) OF *desmaiier*, fr. OF *des-* + *-maiier* (as in *esmaiier* to dismay), fr. (assumed) VL *-magare*, of Gmc origin] : to deprive of courage, resolution, and initiative through the pressure of sudden fear or anxiety or great perplexity ⟨~*ed* at the size of his adversary⟩ — **dis·may·ing·ly** \-iŋ-lē\ *adv*

syn DISMAY, APPALL, HORRIFY, DAUNT *shared meaning element* : to unnerve and check by arousing fear, apprehension, or aversion **ant** cheer

[2]**dismay** *n* **1** : sudden loss of courage or resolution from alarm or fear **2 a** : sudden disappointment **b** : PERTURBATION

disme \ˈdīm\ *n* [obs. E, tenth, fr. obs. F, fr. MF *disme, dime* — more at DIME] : a U.S. 10-cent coin struck in 1792

dis·mem·ber \(ˈ)dis-ˈmem-bər\ *vt* **dis·mem·bered; dis·mem·ber·ing** \-b(ə-)riŋ\ [ME *dismembren*, fr. OF *desmembrer*, fr. *des-* + *membre* member] **1** : to cut off or disjoin the limbs, members, or parts of **2** : to break up or tear into pieces — **dis·mem·ber·ment** \-bər-mənt\ *n*

dis·miss \dis-ˈmis\ *vt* [modif. of L *dimissus*, pp. of *dimittere*, fr. *dis-* apart + *mittere* to send — more at DIS-, SMITE] **1** : to permit or cause to leave ⟨~*ed* his visitor⟩ **2** : to remove from position or service : DISCHARGE **3 a** : to bar from attention or serious consideration ⟨~*ed* the thought⟩ **b** : to put out of judicial consideration ⟨~*ed* all charges⟩ **syn** see EJECT

dis·miss·al \-ˈmis-əl\ *n* : the act of dismissing : the fact or state of being dismissed

dis·mis·sion \-ˈmish-ən\ *n* : DISMISSAL

dis·mis·sive \dis-ˈmis-iv\ *adj* : giving dismissal : serving to dismiss

[1]**dis·mount** \(ˈ)dis-ˈmau̇nt\ *vb* [prob. modif. of MF *desmonter*, fr. *des-* + *monter* to mount] *vi* **1** *obs* : DESCEND **2** : to alight from an elevated position (as on a horse) ~ *vt* **1** : to throw down or remove from a mount or an elevated position; *esp* : UNHORSE **2** : DISASSEMBLE

[2]**dismount** *n* : the act of dismounting

dis·obe·di·ence \ˌdis-ə-ˈbēd-ē-ən(t)s\ *n* : refusal or neglect to obey

dis·obe·di·ent \-ənt\ *adj* [ME, fr. MF *desobedient*, fr. *des-* + *obedient*] : refusing or neglecting to obey — **dis·obe·di·ent·ly** *adv*

dis·obey \ˌdis-ə-ˈbā\ *vb* [ME *disobeyen*, fr. MF *desobeir*, fr. *des-* + *obeir* to obey] *vt* : to fail to obey ~ *vi* : to be disobedient — **dis·obey·er** *n*

dis·oblige \ˌdis-ə-ˈblīj\ *vt* [F *désobliger*, fr. MF, fr. *des-* + *obliger* to oblige] **1** : to go counter to the wishes of **2** : to put out : INCONVENIENCE

di·so·di·um phosphate \(ˌ)dī-ˌsōd-ē-əm-\ *n* : a sodium phosphate Na_2HPO_4

di·so·mic \(ˈ)dī-ˈsō-mik\ *adj* [*di-* + *-somic*] : having one or more chromosomes duplicated but not an entire genome duplicated

[1]**dis·or·der** \(ˈ)dis-ˈȯrd-ər, diz-\ *vt* **1** : to disturb the order of **2** : to disturb the regular or normal functions of

[2]**disorder** *n* **1** : lack of order ⟨clothes in ~⟩ **2** : breach of the peace or public order ⟨troubled times marked by social ~*s*⟩ **3** : an abnormal physical or mental condition : AILMENT

dis·or·dered *adj* **1** *obs* **a** : morally reprehensible **b** : UNRULY **2 a** : marked by disorder **b** : not functioning in a normal orderly healthy way — **dis·or·dered·ly** *adv* — **dis·or·dered·ness** *n*

[1]**dis·or·der·ly** \-ˈȯrd-ər-lē\ *adv*, *archaic* : in a disorderly manner

[2]**disorderly** *adj* **1** : characterized by disorder ⟨a ~ pile of clothes⟩ **2** : engaged in conduct offensive to public order ⟨charged with being drunk and ~⟩ — **dis·or·der·li·ness** *n*

disorderly conduct *n* : a petty offense chiefly against public order and decency that falls short of an indictable misdemeanor

dis·or·ga·nize \(ˈ)dis-ˈȯr-gə-ˌnīz\ *vt* [F *désorganiser*, fr. *dés-* dis- + *organiser* to organize] : to destroy or interrupt the orderly structure or function of — **dis·or·ga·ni·za·tion** \(ˌ)dis-ˌȯrg-(ə-)nə-ˈzā-shən\ *n*

dis·or·ga·nized *adj* : lacking coherence, system, or central guiding agency ⟨~ work habits⟩

dis·ori·ent \(ˈ)dis-ˈōr-ē-ˌent, -ˈȯr-\ *vt* [F *désorienter*, fr. *dés-* dis- + *orienter* to orient, fr. MF, fr. *orient*, n.] **1 a** : to cause to lose bearings : displace from normal position or relationship **b** : to cause to lose the sense of time, place, or identity **2** : CONFUSE

dis·ori·en·tate \-ē-ən-ˌtāt, -ē-ˌen-\ *vt* : DISORIENT — **dis·ori·en·ta·tion** \(ˌ)dis-ˌōr-ē-ən-ˈtā-shən, -ˌȯr-, -ē-ˌen-\ *n*

dis·own \(ˈ)dis-ˈōn\ *vt* **1** : to refuse to acknowledge as one's own **2 a** : to repudiate any connection or identification with **b** : to deny the validity or authority of — **dis·own·ment** \-mənt\ *n*

disp *abbr* dispensary

dis·par·age \dis-ˈpar-ij\ *vt* **-aged; -ag·ing** [ME *disparagen* to degrade by marriage below one's class, disparage, fr. MF *desparagier* to marry below one's class, fr. OF, fr. *des-* dis- + *parage* extraction, lineage, fr. *per* peer] **1** : to lower in rank or reputation : DEGRADE **2** : to depreciate by indirect means (as invidious comparison) : speak slightingly about **syn** see DECRY **ant** applaud — **dis·par·age·ment** \-ij-mənt\ *n* — **dis·par·ag·er** *n* — **dis·par·ag·ing** *adj* — **dis·par·ag·ing·ly** \-ij-iŋ-lē\ *adv*

dis·pa·rate \dis-ˈpar-ət, ˈdis-p(ə-)rət\ *adj* [L *disparatus*, pp. of *disparare* to separate, fr. *dis-* + *parare* to prepare — more at PARE] **1** : markedly distinct in quality or character **2** : containing or made up of fundamentally different and often incongruous elements **syn** see DIFFERENT **ant** comparable, analogous — **dis·pa·rate·ly** *adv* — **dis·pa·rate·ness** *n*

dis·par·i·ty \dis-ˈpar-ət-ē\ *n*, *pl* **-ties** [MF *desparité*, fr. LL *disparitat-*, *disparitas*, fr. L *dis-* + LL *paritat-*, *paritas* parity] : the state of being disparate : DIFFERENCE

dis·part \(ˈ)dis-ˈpärt\ *vb* [It & L; It *dispartire*, fr. L, fr. *dis-* + *partire* to divide — more at PART] *archaic* : SEPARATE, DIVIDE

dis·pas·sion \(ˈ)dis-ˈpash-ən\ *n* : absence of passion : COOLNESS

dis·pas·sion·ate \-(ə-)nət\ *adj* : not influenced by strong feeling; *esp* : not affected by personal or emotional involvement ⟨a ~ critic⟩ ⟨a ~ approach to a problem⟩ **syn** see FAIR — **dis·pas·sion·ate·ly** *adv* — **dis·pas·sion·ate·ness** *n*

[1]**dis·patch** \dis-ˈpach\ *vb* [Sp *despachar* or It *dispacciare*, fr. Prov *despachar* to get rid of, fr. MF *despeechier* to set free, fr. OF, fr. *des-* + *-peechier* (as in *empeechier* to hinder) — more at IMPEACH] *vt* **1** : to send off or away with promptness or speed esp. on official business **2 a** : to kill with quick efficiency ⟨~ an injured dog⟩ **b** *obs* : DEPRIVE **3** : to dispose of (as a task) rapidly or efficiently ~ *vi*, *archaic* : to make haste : HURRY **syn** see KILL — **dis·patch·er** *n*

[2]**dispatch** *n* **1** : the act of dispatching: as **a** *obs* : DISMISSAL **b** : the act of killing **c** (1) : prompt settlement (as of an item of business) (2) : quick riddance **d** : a sending off : SHIPMENT **2 a** : a message sent with speed; *esp* : an important official message sent by a diplomatic, military, or naval officer ⟨sent a ~ to the war department⟩ ⟨his military record brought him three mentions in ~*es* —*Current Biog.*⟩ **b** : a news item sent in by a correspondent to a newspaper **3** : promptness and efficiency in performance or transmission **syn** see HASTE

dispatch case *n* : a case for carrying papers

dis·pel \dis-ˈpel\ *vt* **dis·pelled; dis·pel·ling** [L *dispellere*, fr. *dis-* + *pellere* to drive, beat — more at FELT] : to drive away by scattering : DISSIPATE **syn** see SCATTER

dis·pens·able \dis-ˈpen(t)-sə-bəl\ *adj* : capable of being dispensed with : UNESSENTIAL — **dis·pens·abil·i·ty** \-ˌpen(t)-sə-ˈbil-ət-ē\ *n*

dis·pen·sa·ry \dis-ˈpen(t)s-(ə-)rē\ *n*, *pl* **-ries** **1** : a place where medical or dental aid is dispensed **2** : a store where liquor is sold under state regulations

dis·pen·sa·tion \ˌdis-pən-ˈsā-shən, -ˌpen-\ *n* **1 a** : a general state or ordering of things; *specif* : a system of revealed commands and promises regulating human affairs **b** : a particular arrangement or provision esp. of providence or nature **2 a** : an exemption from a law or from an impediment, vow, or oath **b** : a formal authorization **3 a** : the act of dispensing **b** : something dispensed or distributed — **dis·pen·sa·tion·al** \-shnəl, -shən-ᵊl\ *adj*

dis·pen·sa·to·ry \dis-ˈpen(t)-sə-ˌtōr-ē, -ˌtȯr-\ *n*, *pl* **-ries** **1** : a medicinal formulary **2** *archaic* : a place for keeping medical supplies

dis·pense \dis-ˈpen(t)s\ *vb* **dis·pensed; dis·pens·ing** [ME *dispensen*, fr. ML & L; ML *dispensare* to grant dispensation, fr. L, to distribute, fr. *dispensus*, pp. of *dispendere* to weigh out, fr. *dis-* + *pendere* to weigh — more at SPAN] *vt* **1 a** : to deal out in portions **b** : ADMINISTER ⟨~ justice⟩ **2** : to give dispensation to : EXEMPT **3** : to prepare and distribute (medication) ~ *vi*, *archaic* : to grant dispensation **syn** see DISTRIBUTE — **dispense with 1** : to suspend the operation of ⟨a people that has *dispensed with* its monarchy⟩ **2** : to do without ⟨could *dispense with* his assistants⟩

dis·pens·er \-ˈpen(t)-sər\ *n* : one that dispenses: as **a** : a container that extrudes, sprays, or feeds out in convenient units **b** : a usu. mechanical device for vending merchandise

dis·peo·ple \(ˈ)dis-ˈpē-pəl\ *vt* : DEPOPULATE

dis·pers·al \dis-ˈpər-səl\ *n* : the act or result of dispersing; *specif* : the process or result of the spreading of organisms from one place to another

dis·per·sant \dis-ˈpər-sənt\ *n* : a dispersing agent; *esp* : a substance for promoting the formation and stabilization of a dispersion of one substance in another — **dispersant** *adj*

dis·perse \dis-ˈpərs\ *vb* **dis·persed; dis·pers·ing** [ME *dysparsen,* fr. MF *disperser,* fr. L *dispersus,* pp. of *dispergere* to scatter, fr. *dis-* + *spargere* to scatter — more at SPARK] *vt* **1 a :** to cause to break up ⟨the meeting was *dispersed*⟩ **b :** to cause to become spread widely **c :** to cause to evaporate or vanish ⟨sunlight *dispersing* the vapor⟩ **2 :** to spread or distribute from a fixed or constant source: as **a** *archaic* **:** DISSEMINATE **b :** to subject (as light) to dispersion **c :** to distribute (as fine particles) more or less evenly throughout a medium ~ *vi* **1 :** to break up in random fashion ⟨the crowd *dispersed* at the policeman's request⟩ **2 a :** to become dispersed **b :** DISSIPATE, VANISH ⟨the fog *dispersed* toward morning⟩ ***syn*** see SCATTER — **dis·persed·ly** \-ˈpər-səd-lē, -ˈpərst-lē\ *adv* — **dis·pers·er** *n* — **dis·pers·ible** \-ˈpər-sə-bəl\ *adj*

disperse system *n* **:** DISPERSION 5b

dis·per·sion \dis-ˈpər-zhən, -shən\ *n* **1** *cap* **:** DIASPORA 1a **2 :** the act or process of dispersing **:** the state of being dispersed **3 :** the scattering of the values of a frequency distribution from an average **4 :** the separation of light into colors by refraction or diffraction with formation of a spectrum; *also* **:** the separation of nonhomogeneous radiation into components in accordance with some characteristic (as energy) **5 a :** a dispersed substance **b :** a system consisting of a dispersed substance and the medium in which it is dispersed **:** COLLOID 1b

dis·per·sive \-ˈpər-siv, -ziv\ *adj* **1 :** of or relating to dispersion ⟨a ~ medium⟩ ⟨the ~ power of a lens⟩ **2 :** tending to disperse — **dis·per·sive·ly** *adv* — **dis·per·sive·ness** *n*

dis·per·soid \-ˈpər-ˌsȯid\ *n* **:** finely divided particles of one substance dispersed in another

dispir·it \(ˈ)dis-ˈpir-ət\ *vt* [*dis-* + *spirit*] **:** to deprive of morale or enthusiasm — **dispir·it·ed** *adj* — **dispir·it·ed·ly** *adv* — **dispir·it·ed·ness** *n*

dis·pit·eous \dis-ˈpit-ē-əs\ *adj* [alter. of *despiteous*] *archaic* **:** CRUEL

dis·place \(ˈ)dis-ˈplās\ *vt* [prob. fr. MF *desplacer,* fr. *des-* dis- + *place*] **1 a :** to remove from the usual or proper place; *specif* **:** to expel or force to flee from home or homeland **b :** to remove from an office **c** *obs* **:** to drive out **:** BANISH **2 a :** to remove physically out of position ⟨water *displaced* by a floating object⟩ **b :** to take the place of (as in a chemical reaction) **:** SUPPLANT ***syn*** see REPLACE — **dis·place·able** \-ˈplā-sə-bəl\ *adj*

dis·place·ment \dis-ˈplā-smənt\ *n* **1 :** the act or process of displacing **:** the state of being displaced **2 a :** the volume or weight of a fluid (as water) displaced by a floating body (as a ship) of equal weight **b :** the difference between the initial position of a body and any later position **c :** the volume displaced by a piston (as in a pump or an engine) in a single stroke; *also* **:** the total volume so displaced by all the pistons in an internal-combustion engine (as in an automobile) **3 :** the substitution of another form of behavior for what is normal or expected esp. when the normal response is nonadaptive

dis·plant \dis-ˈplant\ *vt* [MF *desplanter,* fr. *des-* + *planter* to plant, fr. LL *plantare*] **1 :** DISPLACE, REMOVE **2 :** SUPPLANT

[1]**dis·play** \dis-ˈplā\ *vb* [ME *displayen,* fr. AF *despleier,* fr. L *displicare* to scatter, fr. *dis-* + *plicare* to fold — more at PLY] *vt* **1 a :** to put or spread before the view in display ⟨~ the flag⟩ **b :** to make evident ⟨~*ed* great skill⟩ **c :** to exhibit ostentatiously ⟨liked to ~ his erudition⟩ **2** *obs* **:** DESCRY ~ *vi* **1** *obs* **:** to show off **2 :** to make a breeding display ⟨penguins ~*ed* and copulated⟩

[2]**display** *n, often attrib* **1 a (1) :** a setting or presentation of something in open view ⟨a fireworks ~⟩ **(2) :** a clear sign or evidence **:** EXHIBITION ⟨a ~ of courage⟩ **b :** ostentatious show **c :** type composition designed to catch the eye; *also* **:** printed matter so composed **d :** an eye-catching arrangement by which something is exhibited **e :** a device (as a cathode-ray tube) that gives information in visual form in communications ⟨a computer ~⟩ ⟨a radar ~⟩ **2 :** a pattern of behavior exhibited esp. by male birds in the breeding season

dis·please \(ˈ)dis-ˈplēz\ *vb* [ME *displesen,* fr. MF *desplaisir,* fr. (assumed) VL *displacēre,* fr. L *dis-* + *placēre* to please] *vt* **1 :** to incur the disapproval of esp. as accompanied by annoyance or dislike ⟨fired any employee who *displeased* him⟩ **2 :** to be offensive to ⟨abstract art ~*s* him⟩ ~ *vi* **:** to give displeasure ⟨signs of inattention calculated to ~⟩

dis·plea·sure \(ˈ)dis-ˈplezh-ər, -ˈplāzh-\ *n* **1 :** the feeling of one that is displeased **:** DISFAVOR **2 :** DISCOMFORT, UNHAPPINESS **3** *archaic* **:** OFFENSE, INJURY

dis·plode \dis-ˈplōd\ *vb* **dis·plod·ed; dis·plod·ing** [L *displodere,* fr. *dis-* + *plaudere* to clap, applaud] *archaic* **:** EXPLODE — **dis·plo·sion** \-ˈplō-zhən\ *n*

[1]**dis·port** \dis-ˈpō(ə)rt, -ˈpȯ(ə)rt\ *n, archaic* **:** SPORT, PASTIME

[2]**disport** *vb* [ME *disporten,* fr. MF *desporter,* fr. *des-* + *porter* to carry] *vt* **1 :** DIVERT, AMUSE **2 :** DISPLAY ~ *vi* **:** to amuse oneself in light or lively fashion **:** FROLIC — **dis·port·ment** \-mənt\ *n*

[1]**dis·pos·able** \dis-ˈpō-zə-bəl\ *adj* **1 :** subject to or available for disposal; *specif* **:** remaining to an individual after deduction of taxes ⟨~ income⟩ **2 :** designed to be used once and then thrown away ⟨~ towels⟩ — **dis·pos·abil·i·ty** \-ˌpō-zə-ˈbil-ət-ē\ *n*

[2]**disposable** *n* **:** something (as a paper blanket) that is disposable

dis·pos·al \dis-ˈpō-zəl\ *n* **1 :** the act or process of disposing: as **a :** orderly placement or distribution **b :** REGULATION, ADMINISTRATION **c :** BESTOWAL **d :** systematic destruction; *esp* **:** destruction or transformation of garbage **2 :** the power or authority to dispose of ⟨the car was at my ~⟩ **3** [*garbage disposal unit*] **:** a device used to reduce waste matter (as by grinding)

[1]**dis·pose** \dis-ˈpōz\ *vb* **dis·posed; dis·pos·ing** [ME *disposen,* fr. MF *disposer,* fr. L *disponere* to arrange (perf. indic. *disposui*), fr. *dis-* + *ponere* to put — more at POSITION] *vt* **1 :** to give a tendency to **:** INCLINE ⟨faulty diet ~*s* one to sickness⟩ **2 a :** to put in place **:** set in readiness **:** ARRANGE ⟨*disposing* troops for withdrawal⟩ **b** *obs* **:** REGULATE **c :** BESTOW ~ *vi* **1 :** to settle a matter finally **2** *obs* **:** to come to terms ***syn*** see INCLINE — **dis·pos·er** *n* — **dispose of 1 :** to place, distribute, or arrange esp. in an orderly way **2 a :** to transfer to the control of another ⟨*disposing of* his personal property⟩ **b (1) :** to get rid of ⟨waste that is hard to *dispose of*⟩ **(2) :** to deal with conclusively ⟨*disposed of* the matter efficiently⟩

[2]**dispose** *n* **1** *obs* **:** DISPOSAL **2** *obs* **a :** DISPOSITION **b :** DEMEANOR

dis·po·si·tion \ˌdis-pə-ˈzish-ən\ *n* [ME, fr. MF, fr. L *disposition-, dispositio,* fr. *dispositus,* pp. of *disponere*] **1 :** the act or the power of disposing or the state of being disposed: as **a :** ADMINISTRATION, CONTROL **b :** final arrangement **:** SETTLEMENT ⟨the ~ of the case⟩ **c (1) :** transfer to the care or possession of another **(2) :** the power of such transferal **d :** orderly arrangement **2 a :** prevailing tendency, mood, or inclination **b :** temperamental makeup **c :** the tendency of something to act in a certain manner under given circumstances
syn DISPOSITION, TEMPERAMENT, TEMPER, CHARACTER, PERSONALITY *shared meaning element* **:** the dominant quality or qualities distinguishing a person or group

dis·pos·i·tive \dis-ˈpäz-ət-iv\ *adj* **:** directed towards or effecting disposition (as of a case) ⟨~ evidence⟩

dis·pos·sess \ˌdis-pə-ˈzes *also* -ˈses\ *vt* [MF *despossesser,* fr. *des-* dis- + *possesser* to possess] **:** to put out of possession or occupancy — **dis·pos·ses·sion** \-ˈzesh-ən *also* -ˈsesh-\ *n* — **dis·pos·ses·sor** \-ˈzes-ər *also* -ˈses-\ *n*

dis·pos·sessed *adj* **:** deprived of homes, possessions, and security

dis·po·sure \dis-ˈpō-zhər\ *n, archaic* **:** DISPOSAL, DISPOSITION

[1]**dis·praise** \(ˈ)dis-ˈprāz\ *vt* [ME *dispraisen,* fr. OF *despreisier,* fr. *des-* dis- + *preisier* to praise] **:** to comment on with disapproval or censure — **dis·prais·er** *n* — **dis·prais·ing·ly** \-ˈprā-ziŋ-lē\ *adv*

[2]**dispraise** *n* **:** an expression of disapproval **:** DISPARAGEMENT

dispread \dis-ˈpred\ *vt* **:** to spread abroad or out

dis·prize \(ˈ)dis-ˈprīz\ *vt* [MF *despriser,* fr. OF *despreisier* to dispraise] *archaic* **:** UNDERVALUE, SCORN

dis·proof \(ˈ)dis-ˈprüf\ *n* **1 :** the action of disproving **2 :** evidence that disproves

[1]**dis·pro·por·tion** \ˌdis-prə-ˈpōr-shən, -ˈpȯr-\ *n* **:** lack of proportion, symmetry, or proper relation **:** DISPARITY; *also* **:** an instance of such disparity — **dis·pro·por·tion·al** \-shnəl, -shən-ᵊl\ *adj*

[2]**disproportion** *vt* **:** to make out of proportion **:** MISMATCH

dis·pro·por·tion·ate \-sh(ə-)nət\ *adj* **:** being out of proportion — **dis·pro·por·tion·ate·ly** *adv*

dis·pro·por·tion·ation \-ˌpōr-shə-ˈnā-shən, -ˌpȯr-\ *n* **:** the transformation of a substance into two or more dissimilar substances usu. by simultaneous oxidation and reduction — **dis·pro·por·tion·ate** \-ˈpōr-shə-ˌnāt, -ˈpȯr-\ *vi*

dis·prove \(ˈ)dis-ˈprüv\ *vt* [ME *disproven,* fr. MF *desprover,* fr. *des-* + *prover* to prove] **:** to prove to be false **:** REFUTE — **dis·prov·able** \-ˈprü-və-bəl\ *adj*
syn DISPROVE, REFUTE, CONFUTE, REBUT, CONTROVERT *shared meaning element* **:** to show or try to show by presenting evidence that something (as a claim, statement, or charge) is not true ***ant*** prove, demonstrate

dis·pu·tant \dis-ˈpyüt-ᵊnt, ˈdis-pyət-ənt\ *n* **:** one that is engaged in a dispute

dis·pu·ta·tion \ˌdis-pyə-ˈtā-shən\ *n* **1 :** the act of disputing **:** DEBATE **2 :** an academic exercise in oral defense of a thesis by formal logic

dis·pu·ta·tious \-shəs\ *adj* **1 :** inclined to dispute **2 :** provoking debate **:** CONTROVERSIAL — **dis·pu·ta·tious·ly** *adv* — **dis·pu·ta·tious·ness** *n*

[1]**dis·pute** \dis-ˈpyüt\ *vb* **dis·put·ed; dis·put·ing** [ME *disputen,* fr. OF *desputer,* fr. L *disputare* to discuss, fr. *dis-* + *putare* to think] *vi* **:** to engage in argument **:** DEBATE; *esp* **:** to argue irritably or with irritating persistence ~ *vt* **1 a :** to make the subject of disputation **b :** to call into question ⟨the honesty of his intent was never *disputed*⟩ **2 a :** to struggle against ⟨*disputed* the advance of the invaders⟩ **b :** to struggle over **:** CONTEST ⟨the defending troops *disputed* every inch of ground⟩ ***syn*** see DISCUSS — **dis·pu·ta·ble** \dis-ˈpyüt-ə-bəl, ˈdis-pyət-\ *adj* — **dis·pu·ta·bly** \-blē\ *adv* — **dis·put·er** *n*

[2]**dis·pute** \dis-ˈpyüt, ˈdis-ˌ\ *n* **1 a :** verbal controversy **:** DEBATE **b :** QUARREL **2** *obs* **:** physical combat

dis·qual·i·fi·ca·tion \(ˌ)dis-ˌkwäl-ə-fə-ˈkā-shən\ *n* **1 :** the act of disqualifying **:** the state of being disqualified ⟨~ from office⟩ **2 :** something that disqualifies or incapacitates

dis·qual·i·fy \(ˈ)dis-ˈkwäl-ə-ˌfī\ *vt* **1 :** to deprive of the required qualities, properties, or conditions **:** make unfit **2 :** to deprive of a power, right, or privilege **3 :** to make ineligible for a prize or for further competition because of violations of the rules

dis·quan·ti·ty \(ˈ)dis-ˈkwän(t)-ət-ē\ *vt, obs* **:** DIMINISH, LESSEN

[1]**dis·qui·et** \(ˈ)dis-ˈkwī-ət\ *vt* **:** to take away the peace or tranquillity of **:** DISTURB, ALARM ***syn*** see DISCOMPOSE ***ant*** tranquilize, soothe — **dis·qui·et·ing** *adj* — **dis·qui·et·ing·ly** \-iŋ-lē\ *adv*

[2]**disquiet** *n* **:** lack of peace or tranquillity **:** ANXIETY

[3]**disquiet** *adj, archaic* **:** UNEASY, DISQUIETED — **dis·qui·et·ly** *adv*

dis·qui·etude \(ˈ)dis-ˈkwī-ə-ˌt(y)üd\ *n* **:** AGITATION, ANXIETY

dis·qui·si·tion \ˌdis-kwə-ˈzish-ən\ *n* [L *disquisition-, disquisitio,* fr. *disquisitus,* pp. of *disquirere* to inquire diligently, fr. *dis-* + *quaerere* to seek — more at QUEST] **:** a formal inquiry into or discussion of a subject **:** DISCOURSE

dis·rate \(ˈ)dis-ˈrāt\ *vt* **:** to reduce in rank **:** DEMOTE ***syn*** see DEGRADE

[1]**dis·re·gard** \ˌdis-ri-ˈgärd\ *vt* **:** to pay no attention to **:** treat as unworthy of regard or notice ***syn*** see NEGLECT

[2]**disregard** *n* **:** the act of disregarding **:** the state of being disregarded **:** NEGLECT — **dis·re·gard·ful** \-fəl\ *adj*

dis·re·lat·ed \ˌdis-ri-ˈlāt-əd\ *adj* **:** not related

dis·re·la·tion \-ˈlā-shən\ *n* **:** lack of a fitting or proportionate connection or relationship

[1]**dis·rel·ish** \(ˈ)dis-ˈrel-ish\ *vt* **:** to find unpalatable or distasteful

ə abut ᵊ kitten ər further a back ā bake ä cot, cart
aú out ch chin e less ē easy g gift i trip ī life
j joke ŋ sing ō flow ȯ flaw ȯi coin th thin *th* this
ü loot ú foot y yet yü few yú furious zh vision

²disrelish *n* : lack of relish : DISTASTE, DISLIKE
dis·re·mem·ber \ˌdis-ri-ˈmem-bər\ *vt* : FORGET ⟨I ~ rightly what I did —Elizabeth C. Gaskell⟩
dis·re·pair \ˌdis-ri-ˈpa(ə)r, -ˈpe(ə)r\ *n* : the state of being in need of repair ⟨a building fallen into ~⟩
dis·rep·u·ta·ble \(ˈ)dis-ˈrep-yət-ə-bəl\ *adj* : not reputable — dis·rep·u·ta·bil·i·ty \(ˌ)dis-ˌrep-yət-ə-ˈbil-ət-ē\ *n* — dis·rep·u·ta·ble·ness \(ˈ)dis-ˈrep-yət-ə-bəl-nəs\ *n* — dis·rep·u·ta·bly \-blē\ *adv*
dis·re·pute \ˌdis-ri-ˈpyüt\ *n* : lack or decline of good reputation : a state of being held in low esteem ⟨the hotel fell into ~ after the bar was added⟩ *syn* see DISGRACE *ant* repute
¹dis·re·spect \ˌdis-ri-ˈspekt\ *vt* : to have disrespect for
²disrespect *n* : lack of respect or reverence — dis·re·spect·ful \-fəl\ *adj* — dis·re·spect·ful·ly \-fə-lē\ *adv* — dis·re·spect·ful·ness *n*
dis·re·spect·able \ˌdis-ri-ˈspek-tə-bəl\ *adj* : not respectable — dis·re·spect·abil·i·ty \-ˌspek-tə-ˈbil-ət-ē\ *n*
dis·robe \(ˈ)dis-ˈrōb\ *vb* [MF *desrober*, fr. *des-* dis- + *robe* garment — more at ROBE] *vt* : to strip of clothing or covering ~ *vi* : to take off one's clothing
dis·rupt \dis-ˈrəpt\ *vt* [L *disruptus*, pp. of *disrumpere*, fr. *dis-* + *rumpere* to break — more at RUPTURE] **1 a** : to break apart : RUPTURE **b** : to throw into disorder ⟨agitators trying to ~ the meeting⟩ **2** : to cause to break down — dis·rupt·er *n* — dis·rup·tion \-ˈrəp-shən\ *n* — dis·rup·tive \-ˈrəp-tiv\ *adj* — dis·rup·tive·ly *adv* — dis·rup·tive·ness *n*
diss *abbr* dissertation
dis·sat·is·fac·tion \(ˌ)dis-ˌ(s)at-əs-ˈfak-shən\ *n* : the quality or state of being dissatisfied : DISCONTENT
dis·sat·is·fac·to·ry \-ˈfak-t(ə-)rē\ *adj* : causing dissatisfaction
dis·sat·is·fy \(ˈ)dis-ˈ(s)at-əs-ˌfī\ *vt* : to fail to satisfy : DISPLEASE
dis·save \(ˈ)dis-ˈ(s)āv\ *vi* : to use savings for current expenses
dis·seat \(ˈ)dis-ˈ(s)ēt\ *vt, archaic* : UNSEAT
dis·sect \dis-ˈekt; dī-ˈsekt, ˈdī-ˌ\ *vb* [L *dissectus*, pp. of *dissecare* to cut apart, fr. *dis-* + *secare* to cut — more at SAW] *vt* **1** : to separate into pieces : expose the several parts of (as an animal) for scientific examination **2** : to analyze and interpret minutely ~ *vi* : to make a dissection *syn* see ANALYZE — dis·sec·tor \-ər\ *n*
dis·sect·ed *adj* **1** : cut deeply into fine lobes ⟨a ~ leaf⟩ **2** : divided into hills and ridges (as by gorges) ⟨a ~ plateau⟩
dis·sec·tion \dis-ˈek-shən; dī-ˈsek-, ˈdī-ˌ\ *n* **1** : the act or process of dissecting : the state of being dissected **2** : an anatomical specimen prepared by dissecting
dis·seise *or* dis·seize \(ˈ)dis-ˈ(s)ēz\ *vt* dis·seised *or* dis·seized; dis·seis·ing *or* dis·seiz·ing [ME *disseisen*, fr. ML *disseisiare* & AF *disseisir*, fr. OF *dessaisir*, fr. *des-* + *saisir* to put in possession of — more at SEIZE] : to deprive esp. wrongfully of seisin : DISPOSSESS
dis·sei·sin *or* dis·sei·zin \-ˈ(s)ēz-ᵊn\ *n* [ME *dysseysyne*, fr. AF *disseisine*, fr. OF *dessaisine*, fr. *des-* dis- + *saisine* seisin] : the act of disseising : the state of being disseised
dis·sem·ble \dis-ˈem-bəl\ *vb* dis·sem·bled; dis·sem·bling \-b(ə-)liŋ\ [alter. of obs. *dissimule*, fr. ME *dissimulen*, fr. MF *dissimuler*, fr. L *dissimulare* — more at DISSIMULATE] *vt* **1** : to hide under a false appearance **2** : to put on the appearance of : SIMULATE ~ *vi* : to put on a false appearance : conceal facts, intentions, or feelings under some pretense *syn* see DISGUISE — dis·sem·bler \-b(ə-)lər\ *n*
dis·sem·i·nate \dis-ˈem-ə-ˌnāt\ *vb* -nat·ed; -nat·ing [L *disseminatus*, pp. of *disseminare*, fr. *dis-* + *seminare* to sow, fr. *semin-*, *semen* seed — more at SEMEN] *vt* **1** : to spread abroad as though sowing seed ⟨~ ideas⟩ **2** : to disperse throughout ~ *vi* : to spread widely — dis·sem·i·na·tion \-ˌem-ə-ˈnā-shən\ *n* — dis·sem·i·na·tor \-ˈem-ə-ˌnāt-ər\ *n*
dis·sem·i·nule \dis-ˈem-ə-ˌn(y)ü(ə)l\ *n* : a part or organ (as a seed or spore) of a plant that ensures propagation
dis·sen·sion *also* dis·sen·tion \dis-ˈen-chən\ *n* [ME, fr. MF, fr. L *dissension-*, *dissensio*, fr. *dissensus*, pp. of *dissentire*] : DISAGREEMENT; *esp* : partisan and contentious quarreling *syn* see DISCORD *ant* accord, comity
¹dis·sent \dis-ˈent\ *vi* [ME *dissenten*, fr. L *dissentire*, fr. *dis-* + *sentire* to feel — more at SENSE] **1** : to withhold assent **2** : to differ in opinion
²dissent *n* : difference of opinion: as **a** : religious nonconformity **b** : a justice's nonconcurrence with a decision of the majority — called also *dissenting opinion*
dis·sent·er \dis-ˈent-ər\ *n* **1** : one that dissents **2** *cap* : an English Nonconformist
dis·sen·tient \dis-ˈen-ch(ē-)ənt\ *adj* [L *dissentient-*, *dissentiens*, prp. of *dissentire*] : expressing dissent — dissentient *n*
dis·sent·ing \dis-ˈent-iŋ\ *adj, often cap* : belonging to the party of English Nonconformists
dis·sep·i·ment \dis-ˈep-ə-mənt\ *n* [L *dissaepimentum* partition, fr. *dissaepire* to divide, fr. *dis-* + *saepire* to fence in — more at SEPTUM] : a dividing tissue : SEPTUM; *esp* : a partition between cells of a compound plant ovary
dis·sert \dis-ˈərt\ *vi* [L *dissertus*, pp. of *disserere*, fr. *dis-* + *serere* to join, arrange — more at SERIES] : DISCOURSE
dis·ser·tate \ˈdis-ər-ˌtāt\ *vi* -tat·ed; -tat·ing [L *dissertatus*, pp. of *dissertare*, fr. *dissertus*] : DISCOURSE — dis·ser·ta·tor \-ˌtāt-ər\ *n*
dis·ser·ta·tion \ˌdis-ər-ˈtā-shən\ *n* : an extended usu. written treatment of a subject; *specif* : one submitted for a doctorate
dis·serve \(ˈ)dis-ˈ(s)ərv\ *vt* : to serve badly or falsely : HARM ⟨*disserving* the very democracy in which he ardently believes —*New Republic*⟩
dis·ser·vice \(ˈ)dis-ˈ(s)ər-vəs\ *n* : ill service : INJURY ⟨they do a great ~ . . . to our society —Howard Kirschenbaum⟩
dis·sev·er \dis-ˈev-ər\ *vb* [ME *disseveren*, fr. OF *dessevrer*, fr. LL *disseparare*, fr. L *dis-* + *separare* to separate] *vt* : SEVER, SEPARATE ~ *vi* : to come apart : DISUNITE — dis·sev·er·ance \-ˈev-(ə-)rən(t)s\ *n* — dis·sev·er·ment \-ˈev-ər-mənt\ *n*
dis·si·dence \ˈdis-əd-ən(t)s\ *n* : DISSENT, DISAGREEMENT ⟨arresting people for political ~ —Peggy Durdin⟩
dis·si·dent \-ənt\ *adj* [L *dissident-*, *dissidens*, prp. of *dissidēre* to sit apart, disagree, fr. *dis-* + *sedēre* to sit — more at SIT] : differing with an opinion or a group : DISAFFECTED — dissident *n*
dis·sim·i·lar \(ˈ)dis-ˈ(s)im-(ə-)lər\ *adj* : UNLIKE — dis·sim·i·lar·i·ty \(ˌ)dis-ˌ(s)im-ə-ˈlar-ət-ē\ *n* — dis·sim·i·lar·ly \(ˈ)dis-ˈ(s)im-(ə-)lər-lē\ *adv*
dis·sim·i·late \(ˈ)dis-ˈim-ə-ˌlāt\ *vb* -lat·ed; -lat·ing [*dis-* + *-similate* (as in *assimilate*)] *vt* : to make dissimilar ~ *vi* : to become dissimilar — dis·sim·i·la·tive \-ˌlāt-iv\ *adj* — dis·sim·i·la·to·ry \-(ə-)lə-ˌtōr-ē, -ˌtȯr-\ *adj*
dis·sim·i·la·tion \(ˌ)dis-ˌim-ə-ˈlā-shən\ *n* : the act of making or the process of becoming dissimilar: as **a** : CATABOLISM **b** : the development of dissimilarity between two identical or closely related sounds in a word
dis·si·mil·i·tude \ˌdis-(s)ə-ˈmil-ə-ˌt(y)üd\ *n* [L *dissimilitudo*, fr. *dissimilis* unlike, fr. *dis-* + *similis* like] : lack of resemblance
dis·sim·u·late \(ˈ)dis-ˈim-yə-ˌlāt\ *vb* -lat·ed; -lat·ing [L *dissimulatus*, pp. of *dissimulare*, fr. *dis-* + *simulare* to simulate] *vt* : to hide under a false appearance : DISSEMBLE ~ *vi* : to engage in dissembling — dis·sim·u·la·tion \(ˌ)dis-ˌim-yə-ˈlā-shən\ *n* — dis·sim·u·la·tor \(ˈ)dis-ˈim-yə-ˌlāt-ər\ *n*
dis·si·pate \ˈdis-ə-ˌpāt\ *vb* -pat·ed; -pat·ing [L *dissipatus*, pp. of *dissipare*, fr. *dis-* + *supare* to throw; akin to ON *svāf* spear, Skt *svapū* broom] *vt* **1 a** : to break up and drive off (as a crowd) **b** : to cause to spread out or spread thin to the point of vanishing : DISSOLVE **c** : to lose (as heat or electricity) irrecoverably : DISPEL **2 a** : to expend aimlessly or foolishly **b** : to use up esp. foolishly or heedlessly ⟨soon *dissipated* his estate⟩ ~ *vi* **1** : to separate into parts and scatter or vanish **2** : to be extravagant or dissolute in the pursuit of pleasure; *esp* : to drink to excess *syn* **1** see SCATTER **2** see WASTE *ant* accumulate, concentrate — dis·si·pat·er *n*
dis·si·pat·ed *adj* : given to or marked by dissipation : DISSOLUTE — dis·si·pat·ed·ly *adv* — dis·si·pat·ed·ness *n*
dis·si·pa·tion \ˌdis-ə-ˈpā-shən\ *n* **1** : the act or process of dissipating : the state of being dissipated: **a** : DISPERSION, DIFFUSION **b** *archaic* : DISSOLUTION, DISINTEGRATION **c** : wasteful expenditure **d** : intemperate living; *esp* : excessive drinking **2** : DIVERSION, AMUSEMENT
dis·si·pa·tive \ˈdis-ə-ˌpāt-iv\ *adj* : relating to dissipation esp. of heat
dis·so·cia·ble \(ˈ)dis-ˈō-sh(ē-)ə-bəl, -sē-ə-\ *adj* : SEPARABLE — dis·so·cia·bil·i·ty \(ˌ)dis-ˌō-sh(ē-)ə-ˈbil-ət-ē, -sē-ə-\ *n*
dis·so·cial \(ˈ)dis-ˈ(s)ō-shəl\ *adj* : UNSOCIAL, SELFISH
dis·so·ciant \dis-ˈō-s(h)ē-ənt, -ˈō-shənt\ *adj* : producing or resulting from dissociation; *specif* : MUTANT
dis·so·ci·ate \(ˈ)dis-ˈō-s(h)ē-ˌāt\ *vb* -at·ed; -at·ing [L *dissociatus*, pp. of *dissociare*, fr. *dis-* + *sociare* to join, fr. *socius* companion — more at SOCIAL] *vt* **1** : to separate from association or union with another : DISCONNECT **2** : DISUNITE; *specif* : to subject to chemical dissociation ~ *vi* **1** : to undergo dissociation **2** : to mutate esp. reversibly
dis·so·ci·a·tion \(ˌ)dis-ˌō-sē-ˈā-shən, -shē-\ *n* **1** : the act or process of dissociating : the state of being dissociated: as **a** : the process by which a chemical combination breaks up into simpler constituents; *esp* : one that results from the action of energy (as heat) on a gas or of a solvent on a dissolved substance **b** : the separation of an idea or activity from the mainstream of consciousness or of behavior esp. as a mechanism of ego defense **2** : the property inherent in some biological stocks (as of certain bacteria) of differentiating into two or more distinct and relatively permanent strains; *also* : such a strain — dis·so·cia·tive \(ˈ)dis-ˈō-s(h)ē-ˌāt-iv, -shət-iv\ *adj*
dis·sol·u·ble \dis-ˈäl-yə-bəl\ *adj* [L *dissolubilis*, fr. *dissolvere* to dissolve] : capable of being dissolved or disintegrated — dis·sol·u·bil·i·ty \-ˌäl-yə-ˈbil-ət-ē\ *n*
dis·so·lute \ˈdis-ə-ˌlüt, -lət\ *adj* [L *dissolutus*, fr. pp. of *dissolvere* to loosen, dissolve] : lacking restraint; *esp* : loose in morals — dis·so·lute·ly *adv* — dis·so·lute·ness *n*
dis·so·lu·tion \ˌdis-ə-ˈlü-shən\ *n* **1** : the act or process of dissolving: as **a** : separation into component parts **b (1)** : DISINTEGRATION, DECAY **(2)** : DEATH ⟨grew convinced of his friend's approaching ~ —Elinor Wylie⟩ **c** : termination or destruction by breaking down, disrupting, or dispersing ⟨the ~ of the republic⟩ **d** : LIQUEFACTION **2** *obs* : PROFLIGACY
¹dis·solve \diz-ˈälv, -ˈȯlv\ *vb* [ME *dissolven*, fr. L *dissolvere*, fr. *dis-* + *solvere* to loosen — more at SOLVE] *vt* **1 a** : to cause to disperse or disappear : DESTROY **b** : to separate into component parts : DISINTEGRATE **c** : to bring to an end : TERMINATE ⟨~ parliament⟩ **2 a** : to cause to pass into solution ⟨~ sugar in water⟩ **b** : MELT, LIQUEFY **c** : to cause to be emotionally moved **d** : to fade out (a motion-picture or television shot) in a dissolve **3** *archaic* : DETACH, LOOSEN **4** : to clear up ⟨~ the mystery⟩ ~ *vi* **1 a** : to become dissipated or decomposed **b** : to break up : DISPERSE **c** : to fade away **2 a** : to become fluid : MELT **b** : to pass into solution **c** : to be overcome emotionally **d** : to resolve itself as if by dissolution *syn* see ADJOURN — dis·solv·able \-ˈäl-və-bəl, -ˈȯl-\ *adj* — dis·solv·er *n*
²dissolve *n* : a gradual superimposing of one motion-picture or television shot upon another on a screen
dis·sol·vent \diz-ˈäl-vənt, -ˈȯl-\ *adj* : SOLVENT 2 — dissolvent *n*
dis·so·nance \ˈdis-ə-nən(t)s\ *n* **1** : a mingling of discordant sounds; *specif* : a clashing musical interval **2** : lack of agreement; *specif* : inconsistency between the beliefs one holds or between one's actions and one's beliefs ⟨cognitive ~⟩ : DISCORD **3** : an unresolved musical note or chord; *specif* : an interval not included in a major or minor triad or its inversions
dis·so·nant \-nənt\ *adj* [MF or L; MF, fr. L *dissonant-*, *dissonans*, prp. of *dissonare* to be discordant, fr. *dis-* + *sonare* to sound — more at SOUND] **1** : marked by dissonance : DISCORDANT **2** : INCONGRUOUS **3** : harmonically unresolved — dis·so·nant·ly *adv*
dis·spir·it \(ˈ)dis-ˈ(s)pir-ət\ *var of* DISPIRIT
dis·suade \dis-ˈwād\ *vt* dis·suad·ed; dis·suad·ing [MF or L; MF *dissuader*, fr. L *dissuadēre*, fr. *dis-* + *suadēre* to urge — more at SUASION] **1 a** *archaic* : to advise against (an action) **b** : to ad-

vise (a person) against something **2** : to turn from something by persuasion ⟨~ a friend from joining the society⟩ — **dis·suad·er** *n*
dis·sua·sion \dis-ˈwā-zhən\ *n* [MF or L; MF, fr. L *dissuasion-, dissuasio,* fr. *dissuasus,* pp. of *dissuadēre*] : the act of dissuading
dis·sua·sive \dis-ˈwā-siv, -ziv\ *adj* : tending to dissuade — **dis·sua·sive·ly** *adv* — **dis·sua·sive·ness** *n*
dis·syl·lab·ic \ˌdis-ə-ˈlab-ik, ˌdī-sə-\, **dis·syl·la·ble** \ˈdis-ˌil-ə-bəl, (ˈ)dis-ˈ(s)il-; ˈdī-ˌsil-, (ˈ)dī-ˈsil-\ *var of* DISYLLABIC, DISYLLABLE
dis·sym·me·try \(ˈ)dis-ˈ(s)im-ə-trē\ *n* : the absence of or the lack of symmetry — **dis·sym·met·ric** \ˌdis-(s)ə-ˈme-trik\ *adj*
dist *abbr* **1** distance **2** district
[1]**dis·taff** \ˈdis-ˌtaf\ *n, pl* **distaffs** \-ˌtafs, -ˌtavz\ [ME *distaf,* fr. OE *distæf,* fr. *dis-* (akin to MLG *dise* bunch of flax) + *stæf* staff] **1 a** : a staff for holding the flax, tow, or wool in spinning **b** : woman's work or domain **2** : the female branch or side of a family
[2]**distaff** *adj* : MATERNAL, FEMALE ⟨the ~ side of the family⟩ — compare SPEAR
dis·tain \dis-ˈtān\ *vt* [ME *disteynen,* fr. MF *desteindre* to take away the color of, fr. OF, fr. *des-* dis- + *teindre* to dye, fr. L *tingere* to wet, dye — more at TINGE] **1** *archaic* : STAIN **2** *archaic* : DISHONOR
dis·tal \ˈdis-tᵊl\ *adj* [*distant* + *-al*] : far from the point of attachment or origin — compare PROXIMAL — **dis·tal·ly** \-tᵊl-ē\ *adv*
distal convoluted tubule *n* : the convoluted portion of the vertebrate nephron that lies between the loop of Henle and the nonsecretory part of the nephron and that is concerned esp. with the concentration of urine

1, distaff 1a

[1]**dis·tance** \ˈdis-tən(t)s\ *n* **1** *obs* : DISCORD **2 a** : separation in time **b** : the degree or amount of separation between two points, lines, surfaces, or objects measured along the shortest path joining them **c** : an extent of area or an advance along a route measured linearly **d** : an extent of advance away or along from a point considered primary or original **e** : EXPANSE **3** : the quality or state of being distant: as **a** : spatial remoteness **b** : RESERVE, COLDNESS **c** : DIFFERENCE, DISPARITY **4** : a distant point or region
[2]**distance** *vt* **dis·tanced; dis·tanc·ing** **1** : to place or keep at a distance **2** : to leave far behind : OUTSTRIP
dis·tant \ˈdis-tənt\ *adj* [ME, fr. MF, fr. L *distant-, distans,* prp. of *distare* to stand apart, be distant, fr. *dis-* + *stare* to stand — more at STAND] **1 a** : separated in space : AWAY **b** : situated at a great distance : FAR-OFF **c** : separated by a great distance from each other : far apart **2** : separated in a relationship other than spatial ⟨a ~ relative⟩ **3** : different in kind **4** : reserved or aloof in personal relationship : COLD ⟨~ politeness⟩ **5 a** : coming from or going to a distance ⟨~ voyages⟩ **b** : concerned with or directed toward things at a distance ⟨~ thoughts⟩ — **dis·tant·ly** *adv* — **dis·tant·ness** *n*
syn DISTANT, FAR, FAR-OFF, FARAWAY, REMOTE, REMOVED *shared meaning element* : not close in space, time, or relationship
[1]**dis·taste** \(ˈ)dis-ˈtāst\ *vt* **1** *archaic* : to feel aversion to **2** *archaic* : OFFEND, DISPLEASE ~ *vi, obs* : to have an offensive taste
[2]**distaste** *n* **1 a** : dislike of food or drink **b** : AVERSION, DISINCLINATION **2** *obs* : ANNOYANCE, DISCOMFORT
dis·taste·ful \(ˈ)dis-ˈtāst-fəl\ *adj* **1 a** : unpleasant to the taste : LOATHSOME **b** : objectionable because offensive to one's personal taste : DISAGREEABLE ⟨boys who find study ~⟩ **2** : showing distaste or aversion ⟨a ~ expression on her face⟩ ***syn*** see REPUGNANT ***ant*** agreeable, palatable — **dis·taste·ful·ly** \-fə-lē\ *adv* — **dis·taste·ful·ness** *n*
[1]**dis·tem·per** \dis-ˈtem-pər\ *vt* [ME *distempren,* fr. LL *distemperare* to temper badly, fr. L *dis-* + *temperare* to temper] **1** : to throw out of order **2** *archaic* : DERANGE, UNSETTLE
[2]**distemper** *n* **1** : bad humor or temper **2** : a disordered or abnormal bodily state esp. of quadruped mammals: as **a** : a highly contagious virus disease esp. of dogs marked by fever and by respiratory and sometimes nervous symptoms **b** : STRANGLES **c** : PANLEUCOPENIA **d** : a severe frequently fatal infectious nasopharyngeal inflammation of rabbits **3** : political or social disorder ⟨in the middle ages . . . resistance was an ordinary remedy for political ~*s* —T. B. Macaulay⟩ — **dis·tem·per·ate** \-p(ə-)rət\ *adj*
[3]**distemper** *vt* [ME *distemperen,* fr. MF *destemprer,* fr. L *dis-* + *temperare*] **1** *obs* : to dilute with or soak, steep, or dissolve in a liquid **2 a** : to mix (ingredients) to produce distemper **b** : to paint in or with distemper
[4]**distemper** *n* **1** : a process of painting in which the pigments are mixed with an emulsion of egg yolk, with size, or with white of egg as a vehicle and which is used for scene painting or mural decoration **2 a** : the paint or the prepared ground used in the distemper process **b** : a painting done in distemper **3** : any of numerous paints using water as a vehicle
dis·tem·per·a·ture \dis-ˈtem-pə(r)-ˌchu̇(ə)r, -p(ə-)rə-, -chər, -ˌt(y)u̇(ə)r\ *n* : a disordered condition
dis·tem·per·oid \dis-ˈtem-pə-ˌrȯid\ *adj* : resembling distemper; *specif* : of, relating to, or being an attenuated canine distemper virus used to develop immunity to natural distemper infection
dis·tend \dis-ˈtend\ *vb* [ME *distenden,* fr. L *distendere,* fr. *dis-* + *tendere* to stretch — more at THIN] *vt* **1** : EXTEND **2** : to enlarge from internal pressure : SWELL ~ *vi* : to become expanded ***syn*** see EXPAND ***ant*** constrict
dis·ten·si·ble \-ˈten(t)-sə-bəl\ *adj* [LL *distensus,* pp. of L *distendere*] : capable of being distended — **dis·ten·si·bil·i·ty** \-ˌten(t)-sə-ˈbil-ət-ē\ *n*
dis·ten·sion *or* **dis·ten·tion** \dis-ˈten-chən\ *n* [L *distention-, distentio,* fr. *distentus,* pp. of *distendere*] : the act of distending or the state of being distended esp. unduly or abnormally
dis·tent \dis-ˈtent\ *adj, obs* : spread out : DISTENDED
dis·tich \ˈdis-(ˌ)tik\ *n* [L *distichon,* fr. Gk, fr. neut. of *distichos* having two rows, fr. *di-* + *stichos* row, verse; akin to Gk *steichein* to go — more at STAIR] : a strophic unit of two lines
dis·ti·chous \ˈdis-ti-kəs\ *adj* [LL *distichus,* fr. Gk *distichos*] **1** : disposed in two vertical rows ⟨~ leaves⟩ **2** : divided into two segments ⟨~ antennae⟩ — **dis·ti·chous·ly** *adv*
dis·till *also* **dis·til** \dis-ˈtil\ *vb* **dis·tilled; dis·till·ing** [ME *distillen,* fr. MF *distiller,* fr. LL *distillare,* alter. of L *destillare,* fr. *de-* + *stillare* to drip, fr. *stilla* drop; akin to OE *stān* stone — more at STONE] *vt* **1** : to let fall, exude, or precipitate in drops or in a wet mist **2 a** : to subject to or transform by distillation **b** : to obtain by or as if by distillation **c** : to extract the essence of : CONCENTRATE ~ *vi* **1 a** : to fall or materialize in drops or in a fine moisture : DROP **b** : to appear slowly or in small quantities at a time **2 a** : to undergo distillation **b** : to condense or drop from a still after distillation
dis·til·late \ˈdis-tə-ˌlāt, -lət; dis-ˈtil-ət\ *n* **1** : a liquid product condensed from vapor during distillation **2** : something resembling a distillate in being a concentration, an abstract, or an essence ⟨this book is a ~ of facts —*N. Y. Times Bk. Rev.*⟩
dis·til·la·tion \ˌdis-tə-ˈlā-shən\ *n* **1** : a process that consists of driving gas or vapor from liquids or solids by heating and condensing to liquid products and that is used esp. for purification, fractionation, or the formation of new substances **2** : DISTILLATE
dis·till·er \dis-ˈtil-ər\ *n* : one that distills esp. alcoholic liquors
dis·till·ery \dis-ˈtil-(ə-)rē\ *n, pl* **-er·ies** : the works where distilling (as of alcoholic liquors) is done
dis·tinct \dis-ˈtiŋ(k)t\ *adj* [ME, fr. MF, fr. L *distinctus,* fr. pp. of *distinguere*] **1** : distinguishable to the eye or mind as discrete ⟨things similar in effect but wholly ~ in motive —Hilaire Belloc⟩ **2** : readily perceptible to the senses or mind : presenting a clear unmistakable impression ⟨a neat ~ handwriting⟩ ⟨the review gives a ~ idea of the book⟩ **3** *archaic* : notably decorated **4 a** : NOTABLE ⟨felt his sobriety a ~ achievement⟩ **b** : DECIDED ⟨there's a ~ possibility of snow⟩ — **dis·tinct·ly** \-ˈtiŋ(k)-tlē, -ˈtiŋ-klē\ *adv* — **dis·tinct·ness** \-ˈtiŋt-nəs, -ˈtiŋk-nəs\ *n*
syn **1** DISTINCT, SEVERAL, SEPARATE, DISCRETE *shared meaning element* : not being each and every one the same
2 see EVIDENT ***ant*** indistinct, nebulous
dis·tinc·tion \dis-ˈtiŋ(k)-shən\ *n* **1 a** *archaic* : DIVISION **b** : CLASS **2 a** : the act of distinguishing a difference : DISCRIMINATION, DIFFERENTIATION **b** : the object or result of distinguishing : CONTRAST **3** : a distinguishing mark **4** : the quality or state of being distinguishable ⟨there is no appreciable ~ between the twins⟩ **5 a** : the quality or state of being distinguished ⟨a man of some ~⟩ **b** : special honor or recognition ⟨graduated from college with ~⟩ **c** : the quality or state of being worthy
dis·tinc·tive \dis-ˈtiŋ(k)-tiv\ *adj* **1 a** : serving to distinguish **b** : having or giving style or distinction **2** : capable of making a segment of utterance different in meaning as well as in sound from an otherwise identical utterance ***syn*** see CHARACTERISTIC ***ant*** typical — **dis·tinc·tive·ly** *adv* — **dis·tinc·tive·ness** *n*
dis·tin·gué \ˌdēs-ˌtaŋ-ˈgā, (ˌ)dis-; di-ˈstaŋ-ˌ\ *adj* [F, fr. pp. of *distinguer*] : distinguished esp. in manner or bearing
dis·tin·guish \dis-ˈtiŋ-(g)wish\ *vb* [MF *distinguer,* fr. L *distinguere,* lit., to separate by pricking, fr. *dis-* + *-stinguere* (akin to L *instigare* to urge on) — more at STICK] *vt* **1** : to perceive as being separate or different ⟨~ the sound of a piano in an orchestra⟩ **2 a** : to mark as separate or different **b** : to separate into kinds, classes, or categories **c** : to set above or apart from others **d** : CHARACTERIZE **3 a** : DISCERN ⟨~*ed* a light in the distance⟩ **b** : to single out ~ *vi* : to perceive a difference — **dis·tin·guish·abil·i·ty** \-ˌtiŋ-(g)wish-ə-ˈbil-ət-ē\ *n* — **dis·tin·guish·able** \-ˈtiŋ-(g)wish-ə-bəl\ *adj* — **dis·tin·guish·ably** \-blē\ *adv*
dis·tin·guished *adj* **1** : marked by eminence, distinction, or excellence **2** : befitting an eminent person ***syn*** see FAMOUS
Distinguished Conduct Medal *n* : a British military decoration awarded for distinguished conduct in the field
Distinguished Flying Cross *n* **1** : a U.S. military decoration awarded for heroism or extraordinary achievement while participating in an aerial flight **2** : a British military decoration awarded for acts of gallantry when flying in operations against an enemy
Distinguished Service Cross *n* **1** : a U.S. Army decoration awarded for extraordinary heroism during operations against an armed enemy **2** : a British military decoration awarded for distinguished service against the enemy
Distinguished Service Medal *n* **1** : a U.S. military decoration awarded for exceptionally meritorious service to the government in a wartime duty of great responsibility **2** : a British military decoration awarded for distinguished conduct in war
Distinguished Service Order *n* : a British military decoration awarded for special services in action
distn *abbr* distillation
di·stome \ˈdī-ˌstōm\ *n* [deriv. of Gk *di-* + *stomat-, stoma* mouth — more at STOMACH] : any of various trematode worms with both oral and ventral suckers
dis·tort \dis-ˈtȯ(ə)rt\ *vt* [L *distortus,* pp. of *distorquēre,* fr. *dis-* + *torquēre* to twist — more at TORTURE] **1** : to twist out of the true meaning or proportion ⟨~*ed* the news to make it sensational⟩ **2** : to twist out of a natural, normal, or original shape or condition ⟨a face ~*ed* by pain⟩ **3** : PERVERT ***syn*** see DEFORM — **dis·tort·er** *n*
dis·tor·tion \dis-ˈtȯr-shən\ *n* **1** : the act of distorting **2** : the quality or state of being distorted : a product of distortion: as **a** : a lack of proportionality in an image resulting from defects in the

ə abut ᵊ kitten ər further a back ā bake ä cot, cart
au̇ out ch chin e less ē easy g gift i trip ī life
j joke ŋ sing ō flow ȯ flaw ȯi coin th thin th this
ü loot u̇ foot y yet yü few yu̇ furious zh vision

optical system **b** : falsified reproduction of an audio or video signal caused by change in the wave form of the original signal — **dis·tor·tion·al** \-shnəl, -shən-ᵊl\ *adj*
distr *abbr* distribute; distribution
1**dis·tract** \dis-ˈtrakt, ˈdis-ˌ\ *adj, archaic* : INSANE, MAD
2**dis·tract** \dis-ˈtrakt\ *vt* [ME *distracten*, fr. L *distractus*, pp. of *distrahere*, lit., to draw apart, fr. *dis-* + *trahere* to draw — more at DRAW] **1 a** : to turn aside : DIVERT **b** : to draw or direct (as one's attention) to a different object or in different directions at the same time **2** : to stir up or confuse with conflicting emotions or motives : HARASS ***syn*** see PUZZLE ***ant*** collect (*as one's thoughts*) — **dis·tract·i·bil·i·ty** \-ˌtrak-tə-ˈbil-ət-ē\ *n* — **dis·tract·ible** \-ˈtrak-tə-bəl\ *adj* — **dis·tract·ing·ly** \-tiŋ-lē\ *adv*
dis·tract·ed·ly *adv* : in the manner of one that is distracted
dis·trac·tion \dis-ˈtrak-shən\ *n* **1** : the act of distracting or the state of being distracted; *esp* : mental confusion **2** : something that distracts; *esp* : AMUSEMENT — **dis·trac·tive** \-ˈtrak-tiv\ *adj*
dis·train \dis-ˈtrān\ *vb* [ME *distreynen*, fr. OF *destreindre*, fr. ML *distringere*, fr. L, to draw apart, detain, fr. *dis-* + *stringere* to bind tight — more at STRAIN] *vt* **1** : to levy a distress upon **2** : to seize by distress ~ *vi* : to levy a distress — **dis·train·able** \-ˈtrā-nə-bəl\ *adj* — **dis·train·er** \-ˈtrā-nər\ *or* **dis·train·or** \-ˈtrā-nər, -ˌtrā-ˈnȯ(ə)r\ *n*
dis·traint \dis-ˈtrānt\ *n* [*distrain* + *-t* (as in *constraint*)] : the act or action of distraining
dis·trait \di-ˈstrā\ *adj* [F, fr. L *distractus*] : ABSENTMINDED; *esp* : inattentive or distracted because of anxiety or apprehension
dis·traught \dis-ˈtrȯt\ *adj* [ME, fr. L *distractus*] **1** : agitated with doubt or mental conflict **2** : CRAZED — **dis·traught·ly** *adv*
1**dis·tress** \dis-ˈtres\ *n* [ME *destresse*, fr. OF, fr. (assumed) VL *districtia*, fr. L *districtus*, pp. of *distringere*] **1 a** : seizure and detention of the goods of another as pledge or to obtain satisfaction of a claim by the sale of the goods seized; *broadly* : an act of distraining **b** : something that is distrained **2** *obs* : CONSTRAINT **3 a** : anguish of body or mind : TROUBLE **b** : a painful situation : MISFORTUNE **4** : a state of danger or desperate need ⟨a ship in ~⟩
syn DISTRESS, SUFFERING, MISERY, AGONY *shared meaning element* : the state of being in trouble or in mental or physical anguish
2**distress** *vt* **1** : to subject to great strain or difficulties **2** : to cause to worry or be troubled : UPSET **3** *archaic* : to force or overcome by inflicting pain **4** : to mar (wood or furniture) deliberately to give an effect of age ⟨~*ed* cherry⟩ ***syn*** see TROUBLE — **dis·tress·ing·ly** \-iŋ-lē\ *adv*
3**distress** *adj* **1** : offered for sale at a loss ⟨~ merchandise⟩ **2** : involving distress goods ⟨a ~ sale⟩
dis·tress·ful \dis-ˈtres-fəl\ *adj* : causing distress : full of distress — **dis·tress·ful·ly** \-fə-lē\ *adv* — **dis·tress·ful·ness** *n*
dis·trib·u·tary \dis-ˈtrib-yə-ˌter-ē\ *n, pl* **-tar·ies** : a river branch flowing away from the main stream
dis·trib·ute \dis-ˈtrib-yət, *Brit also* ˈdis-trib-ˌyüt\ *vt* **-ut·ed; -ut·ing** [ME *distributen*, fr. L *distributus*, pp. of *distribuere*, fr. *dis-* + *tribuere* to allot — more at TRIBUTE] **1** : to divide among several or many : APPORTION **2 a** : to spread out so as to cover something : SCATTER **b** : SUPPLY ⟨~ magazines to subscribers⟩ **c** : to use (a term) so as to convey information about every member of the class named ⟨the proposition "all men are mortal" ~*s* "man" but not "mortal"⟩ **3 a** : to divide or separate esp. into kinds **b** : to return the units of (as typeset matter) to the proper storage places — **dis·trib·u·tee** \dis-ˌtrib-yə-ˈtē\ *n*
syn DISTRIBUTE, DISPENSE, DIVIDE, DEAL, DOLE *shared meaning element* : to give out, usu. in shares, to each member of a group ***ant*** collect (*as supplies*), amass (*as wealth*)
dis·trib·ut·ed *adj* : characterized by a statistical distribution of a particular kind ⟨a normally ~ random variable⟩
dis·tri·bu·tion \ˌdis-trə-ˈbyü-shən\ *n* **1 a** : the act or process of distributing **b** : the apportionment by a court of the personal property of an intestate **2 a** : the position, arrangement, or frequency of occurrence (as of the members of a group) over an area or throughout a space or unit of time **b** : the natural geographic range of an organism **3 a** : something distributed **b** (1) : FREQUENCY DISTRIBUTION (2) : PROBABILITY FUNCTION (3) : PROBABILITY DENSITY FUNCTION 2 **4 a** : a device by which something is distributed **b** : the pattern of branching and termination of a ramifying structure (as a nerve) **5** : the marketing or merchandising of commodities — **dis·tri·bu·tion·al** \-shnəl, -shən-ᵊl\ *adj*
distribution function *n* : a function that gives the probability that a random variable is less than or equal to the independent variable of the function
dis·trib·u·tive \dis-ˈtrib-yət-iv\ *adj* **1** : of or relating to distribution: as **a** : dealing a proper share to each of a group **b** : diffusing more or less evenly **2** *of a word* : referring singly and without exception to the members of a group ⟨*each, either*, and *none* are ~⟩ **3** : producing the same element when operating on a whole as when operating on each part and collecting the results ⟨multiplication is ~ relative to addition since $a(b + c) = ab + ac$⟩ — **dis·trib·u·tive·ly** *adv* — **dis·trib·u·tive·ness** *n* — **dis·trib·u·tiv·i·ty** \-ˌtrib-yə-ˈtiv-ət-ē\ *n*
distributive education *n, often cap D & E* : a vocational program set up between schools and employers in which the student receives both classroom instruction and on-the-job training
dis·trib·u·tor \dis-ˈtrib-yət-ər\ *n* **1** : one that distributes **2** : one that markets a commodity; *esp* : WHOLESALER **3** : an apparatus for directing the secondary current from the induction coil to the various spark plugs of an engine in their proper firing order
1**dis·trict** \ˈdis-(ˌ)trikt\ *n, often attrib* [F, fr. ML *districtus* jurisdiction, district, fr. *districtus*, pp. of *distringere* to distrain — more at DISTRAIN] **1** : a territorial division (as for administrative or electoral purposes) **2** : an area, region, or section with a distinguishing character
2**district** *vt* : to divide or organize into districts
district attorney *n* : the prosecuting officer of a judicial district
district court *n* : a trial court that has jurisdiction over certain cases within a specific judicial district
district superintendent *n* : a church official supervising a district
1**dis·trust** \(ˈ)dis-ˈtrəst\ *vt* : to have no trust or confidence in
2**distrust** *n* : the lack or absence of trust : SUSPICION, WARINESS
dis·trust·ful \-ˈtrəst-fəl\ *adj* : having or showing distrust — **dis·trust·ful·ly** \-fə-lē\ *adv* — **dis·trust·ful·ness** *n*
dis·turb \dis-ˈtərb\ *vb* [ME *disturben, destourben*, fr. OF & L; OF *destourber*, fr. L *disturbare*, fr. *dis-* + *turbare* to throw into disorder — more at TURBID] *vt* **1 a** : to interfere with : INTERRUPT **b** : to alter the position or arrangement of **2 a** : to destroy the tranquillity or composure of **b** : to throw into disorder **c** : ALARM **d** : to put to inconvenience ~ *vi* : to cause disturbance ***syn*** see DISCOMPOSE — **dis·turb·er** *n* — **dis·turb·ing·ly** \-ˈtər-biŋ-lē\ *adv*
dis·tur·bance \dis-ˈtər-bən(t)s\ *n* **1** : the act of disturbing : the state of being disturbed **2** : a local variation from the average or normal wind conditions
dis·turbed *adj* **1** : showing symptoms of emotional illness **2** : designed for or occupied by disturbed patients ⟨~ wards⟩
di·sub·sti·tut·ed \(ˈ)dī-ˈsəb-stə-ˌt(y)üt-əd\ *adj* : having two substituent atoms or groups in a molecule
di·sul·fide \(ˈ)dī-ˈsəl-ˌfīd\ *n* **1** : a compound containing two atoms of sulfur combined with an element or radical **2** : an organic compound containing the bivalent group SS composed of two sulfur atoms
di·sul·fi·ram \dī-ˈsəl-fə-ˌram\ *n* [*disulf*ide + *thi*ourea + *amyl*] : a compound $C_{10}H_{20}N_2S_4$ that causes a severe physiological reaction to alcohol and is used in the treatment of alcoholism
di·sul·fo·ton \dī-ˈsəl-fə-ˌtän\ *n* [*di*ethyl + *sulfo-* + *-ton* (prob. fr. *thionate*)] : an organophosphorus systemic insecticide $C_8H_{19}O_2PS_3$
dis·union \dish-ˈü-nyən, (ˈ)dis(h)-ˈyü-\ *n* **1** : the termination or destruction of union : SEPARATION **2** : DISUNITY
dis·union·ist \-nyə-nəst\ *n* : one who favors disunion; *specif* : an American secessionist
dis·unite \ˌdish-ü-ˈnīt, ˌdis(h)-yü-\ *vt* : DIVIDE, SEPARATE
dis·uni·ty \dish-ˈü-nət-ē, (ˈ)dis(h)-ˈyü-\ *n* : lack of unity; *esp* : DISSENSION
1**dis·use** \dish-ˈüz, (ˈ)dis(h)-ˈyüz\ *vt* : to discontinue the use or practice of
2**dis·use** \-ˈüs, -ˈyüs\ *n* : cessation of use or practice
dis·util·i·ty \ˌdish-ü-ˈtil-ət-ē, ˌdis(h)-yü-\ *n* : ability to cause fatigue, inconvenience, discomfort, or pain ⟨~ of labor⟩
1**dis·val·ue** \(ˈ)dis-ˈval-(ˌ)yü, -yə(-w)\ *vt* **1** *archaic* : UNDERVALUE, DEPRECIATE **2** : to consider of little value
2**disvalue** *n* **1** *obs* : DISREGARD, DISESTEEM **2** : a negative value
di·syl·la·ble \ˈdī-ˌsil-ə-bəl, (ˈ)dī-ˈsil-; ˈdis-ˌil-, (ˈ)dis-ˈ(s)il-\ *n* [part trans. of MF *dissilabe*, fr. L *disyllabus* having two syllables, fr. Gk *disyllabos*, fr. *di-* + *syllabē* syllable] : a linguistic form consisting of two syllables — **di·syl·lab·ic** \ˌdī-sə-ˈlab-ik, ˌdis-(s)ə-\ *adj*
dit \ˈdit\ *n* [imit.] : a dot in radio or telegraphic code
1**ditch** \ˈdich\ *n* [ME *dich*, fr. OE *dīc* dike, ditch] : a long narrow excavation dug in the earth (as for defense, drainage, or irrigation)
2**ditch** *vt* **1 a** : to enclose with a ditch **b** : to dig a ditch in **2 a** : to cause (a train) to derail **b** : to drive (a car) into a ditch **c** : to make a forced landing of (an airplane) on water **3** : to get rid of : DISCARD
ditch·dig·ger \-ˌdig-ər\ *n* **1** : one that digs ditches **2** : one employed at menial and usu. hard physical labor
ditch reed *n* : a tall No. American reed (*Phragmites communis*) with broad flat leaves
dite \ˈdīt\ *n* [alter. of *doit*] *dial* : MITE, BIT
1**dith·er** \ˈdith-ər\ *vi* **dith·ered; dith·er·ing** \-(ə-)riŋ\ [ME *didderen*] **1** : SHIVER, TREMBLE ⟨the ~*ing* of grass —Wallace Stevens⟩ **2** : to act nervously or indecisively : VACILLATE — **dith·er·er** \-ər-ər\ *n*
2**dither** *n* : a highly nervous, excited, or agitated state : EXCITEMENT, CONFUSION — **dith·ery** \ˈdith-ə-rē\ *adj*
dithi- *or* **dithio-** *comb form* [ISV *di-* + *thi-*] : containing two atoms of sulfur usu. in place of two oxygen atoms
di·thi·ol \(ˈ)dī-ˈthī-ˌȯl, -ˌōl\ *adj* : containing two SH groups composed of sulfur and hydrogen
dith·y·ramb \ˈdith-i-ˌram(b)\ *n, pl* **-rambs** \-ˌramz\ [Gk *dithyrambos*] **1** : a usu. short poem in an inspired wild irregular strain **2** : a statement or writing in an exalted or enthusiastic vein — **dith·y·ram·bic** \ˌdith-i-ˈram-bik\ *adj* — **dith·y·ram·bi·cal·ly** \-bi-k(ə-)lē\ *adv*
dit·ta·ny \ˈdit-ᵊn-ē\ *n, pl* **-nies** [ME *ditoyne*, fr. MF *ditayne*, fr. L *dictamnum*, fr. Gk *diktamnon*] **1** : a pink-flowered herb (*Origanum dictamnus*) that is native to Crete **2** : an American herb (*Conila origanoides*) of the mint family that has much-branched stems
1**dit·to** \ˈdit-(ˌ)ō\ *n, pl* **dittos** [It dial., pp. of It *dire* to say, fr. L *dicere* — more at DICTION] **1** : a thing mentioned previously or above — used to avoid repeating a word; often symbolized by inverted commas or apostrophes **2** : a ditto mark
2**ditto** *vt* **1** : to repeat the action or statement of **2** [fr. *Ditto*, a trademark] : to copy (as printed matter) on a duplicator
3**ditto** *adv* : as before or aforesaid : in the same manner
4**ditto** *adj* : having the same characteristics : SIMILAR
dit·ty \ˈdit-ē\ *n, pl* **ditties** [ME *ditee*, fr. OF *ditié* poem, fr. pp. of *ditier* to compose, fr. L *dictare* to dictate, compose] : an esp. simple and unaffected song
dit·ty bag \ˈdit-ē-\ *n* [origin unknown] : a bag used esp. by sailors to hold small articles of gear (as thread, needles, and tape)
ditty box *n* : a box used for the same purpose as a ditty bag
di·ure·sis \ˌdī-(y)ə-ˈrē-səs\ *n, pl* **di·ure·ses** \-ˌsēz\ [NL] : an increased excretion of urine
di·uret·ic \ˌdī-(y)ə-ˈret-ik\ *adj* [ME, fr. MF or LL; MF *diuretique*, fr. LL *diureticus*, fr. Gk *diourētikos*, fr. *diourein* to urinate, fr. *dia-* + *ourein* to urinate — more at URINE] : tending to increase the flow of urine — **diuretic** *n* — **di·uret·i·cal·ly** \-i-k(ə-)lē\ *adv*
1**di·ur·nal** \dī-ˈərn-ᵊl\ *adj* [ME, fr. L *diurnalis* — more at JOURNAL] **1 a** : recurring every day ⟨~ task⟩ **b** : having a daily cycle ⟨~ tides⟩ **2 a** : of, relating to, or occurring in the daytime ⟨the city's

~ noises⟩ **b** : opening during the day and closing at night ⟨~ flowers⟩ ***syn*** see DAILY — **di·ur·nal·ly** \-ᵊl-ē\ *adv*

²diurnal *n* **1** *archaic* : DAYBOOK, DIARY **2** *archaic* : JOURNAL

di·u·ron \'dī-(y)ə-ˌrän\ *n* [*dichlor-* + *urea* + ¹*-on*] : a persistent herbicide $C_9H_{10}Cl_2N_2O$ used esp. to control annual weeds

div *abbr* **1** divided **2** dividend **3** division **4** divorced

di·va \'dē-və\ *n, pl* **divas** *or* **di·ve** \-(ˌ)vā\ [It, lit., goddess, fr. L, fem. of *divus* divine, god — more at DEITY] : PRIMA DONNA 1

di·va·gate \'dī-və-ˌgāt, 'div-ə-\ *vi* **-gat·ed; -gat·ing** [LL *divagatus*, pp. of *divagari*, fr. L *dis-* + *vagari* to wander — more at VAGARY] **1** : to wander about **2** : DIVERGE — **di·va·ga·tion** \ˌdī-və-'gā-shən, ˌdiv-ə-\ *n*

di·va·lent \(ˈ)dī-'vā-lənt\ *adj* : BIVALENT

di·van \'dī-ˌvan, *esp in senses other than 3 also* di-'van, di-'vän, dī-'van\ *n* [Turk, fr. Per *dīwān* account book] **1** **a** : the privy council of the Ottoman Empire **b** : COUNCIL **2** **a** : a council chamber **b** : a smoking room **3** : a large couch or sofa usu. without back or arms often designed for use as a bed **4** : a collection of poems in Persian or Arabic usu. by one author

di·var·i·cate \dī-'var-ə-ˌkāt, də-\ *vt* **-cat·ed; -cat·ing** [L *divaricatus*, pp. of *divaricare*, fr. *dis-* + *varicare* to straddle — more at PREVARICATE] : to spread apart : branch off : DIVERGE

di·var·i·ca·tion \(ˌ)dī-ˌvar-ə-'kā-shən, də-\ *n* **1** : the action, process, or fact of divaricating **2** : a divergence of opinion

¹dive \'dīv\ *vb* **dived** \'dīvd\ *or* **dove** \'dōv\; **dived; div·ing** [ME *diven, duven*, fr. OE *dȳfan* to dip & *dūfan* to dive; akin to OE *dyppan* to dip — more at DIP] *vi* **1** **a** : to plunge into water headfirst; *specif* : to execute a dive **b** : SUBMERGE **2** **a** : to descend or fall precipitously **b** : to plunge one's hand into something **c** *of an airplane* : to descend in a dive **3** **a** : to plunge into some matter or activity **b** : LUNGE ~ *vt* **1** : to thrust into something **2** : to cause to descend ***syn*** see PLUNGE

²dive *n* **1** : the act or an instance of diving: as **a** (1) : a plunge into water executed in a prescribed manner (2) : a submerging of a submarine (3) : a steep descent of an airplane at greater than the maximum horizontal speed **b** : a sharp decline **2** : a disreputable bar **3** : a faked knockout — usu. used in the phrase *take a dive* **4** : an offensive play in football in which the ballcarrier plunges into the line for short yardage

dive–bomb \'dīv-ˌbäm\ *vt* : to bomb from an airplane by making a steep dive toward the target before releasing the bomb — **dive–bomb·er** *n*

div·er \'dī-vər\ *n* **1** : one that dives **2** **a** : a person who stays underwater for long periods by having air supplied from the surface or by carrying a supply of compressed air **b** : any of various diving birds; *esp* : LOON

di·verge \də-'vərj, dī-\ *vb* **di·verged; di·verg·ing** [ML *divergere*, fr. L *dis-* + *vergere* to incline — more at WRENCH] *vi* **1** **a** : to move or extend in different directions from a common point : draw apart ⟨*diverging* rays of light⟩ **b** : to become or be different in character or form : differ in opinion **2** : to turn aside from a path or course : DEVIATE **3** : to be mathematically divergent ~ *vt* : DEFLECT ***syn*** see SWERVE

di·ver·gence \-'vər-jən(t)s\ *n* **1** **a** : a drawing apart (as of lines extending from a common center) **b** : DIFFERENCE, DISAGREEMENT **c** : the acquisition of dissimilar characters by related organisms in unlike environments **2** : a deviation from a course or standard **3** : the state of being mathematically divergent

di·ver·gen·cy \-jən-sē\ *n, pl* **-cies** : DIVERGENCE

di·ver·gent \-jənt\ *adj* [L *divergent-, divergens*, prp. of *divergere*] **1** **a** : diverging from each other **b** : differing from each other or from a standard : DEVIANT ⟨the ~ interests of capital and labor⟩ **2** : relating to or being an infinite sequence that does not have a limit or an infinite series whose partial sums do not have a limit **3** : causing divergence of rays ⟨a ~ lens⟩ ***syn*** see DIFFERENT ***ant*** convergent — **di·ver·gent·ly** *adv*

di·vers \'dī-vərz\ *adj* [ME *divers, diverse*] : VARIOUS

di·verse \dī-'vərs, də-', 'dī-ˌ\ *adj* [ME *divers, diverse*, fr. OF & L; OF *divers*, fr. L *diversus*, fr. pp. of *divertere*] **1** : differing from one another : UNLIKE **2** : having various forms or qualities ***syn*** see DIFFERENT ***ant*** identical, selfsame — **di·verse·ly** *adv* — **di·verse·ness** *n*

di·ver·si·fy \də-'vər-sə-ˌfī, dī-\ *vb* **-fied; -fy·ing** *vt* **1** : to make diverse : give variety to ⟨~ a course of study⟩ **2** : to balance (as an investment portfolio) defensively by dividing funds among securities of different industries or of different classes **3** : to increase the variety of the products of ~ *vi* **1** : to produce variety **2** : to engage in varied operations — **di·ver·si·fi·ca·tion** \-ˌvər-sə-fə-'kā-shən\ *n* — **di·ver·si·fi·er** \-'vər-sə-ˌfī(-ə)r\ *n*

di·ver·sion \də-'vər-zhən, dī-, -shən\ *n* **1** : the act or an instance of diverting from a course, activity, or use : DEVIATION **2** : something that diverts or amuses : PASTIME **3** : an attack or feint that draws the attention and force of an enemy from the point of the principal operation — **di·ver·sion·ary** \-zhə-ˌner-ē, -shə-\ *adj*

di·ver·sion·ist \-zhə-nəst, -shə-\ *n* **1** : one characterized by political deviation **2** : one engaged in diversionary activities

di·ver·si·ty \də-'vər-sət-ē, dī-\ *n, pl* **-ties** **1** : the condition of being different **2** : an instance or a point of difference

di·vert \də-'vərt, dī-\ *vb* [ME *diverten*, fr. MF & L; MF *divertir*, fr. L *divertere* to turn in opposite directions, fr. *dis-* + *vertere* to turn — more at WORTH] *vi* : to turn aside : DEVIATE ⟨was trained as a doctor but ~*ed* to diplomacy⟩ ~ *vt* **1** **a** : to turn from one course or use to another : DEFLECT **b** : DISTRACT **2** : to give pleasure to esp. by distracting the attention from what burdens or distresses ***syn*** see AMUSE

di·ver·tic·u·li·tis \ˌdī-vər-ˌtik-yə-'līt-əs\ *n* : inflammation of a diverticulum

di·ver·tic·u·lo·sis \-'lō-səs\ *n* : an intestinal disorder characterized by the presence of many diverticula

di·ver·tic·u·lum \ˌdī-vər-'tik-yə-ləm\ *n, pl* **-la** \-lə\ [NL, fr. L, bypath, prob. alter. of *deverticulum*, fr. *devertere* to turn aside, fr. *de-* + *vertere*] **1** : a pocket or closed branch opening off a main passage **2** : an abnormal pouch or sac opening from a hollow organ (as the intestine or bladder)

di·ver·ti·men·to \di-ˌvərt-ə-'ment-(ˌ)ō, -ˌvert-\ *n, pl* **-men·ti** \-'ment-(ˌ)ē\ *or* **-mentos** [It, lit., diversion, fr. *divertire* to divert, amuse, fr. F *divertir*] **1** : an instrumental chamber work in several movements **2** : DIVERTISSEMENT 1

di·ver·tisse·ment \di-'vərt-əs-mənt, -əz-, F dē-ver-tē-smäⁿ\ *n, pl* **divertissements** \-mən(t)s, -smäⁿ(z)\ [F, lit., diversion, fr. *divertiss-* (stem of *divertir*)] **1** : a ballet suite used as an interlude **2** : DIVERTIMENTO 1 **3** : DIVERSION, ENTERTAINMENT

Di·ves \'dī-(ˌ)vēz\ *n* [ME, fr. L, rich, rich man; misunderstood as a proper name in Lk 16:19] : a rich man

di·vest \dī-'vest, də-\ *vt* [alter. of *devest*] **1** **a** : to undress or strip esp. of clothing, ornament, or equipment **b** : to deprive or dispossess esp. of property, authority, or title **c** : RID, FREE **2** : to take away from a person — **di·vest·ment** \-'ves(t)-mənt\ *n*

di·ves·ti·ture \dī-'ves-tə-ˌchu̇(ə)r, -chər, -t(y)u̇(ə)r, də-\ *n* [*divest* + *-iture* (as in *investiture*)] **1** : the act of divesting **2** : the compulsory transfer of title or disposal of interests (as stock in a corporation) upon government order

¹di·vide \də-'vīd\ *vb* **di·vid·ed; di·vid·ing** [ME *dividen*, fr. L *dividere*, fr. *dis-* + *-videre* to separate — more at WIDOW] *vt* **1** **a** : to separate into two or more parts, areas, or groups **b** : to separate into classes, categories, or divisions **c** : CLEAVE, PART **2** **a** : to separate into portions and give out in shares : DISTRIBUTE **b** : to possess, enjoy, or make use of in common **c** : APPORTION **3** **a** : to cause to be separate, distinct, or apart from one another **b** : to separate into opposing sides or parties **c** : to cause (a parliamentary body) to vote by division **4** **a** : to mark divisions on : GRADUATE ⟨~ a sextant⟩ **b** (1) : to subject (a number or quantity) to the operation of finding how many times it contains another number or quantity ⟨~ 42 by 14⟩ (2) : to use as a divisor — used with *into* ⟨~ 14 into 42⟩ (3) : to locate one or more points on (a line or its extension) ~ *vi* **1** : to perform mathematical division **2** **a** (1) : to become separated into parts (2) : to branch out **b** : to become separated or disunited esp. in opinion or interest **c** : to vote by division ***syn*** **1** see SEPARATE ***ant*** unite **2** see DISTRIBUTE — **di·vid·able** \-'vīd-ə-bəl\ *adj*

²divide *n* **1** : an act of dividing **2** **a** : a dividing ridge between drainage areas : WATERSHED **b** : a point or line of division

di·vid·ed *adj* **1** **a** : separated into parts or pieces **b** *of a leaf* : cut into distinct parts by incisions extending to the base or to the midrib **c** : having the opposing streams of traffic separated (as by a median strip) ⟨a ~ highway⟩ **2** **a** : disagreeing with each other : DISUNITED **b** : directed or moved toward conflicting interests, states, or objects **3** : separated by distance ⟨familiar objects from which she had never dreamed of being ~ —James Joyce⟩

div·i·dend \'div-ə-ˌdend, -əd-ənd\ *n* [ME *divident*, fr. L *dividendus*, gerundive of *dividere*] **1** : an individual share of something distributed: as **a** : a share in a pro rata distribution (as of profits) to stockholders **b** : a share of surplus allocated to a policyholder in a participating insurance policy **2** : BONUS **3** **a** : a number to be divided **b** : a sum or fund to be divided and distributed

di·vid·er \də-'vīd-ər\ *n* **1** : one that divides **2** *pl* : an instrument for measuring or marking (as in dividing lines) **3** : something serving as a partition between separate spaces within a larger area

di·vi–di·vi \ˌdē-vē-'dē-vē, ˌdiv-ē-'div-ē\ *n* [Sp *dividivi* of Cariban origin; akin to Cumanagoto *diwidiwi* divi-divi] : a small leguminous tree (*Caesalpinia coriaria*) of tropical America with twisted astringent pods that contain a large proportion of tannin

div·i·na·tion \ˌdiv-ə-'nā-shən\ *n* [ME *divinacioun*, fr. L *divination-, divinatio*, fr. *divinatus*, pp. of *divinare*] **1** : the art or practice that seeks to foresee or foretell future events or discover hidden knowledge usu. by the interpretation of omens or by the aid of supernatural powers **2** : unusual insight : intuitive perception — **di·vi·na·to·ry** \də-'vin-ə-ˌtōr-ē, də-'vī-nə-, 'div-ə-nə-, -ˌtȯr-\ *adj*

¹di·vine \də-'vīn\ *adj* **di·vin·er; -est** [ME *divin*, fr. MF, fr. L *divinus*, fr. *divus* god — more at DEITY] **1** **a** : of, relating to, or proceeding directly from God or a god ⟨the ~ right of kings⟩ **b** : being a deity ⟨the ~ Savior⟩ **c** : directed to a deity ⟨~ worship⟩ **2** **a** : supremely good : SUPERB ⟨her pies were simply ~⟩ **b** : HEAVENLY, GODLIKE — **di·vine·ly** *adv*

²divine *n* [ME, fr. ML *divinus*, fr. L, soothsayer, fr. *divinus*, adj.] **1** : CLERGYMAN **2** : THEOLOGIAN

³divine *vb* **di·vined; di·vin·ing** [ME *divinen*, fr. MF & L; MF *diviner*, fr. L *divinare*, fr. *divinus*, n.] *vt* **1** : to discover intuitively : INFER **2** : to discover or locate (as water) by means of a divining rod ~ *vi* **1** : to practice divination : PROPHESY **2** : to perceive intuitively ***syn*** see FORESEE

Divine Liturgy *n* : the Eastern Orthodox eucharistic rite

Divine Office *n* : the office for the canonical hours of prayer that priests and religious say daily

di·vin·er \də-'vī-nər\ *n* **1** : one that practices divination : SOOTHSAYER **2** : one that seeks to discover the location of water or minerals underground with the aid of a divining rod

divine right *n* : the right of a sovereign to rule as set forth by the theory of government that holds that a monarch receives his right to rule directly from God and not from the people

divine service *n* : a service of Christian worship; *specif* : such a service that is not sacramental in character

diving bell *n* : a diving apparatus consisting of a container open only at the bottom and supplied with compressed air by a hose

diving duck *n* : any of various ducks (as a bufflehead) that frequent deep waters and obtain their food by diving

diving suit *n* : a waterproof suit with a helmet that is supplied with air pumped through a tube

divining rod *n* : a forked rod believed to indicate the presence of water or minerals by dipping downward when held over a vein

ə abut ᵊ kitten ər further a back ā bake ä cot, cart
au̇ out ch chin e less ē easy g gift i trip ī life
j joke ŋ sing ō flow ȯ flaw ȯi coin th thin t͟h this
ü loot u̇ foot y yet yü few yu̇ furious zh vision

di·vin·i·ty \də-'vin-ət-ē\ *n, pl* **-ties** **1** : the quality or state of being divine **2** *often cap* : a divine being: as **a** : GOD 1 **b** (1) : GOD 2 (2) : GODDESS **3** : THEOLOGY **4** : fudge made of whipped egg whites, sugar, and nuts

divinity school *n* : a professional school having a religious curriculum esp. for ministerial candidates

di·vis·i·bil·i·ty \də-ˌviz-ə-'bil-ət-ē\ *n* : the state of being divisible

di·vis·i·ble \də-'viz-ə-bəl\ *adj* : capable of being divided

di·vi·sion \də-'vizh-ən\ *n* [ME, fr. MF, fr. L *division-, divisio,* fr. *divisus,* pp. of *dividere* to divide] **1 a** : the act or process of dividing : the state of being divided **b** : the act, process, or an instance of distributing among a number : DISTRIBUTION *obs* : a method of arranging or disposing (as troops) **2** : one of the parts, sections, or groupings into which a whole is divided or is divisible **3 a** : a major military unit that contains the necessary tactical and administrative services to function as a self-contained unit capable of independent action **b** : a military unit made up normally of five battle groups **c** (1) : the basic unit of men for administration aboard ship and ashore (2) : a tactical subdivision of a squadron of ships **d** : a unit of the U. S. Air Force higher than a wing and lower than an air force **4 a** : a portion of a territorial unit marked off for a particular purpose (as administrative or judicial functions) **b** : an administrative or operating unit of a governmental, business, or educational organization **5** : a group of organisms forming part of a larger group; *specif* : a primary category of the plant kingdom **6** : competitive class or category (as in boxing or wrestling) **7 a** : something that divides, separates, or marks off **b** : the act, process, or an instance of separating or keeping apart : SEPARATION **8** : the condition or an instance of being divided in opinion or interest : DISAGREEMENT, DISUNITY ⟨exploited the ~s between the two countries⟩ **9** : the physical separation into different lobbies of the members of a parliamentary body voting for and against a question **10** : the mathematical operation of dividing **11** : plant propagation by dividing parts and planting segments capable of producing roots and shoots *syn* see PART — **di·vi·sion·al** \-'vizh-nəl, -ən-ᵊl\ *adj*

di·vi·sion·ism \-'vizh-ə-ˌniz-əm\ *n, often cap* : POINTILLISM — **di·vi·sion·ist** \-'vizh-(ə-)nəst\ *n or adj*

division of labor : the breakdown of labor into its components and their distribution among different persons, groups, or machines to increase productive efficiency

division sign *n* **1** : the symbol ÷ used to indicate division **2** : the diagonal / used to indicate a fraction

di·vi·sive \də-'vī-siv *also* -'vis-iv *or* -'viz-iv *or* -'vī-ziv\ *adj* : creating disunity or dissension — **di·vi·sive·ly** *adv* — **di·vi·sive·ness** *n*

di·vi·sor \də-'vī-zər\ *n* : the number by which a dividend is divided

¹di·vorce \də-'vō(ə)rs, -'vȯ(ə)rs *also* dī-\ *n* [ME *divorse,* fr. MF, fr. L *divortium,* fr. *divertere, divortere* to divert, to leave one's husband] **1** : a legal dissolution of a marriage **2** : SEPARATION, SEVERANCE

²divorce *vb* **di·vorced; di·vorc·ing** **1 a** : to end marriage with (one's spouse) by divorce **b** : to dissolve the marriage contract between **2** : to terminate an existing relationship or union : SEPARATE ⟨~ church from state⟩ *syn* see SEPARATE

di·vor·cée \də-ˌvȯr-'sā, -ˌvō-, -'sē, -vȯr-\ *n* [F, fr. fem. of *divorcé,* pp. of *divorcer* to divorce, fr. MF *divorse*] : a divorced woman

di·vorce·ment \də-'vȯr-smənt, -'vȯr- *also* dī-\ *n* : DIVORCE 2

div·ot \'div-ət\ *n* [origin unknown] **1** *Scot* : a square of turf or sod **2** : a piece of turf dug from a golf fairway in making a shot

di·vulge \də-'vəlj, dī-\ *vt* **di·vulged; di·vulg·ing** [ME *divulgen,* fr. L *divulgare,* fr. *dis-* + *vulgare* to make known] **1** *archaic* : to make public : PROCLAIM **2** : to make known (as a confidence or secret) *syn* see REVEAL — **di·vul·gence** \-'vəl-jən(t)s\ *n*

di·vul·sion \-'vəl-shən\ *n* [L *divulsion-, divulsio,* fr. *divulsus,* pp. of *divellere* to tear apart, fr. *dis-* + *vellere* to pluck — more at VULNERABLE] : a tearing apart

div·vy \'div-ē\ *vt* **div·vied; div·vy·ing** [by shortening & alter. fr. *divide*] : DIVIDE, SHARE — often used with *up* ⟨divvied up the candy⟩

Dix·ie \'dik-sē\ *n* [name for the Southern states in the song *Dixie* (1859) by Daniel D. Emmett] : the Southern states of the U.S.

Dix·ie·crat \-ˌkrat\ *n* : a dissident southern Democrat; *specif* : a supporter of a 1948 presidential ticket opposing the civil rights stand of the Democrats — **Dix·ie·crat·ic** \ˌdik-sē-'krat-ik\ *adj*

dix·ie·land \-ˌland\ *n* [prob. fr. the *Original Dixieland Jazz Band*] : jazz music in duple time usu. played by a small band and characterized by ensemble and solo improvisation

di·zen \'dīz-ᵊn, 'diz-ᵊn\ *vt* [earlier *disen* to dress a distaff with flax, fr. MD] *archaic* : BEDIZEN

di·zy·got·ic \ˌdī-zī-'gät-ik\ *also* **di·zy·gous** \(')dī-'zī-gəs\ *adj* [*di-* + *zygotic, -zygous*] *of twins* : FRATERNAL

diz·zi·ness \'diz-ē-nəs\ *n* : the condition of being dizzy : VERTIGO

¹diz·zy \'diz-ē\ *adj* **diz·zi·er; -est** [ME *disy,* fr. OE *dysig* stupid; akin to OHG *tusig* stupid, L *furere* to rage — more at DUST] **1** : FOOLISH, SILLY **2 a** : having a whirling sensation in the head with a tendency to fall **b** : mentally confused **3 a** : causing giddiness or mental confusion **b** : caused by or marked by giddiness **c** : extremely rapid — **diz·zi·ly** \'diz-ə-lē\ *adv*

²dizzy *vt* **diz·zied; diz·zy·ing** **1** : to make dizzy or giddy **2** : BEWILDER ⟨prospects so brilliant as to ~ the mind⟩ — **diz·zy·ing·ly** \-ē-in-lē\ *adv*

DJ *abbr* **1** disc jockey **2** district judge **3** doctor of jurisprudence **4** dust jacket

djel·la·ba *also* **djel·la·bah** \jə-'läb-ə\ *n* [F *djellaba,* fr. Ar *jallabah*] : a long loose garment with full sleeves and a hood

DJIA *abbr* Dow-Jones Industrial Average

djin *or* **djinn** \'jin\ *or* **djin·ni** *var of* JINN

dk *abbr* **1** dark **2** deck **3** dock

dkg *abbr* dekagram

dkl *abbr* dekaliter

dkm *abbr* dekameter

dks *abbr* dekastere

dl *abbr* deciliter

dl- \(')dē-'el, 'dē-ˌ\ *prefix* **1** *also* **d,l-** : consisting of equal amounts of the dextro and levo forms of a specified compound ⟨*dl*-tartaric

acid⟩ **2** : consisting of equal amounts of the D- and L- forms of a specified compound ⟨DL-fructose⟩

D layer *n* : a layer that may exist within the D region of the ionosphere; *also* : D REGION

DLitt *or* **DLit** *abbr* [L *doctor litterarum*] doctor of letters; doctor of literature

DLO *abbr* **1** dead letter office **2** dispatch loading only

DLS *abbr* doctor of library science

dm *abbr* decimeter

DM *abbr* deutsche mark

DMD *abbr* [NL *dentariae medicinae doctor*] doctor of dental medicine

DML *abbr* doctor of modern languages

DMn *abbr* doctor of ministry

DMSO \ˌdē-ˌem-ˌes-'ō\ *n* : DIMETHYLSULFOXIDE

DMZ *abbr* demilitarized zone

dn *abbr* down

DNA \ˌdē-ˌen-'ā\ *n* [deoxyribonucleic acid] : any of various nucleic acids that are localized esp. in cell nuclei, are the molecular basis of heredity in many organisms, and are constructed of a double helix held together by hydrogen bonds between purine and pyrimidine bases which project inward from two chains containing alternate links of deoxyribose and phosphate

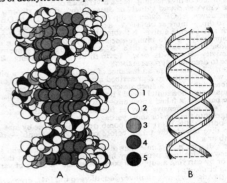

DNA: *A* molecular model, *1* hydrogen, *2* oxygen, *3* carbon in the helical phosphate ester chains, *4* carbon and nitrogen in the cross-linked purine and pyrimidine bases, *5* phosphorus; *B* double helix

DN·ase \(')dē-'en-ˌās, -ˌāz\ *also* **DNA·ase** \(ˌ)dē-ˌen-'ā-ˌās, -ˌāz\ *n* : DEOXYRIBONUCLEASE

DNB *abbr* Dictionary of National Biography

¹do \(')dü\ *vb* **did** \(')did, dəd\; **done** \'dən\; **do·ing** \'dü-in\; **does** \(')dəz\ [ME *don,* fr. OE *dōn;* akin to OHG *tuon* to do, L *-dere* to put, *facere* to make, do, Gk *tithenai* to place, set] *vt* **1** : to bring to pass : carry out **2** : PUT — used chiefly in *do to death* **3 a** : PERFORM, EXECUTE ⟨~ some work⟩ ⟨did his duty⟩ **b** : COMMIT ⟨crimes *done* deliberately⟩ **4 a** : to bring about : EFFECT ⟨sleep will ~ you good⟩ **b** : to give freely : PAY ⟨~ honor to his memory⟩ **5** : to bring to an end : FINISH — used in the past participle ⟨the job is finally *done*⟩ **6** : to put forth : EXERT ⟨did his best to win the race⟩ **7** : to wear out esp. by physical exertion : EXHAUST ⟨at the end of the race the boys were pretty well *done*⟩ **8** : to bring into existence : PRODUCE ⟨~ a biography on the general⟩ **9** : to play the part of ⟨did the main character in several movies⟩ **10** : to treat unfairly; *esp* : CHEAT ⟨did him out of his inheritance⟩ **11** : to treat or deal with in any way typically with the sense of preparation or with that of care or attention: **a** (1) : to put in order : CLEAN ⟨was ~ing the kitchen when the phone rang⟩ (2) : to make ready for use : WASH ⟨did the dishes right after supper⟩ **b** : COOK ⟨likes his steak *done* rare⟩ **c** : SET, ARRANGE ⟨had her hair *done* in a style he didn't like⟩ **d** : to apply cosmetics to ⟨took half an hour to ~ her face⟩ **e** : DECORATE, FURNISH ⟨did the living room in Early American⟩ **12 a** : to work at esp. as a vocation ⟨what to ~ after college⟩ **b** : to prepare or work out esp. by studying ⟨~ing his homework⟩ **13 a** : to pass over (as distance) : TRAVERSE **b** : to travel at a speed of ⟨~ing 80 on the turnpike⟩ **14** : TOUR ⟨~ing 12 countries in 12 days⟩ **15** : to serve out (as a term) in prison **16** : to serve the needs of : SUIT ⟨worms will ~ us for bait⟩ **17** : to approve esp. by custom, opinion, or propriety ⟨you oughtn't to say a thing like that . . . it's not *done* —Dorothy Sayers⟩ **18** — used as a substitute verb to avoid repetition ⟨if you must make such a racket, ~ it somewhere else⟩ ~ *vi* **1** : ACT, BEHAVE ⟨~ as I say⟩ **2 a** : to get along : FARE ⟨~ well in school⟩ **b** : to carry on business or affairs : MANAGE ⟨we can ~ without your help⟩ **c** : to make good use ⟨~ with a cup of coffee⟩ **3** : to take place : HAPPEN ⟨what's ~ing across the street⟩ **4** : to come to or make an end : FINISH — used in the past participle **5** : to be active or busy ⟨let us then be up and ~ing —H. W. Longfellow⟩ **6** : to be adequate or sufficient : SERVE ⟨half of that will ~⟩ **7** : to be fitting : conform to custom or propriety ⟨won't ~ to be late⟩ **8** — used as a substitute verb to avoid repetition ⟨wanted to run and play as children ~⟩ **9** — used in the imperative after an imperative to add emphasis ⟨be quiet ~⟩ ~ *verbal auxiliary* **1 a** — used with the infinitive without *to* to form present and past tenses in legal and parliamentary language ⟨~ hereby bequeath⟩ and in poetry ⟨give what she *did* crave —Shak.⟩ **b** — used with the infinitive without *to* to form present and past tenses in declarative sentences with inverted word order ⟨fervently ~ we pray —Abraham Lincoln⟩, in interrogatory sentences ⟨*did* you hear that⟩, and in negative sentences ⟨we *don't* know⟩ ⟨*don't* go⟩ **2** — used with the infinitive without *to* to form present and past tenses expressing emphasis ⟨I ~ say⟩ ⟨~ be careful⟩ — **do away with** 1 : to put an end to : ABOLISH 2 : to put to death : KILL — **do by** : to deal with : TREAT — **do for** 1 : to attend to the wants and needs of : take care of ⟨*did for* her while she was sick⟩ 2 : to bring about the death or ruin of — **do one's thing** : to do what is personally satisfying — **do proud** : to give cause for pride or gratification — **to do** : necessary to be done ⟨ten thousand times I've done my best and all's *to do* again —A. E. Housman⟩

²**do** \ˈdü\ *n, pl* **dos** *or* **do's** \ˈdüz\ 1 *chiefly dial* : FUSS, ADO 2 *archaic* : DEED, DUTY 3 *chiefly Brit* a : a festive get-together : AFFAIR, PARTY b : BATTLE 4 : a command or entreaty to do something ⟨consider all the ~s and don'ts of the problem⟩ 5 *Brit* : CHEAT, SWINDLE

³**do** \ˈdō\ *n* [It] : the 1st tone of the diatonic scale in solmization

⁴**do** *abbr* ditto

DO *abbr* 1 defense order 2 doctor of osteopathy

DOA *abbr* dead on arrival

do·able \ˈdü-ə-bəl\ *adj* : capable of being done : PRACTICABLE

DOB *abbr* date of birth

dob·bin \ˈdäb-ən\ *n* [*Dobbin,* nickname for *Robert*] 1 : a farm horse 2 : a quiet plodding horse

Do·bell's solution \ˌdō-ˌbelz-, dō-ˌ\ *n* [Horace B. *Dobell* †1917 E physician] : an aqueous solution of borate of sodium, sodium bicarbonate, glycerin, and phenol used as a nose or throat spray

Do·ber·man pin·scher \ˌdō-bər-mən-ˈpin-chər\ *n* [G *Dobermann-pinscher,* fr. Ludwig *Dobermann,* 19th cent. G dog breeder + G *pinscher,* a breed of hunting dog] : a short-haired medium-sized dog of a breed of German origin

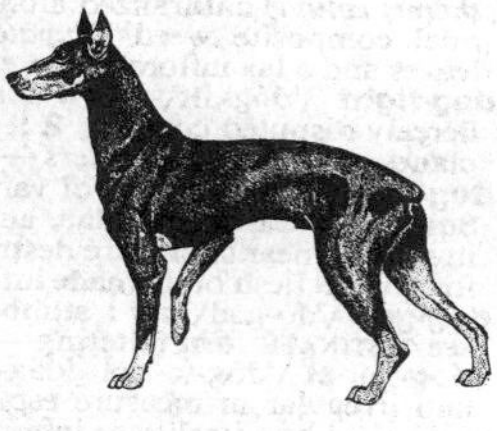

Doberman pinscher

dob·son \ˈdäb-sən\ *n* [prob. fr. the name *Dobson*] : HELLGRAMMITE

dob·son·fly \-ˌflī\ *n* : a winged megalopterous insect (family Corydalidae) with very long slender mandibles in the male and a large carnivorous aquatic larva — compare HELLGRAMMITE

doc *abbr* document

do·cent \ˈdōs-ᵊnt, dō(t)-ˈsent\ *n* [obs. G (now *dozent*), fr. L *docent-, docens,* prp. of *docēre*] 1 : a college or university teacher or lecturer 2 : a person who conducts groups through a museum or art gallery

do·ce·tic \dō-ˈsēt-ik, -ˈset-\ *adj, often cap* [Gk *Dokētai* Docetists, fr. *dokein* to seem — more at DECENT] : of or relating to Docetism or the Docetists

Do·ce·tism \dō-ˈsēt-ˌiz-əm, ˈdō-sə-ˌtiz-\ *n* : a belief opposed as heresy in early Christianity that Christ only seemed to have a human body and to suffer and die on the cross — **Do·ce·tist** \-ˈsēt-əst, -sət-əst\ *n*

doch-an-dor·rach \ˌdäk-ən-ˈdȯr-ək\ *or* **doch-an-dor·ris** \-ˈdȯr-əs\ *n* [ScGael & IrGael *deoch an doruis,* lit., drink of the door] *Scot & Irish* : a parting drink : STIRRUP CUP

doc·ile \ˈdäs-əl *also* -ˌīl, *esp Brit* ˈdō-ˌsīl\ *adj* [L *docilis,* fr. *docēre* to teach; akin to L *decēre* to be fitting — more at DECENT] 1 : easily taught : TEACHABLE 2 : easily led or managed : TRACTABLE *syn* see OBEDIENT *ant* indocile, unruly, ungovernable — **doc·ile·ly** \ˈdäs-ə(l)-lē\ *adv* — **do·cil·i·ty** \dä-ˈsil-ət-ē, dō-\ *n*

¹**dock** \ˈdäk\ *n* [ME, fr. OE *docce;* akin to MD *docke* dock, ScGael *dogha* burdock] 1 : any of a genus (*Rumex*) of the buckwheat family of coarse weedy plants that have long taproots and are used as potherbs and in folk medicine 2 : any of several usu. broad-leaved weedy plants

²**dock** *n* [ME *dok,* fr. OE *-docca* (as in *fingirdocca* finger muscle); akin to OHG *tocka* doll, ON *dokka* bundle] 1 : the solid part of an animal's tail as distinguished from the hair 2 : the cropped tail of an animal after clipping the hair or cropping the end

³**dock** *vt* 1 a : to cut off the end of a body part of; *specif* : to remove part of the tail of b : to cut (as ears or a tail) short 2 a : to take away a part of : ABRIDGE b : to subject (as wages) to a deduction 3 : to deprive of a benefit ordinarily due esp. as a penalty for a fault ⟨~*ed* for tardiness⟩

⁴**dock** *n* [prob. fr. MD *docke* dock, ditch, fr. L *duction-, ductio* act of leading — more at DOUCHE] 1 : a usu. artificial basin or enclosure for the reception of ships that is equipped with means for controlling the water height 2 : the waterway extending between two piers for the reception of ships 3 : a place (as a wharf or platform) for the loading or unloading of materials 4 : scaffolding for the inspection and repair of aircraft; *broadly* : HANGAR

⁵**dock** *vt* 1 : to haul or guide into a dock 2 : to join (as two spacecraft) mechanically while in space ~ *vi* 1 : to come into dock 2 : to become docked

⁶**dock** *n* [Flem *docke* cage] : the place in a criminal court where a prisoner stands or sits during trial — **in the dock** : on trial ⟨soon found himself *in the dock* for robbery⟩

dock·age \ˈdäk-ij\ *n* 1 : a charge for the use of a dock 2 : docking facilities 3 : the docking of ships

¹**dock·er** \ˈdäk-ər\ *n* : one that docks the tails of animals

²**docker** *n* : one connected with docks; *esp* : LONGSHOREMAN

¹**dock·et** \ˈdäk-ət\ *n* [ME *doggette*] 1 : a brief written summary of a document : ABSTRACT 2 a (1) : a formal abridged record of the proceedings in a legal action (2) : a register of such records b (1) : a list of legal causes to be tried (2) : a calendar of business matters to be acted on : AGENDA 3 : an identifying statement about a document placed on its outer surface or cover

²**docket** *vt* 1 : to inscribe (as a document) with an identifying statement 2 : to make a brief abstract of (as a legal matter) and inscribe it in a list 3 : to place on the docket for legal action

dock·hand \ˈdäk-ˌhand\ *n* : LONGSHOREMAN

dock·land \-ˌland\ *n, Brit* : the part of a port occupied by docks; *also* : a residential section adjacent to docks

dock·side \-ˌsīd\ *n* : the shore or area adjacent to a dock

dock·work·er \-ˌwər-kər\ *n* : LONGSHOREMAN

dock·yard \-ˌyärd\ *n* 1 : SHIPYARD 2 *Brit* : NAVY YARD

¹**doc·tor** \ˈdäk-tər\ *n* [ME *doctour* teacher, doctor, fr. MF & ML; MF, fr. ML *doctor,* fr. L, teacher, fr. *doctus,* pp. of *docēre* to teach — more at DOCILE] 1 a : an eminent theologian declared a sound expounder of doctrine by the Roman Catholic Church — called also *doctor of the church* b : a learned or authoritative teacher c : a person who has earned one of the highest academic degrees (as a PhD) conferred by a university d : a person awarded an honorary doctorate (as an LLD or LittD) by a college or university 2 a : one skilled or specializing in healing arts; *esp* : a physician, surgeon, dentist, or veterinarian licensed to practice his profession b : MEDICINE MAN 3 a : material added (as to food) to produce a desired effect b : a blade (as of metal) for spreading a coating or scraping a surface 4 : a usu. makeshift and emergency mechanical contrivance or attachment for remedying a difficulty 5 : any of several brightly colored artificial flies — **doc·tor·al** \-t(ə-)rəl\ *adj* — **doc·tor·less** \-tər-ləs\ *adj* — **doc·tor·ship** \-ˌship\ *n*

²**doctor** *vb* **doc·tored; doc·tor·ing** \-t(ə-)riŋ\ *vt* 1 a : to give medical treatment to b : to restore to good condition : REPAIR ⟨~ an old clock⟩ 2 a : to adapt or modify for a desired end by alteration or special treatment ⟨~*ed* the play to suit the audience⟩ b : to alter deceptively ⟨accused of ~*ing* the election returns⟩ ~ *vi* 1 : to practice medicine 2 *dial* : to take medicine

doc·tor·ate \ˈdäk-t(ə-)rət\ *n* : the degree, title, or rank of a doctor

doctor book *n* : a book intended to supplement the knowledge of the individual in matters of home medication

¹**doc·tri·naire** \ˌdäk-trə-ˈna(ə)r, -ˈne(ə)r\ *n* [F, fr. *doctrine*] : one who attempts to put into effect an abstract doctrine or theory with little or no regard for practical difficulties

²**doctrinaire** *adj* : of, relating to, or characteristic of a doctrinaire : DOGMATIC *syn* see DICTATORIAL — **doc·tri·nair·ism** \-ˈna(ə)r-ˌiz-əm, -ˈne(ə)r-\ *n*

doc·tri·nal \ˈdäk-trən-ᵊl, *esp Brit* däk-ˈtrīn-\ *adj* : of, relating to, or preoccupied with doctrine — **doc·tri·nal·ly** \-ᵊl-ē\ *adv*

doc·trine \ˈdäk-trən\ *n* [ME, fr. MF & L; MF, fr. L *doctrina,* fr. *doctor*] 1 *archaic* : TEACHING, INSTRUCTION 2 a : something that is taught b : a principle or position or the body of principles in a branch of knowledge or system of belief : DOGMA c : a principle of law established through past decisions d : a statement of fundamental government policy esp. in international relations *syn* DOCTRINE, DOGMA, TENET *shared meaning element* : a principle accepted as valid and authoritative

doctrine of descent : a theory in biology: all animals and plants are direct descendants of previous animals or plants

¹**doc·u·ment** \ˈdäk-yə-mənt\ *n* [ME, fr. MF, fr. LL & L; LL *documentum* official paper, fr. L, lesson, proof, fr. *docēre* to teach — more at DOCILE] 1 a *archaic* : PROOF, EVIDENCE b : an original or official paper relied on as the basis, proof, or support of something 2 a : a writing conveying information b : a material substance (as a coin or stone) having on it a representation of the thoughts of men by means of some conventional mark or symbol c : DOCUMENTARY — **doc·u·men·tal** \ˌdäk-yə-ˈment-ᵊl\ *adj*

²**doc·u·ment** \ˈdäk-yə-ˌment\ *vt* 1 : to furnish documentary evidence of 2 : to furnish with documents 3 a : to provide with factual or substantial support for statements made or a hypothesis proposed; *esp* : to equip with exact references to authoritative supporting information ⟨the thesis was well ~*ed* with footnotes on every page⟩ b : to construct or produce (as a movie or novel) with a high proportion of details closely reproducing authentic situations or events ⟨his film ~*ed* the living conditions in the ghetto⟩ 4 : to furnish (a ship) with ship's papers as required by law for the manifesting of ownership and cargo — **doc·u·ment·able** \-ə-bəl, ˌdäk-yə-ˈ\ *adj* — **doc·u·ment·er** \ˈdäk-yə-ˌment-ər\ *n*

doc·u·men·tal·ist \ˌdäk-yə-ˈment-ᵊl-əst\ *n* : a specialist in documentation

doc·u·men·tar·i·an \ˌdäk-yə-mən-ˈter-ē-ən, -ˌmen-\ *n* [²*documentary*] : one who employs or advocates documentary presentation (as in photographic art or fiction)

doc·u·men·ta·rist \-ˈment-ə-rəst\ *n* [²*documentary*] : DOCUMENTARIAN

¹**doc·u·men·ta·ry** \ˌdäk-yə-ˈment-ə-rē, -ˈmen-trē\ *adj* 1 : being or consisting of documents : contained or certified in writing ⟨~ evidence⟩ 2 : of, relating to, or employing documentation in literature or art; *broadly* : FACTUAL, OBJECTIVE ⟨a ~ film of the war⟩ — **doc·u·men·tar·i·ly** \-mən-ˈter-ə-lē, -ˌmen-\ *adv*

²**documentary** *n, pl* **-ries** : a documentary presentation (as a film or novel)

doc·u·men·ta·tion \ˌdäk-yə-mən-ˈtā-shən, -ˌmen-\ *n* 1 : the act or an instance of furnishing or authenticating with documents 2 a : the provision of documents in substantiation; *also* : documentary evidence b (1) : the use of historical documents (2) : conformity to historical or objective facts (3) : the provision of footnotes, appendices, or addenda referring to or containing documentary evidence 3 : INFORMATION SCIENCE — **doc·u·men·ta·tion·al** \-shnəl, -shən-ᵊl\ *adj*

DOD *abbr* Department of Defense

¹**dod·der** \ˈdäd-ər\ *n* [ME *doder;* akin to OE *dydring* yolk, Norw *dudra* to tremble, L *fumus* smoke — more at FUME] : any of a genus (*Cuscuta*) of dicotyledonous leafless elongated wiry herbs that are deficient in chlorophyll and are parasitic on other plants

²**dodder** *vi* **dod·dered; dod·der·ing** \ˈdäd-(ə-)riŋ\ [ME *dadiren*] 1 : to tremble or shake from weakness or age 2 : to progress feebly

ə abut ᵊ kitten ər further a back ā bake ä cot, cart
aů out ch chin e less ē easy g gift i trip ī life
j joke ŋ sing ō flow ȯ flaw ȯi coin th thin t͟h this
ü loot ů foot y yet yü few yů furious zh vision

and unsteadily ⟨an old man ~*ing* down the walk⟩ — **dod·der·er** \-ər-ər\ *n*

dod·dered \ˈdäd-ərd\ *adj* [prob. alter. of *dodded,* fr. pp. of E dial. *dod* to lop, fr. ME *dodden*] **1 :** deprived of branches through age or decay ⟨a ~ oak⟩ **2 :** INFIRM, ENFEEBLED

dod·der·ing \ˈdäd-(ə-)riŋ\ *adj* **:** FOOLISH, SENILE ⟨a ~ old man⟩

dod·dery \-(ə-)rē\ *adj* **:** DODDERED, DODDERING

dodeca- *or* **dodec-** *comb form* [L, fr. Gk *dōdeka-, dōdek-,* fr. *dōdeka, dyōdeka,* fr. *dyō, dyo* two + *deka* ten] **:** twelve ⟨*dodecaphonic*⟩

do·deca·gon \dō-ˈdek-ə-ˌgän\ *n* [Gk *dōdekagōnon,* fr. *dōdeka-* + *-gōnon* -gon] **:** a polygon of 12 angles and 12 sides

do·deca·he·dron \(ˌ)dō-ˌdek-ə-ˈhē-drən\ *n, pl* **-drons** *or* **-dra** \-drə\ [Gk *dōdekaedron,* fr. *dōdeka-* + *-edron* -hedron] **:** a solid having 12 plane faces — **do·deca·he·dral** \-drəl\ *adj*

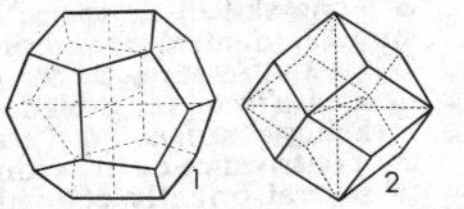

dodecahedrons: *1* pentagonal, *2* rhomboid

do·deca·phon·ic \(ˌ)dō-ˌdek-ə-ˈfän-ik\ *adj* [*dodeca-* + *phon-* + *-ic*] **:** TWELVE-TONE — **do·deca·phon·i·cal·ly** \-i-k(ə-)lē\ *adv* — **do·deca·pho·nist** \dō-ˈdek-ə-fə-nəst, -ˌfō-; ˌdōd-i-ˈkaf-ə-nəst\ *n* — **do·deca·pho·ny** \-nē\ *n*

[1]**dodge** \ˈdäj\ *vb* **dodged; dodg·ing** [origin unknown] *vi* **1 :** to evade a responsibility or a duty esp. by trickery or deceit **2 a :** to move to and fro or from place to place usu. in an irregular course ⟨*dodged* through the crowd⟩ **b :** to make a sudden movement in a new direction (as to evade a blow) ⟨*dodged* behind the door⟩ ~ *vt* **1 :** to evade (as a duty) usu. indirectly and by trickery ⟨*dodged* the draft by leaving the country⟩ **2 a :** to evade by a sudden or repeated shift of position **b :** to avoid an encounter with **3 :** to reduce the intensity of (a portion of a photograph) by selectively shading during printing

[2]**dodge** *n* **1 :** an act of evading by sudden bodily movement **2 a :** an artful device to evade, deceive, or trick **b :** EXPEDIENT

dodge ball *n* **:** a game in which players stand in a circle and try to hit opponents within the circle with a large inflated ball

dodg·er \ˈdäj-ər\ *n* **1 :** one that dodges; *esp* **:** one who uses tricky devices **2 :** a small leaflet **:** CIRCULAR **3 :** CORN DODGER

dodg·ery \ˈdäj-(ə-)rē\ *n, pl* **-er·ies :** EVASION, TRICKERY

dodgy \ˈdäj-ē\ *adj, chiefly Brit* **:** EVASIVE, TRICKY

do·do \ˈdōd-(ˌ)ō\ *n, pl* **dodoes** *or* **dodos** [Pg *doudo,* fr. *doudo* silly, stupid] **1 a :** an extinct heavy flightless bird (*Raphus cucullatus,* syn. *Didus ineptus*) related to the pigeons but larger than a turkey formerly present on the island of Mauritius **b :** an extinct bird of the island of Réunion similar to and apparently closely related to the dodo **2 a :** one hopelessly behind the times **b :** a stupid person

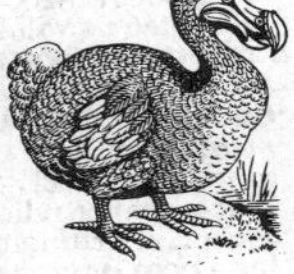
dodo 1a

doe \ˈdō\ *n, pl* **does** *or* **doe** [ME *do,* fr. OE *dā;* akin to G dial. *tē* doe] **:** the adult female fallow deer; *broadly* **:** the female esp. when adult of any of various mammals of which the male is called buck

do·er \ˈdü-ər\ *n* **:** one that takes an active part ⟨a thinker or a ~⟩

does *pres 3d sing of* DO

doe·skin \ˈdō-ˌskin\ *n* **1 :** the skin of does or leather made of it; *also* **:** soft leather from sheep or lambskins **2 :** a compact coating and sportswear fabric napped and felted for a smooth surface

doesn't \ˈdəz-ᵊnt\ **:** does not

do·est \ˈdü-əst\ *archaic pres 2d sing of* DO

do·eth \ˈdü-əth\ *archaic pres 3d sing of* DO

doff \ˈdäf, ˈdȯf\ *vt* [ME *doffen,* fr. *don* to do + *of* off] **1 a :** to remove (an article of wear) from the body **b :** to take off (the hat) in greeting or as a sign of respect **2 :** to rid oneself of **:** put aside ⟨among his intimate friends his studied reserve was ~*ed* —W. J. Ghent⟩

[1]**dog** \ˈdȯg\ *n, often attrib* [ME, fr. OE *docga*] **1 a :** a highly variable carnivorous domesticated mammal (*Canis familiaris*) prob. descended from the common wolf **b :** any of a family (Canidae, the dog family) of carnivores to which the dog belongs **c :** a male dog **2 a :** a worthless person **b :** FELLOW, CHAP ⟨a lazy ~⟩ **3 a :** any of various usu. simple mechanical devices for holding, gripping, or fastening that consist of a spike, rod, or bar **b :** ANDIRON **4 a :** SUN DOG **b :** FOGBOW **5 :** affected stylishness or dignity ⟨liked to put on the ~⟩ **6** *cap* **:** either of the constellations Canis Major or Canis Minor **7** *pl* **:** FEET **8 :** something inferior of its kind **9** *pl* **:** RUIN ⟨go to the ~*s*⟩ **10 a :** an investment (as a stock or bond) not worth its price **b :** a slow-moving or undesirable piece of merchandise **11 :** an unattractive woman or girl **12 :** a theatrical or musical flop **13 :** [1]HOT DOG — **dog·like** \ˈdȯ-ˌglīk\ *adj*

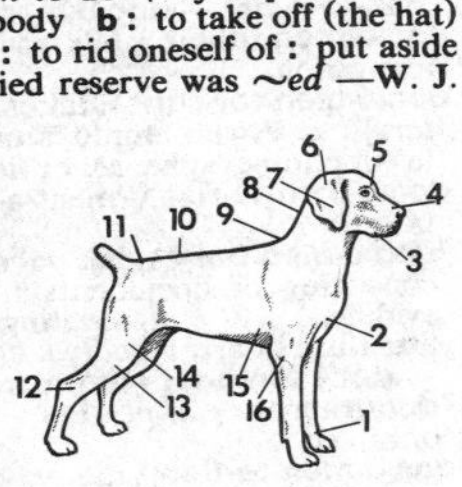

dog: *1* pastern, *2* chest, *3* flews, *4* muzzle, *5* stop, *6* occiput, *7* leather, *8* crest, *9* withers, *10* loin, *11* rump, *12* hock, *13* knee, *14* stifle, *15* brisket, *16* elbow

[2]**dog** *vt* **dogged; dog·ging 1 a :** to hunt or track like a hound **b :** to worry as if by dogs **:** HOUND **2 :** to fasten with a dog — **dog it :** to fail to do one's best **:** GOLDBRICK

[3]**dog** *adv* **:** EXTREMELY, UTTERLY ⟨*dog*-tired⟩

[4]**dog** *adj* **1 :** CANINE **2 :** SPURIOUS; *esp* **:** unlike that used by native speakers or writers ⟨~ Latin⟩ ⟨~ French⟩

dog·bane \ˈdȯg-ˌbān\ *n* **:** any of a genus (*Apocynum* of the family Apocynaceae, the dogbane family) comprising chiefly tropical and often poisonous plants with milky juice and usu. showy flowers

dog·ber·ry \-ˌber-ē\ *n* **:** any of several plants bearing unpalatable fruit: as **a :** a prickly wild gooseberry (*Ribes cynosbati*) **b :** a mountain ash (*Pyrus americana*) of the eastern U.S. and Canada

dog biscuit *n* **1 :** a hard dry cracker for dogs **2 :** a hard coarse cracker (as hardtack) for human consumption

dog·cart \ˈdȯg-ˌkärt\ *n* **1 :** a cart drawn by a dog **2 :** a light two-wheeled carriage with two transverse seats set back to back

dog·catch·er \-ˌkach-ər, -ˌkech-\ *n* **:** a community official assigned to catch and dispose of stray dogs

dog collar *n* **1 :** a collar for a dog **2** *slang* **:** CLERICAL COLLAR **3 :** a wide flexible snug-fitting necklace

dog days *n pl* [fr. their being reckoned from the heliacal rising of the Dog Star (Sirius)] **1 :** the period between early July and early September when the hot sultry weather of summer usu. occurs in the northern hemisphere **2 :** a period of stagnation or inactivity

dog·dom \ˈdȯg-dəm\ *n* **:** the world of dogs or of dog fanciers ⟨the elite of pure-bred ~ —W. R. Fletcher⟩

doge \ˈdōj\ *n* [It dial., fr. L *duc-, dux* leader — more at DUKE] **:** the chief magistrate in the republics of Venice and Genoa

dog–ear \ˈdȯ-ˌgi(ə)r\ *n* **:** the turned-down corner of a page esp. of a book — **dog–ear** *vt*

dog–eared \ˈdȯ-ˌgi(ə)rd\ *adj* **1 :** having dog-ears ⟨a ~ book⟩ **2 :** SHABBY, WORN

dog–eat–dog \ˌdȯ-ˌgēt-ˈdȯg\ *adj* **:** marked by ruthless self-interest ⟨~ competition⟩

dog·face \ˈdȯg-ˌfās\ *n* **:** SOLDIER; *esp* **:** INFANTRYMAN

dog fennel *n* **1 :** a strong-scented European chamomile (*Anthemis cotula*) naturalized along roadsides in the U.S. **2 :** an annual composite weed (*Eupatorium capillifolium*) with dissected leaves and a lax inflorescence

dog·fight \ˈdȯg-ˌfīt\ *n* **1 :** a fight between dogs; *broadly* **:** a fiercely disputed contest **2 :** a fight between two or more fighter planes usu. at close quarters — **dogfight** *vi*

dog·fish \-ˌfish\ *n* **:** any of various small sharks (as of the families Squalidae, Carcharhinidae, and Scyliorhinidae) that often appear in schools near shore, are destructive to fish, and have livers valued for oil and flesh often made into fertilizer

dog·ged \ˈdȯ-gəd\ *adj* **:** stubbornly determined **:** TENACIOUS ***syn*** see OBSTINATE ***ant*** faltering — **dog·ged·ly** *adv* — **dog·ged·ness** *n*

[1]**dog·ger·el** \ˈdȯg-(ə-)rəl, ˈdäg-\ *adj* [ME *dogerel*] **:** loosely styled and irregular in measure esp. for burlesque or comic effect; *also* **:** marked by triviality or inferior worth ⟨~ lines of verse⟩

[2]**doggerel** *n* **1 :** doggerel verse **2 :** an example of doggerel verse

dog·gery \ˈdȯ-gə-rē\ *n, pl* **-ger·ies :** a cheap saloon **:** DIVE

dog·gie bag \ˈdȯ-gē-\ *n* [[2]*doggy;* fr. the presumption that such leftovers are intended for a pet dog] **:** a bag used for carrying home leftover food and esp. meat from a meal eaten at a restaurant

dog·gish \ˈdȯ-gish\ *adj* **1 :** CANINE **2 :** stylish in a showy way — **dog·gish·ly** *adv* — **dog·gish·ness** *n*

dog·go \ˈdȯ-(ˌ)gō\ *adv* [prob. fr. [1]*dog*] **:** in hiding — used chiefly in the phrase *to lie doggo*

[1]**dog·gone** \ˈdäg-ˈgän, ˈdȯg-ˈgȯn\ *vb* **dog·goned; dog·gon·ing** [euphemism for *God damn*] **:** DAMN

[2]**doggone** *n* **:** DAMN

dog·goned *or* **dog·gone** \ˌdäg-ˌgän(d), ˌdȯg-ˌgȯn(d)\ *adj or adv* **:** DAMNED

[1]**dog·gy** \ˈdȯ-gē\ *adj* **dog·gi·er; -est 1 :** resembling or suggestive of a dog ⟨a ~ odor⟩ **2 :** concerned with or fond of dogs ⟨a book for ~ experts⟩ **3 :** STYLISH, SHOWY

[2]**dog·gy** *or* **dog·gie** \ˈdȯ-gē\ *n, pl* **doggies 1 :** a small dog **2 —** used as a pet name or calling name for any dog

dog·house \ˈdȯg-ˌhau̇s\ *n* **:** a shelter for a dog — **in the doghouse :** in a state of disfavor

do·gie \ˈdō-gē\ *n* [origin unknown] *chiefly West* **:** a motherless calf in a range herd

dog in the manger [fr. the fable of the dog who prevented an ox from eating hay which he did not want himself] **:** a person who selfishly withholds from others something useless to himself

[1]**dog·leg** \ˈdȯ-ˌgleg, -ˌglāg\ *n* **1 a :** something having an abrupt angle **b :** a sharp bend (as in a road) **2 :** a golf hole having an angled fairway

[2]**dogleg** *adj* **:** crooked or bent like a dog's hind leg

[3]**dogleg** *vi* **:** to proceed along a dogleg course ⟨the single narrow street that ~*s* through town —Russ Leadabrand⟩

dog·ma \ˈdȯg-mə, ˈdäg-\ *n* [L *dogmat-, dogma,* fr. Gk, fr. *dokein* to seem — more at DECENT] **1 a :** something held as an established opinion; *esp* **:** a definite authoritative tenet **b :** a code of such tenets ⟨pedagogical ~⟩ **c :** a point of view or tenet put forth as authoritative without adequate grounds **2 :** a doctrine or body of doctrines concerning faith or morals formally stated and authoritatively proclaimed by a church ***syn*** see DOCTRINE

dog·mat·ic \dȯg-ˈmat-ik, däg-\ *adj* **1 :** characterized by or given to the use of dogmatism ⟨a ~ critic⟩ **2 :** of or relating to dogma ***syn*** see DICTATORIAL — **dog·mat·i·cal** \-i-kəl\ *adj* — **dog·mat·i·cal·ly** \-i-k(ə-)lē\ *adv* — **dog·mat·i·cal·ness** \-i-kəl-nəs\ *n*

dog·mat·ics \-iks\ *n pl but sing or pl in constr* **:** a branch of theology that seeks to interpret the dogmas of a religious faith

dogmatic theology *n* **:** DOGMATICS

dog·ma·tism \ˈdȯg-mə-ˌtiz-əm, ˈdäg-\ *n* **1 :** positiveness in assertion of opinion esp. when unwarranted or arrogant **2 :** a viewpoint or system of ideas based on insufficiently examined premises

dog·ma·tist \-mət-əst\ *n* **:** one who dogmatizes

dog·ma·tize \ˈdȯg-mə-ˌtīz, ˈdäg-\ *vb* **-tized; -tiz·ing** [F *dogmatiser,* fr. LL *dogmatizare,* fr. Gk *dogmatizein,* fr. *dogmat-, dogma*] *vi* **:** to speak or write dogmatically ~ *vt* **:** to state as a dogma or in a dogmatic manner — **dog·ma·ti·za·tion** \ˌdȯg-mət-ə-ˈzā-shən, ˌdäg-\ *n* — **dog·ma·tiz·er** *n*

dog·nap \ˈdȯg-ˌnap\ *vt* **-napped** *or* **-naped** \-ˌnapt\; **-nap·ping** *or* **-nap·ing** \-ˌnap-iŋ\ [[1]*dog* + *-nap* (as in *kidnap*)] **:** to steal (a dog) often for the purpose of selling to a scientific laboratory — **dog·nap·per** *or* **dog·nap·er** *n*

do–good \ˈdü-ˌgu̇d\ *adj* **:** designed sometimes impracticably and too zealously toward bettering the conditions under which others live — **do–good·ism** \-ˌiz-əm\ *n*

do–good·er \-ər\ *n* : an earnest usu. impractical and often naive and ineffectual humanitarian or reformer
do–good·ing \-iŋ\ *n* : the activities of a do-gooder
dog paddle *n* : an elementary form of swimming in which the arms paddle in the water and the legs maintain a kicking motion — **dog–pad·dle** *vi*
dogs·body \'dȯgz-ˌbäd-ē\ *n* [Brit naval slang *dogsbody* pudding made of peas, junior officer] *chiefly Brit* : DRUDGE
dog's chance *n* : a bare chance in one's favor ⟨didn't have a *dog's chance*⟩
dog·sled \'dȯg-ˌsled\ *n* : a sled drawn by dogs
dog's life *n* : a miserable drab existence
Dog Star *n* **1** : SIRIUS **2** : PROCYON
dog tag *n* **1** : a metal disk or plate on a dog collar bearing a license registration number **2** : a military identification tag
dog·tooth \'dȯg-ˌtüth\ *n* **1** : CANINE 1, EYETOOTH **2** : an architectural ornament common in early English Gothic consisting usu. of four leaves radiating from a raised point at the center
dogtooth violet *n* : any of a genus (*Erythronium*) of small spring-flowering bulbous herbs of the lily family
[1]**dog·trot** \'dȯg-ˌträt\ *n* **1** : a quick easy gait suggesting that of a dog **2** *South & Midland* : a roofed passage similar to a breezeway; *esp* : one connecting two parts of a cabin
[2]**dogtrot** *vi* : to move or progress at a dogtrot
dog·watch \'dȯ-ˌgwäch\ *n* **1** : either of two watches of two hours on shipboard that extend from 4 to 6 and 6 to 8 p.m. **2** : any of various night shifts; *esp* : the last shift
dog·wood \'dȯ-ˌgwu̇d\ *n* : any of a genus (*Cornus*) of trees and shrubs (family Cornaceae, the dogwood family) with heads of small flowers and often showy involucres
doi·ly \'dȯi-lē\ *n, pl* **doilies** [*Doily* or *Doyley* *fl* 1712 London draper] **1** : a small napkin **2** : a small often decorative mat
do in *vt* **1** **a** : to bring about the defeat or destruction of : RUIN ⟨the financial loss *did* him *in*⟩ **b** : to bring about the death of : KILL ⟨tried to *do* him *in* with a club⟩ **c** : to wear out ⟨walking all day nearly *did* us *in*⟩ **2** : CHEAT
do·ing \'dü-iŋ\ *n* **1** : the act of performing or executing : ACTION ⟨that will take a great deal of ∼⟩ **2** *pl* **a** : things that are done or that occur ⟨everyday ∼*s*⟩ **b** : social activities
doit \'dȯit\ *n* [D *duit;* akin to ON *thveiti* small coin, *thveita* to hew] **1** : an old Dutch coin equal to about 1/4 stiver **2** : TRIFLE 1
do–it–yourself \ˌdü-ə-chər-'self\ *adj* : of, relating to, or designed for use by or as if by an amateur or hobbyist ⟨∼ tools⟩ ⟨∼ car model kit⟩ — **do–it–your·self·er** \-'sel-fər\ *n*
do·jo \'dō-(ˌ)jō\ *n, pl* **dojos** [Jap *dōjō,* fr. *dō* way, art + *-jō* ground] : a school for training in various arts of self-defense (as judo and karate)
dol *abbr* dollar
dol·ce \'dōl-(ˌ)chā\ *adj or adv* [It, lit., sweet, fr. L *dulcis* — more at DULCET] : SOFT, SMOOTH — used as a direction in music
dol·ce far nien·te \'dōl-chē-ˌfär-nē-'ent-ē\ *n* [It, lit., sweet doing nothing] : pleasant relaxation in carefree idleness
dol·ce vi·ta \ˌdōl-chā-'vē-(ˌ)tä\ *n* [It, lit., sweet life] : a life of indolence and self-indulgence
dol·drums \'dōl-drəmz, 'däl-, 'dȯl-\ *n pl* [prob. akin to OE *dol* foolish] **1** : a spell of listlessness or despondency : BLUES **2** : a part of the ocean near the equator abounding in calms, squalls, and light shifting winds **3** : a state of inactivity, stagnation, or slump
[1]**dole** \'dōl\ *n* [ME, fr. OE *dāl* portion] **1** *archaic* : one's allotted share, portion, or destiny **2** **a** (1) : a giving or distribution of food, money, or clothing to the needy (2) : a grant of government funds to the unemployed **b** : something distributed at intervals to the needy **c** : something portioned out and distributed usu. grudgingly or bit by bit ***syn*** see RATION
[2]**dole** *vt* **doled; dol·ing** **1** : to give or distribute as a charity **2** : to give or deliver in small portions : PARCEL — used with *out* ***syn*** see DISTRIBUTE
[3]**dole** *n* [ME *dol,* fr. OF, fr. LL *dolus,* alter. of L *dolor*] *archaic* : GRIEF, SORROW
dole·ful \'dōl-fəl\ *adj* **1** : causing grief or affliction ⟨a ∼ loss⟩ **2** : full of grief : CHEERLESS ⟨a ∼ face⟩ **3** : expressing grief : SAD ⟨a ∼ melody⟩ — **dole·ful·ly** \-fə-lē\ *adv* — **dole·ful·ness** *n*
dol·er·ite \'däl-ə-ˌrīt\ *n* [F *dolérite,* fr. Gk *doleros* deceitful, fr. *dolos* deceit; fr. its being easily mistaken for diorite — more at TALE] **1** : any of various coarse basalts **2** *Brit* : DIABASE 3 **3** : any of various dark igneous rocks whose constituents are not determinable megascopically — **dol·er·it·ic** \ˌdäl-ə-'rit-ik\ *adj*
dole·some \'dōl-səm\ *adj* : DOLEFUL
dolich- *or* **dolicho-** *comb form* [Gk, fr. *dolichos* — more at LONG] : long
dol·i·cho·ce·phal·ic \ˌdäl-i-kō-sə-'fal-ik\ *adj* [NL *dolichocephalus* dolichocephalic individual, fr. *dolich-* + *-cephalus* (fr. Gk *kephalē* head) — more at CEPHALIC] : having a relatively long head with cephalic index of less than 75 — **dol·i·cho·ceph·a·lism** \-'sef-ə-ˌliz-əm\ *n* — **dol·i·cho·ceph·a·ly** \-'sef-ə-lē\ *n*
dol·i·cho·cra·ni·al \-'krā-nē-əl\ *also* **dol·i·cho·cra·nic** \-nik\ *adj* [ISV] : having a relatively long head with a cranial index of less than 75 — **dol·i·cho·cra·ny** \'däl-i-kō-ˌkrā-nē\ *n*
doll \'däl, 'dȯl\ *n* [prob. fr. *Doll,* nickname for *Dorothy*] **1** : a small-scale figure of a human being used esp. as a child's plaything **2** **a** (1) : a pretty but often empty-headed young woman (2) : WOMAN **b** : DARLING, SWEETHEART **c** : an attractive person — **doll·ish** \-ish\ *adj* — **doll·ish·ly** *adv* — **doll·ish·ness** *n*
dol·lar \'däl-ər\ *n, often attrib* [D or LG *daler,* fr. G *taler,* short for *joachimstaler,* fr. Sankt *Joachimsthal,* Bohemia, where talers were first made] **1** : TALER **2** : any of numerous coins patterned after the taler (as a Spanish peso) **3** **a** : any of various basic monetary units (as in the U.S. and Canada) — see MONEY table **b** : a coin, note, or token representing one dollar
dollar averaging *n* : investment in a security at regular intervals of a uniform sum regardless of the price level in order to obtain an overall reduction in cost per unit — called also *dollar cost averaging*
dollar–a–year *adj* : compensated by a token salary usu. for government service ⟨a ∼ man⟩
dollar day *n* : a day on which a merchant makes special offerings of goods and services for one dollar; *broadly* : a day on which bargain prices in many lines are offered
dollar diplomacy *n* **1** : diplomacy used by a country to promote its financial or commercial interests abroad **2** : diplomacy that seeks to strengthen the power of a country or effect its purposes in foreign relations by the use of its financial resources
dollar gap *n* : the amount of additional dollar receipts required by a country to meet dollar obligations
dollar sign *n* : a mark $ placed before a number to indicate that it stands for dollars — called also *dollar mark*
doll·house \'däl-ˌhau̇s, 'dȯl-\ *n* **1** : a child's small-scale toy house **2** : a dwelling so small as to suggest resemblance to a house for dolls
dol·lop \'däl-əp\ *n* [origin unknown] **1** **a** : a lump or blob of a usu. semiliquid substance ⟨a ∼ of jelly⟩ **b** : an unmeasured amount (as of hard liquor) : DASH ⟨coffee laced with a ∼ of brandy⟩ **2** : a small amount or admixture ⟨prose without one ∼ of sentimentality —Ann Currah⟩
doll up *vt* **1** : to dress elegantly or extravagantly **2** : to make more attractive (as by addition of decorative details)
[1]**dol·ly** \'däl-ē, 'dȯ-lē\ *n, pl* **dollies** **1** : DOLL **2** **a** : a wooden-pronged instrument for beating and stirring clothes in the process of washing them in a tub **b** : a device turning on a vertical axis by a handle or winch for stirring ore to be washed **3** : a heavy bar with a cupped head for holding against the head of a rivet while the other end is being headed **4** : a compact narrow-gauge railroad locomotive for moving construction trains and for switching **5** **a** : a platform on a roller or on wheels or casters for moving heavy objects **b** : a wheeled platform for a television or motion-picture camera
[2]**dolly** *vb* **dol·lied; dol·ly·ing** *vt* **1** : to treat with a dolly **2** : to move or convey on a dolly ∼ *vi* : to move a motion-picture or television camera about on a dolly while shooting a scene
dol·man \'dōl-mən, 'dȯl-, 'däl-\ *n, pl* **dolmans** [F *doliman,* fr. Turk *dolama,* a Turkish robe] : a woman's coat made with dolman sleeves
dolman sleeve *n* : a sleeve very wide at the armhole and tight at the wrist often cut in one piece with the bodice
dol·men \'dōl-mən, 'dȯl-, 'däl-\ *n* [F, fr. Bret *tolmen,* fr. *tol* table + *men* stone] : a prehistoric monument of two or more upright stones supporting a horizontal stone slab found esp. in Britain and France and thought to be a tomb

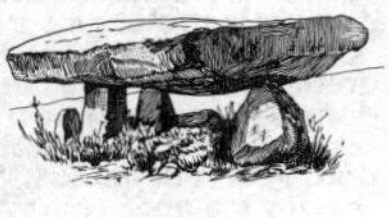
dolmen

do·lo·mite \'dō-lə-ˌmīt, 'däl-ə-\ *n* [F, fr. Déodat de *Dolomieu* †1801 F geologist] **1** : a mineral $CaMg(CO_3)_2$ consisting of a calcium magnesium carbonate found in crystals and in extensive beds as a compact limestone **2** : a limestone or marble rich in magnesium carbonate — **do·lo·mit·ic** \ˌdō-lə-'mit-ik, ˌdäl-ə-\ *adj*
do·lo·mi·tize \'dō-lə-mə-ˌtīz, 'däl-ə-\ *vt* **-tized; -tiz·ing** : to convert into dolomite — **do·lo·mi·ti·za·tion** \ˌdō-lə-mət-ə-'zā-shən, ˌdäl-ə-, -ˌmīt-\ *n*
do·lor \'dō-lər, 'däl-ər\ *n* [ME *dolour,* fr. MF, fr. L *dolor* pain, grief, fr. *dolēre* to feel pain, grieve — more at CONDOLE] : mental suffering or anguish : SORROW
do·lor·ous \'dō-lə-rəs, 'däl-ə-\ *adj* : causing, marked by, or expressive of misery or grief — **do·lor·ous·ly** *adv* — **do·lor·ous·ness** *n*
do·lour *chiefly Brit var of* DOLOR
dol·phin \'däl-fən, 'dȯl-\ *n* [ME, fr. MF *dophin, daufin,* fr. OF *dalfin,* fr. OProv, fr. ML *dalfinus,* alter. of L *delphinus,* fr. Gk *delphin-, delphis;* akin to Gk *delphys* womb, Skt *garbha*] **1** **a** : any of various small toothed whales (family Delphinidae) with the snout more or less elongated into a beak and the neck vertebrae partially fused **b** : PORPOISE 1 **2** : either of two active pelagic percoid food fishes (genus *Coryphaena*) of tropical and temperate seas **3** *cap* : DELPHINUS **4** : a spar or buoy for mooring boats; *also* : a cluster of closely driven piles used as a fender for a dock or as a mooring or guide for boats

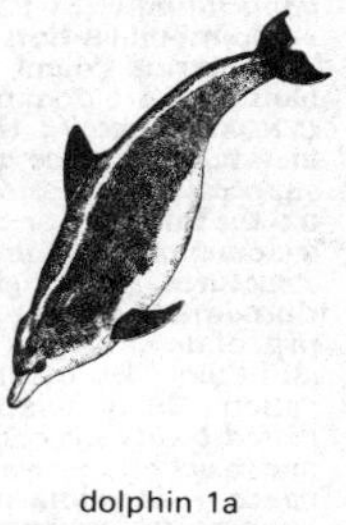
dolphin 1a

dolphin striker *n* : a vertical spar under the end of the bowsprit of a sailboat to extend and support the martingale
dolt \'dōlt\ *n* [prob. akin to OE *dol* foolish] : a stupid fellow — **dolt·ish** \'dōl-tish\ *adj* — **dolt·ish·ly** *adv* — **dolt·ish·ness** *n*
dom *abbr* **1** domestic **2** dominant **3** dominion
Dom [L *dominus* master] **1** \(ˌ)däm\ — used as a title for some monks and canons regular **2** \(ˌ)dōⁿ\ — used as a title prefixed to the Christian name of a Portuguese or Brazilian man of rank
DOM *abbr* [ML *Deo optimo maximo*] to God, the best and greatest
-dom \dəm\ *n suffix* [ME, fr. OE *-dōm;* akin to OHG *-tuom* -dom, OE *dōm* judgment — more at DOOM] **1** **a** : dignity : office ⟨duke*dom*⟩ **b** : realm : jurisdiction ⟨king*dom*⟩ **2** : state or fact of being ⟨free*dom*⟩ **3** : those having a (specified) office, occupation, interest, or character ⟨official*dom*⟩
do·main \dō-'mān, də-\ *n* [MF *domaine, demaine,* fr. L *dominium,* fr. *dominus*] **1** **a** : complete and absolute ownership of land — compare EMINENT DOMAIN **b** : land so owned **2** : a territory over which dominion is exercised **3** : a region distinctively marked by

some physical feature ⟨the ~ of rushing streams, tall trees, and lakes⟩ **4 :** a sphere of influence or activity ⟨the ~ of art⟩ **5 :** the set of elements to which a mathematical or logical variable is limited; *specif* **:** the set on which a function is defined **6 :** any of the small randomly oriented regions of uniform magnetization in a ferromagnetic substance **7 :** INTEGRAL DOMAIN

1dome \'dōm\ *n* [F, It, & L; F *dôme* dome, cathedral, fr. It *duomo* cathedral, fr. ML *domus* church, fr. L, house — more at TIMBER] **1** *archaic* **:** a stately building **:** MANSION **2 :** a large hemispherical roof or ceiling **3 :** a natural formation or other structure that resembles the dome or cupola of a building **4 :** a form of crystal composed of planes parallel to a lateral axis that meet above in a horizontal edge like a roof — **dom·al** \'dō-məl\ *adj*

2dome *vb* **domed; dom·ing** *vt* **1 :** to cover with a dome **2 :** to form into a dome ~ *vi* **:** to swell upward or outward like a dome

Domes·day Book \'dümz-,dā-, 'dōmz-\ *n* [ME, fr. *domesday* doomsday] **:** a record of a survey of English lands made by order of William the Conqueror about 1086

1do·mes·tic \də-'mes-tik\ *adj* [MF *domestique*, fr. L *domesticus*, fr. *domus*] **1 :** of or relating to the household or the family **2 :** of, relating to, or carried on within one and esp. one's own country ⟨~ politics⟩ ⟨~ wines⟩ **3 :** INDIGENOUS **4 a :** living near or about the habitations of man **b :** TAME, DOMESTICATED **5 :** devoted to home duties and pleasures — **do·mes·ti·cal·ly** \-ti-k(ə-)lē\ *adv*

2domestic *n* **1 :** a household servant **2 :** an article of domestic manufacture — usu. used in pl.

domestic animal *n* **:** any of various animals (as the horse or sheep) domesticated by man so as to live and breed in a tame condition

1do·mes·ti·cate \də-'mes-ti-,kāt\ *vt* **-cat·ed; -cat·ing 1 :** to bring into domestic use **:** ADOPT **2 :** to fit for domestic life **3 :** to adapt (an animal or plant) to life in intimate association with and to the advantage of man **4 :** to bring to the level of ordinary people **:** FAMILIARIZE — **do·mes·ti·ca·tion** \-,mes-ti-'kā-shən\ *n*

2do·mes·ti·cate \-kət, -,kāt\ *n* **:** a domesticated animal or plant

domestic fowl *n* **1 :** POULTRY **2 :** a bird of one of the breeds developed from the jungle fowl (*Gallus gallus*) esp. for meat or egg production **:** CHICKEN

do·mes·tic·i·ty \,dō-,mes-'tis-ət-ē, -məs-; ,däm-əs-, -,es-; də-,mes-\ *n, pl* **-ties 1 :** the quality or state of being domestic or domesticated **2 :** domestic activities or life **3** *pl* **:** domestic affairs

domestic prelate *n* **:** a priest having permanent honorary membership in the papal household

domestic relations court *n* **:** COURT OF DOMESTIC RELATIONS

domestic science *n* **:** instruction and training in domestic management and the household arts (as cooking and sewing)

dom·i·cal \'dō-mi-kəl, 'däm-i-\ *adj* **:** relating to, shaped like, or having a dome

1do·mi·cile \'däm-ə-,sīl, 'dō-mə-; 'däm-ə-səl\ *also* **dom·i·cil** \'däm-ə-səl\ *n* [MF, fr. L *domicilium*, fr. *domus*] **1 :** a dwelling place **:** place of residence **:** HOME **2 a :** a person's fixed, permanent, and principal home for legal purposes **b :** RESIDENCE 2b

2domicile *vt* **-ciled; -cil·ing :** to establish in or provide with a domicile

do·mi·cil·i·ary \,däm-ə-'sil-ē-,er-ē, ,dō-mə-\ *adj* **:** of, relating to, or constituting a domicile: as **a :** provided or taking place in the home ⟨~ meal service for elderly and housebound people⟩ **b :** providing care and living space for persons (as veterans) so disabled as to be unable to live independently ⟨the ~ section of the state hospital⟩

do·mi·cil·i·ate \,däm-ə-'sil-ē-,āt, ,dō-mə-\ *vb* **-at·ed; -at·ing** [L *domicilium*] *vt* **1 :** DOMICILE **2 :** DOMESTICATE 3, 4 ~ *vi* **:** RESIDE — **do·mi·cil·i·a·tion** \-,sil-ē-'ā-shən\ *n*

dom·i·nance \'däm(-ə)-nən(t)s\ *n* **:** the fact or state of being dominant: as **a :** dominant position in an order of forcefulness **:** ASCENDANCY; *specif* **:** the relative position of an individual in a social hierarchy **b :** the quality of one of a pair of alleles or traits that suppresses expression of the other in the heterozygous condition **c :** the influence or control over ecological communities exerted by a dominant **d :** functional asymmetry between a pair of bodily structures (as the right and left hands)

1dom·i·nant \-nənt\ *adj* [MF or L; MF, fr. L *dominant-, dominans*, prp. of *dominari*] **1 :** commanding, controlling, or prevailing over all others **2 :** overlooking and commanding from a superior elevation **3 :** of, relating to, or exerting ecological dominance **4** *of paired bodily structures* **:** being the more effective or predominant one in action ⟨~ eye⟩ **5 :** of, relating to, or exerting genetic dominance — **dom·i·nant·ly** *adv*

syn DOMINANT, PREDOMINANT, PARAMOUNT, PREPONDERANT, SOVEREIGN *shared meaning element* **:** superior to all others in power, influence, or importance ***ant*** subordinate

2dominant *n* **1 a :** a dominant genetic character or factor **b :** any of one or more kinds of organism (as a species) in an ecological association that exerts a controlling influence on the environment and thereby largely determines what other kinds of organisms share in the association **c :** a dominant individual in a social hierarchy **2 :** the fifth note of a diatonic scale

dom·i·nate \'däm-ə-,nāt\ *vb* **-nat·ed; -nat·ing** [L *dominatus*, pp. of *dominari*, fr. *dominus* master — more at DAME] *vt* **1 :** RULE, CONTROL **2 :** to exert the supreme determining or guiding influence on **3 :** to overlook from a superior elevation or command because of superior height **4 :** to have a commanding or preeminent place or position in ⟨name brands ~ the market⟩ ~ *vi* **1 :** to have or exert mastery, control, or preeminence **2 :** to occupy a more elevated or superior position — **dom·i·na·tive** \-,nāt-iv\ *adj* — **dom·i·na·tor** \-,nāt-ər\ *n*

dom·i·na·tion \,däm-ə-'nā-shən\ *n* **1 :** supremacy or preeminence over another **2 :** exercise of mastery or preponderant influence **3** *pl* **:** DOMINION 3

dom·i·neer \,däm-ə-'ni(ə)r\ *vb* [D *domineren*, fr. F *dominer*, fr. L *dominari*] *vi* **:** to exercise arbitrary or overbearing control ~ *vt* **:** to tyrannize over

dom·i·neer·ing *adj* **:** inclined to domineer ***syn*** see MASTERFUL ***ant*** subservient — **dom·i·neer·ing·ly** \-iŋ-lē\ *adv* — **dom·i·neer·ing·ness** *n*

do·min·i·cal \də-'min-i-kəl\ *adj* [LL *dominicalis*, fr. *dominicus* (*dies*) the Lord's day, fr. L *dominicus* of a lord, fr. *dominus* lord, master] **1 :** of or relating to Jesus Christ as Lord **2 :** of or relating to the Lord's day

dominical letter *n* **:** the letter designating Sundays in a given year (as for finding the date of Easter) when the first seven letters of the alphabet are applied consecutively to the days of the year beginning with *A* on Jan. 1 and skipping the intercalary day in leap year

Do·min·i·can \də-'min-i-kən\ *n* [St. *Dominic*] **:** a member of a mendicant order of friars founded by St. Dominic in 1215 and dedicated esp. to preaching — **Dominican** *adj*

dom·i·nick \'däm-ə-(,)nik, -,nek\ *or* **dom·i·nick·er** \-,nek-ər, -,nik-\ *n, often cap* **:** DOMINIQUE

do·mi·nie *1 oftenest* 'däm-ə-nē, *2 oftenest* 'dō-mə-\ *n* [L *domine*, voc. of *dominus*] **1 :** PEDAGOGUE **2 :** CLERGYMAN

do·min·ion \də-'min-yən\ *n* [ME *dominioun*, fr. MF *dominion*, modif. of L *dominium*, fr. *dominus*] **1 :** supreme authority **:** SOVEREIGNTY **2 :** DOMAIN **3** *pl* **:** an order of angels — see CELESTIAL HIERARCHY **4** *often cap* **:** a self-governing nation of the British Commonwealth other than the United Kingdom that acknowledges the British monarch as chief of state **5 :** absolute ownership

Dominion Day *n* **:** July 1 observed as a legal holiday in Canada in commemoration of the proclamation of dominion status in 1867

dom·i·nique \'däm-ə-(,)nik, -,nək\ *n* [*Dominique* (Dominica), one of the Windward islands, West Indies] **:** any of an American breed of domestic fowl with a rose comb, yellow legs, and barred plumage; *broadly* **:** a barred fowl

dom·i·no \'däm-ə-,nō\ *n, pl* **-noes** *or* **-nos** [F, prob. fr. L (in the ritual formula *benedicamus Domino* let us bless the Lord)] **1 a** (1) **:** a long loose hooded cloak usu. worn with a half mask as a masquerade costume (2) **:** a half mask worn with a masquerade costume **b :** a person wearing a domino **2** [F, fr. It] **a :** a flat rectangular block (as of wood or plastic) whose face is divided into two equal parts that are blank or bear from one to usu. six dots arranged as on dice faces **b** *pl but usu sing in constr* **:** any of several games played with a set of usu. 28 dominoes

domino theory *n* [fr. the fact that if a number of dominoes are stood on end one behind the other with slight intervening spaces, a slight push on the first will result in the toppling of all the others] **:** a theory that if one nation in Southeast Asia becomes Communist-controlled the neighboring nations will also become Communist-controlled

1don \'dän\ *n* [Sp, fr. L *dominus* master — more at DAME] **1 :** a Spanish nobleman or gentleman — used as a title prefixed to the Christian name **2** *archaic* **:** a person of consequence **:** GRANDEE **3 :** a head, tutor, or fellow in a college of Oxford or Cambridge University; *broadly* **:** a college or university professor

2don \'dän\ *vt* **donned; don·ning** [*do* + *on*] **1 :** to put on (an article of wear) **2 :** to envelop oneself in **:** ASSUME

Don *abbr* Donegal

do·na \,dō-nə\ *n* [Pg, fr. L *domina*] **:** a Portuguese or Brazilian woman of rank — used as a title prefixed to the Christian name

do·ña \,dō-nyə\ *n* [Sp, fr. L *domina* lady] **:** a Spanish woman of rank — used as a title prefixed to the Christian name

do·nate \'dō-,nāt, dō-'\ *vb* **do·nat·ed; do·nat·ing** [back-formation fr. *donation*] *vt* **1 :** to make a gift of; *esp* **:** to contribute to a public or charitable cause ⟨~ a site for a park⟩ **2 :** to give off or transfer (as electrons) ~ *vi* **:** to make a donation ***syn*** see GIVE

do·na·tion \dō-'nā-shən\ *n* [ME *donatyowne*, fr. L *donation-, donatio*, fr. *donatus*, pp. of *donare* to present, fr. *donum* gift; akin to L *dare* to give — more at DATE] **1 :** the action of making a gift esp. to a charity or public institution **2 :** a free contribution **:** GIFT

Do·na·tism \'dō-nə-,tiz-əm, 'dän-ə-\ *n* [*Donatus*, 4th cent. bishop of Carthage] **:** the doctrines of a Christian sect arising in No. Africa in 311 and holding that sanctity is essential for the administration of sacraments and church membership — **Do·na·tist** \-təst\ *n*

1do·na·tive \'dō-nət-iv, 'dän-ət-\ *n* **:** a special gift or donation

2do·na·tive *same or* 'dō-,nāt-, dō-'\ *adj* [L *donativus*, fr. *donatus*] **:** characterized by, capable of, or subject to donation ⟨a ~ trust⟩

do·na·tor \'dō-,nāt-ər, dō-'\ *n* **:** DONOR

1done \'dən\ *past part of* DO

2done *adj* **1 :** conformable to social convention **2 :** arrived at or brought to an end **:** THROUGH **3 :** physically exhausted **:** SPENT **4 :** gone by **:** OVER **5 :** doomed to failure, defeat, or death **6 :** cooked sufficiently

do·nee \dō-'nē\ *n* [*donor*] **:** a recipient of a gift

done for \'dən-,fō(ə)r\ *adj* **1 :** mortally stricken **:** DOOMED **2 :** left with no capacity or opportunity for recovery **:** RUINED **3 :** sunk in defeat **:** BEATEN

done·ness \'dən-nəs\ *n* **:** the condition of being cooked to the desired degree

1dong \'dȯŋ, 'däŋ\ *n* [origin unknown] **:** PENIS — usu. considered vulgar

2dong *n* [Annamese] **1** — see MONEY table **2 :** a coin of South Vietnam worth one piaster

don·jon \'dän-jən, 'dən-\ *n* [ME — more at DUNGEON] **:** a massive inner tower in a medieval castle

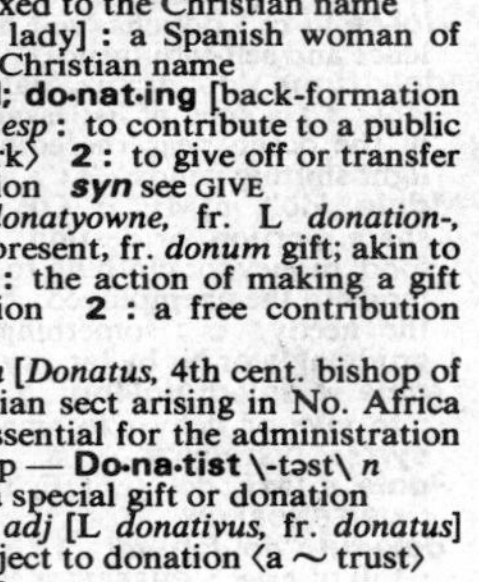

1 donjon

Don Juan \(')dän-'(h)wän, dän-'jü-ən\ *n* [Sp] **1 :** a legendary Spaniard proverbial for his seduction of women **2 :** LIBERTINE, RAKE

don·key \'däŋ-kē, 'dəŋ-, 'dȯŋ-\ *n, pl* **donkeys** [perh. fr. 1*dun* + *-key* (as in *monkey*)] **1 :** the domestic ass (*Equus asinus*) **2 :** a stupid or obstinate person

donkey engine *n* **1 :** a small usu. portable auxiliary engine **2 :** a small locomotive used in switching

donkey's years *n pl* **:** a very long time ⟨place where there'd been no fires for *donkey's years* —Malcolm Lowry⟩

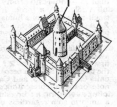

don·key·work \ˈdäŋ-kē-ˌwərk, ˈdəŋ-, ˈdȯŋ-\ n : monotonous and routine work : DRUDGERY

don·na \ˈdän-ə, ˈdȯn-\ n, pl **don·ne** \-(ˌ)ā\ [It., fr. L domina] : an Italian woman esp. of rank — used as a title prefixed to the Christian name

don·née \dȯ-ˈnā, (ˌ)də-\ n, pl **données** \-ˈnā(z)\ [F, fr. fem. of donné, pp. of donner to give, fr. L donare to donate] : the set of assumptions upon which a work of fiction or drama proceeds

don·nish \ˈdän-ish\ adj : of, relating to, or characteristic of a university don : PEDANTIC — **don·nish·ly** adv — **don·nish·ness** n

don·ny·brook \ˈdän-ē-ˌbrůk\ n, often cap [Donnybrook Fair, annual Irish event known for its brawls] : an uproarious brawl : FREE-FOR-ALL

do·nor \ˈdō-nər, -ˌnȯ(ə)r\ n [MF doneur, fr. L donator, fr. donatus] 1 : one that gives, donates, or presents 2 : one used as a source of biological material 3 : a compound capable of giving up a part (as an atom, radical, or elementary particle) for combination with an acceptor b : an impurity that is added to a semiconductor to increase the number of mobile electrons

¹do·noth·ing \ˈdü-ˌnəth-iŋ\ n : a shiftless or habitually lazy person

²do-nothing adj : marked by inactivity; specif : marked by lack of initiative, disinclination to disturb the status quo, or failure to make positive progress — **do-noth·ing·ism** \-ˌiz-əm\ n

Don Qui·xote \ˌdän-kē-ˈ(h)ōt-ē, ˌdän-; dän-ˈkwik-sət\ n [Sp] : the idealistic and impractical hero of Cervantes' Don Quixote

don·sie or **don·sy** \ˈdän(t)-sē\ adj [perh. fr. ScGael donas evil, harm] 1 dial Brit : UNLUCKY 2 Scot a : RESTIVE b : SAUCY

¹don't \(ˈ)dōnt\ : do not 2 : does not — often used by educated speakers though the construction is sometimes objected to ⟨there are simply certain things he ~ know —Ezra Pound⟩

²don't n : a command or entreaty not to do something : PROHIBITION ⟨a long list of ~s⟩

donut var of DOUGHNUT

doo·dad \ˈdü-ˌdad\ n [origin unknown] 1 : a small article whose common name is unknown or forgotten : GADGET 2 : an ornamental attachment or decoration ⟨a mantelpiece cluttered up with all kinds of ~s⟩

¹doo·dle \ˈdüd-ᵊl\ vb **doo·dled; doo·dling** \ˈdüd-liŋ, -ᵊl-iŋ\ [perh. fr. doodle (to ridicule)] vi 1 : to make a doodle 2 : DAWDLE, TRIFLE ~ vt : to produce by doodling — **doo·dler** \ˈdüd-lər, -ᵊl-ər\ n

²doodle n : an aimless scribble, design, or sketch

doo·dle·bug \ˈdüd-ᵊl-ˌbag\ n [prob. fr. doodle (fool) + bug] 1 : the larva of an ant lion; also : any of several other insects 2 : a device (as a divining rod) used in attempting to locate underground gas, water, oil, or ores 3 : any of several small vehicles

doo·hick·ey \ˈdü-ˌhik-ē\ n [prob. fr. doodad + hickey] : DOODAD 1

¹doom \ˈdüm\ n [ME, fr. OE dōm; akin to OHG tuom condition, state, OE dōn to do] 1 : a law or ordinance esp. in Anglo-Saxon England 2 a : JUDGMENT, DECISION; esp : a judicial condemnation or sentence b (1) : JUDGMENT 3a (2) : JUDGMENT DAY 1 3 a : DESTINY; esp : unhappy destiny b : DEATH, RUIN syn see FATE

²doom vt 1 : to give judgment against : CONDEMN 2 a : to fix the fate of : DESTINE b : to make certain the failure or destruction of

doom·ful \ˈdüm-fəl\ adj : presaging doom : OMINOUS — **doom·ful·ly** \-fə-lē\ adv

doom·say·er \ˈdüm-ˌsā-ər\ n : one given to forebodings and predictions of impending calamity

dooms·day \ˈdümz-ˌdā\ n : JUDGMENT DAY

doom·ster \ˈdüm(p)-stər\ n 1 : JUDGE 2 : DOOMSAYER

door \ˈdō(ə)r, ˈdȯ(ə)r\ n, often attrib [ME dure, dor, fr. OE duru door & dor gate; akin to OHG turi door, L fores, Gk thyra] 1 : a usu. swinging or sliding barrier by which an entry is closed and opened; also : a similar part of a piece of furniture 2 : DOORWAY 3 : a means of access ⟨~ to success⟩ — **door·less** \-ləs\ adj — at one's door : as a charge against one as being responsible ⟨laid the blame at our door⟩

door·jamb \ˈdō(ə)r-ˌjam, ˈdȯ(ə)r-\ n : an upright piece forming the side of a door opening

door·keep·er \-ˌkē-pər\ n : one that tends a door

door·knob \-ˌnäb\ n : a knob that when turned releases a door latch

door·man \-ˌman, -mən\ n : one that tends the door of a building (as a hotel or theater) and assists people (as in calling taxis)

door·mat \-ˌmat\ n 1 : a mat placed before or inside a door for wiping dirt from the shoes 2 : one that submits without protest to abuse or indignities

door·nail \-ˌnāl, -ᵊl\ n : a large-headed nail — used chiefly in the phrase dead as a doornail

door·plate \-ˌplāt\ n : a nameplate on a door

door·post \-ˌpōst\ n : DOORJAMB

door prize n : a prize awarded to the holder of a winning ticket passed out at the entrance to an entertainment or function

door·sill \ˈdō(ə)r-ˌsil, ˈdȯ(ə)r-\ n : SILL 1b

door·step \-ˌstep\ n : a step before an outer door

door·stop \-ˌstäp\ n 1 : a device (as a wedge or weight) for holding a door open 2 : a projection attached to a wall or floor and usu. having a rubber-tipped end for preventing damaging contact between an opened door and the wall

door–to–door \ˌdȯrt-ə-ˈdō(ə)r, ˌdȯrt-ə-ˈdȯ(ə)r\ adj 1 : being or making a usu. unsolicited call (as for selling or canvassing) at every residence in an area 2 : providing delivery to a specified address ⟨direct ~ service⟩

door·way \ˈdō(ə)r-ˌwā, ˈdȯ(ə)r-\ n 1 : the opening that a door closes; esp : an entrance into a building or room 2 : a means of gaining access ⟨exercise is a ~ to good health⟩

door·yard \-ˌyärd\ n : a yard about the door of a house

do·pa \ˈdō-pə, -(ˌ)pä\ n [dihydroxyphenylalanine] : an amino acid $C_9H_{11}NO_4$ that in the levorotatory form is found in the broad bean and is used in the treatment of Parkinson's disease

do·pa·mine \ˈdō-pə-ˌmēn\ n [dopa + amine] : a decarboxylated form of dopa found esp. in the adrenal glands; also : DOPA

dop·ant \ˈdō-pənt\ n [²dope] : an impurity added usu. in minute amounts to a pure substance to alter its properties

¹dope \ˈdōp\ n [D doop sauce, fr. dopen to dip; akin to OE dyppan to dip — more at DIP] 1 a : a thick liquid or pasty preparation b : a preparation for giving a desired quality to a substance or surface; specif : an antiknock added to gasoline 2 : absorbent material used in various manufacturing processes (as the making of dynamite) 3 a (1) : a narcotic preparation (as opium or heroin) (2) : a preparation given to a racehorse to stimulate it temporarily b chiefly South : a cola drink c (1) : a narcotic addict (2) : a stupid person 4 : information esp. from a reliable source ⟨inside ~ on the scandal⟩

²dope vb **doped; dop·ing** vt 1 : to treat or affect with dope; specif : to give a narcotic to 2 : to find a solution for ~ vi : to take dope — **dop·er** n

dope·ster \ˈdōp-stər\ n : a forecaster of the outcome of future events (as sports contests or elections)

dop·ey or **dopy** \ˈdō-pē\ adj **dop·i·er; -est** 1 a : dulled by alcohol or a narcotic b : SLUGGISH, STUPEFIED 2 : DULL, STUPID — **dop·i·ness** n

dop·pel·gäng·er or **dop·pel·gang·er** \ˈdäp-əl-ˌgeŋ-ər, ˌdäb-əl-ˈgaŋ-\ n [G doppelgänger, fr. doppel- double + -gänger goer] : a ghostly counterpart of a living person

Dopp·ler \ˈdäp-lər\ adj : of, relating to, or utilizing a shift in frequency in accordance with the Doppler effect; also : of or relating to Doppler radar

Doppler effect n [Christian J. Doppler] : a change in the frequency with which waves (as sound, light, or radio waves) from a given source reach an observer when the source and the observer are in rapid motion with respect to each other so that the frequency increases or decreases according to the speed at which the distance is decreasing or increasing

Doppler radar n : a radar system that utilizes the Doppler effect for measuring velocity

dor·bee·tle \ˈdȯr-ˌbēt-ᵊl\ n [dor (buzzing insect)] : any of various beetles that fly with a buzzing sound; specif : a common European dung beetle (Geotrupes stercorarius)

Dor·cas \ˈdȯr-kəs\ n [Gk Dorkas] : a Christian woman of New Testament times who made clothing for the poor

dor·hawk \ˈdȯ(ə)r-ˌhȯk\ n [dor (buzzing insect); fr. its diet] : the common European nightjar (Caprimulgus europaeus)

Do·ri·an \ˈdȯr-ē-ən, ˈdōr-\ n [L dorius from Doris, fr. Gk dōrios, fr. Dōris, region of ancient Greece] : one of an ancient Hellenic race that completed the overthrow of Mycenaean civilization and settled esp. in the Peloponnesus and Crete — **Dorian** adj

¹Dor·ic \ˈdȯr-ik, ˈdär-\ adj 1 : of, relating to, or constituting Doric 2 : of, relating to, or characteristic of the Dorians 3 : belonging to the oldest and simplest Greek architectural order

²Doric n : a dialect of ancient Greek spoken esp. in the Peloponnesus, Crete, Sicily, and southern Italy

dorm \ˈdȯrm\ n : DORMITORY

dor·man·cy \ˈdȯr-mən-sē\ n : the quality or state of being dormant

dor·mant \ˈdȯr-mənt\ adj [ME, fixed, stationary, fr. MF, fr. prp. of dormir to sleep, fr. L dormire; akin to Skt drāti he sleeps] 1 : represented on a coat of arms in a lying position with the head on the forepaws 2 : marked by a suspension of activity: as a : temporarily devoid of external activity ⟨a ~ volcano⟩ b : temporarily in abeyance yet capable of being activated or resumed ⟨a ~ judgment⟩ 3 a : ASLEEP, INACTIVE b : having the faculties suspended : SLUGGISH c : having biological activity suspended: as (1) : being in a state of suspended animation (2) : not actively growing but protected (as by bud scales) from the environment — used of plant parts 4 : associated with, carried out, or applied during dormancy ⟨~ grafting⟩ syn see LATENT ant active

dor·mer \ˈdȯr-mər\ n [MF dormeor dormitory, fr. L dormitorium] : a window set vertically in a structure projecting through a sloping roof; also : the roofed structure containing such a window

dor·mie or **dor·my** \ˈdȯr-mē\ adj [origin unknown] : being ahead by as many holes in golf as remain to be played

dor·min \ˈdȯr-mən\ n [dormancy + -in] : ABSCISIC ACID

dor·mi·to·ry \ˈdȯr-mə-ˌtōr-ē, -ˌtȯr-\ n, pl **-ries** [L dormitorium, fr. dormitus, pp. of dormire] 1 : a room for sleeping; esp : a large room containing numerous beds 2 : a residence hall providing rooms for individuals or for groups usu. without private baths 3 : a residential community from which the inhabitants commute to their places of employment

dor·mouse \ˈdō(ə)r-ˌmaůs\ n [ME dormowse, perh. fr. MF dormir + ME mous mouse] : any of numerous small Old World rodents (family Gliridae) that resemble small squirrels

dor·nick \ˈdȯr-nik, ˈdän-ik\ n [prob. fr. IrGael dornóg] : small stone or chunk of rock

do·ron·i·cum \də-ˈrän-i-kəm\ n [NL, genus name, fr. Ar darūnaj, a plant of this genus] : any of a genus (Doronicum) of Eurasian perennial composite herbs including several cultivated for their showy yellow flower heads

dormouse

dorp \ˈdȯ(ə)rp\ n [D, fr. MD; akin to OHG dorf village — more at THORP] : VILLAGE

dor·per \ˈdȯr-pər\ n [Dorset Horn + Blackhead Persian (a breed of sheep)] : any of a breed of mutton-producing sheep with white body and black face developed in southern Africa

Dors abbr Dorset

dors- or **dorsi-** or **dorso-** comb form [LL dors-, fr. L dorsum] 1 : back ⟨dorsad⟩ 2 : dorsal and ⟨dorsolateral⟩

ə abut	ᵊ kitten	ər further	a back	ā bake	ä cot, cart
aů out	ch chin	e less	ē easy	g gift	i trip	ī life
j joke	ŋ sing	ō flow	ȯ flaw	ȯi coin	th thin	th this
ü loot	ů foot	y yet	yü few	yů furious	zh vision

dor·sad \'dȯ(ə)r-,sad\ *adv* : toward the back : DORSALLY
1dor·sal \'dȯr-səl\ *adj* [LL *dorsalis*, fr. L *dorsum* back] **1** : relating to or situated near or on the back esp. of an animal or of one of its parts **2** : ABAXIAL — **dor·sal·ly** \-sə-lē\ *adv*
2dorsal *n* : a dorsally located part; *esp* : a thoracic vertebra
dorsal lip *n* : the margin of the fold of blastula wall that delineates the dorsal limit of the blastopore, constitutes the primary organizer, and forms the point of origin of chordamesoderm
dorsal root *n* : the one of the two roots of a spinal nerve that passes dorsally to the spinal cord and consists of sensory fibers
dor·set horn \'dȯr-sət-\ *n, often cap D&H* [*Dorset*, England] : any of an English breed of sheep that have very large horns
dor·si·ven·tral \,dȯr-si-'ven-trəl\ *adj* **1** : having distinct dorsal and ventral surfaces **2** : DORSOVENTRAL 1 — **dor·si·ven·tral·i·ty** \-ven-'tral-ət-ē\ *n* — **dor·si·ven·tral·ly** \-'ven-trə-lē\ *adv*
dor·so·lat·er·al \,dȯr-sō-'lat-ə-rəl, -'la-trəl\ *adj* : of, relating to, or involving both the back and the sides
dor·so·ven·tral \-'ven-trəl\ *adj* [ISV] **1** : extending from the dorsal toward the ventral side **2** : DORSIVENTRAL 1 — **dor·so·ven·tral·i·ty** \-ven-'tral-ət-ē\ *n* — **dor·so·ven·tral·ly** \-trə-lē\ *adv*
dor·sum \'dȯr-səm\ *n, pl* **dor·sa** \-sə\ [L] **1** : BACK; *esp* : the entire dorsal surface of an animal **2** : the upper surface of an appendage or part
do·ry \'dȯr-ē, 'dȯr-\ *n, pl* **dories** [Miskito *dóri* dugout] : a flat-bottomed boat with high flaring sides, sharp bow, and deep V-shaped transom
dos·age \'dō-sij\ *n* **1 a** : the amount of a therapeutic dose **b** (1) : the giving of such a dose (2) : regulation or determination of doses **2 a** : the addition of an ingredient or the application of an agent in a measured dose **b** : the presence and relative representation or strength of a factor or agent **3** : a dealing out of or an exposure to some experience in or as if in measured portions
1dose \'dōs\ *n* [F, fr. LL *dosis*, fr. Gk, lit., act of giving, fr. *didonai* to give — more at DATE] **1 a** : the measured quantity of a therapeutic agent to be taken at one time **b** : the quantity of radiation administered or absorbed **2** : a portion of a substance added during a process **3** : a part of an experience to which one is exposed ⟨a ~ of hard work⟩ **4** : a gonorrheal infection
2dose *vt* **dosed; dos·ing** **1** : to divide (as a medicine) into doses **2** : to give a dose to; *esp* : to give medicine to **3** : to treat with an application or agent
do–si–do \,dō-(,)sē-'dō\ *n, pl* **do–si–dos** [F *dos-à-dos* back to back] : a square-dance figure: **a** : a figure in which the dancers pass each other right shoulder to right shoulder and circle each other back to back **b** : a figure in which the woman moves in a figure circling first her partner and then the man on her right
do·sim·e·ter \dō-'sim-ət-ər\ *n* [LL *dosis* + ISV *-meter*] : a device for measuring doses of X rays or of radioactivity — **do·si·met·ric** \,dō-sə-'me-trik\ *adj* — **do·sim·e·try** \dō-'sim-ə-trē\ *n*
1doss \'däs\ *n* [origin unknown] *chiefly Brit* : a crude or makeshift bed
2doss *vi, chiefly Brit* : to sleep or bed down in a convenient place
dos·sal \'däs-əl\ *or* **dor·sal** \'dȯr-səl\ *or* **dos·sel** \'däs-əl\ *n* [ML *dossale, dorsale*, fr. neut. of LL *dorsalis* dorsal] : an ornamental cloth hung behind and above an altar
dos·sier \'dȯs-,yā, 'dȯs-ē-,ā, 'däs-\ *n* [F, bundle of documents labeled on the back, dossier, fr. *dos* back, fr. L *dorsum*] : a file of papers containing a detailed report or detailed information
dost \(')dəst\ *archaic pres 2d sing of* DO
1dot \'dät\ *n* [(assumed) ME, fr. OE *dott* head of a boil; akin to OHG *tutta* nipple] **1** : a small spot : SPECK **2 a** (1) : a small point made with a pointed instrument ⟨a ~ on the chart marked the ship's position⟩ (2) : a small round mark used in orthography or punctuation ⟨put a ~ over the *i*⟩ **b** : a centered point used as a multiplication sign **c** (1) : a point after a note or rest in music indicating augmentation of the time value by one half (2) : a point over or under a note indicating that it is to be played staccato **3** : a precise point esp. in time ⟨arrived at six on the ~⟩ **4** : a short click or buzz forming a letter or part of a letter (as in the Morse code)
2dot *vb* **dot·ted; dot·ting** *vt* **1** : to mark with a dot **2** : to intersperse with dots or objects scattered at random ⟨boats *dotting* the lake⟩ ~ *vi* : to make a dot — **dot·ter** *n*
3dot \'dät\ *n* [F, fr. L *dot-, dos* dowry] : DOWRY 2a
dot·age \'dōt-ij\ *n* : a state or period of senile decay marked by decline of mental poise and alertness — called also *second childhood*
do·tal \'dōt-ᵊl\ *adj* [L *dotalis*, fr. *dot-, dos*] : of or relating to a woman's marriage dowry
dot·ard \'dōt-ərd\ *n* : a person in his dotage
dote \'dōt\ *vi* **dot·ed; dot·ing** [ME *doten*; akin to MLG *dotten* to be foolish] **1** : to exhibit mental decline of or like that of old age : be in one's dotage **2** : to show excessive or foolish affection or fondness — used esp. with *on* ⟨*doted* on her only grandchild⟩ — **dot·er** *n* — **dot·ing·ly** \'dōt-iŋ-lē\ *adv*
doth \(')dəth\ *archaic pres 3d sing of* DO
dot product *n* [1*dot*; fr. its being commonly written *A·B*] : SCALAR PRODUCT
dotted swiss *n* : a sheer light muslin ornamented with evenly spaced raised dots
dot·ter·el \'dät-ə-rəl, 'dä-trəl\ *n* [ME *dotrelle*, irreg. fr. *doten* to dote] : a Eurasian plover (*Charadrius morinellus*) formerly common in England; *also* : any of various congeners chiefly of eastern Asia, Australia, and So. America
dot·tle \'dät-ᵊl\ *n* [ME *dottel* plug, fr. (assumed) ME *dot*] : unburned and partially burned tobacco caked in the bowl of a pipe
1dot·ty \'dät-ē\ *adj* : composed of or marked by dots
2dotty *adj* **dot·ti·er; -est** [alter. of Sc *dottle* fool, fr. ME *dotel*, fr. *doten*] **1** : being obsessed or infatuated **2 a** : mentally unbalanced : CRAZY ⟨thought the man was ~ for paying the boys so much money⟩ **b** : amiably eccentric ⟨an absentminded ~ old man⟩ **3** : amusingly absurd : RIDICULOUS ⟨some sublimely ~ exchanges of letters⟩ — **dot·ti·ly** \'dät-ᵊl-ē\ *adv* — **dot·ti·ness** \'dät-ē-nəs\ *n*

Dou·ay Version \dü-'ā-\ *n* [*Douay*, France] : an English translation of the Vulgate used by Roman Catholics
1dou·ble \'dəb-əl\ *adj* [ME, fr. OF, fr. L *duplus*, fr. *duo* two + *-plus* multiplied by; akin to Gk *diploos* double, OE *fealdan* to fold — more at TWO, FOLD] **1** : having a twofold relation or character : DUAL **2** : consisting of two usu. combined members or parts ⟨an egg with a ~ yolk⟩ **3 a** : being twice as great or as many ⟨~ the number of expected applicants⟩ **b** *of a coin* : worth two of the specified amount ⟨~ eagle⟩ ⟨~ crown⟩ **4** : marked by duplicity : DECEITFUL **5** : folded in two **6** : of extra size, strength, or value ⟨a ~ martini⟩ **7** : having more than the normal number of floral leaves often at the expense of the sporophylls **8** *of rhyme* : involving correspondence of two syllables (as in *exciting* and *inviting*) — **dou·ble·ness** *n*
2double *n* **1** : something twice the usual size, strength, speed, quantity, or value: as **a** : a double amount **b** : a base hit in baseball that enables the batter to reach second base **2** : one that is the counterpart of another : DUPLICATE: as **a** : a living person that closely resembles another living person **b** : WRAITH **c** (1) : UNDERSTUDY (2) : one who resembles an actor and takes his place in scenes calling for special skills (3) : an actor who plays more than one role in a production **3 a** : a sharp turn (as in running) : REVERSAL **b** : an evasive shift **4** : something consisting of two paired members: as **a** : FOLD **b** : a combined bet placed on two different contests **c** : two consecutive strikes in bowling **5** *pl* : a game between two pairs of players **6** : an act of doubling in a card game
3double *adv* **1** : to twice the extent or amount **2** : two together
4double *vb* **dou·bled; dou·bling** \'dəb-(ə-)liŋ\ *vt* **1** : to make twice as great or as many: as **a** : to increase by adding an equal amount **b** : to amount to twice the number of **c** : to make a call in bridge that increases the value of odd tricks or undertricks at (an opponent's bid) **2 a** : to make of two thicknesses : FOLD **b** : CLENCH ⟨*doubled* his fist⟩ **c** : to cause to stoop **3** : to avoid by doubling : ELUDE **4 a** : to replace in a dramatic role **b** : to play (dramatic roles) by doubling **5 a** (1) : to advance or score (a base runner) by a double (2) : to bring about the scoring of (a run) by a double **b** : to put out (a base runner) in completing a double play ~ *vi* **1 a** : to become twice as much or as many **b** : to double a bid (as in bridge) **2 a** : to turn sharply and suddenly; *esp* : to turn back on one's course **b** : to follow a circuitous course **3** : to become bent or folded usu. in the middle — usu. used with *up* ⟨he *doubled* up in pain⟩ **4 a** : to serve an additional purpose or perform an additional duty **b** : to play a dramatic role as a double **5** : to make a double in baseball — **dou·bler** \-(ə-)lər\ *n*
double agent *n* : a spy pretending to serve one government while actually serving another
double bar *n* : two adjacent vertical lines or a heavy single line separating principal sections of a musical composition
dou·ble–bar·rel \,dəb-əl-'bar-əl\ *n* : a double-barreled gun
dou·ble–bar·reled \-əld\ *adj* **1** *of a firearm* : having two barrels mounted side by side **2** : TWOFOLD; *esp* : having a double purpose ⟨asked a ~ question⟩
double bass *n* : the largest instrument in the violin family tuned a fifth below the cello — **double bass·ist** \-'bā-səst\ *n*
double bassoon *n* : CONTRABASSOON

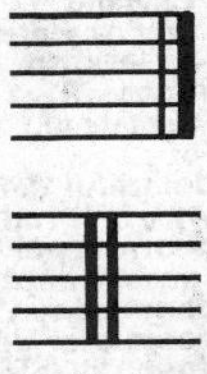
double bars

double bed *n* : a bed designed to sleep two persons
double bill *n* : a bill (as at a theatre) offering two principal features
double bind *n* : a psychological dilemma in which a usu. dependent person (as a child) receives conflicting interpersonal communications from a single source or faces disparagement no matter what his response to a situation
dou·ble–blind \,dəb-əl-'blīnd\ *adj* : of, relating to, or being an experimental procedure in which neither the subjects nor the experimenters know the makeup of the test and control groups during the actual course of the experiments — compare SINGLE-BLIND
double boiler *n* : a cooking utensil consisting of two saucepans fitting into each other so that the contents of the upper can be cooked or heated by boiling water in the lower
double bond *n* : a chemical bond consisting of two covalent bonds between two atoms in a molecule
dou·ble–breast·ed \,dəb-əl-'bres-təd\ *adj* : having one half of the front lapped over the other and usu. a double row of buttons and a single row of buttonholes ⟨a ~ coat⟩ **2** : having a double-breasted coat ⟨a ~ suit⟩
double–check \,dəb-əl-'chek, 'dəb-əl-,\ *vt* : to subject to a double check ⟨an article ~*ed* for accuracy⟩ ~ *vi* : to make a double check

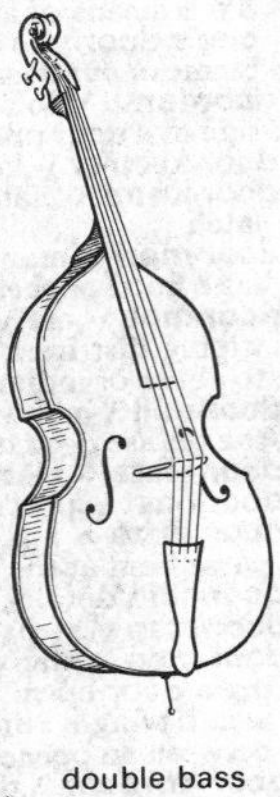
double bass

double check *n* : a careful checking to determine accuracy, condition, or progress esp. of something already checked
double counterpoint *n* : two-part counterpoint so constructed that either part may be played above or below the other
dou·ble–cov·er \,dəb-əl-'kəv-ər\ *vt* : DOUBLE-TEAM
dou·ble–cross \,dəb-əl-'krȯs\ *vt* : to deceive by double-dealing : BETRAY — **dou·ble–cross·er** *n*
double cross *n* **1 a** : an act of winning or trying to win a fight or match after agreeing to lose it **b** : an act of betraying or cheating an associate **2** : a cross between first-generation hybrids of four separate inbred lines (as in the production of hybrid seed corn)
double dagger *n* : the character ‡ used commonly as the third in the series of reference marks — called also *diesis*

dou·ble date *n* : a date participated in by two couples — **dou·ble-date** *vi*
dou·ble-deal·er \ˌdəb-əl-'dē-lər\ *n* : one who practices double-dealing
¹**dou·ble-deal·ing** \-'dē-liŋ\ *n* : action contradictory to a professed attitude : DUPLICITY
²**double-dealing** *adj* : given to or marked by duplicity
dou·ble-deck \ˌdəb-əl-ˌdek\ *or* **dou·ble-decked** \-'dekt\ *adj* : having two decks, levels, or layers ⟨a ~ bus⟩ ⟨a ~ sandwich⟩
dou·ble-deck·er \-'dek-ər\ *n* : something that is double-deck
double decomposition *n* : METATHESIS b
dou·ble-dome \'dəb-əl-ˌdōm\ *n* : EGGHEAD
double door *n* : an opening with two vertical doors that meet in the middle of the opening when closed — compare DUTCH DOOR
double dribble *n* : an illegal action in basketball made when a player dribbles the ball with two hands simultaneously or continues to dribble after allowing the ball to come to rest in one or both hands
dou·ble-edged \ˌdəb-ə-'lejd\ *adj* **1** : having two cutting edges **2 a** : having a dual purpose or effect ⟨a spy with a ~ mission⟩ **b** : capable of being understood or interpreted in two ways ⟨a ~ slur⟩
dou·ble-end·ed \ˌdəb-ə-'len-dəd\ *adj* : similar at both ends ⟨a ~ bolt⟩
dou·ble-end·er \-'dər\ *n* : a ship with bow and stern of similar shape
dou·ble en·ten·dre \ˌdüb-(ə)-ˌlän(n)-'tän(n)dr², ˌdəb-ə-, -'tän(n)d(-rə)\ *n, pl* **double entendres** \-'tän(n)drᶻ, -'tän(n)d-rəz, -'tän(n)d(ᶻ)\ [obs. F, lit., double meaning] **1** : ambiguity of meaning arising from language that lends itself to more than one interpretation **2** : a word or expression capable of two interpretations one of which often has a risqué connotation
double entry *n* : a method of bookkeeping that recognizes both the receiving and the giving sides of a business transaction by debiting the amount of the transaction to one account and crediting it to another account so that the total debits equal the total credits
dou·ble-faced \ˌdəb-əl-'fāst\ *adj* **1** : having two faces or sides ⟨a ~ bookshelf⟩ **2** : TWO-FACED, HYPOCRITICAL
dou·ble-fault \-'fȯlt\ *vi* : to lose a point in tennis by making two consecutive faults while serving
double feature *n* : a movie program consisting of two main films
double fertilization *n* : fertilization characteristic of seed plants in which one sperm nucleus fuses with the egg nucleus to form an embryo and another fuses with polar nuclei to form endosperm
dou·ble-head·er \ˌdəb-əl-'hed-ər\ *n* **1** : a train pulled by two locomotives **2** : two games, contests, or events held consecutively on the same program
double hyphen *n* : a punctuation mark ⸗ used in place of a hyphen at the end of a line to indicate that the word so divided is normally hyphenated
double indemnity *n* : a provision in a life-insurance or accident policy whereby the company agrees to pay twice the face of the contract in case of accidental death
double jeopardy *n* : the putting of a person on trial for an offense for which he has previously been put on trial under a valid charge : two adjudications for one offense
dou·ble-joint·ed \ˌdəb-əl-'jȯint-əd\ *adj* : having a joint that permits an exceptional degree of freedom of motion of the parts joined
double knit *n* : a knitted fabric (as wool) made with a double set of needles to produce a double thickness of fabric with each thickness joined by interlocking stitches
double negative *n* : a now substandard syntactic construction containing two negatives and having a negative meaning ⟨"I didn't hear nothing" is a *double negative*⟩
dou·ble-park \ˌdəb-əl-'pärk\ *vi* : to double-park a vehicle ~ *vt* : to park (a vehicle) beside a row of automobiles already parked parallel to the curb
double play *n* : a play in baseball by which two players are put out
double precision *n* : the use of two computer words rather than one to represent a number
dou·ble-quick \ˌdəb-əl-ˌkwik\ *n* : DOUBLE TIME — **double-quick** *vi*
double reed *n* : two cane reeds bound and vibrating against each other and used as the mouthpiece of certain woodwind instruments
double refraction *n* : BIREFRINGENCE
dou·ble-ring \ˌdəb-əl-ˌriŋ\ *adj* : of or relating to a wedding ceremony in which each partner ceremonially gives the other a wedding ring while formally declaring wedded commitment
double salt *n* **1** : a salt (as an alum) yielding on hydrolysis two different cations or anions **2** : a salt regarded as a molecular combination of two distinct salts
dou·ble-space \ˌdəb-əl-'spās\ *vt* : to type (copy) leaving alternate lines blank ~ *vi* : to type on every other line
dou·ble-speak \'dəb-əl-ˌspēk\ *n* : DOUBLE-TALK 2
double standard *n* **1** : BIMETALLISM **2** : a set of principles that applies differently and usu. more rigorously to one group of people or circumstances than to another; *esp* : a code of morals that applies different and more severe standards of sexual behavior to women than to men
double star *n* **1** : BINARY STAR **2** : two stars in very nearly the same line of sight but seen as physically separate by means of a telescope
double sugar *n* : DISACCHARIDE
dou·blet \'dəb-lət\ *n* [ME, fr. MF, fr. *double*] **1** : a man's close-fitting jacket worn in Europe esp. during the Renaissance **2** : something consisting of two identical or similar parts: as **a** : a lens consisting of two components; *specif* : a small magnifying hand lens consisting of two single lenses in a metal cylinder **b** : a spectrum line having two close components **c** : a domino with the same number of spots on each end **3** : a set of two identical or similar things; *specif* : two thrown dice with the same number of spots on the upper face **4** : one of a pair; *specif* : one of two or more words (as *guard* and *ward*) in the same language derived by different routes of transmission from the same source

dou·ble take \ˌdəb-əl-'tāk\ *n* : a delayed reaction to a surprising or significant situation after an initial failure to notice anything unusual — usu. used in the phrase *do a double take*
dou·ble-talk \-ˌtȯk\ *n* **1** : language that appears to be earnest and meaningful but in fact is a mixture of sense and nonsense **2** : inflated, involved, and often deliberately ambiguous language — **double-talk** *vi* — **dou·ble-talk·er** *n*
dou·ble-team \-ˌtēm\ *vt* : to block or guard (an opponent) with two players at one time
Double Ten *n* [trans. of Chin (Pek) *shuang² shih²*; fr. its being the tenth day of the tenth month] : October 10 observed by Nationalist China in commemoration of the revolution of 1911
dou·ble-think \'dəb-əl-ˌthiŋk\ *n* : a simultaneous belief in two contradictory ideas
dou·ble-time \'dəb-əl-ˌtīm\ *vi* : to move at double time
double time *n* **1** : a marching cadence of 180 36-inch steps per minute **2** : payment of a worker at twice his regular wage rate
dou·ble-tongue \ˌdəb-əl-ˌtəŋ\ *vi* : to cause the tongue to alternate rapidly between the positions for *t* and *k* so as to produce a fast succession of detached notes on a wind instrument
dou·ble-tree \'dəb-əl-(ˌ)trē\ *n* : an equalizing bar for use with a two-horse team
double twill *n* : a twill weave with intersecting diagonal lines going in opposite directions
dou·ble-u *as at* w\ *n* : the letter w
double up *vi* : to share accommodations designed for one
double vision *n* : DIPLOPIA
dou·bloon \ˌdəb-'lün\ *n* [Sp *doblón*, aug. of *dobla*, an old Spanish coin, fr. L *dupla*, fem. of *duplus* double — more at DOUBLE]: an old gold coin of Spain and Spanish America
dou·bly \'dəb-(ə-)lē\ *adv* **1** : to twice the degree **2** : in a twofold manner
¹**doubt** \'daut\ *vb* [ME *douten*, fr. OF *douter* to doubt, fr. L *dubitare*; akin to L *dubius* dubious — more at DUBIOUS] *vt* **1** *archaic* : FEAR **2** : to be in doubt about ⟨he ~s everyone's word⟩ **3 a** : to lack confidence in : DISTRUST ⟨find myself ~ing him even when I know that he is honest —H. L. Mencken⟩ **b** : to consider unlikely ⟨I ~ that it is authentic⟩ ~ *vi* : to be uncertain — **doubt·able** \-ə-bəl\ *adj* — **doubt·er** *n* — **doubt·ing·ly** \-in-lē\ *adv*
²**doubt** *n* **1 a** : uncertainty of belief or opinion that often interferes with decision-making **b** : a deliberate suspension of judgment **2** : a state of affairs giving rise to uncertainty, hesitation, or suspense **3 a** : a lack of confidence : DISTRUST **b** : an inclination not to believe or accept *syn* see UNCERTAINTY *ant* certitude, confidence — **no doubt** : ¹DOUBTLESS
doubt·ful \'daut-fəl\ *adj* **1** : giving rise to doubt : open to question ⟨it is ~ that they ever knew what happened⟩ ⟨a ~ proposition⟩ **2 a** : lacking a definite opinion, conviction, or determination ⟨they were ~ about the advantages of the new system⟩ **b** : uncertain in outcome : UNDECIDED ⟨a ~ progress⟩ ⟨the outcome of the election remains ~⟩ **3** : marked by qualities that raise doubts about worth, honesty, or validity — **doubt·ful·ly** \-fə-lē\ *adv* — **doubt·ful·ness** \-fəl-nəs\ *n*
syn DOUBTFUL, DUBIOUS, PROBLEMATIC, QUESTIONABLE *shared meaning element* : not affording assurance of the worth, soundness, success, or certainty of something or someone. *Doubtful* and *dubious* are sometimes used with little distinction ⟨a *doubtful* (or *dubious*) reputation⟩ ⟨we are *doubtful* (or *dubious*) about their chances of success⟩ but DOUBTFUL may positively impute worthlessness, unsoundness, failure, or uncertainty ⟨their future prospects are very *doubtful*⟩ ⟨his title to the property is *doubtful*⟩ while DUBIOUS can stress hesitation, mistrust, or suspicion (as in accepting or following); thus, a *doubtful* adherent to a party is one who cannot be counted on while a *dubious* adherent is less than wholeheartedly so because of uncertainties in his own mind; *doubtful* friends are probably not real friends while *dubious* friends give grounds for suspicion as to their worth or probity. PROBLEMATIC is applicable to any situation whose outcome is quite unpredictable ⟨success in the control of inflation remains *problematic*⟩ QUESTIONABLE may imply little more than the existence of doubt ⟨the legality of his action is *questionable*⟩ or it may stress doubt about propriety and imply strong or well-grounded suspicion ⟨*questionable* behavior⟩ ⟨a man of *questionable* reputation⟩ *ant* positive
doubting Thom·as \-'täm-əs\ *n* [*Thomas*, apostle of Jesus who doubted Jesus' resurrection until he had proof of it (Jn 20:24–29)] : a habitually doubtful person
¹**doubt·less** \'daut-ləs\ *adv* **1** : without doubt **2** : PROBABLY
²**doubtless** *adj* : free from doubt : CERTAIN — **doubt·less·ly** *adv* — **doubt·less·ness** *n*
douce \'düs\ *adj* [ME, sweet, pleasant, fr. MF, fr. fem. of *douz*, fr. L *dulcis*] *chiefly Scot* : SOBER, SEDATE ⟨the ~ faces of the mourners —L. J. A. Bell⟩ — **douce·ly** *adv, chiefly Scot*
dou·ceur \dü-'sər\ *n* [F, pleasantness, fr. LL *dulcor* sweetness, fr. L *dulcis* sweet] : a conciliatory gift
douche \'düsh\ *n* [F, fr. It *doccia*, fr. *docciare* to douche, fr. *doccia* water pipe, prob. back-formation fr. *doccione* conduit, fr. L *duction-, ductio* action of leading, fr. *ductus*, pp. of *ducere* to lead — more at TOW] **1 a** : a jet or current esp. of water directed against a part or into a cavity of the body **b** : an act of cleansing with a douche **2** : a device for giving douches — **douche** *vb*
dough \'dō\ *n* [ME *dogh*, fr. OE *dāg*; akin to OHG *teic* dough, L *fingere* to shape, Gk *teichos* wall] **1** : a mixture of flour and other ingredients stiff enough to knead or roll **2** : something resembling dough esp. in consistency **3** : MONEY **4** : DOUGHBOY — **dough·like** \-ˌlīk\ *adj*

dough·boy \-ˌbȯi\ *n* : an American infantryman esp. in World War I

dough·face \-ˌfās\ *n* : a northern congressman not opposed to slavery in the South before or during the Civil War; *also* : a northerner sympathetic to the South during the same period — **dough-faced** \-ˌfāst\ *adj*

dough·foot \-ˌfu̇t\ *n, pl* **dough-feet** \-ˌfēt\ *or* **doughfoots** : INFANTRYMAN

dough·nut \-(ˌ)nət\ *n* 1 : a small usu. ring-shaped cake fried in fat 2 : something that resembles a doughnut esp. in shape; *specif* : TORUS 4

dough·ty \ˈdau̇t-ē\ *adj* **dough-ti·er; -est** [ME, fr. OE *dohtig*; akin to OHG *toug* is useful, Gk *teuchein* to make] : marked by fearless resolution : VALIANT — **dough·ti·ly** \ˈdau̇t-ᵊl-ē\ *adv* — **dough·ti·ness** \ˈdau̇t-ē-nəs\ *n*

doughy \ˈdō-ē\ *adj* **dough-i·er; -est** : resembling dough: as a : not thoroughly baked b : unhealthily pale : PASTY ⟨a ~ complexion⟩

Doug·las fir \ˈdəg-ləs-\ *n* [David *Douglas* †1834 Sc botanist] : a tall evergreen timber tree (*Pseudotsuga taxifolia*) of the western U.S. having thick bark, pitchy wood, and pendulous cones — called also *Douglas spruce*

Dou·kho·bor \ˈdü-kə-ˌbȯ(ə)r\ *n* [Russ *dukhoborets*, fr. *dukh* spirit + *borets* wrestler] : a member of a Christian sect of 18th century Russian origin emphasizing the duty of obeying the inner light and rejecting church or civil authority

do up *vt* 1 a : to clean and make ready for use or wear : LAUNDER ⟨*do up* a shirt⟩ b : to put in order ⟨the maid will *do up* your room⟩ c : REPAIR, RENOVATE ⟨*do up* old furniture⟩ 2 a : to wrap up ⟨*do up* a package⟩ b : to put up : CAN 3 : to deck out : CLOTHE 4 : to wear out : EXHAUST

dour \ˈdau̇(ə)r, ˈdu̇(ə)r\ *adj* [ME, fr. L *durus* hard — more at DURING] 1 : STERN, HARSH 2 : OBSTINATE, UNYIELDING 3 : GLOOMY, SULLEN — **dour·ly** *adv* — **dour·ness** *n*

¹**douse** \ˈdüs, ˈdau̇s\ *n* [origin unknown] *Brit* : BLOW, STROKE

²**douse** \ˈdau̇s\ *vt* **doused; dous·ing** 1 a : to take in ⟨~ a sail⟩ b : SLACKEN ⟨~ a rope⟩ 2 : DOFF ⟨doused my cap on entering the porch —W. M. Thackeray⟩

³**douse** \ˈdau̇s *also* ˈdau̇z\ *vb* **doused; dous·ing** [prob. fr. obs. E *douse* (to smite), fr. ¹*douse*] *vt* 1 : to plunge into water 2 a : to throw a liquid on : DRENCH b : SLOSH 3 : EXTINGUISH ⟨~ the lights⟩ ~ *vi* : to fall or become plunged into water — **dous·er** *n*

⁴**douse** \ˈdau̇s *also* ˈdau̇z\ *n* : a heavy drenching

¹**dove** \ˈdəv\ *n* [ME, fr. (assumed) OE *dūfe*; akin to OHG *tūba* dove, and prob. to OE *dēaf* deaf] 1 : any of numerous pigeons; *esp* : a small wild pigeon 2 : a gentle woman or child 3 : an individual who takes a conciliatory attitude (as in a dispute) and advocates negotiations and compromise; *esp* : an opponent of war — compare HAWK — **dove·ish** \ˈdəv-ish\ *adj* — **dov·ish·ness** *n*

²**dove** \ˈdōv\ *past of* DIVE

dove·cote \ˈdəv-ˌkōt, -ˌkät\ *or* **dove·cot** \-ˌkät\ *n* 1 : a small compartmented raised house or box for domestic pigeons 2 : a settled or harmonious group or organization ⟨theological ~s throughout the world were set in an uproar —Cecil Roth⟩

dove·kie \ˈdəv-kē\ *n* [dim. of *dove*] : a small short-billed auk (*Plautus alle*) breeding on arctic coasts and ranging south in winter

doven *var of* DAVEN

Do·ver's powder \ˌdō-vərz-\ *n* [Thomas *Dover* †1742 E physician] : a powder of ipecac and opium compounded in the U.S. with lactose and in England with potassium sulfate and used as an anodyne and diaphoretic

¹**dove·tail** \ˈdəv-ˌtāl\ *n* : something resembling a dove's tail; *esp* : a flaring tenon and a mortise into which it fits tightly making an interlocking joint between two pieces (as of wood)

²**dovetail** *vt* 1 a : to join by means of dovetails 2 a : to cut to a dovetail b : to fit skillfully to form a whole b : to fit together with ~ *vi* : to fit together into a whole

dovetail: *1* mortises, *2* tenons, *3* joint

dow \ˈdau̇\ *vi* **dought** \ˈdau̇t\ *or* **dowed** \ˈdau̇d\; **dow·ing** [ME *dow, deih* have worth, am able, fr. OE *dēah, dēag*; akin to OHG *toug* is worthy, is useful — more at DOUGHTY] *chiefly Scot* : to be able or capable

Dow \ˈdau̇\ *n* : DOW-JONES AVERAGE

dow·a·ger \ˈdau̇-i-jər\ *n* [MF *douagiere*, fr. *douage* dower, fr. *douer* to endow, fr. L *dotare*, fr. *dot-, dos* gift, dower — more at DOWRY] 1 : a widow holding property or a title received from her deceased husband 2 : a dignified elderly woman

¹**dow·dy** \ˈdau̇d-ē\ *n, pl* **dowd·ies** 1 [dim. of *dowd* (dowdy), fr. ME *doude*] *archaic* : a slovenly woman 2 : PANDOWDY

²**dowdy** *adj* **dowd·i·er; -est** 1 : not neat or becoming in appearance : SHABBY 2 a : lacking smartness or taste b : OLD-FASHIONED — **dowd·i·ly** \ˈdau̇d-ᵊl-ē\ *adv* — **dowd·i·ness** \ˈdau̇d-ē-nəs\ *n* — **dowd·y·ish** \-ish\ *adj*

¹**dow·el** \ˈdau̇(-ə)l\ *n* [ME *dowle*; akin to OHG *tubili* plug, LGk *typhos* wedge] 1 : a pin fitting into a hole in an abutting piece to prevent motion or slipping; *also* : a round rod or stick used esp. for cutting up into dowels 2 : a piece of wood driven into a wall so that other pieces can be nailed to it

²**dowel** *vt* **-eled** *or* **-elled; -el·ing** *or* **-el·ling** : to fasten by or furnish with dowels

¹**dow·er** \ˈdau̇(-ə)r\ *n* [ME *dowere*, fr. MF *douaire*, modif. of ML *dotarium* — more at DOWRY] 1 : the part of or interest in the real estate of a deceased husband given by law to his widow during her life 2 : DOWRY

²**dower** *vt* : to supply with a dower or dowry : ENDOW

dow·itch·er \ˈdau̇-i-chər\ *n, pl* **dowitchers** *also* **dowitcher** [of Iroquoian origin; akin to Mohawk *tawis* dowitcher] : a long-billed snipe (*Limnodromus griseus*) intermediate in characters between the typical snipes (genus *Capella*) and the sandpipers

Dow–Jones average \ˌdau̇-ˌjōnz-\ *n* [Charles H. *Dow* †1902 & Edward D. *Jones* †1920 Am financial statisticians] : an index of the relative price of securities based on the daily average price of selected lists of industrial, transportation, and utility common stocks

¹**down** \ˈdau̇n\ *n* [ME *doun* hill, fr. OE *dūn*; akin to ON *dūnn* down of feathers] 1 : an undulating usu. treeless upland with sparse soil — usu. used in pl. 2 *often cap* : a sheep of any breed originating in the downs of southern England

²**down** *adv* [ME *doun*, fr. OE *dūne*, short for *adūne*, of *dūne*, fr. a- (fr. *of*), off, from + *dūne*, dat. of *dūn* hill] 1 a (1) : toward or in a lower physical position (2) : to a lying or sitting position (3) : toward or to the ground, floor, or bottom b : on the spot : in cash ⟨paid $10 ~⟩ c : on paper ⟨put ~ what he says⟩ 2 : in a direction that is the opposite of up: as a : SOUTHWARD b : to or toward a point away from the speaker or the speaker's point of reference 3 : often used as an intensive ⟨cool ~ tensions and hostilities⟩ ⟨had the subject ~ pat⟩ 4 : to or toward a lower position in a series 5 : to or in a lower or worse condition or status 6 : from a past time 7 : to or in a state of less activity or prominence 8 : to a concentrated state ⟨got his report ~ to three pages⟩ ⟨boiled the sap ~ into syrup⟩ — **down to the ground** : PERFECTLY, COMPLETELY ⟨that suits me *down to the ground*⟩

³**down** *adj* 1 a (1) : occupying a low position; *specif* : lying on the ground ⟨~ timber⟩ (2) : directed or going downward b : lower in price c : not being in play in football because of wholly stopped progress or because the officials stop the play ⟨marked the ball ~ on the 15-yard line⟩ d : defeated or trailing an opponent (as in points scored) ⟨~ two tricks⟩ ⟨~ by two touchdowns⟩ e : *baseball* : OUT 2 a : being in a state of reduced or low activity b (1) : DEPRESSED, DEJECTED (2) : SICK ⟨~ with flu⟩ 3 : FINISHED, DONE ⟨eight ~ and two to go⟩ — **down on** : having a low opinion of or dislike for ⟨~ on him⟩

⁴**down** \(ˈ)dau̇n\ *prep* : down along, around, through, toward, in, into, or on

⁵**down** \ˈdau̇n\ *n* 1 : DESCENT, DEPRESSION 2 : an instance of putting down 3 a : a complete drive to advance the ball in football b : one of a series of four attempts to advance a football 10 yards 4 : DISLIKE, GRUDGE 5 : DOWNER 1

⁶**down** *vt* 1 : to cause to go or come down 2 : to cause (a football) to be out of play 3 : DEFEAT ~ *vi* : to go down

⁷**down** *n* [ME *doun*, fr. ON *dūnn*] 1 : a covering of soft fluffy feathers 2 : something soft and fluffy like down

down–and–out \ˌdau̇n-ᵊn-\ *adj* 1 : physically weakened or incapacitated 2 : DESTITUTE, IMPOVERISHED

¹**down·beat** \ˈdau̇n-ˌbēt\ *n* 1 : the downward stroke of a conductor indicating the principally accented note of a measure of music; *also* : the first beat of a measure 2 : a decline in activity or prosperity

²**downbeat** *adj* : PESSIMISTIC, GLOOMY

down–bow \ˈdau̇n-ˌbō\ *n* : a stroke in playing a bowed instrument (as a violin) in which the bow is drawn across the strings from the heel to the tip

down·cast \ˈdau̇n-\ *adj* 1 : low in spirit : DEJECTED 2 : directed downward ⟨with ~ eyes⟩

down·court \-ˈkō(ə)rt, -ˈkȯ(ə)rt\ *adv or adj* : in or into the opposite end of the court (as in basketball)

down east *adv or adj, often cap D & E* : in or into the northeast coastal section of the U.S. and parts of the Maritime Provinces of Canada; *specif* : in or into coastal Maine

down·er \ˈdau̇-nər\ *n* 1 : a depressant drug; *esp* : BARBITURATE 2 : a depressing experience or situation

down·fall \ˈdau̇n-ˌfȯl\ *n* 1 a : a sudden fall (as from high rank or power) b : a fall (as of snow or rain) esp. when sudden or heavy 2 : something that causes a downfall (as of a person) ⟨drink was his ~⟩ — **down·fall·en** \-ˌfȯ-lən\ *adj*

down·field \-ˈfē(ə)ld\ *adv or adj* : in or into the part of the field toward which the offensive team is headed

¹**down·grade** \ˈdau̇n-ˌgrād\ *n* 1 : a downward grade (as of a road) 2 : a descent toward an inferior state — used esp. in the phrase *on the downgrade*

²**downgrade** *vt* 1 : MINIMIZE, DEPRECIATE 2 : to alter the status of (a job) so as to lower the rate of pay

down·haul \ˈdau̇n-ˌhȯl\ *n* : a rope or line for hauling down or holding down a sail or spar

down·heart·ed \-ˈhärt-əd\ *adj* : DOWNCAST, DEJECTED — **down·heart·ed·ly** *adv* — **down·heart·ed·ness** *n*

¹**down·hill** \ˈdau̇n-ˌhil\ *n* 1 : a descending gradient 2 : a skiing race against time down a trail

²**down·hill** \-ˈhil\ *adv* 1 : toward the bottom of a hill 2 : toward a lower or inferior state or level — used esp. in the phrase *go downhill*

³**down·hill** \-ˈhil\ *adj* 1 : sloping downhill 2 : of or relating to skiing downhill 3 : being the lower one or part esp. of a set; *specif* : being nearer the bottom of an incline ⟨your ~ ski, knee, hip and shoulder are angled slightly lower —Perry Fairbank⟩ 4 : not difficult : EASY ⟨had solved the biggest problems and the rest was ~⟩

down–home \ˌdau̇n-ˌhōm\ *adj* : of, relating to, or characteristic of the southern U.S. ⟨a ~ drawl⟩ ⟨traveled widely through the South in rhythm-and-blues bands . . . and this ~ element has never left his music —A. B. Spellman⟩

down payment *n* : a part of the full price paid at the time of purchase or delivery with the balance to be paid later

down·play \ˈdau̇n-ˌplā\ *vt* : to play down : DE-EMPHASIZE

down·pour \-ˌpō(ə)r, -ˌpȯ(ə)r\ *n* : a pouring or streaming downward; *esp* : a heavy rain

down·range \-ˈrānj\ *adv* : away from a launching site and along the course of a test range ⟨a missile landing 5000 miles ~⟩ — **down·range** *adj*

¹**down·right** \-ˌrīt\ *adv* 1 *archaic* : straight down 2 : THOROUGHLY, OUTRIGHT ⟨~ mean⟩ 3 : with straightforward directness

²downright *adj* **1** *archaic* : directed vertically downward **2** : ABSOLUTE, THOROUGH ⟨a ~ lie⟩ **3** : PLAIN, BLUNT ⟨a ~ man⟩ — **down·right·ly** *adv* — **down·right·ness** *n*
down·riv·er \'daùn-'riv-ər\ *adv or adj* : toward or at a point nearer the mouth of a river
down·shift \-ˌshift\ *vi* : to shift an automotive vehicle into a lower gear — **downshift** *n*
Down's syndrome \'daùnz-\ *n* [J. L. H. *Down* †1896 E physician] : MONGOLISM
¹down·stage \'daùn-'stāj\ *adv or adj* **1** : toward or at the front of a theatrical stage **2** : toward a motion-picture or television camera
²down·stage \-ˌstāj\ *n* : the part of a stage that is nearest the audience or camera
¹down·stairs \'daùn-'sta(ə)rz, -'ste(ə)rz\ *adv* : down the stairs : on or to a lower floor
²downstairs \ˌdaùn-ˌsta(ə)rz, -ˌste(ə)rz\ *adj* : situated on the main, lower, or ground floor of a building
³downstairs \'daùn-', 'daùn-ˌ\ *n pl but sing or pl in constr* : the lower floor of a building
down·state \-ˌstāt\ *n* : the chiefly southerly sections of a state of the U.S. as distinguished from a northerly part and esp. a metropolitan region often designated as *upstate* — **down·state** \-'stāt\ *adv or adj* — **down·stat·er** \-'stāt-ər\ *n*
down·stream \'daùn-'strēm\ *adv or adj* : in the direction of the flow of a stream
down·stroke \-ˌstrōk\ *n* : a stroke made in a downward direction
down·swing \-ˌswiŋ\ *n* **1** : a downward swing **2** : a downward trend esp. in business activity
down–the–line *adj* : all the way : COMPLETE ⟨a ~ union supporter⟩
down·time \'daùn-ˌtīm\ *n* : time during which a machine, department, or factory is inactive during normal operating hours
down–to–earth \ˌdaùn-tə-'(w)ərth\ *adj* : PRACTICAL, REALISTIC ⟨a ~ appraisal of the situation⟩ — **down–to–earth·ness** *n*
¹down·town \'daùn-'taùn\ *adv* : to, toward, or in the lower part of a town or city; *esp* : to, toward, or in the main business district — **downtown** \ˌdaùn-ˌtaùn\ *adj*
²downtown \'daùn-ˌtaùn\ *n* : the section of a town or city located downtown
down·trend \-ˌtrend\ *n* : a downturn esp. in business and economic activity
down·trod·den \'daùn-'träd-ᵊn\ *adj* : oppressed by superior power ⟨the ~ peasants⟩
down·turn \-ˌtərn\ *n* : a downward turn esp. toward a decline in business activity
down under *adv* : into or in Australia or New Zealand
¹down·ward \'daùn-wərd\ *or* **down·wards** \-wərdz\ *adv* **1 a** : from a higher to a lower place **b** : toward a direction that is the opposite of up **2** : from a higher to a lower condition **3 a** : from an earlier time **b** : from an ancestor or predecessor
²downward *adj* **1** : moving or extending downward **2** : descending from a head, origin, or source — **down·ward·ly** *adv* — **down·ward·ness** *n*
down·wind \'daùn-'wind\ *adv or adj* : in the direction that the wind is blowing
downy \'daù-nē\ *adj* **down·i·er; -est** **1** : resembling a bird's down **2** : covered with down **3** : made of down **4** : SOFT, SOOTHING ⟨shake off this ~ sleep, death's counterfeit —Shak.⟩
downy mildew *n* **1** : any of various parasitic lower fungi (family Peronosporaceae) that produce whitish masses of sporangiophores or conidiophores on the undersurface of the leaves of the host **2** : a plant disease caused by a downy mildew
downy woodpecker *n* : a small black-and-white woodpecker (*Dendrocopos pubescens*) of No. America that has a white back and is smaller than the hairy woodpecker
dow·ry \'daù(ə)r-ē\ *n, pl* **dowries** [ME *dowarie*, fr. AF, irreg. fr. ML *dotarium*, fr. L *dot-*, *dos* gift, marriage portion; akin to L *dare* to give — more at DATE] **1** *archaic* : DOWER 1 **2 a** : the money, goods, or estate that a woman brings to her husband in marriage **b** : a sum of money or its equivalent required of postulants by some orders of cloistered nuns **3** : a gift of money or property by a man to or for his bride **4** : a natural gift : TALENT
dow·sa·bel \'daù-sə-ˌbel, -zə-\ *n* [*Dowsabel*, fem. name] *obs* : SWEETHEART
¹dowse *var of* DOUSE
²dowse \'daùz\ *vb* **dowsed; dows·ing** [origin unknown] *vi* : to use a divining rod ~ *vt* : to find (as water) by dowsing
dows·er \'daù-zər\ *n* : DIVINING ROD; *also* : a person who uses it
Dow theory *n* : a system of stock-market forecasting based on the observed swings of the market itself
dox·ol·o·gy \däk-'säl-ə-jē\ *n, pl* **-gies** [ML *doxologia*, fr. LGk, fr. Gk *doxa* opinion, glory (fr. *dokein* to seem, seem good) + *-logia* -logy — more at DECENT] : a usu. liturgical expression of praise to God
doxy \'däk-sē\ *n, pl* **dox·ies** [perh. modif. of obs. D *docke* doll, fr. MD] **1** : a woman of loose morals : PROSTITUTE **2** : MISTRESS 5a
doy·en \'dòi-ən, -(y)en; 'dwä-ˌyaⁿ(n)\ *n* [F, fr. LL *decanus* dean — more at DEAN] **1 a** : the senior man of a body or group **b** : a person uniquely skilled by long experience in some field of endeavor **2** : the oldest example of a category ⟨the ~ of the country's newspapers⟩
doy·enne \dòi-'(y)en, dwä-'yen\ *n* [F, fem. of *doyen*] : a female doyen
doy·ley *var of* DOILY
doz *abbr* dozen
¹doze \'dōz\ *vb* **dozed; doz·ing** [prob. of Scand origin; akin to ON *dūsa* to doze] *vt* : to pass (as time) drowsily ⟨*dozing* his life away⟩ ~ *vi* **1 a** : to sleep lightly **b** : to fall into a light sleep — usu. used with *off* **2** : to be in a dull or stupefied condition — **doze** *n* — **doz·er** *n*
²doze *vt* **dozed; doz·ing** [prob. back-formation fr. *dozer* (bulldozer)] : BULLDOZE 2 — **doz·er** *n*
doz·en \'dəz-ᵊn\ *n, pl* **dozens** *or* **dozen** [ME *dozeine*, fr. OF *dozaine*, fr. *doze* twelve, fr. L *duodecim*, fr. *duo* two + *decem* ten — more at TWO, TEN] **1** : a group of 12 **2** : an indefinitely large number ⟨I've ~s of things to do⟩ — **dozen** *adj* — **doz·enth** \-ᵊn(t)th\ *adj*
dozy \'dō-zē\ *adj* **doz·i·er; -est** : DROWSY, SLEEPY — **doz·i·ness** *n*
¹DP \'dē-'pē\ *n, pl* **DP's** *or* **DPs** : DISPLACED PERSON
²DP *abbr* **1** data processing **2** degree of polymerization **3** dew point **4** doctor of podiatry **5** double play
DPE *abbr* doctor of physical education
DPh *abbr* doctor of philosophy
DPH *abbr* **1** department of public health **2** doctor of public health
DPN \ˌdē-ˌpē-'en\ *n* [*d*i*p*hosphopyridine *n*ucleotide] : NAD
dpt *abbr* **1** department **2** deponent
DPT *abbr* diphtheria, pertussis, tetanus
dr *abbr* **1** debtor **2** drachma **3** dram **4** drive **5** drum
Dr *abbr* doctor
DR *abbr* **1** dead reckoning **2** dining room
¹drab \'drab\ *n* [origin unknown] **1** : SLATTERN **2** : HARLOT
²drab *vi* **drabbed; drab·bing** : to associate with prostitutes
³drab *n* [MF *drap* cloth, fr. LL *drappus*] **1** : any of various cloths of a dull brown or gray color; *esp* : a thick woolen coating or a heavy cotton **2 a** : a light olive brown **b** : a dull, lifeless, or faded appearance or quality
⁴drab *adj* **drab·ber; drab·best** **1 a** : of the dull brown color of drab **b** : of the color drab **2** : characterized by dullness and monotony : CHEERLESS ⟨formal engagements are generally ~ and boring —Andrew Duncan⟩ — **drab·ly** *adv* — **drab·ness** *n*
⁵drab *n* [prob. alter. of *drib*] : a small amount — usu. used in the phrase *dribs and drabs*
drab·bet \'drab-ət\ *n* [³*drab* + *-et*] *dial Eng* : a coarse unbleached linen fabric
drab·ble \'drab-əl\ *vb* **drab·bled; drab·bling** \-(ə-)liŋ\ [ME *drabelen*] *vt* : DRAGGLE ~ *vi* : to become wet and muddy
dra·cae·na \drə-'sē-nə\ *n* [NL, fr. LL, she-serpent, fr. Gk *drakaina*, fem. of *drakōn* serpent — more at DRAGON] : any of two genera (*Dracaena* and *Cordyline*) of Old World tropical shrubs or trees of the lily family with naked branches ending in tufts of sword-shaped leaves
drachm \'dram\ *n* [alter. of ME *dragme* — more at DRAM] **1** : DRACHMA **2** : DRAM
drach·ma \'drak-mə\ *n, pl* **drach·mas** *or* **drach·mae** \-(ˌ)mē, -ˌmī\ *or* **drach·mai** \-ˌmī\ [L, fr. Gk *drachmē*— more at DRAM] **1 a** : any of various ancient Greek units of weight **b** : any of various modern units of weight; *esp* : DRAM 1 **2 a** : an ancient Greek silver coin equivalent to 6 obols **b** — see MONEY table
Dra·co \'drā-(ˌ)kō\ *n* [L (gen. *Draconis*), lit., dragon — more at DRAGON] : a northern circumpolar constellation within which is the north pole of the ecliptic
dra·co·ni·an \drā-'kō-nē-ən, drə-\ *adj, often cap* [L *Dracon-*, *Draco*] **1** : of, relating to, or characteristic of Draco or the severe code of laws held to have been framed by him **2** : extremely harsh or cruel : RIGOROUS
¹dra·con·ic \drə-'kän-ik\ *adj* [L *dracon-*, *draco*] : of or relating to a dragon
²dra·con·ic \drā-'kän-ik, drə-\ *adj* : DRACONIAN
¹draft \'draft, 'dräft\ *n* [ME *draght*; akin to OE *dragan* to draw — more at DRAW] **1** : the act of drawing a net; *also* : the quantity of fish taken at one drawing **2 a** : the act of moving loads by drawing or pulling : PULL **b** : a team of animals together with what they draw **3 a** : the force required to pull an implement **b** : load or load-pulling capacity **4 a** : the act or an instance of drinking or inhaling; *also* : the portion drunk or inhaled in one such act **b** : a portion poured out or mixed for drinking : DOSE **5 a** : DELINEATION, REPRESENTATION; *specif* : a construction plan ⟨the ~ of a future building⟩ **b** : SCHEME, DESIGN **c** : a preliminary sketch, outline, or version ⟨the author's first ~⟩ **6** : the act, result, or plan of drawing out or stretching **7 a** : the act of drawing (as from a cask) **b** : a portion of liquid so drawn ⟨a ~ of beer⟩ **8** : an allowance granted a buyer for loss in weight **9** : the depth of water a ship draws esp. when loaded **10 a** (1) : a system or method for detaching or selecting individuals from a group (as for compulsory military service) (2) : an act or process of selecting an individual (as for political candidacy) without his expressed consent **b** : a group of individuals selected esp. by military draft **11 a** : an order for the payment of money drawn by one person or bank on another **b** : the act or an instance of drawing from or making demands upon something : DEMAND **12 a** : a current of air in a closed-in space **b** : a device for regulating the flow of air (as in a fireplace) **13** : ANGLE, TAPER; *specif* : the taper given to a pattern or die so that the work can be easily withdrawn **14** : a narrow border along the edge of a stone or across its face serving as a stonecutter's guide **15** : a system whereby exclusive rights to selected new players are apportioned among professional teams — **on draft** : ready to be drawn from a receptacle ⟨beer *on draft*⟩
²draft *adj* **1** : used for drawing loads ⟨~ animals⟩ **2** : constituting a preliminary or tentative version, sketch, or outline ⟨a ~ treaty⟩ **3** : being on draft ⟨~ beer⟩
³draft *vt* **1** : to detach or select for some purpose: as **a** : to conscript for military service **b** : to select (a professional athlete) by draft **2 a** : to draw the preliminary sketch, version, or plan of **b** : COMPOSE, PREPARE **3** : to draw off or away ⟨water ~*ed* by pumps⟩ **4** : to mark (as a stone) with a draft in masonry ~ *vi* **1** : to practice draftsmanship **2** : to drive close behind another car while racing at high speed in order to take advantage of the reduced air pressure created by the leading car — **draft·able** \'draf-

ə abut ᵊ kitten ər further a back ā bake ä cot, cart
aù out ch chin e less ē easy g gift i trip ī life
j joke ŋ sing ō flow ȯ flaw ȯi coin th thin t͟h this
ü loot ù foot y yet yü few yù furious zh vision

tə-bəl, ˈdráf-\ *adj* — **draft·ee** \draf-ˈtē, dráf-\ *n* — **draft·er** \ˈdraf-tər, ˈdráf-\ *n*

draft board *n* **:** a civilian board that registers, classifies, and selects men for compulsory military service

drafts·man \ˈdraf(t)-smən, ˈdráf(t)-\ *n* **1 :** one who draws legal documents or other writings **2 :** one who draws plans and sketches (as of machinery or structures) **3 :** an artist who excels in drawing — **drafts·man·ship** \-,ship\ *n*

drafty \ˈdraf-tē, ˈdráf-\ *adj* **draft·i·er; -est :** of, relating to, or having a draft — **draft·i·ly** \-tə-lē\ *adv* — **draft·i·ness** \-tē-nəs\ *n*

[1]**drag** \ˈdrag\ *n* **1 :** something that is dragged, pulled, or drawn along or over a surface: as **a :** HARROW **b :** a sledge for conveying heavy bodies **c :** CONVEYANCE **2 :** something used to drag with; *esp* **:** a device for dragging under water to detect or obtain objects **3 a :** something that retards motion or action **b (1) :** the retarding force acting on a body (as an airplane) moving through a fluid (as air) parallel and opposite to the direction of motion **(2) :** friction between engine parts; *also* **:** retardation due to friction **c :** BURDEN, ENCUMBRANCE ⟨the ~ of population growth on living standards⟩ **4 a :** an object drawn over the ground to leave a scented trail **b :** a clog fastened to a trap to prevent the escape of a trapped animal **5 a :** the act or an instance of dragging or drawing: as **(1) :** a drawing along or over a surface with effort or pressure **(2) :** motion effected with slowness or difficulty; *also* **:** the condition of having or seeming to have such motion **(3) :** a draw on a pipe, cigarette, or cigar **:** PUFF; *also* **:** a draft of liquid **b :** a movement, inclination, or retardation caused by or as if by dragging **c** *slang* **:** influence securing special favor **6 :** STREET, ROAD ⟨the main ~⟩ **7** *slang* **:** a girl that one is escorting **8 :** woman's dress worn by a man — often used in the phrase *in drag* **9 :** DRAG RACE **10 :** one that is boring ⟨school is a ~ for some youngsters⟩

[2]**drag** *vb* **dragged; drag·ging** [ME *draggen,* fr. ON *draga* or OE *dragan* — more at DRAW] *vt* **1 a (1) :** to draw slowly or heavily **:** HAUL **(2) :** to cause to move with painful or undue slowness or difficulty ⟨*dragging* the musical tempo⟩ **(3) :** to cause to trail along a surface ⟨*dragged* his feet in the water⟩ **b :** to bring by force or compulsion ⟨had to ~ her husband to the opera⟩ **c (1) :** to pass (time) in lingering pain, tedium, or unhappiness **(2) :** PROTRACT ⟨~ a story out⟩ **2 a :** to explore with a drag **b :** to catch with a dragnet or trawl **3 :** to hit (a bunt) by trailing the bat while moving toward first base ~ *vi* **1 :** to hang or lag behind **2 :** to fish or search with a drag **3 :** to trail along on the ground **4 :** to move on or proceed laboriously or tediously ⟨the book ~*s*⟩ **5 :** DRAW ⟨~ on a cigarette⟩ **6 :** to make a plucking or pulling movement **7 :** to participate in a drag race ***syn*** see PULL — **drag·ging·ly** \ˈdraj-iŋ-lē\ *adv* — **drag one's feet** *or* **drag one's heels :** to act in a deliberately slow, dilatory, or ineffective manner

drag bunt *n* **:** a bunt in baseball made by a left-handed batter by trailing the bat while moving toward first base; *broadly* **:** a bunt made with the object of getting on base safely rather than sacrificing

dra·gée \dra-ˈzhā\ *n* [F, fr. MF *dragie* — more at DREDGE] **1 a :** a sugar-coated nut **b :** a silver-coated candy for decorating cakes **2 :** a sugar-coated medicated confection

drag·ger \ˈdrag-ər\ *n* **:** one that drags; *specif* **:** a fishing boat operating a trawl or dragnet

drag·gle \ˈdrag-əl\ *vb* **drag·gled; drag·gling** \-(ə-)liŋ\ [freq. of *drag*] *vt* **:** to make wet and dirty by dragging ~ *vi* **1 :** to trail on the ground **2 :** STRAGGLE

drag·gle–tail \ˈdrag-əl-,tāl\ *n* **:** SLATTERN

drag·gy \ˈdrag-ē\ *adj* **drag·gi·er; -est :** SLUGGISH, DULL

drag·line \ˈdrag-,līn\ *n* **1 :** a line used in or for dragging **2 :** an excavating machine in which the bucket is attached by cables and operates by being drawn toward the machine

drag·net \ˈdrag-,net\ *n* **1 a :** a net drawn along the bottom of a body of water **:** TRAWL **b :** a net used on the ground (as to capture small game) **2 :** a network of measures for apprehension (as of criminals)

drag·o·man \ˈdrag-ə-mən\ *n, pl* **-mans,** *or* **-men** \-mən\ [ME *drogman,* fr. MF, fr. OIt *dragomanno,* fr. MGk *dragomanos,* fr. Ar *tarjumān,* fr. Aram *tūrgĕmānā*] **:** an interpreter chiefly of Arabic, Turkish, or Persian employed esp. in the Near East

drag·on \ˈdrag-ən\ *n* [ME, fr. OF, fr. L *dracon-, draco* serpent, dragon, fr. Gk *drakōn* serpent; akin to OE *torht* bright, Gk *derkesthai* to see, look at] **1** *archaic* **:** a huge serpent **2 :** a fabulous animal usu. represented as a monstrous winged and scaly serpent or saurian with a crested head and enormous claws **3 :** a violent, combative, or very strict person **4 a :** a short musket formerly carried hooked to a soldier's belt; *also* **:** a soldier carrying such a musket **b :** an artillery tractor **5 :** any of numerous small brilliantly colored arboreal lizards (genus *Draco*) of the East Indies and southern Asia having the hind ribs on each side prolonged and covered with a web of skin **6** *cap* **:** DRACO **7 :** a formidable or baneful figure — **drag·on·ish** \-ə-nish\ *adj*

drag·on·et \,drag-ə-ˈnet, ˈdrag-ə-nət\ *n* **1 :** a little dragon **2 :** any of various small often brightly colored scaleless marine fishes constituting a family (Callionymidae); *esp* **:** a European fish (*Callionymus lyra*) sometimes used as food

drag·on·fly \ˈdrag-ən-,flī\ *n* **:** any of a suborder (Anisoptera) of odonate insects that are larger and stouter than damselflies, hold the wings horizontal in repose, and have rectal gills during the naiad stage; *broadly* **:** ODONATE

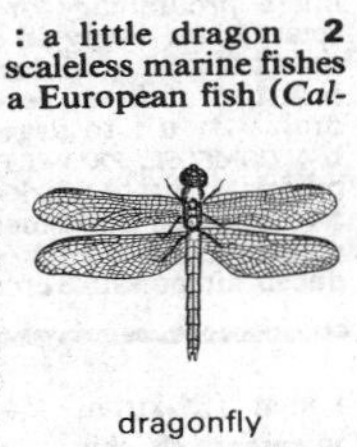
dragonfly

drag·on·head \-,hed\ *n* **:** any of several mints (genus *Dracocephalum*) often grown for their showy flower heads; *esp* **:** a No. American plant (*D. parviflorum*)

dragon lizard *n* **:** an Indonesian monitor lizard (*Varanus komodoensis*) that is the largest of all known lizards and reaches 11 feet in length

dragon's blood *n* **:** any of several resinous mostly dark-red plant products; *specif* **:** a resin from the fruit of a palm (genus *Daemonorops*) used for coloring varnish and in photoengraving

dragon's teeth *n pl* [fr. the dragon's teeth sown by Cadmus which sprang up as armed warriors who killed one another off] **1 :** seeds of strife **2 :** wedge-shaped concrete antitank barriers laid in multiple rows

[1]**dra·goon** \drə-ˈgün, dra-\ *n* [F *dragon* dragon, dragoon, fr. MF] **:** a member of a European military unit formerly composed of heavily armed mounted troops

[2]**dragoon** *vt* **1 :** to reduce to subjection or persecute by harsh use of troops **2 :** to force or attempt to force into submission by violent measures **:** HARASS

drag race *n* **:** an acceleration contest between vehicles (as automobiles) — **drag racing** *n*

drag·rope \ˈdrag-,rōp\ *n* **:** a rope that drags or is used for dragging

drag·ster \ˈdrag-stər\ *n* **1 :** a vehicle (as an automobile) built or modified for use in a drag race **2 :** one who participates in a drag race

drag strip *n* **:** the site of a drag race; *specif* **:** a narrow strip of pavement with a racing area at least ¼ mile long

drail \ˈdrā(ə)l\ *n* [obs. E *drail* to drag, trail] **:** a heavy fishhook used in trolling

[1]**drain** \ˈdrān\ *vb* [ME *draynen,* fr. OE *drēahnian*] *vt* **1** *obs* **:** FILTER **2 a :** to draw off (liquid) gradually or completely ⟨~*ed* all the water out⟩ **b :** to cause the gradual disappearance of **c :** to exhaust physically or emotionally **3 a :** to make gradually dry ⟨~ a swamp⟩ **b :** to carry away the surface water of ⟨the river that ~*s* the valley⟩ **c :** to deplete or empty by or as if by drawing off by degrees or in increments ⟨war that ~*s* a nation of youth and wealth⟩ **d :** to empty by drinking the contents of ⟨~ a glass of beer⟩ ~ *vi* **1 a :** to flow off gradually **b :** to disappear gradually **:** DWINDLE ⟨money ~*ing* away in expenses⟩ **2 :** to become emptied or freed of liquid by its flowing or dropping **3 :** to discharge surface or surplus water ***syn*** see DEPLETE — **drain·er** *n*

[2]**drain** *n* **1 :** a means (as a pipe) by which usu. liquid matter is drained **2 a :** the act of draining **b :** a gradual outflow or withdrawal **:** DEPLETION ⟨a ruinous dollar ~⟩ **3 :** something that causes depletion **:** BURDEN ⟨a ~ on the national resources⟩ — **down the drain :** being used wastefully or brought to nothing ⟨years of work went *down the drain* in the fire⟩

drain·age \ˈdrā-nij\ *n* **1 :** the act, process, or mode of draining; *also* **:** something drained off **2 :** a device for draining **:** DRAIN; *also* **:** a system of drains **3 :** an area or district drained

drain·pipe \ˈdrān-,pīp\ *n* **:** a pipe for drainage

[1]**drake** \ˈdrāk\ *n* [ME, dragon, fr. OE *draca;* akin to ON *dreki* dragon; both fr. a prehistoric WGmc-NGmc word borrowed fr. L *draco* dragon — more at DRAGON] **1 :** a small piece of artillery of the 17th and 18th centuries **2 :** MAYFLY

[2]**drake** *n* [ME; akin to OHG an*trahho* drake] **:** a male duck

[1]**dram** \ˈdram\ *n* [ME *dragme,* fr. MF & LL; MF, dram, drachma, fr. LL *dragma,* fr. L *drachma,* fr. Gk *drachmē,* lit., handful, fr. *drassesthai* to grasp] **1 a —** see WEIGHT table **b :** FLUIDRAM **2 a :** a small portion of something to drink **b :** a small amount

[2]**dram** *abbr* **1** dramatic **2** dramatist

dra·ma \ˈdräm-ə, ˈdram-\ *n* [LL *dramat-, drama,* fr. Gk, deed, drama, fr. *dran* to do, act; prob. akin to Lith *daryti* to do] **1 :** a composition in verse or prose intended to portray life or character or to tell a story usu. involving conflicts and emotions through action and dialogue and typically designed for theatrical performance **:** PLAY — compare CLOSET DRAMA **2 :** dramatic art, literature, or affairs **3 a :** a state, situation, or series of events involving interesting or intense conflict of forces **b :** dramatic state, effect, or quality ⟨the ~ of the courtroom proceedings⟩

dra·ma·logue \-,lȯg, -,läg\ *n* [*drama* + mono*logue*] **:** a reading of a play to an audience

Dram·a·mine \ˈdram-ə-,mēn\ *trademark* — used for dimenhydrinate

dra·mat·ic \drə-ˈmat-ik\ *adj* **1 :** of or relating to the drama **2 a :** suitable to or characteristic of the drama **:** VIVID **b :** striking in appearance or effect **3** *of an opera singer* **:** having a powerful voice and a declamatory style — compare LYRIC — **dra·mat·i·cal·ly** \-i-k(ə-)lē\ *adv*

dramatic irony *n* **:** IRONY 3b

dramatic monologue *n* **:** a literary work in which a character reveals himself in a monologue usu. addressed to a second person

dra·mat·ics \drə-ˈmat-iks\ *n pl but sing or pl in constr* **1 :** the study or practice of theatrical arts (as acting and stagecraft) **2 :** dramatic behavior or expression

dramatic unities *n pl* **:** the unities of time, place, and action that are observed in classical drama

dra·ma·tis per·so·nae \,dram-ət-ə-spər-ˈsō-(,)nē, ,dräm-, -,nī\ *n pl* [NL] **1 :** the characters or actors in a drama **2** *sing in constr* **:** a list of the characters or actors in a drama

dra·ma·tist \ˈdram-ət-əst, ˈdräm-\ *n* **:** PLAYWRIGHT

dra·ma·ti·za·tion \,dram-ət-ə-ˈzā-shən, ,dräm-\ *n* **1 :** the act or process of dramatizing **2 :** a dramatized version (as of a novel)

dra·ma·tize \ˈdram-ə-,tīz, ˈdräm-\ *vb* **-tized; -tiz·ing** *vt* **1 :** to adapt (as a novel) for theatrical presentation **2 :** to present or represent in a dramatic manner ~ *vi* **1 :** to be suitable for dramatization **2 :** to behave dramatically **:** put on an act — **dra·ma·tiz·able** \-,tī-zə-bəl\ *adj*

dra·ma·turge \ˈdram-ə-,tərj, ˈdräm-\ *n* **:** a specialist in dramaturgy

dra·ma·tur·gy \ˈdram-ə-,tər-jē, ˈdräm-\ *n* [G *dramaturgie,* fr. Gk *dramatourgia* dramatic composition, fr. *dramatourgos* dramatist, fr. *dramat-, drama* + *-ourgos* worker, fr. *ergon* work — more at WORK] **:** the art or technique of dramatic composition and theatrical representation — **dra·ma·tur·gic** \,dram-ə-ˈtər-jik, ,dräm-\ *or* **dra·ma·tur·gi·cal** \-ji-kəl\ *adj* — **dra·ma·tur·gi·cal·ly** \-ji-k(ə-)lē\ *adv*

dram·mock \ˈdram-ək\ *n* [ScGael *dramag* foul mixture] *chiefly Scot* **:** raw oatmeal mixed with cold water

dram·shop \ˈdram-,shäp\ *n* **:** BARROOM

drank *past of* DRINK

1drape \'drāp\ *vb* **draped; drap·ing** [ME *drapen* to weave, fr. MF *draper,* fr. *drap* cloth — more at DRAB] *vt* **1** : to cover or adorn with or as if with folds of cloth **2** : to cause to hang or stretch out loosely or carelessly ⟨*draped* his legs over the chair⟩ **3** : to arrange in flowing lines or folds ⟨a cleverly *draped* suit⟩ ~ *vi* : to become arranged in folds ⟨this silk ~*s* beautifully⟩ — **drap·able** *also* **drape·able** \'drā-pə-bəl\ *adj* — **drap·abil·i·ty** *also* **drape·abil·i·ty** \ˌdrā-pə-'bil-ət-ē\ *n*

2drape *n* **1 a** : a drapery esp. for a window : CURTAIN **b** : a sterile covering used in an operating room — usu. used in pl. **2** : arrangement in or of folds **3** : the cut or hang of clothing

drap·er \'drā-pər\ *n, chiefly Brit* : a dealer in cloth and sometimes also in clothing and dry goods

drap·ery \'drā-p(ə-)rē\ *n, pl* **-er·ies** **1** *Brit* : DRY GOODS **2 a** : a decorative piece of material usu. hung in loose folds and arranged in a graceful design **b** : hangings of heavy fabric for use as a curtain **3** : the draping or arranging of materials

dras·tic \'dras-tik\ *adj* [Gk *drastikos,* fr. *dran* to do] **1** : acting rapidly or violently ⟨a ~ purgative⟩ **2** : radical in effect or action : SEVERE ⟨~ measures⟩ — **dras·ti·cal·ly** \-ti-k(ə-)lē\ *adv*

drat \'drat\ *vb* **drat·ted; drat·ting** [prob. euphemistic alter. of *God rot*] : DAMN — used as a mild oath

draught \'draft\ *chiefly Brit var of* DRAFT

draughts \'draf(t)s\ *n pl but sing or pl in constr* [ME *draghtes,* fr. pl. of *draght* draft, move in chess] *Brit* : CHECKERS

draughts·man *chiefly Brit var of* DRAFTSMAN

Dra·vid·i·an \drə-'vid-ē-ən\ *n* [Skt *Drāviḍa*] **1** : a member of an ancient Australoid race of southern India **2** : DRAVIDIAN LANGUAGES — **Dravidian** *adj*

Dravidian languages *n pl* : a language family of India, Ceylon, and Pakistan that includes Tamil, Telugu, Gondi, and Malayalam

1draw \'drȯ\ *vb* **drew** \'drü\; **drawn** \'drȯn\; **draw·ing** [ME *drawen, dragen,* fr. OE *dragan;* akin to ON *draga* to draw, drag and perh. to L *trahere* to pull, draw] *vt* **1** : to cause to move continuously toward or after a force applied in advance : HAUL, DRAG **2** : to cause to go in a certain direction (as by leading) ⟨*drew* him aside⟩ **3 a** : to bring by inducement or allure : ATTRACT ⟨honey ~*s* flies⟩ **b** : to bring in or gather from a specified group or area ⟨a college that ~*s* its students from many states⟩ **c** : to bring on oneself : PROVOKE ⟨*drew* enemy fire⟩ **d** : to bring out by way of response : ELICIT ⟨*drew* cheers from the audience⟩ **4** : INHALE ⟨*drew* a deep breath⟩ **5 a** : to bring or pull out by effort ⟨~ a knife⟩ **b** : to extract the essence from ⟨~ tea⟩ **c** : EVISCERATE ⟨plucking and ~*ing* a goose before cooking⟩ **d** : to derive to one's benefit ⟨*drew* inspiration from the old masters⟩ **6** : to require (a specified depth) to float in ⟨a ship that ~*s* 12 feet of water⟩ **7 a** : ACCUMULATE, GAIN ⟨~*ing* interest⟩ **b** : to take (money) from a place of deposit **c** : to use in making a cash demand ⟨~*ing* a check against his account⟩ **d** : to receive regularly or in due course ⟨~ a salary⟩ **8 a** : to take (cards) from a stack or from the dealer **b** : to receive or take at random ⟨*drew* a winning number⟩ **9** : to bend (a bow) by pulling back the string **10** : to cause to shrink or tighten **11** : to strike (a ball) so as to impart a backward spin **12** : to leave (a contest) undecided : TIE **13 a (1)** : to produce a likeness of by making lines on a surface **(2)** : to give a portrayal of : DELINEATE ⟨a writer who ~*s* his characters well⟩ **b** : to write out in due form ⟨~ a will⟩ **c** : to design or describe in detail : FORMULATE ⟨~ comparisons⟩ **14** : to infer from evidence or premises ⟨~ a conclusion⟩ **15** : to spread or elongate (metal) by hammering or by pulling through dies; *also* : to shape (plastic) by stretching or by drawing through dies ~ *vi* **1** : to come or go steadily or gradually ⟨night ~*s* near⟩ **2 a** : to move something by pulling ⟨~*ing* at the well⟩ **b** : to exert an attractive force ⟨the play is ~*ing* well⟩ **3 a** : to pull back a bowstring **b** : to bring out a weapon ⟨*drew,* aimed, and fired⟩ **4 a** : to produce or allow a draft ⟨the chimney ~*s* well⟩ **b** : to swell out in a wind ⟨all sails ~*ing*⟩ **5 a** : to wrinkle or tighten up : SHRINK **b** : to change shape by pulling or stretching **6 a** : to cause blood or pus to localize at one point **b** : STEEP ⟨give the tea time to ~⟩ **7** : to create a likeness or a picture in outlines : SKETCH **8** : to come out even in a contest **9 a** : to make a written demand for payment of money on deposit **b** : to obtain resources (as of information) ⟨~*ing* from a common fund of knowledge⟩ ***syn*** see PULL — **draw·able** \-ə-bəl\ *adj* — **draw a bead on** : to take aim at — **draw a blank** : to fail to gain a desired object (as information sought) — **draw on** *or* **draw upon** : to use as a source of supply ⟨*drawing on* the whole community for support⟩ — **draw straws** : to decide an issue by lottery in which straws of unequal length are used — **draw the line** *or* **draw a line** **1** : to fix an arbitrary boundary between things that tend to intermingle ⟨the difficulty of *drawing a line* between art and pornography⟩ **2** : to fix a boundary excluding what one will not tolerate or engage in

2draw *n* **1** : the act or process of drawing: as **a** : a sucking pull on something held with the lips ⟨take a ~ on his pipe⟩ **b** : a removal of a handgun from its holster ⟨the sheriff was quicker on the ~⟩ **c** : backward spin given to a ball by striking it below center — compare FOLLOW **2** : something that is drawn: as **a** : a card drawn to replace a discard in poker **b** : a lot or chance drawn at random **c** : the movable part of a drawbridge **3** : a contest left undecided or deadlocked : TIE **4** : something that draws attention or patronage **5 a** : the distance from the string to the back of a drawn bow **b** : the force required to draw a bow fully **6** : a gully shallower than a ravine **7** : the deal in draw poker to improve the players' hands after discarding **8** : a football play in which the quarterback drops back as if to pass and then hands off to a back moving straight ahead — compare BOOTLEG 3

draw away *vi* : to move ahead (as of an opponent in a race)

draw·back \'drȯ-ˌbak\ *n* **1** : a refund of duties esp. on an imported product subsequently exported or used to produce a product for export **2** : an objectionable feature : HINDRANCE

draw back \drȯ-'bak\ *vi* : to avoid an issue or commitment : RETREAT

draw·bar \'drȯ-ˌbär\ *n* **1** : a railroad coupler **2** : a beam across the rear of a tractor to which implements are hitched

draw·bridge \-ˌbrij\ *n* : a bridge made to be raised up, let down, or drawn aside so as to permit or hinder passage

draw·down \-ˌdau̇n\ *n* **1** : a lowering of a water level (as in a reservoir) **2** : the process of depleting

draw down \(ˌ)drȯ-'dau̇n\ *vt* : to deplete by using or spending ⟨an unfavorable trade balance *draws down* gold reserves⟩

draw·ee \drȯ-'ē\ *n* : the person on whom an order or bill of exchange is drawn

draw·er \'drȯ(-ə)r\ *n* **1** : one that draws: as **a** : a person who draws liquor **b** : DRAFTSMAN **c** : one who draws a bill of exchange or order for payment or makes a promissory note **2** : a sliding box or receptacle opened by pulling out and closed by pushing in **3** *pl* : an article of clothing (as underwear) for the lower body — **drawer·ful** \-ˌfu̇l\ *n*

draw in *vt* **1** : to cause or entice to enter or participate ⟨heard the argument but would not be *drawn in*⟩ **2** : to sketch roughly ⟨*drawing in* the first outlines⟩ ~ *vi* **1 a** : to draw to an end ⟨the day *drew in*⟩ **b** : to shorten seasonally ⟨the evenings are already *drawing in*⟩ **2** : to become more cautious or economical

draw·ing \'drȯ(-)iŋ\ *n* **1** : an act or instance of drawing; *specif* : the process of deciding something by drawing lots **2** : the art or technique of representing an object or outlining a figure, plan, or sketch by means of lines **3** : something drawn or subject to drawing: as **a** : an amount drawn from a fund **b** : a representation formed by drawing : SKETCH

drawing account *n* : an account showing payments made to an employee (as a salesman) in advance of actual earnings or for traveling expenses

drawing board *n* **1** : a board used as a base for drafting on paper **2** : a planning stage ⟨a project still on the *drawing boards*⟩

drawing card *n* : something that attracts attention or patronage

drawing pin *n, Brit* : THUMBTACK

drawing room *n* [short for *withdrawing room*] **1 a** : a formal reception room **b** : a private room on a railroad passenger car with three berths and an enclosed toilet **2** : a formal reception

drawing table *n* : a table with a surface adjustable for elevation and angle of incline

draw·knife \'drȯ-ˌnīf\ *n* : a woodworker's tool having a blade with a handle at each end for use in shaving off surfaces — called also *drawshave*

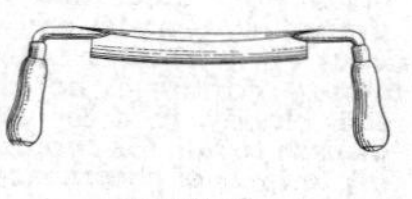

drawknife

1drawl \'drȯl\ *vb* [prob. freq. of *draw*] *vi* : to speak slowly with vowels greatly prolonged ~ *vt* : to utter in a slow lengthened tone — **drawl·er** *n* — **drawl·ing·ly** \'drȯ-liŋ-lē\ *adv*

2drawl *n* : a drawling manner of speaking — **drawly** \'drȯ-lē\ *adj*

drawn butter *n* : melted butter often with seasoning

drawn·work \'drȯn-ˌwərk\ *n* : decoration on cloth made by drawing out threads according to a pattern

draw off *vt* : REMOVE, WITHDRAW ~ *vi* : to move apart : REGROUP ⟨the enemies' losses forced them to *draw off*⟩

draw on *vi* : APPROACH ⟨night *draws on*⟩ ~ *vt* : to bring on : CAUSE

draw out *vt* **1** : REMOVE, EXTRACT **2** : to extend beyond a minimum in time : PROTRACT 2 **3** : to cause to speak freely ⟨a reporter's ability to *draw* a person *out*⟩

draw·plate \'drȯ-ˌplāt\ *n* : a die with holes through which wires are drawn

draw play *n* : DRAW 8

draw poker *n* : poker in which each player is dealt five cards face down and after betting may discard cards and get replacements

draw·shave \'drȯ-ˌshāv\ *n* : DRAWKNIFE

draw shot *n* : a shot in billiards or pool made by striking the cue ball below its center to cause it to move back after striking the object ball

draw·string \'drȯ-ˌstriŋ\ *n* : a string, cord, or tape inserted into hems or casings or laced through eyelets for use in closing a bag or controlling fullness in garments or curtains

draw·tube \-'t(y)üb\ *n* : a telescoping tube (as for the eyepiece of a microscope)

draw up *vt* **1** : to bring (as troops) into array **2** : to draft in due form **3** : to straighten (oneself) to an erect posture esp. as an assertion of dignity or resentment **4** : to bring to a halt ~ *vi* : to come to a halt

1dray \'drā\ *n* [ME *draye,* a wheelless vehicle, fr. OE *dræge* dragnet; akin to OE *dragan* to pull — more at DRAW] : a vehicle used to haul goods; *specif* : a strong low cart or wagon without sides

2dray *vt* : to haul on a dray : CART

dray·age \'drā-ij\ *n* : the work or cost of hauling by dray

dray·man \'drā-mən\ *n* : one whose work is hauling by dray

1dread \'dred\ *vb* [ME *dreden,* fr. OE *drǣdan*] *vt* **1 a** : to fear greatly **b** *archaic* : to regard with awe **2** : to feel extreme reluctance to meet or face ~ *vi* : to be apprehensive or fearful

2dread *n* **1 a** : great fear esp. in the face of impending evil **b** : extreme uneasiness in the face of a disagreeable prospect ⟨his ~ of paperwork⟩ **c** *archaic* : AWE **2** : one causing fear or awe ⟨fire was an omnipresent ~ —F. W. Saunders⟩ ***syn*** see FEAR

3dread *adj* **1** : causing great fear or anxiety **2** : inspiring awe

1dread·ful \'dred-fəl\ *adj* **1 a** : inspiring dread : causing great and oppressive fear **b** : inspiring awe or reverence **2** : extremely distasteful, unpleasant, or shocking **3** : EXTREME ⟨~ disorder⟩ ***syn*** see FEARFUL — **dread·ful·ly** \-f(ə-)lē\ *adv* — **dread·ful·ness** \-fəl-nəs\ *n*

2dreadful *n* : a cheap and sensational story or periodical

ə abut	ᵊ kitten	ər further	a back	ā bake	ä cot, cart	
au̇ out	ch chin	e less	ē easy	g gift	i trip	ī life
j joke	ŋ sing	ō flow	ȯ flaw	ȯi coin	th thin	th this
ü loot	u̇ foot	y yet	yü few	yu̇ furious	zh vision	

dread·nought \'dred-,nȯt, -,nät\ *n* **1 :** a warm garment of thick cloth; *also* **:** the cloth **2** [*Dreadnought,* Brit. battleship] **:** a battleship whose main armament consists of big guns of the same caliber

[1]**dream** \'drēm\ *n, often attrib* [ME *dreem,* fr. OE *drēam* noise, joy] **1 :** a series of thoughts, images, or emotions occurring during sleep **2 :** an experience of waking life having the characteristics of a dream: as **a :** a visionary creation of the imagination **:** DAYDREAM **b :** a state of mind marked by abstraction or release from reality **:** REVERIE **c :** an object seen in a dreamlike state **:** VISION **3 :** something notable for its beauty, excellence, or enjoyable quality ⟨the new car is a ~ to operate⟩ **4 a :** a strongly desired goal or purpose ⟨his ~ of becoming president⟩ **b :** something that fully satisfies a wish **:** IDEAL ⟨a meal that was a gourmet's ~⟩ — **dream·ful** \-fəl\ *adj* — **dream·ful·ly** \-fə-lē\ *adv* — **dream·ful·ness** *n* — **dream·like** \'drēm-,līk\ *adj*

[2]**dream** \'drēm\ *vb* **dreamed** \'drem(p)t, 'drēmd\ *or* **dreamt** \'drem(p)t\; **dream·ing** \'drē-miŋ\ *vi* **1 :** to have a dream **2 :** to indulge in daydreams or fantasies ⟨~*ing* of a better future⟩ **3 :** to appear tranquil or dreamy ⟨houses ~*ing* in leafy shadows — Gladys Taber⟩ ~ *vt* **1 :** to have a dream of **2 :** to consider as a possibility **:** IMAGINE **3 :** to pass (time) in reverie or inaction — usu. used with *away* ⟨~*ing* the hours away⟩ — **dream of :** to consider possible or fitting ⟨wouldn't *dream of* disturbing you⟩

dream·er \'drē-mər\ *n* **1 :** one that dreams **2 a :** one who lives in a world of fancy and imagination **b :** one who has ideas or conceives projects regarded as impractical **:** VISIONARY

dream·land \'drēm-,land\ *n* **:** an unreal delightful country existing only in imagination or in dreams **:** NEVER-NEVER LAND

dream·less \-ləs\ *adj* **:** having or evidencing no dreams ⟨a ~ sleep⟩ — **dream·less·ly** *adv* — **dream·less·ness** *n*

dream up *vt* **:** DEVISE, CONCOCT

dream vision *n* **:** a usu. medieval poem having a framework in which the poet pictures himself as falling asleep and envisioning in his dream a series of allegorical people and events

dream·world \'drēm-,wərld\ *n* **:** a world of illusion or fantasy

dreamy \'drē-mē\ *adj* **dream·i·er; -est 1 a :** full of dreams ⟨a ~ night's sleep⟩ **b :** pleasantly abstracted from immediate reality **2 :** given to dreaming or fantasy ⟨a ~ child⟩ **3 a :** suggestive of a dream in vague or visionary quality ⟨a ~ recollection of the incident⟩ **b :** quiet and soothing **c :** DELIGHTFUL, PLEASING — **dream·i·ly** \-mə-lē\ *adv* — **dream·i·ness** \-mē-nəs\ *n*

drear \'dri(ə)r\ *adj* **:** DREARY

drea·ry \'dri(ə)r-ē\ *adj* **drea·ri·er; -est** [ME *drery,* fr. OE *drēorig* sad, bloody, fr. *drēor* gore; akin to OHG *trūrēn* to be sad, Goth *driusan* to fall, Gk *thrauein* to shatter] **1 :** SAD, DOLEFUL **2 :** causing feelings of cheerlessness **:** GLOOMY — **drea·ri·ly** \'drir-ə-lē\ *adv* — **drear·i·ness** \'drir-ē-nəs\ *n*

dreck \'drek\ *n* [Yiddish *drek* & G *dreck,* fr. MHG *drec;* akin to OE *threax* rubbish, L *stercus* excrement] **:** TRASH, RUBBISH

[1]**dredge** \'drej\ *n* [prob. fr. Sc *dreg-* (in *dregbot* dredge boat)] **1 :** an apparatus usu. in the form of an oblong iron frame with an attached bag net used esp. for gathering fish and shellfish **2 :** a machine for removing earth usu. by buckets on an endless chain or a suction tube **3 :** a barge used in dredging

[2]**dredge** *vb* **dredged; dredg·ing** *vt* **1 a :** to dig, gather, or pull out with a dredge **b :** to deepen (as a waterway) with a dredging machine — often used with *up* **2 :** to bring to light by deep searching ⟨*dredging* up memories⟩ ~ *vi* **1 :** to use a dredge **2 :** to search deeply — **dredg·er** *n*

[3]**dredge** *vt* **dredged; dredg·ing** [obs. *dredge,* n., sweetmeat, fr. ME *drage, drege,* fr. MF *dragie,* modif. of L *tragemata* sweetmeats, fr. Gk *tragēmata,* pl. of *tragēma* sweetmeat, fr. *trōgein* to gnaw — more at TERSE] **:** to coat (food) by sprinkling (as with flour) — **dredg·er** *n*

dree \'drē\ *vt* **dreed; dree·ing** [ME *dreen,* fr. OE *drēogan* — more at DRUDGE] *chiefly Scot* **:** ENDURE, SUFFER

dreg \'dreg\ *n* [ME, fr. ON *dregg;* akin to L *fraces* dregs of oil, Gk *thrassein* to trouble] **1 :** sediment contained in a liquid or precipitated from it **:** LEES — usu. used in pl. **2 :** the most undesirable part — usu. used in pl. ⟨the ~*s* of society⟩ **3 :** the last remaining part **:** VESTIGE

D region *n* **:** the lowest part of the ionosphere occurring between 25 and 40 miles above the surface of the earth

dreich \'drēk\ *adj* [ME, of Scand origin; akin to ON *drjūgr* lasting] *chiefly Scot* **:** DREARY

drei·del *also* **dreidl** \'drād-ᵊl\ *n* [Yiddish *dreidl,* fr. *dreien* to turn, fr. MHG *dræjen,* fr. OHG *drāen* — more at THROW] **1 :** a 4-sided toy marked with Hebrew letters and spun like a top in a game of chance **2 :** a children's game of chance played esp. at Hanukkah with a dreidel

[1]**drench** \'drench\ *n* **1 :** a poisonous or medicinal drink; *specif* **:** a large dose of medicine mixed with liquid and put down the throat of an animal **2 a :** something that drenches **b :** a quantity sufficient to drench or saturate

[2]**drench** *vt* [ME *drenchen,* fr. OE *drencan;* akin to OE *drincan* to drink] **1 a** *archaic* **:** to force to drink **b :** to administer a drench to (an animal) **2 :** to wet thoroughly (as by soaking or immersing in liquid) ⟨desserts ~*ed* with brandy⟩ **3 :** to soak or cover thoroughly with liquid that falls or is precipitated **4 :** to fill completely as if by soaking or precipitation **:** SATURATE ⟨a mind ~*ed* with esoteric lore⟩ ***syn*** see SOAK — **drench·er** *n*

[1]**dress** \'dres\ *vb* [ME *dressen,* fr. MF *dresser,* fr. OF *drecier,* fr. (assumed) VL *directiare,* fr. L *directus* direct, pp. of *dirigere* to direct, fr. *dis-* + *regere* to lead straight — more at RIGHT] *vt* **1 a :** to make or set straight **b :** to arrange (as troops) in a straight line and at proper intervals **2** *archaic* **:** to dress down **3 a :** to put clothes on **b :** to provide with clothing **4 :** to add decorative details or accessories to **:** EMBELLISH **5 :** to prepare for use or service **6 a :** to apply dressings or medicaments to **b** (1) **:** to arrange (the hair) by combing, brushing, or curling (2) **:** to groom and curry (an animal) **c :** to kill and prepare for market **d :** CULTIVATE, TEND; *esp* **:** to apply manure or fertilizer to **e :** to put through a finishing process; *specif* **:** to make (as lumber or stone) trim and smooth ~ *vi* **1 a :** to put on clothing **b :** to put on or wear formal, elaborate, or fancy clothes ⟨guests were expected to ~ for dinner⟩ **2** *of a food animal* **:** to weigh after being dressed **3 :** to align oneself with the next soldier in a line to make the line straight — **dress ship :** to ornament a ship for a celebration by hoisting national ensigns at the mastheads and running a line of signal flags and pennants from bow to stern

[2]**dress** *n* **1 :** APPAREL, CLOTHING **2 :** an outer garment usu. for a woman or a girl **3 :** covering, adornment, or appearance appropriate or peculiar to a particular time **4 :** a particular form of presentation **:** GUISE

[3]**dress** *adj* **1 :** relating to or used for a dress **2 :** suitable for a formal occasion **3 :** requiring or permitting formal dress ⟨a ~ affair⟩

dres·sage \drə-'säzh, dre-\ *n* **:** the execution by a horse of complex maneuvers in response to barely perceptible movements of a rider's hands, legs, and weight

dress circle *n* **:** the first or lowest curved tier of seats in a theater

dress down *vt* **:** to reprove severely

[1]**dress·er** \'dres-ər\ *n* **1** *obs* **:** a table or sideboard for preparing and serving food **2 :** a cupboard to hold dishes and cooking utensils **3 :** a chest of drawers or bureau with a mirror

[2]**dresser** *n* **:** one that dresses ⟨a fashionable ~⟩

dresser set *n* **:** a set of toilet articles including hairbrush, comb, and mirror for use at a dresser or dressing table

dress·ing *n* **1 a :** the act or process of one who dresses **b :** an instance of such act or process **2 a :** a sauce for adding to a dish (as a salad) **b :** a seasoned mixture usu. used as a stuffing (as for poultry) **3 a :** material applied to cover a lesion **b :** fertilizing material (as manure or compost)

dressing glass *n* **:** a small mirror set to swing in a standing frame and used at a dresser or dressing table

dressing gown *n* **:** a robe (as of silk) worn esp. while dressing or resting

dressing room *n* **:** a room used chiefly for dressing; *esp* **:** a room in a theater for changing costumes and makeup

dressing station *n* **:** a station for giving first aid to the wounded

dressing table *n* **:** a table often fitted with drawers and a mirror in front of which one sits while dressing and grooming oneself

[1]**dress·mak·er** \'dres-,mā-kər\ *n* **:** one that does dressmaking

[2]**dressmaker** *adj, of women's clothes* **:** having softness, rounded lines, and intricate detailing ⟨a ~ suit⟩

dress·mak·ing \-,mā-kiŋ\ *n* **:** the process or occupation of making dresses

dress rehearsal *n* **:** a full rehearsal of a play in costume and with stage properties shortly before the first performance

dress shirt *n* **:** a man's shirt esp. for wear with evening dress

dress suit *n* **:** a suit worn for full dress

dress uniform *n* **:** a uniform for formal wear

dress up *vt* **1 a :** to attire in best or formal clothes **b :** to attire in clothes suited to a particular role **2 :** to present or cause to appear in a certain light (as by distortion or exaggeration) ⟨*dressed up* his story to make himself appear a hero⟩ ~ *vi* **:** to get dressed up

dressy \'dres-ē\ *adj* **dress·i·er; -est 1 :** showy in dress **2 :** STYLISH, SMART — **dress·i·ness** *n*

drew *past of* DRAW

Drey·fu·sard \,drī-f(y)ə-'sär(d), ,drā-, -'zär(d)\ *n* [F] **:** a defender or partisan of Alfred Dreyfus

drib \'drib\ *n* [prob. back-formation fr. *dribble* & *driblet*] **:** a small amount — usu. used in the phrase *dribs and drabs*

[1]**drib·ble** \'drib-əl\ *vb* **drib·bled; drib·bling** \-(ə-)liŋ\ [freq. of *drib* (to dribble)] *vi* **1 :** to fall or flow in drops or in a thin intermittent stream **:** TRICKLE **2 :** to let saliva trickle from a corner of the mouth **:** DROOL **3 :** to come or issue in piecemeal or desultory fashion **4 a :** to dribble a ball or puck **b :** to proceed by dribbling **c** *of a ball* **:** to move with short bounces ~ *vt* **1 :** to let or cause to fall in drops little by little **2 :** to issue sporadically and in small bits **3 a :** to propel by successive slight taps or bounces with hand, foot, or stick **b :** to hit (as a baseball) so as to cause a slow bouncing — **drib·bler** \-(ə-)lər\ *n*

[2]**dribble** *n* **1 a :** a small trickling stream or flow **b :** a drizzling shower **2 :** a tiny or insignificant bit or quantity **3 :** an act or instance of dribbling a ball or puck

drib·let \'drib-lət\ *n* **1 :** a trifling sum or part **2 :** a drop of liquid

dried–fruit beetle *n* **:** a small broad brown beetle (*Carpophilus hemipterus*) that is a cosmopolitan pest on stored products

dried–up \'drī-'dəp\ *adj* **:** being wizened and shrivelled

[1]**drier** *comparative of* DRY

[2]**dri·er** *also* **dry·er** \'drī(-ə)r\ *n* **1 :** something that extracts or absorbs moisture **2 :** a substance that accelerates drying (as of oils, paints, and printing inks) **3** *usu dryer* **:** a device for drying

driest *superlative of* DRY

[1]**drift** \'drift\ *n* [ME; akin to OE *drifan* to drive — more at DRIVE] **1 a :** the act of driving something along **b :** the flow or the velocity of the current of a river or ocean stream **2 :** something driven, propelled, or urged along or drawn together in a clump by or as if by a natural agency: as **a :** wind-driven snow, rain, cloud, dust, or smoke usu. at or near the ground surface **b** (1) **:** a mass of matter (as sand) deposited together by or as if by wind or water (2) **:** a helter-skelter accumulation **c :** DROVE, FLOCK **d :** something (as driftwood) washed ashore **e :** rock debris deposited by natural agents; *specif* **:** a deposit of clay, sand, gravel, and boulders transported by a glacier or by running water from a glacier **3 a :** a general underlying design or tendency **b :** the underlying meaning, import, or purport of what is spoken or written **4 :** something driven down upon or forced into a body: as **a :** a tool for ramming down or driving something **b :** a pin for stretching and aligning rivet holes **5 :** the motion or action of drifting esp. spatially and usu. under external influence: as **a :** a ship's deviation from its course caused by currents **b :** one of the slower movements of oceanic circulation **c :** the lateral motion of an airplane due to air currents **d :** an easy moderate more or less steady flow or sweep along a spatial course **e :** a gradual shift in

attitude, opinion, or position **f** : an aimless course; *esp* : a foregoing of any attempt at direction or control **g** : a deviation from a true reproduction, representation, or reading **6 a** : a nearly horizontal mine passageway driven on or parallel to the course of a vein or rock stratum **b** : a small crosscut in a mine connecting two larger tunnels **7 a** : an assumed trend toward a general change in the structure of a language over a period of time **b** : GENETIC DRIFT **c** : a gradual change in the zero reading of an instrument or in any quantitive characteristic that is supposed to remain constant ***syn*** see TENDENCY

[2]drift *vi* **1 a** : to become driven or carried along by a current of water, wind, or air **b** : to move or float smoothly and effortlessly **2 a** : to move along a line of least resistance **b** : to move in a random or casual way **c** : to become carried along subject to no guidance or control ⟨the conversation ~*ed* from one topic to another⟩ **3 a** : to accumulate in a mass or become piled up in heaps by wind or water **b** : to become covered with a drift **4** : to vary or deviate from a set adjustment ~ *vt* **1 a** : to cause to be driven in a current **b** *West* : to drive (livestock) slowly esp. to allow grazing **2 a** : to pile in heaps **b** : to cover with drifts ⟨slopes that are heavily ~*ed* during the winter⟩ — **drift·ing·ly** \'drif-tiŋ-lē\ *adv*

drift·age \'drif-tij\ *n* **1** : a drifting of some object esp. through the action of wind or water **2** : deviation from a set course due to drifting **3** : drifted material ⟨seaweed and other ~⟩

drift·er \'drif-tər\ *n* : one that drifts; *esp* : one that travels or moves about aimlessly

drift fence *n* : a stretch of fence on range land esp. in the western U.S. for preventing cattle from drifting from their home range

drift·weed \'drif-,twēd\ *n* : a seaweed (as of the genus *Laminaria*) that tends to break free and drift ashore

drift·wood \'drif-,twu̇d\ *n* **1** : wood drifted or floated by water **2** : FLOTSAM 2

drifty \'drif-tē\ *adj* **drift·i·er; -est** : exhibiting or tending to form drifts

[1]drill \'dril\ *vb* [D *drillen;* akin to OHG *drāen* to turn — more at THROW] *vt* **1 a** (1) : to bore or drive a hole in (2) : to make by piercing action ⟨~*ed* holes an inch apart⟩ **b** : to hit with piercing effect ⟨~*ed* a single to right field⟩ **2 a** : to fix something in the mind or habit pattern of by repetitive instruction ⟨~ pupils in spelling⟩ **b** : to impart or communicate by repetition ⟨impossible to ~ the simplest idea into some people⟩ **c** : to train or exercise in military drill ~ *vi* **1** : to make a hole with a drill **2** : to engage in an exercise **3** : to act on with penetrating effect ***syn*** see PRACTICE — **drill·abil·i·ty** \,dril-ə-'bil-ət-ē\ *n* — **drill·able** \-ə-bəl\ *adj* — **drill·er** \'dril-ər\ *n*

[2]drill *n* **1** : an instrument with an edged or pointed end for making holes in hard substances by revolving or by a succession of blows; *also* : such an instrument with a machine for operating it **2** : the act or exercise of training soldiers in marching and the manual of arms **3 a** : a physical or mental exercise aimed at perfecting facility and skill esp. by regular practice **b** : a formal exercise by a team of marchers **c** *chiefly Brit* : the approved or correct procedure for accomplishing something efficiently **4 a** : a marine snail (*Urosalpinx cinerea*) destructive to oysters by boring through their shells and feeding on the soft parts **b** : any of several mollusks related to the drill **5** : a drilling sound

[3]drill *n* [prob. native name in West Africa] : a West African baboon (*Mandrillus leucophaeus*) closely related to the typical mandrills

[4]drill *n* [perh. fr. *drill* (rill)] **1 a** : a shallow furrow or trench into which seed is sown **b** : a row of seed sown in such a furrow **2** : a planting implement that makes holes or furrows, drops in the seed and sometimes fertilizer, and covers them with earth

[5]drill *vt* **1** : to sow (seeds) by dropping along a shallow furrow **2 a** : to sow with seed or set with seedlings inserted in drills **b** : to distribute seed or fertilizer in by means of a drill

[6]drill *n* [short for *drilling*] : a durable cotton fabric in twill weave

dril·ling \'dril-iŋ\ *n* [modif. of G *drillich,* fr. MHG *drilich* fabric woven with a threefold thread, fr. OHG *drilīh* made up of three threads, fr. L *trilic-, trilix,* fr. *tri-* + *licium* thread] : [6]DRILL

drill·mas·ter \'dril-,mas-tər\ *n* **1** : an instructor in military drill **2** : an instructor or director who maintains severe discipline and who often stresses the trivial and unimportant

drill press *n* : an upright drilling machine in which the drill is pressed to the work by a hand lever or by power

drill team *n* : an exhibition marching team that engages in precision drill

drily *var of* DRYLY

[1]drink \'driŋk\ *vb* **drank** \'draŋk\; **drunk** \'drəŋk\ *or* **drank; drink·ing** [ME *drinken,* fr. OE *drincan;* akin to OHG *trinkan* to drink] *vt* **1 a** : SWALLOW, IMBIBE **b** : to take in or suck up : ABSORB ⟨~*ing* air into his lungs⟩ **c** : to take in or receive avidly — usu. used with *in* ⟨*drank* in every word of the lecture⟩ **2** : to join in (a toast) **3** : to bring to a specified state by taking drink ⟨*drank* himself into oblivion⟩ ⟨~*ing* his troubles away⟩ ~ *vi* **1 a** : to take liquid into the mouth for swallowing **b** : to receive into one's consciousness **2** : to partake of alcoholic beverages **3** : to join in a toast

[2]drink *n* **1 a** : liquid suitable for swallowing **b** : alcoholic liquor **2** : a draft or portion of liquid **3** : excessive consumption of alcoholic beverages **4** : a sizable body of water — used with *the*

[1]drink·able \'driŋ-kə-bəl\ *adj* : suitable or safe for drinking — **drink·abil·i·ty** \,driŋ-kə-'bil-ət-ē\ *n*

[2]drinkable *n* : a liquid suitable for drinking : BEVERAGE

drink·er \'driŋ-kər\ *n* **1 a** : one that drinks **b** : one that drinks alcoholic beverages esp. to excess **2** : a device that provides water for domestic animals or poultry

drinking fountain *n* : a fixture with nozzle that delivers a stream of water for drinking

drinking song *n* : a song on a convivial theme appropriate for a group engaged in social drinking

[1]drip \'drip\ *vb* **dripped; drip·ping** [ME *drippen,* fr. OE *dryppan;* akin to OE *dropa* drop] *vt* **1** : to let fall in drops **2** : to spill or let out copiously ⟨her voice *dripping* sarcasm⟩ ~ *vi* **1 a** : to let fall drops of moisture or liquid **b** : to overflow with or as if with moisture ⟨a uniform *dripping* with gold braid⟩ ⟨a novel that ~*s* with sentimentality⟩ **2** : to fall in or as if in drops **3** : to waft or pass gently — **drip·per** *n*

[2]drip *n* **1 a** : a falling in drops **b** : liquid that falls, overflows, or is extruded in drops **2** : the sound made by or as if by falling drops **3** : a part of a cornice or other member that projects to throw off rainwater; *also* : an overlapping metal strip serving the same purpose **4** : a device for the administration of a fluid at a slow rate esp. into a vein; *also* : a material so administered **5** *slang* : a dull or unattractive person

drip coffee *n* : coffee made by letting boiling water drip slowly through finely ground coffee

[1]drip–dry \'drip-'drī\ *vi* : to dry with few or no wrinkles when hung dripping wet

[2]drip–dry *adj* : made of a washable fabric that drip-dries

[3]drip–dry *n* : a drip-dry garment

drip·less \'drip-ləs\ *adj* : designed not to drip ⟨~ candles⟩

drip pan *n* : a pan for catching drippings — called also *dripping pan*

[1]drip·ping \'drip-iŋ\ *n* : fat and juices drawn from meat during cooking — often used in pl.

[2]dripping *adv* : EXTREMELY — usu. used in the phrase *dripping wet*

drip pot *n* : a pot for making drip coffee

drip·py \'drip-ē\ *adj* **drip·pi·er; -est** **1** : RAINY, DRIZZLY **2** : MAWKISH 2

drip·stone \'drip-,stōn\ *n* **1** : a stone drip (as over a window) **2** : calcium carbonate in the form of stalactites or stalagmites

[1]drive \'drīv\ *vb* **drove** \'drōv\; **driv·en** \'driv-ən\; **driv·ing** \'drī-viŋ\ [ME *driven,* fr. OE *drīfan;* akin to OHG *trīban* to drive] *vt* **1 a** : to impart a forward motion to by physical force ⟨waves *drove* the boat against the shore⟩ **b** : to repulse, remove, or cause to go by force, authority, or influence ⟨~ the enemy back⟩ **c** : to set or keep in motion or operation ⟨~ machinery by electricity⟩ **2 a** : to direct the motions and course of (a draft animal) **b** : to operate the mechanism and controls and direct the course of (as a vehicle) **c** : to convey in a vehicle **d** : to float (logs) down a stream **3** : to carry on or through energetically ⟨*driving* a hard bargain⟩ **4 a** : to exert inescapable or coercive pressure on : FORCE **b** : to compel to undergo or suffer a change (as in situation, awareness, or emotional state) ⟨*drove* him crazy⟩ **c** : to urge relentlessly to continuous exertion ⟨the sergeant *drove* his recruits⟩ **d** : to press or force into an activity, course, or direction ⟨the expensive drug habit that ~*s* addicts to steal⟩ **e** : to project, inject, or impress incisively ⟨*drove* his point home⟩ **5 a** : to cause (as game or cattle) to move in a desired direction **b** : to search (a district) for game **6** : to force (a passage) by pressing or digging **7 a** : to propel (an object of play) swiftly **b** : to hit (a golf ball) from the tee esp. with a driver **c** : to cause (a run or runner) to be scored in baseball — usu. used with *in* ~ *vi* **1 a** : to dash, plunge, or surge ahead rapidly or violently **b** : to rush along with force against an obstruction ⟨rain *driving* against the windshield⟩ **c** : to progress with strong momentum ⟨the rain was *driving* hard⟩ **2 a** : to operate a vehicle; *also* : HANDLE ⟨an auto that ~*s* well⟩ **b** : to have oneself carried in a vehicle **3** : to drive an object of play ***syn*** see MOVE — **driv·able** *also* **drive·able** \'drī-və-bəl\ *adj* — **drive at** : to have as an ultimate meaning or conclusion ⟨did not understand what she was *driving at* —Eric Goldman⟩

[2]drive *n* **1** : an act of driving: **a** : a trip in a carriage or automobile **b** : a collection and driving together of animals; *also* : the animals gathered **c** : a driving of cattle or sheep overland **d** : a hunt or shoot in which the game is driven within the hunter's range **e** : the guiding of logs downstream to a mill; *also* : the floating logs amassed in a drive **f** (1) : the act or an instance of driving an object of play (2) : the flight of a ball **2 a** : a private road : DRIVEWAY 2 **b** : a public road for driving (as in a park) **3** : an offensive, aggressive, or expansionist move; *esp* : a strong military attack against enemy-held terrain **4** : the state of being hurried and under pressure **5 a** : a strong systematic group effort : CAMPAIGN **b** : a sustained offensive effort ⟨the ~ that ended in a touchdown⟩ **6 a** : an urgent, basic, or instinctual need : a motivating physiological condition of the organism ⟨a sexual ~⟩ **b** : an impelling culturally acquired concern, interest, or longing ⟨enslaved by a ~ for perfection⟩ **c** : dynamic quality **7 a** : the means for giving motion to a machine or machine part **b** : the means by which the propulsive power of an automobile is applied to the road ⟨front wheel ~⟩ **c** : the means by which the propulsion of an automotive vehicle is controlled and directed ⟨a left-hand ~⟩ **8** : a device including a transport and heads for reading or writing tape and esp. magnetic tape — **drive** *adj*

[1]drive–in \'drī-,vin\ *n* : a place of business (as a theater or restaurant) so laid out that patrons can be accommodated while remaining in their automobiles

[2]drive–in *adj* : laid out as a drive-in

[1]driv·el \'driv-əl\ *vb* **-eled** *or* **-elled; -el·ing** *or* **-el·ling** \-(ə-)liŋ\ [ME *drivelen,* fr. OE *dreflian;* akin to ON *draf* malt dregs, OE *deorc* dark] *vi* **1** : to let saliva dribble from the mouth : SLAVER **2** : to talk stupidly and carelessly ~ *vt* **1** : to utter in an infantile or imbecilic way **2** : to waste or fritter in a childish fashion — **driv·el·er** \-(ə-)lər\ *n*

[2]drivel *n* **1** *archaic* : saliva trickling from the mouth **2** : NONSENSE

drive·line \'drīv-,līn\ *n* : the parts including the universal joint and the drive shaft that connect the transmission with the driving axles of an automobile

driv·en *adj* : having a compulsive or urgent quality ⟨a ~ sense of obligation⟩ — **driv·en·ness** \ˈdriv-ən-nəs\ *n*
driv·er \ˈdrī-vər\ *n* : one that drives: as **a** : COACHMAN **b** : the operator of a motor vehicle **c** : an implement (as a hammer) for driving **d** : a mechanical piece for imparting motion to another piece **e** : a golf club with a wooden head and nearly straight face used in driving — **driv·er·less** \-ləs\ *adj*
driver ant *n* : ARMY ANT; *specif* : any of various African and Asian ants (*Dorylus* or related genera) that move in vast armies
driver's license *n* : a license issued under governmental authority that permits the holder to operate a motor vehicle
driver's seat *n* : the position of top authority or dominance
drive shaft *n* : a shaft that transmits mechanical power
drive·way \ˈdrīv-ˌwā\ *n* **1** : a road or way along which animals are driven **2** : a private road giving access from a public way to a building on abutting grounds
driv·ing *adj* **1 a** : communicating force ⟨a ~ wheel⟩ **b** : exerting pressure ⟨a ~ influence⟩ **2 a** : having great force ⟨a ~ rain⟩ **b** : acting with vigor : ENERGETIC ⟨a hard-*driving* worker⟩
driving range *n* : an area equipped with distance markers, clubs, balls, and tees for practicing golf drives
[1]**driz·zle** \ˈdriz-əl\ *vb* **driz·zled; driz·zling** \-(ə-)liŋ\ [perh. alter. of ME *drysnen* to fall, fr. OE *-drysnian* to disappear; akin to Goth *driusan* to fall] *vi* : to rain in very small drops or very lightly : SPRINKLE ~ *vt* **1** : to shed or let fall in minute drops or particles **2** : to make wet with minute drops — **driz·zling·ly** \-(ə-)liŋ-lē\ *adv*
[2]**drizzle** *n* : a fine misty rain — **driz·zly** \ˈdriz-(ə-)lē\ *adj*
drogue \ˈdrōg\ *n* [prob. alter. of [1]*drag*] **1** : SEA ANCHOR **2 a** : a cylindrical or funnel-shaped device towed as a target by an airplane **b** : a small parachute for stabilizing or decelerating something (as an astronaut's capsule) or for pulling a larger parachute out of stowage **3** : a funnel-shaped device which is attached to the end of a long flexible hose suspended from a tanker airplane in flight and into which the probe of another airplane in flight is fitted so as to receive fuel from the tanker airplane
droit \ˈdrȯit, drə-ˈwä\ *n* [MF, fr. ML *directum*, fr. LL, neut. of *directus* just, fr. L, direct] : a legal right ⟨~s of admiralty⟩
droit du sei·gneur \drwä-dūē-se-nʸœr\ *n* [F, right of the lord] : a supposed legal or customary right of a feudal lord to have sexual relations with a vassal's bride on her wedding night
[1]**droll** \ˈdrōl\ *adj* [F *drôle*, fr. *drôle* scamp, fr. MF *drolle*, fr. MD, imp] : having a humorous, whimsical, or odd quality **syn** see LAUGHABLE — **droll·ness** *n* — **drol·ly** \ˈdrō(l)-lē\ *adv*
[2]**droll** *n* : one that amuses or diverts : JESTER, COMEDIAN
[3]**droll** *vi, archaic* : to make fun : JEST, SPORT
droll·ery \ˈdrōl-(ə-)rē\ *n, pl* **-er·ies** **1** : something that is droll: as **a** : a comic picture or drawing **b** : a usu. brief comic show or entertainment **c** : an amusing story : JEST **2** : the act or an instance of jesting or burlesquing **3** : whimsical humor
-drome \ˌdrōm\ *n comb form* [*hippodrome*] **1** : racecourse ⟨motor*drome*⟩ **2** : large specially prepared place ⟨aero*drome*⟩
drom·e·dary \ˈdräm-ə-ˌder-ē *also* ˈdrəm-\ *n, pl* **-dar·ies** [ME *dromedarie*, fr. MF *dromedaire*, fr. LL *dromedarius*, fr. L *dromad-, dromas*, fr. Gk, running; akin to Gk *dramein* to run, *dromos* racecourse, OE *treppan* to tread] **1** : a camel of unusual speed bred and trained esp. for riding **2** : the one-humped camel (*Camelus dromedarius*) of western Asia and northern Africa
drom·ond \ˈdräm-ənd\ *n* [ME, fr. MF *dromont*, fr. LL *dromon-, dromo* light ship, fr. Gk *dromōn*, fr. *dramein* to run] : a large fast-sailing galley or cutter of medieval times
-d·ro·mous \d-rə-məs\ *adj comb form* [NL *-dromus*, fr. Gk *-dromos* (akin to Gk *dramein*)] : running ⟨cata*dromous*⟩
[1]**drone** \ˈdrōn\ *n* [ME, fr. OE *drān*; akin to OHG *treno* drone] **1** : the male of a bee (as the honeybee) that has no sting and gathers no honey — see HONEYBEE illustration **2** : one that lives on the labors of others : PARASITE **3** : a pilotless airplane, helicopter, or ship controlled by radio signals
[2]**drone** *vb* **droned; dron·ing** *vi* **1 a** : to make a sustained deep murmuring, humming, or buzzing sound **b** : to talk in a persistently dull or monotonous tone **2** : to pass, proceed, or act in a dull, drowsy, or indifferent manner ⟨the trial *droned* on for months⟩ ~ *vt* **1** : to utter or pronounce with a drone **2** : to pass or spend in dull or monotonous activity or in idleness ⟨*droned* away the precious years of youth⟩ — **dron·er** *n* — **dron·ing·ly** \ˈdrō-niŋ-lē\ *adv*
[3]**drone** *n* **1** : one of the usu. three pipes on a bagpipe that sound fixed continuous tones **2** : a deep sustained or monotonous sound : HUM **3** : an unvarying sustained bass note often serving as the tonic in a musical composition
[1]**drool** \ˈdrül\ *vb* [perh. alter. of *drivel*] *vi* **1 a** : to secrete saliva in anticipation of food **b** : DRIVEL 1 **2** : to make an effusive show of pleasure **3** : to talk nonsense ~ *vt* : to express sentimentally or effusively
[2]**drool** *n* : DRIVEL
[1]**droop** \ˈdrüp\ *vb* [ME *drupen*, fr. ON *drūpa*; akin to OE *dropa* drop — more at DROP] *vi* **1** : to hang or incline downward **2** : to sink gradually **3** : to become depressed or weakened : LANGUISH ~ *vt* : to let droop — **droop·ing·ly** \ˈdrü-piŋ-lē\ *adv*
[2]**droop** *n* : the condition or appearance of drooping
droopy \ˈdrü-pē\ *adj* **droop·i·er; -est** **1** : drooping or tending to droop **2** : GLOOMY
[1]**drop** \ˈdräp\ *n, often attrib* [ME, fr. OE *dropa*; akin to Goth *driusan* to fall — more at DREARY] **1 a** (1) : the quantity of fluid that falls in one spherical mass (2) *pl* : a dose of medicine measured by drops; *specif* : a solution for dilating the pupil of the eye **b** : a minute quantity or degree of something nonmaterial or intangible **c** : a small quantity of drink **d** : the smallest practical unit of liquid measure **2** : something that resembles a liquid drop: as **a** : a pendent ornament attached to a piece of jewelry; *also* : an earring with such a pendant **b** : a small globular cookie or candy **3** [[2]*drop*] **a** : the act or an instance of dropping : FALL **b** : a decline in quantity or quality **c** : a descent by parachute; *also* : the men or equipment dropped by parachute **d** : a central point or depository to which something (as mail) is brought for distribution or transmission **e** : a place used for the deposit and distribution of stolen or illegal goods **4 a** : the distance from a higher to a lower level or through which something drops **b** : a fall of electric potential **5** : a slot into which something is to be dropped **6** [[2]*drop*] : something that drops, hangs, or falls: as **a** : a movable plate that covers the keyhole of a lock **b** : an unframed piece of cloth stage scenery; *also* : DROP CURTAIN **c** : a hinged platform on a gallows **d** : a fallen fruit **7** : the advantage of having an opponent covered with a firearm; *broadly* : ADVANTAGE, SUPERIORITY — usu. used in the phrase *get the drop on*
[2]**drop** *vb* **dropped; drop·ping** *vi* **1** : to fall in drops **2 a** (1) : to fall unexpectedly or suddenly (2) : to descend from one line or level to another **b** : to fall in a state of collapse or death **c** *of a card* : to become played by reason of the obligation to follow suit **d** *of a ball* : to roll into a hole or basket **3** : to move with a favoring wind or current — usu. used with *down* **4** : to enter as if without conscious effort of will into some state, condition, or activity ⟨*dropped* into sleep⟩ **5 a** : to cease to be of concern : LAPSE ⟨let the matter ~⟩ **b** to become less ⟨production *dropped*⟩ — often used with *off* ~ *vt* **1** : to let fall : cause to fall **2 a** : to lower or cause to descend from one level or position to another **b** : to lower (wheels) in preparation for landing an airplane **c** : to cause to lessen or decrease : REDUCE ⟨*dropped* his speed⟩ **3** : to set down from a ship or vehicle : UNLOAD; *also* : AIR-DROP **4** : to cause (the voice) to be less loud **5 a** : to bring down with a shot or a blow **b** : to cause (a high card) to fall **c** : to toss or roll (a ball) into a hole or basket **6 a** : to give up (as an idea) **b** : to leave incomplete ⟨*dropped* what he was doing⟩ **c** : to break off an association or connection with : DISMISS ⟨~ a failing student⟩ **7 a** : to leave (a letter representing a speech sound) unsounded ⟨~ the g in *running*⟩ **b** : to leave out in writing **8 a** : to utter or mention in a casual way ⟨~ a suggestion⟩ **b** : WRITE ⟨~ us a line soon⟩ **9** *of an animal* : to give birth to **10** : LOSE ⟨*dropped* 3 games⟩ ⟨*dropped* $50 in a poker game⟩ **11** : to take (a drug) orally : SWALLOW ⟨~ acid⟩ — **drop back** **1** : to move toward the rear of an advancing line or column **2** : to move straight back from the line of scrimmage — used of a back in football — **drop behind** : to fail to keep up — **drop by** : to pay a brief casual visit — **drop in** : to pay an unexpected visit
drop cloth *n* : a protective sheet (as of cloth or plastic) used esp. by painters to cover floors and furniture
drop curtain *n* : a stage curtain that can be lowered and raised
drop–forge \ˈdräp-ˈfō(ə)rj, -ˈfȯ(ə)rj\ *vt* : to forge between dies by a drop hammer or punch press — **drop forger** *n*
drop forging *n* : a forging made by the force of a dropped weight
drop front *n* : a hinged cover on the front of a desk that may be lowered to provide a surface for writing
drop hammer *n* : a power hammer raised and then released to drop (as on metal resting on an anvil or die)
drop·head \ˈdräp-ˌhed\ *n* **1** : a device for a desk or table that enables an attached typewriter or sewing machine to be swung or dropped down to leave a flat table top **2** *Brit* : a convertible automobile
drop–in \ˈdräp-ˌin\ *n* **1** : one who drops in : a casual visitor **2** : an informal social gathering at which guests are invited to drop in
drop·kick \-ˈkik\ *n* : a kick made by dropping a football to the ground and kicking it at the moment it starts to rebound
drop–kick \-ˈkik\ *vi* : to make a dropkick ~ *vt* : to score (a goal) with a dropkick — **drop·kick·er** *n*
drop leaf *n* : a hinged leaf on the side or end of a table that can be folded down
drop·let \ˈdräp-lət\ *n* : a tiny drop (as of a liquid)
droplet infection *n* : infection transmitted by airborne droplets of sputum containing infectious organisms
drop letter *n* : a letter to be delivered from the office where mailed
drop·light \ˈdräp-ˌlīt\ *n* : an electric light suspended by a cord
drop–off \ˈdräp-ˌȯf\ *n* **1** : a very steep or perpendicular descent **2** : a marked dwindling or decline ⟨a ~ in attendance⟩
drop off \dräp-ˈȯf\ *vi* : to fall asleep
drop·out \ˈdräp-ˌau̇t\ *n* **1** : one who drops out of school **2** : one who drops out of conventional society **3** : a spot on a magnetic tape from which data has disappeared
drop out \dräp-ˈau̇t\ *vi* : to withdraw from participation or membership : QUIT; *esp* : to withdraw from conventional society because of disenchantment with its values and mores
drop·page \ˈdräp-ij\ *n* : the part of a fruit crop that falls from the tree before it is ready for picking
drop pass *n* : a pass in ice hockey in which the dribbler skates past the puck leaving it for a teammate following close behind
dropped egg *n* : a poached egg
drop·per \ˈdräp-ər\ *n* **1** : one that drops **2** : a short glass tube fitted with a rubber bulb and used to measure liquids by drops — called also *eyedropper, medicine dropper* — **drop·per·ful** \-ˌfu̇l\ *n*
drop·ping *n* **1** : something dropped **2** *pl* : animal dung
drop seat *n* **1** : a hinged seat (as in a taxi) that may be dropped down **2** : a seat (as in an undergarment) that falls down when unbuttoned
drop·shot \ˈdräp-ˌshät\ *n* : a delicately hit ball or shuttlecock (as in tennis, badminton, or rackets) that drops quickly after crossing the net or dies after hitting a wall
drop·si·cal \ˈdräp-si-kəl\ *adj* **1** : relating to or affected with dropsy **2** : TURGID, SWOLLEN — **drop·si·cal·ly** \-k(ə-)lē\ *adv* — **drop·si·cal·ness** \-kəl-nəs\ *n*
drop·sonde \ˈdräp-ˌsänd\ *n* [*drop* + radio*sonde*] : a radiosonde dropped by parachute from a high-flying airplane
drop·sy \ˈdräp-sē\ *n* [ME *dropesie*, short for *ydropesie*, fr. OF, fr. L *hydropisis*, modif. of Gk *hydrōps*, fr. *hydōr* water — more at WATER] : EDEMA
drop zone *n* : the area in which troops, supplies, or equipment are to be air-dropped; *also* : the target on which a skydiver lands
dros·era \ˈdräs-ə-rə\ *n* [NL, genus name, fr. Gk, fem. of *droseros* dewy, fr. *drosos* dew] : SUNDEW

drosh·ky \'dräsh-kē\ *also* **dros·ky** \'dräs-kē\ *n, pl* **droshkies** *also* **droskies** [Russ *drozhki,* fr. *droga* pole of a wagon] : any of various 2- or 4-wheeled carriages used esp. in Russia

dro·soph·i·la \drō-'säf-ə-lə\ *n* [NL, genus name, fr. Gk *drosos* + NL *-phila,* fem. of *-philus* -phil] : any of a genus (*Drosophila*) of small two-winged flies used in genetic research

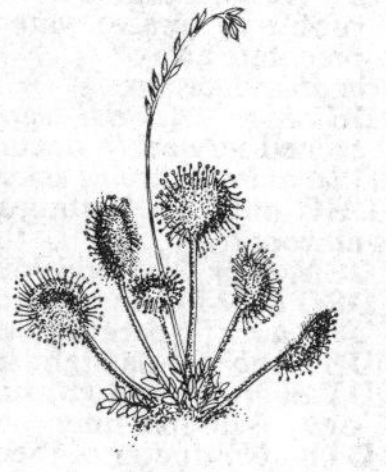

drosera

dross \'dräs, 'drȯs\ *n* [ME *dros,* fr. OE *drōs* dregs] **1** : the scum that forms on the surface of molten metal **2** : waste or foreign matter : IMPURITY — **drossy** \-ē\ *adj*

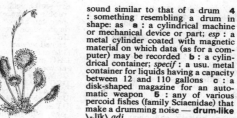

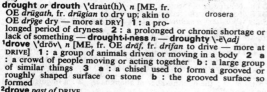

drought *or* **drouth** \'draůt(h)\ *n* [ME, fr. OE *drūgath,* fr. *drūgian* to dry up; akin to OE *drȳge* dry — more at DRY] **1** : a prolonged period of dryness **2** : a prolonged or chronic shortage or lack of something — **drought·i·ness** *n* — **droughty** \-ē\ *adj*

¹drove \'drōv\ *n* [ME, fr. OE *drāf,* fr. *drīfan* to drive — more at DRIVE] **1** : a group of animals driven or moving in a body **2** **a** : a crowd of people moving or acting together **b** : a large group of similar things **3** **a** : a chisel used to form a grooved or roughly shaped surface on stone **b** : the grooved surface so formed

²drove *past of* DRIVE

drov·er \'drō-vər\ *n* : one that drives cattle or sheep

drown \'draůn\ *or substand* **drownd** \'draůnd\ *vb* **drowned** \'draůnd\ *or substand* **drownd·ed** \'draůn-dəd\; **drown·ing** \'draů-niŋ\ *or substand* **drownd·ing** \'draůn-diŋ\ [ME *drounen*] *vi* : to become drowned ~ *vt* **1** **a** : to suffocate by submersion esp. in water **b** : to submerge esp. by a rise in the water level **c** : to wet thoroughly ⟨~*ed* the french fries with catsup⟩ **2** : to engage (oneself) deeply and strenuously ⟨~*ed* himself in work⟩ **3** : to cause (a sound) not to be heard by making a loud noise ⟨his speech was ~*ed* out by . . . boos —*New Yorker*⟩ **4** : to drive out (as a sensation or an idea) ⟨~*ed* his sorrows in liquor⟩

¹drowse \'draůz\ *vb* **drowsed; drows·ing** [prob. akin to Goth *driusan* to fall — more at DREARY] *vi* **1** : to fall into a light slumber **2** : to be inactive ~ *vt* **1** : to make drowsy or inactive **2** : to pass (time) drowsily or in drowsing

²drowse *n* : the act or an instance of drowsing : DOZE

drowsy \'draů-zē\ *adj* **drows·i·er; -est** **1** **a** : ready to fall asleep **b** : tending to induce drowsiness **c** : INDOLENT, LETHARGIC **2** : giving the appearance of peaceful inactivity **syn** see SLEEPY — **drows·i·ly** \-zə-lē\ *adv* — **drows·i·ness** \-zē-nəs\ *n*

drub \'drəb\ *vb* **drubbed; drub·bing** [perh. fr. Ar *daraba*] *vt* **1** : to beat severely (as with a cudgel) **2** : to abuse with words : BERATE ⟨the book was *drubbed* by every critic⟩ **3** : to defeat decisively ~ *vi* : DRUM, STAMP — **drub·ber** *n*

¹drudge \'drəj\ *vb* **drudged; drudg·ing** [ME *druggen;* prob. akin to OE *drēogan* to work, endure, L *firmus* firm] *vi* : to do hard, menial, or monotonous work ~ *vt* : to force to do hard, menial, or monotonous work — **drudg·er** *n*

²drudge *n* **1** : one who is obliged to do menial work **2** : one whose work is routine and boring

drudg·ery \'drəj-(ə-)rē\ *n, pl* **-er·ies** : dull, irksome, and distasteful work : uninspiring or menial labor **syn** see WORK

drudg·ing \'drəj-iŋ\ *adj* : MONOTONOUS, TIRING — **drudg·ing·ly** \-iŋ-lē\ *adv*

¹drug \'drəg\ *n* [ME *drogge*] **1** **a** *obs* : a substance used in dyeing or chemical operations **b** : a substance used as a medication or in the preparation of medication **c** *according to the Food, Drug, and Cosmetic Act* (1) : a substance recognized in an official pharmacopoeia or formulary (2) : a substance intended for use in the diagnosis, cure, mitigation, treatment, or prevention of disease (3) : a substance other than food intended to affect the structure or function of the body (4) : a substance intended for use as a component of a medicine but not a device or a component, part, or accessory of a device **2** : a commodity that is not salable or for which there is no demand — used in the phrase *drug on the market* **3** : a substance that causes addiction or habituation

²drug *vb* **drugged; drug·ging** *vt* **1** : to affect with a drug; *esp* : to stupefy by a narcotic drug **2** : to administer a drug to **3** : to lull or stupefy as if with a drug ~ *vi* : to take drugs for narcotic effect

drug·get \'drəg-ət\ *n* [MF *droguet,* dim. of *drogue* trash, drug] **1** : a wool or partly wool fabric formerly used for clothing **2** : a coarse durable cloth used chiefly as a floor covering **3** : a rug having a cotton warp and a wool filling

drug·gist \'drəg-əst\ *n* : one who sells or dispenses drugs and medicines: as **a** : PHARMACIST **b** : one who owns or manages a drugstore

drug·mak·er \'drəg-,mā-kər\ *n* : one that manufactures pharmaceuticals

drug·store \-,stō(ə)r, -,stȯ(ə)r\ *n* : a retail store where medicines and miscellaneous articles (as food, cosmetics, and film) are sold : PHARMACY

drugstore cowboy *n* **1** : one who wears cowboy clothes but has had no experience as a cowboy **2** : one who loafs on street corners and in drugstores

dru·id \'drü-əd\ *n, often cap* [L *druides, druidae,* pl. fr. Gaulish *druides;* akin to OE *trēow* tree] : one of an ancient Celtic priesthood appearing in Irish and Welsh sagas and Christian legends as magicians and wizards — **dru·id·ess** \-əs\ *n, often cap* — **dru·id·ic** \drü-'id-ik\ *or* **dru·id·i·cal** \-i-kəl\ *adj, often cap*

dru·id·ism \'drü-ə-,diz-əm\ *n, often cap* : the system of religion, philosophy, and instruction of the druids

¹drum \'drəm\ *n* [prob. fr. D *trom;* akin to MHG *trumme* drum] **1** : a percussion instrument usu. consisting of a hollow cylinder with a drumhead stretched over each end that is beaten with a stick or a pair of sticks in playing; *broadly* : a nonmetallic hollow instrument or device beaten to produce a deep-toned rumbling or booming sound **2** : TYMPANIC MEMBRANE **3** : the sound of a drum; *also* : a sound similar to that of a drum **4** : something resembling a drum in shape: as **a** : a cylindrical machine or mechanical device or part; *esp* : a metal cylinder coated with magnetic material on which data (as for a computer) may be recorded **b** : a cylindrical container; *specif* : a usu. metal container for liquids having a capacity between 12 and 110 gallons **c** : a disk-shaped magazine for an automatic weapon **5** : any of various percoid fishes (family Sciaenidae) that make a drumming noise — **drum·like** \-,līk\ *adj*

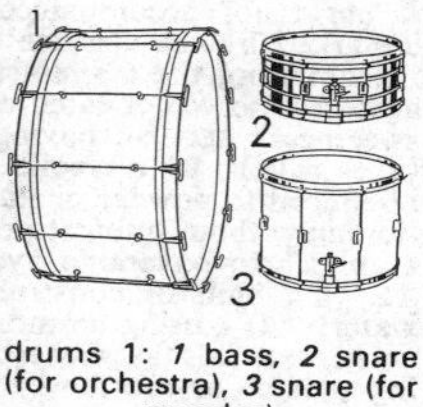

drums 1: *1* bass, *2* snare (for orchestra), *3* snare (for parades)

²drum *vb* **drummed; drum·ming** *vi* **1** : to beat a drum **2** : to make a succession of strokes or vibrations that produce sounds like drumbeats **3** : to throb or sound rhythmically **4** : to stir up interest : SOLICIT ~ *vt* **1** : to summon or enlist by or as if by beating a drum ⟨*drummed* into service⟩ **2** : to dismiss ignominiously : EXPEL — usu. used with *out* **3** : to drive or force by steady effort or reiteration ⟨*drummed* the speech into her head⟩ **4** **a** : to strike or tap repeatedly **b** : to produce (rhythmic sounds) by such action

³drum *n* [ScGael *druim* back, ridge, fr. OIr *druimm*] **1** *chiefly Scot* : a long narrow hill or ridge **2** : DRUMLIN

drum·beat \'drəm-,bēt\ *n* **1** : a stroke on a drum or its sound **2** : a cause advocated vociferously

drum·beat·er \-ər\ *n* : a vociferous supporter of a cause — **drum·beat·ing** \-iŋ\ *n*

drum·fire \'drəm-,fī(ə)r\ *n* **1** : artillery firing so continuous as to sound like a drumroll **2** : something suggestive of drumfire in intensity ⟨a ~ of publicity⟩

drum·head \-,hed\ *n* **1** : the material (as skin or plastic) stretched over each end of a drum **2** : the top of a capstan that is pierced with sockets for the levers used in turning it

drumhead court-martial *n* [fr. the use of a drumhead as a table] : a summary court-martial that tries offenses on the battlefield

drum·lin \'drəm-lən\ *n* [IrGael *druim* back, ridge (fr. OIr *druimm*) + E *-lin* (alter. of *-ling*)] : an elongate or oval hill or glacial drift

drum major *n* : the marching leader of a band

drum ma·jor·ette \,drəm-,mā-jə-'ret\ *n* **1** : a female drum major **2** : a baton twirler who accompanies a marching band

drum·mer \'drəm-ər\ *n* **1** : one that plays a drum **2** : TRAVELING SALESMAN

drum printer *n* : a line printer in which the printing element is a revolving drum

drum·roll \'drəm-,rōl\ *n* : a roll on a drum or its sound

drum·stick \-,stik\ *n* **1** : a stick for beating a drum **2** : the segment of a fowl's leg between the thigh and tarsus

drum up *vt* **1** : to bring about by persistent effort ⟨*drum up* some business⟩ **2** : INVENT, ORIGINATE ⟨*drum up* a new time-saving method⟩

¹drunk *past part of* DRINK

²drunk \'drəŋk\ *adj* [ME *drunke,* alter. of *drunken*] **1** : having the faculties impaired by alcohol **2** : dominated by an intense feeling ⟨~ with power⟩ **3** : of, relating to, or caused by intoxication : DRUNKEN

³drunk *n* **1** : a period of excessive drinking **2** : DRUNKARD

drunk·ard \'drəŋ-kərd\ *n* : one who is habitually drunk

drunk·en \'drəŋ-kən\ *adj* [ME, fr. OE *druncen,* fr. pp. of *drincan* to drink] **1** : DRUNK 1 **2** *obs* : saturated with liquid **3** **a** : given to habitual excessive use of alcohol **b** : of, relating to, or characterized by intoxication ⟨they come from . . . broken homes, ~ homes —P. B. Gilliam⟩ **c** : resulting from or as if from intoxication ⟨a ~ brawl⟩ **4** : unsteady or lurching as if from alcoholic intoxication — **drunk·en·ly** *adv* — **drunk·en·ness** \-kən-nəs\ *n*

drunk·o·me·ter \,drəŋ-'käm-ət-ər, 'drəŋ-kə-,mēt-\ *n* : a device for measuring alcohol content of the blood by chemical analysis of the breath

dru·pa·ceous \drü-'pā-shəs\ *adj* **1** : of or relating to a drupe **2** : bearing drupes

drupe \'drüp\ *n* [NL *drupa,* fr. L overripe olive, fr. Gk *dryppa* olive] : a one-seeded indehiscent fruit having a hard bony endocarp, a fleshy mesocarp, and a thin exocarp that is flexible (as in the cherry) or dry and almost leathery (as in the almond)

drupe·let \'drü-plət\ *n* : a small drupe; *specif* : one of the individual parts of an aggregate fruit (as the raspberry)

druth·ers \'drəth-ərz\ *n pl* [*druther,* alter. of *would rather*] *dial* : free choice : PREFERENCE — used in the phrase *if one had one's druthers*

Druze *or* **Druse** \'drüz\ *n* [Ar *Durūz,* pl., fr. Muḥammed ibn-Ism'aīlal-*Darazīy* †1019 Muslim religious leader] : a member of a religious sect originating among Muslims and centered in the mountains of Lebanon and Syria

¹dry \'drī\ *adj* **dri·er** \'drī(-ə)r\; **dri·est** \'drī-əst\ [ME, fr. OE *drȳge;* akin to OHG *truckan* dry] **1** **a** : free or relatively free from a liquid and esp. water **b** : not being in or under water ⟨~ land⟩ **c** : lacking precipitation or humidity ⟨~ climate⟩ **2** **a** : characterized by exhaustion of a supply of water or liquid ⟨a ~ well⟩ ⟨the fountain pen ran ~⟩ **b** : devoid of running water ⟨a ~ ravine⟩ **c** : devoid of natural moisture ⟨my throat was ~ after the long hike⟩ **d** : no longer sticky or damp ⟨the paint is ~⟩ **e** : not giving milk ⟨a ~ cow⟩ **f** : lacking freshness : STALE **g** : ANHYDROUS **3** **a** : marked by the absence or scantiness of secretions ⟨a ~ cough⟩ **b** : not shedding or accompanied by tears ⟨a ~ sob⟩

ə abut ᵊ kitten ər further a back ā bake ä cot, cart
aů out ch chin e less ē easy g gift i trip ī life
j joke ŋ sing ō flow ȯ flaw ȯi coin th thin t͟h this
ü loot ů foot y yet yü few yů furious zh vision

4 *obs* : not accompanied by bloodshed or drowning **5 a** : marked by the absence of alcoholic beverages ⟨a ~ party⟩ **b** : prohibiting the manufacture or distribution of alcoholic beverages **6** : served or eaten without butter ⟨~ toast⟩ **7 a** : lacking sweetness : SEC **b** : having all or most sugar fermented to alcohol ⟨a ~ wine⟩ **8 a** : solid as opposed to liquid ⟨~ groceries⟩ **b** : reduced to powder or flakes : DEHYDRATED ⟨~ milk⟩ **9** : functioning without lubrication ⟨a ~ clutch⟩ **10** *of natural gas* : containing no recoverable hydrocarbon (as gasoline) **11** : SLACK 6 **12 a** : built or constructed without a process which requires water: (1) : using no mortar ⟨~ masonry⟩ (2) : using prefabricated materials (as plasterboard) rather than a construction involving plaster or mortar ⟨~ wall construction⟩ **b** : requiring no liquid in preparation or operation ⟨a ~ copy of the page⟩ **13 a** : not showing or communicating warmth, enthusiasm, or tender feeling : SEVERE ⟨a ~ style of painting⟩ **b** : WEARISOME, UNINTERESTING ⟨~ passages of description⟩ **c** : lacking embellishment : PLAIN ⟨the ~ facts⟩ **14 a** : not yielding what is expected or desired : UNPRODUCTIVE **b** : having no personal bias or emotional concern ⟨the ~ light of reason⟩ **c** : RESERVED, ALOOF **15** : marked by matter-of-fact, ironic, or terse manner of expression ⟨~ wit⟩ **16** : lacking smooth sound qualities ⟨a ~ rasping voice⟩ **17** : being a dry run ⟨a ~ rehearsal⟩ — **dry·ly** *adv* — **dry·ness** *n*
syn DRY, ARID *shared meaning element* : lacking or deficient in moisture **ant** wet

²dry *vb* **dried; dry·ing** *vt* : to make dry ~ *vi* : to become dry — **dry·able** \'drī-ə-bəl\ *adj*
³dry *n, pl* **drys 1** : the condition of being dry : DRYNESS **2** : something dry; *esp* : a dry place **3** : PROHIBITIONIST
dry·ad \'drī-əd, -,ad\ *n* [L *dryad-, dryas,* fr. Gk, fr. *drys* tree — more at TREE] : WOOD NYMPH
dry-as-dust \'drī-əz-,dəst\ *adj* : BORING — **dryasdust** *n*
dry cell *n* : a battery whose contents are not spillable
dry-clean \'drī-,klēn\ *vt* : to subject to dry cleaning ~ *vi* : to undergo dry cleaning — **dry-clean·able** \-,klē-nə-bəl\ *adj*
dry cleaner *n* : one that does dry cleaning
dry cleaning *n* **1** : the cleansing of fabrics with substantially nonaqueous organic solvents **2** : something that is dry-cleaned
dry–dock *vt* : to place in a dry dock
dry dock *n* : a dock that can be kept dry for use during the construction or repairing of ships
dry·er *var of* DRIER
dry farming *n* : farming that is engaged in on nonirrigated land with little rainfall and that relies on moisture-conserving tillage and drought-resistant crops — **dry farm** *n* — **dry–farm** *vt* — **dry farmer** *n*
dry fly *n* : an artificial angling fly designed to float upon the surface of the water
dry gangrene *n* : gangrene that develops in the presence of arterial obstruction, is sharply localized, and is characterized by dryness of the dead tissue which is sharply demarcated from adjacent tissue by a line of inflammation
dry goods \'drī-,gŭdz\ *n pl* : textiles, ready-to-wear clothing, and notions as distinguished esp. from hardware and groceries
dry ice *n* : solidified carbon dioxide usu. in the form of blocks that at −78.5°C changes directly to a gas and that is used chiefly as a refrigerant
drying oil *n* : an oil (as linseed oil) that changes readily to a hard tough elastic substance when exposed in a thin film to air
dry kiln *n* : a heated chamber for drying and seasoning cut lumber
dry·lot \'drī-,lät\ *n* : an enclosure of limited size usu. free of vegetation and used for fattening livestock
dry measure *n* : a series of units of capacity for dry commodities — see METRIC SYSTEM table, WEIGHT table
dry mop *n* : a long-handled mop for dusting floors — called also *dust mop*
dry–nurse *vt* **1** : to act as dry nurse to **2** : to give unnecessary supervision to
dry nurse *n* : a nurse who takes care of but does not breast-feed another woman's baby
dryo·pith·e·cine \,drī-ō-'pith-ə-,sīn\ *n* [deriv. of Gk *drys* tree + *pithēkos* ape] : any of a subfamily (Dryopithecinae) of Miocene and Pliocene Old World anthropoid apes sometimes regarded as ancestors of both man and modern anthropoids — **dryopithecine** *adj*
dry out *vi* : to take a cure for alcoholism
dry pleurisy *n* : pleurisy in which exudation is mainly fibrinous
dry–point \'drī-,pöint\ *n* : an engraving made with a steel or jeweled point instead of a burin directly into the metal plate without the use of acid as in etching; *also* : a print made from such an engraving
dry–rot *vt* : to affect with dry rot ~ *vi* : to become affected with dry rot
dry rot *n* **1 a** : a decay of seasoned timber caused by fungi that consume the cellulose of wood leaving a soft skeleton which is readily reduced to powder **b** : a fungous rot of plant tissue in which the affected areas are dry and often firmer than normal or more or less mummified **2** : a fungus causing dry rot **3** : decay from within caused esp. by resistance to new forces ⟨art . . . infected by the *dry rot* of formalism —D. G. Mandelbaum⟩
dry run *n* **1** : a practice firing without ammunition **2** : a practice exercise : REHEARSAL, TRIAL
dry–salt·er \'drī-,sòl-tər\ *n, Brit* : a dealer in crude dry chemicals and dyes — **dry–salt·ery** \-tə-rē\ *n, Brit*
dry–shod \'drī-'shäd\ *adj* : having dry shoes or feet
dry socket *n* : a tooth socket in which after extraction a blood clot fails to form or disintegrates without organizing
dry up *vi* **1** : to disappear as if by evaporation, draining, or cutting off of a source of supply **2** : to wither or die through gradual loss of vitality **3** : to stop talking ⟨wished his buddy would *dry up*⟩
dry wash *n* **1** : laundry washed and dried but not ironed **2** *West* : WASH 3d

dry well *n* : a hole made in porous ground and filled with gravel or rubble to receive water (as drainage from a roof) and allow it to percolate away
ds *abbr* decistere
DS *abbr* **1** [It *dal segno*] from the sign **2** days after sight **3** detached service **4** document signed **5** drop siding
DSc *abbr* doctor of science
DSC *abbr* **1** Distinguished Service Cross **2** doctor of surgical chiropody
DSM *abbr* Distinguished Service Medal
DSO *abbr* Distinguished Service Order
DSP *abbr* [L *decessit sine prole*] died without issue
DST *abbr* **1** daylight saving time **2** doctor of sacred theology
DT *abbr* **1** daylight time **2** delirium tremens **3** doctor of theology **4** double time
DTh *abbr* doctor of theology
DTP *abbr* diphtheria, tetanus, pertussis
d.t.'s \(')dē-'tēz\ *n pl, often cap D&T* : DELIRIUM TREMENS
Du *abbr* Dutch
du·ad \'d(y)ü-,ad\ *n* [irreg. fr. Gk *dyad-, dyas* — more at DYAD] : PAIR
¹du·al \'d(y)ü-əl\ *adj* [L *dualis,* fr. *duo* two — more at TWO] **1** *of grammatical number* : denoting reference to two **2 a** : consisting of two parts or elements or having two like parts : DOUBLE **b** : having a double character or nature — **du·al·ly** \-ə(l)-lē\ *adv*
²dual *n* **1** : the dual number of a language **2** : a linguistic form in the dual
dual citizenship *n* : the status of an individual who is a citizen of two or more nations
du·al·ism \'d(y)ü-ə-,liz-əm\ *n* **1** : a theory that considers reality to consist of two irreducible elements or modes **2** : the quality or state of being dual **3 a** : a doctrine that the universe is under the dominion of two opposing principles one of which is good and the other evil **b** : a view of man as constituted of two irreducible elements — **du·al·ist** \-ləst\ *n* — **du·al·is·tic** \,d(y)ü-ə-'lis-tik\ *adj* — **du·al·is·ti·cal·ly** \-ti-k(ə-)lē\ *adv*
du·al·i·ty \d(y)ü-'al-ət-ē\ *n, pl* **-ties** : DUALISM, DICHOTOMY
du·al·ize \'d(y)ü-ə-,līz\ *vt* **-ized; -iz·ing** : to make dual
dual–purpose *adj* : intended for or serving two purposes ⟨~ cattle bred for milk and meat⟩
dual–purpose fund *n* : a closed-end investment company with two classes of shares one of which is entitled to all dividend income and the other to all gains from capital appreciation
¹dub \'dəb\ *vb* **dubbed; dub·bing** [ME *dubben,* fr. OE *dubbian;* akin to ON *dubba* to dub, OHG *tubili* plug] *vt* **1 a** : to confer knighthood on **b** : to dignify or give new character to **c** : to call by a descriptive name or epithet : NICKNAME **2** : to trim or remove the comb and wattles of **3 a** : to hit (a golf ball) poorly **b** : to execute poorly ~ *vi* : THRUST, POKE — **dub·ber** *n*
²dub *n* : a clumsy person : DUFFER
³dub *n* [ME (Sc dial.) *dubbe*] *chiefly Scot* : POOL, PUDDLE
⁴dub *vt* **dubbed; dub·bing** [by shortening & alter. fr. *double*] **1** : to provide (a motion-picture film) with a new sound track **2** : to add (sound effects) to a film or to a radio or television production — usu. used with *in* **3** : to transpose (sound already recorded) to a new record — **dub·ber** *n*
Dub *abbr* Dublin
dub·bin \'dəb-ən\ *also* **dub·bing** \-ən, -iŋ\ *n* [*dubbing,* gerund of *dub* (to dress leather)] : a dressing of oil and tallow for leather
du·bi·e·ty \d(y)ü-'bī-ət-ē\ *n, pl* **-eties** [LL *dubietas,* fr. L *dubius*] **1** : a usu. hesitant uncertainty or doubt that tends to cause vacillation **2** : a matter of doubt **syn** see UNCERTAINTY **ant** decision
du·bi·os·i·ty \d(y)ü-bē-'äs-ət-ē\ *n, pl* **-ties** : DOUBT
du·bi·ous \'d(y)ü-bē-əs\ *adj* [L *dubius,* fr. *dubare* to vacillate; akin to L *duo* two — more at TWO] **1** : giving rise to doubt : EQUIVOCAL ⟨they felt our scheme a little ~⟩ **2** : unsettled in opinion : UNDECIDED ⟨they were a little ~ about our plan⟩ **3** : of doubtful promise or uncertain outcome ⟨this seemed the most promising of all the ~ solutions proposed⟩ **4** : questionable as to value, quality, or origin ⟨persons of ~ reliability and patriotism⟩ **syn** see DOUBTFUL **ant** reliable, trustworthy — **du·bi·ous·ly** *adv* — **du·bi·ous·ness** *n*
du·bi·ta·ble \'d(y)ü-bət-ə-bəl\ *adj* [L *dubitabilis,* fr. *dubitare* to doubt — more at DOUBT] : open to doubt or question
du·bi·ta·tion \,d(y)ü-bə-'tā-shən\ *n, archaic* : DOUBT
Du·bon·net \,d(y)ü-bə-'nā\ *trademark* — used for an aperitif wine
du·cal \'d(y)ü-kəl\ *adj* [MF, fr. LL *ducalis* of a leader, fr. L *duc-, dux* leader — more at DUKE] : of or relating to a duke or dukedom — **du·cal·ly** \-kə-lē\ *adv*
duc·at \'dək-ət\ *n* [ME, fr. MF, fr. OIt *ducato* coin with the doge's portrait on it, fr. *duca* doge, fr. LGk *douk-, doux* leader, fr. L *duc-, dux*] : a usu. gold coin formerly used in various European countries
du·ce \'dü-(,)chā\ *n* [It *(Il) Duce,* lit., the leader, title of Benito Mussolini, fr. L *duc-, dux*] : LEADER 2c(5)
duch·ess \'dəch-əs\ *n* [ME *duchesse,* fr. MF, fr. *duc* duke] **1** : the wife or widow of a duke **2** : a woman who holds a ducal title in her own right
duchy \'dəch-ē\ *n, pl* **duch·ies** [ME *duche,* fr. MF *duché,* fr. *duc*] : the territory of a duke or duchess : DUKEDOM
¹duck \'dək\ *n, pl* **ducks** *often attrib* [ME *doke,* fr. OE *dūce*] **1** *or pl* **duck a** : any of various swimming birds (family Anatidae, the duck family) in

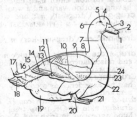

duck: 1 bean, 2 bill, 3 nostril, 4 head, 5 eye, 6 ear, 7 neck, 8 cape, 9 shoulder, 10 coverts, 11 flight coverts, 12 saddle, 13 secondaries, 14 primaries, 15 rump, 16 tail coverts, 17 drake feathers, 18 tail, 19 fluff, 20 shank, 21 web, 22 breast, 23 wing front, 24 wing bow

which the neck and legs are short, the body more or less depressed, the bill often broad and flat, and the sexes almost always different from each other in plumage **b :** the flesh of any of these birds used as food **2 :** a female duck — compare DRAKE **3** *chiefly Brit* **:** DARLING — often used in pl. but sing. in constr. **4 :** PERSON, CREATURE

²duck *vb* [ME *douken;* akin to OHG *tūhhan* to dive, OE *dūce* duck] *vt* **1 :** to thrust under water **2 :** to lower (as the head) quickly **:** BOW **3 :** AVOID, EVADE ⟨~ the issue⟩ **~** *vi* **1 a :** to plunge under the surface of water **b :** to descend suddenly **:** DIP **2 a :** to move (as the head or body) suddenly **:** DODGE **b :** BOW, BOB **3 :** to evade a duty, question, or responsibility **:** back out — **duck·er** *n*

³duck *n* **:** an instance of ducking

⁴duck *n* [D *doek* cloth; akin to OHG *tuoh* cloth, and perh. to Skt *dhvaja* flag] **1 :** a durable closely woven usu. cotton fabric **2** *pl* **:** light clothes made of duck

⁵duck *n* [*DUKW,* its code designation] **:** an amphibious truck

duck·bill \ˈdək-ˌbil\ *n* **1 :** PLATYPUS **2 :** an edible paddlefish (*Polyodon spathula*) of the Mississippi river and its tributaries

duck·board \-ˌbō(ə)rd, -ˌbȯ(ə)rd\ *n* **:** a boardwalk or slatted flooring laid on a wet, muddy, or cold surface — usu. used in pl.

duck call *n* **:** a device for imitating the calls of ducks

duck-foot·ed \ˈdək-ˈfu̇t-əd\ *adv* **:** with feet pointed outward **:** FLAT-FOOTED

ducking stool *n* **:** a seat attached to a plank and formerly used to plunge culprits tied to it into water

duck·ling \ˈdək-liŋ\ *n* **:** a young duck

duck·pin \-ˌpin\ *n* **1 :** a small bowling pin shorter than a tenpin but proportionately wider at mid-diameter **2** *pl but sing in constr* **:** a bowling game using duckpins

ducks and drakes *or* **duck and drake** *n* **:** the pastime of skimming flat stones or shells along the surface of calm water — **play ducks and drakes with** *or* **make ducks and drakes of :** to use recklessly **:** SQUANDER ⟨*played ducks and drakes with* his money⟩

duck sickness *n* **:** a highly destructive botulism affecting esp. wild ducks in the western U.S.

duck soup *n* **:** something easy to do

duck·weed \ˈdək-ˌwēd\ *n* **:** a small floating aquatic monocotyledonous plant (family Lemnaceae, the duckweed family)

ducky \ˈdək-ē\ *adj* **duck·i·er; -est 1 :** SATISFACTORY, FINE ⟨everything is just ~⟩ **2 :** DARLING, CUTE ⟨a ~ little tearoom⟩

¹duct \ˈdəkt\ *n* [NL *ductus,* fr. ML, aqueduct, fr. L, act of leading, fr. *ductus,* pp. of *ducere* to lead — more at TOW] **1 :** a bodily tube or vessel esp. when carrying the secretion of a gland **2 a :** a pipe, tube, or channel that conveys a substance **b :** a pipe or tubular runway for carrying an electric power line, telephone cables, or other conductors **3 a :** a continuous tube formed in plant tissue by a row of elongated cells that have lost their intervening end walls **b :** an elongated cavity (as a resin canal of a conifer) formed by disintegration or separation of cells **4 :** a layer (as in the atmosphere or the ocean) which occurs under usu. abnormal conditions and in which radio or sound waves are confined to a restricted path — **duct·less** \ˈdək-tləs\ *adj*

²duct *vt* **:** to convey (as a gas) through a duct; *also* **:** to propagate (as radio waves) through a duct

duc·tile \ˈdək-tᵊl, -ˌtīl\ *adj* [MF & L; MF, fr. L *ductilis,* fr. *ductus,* pp.] **1 :** capable of being fashioned into a new form **2 :** capable of being drawn out or hammered thin ⟨~ metal⟩ **3 :** easily led or influenced ⟨the ~ masses⟩ ***syn*** see PLASTIC — **duc·til·i·ty** \ˌdək-ˈtil-ət-ē\ *n*

duct·ing \ˈdək-tiŋ\ *n* **:** a system of ducts; *also* **:** the material composing a duct

ductless gland *n* **:** ENDOCRINE GLAND

duct·ule \ˈdək-(ˌ)t(y)ü(ə)l\ *n* **:** a small duct

duc·tus ar·te·ri·o·sus \ˈdək-təs-är-ˌtir-ē-ˈō-səs\ *n* [NL, lit., arterial duct] **:** a short broad vessel in the fetus that connects the pulmonary artery with the aorta and conducts most of the blood directly from the right ventricle to the aorta bypassing the lungs

¹dud \ˈdəd\ *n* [ME *dudde*] **1** *pl* **a :** CLOTHES **b :** personal belongings **2 a :** FAILURE ⟨the movie proved a box-office ~⟩ **b :** MISFIT **3 :** a bomb or missile that fails to explode

²dud *adj* **:** of little or no worth **:** VALUELESS ⟨~ checks⟩

dud·die *or* **dud·dy** \ˈdəd-ē\ *adj, Scot* **:** RAGGED, TATTERED

dude \ˈd(y)üd\ *n* [origin unknown] **1 :** a man extremely fastidious in dress and manner **:** DANDY **2 :** a city man; *esp* **:** an Easterner in the West **3 :** FELLOW, GUY — **dud·ish** \ˈd(y)üd-ish\ *adj* — **dud·ish·ly** *adv*

du·deen \dü-ˈdēn\ *n* [IrGael *dūidīn,* dim. of *dūd* pipe] **:** a short tobacco pipe made of clay

dude ranch *n* **:** a vacation resort offering activities (as horseback riding) typical of western ranches

¹dud·geon \ˈdəj-ən\ *n* [ME *dogeon,* fr. AF *digeon*] **1** *obs* **:** a wood used esp. for dagger hilts **2 a** *archaic* **:** a dagger with a handle of dudgeon **b** *obs* **:** a haft made of dudgeon

²dudgeon *n* [origin unknown] **:** a fit or state of angry indignation usu. provoked by opposition ⟨she stalked out in a ~ when her plan was rejected⟩ ***syn*** see OFFENSE

¹due \ˈd(y)ü\ *adj* [ME, fr. MF *deu,* pp. of *devoir* to owe, fr. L *debēre* — more at DEBT] **1 :** owed or owing as a debt **2 a :** owed or owing as a natural or moral right ⟨everyone's right to dissent . . . is ~ the full protection of the Constitution —Nat Hentoff⟩ **b :** according to accepted notions or procedures **:** APPROPRIATE **3 a :** satisfying or capable of satisfying a need, obligation, or duty **:** ADEQUATE **b :** REGULAR, LAWFUL ⟨~ proof of loss⟩ **4 :** capable of being attributed **:** ASCRIBABLE — used with *to* ⟨this advance is partly ~ to a few men of genius —A. N. Whitehead⟩ **5 :** having reached the date at which payment is required **:** PAYABLE **6 :** required or expected in the prescribed, normal, or logical course of events **:** SCHEDULED — **due·ness** *n*

²due *n* **:** something due or owed: as **a :** something that rightfully belongs to one ⟨the artist has finally been accorded something of his ~⟩ **b :** a payment or obligation required by law or custom **:** DEBT **c** *pl* **:** FEES, CHARGES

³due *adv* **1** *obs* **:** DULY **2 :** DIRECTLY, EXACTLY ⟨~ north⟩

¹du·el \ˈd(y)ü-əl\ *n* [ML *duellum,* fr. OL, war] **1 :** a combat between two persons; *specif* **:** a formal combat with weapons fought between two persons in the presence of witnesses **2 :** a conflict between antagonistic persons, ideas, or forces

²duel *vb* **du·eled** *or* **du·elled; du·el·ing** *or* **du·el·ling** *vi* **:** to fight a duel **~** *vt* **:** to encounter (an opponent) in a duel — **du·el·er** *n* — **du·el·ist** \ˈd(y)ü-ə-ləst\ *n*

du·el·lo \d(y)ü-ˈel-(ˌ)ō\ *n, pl* **-los** [It, fr. ML *duellum*] **1 :** the rules or practice of dueling **2 :** DUEL

du·en·de \dü-ˈen-(ˌ)dā\ *n* [Sp dial., charm, fr. Sp, ghost, goblin, fr. *duen de casa,* prob. fr. *dueño de casa* owner of a house] **:** the power to attract through personal magnetism and charm

du·en·na \d(y)ü-ˈen-ə\ *n* [Sp *dueña,* fr. L *domina* mistress] **1 :** an elderly woman serving as governess and companion to the younger ladies in a Spanish or a Portuguese family **2 :** CHAPERON — **du·en·na·ship** \-ˌship\ *n*

due process *n* **:** a course of legal proceedings carried out regularly and in accordance with established rules and principles — called also *due process of law*

¹du·et \d(y)ü-ˈet\ *n* [It *duetto,* dim. of *duo*] **:** a composition for two performers

²duet *vi* **du·et·ted; du·et·ting :** to perform a duet

due to *prep* **:** because of

duff \ˈdəf\ *n* [E dial., alter. of *dough*] **1 :** a steamed pudding usu. containing raisins and currants **2 :** the partly decayed organic matter on the forest floor **3 :** fine coal **:** SLACK

duf·fel *or* **duf·fle** \ˈdəf-əl\ *n* [D *duffel,* fr. *Duffel,* Belgium] **1 :** a coarse heavy woolen material with a thick nap **2 :** transportable personal belongings, equipment, and supplies **3 :** DUFFEL BAG

duffel bag *n* **:** a large cylindrical fabric bag for personal belongings

duf·fer \ˈdəf-ər\ *n* [origin unknown] **1 a :** a peddler esp. of cheap flashy articles **b :** something counterfeit or worthless **2 :** an incompetent, ineffectual, or clumsy person **3** *Austral* **:** a cattle rustler

¹dug *past of* DIG

²dug \ˈdəg\ *n* [perh. of Scand origin; akin to OSw *dæggia* to suckle; akin to OE *delu* nipple] **:** UDDER; *also* **:** TEAT — usu. used of a suckling animal but vulgar when used of a woman

du·gong \ˈdü-ˌgäŋ, -ˌgȯŋ\ *n* [NL, genus name, fr. Malay & Tag *duyong* sea cow] **:** an aquatic herbivorous mammal of a monotypic genus (*Dugong*) that has a bilobate tail and in the male upper incisors altered into tusks and that is related to the manatee — called also *sea cow*

dugong

dug·out \ˈdəg-ˌau̇t\ *n* **1 :** a boat made by hollowing out a large log **2 a :** a shelter dug in a hillside; *also* **:** a shelter dug in the ground and roofed with sod **b :** an area in the side of a trench for quarters, storage, or protection **3 :** either of two low shelters on either side of and facing a baseball diamond that contain the players' benches

dui·ker \ˈdī-kər\ *n* [Afrik, lit., diver, fr. *duik* to dive, fr. MD *dūken;* akin to OHG *tūhhan* to dive — more at DUCK] **:** any of several small African antelopes (*Cephalophus* or related genera)

duke \ˈd(y)ük\ *n* [ME, fr. OF *duc,* fr. L *duc-, dux,* fr. *ducere* to lead — more at TOW] **1 :** a sovereign ruler of a continental European duchy **2 :** a nobleman of the highest hereditary rank; *esp* **:** a member of the highest grade of the British peerage **3** *slang* **:** FIST, HAND — usu. used in pl. **4 :** any of several cultivated cherries between sweet cherries and sour cherries in character and prob. of hybrid origin — **duke·dom** \-dəm\ *n*

Du·kho·bor *var of* DOUKHOBOR

dul·cet \ˈdəl-sət\ *adj* [ME *doucet,* fr. MF, fr. *douz* sweet, fr. L *dulcis*] **1 :** sweet to the taste **:** LUSCIOUS **2 a :** sweet to the ear **:** MELODIOUS **b :** AGREEABLE, SOOTHING ⟨could not . . . expect such ~ weather to last —Victoria Sackville-West⟩ — **dul·cet·ly** *adv*

dul·ci·fy \ˈdəl-sə-ˌfī\ *vt* **-fied; -fy·ing** [LL *dulcificare,* fr. L *dulcis*] **1 :** to make sweet **2 :** to make agreeable **:** MOLLIFY

dul·ci·mer \ˈdəl-sə-mər\ *n* [ME *dowcemere,* fr. MF *doulcemer,* fr. OIt *dolcimelo*] **1 :** a stringed instrument of trapezoidal shape played with light hammers held in the hands **2** *or* **dul·ci·more** \-ˌmō(ə)r, -ˌmȯ(ə)r\ **:** an American folk instrument with three or four strings stretched over an elongate fretted sound box held on the lap and played by plucking or strumming

dul·ci·nea \ˌdəl-sə-ˈnē-ə, -ˈsin-ē-ə\ *n* [Sp, fr. *Dulcinea* del Toboso, beloved of Don Quixote] **:** MISTRESS, SWEETHEART

¹dull \ˈdəl\ *adj* [ME *dul;* akin to OE *dol* foolish and prob. to L *fumus* smoke — more at FUME] **1 :** mentally slow **:** STUPID **2 a :** slow in perception or sensibility **:** INSENSIBLE **b :** lacking zest or vivacity **:** LISTLESS **3 a :** slow in action **:** SLUGGISH **b :** marked by little business activity ⟨a ~ season⟩ **4 :** lacking sharpness of edge or point **5 :** lacking brilliance or luster **6 :** lacking in force or intensity: as **a :** not clear **:** INDISTINCT ⟨the kerosine lamp gave a ~ light⟩ **b :** not resonant or ringing ⟨a ~ booming sound⟩ **7** *of a color* **:** low in saturation and low in lightness **8 :** CLOUDY, OVERCAST **9 :** TEDIOUS, UNINTERESTING — **dull·ness** *or* **dul·ness** \ˈdəl-nəs\ *n* — **dul·ly** \ˈdəl-(l)ē\ *adv*

syn* 1** see STUPID ***ant clever, bright

2 DULL, BLUNT, OBTUSE *shared meaning element* **:** not sharp, keen, or acute ***ant*** sharp (*as of an edge or point*), poignant (*as of sensations or emotions*), lively (*as of action or activity*)

ə abut	ᵊ kitten	ər further	a back	ā bake	ä cot, cart
au̇ out	ch chin	e less	ē easy	g gift	i trip	ī life
j joke	ŋ sing	ō flow	ȯ flaw	ȯi coin	th thin	t͟h this
ü loot	u̇ foot	y yet	yü few	yu̇ furious	zh vision

²dull vt : to make dull ⟨eyes and ears ~ed by age⟩ ~ vi : to become dull

dull-ard \'dəl-ərd\ n : one that is stupid or insensitive

dull-ish \'dəl-ish\ adj : somewhat dull — **dull-ish-ly** adv

dulls-ville \'dəlz-ˌvil\ n [¹dull + -sville (as in Huntsville)] slang : something that is dull or boring; also : BOREDOM

dulse \'dəls\ n [ScGael & IrGael duileasg; akin to W delysg dulse] : any of several coarse red seaweeds (esp. Rhodymenia palmata) found esp. in northern latitudes and used as a food condiment

du-ly \'d(y)ü-lē\ adv : in a due manner, time, or degree : PROPERLY

du-ma \'dü-mə, -(ˌ)mä\ n [Russ., of Gmc origin; akin to OE dōm judgment — more at DOOM] : a representative council in Russia; specif : the principal legislative assembly in czarist Russia

¹dumb \'dəm\ adj [ME, fr. OE; akin to OHG tumb mute, OE dēaf deaf — more at DEAF] 1 : devoid of the power of speech ⟨deaf and ~ from birth⟩ 2 : naturally incapable of speech ⟨~ animals⟩ 3 : not expressed in uttered words ⟨~ grief⟩ 4 a : not willing to speak b : not having the usual accompaniment of speech or sound 5 : lacking some usual attribute or accompaniment; esp : having no means of self-propulsion ⟨~ barge⟩ 6 : markedly lacking in intelligence : exasperatingly obtuse syn see STUPID ant articulate — **dumb-ly** \'dəm-lē\ adv — **dumb-ness** n

²dumb vt : to make silent : DEADEN ⟨would lie around, ~ed by the drugs —Norman Mailer⟩

Dumb abbr Dumbartonshire

dumb-bell \'dəm-ˌbel\ n 1 : a short bar with two identical spheres or with adjustable weighted disks attached to each end and used usu. in pairs for calisthenic exercise 2 : one that is dull and stupid : DUMMY

dumb-found or **dum-found** \ˌdəm-'faúnd\ vt [dumb + -found (as in confound)] : to confound briefly and usu. with astonishment syn see PUZZLE

dumb-foun-der or **dum-foun-der** \-'faún-dər\ vt : DUMBFOUND

dumb show n 1 : a part of a play presented in pantomime 2 : signs and gestures without words : PANTOMIME

dumb-struck \'dəm-ˌstrək\ adj : made silent by astonishment

dumb-wait-er \'dəm-ˌwāt-ər\ n 1 : a portable serving table or stand 2 : a small elevator used for conveying food and dishes from one story of a building to another

dum-dum \'dəm-ˌdəm\ n [Dum-Dum, arsenal near Calcutta, India] : a bullet (as one with vertical cuts made in its point) that expands upon hitting an object

Dumf abbr Dumfriesshire

dum-ka \'dúm-kə\ n, pl **dum-ky** \-kē\ [Czech, elegy, of Gmc origin; akin to Goth dōms judgment, OE dōm doom] : a Slavic folk ballad usu. melancholy but often alternately melancholy and gay

dumm-kopf \'dúm-ˌkópf\ n [G, fr. dumm stupid + kopf head] : BLOCKHEAD

¹dum-my \'dəm-ē\ n, pl **dummies** [¹dumb + -y] 1 a : one who is incapable of speaking b : one who is habitually silent : one who is stupid 2 a : the exposed hand in bridge played by the declarer in addition to his own hand b : a bridge player whose hand is a dummy 3 : an imitation, copy, or likeness of something used as a substitute 4 : one seeming to act for himself but in reality acting for or at the direction of another 5 : something usu. mechanically operated that serves to replace or aid a human being's work 6 : a pattern arrangement of matter to be reproduced esp. by printing

²dummy adj 1 a : having the appearance of being real but lacking capacity to function : ARTIFICIAL b : existing in name only : FICTITIOUS ⟨bank accounts held in ~ names⟩ 2 : apparently acting for oneself while really acting for or at the direction of another ⟨a ~ director⟩

³dummy vb **dum-mied; dum-my-ing** vt : to make a dummy of ⟨the book was dummied and ready to go to press⟩ — often used with up ⟨the editor dummied up the front page⟩ ~ vi, slang : to refuse to talk — used with up

dummy variable n : an arbitrary mathematical symbol or variable that can be replaced by another without affecting the value of the expression in which it occurs ⟨the variable of integration in a definite integral is a dummy variable⟩

du-mor-tier-ite \d(y)ü-'mórt-ē-ə-ˌrīt\ n [F dumortiérite, fr. Eugène Dumortier †1876 F paleontologist] : a bright blue or greenish blue mineral consisting of a silicate of aluminum and used esp. for jewelry

¹dump \'dəmp\ vb [perh. fr. D dompen to immerse, topple; akin to OE dyppan to dip — more at DIP] vt 1 a : to let fall in a heap or mass b : to get rid of unceremoniously or irresponsibly c : JETTISON ⟨an airplane ~ing gasoline⟩ 2 slang : to knock down : BEAT ⟨the man rushed out and ~ed him —John Corry⟩ 3 : to sell in quantity at a very low price; specif : to sell abroad at less than the market price at home 4 : to copy (data in a computer's internal storage) onto an external storage medium ~ vi 1 : to fall abruptly : PLUNGE 2 : to dump refuse — **dump-er** n

²dump n 1 a : an accumulation of refuse or other discarded materials b : a place where such materials are dumped 2 a : a quantity of reserve materials accumulated at one place b : a place where such materials are stored; esp : a place for the temporary storage of military supplies in the field ⟨ammunition ~⟩ 3 : a disorderly, slovenly, or dilapidated place 4 : an instance of dumping data stored in a computer

dump-ing n : the act of one that dumps; esp : the selling of goods in quantity at below market price (as to dispose of a surplus or to break down competition) esp. in international trade

dump-ish \'dəm-pish\ adj [dumps] : SAD, MELANCHOLY ⟨remembrances . . . that . . . cheer and uplift the ~ heart of man —Douglas Jerrold⟩

dump-ling \'dəm-plin\ n [perh. alter. of lump] 1 a : a small mass of leavened dough cooked by boiling or steaming b : a dessert made by wrapping fruit in biscuit dough and baking 2 a : one that is shaped like a dumpling b : a short fat person or animal

dumps \'dəm(p)s\ n pl [prob. fr. D domp haze, fr. MD damp] : a gloomy state of mind : DESPONDENCY ⟨in the ~⟩

dump truck n : a motor or hand-propelled truck for transporting and dumping loose materials

dumpy \'dəm-pē\ adj **dump-i-er; -est** [E dial. dump (lump)] : being short and thick in build : SQUAT — **dump-i-ly** \-pə-lē\ adv — **dump-i-ness** \-pē-nəs\ n

dumpy level n : a surveyor's level with a short usu. inverting telescope rigidly fixed and rotating only in a horizontal plane

¹dun \'dən\ adj [ME, fr. OE dunn — more at DUSK] 1 a : having a dun color b of a horse : exhibiting reduced hair pigmentation 2 : marked by dullness and drabness — **dun-ness** \'dən-nəs\ n

²dun n 1 : a dun horse 2 : a variable color averaging a nearly neutral slightly brownish dark gray 3 a : a subadult mayfly; also : an artificial fly tied to imitate such an insect b : CADDIS FLY

³dun vt **dunned; dun-ning** [origin unknown] 1 : to make persistent demands upon for payment 2 : to plague or pester constantly

⁴dun n 1 : one who duns 2 : an urgent request; esp : a demand for payment

Dun-can Phyfe \ˌdən-kən-'fīf\ adj : of, relating to, or constituting furniture designed and built by or in the style of Duncan Phyfe

dunce \'dən(t)s\ n [John Duns Scotus, whose once accepted writings were ridiculed in the 16th cent.] : one who is dull-witted or stupid

dunce cap n : a conical cap formerly used as a punishment for slow learners at school — called also dunce's cap

dun-der-head \'dən-dər-ˌhed\ n [perh. fr. D donder thunder + E head; akin to OHG thonar thunder — more at THUNDER] : DUNCE, BLOCKHEAD — **dun-der-head-ed** \-ˌhed-əd\ adj

dun-drea-ries \ˌdən-'dri(ə)r-ēz\ n pl, often cap [Lord Dundreary, character in the play Our American Cousin (1858), by Tom Taylor] : long flowing sideburns

dune \'d(y)ün\ n [F, fr. OF, fr. MD; akin to OE dūn down — more at DOWN] : a hill or ridge of sand piled up by the wind — **dune-like** \-ˌlīk\ adj

dune buggy n : BEACH BUGGY

dune-land \'d(y)ün-ˌland\ n : an area having many dunes

¹dung \'dən\ n [ME, fr. OE; akin to ON dyngja manure pile, Lith dengti to cover] 1 : the excrement of an animal : MANURE 2 : something repulsive — **dungy** \'dən-ē\ adj

²dung vt : to fertilize or dress with manure

dun-ga-ree \ˌdən-gə-'rē, 'dən-gə-\ n [Hindi dūgrī] 1 : a heavy coarse durable cotton twill woven from colored yarns; specif : blue denim 2 pl : heavy cotton work clothes made usu. of blue dungaree

dung beetle n : a beetle (as a dorbeetle or tumblebug) that rolls balls of dung in which to lay eggs and on which the larvae feed

dun-geon \'dən-jən\ n [ME donjon, fr. MF, fr. (assumed) ML dominion-, dominio, fr. L dominus lord — more at DAME] 1 : DONJON 2 : a dark usu. underground prison or vault

dung-hill \'dən-ˌhil\ n 1 : a heap of dung 2 : something (as a situation or condition) that is repulsive or degraded

du-nite \'dü-ˌnīt, 'dən-ˌīt\ n [Mt. Dun, New Zealand] : a granitoid igneous rock consisting chiefly of olivine — **du-nit-ic** \dü-'nit-ik, ˌdən-'it-ik\ adj

¹dunk \'dənk\ vb [PaG dunke, fr. MHG dunken, fr. OHG dunkōn] vt 1 : to dip (as a piece of bread) into liquid (as milk) while eating 2 : to dip or submerge temporarily in liquid ⟨~ed her in the swimming pool⟩ 3 : to throw (a basketball) into the basket from above the rim ~ vi 1 : to submerge oneself in water 2 : to make a dunk shot in basketball

²dunk n : the act or action of dunking; esp : DUNK SHOT

Dun-ker \'dən-kər\ or **Dun-kard** \-kərd\ n [PaG Dunker, fr. dunke] : a member of the Church of the Brethren or any of several other orig. German Baptist denominations practicing trine immersion and love feasts and refusing to take oaths or to perform military service

dunk shot n : a shot in basketball made by jumping high into the air and throwing the ball down through the basket

dun-lin \'dən-lən\ n, pl **dunlins** or **dunlin** [¹dun + -lin (alter. of -ling)] : a small widely distributed sandpiper (Calidris alpina) largely cinnamon to rusty brown above and white below

dun-nage \'dən-ij\ n [origin unknown] 1 : loose materials used around a cargo to prevent damage; also : padding in a shipping container to protect contents against breakage 2 : BAGGAGE

duo \'d(y)ü-(ˌ)ō\ n, pl **du-os** [It, fr. L, two — more at TWO] 1 : DUET 2 : PAIR

duo- comb form [L duo] : two

duo-de-cil-lion \ˌd(y)ü-ō-di-'sil-yən\ n, often attrib [L duodecim twelve + E -illion (as in million)] — see NUMBER table

duo-dec-i-mal \ˌd(y)ü-ə-'des-ə-məl\ adj [L duodecim — more at DOZEN] : of, relating to, or proceeding by twelve or the scale of twelves — **duodecimal** n

duo-dec-i-mo \-ˌmō\ n, pl **-mos** [L, abl. of duodecimus twelfth, fr. duodecim] : TWELVEMO

duoden- or **duodeno-** comb form [NL, fr. ML duodenum] : duodenum ⟨duodenitis⟩ ⟨duodenogram⟩

du-o-de-num \ˌd(y)ü-ə-'dē-nəm, d(y)ü-'äd-ᵊn-əm\ n, pl **-de-na** \-'dē-nə, -ᵊn-ə\ or **-denums** [ME, fr. ML, fr. L duodeni twelve each, fr. duodecim twelve; fr. its length, about 12 fingers' breadth] : the first part of the small intestine extending from the pylorus to the jejunum — **du-o-de-nal** \-'dē-nᵊl, -'äd-ᵊn-əl\ adj

duo-logue \'d(y)ü-ə-ˌlóg, -ˌläg\ n : a dialogue between two persons

duo-mo \'dwò-(ˌ)mō\ n, pl **duomos** [It — more at DOME] : CATHEDRAL

du-op-o-ly \d(y)ü-'äp-ə-lē\ n, pl **-lies** [duo- + -poly (as in monopoly)] 1 : an oligopoly limited to two sellers 2 : hegemony exercised by two great powers — **du-op-o-lis-tic** \-ˌäp-ə-'lis-tik\ adj

¹dup \'dəp\ vt [contr. of do up] archaic : OPEN

²dup abbr 1 duplex 2 duplicate

¹dupe \'d(y)üp\ n [F, fr. MF duppe, prob. alter. of huppe hoopoe] : one that is easily deceived or cheated : FOOL

²dupe vt **duped; dup-ing** : to make a dupe of : DECEIVE — **dup-er** n

syn DUPE, GULL, TRICK, HOAX *shared meaning element* : to delude by underhand methods or for one's own ends

[3]dupe *n or vb* : DUPLICATE

dup·ery \'d(y)ü-p(ə-)rē\ *n, pl* **-er·ies** **1** : the act or practice of duping **2** : the condition of being duped

du·ple \'d(y)ü-pəl\ *adj* [L *duplus* double — more at DOUBLE] **1** : having two elements **2 a** : marked by two or a multiple of two beats per measure of music ⟨~ time⟩ **b** *of rhythm* : consisting of a meter based on disyllabic feet

[1]du·plex \'d(y)ü-ˌpleks\ *adj* [L, fr. *duo* two + *-plex* -fold — more at TWO, SIMPLE] **1** : DOUBLE, TWOFOLD; *specif* : having two parts that operate at the same time or in the same way ⟨a ~ lathe⟩ **2** : allowing telecommunication in opposite directions simultaneously

[2]duplex *n* : something duplex; *esp* : a two-family house

[3]duplex *vt* : to make duplex

duplex apartment *n* : an apartment having rooms on two floors

du·plex·er \'d(y)ü-ˌplek-sər\ *n* : a switching device that permits alternate transmission and reception with the same radio antenna

[1]du·pli·cate \'d(y)ü-pli-kət\ *adj* [ME, fr. L *duplicatus*, pp. of *duplicare* to double, fr. *duplic-, duplex*] **1 a** : consisting of or existing in two corresponding or identical parts or examples ⟨~ invoices⟩ **b** : being the same as another **2** : being a card game in which players play identical hands in order to compare scores ⟨~ bridge⟩

[2]duplicate *n* **1** : either of two things that exactly resemble or correspond to each other; *specif* : a legal instrument that is essentially identical with another and has equal validity as an original **2** : COPY, COUNTERPART **3** : two copies both alike — used with *in* ⟨typed in ~⟩

[3]du·pli·cate \'d(y)ü-pli-ˌkāt\ *vb* **-cat·ed; -cat·ing** *vt* **1** : to make double or twofold ⟨the walls should be *duplicated* . . . in order to have a second line of defense —J. A. Steers⟩ **2 a** : to make an exact copy of ⟨~ the document⟩ **b** : to be a match for : EQUAL ⟨a feat that can never be *duplicated*⟩ ~ *vi* : to become duplicate : REPLICATE ⟨DNA in chromosomes ~*s*⟩ — **du·pli·ca·tive** \-ˌkāt-iv\ *adj*

du·pli·ca·tion \ˌd(y)ü-pli-'kā-shən\ *n* **1** : the act or process of duplicating : the quality or state of being duplicated **2** : DUPLICATE, COUNTERPART **3** : a chromosomal aberration in which a segment of genetic material is repeated

du·pli·ca·tor \'d(y)ü-pli-ˌkāt-ər\ *n* : one that duplicates; *specif* : a machine for making copies of typed, drawn, or printed matter

du·plic·i·tous \d(y)ü-'plis-ət-əs\ *adj* : marked by duplicity — **du·plic·i·tous·ly** *adv*

du·plic·i·ty \d(y)ü-'plis-ət-ē\ *n, pl* **-ties** **1** : contradictory doubleness of thought, speech, or action; *esp* : the belying of one's true intentions by deceptive words or action **2** : the quality or state of being double or twofold **3** : the technically incorrect use of two or more distinct items (as claims, charges, or defenses) in a single legal action

Dur *abbr* Durham

du·ra·ble \'d(y)u̇r-ə-bəl\ *adj* [ME, fr. MF, fr. L *durabilis*, fr. *durare* to last — more at DURING] : able to exist for a long time without significant deterioration; *also* : designed to be durable ⟨~ goods⟩ ***syn*** see LASTING — **du·ra·bil·i·ty** \ˌd(y)u̇r-ə-'bil-ət-ē\ *n* — **du·ra·ble·ness** \'d(y)u̇r-ə-bəl-nəs\ *n* — **du·ra·bly** \-blē\ *adv*

durable press *n* **1** : the process of treating a fabric with a chemical (as a resin) and heat for setting the shape and for aiding wrinkle resistance **2** : material treated by durable press **3** : the condition of material treated by durable press

du·ra·bles \'d(y)u̇r-ə-bəlz\ *n pl* : consumer goods (as vehicles and household appliances) that are typically used repeatedly over a period of years

du·ral·u·min \d(y)u̇-'ral-yə-mən\ *n* [fr. *Duralumin*, a trademark] : an alloy of aluminum, copper, manganese, and magnesium comparable in strength and hardness to soft steel

du·ra ma·ter \'d(y)u̇r-ə-ˌmāt-ər, -ˌmät-\ *n* [ME, fr. ML, lit., hard mother] : the tough fibrous membrane that envelops the brain and spinal cord external to the arachnoid and pia mater

du·ra·men \d(y)u̇-'rā-mən\ *n* [NL, fr. L, hardness, fr. *durare* to harden — more at DURING] : HEARTWOOD

du·rance \'d(y)u̇r-ən(t)s\ *n* [MF, fr. *durer* to endure] **1** *archaic* : ENDURANCE **2** : IMPRISONMENT — often used in the phrase *durance vile* ⟨after ~ vile of ten days he was released —J. E. Davies⟩

du·ra·tion \d(y)u̇-'rā-shən\ *n* **1** : continuance in time **2** : the time during which something exists or lasts ⟨was in the army for the ~ of the war⟩

dur·bar \'dər-ˌbär, ˌdər-'\ *n* [Hindi *darbār*, fr. Per, fr. *dar* door + *bār* admission, audience] **1** : court held by an Indian prince **2** : a formal reception marked by pledges of fealty given to an Indian or African prince by his subjects or to the British monarch by native princes

du·ress \d(y)u̇-'res\ *n* [ME *duresse*, fr. MF *duresce* hardness, severity, fr. L *duritia*, fr. *durus*] **1** : forcible restraint or restriction **2** : compulsion by threat; *specif* : unlawful constraint

Dur·ham \'dər-əm, 'də-rəm, 'du̇r-əm\ *n* [County *Durham*, England] : SHORTHORN

Durham Rule *n* [Monte *Durham*, 20th cent. Am litigant] : a legal hypothesis under which a person is not judged responsible for a criminal act that is attributed to a mental disease or defect

du·ri·an \'d(y)u̇r-ē-ən, -ē-ˌän\ *n* [Malay] **1** : a large oval tasty but foul-smelling fruit with a prickly rind **2** : an East Indian tree (*Durio zibethinus*) of the silk-cotton family that bears durians

dur·ing \ˌd(y)u̇r-iŋ\ *prep* [ME, fr. prp. of *duren* to last, fr. OF *durer*, fr. L *durare* to harden, endure, fr. *durus* hard; perh. akin to Skt *dāru* wood — more at TREE] **1** : throughout the duration of ⟨swims every day ~ the summer⟩ **2** : at a point in the course of : IN ⟨takes his vacation ~ July⟩

dur·mast \'dər-ˌmast\ *n* [perh. alter. of *dun mast*, fr. [1]*dun* + *mast*] : a European oak (*Quercus sessiliflora* or *Q. petraea*) valued esp. for its dark heavy tough elastic wood

durn \'dərn\, **durned** \'dərn(d)\ *var of* DARN, DARNED

du·ro \'du̇(ə)r-(ˌ)ō\ *n, pl* **duros** [Sp, short for *peso duro* hard peso] : a Spanish or Spanish American peso or silver dollar

du·roc \'d(y)u̇(ə)r-ˌäk\ *n* [*Duroc*, 19th cent. Am stallion] *often cap* : any of a breed of large vigorous red American hogs

du·rom·e·ter \d(y)u̇-'räm-ət-ər\ *n* [L *durus* hard] : an instrument for measuring hardness

dur·ra *also* **du·ra** \'du̇r-ə\ *n* [Ar *dhurah*] : any of several grain sorghums widely grown in warm dry regions

du·rum wheat \ˌd(y)u̇r-əm-, ˌdər-əm-, ˌdə-rəm-\ *n* [NL *durum*, fr. L, neut. of *durus* hard] : a wheat (*Triticum durum*) that yields a glutenous flour used esp. in macaroni and spaghetti — called also *durum*

[1]dusk \'dəsk\ *adj* [ME *dosk*, alter. of OE *dox*; akin to L *fuscus* dark brown, OE *dunn* dun, *dūst* dust] : DUSKY

[2]dusk *vi* : to become dark ~ *vt* : to make dark or gloomy ⟨a gray light ~*ed* the room —William Sansom⟩

[3]dusk *n* **1** : the darker part of twilight esp. at night **2** : darkness or semidarkness caused by the shutting out of light

dusky \'dəs-kē\ *adj* **dusk·i·er; -est** **1** : somewhat dark in color; *specif* : having dark skin **2** : marked by slight or deficient light : SHADOWY — **dusk·i·ly** \-kə-lē\ *adv* — **dusk·i·ness** \-kē-nəs\ *n*

***syn* 1** see DARK

2 DUSKY, SWARTHY, TAWNY *shared meaning element* : tending toward darkness and dullness — used esp. in the description of human appearance ***ant*** light, bright

[1]dust \'dəst\ *n* [ME, fr. OE *dūst*; akin to L *furere* to rage, Gk *thyein*] **1** : fine dry pulverized particles of matter and esp. earth **2** : the particles into which something disintegrates **3 a** : something worthless **b** : a state of humiliation **4 a** : the earth esp. as a place of burial **b** : the surface of the ground **5 a** : a cloud of dust ⟨a thin ~ rising from the hooves —H. V. Morton⟩ **b** : CONFUSION, DISTURBANCE **6** *archaic* : a single particle (as of earth) **7** *Brit* : refuse (as sweepings) ready for collection — **dust·less** \-ləs\ *adj* — **dust·like** \-ˌlīk\ *adj*

[2]dust *vt* **1** *archaic* : to make dusty **2 a** : to make free of dust **b** : to prepare to use again **3 a** : to sprinkle with fine particles **b** : to sprinkle in the form of dust ~ *vi* **1** *of a bird* : to work dust into the feathers **2** : to remove dust **3** : to give off dust

dust·bin \'dəs(t)-ˌbin\ *n, Brit* : a can for trash or garbage

dust bowl *n* : a region that suffers from prolonged droughts and dust storms

dust bowl·er \'dəs(t)-ˌbō-lər\ *n* : a resident of a dust bowl

dust·cov·er \-ˌkəv-ər\ *n* **1** : a cover (as of cloth or plastic) used to protect furniture or equipment from dust **2** : DUST JACKET

dust devil *n* : a small whirlwind containing sand or dust

dust·er \'dəs-tər\ *n* **1** : one that removes dust **2 a** : a lightweight overgarment to protect clothing from dust **b** : a dress-length housecoat **3** : one that scatters fine particles; *specif* : a device for applying insecticidal or fungicidal dusts to crops **4** : DUST STORM

dust·heap \'dəst-ˌ(h)ēp\ *n* **1** : a pile of refuse **2** : a category of forgotten items ⟨the ~ of history —*New Republic*⟩

dust jacket *n* : a paper cover for a book

dust·man \'dəs(t)-mən\ *n, Brit* : a collector of trash or garbage

dust mop *n* : DRY MOP

dust·pan \'dəs(t)-ˌpan\ *n* : a shovel-shaped pan for sweepings

dust storm *n* **1** : a dust-laden whirlwind that moves across an arid region and is usu. associated with hot dry air and marked by high electrical tension **2** : strong winds bearing clouds of dust

dust·up \'dəs-ˌtəp\ *n* : QUARREL, ROW

dust wrapper *n* : DUST JACKET

dusty \'dəs-tē\ *adj* **dust·i·er; -est** **1** : covered or abounding with dust **2** : consisting of dust : POWDERY **3** : resembling dust **4** : lacking vitality : DRY ⟨~ scholarship⟩ — **dust·i·ly** \'dəs-tə-lē\ *adv* — **dust·i·ness** \-tē-nəs\ *n*

dusty miller *n* : any of several plants (as a mullein pink) having ashy-gray or white tomentose leaves

dutch \'dəch\ *adv, often cap* : with each person paying his own way

[1]Dutch \'dəch\ *adj* [ME *Duch*, fr. MD *duutsch*; akin to OHG *diutisc* German, Goth *thiudisko* as a gentile, *thiuda* people, Oscan *touto* city] **1 a** *archaic* : of or relating to the Germanic peoples of Germany, Austria, Switzerland, and the Low Countries **b** : of or relating to the Netherlands or its inhabitants **c** : GERMAN **2 a** *archaic* : of, relating to, or in any of the Germanic languages of Germany, Austria, Switzerland, and the Low Countries **b** : of, relating to, or in the Dutch of the Netherlands **3** : of or relating to the Pennsylvania Dutch or their language — **Dutch·ly** *adv*

[2]Dutch *n* **1 a** *archaic* (1) : any of the Germanic languages of Germany, Austria, Switzerland, and the Low Countries (2) : GERMAN 2 **b** : the Germanic language of the Netherlands **2 Dutch** *pl* **a** *archaic* : the Germanic peoples of Germany, Austria, Switzerland, and the Low Countries **b** *archaic* : people of Germanic descent **c** : the people of the Netherlands **3** : PENNSYLVANIA DUTCH **4** : DANDER ⟨his ~ is up⟩ **5** : DISFAVOR, TROUBLE ⟨in ~ with his boss⟩

Dutch cheese *n* : COTTAGE CHEESE

Dutch clover *n* : WHITE DUTCH CLOVER

Dutch Colonial *adj* : characterized by a gambrel roof with overhanging eaves ⟨four-bedroom house . . . built in *Dutch Colonial* style —William Robbins⟩

Dutch courage *n* : courage due to intoxicants

Dutch door *n* : a door divided horizontally so that the lower or upper part can be shut separately

Dutch elm disease *n* : a disease of elms caused by an ascomycetous fungus (*Ceratostomella ulmi*) and characterized by yellowing of the foliage, defoliation, and death

Dutch hoe *n* : SCUFFLE HOE

ə abut	ᵊ kitten	ər further	a back	ā bake	ä cot, cart
au̇ out	ch chin	e less	ē easy	g gift	i trip	ī life
j joke	ŋ sing	ō flow	ȯ flaw	ȯi coin	th thin	t͟h this
ü loot	u̇ foot	y yet	yü few	yu̇ furious	zh vision

dutch·man \'dəch-mən\ *n* **1** *cap* **a** *archaic* : a member of any of the Germanic peoples of Germany, Austria, Switzerland, and the Low Countries **b** : a native or inhabitant of the Netherlands **c** : a person of Dutch descent **d** : GERMAN 1a, 1b **2** : a device for hiding or counteracting structural defects

Dutch·man's–breech·es \,dəch-mənz-'brich-əz\ *n pl but sing or pl in constr* : a delicate spring-flowering herb (*Dicentra cucullaria*) of the fumitory family occurring in the eastern U.S. and having finely divided leaves and cream-white double-spurred flowers

Dutchman's-breeches

Dutchman's–pipe \-'pīp\ *n, pl* **Dutch·man's–pipes** \-'pīps\ : a vine (*Aristolochia durior*) with large leaves and early summer flowers having the tube of the calyx curved like the bowl of a pipe

Dutch oven *n* **1** : a metal shield for roasting before an open fire **2** : a brick oven in which cooking is done by the preheated walls **3 a** : a cast-iron kettle with a tight cover that is used for baking in an open fire **b** : a heavy pot with a tight-fitting domed cover

dutch treat *adv* : on the basis of a Dutch treat ⟨go *dutch treat*⟩

Dutch treat *n* : a meal or other entertainment for which each person pays his own way

Dutch uncle *n* : one who admonishes sternly and bluntly

du·te·ous \'d(y)üt-ē-əs\ *adj* [irreg. fr. *duty*] : DUTIFUL, OBEDIENT

du·ti·able \'d(y)üt-ē-ə-bəl\ *adj* : subject to a duty ⟨~ imports⟩

du·ti·ful \'d(y)üt-i-fəl\ *adj* **1** : filled with or motivated by a sense of duty ⟨a ~ son⟩ **2** : proceeding from or expressive of a sense of duty ⟨~ affection⟩ — **du·ti·ful·ly** \-f(ə-)lē\ *adv* — **du·ti·ful·ness** \-fəl-nəs\ *n*

du·ty \'d(y)üt-ē\ *n, pl* **duties** [ME *duete,* fr. AF *dueté,* fr. OF *deu* due] **1** : conduct due to parents and superiors : RESPECT **2 a** : obligatory tasks, conduct, service, or functions that arise from one's position (as in life or in a group) **b** : assigned service or business; *specif* : active military service **3 a** : a moral or legal obligation **b** : the force of moral obligation **4** : TAX; *esp* : a tax on imports **5 a** (1) : the work done by a machine under given conditions (2) : a measure of efficiency expressed in terms of the amount of work done in relation to the energy consumed **b** (1) : the service required (as of an electrical machine) under specified conditions of load and rest (2) : functional application : USE; *esp* : use as a substitute ⟨making the word do ~ for the thing —Edward Sapir⟩ **6** : the quantity of irrigation water required to fill the needs of the area of a particular crop ***syn*** see FUNCTION, TASK

du·um·vir \d(y)ü-'əm-vər\ *n* [L, fr. *duum* (gen. of *duo* two) + *vir* man] **1** : one of two Roman officers or magistrates constituting a board or court **2** : one of two men jointly holding power

du·um·vi·rate \-və-rət\ *n* **1** : two people associated in high office **2** : government or control by two people

duve·tyn \'d(y)ü-və-,tēn, 'dəv-,tēn\ *n* [F *duvetine,* fr. *duvet* down, fr. MF, alter. of (assumed) MF *dumet,* dim. of OF *dun, dum* down, fr. ON *dūnn* — more at DOWN] : a smooth lustrous velvety fabric

DV *abbr* **1** [L *Deo volente*] God willing **2** Douay Version

DVM *abbr* doctor of veterinary medicine

DW *abbr* **1** deadweight **2** delayed weather **3** distilled water **4** dust wrapper

1**dwarf** \'dwȯ(ə)rf\ *n, pl* **dwarfs** \'dwȯ(ə)rfs\ *or* **dwarves** \'dwȯ(ə)rvz\ *often attrib* [ME *dwerg, dwerf,* fr. OE *dweorg, dweorh;* akin to OHG *twerg* dwarf] **1** : a person of unusually small stature; *esp* : one whose bodily proportions are abnormal **2** : an animal or plant much below normal size **3** : a small legendary manlike being who is usu. misshapen and ugly and skilled as an artificer **4** : a star (as the sun) of ordinary or low luminosity and relatively small mass and size — **dwarf·ish** \'dwȯr-fish\ *adj* — **dwarf·ish·ly** *adv* — **dwarf·ish·ness** *n* — **dwarf·like** \'dwȯr-,flīk\ *adj* — **dwarf·ness** \'dwȯrf-nəs\ *n*

2**dwarf** *vt* **1** : to restrict the growth of : STUNT ⟨children ~*ed* by malnutrition⟩ **2** : to cause to appear smaller ⟨the other buildings are ~*ed* by the skyscraper⟩ ~ *vi* : to become smaller

dwarf·ism \'dwȯr-,fiz-əm\ *n* : the condition of stunted growth

dwell \'dwel\ *vi* **dwelt** \'dwelt\ *or* **dwelled** \'dweld, 'dwelt\; **dwell·ing** [ME *dwellen,* fr. OE *dwellan* to go astray, hinder; akin to OHG *twellen* to tarry] **1** : to remain for a time **2 a** : to live as a resident **b** : EXIST, LIE **3 a** : to keep the attention directed — used with *on* or *upon* ⟨won't ~ on familiar material⟩ **b** : to expatiate insistently — used with *on* or *upon* ⟨*dwelt* on the weaknesses in this theory⟩ ***syn*** see RESIDE — **dwell·er** *n*

dwell·ing *n* : a building or other shelter in which people live : HOUSE

DWI *abbr* Dutch West Indies

dwin·dle \'dwin-dᵊl\ *vb* **dwin·dled; dwin·dling** \-(d)liŋ, -dᵊl-iŋ\ [prob. freq. of *dwine* (to waste away)] *vi* : to become steadily less : SHRINK ~ *vt* : to make steadily less ***syn*** see DECREASE

dwt *abbr* pennyweight

DX \(')dē-'eks\ *n* : DISTANCE — used of long-distance radio transmission

dy *abbr* **1** delivery **2** deputy **3** duty

Dy *symbol* dysprosium

dy- *or* **dyo-** *comb form* [LL, fr. Gk, fr. *dyo* — more at TWO] : two ⟨*dy*archy⟩

dy·ad \'dī-,ad, -əd\ *n* [LL *dyad-, dyas,* fr. Gk, fr. *dyo*] **1** : PAIR; *specif* : two individuals (as husband and wife) maintaining a sociologically significant relationship **2** : a meiotic chromosome after separation of the two homologous members of a tetrad **3** : an operator indicated by writing the symbols of two vectors without a dot or cross between (as AB) — **dy·ad·ic** \dī-'ad-ik\ *adj* — **dy·ad·i·cal·ly** \-i-k(ə-)lē\ *adv*

dy·ad·ic \dī-'ad-ik\ *n* : a sum of mathematical dyads

Dy·ak *var of* DAYAK

dy·ar·chy \'dī-,är-kē\ *n, pl* **-chies** : a government in which power is vested in two rulers or authorities

dyb·buk \'dib-ək\ *n, pl* **dyb·bu·kim** \,dib-ü-'kēm\ *also* **dybbuks** [LHeb *dibbūq*] : a wandering soul believed in Jewish folklore to enter the body of a man and control his actions until exorcised by a religious rite

1**dye** \'dī\ *n* [ME *dehe,* fr. OE *dēah, dēag;* akin to L *fumus* smoke — more at FUME] **1** : color from dyeing **2** : a soluble or insoluble coloring matter

2**dye** *vb* **dyed; dye·ing** *vt* **1** : to impart a new and often permanent color to esp. by impregnating with a dye **2** : to impart (a color) by dyeing ⟨~*ing* blue on yellow⟩ ~ *vi* : to take up or impart color in dyeing — **dye·abil·i·ty** \,dī-ə-'bil-ət-ē\ *n* — **dye·able** \'dī-ə-bəl\ *adj* — **dy·er** \'dī(-ə)r\ *n*

dyed–in–the–wool \,dīd-ᵊn-thə-'wu̇l\ *adj* : THOROUGHGOING, UNCOMPROMISING ⟨a ~ conservative⟩

dy·er's–broom \'dī(-ə)rz-'brüm, -'bru̇m\ *n, pl* **dyer's–brooms** : WOODWAXEN

dye·stuff \'dī-,stəf\ *n* : DYE 2

dye·wood \-,wu̇d\ *n* : a wood (as logwood or fustic) from which coloring matter is extracted for dyeing

dying *pres part of* DIE

dyke *var of* DIKE

dynam *abbr* dynamics

1**dy·nam·ic** \dī-'nam-ik\ *adj* [F *dynamique,* fr. Gk *dynamikos* powerful, fr. *dynamis* power, fr. *dynasthai* to be able] **1 a** : of or relating to physical force or energy **b** : of or relating to dynamics : ACTIVE **2 a** : marked by continuous usu. productive activity or change ⟨a ~ population⟩ **b** : marked by energy : FORCEFUL ⟨a ~ personality⟩ — **dy·nam·i·cal** \-i-kəl\ *adj* — **dy·nam·i·cal·ly** \-i-k(ə-)lē\ *adv*

2**dynamic** *n* **1** : a dynamic force **2** : DYNAMICS 2

dy·nam·ics \dī-'nam-iks\ *n pl but sing or pl in constr* **1** : a branch of mechanics that deals with forces and their relation primarily to the motion but sometimes also to the equilibrium of bodies **2** : the pattern of change or growth of an object or phenomenon ⟨personality ~⟩ ⟨population ~⟩ **3** : variation and contrast in force or intensity (as in music)

dy·na·mism \'dī-nə-,miz-əm\ *n* **1 a** : a theory that explains the universe in terms of forces and their interplay **b** : DYNAMICS 2 **2** : a dynamic or expansionist quality — **dy·na·mist** \-məst\ *n* — **dy·na·mis·tic** \,dī-nə-'mis-tik\ *adj*

1**dy·na·mite** \'dī-nə-,mīt\ *n* **1** : a blasting explosive that is made of nitroglycerin absorbed in a porous material and that sometimes contains ammonium nitrate or cellulose nitrate; *also* : a blasting explosive that contains no nitroglycerin **2** : one that has explosive force ⟨this letter is ~ —Erle Stanley Gardner⟩ — **dy·na·mit·ic** \,dī-nə-'mit-ik\ *adj*

2**dynamite** *vt* **-mit·ed; -mit·ing** **1** : to blow up with dynamite **2** : to cause the complete failure or destruction of — **dy·na·mit·er** *n*

dy·na·mo \'dī-nə-,mō\ *n, pl* **-mos** [short for *dynamoelectric machine*] **1** : GENERATOR 3 **2** : a forceful energetic individual

dy·na·mom·e·ter \,dī-nə-'mäm-ət-ər\ *n* [F *dynamomètre,* fr. Gk *dynamis* power + F *-mètre* -meter] **1** : an instrument for measuring mechanical force **2** : an apparatus for measuring mechanical power (as of an engine) — **dy·na·mo·met·ric** \-mō-'me-trik\ *adj* — **dy·na·mom·e·try** \-'mäm-ə-trē\ *n*

dy·na·mo·tor \'dī-nə-,mōt-ər\ *n* [*dynamo* + *motor*] : a motor generator combining the electric motor and generator

dy·nap·o·lis \dī-'nap-ə-ləs\ *n* [NGk, fr. *dyna*mikos dynamic (fr. Gk, powerful) + Gk *polis* city — more at POLICE] : a city planned for orderly growth along a major traffic artery

dy·nast \'dī-,nast, -nəst\ *n* [L *dynastes,* fr. Gk *dynastēs,* fr. *dynasthai* to be able, have power] : RULER

dy·nas·ty \'dī-nə-stē *also* -,nas-tē, *esp Brit* 'din-ə-stē\ *n, pl* **-ties** **1** : a succession of rulers of the same line of descent **2** : a powerful group or family that maintains its position for a considerable time — **dy·nas·tic** \dī-'nas-tik\ *adj* — **dy·nas·ti·cal·ly** \-ti-k(ə-)lē\ *adv*

dy·na·tron \'dī-nə-,trän\ *n* [Gk *dynamis* power] : a vacuum tube in which the secondary emission of electrons from the plate results in a decrease in the plate current as the plate voltage increases

dyne \'dīn\ *n* [F, fr. Gk *dynamis*] : the unit of force in the cgs system equal to the force that would give a free mass of one gram an acceleration of one centimeter per second per second

dy·node \'dī-,nōd\ *n* [Gk *dynamis*] : an electrode in an electron tube that functions to produce secondary emission of electrons

dys- *prefix* [ME *dis-* bad, difficult, fr. MF & L; MF *dis-,* fr. L *dys-,* fr. Gk; akin to OE *tō-, te-* apart, Skt *dus-* bad, difficult] **1** : abnormal ⟨*dys*hidrosis⟩ **2** : difficult ⟨*dys*phagia⟩ — compare EU- **3** : impaired ⟨*dys*function⟩ **4** : bad ⟨*dys*logistic⟩ — compare EU-

dys·cra·sia \dis-'krā-zh(ē-)ə\ *n* [NL, fr. ML, bad mixture of humors, fr. Gk *dyskrasia,* fr. *dys-* + *krasis* mixture — more at CRASIS] : an abnormal condition of the body

dys·en·ter·ic \,dis-ᵊn-'ter-ik\ *adj* : of or relating to dysentery

dys·en·tery \'dis-ᵊn-,ter-ē\ *n, pl* **-ter·ies** [ME *dissenterie,* fr. L *dysenteria,* fr. Gk, fr. *dys-* + *enteron* intestine — more at INTER-] **1** : a disease characterized by severe diarrhea with passage of mucus and blood and usu. caused by infection **2** : DIARRHEA

dys·func·tion \(')dis-'fəŋ(k)-shən\ *n* : impaired or abnormal functioning — **dys·func·tion·al** \-shnəl, -shən-ᵊl\ *adj*

dys·gen·e·sis \(')dis-'jen-ə-səs\ *n* [NL] : defective development esp. of the gonads (as in Klinefelter's syndrome or Turner's syndrome)

dys·gen·ic \(')dis-'jen-ik\ *adj* **1** : detrimental to the hereditary qualities of a stock **2** : biologically defective or deficient

dys·gen·ics \-iks\ *n pl but sing in constr* : the study of racial degeneration

dys·lex·ia \dis-'lek-sē-ə\ *n* [NL, fr. *dys-* + Gk *lexis* word, speech] : a disturbance of the ability to read — **dys·lex·ic** \-sik\ *adj*

dys·lo·gis·tic \,dis-lə-'jis-tik\ *adj* [*dys-* + *-logistic* (as in *eulogistic*)] : UNCOMPLIMENTARY — **dys·lo·gis·ti·cal·ly** \-ti-k(ə-)lē\ *adv*

dys·men·or·rhea \(,)dis-,men-ə-'rē-ə\ *n* [NL] : painful menstruation — **dys·men·or·rhe·al** \-'rē-əl\ *or* **dys·men·or·rhe·ic** \-'rē-ik\ *adj*

dys·pep·sia \dis-'pep-shə, -sē-ə\ n [L, fr. Gk, fr. dys- + pepsis diges-tion, fr. peptein, pessein to cook, digest — more at COOK] : INDIGES-TION

¹dys·pep·tic \-'pep-tik\ adj **1** : relating to or having dyspepsia **2** : showing a sour disposition — **dys·pep·ti·cal·ly** \-ti-k(ə-)lē\ adv

²dyspeptic n : a person having dyspepsia

dys·pha·gia \dis-'fā-j(ē-)ə\ n [NL] : difficulty in swallowing — **dys·phag·ic** \-'faj-ik\ adj

dys·pha·sia \dis-'fā-zh(ē-)ə\ n [NL] : loss of or deficiency in the power to use or understand language as a result of injury to or disease of the brain — **dys·pha·sic** \-'fā-zik\ n or adj

dys·pho·nia \dis-'fō-nē-ə\ n [NL] : defective use of the voice — **dys·phon·ic** \-'fän-ik\ adj

dys·pho·ria \dis-'fōr-ē-ə, -'fȯr-\ n [NL, fr. Gk, fr. dysphoros hard to bear, fr. dys- + pherein to bear — more at BEAR] : a state of feeling unwell or unhappy — **dys·phor·ic** \-'fōr-ik, -'fär-\ adj

dys·pla·sia \dis-'plā-zh(ē-)ə\ n [NL] : abnormal growth or devel-opment (as of organs or cells); broadly : abnormal anatomic struc-ture due to such growth — **dys·plas·tic** \-'plas-tik\ adj

dys·pnea \'dis(p)-nē-ə\ n [L dyspnoea, fr. Gk dyspnoia, fr. dyspnoos

short of breath, fr. dys- + pnein, to breathe — more at SNEEZE] : difficult or labored respiration — **dys·pne·ic** \-nē-ik\ adj

dys·pro·si·um \dis-'prō-zē-əm, -zh(ē-)əm\ n [NL, fr. Gk dysprositos hard to get at, fr. dys- + prositos approachable, fr. prosienai to approach, fr. pros- + ienai to go — more at ISSUE] : an element of the rare-earth group that forms highly magnetic compounds — see ELEMENT table

dys·to·pia \(')dis-'tō-pē-ə\ n [NL, fr. dys- + -topia (as in utopia)] : an imaginary place which is depressingly wretched and whose people lead a fearful existence — **dys·to·pi·an** \-pē-ən\ adj

dys·tro·phic \dis-'trō-fik\ adj **1** : relating to or caused by faulty nutrition **2** of a lake : brownish with much dissolved humic mat-ter, a sparse bottom fauna, and a high oxygen consumption

dys·tro·phy \'dis-trə-fē\ n, pl -phies [NL dystrophia, fr. dys- + -trophia -trophy] : imperfect nutrition; specif : any of several neu-romuscular disorders — compare MUSCULAR DYSTROPHY

dys·uria \dish-'(y)ūr-ē-ə, dis-'yūr-\ n [NL, fr. Gk dysouria, fr. dys- + -ouria -uria] : difficult or painful discharge of urine

dz abbr dozen

E

¹e \'ē\ n, pl e's or es \'ēz\ often cap, often attrib **1 a** : the 5th letter of the English alphabet **b** : a graphic representation of this letter **c** : a speech counterpart of orthographic e **2** : the 3d tone of a C-major scale **3 a** : a graphic device for reproducing the letter e **4** : one designated e esp. as the 5th in order or class; specif : the base of the system of natural logarithms having the approximate numerical value 2.71828 **5 a** : a grade rating a stu-dent's work as poor and usu. constituting a conditional pass **b** : a grade rating a stu-dent's work as failing **c** : one graded or rated with an E **6** : something shaped like the letter E

²e abbr, often cap **1** earth **2** east; easterly; eastern **3** edge **4** eldest **5** ell **6** empty **7** end **8** energy **9** erg **10** error **11** excellent

³e symbol **1** charge of an electron **2** eccentricity of a conic section

E symbol **1** einsteinium **2** energy

e- \(')ē, i\ prefix [ME, fr. OF & L; OF, out, forth, away, fr. L, fr. ex-] **1 a** : not ⟨ecarinate⟩ **b** : missing : absent ⟨edental⟩ **2** : out : on the outside ⟨escribe⟩ **3** : thoroughly ⟨evaporize⟩ **4** : forth ⟨eradiate⟩ **5** : away ⟨eluvium⟩

ea abbr each

EA abbr enemy aircraft

¹each \'ēch\ adj [ME ech, fr. OE ǣlc; akin to OHG iogilih each; both fr. a prehistoric WGmc compound whose first and second constituents respectively are represented by OE ā always and by OE gelic alike] : being one of two or more distinct individuals hav-ing a similar relation and often constituting an aggregate

²each pron : each one

³each adv : to or for each : APIECE

each other pron : each of two or more in reciprocal action or rela-tion ⟨looked at each other in surprise⟩

ea·ger \'ē-gər\ adj [ME egre, fr. OF aigre, fr. L acer — more at EDGE] **1 a** archaic : SHARP **b** obs : SOUR **2** : marked by keen, enthusiastic, or impatient desire or interest — **ea·ger·ly** adv — **ea·ger·ness** n

syn EAGER, AVID, KEEN, ANXIOUS, ATHIRST shared meaning element : moved by a strong and urgent desire or interest **ant** listless

eager beaver n : one who is extremely zealous in performing his assigned duties and in volunteering for more

ea·gle \'ē-gəl\ n [ME egle, fr. OF aigle, fr. L aquila] **1** : any of various large diurnal birds of prey of the accipiter family noted for their strength, size, gracefulness, keenness of vision, and powers of flight **2** : any of various esp. emblematic or symbolic figures or representations of an eagle: as **a** : the standard of the ancient Romans **b** : the seal or standard of a nation (as the U.S.) having an eagle as emblem **c** : one of a pair of silver insignia of rank worn by a military colonel or a navy captain **3** : a ten-dollar gold coin of the U.S. bearing an eagle on the reverse **4** : a golf score of two strokes less than par on a hole — compare BIRDIE **5** cap [Fra-ternal Order of Eagles] : a member of a major fraternal order

eagle eye n **1** : the ability to see or observe with exceptional keen-ness **2** : one that sees or observes keenly

eagle ray n : any of several widely distributed large active sting-rays (family Myliobatidae) with broad pectoral fins like wings

ea·glet \'ē-glət\ n : a young eagle

ea·gre \'ē-gər\ n [origin unknown] : a tidal bore

eal·dor·man \'al-dər-mən\ n [OE — more at ALDERMAN] : the chief officer in a district (as a shire) in Anglo-Saxon England

-ean — see -AN

E and OE abbr errors and omissions excepted

¹ear \'i(ə)r\ n [ME ere, fr. OE ēare; akin to OHG ōra ear, L auris, Gk ous] **1 a** : the characteristic vertebrate organ of hearing and equilibrium consisting in the typical mammal of a sound-collecting outer ear separated by a membranous drum from a sound-transmitting middle ear that in turn is separated from a sensory inner ear by membranous fenestrae **b** : any of various organs capable of detecting vibratory motion **2** : the external ear of man and most mammals **3 a** : the sense or act of hearing **b** : acuity of hearing **c** : sensitivity to musical tone and pitch **4** : some-thing resembling a mammalian ear in shape or position: as **a** : a projecting part (as a lug or handle) **b** : either of a pair of tufts of lengthened feathers on the head of some birds **5 a** : sympathetic attention **b** : NOTICE, AWARENESS **6** : a space in the upper corner of a periodical (as a newspaper) usu. containing advertising for the periodical itself or a weather forecast — **by ear** : without reference to or memorization of written music : EXTEMPORANEOUSLY — **in one ear and out the other** : through one's mind without making an impression ⟨everything you say to him goes in one ear and out the other⟩ — **on one's ear** : in or into a state of irritation, shock, or discord ⟨his insults really put me on my ear⟩ ⟨he set the racing world on its ear by breaking 50 world records⟩ — **up to one's ears** : deeply involved : heavily implicated ⟨up to his ears in the conspir-acy⟩

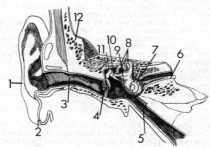

ear 1a: 1 pinna, 2 lobe, 3 auditory meatus, 4 tympanic mem-brane, 5 eustachian tube, 6 auditory nerve, 7 cochlea, 8 semicir-cular canals, 9 stapes, 10 incus, 11 malleus, 12 bones of skull

²ear n [ME er, fr. OE ēar; akin to OHG ahir ear, OE ecg edge — more at EDGE] : the fruiting spike of a cereal (as Indian corn) in-cluding both the seeds and protective structures

³ear vi : to form ears in the course of growing — often used with up ⟨the rye should be ~ing up⟩

ear·ache \'i(ə)r-,āk\ n : an ache or pain in the ear

ear·drop \-,dräp\ n : EARRING; esp : one with a pendant

ear·drum \-,drəm\ n : TYMPANIC MEMBRANE

eared \'i(ə)rd\ adj : having ears esp. of a specified kind or number ⟨a big-eared man⟩ ⟨golden-eared corn⟩

eared seal n : any of a family (Otariidae) of seals including the sea lions and fur seals and having independent mobile hind limbs and small well-developed external ears

ear·flap n : a warm covering for the ears; esp : an extension on the lower edge of a cap that may be folded up or down

---

ə abut	ᵉ kitten	ər further	a back	ā bake ä cot, cart
aù out	ch chin	e less	ē easy	g gift i trip ī life
j joke	ŋ sing	ō flow	ȯ flaw	ȯi coin th thin t͟h this
ü loot	ù foot	y yet	yü few	yù furious zh vision

ear·ful \ˈi(ə)r-ˌfu̇l\ *n* **1 :** an outpouring of news or gossip **2 :** a sharp reprimand
ear·ing \ˈi(ə)r-iŋ\ *n* [perh. fr. [1]*ear*] **:** a line used to fasten a corner of a sail to the yard or gaff or to haul a reef cringle to the yard
earl \ˈər(-ə)l\ *n* [ME *erl,* fr. OE *eorl* warrior, nobleman; akin to ON *jarl* warrior, nobleman] **:** a member of the British peerage ranking below a marquess and above a viscount — **earl·dom** \-dəm\ *n*
ear·less seal \ˌi(ə)r-ləs-\ *n* **:** any of a family (Phocidae, the earless seal family) of seals including the hair seals and having the hind limbs reduced to swimming flippers and no external ears
earlier on *adv* **:** PREVIOUSLY ⟨discussed the matter *earlier on*⟩
earl marshal *n* **:** an officer of state in England serving chiefly as a royal attendant on ceremonial occasions, as marshal of state processions, and as head of the College of Arms
ear·lobe \ˈi(ə)r-ˌlōb\ *n* **:** the pendent part of the ear of man or some fowls
ear·lock \-ˌläk\ *n* **:** a curl of hair hanging in front of the ear
[1]**ear·ly** \ˈər-lē\ *adv* **ear·li·er; -est** [ME *erly,* fr. OE *ǣrlīce,* fr. *ǣr* early, soon — more at ERE] **1 :** near the beginning of a period of time or of a process or series **2 a :** before the usual time **b** *archaic* **:** SOON **c :** sooner than related forms ⟨these apples bear ~⟩
[2]**early** *adj* **ear·li·er; -est 1 a :** of, relating to, or occurring near the beginning of a period of time, a development, or a series **b** (1) **:** distant in past time (2) **:** PRIMITIVE **2 a :** occurring before the usual time **b :** occurring in the near future **c :** maturing or producing sooner than related forms ⟨an ~ peach⟩ — **ear·li·ness** *n*
Early American *n* **:** a style of furniture, architecture, or fabric originating in or characteristic of colonial America
early bird *n* [fr. the proverb, "the early bird catches the worm"] **1 :** an early riser **2 :** one that arrives early and esp. before possible competitors
early on *adv* **:** at or during an early point or stage ⟨the reasons were obvious *early on* in the experiment⟩
ear·ly·wood \ˈər-lē-ˌwu̇d\ *n* **:** SPRINGWOOD
[1]**ear·mark** \ˈi(ə)r-ˌmärk\ *n* **1 :** a mark of identification on the ear of an animal **2 :** a distinguishing mark ⟨all the ~*s* of poverty⟩
[2]**earmark** *vt* **1 a :** to mark (livestock) with an earmark **b :** to mark in a distinguishing manner ⟨dissipation ~*s* a man⟩ **2 :** to designate (as funds) for a specific use or owner
ear·muff \ˈi(ə)r-ˌməf\ *n* **:** one of a pair of ear coverings connected by a flexible band and worn as protection against cold or noises
[1]**earn** \ˈərn\ *vt* [ME *ernen,* fr. OE *earnian*] **1 a :** to receive as return for effort and esp. for work done or services rendered **b :** to bring in by way of return ⟨bonds ~*ing* 10% interest⟩ **2 a :** to come to be duly worthy of or entitled or suited to ⟨he had ~*ed* a promotion by his devotion to duty⟩ **b :** to make worthy of or obtain for ⟨his devotion to duty had ~*ed* him a promotion⟩ ***syn*** see GET — **earn·er** *n*
[2]**earn** *vi* [prob. alter. of *yearn*] *obs* **:** GRIEVE
earned run *n* **:** a run in baseball that scores without benefit of an error before the fielding team has had a chance to make the third putout of the inning
earned run average *n* **:** the average number of earned runs per game scored against a pitcher in baseball determined by dividing the total of earned runs scored against him by the total number of innings pitched and multiplying by nine
[1]**ear·nest** \ˈər-nəst\ *n* [ME *ernest,* fr. OE *eornost;* akin to OHG *ernust* earnest] **:** a serious and intent mental state ⟨in ~⟩
[2]**earnest** *adj* **1 :** characterized by or proceeding from an intense and serious state of mind **2 :** GRAVE, IMPORTANT ***syn*** see SERIOUS ***ant*** frivolous — **ear·nest·ly** *adv* — **ear·nest·ness** \-nəs(t)-nəs\ *n*
[3]**earnest** *n* [ME *ernes, ernest,* fr. OF *erres,* pl. of *erre* earnest, fr. L *arra,* short for *arrabo,* fr. Gk *arrhabōn,* fr. Heb *ʽērābhōn*] **1 :** something of value given by a buyer to a seller to bind a bargain **2 :** a token of what is to come **:** PLEDGE
earn·ings \ˈər-niŋz\ *n pl* **1 :** something earned **2 :** the balance of revenue after deduction of costs and expenses
ear·phone \ˈi(ə)r-ˌfōn\ *n* **:** a device that converts electrical energy into sound waves and is worn over or inserted into the ear
ear pick *n* **:** a device often of precious metal for removing wax or foreign bodies from the ear
ear·piece \ˈi(ə)r-ˌpēs\ *n* **1 :** a part of an instrument (as a stethoscope or hearing aid) to which the ear is applied; *esp* **:** EARPHONE **2 :** one of the two sidepieces that support eyeglasses by passing over or behind the ears
ear·plug \-ˌpləg\ *n* **:** a device of pliable material for insertion into the outer opening of the ear (as for protection against water or to deaden sound)
ear·ring \ˈi(ə)r-(ˌ)iŋ, -ˌriŋ\ *n* **:** an ornament for the earlobe
ear rot *n* **:** a condition of Indian corn that is characterized by molding and decay of the ears and that is caused by fungi (genera *Diplodia, Fusarium,* or *Gibberella*)
ear shell *n* **:** ABALONE
ear·shot \ˈi(ə)r-ˌshät\ *n* **:** the range within which the unaided voice may be heard
ear·split·ting \-ˌsplit-iŋ\ *adj* **:** distressingly loud or shrill
[1]**earth** \ˈərth\ *n* [ME *erthe,* fr. OE *eorthe;* akin to OHG *erda* earth, Gk *eraze* to the ground] **1 :** the fragmental material composing part of the surface of the globe; *esp* **:** cultivable soil **2 :** the sphere of mortal life as distinguished from spheres of spirit life — compare HEAVEN, HELL **3 a :** areas of land as distinguished from sea and air **b :** the solid footing formed of soil **:** GROUND **4** *often cap* **:** the planet on which we live that is third in order from the sun — see PLANET table **5 a :** the people of the planet Earth **b :** the mortal body of man **c :** the pursuits and interests and pleasures of earthly life as distinguished from spiritual concerns **6 :** the lair of a burrowing animal **7 :** a difficultly reducible metallic oxide (as alumina) formerly classed as an element — **earth·like** \-ˌlīk\ *adj*
syn EARTH, WORLD, UNIVERSE *shared meaning element* **:** the entire area in which man thinks of himself as living and acting — **on earth :** among many possibilities — used as an intensive
[2]**earth** *vt* **1 :** to drive to hiding in the earth **2 :** to draw soil about (plants) **3** *chiefly Brit* **:** GROUND 3 ~ *vi, of a hunted animal* **:** to hide in the ground
earth·born \ˈərth-ˌbȯ(ə)rn\ *adj* **1 :** born on this earth **:** MORTAL **2 :** associated with earthly life ⟨~ cares⟩
earth·bound \-ˌbau̇nd\ *adj* **1 a :** fast in or to the soil ⟨~ roots⟩ **b :** restricted to land or to the surface of the earth **2 a :** bound by earthly interests **b :** PEDESTRIAN, UNIMAGINATIVE
earth·en \ˈər-thən, -t͟hən\ *adj* **1 :** made of earth **2 :** EARTHLY
earth·en·ware \-ˌwa(ə)r, -ˌwe(ə)r\ *n* **:** ceramic ware made of slightly porous opaque clay fired at low heat
earth·i·ly \ˈər-thə-lē, -t͟hə-\ *adv* **:** in an earthy manner
earth·ling \ˈərth-liŋ\ *n* **1 :** an inhabitant of the earth **2 :** WORLDLING
earth·ly \ˈərth-lē\ *adj* **1 a :** characteristic of or belonging to this earth **b :** relating to man's actual life on this earth **2 :** POSSIBLE ⟨there is no ~ reason for such behavior⟩ — **earth·li·ness** *n*
syn EARTHLY, TERRESTRIAL, MUNDANE, WORLDLY *shared meaning element* **:** belonging to or characteristic of the earth ***ant*** heavenly
earth mother *n, often cap E & M* **1 :** the earth viewed (as in primitive theology) as the divine source of terrestrial life **2 :** the female principle of fertility
earth·quake \ˈərth-ˌkwāk\ *n* **:** a shaking or trembling of the earth that is volcanic or tectonic in origin
earth science *n* **:** any of the sciences (as geology, meteorology, or oceanography) that deal with the earth or with one or more of its parts
earth·shak·er \ˈərth-ˌshā-kər\ *n* **:** something earthshaking
earth·shak·ing \-kiŋ\ *adj* **:** of fundamental importance — **earth·shak·ing·ly** \-kiŋ-lē\ *adv*
earth·shine \ˈərth-ˌshīn\ *n* **:** sunlight reflected by the earth that illuminates the dark part of the moon — called also *earthlight*
earth·star \-ˌstär\ *n* **:** a globose fungus (genus *Geastrum*) with a double wall whose outer layer splits into the shape of a star
earth·ward \-wərd\ *or* **earth·wards** \-wərdz\ *adv* **:** toward the earth
earth·work \ˈərth-ˌwərk\ *n* **1 :** an embankment or other construction made of earth; *esp* **:** one used as a field fortification **2 :** the operations connected with excavations and embankments of earth
earth·worm \-ˌwərm\ *n* **:** a terrestrial annelid worm (class Oligochaeta); *esp* **:** any of a family (Lumbricidae) of numerous widely distributed hermaphroditic worms that move through the soil by means of setae — see ANNELID illustration
earthy \ˈər-thē, -t͟hē\ *adj* **earth·i·er; -est 1 :** consisting of, resembling, or suggesting earth ⟨an ~ flavor⟩ **2** *archaic* **:** EARTHLY, WORLDLY **3 a :** DOWN-TO-EARTH, PRACTICAL **b :** CRUDE, GROSS ⟨~ humor⟩ — **earth·i·ness** *n*
ear·wax \ˈi(ə)r-ˌwaks\ *n* **:** CERUMEN
[1]**ear·wig** \-ˌwig\ *n* [ME *erwigge,* fr. OE *ēarwicga,* fr. *ēare* ear + *wicga* insect — more at VETCH] **:** any of numerous insects (order Dermaptera) having slender many-jointed antennae and a pair of cerci resembling forceps at the end of the body

earwig

[2]**earwig** *vt* **ear·wigged; ear·wig·ging :** to annoy or attempt to influence by private talk
ear·wit·ness \ˈi(ə)r-ˈwit-nəs\ *n* **:** one who overhears something; *esp* **:** one who gives a report on what he has heard
ear·worm \-ˌwərm\ *n* **:** CORN EARWORM
[1]**ease** \ˈēz\ *n* [ME *ese,* fr. OF *aise* convenience, comfort, fr. L *adjacent-, adjacens* neighborhood, fr. neut. of prp. of *adjacēre* to lie near — more at ADJACENT] **1 :** the state of being comfortable: as **a :** freedom from pain or discomfort **b :** freedom from care **c :** freedom from labor or difficulty **d :** freedom from embarrassment or constraint **:** NATURALNESS **2 :** relief from discomfort or obligation **3 :** FACILITY, EFFORTLESSNESS **4 :** an act of easing or a state of being eased; *esp* **:** a lowering trend in prices — **ease·ful** \-fəl\ *adj* — **ease·ful·ly** \-fə-lē\ *adv* — **at ease 1 :** free from pain or discomfort **2 a :** free from restraint or formality **b :** standing silently (as in a military formation) with the feet apart, the right foot in place, and one or both hands behind the body — often used as a command
[2]**ease** *vb* **eased; eas·ing** *vt* **1 :** to free from something that pains, disquiets, or burdens **2 :** to make less painful **:** ALLEVIATE ⟨~ his suffering⟩ **3 a :** to lessen the pressure or tension of esp. by slackening, lifting, or shifting **b :** to moderate or reduce esp. in amount or intensity **4 :** to make less difficult ⟨~ credit⟩ **5 a :** to put the helm of (a ship) alee **b :** to let (a helm or rudder) come back a little after having been put hard over ~ *vi* **1 :** to give freedom or relief **2 :** to move or pass with freedom **3 :** MODERATE, SLACKEN
ea·sel \ˈē-zəl\ *n* [D *ezel* ass; akin to OE *esol* ass; both fr. a prehistoric EGmc-WGmc word borrowed fr. L *asinus* ass] **:** a frame for supporting something (as an artist's canvas)
ease·ment \ˈēz-mənt\ *n* **1 :** an act or means of easing or relieving (as from discomfort) **2 :** an interest in land owned by another that entitles its holder to a specific limited use or enjoyment
eas·i·ly \ˈēz-(ə-)lē\ *adv* **1 :** in an easy manner **2 :** by far
[1]**east** \ˈēst\ *adv* [ME *est,* fr. OE *ēast;* akin to OHG *ōstar* to the east, L *aurora* dawn, Gk *ēōs, heōs*] **:** to, toward, or in the east
[2]**east** *adj* **1 :** situated toward or at the east ⟨an ~ window⟩ **2 :** coming from the east ⟨an ~ wind⟩
[3]**east** *n* **1 a :** the general direction of sunrise **:** the direction toward the right of one facing north **b :** the place on the horizon where the sun rises when it is near one of the equinoxes **c :** the compass point directly opposite to west **2** *cap* **a :** regions lying to the east of a specified or implied point of orientation **b :** regions having a culture derived from ancient non-European esp. Asiatic areas **3 :** the altar end of a church **4** *often cap* **a :** the one of four positions at 90-degree intervals that lies to the east or to the right of South **b :** a person (as a bridge player) occupying this position in the course of a specified activity

east·bound \'ēs(t)-ˌbaund\ *adj* : traveling or heading east

east by north : a compass point that is one point north of due east : N78°45'E

east by south : a compass point that is one point south of due east : S78°45'E

east·er \'ē-stər\ *n* : an easterly wind; *esp* : a storm coming from the east

Eas·ter \'ē-stər\ *n* [ME *estre*, fr. OE *ēastre*; akin to OHG *ōstarun* (pl.) Easter; both fr. the prehistoric WGmc name of a pagan spring festival akin to OE *ēast* east] : a feast that commemorates Christ's resurrection and is observed with variations of date due to different calendars on the first Sunday after the full moon on or next after March 21 or one week later if the full moon falls on Sunday

EASTER DATES

YEAR	ASH WEDNESDAY	EASTER	YEAR	ASH WEDNESDAY	EASTER
1973	Mar 7	Apr 22	1983	Feb 16	Apr 3
1974	Feb 27	Apr 14	1984	Mar 7	Apr 22
1975	Feb 12	Mar 30	1985	Feb 20	Apr 7
1976	Mar 3	Apr 18	1986	Feb 12	Mar 30
1977	Feb 23	Apr 10	1987	Mar 4	Apr 19
1978	Feb 8	Mar 26	1988	Feb 17	Apr 3
1979	Feb 28	Apr 15	1989	Feb 8	Mar 26
1980	Feb 20	Apr 6	1990	Feb 28	Apr 15
1981	Mar 4	Apr 19	1991	Feb 13	Mar 31
1982	Feb 24	Apr 11	1992	Mar 4	Apr 19

Easter egg *n* : an egg that is dyed bright colors and that is associated with the celebration of Easter

Easter lily *n* : any of several white cultivated lilies (esp. *Lilium longiflorum*) that bloom in early spring

¹east·er·ly \'ē-stər-lē\ *adj or adv* [obs. *easter* (eastern)] **1** : situated toward or belonging to the east (the ~ shore of the lake) **2** : coming from the east (an ~ storm)

²easterly *n, pl* **-lies** : a wind from the east

Easter Monday *n* : the Monday after Easter observed as a legal holiday in parts of the British Commonwealth and in No. Carolina

east·ern \'ē-stərn\ *adj* [ME *estern*, fr. OE *ēasterne*; akin to OHG *ōstrōni* eastern, OE *ēast* east] **1** *cap* : of, relating to, or characteristic of a region conventionally designated East **2** *cap* **a** : of, relating to, or being the Christian churches originating in the church of the Eastern Roman Empire **b** : Eastern Orthodox **3 a** : lying toward the east **b** : coming from the east (an ~ wind) — **east·ern·most** \-ˌmōst\ *adj*

East·ern·er \'ē-stə(r)-nər\ *n* : a native or inhabitant of the East; *esp* : a native or resident of the eastern part of the U.S.

eastern hemisphere *n* : the half of the earth to the east of the Atlantic ocean including Europe, Asia, and Africa

east·ern·ize \'ē-stər-ˌnīz\ *vt* **-ized; -iz·ing** **1** : to imbue with qualities native to or associated with residents of the eastern U.S. **2** : ORIENTALIZE

Eastern Orthodox *adj* : of or consisting of the Eastern churches that form a loose federation according primacy of honor to the patriarch of Constantinople and adhering to the decisions of the first seven ecumenical councils and to the Byzantine rite

eastern time *n, often cap E* : the time of the time zone west of Greenwich that includes the eastern U.S. — see TIME ZONE illustration

eastern white pine *n* : WHITE PINE 1a

Eas·ter·tide \'ē-stər-ˌtīd\ *n* : the period from Easter to Ascension Day, to Whitsunday, or to Trinity Sunday

East Germanic *n* : a subdivision of the Germanic languages that includes Gothic — see INDO-EUROPEAN LANGUAGES table

east·ing \'ē-stiŋ\ *n* **1** : difference in longitude to the east from the last preceding point of reckoning **2** : easterly progress

east–northeast *n* : a compass point that is two points north of due east : N67°30'E

east–southeast *n* : a compass point that is two points south of due east : S67°30'E

¹east·ward \'ēs-twərd\ *adv or adj* : toward the east — **east·wards** \-twərdz\ *adv*

²eastward *n* : eastward direction or part (sail to the ~)

¹easy \'ē-zē\ *adj* **eas·i·er; -est** [ME *esy*, fr. OF *aaisié*, pp. of *aaisier* to ease, fr. a- ad- (fr. L *ad-*) + *aise* ease] **1** : causing or involving little difficulty or discomfort (an ~ problem) **2 a** : not severe : LENIENT **b** : not steep or abrupt (~ slopes) **c** : not difficult to endure or undergo (an ~ penalty) **d** : readily prevailed on (~ prey) **e** (1) : plentiful in supply at low or declining interest rates (~ money) (2) : less in demand and usu. lower in price (bonds were *easier*) **3 a** : marked by peace and comfort (the ~ course of his life) **b** : not hurried or strenuous (~ pace) **4 a** : free from pain, annoyance, or anxiety (did all she could to make him *easier*) **b** : marked by social ease (~ manners) **c** : showing a disinclination to energetic individual action or resolute independent thought (an ~ disposition) **5 a** : giving ease, comfort, or relaxation (~ chairs) **b** : not burdensome or straitened (bought on ~ terms) (living in ~ circumstances) **c** : fitting comfortably (an ~ shoe) **d** : marked by ready facility (an ~ flowing style) **e** : felt or attained to readily, naturally, and spontaneously (~ emotions) *syn* see COMFORTABLE — **eas·i·ness** *n*

²easy *adv* **eas·i·er; -est** **1** : EASILY (promises come ~) **2** : without undue speed or excitement : SLOWLY, CAUTIOUSLY (take it ~)

easy·go·ing \ˌē-zē-ˈgō-iŋ, -ˈgó-(ˌ)iŋ\ *adj* **1** : taking life easy: as **a** : PLACID (an ~ man) **b** : indolent and careless (his inertia, his laziness, his ~ ways —*Times Lit. Supp.*) **c** : morally lax **2** : UNHURRIED, COMFORTABLE (an ~ pace) — **easy·go·ing·ness** *n*

easy mark *n* : one easily imposed upon, duped, or overcome : PATSY

easy street *n* : a situation with no financial worries

easy virtue *n* : sexually promiscuous behavior or habits (a woman of *easy virtue*)

eat \'ēt\ *vb* **ate** \'āt, *chiefly Brit or substand* 'et\; **eat·en** \'ēt-ⁿn\; **eat·ing** [ME *eten*, fr. OE *etan*; akin to OHG *ezzan* to eat, L *edere*, Gk *edmenai*] *vt* **1** : to take in through the mouth as food : ingest, chew, and swallow in turn **2** : to destroy, use up, or waste by or as if by eating : DEVOUR (locusts *ate* the country bare) **3 a** : to consume gradually : CORRODE **b** : to consume with vexation : BOTHER (what's ~*ing* her now) ~ *vi* **1** : to take food or a meal **2** : to affect something by gradual destruction or consumption — used with *into* — **eat·er** *n* — **eat crow** : to accept what one has fought against — **eat humble pie** : to apologize or retract under pressure — **eat one's heart out** : to grieve bitterly — **eat one's words** : to retract what one has said — **eat out of one's hand** : to accept the domination of another

¹eat·able \'ēt-ə-bəl\ *adj* : fit to be eaten

²eatable *n* **1** : something to eat **2** *pl* : FOOD

eat·ery \'ēt-ə-rē\ *n, pl* **-er·ies** : LUNCHEONETTE, RESTAURANT

eath \'ēth\ *adv or adj* [ME *ethe*, fr. OE *ēathe*; akin to OHG *ōdi* easy and perh. to L *avēre* to long for — more at AVID] *Scot* : EASY

eat·ing \'ēt-iŋ\ *adj* **1** : used for eating **2** : fit to be eaten raw (makes a better cooking than ~ apple)

eat out *vi* : to eat away from home and esp. at a restaurant

eau de co·logne \ˌōd-ə-kə-ˈlōn\ *n, pl* **eaux de cologne** \ˌō(z)d-ə-\ [F, lit., Cologne water, fr. *Cologne*, Germany] : COLOGNE

eau–de–vie \ˌōd-ə-ˈvē\ *n, pl* **eaux–de–vie** \ˌō(z)d-ə-\ [F, lit., water of life, trans. of ML *aqua vitae*] : BRANDY

eaves \'ēvz\ *n pl* [ME *eves* (sing.), fr. OE *efes*; akin to OHG *obasa* portico, OE *ūp* up — more at UP] **1** : the lower border of a roof that overhangs the wall **2** : a projecting edge (as of a hill)

eaves·drop \'ēvz-ˌdräp\ *vi* [prob. back-formation fr. *eavesdropper*, lit., one standing under the drip from the eaves] : to listen secretly to what is said in private — **eaves·drop·per** *n*

EB *abbr* eastbound

¹ebb \'eb\ *n* [ME *ebbe*, fr OE *ebba*; akin to MD *ebbe* ebb, OE *of* from — more at OF] **1** : the reflux of the tide toward the sea **2** : a point or condition of decline (relations were at a low ~)

²ebb *vi* **1** : to recede from the flood **2** : to fall from a higher to a lower level or from a better to a worse state *syn* see ABATE *ant* flow (as the tide)

eb·bet \'eb-ət\ *n* [ME *evete*, fr. OE *efete*] : a common green newt (*Triturus viridescens*) of the eastern U.S.

ebb tide *n* **1** : the tide while ebbing or at ebb **2** : a period or state of decline

eb·on \'eb-ən\ *adj* : EBONY

eb·o·nite \'eb-ə-ˌnīt\ *n* : hard rubber esp. when black or unfilled

eb·o·nize \-ˌnīz\ *vt* **-nized; -niz·ing** : to stain black in imitation of ebony

¹eb·o·ny \'eb-ə-nē\ *n, pl* **-nies** [prob. fr. LL *hebeninus* of ebony, fr. Gk *ebeninos*, fr. *ebenos* ebony, fr. Egypt *hbnj*] **1** : a hard heavy wood yielded by various Old World tropical dicotyledonous trees (genus *Diospyros*) of the ebony family (Ebonaceae) **2 a** : a tree yielding ebony **b** : any of several trees yielding wood resembling ebony

²ebony *adj* **1** : made of or resembling ebony **2** : BLACK, DARK

ebul·lience \i-ˈbul-yən(t)s, -ˈbəl-\ *n* : the quality of lively or enthusiastic expression of thoughts or feelings : EXUBERANCE

ebul·lien·cy \-yən-sē\ *n* : EBULLIENCE

ebul·lient \-yənt\ *adj* [L *ebullient-*, *ebulliens*, prp. of *ebullire* to bubble out, fr. e- + *bullire* to bubble, boil — more at BOIL] **1** : BOILING, AGITATED **2** : characterized by ebullience — **ebul·lient·ly** *adv*

eb·ul·li·tion \ˌeb-ə-ˈlish-ən\ *n* **1** : the act, process, or state of boiling or bubbling up **2** : a sudden violent outburst or display

ec- or **eco-** *comb form* [LL *oeco-* household, fr. Gk *oiko-*, *oiko-*, fr. *oikos* house — more at VICINITY] **1** : habitat or environment (ecospecies) **2** : ecology

¹ec·cen·tric \ik-ˈsen-trik, ek-\ *adj* [ML *eccentricus*, fr. Gk *ekkentros*, fr. *ex* out of + *kentron* center] **1** : not having the same center (~ spheres) **2** : deviating from an established pattern or from accepted usage or conduct **3 a** : deviating from a circular path (an ~ orbit) **b** : located elsewhere than at the geometrical center; *also* : having the axis or support so located (an ~ wheel) — **ec·cen·tri·cal·ly** \-tri-k(ə-)lē\ *adv*

²eccentric *n* **1** : a mechanical device consisting of a disk through which a shaft is keyed eccentrically and a circular strap which works freely round the rim of the disk for communicating its motion to one end of a rod whose other end is constrained to move in a straight line so as to produce reciprocating motion **2** : an eccentric person

ec·cen·tric·i·ty \ˌek-ˌsen-ˈtris-ət-ē\ *n, pl* **-ties** **1 a** : the quality or state of being eccentric **b** : deviation from an established pattern, rule, or norm; *esp* : odd or whimsical behavior **2** : a mathematical constant that for a given conic section is the ratio of the distances from any point of the conic section to a focus and the corresponding directrix

syn ECCENTRICITY, IDIOSYNCRASY *shared meaning element* : singularity of behavior or an instance of this

ec·chy·mo·sis \ˌek-i-ˈmō-səs\ *n, pl* **-mo·ses** \-ˌsēz\ [NL, fr. Gk *ekchymōsis*, fr. *ekchymousthai* to extravasate blood, fr. *ex-* + *chymos* juice — more at CHYME] : the escape of blood into the tissues from ruptured blood vessels — **ec·chy·mot·ic** \-ˈmät-ik\ *adj*

eccl *abbr* ecclesiastic; ecclesiastical

Eccles *abbr* Ecclesiastes

ə abut	⁹ kitten	ər further	a back	ā bake	ä cot, cart
au out	ch chin	e less	ē easy	g gift	i trip	ī life
j joke	ŋ sing	ō flow	ȯ flaw	ȯi coin	th thin	th this
ü loot	u̇ foot	y yet	yü few	yu̇ furious	zh vision	

ecclesi- *or* **ecclesio-** *comb form* [ME *ecclesi-*, fr. LL *ecclesia*, fr. Gk *ekklēsia* assembly of citizens, church, fr. *ekkalein* to call forth, summon, fr. *ex-* + *kalein* to call]: church ⟨*ecclesiography*⟩

ec-cle-si-al \ik-ˈlē-zē-əl, e-ˈklē-\ *adj*: of or relating to a church

Ec-cle-si-as-tes \ik-ˌlē-zē-ˈas-(ˌ)tēz, e-ˌklē-\ *n* [Gk *Ekklēsiastēs*, lit., preacher (trans. of Heb *Qōheleth*), fr. *ekklēsiastēs* member of an assembly]: a book of wisdom literature in canonical Jewish and Christian Scripture — see BIBLE table

¹ec-cle-si-as-tic \-ˈas-tik\ *adj*: ECCLESIASTICAL

²ecclesiastic *n*: CLERGYMAN

ec-cle-si-as-ti-cal \-ti-kəl\ *adj* [ecclesiastical fr. ME, fr. LL *ecclesiasticus*; ecclesiastic fr. MF *ecclesiastique*, fr. LL *ecclesiasticus*, fr. LGk *ekklēsiastikos*, fr. Gk, of an assembly of citizens, fr. *ekklēsiastēs* member of an assembly, fr. *ekklēsia*] **1**: of or relating to a church esp. as a formal and established institution ⟨~ law⟩ **2**: suitable for use in a church ⟨~ vestments⟩ — **ec-cle-si-as-ti-cal-ly** \-ti-(ə-)lē\ *adv*

ec-cle-si-as-ti-cism \-tə-ˌsiz-əm\ *n*: excessive attachment to ecclesiastical forms and practices

Ec-cle-si-as-ti-cus \-ti-kəs\ *n* [LL, fr. *ecclesiasticus* ecclesiastic]: a didactic book included in the Roman Catholic canon of the Old Testament and in the Protestant Apocrypha — see BIBLE table

ec-cle-si-ol-o-gy \ik-ˌlē-zē-ˈäl-ə-jē, e-ˌklē-\ *n, pl* **-gies 1**: the study of church architecture and adornment **2**: theological doctrine relating to the church — **ec-cle-si-o-log-i-cal** \-zē-ə-ˈläj-i-kəl\ *adj*

Ecclus *abbr* Ecclesiasticus

ec-crine \ˈek-rən, -ˌrīn, -ˌrēn\ *adj* [ISV *ec-* (fr. Gk *ex* out) + Gk *krinein* to separate — more at CERTAIN]: producing a fluid secretion without removing cytoplasm from the secreting cells; *also*: produced by an eccrine gland

eccrine gland *n*: any of the rather small sweat glands that produce an eccrine secretion and that are restricted to the human skin — called *also eccrine sweat gland*

ec-dys-i-ast \ek-ˈdiz-ē-ˌast, -ē-əst\ *n*: STRIPTEASER

ec-dy-sis \ˈek-də-səs\ *n, pl* **ec-dy-ses** \-də-ˌsēz\ [NL, fr. Gk *ekdysis* act of getting out]: the act of molting or shedding an outer cuticular layer (as in insects and crustaceans)

ec-dy-sone \ˈek-də-ˌsōn\ *also* **ec-dy-son** \-ˌsän\ *n* [ISV *ecdysis* + hormone]: any of several arthropod hormones that in insects are produced by the prothoracic gland and that trigger molting and metamorphosis

ece-sis \i-ˈsē-səs, -ˈkē-\ *n* [NL, fr. Gk *oikēsis* inhabitation]: the establishment of a plant or animal in a new habitat

ECG *abbr* electrocardiogram

ech *abbr* echelon

¹ech-e-lon \ˈesh-ə-ˌlän\ *n* [F *échelon*, lit., rung of a ladder] **1 a** (1): an arrangement of a body of troops with its units each somewhat to the left or right of the one in the rear like a series of steps (2): a formation of units or individuals resembling such an echelon (3): a flight formation in which each airplane flies at a certain elevation above or below and at a certain distance behind and to the right or left of the airplane ahead **b**: any of several military units in echelon formation **2 a**: one of a series of levels or grades (as of leadership or responsibility) in an organization or field of activity **b**: a group of individuals having a particular responsibility or occupying a particular level or grade

²echelon *vt*: to form or arrange in an echelon ~ *vi*: to take position in an echelon

ech-e-ve-ria \ˌech-ə-və-ˈrē-ə\ *n* [NL, genus name, fr. *Echeveria*, 19th cent. Mex botanical illustrator]: any of a large genus (*Echeveria*) of tropical American succulent plants of the orpine family that have showy rosettes of often plushy basal leaves and axillary clusters of flowers with erect petals spreading only at the tips and that are often grown in warm regions as ornamentals

echid-na \i-ˈkid-nə\ *n* [NL, fr. L, viper, fr. Gk]: an oviparous spiny-coated toothless burrowing nocturnal mammal (*Tachyglossus aculeatus*) of Australia, Tasmania, and New Guinea that has a long extensile tongue and long heavy claws and that feeds chiefly on ants — called also *spiny anteater*

echidna

echin- *or* **echino-** *comb form* [L, fr. Gk, fr. *echinos* sea urchin] **1**: prickle ⟨*Echino*dermata⟩ **2**: sea urchin ⟨*echin*ite⟩

echi-no-coc-co-sis \i-ˌkī-nə-kä-ˈkō-səs\ *n, pl* **-co-ses** \-ˌsēz\ [NL]: infestation with or disease caused by a small tapeworm (*Echinococcus granulosus*)

echi-no-coc-cus \i-ˌkī-nə-ˈkäk-əs\ *n, pl* **-coc-ci** \-ˈkäk-ˌ(s)ī, -ˈkäk-(ˌ)(s)ē\ [NL, genus name]: any of a genus (*Echinococcus*) of tapeworms that alternate a minute adult living as a commensal in the intestine of carnivores with a hydatid larva invading tissues esp. of the liver of cattle, sheep, swine, and man and acting as a dangerous pathogen

echi-no-derm \i-ˈkī-nə-ˌdərm\ *n* [NL *Echinodermata*, phylum name, fr. *echino-* + *-dermata* (fr. Gk *derma* skin)]: any of a phylum (Echinodermata) of radially symmetrical coelomate marine animals consisting of the starfishes, sea urchins, and related forms — **echi-no-der-ma-tous** \-ˌkī-nə-ˈdər-mət-əs\ *adj*

echi-noid \i-ˈkī-ˌnóid, ˈek-ə-ˌnóid\ *n*: SEA URCHIN

echi-nu-late \i-ˈkin-yə-lət, -ˈkīn-, -ˌlāt\ *adj*: set with small spines or prickles — **echi-nu-la-tion** \-ˌkin-yə-ˈlā-shən, -ˌkīn-\ *n*

echi-nus \i-ˈkī-nəs\ *n, pl* **-ni** \-ˌnī\ [ME, fr. L, fr. Gk *echinos* hedgehog, sea urchin, architectural echinus] **1**: SEA URCHIN **2 a**: the rounded molding forming the bell of the capital in the Greek Doric order **b**: a similar member in other orders

echi-uroid \ˌek-i-ˈyü-(ˌ)ȯr-ˌȯid\ *n* [NL *Echiuroidea*, group name, deriv. of Gk *echis* viper + *oura* tail]: any of a group (Echiuroidea) of marine worms of uncertain taxonomic affinities that have a sensitive but nonretractile proboscis above the mouth

¹echo \ˈmu-ə\ *n, pl* **ech-oes** [ME *ecco*, fr. MF & L; MF *echo*, fr. L, fr. Gk *ēchō*; akin to L *vagire* to wail, Gk *ēchē* sound] **1 a**: the repetition of a sound caused by reflection of sound waves **b**: the sound due to such reflection **2 a**: a repetition or imitation of another : REFLECTION **b**: REPERCUSSION, RESULT **c**: TRACE, VESTIGE **d**: RESPONSE **3**: one who closely imitates or repeats another's words, ideas, or acts **4**: a soft repetition of a musical phrase **5 a**: the repetition of a received radio signal due esp. to reflection of part of the wave from an ionized layer of the atmosphere **b** (1): the reflection of transmitted radar signals by an object (2): the visual indication of this reflection on a radarscope — **echo-ey** \ˈek-ˌō-ē\ *adj*

²echo *vb* **ech-oed; echo-ing** \ˈek-(ˌ)ō-iŋ, ˈek-ə-wiŋ\ *vi* **1**: to resound with echoes **2**: to produce an echo ~ *vt* **1**: REPEAT, IMITATE **2**: to send back or repeat (a sound) by the reflection of sound waves

¹Echo *n* [Gk *Ēchō*]: a nymph in Greek legend who pined away for love of Narcissus until nothing was left of her but her voice

²Echo — a communications code word for the letter *e*

echo chamber *n*: a room with sound-reflecting walls used for producing hollow or echoing sound effects esp. in radio broadcasting

echo-en-ceph-a-log-ra-phy \ˌek-ō-in-ˌsef-ə-ˈläg-rə-fē\ *n*: the use of ultrasound in the examination and measurement of internal structures (as the ventricles) of the skull and in the diagnosis of abnormalities

echo-ic \e-ˈkō-ik, e-\ *adj* **1**: of or relating to an echo **2**: formed in imitation of some natural sound : ONOMATOPOEIC

echo-la-lia \ˌek-ō-ˈlā-lē-ə\ *n* [NL]: the often pathological repetition of what is said by other people as if echoing them — **echo-lal-ic** \-ˈlal-ik\ *adj*

echo-lo-ca-tion \ˌek-ō-lō-ˈkā-shən\ *n*: a process for locating distant or invisible objects (as prey) by means of sound waves reflected back to the emitter (as a bat or submarine) by the objects

echo sounder *n*: an instrument for determining the depth of a body of water or of an object below the surface by means of sound waves

echo-vi-rus \ˈek-ō-ˌvī-rəs\ *n* [*enteric cytopathogenic human orphan* + *virus*]: any of a group of picornaviruses that are found in the gastrointestinal tract, that cause cytopathic changes in cells in tissue culture, and that are sometimes associated with respiratory ailments and meningitis

éclair \ā-ˈkla(ə)r, i-, -ˈkle(ə)r, ˈā-ˌ, ˈē-ˌ\ *n* [F, lit., lightning]: a usu. chocolate-frosted oblong cream puff with whipped cream or custard filling

éclair-cis-se-ment \ā-kler-sēs-(ə-)mäⁿ\ *n, pl* **éclaircissements** \-mäⁿ(z)\ [F]: ENLIGHTENMENT, CLARIFICATION

eclamp-sia \i-ˈklam(p)-sē-ə\ *n* [NL, fr. Gk *eklampsis* sudden flashing, fr. *eklampein* to shine forth, fr. *ex* out + *lampein* to shine]: a convulsive state; *esp*: an attack of convulsions during pregnancy or parturition — **eclamp-tic** \-ˈklam(p)-tik\ *adj*

éclat \ā-ˈklä, ˈā-ˌ\ *n* [F, splinter, burst, éclat] **1**: dazzling effect : BRILLIANCE **2 a**: ostentatious display : PUBLICITY **b** *archaic* : NOTORIETY **3 a**: brilliant or conspicuous success : ACCLAIM, APPLAUSE

¹eclec-tic \e-ˈklek-tik, i-\ *adj* [Gk *eklektikos*, fr. *eklegein* to select, fr. *ex* + *legein* to gather — more at LEGEND] **1**: selecting what appears to be best in various doctrines, methods, or styles **2**: composed of elements drawn from various sources — **eclec-ti-cal-ly** \-ti-k(ə-)lē\ *adv*

²eclectic *n*: one who uses an eclectic method or approach

eclec-ti-cism \-ˈklek-tə-ˌsiz-əm\ *n*: the theory or practice of an eclectic method

¹eclipse \i-ˈklips\ *n* [ME, fr. OF, fr. L *eclipsis*, fr. Gk *ekleipsis*, fr. *ekleipein* to omit, fail, suffer eclipse, fr. *ex* + *leipein* to leave — more at LOAN] **1 a**: the total or partial obscuring of one celestial body by another **b**: the passing into the shadow of a celestial body — compare OCCULTATION, TRANSIT **2**: a falling into obscurity or decline : DISGRACE **3**: the state of being in eclipse plumage

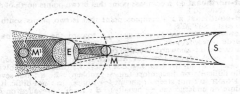

eclipse 1a: *S* sun; *E* earth; *M* moon in solar eclipse; *M¹* moon in lunar eclipse

²eclipse *vt* **eclipsed; eclips-ing**: to cause an eclipse of: as **a**: OBSCURE, DARKEN **b**: to reduce in importance or repute : DISGRACE **c**: SURPASS

eclipse plumage *n*: comparatively dull plumage that is usu. of seasonal occurrence in birds which exhibit a distinct nuptial plumage

¹eclip-tic \i-ˈklip-tik\ *n* [ME *ecliptik*, fr. LL *ecliptica linea*, lit., line of eclipses] **1**: the great circle of the celestial sphere that is the apparent path of the sun among the stars or of the earth as seen from the sun : the plane of the earth's orbit extended to meet the celestial sphere **2**: a great circle drawn on a terrestrial globe making an angle of about 23° 27' with the equator and used for illustrating and solving astronomical problems

²ecliptic *adj*: of or relating to the ecliptic or an eclipse

ec-logue \ˈek-ˌlȯg, -ˌläg\ *n* [ME *eclog*, fr. L *Eclogae*, title of Vergil's pastorals, lit., selections, pl. of *ecloga*, fr. Gk *eklogē*, fr. *eklegein* to select]: a poem in which shepherds converse

eclo·sion \i-ˈklō-zhən\ *n* [F *éclosion*] *of an insect* **:** the act of emerging from the pupal case or hatching from the egg
ECM *abbr* European Common Market
eco- — see EC-
ecol *abbr* ecological; ecology
ecol·o·gy \i-ˈkäl-ə-jē, e-\ *n, pl* **-gies** [G *ökologie*, fr. *ök-* ec- + *-logie* -logy] **1 :** a branch of science concerned with the interrelationship of organisms and their environments **2 :** the totality or pattern of relations between organisms and their environment **3 :** HUMAN ECOLOGY — **eco·log·i·cal** \ˌē-kə-ˈläj-i-kəl, ˌek-ə-\ *also* **eco·log·ic** \-ik\ *adj* — **eco·log·i·cal·ly** \-i-k(ə-)lē\ *adv* — **ecol·o·gist** \i-ˈkäl-ə-jəst, e-\ *n*
econ *abbr* economics; economist; economy
econo·met·rics \i-ˌkän-ə-ˈme-triks\ *n pl but sing in constr* [blend of *economics* and *metric*] **:** the application of statistical methods to the study of economic data and problems — **econo·met·ric** \-trik\ *adj* — **econo·met·ri·cal·ly** \-tri-k(ə-)lē\ *adv* — **econo·me·tri·cian** \-mə-ˈtrish-ən\ *n* — **econo·met·rist** \-ˈme-trəst\ *n*
eco·nom·ic \ˌek-ə-ˈnäm-ik, ˌē-kə-\ *adj* **1** *archaic* **:** of or relating to a household or its management **2 :** ECONOMICAL 2 **3 a :** of or relating to economics **b :** of, relating to, or based on the production, distribution, and consumption of goods and services **c :** of or relating to an economy **4 :** having practical or industrial significance or uses **:** affecting material resources **5 :** PROFITABLE
eco·nom·i·cal \-ˈnäm-i-kəl\ *adj* **1** *archaic* **:** ECONOMIC 1 **2 :** marked by careful, efficient, and prudent use of resources **:** THRIFTY **3 :** operating with little waste or at a saving ***syn*** see SPARING ***ant*** extravagant — **eco·nom·i·cal·ly** \-i-k(ə-)lē\ *adv*
economic rent *n* **:** the return for the use of a factor in excess of the minimum required to bring forth its service
eco·nom·ics \ˌek-ə-ˈnäm-iks, ˌē-kə-\ *n pl but sing or pl in constr* **1 :** a social science concerned chiefly with description and analysis of the production, distribution, and consumption of goods and services **2 :** economic aspect or significance
econ·o·mist \i-ˈkän-ə-məst\ *n* **1** *archaic* **:** one who practices economy **2 :** a specialist in economics
econ·o·mize \-ˌmīz\ *vb* **-mized; -miz·ing** *vi* **:** to practice economy **:** be frugal **~** *vt* **:** to use more economically **:** SAVE — **econ·o·miz·er** *n*
¹econ·o·my \i-ˈkän-ə-mē\ *n, pl* **-mies** [MF *yconomie*, fr. ML *oeconomia*, fr. Gk *oikonomia*, fr. *oikonomos* household manager, fr. *oikos* house + *nemein* to manage — more at VICINITY, NIMBLE] **1** *archaic* **:** the management of household or private affairs and esp. expenses **2 a :** thrifty and efficient use of material resources **:** frugality in expenditures; *also* **:** an instance or a means of economizing **b :** efficient and concise use of nonmaterial resources (as effort, language, or motion) for the end proposed **3 :** the arrangement or mode of operation of something **:** ORGANIZATION **4 :** the structure of economic life in a country, area, or period; *specif* **:** an economic system
²economy *adj* **:** designed to save money ⟨~ cars⟩ ⟨~ measures⟩
eco·phys·i·ol·o·gy \ˌē-kō-ˌfiz-ē-ˈäl-ə-jē, ˌek-ō-\ *n* **:** the science of the interrelationships between the physiology of organisms and their environment — **eco·phys·i·o·log·i·cal** \-ē-ə-ˈläj-i-kəl\ *adj*
eco·spe·cies \ˈē-kō-ˌspē-(ˌ)shēz, ˌek-ō-, -(ˌ)sēz\ *n, pl* **ecospecies :** a subdivision of a cenospecies capable of free gene interchange between its members without impairment of fertility but less capable of fertile crosses with members of other subdivisions and typically more or less equivalent to the taxonomic species — **eco·spe·cif·ic** \ˌē-kō-spi-ˈsif-ik, ˌek-ō-\ *adj*
eco·sphere \ˈē-kō-ˌsfi(ə)r, ˈek-ō-\ *n* **:** the parts of the universe habitable by living organisms; *esp* **:** BIOSPHERE 1
eco·sys·tem \-ˌsis-təm\ *n* **:** the complex of a community and its environment functioning as an ecological unit in nature
eco·tone \ˈē-kə-ˌtōn, ˈek-ə-\ *n* [*ec-* + Gk *tonos* tension — more at TONE] **:** a transition area between two adjacent ecological communities usu. exhibiting competition between organisms common to both
eco·type \-ˌtīp\ *n* **:** a subdivision of an ecospecies that comprises individuals interfertile with each other and with members of other ecotypes of the same ecospecies but surviving as a distinct group through environmental selection and isolation and that is comparable with a taxonomic subspecies — **eco·typ·ic** \ˌē-kə-ˈtip-ik, ˌek-ə-\ *adj* — **eco·typ·i·cal·ly** \-i-k(ə-)lē\ *adv*
ecru \ˈek-(ˌ)rü, ˈā-(ˌ)krü\ *n* [F *écru* unbleached, fr. OF *escru*, fr. *es-* completely (fr. L *ex-*) + *cru* raw, fr. L *crudus* — more at RAW] **:** BEIGE 2
ec·sta·sy \ˈek-stə-sē\ *n, pl* **-sies** [ME *extasie*, fr. MF, fr. LL *ecstasis*, fr. Gk *ekstasis*, fr. *existanai* to derange, fr. *ex* out + *histanai* to cause to stand — more at EX-, STAND] **1 a :** a state of being beyond reason and self-control **b** *archaic* **:** SWOON **2 :** a state of overwhelming emotion; *esp* **:** rapturous delight **3 :** TRANCE; *esp* **:** a mystic or prophetic trance
syn ECSTASY, RAPTURE, TRANSPORT *shared meaning element* **:** intense exaltation of mind and feelings
¹ec·stat·ic \ek-ˈstat-ik, ik-ˈstat-\ *adj* [ML *ecstaticus*, fr. Gk *ekstatikos*, fr. *existanai*] **:** of, relating to, or marked by ecstasy — **ec·stat·i·cal·ly** \-ˈstat-i-k(ə-)lē\ *adv*
²ecstatic *n* **:** one that is subject to ecstasies
ect- *or* **ecto-** *comb form* [NL, fr. Gk *ekto-*, fr. *ektos*, fr. *ex* out — more at EX-] **:** outside **:** external ⟨*ecto*mere⟩ — compare END-, EXO-
ec·to·blast \ˈek-tə-ˌblast\ *n* [ISV] **:** EPIBLAST — **ec·to·blas·tic** \ˌek-tə-ˈblas-tik\ *adj*
ec·to·com·men·sal \ˌek-tō-kə-ˈmen(t)-səl\ *n* **:** an organism that lives as a commensal on the body surface of another
ec·to·derm \ˈek-tə-ˌdərm\ *n* [ISV *ect-* + Gk *derma* skin — more at DERM-] **1 :** the outer cellular membrane of a diploblastic animal (as a jellyfish) **2 a :** the outermost of the three primary germ layers of an embryo **b :** a tissue (as neural tissue) derived from this germ layer — **ec·to·der·mal** \ˌek-tə-ˈdər-məl\ *or* **ec·to·der·mic** \-mik\ *adj*
ec·to·gen·ic \ˌek-tə-ˈjen-ik\ *adj* **:** ECTOGENOUS
ec·tog·e·nous \ek-ˈtäj-ə-nəs\ *adj* **:** capable of development apart from the host — used chiefly of pathogenic bacteria
ec·to·mere \ˈek-tə-ˌmi(ə)r\ *n* **:** a blastomere destined to form ectoderm — **ec·to·mer·ic** \ˌek-tə-ˈmer-ik, -ˈmi(ə)r-\ *adj*
ec·to·morph \ˈek-tə-ˌmȯrf\ *n* [*ecto*derm + *-morph*] **:** an ectomorphic individual
ec·to·mor·phic \ˌek-tə-ˈmȯr-fik\ *adj* [*ecto*derm + *-morphic;* fr. the predominance in such types of structures developed from the ectoderm] **1 :** of or relating to the component in W. H. Sheldon's classification of body types that measures the body's degree of slenderness, angularity, and fragility **2 :** having a light body build
-ec·to·my \ˈek-tə-mē\ *n comb form* [NL *-ectomia*, fr. Gk *ektemnein* to cut out, fr. *ex* out + *temnein* to cut — more at TOME] **:** surgical removal ⟨gastr*ectomy*⟩
ec·to·par·a·site \ˌek-tō-ˈpar-ə-ˌsīt\ *n* [ISV] **:** a parasite that lives on the exterior of its host — **ec·to·par·a·sit·ic** \-ˌpar-ə-ˈsit-ik\ *adj*
ec·top·ic \ek-ˈtäp-ik\ *adj* [Gk *ektopos* out of place, fr. *ex-* out + *topos* place — more at TOPIC] **:** occurring in an abnormal position or in an unusual manner or form ⟨~ lesions⟩ ⟨~ heartbeat⟩
ectopic pregnancy *n* **:** gestation elsewhere than in the uterus (as in a fallopian tube or in the peritoneal cavity)
ec·to·plasm \ˈek-tə-ˌplaz-əm\ *n* **1 :** the outer relatively rigid granule-free layer of the cytoplasm usu. held to be a reversible gel **2 :** a substance held to produce spirit materialization and telekinesis — **ec·to·plas·mic** \ˌek-tə-ˈplaz-mik\ *adj*
ec·to·therm \ˈek-tə-ˌthərm\ *n* **:** a cold-blooded animal **:** POIKILOTHERM — **ec·to·ther·mic** \ˌek-tə-ˈthər-mik\ *adj*
ec·to·tro·phic \ˌek-tə-ˈtrō-fik\ *also* **ec·to·tro·pic** \-ˈtrō-pik, -ˈträp-ik\ *adj, of a mycorrhiza* **:** growing in a close web on the surface of the associated root — compare ENDOTROPHIC
ecu \ˈā-ˌkyü, ā-ˈkue̅\ *n, pl* **ecus** \-ˌkyüz, -ˈkue̅\ [MF, lit., shield, fr. OF *escu*, fr. L *scutum;* from the device of a shield on the coin — more at ESQUIRE] **:** any of various old French units of value; *also* **:** a coin representing this
Ecua *abbr* Ecuador
ec·u·men·i·cal \ˌek-yə-ˈmen-i-kəl\ *adj* [LL *oecumenicus*, fr. LGk *oikoumenikos*, fr. Gk *oikoumenē* the inhabited world, fr. fem. of *oikoumenos*, pres. pass. part. of *oikein* to inhabit, fr. *oikos* house — more at VICINITY] **1 :** worldwide or general in extent, influence, or application **2 a :** of, relating to, or representing the whole of a body of churches **b :** promoting or tending toward worldwide Christian unity or cooperation — **ec·u·men·i·cal·ly** \-k(ə-)lē\ *adv*
ec·u·men·i·cal·ism \-ˈmen-i-kə-ˌliz-əm\ *n* **:** ECUMENISM
ecumenical patriarch *n* **:** the patriarch of Constantinople as the dignitary given first honor in the Eastern Orthodox Church
ec·u·men·i·cism \ˌek-yə-ˈmen-ə-ˌsiz-əm\ *n* **:** ECUMENISM — **ec·u·men·i·cist** \-səst\ *n*
ec·u·me·nic·i·ty \ˌek-yə-mə-ˈnis-ət-ē, -me-\ *n* **:** the quality or state of being drawn close to others esp. through Christian ecumenical feeling or action
e·cu·men·ics \-ˈmen-iks\ *n pl but sing in constr* **:** the study of the nature, mission, problems, and strategy of the Christian church from the perspective of its ecumenical character
ecu·me·nism \e-ˈkyü-mə-ˌniz-əm, i- *also* ˈek-yə-mə-ˌniz- *or* ˌek-yə-ˈmen-ˌiz-\ *n* **:** ecumenical principles and practices esp. as exemplified among religious groups (as Christian denominations) — **ecu·me·nist** \e-ˈkyü-mə-nəst, i- *also* ˈek-yə-mə-nəst *or* ˌek-yə-ˈmen-əst\ *n*
ec·ze·ma \ig-ˈzē-mə, ˈeg-zə-mə, ˈek-sə-\ *n* [NL, fr. Gk *ekzema*, fr. *ekzein* to erupt, fr. *ex* out + *zein* to boil — more at EX-, YEAST] **:** an inflammatory condition of the skin characterized by redness, itching, and oozing vesicular lesions which become scaly, crusted, or hardened — **ec·zem·a·tous** \ig-ˈzem-ət-əs\ *adj*
ed *abbr* **1** edited; edition; editor **2** education
ED *abbr* extra duty
¹-ed \d *after a vowel or* b, g, j, l, m, n, ŋ, r, th, v, z, zh; əd, id *after* d, t; t *after other sounds; exceptions are pronounced at their subentries or entries*\ *vb suffix or adj suffix* [ME, fr. OE *-ed, -od, -ad;* akin to OHG *-t*, pp. ending, L *-tus*, Gk *-tos*, suffix forming verbals] **1 —** used to form the past participle of regular weak verbs ⟨end*ed*⟩ ⟨fad*ed*⟩ ⟨tri*ed*⟩ ⟨patt*ed*⟩ **2 —** used to form adjectives of identical meaning from Latin-derived adjectives ending in *-ate* ⟨crenulat*ed*⟩ **3 a :** having **:** characterized by ⟨cultur*ed*⟩ ⟨two-legg*ed*⟩ **b :** having the characteristics of ⟨bigot*ed*⟩
²-ed *vb suffix* [ME *-ede, -de*, fr. OE *-de, -ede, -ode, -ade;* akin to OHG *-ta*, past ending (1st sing.) and prob. to OHG *-t*, pp. ending] — used to form the past tense of regular weak verbs ⟨judg*ed*⟩ ⟨deni*ed*⟩ ⟨dropp*ed*⟩
eda·cious \i-ˈdā-shəs\ *adj* [L *edac-*, *edax*, fr. *edere* to eat — more at EAT] **1** *archaic* **:** of or relating to eating **2 :** VORACIOUS — **edac·i·ty** \-ˈdas-ət-ē\ *n*
Edam \ˈēd-əm, ˈē-ˌdam\ *n* [*Edam*, Netherlands] **:** a yellow pressed cheese of Dutch origin usu. made in flattened balls and often coated with red wax
edaph·ic \i-ˈdaf-ik\ *adj* [Gk *edaphos* bottom, ground] **1 :** of or relating to the soil **2 a :** resulting from or influenced by the soil rather than the climate **b :** AUTOCHTHONOUS — **edaph·i·cal·ly** \-ˈdaf-i-k(ə-)lē\ *adv*
edaphic climax *n* **:** an ecological climax resulting from soil factors and commonly persisting through cycles of climactic and physiographic change — compare PHYSIOGRAPHIC CLIMAX
EDD *abbr* English Dialect Dictionary
Ed·dic \ˈed-ik\ *adj* [ON *Edda*] **:** of, relating to, or resembling the Old Norse *Edda* which is a 13th century collection of mythological, heroic, and aphoristic poems in alliterative verse
¹ed·dy \ˈed-ē\ *n, pl* **eddies** [ME (Sc dial.) *ydy*, prob. fr. ON *itha;* akin to OHG *ith-* again, L *et* and] **1 a :** a current of water or air

ə abut ᵊ kitten ər further a back ā bake ä cot, cart
au̇ out ch chin e less ē easy g gift i trip ī life
j joke ŋ sing ō flow ȯ flaw ȯi coin th thin th this
ü loot u̇ foot y yet yü few yu̇ furious zh vision

running contrary to the main current; *esp* : a small whirlpool **b** : something moving similarly ⟨little *eddies* of people were dancing with each other in the streets —L. C. Stevens⟩ **2** : a contrary or circular current (as of thought or policy)

[2]**eddy** *vb* **ed·died; ed·dy·ing** *vt* : to cause to move in an eddy ~ *vi* : to move in an eddy or in the manner of an eddy ⟨the crowd frantically *eddied* in a half-moon shape —*Walker Report*⟩

eddy current *n* : an electric current induced by an alternating magnetic field

edel·weiss \ˈād-ᵊl-ˌwīs, -ˌvīs\ *n* [G, fr. *edel* noble + *weiss* white] : a small perennial composite herb (*Leontopodium alpinum*) having a dense woolly white pubescence and growing high in the Alps

ede·ma \i-ˈdē-mə\ *n* [NL, fr. Gk *oidēma* swelling, fr. *oidein* to swell; akin to OE *ātor* pus] **1** : an abnormal excess accumulation of serous fluid in connective tissue or in a serous cavity **2 a** : watery swelling of plant organs or parts **b** : any of various plant diseases characterized by such swellings — **edem·a·tous** \-ˈdem-ət-əs\ *adj*

Eden \ˈēd-ᵊn\ *n* [LL, fr. Heb *ʽEdhen*] **1** : the garden where according to the account in Genesis Adam and Eve first lived **2** : PARADISE 2 — **Eden·ic** \i-ˈden-ik\ *adj*

[1]**eden·tate** \(ˈ)ē-ˈden-ˌtāt\ *adj* [L *edentatus*, pp. of *edentare* to make toothless, fr. *e-* + *dent-, dens* tooth — more at TOOTH] **1** : lacking teeth **2** : being an edentate

[2]**edentate** *n* : any of an order (Edentata) of mammals having few or no teeth and including the sloths, armadillos, and New World anteaters and formerly also the pangolins and the aardvark

eden·tu·lous \(ˈ)ē-ˈden-chə-ləs\ *adj* [L *edentulus*, fr. *e-* + *dent-, dens*] : TOOTHLESS

Ed·gar \ˈed-gər\ *n* [*Edgar Allan Poe*, regarded as father of the detective story] : a statuette awarded annually by a professional organization for notable achievement in mystery-novel writing

[1]**edge** \ˈej\ *n* [ME *egge*, fr. OE *ecg*; akin to L *acer* sharp, Gk *akmē* point] **1 a** : the cutting side of a blade **b** : the sharpness of a blade **c** : penetrating power : KEENNESS ⟨an ~ of sarcasm in his voice⟩ ⟨took the ~ off the proposal⟩ **2 a** : the line where an object or area begins or ends : BORDER ⟨the town stands on the ~ of a plain⟩ **b** : the narrow part adjacent to a border ⟨walk on the ~ of the deck⟩ **c** : a point near the beginning or the end ⟨on the ~ of disaster⟩ **d** : a favorable margin : ADVANTAGE ⟨had the ~ on the competition⟩ **3** : a line or line segment that is the intersection of two plane faces (as of a pyramid) or of two planes ***syn*** see BORDER — **on edge** : ANXIOUS, NERVOUS

[2]**edge** *vb* **edged; edg·ing** *vt* **1 a** : to give an edge to **b** : to be on an edge of ⟨grew up in a community still *edging* the wilderness —H. M. Kallen⟩ **2** : to move or force gradually ⟨*edged* him off the road⟩ **3** : to incline (a ski) sideways so that one edge cuts into the snow **4** : to defeat by a small margin — usu. used with *out* ⟨*edged* out the opposing team by one point⟩ ~ *vi* : to advance by short moves ⟨the climbers *edged* along the cliff⟩

edged \ˈejd\ *adj* **1** : having a specified kind of edge, boundary, or border or a specified number of edges ⟨rough-*edged*⟩ ⟨two-*edged*⟩ **2** : SHARP, CUTTING ⟨an ~ knife⟩ ⟨an ~ remark⟩

edge effect *n* : the result of the presence of two adjoining plant communities (as in an ecotone) on the numbers and kinds of animals present in the immediate vicinity

edge–grain \ˌej-ˌgrān\ *or* **edge–grained** \ˈej-ˈgrānd\ *adj* : QUARTERSAWED

edge in *vt* : to work in : INTERPOLATE ⟨had difficulty *edging in* a word of his own⟩

edge·less \ˈej-ləs\ *adj* : lacking an edge : DULL

edg·er \ˈej-ər\ *n* : one that edges; *esp* : a tool used to trim the edge of a lawn along a sidewalk or curb

edge tool *n* : a tool with a sharp cutting edge

edge·ways \ˈej-ˌwāz\ *adv* : SIDEWAYS

edge·wise \-ˌwīz\ *adv* : EDGEWAYS

edg·ing *n* : something that forms an edge or border

edgy \ˈej-ē\ *adj* **edg·i·er; -est** **1** : having an edge : SHARP ⟨often displayed a perceptive, ~ wit —*New Yorker*⟩ **2** : being on edge : TENSE, IRRITABLE — **edg·i·ly** \ˈej-ə-lē\ *adv* — **edg·i·ness** \ˈej-ē-nəs\ *n*

edh \ˈeth\ *n* [Icel *eth*] : a letter ð used in Old English and in Icelandic to represent an interdental fricative and in some phonetic alphabets to represent the voiced interdental fricative (as in *then*)

ed·i·ble \ˈed-ə-bəl\ *adj* [LL *edibilis*, fr. L *edere* to eat — more at EAT] : fit to be eaten : EATABLE — **ed·i·bil·i·ty** \ˌed-ə-ˈbil-ət-ē\ *n* — **edible** *n* — **ed·i·ble·ness** \ˈed-ə-bəl-nəs\ *n*

edict \ˈē-ˌdikt\ *n* [L *edictum*, fr. neut. of *edictus*, pp. of *edicere* to decree, fr. *e-* + *dicere* to say — more at DICTION] **1** : an official public proclamation having the force of law **2** : ORDER, COMMAND ⟨we held firm to Grandmother's ~ —M. F. K. Fisher⟩ — **edic·tal** \i-ˈdik-tᵊl\ *adj*

ed·i·fi·ca·tion \ˌed-ə-fə-ˈkā-shən\ *n* : an act or process of edifying

edif·i·ca·to·ry \i-ˈdif-ə-kə-ˌtōr-ē, -ˌtȯr-\ *adj* : intended or suitable for edification

ed·i·fice \ˈed-ə-fəs\ *n* [ME, fr. MF, fr. L *aedificium*, fr. *aedificare*] **1** : BUILDING; *esp* : a large or massive structure **2** : a large abstract structure ⟨the keystone which holds together the social ~ —R. H. Tawney⟩

ed·i·fy \ˈed-ə-ˌfī\ *vt* **-fied; -fy·ing** [ME *edifien*, fr. MF *edifier*, fr. LL & L; LL *aedificare* to instruct or improve spiritually, fr. L, to erect a house, fr. *aedes* temple, house; akin to OE *ād* funeral pyre, L *aestas* summer] **1** *archaic* **a** : BUILD **b** : ESTABLISH **2** : to instruct and improve esp. in moral and religious knowledge : ENLIGHTEN

[1]**ed·it** \ˈed-ət\ *vt* **1 a** : to prepare an edition of ⟨~*ed* Poe's works⟩ **b** : to assemble (as a moving picture or tape recording) by cutting and rearranging **c** : to alter, adapt, or refine esp. to bring about conformity to a standard or to suit a particular purpose ⟨carefully ~*ed* his speech⟩ **2** : to direct the publication of ⟨~*s* the daily newspaper⟩ **3** : DELETE — usu. used with *out* — **ed·it·able** \-ə-bəl\ *adj*

[2]**edit** *n* : an instance of editing

edi·tion \i-ˈdish-ən\ *n* [MF, fr. L *edition-, editio* publication, edition, fr. *editus*, pp. of *edere* to bring forth, publish, fr. *e-* + *-dere* to put or *-dere* (fr. *dare* to give) — more at DO, DATE] **1 a** : the form in which a text (as a printed book) is published **b** (1) : the whole number of copies published at one time (2) : the usu. special issue of a newspaper for a particular day ⟨the Sunday ~⟩ (3) : one of the several issues of a newspaper for a single day ⟨the late afternoon ~⟩ **2 a** : one of the forms in which something is presented ⟨this year's ~ of the annual charity ball⟩ **b** : the whole number of articles of one style put out at one time ⟨a limited ~ of collectors' pieces⟩ **3** : COPY, VERSION

edi·tio prin·ceps \ā-ˌdit-ē-(ˌ)ō-ˈprin-ˌkeps, i-ˌdish-ē-(ˌ)ō-ˈprin-ˌseps\ *n, pl* **edi·ti·o·nes prin·ci·pes** \ā-ˌdit-ē-ˈō-ˌnās-ˈpriŋ-kə-ˌpās, i-ˌdish-ē-ˈō-(ˌ)nēz-ˈprin(t)-sə-ˌpēz\ [NL, lit., first edition] : the first printed edition esp. of a work that circulated in manuscript before printing became common

ed·i·tor \ˈed-ət-ər\ *n* **1** : one that edits esp. as an occupation **2** : a person who writes editorials **3** : a device used in editing motion-picture film or magnetic tape — **ed·i·tor·ship** \-ˌship\ *n*

[1]**ed·i·to·ri·al** \ˌed-ə-ˈtōr-ē-əl, -ˈtȯr-\ *adj* **1** : of or relating to an editor ⟨an ~ office⟩ **2** : being or resembling an editorial ⟨an ~ statement⟩ — **ed·i·to·ri·al·ly** \-ē-ə-lē\ *adv*

[2]**editorial** *n* : a newspaper or magazine article that gives the opinions of the editors or publishers; *also* : an expression of opinion that resembles such an article ⟨a television ~⟩

ed·i·to·ri·al·ist \-ē-ə-ləst\ *n* : a writer of editorials

ed·i·to·ri·al·ize \ˌed-ə-ˈtōr-ē-ə-ˌlīz, -ˈtȯr-\ *vi* **-ized; -iz·ing** **1** : to express an opinion in the form of an editorial **2** : to introduce opinion into the reporting of facts **3** : to express an opinion (as on a controversial issue) — **ed·i·to·ri·al·iza·tion** \-ˌtōr-ē-ə-lə-ˈzā-shən, -ˌtȯr-\ *n* — **ed·i·to·ri·al·iz·er** *n*

editor in chief *n* : an editor who is the head of an editorial staff (as of a publication)

ed·i·tress \ˈed-ə-trəs\ *n* : a female editor

EdM [NL *educationis magister*] *abbr* master of education

Edom·ite \ˈēd-ə-ˌmīt\ *n* [*Edom* (Esau), ancestor of the Edomites] : a member of a Semitic people living south of the Dead sea in biblical times

EDP *abbr* electronic data processing

EDT *abbr* eastern daylight time

EDTA \ˌē-ˌdē-ˌtē-ˈā\ *n* [ethylene*d*iamine*t*etra*a*cetic acid] : a white crystalline acid $C_{10}H_{16}N_2O_8$ used esp. as a chelating agent and in medicine as an anticoagulant and in the treatment of lead poisoning

educ *abbr* education; educational

[1]**ed·u·ca·ble** \ˈej-ə-kə-bəl\ *adj* : capable of being educated; *specif* : capable of some degree of learning — **ed·u·ca·bil·i·ty** \ˌej-ə-kə-ˈbil-ət-ē\ *n*

[2]**educable** *n* : a mildly retarded person : MORON

ed·u·cate \ˈej-ə-ˌkāt\ *vb* **-cat·ed; -cat·ing** [ME *educaten* to rear, fr. L *educatus*, pp. of *educare* to rear, educate] *vt* **1** : to provide schooling for **2** : to develop mentally or morally esp. by instruction ~ *vi* : to educate a person or thing ***syn*** see TEACH

ed·u·cat·ed *adj* **1** : having an education; *esp* : having an education beyond the average **2 a** : giving evidence of training or practice : SKILLED ⟨Doc worked over him with his ~ fingers —Budd Schulberg⟩ **b** : befitting one that is educated ⟨~ conversation⟩ **c** : based on some knowledge of fact ⟨an ~ guess⟩ — **ed·u·cat·ed·ly** *adv* — **ed·u·cat·ed·ness** *n*

ed·u·ca·tion \ˌej-ə-ˈkā-shən\ *n* **1 a** : the action or process of educating or of being educated; *also* : a stage of such a process **b** : the knowledge and development resulting from an educational process ⟨a man of little ~⟩ **2** : the field of study that deals mainly with methods of teaching and learning in schools — **ed·u·ca·tion·al** \-shnəl, -shən-ᵊl\ *adj* — **ed·u·ca·tion·al·ly** \-ē\ *adv*

educational park *n* : a large centralized educational complex of elementary and secondary schools

educational psychology *n* : psychology concerned with human maturation, school learning, teaching methods, guidance, and evaluation of aptitude and progress by standardized tests — **educational psychologist** *n*

educational television *n* **1** : PUBLIC TELEVISION **2** : television that provides instruction esp. for students and sometimes by closed circuit

ed·u·ca·tion·ist \ˌej-ə-ˈkā-sh(ə-)nəst\ *also* **ed·u·ca·tion·al·ist** \-shnə-ləst, -shən-ᵊl-əst\ *n* **1** *chiefly Brit* : a professional educator **2** : an educational theorist

ed·u·ca·tive \ˈej-ə-ˌkāt-iv\ *adj* **1** : tending to educate : INSTRUCTIVE **2** : of or relating to education

ed·u·ca·tor \ˈej-ə-ˌkāt-ər\ *n* **1** : one skilled in teaching : TEACHER **2 a** : a student of the theory and practice of education : EDUCATIONIST 2 **b** : an administrator in education

educe \i-ˈd(y)üs\ *vt* **educed; educ·ing** [L *educere* to draw out, fr. *e-* + *ducere* to lead — more at TOW] **1** : to bring out (as something latent) **2** : DEDUCE — **educ·ible** \-ˈd(y)ü-sə-bəl\ *adj* — **educ·tion** \-ˈdək-shən\ *n*

syn EDUCE, EVOKE, ELICIT, EXTRACT, EXTORT *shared meaning element* : to draw out something hidden, latent, or reserved

educ·tor \i-ˈdək-tər\ *n* [LL, one that leads out, fr. L *eductus*, pp. of *educere*] **1** : one that educes; *specif* : EJECTOR 2 **2** : a device similar to an ejector for mixing two fluids

edul·co·rate \i-ˈdəl-kə-ˌrāt\ *vb* **-rat·ed; -rat·ing** [NL *edulcoratus*, pp. of *edulcorare*, fr. L *e-* + *dulcor* sweetness, fr. *dulcis* sweet] *vt* : to free from harshness (as of attitude) : make pleasant ~ *vi* : to make something more pleasant

Ed·war·di·an \e-ˈdwärd-ē-ən, -ˈdwȯrd-\ *adj* : of, relating to, or characteristic of Edward VII of England or his age: as **a** : characterized by opulence and a complacent sense of material security **b** *of clothing* : marked by the hourglass silhouette for women and long narrow fitted suits for men

EE *abbr* electrical engineer

[1]**-ee** \ˈē, ˌē, ē\ *n suffix* [ME *-e*, fr. MF *-é*, fr. *-é*, pp. ending, fr. L *-atus*] **1** : recipient or beneficiary of (a specified action) ⟨appointee⟩

⟨grantee⟩ **2 :** person furnished with (a specified thing) ⟨patentee⟩ **3 :** person that performs (a specified action) ⟨escapee⟩

²-ee *n suffix* [prob. alter. of *-y*] **1 :** one associated with ⟨bargee⟩ **2 :** a particular esp. small kind of ⟨bootee⟩ **3 :** one resembling or suggestive of ⟨goatee⟩

EEC *abbr* European Economic Community

EEG *abbr* electroencephalogram; electroencephalograph

eel \ˈē(ə)l\ *n* [ME *ele*, fr. OE *ǣl*; akin to OHG *āl* eel] **1 a :** any of numerous voracious elongate snakelike teleost fishes (order Apodes) that have a smooth slimy skin, lack pelvic fins, and have the median fins confluent around the tail **b :** any of numerous other elongate fishes (as of the order Symbranchii) **2 :** any of various nematodes — **eel·like** \ˈē(ə)l-ˌlīk\ *adj* — **eely** \ˈē-lē\ *adj*

eel·grass \ˈē(ə)l-ˌgras\ *n* **1 :** a submerged marine plant (*Zostera marina*) that has very long narrow leaves, is abundant along the No. Atlantic coast, and with related forms constitutes a monocotyledonous family (Zosteraceae, the eelgrass family) **2 :** TAPE GRASS

eel·pout \-ˌpau̇t\ *n* **1 :** any of various marine fishes resembling blennies (family Zoarcidae) **2 :** BURBOT

eel·worm \-ˌwərm\ *n* **:** a nematode worm; *esp* **:** any of various small free-living or plant-parasitic roundworms

-een \ˈēn\ *n suffix* [prob. fr. *ratteen*] **:** inferior fabric resembling (a specified fabric) **:** imitation ⟨velveteen⟩

e'en \(ˈ)ēn\ *adv* **:** EVEN

EENT *abbr* eye, ear, nose, and throat

-eer \ˈi(ə)r\ *n suffix* [MF *-ier*, fr. L *-arius* — more at -ARY] **1 :** one that is concerned with professionally, conducts, or produces ⟨auctioneer⟩ ⟨pamphleteer⟩ — often in words with derogatory meaning ⟨profiteer⟩ **2 :** contemptible one ⟨patrioteer⟩

e'er \(ˈ)e(ə)r, (ˈ)a(ə)r\ *adv* **:** EVER

ee·rie *also* **ee·ry** \ˈi(ə)r-ē\ *adj* **ee·ri·er; -est** [ME *eri*, fr. OE *earg* cowardly, wretched] **1** *chiefly Scot* **:** affected with fright **:** SCARED **2 a :** frightening because of strangeness or gloominess **b :** notably strange and mysterious **:** BAFFLING ⟨the *eeriest* mystery in modern court records — a persistent riddle —*Life*⟩ ***syn*** see WEIRD — **ee·ri·ly** \ˈir-ə-lē\ *adv* — **ee·ri·ness** \ˈir-ē-nəs\ *n*

ef \ˈef\ *n* **:** the letter *f*

eff *abbr* efficiency

ef·face \i-ˈfās, e-\ *vt* **ef·faced; ef·fac·ing** [MF *effacer*, fr. *ex-* + *face*] **1 :** to eliminate or make indistinct by or as if by wearing away a surface ⟨coins with dates *effaced* by wear⟩ ⟨regrowth has *effaced* the worst scars from the fire⟩ **2 :** to make (oneself) modestly or shyly inconspicuous ***syn*** see ERASE — **ef·face·able** \-ˈfā-sə-bəl\ *adj* — **ef·face·ment** \-ˈfā-smənt\ *n* — **ef·fac·er** *n*

¹ef·fect \i-ˈfekt\ *n* [ME, fr. MF & L; MF, fr. L *effectus*, fr. *effectus*, pp. of *efficere* to bring about, fr. *ex-* + *facere* to make, do — more at DO] **1 :** something that inevitably follows an antecedent (as a cause or agent) **2 a :** PURPORT, INTENT **b :** basic meaning **:** ESSENCE **3 :** an outward sign **:** APPEARANCE **4 :** ACCOMPLISHMENT, FULFILLMENT **5 :** power to bring about a result **:** INFLUENCE **6** *pl* **:** movable property **:** GOODS ⟨personal ~*s*⟩ **7 a :** a distinctive impression ⟨the color gives the ~ of being warm⟩ **b :** the creation of a desired impression ⟨her tears were purely for ~⟩ **c :** something designed to produce a distinctive or desired impression ⟨special lighting ~*s*⟩ **8 :** the quality or state of being operative **:** OPERATION ⟨the law goes into ~ next week⟩

syn EFFECT, RESULT, CONSEQUENCE, EVENT, ISSUE, OUTCOME *shared meaning element* **:** a condition or occurrence traceable to a cause ***ant*** cause

— **in effect :** in substance **:** VIRTUALLY ⟨the . . . committee agreed to what was *in effect* a reduction in the hourly wage —*Current Biog.*⟩ — **to the effect :** with the meaning ⟨issued a statement *to the effect* that he would resign⟩

²effect *vt* **1 :** to cause to come into being **2 a :** to bring about often by surmounting obstacles **:** ACCOMPLISH ⟨~ a settlement of a dispute⟩ **b :** to put into effect ⟨the duty of the legislature to ~ the will of the citizens⟩

¹ef·fec·tive \i-ˈfek-tiv\ *adj* **1 a :** producing a decided, decisive, or desired effect **b :** IMPRESSIVE, STRIKING ⟨they did . . . develop sharply ~ criticisms of the monstrosities of social and economic inequality —R. L. Hoffman⟩ **2 :** ready for service or action ⟨~ manpower⟩ **3 :** ACTUAL ⟨the need to increase ~ demand for goods⟩ **4 :** being in effect **:** OPERATIVE ⟨the tax becomes ~ next year⟩ — **ef·fec·tive·ly** *adv* — **ef·fec·tive·ness** *n*

syn EFFECTIVE, EFFECTUAL, EFFICIENT, EFFICACIOUS *shared meaning element* **:** producing or capable of producing a result. EFFECTIVE emphasizes the actual production of or the power to produce an effect ⟨*effective* thinking⟩ ⟨an *effective* rebuke⟩ EFFECTUAL suggests the accomplishment of a desired result or the fulfillment of a purpose or intent esp. as viewed after the event ⟨the remedy proved *effectual* and relieved her distress⟩ EFFICIENT may apply to what is actually operative and producing a result ⟨the *efficient* cause of an end result⟩ or it may suggest an acting or a potential for action or use in such a way as to avoid loss or waste of energy in effecting, producing, or functioning ⟨an *efficient* little car⟩ ⟨a very *efficient* worker⟩ EFFICACIOUS implies possession of a special quality or virtue that gives effective power ⟨quinine is still one of the most *efficacious* drugs for the control of malaria⟩ ***ant*** ineffective, futile

²effective *n* **:** one that is effective; *esp* **:** a soldier equipped for duty

ef·fec·tiv·i·ty \ˌef-ˌek-ˈtiv-ət-ē, i-ˌfek-\ *n* **:** the quality or state of being effective **:** EFFECTIVENESS

ef·fec·tor \i-ˈfek-tər, -ˌtȯ(ə)r\ *n* **1 :** a bodily organ (as a gland or muscle) that becomes active in response to stimulation **2 :** a substance that induces protein synthesis by combining allosterically with a genetic repressor

ef·fec·tu·al \i-ˈfek-chə(-wə)l, -ˈfeksh-wəl\ *adj* **:** producing or able to produce a desired effect **:** ADEQUATE ***syn*** see EFFECTIVE ***ant*** ineffectual, fruitless — **ef·fec·tu·al·i·ty** \-ˌfek-chə-ˈwal-ət-ē\ *n* — **ef·fec·tu·al·ness** \-ˈfek-chə(-wə)l-nəs, -ˈfeksh-wəl-\ *n*

ef·fec·tu·al·ly \i-ˈfek-chə(-wə)-lē, -ˈfeksh-wə-\ *adv* **1 :** in an effectual manner **2 :** with great effect **:** COMPLETELY

ef·fec·tu·ate \i-ˈfek-chə-ˌwāt\ *vt* **-at·ed; -at·ing :** EFFECT 2 — **ef·fec·tu·a·tion** \-ˌfek-chə-ˈwā-shən\ *n*

ef·fem·i·na·cy \ə-ˈfem-ə-nə-sē\ *n* **:** the quality of being effeminate

¹ef·fem·i·nate \-nət\ *adj* [ME, fr. L *effeminatus*, fr. pp. of *effeminare* to make effeminate, fr. *ex-* + *femina* woman — more at FEMININE] **1 :** having feminine qualities (as weakness or softness) inappropriate to a man **:** not manly in appearance or manner **2 :** marked by an unbecoming delicacy or overrefinement ⟨~ art⟩ ⟨an ~ civilization⟩

²effeminate *n* **:** an effeminate person

ef·fen·di \e-ˈfen-dē, ə-\ *n* [Turk *efendi* master, fr. NGk *aphentēs*, alter. of Gk *authentēs* — more at AUTHENTIC] **:** a man of property, authority, or education in an eastern Mediterranean country

ef·fer·ent \ˈef-ə-rənt; ˈef-ˌer-ənt, ˈē-ˌfer-\ *adj* [F *efférent*, fr. L *efferent-, efferens*, prp. of *efferre* to carry outward, fr. *ex-* + *ferre* to carry — more at BEAR] **:** conducting outward from a part or organ; *specif* **:** conveying nervous impulses to an effector — compare AFFERENT — **efferent** *n* — **ef·fer·ent·ly** *adv*

ef·fer·vesce \ˌef-ər-ˈves\ *vi* **-vesced; -vesc·ing** [L *effervescere*, fr. *ex-* + *fervescere* to begin to boil, fr. *fervēre* to boil — more at BURN] **1 :** to bubble, hiss, and foam as gas escapes **2 :** to show liveliness or exhilaration — **ef·fer·ves·cence** \-ˈves-ᵊn(t)s\ *n* — **ef·fer·ves·cent** \-ᵊnt\ *adj* — **ef·fer·ves·cent·ly** *adv*

ef·fete \e-ˈfēt, i-\ *adj* [L *effetus*, fr. *ex-* + *fetus* fruitful — more at FEMININE] **1 :** no longer fertile **2 a :** worn out with age **:** EXHAUSTED **b :** marked by weakness or decadence **c :** OUTMODED ⟨an old but by no means ~ statute —Edward Jenks⟩ **3 :** EFFEMINATE ⟨a good humored, ~ boy brought up by maiden aunts —Herman Wouk⟩ — **ef·fete·ly** *adv* — **ef·fete·ness** *n*

ef·fi·ca·cious \ˌef-ə-ˈkā-shəs\ *adj* [L *efficac-, efficax*, fr. *efficere*] **:** having the power to produce a desired effect ***syn*** see EFFECTIVE ***ant*** inefficacious, powerless — **ef·fi·ca·cious·ly** *adv* — **ef·fi·ca·cious·ness** *n*

ef·fi·cac·i·ty \ˌef-ə-ˈkas-ət-ē\ *n* **:** EFFICACY

ef·fi·ca·cy \ˈef-i-kə-sē\ *n, pl* **-cies :** the power to produce an effect

ef·fi·cien·cy \i-ˈfish-ən-sē\ *n, pl* **-cies 1 :** the quality or degree of being efficient **2 a :** efficient operation **b (1) :** effective operation as measured by a comparison of production with cost (as in energy, time, and money) **(2) :** the ratio of the useful energy delivered by a dynamic system to the energy supplied to it **3 :** EFFICIENCY APARTMENT

efficiency apartment *n* **:** a small usu. furnished apartment with minimal kitchen and bath facilities

efficiency engineer *n* **:** one who analyzes methods, procedures, and jobs in order to secure maximum efficiency — called also *efficiency expert*

ef·fi·cient \i-ˈfish-ənt\ *adj* [ME, fr. MF or L; MF, fr. L *efficient-, efficiens*, fr. prp. of *efficere* to bring about] **1 :** being or involving the immediate agent in producing an effect ⟨the ~ action of heat in changing water to steam⟩ **2 :** productive of desired effects; *esp* **:** productive without waste ***syn*** see EFFECTIVE ***ant*** inefficient — **ef·fi·cient·ly** *adv*

ef·fi·gy \ˈef-ə-jē\ *n, pl* **-gies** [ME *effigie*, fr. L *effigies*, fr. *effingere* to form, fr. *ex-* + *fingere* to shape — more at DOUGH] **:** an image or representation esp. of a person; *specif* **:** a crude figure representing a hated person — **in effigy :** publicly in the form of an effigy ⟨the football coach was burned *in effigy*⟩

ef·flo·resce \ˌef-lə-ˈres\ *vi* **-resced; -resc·ing** [L *efflorescere*, fr. *ex-* + *florescere* to begin to blossom — more at FLORESCENCE] **1 :** to burst forth **:** BLOOM **2 a :** to change to a powder from loss of water of crystallization **b :** to form or become covered with a powdery crust ⟨bricks may ~ owing to the deposition of soluble salts⟩

ef·flo·res·cence \-ˈres-ᵊn(t)s\ *n* **1 :** the period or state of flowering **2 a :** the action or process of developing and unfolding as if coming into flower **:** BLOSSOMING ⟨periods of . . . intellectual and artistic ~ —Julian Huxley⟩ **b :** an instance of such development **c :** fullness of manifestation **:** CULMINATION **3 :** the process or product of efflorescing chemically **4 :** a redness of the skin **:** ERUPTION — **ef·flo·res·cent** \-ᵊnt\ *adj*

ef·flu·ence \ˈef-ˌlü-ən(t)s; e-ˈflü-, ə-ˈ\ *n* **1 :** something that flows out **2 :** an action or process of flowing out

¹ef·flu·ent \-ənt\ *adj* [L *effluent-, effluens*, prp. of *effluere* to flow out, fr. *ex-* + *fluere* to flow — more at FLUID] **:** flowing out **:** EMANATING, OUTGOING ⟨an ~ river⟩

²effluent *n* **:** something that flows out: as **a :** an outflowing branch of a main stream or lake **b :** waste material (as smoke, liquid industrial refuse, or sewage) discharged into the environment esp. when serving as a pollutant

ef·flu·vi·um \e-ˈflü-vē-əm\ *n, pl* **-via** \-vē-ə\ *often sing in constr or* **-vi·ums** [L *effluvium* act of flowing out, fr. *effluere*] **1 :** an invisible emanation; *esp* **:** an offensive exhalation or smell **2 :** a by-product esp. in the form of waste

ef·flux \ˈef-ˌləks\ *n* [L *effluxus*, pp. of *effluere*] **1 :** EFFLUENCE **2 :** a passing away **:** EXPIRATION — **ef·flux·ion** \e-ˈflək-shən\ *n*

ef·fort \ˈef-ərt, -ˌȯ(ə)rt\ *n* [MF, fr. OF *esfort*, fr. *esforcier* to force, fr. *ex-* + *forcier* to force] **1 :** conscious exertion of power **2 :** a serious attempt **:** TRY **3 :** something produced by exertion or trying ⟨the novel was his most ambitious ~⟩ **4 :** effective force as distinguished from the possible resistance called into action by such a force **5 :** the total work done to achieve a particular end ⟨the war ~⟩

syn EFFORT, EXERTION, PAINS, TROUBLE *shared meaning element* **:** the active use of energy in producing a result ***ant*** ease

ef·fort·ful \-ərt-fəl\ *adj* **:** showing or requiring effort — **ef·fort·ful·ly** \-fə-lē\ *adv*

ef·fort·less \-ərt-ləs\ *adj* **:** showing or requiring little or no effort — **ef·fort·less·ly** *adv* — **ef·fort·less·ness** *n*

ə abut	ᵊ kitten	ər further	a back	ā bake	ä cot, cart
au̇ out	ch chin	e less	ē easy	g gift	i trip ī life
j joke	ŋ sing	ō flow	ȯ flaw	ȯi coin	th thin t͟h this
ü loot	u̇ foot	y yet	yü few	yu̇ furious	zh vision

ef·fron·tery \i-'frənt-ə-rē, e-\ *n, pl* **-ter·ies** [F *effronterie,* deriv. of LL *effront-, effrons* shameless, fr. L *ex- + front-, frons* forehead — more at BRINK] : shameless boldness : INSOLENCE (the ~ to propound three such heresies —*Times Lit. Supp.*⟩ *syn* see TEMERITY

ef·ful·gence \i-'fu̇l-jən(t)s, e-\ *n* [LL *effulgentia,* fr. L *effulgent-, effulgens,* prp. of *effulgēre* to shine forth, fr. *ex- + fulgēre* to shine — more at FULGENT] : radiant splendor : BRILLIANCE — **ef·ful·gent** \-jənt\ *adj*

¹ef·fuse \i-'fyüz, e-\ *vb* **ef·fused; ef·fus·ing** [L *effusus,* pp. of *effundere,* fr. *ex- + fundere* to pour — more at FOUND] *vt* **1** : to pour out (a liquid) **2** : to give off : RADIATE ~ *vi* : to flow out : EMANATE

²ef·fuse \-'fyüs\ *adj* **1** : poured out freely : OVERFLOWING **2** : DIFFUSE; *specif* : spread out flat without definite form ⟨~ lichens⟩

ef·fu·sion \i-'fyü-zhən, e-\ *n* **1** : an act of effusing **2** : unrestrained expression of words or feelings ⟨greeted her with great ~ —Olive H. Prouty⟩ **3 a** (1) : the escape of a fluid from anatomical vessels by rupture or exudation (2) : the flow of a gas through an aperture whose diameter is small as compared with the distance between the molecules of the gas **b** : the fluid that escapes

ef·fu·sive \i-'fyü-siv, e-, -ziv\ *adj* **1** *archaic* : pouring freely **2** : excessively demonstrative : GUSHING **3** : characterized by or formed by a nonexplosive outpouring of lava ⟨~ rocks⟩ — **ef·fu·sive·ly** *adv* — **ef·fu·sive·ness** *n*

eft \'eft\ *n* [ME *evete, ewte,* fr. OE *efete*] : NEWT

eft·soons \eft-'sünz\ *adv* [ME *eftsones,* fr. *eft* after (fr. OE) + *sone* soon + *-s,* adv. suffix; akin to OE *æfter* after] *archaic* : soon after

e.g. \(f(ə-)'zam-pəl, (ˌ)ē-'jē\ *abbr* [L *exempli gratia*] for example

Eg *abbr* Egypt; Egyptian

egad \i-'gad\ *or* **egads** \-'gadz\ *interj* [prob. euphemism for *oh God*] — used as a mild oath

egal \'ē-gəl\ *adj* [ME, fr. MF, fr. L *aequalis*] *obs* : EQUAL

egal·i·tar·i·an \i-ˌgal-ə-'ter-ē-ən\ *adj* [F *égalitaire,* fr. *égalité* equality, fr. L *aequalitat-, aequalitas,* fr. *aequalis*] : asserting, promoting, or marked by egalitarianism — **egalitarian** *n*

egal·i·tar·i·an·ism \-ē-ə-ˌniz-əm\ *n* **1** : a belief in human equality esp. with respect to social, political, and economic rights and privileges **2** : a social philosophy advocating the removal of inequalities among men

éga·li·té \ā-gä-lē-tā\ *n* [F] : social or political equality

EGD *abbr* electrogasdynamics

eger *var of* EAGRE

Ege·ria \i-'jir-ē-ə\ *n* [L, a nymph who advised the legendary Roman king Numa Pompilius] : a woman adviser or companion

egest \i-'jest\ *vt* [L *egestus,* pp. of *egerere* to carry outside, discharge, fr. *e- + gerere* to carry — more at CAST] : DEFECATE; *broadly* : to rid the body of (waste material) — **eges·tion** \-'jes(h)-chən\ *n* — **eges·tive** \-'jes-tiv\ *adj*

eges·ta \i-'jes-tə\ *n pl* [NL, fr. L, neut. pl. of *egestus*] : something egested

¹egg \'eg, 'āg\ *vt* [ME *eggen,* fr. ON *eggja;* akin to OE *ecg* edge — more at EDGE] : to incite to action — usu. used with *on* ⟨~ed the mob on to riot⟩

²egg *n, often attrib* [ME *egge,* fr. ON *egg;* akin to OE *ǣg* egg, L *ovum,* Gk *ōion*] **1 a** : the hard-shelled reproductive body produced by a bird and esp. by domestic poultry **b** : an animal reproductive body consisting of an ovum together with its nutritive and protective envelopes and having the capacity to develop into a new individual capable of independent existence **c** : OVUM **2** : something resembling an egg **3** : FELLOW, GUY ⟨he's a good ~⟩

³egg *vt* **1** : to cover with egg **2** : to pelt with eggs

egg and dart *n* : a carved ornamental design in relief consisting of an egg-shaped figure alternating with a figure somewhat like an elongated javelin or arrowhead

egg-beat·er \'eg-ˌbēt-ər, 'āg-\ *n* **1** : a hand-operated kitchen utensil used for beating, stirring, or whipping; *esp* : a rotary device for these purposes **2** : HELICOPTER

egg case *n* : a protective case enclosing eggs : OOTHECA — called also *egg capsule*

egg cell *n* : OVUM

egg-cup \'eg-ˌkəp, 'āg-\ *n* : a cup for holding an egg that is to be eaten from the shell

egg·head \-ˌhed\ *n* : INTELLECTUAL, HIGHBROW ⟨practical men who disdain the schemes and dreams of ~s —W. L. Miller⟩

egg·head·ed \-'hed-əd\ *adj* : having the characteristics of an egghead — **egg·head·ed·ness** *n*

egg·nog \-ˌnäg\ *n* : a drink consisting of eggs beaten up with sugar, milk or cream, and often alcoholic liquor

egg·plant \-ˌplant\ *n* **1** : a widely cultivated perennial herb (*Solanum melongena*) yielding edible fruit **b** : the usu. smooth ovoid fruit of the eggplant **2** : a dark grayish or blackish purple

egg roll *n* : a thin egg-dough casing filled with minced vegetables and often bits of meat (as shrimp or chicken) and usu. fried in deep fat

eggs Ben·e·dict \-'ben-ə-ˌdikt\ *n pl but sing or pl in constr* [prob. fr. the name *Benedict*] : poached eggs and broiled ham placed on toasted halves of English muffin and covered with hollandaise sauce

¹egg·shell \'eg-ˌshel, 'āg-\ *n* **1** : the hard exterior covering of an egg **2** : something resembling an eggshell esp. in fragility

²eggshell *adj* **1** : thin and fragile **2** : slightly glossy

egg timer *n* : a small sandglass running about three minutes for timing the boiling of eggs

egg 1a: *1* inner shell membrane, *2* outer shell membrane, *3* shell, *4* albumen or white, *5* chalazae, *6* yolk, *7* blastodisc, *8* air space

egg tooth *n* : a hard sharp prominence on the beak of an unhatched bird or the nose of an unhatched reptile that is used to break through the eggshell

egis \'ē-jəs\ *var of* AEGIS

eg·lan·tine \'eg-lən-ˌtīn, -ˌtēn\ *n* [ME *eglentyn,* fr. MF *aiglent,* fr. (assumed) VL *aculentum,* fr. L *acus* needle; akin to L *acer* sharp — more at EDGE] : SWEETBRIER

ego \'ē-(ˌ)gō *also* 'eg-(ˌ)ō\ *n, pl* **egos** [NL, fr. L, I — more at I] **1** : the self esp. as contrasted with another self or the world **2 a** : EGOTISM **b** : SELF-ESTEEM 1 **3** : the one of the three divisions of the psyche in psychoanalytic theory that serves as the organized conscious mediator between the person and reality esp. by functioning both in the perception of and adaptation to reality — compare ¹ID, SUPEREGO

ego·cen·tric \ˌē-gō-'sen-trik *also* ˌeg-ō-\ *adj* **1** : concerned with the individual rather than society **2** : taking the ego as the starting point in philosophy **3 a** : limited in outlook or concern to one's own activities or needs **b** : SELF-CENTERED, SELFISH — **egocentric** *n* — **ego·cen·tri·cal·ly** \-tri-k(ə-)lē\ *adv* — **ego·cen·tric·i·ty** \-ˌsen-'tris-ət-ē\ *n* — **ego·cen·trism** \-'sen-ˌtriz-əm\ *n*

ego–defense \ˌē-(ˌ)gō-di-'fen(t)s *also* ˌeg-(ˌ)ō-\ *n* : a psychological mechanism designed consciously or unconsciously to protect one's self-image or self-esteem

ego ideal *n* : the positive standards, ideals, and ambitions that according to psychoanalytic theory are assimilated from the superego

ego–in·volve·ment \-in-'välv-mənt, -'võlv-\ *n* : an involvement of one's self-esteem in the performance of a task or in an object

ego·ism \'ē-gə-ˌwiz-əm *also* 'eg-ə-\ *n* **1** : a doctrine that all the elements of knowledge are in the ego and its relations **2 a** : an ethical doctrine that individual self-interest is the actual motive of all conscious action **b** : an ethical doctrine that individual self-interest is the valid end of all actions **3** : EGOTISM

ego·ist \-wəst\ *n* **1** : a believer in egoism **2** : an egocentric or egotistic person — **ego·is·tic** \ˌē-gə-'wis-tik *also* ˌeg-ə-\ *also* **ego·is·ti·cal** \-ti-kəl\ *adj* — **ego·is·ti·cal·ly** \-ti-k(ə-)lē\ *adv*

egoistic hedonism *n* : the ethical theory that the valid aim of right conduct is one's own happiness

ego·ma·nia \ˌē-gō-'mā-nē-ə, -nyə\ *n* : the quality or state of being extremely egocentric

ego·ma·ni·ac \-nē-ˌak\ *n* : one characterized by egomania — **ego·ma·ni·a·cal** \-mə-'nī-ə-kəl\ *adj* — **ego·ma·ni·a·cal·ly** \-k(ə-)lē\ *adv*

ego·tism \'ē-gə-ˌtiz-əm *also* 'eg-ə-\ *n* [L *ego* + E *-tism* (as in *idiotism*)] **1 a** : excessive use of the first person singular personal pronoun **b** : the practice of talking about oneself too much **2** : an exaggerated sense of self-importance : CONCEIT

ego·tist \-təst\ *n* : one characterized by egotism — **ego·tis·tic** \ˌē-gə-'tis-tik *also* ˌeg-ə-\ *or* **ego·tis·ti·cal** \-'tis-ti-kəl\ *adj* — **ego·tis·ti·cal·ly** \-'tis-ti-k(ə-)lē\ *adv*

ego–trip \'ē-gō-ˌtrip *also* 'eg-ō-\ *vi* : to behave in a self-seeking manner ⟨never overplayed, never *ego-tripped,* never grabbed the spotlight —Bob Palmer⟩

ego trip *n* : an act that enhances and satisfies one's ego

egre·gious \i-'grē-jəs\ *adj* [L *egregius,* fr. *e- + greg-, grex* herd — more at GREGARIOUS] **1** *archaic* : DISTINGUISHED **2** : conspicuously bad : FLAGRANT ⟨an ~ mistake⟩ — **egre·gious·ly** *adv* — **egre·gious·ness** *n*

¹egress \'ē-ˌgres\ *n* [L *egressus,* fr. *egressus,* pp. of *egredi* to go out, fr. *e- + gradi* to go — more at GRADE] **1** : the act or right of going or coming out; *specif* : the emergence of a celestial object from eclipse, occultation, or transit **2** : a place or means of going out : EXIT

²egress \ē-'gres\ *vi* : to go out : ISSUE

egres·sion \ē-'gresh-ən\ *n* : EGRESS, EMERGENCE

egret \'ē-grət, i-'gret, 'ē-ˌgret, 'eg-rət\ *n* [ME, fr. MF *aigrette,* fr. OProv *aigreta,* of Gmc origin; akin to OHG *heigaro* heron] : any of various herons that bear long plumes during the breeding season

Egypt *abbr* Egyptian

¹Egyp·tian \i-'jip-shən\ *adj* : of, relating to, or characteristic of Egypt or the Egyptians

²Egyptian *n* **1** : a native or inhabitant of Egypt **2** : the Afro-Asiatic language of the ancient Egyptians from earliest times to about the 3d century A.D. **3** *often not cap* : a typeface having little contrast between thick and thin strokes and squared serifs

egret

Egyptian clover *n* : BERSEEM

Egyptian cotton *n* : a fine long-staple often somewhat brownish cotton grown chiefly in Egypt

Egypto- *comb form* [prob. fr. F *Égypto-,* fr. Gk *Aigypto-,* fr. *Aigyptos*] : Egypt ⟨*Egyptology*⟩

Egyp·tol·o·gy \ˌē-(ˌ)jip-'täl-ə-jē\ *n* : the study of Egyptian antiquities — **Egyp·tol·o·gist** \-jəst\ *n*

eh \'ā, 'e, 'a(i), *also with* h preceding and/or with nasalization\ *interj* [ME *ey*] — used to ask for confirmation or to express inquiry

EHF *abbr* extremely high frequency

EHP *abbr* **1** effective horsepower **2** electric horsepower

EHV *abbr* extra high voltage

ei·der \'īd-ər\ *n* [D, G, or Sw, fr. Icel *æthur,* fr. ON *æthr*] **1** : any of several large northern sea ducks (*Somateria* or related genera) having fine soft down that is used by the female for lining the nest — called also *eider duck* **2** : EIDERDOWN 1

ei·der·down \-ˌdau̇n\ *n* [prob. fr. G *eiderdaune,* fr. Icel *æthardūnn,* fr. *æthur + dūnn* down] **1** : the down of the eider **2** : a com-

EGYPTIAN

forter filled with eiderdown **3 :** a soft lightweight clothing fabric knitted or woven and napped on one or both sides

ei·det·ic \ī-'det-ik\ *adj* [Gk *eidētikos* of a form, fr. *eidos* form — more at WISE] : marked by or involving extraordinarily accurate and vivid recall esp. of visual images ⟨an ~ memory⟩ — **ei·det·i·cal·ly** \-i-k(ə-)lē\ *adv*

ei·do·lon \ī-'dō-lən\ *n, pl* **-lons** \-lənz\ *or* **-la** \-lə\ [Gk *eidōlon*] **1 :** an unsubstantial image : PHANTOM **2 :** IDEAL

ei·gen·val·ue \'ī-gən-ˌval-(ˌ)yü, -yə(-w)\ *n* [part trans. of G *eigenwert,* fr. *eigen* own, peculiar, characteristic (fr. OHG *eigan*) + *wert* value — more at OWN] : CHARACTERISTIC ROOT

ei·gen·vec·tor \-ˌvek-tər\ *n* [ISV *eigen-* (fr. G *eigen*) + *vector*] : CHARACTERISTIC VECTOR

eight \'āt\ *n* [ME *eighte,* fr. *eighte,* adj., fr. OE *eahta;* akin to OHG *ahto* eight, L *octo,* Gk *oktō*] **1** — see NUMBER table **2 :** the eighth in a set or series ⟨sat in row ~⟩ **3 :** something having eight units or members: as **a :** an 8-oared racing boat or its crew **b :** an 8-cylinder engine or automobile — **eight** *adj or pron*

eight ball *n* **1 :** a black pool ball numbered 8 **2 :** MISFIT ⟨tried to weed out the *eight balls*⟩ — **behind the eight ball :** in a highly disadvantageous position or baffling situation

eigh·teen \(ˈ)ā(t)-'tēn\ *n* [ME *eightetene,* adj., fr. OE *eahtatīene;* akin to OE *tīen* ten] — see NUMBER table — **eighteen** *adj or pron* — **eigh·teenth** \-'tēn(t)th\ *adj or n*

eigh·teen·mo \ā(t)-'tēn-(ˌ)mō\ *n, pl* **-mos :** the size of a piece of paper cut 18 from a sheet; *also* **:** a book, a page, or paper of this size

eight·fold \'āt-ˌfōld, -'fōld\ *adj* **1 :** having eight units or members **2 :** being eight times as great or as many — **eight·fold** \-'fōld\ *adv*

eighth \'ātth, *nonstand* 'āth\ *n* **1** — see NUMBER table **2 :** OCTAVE — **eighth** *adj or adv*

eighth note *n* **:** a musical note with the time value of 1/8 of a whole note — see NOTE illustration

eighth rest *n* **:** a musical rest corresponding in time value to an eighth note

eight·pen·ny nail \ˌāt-ˌpen-ē-\ *n* [eight + *-penny*] : a nail typically 2 1/2 inches long

eighty \'āt-ē\ *n, pl* **eight·ies** [ME *eighty,* adj., fr. OE *eahtatig,* short for *hundeahtatig,* n., group of eighty, fr. *hund* hundred + *eahta* eight + *-tig* group of ten; akin to OE *tīen* ten] **1** — see NUMBER table **2** *pl* **:** the numbers 80 to 89; *specif* **:** the years 80 to 89 in a lifetime or century — **eight·i·eth** \'āt-ē-əth\ *adj or n* — **eighty** *adj or pron*

-ein *or* **-eine** *n suffix* [ISV, alter. of *-in, -ine*] : compound distinguished from a compound with a similar name ending in *-in* or *-ine* ⟨phthalein⟩

ein·korn \'īn-ˌkȯ(ə)rn\ *n* [G, fr. OHG *ein* one + *korn* grain — more at ONE, CORN] : a one-grained wheat (*Triticum monococum*) that is sometimes considered the most primitive wheat and is grown esp. in poor soils in central Europe — called also *einkorn wheat*

Ein·stein·ian \īn-'stī-nē-ən\ *adj* **:** of or relating to Albert Einstein or his theories

ein·stei·ni·um \-nē-əm\ *n* [NL, fr. Albert *Einstein* †1955 Am physicist & mathematician] : a radioactive element produced artificially — see ELEMENT table

ei·re·nic *var of* IRENIC

ei·ren·i·con \ī-'ren-i-ˌkän\ *n* [LGk *eirēnikon,* fr. neut. of Gk *eirēnikos* irenic — more at IRENIC] : a statement that attempts to harmonize conflicting doctrines : RECONCILIATION

eis·ege·sis \ˌī-sə-'jē-səs\ *n, pl* **-ege·ses** \-ˌsēz\ [Gk *eis* into + E *exegesis;* akin to Gk *en* in — more at IN] : the interpretation of a text (as of the Bible) by reading into it one's own ideas — compare EXEGESIS

ei·stedd·fod \ī-'steth-ˌvȯd, ā-\ *n* [W, lit., session, fr. *eistedd* to sit + *bod* being] : a Welsh competitive festival of the arts esp. in singing — **ei·stedd·fod·ic** \ˌī-ˌsteth-'vȯd-ik, ˌā-\ *adj*

¹ei·ther \'ē-thər *also* 'ī-\ *adj* [ME, fr. OE *ǣghwæther* both, each, fr. *ā* always + *ge-,* collective prefix + *hwæther* which of two, whether — more at AYE, CO-] **1 :** being the one and the other of two : EACH ⟨flowers blooming on ~ side of the walk⟩ **2 :** being the one or the other of two ⟨take ~ road⟩

²either *pron* **:** the one or the other

³either *conj* — used as a function word before two or more coordinate words, phrases, or clauses joined usu. by *or* to indicate that what immediately follows is the first of two or more alternatives

⁴either *adv* **1 :** LIKEWISE, MOREOVER — used for emphasis after a negative ⟨not wise or handsome ~⟩ **2 :** for that matter — used for emphasis after an alternative following a question or conditional clause esp. where negation is implied ⟨who answers for the Irish parliament? or army ~? —Robert Browning⟩

¹either–or \ˌē-thə-'rȯ(ə)r *also* ˌī-\ *adj* **:** of or marked by either-or : BLACK-AND-WHITE

²either–or *n* **:** an unavoidable choice or exclusive division between only two alternatives : DICHOTOMY ⟨never a matter of knowledge versus proficiency, never a simple ~ — H. J. Muller⟩

¹ejac·u·late \i-'jak-yə-ˌlāt\ *vb* **-lat·ed; -lat·ing** [L *ejaculatus,* pp. of *ejaculari* to throw out, fr. *e-* + *jaculari* to throw, fr. *jaculum* dart, fr. *jacere* to throw — more at JET] *vt* **1 :** to eject from a living body; *specif* **:** to eject (semen) in orgasm **2 :** to utter suddenly and vehemently ~ *vi* **:** to eject a fluid

²ejac·u·late \-lət\ *n* **:** the semen released by one ejaculation

ejac·u·la·tion \i-ˌjak-yə-'lā-shən\ *n* **1 :** an act of ejaculating; *specif* **:** a sudden discharging of a fluid from a duct **2 :** something ejaculated; *esp* **:** a short sudden emotional utterance

ejac·u·la·to·ry \i-'jak-yə-lə-ˌtōr-ē, -ˌtȯr-\ *adj* **1 :** casting or throwing out; *specif* **:** associated with or concerned in physiological ejaculation ⟨~ vessels⟩ **2 :** marked by or given to vocal ejaculation

ejaculatory duct *n* **:** a duct through which semen is ejaculated; *specif* **:** either of the paired ducts in man that are formed by the junction of the duct from the seminal vesicle with the vas deferens, pass through the prostate, and open into or close to the prostatic utricle

eject \i-'jekt\ *vt* [ME *ejecten,* fr. L *ejectus,* pp. of *eicere,* fr. *e-* + *jacere*] **1 a :** to drive out esp. by physical force **b :** to evict from property **2 :** to throw out or off from within ⟨~*s* the empty cartridges⟩ — **eject·able** \-'jek-tə-bəl\ *adj* — **ejec·tion** \-'jek-shən\ *n* — **ejec·tive** \-'jek-tiv\ *adj*

syn EJECT, EXPEL, OUST, EVICT, DISMISS *shared meaning element* **:** to drive or force out *ant* admit

ejec·ta \i-'jek-tə\ *n pl but sing or pl in constr* [NL, fr. L, neut. pl. of *ejectus*] : material thrown out (as from a volcano)

ejection seat *n* **:** an emergency escape seat for propelling an occupant out and away from an airplane by means of an explosive charge

eject·ment \i-'jek(t)-mənt\ *n* **1 :** DISPOSSESSION **2 :** an action for the recovery of possession of real property and damages and costs

ejec·tor \i-'jek-tər\ *n* **1 :** one that ejects **2 :** a jet pump for withdrawing a gas, fluid, or powdery substance from a space

eka- \ˌek-ə, ˌā-kə\ *comb form* [Skt *eka* one — more at ONE] : standing or assumed to stand next in order beyond (a specified element) in the same family of the periodic table — in names of chemical elements esp. when not yet discovered ⟨*eka*cesium (now called francium)⟩

¹eke \'ēk\ *adv* [ME, fr. OE *ēac;* akin to OHG *ouh* also, L *aut* or, Gk *au* again] *archaic* **:** ALSO

²eke *vt* **eked; ek·ing** [ME *eken,* fr. OE *īecan, ēcan;* akin to OHG *ouhhōn* to add, L *augēre* to increase, Gk *auxein*] *archaic* **:** INCREASE, LENGTHEN

eke out *vt* **1 a :** to make up for the deficiencies of : SUPPLEMENT ⟨*eked out* his income by getting a second job⟩ **b :** to make (a supply) last by economy **2 :** to make (as a living) by laborious or precarious means

EKG *abbr* [G *elektrokardiogramm*] electrocardiogram; electrocardiograph

ekis·tics \i-'kis-tiks\ *n pl but sing in constr* [NGk *oikistikē,* fr. fem. of *oikistikos* relating to settlement, fr. Gk, fr. *oikizein* to settle, colonize, fr. *oikos* house — more at VICINITY] : a science dealing with human settlements and drawing on the research and experience of professionals in various fields (as architecture, engineering, city planning, and sociology) — **ekis·tic** \-tik\ *adj*

Ek·man dredge \ˌek-mən-\ *n* [prob. fr. V. W. *Ekman* †1954 Sw oceanographer] : a dredge that has opposable jaws operated by a messenger traveling down a cable to release a spring catch and that is used in ecology for sampling the bottom of a body of water

ekt·ex·ine \(ˈ)ek-'tek-ˌsēn, -ˌsīn\ *n* [Gk *ekto-* outside + E *exine* — more at ECT-] : a structurally variable outer layer of the exine

¹el \'el\ *n* **:** the letter *l*

²el *n, often cap* **:** ELEVATED RAILROAD

³el *abbr* elevation

¹elab·o·rate \i-'lab-(ə-)rət\ *adj* [L *elaboratus,* fr. pp. of *elaborare* to work out, acquire by labor, fr. *e-* + *laborare* to work — more at LABORATORY] **1 :** planned or carried out with great care : DETAILED ⟨~ calculations⟩ **2 :** marked by complexity, fullness of detail, or ornateness : INTRICATE ⟨a highly ~ coiffure⟩ **3 :** marked by painstaking diligence — **elab·o·rate·ly** *adv* — **elab·o·rate·ness** *n*

²elab·o·rate \i-'lab-ə-ˌrāt\ *vb* **-rat·ed; -rat·ing** *vt* **1 :** to produce by labor **2 :** to build up (complex organic compounds) from simple ingredients **3 :** to work out in detail : DEVELOP ~ *vi* **1 :** to become elaborate **2 :** to expand something in detail ⟨would you care to ~ on that statement⟩ — **elab·o·ra·tion** \-ˌlab-ə-'rā-shən\ *n* — **elab·o·ra·tive** \-'lab-ə-ˌrāt-iv\ *adj*

Elaine \i-'lān\ *n* **:** any of several women in Arthurian legend; *esp* **:** one who dies for unrequited love of Lancelot

Elam·ite \'ē-lə-ˌmīt\ *n* **:** a language of unknown affinities used in Elam approximately from the 25th to the 4th centuries B.C.

élan \ā-läⁿ\ *n* [F, fr. MF *eslan* rush, fr. *(s')eslancer* to rush, fr. *ex-* + *lancer* to hurl — more at LANCE] : vigorous spirit or enthusiasm typically revealed by poise, verve, or liveliness of imagination

eland \'ē-lənd, -ˌland\ *n* [Afrik, elk, fr. D, fr. obs. G *elend,* fr. Lith *elnis;* akin to OHG *elaho* elk — more at ELK] : either of two large African antelopes (*Taurotragus oryx* and *T. derbianus*) bovine in form with short spirally twisted horns in both sexes

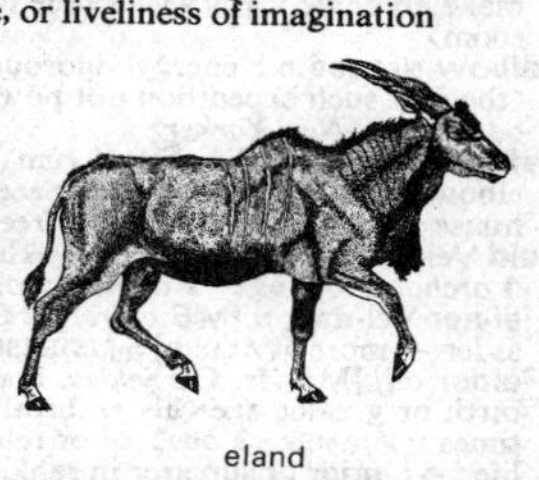
eland

élan vi·tal \ā-läⁿ-vē-tàl\ *n* [F] **:** the vital force or impulse of life; *specif* **:** a creative principle held by Bergson to be immanent in all organisms and responsible for evolution

el·a·pid \'el-ə-pəd\ *n* [NL *Elap-, Elaps,* genus of snakes, fr. MGk, a fish, alter. of Gk *elops*] : any of a family (Elapidae) of venomous snakes with grooved fangs

¹elapse \i-'laps\ *vi* **elapsed; elaps·ing** [L *elapsus,* pp. of *elabi,* fr. *e-* + *labi* to slip — more at SLEEP] : to slip or glide away : PASS ⟨four years *elapsed* before he returned⟩

²elapse *n* **:** PASSAGE ⟨went back to college after an ~ of 15 years⟩

elapsed time *n* **:** the actual time taken (as by a boat or automobile) to travel over a specified course (as in racing)

elas·mo·branch \i-'laz-mə-ˌbraŋk\ *n, pl* **-branchs** [deriv. of Gk *elasmos* metal plate (fr. *elaunein*) + L *branchia* gill] : any of a class (Chondrichthyes) of fishes with lamellate gills that comprise the sharks, rays, chimaeras, and various extinct related fishes — **elasmobranch** *adj*

ə abut ᵊ kitten ər further a back ā bake ä cot, cart
aù out ch chin e less ē easy g gift i trip ī life
j joke ŋ sing ō flow ȯ flaw ȯi coin th thin th this
ü loot ù foot y yet yü few yù furious zh vision

elas·tase \i-ˈlas-ˌtās, -ˌtāz\ *n* : an enzyme esp. of pancreatic juice that digests elastin

1elas·tic \i-ˈlas-tik\ *adj* [NL *elasticus,* fr. LGk *elastos* ductile, beaten, fr. Gk *elaunein* to drive, beat out; akin to OIr *luid* he went] **1 a** *of a solid* : capable of recovering size and shape after deformation **b** *of a gas* : capable of indefinite expansion **2** : capable of recovering quickly esp. from depression or disappointment **3** : capable of being easily stretched or expanded and resuming former shape : FLEXIBLE **4 a** : capable of ready change or easy expansion or contraction **b** : receptive to new ideas : ADAPTABLE — **elas·ti·cal·ly** \-ti-k(ə-)lē\ *adv*

2elastic *n* **1 a** : an elastic fabric usu. made of yarns containing rubber **b** : something made from this fabric **2 a** : easily stretched rubber usu. prepared in cords, strings, or bands **b** : RUBBER BAND

elastic clause *n* : a clause in the U.S. Constitution that provides the Constitutional basis for the implied or potential powers of Congress

elastic collision *n* : a collision in which the total kinetic energy of the colliding particles remains unchanged

elas·tic·i·ty \i-ˌlas-ˈtis-ət-ē, ˌē-ˌlas-, -ˈtis-tē\ *n, pl* **-ties** : the quality or state of being elastic: as **a** : the capability of a strained body to recover its size and shape after deformation : SPRINGINESS **b** : RESILIENCE **c** : the quality of being adaptable

elas·ti·cized \i-ˈlas-tə-ˌsīzd\ *adj* : made with elastic thread or inserts

elastic scattering *n* : a scattering of particles as the result of elastic collision

elas·tin \i-ˈlas-tən\ *n* [ISV, fr. NL *elasticus*] : a protein that is similar to collagen and is the chief constituent of elastic fibers

elas·to·mer \-tə-mər\ *n* [*elastic* + *-o-* + Gk *meros* part — more at MERIT] : any of various elastic substances resembling rubber ⟨polyvinyl ~*s*⟩ — **elas·to·mer·ic** \i-ˌlas-tə-ˈmer-ik\ *adj*

1elate \i-ˈlāt\ *adj* : ELATED

2elate *vt* **elat·ed; elat·ing** [L *elatus* (pp. of *efferre* to carry out, elevate), fr. *e-* + *latus,* pp. of *ferre* to carry — more at TOLERATE, BEAR] : to fill with joy or pride

elat·ed *adj* : marked by high spirits : EXULTANT — **elat·ed·ly** *adv* — **elat·ed·ness** *n*

el·a·ter \ˈel-ət-ər\ *n* [NL, genus of beetles, fr. Gk *elatēr* driver, fr. *elaunein*] **1** : CLICK BEETLE **2** : a plant structure functioning in the distribution of spores: as **a** : one of the elongated filaments among the spores in the capsule of a liverwort **b** : one of the filamentous appendages of the spores in the scouring rushes

elat·er·ite \i-ˈlat-ə-ˌrīt\ *n* [G *elaterit,* fr. Gk *elatēr*] : a dark brown elastic mineral resin occurring in soft flexible masses

ela·tion \i-ˈlā-shən\ *n* **1** : the quality or state of being elated **2** : pathological euphoria

E layer *n* : a layer of the ionosphere occurring at about 60 miles above the earth's surface and capable of reflecting radio waves

1el·bow \ˈel-ˌbō\ *n* [ME *elbowe,* fr. OE *elboga;* akin to OHG *elinbogo* elbow; both fr. a prehistoric NGmc-WGmc compound whose constituents are akin to OE *eln* ell & OE *boga* bow — more at ELL, BOW] **1 a** : the joint of the arm **b** : a corresponding joint in the anterior limb of a lower vertebrate **2** : something resembling an elbow; *specif* : an angular pipe fitting — **out at elbows 1** : shabbily dressed **2** : short of funds

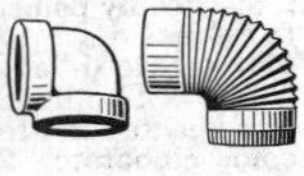

elbows 2

2elbow *vt* **1 a** : to push with the elbow : JOSTLE **b** : to shove aside by pushing with the elbow **2 a** : to force (as one's way) by pushing with the elbow ⟨~*ing* our way through the crowd⟩ **b** : to force (as one's way) rudely or forwardly ⟨~*s* her way into the best circles⟩ ~ *vi* **1** : to advance by pushing with the elbow **2** : to make an angle : TURN ⟨here the passage ~*s* and we are in another room⟩

elbow grease *n* : energy vigorously exerted esp. in physical labor ⟨the first such expedition not powered solely by the *elbow grease* of oarsmen —*New Yorker*⟩

el·bow·room \ˈel-ˌbō-ˌrüm, -ˌrům\ *n* **1 a** : room for moving the elbows freely **b** : adequate space for work or operation ⟨the large house gives plenty of ~⟩ **2** : free scope

eld \ˈeld\ *n* [ME, fr. OE *ieldo;* akin to OE *eald* old — more at OLD] **1** *archaic* : old age **2** *archaic* : old times : ANTIQUITY

1el·der \ˈel-dər\ *n* [ME *eldre,* fr. OE *ellærn;* prob. akin to OE *alor* alder — more at ALDER] : ELDERBERRY 2

2elder *adj* [ME, fr. OE *ieldra,* compar. of *eald* old] **1** : of earlier birth or greater age ⟨his ~ brother⟩ **2** : of or relating to earlier times : FORMER **3** *obs* : of or relating to a more advanced time of life **4** : prior or superior in rank, office, or validity

3elder *n* **1** : one living in an earlier period **2 a** : one who is older : SENIOR ⟨the child trying to please his ~*s*⟩ **b** *archaic* : an aged person **3** : one having authority by virtue of age and experience ⟨the village ~*s*⟩ **4** : any of various church officers: as **a** : PRESBYTER 1 **b** : a permanent officer elected by a Presbyterian congregation and ordained to serve on the session and assist the pastor at communion **c** : MINISTER 2a, 2b **d** : a Mormon ordained to the Melchizedek priesthood — **el·der·ship** \-ˌship\ *n*

el·der·ber·ry \ˈel-də(r)-ˌber-ē\ *n* **1** : the edible black or red berrylike drupe of any of a genus (*Sambucus*) of shrubs or trees of the honeysuckle family bearing flat clusters of small white or pink flowers **2** : a tree or shrub bearing elderberries

el·der·ly \ˈel-dər-lē\ *adj* **1 a** : rather old; *specif* : being past middle age **b** : OLD-FASHIONED **2** : of, relating to, or characteristic of later life — **el·der·li·ness** *n*

elder statesman *n* : an eminent senior member of a group or organization; *esp* : a retired statesman who unofficially advises current leaders

el·dest \ˈel-dəst\ *adj* : of the greatest age or seniority : OLDEST

eldest hand *n* : the card player who first receives cards in the deal

El Do·ra·do \ˌel-də-ˈräd-(ˌ)ō, -ˈrād-\ *n* [Sp, lit., the gilded one] **1** : a city or country of fabulous riches held by 16th century explorers to exist in So. America **2** : a place of fabulous wealth, abundance, or opportunity

el·dritch \ˈel-drich\ *adj* [perh. fr. (assumed) ME *elfriche* fairyland, fr. ME *elf* + *riche* kingdom, fr. OE *rice* — more at RICH] : WEIRD, EERIE

El·e·at·ic \ˌel-ē-ˈat-ik\ *adj* [L *Eleaticus,* fr. Gk *Eleatikos,* fr. *Elea* (Velia), ancient town in So. Italy] : of or relating to a school of Greek philosophers founded by Parmenides and developed by Zeno and marked by belief in the unity of being and the unreality of motion or change — **Eleatic** *n* — **El·e·at·i·cism** \-ˈat-ə-ˌsiz-əm\ *n*

elec *abbr* electric; electrical; electricity

ele·cam·pane \ˌel-i-ˌkam-ˈpān\ *n* [ME *elena campana,* fr. ML *enula campana,* lit., field elecampane, fr. *inula, enula* elecampane + *campana* of the field] : a large coarse European composite herb (*Inula helenium*) with yellow ray flowers naturalized in the U.S.

1elect \i-ˈlekt\ *adj* [ME, fr. L *electus* choice, fr. pp. of *eligere* to select, fr. *e-* + *legere* to choose — more at LEGEND] **1** : carefully selected : CHOSEN **2** : chosen for salvation through divine mercy **3 a** : chosen for office or position but not yet installed ⟨the president-*elect*⟩ **b** : chosen for marriage at some future time to a specific person ⟨the bride-*elect*⟩

2elect *n, pl* **elect 1** : one chosen or set apart (as by divine favor) **2** *pl* : a select or exclusive group of people

3elect *vt* **1** : to select by vote for an office, position, or membership ⟨~*ed* him class president⟩ **2** : to make a selection of ⟨will ~ a heavy academic program⟩ **3** : to choose esp. by preference : decide on ⟨might ~ to sell the business⟩ ~ *vi* : to make a selection

elect·able \i-ˈlek-tə-bəl\ *adj* : capable of being elected; *specif* : eminently qualified to be elected to office — **elect·abil·i·ty** \-ˌlek-tə-ˈbil-ət-ē\ *n*

elec·tion \i-ˈlek-shən\ *n* **1 a** : an act or process of electing **b** : the fact of being elected **2** : predestination to eternal life **3** : the right, power, or privilege of making a choice *syn* see CHOICE

Election Day *n* : a day legally established for the election of public officials; *esp* : the first Tuesday after the first Monday in November in an even year designated for national elections in the U.S. and observed as a legal holiday in many states

elec·tion·eer \i-ˌlek-shə-ˈni(ə)r\ *vi* [*election* + *-eer* (as in *auctioneer,* v.)] : to take an active part in an election; *specif* : to work for the election of a candidate or party — **elec·tion·eer·er** *n*

1elec·tive \i-ˈlek-tiv\ *adj* **1 a** : chosen or filled by popular election ⟨an ~ official⟩ **b** : of or relating to election **c** : based on the right or principle of election ⟨the presidency is an ~ office⟩ **2** : permitting a choice : OPTIONAL ⟨an ~ course in school⟩ **3 a** : tending to operate on one substance rather than another **b** : favorably inclined : SYMPATHETIC — **elec·tive·ly** *adv* — **elec·tive·ness** *n*

2elective *n* : an elective course or subject

elec·tor \i-ˈlek-tər, -ˌtȯ(ə)r\ *n* **1** : one qualified to vote in an election **2** : one entitled to participate in an election: as **a** : one of the German princes entitled to take part in choosing the Holy Roman Emperor **b** : a member of the electoral college in the U.S.

elec·tor·al \i-ˈlek-t(ə-)rəl\ *adj* **1** : of or relating to an elector ⟨the ~ vote⟩ **2** : of or relating to election ⟨an ~ system⟩

electoral college *n* : a body of electors; *esp* : one that elects the president and vice-president of the U.S.

elec·tor·ate \i-ˈlek-t(ə-)rət\ *n* **1** : the territory, jurisdiction, or dignity of a German elector **2** : a body of people entitled to vote

electr- *or* **electro-** *comb form* [NL *electricus*] **1 a** : electricity ⟨*electro*meter⟩ **b** : electric ⟨*electr*ode⟩ : electric and ⟨*electro*chemical⟩ : electrically ⟨*electro*positive⟩ **2** : electrolytic ⟨*electro*analysis⟩ **3** : electron ⟨*electro*valence⟩

Elec·tra \i-ˈlek-trə\ *n* [L, fr. Gk *Ēlektra*] : a sister of Orestes who aids him in killing their mother Clytemnestra to avenge their murdered father Agamemnon

Electra complex *n* : the Oedipus complex when it occurs in a female

elec·tress \i-ˈlek-trəs\ *n* : the wife or widow of a German elector

elec·tret \i-ˈlek-trət, -ˌtret\ *n* [*electricity* + *magnet*] : a dielectric body in which a permanent state of electric polarization has been set up

1elec·tric \i-ˈlek-trik\ *adj* [NL *electricus* produced from amber by friction, electric, fr. ML, of amber, fr. L *electrum* amber, electrum, fr. Gk *ēlektron;* akin to Gk *ēlektōr* beaming sun, Skt *ulkā* meteor] **1** : of, relating to, or operated by electricity **2** : producing an intensely stimulating effect : THRILLING ⟨an ~ performance⟩ **3 a** : ELECTRONIC 3a **b** : electronically amplifying sound — used of a musical instrument ⟨an ~ guitar⟩ — **elec·tri·cal** \-tri-kəl\ *adj* — **elec·tri·cal·ly** \-k(ə-)lē\ *adv* — **elec·tri·cal·ness** \-kəl-nəs\ *n*

2electric *n* **1** *archaic* : a nonconductor of electricity used to excite or accumulate electricity **2** : something (as a light, automobile, or train) operated by electricity

electrical storm *n* : THUNDERSTORM — called also *electric storm*

electrical transcription *n* **1** : a phonograph record or tape recording esp. designed for use in radiobroadcasting **2** : a radio program broadcast from an electrical transcription

electric chair *n* **1** : a chair used in legal electrocution **2** : the penalty of death by electrocution

electric eel *n* : a large eel-shaped fish (*Electrophorus electricus*) of the Orinoco and Amazon basins that is capable of giving a severe shock with its electric organs

electric eye *n* **1** : PHOTOELECTRIC CELL **2** : a miniature cathode-ray tube used to determine a condition (as of radio tuning)

elec·tri·cian \i-ˌlek-ˈtrish-ən\ *n* **1** : a specialist in electricity **2** : one who installs, maintains, operates, or repairs electrical equipment

elec·tric·i·ty \i-ˌlek-ˈtris-ət-ē, -ˈtris-tē\ *n, pl* **-ties 1 a** : a fundamental entity of nature consisting of negative and positive kinds composed respectively of electrons and protons or possibly of electrons and positrons, observable in the attractions and repulsions of bodies electrified by friction and in natural phenomena (as lightning or the aurora borealis), and usu. utilized in the form of electric currents **b** : electric current **2** : a science that deals with the phenomena and laws of electricity **3 :** keen contagious excitement

electric organ *n* **:** a specialized tract of tissue (as in the electric eel) in which electricity is generated

electric ray *n* **:** any of various round-bodied short-tailed rays (family Torpedinidae) of warm seas with a pair of electric organs

elec·tri·fi·ca·tion \i-ˌlek-trə-fə-ˈkā-shən\ *n* **1 :** an act or process of electrifying **2 :** the state of being electrified

elec·tri·fy \i-ˈlek-trə-ˌfī\ *vt* **-fied; -fy·ing** **1 a :** to charge with electricity **b** (1) **:** to equip for use of electric power (2) **:** to supply with electric power (3) **:** to amplify (music) electronically **2 :** to excite intensely or suddenly as if by an electric shock ***syn*** see THRILL

elec·tro·acous·tics \i-ˌlek-trō-ə-ˈkü-stiks\ *n pl but sing in constr* **:** a science that deals with the transformation of acoustic energy into electric energy or vice versa — **elec·tro·acous·tic** \-tik\ *adj* — **elec·tro·acous·ti·cal·ly** \-ti-k(ə-)lē\ *adv*

elec·tro·anal·y·sis \-ə-ˈnal-ə-səs\ *n* **:** chemical analysis by electrolytic methods — **elec·tro·an·a·lyt·ic** \-ˌan-ᵊl-ˈit-ik\ *or* **elec·tro·an·a·lyt·i·cal** \-ˈit-i-kəl\ *adj*

elec·tro·car·dio·gram \-ˈkärd-ē-ə-ˌgram\ *n* **:** the tracing made by an electrocardiograph

elec·tro·car·dio·graph \-ˌgraf\ *n* **:** an instrument for recording the changes of electrical potential occurring during the heartbeat used esp. in diagnosing abnormalities of heart action — **elec·tro·car·dio·graph·ic** \-ˌkärd-ē-ə-ˈgraf-ik\ *adj* — **elec·tro·car·dio·graph·i·cal·ly** \-i-k(ə-)lē\ *adv* — **elec·tro·car·di·og·ra·phy** \-ē-ˈäg-rə-fē\ *n*

elec·tro·chem·is·try \-ˈkem-ə-strē\ *n* **:** a science that deals with the relation of electricity to chemical changes and with the interconversion of chemical and electrical energy — **elec·tro·chem·i·cal** \-ˈkem-i-kəl\ *adj* — **elec·tro·chem·i·cal·ly** \-k(ə-)lē\ *adv*

elec·tro·con·vul·sive \i-ˌlek-trō-kən-ˈvəl-siv\ *adj* **:** of, relating to, or involving convulsive response to electroshock ⟨impaired learning ability in rats due to ~ shocks⟩

electroconvulsive therapy *n* **:** ELECTROSHOCK THERAPY

elec·tro·cor·ti·co·gram \i-ˌlek-trō-ˈkȯrt-i-kə-ˌgram\ *n* [*electr-* + *cortico-* (fr. L *cortic- cortex* cortex) + *-gram*] **:** an electroencephalogram made with the electrodes in direct contact with the brain

elec·tro·cute \i-ˈlek-trə-ˌkyüt\ *vt* **-cut·ed; -cut·ing** [*electr-* + *-cute* (as in *execute*)] **1 :** to execute (a criminal) by electricity **2 :** to kill by electric shock — **elec·tro·cu·tion** \-ˌlek-trə-ˈkyü-shən\ *n*

elec·trode \i-ˈlek-ˌtrōd\ *n* **:** a conductor used to establish electrical contact with a nonmetallic part of a circuit

[1]elec·tro·de·pos·it \i-ˌlek-trō-di-ˈpäz-ət\ *n* **:** a deposit formed in or at an electrode by electrolysis

[2]electrodeposit *vt* **:** to deposit (as a metal or rubber) by electrolysis — **elec·tro·de·po·si·tion** \-ˌdep-ə-ˈzish-ən, -ˌdē-pə-\ *n*

elec·tro·di·al·y·sis \i-ˌlek-trō-dī-ˈal-ə-səs\ *n* **:** dialysis accelerated by an electromotive force applied to electrodes adjacent to the membranes — **elec·tro·di·a·lyt·ic** \-ˌdī-ə-ˈlit-ik\ *adj* — **elec·tro·di·a·lyze** \-ˈdī-ə-ˌlīz\ *vt* — **elec·tro·di·a·lyz·er** *n*

elec·tro·dy·nam·ics \-dī-ˈnam-iks\ *n pl but sing in constr* **:** a branch of physics that deals with the effects arising from the interactions of electric currents with magnets, with other currents, or with themselves — **elec·tro·dy·nam·ic** \-ik\ *adj*

elec·tro·dy·na·mom·e·ter \-ˌdī-nə-ˈmäm-ət-ər\ *n* [ISV] **:** an instrument that measures current by indicating the strength of the forces between a current flowing in fixed coils and one flowing in movable coils

elec·tro·en·ceph·a·lo·gram \-in-ˈsef-ə-lə-ˌgram\ *n* [ISV] **:** the tracing of brain waves made by an electroencephalograph

elec·tro·en·ceph·a·lo·graph \-ˌgraf\ *n* [ISV] **:** an apparatus for detecting and recording brain waves — **elec·tro·en·ceph·a·lo·graph·ic** \-ˌsef-ə-lə-ˈgraf-ik\ *adj* — **elec·tro·en·ceph·a·log·ra·phy** \-ˈläg-rə-fē\ *n*

elec·tro·fish·ing \i-ˈlek-trō-ˌfish-iŋ\ *n* **:** the taking of fish by a system based on their tendency to respond positively to a source of direct electric current

elec·tro·form \i-ˈlek-trə-ˌfȯrm\ *vt* **:** to form (shaped articles) by electrodeposition on a mold

elec·tro·gen·e·sis \i-ˌlek-trə-ˈjen-ə-səs\ *n* **:** the production of electrical activity esp. in living tissue

elec·tro·gen·ic \-ˈjen-ik\ *adj* **:** of or relating to the production of electricity in living tissue ⟨an ~ pump causing movement of sodium ions across a membrane⟩

elec·tro·gram \i-ˈlek-trə-ˌgram\ *n* **:** a tracing of the electrical potentials of a tissue (as the brain or heart) made by means of electrodes placed directly in the tissue instead of on the surface of the body

elec·tro·hy·drau·lic \i-ˌlek-trō-hī-ˈdrȯ-lik\ *adj* **1 :** of or relating to a combination of electric and hydraulic mechanisms **2 :** involving or produced by the action of very brief but powerful pulse discharges of electricity under a liquid resulting in the generation of shock waves and highly reactive chemical species ⟨an ~ effect⟩ — **elec·tro·hy·drau·li·cal·ly** \-li-k(ə-)lē\ *adv*

elec·tro·jet \i-ˈlek-trə-ˌjet\ *n* **:** an overhead concentration of electric current found in the regions of strong auroral displays and along the magnetic equator

elec·tro·ki·net·ic \i-ˌlek-trō-kə-ˈnet-ik, -kī-\ *adj* **:** of or relating to the motion of particles or liquids that results from or produces a difference of electric potential

elec·tro·ki·net·ics \-iks\ *n pl but sing in constr* **:** a branch of physics that deals with electrokinetic phenomena

elec·tro·less \i-ˈlek-ˌtrō-ləs, -trə-\ *adj* **:** being or involving chemical deposition of metal instead of electrodeposition

elec·trol·o·gist \i-ˌlek-ˈträl-ə-jəst\ *n* [blend of *electrolysis* and *-logist* (fr. *-logy* + *-ist*)] **:** one that removes hair, warts, moles, and birthmarks by means of an electric current applied to the body with a needle-shaped electrode

elec·tro·lu·mi·nes·cence \i-ˌlek-trō-ˌlü-mə-ˈnes-ᵊn(t)s\ *n* **:** luminescence resulting from a high-frequency discharge through a gas or from application of an alternating current to a layer of phosphor — **elec·tro·lu·mi·nes·cent** \-ᵊnt\ *adj*

elec·trol·y·sis \i-ˌlek-ˈträl-ə-səs\ *n* **1 a :** the producing of chemical changes by passage of an electric current through an electrolyte **b :** subjection to this action **2 :** the destruction of hair roots with an electric current

elec·tro·lyte \i-ˈlek-trə-ˌlīt\ *n* **1 :** a nonmetallic electric conductor in which current is carried by the movement of ions **2 :** a substance that when dissolved in a suitable solvent or when fused becomes an ionic conductor

elec·tro·lyt·ic \i-ˌlek-trə-ˈlit-ik\ *adj* **:** of or relating to electrolysis or an electrolyte; *also* **:** involving or produced by electrolysis — **elec·tro·lyt·i·cal·ly** \-i-k(ə-)lē\ *adv*

elec·tro·lyze \i-ˈlek-trə-ˌlīz\ *vt* **-lyzed; -lyz·ing :** to subject to electrolysis

elec·tro·mag·net \i-ˌlek-trō-ˈmag-nət\ *n* **:** a core of magnetic material surrounded by a coil of wire through which an electric current is passed to magnetize the core

elec·tro·mag·net·ic \-mag-ˈnet-ik\ *adj* **:** of, relating to, or produced by electromagnetism — **elec·tro·mag·net·i·cal·ly** \-i-k(ə-)lē\ *adv*

electromagnetic radiation *n* **:** a series of electromagnetic waves

electromagnetic spectrum *n* **:** the entire range of wavelengths or frequencies of electromagnetic radiation extending from gamma rays to the longest radio waves and including visible light

electromagnetic unit *n* **:** any of a system of electrical units based primarily on the magnetic properties of electrical currents

electromagnetic wave *n* **:** one of the waves that are propagated by simultaneous periodic variations of electric and magnetic field intensity and that include radio waves, infrared, visible light, ultraviolet, X rays, and gamma rays

elec·tro·mag·ne·tism \i-ˌlek-trō-ˈmag-nə-ˌtiz-əm\ *n* **1 :** magnetism developed by a current of electricity **2 :** a branch of physical science that deals with the physical relations between electricity and magnetism

elec·tro·me·chan·i·cal \-mə-ˈkan-i-kəl\ *adj* **:** of or relating to a mechanical process or device actuated or controlled electrically; *specif* **:** being a transducer for converting mechanical energy to electrical energy or vice versa — **elec·tro·me·chan·i·cal·ly** \-k(ə-)lē\ *adv*

elec·tro·met·al·lur·gy \-ˈmet-ᵊl-ˌər-jē, *esp Brit* -mə-ˈtal-ər-\ *n* **:** a branch of metallurgy that deals with the application of electric current either for electrolytic deposition or as a source of heat

elec·trom·e·ter \i-ˌlek-ˈträm-ət-ər\ *n* **:** any of various instruments for detecting or measuring electric-potential differences or ionizing radiations by means of the forces of attraction or repulsion between charged bodies

electromotive force *n* **:** something that moves or tends to move electricity **:** the amount of energy derived from an electrical source per unit quantity of electricity passing through the source (as a cell or generator)

elec·tro·myo·gram \i-ˈlek-trō-ˈmī-ə-ˌgram\ *n* **:** a tracing made with an electromyograph

elec·tro·myo·graph \-ˌgraf\ *n* [*electr-* + *my-* + *-graph*] **:** an instrument for the simultaneous recording of a visual and sound record of electric waves associated with activity of skeletal muscle that is used in the diagnosis of neuromuscular disorders — **elec·tro·myo·graph·ic** \-ˌmī-ə-ˈgraf-ik\ *also* **elec·tro·myo·graph·i·cal** \-i-kəl\ *adj* — **elec·tro·myo·graph·i·cal·ly** \-i-k(ə-)lē\ *adv* — **elec·tro·my·og·ra·phy** \-mī-ˈäg-rə-fē\ *n*

elec·tron \i-ˈlek-ˌträn\ *n* [*electr-* + *-on*] **:** an elementary particle consisting of a charge of negative electricity equal to about 1.602 $\times 10^{-19}$ coulomb and having a mass when at rest of about 9.107 $\times 10^{-28}$ gram or 1/1837 that of a proton

elec·tro·neg·a·tive \i-ˌlek-trō-ˈneg-ət-iv\ *adj* **1 :** charged with negative electricity **2 :** capable of acting as the negative electrode of a voltaic cell **3 :** having a tendency to attract electrons — **elec·tro·neg·a·tiv·i·ty** \-ˌneg-ə-ˈtiv-ət-ē\ *n*

electron gas *n* **:** a population of free electrons in a vacuum or in a metallic conductor

electron gun *n* **:** the electron-emitting cathode and its surrounding assembly in a cathode-ray tube for directing, controlling, and focusing the stream of electrons to a spot of desired size

[1]elec·tron·ic \i-ˌlek-ˈträn-ik\ *adj* **1 :** of or relating to electrons **2 :** of, relating to, or utilizing devices constructed or working by the methods or principles of electronics **3 a :** generating music by electronic means ⟨an ~ organ⟩ **b :** of, relating to, or being music that consists of sounds electronically generated or modified

[2]electronic *n* **:** an electronic circuit or device

elec·tron·ics \i-ˌlek-ˈträn-iks\ *n pl but sing in constr* **:** a branch of physics that deals with the emission, behavior, and effects of electrons (as in electron tubes and transistors) and with electronic devices

electron lens *n* **:** a device for converging or diverging a beam of electrons by means of an electric or a magnetic field

electron microscope *n* **:** an electron-optical instrument in which a beam of electrons focused by means of an electron lens is used to produce an enlarged image of a minute object on a fluorescent screen or photographic plate — **electron microscopist** *n* — **electron microscopy** *n*

electron multiplier *n* **:** a device utilizing secondary emission of electrons for amplifying a current of electrons

electron optics *n pl but sing in constr* **:** a branch of electronics that deals with those properties of beams of electrons that are analogous to the properties of rays of light

electron transport *n* **:** the sequential transfer of electrons esp. by cytochromes in cellular respiration from an oxidizable substrate to molecular oxygen by a series of oxidation-reduction reactions

ə abut	ᵊ kitten	ər further	a back	ā bake	ä cot, cart
au̇ out	ch chin	e less	ē easy	g gift	i trip	ī life
j joke	ŋ sing	ō flow	ȯ flaw	ȯi coin	th thin	t͟h this
ü loot	u̇ foot	y yet	yü few	yu̇ furious	zh vision

electron tube *n* : an electronic device in which conduction by electrons takes place through a vacuum or a gaseous medium within a sealed glass or metal container and which has various common uses based on the controlled flow of electrons

electron volt *n* : a unit of energy equal to the energy gained by an electron in passing from a point of low potential to a point one volt higher in potential : 1.60×10^{-12} erg

elec·tro·oc·u·lo·gram \i-,lek-trō-'äk-yə-lə-,gram\ *n* [*electr-* + *ocul-* + *-gram*] : a record of the standing voltage between the front and back of the eye that is correlated with eyeball movement (as in sleep) and obtained by electrodes suitably placed on the skin near the eye

elec·tro·op·tics \-trō-'äp-tiks\ *n pl but sing in constr* : a branch of physics that deals with the effects of an electric field on light traversing it — **elec·tro·op·tic** \-tik\ *or* **elec·tro·op·ti·cal** \-ti-kəl\ *adj* — **elec·tro·op·ti·cal·ly** \-ti-k(ə-)lē\ *adv*

elec·tro·phil·ic \i-,lek-trō-'fil-ik\ *adj* : involving or having an affinity for electrons : electron-seeking ⟨~ reagents⟩ — **elec·tro·phi·lic·ity** \-trō-fil-'is-ət-ē\ *n*

elec·tro·pho·re·sis \i-,lek-trə-fə-'rē-səs\ *n* [NL] : the movement of suspended particles through a fluid under the action of an electromotive force applied to electrodes in contact with the suspension — **elec·tro·pho·ret·ic** \-'ret-ik\ *adj* — **elec·tro·pho·ret·i·cal·ly** \-i-k(ə-)lē\ *adv*

elec·tro·pho·re·to·gram \-'ret-ə-,gram\ *n* [*electrophoretic* + *-o-* + *-gram*] : a record that consists of the separated components of a mixture (as of proteins) produced by electrophoresis in a supporting medium (as filter paper)

elec·troph·o·rus \i-,lek-'träf-ə-rəs\ *n, pl* **-ri** \-,rī, -,rē\ [NL, fr. *electr-* + *-phorus* -phore (fr. Gk *-phoros*)] : an instrument for the production of electric charges by induction consisting of a disk that is negatively electrified by friction and a metal plate that becomes charged by induction when placed on the disk

elec·tro·pho·tog·ra·phy \i-,lek-trō-fə-'täg-rə-fē\ *n* : photography in which images are produced by electrical means (as in xerography) — **elec·tro·pho·to·graph·ic** \-trə-,fōt-ə-'graf-ik\ *adj*

elec·tro·phys·i·ol·o·gy \i-,lek-trō-,fiz-ē-'äl-ə-jē\ *n* 1 : physiology that is concerned with the electrical aspects of physiological phenomena 2 : electrical phenomena associated with a physiological process (as the function of a body or bodily part) ⟨~ of the eye⟩ — **elec·tro·phys·i·o·log·i·cal** \-ē-ə-'läj-i-kəl\ *also* **elec·tro·phys·i·o·log·ic** \-ik\ *adj* — **elec·tro·phys·i·o·log·i·cal·ly** \-i-k(ə-)lē\ *adv* — **elec·tro·phys·i·ol·o·gist** \-ē-'äl-ə-jəst\ *n*

elec·tro·plate \i-'lek-trə-,plāt\ *vt* 1 : to plate with an adherent continuous coating by electrodeposition 2 : ELECTROTYPE

elec·tro·pos·i·tive \i-,lek-trō-'päz-ət-iv, -'päz-tiv\ *adj* 1 a : charged with positive electricity b : capable of acting as the positive electrode of a voltaic cell 2 : having a tendency to release electrons

elec·tro·ret·i·no·gram \-'ret-ᵊn-ə-,gram\ *n* : a graphic record of electrical activity of the retina used esp. in the diagnosis of retinal conditions

elec·tro·ret·i·no·graph \-,graf\ *n* : an instrument for recording electrical activity in the retina — **elec·tro·ret·i·no·graph·ic** \-,ret-ᵊn-ə-'graf-ik\ *adj* — **elec·tro·ret·i·nog·ra·phy** \-ᵊn-'äg-rə-fē\ *n*

elec·tro·scope \i-'lek-trə-,skōp\ *n* [prob. fr. F *électroscope*] : any of various instruments for detecting the presence of an electric charge on a body, for determining whether the charge is positive or negative, or for indicating and measuring intensity of radiation

elec·tro·shock \-trō-,shäk\ *n* 1 : ³SHOCK 5 2 : ELECTROSHOCK THERAPY

electroshock therapy *n* : the treatment of mental disorder by the induction of coma through the use of an electric current — called also *electroconvulsive therapy*

elec·tro·stat·ic \i-,lek-trə-'stat-ik\ *adj* [ISV] 1 : of or relating to static electricity or electrostatics 2 : of or relating to painting with a spray that utilizes electrically charged particles to ensure complete coating — **elec·tro·stat·i·cal·ly** \-'stat-i-k(ə-)lē\ *adv*

electrostatic generator *n* : an apparatus for the production of electrical discharges at high voltage commonly consisting of an insulated hollow conducting sphere that accumulates in its interior the charge continuously conveyed from a source of direct current by an endless belt of flexible nonconducting material

electrostatic printing *n* : a process (as xerography) for printing or copying in which electrostatic forces are used to form the image (as with powder or ink) directly on a surface

elec·tro·stat·ics \i-,lek-trə-'stat-iks\ *n pl but sing in constr* : physics that deals with phenomena due to attractions or repulsions of electric charges but not dependent upon their motion

electrostatic unit *n* : any of a system of electrical units based primarily on forces of interaction between electric charges — abbr. *esu*

elec·tro·sur·gery \i-,lek-trō-'sərj-(ə-)rē\ *n* : surgery by means of diathermy — **elec·tro·sur·gi·cal** \-'sər-ji-kəl\ *adj*

elec·tro·ther·a·py \-'ther-ə-pē\ *n* : treatment of disease by means of electricity (as in diathermy)

elec·tro·ther·mal \-'thər-məl\ *or* **elec·tro·ther·mic** \-mik\ *adj* : relating to or combining electricity and heat; *specif* : relating to the generation of heat by electricity — **elec·tro·ther·mal·ly** \-mə-lē\ *adv*

elec·trot·o·nus \i-,lek-'trät-ᵊn-əs\ *n* [NL] : the altered sensitivity of a nerve when a constant current of electricity passes through any part of it — **elec·tro·ton·ic** \i-,lek-trə-'tän-ik\ *adj*

¹elec·tro·type \i-'lek-trə-,tīp\ *n* 1 : a duplicate printing surface made by pressure molding in a plastic material the surface to be reproduced and electrodepositing on it a thin shell that is then backed up with lead 2 : a copy of a coin made by an electroplating process

²electrotype *vt* : to make an electrotype from (a printing surface) ~ *vi* : to be reproducible by electrotyping — **elec·tro·typ·er** *n*

elec·tro·va·lence \i-,lek-trō-'vā-lən(t)s\ *n* : valence characterized by the transfer of electrons from one atom to another with the formation of ions; *also* : the number of charges acquired by an atom by the loss or gain of electrons — **elec·tro·va·lent** \-'lənt\ *adj*

elec·tro·va·len·cy \-lən-sē\ *n* : ELECTROVALENCE

electrovalent bond *n* : a chemical bond formed between ions of opposite charge

elec·tro·win·ning \i-'lek-trō-,win-iŋ\ *n* : the recovery esp. of metals from solutions by electrolysis

elec·trum \i-'lek-trəm\ *n* [ME, fr. L — more at ELECTRIC] : a natural pale yellow alloy of gold and silver

elec·tu·ary \i-'lek-chə-,wer-ē\ *n, pl* **-ar·ies** [ME *electuarie*, fr. L *electuarium*, prob. fr. Gk *ekleikton*, fr. *ekleichein* to lick up, fr. *ex-* + *leichein* to lick — more at LICK] : CONFECTION 2b

el·e·doi·sin \,el-ə-'dóis-ᵊn\ *n* [irreg. fr. NL *Eledone*, genus name] : a small protein $C_{54}H_{85}N_{13}O_{15}S$ from the salivary glands of several octopuses (genus *Eledone*) that is a powerful vasodilator and hypotensive agent

el·ee·mos·y·nary \,el-i-'mäs-ᵊn-,er-ē, -'mäz-\ *adj* [ML *eleemosynarius*, fr. LL *eleemosyna* alms — more at ALMS] : of, relating to, or supported by charity

el·e·gance \'el-i-gən(t)s\ *n* 1 a : refined grace or dignified propriety : URBANITY b : tasteful richness of design or ornamentation ⟨the sumptuous ~ of the furnishings⟩ c : dignified gracefulness or restrained beauty of style : POLISH ⟨the essay is marked by lucidity, wit, and ~⟩ d : scientific precision, neatness, and simplicity ⟨the ~ of a mathematical proof⟩ 2 : something that is elegant

el·e·gan·cy \-gən-sē\ *n, pl* **-cies** : ELEGANCE

el·e·gant \'el-i-gənt\ *adj* [MF or L; MF, fr. L *elegant-*, *elegans*; akin to L *eligere* to select — more at ELECT] 1 : marked by elegance 2 : of a high grade or quality : SPLENDID ⟨~ gems priced at hundreds of thousands of dollars⟩ *syn* see CHOICE — **el·e·gant·ly** *adv*

el·e·gi·ac \,el-ə-'jī-ək, -,ak *also* i-'lē-jē-,ak\ *also* **el·e·gi·a·cal** \,el-ə-'jī-ə-kəl\ *adj* [LL *elegiacus*, fr. Gk *elegeiakos*, fr. *elegeion*] 1 a : of, relating to, or consisting of two dactylic hexameter lines the second of which lacks the arses in the third and sixth feet b (1) : written in or consisting of elegiac couplets (2) : noted for having written poetry in such couplets c : of or relating to the period in Greece about the seventh century B.C. when poetry written in such couplets flourished 2 : of, relating to, or comprising elegy or an elegy; *esp* : expressing sorrow often for something now past ⟨an ~ lament for departed youth⟩ — **elegiac** *n* — **el·e·gi·a·cal·ly** \,el-ə-'jī-ə-k(ə-)lē\ *adv*

elegiac stanza *n* : a quatrain in iambic pentameter with a rhyme scheme of *abab*

el·e·git \i-'lē-jət\ *n* [L, he has chosen, fr. *eligere*] : a judicial writ of execution by which a defendant's goods and if necessary his lands are delivered for debt to the plaintiff until the debt is paid

el·e·gize \'el-ə-,jīz\ *vb* **-gized; -giz·ing** *vi* : to lament or celebrate in an elegy ~ *vt* : to write an elegy on

el·e·gy \'el-ə-jē\ *n, pl* **-gies** [L *elegia* poem in elegiac couplets, fr. Gk *elegeia*, *elegeion*, fr. *elegos* song of mourning] 1 a : a song or poem expressing sorrow or lamentation esp. for one who is dead b : something (as a speech) resembling such a song or poem 2 : a poem in elegiac couplets 3 a : a pensive or reflective poem that is usu. nostalgic or melancholy b : a short pensive musical composition

elem *abbr* elementary

el·e·ment \'el-ə-mənt\ *n* [ME, fr. OF & L; OF, fr. L *elementum*] 1 a : one of the four substances air, water, fire, and earth formerly believed to compose the physical universe b *pl* : weather conditions caused by activities of the elements; *esp* : violent or severe weather c : the state or sphere natural or suited to a person or thing ⟨at school she was in her ~⟩ 2 : a constituent part: as a *pl* : the simplest principles of a subject of study : RUDIMENTS b (1) : a part of a geometric magnitude ⟨an infinitesimal ~ of volume⟩ (2) : a generator of a geometric figure (3) : a basic member of a mathematical class or set c : one of a number of distinct groups composing a human community ⟨the criminal ~ in the city⟩ d (1) : one of the necessary data or values on which calculations or conclusions are based (2) : one of the factors determining the outcome of a process e : any of more than 100 fundamental substances that consist of atoms of only one kind and that singly or in combination constitute all matter f : a distinct part of a composite device g : a subdivision of a military unit h : MEMBER 4d 3 *pl* : the bread and wine used in the Eucharist
syn ELEMENT, COMPONENT, CONSTITUENT, INGREDIENT, FACTOR *shared meaning element* : one of the parts, substances, or principles that make up a compound or complex whole *ant* compound, composite

CHEMICAL ELEMENTS

ELEMENT & SYMBOL	ATOMIC NUMBER	ATOMIC WEIGHT (C = 12)
actinium (Ac)	89	
aluminum (Al)	13	26.9815
americium (Am)	95	
antimony (Sb)	51	121.75
argon (Ar)	18	39.948
arsenic (As)	33	74.9216
astatine (At)	85	
barium (Ba)	56	137.34
berkelium (Bk)	97	
beryllium (Be)	4	9.01218
bismuth (Bi)	83	208.9806
boron (B)	5	10.81
bromine (Br)	35	79.904
cadmium (Cd)	48	112.40
calcium (Ca)	20	40.08
californium (Cf)	98	
carbon (C)	6	12.011
cerium (Ce)	58	140.12
cesium (Cs)	55	132.9055
chlorine (Cl)	17	35.453
chromium (Cr)	24	51.996
cobalt (Co)	27	58.9332

ELEMENT & SYMBOL	ATOMIC NUMBER	ATOMIC WEIGHT (C = 12)
columbium (Cb)	(see niobium)	
copper (Cu)	29	63.546
curium (Cm)	96	
dysprosium (Dy)	66	162.50
einsteinium (Es)	99	
erbium (Er)	68	167.26
europium (Eu)	63	151.96
fermium (Fm)	100	
fluorine (F)	9	18.9984
francium (Fr)	87	
gadolinium (Gd)	64	157.25
gallium (Ga)	31	69.72
germanium (Ge)	32	72.59
gold (Au)	79	196.9665
hafnium (Hf)	72	178.49
helium (He)	2	4.00260
holmium (Ho)	67	164.9303
hydrogen (H)	1	1.0080
indium (In)	49	114.82
iodine (I)	53	126.9045
iridium (Ir)	77	192.22
iron (Fe)	26	55.847
krypton (Kr)	36	83.80
lanthanum (La)	57	138.9055
lawrencium (Lr)	103	
lead (Pb)	82	207.2
lithium (Li)	3	6.941
lutetium (Lu)	71	174.97
magnesium (Mg)	12	24.305
manganese (Mn)	25	54.9380
mendelevium (Md)	101	
mercury (Hg)	80	200.59
molybdenum (Mo)	42	95.94
neodymium (Nd)	60	144.24
neon (Ne)	10	20.179
neptunium (Np)	93	237.0482
nickel (Ni)	28	58.71
niobium (Nb)	41	92.9064
nitrogen (N)	7	14.0067
nobelium (No)	102	
osmium (Os)	76	190.2
oxygen (O)	8	15.9994
palladium (Pd)	46	106.4
phosphorus (P)	15	30.9738
platinum (Pt)	78	195.09
plutonium (Pu)	94	
polonium (Po)	84	
potassium (K)	19	39.102
praseodymium (Pr)	59	140.9077
promethium (Pm)	61	
protactinium (Pa)	91	231.0359
radium (Ra)	88	226.0254
radon (Rn)	86	
rhenium (Re)	75	186.2
rhodium (Rh)	45	102.9055
rubidium (Rb)	37	85.4678
ruthenium (Ru)	44	101.07
samarium (Sm)	62	150.4
scandium (Sc)	21	44.9559
selenium (Se)	34	78.96
silicon (Si)	14	28.086
silver (Ag)	47	107.868
sodium (Na)	11	22.9898
strontium (Sr)	38	87.62
sulfur (S)	16	32.06
tantalum (Ta)	73	180.9479
technetium (Tc)	43	98.9062
tellurium (Te)	52	127.60
terbium (Tb)	65	158.9254
thallium (Tl)	81	204.37
thorium (Th)	90	232.0381
thulium (Tm)	69	168.9342
tin (Sn)	50	118.69
titanium (Ti)	22	47.90
tungsten (W)	74	183.85
uranium (U)	92	238.029
vanadium (V)	23	50.9414
wolfram (W)	(see tungsten)	
xenon (Xe)	54	131.30
ytterbium (Yb)	70	173.04
yttrium (Y)	39	88.9059
zinc (Zn)	30	65.37
zirconium (Zr)	40	91.22

el·e·men·tal \,el-ə-'ment-ᵊl\ *adj* **1 a** : of, relating to, or being an element; *specif* : existing as an uncombined chemical element **b** : of, relating to, or being the basic or ultimate constituent of something : FUNDAMENTAL ⟨certain ~ biological and social realities⟩ **c** : of, relating to, or dealing with the rudiments of something : ELEMENTARY ⟨taught ~ arts and crafts to the children⟩ **d** : forming an integral part : INHERENT ⟨an ~ sense of rhythm⟩ **2** : of, relating to, or resembling a great force of nature ⟨the rains come with ~ violence⟩ ⟨~ passions⟩ — **elemental** *n* — **el·e·men·tal·ly** \-'ᵊl-ē-ē\ *adv*
el·e·men·ta·ry \,el-ə-'ment-ə-rē, -'men-trē\ *adj* **1 a** : of, relating to, or dealing with the simplest elements or principles of something ⟨can't handle the most ~ decision-making⟩ **b** : of or relating to an elementary school ⟨an ~ curriculum⟩ **2** : ELEMENTAL 1a, 1b **3** : ELEMENTAL 2 — **el·e·men·ta·ri·ly** \-,men-'ter-ə-lē, -'men-trə-lē\ *adv* — **el·e·men·ta·ri·ness** \-'ment-ə-rē-nəs, -'men-trē-\ *n*
elementary body *n* : a distinguishable unit that makes up an inclusion body and probably is the infective particle of some viruses

elementary particle *n* **1** : any of the submicroscopic constituents of matter and energy (as the electron, proton, or photon) whose existence has not been attributed to the combination of other more fundamental entities **2** : OXYSOME
elementary school *n* : a school usu. including the first six or the first eight grades
el·e·mi \'el-ə-mē\ *n* [NL *elimi*] : any of various fragrant oleoresins obtained from tropical trees (family Burseraceae) and used chiefly in varnishes, lacquers, and printing inks
elen·chus \i-'leŋ-kəs\ *n, pl* **-chi** \-,kī, -,kē\ [L, fr. Gk *elenchos*] : REFUTATION; *esp* : one in syllogistic form
el·e·phant \'el-ə-fənt\ *n, often attrib* [ME, fr. OF & L; OF *olifant*, fr. L *elephantus*, fr. Gk *elephant-, elephas*] : any of various thickset mostly very large nearly hairless four-footed mammals that constitute with related extinct forms a family (Elephantidae, the elephant family) and have the snout prolonged into a muscular trunk and two incisors in the upper jaw developed esp. in the male into long tusks which furnish ivory; *broadly* : a related animal or fossil

elephants: *1* Indian, *2* African

elephant grass *n* **1** : an Old World cattail (*Typha elephantina*) used esp. in making baskets **2** : NAPIER GRASS
el·e·phan·ti·a·sis \,el-ə-fən-'tī-ə-səs, -,fan-\ *n, pl* **-a·ses** \-,sēz\ [NL, fr. L, a kind of leprosy, fr. Gk, fr. *elephant-, elephas*] **1** : enlargement and thickening of tissues; *specif* : the enormous enlargement of a limb or the scrotum caused by obstruction of lymphatics by filarial worms **2** : an undesirable usu. enormous growth, enlargement, or overdevelopment ⟨~ of intellect and atrophy of emotion —Michael Lerner⟩
el·e·phan·tine \,el-ə-'fan-,tēn, -,tīn, 'el-ə-fən-\ *adj* **1 a** : having enormous size or strength : MASSIVE **b** : CLUMSY, PONDEROUS **2** : of or relating to an elephant
elephant seal *n* : a nearly extinct large seal (*Mirounga angustirostris*) with a long inflatable proboscis that was formerly abundant along the coasts of California and Lower California; *also* : a related seal (*M. leonina*) formerly abundant on coasts of the southern hemisphere
El·eu·sin·i·an mysteries \,el-yù-,sin-ē-ən-\ *n pl* : religious mysteries celebrated at ancient Eleusis in worship of Demeter and Persephone
elev *abbr* elevation
¹el·e·vate \'el-ə-,vāt, -vət\ *adj, archaic* : ELEVATED
²el·e·vate \-,vāt\ *vt* **-vat·ed; -vat·ing** [ME *elevaten*, fr. L *elevatus*, pp. of *elevare*, fr. *e-* + *levare* to raise — more at LEVER] **1** : to lift up : RAISE **2** : to raise in rank or status : EXALT **3** : to improve morally, intellectually, or culturally **4** : to raise the spirits of : ELATE *syn* see LIFT *ant* lower
el·e·vat·ed \-,vāt-əd\ *adj* **1** : raised esp. above the ground or other surface ⟨an ~ highway⟩ **2 a** : morally or intellectually on a high plane ⟨an ~ mind⟩ **b** : FORMAL, DIGNIFIED ⟨~ diction⟩ **3** : exhilarated in mood or feeling
elevated railroad *n* : an urban or interurban railroad operating chiefly on an elevated structure — called also *elevated railway*
el·e·va·tion \,el-ə-'vā-shən\ *n* **1** : the height to which something is elevated: as **a** : the angular distance of a celestial object above the horizon **b** : the degree to which a gun is aimed above the horizon **c** : the height above the level of the sea : ALTITUDE **2** : a ballet dancer's or a skater's leap and seeming suspension in the air; *also* : the ability to achieve an elevation **3** : an act or instance of elevating **4** : something that is elevated: as **a** : an elevated place **b** : a swelling esp. on the skin **5** : the quality or state of being elevated **6** : a geometrical projection (as of a building) on a vertical plane *syn* see HEIGHT
el·e·va·tor \'el-ə-,vāt-ər\ *n* **1** : one that raises or lifts something up: as **a** : an endless belt or chain conveyor with cleats, scoops, or buckets for raising material **b** : a cage or platform and its hoisting machinery for conveying something to different levels **c** : a building for elevating, storing, discharging, and sometimes processing grain **2** : a movable auxiliary airfoil usu. attached to the tail plane of an airplane for producing motion up or down — see AIRPLANE illustration
elev·en \i-'lev-ən\ *n* [ME *enleven*, fr. *enleven*, adj., fr. OE *endleofan*; akin to OHG *einlif* eleven; both fr. a prehistoric Gmc compound whose first element is akin to OE *ān* one, and whose second element is prob. akin to OE *lēon* to lend] **1** — see NUMBER table **2** : the 11th in a set or series **3** : something having 11 units or members; *esp* : a football team — **eleven** *adj or pron* — **elev·enth** \-ən(t)th\ *adj or n*

ə abut	ᵊ kitten	ər further	a back	ā bake	ä cot, cart
aú out	ch chin	e less	ē easy	g gift	i trip	ī life
j joke	ŋ sing	ō flow	ȯ flaw	ȯi coin	th thin	th this
ü loot	u̇ foot	y yet	yü few	yu̇ furious	zh vision	

elev·ens·es \-ən-zəz\ *n pl but sometimes sing in constr* [irreg. pl. of *eleven* (o'clock)] *Brit* : a light lunch or sometimes only coffee or tea taken around the middle of the morning

eleventh hour *n* : the latest possible time ⟨won his reprieve at the *eleventh hour*⟩

el·e·von \'el-ə-,vän\ *n* [*elev*ator + ailer*on*] : an airplane control surface that combines the functions of elevator and aileron

elf \'elf\ *n, pl* **elves** \'elvz\ [ME, fr. OE *ælf*; akin to ON *alfr* elf] **1** : a small often mischievous fairy **2 a** : a small creature; *esp* : a mischievous child **b** : a mischievous or malicious person — **elf·ish** \'el-fish\ *adj* — **elf·ish·ly** *adv*

ELF *abbr* extremely low frequency

elf·in \'el-fən\ *adj* [irreg. fr. *elf*] **1 a** : of, relating to, or produced by an elf **b** : resembling an elf **2** : having an otherworldly or magical quality or charm

elf·lock \'el-,fläk\ *n* : hair matted as if by elves — usu. used in pl.

Eli \'ē-,lī\ *n* [Heb *'Ēlī*] : a judge and priest of Israel who according to the account in I Samuel was entrusted with the care of the boy Samuel

Eli·as \i-'lī-əs\ *n* [LL, fr. Gk *Ēlias*, fr. Heb *Ēlīyāh*] : ELIJAH

elic·it \i-'lis-ət\ *vt* [L *elicitus*, pp. of *elicere*, fr. *e-* + *lacere* to allure — more at DELIGHT] **1 a** : to draw forth or bring out (something latent or potential) **b** : to derive (as a truth) by logical processes **2** : to call forth or draw out (a response or reaction) ***syn*** see EDUCE — **elic·i·ta·tion** \ i-,lis-ə-'tā-shən, ,ē-\ *n* — **elic·i·tor** \i-'lis-ət-ər\ *n*

elide \i-'līd\ *vt* **elid·ed; elid·ing** [L *elidere* to strike out, fr. *e-* + *laedere* to injure by striking] **1 a** : to suppress or alter (as a vowel or syllable) by elision **b** : to strike out (as a written word or passage) **2 a** : to leave out of consideration : OMIT **b** : CURTAIL, ABRIDGE

el·i·gi·ble \'el-ə-jə-bəl\ *adj* [ME, fr. MF & LL; MF, fr. LL *eligibilis*, fr. L *eligere* to choose — more at ELECT] **1 a** : qualified to be chosen : ENTITLED ⟨~ for sophomore standing⟩ ⟨~ to retire⟩ **b** : permitted under football rules to catch a forward pass ⟨an ~ receiver⟩ **2** : worthy of being chosen : DESIRABLE ⟨an ~ young bachelor⟩ — **el·i·gi·bil·i·ty** \,el-ə-jə-'bil-ət-ē\ *n* — **eligible** *n* — **el·i·gi·bly** \'el-ə-jə-blē\ *adv*

Eli·jah \i-'lī-jə\ *n* [Heb *Ēlīyāh*] : a Hebrew prophet of the 9th century B.C. who according to the account in I Kings championed the worship of Jehovah as against Baal

elim·i·nate \i-'lim-ə-,nāt\ *vt* **-nat·ed; -nat·ing** [L *eliminatus*, pp. of *eliminare*, fr. *e-* + *limin-, limen* threshold] **1 a** : to cast out or get rid of : REMOVE, ERADICATE ⟨the need to ~ poverty⟩ **b** : to set aside as unimportant : IGNORE **2** : to expel (as waste) from the living body **3** : to cause to disappear by combining two or more equations ***syn*** see EXCLUDE — **elim·i·na·tion** \-,lim-ə-'nā-shən\ *n* — **elim·i·na·tive** \-'lim-ə-,nāt-iv\ *adj* — **elim·i·na·tor** \-,nāt-ər\ *n*

Eli·sha \i-'lī-shə\ *n* [Heb *Ēlīshā'*] : a Hebrew prophet and disciple and successor of Elijah

eli·sion \i-'lizh-ən\ *n* [LL *elision-, elisio*, fr. L *elisus*, pp. of *elidere*] **1 a** : the use of a speech form that lacks a final or initial sound which a variant speech form has ⟨the use of *'s* instead of *is* in English *there's* is an example of ~⟩ **b** : the omission of an unstressed vowel or syllable in a verse to achieve a uniform metrical pattern **2** : the act or an instance of dropping out or omitting something : OMISSION

elite \ā-'lēt, i-\ *n* [F *élite*, fr. OF *eslite*, fr. fem. of *eslit*, pp. of *eslire* to choose, fr. L *eligere*] **1 a** : the choice part; *esp* : a socially superior group **b** : a powerful minority group ⟨a power ~ inside the government⟩ **2** : a typewriter type providing 12 characters to the linear inch — **elite** *adj*

elit·ism \-'lēt-,iz-əm\ *n* **1 a** : leadership or rule by an elite **b** : belief in or advocacy of such elitism **2** : consciousness of being or belonging to an elite — **elit·ist** \-'lēt-əst\ *n or adj*

elix·ir \i-'lik-sər\ *n* [ME, fr. ML, fr. Ar *al-iksīr* the elixir, fr. *al* the + *iksīr* elixir, prob. fr. Gk *xērion* desiccative powder, fr. *xēros* dry] **1 a** : a substance held capable of changing base metals into gold : PHILOSOPHERS' STONE **b** (1) : a substance held capable of prolonging life indefinitely (2) : CURE-ALL (3) : a sweetened liquid usu. containing alcohol that is used as a vehicle for medicinal agents **2** : the essential principle

Eliz *abbr* Elizabethan

Eliz·a·be·than \i-,liz-ə-'bē-thən\ *adj* : of, relating to, or characteristic of Elizabeth I of England or her age — **Elizabethan** *n*

elk \'elk\ *n, pl* **elks** [ME, prob. fr. OE *eolh*; akin to OHG *elaho* elk, Gk *elaphos* deer] **1** *pl usu* **elk a** : the largest existing deer (*Alces alces*) of Europe and Asia resembling but not so large as the moose of No. America **b** : WAPITI **c** : any of various large Asiatic deer **2** : soft tanned rugged leather **3** *cap* [Benevolent and Protective Order of *Elks*] : a member of a major benevolent and fraternal order

elk·hound \'elk-,haund, 'el-,kaund\ *n* : NORWEGIAN ELKHOUND

¹ell \'el\ *n* [ME *eln*, fr. OE] **1** : a former English unit of length (as for cloth) equal to 45 inches **2** : any of various units of length similar in use to the English ell

²ell *n* [alter. of ¹*el*] **1** : an extension at right angles to the length of a building **2** : an elbow in a pipe or conduit

el·lag·ic acid \ə-,laj-ik-, e-\ *n* [F *ellagique*, fr. *ellag*, anagram of *galle* gall] : a crystalline phenolic compound $C_{14}H_6O_8$ with two lactone groupings that is obtained esp. from oak galls and some tannins

el·lipse \i-'lips, e-\ *n* [Gk *elleipsis*] **1 a** : OVAL **b** : a closed plane curve generated by a point moving in such a way that the sums of its distances from two fixed points is a constant: a plane section of a right circular cone that is a closed curve **2** : ELLIPSIS

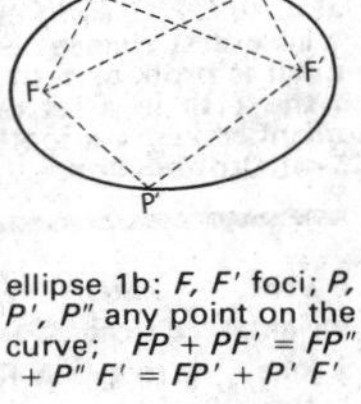

ellipse 1b: *F, F'* foci; *P, P', P''* any point on the curve; *FP* + *PF'* = *FP''* + *P'' F'* = *FP'* + *P' F'*

el·lip·sis \i-'lip-səs, e-\ *n, pl* **el·lip·ses** \-,sēz\ [L, fr. Gk *elleipsis* ellipsis, ellipse, fr. *elleipein* to leave out, fall short, fr. *en* in + *leipein* to leave — more at IN, LOAN] **1 a** : the omission of one or more words that are obviously understood but that must be supplied to make a construction grammatically complete ⟨"the man that he sees" may be changed by ~ to "the man he sees"⟩ **b** : a leap or sudden passage without logical connectives from one topic to another **2** : marks or a mark (as . . . or *** or —) indicating the omission esp. of letters or words

el·lip·soid \i-'lip-,sȯid, e-\ *n* : a surface all plane sections of which are ellipses or circles — **ellipsoid** *or* **el·lip·soi·dal** \i-,lip-'sȯid-ᵊl, (,)e-\ *adj*

el·lip·tic \i-'lip-tik, e-\ *or* **el·lip·ti·cal** \-ti-kəl\ *adj* [Gk *elleiptikos* defective, marked by ellipsis, fr. *elleipein*] **1 a** : of, relating to, or shaped like an ellipse **b** : of, relating to, or being a space in which no line parallel to a given line passes through a point not on the line **2 a** : of, relating to, or marked by ellipsis or an ellipsis **b** (1) : of, relating to, or marked by extreme economy of speech or writing (2) : of or relating to studied obscurity of literary style — **el·lip·ti·cal·ly** \-ti-k(ə-)lē\ *adv*

el·lip·tic·i·ty \i-,lip-'tis-ət-ē, (,)e-\ *n* : deviation of an ellipse or a spheroid from the form of a circle or a sphere

elm \'elm\ *n* [ME, fr. OE; akin to OHG *elme* elm, L *ulmus*] **1** : any of a genus (*Ulmus* of the family Ulmaceae, the elm family) comprising large graceful trees with alternate stipulate leaves and small apetalous flowers **2** : the wood of an elm

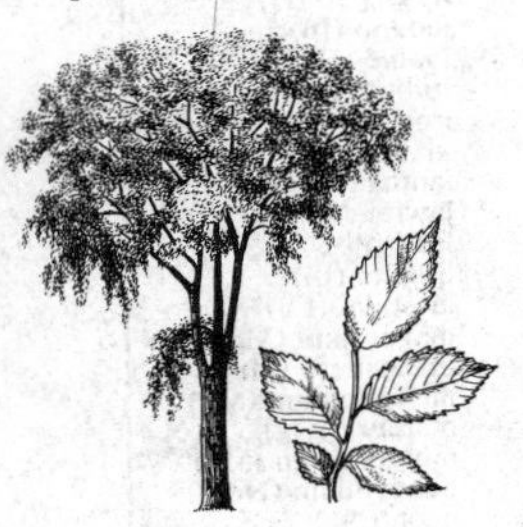

elm 1

elm bark beetle *n* : either of two beetles that are vectors for the fungus causing Dutch elm disease: **a** : a beetle (*Hylurgopinus rufipes*) native to eastern No. America **b** : a European beetle (*Scolytus multistriatus*) that is established in eastern No. America

elm blight *n* : DUTCH ELM DISEASE

elm leaf beetle *n* : a small orange-yellow black-striped Old World chrysomelid beetle (*Pyrrhalta luteola*) that is a leaf-eating pest of elms in eastern No. America as a larva and as an adult

el·o·cu·tion \,el-ə-'kyü-shən\ *n* [ME *elocucioun*, fr. L *elocution-, elocutio*, fr. *elocutus*, pp. of *eloqui*] **1** : the art of effective public speaking **2** : a style of speaking esp. in public — **el·o·cu·tion·ary** \-shə-,ner-ē\ *adj* — **el·o·cu·tion·ist** \-sh(ə-)nəst\ *n*

elo·dea \i-'lōd-ē-ə\ *n* [NL, genus name, fr. Gk *helōdēs* marshy, fr. *helos* marsh; akin to Skt *saras* pond] : any of a small American genus (*Elodea*) of submerged aquatic monocotyledonous herbs

eloign \i-'lȯin\ *vt* [ME *eloynen*, fr. MF *esloigner*, fr. OF, fr. *es-* ex- (fr. L *ex-*) + *loing* (adv.) far, fr. L *longe*, fr. *longus* long] **1** *archaic* : to take (oneself) far away **2** *archaic* : to remove to a distant or unknown place : CONCEAL

¹elon·gate \i-'lȯŋ-,gāt\ *vb* **-gat·ed; -gat·ing** [LL *elongatus*, pp. of *elongare*, to withdraw, fr. L *e-* + *longus* long] *vt* : to extend the length of ~ *vi* : to grow in length ***syn*** see EXTEND ***ant*** abbreviate, shorten

²elongate *adj* **1** : stretched out : LENGTHENED **2** : long in proportion to width : SLENDER

elon·gat·ed *adj* : ELONGATE

elon·ga·tion \(,)ē-,lȯŋ-'gā-shən\ *n* [LL *elongare* to withdraw] **1 a** : the angular distance of a celestial body from another around which it revolves or from a particular point in the sky **b** : the daily extreme east or west position of a star with reference to the north celestial pole **2 a** : the state of being elongated or lengthened **b** : something that is elongated

elope \i-'lōp\ *vi* **eloped; elop·ing** [AF *aloper*] **1 a** : to run away from one's husband with a lover **b** : to run away secretly with the intention of getting married usu. without parental consent **2** : to slip away : ESCAPE — **elope·ment** \-'lōp-mənt\ *n* — **elop·er** *n*

el·o·quence \'el-ə-kwən(t)s\ *n* : discourse marked by force and persuasiveness; *also* : the art or power of using such discourse

el·o·quent \-kwənt\ *adj* [ME, fr. MF, fr. L *eloquent-, eloquens*, fr. prp. of *eloqui* to speak out, fr. *e-* + *loqui* to speak] **1** : marked by forceful and fluent expression ⟨an ~ preacher⟩ **2** : vividly or movingly expressive or revealing ⟨put his arm around her in an ~ gesture of reassurance⟩ — **el·o·quent·ly** *adv*

¹else \'els\ *adv* [ME *elles*, fr. OE; akin to L *alius* other, *alter* other of two, Gk *allos* other] **1 a** : in a different manner or place or at a different time ⟨how ~ could he have acted⟩ ⟨here and nowhere ~⟩ **b** : in an additional manner or place or at an additional time ⟨where ~ is gold found⟩ **2** : if the facts are or were different : if not : OTHERWISE ⟨do what you are told or ~ you'll be sorry⟩ — used absolutely to express a threat ⟨do what I tell you or ~⟩

²else *adj* : OTHER: **a** : being different in identity ⟨it must have been somebody ~⟩ **b** : being in addition ⟨what ~ did he say⟩

else·where \-,(h)we(ə)r, -,(h)wa(ə)r\ *adv* : in or to another place ⟨took his business ~⟩

ELSS *abbr* extravehicular life support system

el·u·ant *or* **el·u·ent** \'el-yə-wənt\ *n* [L *eluent-, eluens*, prp. of *eluere*] : a solvent used in eluting

el·u·ate \'el-yə-wət, -,wāt\ *n* [L *eluere* + E *-ate*] : the washings obtained by eluting

elu·ci·date \i-'lü-sə-,dāt\ *vb* **-dat·ed; -dat·ing** [LL *elucidatus*, pp. of *elucidare*, fr. L *e-* + *lucidus* lucid] *vt* : to make lucid esp. by explanation ~ *vi* : to give a clarifying explanation ***syn*** see EXPLAIN — **elu·ci·da·tion** \-,lü-sə-'dā-shən\ *n* — **elu·ci·da·tive** \-'lü-sə-,dāt-iv\ *adj* — **elu·ci·da·tor** \-,dāt-ər\ *n*

elu·cu·brate \i-'lü-k(y)ə-,brāt\ *vt* **-brat·ed; -brat·ing** [L *elucubratus*, pp. of *elucubrare* to compose by lamplight, fr. *e-* + *lucubrare* to work by lamplight — more at LUCUBRATION] : to work out or express by studious effort — **elu·cu·bra·tion** \-,lü-k(y)ə-'brā-shən\ *n*

elude \ē-'lüd\ *vt* **elud·ed; elud·ing** [L *eludere*, fr. *e-* + *ludere* to play — more at LUDICROUS] **1** : to avoid adroitly : EVADE **2** : to escape the notice of ***syn*** see ESCAPE

Elul \e-ˈlül\ *n* [Heb *Ĕlūl*] **:** the 12th month of the civil year or the 6th month of the ecclesiastical year in the Jewish calendar — see MONTH table

elu·sion \ē-ˈlü-zhən\ *n* [ML *elusion-, elusio,* fr. LL, deception, fr. L *elusus,* pp. of *eludere*] **:** an act of eluding: as **a :** an adroit escape **b :** an evasion esp. of a problem or an order

elu·sive \ē-ˈlü-siv, -ˈlü-ziv\ *adj* **:** tending to elude: as **a :** tending to evade grasp or pursuit ⟨an eligible though ~ bachelor⟩ **b :** hard to comprehend or define ⟨an ~ concept that means many things to many people⟩ **c :** hard to isolate or identify ⟨a haunting ~ aroma⟩ — **elu·sive·ly** *adv* — **elu·sive·ness** *n*

elute \ē-ˈlüt\ *vt* **elut·ed; elut·ing** [L *elutus,* pp. of *eluere* to wash out, fr. *e-* + *lavere* to wash — more at LYE] **:** EXTRACT; *specif* **:** to remove (adsorbed material) from an adsorbent by means of a solvent — **elu·tion** \-ˈlü-shən\ *n*

elu·tri·ate \ē-ˈlü-trē-ˌāt\ *vt* **-at·ed; -at·ing** [L *elutriatus,* pp. of *elutriare,* irreg. fr. *elutus*] **:** to purify, separate, or remove by washing — **elu·tri·a·tor** \-ˌāt-ər\ *n*

elu·vi·al \ē-ˈlü-vē-əl\ *adj* **1 :** of, relating to, or composed of eluvium **2 :** of or relating to eluviation or to eluviated materials or areas

elu·vi·ate \-vē-ˌāt\ *vi* **-at·ed; -at·ing :** to undergo eluviation

elu·vi·a·tion \(ˌ)ē-ˌlü-vē-ˈā-shən\ *n* **:** the transportation of dissolved or suspended material within the soil by the movement of water when rainfall exceeds evaporation

elu·vi·um \ē-ˈlü-vē-əm\ *n* [NL, fr. L *eluere* to wash out] **1 :** rock debris produced by the weathering and disintegration of rock in situ **2 :** fine soil or sand deposited by wind

el·ver \ˈel-vər\ *n* [alter. of *eelfare* (migration of eels)] **:** a young eel

elves *pl of* ELF

el·vish \ˈel-vish\ *adj* **1 :** of or relating to elves **2 :** MISCHIEVOUS

ely·sian \i-ˈlizh-ən\ *adj, often cap* **1 :** of or relating to Elysium **2 :** BLISSFUL, DELIGHTFUL

elysian fields *n pl, often cap E* **:** ELYSIUM

Ely·si·um \i-ˈliz(h)-ē-əm\ *n, pl* **-si·ums** *or* **-sia** \-ē-ə\ [L, fr. Gk *Elysion*] **1 :** the abode of the blessed after death in classical mythology **2 :** PARADISE 2

elytr- *or* **elytri-** *or* **elytro-** *comb form* [NL *elytron*] **:** elytron ⟨*elytroid*⟩ ⟨*elytriferous*⟩

el·y·tron \ˈel-ə-ˌträn\ *also* **el·y·trum** \-trəm\ *n, pl* **-tra** \-trə\ [NL, fr. Gk *elytron* sheath, wing cover, fr. *eilyein* to roll, wrap — more at VOLUBLE] **:** one of the anterior wings in beetles and some other insects that serve to protect the posterior pair of functional wings

em \ˈem\ *n* **1 :** the letter *m* **2 :** the set dimension of an em quad used as a unit of measure **3 :** ¹PICA 2

EM *abbr* **1** electromagnetic **2** end matched **3** engineer of mines **4** enlisted man

em- — see EN-

ema·ci·ate \i-ˈmā-shē-ˌāt\ *vb* **-at·ed; at·ing** [L *emaciatus,* pp. of *emaciare,* fr. *e-* + *macies* leanness, fr. *macer* lean — more at MEAGER] *vt* **1 :** to cause to lose flesh so as to become very thin **2 :** to make feeble ~ *vi* **:** to waste away physically — **ema·ci·a·tion** \-ˌmā-s(h)ē-ˈā-shən\ *n*

em·a·nate \ˈem-ə-ˌnāt\ *vb* **-nat·ed; -nat·ing** [L *emanatus,* pp. of *emanare,* fr. *e-* + *manare* to flow] *vi* **:** to come out from a source ~ *vt* **:** to give out **:** EMIT ***syn*** see SPRING

em·a·na·tion \ˌem-ə-ˈnā-shən\ *n* **1 a :** the action of emanating **b :** the origination of the world by a series of hierarchically descending radiations from the Godhead through intermediate stages to matter **2 a :** something that emanates or is produced by emanation **:** EFFLUENCE **b :** a heavy gaseous element produced by radioactive disintegration ⟨radium ~⟩ — **em·a·na·tion·al** \-shnəl, -shən-ᵊl\ *adj* — **em·a·na·tive** \ˈem-ə-ˌnāt-iv\ *adj*

eman·ci·pate \i-ˈman(t)-sə-ˌpāt\ *vt* **-pat·ed; -pat·ing** [L *emancipatus,* pp. of *emancipare,* fr. *e-* + *mancipare* to transfer ownership of, fr. *mancip-, manceps* purchaser, fr. *manus* hand + *capere* to take — more at MANUAL, HEAVE] **1 :** to release from paternal care and responsibility and make sui juris **2 :** to free from restraint, control, or the power of another; *esp* **:** to free from bondage ***syn*** see FREE — **eman·ci·pa·tor** \-ˌpāt-ər\ *n*

eman·ci·pa·tion \i-ˌman(t)-sə-ˈpā-shən\ *n* **:** the act or process of emancipating — **eman·ci·pa·tion·ist** \-sh(ə-)nəst\ *n*

emar·gin·ate \(ˈ)ē-ˈmär-jə-nət, -ˌnāt\ *adj* [L *emarginatus,* pp. of *emarginare* to deprive of a margin, fr. *e-* + *margin-, margo* margin] **:** having the margin notched — **emar·gi·na·tion** \(ˌ)ē-ˌmär-jə-ˈnā-shən\ *n*

emas·cu·late \i-ˈmas-kyə-ˌlāt\ *vt* **-lat·ed; -lat·ing** [L *emasculatus,* pp. of *emasculare,* fr. *e-* + *masculus* male — more at MALE] **1 :** to deprive of virile or procreative power **:** CASTRATE **2 :** to deprive of masculine vigor or spirit **:** WEAKEN **3 :** to remove the androecium of (a flower) in the process of artificial cross-pollination ***syn*** see UNNERVE — **emas·cu·late** \-lət\ *adj* — **emas·cu·la·tion** \-ˌmas-kyə-ˈlā-shən\ *n* — **emas·cu·la·tor** \-ˈmas-kyə-ˌlāt-ər\ *n*

em·balm \im-ˈbäm, -ˈbälm\ *vt* [ME *embaumen,* fr. MF *embaumer,* fr. OF *embasmer,* fr. *en-* + *basme* balm — more at BALM] **1 :** to treat (a dead body) so as to protect from decay **2 :** to fill with sweet odors **:** PERFUME **3 :** to protect from decay or oblivion **:** PRESERVE — **em·balm·er** *n* — **em·balm·ment** \-ˈbä(l)m-mənt\ *n*

em·bank \im-ˈbaŋk\ *vt* **:** to enclose or confine by an embankment

em·bank·ment \-mənt\ *n* **1 :** the action of embanking **2 :** a raised structure to hold back water or to carry a roadway

em·bar·ca·de·ro \(ˌ)em-ˌbär-kə-ˈde(ə)r-(ˌ)ō\ *n, pl* **-ros** [Sp, fr. *embarcado,* pp. of *embarcar* to embark] *West* **:** a landing place esp. on an inland waterway

¹em·bar·go \im-ˈbär-(ˌ)gō\ *n, pl* **-goes** [Sp, fr. *embargar* to bar, fr. (assumed) VL *imbarricare,* fr. L *in-* + (assumed) VL *barra* bar] **1 :** an order of a government prohibiting the departure of commercial ships from its ports **2 :** a legal prohibition on commerce ⟨an ~ on arms shipments⟩ **3 :** STOPPAGE, IMPEDIMENT; *esp* **:** PROHIBITION ⟨I lay no ~ on anybody's words —Jane Austen⟩ **4 :** a common carrier or public regulatory agency order prohibiting or restricting freight transportation

²embargo *vt* **-goed; -go·ing :** to place an embargo on (as ships or commerce)

em·bark \im-ˈbärk\ *vb* [MF *embarquer,* fr. OProv *embarcar,* fr. *em-* (fr. L *im-*) + *barca* bark] *vt* **1 :** to cause to go on board a boat or airplane **2 :** to engage, enlist, or invest in an enterprise ~ *vi* **1 :** to go on board a boat or airplane for transportation **2 :** to make a start **:** COMMENCE ⟨~*ed* on a new career⟩ — **em·bar·ka·tion** \ˌem-ˌbär-ˈkā-shən, -bər-\ *n* — **em·bark·ment** \im-ˈbärk-mənt\ *n*

em·bar·rass \im-ˈbar-əs\ *vt* [F *embarrasser,* fr. Sp *embarazar,* fr. Pg *embaraçar*] **1 a :** to hamper the movement of **b :** HINDER, IMPEDE **2 a :** to place in doubt, perplexity, or difficulties **b :** to involve in financial difficulties **c :** to cause to experience a state of self-conscious distress ⟨bawdy stories ~*ed* her ⟩ **3 :** to make intricate **:** COMPLICATE **4 :** to impair the activity of (a bodily function) or the function of (a bodily part) ⟨digestion ~*ed* by overeating⟩ — **em·bar·rass·able** \-ə-bəl\ *adj*

syn EMBARRASS, DISCOMFIT, ABASH, DISCONCERT, RATTLE, FAZE *shared meaning element* **:** to distress by confusing or confounding

em·bar·rassed·ly \-əst-lē, -ə-səd-lē\ *adv* **:** with embarrassment ⟨giggled ~⟩

em·bar·rass·ing·ly \-ə-siŋ-lē\ *adv* **:** to an embarrassing degree

em·bar·rass·ment \im-ˈbar-ə-smənt\ *n* **1 :** the state of being embarrassed: as **a :** confusion or disturbance of mind **b :** difficulty arising from the want of money to pay debts **c :** difficulty in functioning as a result of disease **2 a :** something that embarrasses **:** IMPEDIMENT **b :** an excessive quantity from which to select — used esp. in the phrase *embarrassment of riches*

em·bas·sage \ˈem-bə-sij\ *n* **1 :** the message or commission entrusted to an ambassador **2** *archaic* **:** EMBASSY

em·bas·sy \ˈem-bə-sē\ *n, pl* **-sies** [MF *ambassee,* of Gmc origin; akin to OHG *ambaht* service] **1 a :** the function or position of an ambassador **b :** a mission abroad undertaken officially esp. by an ambassador **2 :** EMBASSAGE 1 **3 :** a body of diplomatic representatives; *specif* **:** one headed by an ambassador **4 :** the official residence and offices of an ambassador

em·bat·tle \im-ˈbat-ᵊl\ *vt* **em·bat·tled; em·bat·tling** \-ˈbat-liŋ, -ᵊl-iŋ\ [ME *embatailen,* fr. MF *embatailler,* fr. *en-* + *batailler* to battle] **1 :** to arrange in order of battle **:** prepare for battle **2 :** FORTIFY

em·bat·tle·ment \-ˈbat-ᵊl-mənt\ *n* **:** BATTLEMENT

em·bay \im-ˈbā\ *vt* **:** to shut or shelter esp. in a bay ⟨an ~*ed* fleet⟩

em·bay·ment \-ˈbā-mənt\ *n* **1 :** formation of a bay **2 :** a bay or a conformation resembling a bay

Emb·den \ˈem-dən\ *n* [*Emden,* Germany] **:** a breed of large white domestic geese with an orange bill and deep orange shanks and toes

em·bed \im-ˈbed\ *vb* **em·bed·ded; em·bed·ding** *vt* **1 a :** to enclose closely in or as if in a matrix **b :** to make something an integral part of **c :** to prepare (a microscopy specimen) for sectioning by infiltrating with and enclosing in a supporting substance **2 :** to place or fix firmly in surrounding matter ⟨dirt *embedded* in a carpet⟩ ~ *vi* **:** to become embedded — **em·bed·ment** \-ˈbed-mənt\ *n*

em·bel·lish \im-ˈbel-ish\ *vt* [ME *embelisshen,* fr. MF *embeliss-,* stem of *embelir,* fr. *en-* + *bel* beautiful — more at BEAUTY] **1 :** to make beautiful with ornamentation **:** DECORATE **2 :** to heighten the attractiveness of by adding ornamental details **:** ENHANCE ⟨events in his life, heavily ~*ed* by his biographers —Marvin Reznikoff⟩ ***syn*** see ADORN — **em·bel·lish·er** *n*

em·bel·lish·ment \-ish-mənt\ *n* **1 :** the act or process of embellishing **2 :** something serving to embellish **3 :** ORNAMENT 5

em·ber \ˈem-bər\ *n* [ME *eymere,* fr. ON *eimyrja;* akin to OE *ǣmerge* ashes] **1 :** a glowing fragment (as of coal) from a fire; *esp* **:** one smoldering in ashes **2** *pl* **:** the smoldering remains of a fire **3** *pl* **:** slowly cooling emotions, memories, ideas, or responses still capable of being enlivened

ember day \ˈem-bər-\ *n* [ME, fr. OE *ymbrendæg,* fr. *ymbrene* circuit, anniversary + *dæg* day] **:** a Wednesday, Friday, or Saturday following the first Sunday in Lent, Whitsunday, September 14, or December 13 and set apart for fasting and prayer in Western churches

em·bez·zle \im-ˈbez-əl\ *vt* **em·bez·zled; em·bez·zling** \-(ə-)liŋ\ [ME *embesilen,* fr. AF *embeseiller,* fr. MF *en-* + *besillier* to destroy] **:** to appropriate (as property entrusted to one's care) fraudulently to one's own use — **em·bez·zle·ment** \-əl-mənt\ *n* — **em·bez·zler** \-(ə-)lər\ *n*

em·bit·ter \im-ˈbit-ər\ *vt* **1 :** to make bitter **2 :** to excite bitter feelings in — **em·bit·ter·ment** \-mənt\ *n*

¹em·blaze \im-ˈblāz\ *vt* **em·blazed; em·blaz·ing** [*en-* + *blaze* (to blazon)] **1** *archaic* **:** EMBLAZON 1 **2 :** to adorn sumptuously ⟨with gems and golden luster rich *emblazed* —John Milton⟩

²emblaze *vt* **em·blazed; em·blaz·ing 1 :** to illuminate esp. by a blaze **2 :** to set ablaze

em·bla·zon \im-ˈblāz-ᵊn\ *vt* **em·bla·zoned; em·bla·zon·ing** \-ˈblāz-niŋ, -ᵊn-iŋ\ **1 :** to inscribe or adorn with heraldic bearings or devices **2 a :** to deck in bright colors **b :** CELEBRATE, EXTOL ⟨have his . . . deeds ~*ed* by a poet —Thomas Nash⟩ — **em·bla·zon·er** \-ˈblāz-nər, -ᵊn-ər\ *n* — **em·bla·zon·ment** \-ˈblāz-ᵊn-mənt\ *n* — **em·bla·zon·ry** \-ᵊn-rē\ *n*

¹em·blem \ˈem-bləm\ *n* [ME, fr. L *emblema* inlaid work, fr. Gk *emblēmat-, emblēma,* fr. *emballein* to insert, fr. *en-* + *ballein* to throw — more at DEVIL] **1 :** a picture with a motto or set of verses intended as a moral lesson **2 :** an object or the figure of an object symbolizing and suggesting another object or an idea **3 a :** a symbolic object used as a heraldic device **b :** a device, symbol, or figure adopted and used as an identifying mark

²emblem *vt* **:** EMBLEMATIZE

ə abut ᵊ kitten ər further a back ā bake ä cot, cart
aù out ch chin e less ē easy g gift i trip ī life
j joke ŋ sing ō flow ȯ flaw ȯi coin th thin t͟h this
ü loot u̇ foot y yet yü few yu̇ furious zh vision

em·blem·at·ic \ˌem-blə-ˈmat-ik\ *also* **em·blem·at·i·cal** \-i-kəl\ *adj* : of, relating to, or constituting an emblem : SYMBOLIC — **em·blem·at·i·cal·ly** \-i-k(ə-)lē\ *adv*
em·blem·a·tize \em-ˈblem-ə-ˌtīz\ *vt* **-tized; -tiz·ing** : to represent by or as if by an emblem : SYMBOLIZE
em·ble·ments \ˈem-blə-mən(t)s\ *n pl* [ME *emblayment*, fr. MF *emblaement*, fr. *emblaer* to sow with grain, fr. *en-* + *blee* grain] : crops from annual cultivation legally belonging to the tenant
em·bodi·ment \im-ˈbäd-i-mənt\ *n* **1** : the act of embodying : the state of being embodied **2** : one that embodies something ⟨the ~ of all our hopes⟩
em·body \im-ˈbäd-ē\ *vt* **em·bod·ied; em·body·ing** **1** : to give a body to (a spirit) : INCARNATE **2 a** : to deprive of spirituality **b** : to make concrete and perceptible **3** : to cause to become a body or part of a body : INCORPORATE **4** : to represent in human or animal form : PERSONIFY ⟨men who greatly *embodied* the idealism of American life —A. M. Schlesinger *b*1917⟩ — **em·bodi·er** *n*
embol- *or* **emboli-** *or* **embolo-** *comb form* [NL, fr. *embolus*] : embolus ⟨*embolectomy*⟩
em·bold·en \im-ˈbōl-dən\ *vt* : to instill with boldness or courage
em·bo·lec·to·my \ˌem-bə-ˈlek-tə-mē\ *n, pl* **-mies** : surgical removal of an embolus
em·bol·ic \em-ˈbäl-ik, im-\ *adj* : of or relating to an embolus or embolism
em·bo·lism \ˈem-bə-ˌliz-əm\ *n* [ME *embolisme*, fr. ML *embolismus*, fr. Gk *embol-* (fr. *emballein* to insert, intercalate) — more at EMBLEM] **1** : the insertion of one or more days in a calendar : INTERCALATION **2 a** : the sudden obstruction of a blood vessel by an embolus **b** : EMBOLUS — **em·bo·lis·mic** \ˌem-bə-ˈliz-mik\ *adj*
em·bo·li·za·tion \ˌem-bə-lə-ˈzā-shən\ *n* : the process or state in which a blood vessel or organ is obstructed by the lodgment of a material mass (as an embolus)
em·bo·lus \ˈem-bə-ləs\ *n, pl* **-li** \-ˌlī\ [NL, fr. Gk *embolos* wedge-shaped object, stopper, fr. *emballein*] : an abnormal particle (as an air bubble) circulating in the blood — compare THROMBUS
em·bo·ly \ˈem-bə-lē\ *n* [Gk *embolē* insertion, fr. *emballein*] : gastrula formation by simple invagination of the blastula wall
em·bon·point \äⁿ-bōⁿ-pwaⁿ\ *n* [F, fr. MF, fr. *en bon point* in good condition] : plumpness of person : STOUTNESS
em·bo·som \im-ˈbu̇z-əm *also* -ˈbüz-\ *vt* **1** *archaic* : to take into or place in the bosom **2** : to shelter closely : ENCLOSE ⟨his house ~*ed* in the grove —Alexander Pope⟩
[1]**em·boss** \im-ˈbäs, -ˈbȯs\ *vt* [ME *embosen* to become exhausted fr. being hunted] *obs* : to drive (as a hunted animal) to bay
[2]**emboss** *vt* [ME *embosen*, fr. MF *embocer*, fr. *en-* + *boce* boss] **1** : to raise the surface of into bosses; *esp* : to ornament with raised work **2** : to raise in relief from a surface **3** : ADORN, EMBELLISH — **em·boss·able** \-ə-bəl\ *adj* — **em·boss·er** \-ər\ *n* — **em·boss·ment** \-mənt\ *n*
em·bou·chure \ˌäm-bu̇-ˈshu̇(ə)r\ *n* [F, fr. (*s'*)*emboucher* to flow into, fr. *en-* + *bouche* mouth — more at DEBOUCH] **1** : the position and use of the lips in producing a musical tone on a wind instrument **2** : the mouthpiece of a musical instrument
em·bowed \im-ˈbōd\ *adj* : bent like a bow: as **a** : ARCHED, VAULTED ⟨an ~ ceiling⟩ **b** : curved outward to form a projecting recess
em·bow·el \im-ˈbau̇(-ə)l\ *vt* **-eled** *or* **-elled; -el·ing** *or* **-el·ling** **1** : DISEMBOWEL **2** *obs* : ENCLOSE
em·bow·er \im-ˈbau̇(-ə)r\ *vt* : to shelter or enclose in a bower ⟨like a rose ~*ed* in its own green leaves —P. B. Shelley⟩
[1]**em·brace** \im-ˈbrās\ *vb* **em·braced; em·brac·ing** [ME *embracen*, fr. MF *embracer*, fr. OF *embracier*, fr. *en-* + *brace* two arms — more at BRACE] *vt* **1 a** : to clasp in the arms : HUG **b** : CHERISH, LOVE **2** : ENCIRCLE, ENCLOSE **3 a** : to take up esp. readily or gladly ⟨~ a cause⟩ **b** : to avail oneself of : WELCOME ⟨*embraced* the opportunity to study further⟩ **4 a** : to take in or include as a part, item, or element of a more inclusive whole ⟨charity ~*s* all acts that contribute to human welfare⟩ **b** : to be equal or equivalent to ⟨his assets *embraced* $10⟩ ~ *vi* : to participate in an embrace ***syn*** **1** see ADOPT ***ant*** spurn **2** see INCLUDE — **em·brace·able** \-ˈbrā-sə-bəl\ *adj* — **em·brace·ment** \-ˈbrā-smənt\ *n* — **em·brac·er** *n* — **em·brac·ing·ly** \-ˈbrā-siŋ-lē\ *adv*
[2]**embrace** *n* **1** : a close encircling with the arms and pressure to the bosom esp. as a sign of affection : HUG **2** : GRIP, ENCIRCLEMENT ⟨helpless in the ~ of terror⟩ **3** : ACCEPTANCE ⟨his ready ~ of new doctrines⟩
em·bra·ceor \im-ˈbrā-sər\ *n* [AF, fr. MF *embraseor* instigator, fr. *embraser* to set on fire, fr. *en-* + *brase, brese* live coals] : one guilty of embracery
em·brac·ery \im-ˈbrās-(ə-)rē\ *n, pl* **-er·ies** [ME, fr. AF *embraceor*] : an attempt to influence a jury corruptly (as by bribes or threats)
em·brac·ive \-ˈbrā-siv\ *adj* **1** : disposed to embrace **2** : INCLUSIVE, COMPREHENSIVE
em·branch·ment \im-ˈbranch-mənt\ *n* [F *embranchement*, fr. (*s'*)*embrancher* to branch out, fr. *en-* + *branche* branch] **1** : a branching off or out (as of a valley) **2** : BRANCH
em·bran·gle \im-ˈbraŋ-gəl\ *vt* **-gled; -gling** \-g(ə-)liŋ\ [*en-* + *brangle* (squabble)] : EMBROIL — **em·bran·gle·ment** \-gəl-mənt\ *n*
em·bra·sure \im-ˈbrā-zhər\ *n* [F, fr. obs. *embraser* to widen an opening] **1** : a recess of a door or window **2** : an opening with sides flaring outward in a wall or parapet of a fortification usu. for allowing the firing of cannon
em·brit·tle \im-ˈbrit-ᵊl\ *vb* **-brit·tled; -brit·tling** \-ˈbrit-liŋ, -ᵊl-iŋ\ *vt* : to make brittle ~ *vi* : to become brittle — **em·brit·tle·ment** \-ˈbrit-ᵊl-mənt\ *n*
em·bro·cate \ˈem-brə-ˌkāt\ *vt* **-cat·ed; -cat·ing** [LL *embrocatus*, pp. of *embrocare*, fr. Gk *embrochē* lotion, fr. *embrechein* to embrocate, fr. *en-* + *brechein* to wet] : to moisten and rub (a part of the body) with a lotion
em·bro·ca·tion \ˌem-brə-ˈkā-shən\ *n* : LINIMENT
embroglio *var of* IMBROGLIO
em·broi·der \im-ˈbrȯid-ər\ *vb* **em·broi·dered; em·broi·der·ing** \-(ə-)riŋ\ [ME *embroderen*, fr. MF *embroder*, fr. *en-* + *broder* to embroider, of Gmc origin; akin to OE *brord* point, *byrst* bristle] *vt* **1 a** : to ornament with needlework **b** : to form with needlework **2** : to elaborate on : EMBELLISH ~ *vi* **1** : to make embroidery **2** : to provide embellishments : ELABORATE — **em·broi·der·er** \-ˈbrȯid-ər-ər\ *n*
em·broi·dery \im-ˈbrȯid-(ə-)rē\ *n, pl* **-der·ies** **1 a** : the art or process of forming decorative designs with hand or machine needlework **b** : a design or decoration so formed **c** : an object decorated with embroidery **2** : elaboration by use of decorative and often fictitious detail **3** : something pleasing or desirable but unimportant ⟨considered the humanities mere educational ~⟩
em·broil \im-ˈbrȯi(ə)l\ *vt* [F *embrouiller*, fr. MF, fr. *en-* + *brouiller* to broil] **1** : to throw into disorder or confusion **2** : to involve in conflict or difficulties — **em·broil·ment** \-mənt\ *n*
em·brown \im-ˈbrau̇n\ *vt* **1** : DARKEN **2** : to cause to turn brown
embrue *var of* IMBRUE
embry- *or* **embryo-** *comb form* [LL, fr. Gk, fr. *embryon*] : embryo ⟨*embryogeny*⟩
em·bryo \ˈem-brē-ˌō\ *n, pl* **em·bry·os** [ML *embryon-*, *embryo*, fr. Gk *embryon*, fr. *en-* + *bryein* to swell; akin to Gk *bryon* moss] **1 a** *archaic* : a vertebrate at any stage of development prior to birth or hatching **b** : an animal in the early stages of growth and differentiation that are characterized by cleavage, the laying down of fundamental tissues, and the formation of primitive organs and organ systems; *esp* : the developing human individual from the time of implantation to the end of the eighth week after conception **2** : the young sporophyte of a seed plant usu. comprising a rudimentary plant with plumule, radicle, and cotyledons **3 a** : something as yet undeveloped **b** : a beginning or undeveloped state of something ⟨productions seen in ~ during their out-of-town tryout period —Henry Hewes⟩
em·bryo·gen·e·sis \ˌem-brē-ō-ˈjen-ə-səs\ *n* : the formation and development of the embryo — **em·bryo·ge·net·ic** \-jə-ˈnet-ik\ *adj*
em·bry·og·e·ny \ˌem-brē-ˈäj-ə-nē\ *n, pl* **-nies** : EMBRYOGENESIS — **em·bryo·gen·ic** \-brē-ō-ˈjen-ik\ adj
embryol *abbr* embryology
em·bry·ol·o·gy \ˌem-brē-ˈäl-ə-jē\ *n* [F *embryologie*] **1** : a branch of biology dealing with embryos and their development **2** : the features and phenomena exhibited in the formation and development of an embryo — **em·bry·o·log·ic** \-brē-ə-ˈläj-ik\ *or* **em·bry·o·log·i·cal** \-i-kəl\ *adj* **em·bry·o·log·i·cal·ly** \-i-k(ə-)lē\ *adv* — **em·bry·ol·o·gist** \-brē-ˈäl-ə-jəst\ *n*
embryon- *or* **embryoni-** *comb form* [ML *embryon-*, *embryo*] : embryo ⟨*embryonic*⟩
em·bry·o·nal \em-ˈbrī-ən-ᵊl\ *adj* : EMBRYONIC 1 — **em·bry·o·nal·ly** \-ˈbrī-ə-nə-lē\ *adv*
em·bry·o·nat·ed \ˈem-brē-ə-ˌnāt-əd\ *adj* : having an embryo
em·bry·on·ic \ˌem-brē-ˈän-ik\ *adj* **1** : of or relating to an embryo **2** : being in an early stage of development : INCIPIENT, RUDIMENTARY — **em·bry·on·i·cal·ly** \-i-k(ə-)lē\ *adv*
embryonic disk *n* **1 a** : BLASTODISC **b** : BLASTODERM **2** : the part of the inner cell mass of a blastocyst from which the embryo of a placental mammal develops — called also *embryonic shield*
embryonic layer *n* : GERM LAYER
embryonic membrane *n* : a structure (as the amnion) that derives from the fertilized ovum but does not form a part of the embryo
em·bryo·phyte \ˈem-brē-ə-ˌfīt\ *n* : a plant (as a fern) producing an embryo and developing vascular tissues
embryo sac *n* : the female gametophyte of a seed plant consisting of a thin-walled sac within the nucellus that contains the egg nucleus and others which give rise to endosperm on fertilization
em·bry·ot·ic \ˌem-brē-ˈät-ik\ *adj* [*embryo* + *-tic* (as in *patriotic*)] : EMBRYONIC 2
[1]**em·cee** \ˈem-ˈsē\ *n* [*M. C.*] : MASTER OF CEREMONIES
[2]**emcee** *vb* **em·ceed; em·cee·ing** *vt* : to act as master of ceremonies of ~ *vi* : to act as master of ceremonies
Em·den *var of* EMBDEN
-eme \ˌēm\ *n suffix* [F *-ème* (fr. *phonème* speech sound, phoneme)] : significantly distinctive unit of language structure ⟨taxeme⟩
emend \ē-ˈmend\ *vt* [ME *emenden*, fr. L *emendare* — more at AMEND] **1** *archaic* : to free from defects **2** : to correct usu. by textual alterations ***syn*** see CORRECT ***ant*** corrupt (*as a text*) — **emend·able** \-ˈmen-də-bəl\ *adj* — **emend·er** *n*
emen·date \ˈē-ˌmen-ˌdāt; ˈem-ən-, -ˌen-\ *vt* **-dat·ed; -dat·ing** : EMEND 2 — **emen·da·tor** \-ˌdāt-ər\ *n* — **emen·da·to·ry** \ē-ˈmen-də-ˌtōr-ē, -ˌtȯr-\ *adj*
emen·da·tion \ˌē-ˌmen-ˈdā-shən; ˌem-ən-, -ˌen-\ *n* **1** : the act of emending **2** : an alteration designed to correct or improve
emer *abbr* emeritus
[1]**em·er·ald** \ˈem-(ə-)rəld\ *n* [ME *emeralde*, fr. MF *esmeralde*, fr. (assumed) VL *smaralda*, fr. L *smaragdus*, fr. Gk *smaragdos*] **1** : a rich green variety of beryl prized as a gemstone **2** : any of various green gemstones (as synthetic corundum or demantoid)
[2]**emerald** *adj* : brightly or richly green
emerald green *n* **1** : a clear bright green resembling that of the emerald **2** : any of various strong greens
emerge \i-ˈmərj\ *vi* **emerged; emerg·ing** [L *emergere*, fr. *e-* + *mergere* to plunge — more at MERGE] **1** : to rise from or as if from an enveloping fluid : come out into view **2** : to become manifest **3** : to rise from an obscure or inferior condition **4** : to come into being through evolution
emer·gence \i-ˈmər-jən(t)s\ *n* **1** : the act or an instance of emerging **2** : any of various superficial outgrowths of plant tissue usu. formed from both epidermis and immediately underlying tissues
emer·gen·cy \i-ˈmər-jən-sē\ *n, pl* **-cies** **1** : an unforeseen combination of circumstances or the resulting state that calls for immediate action **2** : a pressing need ***syn*** see JUNCTURE
[1]**emer·gent** \i-ˈmər-jənt\ *adj* [ME, fr. L *emergent-*, *emergens*, prp. of *emergere*] **1** : rising out of or as out of a fluid **2 a** : arising unexpectedly **b** : calling for prompt action : URGENT **3** : arising as a natural or logical consequence **4** : newly formed ⟨the ~ nations of Africa⟩
[2]**emergent** *n* **1** : something emergent **2 a** : a tree that rises above the surrounding forest **b** : a plant rooted in shallow water and having most of the vegetative growth above water

emergent evolution *n* : a biological and philosophical theory that new characters and qualities (as life and consciousness) appear in the evolutionary process at more complex organizational levels (as that of the molecule, the cell, and the organism) which cannot be predicted solely by studying less complex levels of organization but which are determined by a rearrangement of preexistent entities

emer·i·ta \i-ˈmer-ət-ə\ *adj* [L, fem. of *emeritus*] : EMERITUS — used of a woman ⟨Professor *Emerita* Mary Smith⟩

[1]**emer·i·tus** \i-ˈmer-ət-əs\ *adj* [L, pp. of *emereri* to serve out one's term, fr. *e-* + *mereri, merēre* to earn, deserve, serve — more at MERIT] **1** : holding after retirement an honorary title corresponding to that held last during active service **2** : retired from an office or position ⟨professor ~⟩ — converted to *emeriti* after a plural substantive ⟨professors *emeriti*⟩

[2]**emeritus** *n, pl* **-i·ti** \-ə-ˌtī, -ˌtē\ : one retired from professional life but permitted to hold the rank of his last office as an honorary title

emersed \(ˈ)ē-ˈmərst\ *adj* : standing out of or rising above a surface (as of a fluid) ⟨~ aquatic weeds⟩

emer·sion \(ˈ)ē-ˈmər-zhən, -shən\ *n* [L *emersus*, pp. of *emergere*] : an act of emerging : EMERGENCE

em·ery \ˈem-(ə-)rē\ *n, pl* **em·er·ies** *often attrib* [ME, fr. MF *emeri*, fr. OIt *smiriglio*, fr. ML *smiriglum*, fr. Gk *smyrid-, smyris*] : a dark granular mineral that consists essentially of corundum and is used for grinding and polishing; *also* : a hard abrasive powder

emery board *n* : a nail file made of cardboard covered with powdered emery

eme·sis \ˈem-ə-səs, i-ˈmē-\ *n, pl* **eme·ses** \-ˌsēz\ [NL, fr. Gk, fr. *emein*] : an act or instance of vomiting

emet·ic \i-ˈmet-ik\ *n* [L *emetica*, fr. Gk *emetikē*, fr. fem. of *emetikos* causing vomiting, fr. *emein* to vomit — more at VOMIT] : an agent that induces vomiting — **emetic** *adj* — **emet·i·cal·ly** \-i-k(ə-)lē\ *adv*

em·e·tine \ˈem-ə-ˌtēn\ *n* : an amorphous alkaloid $C_{29}H_{40}N_2O_4$ extracted from ipecac root and used as an emetic and expectorant

émeute \ā-mœ̄t\ *n, pl* **émeutes** *same*\ [F] : an outbreak of disorder or violence; *esp* : a popular uprising

EMF *abbr* electromotive force

-emia *or* **-ae·mia** \ˈē-mē-ə\ *also* **-he·mia** *or* **-hae·mia** \ˈhē-\ *n comb form* [NL *-emia, -aemia*, fr. Gk *-aimia*, fr. *haima* blood — more at HEM-] **1** : condition of having (such) blood ⟨leuk*emia*⟩ **2** : condition of having (a specified thing) in the blood ⟨ur*emia*⟩

[1]**em·i·grant** \ˈem-i-grənt\ *n* **1** : one who emigrates **2** : a migrant plant or animal

syn EMIGRANT, IMMIGRANT *shared meaning element* : one that leaves one place to settle in another

[2]**emigrant** *adj* : departing from a country to settle elsewhere

em·i·grate \ˈem-ə-ˌgrāt\ *vi* **-grat·ed; -grat·ing** [L *emigratus*, pp. of *emigrare*, fr. *e-* + *migrare* to migrate] : to leave one's place of abode or country for life or residence elsewhere — **em·i·gra·tion** \ˌem-ə-ˈgrā-shən\ *n*

émi·gré *or* **emi·gré** \ˈem-i-ˌgrā, ˌem-i-ˈ\ *n* [F *émigré*, fr. pp. of *émigrer* to emigrate, fr. L *emigrare*] : EMIGRANT; *esp* : a person forced to emigrate for political reasons

em·i·nence \ˈem-ə-nən(t)s\ *n* **1** : a position of prominence or superiority — used as a title for a cardinal **2** : something eminent, prominent, or lofty: as **a** : a person of high rank or attainments **b** : a natural elevation

émi·nence grise \ā-mē-näⁿ-sə-grēz\ *n, pl* **éminences grises** *same*\ [F, lit., gray eminence, nickname of Père Joseph (François du Tremblay) †1638 F monk and diplomat, confidant of Cardinal Richelieu who was known as *Éminence Rouge* red eminence; fr. the colors of their respective habits] : a confidential agent; *esp* : one exercising unsuspected or unofficial power

em·i·nen·cy \ˈem-ə-nən-sē\ *n, pl* **-cies** : EMINENCE

em·i·nent \ˈem-ə-nənt\ *adj* [ME, fr. MF or L; MF, fr. L *eminent-, eminens*, prp. of *eminēre* to stand out, fr. *e-* + *-minēre* (akin to L *mont-, mons* mountain] **1** : standing out so as to be readily perceived or noted : CONSPICUOUS **2 a** : jutting out : PROJECTING **b** : LOFTY, TOWERING **3** : exhibiting eminence esp. in standing above others in some quality or position : PROMINENT ***syn*** see FAMOUS — **em·i·nent·ly** *adv*

eminent domain *n* : a right of a government to take private property for public use by virtue of the superior dominion of the sovereign power over all lands within its jurisdiction

emir \i-ˈmi(ə)r, ā-\ *n* [Ar *amīr* commander] : a native ruler in parts of Asia and Africa

emir·ate \i-ˈmir-ət, ā-, -ˈmi(ə)r-ˌāt\ *n* : the state or jurisdiction of an emir

em·is·sary \ˈem-ə-ˌser-ē\ *n, pl* **-sar·ies** [L *emissarius*, fr. *emissus*, pp. of *emittere*] **1** : one sent on a mission as the agent of another **2** : a secret agent

emis·sion \ē-ˈmish-ən\ *n* **1 a** : an act or instance of emitting : EMANATION **b** *archaic* : PUBLICATION **c** : a putting into circulation **2 a** : something sent forth by emitting: as (1) : electrons discharged from a surface (2) : electromagnetic waves radiated by an antenna or a celestial body (3) : substances discharged into the air (as by a smokestack or an automobile gasoline engine) **b** : EFFLUVIUM — **emis·sive** \-ˈmis-iv\ *adj*

emis·siv·i·ty \ˌem-ə-ˈsiv-ət-ē, ˌē-ˌmis-ˈiv-\ *n, pl* **-ties** : the relative power of a surface to emit heat by radiation : the ratio of the radiant energy emitted by a surface to that emitted by a blackbody at the same temperature

emit \ē-ˈmit\ *vt* **emit·ted; emit·ting** [L *emittere* to send out, fr. *e-* + *mittere* to send — more at SMITE] **1 a** : to throw or give off or out (as light) **b** : to send out : EJECT **2 a** : to issue with authority; *esp* : to put (as money) into circulation **b** *obs* : PUBLISH **3** : to give utterance or voice to ⟨*emitted* a groan⟩ — **emit·ter** *n*

em·men·a·gogue \ə-ˈmen-ə-ˌgäg, e-\ *n* [Gk *emmēna* menses (fr. neut. pl. of *emmēnos* monthly, fr. *en-* + *mēn* month) + E *-agogue* — more at MOON] : an agent that promotes the menstrual discharge

Em·men·ta·ler *or* **Em·men·tha·ler** \ˈem-ən-ˌtäl-ər\ *or* **Em·men·thal** \-ˌtäl\ *n* [G, fr. *Emmenthal*, Switzerland] : SWISS CHEESE

em·mer \ˈem-ər\ *n* [G, fr. OHG *amari*] : a hard red wheat (*Triticum dicoccum*) having spikelets with two kernels that remain in the glumes after threshing; *broadly* : a tetraploid wheat — called also *emmer wheat*

em·met \ˈem-ət\ *n* [ME *emete*] *chiefly dial* : ANT

Em·my \ˈem-ē\ *n, pl* **Emmys** [fr. alter. of *Immy*, nickname for *image orthicon* (a camera tube used in television)] : a statuette awarded annually by a professional organization for notable achievement in television

em·o·din \ˈem-ə-dən\ *n* [ISV *emodi-* (fr. NL *Rheum emodi*, species of rhubarb) + *-in*] : an orange crystalline phenolic compound $C_{15}H_{10}O_5$ that is obtained from plants (as rhubarb and cascara buckthorn) and is used as a laxative

[1]**emol·lient** \i-ˈmäl-yənt\ *adj* [L *emollient-, emolliens*, prp. of *emollire* to soften, fr. *e-* + *mollis* soft — more at MELT] **1** : making soft or supple; *also* : soothing esp. to the skin or mucous membrane **2** : making less intense or harsh : MOLLIFYING ⟨soothe us in our agonies with ~ words —H. L. Mencken⟩

[2]**emollient** *n* : something that softens or soothes

emol·u·ment \i-ˈmäl-yə-mənt\ *n* [ME, fr. L *emolumentum*, lit., miller's fee, fr. *emolere* to grind up, fr. *e-* + *molere* to grind — more at MEAL] **1** : the returns arising from office or employment usu. in the form of compensation or perquisites **2** *archaic* : ADVANTAGE ***syn*** see WAGE

emote \i-ˈmōt\ *vt* **emot·ed; emot·ing** [back-formation fr. *emotion*] : to give expression to emotion esp. in or as if in a play or movie

emo·tion \i-ˈmō-shən\ *n* [MF, fr. *emouvoir* to stir up, fr. L *exmovēre* to move away, disturb, fr. *ex-* + *movēre* to move] **1 a** *obs* : DISTURBANCE **b** : EXCITEMENT **2 a** : the affective aspect of consciousness : FEELING **b** : a state of feeling **c** : a psychic and physical reaction (as anger or fear) subjectively experienced as strong feeling and physiologically involving changes that prepare the body for immediate vigorous action ***syn*** see FEELING

emo·tion·al \-shnəl, -shən-ᵊl\ *adj* **1** : of or relating to emotion ⟨an ~ disorder⟩ **2** : dominated by or prone to emotion ⟨an ~ person⟩ **3** : appealing to or arousing emotion ⟨an ~ sermon⟩ **4** : markedly aroused or agitated in feeling or sensibilities ⟨gets ~ at weddings⟩ — **emo·tion·al·i·ty** \-ˌmō-shə-ˈnal-ət-ē\ *n* — **emo·tion·al·ly** \-ē\ *adv*

emo·tion·al·ism \i-ˈmō-shnə-ˌliz-əm, -shən-ᵊl-ˌiz-\ *n* **1** : undue indulgence in or display of emotion **2** : a tendency to regard things emotionally

emo·tion·al·ist \-shnə-ləst, -shən-ᵊl-əst\ *n* **1** : one who tends to rely on emotion as opposed to reason; *esp* : one who bases a theory or policy on an emotional conviction **2** : one given to emotionalism — **emo·tion·al·is·tic** \-ˌmō-shnə-ˈlis-tik, -shən-ᵊl-ˈis-\ *adj*

emo·tion·al·ize \i-ˈmō-shnə-ˌlīz, -shən-ᵊl-ˌīz\ *vt* **-ized; -iz·ing** : to give an emotional quality to

emo·tion·less \i-ˈmō-shən-ləs\ *adj* : showing or expressing no emotion ⟨the colonel's words were short and ~ —*Infantry Jour.*⟩ — **emo·tion·less·ness** *n*

emo·tive \i-ˈmōt-iv\ *adj* **1** : of or relating to the emotions **2** : appealing to or expressing emotion ⟨the ~ use of language⟩ — **emo·tive·ly** *adv* — **emo·tiv·i·ty** \i-ˌmō-ˈtiv-ət-ē, ˌē-ˌmō-\ *n*

emp *abbr* emperor; empress

empanel *var of* IMPANEL

em·pa·thet·ic \ˌem-pə-ˈthet-ik\ *adj* : EMPATHIC — **em·pa·thet·i·cal·ly** \-i-k(ə-)lē\ *adv*

em·path·ic \em-ˈpath-ik, im-\ *adj* : involving, characterized by, or based on empathy

em·pa·thize \ˈem-pə-ˌthīz\ *vi* **-thized; -thiz·ing** : to experience empathy ⟨adults unable to ~ with the frustrations of children⟩

em·pa·thy \ˈem-pə-thē\ *n* **1** : the imaginative projection of a subjective state into an object so that the object appears to be infused with it **2** : the capacity for participation in another's feelings or ideas ***syn*** see SYMPATHY

em·pen·nage \ˌäm-pə-ˈnäzh, ˌem-\ *n* [F, feathers of an arrow, empennage] : the tail assembly of an airplane

em·per·or \ˈem-pər-ər, -prər\ *n* [ME, fr. OF *empereor*, fr. L *imperator*, lit., commander, fr. *imperatus*, pp. of *imperare* to command, fr. *in-* + *parare* to prepare, order — more at PARE] : the sovereign or supreme monarch of an empire — **em·per·or·ship** \-ˌship\ *n*

em·pery \ˈem-p(ə-)rē\ *n, pl* **em·per·ies** [ME *emperie*, fr. OF, fr. *emperer* to command, fr. L *imperare*] : wide dominion : EMPIRE

em·pha·sis \ˈem(p)-fə-səs\ *n, pl* **em·pha·ses** \-ˌsēz\ [L, fr. Gk, exposition, emphasis, fr. *emphainein* to indicate, fr. *en-* + *phainein* to show — more at FANCY] **1 a** : force or intensity of expression that gives special impressiveness or importance to something ⟨writing with ~ on the need for reform⟩ **b** : a particular prominence given in reading or speaking to one or more words or syllables **2** : special consideration of or stress or insistence on something ⟨the school's ~ on discipline⟩

em·pha·size \ˈem(p)-fə-ˌsīz\ *vt* **-sized; -siz·ing** : to give emphasis to : place emphasis on : STRESS ⟨*emphasized* the need for reform⟩

em·phat·ic \im-ˈfat-ik, em-\ *adj* [Gk *emphatikos*, fr. *emphainein*] **1** : uttered with or marked by emphasis **2** : tending to express oneself in forceful speech or to take decisive action **3** : attracting special attention **4** : constituting or belonging to a set of tense forms in English consisting of the auxiliary *do* followed by an infinitive without *to* that are used to facilitate rhetorical inversion or to emphasize — **em·phat·i·cal·ly** \-ˈfat-i-k(ə-)lē\ *adv*

em·phy·se·ma \ˌem(p)-fə-ˈzē-mə, -ˈsē-\ *n* [NL, fr. Gk *emphysēma* bodily inflation] : a condition characterized by air-filled expansions of body tissues; *specif* : a condition of the lung marked by distension and frequently by impairment of heart action — **em·phy·se·ma·tous** \-ˈzem-ət-əs, -ˈsem-, -ˈzēm-, -ˈsēm-\ *adj*

em·pire \'em-ˌpī(ə)r\ *n* [ME, fr. OF *empire, empirie,* fr. L *imperium* absolute authority, empire, fr. *imperare* to command] **1 a** (1) : a major political unit having a territory of great extent or a number of territories or peoples under a single sovereign authority; *esp* : one having an emperor as chief of state (2) : the territory of such a political unit **b** : something held to resemble a political empire; *esp* : an extensive territory or enterprise under single domination or control ⟨the beautiful heiress to a meat-packing ~ —*Punch*⟩ **2** : imperial sovereignty, rule, or dominion

Em·pire \'äm-ˌpi(ə)r, 'em-ˌpī(ə)r\ *adj* [F, fr. (*le premier*) *Empire* the first Empire of France] : of, relating to, or characteristic of a style (as of clothing or furniture) popular in early 19th century France

Em·pire Day \'em-ˌpī(ə)r-\ *n* : COMMONWEALTH DAY — used before the official adoption of *Commonwealth Day* in 1958

em·pir·ic \im-'pir-ik, em-\ *n* [L *empiricus,* fr. Gk *empeirikos* doctor relying on experience alone, fr. *empeiria* experience, fr. *en-* + *peiran* to attempt — more at FEAR] **1** *archaic* : CHARLATAN **2** : one who relies on practical experience

em·pir·i·cal \-i-kəl\ *also* **em·pir·ic** \-ik\ *adj* **1** : relying on experience or observation alone often without due regard for system and theory **2** : originating in or based on observation or experience ⟨~ data⟩ **3** : capable of being verified or disproved by observation or experiment ⟨~ laws⟩ — **em·pir·i·cal·ly** \-i-k(ə-)lē\ *adv*

empirical formula *n* : a chemical formula showing the simplest ratio of elements in a compound rather than the total number of atoms in the molecule ⟨CH_2O is the *empirical formula* for glucose⟩

em·pir·i·cism \im-'pir-ə-ˌsiz-əm, em-\ *n* **1 a** : a former school of medical practice founded on experience without the aid of science or theory **b** : QUACKERY, CHARLATANRY **2 a** : the practice of relying on observation and experiment esp. in the natural sciences **b** : a tenet arrived at empirically **3 a** : a theory that all knowledge originates in experience **b** : LOGICAL POSITIVISM — **em·pir·i·cist** \-səst\ *n*

em·place \im-'plās\ *vt* [back-formation fr. *emplacement*] : to put into position ⟨missiles *emplaced* around the city⟩

em·place·ment \-'plā-smənt\ *n* [F, fr. MF *emplacer* to emplace, fr. *en-* + *place*] **1** : the situation or location of something **2** : a prepared position for weapons or military equipment ⟨radar ~*s*⟩ **3** : a putting into position : PLACEMENT

em·plane \im-'plān\ *var of* ENPLANE

¹em·ploy \im-'plȯi\ *vt* [ME *emploien,* fr. MF *emploier,* fr. L *implicare* to enfold, involve, implicate, fr. *in-* + *plicare* to fold — more at PLY] **1 a** : to make use of (someone or something inactive) ⟨~ a fine pen to fill in the details⟩ **b** : to occupy (as time) advantageously **c** (1) : to use or engage the services of (2) : to provide with a job that pays wages or a salary **2** : to devote to or direct toward a particular activity or person ⟨~*ed* all her wiles to get him to propose⟩ ***syn*** see USE — **em·ploy·er** *n*

²employ *n* **1** *archaic* **a** : USE **b** : OCCUPATION **2** : the state of being employed esp. for wages or a salary ⟨in the government's ~⟩

¹em·ploy·able \im-'plȯi-ə-bəl\ *adj* : capable of being employed — **em·ploy·abil·i·ty** \-ˌplȯi-ə-'bil-ət-ē\ *n*

²employable *n* : one who is employable

em·ploy·ee *or* **em·ploye** \im-ˌplȯ(i)-'ē, (ˌ)em-; im-'plȯ(i)-ˌē, em-\ *n* : one employed by another usu. for wages or salary and in a position below the executive level

em·ploy·ment \im-'plȯi-mənt\ *n* **1** : USE, PURPOSE **2 a** : activity in which one engages or is employed ⟨suitable ~ was hard to find⟩ **b** : an instance of such activity **3** : the act of employing : the state of being employed

employment agency *n* : an agency whose business is to find jobs for people seeking them or to find people to fill jobs that are open

em·poi·son \im-'pȯiz-ᵊn\ *vt* [ME *empoysonen,* fr. MF *empoisoner,* fr. *en-* + *poison*] **1** *archaic* : POISON **2** : EMBITTER ⟨a look of ~*ed* acceptance —Saul Bellow⟩ — **em·poi·son·ment** \-mənt\ *n*

em·po·ri·um \im-'pōr-ē-əm, em-, -'pȯr-\ *n, pl* **-ri·ums** *also* **-ria** \-ē-ə\ [L, fr. Gk *emporion,* fr. *emporos* traveler, trader, fr. *en* in + *poros* passage, journey — more at IN, FARE] **1 a** : a place of trade; *esp* : a commercial center **b** : a usu. sizable place of business that serves customers **2** : a store carrying a diversity of merchandise

em·pow·er \im-'pau̇(-ə)r\ *vt* : to give official authority or legal power to ***syn*** see ENABLE — **em·pow·er·ment** \-mənt\ *n*

em·press \'em-prəs\ *n* [ME *emperesse,* fr. OF, fem. of *empereor* emperor] **1** : the wife or widow of an emperor **2** : a woman who holds an imperial title in her own right

em·presse·ment \äⁿ-pres-(ə-)mäⁿ\ *n* [F, fr. (*s'*)*empresser* to hurry, fr. *en-* + *presser* to press] : demonstrative warmth or cordiality

em·prise \em-'prīz\ *n* [ME, fr. MF, fr. OF, fr. *emprendre* to undertake, fr. (assumed) VL *imprehendere,* fr. L *in-* + *prehendere* to seize] : UNDERTAKING, ENTERPRISE; *esp* : an adventurous, daring, or chivalric enterprise

¹emp·ty \'em(p)-tē\ *adj* [ME, fr. OE *ǣmettig* unoccupied, fr. *ǣmetta* leisure, fr. *ǣ-* without + *-metta* (fr. *mōtan* to have to) — more at MUST] **1 a** : containing nothing **b** : not occupied or inhabited **c** : UNFREQUENTED **d** : not pregnant ⟨~ heifer⟩ **e** : NULL 4a ⟨the ~ set⟩ **2 a** : lacking reality, substance, or value : HOLLOW ⟨an ~ pleasure⟩ **b** : destitute of effect or force **c** : devoid of sense : FOOLISH **3** : HUNGRY **4 a** : IDLE ⟨~ hours⟩ **b** : having no purpose or result : USELESS **5** : marked by the absence of human life, activity, or comfort — **emp·ti·ly** \-tə-lē\ *adv* — **emp·ti·ness** \-tē-nəs\ *n*

syn **1** EMPTY, VACANT, BLANK, VOID, VACUOUS *shared meaning element* : lacking contents which could or should be present. EMPTY implies a complete absence of contents, especially of usual or normal contents; VACANT, an absence of appropriate contents or occupants ⟨an *empty* bucket⟩ ⟨his purse was *empty*⟩ ⟨a *vacant* apartment⟩ ⟨*vacant* professorships⟩ BLANK stresses the absence of any significant, relieving, or intelligible features on a surface ⟨the window faced a *blank* wall⟩ Sometimes the word implies a vacancy intended to be filled; thus, a *blank* sheet of paper is one available for writing on. VOID implies absolute emptiness to the senses ⟨the *void,* hollow, universal air —P. B. Shelley⟩ VACUOUS suggests the emptiness of a vacuum and is often applied hyperbolically to what lacks intelligence or significance ⟨there was nothing to be read in the *vacuous* face, blank as a school notice-board out of term —Graham Greene⟩ ***ant*** full
2 see VAIN

²empty *vb* **emp·tied; emp·ty·ing** *vt* **1 a** : to make empty : remove the contents of **b** : DEPRIVE, DIVEST **c** : to discharge (itself) of contents **2** : to remove from what holds or encloses **3** : to transfer by emptying ~ *vi* **1** : to become empty **2** : to discharge its contents ⟨the river *empties* into the ocean⟩

³empty *n, pl* **empties** : something that is empty: as **a** : an empty container **b** : an unoccupied vehicle

emp·ty–hand·ed \ˌem(p)-tē-'han-dəd\ *adj* **1** : having or bringing nothing **2** : having acquired or gained nothing ⟨came back ~⟩

emp·ty–head·ed \-'hed-əd\ *adj* : SCATTERBRAINED

em·pur·ple \im-'pər-pəl\ *vb* **em·pur·plied; em·pur·pling** \-'pər-p(ə-)liŋ\ *vt* : to tinge or color purple ~ *vi* : to become purple

em·py·ema \ˌem-ˌpī-'ē-mə\ *n, pl* **-ema·ta** \-mət-ə\ *or* **-emas** [LL, fr. Gk *empyēma*] : the presence of pus in a bodily cavity — **em·py·emic** \-mik\ *adj*

em·py·re·al \ˌem-ˌpī-'rē-əl, -pə-; em-'pir-ē-əl, -'pī-rē-\ *adj* [LL *empyrius, empyreus,* fr. LGk *empyrios,* fr. Gk *en* in + *pyr* fire] **1** : of or relating to the empyrean : CELESTIAL **2** : SUBLIME

¹em·py·re·an \-ən\ *adj* : EMPYREAL

²empyrean *n* **1 a** : the highest heaven or heavenly sphere in ancient and medieval cosmology usu. consisting of fire or light **b** : the true and ultimate heavenly paradise **2** : FIRMAMENT, HEAVENS

em quad *n* [fr. its use for the letter *m*] : a quad whose point dimension and set dimension are the same or very nearly the same : a quad with a square or almost square body

¹emu \'ē-(ˌ)myü\ *n* [modif. of Pg *ema* rhea] **1** : a swift-running Australian bird (*Dromiceius novae-hollandiae*) with undeveloped wings that is related to and smaller than the ostrich **2** : any of various tall flightless birds (as the rhea)

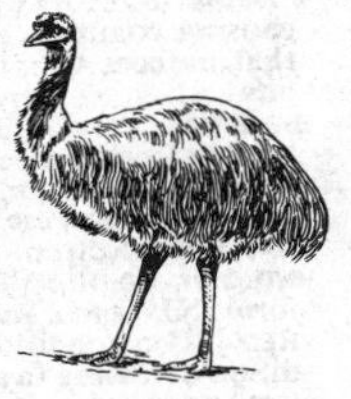

emu 1

²emu *abbr* electromagnetic unit

¹em·u·late \'em-yə-ˌlāt\ *vt* **-lat·ed; -lat·ing** [L *aemulatus,* pp. of *aemulari,* fr. *aemulus* rivaling] **1 a** : to strive to equal or excel **b** : IMITATE; *specif* : to imitate by means of an emulator **2** : to equal or approach equality with ***syn*** see RIVAL

²em·u·late \-lət\ *adj, obs* : EMULOUS 1a ⟨pricked on by a most ~ pride —Shak.⟩

em·u·la·tion \ˌem-yə-'lā-shən\ *n* **1** : ambition or endeavor to equal or excel others (as in achievement) **2 a** : IMITATION **b** : the use of or technique of using an emulator **3** *obs* : ambitious or envious rivalry — **em·u·la·tive** \'em-yə-ˌlāt-iv\ *adj* — **em·u·la·tive·ly** *adv*

em·u·la·tor \'em-yə-ˌlāt-ər\ *n* **1** : one that emulates **2** : a hardware device or a combination of hardware and software that permits programs written for one computer to be run on another usu. newer computer

em·u·lous \'em-yə-ləs\ *adj* **1 a** : ambitious or eager to emulate **b** : inspired by or deriving from a desire to emulate **2** *obs* : JEALOUS — **em·u·lous·ly** *adv* — **em·u·lous·ness** *n*

emul·si·ble \i-'məl-sə-bəl\ *adj* [L *emulsus,* pp., + E *-ible*] : capable of being emulsified

emul·si·fi·er \i-'məl-sə-ˌfī(-ə)r\ *n* : one that emulsifies; *esp* : a surface-active agent (as a soap) promoting the formation and stabilization of an emulsion

emul·si·fy \-ˌfī\ *vt* **-fied; -fy·ing** : to convert (as an oil) into an emulsion — **emul·si·fi·able** \-ˌfī-ə-bəl\ *adj* — **emul·si·fi·ca·tion** \i-ˌməl-sə-fə-'kā-shən\ *n*

emul·sion \i-'məl-shən\ *n* [NL *emulsion-, emulsio,* fr. L *emulsus,* pp. of *emulgēre* to milk out, fr. *e-* + *mulgēre* to milk; akin to OE *melcan* to milk, Gk *amelgein*] **1 a** : a system (as fat in milk) consisting of a liquid dispersed with or without an emulsifier in an immiscible liquid usu. in droplets of larger than colloidal size **b** : the state of such a system **2** : SUSPENSION 2b(3); *esp* : a suspension of a sensitive silver salt or a mixture of silver halides in a viscous medium (as a gelatin solution) forming a coating on photographic plates, film, or paper — **emul·sive** \-'məl-siv\ *adj*

emul·soid \i-'məl-ˌsȯid\ *n* **1** : a colloidal system consisting of a liquid dispersed in a liquid **2** : a lyophilic sol (as a gelatin solution) — **emul·soi·dal** \-ˌməl-'sȯid-ᵊl\ *adj*

emunc·to·ry \i-'məŋ(k)-t(ə-)rē\ *n, pl* **-ries** [NL *emunctorium,* fr. L *emunctus,* pp. of *emungere* to clean the nose, fr. *e-* + *-mungere* (akin to *mucus*)] : an organ (as a kidney) or part of the body (as the skin) that carries off body wastes

en \'en\ *n* **1** : the letter *n* **2** : the set dimension of an en quad

¹en- *also* **em-** \e *also occurs in these prefixes although only* i *may be shown as in "engage"*\ *prefix* [ME, fr. OF, fr. L *in-, im-,* fr. *in*] **1** : put into or on to ⟨*en*cradle⟩ ⟨*en*throne⟩ : cover with ⟨*en*verdure⟩ : go into or on to ⟨*em*bus⟩ — in verbs formed from nouns **2** : cause to be ⟨*en*slave⟩ — in verbs formed from adjectives or nouns **3** : provide with ⟨*em*power⟩ — in verbs formed from nouns **4** : so as to cover ⟨*en*wrap⟩ : thoroughly ⟨*en*tangle⟩ — in verbs formed from verbs; in all senses usu. *em-* before *b, m,* or *p*

²en- *also* **em-** *prefix* [ME, fr. L, fr. Gk, fr. *en* in — more at IN] : in : within ⟨*en*zootic⟩ — usu. *em-* before *b, m,* or *p* ⟨*em*pathy⟩

³en- *comb form* [ISV, fr. *-ene*] : chemically unsaturated; *esp* : having one double bond ⟨*en*amine⟩

¹-en \ən, ᵊn\ *also* **-n** \n\ *adj suffix* [ME, fr. OE; akin to OHG *-īn* made of, L *-inus* of or belonging to, Gk *-inos* made of, of or belonging to] : made of : consisting of ⟨earth*en*⟩ ⟨silver*n*⟩

²-en *vb suffix* [ME *-nen,* fr. OE *-nian;* akin to OHG *-inōn* -en] **1 a** : cause to be ⟨sharp*en*⟩ **b** : cause to have ⟨length*en*⟩ **2 a** : come to be ⟨steep*en*⟩ **b** : come to have ⟨length*en*⟩

en·able \in-'ā-bəl\ *vt* **en·abled; en·abling** \-b(ə-)liŋ\ **1 a** : to provide with the means or opportunity ⟨training that ~*s* men to earn a living⟩ **b** : to make possible, practical, or easy **2** : to give legal power, capacity, or sanction to ⟨legislation *enabling* the admission of a state⟩

syn ENABLE, EMPOWER *shared meaning element* : to make one able to do something

en·act \in-'akt\ *vt* **1** : to establish by legal and authoritative act; *specif* : to make (as a bill) into law **2** : to act out : REPRESENT ⟨~ a role⟩ — **en·ac·tor** \-'ak-tər\ *n*

en·act·ment \-'ak(t)-mənt\ *n* **1** : the act of enacting : the state of being enacted **2** : something (as a law) that has been enacted

¹enam·el \in-'am-əl\ *vt* **-eled** *or* **-elled; -el·ing** *or* **-el·ling** \-(ə-)liŋ\ [ME *enamelen*, fr. MF *enamailler*, fr. *en-* + *esmail* enamel, of Gmc origin; akin to OHG *smelzan* to melt — more at SMELT] **1** : to cover, inlay, or decorate with enamel **2** : to beautify with a colorful surface **3** : to form a glossy surface on (as paper, leather, or cloth) — **enam·el·er** \-(ə-)lər\ *n* — **enam·el·ist** \-ə-ləst\ *n*

²enamel *n* **1** : a usu. opaque vitreous composition applied by fusion to the surface of metal, glass, or pottery **2** : a surface or outer covering that resembles enamel **3 a** : something that is enameled **b** : ENAMELWARE **4** : a cosmetic intended to give a smooth or glossy appearance **5** : a calcareous substance that forms a thin layer capping the teeth **6** : a paint that flows out to a smooth coat when applied and that dries with a glossy appearance

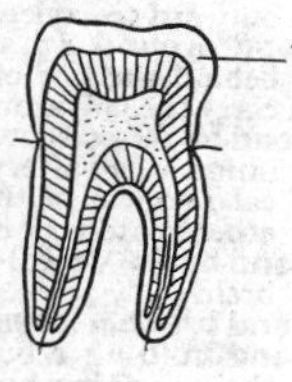

1, enamel 5

enam·el·ware \in-'am-əl-ˌwa(ə)r, -ˌwe(ə)r\ *n* : metalware (as kitchen utensils) coated with enamel

en·amine \'en-ə-ˌmēn\ *n* : an amine containing the double bond linkage C=C—N

en·am·or \in-'am-ər\ *vt* **en·am·ored; en·am·or·ing** \-(ə-)riŋ\ [ME *enamouren*, fr. OF *enamourer*, fr. *en-* + *amour* love — more at AMOUR] : to inflame with love : CHARM — usu. used in the passive with *of*

en·am·our *chiefly Brit var of* ENAMOR

en·an·tio·mer \in-'ant-ē-ə-mər\ *n* [Gk *enantios* + E *-mer*] : ENANTIOMORPH — **en·an·tio·mer·ic** \-ˌant-ē-ə-'mer-ik\ *adj*

en·an·tio·morph \in-'ant-ē-ə-ˌmȯrf\ *n* [Gk *enantios* opposite (fr. *enanti* facing, fr. *en* in + *anti* against) + ISV *-morph*] : either of a pair of chemical compounds or crystals whose molecular structures have a mirror-image relationship to each other — **en·an·tio·mor·phic** \-ˌant-ē-ə-'mȯr-fik\ *adj* — **en·an·tio·mor·phism** \-'mȯr-ˌfiz-əm\ *n* — **en·an·tio·mor·phous** \-'mȯr-fəs\ *adj*

en·ar·thro·sis \ˌen-ˌär-'thrō-səs\ *n, pl* **-thro·ses** \-ˌsēz\ [NL, fr. Gk *enarthrōsis*] : BALL-AND-SOCKET JOINT 2

ena·tion \i-'nā-shən\ *n* [L *enatus*, pp. of *enasci* to rise out of, fr. *e-* + *nasci* to be born — more at NATION] : an outgrowth from the surface of an organ ⟨a plant virus forming ~s on leaves⟩

en bloc \äⁿ-'bläk\ *adv or adj* [F] : as a whole : in a mass ⟨forced the islanders . . . to move *en bloc* —D. B. Forrester⟩

enc *or* **encl** *abbr* enclosure

En·cae·nia \en-'sē-nyə\ *n pl but sing or pl in constr* [NL, fr. L, dedication festival, fr. Gk *enkainia*, fr. *en* in + *kainos* new — more at IN, RECENT] : an annual university ceremony (as at Oxford) of commemoration with recital of poems and essays and conferring of degrees

en·cage \in-'kāj\ *vt* : CAGE 1

en·camp \in-'kamp\ *vt* : to place or establish in a camp ~ *vi* : to set up or occupy a camp

en·camp·ment \-mənt\ *n* **1** : the act of encamping : the state of being encamped **2 a** : the place where a group (as a body of troops) is encamped **b** : the individuals that make up an encampment

en·cap·su·late \in-'kap-sə-ˌlāt\ *vb* **-lat·ed; -lat·ing** *vt* **1** : to enclose in or as if in a capsule **2** : EPITOMIZE, CONDENSE ⟨~ a period of history⟩ ~ *vi* : to become encapsulated — **en·cap·su·la·tion** \-ˌkap-sə-'lā-shən\ *n*

en·cap·su·lat·ed *adj* : surrounded by a gelatinous or membranous envelope ⟨~ water bacteria⟩

en·cap·sule \in-'kap-səl, -(ˌ)sül\ *vt* **-suled; -sul·ing** : ENCAPSULATE

en·case \in-'kās\ *vt* : to enclose in or as if in a case

en·case·ment \in-'kā-smənt\ *n* **1 a** : the act or process of encasing : the state of being encased **b** : CASE, COVERING **2** : the supposed enclosure in a living germ of the germs of all future generations that might develop from it

en·cash \in-'kash\ *vt, Brit* : CASH — **en·cash·ment** \-mənt\ *n, Brit*

en·caus·tic \in-'kȯ-stik\ *n* [*encaustic*, adj., fr. L *encausticus*, fr. Gk *enkaustikos*, fr. *enkaiein* to burn in, fr. *en-* + *kaiein* to burn — more at CAUSTIC] **1** : a paint made from pigment mixed with melted beeswax and resin and after application fixed by heat **2** : the method involving the use of encaustic; *also* : a work produced by this method — **encaustic** *adj*

-ence \ən(t)s, ᵊn(t)s\ *n suffix* [ME, fr. OF, fr. L *-entia*, fr. *-ent-*, *-ens*, prp. ending + *-ia* -y] **1** : action or process ⟨emer*gence*⟩ : instance of an action or process ⟨refer*ence*⟩ **2** : quality or state ⟨despond*ence*⟩

¹en·ceinte \äⁿ(n)-'sant\ *adj* [MF, fr. (assumed) VL *incienta*, alter. of L *incient-*, *inciens* being with young, fr. *in* + *-cient*, *-ciens* (akin to Gk *kyein* to be pregnant) — more at CAVE] : being with child : PREGNANT

²enceinte *n* [F, fr. OF, enclosing wall, fr. *enceindre* to surround, fr. L *incingere*, fr. *in-* + *cingere* to gird — more at CINCTURE] : a line of fortification enclosing a castle or town; *also* : the area or town so enclosed

encephal- *or* **encephalo-** *comb form* [F *encéphal-*, fr. Gk *enkephal-*, fr. *enkephalos*] : brain ⟨*encephal*itis⟩ ⟨*encephalo*cele⟩

en·ce·phal·ic \ˌen(t)-sə-'fal-ik\ *adj* : of or relating to the brain; *also* : lying within the cranial cavity

en·ceph·a·li·tis \in-ˌsef-ə-'līt-əs\ *n, pl* **-lit·i·des** \-'lit-ə-ˌdēz\ : inflammation of the brain — **en·ceph·a·lit·ic** \-'lit-ik\ *adj*

en·ceph·a·li·to·gen·ic \-ˌlīt-ə-'jen-ik\ *adj* : tending to cause encephalitis ⟨an ~ strain of a virus⟩

en·ceph·a·lo·gram \in-'sef-ə-lə-ˌgram\ *n* [ISV] : an X-ray picture of the brain made by encephalography

en·ceph·a·lo·graph \-ˌgraf\ *n* **1** : ENCEPHALOGRAM **2** : ELECTROENCEPHALOGRAPH

en·ceph·a·log·ra·phy \in-ˌsef-ə-'läg-rə-fē\ *n* [ISV] : roentgenography of the brain after the cerebrospinal fluid has been replaced by a gas (as air)

en·ceph·a·lo·my·eli·tis \in-ˌsef-ə-lō-ˌmī-ə-'līt-əs\ *n* [NL] : concurrent inflammation of the brain and spinal cord; *specif* : any of several virus diseases of horses

en·ceph·a·lo·myo·car·di·tis \-ˌmī-ə-kär-'dīt-əs\ *n* : an acute febrile virus disease characterized by degeneration and inflammation of skeletal and cardiac muscle and lesions of the central nervous system

en·ceph·a·lon \in-'sef-ə-ˌlän, -lən\ *n, pl* **-la** \-lə\ [NL, fr. Gk *enkephalos*, fr. *en* in + *kephalē* head — more at IN, CEPHALIC] : the vertebrate brain

en·ceph·a·lop·a·thy \in-ˌsef-ə-'läp-ə-thē\ *n* : a disease of the brain; *esp* : one involving alterations of brain structure — **en·ceph·a·lo·path·ic** \-lə-'path-ik\ *adj*

en·chain \in-'chān\ *vt* [ME *encheynen*, fr. MF *enchainer*, fr. OF, fr. *en-* + *chaeine* chain] : to bind or hold with or as if with chains — **en·chain·ment** \-mənt\ *n*

en·chant \in-'chant\ *vt* [ME *enchanten*, fr. MF *enchanter*, fr. L *incantare*, fr. *in-* + *cantare* to sing — more at CHANT] **1** : to influence by charms and incantation : BEWITCH **2** : to attract and move deeply : rouse to ecstatic admiration ⟨the scene ~*ed* her to the point of tears —Elinor Wylie⟩ ***syn*** see ATTRACT ***ant*** disenchant

en·chant·er *n* : one that enchants; *esp* : SORCERER

en·chant·ing *adj* : CHARMING — **en·chant·ing·ly** \-iŋ-lē\ *adv*

en·chant·ment \in-'chant-mənt\ *n* **1 a** : the act or art of enchanting **b** : the quality or state of being enchanted **2** : something that enchants

en·chant·ress \in-'chan-trəs\ *n* **1** : a woman who practices magic : SORCERESS **2** : a fascinating woman

en·chase \in-'chās\ *vt* **en·chased; en·chas·ing** [ME *enchasen* to emboss, fr. MF *enchasser* to enshrine, set, fr. *en-* + *chasse* reliquary, fr. L *capsa* case — more at CASE] **1** : SET ⟨~ a gem⟩ **2** : ORNAMENT: as **a** : to cut or carve in relief **b** : INLAY

en·chi·la·da \ˌen-chə-'läd-ə\ *n* [AmerSp] : a tortilla on which meat filling is spread and which is rolled up and covered with chili-seasoned tomato sauce

en·chi·rid·i·on \ˌen-ˌkī-rid-ē-ən\ *n, pl* **-rid·ia** \-ē-ə\ [LL, fr. Gk *encheiridion*, fr. *en* in + *cheir* hand — more at IN, CHIR-] : HANDBOOK, MANUAL

-en·chy·ma \'eŋ-kə-mə\ *n comb form, pl* **-en·chy·ma·ta** \ən-'kim-ət-ə, -'kī-mət-\ *or* **-enchymas** [NL, fr. *parenchyma*] : cellular tissue ⟨coll*enchyma*⟩

en·ci·pher \in-'sī-fər, en-\ *vt* : to convert (a message) into cipher — **en·ci·pher·er** \-fər-ər\ *n* — **en·ci·pher·ment** \-fər-mənt\ *n*

en·cir·cle \in-'sər-kəl\ *vt* **1** : to form a circle around : SURROUND **2** : to pass completely around — **en·cir·cle·ment** \-mənt\ *n*

en·clasp \in-'klasp\ *vt* : to seize and hold : EMBRACE

en·clave \'en-ˌklāv; 'än-ˌklāv, 'äŋ-, -ˌkläv\ *n* [F, fr. MF, fr. *enclaver* to enclose, fr. (assumed) VL *inclavare* to lock up, fr. L *in-* + *clavis* key — more at CLAVICLE] **1** : a territorial or culturally distinct unit enclosed within foreign territory ⟨ethnic ~*s*⟩ **2** : a small often relict community of one kind of plant in an opening of a larger plant community

en·clit·ic \en-'klit-ik\ *adj* [LL *encliticus*, fr. Gk *enklitikos*, fr. *enklinesthai* to lean on, fr. *en-* + *klinein* to lean — more at LEAN] *of a word or particle* : being without independent accent and treated in pronunciation as forming a part of the preceding word ⟨*thee* in *prithee* and *not* in *cannot* are ~⟩ — **enclitic** *n*

en·close \in-'klōz\ *vt* [ME *enclosen*, prob. fr. *enclos* enclosed, fr. MF, pp. of *enclore* to enclose, fr. (assumed) VL *inclaudere*, alter. of L *includere* — more at INCLUDE] **1 a** (1) : to close in : SURROUND ⟨~ a porch with glass⟩ (2) : to fence off (common land) for individual use **b** : to hold in : CONFINE **2** : to include along with something else in a parcel or envelope ⟨a check is *enclosed* herewith⟩

en·clo·sure \in-'klō-zhər\ *n* **1** : the act or action of enclosing : the quality or state of being enclosed **2** : something that encloses **3** : something enclosed ⟨a letter with two ~*s*⟩

en·code \in-'kōd, en-\ *vt* : to convert (as a body of information) from one system of communication into another; *esp* : to convert (a message) into code — **en·cod·er** *n*

en·co·mi·ast \en-'kō-mē-ˌast, -mē-əst\ *n* [Gk *enkōmiastēs*, fr. *enkōmiazein* to praise, fr. *enkōmion*] : one that praises : EULOGIST — **en·co·mi·as·tic** \-ˌkō-mē-'as-tik\ *adj*

en·co·mi·um \en-'kō-mē-əm\ *n, pl* **-mi·ums** *or* **-mia** \-mē-ə\ [L, fr. Gk *enkōmion*, fr. *en* in + *kōmos* revel, celebration — more at IN, COMEDY] : glowing and warmly enthusiastic praise; *also* : an expression of this

syn ENCOMIUM, EULOGY, PANEGYRIC, TRIBUTE, CITATION *shared meaning element* : a formal expression of praise

en·com·pass \in-'kəm-pəs *also* -'käm-\ *vt* **1 a** : to form a circle about : ENCLOSE **b** *obs* : to go completely around **2 a** : ENVELOP **b** : INCLUDE ⟨a plan that ~*es* a number of aims⟩ **3** : to bring about : ACCOMPLISH ⟨~ a task⟩ — **en·com·pass·ment** \-pə-smənt\ *n*

¹en·core \'än-ˌkō(ə)r, -ˌkȯ(ə)r\ *n* [F, still, again] : a demand for repetition or reappearance made by an audience; *also* : a reappearance or additional performance in response to such a demand

²encore *vt* **en·cored; en·cor·ing** : to request an encore of or by

¹en·coun·ter \in-'kau̇nt-ər\ *vb* **en·coun·tered; en·coun·ter·ing** \-'kau̇nt-ə-riŋ, -'kau̇n-triŋ\ [ME *encountren*, fr. OF *encontrer*, fr.

ə abut ᵊ kitten ər further a back ā bake ä cot, cart
au̇ out ch chin e less ē easy g gift i trip ī life
j joke ŋ sing ō flow ȯ flaw ȯi coin th thin th this
ü loot u̇ foot y yet yü few yu̇ furious zh vision

ML *incontrare,* fr. LL *incontra* toward, fr. L *in-* + *contra* against — more at COUNTER] *vt* **1 a :** to meet as an adversary or enemy **b :** to engage in conflict with **2 :** to come upon face to face **3 :** to come upon unexpectedly ~ *vi* **:** to meet esp. by chance

²**encounter** *n* **1 a :** a meeting between hostile factions or persons **b :** a sudden often violent clash : COMBAT **2 a :** a chance meeting **b :** a direct often momentary meeting **3 :** a coming into the vicinity of a celestial body ⟨the Martian ~ of a spacecraft⟩

encounter group *n* **:** a usu. leaderless and unstructured group that seeks to develop the capacity of the individual to openly express human feelings and to form close emotional ties by more or less unrestrained confrontation of individuals (as by physical contact, uninhibited verbalization, or nudity)

en·cour·age \in-'kər-ij, -'kə-rij\ *vt* **-aged; -ag·ing** [ME *encoragen,* fr. MF *encoragier,* fr. OF, fr. *en-* + *corage* courage] **1 :** to inspire with courage, spirit, or hope : HEARTEN **2 :** to spur on : STIMULATE **3 :** to give help or patronage to : FOSTER — **en·cour·ag·er** *n*

en·cour·age·ment \-ij-mənt, -rij-\ *n* **1 :** the act of encouraging **:** the state of being encouraged **2 :** something that encourages

en·cour·ag·ing *adj* **:** giving hope or promise : INSPIRITING — **en·cour·ag·ing·ly** \-iŋ-lē\ *adv*

en·crim·son \in-'krim-zən\ *vt* **:** to make or dye crimson

en·croach \in-'krōch\ *vi* [ME *encrochen* to get, seize, fr. MF *encrochier,* fr. OF, fr. *en-* + *croc, croche* hook — more at CROCHET] **1 :** to enter by gradual steps or by stealth into the possessions or rights of another **2 :** to advance beyond the usual or proper limits ⟨the gradually ~*ing* sea⟩ ***syn*** see TRESPASS — **en·croach·er** *n* — **en·croach·ment** \-'krōch-mənt\ *n*

en·crust \in-'krəst\ *vb* [prob. fr. L *incrustare,* fr. *in-* + *crusta* crust] *vt* **:** to cover, line, or overlay with a crust ~ *vi* **:** to form a crust

en·crus·ta·tion \(,)in-,krəs-'tā-shən, ,en-\ *var of* INCRUSTATION

en·crypt \in-'kript, en-\ *vt* **1 :** ENCIPHER **2 :** ENCODE — **en·cryp·tion** \-'krip-shən\ *n*

en·cum·ber \in-'kəm-bər\ *vt* **en·cum·bered; en·cum·ber·ing** \-b(ə-)riŋ\ [ME *encombren,* fr. MF *encombrer,* fr. OF, fr. *en-* + (assumed) OF *combre* abatis] **1 :** to weigh down : BURDEN **2 :** to impede or hamper the function or activity of : HINDER **3 :** to burden with a legal claim (as a mortgage) ⟨~ an estate⟩

en·cum·brance \in-'kəm-brən(t)s\ *n* **1 :** something that encumbers : IMPEDIMENT **2 :** a claim (as a mortgage) against property

en·cum·branc·er \-brən-sər\ *n* **:** one that holds an encumbrance

ency *or* **encyc** *abbr* encyclopedia

-en·cy \ən-sē, ᵊn-\ *n suffix* [ME *-encie,* fr. L *-entia* — more at -ENCE] **:** quality or state ⟨despond*ency*⟩

¹**en·cyc·li·cal** \in-'sik-li-kəl, en-\ *adj* [LL *encyclicus,* fr. Gk *enkyklios* circular, general, fr. *en* in + *kyklos* circle — more at IN, WHEEL] **:** addressed to all the individuals of a group : GENERAL

²**encyclical** *n* **:** an encyclical letter; *specif* **:** a papal letter to the bishops of the church as a whole or to those in one country

en·cy·clo·pe·dia *also* **en·cy·clo·pae·dia** \in-,sī-klə-'pēd-ē-ə\ *n* [ML *encyclopaedia* course of general education, fr. Gk *enkyklios paideia* general education] **:** a work that contains information on all branches of knowledge or treats comprehensively a particular branch of knowledge usu. in articles arranged alphabetically by subject

en·cy·clo·pe·dic *also* **en·cy·clo·pae·dic** \-'pēd-ik\ *adj* **:** of, relating to, or suggestive of an encyclopedia or its methods of treating or covering a subject : COMPREHENSIVE ⟨an ~ mind⟩ — **en·cy·clo·pe·di·cal·ly** \-i-k(ə-)lē\ *adv*

en·cy·clo·pe·dism \-'pē-,diz-əm\ *n* **:** encyclopedic knowledge

en·cy·clo·pe·dist \-'pēd-əst\ *n* **1 :** one who compiles or writes for an encyclopedia **2** *often cap* **:** one of the writers of a French encyclopedia (1751-80) who were identified with the Enlightenment and advocated deism and scientific rationalism

en·cyst \in-'sist, en-\ *vt* **:** to enclose in or as if in a cyst ~ *vi* **:** to form or become enclosed in a cyst — **en·cyst·ment** \-'sis(t)-mənt\ *n*

en·cys·ta·tion \,en-,sis-'tā-shən\ *n* **:** the process of forming a cyst or becoming enclosed in a capsule

¹**end** \'end\ *n* [ME *ende,* fr. OE; akin to OHG *enti* end, L *ante* before, Gk *anti* against] **1 a :** the part of an area that lies at the boundary **b** (1) **:** a point that marks the extent of something (2) **:** the point where something ceases to exist ⟨world without ~⟩ **c :** the extreme or last part lengthwise : TIP **d :** the terminal unit of something spatial that is marked off by units **e :** a player stationed at the extremity of a line (as in football) **2 a :** cessation of a course of action, pursuit, or activity **b :** DEATH, DESTRUCTION **c** (1) **:** the ultimate state (2) **:** RESULT, ISSUE **d :** the complex of events, parts, or sections that forms an extremity, termination, or finish **3 :** something incomplete, fragmentary, or undersized **:** REMNANT **4 a :** the goal toward which an agent acts or should act **b :** the object by virtue of or for the sake of which an event takes place **5 a :** a share in an undertaking ⟨kept his ~ up⟩ **b :** a particular phase of an undertaking or organization ⟨the advertising ~ of a business⟩ **6 :** something that is extreme : ULTIMATE — used with *the* **7 :** a period of action or activity in any of various sports events; *specif* **:** a turn for an individual or team — **end·ed** \'en-dəd\ *adj*

syn **1** END, TERMINATION, ENDING, TERMINUS *shared meaning element* **:** the point or line beyond which something does not or cannot go ***ant*** beginning

2 see INTENTION

— **in the end :** after all : ULTIMATELY — **no end :** EXCEEDINGLY — **on end 1 :** with the end down : UPRIGHT ⟨turn a box *on end*⟩ **2 :** without a stop or letup ⟨it rained for days *on end*⟩

²**end** *vt* **1 a :** to bring to an end **b :** DESTROY **2 :** to make up the end of ~ *vi* **1 a :** to come to an end **b :** to reach a specified ultimate rank or situation — often used with *up* ⟨~*ed* up as a colonel⟩ **2 :** DIE ***syn*** see CLOSE ***ant*** begin

³**end** *vt* [prob. alter. of E dial. *in* (to harvest)] *dial Eng* **:** to put (grain or hay) into a barn or stack

⁴**end** *adj* **:** FINAL, ULTIMATE ⟨~ results⟩ ⟨~ markets⟩ ⟨~ user⟩

end- *or* **endo-** *comb form* [F, fr. Gk, fr. *endon* within, fr. *en* in + *-don* (akin to L *domus* house) — more at IN, TIMBER] **1 :** within **:** inside ⟨*endo*skeleton⟩ — compare ECT-, EXO- **2 :** taking in ⟨*endo*thermal⟩ **3** *endo-* **:** forming a bridge between two atoms in a cyclic system

en·dam·age \in-'dam-ij\ *vt* **:** to cause loss or damage to

end·amoe·ba \,en-də-'mē-bə\ *n* [NL, genus name] **:** any of a genus (*Endamoeba*) comprising amoebas parasitic in the intestines of insects and in some classifications various parasites of vertebrates including the amoeba (*E. histolytica*) that causes amebic dysentery in man — **end·amoe·bic** \-bik\ *adj*

en·dan·ger \in-'dān-jər\ *vt* **en·dan·gered; en·dan·ger·ing** \-'dānj-(ə-)riŋ\ **:** to bring into danger or peril — **en·dan·ger·ment** \-'dān-jər-mənt\ *n*

en·dan·gered *adj* **:** threatened with extinction ⟨~ species⟩

en·darch \'en-,därk\ *adj* **:** formed or taking place from the center outward ⟨~ xylem⟩ — **en·dar·chy** \-,där-kē\ *n*

end around *n* **:** a football play in which an offensive end comes behind the line of scrimmage to take a handoff and attempts to carry the ball around the opposite flank

end·ar·ter·ec·to·my \,en-,därt-ə-'rek-tə-mē\ *n* [NL *endarterium* intima of an artery (fr. *end-* + *arteria* artery) + E *-ectomy*] **:** surgical removal of the inner layer of an artery when thickened and atheromatous or occluded (as by intimal plaques)

end·brain \'en(d)-,brān\ *n* **:** the anterior subdivision of the forebrain

end brush *n* **:** END PLATE

end bulb *n* **:** a bulbous termination of a sensory nerve fiber (as in the skin or in a mucous membrane)

en·dear \in-'di(ə)r\ *vt* **1** *obs* **:** to make higher in cost, value, or estimation **2 :** to cause to become beloved or admired — **en·dear·ing·ly** \-iŋ-lē\ *adv*

en·dear·ment \in-'di(ə)r-mənt\ *n* **1 :** the act or process of endearing **2 :** a word or an act (as a caress) expressing affection

¹**en·deav·or** \in-'dev-ər\ *vb* **en·deav·ored; en·deav·or·ing** \-(ə-)riŋ\ [ME *endeveren* to exert oneself, fr. *en-* + *dever* duty — more at DEVOIR] *vt* **1** *archaic* **:** to strive to achieve or reach **2 :** to attempt (as the fulfillment of an obligation) by exertion of effort ⟨~*ing* to control her disgust⟩ ~ *vi* **:** to work with set purpose ***syn*** see ATTEMPT

²**endeavor** *n* **:** serious determined effort ⟨fields of ~⟩; *also* **:** an instance of this

¹**en·dem·ic** \en-'dem-ik, in-\ *adj* [F *endémique,* fr. *endémie* endemic disease, fr. Gk *endēmia* action of dwelling, fr. *endēmos* endemic, fr. *en* in + *dēmos* people, populace — more at DEMAGOGUE] **1 :** belonging or native to a particular people or country **2 :** restricted or peculiar to a locality or region ⟨~ diseases⟩ ⟨an ~ species⟩ ***syn*** see NATIVE ***ant*** exotic, pandemic — **en·dem·i·cal·ly** \-dem-i-k(ə-)lē\ *adv* — **en·de·mic·i·ty** \,en-,dem-'is-ət-ē, -də-'mis-\ *n* — **en·de·mism** \'en-də-,miz-əm\ *n*

²**endemic** *n* **:** NATIVE 2b

end·er·gon·ic \,en-,dər-'gän-ik\ *adj* [*end-* + Gk *ergon* work — more at WORK] **:** requiring expenditure of energy ⟨~ biochemical reactions⟩

en·der·mic \en-'dər-mik\ *adj* **:** acting through the skin or by direct application to the skin — **en·der·mi·cal·ly** \-mi-k(ə-)lē\ *adv*

end·ex·ine \(')en-'dek-,sēn, -,sīn\ *n* **:** an inner membranous layer of the exine

end game *n* **:** the last stage in various games; *esp* **:** the stage of a chess game following serious reduction of forces

end·ing \'en-diŋ\ *n* **:** a thing that constitutes an end; *esp* **:** one or more letters or syllables added to a word base esp. in inflection ***syn*** see END ***ant*** beginning

endite *archaic var of* INDITE

en·dive \'en-,dīv\ *n* [ME, fr. MF, fr. LL *endivia,* fr. LGk *entubion,* fr. L *intubus*] **1 :** an annual or biennial composite herb (*Cichorium endivia*) widely cultivated as a salad plant — called also *escarole* **2 :** the developing crown of chicory when blanched for use as salad by growing in darkness or semidarkness

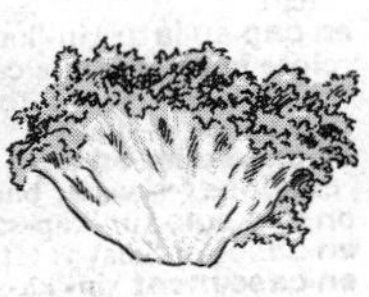

endive 1

end·leaf \'en-,dlēf\ *n* **:** ENDPAPER

end·less \'en-(d)ləs\ *adj* **1 :** being or seeming to be without end **2 :** extremely numerous **3 :** joined at the ends ⟨an ~ chain⟩ — **end·less·ly** *adv* — **end·less·ness** *n*

end line *n* **:** a line marking an end or boundary esp. of a playing area: as **a :** a line at either end of a football field 10 yards beyond and parallel to the goal line **b :** a line at either end of a court (as in basketball or tennis) perpendicular to the sidelines

end·long \'en-,dlȯŋ\ *adv* [ME *endelong,* alter. of *andlong,* fr. OE *andlang* along, fr. *andlang,* prep. — more at ALONG] *archaic* **:** LENGTHWISE

end man *n* **:** a man at each end of the line of performers in a minstrel show who engages in comic repartee with the interlocutor

end·most \'en(d)-,mōst\ *adj* **:** situated at the very end : FARTHEST

en·do·bi·ot·ic \,en-dō-,bī-'ät-ik, -bē-\ *adj* [ISV] **:** dwelling within the tissues of a host

en·do·blast \'en-də-,blast\ *n* [ISV] **:** HYPOBLAST — **en·do·blas·tic** \,en-də-'blas-tik\ *adj*

en·do·car·di·al \,en-dō-'kärd-ē-əl\ *adj* **1 :** situated within the heart **2 :** of or relating to the endocardium

en·do·car·di·tis \-,kär-'dīt-əs\ *n* **:** inflammation of the lining of the heart and its valves

en·do·car·di·um \-'kärd-ē-əm\ *n, pl* **-dia** [NL, fr. *end-* + Gk *kardia* heart] **:** a thin serous membrane lining the cavities of the heart

en·do·carp \'en-də-,kärp\ *n* [F *endocarpe*] **:** the inner layer of the pericarp of a fruit (as an apple or orange) when it consists of two or more layers of different texture or consistency — **en·do·car·pal** \,en-də-'kär-pəl\ *adj*

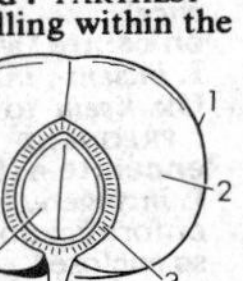

vertical section of a cherry, showing *1* exocarp, *2* mesocarp, *3* endocarp, *4* seed; *1, 2,* and *3* together form the pericarp

en·do·chon·dral \ˌen-də-ˈkän-drəl\ *adj* : occurring within the substance of cartilage ⟨~ calcification⟩

en·do·cra·ni·al cast \ˌen-də-ˌkrā-nē-əl-\ *n* : a cast of the cranial cavity showing the approximate shape of the brain

¹en·do·crine \ˈen-də-krən, -ˌkrīn, -ˌkrēn\ *adj* [ISV *end-* + Gk *krinein* to separate — more at CERTAIN] **1 a** : secreting internally; *specif* : producing secretions that are distributed in the body by way of the bloodstream ⟨an ~ system⟩ **b** : of, relating to, or resembling that of an endocrine gland ⟨~ tumors⟩ **2** : HORMONAL

²endocrine *n* **1** : HORMONE **2** : ENDOCRINE GLAND

endocrine gland *n* : a gland (as the thyroid or the pituitary) that produces an endocrine secretion — called also *ductless gland*

en·do·cri·no·log·ic \ˌen-də-ˌkrin-ᵊl-ˈäj-ik, -ˌkrīn-, -ˌkrēn-\ *or* **en·do·cri·no·log·i·cal** \-i-kəl-\ *adj* : involving or relating to the endocrine glands or secretions or to endocrinology

en·do·cri·nol·o·gy \ˌen-də-kri-ˈnäl-ə-jē, -ˌkrī-\ *n* [ISV] : a science dealing with the endocrine glands — **en·do·cri·nol·o·gist** \-jəst\ *n*

en·do·cyt·ic \ˌen-də-ˈsit-ik\ *adj* : of or relating to endocytosis : ENDOCYTOTIC

en·do·cy·to·sis \-sī-ˈtō-səs\ *n* [NL, fr. *end-* + *-cytosis* (as in *phagocytosis*)] : incorporation of substances into a cell by phagocytosis or pinocytosis — **en·do·cy·tot·ic** \-ˈtät-ik\ *adj*

en·do·derm \ˈen-də-ˌdərm\ *n* [F *endoderme*, fr. *end-* + Gk *derma* skin — more at DERM-] : the innermost of the germ layers of an embryo that is the source of the epithelium of the digestive tract and its derivatives : HYPOBLAST; *also* : a tissue that is derived from this germ layer — **en·do·der·mal** \ˌen-də-ˈder-məl\ *adj*

en·do·der·mis \ˌen-də-ˈdər-məs\ *n* [NL] : the innermost tissue of the cortex in many roots and stems

end·odon·tia \ˌen-də-ˈdän-ch(ē-)ə\ *n* [NL, fr. *end-* + *-odontia*] : a branch of dentistry concerned with diseases of the pulp — **end·odon·tic** \-ˈdänt-ik\ *adj* — **end·odon·ti·cal·ly** \-ˈdänt-i-k(ə-)lē\ *adv* — **end·odon·tist** \-ˈdänt-əst\ *n*

end·odon·tics \-ˈdänt-iks\ *n pl but sing in constr* : ENDODONTIA

en·do·en·zyme \ˌen-dō-ˈen-ˌzīm\ *n* [ISV] : an enzyme that functions inside the cell

en·do·er·gic \ˌen-dō-ˈər-jik\ *adj* : absorbing energy : ENDOTHERMIC ⟨~ nuclear reactions⟩

en·do·eryth·ro·cyt·ic \ˌen-dō-i-ˌrith-rə-ˈsit-ik\ *adj* : occurring within red blood cells — used chiefly of stages of malaria parasites

en·dog·a·my \en-ˈdäg-ə-mē\ *n* **1** : marriage within a specific group as required by custom or law **2** : sexual reproduction between near relatives; *esp* : pollination of a flower by pollen from another flower of the same plant — compare AUTOGAMY — **en·dog·a·mous** \-məs\ *or* **en·do·gam·ic** \ˌen-də-ˈgam-ik\ *adj*

en·do·gen \ˈen-də-jən\ *n* [F *endogène*, fr. *end-* + *-gène* -gen] : a plant that develops by endogenous growth

en·dog·e·nous \en-ˈdäj-ə-nəs\ *also* **en·do·gen·ic** \ˌen-də-ˈjen-ik\ *adj* **1 a** : growing from or on the inside : developing within the cell wall **b** : originating within the body **2** : constituting or relating to metabolism of the nitrogenous constituents of cells and tissues — **en·dog·e·nous·ly** *adv*

en·dog·e·ny \en-ˈdäj-ə-nē\ *n* : growth from within or from a deep layer

en·do·lymph \ˈen-də-ˌlim(p)f\ *n* [ISV] : the watery fluid in the membranous labyrinth of the ear — **en·do·lym·phat·ic** \ˌen-də-lim-ˈfat-ik\ *adj*

en·do·me·tri·o·sis \ˌen-dō-ˌmē-trē-ˈō-səs\ *n* : the presence of functioning endometrial tissue in places where it is not normally found

en·do·me·tri·um \-ˈmē-trē-əm\ *n, pl* **-tria** \-trē-ə\ [NL, fr. *end-* + Gk *mētra* uterus, fr. *mētr-*, *mētēr* mother — more at MOTHER] : the mucous membrane lining the uterus — **en·do·me·tri·al** \-trē-əl\ *adj*

en·do·mi·to·sis \-mī-ˈtō-səs\ *n* : division of chromosomes that is not followed by nuclear division and that results in an increased number of chromosomes in the cell

en·do·mix·is \-ˈmik-səs\ *n* [NL, fr. *end-* + Gk *mixis* act of mixing, fr. *mignynai* to mix — more at MIX] : a periodic nuclear reorganization in ciliated protozoans

en·do·morph \ˈen-də-ˌmȯrf\ *n* [ISV] **1** : a crystal of one species enclosed in one of another **2** [*endo*derm + *-morph*] : an endomorphic individual

en·do·mor·phic \ˌen-də-ˈmȯr-fik\ *adj* **1 a** : of or relating to an endomorph **b** : of, relating to, or produced by endomorphism **2** [*endo*derm + *-morphic*; fr. the predominance in such types of structures developed from the endoderm] **a** : of or relating to the component in W. H. Sheldon's classification of body types that measures the massiveness of the digestive viscera and the body's degree of roundedness and softness **b** : having a heavy rounded body build often with a marked tendency to become fat — **en·do·mor·phy** \ˈen-də-ˌmȯr-fē\ *n*

en·do·mor·phism \ˌen-də-ˈmȯr-ˌfiz-əm\ *n* **1** : a change produced in an intrusive rock by reaction with the wall rock **2** : a homomorphism that maps a mathematical set into itself — compare ISOMORPHISM

en·do·nu·cle·ase \ˌen-dō-ˈn(y)ü-klē-ˌās, -ˌāz\ *n* : an enzyme that breaks down a chain of nucleotides (as a nucleic acid) at points not adjacent to the end and thereby produces two or more shorter nucleotide chains — compare EXONUCLEASE

en·do·par·a·site \-ˈpar-ə-ˌsīt\ *n* [ISV] : a parasite that lives in the internal organs or tissues of its host — **en·do·par·a·sit·ism** \-ˌsīt-ˌiz-əm, -sə-ˌtiz-\ *n*

en·do·pep·ti·dase \-ˈpep-tə-ˌdās, -ˌdāz\ *n* : any of a group of enzymes that hydrolyze peptide bonds inside the long chains of protein molecules : PROTEINASE — compare EXOPEPTIDASE

en·doph·a·gous \en-ˈdäf-ə-gəs\ *adj* : feeding from within; *esp* : consuming vegetation or plant debris by burrowing in and disintegrating plant structures

en·do·phyte \ˈen-də-ˌfīt\ *n* [ISV] : a plant living within another plant — **en·do·phyt·ic** \ˌen-də-ˈfit-ik\ *adj*

en·do·plasm \ˈen-də-ˌplaz-əm\ *n* [ISV] : the inner relatively fluid part of the cytoplasm — **en·do·plas·mic** \ˌen-də-ˈplaz-mik\ *adj*

endoplasmic reticulum *n* : a system of interconnected vesicular and lamellar cytoplasmic membranes that functions esp. in the transport of materials within the cell and that is studded with ribosomes in some places

en·dop·o·dite \en-ˈdäp-ə-ˌdīt\ *n* [ISV] : the mesial or internal branch of a typical limb of a crustacean — **en·dop·o·dit·ic** \(ˌ)en-ˌdäp-ə-ˈdit-ik\ *adj*

en·do·poly·ploid \ˌen-dō-ˈpäl-i-ˌplȯid\ *adj* : of or relating to a polyploid state in which the chromosomes have divided repeatedly without subsequent division of the nucleus or cell — **en·do·poly·ploi·dy** \-ˌplȯid-ē\ *n*

en·do·ra·dio·sonde \-ˈrād-ē-ō-ˌsänd\ *n* : a microelectronic device introduced into the body to record physiological data not otherwise obtainable

end organ *n* : a structure forming the end of a neural path and consisting of an effector or a receptor with its associated nerve terminations

en·dorse \in-ˈdȯ(ə)rs\ *vt* **en·dorsed; en·dors·ing** [alter. of obs. *endoss*, fr. ME *endosen*, fr. MF *endosser*, fr. OF, to put on the back, fr. *en-* + *dos* back, fr. L *dorsum*] **1 a** : to write on the back of; *esp* : to sign one's name as payee on the back of (a check) in order to obtain the cash or credit represented on the face **b** : to inscribe (one's signature) on a check, bill, or note **c** : to inscribe (as an official document) with a title or memorandum **d** : to make over to another (the value represented in a check, bill, or note) by inscribing one's name on the document **e** : to acknowledge receipt of (a sum specified) by one's signature on a document **2** : to express approval of publicly and definitely ⟨~ a mayoral candidate⟩ *syn* see APPROVE — **en·dors·able** \-ˈdȯr-sə-bəl\ *adj* — **en·dors·ee** \in-ˌdȯr-ˈsē, ˌen-\ *n* — **en·dors·er** \in-ˈdȯr-sər\ *n*

en·dorse·ment \in-ˈdȯr-smənt\ *n* **1** : the act or process of endorsing **2 a** : something that is written in the process of endorsing **b** : a provision added to an insurance contract altering its scope or application **3** : SANCTION, APPROVAL

en·do·scope \ˈen-də-ˌskōp\ *n* [ISV] : an instrument for visualizing the interior of a hollow organ (as the rectum or urethra) — **en·dos·co·py** \en-ˈdäs-kə-pē\ *n*

en·do·scop·ic \ˌen-də-ˈskäp-ik\ *adj* : of, relating to, or performed by means of the endoscope or endoscopy — **en·do·scop·i·cal·ly** \-i-k(ə-)lē\ *adv*

en·do·skel·e·ton \ˌen-dō-ˈskel-ət-ᵊn\ *n* : an internal skeleton or supporting framework in an animal — **en·do·skel·e·tal** \-ət-ᵊl\ *adj*

end·os·mo·sis \ˌen-ˌdäs-ˈmō-səs, -ˌdäz-\ *n* [alter. of obs. *endosmose*, fr. F, fr. *end-* + Gk *ōsmos* act of pushing, fr. *ōthein* to push; akin to Skt *vadhati* he strikes] : passage (as of a surface-active substance) through a membrane from a region of lower to a region of higher concentration — **end·os·mot·ic** \-ˈmät-ik\ *adj* — **end·os·mot·i·cal·ly** \-i-k(ə-)lē\ *adv*

en·do·sperm \ˈen-də-ˌspərm\ *n* [F *endosperme*, fr. *end-* + Gk *sperma* seed — more at SPERM] : a nutritive tissue in seed plants formed within the embryo sac — **en·do·sper·mic** \ˌen-də-ˈspər-mik\ *adj* — **en·do·sper·mous** \-məs\ *adj*

endosperm nucleus *n* : the triploid nucleus formed in the embryo sac of a seed plant by fusion of a sperm nucleus with two polar nuclei or with a nucleus formed by their prior fusion

en·do·spore \ˈen-də-ˌspō(ə)r, -ˌspȯ(ə)r\ *n* [ISV] : an asexual spore developed within the cell esp. in bacteria — **en·do·spor·ic** \ˌen-də-ˈspōr-ik, -ˈspȯr-\ *adj* — **en·do·spo·rous** \-əs; en-ˈdäs-pə-rəs\ *adj*

end·os·te·al \en-ˈdäs-tē-əl\ *adj* **1** : of or relating to the endosteum **2** : located within bone or cartilage — **end·os·te·al·ly** \-ə-lē\ *adv*

en·do·ster·nite \ˌen-dō-ˈstər-ˌnīt\ *n* [ISV *end-* + *sternum* + *-ite*] : a segment of the endoskeleton of an arthropod

end·os·te·um \en-ˈdäs-tē-əm\ *n, pl* **-tea** \-tē-ə\ [NL, fr. *end-* + Gk *osteon* bone — more at OSSEOUS] : the layer of vascular connective tissue lining the medullary cavities of bone

en·do·style \ˈen-də-ˌstīl\ *n* [ISV *end-* + Gk *stylos* pillar — more at STEER] : a pair of parallel longitudinal folds projecting into the pharyngeal cavity and bounding a furrow lined with glandular ciliated cells in lower chordates (as the tunicates)

en·do·sul·fan \ˌen-də-ˈsəl-fən, -ˌfan\ *n* [*endo-* + *sulf-* + *-an*] : a brownish crystalline insecticide $C_9H_6Cl_6O_3S$ that is used in the control of numerous crop insects and some mites

en·do·sym·bi·o·sis \ˌen-dō-ˌsim-bī-ˈō-səs, -bē-\ *n* : symbiosis in which a symbiont dwells within the body of its symbiotic partner

en·do·the·ci·um \ˌen-dō-ˈthē-s(h)ē-əm\ *n, pl* **-cia** \-s(h)ē-ə\ [NL] : the inner lining of a mature anther

endotheli- *or* **endothelio-** *comb form* [ISV, fr. NL *endothelium*] : endothelium ⟨*endothelio*ma⟩

en·do·the·li·o·ma \-ˌthē-lē-ˈō-mə\ *n, pl* **-o·mas** *or* **-o·ma·ta** \-mət-ə\ [NL] : a tumor developing from endothelial tissue

en·do·the·li·um \ˌen-də-ˈthē-lē-əm\ *n, pl* **-lia** \-lē-ə\ [NL, fr. *end-* + *epithelium*] **1** : an epithelium of mesoblastic origin composed of a single layer of thin flattened cells that lines internal body cavities **2** : the inner layer of the seed coat of some plants — **en·do·the·li·al** \-lē-əl\ *adj* — **en·do·the·loid** \-ˈthē-ˌlȯid\ *adj*

en·do·therm \ˈen-də-ˌthərm\ *n* : a warm-blooded animal

en·do·ther·mic \ˌen-də-ˈthər-mik\ *or* **en·do·ther·mal** \-məl\ *adj* [ISV] **1** : characterized by or formed with absorption of heat **2** : WARM-BLOODED

en·do·tox·in \ˌen-dō-ˈtäk-sən\ *n* [ISV] : a toxin of internal origin; *specif* : a poisonous substance present in bacteria (as of typhoid fever) but separable from the cell body only on its disintegration — **en·do·tox·ic** \-sik\ *adj*

en·do·tra·che·al \-ˈtrā-kē-əl\ *adj* **1** : placed within the trachea ⟨an ~ tube⟩ **2** : applied or effected through the trachea

en·do·tro·phic \ˌen-də-ˈtrō-fik\ *also* **en·do·tro·pic** \-ˈtrō-pik, -ˈträp-ik\ *adj, of a mycorrhiza* : penetrating into the associated root and ramifying between the cells — compare ECTOTROPHIC

ə abut ᵊ kitten ər further a back ā bake ä cot, cart
aù out ch chin e less ē easy g gift i trip ī life
j joke ŋ sing ō flow ȯ flaw ȯi coin th thin t͟h this
ü loot ú foot y yet yü few yú furious zh vision

en·dow \in-'dau̇\ *vt* [ME *endowen,* fr. AF *endouer,* fr. MF *en-* + *douer* to endow, fr. L *dotare,* fr. *dot-, dos* gift, dowry — more at DOWRY] **1** : to furnish with a dower **2** : to furnish with an income ⟨~ a hospital⟩ **3** **a** : to provide or equip gratuitously : ENRICH **b** : CREDIT 5a
en·dow·ment \-mənt\ *n* **1** : the act or process of endowing **2** : something that is endowed; *specif* : the part of an institution's income derived from donations **3** : natural capacity, power, or ability
en·do·zo·ic \,en-də-'zō-ik\ *adj* [ISV] : living within or involving passage through an animal ⟨~ distribution of weeds⟩
end·pa·per \'en(d)-,pā-pər\ *n* : a once-folded sheet of paper having one leaf pasted flat against the inside of the front or back cover of a book and the other pasted at the base to the first or last page
end plate *n* : a flat plate or structure at the end of something; *specif* : a complex terminal arborization of a motor nerve fiber
end point *n* **1** : a point marking the completion of a process or stage of a process **2** *usu* **end·point** : either of two points or values that mark the ends of a line segment or interval; *also* : a point that marks the end of a ray
end product *n* : the final product of a series of processes or activities
en·drin \'en-drən\ *n* [blend of *end-* and *dieldrin*] : a chlorinated hydrocarbon insecticide $C_{12}H_8Cl_6O$ that is a stereoisomer of dieldrin and resembles dieldrin in toxicity
end run *n* **1** : a football play in which the ballcarrier attempts to run wide around his own end **2** : an evasive trick
end–stopped \'en(d)-,stäpt\ *adj* : marked by a logical or rhetorical pause at the end ⟨an ~ line of verse⟩ — compare RUN-ON
end table *n* : a small table that is usu. about the height of the arm of a chair and is used beside a larger piece of furniture (as a sofa)
en·due \in-'d(y)ü\ *vt* **en·dued; en·du·ing** [ME *enduen,* fr. MF *enduire* to bring in, introduce, fr. L *inducere* — more at INDUCE] **1** **a** : PROVIDE, ENDOW **b** : IMBUE, TRANSFUSE **2** [ME *enduen,* fr. L *induere,* fr. *ind-* in (fr. OL *indu*) + *-uere* to put on — more at INDIGENOUS, EXUVIAE] : to put on : DON
en·dur·able \in-'d(y)u̇r-ə-bəl\ *adj* : capable of being endured : BEARABLE — **en·dur·ably** \-blē\ *adv*
en·dur·ance \in-'d(y)u̇r-ən(t)s\ *n* **1** : PERMANENCE, DURATION **2** : the ability to withstand hardship, adversity, or stress **3** : SUFFERING, TRIAL
en·dure \in-'d(y)u̇(ə)r\ *vb* **en·dured; en·dur·ing** [ME *enduren,* fr. MF *endurer,* fr. (assumed) VL *indurare,* fr. L, to harden, fr. *in-* + *durare* to harden, endure — more at DURING] *vi* **1** : to continue in the same state : LAST **2** : to remain firm under suffering or misfortune without yielding ~ *vt* **1** : to undergo (as a hardship) esp. without giving in : SUFFER **2** : TOLERATE, PERMIT ***syn*** see BEAR, CONTINUE
en·dur·ing *adj* : LASTING, DURABLE — **en·dur·ing·ly** \-'d(y)u̇r-iŋ-lē\ *adv* — **en·dur·ing·ness** *n*
en·duro \in-'d(y)u̇(ə)r-(,)ō\ *n, pl* **en·dur·os** [irreg. fr. *endurance*] : a long race (as for automobiles or motorcycles) stressing endurance rather than speed
end·ways \'en-,dwāz\ *adv or adj* **1** : with the end forward (as toward the observer) **2** : in or toward the direction of the ends : LENGTHWISE ⟨~ pressure⟩ **3** : on end : UPRIGHT ⟨boxes set ~⟩
end·wise \'en-,dwīz\ *adv or adj* : ENDWAYS
En·dym·i·on \en-'dim-ē-ən\ *n* [L, fr. Gk *Endymiōn*] : a beautiful youth loved by Selene
end zone *n* : the area at either end of a football field between the goal line and the end line
ENE *abbr* east-northeast
-ene \,ēn\ *n suffix* [ISV, fr. Gk *-ēnē,* fem. of *-ēnos,* adj. suffix] : unsaturated carbon compound ⟨benzene⟩; *esp* : carbon compound with one double bond ⟨eth*ylene*⟩
en·e·ma \'en-ə-mə\ *n, pl* **enemas** *also* **ene·ma·ta** \,en-ə-'mät-ə, 'en-ə-mə-tə\ [LL, fr. Gk, fr. *enienai* to inject, fr. *en-* + *hienai* to send — more at JET] **1** : the injection of liquid into the intestine by way of the anus **2** : material for injection as an enema
en·e·my \'en-ə-mē\ *n, pl* **-mies** [ME *enemi,* fr. OF, fr. L *inimicus,* fr. *in-* [1]in- + *amicus* friend — more at AMIABLE] **1** : one that is antagonistic to another; *esp* : one seeking to injure, overthrow, or confound an opponent **2** : something harmful or deadly **3** **a** : a military adversary **b** : a hostile unit or force
syn ENEMY, FOE *shared meaning element* : one who shows hostility or ill will
en·er·get·ic \,en-ər-'jet-ik\ *adj* [Gk *energētikos,* fr. *energein* to be active, fr. *energos*] **1** : marked by energy : STRENUOUS **2** : operating with vigor or effect **3** : of or relating to energy ⟨~ equation⟩ — **en·er·get·i·cal·ly** \-i-k(ə-)lē\ *adv*
en·er·get·ics \-iks\ *n pl but sing in constr* **1** : a branch of mechanics that deals primarily with energy and its transformations **2** : the total energy relations and transformations of a system (as a chemical reaction or an ecological community) ⟨~ of muscular contraction⟩
en·er·gid \'en-ər-jəd, -jid\ *n* [ISV, fr. Gk *energos*] : a nucleus and the body of cytoplasm with which it interacts
en·er·gize \'en-ər-,jīz\ *vb* **-gized; -giz·ing** *vi* : to put forth energy : ACT ~ *vt* **1** : to impart energy to **2** : to make energetic or vigorous **3** : to apply voltage to ***syn*** see VITALIZE
en·er·giz·er \-,jī-zər\ *n* : one that energizes; *esp* : ANTIDEPRESSANT
en·er·gy \'en-ər-jē\ *n, pl* **-gies** [LL *energia,* fr. Gk *energeia* activity, fr. *energos* active, fr. *en* in + *ergon* work — more at WORK] **1** : the capacity of acting or being active ⟨intellectual ~⟩ **2** : natural power vigorously exerted ⟨work with ~⟩ **3** : the capacity for doing work
energy level *n* : one of the stable states of constant energy that may be assumed by a physical system — used esp. of the quantum states of electrons in atoms and of nuclei; called also *energy state*
[1]**ener·vate** \i-'nər-vət\ *adj* : lacking physical, mental, or moral vigor : ENERVATED
[2]**en·er·vate** \'en-ər-,vāt\ *vt* **-vat·ed; -vat·ing** [L *enervatus,* pp. of *enervare,* fr. *e-* + *nervus* sinew — more at NERVE] **1** : to lessen the vitality or strength of **2** : to reduce the mental or moral vigor of ***syn*** see UNNERVE — **en·er·va·tion** \,en-ər-'vā-shən\ *n* — **en·er·va·tive** \'en-ər-,vāt-iv\ *adj*
en·fant ter·ri·ble \äⁿ-fäⁿ-te-rēblᵊ\ *n, pl* **enfants terribles** *same*\ [F, lit., terrifying child] : one whose inopportune remarks or unconventional actions cause embarrassment
en·fee·ble \in-'fē-bəl\ *vt* **en·fee·bled; en·fee·bling** \-b(ə-)liŋ\ [ME *enfeblen,* fr. MF *enfeblir,* fr. OF, fr. *en-* + *feble* feeble] : to make feeble : deprive of strength ***syn*** see WEAKEN ***ant*** fortify — **en·fee·ble·ment** \-bəl-mənt\ *n*
en·feoff \in-'fef, -'fēf\ *vt* [ME *enfeoffen,* fr. AF *enfeoffer,* fr. OF *en-* + *fief*] : to invest with a fief, fee, or other possession — **en·feoff·ment** \-mənt\ *n*
en·fet·ter \in-'fet-ər\ *vt* : to bind in fetters : ENCHAIN
en·fe·ver \in-'fē-vər\ *vt* : FEVER
En·field rifle \,en-,fēld-\ *n* [*Enfield,* England] : a .30 caliber bolt-operated repeating rifle used by U.S. and British troops in World War I
[1]**en·fi·lade** \'en-fə-,lād, -,läd\ *n* [F, fr. *enfiler* to thread, enfilade, fr. OF, to thread, fr. *en-* + *fil* thread — more at FILE] **1** : an arrangement (as of rooms) in opposite and parallel rows **2** : gunfire directed along the length of an enemy battle line
[2]**enfilade** *vt* **-lad·ed; -lad·ing** : to rake or be in a position to rake with gunfire in a lengthwise direction
enflame *var of* INFLAME
en·fleu·rage \,äⁿ-,flər-'äzh\ *n* [F] : a process of extracting perfumes by exposing absorbents to the exhalations of flowers
en·fold \in-'fōld\ *vt* **1** **a** : to cover with folds : ENVELOP **b** : to surround with a covering : CONTAIN **2** : to clasp within the arms : EMBRACE
en·force \in-'fō(ə)rs, -'fȯ(ə)rs\ *vt* [ME *enforcen,* fr. MF *enforcier,* fr. OF, fr. *en-* + *force*] **1** : to give force to : STRENGTHEN **2** : to urge with energy **3** : CONSTRAIN, COMPEL **4** *obs* : to effect or gain by force **5** : to carry out effectively ⟨~ laws⟩ — **en·force·abil·i·ty** \-,fōr-sə-'bil-ət-ē, -,fȯr-\ *n* — **en·force·able** \-'fōr-sə-bəl, -'fȯr-\ *adj* — **en·force·ment** \-'fōr-smənt, -'fȯr-\ *n* — **en·forc·er** *n*
en·fran·chise \in-'fran-,chīz\ *vt* **-chised; -chis·ing** [ME *enfranchisen,* fr. MF *enfranchiss-,* stem of *enfranchir,* fr. OF, fr. *en-* + *franc* free — more at FRANK] **1** : to set free (as from slavery) **2** : to endow with a franchise: as **a** : to admit to the privileges of a citizen; *specif* : to admit to the right of suffrage **b** : to admit (a municipality) to political privileges or rights — **en·fran·chise·ment** \-,chīz-mənt, -chəz-\ *n*
eng *abbr* engine; engineer; engineering
Eng *abbr* England; English
en·gage \in-'gāj\ *vb* **en·gaged; en·gag·ing** [ME *engagen,* fr. MF *engagier,* fr. OF, fr. *en-* + *gage*] *vt* **1** : to offer (as one's word) as security for a debt or cause **2** **a** *obs* : to entangle or entrap in or as if in a snare or bog **b** : to attract and hold by influence or power **c** : to interlock with : MESH; *also* : to cause (mechanical parts) to mesh **3** : to bind (as oneself) to do something; *esp* : to bind by a pledge to marry **4** **a** : to provide occupation for : INVOLVE ⟨~ him in a new project⟩ **b** : to arrange to obtain the use or services of : HIRE **5** **a** : to hold the attention of : ENGROSS ⟨her work ~*s* her completely⟩ **b** : to induce to participate ⟨*engaged* the shy boy in conversation⟩ **6** **a** : to enter into contest with **b** : to bring together or interlock (weapons) ~ *vi* **1** **a** : to pledge oneself : PROMISE **b** : GUARANTEE ⟨he ~*s* for the honesty of his brother⟩ **2** **a** : to begin and carry on an enterprise ⟨he *engaged* in trade for a number of years⟩ **b** : to take part : PARTICIPATE ⟨at college he *engaged* in gymnastics⟩ **3** : to enter into conflict **4** : to be or become in gear
en·ga·gé \,äⁿ-,gäzh-'ā\ *adj* [F, pp. of *engager* to engage, fr. MF *engagier*] : being actively involved in or committed esp. to political concerns
en·gaged \in-'gājd\ *adj* **1** : involved in activity : OCCUPIED **2** : pledged to be married : BETROTHED **3** : greatly interested : COMMITTED **4** : involved esp. in a hostile encounter **5** : partly embedded in a wall ⟨an ~ column⟩ **6** : being in gear : MESHED
en·gage·ment \in-'gāj-mənt\ *n* **1** **a** : the act of engaging : the state of being engaged **b** : BETROTHAL **2** : something that engages : PLEDGE **3** **a** : a promise to be present at a specified time and place **b** : employment esp. for a stated time **4** : the state of being in gear **5** : a hostile encounter between military forces ***syn*** see BATTLE
en·gag·ing *adj* : tending to draw favorable attention : ATTRACTIVE ***syn*** see SWEET ***ant*** loathsome — **en·gag·ing·ly** \-'gā-jiŋ-lē\ *adv*
en·gar·land \in-'gär-lənd\ *vt* : to adorn with or as if with a garland
En·gel·mann spruce \,eŋ-gəl-mən-\ *n* [George *Engelmann* †1884 Am botanist] : a large spruce (*Picea engelmannii*) of the Rocky mountain region and British Columbia that yields a light-colored wood
en·gen·der \in-'jen-dər\ *vb* **en·gen·dered; en·gen·der·ing** \-d(ə-)riŋ\ [ME *engendren,* fr. MF *engendrer,* fr. L *ingenerare,* fr. *in-* + *generare* to generate] *vt* **1** : BEGET, PROCREATE **2** : to cause to exist or to develop : PRODUCE ⟨angry words ~ strife⟩ ~ *vi* : to assume form : ORIGINATE
en·gild \in-'gild\ *vt* : to make bright with or as if with light
[1]**en·gine** \'en-jən\ *n* [ME *engin,* fr. OF, fr. L *ingenium* natural disposition, talent, fr. *in-* + *gignere* to beget — more at KIN] **1** *obs* **a** : INGENUITY **b** : evil contrivance : WILE **2** : something used to effect a purpose : AGENT, INSTRUMENT ⟨mournful and terrible ~ of horror and of crime —E. A. Poe⟩ **3** **a** : a mechanical tool: as (1) : an instrument or machine of war (2) *obs* : a torture implement **b** : MACHINERY **c** : any of various mechanical appliances — compare FIRE ENGINE **4** : a machine for converting any of various forms of energy into mechanical force and motion **5** : a railroad locomotive
[2]**engine** *vt* **en·gined; en·gin·ing** : to equip with engines
-en·gined \'en-jənd\ *adj comb form* : having (such or so many) engines ⟨front-*engined* cars⟩ ⟨four-*engined* planes⟩
[1]**en·gi·neer** \,en-jə-'ni(ə)r\ *n* **1** : a member of a military group devoted to engineering work **2** *obs* : a crafty schemer : PLOTTER **3** **a** : a designer or builder of engines **b** : a person who is trained in or follows as a profession a branch of engineering **c** : a person

who carries through an enterprise by skillful or artful contrivance **4** : a person who runs or supervises an engine or an apparatus

²engineer *vt* **1** : to lay out, construct, or manage as an engineer **2 a** : to contrive or plan out usu. with more or less subtle skill and craft **b** : to guide the course of ***syn*** see GUIDE

en·gi·neer·ing *n* **1** : the art of managing engines **2** : the application of science and mathematics by which the properties of matter and the sources of energy in nature are made useful to man in structures, machines, products, systems, and processes

en·gine·ry \ˈen-jən-rē\ *n* **1** : instruments of war **2** : machines and tools : MACHINERY

en·gird \in-ˈgərd\ *vt* : GIRD, ENCOMPASS

en·gir·dle \in-ˈgərd-ᵊl\ *vt* : to encircle with or as if with a girdle

en·gla·cial \en-ˈglā-shəl\ *adj* : embedded in a glacier

¹En·glish \ˈiŋ-glish *also* ˈiŋ-lish\ *adj* [ME, fr. OE *englisc,* fr. *Engle* (pl.) Angles] : of, relating to, or characteristic of England, the English people, or the English language

²English *n* **1 a** : the language of the people of England and the U.S. and many areas now or formerly under British control **b** : a particular variety of English distinguished by peculiarities (as of pronunciation) **c** : English language, literature, or composition when a subject of study **2** *pl in constr* : the people of England **3 a** : an English translation **b** : idiomatic or intelligible English **4** : spin around the vertical axis given to a ball by striking it to right or left of center (as in pool) or by the manner of releasing it (as in bowling) — compare DRAW, FOLLOW; BODY ENGLISH

³English *vt* **1** : to translate into English **2** : to adopt into English : ANGLICIZE

English breakfast tea *n* : CONGOU; *broadly* : any similar black tea

English cocker spaniel *n* : any of a breed of spaniels that have square muzzles, wide well-developed noses, and distinctive heads which are ideally half muzzle and half skull with the forehead and skull arched and slightly flattened

English daisy *n* : DAISY 1a

English foxhound *n* : any of a breed of foxhounds developed in England and characterized by a large heavily boned form, rather short ears, and lightly fringed tail

English horn *n* [trans. of It *corno inglese*] : a double-reed woodwind instrument resembling the oboe in design but having a longer tube and a range a fifth lower than that of the oboe

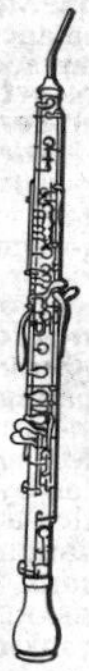

English horn

En·glish·man \ˈiŋ-glish-mən *also* ˈiŋ-lish-\ *n* : a native or inhabitant of England

English muffin *n* : bread dough rolled and cut into rounds, baked on a griddle, and split and toasted just before eating

En·glish·ness \ˈiŋ-glish-nəs *also* ˈiŋ-lish-\ *n* : the distinctive qualities or characteristics of the English people, their works, or their institutions

English rabbit *n* : any of a breed of white domestic rabbits having distinctive dark markings

English saddle *n* : a saddle with long side bars, steel cantle and pommel, no horn, and a leather seat supported by webbing stretched between the saddlebow and cantle

English setter *n* : any of a breed of bird dogs characterized by a moderately long flat silky coat of white or white with color and by feathering on the tail and legs

English shepherd *n* : any of a breed of vigorous medium-sized working dogs with a long and glossy black coat usu. with tan to brown markings that was developed in England for herding sheep and cattle

English sonnet *n* : a sonnet consisting of three quatrains and a couplet with a rhyme scheme of *abab cdcd efef gg* — called also *Shakespearean sonnet*

English sparrow *n* : a sparrow (*Passer domesticus*) native to most of Europe and parts of Asia that has been intentionally introduced into America, Australia, New Zealand and elsewhere to destroy insects although it feeds largely on grain seeds — called also *house sparrow*

English springer spaniel *n* : any of a breed of springer spaniels that may have originated in Spain and are characterized by deep-bodied muscular build and a moderately long straight or slightly wavy silky coat usu. of black and white hair — called also *English springer*

English toy spaniel *n* : any of a breed of small blocky spaniels with well-rounded upper skull projecting forward toward the short turned-up nose

English walnut *n* : a Eurasian walnut (*Juglans regia*) valued for its large edible nut and its hard richly figured wood; *also* : its nut

En·glish·wom·an \ˈiŋ-glish-ˌwu̇m-ən *also* ˈiŋ-lish-\ *n* : a woman of English birth, nationality, or origin

English yew *n* : YEW 1a

en·glut \in-ˈglət\ *vt* **en·glut·ted; en·glut·ting** [MF *engloutir,* fr. LL *inglutire,* fr. L *in-* + *gluttire* to swallow — more at GLUTTON] : to gulp down : SWALLOW

en·gorge \in-ˈgȯ(ə)rj\ *vb* [MF *engorgier,* fr. OF, to devour, fr. *en-* + *gorge* throat — more at GORGE] *vt* : GORGE, GLUT; *specif* : to fill with blood to the point of congestion ~ *vi* : to suck blood to the limit of body capacity — **en·gorge·ment** \-mənt\ *n*

engr *abbr* **1** engineer **2** engraved; engraver; engraving

en·graft \in-ˈgraft\ *vt* **1** : GRAFT 1, 3 ⟨~*ed* embryonic gill tissue into the back⟩ **2** : to join or fasten as if by grafting

en·grailed \in-ˈgrā(ə)ld\ *adj* [ME *engreled,* fr. MF *engreslé,* fr. *en-* + *gresle* slender, fr. L *gracilis*] **1** : indented with small concave curves ⟨an ~ heraldic bordure⟩ **2** : made of or bordered by a circle of raised dots ⟨an ~ coin⟩

en·grain \in-ˈgrān\ *vt* : INGRAIN

en·gram *also* **en·gramme** \ˈen-ˌgram\ *n* [ISV] : MEMORY TRACE; *specif* : a hypothetical change in neural tissue postulated in order to account for persistence of memory — **en·gram·mic** \en-ˈgram-ik\ *adj*

en·grave \in-ˈgrāv\ *vt* **en·graved; en·grav·ing** [MF *engraver,* fr. *en-* + *graver* to grave, of Gmc origin; akin to OE *grafan* to grave] **1 a** : to form by incision (as on wood or metal) **b** : to impress deeply as if with a graver ⟨the incident was *engraved* in his memory⟩ **2 a** : to cut figures, letters, or devices on for printing; *also* : to print from an engraved plate **b** : PHOTOENGRAVE — **en·grav·er** *n*

en·grav·ing *n* **1** : the act or process of one that engraves **2** : something that is engraved: as **a** : an engraved printing surface **b** : engraved work **3** : an impression from an engraved printing surface

en·gross \in-ˈgrōs\ *vt* [ME *engrossen,* fr. AF *engrosser,* prob. fr. ML *ingrossare,* fr. L *in* + ML *grossa* large handwriting, fr. L, fem. of *grossus* thick] **1 a** : to copy or write in a large hand **b** : to prepare the usu. final handwritten or printed text of (an official document) **2** [ME *engrossen,* fr. MF *en gros* in large quantities] **a** : to purchase large quantities of (as for speculation) **b** *archaic* : AMASS, COLLECT **c** : to take or occupy the whole of ⟨ideas that have ~*ed* the minds of scholars for generations⟩ ***syn*** see MONOPOLIZE — **en·gross·er** *n*

en·grossed \-ˈgrōst\ *adj* : completely occupied or absorbed ⟨a scholar ~ in his research⟩ — **en·grossed·ly** \-ˈgrō-səd-lē, -ˈgrōst-lē\ *adv*

en·gross·ing \-ˈgrō-siŋ\ *adj* : taking up the attention completely : ABSORBING — **en·gross·ing·ly** \-siŋ-lē\ *adv*

en·gross·ment \in-ˈgrō-smənt\ *n* **1** : the act of engrossing **2** : the state of being absorbed or occupied : PREOCCUPATION

en·gulf \in-ˈgəlf\ *vt* **1** : to flow over and enclose : OVERWHELM ⟨the mounting seas threatened to ~ the island⟩ **2** : to take in (food) by or as if by flowing over and enclosing — **en·gulf·ment** \-mənt\ *n*

en·ha·lo \in-ˈhā-(ˌ)lō\ *vt* : to surround with or as if with a halo

en·hance \in-ˈhan(t)s\ *vt* **en·hanced; en·hanc·ing** [ME *enhauncen,* fr. AF *enhauncer,* alter. of OF *enhaucier,* fr. (assumed) VL *inaltiare,* fr. L *in* + *altus* high — more at OLD] **1** *obs* : RAISE **2** : to make greater (as in value, desirability, or attractiveness) : HEIGHTEN ⟨a hillside location *enhanced* by a broad vista⟩ ***syn*** see INTENSIFY — **en·hance·ment** \-ˈhan(t)-smənt\ *n*

en·har·mon·ic \ˌen-(ˌ)här-ˈmän-ik\ *adj* [F *enharmonique,* fr. MF, of a scale employing quarter tones, fr. Gk *enarmonios,* fr. *en* in + *harmonia* harmony, scale] : of, relating to, or being notes that are written differently (as A flat and G sharp) but sound the same — **en·har·mon·i·cal·ly** \-i-k(ə-)lē\ *adv*

enig·ma \i-ˈnig-mə\ *n* [L *aenigma,* fr. Gk *ainigmat-, ainigma,* fr. *ainissesthai* to speak in riddles, fr. *ainos* fable] **1** : an obscure speech or writing **2** : something hard to understand or explain **3** : an inscrutable or mysterious person ***syn*** see MYSTERY

enig·mat·ic \ˌen-(ˌ)ig-ˈmat-ik *also* ˌē-(ˌ)nig-\ *adj* : of, relating to, or resembling an enigma : PUZZLING ***syn*** see OBSCURE ***ant*** explicit — **enig·mat·i·cal** \-i-kəl\ *adj* — **enig·mat·i·cal·ly** \-i-k(ə-)lē\ *adv*

en·isle \in-ˈī(ə)l\ *vt* **1** : to place apart : ISOLATE **2** : to make an island of

en·jamb·ment \in-ˈjam-mənt\ *or* **en·jambe·ment** *same, or* än-zhäⁿb(-ə)mäⁿ\ *n* [F *enjambement,* fr. MF, encroachment, fr. *enjamber* to straddle, encroach on, fr. *en-* + *jambe* leg — more at JAMB] : the running over of a sentence from one verse or couplet into another so that closely related words fall in different lines — compare RUN-ON

en·join \in-ˈjȯin\ *vt* [ME *enjoinen,* fr. OF *enjoindre,* fr. L *injungere,* fr. *in-* + *jungere* to join — more at YOKE] **1** : to direct or impose by authoritative order or with urgent admonition **2** : FORBID, PROHIBIT ⟨was ~*ed* by conscience from telling a lie⟩ ***syn*** see COMMAND

en·joy \in-ˈjȯi\ *vt* [MF *enjoir,* fr. OF, fr. *en-* + *joir* to enjoy, fr. L *gaudēre* to rejoice — more at JOY] **1** : to take pleasure or satisfaction in **2** : to have for one's use, benefit, or lot ***syn*** see HAVE — **en·joy·able** \-ə-bəl\ *adj* — **en·joy·able·ness** *n* — **en·joy·ably** \-blē\ *adv*

en·joy·ment \in-ˈjȯi-mənt\ *n* **1 a** : the action or state of enjoying **b** : possession and use ⟨the ~ of civic rights⟩ **2** : something that gives keen satisfaction

en·kin·dle \in-ˈkin-dᵊl\ *vt* **1** : to set (as fuel) on fire **2** : to make bright and glowing ~ *vi* : to take fire : FLAME

enl *abbr* **1** enlarged **2** enlisted

en·lace \in-ˈlās\ *vt* [ME *enlacen,* fr. MF *enlacier,* fr. OF, fr. *en-* + *lacier* to lace] **1** : ENCIRCLE, ENFOLD **2** : ENTWINE, INTERLACE

en·lace·ment \in-ˈlā-smənt\ *n* **1** : the process or result of interlacing **2** : a pattern of interlacing elements

en·large \in-ˈlärj\ *vb* **en·larged; en·larg·ing** [ME *enlargen,* fr. MF *enlargier,* fr. OF, fr. *en-* + *large*] *vt* **1** : to make larger : EXTEND **2** : to give greater scope to : EXPAND **3** : to set free (as a captive) ~ *vi* **1** : to grow larger **2** : to speak or write at length : ELABORATE ⟨let me ~ upon that point⟩ ***syn*** see INCREASE — **en·large·able** \-ˈlär-jə-bəl\ *adj* — **en·larg·er** *n*

en·large·ment \in-ˈlärj-mənt\ *n* **1** : an act or instance of enlarging : the state of being enlarged **2** : a photographic print that is larger than the negative and that is made by projecting through a lens an image of the negative upon a photographic printing surface

en·light·en \in-ˈlīt-ᵊn\ *vt* **en·light·ened; en·light·en·ing** \-ˈlīt-niŋ, -ᵊn-iŋ\ **1** *archaic* : ILLUMINATE **2 a** : to furnish knowledge to : INSTRUCT **b** : to give spiritual insight to

en·light·ened *adj* **1** : freed from ignorance and misinformation ⟨an ~ people⟩ **2** : based on full comprehension of the problems involved ⟨issued an ~ ruling⟩

en·light·en·ment \in-ˈlīt-ᵊn-mənt\ *n* **1** : the act or means of enlightening : the state of being enlightened **2** *cap* : a philosophic movement of the 18th century marked by questioning of traditional doctrines and values, a tendency toward individualism, and

ə abut	ᵊ kitten	ər further	a back	ā bake	ä cot, cart
au̇ out	ch chin	e less	ē easy	g gift	i trip	ī life
j joke	ŋ sing	ō flow	ȯ flaw	ȯi coin	th thin	t͟h this
ü loot	u̇ foot	y yet	yü few	yu̇ furious	zh vision

an emphasis on the idea of universal human progress, the empirical method in science, and the free use of reason — used with *the* **3** *Buddhism* : a final blessed state marked by the absence of desire or suffering

en·list \in-'list\ *vt* **1** : to engage (a person) for duty in the armed forces **2 a** : to secure the support and aid of : employ in advancing an interest ⟨~ all the available resources⟩ ⟨~ the community in an experiment⟩ **b** : to win over : ATTRACT ⟨trying to ~ my sympathies⟩ ~ *vi* **1** : to enroll oneself in the armed forces **2** : to participate heartily (as in a cause, drive, or crusade) — **en·list·ee** \-,lis-'tē\ *n* — **en·list·ment** \-'lis(t)-mənt\ *n*

en·list·ed \-'lis-təd\ *adj* : of, relating to, or constituting the part of a military or naval force below commissioned or warrant officers

enlisted man *n* : a man or woman in the armed forces ranking below a commissioned or warrant officer; *specif* : an enlisted man ranking below a noncommissioned officer or petty officer

en·liv·en \in-'lī-vən\ *vt* : to give life, action, or spirit to : ANIMATE **syn** see QUICKEN **ant** deaden, subdue

en masse \äⁿ(n)-'mas\ *adv* [F] : in a body : as a whole

en·mesh \in-'mesh\ *vt* : to catch or entangle in or as if in meshes — **en·mesh·ment** \-mənt\ *n*

en·mi·ty \'en-mət-ē\ *n, pl* **-ties** [ME *enmite,* fr. MF *enemité,* fr. OF *enemisté,* irreg. fr. *enemi* enemy] : positive, active, and typically mutual hatred or ill will

syn ENMITY, HOSTILITY, ANTIPATHY, ANTAGONISM, RANCOR, ANIMOSITY, ANIMUS *shared meaning element* : deep-seated dislike or ill will or a manifestation of such feeling **ant** amity

en·ne·ad \'en-ē-,ad\ *n* [Gk *ennead-, enneas,* fr. *ennea* nine — more at NINE] : a group of nine

en·no·ble \in-'ō-bəl\ *vt* **en·no·bled; en·no·bling** \-b(ə-)liŋ\ [ME *ennobelen,* fr. MF *ennoblir,* fr. OF, fr. *en-* + *noble*] **1** : to make noble : ELEVATE ⟨believes that hard work ~s the human spirit⟩ **2** : to raise to the rank of nobility — **en·no·ble·ment** \-bəl-mənt\ *n* — **en·no·bler** \-b(ə-)lər\ *n*

en·nui \'än-'wē\ *n* [F, fr. OF *enui* annoyance, fr. *enuier* to annoy] : a feeling of weariness and dissatisfaction : BOREDOM

Enoch \'ē-nək, -nik\ *n* [Gk *Enōch,* fr. Heb *Ḥănōkh*] : an Old Testament patriarch and father of Methuselah

enol \'ē-,nȯl, -,nōl\ *n* [ISV *ene-* (fr. *-ene*) + *-ol*] : an organic compound that contains a hydroxyl group bonded to a carbon atom having a double bond and that is usu. characterized by the grouping C=C(OH) — **eno·lic** \ē-'nō-lik, -'näl-ik\ *adj*

eno·lase \'ē-nə-,lās, -,lāz\ *n* [ISV *enol* + *-ase*] : a crystalline enzyme that is found esp. in muscle and yeast and is important in the metabolism of carbohydrates

enol·o·gy \ē-'näl-ə-jē\ *n* [Gk *oinos* wine + E *-logy* — more at WINE] : a science that deals with wine and wine making — **enol·o·gist** \-jəst\ *n*

enor·mi·ty \i-'nȯr-mət-ē\ *n, pl* **-ties** **1** : the quality or state of being immoderate, monstrous, or outrageous; *esp* : great wickedness **2** : a grave offense against order, right, or decency **3** : the quality or state of being huge : IMMENSITY ⟨the ~ of the task of teachers in slum schools —J. B. Conant⟩

enor·mous \i-'nȯr-məs\ *adj* [L *enormis,* fr. *e, ex* out of + *norma* rule] **1 a** *archaic* : ABNORMAL, INORDINATE **b** : exceedingly wicked : SHOCKING ⟨an ~ sin⟩ **2** : marked by extraordinarily great size, number, or degree; *esp* : exceeding usual bounds or accepted notions **syn** see HUGE — **enor·mous·ly** *adv* — **enor·mous·ness** *n*

¹enough \i-'nəf; *after* t, d, s, z *often* ᵊn-'əf\ *adj* [ME *ynough,* fr. OE *genōg;* akin to OHG *ginuog* enough; both fr. a prehistoric Gmc compound whose first constituent is represented by OE *ge-* (perfective prefix) and whose second constituent is akin to L *nancisci* to get, Gk *enenkein* to carry] : occurring in such quantity, quality, or scope as to fully satisfy demands or needs **syn** see SUFFICIENT

²enough *adv* **1** : in or to a degree or quantity that satisfies or that is sufficient or necessary for satisfaction : SUFFICIENTLY **2** : FULLY, QUITE **3** : in a tolerable degree

³enough *pron* : a sufficient number, quantity, or amount ⟨~ were present to constitute a quorum⟩ ⟨had ~ of their foolishness⟩

enounce \ē-'naů(n)s\ *vt* **enounced; enounc·ing** [F *énoncer,* fr. L *enuntiare* to report — more at ENUNCIATE] **1** : to set forth or state (as a proposition) **2** : to pronounce distinctly : ARTICULATE

enow \i-'naů\ *adv or adj* [ME *inow,* fr. OE *genōg*] *archaic* : ENOUGH

en pas·sant \,äⁿ-,pä-'säⁿ, -pə-\ *adv* [F] : in passing — used in chess of the capture of a pawn as it makes a first move of two squares by an enemy pawn in a position to threaten the first of these squares

en·phy·tot·ic \,en-fī-'tät-ik\ *adj* [²*en-* + *phyt-* + *-otic*] *of a plant disease* : occurring regularly in a district but only in moderate severity — **enphytotic** *n*

en·plane \in-'plān\ *vi* : to board an airplane

en prise \äⁿ-prēz\ *adj* [F] *of a chess piece* : exposed to capture

en quad *n* [fr. its use for the letter *n*] : a quad whose set dimension is one half that of an em quad

en·quire \in-'kwī(ə)r\, **en·qui·ry** \'in-,kwī(ə)r-ē, in-'; 'in-kwə-rē, 'iŋ-\ *var of* INQUIRE, INQUIRY

en·rage \in-'rāj\ *vt* [MF *enrager* to become mad, fr. OF *enragier,* fr. *en-* + *rage*] : to fill with rage : ANGER

en rap·port \,äⁿ-rə-'pō(ə)r, -'pȯ(ə)r\ *adj* [F] : being in a state of mutual accord and harmony ⟨we finished the drive in silence; spiritually we were not *en rapport* —W. A. Percy⟩

en·rapt \in-'rapt\ *adj* : wholly absorbed : RAPT; *also* : filled with delight

en·rap·ture \in-'rap-chər\ *vt* **en·rap·tured; en·rap·tur·ing** \-'rap-chə-riŋ, -'rap-shriŋ\ : to fill with delight **syn** see TRANSPORT

en·reg·is·ter \in-'rej-ə-stər\ *vt* [MF *enregistrer,* fr. OF, fr. *en-* + *registre* register] : to put on record

en·rich \in-'rich\ *vt* [ME *enrichen,* fr. MF *enrichir,* fr. OF, fr. *en-* + *riche* rich] **1** : to make rich or richer ⟨~*ing* himself in the stock market⟩ ⟨~*es* his cultural life by going to museums, concerts, and plays⟩ **2** : ADORN, ORNAMENT ⟨~*ing* the ceiling with frescoes⟩ **3 a** : to make richer in some quality ⟨~ the gravy with a little flour browned in butter⟩ **b** : to make (soil) more fertile **c** : to improve (a food) in nutritive value by adding nutrients (as vitamins or amino acids) and esp. by restoring part of the nutrients wasted in processing **d** : to increase the proportion of a valuable or desirable ingredient in ⟨~ uranium in uranium 235⟩; *also* : to add a desirable substance to ⟨~ natural gas⟩ **4** : to expand (a course of study) by increasing the variety of subjects and the depth of treatment ⟨an ~*ed* curriculum for the brighter students⟩ — **en·rich·er** *n* — **en·rich·ment** \-'rich-mənt\ *n*

en·robe \in-'rōb\ *vt* : to invest or adorn with or as if with a robe

en·roll *or* **en·rol** \in-'rōl\ *vb* **en·rolled; en·roll·ing** [ME *enrollen,* fr. MF *enroller,* fr. *en-* + *rolle* roll, register] *vt* **1** : to insert, register, or enter in a list, catalog, or roll ⟨the school ~*s* about 800 pupils⟩ **2** : to prepare a final perfect copy of (a bill passed by a legislature) in written or printed form **3** : to roll or wrap up ~ *vi* : to enroll oneself or cause oneself to be enrolled ⟨he ~*ed* in the history course⟩ — **en·roll·ee** \-rō-'lē\ *n* — **en·roll·ment** \-'rōl-mənt\ *n*

en·root \in-'rüt, -'růt\ *vt* : to fix or implant by or as if by roots : ESTABLISH

en route \äⁿ(n)-'rüt, en-, in-\ *adv or adj* [F] : on or along the way ⟨he reads *en route*⟩ ⟨arrived early in spite of *en route* delays⟩

ENS *abbr* ensign

en·sam·ple \in-'sam-pəl\ *n* [ME, fr. MF *ensample, example*] : EXAMPLE, INSTANCE

en·san·guine \in-'saŋ-gwən\ *vt* **-guined; -guin·ing** **1** : to make bloody **2** : CRIMSON

en·sconce \in-'skän(t)s\ *vt* **en·sconced; en·sconc·ing** **1** : SHELTER, CONCEAL **2** : to settle comfortably or snugly ⟨*ensconced* herself before the blazing hearth⟩

enscroll *var of* INSCROLL

en·sem·ble \äⁿ(n)-'säm-bəl\ *n* [F, fr. *ensemble* together, fr. L *insimul* at the same time, fr. *in-* + *simul* at the same time — more at SAME] : a group constituting an organic whole or producing together a single effect: as **a** : concerted music of two or more parts **b** : a complete costume of harmonizing or complementary pieces **c (1)** : the musicians engaged in the performance of a musical ensemble **c (2)** : a group of supporting players, singers, or dancers; *esp* : CORPS DE BALLET

ensemble acting *n* : a system of theatrical presentation in which balanced casting and careful integration of the whole performance replace the star system

en·serf \in-'sərf\ *vt* : to deprive of liberty and personal rights — **en·serf·ment** \-mənt\ *n*

en·sheathe \in-'shēth\ *vt* : to cover with or as if with a sheath

en·shrine \in-'shrīn, *esp South* -'srīn\ *vt* **1** : to enclose in or as if in a shrine **2** : to preserve or cherish as sacred — **en·shrine·ment** \-mənt\ *n*

en·shroud \in-'shraůd, *esp South* -'sraůd\ *vt* : to cover or enclose with or as if with a shroud

en·si·form \'en(t)-sə-,fȯrm\ *adj* [F *ensiforme,* fr. L *ensis* sword + F *-forme* -form; akin to Skt *asi* sword] : having sharp edges and tapering to a slender point ⟨~ leaves of the gladiolus⟩

en·sign \'en(t)-sən, *also* 'en-,sīn *for 1, 2, & 3a*\ *n* [ME *ensigne,* fr. MF *enseigne,* fr. L *insignia* insignia, flags] **1** : a flag that is flown (as by a ship) as the symbol of nationality and that may also be flown with a distinctive badge added to its design (as by an organization having nautical associations) **2 a** : a badge of office, rank, or power **b** : EMBLEM, SIGN **3 a** *archaic* : STANDARD-BEARER **b** : a commissioned officer in the navy or coast guard ranking above a chief warrant officer and below a lieutenant junior grade

en·si·lage \'en(t)-s(ə-)lij, *for 1 also* in-'sī-lij\ *n* **1** : the process of preserving fodder by ensiling **2** : SILAGE

en·sile \en-'sī(ə)l, in-\ *vt* **en·siled; en·sil·ing** [F *ensiler,* fr. *en-* + *silo,* fr. Sp] : to prepare and store (fodder) for silage in a tight silo or pit

en·sky \in-'skī\ *vt* : to lift to or as if to the skies or heaven : EXALT

en·slave \in-'slāv\ *vt* : to reduce to or as if to slavery : SUBJUGATE — **en·slave·ment** \-mənt\ *n* — **en·slav·er** *n*

en·snare \in-'sna(ə)r, -'sne(ə)r\ *vt* : to take in or as if in a snare **syn** see CATCH

en·snarl \in-'snär(ə)l\ *vt* : to involve in a snarl

en·soul \in-'sōl\ *vt* : to endow or imbue with a soul

en·sphere \in-'sfi(ə)r\ *vt* : to enclose in or as if in a sphere

en·sue \in-'sü\ *vb* **en·sued; en·su·ing** [ME *ensuen,* fr. MF *ensuivre,* fr. OF, fr. *en-* + *suivre* to follow — more at SUE] *vt* : to strive to attain : PURSUE ⟨I wander, seeking peace, and *ensuing* it —Rupert Brooke⟩ ~ *vi* : to take place afterward or as a result **syn** see FOLLOW

en suite \äⁿ-'swēt\ *adv or adj* [F] : in a succession, series, or set

en·sure \in-'shů(ə)r\ *vt* **en·sured; en·sur·ing** [ME *ensuren,* fr. AF *enseurer,* prob. alter. of OF *aseürer* — more at ASSURE] : to make sure, certain, or safe : GUARANTEE

syn ENSURE, INSURE, ASSURE, SECURE *shared meaning element* : to make an outcome sure

en·swathe \in-'swāth, -'swōth, -'swäth\ *vt* : to enfold or enclose with or as if with a covering : SWATHE

ent- *or* **ento-** *comb form* [NL, fr. Gk *entos* within; akin to L *intus* within, Gk *en* in — more at IN] : inner : within ⟨*ento*blast⟩

en·tab·la·ture \in-'tab-lə-,chů(ə)r, -chər, -,t(y)ů(ə)r\ *n* [obs. F, modif. of It *intavolatura,* fr. *intavolare* to put on a board or table, fr. *in-* (fr. L) + *tavola* board, table, fr. L *tabula* — more at TABLE] : the upper section of a wall or story that is usu. supported on columns or pilasters and that in classical orders consists of architrave, frieze, and cornice; *also* : a similar part (as an elevated support for a machine part)

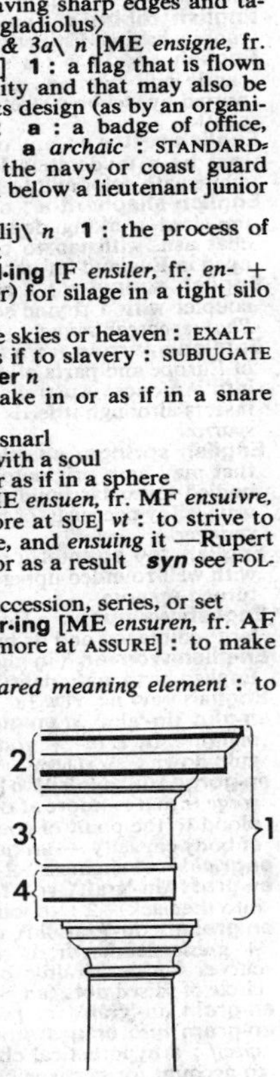

1 entablature, *2* cornice, *3* frieze, *4* architrave

en·ta·ble·ment \in-'tā-bəl-mənt, äⁿ-tä-blə-mäⁿ\ *n* [F, fr. OF, fr. *en-* + *table*]

: a platform that supports a statue and that is placed above the dado

¹en·tail \in-ˈtā(ə)l\ *vt* **1** : to restrict (property) by limiting the inheritance to the owner's lineal descendants or to a particular class thereof (as his male children) **2 a** : to confer, assign, or transmit as if by entail : FASTEN ⟨~*ed* on them indelible disgrace —Robert Browning⟩ **b** : to fix (a person) permanently in some condition or status ⟨~ him and his heirs unto the crown —Shak.⟩ **3** : to impose, involve, or imply as a necessary accompaniment or result ⟨the project will ~ considerable expense⟩ — **en·tail·er** \-ˈtā-lər\ *n* — **en·tail·ment** \-ˈtā(ə)l-mənt\ *n*

²en·tail \ˈen-ˌtāl, in-ˈtā(ə)l\ *n* **1 a** : an entailing esp. of lands **b** : an entailed estate **c** : the rule fixing the descent **2** : something (as a quality) transmitted as if by entail

ent·amoe·ba \ˌent-ə-ˈmē-bə\ *n* : an endamoeba esp. of a vertebrate

en·tan·gle \in-ˈtaŋ-gəl\ *vt* **1** : to make tangled, complicated, or confused ⟨his explanation only served to ~ the question further⟩ **2** : to involve in a tangle ⟨become *entangled* in a ruinous lawsuit⟩ — **en·tan·gler** \-g(ə-)lər\ *n*

en·tan·gle·ment \in-ˈtaŋ-gəl-mənt\ *n* **1 a** : the action of entangling : the state of being entangled **b** : something that entangles, confuses, or ensnares **2** : the condition of being deeply involved

en·tel·e·chy \en-ˈtel-ə-kē, in-\ *n, pl* **-chies** [LL *entelechia*, fr. Gk *entelecheia*] **1** : the realization of form-giving cause as contrasted with potential existence **2** : a hypothetical agency that in some vitalist doctrines is considered inherent in living substances and regulates or directs the vital processes of an organism but is not discoverable by scientific investigation

en·tente \än-ˈtänt\ *n* [F, fr. OF, intent, understanding — more at INTENT] **1** : an international understanding providing for a common course of action **2** : a coalition of parties to an entente

en·ter \ˈent-ər\ *vb* **en·tered; en·ter·ing** \ˈent-ə-riŋ, ˈen-triŋ\ [ME *entren*, fr. OF *entrer*, fr. L *intrare*, fr. *intra* within; akin to L *inter* between — more at INTER-] *vi* **1** : to go or come in **2** : to come or gain admission into a group : JOIN **3 a** : to make a beginning ⟨~*ing* upon a career⟩ **b** : to begin to consider a subject **4** : to go upon land for the purpose of taking possession **5** : to play a part : be a factor ⟨~ into a conversation⟩ ~ *vt* **1** : to come or go into ⟨~ a room⟩ **2** : INSCRIBE, REGISTER ⟨~ the names of qualified voters⟩ **3** : to cause to be received or admitted ⟨~ a boy at a school⟩ **4** : to put in : INSERT **5 a** : to make a beginning in : take up ⟨~ politics⟩ **b** : to pass within the limits of (a particular period of time) ⟨was famous by the time he ~*ed* his early thirties⟩ **6** : to become a member of or an active participant in ⟨~ the university⟩ ⟨~ a race⟩ **7** : to make report of (a ship or her cargo) to customs authorities **8** : to place in proper form before a court of law or upon record ⟨~ a writ⟩ **9** : to go into or upon and take actual possession of (as land) **10** : to put formally on record ⟨~*ing* a complaint against his business partner⟩ — **en·ter·able** \ˈent-ə-rə-bəl, ˈen-trə-\ *adj*

syn ENTER, PENETRATE, PIERCE, PROBE *shared meaning element* : to make way into something ***ant*** issue (*from or out*)

— **enter into** **1** : EXAMINE, CONSIDER ⟨the book doesn't *enter into* the moral aspect of the issue⟩ **2** : to make oneself a party to or in ⟨*enter into* an important agreement⟩ **3** : to form a constituent part of ⟨tin *enters into* the composition of pewter⟩ **4 a** : to participate or share in ⟨cheerfully *entering into* the household tasks⟩ **b** : to be in tune or sympathy with ⟨couldn't *enter into* the festive spirit of the occasion⟩

enter- *or* **entero-** *comb form* [Gk, fr. *enteron*] : intestine ⟨*enter*itis⟩

en·ter·al \ˈent-ə-rəl\ *adj* : ENTERIC — **en·ter·al·ly** \-rə-lē\ *adv*

en·ter·ic \en-ˈter-ik, in-\ *adj* **1** : of or relating to the intestines; *broadly* : ALIMENTARY **2** : of, relating to, or being a medicinal preparation treated to pass through the stomach unaltered and disintegrate in the intestines

en·ter·it·i·dis \ˌent-ə-ˈrit-əd-əs, -ˈrīt-\ *n* [NL (*Salmonella*) *enteritidis*, species of bacteria] : enteritis esp. in young animals

en·ter·i·tis \ˌent-ə-ˈrīt-əs\ *n* **1** : inflammation of the intestines and esp. of the human ileum **2** : a disease of domestic animals (as panleucopenia of cats) marked by enteritis and diarrhea

en·tero·bac·te·ri·um \ˌent-ə-rō-bak-ˈtir-ē-əm\ *n* : any of a family (Enterobacteriaceae) of gram-negative straight rod bacteria (as a salmonella or a colon bacillus) that ferment glucose and include saprophytes as well as some serious pathogens of man, lower animals, and plants — **en·tero·bac·te·ri·al** \-ē-əl\ *adj*

en·tero·bi·a·sis \-ˈbī-ə-səs\ *n, pl* **-a·ses** \-ˌsēz\ [NL, fr. *Enterobius*, genus name + *-iasis*] : infestation with or disease caused by pinworms (genus *Enterobius*) that occurs esp. in children

en·tero·chro·maf·fin \-ˈkrō-mə-fən\ *adj* [*enter-* + *chromaffin*] : of or relating to epithelial cells of the intestinal mucosa that stain esp. with chromium salts and usu. contain serotonin

en·tero·coc·cus \-ˈkäk-əs\ *n*, **-coc·ci** \-ˈkäk-ˌ(s)ī, -ˈkäk-(ˌ)(s)ē\ [NL, genus name] : STREPTOCOCCUS; *esp* : a streptococcus (as *Streptococcus faecalis*) normally present in the intestine — **en·tero·coc·cal** \-ˈkäk-əl\ *adj*

en·tero·coele *or* **en·tero·coel** \ˈent-ə-rō-ˌsēl\ *n* : a coelom originating by outgrowth from the archenteron — **en·tero·coe·lic** \ˌent-ə-rō-ˈsē-lik\ *adj* — **en·tero·coe·lous** \-ləs\ *adj*

en·tero·co·li·tis \ˌent-ərō-kə-ˈlīt-əs\ *n* [NL] : enteritis affecting both the large and small intestine

en·tero·gas·trone \-ˈgas-ˌtrōn\ *n* [*enter-* + *gastr-* + *hormone*] : a hormone that is produced by the duodenal mucosa and has an inhibitory action on gastric motility and secretion

en·tero·hep·a·ti·tis \-ˌhep-ə-ˈtīt-əs\ *n* [NL] : BLACKHEAD 2

en·tero·ki·nase \ˌent-ə-rō-ˈkī-ˌnās, -ˌnāz\ *n* [ISV] : an enzyme esp. of the upper intestinal mucosa that activates trypsinogen by converting it to trypsin

en·ter·on \ˈent-ə-ˌrän, -rən\ *n* [NL, fr. Gk, intestine — more at INTER-] : the alimentary canal or system — used esp. of the embryo

en·tero·patho·gen·ic \ˌent-ə-rō-ˌpath-ə-ˈjen-ik\ *adj* : tending to produce disease in the intestinal tract ⟨~ bacteria⟩

en·ter·op·a·thy \ˌent-ə-ˈräp-ə-thē\ *n* : a disease of the intestinal tract

en·ter·os·to·my \ˌent-ə-ˈräs-tə-mē\ *n, pl* **-mies** [ISV] : a surgical formation of an opening into the intestine through the abdominal wall

en·tero·tox·in \ˌent-ə-rō-ˈtäk-sən\ *n* : a toxic substance that is produced by microorganisms (as some staphylococci) and is responsible for the gastrointestinal symptoms of some forms of food poisoning

en·tero·vi·rus \-ˈvī-rəs\ *n* [NL] : any of a group of picornaviruses (as a Coxsackie virus) that typically occur in the gastrointestinal tract but may be involved in respiratory ailments, meningitis, and neurological disorders — **en·tero·vi·ral** \-rəl\ *adj*

en·ter·prise \ˈent-ə(r)-ˌprīz\ *n* [ME *enterprise*, fr. MF *entreprise*, fr. *entreprendre* to undertake, fr. *entre-* inter- + *prendre* to take — more at PRIZE] **1** : a project or undertaking that is esp. difficult, complicated, or risky **2 a** : a unit of economic organization or activity; *esp* : a business organization **b** : a systematic purposeful activity ⟨agriculture is the main economic ~ among these people⟩ **3** : readiness to engage in daring action : INITIATIVE

en·ter·pris·er \-ˌprī-zər\ *n* : one who undertakes an enterprise; *specif* : ENTREPRENEUR

en·ter·pris·ing \-ˌprī-ziŋ\ *adj* : marked by an independent energetic spirit and by readiness to undertake or experiment

en·ter·tain \ˌent-ər-ˈtān\ *vb* [ME *entertinen*, fr. MF *entretenir*, fr. *entre-* inter- + *tenir* to hold — more at TENABLE] *vt* **1 a** *archaic* : MAINTAIN **b** *obs* : RECEIVE **2** : to show hospitality to **3 a** : to keep, hold, or maintain in the mind : HARBOR ⟨I ~ grave doubts about her sincerity⟩ **b** (1) : to receive and take into consideration ⟨he refused to ~ her plea⟩ (2) : TREAT, CONSIDER ⟨~ a subject⟩ **4** : to provide entertainment for **5** : to play against (an opposing team) on one's home field or court ~ *vi* : to provide entertainment esp. for guests ***syn*** see AMUSE — **en·ter·tain·er** *n*

en·ter·tain·ing *adj* : providing entertainment : DIVERTING — **en·ter·tain·ing·ly** \-ˈtā-niŋ-lē\ *adv*

en·ter·tain·ment \ˌent-ər-ˈtān-mənt\ *n* **1** : the act of entertaining **2 a** *archaic* : MAINTENANCE, PROVISION **b** *obs* : EMPLOYMENT **3** : something diverting or engaging: as **a** : a public performance **b** : a usu. light comic or adventure novel

en·thal·py \ˈen-ˌthal-pē, en-ˈ\ *n* [*en-* + Gk *thalpein* to heat] : the sum of the internal energy of a body and the product of its volume multiplied by the pressure

en·thrall *or* **en·thral** \in-ˈthrȯl\ *vt* **en·thralled; en·thrall·ing** **1** : to hold in or reduce to slavery **2** : to hold spellbound : CHARM — **en·thrall·ment** *or* **en·thral·ment** \-ˈthrȯl-mənt\ *n*

en·throne \in-ˈthrōn\ *vt* **1 a** : to seat ceremonially on a throne **b** : to seat in a place associated with a position of authority or influence **2** : to assign supreme virtue or value to : EXALT — **en·throne·ment** \-mənt\ *n*

en·thuse \in-ˈth(y)üz\ *vb* **en·thused; en·thus·ing** [back-formation fr. *enthusiasm*] *vt* : to make enthusiastic ⟨proposals which . . . shocked the orthodox and *enthused* the rebellious —*Times Lit. Supp.*⟩ ~ *vi* : to show enthusiasm ⟨tourists *enthusing* over a moribund culture —R. J. Clements⟩ ***syn*** see THRILL

en·thu·si·asm \in-ˈth(y)ü-zē-ˌaz-əm\ *n* [Gk *enthousiasmos*, fr. *enthousiazein* to be inspired, fr. *entheos* inspired, fr. *en-* + *theos* god] **1 a** : belief in special revelations of the Holy Spirit **b** : religious fanaticism **2 a** : strong excitement of feeling : ARDOR **b** : something inspiring zeal or fervor ***syn*** see PASSION

en·thu·si·ast \-ˌast, -əst\ *n* : a person filled with enthusiasm: as **a** : one who is ardently attached to a cause, object, or pursuit ⟨he's a sports car ~⟩ **b** : one who tends to give himself completely to whatever engages his interest

en·thu·si·as·tic \in-ˌth(y)ü-zē-ˈas-tik\ *adj* : filled with or marked by enthusiasm — **en·thu·si·as·ti·cal·ly** \-ti-k(ə-)lē\ *adv*

en·thy·meme \ˈen(t)-thi-ˌmēm\ *n* [L *enthymema*, fr. Gk *enthymēma*, fr. *enthymeisthai* to keep in mind, fr. *en-* + *thymos* mind, soul — more at FUME] : a syllogism in which one of the premises is implicit

en·tice \in-ˈtīs\ *vt* **en·ticed; en·tic·ing** [ME *enticen*, fr. OF *enticier*, fr. (assumed) VL *intitiare*, fr. L *in-* + *titio* firebrand] : to draw on artfully or adroitly or by arousing hope or desire : TEMPT ***syn*** see LURE ***ant*** scare — **en·tice·ment** \-ˈtī-smənt\ *n*

¹en·tire \in-ˈtī(ə)r, ˈen-ˌ\ *adj* [ME, fr. MF *entir*, fr. L *integer*, lit., untouched, fr. *in-* + *tangere* to touch — more at TANGENT] **1** : having no element or part left out : WHOLE ⟨was alone the ~ day⟩ **2** : complete in degree : TOTAL ⟨his ~ devotion to his family⟩ **3 a** : consisting of one piece **b** : HOMOGENEOUS, UNMIXED **c** : INTACT ⟨strove to keep the collection ~⟩ **4** : not castrated **5** : having the margin continuous or free from indentations ⟨an ~ leaf⟩ — **entire** *adv* — **en·tire·ness** *n*

²entire *n* **1** *archaic* : the whole : ENTIRETY **2** : STALLION

en·tire·ly *adv* **1** : in a whole, complete, or full manner ⟨agreed with me ~⟩ ⟨you are ~ welcome⟩ **2** : in an exclusive manner : SOLELY ⟨it is his fault ~⟩

en·tire·ty \in-ˈtī-rət-ē, -ˈtī-(ə)rt-ē\ *n, pl* **-ties** **1** : the state of being entire or complete **2** : SUM TOTAL, WHOLE

en·ti·tle \in-ˈtīt-ᵊl\ *vt* **en·ti·tled; en·ti·tling** \-ˈtīt-liŋ, -ᵊl-iŋ\ [ME *entitlen*, fr. MF *entituler*, fr. LL *intitulare*, fr. L *in-* + *-titulus* title] **1** : to give a title to : DESIGNATE **2** : to furnish with proper grounds for seeking or claiming something ⟨this ticket ~*s* the bearer to free admission⟩ — **en·ti·tle·ment** \-ˈtīt-ᵊl-mənt\ *n*

en·ti·ty \ˈen(t)-ət-ē\ *n, pl* **-ties** [ML *entitas*, fr. L *ent-*, *ens* existing thing, fr. coined prp. of *esse* to be — more at IS] **1 a** : BEING, EXISTENCE; *esp* : independent, separate, or self-contained existence **b** : the existence of a thing as contrasted with its attributes **2** : something that has separate and distinct existence and objective or conceptual reality

ə abut ᵊ kitten ər further a back ā bake ä cot, cart
au̇ out ch chin e less ē easy g gift i trip ī life
j joke ŋ sing ō flow ȯ flaw ȯi coin th thin t͟h this
ü loot u̇ foot y yet yü few yu̇ furious zh vision

ento- — see ENT-

en·to·blast \ˈent-ə-ˌblast\ *n* **1 :** HYPOBLAST **2 :** a blastomere producing endoderm — **en·to·blas·tic** \ˌent-ə-ˈblas-tik\ *adj*

en·to·derm \ˈent-ə-ˌdərm\ *n* **:** ENDODERM — **en·to·der·mal** \ˌent-ə-ˈdər-məl\ *or* **en·to·der·mic** \-mik\ *adj*

en·toil \in-ˈtȯi(ə)l\ *vt* **:** ENTRAP, ENMESH

entom *or* **entomol** *abbr* entomological; entomology

entom- *or* **entomo-** *comb form* [F, fr. Gk *entomon*] **:** insect ⟨*entomophagous*⟩

en·tomb \in-ˈtüm\ *vt* [ME *entoumben*, fr. MF *entomber*, fr. *en-* + *tombe* tomb] **1 :** to deposit in a tomb **:** BURY **2 :** to serve as a tomb for — **en·tomb·ment** \-ˈtüm-mənt\ *n*

en·to·mo·fau·na \ˌent-ə-mō-ˈfȯn-ə, -ˈfän-\ *n* [NL] **:** a fauna of insects **:** the insects of an environment or region

en·to·mol·o·gy \ˌent-ə-ˈmäl-ə-jē\ *n* [F *entomologie*, fr. Gk *entomon* insect (fr. neut. of *entomos* cut up, fr. *en-* + *temnein* to cut) + F *-logie* -logy — more at TOME] **:** a branch of zoology that deals with insects — **en·to·mo·log·i·cal** \-mə-ˈläj-i-kəl\ *adj* — **en·to·mo·log·i·cal·ly** \-k(ə-)lē\ *adv* — **en·to·mol·o·gist** \ˌent-ə-ˈmäl-ə-jəst\ *n*

en·to·moph·a·gous \ˌent-ə-ˈmäf-ə-gəs\ *adj* **:** feeding on insects

en·to·moph·i·lous \ˌent-ə-ˈmäf-ə-ləs\ *adj* **:** being normally pollinated by insects — compare ZOOPHILOUS — **en·to·moph·i·ly** \-lē\ *n*

en·to·mos·tra·can \ˌent-ə-ˈmäs-tri-kən\ *n* [deriv. of *entom-* + Gk *ostrakon* shell — more at OYSTER] **:** any of numerous simple typically small crustaceans (as branchiopods, ostracods, copepods, and barnacles) sometimes placed in a subclass (Entomostraca) — **entomostracan** *or* **en·to·mos·tra·cous** \-kəs\ *adj*

en·to·proct \ˈent-ə-ˌpräkt\ *n* [deriv. of *ent-* + Gk *prōktos* anus] **:** any of a phylum (Entoprocta) of animals lacking a true coelom and having the anus adjacent to the mouth — **entoproct** *or* **en·to·proc·tous** \ˌent-ə-ˈpräk-təs\ *adj*

en·tou·rage \ˌän-tü-ˈräzh\ *n* [F, fr. MF, fr. *entourer* to surround, fr. *entour* around, fr. *en* in (fr. L *in*) + *tour* circuit — more at TURN] **1 :** one's attendants or associates **2 :** SURROUNDINGS

en·to·zoa \ˌent-ə-ˈzō-ə\ *n pl* [NL] **:** internal animal parasites; *esp* **:** the intestinal worms — **en·to·zo·an** \-ˈzō-ən\ *adj or n*

en·to·zo·ic \-ˈzō-ik\ *adj* **:** living within an animal ⟨an ~ ameba⟩

en·tr'acte \ˈäⁿ(n)-ˌtrakt, -ˌträkt, äⁿ(n)-ˈ\ *n* [F, fr. *entre-* inter- + *acte* act] **1 :** the interval between two acts of a play **2 :** a dance, piece of music, or interlude performed between two acts of a play

en·trails \ˈen-trəlz, -ˌtrālz\ *n pl* [ME *entrailles*, fr. MF, fr. ML *intralia*, alter. of L *interanea*, pl. of *interaneum* intestine, fr. neut. of *interaneus* interior] **:** GUTS, VISCERA; *broadly* **:** internal parts

¹en·train \in-ˈtrān\ *vt* [MF *entrainer*, fr. *en-* + *trainer* to draw, drag — more at TRAIN] **1 :** to draw along with or after oneself **2 :** to draw in and transport (as solid particles or gas) by the flow of a fluid **3 :** to incorporate (air bubbles) into concrete **4 :** to determine or modify the phase or period of ⟨circadian rhythms ~*ed* by a light cycle⟩ — **en·train·er** *n* — **en·train·ment** \-ˈtrān-mənt\ *n*

²entrain *vt* **:** to put aboard a train ~ *vi* **:** to go aboard a train

¹en·trance \ˈen-trən(t)s\ *n* **1 :** the act of entering **2 :** the means or place of entry **3 :** power or permission to enter **:** ADMISSION **4 :** the point at which a voice or instrument part begins in ensemble music **5 :** the first appearance of an actor in a scene

²en·trance \in-ˈtran(t)s\ *vt* **en·tranced; en·tranc·ing** **1 :** to put into a trance **2 :** to carry away with delight, wonder, or rapture *syn* see TRANSPORT — **en·trance·ment** \-ˈtran(t)-smənt\ *n*

en·trant \ˈen-trənt\ *n* **:** one that enters; *esp* **:** one that enters a contest

en·trap \in-ˈtrap\ *vt* [MF *entraper*, fr. *en-* + *trape* trap] **1 :** to catch in or as if in a trap **2 :** to lure into a compromising statement or act *syn* see CATCH — **en·trap·ment** \-mənt\ *n*

en·treat \in-ˈtrēt\ *vb* [ME *entreten*, fr. MF *entraitier*, fr. *en-* + *traitier* to treat — more at TREAT] *vt* **1** *archaic* **:** to deal with **:** TREAT **2 :** to plead with esp. in order to persuade **:** ask urgently ⟨~*ed* his boss for another chance⟩ ~ *vi* **1** *obs* **a :** NEGOTIATE **b :** INTERCEDE **2 :** to make an earnest request **:** PLEAD *syn* see BEG — **en·treat·ing·ly** \-iŋ-lē\ *adv* — **en·treat·ment** \-mənt\ *n*

en·treaty \in-ˈtrēt-ē\ *n, pl* **-treat·ies** **:** an act of entreating **:** PLEA

en·tre·chat \ˈäⁿ(n)-trə-ˌshä\ *n* [F] **:** a leap in which a ballet dancer repeatedly crosses the legs and sometimes beats them together

en·trée *or* **en·tree** \ˈän-ˌtrā *also* än-ˈ\ *n* [F *entrée*, fr. OF] **1 a :** the act or manner of entering **:** ENTRANCE **b :** freedom of entry or access ⟨had ~ into the best circles⟩ **2 :** the principal dish of the meal in the U.S.

en·tre·mets *as sing*, ˌäⁿ(n)-trə-ˈmā, *as pl* -ˈmā(z)\ *n pl but sing or pl in constr* [F, fr. OF *entremes*, fr. L *intermissus*, pp. of *intermittere* to intermit] **:** dishes served in addition to the main course of a meal

en·trench \in-ˈtrench\ *vt* **1 a :** to place within or surround with a trench esp. for defense **b :** to place (oneself) in a strong defensive position **c :** to establish solidly **:** CONFIRM ⟨pity only ~*es* him in his misery⟩ **2 :** to cut into **:** FURROW; *specif* **:** to erode downward so as to form a trench ~ *vi* **1 :** to dig or occupy a trench for defensive purposes **2 :** to enter upon or take over something unfairly, improperly, or unlawfully **:** ENCROACH — used with *on* or *upon* *syn* see TRESPASS — **en·trench·ment** \-mənt\ *n*

en·tre·pôt \ˈäⁿ(n)-trə-ˌpō\ *n* [F] **:** an intermediary center of trade and transshipment

en·tre·pre·neur \ˌäⁿn-trə-p(r)ə-ˈnər, -ˈn(y)u̇(ə)r\ *n* [F, fr. OF, fr. *entreprendre* to undertake] **:** one who organizes, manages, and assumes the risks of a business or enterprise — **en·tre·pre·neur·ial** \-ˈn(y)u̇r-ē-əl, -ˈnər-\ *adj* — **en·tre·pre·neur·ship** \-ˈnər-ˌship, -ˈn(y)u̇(ə)r-\ *n*

en·tre·sol \ˈäⁿ(n)-trə-ˌsäl, -ˌsȯl\ *n* [F] **:** MEZZANINE

en·tro·py \ˈen-trə-pē\ *n, pl* **-pies** [G *entropie*, fr. Gk *en-* + *trepein* to turn, change — more at TROPE] **1 a :** a measure of the unavailable energy in a closed thermodynamic system so related to the state of the system that a change in the measure varies with change in the ratio of the increment of heat taken in to the absolute temperature at which it is absorbed **b :** a measure of the disorder of a closed thermodynamic system in terms of a constant multiple of the natural logarithm of the probability of the occurrence of a particular molecular arrangement of the system that by suitable choice of a constant reduces to the measure of unavailable energy **2 :** a measure of the amount of information in a message that is based on the logarithm of the number of possible equivalent messages **3 :** the degradation of the matter and energy in the universe to an ultimate state of inert uniformity

en·trust \in-ˈtrəst\ *vt* **1 :** to confer a trust on; *esp* **:** to deliver something in trust to **2 :** to commit to another with confidence *syn* see COMMIT — **en·trust·ment** \-ˈtrəs(t)-mənt\ *n*

en·try \ˈen-trē\ *n, pl* **entries** [ME *entre*, fr. OF *entree*, fr. fem. of *entré*, pp. of *entrer* to enter] **1 :** the act of entering **:** ENTRANCE **2 :** the right or privilege of entering **:** ENTRÉE **3 :** a place of entrance: as **a :** VESTIBULE, PASSAGE **b :** DOOR, GATE **4 a :** the act of making or entering a record **b :** something entered: as (1) **:** a record or notation of an occurrence, transaction, or proceeding (2) **:** a descriptive record (as in a card catalog or an index) (3) **:** HEADWORD (4) **:** a headword with its definition or identification (5) **:** VOCABULARY ENTRY **5 :** a person, thing, or group entered in a contest

en·try·way \-trē-ˌwā\ *n* **:** a passage for entrance

entry word *n* **:** HEADWORD

en·twine \in-ˈtwīn\ *vt* **:** to twine together or around ~ *vi* **:** to become twisted or twined

en·twist \in-ˈtwist\ *vt* **:** ENTWINE

enu·cle·ate \(ˈ)ē-ˈn(y)ü-klē-ˌāt\ *vt* **-at·ed; -at·ing** [L *enucleatus*, pp. of *enucleare*, lit., to remove the kernel from, fr. *e-* + *nucleus* kernel — more at NUCLEUS] **1** *archaic* **:** EXPLAIN **2 :** to deprive of a nucleus **3 :** to remove without cutting into ⟨~ a tumor⟩ — **enu·cle·ation** \(ˌ)ē-ˌn(y)ü-klē-ˈā-shən\ *n*

enu·mer·a·ble \i-ˈn(y)üm-(ə-)rə-bəl\ *adj* **:** DENUMERABLE — **enu·mer·a·bil·i·ty** \-ˌn(y)üm-(ə-)rə-ˈbil-ət-ē\ *n*

enu·mer·ate \i-ˈn(y)ü-mə-ˌrāt\ *vt* **-at·ed; -at·ing** [L *enumeratus*, pp. of *enumerare*, fr. *e-* + *numerare* to count, fr. *numerus* number — more at NIMBLE] **1 :** to ascertain the number of **:** COUNT **2 :** to specify one after another **:** LIST — **enu·mer·a·tion** \-ˌn(y)ü-mə-ˈrā-shən\ *n* — **enu·mer·a·tive** \-ˈn(y)ü-mə-ˌrāt-iv, -ˈn(y)üm-(ə-)rət-\ *adj* — **enu·mer·a·tor** \-ˈn(y)ü-mə-ˌrāt-ər\ *n*

enun·ci·ate \ē-ˈnən(t)-sē-ˌāt\ *vb* **-at·ed; -at·ing** [L *enuntiatus*, pp. of *enuntiare* to report, declare, fr. *e-* + *nuntiare* to report — more at ANNOUNCE] *vt* **1 a :** to make a definite or systematic statement of **:** FORMULATE **b :** ANNOUNCE, PROCLAIM ⟨*enunciated* the principles to be followed by the new administration⟩ **2 :** ARTICULATE, PRONOUNCE ⟨~ your words clearly⟩ ~ *vi* **:** to utter articulate sounds — **enun·cia·ble** \-ˈnən(t)-sē-ə-bəl, -ˈnən-ch(ē-)ə-\ *adj* — **enun·ci·a·tion** \-ˌnən(t)-sē-ˈā-shən\ *n* — **enun·ci·a·tor** \-ˈnən(t)-sē-ˌāt-ər\ *n*

enure *var of* INURE

en·ure·sis \ˌen-yu̇-ˈrē-səs\ *n* [NL, fr. Gk *enourein* to urinate in, wet the bed, fr. *en-* + *ourein* to urinate] **:** an involuntary discharge of urine **:** incontinence of urine — **en·uret·ic** \-ˈret-ik\ *adj or n*

env *abbr* envelope

en·vel·op \in-ˈvel-əp\ *vt* [ME *envolupen*, fr. MF *envoluper*, *enveloper*, fr. OF *envoloper*, fr. *en-* + *voloper* to wrap] **1 :** to enclose or enfold completely with or as if with a covering **2 :** to mount an attack on (an enemy's flank) — **en·vel·op·ment** \-mənt\ *n*

en·ve·lope \ˈen-və-ˌlōp, ˈän-\ *n* **1 :** something that envelops **:** WRAPPER ⟨the ~ of air around the earth⟩ **2 :** a flat usu. paper container (as for a letter) **3 a :** the outer covering of an aerostat **b :** the bag containing the gas in a balloon or airship **4 :** a natural enclosing covering (as a membrane, shell, or integument) **5 a :** a curve tangent to each of a family of curves **b :** a surface tangent to each of a family of surfaces

en·ven·om \in-ˈven-əm\ *vt* [ME *envenimen*, fr. OF *envenimer*, fr. *en-* + *venim* venom] **1 :** to make poisonous **2 :** EMBITTER ⟨jealousy ~*ing* his mind⟩

en·ven·om·iza·tion \in-ˌven-ə-mə-ˈzā-shən\ *n* **:** a poisoning caused by a bite or sting

en·vi·able \ˈen-vē-ə-bəl\ *adj* **:** highly desirable — **en·vi·able·ness** *n* — **en·vi·ably** \-blē\ *adv*

en·vi·er \ˈen-vē-ər\ *n* **:** one that envies

en·vi·ous \ˈen-vē-əs\ *adj* **1 :** feeling or showing envy ⟨~ of her neighbor's success⟩ ⟨~ looks⟩ **2** *archaic* **a :** EMULOUS **b :** ENVIABLE — **en·vi·ous·ly** *adv* — **en·vi·ous·ness** *n*

syn ENVIOUS, JEALOUS *shared meaning element* **:** begrudging another possession of something. In spite of their shared element of meaning, these words are not close synonyms and can rarely be interchanged without loss of precision or alteration of emphasis. ENVIOUS stresses a coveting of something (as riches or attainments) which belongs to another or of something (as success or good luck) which has come to another; it may imply an urgent, even malicious desire to see him dispossessed ⟨some *envious* hand has sprinkled ashes just to spoil our slide —Eugene Field⟩ or no more than a mild innocuous coveting ⟨we are all *envious* of your new coat⟩ JEALOUS is likely to stress intolerance of a rival for possession of what one regards as peculiarly one's own possession or due, or it may imply intensely zealous efforts to keep what one treasures. The term can be used without derogation ⟨thou shalt have no other gods before me . . . for I the Lord thy God am a *jealous* God —Exod 20:3–5(AV)⟩ but more often it carries a strong implication of distrust, suspicion, enviousness, or sometimes anger ⟨stabbed by a *jealous* lover⟩ ⟨a *jealous* rage⟩

en·vi·ron \in-ˈvī-rən, -ˈvī(-ə)rn\ *vt* [ME *envirounen*, fr. MF *environner*, fr. *environ* around, fr. *en* in (fr. L *in*) + *viron* circle, fr. *virer* to turn, fr. (assumed) VL *virare*] **:** ENCIRCLE, SURROUND

en·vi·ron·ment \in-ˈvī-rən-mənt, -ˈvī(-ə)rn-\ *n* **1 :** the circumstances, objects, or conditions by which one is surrounded **2 a :** the complex of climatic, edaphic, and biotic factors that act upon an organism or an ecological community and ultimately determine its form and survival **b :** the aggregate of social and cultural conditions that influence the life of an individual or community **3 :** an artistic or theatrical work that involves or encompasses the spectator — **en·vi·ron·men·tal** \-ˌvī-rən-ˈment-ᵊl, -ˌvī(-ə)rn-\ *adj* — **en·vi·ron·men·tal·ly** \-ᵊl-ē\ *adv*

en·vi·ron·men·tal·ism \-ˌvī-rən-ˈment-ᵊl-ˌiz-əm, -ˌvī(-ə)rn-\ *n* **:** a theory that views environment rather than heredity as the important factor in the development and esp. the cultural and intellectual development of an individual or group

en·vi·ron·men·tal·ist \-ᵊl-əst\ *n* **1 :** an advocate of environmentalism **2 :** one concerned about the quality of the human environment; *specif* **:** a specialist in human ecology

en·vi·rons \in-ˈvī-rənz, -ˈvī(-ə)rnz\ *n pl* **1 :** the districts around a city **2 a :** environing things **:** SURROUNDINGS **b :** an adjoining region or space **:** VICINITY

en·vis·age \in-ˈviz-ij\ *vt* **-aged; -ag·ing** [F *envisager,* fr. *en-* + *visage*] **1 :** to view or regard in a certain way ⟨~*s* himself as a sincere young man⟩ **2 :** to have a mental picture of esp. in advance of realization ⟨~*s* an entirely new system of education⟩ ***syn*** see THINK

en·vi·sion \in-ˈvizh-ən\ *vt* **:** to picture to oneself ⟨~*s* a career dedicated to promoting peace⟩ ***syn*** see THINK

en·voi *or* **en·voy** \ˈen-ˌvȯi, ˈän-\ *n* [F *envoi,* lit., message, fr. OF *envei,* fr. *envoier* to send on one's way, fr. (assumed) VL *inviare,* fr. L *in-* + *via* way — more at VIA] **:** the usu. explanatory or commendatory concluding remarks to a poem, essay, or book; *specif* **:** a short fixed final stanza of a ballade serving as a summary or dedication

en·voy \ˈen-ˌvȯi, ˈän-\ *n* [F *envoyé,* fr. pp. of *envoyer* to send, fr. OF *envoier*] **1 a :** a minister plenipotentiary accredited to a foreign government who ranks between an ambassador and a minister resident — called also *envoy extraordinary* **b :** a person delegated to represent one government in its dealings with another **2 :** MESSENGER, REPRESENTATIVE

¹en·vy \ˈen-vē\ *n, pl* **envies** [ME *envie,* fr. OF, fr. L *invidia,* fr. *invidus* envious, fr. *invidēre* to look askance at, envy, fr. *in-* + *vidēre* to see — more at WIT] **1** *obs* **:** MALICE **2 :** painful or resentful awareness of an advantage enjoyed by another joined with a desire to possess the same advantage **3 :** an object of envious notice or feeling ⟨his beautiful wife made him the ~ of his friends⟩

²envy *vb* **en·vied; en·vy·ing** *vt* **1 :** to feel envy toward or on account of **2** *obs* **:** BEGRUDGE ~ *vi, obs* **:** to feel or show envy — **en·vy·ing·ly** \-vē-iŋ-lē\ *adv*

en·wheel \in-ˈhwē(ə)l, -ˈwē(ə)l\ *vt, obs* **:** ENCIRCLE

en·wind \in-ˈwīnd\ *vt* **en·wound** \-ˈwau̇nd\; **en·wind·ing :** to wind in or about **:** ENFOLD

en·womb \in-ˈwüm\ *vt* **:** to shut up as if in a womb

en·wrap \in-ˈrap\ *vt* **1 :** to wrap in a covering **:** ENFOLD **2 a :** ENVELOP **b :** to preoccupy or absorb mentally **:** ENGROSS

en·wreathe \in-ˈrēth\ *vt* **:** to encircle with or as if with a wreath **:** ENVELOP

en·zo·ot·ic \ˌen-zə-ˈwät-ik\ *adj* [*en-* + *zo-*] *of animal diseases* **:** peculiar to or constantly present in a locality — **enzootic** *n*

en·zy·got·ic \ˌen-zī-ˈgät-ik\ *adj* [*en-* + *zyg-*] *of twins* **:** IDENTICAL

en·zy·mat·ic \ˌen-zə-ˈmat-ik\ *also* **en·zy·mic** \en-ˈzī-mik\ *adj* **:** of, relating to, or produced by an enzyme — **en·zy·mat·i·cal·ly** \-ˈmat-i-k(ə-)lē\ *also* **en·zy·mi·cal·ly** \-ˈzī-mi-k(ə-)lē\ *adv*

en·zyme \ˈen-ˌzīm\ *n* [G *enzym,* fr. MGk *enzymos* leavened, fr. Gk *en-* + *zymē* leaven] **:** any of numerous complex proteins that are produced by living cells and catalyze specific biochemical reactions at body temperatures

en·zy·mol·o·gy \ˌen-zə-ˈmäl-ə-jē\ *n* [ISV] **:** a branch of science that deals with enzymes, their nature, activity, and significance — **en·zy·mol·o·gist** \-jəst\ *n*

EO *abbr* executive order

eo- *comb form* [Gk *ēō-* dawn, fr. *ēōs*] **:** earliest **:** oldest ⟨eolithic⟩

Eo·cene \ˈē-ə-ˌsēn\ *adj* **:** of, relating to, or being an epoch of the Tertiary between the Paleocene and the Oligocene or the corresponding system of rocks — **Eocene** *n*

eo·hip·pus \ˌē-ō-ˈhip-əs\ *n* [NL, genus name, fr. *eo-* + Gk *hippos* horse — more at EQUINE] **:** any of a genus (*Eohippus*) of small primitive 4-toed horses from the Lower Eocene of the western U.S.

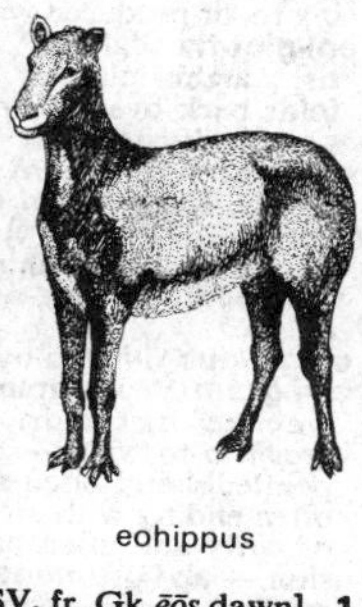
eohippus

eo·lian \ē-ˈō-lē-ən, -ˈōl-yən\ *adj* [L *Aeolus,* god of the winds] **:** borne, deposited, produced, or eroded by the wind

eo·lith \ˈē-ə-ˌlith\ *n* **:** a very crudely chipped flint

Eo·lith·ic \ˌē-ə-ˈlith-ik\ *adj* **:** of or relating to the early period of the Stone Age marked by the use of eoliths

EOM *abbr* end of month

eon \ˈē-ən, ˈē-ˌän\ *var of* AEON

eo no·mi·ne \ˌē-ō-ˈnäm-ə-nē\ [L] **:** by or under that name

Eos \ˈē-ˌäs\ *n* [Gk *Ēōs*] **:** the Greek goddess of dawn — compare AURORA

eo·sin \ˈē-ə-sən\ *or* **eo·sine** \-sən, -ˌsēn\ *n* [ISV, fr. Gk *ēōs* dawn] **1 :** a red fluorescent dye $C_{20}H_8Br_4O_5$ obtained by the action of bromine on fluorescein and used esp. in cosmetics and as a toner; *also* **:** its red to brown sodium or potassium salt used esp. as a biological stain for cytoplasmic structures **2 :** any of several dyes related to eosin

¹eo·sin·o·phil \ˌē-ə-ˈsin-ə-ˌfil\ *or* **eo·sin·o·phile** \-ˌfīl\ *n* **:** a leukocyte or other granulocyte with cytoplasmic inclusions readily stained by eosin

²eosinophil *or* **eosinophile** *adj* **:** EOSINOPHILIC 1

eo·sin·o·phil·ia \-ˈfil-ē-ə\ *n* **:** abnormal increase in the number of eosinophils in the blood that is characteristic of allergic states and various parasitic infections

eo·sin·o·phil·ic \ˌē-ə-ˌsin-ə-ˈfil-ik\ *adj* **1 :** staining readily with eosin **2 :** of, relating to, or characterized by eosinophilia

Eo·zo·ic \ˌē-ə-ˈzō-ik\ *adj or n* **1 :** PRECAMBRIAN **2 :** PROTEROZOIC

EP *abbr* **1** estimated position **2** European plan **3** extended play

epact \ˈē-ˌpakt, ˈep-ˌakt\ *n* [MF *epacte,* fr. LL *epacta,* fr. Gk *epaktē,* fr. *epagein* to bring in, intercalate, fr. *epi-* + *agein* to drive — more at AGENT] **:** a period added to harmonize the lunar with the solar calendar

ep·ar·chy \ˈep-ˌär-kē\ *n, pl* **-chies** [Gk *eparchia* province, fr. *eparchos* prefect, fr. *epi-* + *archos* ruler — more at ARCH-] **:** a diocese of an Eastern church

ep·au·let *also* **ep·au·lette** \ˌep-ə-ˈlet; ˈep-ə-ˌlet, -lət\ *n* [F *épaulette,* dim. of *épaule* shoulder, fr. LL *spatula* shoulder blade, spoon, dim. of L *spatha* spoon, sword — more at SPADE] **1 :** something that ornaments or protects the shoulder; *specif* **:** an ornamental fringed shoulder pad formerly worn as part of a military uniform **2 :** a 5-sided step cut of a gem

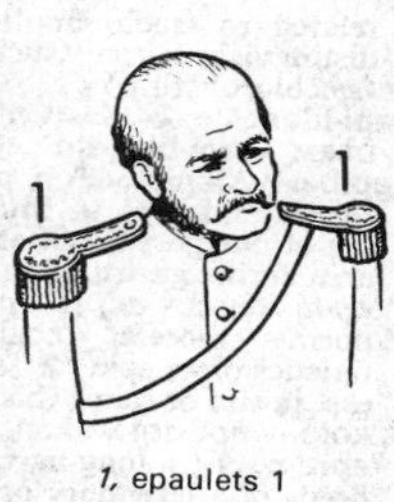
1, epaulets 1

épée \ˈep-ˌā, ā-ˈpā\ *n* [F, fr. L *spatha*] **1 :** a fencing or dueling sword having a bowl-shaped guard and a rigid blade of triangular section with no cutting edge that tapers to a sharp point blunted for fencing — compare FOIL, SABER **2 :** the art or sport of fencing with the épée

épée·ist \-əst\ *n* **:** one who fences with an épée

ep·ei·rog·e·ny \ˌep-ˌī-ˈräj-ə-nē\ *n, pl* **-nies** [Gk *ēpeiros* mainland, continent + E *-geny*] **:** the deformation of the earth's crust by which the broader features of relief are produced — **epei·ro·gen·ic** \i-ˌpī-rə-ˈjen-ik\ *adj* — **epei·ro·gen·i·cal·ly** \-i-k(ə-)lē\ *adv*

epen·the·sis \i-ˈpen(t)-thə-səs, e-\ *n, pl* **-the·ses** \-ˌsēz\ [LL, fr. Gk, fr. *epentithenai* to insert a letter, fr. *epi-* + *entithenai* to put in, fr. *en-* + *tithenai* to put — more at DO] **:** the insertion or development of a sound or letter in the body of a word (as \ə\ in \ˈath-ə-ˌlēt\ *athlete*) — **ep·en·thet·ic** \ˌep-ən-ˈthet-ik\ *adj*

epergne \i-ˈpərn, ā-\ *n* [prob. fr. F *épargne* saving] **:** an often ornate tiered centerpiece consisting typically of a frame of wrought metal (as silver or gold) bearing dishes, vases, or candle holders or a combination of these

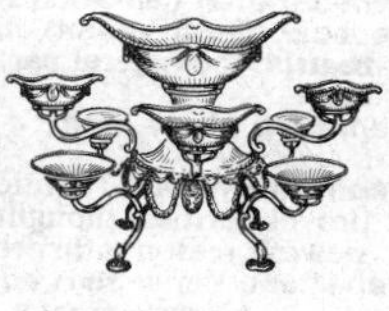
epergne

ep·ex·e·ge·sis \ˌep-ˌek-sə-ˈjē-səs\ *n, pl* **-ge·ses** \-ˌsēz\ [Gk *epexēgēsis,* fr. *epi-* + *exēgēsis*] **:** additional explanation or explanatory matter — **ep·ex·e·get·i·cal** \-ˈjet-i-kəl\ *or* **ep·ex·e·get·ic** \-ˈjet-ik\ *adj* — **ep·ex·e·get·i·cal·ly** \-ˈjet-i-k(ə-)lē\ *adv*

Eph *or* **Ephes** *abbr* Ephesians

ephah \ˈē-fə, ˈef-ə\ *n* [Heb *ēphāh,* fr. Egypt *ipt*] **:** an ancient Hebrew unit of dry measure equal to $^1/_{10}$ homer or a little over a bushel

ephebe \ˈef-ˌēb, i-ˈfēb\ *n* [L *ephebus*] **:** a young man; *esp* **:** EPHEBUS

ephe·bic \-ˈbik\ *adj* **:** of or relating to the ephebi ⟨~ education⟩

ephe·bus \i-ˈfē-bəs, e-\ *n, pl* **-bi** \-ˌbī\ [L, fr. Gk *ephēbos,* fr. *epi-* + *hēbē* youth, puberty] **:** a youth of ancient Greece; *esp* **:** an Athenian 18 or 19 years old in training for full citizenship

ephe·dra \i-ˈfed-rə, ˈef-ə-drə\ *n* [NL, genus name] **:** any of a large genus (*Ephedra* of the family Gnetaceae) of jointed nearly leafless desert shrubs with the leaves reduced to scales at the nodes

ephed·rine \i-ˈfed-rən\ *n* [NL *Ephedra,* genus of shrubs, fr. L, horsetail plant, fr. Gk, fr. *ephedros* sitting upon, fr. *epi-* + *hedra* seat — more at SIT] **:** a crystalline alkaloid $C_{10}H_{15}NO$ extracted from Chinese ephedras or synthesized and used in the form of a salt for relief of hay fever, asthma, and nasal congestion

¹ephem·er·al \i-ˈfem-(ə-)rəl\ *adj* [Gk *ephēmeros* lasting a day, daily, fr. *epi-* + *hēmera* day] **1 :** lasting one day only ⟨an ~ fever⟩ **2 :** lasting a very short time ⟨~ pleasures⟩ ***syn*** see TRANSIENT — **ephem·er·al·ly** \-rə-lē\ *adv*

²ephemeral *n* **:** something ephemeral; *specif* **:** a plant that grows, flowers, and dies in a few days

ephem·er·al·i·ty \i-ˌfem-ə-ˈral-ət-ē\ *n, pl* **-ties** **1 :** the quality or state of being ephemeral **2** *pl* **:** ephemeral things

ephem·er·id \i-ˈfem-ə-rəd\ *n* [deriv. of Gk *ephēmeron*] **:** MAYFLY — **ephemerid** *adj*

ephem·er·is \-ə-rəs\ *n, pl* **eph·e·mer·i·des** \ˌef-ə-ˈmer-ə-ˌdēz\ [L, diary, ephemeris, fr. Gk *ephēmeris,* fr. *ephēmeros*] **1 :** a tabular statement of the assigned places of a celestial body for regular intervals **2 :** EPHEMERAL

ephemeris time *n* **:** a uniform measure of time defined by the orbital motions of the planets

ephem·er·on \i-ˈfem-ə-ˌrän\ *n, pl* **ephem·era** \-ˈfem-(ə-)rə\ *also* **ephem·er·ons** \-ˈfem-ə-ˌränz\ [NL, fr. Gk *ephēmeron* mayfly, fr. neut. of *ephēmeros*] **1 :** EPHEMERID **2 :** EPHEMERAL

ephem·er·ous \i-ˈfem-(ə-)rəs\ *adj* **:** EPHEMERAL

Ephe·sians \i-ˈfē-zhənz\ *n pl but sing in constr* [short for *Epistle to the Ephesians*] **:** a letter addressed to early Christians and included as a book in the New Testament — see BIBLE table

eph·od \ˈef-ˌäd, ˈē-ˌfäd\ *n* [Heb *ēphōdh*] **1 :** a linen apron worn in ancient Hebrew rites; *esp* **:** a vestment for the high priest **2 :** an ancient Hebrew instrument of priestly divination

eph·or \ˈef-ər, -ˌȯ(ə)r\ *n* [L *ephorus,* fr. Gk *ephoros,* fr. *ephoran* to oversee, fr. *epi-* + *horan* to see — more at WARY] **1 :** one of five ancient Spartan magistrates having power over the king **2 :** a government official in modern Greece; *esp* **:** one who oversees public works — **eph·or·ate** \ˈef-ə-ˌrāt\ *n*

Ephra·im \ˈē-frē-əm\ *n* [Heb *Ephrayim*] **:** a son of Joseph and the traditional eponymous ancestor of one of the tribes of Israel

Ephra·im·ite \-ə-ˌmīt\ *n* **1 :** a member of the Hebrew tribe of Ephraim **2 :** a native or inhabitant of the biblical northern kingdom of Israel

epi- *or* **ep-** *prefix* [ME, fr. MF & L; MF, fr. L, fr. Gk, fr. *epi* on, at, besides, after; akin to OE *eofot* crime] **1 :** upon ⟨*epi*phyte⟩ **:** besides ⟨*epi*phenomenon⟩ **:** attached to ⟨*epi*didymis⟩ **:** over ⟨*epi*center⟩ **:** outer ⟨*epi*blast⟩ **:** after ⟨*epi*genesis⟩ **2 a :** chemical entity

ə abut ᵊ kitten ər further a back ā bake ä cot, cart
au̇ out ch chin e less ē easy g gift i trip ī life
j joke ŋ sing ō flow ȯ flaw ȯi coin th thin th this
ü loot u̇ foot y yet yü few yu̇ furious zh vision

related to (such) another ⟨epicholesterol⟩ **b** : chemical entity distinguished from (such) another by having a bridge connection ⟨epichlorohydrin⟩

epi·blast \'ep-ə-,blast\ *n* : the outer layer of the blastoderm — ECTODERM — **epi·blas·tic** \,ep-ə-'blas-tik\ *adj*

epib·o·ly \i-'pib-ə-lē\ *n, pl* **-lies** [Gk *epibolē* addition, fr. *epiballein* to throw on, fr. *epi-* + *ballein* to throw — more at DEVIL] : the growing of one part about another; *esp* : such growth of the dorsal lip area during gastrulation — **epi·bol·ic** \,ep-ə-'bäl-ik\ *adj*

¹ep·ic \'ep-ik\ *adj* [L *epicus*, fr. Gk *epikos*, fr. *epos* word, speech, poem — more at VOICE] **1** : of, relating to, or having the characteristics of an epic **2 a** : extending beyond the usual or ordinary esp. in size or scope ⟨his genius was ~ —*Times Lit. Supp.*⟩ **b** : HEROIC — **ep·i·cal** \-i-kəl\ *adj* — **ep·i·cal·ly** \-i-k(ə-)lē\ *adv*

²epic *n* **1** : a long narrative poem in elevated style recounting the deeds of a legendary or historical hero ⟨the *Iliad* and the *Odyssey* are ~s⟩ **2** : a work of art (as a novel or drama) that resembles or suggests an epic **3** : a series of events or body of legend or tradition thought to form the proper subject of an epic ⟨the winning of the West was a great American ~⟩

epi·ca·lyx \,ep-i-'kā-liks *also* -'kal-iks\ *n* : an involucre resembling the calyx but consisting of a whorl of bracts that is exterior to the calyx or results from the union of the sepal appendages

epi·can·thic fold \,ep-ə-,kan(t)-thik-\ *n* [NL *epicanthus* epicanthic fold, fr. *epi-* + *canthus*] : a prolongation of a fold of the skin of the upper eyelid over the inner angle or both angles of the eye — called also Mongolian fold

epi·car·di·al \,ep-i-'kärd-ē-əl\ *adj* : of or relating to the epicardium

epi·car·di·um \-ē-əm\ *n, pl* **-dia** \-ē-ə\ [NL, fr. *epi-* + Gk *kardia* heart] : the visceral part of the pericardium that closely invests the heart

epi·carp \'ep-i-,kärp\ *n* [F *épicarpe*, fr. *épi-* epi- + -*carpe* -carp] : EXOCARP

epic drama *n* : twentieth century narrative drama that seeks to provoke critical thought about social problems by appealing to the viewer's reason rather than to his emotions

ep·i·cene \'ep-ə-,sēn\ *adj* [ME, fr. L *epicoenus*, fr. Gk *epikoinos*, fr. *epi-* + *koinos* common — more at CO-] **1** *of a noun* : having but one form to indicate either sex **2 a** : having characteristics typical of the other sex : INTERSEXUAL **b** : EFFEMINATE **3** : lacking characteristics of either sex — **epicene** *n* — **ep·i·cen·ism** \-,sē-,niz-əm, ,ep-ə-'\ *n*

epi·cen·ter \'ep-i-,sent-ər\ *n* [NL *epicentrum*, fr. *epi-* + L *centrum* center] **1** : the part of the earth's surface directly above the focus of an earthquake **2** : CENTER 2a, 2c — **epi·cen·tral** \,ep-i-'sen-trəl\ *adj*

epi-chlo·ro·hy·drin \,ep-i-,klōr-ə-'hī-drən, -,klȯr-\ *n* : a volatile liquid toxic epoxide C_3H_5ClO having a chloroform odor and used esp. in making epoxy resins and rubbers

epi·con·ti·nen·tal \,ep-i-,känt-ᵊn-'ent-ᵊl\ *adj* : lying upon a continent or a continental shelf ⟨~ seas⟩

epi·cot·yl \'ep-i-,kät-ᵊl\ *n* [*epi-* + *cotyl*edon] : the portion of the axis of a plant embryo or seedling above the cotyledonary node

epi·cra·ni·al \,ep-i-'krā-nē-əl\ *adj* : situated on the cranium

ep·i·crit·ic \,ep-ə-'krit-ik\ *adj* [Gk *epikritikos* determinative, fr. *epikrinein* to decide, fr. *epi-* + *krinein* to judge — more at CERTAIN] : of, relating to, or being cutaneous sensory reception marked by accurate discrimination between small degrees of sensation

epic simile *n* : an extended simile that is used typically in epic poetry to intensify the heroic stature of the subject and to serve as decoration

epic theater *n* : theater that employs epic drama

ep·i·cure \'ep-i-,kyu̇(ə)r\ *n* [*Epicurus*] **1** *archaic* : one devoted to sensual pleasure : SYBARITE **2** : one with sensitive and discriminating tastes esp. in food or wine

syn EPICURE, BON VIVANT, GOURMET, GOURMAND, GLUTTON *shared meaning element* : one who takes pleasure in eating and drinking

epi·cu·re·an \,ep-i-kyu̇-'rē-ən, -'kyu̇r-ē-\ *adj* **1** *cap* : of or relating to Epicurus or Epicureanism **2** : of, relating to, or suited to an epicure

Epicurean *n* **1** : a follower of Epicurus **2** *often not cap* : EPICURE 2

ep·i·cu·re·an·ism \-ə-,niz-əm\ *n* **1** *cap* **a** : the philosophy of Epicurus who subscribed to a hedonistic ethics that considered an imperturbable emotional calm the highest good, held intellectual pleasures superior to others, and advocated the renunciation of momentary in favor of more permanent pleasures **b** : a mode of life in consonance with Epicureanism **2** : EPICURISM

ep·i·cur·ism \'ep-i-,kyu̇(ə)r-,iz-əm, ,ep-i-'\ *n* : the practices or tastes of an epicure or an epicurean

epi·cu·ti·cle \,ep-i-'kyüt-i-kəl\ *n* : an outermost waxy layer of the insect exoskeleton — **epi·cu·tic·u·lar** \-kyü-'tik-yə-lər\ *adj*

epi·cy·cle \'ep-ə-,sī-kəl\ *n* [ME *epicicle*, fr. LL *epicyclus*, fr. Gk *epikyklos*, fr. *epi-* + *kyklos* circle — more at WHEEL] **1** *in Ptolemaic astron* : a circle in which a planet moves and which has a center that is itself carried around at the same time on the circumference of a larger circle **2** : a process going on within a larger one — **epi·cy·clic** \,ep-ə-'sī-klik, -'sik-lik\ *adj*

epicyclic train *n* : a train (as of gear wheels) designed to have one or more parts travel around the circumference of another fixed or revolving part

epi·cy·cloid \,ep-ə-'sī-,klȯid\ *n* : a curve traced by a point on a circle that rolls on the outside of a fixed circle

¹ep·i·dem·ic \,ep-ə-'dem-ik\ *adj* [F *épidémique*, fr. MF, fr. *epidemie*, n., epidemic, fr. LL *epidemia*, fr. Gk *epidēmia* visit, epidemic, fr. *epidēmos* visiting, epidemic, fr. *epi-* + *dēmos* people] **1** : affecting or tending to affect many individuals within a population, community, or region at the same time ⟨typhoid was ~⟩ **2 a** : excessively prevalent **b** : CONTAGIOUS 4 ⟨an ~ personality⟩ **3** : of, relating to, or constituting an epidemic ⟨the practice had reached ~ proportions⟩ — **ep·i·dem·i·cal** \-i-kəl\ *adj* — **ep·i·dem·i·cal·ly** \-i-k(ə-)lē\ *adv* — **ep·i·de·mic·i·ty** \-də-'mis-ət-ē\ *n*

²epidemic *n* **1** : an outbreak of epidemic disease **2** : an outbreak or product of sudden rapid spread, growth, or development; *specif* : a natural population suddenly and greatly enlarged

ep·i·de·mi·ol·o·gy \,ep-ə-,dē-mē-'äl-ə-jē, -,dem-ē-\ *n* [LL *epidemia* + ISV -*logy*] **1** : a branch of medical science that deals with the incidence, distribution, and control of disease in a population **2** : the sum of the factors controlling the presence or absence of a disease or pathogen — **ep·i·de·mi·o·log·ic** \-,dē-mē-ə-'läj-ik, -,dem-ē-\ *or* **ep·i·de·mi·o·log·i·cal** \-i-kəl\ *adj* — **ep·i·de·mi·o·log·i·cal·ly** \-i-k(ə-)lē\ *adv* — **ep·i·de·mi·ol·o·gist** \-,dē-mē-'äl-ə-jəst, -,dem-ē-\ *n*

epi·den·drum \,ep-ə-'den-drəm\ *or* **-dron** \-drän\ *n* [NL, genus name, fr. Gk *epi-* + *dendron* tree — more at DENDR-] : any of a large genus (*Epidendrum*) of chiefly epiphytic and tropical American orchids

epiderm- *or* **epidermo-** *comb form* [*epidermis*] : epidermis ⟨*epidermal*⟩

epi·der·mal \,ep-ə-'dər-məl\ *also* **epi·der·mic** \-mik\ *adj* : of, relating to, or arising from the epidermis

epi·der·mis \-məs\ *n* [LL, fr. Gk, fr. *epi-* + *derma* skin] **1 a** : the outer epithelial layer of the external integument of the animal body that is derived from the embryonic epiblast; *specif* : the outer nonsensitive and nonvascular layer of the skin of a vertebrate that overlies the dermis **b** : any of various animal integuments **2 a** : a thin surface layer of tissue in higher plants formed by growth of a primary meristem

epi·der·moid \-,mȯid\ *also* **epi·der·moi·dal** \-,dər-'mȯid-ᵊl\ *adj* : resembling epidermis or epidermal cells : made up of elements like those of epidermis ⟨~ neoplasms⟩

epi·dia·scope \,ep-ə-'dī-ə-,skōp\ *n* [ISV] **1** : a projector for images of opaque objects or for images or transparencies **2** : EPISCOPE

ep·i·did·y·mis \,ep-ə-'did-ə-məs\ *n, pl* **-mi·des** \-mə-,dēz\ [NL, fr. Gk, fr. *epi-* + *didymos* testicle — more at DIDYMOUS] : an elongated mass of convoluted efferent tubes at the back of the testis — **ep·i·did·y·mal** \-məl\ *adj*

ep·i·dote \'ep-ə-,dōt\ *n* [F *épidote*, fr. Gk *epididonai* to give in addition, fr. *epi-* + *didonai* to give — more at DATE] : a yellowish green mineral $Ca_2(Al,Fe)_3Si_3O_{12}OH$ usu. occurring in grains or columnar masses and sometimes used as a gemstone

epi·du·ral \,ep-i-'d(y)u̇r-əl\ *adj* : situated upon or administered outside the dura mater ⟨~ anesthesia⟩ ⟨~ structures⟩

epi·fau·na \-'fȯn-ə, -'fän-\ *n* [NL] : benthic fauna living on the substrate and esp. on a hard sea floor — compare INFAUNA — **epi·fau·nal** \-'fȯn-ᵊl, -'fän-\ *adj*

epi·gas·tric \,ep-i-'gas-trik\ *adj* **1** : lying upon or over the stomach **2** : of or relating to the anterior walls of the abdomen

epi·ge·al \,ep-i-'jē-əl\ *or* **epi·ge·ous** \-'jē-əs\ *adj* [Gk *epigaios* upon the earth, fr. *epi-* + *gē* earth] **1** : growing above the surface of the ground **2** *of a cotyledon* : forced above ground by elongation of the hypocotyl **b** : marked by the production of epigeal cotyledons ⟨~ germination⟩

epi·gen·e·sis \,ep-ə-'jen-ə-səs\ *n* [NL] **1** : development of new characters (as of a whole new plant) in an initially undifferentiated entity (as a fertilized egg or spore) **2** : change in the mineral character of a rock owing to outside influences

epi·ge·net·ic \-jə-'net-ik\ *adj* **1** : of, relating to, or produced by epigenesis ⟨genetic versus ~ influences⟩ **2** *or* **epi·gen·ic** \-'jen-ik\ *of deposit or structure* : formed after the laying down of the enclosing rock

epi·glot·tal \,ep-ə-'glät-ᵊl\ *also* **epi·glot·tic** \-'glät-ik\ *adj* : of, relating to, or produced with the aid of the epiglottis

epi·glot·tis \-'glät-əs\ *n* [NL, fr. Gk *epiglōttis*, fr. *epi-* + *glōttis* glottis] : a thin plate of flexible cartilage in front of the glottis that folds back over and protects the glottis during swallowing — see LARYNX illustration

ep·i·gone \'ep-ə-,gōn\ *n* [G, fr. L *epigonus* successor, fr. Gk *epigonos*, fr. *epigignesthai* to be born after, fr. *epi-* + *gignesthai* to be born — more at KIN] : an imitative follower; *esp* : an inferior imitator of a creative thinker or artist — **epi·gon·ic** \,ep-ə-'gän-ik\ *or* **epig·o·nous** \i-'pig-ə-nəs, e-\ *adj* — **epig·o·nism** \-'pig-ə-,niz-əm\ *n*

epig·o·nus \i-'pig-ə-nəs, e-\ *n, pl* **-ni** \-,nī, -,nē\ [L] : EPIGONE

ep·i·gram \'ep-ə-,gram\ *n* [ME *epigrame*, fr. L *epigrammat-*, *epigramma*, fr. Gk, fr. *epigraphein* to write on, inscribe, fr. *epi-* + *graphein* to write — more at CARVE] **1** : a concise poem dealing pointedly and often satirically with a single thought or event and often ending with an ingenious turn of thought **2** : a terse, sage, or witty and often paradoxical saying **3** : epigrammatic expression — **ep·i·gram·ma·tism** \,ep-ə-'gram-ə-,tiz-əm\ *n* — **ep·i·gram·ma·tist** \-'gram-ət-əst\ *n*

ep·i·gram·mat·ic \,ep-ə-grə-'mat-ik\ *adj* **1** : of, relating to, or resembling an epigram **2** : marked by or given to the use of epigrams — **ep·i·gram·mat·i·cal** \-i-kəl\ *adj* — **ep·i·gram·mat·i·cal·ly** \-i-k(ə-)lē\ *adv*

ep·i·gram·ma·tize \-'gram-ə-,tīz\ *vb* **-tized; -tiz·ing** *vt* **1** : to express in the form of an epigram **2** : to make an epigram about ~ *vi* : to make an epigram — **ep·i·gram·ma·tiz·er** *n*

ep·i·graph \'ep-ə-,graf\ *n* [Gk *epigraphē*, fr. *epigraphein*] **1** : an engraved inscription **2** : a quotation set at the beginning of a literary work or a division of it to suggest its theme

epig·ra·pher \i-'pig-rə-fər, e-\ *n* : EPIGRAPHIST

ep·i·graph·ic \,ep-ə-'graf-ik\ *also* **ep·i·graph·i·cal** \-i-kəl\ *adj* : of or relating to epigraphs or epigraphy — **ep·i·graph·i·cal·ly** \-i-k(ə-)lē\ *adv*

epig·ra·phist \i-'pig-rə-fəst, e-\ *n* : a specialist in epigraphy

epig·ra·phy \-fē\ *n* **1** : EPIGRAPHS, INSCRIPTIONS **2** : the study of inscriptions; *esp* : the deciphering of ancient inscriptions

epig·y·nous \i-'pij-ə-nəs, e-\ *adj* **1** *of a floral organ* : adnate to the surface of the ovary and appearing to grow from the top of it **2** : having epigynous floral organs — **epig·y·ny** \-nē\ *n*

epil *abbr* **1** epilepsy **2** epileptic

ep·i·la·tion \,ep-ə-'lā-shən\ *n* [F *épilation*, fr. *épiler* to remove hair, fr. *é- e-* + L *pilus* hair — more at PILE] : the loss or removal of hair

ep·i·lep·sy \'ep-ə-,lep-sē\ *n, pl* **-sies** [MF *epilepsie,* fr. LL *epilepsia,* fr. Gk *epilēpsia,* fr. *epilambanein* to seize, fr. *epi-* + *lambanein* to take, seize — more at LATCH] : any of various disorders marked by disturbed electrical rhythms of the central nervous system and typically manifested by convulsive attacks usu. with clouding of consciousness

epilept- *or* **epilepti-** *or* **epilepto-** *comb form* [Gk *epilēpt-,* fr. *epilēptos* seized by epilepsy, fr. *epilambanein*] : epilepsy ⟨*epileptoid*⟩

ep·i·lep·tic \,ep-ə-'lep-tik\ *adj* : relating to, affected with, or having the characteristics of epilepsy — **epileptic** *n* — **ep·i·lep·ti·cal·ly** \-ti-k(ə-)lē\ *adv*

ep·i·lep·ti·form \-'lep-tə-,fȯrm\ *adj* : resembling that of epilepsy ⟨an ~ convulsion⟩

ep·i·lep·to·gen·ic \-,lep-tə-'jen-ik\ *adj* : inducing or tending to induce epilepsy

ep·i·lep·toid \-'lep-,tȯid\ *adj* **1** : EPILEPTIFORM **2** : exhibiting symptoms resembling those of epilepsy ⟨the ~ person⟩

epi·lim·ni·on \,ep-ə-'lim-nē-,än, -nē-ən\ *n* [NL, fr. *epi-* + Gk *limnion,* dim. of *limnē* marshy lake — more at LIMNETIC] : the water layer overlying the thermocline of a lake

ep·i·logue \'ep-ə-,lȯg, -,läg\ *n* [ME *epiloge,* fr. MF *epilogue,* fr. L *epilogus,* fr. Gk *epilogos,* fr. *epilegein* to say in addition, fr. *epi-* + *legein* to say — more at LEGEND] **1** : a concluding section that rounds out the design of a literary work **2 a** : a speech often in verse addressed to the audience by an actor at the end of a play **b** : the actor speaking such an epilogue **c** : the final scene of a play that comments on or summarizes the main action **3** : the concluding section of a musical composition : CODA

epi·mer \'ep-i-mər\ *n* [*epi-* + *isomer*] : either of the stereoisomers of a sugar or sugar derivative that differ in the arrangement of the hydrogen atom and the hydroxyl group on the last asymmetric carbon atom of a chain — **epi·mer·ic** \,ep-i-'mer-ik\ *adj*

epim·er·ase \i-'pim-ə-,rās, e-, -,rāz\ *n* : any of various isomerases that catalyze the inversion of asymmetric groups in a substrate with several centers of asymmetry

ep·i·mere \'ep-ə-,mi(ə)r\ *n* [ISV] : the dorsal part of a mesodermal segment of a chordate embryo

epi·mor·pho·sis \,ep-ə-'mȯr-fə-səs\ *n* [NL, fr. *epi-* + Gk *morphōsis* formation, fr. *morphoun* to form, fr. *morphē* form — more at FORM] : regeneration of a part or organism involving extensive cell proliferation followed by differentiation

epi·my·si·um \,ep-ə-'miz(h)-ē-əm\ *n, pl* **-sia** \-ē-ə\ [NL, fr. *epi-* + Gk *mys* mouse, muscle — more at MOUSE] : the external connective-tissue sheath of a muscle

epi·nas·ty \'ep-ə-,nas-tē\ *n* : a nastic movement in which a plant part (as a flower petal) is bent outward and often downward

epi·neph·rine *also* **epi·neph·rin** \,ep-ə-'nef-rən\ *n* [ISV *epi-* + Gk *nephros* kidney — more at NEPHRITIS] : a colorless crystalline feebly basic sympathomimetic adrenal hormone $C_9H_{13}NO_3$ used medicinally esp. as a heart stimulant, a vasoconstrictor, and a muscle relaxant — called also *adrenaline*

epi·neu·ri·um \,ep-ə-'n(y)u̇r-ē-əm\ *n* [NL] : the external connective-tissue sheath of a nerve trunk

epi·pe·lag·ic \,ep-i-pə-'laj-ik\ *adj* : of, relating to, or constituting the part of the oceanic zone into which enough light penetrates for photosynthesis

ep·i·phan·ic \,ep-ə-'fan-ik\ *adj* : of or having the character of an epiphany

epiph·a·nous \i-'pif-ə-nəs\ *adj* : EPIPHANIC

epiph·a·ny \i-'pif-ə-nē\ *n, pl* **-nies** [ME *epiphanie,* fr. MF, fr. LL *epiphania,* fr. LGk, pl., prob. alter. of Gk *epiphaneia* appearance, manifestation, fr. *epiphainein* to manifest, fr. *phainein* to show — more at FANCY] **1** *cap* : January 6 observed as a church festival in commemoration of the coming of the Magi as the first manifestation of Christ to the Gentiles or in the Eastern Church in commemoration of the baptism of Christ **2** : an appearance or manifestation esp. of a divine being **3 a** (1) : a usu. sudden manifestation or perception of the essential nature or meaning of something (2) : an intuitive grasp of reality through something (as an event) usu. simple and striking **b** : a literary representation of an epiphany

epi·phe·nom·e·nal \,ep-i-fi-'näm-ən-ᵊl\ *adj* : of or relating to an epiphenomenon : DERIVATIVE — **epi·phe·nom·e·nal·ly** \-ᵊl-ē\ *adv*

epi·phe·nom·e·nal·ism \-ᵊl-,iz-əm\ *n* : a doctrine that mental processes are epiphenomena of brain processes

epi·phe·nom·e·non \-'näm-ə-,nän, -nən\ *n* : a secondary phenomenon accompanying another and caused by it

ep·i·phragm \'ep-ə-,fram\ *n* [Gk *epiphragma* covering] : a closing membrane or septum (as of a snail shell or a moss capsule)

epiph·y·se·al \i-,pif-ə-'sē-əl\ *also* **ep·i·phys·i·al** \,ep-ə-'fiz-ē-əl\ *adj* : of or relating to an epiphysis

epiph·y·sis \i-'pif-ə-səs\ *n, pl* **-y·ses** \-,sēz\ [NL, fr. Gk, growth, fr. *epiphyesthai* to grow on, fr. *epi-* + *phyesthai* to grow, pass. of *phyein* to bring forth — more at BE] **1** : a part or process of a bone that ossifies separately and later becomes ankylosed to the main part of the bone; *esp* : an end of a long bone **2** : PINEAL BODY

epi·phyte \'ep-ə-,fīt\ *n* : a plant that derives its moisture and nutrients from the air and rain and grows usu. on another plant

epi·phyt·ic \,ep-ə-'fit-ik\ *adj* **1** : of, relating to, or being an epiphyte **2** : living on the surface of plants — **epi·phyt·i·cal·ly** \-'fit-i-k(ə-)lē\ *adv*

ep·i·phy·tol·o·gy \,ep-ə-,fī-'täl-ə-jē\ *n* [*epiphytotic* + *-logy*] **1** : a science that deals with character, ecology, and causes of outbreak of plant diseases **2** : the sum of the factors controlling the occurrence of a disease or pathogen of plants

ep·i·phy·tot·ic \-'tät-ik\ *adj* [*epi-* + Gk *phyton* plant] : of, relating to, or being a plant disease that tends to recur sporadically and to affect large numbers of susceptible plants — **epiphytotic** *n*

epi·ro·gen·ic, ep·i·rog·e·ny *var of* EPEIROGENIC, EPEIROGENY

Episc *abbr* Episcopal

epi·scia \i-'pish-(ē-)ə\ *n* [NL, genus name, fr. Gk *episkios* shaded, fr. *epi-* + *skia* shadow — more at SHINE] : any of a genus (*Episcia*) of tropical American herbs that have hairy foliage and are related to the African violet

epis·co·pa·cy \i-'pis-kə-pə-sē\ *n, pl* **-cies** **1** : government of the church by bishops or by a hierarchy **2** : EPISCOPATE

epis·co·pal \i-'pis-kə-pəl\ *adj* [ME, fr. LL *episcopalis,* fr. *episcopus* bishop — more at BISHOP] **1** : of or relating to a bishop **2** : of, having, or constituting government by bishops **3** *cap* : of or relating to the Protestant Episcopal Church representing the Anglican communion in the U.S. — **epis·co·pal·ly** \-p(ə-)lē\ *adv*

Episcopal *n* : EPISCOPALIAN

Epis·co·pa·lian \i-,pis-kə-'pāl-yən\ *n* **1** : an adherent of the episcopal form of church government **2** : a member of an episcopal church (as the Protestant Episcopal Church) — **Episcopalian** *adj* — **Epis·co·pa·lian·ism** \-yə-,niz-əm\ *n*

epis·co·pate \i-'pis-kə-pət, -,pāt\ *n* **1** : the rank, office, or term of bishop **2** : DIOCESE **3** : the body of bishops (as in a country)

epi·scope \'ep-ə-,skōp\ *n* [ISV *epi-* + *-scope*] : a projector for images of opaque objects (as photographs)

epis·i·ot·o·my \i-,piz-ē-'ät-ə-mē\ *n* [NL *episio-* vulva, fr. Gk *epision* pubic region] : surgical enlargement of the vulval orifice for obstetrical purposes during parturition

ep·i·sode \'ep-ə-,sōd *also* -,zōd\ *n* [Gk *epeisodion,* fr. neut. of *epeisodios* coming in besides, fr. *epi-* + *eisodios* coming in, fr. *eis* into (akin to Gk *en* in) + *hodos* road, journey — more at IN, CEDE] **1** : a usu. brief unit of action in a dramatic or literary work: as **a** : the part of an ancient Greek tragedy between two choric songs **b** : a developed situation that is integral to but separable from a continuous narrative : INCIDENT **c** : one of a series of loosely connected stories or scenes **d** : the part of a serial presented at one performance **2** : an event that is distinctive and separate although part of a larger series **3** : a digressive subdivision in a musical composition ***syn*** see OCCURRENCE

ep·i·sod·ic \,ep-ə-'säd-ik *also* -'zäd-\ *also* **ep·i·sod·i·cal** \-i-kəl\ *adj* **1** : made up of separate esp. loosely connected episodes **2** : having the form of an episode **3** : of or limited in duration or significance to a particular episode : TEMPORARY ⟨may be able to establish whether the sea-floor spreading is continuous or ~ —A. I. Hammond⟩ **4** : occurring, appearing, or changing at usu. irregular intervals : OCCASIONAL, CAPRICIOUS ⟨~ care of his patients⟩ — **ep·i·sod·i·cal·ly** \-i-k(ə-)lē\ *adv*

epi·some \'ep-ə-,sōm, -,zōm\ *n* : a genetic determinant (as the DNA of some bacteriophages) that can replicate autonomously in bacterial cytoplasm or as an integral part of the chromosomes — **epi·som·al** \,ep-ə-'sō-məl, -'zō-\ *adj* — **epi·som·al·ly** \-mə-lē\ *adv*

epis·ta·sis \i-'pis-tə-səs\ *or* **epis·ta·sy** \-sē\ *n, pl* **-ta·ses** \-,sēz\ *or* **-ta·sies** \-sēz\ [NL *epistasis,* fr. Gk, act of stopping, fr. *ephistanai* to stop, fr. *epi-* + *histanai* to cause to stand — more at STAND] : suppression of the effect of a gene by a nonallelic gene — **ep·i·stat·ic** \,ep-ə-'stat-ik\ *adj*

ep·i·stax·is \,ep-ə-'stak-səs\ *n, pl* **-stax·es** \-,sēz\ [NL, fr. Gk, fr. *epistazein* to drip on, to bleed at the nose again, fr. *epi-* + *stazein* to drip — more at STAGNATE] : NOSEBLEED

ep·i·ste·mic \,ep-ə-'stē-mik, -'stem-ik\ *adj* : of or relating to knowledge or knowing : COGNITIVE — **ep·i·ste·mi·cal·ly** \-(m)i-k(ə-)lē\ *adv*

epis·te·mol·o·gy \i-,pis-tə-'mäl-ə-jē\ *n* [Gk *epistēmē* knowledge, fr. *epistanai* to understand, know, fr. *epi-* + *histanai* to cause to stand — more at STAND] : the study or a theory of the nature and grounds of knowledge esp. with reference to its limits and validity — **epis·te·mo·log·i·cal** \-mə-'läj-i-kəl\ *adj* — **epis·te·mo·log·i·cal·ly** \-k(ə-)lē\ *adv* — **epis·te·mol·o·gist** \-'mäl-ə-jəst\ *n*

epi·ster·num \,ep-i-'stər-nəm\ *n* [NL] **1** : an anterior element of or associated with the sternum: as **a** : INTERCLAVICLE **b** : MANUBRIUM **2** : a lateral division or piece of a somite of an arthropod

epis·tle \i-'pis-əl\ *n* [ME, letter, Epistle, fr. OF, fr. L *epistula, epistola* letter, fr. Gk *epistolē* message, letter, fr. *epistellein* to send to, fr. *epi-* + *stellein* to send — more at STALL] **1** *cap* **a** : one of the letters adopted as books of the New Testament **b** : a liturgical lection usu. from one of the New Testament Epistles **2 a** : LETTER; *esp* : a formal or elegant letter **b** : a composition in the form of a letter — **epis·tler** \-'pis-(ə-)lər\ *n*

epistle side *n, often cap E* [fr. the custom of reading the Epistle from this side] : the right side of an altar or chancel as one faces it

[1]**epis·to·lary** \i-'pis-tə-,ler-ē\ *adj* **1** : of, relating to, or suitable to a letter **2** : contained in or carried on by letters ⟨an endless sequence of . . . ~ love affairs —*Times Lit. Supp.*⟩ **3** : written in the form of a series of letters ⟨~ novel⟩

[2]**epistolary** *n, pl* **-lar·ies** : a lectionary containing a body of liturgical epistles

epis·to·ler \i-'pis-tə-lər\ *n* : the reader of the liturgical Epistle esp. in Anglican churches

epis·tro·phe \i-'pis-trə-(,)fē\ *n* [Gk *epistrophē,* lit., turning about, fr. *epi-* + *strophē* turning — more at STROPHE] : repetition of the same word or expression at the end of successive phrases, clauses, or sentences for rhetorical effect ⟨Lincoln's "of the people, by the people, for the people" is an example of ~⟩ — compare ANAPHORA

epi·style \'ep-ə-,stīl\ *n* [L *epistylium,* fr. Gk *epistylion,* fr. *epi-* + Gk *stylos* pillar — more at STEER] : ARCHITRAVE 1

ep·i·taph \'ep-ə-,taf\ *n* [ME *epitaphe,* fr. MF, fr. ML *epitaphium,* fr. L, funeral oration, fr. Gk *epitaphion,* fr. *epi-* + *taphos* tomb, funeral; akin to Gk *thaptein* to bury, Arm *damban* grave] **1** : an inscription on or at a tomb or a grave in memory of the one buried there **2** : a brief statement commemorating or epitomizing a deceased person or something past — **ep·i·taph·ial** \,ep-ə-'taf-ē-əl\ *or* **ep·i·taph·ic** \-'taf-ik\ *adj*

epit·a·sis \i-'pit-ə-səs\ *n, pl* **-a·ses** \-,sēz\ [Gk, increased intensity, fr. *epiteinein* to stretch tighter, fr. *epi-* + *teinein* to stretch — more

ə abut	ᵊ kitten	ər further	a back	ā bake	ä cot, cart
au̇ out	ch chin	e less	ē easy	g gift	i trip	ī life
j joke	ŋ sing	ō flow	ȯ flaw	ȯi coin	th thin	th this
ü loot	u̇ foot	y yet	yü few	yu̇ furious	zh vision

at THIN] : the part of a play developing the main action and leading to the catastrophe

ep·i·taxy \ˈep-ə-ˌtak-sē\ *n* [*epi-* + *-taxy* (fr. Gk *-taxia* -taxis)] : the growth on a crystalline substrate of a crystalline substance that mimics the orientation of the substrate — **ep·i·tax·i·al** \ˌep-ə-ˈtak-sē-əl\ *adj* — **ep·i·tax·i·al·ly** \-sē-ə-lē\ *adv*

ep·i·tha·la·mi·um \ˌep-ə-thə-ˈlā-mē-əm\ *or* **ep·i·tha·la·mi·on** \-mē-ən\ *n, pl* **-mi·ums** *or* **-mia** \-mē-ə\ [L & Gk; L *epithalamium,* fr. Gk *epithalamion,* fr. *epi-* + *thalamos* room, bridal chamber] : a song or poem in honor of a bride and bridegroom

epitheli- *or* **epithelio-** *comb form* [NL *epithelium*] : epithelium

ep·i·the·li·al \ˌep-ə-ˈthē-lē-əl\ *adj* : of or relating to epithelium

ep·i·the·li·oid \-lē-ˌȯid\ *adj* : resembling epithelium ⟨~ cells⟩

ep·i·the·li·o·ma \-ˌthē-lē-ˈō-mə\ *n* : a benign or malignant tumor derived from epithelial tissue — **ep·i·the·li·o·ma·tous** \-mət-əs\ *adj*

ep·i·the·li·um \ˌep-ə-ˈthē-lē-əm\ *n, pl* **-lia** \-lē-ə\ [NL, fr. *epi-* + Gk *thēlē* nipple — more at FEMININE] **1** : a membranous cellular tissue that covers a free surface or lines a tube or cavity of an animal body and serves esp. to enclose and protect the other parts of the body, to produce secretions and excretions, and to function in assimilation **2** : a usu. thin layer of parenchyma that lines a cavity or tube of a plant

ep·i·the·lize \ˌep-ə-ˈthē-ˌlīz\ *also* **ep·i·the·li·al·ize** \-lē-ə-ˌlīz\ *vt* **-lized; -liz·ing** : to cover with or convert to epithelium ⟨*epithelized* lesions⟩

ep·i·thet \ˈep-ə-ˌthet *also* -thət\ *n* [L *epitheton,* fr. Gk, fr. neut. of *epithetos* added, fr. *epitithenai* to put on, add, fr. *epi-* + *tithenai* to put — more at DO] **1 a** : a characterizing word or phrase accompanying or occurring in place of the name of a person or thing **b** : a disparaging or abusive word or phrase **c** : the part of a taxonomic name identifying a subordinate unit within a genus **2** *obs* : EXPRESSION — **ep·i·thet·ic** \ˌep-ə-ˈthet-ik\ *or* **ep·i·thet·i·cal** \-i-kəl\ *adj*

epit·o·me \i-ˈpit-ə-mē\ *n* [L, fr. Gk *epitomē,* fr. *epitemnein* to cut short, fr. *epi-* + *temnein* to cut — more at TOME] **1 a** : a summary of a written work **b** : a brief presentation or statement of something **2** : a typical or ideal example : EMBODIMENT ⟨the British monarchy itself is the ~ of tradition —Richard Joseph⟩ **3** : brief or miniature form — usu. used with *in* ***syn*** see ABRIDGMENT

epit·o·mize \-ˌmīz\ *vt* **-mized; -miz·ing** **1** : to make or give an epitome of **2** : to serve as the typical or ideal example of

epi·zo·ic \ˌep-ə-ˈzō-ik\ *adj* : dwelling upon the body of an animal ⟨an ~ plant⟩ — **epi·zo·ism** \-ˌiz-əm\ *n* — **epi·zo·ite** \-ˌīt\ *n*

¹epi·zo·ot·ic \ˌep-ə-zə-ˈwät-ik\ *adj* : of, relating to, or being a disease that affects many animals of one kind at the same time — **epi·zo·ot·i·cal·ly** \-i-k(ə-)lē\ *adv*

²epizootic *n* : an epizootic disease

epi·zo·ot·i·ol·o·gy \ˌep-ə-zə-ˌwät-ē-ˈäl-ə-jē\ *or* **epi·zo·otol·o·gy** \-ˌzō-ə-ˈtäl-ə-jē\ *or* **epi·zo·ol·o·gy** \-zə-ˈwäl-ə-jē\ *n* **1** : a science that deals with the character, ecology, and causes of outbreaks of animal diseases **2** : the sum of the factors controlling the occurrence of a disease or pathogen of animals — **epi·zo·oti·o·log·i·cal** \-zə-ˌwōt-ē-ə-ˈläj-i-kəl, -ˌwät-\ *also* **epi·zo·oti·o·log·ic** \-ik\ *adj* — **epi·zo·oti·o·log·i·cal·ly** \-i-k(ə-)lē\ *adv*

e plu·ri·bus unum \ˌē-ˌplu̇r-ə-bəs-ˈyü-nəm; ˌā-ˌplu̇r-, -bə-ˈsü-\ [L, one out of many] : one composed of many; *specif* : a national government formed by uniting many states — used on the seal of the U.S. and on several U.S. coins

ep·och \ˈep-ək, ˈep-ˌäk *also* ˈē-ˌpäk\ *n* [ML *epocha,* fr. Gk *epochē* cessation, fixed point, fr. *epechein* to pause, hold back, fr. *epi-* + *echein* to hold — more at SCHEME] **1** : an instant of time or a date selected as a point of reference (as in astronomy) **2 a** : an event or a time marked by an event that begins a new period or development **b** : a memorable event or date **3 a** : an extended period of time usu. characterized by a distinctive development or by a memorable series of events **b** : a division of geologic time less than a period and greater than an age ***syn*** see PERIOD

ep·och·al \ˈep-ə-kəl, ˈep-ˌäk-əl\ *adj* **1** : of or relating to an epoch **2** : uniquely or highly significant : MOMENTOUS ⟨his fights to advance . . . democracy during his three ~ years in the assembly —C. G. Bowers⟩; *also* : UNPARALLELED ⟨the . . . delegates . . . have fallen for it out of their almost ~ dumbness —J. T. Flynn⟩ — **ep·och·al·ly** \-ē\ *adv*

ep·ode \ˈep-ˌōd\ *n* [L *epodos,* fr. Gk *epōidos,* fr. *epōidos* sung or said after, fr. *epi-* + *aidein* to sing — more at ODE] **1** : a lyric poem in which a long verse is followed by a shorter one **2** : the third part of a triadically constructed Greek ode following the strophe and the antistrophe

ep·onym \ˈep-ə-ˌnim\ *n* [Gk *epōnymos,* fr. *epōnymos* eponymous, fr. *epi-* + *onyma* name — more at NAME] **1** : the person for whom something is or is believed to be named **2** : a name (as of a drug or a disease) based on or derived from an eponym — **ep·onym·ic** \ˌep-ə-ˈnim-ik\ *adj*

epon·y·mous \i-ˈpän-ə-məs, e-\ *adj* : of, relating to, or being the person for whom something is or is believed to be named

epon·y·my \-mē\ *n, pl* **-mies** : the explanation of a proper name (as of a town or tribe) by supposing a fictitious eponym

ep·o·pee \ˈep-ə-ˌpē\ *n* [F *épopée,* fr. Gk *epopoiia,* fr. *epos* + *poiein* to make — more at POET] : EPIC; *esp* : an epic poem

ep·os \ˈep-ˌäs\ *n* [Gk, word, epic poem] **1** : a number of poems that treat an epic theme but are not formally united **2** : EPIC

ep·ox·ide \(ˈ)ep-ˈäk-ˌsīd\ *n* : an epoxy compound

ep·ox·i·dize \-sə-ˌdīz\ *vt* **-dized; -diz·ing** : to convert into an epoxide ⟨*epoxidized* oils⟩

¹ep·oxy \ˈep-ˌäk-sē, ep-ˈ\ *adj* **1** : containing oxygen attached to two different atoms already united in some other way; *specif* : containing a 3-membered ring consisting of one oxygen and two carbon atoms **2** : of or relating to an epoxide

²epoxy *vt* **ep·ox·ied** *or* **ep·oxyed; ep·oxy·ing** : to glue with epoxy resin

epoxy resin *n* : a flexible usu. thermosetting resin made by polymerization of an epoxide and used chiefly in coatings and adhesives — called also *epoxy*

ep·si·lon \ˈep-sə-ˌlän, -lən\ *n* [Gk *e psilon,* lit., simple e] **1** : the 5th letter of the Greek alphabet — see ALPHABET table **2** : an arbitrarily small positive quantity in mathematical analysis

Ep·som salt \ˌep-səm-\ *n* : EPSOM SALTS

Epsom salts *n pl but sing in constr* [*Epsom,* England] : a bitter colorless or white crystalline salt $MgSO_4 \cdot 7H_2O$ that is a hydrated magnesium sulfate with cathartic properties

eq *abbr* **1** equal **2** equation

equa·ble \ˈek-wə-bəl, ˈē-kwə-\ *adj* [L *aequabilis,* fr. *aequare* to make level or equal, fr. *aequus*] **1** : marked by lack of variation or change : UNIFORM **2** : marked by lack of noticeable, unpleasant, or extreme variation or inequality ***syn*** see STEADY ***ant*** variable, changeable — **equa·bil·i·ty** \ˌek-wə-ˈbil-ət-ē, ˌē-kwə-\ *n* — **equa·ble·ness** \ˈek-wə-bəl-nəs, ˈē-kwə-\ *n* — **equa·bly** \-blē\ *adv*

¹equal \ˈē-kwəl\ *adj* [ME, fr. L *aequalis,* fr. *aequus* level, equal] **1 a** (1) : of the same measure, quantity, amount, or number as another (2) : identical in mathematical value or logical denotation : EQUIVALENT **b** : like in quality, nature, or status **c** : like for each member of a group, class, or society ⟨provide ~ employment opportunities⟩ **2** : regarding or affecting all objects in the same way : IMPARTIAL **3** : free from extremes: as **a** : tranquil of mind or mood **b** : not showing variation in appearance, structure, or proportion **4 a** : capable of meeting the requirements of a situation or a task **b** : SUITABLE ⟨bored with work not ~ to his abilities⟩ ***syn*** see SAME ***ant*** unequal

²equal *n* **1** : one that is equal ⟨insists that women can be absolute ~s with men —Anne Bernays⟩ **2** : an equal quantity

³equal *vt* **equaled** *or* **equalled; equal·ing** *or* **equal·ling** **1** *archaic* : EQUALIZE **2** : to be equal to; *esp* : to be identical in value to **3** : to make or produce something equal to ***syn*** see MATCH

equal–area *adj, of a map projection* : maintaining constant ratio of size between quadrilaterals formed by the meridians and parallels and the quadrilaterals of the globe thereby preserving true areal extent of forms represented

equal·i·tar·i·an \i-ˌkwäl-ə-ˈter-ē-ən\ *adj or n* : EGALITARIAN — **equal·i·tar·i·an·ism** \-ē-ə-ˌniz-əm\ *n*

equal·i·ty \i-ˈkwäl-ət-ē\ *n, pl* **-ties** **1** : the quality or state of being equal **2** : EQUATION 2a

equal·ize \ˈē-kwə-ˌlīz\ *vt* **-ized; -iz·ing** **1** : to make equal **2 a** : to compensate for **b** : to make uniform; *specif* : to distribute evenly or uniformly ⟨~ the tax burden⟩ **c** : to adjust or correct the frequency characteristics of (an electronic signal) by restoring to their original level high frequencies that have been attenuated — **equal·iza·tion** \ˌē-kwə-lə-ˈzā-shən\ *n*

equal·iz·er \-ˌlī-zər\ *n* : one that equalizes: as **a** : a device that provides for equal distribution (as of force) **b** : a score that ties a game

equal·ly \ˈē-kwə-lē\ *adv* **1** : in an equal or uniform manner : EVENLY **2** : to an equal degree : ALIKE ⟨respected ~ by young and old⟩

equal opportunity employer *n* : an employer who agrees not to discriminate against any employee or job applicant because of race, color, religion, sex, or national origin

equal sign *n* : a sign = indicating mathematical or logical equivalence — called also *equality sign, equals sign*

equa·nim·i·ty \ˌē-kwə-ˈnim-ət-ē, ˌek-wə-\ *n, pl* **-ties** [L *aequanimitas,* fr. *aequo animo* with even mind] **1** : evenness of mind esp. under stress **2** : right disposition : BALANCE

syn EQUANIMITY, COMPOSURE, SANGFROID, PHLEGM *shared meaning element* : the characteristic quality of one who is self-possessed and not easily disturbed or perturbed

equate \i-ˈkwāt, ˈē-ˌ\ *vb* **equat·ed; equat·ing** [ME *equaten,* fr. L *aequatus,* pp. of *aequare*] *vt* **1 a** : to make equal : EQUALIZE **b** : to make such an allowance or correction in as will reduce to a common standard or obtain a correct result **2** : to treat, represent, or regard as equal, equivalent, or comparable ⟨~s disagreement with disloyalty⟩ ~ *vi* : to correspond as equal

equa·tion \i-ˈkwā-zhən *also* -shən\ *n* **1 a** : the act or process of equating **b** (1) : an element affecting a process : FACTOR (2) : a complex of variable factors **c** : a state of being equated; *specif* : a state of association or identification of two or more things ⟨bring governmental enterprises and payment for them into immediate ~ —R. G. Tugwell⟩ **2 a** : a usu. formal statement of the equality or equivalence of mathematical or logical expressions **b** : an expression representing a chemical reaction quantitatively by means of chemical symbols

equa·tion·al \i-ˈkwāzh-nəl, -ən-ᵊl *also* -ˈkwāsh-\ *adj* **1** : of, using, or involving equation or equations **2** : dividing into two equal parts — used esp. of the mitotic cell division usu. following reduction in meiosis — **equa·tion·al·ly** \-ē\ *adv*

equation of time : the difference between mean time and apparent time usu. expressed as a correction which is to be added to apparent time to give local mean solar time

equa·tor \i-ˈkwāt-ər, ˈē-ˌ\ *n* [ME, fr. ML *aequator,* lit., equalizer, fr. L *aequatus;* fr. its containing the equinoxes] **1** : the great circle of the celestial sphere whose plane is perpendicular to the axis of the earth **2** : a great circle of the earth that is everywhere equally distant from the two poles and divides the earth's surface into the northern and southern hemispheres **3** : a circle or circular band dividing the surface of a body into two usu. equal and symmetrical parts ⟨the ~ of a dividing cell⟩ **4** : GREAT CIRCLE

¹equa·to·ri·al \ˌē-kwə-ˈtōr-ē-əl, ˌek-wə-, -ˈtȯr-\ *adj* **1 a** : of, relating to, or located at the equator or an equator; *also* : being in the plane of the equator ⟨an ~ orbit of a satellite⟩ **b** : of, originating in, or suggesting the region around the geographic equator **2 a** : being or having a support that includes two axles at right angles to each other with one parallel to the earth's axis of rotation ⟨an ~ telescope⟩ **b** : extending in a direction essentially in the plane of a cyclic structure (as of cyclohexane) ⟨~ hydrogens⟩ — compare AXIAL

²equatorial *n* : an equatorial telescope

equatorial plane *n* **:** the plane perpendicular to the spindle of a dividing cell and midway between the poles
equatorial plate *n* **1 :** EQUATORIAL PLANE **2 :** METAPHASE PLATE
[1]**equa·tor·ward** \i-ˈkwāt-ər-wərd\ *adv* **:** toward the equator ⟨currents flowing ~⟩
[2]**equatorward** *adj* **:** lying near or moving toward the equator ⟨~ winds⟩
equer·ry \ˈek-wə-rē, i-ˈkwer-ē\ *n, pl* **-ries** [obs. *escuirie, equerry* stable, fr. MF *escuirie* office of a squire, stable, fr. *escuier* squire — more at ESQUIRE] **1 :** an officer of a prince or noble charged with the care of horses **2 :** one of the officers of the British royal household in personal attendance on the sovereign or another member of the royal family
[1]**eques·tri·an** \i-ˈkwes-trē-ən\ *adj* [L *equestr-, equester* of a horseman, fr. *eques* horseman, fr. *equus* horse — more at EQUINE] **1 a :** of, relating to, or featuring horseback riding **b** *archaic* **:** riding on horseback **:** MOUNTED **c :** representing a person on horseback ⟨an ~ statue⟩ **2 :** of, relating to, or composed of knights
[2]**equestrian** *n* **:** one who rides on horseback
eques·tri·enne \i-ˌkwes-trē-ˈen\ *n* [[2]*equestrian* + *-enne* (as in *tragedienne*)] **:** a female equestrian
equi- *comb form* [ME, fr. MF, fr. L *aequi-*, fr. *aequus* equal] **:** equal ⟨*equi*poise⟩ **:** equally ⟨*equi*probable⟩
equi·an·gu·lar \ˌē-kwi-ˈaŋ-gyə-lər, ˌek-wi-\ *adj* **:** having all or corresponding angles equal ⟨an ~ triangle⟩ ⟨~ polygons⟩
equi·ca·lor·ic \ˌē-kwə-kə-ˈlȯr-ik, ˌek-wə-, -ˈlär-\ *adj* **:** capable of yielding equal amounts of energy in the body ⟨~ diets⟩
equi·dis·tance \-ˈdis-tən(t)s\ *n* **:** equal distance
equi·dis·tant \-tənt\ *adj* [MF or LL; MF, fr. LL *aequidistant-, aequidistans,* fr. L *aequi-* + *distant-, distans,* prp. of *distare* to stand apart] **1 :** equally distant **2 :** representing map distances true to scale in all directions — **equi·dis·tant·ly** *adv*
equi·lat·er·al \ˌē-kwə-ˈlat-ə-rəl, ˌek-wə-, -ˈla-trəl\ *adj* [LL *aequilateralis,* fr. L *aequi-* + *later-, latus* side — more at LATERAL] **1 a :** having all sides equal ⟨~ triangle⟩ **b :** having all the faces equal ⟨~ polyhedron⟩ **2 :** bilaterally symmetrical
equilateral hyperbola *n* **:** a hyperbola with its asymptotes at right angles
equil·i·brate \i-ˈkwil-ə-ˌbrāt\ *vb* **-brat·ed; -brat·ing** *vt* **:** to bring into or keep in equilibrium **:** BALANCE **~** *vi* **:** to bring about, come to, or be in equilibrium — **equil·i·bra·tion** \-ˌkwil-ə-ˈbrā-shən\ *n* — **equil·i·bra·tor** \-ˈkwil-ə-ˌbrāt-ər\ *n* — **equil·i·bra·to·ry** \-brə-ˌtōr-ē, -ˌtȯr-\ *adj*
equi·li·brist \ˌē-kwə-ˈlib-rəst, ˌek-wə-; i-ˈkwil-ə-brəst\ *n* **:** one who balances himself in unnatural positions and hazardous movements — **equil·i·bris·tic** \i-ˌkwil-ə-ˈbris-tik\ *adj*
equi·lib·ri·um \ˌē-kwə-ˈlib-rē-əm, ˌek-wə-\ *n, pl* **-ri·ums** *or* **-ria** \-rē-ə\ [L *aequilibrium,* fr. *aequilibris* being in equilibrium, fr. *aequi-* + *libra* weight, balance] **1 :** a state of balance between opposing forces or actions that is either static (as in a body acted on by forces whose resultant is zero) or dynamic (as in a reversible chemical reaction when the velocities in both directions are equal) **2 a :** a state of adjustment between opposing or divergent influences or elements **b :** a state of intellectual or emotional balance **:** POISE **3 :** the normal oriented state of the animal body in respect to its substrate that involves adjustment to changing gravitational and spatial relationships
equi·mo·lal \-ˈmō-ləl\ *adj* **1 :** having equal molal concentration **2 :** EQUIMOLAR 1
equi·mo·lar \-ˈmō-lər\ *adj* **1 :** of or relating to an equal number of moles ⟨an ~ mixture⟩ **2 :** having equal molar concentration
equine \ˈē-ˌkwīn, ˈek-ˌwīn\ *adj* [L *equinus,* fr. *equus* horse; akin to OE *eoh* horse, Gk *hippos*] **:** of, relating to, or resembling a horse or the horse family — **equine** *n* — **equine·ly** *adv*
[1]**equi·noc·tial** \ˌē-kwə-ˈnäk-shəl, ˌek-wə-\ *adj* **1 :** relating to an equinox or to a state or the time of equal day and night **2 :** relating to the regions or climate of the equinoctial line or equator **3 :** relating to the time when the sun passes an equinoctial point
[2]**equinoctial** *n* **1 :** EQUATOR 1 **2 :** an equinoctial storm
equinoctial circle *n* **:** EQUATOR 1 — called also *equinoctial line*
equi·nox \ˈē-kwə-ˌnäks, ˈek-wə-\ *n* [ME, fr. MF or ML; MF *equinoxe,* fr. ML *equinoxium,* alter. of L *aequinoctium,* fr. *aequi-* equi- + *noct-, nox* night — more at NIGHT] **1 :** either of the two times each year when the sun crosses the equator and day and night are everywhere of equal length, being about March 21 and September 23 **2 :** either of the two points on the celestial sphere where the celestial equator intersects the ecliptic
[1]**equip** \i-ˈkwip\ *vt* **equipped; equip·ping** [MF *equiper,* of Gmc origin; akin to OE *scip* ship] **1 :** to furnish for service or action **:** make ready by appropriate provisioning **2 :** DRESS, ARRAY ***syn*** see FURNISH
[2]**equip** *abbr* equipment
eq·ui·page \ˈek-wə-pij\ *n* **1 a :** material or articles used in equipment **:** OUTFIT **b** *archaic* (1) **:** a set of small articles (as for table service) (2) **:** ETUI **c :** TRAPPINGS **2** *archaic* **:** RETINUE **3 :** a horse-drawn carriage with its servants; *also* **:** such a carriage alone
equip·ment \i-ˈkwip-mənt\ *n* **1 a :** the equipping of a person or thing **b :** the state of being equipped **2 a :** the set of articles or physical resources serving to equip a person or thing: as (1) **:** the implements used in an operation or activity **:** APPARATUS (2) **:** all the fixed assets other than land and buildings of a business enterprise (3) **:** the rolling stock of a railway **b :** a piece of such equipment **3 :** mental or emotional traits or resources **:** ENDOWMENT
[1]**equi·poise** \ˈek-wə-ˌpȯiz, ˈē-kwə-\ *n* **1 :** a state of equilibrium **2 :** COUNTERBALANCE
[2]**equipoise** *vt* **1 :** to serve as an equipoise to **2 :** to put or hold in equipoise
equi·pol·lence \ˌē-kwə-ˈpäl-ən(t)s, ˌek-wə-\ *n* **:** the quality of being equipollent
equi·pol·lent \-ənt\ *adj* [ME, fr. MF, fr. L *aequipollent-, aequipollens,* fr. *aequi-* equi- + *pollent-, pollens,* prp. of *pollēre* to be able] **1 :** equal in force, power, or validity **2 :** the same in effect or signification — **equipollent** *n* — **equi·pol·lent·ly** *adv*
equi·pon·der·ant \-ˈpän-d(ə-)rənt\ *adj* **:** evenly balanced
equi·pon·der·ate \-ˈpän-də-ˌrāt\ *vb* **-at·ed; -at·ing** [ML *aequiponderatus,* pp. of *equiponderare,* fr. L *aequi-* + *ponderare* to weigh, ponder] *vi* **:** to be equal in weight or force **~** *vt* **:** to equal or make equal in weight
equi·po·tent \ˌē-kwə-ˈpōt-ᵊnt, ˌek-wə-\ *adj* **:** having equal effects or capacities for development ⟨~ genes⟩ ⟨~ regions of an egg⟩
equi·po·ten·tial \-pə-ˈten-chəl\ *adj* **:** having the same potential **:** of uniform potential throughout ⟨~ points⟩ ⟨an ~ surface⟩
equi·prob·a·ble \-ˈpräb-(ə-)bəl\ *adj* **:** having the same degree of logical or mathematical probability ⟨~ alternatives⟩
eq·ui·se·tum \ˌek-wə-ˈsēt-əm\ *n, pl* **-se·tums** *or* **-se·ta** \-ˈsēt-ə\ [NL, genus name, fr. L *equisaetum* horsetail (plant), fr. *equus* horse + *saeta* bristle] **:** any of a genus (*Equisetum*) of lower tracheophytes comprising perennial plants that spread by creeping rhizomes, are homosporous and asexual, and have leaves reduced to nodal sheaths on the hollow jointed grooved shoots — called also *scouring rush*

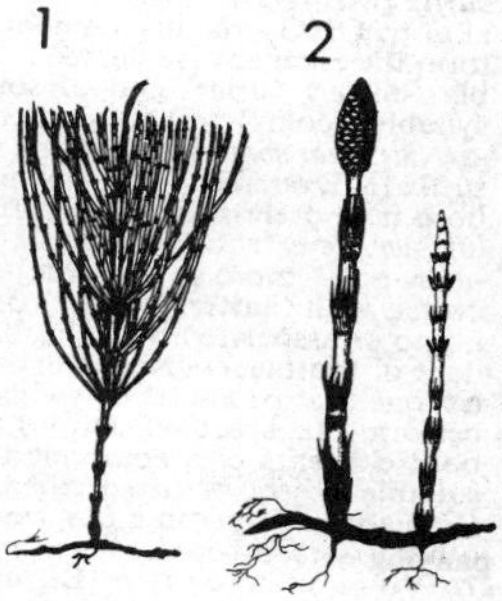

equisetum: *1* sterile stem, *2* fertile stem

eq·ui·ta·ble \ˈek-wət-ə-bəl\ *adj* **1 :** having or exhibiting equity **:** dealing fairly and equally with all concerned **2 :** existing or valid in equity as distinguished from law ***syn*** see FAIR ***ant*** inequitable — **eq·ui·ta·bil·i·ty** \ˌek-wət-ə-ˈbil-ət-ē\ *n* — **eq·ui·ta·ble·ness** \ˈek-wət-ə-bəl-nəs\ *n* — **eq·ui·ta·bly** \-blē\ *adv*
eq·ui·tant \ˈek-wət-ənt\ *adj* [L *equitant-, equitans,* prp. of *equitare* to ride on horseback, fr. *equit-, eques* horseman — more at EQUESTRIAN] *of leaves* **:** overlapping each other transversely at the base (as in an iris)
eq·ui·ta·tion \ˌek-wə-ˈtā-shən\ *n* **:** the act or art of riding on horseback
eq·ui·ty \ˈek-wət-ē\ *n, pl* **-ties** [ME *equite,* fr. MF *equité,* fr. L *aequitat-, aequitas,* fr. *aequus* equal, fair] **1 a :** justice according to natural law or right; *specif* **:** freedom from bias or favoritism **b :** something that is equitable **2 a :** a system of law originating in the English chancery and comprising a settled and formal body of legal and procedural rules and doctrines that supplement, aid, or override common and statute law and are designed to protect rights and enforce duties fixed by substantive law **b :** trial or remedial justice under or by the rules and doctrines of equity **c :** a body of legal doctrines and rules developed to enlarge, supplement, or override a narrow rigid system of law **3 a :** a right, claim, or interest existing or valid in equity **b :** the money value of a property or of an interest in a property in excess of claims or liens against it **c :** a risk interest or ownership right in property
equity capital *n* **:** VENTURE CAPITAL
equiv *abbr* equivalency; equivalent
equiv·a·lence \i-ˈkwiv(-ə)-lən(t)s\ *n* **1 a :** the state or property of being equivalent **b** (1) **:** the relation holding between two statements if they are either both true or both false (2) **:** the relation holding between two statements if to affirm one and to deny the other would result in a contradiction **2 :** a presentation of terms as equivalent **3 :** equality in metrical value of a regular foot and one in which there are substitutions
equivalence class *n* **:** a set for which an equivalence relation holds between every pair of elements
equivalence relation *n* **:** a relation (as equality) between elements of a set (as the real numbers) that is symmetric, reflexive, and transitive and for any two elements either holds or does not hold
equiv·a·len·cy \i-ˈkwiv(-ə)-lən-sē\ *n, pl* **-cies :** EQUIVALENCE
equiv·a·lent \-lənt\ *adj* [ME, fr. MF or LL; MF, fr. LL *aequivalent-, aequivalens,* prp. of *aequivalēre* to have equal power, fr. L *aequi-* + *valēre* to be strong — more at WIELD] **1 :** equal in force, amount, or value; *also* **:** equal in area or volume but not admitting of superposition ⟨a square ~ to a triangle⟩ **2 :** like in signification or import **3 :** corresponding or virtually identical esp. in effect or function **4** *obs* **:** equal in might or authority **5 :** having the same chemical combining capacity ⟨~ quantities of two elements⟩ **6 a :** having the same solution set ⟨~ equations⟩ **b :** capable of being placed in one-to-one correspondence ⟨~ sets⟩ **c :** related by an equivalence relation ***syn*** see SAME ***ant*** different — **equivalent** *n* — **equiv·a·lent·ly** *adv*
equivalent weight *n* **:** the weight of a substance esp. in grams that combines with or is chemically equivalent to eight grams of oxygen or one gram of hydrogen **:** the atomic or molecular weight divided by the valence
equiv·o·cal \i-ˈkwiv-ə-kəl\ *adj* [LL *aequivocus,* fr. *aequi-* equi- + *voc-, vox* voice — more at VOICE] **1 a :** subject to two or more interpretations and usu. used to mislead or confuse ⟨he did not lie but his story of the party was certainly ~⟩ **b :** uncertain as an indication or sign **2 a :** of uncertain nature or classification **b :** of uncertain disposition toward a person or thing **:** UNDECIDED **c :** of doubtful advantage, genuineness, or moral rectitude ⟨~ behavior⟩ ***syn*** see OBSCURE ***ant*** unequivocal — **equiv·o·cal·i·ty**

ə abut ᵊ kitten ər further a back ā bake ä cot, cart
au̇ out ch chin e less ē easy g gift i trip ī life
j joke ŋ sing ō flow ȯ flaw ȯi coin th thin t͟h this
ü loot u̇ foot y yet yü few yu̇ furious zh vision

\-ˌkwiv-ə-ˈkal-ət-ē\ *n* — **equiv·o·cal·ly** \-ˈkwiv-ə-k(ə-)lē\ *adv* — **equiv·o·cal·ness** \-kəl-nəs\ *n*

equiv·o·cate \i-ˈkwiv-ə-ˌkāt\ *vi* **-cat·ed; -cat·ing** **1** : to use equivocal language esp. with intent to deceive **2** : to avoid committing oneself in what one says ***syn*** see LIE — **equiv·o·ca·tion** \-ˌkwiv-ə-ˈkā-shən\ *n* — **equiv·o·ca·tor** \-ˈkwiv-ə-ˌkāt-ər\ *n*

equi·voque *also* **equi·voke** \ˈek-wə-ˌvōk, ˈē-kwə-\ *n* [F *équivoque,* fr. *équivoque* equivocal, fr. LL *aequivocus*] **1** : an equivocal word or phrase; *specif* : PUN **2 a** : double meaning **b** : WORDPLAY

Er *symbol* erbium

ER *abbr* earned run

¹-er \ər; *after some vowels, often* r; *after* ŋ, *usu* gər\ *adj suffix or adv suffix* [ME *-er, -ere, -re,* fr. OE *-ra* (in adjectives), *-or* (in adverbs); akin to OHG *-iro,* adj. compar. suffix, L *-ior,* Gk *-iōn*] — used to form the comparative degree of adjectives and adverbs of one syllable ⟨hott*er*⟩ ⟨dri*er*⟩ and of some adjectives and adverbs of two syllables ⟨complet*er*⟩ and sometimes of longer ones ⟨divineli*er*⟩

²-er \ər; *after some vowels, often* r\ *also* **-ier** \ē-ər, yər\ *or* **-yer** \yər\ *n suffix* [ME *-er, -ere, -ier, -iere;* partly fr. OE *-ere* (akin to OHG *-āri;* both fr. a prehistoric Gmc suffix borrowed fr. L *-arius*); partly fr. OF *-ier, -iere,* fr. L *-arius, -aria, -arium* -ary; partly fr. MF *-ere,* fr. L *-ator* -or — more at -ARY, -OR] **1 a** : person occupationally connected with ⟨hatt*er*⟩ ⟨furri*er*⟩ ⟨lawy*er*⟩ **b** : person or thing belonging to or associated with ⟨head*er*⟩ ⟨old-tim*er*⟩ **c** : native of : resident of ⟨cottag*er*⟩ ⟨New York*er*⟩ **d** : one that has ⟨three-deck*er*⟩ **e** : one that produces or yields ⟨pork*er*⟩ **2 a** : one that does or performs (a specified action) ⟨report*er*⟩ — sometimes added to both elements of a compound ⟨build*er*-upp*er*⟩ **b** : one that is a suitable object of (a specified action) ⟨broil*er*⟩ **3** : one that is ⟨foreign*er*⟩ — *-yer* in a few words after *w, -ier* in a few words after other letters, otherwise *-er*

era \ˈir-ə, ˈer-ə, ˈē-rə\ *n* [LL *aera,* fr. L, counters, pl. of *aer-, aes* copper, money — more at ORE] **1** : a system of chronological notation computed from a given date as basis **2 a** : a fixed point in time from which a series of years is reckoned **b** : a memorable or important date or event; *esp* : one that begins a new period in the history of a person or thing **3 a** : a period set off or typified by some prominent figure or characteristic feature **b** : a stage in the development of a person or thing; *esp* : one of the five major divisions of geologic time ⟨Paleozoic ∼⟩ ***syn*** see PERIOD

ERA *abbr* **1** earned run average **2** Equal Rights Amendment

erad·i·cate \i-ˈrad-ə-ˌkāt\ *vt* **-cat·ed; -cat·ing** [L *eradicatus,* pp. of *eradicare,* fr. *e-* + *radic-, radix* root — more at ROOT] **1** : to pull up by the roots **2** : to do away with as if by pulling up by the roots ⟨∼ ignorance by better teaching⟩ ***syn*** see EXTERMINATE — **erad·i·ca·ble** \-ˈrad-i-kə-bəl\ *adj* — **erad·i·ca·tion** \-ˌrad-ə-ˈkā-shən\ *n* — **erad·i·ca·tive** \-ˈrad-ə-ˌkāt-iv\ *adj* — **erad·i·ca·tor** \-ˌkāt-ər\ *n*

erase \i-ˈrās, *Brit* -ˈrāz\ *vb* **erased; eras·ing** [L *erasus,* pp. of *eradere,* fr. *e-* + *radere* to scratch, scrape — more at RAT] *vt* **1 a** : to rub or scrape out (as written, painted, or engraved letters) **b** : to remove (recorded matter) from a magnetic tape or wire **c** : to delete from a computer storage device **2 a** : to remove from existence or memory as if by erasing **b** : to nullify the effect or force of ∼ *vi* : to yield to being erased — **eras·abil·i·ty** \-ˌrā-sə-ˈbil-ət-ē\ *n* — **eras·able** \-ˈrā-sə-bəl\ *adj*

syn ERASE, EXPUNGE, CANCEL, EFFACE, OBLITERATE, BLOT OUT, DELETE *shared meaning element* : to eradicate something so that it no longer has effect or existence

eras·er \i-ˈrā-sər\ *n* : one that erases; *specif* : a device (as a sharp instrument, a piece of rubber, or a felt pad) used to erase marks (as of ink or chalk)

Eras·tian \i-ˈras-tē-ən, -ˈras-chən\ *adj* [Thomas *Erastus* †1583 German-Swiss physician and Zwinglian theologian] : of, characterized by, or advocating the doctrine of state supremacy in ecclesiastical affairs — **Erastian** *n* — **Eras·tian·ism** \-ˌiz-əm\ *n*

era·sure \i-ˈrā-shər *also* -zhər\ *n* : an act or instance of erasing

Er·a·to \ˈer-ə-ˌtō\ *n* [Gk *Eratō*] : the Greek Muse of lyric and love poetry

er·bi·um \ˈər-bē-əm\ *n* [NL, fr. *Ytterby,* Sweden] : a metallic element of the rare-earth group that occurs with yttrium — see ELEMENT table

¹ere \(ˌ)e(ə)r, (ˌ)a(ə)r\ *prep* [ME *er,* fr. OE *ǣr,* fr. *ǣr,* adv., early, soon; akin to OHG *ēr* earlier, Gk *ēri* early] : ²BEFORE 2 ⟨contrived ∼ the beginning of the world —Norman Douglas⟩

²ere *conj* : ³BEFORE ⟨I will be thrown into Etna . . . ∼ I will leave her —Shak.⟩

Er·e·bus \ˈer-ə-bəs\ *n* [L, fr. Gk *Erebos*] **1** : a personification of darkness in Greek mythology **2** : a place of darkness in the underworld on the way to Hades

¹erect \i-ˈrekt\ *adj* [ME, fr. L *erectus,* pp. of *erigere* to erect, fr. *e-* + *regere* to lead straight, guide — more at RIGHT] **1 a** : vertical in position; *specif* : not spread out or lying down **b** : standing up or out from the body ⟨∼ hairs⟩ **c** : characterized by firm or rigid straightness in bodily posture ⟨an ∼ bearing⟩ **2** *archaic* : directed upward **3** *obs* : ALERT, WATCHFUL **4** : being in a state of physiological erection — **erect·ly** \-ˈrek-(t)lē\ *adv* — **erect·ness** \-ˈrek(t)-nəs\ *n*

²erect *vt* **1 a** (1) : to put up by the fitting together of materials or parts : BUILD (2) : to fix in an upright position (3) : to cause to stand up or out **b** *archaic* : to direct upward **c** : to change (an image) from an inverted to a normal position **2** : to elevate in status **3** : to set up : ESTABLISH **4** *obs* : ENCOURAGE, EMBOLDEN **5** : to construct (as a perpendicular) upon a given base — **erect·able** \-ˈrek-tə-bəl\ *adj*

erec·tile \i-ˈrek-tᵊl, -ˌtīl\ *adj* : capable of being raised to an erect position; *esp* : CAVERNOUS 3 — **erec·til·i·ty** \-ˌrek-ˈtil-ət-ē\ *n*

erec·tion \i-ˈrek-shən\ *n* **1** : the act or process of erecting : CONSTRUCTION **2 a** : the state marked by firm turgid form and erect position of a previously flaccid bodily part containing cavernous tissue when that tissue becomes dilated with blood **b** : an occurrence of such a state in the penis or clitoris **3** : something erected

erec·tor \i-ˈrek-tər\ *n* : one that erects; *esp* : a muscle that raises or keeps a part erect

E region *n* : the part of the ionosphere occurring between 40 and 90 miles above the surface of the earth and containing the daytime E layer and the sporadic E layer

ere·long \e(ə)r-ˈlȯŋ, a(ə)r-\ *adv* : before long : SOON

er·e·mite \ˈer-ə-ˌmīt\ *n* [ME — more at HERMIT] : HERMIT; *esp* : a religious recluse — **er·e·mit·ic** \ˌer-ə-ˈmit-ik\ *or* **er·e·mit·i·cal** \-i-kəl\ *adj* — **er·e·mit·ism** \ˈer-ə-ˌmīt-ˌiz-əm\ *n*

er·em·urus \ˌer-ə-ˈmyu̇r-əs\ *n, pl* **-uri** \-ˈmyu̇(ə)r-ˌī\ [NL, genus name, fr. Gk *erēmos* solitary + *oura* tail — more at RETINA, SQUIRREL] : FOXTAIL LILY

ere·now \e(ə)r-ˈnau̇, a(ə)r-\ *adv* : before now : HERETOFORE

erep·sin \i-ˈrep-sən\ *n* [ISV *er-* (prob. fr. L *eripere* to sweep away, fr. *e-* + *rapere* to sweep) + *pepsin* — more at RAPID] : a proteolytic fraction obtained esp. from the intestinal juice and known to be a mixture of exopeptidases

er·e·thism \ˈer-ə-ˌthiz-əm\ *n* [F *éréthisme,* fr. Gk *erethismos* irritation, fr. *erethizein* to irritate; akin to Gk *ornynai* to rouse — more at RISE] : abnormal irritability or responsiveness to stimulation — **er·e·this·mic** \ˌer-ə-ˈthiz-mik\ *adj*

ere·while \e(ə)r-ˈ(h)wī(ə)l, a(ə)r-\ *also* **ere·whiles** \-ˈ(h)wī(ə)lz\ *adv, archaic* : HERETOFORE

erg \ˈərg\ *n* [Gk *ergon* work — more at WORK] : a cgs unit of work equal to the work done by a force of one dyne acting through a distance of one centimeter

erg- *or* **ergo-** *comb form* [Gk, fr. *ergon*] : work ⟨*ergo*phobia⟩

er·gas·tic \(ˌ)ər-ˈgas-tik\ *adj* [Gk *ergastikos* able to work, fr. *ergazesthai* to work, fr. *ergon* work] : constituting the nonliving by-products of protoplasmic activity

er·gas·to·plasm \-tə-ˌplaz-əm\ *n* [ISV *ergastic* + *-o-* + *-plasm*] : ribosome-studded endoplasmic reticulum — **er·gas·to·plas·mic** \-ˌgas-tə-ˈplaz-mik\ *adj*

er·go \ˈe(ə)r-(ˌ)gō, ˈər-\ *adv* [L, fr. OL, because of, fr. (assumed) OL *e rogo* from the direction (of)] : THEREFORE, HENCE

ergo- *comb form* [F, fr. *ergot*] : ergot ⟨*ergo*sterol⟩

er·go·dic \(ˌ)ər-ˈgäd-ik, -ˈgōd-\ *adj* [G *ergodenhypothese,* lit., hypothesis of the path of energy, fr. *erg-* + Gk *hodos* path, road] **1** : of or relating to a process in which every sequence or sizable sample is equally representative of the whole (as in regard to a statistical parameter) **2** : involving or relating to the probability that any state will recur; *esp* : having zero probability that any state will never recur — **er·go·dic·i·ty** \ˌər-gə-ˈdis-ət-ē\ *n*

er·go·graph \ˈər-gə-ˌgraf\ *n* [ISV] : an apparatus for measuring the work capacity of a muscle

er·gom·e·ter \(ˌ)ər-ˈgäm-ət-ər\ *n* : an apparatus for measuring the work performed by a group of muscles — **er·go·met·ric** \ˌər-gə-ˈme-trik\ *adj*

er·go·nom·ic \ˌər-gə-ˈnäm-ik\ *adj* [*erg-* + *economic*] : of or relating to biotechnology

er·go·nom·ics \-iks\ *n pl but sing or pl in constr* [*erg-* + *economics*] : BIOTECHNOLOGY

er·gon·o·mist \(ˌ)ər-ˈgän-ə-məst\ *n* : a specialist in biotechnology

er·go·no·vine \ˌər-gə-ˈnō-ˌvēn\ *n* [*ergo-* + L *novus* new — more at NEW] : an alkaloid $C_{19}H_{23}N_3O_2$ from ergot with similar pharmacological action but reduced toxicity

er·gos·ter·ol \(ˌ)ər-ˈgäs-tə-ˌrōl, -ˌrȯl\ *n* [ISV] : a crystalline steroid alcohol $C_{28}H_{44}O$ that occurs esp. in yeast, molds, and ergot and is converted by ultraviolet irradiation ultimately into vitamin D_2

er·got \ˈər-gət, -ˌgät\ *n* [F, lit., cock's spur] **1** : the black or dark purple sclerotium of fungi (genus *Claviceps*) that occurs as a club-shaped body replacing the seed of a grass (as rye); *also* : a fungus bearing ergots **2** : a disease of rye and other cereals caused by an ergot fungus **3 a** : the dried sclerotia of an ergot fungus grown on rye and containing several alkaloids (as ergonovine and ergotamine) **b** : any of such alkaloids used medicinally for their contractile effect on smooth muscle (as of peripheral arterioles) — **er·got·ic** \(ˌ)ər-ˈgät-ik\ *adj*

er·got·a·mine \(ˌ)ər-ˈgät-ə-ˌmēn\ *n* [ISV] : an alkaloid $C_{33}H_{35}N_5O_5$ from ergot that has the pharmacological action of ergot and is used esp. in treating migraine

er·got·ism \ˈər-gət-ˌiz-əm\ *n* : a toxic condition produced by eating grain, grain products (as rye bread), or grasses infected with ergot fungus or by chronic excessive use of an ergot drug

er·got·ized \-ˌīzd\ *adj* : containing ergot ⟨∼ grain⟩

ERIC *abbr* educational resources information center

er·i·ca \ˈer-i-kə\ *n* [NL, genus name, fr. L *erice* heather, fr. Gk *ereikē*] : any of a large genus (*Erica*) of the heath family of low much-branched evergreen shrubs

er·i·ca·ceous \ˌer-ə-ˈkā-shəs\ *adj* : of, relating to, or being a heath or the heath family

er·i·coid \ˈer-ə-ˌkȯid\ *adj* : resembling heath

Erie \ˈi(ə)r-ē\ *n* **1** : a member of an Amerindian people of the Lake Erie region **2** : the language of the Erie people

erig·er·on \ə-ˈrij-ə-ˌrän\ *n* [NL, genus name, fr. L, groundsel, fr. Gk *ērigerōn,* fr. *ēri* early + *gerōn* old man; fr. the hoary down of some species — more at ERE, GERONT-] : any of a widely distributed genus (*Erigeron*) of composite herbs with flower heads that resemble asters but have fewer and narrower involucral bracts

Er·in \ˈer-ən\ *n* [OIr *Ērinn,* dat. of *Ēriu* Ireland] : Ireland

Eri·nys \i-ˈrin-əs, -ˈrī-nəs\ *n, pl* **Eriny·es** \-ˈrin-ē-ˌēz\ [Gk] : FURY 2a

er·i·o·phy·id \ˌer-ē-ˈäf-ē-əd, -ē-ə-ˈfī-əd\ *n* [deriv. of Gk *erion* wool + *phyē* growth; akin to Gk *physis* growth — more at PHYSICS] : any of a large family (Eriophyidae) of minute plant-feeding mites that have two pairs of legs placed far anterior and lack a respiratory system — **eriophyid** *adj*

¹eris·tic \i-ˈris-tik, e-\ *also* **eris·ti·cal** \-ti-kəl\ *adj* [Gk *eristikos* fond of wrangling, fr. *erizein* to wrangle, fr. *eris* strife] : characterized by disputatious and often subtle and specious reasoning — **eris·ti·cal·ly** \-ti-k(ə-)lē\ *adv*

²eristic *n* **1** : a person devoted to logical disputation **2** : the art or practice of disputation and polemics

Er·len·mey·er flask \ˌər-lən-ˌmī(-ə)r-, ˌer-lən-\ *n* [Emil *Erlenmeyer*] : a flat-bottomed conical laboratory flask

er·mine \ˈər-mən\ *n, pl* **ermines** [ME, fr. OF, of Gmc origin; akin to OHG *harmo* weasel; akin to Lith *šarmuō* weasel] **1** *or pl* **er-**

mine **a** : any of several weasels that assume white winter pelage usu. with more or less black on the tail; *esp* : a large European weasel (*Mustela erminea*) **b** : the white fur of the ermine in winter pelage **2** : a rank or office whose ceremonial or official robe is ornamented with ermine

er·mined \-mənd\ *adj* : clothed or adorned with ermine

erne *or* **ern** \'ərn, 'e(ə)rn\ *n* [ME, fr. OE *earn;* akin to OHG *arn* eagle, Gk *ornis* bird] : EAGLE; *esp* : WHITE-TAILED SEA EAGLE

erode \i-'rōd\ *vb* **erod·ed; erod·ing** [L *erodere* to eat away, fr. *e-* + *rodere* to gnaw — more at RAT] *vt* **1** : to diminish or destroy by degrees: **a** : to eat into or away by slow destruction of substance : CORRODE **b** : to wear away by the action of water, wind, or glacial ice **c** : to cause to deteriorate or disappear as if by eating or wearing away ⟨buying power is *eroded* with each inflationary year —R. H. McDonough⟩ **2** : to produce or form by eroding ⟨glaciers ~ U-shaped valleys⟩ ~ *vi* : to undergo erosion — **erod·ibil·i·ty** \-,rōd-ə-'bil-ət-ē\ *n* — **erod·ible** \-'rōd-ə-bəl\ *adj*

erog·e·nous \i-'räj-ə-nəs\ *also* **er·o·gen·ic** \,er-ə-'jen-ik\ *adj* [Gk *erōs* + E *-genous, -genic*] **1** : producing sexual excitement or libidinal gratification when stimulated : sexually sensitive **2** : of, relating to, or arousing sexual feelings

Eros \'e(ə)r-,äs, 'i(ə)r-\ *n* [Gk *Erōs,* fr. *erōs* love; akin to Gk *erasthai* to love, desire] **1** : a son of Aphrodite who excites erotic love in gods and men with his arrows and torches — compare CUPID **2** : the aggregate of pleasure-directed life instincts whose energy is derived from libido — compare THANATOS **3** *often not cap* : love directed toward self-realization

erose \i-'rōs\ *adj* [L *erosus,* pp. of *erodere*] : IRREGULAR, UNEVEN; *specif* : having the margin irregularly notched as if gnawed ⟨an ~ leaf⟩ ⟨an ~ edge of a bacterial colony⟩ — **erose·ly** *adv*

ero·si·ble \i-'rō-zə-bəl, -'rō-sə-\ *adj* : capable of being eroded

ero·sion \i-'rō-zhən\ *n* **1** **a** : the action or process of eroding **b** : the state of being eroded **2** : an instance or product of erosive action — **ero·sion·al** \-'rōzh-nəl, -'rō-zhən-ᵊl\ *adj* — **ero·sion·al·ly** \-ē\ *adv*

ero·sive \i-'rō-siv, -ziv\ *adj* : tending to erode or to induce or permit erosion — **ero·sive·ness** *n* — **ero·siv·i·ty** \i-,rō-'siv-ət-ē\ *n*

erot·ic \i-'rät-ik\ *adj* [Gk *erōtikos,* fr. *erōt-, erōs*] **1** : of, devoted to, or tending to arouse sexual love or desire ⟨~ art⟩ **2** : strongly affected by sexual desire — **erotic** *n* — **erot·i·cal** \-i-kəl\ *adj* — **erot·i·cal·ly** \-i-k(ə-)lē\ *adv*

erot·i·ca \i-'rät-i-kə\ *n pl but sing or pl in constr* [NL, fr. Gk *erōtika,* neut. pl. of *erōtikos*] : literary or artistic works having an erotic theme or quality

erot·i·cism \i-'rät-ə-,siz-əm\ *n* **1** : an erotic theme or quality **2** : a state of sexual arousal **3** : sexual impulse or desire esp. when abnormally insistent — **erot·i·cist** \-səst\ *n*

erot·i·cize \-,sīz\ *vt* **-cized; -ciz·ing** : to make erotic ⟨a film version that ~s the original story⟩ — **erot·i·ci·za·tion** \i-,rät-ə-sə-'zā-shən\ *n*

er·o·tism \'er-ə-,tiz-əm\ *n* [Gk *erōt-, erōs* + E *-ism*] : EROTICISM

ero·to·gen·ic \i-,rōt-ə-'jen-ik, -,rät-\ *adj* : EROGENOUS

err \'e(ə)r, 'ər\ *vi* [ME *erren,* fr. OF *errer,* fr. L *errare;* akin to OE *ierre* wandering, angry, ON *rās* race — more at RACE] **1** *archaic* : STRAY **2** **a** : to make a mistake **b** : to violate an accepted standard of conduct

er·ran·cy \'er-ən-sē\ *n, pl* **-cies** : the state or an instance of erring

er·rand \'er-ənd\ *n* [ME *erend* message, business, fr. OE *ǣrend;* akin to OHG *ārunti* message] **1** *archaic* **a** : an oral message entrusted to a person **b** : EMBASSY, MISSION **2** **a** : a short trip taken to attend to some business often for another ⟨was on an ~ for his mother⟩ **b** : the object or purpose of such a trip

er·rant \'er-ənt\ *adj* [ME *erraunt,* fr. MF *errant,* prp. of *errer* to err & *errer* to travel, fr. ML *iterare,* fr. L *iter* road, journey — more at ITINERANT] **1** : traveling or given to traveling ⟨an ~ knight⟩ **2** **a** : straying outside the proper path or bounds ⟨an ~ calf⟩ **b** : moving about aimlessly or irregularly ⟨an ~ breeze⟩ **c** : deviating from a standard (as of truth or propriety) ⟨an ~ child⟩ **3** *obs* : ARRANT — **errant** *n* — **er·rant·ly** *adv*

er·rant·ry \'er-ən-trē\ *n, pl* **-ries** : the quality, condition, or fact of wandering; *esp* : a roving in search of chivalrous adventure

er·ra·ta \e-'rät-ə, -'rāt-, -'rat-\ *n* [fr. pl. of *erratum*] : a list of corrigenda; *also* : a page bearing such a list

¹er·rat·ic \ir-'at-ik\ *adj* [ME, fr. MF or L; MF *erratique,* fr. L *erraticus,* fr. *erratus,* pp. of *errare*] **1** **a** : having no fixed course : WANDERING ⟨an ~ comet⟩ **b** *archaic* : NOMADIC **2** : transported from an original resting place esp. by a glacier ⟨~ boulder⟩ **3** **a** : characterized by lack of consistency, regularity, or uniformity **b** : deviating from what is ordinary or standard : ECCENTRIC ⟨an ~ genius⟩ — **er·rat·i·cal** \-i-kəl\ *adj* — **er·rat·i·cal·ly** \-i-k(ə-)lē\ *adv* — **er·rat·i·cism** \-'at-ə-,siz-əm\ *n*

²erratic *n* : one that is erratic; *esp* : an erratic boulder or block of rock

er·ra·tum \e-'rät-əm, -'rāt-, -rat-\ *n, pl* **-ta** \-ə\ [L, fr. neut. of *erratus*] : CORRIGENDUM

er·ro·ne·ous \ir-'ō-nē-əs, e-'rō-\ *adj* [ME, fr. L *erroneus,* fr. *erron-, erro* wanderer, fr. *errare*] **1** *archaic* : WANDERING **2** : containing or characterized by error : MISTAKEN ⟨~ assumptions⟩ — **er·ro·ne·ous·ly** *adv* — **er·ro·ne·ous·ness** *n*

er·ror \'er-ər\ *n* [ME *errour,* fr. OF, fr. L *error,* fr. *errare*] **1** **a** : an act or condition of ignorant or imprudent deviation from a code of behavior **b** : an act involving an unintentional deviation from truth or accuracy **c** : an act that through ignorance, deficiency, or accident departs from or fails to achieve what should be done: as (1) : a defensive misplay other than a wild pitch or passed ball made by a baseball player when normal play would have resulted in an out or prevented an advance by a base runner (2) : the failure of a player (as in tennis) to make a successful return of a ball during play **d** : a mistake in the proceedings of a court of record in matters of law or of fact **2** **a** : the quality or state of erring **b** *Christian Science* : illusion about the nature of reality that is the cause of human suffering : the contradiction of truth **c** : an instance of false belief **3** : something produced by mistake **4** **a** : the difference between an observed or calculated value and a true value; *specif* : variation in measurements, calculations, or observations of a quantity due to mistakes or to uncontrollable factors **b** : the amount of deviation from a standard or specification — **er·ror·less** \'er-ər-ləs\ *adj*

syn ERROR, MISTAKE, SLIP, BLUNDER, LAPSE *shared meaning element* : a departure from what is true, right, or proper. ERROR suggests the existence of a standard or guide and a straying from the right course through failure to make effective use of this; thus, an *error* in addition involves some failure in following the rules of addition; an *error* in conduct is an infraction of an accepted code of morals or manners. MISTAKE implies misconception or inadvertence and usually expresses less severe criticism than *error* ⟨willing to learn from his *mistakes*⟩ BLUNDER regularly imputes stupidity or ignorance as a cause and connotes some degree of culpability ⟨we usually call our *blunders* mistakes, and our friends style our mistakes *blunders* —H. B. Wheatley⟩ SLIP stresses inadvertence or accident and applies especially to trivial but embarrassing mistakes ⟨a social *slip* which makes us feel hot all over —L. P. Smith⟩ LAPSE, sometimes interchangeable with *slip,* is more likely to stress forgetfulness, weakness, or inattention as a cause ⟨forever chiding him for his grammatical *lapses* —William Styron⟩

er·satz \'e(ə)r-,zäts, er-'\ *adj* [G *ersatz-,* fr. *ersatz,* n., substitute] : being a usu. artificial and inferior substitute ⟨~ flour made from potatoes⟩ ***syn*** see ARTIFICIAL — **ersatz** *n*

Erse \'ərs\ *n* [ME (Sc) *Erisch,* adj., Irish, alter. of *Irish*] **1** : SCOTTISH GAELIC **2** : IRISH GAELIC — **Erse** *adj*

erst \'ərst\ *adv* [ME *erest* earliest, formerly, fr. OE *ǣrest,* superl. of *ǣr* early — more at ERE] *archaic* : ERSTWHILE

¹erst·while \'ərst-,(h)wīl\ *adv* : in the past : FORMERLY ⟨cultures, ~ unknown to each other — Robert Plank⟩

²erstwhile *adj* : FORMER, PREVIOUS ⟨his ~ students⟩

eru·cic acid \i-,rü-sik-\ *n* [NL *Eruca,* genus of herbs, fr. L, caterpillar, garden rocket] : a crystalline fatty acid $C_{22}H_{42}O_2$ found in the form of glycerides esp. in rapeseed oil

eruct \i-'rəkt\ *vb* [L *eructare,* fr. *e-* + *ructare* to belch, fr. *-ructus,* pp. of *-rugere* to belch; akin to L *rugire* to roar] : BELCH

eruc·ta·tion \i-,rək-'tā-shən, ,ē-\ *n* : an act or instance of belching

er·u·dite \'er-(y)ə-,dīt\ *adj* [ME *erudit,* fr. L *eruditus,* fr. pp. of *erudire* to instruct, fr. *e-* + *rudis* rude, ignorant] : possessing or displaying erudition : LEARNED ⟨an ~ scholar⟩ — **er·u·dite·ly** *adv*

er·u·di·tion \,er-(y)ə-'dish-ən\ *n* : extensive knowledge acquired chiefly from books : profound, recondite, or bookish learning ***syn*** see KNOWLEDGE

erum·pent \i-'rəm-pənt\ *adj* [L *erumpent-, erumpens,* prp. of *erumpere*] : bursting forth ⟨~ fungi⟩

erupt \i-'rəpt\ *vb* [L *eruptus,* pp. of *erumpere* to burst forth, fr. *e-* + *rumpere* to break — more at REAVE] *vi* **1** **a** : to force out or release suddenly and often violently something (as lava or steam) that is pent up **b** (1) : to burst from limits or restraint (2) *of a tooth* : to emerge through the gum **c** : to become active or violent : EXPLODE ⟨violence ~*ed* in the ghetto⟩ **2** : to break out (as with a skin eruption) ~ *vt* : to force out or release usu. suddenly and violently — **erupt·ible** \-'rəp-tə-bəl\ *adj* — **erup·tive** \-tiv\ *adj* — **erup·tive·ly** *adv*

erup·tion \i-'rəp-shən\ *n* **1** **a** : an act, process, or instance of erupting **b** : the breaking out of a rash on the skin or mucous membrane **2** : a product of erupting (as a skin rash)

-ery \(ə-)rē\ *n suffix* [ME *-erie,* fr. OF, fr. *-ier* -er + *-ie* -y] **1** : qualities collectively : character : -NESS ⟨snobb*ery*⟩ **2** : art : practice ⟨quack*ery*⟩ **3** : place of doing, keeping, producing, or selling (the thing specified) ⟨fish*ery*⟩ ⟨bak*ery*⟩ **4** : collection : aggregate ⟨fin*ery*⟩ **5** : state or condition ⟨slav*ery*⟩

eryn·go \i-'riŋ-(,)gō\ *n, pl* **-goes** *or* **-gos** [modif. of L *eryngion* sea holly, fr. Gk *ēryngion*] **1** *obs* : candied sea-holly root made to be used as an aphrodisiac **2** : any of various plants (genus *Eryngium*) that have elongate spinulose-margined leaves and flowers in dense bracted heads

ery·sip·e·las \,er-ə-'sip-(ə-)ləs, ,ir-\ *n* [ME *erisipila,* fr. L *erysipelas,* fr. Gk, fr. *erysi-* (akin to Gk *erythros* red) + *-pelas* (akin to L *pellis* skin) — more at RED, FELL] : an acute febrile disease associated with intense edematous local inflammation of the skin and subcutaneous tissues caused by a hemolytic streptococcus

er·y·the·ma \,er-ə-'thē-mə\ *n* [NL, fr. Gk *erythēma,* fr. *erythainein* to redden, fr. *erythros*] : abnormal redness of the skin due to capillary congestion (as in inflammation) — **er·y·them·a·tous** \-'them-ət-əs\ *adj*

er·y·thor·bate \,er-ə-'thór-,bāt\ *n* : a salt of erythorbic acid that is used in foods as an antioxidant

er·y·thor·bic acid \-,thór-bik-\ *n* [*erythr-* + *ascorbic acid*] : an optical isomer of ascorbic acid

erythr- *or* **erythro-** *comb form* [Gk, fr. *erythros* — more at RED] **1** : red ⟨*erythro*cyte⟩ **2** : erythrocyte ⟨*erythr*oid⟩

er·y·thre·mia \,er-ə-'thrē-mē-ə\ *n* [NL] : POLYCYTHEMIA VERA

er·y·thrism \'er-ə-,thriz-əm\ *n* : a condition marked by exceptional prevalence of red pigmentation (as in skin or hair) — **er·y·thris·mal** \,er-ə-'thriz-məl\ *adj* — **er·y·thris·tic** \-'thris-tik\ *adj*

er·y·thrite \'er-ə-,thrīt\ *n* : a mineral $Co_3(AsO_4)_2.8H_2O$ consisting of a hydrous cobalt arsenate occurring esp. in monoclinic crystals

eryth·ro·blast \i-'rith-rə-,blast\ *n* [ISV] : a polychromatic nucleated cell of red marrow that is the first specifically identifiable stage in red blood cell formation; *broadly* : a cell ancestral to red blood cells — **eryth·ro·blas·tic** \-,rith-rə-'blas-tik\ *adj*

eryth·ro·blas·to·sis \i-,rith-rə-,blas-'tō-səs\ *n, pl* **-to·ses** \-,sēz\ [NL] : abnormal presence of erythroblasts in the circulating blood; *esp* : ERYTHROBLASTOSIS FETALIS

ə abut	ᵊ kitten	ər further	a back	ā bake	ä cot, cart
aù out	ch chin	e less	ē easy	g gift	i trip
ī life	j joke	ŋ sing	ō flow	ȯ flaw	ȯi coin
th thin	t͟h this	ü loot	u̇ foot	y yet	yü few
yu̇ furious	zh vision				

erythroblastosis fe·ta·lis \-fi-'tal-əs\ *n* [NL, fetal erythroblastosis] : a hemolytic disease of the fetus and newborn that is characterized by destruction of circulating erythrocytes, increase in circulating erythroblasts, and jaundice and that is usu. associated with Rh= factor incompatibility

eryth·ro·cyte \i-'rith-rə-,sīt\ *n* [ISV] : RED BLOOD CELL — **eryth·ro·cyt·ic** \-,rith-rə-'sit-ik\ *adj*

eryth·ro·cy·tom·e·ter \i-,rith-rə-sī-'täm-ət-ər\ *n* : HEMACYTOMETER

ery·throid \i-'rith-,rȯid, 'er-ə-,thrȯid\ *adj* : relating to erythrocytes or their precursors

eryth·ro·my·cin \i-,rith-rə-'mīs-ᵊn\ *n* : an antibiotic that is produced by an actinomycete (*Streptomyces erythreus*) and that is effective against amebiasis

er·y·thron \'er-ə-,thrän\ *n* [NL, fr. Gk, neut. of *erythros*] : the red blood cells and their precursors in the bone marrow

eryth·ro·poi·e·sis \i-,rith-rō-pȯi-'ē-səs\ *n* [NL, fr. *erythr-* + Gk *poiēsis* creation] : the production of red blood cells (as from the bone marrow) — **eryth·ro·poi·et·ic** \-'et-ik\ *adj*

eryth·ro·poi·e·tin \-'pȯi-ət-ᵊn\ *n* [*erythropoietic* + *-in*] : a hormonal substance that is prob. formed in the kidney and stimulates red blood cell formation

eryth·ro·sin \i-'rith-rə-sən\ *also* **eryth·ro·sine** \-sən, -,sēn\ *n* [ISV *erythr-* + *eosin*] : any of several dyes made by iodination of fluorescein that yield reddish shades

Es *symbol* einsteinium

¹-es \əz, iz *after* s, z, sh, ch; z *after* v *or a vowel*\ *n pl suffix* [ME *-es*, *-s* — more at ¹-s] **1** — used to form the plural of most nouns that end in *s* ⟨glass*es*⟩, *z* ⟨fuzz*es*⟩, *sh* ⟨bush*es*⟩, *ch* ⟨peach*es*⟩, or a final *y* that changes to *i* ⟨lad*ies*⟩ and of some nouns ending in *f* that changes to *v* ⟨loav*es*⟩; compare ¹-s 1 **2** : ¹-s 2

²-es *vb suffix* [ME — more at ²-s] — used to form the third person singular present of most verbs that end in *s* ⟨bless*es*⟩, *z* ⟨fizz*es*⟩, *sh* ⟨hush*es*⟩, *ch* ⟨catch*es*⟩, or a final *y* that changes to *i* ⟨def*ies*⟩ ; — compare ²-s

Esau \'ē-(,)sȯ\ *n* [L, fr. Gk *Ēsau*, fr. Heb *'Ēsāw*] : the elder son of Isaac and Rebekah who sold his birthright to his twin brother Jacob

es·ca·drille \'es-kə-,dril, -,drē\ *n* [F, flotilla, escadrille, fr. Sp *escuadrilla*, dim. of *escuadra* squadron, squad — more at SQUAD] : a unit of a European air command containing usu. six airplanes

es·ca·lade \'es-kə-,lād, -,läd\ *n* [F, fr. It *scalata*, fr. *scalare* to scale, fr. *scala* ladder, fr. LL — more at SCALE] : an act of scaling esp. the walls of a fortification — **escalade** *vt* — **es·ca·lad·er** *n*

es·ca·late \'es-kə-,lāt, *nonstand* -kyə-\ *vb* **-lat·ed; -lat·ing** [back= formation fr. *escalator*] *vi* : to increase in extent, volume, number, amount, intensity, or scope ⟨a little war threatens to ~ into a huge ugly one —Arnold Abrams⟩ ~ *vt* : EXPAND 1 — **es·ca·la·tion** \,es-kə-'lā-shən, *nonstand* -kyə-\ *n* — **es·ca·la·to·ry** \'es-kə-lə-,tōr-ē, -,tȯr-, *nonstand* -kyə-\ *adj*

¹es·ca·la·tor \'es-kə-,lāt-ər, *nonstand* -kyə-\ *n* [fr. *Escalator*, a trademark] **1 a** : a power-driven set of stairs arranged like an endless belt that ascend or descend continuously **b** : an upward course suggestive of an escalator ⟨a never-stopping ~ of economic progress —D. W. Brogan⟩ **2** : an escalator clause or provision

²escalator *adj* : providing for a periodic proportional upward or downward adjustment (as of prices or wages) ⟨an ~ arrangement tying the base pay . . . to living costs —*N.Y. Times*⟩

es·cal·lop \is-'käl-əp, -'kal-\ *var of* SCALLOP

es·cap·able \is-'kā-pə-bəl\ *adj* : capable of being escaped : AVOIDABLE

es·ca·pade \'es-kə-,pād\ *n* [MF, fr. OIt *scappata*, fr. *scappare* to escape, fr. (assumed) VL *excappare*] : a usu. adventurous action that runs counter to approved or conventional conduct ⟨childish ~s⟩

¹es·cape \is-'kāp\ *vb* **es·caped; es·cap·ing** [ME *escapen*, fr. ONF *escaper*, fr. (assumed) VL *excappare*, fr. L *ex-* + LL *cappa* head covering, cloak] *vi* **1 a** : to get away (as by flight) ⟨*escaped* from prison⟩ **b** : to issue from confinement ⟨gas is *escaping*⟩ **c** *of a plant* : to run wild from cultivation **2** : to avoid a threatening evil ~ *vt* **1** : to get or stay out of the way of : AVOID **2** : to fail to be noticed or recallable by ⟨his name ~*s* me⟩ **3 a** : to issue from **b** : to be uttered involuntarily by — **es·cap·er** *n*

syn ESCAPE, AVOID, EVADE, ELUDE, SHUN, ESCHEW *shared meaning element* : to get away or keep away from something one does not want to incur, endure, or encounter

²escape *n* **1** : an act or instance of escaping: as **a** : flight from confinement **b** : evasion of something undesirable **c** : leakage or outflow esp. of a fluid **d** : distraction or relief from routine or reality **2** : a means of escape **3** : a cultivated plant run wild

³escape *adj* **1** : providing a means of escape ⟨an ~ hatch⟩ ⟨~ literature⟩ **2** : providing a means of evading a regulation, claim, or commitment ⟨an ~ clause in a contract⟩

escape artist *n* : one (as a showman or criminal) unusually adept at escaping from confinement

es·cap·ee \is-,kā-'pē, ,es-(,)kā-, ,es-kə-\ *n* : one that has escaped; *esp* : an escaped prisoner

escape mechanism *n* : a mode of behavior or thinking adopted to evade unpleasant facts or responsibilities

es·cape·ment \is-'kāp-mənt\ *n* **1 a** : a device in a timepiece which controls the motion of the train of wheelwork and through which the energy of the power source is delivered to the pendulum or balance by means of impulses that permit a tooth to escape from a pallet at regular intervals **b** : a ratchet device (as the spacing mechanism of a typewriter) that permits motion in one direction only in equal steps **2 a** : the act of escaping **b** : a way of escape : VENT

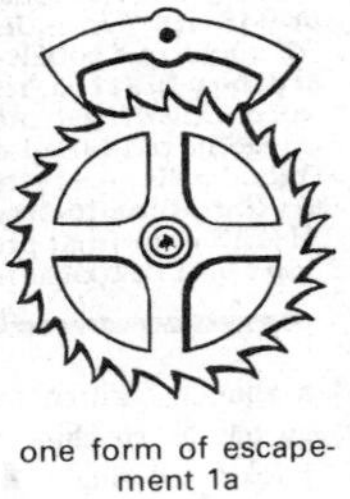
one form of escapement 1a

escape velocity *n* : the minimum velocity that a moving body (as a rocket) must have to escape from the gravitational field of the earth or of a celestial body and move outward into space

es·cap·ism \is-'kā-,piz-əm\ *n* : habitual diversion of the mind to purely imaginative activity or entertainment as an escape from reality or routine — **es·cap·ist** \-pəst\ *adj or n*

es·cap·ol·o·gy \is-,kā-'päl-ə-jē, ,es-(,)\ *n* : the art or practice of escaping — **es·cap·ol·o·gist** \-jəst\ *n*

es·car·got \,es-,kär-'gō\ *n, pl* **-gots** \-'gō(z)\ [F, fr. MF, fr. OProv *escaragol*] : a snail prepared for use as food

es·ca·role \'es-kə-,rōl\ *n* [F, fr. LL *escariola*, fr. L *escarius* of food, fr. *esca* food, fr. *edere* to eat — more at EAT] : ENDIVE 1

es·carp \is-'kärp\ *n or vt* [F *escarpe*, n., fr. It *scarpa*] : SCARP

es·carp·ment \-mənt\ *n* **1** : a steep slope in front of a fortification **2** : a long cliff or steep slope separating two comparatively level or more gently sloping surfaces and resulting from erosion or faulting

-es·cence \'es-ᵊn(t)s\ *n suffix* [MF, fr. L *-escentia*, fr. *-escent-*, *-escens* + *-ia* -y] : process of becoming ⟨hyal*escence*⟩

-es·cent \'es-ᵊnt\ *adj suffix* [MF, fr. L *-escent-*, *-escens*, prp. suffix of incho. verbs in *-escere*] **1** : beginning : beginning to be : slightly ⟨alkal*escent*⟩ **2** : reflecting or emitting light (in a specified way) ⟨fluor*escent*⟩

esch·a·lot \'esh-ə-,lät\ *n* [F *échalote*] : SHALLOT

¹es·char \'es-,kär\ *n* [ME *escare* — more at SCAR] : a scab formed esp. after a burn

²es·char \'es-kər\ *var of* ESKER

es·cha·rot·ic \,es-kə-'rät-ik\ *adj* [F or LL; F *escharotique*, fr. LL *escharoticus*, fr. Gk *escharōtikos*, fr. *escharoun* to form an eschar, fr. *eschara* eschar] : producing an eschar — **escharotic** *n*

es·cha·to·log·i·cal \(,)es-,kat-ᵊl-'äj-i-kəl, ,es-kət-\ *adj* **1** : of or relating to eschatology or an eschatology **2** : of or relating to the end of the world or the events associated with it in eschatology — **es·cha·to·log·i·cal·ly** \-i-k(ə-)lē\ *adv*

es·cha·tol·o·gy \,es-kə-'täl-ə-jē\ *n, pl* **-gies** [Gk *eschatos* last, farthest] **1** : a branch of theology concerned with the final events in the history of the world or of mankind **2** : a particular religious or mythological belief concerning the end of the world or of human history ⟨Navaho ~⟩; *specif* : any of various Christian doctrines concerning the second coming of Christ, the resurrection of the dead, the Last Judgment, or the nature of human existence upon the completion of history

¹es·cheat \is(h)-'chēt\ *n* [ME *eschete*, fr. OF, reversion of property, fr. *escheoir* to fall, devolve, fr. (assumed) VL *excadēre*, fr. L *ex-* + (assumed) VL *cadēre* to fall, fr. L *cadere* — more at CHANCE] **1** : escheated property **2 a** : the reversion of lands in English feudal law to the lord of the fee upon the failure of heirs capable of inheriting under the original grant **b** : the reversion of property to the crown in England or to the state in the U.S. by failure of persons legally entitled to hold the property

²escheat *vt* : to cause to revert by escheat ~ *vi* : to revert by escheat — **es·cheat·able** \-ə-bəl\ *adj*

es·chew \is(h)-'chü\ *vt* [ME *eschewen*, fr. MF *eschiuver*, of Gmc origin; akin to OHG *sciuhen* to frighten off — more at SHY] : to avoid habitually esp. on moral or practical grounds : SHUN *syn* see ESCAPE — **es·chew·al** \-əl\ *n*

es·co·lar \,es-kə-'lär\ *n, pl* **escolar** *or* **escolars** [Sp, lit., scholar, fr. ML *scholaris*] : a large widely distributed rough-scaled fish (*Ruvettus pretiosus*) that resembles a mackerel

¹es·cort \'es-,kȯ(ə)rt\ *n* [F *escorte*, fr. It *scorta*, fr. *scorgere* to guide, fr. (assumed) VL *excorrigere*, fr. L *ex-* + *corrigere* to make straight, correct — more at CORRECT] **1 a** (1) : a person or group of persons accompanying another to give protection or show courtesy (2) : the man who goes on a date with a woman **b** : a protective screen of warships or fighter planes or a single ship or plane used to fend off enemy attack from one or more vulnerable craft **2** : accompaniment by a person or an armed protector (as a ship)

²es·cort \is-'kȯ(ə)rt, es-, 'es-,\ *vt* : to accompany as an escort *syn* see ACCOMPANY

es·cot \is-'kät\ *vt* [MF *escoter*, fr. *escot* contribution, of Gmc origin; akin to ON *skot* contribution] *obs* : SUPPORT, MAINTAIN

es·cri·toire \'es-krə-,twär\ *n* [obs. F, writing desk, scriptorium, fr. ML *scriptorium*] : a writing table or desk; *specif* : SECRETARY 4b

¹es·crow \'es-,krō, es-'\ *n* [MF *escroue* scroll] **1** : a deed, a bond, money, or a piece of property delivered to a third person to be delivered by him to the grantee only upon the fulfillment of a condition **2** : a fund or deposit designed to serve as an escrow — **in escrow** : in trust as an escrow ⟨have over $1000 *in escrow* to pay taxes⟩

²es·crow \es-'krō, 'es-,\ *vt* : to place in escrow

es·cu·do \is-'küd-(,)ō\ *n, pl* **-dos** [Sp & Pg, lit., shield, fr. L *scutum*] **1** : any of various former gold or silver coins of Hispanic countries **2** — see MONEY table

es·cu·lent \'es-kyə-lənt\ *adj* [L *esculentus*, fr. *esca* food, fr. *edere* to eat — more at EAT] : EDIBLE — **esculent** *n*

es·cutch·eon \is-'kəch-ən\ *n* [ME *escochon*, fr. MF *escuchon*, fr. (assumed) VL *scution-*, *scutio*, fr. L *scutum* shield — more at ESQUIRE] **1** : a defined area on which armorial bearings are displayed and which usu. consists of a shield **2** : a protective or ornamental shield (as around a keyhole) **3** : the part of a ship's stern on which the name is displayed

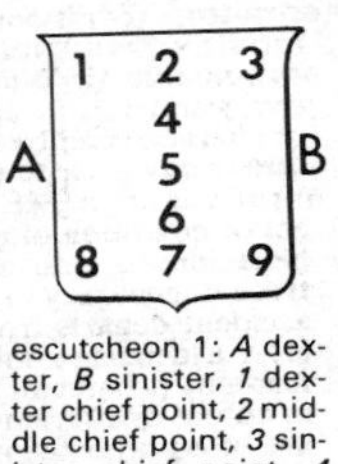

escutcheon 1: *A* dexter, *B* sinister, *1* dexter chief point, *2* middle chief point, *3* sinister chief point, *4* honor point, *5* fess point, *6* nombril, *7* middle base point, *8* dexter base point, *9* sinister base point

Esd *abbr* Esdras

Es·dras \'ez-drəs\ *n* [LL, fr. Gk, fr. Heb *'Ezrā*] **1** : either of two books of the Roman Catholic canon of the Old Testament — see BIBLE table **2** : either of two noncanonical books of Scripture included in the Protestant Apocrypha — see BIBLE table

ESE *abbr* east-southeast

¹-ese \'ēz, 'ēs\ *adj suffix* [Pg *-ês* & It *-ese*, fr. L *-ensis*] : of, relating to, or originating in (a certain place or country) ⟨Japan*ese*⟩

[2]-ese *n suffix, pl* **-ese** **1 :** native or resident of (a specified place or country) ⟨Chin*ese*⟩ **2 a :** language of (a particular place, country, or nationality) ⟨Siam*ese*⟩ **b :** speech, literary style, or diction peculiar to (a specified place, person, or group) — usu. in words applied in depreciation ⟨journal*ese*⟩

es·em·plas·tic \ˌes-ˌem-ˈplas-tik, -əm-\ *adj* [Gk *es hen* into one + E *plastic*] **:** shaping or having the power to shape disparate things into a unified whole ⟨the ~ power of the poetic imagination —W. H. Gardner⟩

es·er·ine \ˈes-ə-ˌrēn\ *n* [F *ésérine*] **:** PHYSOSTIGMINE

Esk *abbr* Eskimo

es·ker \ˈes-kər\ *n* [IrGael *eiscir* ridge] **:** a long narrow ridge or mound of sand, gravel, and boulders deposited by a stream flowing on, within, or beneath a stagnant glacier

Es·ki·mo \ˈes-kə-ˌmō\ *n* [Dan, of Algonquian origin; akin to Cree *askimowew* he eats it raw] **1** *pl* **Eskimo** *or* **Eskimos a :** a group of peoples of northern Canada, Greenland, Alaska, and eastern Siberia **b :** a member of such people **2 :** the language of the Eskimo people — **Es·ki·mo·an** \ˌes-kə-ˈmō-ən\ *adj*

Eskimo dog *n* **1 :** a broad-chested powerful dog of a breed native to Greenland and Labrador characterized by a long and shaggy outer coat and a soft dense woolly inner coat **2 :** a sled dog of American origin

ESL *abbr* English as a second language

esophag- *or* **esophago-** *comb form* **:** esophagus ⟨*esophag*ectomy⟩ **:** esophageal and ⟨*esophago*gastric⟩

esoph·a·ge·al \i-ˌsäf-ə-ˈjē-əl\ *adj* **:** of or relating to the esophagus

esoph·a·gus \i-ˈsäf-ə-gəs\ *n, pl* **-gi** \-ˌgī, -ˌjī\ [ME *ysophagus,* fr. Gk *oisophagos,* fr. *oisein* to be going to carry + *phagein* to eat — more at BAKSHEESH] **:** a muscular tube that leads from the pharynx to the stomach, passes down the neck between the trachea and the spinal column, and in man is about nine inches long — see LARYNX illustration

es·o·ter·ic \ˌes-ə-ˈter-ik\ *adj* [LL *esotericus,* fr. Gk *esōterikos,* fr. *esōterō,* compar. of *eisō, esō* within, fr. *eis* into, fr. *en* in — more at IN] **1 a :** designed for or understood by the specially initiated alone ⟨a body of ~ legal doctrine —B. N. Cardozo⟩ **b :** of or relating to knowledge that is restricted to a small group **2 a :** limited to a small circle ⟨~ pursuits⟩ **b :** PRIVATE, CONFIDENTIAL ⟨an ~ purpose⟩ — **es·o·ter·i·cal·ly** \-i-k(ə-)lē\ *adv*

es·o·ter·i·ca \-i-kə\ *n pl* [NL, fr. Gk *esōterika,* neut. pl. of *esōterikos*] **:** esoteric items

es·o·ter·i·cism \-ˈter-ə-ˌsiz-əm\ *n* **1 :** esoteric doctrines or practices **2 :** the quality or state of being esoteric

esp *abbr* especially

ESP \ˌē-ˌes-ˈpē\ *n* [extrasensory perception] **:** extrasensory perception

es·pa·drille \ˈes-pə-ˌdril\ *n* [F] **:** a flat sandal usu. having a fabric upper and a flexible sole

[1]es·pal·ier \is-ˈpal-yər, -ˌyā\ *n* [F, deriv. of It *spalla* shoulder, fr. LL *spatula* shoulder blade — more at EPAULET] **1 :** a plant (as a fruit tree) trained to grow flat against a support (as a wall or trellis) **2 :** a railing or trellis on which fruit trees or shrubs are trained to grow flat

[2]espalier *vt* **1 :** to train as an espalier **2 :** to furnish with an espalier

es·par·to \is-ˈpärt-(ˌ)ō\ *n, pl* **-tos** [Sp, fr. L *spartum,* fr. Gk *sparton* — more at SPIRE] **:** either of two Spanish and Algerian grasses (*Stipa tenacissima* and *Lygeum spartum*) used esp. to make cordage, shoes, and paper

es·pe·cial \is-ˈpesh-əl\ *adj* [ME, fr. MF — more at SPECIAL] **:** being distinctive: as **a :** directed toward a particular individual, group, or end ⟨sent ~ greetings to his son⟩ ⟨took ~ care to speak clearly⟩ **b :** of special note or importance **:** unusually great or significant ⟨a decision of ~ relevance⟩ ⟨illness puts an ~ burden on modest resources⟩ **c :** highly distinctive or personal **:** PECULIAR ⟨had an ~ dislike for music⟩ **d :** CLOSE, INTIMATE ⟨his ~ crony⟩ **e :** capable of being specifically identified ⟨had no ~ destination in mind⟩ ***syn*** see SPECIAL — **es·pe·cial·ly** \-ˈpesh-(ə-)lē\ *adv* — **in especial :** in particular

es·per·ance \ˈes-p(ə-)rən(t)s\ *n* [ME *esperaunce,* fr. MF *esperance*] *obs* **:** HOPE, EXPECTATION

Es·pe·ran·to \ˌes-pə-ˈrant-(ˌ)ō, -ˈrän-(ˌ)tō\ *n* [Dr. *Esperanto,* pseudonym of L. L. Zamenhof †1917 Pol oculist, its inventor] **:** an artificial international language based as far as possible on words common to the chief European languages

es·pi·al \is-ˈpī(-ə)l\ *n* **1 :** OBSERVATION **2 :** an act of noticing **:** DISCOVERY

es·piè·gle \es-pyeglᵊ\ *adj* [F] **:** FROLICSOME, ROGUISH

es·piè·gle·rie \es-pyeg-lə-rē\ *n* [F, fr. *espiègle*] **:** the quality or state of being roguish or frolicsome

es·pi·o·nage \ˈes-pē-ə-ˌnäzh, -nij, -ˌnäj; is-ˈpē-ə-nij\ *n* [F *espionnage,* fr. MF, fr. *espionner* to spy, fr. *espion* spy, fr. OIt *spione,* fr. *spia,* of Gmc origin; akin to OHG *spehōn* to spy — more at SPY] **:** the practice of spying or the use of spies to obtain information about the plans and activities esp. of a foreign government or a competing company ⟨industrial ~⟩

es·pla·nade \ˈes-plə-ˌnäd, -ˌnād\ *n* [F, fr. It *spianata,* fr. *spianare* to level, fr. L *explanare* — more at EXPLAIN] **:** a level open stretch of paved or grassy ground; *esp* **:** one designed for walking or driving along a shore

es·pous·al \is-ˈpau̇-zəl *also* -səl\ *n* **1 a :** BETROTHAL **b :** WEDDING **c :** MARRIAGE **2 :** a taking up or adopting of a cause or belief

es·pouse \is-ˈpau̇z *also* -ˈpau̇s\ *vt* **es·poused; es·pous·ing** [ME *espousen,* fr. MF *espouser,* fr. LL *sponsare* to betroth, fr. L *sponsus,* pp. of *spondēre* to promise, betroth — more at SPOUSE] **1 :** MARRY **2 :** to take up and support as a cause **:** become attached to ⟨~ the problems of minority groups⟩ ***syn*** see ADOPT — **es·pous·er** *n*

espres·so \e-ˈspres-(ˌ)ō\ *n, pl* **-sos** [It (*caffè*) *espresso,* lit., pressed out coffee] **:** coffee brewed by forcing steam through finely ground darkly roasted coffee beans

es·prit \is-ˈprē\ *n* [F, fr. L *spiritus* spirit] **1 :** vivacious cleverness or wit **2 :** ESPRIT DE CORPS

es·prit de corps \is-ˌprēd-ə-ˈkō(ə)r, -ˈkȯ(ə)r\ *n* [F] **:** the common spirit existing in the members of a group and inspiring enthusiasm, devotion, and strong regard for the honor of the group

es·py \is-ˈpī\ *vt* **es·pied; es·py·ing** [ME *espien,* fr. OF *espier* — more at SPY] **:** to catch sight of ⟨among the several horses . . . she *espied* the white mustang —Zane Grey⟩

Esq *or* **Esqr** *abbr* esquire

-esque \ˈesk\ *adj suffix* [F, fr. It *-esco,* of Gmc origin; akin to OHG *-isc* -ish — more at -ISH] **:** in the manner or style of **:** like ⟨statu*esque*⟩

Es·qui·mau \ˈes-kə-ˌmō\ *n, pl* **Esquimau** *or* **Es·qui·maux** \-ˌmō(z)\ [F, of Algonquian origin] **:** ESKIMO

es·quire \ˈes-ˌkwī(ə)r, is-ˈ\ *n* [ME, fr. MF *esquier* squire, fr. LL *scutarius,* fr. L *scutum* shield; akin to OHG *sceida* sheath] **1 :** a member of the English gentry ranking below a knight **2 :** a candidate for knighthood serving as shield bearer and attendant to a knight **3 —** used as a title of courtesy usu. placed in its abbreviated form after the surname ⟨John R. Smith, *Esq.*⟩ **4** *archaic* **:** a landed proprietor

ess \ˈes\ *n* **1 :** the letter *s* **2 :** something resembling the letter *S* in shape; *esp* **:** an S-shaped curve in a road

-ess \əs, is *also* ˌes\ *n suffix* [ME *-esse,* fr. OF, fr. LL *-issa,* fr. Gk] **:** female ⟨gian*tess*⟩

[1]es·say \e-ˈsā, ˈes-ˌā\ *vt* **1 a :** to put to a test **b :** [2]ASSAY 2a **2 :** to make an often tentative or experimental effort to perform ***syn*** see ATTEMPT — **es·say·er** *n*

[2]es·say *in sense 2* ˈes-ˌā, *in other senses also* e-ˈsā\ *n* [MF *essai,* fr. LL *exagium* act of weighing, fr. *ex-* + *agere* to drive — more at AGENT] **1 a :** EFFORT, ATTEMPT; *esp* **:** an initial tentative effort **b :** the result or product of an attempt **2 a :** an analytic or interpretative literary composition usu. dealing with its subject from a limited or personal point of view **b :** something resembling such a composition ⟨a photographic ~⟩ **3 :** TRIAL, TEST **4 :** a proof of an unaccepted design for a stamp or piece of paper money

es·say·ist \ˈes-ˌā-əst\ *n* **:** a writer of essays

es·say·is·tic \ˌes-(ˌ)ā-ˈis-tik\ *adj* **1 :** of or relating to an essay or an essayist **2 :** resembling an essay in quality or character

essay question *n* **:** an examination question that requires an answer in a sentence, paragraph, or short composition

essay test *n* **:** a test made up of essay questions — compare OBJECTIVE TEST

es·sence \ˈes-ᵊn(t)s\ *n* [ME, fr. MF & L; MF, fr. L *essentia,* fr. *esse* to be — more at IS] **1 a :** the permanent as contrasted with the accidental element of being **b :** the individual, real, or ultimate nature of a thing esp. as opposed to its existence **c :** the properties or attributes by means of which something can be placed in its proper class or identified as being what it is **2 :** something that exists **:** ENTITY **3 a** (1) **:** a volatile substance or constituent (as of perfume) (2) **:** a constituent or derivative (as an extract or essential oil) possessing the special qualities (as of a plant or drug) in concentrated form; *also* **:** a preparation (as an alcoholic solution) of such an essence or a synthetic substitute **b :** ODOR, PERFUME **c :** something that resembles an extract in possessing a quality in concentrated form — **in essence :** in or by its very nature **:** ESSENTIALLY, BASICALLY ⟨accusations which *in essence* are well-founded —*Times Lit. Supp.*⟩ — **of the essence :** of the utmost importance **:** ESSENTIAL ⟨time was *of the essence*⟩

Es·sene \is-ˈēn, ˈes-ˌēn\ *n* [Gk *Essēnos*] **:** a member of a monastic brotherhood of Jews in Palestine from the 2d century B.C. to the 2d century A.D. — **Es·se·ni·an** \is-ˈē-nē-ən, es-\ *or* **Es·se·nic** \-ˈen-ik, -ˈē-nik\ *adj* — **Essenism** *n*

[1]es·sen·tial \i-ˈsen-chəl\ *adj* **1 :** of, relating to, or constituting essence **:** INHERENT **2 :** of the utmost importance **:** BASIC, INDISPENSABLE, NECESSARY ⟨~ foods⟩ ⟨an ~ requirement for admission to college⟩ **3 :** IDIOPATHIC ⟨~ disease⟩ — **es·sen·ti·al·i·ty** \-ˌsen-chē-ˈal-ət-ē\ *n* — **es·sen·tial·ly** \-ˈsench-(ə-)lē\ *adv* — **es·sen·tial·ness** \-ˈsen-chəl-nəs\ *n*

syn ESSENTIAL, FUNDAMENTAL, VITAL, CARDINAL *shared meaning element* **:** so important as to be indispensable

[2]essential *n* **1 :** something basic ⟨the ~s of astronomy⟩ **2 :** something necessary, indispensable, or unavoidable

essential amino acid *n* **:** an amino acid (as lysine) that is required for normal health and growth, is manufactured in the body in insufficient quantities or not at all, and is usu. supplied by dietary protein

es·sen·tial·ism \i-ˈsen-chə-ˌliz-əm\ *n* **1 :** an educational theory that ideas and skills basic to a culture should be taught to all alike by time-tested methods — compare PROGRESSIVISM **2 a :** REALISM **b :** a theory that gives priority to essence over existence — compare EXISTENTIALISM — **es·sen·tial·ist** \-ləst\ *adj or n*

es·sen·ti·al·i·ty \i-ˌsen-chē-ˈal-ət-ē\ *n, pl* **-ties 1 :** the quality or state of being essential ⟨the ~ of freedom and justice —P. G. Hoffman⟩ **2 a :** essential nature **:** ESSENCE **b :** an essential quality, property, or aspect

essential oil *n* **:** any of a class of volatile oils that impart the characteristic odors to plants and are used esp. in perfumes and flavorings — compare FIXED OIL

es·soin \is-ˈȯin\ *n* [ME *essoine,* fr. MF, fr. ML *essonium,* fr. L *ex-* + LL *sonium* care, worry] **1 :** an excuse for not appearing in an English law court at the appointed time **2** *obs* **:** EXCUSE, DELAY

es·so·nite \ˈes-ᵊn-ˌīt\ *n* [F, fr. Gk *hēsson* inferior; fr. its being less hard than true hyacinth] **:** a yellow to brown garnet

est *abbr* **1** established **2** estimate; estimated

EST *abbr* eastern standard time

[1]-est \əst, ist\ *adj suffix or adv suffix* [ME, fr. OE *-st, -est, -ost;* akin to OHG *-isto* (adj. superl. suffix), Gk *-istos*] — used to form the

ə abut	ᵊ kitten	ər further	a back	ā bake	ä cot, cart
au̇ out	ch chin	e less	ē easy	g gift	i trip	ī life
j joke	ŋ sing	ō flow	ȯ flaw	ȯi coin	th thin	t͟h this
ü loot	u̇ foot	y yet	yü few	yu̇ furious	zh vision

superlative degree of adjectives and adverbs of one syllable ⟨fatt*est*⟩ ⟨lat*est*⟩, of some adjectives and adverbs of two syllables ⟨luck*iest*⟩ ⟨oft*enest*⟩, and less often of longer ones ⟨beggarli*est*⟩
²-est \əst, ist\ *or* **-st** \st\ *vb suffix* [ME, fr. OE *-est, -ast, -st;* akin to OHG *-ist, -ōst, -ēst*, 2d sing. ending] — used to form the archaic 2d person singular of English verbs (with *thou*) ⟨get*test*⟩ ⟨di*dst*⟩
es·tab·lish \is-ˈtab-lish\ *vb* [ME *establissen*, fr. MF *establiss-*, stem of *establir*, fr. L *stabilire*, fr. *stabilis* stable] *vt* **1** : to make firm or stable **2** : to institute (as a law) permanently by enactment or agreement **3** *obs* : SETTLE 7 **4 a** : to bring into existence : FOUND ⟨~*ed* a republic⟩ **b** : to bring about : EFFECT ⟨~*ed* friendly relations⟩ **5 a** : to set on a firm basis ⟨~ his son in business⟩ **b** : to put into a favorable position **c** : to gain full recognition or acceptance of **6** : to make (a church) a national institution **7** : to put beyond doubt : PROVE ⟨~*ed* his innocence⟩ ~ *vi, of a plant* : to become naturalized ⟨a grass that ~*es* on poor soil⟩ ***syn*** see SET ***ant*** uproot (*as a plant or a practice*), abrogate (*as a privilege*) — **es·tab·lish·able** \-ə-bəl\ *adj* — **es·tab·lish·er** *n*
established church *n* : a church recognized by law as the official church of a nation and supported by civil authority
es·tab·lish·ment \is-ˈtab-lish-mənt\ *n* **1** : something established: as **a** : a settled arrangement; *esp* : a code of laws **b** : ESTABLISHED CHURCH **c** : a permanent civil or military organization **d** : a place of business or residence with its furnishings and staff **e** : a public or private institution **2** : an established order of society: as **a** *often cap* : a group of social, economic, and political leaders who form a ruling class (as of a nation) **b** *often cap* : a controlling group ⟨the literary ~⟩ **3 a** : the act of establishing **b** : the state of being established
es·tab·lish·men·tar·i·an \is-ˌtab-lish-mən-ˈter-ē-ən, -ˌmen-\ *adj* : of, relating to, or favoring the social or political establishment — **establishmentarian** *n* — **es·tab·lish·men·tar·i·an·ism** \-ē-ə-ˌniz-əm\ *n*
es·ta·mi·net \e-stȧ-mē-nā\ *n, pl* **-nets** \-nā(z)\ [F] : a small café : BISTRO
es·tate \is-ˈtāt\ *n* [ME *estat*, fr. MF — more at STATE] **1** : STATE, CONDITION **2** : social standing or rank esp. of a high order **3** : a social or political class; *specif* : one of the great classes (as the nobility, the clergy and the commons) formerly vested with distinct political powers **4 a** : the degree, quality, nature, and extent of one's interest in land or other property **b** (1) : POSSESSIONS, PROPERTY; *esp* : a person's property in land and tenements ⟨a man of small ~⟩ (2) : the assets and liabilities left by a person at death **c** : a landed property usu. with a large house on it **5** *Brit* : ESTATE CAR
estate agent *n, Brit* : a real estate broker or manager
estate car *n, Brit* : STATION WAGON
estate tax *n* : an excise in the form of a percentage of the net estate that is levied on the privilege of an owner of property of transmitting his property to others after his death — compare INHERITANCE TAX 1
¹es·teem \is-ˈtēm\ *n* **1** *archaic* : WORTH, VALUE **2** *archaic* : OPINION, JUDGMENT **3** : high regard ⟨held in ~ by his colleagues⟩
²esteem *vt* [ME *estemen* to estimate, fr. MF *estimer*, fr. L *aestimare*] **1** *archaic* : APPRAISE **2 a** : to view as : CONSIDER ⟨~ it a privilege⟩ **b** : THINK, BELIEVE **3** : to set a high value on : regard highly and prize accordingly ***syn*** see REGARD ***ant*** abominate
es·ter \ˈes-tər\ *n* [G, fr. *essigäther* ethyl acetate, fr. *essig* vinegar + *äther* ether] : an often fragrant compound formed by the reaction between an acid and an alcohol usu. with elimination of water
es·ter·ase \ˈes-tə-ˌrās, -ˌrāz\ *n* : an enzyme that accelerates the hydrolysis or synthesis of esters
es·ter·i·fy \e-ˈster-ə-ˌfī\ *vt* **-fied; -fy·ing** : to convert into an ester — **es·ter·i·fi·ca·tion** \-ˌster-ə-fə-ˈkā-shən\ *n*
Esth *abbr* Esther
Es·ther \ˈes-tər\ *n* [L, fr. Heb *Estēr*] **1** : the Jewish heroine of the Old Testament book of Esther **2** : a narrative book of canonical Jewish and Christian Scripture — see BIBLE table
es·the·sia \es-ˈthē-zh(ē-)ə\ *n* [NL, back-formation fr. *anesthesia*] : capacity for sensation and feeling : SENSIBILITY
esthesio- *or* **aesthesio-** *comb form* [Gk *aisthēsis*] : sensation ⟨*esthesio*logy⟩
es·the·si·om·e·ter \es-ˌthē-zē-ˈäm-ət-ər, -ˌthē-sē-\ *n* : an instrument for measuring sensory discrimination; *esp* : one for determining the distance by which two points pressed against the skin must be separated in order that they may be felt as separate
es·the·sis \es-ˈthē-səs\ *n* [NL, fr. Gk *aisthēsis*, fr. *aisthanesthai* to perceive — more at AUDIBLE] : SENSATION; *esp* : rudimentary sensation
esthete, esthetic, esthetics *var of* AESTHETE, AESTHETIC, AESTHETICS
es·ti·ma·ble \ˈes-tə-mə-bəl\ *adj* **1** *archaic* : VALUABLE **2** : worthy of esteem **3** : capable of being estimated — **es·ti·ma·ble·ness** *n*
¹es·ti·mate \ˈes-tə-ˌmāt\ *vt* **-mat·ed; -mat·ing** [L *aestimatus*, pp. of *aestimare* to value, estimate] **1** *archaic* **a** : ESTEEM **b** : APPRAISE **2 a** : to judge tentatively or approximately the value, worth, or significance of **b** : to determine roughly the size, extent, or nature of **c** : to produce a statement of the approximate cost of **3** : JUDGE, CONCLUDE — **es·ti·ma·tive** \-ˌmāt-iv\ *adj*
syn ESTIMATE, APPRAISE, EVALUATE, VALUE, RATE, ASSESS *shared meaning element* : to judge something with respect to its worth or significance
²es·ti·mate \ˈes-tə-mət\ *n* **1** : the act of appraising or valuing : CALCULATION **2** : an opinion or judgment of the nature, character, or quality of a person or thing ⟨an ~ of a man⟩ **3 a** : a rough or approximate calculation **b** : a numerical value obtained from a statistical sample and assigned to a population parameter **4** : a statement of the cost of a job
es·ti·ma·tion \ˌes-tə-ˈmā-shən\ *n* **1** : JUDGMENT, OPINION **2 a** : the act of estimating **b** : the value, amount, or size arrived at in an estimate **3** : ESTEEM, HONOR
es·ti·ma·tor \ˈes-tə-ˌmāt-ər\ *n* **1** : one that estimates **2** : ESTIMATE 3b; *also* : a statistical function whose value for a sample furnishes an estimate of a population parameter
estival, estivate, estivation *var of* AESTIVAL, AESTIVATE, AESTIVATION
Es·to·nian \e-ˈstō-nē-ən, -nyən\ *n* **1** : a member of a Finno-Ugric-speaking people of Estonia **2** : the Finno-Ugric language of the Estonian people — **Estonian** *adj*
es·top \e-ˈstäp\ *vt* **es·topped; es·top·ping** [ME *estoppen*, fr. MF *estouper*] **1** *archaic* : to stop up **2** : STOP, BAR; *specif* : to impede by estoppel
es·top·pel \e-ˈstäp-əl\ *n* [prob. fr. MF *estoupail* bung, fr. *estouper*] : a bar to alleging or denying a fact because of one's own previous actions or words to the contrary
estr- *or* **estro-** *or* **oestr-** *or* **oestro-** *comb form* : estrus ⟨*estro*gen⟩
es·tra·di·ol \ˌes-trə-ˈdī-ˌȯl, -ˌōl\ *n* [ISV *estra-* (fr. *estrin*) + *di-* + *-ol*] : an estrogenic hormone that is a phenolic steroid alcohol $C_{18}H_{24}O_2$ usu. made synthetically and that is often used combined as an ester esp. in treating menopausal symptoms
es·tral \ˈes-trəl\ *adj* : ESTROUS
estral cycle *n* : ESTROUS CYCLE
es·trange \is-ˈtrānj\ *vt* **es·tranged; es·trang·ing** [MF *estranger*, fr. ML *extraneare*, fr. L *extraneus* strange — more at STRANGE] **1** : to remove from customary environment or associations **2** : to arouse esp. mutual enmity or indifference in where there had formerly been love, affection, or friendliness : ALIENATE — **es·trange·ment** \-ˈtrānj-mənt\ *n* — **es·trang·er** *n*
syn ESTRANGE, ALIENATE, DISAFFECT, WEAN *shared meaning element* : to cause one to break a bond of affection or loyalty ***ant*** reconcile
¹es·tray \is-ˈtrā\ *vi* [MF *estraier*] *archaic* : STRAY
²estray *n* : STRAY 1
es·trin \ˈes-trən\ *n* [NL *estrus*] : an estrogenic hormone; *esp* : ESTRONE
es·tri·ol \ˈes-ˌtrī-ˌȯl, e-ˈstrī-, -ˌōl\ *n* [*estrin* + *tri-* + *-ol*] : a crystalline estrogenic hormone that is a glycol $C_{18}H_{24}O_3$ usu. obtained from the urine of pregnant women
es·tro·gen \ˈes-trə-jən\ *n* [NL *estrus* + ISV *-o-* + *-gen*] : a substance (as a sex hormone) tending to promote estrus and stimulate the development of secondary sex characteristics in the female
es·tro·gen·ic \ˌes-trə-ˈjen-ik\ *adj* **1** : promoting estrus **2** : of, relating to, or caused by an estrogen — **es·tro·gen·i·cal·ly** \-i-k(ə-)lē\ *adv*
es·trone \ˈes-ˌtrōn\ *n* [ISV, fr. *estrin*] : an estrogenic hormone that is a ketone $C_{18}H_{22}O_2$ is usu. obtained from the urine of pregnant females, and is used similarly to estradiol
es·trous \ˈes-trəs\ *adj* **1** : of, relating to, or characteristic of estrus **2** : being in heat
estrous cycle *n* : the correlated phenomena of the endocrine and generative systems of a female mammal from the beginning of one period of estrus to the beginning of the next — called also *estral cycle*
es·tru·al \ˈes-trə-wəl\ *adj* : ESTROUS
es·trus \ˈes-trəs\ *or* **es·trum** \-trəm\ *n* [NL, fr. L *oestrus* gadfly, frenzy, fr. Gk *oistros* — more at IRE] **1 a** : a regularly recurrent state of sexual excitability during which the female of most mammals will accept the male and is capable of conceiving : HEAT **b** : a single occurrence of this state **2** : ESTROUS CYCLE
es·tu·ar·i·al \ˌes(h)-chə-ˈwer-ē-əl\ *adj* : ESTUARINE
es·tu·a·rine \ˈes(h)-chə-wə-ˌrīn, -ˌrēn\ *adj* : of, relating to, or formed in an estuary ⟨~ currents⟩ ⟨~ animals⟩ ⟨~ environment⟩
es·tu·ary \ˈes(h)-chə-ˌwer-ē\ *n, pl* **-ar·ies** [L *aestuarium*, fr. *aestus* boiling, tide; akin to L *aestas* summer — more at AESTIVAL] : a water passage where the tide meets a river current; *esp* : an arm of the sea at the lower end of a river
ESU *abbr* electrostatic unit
esu·ri·ence \i-ˈsu̇r-ē-ən(t)s, -ˈzu̇r-\ *n* : the quality or state of being esurient
esu·ri·en·cy \-ən-sē\ *n* : ESURIENCE
esu·ri·ent \-ənt\ *adj* [L *esurient-*, *esuriens*, prp. of *esurire* to be hungry] : HUNGRY, GREEDY — **esu·ri·ent·ly** *adv*
ESV *abbr* earth satellite vehicle
et \ˈet\ *dial past of* EAT
Et *symbol* ethyl
ET *abbr* eastern time
-et \ˈet, ˌet, ət, it\ *n suffix* [ME, fr. OF *-et*, masc., & *-ete*, fem., fr. LL *-itus* & *-ita*] **1** : small one ⟨baron*et*⟩ ⟨cellar*et*⟩ **2** : group ⟨oct*et*⟩
eta \ˈāt-ə, ˈēt-ə\ *n* [LL, fr. Gk *ēta*, of Sem origin; akin to Heb *ḥēth* heth] : the 7th letter of the Greek alphabet — see ALPHABET table
ETA *abbr* estimated time of arrival
éta·gère *or* **eta·gere** \ˌā-ˌtä-ˈzhe(ə)r, ˌāt-ə-\ *n* [F *étagère*] : an elaborate whatnot often with a large mirror at the back and sometimes with an enclosed cabinet as a base

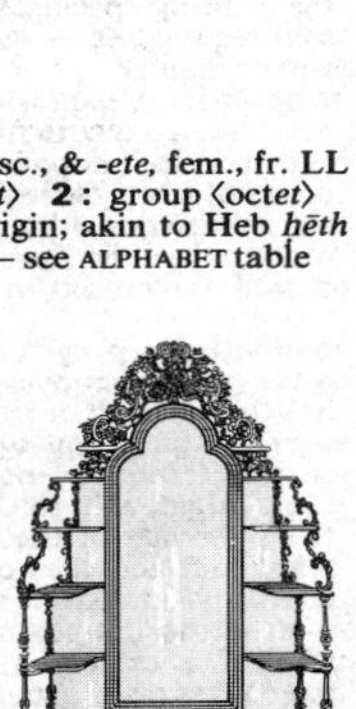

étagère

et al \et-ˈal, -ˈōl\ *abbr* [L *et alii* (masc.), *et aliae* (fem.), or *et alia* (neut.)] and others
eta·mine \ˈāt-ə-ˌmēn\ *n* [F *étamine*] : a light cotton or worsted fabric with an open mesh
etat·ism \ā-ˈtät-ˌiz-əm\ *n* [F *étatisme*, fr. *état* state, fr. OF *estat*] : STATE SOCIALISM — **etat·ist** \-ˈtät-əst\ *adj*
etc \ən-ˈsō-ˌfōrth, -ˌfȯrth; et-ˈset-ə-rə, -ˈse-trə\ *abbr* et cetera
et·cet·era \et-ˈset-ə-rə, -ˈse-trə\ *n* **1** : a number of unspecified additional persons or things **2** *pl* : unspecified additional items : ODDS AND ENDS
et cet·era \et-ˈset-ə-rə, -ˈse-trə\ [L] : and others esp. of the same kind : and so forth
¹etch \ˈech\ *vb* [D *etsen*, fr. G *ätzen*, lit., to feed, fr. OHG *azzen*; akin to OHG *ezzan* to eat — more at EAT] *vt* **1 a** : to produce esp. on metal or glass by the corrosive action of an acid **b** : to subject to such etching **2** : to delineate or impress clearly ⟨scenes that are indelibly ~*ed* in our minds⟩ ~ *vi* : to practice etching — **etch·er** *n*

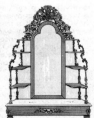

2etch *n* **1 :** the action or effect of an etching acid on a surface **2 :** a chemical agent used in etching
etch·ing *n* **1 a :** the act or process of etching **b :** the art of producing pictures or designs by printing from an etched metal plate **2 a :** an etched design **b :** an impression from an etched plate
ETD *abbr* estimated time of departure
1eter·nal \i-ˈtərn-ᵊl\ *adj* [ME, fr. MF, fr. LL *aeternalis,* fr. L *aeternus* eternal; akin to L *aevum* age, eternity — more at AYE] **1 a :** having infinite duration : EVERLASTING **b :** of or relating to eternity **c :** characterized by abiding fellowship with God ⟨good teacher, what must I do to inherit ~ life? —Mk 10:17 (RSV)⟩ **2 a :** continued without intermission : PERPETUAL **b :** seemingly endless **3** *archaic* : INFERNAL **4 :** valid or existing at all times : TIMELESS ⟨~ verities⟩ — **eter·nal·ize** \-ᵊl-ˌīz\ *vt* — **eter·nal·ly** \-ᵊl-ē\ *adv* — **eter·nal·ness** *n*
2eternal *n* **1** *cap* : GOD 1 — used with *the* **2 :** something eternal
eterne \i-ˈtərn\ *adj* [ME, fr. MF, fr. L *aeternus*] *archaic* : ETERNAL
eter·ni·ty \i-ˈtər-nət-ē\ *n, pl* **-ties** [ME *eternite,* fr. MF *eternité,* fr. L *aeternitat-, aeternitas,* fr. *aeternus*] **1 :** the quality or state of being eternal **2 :** infinite time **3** *pl* : AGE 2c **4 :** the state after death : IMMORTALITY **5 :** a seemingly endless or immeasurable time ⟨he posed motionless for a seeming ~ as the crowd roared with laughter and encouragement —J. W. Cross⟩
eter·nize \i-ˈtər-ˌnīz\ *vt* **-nized; -niz·ing** **1 a :** to make eternal **b :** to prolong indefinitely **2 :** IMMORTALIZE — **eter·ni·za·tion** \-ˌtər-nə-ˈzā-shən\ *n*
ete·sian \i-ˈtē-zhən\ *adj, often cap* [L *etesius,* fr. Gk *etēsios,* fr. *etos* year — more at WETHER] : recurring annually — used of summer winds that blow over the Mediterranean — **etesian** *n, often cap*
eth \ˈet͟h\ *var of* EDH
eth- *or* **etho-** *comb form* [ISV] : ethyl ⟨*eth*aldehyde⟩ ⟨*etho*chloride⟩
1-eth \əth, ith\ *or* **-th** \th\ *vb suffix* [ME, fr. OE *-eth, -ath, -th;* akin to OHG *-it, -ōt, -ēt,* 3d sing. ending, L *-t, -it*] — used to form the archaic third person singular present of verbs ⟨go*eth*⟩ ⟨do*th*⟩
2-eth — see -TH
eth·a·cryn·ic acid \ˌeth-ə-ˌkrin-ik-\ *n* [perh. fr. *eth-* + acetic + buty*ryl* + phe*nol*] : a diuretic $C_{13}H_{12}Cl_2O_4$ used esp. in the treatment of edema
eth·am·bu·tol \eth-ˈam-byü-ˌtȯl, -ˌtōl\ *n* [*eth*ylene + *am*ine + *but*an*ol*] : a compound $C_{10}H_{24}N_2O_2$ used esp. in the treatment of tuberculosis
eth·ane \ˈeth-ˌān\ *n* [ISV, fr. *ethyl*] : a colorless odorless gaseous hydrocarbon C_2H_6 found in natural gas and used esp. as a fuel
eth·a·nol \ˈeth-ə-ˌnȯl, -ˌnōl\ *n* : ALCOHOL 1
eth·a·nol·amine \ˌeth-ə-ˈnäl-ə-ˌmēn, -ˈnōl-\ *n* : a colorless liquid amino alcohol C_2H_7NO used esp. as a solvent and in scrubbing gases
eth·ene \ˈeth-ˌēn\ *n* : ETHYLENE
ether \ˈē-thər\ *n* [ME, fr. L *aether,* fr. Gk *aithēr,* fr. *aithein* to ignite, blaze] **1 a :** the rarefied element formerly believed to fill the upper regions of space **b :** the upper regions of space : HEAVENS **2 a :** a medium that in the undulatory theory of light permeates all space and transmits transverse waves **b :** the medium that transmits radio waves **3 a :** a light volatile flammable liquid $C_4H_{10}O$ used chiefly as a solvent and anesthetic **b :** any of various organic compounds characterized by an oxygen atom attached to two carbon atoms — **ether·ish** \-thə-rish\ *adj* — **ether·like** \-thər-ˌlīk\ *adj*
ethe·re·al \i-ˈthir-ē-əl\ *adj* **1 a :** of or relating to the regions beyond the earth **b :** CELESTIAL, HEAVENLY **c :** UNWORLDLY, SPIRITUAL **2 a :** lacking material substance : IMMATERIAL, INTANGIBLE **b :** marked by unusual delicacy and refinement ⟨this smallest, most ~, and daintiest of birds —William Beebe⟩ **3 :** relating to, containing, or resembling a chemical ether — **ethe·re·al·i·ty** \-ˌthir-ē-ˈal-ət-ē\ *n* — **ethe·re·al·iza·tion** \-ē-ə-lə-ˈzā-shən\ *n* — **ethe·re·al·ize** \-ˈthir-ē-ə-ˌlīz\ *vt* — **ethe·re·al·ly** \-ē-ə-lē\ *adv* — **ethe·re·al·ness** *n*
ether extract *n* : the part of a complex organic material that is soluble in ether and consists chiefly of fats and fatty acids
ethe·ric \i-ˈther-ik, -ˈthir-\ *adj* : ETHEREAL
ether·ize \ˈē-thə-ˌrīz\ *vt* **-ized; -iz·ing** **1 :** to treat or anesthetize with ether **2 :** to make numb as if by anesthetizing — **ether·iza·tion** \ˌē-thə-rə-ˈzā-shən\ *n* — **ether·iz·er** *n*
eth·ic \ˈeth-ik\ *n* [ME *ethik,* fr. MF *ethique,* fr. L *ethice,* fr. Gk *ēthikē,* fr. *ēthikos*] **1** *pl but sing or pl in constr* : the discipline dealing with what is good and bad and with moral duty and obligation **2 a :** a set of moral principles or values **b :** a theory or system of moral values ⟨the present-day materialistic ~⟩ **c** *pl but sing or pl in constr* : the principles of conduct governing an individual or a group ⟨professional ~*s*⟩
1eth·i·cal \ˈeth-i-kəl\ *also* **eth·ic** \-ik\ *adj* [ME *etik,* fr. L *ethicus,* fr. Gk *ēthikos,* fr. *ēthos* character] **1 :** of or relating to ethics **2 :** conforming to accepted professional standards of conduct **3** *of a drug* : restricted to sale only on a doctor's prescription ***syn*** see MORAL ***ant*** unethical — **eth·i·cal·i·ty** \ˌeth-ə-ˈkal-ət-ē\ *n* — **eth·i·cal·ly** \ˈeth-i-k(ə-)lē\ *adv* — **eth·i·cal·ness** \-kəl-nəs\ *n*
2ethical *n* : an ethical drug
ethi·cian \e-ˈthish-ən\ *n* : ETHICIST
eth·i·cist \ˈeth-ə-səst\ *n* : a specialist in ethics
eth·i·on \ˈeth-ē-ˌän\ *n* [blend of *eth-* and *thion-*] : an organophosphate $C_9H_{22}O_4P_2S_4$ used as a pesticide
eth·i·on·amide \ˌeth-ē-ˈän-ə-ˌmīd\ *n* [*eth-* + *thion-* + *amide*] : a compound $C_8H_{10}N_2S$ used against mycobacteria (as in tuberculosis and leprosy)
ethi·o·nine \e-ˈthī-ə-ˌnēn\ *n* [*eth-* + *thion-* + *-ine*] : an amino acid $C_6H_{13}NO_2S$ that is the ethyl homologue of methionine and is biologically antagonistic to methionine
Ethi·op \ˈē-thē-ˌäp\ *or* **Ethi·ope** \-ˌōp\ *n* [ME *Ethiope,* fr. L *Aethiops,* fr. Gk *Aithiops*] *archaic* : ETHIOPIAN
1Ethi·o·pi·an \ˌē-thē-ˈō-pē-ən\ *n* **1 :** a member of any of the mythical or actual peoples usu. described by the ancient Greeks as dark-skinned and living far to the south **2 :** NEGRO **3 :** a native or inhabitant of Ethiopia
2Ethiopian *adj* **1 :** of, relating to, or characteristic of the inhabitants or the country of Ethiopia **2 :** of, relating to, or being the biogeographic region that includes Africa south of the Sahara, southern Arabia, and sometimes Madagascar and the adjacent islands
1Ethi·o·pic \-ˈäp-ik, -ˈō-pik\ *adj* **1 :** ETHIOPIAN **2 a :** of, relating to, or constituting Ethiopic **b :** of, relating to, or constituting a group of related Semitic languages spoken in Ethiopia
2Ethiopic *n* **1 :** a Semitic language formerly spoken in Ethiopia and still used as the liturgical language of the Christian church in Ethiopia **2 :** the Ethiopic group of Semitic languages
eth·moid \ˈeth-ˌmȯid\ *or* **eth·moi·dal** \eth-ˈmȯid-ᵊl\ *adj* [F *ethmoïde,* fr. Gk *ēthmoeidēs,* lit., like a strainer, fr. *ēthmos* strainer] : of, relating to, adjoining, or being one or more bones of the walls and septum of the nasal cavity — **ethmoid** *n*
1eth·nic \ˈeth-nik\ *adj* [ME, fr. LL *ethnicus,* fr. Gk *ethnikos* national, gentile, fr. *ethnos* nation, people] **1 :** HEATHEN **2 :** of or relating to races or large groups of people classed according to common traits and customs ⟨the changing ~ composition of the city —Leonard Buder⟩
2ethnic *n* : a member of an ethnic group; *esp* : a member of a minority group who retains the customs, language, or social views of his group
eth·ni·cal \ˈeth-ni-kəl\ *adj* **1 :** ETHNIC **2 :** of or relating to ethnology : ETHNOLOGIC — **eth·ni·cal·ly** \-k(ə-)lē\ *adv*
eth·nic·i·ty \eth-ˈnis-ət-ē\ *n* : ethnic quality or affiliation
ethno- *comb form* [F, fr. Gk *ethno-, ethn-,* fr. *ethnos*] : race : people : cultural group ⟨*ethno*centric⟩
eth·no·bi·ol·o·gy \ˌeth-nō-bī-ˈäl-ə-jē\ *n* : a branch of biology dealing with the relation between usu. primitive human societies and the plants and animals of their environment — **eth·no·bi·o·log·i·cal** \-ˌbī-ə-ˈläj-i-kəl\ *adj*
eth·no·cen·tric \ˌeth-nō-ˈsen-trik\ *adj* **1 :** having race as a central interest **2 :** characterized by or based on the attitude that one's own group is superior — **eth·no·cen·tri·cal·ly** \-tri-k(ə-)lē\ *adv* — **eth·no·cen·tric·i·ty** \-sen-ˈtris-ət-ē\ *n* — **eth·no·cen·trism** \-ˈsen-ˌtriz-əm\ *n*
eth·nog·ra·phy \eth-ˈnäg-rə-fē\ *n* [F *ethnographie,* fr. *ethno-* + *-graphie* -graphy] : ETHNOLOGY; *specif* : descriptive anthropology — **eth·nog·ra·pher** \-fər\ *n* — **eth·no·graph·ic** \ˌeth-nə-ˈgraf-ik\ *or* **eth·no·graph·i·cal** \-i-kəl\ *adj* — **eth·no·graph·i·cal·ly** \-i-k(ə-)lē\ *adv*
ethnol *abbr* ethnologist; ethnology
eth·nol·o·gy \eth-ˈnäl-ə-jē\ *n* **1 :** a science that deals with the division of mankind into races and their origin, distribution, relations, and characteristics **2 :** anthropology dealing chiefly with the comparative and analytical study of cultures : CULTURAL ANTHROPOLOGY — **eth·no·log·ic** \ˌeth-nə-ˈläj-ik\ *or* **eth·no·log·i·cal** \-i-kəl\ *adj* — **eth·no·log·i·cal·ly** \-i-k(ə-)lē\ *adv* — **eth·nol·o·gist** \eth-ˈnäl-ə-jəst\ *n*
eth·no·mu·si·col·o·gy \ˌeth-nō-ˌmyü-zi-ˈkäl-ə-jē\ *n* : a study of the music of non-European cultures — **eth·no·mu·si·co·log·i·cal** \-kə-ˈläj-i-kəl\ *adj* — **eth·no·mu·si·col·o·gist** \-ˈkäl-ə-jəst\ *n*
eth·no·sci·ence \ˈeth-nō-ˌsī-ən(t)s\ *n* : the nature lore (as folk taxonomy of plants and animals) of primitive peoples
ethol·o·gy \ē-ˈthäl-ə-jē\ *n* **1 :** a branch of knowledge dealing with human ethos and with its formation and evolution **2 :** the scientific and objective study of animal behavior — **etho·log·i·cal** \ˌē-thə-ˈläj-i-kəl, ˌeth-ə-\ *adj* — **ethol·o·gist** \ē-ˈthäl-ə-jəst\ *n*
ethos \ˈē-ˌthäs\ *n* [NL, fr. Gk *ēthos* custom, character] : the distinguishing character, sentiment, moral nature, or guiding beliefs of a person, group, or institution ⟨the ~ of thrift, hard work, and wealth —N. P. Hurley⟩
eth·oxy \e-ˈthäk-sē\ *adj* : relating to or containing ethoxyl
eth·ox·yl \e-ˈthäk-səl\ *n* [ISV *eth-* + *ox-* + *-yl*] : the univalent radical C_2H_5O composed of ethyl united with oxygen
eth·yl \ˈeth-əl\ *n* [ISV *ether* + *-yl*] : a univalent hydrocarbon radical C_2H_5 — **eth·yl·ic** \e-ˈthil-ik\ *adj*
ethyl acetate *n* : a colorless fragrant volatile flammable liquid ester $C_4H_8O_2$ used esp. as a solvent
ethyl alcohol *n* : ALCOHOL 1
eth·yl·ate \ˈeth-ə-ˌlāt\ *vt* **-at·ed; -at·ing** : to introduce the ethyl group into (a compound) — **eth·yl·ation** \ˌeth-ə-ˈlā-shən\ *n*
ethyl cellulose *n* : any of various thermoplastic substances used esp. in plastics and lacquers
ethyl chloride *n* : a colorless pungent flammable gaseous or volatile liquid C_2H_5Cl used esp. as a local surface anesthetic
eth·yl·ene \ˈeth-ə-ˌlēn\ *n* **1 :** a colorless flammable gaseous unsaturated hydrocarbon C_2H_4 found in coal gas or obtained by pyrolysis of petroleum hydrocarbons **2 :** a bivalent hydrocarbon radical C_2H_4 derived from ethane — **eth·yl·enic** \ˌeth-ə-ˈlē-nik, -ˈlen-ik\ *adj* — **eth·yl·eni·cal·ly** \-(n)i-k(ə-)lē\ *adv*
ethylene glycol *n* : a thick liquid alcohol $C_2H_6O_2$ used esp. as an antifreeze
ethylene oxide *n* : a colorless flammable toxic gaseous or liquid compound C_2H_4O used esp. in synthesis (as of ethylene glycol) and in sterilization and fumigation
ethyl ether *n* : ETHER 3a
ethy·nyl *or* **ethi·nyl** \e-ˈthīn-ᵊl, ˈeth-ə-ˌnil\ *n* [*ethyne, ethine* (acetylene) (fr. *ethyl* + *-ine*) + *-yl*] : a univalent unsaturated radical $HC{\equiv}C$ derived from acetylene by removal of one hydrogen
-et·ic \ˈet-ik\ *adj suffix* [L & Gk; L *-eticus,* fr. Gk *-etikos, -ētikos,* fr. *-etos, -ētos,* ending of certain verbals] : -IC ⟨limn*etic*⟩ — often in adjectives corresponding to nouns ending in *-esis* ⟨gen*etic*⟩
eti·o·late \ˈēt-ē-ə-ˌlāt\ *vt* **-lat·ed; -lat·ing** [F *étioler*] **1 :** to bleach and alter the natural development of (a green plant) by excluding

ə abut ᵊ kitten ər further a back ā bake ä cot, cart
au̇ out ch chin e less ē easy g gift i trip ī life
j joke ŋ sing ō flow ȯ flaw ȯi coin th thin t͟h this
ü loot u̇ foot y yet yü few yu̇ furious zh vision

sunlight **2 a :** to make pale and sickly **b :** to take away the natural vigor or inhibit the potential for growth of (as by undue sheltering or pampering) — **eti·o·la·tion** \ˌēt-ē-ə-ˈlā-shən\ *n*

eti·o·log·ic \ˌēt-ē-ə-ˈläj-ik\ *or* **eti·o·log·i·cal** \-i-kəl\ *adj* **1 :** assigning or seeking to assign a cause **2 :** of or relating to etiology — **eti·o·log·i·cal·ly** \-i-k(ə-)lē\ *adv*

eti·ol·o·gy \ˌēt-ē-ˈäl-ə-jē\ *n* [ML *aetiologia* statement of causes, fr. Gk *aitiologia*, fr. *aitia* cause; akin to L *aemulus* rivaling] **1 :** CAUSE, ORIGIN; *specif* **:** all of the causes of a disease or abnormal condition **2 :** a branch of knowledge dealing with causes

et·i·quette \ˈet-i-kət, -ˌket\ *n* [F *étiquette*, lit., ticket — more at TICKET] **:** the forms required by good breeding or prescribed by authority to be observed in social or official life ⟨the hauteur of Spanish court ~ —G. C. Sellery⟩

ETO *abbr* European theater of operations

Eton collar \ˌēt-ᵊn-\ *n* [*Eton* College, English public school] **:** a large stiff turnover collar

Eton jacket *n* **:** a short black jacket with long sleeves, wide lapels, and an open front

Etru·ri·an \i-ˈtru̇r-ē-ən\ *n* [*Etruria*] **:** ETRUSCAN — **Etrurian** *adj*

¹Etrus·can \i-ˈtrəs-kən\ *adj* [L *etruscus*; akin to L *Etruria*, ancient country] **:** of, relating to, or characteristic of Etruria, the Etruscans, or the Etruscan language

²Etruscan *n* **1 :** a native or inhabitant of ancient Etruria **2 :** the language of the Etruscans which is of unknown affiliation

et seq *abbr* **1** [L *et sequens*] and the following one **2** [L *et sequentes* (masc. & fem. pl.), or *et sequentia* (neut. pl.)] and the following ones

-ette \ˈet, ˌet, ət, it\ *n suffix* [ME, fr. MF, fem. dim. suffix, fr. OF *-ete* — more at -ET] **1 :** little one ⟨kitchen*ette*⟩ **2 :** group ⟨oct*ette*⟩ **3 :** female ⟨farmer*ette*⟩ **4 :** imitation ⟨beaver*ette*⟩

étude \ˈā-ˌt(y)üd\ *n* [F, lit., study, fr. MF *estude, estudie*] **1 :** a piece of music for the practice of a point of technique **2 :** a composition built on a technical motive but played for its artistic value

etui \ā-ˈtwē, ˈā-ˌ\ *n, pl* **etuis** [F *étui*] **:** a small ornamental case

ETV *abbr* educational television

et·y·mol·o·gist \ˌet-ə-ˈmäl-ə-jəst\ *n* **:** a specialist in etymology

et·y·mol·o·gize \-ˌjīz\ *vb* **-gized; -giz·ing** *vt* **:** to discover, formulate, or state an etymology for ~ *vi* **:** to study or formulate etymologies

et·y·mol·o·gy \-jē\ *n, pl* **-gies** [ME *ethimologie*, fr. L *etymologia*, fr. Gk, fr. *etymon* + *-logia* -logy] **1 :** the history of a linguistic form (as a word) shown by tracing its development since its earliest recorded occurrence in the language where it is found, by tracing its transmission from one language to another, by analyzing it into its component parts, by identifying its cognates in other languages, or by tracing it and its cognates to a common ancestral form in an ancestral language **2 :** a branch of linguistics concerned with etymologies — **et·y·mo·log·i·cal** \-mə-ˈläj-i-kəl\ *adj* — **et·y·mo·log·i·cal·ly** \-k(ə-)lē\ *adv*

et·y·mon \ˈet-ə-ˌmän\ *n, pl* **-ma** \-mə\ *also* **-mons** [L, fr. Gk, literal meaning of a word according to its origin, fr. *etymos* true; akin to Gk *eteos* true] **1 a :** an earlier form of a word in the same language or an ancestral language **b :** a word in a foreign language that is the source of a particular loanword **2 :** a word or morpheme from which words are formed by composition or derivation

Eu *symbol* europium

eu- *comb form* [ME, fr. L, fr. Gk, fr. *ey, eu*, fr. neut. of *eys* good; akin to Hitt *asus* good and perh. to L *esse* to be] **1 a :** well **:** easily ⟨*eu*plastic⟩ — compare DYS- **b :** good ⟨*eu*daemon⟩ — compare DYS- **2 a :** true ⟨*eu*chromosome⟩ ⟨*eu*globulin⟩ **b :** truly ⟨*eu*coelomate⟩

eu·ca·lypt \ˈyü-kə-ˌlipt\ *n* **:** EUCALYPTUS

eu·ca·lyp·tol *also* **eu·ca·lyp·tole** \ˌyü-kə-ˈlip-ˌtȯl, -ˌtōl\ *n* **:** CINEOLE

eu·ca·lyp·tus \ˌyü-kə-ˈlip-təs\ *n, pl* **-ti** \-ˌtī, -ˌtē\ *or* **-tus·es** [NL, genus name, fr. *eu-* + Gk *kalyptos* covered, fr. *kalyptein* to conceal; fr. the conical covering of the buds — more at HELL] **:** any of a genus (*Eucalyptus*) of mostly Australian evergreen trees or rarely shrubs of the myrtle family that have rigid entire leaves and umbellate flowers and are widely cultivated for their gums, resins, oils, and useful woods

eu·cary·ote *or* **eu·kary·ote** \(ˈ)yü-ˈkar-ē-ˌōt, -ē-ət\ *n* [*eu-* + *kary-* + *-ote* (as in *zygote*)] **:** an organism composed of one or more cells with visibly evident nuclei — compare PROCARYOTE — **eu·cary·ot·ic** \(ˌ)yü-ˌkar-ē-ˈät-ik\ *adj*

Eu·cha·rist \ˈyü-k(ə-)rəst\ *n* [ME *eukarist*, fr. MF *eucariste*, fr. LL *eucharistia*, fr. Gk, Eucharist, gratitude, fr. *eucharistos* grateful, fr. *eu-* + *charizesthai* to show favor, fr. *charis* favor, grace, gratitude; akin to Gk *chairein* to rejoice — more at YEARN] **1 :** COMMUNION 2a **2** *Christian Science* **:** spiritual communion with God — **eu·cha·ris·tic** \ˌyü-kə-ˈris-tik\ *adj, often cap*

¹eu·chre \ˈyü-kər\ *n* [origin unknown] **1 :** a card game in which each player is dealt five cards and the player making trump must take three tricks to win a hand **2 :** the action of euchring an opponent

²euchre *vt* **eu·chred; eu·chring** \-k(ə-)riŋ\ **1 :** to prevent from winning three tricks in euchre **2 :** CHEAT, TRICK ⟨*euchred* out of their life savings —Pete Martin⟩

eu·chro·ma·tin \(ˈ)yü-ˈkrō-mət-ən\ *n* [G, fr. *eu-* + *chromatin*] **:** the genetically active portion of chromatin that is largely composed of genes — **eu·chro·mat·ic** \ˌyü-krō-ˈmat-ik\ *adj*

eu·cil·i·ate \yü-ˈsil-ē-ət\ *n* [deriv. of NL *eu-* + *cilium*] **:** any of a subclass (Euciliata) of ciliated protozoans with a trophic macronucleus and a reproductive micronucleus — **euciliate** *adj*

eu·clase \ˈyü-ˌklās, -ˌklāz\ *n* [F, fr. *eu-* (fr. L) + Gk *klasis* breaking, fr. *klan* to break — more at HALT] **:** a mineral $BeAlSiO_4(OH)$ that consists of a brittle silicate of beryllium and aluminum in pale yellow, green, or blue prismatic crystals and is used esp. as a gemstone

eu·clid·e·an *also* **eu·clid·i·an** \yü-ˈklid-ē-ən\ *adj, often cap* **:** of or relating to the geometry of Euclid or a geometry based on similar axioms

euclidean algorithm *n, often cap E* **:** a method of finding the greatest common divisor of two numbers by dividing the first by the second, the second by the remainder, the first remainder by the second remainder, and so on until exact division is obtained whence the greatest common divisor is the exact divisor

euclidean geometry *n, often cap E* **1 :** geometry based on Euclid's axioms **2 :** the geometry of a euclidean space

euclidean space *n, often cap E* **:** a space in which Euclid's axioms and definitions (as of straight and parallel lines and angles of plane triangles) apply

eu·clid's algorithm \ˌyü-klədz-\ *n, often cap E* **:** EUCLIDEAN ALGORITHM

eu·crite \ˈyü-ˌkrīt\ *n* [G *eukrit*, fr. Gk *eukritos* easily discerned] **1 :** a meteorite composed essentially of anorthite and augite **2 :** a rock consisting of a very basic gabbro — **eu·crit·ic** \yü-ˈkrit-ik\ *adj*

eu·dae·mo·nism \yu̇-ˈdē-mə-ˌniz-əm\ *or* **eu·dai·mo·nism** \-ˈdī-\ *n* [Gk *eudaimonia* happiness, fr. *eudaimōn* having a good attendant spirit, happy, fr. *eu-* + *daimōn* spirit] **:** a theory that defines moral obligation by reference to personal well-being through a life governed by reason — **eu·dae·mo·nist** \-nəst\ *n* — **eu·dae·mo·nis·tic** \-ˌdē-mə-ˈnis-tik\ *adj*

eu·di·om·e·ter \ˌyüd-ē-ˈäm-ət-ər\ *n* [It *eudiometro*, fr. Gk *eudia* fair weather (fr. *eu-* + *-dia* weather — akin to L *dies* day) + It *-metro* -meter, fr. Gk *metron* measure] **:** an instrument for the volumetric measurement and analysis of gases — **eu·dio·met·ric** \ˌyüd-ē-ə-ˈme-trik\ *adj* — **eu·dio·met·ri·cal·ly** \-tri-k(ə-)lē\ *adv*

eu·gen·ic \yu̇-ˈjen-ik\ *adj* [Gk *eugenēs* wellborn, fr. *eu-* + *-genēs* born — more at -GEN] **1 :** relating to or fitted for the production of good offspring **2 :** of or relating to eugenics — **eu·gen·i·cal·ly** \-i-k(ə-)lē\ *adv*

eu·gen·i·cist \-ˈjen-ə-səst\ *n* **:** a student or advocate of eugenics

eu·gen·ics \yu̇-ˈjen-iks\ *n pl but sing or pl in constr* **:** a science that deals with the improvement (as by control of human mating) of hereditary qualities of a race or breed

eu·ge·nol \ˈyü-jə-ˌnȯl, -ˌnōl\ *n* [F *eugénol*, fr. NL *Eugenia*, genus of tropical trees] **:** a colorless aromatic liquid phenol $C_{10}H_{12}O_2$ found esp. in clove oil and used chiefly in flavors and perfumes

eu·geo·syn·cline \(ˌ)yü-ˌjē-ō-ˈsin-ˌklīn\ *n* **:** a narrow rapidly subsiding geosyncline usu. with volcanic materials mingled with clastic sediments — **eu·geo·syn·cli·nal** \-(ˌ)sin-ˈklīn-ᵊl\ *adj*

eu·gle·na \yu̇-ˈglē-nə\ *n* [NL, genus name, fr. *eu-* + Gk *glēnē* eyeball, socket of a joint; prob. akin to Gk *glainoi* ornaments — more at CLEAN] **:** any of a genus (*Euglena*) of green freshwater flagellates often classed as algae

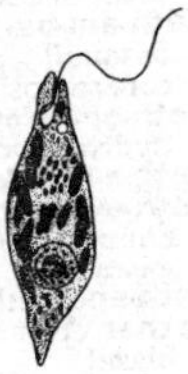

euglena

eu·gle·noid \-ˌnȯid\ *n* **:** any of a taxon (Euglenoidina or Euglenophyta) of varied flagellates (as a euglena) that are typically green or colorless stigma-bearing solitary organisms with one or two flagella emerging from a well-defined gullet — **euglenoid** *adj*

euglenoid movement *n* **:** writhing usu. nonprogressive protoplasmic movement of plastic-bodied euglenoid flagellates

eu·glob·u·lin \yü-ˈgläb-yə-lən\ *n* [ISV *eu-* + *globulin*] **:** a simple protein that does not dissolve in pure water

eu·he·mer·ism \yu̇-ˈhē-mə-ˌriz-əm, -ˈhem-ə-\ *n* [*Euhemerus*, 4th cent. B.C. Gk mythographer] **:** interpretation of myths as traditional accounts of historical persons and events — **eu·he·mer·ist** \-rəst\ *n* — **eu·he·mer·is·tic** \-ˌhē-mə-ˈris-tik, -ˌhem-ə-\ *adj* — **eu·he·mer·is·ti·cal·ly** \-ti-k(ə-)lē\ *adv* — **eu·he·mer·ize** \-ˈhē-mə-ˌrīz, -ˈhem-ə-\ *vt*

eu·la·chon \ˈyü-lə-ˌkän, -li-kən\ *n, pl* **eulachon** *or* **eulachons** [Chinook Jargon *ulâkân*] **:** a marine food fish (*Thaleichthys pacificus*) of the north Pacific coast related to the smelt — called also *candlefish*

eu·la·mel·li·branch \ˌyü-lə-ˈmel-ə-ˌbraŋk\ *n, pl* **-branchs** [NL *Eulamellibranchia*, order name, fr. *eu-* + *Lamellibranchia*, class of mollusks — more at LAMELLIBRANCH] **:** any of an order (Eulamellibranchia) of lamellibranchiate bivalve mollusks with filamentous gills forming two continuous flattened layers on each side of the body — **eu·la·mel·li·bran·chi·ate** \-ˌmel-ə-ˈbraŋ-kē-ət\ *adj or n*

eu·lo·gist \ˈyü-lə-jəst\ *n* **:** one who eulogizes

eu·lo·gi·um \yu̇-ˈlō-jē-əm\ *n, pl* **-gia** \-jē-ə\ *or* **-gi·ums** [ML] **:** EULOGY

eu·lo·gize \ˈyü-lə-ˌjīz\ *vt* **-gized; -giz·ing :** to speak or write in high praise of **:** EXTOL — **eu·lo·giz·er** *n*

eu·lo·gy \ˈyü-lə-jē\ *n, pl* **-gies** [ME *euloge*, fr. ML *eulogium*, fr. Gk *eulogia* praise, fr. *eu-* + *-logia* -logy] **1 :** a commendatory formal statement or set oration **2 :** high praise ***syn*** see ENCOMIUM ***ant*** calumny, tirade — **eu·lo·gis·tic** \ˌyü-lə-ˈjis-tik\ *adj* — **eu·lo·gis·ti·cal·ly** \-ti-k(ə-)lē\ *adv*

Eu·men·i·des \yu̇-ˈmen-ə-ˌdēz\ *n pl* [L, fr. Gk] **:** the Furies in Greek mythology

eu·mor·phic \(ˈ)yü-ˈmȯr-fik\ *adj* **:** MESOMORPHIC, ATHLETIC 3

eu·nuch \ˈyü-nək, -nik\ *n* [ME *eunuk*, fr. L *eunuchus*, fr. Gk *eunouchos*, fr. *eunē* bed + *echein* to have, have charge of — more at SCHEME] **1 :** a castrated man placed in charge of a harem or employed as a chamberlain in a palace **2 :** a man or boy deprived of the testes or external genitals — **eu·nuch·ism** \-ˌiz-əm\ *n*

eu·nuch·oid \-ˌȯid\ *n* **:** a sexually deficient individual; *esp* **:** one lacking in sexual differentiation and tending toward the intersex state — **eunuchoid** *adj*

eu·on·y·mus \yu̇-ˈän-ə-məs\ *n* [NL, genus name, fr. L *euonymos* spindle tree, fr. Gk *euōnymos*, fr. *euōnymos* having an auspicious name, fr. *eu-* + *onyma* name — more at NAME] **:** any of a genus (*Euonymus*) of often evergreen shrubs, small trees, or vines of the staff tree family — called also *spindle tree*

eu·pa·trid \yu̇-ˈpa-trəd, ˈyü-pə-\ *n, pl* **eu·pat·ri·dae** \yu̇-ˈpa-trə-ˌdē\ *often cap* [Gk *eupatridēs*, fr. *eu-* + *patr-, patēr* father — more at FATHER] **:** one of the hereditary aristocrats of ancient Athens

eu·pep·sia \yu̇-ˈpep-shə, -sē-ə\ *n* [NL, fr. *eu-* + *-pepsia* (as in *dyspepsia*)] **:** good digestion

eu·pep·tic \-ˈpep-tik\ *adj* **1 :** of, relating to, or having good digestion **2 :** CHEERFUL, OPTIMISTIC — **eu·pep·ti·cal·ly** \-ti-k(ə-)lē\ *adv*

eu·phau·si·id \yu̇-ˈfȯ-zē-əd\ *n* [NL *Euphausia*, genus of crustaceans] : any of an order (Euphausiacea) of small usu. luminescent malacostracan crustaceans that resemble shrimps and in some areas form an important element in marine plankton — **euphausiid** *adj*

eu·phe·mism \ˈyü-fə-ˌmiz-əm\ *n* [Gk *euphēmismos*, fr. *euphēmos* auspicious, sounding good, fr. *eu-* + *phēmē* speech, fr. *phanai* to speak — more at BAN] : the substitution of an agreeable or inoffensive expression for one that may offend or suggest something unpleasant; *also* : the expression so substituted ⟨that vandalism which goes under the ∼ of souvenir hunting —*Saturday Rev.*⟩ — **eu·phe·mis·tic** \ˌyü-fə-ˈmis-tik\ *adj* — **eu·phe·mis·ti·cal·ly** \-ti-k(ə-)lē\ *adv*

eu·phe·mize \ˈyü-fə-ˌmīz\ *vb* **-mized; -miz·ing** *vt* : to express by a euphemism ⟨the uneasy effort in America to ∼ death —W. J. Fisher⟩ ∼ *vi* : to make use of euphemistic expressions — **eu·phe·miz·er** *n*

eu·phen·ics \yu̇-ˈfen-iks\ *n pl but sing in constr* [*eu-* + *phen-* (fr. *phenotype*) + *-ics*; after E *genotype*: *eugenics*] : a science that deals with the biological improvement of human beings after birth — **euphen·ic** \-ik\ *adj*

eu·pho·ni·ous \yu̇-ˈfō-nē-əs\ *adj* : pleasing to the ear — **eu·pho·ni·ous·ly** *adv* — **eu·pho·ni·ous·ness** *n* — **eu·pho·nize** \ˈyü-fə-ˌnīz\ *vt*

eu·pho·ni·um \yu̇-ˈfō-nē-əm\ *n* [Gk *euphōnia* + E *-ium* (as in *harmonium*)] : a brass instrument having a conical bore, a cup-shaped mouthpiece, and a range from B flat below the bass staff upward for three octaves

eu·pho·ny \ˈyü-fə-nē\ *n, pl* **-nies** [F *euphonie*, fr. LL *euphonia*, fr. Gk *euphōnia*, fr. *euphōnos* sweet-voiced, musical, fr. *eu-* + *phōnē* voice — more at BAN] **1** : pleasing or sweet sound; *esp* : the acoustic effect produced by words so formed or combined as to please the ear **2** : a harmonious succession of words having a pleasing sound — **eu·phon·ic** \yu̇-ˈfän-ik\ *adj* — **eu·phon·i·cal·ly** \-i-k(ə-)lē\ *adv*

eu·phor·bia \yu̇-ˈfȯr-bē-ə\ *n* [NL. genus name, alter. of L *euphorbea* euphorbia, fr. *Euphorbus*, 1st cent. A.D. physician] : any of a large genus (*Euphorbia* of the family Euphorbiaceae) of plants that have a milky juice and flowers lacking a calyx and included in an involucre which surrounds a group of several staminate flowers and a central pistillate flower with 3-lobed pistils; *broadly* : SPURGE

eu·pho·ria \yu̇-ˈfȯr-ē-ə, -ˈfȯr-\ *n* [NL, fr. Gk, fr. *euphoros* healthy, fr. *eu-* + *pherein* to bear — more at BEAR] : a feeling of well-being or elation — **eu·phor·ic** \-ˈfȯr-ik, -ˈfär-\ *adj* — **eu·phor·i·cal·ly** \-i-k(ə-)lē\ *adv*

eu·pho·tic \yü-ˈfōt-ik\ *adj* [ISV] : of, relating to, or constituting the upper layers of a body of water into which sufficient light penetrates to permit growth of green plants

Eu·phros·y·ne \yu̇-ˈfräs-ᵊn-(ˌ)ē\ *n* [L, fr. Gk *Euphrosynē*] : one of the three Graces

eu·phu·ism \ˈyü-fyə-ˌwiz-əm\ *n* [*Euphues*, character in prose romances by John Lyly] **1** : an elegant Elizabethan literary style marked by excessive use of balance, antithesis, and alliteration and by frequent use of similes drawn from mythology and nature **2** : artificial elegance of language — **eu·phu·ist** \-wəst\ *n* — **eu·phu·is·tic** \ˌyü-fyə-ˈwis-tik\ *adj* — **eu·phu·is·ti·cal·ly** \-ti-k(ə-)lē\ *adv*

eu·plas·tic \yü-ˈplas-tik\ *adj* : adapted to the formation of tissue : BLASTEMATIC

eu·ploid \ˈyü-ˌplȯid\ *adj* [ISV] : having a chromosome number that is an exact multiple of the monoploid number — compare ANEUPLOID — **euploid** *n* — **eu·ploi·dy** \-ˌplȯid-ē\ *n*

eup·nea *also* **eup·noea** \yüp-nē-ə\ *n* [NL, fr. Gk *eupnoia*, fr. *eupnous* breathing freely, fr. *eu-* + *pnein* to breathe — more at SNEEZE] : normal respiration — **eup·ne·ic** \-nē-ik\ *adj*

Eur *abbr* Europe; European

Eur- *or* **Euro-** *comb form* [*Europe*] : European and (*Euramerican*)

Eur·amer·i·can \ˌyu̇r-ə-ˈmer-ə-kən\ *or* **Eu·ro-Amer·i·can** \ˌyu̇r-ō-ə-ˈmer-\ *adj* : common to Europe and America ⟨culture patterns that are variants of our common ∼ culture —W. H. Wickwar⟩

Eur·asian \yu̇-ˈrā-zhən, -shən\ *adj* **1** : of or relating to Europe and Asia **2** : of a mixed European and Asiatic origin — **Eur·asian** *n*

eu·re·ka \yu̇-ˈrē-kə\ *interj* [Gk *heurēka* I have found, fr. *heuriskein* to find; fr. the exclamation attributed to Archimedes on discovering a method for determining the purity of gold — more at HEURISTIC] — used to express triumph on a discovery

eu·ro \ˈyu̇(ə)r-(ˌ)ō\ *n, pl* **euros** [native name in Australia] : a large reddish gray kangaroo (*Macrobus robustus*)

Eu·ro·bond \ˈyu̇r-ō-ˌbänd\ *n* [*Europe* + *bond*] : a bond of a U.S. corporation that is sold outside the U.S. and that is denominated and paid for in dollars and yields interest in dollars

Eu·ro·crat \ˈyu̇r-ə-ˌkrat\ *n* [*European Common Market* + *-crat* (as in *bureaucrat*)] : a staff member of the administrative commission of the European Common Market

Eu·ro·dol·lar \ˈyu̇r-ō-ˌdäl-ər\ *n* [*Europe* + *dollar*] : a U.S. dollar held (as by a bank) outside the U.S. and esp. in Europe

Eu·ro·pa \yu̇-ˈrō-pə\ *n* [L, fr. Gk *Europē*] : a Phoenician princess carried off by Zeus in the form of a white bull and by him mother of Minos, Rhadamanthus, and Sarpedon

Eu·ro·pe·an \ˌyu̇r-ə-ˈpē-ən\ *n* **1** : a native or inhabitant of Europe **2** : a person of European descent — **European** *adj* — **Eu·ro·pe·an·iza·tion** \-ˌpē-ə-nə-ˈzā-shən\ *n* — **Eu·ro·pe·an·ize** \-ˈpē-ə-ˌnīz\ *vt*

European chafer *n* : an Old World beetle (*Amphimallon majalis*) now established in parts of eastern No. America where its larva is a destructive pest on the roots of turf grasses

European corn borer *n* : an Old World moth (*Ostrinia nubilalis*) that is widespread in eastern No. America where its larva is a major pest esp. in the stems and crowns of Indian corn, dahlias, and potatoes

European plan *n* : a hotel plan whereby the daily rates cover only the cost of the room — compare AMERICAN PLAN

European red mite *n* : a small bright or brownish red oval mite (*Panonychus ulmi*) that is a destructive orchard pest

eu·ro·pi·um \yu̇-ˈrō-pē-əm\ *n* [NL, fr. *Europa* Europe] : a bivalent and trivalent metallic element of the rare-earth group found in monazite sand — see ELEMENT table

Eu·ro·po·cen·tric \yu̇-ˌrō-pə-ˈsen-trik\ *adj* [*Europe* + E *-o-* + *-centric*] : centered on Europe and the Europeans ⟨world history texts . . . showed a markedly ∼ orientation —J. W. Hall⟩ — **Eu·ro·po·cen·trism** \-ˌtriz-əm\ *n*

eury- *comb form* [NL, fr. Gk, fr. *eurys*; akin to Skt *uru* broad, wide] : broad : wide ⟨*euryhaline*⟩

eu·ry·bath·ic \ˌyu̇r-i-ˈbath-ik\ *adj* [*eury-* + Gk *bathos* depth] : capable of living on the bottom in both deep and shallow water ⟨∼ gastropods⟩

Eu·ryd·i·ce \yu̇-ˈrid-ə-(ˌ)sē\ *n* [L, fr. Gk *Eurydikē*] : the wife of Orpheus whom according to Greek myth he nearly succeeds in bringing back from Hades to the land of the living

eu·ry·ha·line \ˌyu̇r-i-ˈhā-ˌlīn, -ˈhal-ˌin\ *adj* [ISV *eury-* + Gk *halinos* of salt, fr. *hals* salt — more at SALT] : able to live in waters of a wide range of salinity

eu·ryp·ter·id \yu̇-ˈrip-tə-rəd\ *n* [deriv. of Gk *eury-* + *pteron* wing — more at FEATHER] : any of an order (Eurypterida) of usu. large aquatic Paleozoic arthropods related to the king crabs — **eurypterid** *adj*

eu·ry·therm \ˈyu̇r-i-ˌthərm\ *n* [prob. fr. G *eurytherm* eurythermal, fr. *eury-* + Gk *thermē* heat] : an organism that tolerates a wide range of temperature — **eu·ry·ther·mal** \ˌyu̇r-i-ˈthər-məl\ *or* **eu·ry·ther·mic** \-mik\ *or* **eu·ry·ther·mous** \-məs\ *adj*

eu·ryth·mic *or* **eu·rhyth·mic** \yu̇-ˈrith-mik\ *adj* **1** : HARMONIOUS **2** : of or relating to eurythmy or eurythmics

eu·ryth·mics *or* **eu·rhyth·mics** \-miks\ *n pl but sing or pl in constr* : the art of harmonious bodily movement esp. through expressive timed movements in response to improvised music

eu·ryth·my *or* **eu·rhyth·my** \-mē\ *n* [G *eurhythmie*, fr. L *eurythmia* rhythmical movement, fr. Gk, fr. *eurythmos* rhythmical, fr. *eu-* + *rhythmos* rhythm] : a system of harmonious body movement to the rhythm of spoken words

eu·ry·top·ic \ˌyu̇r-i-ˈtäp-ik\ *adj* [prob. fr. G *eurytop*, fr. *eury-* + Gk *topos* place] : tolerant of wide variation in one or more physical factors of the environment — **eu·ry·to·pic·i·ty** \-tō-ˈpis-ət-ē, -tä-\ *n*

eu·sta·chian tube \yu̇-ˌstā-sh(ē-)ən- *also* -ˌstā-kē-ən-\ *n, often cap E* [Bartolommeo *Eustachio*] : a bony and cartilaginous tube connecting the middle ear with the nasopharynx and equalizing air pressure on both sides of the tympanic membrane — see EAR illustration

eu·stat·ic \yu̇-ˈstat-ik\ *adj* [ISV] : relating to or characterized by worldwide change of sea level

eu·stele \ˈyü-ˌstēl, yü-ˈstē-lē\ *n* : a stele in which the vascular cylinder is broken at leaf emergences and by interfascicular areas

eu·tec·tic \yü-ˈtek-tik\ *adj* [Gk *eutēktos* easily melted, fr. *eu-* + *tēktos* melted, fr. *tēkein* to melt — more at THAW] **1** *of an alloy or solution* : having the lowest melting point possible **2** : of or relating to a eutectic alloy or solution or its melting or freezing point — **eutectic** *n* — **eu·tec·toid** \-ˌtȯid\ *adj or n*

Eu·ter·pe \yu̇-ˈtər-pē\ *n* [L, fr. Gk *Euterpē*] : the Greek Muse of music

eu·tha·na·sia \ˌyü-thə-ˈnā-zh(ē-)ə\ *n* [Gk, easy death, fr. *eu-* + *thanatos* death — more at THANATOS] : the act or practice of killing individuals (as persons or domestic animals) that are hopelessly sick or injured for reasons of mercy — **eu·tha·na·sic** \-zik, -sik\ *adj*

eu·then·ics \yu̇-ˈthen-iks\ *n pl but sing or pl in constr* [Gk *euthenein* to thrive, fr. *eu-* + *-thenein* (akin to Skt *āhanas* swelling)] : a science that deals with development of human well-being by improvement of living conditions — **eu·the·nist** \yu̇-ˈthen-əst, ˈyü-thə-nəst\ *n*

eu·the·ri·an \yu̇-ˈthir-ē-ən\ *adj* [deriv. of NL *eu-* + Gk *thērion* beast — more at TREACLE] : of or relating to a major division (Eutheria) of mammals comprising the placental mammals — **eutherian** *n*

eu·thy·roid \(ˈ)yü-ˈthī-ˌrȯid\ *adj* : characterized by normal thyroid function

eu·tro·phic \yu̇-ˈtrō-fik\ *adj* [prob. fr. G *eutroph* eutrophic, fr. *eutrophos* well nourished, nourishing, fr. *eu-* + *trephein* to nourish — more at ATROPHY] *of a body of water* : rich in dissolved nutrients (as phosphates) but often shallow and seasonally deficient in oxygen — compare MESOTROPHIC, OLIGOTROPHIC — **eu·tro·phi·ca·tion** \-ˌtrō-fə-ˈkā-shən\ *n* — **eu·tro·phy** \ˈyü-trə-fē\ *n*

EV *abbr* electron volt

EVA *abbr* extravehicular activity

evac·u·ate \i-ˈvak-yə-ˌwāt\ *vb* **-at·ed; -at·ing** [L *evacuatus*, pp. of *evacuare*, fr. *e-* + *vacuus* empty — more at VACUUM] *vt* **1** : to remove the contents of : EMPTY **2** : to discharge from the body as waste : VOID **3** : to remove something (as gas or water) from esp. by pumping **4 a** : to remove esp. from a military zone or dangerous area **b** : to withdraw from military occupation of **c** : VACATE ⟨were ordered to ∼ the building⟩ ∼ *vi* **1** : to withdraw from a place in an organized way esp. for protection **2** : to pass urine or feces from the body — **evac·u·a·tive** \-ˌwāt-iv\ *adj*

evac·u·a·tion \i-ˌvak-yə-ˈwā-shən\ *n* **1** : the act or process of evacuating **2** : something evacuated or discharged
evac·u·ee \i-ˌvak-yə-ˈwē\ *n* : an evacuated person
evade \i-ˈvād\ *vb* **evad·ed; evad·ing** [MF & L; MF *evader,* fr. L *evadere,* fr. *e-* + *vadere* to go, walk — more at WADE] *vi* **1** : to slip away **2** : to take refuge in evasion ~ *vt* **1** : to elude by dexterity or stratagem **2 a** : to avoid facing up to ⟨*evaded* the real issues⟩ **b** : to avoid the performance of : DODGE, CIRCUMVENT; *esp* : to fail to pay (taxes) **c** : to avoid answering directly : turn aside **3** : to be elusive to : BAFFLE ⟨the simple, personal meaning *evaded* them —C. D. Lewis⟩ ***syn*** see ESCAPE — **evad·able** \-ˈvād-ə-bəl\ *adj* — **evad·er** *n*
evag·i·na·tion \i-ˌvaj-ə-ˈnā-shən\ *n* [LL *evagination-, evaginatio,* act of unsheathing, fr. L *evaginare* to unsheathe, fr. *e-* + *vagina* sheath] **1** : an act or instance of everting **2** : a product of eversion : OUTGROWTH
eval·u·ate \i-ˈval-yə-ˌwāt\ *vt* **-at·ed; -at·ing** [back-formation fr. *evaluation*] **1** : to determine or fix the value of **2** : to determine the significance or worth of usu. by careful appraisal and study ⟨~ a new antibiotic⟩ ***syn*** see ESTIMATE — **eval·u·a·tion** \-ˌval-yə-ˈwā-shən\ *n* — **eval·u·a·tive** \-ˈval-yə-ˌwāt-iv\ *adj* — **eval·u·a·tor** \-ˌwāt-ər\ *n*
ev·a·nesce \ˌev-ə-ˈnes\ *vi* **-nesced; -nesc·ing** [L *evanescere* — more at VANISH] : to dissipate like vapor
ev·a·nes·cence \ˌev-ə-ˈnes-ᵊn(t)s\ *n* **1** : the process or fact of evanescing **2** : evanescent quality
ev·a·nes·cent \-ᵊnt\ *adj* [L *evanescent-, evanescens,* prp. of *evanescere*] : tending to vanish like vapor ***syn*** see TRANSIENT
¹**evan·gel** \i-ˈvan-jəl\ *n* [ME *evangile,* fr. MF, fr. LL *evangelium,* fr. Gk *euangelion* good news, gospel, fr. *euangelos* bringing good news, fr. *eu-* + *angelos* messenger] : GOSPEL
²**evangel** *n* : EVANGELIST
evan·gel·i·cal \ˌē-ˌvan-ˈjel-i-kəl, ˌev-ən-\ *also* **evan·gel·ic** \-ik\ *adj* **1** : of, relating to, or being in agreement with the Christian gospel esp. as it is presented in the four Gospels **2** : PROTESTANT **3** : emphasizing salvation by faith in the atoning death of Jesus Christ through personal conversion, the authority of Scripture, and the importance of preaching as contrasted with ritual **4 a** *cap* : of or relating to the Evangelical Church in Germany **b** *often cap* : of, adhering to, or marked by fundamentalism : FUNDAMENTALIST **c** *often cap* : Low Church **5** : marked by militant or crusading zeal : EVANGELISTIC, ZEALOUS ⟨the ~ ardor of the movement's leaders —Amos Vogel⟩ — **Evan·gel·i·cal·ism** \-i-kə-ˌliz-əm\ *n* — **evan·gel·i·cal·ly** \-i-k(ə-)lē\ *adv*
Evangelical *n* : one holding evangelical principles or belonging to an evangelical party or church
evan·ge·lism \i-ˈvan-jə-ˌliz-əm\ *n* **1** : the winning or revival of personal commitments to Christ **2** : militant or crusading zeal — **evan·ge·lis·tic** \-ˌvan-jə-ˈlis-tik\ *adj* — **evan·ge·lis·ti·cal·ly** \-ti-k(ə-)lē\ *adv*
evan·ge·list \i-ˈvan-jə-ləst\ *n* **1** *often cap* : a writer of any of the four Gospels **2** : one who evangelizes; *specif* : a Protestant minister or layman who preaches at special services
evan·ge·lize \i-ˈvan-jə-ˌlīz\ *vb* **-lized; -liz·ing** *vt* **1** : to preach the gospel to **2** : to convert to Christianity ~ *vi* : to preach the gospel — **evan·ge·li·za·tion** \-ˌvan-jə-lə-ˈzā-shən\ *n*
evan·ish \i-ˈvan-ish\ *vi* [ME *evanisshen,* fr. MF *evaniss-,* stem of *evanir*] : VANISH — **evan·ish·ment** \-mənt\ *n*
evap *abbr* evaporate
evap·o·rate \i-ˈvap-ə-ˌrāt\ *vb* **-rat·ed; -rat·ing** [ME *evaporaten,* fr. L *evaporatus,* pp. of *evaporare,* fr. *e-* + *vapor* steam, vapor] *vi* **1 a** : to pass off in vapor or in invisible minute particles **b** (1) : to pass off or away : DISAPPEAR ⟨my despair *evaporated* —J. F. Wharton⟩ (2) : to diminish quickly **2** : to give forth vapor ~ *vt* **1 a** : to convert into vapor; *also* : to dissipate or draw off in vapor or fumes **b** : to deposit (as a metal) in the form of a film by sublimation **2 a** : to expel moisture from **b** : EXPEL ⟨~ electrons from a hot wire⟩ — **evap·o·ra·tion** \-ˌvap-ə-ˈrā-shən\ *n* — **evap·o·ra·tive** \-ˈvap-ə-ˌrāt-iv\ *adj* — **evap·o·ra·tive·ly** *adv* — **evap·o·ra·tiv·i·ty** \-ˌvap-ə-rə-ˈtiv-ət-ē\ *n* — **evap·o·ra·tor** \-ˈvap-ə-ˌrāt-ər\ *n*
evaporated milk *n* : milk concentrated by evaporation without the addition of sugar to one half or less of its bulk and usu. to a specified amount of milk fat and milk solids
evap·o·rite \i-ˈvap-ə-ˌrīt\ *n* [*evaporation* + *-ite*] : a sedimentary rock (as gypsum) that originates by evaporation of sea water in an enclosed basin — **evap·o·rit·ic** \-ˌvap-ə-ˈrit-ik\ *adj*
evapo·trans·pi·ra·tion \i-ˈvap-ō-ˌtran(t)-spə-ˈrā-shən\ *n* [*evaporation* + *transpiration*] : loss of water from the soil both by evaporation and by transpiration from the plants growing thereon
eva·sion \i-ˈvā-zhən\ *n* [ME, fr. MF or LL; MF, fr. LL *evasion-, evasio,* fr. L *evasus,* pp. of *evadere* to evade] **1** : the act or an instance of evading : ESCAPE ⟨suspected of tax ~⟩ **2** : a means of evading : DODGE
eva·sive \i-ˈvā-siv, -ziv\ *adj* : tending or intended to evade : EQUIVOCAL ⟨~ answers⟩ — **eva·sive·ly** *adv* — **eva·sive·ness** *n*
eve \ˈēv\ *n* [ME *eve, even*] **1** : EVENING **2** : the evening or the day before a special day **3** : the period immediately preceding
Eve \ˈēv\ *n* [OE *Ēfe,* fr. LL *Eva,* fr. Heb *Ḥawwāh*] : the first woman and wife of Adam
evec·tion \i-ˈvek-shən\ *n* [L *evection-, evectio* rising, fr. *evectus,* pp. of *evehere* to carry out, raise up, fr. *e-* + *vehere* to carry — more at WAY] : perturbation of the moon's orbital motion due to the attraction of the sun
¹**even** \ˈē-vən\ *n* [ME, *even, eve,* fr. OE *ǣfen*] *archaic* : EVENING
²**even** *adj* [ME, fr. OE *efen;* akin to OHG *eban* even] **1 a** : having a horizontal surface : FLAT ⟨~ ground⟩ **b** : being without break, indentation, roughness, or other irregularity : SMOOTH **c** : being in the same plane or line **2 a** : free from irregularity or variation : UNIFORM ⟨his disposition was ~⟩ **b** : LEVEL 4 **3 a** *obs* : CANDID **b** : EQUAL, FAIR ⟨an ~ exchange⟩ **c** (1) : leaving nothing due on either side : SQUARE ⟨we will not be ~ until you repay my visit⟩ (2) : fully revenged **d** : being in equilibrium : BALANCED; *specif* : showing neither profit nor loss **4 a** : being one of the sequence of natural numbers beginning with two and counting by twos that are exactly divisible by two **b** : marked by an even number **5** : EXACT, PRECISE ⟨an ~ dollar⟩ **6** : as likely as not : FIFTY-FIFTY ⟨he stands an ~ chance of winning⟩ ***syn* 1** see LEVEL ***ant*** uneven **2** see STEADY ***ant*** uneven — **even·ly** *adv* — **even·ness** \-vən-nəs\ *n*
³**even** *adv* [ME, fr. OE *efne,* fr. *efen,* adj.] **1 a** : EXACTLY, PRECISELY **b** : to a degree that extends : FULLY, QUITE ⟨faithful ~ unto death⟩ **c** : at the very time **2 a** — used as an intensive to emphasize the identity or character of something ⟨he looked content, ~ happy⟩ **b** — used as an intensive to indicate something unexpected ⟨refused ~ to look at her⟩ **c** — used as an intensive to stress the comparative degree ⟨he did ~ better⟩
⁴**even** *vb* **evened; even·ing** \ˈēv-(ə-)niŋ\ *vt* : to make even ~ *vi* : to become even — **even·er** \-(ə-)nər\ *n*
even·fall \ˈē-vən-ˌfȯl\ *n* : the beginning of evening : DUSK
even function *n* : a function such that $f(x) = f(-x)$ where the value remains unchanged if the sign of the independent variable is reversed
even·hand·ed \ˌē-vən-ˈhan-dəd\ *adj* : FAIR, IMPARTIAL — **even·hand·ed·ly** *adv* — **even·hand·ed·ness** *n*
eve·ning \ˈēv-niŋ\ *n, often attrib* [ME, fr. OE *ǣfnung,* fr. *ǣfnian* to grow toward evening, fr. *ǣfen* evening; akin to OHG *āband* evening and perh. to Gk *epi* on] **1 a** : the latter part and close of the day and early part of the night **b** *chiefly South & Midland* : AFTERNOON **c** : the period from sunset or the evening meal to bedtime **2** : the latter portion **3** : the period of an evening's entertainment
evening dress *n* : dress for evening social occasions
evening prayer *n, often cap E & P* : the daily evening office of the Anglican liturgy
evening primrose *n* : any of several dicotyledonous plants of a family (Onagraceae, the evening-primrose family) and esp. of the type genus (*Oenothera*); *esp* : a coarse biennial herb (*O. biennis*) with yellow flowers that open in the evening
eve·nings \ˈēv-niŋz\ *adv* : in the evening repeatedly : on any evening ⟨goes bowling ~⟩
evening star *n* **1** : a bright planet (as Venus) seen esp. in the western sky at or after sunset **2** : a planet that rises before midnight
even permutation *n* : a permutation that is produced by the successive application of an even number of interchanges of pairs of elements
even·song \ˈē-vən-ˌsȯŋ\ *n, often cap* [ME, fr. OE *ǣfensang,* fr. *ǣfen* even + *sang* song] **1** : VESPERS 1 **2** : EVENING PRAYER
event \i-ˈvent\ *n* [MF or L; MF, fr. L *eventus,* fr. *eventus,* pp. of *evenire* to happen, fr. *e-* + *venire* to come — more at COME] **1 a** : something that happens : OCCURRENCE **b** : a noteworthy happening **c** : a social occasion or activity **2 a** *archaic* : OUTCOME **b** : the issue of a legal action as finally determined **c** : a postulated outcome, condition, or eventuality ⟨in the ~ that I am not there, call the house⟩ **3** : any of the contests in a program of sports **4** : the fundamental entity of observed physical reality represented by a point designated by three coordinates of place and one of time in the space-time continuum postulated by the theory of relativity **5** : a subset of the possible outcomes of an experiment ⟨7 is an ~ in the throwing of two dice⟩ ***syn*** see EFFECT, OCCURRENCE — **event·less** \-ləs\ *adj* — **at all events** : in any case — **in any event** : in any case — **in the event** *Brit* : as it turns out
event·ful \i-ˈvent-fəl\ *adj* **1** : full of or rich in events **2** : MOMENTOUS — **event·ful·ly** \-fə-lē\ *adv* — **event·ful·ness** *n*
even·tide \ˈē-vən-ˌtīd\ *n* : the time of evening : EVENING
even·tu·al \i-ˈvench-(ə-)wəl, -ˈven-chəl\ *adj* **1** *archaic* : CONTINGENT, CONDITIONAL **2** : taking place at an unspecified later time : ultimately resulting ⟨they counted on his ~ success⟩ ***syn*** see LAST — **even·tu·al·ly** \-ē\ *adv*
even·tu·al·i·ty \i-ˌven-chə-ˈwal-ət-ē\ *n, pl* **-ties** : a possible event or outcome : POSSIBILITY
even·tu·ate \i-ˈven-chə-ˌwāt\ *vi* **-at·ed; -at·ing** : to come out finally : RESULT ⟨emotional growth . . . ~s in balance and control — *Encyc. Americana*⟩
ev·er \ˈev-ər\ *adv* [ME, fr. OE *ǣfre*] **1** : ALWAYS ⟨~ striving to improve⟩ ⟨the *ever*-increasing population⟩ **2 a** : at any time ⟨more than ~ before⟩ **b** : in any way ⟨how can I ~ thank you⟩ **3** — used as an intensive esp. with *so* ⟨looks ~ so angry⟩
ev·er·bloom·ing \ˌev-ər-ˈblü-miŋ\ *adj* : blooming more or less continuously throughout the growing season
ev·er·glade \ˈev-ər-ˌglād\ *n* [the *Everglades,* Fla.] : a swampy grassland esp. in southern Florida usu. containing sawgrass and at least seasonally covered by slowly moving water — usu. used in pl.
¹**ev·er·green** \ˈev-ər-ˌgrēn\ *adj* **1** : having foliage that remains green and functional through more than one growing season — compare DECIDUOUS **2** : ever retaining its freshness, interest, or popularity : PERENNIAL, ENDURING ⟨the ~ hope of discovering the consummate woman —A. L. Burt⟩
²**evergreen** *n* **1** : an evergreen plant; *also* : CONIFER **2** *pl* : twigs and branches of evergreen plants used for decoration **3** : something that retains its freshness, interest, or popularity
evergreen oak *n* : any of various oaks (as a holm oak or tan oak) with foliage that persists for two years so that the plant is more or less continuously green
¹**ev·er·last·ing** \ˌev-ər-ˈlas-tiŋ\ *adj* **1** : lasting or enduring through all time : ETERNAL **2 a** (1) : continuing long or indefinitely (2) *of a plant* : retaining its form or color for a long time when dried **b** : tediously persistent ⟨the ~ sympathy-seeker who demands attention —H. A. Overstreet⟩ **3** : wearing indefinitely — **ev·er·last·ing·ly** \-tiŋ-lē\ *adv* — **ev·er·last·ing·ness** *n*
²**everlasting** *n* **1** *cap* : GOD 1 — used with *the* **2** : ETERNITY ⟨from ~⟩ **3 a** : any of several chiefly composite plants (as cudweed) with flowers that can be dried without loss of form or color **b** : the flower of an everlasting
ev·er·more \ˌev-ər-ˈmō(ə)r, -ˈmȯ(ə)r\ *adv* **1** : ALWAYS, FOREVER **2** : in the future

evert \i-ˈvərt\ *vt* [L *evertere,* fr. *e-* + *vertere* to turn — more at WORTH] **1** : OVERTHROW, UPSET **2** : to turn outward or inside out — **ever·si·ble** \-ˈvər-sə-bəl\ *adj* — **ever·sion** \-zhən, -shən\ *n*

ev·ery \ˈev-rē\ *adj* [ME *everich, every,* fr. OE *ǣfre ǣlc,* fr. *ǣfre* ever + *ǣlc* each] **1** : being each individual or part of a group without exception **2** *obs* : being all taken severally **3** : being each within a range of possibilities ⟨was given ~ chance⟩ **4** : COMPLETE, ENTIRE — **every now and then** *or* **every now and again** *or* **every so often** : at intervals : OCCASIONALLY

ev·ery·body \ˈev-ri-ˌbäd-ē, -bəd-\ *pron* : every person : EVERYONE

ev·ery·day \ˌev-rē-ˌdā\ *adj* : encountered or used routinely or typically : ORDINARY ⟨clothes for ~ wear⟩ — **ev·ery·day·ness** \-ˈdā-nəs\ *n*

ev·ery·man \ˈev-rē-ˌman\ *n* [*Everyman,* allegorical character in *The Summoning of Everyman,* 15th cent. E morality play] *often cap* : the typical or ordinary man ⟨an *Everyman,* always tempted, always guileless, always rueful —Walter Terry⟩

ev·ery·one \-(ˌ)wən\ *pron* : EVERYBODY

ev·ery·place \-ˌplās\ *adv* : EVERYWHERE

ev·ery·thing \ˈev-rē-ˌthiŋ\ *pron* **1 a** : all that exists **b** : all that relates to the subject **2** : something that is most important or excellent : all that counts ⟨he meant ~ to her⟩

ev·ery·where \ˈev-rē-ˌ(h)we(ə)r, -ˌ(h)wa(ə)r\ *adv* : in every place or part

every which way \ˌev-rē-ˈhwich-ˌwā, -ˈwich-\ *adv* [prob. by folk etymology fr. ME *everich way* every way] **1** : in every direction **2** : in a disorderly manner : IRREGULARLY ⟨toys scattered about *every which way*⟩

evg *abbr* evening

evict \i-ˈvikt\ *vt* [ME *evicten,* fr. LL *evictus,* pp. of *evincere,* fr. L, to vanquish, win a point — more at EVINCE] **1 a** : to recover (property) from a person by legal process **b** : to put (a tenant) out by legal process **2** : to force out : EXPEL *syn* see EJECT — **evic·tion** \-ˈvik-shən\ *n* — **evic·tor** \-ˈvik-tər\ *n*

evict·ee \i-ˌvik-ˈtē\ *n* : an evicted person

[1]**ev·i·dence** \ˈev-əd-ən(t)s, -ə-ˌden(t)s\ *n* **1 a** : an outward sign : INDICATION **b** : something that furnishes proof : TESTIMONY; *specif* : something legally submitted to a tribunal to ascertain the truth of a matter **2** : one who bears witness; *esp* : one who voluntarily confesses a crime and testifies for the prosecution against his accomplices — **in evidence 1** : to be seen : CONSPICUOUS ⟨trim lawns . . . are everywhere *in evidence* —*Amer. Guide Series: N.C.*⟩ **2** : as evidence

[2]**evidence** *vt* **-denced; -denc·ing** : to offer evidence of : PROVE, EVINCE *syn* see SHOW

ev·i·dent \ˈev-əd-ənt, -ə-ˌdent\ *adj* [ME, fr. MF, fr. L *evident-, evidens,* fr. *e-* + *vident-, videns,* prp. of *vidēre* to see — more at WIT] : clear to the vision or understanding

syn EVIDENT, MANIFEST, PATENT, DISTINCT, OBVIOUS, APPARENT, PLAIN, CLEAR *shared meaning element* : readily perceived or apprehended. EVIDENT implies the presence of signs that point unmistakably to a conclusion ⟨her enjoyment of the music was *evident*⟩ MANIFEST implies signs so evident that little or no inference is needed ⟨the verdict is against the *manifest* weight of the evidence —L. B. Howard⟩ PATENT applies to a cause, effect, or significant feature that is clear and unmistakable once attention is drawn to it ⟨*patent* defects are those readily perceptible on inspection⟩ ⟨a *patent* lie⟩ DISTINCT implies such sharpness of outline or definition as makes discernment or identification easy ⟨a neat *distinct* handwriting⟩ OBVIOUS implies such ease in discovering or accounting for as may suggest conspicuity in the thing or little need of perspicuity in the observer ⟨his guilt was *obvious* to all⟩ APPARENT may add to *evident* the notion of recognition through more or less elaborate reasoning ⟨it is *apparent* from comparison of their stories that one of them is lying⟩ *Plain* and *clear* both apply to something that is immediately apprehended or unmistakably understood, but PLAIN implies lack of complexity or elaboration and CLEAR, an absence of anything that confuses or obscures ⟨told the *plain* truth⟩ ⟨gave a *clear* account of the accident⟩

ev·i·den·tial \ˌev-ə-ˈden-chəl\ *adj* : being, relating to, or affording evidence ⟨photographs of ~ value⟩ — **ev·i·den·tial·ly** \-ˈdench-(ə-)lē\ *adv*

ev·i·den·tia·ry \ˌev-ə-ˈden-chə-rē, -chē-ˌer-ē\ *adj* **1** : EVIDENTIAL **2** : conducted so that evidence may be presented ⟨an ~ hearing⟩

ev·i·dent·ly \ˈev-əd-ənt-lē, -ə-ˌdent-, *esp for 2 often* ˌev-ə-ˈdent-\ *adv* **1** : in an evident manner : CLEARLY, OBVIOUSLY ⟨any style that is . . . so ~ bad or second-rate —T. S. Eliot⟩ **2** : on the basis of available evidence ⟨he was born . . . ~ in Texas —Robert Coughlan⟩

[1]**evil** \ˈē-vəl\ *adj* **evil·er** *or* **evil·ler; evil·est** *or* **evil·lest** [ME, fr. OE *yfel;* akin to OHG *ubil* evil] **1 a** : morally reprehensible : SINFUL, WICKED ⟨an ~ impulse⟩ **b** : arising from actual or imputed bad character or conduct ⟨a man of ~ reputation⟩ **2 a** *archaic* : INFERIOR **b** : causing discomfort or repulsion : OFFENSIVE ⟨an ~ odor⟩ **c** : DISAGREEABLE ⟨woke late and in an ~ temper⟩ **3 a** : causing harm : PERNICIOUS ⟨the ~ institution of slavery⟩ **b** : marked by misfortune : UNLUCKY *syn* see BAD *ant* exemplary, salutary — **evil** *adv, archaic* — **evil·ly** \-və(l)-lē\ *adv* — **evil·ness** \-vəl-nəs\ *n*

[2]**evil** *n* **1** : something that brings sorrow, distress, or calamity **2 a** : the fact of suffering, misfortune, and wrongdoing **b** : a cosmic evil force

evil·do·er \ˌē-vəl-ˈdü-ər\ *n* : one who does evil

evil·do·ing \-ˈdü-iŋ\ *n* : the act or action of doing evil

evil eye *n* : an eye or glance held capable of inflicting harm; *also* : a person believed to have such an eye or glance

evil–mind·ed \ˌē-vəl-ˈmīn-dəd\ *adj* : having an evil disposition or evil thoughts — **evil–mind·ed·ly** *adv* — **evil–mind·ed·ness** *n*

evince \i-ˈvin(t)s\ *vt* **evinced; evinc·ing** [L *evincere* to vanquish, win a point, fr. *e-* + *vincere* to conquer — more at VICTOR] **1** : to constitute outward evidence of **2** : to display clearly : REVEAL *syn* see SHOW — **evinc·ible** \-ˈvin(t)-sə-bəl\ *adj*

evis·cer·ate \i-ˈvis-ə-ˌrāt\ *vb* **-at·ed; -at·ing** [L *evisceratus,* pp. of *eviscerare,* fr. *e-* + *viscera*] *vt* **1 a** : to take out the entrails of : DISEMBOWEL **b** : to deprive of vital content or force **2** : to remove an organ from (a patient) or the contents of (an organ) ~ *vi* : to protrude through a surgical incision or suffer protrusion of a part through an incision — **evis·cer·a·tion** \-ˌvis-ə-ˈrā-shən\ *n*

ev·i·ta·ble \ˈev-ət-ə-bəl\ *adj* [L *evitabilis,* fr. *evitare* to avoid, fr. *e-* + *vitare* to shun] : capable of being avoided

evo·ca·ble \ˈev-ə-kə-bəl, i-ˈvō-kə-\ *adj* : capable of being evoked

evo·ca·tion \ˌē-vō-ˈkā-shən, ˌev-ə-\ *n* [L *evocation-, evocatio,* fr. *evocatus,* pp. of *evocare*] **1** : the act or fact of evoking : SUMMONING: as **a** : the summoning of a spirit **b** : imaginative recreation ⟨a contemporary film rather than an ~ of the past —R. M. Coles⟩ **2** : INDUCTION 4e; *specif* : initiation of development of a primary embryonic axis — **evo·ca·tor** \ˈē-vō-ˌkāt-ər, ˈev-ə-\ *n*

evoc·a·tive \i-ˈväk-ət-iv\ *adj* : tending or serving to evoke ⟨settings . . . so ~ that they bring tears to the eyes —Eric Malpass⟩ — **evoc·a·tive·ly** *adv* — **evoc·a·tive·ness** *n*

evoke \i-ˈvōk\ *vt* **evoked; evok·ing** [F *évoquer,* fr. L *evocare,* fr. *e-* + *vocare* to call — more at VOCATION] **1** : to call forth or up: as **a** : CONJURE 2a ⟨~ evil spirits⟩ **b** : to cite esp. with approval or for support : INVOKE **c** : to bring to mind or recollection ⟨this place ~*s* memories of happier years⟩ **2** : to re-create imaginatively *syn* see EDUCE

evo·lute \ˈev-ə-ˌlüt *also* ˈē-və-\ *n* : the locus of the center of curvature or the envelope of the normals of a curve

evo·lu·tion \ˌev-ə-ˈlü-shən *also* ˌē-və-\ *n* [L *evolution-, evolutio* unrolling, fr. *evolutus,* pp. of *evolvere*] **1 a** : a process of change in a certain direction : UNFOLDING **b** : the action or an instance of forming and giving something off : EMISSION **c** (1) : a process of continuous change from a lower, simpler, or worse to a higher, more complex, or better state : GROWTH (2) : a process of gradual and relatively peaceful social, political, and economic advance **d** : something evolved **2** : one of a set of prescribed movements **3** : the process of working out or developing **4** : the extraction of a mathematical root **5 a** : the historical development of a biological group (as a race or species) : PHYLOGENY **b** : a theory that the various types of animals and plants have their origin in other preexisting types and that the distinguishable differences are due to modifications in successive generations **6** : a process in which the whole universe is a progression of interrelated phenomena — **evo·lu·tion·ari·ly** \-shə-ˌner-ə-lē\ *adv* — **evo·lu·tion·ary** \-shə-ˌner-ē\ *adj* — **evo·lu·tion·ism** \-shə-ˌniz-əm\ *n* — **evo·lu·tion·ist** \-sh(ə-)nəst\ *n or adj*

evolve \i-ˈvälv, -ˈvȯlv\ *vb* **evolved; evolv·ing** [L *evolvere* to unroll, fr. *e-* + *volvere* to roll — more at VOLUBLE] *vt* **1** : to give off : EMIT **2 a** : DERIVE, EDUCE **b** : to work out : DEVELOP ⟨~ social, political, and literary philosophies —L. W. Doob⟩ **c** : to produce by natural evolutionary processes ~ *vi* : to undergo evolutionary change — **evolv·able** \-ˈväl-və-bəl, -ˈvȯl-\ *adj* — **evolve·ment** \-ˈvälv-mənt, -ˈvȯlv-\ *n*

evon·y·mus \i-ˈvän-ə-məs, e-\ *n* : EUONYMUS

EVR *abbr* electronic video recorder, electronic video recording

evul·sion \i-ˈvəl-shən\ *n* [L *evulsion-, evulsio,* fr. *evulsus,* pp. of *evellere* to pluck out, fr. *e-* + *vellere* to pluck — more at VULNERABLE] : EXTRACTION

ev·zone \ˈev-ˌzōn\ *n* [NGk *euzōnos,* fr. Gk, active, lit., well girt, fr. *eu-* + *zōnē* girdle — more at ZONE] : a member of a select Greek infantry unit

EW *abbr* enlisted woman

ewe \ˈyü, ˈyō\ *n* [ME, fr. OE *ēowu*] : the female of the sheep esp. when mature; *also* : the female of various related animals

Ewe \ˈā-ˌwā, ˈā-ˌvā\ *n* : a Kwa language of Ghana and Togo

ewe–neck \-ˈnek\ *n* : a thin neck having an insufficient, faulty, or concave arch and occurring as a defect in dogs and horses — **ewe–necked** \-ˈnekt\ *adj*

ew·er \ˈyü-ər, ˈyu̇(-ə)r\ *n* [ME, fr. AF, fr. OF *evier,* fr. (assumed) VL *aquarium,* fr. L, neut. of *aquarius* of water, fr. *aqua* water — more at ISLAND] : a vase-shaped pitcher or jug

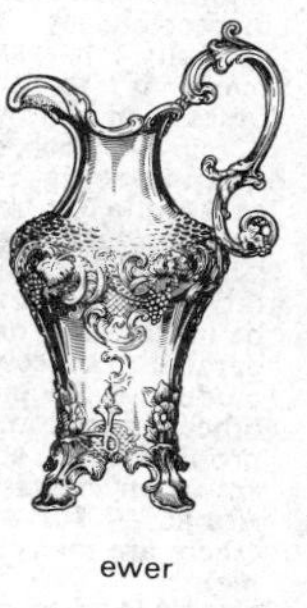

ewer

[1]**ex** \ˈeks\ *n* [[1]*ex-*] : one that formerly held a specified position or place; *esp* : a former spouse

[2]**ex** \(ˌ)eks\ *prep* [L] **1** : out of : FROM: as **a** : from a specified place or source **b** : from a specified dam ⟨a promising calf by Eric XVI ~ Heatherbell⟩ **2** : free from : WITHOUT: as **a** : without an indicated value or right — used esp. of securities **b** : free of charges precedent to removal from the specified place with purchaser to provide means of subsequent transportation ⟨~ dock⟩

[3]**ex** \ˈeks\ *n* : the letter *x*

[4]**ex** *abbr* **1** example **2** exchange **3** executive **4** express **5** extra

Ex *abbr* Exodus

[1]**ex-** \e *also occurs in this prefix where only* i *is shown below (as in "express") and* ks *sometimes occurs where only* gz *is shown (as in "exact")*\ *prefix* [ME, fr. OF & L; OF, fr. L (also, intensive prefix), fr. *ex* out of, from; akin to Gk *ex, ex-* out of, from, OSlav *iz*] **1** : out of : outside ⟨exclave⟩ **2** : not ⟨exstipulate⟩ **3** \(ˌ)eks, ˈeks\ [ME, fr. LL, fr. L] : former ⟨*ex*-president⟩ ⟨*ex*-child actor⟩

[2]**ex-** — see EXO-

ex·ac·er·bate \ig-ˈzas-ər-ˌbāt\ *vt* **-bat·ed; -bat·ing** [L *exacerbatus,* pp. of *exacerbare,* fr. *ex-* + *acerbus* harsh, bitter, fr. *acer* sharp — more at EDGE] : to make more violent, bitter, or severe ⟨the proposed shutdown . . . would ~ unemployment problems —*Science*⟩ — **ex·ac·er·ba·tion** \-ˌzas-ər-ˈbā-shən\ *n*

ə abut   ᵊ kitten   ər further   a back   ā bake   ä cot, cart
au̇ out   ch chin   e less   ē easy   g gift   i trip   ī life
j joke   ŋ sing   ō flow   ȯ flaw   ȯi coin   th thin   t͟h this
ü loot   u̇ foot   y yet   yü few   yu̇ furious   zh vision

1ex·act \ig-ˈzakt\ *vt* [ME *exacten,* fr. L *exactus,* pp. of *exigere* to drive out, demand, measure, fr. *ex-* + *agere* to drive — more at AGENT] **1 :** to call for forcibly or urgently and obtain : press for ⟨from them has been ~*ed* the ultimate sacrifice —D. D. Eisenhower⟩ **2 :** to call for as necessary, appropriate, or desirable ***syn*** see DEMAND — **ex·act·able** \-ˈzak-tə-bəl\ *adj* — **ex·ac·tor** *also* **ex·act·er** \-ˈzak-tər\ *n*

2exact *adj* [L *exactus,* fr. pp. of *exigere*] **1 :** exhibiting or marked by strict, particular, and complete accordance with fact **2 :** marked by thorough consideration or minute measurement of small factual details ***syn*** see CORRECT ***ant*** inexact — **exact·ness** \-ˈzak(t)-nəs\ *n*

ex·ac·ta \ig-ˈzak-tə\ *n* [AmerSp *quiniela exacta* exact quiniela] : PERFECTA

exact differential *n* : a differential expression of the form $X_1dx_1 + \ldots + X_ndx_n$ where the X's are the partial derivatives of a function $f(x_1, \ldots, x_n)$ with respect to $x_1, \ldots, x_n$ respectively

ex·act·ing \ig-ˈzak-tiŋ\ *adj* **1 :** tryingly or unremittingly severe in making demands **2 :** requiring careful attention and precise accuracy ***syn*** see ONEROUS — **ex·act·ing·ly** \-tiŋ-lē\ *adv* — **ex·act·ing·ness** *n*

ex·ac·tion \ig-ˈzak-shən\ *n* **1 a :** the act or process of exacting **b :** EXTORTION **2 :** something exacted; *esp* : a fee, reward, or contribution demanded or levied with severity or injustice

ex·ac·ti·tude \ig-ˈzak-tə-ˌt(y)üd\ *n* : the quality or an instance of being exact : EXACTNESS

ex·act·ly \ig-ˈzak-(t)lē\ *adv* **1 a :** in an exact manner : PRECISELY **b :** ALTOGETHER, ENTIRELY ⟨not ~ what I had in mind⟩ **2 :** quite so — used to express agreement

ex·ag·ger·ate \ig-ˈzaj-ə-ˌrāt\ *vb* **-at·ed; -at·ing** [L *exaggeratus,* pp. of *exaggerare,* lit., to heap up, fr. *ex-* + *agger* heap, fr. *aggerere* to carry toward, fr. *ad-* + *gerere* to carry — more at CAST] *vt* **1 :** to enlarge beyond bounds or the truth : OVERSTATE ⟨a friend ~*s* a man's virtues —Joseph Addison⟩ **2 :** to enlarge or increase esp. beyond the normal : OVEREMPHASIZE ~ *vi* : to make an overstatement — **ex·ag·ger·at·ed·ly** *adv* — **ex·ag·ger·at·ed·ness** *n* — **ex·ag·ger·a·tion** \-ˌzaj-ə-ˈrā-shən\ *n* — **ex·ag·ger·a·tive** \-ˈzaj-ə-ˌrāt-iv, ˈ-zaj-(-ə-)rət-\ *adj* — **ex·ag·ger·a·tor** \-ˈzaj-ə-rāt-ər\ *n* — **ex·ag·ger·a·to·ry** \-ˈzaj-(ə-)rə-ˌtōr-ē, -ˌtȯr-\ *adj*

ex·alt \ig-ˈzȯlt\ *vb* [ME *exalten,* fr. MF & L; MF *exalter,* fr. L *exaltare,* fr. *ex-* + *altus* high — more at OLD] *vt* **1 :** to raise high : ELEVATE **2 :** to raise in rank, power, or character **3 :** to elevate by praise or in estimation : GLORIFY **4** *obs* : ELATE **5 :** to enhance the activity of : INTENSIFY ⟨rousing and ~*ing* the imagination —George Eliot⟩ ~ *vi* : to induce exaltation — **ex·alt·ed·ly** *adv* — **ex·alt·er** *n*

ex·al·ta·tion \ˌeg-ˌzȯl-ˈtā-shən, ˌek-ˌsȯl-\ *n* **1 :** an act of exalting : the state of being exalted **2 :** an excessively intensified sense of well-being, power, or importance ⟨pursued ~ through drink and sex —Howard Kaye⟩ **3 :** an increase in degree or intensity ⟨~ of virulence of a virus⟩

ex·am \ig-ˈzam\ *n* : EXAMINATION

ex·a·men \ig-ˈzā-mən\ *n* [L, tongue of a balance, examination, fr. *exigere* — more at EXACT] **1 :** EXAMINATION **2 :** a critical study

ex·am·i·nant \-ˈzam-ə-nənt\ *n* **1 :** one who examines : EXAMINER **2 :** EXAMINEE

ex·am·i·na·tion \ig-ˌzam-ə-ˈnā-shən\ *n* **1 :** the act or process of examining : the state of being examined **2 :** an exercise designed to examine progress or test qualification or knowledge **3 :** a formal interrogation — **ex·am·i·na·tion·al** \-shnəl, -shən-ᵊl\ *adj*

ex·am·i·na·to·ri·al \-nə-ˈtōr-ē-əl, -ˈtȯr-\ *adj* : of or relating to an examiner or examination

ex·am·ine \ig-ˈzam-ən\ *vt* **ex·am·ined; ex·am·in·ing** \-(ə-)niŋ\ [ME *examinen,* fr. MF *examiner,* fr. L *examinare,* fr. *examen*] **1 a :** to inspect closely **b :** to test the condition of **c :** to inquire into carefully : INVESTIGATE **2 a :** to interrogate closely ⟨~ a prisoner⟩ **b :** to test by questioning in order to determine progress, fitness, or knowledge ***syn*** see SCRUTINIZE — **ex·am·in·able** \-ˈzam-ə-nə-bəl\ *adj* — **ex·am·in·er** \-ˈzam-(ə-)nər\ *n*

ex·am·in·ee \ig-ˌzam-ə-ˈnē\ *n* : a person who is examined

1ex·am·ple \ig-ˈzam-pəl\ *n* [ME, fr. MF, fr. L *exemplum,* fr. *eximere* to take out, fr. *ex-* + *emere* to take — more at REDEEM] **1 :** a particular single item, fact, incident, or aspect that is representative of all of a group or type **2 :** one that serves as a pattern to be imitated or not to be imitated ⟨a good ~⟩ ⟨a bad ~⟩ **3 :** a parallel or closely similar case esp. when serving as a precedent or model **4 :** a punishment inflicted on someone as a warning to others; *also* : an individual so punished **5 :** an instance (as a problem to be solved) serving to illustrate a rule or precept or to act as an exercise in the application of a rule ***syn*** see INSTANCE, MODEL — **for example** \fər-ig-ˈzam-pəl, frig-\ : as an example ⟨there are many sources of air pollution; exhaust fumes, *for example*⟩

2example *vt* **ex·am·pled; ex·am·pling** \-p(ə-)liŋ\ **1 :** to serve or use as an example of **2** *archaic* : to be or set an example to

ex·an·i·mate \eg-ˈzan-ə-mət\ *adj* [L *exanimatus,* pp. of *exanimare* to deprive of life or spirit, fr. *ex-* + *anima* breath, soul — more at ANIMATE] **1 :** lacking animation : SPIRITLESS **2 :** lifeless or appearing lifeless

ex·an·them \eg-ˈzan(t)-thəm, ˈek-ˌsan-ˌthem\ *also* **ex·an·the·ma** \ˌeg-ˌzan-ˈthē-mə\ *n, pl* **exanthems** *also* **ex·an·them·a·ta** \ˌeg-ˌzan-ˈthem-ət-ə\ *or* **exanthemas** [LL *exanthema,* fr. Gk *exanthēma,* fr. *exanthein* to bloom, break out, fr. *ex-* + *anthos* flower — more at ANTHOLOGY] : an eruptive disease (as measles) or its symptomatic eruption — **ex·an·them·a·tous** \ˌeg-ˌzan-ˈthem-ət-əs\ *adj*

1ex·arch \ˈek-ˌsärk\ *n* [LL *exarchus,* fr. LGk *exarchos,* fr. Gk, leader, fr. *exarchein* to begin, take the lead, fr. *ex-* + *archein* to rule, begin — more at ARCH-] **1 :** a Byzantine viceroy **2 :** an Eastern bishop ranking below a patriarch and above a metropolitan; *specif* : the head of an independent church — **ex·ar·chal** \ek-ˈsär-kəl\ *adj* — **ex·arch·ate** \ˈek-ˌsär-kət\ *n* — **ex·ar·chy** \ˈek-ˌsär-kē\ *n*

2exarch *adj* [*exo-* + *-arch*] : formed or taking place from the periphery toward the center ⟨~ xylem⟩

1ex·as·per·ate \ig-ˈzas-pə-ˌrāt\ *vt* **-at·ed; -at·ing** [L *exasperatus,* pp. of *exasperare,* fr. *ex-* + *asper* rough] **1 a :** to excite or inflame the anger of : ENRAGE **b :** to cause irritation or annoyance to **2** *obs* : to make grievous or more grievous or malignant ***syn*** see IRRITATE — **ex·as·per·at·ed·ly** *adv* — **ex·as·per·at·ing·ly** \-ˌrāt-iŋ-lē\ *adv*

2ex·as·per·ate \-p(ə-)rət\ *adj* **1 :** irritated or annoyed esp. to the point of injudicious action : EXASPERATED **2 :** roughened with irregular prickles or elevations ⟨~ seed coats⟩

ex·as·per·a·tion \ig-ˌzas-pə-ˈrā-shən\ *n* **1 :** the state of being exasperated **2 :** the act or an instance of exasperating

exc *abbr* **1** excellent **2** except

Ex·cal·i·bur \ek-ˈskal-ə-bər\ *n* [OF *Escalibor,* fr. ML *Caliburnus*] : the legendary sword of King Arthur

ex·car·di·na·tion \(ˌ)ek-ˌskärd-ᵊn-ˈā-shən\ *n* [1*ex-* + *-cardination* (as in *incardination*)] : the transfer of a clergyman from one diocese to another

ex ca·the·dra \ˌek-skə-ˈthē-drə\ *adv or adj* [NL, lit., from the chair] : by virtue of or in the exercise of one's office ⟨*ex cathedra* pronouncements⟩

ex·ca·vate \ˈek-skə-ˌvāt\ *vb* **-vat·ed; -vat·ing** [L *excavatus,* pp. of *excavare,* fr. *ex-* + *cavare* to make hollow — more at CAVATINA] *vt* **1 :** to form a cavity or hole in **2 :** to form by hollowing **3 :** to dig out and remove **4 :** to expose to view by digging away a covering ~ *vi* : to make excavations

ex·ca·va·tion \ˌek-skə-ˈvā-shən\ *n* **1 :** the action or process of excavating **2 :** a cavity formed by cutting, digging, or scooping — **ex·ca·va·tion·al** \-shnəl, -shən-ᵊl\ *adj*

ex·ca·va·tor \ˈek-skə-ˌvāt-ər\ *n* : one that excavates; *esp* : a power-operated shovel

ex·ceed \ik-ˈsēd\ *vb* [ME *exceden,* fr. MF *exceder,* fr. L *excedere,* fr. *ex-* + *cedere* to go — more at CEDE] *vt* **1 :** to extend outside of ⟨the river will ~ its banks⟩ **2 :** to be greater than or superior to **3 :** to go beyond a limit set by ⟨~*ed* his authority⟩ ~ *vi* **1** *obs* : OVERDO **2 :** PREDOMINATE

syn EXCEED, SURPASS, TRANSCEND, EXCEL, OUTDO, OUTSTRIP *shared meaning element* : to go or be beyond a stated or implied limit, measure, or degree

ex·ceed·ing *adj* : exceptional in amount, quality, or degree ⟨the ~ darkness which surrounds man's existence —L. H. Harshbarger⟩

ex·ceed·ing·ly \-iŋ-lē\ *or* **ex·ceed·ing** *adv* : to an extreme degree : EXTREMELY

ex·cel \ik-ˈsel\ *vb* **ex·celled; ex·cel·ling** [ME *excellen,* fr. L *excellere,* fr. *ex-* + *-cellere* to rise, project; akin to L *collis* hill — more at HILL] *vt* : to be superior to : surpass in accomplishment or achievement ~ *vi* : to be distinguishable by superiority : surpass others ⟨~ in mathematics⟩ ***syn*** see EXCEED

ex·cel·lence \ˈek-s(ə-)lən(t)s\ *n* **1 :** the quality of being excellent **2 :** an excellent or valuable quality : VIRTUE **3 :** EXCELLENCY 2

ex·cel·len·cy \-s(ə-)lən-sē\ *n, pl* **-cies** **1 :** EXCELLENCE; *esp* : outstanding or valuable quality — usu. used in pl. ⟨so crammed, as he thinks, with *excellencies* —Shak.⟩ **2** — used as a title for certain high dignitaries of state (as a governor or an ambassador) and church (as a Roman Catholic archbishop or bishop)

ex·cel·lent \ˈek-s(ə-)lənt\ *adj* [ME, fr. MF, fr. L *excellent-, excellens,* fr. prp. of *excellere*] **1** *archaic* : SUPERIOR **2 :** very good of its kind : eminently good : FIRST-CLASS — **ex·cel·lent·ly** *adv*

ex·cel·si·or \ik-ˈsel-sē-ər\ *n* [trade name, fr. L, higher, compar. of *excelsus* high, fr. pp. of *excellere*] : fine curled wood shavings used esp. for packing fragile items

1ex·cept \ik-ˈsept\ *vb* [ME *excepten,* fr. MF *excepter,* fr. L *exceptare,* fr. *exceptus,* pp. of *excipere* to take out, except, fr. *ex-* + *capere* to take — more at HEAVE] *vt* : to take or leave out from a number or a whole : EXCLUDE ~ *vi* : to take exception : OBJECT

2except *also* **ex·cept·ing** *prep* : with the exclusion or exception of ⟨daily ~ Sundays⟩

3except *also* **excepting** *conj* **1 :** on any other condition than that : UNLESS ⟨~ you repent⟩ **2 :** ONLY ⟨I would go ~ it's too far⟩

except for *prep* : but for ⟨*except for* you I would be dead⟩

ex·cep·tion \ik-ˈsep-shən\ *n* **1 :** the act of excepting : EXCLUSION **2 :** one that is excepted; *esp* : a case to which a rule does not apply **3 :** QUESTION, OBJECTION ⟨witnesses whose authority is beyond ~ —T. B. Macaulay⟩ **4 :** an oral or written legal objection (as to a court's ruling)

ex·cep·tion·able \ik-ˈsep-sh(ə-)nə-bəl\ *adj* : being likely to cause objection : OBJECTIONABLE ⟨visitors even drink the ~ beer —W. D. Howells⟩ — **ex·cep·tion·abil·i·ty** \-ˌsep-sh(ə-)nə-ˈbil-ət-ē\ *n* — **ex·cep·tion·ably** \-ˈsep-sh(ə-)nə-blē\ *adv*

ex·cep·tion·al \ik-ˈsep-shnəl, -shən-ᵊl\ *adj* **1 :** forming an exception : RARE ⟨an ~ number of rainy days⟩ **2 :** better than average : SUPERIOR **3 :** deviating from the norm; *esp* : below average ⟨schools for ~ children⟩ — **ex·cep·tion·al·i·ty** \-ˌsep-shə-ˈnal-ət-ē\ *n* — **ex·cep·tion·al·ly** \-ˈsep-shnə-lē, -shən-ᵊl-ē\ *adv* — **ex·cep·tion·al·ness** *n*

ex·cep·tive \ik-ˈsep-tiv\ *adj* **1 :** relating to, containing, or constituting exception **2** *archaic* : CAPTIOUS

1ex·cerpt \ek-ˈsərpt, eg-ˈzərpt, ˈek-ˌ, ˈeg-ˌ\ *vt* [L *excerptus,* pp. of *excerpere,* fr. *ex-* + *carpere* to gather, pluck — more at HARVEST] **1 :** to select (a passage) for quoting : EXTRACT **2 :** to take extracts from (as a book) — **ex·cerpt·er** *also* **ex·cerp·tor** *n* — **ex·cerp·tion** \ek-ˈsərp-shən, eg-ˈzərp-\ *n*

2ex·cerpt \ˈek-ˌsərpt, ˈeg-ˌzərpt\ *n* : a passage (as from a book or musical composition) selected, performed, or copied : EXTRACT

1ex·cess \ik-ˈses, ˈek-ˌ\ *n* [ME, fr. MF or LL; MF *exces,* fr. LL *excessus,* fr. L, departure, projection, fr. *excessus,* pp. of *excedere* to exceed] **1 a :** the state or an instance of surpassing usual, proper, or specified limits : SUPERFLUITY **b :** the amount or degree by which one thing or quantity exceeds another ⟨an ~ of ten bushels⟩ **2 :** undue or immoderate indulgence : INTEMPERANCE ⟨prevent ~*es* and abuses by newly created local powers —Albert Shanker⟩ — **in excess of :** to an amount or degree beyond : OVER

2excess *adj* : more than the usual, proper, or specified amount ⟨charges for ~ baggage⟩

ex·ces·sive \ik-ˈses-iv\ *adj* : exceeding the usual, proper, or normal — **ex·ces·sive·ly** *adv* — **ex·ces·sive·ness** *n*
syn EXCESSIVE, IMMODERATE, INORDINATE, EXTRAVAGANT, EXORBITANT, EXTREME *shared meaning element* : going beyond a normal or acceptable limit ***ant*** deficient

exch *abbr* exchange; exchanged

[1]**ex·change** \iks-ˈchānj, ˈeks-ˌ\ *n, often attrib* [ME *exchaunge*, fr. MF *eschange*, fr. *eschangier* to exchange, fr. (assumed) VL *excambiare*, fr. L *ex-* + *cambiare* to exchange — more at CHANGE] **1** : the act of giving or taking one thing in return for another : TRADE ⟨an ~ of prisoners⟩ **2 a** : the act of substituting one thing for another **b** : reciprocal giving and receiving **3** : something offered, given, or received in an exchange; *also* : an item or article reprinted from a newspaper **4 a** : funds payable currently at a distant point either in a foreign currency or in domestic currency **b** (1) : interchange or conversion of the money of two countries or of current and uncurrent money with allowance for difference in value (2) : EXCHANGE RATE (3) : the amount of the difference in value between two currencies or between values of a particular currency at two places **c** : instruments (as checks or bills of exchange) presented in a clearinghouse for settlement **5** : a place where things or services are exchanged: as **a** : an organized market or center for trading in securities or commodities **b** : a store or shop specializing in merchandise usu. of a particular type **c** : a cooperative store or society **d** : a central office in which telephone lines are connected to permit communication

[2]**exchange** *vb* **ex·changed; ex·chang·ing** *vt* **1 a** : to part with, give, or transfer in consideration of something received as an equivalent **b** : to have replaced by other merchandise ⟨*exchanged* the shirt for one in a larger size⟩ **2** : to part with for a substitute ⟨*exchanging* future security for immediate pleasure⟩ **3** : BARTER, SWAP ~ *vi* **1** : to pass or become received in exchange **2** : to engage in an exchange — **ex·change·abil·i·ty** \iks-ˌchān-jə-ˈbil-ət-ē\ *n* — **ex·change·able** \iks-ˈchān-jə-bəl\ *adj* — **ex·chang·er** \iks-ˈchān-jər, eks-ˌ\ *n*

ex·chang·ee \iks-ˌchān-ˈjē, ˌeks-\ *n* : a participant (as a student or teacher) in an exchange program

exchange rate *n* : the ratio at which the principal unit of two currencies may be traded

exchange student *n* : a student from one country received into an institution in another country in exchange for one sent to an institution in the home country of the first

Ex·chang·ite \iks-ˈchān-ˌjīt\ *n* [(*National*) *Exchange* (*club*)] : a member of a major national service club

ex·che·quer \ˈeks-ˌchek-ər, iks-ˈ\ *n* [ME *escheker*, fr. AF, fr. OF *eschequier* chessboard, counting table — more at CHECKER] **1** *cap* : a department or office of state in medieval England charged with the collection and management of the royal revenue and judicial determination of all revenue causes **2** *cap* : a former superior court having jurisdiction in England and Wales primarily over revenue matters and now merged with King's Bench **3** *often cap* **a** : the department or office of state in Great Britain and Northern Ireland charged with the receipt and care of the national revenue **b** : the national banking account of this realm **4** : TREASURY; *esp* : a national or royal treasury **5** : pecuniary resources : FUNDS

ex·cide \ek-ˈsīd\ *vt* **ex·cid·ed; ex·cid·ing** [L *excidere*] : to cut out : EXCISE

ex·cip·i·ent \ik-ˈsip-ē-ənt\ *n* [L *excipient-*, *excipiens*, prp. of *excipere* to take out, take up — more at EXCEPT] : an inert substance (as gum arabic or starch) that forms a vehicle (as for a drug)

ex·ci·ple \ˈek-sə-pəl\ *n* [NL *excipulum*, fr. L, receptacle, fr. *excipere*] : a saucer-shaped rim around the hymenium of various lichens

ex·cis·able \ˈek-ˌsī-zə-bəl, -ˌsī-sə-, ek-ˈ\ *adj* : subject to excise

[1]**ex·cise** \ˈek-ˌsīz, -ˌsīs\ *n* [obs. D *excijs* (now *accijus*), fr. MD, prob. modif. of OF *assise* session, assessment — more at ASSIZE] **1** : an internal tax levied on the manufacture, sale, or consumption of a commodity within a country **2** : any of various taxes on privileges often assessed in the form of a license or other fee

[2]**excise** *vt* **ex·cised; ex·cis·ing** : to impose an excise on

[3]**ex·cise** \ik-ˈsīz\ *vt* **ex·cised; ex·cis·ing** [L *excisus*, pp. of *excidere*, fr. *ex-* + *caedere* to cut — more at CONCISE] : to remove by or as if by cutting out — **ex·ci·sion** \-ˈsizh-ən\ *n*

ex·cise·man \ˈek-ˌsīz-mən, -ˌsīs-, -ˌman, ek-ˈ\ *n* : an officer who inspects and rates articles liable to excise under British law

ex·cit·able \ik-ˈsīt-ə-bəl\ *adj* : capable of being readily roused into action or a state of excitement or irritability; *specif* : capable of being activated by and reacting to stimuli — **ex·cit·abil·i·ty** \-ˌsīt-ə-ˈbil-ət-ē\ *n* — **ex·cit·able·ness** \-ˈsīt-ə-bəl-nəs\ *n*

ex·ci·tant \ik-ˈsīt-ᵊnt, ˈek-sət-ənt\ *adj* : tending to excite or augment ⟨~ drugs⟩ — **excitant** *n*

ex·ci·ta·tion \ˌek-ˌsī-ˈtā-shən, ˌek-sə-\ *n* : EXCITEMENT; *esp* : the disturbed or altered condition resulting from stimulation of an individual, organ, tissue, or cell

ex·cit·ative \ik-ˈsīt-ət-iv\ *adj* : tending or able to excite

ex·cit·ato·ry \ik-ˈsīt-ə-ˌtōr-ē, -ˌtȯr-\ *adj* **1** : EXCITATIVE **2** : exhibiting or marked by excitement or excitation

ex·cite \ik-ˈsīt\ *vt* **ex·cit·ed; ex·cit·ing** [ME *exciten*, fr. MF *exciter*, fr. L *excitare*, fr. *ex-* + *citare* to rouse — more at CITE] **1 a** : to call to activity **b** : to rouse to feeling usu. by a profound moving ⟨scenes to ~ the hardest man to pity and help⟩ **c** : to arouse (as an emotional response) by appropriate stimuli ⟨~ enthusiasm for the new regime —Arthur Knight⟩ **2 a** : ENERGIZE ⟨~ an electromagnet⟩ **b** : to produce a magnetic field in ⟨~ a dynamo⟩ **3** : to increase the activity of (as a living organism) : STIMULATE **4** : to raise (as an atomic nucleus, an atom, or a molecule) to a higher energy level ***syn*** see PROVOKE ***ant*** soothe, quiet (*as persons*), allay (*as fears*)

ex·cit·ed *adj* : having or showing strong feelings — **ex·cit·ed·ly** *adv*

excited state *n* : a state of a physical system (as an atomic nucleus, an atom, or a molecule) that is higher in energy than the ground state

ex·cite·ment \ik-ˈsīt-mənt\ *n* **1** : the action of exciting : the state of being excited **2** : something that excites or rouses

ex·cit·er \ik-ˈsīt-ər\ *n* **1** : one that excites **2 a** : a dynamo or battery that supplies the electric current used to produce the magnetic field in another dynamo or motor **b** : an electrical oscillator that generates the carrier frequency (as for a radio transmitter)

ex·cit·ing \ik-ˈsīt-iŋ\ *adj* : producing excitement — **ex·cit·ing·ly** \-iŋ-lē\ *adv*

ex·ci·ton \ˈek-sə-ˌtän, -ˌsī-\ *n* [ISV *excitation* + *-on*] : a mobile combination of an electron and a hole in an excited crystal (as of a semiconductor) — **ex·ci·ton·ic** \ˌek-sə-ˈtän-ik, -ˌsī-\ *adj*

ex·ci·tor \ik-ˈsīt-ər\ *n, archaic* : EXCITER

ex·claim \iks-ˈklām\ *vb* [MF *exclamer*, fr. L *exclamare*, fr. *ex-* + *clamare* to cry out — more at CLAIM] *vi* **1** : to cry out or speak in strong or sudden emotion ⟨~*ed* in delight⟩ **2** : to speak loudly or vehemently ⟨~*ed* against immorality⟩ ~ *vt* : to utter sharply, passionately, or vehemently : PROCLAIM — **ex·claim·er** *n*

ex·cla·ma·tion \ˌeks-klə-ˈmā-shən\ *n* **1** : a sharp or sudden utterance **2** : vehement expression of protest or complaint

exclamation point *n* : a mark ! used esp. after an interjection or exclamation to indicate forceful utterance or strong feeling

ex·clam·a·to·ry \iks-ˈklam-ə-ˌtōr-ē, -ˌtȯr-\ *adj* : containing, expressing, using, or relating to exclamation ⟨an ~ phrase⟩

ex·clave \ˈeks-ˌklāv, -ˌkläv\ *n* [*ex-* + *-clave* (as in *enclave*)] : a portion of a country separated from the main part and constituting an enclave in respect to the surrounding territory

ex·clo·sure \eks-ˈklō-zhər\ *n* [*ex-* + *-closure* (as in *enclosure*)] : an area from which intruders (as animals) are excluded esp. by fencing

ex·clud·able *or* **ex·clud·ible** \iks-ˈklüd-ə-bəl\ *adj* : subject to exclusion ⟨~ income⟩ — **ex·clud·abil·i·ty** \-ˌklüd-ə-ˈbil-ət-ē\ *n*

ex·clude \iks-ˈklüd\ *vt* **ex·clud·ed; ex·clud·ing** [ME *excluden*, fr. L *excludere*, fr. *ex-* + *claudere* to close — more at CLOSE] **1 a** : to shut out **b** : to bar from participation, consideration, or inclusion **2** : to expel esp. from a place or position previously occupied — **ex·clud·er** *n*
syn EXCLUDE, DEBAR, ELIMINATE, SUSPEND *shared meaning element* : to shut or put out ***ant*** admit (*persons*), include (*things*)

ex·clu·sion \iks-ˈklü-zhən\ *n* [L *exclusion-*, *exclusio*, fr. *exclusus*, pp. of *excludere*] **1** : the act or an instance of excluding **2** : the state of being excluded — **ex·clu·sion·ary** \-zhə-ˌner-ē\ *adj*

ex·clu·sion·ist \iks-ˈklüzh-(ə-)nəst\ *n* : one who would exclude another from some right or privilege — **exclusionist** *adj*

exclusion principle *n* : a principle in physics: no two electrons in an atom or molecule will be exactly equivalent

[1]**ex·clu·sive** \iks-ˈklü-siv, -ziv\ *adj* **1 a** : excluding or having power to exclude **b** : limiting or limited to possession, control, or use by a single individual or group **2 a** : excluding others from participation **b** : snobbishly aloof **3 a** : accepting or soliciting only a socially restricted patronage (as of the upper class) **b** : STYLISH, FASHIONABLE **c** : restricted in distribution, use, or appeal because of expense **4 a** : SINGLE, SOLE ⟨~ jurisdiction⟩ **b** : WHOLE, UNDIVIDED ⟨his ~ attention⟩ — **ex·clu·sive·ly** *adv* — **ex·clu·sive·ness** *n*

[2]**exclusive** *n* : something exclusive: as **a** : a newspaper story at first released to or printed by only one newspaper **b** : an exclusive right (as to sell a particular product in a certain area)

exclusive disjunction *n* : a statement of a logical proposition expressing alternatives usu. taking the form $p + q$ meaning p or q but not both — see TRUTH TABLE table

exclusive of *prep* : not taking into account ⟨there were four of us *exclusive of* the guide⟩

ex·clu·siv·i·ty \ˌeks-ˌklü-ˈsiv-ət-ē, iks-, -ˈziv-\ *n, pl* **-ties** **1** : the quality or state of being exclusive **2** : exclusive rights or services

ex·cog·i·tate \ek-ˈskäj-ə-ˌtāt\ *vt* [L *excogitatus*, pp. of *excogitare*, fr. *ex-* + *cogitare* to cogitate] : to think out : DEVISE — **ex·cog·i·ta·tion** \(ˌ)ek-ˌskäj-ə-ˈtā-shən\ *n* — **ex·cog·i·ta·tive** \ek-ˈskäj-ə-ˌtāt-iv\ *adj*

[1]**ex·com·mu·ni·cate** \ˌek-skə-ˈmyü-nə-ˌkāt\ *vt* [ME *excommunicaten*, fr. LL *excommunicatus*, pp. of *excommunicare*, fr. L *ex-* + LL *communicare* to communicate] : to subject to excommunication — **ex·com·mu·ni·ca·tor** \-ˌkāt-ər\ *n*

[2]**ex·com·mu·ni·cate** \-ni-kət\ *adj* : interdicted from the rites of the church : EXCOMMUNICATED — **excommunicate** *n*

ex·com·mu·ni·ca·tion \-ˌmyü-nə-ˈkā-shən\ *n* **1** : an ecclesiastical censure depriving a person of the rights of church membership **2** : exclusion from fellowship in a group or community — **ex·com·mu·ni·ca·tive** \-ˈmyü-nə-ˌkāt-iv, -ni-kət-\ *adj*

ex·co·ri·ate \ek-ˈskōr-ē-ˌāt, -ˈskȯr-\ *vt* **-at·ed; -at·ing** [ME *excoriaten*, fr. LL *excoriatus*, pp. of *excoriare*, fr. L *ex-* + *corium* skin, hide — more at CUIRASS] **1** : to wear off the skin of : ABRADE **2** : to censure scathingly ⟨we ~ and scorn the public servant who takes a bribe —Estes Kefauver⟩ — **ex·co·ri·a·tion** \(ˌ)ek-ˌskōr-ē-ˈā-shən, -ˌskȯr-\ *n*

ex·cre·ment \ˈek-skrə-mənt\ *n* [L *excrementum*, fr. *excernere*] : waste matter discharged from the body; *esp* : waste discharged from the alimentary canal — **ex·cre·men·tal** \ˌek-skrə-ˈment-ᵊl\ *adj* — **ex·cre·men·ti·tious** \-ˌmen-ˈtish-əs, -mən-\ *adj*

ex·cres·cence \ik-ˈskres-ᵊn(t)s\ *n* : an often excessive or abnormal outgrowth or enlargement

ex·cres·cen·cy \-ᵊn-sē\ *n, pl* **-cies** : EXCRESCENCE

ex·cres·cent \-ᵊnt\ *adj* [L *excrescent-*, *excrescens*, prp. of *excrescere* to grow out, fr. *ex-* + *crescere* to grow — more at CRESCENT] **1** : forming an abnormal, excessive, or useless outgrowth **2** : of, relating to, or constituting epenthesis — **ex·cres·cent·ly** *adv*

ex·cre·ta \ik-ˈskrēt-ə\ *n pl* [NL, fr. L, neut. pl. of *excretus*] : waste matter eliminated or separated from an organism; *esp* : EXCRETIONS — **ex·cre·tal** \-ˈskrēt-ᵊl\ *adj*

ə abut ᵊ kitten ər further a back ā bake ä cot, cart
aú out ch chin e less ē easy g gift i trip ī life
j joke ŋ sing ō flow ȯ flaw ȯi coin th thin t͟h this
ü loot u̇ foot y yet yü few yu̇ furious zh vision

ex·crete \ik-ˈskrēt\ *vt* **ex·cret·ed; ex·cret·ing** [L *excretus,* pp. of *excernere* to sift out, discharge, fr. *ex-* + *cernere* to sift — more at CERTAIN] : to separate and eliminate or discharge (waste) from the blood or tissues or from the active protoplasm — **ex·cret·er** *n*

ex·cre·tion \ik-ˈskrē-shən\ *n* **1** : the act or process of excreting **2** : something excreted; *esp* : useless, superfluous, or harmful material (as urea) that is eliminated from the body and that differs from a secretion in not being produced to perform a useful function

ex·cre·to·ry \ˈek-skrə-ˌtōr-ē, -ˌtȯr-\ *adj* : of, relating to, or functioning in excretion ⟨~ ducts⟩

ex·cru·ci·ate \ik-ˈskrü-shē-ˌāt\ *vt* **-at·ed; -at·ing** [L *excruciatus,* pp. of *excruciare,* fr. *ex-* + *cruciare* to crucify, fr. *cruc-, crux* cross — more at RIDGE] **1** : to inflict intense pain on : TORTURE **2** : to subject to intense mental distress

ex·cru·ci·at·ing *adj* **1** : causing great pain or anguish : AGONIZING ⟨the nation's most ~ dilemma —W. H. Ferry⟩ **2** : very intense : EXTREME ⟨~ pain⟩ ⟨the characters are paired off with an ~ regard for balance —Douglas Watt⟩ — **ex·cru·ci·at·ing·ly** \-ˌāt-iŋ-lē\ *adv*

ex·cru·ci·a·tion \ik-ˌskrü-s(h)ē-ˈā-shən\ *n* : the act of excruciating : the state or an instance of being excruciated

ex·cul·pate \ˈek-(ˌ)skəl-ˌpāt, (ˈ)ek-ˈ\ *vt* **-pat·ed; -pat·ing** [(assumed) ML *exculpatus,* pp. of *exculpare,* fr. L *ex* + *culpa* blame] : to clear from alleged fault or guilt — **ex·cul·pa·tion** \ˌek-(ˌ)skəl-ˈpā-shən\ *n*

ex·cul·pa·to·ry \ek-ˈskəl-pə-ˌtōr-ē, -ˌtȯr-\ *adj* : tending or serving to exculpate

ex·cur·rent \(ˈ)ek-ˈskər-ənt, -ˈskə-rənt\ *adj* [L *excurrent-, excurrens,* prp. of *excurrere* to run out, extend, fr. *ex-* + *currere* to run — more at CAR] : running or flowing out: as **a** (1) : having the axis prolonged to form an undivided main stem or trunk (as in conifers) **a** (2) : projecting beyond the apex — used esp. of the midrib of a mucronate leaf **b** : characterized by a current that flows outward ⟨~ canals of a sponge⟩

ex·cur·sion \ik-ˈskər-zhən\ *n* [L *excursion-, excursio,* fr. *excursus,* pp. of *excurrere*] **1 a** : a going out or forth : EXPEDITION **b** (1) : a usu. brief pleasure trip (2) : a trip at special reduced rates **2** : deviation from a direct, definite, or proper course; *esp* : DIGRESSION ⟨needless ~s into abstruse theory⟩ **3 a** : a movement outward and back or from a mean position or axis; *also* : the distance traversed : AMPLITUDE ⟨the ~ of a piston⟩ **b** : one complete movement of expansion and contraction of the lungs and their membranes (as in breathing)

ex·cur·sion·ist \-ˈskərzh-(ə-)nəst\ *n* : a person who goes on an excursion

ex·cur·sive \-ˈskər-siv\ *adj* : constituting a digression : characterized by digression — **ex·cur·sive·ly** *adv* — **ex·cur·sive·ness** *n*

ex·cur·sus \ik-ˈskər-səs\ *n, pl* **ex·cur·sus·es** *also* **ex·cur·sus** \-səs, -ˌsüs\ [L, digression, fr. *excursus,* pp.] : an appendix or digression that contains further exposition of some point or topic

ex·cu·sa·to·ry \-zə-ˌtōr-ē, -ˌtȯr-\ *adj* : making or containing excuse

¹ex·cuse \ik-ˈskyüz, *imperatively often without* ik-\ *vt* **ex·cused; ex·cus·ing** [ME *excusen,* fr. OF *excuser,* fr. L *excusare,* fr. *ex-* + *causa* cause, explanation] **1 a** : to make apology for ⟨quietly *excused* his clumsiness⟩ **b** : to try to remove blame from ⟨*excused* himself for being so careless⟩ **2** : to forgive entirely or overlook as of trivial import : regard as excusable ⟨she graciously *excused* his thoughtlessness⟩ **3** : to grant exemption or release to ⟨the class was *excused*⟩ **4** : to serve as excuse for : JUSTIFY ⟨nothing can ~ such heedlessness⟩ — **ex·cus·able** \ik-ˈskyü-zə-bəl\ *adj* — **ex·cus·able·ness** *n* — **ex·cus·ably** \-blē\ *adv* — **ex·cus·er** *n*

syn EXCUSE, CONDONE, PARDON, FORGIVE *shared meaning element* : to exact neither punishment nor redress for (an offense) or from (an offender). Both *excuse* and *condone* imply a passing over without censure or meet punishment. Distinctively, one may EXCUSE specific acts especially in social or conventional situations or the person responsible for these ⟨*excuse* an interruption⟩ ⟨always ready to *excuse* her children for little faults⟩ Often the term implies extenuating circumstances ⟨injustice *excuses* strong responses⟩ or in some contexts self-justification ⟨always ready to *excuse* himself from any responsibility for the results of his behavior⟩ One more often CONDONES a kind of behavior (as dishonesty, folly, or violence) and especially one that constitutes a grave breach (as of a moral or legal code) or a person or institution responsible for such behavior ⟨a culture that *condones* drink but not drugs⟩ *Pardon* and *forgive* are often interchangeable, but their implications can be distinct. One PARDONS when one remits a penalty rightfully due for an admitted or established offense ⟨*pardon* a criminal⟩ ⟨*pardon* the noisy enthusiasm of a child⟩ One FORGIVES when one gives up all claim to requital and to resentment or vengeful feelings ⟨to err is human, to *forgive* divine —Alexander Pope⟩ ***ant*** punish

²excuse \ik-ˈskyüs\ *n* **1** : the act of excusing **2 a** : something offered as justification or as grounds for being excused **b** *pl* : an expression of regret for failure to do something **c** : a note of explanation of an absence **3** : JUSTIFICATION, REASON ***syn*** see APOLOGY

ex–di·rec·to·ry \ˌeks-də-ˈrek-t(ə-)rē, -dī-\ *adj* [L *ex* out of — more at EX-] *Brit* : not listed in a telephone directory : UNLISTED

¹ex·ec \ig-ˈzek\ *n* : EXECUTIVE OFFICER

²exec *abbr* executive

ex·e·cra·ble \ˈek-si-krə-bəl\ *adj* **1** : deserving to be execrated : DETESTABLE ⟨~ crimes⟩ **2** : very bad : WRETCHED ⟨~ hotel food⟩ — **ex·e·cra·ble·ness** *n* — **ex·e·cra·bly** \-blē\ *adv*

ex·e·crate \ˈek-sə-ˌkrāt\ *vt* **-crat·ed; -crat·ing** [L *exsecratus,* pp. of *exsecrari* to put under a curse, fr. *ex* + *sacr-, sacer* sacred] **1** : to declare to be evil or detestable : DENOUNCE **2** : to detest utterly — **ex·e·cra·tive** \-ˌkrāt-iv\ *adj* — **ex·e·cra·tor** \-ˌkrāt-ər\ *n*

syn EXECRATE, CURSE, DAMN, ANATHEMATIZE *shared meaning element* : to denounce violently

ex·e·cra·tion \ˌek-sə-ˈkrā-shən\ *n* **1** : the act of cursing or denouncing; *also* : the curse so uttered **2** : an object of curses : something detested

ex·ec·u·tant \ig-ˈzek-(y)ət-ənt\ *n* : one who executes or performs; *esp* : one skilled in the technique of an art : PERFORMER

ex·e·cute \ˈek-si-ˌkyüt\ *vt* **-cut·ed; -cut·ing** [ME *executen,* fr. MF *executer,* back-formation fr. *execution*] **1** : to carry out fully : put completely into effect ⟨is a soldier morally responsible for a command that he ~s⟩ **2** : to do what is provided or required by ⟨~ a decree⟩ **3** : to put to death esp. in compliance with a legal sentence **4** : to make or produce (as a work of art) esp. by carrying out a design **5** : to perform what is required to give validity to ⟨~ a deed⟩ **6** : PLAY ⟨~ a piece of music⟩ — **ex·e·cut·able** \-ˌkyüt-ə-bəl\ *adj*

syn **1** see PERFORM

2 EXECUTE, ADMINISTER *shared meaning element* : to carry out the declared intent of another

3 see KILL

ex·e·cu·tion \ˌek-si-ˈkyü-shən\ *n* [ME, fr. MF, fr. L *exsecution-, exsecutio,* fr. *exsecutus,* pp. of *exsequi* to execute, fr. *ex-* + *sequi* to follow — more at SUE] **1** : the act or process of executing : PERFORMANCE **2** : a putting to death esp. as a legal penalty **3** : a judicial writ empowering an officer to carry out a judgment **4** : the act or mode or result of performance **5** : effective or destructive action ⟨his brandished steel, which smoked with bloody ~ —Shak.⟩ — usu. used with *do* ⟨as soon as day came, we went out to see what ~ we had done —Daniel Defoe⟩

ex·e·cu·tion·er \-sh(ə-)nər\ *n* : one who executes; *esp* : one who puts to death

¹ex·ec·u·tive \ig-ˈzek-(y)ət-iv\ *adj* **1** : designed for or relating to execution or carrying into effect ⟨~ board⟩ **2 a** : of or relating to the execution of the laws and the conduct of public and national affairs **b** : belonging to the branch of government that is charged with such powers as diplomatic representation, superintendence of the execution of the laws, and appointment of officials and that usu. has some power over legislation (as through veto) — compare JUDICIAL, LEGISLATIVE **3** : of or relating to an executive ⟨the ~ offices⟩

²executive *n* **1** : the executive branch of a government; *also* : the persons who constitute the executive magistracy of a state **2** : an individual or group constituting the agency that controls or directs an organization **3** : one who holds a position of administrative or managerial responsibility

executive agreement *n* : an agreement between the U.S. and a foreign government made by the executive branch of the government alone and dealing usu. with routine matters

executive council *n* **1** : a council constituted to advise or share in the functions of a political executive **2** : a council that exercises supreme executive power

executive officer *n* : the officer second in command of a military or naval organization

executive order *n* : REGULATION 2b

executive secretary *n* : a secretary having administrative duties; *specif* : a paid full-time official who is responsible for organizing and administering the activities and business affairs of an organization or association

executive session *n* : a usu. closed session (as of a legislative body) that functions as an executive council (as of the U.S. Senate when considering appointments or the ratification of treaties)

ex·ec·u·tor \ig-ˈzek-(y)ət-ər *or in sense 1* ˈek-sə-ˌkyüt-\ *n* [ME, fr. OF, fr. L *exsecutor,* fr. *exsecutus*] **1 a** : one who executes something **b** *obs* : EXECUTIONER **2** : the person appointed by a testator to execute his will — **ex·ec·u·to·ri·al** \ig-ˌzek-(y)ə-ˈtōr-ē-əl, -ˈtȯr-\ *adj*

ex·ec·u·to·ry \ig-ˈzek-(y)ə-ˌtōr-ē, -ˌtȯr-\ *adj* **1** : relating to administration **2** : designed or of such a nature as to be executed in time to come or to take effect on a future contingency ⟨an agreement to sell is an ~ contract⟩

ex·ec·u·trix \ig-ˈzek-(y)ə-(ˌ)triks\ *n, pl* **ex·ec·u·tri·ces** \-ˌzek-(y)ə-ˈtrī-(ˌ)sēz\ *or* **ex·ec·u·trix·es** \-ˈzek-(y)ə-ˌtrik-səz\ : a female executor

ex·e·dra \ˈek-sə-drə\ *n, pl* **-drae** \-ˌdrē, -ˌdrī\ [L, fr. Gk, fr. *ex-* + *hedra* seat — more at SIT] **1** *in ancient Greece and Rome* : a room for conversation formed by an open or columned recess often semicircular in shape and furnished with seats **2** : a large outdoor nearly semicircular seat with a solid back

ex·e·ge·sis \ˌek-sə-ˈjē-səs\ *n, pl* **-ge·ses** \-ˈjē-(ˌ)sēz\ [NL, fr. Gk *exēgēsis,* fr. *exēgeisthai* to explain, interpret, fr. *ex-* + *hēgeisthai* to lead — more at SEEK] : EXPOSITION, EXPLANATION; *esp* : an explanation or critical interpretation of a text

ex·e·gete \ˈek-sə-ˌjēt\ *n* [Gk *exēgētēs,* fr. *exēgeisthai*] : one who practices exegesis

ex·e·get·i·cal \ˌek-sə-ˈjet-i-kəl\ *or* **ex·e·get·ic** \-ik\ *adj* [Gk *exēgētikos,* fr. *exēgeisthai*] : of or relating to exegesis : EXPLANATORY — **ex·e·get·i·cal·ly** \-i-k(ə-)lē\ *adv*

ex·e·get·ist \-ˈjet-əst\ *n* : EXEGETE

ex·em·plar \ig-ˈzem-ˌplär, -plər\ *n* [ME, fr. L, fr. *exemplum* example] : something that serves as a model or example: as **a** : an ideal model **b** : a typical or standard specimen **c** : a copy of a book or writing **d** : IDEA 1a ***syn*** see MODEL

ex·em·pla·ry \ig-ˈzem-plə-rē\ *adj* **1 a** : serving as a pattern **b** : deserving imitation : COMMENDABLE ⟨his courage was ~⟩ **2** : serving as a warning : MONITORY **3** : serving as an example, instance, or illustration — **ex·em·plar·i·ly** \ˌeg-ˌzem-ˈpler-ə-lē\ *adv* — **ex·em·pla·ri·ness** \ig-ˈzem-plə-rē-nəs\ *n* — **ex·em·plar·i·ty** \ˌeg-ˌzem-ˈplar-ət-ē\ *n*

ex·em·pli·fi·ca·tion \ig-ˌzem-plə-fə-ˈkā-shən\ *n* **1** : an exemplified copy of a document **2 a** : the act or process of exemplifying **b** : a case in point : EXAMPLE

ex·em·pli·fy \ig-ˈzem-plə-ˌfī\ *vt* **-fied; -fy·ing** [ME *exemplifien,* fr. MF *exemplifier,* fr. ML *exemplificare,* fr. L *exemplum*] **1** : to show or illustrate by example **2** : to make an attested copy or transcript of (a document) under seal **3 a** : to be an instance of or serve as an example : EMBODY **b** : to be typical of

ex·em·pli gra·tia \ig-ˌzem-(ˌ)plē-ˈgrät-ē-ˌä\ *adv* [L] : for example

ex·em·plum \ig-ˈzem-pləm\ *n, pl* **-pla** \-plə\ [L] **1** : EXAMPLE, MODEL **2** : an anecdote or short narrative used to point a moral or sustain an argument

1ex·empt \ig-ˈzem(p)t\ *adj* [ME, fr. L *exemptus,* pp. of *eximere* to take out — more at EXAMPLE] **1** *obs* : set apart **2** : free or released from some liability or requirement to which others are subject ⟨was ~ from jury duty⟩

2exempt *n* : one exempted or freed from duty

3exempt *vt* **1** *obs* : to set apart **2** : to release or deliver from some liability or requirement to which others are subject : EXCUSE ⟨a man ~*ed* from military service⟩

ex·emp·tion \ig-ˈzem(p)-shən\ *n* **1** : the act of exempting or state of being exempt : IMMUNITY **2** : one that exempts or is exempted; *esp* : a source or amount of income exempted from taxation

ex·en·ter·ate \ig-ˌzent-ə-ˌrāt\ *vt* **-at·ed; -at·ing** [L *exenteratus,* pp. of *exenterare* to disembowel, modif. of Gk *exenterizein,* fr. *ex-* + *enteron* intestine — more at INTER-] : to remove the contents of (as the orbit or pelvis) — **ex·en·ter·a·tion** \-ˌzent-ə-ˈrā-shən\ *n*

1ex·er·cise \ˈek-sər-ˌsīz\ *n* [ME, fr. MF *exercice,* fr. L *exercitium,* fr. *exercitus,* pp. of *exercēre* to drive on, keep busy, fr. *ex-* + *arcēre* to enclose, hold off — more at ARK] **1 a** : the act of bringing into play or realizing in action : USE **b** : the discharge of an official function or professional occupation **2 a** : regular or repeated use of a faculty or bodily organ **b** : bodily exertion for the sake of developing and maintaining physical fitness **3** : something performed or practiced in order to develop, improve, or display a specific power or skill ⟨arithmetic ~*s*⟩ **4** : a performance having a strongly marked secondary or ulterior aspect ⟨party politics has always been an ~ in compromise —H.S. Ashmore⟩ **5 a** : a maneuver, operation, or drill carried out for training and discipline **b** *pl* : a program including speeches, announcements of awards and honors, and various traditional practices of secular or religious character ⟨commencement ~*s*⟩

2exercise *vb* **-cised; -cis·ing** *vt* **1 a** : to make effective in action : USE ⟨didn't ~ good judgment⟩ **b** : to bring to bear : EXERT ⟨~ influence⟩ **2 a** : to use repeatedly in order to strengthen or develop **b** : to train (as troops) by drills and maneuvers **c** : to put through exercises ⟨~ the horses⟩ **3 a** : to engage the attention and effort of **b** : to cause anxiety, alarm, or indignation in ⟨citizens *exercised* about pollution⟩ ~ *vi* : to take exercise ***syn*** see PRACTICE — **ex·er·cis·able** \-ˌsī-zə-bəl\ *adj* — **ex·er·cis·er** *n*

ex·er·ci·ta·tion \ig-ˌzər-sə-ˈtā-shən\ *n* [ME *exercitacioun,* fr. L *exercitation-, exercitatio,* fr. *exercitatus,* pp. of *exercitare* to exercise diligently, fr. *exercitus,* pp. of *exercēre*] : EXERCISE

ex·er·gon·ic \ˌek-(ˌ)sər-ˈgän-ik\ *adj* [*exo-* + Gk *ergon* work — more at WORK] : liberating energy ⟨an ~ biochemical reaction⟩

ex·ergue \ˈek-ˌsərg, ˈeg-ˌzərg\ *n* [F, fr. NL *exergum,* fr. Gk *ex* out of + *ergon* work] : a space on a coin, token, or medal usu. on the reverse below the central part of the design

ex·ert \ig-ˈzərt\ *vt* [L *exsertus,* pp. of *exserere* to thrust out, fr. *ex-* + *serere* to join — more at SERIES] **1 a** : to put forth (as strength) **b** : to put (oneself) into action or to tiring effort **2** : to bring to bear esp. with sustained effort or lasting effect **3** : EMPLOY, WIELD ⟨~*ed* his leadership abilities intelligently⟩

ex·er·tion \ig-ˈzər-shən\ *n* : the act or an instance of exerting; *esp* : a laborious or perceptible effort ***syn*** see EFFORT

ex·e·unt \ˈek-sē-(ˌ)ənt, -ˌu̇nt\ [L, they go out, fr. *exire* to go out — more at EXIT] — used as a stage direction to specify that all or certain named characters leave the stage

ex·fo·li·ate \(ˈ)eks-ˈfō-lē-ˌāt\ *vb* **-at·ed; -at·ing** [LL *exfoliatus,* pp. of *exfoliare* to strip of leaves, fr. L *ex-* + *folium* leaf — more at BLADE] *vt* **1** : to cast off in scales, laminae, or splinters **2** : to remove the surface of in scales or laminae **3** : to spread or extend by or as if by opening out leaves ~ *vi* **1** : to split into or give off scales, laminae, or body cells **2** : to come off in a thin piece **3** : to grow by or as if by producing or unfolding leaves — **ex·fo·li·a·tion** \(ˌ)eks-ˌfō-lē-ˈā-shən\ *n* — **ex·fo·li·a·tive** \eks-ˈfō-lē-ˌāt-iv\ *adj*

ex gra·tia \(ˈ)eks-ˈgrā-sh(ē-)ə\ *adj or adv* [NL] : as a favor : not compelled by legal right ⟨*ex gratia* pension payments⟩

ex·hal·ant *or* **ex·hal·ent** \eks-ˈ(h)ā-lənt\ *adj* : bearing out or outward : EMISSIVE ⟨an ~ siphon of a clam⟩

ex·ha·la·tion \ˌeks-(h)ə-ˈlā-shən\ *n* **1** : an act of exhaling **2** : something exhaled or given off : EMANATION

ex·hale \eks-ˈ(h)ā(ə)l\ *vb* **ex·haled; ex·hal·ing** [ME *exalen,* fr. L *exhalare,* fr. *ex-* + *halare* to breathe; akin to L *anima* breath — more at ANIMATE] *vt* **1 a** : to breathe out **b** : to give forth (gaseous matter) : EMIT **2** *archaic* : to cause to be emitted in vapor ~ *vi* **1** : to rise or be given off as vapor **2** : to emit breath or vapor

1ex·haust \ig-ˈzȯst\ *vb* [L *exhaustus,* pp. of *exhaurire,* fr. *ex-* + *haurire* to draw; akin to MHG *œsen* to empty, Gk *auein* to take] *vt* **1 a** : to draw off or let out completely **b** : to empty by drawing off the contents; *specif* : to create a vacuum in **2 a** : to use up : consume entirely ⟨~*ed* our funds in a week⟩ **b** : to tire extremely or completely ⟨~*ed* by overwork⟩ **c** : to deprive of a valuable quality or constituent ⟨~ a photographic developer⟩ ⟨~ a soil of fertility⟩ **3 a** : to develop (a subject) completely **b** : to try out the whole number of ⟨~*ed* all the possibilities⟩ ~ *vi* : DISCHARGE, EMPTY ⟨the engine ~*s* through the muffler⟩ ***syn*** see DEPLETE, TIRE — **ex·haust·er** *n* — **ex·haust·ibil·i·ty** \-ˌzȯ-stə-ˈbil-ət-ē\ *n* — **ex·haust·ible** \-ˈzȯ-stə-bəl\ *adj*

2exhaust *n* **1 a** : the escape of used gas or vapor from an engine **b** : the gas or vapor thus escaping **2 a** : the conduit through which used gases escape **b** : an arrangement for withdrawing fumes, dusts, or odors from an enclosure **3** : EXHAUSTION

ex·haus·tion \ig-ˈzȯs-chən\ *n* : the act or process of exhausting : the state of being exhausted

ex·haus·tive \ig-ˈzȯ-stiv\ *adj* **1** : serving or tending to exhaust **2** : testing all possibilities or considering all elements : THOROUGH ⟨conducted an ~ investigation⟩ — **ex·haus·tive·ly** *adv* — **ex·haus·tive·ness** *n* — **ex·haus·tiv·i·ty** \-ˌzȯ-ˈstiv-ət-ē\ *n*

ex·haust·less \ig-ˈzȯst-ləs\ *adj* : not to be exhausted : INEXHAUSTIBLE — **ex·haust·less·ly** *adv* — **ex·haust·less·ness** *n*

exhbn *abbr* exhibition

1ex·hib·it \ig-ˈzib-ət\ *vb* [ME *exhibiten,* fr. L *exhibitus,* pp. of *exhibēre,* fr. *ex-* + *habēre* to have, hold — more at GIVE] *vt* **1** : to present to view: as **a** : to show or display outwardly esp. by visible signs or actions ⟨~*ed* no fear⟩ **b** : to have as a readily discernible quality or feature ⟨in all cultures we know, men ~ an aesthetic sense —H. J. Muller⟩ **c** : to show publicly esp. for purposes of competition or demonstration **2** : to submit (as a document) to a court or officer in course of proceedings; *also* : to present or offer officially or in legal form **3** : to administer for medical purposes ⟨the patient should fast . . . before chloroform is ~*ed* —A. B. Garrod⟩ ~ *vi* : to display something for public inspection — **ex·hib·i·tive** \-ət-iv\ *adj* — **ex·hib·i·tor** \-ət-ər\ *n* — **ex·hib·i·to·ry** \-ə-ˌtōr-ē, -ˌtȯr-\ *adj*

2exhibit *n* **1** : an act or instance of exhibiting **2** : something exhibited **3** : a document or material object produced and identified in court or before an examiner for use as evidence

ex·hi·bi·tion \ˌek-sə-ˈbish-ən\ *n* **1** : an act or instance of exhibiting **2** *Brit* : a grant drawn from the funds of a school or university to help maintain a student **3** : a public showing (as of works of art, objects of manufacture, or athletic skill)

ex·hi·bi·tion·er \-ˈbish-(ə-)nər\ *n, Brit* : one who holds a grant from a school or university

ex·hi·bi·tion·ism \-ˈbish-ə-ˌniz-əm\ *n* **1 a** : a perversion marked by a tendency to indecent exposure **b** : an act of such exposure **2** : the act or practice of behaving so as to attract attention to oneself — **ex·hi·bi·tion·ist** \-ˈbish-(ə-)nəst\ *n or adj* — **ex·hi·bi·tion·is·tic** \-ˌbish-ə-ˈnis-tik\ *adj*

ex·hil·a·rant \ig-ˈzil-ə-rənt\ *adj* : EXHILARATING

ex·hil·a·rate \ig-ˈzil-ə-ˌrāt\ *vt* **-rat·ed; -rat·ing** [L *exhilaratus,* pp. of *exhilarare,* fr. *ex-* + *hilarare* to gladden, fr. *hilarus* cheerful — more at HILARIOUS] **1 a** : to make cheerful **b** : ENLIVEN, EXCITE **2** : REFRESH, STIMULATE — **ex·hil·a·ra·tive** \-ˌrāt-iv\ *adj*

ex·hil·a·rat·ing \-ˌrāt-iŋ\ *adj* : that exhilarates ⟨~ effect of mountain air⟩ — **ex·hil·a·rat·ing·ly** \-iŋ-lē\ *adv*

ex·hil·a·ra·tion \ig-ˌzil-ə-ˈrā-shən\ *n* **1** : the action of exhilarating **2** : the feeling or the state of being exhilarated

ex·hort \ig-ˈzȯ(ə)rt\ *vb* [ME *exhorten,* fr. MF *exhorter,* fr. L *exhortari,* fr. *ex-* + *hortari* to incite — more at YEARN] *vt* : to incite by argument or advice : urge strongly ~ *vi* : to give warnings or advice : make urgent appeals — **ex·hort·er** *n*

ex·hor·ta·tion \ˌeks-ˌȯr-ˈtā-shən, ˌegz-, -ər-\ *n* **1** : an act or instance of exhorting **2** : language intended to incite and encourage

ex·hor·ta·tive \ig-ˈzȯrt-ət-iv\ *adj* : serving to exhort

ex·hor·ta·to·ry \-ə-ˌtōr-ē, -ˌtȯr-\ *adj* : using exhortation : EXHORTATIVE

ex·hume \igz-ˈ(y)üm, iks-ˈ(h)yüm\ *vt* **ex·humed; ex·hum·ing** [F or ML; F *exhumer,* fr. ML *exhumare,* fr. L *ex* out of + *humus* earth — more at EX-, HUMBLE] **1** : DISINTER **2** : to bring back from neglect or obscurity — **ex·hu·ma·tion** \ˌeks-(h)yü-ˈmā-shən, ˌegz-(y)ü-\ *n* — **ex·hum·er** \igz-ˈ(y)ü-mər, iks-ˈ(h)yü-\ *n*

ex·i·gence \ˈek-sə-jən(t)s\ *n* : EXIGENCY

ex·i·gen·cy \ˈek-sə-jən-sē, ig-ˈzij-ən-\ *n, pl* **-cies** **1 a** : the quality or state of being exigent **b** : a state of affairs that makes urgent demands ⟨the president must be free to act in any sudden ~⟩ **2** : such need or necessity as belongs to the occasion : that which is required in a particular situation — usu. used in pl. ***syn*** see JUNCTURE, NEED

ex·i·gent \ˈek-sə-jənt\ *adj* [L *exigent-, exigens,* prp. of *exigere* to demand — more at EXACT] **1** : requiring immediate aid or action **2** : requiring or calling for much : DEMANDING — **ex·i·gent·ly** *adv*

ex·i·gu·ity \ˌeg-zi-ˈgyü-ət-ē\ *n, pl* **-ities** : the quality or state of being exiguous : SCANTINESS

ex·ig·u·ous \ig-ˈzig-yə-wəs\ *adj* [L *exiguus,* fr. *exigere*] : excessively scanty : INADEQUATE ⟨attempting to build up their ~ navy⟩ ***syn*** see MEAGER ***ant*** capacious, ample — **ex·ig·u·ous·ly** *adv* — **ex·ig·u·ous·ness** *n*

1ex·ile \ˈeg-ˌzīl, ˈek-ˌsīl\ *n* [ME *exil,* fr. MF, fr. L *exilium*] **1 a** : forced removal from one's country or home **b** : voluntary absence from one's country or home **2 a** : a person expelled from his country or home by authority **b** : one who separates himself from his home

2exile *vt* **ex·iled; ex·il·ing** : to banish or expel from one's own country or home ***syn*** see BANISH

ex·il·ic \eg-ˈzil-ik\ *adj* : of or relating to exile (as that of the Jews in Babylon)

ex·im·i·ous \eg-ˈzim-ē-əs\ *adj* [L *eximius,* fr. *eximere* to take out — more at EXAMPLE] *archaic* : CHOICE, EXCELLENT

ex·ine \ˈek-ˌsēn, -ˌsīn\ *n* [prob. fr. G, fr. *ex-* + NL *in-* fibrous tissue, fr. Gk *in-, is* tendon] : the outer of the two major layers forming the walls of some spores and esp. pollen grains

ex·ist \ig-ˈzist\ *vi* [L *exsistere* to come into being, exist, fr. *ex-* + *sistere* to stand; akin to L *stare* to stand — more at STAND] **1 a** : to have real being whether material or spiritual ⟨do unicorns ~⟩ **b** : to have being in space and time ⟨the greatest poet who ever ~*ed*⟩ **c** : to have being in a specified place or with respect to understood limitations or conditions ⟨strange ideas ~*ed* in his mind⟩ **2** : to continue to be ⟨racism still ~*s* to varying degrees⟩ **3 a** : to have life or the functions of vitality ⟨man cannot ~ without oxygen⟩ **b** : to live at an inferior level or under adverse circumstances ⟨starving people ~*ing* from one day to the next⟩ **4** *in existentialism* : to have contingent but free and responsible being

ex·is·tence \ig-ˈzis-tən(t)s\ *n* **1 a** *obs* : reality as opposed to appearance **b** : reality as presented in experience **c (1)** : the totality of existent things **(2)** : a particular being ⟨all the fair ~*s* of heaven —John Keats⟩ **d** : sentient or living being : LIFE **2 a** : the state or fact of having being esp. independently of human consciousness and as contrasted with nonexistence **b :** the manner of being that is common to every mode of being **c :** being with respect to a limiting condition or under a particular aspect **3 :** continued or repeated manifestation **4** *in existentialism* **:** the condition of a person aware of his radically contingent yet free and responsible nature

ex·is·tent \-tənt\ *adj* [L *exsistent-, exsistens,* prp. of *exsistere*] **1 :** having being **:** EXISTING **2 :** existing now **:** PRESENT — **existent** *n*

ex·is·ten·tial \ˌeg-(ˌ)zis-ˈten-chəl, ˌek-(ˌ)sis-\ *adj* **1 :** of, relating to, or affirming existence ⟨~ propositions⟩ **2 a :** grounded in existence or the experience of existence **:** EMPIRICAL **b :** having being in time and space **3** [trans. of Dan *eksistentiel* & G *existential*] **a :** concerned with or involving an individual as radically free and responsible **b :** EXISTENTIALIST — **ex·is·ten·tial·ly** \-ˈtench-(ə-)lē\ *adv*

ex·is·ten·tial·ism \-ˈten-chə-ˌliz-əm\ *n* **:** a chiefly 20th century philosophy that is centered upon the analysis of existence and of the way man finds himself existing in the world, that regards human existence as not exhaustively describable or understandable in scientific terms, and that stresses the freedom and responsibility of the individual, the irreducible uniqueness of an ethical or religious situation, and usu. the isolation and subjective experiences (as of anxiety, guilt, dread, anguish) of an individual therein

¹ex·is·ten·tial·ist \-ləst\ *n* **:** an adherent of existentialism

²existentialist *adj* **1 :** of or relating to existentialism or existentialists **2 :** EXISTENTIAL 3a — **ex·is·ten·tial·is·tic** \-ˌten-chə-ˈlis-tik\ *adj* — **ex·is·ten·tial·is·ti·cal·ly** \-ti-k(ə-)lē\ *adv*

existential quantifier *n* **:** a quantifier that asserts that there exists at least one value of a variable — called also *existential operator*

¹ex·it \ˈeg-zət, ˈek-sət\ [L, he goes out, fr. *exire* to go out, fr. *ex-* + *ire* to go — more at ISSUE] — used as a stage direction to specify who goes off stage

²exit *n* [L *exitus,* fr. *exitus,* pp. of *exire*] **1** [¹*exit*] **:** a departure from a stage **2 a :** the act of going out or going away **b :** DEATH **3 :** a way out of an enclosed place or space — **exit** *vi*

ex li·bris \ek-ˈslē-brəs, -ˌbrēs\ *n, pl* **ex libris** [NL, from the books; used before the owner's name on bookplates] **:** BOOKPLATE

Ex·moor \ˈek-ˌsmu̇(ə)r, -ˌsmō(ə)r, -ˌsmȯ(ə)r\ *n* [*Exmoor,* England] **1 :** any of a breed of horned sheep of Devonshire in England valued esp. for mutton **2 :** any of a breed of hardy heavy-maned ponies native to the Exmoor district

ex ni·hi·lo \(ˈ)eks-ˈnē-(h)ə-ˌlō, -ˈni-, -ˈnī-\ *adv or adj* [L] **:** from or out of nothing ⟨creation *ex nihilo*⟩

exo- *or* **ex-** *comb form* [Gk *exō* out, outside, fr. *ex* out of — more at EX-] **1 :** outside ⟨*exo*gamy⟩ **:** outer ⟨*exo*skeleton⟩ — compare ECT-, END- **2 :** turning out ⟨*exo*ergic⟩

exo·bi·ol·o·gy \ˌek-sō-bī-ˈäl-ə-jē\ *n* **:** extraterrestrial biology — **exo·bi·o·log·i·cal** \-ˌbī-ə-ˈläj-i-kəl\ *adj* — **exo·bi·ol·o·gist** \-bī-ˈäl-ə-jəst\ *n*

exo·carp \ˈek-sō-ˌkärp\ *n* [ISV] **:** the outermost layer of the pericarp of a fruit — see ENDOCARP illustration

exo·crine \ˈek-sə-krən, -ˌkrīn, -ˌkrēn\ *adj* [ISV *exo-* + Gk *krinein* to separate — more at CERTAIN] **:** secreting externally ⟨~ pancreatic cells⟩

exocrine gland *n* **:** a gland (as a sweat gland or a kidney) that releases a secretion external to or at the surface of an organ by means of a canal or duct

exo·cy·clic \ˌek-sō-ˈsī-klik, -ˈsik-lik\ *adj* **:** situated outside of a ring in a chemical structure

Exod *abbr* Exodus

exo·der·mis \ˌek-sō-ˈdər-məs\ *n* [NL] **:** a layer of the outer living cortical cells that takes over the functions of the epidermis in roots lacking secondary thickening

ex·odon·tia \ˌek-sə-ˈdän-ch(ē-)ə\ *n* [NL, fr. *ex-* + *-odontia*] **:** a branch of dentistry that deals with the extraction of teeth — **ex·odon·tist** \-ˈdänt-əst\ *n*

ex·o·dus \ˈek-səd-əs, ˈeg-zəd-\ *n* [L, fr. Gk *Exodos,* lit., road out, fr. *ex-* + *hodos* road — more at CEDE] **1** *cap* **:** the mainly narrative second book of canonical Jewish and Christian Scripture — see BIBLE table **2 :** a mass departure **:** EMIGRATION

exo·en·zyme \ˌek-sō-ˈen-ˌzīm\ *n* [ISV] **:** an extracellular enzyme

exo·er·gic \ˌek-sō-ˈər-jik\ *adj* **:** releasing energy **:** EXOTHERMIC ⟨~ nuclear reaction⟩

exo·eryth·ro·cyt·ic \ˌek-sō-i-ˌrith-rə-ˈsit-ik\ *adj* **:** occurring outside the red blood cells — used of stages of malaria parasites

ex of·fi·cio \ˌek-sə-ˈfish-ē-ˌō\ *adv or adj* [LL] **:** by virtue or because of an office ⟨the Vice President serves *ex officio* as president of the Senate⟩

ex·og·a·my \ek-ˈsäg-ə-mē\ *n, pl* **-mies** **1 :** marriage outside of a specific group esp. as required by custom or law **2 :** sexual reproduction between organisms that are not closely related — **ex·og·a·mous** \ek-ˈsäg-ə-məs\ *or* **exo·gam·ic** \ˌek-sə-ˈgam-ik\ *adj*

ex·og·e·nous \ek-ˈsäj-ə-nəs\ *adj* [F *exogène* exogenous, fr. *exo-* + *-gène* (fr. Gk *-genēs* born) — more at -GEN] **:** originating from or due to external causes: as **a :** growing from or on the outside ⟨~ spores⟩ **b (1) :** caused by a factor (as food) or an agent from outside the organism ⟨~ obesity⟩ ⟨~ infection⟩ **b (2) :** introduced from or produced outside the organism ⟨~ supply of a vitamin⟩ **c :** of, relating to, or produced by the metabolism of nitrogenous substances obtained from food — **ex·og·e·nous·ly** *adv*

ex·on·er·ate \ig-ˈzän-ə-ˌrāt\ *vt* **-at·ed; -at·ing** [ME *exoneraten,* fr. L *exoneratus,* pp. of *exonerare* to unburden, fr. *ex-* + *oner-, onus* load] **1 :** to relieve of a responsibility, obligation, or hardship **2 :** to clear from accusation or blame — **ex·on·er·a·tion** \-ˌzän-ə-ˈrā-shən\ *n* — **ex·on·er·a·tive** \-ˈzän-ə-ˌrāt-iv\ *adj*

exo·nu·cle·ase \ˌek-sō-ˈn(y)ü-klē-ˌās, -ˌāz\ *n* [*exo-* + *nucle-* + *-ase*] **:** an enzyme that breaks down a nucleic acid by removing nucleotides one by one from the end of a chain — compare ENDONUCLEASE

exo·pep·ti·dase \-ˈpep-tə-ˌdās, -ˌdāz\ *n* [*exo-* + *peptide* + *-ase*] **:** any of a group of enzymes that hydrolyze peptide bonds formed by the terminal amino acids of peptide chains **:** PEPTIDASE — compare ENDOPEPTIDASE

ex·oph·thal·mos *also* **ex·oph·thal·mus** \ˌek-säf-ˈthal-məs, -səf-, -säp-\ *n* [NL, fr. Gk *exophthalmos* having prominent eyes, fr. *ex* out + *ophthalmos* eye] **:** abnormal protrusion of the eyeball — **ex·oph·thal·mic** \-mik\ *adj*

exor *abbr* executor

ex·or·bi·tance \ig-ˈzȯr-bət-ən(t)s\ *n* **1 :** an exorbitant action or procedure; *esp* **:** excessive or gross deviation from rule, right, or propriety **2 :** the tendency or disposition to be exorbitant

ex·or·bi·tant \-ənt\ *adj* [ME, fr. MF, fr. LL *exorbitant-, exorbitans,* prp. of *exorbitare* to deviate, fr. L *ex-* + *orbita* track, rut — more at ORB] **1 :** not coming within the orbit or scope of the law **2 :** exceeding in intensity, quality, or size the customary or appropriate limits **syn** see EXCESSIVE **ant** just (*price, charge*) — **ex·or·bi·tant·ly** *adv*

ex·or·cise \ˈek-ˌsȯr-ˌsīz, -sər-\ *vt* **-cised; -cis·ing** [ME *exorcisen,* fr. MF *exorciser,* fr. LL *exorcizare,* fr. Gk *exorkizein,* fr. *ex-* + *horkizein* to bind by oath, adjure, fr. *horkos* oath; akin to Gk *herkos* fence, L *sarcire* to mend] **1 a :** to expel (an evil spirit) by adjuration **b :** to get rid of (something troublesome, menacing, or oppressive) **2 :** to free of an evil spirit — **ex·or·cis·er** *n*

ex·or·cism \-ˌsiz-əm\ *n* **1 :** the act or practice of exorcising **2 :** a spell or formula used in exorcising — **ex·or·cist** \-ˌsist, -səst\ *n* — **ex·or·cis·ti·cal** \ˌek-ˌsȯr-ˈsis-ti-kəl, -sər-\ *or* **ex·or·cis·tic** \-tik\ *adj*

ex·or·di·um \eg-ˈzȯrd-ē-əm\ *n, pl* **-diums** *or* **-dia** \-ē-ə\ [L, fr. *exordiri* to begin, fr. *ex-* + *ordiri* to begin — more at ORDER] **:** a beginning or introduction esp. to a discourse or composition — **ex·or·di·al** \-ē-əl\ *adj*

exo·skel·e·ton \ˌek-sō-ˈskel-ət-ᵊn\ *n* **1 :** an external supportive covering of an animal **2 :** bony or horny parts of a vertebrate produced from epidermal tissues — **exo·skel·e·tal** \-ət-ᵊl\ *adj*

ex·os·mo·sis \ˌek-(ˌ)säs-ˈmō-səs, -(ˌ)säz-\ *n* [alter. of obs. *exosmose,* fr. F, fr. *ex-* + Gk *ōsmos* act of pushing — more at ENDOSMOSIS] **:** passage of material through a membrane from a region of higher to a region of lower concentration — **ex·os·mot·ic** \-ˈmät-ik\ *adj*

exo·sphere \ˈek-sō-ˌsfi(ə)r\ *n* [ISV] **:** the outer fringe region of the atmosphere of the earth or a planet — **exo·spher·ic** \ˌek-sō-ˈsfi(ə)r-ik, -ˈsfer-\ *adj*

exo·spore \ˈek-sə-ˌspō(ə)r, -ˌspȯ(ə)r\ *n* [ISV] **:** an asexual spore formed by abstriction from a parent cell

ex·os·to·sis \ˌek-(ˌ)säs-ˈtō-səs\ *n, pl* **-to·ses** \-ˌsēz\ [NL, fr. Gk *exostōsis,* fr. *ex* out of + *osteon* bone — more at EX-, OSSEOUS] **:** a spur or bony outgrowth from a bone or the root of a tooth

ex·o·ter·ic \ˌek-sə-ˈter-ik\ *adj* [L & Gk; L *exotericus,* fr. Gk *exōterikos,* lit., external, fr. *exōterō* more outside, compar. of *exō* outside — more at EXO-] **1 a :** suitable to be imparted to the public ⟨the ~ doctrine⟩ — compare ESOTERIC **b :** belonging to the outer or less initiate circle **2 :** relating to the outside **:** EXTERNAL — **ex·o·ter·i·cal·ly** \-i-k(ə-)lē\ *adv*

exo·ther·mic \ˌek-sō-ˈthər-mik\ *or* **exo·ther·mal** \-məl\ *adj* [ISV] **:** characterized by or formed with evolution of heat — **exo·ther·mi·cal·ly** \-mi-k(ə-)lē\ *adv*

¹ex·ot·ic \ig-ˈzät-ik\ *adj* [L *exoticus,* fr. Gk *exōtikos,* fr. *exō*] **1 :** introduced from another country **:** not native to the place where found **2** *archaic* **:** OUTLANDISH, ALIEN **3 :** strikingly or excitingly different or unusual **4 :** of or relating to striptease ⟨~ dancing⟩ — **ex·ot·i·cal·ly** \-i-k(ə-)lē\ *adv* — **ex·ot·ic·ness** \-ik-nəs\ *n*

²exotic *n* **:** one that is exotic; *also* **:** STRIPTEASER

ex·ot·i·ca \ig-ˈzät-i-kə\ *n pl* [NL, fr. L, neut. pl. of *exoticus*] **:** things excitingly different or unusual; *esp* **:** literary or artistic items having an exotic theme or nature

ex·ot·i·cism \ig-ˈzät-ə-ˌsiz-əm\ *also* **ex·o·tism** \ˈeg-zə-ˌtiz-əm, ˈek-sə-\ *n* **:** the quality or state of being exotic

exo·tox·in \ˌek-sō-ˈtäk-sən\ *n* [ISV] **:** a soluble poisonous substance given off during growth of a microorganism

exp *abbr* **1** expense **2** experiment; experimental **3** export **4** express

ex·pand \ik-ˈspand\ *vb* [ME *expaunden,* fr. L *expandere,* fr. *ex-* + *pandere* to spread — more at FATHOM] *vt* **1 :** to increase the extent, number, volume, or scope of **:** ENLARGE **2 a :** to express fully or in detail **b :** to write out in full **c :** to state in enlarged form **:** develop in a mathematical series **~** *vi* **1 :** to open out **2 :** to increase in extent, number, volume, or scope **3 :** to speak or write fully or in detail ⟨intend to ~ on this theme tomorrow⟩ **4 :** to feel generous or optimistic — **ex·pand·able** \-ˈspan-də-bəl\ *adj*

syn EXPAND, AMPLIFY, SWELL, DISTEND, INFLATE, DILATE *shared meaning element* **:** to increase in size or volume **ant** contract, abridge

expanded metal *n* **:** sheet metal cut and expanded into a lattice and used esp. as lath

expanded plastic *n* **:** lightweight cellular plastic used esp. as insulation and protective packing material — called also *foamed plastic, plastic foam*

ex·pand·er \ik-ˈspan-dər\ *n* **:** one that expands; *specif* **:** any of several colloidal substances of high molecular weight used as a blood or plasma substitute for increasing the blood volume

ex·panse \ik-ˈspan(t)s\ *n* [NL *expansum,* fr. L, neut. of *expansus,* pp. of *expandere*] **:** something spread out typically over a wide area: as **a :** FIRMAMENT **b :** an extensive stretch of land or sea

ex·pan·si·ble \ik-ˈspan(t)-sə-bəl\ *adj* **:** capable of being expanded — **ex·pan·si·bil·i·ty** \-ˌspan(t)-sə-ˈbil-ət-ē\ *n*

ex·pan·sile \ik-ˈspan(t)-səl, -ˈspan-ˌsīl\ *adj* **:** of, relating to, or capable of expansion

ex·pan·sion \ik-ˈspan-chən\ *n* **1 :** the act or process of expanding ⟨territorial ~⟩ **2 :** the quality or state of being expanded **3 :** EXPANSE **4 :** the increase in volume of working fluid (as steam) in an engine cylinder after cutoff or in an internal-combustion engine after explosion **5 a :** an expanded part **b :** something that results from an act of expanding ⟨the book is an ~ of a lecture series⟩ **6 :** the result of carrying out an indicated mathematical operation **:** the expression of a function in the form of a series — **ex·pan·sion·al** \-ˈpanch-nəl, -ən-ᵊl\ *adj*

ex·pan·sion·ary \ik-ˈspan-chə-ˌner-ē\ *adj* **:** tending toward expansion ⟨an ~ economy⟩

ex·pan·sion·ism \ik-ˈspan-chə-ˌniz-əm\ *n* **:** a policy or practice of usu. territorial expansion by a nation — **ex·pan·sion·ist** \-ˈspanch-(ə-)nəst\ *n* — **expansionist** *or* **ex·pan·sion·is·tic** \-ˌspan-chə-ˈnis-tik\ *adj*

ex·pan·sive \ik-ˈspan(t)-siv\ *adj* **1 :** having a capacity or a tendency to expand **2 :** causing or tending to cause expansion **3 a :** characterized by high spirits or benevolent inclinations ⟨he grew ~ after dinner⟩ **b :** marked by or indicative of exaggerated euphoria and delusions of self-importance **4 :** having considerable extent **5 :** characterized by largeness or magnificence of scale ⟨~ living⟩ — **ex·pan·sive·ly** *adv* — **ex·pan·sive·ness** *n*

ex·pan·siv·i·ty \ˌek-ˌspan-ˈsiv-ət-ē, ik-\ *n* **:** the quality or state of being expansive; *esp* **:** the capacity to expand

ex par·te \(ˈ)ek-ˈspärt-ē\ *adv or adj* [ML] **1 :** on or from one side only — used of legal proceedings **2 :** from a one-sided or partisan point of view

ex·pa·ti·ate \ek-ˈspā-shē-ˌāt\ *vi* **-at·ed; -at·ing** [L *exspatiatus,* pp. of *exspatiari* to wander, digress, fr. *ex-* + *spatium* space, course — more at SPEED] **1 :** to move about freely or at will **:** WANDER **2 :** to speak or write at length or in detail ⟨was *expatiating* upon the value of the fabric —Thomas Hardy⟩ — **ex·pa·ti·a·tion** \(ˌ)ek-ˌspā-shē-ˈā-shən\ *n*

¹ex·pa·tri·ate \ek-ˈspā-trē-ˌāt\ *vb* **-at·ed; -at·ing** [ML *expatriatus,* pp. of *expatriare* to leave one's own country, fr. L *ex-* + *patria* native country, fr. fem. of *patrius* of a father, fr. *patr-, pater* father — more at FATHER] *vt* **1 :** to drive into exile **:** BANISH **2 :** to withdraw (oneself) from residence in or allegiance to one's native country ~ *vi* **:** to leave one's native country; *specif* **:** to renounce allegiance to one's native country — **ex·pa·tri·a·tion** \(ˌ)ek-ˌspā-trē-ˈā-shən\ *n*

²ex·pa·tri·ate \ek-ˈspā-trē-ˌāt, -trē-ət\ *adj* **:** living in a foreign country **:** EXPATRIATED

³ex·pa·tri·ate \-ˌāt, -ət\ *n* **:** one who lives in a foreign country; *specif* **:** one who has renounced his native country

ex·pect \ik-ˈspekt\ *vb* [L *exspectare* to look forward to, fr. *ex-* + *spectare* to look at, fr. *spectus,* pp. of *specere* to look — more at SPY] *vi* **1** *archaic* **:** WAIT, STAY **2 :** to look forward **3 :** to be pregnant ~ *vt* **1** *archaic* **:** to wait for **2 :** SUPPOSE, THINK **3 :** to anticipate or look forward to the coming or occurrence of ⟨~*ed* a telephone call⟩ **4 a :** to consider probable or certain ⟨~ to be forgiven⟩ **b :** to consider reasonable, due, or necessary ⟨he ~*ed* respect from his students⟩ **c :** to consider bound in duty or obligated ⟨they ~*ed* him to pay his dues⟩ — **ex·pect·able** \-ˈspek-tə-bəl\ *adj* — **ex·pect·ably** \-blē\ *adv* — **ex·pect·ed·ly** *adv* — **ex·pect·ed·ness** *n*

syn EXPECT, LOOK, HOPE, AWAIT *shared meaning element* **:** to anticipate in the mind some occurrence or outcome ***ant*** despair (*of*)

ex·pec·tance \ik-ˈspek-tən(t)s\ *n* **:** EXPECTANCY

ex·pec·tan·cy \-tən-sē\ *n, pl* **-cies 1 a :** the act, action, or state of expecting **b :** the state of being expected **2 a :** something expected **b :** the expected amount (as of the number of years of life) based on statistical probability

¹ex·pec·tant \-tənt\ *adj* **1 :** characterized by expectation **2 :** expecting the birth of a child — **ex·pec·tant·ly** *adv*

²expectant *n* **:** one who is expectant; *esp* **:** a candidate for a position

ex·pec·ta·tion \ˌek-ˌspek-ˈtā-shən, ik-\ *n* **1 :** the act or state of expecting **:** ANTICIPATION ⟨had given rise to a general ~ of their marriage —Jane Austen⟩ **2 a :** something expected **b :** prospects of inheritance — usu. used in pl. **3 :** the state of being expected **4 a :** EXPECTANCY 2b **b :** EXPECTED VALUE

ex·pec·ta·tive \ik-ˈspek-tət-iv\ *adj* **:** of, relating to, or constituting an object of expectation

expected value *n* **:** the mean value of a random variable

ex·pec·to·rant \ik-ˈspek-t(ə-)rənt\ *adj* **:** tending to promote discharge of mucus from the respiratory tract — **expectorant** *n*

ex·pec·to·rate \-tə-ˌrāt\ *vb* **-rat·ed; -rat·ing** [prob. fr. (assumed) NL *expectoratus,* pp. of *expectorare,* fr. L, to cast out of the mind, fr. *ex-* + *pector-, pectus* breast, soul — more at PECTORAL] *vt* **1 :** to eject from the throat or lungs by coughing or hawking and spitting **2 :** SPIT ~ *vi* **1 :** to discharge matter from the throat or lungs by coughing or hawking and spitting **2 :** SPIT — **ex·pec·to·ra·tion** \-ˌspek-tə-ˈrā-shən\ *n*

ex·pe·di·ence \ik-ˈspēd-ē-ən(t)s\ *n* **:** EXPEDIENCY

ex·pe·di·en·cy \-ən-sē\ *n, pl* **-cies 1** *obs* **:** HASTE, DISPATCH **2 :** the quality or state of being suited to the end in view **:** SUITABILITY, FITNESS **3 :** cultivation of or adherence to expedient means and methods ⟨put more emphasis on ~ than on principle —W. H. Jones⟩ **4 :** a means of achieving a particular end **:** EXPEDIENT — **ex·pe·di·en·tial** \-ˌspēd-ē-ˈen-chəl\ *adj*

¹ex·pe·di·ent \ik-ˈspēd-ē-ənt\ *adj* [ME, fr. MF or L; MF, fr. L *expedient-, expediens* prp. of *expedire* to extricate, arrange, be advantageous, fr. *ex-* + *ped-, pes* foot — more at FOOT] **1 :** suitable for achieving a particular end **2 :** characterized by concern with what is opportune; *specif* **:** governed by self-interest — **ex·pe·di·ent·ly** *adv*

syn EXPEDIENT, POLITIC, ADVISABLE *shared meaning element* **:** dictated by practical or prudential motives ***ant*** inexpedient

²expedient *n* **1 :** something expedient **:** a means to an end **2 :** a means devised or used in an exigency **:** MAKESHIFT ***syn*** see RESOURCE

ex·pe·dite \ˈek-spə-ˌdīt\ *vt* **-dit·ed; -dit·ing** [L *expeditus,* pp. of *expedire*] **1 :** to execute promptly **2 :** to accelerate the process or progress of **:** FACILITATE ⟨the new representatives should ~ the passage of the bill⟩ **3 :** to send out **:** DISPATCH

ex·pe·dit·er *also* **ex·pe·di·tor** \-ˌdīt-ər\ *n* **:** one that expedites; *specif* **:** one employed to ensure adequate supplies of raw materials and equipment or to coordinate the flow of materials, tools, parts, and processed goods within a plant

ex·pe·di·tion \ˌek-spə-ˈdish-ən\ *n* **1 a :** a journey or excursion undertaken for a specific purpose **b :** the group of persons making such a journey **2 :** efficient promptness **:** SPEED **3 :** a sending or setting forth ***syn*** see HASTE ***ant*** procrastination

ex·pe·di·tion·ary \-ˈdish-ə-ˌner-ē\ *adj* **:** of, relating to, or constituting an expedition; *also* **:** sent on military service abroad ⟨an ~ force⟩

ex·pe·di·tious \ˌek-spə-ˈdish-əs\ *adj* **:** characterized by or acting with promptness and efficiency **:** SPEEDY ***syn*** see FAST ***ant*** sluggish — **ex·pe·di·tious·ly** *adv* — **ex·pe·di·tious·ness** *n*

ex·pel \ik-ˈspel\ *vt* **ex·pelled; ex·pel·ling** [ME *expellen,* fr. L *expellere,* fr. *ex-* + *pellere* to drive — more at FELT] **1 :** to force out from or as if from a receptacle ⟨the well *expelled* great quantities of gas⟩ **2 :** to drive away; *esp* **:** DEPORT **3 :** to cut off from membership ⟨*expelled* from college⟩ ***syn*** see EJECT ***ant*** admit — **ex·pel·la·ble** \-ˈspel-ə-bəl\ *adj* — **ex·pel·ler** *n*

ex·pel·lee \ˌek-ˌspel-ˈē, ik-\ *n* **:** one who is expelled; *specif* **:** one transferred from the country of residence for resettlement in the country with which he is ethnically associated

ex·pend \ik-ˈspend\ *vt* [ME *expenden,* fr. L *expendere* to weigh out, expend, fr. *ex-* + *pendere* to weigh — more at SPAN] **1 :** to pay out **:** SPEND ⟨the social services upon which public revenue is ~*ed* — J. A. Hobson⟩ **2 :** to consume by use **:** use up ⟨projects on which he ~*ed* great energy⟩ — **ex·pend·er** *n*

¹ex·pend·able \ik-ˈspen-də-bəl\ *adj* **:** that may be expended: as **a :** normally used up or consumed in service ⟨~ supplies like pencils and paper⟩ **b :** more economically replaced than rescued, salvaged, or protected — **ex·pend·abil·i·ty** \-ˌspen-də-ˈbil-ət-ē\ *n*

²expendable *n* **:** one that is expendable — usu. used in pl.

ex·pen·di·ture \ik-ˈspen-di-chər, -də-ˌchu̇(ə)r, -də-ˌt(y)u̇(ə)r\ *n* [irreg. fr. *expend*] **1 :** the act or process of expending ⟨renovations required an ~ of several thousand dollars⟩ **2 :** something expended **:** DISBURSEMENT, EXPENSE

¹ex·pense \ik-ˈspen(t)s\ *n* [ME, fr. AF or LL; AF, fr. LL *expensa,* fr. L, fem. of *expensus,* pp. of *expendere*] **1 a** *archaic* **:** the act or practice of expending money **:** SPENDING **b (1)** *archaic* **:** the act or process of using up **:** CONSUMPTION **(2)** *obs* **:** LOSS **2 a :** something expended to secure a benefit or bring about a result **b :** financial burden or outlay **:** COST ⟨he built the monument at his own ~⟩ **c :** the charges incurred by an employee in connection with the performance of his duties — usu. used in pl. **d :** an item of business outlay chargeable against revenue for a specific period **3 :** a cause or occasion of expenditure ⟨an estate is a great ~⟩ **4 :** SACRIFICE — usu. used in the phrase *at the expense of* ⟨develop a boy's physique at the ~ of his intelligence —Bertrand Russell⟩

²expense *vt* **ex·pensed; ex·pens·ing 1 :** to charge with expenses **2 a :** to charge to an expense account **b :** to write off as an expense

expense account *n* **:** an account of expenses reimbursable to an employee

ex·pen·sive \ik-ˈspen(t)-siv\ *adj* **1 :** involving expense ⟨an ~ hobby⟩ **2 :** commanding a high price and esp. one that is not based on intrinsic worth or is beyond a prospective buyer's means ***syn*** see COSTLY ***ant*** inexpensive — **ex·pen·sive·ly** *adv* — **ex·pen·sive·ness** *n*

¹ex·pe·ri·ence \ik-ˈspir-ē-ən(t)s\ *n* [ME, fr. MF, fr. L *experientia* act of trying, fr. *experient-, experiens,* prp. of *experiri* to try, fr. *ex-* + *-periri* (akin to *periculum* attempt) — more at FEAR] **1 a :** the usu. conscious perception or apprehension of reality or of an external, bodily, or psychic event **b :** facts or events or the totality of facts or events observed **2 a :** direct participation in events **b :** the state or result of being engaged in an activity or in affairs ⟨business ~⟩ **c :** knowledge, skill, or practice derived from direct observation of or participation in events **3 a :** the conscious events that make up an individual life **b :** the events that make up the conscious past of a community or nation or mankind generally **4 :** something personally encountered, undergone, or lived through

²experience *vt* **-enced; -enc·ing 1 :** to have experience of **:** UNDERGO ⟨*experienced* severe hardships as a child⟩ **2 :** to learn by experience ⟨I have *experienced* that a landscape and the sky unfold the deepest beauty —Nathaniel Hawthorne⟩ — **experience religion :** to undergo religious conversion

ex·pe·ri·enced \-ən(t)st\ *adj* **:** made skillful or wise through observation of or participation in a particular activity or in affairs generally **:** PRACTICED ⟨an ~ driver⟩

ex·pe·ri·en·tial \ik-ˌspir-ē-ˈen-chəl\ *adj* **:** derived from, based on, or relating to experience **:** EMPIRICAL — **ex·pe·ri·en·tial·ly** \-ˈench-(ə-)lē\ *adv*

¹ex·per·i·ment \ik-ˈsper-ə-mənt *also* -ˈspir-\ *n* [ME, fr. MF, fr. L *experimentum,* fr. *experiri*] **1 a :** TEST, TRIAL ⟨make another ~ of his suspicion —Shak.⟩ **b :** a tentative procedure or policy **c :** an operation carried out under controlled conditions in order to discover an unknown effect or law, to test or establish a hypothesis, or to illustrate a known law **2** *obs* **:** EXPERIENCE **3 :** the process of testing **:** EXPERIMENTATION

²ex·per·i·ment \-ˌment\ *vi* **:** to carry out experiments — **ex·per·i·men·ta·tion** \ik-ˌsper-ə-mən-ˈtā-shən, -ˌmen- *also* -ˌspir-\ *n* — **ex·per·i·ment·er** \-ˈsper-ə-ˌment-ər *also* -ˈspir-\ *n*

ex·per·i·men·tal \ik-ˌsper-ə-ˈment-ᵊl *also* -ˌspir-\ *adj* **1 :** of, relating to, or based on experience **:** EMPIRICAL **2 :** founded on or derived from experiment ⟨the heart of the ~ method is the direct control of the thing studied —B. F. Skinner⟩ **3 a :** serving the ends of or used as a means of experimentation ⟨an ~ school⟩ **b :** relating to or having the characteristics of experiment **:** TENTATIVE ⟨still in the ~ stage⟩ — **ex·per·i·men·tal·ly** \-ᵊl-ē\ *adv*

ex·per·i·men·tal·ism \-ᵊl-ˌiz-əm\ *n* **:** reliance on or advocacy of experimental or empirical principles and procedures; *specif* **:** INSTRUMENTALISM

ə abut	ᵊ kitten	ər further	a back	ā bake	ä cot, cart
au̇ out	ch chin	e less	ē easy	g gift	i trip	ī life
j joke	ŋ sing	ō flow	ȯ flaw	ȯi coin	th thin	t͟h this
ü loot	u̇ foot	y yet	yü few	yu̇ furious	zh vision

ex·per·i·men·tal·ist \-ᵊl-əst\ *n* : one who experiments; *specif* : a person conducting scientific experiments

experiment station *n* : an establishment for scientific research (as in agriculture) where experiments are carried out, studies of practical application are made, and information is disseminated

¹ex·pert \'ek-,spərt, ik-'\ *adj* [ME, fr. MF & L; MF, fr. L *expertus*, fr. pp. of *experiri*] **1** *obs* : EXPERIENCED **2** : having, involving, or displaying special skill or knowledge derived from training or experience **syn** see PROFICIENT **ant** amateurish — **ex·pert·ly** *adv* — **ex·pert·ness** *n*

²ex·pert \'ek-,spərt\ *n* [F, fr. *expert*, adj.] : one who has acquired special skill in or knowledge of a particular subject : AUTHORITY

³ex·pert \'ek-,spərt\ *vt* : to serve as an expert for ~ *vi* : to serve as an expert

ex·per·tise \,ek-(,)spər-'tēz *also* -'tēs\ *n* [F, fr. MF, expertness, fr. *expert*] **1** : expert opinion or commentary **2** : skill in a particular field : KNOW-HOW ⟨technical ~⟩

ex·pert·ism \'ek-,spərt-,iz-əm\ *n* : EXPERTISE 2

ex·pert·ize \'ek-spər-,tīz\ *vb* **-ized; -iz·ing** *vi* : to give a professional opinion usu. after careful study ~ *vt* : to examine and give expert judgment on

ex·pi·a·ble \'ek-spē-ə-bəl\ *adj* : capable of being expiated

ex·pi·ate \'ek-spē-,āt\ *vb* **-at·ed; -at·ing** [L *expiatus*, pp. of *expiare* to atone for, fr. *ex-* + *piare* to atone for, appease — more at PIOUS] *vt* **1** *obs* : to put an end to **2 a** : to extinguish the guilt incurred by **b** : to pay the penalty for **c** : to make amends for ⟨permission to ~ their offences by their assiduous labours —Francis Bacon⟩ ~ *vi* : to make expiation — **ex·pi·a·tor** \-,āt-ər\ *n*

ex·pi·a·tion \,ek-spē-'ā-shən\ *n* **1** : the act of making atonement **2** : the means by which atonement is made

ex·pi·a·to·ry \'ek-spē-ə-,tōr-ē, -,tōr-\ *adj* : serving to expiate

ex·pi·ra·tion \,ek-spə-'rā-shən\ *n* **1 a** : the act or process of releasing air from the lungs through the nose or mouth **b** *archaic* : the last emission of breath : DEATH **2** : the fact of coming to an end : TERMINATION **3** : something produced by breathing out

ex·pi·ra·to·ry \ik-'spī-rə-,tōr-ē, ek-', -,tōr-; 'ek-sp(ə-)rə-\ *adj* : of, relating to, or employed in the expiration of air from the lungs

ex·pire \ik-'spī(ə)r, *oftenest for vi 3 and vt 2* ek-'\ *vb* **ex·pired; ex·pir·ing** [ME *expiren*, fr. MF or L; MF *expirer*, fr. L *exspirare*, fr. *ex-* + *spirare* to breathe — more at SPIRIT] *vi* **1** : to breathe one's last breath : DIE **2** : to come to an end ⟨his term of office ~s this year⟩ **3** : to emit the breath ~ *vt* **1** *obs* : CONCLUDE **2** : to breathe out from or as if from the lungs **3** *archaic* : to give out

ex·pi·ry \ik-'spī(ə)r-ē, 'ek-spə-rē\ *n, pl* **-ries 1 a** : exhalation of breath : DEATH **2** : TERMINATION; *esp* : the termination of a time or period fixed by law, contract, or agreement

ex·plain \ik-'splān\ *vb* [ME *explanen*, fr. L *explanare*, lit., to make level, fr. *ex-* + *planus* level, flat — more at FLOOR] *vt* **1** : to make plain or understandable ⟨a commentary that ~s the more difficult passages of the poem⟩ **2** : to give the reason for or cause of ⟨unable to ~ his conduct⟩ **3** : to show the logical development or relationships of ~ *vi* : to make something plain or understandable — **ex·plain·able** \-'splā-nə-bəl\ *adj* — **ex·plain·er** *n* **syn** EXPLAIN, EXPOUND, EXPLICATE, ELUCIDATE, INTERPRET *shared meaning element* : to make something clear or understandable — **explain oneself** : to clarify one's statements or the reasons for one's conduct

explain away *vt* **1** : to get rid of by or as if by explanation **2** : to minimize the significance of by or as if by explanation ⟨evidence which it was hard to *explain away* —A. G. N. Flew⟩

ex·pla·na·tion \,ek-splə-'nā-shən\ *n* **1** : the act or process of explaining **2** : something that explains ⟨the ~s offered for mistakes followed a set pattern —V. G. Heiser⟩ **3** : a mutual discussion designed to correct a misunderstanding or reconcile differences

ex·plan·a·tive \ik-'splan-ət-iv\ *adj* : EXPLANATORY — **ex·plan·a·tive·ly** *adv*

ex·plan·a·to·ry \ik-'splan-ə-,tōr-ē, -,tōr-\ *adj* : serving or disposed to explain ⟨~ notes⟩ — **ex·plan·a·to·ri·ly** \-,splan-ə-'tōr-ə-lē, -'tōr-\ *adv*

¹ex·plant \(')ek-'splant\ *vt* [*ex-* + *-plant* (as in *implant*)] : to remove (living tissue) esp. to a medium for tissue culture — **ex·plan·ta·tion** \,ek-,splan-'tā-shən\ *n*

²ex·plant \'ek-,splant\ *n* : living tissue removed from an organism and placed in a medium for tissue culture

¹ex·ple·tive \'ek-splət-iv\ *adj* [LL *expletivus*, fr. L *expletus*, pp. of *explēre* to fill out, fr. *ex-* + *plēre* to fill — more at FULL] **1** : serving to fill up ⟨~ phrases⟩ **2** : marked by the use of expletives

²expletive *n* **1 a** : a syllable, word, or phrase inserted to fill a vacancy (as in a sentence or a metrical line) without adding to the sense; *esp* : a word (as *it* in "make it clear which you prefer") that occupies the position of the subject or object of a verb in normal English word order and anticipates a subsequent word or phrase that supplies the needed meaningful content **b** : an exclamatory word or phrase; *esp* : one that is obscene or profane **2** : one that serves as a filler

ex·ple·to·ry \'ek-splə-,tōr-ē, -,tōr-\ *adj* : EXPLETIVE

ex·pli·ca·ble \ek-'splik-ə-bəl, 'ek-splik-\ *adj* : capable of being explained — **ex·pli·ca·bly** \-blē\ *adv*

ex·pli·cate \'ek-splə-,kāt\ *vt* **-cat·ed; -cat·ing** [L *explicatus*, pp. of *explicare*, lit., to unfold, fr. *ex-* + *plicare* to fold — more at PLY] **1** : to give a detailed explanation of **2** : to develop the implications of : analyze logically **syn** see EXPLAIN — **ex·pli·ca·tion** \,ek-splə-'kā-shən\ *n* — **ex·pli·ca·tor** \'ek-splə-,kāt-ər\ *n*

ex·pli·ca·tion de texte \,ek-splē-,kä-syōⁿ-də-'tekst\ *n, pl* **explications de texte** *same*\ [F, lit., explanation of text] : a method of literary criticism involving a detailed analysis of each part of a work

¹ex·pli·ca·tive \ek-'splik-ət-iv, 'ek-splə-,kāt-\ *adj* : serving to explicate : EXPLANATORY; *specif* : serving to explain logically what is contained in the subject ⟨an ~ proposition⟩ — **ex·pli·ca·tive·ly** *adv*

²explicative *n* : an explicative expression

ex·pli·ca·to·ry \ek-'splik-ə-,tōr-ē, -,tōr-, 'ek-(,)splik-, -,tōr-\ *adj* : EXPLICATIVE

ex·plic·it \ik-'splis-ət\ *adj* [F or ML; F *explicite*, fr. ML *explicitus*, fr. L, pp. of *explicare*] **1 a** : free from all vagueness and ambiguity ⟨an ~ statement of the problem⟩ **b** : fully developed or formulated ⟨an ~ statement of his objectives⟩ **2** : unreserved and unambiguous in expression **3** : externally visible **4** : involving direct payment ⟨~ costs⟩ — **ex·plic·it·ly** *adv* — **ex·plic·it·ness** *n* **syn** EXPLICIT, EXPRESS, SPECIFIC, DEFINITE *shared meaning element* : perfectly clear and unambiguous **ant** ambiguous

explicit function *n* : a mathematical function defined by an expression containing only independent variables — compare IMPLICIT FUNCTION

ex·plode \ik-'splōd\ *vb* **ex·plod·ed; ex·plod·ing** [L *explodere* to drive off the stage by clapping, fr. *ex-* + *plaudere* to clap] *vt* **1** *archaic* : to drive from the stage by noisy disapproval **2** : to bring into disrepute or discredit ⟨~ a rumor⟩ **3** : to cause to explode or burst noisily ⟨~ dynamite⟩ ⟨~ a bomb⟩ ~ *vi* **1** : to burst forth with sudden violence or noise ⟨~ with anger⟩ **2 a** : to undergo a rapid chemical or nuclear reaction with the production of noise, heat, and violent expansion of gases ⟨dynamite ~s⟩ ⟨an atomic bomb ~s⟩ **b** : to burst violently as a result of pressure from within — **ex·plod·er** *n*

ex·plod·ed *adj* : showing the parts separated but in correct relationship to each other ⟨an ~ view of a carburetor⟩

ex·plod·ent \ik-'splōd-ᵊnt\ *n* [L *explodent-, explodens*, prp. of *explodere*] : EXPLOSIVE

¹ex·ploit \'ek-,splȯit, ik-'\ *n* [ME, outcome, success, fr. OF, fr. L *explicitum*, neut. of *explicitus*, pp.] : DEED, ACT; *esp* : a notable or heroic act **syn** see FEAT

²ex·ploit \ik-'splȯit, 'ek-,\ *vt* **1 a** : to turn to economic account ⟨~ a mine⟩ **b** : to take advantage of : UTILIZE ⟨~ing the qualities of the material⟩ **2** : to make use of meanly or unjustly for one's own advantage ⟨~s his friends⟩ — **ex·ploit·able** \-ə-bəl\ — **ex·ploit·er** *n*

ex·ploi·ta·tion \,ek-,splȯi-'tā-shən\ *n* **1** : an act of exploiting: as **a** : utilization or working of a natural resource **b** : an unjust or improper use of another person for one's own profit or advantage **c** : coaction between organisms in which one is benefited at the expense of the other **2** : PUBLICITY, ADVERTISING — **ex·ploit·ative** \ik-'splȯit-ət-iv\ *adj* — **ex·ploit·ative·ly** *adv*

ex·ploit·ive \ik-'splȯit-iv\ *adj* : of or relating to exploitation

ex·plo·ra·tion \,ek-splə-'rā-shən, -,splō-\ *n* : the act or an instance of exploring — **ex·plo·ra·tion·al** \-shnəl, -shən-ᵊl\ *adj*

ex·plor·a·tive \ik-'splȯr-ət-iv, -'splȯr-\ *adj* : EXPLORATORY — **ex·plor·a·tive·ly** *adv*

ex·plor·a·to·ry \-ə-,tōr-ē, -,tōr-\ *adj* : of or relating to exploration ⟨~ surgery⟩

ex·plore \ik-'splō(ə)r, -'splȯ(ə)r\ *vb* **ex·plored; ex·plor·ing** [L *explorare*, fr. *ex-* + *plorare* to cry out; prob. fr. the outcry of hunters on sighting game] *vt* **1** *obs* : to seek for or after **2 a** : to search through or into ⟨~ the possibilities of reaching an agreement⟩ **b** : to examine minutely esp. for diagnostic purposes **c** : to penetrate into or range over for purposes of geographical discovery ~ *vi* : to make or conduct a systematic search ⟨~ for oil⟩

ex·plor·er \ik-'splōr-ər, -'splȯr-\ *n* : one that explores; *esp* : a person who travels in search of geographical or scientific information

ex·plo·si·ble \ik-'splō-zə-bəl, -'splō-sə-\ *adj* : capable of being exploded — **ex·plo·si·bil·i·ty** \-,splō-zə-'bil-ət-ē, -sə-\ *n*

ex·plo·sion \ik-'splō-zhən\ *n* [L *explosion-, explosio* act of driving off by clapping, fr. *explosus*, pp. of *explodere*] **1** : the act or an instance of exploding: as **a** : a large-scale, rapid, and spectacular expansion, outbreak, or upheaval ⟨the population ~⟩ **b** : a violent outburst of feeling **2** : the release of occluded breath that occurs in one kind of articulation of stop consonants

¹ex·plo·sive \ik-'splō-siv, -ziv\ *adj* **1** : relating to, characterized by, or operated by explosion ⟨an ~ engine⟩ **2** : tending to explode ⟨an ~ person⟩ — **ex·plo·sive·ly** *adv* — **ex·plo·sive·ness** *n*

²explosive *n* **1** : an explosive substance **2** : a consonant characterized by explosion in its articulation when it occurs in certain environments : STOP

ex·po \'ek-(,)spō\ *n, pl* **expos** : EXPOSITION 3b

ex·po·nent \ik-'spō-nənt, 'ek-,\ *n* [L *exponent-, exponens*, prp. of *exponere*] **1** : a symbol written above and to the right of a mathematical expression to indicate the operation of raising to a power ⟨in the expression a^3, the ~ 3 indicates that a is to be multiplied by itself twice⟩ **2 a** : one that expounds or interprets **b** : one that champions, advocates, or exemplifies

ex·po·nen·tial \,ek-spə-'nen-chəl\ *adj* **1** : of or relating to an exponent **2** : involving a variable in an exponent ⟨10^x is an ~ expression⟩ **3** : expressible or approximately expressible by an exponential equation ⟨an ~ growth rate⟩ — **ex·po·nen·tial·ly** \-'nench-(ə-)lē\ *adv*

exponential equation *n* : an equation involving an exponential function of a variable

exponential function *n* : a mathematical function in which an independent variable appears in one of the exponents — called also *exponential*

ex·po·nen·ti·a·tion \,ek-spə-,nen-chē-'ā-shən\ *n* [*exponent* + *-iation* (as in *differentiation*)] : INVOLUTION 2

¹ex·port \ek-'spō(ə)rt, -'spȯ(ə)rt, 'ek-,\ *vb* [L *exportare*, fr. *ex-* + *portare* to carry — more at FARE] *vt* **1** : to carry away : REMOVE **2** : to carry or send (as a commodity) to some other place (as another country) ~ *vi* : to export something abroad — **ex·port·abil·i·ty** \(,)ek-,spȯrt-ə-'bil-ət-ē, -,spȯrt-\ *n* — **ex·port·able** \ek-'spȯrt-ə-bəl, -'spȯrt-, 'ek-,\ *adj*

²ex·port \'ek-,spō(ə)rt, -,spȯ(ə)rt\ *n* **1** : something exported; *specif* : a commodity conveyed from one country or region to another for purposes of trade **2** : an act of exporting : EXPORTATION ⟨the ~ of wheat⟩

³export \'ek-,\ *adj* : of or relating to exportation or exports ⟨~ duties⟩

ex·por·ta·tion \,ek-,spȯr-'tā-shən, -,spȯr-, -spər-\ *n* : an act of exporting; *also* : a commodity exported

ex·port·er \ek-ˈspōrt-ər, -ˈspȯrt-, ˈek-ˌ\ *n* : one that exports; *specif* : a wholesaler who sells to merchants or industrial consumers in foreign countries
ex·pose \ik-ˈspōz\ *vt* **ex·posed; ex·pos·ing** [ME *exposen,* fr. MF *exposer,* fr. L *exponere* to set forth, explain (perf. indic. *exposui*), fr. *ex-* + *ponere* to put, place — more at POSITION] **1 a** : to deprive of shelter, protection, or care ⟨~ troops needlessly⟩ **b** : to submit or subject to an action or influence; *specif* : to subject (a sensitive photographic film, plate, or paper) to the action of radiant energy **c** : to abandon (an infant) esp. by leaving in the open : DESERT **2** : to lay open to view: as **a** : to offer publicly for sale **b** : to exhibit for public veneration **c** : to reveal the face of (a playing card) **3 a** : to bring to light (as something shameful) : UNMASK **b** : to disclose the faults or crimes of ⟨~ a murderer⟩ — **ex·pos·er** *n*
ex·po·sé *or* **ex·po·se** \ˌek-spō-ˈzā, -spə-\ *n* [F *exposé,* fr. pp. of *exposer*] **1** : a formal recital or exposition of facts : STATEMENT **2** : an exposure of something discreditable ⟨a newspaper ~ of crime conditions⟩
ex·posed \ik-ˈspōzd\ *adj* **1** : open to view ⟨an ~ card⟩ **2** : not shielded or protected ⟨an ~ electric wire⟩
ex·pos·it \ik-ˈspäz-ət\ *vt* [L *expositus,* pp. of *exponere*] : EXPOUND
ex·po·si·tion \ˌek-spə-ˈzish-ən\ *n* **1** : a setting forth of the meaning or purpose (as of a writing) **2 a** : discourse or an example of it designed to convey information or explain what is difficult to understand **b** (1) : the first part of a musical composition in sonata form in which the thematic material of the movement is presented (2) : the opening section of a fugue **3** : an act or an instance of exposing: as **a** : abandonment of an infant **b** : a public exhibition or show — **ex·po·si·tion·al** \-ˈzish-nəl, -ən-ᵊl\ *adj*
ex·pos·i·tive \ik-ˈspäz-ət-iv\ *adj* : DESCRIPTIVE, EXPOSITORY
ex·pos·i·tor \-ət-ər\ *n* [ME *expositour,* fr. MF *expositeur,* fr. LL *expositor,* fr. L *expositus*] : one who expounds or explains : COMMENTATOR
ex·pos·i·to·ry \-ə-ˌtōr-ē, -ˌtȯr-\ *adj* : of, relating to, or containing exposition ⟨~ writing⟩
¹ex post fac·to \ˌek-ˌspōst-ˈfak-(ˌ)tō\ *adj* [LL, from a thing done afterward] **1** : done, made, or formulated after the fact ⟨*ex post facto* approval⟩ **2** : disregarding or altering the previous status or setting of the event or thing concerning which a conclusion is reached or at which action is directed ⟨*ex post facto* laws⟩
²ex post facto *adv* : after the fact : RETROACTIVELY
ex·pos·tu·late \ik-ˈspäs-chə-ˌlāt\ *vb* [L *expostulatus,* pp. of *expostulare* to demand, dispute, fr. *ex-* + *postulare* to ask for — more at POSTULATE] *vt, obs* : DISCUSS, EXAMINE ~ *vi* : to reason earnestly with a person for purposes of dissuasion or remonstrance ***syn*** see OBJECT
ex·pos·tu·la·tion \-ˌspäs-chə-ˈlā-shən\ *n* : an act or an instance of expostulating : REMONSTRANCE ⟨all his ~*s* proved futile⟩ — **ex·pos·tu·la·to·ry** \-ˈspäs-chə-lə-ˌtōr-ē, -ˌtȯr-\ *adj*
ex·po·sure \ik-ˈspō-zhər\ *n* **1** : the act or an instance of exposing: as **a** : disclosure to view ⟨skillful ~ of goods in a store window⟩ **b** (1) : a disclosure esp. of a weakness or something shameful or criminal : UNMASKING ⟨continued his ~ of electoral frauds⟩ (2) : PRESENTATION, EXPOSITION **c** : an act of abandoning esp. in the open **d** (1) : the act of exposing a sensitized photographic material (2) : a section of a film for an individual picture (3) : the total amount of light or other radiant energy received per unit area on the sensitized material usu. expressed for cameras in terms of the time and the lens *f*-number **2 a** : a condition or an instance of being exposed; *specif* : the condition of being exposed to the elements **b** : a position with respect to the points of the compass or to climatic or weather influences ⟨a house with a western ~⟩
exposure meter *n* : a device for indicating correct photographic exposure under varying conditions of illumination
ex·pound \ik-ˈspau̇nd\ *vb* [ME *expounden,* fr. MF *expondre,* fr. L *exponere* to explain — more at EXPOSE] *vt* **1 a** : to set forth : STATE **b** : to defend with argument **2** : to explain by setting forth in careful and often elaborate detail ⟨~ a law⟩ ~ *vi* : to make a statement ***syn*** see EXPLAIN — **ex·pound·er** *n*
¹ex·press \ik-ˈspres\ *adj* [ME, fr. MF *expres,* fr. L *expressus,* pp. of *exprimere* to press out, express, fr. *ex-* + *premere* to press — more at PRESS] **1 a** : directly, firmly, and explicitly stated ⟨he disobeyed my ~ orders⟩ **b** : EXACT, PRECISE **2 a** : designed for or adapted to its purpose **b** : of a particular sort : SPECIFIC ⟨he came for that ~ purpose⟩ **3 a** : traveling at high speed; *specif* : traveling with few or no stops along the way ⟨~ train⟩ **b** : adapted or suitable for travel at high speed ⟨an ~ highway⟩ **c** *Brit* : designated to be delivered without delay by special messenger ⟨~ mail⟩ ***syn*** see EXPLICIT
²express *adv* **1** *obs* : EXPRESSLY **2** : by express ⟨send a package ~⟩
³express *n* **1 a** *Brit* : a messenger sent on a special errand **b** *Brit* : a dispatch conveyed by a special messenger **c** (1) : a system for the prompt and safe transportation of parcels, money, or goods at rates higher than standard freight charges (2) : a company operating such a merchandise freight service (3) : the goods or shipments so transported **d** *Brit* : SPECIAL DELIVERY **2** : an express vehicle
⁴express *vt* [ME *expressen,* fr. MF & L; MF *expresser,* fr. OF, fr. *expres,* adj., fr. L *expressus,* pp.] **1 a** : DELINEATE, DEPICT **b** : to represent in words : STATE **c** : to give or convey a true impression of : SHOW, REFLECT **d** : to make known the opinions or feelings of (oneself) ⟨~*ed* himself very strongly on that subject⟩ **e** : to give expression to the artistic or creative impulses or abilities of (oneself) **f** : to represent by a sign or symbol : SYMBOLIZE **2 a** : to force out (as the juice of a fruit) by pressure **b** : to subject to pressure so as to extract something **3** : to send by express — **ex·press·er** *n* — **ex·press·ible** \-ə-bəl\ *adj*
syn EXPRESS, VENT, UTTER, VOICE, BROACH, AIR *shared meaning element* : to let out what one thinks or feels ***ant*** imply
ex·press·age \ik-ˈspres-ij\ *n* : a carrying of parcels by express; *also* : a charge for such carrying
ex·pres·sion \ik-ˈspresh-ən\ *n* **1 a** : an act, process, or instance of representing in a medium (as words) : UTTERANCE ⟨freedom of ~⟩ **b** (1) : something that manifests, embodies, or symbolizes something else ⟨this gift is an ~ of my admiration for you⟩ (2) : a significant word or phrase (3) : a mathematical or logical symbol or a meaningful combination of symbols (4) : the detectable effect of a gene; *also* : EXPRESSIVITY **2 a** : a mode, means, or use of significant representation or symbolism; *esp* : felicitous or vivid indication or depiction of mood or sentiment ⟨read the poem with ~⟩ **b** (1) : the quality or fact of being expressive (2) : facial aspect or vocal intonation as indicative of feeling **3** : an act or product of pressing out — **ex·pres·sion·al** \-ˈspresh-nəl, -ən-ᵊl\ *adj*
ex·pres·sion·ism \ik-ˈspresh-ə-ˌniz-əm\ *n* : a theory or practice in art of seeking to depict not objective reality but the subjective emotions and responses that objects and events arouse in the artist — **ex·pres·sion·ist** \-ˈspresh-(ə-)nəst\ *n or adj* — **ex·pres·sion·is·tic** \-ˌspresh-ə-ˈnis-tik\ *adj* — **ex·pres·sion·is·ti·cal·ly** \-ti-k(ə-)lē\ *adv*
ex·pres·sion·less \ik-ˈspresh-ən-ləs\ *adj* : lacking expression ⟨an ~ face⟩ — **ex·pres·sion·less·ly** *adv* — **ex·pres·sion·less·ness** *n*
ex·pres·sive \ik-ˈspres-iv\ *adj* **1** : of or relating to expression ⟨the ~ function of language⟩ **2** : serving to express, utter, or represent ⟨he used foul and novel terms ~ of rage —H. G. Wells⟩ **3** : full of expression : SIGNIFICANT ⟨an ~ silence⟩ — **ex·pres·sive·ly** *adv* — **ex·pres·sive·ness** *n*
ex·pres·siv·i·ty \ˌek-ˌspres-ˈiv-ət-ē\ *n, pl* **-ties** **1** : the relative capacity of a gene to affect the phenotype of the organism of which it is a part **2** : the quality of being expressive
ex·press·ly \ik-ˈspres-lē\ *adv* **1** : in an express manner : EXPLICITLY ⟨he ~ rejected socialism⟩ **2** : for the express purpose : PARTICULARLY ⟨needed a clinic ~ for the treatment of addicts⟩
ex·press·man \ik-ˈspres-ˌman, -mən\ *n* : a person employed in the express business
ex·press·way \ik-ˈspres-ˌwā\ *n* : a high-speed divided highway for through traffic with access partially or fully controlled and grade separations at important intersections with other roads
ex·pro·pri·ate \ek-ˈsprō-prē-ˌāt\ *vt* **-at·ed; -at·ing** [ML *expropriatus,* pp. of *expropriare,* fr. L *ex-* + *proprius* own] **1** : to deprive of possession or proprietary rights **2** : to transfer (the property of another) to one's own possession ⟨*expropriated* all the land within a 10 mile radius⟩ — **ex·pro·pri·a·tor** \-ˌāt-ər\ *n*
ex·pro·pri·a·tion \(ˌ)ek-ˌsprō-prē-ˈā-shən\ *n* : the act of expropriating or the state of being expropriated; *specif* : the action of the state in taking or modifying the property rights of an individual in the exercise of its sovereignty
expt *abbr* experiment
exptl *abbr* experimental
ex·pulse \ik-ˈspəls\ *vt* **ex·pulsed; ex·puls·ing** : EXPEL
ex·pul·sion \ik-ˈspəl-shən\ *n* [ME, fr. L *expulsion-, expulsio,* fr. *expulsus,* pp. of *expellere* to expel] : the act of expelling : the state of being expelled — **ex·pul·sive** \-ˈpəl-siv\ *adj*
ex·punc·tion \ik-ˈspəŋ(k)-shən\ *n* [L *expunctus,* pp. of *expungere*] : the act of expunging : the state of being expunged : ERASURE
ex·punge \ik-ˈspənj\ *vt* **ex·punged; ex·pung·ing** [L *expungere* to mark for deletion by dots, fr. *ex-* + *pungere* to prick — more at PUNGENT] **1** : to strike out, obliterate, or mark for deletion **2** : to efface completely : DESTROY ***syn*** see ERASE — **ex·pung·er** *n*
ex·pur·gate \ˈek-spər-ˌgāt\ *vt* **-gat·ed; -gat·ing** [L *expurgatus,* pp. of *expurgare,* fr. *ex-* + *purgare* to purge] : to cleanse of something morally harmful, offensive, or erroneous; *esp* : to expunge objectionable parts from before publication or presentation ⟨~ a book⟩ — **ex·pur·ga·tion** \ˌek-spər-ˈgā-shən\ *n* — **ex·pur·ga·tor** \ˈek-spər-ˌgāt-ər\ *n*
ex·pur·ga·to·ri·al \(ˌ)ek-ˌspər-gə-ˈtōr-ē-əl, -ˈtȯr-\ *adj* : relating to expurgation or an expurgator : EXPURGATORY
ex·pur·ga·to·ry \ek-ˈspər-gə-ˌtōr-ē, -ˌtȯr-\ *adj* : serving to purify from something morally harmful, offensive, or erroneous
expy *abbr* expressway
¹ex·qui·site \ek-ˈskwiz-ət, ˈek-(ˌ)\ *adj* [ME *exquisit,* fr. L *exquisitus,* fr. pp. of *exquirere* to search out, fr. *ex-* + *quaerere* to seek] **1** : carefully selected : CHOICE **2** *archaic* : ACCURATE **3 a** : marked by flawless craftsmanship or by beautiful, ingenious, delicate, or elaborate execution **b** : keenly appreciative : DISCRIMINATING ⟨~ taste⟩ **c** : ACCOMPLISHED, PERFECTED ⟨an ~ gentleman⟩ **4 a** : pleasing through beauty, fitness, or perfection ⟨an ~ white blossom⟩ **b** : ACUTE, INTENSE ⟨~ pain⟩ **c** : having uncommon or esoteric appeal ***syn*** see CHOICE — **ex·qui·site·ly** *adv* — **ex·qui·site·ness** *n*
²exquisite *n* : one who is overly fastidious in dress or ornament
exrx *abbr* executrix
ex·san·gui·nate \ek(s)-ˈsaŋ-gwə-ˌnāt\ *vt* **-nat·ed; -nat·ing** [L *exsanguinatus* bloodless, fr. *ex-* + *sanguin-, sanguis* blood] : to drain of blood — **ex·san·gui·na·tion** \(ˌ)ek(s)-ˌsaŋ-gwə-ˈnā-shən\ *n*
ex·scind \ek-ˈsind\ *vt* [L *exscindere,* fr. *ex-* + *scindere* to cut, tear — more at SHED] : to cut off or out : EXCISE
ex·sert \ek-ˈsərt\ *vt* [L *exsertus,* pp. of *exserere* — more at EXERT] : to thrust out — **ex·ser·tile** \-ˈsərt-ᵊl, -ˈsər-ˌtīl\ *adj* — **ex·ser·tion** \-ˈsər-shən\ *n*
ex·sert·ed *adj* : projecting beyond an enclosing organ or part
ex·sic·cate \ˈek-si-ˌkāt\ *vt* **-cat·ed; -cat·ing** [L *exsiccatus,* pp. of *exsiccare,* fr. *ex-* + *siccare* to dry, fr. *siccus* dry — more at SACK] : to remove moisture from : DRY — **ex·sic·ca·tion** \ˌek-si-ˈkā-shən\ *n*
ex·stip·u·late \(ˈ)ek(s)-ˈstip-yə-lət\ *adj* : having no stipules
ext *abbr* **1** extension **2** exterior **3** external **4** externally **5** extra **6** extract

ex·tant \ˈek-stənt; ek-ˈstant, ˈek-,\ *adj* [L *exstant-, exstans,* prp. of *exstare* to stand out, be in existence, fr. *ex-* + *stare* to stand — more at STAND] **1** *archaic* : standing out or above **2 a** : currently or actually existing ⟨~ and projected programs⟩ ⟨the most charming writer ~ —G. W. Johnson⟩ **b** : not destroyed or lost ⟨~ manuscripts⟩

ex·tem·po·ral \ek-ˈstem-p(ə-)rəl\ *adj* [L *extemporalis,* fr. *ex tempore*] *archaic* : EXTEMPORANEOUS — **ex·tem·po·ral·ly** \-ē\ *adv*

ex·tem·po·ra·ne·ity \(ˌ)ek-ˌstem-pə-rə-ˈnē-ət-ē, -ˈnā-\ *n* : the quality or state of being extemporaneous

ex·tem·po·ra·ne·ous \(ˌ)ek-ˌstem-pə-ˈrā-nē-əs\ *adj* [LL *extemporaneus,* fr. L *ex tempore*] **1 a** (1) : composed, performed, or uttered on the spur of the moment : IMPROMPTU (2) : carefully prepared but delivered without notes or text **b** : skilled at or given to extemporaneous utterance **c** : happening suddenly and often unexpectedly and usu. without clearly known causes or relationships ⟨a great deal of criminal and delinquent behavior is . . . ~ —W. C. Reckless⟩ **2** : provided, made, or put to use as an expedient : MAKESHIFT — **ex·tem·po·ra·ne·ous·ly** *adv* — **ex·tem·po·ra·ne·ous·ness** *n*

ex·tem·po·rary \ik-ˈstem-pə-ˌrer-ē\ *adj* : EXTEMPORANEOUS — **ex·tem·po·rar·i·ly** \-ˌstem-pə-ˈrer-ə-lē\ *adv*

ex·tem·po·re \ik-ˈstem-pə-(ˌ)rē\ *adv* [L *ex tempore,* fr. *ex* + *tempore,* abl. of *tempus* time] : in an extemporaneous manner ⟨speaking ~⟩

ex·tem·po·ri·za·tion \ik-ˌstem-pə-rə-ˈzā-shən\ *n* **1** : the act of extemporizing : IMPROVISATION **2** : something extemporized

ex·tem·po·rize \ik-ˈstem-pə-ˌrīz\ *vb* **-rized; -riz·ing** *vi* **1** : to do something extemporaneously : IMPROVISE; *esp* : to speak extemporaneously **2** : to get along in a makeshift manner ~ *vt* : to compose, perform, or utter extemporaneously : IMPROVISE — **ex·tem·po·riz·er** *n*

ex·tend \ik-ˈstend\ *vb* [ME *extenden,* fr. MF or L; MF *estendre,* fr. L *extendere,* fr. *ex-* + *tendere* to stretch — more at THIN] *vt* **1** [ME *extenden,* fr. ML *extendere* (fr. L) or AF *estendre,* fr. OF] **a** *Brit* : to take possession of (as lands) by a writ of extent **b** *obs* : to take by force **2** : to spread or stretch forth : UNBEND ⟨~*ed* both her arms⟩ **3 a** : to stretch out to fullest length **b** : to cause (as a horse) to move at full stride **c** : to exert (oneself) to full capacity ⟨could work long and hard without seeming to ~ himself⟩ **d** (1) : to increase the bulk of (as by the addition of a cheaper substance or a modifier) (2) : ADULTERATE **4 a** : to make the offer of : PROFFER ⟨~*ing* aid to the needy⟩ **b** : to make available ⟨~*ing* credit to customers⟩ **5 a** : to cause to reach (as in distance or scope) ⟨national authority was ~*ed* over new territories⟩ **b** : to cause to be longer : prolong in time ⟨~*ed* their visit another day⟩; *esp* : to prolong the time of payment of **c** : ADVANCE, FURTHER ⟨~*ing* his potential through job training⟩ **6 a** : to cause to be of greater area or volume : ENLARGE **b** : to increase the scope, meaning, or application of : BROADEN ⟨beauty, I suppose, opens the heart, ~*s* the consciousness —Algernon Blackwood⟩ **c** *archaic* : EXAGGERATE ~ *vi* **1** : to stretch out in distance, space, or time : REACH ⟨his jurisdiction ~*ed* over the whole area⟩ **2** : to reach in scope or application ⟨his concern ~*s* beyond mere business to real service to his customers⟩ — **ex·tend·able** *or* **ex·tend·ible** \-ˈsten-də-bəl\ *adj*

syn EXTEND, LENGTHEN, ELONGATE, PROLONG, PROTRACT *shared meaning element* : to draw out or add to so as to increase in length ***ant*** abridge, shorten

ex·tend·ed *adj* **1** : INTENSIVE ⟨~ efforts⟩ **2** : having spatial magnitude : being larger than a point ⟨an ~ source of light⟩ **3** : EXTENSIVE ⟨made available ~ information —Ruth G. Strickland⟩ **4** : DERIVATIVE 1, SECONDARY 2a ⟨an ~ sense of a word⟩ — **ex·tend·ed·ly** *adv* — **ex·tend·ed·ness** *n*

extended family *n* : a family that includes in one household near relatives in addition to a nuclear family

extended play *n* : a 45-rpm phonograph record with a playing time of about 6 to 8 minutes

ex·tend·er \ik-ˈsten-dər\ *n* : one that extends; *esp* : a substance added to a product esp. in the capacity of a diluent, adulterant, or modifier

ex·ten·si·ble \ik-ˈsten(t)-sə-bəl\ *adj* : capable of being extended — **ex·ten·si·bil·i·ty** \-ˌsten(t)-sə-ˈbil-ət-ē\ *n*

ex·ten·sile \ik-ˈsten(t)-səl, -ˈsten-ˌsīl\ *adj* : EXTENSIBLE

ex·ten·sion \ik-ˈsten-chən\ *n* [ME, fr. MF or LL; MF, fr. LL *extension-, extensio,* fr. L *extensus,* pp. of *extendere*] **1 a** : the action of extending : state of being extended **b** : an enlargement in scope or operation ⟨tools are ~*s* of human hands⟩ **2 a** : the total range over which something extends : COMPASS **b** : DENOTATION 2 **3 a** : the stretching of a fractured or luxated limb so as to restore it to its natural position **b** : the unbending of a joint between the bones of a limb by which the angle between the bones is increased — compare FLEXION **4** : a property whereby something occupies space **5** : an increase in length of time; *specif* : an increase in time allowed under agreement or concession ⟨was granted an ~⟩ **6** : a program that geographically extends the educational resources of an institution by special arrangements (as correspondence courses) to persons otherwise unable to take advantage of such resources **7 a** : a part constituting an addition **b** : a section forming an additional length **c** : an extra telephone connected to the principal line **8** : a mathematical set (as a field or group) that includes a given and similar set as a subset

ex·ten·sion·al \ik-ˈstench-nəl, -ˈsten-chən-ᵊl\ *adj* **1** : of, relating to, or marked by extension; *specif* : DENOTATIVE **2** : concerned with objective reality — **ex·ten·sion·al·i·ty** \-ˌsten-chə-ˈnal-ət-ē\ *n* — **ex·ten·sion·al·ly** \-ˈstench-nə-lē, -ˈsten-chən-ᵊl-ē\ *adv*

extension cord *n* : CORD 3b

ex·ten·si·ty \ik-ˈsten(t)-sət-ē\ *n, pl* **-ties 1 a** : the quality of having extension **b** : degree of extension : RANGE **2** : an attribute of sensation whereby space or size is perceived

ex·ten·sive \ik-ˈsten(t)-siv\ *adj* **1** : EXTENSIONAL **2** : having wide or considerable extent ⟨~ reading⟩ **3** : of, relating to, or constituting farming in which large areas of land are utilized with minimum outlay and labor — **ex·ten·sive·ly** *adv* — **ex·ten·sive·ness** *n*

ex·ten·som·e·ter \ˌek-ˌsten-ˈsäm-ət-ər\ *n* [*extension* + *-o-* + *-meter*] : an instrument for measuring minute deformations of test specimens caused by tension, compression, bending, or twisting

ex·ten·sor \ik-ˈsten(t)-sər\ *n* : a muscle serving to extend a bodily part (as a limb)

ex·tent \ik-ˈstent\ *n* [ME, fr. AF & MF; AF *extente* land valuation, fr. MF, area, surveying of land, fr. *extendre* to extend] **1** *archaic* : valuation (as of land) in Great Britain esp. for taxation **2 a** : seizure (as of land) in execution of a writ of extent in Great Britain : the condition of being so seized **b** : a writ giving to a creditor temporary possession of his debtor's property **3 a** : the range over which something extends : SCOPE ⟨the ~ of his authority⟩ **b** : the point, degree, or limit to which something extends ⟨using talents to the greatest ~⟩ **c** : the amount of space or surface that something occupies or the distance over which it extends : MAGNITUDE ⟨the ~ of the forest⟩

ex·ten·u·ate \ik-ˈsten-yə-ˌwāt\ *vt* **-at·ed; -at·ing** [L *extenuatus,* pp. of *extenuare,* fr. *ex-* + *tenuis* thin — more at THIN] **1 a** *archaic* : to make light of **b** : to lessen or to try to lessen the seriousness or extent of by making partial excuses : MITIGATE **c** *obs* : DISPARAGE **2 a** *archaic* : to make thin or emaciated **b** : to lessen the strength or effect of — **ex·ten·u·a·tor** \-ˌwāt-ər\ *n* — **ex·ten·u·a·to·ry** \-wə-ˌtōr-ē, -ˌtȯr-\ *adj*

ex·ten·u·a·tion \ik-ˌsten-yə-ˈwā-shən\ *n* **1** : the act of extenuating or state of being extenuated; *esp* : partial justification **2** : something extenuating; *esp* : a partial excuse

[1]**ex·te·ri·or** \ek-ˈstir-ē-ər\ *adj* [L, compar. of *exter, exterus* being on the outside, foreign, fr. *ex*] **1** : being on an outside surface : situated on the outside **2** : observable by outward signs ⟨his ~ quietness is belied by an occasional nervous twitch —*Current Biog.*⟩ **3** : suitable for use on outside surfaces — **ex·te·ri·or·ly** *adv*

[2]**exterior** *n* **1 a** : an exterior part or surface : OUTSIDE **b** : outward manner or appearance **2** : a representation of an outdoor scene

exterior angle *n* **1** : the angle between a side of a polygon and an extended adjacent side **2** : an angle between a line crossing two parallel lines and either of the latter on the outside

ex·te·ri·or·i·ty \(ˌ)ek-ˌstir-ē-ˈȯr-ət-ē, -ˈär-\ *n* : the quality or state of being exterior or exteriorized : EXTERNALITY

ex·te·ri·or·ize \ek-ˈstir-ē-ə-ˌrīz\ *vt* **-ized; -iz·ing 1** : EXTERNALIZE **2** : to bring out of the abdomen (as for surgery) — **ex·te·ri·or·iza·tion** \-ˌstir-ē-ə-rə-ˈzā-shən\ *n*

ex·ter·mi·nate \ik-ˈstər-mə-ˌnāt\ *vt* **-nat·ed; -nat·ing** [L *exterminatus,* pp. of *exterminare,* fr. *ex-* + *terminus* boundary — more at TERM] : to get rid of completely usu. by killing off ⟨~ crabgrass from a lawn⟩ — **ex·ter·mi·na·tion** \-ˌstər-mə-ˈnā-shən\ *n* — **ex·ter·mi·na·tor** \-ˈstər-mə-ˌnāt-ər\ *n*

syn EXTERMINATE, EXTIRPATE, ERADICATE, UPROOT *shared meaning element* : to effect the destruction or abolition of

ex·ter·mi·na·to·ry \ik-ˈstərm-(ə-)nə-ˌtōr-ē, -ˌtȯr-\ *adj* : of, relating to, or marked by extermination

ex·ter·mine \ik-ˈstər-mən\ *vt* **-mined; -min·ing** *obs* : EXTERMINATE

[1]**ex·tern** \ek-ˈstərn, ˈek-ˌ\ *adj* [MF or L; MF *externe,* fr. L *externus*] *archaic* : EXTERNAL

[2]**ex·tern** *also* **ex·terne** \ˈek-ˌstərn\ *n* : a person connected with an institution but not living or boarding in it; *specif* : a nonresident doctor or medical student at a hospital — **ex·tern·ship** \-ˌship\ *n*

[1]**ex·ter·nal** \ek-ˈstərn-ᵊl\ *adj* [ME, fr L *externus* external, fr. *exter*] **1 a** : capable of being perceived outwardly ⟨~ signs of a disease⟩ ⟨~ reality⟩ **b** (1) : having merely the outward appearance of something : SUPERFICIAL (2) : not intrinsic or essential ⟨~ circumstances⟩ **2 a** : of, relating to, or connected with the outside or an outer part **b** : applied or applicable to the outside **3 a** (1) : situated outside, apart, or beyond; *specif* : situated away from the mesial plane (2) : arising or acting from outside ⟨~ force⟩ **b** : of or relating to dealings or relationships with foreign countries **c** : having existence independent of the mind ⟨~ reality⟩ — **ex·ter·nal·ly** \-ᵊl-ē\ *adv*

[2]**external** *n* : something that is external: as **a** *archaic* : an outer part **b** : an external feature or aspect — usu. used in pl. ⟨the ~*s* of religion⟩

external–combustion engine *n* : a heat engine (as a steam engine) that derives its heat from fuel consumed outside the engine cylinder

ex·ter·nal·ism \ek-ˈstərn-ᵊl-ˌiz-əm\ *n* **1** : EXTERNALITY 1 **2** : attention to externals; *esp* : excessive preoccupation with externals

ex·ter·nal·i·ty \ˌek-ˌstər-ˈnal-ət-ē\ *n, pl* **-ties 1** : the quality or state of being external or externalized **2** : something that is external

ex·ter·nal·iza·tion \ek-ˌstərn-ᵊl-ə-ˈzā-shən\ *n* **1 a** : the action or process of externalizing **b** : the quality or state of being externalized **2** : something externalized : EMBODIMENT

ex·ter·nal·ize \ek-ˈstərn-ᵊl-ˌīz\ *vt* **-ized; iz·ing 1** : to make external or externally manifest : EMBODY **2** : to attribute to causes outside the self : RATIONALIZE ⟨~ his failure⟩

external respiration *n* : exchange of gases between the external environment and a distributing system of the animal body (as the lungs of higher vertebrates or the tracheal tubes of insects) or between the alveoli of the lungs and the blood

ex·tero·cep·tive \ˌek-stə-rō-ˈsep-tiv\ *adj* [L *exter* + E *-o-* + *-ceptive* (as in *receptive*)] : activated by, relating to, or being stimuli received by an organism from outside

ex·tero·cep·tor \-tər\ *n* [NL, fr. L *exter* + NL *-o-* + *-ceptor* (as in *receptor*)] : a sense organ excited by exteroceptive stimuli

ex·ter·ri·to·ri·al \ˌek-ˌster-ə-ˈtōr-ē-əl, -ˈtȯr-\ *adj* : EXTRATERRITORIAL — **ex·ter·ri·to·ri·al·i·ty** \-ˌtōr-ē-ˈal-ət-ē, -ˌtȯr-\ *n*

extg *abbr* extracting

[1]**ex·tinct** \ik-ˈstiŋ(k)t, ˈek-ˌ\ *adj* [ME, fr. L *exstinctus,* pp. of *exstinguere*] **1 a** : no longer burning **b** : no longer active ⟨an ~ volcano⟩ **2** : no longer existing ⟨an ~ animal⟩ **3 a** : gone out of use : SUPERSEDED **b** : having no qualified claimant ⟨an ~ title⟩

[2]**extinct** *vt, archaic* : EXTINGUISH

ex·tinc·tion \ik-ˈstiŋ(k)-shən\ *n* **1** : the act of making extinct or causing to be extinguished **2** : the condition or fact of being extinct or extinguished **3 :** the process of eliminating or reducing a conditioned response by not reinforcing it

ex·tinc·tive \ik-ˈstiŋ(k)-tiv\ *adj* **:** tending or serving to extinguish or make extinct

ex·tin·guish \ik-ˈstiŋ-(g)wish\ *vt* [L *exstinguere* (fr. *ex-* + *stinguere* to extinguish) + E *-ish* (as in *abolish*); akin to L *instigare* to incite — more at STICK] **1 a :** to cause to cease burning **:** QUENCH **b** (1) **:** to bring to an end **:** make an end of ⟨hope for their safety was slowly *~ed*⟩ (2) **:** to reduce to silence or ineffectiveness **c :** to cause extinction of (a conditioned response) **d :** to dim the brightness of **:** ECLIPSE **2 a :** to cause to be void **:** NULLIFY ⟨~ a claim⟩ **b :** to get rid of usu. by payment ⟨~ a debt⟩ ***syn* 1** see CRUSH ***ant*** inflame **2** see ABOLISH — **ex·tin·guish·able** \-ə-bəl\ *adj* — **ex·tin·guish·er** \-ər\ *n* — **ex·tin·guish·ment** \-mənt\ *n*

ex·tir·pate \ˈek-stər-ˌpāt\ *vt* **-pat·ed; -pat·ing** [L *exstirpatus*, pp. *exstirpare*, fr. *ex-* + *stirp-*, *stirps* trunk, root — more at TORPID] **1 a :** to pull up by the root **b :** to destroy completely **:** wipe out **2 :** to cut out by surgery ***syn*** see EXTERMINATE — **ex·tir·pa·tion** \ˌek-stər-ˈpā-shən\ *n* — **ex·tir·pa·tive** \ˈek-stər-ˌpāt-iv, ek-ˈstər-pət-\ *adj* — **ex·tir·pa·tor** \ˈek-stər-ˌpāt-ər\ *n*

ex·tol *also* **ex·toll** \ik-ˈstōl\ *vt* **ex·tolled; ex·tol·ling** [ME *extollen*, fr. L *extollere*, fr. *ex-* + *tollere* to lift up — more at TOLERATE] **:** to praise highly **:** GLORIFY — **ex·tol·ler** *n* — **ex·tol·ment** \-ˈstōl-mənt\ *n*

ex·tor·sion \ek-ˈstȯr-shən, ˈek-ˌ\ *n* **:** outward rotation (as of a body part) about an axis or fixed point

ex·tort \ik-ˈstȯ(ə)rt\ *vt* [L *extortus*, pp. of *extorquēre* to wrench out, extort, fr. *ex-* + *torquēre* to twist — more at TORTURE] **:** to obtain from a person by force or undue or illegal power or ingenuity **:** WRING ***syn*** see EDUCE — **ex·tort·er** *n* — **ex·tor·tive** \-ˈstȯrt-iv\ *adj*

ex·tor·tion \ik-ˈstȯr-shən\ *n* **1 :** the act or practice of extorting esp. money or other property; *specif* **:** the offense committed by an official engaging in such practice **2 :** something extorted; *esp* **:** a gross overcharge — **ex·tor·tion·er** \-sh(ə-)nər\ *n* — **ex·tor·tion·ist** \-sh(ə-)nəst\ *n*

ex·tor·tion·ary \-shə-ˌner-ē\ *adj, archaic* **:** EXTORTIONATE 1

ex·tor·tion·ate \ik-ˈstȯr-sh(ə-)nət\ *adj* **1 :** characterized by extortion **2 :** EXCESSIVE, EXORBITANT — **ex·tor·tion·ate·ly** *adv*

[1]**ex·tra** \ˈek-strə\ *adj* [prob. short for *extraordinary*] **1 a :** more than is due, usual, or necessary **:** ADDITIONAL ⟨~ work⟩ **b :** subject to an additional charge ⟨room service is ~⟩ **2 :** SUPERIOR ⟨~ quality⟩

[2]**extra** *n* **1 :** something extra or additional: as **a :** an added charge **b :** a special edition of a newspaper **c :** an additional worker; *specif* **:** one hired to act in a group scene in a motion picture or stage production **2 :** something of superior quality or grade

[3]**extra** *adv* **:** beyond the usual size, extent, or degree ⟨~ large⟩

extra- *prefix* [ME, fr. L, fr. *extra*, adv. & prep., outside, except, beyond, fr. *exter* being on the outside — more at EXTERIOR] **:** outside **:** beyond ⟨*extra*judicial⟩

extra–base hit *n* **:** a hit in baseball good for more than one base

ex·tra·cel·lu·lar \ˌek-strə-ˈsel-yə-lər\ *adj* **:** situated or occurring outside a cell or the cells of the body ⟨~ digestion⟩ ⟨~ enzymes⟩ — **ex·tra·cel·lu·lar·ly** *adv*

ex·tra·chro·mo·som·al \-ˌkrō-mə-ˈsō-məl, -ˈzō-\ *adj* **:** situated or controlled by factors outside the chromosome ⟨~ inheritance⟩

ex·tra·cor·po·re·al \-kȯr-ˈpōr-ē-əl, -ˈpȯr-\ *adj* **:** occurring or based outside the living body ⟨heart surgery employing ~ circulation⟩ — **ex·tra·cor·po·re·al·ly** \-ē-ə-lē\ *adv*

ex·tra·cra·ni·al \-ˈkrā-nē-əl\ *adj* **:** situated or occurring outside the cranium

[1]**ex·tract** \ik-ˈstrakt, *oftenest in sense* 5 ˈek-ˌ\ *vt* [ME *extracten*, fr. L *extractus*, pp. of *extrahere*, fr. *ex-* + *trahere* to draw — more at DRAW] **1 a :** to draw forth (as by research) ⟨~ data⟩ **b :** to pull or take out forcibly ⟨*~ed* a wisdom tooth⟩ **c :** to obtain by much effort from someone unwilling ⟨*~ed* a confession⟩ **2 :** to withdraw (as a juice or fraction) by physical or chemical process; *also* **:** to treat with a solvent so as to remove a soluble substance **3 :** to separate (a metal) from an ore **4 :** to determine (a mathematical root) by calculation **5 :** to select (excerpts) and copy out or cite ***syn*** see EDUCE — **ex·tract·abil·i·ty** \ik-ˌstrak-tə-ˈbil-ət-ē, (ˌ)ek-\ *n* — **ex·tract·able** *or* **ex·tract·ible** \ik-ˈstrak-tə-bəl, ˈek-ˌ\ *adj* — **ex·trac·tor** \ik-ˈstrak-tər, ˈek-ˌ\ *n*

[2]**ex·tract** \ˈek-ˌstrakt\ *n* **1 :** a selection from a writing or discourse **:** EXCERPT **2 :** a product (as an essence or concentrate) prepared by extracting; *esp* **:** a solution (as in alcohol) of essential constituents of a complex material (as meat or an aromatic plant) ⟨beef ~⟩ ⟨lemon ~⟩

ex·trac·tion \ik-ˈstrak-shən\ *n* **1 :** the act or process of extracting **2 :** ORIGIN, LINEAGE **3 :** something extracted

[1]**ex·trac·tive** \ik-ˈstrak-tiv, ˈek-ˌ\ *adj* **1 a :** of, relating to, or involving extraction ⟨~ processes⟩ **b :** tending toward or resulting in withdrawal of natural resources by extraction with no provision for replenishment ⟨~ agriculture⟩ **2 :** capable of being extracted — **ex·trac·tive·ly** *adv*

[2]**extractive** *n* **:** something extracted or extractable **:** EXTRACT

ex·tra·cur·ric·u·lar \ˌek-strə-kə-ˈrik-yə-lər\ *adj* **1 :** not falling within the scope of a regular curriculum; *specif* **:** of or relating to officially or semiofficially approved and usu. organized student activities (as athletics) connected with school and usu. carrying no academic credit **2 :** lying outside one's regular duties or routine ⟨worked extra hours on ~ tasks⟩

ex·tra·dit·able \ˈek-strə-ˌdīt-ə-bəl\ *adj* **1 :** subject or liable to extradition **2 :** making liable to extradition ⟨an ~ offense⟩

ex·tra·dite \ˈek-strə-ˌdīt\ *vt* **-dit·ed; -dit·ing** [back-formation fr. *extradition*] **1 :** to deliver up to extradition **2 :** to obtain the extradition of

ex·tra·di·tion \ˌek-strə-ˈdish-ən\ *n* [F, fr. *ex-* + L *tradition-*, *traditio* act of handing over — more at TRADITION] **:** the surrender of an alleged criminal usu. under the provisions of a treaty or statute by one state or other authority to another having jurisdiction to try the charge

ex·tra·dos \ˈek-strə-ˌdäs, -ˌdō; ek-ˈstrā-ˌdäs\ *n, pl* **ex·tra·dos** \-ˌdōz, -ˌdäs\ *or* **ex·tra·dos·es** \-ˌdäs-əz\ [F, fr. L *extra* + F *dos* back — more at DOSSIER] **:** the exterior curve of an arch

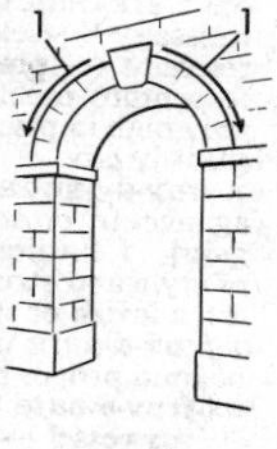

1 extrados

ex·tra·ga·lac·tic \ˌek-strə-gə-ˈlak-tik\ *adj* [ISV] **:** lying or coming from outside the Milky Way

ex·tra·he·pat·ic \-hi-ˈpat-ik\ *adj* **:** situated or originating outside the liver

ex·tra·ju·di·cial \-jü-ˈdish-əl\ *adj* **1 a :** not forming a valid part of regular legal proceedings ⟨an ~ investigation⟩ **b :** delivered without legal authority **:** PRIVATE 2a(2) ⟨the judge's ~ statements⟩ **2 :** done in contravention of due process of law ⟨an ~ execution⟩ — **ex·tra·ju·di·cial·ly** \-ˈdish-(ə-)lē\ *adv*

ex·tra·le·gal \ˌek-strə-ˈlē-gəl\ *adj* **:** not regulated or sanctioned by law — **ex·tra·le·gal·ly** \-gə-lē\ *adv*

ex·tra·lim·it·al \-ˈlim-ət-ᵊl\ *adj* **:** not present in a given area — used of kinds of organisms (as species)

ex·tra·lin·guis·tic \-liŋ-ˈgwis-tik\ *adj* **:** lying outside the province of linguistics — **ex·tra·lin·guis·ti·cal·ly** \-ti-kə-lē\ *adv*

ex·tral·i·ty \ek-ˈstral-ət-ē\ *n* [by contr.] **:** EXTRATERRITORIALITY

ex·tra·mar·i·tal \ˌek-strə-ˈmar-ət-ᵊl\ *adj* **:** of or relating to a married person's sexual intercourse with other than his or her spouse **:** ADULTEROUS

ex·tra·mun·dane \ˌek-strə-ˌmən-ˈdān, -ˈmən-ˌ\ *adj* [LL *extramundanus*, fr. L *extra* + *mundus* the world] **:** situated in or relating to a region beyond the material world

ex·tra·mu·ral \-ˈmyu̇r-əl\ *adj* **1 :** existing or functioning outside or beyond the walls, boundaries, or precincts of an organized unit ⟨~ medical care provided by hospital personnel⟩ **2** *chiefly Brit* **:** of, relating to, or taking part in extension courses or facilities — **ex·tra·mu·ral·ly** \-ə-lē\ *adv*

ex·tra·mu·si·cal \-ˈmyü-zi-kəl\ *adj* **:** lying outside the province of music

ex·tra·ne·ous \ek-ˈstrā-nē-əs\ *adj* [L *extraneus* — more at STRANGE] **1 :** existing on or coming from the outside **2 a :** not forming an essential or vital part ⟨an ~ scene that added nothing to the play⟩ **b :** having no relevance ⟨~ points that do not serve his argument⟩ **3 :** being a number obtained in solving an equation that is not a solution of the equation ⟨~ roots⟩ ***syn*** see EXTRINSIC ***ant*** relevant — **extra·ne·ous·ly** *adv* — **ex·tra·ne·ous·ness** *n*

ex·tra·nu·cle·ar \ˌek-strə-ˈn(y)ü-klē-ər\ *adj* **1 :** situated in or affecting the parts of a cell external to the nucleus **:** CYTOPLASMIC **2 :** situated outside the nucleus of an atom

extraocular muscle \ˌek-strə-ˈäk-yə-lər-\ *n* **:** any of six small voluntary muscles that pass between the eyeball and the orbit and control the movement of the eyeball in relation to the orbit

ex·traor·di·nary \ik-ˈstrȯrd-ᵊn-ˌer-ē, ˌek-strə-ˈȯrd-\ *adj* [ME *extraordinarie*, fr. L *extraordinarius*, fr. *extra ordinem* out of course, fr. *extra* + *ordinem*, acc. of *ordin-*, *ordo* order] **1 a :** going beyond what is usual, regular, or customary ⟨~ powers⟩ **b :** exceptional to a very marked extent **:** REMARKABLE ⟨~ beauty⟩ **2 :** employed for or sent on a special function or service ⟨an ambassador ~⟩ — **ex·traor·di·nari·ly** \ik-ˌstrȯrd-ᵊn-ˈer-ə-lē, ˌek-strə-ˌȯrd-\ *adv* — **ex·traor·di·nari·ness** \ik-ˈstrȯrd-ᵊn-ˌer-ē-nəs, ˌek-strə-ˈȯrd-\ *n*

extra point *n* **:** a point gained on a conversion in football

ex·trap·o·late \ik-ˈstrap-ə-ˌlāt\ *vb* **-lat·ed; -lat·ing** [L *extra* outside + E *-polate* (as in *interpolate*) — more at EXTRA-] *vt* **1 :** to infer (values of a variable in an unobserved interval) from values within an already observed interval **2 a :** to project, extend, or expand (known data or experience) into an area not known or experienced so as to arrive at a usu. conjectural knowledge of the unknown area ⟨*~s* present trends to construct an image of the future⟩ **b :** to predict by projecting past experience or known data ⟨~ public sentiment on one issue from known public reaction on others⟩ ~ *vi* **:** to perform the act or process of extrapolating — **ex·trap·o·la·tion** \-ˌstrap-ə-ˈlā-shən\ *n* — **ex·trap·o·la·tive** \-ˈstrap-ə-ˌlāt-iv\ *adj* — **ex·trap·o·la·tor** \-ˌlāt-ər\ *n*

ex·tra·sen·so·ry \ˌek-strə-ˈsen(t)s-(ə-)rē\ *adj* **:** residing beyond or outside the ordinary senses ⟨instances of ~ perception⟩

ex·tra·sys·to·le \-ˈsis-tə-(ˌ)lē\ *n* [NL] **:** a premature beat of one of the chambers of the heart that leads to momentary arrhythmia — **ex·tra·sys·tol·ic** \-sis-ˈtäl-ik\ *adj*

[1]**ex·tra·ter·res·tri·al** \-tə-ˈres-trē-əl, -ˈres(h)-chəl\ *adj* **:** originating or existing outside the earth or its atmosphere ⟨~ life⟩; *also* **:** of or relating to extraterrestrial space ⟨~ exploration⟩

[2]**extraterrestrial** *n* **:** an extraterrestrial being

ex·tra·ter·ri·to·ri·al \-ˌter-ə-ˈtōr-ē-əl, -ˈtȯr-\ *adj* **:** existing or taking place outside the territorial limits of a jurisdiction

ex·tra·ter·ri·to·ri·al·i·ty \-ˌtōr-ē-ˈal-ət-ē, -ˌtȯr-\ *n* **:** exemption from the application or jurisdiction of local law or tribunals

ex·tra·trop·i·cal cyclone \ˌek-strə-ˌträp-i-kəl-\ *n* **:** a cyclone in the middle latitudes often being 1500 miles in diameter and usu. containing a cold front that extends toward the equator for hundreds of miles

ex·tra·uter·ine \ˌek-strə-ˈyüt-ə-rən, -ˌrīn\ *adj* [ISV] **:** situated or occurring outside the uterus ⟨~ pregnancy⟩

ex·trav·a·gance \ik-ˈstrav-i-gən(t)s\ *n* **1 a :** an instance of excess or prodigality; *specif* **:** an excessive outlay of money **b :** something extravagant **2 :** the quality or fact of being extravagant

ex·trav·a·gan·cy \-gən-sē\ *n, pl* **-cies :** EXTRAVAGANCE

ex·trav·a·gant \ik-ˈstrav-i-gənt\ *adj* [ME, fr. MF, fr. ML *extravagant-*, *extravagans*, fr. L *extra-* + *vagant-*, *vagans*, prp. of *vagari* to wander about — more at VAGARY] **1 a** *archaic* : WANDERING **b** *obs* : STRANGE, CURIOUS **2 a** : exceeding the limits of reason or necessity ⟨~ claims⟩ **b** : lacking in moderation, balance, and restraint ⟨~ praise⟩ **c** : extremely or excessively elaborate **3 a** : spending much more than necessary **b** : PROFUSE **4** : unreasonably high in price ***syn*** see EXCESSIVE ***ant*** restrained — **ex·trav·a·gant·ly** *adv*

ex·trav·a·gan·za \ik-ˌstrav-ə-ˈgan-zə\ *n* [It *estravaganza*, lit., extravagance, fr. *estravagante* extravagant, fr. ML *extravagant-, extravagans*] **1** : a literary or musical work marked by extreme freedom of style and structure and usu. by elements of burlesque or parody **2** : a lavish or spectacular show or event

ex·trav·a·gate \ik-ˈstrav-ə-ˌgāt\ *vi* **-gat·ed; -gat·ing** *archaic* : to go beyond proper limits

1ex·trav·a·sate \ik-ˈstrav-ə-ˌsāt, -ˌzāt\ *vb* **-sat·ed; -sat·ing** [L *extra* + *vas* vessel — more at VASE] *vt* : to force out or cause to escape from a proper vessel or channel ~ *vi* **1** : to pass by infiltration or effusion from a proper vessel or channel (as a blood vessel) into surrounding tissue **2** : to erupt in liquid form from a vent — **ex·trav·a·sa·tion** \-ˌstrav-ə-ˈsā-shən, -ˈzā-\ *n*

2extravasate *n* : an extravasated fluid (as blood)

ex·tra·vas·cu·lar \ˌek-strə-ˈvas-kyə-lər\ *adj* : destitute of or not contained in body vessels ⟨~ plant fibers⟩ ⟨~ tissue fluids⟩

ex·tra·ve·hic·u·lar \-vē-ˈhik-yə-lər\ *adj* : taking place outside a vehicle (as a spacecraft) ⟨~ activity⟩

ex·tra·ver·sion *or* **ex·tro·ver·sion** \ˌek-strə-ˈvər-zhən, -shən\ *n* [G, fr. *extra-* or *extro-* + L *versus*, pp. of *vertere* to turn] : the act, state, or habit of directing attention toward and obtaining gratification from what is outside the self — **ex·tra·ver·sive** \-siv, -ziv\ *adj*

1ex·tra·vert *or* **ex·tro·vert** \ˈek-strə-ˌvərt\ *adj* [modif. of G *extravertiert, extrovertiert*, fr. *extra-* or *extro-* + L *vertere*] : EXTRAVERTED

2extravert *or* **extrovert** *n* : one whose attention and interests are directed wholly or predominantly toward what is outside the self

ex·tra·vert·ed *or* **ex·tro·vert·ed** \-ˌvərt-əd\ *adj* : marked by extraversion

1ex·treme \ik-ˈstrēm\ *adj* [ME, fr. MF, fr. L *extremus*, superl. of *exter, exterus* being on the outside — more at EXTERIOR] **1 a** : existing in a very high degree ⟨~ poverty⟩ **b** : going to great or exaggerated lengths ⟨went on an ~ diet⟩ **c** : exceeding the ordinary, usual, or expected **2** *archaic* : LAST **3** : situated at the farthest possible point from a center ⟨the country's ~ north⟩ **4 a** : most advanced or thoroughgoing ⟨the ~ political left⟩ **b** : MAXIMUM ***syn*** see EXCESSIVE — **ex·treme·ness** *n*

2extreme *n* **1 a** : something situated at or marking one end or the other of a range ⟨~*s* of heat and cold⟩ **b** : the first term or the last term of a mathematical proportion **c** : the major term or minor term of a syllogism **2 a** : a very pronounced or excessive degree ⟨his enthusiasm was carried to an ~⟩ **b** : highest degree : MAXIMUM **3** : an extreme measure or expedient ⟨going to ~*s*⟩ — **in the extreme** : to the greatest possible extent ⟨find the task wearisome *in the extreme* —L. R. McColvin⟩

ex·treme·ly *adv* **1** : in an extreme manner **2** : to an extreme extent

extremely high frequency *n* : a radio frequency in the highest range of the radio spectrum — see RADIO FREQUENCY table

extremely low frequency *n* : a radio frequency in the lowest range of the radio spectrum — see RADIO FREQUENCY table

extreme unction \ik-ˌstrē-ˈməŋ(k)-shən, ˌek-(ˌ)strē-\ *n* : a sacrament in which a priest anoints a critically ill or injured person and prays for his recovery and salvation

ex·trem·ism \ik-ˈstrē-ˌmiz-əm\ *n* : the quality or state of being extreme; *esp* : advocacy of extreme political measures : RADICALISM — **ex·trem·ist** \-məst\ *n or adj*

ex·trem·i·ty \ik-ˈstrem-ət-ē\ *n, pl* **-ties** **1 a** : the farthest or most remote part, section, or point **b** : a limb of the body; *esp* : a human hand or foot **2 a** : extreme danger or critical need **b** : a moment marked by imminent destruction or death **3 a** : an intense degree ⟨the ~ of his participation — *Saturday Rev.*⟩ **b** : the utmost degree (as of emotion or pain) **4** : a drastic or desperate act or measure ⟨driven to *extremities*⟩

ex·tre·mum \ik-ˈstrē-məm\ *n, pl* **-ma** \-mə\ [NL, fr. L, neut. of *extremus*] : a maximum or a minimum of a mathematical function

ex·tri·cate \ˈek-strə-ˌkāt\ *vt* **-cat·ed; -cat·ing** [L *extricatus*, pp. of *extricare*, fr. *ex-* + *tricae* trifles, perplexities] **1 a** *archaic* : UNRAVEL **b** : to distinguish from a related thing **2** : to free or remove from an entanglement or difficulty — **ex·tri·ca·ble** \ik-ˈstrik-ə-bəl, ek-ˈ; ˈek-(ˌ)\ *adj* — **ex·tri·ca·tion** \ˌek-strə-ˈkā-shən\ *n*

syn EXTRICATE, DISENTANGLE, UNTANGLE, DISENCUMBER, DISEMBARRASS *shared meaning element* : to free from what binds or holds back

ex·trin·sic \ek-ˈstrin-zik, -ˈstrin(t)-sik\ *adj* [F & LL; F *extrinsèque*, fr. LL *extrinsecus*, fr. L, adv., from without; akin to L *exter* outward and to L *sequi* to follow — more at EXTERIOR, SUE] **1 a** : not forming part of or belonging to a thing : EXTRANEOUS **b** : originating from or on the outside; *esp* : originating outside a part and acting upon the part as a whole **2** : EXTERNAL — **ex·trin·si·cal·ly** \-zi-k(ə-)lē, -si-\ *adv*

syn EXTRINSIC, EXTRANEOUS, FOREIGN, ALIEN *shared meaning element* : external to a thing, its essential nature, or original character ***ant*** intrinsic

extrinsic factor *n* : VITAMIN B_{12}

extro- *prefix* [alter. of L *extra-*] : outward ⟨*extro*vert⟩ — compare INTRO-

ex·trorse \ˈek-ˌstrȯ(ə)rs\ *adj* [prob. fr. (assumed) NL *extrorsus*, fr. LL, adv., outward, fr. L *extra-* + *-orsus* (as in *introrsus*) — more at INTRORSE] : turned away from the axis of growth ⟨an ~ anther⟩ — **ex·trorse·ly** *adv*

extroversion, extrovert *var of* EXTRAVERSION, EXTRAVERT

ex·trude \ik-ˈstrüd\ *vb* **ex·trud·ed; ex·trud·ing** [L *extrudere*, fr. *ex-* + *trudere* to thrust] *vt* **1** : to force, press, or push out **2** : to shape (as metal or plastic) by forcing through a die ~ *vi* : to become extruded — **ex·trud·abil·i·ty** \-ˌstrüd-ə-ˈbil-ət-ē\ *n* — **ex·trud·able** \-ˈstrüd-ə-bəl\ *adj* — **ex·trud·er** \-ˈstrüd-ər\ *n*

ex·tru·sion \ik-ˈstrü-zhən\ *n* [ML *extrusion-, extrusio*, fr. L *extrusus*, pp. of *extrudere*] : the act or process of extruding; *also* : a form or product produced by this process

ex·tru·sive \ik-ˈstrü-siv, -ziv\ *adj* : formed by crystallization of lava poured out at the earth's surface ⟨~ rock⟩

ex·u·ber·ance \ig-ˈzü-b(ə-)rən(t)s\ *n* **1** : the quality or state of being exuberant **2** : an exuberant act or expression

ex·u·ber·ant \-b(ə-)rənt\ *adj* [ME, fr. MF, fr. L *exuberant-, exuberans*, prp. of *exuberare* to be abundant, fr. *ex-* + *uber* fruitful, fr. *uber* udder — more at UDDER] **1 a** : joyously unrestrained and enthusiastic **b** : lacking compactness and discipline : flamboyantly overdone ⟨writing spoiled by ~ overdrawn metaphors⟩ **2** : extreme or excessive in degree, size, or extent **3** : produced in extreme abundance : PLENTIFUL ***syn*** see PROFUSE ***ant*** austere, sterile — **ex·u·ber·ant·ly** *adv*

ex·u·ber·ate \-bə-ˌrāt\ *vi* **-at·ed; -at·ing** **1** *archaic* : to have something in abundance : OVERFLOW **2** : to become exuberant : show exuberance ⟨*exuberated* over his victory⟩

ex·u·date \ˈek-s(y)ü-ˌdāt, -shü-\ *n* : exuded matter

ex·u·da·tion \ˌek-s(y)ü-ˈdā-shən, -shü-\ *n* **1** : the process of exuding **2** : EXUDATE — **ex·u·da·tive** \ig-ˈzüd-ət-iv; ˈek-s(y)ü-ˌdāt-iv, -shü-\ *adj*

ex·ude \ig-ˈzüd\ *vb* **ex·ud·ed; ex·ud·ing** [L *exsudare*, fr. *ex-* + *sudare* to sweat — more at SWEAT] *vi* **1** : to ooze out **2** : to undergo diffusion ~ *vt* **1** : to cause to ooze or spread out in all directions **2** : to display conspicuously or abundantly ⟨~*s* charm⟩

ex·ult \ig-ˈzəlt\ *vi* [MF *exulter*, fr. L *exsultare*, lit., to leap up, fr. *ex-* + *saltare* to leap — more at SALTATION] **1** *obs* : to leap for joy **2** : to be extremely joyful : REJOICE — **ex·ult·ing·ly** \-ˈzəl-tiŋ-lē\ *adv*

ex·ul·tance \ig-ˈzəlt-ᵊn(t)s\ *n* : EXULTATION

ex·ul·tan·cy \-ˈzəlt-ᵊn-sē\ *n* : EXULTATION

ex·ul·tant \ig-ˈzəlt-ᵊnt\ *adj* : filled with or expressing great joy or triumph : JUBILANT — **ex·ul·tant·ly** *adv*

ex·ul·ta·tion \ˌek-(ˌ)səl-ˈtā-shən, ˌeg-(ˌ)zəl-\ *n* : the act of exulting : the state of being exultant

ex·urb \ˈek-ˌsərb, ˈeg-ˌzərb\ *n* [*ex-* + *-urb* (as in *suburb*)] : a region or district that lies outside a city and usu. beyond its suburbs and that is inhabited chiefly by well-to-do families — **ex·ur·ban** \ek-ˈsər-bən; eg-ˈzər-, ig-\ *adj*

ex·ur·ban·ite \ek-ˈsər-bə-ˌnīt; eg-ˈzər-, ig-\ *n* : one who lives in an exurb

ex·ur·bia \-bē-ə\ *n* : the generalized region of exurbs

ex·u·vi·ae \ig-ˈzü-vē-ˌē, -vē-ˌī\ *n pl* [L, fr. *exuere* to take off, fr. *ex-* + *-uere* to put on; akin to ORuss *izuti* to take off footwear] : the natural coverings of animals (as the skins of snakes) after they have been sloughed off — **ex·u·vi·al** \-vē-əl\ *adj*

ex·u·vi·a·tion \-ˌzü-vē-ˈā-shən\ *n* : the process of molting

1ex–vo·to \(ˈ)eks-ˈvōt-(ˌ)ō\ *n, pl* **ex–votos** [L *ex voto* according to a vow] : a votive offering

2ex–voto *adj* : VOTIVE

-ey — see -Y

ey·as \ˈī-əs\ *n* [ME, alter. (by incorrect division of *a neias*) of *neias*, fr. MF *niais* fresh from the nest, fr. (assumed) VL *nidax* nestling, fr. L *nidus* nest — more at NEST] : an unfledged bird; *specif* : a nestling hawk

1eye \ˈī\ *n* [ME, fr. OE *ēage*; akin to OHG *ouga* eye, L *oculus*, Gk *ōps* eye, face] **1 a** : an organ of sight; *esp* : a nearly spherical hollow organ that is lined with a sensitive retina, is lodged in a bony orbit in the skull, is the vertebrate organ of sight, and is normally paired **b** : all the visible structures within and surrounding the orbit and including eyelids, eyelashes, and eyebrows **c** (1) : the faculty of seeing with eyes (2) : the faculty of intellectual or aesthetic perception or appreciation ⟨an ~ for beauty⟩ **d** : LOOK, GLANCE ⟨caught his ~⟩ **e** : an attentive look ⟨kept an ~ on his valuables⟩ **f** : POINT OF VIEW, JUDGMENT ⟨beauty is in the ~ of the beholder⟩ — often used in pl. ⟨an offender in the ~*s* of the law⟩ **2** : something having an appearance suggestive of an eye: as **a** : the hole through the head of a needle **b** : a usu. circular marking (as on a peacock's tail) **c** : LOOP; *esp* : a loop or other catch to receive a hook **d** : an undeveloped bud (as on a potato) **e** : an area like a hole in the center of a tropical cyclone marked by only light winds or complete calm with no precipitation **f** : the center of a flower esp. when differently colored or marked; *specif* : the disk of a composite **g** (1) : a triangular piece of beef cut from between the top and bottom of a round (2) : the chief muscle of a chop (3) : a compact mass of muscular tissue usu. embedded in fat in a rib or loin cut of meat **h** : a device (as a photoelectric cell) that functions in a manner analogous to human vision **3** : something central : CENTER ⟨the ~ of the problem —Norman Mailer⟩ **4** : the direction from which the wind is blowing — **eye·less** \ˈī-ləs\ *adj* — **eye·like** \-ˌlīk\ *adj* — **my eye** — used to express mild disagreement or sometimes surprise ⟨a diamond, *my eye!* That's glass⟩ — **with an eye to** : with a view to

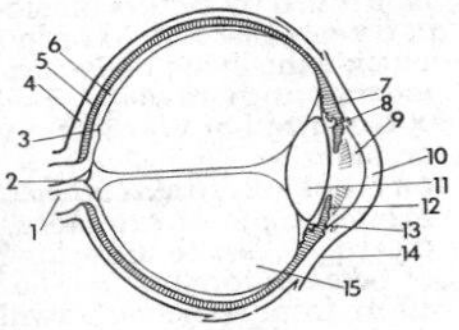

eye 1a: *1* optic nerve, *2* blind spot, *3* fovea, *4* sclera, *5* choroid, *6* retina, *7* ciliary body, *8* posterior chamber, *9* anterior chamber, *10* cornea, *11* lens, *12* iris, *13* suspensory ligament, *14* conjunctiva, *15* vitreous humor

2eye *vb* **eyed; eye·ing** *or* **ey·ing** *vt* **1 a** : to fix the eyes on **b** : to watch sharply **2** : to furnish with an eye ~ *vi, obs* : SEEM, LOOK — **ey·er** \ˈī(-ə)r\ *n*

1eye·ball \ˈī-ˌbȯl\ *n* : the more or less globular capsule of the vertebrate eye formed by the sclera and cornea together with their contained structures

2eyeball *vt* : to look at intently

eyeball–to–eyeball *adj* : FACE-TO-FACE

eye bank *n* : a storage place for human corneas from the newly dead for transplanting to the eyes of those blind through corneal defects

eye·bolt \'ī-ˌbōlt\ *n* : a bolt with a looped head

eye·bright \'ī-ˌbrīt\ *n* : any of several herbs (genus *Euphrasia*) of the figwort family with opposite toothed or cut leaves

eye·brow \'ī-ˌbrau̇\ *n* : the ridge over the eye or hair growing on it

eyebrow pencil *n* : a cosmetic pencil for the eyebrows

eye–catch·er \'ī-ˌkach-ər, -ˌkech-\ *n* : something strongly attracting the eye — **eye–catch·ing** \-iŋ\ *adj*

eye·cup \'ī-ˌkəp\ *n* : a small oval cup with a rim curved to fit the orbit of the eye used for applying liquid remedies to the eyes

eyed \'īd\ *adj* : having an eye or eyes esp. of a specified kind or number — often used in combination ⟨an almond-*eyed* girl⟩

eye dialect *n* : the use of pronunciation-based spellings (as *sez* for *says*) in the representation of speech esp. to convey an impression of illiteracy

eyed·ness \'īd-nəs\ *n* [-*eyed* (as in *right-eyed, left-eyed*)] : preference (as in using a monocular microscope) for the use of one eye instead of the other

eye·drop·per \'ī-ˌdräp-ər\ *n* : DROPPER 2 — **eye·drop·per·ful** \-ˌful\ *n*

eye·ful \'ī-ˌful\ *n* 1 : a full or completely satisfying view 2 : one that is visually attractive; *esp* : a strikingly beautiful woman

eye·glass \'ī-ˌglas\ *n* 1 **a** : EYEPIECE **b** : a lens worn to aid vision; *specif* : MONOCLE **c** *pl* : GLASSES, SPECTACLES 2 : EYECUP

eye·hole \'ī-ˌhōl\ *n* 1 : ORBIT 1 2 : PEEPHOLE

eye·lash \'ī-ˌlash\ *n* : the fringe of hair edging the eyelid; *esp* : a single hair of this fringe

eye lens *n* : the lens nearest the eye in an eyepiece

eye·let \'ī-lət\ *n* [ME, fr. MF *oillet*, dim. of *oil* eye, fr. L *oculus*] 1 **a** : a small hole designed to receive a cord or used for decoration (as in embroidery) **b** : a small typically metal ring to reinforce an eyelet : GROMMET 2 : an aperture for observing : PEEPHOLE, LOOPHOLE

eye·lid \'ī-ˌlid\ *n* : one of the movable lids of skin and muscle that can be closed over the eyeball

eye·lin·er \'ī-ˌlī-nər\ *n* : makeup used to emphasize the contour of the eyes

ey·en \'ī-(ə)n\ *archaic pl of* EYE

eye–open·er \'ī-ˌōp(-ə)-nər\ *n* 1 : a drink intended to wake one up 2 : something startling or surprising — **eye–open·ing** \-niŋ\ *adj*

eye·piece \'ī-ˌpēs\ *n* : the lens or combination of lenses at the far end of an optical instrument

eye·point \'ī-ˌpȯint\ *n* : the point at which the eye is placed in using an optical instrument (as a microscope)

eye·pop·per \'ī-ˌpäp-ər\ *n* : something that excites or astonishes — **eye–pop·ping** \-ˌpäp-iŋ\ *adj*

eye rhyme *n* : an imperfect rhyme that appears to have identical vowel sounds from similarity of spelling (as *move* and *love*)

eye·shade \'ī-ˌshād\ *n* : a visor that shields the eyes from strong light and is fastened on with a headband

eye shadow *n* : a cosmetic cream or powder in one of various colors that is applied to the eyelids to accent the eyes

eye·shot \'ī-ˌshät\ *n* : the range of the eye : VIEW

eye·sight \'ī-ˌsīt\ *n* 1 : SIGHT 4a 2 *archaic* : OBSERVATION 1

eye·sore \'ī-ˌsō(ə)r, -ˌsȯ(ə)r\ *n* : something offensive to the sight

eye·spot \'ī-ˌspät\ *n* 1 **a** : a simple visual organ of pigment or pigmented cells covering a sensory termination : OCELLUS **b** : a small pigmented body of various unicellular algae 2 : a spot of color

eye·stalk \'ī-ˌstȯk\ *n* : one of the movable peduncles bearing an eye at the tip in a decapod crustacean

eye·strain \'ī-ˌstrān\ *n* : weariness or a strained state of the eye

eye·strings \'ī-ˌstriŋz\ *n pl, obs* : organic eye attachments formerly believed to break at death or blindness

eye·tooth \'ī-ˌtüth\ *n* : a canine tooth of the upper jaw

eye·wash \'ī-ˌwȯsh, -ˌwäsh\ *n* 1 : an eye lotion 2 : misleading or deceptive statements, actions, or procedures

eye·wink \'ī-ˌwiŋk\ *n* 1 : a wink of the eye 2 *obs* : LOOK, GLANCE

eye·wit·ness \'ī-ˈwit-nəs\ *n* : one who sees an occurrence or an object; *esp* : one who gives a report on what he has seen

eyre \'a(ə)r, 'e(ə)r\ *n* [ME *eire*, fr. AF, fr. OF *erre* trip, fr. *errer* to travel — more at ERRANT] 1 : periodic circuit ⟨medieval English justices in ∼⟩ 2 : a medieval English court held by itinerant royal justices

ey·rie \'ī(ə)r-ē, *or like* AERIE\ *var of* AERIE

ey·rir \'ā-ˌri(ə)r\ *n, pl* **au·rar** \'au̇-ˌrär, 'ȯi-\ [Icel, fr. ON, money (in pl.)] — see *krona* at MONEY table

Ez *or* **Ezr** *abbr* Ezra

Ezech *abbr* Ezechiel

Eze·chiel \i-ˈzē-kyəl, -kē-əl\ *n* [LL] : EZEKIEL

Ezek *abbr* Ezekiel

Eze·kiel \i-ˈzē-kyəl, -kē-əl\ *n* [LL *Ezechiel*, fr. Heb *Yĕḥezqēl*] 1 : a Hebrew priest and prophet of the 6th century B.C. 2 : a prophetic book of canonical Jewish and Christian Scripture written by Ezekiel — see BIBLE table

Ez·ra \'ez-rə\ *n* [LL, fr. Heb *'Ezrā*] 1 : a Hebrew priest, scribe, and reformer of Judaism of the 5th century B.C. in Babylon and Jerusalem 2 : a narrative book of canonical Jewish and Christian Scripture — see BIBLE table

---

¹f \'ef\ *n, pl* **f's** *or* **fs** \'efs\ *often cap, often attrib* 1 **a** : the 6th letter of the English alphabet **b** : a graphic representation of this letter **c** : a speech counterpart of orthographic *f* 2 : the 4th tone of a C-major scale 3 : a graphic device for reproducing the letter *f* 4 : one designated *f* esp. as the 6th in order or class 5 **a** : a grade rating a student's work as failing **b** : one graded or rated with an F 6 : something shaped like the letter F

²f *abbr, often cap* 1 Fahrenheit 2 failure 3 false 4 family 5 farad 6 feast 7 female 8 feminine 9 femto- 10 fermi 11 fine 12 finish 13 fluid; fluidness 14 following] and the following one 15 force 16 forte 17 fragile 18 French 19 frequency 20 from 21 full

³f *symbol* 1 faraday 2 focal length 3 the relative aperture of a photographic lens — often written *f/* 4 function ⟨*y = f(x)*⟩

F *symbol* fluorine

fa \'fä\ *n* [ME, fr. ML, fr. the syllable sung to this note in a medieval hymn to St. John the Baptist] : the 4th tone of the diatonic scale in solmization

FA *abbr* 1 field artillery 2 fielding average 3 football association

FAA *abbr* 1 Federal Aviation Administration 2 free of all average

fa·ba·ceous \fə-ˈbā-shəs\ *adj* [NL *Fabaceae*, family of legumes, fr. *Faba*, type genus, fr. L, bean] 1 : of or relating to the legume family : LEGUMINOUS 2 : relating to, resembling, or being a bean

Fa·bi·an \'fā-bē-ən\ *adj* 1 **a** : of, relating to, or in the manner of the Roman general Quintus Fabius Maximus known for his defeat of Hannibal in the Second Punic War by the avoidance of decisive contests **b** : CAUTIOUS, DILATORY 2 [the *Fabian* Society; fr. the members' belief in slow rather than revolutionary change in government] : of, relating to, or being a society of socialists organized in England in 1884 to spread socialist principles gradually — **Fabian** *n* — **Fa·bi·an·ism** \-ˌniz-əm\ *n*

¹fa·ble \'fā-bəl\ *n* [ME, fr. MF, fr. L *fabula* conversation, story, play, fr. *fari* to speak — more at BAN] : a fictitious narrative or statement: as **a** : a legendary story of supernatural happenings **b** : a narration intended to enforce a useful truth; *esp* : one in which animals speak and act like human beings **c** : FALSEHOOD, LIE

²fable *vb* **fa·bled; fa·bling** \-b(ə-)liŋ\ *vi, archaic* : to tell fables ∼ *vt* : to talk or write about as if true — **fa·bler** \-b(ə-)lər\ *n*

fa·bled \'fā-bəld\ *adj* 1 : FICTITIOUS 2 : told or celebrated in fables

fab·li·au \'fab-lē-ˌō\ *n, pl* **-aux** \-ˌō(z)\ [F, fr. OF, dim. of *fable*] : a short usu. comic, frankly coarse, and often cynical tale in verse popular in the 12th and 13th centuries

fab·ric \'fab-rik\ *n* [MF *fabrique*, fr. L *fabrica* workshop, structure — more at FORGE] 1 **a** : STRUCTURE, BUILDING **b** : underlying structure : FRAMEWORK ⟨the ∼ of society⟩ 2 : an act of constructing : ERECTION; *specif* : the construction and maintenance of a church building 3 **a** : structural plan or style of construction **b** : TEXTURE, QUALITY — used chiefly of textiles **c** : the arrangement of physical components (as of soil) in relation to each other 4 **a** : CLOTH 1a **b** : a material that resembles cloth 5 : the appearance or pattern produced by the shapes and arrangement of the crystal grains in a rock

fab·ri·cant \'fab-ri-kənt\ *n* : MANUFACTURER

fab·ri·cate \'fab-ri-ˌkāt\ *vt* **-cat·ed; -cat·ing** [ME *fabricaten*, fr. L *fabricatus*, pp. of *fabricari*, fr. *fabrica*] 1 : CONSTRUCT, MANUFACTURE; *specif* : to construct from diverse and usu. standardized parts 2 : INVENT, CREATE 3 : to make up for the purpose of deception *syn* see MAKE — **fab·ri·ca·tion** \ˌfab-ri-ˈkā-shən\ *n* — **fab·ri·ca·tor** \'fab-ri-ˌkāt-ər\ *n*

fab·u·lar \'fab-yə-lər\ *adj* : of, relating to, or having the form of a fable

fab·u·list \'fab-yə-ləst\ *n* 1 : a creator or writer of fables 2 : LIAR

fab·u·lous \'fab-yə-ləs\ *adj* [L *fabulosus*, fr. *fabula*] 1 : resembling a fable esp. in incredible, marvelous, or exaggerated quality 2 : told in or based on fable *syn* see FICTITIOUS — **fab·u·lous·ly** *adv* — **fab·u·lous·ness** *n*

fac *abbr* 1 facsimile 2 faculty

ə abut	ᵊ kitten	ər further	a back	ā bake	ä cot, cart
au̇ out	ch chin	e less	ē easy	g gift	i trip	ī life
j joke	ŋ sing	ō flow	ȯ flaw	ȯi coin	th thin	th̶ this
ü loot	u̇ foot	y yet	yü few	yu̇ furious	zh vision	

fa·cade *also* **fa·çade** \fə-'säd\ *n* [F *façade*, fr. It *facciata*, fr. *faccia* face, fr. (assumed) VL *facia*] **1 :** the front of a building; *also* **:** any other face (as on a street or court) of a building given special architectural treatment **2 :** a false, superficial, or artificial appearance or effect **:** FACE

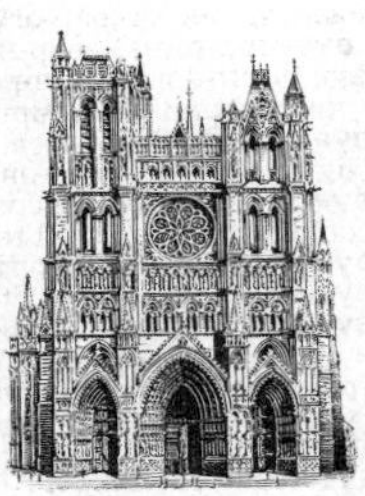

facade 1

¹face \'fās\ *n, often attrib* [ME, fr. OF, fr. (assumed) VL *facia*, fr. L *facies* make, form, face, fr. *facere* to make, do — more at DO] **1 :** the front part of the human head including the chin, mouth, nose, cheeks, eyes, and usu. the forehead **2** *archaic* **:** PRESENCE, SIGHT **3 a :** facial expression **b :** GRIMACE **c :** MAKEUP 3a **4 a :** outward appearance ⟨suspicious on the ~ of it⟩ **b :** DISGUISE, PRETENSE **c** (1) **:** ASSURANCE, CONFIDENCE ⟨maintaining a firm ~ in spite of adversity⟩ (2) **:** EFFRONTERY ⟨how anyone could have the ~ to ask that question⟩ **d :** DIGNITY, PRESTIGE ⟨afraid to lose ~⟩ **5 :** SURFACE: **a** (1) **:** a front, upper, or outer surface (2) **:** the front of something having two or four sides (3) **:** FACADE (4) **:** an exposed surface of rock (5) **:** any of the plane surfaces that bound a geometric solid **b :** a surface specially prepared: as (1) **:** the principal dressed surface (as of a disk) (2) **:** the right side (as of cloth or leather) (3) **:** an inscribed, printed, or marked side **c** (1) **:** the surface (as of type) that receives the ink and transfers it to the paper — see TYPE illustration (2) **:** a style of type **6 :** the end or wall of a mine tunnel, drift, or excavation at which work is progressing — **face·less** \-ləs\ *adj* — **face·less·ness** *n* — **face to face 1 :** within each other's sight or presence **:** in person ⟨we met *face to face* for the first time⟩ **2 :** under the necessity of having to make a decision or to take action ⟨finally came *face to face* with the problem⟩ — **in the face of** *or* **in face of :** in opposition to **:** DESPITE ⟨succeed *in the face of* great difficulties⟩ — **to one's face :** in one's presence or so that one is fully aware of what is going on **:** FRANKLY

²face *vb* **faced; fac·ing** *vt* **1 :** to confront impudently **2 a :** to line near the edge esp. with a different material **b :** to cover the front or surface of ⟨*faced* the building with marble⟩ **3 :** to bring face-to-face **4 a :** to stand or sit with the face toward **b :** to front on ⟨a house *facing* the park⟩ **5 a :** to meet firmly and without evasion ⟨~ the facts⟩ **b :** to master by confronting with determination — used with *down* ⟨*faced* down the critics of his policy⟩ **6 :** to turn (as a playing card) face-up **7 :** to make the surface of (as a stone) flat or smooth **8 :** to cause (troops) to face in a particular direction on command **~** *vi* **1 :** to have the face or front turned in a specified direction **2 :** to turn the face in a specified direction — **face the music :** to meet an unpleasant situation, a danger, or the consequences of one's actions

face angle *n* **:** an angle formed by two edges of a polyhedral angle

face card *n* **:** a king, queen, or jack in a deck of cards

face·cloth \'fās-,klȯth\ *n* **:** WASHCLOTH

-faced \'fāst\ *adj comb form* **:** having (such) a face or (so many) faces ⟨rosy-*faced*⟩ ⟨two-*faced*⟩

face·down \'fās-'daủn\ *adv* **:** with the face down ⟨sliding ~⟩

face fly *n* **:** a European fly (*Musca autumnalis*) that is similar to the house fly, is widely established in No. America, and causes great distress in livestock by clustering about the face

face–hard·en \'fās-,härd-ᵊn\ *vt* **:** to harden the surface of (as steel)

face–lift·ing \'fā-,slif-tiŋ\ *n* **1 :** a plastic operation for removal of facial defects (as wrinkles) typical of aging **2 :** an alteration or restyling intended to modernize

face–off \'fā-,sȯf\ *n* **1 :** a method of putting a puck in play in ice hockey by dropping it between two opposing players each of whom attempts to gain control of the puck or hit it to a teammate **2 :** CONFRONTATION

face·plate \'fā-,splāt\ *n* **1 :** a disk fixed with its face at right angles to the live spindle of a lathe for the attachment of the work **2 :** a protective cover for the human face (as of a diver) **3 :** the glass front of a kinescope on which the image is seen

fac·er \'fā-sər\ *n* **1 :** a stunning check or defeat **2 :** one that faces; *specif* **:** a cutter for facing a surface

face–sav·er \'fās-,sā-vər\ *n* **:** something (as a compromise) that saves face

face–sav·ing \-,sā-viŋ\ *n* **:** the act or an instance of preserving one's prestige or dignity

fac·et \'fas-ət\ *n* [F *facette*, dim. of *face*] **1 :** a small plane surface (as on a cut gem) — see BRILLIANT illustration **2 :** any of the definable aspects that make up a subject (as of contemplation) or an object (as of consideration) **3 :** the external corneal surface of an ommatidium **4 :** a smooth flat circumscribed anatomical surface **5 :** a fillet between the flutes of a column ***syn*** see PHASE — **fac·et·ed** *or* **fac·et·ted** \'fas-ət-əd\ *adj*

fa·cete \fə-'sēt\ *adj* [L *facetus*] *archaic* **:** FACETIOUS, WITTY

fa·ce·ti·ae \fə-'sē-shē-,ē\ *n pl* [L, fr. pl. of *facetia* jest, fr. *facetus*] **:** witty or humorous writings or sayings

fa·ce·tious \fə-'sē-shəs\ *adj* [MF *facetieux*, fr. *facetie* jest, fr. L *facetia*] **1 :** jocular in an often clumsy or inappropriate manner **2 :** characterized by pleasantry or levity **:** JOCOSE ⟨a ~ remark⟩ ***syn*** see WITTY ***ant*** lugubrious — **fa·ce·tious·ly** *adv* — **fa·ce·tious·ness** *n*

face–to–face *adv or adj* **:** within each other's sight or presence ⟨met and talked ~ for the first time⟩

face·up \'fā-'səp\ *adv* **:** with the face up

face up *vi* **:** to meet without shrinking — usu. used with *to* ⟨*faced up* to the situation⟩

face value *n* **1 :** the value indicated on the face (as of a postage stamp or a stock certificate) **2 :** the apparent value or significance ⟨if their results may be taken at *face value*⟩

fa·cia \'fāsh-(ē-)ə\ *var of* FASCIA

¹fa·cial \'fā-shəl\ *adj* **1 :** of or relating to the face **2 :** concerned with or used in improving the appearance of the face — **fa·cial·ly** \-shə-lē\ *adv*

²facial *n* **:** a facial treatment

facial index *n* **:** the ratio of the breadth of the face to its length multiplied by 100

facial nerve *n* **:** either of the seventh pair of cranial nerves that supply motor fibers esp. to the muscles of the face and jaw and send a separate mixed branch to the tongue

-fa·cient \'fā-shənt\ *adj comb form* [L *-facient-*, *-faciens* (as in *calefacient-*, *calefaciens* making warm, prp. of *calefacere* to warm) — more at CHAFE] **:** making **:** causing ⟨somni*facient*⟩

fa·cies \'fā-sh(ē-,)ēz\ *n, pl* **facies** [NL, fr. L, face] **1 :** an appearance and expression of the face characteristic of a particular condition **2 a :** general appearance ⟨a plant species with a particularly distinct ~⟩ **b :** a particular local aspect or modification of an ecological community **3 :** a rock or group of rocks that differs from comparable rocks (as in composition, age, or fossil content)

fac·ile \'fas-əl\ *adj* [MF, fr. L *facilis*, fr. *facere* to do — more at DO] **1 a** (1) **:** easily accomplished or attained ⟨a ~ victory⟩ (2) **:** SPECIOUS, SUPERFICIAL ⟨I am not concerned . . . with offering any ~ solution for so complex a problem —T. S. Eliot⟩ **b :** used or comprehended with ease **c :** readily manifested and often lacking sincerity or depth ⟨~ tears⟩ **2** *archaic* **:** mild or pleasing in manner or disposition **3 a :** READY, FLUENT ⟨~ prose⟩ **b :** ASSURED, POISED — **fac·ile·ly** \-ə(l)-lē\ *adv* — **fac·ile·ness** \-əl-nəs\ *n*

fa·cil·i·tate \fə-'sil-ə-,tāt\ *vt* **-tat·ed; -tat·ing :** to make easier — **fa·cil·i·ta·tive** \-,tāt-iv\ *adj* — **fa·cil·i·ta·tor** \-,tāt-ər\ *n*

fa·cil·i·ta·tion \fə-,sil-ə-'tā-shən\ *n* **1 :** the act of facilitating **:** the state of being facilitated **2 :** the lowering of the threshold for reflex conduction along a particular neural pathway esp. from repeated use of that pathway

fa·cil·i·ty \fə-'sil-ət-ē\ *n, pl* **-ties 1 :** the quality of being easily performed **2 :** ease in performance **:** APTITUDE **3 :** readiness of compliance **4 a :** something that promotes the ease of an action, operation, or course of conduct — usu. used in pl. ⟨provide books and other *facilities* for independent study⟩ **b :** something (as a hospital) that is built, installed, or established to serve a particular purpose

fac·ing \'fā-siŋ\ *n* **1 a :** a lining at the edge esp. of a garment **b** *pl* **:** the collar, cuffs, and trimmings of a uniform coat **2 :** an ornamental or protective layer **3 :** material for facing

fac·sim·i·le \fak-'sim-ə-lē\ *n* [L *fac simile* make similar] **1 :** an exact copy **2 :** the transmission of graphic matter (as printing or still pictures) by wire or radio and its reproduction — **facsimile** *vt*

fact \'fakt\ *n* [L *factum*, fr. neut. of *factus*, pp. of *facere*] **1 :** a thing done: as **a :** CRIME ⟨accessory after the ~⟩ **b** *obs* **:** FEAT **c** *archaic* **:** ACTION **2** *archaic* **:** PERFORMANCE, DOING **3 :** the quality of being actual **:** ACTUALITY ⟨a question of ~ brings on actual evidence⟩ **4 a :** something that has actual existence ⟨space travel is now a ~⟩ **b :** an actual occurrence **:** EVENT ⟨the ~ of his presence is proven by witnesses⟩ **5 :** a piece of information presented as having objective reality — **fac·tic·i·ty** \fak-'tis-ət-ē\ *n* — **in fact :** in truth **:** ACTUALLY

fact finder *n* **:** one that tries to determine the realities of a case, situation, or relationship; *esp* **:** an impartial examiner designated by a government agency to appraise the facts underlying a particular matter (as a labor dispute) — **fact–find·ing** *n*

fac·tion \'fak-shən\ *n* [MF & L; MF, fr. L *faction-*, *factio* act of making, faction — more at FASHION] **1 :** a party or group (as within a government) that is often contentious or self-seeking **:** CLIQUE **2 :** party spirit esp. when marked by dissension — **fac·tion·al** \-shnəl, -shən-ᵊl\ *adj* — **fac·tion·al·ism** \-shnə-,liz-əm, -shən-ᵊl-,iz-\ *n* — **fac·tion·al·ly** \-ē\ *adv*

-fac·tion \'fak-shən\ *n comb form* [ME *-faccioun*, fr. MF & L; MF *-faction*, fr. L *-faction-*, *-factio* (as in *satisfaction-*, *satisfactio* satisfaction)] **:** making **:** -FICATION ⟨petri*faction*⟩

fac·tious \'fak-shəs\ *adj* [MF or L; MF *factieux*, fr. L *factiosus*, fr. *factio*] **:** of or relating to faction: as **a :** caused by faction ⟨~ disputes⟩ **b :** inclined to faction or the formation of factions **c :** SEDITIOUS — **fac·tious·ly** *adv* — **fac·tious·ness** *n*

fac·ti·tious \fak-'tish-əs\ *adj* [L *facticius*, fr. *factus*, pp. of *facere* to make, do — more at DO] **1 :** produced by man rather than by natural forces **2 a :** formed by or adapted to an artificial or conventional standard **b :** produced by special effort **:** SHAM ⟨created a ~ demand by spreading rumors of shortage⟩ ***syn*** see ARTIFICIAL ***ant*** bona fide, veritable — **fac·ti·tious·ly** *adv* — **fac·ti·tious·ness** *n*

fac·ti·tive \'fak-tət-iv\ *adj* [NL *factitivus*, irreg. fr. L *factus*] **:** of or relating to a transitive verb that in some constructions requires an objective complement as well as an object — **fac·ti·tive·ly** *adv*

-fac·tive \'fak-tiv\ *adj comb form* [MF *-factif*, fr. *-faction*] **:** making **:** causing ⟨petri*factive*⟩

fact of life 1 *pl* **:** the fundamental physiological processes and behavior involved in sex and reproduction **2 :** something that exists and must be taken into consideration

¹fac·tor \'fak-tər\ *n* [ME, fr. MF *facteur*, fr. L *factor* doer, fr. *factus*] **1 :** one who acts or transacts business for another: as **a :** COMMISSION MERCHANT **b :** one that lends money to producers and dealers (as on the security of accounts receivable) **2 a :** something that actively contributes to the production of a result **:** INGREDIENT **b :** a good or service used in the process of production **3 :** GENE **4 a :** any of the numbers or symbols in mathematics that when multiplied together form a product; *also* **:** a number or symbol that divides another number or symbol **b :** a quantity by which a given quantity is multiplied or divided in order to indicate a difference in measurement **c :** the number by which a given time is multiplied in photography to give the complete time for exposure or development ***syn*** see ELEMENT — **fac·tor·ship** \-,ship\ *n*

²factor *vb* **fac·tored; fac·tor·ing** \-t(ə-)riŋ\ *vt* **:** to resolve into factors **~** *vi* **:** to work as a factor — **fac·tor·able** \-t(ə-)rə-bəl\ *adj*

fac·tor·age \-t(ə-)rij\ *n* **1 :** the charges made by a factor for his services **2 :** the business of a factor

factor analysis *n* **:** the transformation of statistical data (as measurements) into linear combinations of variables that are usu. not correlated — **factor analytic** *adj*

[1]**fac·to·ri·al** \fak-ˈtōr-ē-əl, -ˈtȯr-\ *n* **1 :** the product of all the positive integers from one to *n* — symbol *n!* **2 :** the quantity *0!* arbitrarily defined as equal to 1
[2]**factorial** *adj* **:** of or relating to a factor or a factorial
fac·tor·ize \ˈfak-tə-ˌrīz\ *vt* **-ized; -iz·ing :** FACTOR — **fac·tor·iza·tion** \ˌfak-tə-rə-ˈzā-shən\ *n*
fac·to·ry \ˈfak-t(ə-)rē\ *n, pl* **-ries 1 :** a station where resident factors trade **2 a :** a building or set of buildings with facilities for manufacturing **b :** the seat of some kind of production ⟨the vice *factories* of the slums⟩
fac·to·tum \fak-ˈtōt-əm\ *n* [NL, lit., do everything, fr. L *fac* do + *totum* everything] **1 :** a person having many diverse activities or responsibilities **2 :** a general servant
fac·tu·al \ˈfak-chə(-wə)l, ˈfaksh-wəl\ *adj* **1 :** of or relating to facts **2 :** restricted to or based on fact — **fac·tu·al·i·ty** \ˌfak-chə-ˈwal-ət-ē\ *n* — **fac·tu·al·ly** \ˈfak-chə(-wə)-lē, ˈfaksh-wə-\ *adv* — **fac·tu·al·ness** *n*
fac·tu·al·ism \ˈfak-chə(-wə)-ˌliz-əm, ˈfaksh-wə-\ *n* **:** adherence or dedication to facts — **fac·tu·al·ist** \-ləst\ *n*
fac·ture \ˈfak-chər\ *n* [ME, fr. MF, fr. L *factura* action of making, fr. *factus*] **:** the manner in which something (as an artistic work) is made **:** EXECUTION ⟨his modelling of faces . . . his delicate yet firm ~ —J. C. Vandyke⟩
fac·u·la \ˈfak-yə-lə\ *n, pl* **-lae** \-ˌlē, -ˌlī\ [NL, fr. L, dim. of *fac-*, *fax* torch] **:** any of the bright regions of the sun's photosphere seen most easily near the sun's edge
fac·ul·ta·tive \ˈfak-əl-ˌtāt-iv\ *adj* **1 a :** of or relating to the grant of permission, authority, or privilege ⟨~ legislation⟩ **b :** OPTIONAL **2 :** of or relating to a mental faculty **3 a :** taking place under some conditions but not under others ⟨~ diapause⟩ ⟨~ parasitism⟩ **b :** showing the typical life style under some environmental conditions but not under others ⟨~ anaerobes⟩ ⟨~ homosexuals⟩ — **fac·ul·ta·tive·ly** *adv*
fac·ul·ty \ˈfak-əl-tē\ *n, pl* **-ties** [ME *faculte*, fr. MF *faculté*, fr. ML & L; ML *facultat-*, *facultas* branch of learning or teaching, fr. L, ability, abundance, fr. *facilis* facile] **1 :** ABILITY, POWER: as **a :** innate or acquired ability to act or do **b :** an inherent capability, power, or function ⟨the ~ of hearing⟩ **c :** one of the powers of the mind formerly held by psychologists to form a basis for the explanation of all mental phenomena **d :** natural aptitude ⟨he has a ~ for saying the right things⟩ **2 a :** a branch of teaching or learning in an educational institution **b** *archaic* **:** something in which one is trained or qualified **3 a :** the members of a profession **b :** the teaching and administrative staff and those members of the administration having academic rank in an educational institution **4 :** power, authority, or prerogative given or conferred ***syn*** see POWER, GIFT
fad \ˈfad\ *n* [origin unknown] **:** a practice or interest followed for a time with exaggerated zeal **:** CRAZE ***syn*** see FASHION — **fad·dish** \ˈfad-ish\ *adj* — **fad·dish·ness** *n* — **fad·dism** \ˈfad-ˌiz-əm\ *n* — **fad·dist** \ˈfad-əst\ *n*
FAD \ˌef-ˌā-ˈdē\ *n* **:** FLAVIN ADENINE DINUCLEOTIDE
[1]**fade** \ˈfād\ *vb* **fad·ed; fad·ing** [ME *faden*, fr. MF *fader*, fr. *fade* feeble, insipid, fr. (assumed) VL *fatidus*, alter. of L *fatuus* fatuous, insipid] *vi* **1 :** to lose freshness or vitality **:** WITHER **2** *of an automobile brake* **:** to lose braking power gradually **3 :** to lose freshness or brilliance of color **4 :** to sink away **:** VANISH **5 :** to change gradually in loudness, strength, or visibility — used of a motion-picture image or of an electronics signal and usu. with *in* or *out* **6 :** to move back from the line of scrimmage — used of a quarterback **~** *vt* **:** to cause to fade
[2]**fade** *n* **1 :** a gradual changing of one picture to another in a motion-picture or television sequence **2 :** a fading of an automobile brake
[3]**fade** \ˈfäd\ *adj* [F, fr. MF] **:** INSIPID, COMMONPLACE
fade·away \ˈfād-ə-ˌwā\ *n* **1 :** an act or instance of fading away **2 a :** SCREWBALL 1 **b :** a slide in which a base runner throws his body sideways to avoid the tag
fad·ed·ly \ˈfād-əd-lē\ *adv* **:** in the manner of one that has faded ⟨a ~ handsome woman⟩
fade·less \ˈfād-ləs\ *adj* **:** not susceptible to fading — **fade·less·ly** *adv*
FADM *abbr* fleet admiral
fa·do \ˈfäth-(ˌ)ü, ˈfath-\ *n, pl* **fados** [Pg, lit., fate, fr. L *fatum*] **:** a plaintive Portuguese folk song
fae·cal, fae·ces *var of* FECAL, FECES
fa·e·na \fä-ˈā-(ˌ)nä\ *n* [Sp, lit., task, fr. obs. Catal, fr. L *facienda* things to be done, fr. *facere* to do — more at DO] **:** a series of final passes leading to the kill made by the matador in a bullfight
fa·er·ie *also* **fa·ery** \ˈfā-(ə-)rē, ˈfa(ə)r-ē, ˈfe(ə)r-ē\ *n, pl* **fa·er·ies** [MF *faerie* — more at FAIRY] **1 :** the realm of fairies **2 :** FAIRY — **faery** *adj*
Faero·ese \ˌfar-ə-ˈwēz, ˌfer-, -ˈwēs\ *n, pl* **Faeroese 1 :** a member of the Germanic people inhabiting the Faeroes **2 :** the Germanic language of the Faeroese people — **Faeroese** *adj*
Faf·nir \ˈfäv-nər, -ˌni(ə)r\ *n* [ON *Fāfnir*] **:** a dragon of Norse myth that guards the Nibelungs' gold hoard until slain by Sigurd
[1]**fag** \ˈfag\ *vb* **fagged; fag·ging** [obs. *fag* to droop, perh. fr. *fag* (fag end)] *vi* **1 :** to work hard **:** TOIL **2 :** to act as a fag esp. in an English public school ⟨*fagging* for older boys during his first year⟩ **~** *vt* **:** to tire by strenuous activity **:** EXHAUST ***syn*** see TIRE
[2]**fag** *n* **1** *chiefly Brit* **:** TOIL, DRUDGERY **2 a :** an English public-school boy who acts as servant to an older schoolmate **b :** DRUDGE
[3]**fag** *n* [*fag end*] **:** CIGARETTE
[4]**fag** *n* [prob. short for *faggot*] **:** HOMOSEXUAL
fag end *n* [earlier *fag*, fr. ME *fagge* flap] **1 a :** the last part or coarser end of a web of cloth **b :** the untwisted end of a rope **2 a :** a poor or worn-out end **:** REMNANT **b :** the extreme end ⟨not quite too late for the *fag end* of lunch —Earle Birney⟩
fag·got \ˈfag-ət\ *n* [origin unknown] **:** HOMOSEXUAL
fa·gin \ˈfā-gən\ *n* [*Fagin*, character in Charles Dickens' *Oliver Twist* (1839)] **:** an adult who instructs others (as children) in crime
FAGO *abbr* Fellow of the American Guild of Organists
[1]**fag·ot** *or* **fag·got** \ˈfag-ət\ *n* [ME *fagot*, fr. MF] **:** BUNDLE: as **a :** a bundle of sticks **b :** a bundle of pieces of wrought iron to be shaped by rolling or hammering at high temperature
[2]**fagot** *or* **faggot** *vt* **:** to make a fagot of **:** bind together into a bundle ⟨~*ed* sticks⟩
fag·ot·ing *or* **fag·got·ing** *n* **1 :** an embroidery produced by pulling out horizontal threads from a fabric and tying the remaining cross threads into groups of an hourglass shape **2 :** an openwork stitch joining hemmed edges

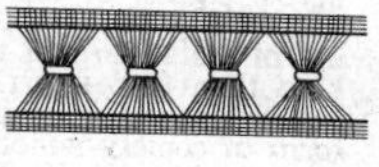

fagoting 1

Fah *or* **Fahr** *abbr* Fahrenheit
Fahr·en·heit \ˈfar-ən-ˌhīt\ *adj* [Gabriel D. *Fahrenheit*] **:** relating or conforming to a thermometric scale on which under standard atmospheric pressure the boiling point of water is at 212 degrees above the zero of the scale, the freezing point is at 32 degrees above zero, and the zero point approximates the temperature produced by mixing equal quantities by weight of snow and common salt — abbr. *F*
fa·ience *or* **fa·ïence** \fā-ˈän(t)s, fī-, -ˈäⁿs\ *n* [F, fr. *Faenza*, Italy] **:** earthenware decorated with opaque colored glazes
[1]**fail** \ˈfā(ə)l\ *vb* [ME *failen*, fr. OF *faillir*, fr. (assumed) VL *fallire*, alter. of L *fallere* to deceive, disappoint; prob. akin to Gk *phēlos* deceitful] *vi* **1 a :** to lose strength **:** WEAKEN ⟨her health was ~*ing*⟩ **b :** to fade or die away ⟨until our family line ~*s*⟩ **c :** to stop functioning ⟨the patient's heart ~*ed*⟩ **2 a :** to fall short ⟨~*ed* in his duty⟩ **b :** to be or become absent or inadequate ⟨the water supply ~*ed*⟩ **c :** to be unsuccessful (as in passing an examination) **d :** to become bankrupt or insolvent **~** *vt* **1 a :** to disappoint the expectations or trust of ⟨his friends ~*ed* him⟩ **b :** to miss performing an expected service or function for ⟨for once his wit ~*ed* him⟩ **2 :** to be deficient in **:** LACK ⟨our youth . . . never ~*ed* an invincible courage —Douglas MacArthur⟩ **3 :** to leave undone **:** NEGLECT **4 a :** to be unsuccessful in passing (as a test) **b :** to grade (as a student) as not passing — **fail·ing·ly** \ˈfā-liŋ-lē\ *adv*
[2]**fail** *n* **1 :** FAILURE — usu. used in the phrase *without fail* **2 :** a failure (as by a security dealer) to deliver or receive securities within a prescribed period after purchase or sale
[1]**fail·ing** \ˈfā-liŋ\ *n* **:** a slight or insignificant defect in character or conduct ***syn*** see FAULT ***ant*** perfection
[2]**failing** *prep* **:** in absence or default of ⟨~ specific instructions, use your own judgment⟩
faille \ˈfī(ə)l\ *n* [F] **:** a somewhat shiny closely woven silk, rayon, or cotton fabric characterized by slight ribs in the weft
fail–safe \ˈfā(ə)l-ˌsāf\ *adj* **1 :** incorporating some feature for automatically counteracting the effect of an anticipated possible source of failure **2 :** being or relating to a safeguard that prevents continuing on a bombing mission according to a preconceived plan
fail·ure \ˈfā(ə)l-yər\ *n* [alter. of earlier *failer*, fr. AF, fr. OF *faillir* to fail] **1 a :** omission of occurrence or performance; *specif* **:** a failing to perform a duty or expected action **b :** a state of inability to perform a normal function ⟨heart ~⟩ **2 a :** lack of success **b :** a failing in business **:** BANKRUPTCY **3 a :** a falling short **:** DEFICIENCY ⟨a crop ~⟩ **b :** DETERIORATION, DECAY **4 :** one that has failed
[1]**fain** \ˈfān\ *adj* [ME *fagen*, *fayn*, fr. OE *fægen*; akin to ON *feginn* happy, OE *fæger* fair] **1** *archaic* **:** HAPPY, PLEASED **2** *archaic* **:** INCLINED, DESIROUS **3** *archaic* **:** WILLING **b :** being obliged or constrained **:** COMPELLED
[2]**fain** *adv* **1** *archaic* **:** with pleasure **2** *archaic* **:** RATHER
[1]**fai·né·ant** \fā-nā-äⁿ\ *n, pl* **fainéants** \-äⁿ(z)\ [F, fr. MF *fait-nient*, lit., does nothing, by folk etymology fr. *faignant*, fr. prp. of *faindre*, *feindre* to feign] **:** an irresponsible idler
[2]**fainéant** \fā-nā-äⁿ\ *or* **fai·ne·ant** \ˈfā-nē-ənt\ *adj* **:** idle and ineffectual **:** INDOLENT
[1]**faint** \ˈfānt\ *adj* [ME *faint*, *feint*, fr. OF, fr. pp. of *faindre*, *feindre* to feign, shirk — more at FEIGN] **1 :** lacking courage and spirit **:** COWARDLY **2 :** weak, dizzy, and likely to faint **3 :** lacking strength or vigor **:** performed, offered, or accomplished weakly or languidly **4 :** producing a sensation of faintness **:** OPPRESSIVE ⟨the ~ atmosphere of a tropical port⟩ **5 :** lacking distinctness **:** DIM — **faint·ish** \-ish\ *adj* — **faint·ish·ness** *n* — **faint·ly** *adv* — **faint·ness** *n*
[2]**faint** *vi* **1** *archaic* **:** to lose courage or spirit **2** *archaic* **:** to become weak **3 :** to lose consciousness because of a temporary decrease in the blood supply to the brain **4 :** to lose brightness
[3]**faint** *n* **:** an act or condition of fainting **:** SYNCOPE
faint·heart·ed \ˈfānt-ˈhärt-əd\ *adj* **:** lacking courage or resolution **:** TIMID — **faint·heart·ed·ly** *adv* — **faint·heart·ed·ness** *n*
[1]**fair** \ˈfa(ə)r, ˈfe(ə)r\ *adj* [ME *fager*, *fair* fr. OE *fæger*; akin to OHG *fagar* beautiful and perh. to Lith *puošti* to decorate] **1 :** pleasing to the eye or mind esp. because of fresh, charming, or flawless quality **2 :** superficially pleasing **:** SPECIOUS ⟨she trusted his ~ promises⟩ **3 a :** CLEAN, PURE ⟨~ sparkling water⟩ ⟨a man of ~ fame⟩ **b :** CLEAR, LEGIBLE **4 :** not stormy or foul **:** FINE ⟨a ~ sky⟩ ⟨~ weather⟩ **5 :** AMPLE ⟨a ~ estate⟩ **6 a :** marked by impartiality and honesty **:** free from self-interest, prejudice, or favoritism ⟨a very ~ man to do business with ⟩ **b :** conforming with the established rules **:** ALLOWED **c :** open to legitimate pursuit or attack ⟨~ game⟩ **7 a :** PROMISING, LIKELY ⟨he was in a ~ way to win⟩ **b :** favorable to a ship's course ⟨a ~ wind⟩ **8** *archaic* **:** free of obstacles **9 :** not dark **:** BLOND **10 :** sufficient but not ample **:** ADEQUATE ⟨a ~ understanding of the work⟩ **11 :** being such to the utmost **:** UTTER ⟨a ~ treat to watch him —*New Republic*⟩ — **fair·ness** *n*

syn **1** see BEAUTIFUL ***ant*** foul, ill-favored
2 FAIR, JUST, EQUITABLE, IMPARTIAL, UNBIASED, DISPASSIONATE, OBJECTIVE *shared meaning element* : free from favor toward either or any side. FAIR implies an elimination of personal feelings, interests, or prejudices so as to achieve a proper balance of conflicting needs, rights, or demands ⟨a *fair* distribution of a treat⟩ ⟨the judge's decision was absolutely *fair*⟩ JUST implies a precise following of a standard of what is right and proper ⟨it is easier to be kind than *just*⟩ EQUITABLE implies a less rigorous standard than *just* and usually a fair and equal treatment of all concerned ⟨a form of society which will provide for an *equitable* distribution of . . . riches —J. W. Krutch⟩ IMPARTIAL stresses absence of favor and prejudice ⟨law shall be uniform and *impartial* —B. N. Cardozo⟩ UNBIASED reinforces the notion of freedom from favoritism and prejudice with that of a firm interest to be fair to all ⟨furnish the cabinet with *unbiased* and helpful advice —R. M. Dawson⟩ DISPASSIONATE stresses freedom from emotional involvement and tends to imply cool detachment in judging ⟨a *dispassionate* appraisal of a health program⟩ OBJECTIVE stresses a tendency to view events or phenomena as apart from oneself and therefore to be judged dispassionately and without reference to personal feelings or interests ⟨we shall be like ice when relating passions and adventures . . . we shall be . . . *objective* and impersonal —William Troy⟩ ***ant*** unfair

²fair *n* **1** *obs* : BEAUTY, FAIRNESS **2** : something that is fair or fortunate **3** *archaic* : WOMAN; *esp* : SWEETHEART — **for fair** : to the greatest extent or degree : FULLY ⟨the rush was on *for fair* —R. L. Neuberger⟩ — **no fair** : something that is not according to the rules ⟨that's *no fair*⟩

³fair *adv* : FAIRLY

⁴fair *vi, of the weather* : CLEAR ~ *vt* : to join so that the external surfaces blend smoothly

⁵fair *n* [ME *feire,* fr. OF, fr. ML *feria* weekday, fair, fr. LL, festal day, fr. L *feriae* (pl.) holidays — more at FEAST] **1** : a gathering of buyers and sellers at a particular place and time for trade **2 a** : a competitive exhibition (as of farm products) usu. with accompanying entertainment and amusements **b** : an exhibition designed to acquaint prospective buyers or the general public with a product **3** : a sale of a collection of articles usu. for a charitable purpose

fair ball *n* : a batted baseball that lands within the foul lines or that is within the foul lines when bounding to the outfield past first or third base or when going beyond the outfield for a home run

fair catch *n* : a catch of a kicked football by a player who gives a prescribed signal, may not advance the ball, and may not be tackled

fair copy *n* : a neat and exact copy esp. of a corrected draft

fair·ground \ˈfa(ə)r-ˌgraůnd, ˈfe(ə)r-\ *n* : an area where outdoor fairs, circuses, or exhibitions are held — often used in pl. with sing. constr. ⟨what a spot for a ~*s* —W. L. Gresham⟩

¹fair·ing \ˈfa(ə)r-iŋ, ˈfe(ə)r-\ *n* **1** *Brit* **a** : a present bought or given at a fair **b** : GIFT **2** *Brit* : ³DESERT 2

²fairing *n* : a member or structure whose primary function is to produce a smooth outline and to reduce drag or air resistance (as on an airplane)

fair·ish \ˈfa(ə)r-ish, ˈfe(ə)r-\ *adj* : fairly good ⟨a ~ wage for those days⟩ — **fair·ish·ly** *adv*

fair·lead \ˈfa(ə)r-ˌlēd, ˈfe(ə)r-\ *n* **1** *also* **fair·lead·er** \-ər\ : a block, ring, or strip of plank with holes that serves as a guide for the running rigging or any ship's rope and keeps it from chafing **2** : a course of running ship's rope that avoids all chafing

fair·ly \ˈfa(ə)r-lē, ˈfe(ə)r-\ *adv* **1** : in a handsome manner ⟨a table ~ set⟩ **2** *obs* **a** : in a gentle manner : QUIETLY **b** : in a courteous manner **3** : in a manner of speaking : QUITE ⟨~ bursting with pride⟩ **4 a** : in a proper or legal manner ⟨~ priced stocks⟩ **b** : without bias or distortion : IMPARTIALLY ⟨a story told ~ and objectively⟩ **5** : to a full degree or extent : PLAINLY, DISTINCTLY ⟨had ~ caught sight of him⟩ **6** : for the most part : RATHER ⟨a ~ easy job⟩

fair–mind·ed \ˈfa(ə)r-ˈmīn-dəd, ˈfe(ə)r-\ *adj* : JUST, UNPREJUDICED — **fair–mind·ed·ness** *n*

fair play *n* : equitable or impartial treatment : JUSTICE

fair shake *n* : a fair chance ⟨give the negative side a *fair shake* —S. L. Payne⟩

fair–spok·en \ˈfa(ə)r-ˈspō-kən, ˈfe(ə)r-\ *adj* : pleasant and courteous in speech ⟨a ~ youth⟩

fair–trade \ˈfa(ə)r-ˈtrād, ˈfe(ə)r-\ *vt* : to market (a commodity) in compliance with the provisions of a fair-trade agreement — **fair trader** *n*

fair trade *n* : trade in conformity with a fair-trade agreement

fair–trade agreement *n* : an agreement between a producer and a seller that commodities bearing a trademark, label, or brand name belonging to the producer be sold at or above a specified price

fair·way \ˈfa(ə)r-ˌwā, ˈfe(ə)r-\ *n* **1 a** : a navigable part of a river, bay, or harbor **b** : an open path or space **2** : the mowed part of a golf course between a tee and a green

fair–weather *adj* **1** : suitable for, done during, or made in fair weather ⟨a ~ sail⟩ **2** : loyal only during a time of success ⟨a ~ friend⟩

fairy \ˈfa(ə)r-ē, ˈfe(ə)r-\ *n, pl* **fairies** [ME *fairie* fairyland, fairy people, fr. OF *faerie,* fr. *feie, fee* fairy, fr. L *Fata,* goddess of fate, fr. *fatum* fate] **1** : a mythical being of folklore and romance usu. having diminutive human form and magic powers **2** : a male homosexual — **fairy** *adj* — **fairy·like** \-ˌlīk\ *adj*

fairy·ism \-ˌiz-əm\ *n, archaic* : the power to enchant

fairy·land \-ˌland\ *n* **1** : the land of fairies **2** : a place of delicate beauty or magical charm

fairy ring *n* [fr. the folk belief that such rings were dancing places of the fairies] **1** : a ring of mushrooms produced at the periphery of a body of mycelium which has grown centrifugally from an initial growth point; *also* : a ring of luxuriant vegetation associated with these mushrooms **2** : a mushroom (esp. *Marasmius oreades*) that commonly grows in fairy rings

fairy shrimp *n* : any of several delicate transparent freshwater branchiopod crustaceans (order Anostraca)

fairy–tale *adj* : characteristic of or suitable to a fairy tale; *esp* : marked by unusual grace or beauty

fairy tale *n* **1** : a narrative of adventures involving fantastic forces and beings (as fairies, wizards, and goblins) — called also *fairy story* **2** : a made-up story usu. designed to mislead

fait ac·com·pli \ˈfāt-ˌak-ˌōⁿ(m)-ˈplē, ˌfe-ˌtak-\ *n, pl* **faits accomplis** *same, or* -ˈplēz\ [F, accomplished fact] : a thing accomplished and presumably irreversible

¹faith \ˈfāth\ *n, pl* **faiths** \ˈfāths, ˈfāthz\ [ME *feith,* fr. OF *feid, foi,* fr. L *fides;* akin to L *fidere* to trust — more at BIDE] **1 a** : allegiance to duty or a person : LOYALTY **b** : fidelity to one's promises **2 a** (1) : belief and trust in and loyalty to God (2) : belief in the traditional doctrines of a religion **b** (1) : firm belief in something for which there is no proof (2) : complete confidence **3** : something that is believed esp. with strong conviction; *esp* : a system of religious beliefs ***syn*** see BELIEF ***ant*** doubt — **in faith** : without doubt or question : VERILY

²faith *vt, archaic* : BELIEVE, TRUST

¹faith·ful \ˈfāth-fəl\ *adj* **1** *obs* : full of faith **2** : steadfast in affection or allegiance : LOYAL **3** : firm in adherence to promises or in observance of duty : CONSCIENTIOUS **4** : given with strong assurance : BINDING ⟨~ promise⟩ **5** : true to the facts or to an original ⟨the portrait is a ~ likeness⟩ — **faith·ful·ly** \-fə-lē\ *adv* — **faith·ful·ness** *n*

syn FAITHFUL, LOYAL, CONSTANT, STAUNCH, STEADFAST, RESOLUTE *shared meaning element* : firm in adherence to whatever one owes allegiance ***ant*** faithless

²faithful *n, pl* **faithful** *or* **faithfuls** : one that is faithful: as **a** : church members in full communion and good standing — used with *the* **b** : the body of adherents of the Muslim religion — used with *the* **c** : a loyal follower or member ⟨party ~*s*⟩

faith healing *n* : a method of treating diseases by prayer and exercise of faith in God — **faith healer** *n*

faith·less \ˈfāth-ləs\ *adj* **1** : not true to allegiance or duty : TREACHEROUS, DISLOYAL ⟨a ~ servant⟩ **2** : not to be relied on : UNTRUSTWORTHY ⟨a ~ tool⟩ — **faith·less·ly** *adv* — **faith·less·ness** *n*

syn FAITHLESS, FALSE, DISLOYAL, TRAITOROUS, TREACHEROUS, PERFIDIOUS *shared meaning element* : untrue to what has a right to one's fidelity or allegiance ***ant*** faithful

fai·tour \ˈfāt-ər\ *n* [ME, fr. AF, fr. OF *faitor* perpetrator, fr. L *factor* doer — more at FACTOR] *archaic* : CHEAT, IMPOSTOR

¹fake \ˈfāk\ *vt* **faked; fak·ing** [ME *faken*] : to coil (as a fire hose) in fakes

²fake *n* : one loop of a coil (as of ship's rope) coiled free for running

³fake *vb* **faked; fak·ing** [origin unknown] *vt* **1** : to alter, manipulate, or treat so as to impart a false character or appearance to **2** : COUNTERFEIT, SIMULATE **3 a** : to deceive (an opponent) in a sports contest by simulated movement **b** : to give a fake to (an opponent) **4** : IMPROVISE, AD-LIB ⟨whistle a few bars . . . and I'll ~ the rest —Robert Sylvester⟩ ~ *vi* **1** : to engage in faking something : PRETEND **2** : to give a fake to an opponent — **fak·er** *n* — **fak·ery** \ˈfā-k(ə-)rē\ *n*

⁴fake *n* : one that is not what it purports to be: as **a** : a worthless imitation passed off as genuine **b** : IMPOSTOR, CHARLATAN **c** : a simulated movement in a sports contest (as a pretended kick, pass, or jump or a quick movement in one direction before going in another) designed to deceive an opponent **d** : a device or apparatus used by a magician to achieve the illusion of magic in a trick ***syn*** see IMPOSTURE

⁵fake *adj* : COUNTERFEIT, SHAM

fa·kir *n* [Ar *faqīr,* lit., poor man] **1** \fə-ˈki(ə)r, fä-, fa-\ **a** : a Muslim mendicant : DERVISH **b** : an itinerant Hindu ascetic or wonder-worker **2** \ˈfā-kər\ : IMPOSTOR; *esp* : SWINDLER

fa la \fä-ˈlä\ *n* [*fa-la,* meaningless syllables often occurring in its refrain] : a 16th and 17th century part-song

Fa·lan·gist \fə-ˈlan-jəst, ˈfā-ˌ\ *n* [Sp *Falangista,* fr. *Falange española* Spanish Phalanx, a fascist organization] : a member of the fascist political party governing Spain after the civil war of 1936–39

fal·cate \ˈfal-ˌkāt, ˈfȯl-\ *also* **fal·cat·ed** \-ˌkāt-əd\ *adj* [L *falcatus,* fr. *falc-, falx* sickle, scythe] : hooked or curved like a sickle

fal·chion \ˈfȯl-chən\ *n* [ME *fauchoun,* fr. OF *fauchon,* fr. *fauchier* to mow, fr. (assumed) VL *falcare,* fr. L *falc-, falx*] **1** : a broad-bladed slightly curved sword of medieval times **2** *archaic* : SWORD

fal·ci·form \ˈfal-sə-ˌfȯrm, ˈfȯl-\ *adj* [L *falc-, falx* + E *-iform*] : having the shape of a scythe or sickle

fal·con \ˈfal-kən *also* ˈfȯl- *sometimes* ˈfȯ-kən\ *n* [ME, fr. OF, fr. LL *falcon-, falco,* prob. of Gmc origin; akin to OHG *falcho* falcon] **1 a** : any of various hawks trained for use in falconry; *esp* : PEREGRINE — used technically only of a female; compare TIERCEL **b** : any of various hawks (family Falconidae) distinguished by long wings and a notch and tooth on the edge of the upper mandible **c** : HAWK 1 **2** : a light cannon used from the 15th to the 17th centuries

fal·con·er \-kə-nər\ *n* **1** : one who hunts with hawks **2** : a breeder or trainer of hawks for hunting

fal·con·et \ˌfal-kə-ˈnet, ˌfȯ(l)-\ *n* **1** : a very small cannon used in the 16th and 17th centuries **2** : any of several very small Asiatic falcons constituting a genus (*Microhierax*)

fal·con–gen·tle \-kən-ˈjent-ᵊl\ *n* [ME *faucon gentil* peregrine falcon, fr. MF, lit., noble falcon] : the female peregrine falcon

fal·con·ry \ˈfal-kən-rē *also* ˈfȯl- *sometimes* ˈfȯ-kən-\ *n* **1** : the art of training falcons to pursue game **2** : the sport of hunting with falcons

fal·de·ral \ˈfäl-də-ˌräl\ *var of* FOLDEROL

fald·stool \ˈfȯl(d)-ˌstül\ *n* [ML *faldistolium,* of Gmc origin; akin to OHG *faltistuol* folding chair, fr. a prehistoric WGmc compound whose first constituent is akin to OHG *faldan* to fold and whose second constituent is repre-

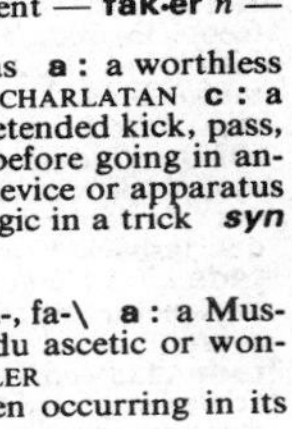

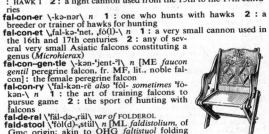

faldstool 1

sented by OHG *stuol* chair — more at FOLD, STOOL] **1 :** a folding stool or chair; *specif* **:** one used by a bishop **2 :** a folding stool or small desk at which one kneels during devotions; *esp* **:** one used by the sovereign of England at his coronation **3 :** the desk from which the litany is read in Anglican churches

[1]**fall** \ˈfȯl\ *vb* **fell** \ˈfel\; **fall·en** \ˈfȯ-lən\; **fall·ing** [ME *fallen,* fr. OE *feallan;* akin to OHG *fallan* to fall and perh. to Lith *pulti*] *vi* **1 a :** to descend freely by the force of gravity **b :** to hang freely ⟨her hair ~*s* over her shoulders⟩ **c :** to drop oneself to a lower position ⟨*fell* to his knees⟩ **d :** to come as if by descending ⟨darkness ~*s* early in the winter⟩ **2 :** to become born — usu. used of lambs **3 a :** to become lower in degree or level ⟨the temperature *fell* 10°⟩ **b :** to drop in pitch or volume ⟨their voices *fell* to a whisper⟩ **c :** ISSUE ⟨wisdom that *fell* from his lips⟩ **d :** to become lowered ⟨her eyes *fell*⟩ **4 a :** to leave an erect position suddenly and involuntarily ⟨slipped and *fell* on the ice⟩ **b :** to enter as if unawares **:** STUMBLE, STRAY ⟨*fell* into error⟩ **c :** to drop down wounded or dead; *esp* **:** to die in battle **d :** to suffer military capture ⟨after a long siege the city *fell*⟩ **e :** to lose office ⟨the party *fell* from power⟩ **f :** to suffer ruin, defeat, or failure ⟨we must stand or ~ together⟩ ⟨the deal *fell* through⟩ **5 :** to commit an immoral act; *esp* **:** to lose one's chastity **6 a :** to move or extend in a downward direction ⟨the land ~*s* away to the east⟩ **b :** SUBSIDE, ABATE ⟨the wind is ~*ing*⟩ **c :** to decline in quality, activity, or quantity ⟨production *fell* off because of the strike⟩ **d :** to lose weight — used with *off* or *away* **e :** to assume a look of shame, disappointment, or dejection ⟨his face *fell*⟩ **f :** to decline in financial value or price ⟨stocks *fell* sharply after the President's speech⟩ **7 a :** to occur at a certain time **b :** to come by chance ⟨it *fell* into my mind to write you⟩ ⟨*fell* in with a fast crowd⟩ **c :** to come or pass by lot, assignment, or inheritance **:** DEVOLVE ⟨it *fell* to him to break the news⟩ **d :** to have the proper place or station ⟨the accent ~*s* on the second syllable⟩ **8 :** to come within the limits, scope, or jurisdiction of something ⟨this word ~*s* into the class of verbs⟩ **9 :** to pass suddenly and passively into a state of body or mind or a new state or condition ⟨~ asleep⟩ ⟨~ in love⟩ ⟨the book *fell* apart⟩ **10 :** to set about heartily or actively ⟨*fell* to work⟩ **11 :** STRIKE, IMPINGE ⟨music ~*ing* on the ear⟩ ~ *vt* **:** FELL 1 — **fall behind 1 :** to lag behind **2 :** to be in arrears — **fall flat :** to produce no response or result ⟨the joke *fell flat*⟩ — **fall for 1 :** to fall in love with **2 :** to become a victim of ⟨he *fell for* the trick⟩ — **fall foul 1 :** to have a collision — used chiefly of ships **2 :** to have a quarrel **:** CLASH — often used with *of* — **fall from grace 1 :** to lapse morally **:** SIN **2 :** BACKSLIDE — **fall home :** to curve inward — used of the timbers or upper parts of a ship's side — **fall into line :** to comply with a certain course of action — **fall on** *or* **fall upon :** to meet with ⟨he *fell on* hard times⟩ — **fall over oneself** *or* **fall over backward :** to display excessive eagerness — **fall short 1 :** to be deficient **2 :** to fail to attain something (as a goal or target)

[2]**fall** *n* **1 :** the act of falling by the force of gravity **2 a :** a falling out, off, or away **:** DROPPING ⟨the ~ of leaves⟩ ⟨a ~ of snow⟩ **b :** the season when leaves fall from trees **:** AUTUMN **c :** a thing or quantity that falls or has fallen ⟨a ~ of rock at the base of the cliff⟩; *specif* **:** one or more meteorites or their fragments that have fallen together **d (1) :** BIRTH **(2) :** the quantity born — usu. used of lambs **3 a :** a costume decoration of lace or thin fabric arranged to hang loosely and gracefully **b :** a very wide turned-down collar worn in the 17th century **c :** the part of a turned-over collar from the crease to the outer edge **d :** a wide front flap on trousers (as those worn by sailors) **e :** the freely hanging lower edge of the skirt of a coat **f :** one of the three outer and often drooping segments of the flower of an iris **g :** long hair overhanging the face of certain terriers **h :** a usu. long straight portion of hair that is attached to a person's own hair **4 :** a hoisting-tackle rope or chain; *esp* **:** the part of it to which the power is applied **5 a :** loss of greatness **:** COLLAPSE ⟨the ~ of the Roman Empire⟩ **b :** the surrender or capture of a besieged place ⟨the ~ of Troy⟩ **c :** lapse or departure from innocence or goodness **d :** loss of a woman's chastity **6 a :** the downward slope (as of a hill) **:** DECLIVITY **b :** a precipitous descent of water **:** WATERFALL — usu. used in pl. but sing. or pl. in constr. **c :** a musical cadence **d :** a falling-pitch intonation in speech **7 :** a decrease in size, quantity, or degree; *specif* **:** a decrease in price or value **8 a :** the distance which something falls **b :** INCLINATION, PITCH **9 a :** the act of felling **b :** the quantity of trees cut down **c (1) :** an act of forcing a wrestler's shoulders to the mat for a specified time (as three seconds) **(2) :** a bout of wrestling **10** *Scot* **:** FORTUNE, LOT

[3]**fall** *adj* **:** of or relating to autumn ⟨a new ~ coat⟩

fal·la·cious \fə-ˈlā-shəs\ *adj* **1 :** embodying a fallacy **2 :** tending to deceive or mislead **:** DELUSIVE — **fal·la·cious·ly** *adv* — **fal·la·cious·ness** *n*

fal·la·cy \ˈfal-ə-sē\ *n, pl* **-cies** [L *fallacia,* fr. *fallac-, fallax* deceitful, fr. *fallere* to deceive — more at FAIL] **1 a** *obs* **:** GUILE, TRICKERY **b :** deceptive appearance **:** DECEPTION **2 a :** a false idea ⟨the popular ~ that poets are impractical⟩ **b :** erroneous or fallacious character **:** ERRONEOUSNESS **3 :** an argument failing to satisfy the conditions of valid or correct inference

fal–lal \fa-ˈlal, ˈfal-ˌ(l)al\ *n* [perh. alter. of *falbala* (furbelow)] **:** a fancy ornament esp. in dress — **fal·lal·ery** \fa-ˈlal-ə-rē\ *n*

fall armyworm *n* **:** a migratory American moth (*Spodoptera frugiperda*) that is esp. destructive to small grains and grasses as a larva

fall away *vi* **1 a :** to withdraw friendship or support **b :** to renounce one's faith **2 a :** to diminish gradually in size **b :** to drift off a course

fall·back \ˈfȯl-ˌbak\ *n* **1 :** something on which one can fall back **:** RESERVE **2 :** a falling back **:** RETREAT **3 :** something that falls back ⟨the ~ from an explosion⟩

fall back \-ˈbak\ *vi* **:** RETREAT, RECEDE — **fall back on** *or* **fall back upon :** to have recourse to ⟨when facts were scarce he *fell back on* his imagination⟩

fall down *vi* **:** to fail to meet expectations or requirements ⟨he *fell down* on the job⟩

fall·er \ˈfȯ-lər\ *n* **1 :** a logger who fells trees **2 :** a machine part that acts by falling

fall·fish \ˈfȯl-ˌfish\ *n* **:** a common cyprinid fish (*Semotilus corporalis*) of the streams of northeastern No. America — compare CHUB

fall guy *n* **1 :** one that is easily duped **2 :** SCAPEGOAT

fal·li·bil·i·ty \ˌfal-ə-ˈbil-ət-ē\ *n* **:** liability to err

fal·li·ble \ˈfal-ə-bəl\ *adj* [ME, fr. ML *fallibilis,* fr. L *fallere*] **1 :** liable to be erroneous ⟨a ~ generalization⟩ **2 :** capable of making a mistake ⟨all men are ~⟩ — **fal·li·bly** \-blē\ *adv*

fall in *vi* **1 :** to sink inward ⟨the roof *fell in*⟩ **2 :** to take one's proper place in a military formation — **fall in with 1 :** to concur with ⟨had to *fall in with* her wishes⟩ **2 :** to harmonize with ⟨it *falls in* exactly *with* my views⟩

falling diphthong *n* **:** a diphthong with less stress on the second element than on the first (as \ȯi\ in \ˈnȯiz\ *noise*)

fall·ing–out \ˌfȯ-liŋ-ˈau̇t\ *n, pl* **fallings–out** *or* **falling–outs :** an instance of falling out **:** QUARREL

falling rhythm *n* **:** rhythm with stress occurring regularly on the first syllable of each foot — compare RISING RHYTHM

falling star *n* **:** METEOR 2a

fall line *n* **1 :** a line joining the waterfalls on numerous rivers that marks the point where each river descends from the upland to the lowland and the limit of the navigability of each river **2 :** the natural downhill course (as for skiing) between two points on a slope

fall·off \ˈfȯ-ˌlȯf\ *n* **:** a decline esp. in quantity or quality ⟨a ~ in exports⟩ ⟨a ~ of light intensity⟩

fall off \(ˈ)fȯ-ˈlȯf\ *vi* **1 :** TREND 1b **2** *of a ship* **:** to deviate to leeward of the point to which the bow was directed

fal·lo·pi·an tube \fə-ˌlō-pē-ən-\ *n, often cap F* [Gabriel *Fallopius* †1562 It anatomist] **:** either of the pair of tubes conducting the egg from the ovary to the uterus

fall·out \ˈfȯ-ˌlau̇t\ *n* **1 a :** the often radioactive particles stirred up by or resulting from a nuclear explosion and descending through the atmosphere; *also* **:** other polluting particles (as volcanic ash) descending likewise **b :** descent (as of fallout) through the atmosphere **2 :** an incidental result or product ⟨the war . . . produced its own literary ~ —a profusion of books —*Newsweek*⟩

fall out \(ˈ)fȯ-ˈlau̇t\ *vi* **1 :** to turn out **:** HAPPEN ⟨as it *fell out* we couldn't have made it on time⟩ **2 :** QUARREL ⟨friends who have *fallen out*⟩ **3 a :** to leave one's place in the ranks **b :** to leave a building in order to take one's place in a military formation

[1]**fal·low** \ˈfal-(ˌ)ō, -ə(-w)\ *adj* [ME *falow,* fr. OE *fealu;* akin to OHG *falo* pale, fallow, L *pallēre* to be pale, Gk *polios* gray] **:** of a light yellowish brown color

[2]**fallow** *n* [ME *falwe, falow,* fr. OE *fealg* — more at FELLY] **1** *obs* **:** plowed land **2 :** usu. cultivated land that is allowed to lie idle during the growing season **3 :** the state or period of being fallow **4 :** the tilling of land without sowing it for a season

[3]**fallow** *vt* **:** to plow, harrow, and break up (land) without seeding to destroy weeds and conserve soil moisture

[4]**fallow** *adj* **1 :** left untilled or unsown after plowing **2 :** DORMANT, INACTIVE — used esp. in the phrase *to lie fallow* ⟨at this very moment there are probably important inventions lying ~ —*Harper's*⟩ — **fal·low·ness** *n*

fallow deer *n* **:** a small European deer (*Dama dama*) with broad antlers and a pale yellow coat spotted with white in the summer

fallow deer

fall to \ˈfȯl-ˈtü\ *vi* **:** to begin doing something (as working or eating) esp. vigorously — often used in invitation or command

[1]**false** \ˈfȯls\ *adj* **fals·er; fals·est** [ME *fals,* fr. OF & L; OF, fr. L *falsus,* fr. pp. of *fallere* to deceive] **1 :** not genuine ⟨~ documents⟩ ⟨~ teeth⟩ **2 a :** intentionally untrue ⟨~ testimony⟩ **b :** adjusted or made so as to deceive ⟨~ scales⟩ ⟨a trunk with a ~ bottom⟩ **c :** tending to mislead ⟨a ~ promise⟩ **3 :** not true ⟨~ concepts⟩ **4 a :** not faithful or loyal **:** TREACHEROUS **b** *obs* **:** not solid **5 a :** not essential or permanent — used of parts of a structure that are temporary or supplemental **b :** fitting over a main part to strengthen it, to protect it, or to disguise its appearance ⟨a ~ ceiling⟩ **c :** appearing forced or artificial **:** UNCONVINCING ⟨a ~ scene in a movie⟩ **6 :** of a kind related to or resembling another kind that is usu. designated by the unqualified vernacular ⟨~ oats⟩ **7 :** inaccurate in pitch ⟨a ~ note⟩ **8 a :** based on mistaken ideas ⟨~ pride⟩ **b :** inconsistent with the true facts ⟨a ~ position⟩ ⟨a ~ sense of security⟩ **9 :** IMPRUDENT, UNWISE ⟨don't make a ~ move⟩ — **false·ly** *adv* — **false·ness** *n*

syn* 1** FALSE, WRONG *shared meaning element* **:** neither true nor right ***ant true
2 see FAITHLESS ***ant*** true

[2]**false** *adv* **:** in a false or faithless manner **:** TREACHEROUSLY ⟨his wife played him ~⟩

false alarm *n* **1 :** an alarm (as a fire or burglar alarm) that is set off needlessly **2 :** one that raises but fails to meet expectations

false arrest *n* **:** an arrest not justifiable under law

false·hood \ˈfȯls-ˌhu̇d\ *n* **1 :** an untrue statement **:** LIE **2 :** absence of truth or accuracy **:** FALSITY **3 :** the practice of lying **:** MENDACITY

false horizon *n* **:** HORIZON 1c

false imprisonment *n* **:** imprisonment of a person contrary to law

false miterwort *n* : FOAMFLOWER
false pregnancy *n* : PSEUDOCYESIS, PSEUDOPREGNANCY
false rib *n* : a rib whose cartilages unite indirectly or not at all with the sternum — compare FLOATING RIB
false Solomon's–seal *n* : any of a genus (*Smilacina*) of herbs of the lily family that differ from Solomon's seal in having flowers in a terminal raceme or panicle
1**fal·set·to** \fȯl-ˈset-(ˌ)ō\ *n, pl* **-tos** [It, fr. dim. of *falso* false, fr. L *falsus*] **1** : an artificially high voice; *specif* : an artificially produced singing voice that overlaps and extends above the range of the full voice esp. of a tenor **2** : a singer who uses falsetto
2**falsetto** *adv* : in falsetto
fals·ie \ˈfȯl-sē\ *n* : a breast-shaped usu. fabric or rubber cup used to pad a brassiere — usu. used in pl.
fal·si·fy \ˈfȯl-sə-ˌfī\ *vb* **-fied; -fy·ing** [ME *falsifien*, fr. MF *falsifier*, fr. ML *falsificare*, fr. L *falsus*] *vt* **1** : to prove or declare false **2** : to make false: as **a** : to make false by mutilation or addition ⟨his accounts were *falsified* to conceal a theft⟩ **b** : to represent falsely : MISREPRESENT **3** : to prove unsound by experience ~ *vi* : to tell lies : LIE ***syn*** see MISREPRESENT — **fal·si·fi·ca·tion** \ˌfȯl-sə-fə-ˈkā-shən\ *n* — **fal·si·fi·er** \ˈfȯl-sə-ˌfī(-ə)r\ *n*
fal·si·ty \ˈfȯl-sət-ē\ *n, pl* **-ties** **1** : something false : LIE **2** : the quality or state of being false
Fal·staff \ˈfȯl-ˌstaf\ *n* : a convivial roguish character in Shakespeare's *Merry Wives of Windsor* and *Henry IV* — **Fal·staff·ian** \fȯl-ˈstaf-ē-ən\ *adj*
falt·boat \ˈfält-ˌbōt, ˈfȯlt-\ *n* [part trans. of G *faltboot* folding boat, fr. *falten* to fold (fr. OHG *faldan*) + *boot* boat] : FOLDBOAT
1**fal·ter** \ˈfȯl-tər\ *vb* **fal·tered; fal·ter·ing** \-t(ə-)riŋ\ [ME *falteren*] *vi* **1 a** : to walk unsteadily : STUMBLE **b** : to give way : TOTTER ⟨could feel his legs ~*ing*⟩ **c** : to move waveringly or hesitatingly ⟨forced to bail out of ~*ing* airplanes —*Nat'l Geographic*⟩ **2** : to speak brokenly or weakly : STAMMER **3 a** : to hesitate in purpose or action : WAVER **b** : to lose drive or effectiveness : FAIL, WEAKEN ⟨the business was ~*ing*⟩ ~ *vt* : to utter hesitatingly or brokenly ***syn*** see HESITATE — **fal·ter·er** \-tər-ər\ *n* — **fal·ter·ing·ly** \-t(ə-)riŋ-lē\ *adv*
2**falter** *n* : an act or instance of faltering
fam *abbr* **1** familiar **2** family
1**fame** \ˈfām\ *n* [ME, fr. OF, fr. L *fama* report, fame; akin to L *fari* to speak — more at BAN] **1 a** : public estimation : REPUTATION **b** : popular acclaim : RENOWN **2** *archaic* : RUMOR
2**fame** *vt* **famed; fam·ing** **1** : REPORT, REPUTE **2** : to make famous
famed \ˈfāmd\ *adj* : known widely and well : FAMOUS ⟨a ~ university⟩
fa·mil·ial \fə-ˈmil-yəl\ *adj* [F, fr. L *familia*] **1** : of, relating to, or characteristic of a family **2** : tending to occur in more members of a family than expected by chance alone ⟨a ~ disorder⟩
1**fa·mil·iar** \fə-ˈmil-yər\ *n* **1** : an intimate associate : COMPANION **2** : a member of the household of a high official **3** : a spirit often embodied in an animal and held to attend and serve or guard a person **4 a** : one who is well acquainted with something **b** : one who frequents a place
2**familiar** *adj* [ME *familier*, fr. OF, fr. L *familiaris*, fr. *familia*] **1** : closely acquainted : INTIMATE ⟨a ~ family friend⟩ **2** *obs* : AFFABLE, SOCIABLE **3 a** : of or relating to a family ⟨remembering past ~ celebrations⟩ **b** : frequented by families ⟨a ~ resort⟩ **4 a** : being free and easy ⟨the ~ association of old friends⟩ **b** : marked by informality ⟨a ~ essay⟩ **c** : overly free and unrestrained : PRESUMPTUOUS ⟨grossly ~ behavior⟩ **d** : moderately tame ⟨~ animals⟩ **5 a** : frequently seen or experienced **b** : of everyday occurrence ***syn*** see COMMON — **fa·mil·iar·ly** *adv* — **fa·mil·iar·ness** *n*
fa·mil·iar·i·ty \fə-ˌmil-ˈyar-ət-ē, -ˌmil-ē-ˈ(y)ar-\ *n, pl* **-ties** **1 a** : the quality or state of being familiar **b** : a state of close relationship : INTIMACY **2 a** : absence of ceremony : INFORMALITY **b** : an unduly informal act or expression : IMPROPRIETY **c** : a sexual liberty **3** : close acquaintance with something ⟨his ~ with American history⟩
fa·mil·iar·ize \fə-ˈmil-yə-ˌrīz\ *vt* **-ized; -iz·ing** **1** : to make known or familiar ⟨Shakespeare . . . ~*s* the wonderful —Samuel Johnson⟩ **2** : to make well acquainted ⟨~ students with good literature⟩ — **fa·mil·iar·iza·tion** \-ˌmil-yə-rə-ˈzā-shən\ *n*
familiar spirit *n* **1** : a spirit or demon that serves or prompts an individual **2** : the spirit of a dead person invoked by a medium to advise or prophesy
1**fam·i·ly** \ˈfam-(ə-)lē\ *n, pl* **-lies** [ME *familie*, fr. L *familia* household (including servants as well as kin of the householder), fr. *famulus* servant; perh. akin to Skt *dhāman* dwelling place] **1 a** : a group of people united by certain convictions (as of religion or philosophy) : FELLOWSHIP **b** : the staff of a high official (as the President) **2 a** : a group of persons of common ancestry : CLAN **b** : a people or group of peoples regarded as deriving from a common stock : RACE **3** : a group of individuals living under one roof and usu. under one head : HOUSEHOLD **4 a** : a group of things related by common characteristics or properties **b** : a closely related series of elements or chemical compounds **c** : a group of soils that have similar profiles and include one or more series **d** : a group of related languages descended from a single ancestral language **5** : the basic unit in society having as its nucleus two or more adults living together and cooperating in the care and rearing of their own or adopted children **6 a** : a group of related plants or animals forming a category ranking above a genus and below an order and usu. comprising several to many genera **b** *in livestock breeding* (1) : the descendants or line of a particular individual esp. of some outstanding female (2) : an identifiable strain within a breed **c** : an ecological community consisting of a single kind of organism and usu. being of limited extent and representing an early stage of a succession **7** : a set of curves or surfaces whose equations differ only in parameters
2**family** *adj* : of or relating to a family
family Bible *n* : a large Bible usu. having special pages for recording births, marriages, and deaths
family circle *n* : a gallery in a theater or opera house usu. located above or behind a gallery containing more expensive seats
family court *n* : COURT OF DOMESTIC RELATIONS
family doctor *n* : a doctor regularly called by a family in time of illness — called also *family physician*
family man *n* **1** : a man with a wife and children dependent on him **2** : a responsible man of domestic habits
family name *n* : SURNAME 2
family planning *n* : a system of controlling family size and approximate birth dates of children by appropriate use of contraceptive techniques
family room *n* : a large room designed as a recreation center for members of a family
family style *adv or adj* : with the food placed on the table in serving dishes from which those eating may help themselves ⟨meals are served *family style*⟩
family tree *n* **1** : GENEALOGY **2** : a genealogical diagram
fam·ine \ˈfam-ən\ *n* [ME, fr. MF, fr. (assumed) VL *famina*, fr. L *fames* hunger] **1** : an extreme scarcity of food **2** *archaic* : STARVATION **3** *archaic* : a ravenous appetite **4** : a great shortage
fam·ish \ˈfam-ish\ *vb* [ME *famishen*, prob. alter. of *famen*, fr. MF *afamer*, fr. (assumed) VL *affamare*, fr. L *ad-* + *fames*] *vt* **1** : to cause to suffer severely from hunger **2** *archaic* : to cause to starve to death ~ *vi* **1** *archaic* : STARVE **2** : to suffer for lack of something necessary ⟨this invention of language, at a moment when French poetry in particular was ~*ing* for such invention —T. S. Eliot⟩ — **fam·ish·ment** \-mənt\ *n*
fa·mous \ˈfā-məs\ *adj* [ME, fr. MF *fameux*, fr. L *famosus*, fr. *fama* fame] **1 a** : widely known **b** : honored for achievement **2** : EXCELLENT, FIRST-RATE ⟨~ weather for a walk⟩ — **fa·mous·ly** *adv* — **fa·mous·ness** *n*
syn FAMOUS, RENOWNED, CELEBRATED, NOTED, DISTINGUISHED, EMINENT, ILLUSTRIOUS *shared meaning element* : known far and wide ***ant*** obscure
fam·u·lus \ˈfam-yə-ləs\ *n, pl* **-li** \-ˌlī, -ˌlē\ [G, assistant to a professor, fr. L, servant] : a private secretary or attendant
1**fan** \ˈfan\ *n* [ME, fr. OE *fann*, fr. L *vannus* — more at WINNOW] **1** : any of various devices for winnowing grain **2** : an instrument for producing a current of air: as **a** : a device for cooling the person that is usu. shaped like a segment of a circle and is composed of material (as feathers or paper) mounted on thin rods or slats moving about a pivot so that the device may be closed compactly when not in use **b** : a device for producing a current of air that consists of a series of vanes radiating from a hub rotated on its axle by a motor **c** *slang* : an airplane propeller **3** : something resembling an open fan — **fan·like** \-ˌlīk\ *adj*
2**fan** *vb* **fanned; fan·ning** *vt* **1 a** : to drive away the chaff of (grain) by means of a current of air **b** : to eliminate (as chaff) by winnowing **2** : to move or impel (air) with a fan **3** : to blow or breathe upon ⟨the breeze *fanning* her hair⟩ **4 a** : to direct a current of air upon with a fan **b** : to stir up to activity as if by fanning : STIMULATE ⟨he was *fanning* her antagonism with insults⟩ **5** *archaic* : WAVE **6** *slang* : SPANK **7** : to spread like a fan ⟨the peacock *fanned* his tail⟩ **8** : to strike (a batter) out in baseball **9** : to fire a series of shots from (a revolver) by holding the trigger back and successively striking the hammer to the rear with the free hand ~ *vi* **1** : to move like a fan : FLUTTER **2** : to spread like a fan — often used with *out* ⟨deputies *fanning* out on the hunt⟩ **3** *of a baseball batter* : to strike out
3**fan** *n* [prob. short for *fanatic*] **1** : an enthusiastic devotee (as of a sport or a performing art) usu. as a spectator **2** : an ardent admirer or enthusiast (as of a celebrity or a pursuit) ⟨science-fiction ~*s*⟩
fa·nat·ic \fə-ˈnat-ik\ *or* **fa·nat·i·cal** \-i-kəl\ *adj* [L *fanaticus* inspired by a deity, frenzied, fr. *fanum* temple — more at FEAST] : marked by excessive enthusiasm and often intense uncritical devotion ⟨he's ~ about politics⟩ — **fanatic** *n* — **fa·nat·i·cal·ly** \fə-ˈnat-i-k(ə-)lē\ *adv* — **fa·nat·i·cal·ness** \-kəl-nəs\ *n*
fa·nat·i·cism \fə-ˈnat-ə-ˌsiz-əm\ *n* : fanatic outlook or behavior
fa·nat·i·cize \-ˌsīz\ *vt* **-cized; -ciz·ing** : to cause to become fanatic
fan·ci·er \ˈfan(t)-sē-ər\ *n* : one that has a special liking or interest; *esp* : a person who breeds or grows a particular animal or plant for points of excellence ⟨a pigeon ~⟩
fan·ci·ful \ˈfan(t)-si-fəl\ *adj* **1** : marked by fancy or unrestrained imagination rather than by reason and experience **2** : existing in fancy only **3** : marked by or as if by fancy or whim ⟨gave ~ names to her children⟩ ***syn*** see IMAGINARY ***ant*** realistic — **fan·ci·ful·ly** \-f(ə-)lē\ *adv* — **fan·ci·ful·ness** \-fəl-nəs\ *n*
fan·ci·ly \ˈfan(t)-sə-lē\ *adv* **1** : with fancy or imagination esp. when studied or affected **2** : in an elaborate or ornate manner ⟨~ dressed⟩
fan·ci·ness \-sē-nəs\ *n* : fancy quality or form
1**fan·cy** \ˈfan(t)-sē\ *n, pl* **fancies** [ME *fantasie, fantsy* fantasy, fancy, fr. MF *fantasie*, fr. L *phantasia*, fr. Gk, appearance, imagination, fr. *phantazein* to present to the mind (middle voice, to imagine), fr. *phainein* to show; akin to OE *gebōned* polished, Gk *phōs* light] **1 a** : a liking formed by caprice rather than reason : INCLINATION ⟨took a ~ to the strange little animal⟩ **b** : amorous fondness : LOVE **2 a** : NOTION, WHIM **b** : an image or representation of something formed in the mind **3** *archaic* : fantastic quality or state **4 a** : imagination esp. of a capricious or delusive sort **b** : the power of conception and representation used in artistic expression (as by a poet) **5** : TASTE, JUDGMENT **6 a** : devotees of some particular art, practice, or amusement **b** : the object of interest of such a fancy; *esp* : PUGILISM ***syn*** see IMAGINATION
2**fancy** *vt* **fan·cied; fan·cy·ing** **1** : to have a fancy for : LIKE **2** : to form a conception of : IMAGINE ⟨~ our embarrassment⟩ **3** : to form an idea about on the basis of inadequate evidence or in the absence of evidence ⟨she *fancied* she had met him before⟩ ***syn*** see THINK
3**fancy** *adj* **fan·ci·er; -est** **1** : dependent or based on fancy : WHIMSICAL **2 a** : not plain : ORNAMENTAL ⟨a ~ hairdo⟩ **b** : of particular excellence or highest grade ⟨~ tuna⟩ **c** *of an animal or plant* : bred esp. for bizarre or ornamental qualities that lack prac-

tical utility **3** : based on conceptions of the fancy ⟨~ sketches⟩ **4** **a** : dealing in fancy goods **b** : above real value or the usual market price; *esp* : EXTRAVAGANT ⟨paying ~ prices for inferior goods⟩ **5** : executed with technical skill and superior grace ⟨~ diving⟩ **6** : PARTI-COLORED ⟨~ carnations⟩

fancy dress *n* : a costume (as for a masquerade) chosen to suit the wearer's fancy

fan·cy–free \ˈfan(t)-sē-ˌfrē\ *adj* **1** : free to imagine or fancy **2** : free from amorous attachment or engagement

fancy man *n* : a woman's paramour; *also* : PIMP

fancy up *vt* : to add superficial adornment to ⟨*fancy up* an old dress with ruffles⟩

fancy woman *n* : a woman of questionable morals; *specif* : PROSTITUTE

fan·cy·work \ˈfan(t)-sē-ˌwərk\ *n* : decorative needlework

F and A *abbr* fore and aft

fan·dan·go \fan-ˈdaŋ-(ˌ)gō\ *n, pl* **-gos** [Sp] **1** : a lively Spanish or Spanish-American dance in triple time that is usu. performed by a man and a woman to the accompaniment of guitar and castanets; *also* : music for this dance **2** : TOMFOOLERY

fan·dom \ˈfan-dəm\ *n* : all the fans (as of a sport)

fane \ˈfān\ *n* [ME, fr. L *fanum* — more at FEAST] **1** : TEMPLE **2** : CHURCH

fan·fare \ˈfan-ˌfa(ə)r, -ˌfe(ə)r\ *n* [F] **1** : a flourish of trumpets **2** : a showy outward display

fan·far·o·nade \ˌfan-ˌfar-ə-ˈnād, -ˈnäd\ *n* [F *fanfaronnade,* fr. Sp *fanfarronada,* fr. *fanfarrón* braggart] : empty boasting : BLUSTER

fan·fold \ˈfan-ˌfōld\ *n* : a business form made from a web of paper folded like a fan both lengthwise and crosswise

fang \ˈfaŋ\ *n* [ME, fr. OE; akin to OHG *fang* seizure, OE *fōn* to seize — more at PACT] **1** **a** : a long sharp tooth: as (1) : one by which an animal's prey is seized and held or torn (2) : one of the long hollow or grooved and often erectile teeth of a venomous snake **b** : one of the chelicerae of a spider at the tip of which a poison gland opens **2** : the root of a tooth or one of the processes or prongs into which a root divides **3** : a projecting tooth or prong — **fanged** \ˈfaŋd\ *adj*

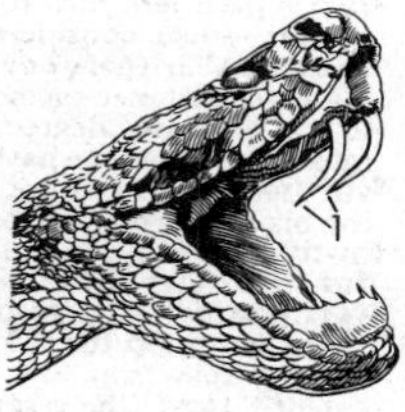

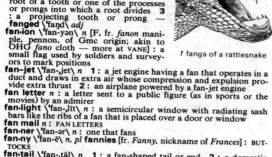

1 fangs of a rattlesnake

fan·ion \ˈfan-yən\ *n* [F, fr. *fanon* maniple, pennon, of Gmc origin; akin to OHG *fano* cloth — more at VANE] : a small flag used by soldiers and surveyors to mark positions

fan–jet \ˈfan-ˌjet\ *n* **1** : a jet engine having a fan that operates in a duct and draws in extra air whose compression and expulsion provide extra thrust **2** : an airplane powered by a fan-jet engine

fan letter *n* : a letter sent to a public figure (as in sports or the movies) by an admirer

fan·light \ˈfan-ˌlīt\ *n* : a semicircular window with radiating sash bars like the ribs of a fan that is placed over a door or window

fan mail *n* : FAN LETTERS

fan·ner \ˈfan-ər\ *n* : one that fans

fan·ny \ˈfan-ē\ *n, pl* **fannies** [fr. *Fanny,* nickname of *Frances*] : BUTTOCKS

fan·tail \ˈfan-ˌtāl\ *n* **1** : a fan-shaped tail or end **2** : a domestic pigeon having a broad rounded tail often with 30 or 40 feathers **3** : an architectural part resembling a fan **4** : a counter or after overhang of a ship shaped like a duck's bill

fan–tan \ˈfan-ˌtan\ *n* [Chin *fan¹-t'an¹*] **1** : a Chinese gambling game in which the banker divides a pile of objects (as beans) into fours and players bet on what number will be left at the end of the count **2** : a card game in which players must build in sequence upon sevens and attempt to be the first one out of cards

fan·ta·sia \fan-ˈtā-zhə, -z(h)ē-ə; ˌfant-ə-ˈzē-ə\ *also* **fan·ta·sie** \ˌfant-ə-ˈzē, ˌfänt-\ *n* [It *fantasia* & G *fantasie,* lit., fancy, fr. L *phantasia* — more at FANCY] **1** **a** : a free instrumental composition not in strict form **b** : a potpourri of operatic arias or familiar airs **2** **a** : a work (as a poem or play) in which the author's fancy roves unrestricted **b** : something possessing grotesque, bizarre, or unreal qualities

fan·ta·sied \ˈfant-ə-sēd, -zēd\ *adj* **1** : existing only in the imagination : FANCIED **2** *obs* : full of fancies or strange whims

fan·ta·sist \-səst, -zəst\ *n* : one who creates fantasias or fantasies

fan·ta·size \-ˌsīz\ *vb* **-sized; -siz·ing** *vt* : FANTASY ⟨likes to ~ herself as very wealthy⟩ ~ *vi* : to indulge in reverie : create or develop imaginative and often fantastic views or ideas ⟨doing things I'd *fantasized* about in my sheltered childhood —Diane Arbus⟩

fantasm *var of* PHANTASM

fan·tast \ˈfan-ˌtast\ *n* [G, fr. ML *fantasta,* prob. back-formation fr. LL *phantasticus*] **1** : VISIONARY **2** : a fantastic or eccentric person **3** : FANTASIST

1**fan·tas·tic** \fan-ˈtas-tik, fən-\ *adj* [ME *fantastic, fantastical,* fr. MF & LL; MF *fantastique,* fr. LL *phantasticus,* fr. Gk *phantastikos* producing mental images, fr. *phantazein* to present to the mind] **1** **a** : based on fantasy : not real **b** : conceived or seemingly conceived by unrestrained fancy **c** : so extreme as to challenge belief : UNBELIEVABLE; *broadly* : excessively large or great **2** : marked by extravagant fantasy or extreme individuality : ECCENTRIC — **fan·tas·ti·cal** \-ti-kəl\ *adj* — **fan·tas·ti·cal·i·ty** \(ˌ)fan-ˌtas-tə-ˈkal-ət-ē, fən-\ *n* — **fan·tas·ti·cal·ly** \fan-ˈtas-ti-k(ə-)lē, fən-\ *adv* — **fan·tas·ti·cal·ness** \-kəl-nəs\ *n*

syn **1** see IMAGINARY
2 FANTASTIC, BIZARRE, GROTESQUE *shared meaning element* : conceived or made or carried out without evident reference to reality, truth, or common sense

2**fantastic** *n* : ECCENTRIC 2

fan·tas·ti·cate \fan-ˈtas-tə-ˌkāt, fən-\ *vt* **-cat·ed; -cat·ing** : to make fantastic — **fan·tas·ti·ca·tion** \(ˌ)fan-ˌtas-tə-ˈkā-shən, fən-\ *n*

fan·tas·ti·co \fan-ˈtas-ti-ˌkō, fən-\ *n, pl* **-coes** [It, fantastic (adj.), fr. LL *phantasticus*] : a ridiculously fantastic individual

1**fan·ta·sy** \ˈfant-ə-sē, -zē\ *n, pl* **-sies** [ME *fantasie* — more at FANCY] **1** *obs* : HALLUCINATION **2** : FANCY; *esp* : the free play of creative imagination **3** : a creation of the imaginative faculty whether expressed or merely conceived: as **a** : a fanciful design or invention **b** : a chimerical or fantastic notion **c** : FANTASIA 1 **d** : imaginative fiction featuring esp. strange settings and grotesque characters — called also *fantasy fiction* **4** : CAPRICE **5** : the power or process of creating esp. unrealistic or improbable mental images in response to psychological need ⟨an object of ~⟩; *also* : a mental image so created : DAYDREAM ⟨sexual *fantasies* of adolescence⟩ **6** : a coin usu. not intended for circulation as currency and often issued by a dubious authority (as a government-in-exile) ***syn*** see IMAGINATION

2**fantasy** *vb* **-sied; -sy·ing** *vt* : to portray in the mind : FANCY ~ *vi* : to indulge in reverie : DAYDREAM

fan·toc·ci·ni \ˌfänt-ə-ˈchē-nē, ˌfant-\ *n pl* [It, pl. of *fantoccino,* dim. of *fantoccio* doll, aug. of *fante* child, fr. L *infant-, infans* infant] **1** : puppets operated by strings or mechanical devices **2** : a puppet show using fantoccini

fan·tod \ˈfan-ˌtäd\ *n* [perh. alter. of E dial. *fantique, fanteeg*] **1** *pl* **a** : a state of irritability and tension **b** : FIDGETS **2** : an emotional outburst : FIT

fantom *var of* PHANTOM

fan tracery *n* : decorative tracery on vaulting in which the ribs diverge like the rays of a fan

fan·wise \ˈfan-ˌwīz\ *adv or adj* : in the manner or position of the slats of an open fan ⟨boats anchored ~ at the pier⟩

FAO *abbr* Food and Agriculture Organization of the United Nations

FAQ *abbr* fair average quality

1**far** \ˈfär\ *adv* **far·ther** \-t͟hər\ *or* **fur·ther** \ˈfər-\; **far·thest** *or* **fur·thest** \-t͟həst\ [ME *fer,* fr. OE *feorr;* akin to OHG *ferro* far, OE *faran* to go — more at FARE] **1** : at or to a considerable distance in space ⟨wandered ~ from home⟩ **2** **a** : by a broad interval : WIDELY ⟨the ~ distant future⟩ **b** : of a distinctly different quality — usu. used with *from* ⟨the trip was ~ from a failure⟩ **3** : to or at a definite distance, point, or degree ⟨as ~ as I know⟩ **4** **a** : to an advanced point or extent ⟨a bright student will go ~⟩ ⟨worked ~ into the night⟩ **b** : to a great extent : MUCH ⟨~ better methods⟩ **5** : at a considerable distance in time ⟨not ~ from the year 1870⟩ — **by far** : far and away ⟨is *by far* the best runner⟩ — **far and away** : by a considerable margin ⟨was *far and away* the superior team⟩ — **how far** : to what extent, degree, or distance ⟨didn't know *how far* to trust him⟩ — **so far** **1** : to a certain extent, degree, or distance ⟨when the water rose *so far,* the villagers sought higher ground⟩ **2** : up to the present ⟨has written just one novel *so far*⟩ — **thus far** : so far ⟨*thus far* our findings have been negative⟩

2**far** *adj* **farther** *or* **further; farthest** *or* **furthest** **1** **a** : remote in space **b** : distinctly different in quality or relationship **c** : remote in time **2** **a** : LONG ⟨a ~ journey⟩ **b** : of notable extent : COMPREHENSIVE ⟨a man of ~ vision⟩ **3** : the more distant of two **4** *of a political position* : EXTREME ⟨the ~ left⟩ ⟨a ~ right organization⟩ ***syn*** see DISTANT ***ant*** near, nigh, nearby

3**far** *abbr* farthing

far·ad \ˈfa(ə)r-ˌad, ˈfar-əd\ *n* [Michael *Faraday*] : the unit of capacitance equal to the capacitance of a capacitor between whose plates there appears a potential of one volt when it is charged by one coulomb of electricity

far·a·day \ˈfar-ə-ˌdā, -əd-ē\ *n* [Michael *Faraday*] : the quantity of electricity transferred in electrolysis per equivalent weight of an element or ion equal to about 96,500 coulombs

fa·rad·ic \fə-ˈrad-ik, far-ˈad-\ *also* **far·a·da·ic** \ˌfar-ə-ˈdā-ik\ *adj* : of or relating to an asymmetric alternating current of electricity produced by an induction coil

far·a·dism \ˈfar-ə-ˌdiz-əm\ *n* : the application of a faradic current of electricity (as for therapeutic purposes)

far·an·dole \ˈfar-ən-ˌdōl\ *n* [F *farandole,* fr. Prov *farandoulo*] **1** : a lively Provençal dance in which men and women hold hands, form a chain, and follow a leader through a serpentine course **2** : music in sextuple time for a farandole

far and wide *adv* : in every direction : EVERYWHERE ⟨advertised the event *far and wide*⟩

far·away \ˌfär-ə-ˌwā\ *adj* **1** : lying at a great distance : REMOTE **2** : DREAMY, ABSTRACTED ⟨a ~ look in her eyes⟩ ***syn*** see DISTANT ***ant*** near, nigh, nearby

1**farce** \ˈfärs\ *vt* **farced; farc·ing** [ME *farsen,* fr. MF *farcir,* fr. L *farcire;* akin to Gk *phrassein* to enclose] **1** : STUFF **2** : to make more acceptable (as a literary work) by padding or spicing

2**farce** *n* [ME *farse,* fr. MF *farce,* fr. (assumed) VL *farsa,* fr. L, fem. of *farsus,* pp. of *farcire*] **1** : a savory stuffing : FORCEMEAT **2** : a light dramatic composition marked by broadly satirical comedy and improbable plot **3** : the broad humor characteristic of farce or pretense **4** **a** : ridiculous or empty show **b** : MOCKERY ⟨the upholding of this law became a ~⟩

far·ceur \fär-ˈsər\ *n* [F, fr. MF, fr. *farcer* to joke, fr. OF, fr. *farce*] **1** : JOKER, WAG **2** : a writer or actor of farce

far·ci *or* **far·cie** \fär-ˈsē\ *adj* [F, fr. pp. of *farcir*] : stuffed esp. with forcemeat ⟨oysters ~⟩

far·ci·cal \ˈfär-si-kəl\ *adj* **1** : of, relating to, or resembling farce : LUDICROUS **2** : laughably inept : ABSURD — **far·ci·cal·i·ty** \ˌfär-sə-ˈkal-ət-ē\ *n* — **far·ci·cal·ly** \ˈfär-si-k(ə-)lē\ *adv*

far·cy \ˈfär-sē\ *n* [ME *farsin, farsi,* fr. MF *farcin,* fr. LL *farcimen,* fr. L, sausage, fr. *farcire*] **1** : GLANDERS; *esp* : cutaneous glanders **2** : a chronic ultimately fatal actinomycosis of cattle

ə abut	ᵊ kitten	ər further	a back	ā bake	ä cot, cart
au̇ out	ch chin	e less	ē easy	g gift	i trip
j joke	ŋ sing	ō flow	ȯ flaw	ȯi coin	th thin
ü loot	u̇ foot	y yet	yü few	yu̇ furious	zh vision

[1]**fard** \ˈfärd\ *vt* [ME *farden,* fr. MF *farder;* akin to OHG *faro* colored — more at PERCH] **1 :** to paint (the face) with cosmetics **2** *archaic* **:** to gloss over

[2]**fard** *n, archaic* **:** paint used on the face

far·del \ˈfärd-ᵊl\ *n* [ME, fr. MF, prob. fr. Ar *fardah*] **1 :** BUNDLE **2 :** BURDEN

[1]**fare** \ˈfa(ə)r, ˈfe(ə)r\ *vi* **fared; far·ing** [ME *faren,* fr. OE *faran;* akin to OHG *faran* to go, L *portare* to carry, Gk *peran* to pass through, *poros* passage, journey] **1 :** GO, TRAVEL **2 :** to get along **:** SUCCEED ⟨how did you ~ on your exam?⟩ **3 :** EAT, DINE

[2]**fare** *n* [ME, journey, passage, supply of food, fr. OE *faru, fær;* akin to OE *faran* to go] **1 a :** the price charged to transport a person **b :** a paying passenger on a public conveyance **2 a :** range of food **:** DIET **b :** material provided for use, consumption, or enjoyment

fare–thee–well \ˌfa(ə)r-(ˌ)thē-ˌwel, ˌfe(ə)r-\ *or* **fare–you–well** \-yə-, -yü-, -yē-\ *n* **1 :** a state of perfection ⟨imitated the speaker's pompous manner to a ~⟩ **2 :** the utmost degree ⟨drubbed the burglar to a ~⟩

[1]**fare·well** \fa(ə)r-ˈwel, fe(ə)r-\ *vb imper* **:** get along well — used interjectionally to or by one departing

[2]**farewell** *n* **1 :** a wish of well-being at parting **:** GOOD-BYE **2 a :** an act of departure **:** LEAVE-TAKING **b :** a formal occasion honoring a person about to leave or retire

[3]**fare·well** \ˌfa(ə)r-ˌwel, ˌfe(ə)r-\ *adj* **:** of or relating to leave-taking **:** FINAL ⟨a ~ appearance⟩

[4]**fare·well** \fa(ə)r-ˈwel, fe(ə)r-\ *vt* **:** to bid farewell

far·fel *or* **far·fal** \ˈfär-fəl\ *n* [Yiddish *farfl* (pl.), fr. MHG *varveln*] **:** noodles in the form of small pellets or granules

far·fetched \ˈfär-ˈfecht\ *adj* **1 :** brought from a remote time or place **2 :** not easily or naturally deduced or introduced **:** IMPROBABLE — **far·fetched·ness** \-ˈfech(t)-nəs, -ˈfech-əd-nəs\ *n*

far–flung \-ˈfləŋ\ *adj* **1 :** widely spread or distributed ⟨~ trading operations⟩ **2 :** REMOTE ⟨~ sections of the city⟩

far–gone \ˈfär-ˈgȯn *also* -ˈgän\ *adj* **:** nearing an end ⟨a nightmare vision of the . . . mother, ~ in pregnancy, clawing with her hands —R. E. Long⟩

fa·ri·na \fə-ˈrē-nə\ *n* [L, meal, flour, fr. *far* spelt — more at BARLEY] **1 :** a fine meal of vegetable matter (as cereal grains) used chiefly for puddings or as a breakfast cereal **2 :** any of various powdery or mealy substances

far·i·na·ceous \ˌfar-ə-ˈnā-shəs\ *adj* **1 :** containing or rich in starch **2 :** having a mealy texture or surface — **far·i·na·ceous·ly** *adv*

fa·ri·nha \fə-ˈrēn-yə\ *n* [Pg, flour, cassava meal, fr. L *farina*] **:** cassava meal

far·kle·ber·ry \ˈfär-kəl-ˌber-ē\ *n* [prob. alter. of *whortleberry*] **:** a shrub or small tree (*Vaccinium arboreum*) of the heath family of the southeastern U.S. having a black berry with stony seeds

farl *or* **farle** \ˈfär(ə)l\ *n* [contr. of Sc *fardel,* lit., fourth part, fr. ME (Sc), fr. *ferde del;* fr. *ferde* fourth + *del* part] *Scot* **:** a small scone

[1]**farm** \ˈfärm\ *n* [ME *ferme* rent, lease, fr. OF, lease, fr. *fermer* to fix, make a contract, fr. L *firmare* to make firm, fr. *firmus* firm] **1** *obs* **:** a sum or due fixed in amount and payable at fixed intervals **2 :** a letting out of revenues or taxes for a fixed sum to one authorized to collect and retain them **3 :** a district or division of a country leased out for the collection of government revenues **4 :** a tract of land devoted to agricultural purposes **5 a :** a plot of land devoted to the raising of animals and esp. domestic livestock **b :** a tract of water reserved for the artificial cultivation of some aquatic life form **6 :** a minor-league baseball club associated with a major-league club as a subsidiary to which recruits are assigned until needed or for further training

[2]**farm** *vt* **1** *obs* **:** RENT **2 :** to collect and take the fees or profits of (an occupation or business) on payment of a fixed sum **3 :** to give up (as an estate or a business) to another on condition of receiving in return a fixed sum **4 a :** to devote to agriculture **b :** to manage and cultivate as a farm ~ *vi* **:** to engage in raising crops or livestock

farm·er \ˈfär-mər\ *n* **1 :** a person who pays a fixed sum for some privilege or source of income **2 :** a person who cultivates land or crops or raises livestock **3 :** YOKEL, BUMPKIN

farmer cheese *n* **:** a pressed unripened cheese similar to but drier and firmer than cottage cheese — called also *farm cheese*

farm·er·ette \ˌfär-mə-ˈret\ *n* **:** a female farmer or farmhand

farm·hand \ˈfärm-ˌhand\ *n* **:** a farm laborer; *esp* **:** a hired laborer on a farm

farm·house \-ˌhau̇s\ *n* **:** a dwelling on a farm

farm·ing *n* **:** the practice of agriculture

farm·land \ˈfärm-ˌland\ *n* **:** land used or suitable for farming

farm out *vt* **1 :** to turn over for performance (as a job) or use usu. on contract **2 a :** to put (as children or prisoners) into the hands of a private individual for care in return for a fee **b :** to send (a baseball player) to a farm team **3 :** to exhaust (land) by farming esp. by continuously raising one crop

farm·stead \ˈfärm-ˌsted\ *also* **farm·stead·ing** \-iŋ\ *n* **:** the buildings and adjacent service areas of a farm

farm·yard \-ˌyärd\ *n* **:** space around or enclosed by farm buildings; *esp* **:** BARNYARD

faro \ˈfa(ə)r-(ˌ)ō, ˈfe(ə)r-\ *n, pl* **faros** [prob. alter. of earlier *pharaoh,* trans. of F *pharaon*] **:** a gambling game in which players bet on cards drawn from a dealing box

Faro·ese *var of* FAEROESE

far–off \ˈfär-ˈȯf\ *adj* **:** remote in time or space ***syn*** see DISTANT ***ant*** near, nigh, nearby

fa·rouche \fə-ˈrüsh\ *adj* [F, wild, shy, fr. LL *forasticus* belonging outside, fr. L *foras* outdoors; akin to L *fores* door — more at DOOR] **:** marked by shyness and lack of polish; *also* **:** WILD

far–out \ˈfär-ˈau̇t\ *adj* **:** marked by a considerable departure from the conventional or traditional **:** EXTREME ⟨~ clothes⟩ — **far–out·ness** *n*

far point *n* **:** the point farthest from the eye at which an object is accurately focused on the retina at full accommodation

far·rag·i·nous \fə-ˈraj-ə-nəs\ *adj* **:** formed of various materials

far·ra·go \fə-ˈräg-(ˌ)ō, -ˈrā-(ˌ)gō\ *n, pl* **-goes** [L *farragin-, farrago* mixed fodder, mixture, fr. *far* spelt — more at BARLEY] **:** a confused collection **:** MIXTURE

far–reach·ing \ˈfär-ˈrē-chiŋ\ *adj* **:** having a wide range or effect

far–red \-ˈred\ *adj* **1 :** lying in the part of the infrared spectrum farthest from the red — used of radiations with wavelengths between 30 and about 1000 microns **2 :** lying in the part of the infrared spectrum nearest to the red — used of radiations with wavelengths starting at about .8 micron

far·ri·er \ˈfar-ē-ər\ *n* [alter. of ME *ferrour,* fr. MF *ferrour* blacksmith, fr. OF *ferreor,* fr. *ferrer* to fit with iron, fr. (assumed) VL *ferrare,* fr. L *ferrum* iron] **:** one that attends to or shoes horses

[1]**far·row** \ˈfar-(ˌ)ō, -ə(-w)\ *vb* [ME *farwen,* fr. (assumed) OE *feargian,* fr. OE *fearh* young pig; akin to OHG *farah* young pig, L *porcus* pig] *vt* **:** to give birth to (a farrow) ~ *vi, of swine* **:** to bring forth young — often used with *down*

[2]**farrow** *n* **1 :** a litter of pigs **2 :** an act of farrowing

[3]**farrow** *adj* [ME (Sc) *ferow;* prob. akin to OE *fearr* bull, ox — more at PARE] *of a cow* **:** not in calf **:** not settled

far·see·ing \ˈfär-ˈsē-iŋ\ *adj* **:** FARSIGHTED 1

far side *n* **:** the farther side — **on the far side of :** BEYOND ⟨just *on the far side of* 40⟩

far·sight·ed \ˈfär-ˈsīt-əd\ *adj* **1 a :** seeing or able to see to a great distance **b :** having foresight or good judgment **:** SAGACIOUS **2 :** affected with hyperopia — **far·sight·ed·ly** *adv*

far·sight·ed·ness *n* **1 :** the quality or state of being farsighted **2 :** HYPEROPIA

[1]**fart** \ˈfärt\ *vi* [ME *ferten, farten;* akin to OHG *ferzan* to break wind, ON *freta,* Gk *perdesthai,* Skt *pardate* he breaks wind] **:** to expel intestinal gas from the anus — usu. considered vulgar

[2]**fart** *n* [ME *fert, fart,* fr. *ferten, farten;* v.] **:** an expulsion of intestinal gas — usu. considered vulgar

[1]**far·ther** \ˈfär-thər\ *adv* [ME *ferther,* alter. of *further*] **1 :** at or to a greater distance or more advanced point ⟨~ down the corridor⟩ **2 :** to a greater degree or extent ⟨we do not extend the one-man idea any ~ than we have to —G. F. Eliot⟩

[2]**farther** *adj* **1 :** more distant **:** REMOTER **2 :** [2]FURTHER 2 ⟨clearing his throat preparatory to ~ revelations —Edith Wharton⟩

far·ther·most \-ˌmōst\ *adj* **:** most distant **:** FARTHEST

[1]**far·thest** \ˈfär-thəst\ *adj* **:** most distant in space or time

[2]**farthest** *adv* **1 :** to or at the greatest distance in space or time ⟨who can jump the ~⟩ **2 :** to the most advanced point ⟨goes ~ toward answering the question⟩ **3 :** by the greatest degree or extent **:** MOST ⟨the essay ~ removed from this reviewer's comprehension —*Saturday Rev.*⟩

far·thing \ˈfär-thiŋ\ *n* [ME *ferthing,* fr. OE *fēorthung;* akin to MHG *vierdunc* fourth part, OE *fēortha* fourth] **1 a :** a former British monetary unit equal to 1/4 of a penny **b :** a coin representing this unit **2 :** something of small value **:** MITE

far·thin·gale \ˈfär-thən-ˌgāl, -thiŋ-\ *n* [modif. of MF *verdugale,* fr. OSp *verdugado,* fr. *verdugo* young shoot of a tree, fr. *verde* green, fr. L *viridis* — more at VERDANT] **:** a support (as of hoops) worn esp. in the 16th century beneath a skirt to expand it at the hip line

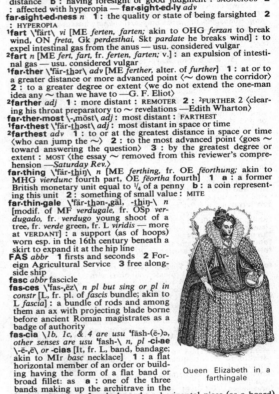

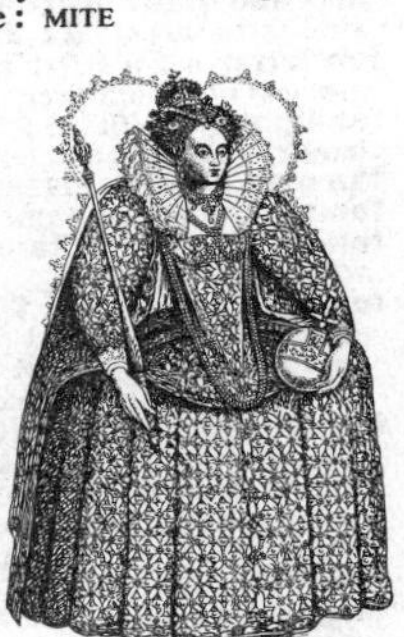
Queen Elizabeth in a farthingale

FAS *abbr* **1** firsts and seconds **2** Foreign Agricultural Service **3** free alongside ship

fasc *abbr* fascicle

fas·ces \ˈfas-ˌēz\ *n pl but sing or pl in constr* [L, fr. pl. of *fascis* bundle; akin to L *fascia*] **:** a bundle of rods and among them an ax with projecting blade borne before ancient Roman magistrates as a badge of authority

fas·cia *1b, 1c, & 4 are usu* ˈfāsh-(ē-)ə, *other senses are usu* ˈfash-\ *n, pl* **-ci·ae** \-ē-ˌē\ *or* **-cias** [It, fr. L, band, bandage; akin to MIr *basc* necklace] **1 :** a flat horizontal member of an order or building having the form of a flat band or broad fillet: as **a :** one of the three bands making up the architrave in the Ionic order **b** *or* **fascia board :** a horizontal piece (as a board) covering the joint between the top of a wall and the projecting eaves **c :** a nameplate over the front of a shop **2 :** a broad and well-defined band of color **3 :** a sheet of connective tissue covering or binding together body structures; *also* **:** tissue of this character **4** *Brit* **:** the dashboard of an automobile — **fas·cial** \ˈfash-(ē-)əl\ *adj*

fas·ci·at·ed \ˈfash-ē-ˌāt-əd\ *adj* **1 :** arranged in fascicles **2 :** exhibiting fasciation

fas·ci·a·tion \ˌfas(h)-ē-ˈā-shən\ *n* **:** a malformation of plant stems commonly manifested as enlargement and flattening as if several were fused

fas·ci·cle \ˈfas-i-kəl\ *n* [L *fasciculus,* dim. of *fascis*] **1 :** a small bundle: as **a :** an inflorescence consisting of a compacted cyme less capitate than a glomerule **b :** FASCICULUS 1 **2 :** one of the divisions of a book published in parts — **fas·ci·cled** \-kəld\ *adj*

fas·cic·u·lar \fə-ˈsik-yə-lər, fa-\ *adj* **:** of, relating to, or consisting of fascicles — **fas·cic·u·lar·ly** *adv*

fas·cic·u·late \-lət\ *adj* **:** FASCICULAR

fas·cic·u·la·tion \fə-ˌsik-yə-ˈlā-shən, fa-\ *n* [NL *fasciculus* + E *-ation* (as in *fibrillation*)] **:** muscular twitching involving contiguous groups of muscle fibers

fas·ci·cule \ˈfas-i-ˌkyü(ə)l\ *n* [F, fr. L *fasciculus*] **:** FASCICLE 2

fas·cic·u·lus \fə-ˈsik-yə-ləs, fa-\ *n, pl* **-li** \-ˌlī\ [NL, fr. L] **1 :** a slender bundle of anatomical fibers **2 :** FASCICLE 2

fas·ci·nate \ˈfas-ᵊn-ˌāt\ *vb* **-nat·ed; -nat·ing** [L *fascinatus,* pp. of *fascinare,* fr. *fascinum* witchcraft] *vt* **1** *obs* **:** BEWITCH **2 a :** to transfix and hold spellbound by an irresistible power ⟨believed that the serpent could ~ its prey⟩ **b :** to command the interest of

: ALLURE ⟨was *fascinated* by her personality⟩ ~ *vi* : to be irresistibly attractive ***syn*** see ATTRACT

fas·ci·nat·ing *adj* : extremely interesting or charming : CAPTIVATING — **fas·ci·nat·ing·ly** \-ˌnāt-iŋ-lē\ *adv*

fas·ci·na·tion \ˌfas-ᵊn-ˈā-shən\ *n* **1** : the quality or power of fascinating **2** : the state of being fascinated

fas·ci·na·tor \ˈfas-ᵊn-ˌāt-ər\ *n* **1** : one that fascinates **2** : a woman's lightweight head scarf usu. of crochet or lace

fas·cine \fa-ˈsēn, fə-\ *n* [F, fr. L *fascina,* fr. *fascis*] : a long bundle of sticks of wood bound together and used for such purposes as filling ditches and making revetments for river banks

fas·ci·o·li·a·sis \fə-ˌsē-ə-ˈlī-ə-səs, -ˌsī-\ *n, pl* **-a·ses** \-ˌsēz\ [NL, fr. *Fasciola,* genus of flukes + *-iasis*] : infestation with or disease caused by liver flukes (genus *Fasciola*)

fas·cism \ˈfash-ˌiz-əm *also* ˈfas-ˌiz-\ *n* [It *fascismo,* fr. *fascio* bundle, fasces, group, fr. L *fascis* bundle & *fasces* fasces] **1** : a political philosophy, movement, or regime (as that of the Fascisti) that exalts nation and race above the individual and that stands for a centralized autocratic government headed by a dictatorial leader, severe economic and social regimentation, and forcible suppression of opposition **2** : a tendency toward or actual exercise of strong autocratic or dictatorial control ⟨early instances of army ~ and brutality —J. W. Aldridge⟩ — **fas·cist** \-əst\ *n or adj, often cap* — **fas·cis·tic** \fa-ˈshis-tik *also* -ˈsis-\ *adj, often cap* — **fas·cis·ti·cal·ly** \-ti-k(ə-)lē\ *adv, often cap*

Fa·sci·sta \fä-ˈshē-(ˌ)stä\ *n, pl* **-sti** \-(ˌ)stē\ [It, fr. *fascio*] : a member of an Italian political organization under Mussolini governing Italy 1922–1943 according to the principles of fascism

fas·cist·ize \ˈfash-ə-ˌstīz *also* ˈfas-ə-\ *vt* **-ized; -iz·ing** : to make over or transform into a Fascista : convert to the principles of fascism — **fas·cist·iza·tion** \ˌfash-ə-stə-ˈzā-shən *also* ˌfas-ə-\ *n*

fash \ˈfash\ *vb* [MF *fascher,* fr. (assumed) VL *fastidiare* to disgust, fr. L *fastidium* disgust — more at FASTIDIOUS] *chiefly Scot* : VEX — **fash** *n, chiefly Scot*

¹**fash·ion** \ˈfash-ən\ *n* [ME *facioun, fasoun* shape, manner, fr. OF *façon,* fr. L *faction-, factio* act of making, faction, fr. *factus,* pp. of *facere* to make — more at DO] **1** **a** : the make or form of something **b** *archaic* : KIND, SORT **2** **a** : an often personal manner or way ⟨he will, after his sour ~, tell you —Shak.⟩ **b** : mode of action or operation ⟨the people assembled in an orderly ~⟩ **3** **a** : a prevailing custom, usage, or style **b** (1) : the prevailing style (as in dress) during a particular time (2) : a garment in such a style ⟨always wears the latest ~*s*⟩ **c** : social standing or prominence esp. as signalized by dress or conduct
syn **1** see METHOD
2 FASHION, STYLE, MODE, VOGUE, FAD, RAGE, CRAZE *shared meaning element* : the choice or usage (as in dressing, decorating, or living) generally accepted by those who regard themselves as up-to-date and sophisticated
— **after a fashion** : in an approximate or rough way ⟨became an artist *after a fashion*⟩

²**fashion** *vt* **fash·ioned; fash·ion·ing** \ˈfash-(ə-)niŋ\ **1** **a** : to give shape or form to : MOLD **b** : ALTER, TRANSFORM **c** : to mold into a particular character by influencing or training **d** : to make or construct usu. with the use of imagination and ingenuity ⟨~ a lamp from an old churn⟩ **2** : FIT, ADAPT **3** *obs* : CONTRIVE ***syn*** see MAKE — **fash·ion·er** \-(ə-)nər\ *n*

¹**fash·ion·able** \ˈfash-(ə-)nə-bəl\ *adj* **1** : conforming to the custom, fashion, or established mode **2** : of or relating to the world of fashion — **fash·ion·abil·i·ty** \ˌfash-(ə-)nə-ˈbil-ət-ē\ *n* — **fash·ion·able·ness** \ˈfash-(ə-)nə-bəl-nəs\ *n* — **fash·ion·ably** \-blē\ *adv*

²**fashionable** *n* : a fashionable person

fash·ion·mon·ger \ˈfash-ən-ˌməŋ-gər, -ˌmäŋ-\ *n* : one that studies, imitates, or sets the fashion

fashion plate *n* **1** : an illustration of a clothing style **2** : a person who dresses in the newest fashion

¹**fast** \ˈfast\ *adj* [ME, fr. OE *fæst;* akin to OHG *festi* firm, ON *fastr,* Arm *hast*] **1** **a** : firmly fixed ⟨roots that are ~ in the ground⟩ **b** : tightly shut ⟨all the drawers were ~⟩ **c** : adhering firmly ⟨the glued sheets became ~⟩ **d** : not easily freed : STUCK ⟨a shell ~ in the chamber of a gun⟩ **e** : STABLE ⟨movable items were made ~ to the deck⟩ **2** : firmly loyal ⟨became ~ friends over the years⟩ **3** **a** : characterized by quick motion, operation, or effect: (1) : moving or able to move rapidly : SWIFT (2) : taking a comparatively short time (3) : imparting quickness of motion ⟨a ~ bowler⟩ (4) : accomplished quickly (5) : agile of mind; *esp* : quick to learn ⟨a special class for ~ students⟩ **b** : conducive to rapidity of play or action ⟨a ~ track⟩ **c** (1) *of a timepiece or weighing device* : indicating in advance of what is correct (2) : according to daylight saving time **d** : contributing to a shortening of exposure time ⟨~ lens⟩ **e** : acquired with unusually little effort and often by shady or dishonest methods ⟨made some ~ money on the numbers⟩ **4** **a** : securely attached ⟨a rope ~ to the wharf⟩ **b** : TENACIOUS ⟨kept a ~ hold on her purse⟩ **5** **a** *archaic* : sound asleep **b** *of sleep* : not easily disturbed **6** : permanently dyed **7** **a** : WILD ⟨runs around with a pretty ~ bunch⟩ **b** : daringly unconventional esp. in sexual matters ⟨a ~ woman⟩ **8** : resistant to change (as from destructive action or fading) — often used in combination ⟨ sun*fast*⟩ ⟨acid-*fast* bacteria⟩
syn FAST, RAPID, SWIFT, FLEET, QUICK, SPEEDY, HASTY, EXPEDITIOUS *shared meaning element* : moving, proceeding, or acting with celerity ***ant*** slow

²**fast** *adv* **1** : in a firm or fixed manner **2** : in a sound manner : DEEPLY ⟨fell ~ asleep⟩ **3** **a** : in a rapid manner : QUICKLY **b** : in quick succession ⟨kaleidoscopic impressions that come so thick and ~ —M. B. Tucker⟩ **4** : in a reckless manner : DISSIPATEDLY **5** : ahead of a correct time or posted schedule **6** *archaic* : CLOSE, NEAR

³**fast** *vi* [ME *fasten,* fr. OE *fæstan*] **1** : to abstain from food **2** : to eat sparingly or abstain from some foods

⁴**fast** *n* **1** : the practice of fasting **2** : a time of fasting

⁵**fast** *n* [alter. of ME *fest,* fr. ON *festr* rope, mooring cable, fr. *fastr* firm] : something that fastens or holds a fastening

fast and loose *adv* **1** : in a craftily deceitful way ⟨manipulated evidence . . . and played *fast and loose* with the truth —C. V. Woodward⟩ **2** : in a reckless or irresponsible manner ⟨playing *fast and loose* with his wife's money⟩

fast·back \ˈfas(t)-ˌbak\ *n* : an automobile roof with a long curving downward slope to the rear; *also* : an automobile with such a roof

fast·ball \ˈfas(t)-ˌbȯl\ *n* : a baseball pitch thrown at full speed and often rising slightly as it nears the plate — compare CURVEBALL, SLIDER, KNUCKLE BALL, CHANGE-UP, SCREWBALL

fast break *n* : a quick offensive drive toward a goal (as in basketball) in an attempt to score before the opponent's defense is set up — **fast–break** *vi*

fas·ten \ˈfas-ᵊn\ *vb* **fas·tened; fas·ten·ing** \ˈfas-niŋ, -ᵊn-iŋ\ [ME *fastnen,* fr. OE *fæstnian* to make fast; akin to OHG *festinōn* to make fast, OE *fæst* fast] *vt* **1** **a** : to attach esp. by pinning, tying, or nailing **b** : to make fast and secure **c** : to fix firmly or securely **d** : to secure against opening **2** : to fix or set steadily ⟨~*ed* his attention on the main problem⟩ **3** : to take a firm grip with ⟨the dog ~*ed* his teeth in the old shoe⟩ **4** **a** : to attach (oneself) persistently and usu. objectionably **b** : IMPOSE ⟨~*ed* the blame on the wrong man⟩ ~ *vi* **1** : to become fast or fixed **2** **a** : to take a firm grip or hold **b** : to focus attention — **fas·ten·er** \ˈfas-nər, -ᵊn-ər\ *n*
syn FASTEN, FIX, ATTACH, AFFIX *shared meaning element* : to make something stay firmly in place ***ant*** unfasten, loosen, loose

fas·ten·ing *n* : something that fastens : FASTENER

fast–food \ˌfas(t)-ˌfüd\ *adj* : specializing in the rapid preparation and service of food (as hamburgers or fried chicken) ⟨a ~ restaurant chain⟩

fas·tid·i·ous \fa-ˈstid-ē-əs, fə-\ *adj* [ME, fr. L *fastidiosus,* fr. *fastidium* disgust, prob. fr. *fastus* arrogance + *taedium* irksomeness; akin to L *fastigium* top] **1** *archaic* : SCORNFUL **2** **a** : having high and often capricious standards : difficult to satisfy or please ⟨must surely give pleasure to the most ~ reader, for her art is scrupulous —Richard Church⟩ **b** : showing or demanding excessive delicacy or care ⟨highbrow critics . . . so ~ that they can talk only to a small circle of initiates —Granville Hicks⟩ **c** : reflecting a meticulous, sensitive, or demanding attitude ⟨~ workmanship⟩ **3** : having complex nutritional requirements ⟨~ microorganisms⟩ ***syn*** see NICE — **fas·tid·i·ous·ly** *adv* — **fas·tid·i·ous·ness** *n*

fas·tig·i·ate \fa-ˈstij-ē-ət\ *adj* [prob. fr. (assumed) NL *fastigiatus,* fr. L *fastigium*] : narrowing toward the top; *esp* : having upright usu. clustered branches — **fas·tig·i·ate·ly** *adv*

fas·tig·i·um \-ē-əm\ *n* [NL, fr. L, top, gable end] : the period of greatest intensity (as of a disease)

fast·ness \ˈfas(t)-nəs\ *n* **1** : the quality or state of being fast: as **a** : the quality or state of being fixed **b** : the quality or state of being swift **c** : colorfast quality **d** : resistance (as of an organism) to the action of a usu. toxic substance **2** **a** : a fortified or secure place **b** : a remote and secluded place ⟨spent the weekend in his mountain ~⟩

Fast of Esther : a Jewish fast day observed the day before Purim in commemoration of a fast proclaimed by Queen Esther

fast–talk \ˈfas(t)-ˈtȯk\ *vt* : to influence or persuade by fluent, facile, and usu. deceptive or tricky talk ⟨~*ed* tribal chieftains . . . out of a parcel of rain-drenched, tropical real estate —*Newsweek*⟩

fas·tu·ous \ˈfas-chə-wəs\ *adj* [L *fastuosus,* fr. *fastus* arrogance — more at FASTIDIOUS] **1** : HAUGHTY, ARROGANT ⟨a ~ air of finality —Carl Van Vechten⟩ **2** : OSTENTATIOUS, SHOWY ⟨a period when ~ living was very much the order of the day —*Times Lit. Supp.*⟩

¹**fat** \ˈfat\ *adj* **fat·ter; fat·test** [ME, fr. OE *fǣtt,* pp. of *fǣtan* to cram; akin to OHG *feizit* fat, L *opimus* fat, copious] **1** : notable for having an unusual amount of fat: **a** : PLUMP **b** : OBESE **c** *of a meat animal* : fattened for market **d** *of food* : OILY, GREASY **2** **a** : well filled out : THICK, BIG ⟨a ~ volume of verse⟩ **b** : FULL, RICH ⟨a gorgeous ~ bass voice —*Irish Digest*⟩ **c** : well stocked ⟨a ~ refrigerator⟩ **d** : PROSPEROUS, WEALTHY ⟨grew ~ on the war —*Time*⟩ **e** : being substantial and impressive ⟨a ~ bank account⟩ **3** **a** : richly rewarding or profitable ⟨a ~ part in a new play⟩ ⟨accepted a ~ contract⟩ **b** : practically nonexistent ⟨a ~ chance⟩ **4** : PRODUCTIVE, FERTILE ⟨a ~ year for crops⟩ **5** **a** *of soil* : containing minerals that cause a greasy feel **b** *of wood* : having a high resin content **6** : STUPID, FOOLISH **7** : SWOLLEN ⟨got a ~ lip from the fight⟩ — **fat·ness** *n*

²**fat** *n* **1** : animal tissue consisting chiefly of cells distended with greasy or oily matter **2** **a** : oily or greasy matter making up the bulk of adipose tissue and often abundant in seeds **b** : any of numerous compounds of carbon, hydrogen, and oxygen that are glycerides of fatty acids, the chief constituents of plant and animal fat, and a major class of energy-rich food, that are soluble in organic solvents (as ether) but not in water, and that are widely used industrially **c** : a solid or semisolid fat as distinguished from an oil **3** : the best or richest part **4** : the condition of fatness : OBESITY **5** : something in excess : SUPERFLUITY

³**fat** *vt* **fat·ted; fat·ting** : to make fat : FATTEN

⁴**fat** *var of* PHAT

fa·tal \ˈfāt-ᵊl\ *adj* [ME, fr. MF & L; MF, fr. L *fatalis,* fr. *fatum*] **1** *obs* : FATED **2** : FATEFUL ⟨a ~ hour⟩ **3** **a** : of or relating to fate **b** : resembling fate in foretelling destiny : PROPHETIC **c** : resembling fate in proceeding according to a fixed sequence **d** : determining one's fate **4** **a** : causing death **b** : bringing ruin ***syn*** see DEADLY

fa·tal·ism \-ˌiz-əm\ *n* : a doctrine that events are fixed in advance for all time in such a manner that human beings are powerless to change them; *also* : a belief in or attitude determined by this doc-

ə abut ᵊ kitten ər further a back ā bake ä cot, cart
au̇ out ch chin e less ē easy g gift i trip ī life
j joke ŋ sing ō flow ȯ flaw ȯi coin th thin t͟h this
ü loot u̇ foot y yet yü few yu̇ furious zh vision

trine — **fa·tal·ist** \-əst\ *n* — **fa·tal·is·tic** \ˌfāt-ᵊl-ˈis-tik\ *adj* — **fa·tal·is·ti·cal·ly** \-ti-k(ə-)lē\ *adv*

fa·tal·i·ty \fā-ˈtal-ət-ē, fə-\ *n, pl* **-ties** **1 :** something established by fate **2 a :** the quality or state of causing death or destruction : DEADLINESS **b :** the quality or condition of being destined for disaster **3 a :** FATE 1 **b :** FATALISM **4 :** the agent or agency of fate **5 a :** death resulting from a disaster **b :** one that experiences or is subject to a fatal outcome ⟨one of the *fatalities* was a small child⟩

fa·tal·ly \ˈfāt-ᵊl-ē\ *adv* **1 :** in a way determined by fate **2 :** in a manner suggesting fate or an act of fate: as **a :** in a manner resulting in death : MORTALLY ⟨~ wounded⟩ **b :** beyond repair : IRREVOCABLY **c :** in a manner resulting in ruin or evil ⟨it is ~ easy to pass off our prejudices as our opinions —W. F. Hambly⟩ **d :** IRRESISTIBLY ⟨thinks she is ~ attractive —J. W. Krutch⟩

fa·ta mor·ga·na \ˌfät-ə-mȯr-ˈgän-ə, -ˈgan-\ *n* [It, lit., Morgan the fay, sorceress of Arthurian legend] **:** MIRAGE

fat·back \ˈfat-ˌbak\ *n* **:** the strip of fat from the back of a hog carcass usu. cured by drying and salting — see PORK illustration

fat body *n* **:** an insect fatty tissue esp. of nearly mature larvae that serves as a food reserve

fat cat *n* **1 a :** a wealthy contributor to a political campaign fund **b :** a wealthy and privileged person **c :** BIG SHOT **2 :** a lethargic, complacent person

¹fate \ˈfāt\ *n* [ME, fr. MF or L; MF, fr. L *fatum,* lit., what has been spoken, fr. neut. of *fatus,* pp. of *fari* to speak — more at BAN] **1 :** the principle or determining cause or will by which things in general are believed to come to be as they are or events to happen as they do : DESTINY **2 a :** an inevitable and often adverse outcome, condition, or end **b :** DISASTER; *esp* : DEATH **3 a :** final outcome **b :** the expected result of normal development ⟨prospective ~ of embryonic cells⟩ **4** *pl, cap* **:** the three goddesses of classical mythology who determine the course of human life

syn FATE, DESTINY, LOT, PORTION, DOOM *shared meaning element* **:** a predetermined state or end

²fate *vt* **fat·ed; fat·ing :** DESTINE; *also* : DOOM ⟨the deep antipathy . . . seeming to ~ them to antagonism —Les Savage⟩

fat·ed *adj* **:** decreed, controlled, or marked by fate

fate·ful \ˈfāt-fəl\ *adj* **1 :** having a quality of ominous prophecy ⟨a ~ remark⟩ **2 a :** involving momentous consequences : DECISIVE ⟨made his ~ decision to declare war —W. L. Shirer⟩ **b :** DEADLY, CATASTROPHIC **3 :** controlled by fate : FOREORDAINED ***syn*** see OMINOUS — **fate·ful·ly** \-fə-lē\ *adv* — **fate·ful·ness** *n*

fath *abbr* fathom

fat·head \ˈfat-ˌhed\ *n* **:** a slow-witted or stupid person : FOOL — **fat·head·ed** \-ˈhed-əd\ *adj* — **fat·head·ed·ly** *adv* — **fat·head·ed·ness** *n*

¹fa·ther \ˈfäth-ər, ˈfȧth-\ *n* [ME *fader,* fr. OE *fæder;* akin to OHG *fater* father, L *pater,* Gk *patēr*] **1 a :** a man who has begotten a child; *also* : SIRE 3 **b** *cap* (1) **:** GOD 1 (2) **:** the first person of the Trinity **2 :** FOREFATHER **3 a :** one related to another in a way suggesting that of father to child **b :** an old man — used as a respectful form of address **4** *often cap* **:** a pre-Scholastic Christian writer accepted by the church as an authoritative witness to its teaching and practice — called also *church father* **5 a :** one that originates or institutes ⟨the ~ of modern science⟩ **b :** SOURCE ⟨the sun, the ~ of warmth and light —Lena M. Whitney⟩ **c :** PROTOTYPE **6 :** a priest of the regular clergy; *broadly* : PRIEST — used esp. as a title **7 :** one of the leading men (as of a city) — usu. used in pl. — **fa·ther·hood** \-ˌhu̇d\ *n* — **fa·ther·less** \-ləs\ *adj*

²father *vb* **fa·thered; fa·ther·ing** \ˈfäth-(ə-)riŋ, ˈfȧth-\ *vt* **1 a :** BEGET **b :** to make oneself the founder, producer, or author of ⟨~*ed* a plan for improving the city's schools⟩ **c :** to accept responsibility for **2 :** to fix the paternity or origin of **3 :** FOIST, IMPOSE ~ *vi* **:** to care for or look after someone as a father might

Father Christmas *n, Brit* **:** SANTA CLAUS

father figure *n* **:** one often of particular power or influence who serves as an emotional substitute for a father

father image *n* **:** an idealization of one's father often projected onto someone to whom one looks for guidance and protection

father-in-law \ˈfäth-(ə-)rən-ˌlȯ, -ərn-ˌlȯ, ˈfȧth-\ *n, pl* **fa·thers-in-law** \-ər-zən-\ **1 :** the father of one's spouse **2 :** STEPFATHER

fa·ther·land \ˈfäth-ər-ˌland, ˈfȧth-\ *n* **1 :** one's native land or country **2 :** the native land or country of one's father or ancestors

fa·ther·like \-ˌlīk\ *adj or adv* **:** FATHERLY

fa·ther·li·ness \-lē-nəs\ *n* **:** paternal quality

fa·ther·ly \ˈfäth-ər-lē, fȧth-\ *adj* **1 :** of, relating to, or befitting a father ⟨~ responsibilities⟩ **2 :** resembling a father (as in affection or care) ⟨a ~ old man⟩ — **fatherly** *adv*

Father's Day *n* **:** the third Sunday in June appointed for the honoring of fathers

¹fath·om \ˈfath-əm\ *n* [ME *fadme,* fr. OE *fæthm* outstretched arms, length of the outstretched arms; akin to ON *fathmr* fathom, L *patēre* to be open, *pandere* to spread out, Gk *petannynai*] **1 :** a unit of length equal to 6 feet used esp. for measuring the depth of water **2 :** COMPREHENSION

²fathom *vt* **1 :** to measure by a sounding line **2 :** to penetrate and come to understand ⟨couldn't ~ the problem⟩ ~ *vi* **1 :** to take soundings **2 :** PROBE — **fath·om·able** \ˈfath-ə-mə-bəl\ *adj*

Fa·thom·e·ter \fa-ˈthäm-ət-ər, ˈfath-ə(m)-ˌmēt-\ *trademark* — used for a sonic depth finder

fath·om·less \ˈfath-əm-ləs\ *adj* **:** incapable of being fathomed — **fath·om·less·ly** *adv* — **fath·om·less·ness** *n*

fa·tid·ic \fā-ˈtid-ik, fə-\ *or* **fa·tid·i·cal** \-i-kəl\ *adj* [L *fatidicus,* fr. *fatum* fate + *dicere* to say — more at DICTION] **:** of or relating to prophecy

fa·ti·ga·bil·i·ty \fə-ˌtē-gə-ˈbil-ət-ē, ˌfat-i-gə-\ *n* **:** susceptibility to fatigue

fa·ti·ga·ble \fə-ˈtē-gə-bəl, ˈfat-i-gə-\ *adj* **:** susceptible to fatigue

¹fa·tigue \fə-ˈtēg\ *n* [F, fr. MF, fr. *fatiguer* to fatigue, fr. L *fatigare;* akin to L *affatim* sufficiently and prob. to L *fames* hunger] **1 a** (1) **:** weariness from labor or exertion (2) **:** nervous exhaustion **b :** the temporary loss of power to respond induced in a sensory receptor or motor end organ by continued stimulation **2 a :** LABOR **b :** manual or menial work performed by military personnel **c** *pl* **:** the uniform or work clothing worn on fatigue and in the field **3 :** the tendency of a material to break under repeated stress

²fatigue *vb* **fa·tigued; fa·tigu·ing** *vt* **1 :** to weary with labor or exertion **2 :** to induce a condition of fatigue in ~ *vi* **:** to suffer fatigue ***syn*** see TIRE — **fa·tigu·ing·ly** \-ˈtē-giŋ-lē\ *adv*

³fatigue *adj* **1 :** consisting of, done, or used in fatigue ⟨~ detail⟩ **2 :** belonging to fatigues ⟨a ~ cap⟩

fat·ling \ˈfat-liŋ\ *n* **:** a young animal fattened for slaughter

fat·ly *adv* **1 :** RICHLY **2 :** in the manner of one that is fat **3 :** in a smug manner : COMPLACENTLY ⟨snickered ~ at his wife's mistake⟩

fats·hed·era \fats-ˈ(h)ed-ə-rə\ *n* [NL *Fatsia,* genus of shrubs + *Hedera,* genus of vines, fr. L, ivy] **:** a vigorous upright hybrid ornamental foliage plant (*Hedera helix* × *Aralia elata*) with glossy deeply lobed palmate leaves

fat·so \ˈfat-(ˌ)sō\ *n, pl* **fatsoes** [prob. fr. *Fats,* nickname for a fat person + *-o*] **:** a fat person — often used as a disparaging form of address

fat-sol·u·ble \ˈfat-ˌsäl-yə-bəl\ *adj* **:** soluble in fats or fat solvents

fat·stock \-ˌstäk\ *n* **:** livestock that is fat and ready for market

fat-tailed sheep \ˌfat-ˌtāld-\ *n* **:** a coarse-wooled mutton sheep that has great quantities of fat on each side of the tail bones

fat·ten \ˈfat-ᵊn\ *vb* **fat·tened; fat·ten·ing** \ˈfat-niŋ, -ᵊn-iŋ\ *vt* **1 a :** to make fat, fleshy, or plump; *esp* : to feed (as a stock animal) for slaughter **b :** to make more substantial **2 :** to make fertile ~ *vi* **:** to become fat — **fat·ten·er** \ˈfat-nər, -ᵊn-ər\ *n*

fat·tish \ˈfat-ish\ *adj* **:** somewhat fat

¹fat·ty \ˈfat-ē\ *adj* **fat·ti·er; -est** **1 :** containing fat esp. in unusual amounts; *also* : unduly stout : CORPULENT **2 :** GREASY **3 :** derived from or chemically related to fat — **fat·ti·ness** *n*

²fatty *n, pl* **fatties :** one that is fat

fatty acid *n* **1 :** any of numerous saturated aliphatic monocarboxylic acids $C_nH_{2n+1}COOH$ (as acetic acid) including many that occur naturally usu. in the form of esters in fats, waxes, and essential oils **2 :** any of the saturated or unsaturated monocarboxylic acids (as palmitic acid) usu. with an even number of carbon atoms that occur naturally in the form of glycerides in fats and fatty oils

fa·tu·ity \fə-ˈt(y)ü-ət-ē, fa-\ *n, pl* **-ities** [MF *fatuité* foolishness, fr. L *fatuitat-, fatuitas,* fr. *fatuus*] **1 a :** something foolish or stupid **b :** STUPIDITY, FOOLISHNESS **2** *archaic* **:** IMBECILITY, DEMENTIA

fat·u·ous \ˈfach-(ə-)wəs\ *adj* [L *fatuus* foolish — more at BATTLE] **:** complacently or inanely foolish : SILLY ***syn*** see SIMPLE ***ant*** sensible — **fat·u·ous·ly** *adv* — **fat·u·ous·ness** *n*

fat-wit·ted \ˈfat-ˈwit-əd\ *adj* **:** STUPID, IDIOTIC

fau·bourg \fō-ˈbu̇(ə)r\ *n* [ME *fabour,* fr. MF *fauxbourg,* alter. of *forsbourg,* fr. OF *forsborc,* fr. *fors* outside + *borc* town] **1 :** SUBURB; *esp* : a suburb of a French city **2 :** a city quarter

fau·ces \ˈfȯ-ˌsēz\ *n pl but sing or pl in constr* [L, pl., throat, fauces] **:** the narrow passage from the mouth to the pharynx situated between the soft palate and the base of the tongue — **fau·cial** \ˈfō-shəl\ *adj*

fau·cet \ˈfȯs-ət, ˈfäs-\ *n* [ME, bung, faucet, fr. MF *fausset* bung, fr. *fausser* to damage, fr. LL *falsare* to falsify, fr. L *falsus* false] **:** a fixture for drawing a liquid from a pipe, cask, or other vessel

faugh *a strong p-sound or lip trill; often read as* ˈfȯ\ *interj* — used to express contempt, disgust, or abhorrence

¹fault \ˈfȯlt\ *n* [ME *faute,* fr. OF, fr. (assumed) VL *fallita,* fr. fem. of *fallitus,* pp. of L *fallere* to deceive, disappoint — more at FAIL] **1** *obs* **:** LACK **2 a :** WEAKNESS, FAILING; *esp* : a moral weakness less serious than a vice **b :** a physical or intellectual imperfection or impairment **c :** an error in a racket game (as tennis) **3 a :** MISDEMEANOR **b :** MISTAKE **4 :** responsibility for wrongdoing or failure ⟨the accident was the driver's ~⟩ **5 :** a fracture in the earth's crust accompanied by a displacement of one side of the fracture with respect to the other and in a direction parallel to the fracture

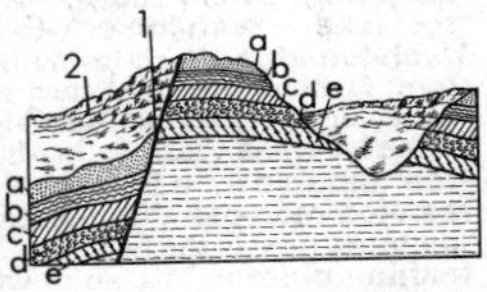

fault 5: *1* fault with strata a,b,c,d,e; parts with the same letter are of the same stratum; *2* scarp

syn FAULT, FAILING, FRAILTY, FOIBLE, VICE *shared meaning element* **:** an imperfection or weakness of character ***ant*** merit

— **at fault** **1 :** unable to find the scent and continue chase : PUZZLED **2 :** open to blame : RESPONSIBLE ⟨couldn't determine who was really *at fault*⟩ — **to a fault :** to an excessive degree ⟨particular *to a fault*⟩

²fault *vi* **1 :** to commit a fault : ERR **2 :** to fracture so as to produce a geologic fault ~ *vt* **1 :** to find a fault in ⟨equally easy to praise this book and to ~ it —H. G. Roepke⟩ **2 :** to produce a geologic fault in **3 :** BLAME, CENSURE ⟨one cannot ~ him for publishing as much as he did —R. M. Elman⟩

fault·find·er \ˈfȯlt-ˌfīn-dər\ *n* **:** one given to faultfinding

¹fault·find·ing \-diŋ\ *n* **:** CRITICISM; *esp* : petty, nagging, or unreasonable censure

²faultfinding *adj* **:** disposed to find fault : captiously critical ***syn*** see CRITICAL

fault·less \ˈfȯlt-ləs\ *adj* **:** having no fault : IRREPROACHABLE ⟨~ workmanship⟩ — **fault·less·ly** *adv* — **fault·less·ness** *n*

faulty \ˈfȯl-tē\ *adj* **fault·i·er; -est :** marked by fault, blemish, or defect : IMPERFECT — **fault·i·ly** \-tə-lē\ *adv* — **fault·i·ness** \-tē-nəs\ *n*

faun \ˈfȯn, ˈfän\ *n* [ME, fr. L *faunus,* fr. *Faunus*] **:** a figure of Roman mythology similar to the satyr

fau·na \ˈfȯn-ə, ˈfän-\ *n, pl* **faunas** *also* **fau·nae** \-ˌē, -ˌī\ [NL, fr. LL *Fauna,* sister of Faunus] **:** animals or animal life: as **a :** the animals or animal life of a region, period, or geological stratum — compare FLORA **b :** the animals or animal life developed or adapted for living in a specified environment — **fau·nal** \-ᵊl\ *adj* — **fau·nal·ly** \-ᵊl-ē\ *adv*

fau·nis·tic \fō-ˈnis-tik, fä-\ *adj* **:** of or relating to zoogeography : FAUNAL — **fau·nis·ti·cal·ly** \-ti-k(ə-)lē\ *adv*

Fau·nus \ˈfȯn-əs, ˈfän-\ *n* [L] **:** the Roman god of animals

Faust \ˈfau̇st\ *or* **Fau·stus** \ˈfau̇-stəs, ˈfȯ-\ *n* [G] **:** a magician of German legend who enters into a compact with the devil

Faust·ian \ˈfau̇-stē-ən, ˈfȯ-\ *adj* **:** of, belonging to, resembling, or befitting Faust or Faustus: as **a :** sacrificing spiritual values for material gains **b :** striving insatiably for knowledge and mastery **c :** constantly troubled and tormented by spiritual dissatisfaction or spiritual striving

faute de mieux \ˌfōt-də-ˈmyə(r), -ˈmyœ\ *adv* [F] **:** for lack of something better or more desirable ⟨sherry made him dopey but he drank it *faute de mieux* —F. T. Marsh⟩

fau·vism \ˈfō-ˌviz-əm\ *n, often cap* [F *fauvisme,* fr. *fauve* wild animal, fr. *fauve* tawny, wild, of Gmc origin; akin to OHG *falo* fallow — more at FALLOW] **:** a movement in painting typified by the work of Matisse and characterized by vivid colors, free treatment of form, and a resulting vibrant and decorative effect — **fau·vist** \-vəst\ *n, often cap*

faux pas \ˈfō-ˈpä\ *n, pl* **faux pas** \-ˈpä(z)\ [F, lit., false step] **:** BLUNDER; *esp* **:** a social blunder

fa·va bean \ˈfäv-ə-\ *n* [It *fava,* fr. L *faba* bean] **:** BROAD BEAN

fa·vo·ni·an \fə-ˈvō-nē-ən\ *adj* [L *favonianus,* fr. *Favonius,* the west wind] **:** of or relating to the west wind **:** MILD

[1]**fa·vor** \ˈfā-vər\ *n* [ME, friendly regard, attractiveness, fr. OF *favor* friendly regard, fr. L, fr. *favēre* to be favorable; akin to OHG *gouma* attention, OSlav *govĕti* to revere] **1** *archaic* **a :** APPEARANCE **b** (1) **:** FACE (2) **:** a facial feature **2 a** (1) **:** friendly regard shown toward another esp. by a superior (2) **:** approving consideration or attention **:** APPROBATION **b :** PARTIALITY **c** *archaic* **:** LENIENCY **d** *archaic* **:** PERMISSION **e :** POPULARITY **3 a :** gracious kindness; *also* **:** an act of such kindness **b** *archaic* **:** HELP, ASSISTANCE **c** *pl* **:** effort in one's behalf or interest **:** ATTENTION **4 a :** a token of love (as a ribbon) usu. worn conspicuously **b :** a small gift or decorative item given out at a party **c :** BADGE **5 a :** a special privilege or right granted or conceded **b :** sexual privileges — usu. used in pl. **6** *archaic* **:** LETTER **7 :** BEHALF, INTEREST

syn FAVOR, GOODWILL, COUNTENANCE *shared meaning element* **:** approving interest ***ant*** disfavor, animus

— **in favor of 1 a :** in accord or sympathy with **b :** for the acquittal of ⟨returned a verdict *in favor of* the accused⟩ **c :** in support of **2 :** to the order of **3 :** in order to choose **:** out of preference for ⟨was offered athletic scholarships . . . but he turned them down *in favor of* a career in professional baseball —*Current Biog.*⟩ — **in one's favor 1 :** in one's good graces ⟨doing extra work to get back *in the teacher's favor*⟩ **2 :** to one's advantage ⟨the odds were *in his favor*⟩ — **out of favor :** UNPOPULAR, DISLIKED ⟨was *out of favor* with his neighbors⟩

[2]**favor** *vt* **fa·vored; fa·vor·ing** \ˈfāv-(ə-)riŋ\ **1 a :** to regard or treat with favor **b** (1) **:** to do a kindness for **:** OBLIGE (2) **:** ENDOW **c :** to treat gently or carefully **:** SPARE ⟨∼*ed* his injured leg⟩ **2 :** to show partiality toward **:** PREFER **3 a :** to give support or confirmation to **:** SUSTAIN **b :** to afford advantages for success to **:** FACILITATE ⟨good weather ∼*ed* the outing⟩ **4 :** to bear a resemblance to ⟨he ∼*s* his father⟩ ***syn*** see OBLIGE — **fa·vor·er** \ˈfā-vər-ər\ *n*

fa·vor·able \ˈfāv-(ə-)rə-bəl, ˈfā-vər-bəl\ *adj* **1 a :** disposed to favor **:** PARTIAL **b :** expressing approval **:** COMMENDATORY **c :** giving a result that is in one's favor ⟨a ∼ comparison⟩ **d :** AFFIRMATIVE **2 :** winning approval **:** PLEASING **3 a :** tending to promote or facilitate **:** ADVANTAGEOUS ⟨∼ wind⟩ **b :** marked by success — **fa·vor·able·ness** *n* — **fa·vor·ably** \-blē\ *adv*

syn FAVORABLE, AUSPICIOUS, PROPITIOUS *shared meaning element* **:** pointing towards a felicitous outcome ***ant*** unfavorable, antagonistic

fa·vored \ˈfā-vərd\ *adj* **1 :** endowed with special advantages or gifts **2 :** having an appearance or features of a particular kind ⟨hard-*favored*⟩ **3 :** providing preferential treatment

[1]**fa·vor·ite** \ˈfāv-(ə-)rət\ *n* [It *favorito,* pp. of *favorire* to favor, fr. *favore* favor, fr. L *favor*] **1 :** one that is treated or regarded with special favor or liking; *specif* **:** one unusually loved, trusted, or provided with favors by a person of high rank or authority **2 :** a competitor (as a horse in a race) judged most likely to win

[2]**favorite** *adj* **:** constituting a favorite; *specif* **:** markedly popular

favorite son *n* **:** one favored by the delegates of his state as presidential candidate at a national political convention

fa·vor·it·ism \ˈfāv-(ə-)rət-ˌiz-əm\ *n* **1 :** the showing of special favor **:** PARTIALITY **2 :** the state or fact of being a favorite

favour *chiefly Brit var of* FAVOR

fa·vus \ˈfā-vəs\ *n* [NL, fr. L, honeycomb] **:** a contagious skin disease caused by a fungus (as *Achorion schoenleinii*) occurring in man and many domestic animals and fowls

[1]**fawn** \ˈfȯn, ˈfän\ *vi* [ME *faunen,* fr. OE *fagnian* to rejoice, fr. *fægen, fagan* glad — more at FAIN] **1 :** to show affection — used esp. of a dog **2 :** to court favor by a cringing or flattering manner **:** GROVEL — **fawn·er** *n* — **fawn·ing·ly** \-iŋ-lē\ *adv*

syn FAWN, TOADY, TRUCKLE, CRINGE, COWER *shared meaning element* **:** to act or behave with abjectness ***ant*** domineer

[2]**fawn** *n* [ME *foun,* fr. MF *feon, faon* young of an animal, fr. (assumed) VL *feton-, feto,* fr. L *fetus* offspring — more at FETUS] **1 :** a young deer; *esp* **:** one still unweaned or retaining a distinctive baby coat **2 :** KID 1 **3 :** a variable color averaging a light grayish brown

fawn lily *n* **:** DOGTOOTH VIOLET

fawny \ˈfȯn-ē, ˈfän-\ *adj* **:** of a color approximating fawn

[1]**fay** \ˈfā\ *vb* [ME *feien,* fr. OE *fēgan;* akin to OHG *fuogen* to fit, L *pangere* to fasten — more at PACT] **:** to fit or join closely or tightly

[2]**fay** *n* [ME *fai, fei,* fr. OF *feid, fei* — more at FAITH] *obs* **:** FAITH

[3]**fay** *n* [ME *faie,* fr. MF *feie, fee* — more at FAIRY] **:** FAIRY, ELF

[4]**fay** *adj* **:** resembling an elf

[5]**fay** *n* **:** OFAY

faze \ˈfāz\ *vt* **fazed; faz·ing** [alter. of *feeze* (to drive away, frighten), fr. ME *fesen,* fr. OE *fēsian* to drive away] **:** to disturb the composure of **:** DISCONCERT, DAUNT ***syn*** see EMBARRASS

FB *abbr* **1** foreign body **2** freight bill

FBA *abbr* Fellow of the British Academy

FBI *abbr* Federal Bureau of Investigation

FBOA *abbr* Fellow of the British Optical Association

FC *abbr* **1** fire control; fire controlman **2** follow copy **3** food control **4** footcandle

FCA *abbr* **1** Farm Credit Administration **2** Fellow of the Chartered Accountants

FCC *abbr* Federal Communications Commission

FCIS *abbr* Fellow of the Chartered Institute of Secretaries

F clef *n* **:** BASS CLEF

fcp *abbr* foolscap

FCS *abbr* Fellow of the Chemical Society

fcy *abbr* fancy

FD *abbr* **1** fire department **2** free dock

FDA *abbr* Food and Drug Administration

FDIC *abbr* Federal Deposit Insurance Corporation

F distribution *n* [Sir Ronald *F*isher †1962 E geneticist and statistician] **:** a probability density function that is used esp. in analysis of variance and is a function of the ratio of two independent random variables (as the variances of two random samples) each of which has a chi-square distribution and is divided by its number of degrees of freedom

Fe *symbol* [L *ferrum*] iron

fe·al·ty \ˈfē-(ə-)l-tē\ *n, pl* **-ties** [alter. of ME *feute,* fr. OF *feelté, fealté,* fr. L *fidelitat-, fidelitas* — more at FIDELITY] **1 a :** the fidelity of a vassal or feudal tenant to his lord **b :** the obligation of such fidelity **2 :** intense and compelling fidelity ***syn*** see FIDELITY ***ant*** perfidy

[1]**fear** \ˈfi(ə)r\ *n* [ME *fer,* fr. OE *fǣr* sudden danger; akin to L *periculum* attempt, peril, Gk *peiran* to attempt, OE *faran* to go — more at FARE] **1 a :** an unpleasant often strong emotion caused by anticipation or awareness of danger **b** (1) **:** an instance of this emotion (2) **:** a state marked by this emotion **2 :** anxious concern **:** SOLICITUDE **3 :** profound reverence and awe esp. toward God **4 :** reason for alarm **:** DANGER

syn* 1** FEAR, DREAD, FRIGHT, ALARM, PANIC, TREPIDATION *shared meaning element* **:** painful agitation in the presence or anticipation of danger ***ant fearlessness

2 see REVERENCE

[2]**fear** *vt* **1** *archaic* **:** FRIGHTEN **2** *archaic* **:** to feel fear in (oneself) **3 :** to have a reverential awe of ⟨∼ God⟩ **4 :** to be afraid of **:** consider or expect with alarm ∼ *vi* **:** to be afraid or apprehensive — **fear·er** *n*

fear·ful \ˈfi(ə)r-fəl\ *adj* **1 :** causing or likely to cause fear, fright, or alarm esp. because of dangerous quality ⟨a ∼ storm⟩ **2 a :** full of fear **b :** indicating or arising from fear ⟨a ∼ glance⟩ **c :** inclined to fear **:** TIMOROUS **3 :** being extreme (as in badness, intensity, or size) ⟨a ∼ waste⟩ ⟨∼ slum conditions⟩ — **fear·ful·ly** \-f(ə-)lē\ *adv* — **fear·ful·ness** \-fəl-nəs\ *n*

syn* 1** FEARFUL, APPREHENSIVE, AFRAID *shared meaning element* **:** disturbed by fear ***ant fearless, intrepid

2 FEARFUL, AWFUL, DREADFUL, FRIGHTFUL, TERRIBLE, TERRIFIC, APPALLING *shared meaning element* **:** of a kind to cause grave distress of mind. Additionally, all these words and their corresponding adverbs have a lighter, chiefly conversational value in which they are used as intensives and mean little more than *extreme* (or *extremely*). Basically, FEARFUL applies to what produces fear, agitation, or loss of courage ⟨our *fearful* trip is done, the ship has weathered every rack —Walt Whitman⟩ AWFUL implies striking with an awareness of transcendent overpowering force, might, or significance ⟨the *awful* arithmetic of the atomic bomb —D. D. Eisenhower⟩ DREADFUL applies to what fills one with dread and suggests a blending of fear and aversion ⟨shuddering at the *dreadful* loss of life⟩ FRIGHTFUL implies a startling or outrageous quality that induces utter consternation or a paralysis of fear ⟨a *frightful* spectacle of poverty, barbarity, and ignorance —T. B. Macaulay⟩ TERRIBLE suggests painfulness too great to be endured or a capacity to induce and prolong intense fear ⟨those five *terrible* days of war —*New Yorker*⟩ TERRIFIC applies to what is intended or fitted to inspire fear ⟨the storm was *terrific* beyond imagining⟩ APPALLING describes something that strikes with dismay as well as fear or horror ⟨taken aback when he grasped the *appalling* risk involved⟩

fear·less \ˈfi(ə)r-ləs\ *adj* **:** free from fear **:** BRAVE — **fear·less·ly** *adv* — **fear·less·ness** *n*

fear·some \ˈfi(ə)r-səm\ *adj* **1 :** causing fear **2 :** TIMID, TIMOROUS — **fear·some·ly** *adv* — **fear·some·ness** *n*

fea·si·ble \ˈfē-zə-bəl\ *adj* [ME *faisible,* fr. MF, fr. *fais-,* stem of *faire* to make, do, fr. L *facere*] **1 :** capable of being done or carried out ⟨a ∼ plan⟩ **2 :** capable of being used or dealt with successfully **:** SUITABLE **3 :** REASONABLE, LIKELY ***syn*** see POSSIBLE ***ant*** unfeasible, infeasible, chimerical *(as a scheme or project)* — **fea·si·bil·i·ty** \ˌfē-zə-ˈbil-ət-ē\ *n* — **fea·si·ble·ness** \ˈfē-zə-bəl-nəs\ *n* — **fea·si·bly** \-blē\ *adv*

[1]**feast** \ˈfēst\ *n* [ME *feste* festival, feast, fr. OF, festival, fr. L *festa,* pl. of *festum* festival, fr. neut. of *festus* solemn, festal; akin to L *feriae* holidays, *fanum* temple, Arm *dikʻ* gods] **1 a :** an elaborate meal often accompanied by a ceremony or entertainment **:** BANQUET **b :** something that gives unusual or abundant pleasure **2 :** a periodic religious observance commemorating an event or honoring a deity, person, or thing

[2]**feast** *vi* **:** to take part in a feast ∼ *vt* **1 :** to give a feast for **2 :** DELIGHT, GRATIFY — **feast·er** *n*

Feast of Tabernacles : SUKKOTH

[1]**feat** \ˈfēt\ *adj* [ME *fete, fayt,* fr. MF *fait,* pp. of *faire*] **1** *archaic* **:** BECOMING, NEAT **2** *archaic* **:** SMART, DEXTEROUS

ə abut	ᵊ kitten	ər further	a back	ā bake	ä cot, cart	
au̇ out	ch chin	e less	ē easy	g gift	i trip	ī life
j joke	ŋ sing	ō flow	ȯ flaw	ȯi coin	th thin	th this
ü loot	u̇ foot	y yet	yü few	yu̇ furious	zh vision	

2feat *n* [ME *fait,* fr. MF, fr. L *factum,* fr. neut. of *factus,* pp. of *facere* to make, do — more at DO] **1 :** ACT, DEED **2 a :** a deed notable esp. for courage **b :** an act or product of skill, endurance, or ingenuity
syn FEAT, EXPLOIT, ACHIEVEMENT *shared meaning element* : a remarkable deed

1feath·er \ˈfeth-ər\ *n* [ME *fether,* fr. OE; akin to OHG *federa* wing, L *petere* to go to, seek, Gk *petesthai* to fly, *piptein* to fall, *pteron* wing] **1 a :** one of the light horny epidermal outgrowths that form the external covering of the body of birds and that consist of a shaft bearing on each side a series of barbs which bear barbules which in turn bear barbicels commonly ending in hooked hamuli and interlocking with the barbules of an adjacent barb to link the barbs into a continuous vane **b :** PLUME **c :** the vane of an arrow **2 a :** PLUMAGE **b :** KIND, NATURE ⟨birds of a ~ flock together⟩ **c :** ATTIRE, DRESS **d :** CONDITION, MOOD **3 :** FEATHERING 2 **4 :** a projecting strip, rib, fin, or flange **5 :** a feathery flaw in the eye or in a precious stone **6 :** the act of feathering an oar — **feath·ered** \-ərd\ *adj* — **a feather in one's cap :** a mark of distinction : HONOR

2feather *vb* **feath·ered; feath·er·ing** \-(ə-)riŋ\ *vt* **1 a :** to furnish (as an arrow) with a feather **b :** to cover, clothe, or adorn with feathers **2 a :** to turn (an oar blade) almost horizontal when lifting from the water at the end of a stroke to reduce air resistance **b** (1) : to change the angle of (airplane propeller blades) so that the chords become approximately parallel to the line of flight; *also* : to change the angle of airplane propeller blades of (an engine) in such a manner (2) : to change the angle of (a rotor blade of a rotary-wing aircraft) periodically in forward flight **3 :** to reduce the edge of to a featheredge **4 :** to cut (as air) with or as if with a wing **5 :** to join by a tongue and groove ~ *vi* **1 :** to grow or form feathers **2 :** to have or take on the appearance of a feather or something feathered **3 :** to soak in and spread : BLUR — used of ink or a printed impression **4 :** to feather an oar or an airplane propeller blade — **feather one's nest :** to provide for oneself esp. while in a position of trust

1feath·er·bed \ˈfeth-ər-ˌbed\ *adj* : calling for, sanctioning, or resulting from featherbedding

2featherbed *vi* **1 a :** to require more workmen than are needed **b :** to limit production under a featherbed rule **2 :** to do featherbed work or put in time under a featherbed rule ~ *vt* **1 :** to bring under a featherbed rule **2 :** to assist (as an industry) by government aid

feather bed *n* **1 :** a feather mattress **2 :** a bed having a feather mattress

feath·er·bed·ding *n* : the requiring of an employer usu. under a union rule or safety statute to hire more employees than are needed or to limit production

feath·er·brain \-ˌbrān\ *n* : a foolish scatterbrained person — **feath·er·brained** \ˌfeth-ər-ˈbrānd\ *adj*

feath·er·edge \ˈfeth-ə-ˌrej, ˌfeth-ə-ˈ\ *n* : a very thin sharp edge; *esp* : one that is easily broken or bent over — **featheredge** *vt*

feath·er·head \ˈfeth-ər-ˌhed\ *n* : FEATHERBRAIN — **feath·er·head·ed** \ˌfeth-ər-ˈhed-əd\ *adj*

feath·er·ing \ˈfeth-(ə-)riŋ\ *n* **1 a :** a covering of feathers : PLUMAGE **b :** a style in which feathers are attached to arrows; *also* : the feathers of an arrow **2 :** a fringe of hair (as on the legs of a dog)

feath·er·less \ˈfeth-ər-ləs\ *adj* : having no feathers

feather star *n* : COMATULID

feath·er·stitch \ˈfeth-ər-ˌstich\ *n* : an embroidery stitch consisting of a line of diagonal blanket stitches worked alternately to the left and right — **featherstitch** *vb*

feath·er·weight \-ˌwāt\ *n* **1 :** one that is very light in weight; *specif* : a boxer who weighs more than 118 but not more than 126 pounds **2 :** a person of limited intelligence or effectiveness

feath·ery \ˈfeth-(ə-)rē\ *adj* : resembling, suggesting, or covered with feathers

1feat·ly \ˈfēt-lē\ *adv* [ME *fetly,* fr. *fete* feat (adj.)] **1 :** SUITABLY, PROPERLY **2 :** in a graceful manner : NIMBLY **3 :** with skill and ingenuity

2featly *adj* : GRACEFUL, NEAT

1fea·ture \ˈfē-chər\ *n* [ME *feture,* fr. MF, fr. L *factura* act of making, fr. *factus,* pp. of *facere* to make — more at DO] **1 a :** the structure, form, or appearance esp. of a person **b** *obs* : physical beauty **2 a :** the makeup or appearance of the face or its parts **b :** a part of the face : LINEAMENT **3 :** a prominent part or characteristic **4 :** a special attraction: as **a :** the principal motion picture shown on a program with other pictures **b :** a distinctive article, story, or special department in a newspaper or magazine **c :** something offered to the public or advertised as particularly attractive

2feature *vb* **fea·tured; fea·tur·ing** \ˈfēch-(ə-)riŋ\ *vt* **1** *chiefly dial* : to resemble in features **2 :** to picture or portray in the mind : IMAGINE **3 a :** to give special prominence to **b :** to have as a characteristic or feature ~ *vi* : to play an important part

fea·tured \ˈfē-chərd\ *adj* **1 :** having facial features of a particular kind — used in combination ⟨a heavy-*featured* man⟩ ⟨a grim-*featured* shrew⟩ **2 :** displayed, advertised, or presented as a special attraction

fea·ture·less \ˈfē-chər-ləs\ *adj* : having no distinctive features

feaze \ˈfēz, ˈfāz\ *var of* FAZE

Feb *abbr* February

febri- *comb form* [LL, fr. L *febris*] : fever ⟨*febri*fic⟩

fe·brif·ic \fi-ˈbrif-ik\ *adj, archaic* : FEVERISH

feb·ri·fuge \ˈfeb-rə-ˌfyüj\ *n* [F *fébrifuge,* prob. fr. (assumed) NL *febrifuga,* fr. LL *febrifuga, febrifugia* centaury, fr. *febri-* + *-fuga* -fuge] : ANTIPYRETIC — **febrifuge** *adj*

fe·brile \-ˌrīl *also* ˈfēb-\ *adj* [ML *febrilis,* fr. L *febris* fever — more at FEVER] : of or relating to fever : FEVERISH

Feb·ru·ary \ˈfeb-(y)ə-ˌwer-ē, ˈfeb-rə-\ *n* [ME *Februarie,* fr. L *Februarius,* fr. *Februa,* pl., feast of purification; perh. akin to L *fumus* smoke] : the 2d month of the Gregorian calendar

fec *abbr* [L *fecit*] he made it

fe·cal \ˈfē-kəl\ *adj* : of, relating to, or constituting feces

fe·ces \ˈfē-(ˌ)sēz\ *n pl* [ME, fr. L *faec-, faex* (sing.) dregs] : bodily waste discharged through the anus : EXCREMENT

feck·less \ˈfek-ləs\ *adj* [Sc, fr. *feck* effect, majority, fr. ME (Sc) *fek,* alter. of ME *effect*] **1 :** INEFFECTUAL, WEAK **2 :** WORTHLESS, IRRESPONSIBLE — **feck·less·ly** *adv* — **feck·less·ness** *n*

feck·ly \ˈfek-lē\ *adv* [Sc, fr. *feck* + *-ly*] *chiefly Scot* : ALMOST, NEARLY

fec·u·lent \ˈfek-yə-lənt\ *adj* [ME, fr. L *faeculentus,* fr. *faec-, faex*] : foul with impurities : FECAL — **fe·cu·lence** \-lən(t)s\ *n*

fe·cund \ˈfek-ənd, ˈfēk-\ *adj* [ME, fr. MF *fecond,* fr. L *fecundus* — more at FEMININE] **1 :** fruitful in offspring or vegetation : PROLIFIC **2 :** intellectually productive or inventive to a marked degree *syn* see FERTILE *ant* barren — **fe·cun·di·ty** \fi-ˈkən-dət-ē, fe-\ *n*

fe·cun·date \ˈfek-ən-ˌdāt, ˈfē-kən-\ *vt* **-dated; -dat·ing** [L *fecundatus,* pp. of *fecundare,* fr. *fecundus*] **1 :** to make fecund **2 :** to make fertile : IMPREGNATE — **fe·cun·da·tion** \ˌfek-ən-ˈdā-shən, ˌfē-kən-\ *n*

1fed \ˈfed\ *n, often cap* : FEDERAL 2

2fed *abbr* federal; federation

fe·da·yee \fi-ˌda-ˈ(y)ē, -ˌdä-\ *n, pl* **fe·da·yeen** \-ˈ(y)ēn\ [Ar *fidāʾī,* lit., one who sacrifices himself] : a member of an Arab commando group operating esp. against Israel

fed·er·al \ˈfed(-ə)-rəl\ *adj* [L *foeder-, foedus* compact, league; akin to L *fidere* to trust — more at BIDE] **1** *archaic* : of or relating to a compact or treaty **2 a :** formed by a compact between political units that surrender their individual sovereignty to a central authority but retain limited residuary powers of government **b :** of or constituting a form of government in which power is distributed between a central authority and a number of constituent territorial units **c :** of or relating to the central government of a federation as distinguished from the governments of the constituent units **3** *cap* : advocating or friendly to the principle of a federal government with strong centralized powers; *esp* : of or relating to the American Federalists **4** *often cap* : of, relating to, or loyal to the federal government or the Union armies of the U.S. in the American Civil War — **fed·er·al·ly** \-rə-lē\ *adv*

Federal *n* **1 :** a supporter of the government of the U.S. in the Civil War; *specif* : a soldier in the federal armies **2 :** a federal agent or officer

federal court *n* : a court established by authority of a federal government; *esp* : one established under the constitution and laws of the U.S.

federal district *n* : a district set apart as the seat of the central government of a federation

federal district court *n* : a district trial court of law and equity that hears cases under federal jurisdiction

fed·er·al·ism \ˈfed(-ə)-rə-ˌliz-əm\ *n* **1 a** *often cap* : the federal principle of organization **b :** support or advocacy of this principle **2** *cap* : the principles of the Federalists

fed·er·al·ist \-ləst\ *n* **1 :** an advocate of federalism: as **a** *often cap* : an advocate of a federal union between the American colonies after the Revolution and of the adoption of the U.S. Constitution **b** *often cap* : WORLD FEDERALIST **2** *cap* : a member of a major political party in the early years of the U.S. favoring a strong centralized national government — **federalist** *adj, often cap*

fed·er·al·iza·tion \ˌfed(-ə)-rə-lə-ˈzā-shən\ *n* **1 :** the act of federalizing **2 :** the state of being federalized

fed·er·al·ize \ˈfed(-ə)-rə-ˌlīz\ *vt* **-ized; -iz·ing 1 :** to unite in or under a federal system **2 :** to bring under the jurisdiction of a federal government

Federal Reserve bank *n* : one of 12 banks set up under the Federal Reserve system to hold reserves and discount commercial paper for affiliated banks in their respective districts

1fed·er·ate \ˈfed(-ə)-rət\ *adj* [L *foederatus,* fr. *foeder-, foedus*] : united in an alliance or federation : FEDERATED

2fed·er·ate \ˈfed-ə-ˌrāt\ *vt* **-at·ed; -at·ing :** to join in a federation

federated church *n* : a local church uniting two or more congregations that maintain different denominational ties

fed·er·a·tion \ˌfed-ə-ˈrā-shən\ *n* **1 :** the act of federating; *esp* : the formation of a federal union **2 :** something formed by federation: as **a :** a federal government **b :** a union of organizations

fed·er·a·tive \ˈfed-ə-ˌrāt-iv, ˈfed(-ə)-rət-\ *adj* : FEDERAL — **fed·er·a·tive·ly** *adv*

fedn *abbr* federation

fe·do·ra \fi-ˈdōr-ə, -ˈdȯr-\ *n* [*Fédora,* drama by V. Sardou] : a low soft felt hat with the crown creased lengthwise

fed up *adj* : tired, sated, or disgusted beyond endurance ⟨*fed up* with things as they are⟩

1fee \ˈfē\ *n* [ME, fr. OF *fé, fief,* of Gmc origin; akin to OE *feoh* cattle, property, OHG *fihu* cattle; akin to L *pecus* cattle, *pecunia* money, *pectere* to comb] **1 a** (1) : an estate in land held in feudal law from a lord on condition of homage and service (2) : a piece of land so held **b :** an inherited or heritable estate in land **2 a** (1) : a fixed charge (2) : a charge for a professional service **b :** TIP *syn* see WAGE — **in fee :** in absolute and legal possession

2fee *vt* **feed; fee·ing 1** *chiefly Scot* : HIRE **2 :** TIP

fee·ble \ˈfē-bəl\ *adj* **fee·bler** \-b(ə-)lər\; **fee·blest** \-b(ə-)ləst\ [ME *feble,* fr. OF, fr. L *flebilis* lamentable, wretched, fr. *flēre* to weep — more at BLEAT] **1 a :** markedly lacking in strength **b :** indicating weakness **2 a :** deficient in qualities or resources that indicate vigor, authority, force, or efficiency **b :** INADEQUATE, INFERIOR *syn* see WEAK *ant* robust — **fee·ble·ness** \-bəl-nəs\ *n* — **fee·bly** \-blē\ *adv*

fee·ble·mind·ed \ˌfē-bəl-ˈmīn-dəd\ *adj* **1** *obs* : IRRESOLUTE, VACILLATING **2 :** mentally deficient **3 :** FOOLISH, STUPID — **fee·ble·mind·ed·ly** *adv* — **fee·ble·mind·ed·ness** *n*

fee·blish \ˈfē-b(ə-)lish\ *adj* : somewhat feeble

1feed \ˈfēd\ *vb* **fed** \ˈfed\; **feed·ing** [ME *feden,* fr. OE *fēdan;* akin to OE *fōda* food — more at FOOD] *vt* **1 a :** to give food to **b :** to give as food **2 :** to furnish something essential to the growth, sustenance, maintenance, or operation of **3 :** to produce or provide food for **4 a :** SATISFY, GRATIFY **b :** SUPPORT, ENCOURAGE **5 a :** to supply for use or consumption **b** (1) : to supply (a signal) to an electronic circuit (2) : to send by wire to a transmitting station for broadcast **6** : to supply with cues and situations that make a role more effective **7** : to pass or throw a ball or puck to (a teammate) esp. for a shot at the goal ~ *vi* **1 a** : to consume food : EAT **b** : PREY — used with *on, upon,* or *off* **2** : to become nourished or satisfied as if by food **3** : to move into a machine or opening in order to be used or processed

²feed *n* **1 a** : an act of eating **b** : MEAL; *esp* : a large meal **2 a** : food for livestock; *specif* : a mixture or preparation for feeding livestock **b** : the amount given at each feeding **3 a** : material supplied (as to a furnace or machine) **b** : a mechanism by which the action of feeding is effected **c** : the motion or process of carrying forward the material to be operated upon (as in a machine) **4** : ASSIST 2

feed·back \ˈfēd-ˌbak\ *n* **1** : the return to the input of a part of the output of a machine, system, or process (as for producing changes in an electronic circuit that improve performance or in an automatic control device that provide self-corrective action) **2 a** : the partial reversion of the effects of a process to its source or to a preceding stage **b** : the return to a point of origin of evaluative or corrective information about an action or process ⟨student ~ was solicited to help revise the curriculum⟩ ⟨we welcome . . . ~ from our readers — brickbats as well as bouquets —*Johns Hopkins Mag.*⟩; *also* : the information so transmitted

feedback inhibition *n* : inhibition of an enzyme controlling an early stage of a series of biochemical reactions by the end product when it reaches a critical concentration

feed·er \ˈfēd-ər\ *n* : one that feeds: as **a** : a device or apparatus for supplying food **b (1)** : TRIBUTARY **b (2)** : a source of supply **b (3)** : a heavy wire conductor supplying electricity at some point of an electric distribution system (as from a substation) **b (4)** : a transmission line running from a radio transmitter to an antenna **b (5)** : a branch transportation line **c** : an animal being fattened or suitable for fattening **d** : an actor or role that serves as a foil for another

feed·lot \ˈfēd-ˌlät\ *n* : a plot of land on which livestock are fattened for market

feed·stock \-ˌstäk\ *n* : raw material supplied to a machine or processing plant

feed·stuff \-ˌstəf\ *n* : FEED 2a; *also* : any of the constituent nutrients of an animal ration

¹feel \ˈfē(ə)l\ *vb* **felt** \ˈfelt\; **feel·ing** [ME *felen,* fr. OE *fēlan;* akin to OHG *fuolen* to feel, L *palpare* to caress, and perh. to Gk *pallein* to brandish — more at POLEMIC] *vt* **1 a** : to handle or touch in order to examine, test, or explore some quality ⟨*felt* the coat to see if it was wet⟩ **b** : to perceive by a physical sensation coming from discrete end organs (as of the skin or muscles) **2 a** : to undergo passive experience of **b** : to have one's sensibilities markedly affected by **3** : to ascertain by cautious trial — often used with *out* **4 a** : to be aware of by instinct or inference **b** : BELIEVE, THINK ~ *vi* **1 a** : to receive or be able to receive a tactile sensation **b** : to search for something by using the sense of touch **2** : to be conscious of an inward impression, state of mind, or physical condition **3** : to seem esp. to the sense of touch **4** : to have sympathy or pity ***syn*** see TOUCH

²feel *n* **1** : the sense of touch **2** : SENSATION, FEELING **3 a** : the quality of a thing as imparted through or as if through touch **b** : typical or peculiar quality or atmosphere **4** : intuitive knowledge or ability

feel·er \ˈfē-lər\ *n* : one that feels: as **a** : a tactile process (as a tentacle) of an animal **b** : something (as a proposal) ventured to ascertain the views of others

¹feel·ing \ˈfē-liŋ\ *n* **1 a (1)** : the one of the basic physical senses of which the skin contains the chief end organs and of which the sensations of touch and temperature are characteristic : TOUCH **(2)** : a sensation experienced through this sense **b** : generalized bodily consciousness or sensation **c** : appreciative or responsive awareness or recognition ⟨experienced a ~ of safety⟩ **2 a** : an emotional state or reaction ⟨had a kindly ~ toward the child⟩ **b** *pl* : susceptibility to impression : SENSITIVITY ⟨the remark hurt her ~*s*⟩ **3 a** : the undifferentiated background of one's awareness considered apart from any identifiable sensation, perception, or thought **b** : the overall quality of one's awareness **c** : conscious recognition : SENSE **4 a** : often unreasoned opinion or belief : SENTIMENT **b** : PRESENTIMENT **5** : capacity to respond emotionally esp. with the higher emotions ⟨a man of noble ~⟩ **6** : the character ascribed to something as a result of one's impression or emotional state : ATMOSPHERE **7 a** : the quality of a work of art that embodies and conveys the emotion of the artist **b** : sympathetic aesthetic response **8** : FEEL 4 ⟨lacks a ~ for words⟩
***syn* 1** see SENSATION
2 FEELING, AFFECTION, EMOTION, SENTIMENT, PASSION *shared meaning element* : subjective response or reaction (as to a person or situation) or an instance of this

²feeling *adj* **1 a** : SENTIENT, SENSITIVE **b** : easily moved emotionally **2** *obs* : deeply felt **3** : expressing emotion or sensitivity — **feel·ing·ly** \-liŋ-lē\ *adv* — **feel·ing·ness** *n*

fee simple *n, pl* **fees simple** : a fee without limitation to any class of heirs or restrictions on transfer of ownership

fee splitting *n* : payment by a specialist (as a doctor or a lawyer) of a part of his fee to the person who made the referral

feet *pl of* FOOT

fee tail *n, pl* **fees tail** : a fee limited to a particular class of heirs

feet·first \ˈfēt-ˈfərst\ *adv* : with the feet foremost ⟨jumped into the water ~⟩

feet of clay [fr. the feet of the idol in Dan 2:33] : a generally concealed or unobserved but marked weakness or frailty ⟨a towering figure, posthumously judged to have *feet of clay* —*Times Lit. Supp.*⟩

feeze \ˈfēz, ˈfāz\ *n* [ME *veze,* fr. *fesen, vesen* to drive away — more at FAZE] **1** *chiefly dial* : RUSH **2** *dial* : a state of alarm or excitement

Feh·ling's solution \ˈfā-liŋz-\ *n* [Hermann *Fehling* †1885 G chemist] : a blue solution of Rochelle salt and copper sulfate used as an oxidizing agent in testing for sugars and aldehydes

feign \ˈfān\ *vb* [ME *feignen,* fr. OF *feign-,* stem of *feindre,* fr. L *fingere* to shape, feign — more at DOUGH] *vt* **1 a** : to give a false appearance of : induce as a false impression ⟨~ death⟩ ⟨he ~*ed* that he believed her story⟩ **b** : to assert as if true : PRETEND **2** *archaic* **a** : INVENT, IMAGINE **b** : to give fictional representation to **3** *obs* : DISGUISE, CONCEAL ~ *vi* : PRETEND, DISSEMBLE ***syn*** see ASSUME — **feign·er** *n*

feigned *adj* **1** : FICTITIOUS **2** : not genuine or real

¹feint \ˈfānt\ *n* [F *feinte,* fr. OF, fr. *feint,* pp. of *feindre*] : something feigned; *specif* : a mock blow or attack on or toward one part in order to distract attention from the point one really intends to attack ***syn*** see TRICK

²feint *vi* : to make a feint ~ *vt* **1** : to lure or deceive with a feint **2** : to make a pretense of

fei·rie \ˈfē-rē\ *adj* [ME (Sc) *fery,* fr. ME *fere* strong, fr. OE *fēre* able to go; akin to OE *faran* to travel, fare] *Scot* : NIMBLE, STRONG

feist \ˈfīst\ *n* [obs. *fisting hound,* fr. obs. *fist* (to break wind)] *chiefly dial* : a small dog

feisty \ˈfī-stē\ *adj* **feist·i·er; -est** : being in a state of excitement or agitation: as **a** : full of nervous energy : FIDGETY **b** : being touchy and quarrelsome ⟨found us irritated, upset, ~ —E. E. Rebstock⟩ **c** : being frisky and exuberant

feld·spar \ˈfel(d)-ˌspär\ *n* [modif. of obs. G *feldspath* (now *feldspat*), fr. G *feld* field + obs. G *spath* (now *spat*) spar] : any of a group of crystalline minerals that consist of aluminum silicates with either potassium, sodium, calcium, or barium and that are an essential constituent of nearly all crystalline rocks (hardness 6–6.5, sp. gr. 2.5–2.9)

feld·spath·ic \fel(d)-ˈspath-ik\ *adj* [*feldspath* (var. of *feldspar*), fr. obs. G] : relating to or containing feldspar — used esp. of a porcelain glaze

fe·li·cif·ic \ˌfē-lə-ˈsif-ik\ *adj* [L *felic-, felix*] : causing or intended to cause happiness

felicific calculus *n* : a method of determining the rightness of an action by balancing the probable pleasures and pains that it would produce

¹fe·lic·i·tate \fi-ˈlis-ə-ˌtāt\ *adj* [LL *felicitatus,* pp. of *felicitare* to make happy, fr. L *felicitas*] *obs* : made happy

²felicitate *vt* **-tat·ed; -tat·ing** **1** *archaic* : to make happy **2 a** : to consider happy or fortunate **b** : to offer congratulations to — **fe·lic·i·ta·tion** \-ˌlis-ə-ˈtā-shən\ *n* — **fe·lic·i·ta·tor** \-ˈlis-ə-ˌtāt-ər\ *n*

fe·lic·i·tous \fi-ˈlis-ət-əs\ *adj* **1** : very well suited or expressed : APT ⟨a ~ remark⟩ **2** : PLEASANT, DELIGHTFUL ***syn*** see FIT ***ant*** infelicitous — **fe·lic·i·tous·ly** *adv* — **fe·lic·i·tous·ness** *n*

fe·lic·i·ty \fi-ˈlis-ət-ē\ *n, pl* **-ties** [ME *felicite,* fr. MF *felicité,* fr. L *felicitat-, felicitas,* fr. *felic-, felix* fruitful, happy — more at FEMININE] **1 a** : the quality or state of being happy; *esp* : great happiness **b** : an instance of happiness **2** : something that causes happiness **3** : a pleasing faculty esp. in art or language : APTNESS **4** : an apt expression

fe·lid \ˈfē-ləd\ *n* [NL *Felidae,* family name, fr. *Felis,* genus of cats, fr. L, cat] : CAT 1b — **felid** *adj*

fe·line \ˈfē-ˌlīn\ *adj* [L *felinus,* fr. *felis*] **1** : of or relating to cats or the cat family **2** : resembling a cat: as **a** : sleekly graceful **b** : SLY, TREACHEROUS **c** : STEALTHY — **feline** *n* — **fe·line·ly** *adv* — **fe·lin·i·ty** \fē-ˈlin-ət-ē\ *n*

feline distemper *n* **1** : PANLEUCOPENIA **2** : a gastrointestinal disease of cats closely related to panleucopenia

¹fell \ˈfel\ *n* [ME, fr. OE; akin to OHG *fel* skin, L *pellis*] : SKIN, HIDE, PELT

²fell *vt* [ME *fellen,* fr. OE *fellan;* akin to OE *feallan* to fall — more at FALL] **1 a** : to cut, beat, or knock down **b** : KILL **2** : to sew (a seam) by folding one raw edge under the other and sewing flat on the wrong side — **fell·able** \ˈfel-ə-bəl\ *adj* — **fell·er** *n*

³fell *past of* FALL

⁴fell *adj* [ME *fel,* fr. OF — more at FELON] **1 a** : FIERCE, CRUEL, TERRIBLE **b** : very destructive or painful : DEADLY **2** *Scot* : SHARP, PUNGENT — **fell·ness** *n* — **fel·ly** \ˈfel-lē\ *adv* — **at one fell swoop** : all at once; *also* : with a single concentrated effort

fel·lah \ˈfel-ə, fə-ˈlä\ *n, pl* **fel·la·hin** *or* **fel·la·heen** \ˌfel-ə-ˈhēn, fə-ˌlä-ˈhēn\ [Ar *fallāḥ*] : a peasant or agricultural laborer in an Arab country (as Egypt)

fel·la·tio \fə-ˈlā-shē-ˌō, fe-, -ˈlät-ē-\ *also* **fel·la·tion** \-ˈlā-shən\ *n* [NL *fellation-, fellatio,* fr. L *fellatus,* pp. of *felare, fellare,* lit., to suck — more at FEMININE] : oral stimulation of the penis

fell·mon·ger \ˈfel-ˌməŋ-gər, -ˌmäŋ-\ *n, Brit* : one who removes hair or wool from hides in preparation for leather making — **fell·mon·gered** \-gərd\ *adj, Brit* — **fell·mon·ger·ing** \-g(ə-)riŋ\ *or* **fell·mon·gery** \-g(ə-)rē\ *n, Brit*

fel·low \ˈfel-(ˌ)ō, -ə(-w)\ *n* [ME *felawe,* fr. OE *fēolaga,* fr. ON *fēlagi,* fr. *fēlag* partnership, fr. *fē* cattle, money + *lag* act of laying] **1** : COMRADE, ASSOCIATE **2 a** : an equal in rank, power, or character : PEER **b** : one of a pair : MATE **3** : a member of a group having common characteristics; *specif* : a member of an incorporated literary or scientific society **4 a** *obs* : a person of one of the lower social classes **b** : a worthless man or boy **c** : MAN, BOY **d** : BOYFRIEND, BEAU **5** : an incorporated member of a college or collegiate foundation esp. in a British university **6** : a person appointed to a position granting a stipend and allowing for advanced study or research

fellow feeling *n* : a feeling of community of interest or of mutual understanding ⟨*fellow feeling* . . . in the face of the impersonality of urban life —Richard Poirier⟩

fel·low·ly \-ō-lē, -ə-lē\ *adj* : SOCIABLE — **fellowly** *adv*

fel·low·man \ˌfel-ō-ˈman, -ə-\ *n* : a kindred human being

ə abut ᵊ kitten ər further a back ā bake ä cot, cart
aü out ch chin e less ē easy g gift i trip ī life
j joke ŋ sing ō flow ȯ flaw ȯi coin th thin t͟h this
ü loot u̇ foot y yet yü few yu̇ furious zh vision

fellow servant *n* **:** an employee working with another employee under such circumstances that each one if negligent may expose the other to harm which the employer cannot reasonably be expected to guard against or be held legally liable for

[1]**fel·low·ship** \ˈfel-ō-ˌship, -ə-\ *n* **1 :** COMPANIONSHIP, COMPANY **2 a :** community of interest, activity, feeling, or experience **b :** the state of being a fellow or associate **3 :** a company of equals or friends **:** ASSOCIATION **4 :** the quality or state of being comradely **5** *obs* **:** MEMBERSHIP, PARTNERSHIP **6 a :** the position of a fellow (as of a university) **b :** the stipend of a fellow **c :** a foundation for the providing of such a stipend

[2]**fellowship** *vb* **-shipped** *also* **-shiped** \-ˌshipt\; **-ship·ping** *also* **-ship·ing** \-ˌship-iŋ\ *vi* **:** to join in fellowship esp. with a church member ~ *vt* **:** to admit to fellowship (as in a church)

fellow traveler *n* [trans. of Russ *poputchik*] **:** one that sympathizes with and often furthers the ideals and program of an organized group (as the Communist party) without membership in the group or regular participation in its activities — **fel·low–trav·el·ing** *adj*

fel·ly \ˈfel-ē\ *or* **fel·loe** \-(ˌ)ō\ *n, pl* **fellies** *or* **felloes** [ME *fely, felive,* fr. OE *felg;* akin to OHG *felga* felly, OE *fealg* piece of plowed land] **:** the exterior rim or a segment of the rim of a wheel supported by the spokes

felo–de–se \ˌfel-ōd-ə-ˈsā, -ˈsē\ *n, pl* **fe·lo·nes–de–se** \fə-ˌlō-(ˌ)nēz-də-\ *or* **felos–de–se** \ˌfel-ōz-də-\ [ML *felo de se, fello de se,* lit., evildoer upon himself] **1 :** one who deliberately kills himself or who dies from the effects of his commission of an unlawful malicious act **2 :** an act of deliberate self-destruction **:** SUICIDE

[1]**fel·on** \ˈfel-ən\ *adj* [ME, fr. OF *felon, fel,* fr. ML *fellon-, fello* evildoer, villain] **1** *archaic* **a :** CRUEL **b :** EVIL **2** *archaic* **:** WILD

[2]**felon** *n* **1 :** one who has committed a felony **2** *archaic* **:** VILLAIN **3 :** a deep usu. suppurative inflammation of the finger or toe esp. near the end or around the nail

fe·lo·ni·ous \fə-ˈlō-nē-əs\ *adj* **1** *archaic* **:** very evil **:** VILLAINOUS **2 :** of, relating to, or having the quality of a felony — **fe·lo·ni·ous·ly** *adv* — **fe·lo·ni·ous·ness** *n*

fel·on·ry \ˈfel-ən-rē\ *n* **:** FELONS; *specif* **:** the convict population of a penal colony

fel·o·ny \ˈfel-ə-nē\ *n, pl* **-nies 1 :** an act on the part of a feudal vassal involving the forfeiture of his fee **2 a :** a grave crime formerly differing from a misdemeanor under English common law by involving forfeiture in addition to any other punishment **b :** a grave crime declared to be a felony by the common law or by statute regardless of the punishment actually imposed **c :** a crime declared a felony by statute because of the punishment imposed **d :** a crime for which the punishment in federal law may be death or imprisonment for more than one year

fel·site \ˈfel-ˌsīt\ *n* [*felspar*] **:** a dense igneous rock that consists almost entirely of feldspar and quartz — **fel·sit·ic** \fel-ˈsit-ik\ *adj*

fel·spar *var of* FELDSPAR

[1]**felt** \ˈfelt\ *n* [ME, fr. OE; akin to OHG *filz* felt, L *pellere* to drive, beat, Gk *pelas* near] **1 a :** a cloth made of wool and fur often mixed with natural or synthetic fibers through the action of heat, moisture, chemicals, and pressure **b :** a firm woven cloth of wool or cotton heavily napped and shrunk **2 :** an article made of felt **3 :** a material resembling felt: as **a :** a heavy paper of organic or asbestos fibers impregnated with asphalt and used in building construction **b :** semirigid pressed fiber insulation used in building

[2]**felt** *vt* **1 :** to make into felt or a similar substance **2 :** to cause to adhere and mat together **3 :** to cover with felt

[3]**felt** *past of* FEEL

felt·ing \ˈfel-tiŋ\ *n* **1 :** the process by which felt is made **2 :** FELT

fe·luc·ca \fə-ˈlü-kə, -ˈlək-ə\ *n* [It *feluca*] **:** a narrow fast lateen-rigged sailing ship chiefly of the Mediterranean area

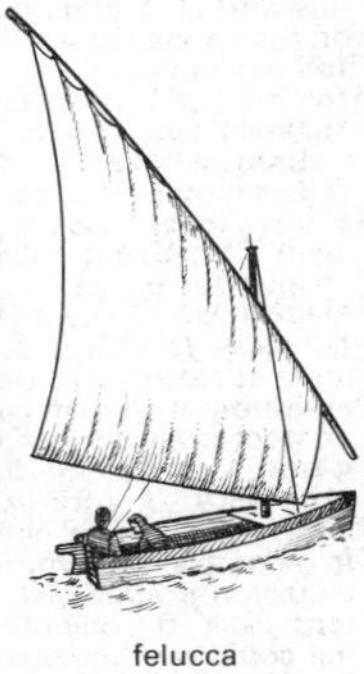
felucca

fem *abbr* **1** female **2** feminine

[1]**fe·male** \ˈfē-ˌmāl\ *n* [ME, alter. of *femel, femelle,* fr. MF & ML; MF *femelle,* fr. ML *femella,* fr. L, girl, dim. of *femina*] **1 :** an individual that bears young or produces eggs as distinguished from one that begets young; *esp* **:** a woman or girl as distinguished from a man or boy **2 :** a pistillate plant

[2]**female** *adj* **1 a :** of, relating to, or being the sex that bears young or produces eggs **b :** PISTILLATE **2 :** having some quality (as gentleness or delicacy) associated with the female sex **3 :** designed with a hollow into which a corresponding male part fits ⟨~ coupling of a hose⟩ — **fe·male·ness** *n*

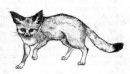

[1]**fem·i·nine** \ˈfem-ə-nən\ *adj* [ME, fr. MF *feminin,* fr. L *femininus,* fr. *femina* woman; akin to OE *delu* nipple, L *filius* son, *felix, fetus, & fecundus* fruitful, *felare* to suck, Gk *thēlē* nipple] **1 :** FEMALE 1a **2 :** characteristic of or appropriate or peculiar to women **3 :** of, relating to, or constituting the gender that ordinarily includes most words or grammatical forms referring to females ⟨a ~ noun⟩ **4 a :** having an unstressed and usu. hypermetric final syllable ⟨~ ending⟩ **b** *of rhyme* **:** having an unstressed final syllable **c :** having the final chord occurring on a weak beat ⟨music in ~ cadences⟩ — **fem·i·nine·ly** *adv* — **fem·i·nine·ness** \-nə(n)-nəs\ *n*

[2]**feminine** *n* **1 :** the female principle ⟨eternal ~⟩ **2 a :** a noun, pronoun, adjective, or inflectional form or class of the feminine gender **b :** the feminine gender

fem·i·nin·i·ty \ˌfem-ə-ˈnin-ət-ē\ *n* **1 :** the quality or nature of the female sex **2 :** EFFEMINACY **3 :** WOMEN, WOMANKIND

fem·i·nism \ˈfem-ə-ˌniz-əm\ *n* **1 :** the theory of the political, economic, and social equality of the sexes **2 :** organized activity on behalf of women's rights and interests — **fem·i·nist** \-nəst\ *n or adj* — **fem·i·nis·tic** \ˌfem-ə-ˈnis-tik\ *adj*

fe·min·i·ty \fe-ˈmin-ət-ē, fə-\ *n* **:** FEMININITY

fem·i·nize \ˈfem-ə-ˌnīz\ *vt* **-nized; -niz·ing 1 :** to give a feminine quality to **2 :** to cause (a male or castrate) to take on feminine characters (as by implantation of ovaries or administration of estrogenic substances) — **fem·i·ni·za·tion** \ˌfem-ə-nə-ˈzā-shən\ *n*

femme fa·tale \ˌfem-fə-ˈtal, ˌfam-, -ˈtäl\ *n, pl* **femmes fa·tales** \-ˈtal(z), -ˈtäl(z)\ [F, lit., disastrous woman] **1 :** a seductive woman who lures men into dangerous or compromising situations **:** SIREN **2 :** a woman who attracts men by an aura of charm and mystery

fem·o·ral \ˈfem-(ə-)rəl\ *adj* **:** of or relating to the femur or thigh

femoral artery *n* **:** the chief artery of the thigh lying in its anterior inner part

fem·to- \ˌfem(p)-tō\ *comb form* [ISV, fr. Dan or Norw *femten* fifteen, fr. ON *fimmtān;* akin to OE *fīftēne* fifteen] **:** one quadrillionth (10^{-15}) part of ⟨*femto*ampere⟩

fe·mur \ˈfē-mər\ *n, pl* **fe·murs** *or* **fem·o·ra** \ˈfem-(ə-)rə\ [NL *femor-, femur,* fr. L, thigh] **1 :** the proximal bone of the hind or lower limb — called also *thighbone* **2 :** the segment of an insect's leg that is third from the body

[1]**fen** \ˈfen\ *n* [ME, fr. OE *fenn;* akin to OHG *fenna* fen, Skt *paṅka* mud] **:** low land covered wholly or partly with water unless artificially drained

[2]**fen** \ˈfən\ *n, pl* **fen** [Chin (Pek) *fên*[1]] — see *yuan* at MONEY table

[1]**fence** \ˈfen(t)s\ *n, often attrib* [ME *fens,* short for *defens* defense] **1** *archaic* **:** a means of protection **:** DEFENSE **2 :** a barrier intended to prevent escape or intrusion or to mark a boundary; *esp* **:** such a barrier made of posts and wire or boards **3 :** FENCING 1 **4 a :** a receiver of stolen goods **b :** a place where stolen goods are bought — **fence·less** \-ləs\ *adj* — **fence·less·ness** *n* — **on the fence :** in a position of neutrality or indecision

[2]**fence** *vb* **fenced; fenc·ing** *vt* **1 a :** to enclose with a fence **b** (1) **:** to keep in or out with a fence (2) **:** to ward off **2 :** to provide a defense for ~ *vi* **1 a :** to practice fencing **b** (1) **:** to use tactics of attack and defense resembling those of fencing (2) **:** to parry arguments by shifting ground **2** *archaic* **:** to provide protection — **fenc·er** *n*

fence–sit·ting \ˈfen(t)s-ˌsit-iŋ\ *n* **:** a state of indecision or neutrality with respect to conflicting positions — **fence sitter** *n*

fenc·ing *n* **1 :** the art or practice of attack and defense with the foil, épee, or saber **2 a** (1) **:** FENCE 2 (2) **:** the fences of a property or region **b :** material used for building fences

[1]**fend** \ˈfend\ *vb* [ME *fenden,* short for *defenden*] *vt* **1 :** DEFEND **2 :** to keep or ward off **:** REPEL — often used with *off* **3** *dial Brit* **:** to provide for **:** SUPPORT ~ *vi* **1** *dial Brit* **:** to make an effort **:** STRUGGLE **2 a :** to try to get along without help **:** SHIFT **b :** to provide a livelihood

[2]**fend** *n, chiefly Scot* **:** an effort or attempt esp. for oneself

fend·er \ˈfen-dər\ *n* **:** a device that protects: as **a :** a cushion (as foam rubber, a bundle of rope, or a wood float) between a boat and a dock or between two boats that lessens shock and prevents chafing **b :** RAILING **c :** a device in front of locomotives and streetcars to lessen injury to animals or pedestrians in case of collision **d :** a guard over the wheel of a motor vehicle **e :** a low metal frame or a screen before an open fireplace **f :** an oblong or triangular shield of leather attached to the stirrup leather of a saddle to protect a rider's legs

fe·nes·tra \fə-ˈnes-trə\ *n, pl* **-trae** \-ˌtrē, -ˌtrī\ [NL, fr. L, window] **1 :** a small opening: as **a :** an oval opening between the middle ear and the vestibule having the base of the stapes or columella attached to its membrane — called also *fenestra ovalis, fenestra vestibuli* **b :** a round opening between the middle ear and the cochlea — called also *fenestra cochleae, fenestra rotunda* **2 :** an opening cut in bone **3 :** a transparent spot (as in the wings of a moth) — **fe·nes·tral** \-trəl\ *adj*

fe·nes·trate \fə-ˈnes-ˌtrāt, ˈfen-ə-ˌstrāt\ *adj* [L *fenestratus,* fr. *fenestra*] **:** FENESTRATED 2

fen·es·trat·ed \ˈfen-ə-ˌstrāt-əd\ *adj* **1 :** provided with or characterized by windows **2 :** having one or more openings or pores ⟨~ blood capillaries⟩

fen·es·tra·tion \ˌfen-ə-ˈstrā-shən\ *n* **1 :** the arrangement, proportioning, and design of windows and doors in a building **2 :** an opening in a surface (as a wall or membrane) **3 :** the operation of cutting an opening in the bony labyrinth between the inner ear and tympanum to replace natural fenestrae that are not functional

Fe·ni·an \ˈfē-nē-ən\ *n* [IrGael *Fēinne,* pl. of *Fiann,* legendary band of Irish warriors] **1 :** one of a legendary band of warriors defending Ireland in the 2d and 3d centuries A.D. **2 :** a member of a secret 19th century Irish and Irish-American organization dedicated to the overthrow of British rule in Ireland — **Fenian** *adj* — **Fe·ni·an·ism** \-ə-ˌniz-əm\ *n*

fen·nec \ˈfen-ik\ *n* [Ar *fanak*] **:** a small pale-fawn African fox (*Fennecus zerda*) with large ears

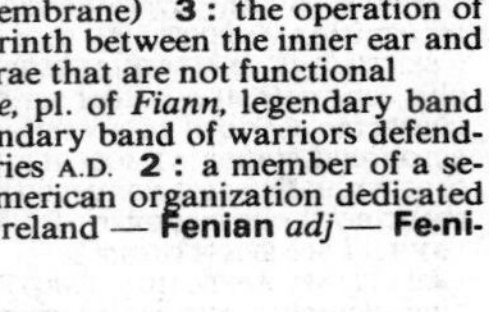
fennec

fen·nel \ˈfen-ᵊl\ *n* [ME *fenel,* fr. OE *finugl,* fr. (assumed) VL *fenuculum,* fr. L *feniculum* fennel, dim. of *fenum* hay; perh. akin to L *fetus* fruitful — more at FEMININE] **:** a perennial European herb (*Foeniculum vulgare*) of the carrot family adventive in No. America and cultivated for its aromatic seeds and its foliage

fen·ny \ˈfen-ē\ *adj* [ME, fr. OE *fennig,* fr. *fenn* fen] **1 :** having the characteristics of a fen **:** BOGGY **2 :** peculiar to or found in a fen

fenu·greek \ˈfen-yə-ˌgrēk\ *n* [ME *fenugrek,* fr. MF *fenugrec,* fr. L *fenum Graecum,* lit., Greek hay] **:** a leguminous annual Asiatic herb (*Trigonella foenumgraecum*) with aromatic seeds

feoff·ee \fe-ˈfē, fē-ˈfē\ *n* **:** the person to whom a feoffment is made

feoff·ment \ˈfef-mənt, ˈfēf-\ *n* [ME *feoffement,* fr. AF, fr. *feoffer* to invest with a fee, fr. OF *fief* fee] **:** the granting of a fee

feof·for \ˈfef-ər, ˈfēf-; fe-ˈfȯ(ə)r, fē-\ *or* **feoff·er** \ˈfef-ər, ˈfēf-\ *n* **:** one who makes a feoffment

FEPA *abbr* Fair Employment Practices Act

FEPC *abbr* Fair Employment Practices Commission

-fer \fər\ *n comb form* [F & L; F *-fère*, fr. L *-fer* bearing, one that bears, fr. *ferre* to carry — more at BEAR] : one that bears ⟨aqui*fer*⟩

FERA *abbr* Federal Emergency Relief Administration

fe·rae na·tu·rae \ˈfer-ˌī-nə-ˈtu̇(ə)r-ˌī\ *adj* [L, of a wild nature] : wild by nature and not usu. tamed

fe·ral \ˈfir-əl, ˈfer-\ *adj* [ML *feralis*, fr. L *fera* wild animal, fr. fem. of *ferus* wild — more at FIERCE] **1** : of, relating to, or suggestive of a wild beast : SAVAGE **2 a** : not domesticated or cultivated : WILD 1a **b** : having escaped from domestication and become wild

fer·bam \ˈfər-ˌbam\ *n* [*fer*ric dimethyl-dithiocar*bam*ate] : an agricultural fungicide $FeC_9H_{18}N_3S_6$ used esp. on fruit trees

fer–de–lance \ˈferd-ᵊl-ˈan(t)s, -ˈän(t)s\ *n, pl* **fer–de–lance** [F, lit., lance iron, spearhead] : a large extremely venomous pit viper (*Bothrops atrox*) of Central and So. America

fere \ˈfi(ə)r\ *n* [ME, fr. OE *gefēra;* akin to OE *faran* to go, travel — more at FARE] **1** *archaic* : COMPANION, COMRADE **2** *archaic* : SPOUSE

¹fe·ria \ˈfir-ē-ə, ˈfer-\ *n* [ML — more at FAIR] : a weekday of a church calendar on which no feast is celebrated — **fe·ri·al** \-ē-əl\ *adj*

²fe·ria \ˈfer-ē-ə, -ē-ˌä\ *n* [Sp, fair, market, fr. ML — more at FAIR] : an Hispanic market festival often in observance of a religious holiday

fe·rine \ˈfi(ə)r-ˌīn\ *adj* [L *ferinus*, fr. *fera*] : FERAL

fer·i·ty \ˈfer-ət-ē\ *n* [L *feritas*, fr. *ferus*] : the quality or state of being feral

fer·lie *also* **fer·ly** \ˈfer-lē\ *n, pl* **ferlies** [ME, fr. *ferly* strange, fr. OE *fǣrlic* unexpected, fr. *fǣr* sudden danger — more at FEAR] *Scot* : WONDER

Ferm *abbr* Fermanagh

fer·ma·ta \fer-ˈmät-ə\ *n* [It, lit., stop, fr. *fermare* to stop, fr. L *firmare* to make firm] : a prolongation at the discretion of the performer of a musical note, chord, or rest beyond its given time value; *also* : the sign denoting such a prolongation

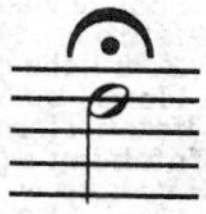

fermata

¹fer·ment \(ˌ)fər-ˈment\ *vi* **1** : to undergo fermentation **2** : to be in a state of agitation or intense activity ~ *vt* **1** : to cause to undergo fermentation **2** : to work up (as into a state of agitation) : FOMENT — **fer·ment·able** \-ə-bəl\ *adj* — **fer·ment·er** *n*

²fer·ment \ˈfər-ˌment *also* (ˌ)fər-ˈ\ *n* [ME, fr. L *fermentum* yeast — more at BARM] **1** : an agent (as an enzyme or an organism) capable of bringing about fermentation **2 a** : FERMENTATION 1 **b** (1) : a state of unrest : AGITATION (2) : a process of active often disorderly development ⟨the great period of creative ~ in literature —William Barrett⟩

fer·men·ta·tion \ˌfər-mən-ˈtā-shən, -ˌmen-\ *n* **1 a** : a chemical change with effervescence **b** : an enzymatically controlled anaerobic breakdown of an energy-rich compound (as a carbohydrate to carbon dioxide and alcohol or to an organic acid); *broadly* : an enzymatically controlled transformation of an organic compound **2** : FERMENT 2b

fer·men·ta·tive \(ˌ)fər-ˈment-ət-iv\ *adj* **1** : causing fermentation **2** : of, relating to, or produced by fermentation **3** : capable of undergoing fermentation

fer·mi \ˈfe(ə)r-(ˌ)mē, ˈfər-\ *n* [Enrico *Fermi*] : a unit of length equal to 10^{-13} centimeter

fer·mi·on \ˈfer-mē-ˌän, ˈfər-\ *n* [Enrico *Fermi* + E ²*-on*] : a particle (as an electron, proton, or neutron) having a half-odd-integer number of units of spin (as $^1/_2$, $^3/_2$, $^5/_2$)

fer·mi·um \ˈfer-mē-əm, ˈfər-\ *n* [Enrico *Fermi*] : a radioactive metallic element artificially produced (as by bombardment of plutonium with neutrons) — see ELEMENT table

fern \ˈfərn\ *n* [ME, fr. OE *fearn;* akin to OHG *farn* fern, Skt *parṇa* wing, leaf] : any of numerous flowerless seedless plants constituting a class (Filicineae) of lower vascular plants; *esp* : any of an order (Filicales) resembling seed plants in being differentiated into root, stem, and leaflike fronds and in having vascular tissue but differing in reproducing by spores — **fern·like** \-ˌlīk\ *adj* — **ferny** \ˈfər-nē\ *adj*

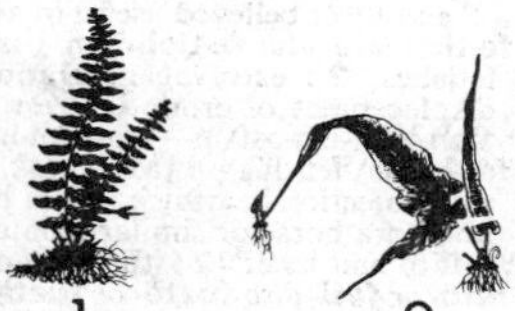

ferns: *1* Christmas fern, *2* walking leaf

fern·ery \ˈfərn-(ə-)rē\ *n, pl* **-er·ies** **1** : a place or stand where ferns grow **2** : a collection of growing ferns

fern seed *n* : the dustlike asexual spores of ferns formerly taken for seeds and thought to make the possessor invisible

fe·ro·cious \fə-ˈrō-shəs\ *adj* [L *feroc-*, *ferox*, lit., fierce looking, fr. *ferus* + *-oc-*, *-ox* (akin to Gk *ōps* eye) — more at EYE] **1** : exhibiting or given to extreme fierceness and unrestrained violence and brutality **2** : unbearably intense : EXTREME ⟨~ heat⟩ ***syn*** see FIERCE — **fe·ro·cious·ly** *adv* — **fe·ro·cious·ness** *n*

fe·roc·i·ty \fə-ˈräs-ət-ē\ *n* : the quality or state of being ferocious

-f·er·ous \f-(ə-)rəs\ *adj comb form* [ME, fr. L *-fer* & MF *-fere* (fr. L *-fer*)] : bearing : producing ⟨carboni*ferous*⟩

fer·rate \ˈfe(ə)r-ˌāt\ *n* [ISV, fr. L *ferrum* iron] : a compound containing iron and oxygen in the anion; *esp* : a red salt analogous to the chromates and sulfates

fer·re·dox·in \ˌfer-ə-ˈdäk-sən\ *n* [L *ferrum* iron + E *redox* + *-in*] : an iron-containing plant protein that functions as an electron carrier in photosynthetic organisms and in some anaerobic bacteria

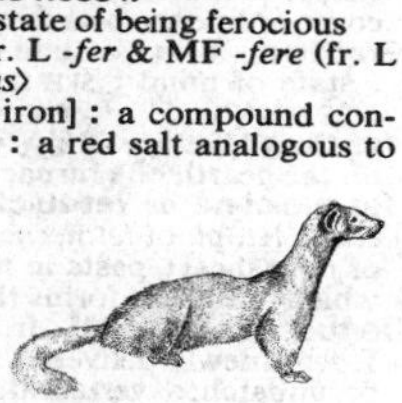

ferret 1

¹fer·ret \ˈfer-ət\ *n* [ME *furet, ferret*, fr. MF *furet*, fr. (assumed) VL *furittus*, lit., little thief, dim. of L *fur* thief] **1** : a partially domesticated usu. albino European polecat that is sometimes classed as a separate species (*Mustela furo*) and is used esp. for hunting rodents **2** : an active and persistent searcher — **fer·rety** \-ət-ē\ *adj*

²ferret *vi* **1** : to hunt with ferrets **2** : to search about ~ *vt* **1 a** (1) : to hunt (as rabbits) with ferrets (2) : to drive esp. from covert **b** : to find and bring to light by searching — usu. used with *out* ⟨~ out the answers⟩ **2** : HARRY, WORRY — **fer·ret·er** *n*

³ferret *n* [prob. modif. of It *fioretti* floss silk, fr. pl. of *fioretto*, dim. of *fiore* flower, fr. L *flor-*, *flos* — more at BLOW] : a narrow cotton, silk, or wool tape — called also *ferreting*

ferri- *comb form* [L, fr. *ferrum*] **1** : iron ⟨*ferri*ferous⟩ **2** : ferric iron ⟨*ferri*cyanic⟩

fer·ri·age \ˈfer-ē-ij\ *n* **1** : the fare paid for a ferry passage **2** : the act or business of transporting by ferry

fer·ric \ˈfer-ik\ *adj* **1** : of, relating to, or containing iron **2** : being or containing iron usu. with a valence of three

ferric ammonium citrate *n* : a complex salt containing varying amounts of iron and used esp. for making blueprints

ferric chloride *n* : a deliquescent dark salt $FeCl_3$ that readily hydrates to the yellow-orange form and that is used in sewage treatment and as an astringent

ferric hydroxide *n* : a hydrate $Fe_2O_3.nH_2O$ of ferric oxide that is capable of acting both as a base and as a weak acid

ferric oxide *n* : the red or black oxide of iron Fe_2O_3 found in nature as hematite and as rust and also obtained synthetically and used as a pigment and for polishing

fer·ri·cy·a·nide \ˌfer-ˌī-ˈsī-ə-ˌnīd, ˌfer-i-\ *n* [ISV] : a complex iron salt containing the trivalent radical $Fe(CN)_6$ and used in making blue pigments

fer·rif·er·ous \fə-ˈrif-(ə-)rəs, fe-\ *adj* : containing or yielding iron

fer·ri·mag·net·ic \ˈfer-ˌī-mag-ˈnet-ik, ˌfer-i-\ *adj* : of or relating to a substance (as ferrite) characterized by magnetization in which one group of magnetic ions is polarized in a direction opposite to the other — **fer·ri·mag·net** \ˈfer-ˌī-ˌmag-nət, ˈfer-i-\ *n* — **fer·ri·mag·net·i·cal·ly** \ˈfer-ˌī-mag-ˈnet-i-k(ə-)lē, ˌfer-i-\ *adv* — **fer·ri·mag·ne·tism** \-ˈmag-nə-ˌtiz-əm\ *n*

Fer·ris wheel \ˈfer-əs-\ *n* [G. W. G. *Ferris* †1896 Am engineer] : an amusement device consisting of a large upright power-driven wheel carrying seats that remain horizontal around its rim

fer·rite \ˈfe(ə)r-ˌīt\ *n* **1** : any of several magnetic substances that consist essentially of an iron oxide combined with one or more metals (as manganese, nickel, or zinc), have high magnetic permeability and high electrical resistivity, and are used esp. in computer memories **2** : a solid solution in which alpha iron is the solvent — **fer·rit·ic** \fə-ˈrit-ik, fe-\ *adj*

fer·ri·tin \ˈfer-ət-ᵊn\ *n* [*ferrite* + *-in*] : a crystalline iron-containing protein that functions in the storage of iron and is found esp. in the liver and spleen

ferro- *comb form* [ML, fr. L *ferrum*] **1** : iron ⟨*ferro*concrete⟩ **2** : iron and ⟨*ferro*nickel⟩ — chiefly in names of alloys **3** : ferrous iron ⟨*ferro*cyanic⟩

fer·ro·cene \ˈfer-ō-ˌsēn\ *n* [*ferro-* + cyclopentadi*ene*] : a crystalline stable organometallic coordination compound $(C_5H_5)_2Fe$; *also* : an analogous compound with a heavy metal (as chromium)

fer·ro·con·crete \ˌfer-ō-ˈkän-ˌkrēt, -kän-ˈ\ *n* : REINFORCED CONCRETE

fer·ro·cy·a·nide \-ˈsī-ə-ˌnīd\ *n* : a complex iron salt containing the tetravalent radical $Fe(CN)_6$ and used in making blue pigments (as Prussian blue)

fer·ro·elec·tric \ˌfer-ō-i-ˈlek-trik\ *adj* : of or relating to crystalline substances having spontaneous electric polarization reversible by an electric field — **ferroelectric** *n* — **fer·ro·elec·tric·i·ty** \-ˌlek-ˈtris-ət-ē, -ˈtris-tē\ *n*

fer·ro·mag·ne·sian \-mag-ˈnē-zhən, -shən\ *adj* : containing iron and magnesium ⟨~ minerals⟩

fer·ro·mag·net·ic \-ˈnet-ik\ *adj* : of or relating to substances with an abnormally high magnetic permeability, a definite saturation point, and appreciable residual magnetism and hysteresis — **ferromagnetic** *n* — **fer·ro·mag·ne·tism** \-ˈmag-nə-ˌtiz-əm\ *n*

¹fer·ro·type \ˈfer-ə-ˌtīp\ *n* **1** : a positive photograph made by a collodion process on a thin iron plate having a darkened surface **2** : the process by which a ferrotype is made

²ferrotype *vt* : to give a gloss to (a photographic print) by squeegeeing facedown while wet on a ferrotype plate and allowing to dry

fer·rous \ˈfer-əs\ *adj* [NL *ferrosus*, fr. L *ferrum*] **1** : of, relating to, or containing iron **2** : being or containing iron with a valence of two

ferrous oxide *n* : a black easily oxidizable powder FeO that is the monoxide of iron

ferrous sulfate *n* : a salt $FeSO_4$; *esp* : COPPERAS

fer·ru·gi·nous \fə-ˈrü-jə-nəs, fe-\ *or* **fer·ru·gin·e·ous** \ˌfer-(y)u̇-ˈjin-ē-əs\ *adj* [L *ferrugineus*, *ferruginus*, fr. *ferrugin-*, *ferrugo* iron rust, fr. *ferrum*] **1** : of, relating to, or containing iron ⟨a ~ soil⟩ **2** : resembling iron rust in color

¹fer·rule \ˈfer-əl\ *n* [alter. of ME *virole*, fr. MF, fr. L *viriola*, dim. of *viria* bracelet, of Celtic origin; akin to OIr *fiar* oblique — more at VEER] **1** : a ring or cap usu. of metal put around a slender shaft (as a cane or a tool handle) to strengthen it or prevent splitting **2** : a short tube or bushing for making a tight joint (as between pipes)

²ferrule *vt* **fer·ruled; fer·rul·ing** : to supply with a ferrule

¹fer·ry \ˈfer-ē\ *vb* **fer·ried; fer·ry·ing** [ME *ferien*, fr. OE *ferian* to carry, convey; akin to OE *faran* to go — more at FARE] *vt* **1 a** : to carry by boat over a body of water **b** : to cross by a ferry **2 a** : to convey (as by aircraft or motor vehicle) from one place to

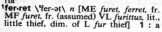

another : TRANSPORT **b** : to fly (an airplane) from the factory or other shipping point to a designated delivery point or from one base to another ~ *vi* : to cross water in a boat

²ferry *n, pl* **ferries** **1** : a place where persons or things are carried across a body of water (as a river) in a boat **2** : FERRYBOAT **3** : a franchise or right to operate a ferry service across a body of water **4** : an organized service and route for flying airplanes esp. across a sea or continent for delivery to the user

fer·ry·boat \ˈfer-ē-ˌbōt\ *n* : a boat used to ferry passengers, vehicles, or goods

fer·ry·man \-mən\ *n* : a person who operates a ferry

fer·tile \ˈfərt-ᵊl\ *adj* [ME, fr. MF & L; MF, fr. L *fertilis*, fr. *ferre* to carry, bear — more at BEAR] **1 a** : producing or bearing fruit in great quantities : PRODUCTIVE **b** : characterized by great resourcefulness of thought or imagination : INVENTIVE ⟨a ~ mind⟩ **c** *obs* : PLENTIFUL **2 a** (1) : capable of sustaining abundant plant growth ⟨~ soil⟩ (2) : affording abundant possibilities for development ⟨a ~ area for research⟩ **b** : capable of growing or developing ⟨~ egg⟩ **c** (1) : capable of producing fruit (2) *of an anther* : containing pollen (3) : developing spores or spore-bearing organs **d** : capable of breeding or reproducing **3** : capable of being converted into fissionable material ⟨~ uranium 238⟩ — **fer·tile·ly** \-ᵊl-(l)ē\ *adv* — **fer·tile·ness** \-ᵊl-nəs\ *n*

syn FERTILE, FECUND, FRUITFUL, PROLIFIC *shared meaning element* : producing or having the power to produce offspring or fruit ***ant*** infertile, sterile

fer·til·i·ty \(ˌ)fər-ˈtil-ət-ē\ *n* **1** : the quality or state of being fertile **2** : the birthrate of a population

fer·til·iza·tion \ˌfərt-ᵊl-ə-ˈzā-shən\ *n* : an act or process of making fertile: as **a** : the application of fertilizer **b** (1) : an act or process of fecundation, insemination, impregnation, or pollination **b** (2) : the process of union of two germ cells whereby the somatic chromosome number is restored and the development of a new individual is initiated — **fer·til·iza·tion·al** \-shnəl, -shən-ᵊl\ *adj*

fer·til·ize \ˈfərt-ᵊl-ˌīz\ *vt* **-ized; -iz·ing** : to make fertile: as **a** : to cause the fertilization of **b** : to apply a fertilizer to ⟨~ land⟩ — **fer·til·iz·able** \-ˌī-zə-bəl\ *adj*

fer·til·iz·er \-ˌī-zər\ *n* : one that fertilizes; *specif* : a substance (as manure or a chemical mixture) used to make soil more fertile

fer·u·la \ˈfer-(y)ə-lə\ *n* [NL, genus name, fr. L, giant fennel] : any of a genus (*Ferula*) of Old World plants of the carrot family yielding various gum resins (as galbanum and asafetida)

fer·ule \ˈfer-əl\ *also* **fer·u·la** \ˈfer-(y)ə-lə\ *n* [L *ferula* giant fennel, ferule] **1** : an instrument (as a flat piece of wood) used to punish children **2** : school discipline

fe·ru·lic acid \fə-ˌrü-lik-\ *n* [*ferula*] : a white crystalline acid that is structurally related to vanillin and is obtained esp. from plant sources (as aspen bark)

fer·ven·cy \ˈfər-vən-sē\ *n, pl* **-cies** : FERVOR

fer·vent \ˈfər-vənt\ *adj* [ME, fr. MF & L; MF, fr. L *fervent-, fervens*, prp. of *fervēre* to boil, glow — more at BURN] **1** : very hot : GLOWING **2** : marked by great warmth of feeling : exhibiting deep sincere emotion ⟨~ prayers⟩ ***syn*** see IMPASSIONED — **fer·vent·ly** *adv*

fer·vid \ˈfər-vəd\ *adj* [L *fervidus*, fr. *fervēre*] **1** : very hot : BURNING **2** : marked by warm spontaneity or sometimes febrile urgency ⟨his ~ manner of lovemaking offended her —Arnold Bennett⟩ ***syn*** see IMPASSIONED — **fer·vid·ly** *adv* — **fer·vid·ness** *n*

fer·vor \ˈfər-vər\ *n* [ME *fervour*, fr. MF & L; MF *ferveur*, fr. L *fervor*, fr. *fervēre*] **1** : intense heat **2** : warm steady intensity of feeling or expression ***syn*** see PASSION

fer·vour *chiefly Brit var of* FERVOR

fes·cen·nine \ˈfes-ᵊn-ˌīn, -ˌēn\ *adj* [L *fescennini (versus)*, ribald songs sung at rustic weddings, prob. fr. *fescinninus* of Fescennium, fr. *Fescennium*, town in Etruria] : SCURRILOUS, OBSCENE

fes·cue \ˈfes-(ˌ)kyü\ *n* [ME *festu* stalk, straw, fr. MF, fr. LL *festucum*, fr. L *festuca*] **1** : a small pointer (as a stick) used to point out letters to children learning to read **2** : any of a genus (*Festuca*) of tufted perennial grasses with panicled spikelets

fescue foot *n* : a disease of the feet of cattle resembling ergotism that is associated with feeding on fescue grasses

¹fess *also* **fesse** \ˈfes\ *n* [ME *fesse*, fr. MF *faisse*, fr. L *fascia* band] **1** : a broad horizontal bar across the middle of a heraldic field **2** : the center point of an armorial escutcheon

²fess \ˈfes\ *vi* [short for *confess*] : to own up : CONFESS — usu. used with *up*

-fest \ˌfest\ *n comb form* [G, fr. *fest* celebration, fr. L *festum*] : meeting or occasion marked by (such) activity ⟨song*fest*⟩

fes·tal \ˈfest-ᵊl\ *adj* [L *festum* festival — more at FEAST] : of or relating to a feast or festival : FESTIVE — **fes·tal·ly** \-ᵊl-ē\ *adv*

¹fes·ter \ˈfes-tər\ *n* [ME, fr. MF *festre*, fr. L *fistula* pipe, fistulous ulcer] : a suppurating sore : PUSTULE

²fester *vb* **fes·tered; fes·ter·ing** \-t(ə-)riŋ\ *vi* **1** : to generate pus **2** : PUTREFY, ROT **3 a** : to cause increasing poisoning or irritation : RANKLE **b** : to undergo or exist in a state of progressive deterioration ~ *vt* : to make inflamed or corrupt

¹fes·ti·nate \ˈfes-tə-nət, -ˌnāt\ *adj* [L *festinatus*, pp. of *festinare* to hasten — more at BORZOI] : HASTY — **fes·ti·nate·ly** *adv*

²fes·ti·nate \-ˌnāt\ *vb* **-nat·ed; -nat·ing** : HASTEN

¹fes·ti·val \ˈfes-tə-vəl\ *adj* [ME, fr. MF, fr. L *festivus* festive] : of, relating to, appropriate to, or set apart as a festival

²festival *n* **1 a** : a time of celebration marked by special observances **b** : FEAST 2 **2** : a periodic season or program of cultural events or entertainment **3** : GAIETY, CONVIVIALITY

fes·ti·val·go·er \-ˌgō(-ə)r\ *n* : one who attends a festival

fes·tive \ˈfes-tiv\ *adj* [L *festivus*, fr. *festum*] **1** : of, relating to, or suitable for a feast or festival **2** : JOYOUS, GAY — **fes·tive·ly** *adv* — **fes·tive·ness** *n*

fes·tiv·i·ty \fes-ˈtiv-ət-ē, fəs-\ *n, pl* **-ties** **1** : FESTIVAL 1 **2** : the quality or state of being festive : GAIETY **3** : festive activity

¹fes·toon \fes-ˈtün\ *n* [F *feston*, fr. It *festone*, fr. *festa* festival, fr. L — more at FEAST] **1** : a decorative chain or strip hanging between two points **2** : a carved, molded, or painted ornament representing a decorative chain **3** : one of the somewhat quadrangular segments bordering the body of some ticks

²festoon *vt* **1** : to hang or form festoons on **2** : to shape into festoons

fes·toon·ery \fes-ˈtü-nə-rē\ *n* : an arrangement of festoons

fest·schrift \ˈfest-ˌshrift\ *n, pl* **fest·schrif·ten** \-ˌshrif-tən\ *or* **fest·schrifts** *often cap* [G, fr. *fest* festival, celebration + *schrift* writing] : a volume of writings by different authors presented as a tribute or memorial esp. to a scholar

fe·ta \ˈfet-ə, ˈfe-ˌtä\ *n* [NGk (*tyri*) *pheta*, fr. *tyri* cheese + *pheta* slice, fr. It *fetta*] : a firm white Greek cheese made of sheep's or goat's milk and cured in brine

fe·tal \ˈfēt-ᵊl\ *adj* : of, relating to, or being a fetus

fetal hemoglobin *n* : a hemoglobin variant that predominates in the blood of a newborn and persists in increased proportions in some forms of anemia (as thalassemia)

fetal position *n* : a resting position in which the body is curved, the legs and arms are bent and drawn toward the chest, and the head is bowed forward and which is assumed in some forms of psychic regression

fe·ta·tion \fē-ˈtā-shən\ *n* : the formation of a fetus : PREGNANCY

¹fetch \ˈfech\ *vb* [ME *fecchen*, fr. OE *fetian, feccan*; akin to OE *fōt* foot — more at FOOT] *vt* **1 a** : to go or come after and bring or take back **b** : DERIVE, DEDUCE **2 a** : to cause to come **b** : to bring in (as a price) : REALIZE **c** : INTEREST, ATTRACT **3 a** : to give (a blow) by striking : DEAL **b** *chiefly dial* : to bring about : ACCOMPLISH **c** (1) : to take in (as a breath) : DRAW (2) : to bring forth (as a sound) : HEAVE ⟨~ a sigh⟩ **4 a** : to reach by sailing esp. against the wind or tide **b** : to arrive at : REACH ~ *vi* **1** : to get and bring something; *specif* : to retrieve killed game **2** : to take a roundabout way : CIRCLE **3 a** : to hold a course on a body of water **b** : VEER — **fetch·er** *n*

²fetch *n* **1** : an act or instance of fetching **2** : TRICK, STRATAGEM **3 a** : the distance along open water or land over which the wind blows **b** : the distance traversed by waves without obstruction

³fetch *n* [origin unknown] **1** : DOPPELGÄNGER **2** : GHOST

fetch·ing *adj* : ATTRACTIVE, PLEASING — **fetch·ing·ly** \-iŋ-lē\ *adv*

fetch up *vt* **1** : to bring up or out : PRODUCE **2** : to make up (as leeway) **3** : to bring to a stop ~ *vi* : to come to a standstill, stopping place, or result : ARRIVE

¹fete *or* **fête** \ˈfāt, ˈfet\ *n* [F *fête*, fr. OF *feste* — more at FEAST] **1** : FESTIVAL **2 a** : a lavish often outdoor entertainment **b** : a large elaborate party

²fete *or* **fête** *vt* **fet·ed** *or* **fêt·ed; fet·ing** *or* **fêt·ing** **1** : to honor or commemorate with a fete **2** : to pay high honor to

fête cham·pê·tre \ˌfāt-ˌshäⁿ(m)-ˈpetrᵊ, ˌfet-\ *n, pl* **fêtes cham·pêtres** *same*\ [F, lit., rural festival] : an outdoor entertainment

fet·er·i·ta \ˌfet-ə-ˈrēt-ə\ *n* [Sudanese Ar] : any of various grain sorghums with compact oval heads of large soft white seeds

fe·ti·cide \ˈfēt-ə-ˌsīd\ *n* : the act of killing a fetus

fet·id \ˈfet-əd, *esp Brit* ˈfē-tid\ *adj* [ME, fr. L *foetidus*, fr. *foetēre* to stink; akin to L *fumus* smoke — more at FUME] : having a heavy offensive smell ***syn*** see MALODOROUS — **fet·id·ly** *adv* — **fet·id·ness** *n*

fe·tish *also* **fe·tich** \ˈfet-ish *also* ˈfēt-\ *n* [F & Pg; F *fétiche*, fr. Pg *feitiço*, fr. *feitiço* artificial, false, fr. L *facticius* factitious] **1 a** : an object believed among a primitive people to have magical power to protect or aid its owner; *broadly* : a material object regarded with superstitious or extravagant trust or reverence **b** : an object of irrational reverence or obsessive devotion : PREPOSSESSION **c** : an object or bodily part whose real or fantasied presence is psychologically necessary for sexual gratification and that is an object of fixation to the extent that it may interfere with complete sexual expression **2** : a rite or cult of fetish worshipers **3** : FIXATION

syn FETISH, TALISMAN, CHARM, AMULET *shared meaning element* : an object believed useful in averting evil or attracting good

fe·tish·ism *also* **fe·tich·ism** \-ish-ˌiz-əm\ *n* **1** : belief in magical fetishes **2** : extravagant irrational devotion **3** : the pathological displacement of erotic interest and satisfaction to a fetish — **fe·tish·ist** \-ish-əst\ *n* — **fe·tish·is·tic** \ˌfet-ish-ˈis-tik *also* ˌfēt-\ *adj*

fet·lock \ˈfet-ˌläk\ *n* [ME *fitlok, fetlak*; akin to OE *fōt* foot] **1 a** : a projection bearing a tuft of hair on the back of the leg above the hoof of a horse or similar animal — see HORSE illustration **b** : the tuft of hair itself **2** : the joint of the limb at the fetlock

feto- *or* **feti-** *also* **foeto-** *or* **foeti-** *comb form* [NL *fetus*] : fetus ⟨*feti*cide⟩ : fetal and ⟨*feto*placental⟩

fe·tol·o·gy \fē-ˈtäl-ə-jē\ *n* : a branch of medical science concerned with the study and treatment of the fetus in the uterus — **fe·tol·o·gist** \-jəst\ *n*

fe·tor \ˈfēt-ər, ˈfē-ˌtȯ(ə)r\ *n* [ME *fetoure*, fr. L *foetor*, fr. *foetēre*] : a strong offensive smell : STENCH

¹fet·ter \ˈfet-ər\ *n* [ME *feter*, fr. OE; akin to OE *fōt* foot] **1** : a chain or shackle for the feet **2** : something that confines : RESTRAINT

²fetter *vt* **1** : to put fetters on : SHACKLE **2** : to restrain from motion or action ***syn*** see HAMPER

¹fet·tle \ˈfet-ᵊl\ *vt* **fet·tled; fet·tling** \ˈfet-liŋ, -ᵊl-iŋ\ [ME *fetlen* to shape, prepare; prob. akin to OE *fæt* vessel — more at VAT] : to cover or line the hearth of (as a reverberatory furnace) with fettling

²fettle *n* **1 a** : a state of physical fitness or order : CONDITION **b** : state of mind : SPIRITS ⟨the good news put him in fine ~⟩ **2** : FETTLING

fet·tling \ˈfet-liŋ, -ᵊl-iŋ\ *n* : loose material (as ore or sand) thrown on the hearth of a furnace to protect it

fet·tuc·ci·ne *or* **fet·tu·ci·ni** \ˌfet-ə-ˈchē-nē\ *n pl but sing or pl in constr* [It, pl. of *fettuccina*, dim. of *fettuccia* small slice, ribbon, dim. of *fetta* slice] : pasta in the form of narrow ribbons; *also* : a dish of which fettuccine forms the base

fe·tus \ˈfēt-əs\ *n* [NL, fr. L, act of bearing young, offspring; akin to L *fetus* newly delivered, fruitful — more at FEMININE] : an unborn or unhatched vertebrate esp. after attaining the basic structural plan of its kind; *specif* : a developing human from usu. three months after conception to birth

1feud \ˈfyüd\ *n* [alter. of ME *feide,* fr. MF, of Gmc origin; akin to OHG *fēhida* hostility, feud, OE *fāh* hostile — more at FOE] **:** a mutual enmity or quarrel that is often prolonged or inveterate; *esp* **:** a lasting state of hostilities between families or clans marked by violent attacks for revenge — **feud** *vi*

2feud *n* [ML *feodum, feudum,* of Gmc origin; akin to OE *feoh* cattle, property — more at FEE] **:** FEE 1a

feu·dal \ˈfyüd-ᵊl\ *adj* **1 :** of, relating to, or having the characteristics of a medieval fee **2 :** of, relating to, or suggestive of feudalism ⟨~ law⟩ — **feu·dal·ly** \-ᵊl-ē\ *adv*

feu·dal·ism \ˈfyüd-ᵊl-ˌiz-əm\ *n* **1 :** the system of political organization prevailing in Europe from the 9th to about the 15th centuries having as its basis the relation of lord to vassal with all land held in fee and as chief characteristics homage, the service of tenants under arms and in court, wardship, and forfeiture **2 :** any of various political or social systems similar to medieval feudalism — **feu·dal·ist** \-ᵊl-əst\ *n* — **feu·dal·is·tic** \ˌfyüd-ᵊl-ˈis-tik\ *adj*

feu·dal·i·ty \fyü-ˈdal-ət-ē\ *n, pl* **-ties 1 :** the quality or state of being feudal **2 :** a feudal holding, domain, or concentration of power

feu·dal·ize \ˈfyüd-ᵊl-ˌīz\ *vt* **-ized; -iz·ing :** to make feudal — **feu·dal·iza·tion** \ˌfyüd-ᵊl-ə-ˈzā-shən\ *n*

1feu·da·to·ry \ˈfyüd-ə-ˌtōr-ē, -ˌtȯr-\ *adj* [ML *feudatorius,* fr. *feudatus,* pp. of *feudare* to enfeoff, fr. *feudum*] **1 :** owing feudal allegiance **2 :** being under the overlordship of a foreign state

2feudatory *n, pl* **-ries 1 :** one holding lands by feudal tenure **2 :** a dependent lordship **:** FEE

1feud·ist \ˈfyüd-əst\ *n* **:** a specialist in feudal law

2feudist *n* **:** one who feuds

feuil·le·ton \ˌfə(r)-yə-ˈtōⁿ, ˌfœ-yə-\ *n* [F, fr. *feuillet* sheet of paper, fr. OF *foillet,* dim. of *foille* leaf — more at FOIL] **1 :** a part of a European newspaper or magazine devoted to material designed to entertain the general reader **2 :** something (as an installment of a novel) printed in a feuilleton **3 a :** a novel printed in installments **b :** a work of fiction catering to popular taste **4 :** a short literary composition often having a familiar tone and reminiscent content — **feuil·le·ton·ism** \-ˈtō(ⁿ)-ˌniz-əm\ *n* — **feuil·le·ton·ist** \-nəst\ *n*

Feul·gen \ˈfȯil-gən\ *adj* **:** of, relating to, utilizing, or staining by the Feulgen reaction ⟨positive ~ mitochondria⟩

Feulgen reaction *n* [Robert *Feulgen* b1884 G physiologist] **:** the development of a brilliant purple color by DNA in a microscopic preparation stained with a modified Schiff's reagent

1fe·ver \ˈfē-vər\ *n* [ME, fr. OE *fēfer,* fr. L *febris;* akin to L *fovēre* to warm] **1 a :** a rise of body temperature above the normal **b :** any of various diseases of which fever is a prominent symptom **2 a :** a state of heightened or intense emotion or activity **b :** a contagious usu. transient enthusiasm **:** CRAZE

2fever *vb* **fe·vered; fe·ver·ing** \ˈfēv-(ə-)riŋ\ *vt* **:** to throw into a fever **:** UPSET ~ *vi* **:** to contract or be in a fever **:** be or become feverish

fever blister *n* **:** COLD SORE

fe·ver·few \ˈfē-vər-ˌfyü\ *n* [ME, fr. (assumed) AF *fevrefue,* fr. LL *febrifugia* centaury — more at FEBRIFUGE] **:** a perennial European composite herb (*Chrysanthemum parthenium*)

fe·ver·ish \ˈfēv-(ə-)rish\ *adj* **1 a :** having the symptoms of a fever **b :** indicating or relating to fever **c :** tending to cause fever **2 :** marked by intense emotion, activity, or instability — **fe·ver·ish·ly** *adv* — **fe·ver·ish·ness** *n*

fe·ver·ous \ˈfēv-(ə-)rəs\ *adj* **:** FEVERISH — **fe·ver·ous·ly** *adv*

fever pitch *n* **:** a state of intense excitement and agitation

fe·ver·root \ˈfē-və(r)-ˌrüt, -ˌru̇t\ *n* **:** FEVERWORT

fever thermometer *n* **:** CLINICAL THERMOMETER

fever tree *n* **:** any of several shrubs or trees that are thought to indicate regions free from fever or that yield remedies for fever: as **a :** a blue gum (*Eucalyptus globulus*) **b :** an ornamental tree (*Pinckneya pubens*) of the southeastern U.S.

fe·ver·wort \ˈfē-vər-ˌwərt, -ˌwȯ(ə)rt\ *n* **:** a coarse American herb (*Triosteum perfoliatum*) of the honeysuckle family — called also *feverroot, horse gentian*

1few \ˈfyü\ *pron, pl in constr* [ME *fewe,* pron. & adj., fr. OE *fēawa;* akin to OHG *fō* little, L *paucus* little, *pauper* poor, Gk *paid-, pais* child, Skt *putra* son] **:** not many persons or things ⟨~ were present⟩ ⟨~ of his stories are true⟩

2few *adj* **1 :** consisting of or amounting to only a small number ⟨one of his ~ pleasures⟩ **2 :** at least some but indeterminately small in number — used with *a* ⟨caught a ~ fish⟩ — **few·ness** *n*

3few *n, pl in constr* **1 :** a small number of units or individuals ⟨a ~ of them⟩ **2 :** a special limited number ⟨the discriminating ~⟩

1few·er *pron, pl in constr* **:** a smaller number of persons or things

2fewer *adj, comparative of* FEW *syn* see LESS

few·trils \ˈfyü-trəlz\ *n pl* [origin unknown] *dial Eng* **:** things of little value **:** TRIFLES

fey \ˈfā\ *adj* [ME *feye,* fr. OE *fǣge;* akin to OHG *feigi* fey and perh. to OE *fāh* hostile, outlawed — more at FOE] **1 a** *chiefly Scot* **:** fated to die **:** DOOMED **b :** marked by a foreboding of death or calamity **2 a :** able to see into the future **:** VISIONARY **b :** marked by an otherworldly air or attitude **c :** CRAZY, TOUCHED — **fey·ness** *n*

fez \ˈfez\ *n, pl* **fez·zes** *also* **fez·es** [F, fr. *Fez,* Morocco] **:** a brimless cone-shaped flat-crowned hat that usu. has a tassel, is usu. made of red felt, and is worn esp. by men in eastern Mediterranean countries

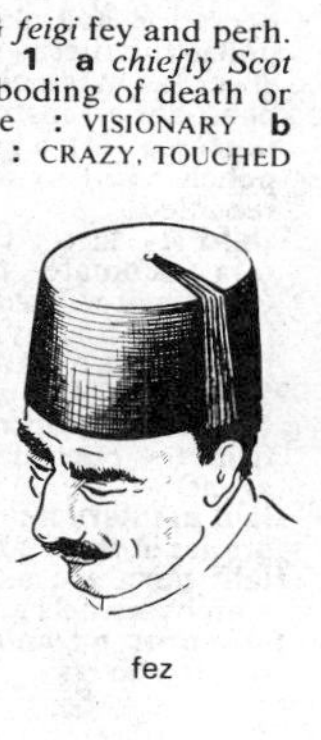
fez

ff *abbr* **1** folios **2** [*f*ollowing] and the following ones **3** fortissimo

FG *abbr* fine grain

FHA *abbr* Federal Housing Administration

FHWA *abbr* Federal Highway Administration

fi·acre \fē-ˈäkrᵊ\ *n, pl* **fi·acres** *same, or* -ˈäk-rəz\ [F, fr. the Hotel St. *Fiacre,* Paris] **:** a small hackney coach

fi·an·cé \ˌfē-ˌän-ˈsā, fē-ˈän-ˌ\ *n* [F, fr. MF, fr. pp. of *fiancer* to promise, betroth, fr. OF *fiancier,* fr. *fiance* promise, trust, fr. *fier* to trust, fr. (assumed) VL *fidare,* alter. of L *fidere* — more at BIDE] **:** a man engaged to be married

fi·an·cée \ˌfē-ˌän-ˈsā, fē-ˈän-ˌ\ *n* [F, fem. of *fiancé*] **:** a woman engaged to be married

fi·an·chet·to \ˌfē-ən-ˈket-(ˌ)ō, -ˈchet-\ *vb* [*fianchetto* (an opening in chess), fr. It, dim. of *fianco* side, flank, fr. OF *flanc*] *vt* **:** to develop (a bishop) in a chess game to the second square on the adjacent knight's file ~ *vi* **:** to fianchetto a bishop in a chess game

fi·as·co *n, pl* **-coes** [It, of Gmc origin; akin to OHG *flaska* bottle] **1** \fē-ˈäs-(ˌ)kō\ *pl also* **fi·as·chi** \-(ˌ)kē\ **:** BOTTLE, FLASK; *esp* **:** a long-necked straw-covered bottle for wine **2** \-ˈas- *also* -ˈäs-\ [F, fr. It] **:** a complete failure

fi·at \ˈfē-ət, -ˌat, -ˌät; ˈfī-ət, -ˌat\ *n* [L, let it be done, 3d sing. pres. subj. of *fieri* to become, be done — more at BE] **1 :** a command or act of will that creates something without or as if without further effort **2 :** an authoritative decision of consciousness ⟨a ~ of conscience⟩ **3 :** an authoritative or arbitrary order **:** DECREE ⟨government by ~⟩

fiat money *n* **:** money (as paper currency) not convertible into coin or specie of equivalent value

1fib \ˈfib\ *n* [perh. by shortening & alter. fr. *fable*] **:** a trivial or childish lie

2fib *vi* **fibbed; fib·bing :** to tell a fib *syn* see LIE — **fib·ber** *n*

3fib *vb* **fibbed; fib·bing** [origin unknown] *Brit* **:** BEAT, PUMMEL

fi·ber *or* **fi·bre** \ˈfī-bər\ *n* [F *fibre,* fr. L *fibra*] **1 :** a thread or a structure or object resembling a thread: as **a** (1) **:** a slender root (as of a grass) (2) **:** an elongated tapering thick-walled plant cell void at maturity that imparts elasticity, flexibility, and tensile strength **b** (1) **:** a strand of nerve tissue **:** AXON, DENDRITE (2) **:** one of the filaments composing most of the intercellular matrix of connective tissue (3) **:** one of the elongated contractile cells of muscle tissue **c :** a slender and greatly elongated natural or synthetic filament (as of wool, cotton, asbestos, gold, glass, or rayon) typically capable of being spun into yarn **2 :** material made of fibers; *specif* **:** VULCANIZED FIBER **3 a :** an element that gives texture or substance **b :** basic toughness **:** STRENGTH, FORTITUDE **c :** essential structure or character ⟨the very ~ of a person's being⟩ — **fi·bered** \-bərd\ *adj*

fi·ber·board \-ˌbō(ə)rd, -ˌbȯ(ə)rd\ *n* **:** a material made by compressing fibers (as of wood) into stiff sheets

fi·ber·glass \-ˌglas\ *n* **:** glass in fibrous form used in making various products (as glass wool, yarns, textiles, and structures) ⟨a ~ boat⟩ ⟨~ insulation⟩

fi·ber·ize \ˈfī-bə-ˌrīz\ *vt* **-ized; -iz·ing :** to break into fibers — **fi·ber·iza·tion** \ˌfī-b(ə-)rə-ˈzā-shən\ *n*

fi·ber–op·tic \ˈfī-bə-ˌräp-tik\ *adj* **:** of, relating to, or using fiber optics

fiber optics *n pl* **1 :** thin transparent fibers of glass or plastic that are enclosed by material of a lower index of refraction and that transmit light throughout their length by internal reflections; *also* **:** a bundle of such fibers used in an instrument (as for viewing body cavities) **2** *sing in constr* **:** the technique of the use of fiber optics

fi·ber·scope \ˈfī-bər-ˌskōp\ *n* **:** a flexible instrument utilizing fiber optics and used esp. in medicine for examination of inaccessible areas (as the stomach)

Fi·bo·nac·ci number \ˌfē-bə-ˌnäch-ē-\ *n* [Leonardo *Fibonacci* †*ab* 1250 It mathematician] **:** an integer in the infinite sequence 1, 1, 2, 3, 5, 8, 13, . . . of which the first two terms are 1 and 1 and each succeeding term is the sum of the two immediately preceding

fibr- *or* **fibro-** *comb form* [L *fibra*] **:** fiber **:** fibrous tissue ⟨*fibr*oid⟩ **:** fibrous and ⟨*fibro*vascular⟩

fi·bril \ˈfīb-rəl, ˈfib-\ *n* [NL *fibrilla,* dim. of L *fibra*] **:** a small filament or fiber: as **a :** ROOT HAIR **b** (1) **:** one of the fine threads into which a striated muscle fiber can be longitudinally split **b** (2) **:** NEUROFIBRIL — **fi·bril·lar** \ˈfib-rə-lər, ˈfīb-\ *adj* — **fi·bril·li·form** \fī-ˈbril-ə-ˌfȯrm, fə-\ *adj* — **fi·bril·lose** \ˈfib-rə-ˌlōs, ˈfīb-\ *adj*

fi·bril·late \ˈfib-rə-ˌlāt, ˈfīb-\ *vb* **-lat·ed; -lat·ing** *vi* **:** to undergo or exhibit fibrillation ~ *vt* **:** to cause to undergo fibrillation ⟨~ plastic film into fibrils⟩

fi·bril·la·tion \ˌfib-rə-ˈlā-shən, ˌfīb-\ *n* **1 :** an act or process of forming fibers or fibrils **2 a :** a muscular twitching involving individual muscle fibers acting without coordination **b :** very rapid irregular contractions of the muscle fibers of the heart resulting in a lack of synchronism between heartbeat and pulse

fi·brin \ˈfī-brən\ *n* **:** a white insoluble fibrous protein formed from fibrinogen by the action of thrombin esp. in the clotting of blood

fi·brin·o·gen \fī-ˈbrin-ə-jən\ *n* [ISV] **:** a globulin that is produced in the liver, that is present esp. in the blood plasma, and that is converted into fibrin during clotting of blood

fi·bri·noid \ˈfīb-rə-ˌnȯid, ˈfīb-\ *n* **:** a homogeneous acidophilic refractile material that somewhat resembles fibrin and is formed in the walls of blood vessels and in connective tissue in some pathological conditions and normally in the placenta

fi·bri·no·ly·sin \ˌfī-brən-ᵊl-ˈīs-ᵊn\ *n* [ISV] **1 :** PLASMIN **2 :** STREPTOKINASE

fi·bri·no·ly·sis \-ˈī-səs, -brə-ˈnäl-ə-səs\ *n* [NL] **:** the usu. enzymatic breakdown of fibrin — **fi·bri·no·lyt·ic** \-brən-ᵊl-ˈit-ik\ *adj*

fi·bri·nous \ˈfīb-rə-nəs, ˈfib-\ *adj* **:** marked by the presence of fibrin

fi·bro·blast \ˈfīb-rə-ˌblast, ˈfib-\ *n* [ISV] **:** a mesenchyme cell giving rise to connective tissue — **fi·bro·blas·tic** \ˌfīb-rə-ˈblas-tik, ˌfib-\ *adj*

fi·bro·cyte \ˈfīb-rə-ˌsīt, ˈfib-\ *n* [ISV] **:** a spindle-shaped cell of fibrous tissue — **fi·bro·cyt·ic** \ˌfīb-rə-ˈsit-ik, ˌfib-\ *adj*

1fi·broid \ˈfīb-ˌrȯid, ˈfib-\ *adj* **:** resembling, forming, or consisting of fibrous tissue

ə abut   ᵊ kitten   ər further   a back   ā bake   ä cot, cart
au̇ out   ch chin   e less   ē easy   g gift   i trip   ī life
j joke   ŋ sing   ō flow   ȯ flaw   ȯi coin   th thin   t͟h this
ü loot   u̇ foot   y yet   yü few   yu̇ furious   zh vision

2**fibroid** *n* : a benign tumor made up of fibrous and muscular tissue that occurs esp. in the uterine wall
fi·bro·in \ˈfī-brə-wən, ˈfib-\ *n* [F *fibroïne*, fr. *fibr-* + *-ine* -in] : an insoluble protein comprising the filaments of the raw silk fiber
fi·bro·ma \fī-ˈbrō-mə\ *n, pl* **-mas** *also* **-ma·ta** \-mət-ə\ : a benign tumor consisting mainly of fibrous tissue — **fi·bro·ma·tous** \-mət-əs\ *adj*
fi·bro·sar·co·ma \ˌfīb-rə-sär-ˈkō-mə, ˌfib-\ *n* : a sarcoma of relatively low malignancy made up chiefly of spindle-shaped cells that tend to form collagenous fibrils
fi·bro·sis \fī-ˈbrō-səs\ *n* : a condition marked by increase of interstitial fibrous tissue — **fi·brot·ic** \-ˈbrät-ik\ *adj*
fi·bro·si·tis \ˌfīb-rə-ˈsīt-əs, ˌfib-\ *n* [NL, fr. *fibrosus* fibrous, fr. ISV *fibrous*] : a rheumatic disorder of fibrous tissue
fi·brous \ˈfī-brəs\ *adj* [F *fibreux*, fr. *fibre* fiber, fr. L *fibra*] **1 a** : containing, consisting of, or resembling fibers **b** : characterized by fibrosis **c** : capable of being separated into fibers ⟨a ~ mineral⟩ **2** : TOUGH, SINEWY ⟨~ texture⟩ — **fi·brous·ly** *adv* — **fi·brous·ness** *n*
fibrous root *n* : a root (as in most grasses) that has no prominent central axis and that branches in all directions
fi·bro·vas·cu·lar \ˈfīb-rō-ˈvas-kyə-lər, ˌfib-\ *adj* : having or consisting of fibers and conducting cells ⟨~ bundles in leaves⟩
fibrovascular bundle *n* : VASCULAR BUNDLE
fib·u·la \ˈfib-yə-lə\ *n, pl* **-lae** \-ˌlē, -ˌlī\ *or* **-las** [L] **1** : a clasp resembling a safety pin used by the ancient Greeks and Romans **2** : the outer and usu. the smaller of the two bones of the hind limb below the knee — **fib·u·lar** \-lər\ *adj*

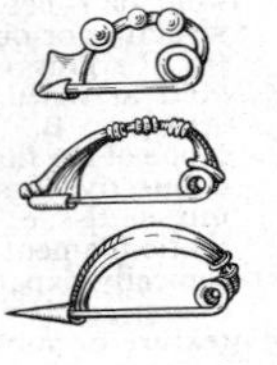
fibulae 1

-fic \fik\ *adj suffix* [MF & L; MF *-fique*, fr. L *-ficus*, fr. *facere* to make — more at DO] : making : causing ⟨feli*cific*⟩
FICA *abbr* Federal Insurance Contributions Act
-fi·ca·tion \fə-ˈkā-shən\ *n comb form* [ME *-ficacioun*, fr. MF & L; MF *-fication*, fr. L *-fication-*, *-ficatio*, fr. *-ficatus*, pp. ending of verbs ending in *-ficare* to make, fr. *-ficus*] : making : production ⟨rei*fication*⟩
fice \ˈfīs\ *var of* FEIST
fiche \ˈfēsh *also* ˈfish\ *n, pl* **fiche** *also* **fiches** : MICROFICHE
fi·chu \ˈfish-(ˌ)ü, ˈfēsh-\ *n* [F, fr. pp. of *ficher* to stick in, throw on, fr. (assumed) VL *figicare*, fr. L *figere* to fasten, pierce — more at DIKE] : a woman's light triangular scarf that is draped over the shoulders and fastened in front or worn to fill in a low neckline
fi·cin \ˈfīs-ᵊn\ *n* [L *ficus* fig] : a proteinase that is obtained from the latex of fig trees and is used as an anthelmintic and protein digestive
fick·le \ˈfik-əl\ *adj* [ME *fikel* deceitful, inconstant, fr. OE *ficol* deceitful; akin to OE *befician* to deceive, L *pigēre* to irk and prob. to OE *fāh* hostile — more at FOE] : marked by lack of steadfastness, constancy, or stability : given to erratic and even perverse changeableness ***syn*** see INCONSTANT ***ant*** constant, true — **fick·le·ness** *n*
fi·co \ˈfē-(ˌ)kō\ *n, pl* **ficoes** [obs. *fico*, obscene gesture of contempt, modif. of It *fica* fig, vulva, gesture of contempt, fr. (assumed) VL *fica* fig — more at FIG] : FIG 2
fict *abbr* **1** fiction **2** fictitious
fic·tile \ˈfik-tᵊl, -ˌtīl\ *adj* [L *fictilis* molded of clay, fr. *fictus*] **1** : molded or moldable of earth, clay, or other soft material **2** : of or relating to pottery
fic·tion \ˈfik-shən\ *n* [ME *ficcioun*, fr. MF *fiction*, fr. L *fiction-*, *fictio* act of fashioning, fiction, fr. *fictus*, pp. of *fingere* to shape, fashion, feign — more at DOUGH] **1 a** : something invented by the imagination or feigned; *specif* : an invented story ⟨distinguish fact from ~⟩ **b** : fictitious literature (as novels or short stories) ⟨a writer of ~⟩ **2** : an assumption of a possibility as a fact irrespective of the question of its truth ⟨a legal ~⟩ **3** : the action of feigning or of creating with the imagination — **fic·tion·al** \-shnəl, -shən-ᵊl\ *adj* — **fic·tion·al·ly** \-ē\ *adv*
fic·tion·al·iza·tion \ˌfik-shnə-lə-ˈzā-shən, -shən-ᵊl-ə-ˈzā-\ *n* : an act, process, or product of fictionalizing
fic·tion·al·ize \ˈfik-shnə-ˌlīz, -shən-ᵊl-ˌīz\ *vt* **-ized; -iz·ing** : to make into or treat in the manner of fiction ⟨~ the diary he kept in prison⟩
fic·tion·eer \ˌfik-shə-ˈni(ə)r\ *n* : one who writes fiction esp. in quantity and without high standards — **fic·tion·eer·ing** *n*
fic·tion·ist \ˈfik-sh(ə-)nəst\ *n* : a writer of fiction; *esp* : NOVELIST
fic·tion·ize \ˈfik-shə-ˌnīz\ *vt* **-ized; -iz·ing** : FICTIONALIZE — **fic·tion·iza·tion** \ˌfik-shə-nə-ˈzā-shən\ *n*
fic·ti·tious \fik-ˈtish-əs\ *adj* [L *ficticius* artificial, feigned, fr. *fictus*] **1** : of, relating to, or characteristic of fiction : IMAGINARY **2 a** : conventionally or hypothetically assumed or accepted ⟨a ~ concept⟩ **b** *of a name* : FALSE, ASSUMED **3** : not genuinely felt : FEIGNED, SIMULATED — **fic·ti·tious·ly** *adv* — **fic·ti·tious·ness** *n*
syn FICTITIOUS, FABULOUS, LEGENDARY, MYTHICAL, APOCRYPHAL *shared meaning element* : being the product of imagination or mental invention ***ant*** historical
fic·tive \ˈfik-tiv\ *adj* **1** : not genuine : FEIGNED **2** : of, relating to, or capable of imaginative creation — **fic·tive·ly** *adv*
fid \ˈfid\ *n* [origin unknown] **1** : a square bar of wood or iron used to support a topmast **2** : a pin usu. of hard wood that tapers to a point and is used in opening the strands of a rope
-fid \fəd, ˌfid\ *adj comb form* [L *-fidus*, fr. *findere* to split — more at BITE] : divided into (so many) parts ⟨sexi*fid*⟩ or (such) parts ⟨pinna*tifid*⟩
1**fid·dle** \ˈfid-ᵊl\ *n* [ME *fidel*, fr. OE *fithele*, prob. fr. ML *vitula*] **1** : VIOLIN **2** : a device (as a slat, rack, or light railing of cords) to keep dishes from sliding off a table aboard ship **3** : FIDDLESTICKS — used as an interjection **4** *Brit* : SWINDLE
2**fiddle** *vb* **fid·dled; fid·dling** \ˈfid-liŋ, -ᵊl-iŋ\ *vi* **1** : to play on a fiddle **2 a** : to move the hands or fingers restlessly **b** : to spend time in aimless or fruitless activity : PUTTER ⟨*fiddled* around with the engine for hours⟩ **c** : MEDDLE, TAMPER ~ *vt* : to play (as a tune) on a fiddle — **fid·dler** \ˈfid-lər, -ᵊl-ər\ *n*
fiddle away *vt* : to fritter away ⟨*fiddled away* his time⟩
fid·dle·back \ˈfid-ᵊl-ˌbak\ *n* : something resembling a fiddle
fid·dle–fad·dle \ˈfid-ᵊl-ˌfad-ᵊl\ *n* [redupl. of *fiddle* (fiddlesticks)] : NONSENSE — often used as an interjection
fid·dle–foot·ed \ˌfid-ᵊl-ˈfu̇t-əd\ *adj* **1** : SKITTISH, JUMPY ⟨a ~ horse⟩ **2** : prone to wander ⟨the nameless ~ drifters, the shifty riders who traveled the back trails —Luke Short⟩
fid·dle·head \ˈfid-ᵊl-ˌhed\ *n* **1** : an ornament on a ship's bow curved like the scroll at the head of a violin **2** : one of the young unfurling fronds of some ferns that are often eaten as greens
fiddler crab *n* : a burrowing crab (genus *Uca*) that has one claw much enlarged in the male
fid·dle·stick \ˈfid-ᵊl-ˌstik\ *n* **1 a** *archaic* : a violin bow **b** *South* : a small stick or switch used to strike the strings of a fiddle in time to the music while the fiddler plays with a bow — usu. used in pl. **2 a** : something of little value : TRIFLE ⟨didn't care a ~ for that⟩ **b** *pl* : NONSENSE — used as an interjection
fid·dling \ˈfid-liŋ, -lən\ *adj* : TRIFLING, PETTY ⟨made some ~ excuse⟩
fi·de·ism \ˈfēd-(ˌ)ā-ˌiz-əm\ *n* [prob. fr. F *fidéisme*, fr. L *fides* faith] : reliance on faith rather than reason esp. in metaphysics — **fi·de·ist** \-ˌā-əst\ *n* — **fi·de·is·tic** \ˌfēd-(ˌ)ā-ˈis-tik\ *adj*
fi·del·i·ty \fə-ˈdel-ət-ē, fī-\ *n, pl* **-ties** [ME *fidelite*, fr. MF *fidelité*, fr. L *fidelitat-*, *fidelitas*, fr. *fidelis* faithful, fr. *fides* faith — more at BIDE] **1 a** : the quality or state of being faithful **b** : accuracy in details : EXACTNESS **2** : the degree to which an electronic device (as a record player, radio, or television) accurately reproduces its effect (as sound or picture)
syn FIDELITY, ALLEGIANCE, FEALTY, LOYALTY, DEVOTION, PIETY *shared meaning element* : faithfulness to something to which one is bound by a pledge, by duty, or by a sense of what is right or appropriate ***ant*** faithlessness, perfidy
fidge \ˈfij\ *vi* **fidged; fidg·ing** [prob. alter. of E dial. *fitch*, fr. ME *fichen*] *chiefly Scot* : FIDGET
1**fid·get** \ˈfij-ət\ *n* [irreg. fr. *fidge*] **1** : uneasiness or restlessness as shown by nervous movements — usu. used in pl. **2** [2*fidget*] : one that fidgets
2**fidget** *vi* : to move or act restlessly or nervously ~ *vt* : to cause to move or act nervously
fid·gety \ˈfij-ət-ē\ *adj* **1** : inclined to fidget **2** : making unnecessary fuss : FUSSY — **fid·get·i·ness** *n*
fi·do \ˈfīd-(ˌ)ō\ *n, pl* **fidos** [*f*reaks + *i*rregulars + *d*efects + *o*ddities] : a coin having a minting error
fi·du·cial \fə-ˈd(y)ü-shəl, fī-\ *adj* **1** : taken as standard of reference ⟨a ~ mark⟩ **2** : founded on faith or trust **3** : having the nature of a trust : FIDUCIARY — **fi·du·cial·ly** \-ˌd(y)üsh-(ə-)lē\ *adv*
1**fi·du·cia·ry** \-ˈd(y)ü-shē-ˌer-ē, -shə-rē\ *n, pl* **-ries** : one that holds a fiduciary relation or acts in a fiduciary capacity
2**fiduciary** *adj* [L *fiduciarius*, fr. *fiducia* confidence, trust, fr. *fidere*] : of, relating to, or involving a confidence or trust: as **a** : held or founded in trust or confidence **b** : holding in trust **c** : depending on public confidence for value or currency ⟨~ fiat money⟩
fie \ˈfī\ *interj* [ME *fi*, fr. OF] — used to express disgust or shock
fief \ˈfēf\ *n* [F — more at FEE] **1** : a feudal estate : FEE **2** : something over which one has rights or exercises control ⟨a politician's ~⟩
fief·dom \ˈfēf-dəm, -təm\ *n* : FIEF
1**field** \ˈfē(ə)ld\ *n* [ME, fr. OE *feld*; akin to OHG *feld* field, OE *flōr* floor] **1 a** : an open land area free of woods and buildings **b** (1) : an area of cleared enclosed land used for cultivation or pasture ⟨a ~ of wheat⟩ (2) : land containing a natural resource ⟨coal ~⟩ **c** : the place where a battle is fought; *also* : BATTLE **d** : a large unbroken expanse (as of ice) **2 a** : an area or division of an activity ⟨a lawyer eminent in his ~⟩ **b** : the sphere of practical operation outside a laboratory, office, or factory ⟨geologists working in the ~⟩ **c** : an area for military exercises or maneuvers **d** (1) : an area constructed, equipped, or marked for sports (2) : the portion of an indoor or outdoor sports area enclosed by the running track and on which are conducted field events (3) : either of the three sections of a baseball outfield ⟨hits to all ~*s*⟩ **3** : a space on which something is drawn or projected: as **a** : the space on the surface of a coin, medal, or seal that does not contain the design **b** : the ground of each division in a flag **c** : the whole surface of an escutcheon **4** : the individuals that make up all or part of the participants in a sports activity; *esp* : all participants with the exception of the favorite or the winner in a contest where more than two are entered **5** : a complex of forces that serve as causative agents in human behavior **6 a** : a set of mathematical elements that is subject to two binary operations the second of which is distributive relative to the first and both of which yield an element and that constitutes a commutative group under the first operation and also under the second if the zero or unit element under the first is omitted **b** : a region or space in which a given effect (as magnetism) exists **7** : the area visible through the lens of an optical instrument **8** : a series of drain tiles and an absorption area **9** : a particular area (as a column or set of columns on a punch card) in which the same type of information is regularly recorded
2**field** *vt* **1 a** : to catch or pick up (a batted ball) and usu. throw to a teammate **b** : to give an impromptu answer or solution to ⟨the senator ~*ed* the reporters' questions⟩ **2** : to put into the field ⟨~ an army⟩ ⟨~ a team⟩; *also* : to enter in competition ~ *vi* : to play as a fielder
3**field** *adj* : of or relating to a field: as **a** : growing in or inhabiting the fields or open country **b** : made, conducted, or used in the field ⟨~ operations⟩ **c** : operating or active in the field ⟨a ~ agent⟩
field artillery *n* : artillery other than antiaircraft artillery used with armies in the field
field corn *n* : an Indian corn (as dent corn or flint corn) with starchy kernels grown for feeding stock or for market grain
field crop *n* : an agricultural crop (as hay, grain, or cotton) grown on large areas

field day *n* **1** **a** : a day for military exercises or maneuvers **b** : an outdoor meeting or social gathering **c** : a day of sports and athletic competition **2** : a time of unusual pleasure or unexpected success ⟨the newspaper had a *field day* with the scandal⟩
field·er \ˈfēl-dər\ *n* : one that fields; *esp* : a defensive player stationed in the field (as in baseball)
fielder's choice *n* : a situation in baseball in which a batter reaches base safely because the fielder attempts to put out another base runner on the play
field event *n* : an event (as weight-throwing or jumping) in a track-and-field meet other than a race
field·fare \ˈfē(ə)l(d)-ˌfa(ə)r, -ˌfe(ə)r\ *n* [ME *feldefare*, fr. OE *feldeware*, fr. *feld* + *-ware* dweller] : a medium-sized Eurasian thrush (*Turdus pilaris*) with ash-colored head and chestnut wings
field glass *n* : a hand-held optical instrument for use outdoors usu. consisting of two telescopes on a single frame with a focusing device — usu. used in pl.
field goal *n* **1** : a score in football made by drop-kicking or place-kicking the ball over the crossbar from ordinary play **2** : a goal in basketball made while the ball is in play
field grade *n* : the rank of a field officer
field hand *n* : an outdoor farm laborer
field hockey *n* : a game played on a turfed field between two teams of 11 players each whose object is to direct a ball into the opponent's goal with a hockey stick
field house *n* **1** : a building at an athletic field for housing equipment or providing dressing facilities **2** : a building enclosing a large area suitable for various forms of athletics and usu. providing seats for spectators
fielding average *n* : the average (as of a baseball fielder) determined by dividing the number of putouts and assists by the number of chances — compare BATTING AVERAGE
field judge *n* : a football official whose duties include covering action on kicks and forward passes and timing intermission periods and time outs
field lens *n* : the lens in a compound eyepiece that is nearer the objective
field magnet *n* : a magnet for producing and maintaining a magnetic field esp. in a generator or electric motor
field marshal *n* : the highest ranking military officer (as in the British army)
field mouse *n* : any of various mice that inhabit fields; *esp* : VOLE
field officer *n* : a commissioned officer in the army, air force, or marine corps of the rank of colonel, lieutenant colonel, or major — called also *field grade officer;* compare COMPANY OFFICER, GENERAL OFFICER
field of force : FIELD 6b
field of honor **1** : a place where a duel is fought **2** : BATTLEFIELD
field of view : FIELD 7
field of vision : VISUAL FIELD
field pea *n* : a small-seeded pea (*Pisum sativum* var. *arvense*) widely grown for forage and food
field·piece \ˈfē(ə)l(d)-ˌpēs\ *n* : a gun or howitzer for use in the field
field spaniel *n* : any of a breed of large usu. black hunting and retrieving spaniels that have a dense flat or slightly waved coat
field·stone \ˈfē(ə)l(d)-ˌstōn\ *n* : stone used as taken from the field (as in building)
field-strip \-ˌstrip\ *vt* : to take apart (a weapon) to the extent authorized for routine cleaning, lubrication, and minor repairs
field–test \-ˌtest\ *vt* : to test (as a procedure or product) in a natural environment for various things (as utility and acceptability by intended users) — **field test** *n*
field theory *n* : a detailed mathematical description of the assumed physical properties of a region under some influence (as gravitation)
field trial *n* : a trial of sporting dogs in actual performance
field trip *n* : a visit made by students and usu. a teacher for purposes of firsthand observation (as to a factory, farm, or museum)
field winding *n* : the winding of the field magnet of a dynamo or motor
field·work \ˈfē(ə)l-ˌdwərk\ *n* **1** : a temporary fortification thrown up by an army in the field **2** : work done in the field (as by students) to gain practical experience through firsthand observation **3** : the gathering of anthropological or sociological data through the interviewing of subjects in the field — **field–work·er** *n*
fiend \ˈfēnd\ *n* [ME, fr. OE *fiend;* akin to OHG *fiant* enemy, Skt *pīyati* he scorns] **1** **a** : DEVIL 1 **b** : DEMON **c** : a person of great wickedness or maliciousness **2** : a person excessively devoted to a pursuit or study : FANATIC ⟨a golf ~⟩ **3** : a person who uses immoderate quantities of something : ADDICT ⟨a dope ~⟩ **4** : a person remarkably clever at something : WIZARD 3 ⟨a ~ at mathematics⟩
fiend·ish \ˈfēn-dish\ *adj* **1** : perversely diabolical ⟨took a ~ pleasure in hurting people⟩ **2** : extremely cruel or wicked ⟨a ~ old man⟩ **3** : excessively bad, unpleasant, or difficult ⟨~ weather⟩ — **fiend·ish·ly** *adv* — **fiend·ish·ness** *n*
fierce \ˈfi(ə)rs\ *adj* **fierc·er; fierc·est** [ME *fiers*, fr. OF, fr. L *ferus* wild, savage; akin to Gk *thēr* wild animal] **1** **a** : violently hostile or aggressive in temperament **b** : given to fighting or killing : PUGNACIOUS **2** **a** : marked by unrestrained zeal or vehemence ⟨a ~ argument⟩ **b** : extremely vexatious, disappointing, or intense ⟨~ pain⟩ **3** : furiously active or determined ⟨make a ~ effort⟩ **4** : wild or menacing in appearance — **fierce·ly** *adv* — **fierce·ness** *n*
syn FIERCE, FEROCIOUS, BARBAROUS, SAVAGE, CRUEL *shared meaning element* : showing fury or malignity in looks or actions *ant* tame, mild
fi·eri fa·cias \ˌfī-(ə-)rē-ˈfā-sh(ē-)əs\ *n* [L, cause (it) to be done] : a writ authorizing the sheriff to obtain satisfaction of a judgment in debt or damages from the goods and chattels of the defendant
fi·ery \ˈfī(-ə)-rē\ *adj* **fi·er·i·er; -est** [ME, fr. *fire*, *fier* fire] **1** **a** : consisting of fire **b** : BURNING, BLAZING ⟨the ~ interior of a furnace⟩ **c** : using or carried out with fire ⟨~ experiments of the alchemists⟩ **d** : liable to catch fire or explode : FLAMMABLE ⟨a ~ vapor⟩ **2** **a** : hot like a fire **b** (1) : being in an inflamed state or condition ⟨a ~ boil⟩ (2) : feverish and flushed ⟨a ~ forehead⟩ **3** **a** : of the color of fire : RED ⟨a ~ sunset⟩ **b** : intensely or unnaturally red ⟨~ lips and fingernails⟩ **4** **a** : full of or exuding emotion or spirit ⟨a ~ sermon⟩ **b** : easily provoked : IRRITABLE — **fi·eri·ly** \-rə-lē\ *adv* — **fi·eri·ness** \-rē-nəs\ *n* — **fiery** *adv*
fi·es·ta \fē-ˈes-tə\ *n* [Sp, fr. L *festa* — more at FEAST] : FESTIVAL; *specif* : a saint's day celebrated in Spain and Latin America with processions and dances
fi fa \ˈfī-ˈfā\ *abbr* fieri facias
fife \ˈfīf\ *n* [G *pfeife* pipe, fife, fr. OHG *pfīfa* — more at PIPE] : a small flute with six to eight finger holes and no keys that is used chiefly to accompany the drum
fife rail *n* : a rail about the mast near the deck to which running rigging is belayed
FIFO *abbr* first in, first out
fif·teen \fif-ˈtēn\ *n* [ME *fiftene*, adj., fr. OE *fīftēne;* akin to OE *tīen* ten] **1** — see NUMBER table **2** : the first point scored by a side in a game of tennis — called also *five* — **fifteen** *adj or pron* — **fifteenth** \-ˈtēn(t)th\ *adj or n*
fifth \ˈfif(t)th\ *n* **1** — see NUMBER table **2** **a** : the musical interval embracing five diatonic degrees **b** : a tone at this interval; *specif* : DOMINANT 2 **c** : the harmonic combination of two tones at this interval **3** : a unit of measure for liquor equal to one fifth of a U.S. gallon **4** *cap* : the Fifth Amendment of the U.S. Constitution — **fifth** *adj or adv* — **fifth·ly** *adv*
fifth column *n* [name applied to rebel sympathizers in Madrid in 1936 when four rebel columns were advancing on the city] : a group of secret sympathizers or supporters of an enemy that engage in espionage or sabotage within defense lines or national borders — **fifth col·um·nism** \-ˈkäl-əm-ˌ(n)iz-əm\ *n* — **fifth col·um·nist** \-(n)əst\ *n*
fifth wheel *n* **1** **a** : a horizontal wheel or segment of a wheel that consists of two parts rotating on each other above the fore axle of a carriage and that forms support to prevent tipping **b** : a similar coupling between tractor and trailer of a semitrailer **2** : a spare wheel **3** : one that is superfluous, unnecessary, or burdensome
fif·ty \ˈfif-tē\ *n, pl* **fifties** [ME, fr. *fifty*, adj., fr. OE *fīftig*, fr. *fīftig*, n., group of 50, fr. *fīf* five + *-tig* group of ten — more at EIGHTY] **1** — see NUMBER table **2** *pl* : the numbers 50 to 59; *specif* : the years 50 to 59 in a lifetime or century **3** : a 50-dollar bill — **fif·ti·eth** \-tē-əth\ *adj or n* — **fifty** *adj or pron*
fif·ty–fif·ty \ˌfif-tē-ˈfif-tē\ *adj* **1** : shared, assumed, or borne equally ⟨a ~ proposition⟩ **2** : half favorable and half unfavorable ⟨a ~ chance⟩ — **fifty–fifty** *adv*
¹fig \ˈfig\ *n* [ME *fige*, fr. OF, fr. OProv *figa*, fr. (assumed) VL *fica*, fr. L *ficus* fig tree, fig] **1** **a** : an oblong or pear-shaped fruit that is a syconium **b** : any of a genus (*Ficus*) of trees of the mulberry family bearing fruits that are syconia; *esp* : a widely cultivated tree (*F. carica*) that produces edible figs **2** : a contemptibly worthless trifle ⟨not worth a ~⟩

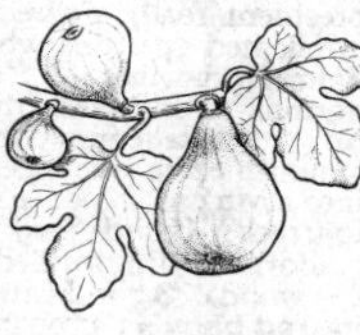

fig: leaves and fruit

²fig *n* [*fig* (to adorn)] : DRESS, ARRAY ⟨a young woman in dazzling royal full ~ —Mollie Panter-Downes⟩
³fig *abbr* **1** figurative; figuratively **2** figure
¹fight \ˈfīt\ *vb* **fought** \ˈfȯt\; **fight·ing** [ME *fighten*, fr. OE *feohtan;* akin to OHG *fehtan* to fight, L *pectere* to comb — more at FEE] *vi* **1** **a** : to contend in battle or physical combat; *esp* : to strive to overcome a person by blows or weapons **b** : to engage in boxing **2** : to put forth a determined effort ~ *vt* **1** **a** (1) : to contend against in or as if in battle or physical combat (2) : to box against in the ring **b** (1) : to attempt to prevent the success or effectiveness of ⟨the company *fought* the strike for months⟩ (2) : to oppose the passage or development of ⟨~ a bad habit⟩ **2** **a** : to carry on : WAGE **b** : to take part in (as a boxing match) **3** : to struggle to endure or surmount ⟨~ out a storm at sea⟩ **4** **a** : to gain by struggle ⟨~*s* his way through⟩ **b** : to resolve by struggle ⟨*fought* out their differences in court⟩ **5** **a** : to manage (a ship) in a battle or storm **b** : to cause to struggle or contend **c** : to manage in an unnecessarily rough or awkward manner — **fight shy of** : to avoid facing or meeting
²fight *n* **1** **a** : a hostile encounter : BATTLE, COMBAT **b** : a boxing match **c** : a verbal disagreement : ARGUMENT **2** : a struggle for a goal or an objective ⟨a ~ for justice⟩ **3** : strength or disposition for fighting : PUGNACITY ⟨still full of ~⟩
fight·er *n* : one that fights: as **a** (1) : WARRIOR, SOLDIER **a** (2) : a pugnacious or game individual **a** (3) : BOXER **b** : an airplane of high speed and maneuverability with armament designed to destroy enemy aircraft
fighting chair *n* : a chair from which a salt-water angler plays a hooked fish
fighting chance *n* : a chance that may be realized by a struggle ⟨the patient had a *fighting chance* to live⟩
fig leaf *n* **1** : the leaf of a fig tree **2** [fr. the use by Adam and Eve of fig leaves to cover their nakedness after eating the forbidden fruit (Gen. 3:7)] : something that conceals or camouflages usu. inadequately or dishonestly
fig marigold *n* : any of several carpetweeds (genus *Mesembryanthemum*) with showy white or pink flowers

ə abut ᵊ kitten ər further a back ā bake ä cot, cart
au̇ out ch chin e less ē easy g gift i trip ī life
j joke ŋ sing ō flow ȯ flaw ȯi coin th thin t͟h this
ü loot u̇ foot y yet yü few yu̇ furious zh vision

fig·ment \ˈfig-mənt\ *n* [ME, fr. L *figmentum,* fr. *fingere* to shape — more at DOUGH] : something made up, fabricated, or contrived ⟨a ~ of the author's imagination⟩

fig·ur·al \ˈfig-(y)ə-rəl\ *adj* : of, relating to, or consisting of human or animal figures ⟨a ~ composition⟩

fig·u·ra·tion \ˌfig-(y)ə-ˈrā-shən\ *n* **1** : the act or process of creating or providing a figure ⟨Dante's unique ~ of the underworld⟩ **2** : FORM, OUTLINE **3** : an act or instance of representation in figures and shapes ⟨cubism was explained as a synthesis of colored ~s of objects —Janet Flanner⟩ **4** : ornamentation of a musical passage by using decorative and usu. repetitive figures

fig·u·ra·tive \ˈfig-(y)ə-rət-iv\ *adj* **1 a** : representing by a figure or resemblance : EMBLEMATIC **b** : of or relating to representation of form or figure in art ⟨~ sculpture⟩ **2 a** : expressing one thing in terms normally denoting another with which it may be regarded as analogous : METAPHORICAL ⟨~ language⟩ **b** : characterized by figures of speech ⟨a ~ description⟩ — **fig·u·ra·tive·ly** *adv* — **fig·u·ra·tive·ness** *n*

¹fig·ure \ˈfig-yər, *esp Brit* ˈfig-ər\ *n* [ME, fr. OF, fr. L *figura,* fr. *fingere*] **1 a** : a number symbol : NUMERAL, DIGIT ⟨a salary running into six ~s⟩ **b** *pl* : arithmetical calculations ⟨good at ~s⟩ **c** : a written or printed character **d** : value esp. as expressed in numbers : PRICE ⟨the house sold at a low ~⟩ **2 a** : bodily shape or form esp. of a person ⟨a slender ~⟩ **b** : an object noticeable only as a shape or form ⟨~s moving in the dusk⟩ **3 a** : the graphic representation of a form esp. of a person **b** : a diagram or pictorial illustration of textual matter **c** : a geometric diagram **4** : a person, thing, or action representative of another **5** : an intentional deviation from the ordinary form or syntactical relation of words **6** : the form of a syllogism with respect to the relative position of the middle term **7** : an often repetitive pattern or design in a manufactured article (as cloth) or natural product (as wood) ⟨a polka-dot ~⟩ **8** : appearance made : impression produced ⟨the couple cut quite a ~⟩ **9 a** : a series of movements in a dance **b** : an outline representation of a form traced by a series of evolutions (as with skates on an ice surface or by an airplane in the air) **10** : a prominent personality : PERSONAGE ⟨great ~s of history⟩ **11** : a short coherent group of tones or chords that may grow into a phrase, theme, or composition ***syn*** see FORM

²figure *vb* **fig·ured; fig·ur·ing** \ˈfig-yə-riŋ, ˈfig(-ə)-\ *vt* **1** : to represent by or as if by a figure or outline : PORTRAY **2** : to decorate with a pattern; *specif* : to write figures over or under (the bass) in order to indicate the accompanying chords **3** : to indicate or represent by numerals **4 a** : CALCULATE **b** : CONCLUDE, DECIDE ⟨he *figured* there was no use in further effort⟩ **c** : REGARD, CONSIDER ⟨backed him because they *figured* him an upright man⟩ ~ *vi* **1 a** : to be or appear important or conspicuous ⟨the vice-president really *figured* in the company⟩ **b** : to be involved or implicated ⟨persons who *figured* in a robbery⟩ **2** : to perform a figure in dancing **3** : COMPUTE, CALCULATE **4** : to seem rational, normal, or expected ⟨that ~s⟩ — **fig·ur·er** \-(y)ər-ər\ *n* — **figure on 1** : to take into consideration (as in planning) ⟨*figuring on* $50 a month extra income⟩ **2** : to rely on **3** : PLAN ⟨I *figure on* going into town⟩

fig·ured \-(y)ərd\ *adj* **1** : being represented : PORTRAYED **2** : adorned with, formed into, or marked with a figure ⟨~ muslin⟩ ⟨~ wood⟩ **3** : indicated by figures

figured bass *n* : CONTINUO

figure eight *n* : something resembling the Arabic numeral eight in form or shape: as **a** : a small knot — see KNOT illustration **b** : an embroidery stitch **c** : a dance pattern **d** : a skater's figure

fig·ure·head \ˈfig-(y)ər-ˌhed\ *n* **1** : the figure on a ship's bow **2** : a head or chief in name only

figurehead 1

figure in *vt* : to include esp. in a reckoning ⟨*figure in* occasional expenses⟩

figure of speech : a form of expression (as a simile or metaphor) used to convey meaning or heighten effect often by comparing or identifying one thing with another that has a meaning or connotation familiar to the reader or listener

figure out *vt* **1** : DISCOVER, DETERMINE ⟨try to *figure out* a way to solve the problem⟩ **2** : SOLVE, FATHOM ⟨*figure out* a problem⟩

figure skating *n* : skating in which the skater describes or outlines prescribed figures

fig·u·rine \ˌfig-(y)ə-ˈrēn\ *n* : a small carved or molded figure : STATUETTE

fig wasp *n* : a minute wasp (*Blastophaga psenes* of the family Agaontidae) that breeds in the caprifig and is the agent of caprification; *broadly* : a wasp of the same family

fig·wort \ˈfig-ˌwərt, -ˌwȯ(ə)rt\ *n* : any of a genus (*Scrophularia* of the family Scrophulariaceae, the figwort family) of chiefly herbaceous plants with leaves having no stipules, an irregular bilabiate corolla, and a 2-celled ovary

Fi·ji·an \ˈfē-(ˌ)jē-ən, fi-ˈ\ *n* **1** : a member of a Melanesian people of the Fiji islands **2** : the Austronesian language of the Fijians — **Fijian** *adj*

fila *pl of* FILUM

fil·a·ment \ˈfil-ə-mənt\ *n* [MF, fr. ML *filamentum,* fr. LL *filare* to spin — more at FILE] : a single thread or a thin flexible threadlike object, process, or appendage: as **a** : a tenuous conductor (as of carbon or metal) made incandescent by the passage of an electric current; *specif* : a cathode in the form of a metal wire in an electron tube **b (1)** : a thin and fine elongated constituent part of a gill **b (2)** : an elongated thin series of cells attached one to another or a very long thin cylindrical single cell (as of some algae, fungi, or bacteria) **c** : the anther-bearing stalk of a stamen — see FLOWER illustration — **fil·a·men·ta·ry** \ˌfil-ə-ˈment-ə-rē, -ˈmen-trē\ *adj* — **fil·a·men·tous** \-ˈment-əs\ *adj*

fi·lar \ˈfī-lər\ *adj* [L *filum* thread] : of or relating to a thread or line; *esp* : having threads across the field of view ⟨a ~ eyepiece⟩

fi·lar·ia \fə-ˈlar-ē-ə, -ˈler-\ *n, pl* **-i·ae** \-ē-ˌē, -ē-ˌī\ [NL, fr. L *filum*] : any of numerous slender filamentous nematodes (of *Filaria* and related genera) that as adults are parasites in the blood or tissues of mammals and as larvae usu. develop in biting insects — **fi·lar·i·al** \-ē-əl\ *adj* — **fi·lar·i·id** \-ē-əd\ *adj or n*

fil·a·ri·a·sis \ˌfil-ə-ˈrī-ə-səs\ *n, pl* **-a·ses** \-ˌsēz\ : infestation with or disease caused by filariae

fil·a·ture \ˈfil-ə-ˌchu̇(ə)r, -chər, -ˌt(y)u̇(ə)r\ *n* [F, fr. LL *filatus,* pp. of *filare*] **1** : the reeling of silk from cocoons **2** : a reel for drawing off silk from cocoons **3** : a factory where silk is reeled

fil·bert \ˈfil-bərt\ *n* [ME, fr. AF *philber,* fr. St. *Philibert* †684 Frankish abbot whose feast day falls in the nutting season] **1** : either of two European hazels (*Corylus avellana pontica* and *C. maxima*); *also* : the sweet thick-shelled nut of the filbert **2** : HAZELNUT

filch \ˈfilch\ *vt* [ME *filchen*] : to appropriate furtively or casually ⟨~ a doughnut from the platter⟩ ***syn*** see STEAL

¹file \ˈfī(ə)l\ *n* [ME, fr. OE *fēol;* akin to OHG *fīla* file] **1** : a tool usu. of hardened steel with cutting ridges for forming or smoothing surfaces esp. of metal **2** : a shrewd or crafty person

²file *vt* **filed; fil·ing** : to rub, smooth, or cut away with or as if with a file

³file *vt* **filed; fil·ing** [ME *filen,* fr. OE *fȳlan,* fr. *fūl* foul] *chiefly dial* : DEFILE, CORRUPT

⁴file *vb* **filed; fil·ing** [ME *filen,* fr. MF *filer* to string documents on a string or wire, fr. *fil* thread, fr. L *filum;* akin to Arm *jil* sinew] *vt* **1** : to arrange in order for preservation and reference ⟨~ letters⟩ **2 a** : to place among official records as prescribed by law ⟨~ a mortgage⟩ **b** : to send (copy) to a newspaper ⟨*filed* a good story⟩ **c** : to return to the office of the clerk of a court without action on the merits **3** : to perform the first act of (as a lawsuit) ⟨threatened to ~ charges against him⟩ ~ *vi* **1** : to register as a candidate esp. in a primary election ⟨~ for county attorney⟩ **2** : to place items (as letters) in a file

⁵file *n* **1** : a device (as a folder, case, or cabinet) by means of which papers are kept in order **2 a** *archaic* : ROLL, LIST **b** : a collection of papers or publications usu. arranged or classified **c** : a collection of related data records (as for a computer) — **on file** : in or as if in a file for ready reference

⁶file *n* [MF, fr. *filer* to spin, fr. LL *filare,* fr. L *filum*] **1** : a row of persons, animals, or things arranged one behind the other **2** : any of the rows of squares that extend across a chessboard from white's side to black's side

⁷file *vi* **filed; fil·ing** : to march or proceed in file

filé \fə-ˈlā, (ˈ)fi-ˈlā, (ˈ)fē-ˈlā\ *n* [AmerF (Louisiana), fr. F, pp. of *filer* to twist, spin] : powdered young leaves of sassafras used to thicken soups or stews

file clerk *n* : a clerk who works on files

file·fish \ˈfī(ə)l-ˌfish\ *n* : any of various plectognath fishes (esp. genera *Aluterus, Cantherhines,* and *Monacanthus* of the family Balistidae) with rough granular leathery skins

fi·let \fi-ˈlā\ *n* [F, lit., net] : a lace with a square mesh and geometric designs

fi·let mi·gnon \ˌfil-(ˌ)ā-mēn-ˈyōⁿ, fi-ˌlā-\ *n, pl* **filets mignons** \-(ˌ)ā-mēn-ˈyōⁿz, -ˌlā-\ [F, lit., dainty fillet] : a fillet of beef cut from the thick end of a beef tenderloin

fili- *or* **filo-** *comb form* [L *filum*] : thread ⟨*fili*form⟩

fil·ial \ˈfil-ē-əl, ˈfil-yəl\ *adj* [ME, fr. LL *filialis,* fr. L *filius* son — more at FEMININE] **1** : of, relating to, or befitting a son or daughter ⟨~ obedience⟩ **2** : having or assuming the relation of a child or offspring — **fil·ial·ly** \-ē-ə-lē, -yə-lē\ *adv*

filial generation *n* : a generation in a breeding experiment that is successive to a parental generation — symbol F_1 for the first, F_2 for the second, etc.

fil·i·a·tion \ˌfil-ē-ˈā-shən\ *n* **1 a** : filial relationship esp. of a son to his father **b** : the adjudication of paternity : AFFILIATION **2** : an offshoot or branch of a culture or language **3 a** : descent or derivation esp. from a culture or language **b** : the act or process of determining such relationship

¹fil·i·bus·ter \ˈfil-ə-ˌbəs-tər\ *n* [Sp *filibustero,* lit., freebooter] **1** : an irregular military adventurer; *specif* : an American engaged in fomenting insurrections in Latin America in the mid-19th century **2** [²*filibuster*] **a** : the use of extreme dilatory tactics in an attempt to delay or prevent action esp. in a legislative assembly **b** : an instance of this practice

²filibuster *vb* **fil·i·bus·tered; fil·i·bus·ter·ing** \-t(ə-)riŋ\ *vi* **1** : to carry out insurrectionist or revolutionary activities in a foreign country **2** : to engage in a filibuster ~ *vt* : to subject to a filibuster — **fil·i·bus·ter·er** \-tər-ər\ *n*

fil·i·form \ˈfil-ə-ˌfȯrm, ˈfī-lə-\ *adj* : shaped like a filament

¹fil·i·gree \ˈfil-ə-ˌgrē\ *n* [F *filigrane,* fr. It *filigrana,* fr. L *filum* + *granum* grain] **1** : ornamental work esp. of fine wire of gold, silver, or copper applied chiefly to gold and silver surfaces **2 a** : ornamental openwork of delicate or intricate design **b** : a pattern or design resembling such openwork ⟨a ~ of frost⟩

²filigree *vt* **fil·i·greed; fil·i·gree·ing** : to adorn with or as if with filigree

fil·ing \ˈfī-liŋ\ *n* **1** : an act or instance of using a file **2** : a fragment rubbed off in filing ⟨iron ~s⟩

fil·io·pi·etis·tic \ˈfil-ē-ō-ˌpī-ə-ˈtis-tik\ *adj* [*fil*ial + *-o-* + *piety* + *-istic*] : of or relating to an often excessive veneration of ancestors or tradition

Fil·i·pi·no \ˌfil-ə-ˈpē-(ˌ)nō\ *n, pl* **Filipinos** [Sp] **1** : a native of the Philippine islands; *specif* : a member of a Christianized Philippine people **2** : a citizen of the Republic of the Philippines — **Filipino** *adj*

¹fill \ˈfil\ *vb* [ME *fillen,* fr. OE *fyllan;* akin to OE *full*] *vt* **1 a** : to put into as much as can be held or conveniently contained ⟨~ a cup with water⟩ **b** : to supply with a full complement ⟨the class is already ~*ed*⟩ **c (1)** : to cause to swell or billow ⟨wind ~*ed* the sails⟩ **(2)** : to trim (a sail) to catch the wind **d** : to raise the level of with fill ⟨~*ed* land⟩ **e** : to repair the cavities of (teeth) **f** : to stop up : OBSTRUCT, PLUG ⟨wreckage ~*ed* the channel⟩ ⟨~ the chink⟩ **g :** to stop up the interstices, crevices, or pores of (as cloth, wood, or leather) with a foreign substance **2 a :** FEED, SATIATE **b :** SATISFY, FULFILL ⟨~*s* all requirements⟩ **c :** to make out : COMPLETE — often used with *out* or *in* ⟨~ out a form⟩ ⟨~ in the blanks⟩ **3 a :** to occupy the whole of ⟨smoke ~*ed* the room⟩ **b :** to spread through **c :** to make full (as the mind or spirit) ⟨a mind ~*ed* with fantasies⟩ **4 a :** to possess and perform the duties of : HOLD ⟨~ an office⟩ **b :** to place a person in ⟨~ a vacancy⟩ **5 :** to supply as directed ⟨~ a prescription⟩ **6 :** to cover the surface of with a layer of precious metal ~ *vi* : to become full ⟨the stadium ~*ed* and overflowed⟩ — **fill one's shoes :** to take over one's job, position, or responsibilities — **fill the bill :** to answer a need

²fill *n* **1 :** a full supply; *esp* : a quantity that satisfies or satiates ⟨eat your ~⟩ **2 :** material used to fill a receptacle, cavity, passage, or low place

fill away *vi* **1 :** to trim a sail to catch the wind **2 :** to proceed on the course esp. after being brought up in the wind

filled milk *n* **:** skim milk with fat content increased by the addition of vegetable oils

¹fill·er \ˈfil-ər\ *n* **:** one that fills: as **a :** a substance added to a product (as to increase bulk, weight, viscosity, opacity, or strength) **b :** a composition used to fill the pores and grain of a wood or other surface before painting or varnishing **c :** a plate or other piece used to cover or fill in a space between two parts of a structure **d :** tobacco used to form the core of a cigar **e :** material (as a brief item of fact) used to fill extra space in a column or page of a newspaper or magazine **f :** a pack of paper used esp. in a loose-leaf notebook

²fil·ler \ˈfil-ˌe(ə)r\ *n, pl* **fillers** *or* **filler** [Hung *fillér*] — see *forint* at MONEY table

¹fil·let \ˈfil-ət, *in sense 2b also* fi-ˈlā, ˈfil-(ˌ)ā\ *also* **fi·let** \fi-ˈlā, ˈfil-(ˌ)ā\ *n* [ME *filet*, fr. MF, dim. of *fil* thread — more at FILE] **1 :** a ribbon or narrow strip of material used esp. as a headband **2 :** a thin narrow strip of material: as **a :** a band of anatomical fibers; *specif* : LEMNISCUS **b :** a piece or slice of boneless meat or fish; *specif* : the tenderloin of beef **3 a :** a concave junction formed where two surfaces meet **b :** a curved strip forming such a junction **4 :** a narrow flat architectural member: **a :** a flat molding separating others **b :** the space between two flutings in a shaft **5 :** a design impressed on a book cover

1, fillet 1

²fil·let \ˈfil-ət, *in sense 2 also* fi-ˈlā, ˈfil-(ˌ)ā\ *vt* **1 :** to bind, furnish, or adorn with or as if with a fillet **2 :** to cut into fillets

fill–in \ˈfil-ˌin\ *n* **:** someone or something that fills in

fill in \(ˈ)fil-ˈin\ *vt* **1 :** to give (a person) necessary or recently acquired information ⟨friends *filled* him *in* on the latest gossip⟩ **2 :** to enrich (as a design) with detail ~ *vi* : to fill a vacancy usu. temporarily : SUBSTITUTE ⟨he often *filled in* in emergencies⟩

fill·ing \ˈfil-iŋ\ *n* **1 :** an act or instance of filling **2 :** something used to fill a cavity, container, or depression ⟨a ~ for a tooth⟩ **3 :** something that completes: as **a :** the yarn interlacing the warp in a fabric; *also* : yarn for the shuttle **b :** a food mixture used to fill pastry or sandwiches

filling station *n* **:** SERVICE STATION 1

¹fil·lip \ˈfil-əp\ *n* [prob. of imit. origin] **1 a :** a blow or gesture made by the sudden forcible straightening of a finger curled up against the thumb **b :** a short sharp blow : BUFFET **2 :** something tending to arouse or excite

²fillip *vt* **1 a :** to strike or tap with a fillip ⟨~*ed* him on the nose⟩ **b :** to make a filliping motion with ⟨~*ed* his fingers toward them⟩ **2 :** to project quickly by or as if by a fillip ⟨~*ed* crumbs off the table⟩ **3 :** STIMULATE ⟨with this to ~ his spirits —Robert Westerby⟩

fill out *vi* **:** to put on flesh

fil·ly \ˈfil-ē\ *n, pl* **fillies** [ME *fyly*, fr. ON *fylja;* akin to OE *fola* foal] **1 :** a young female horse usu. of less than four years **2 :** a young woman : GIRL

¹film \ˈfilm\ *n, often attrib* [ME *filme*, fr. OE *filmen;* akin to Gk *pelma* sole of the foot, OE *fell* skin — more at FELL] **1 a :** a thin skin or membranous covering : PELLICLE **b :** an abnormal growth on or in the eye **2 :** a thin covering or coating ⟨a ~ of ice on the pond⟩ **3 a :** an exceedingly thin layer : LAMINA **b** (1) **:** a thin flexible transparent sheet (as of plastic) used as a wrapping (2) **:** such a sheet of cellulose acetate or cellulose nitrate coated with a light-sensitive emulsion for taking photographs **4 :** MOTION PICTURE

²film *vt* **1 :** to cover with or as if with a film **2 :** to make a motion picture of or from ⟨~ a scene⟩ ⟨~ a novel⟩ ~ *vi* **1 :** to become covered or obscured with or as if with a film **2 a :** to be suitable for photographing ⟨a scene that would ~ well⟩ **b :** to make a motion picture ⟨~*ing* on location⟩

film badge *n* **:** a small pack of sensitive photographic film worn as a badge for indicating exposure to radiation

film·card \ˈfilm-ˌkärd\ *n* **:** MICROFICHE

film·dom \ˈfilm-dəm\ *n* **1 :** the motion-picture industry **2 :** the personnel of the motion-picture industry

film·ic \ˈfil-mik\ *adj* **:** of, relating to, or resembling motion pictures — **film·i·cal·ly** \-mi-k(ə-)lē\ *adv*

film·mak·er \ˈfilm-ˌmā-kər\ *n* **:** MOVIEMAKER

film·mak·ing \-ˌmā-kiŋ\ *n* **:** the making of movies

film·og·ra·phy \fil-ˈmäg-rə-fē\ *n, pl* **-phies** [*film* + *-ography* (as in *bibliography*)] **:** a list of motion pictures featuring the work of a prominent film figure (as an actor) or relating to a particular topic

film·set·ting \ˈfilm-ˌset-iŋ\ *n* **:** PHOTOCOMPOSITION — **film·set** *adj* — **filmset** *vt* — **film·set·ter** *n*

film·strip \ˈfilm-ˌstrip\ *n* **:** a strip of usu. 35 millimeter film bearing photographs, diagrams, or graphic matter for still projection

filmy \ˈfil-mē\ *adj* **film·i·er; -est 1 :** of, resembling, or composed of film : GAUZY ⟨~ draperies⟩ **2 :** covered with a haze or film — **film·i·ly** \-mə-lē\ *adv* — **film·i·ness** \-mē-nəs\ *n*

filo- — see FILI-

fils \ˈfils\ *n, pl* **fils** [Ar] — see *dinar* at MONEY table

¹fil·ter \ˈfil-tər\ *n* [ME *filtre*, fr. ML *filtrum*, piece of felt used as a filter, of Gmc origin; akin to OHG *filz* felt — more at FELT] **1 :** a porous article or mass (as of paper or sand) through which a gas or liquid is passed to separate out matter in suspension **2 :** an apparatus containing a filter medium **3 a :** a device or material for suppressing or minimizing waves or oscillations of certain frequencies (as of electricity, light, or sound) **b :** a transparent material (as colored glass) that absorbs light of certain wavelengths or colors selectively and is used for modifying light that reaches a sensitized photographic material — called also *color filter*

²filter *vb* **fil·tered; fil·ter·ing** \-t(ə-)riŋ\ *vt* **1 :** to subject to the action of a filter **2 :** to remove by means of a filter ~ *vi* **1 :** to pass or move through or as if through a filter **2 :** to enter or cross over in small units over a period of time ⟨people began ~*ing* into the hall⟩

fil·ter·able *also* **fil·tra·ble** \ˈfil-t(ə-)rə-bəl\ *adj* **:** capable of being filtered or of passing through a filter — **fil·ter·abil·i·ty** \ˌfil-t(ə-)rə-ˈbil-ət-ē\ *n*

filterable virus *n* **:** a virus so small that a fluid containing it remains virulent after passing through a filter

filter bed *n* **:** a bed of sand or gravel for filtering water or sewage

filter feeder *n* **:** an animal that obtains its food by filtering organic matter or minute organisms from a current of water that passes through some part of its system

filter paper *n* **:** porous unsized paper used esp. for filtering

filter tip *n* **:** a cigar or cigarette tip designed to filter the smoke before it enters the smoker's mouth; *also* : a cigar or cigarette provided with such a tip — **fil·ter–tipped** \ˌfil-tər-ˈtipt\ *adj*

filth \ˈfilth\ *n* [ME, fr. OE *fȳlth*, fr. *fūl* foul] **1 :** foul or putrid matter; *esp* : loathsome dirt or refuse **2 a :** moral corruption or defilement **b :** something that tends to corrupt or defile : OBSCENITY

filthy \ˈfil-thē\ *adj* **filth·i·er; -est 1 :** covered with or containing filth : offensively dirty **2 a :** UNDERHAND, VILE **b :** OBSCENE ***syn*** see DIRTY — **filth·i·ly** \-thə-lē\ *adv* — **filth·i·ness** \-thē-nəs\ *n*

¹fil·trate \ˈfil-ˌtrāt\ *vb* **fil·trat·ed; fil·trat·ing** [ML *filtratus*, pp. of *filtrare*, fr. *filtrum*] **:** FILTER

²filtrate *n* **:** material that has passed through a filter

fil·tra·tion \fil-ˈtrā-shən\ *n* **1 :** the process of filtering **2 :** the process of passing through or as if through a filter; *also* : DIFFUSION ⟨the kidney produces urine by ~⟩

fi·lum \ˈfī-ləm\ *n, pl* **fi·la** \-lə\ [NL, fr. L — more at FILE] **:** filamentous structure : FILAMENT

fim·bria \ˈfim-brē-ə\ *n, pl* **-bri·ae** \-brē-ˌē, -ˌī\ [NL, fr. L, fringe] **:** a bordering fringe esp. at the entrance of the fallopian tubes — **fim·bri·al** \-brē-əl\ *adj*

fim·bri·ate \-ˌāt\ *or* **fim·bri·at·ed** \-ˌāt-əd\ *adj* **:** having the edge or extremity bordered by slender processes : FRINGED — **fim·bri·a·tion** \ˌfim-brē-ˈā-shən\ *n*

¹fin \ˈfin\ *n* [ME *finn*, fr. OE; akin to L *spina* thorn, spine] **1 :** an external membranous process of an aquatic animal (as a fish) used in propelling or guiding the body — see FISH illustration **2 :** something resembling a fin esp. in appearance or function: **a :** HAND, ARM **b** (1) **:** an appendage of a boat (as a submarine) (2) **:** an airfoil attached to an airplane for directional stability **c :** FLIPPER 1b **d :** any of the projecting ribs on a radiator or an engine cylinder — **fin·like** \-ˌlīk\ *adj* — **finned** \ˈfind\ *adj*

²fin *vb* **finned; fin·ning** *vi* **:** to show the fins above the water ~ *vt* **:** to equip with fins

³fin *n* [Yiddish *finf* five, fr. OHG] *slang* **:** a 5-dollar bill

⁴fin *abbr* **1** finance; financial **2** finish

fi·na·gle \fə-ˈnā-gəl\ *vb* **fi·na·gled; fi·na·gling** \-g(ə-)liŋ\ [perh. alter. of *fainaigue* (to renege)] *vt* **1 :** to obtain by indirect or involved means **2 :** to obtain by trickery : SWINDLE ~ *vi* : to use devious and often dishonest methods to achieve one's ends — **fi·na·gler** \-g(ə-)lər\ *n*

¹fi·nal \ˈfīn-ᵊl\ *adj* [ME, fr. MF, fr. L *finalis*, fr. *finis* boundary, end] **1 a :** not to be altered or undone : CONCLUSIVE **b :** of or relating to a concluding court action or proceeding ⟨~ decree⟩ **2 :** being the last : constituting the closing element in a series, process, or progress ⟨the ~ chapter of a book⟩ **3 :** of or relating to the ultimate purpose or result of a process ⟨the ~ goal of life⟩ **4 :** relating to or occurring at the end or conclusion ***syn*** see LAST — **fi·nal·ly** \ˈfīn-ᵊl-ē, ˈfīn-lē\ *adv*

²final *n* **:** something that is final: as **a :** a deciding match, game, heat, or trial **b :** the last examination in a course

fi·na·le \fə-ˈnal-ē, fi-ˈnäl-\ *n* [It, fr. *finale*, adj., final, fr. L *finalis*] **:** the close or termination of something: as **a :** the last section of an instrumental musical composition **b :** the closing part, scene, or number in a public performance **c :** the last and often climactic event or item in a sequence

fi·nal·ist \ˈfīn-ᵊl-əst\ *n* **:** a contestant in the finals of a competition

fi·nal·i·ty \fī-ˈnal-ət-ē, fə-\ *n, pl* **-ties 1 a :** the character or condition of being final, settled, irrevocable, or complete **b :** the condition of being at an ultimate point esp. of development or authority **2 :** something final; *esp* : a fundamental fact, action, or belief

fi·nal·ize \ˈfīn-ᵊl-ˌīz\ *vt* **-ized; -iz·ing 1 :** to put in final or finished form ⟨soon my conclusion will be *finalized* —D. D. Eisenhower⟩ **2 :** to give final approval to ⟨ties up the day's loose ends, *finalizing* the papers prepared and presented by his staff —*Newsweek*⟩ — **fi·nal·iza·tion** \ˌfīn-ᵊl-ə-ˈzā-shən\ *n*

¹fi·nance \fə-ˈnan(t)s, ˈfī-ˌ, fī-ˈ\ *n* [ME, payment, ransom, fr. MF, fr. *finer* to end, pay, fr. *fin* end — more at FINE] **1** *pl* **:** money or other liquid resources of a government, business, group, or individual **2** : the system that includes the circulation of money, the granting of credit, the making of investments, and the provision of banking facilities **3** : the science or study of the management of funds **4** : the obtaining of funds or capital : FINANCING

[2]**finance** *vt* **fi·nanced; fi·nanc·ing** **1 a** : to raise or provide funds or capital for ⟨~ a new house⟩ **b** : to furnish with necessary funds ⟨~ a son through college⟩ **2** : to sell something to on credit : provide with credit ⟨auto producers unable to ~ their dealers⟩

fi·nan·cial \fə-ˈnan-chəl, fī-\ *adj* : relating to finance or financiers — **fi·nan·cial·ly** \-ˈnanch-(ə-)lē\ *adv*

syn FINANCIAL, MONETARY, PECUNIARY, FISCAL *shared meaning element* : of or relating to money and its use and distribution

[1]**fi·nan·cier** \ˌfin-ən-ˈsi(ə)r; fə-ˌnan-, ˌfī-\ *n* **1** : one who specializes in raising and expending public moneys **2** : one who deals with finance and investment on a large scale

[2]**financier** *vi* : to conduct financial operations often by sharp or reprehensible practices

fi·nanc·ing *n* : the act or process or an instance of raising or providing funds; *also* : the funds thus raised or provided

fin·back \ˈfin-ˌbak\ *n* : a common whalebone whale (*Balaenoptera physalus*) of the Atlantic coast of the U.S. that attains a length of over 60 feet; *broadly* : RORQUAL

finch \ˈfinch\ *n* [ME, fr. OE *finc*; akin to OHG *fincho* finch, Gk *spiza* chaffinch] : any of numerous songbirds (as the sparrows, grosbeaks, crossbills, goldfinches, linnets, and buntings of the family Fringillidae) having a short stout conical bill adapted for crushing seeds

[1]**find** \ˈfīnd\ *vb* **found** \ˈfau̇nd\; **find·ing** [ME *finden*, fr. OE *findan*; akin to OHG *findan* to find, L *pont-, pons* bridge, Gk *pontos* sea, Skt *patha* way, course] *vt* **1 a** : to come upon often accidentally : ENCOUNTER **b** : to meet with (a particular reception) ⟨hoped to ~ favor⟩ **2 a** : to come upon by searching or effort ⟨the committee must ~ a suitable person for the job⟩ **b** : to discover by study or experiment ⟨~ an answer to a problem⟩ **c** : to obtain by effort or management ⟨~ the time to study⟩ **d** : ATTAIN, REACH ⟨the bullet *found* its mark⟩ **e** : to discover by sounding ⟨~ bottom in a lake⟩ **3 a** : EXPERIENCE, DETECT ⟨~ much pleasure in his company⟩ **b** : to perceive (oneself) to be in a certain place or condition ⟨*found* himself in a dilemma⟩ **c** : to gain or regain the use or power of ⟨trying to ~ his tongue⟩ **d** : to bring (oneself) to a realization of one's powers or of one's proper sphere of activity ⟨must help the student to ~ himself as an individual —N. M. Pusey⟩ **4 a** : PROVIDE, SUPPLY **b** : to furnish (room and board) esp. as a condition of employment **5** : to settle upon and make a statement about (as a conclusion) ⟨~ a verdict⟩ ~ *vi* : to determine a case judicially by a verdict ⟨~ for the defendant⟩ — **find fault** : to criticize unfavorably

[2]**find** *n* **1** : an act or instance of finding **2** : something found: as **a** : a valuable item ⟨an archaeological ~⟩ **b** : a person whose ability proves to be unexpectedly great ⟨the young actress was the theatrical ~ of the year⟩

find·er \ˈfīn-dər\ *n* **1** : one that finds **2** : a small astronomical telescope of low power and wide field attached to a larger telescope for finding an object **3** : a device on a camera for showing the area of the subject to be included in the picture

fin de siè·cle \ˌfaⁿ-də-sē-ˈekl[ə]\ *adj* [F, end of the century] : of, relating to, or characteristic of the close of the 19th century and esp. its literary and artistic climate of sophistication, world-weariness, and fashionable despair

find·ing \ˈfīn-diŋ\ *n* **1 a** : the act of one that finds **b** : FIND 2 **2** *pl* : small tools and supplies used by an artisan (as a dressmaker, jeweler, or shoemaker) **3 a** : the result of a judicial examination or inquiry **b** : the results of an investigation — usu. used in pl. ⟨basic research ~*s*⟩

find out *vt* **1** : to learn by study, observation, or search : DISCOVER **2 a** : to catch in an offense (as a crime) ⟨the culprits were soon *found out*⟩ **b** : to ascertain the true character or identity of : UNMASK ⟨if you pretend, you may be *found out*⟩ ~ *vi* : to discover, learn, or verify something ⟨I don't know, but I'll *find out* for you⟩

[1]**fine** \ˈfīn\ *n* [ME, fr. OF *fin*, fr. L *finis* boundary, end] **1** *obs* : END, CONCLUSION **2** : a compromise of a fictitious suit used as a form of conveyance of lands **3 a** : a sum imposed as punishment for an offense **b** : a forfeiture or penalty paid to an injured party in a civil action — **in fine** : in short

[2]**fine** *vt* **fined; fin·ing** : to impose a fine on : punish by a fine

[3]**fine** *adj* **fin·er; fin·est** [ME *fin*, fr. OF, fr. L *finis*, n., end, limit] **1 a** : free from impurity **b** *of a metal* : having a stated proportion of pure metal in the composition **2 a** (1) : very thin in gauge or texture ⟨~ thread⟩ (2) : not coarse ⟨~ sand⟩ (3) : very small ⟨~ print⟩ (4) : KEEN ⟨a knife with a ~ edge⟩ **b** : physically trained or hardened close to the limit of efficiency — used of an athlete or animal **3 a** (1) : having a delicate or subtle quality ⟨a wine of ~ bouquet⟩ (2) : subtle or sensitive in perception or discrimination ⟨a ~ distinction⟩ **b** : performed with extreme care and accuracy ⟨a ~ adjustment⟩ **4** : superior in quality, conception, or appearance : EXCELLENT ⟨a ~ musician⟩ ⟨a ~ view⟩ **5** : marked by or affecting elegance or refinement ⟨~ manners⟩ **6** : very well ⟨feel ~⟩ **7** : AWFUL — used as an intensive ⟨the leader, in a ~ frenzy, beheaded one of his wives —Brian Crozier⟩ — **fine·ness** \ˈfīn-nəs\ *n*

[4]**fine** *adv* : FINELY

[5]**fine** *vb* **fined; fin·ing** *vt* **1** : PURIFY, CLARIFY ⟨~ and filter wine⟩ **2** : to make finer in quality or size ~ *vi* **1** : to become pure or clear ⟨the ale will ~⟩ **2** : to become smaller in lines or proportions : DIMINISH

[6]**fi·ne** \ˈfē-(ˌ)nā\ *n* [It, fr. L *finis* end] : END — used as a direction in music to mark the closing point after a repeat

fine art *n* **1 a** : art (as painting, sculpture, or music) concerned primarily with the creation of beautiful objects — usu. used in pl. **b** : objects of fine art **2** : an activity requiring a fine skill ⟨the *fine art* of making friends⟩

fine·ly \ˈfīn-lē\ *adv* : in a fine manner: as **a** : extremely well : EXCELLENTLY ⟨you did ~⟩ **b** : with close discrimination : PRECISELY **c** : with delicacy or subtlety : SENSITIVELY ⟨a leader ~ attuned to the needs of his people⟩ **d** : MINUTELY ⟨~ ground meal⟩

fine print *n* : something thoroughly and often deliberately obscure; *esp* : a part of an agreement (as a contract) spelling out restrictions and limitations often in small type or obscure language

fin·ery \ˈfīn-(ə-)rē\ *n, pl* **-er·ies** : ORNAMENT, DECORATION; *esp* : dressy or showy clothing and jewels

fines \ˈfīnz\ *n pl* [[3]*fine*] : finely crushed or powdered material (as ore or coal); *also* : very small particles in a mixture of various sizes

fines herbes \fēn-ˈze(ə)rb, fē-ˈne(ə)rb\ *n pl* [F, lit., fine herbs] : a mixture of herbs (as parsley, chives, and tarragon) used as a seasoning or garnish

fine·spun \ˈfīn-ˈspən\ *adj* : developed with extreme care or delicacy; *also* : developed in excessively fine or subtle detail

[1]**fi·nesse** \fə-ˈnes\ *n* [ME, fr. MF, fr. *fin*] **1** : refinement or delicacy of workmanship, structure, or texture **2** : skillful handling of a situation : adroit maneuvering ⟨accomplish by ~ what could not have been accomplished by force⟩ **3** : the withholding of one's highest card or trump in the hope that a lower card will take the trick because the only opposing higher card is in the hand of an opponent who has already played

[2]**finesse** *vb* **fi·nessed; fi·ness·ing** *vi* : to make a finesse in playing cards — sometimes used with *for* or *against* ⟨~ for the jack⟩ ⟨~ against the queen⟩ ~ *vt* **1** : to play (a card) in a finesse **2 a** : to bring about or manage by adroit maneuvering ⟨~ his way through tight places —Marquis James⟩ **b** : EVADE, TRICK ⟨trying to ~ an eagle-eyed editor —J. C. G. Conniff⟩

fin·est \ˈfī-nəst\ *n, pl in constr* [superl. of [3]*fine*] : POLICEMEN — usu. used with the possessive form of a city or area ⟨the city's ~⟩

fine structure *n* : microscopic structure of a biological entity or one of its parts esp. as studied in preparations for the electron microscope — **fine structural** *adj*

fine-tooth comb \ˌfīn-ˌtüth-\ *n* **1** : a comb with close-set teeth used esp. for clearing parasites or foreign matter from the hair **2** : an attitude or system of thorough searching or scrutinizing ⟨went over the report with a *fine-tooth comb* without finding any discrepancies⟩

fin·fish \ˈfin-ˌfish\ *n* : a true fish — compare SHELLFISH

[1]**fin·ger** \ˈfiŋ-gər\ *n* [ME, fr. OE; akin to OHG *fingar* finger] **1** : one of the five terminating members of the hand : a digit of the forelimb; *esp* : one other than the thumb **2 a** : something that resembles a finger ⟨a narrow ~ of land extending into the sea⟩ **b** : a part of a glove into which a finger is inserted **c** : a projecting piece (as a pawl for a ratchet) brought into contact with an object to affect its motion **3** : the breadth of a finger **4** : INTEREST, SHARE — often used in the phrase *to have a finger in the pie* — **fin·ger·like** \-ˌlīk\ *adj*

[2]**finger** *vb* **fin·gered; fin·ger·ing** \-g(ə-)riŋ\ *vt* **1 a** : to play (a musical instrument) with the fingers **b** : to play (as notes or chords) with a specific fingering **c** : to mark the notes of (a music score) as a guide in playing **2** : to touch or feel with the fingers : HANDLE **3** : to point out : IDENTIFY **4** : to extend into or penetrate in the shape of a finger ~ *vi* **1** : to touch or handle something ⟨~*s* through the cards⟩ **2 a** : to use the fingers in playing a musical instrument **b** : to have a certain fingering — used of a musical instrument ⟨~*s* like a clarinet⟩ **3** : to extend in the shape or manner of a finger

fin·ger·board \ˈfiŋ-gər-ˌbō(ə)rd, -ˌbȯ(ə)rd\ *n* : the part of a stringed instrument against which the fingers press the strings to vary the pitch — see VIOLIN illustration

finger bowl *n* : a small water bowl for rinsing the fingers at the table

fin·gered \ˈfiŋ-gərd\ *adj* **1** : having fingers esp. of a specified kind or number — used in combination ⟨stubby-*fingered*⟩ ⟨five-*fingered*⟩ **2** : having projections or processes like fingers ⟨a ~ cranberry scoop⟩

finger hole *n* **1** : any of several holes in the side of a wind instrument (as a recorder) which may be covered or left open by the fingers to change the pitch of the tone **2** : a hole (as in a telephone dial or a bowling ball) into which the finger is placed to provide a grip

fin·ger·ing \ˈfiŋ-g(ə-)riŋ\ *n* **1** : the act or process of handling or touching with the fingers **2 a** : the act or method of using the fingers in playing an instrument **b** : the marking (as by figures on a musical score) of the method of fingering

fin·ger·ling \ˈfiŋ-gər-liŋ\ *n* : a small fish esp. up to one year of age

fin·ger·nail \ˈfiŋ-gər-ˌnāl, ˌfiŋ-gər-ˈnā(ə)l\ *n* : the nail of a finger

finger painting *n* **1** : a technique of spreading pigment on wet paper chiefly with the fingers **2** : a picture produced by finger painting

fin·ger·post \ˈfiŋ-gər-ˌpōst\ *n* **1** : a post bearing one or more signs often terminating in a pointing finger **2** : something serving as a guide to understanding or knowledge

fin·ger·print \-ˌprint\ *n* **1** : the impression of a fingertip on any surface; *esp* : an ink impression of the lines upon the fingertip taken for purpose of identification **2** : the chromatogram or electrophoretogram obtained by cleaving a protein by enzymatic action and subjecting the resulting collection of peptides to two-dimensional chromatography or electrophoresis — **fingerprint** *vt* — **fin·ger·print·ing** *n*

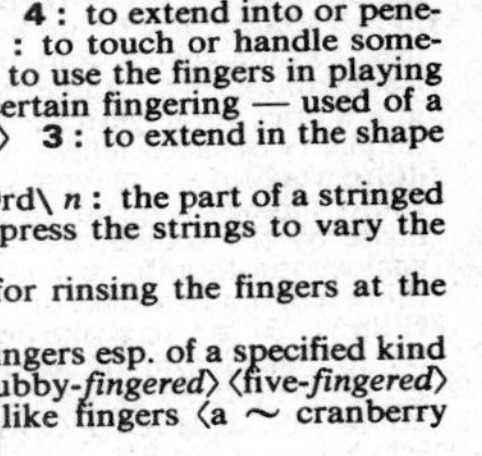

fingerprints 1: *1* arch, *2* loop, *3* whorl, *4* composite

[1]**fin·ger·tip** \-ˌtip\ *n* **1** : the tip of a finger **2** : a protective covering for the end of a finger — **at one's fingertips** : instantly or readily available

[2]**fingertip** *adj* **1** : extending from head or shoulders to mid-thigh —

used of clothing **2 :** readily accessible : being in close proximity ⟨~ information⟩ ⟨~ controls⟩
finger wave *n* **:** a method of setting hair by dampening with water or wave solution and forming waves or curls with the fingers and a comb
fin·i·al \ˈfin-ē-əl\ *n* [ME, fr. *final, finial* final] **1 :** a usu. foliated ornament forming an upper extremity esp. in Gothic architecture **2 :** a crowning ornament or detail (as a decorative knob)

finial 2

fin·i·cal \ˈfin-i-kəl\ *adj* [prob. fr. [3]*fine*] **:** FINICKY ***syn*** see NICE — **fin·i·cal·ly** \-k(ə-)lē\ *adv* — **fin·i·cal·ness** \-kəl-nəs\ *n*
fin·ick·ing \-kiŋ, -kən\ *adj* [alter. of *finical*] **:** FINICKY
fin·icky \ˈfin-i-kē\ *adj* [alter. of *finicking*] **:** excessively nice, exacting, or meticulous in taste or standards ***syn*** see NICE — **fin·icki·ness** *n*
fi·nis \ˈfin-əs, ˈfī-nəs\ *n* [ME, fr. L] **:** END, CONCLUSION
[1]**fin·ish** \ˈfin-ish\ *vb* [ME *finisshen,* fr. MF *finiss-,* stem of *finir,* fr. L *finire,* fr. *finis*] *vt* **1 a :** to bring to an end **:** TERMINATE ⟨~*ed* his speech and sat down⟩ **b :** to use or dispose of entirely ⟨her sandwich ~*ed* the loaf⟩ **2 a :** to bring to completion or issue **:** PERFECT ⟨hope to ~ their new home before winter⟩ **b :** to provide with a finish; *esp* **:** to put a final coat or surface on ⟨~ a table with varnish⟩ **3 a :** to bring to an end the significance or effectiveness of ⟨the scandal ~*ed* his career⟩ **b :** to bring about the death of ~ *vi* **1 :** to come to an end **:** TERMINATE **2 :** to come to the end of a course, task, or undertaking **3 :** to end a competition in a specified manner or position ⟨~*ed* third in the race⟩ ***syn*** see CLOSE — **fin·ish·er** *n*
[2]**finish** *n* **1 a :** the final stage **:** END **b :** the cause of one's ruin **2 :** something that completes or perfects: as **a :** the fine or decorative work required for a building or one of its parts **b :** a finishing material used in painting **c :** the final treatment or coating of a surface **3 :** the result or product of a finishing process **4 :** the quality or state of being perfected
fin·ished *adj* **:** marked by the highest quality **:** CONSUMMATE
finishing school *n* **:** a private school for girls that emphasizes cultural studies and prepares students esp. for social activities
finish line *n* **:** a line marking the end of a racecourse
fi·nite \ˈfī-ˌnīt\ *adj* [ME *finit,* fr. L *finitus,* pp. of *finire*] **1 a :** having definite or definable limits ⟨~ number of possibilities⟩ ⟨a ~ community⟩ **b :** having a limited nature of existence ⟨~ beings⟩ **2 :** completely determinable in theory or in fact by counting, measurement, or thought **:** neither infinite nor infinitesimal ⟨a ~ distance⟩ ⟨the ~ velocity of light⟩ **3 a :** less than an arbitrary positive integer and greater than the negative of that integer **b :** having a finite number of elements ⟨a ~ set⟩ **4 :** showing distinction of grammatical person and number in a verb or verb form — **finite** *n* — **fi·nite·ly** *adv* — **fi·nite·ness** *n*
fi·ni·tude \ˈfī-nə-ˌt(y)üd, ˈfin-ə-\ *n* **:** finite quality or state
fink \ˈfiŋk\ *n* [origin unknown] **1 :** INFORMER 2 **2 :** STRIKEBREAKER **3 :** one who is disapproved of or is held in contempt
fink out *vi* **1 :** to fail miserably **2 :** to back out **:** cop out
[1]**Finn** \ˈfin\ *n* [Sw *Finne*] **1 :** a member of a people speaking Finnish or a Finnic language **2 a :** a native or inhabitant of Finland **b :** one who is of Finnish descent
[2]**Finn** *abbr* Finnish
fin·nan had·die \ˌfin-ən-ˈhad-ē\ *n* [*finnan* alter. of *findon,* fr. *Findon,* Scotland] **:** smoked haddock — called also *finnan haddock*
Fin·nic \ˈfin-ik\ *adj* **1 :** of or relating to the Finns **2 :** of, relating to, or constituting the branch of the Finno-Ugric subfamily of the Uralic family of languages that includes Finnish, Estonian, and Lapp
[1]**Finn·ish** \ˈfin-ish\ *adj* **:** of, relating to, or characteristic of Finland, the Finns, or Finnish
[2]**Finnish** *n* **:** a Finno-Ugric language spoken in Finland, Karelia, and small areas of Sweden and Norway
Fin·no–Ugric \ˌfin-ō-ˈ(y)ü-grik\ *adj* **1 :** of or relating to any of various peoples of northern and eastern Europe and northwestern Siberia speaking related languages and including the Finnish, Hungarian, and Bulgarian peoples and the Lapps and Estonians **2 :** of, relating to, or constituting a subfamily of the Uralic family of languages comprising various languages spoken in Hungary, Lapland, Finland, Estonia, and northwestern U.S.S.R. — **Finno–Ugric** *n*
fin·ny \ˈfin-ē\ *adj* **1 :** provided with or characterized by fins **2 :** relating to or being fish
fin sec *abbr* financial secretary
FIO *abbr* free in and out
fiord *var of* FJORD
fio·ri·tu·ra \fē-ˌȯr-ə-ˈtu̇r-ə\ *n, pl* **-tu·re** \-ˈtu̇r-ē\ [It, lit., flowering, fr. *fiorito,* pp. of *fiorire* to flower, fr. (assumed) VL *florire* — more at FLOURISH] **:** ORNAMENT 5
fip·ple flute \ˌfip-əl-\ *n* [origin unknown] **:** a tubular wind instrument (as a flageolet, pipe, or recorder) characterized mainly by a whistle mouthpiece and finger holes
[1]**fir** \ˈfər\ *n* [ME, fr. OE *fyrh;* akin to OHG *forha* fir, L *quercus* oak] **1 :** any of a genus (*Abies*) of north temperate evergreen trees of the pine family that have flattish leaves, smooth circular leaf scars, and erect cones and are valued for their wood; *also* **:** any of various conifers (as the Douglas fir) of other genera **2 :** the wood of a fir
[2]**fir** *abbr* firkin
[1]**fire** \ˈfī(ə)r\ *n, often attrib* [ME, fr. OE *fȳr;* akin to OHG *fiur* fire, Gk *pyr*] **1 a** (1) **:** the phenomenon of combustion manifested in light, flame, and heat (2) **:** one of the four elements of the alchemists **b** (1) **:** burning passion **:** ARDOR (2) **:** liveliness of imagination **:** INSPIRATION **2 :** fuel in a state of combustion (as on a hearth) **3 a :** a destructive burning (as of a building) **b** (1) **:** death or torture by fire (2) **:** severe trial or ordeal **4 :** BRILLIANCY, LUMINOSITY ⟨the ~ of a gem⟩ **5 a :** the discharge of firearms **b :** intense verbal attack **c :** a rapidly delivered series (as of remarks) — **fire·less** \-ləs\ *adj* — **on fire :** EAGER, BURNING — **under fire 1 :** exposed to the firing of an enemy's weapons **2 :** under attack
[2]**fire** *vb* **fired; fir·ing** *vt* **1 a :** to set on fire **:** KINDLE; *also* **:** IGNITE ⟨~ a rocket engine⟩ **b** (1) **:** to give life or spirit to **:** INSPIRE (2) **:** to fill with passion **:** INFLAME **c :** to light up as if by fire **2 a :** to drive out or away by or as if by fire **b :** to dismiss from a position **3 a** (1) **:** to cause to explode **:** DETONATE (2) **:** to propel from or as if from a gun **:** DISCHARGE, LAUNCH ⟨~ a rocket⟩ (3) **:** to score (a number) in a game or contest **b :** to throw with speed **:** HURL **c :** to utter with force and rapidity **4 :** to apply fire or fuel to: as **a :** to process by applying heat **b :** to feed or serve the fire of ~ *vi* **1 a :** to take fire **:** KINDLE, IGNITE **b** *of an internal-combustion engine* **:** to have the explosive charge ignite at the proper time **2 a :** to become irritated or angry — often used with *up* **b :** to become filled with excitement or enthusiasm **3 a :** to discharge a firearm **b :** to emit or let fly an object **4 :** to tend a fire ***syn*** see LIGHT — **fir·er** *n*
fire ant *n* **:** any of a genus (*Solenopsis*) of fiercely stinging omnivorous ants; *esp* **:** IMPORTED FIRE ANT
fire·arm \ˈfī(ə)r-ˌärm\ *n* **:** a weapon from which a shot is discharged by gunpowder — usu. used only of small arms
fire·ball \ˈfī(ə)r-ˌbȯl\ *n* **1 :** a ball of fire; *also* **:** something resembling such a ball ⟨the primordial ~ associated with the beginning of the universe —*Scientific American*⟩ **2 :** a brilliant meteor that may trail bright sparks **3 :** the highly luminous cloud of vapor and dust created by a nuclear explosion **4 :** a highly energetic person **:** HUSTLER
fire·bird \-ˌbərd\ *n* **:** any of several small birds (as the Baltimore oriole or the scarlet tanager) having brilliant orange or red plumage
fire blight *n* **:** a destructive highly infectious disease of apples, pears, and related fruits caused by a bacterium (*Erwinia amylovora*)
fire·boat \ˈfī(ə)r-ˌbōt\ *n* **:** a ship equipped with fire-fighting apparatus
fire·bomb \-ˌbäm\ *n* **:** an incendiary bomb — **firebomb** *vt*
fire·box \-ˌbäks\ *n* **1 :** a chamber (as of a furnace or steam boiler) that contains a fire **2 :** a box containing an apparatus for transmitting an alarm to a fire station
fire·brand \-ˌbrand\ *n* **1 :** a piece of burning wood **2 :** one that creates unrest or strife **:** AGITATOR
fire·break \-ˌbrāk\ *n* **:** a barrier of cleared or plowed land intended to check a forest or grass fire
fire·brick \-ˌbrik\ *n* **:** a refractory brick capable of sustaining high temperature that is used esp. for lining furnaces or fireplaces
fire brigade *n* **:** a body of fire fighters: as **a :** a private, institutional, or temporary fire-fighting organization **b** *Brit* **:** FIRE DEPARTMENT
fire·bug \ˈfī(ə)r-ˌbəg\ *n* **:** INCENDIARY, PYROMANIAC
fire·clay \-ˌklā\ *n* **:** clay capable of withstanding high temperatures that is used esp. for firebrick and crucibles
fire control *n* **1 :** the planning, preparation, and delivery of gunfire on targets **2 :** the control or extinction of fires
fire·crack·er \ˈfī(ə)r-ˌkrak-ər\ *n* **:** a usu. paper cylinder containing an explosive and a fuse and usu. discharged to make a noise
fire–cured \-ˈkyu̇(ə)rd\ *adj* **:** cured over open fires in direct contact with the smoke ⟨~ tobacco⟩ — compare FLUE-CURED
fire·damp \-ˌdamp\ *n* **:** a combustible mine gas that consists chiefly of methane; *also* **:** the explosive mixture of this gas with air
fire department *n* **1 :** an organization for preventing or extinguishing fires; *esp* **:** a government division (as in a municipality) having these duties **2 :** the members of a fire department
fire·drake \ˈfī(ə)r-ˌdrāk\ *n* [ME *firdrake,* fr. OE *fȳrdraca,* fr. *fȳr* + *draca* dragon — more at DRAKE] **:** a fire-breathing dragon esp. in Teutonic mythology
fire drill *n* **:** a practice drill in extinguishing fires or in the conduct and manner of exit in case of fire
fire–eat·er \ˈfī(ə)r-ˌēt-ər\ *n* **1 :** a performer who pretends to eat fire **2 a :** a violent or pugnacious person **b :** one who displays very militant or aggressive partisanship (as on political questions)
fire–eat·ing \-ˌēt-iŋ\ *adj* **:** violent or highly militant in disposition, bearing, or policy ⟨a ~ radical⟩
fire engine *n* **:** a usu. mobile apparatus for directing an extinguishing agent upon fires
fire escape *n* **:** a device for escape from a burning building; *esp* **:** a metal stairway attached to the outside of a building
fire extinguisher *n* **:** a portable or wheeled apparatus for putting out small fires by ejecting fire-extinguishing chemicals
fire·fight \ˈfī(ə)r-ˌfīt\ *n* **:** an often spontaneous exchange of fire between opposing military units
fire fighter *n* **:** one who fights fires **:** FIREMAN 1 — **fire fighting** *n*
fire·fly \ˈfī(ə)r-ˌflī\ *n* **:** any of various winged nocturnal beetles (esp. family Lampyridae) that produce a bright soft intermittent light by oxidation of luciferin esp. for courtship purposes
fire·guard \-ˌgärd\ *n* **1 :** FIRE SCREEN **2 :** FIREBREAK **3 :** one who watches for the outbreak of fire; *also* **:** one whose duty is to extinguish fires
fire hall *n* **:** FIRE STATION
fire·house \ˈfī(ə)r-ˌhau̇s\ *n* **:** FIRE STATION
fire irons *n pl* **:** utensils (as tongs) for tending a fire esp. in a fireplace
fire·light \ˈfī(ə)r-ˌlīt\ *n* **:** the light of a fire (as in a fireplace)
fire·lock \-ˌläk\ *n* **1 :** a gunlock employing a slow match to ignite the powder charge; *also* **:** a gun having such a lock **2 a :** FLINTLOCK **b :** WHEEL LOCK
fire·man \-mən\ *n* **1 :** a member of a company organized to fight fires **:** FIRE FIGHTER **2 :** one who tends or feeds fires **:** STOKER **3**

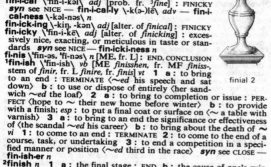

: an enlisted man in the navy who works with engineering machinery **4** : a relief pitcher in baseball
fire opal *n* : GIRASOL 2
fire·place \ˈfī(ə)r-ˌplās\ *n* **1** : a framed opening made in a chimney to hold an open fire : HEARTH; *also* : a metal container with a smoke pipe used for the same purpose **2** : an outdoor structure of brick, stone, or metal for an open fire
fire·plug \-ˌpləg\ *n* : HYDRANT
fire·pow·er \-ˌpau̇(-ə)r\ *n* **1** : the capacity (as of a military unit) to deliver effective fire on a target **2** : the aggregate of effective missiles that can be placed upon a target **3** : the scoring action or potential of a team
[1]**fire·proof** \-ˈprüf\ *adj* : proof against or resistant to fire
[2]**fireproof** *vt* : to make fireproof
fire·room \ˈfī(ə)r-ˌrüm, -ˌru̇m\ *n* : STOKEHOLD 2
fire sale *n* : a sale of merchandise damaged in a fire
fire screen *n* : a protective and often ornamental screen before a fireplace
fire ship *n* : a ship carrying combustibles or explosives sent among the enemy's ships or works to set them on fire
[1]**fire·side** \ˈfī(ə)r-ˌsīd\ *n* **1** : a place near the fire or hearth **2** : HOME
[2]**fireside** *adj* : having an informal or intimate quality ⟨a report written in ~ language⟩ ⟨a ~ chat⟩
fire station *n* : a building housing fire apparatus and usu. firemen
fire·stone \ˈfī(ə)r-ˌstōn\ *n* **1** : pyrite formerly used for striking fire; *also* : FLINT **2** : a stone that will endure high heat
fire–stop \-ˌstäp\ *n* : material used to close open parts of a structure (as a building) for preventing the spread of fire — **fire–stop** *vt*
fire tower *n* : a tower (as in a forest) from which a watch for fires is maintained
fire·trap \ˈfī(ə)r-ˌtrap\ *n* : a place (as a building) apt to catch on fire or difficult to escape from in case of fire
fire truck *n* : an automotive vehicle equipped with fire-fighting apparatus
fire wall *n* : a wall constructed to prevent the spread of fire
fire·wa·ter \ˈfī(ə)r-ˌwȯt-ər, -ˌwät-\ *n* : strong alcoholic beverage
fire·weed \-ˌwēd\ *n* : any of several plants that grow esp. in clearings or burned districts: as **a** : a weedy composite (*Erechtites hieracifolia*) that has clusters of brush-shaped flower heads with no ray flowers **b** : a tall perennial (*Epilobium angustifolium*) of the evening-primrose family that has long spikes of pinkish purple flowers and is an important honey plant in some areas — called also *willow herb*
fire·wood \-ˌwu̇d\ *n* : wood cut for fuel
fire·work \-ˌwərk\ *n* **1** : a device for producing a striking display (as of light, noise, or smoke) by the combustion of explosive or flammable compositions **2** *pl* : a display of fireworks **3** *pl* **a** : a display of temper or intense conflict **b** : a spectacular display (as of artistic brilliance) ⟨~*s* of virtuosity⟩
fir·ing \ˈfī(ə)r-iŋ\ *n* **1** : the act or process of one that fires **2** : the process of maturing ceramic products by the application of heat **3** : FIREWOOD, FUEL **4** : the scorching of plants esp. by unfavorable soil conditions
firing line *n* **1** : a line from which fire is delivered against a target **2** : the forefront of an activity — used esp. in the phrase *on the firing line*
firing pin *n* : the pin that strikes the cartridge primer in the breech mechanism of a firearm
firing squad *n* **1** : a detachment detailed to fire volleys over the grave of one buried with military honors **2** : a detachment detailed to carry out a sentence of death by shooting
fir·kin \ˈfər-kən\ *n* [ME, deriv. of MD *veerdel* fourth] **1** : a small wooden vessel or cask **2** : any of various British units of capacity usu. equal to ¼ barrel
[1]**firm** \ˈfərm\ *adj* [ME *ferm*, fr. MF, fr. L *firmus*; akin to Gk *thronos* chair, throne] **1 a** : securely or solidly fixed in place **b** : not weak or uncertain : VIGOROUS **c** : having a solid or compact structure that resists stress or pressure **2 a** (1) : not subject to change or revision : SET, DEFINITE ⟨they gave us a ~ price⟩ (2) : not subject to price weakness : STEADY **b** : not easily moved or disturbed : STEADFAST **c** : WELL-FOUNDED **3** : indicating firmness or resolution ⟨a ~ mouth⟩ — **firm·ly** *adv* — **firm·ness** *n*
syn FIRM, HARD, SOLID *shared meaning element* : having a texture or consistency that resists deformation. FIRM implies such compactness and coherence and often elasticity of substance as provides resistance to pulling, distorting, cutting, or displacement ⟨a *firm* close-woven cloth⟩ ⟨*firm* healthy flesh⟩ ⟨the ground was *firm* enough to walk on⟩ HARD implies inpenetrability or strong resistance to pressure or tension but not elasticity ⟨diamond is one of the *hardest* of substances⟩ SOLID implies such density and coherence as enable a thing to maintain a fixed form in spite of external deforming forces ⟨ice is a *solid* form of water⟩ In extended use FIRM stresses stability, fixedness, or resolution ⟨a *firm* disciplinarian⟩ ⟨his purpose is *firm*⟩ HARD implies obduracy or lack of normal responsiveness ⟨a *hard* man to do business with⟩ SOLID typically implies substantiality or genuineness ⟨demand *solid* facts⟩ ⟨lived in *solid* comfort⟩ or it may imply complete reliability ⟨one of the most *solid* citizens of the community⟩ or sometimes unbroken continuity (as in time, feeling, or opinion) ⟨there had been a *solid* week of rain⟩ ***ant*** loose, flabby
[2]**firm** *vt* **1 a** : to make secure or fast : TIGHTEN ⟨~*ing* his grip on the racquet⟩ — often used with *up* **b** : to make solid or compact ⟨~ the soil⟩ **2** : to put into final form : SETTLE ⟨~ a contract⟩ — often used with *up* **3** : to give additional support to : STRENGTHEN — usu. used with *up* ⟨help ~ up the French franc — Herbert Harris⟩ ~ *vi* **1** : to become firm : HARDEN ⟨his face ~*ed* and he spoke with restrained anger⟩ — often used with *up* ⟨his opinions have not yet ~*ed* up⟩ **2** : to recover from a decline : IMPROVE ⟨the market ~*ed* slightly⟩ — often used with *up*
[3]**firm** *n* [G *firma*, fr. It, signature, deriv. of L *firmare* to make firm, confirm, fr. *firmus*] **1** : the name or title under which a company transacts business **2** : a partnership of two or more persons not recognized as a legal person distinct from the members composing it **3** : a business unit or enterprise
fir·ma·ment \ˈfər-mə-mənt\ *n* [ME, fr. LL & L; LL *firmamentum*, fr. L, support, fr. *firmare*] **1** : the vault or arch of the sky : HEAVENS **2** *obs* : BASIS — **fir·ma·men·tal** \ˌfər-mə-ˈment-ᵊl\ *adj*
fir·mer chisel \ˈfər-mər-\ *n* [F *fermoir* chisel, alter. of MF *formoir*, fr. *former* to form] : a woodworking chisel with a thin flat blade — see CHISEL illustration
firn \ˈfi(ə)rn\ *n* [G] : NÉVÉ
[1]**first** \ˈfərst\ *adj* [ME, fr. OE *fyrst*; akin to OHG *furist* first, OE *faran* to go — more at FARE] : preceding all others in time, order, or importance: as **a** : EARLIEST **b** : being the lowest forward gear or speed of a motor vehicle **c** : relating to or having the highest or most prominent part among a group of similar voices or instruments in concerted or ensemble music ⟨~ tenor⟩ ⟨~ violins⟩
[2]**first** *adv* **1 a** : before another in time, space, or importance ⟨~ we had cocktails⟩ — often used with *off* ⟨~ off he thanked us for the invitation⟩ **b** : for the first time **2** : in preference to something else : SOONER
[3]**first** *n* **1** — see NUMBER table **2** : something that is first: as **a** : the first occurrence or item of a kind **b** : the first forward gear or speed of a motor vehicle **c** : the highest or chief voice or instrument of a group **d** : an article of commerce of the finest grade **e** : the winning or highest place in a competition, examination, or contest **3** : FIRST BASE — **at first** : at the beginning : INITIALLY
first aid *n* : emergency care or treatment given to an ill or injured person before regular medical aid can be obtained
first base *n* **1** : the base that must be touched first by a base runner in baseball **2** : the player position for defending the area around first base **3** : the first step or stage in a course of action ⟨plan never got to *first base*⟩ — **first base·man** \-ˈbā-smən\ *n*
first·born \ˈfərs(t)-ˈbȯ(ə)rn\ *adj* : first brought forth : ELDEST — **firstborn** *n*
first cause *n* : the self-created source of all causality
first class *n* : the first or highest group in a classification: as **a** : the highest of usu. three classes of travel accommodations **b** : a class of mail that comprises letters, postcards, or matter sealed against inspection — **first–class** *adj or adv*
first class·man \ˈfərs(t)-ˈklas-mən\ *n* : a fourth-year student in a military school (as West Point)
first consonant shift *n* : CONSONANT SHIFT a
first day cover *n* : a philatelic cover franked with a newly issued postage stamp and postmarked on the first day of issue at a city officially chosen for first day sale
first–degree burn *n* : a mild burn characterized by heat, pain, and reddening of the burned surface but not exhibiting blistering or charring of tissues
first down *n* **1** : the first of a series of four downs in which a football team must net a 10-yard gain to retain possession of the ball **2** : a gain of a total of 10 or more yards within four downs giving the team the right to start a new series of downs
first edition *n* **1 a** : the copies of a literary work first printed from the same type and issued at the same time **b** : the first press-run of a newspaper for a given date **2** : a single copy from a first edition
first estate *n, often cap F&E* : the first of the traditional political estates; *specif* : CLERGY
first floor *n* **1** : GROUND FLOOR **2** *Brit* : the floor next above the ground floor
first·fruits \ˈfərs(t)-ˈfrüts\ *n pl* **1** : the earliest gathered fruits offered to the Deity in acknowledgment of the gift of fruitfulness **2** : the earliest products or results of an endeavor
first·hand \ˈfərst-ˈhand\ *adj* : coming directly from the original source — **firsthand** *adv*
first lady *n, often cap F&L* **1** : the wife or hostess of the chief executive of a country or jurisdiction **2** : the leading woman of an art or profession
first lieutenant *n* **1** : a commissioned officer in the army, air force, or marine corps ranking above a second lieutenant and below a captain **2** : a naval officer responsible for a ship's upkeep
first·ling \ˈfərst-liŋ\ *n* **1** : the first of a class or kind **2** : the first produce or result of something
first·ly \-lē\ *adv* : in the first place : FIRST
first mortgage *n* : a mortgage that has priority as a lien over all mortgages and liens except those imposed by law
first name *n* : the name that stands first in one's full name
first night *n* **1** : the night on which a theatrical production is first performed at a given place **2** : the performance given on a first night
first–night·er \ˈfərs(t)-ˈnīt-ər\ *n* : a spectator at a first-night performance
first offender *n* : one legally convicted of an offense for the first time
first papers *n pl* : papers declaring intention filed by an applicant for citizenship as the first step in the naturalization process
first person *n* **1 a** : a set of linguistic forms (as verb forms, pronouns, and inflectional affixes) referring to the speaker or writer of the utterance in which they occur **b** : a linguistic form belonging to such a set **c** : reference of a linguistic form to the speaker or writer of the utterance in which it occurs **2** : a style of discourse marked by general use of verbs and pronouns of the first person ⟨a novel narrated in the *first person*⟩
[1]**first–rate** \ˈfərs(t)-ˈstrāt\ *adj* : of the first order of size, importance, or quality — **first–rate·ness** *n* — **first–rat·er** \-ˈstrāt-ər\ *n*
[2]**first–rate** *adv* : very well
First Reader *n* : a Christian Scientist chosen to conduct meetings for a specified time and specif. to read aloud from the writings of Mary Baker Eddy
first reading *n* : the first submitting of a bill before a quorum of a legislative assembly usu. by title or number only
first sergeant *n* **1** : a noncommissioned officer serving as the chief assistant to the commander of a military unit (as a company or squadron) **2** : the rank of a first sergeant; *specif* : a rank in the army above a platoon sergeant and below a command sergeant

major and in the marine corps above a gunnery sergeant and below a sergeant major

first–string \'fərs(t)-'striŋ\ adj **1 :** being a regular as distinguished from a substitute (as on a football team) **2 :** FIRST-RATE

first water n **1 :** the purest luster — used of gems **2 :** the highest grade, degree, or quality ⟨this is choral music of the *first water* —P. H. Lang⟩

firth \'fərth\ n [ME, fr. ON *fjörthr*] : ESTUARY

fisc \'fisk\ n [L *fiscus*] : a state or royal treasury

¹fis·cal \'fis-kəl\ adj [L *fiscalis*, fr. *fiscus* basket, treasury; akin to Gk *pithos* wine jar] **1 :** of or relating to taxation, public revenues, or public debt ⟨~ policy⟩ **2 :** of or relating to financial matters ⟨~ agent⟩ **syn** see FINANCIAL — **fis·cal·ly** \-kə-lē\ adv

²fiscal n : REVENUE STAMP

fiscal year n : an accounting period of 12 months

¹fish \'fish\ n, pl **fish** or **fish·es** often attrib [ME, fr. OE *fisc*; akin to OHG *fisc* fish, L *piscis*] **1 a :** an aquatic animal — usu. used in combination ⟨star*fish*⟩ ⟨cuttle*fish*⟩ **b :** any of numerous cold-blooded strictly aquatic craniate vertebrates that have typically an elongated somewhat spindle-shaped body terminating in a broad caudal fin, limbs in the form of fins when present at all, and a 2-chambered heart by which blood is sent through thoracic gills to be oxygenated **c** *fishes* pl, *cap* : PISCES **2 :** the flesh of fish used as food **3 :** FELLOW, CHAP ⟨a queer ~⟩ **4 :** something that resembles a fish: as **a :** a purchase used to fish the anchor **b :** a piece of wood or iron fastened alongside another member to strengthen it — **fish·less** \'fish-ləs\ adj — **fish·like** \-,līk\ adj — **fish out of water :** a person who is out of his proper sphere or element — **neither fish nor fowl :** one that does not belong to a particular class or category

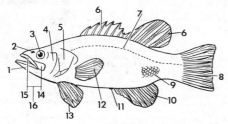

fish 1b: *1* mandible, *2* external naris, *3* eye, *4* cheek, *5* operculum, *6* dorsal fins, *7* lateral line, *8* caudal fin, *9* scales, *10* anal fin, *11* anus, *12* pectoral fin, *13* pelvic fin, *14* maxilla, *15* premaxilla, *16* upper jaw

²fish vi **1 :** to attempt to catch fish **2 :** to seek something by round-about means ⟨~ing for praise⟩ **3 a :** to search for something underwater (as with a dredge) ⟨~ for pearls⟩ **b :** to engage in a search by groping or feeling ⟨~ing around in her purse for her keys⟩ ~ vt **1 a :** to try to catch fish in ⟨~ the stream⟩ **b :** to fish with : use (as a boat, net, or bait) in fishing **2 a :** to catch or try to catch **b :** to draw forth as if fishing ⟨~ed the ball from under the car⟩ — **fish or cut bait :** to make a choice between alternatives

fish·able \'fish-ə-bəl\ adj : suitable, promising, or legally open for fishing — **fish·abil·i·ty** \,fish-ə-'bil-ət-ē\ n

fish–and–chips \,fish-ən-'chips\ n pl : fried fish and french fried potatoes

fish·bone \'fish-,bōn\ n : a bone of a fish

fish·bowl \-,bōl\ n **1 :** a bowl for the keeping of live fish **2 :** a place or condition that affords no privacy

fish cake n : a round fried cake made of shredded fish and mashed potato

fish duck n : MERGANSER

fish·er \'fish-ər\ n **1 :** one that fishes **2 a :** a large dark brown No. American arboreal carnivorous mammal (*Martes pennanti*) related to the weasels **b :** the fur or pelt of this animal

fish·er·man \-mən\ n **1 :** one who engages in fishing as an occupation or for pleasure **2 :** a ship used in commercial fishing

fisherman's bend n : a knot made by passing the end twice round a spar or through a ring and then back under both turns — see KNOT illustration

fish·ery \'fish-(ə-)rē\ n, pl **-er·ies 1 :** the act, process, occupation, or season of taking fish or other sea animals (as sponges or seals) : FISHING **2 :** a place for catching fish or taking other sea animals (as sponges or seals) **3 :** a fishing establishment; *also* : its fishermen **4 :** the legal right to take fish at a particular place or in particular waters **5 :** the technology of fishery — usu. used in pl.

fisher 2a

fish–eye \'fish-,ī\ adj : being, having, or produced by a wide-angle photographic lens that has a highly curved protruding front, that covers an angle of about 180 degrees, and that gives a circular image ⟨a ~ lens⟩

fish fry n **1 :** a meal (as a picnic) featuring fried fish **2 :** fried fish

fish hawk n : OSPREY 1

fish·hook \'fish-,hůk\ n : a usu. barbed hook for catching fish

fish·ing n **1 :** the sport or business of catching fish **2 :** a place for catching fish

fishing expedition n **1 :** a legal interrogation or examination to discover information for a later proceeding **2 :** an investigation

that does not stick to a stated objective and that uses questionable methods (as the irrelevant questioning of witnesses) in hope of uncovering incriminating or newsworthy evidence

fish joint n : a butt joint of timbers or rails in which the two abutting members are held in alignment by one or more fishplates

fish ladder n : a series of pools arranged like steps by which fishes can pass over a dam in going upstream

fish meal n : ground dried fish and fish waste used as fertilizer and animal food

fish·mong·er \'fish-,məŋ-gər, -,mäŋ-\ n, chiefly Brit : a fish dealer

fish·net \-,net\ n **1 :** netting fitted with floats and weights or a supporting frame for catching fish **2 :** a coarse open-mesh fabric

fish out vt : to exhaust the supply of fish in by fishing ⟨this lake has been *fished out*⟩

fish·plate \-,plāt\ n : a steel plate used to lap a butt joint

fish protein concentrate n : a protein-rich food additive obtained as a nearly colorless and tasteless powder from ground whole fish — abbr. FPC

fish stick n : a small elongated breaded fillet of fish

fish story n [fr. the traditional exaggeration by fishermen of the size of fish almost caught] : an extravagant or incredible story

fish·tail \'fish-,tāl\ vi **1 :** to swing the tail of an airplane from side to side to reduce speed esp. when landing **2 :** to have the rear end slide from side to side out of control while moving forward ⟨the car ~ed on the icy curve⟩

fish·way \-,wā\ n : a contrivance enabling fish to pass around a fall or dam in a stream; *specif* : FISH LADDER

fish·wife \-,wīf\ n **1 :** a woman who sells fish **2 :** a vulgar abusive woman

fishy \'fish-ē\ adj **fish·i·er; -est 1 :** of or resembling fish esp. in taste or odor **2 :** creating doubt or suspicion : QUESTIONABLE

fishy·back \-,bak\ n [*fish* + *-y* + *-back* (as in *piggyback*)] : the movement of truck trailers or freight containers by barge or ship — compare BIRDYBACK, PIGGYBACK

fis·sile \'fis-əl, 'fis-,il\ adj **1 :** capable of being split or divided in the direction of the grain or along natural planes of cleavage ⟨~ wood⟩ ⟨~ crystals⟩ **2 :** FISSIONABLE — **fis·sil·i·ty** \fis-'il-ət-ē\ n

¹fis·sion \'fish-ən also 'fizh-\ n [L *fission-, fissio*, fr. *fissus*, pp. of *findere* to split — more at BITE] **1 :** a splitting or breaking up into parts **2 :** reproduction by spontaneous division of the body into two or more parts each of which grows into a complete organism **3 a :** the splitting of a molecule into simpler molecules **b :** the splitting of an atomic nucleus resulting in the release of large amounts of energy — **fis·sion·al** \-'l\ adj

²fission vb **fis·sioned; fis·sion·ing** \'fish-(ə-)niŋ, 'fizh-\ vt : to cause to undergo fission ~ vi : to undergo fission

fis·sion·able \'fish-(ə-)nə-bəl, 'fizh-\ adj : capable of undergoing fission — **fis·sion·abil·i·ty** \,fish-(ə-)nə-'bil-ət-ē, ,fizh-\ n — **fis·sionable** n

fission bomb n : ATOM BOMB 1

fis·sip·a·rous \fis-'ip-ə-rəs\ adj [L *fissus* + E *-parous*] **1 :** producing new biological units or individuals by fission **2 :** tending to break up into parts : DIVISIVE ⟨he knows how to reconcile ~ elements in his party —W. H. Stevenson⟩ — **fis·sip·a·rous·ly** adv — **fis·sip·a·rous·ness** n

fis·si·ped \'fis-ə-,ped\ adj [LL *fissiped-, fissipes*, fr. L *fissus* + *ped-, pes* foot — more at FOOT] : of or relating to a suborder (Fissipeda) of carnivores (as cats, dogs, and bears) — **fissiped** n

¹fis·sure \'fish-ər\ n **1 :** a narrow opening or crack of considerable length and depth usu. occurring from some breaking or parting **2 :** a separation or disagreement in thought or viewpoint : SCHISM ⟨~s in a political party⟩ **3 a :** a natural cleft between body parts or in the substance of an organ **b :** a break or lesion in tissue usu. at the junction of skin and mucous membrane

²fissure vb **fis·sured; fis·sur·ing** vt : to break into fissures : CLEAVE ~ vi : CRACK, DIVIDE

¹fist \'fist\ n [ME, fr. OE *fyst*; akin to OHG *fūst* fist, OSlav *pęsti*] **1 :** the hand clenched with the fingers doubled into the palm and the thumb doubled inward across the fingers ⟨~ in grasping : CLUTCH **3 :** INDEX 5

²fist vt **1 :** to clench into a fist **2 :** to grip with the fist : HANDLE

-fist·ed \'fis-təd\ comb form : having (such or so many) fists ⟨two=fisted⟩ ⟨tight*fisted*⟩

fist·fight \'fist-,fīt\ n : a usu. spontaneous fight with bare fists

fist·ful \-,ful\ n **1 :** HANDFUL ⟨a ~ of coins⟩ **2 :** a considerable number ⟨a whole ~ of musicians —Thomas Lask⟩

fist·ic \'fis-tik\ adj : of or relating to boxing or to fighting with the fists

fist·i·cuffs \'fis-ti-,kəfs\ n pl [alter. of *fisty cuff*, fr. *fisty* (fistic) + *cuff*] : a fight with the fists

fist·note \'fis(t)-,nōt\ n : matter in a text to which attention is directed by means of an index mark

fis·tu·la \'fis(h)-chə-lə\ n, pl **-las** or **-lae** \-,lē, -,lī\ [ME, fr. L, pipe, fistula] : an abnormal passage leading from an abscess or hollow organ to the body surface or from one hollow organ to another

fis·tu·lous \-ləs\ adj **1 :** of, relating to, or having the form or nature of a fistula **2 :** hollow like a pipe or reed

fistulous withers n pl but sing or pl in constr : a deep-seated chronic inflammation of the withers of the horse in which bloody fluid is discharged

¹fit \'fit\ n [ME, fr. OE *fitt*; akin to OS *fittea* division of a poem, OHG *fizza* skein] archaic : a division of a poem or song

²fit n [ME, fr. OE *fitt* strife] **1 a :** a sudden violent attack of a disease (as epilepsy) esp. when marked by convulsions or unconsciousness : PAROXYSM **b :** a sudden but transient attack of a physical disturbance **2 :** a sudden burst or flurry (as of activity)

⟨in a ~ of efficiency he answered all his mail in an hour⟩ **3** : an emotional outburst ⟨a ~ of anger⟩ — **by fits** *or* **by fits and starts** : in an impulsive and irregular manner

3fit *adj* **fit·ter; fit·test** [ME; akin to ME *fitten*] **1 a** (1) : adapted to an end or design : suitable by nature or by art (2) : adapted to the environment so as to be capable of surviving **b** : acceptable from a particular viewpoint (as of competence or morality) ⟨not ~ to be a father⟩ **2 a** : put into a suitable state : made ready ⟨get the house ~ for company⟩ **b** : being in such a state as to be ready to do or suffer something ⟨fair ~ to cry I was —Bryan MacMahon⟩ **3** : COMPETENT, QUALIFIED **4** : sound physically and mentally : HEALTHY — **fit·ly** *adv* — **fit·ness** *n*
syn FIT, SUITABLE, MEET, PROPER, APPROPRIATE, FITTING, APT, HAPPY, FELICITOUS *shared meaning element* : right with respect to some end, need, use, or circumstance ***ant*** unfit
— **fit to be tied** : extremely angry or irritated

4fit *vb* **fit·ted** *also* **fit; fit·ting** [ME *fitten*, fr. or akin to MD *vitten* to be suitable; akin to OHG *fizza* skein] *vt* **1 a** : to be suitable for or to : harmonize with **b** *archaic* : to be seemly or proper for ⟨it ~*s* us then to be as provident as fear may teach us —Shak.⟩ **2 a** : to be correctly adjusted to or shaped for **b** : to insert or adjust until correctly in place **c** : to make a place or room for : ACCOMMODATE **3** : to be in agreement or accord with ⟨the theory ~*s* all the facts⟩ **4 a** : to put into a condition of readiness **b** : to bring to a required form and size : ADJUST **c** : to cause to conform to or suit something **5** : SUPPLY, EQUIP ⟨*fitted* the ship with new engines⟩ — often used with *out* **6** : to adjust (a smooth curve of a specified type) to a given set of points ~ *vi* **1** *archaic* : to be seemly, proper, or suitable **2** : to conform to a particular shape or size **3** : to be in harmony or accord : BELONG ***syn*** see PREPARE — **fit·ter** *n*

5fit *n* **1** : the quality, state, or manner of being fitted or adapted **2** : the manner in which clothing fits the wearer **3** : the degree of closeness with which surfaces are brought together in an assembly of parts **4** : the conformity between an experimental result and theoretical expectation or between data and an approximating curve ⟨a statistical test of goodness of ~⟩

6fit *dial past of* FIGHT

fitch \ˈfich\ *or* **fitch·ew** \ˈfich-(ˌ)ü\ *n* [ME *fiche, ficheux*, fr. MF or MD; MF *fichau*, fr. MD *vitsau*] **1** : POLECAT 1 **2** : the fur or pelt of the polecat

fitch·et \ˈfich-ət\ *n* : POLECAT 1

fit·ful \ˈfit-fəl\ *adj* **1** *obs* : characterized by fits or paroxysms **2** : having a spasmodic or intermittent character : IRREGULAR ⟨~ sleep⟩ — **fit·ful·ly** \-fə-lē\ *adv* — **fit·ful·ness** *n*
syn FITFUL, SPASMODIC, CONVULSIVE *shared meaning element* : lacking steadiness or regularity (as in course, movement, or activity) ***ant*** constant

fit·ment \ˈfit-mənt\ *n* [4*fit*] **1** : EQUIPMENT **2** *pl* : FITTINGS

1fit·ting \ˈfit-iŋ\ *adj* : of a kind appropriate to the situation ⟨made a ~ answer⟩ ***syn*** see FIT ***ant*** unfitting — **fit·ting·ly** \-iŋ-lē\ *adv* — **fit·ting·ness** *n*

2fitting *n* **1** : an action or act of one that fits; *specif* : a trying on of clothes which are in the process of being made or altered **2** : a small often standardized accessory part ⟨an electrical ~⟩

five \ˈfīv\ *n* [ME, fr. *five*, adj., fr. OE *fīf*; akin to OHG *finf* five, L *quinque*, Gk *pente*] **1** — see NUMBER table **2** : the fifth in a set or series ⟨the ~ of clubs⟩ **3** : something having five units or members; *esp* : a basketball team **4** : a 5-dollar bill **5** : FIFTEEN 2 — **five** *adj or pron*

five-and-ten \ˌfī-vən-ˈten\ *also* **five-and-dime** \-ˈdīm\ *n* [fr. the fact that all articles in such stores were formerly priced at either 5 or 10 cents] : a variety store that carries chiefly inexpensive items

five-fin·ger \ˈfīv-ˌfiŋ-gər\ *n* : CINQUEFOIL 1

five·fold \ˈfīv-ˌfōld, -ˈfōld\ *adj* **1** : having five units or members **2** : being five times as great or as many — **five·fold** \-ˈfōld\ *adv*

five of a kind : four cards of the same rank plus a wild card in one hand — see POKER illustration

fiv·er \ˈfī-vər\ *n* **1** *slang* : a 5-dollar bill **2** *slang* : a 5-pound note

five-star \ˌfīv-ˈstär\ *adj* : of first class or quality ⟨there are not enough ~ works of art to go around —J. T. Soby⟩

1fix \ˈfiks\ *vb* [ME *fixen*, fr. L *fixus*, pp. of *figere* to fasten — more at DIKE] *vt* **1 a** : to make firm, stable, or stationary **b** : to give a permanent or final form to: as (1) : to change into a stable compound or available form ⟨bacteria that ~ nitrogen⟩ (2) : to kill, harden, and preserve for microscopic study (3) : to make the image of (a photographic film) permanent by removing unused salts **c** : AFFIX, ATTACH **2** : to hold or direct steadily ⟨~*es* his eyes on the horizon⟩ **3 a** : to set or place definitely : ESTABLISH **b** : ASSIGN ⟨~ the blame⟩ **4** : to set in order : ADJUST **5** : to get ready : PREPARE ⟨~ lunch⟩ **6 a** : REPAIR, MEND ⟨~ the clock⟩ **b** : RESTORE, CURE ⟨the doctor ~*ed* him up⟩ **c** : SPAY, CASTRATE **7 a** : to get even with **b** : to influence the actions, outcome, or effect of by improper or illegal methods ⟨the jury had been ~*ed*⟩ ~ *vi* **1** : to become firm, stable, or fixed **2** : to get set : be about to ⟨we're ~*ing* to leave soon⟩ ***syn*** **1** see SET ***ant*** alter, abrogate (*as a rule*) **2** see FASTEN — **fix·able** \ˈfik-sə-bəl\ *adj*

2fix *n* **1** : a position of difficulty or embarrassment : a trying predicament **2 a** : the position (as of a ship) determined by bearings, observations, or radio **b** : a determination of one's position **3** : an act of obtaining special privilege or immunity from the law by bribery or collusion; *also* : the money paid to obtain such privilege **4** : a shot of a narcotic **5** : FIXATION

fix·ate \ˈfik-ˌsāt\ *vb* **fix·at·ed; fix·at·ing** *vt* **1** : to make fixed, stationary, or unchanging **2** : to focus one's gaze on **3** : to direct (the libido) toward an infantile form of gratification ~ *vi* **1** : to focus or concentrate one's gaze or attention **2** : to undergo arrestment at a stage of development

fix·a·tion \fik-ˈsā-shən\ *n* : the act, process, or result of fixing or fixating: as **a** : a persistent concentration of libidinal energies upon objects characteristic of psychosexual stages of development preceding the genital stage **b** : stereotyped behavior (as in response to frustration) **c** : an obsessive or unhealthy preoccupation or attachment

fix·a·tive \ˈfik-sət-iv\ *n* : something that fixes or sets: as **a** : a substance added to a perfume esp. to prevent too rapid evaporation **b** : a varnish used esp. for the protection of crayon drawings **c** : a substance used to fix living tissue — **fixative** *adj*

fixed \ˈfikst\ *adj* **1 a** : securely placed or fastened : STATIONARY **b** (1) : NONVOLATILE (2) : formed into a chemical compound **c** (1) : not subject to change or fluctuation : SETTLED ⟨a ~ income⟩ (2) : firmly set in the mind ⟨a ~ idea⟩ (3) : having a final or crystallized form or character (4) : recurring on the same date from year to year ⟨~ holidays⟩ **d** : IMMOBILE, CONCENTRATED ⟨a ~ stare⟩ **2** : supplied with something (as money) needed or desirable ⟨comfortably ~ by the standards of his class — Frederick Lane⟩ — **fixed·ly** \ˈfik-səd-lē, ˈfiks-tlē\ *adv* — **fixed·ness** \ˈfik-səd-nəs, ˈfiks(t)-nəs\ *n*

fixed charge *n* **1** : a regularly recurring expense (as rent, taxes, or interest) that must be met when due **2** : FIXED COST

fixed cost *n* : an indirect cost (as maintenance) that continues with little variation irrespective of the level of production

fixed oil *n* : a nonvolatile oil; *esp* : a fatty oil — compare ESSENTIAL OIL

fixed-point *adj* : involving or being a mathematical notation (as in a decimal system) in which the point separating whole numbers and fractions is fixed — compare FLOATING-POINT

fixed star *n* : a star so distant that its motion can be measured only by very precise observations over long periods

fix·er \ˈfik-sər\ *n* : one that fixes: as **a** : one that intervenes to enable a person to circumvent the law or obtain a political favor **b** : one that adjusts matters or disputes by negotiation

fix·ing \-siŋ\ *n* **1** : the act or process of one that fixes **2** *pl* *often* -sənz\ : TRIMMINGS ⟨a turkey dinner with all the ~*s*⟩

fix·i·ty \ˈfik-sət-ē\ *n*, *pl* **-ties** **1** : the quality or state of being fixed or stable **2** : something that is fixed : FIXTURE

fix·ture \ˈfiks-chər\ *n* [modif. of LL *fixura*, fr. L *fixus*] **1** : the act or process of fixing : the state of being fixed **2 a** : something that is fixed or attached (as to a building) as a permanent appendage or as a structural part ⟨a fluorescent lighting ~⟩ ⟨a plumbing ~⟩ **b** : a device for supporting work during machining **c** : a chattel so annexed to realty that it may be regarded as legally a part of it **3** : a familiar or invariably present element or feature in some particular setting; *esp* : a person long associated with a place or activity **4** : a settled date or time esp. for a sporting or festive event; *also* : such an event esp. as a regularly scheduled affair

1fizz \ˈfiz\ *vi* [prob. of imit. origin] **1** : to make a hissing or sputtering sound : EFFERVESCE **2** : to exhibit excitement or exhilaration

2fizz *n* **1 a** : a hissing sound **b** : SPIRIT, LIVELINESS **2** : an effervescent beverage — **fizzy** \-ē\ *adj*

1fiz·zle \ˈfiz-əl\ *vi* **fiz·zled; fiz·zling** \-(ə-)liŋ\ [prob. alter. of *fist* (to break wind)] **1** : FIZZ **2** : to fail or end feebly esp. after a promising start — often used with *out*

2fizzle *n* : an abortive effort : FAILURE

fjeld \fē-ˈel\ *n* [Dan] : a barren plateau of the Scandinavian upland

fjord \fē-ˈȯ(ə)rd\ *n* [Norw *fjord*, fr. ON *fjǫrthr* — more at FORD] : a narrow inlet of the sea between cliffs or steep slopes

FJP *abbr* Federation of Jewish Philanthropies of New York

fl *abbr* **1** floor **2** florin **3** [L *floruit*] flourished **4** fluid

FL *abbr* **1** Florida **2** focal length **3** foreign language

Fla *abbr* Florida

flab \ˈflab\ *n* [back-formation fr. *flabby*] : soft flabby body tissue

flab·ber·gast \ˈflab-ər-ˌgast\ *vt* [origin unknown] : to overwhelm with shock, surprise, or wonder : DUMBFOUND ***syn*** see SURPRISE — **flab·ber·gast·ing·ly** \-ˌgas-tiŋ-lē\ *adv*

flab·by \ˈflab-ē\ *adj* **flab·bi·er; -est** [alter. of *flappy*] **1** : lacking resilience or firmness : FLACCID **2** : weak and ineffective : FEEBLE ***syn*** see LIMP ***ant*** firm — **flab·bi·ly** \ˈflab-ə-lē\ *adv* — **flab·bi·ness** \ˈflab-ē-nəs\ *n*

fla·bel·late \flə-ˈbel-ət, ˈflab-ə-ˌlāt\ *adj* : shaped like a fan

flabelli- *comb form* [L, fr. *flabellum*] : fan ⟨*flabelli*form⟩

fla·bel·li·form \flə-ˈbel-ə-ˌfȯrm\ *adj* : FLABELLATE

fla·bel·lum \flə-ˈbel-əm\ *n*, *pl* **-la** \-ə\ [NL, fr. L, fan] : a body organ or part resembling a fan

flac·cid \ˈflak-səd, ˈflas-əd\ *adj* [L *flaccidus*, fr. *flaccus* flabby] **1 a** : lacking normal or youthful firmness : FLABBY ⟨~ muscles⟩ **b** *of a plant part* : deficient in turgor **2** : lacking vigor or force ⟨~ leadership⟩ ***syn*** see LIMP ***ant*** resilient — **flac·cid·i·ty** \fla(k)-ˈsid-ət-ē\ *n* — **flac·cid·ly** \ˈflak-səd-lē, ˈflas-əd-\ *adv*

1flack \ˈflak\ *n* [origin unknown] : one who provides publicity; *esp* : PRESS AGENT

2flack *var of* FLAK

fla·con \ˈflak-ən, -ˌän; fla-ˈkōⁿ\ *n* [F, fr. MF, bottle — more at FLAGON] : a small usu. ornamental bottle with a tight cap

1flag \ˈflag\ *n* [ME *flagge* reed, rush] : any of various monocotyledonous plants with long ensiform leaves: as **a** : IRIS; *esp* : a wild iris **b** : SWEET FLAG **c** : CATTAIL

2flag *n* [ME *flagge*, fr. ON *flaga* slab; akin to OE *flēan* to flay — more at FLAY] : a hard evenly stratified stone that splits into flat pieces suitable for paving; *also* : a piece of such stone

3flag *vt* **flagged; flag·ging** : to lay (as a pavement) with flags

4flag *n*, *often attrib* [perh. fr. 1*flag*] **1** : a usu. rectangular piece of fabric of distinctive design that is used as a symbol (as of a nation) or as a signaling device **2 a** : something used like a flag to signal or attract attention **b** : one of the cross strokes of a musical note less than a quarter note in value **c** : MASTHEAD 2b **3 a** : FLAGSHIP **b** : an admiral functioning in his office of command **c** : NATIONALITY; *esp* : the nationality of registration of a ship or aircraft

5flag *vt* **flagged; flag·ging** **1** : to put a flag on (as for identification) ⟨*flagged* the important pages by clipping red tabs to the margin⟩ **2** : to signal with or as if with a flag; *esp* : to signal to stop ⟨*flagged* the train⟩

6flag *vi* **flagged; flag·ging** [origin unknown] **1 a** : to hang loose without stiffness **b** *of a plant* : to droop esp. from lack of water **2 a** : to become unsteady, feeble, or spiritless : DROOP ⟨his interest *flagged*⟩ **b** : to decline in interest or attraction ⟨when everyone had had a say the topic *flagged*⟩

flag day n **1** cap F&D : June 14 observed in various states in commemoration of the adoption in 1777 of the official U.S. flag **2** Brit : a day on which charitable contributions are solicited in exchange for small flags

fla·gel·lant \'flaj-ə-lənt, flə-'jel-ənt\ n : one that whips: as **a** : a person who scourges himself as a public penance **b** : a person who responds sexually to being beaten by or to beating another person — **flagellant** adj — **fla·gel·lant·ism** \-,iz-əm\ n

fla·gel·lar \flə-'jel-ər, 'flaj-ə-lər\ adj : of or relating to a flagellum

¹fla·gel·late \'flaj-ə-,lāt\ vt **-lat·ed; -lat·ing** [L flagellatus, pp. of flagellare, fr. flagellum, dim. of flagrum whip; akin to ON blaka to wave] **1** : WHIP, SCOURGE **2** : to drive or punish as if by whipping

²fla·gel·late \'flaj-ə-lət, -,lāt; flə-'jel-ət\ adj [NL flagellatus, fr. flagellum] **1** a or **flag·el·lat·ed** \'flaj-ə-,lāt-əd\ : having flagella **b** : shaped like a flagellum **2** [³flagellate] : of, relating to, or caused by flagellates ⟨~ diarrhea⟩

³flagellate \like] n [NL Flagellata, class of unicellular organisms, fr. neut. pl. of flagellatus] : a flagellate protozoan or alga

flag·el·la·tion \,flaj-ə-'lā-shən\ n : the act or practice of flagellating; esp : the practice of a flagellant

fla·gel·la·tion : the formation or arrangement of flagella

fla·gel·lum \flə-'jel-əm\ n, pl **-la** \-ə\ also **-lums** [NL, fr. L, whip, shoot of a plant] : any of various elongated filiform appendages of plants or animals: as **a** : the slender distal part of an antenna **b** : a long tapering process that projects singly or in groups from a cell and is the primary organ of motion of many microorganisms **c** : a long slender shoot

fla·geo·let \,flaj-ə-'let, -'lā\ n [F, fr. OF flajolet, fr. flajol flute, fr. (assumed) VL flabeolum, fr. L flare to blow — more at BLOW] : a small fipple flute resembling the treble recorder

flag football n : a variation of football in which a player must remove a flag attached to the ballcarrier's clothing to stop the play

¹flag·ging \'flag-iŋ\ adj **1** : LANGUID, WEAK **2** : becoming progressively less : DWINDLING — **flag·ging·ly** \-iŋ-lē\ adv

²flagging n : a pavement or walk of flagstones

fla·gi·tious \flə-'jish-əs\ adj [ME flagicious, fr. L flagitiosus, fr. flagitium shameful thing; akin to L flagrum whip] : marked by outrageous or scandalous crime or vice : VILLAINOUS syn see VICIOUS — **fla·gi·tious·ly** adv — **fla·gi·tious·ness** n

flag·man \'flag-mən\ n : one who signals with or as if with a flag

flag officer n [fr. his being entitled to display a flag with one or more stars indicating his rank] : any of the officers in the navy or coast guard above captain — compare GENERAL OFFICER

flag of truce : a white flag carried or displayed to an enemy as an invitation to conference or parley

flag·on \'flag-ən\ n [ME, fr. MF flascon, flacon bottle, fr. LL flascon-, flasco — more at FLASK] **1 a** : a large usu. metal or pottery vessel with handle and spout and often a lid **b** : a large bulging short-necked bottle **2** : the contents of a flagon

flag·pole \'flag-,pōl\ n : a pole on which to raise a flag

fla·grance \'flā-grən(t)s also 'flag-rən(t)s\ n : FLAGRANCY

fla·gran·cy \'flā-grən-sē also 'flag-rən-\ n : the quality or state of being flagrant

flag rank n : the rank of a flag officer

fla·grant \'flā-grənt also 'flag-rənt\ adj [L flagrant-, flagrans, prp. of flagrare to burn — more at BLACK] **1** archaic : FLAMING, GLOWING **2** : extremely or purposefully conspicuous usu. because of uncommon objectionableness or evil — **fla·grant·ly** adv

flagon 1a

syn FLAGRANT, GLARING, GROSS, RANK shared meaning element : conspicuously bad or objectionable. FLAGRANT applies usually to offenses or errors so bad that they can neither escape notice nor be condoned ⟨open and flagrant mutiny⟩ ⟨flagrant abuse of his office⟩ GLARING implies painful or damaging obtrusiveness of something that is conspicuously wrong, faulty, or improper ⟨this evil is so glaring, so inexcusable — G. B. Shaw⟩ ⟨a glaring inconsistency in his argument⟩ GROSS, more likely to apply to attitudes, qualities, or faults than to specific evil acts or offenses, attributes an unbounded and inexcusable badness to what it describes ⟨gross carelessness⟩ ⟨gross stupidity⟩ RANK applies to what is openly and extremely objectionable and utterly condemned ⟨O, my offense is rank, it smells to heaven — Shak.⟩

fla·gran·te de·lic·to \flə-,grant-ē-di-'lik-(,)tō\ adv [ML, lit., while the crime is blazing] : in the very act of committing a misdeed : RED-HANDED

flag·ship \'flag-,ship\ n **1** : the ship that carries the commander of a fleet or subdivision thereof and flies his flag **2** : the finest, largest, or most important one esp. in a fleet of ships, a radio network, or a chain of newspapers ⟨the editorial tone of the fiercely conservative chain is set by the ~ paper — J. C. Goulden⟩

flag·staff \-,staf\ n : a staff on which a flag is hoisted

flag·stick \-,stik\ n : a stick for a flag marking the location of a golf cup

flag·stone \-,stōn\ n : ²FLAG

flag stop n : a point at which a vehicle in public transportation stops only on prearrangement or signal

flag-wav·ing \'flag-,wā-viŋ\ n : passionate appeal to patriotic or partisan sentiment : CHAUVINISM

¹flail \'flā(ə)l\ n [ME fleil, flail, partly fr. (assumed) OE flegel (akin to OHG flegil flail; both fr. a prehistoric WGmc word borrowed fr. LL flagellum flail, fr. L, whip) & partly fr. MF flaiel, fr. LL flagellum — more at FLAGELLATE] : a hand threshing implement consisting of a wooden handle at the end of which a stouter and shorter stick is so hung as to swing freely

flail

²flail vt **1 a** : to strike with or as if with a flail ⟨his arms ~ing the water⟩ **b** : to move, swing, or beat as though wielding a flail

with a flail ~ vi **2** : to thresh (grain) **2** : to engage in flailing : THRASH ⟨~ed away at each other⟩

flair \'fla(ə)r, 'fle(ə)r\ n [F, lit., sense of smell, fr. OF, odor, fr. flairier to give off an odor, fr. LL flagrare, fr. L fragrare — more at FRAGRANT] **1** : instinctive attraction to and keen discernment about something ⟨a woman with a ~ for style⟩ **2** : natural aptitude : BENT **3** : a uniquely attractive quality (as elegance, smartness, or sophistication) ⟨fashionable dresses with a ~ all their own⟩ syn see LEANING

flak \'flak\ n, pl **flak** [G, fr. Fliegerabwehrkanonen, fr. flieger flyer + abwehr defense + kanonen cannons] **1** : antiaircraft guns **2** : the bursting shells fired from flak **3** : agitated discussion, opposition, or accusation : DISSENSION ⟨this modest proposal ran into ~ — Charles MacDonald⟩

¹flake \'flāk\ n [ME, hurdle, fr. ON flaki; akin to OHG flah smooth, Gk pelagos sea, L placēre to please — more at PLEASE] : a stage, platform, or tray for drying fish or produce

²flake n [ME, of Scand origin; akin to Norw flak disk] **1** : a small loose mass or bit **2** : a thin flattened piece or layer : CHIP

³flake vb **flaked; flak·ing** vi **1** : to separate into flakes ~ vt **1** : to form into flakes : CHIP **2** : to cover with or as if with flakes — **flak·er** n

flak jacket n : a jacket of heavy fabric containing metal plates for protection against flak — called also flak vest

flaky \'flā-kē\ adj **flak·i·er; -est 1** : consisting of flakes ⟨~ snow⟩ **2** : tending to flake ⟨a ~ piecrust⟩ **3** slang : slightly eccentric : SCREWY ⟨the rock writer's ~, half-literate idiom — Benjamin De Mott⟩ — **flak·i·ness** n

¹flam \'flam\ n [prob. short for flimflam] **1** : FALSEHOOD, TRICK **2** : HUMBUG, NONSENSE

²flam n [prob. imit.] : a drumbeat of two strokes of which the first is a very quick grace note

¹flam·bé \fläm-'bā, flä-\ adj [F flambé, fr. pp. of flamber to flame, singe, fr. OF, fr. flambe flame] : dressed or served covered with flaming liquor — usu. used postpositively ⟨chicken ~⟩ ⟨crepe suzettes ~⟩

²flambé vt **flam·béed; flam·bé·ing** : to douse with a liqueur (as brandy, rum, or cognac) and ignite ⟨pineapple flambéed with kirsch⟩

flam·beau \'flam-,bō\ n, pl **flam·beaux** \-,bōz\ or **flambeaus** [F, fr. MF, fr. flambe flame] : a flaming torch; broadly : TORCH

flam·boy·ance \flam-'bȯi-ən(t)s\ n : the quality or state of being flamboyant

flam·boy·an·cy \-ən-sē\ n : FLAMBOYANCE

¹flam·boy·ant \-ənt\ adj [F, fr. prp. of flamboyer to flame, fr. OF, fr. flambe] **1** often cap : characterized by waving curves suggesting flames ⟨windows ornamented with ~ tracery⟩ **2** : FLORID, ORNATE; also : RESPLENDENT **3** : given to dashing display : SHOWY — **flam·boy·ant·ly** adv

²flamboyant n : ROYAL POINCIANA

¹flame \'flām\ n [ME flaume, flaumbe, fr. MF flamme (fr. L flamma) & flambe, fr. OF, fr. flamble, fr. L flammula, dim. of flamma flame; akin to L flagrare to burn — more at BLACK] **1** : the glowing gaseous part of a fire **2 a** : state of blazing combustion ⟨the car burst into ~⟩ **b** : a condition or appearance suggesting a flame ⟨~ : BRILLIANCE, BRIGHTNESS⟩ **3** : burning zeal or passion **4** : SWEETHEART syn see BLAZE

²flame vb **flamed; flam·ing** vi **1** : to burn with a flame : BLAZE **2** : to burst or break out violently or passionately ⟨flaming with indignation⟩ **3** : to shine brightly : GLOW ⟨color flaming up in her cheeks⟩ ~ vt **1** : to send or convey by means of flame ⟨a message by signal fires⟩ **2** : to treat or affect with flame: as **a** : to cleanse, sterilize, or destroy by fire **b** : to dress food with flaming liquor ⟨~ pork chops at the table⟩ — **flam·er** n

flame cell n : a hollow cell that has a tuft of vibratile cilia and is part of the excretory system of various lower invertebrates (as a flatworm)

flame cultivator n : a flamethrower to destroy small weeds

fla·men \'flā-mən\ n, pl **flamens** or **flam·i·nes** \'flam-ə-,nēz\ [ME flamin, fr. L flamin-, flamen] : PRIEST; esp : a priest of a Roman god

fla·men·co \flə-'meŋ-(,)kō\ n, pl **-cos** [Sp, Flemish, like a gypsy, fr. MD Vlaminc Fleming] **1** : a vigorous rhythmic dance style of the Andalusian gypsies; also : a dance in flamenco style **2** : music or song suitable to accompany a flamenco dance

flame-out \'flā-,maut\ n : the unintentional cessation of operation of a jet airplane engine

flame photometer n : a spectrophotometer in which a spray of metallic salts in solution is vaporized in a very hot flame and subjected to quantitative analysis by measuring the intensities of the spectrum lines of the metals present — **flame photometric** adj — **flame photometry** n

flame-proof \'flām-'prüf\ adj **1** : resistant to the action of flame **2** : not burning on contact with flame — **flameproof** vt — **flame-proof·er** n

flame-throw·er \-,thrō-(ə)r\ n : a device that expels from a nozzle a burning stream of liquid or semiliquid fuel under pressure

flame tree n : any of several trees or shrubs with showy scarlet or yellow flowers: as **a** : a tree (Brachychiton acerifolium) of southern Australia with panicles of brilliant scarlet flowers **b** : ROYAL POINCIANA

flam·ing \'flā-miŋ\ adj **1** : being on fire : BLAZING **2** : resembling or suggesting a flame in color, brilliance, or wavy outline ⟨the ~ sunset sky⟩ ⟨~ red hair⟩ **3** : ARDENT, PASSIONATE ⟨~ youth⟩ — **flam·ing·ly** \-miŋ-lē\ adv

fla·min·go \flə-'miŋ-(,)gō\ *n, pl* **-gos** *also* **-goes** [Pg, fr. Sp *flamenco,* prob. fr. OProv *flamenc,* fr. *flama* flame (fr. L *flamma*) + *-enc* 2-ing] : any of several aquatic birds (family Phoenicopteridae) with long legs and neck, webbed feet, a broad lamellate bill resembling that of a duck but abruptly bent downward, and usu. rosy-white plumage with scarlet wing coverts and black wing quills

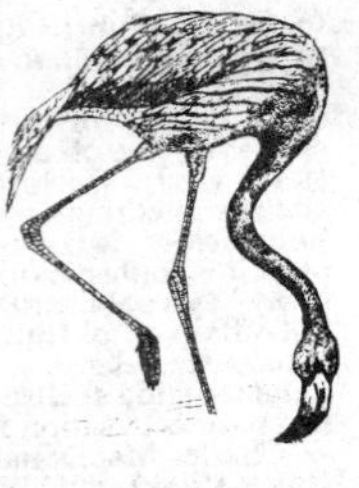

flamingo

flam·ma·bil·i·ty \,flam-ə-'bil-ət-ē\ *n* : ability to support combustion; *esp* : a high capacity for combustion

flam·ma·ble \'flam-ə-bəl\ *adj* [L *flammare* to flame, set on fire, fr. *flamma*] : capable of being easily ignited and of burning with extreme rapidity — **flammable** *n*

flan \'flan, 'flän(n)\ *n* [F, fr. OF *flaon,* fr. LL *fladon-, flado* flat cake] **1** : a large usu. straight-sided open pie **2** : the metal disk of a coin, token, or medal as distinguished from the design and lettering stamped on it

flâ·ne·rie \,flän-(ə-)'rē\ *n* [F] : the state of being aimless : IDLENESS

flâ·neur \flä-'nər\ *n* [F *flâneur* idler] : an aimless person: as **a** : MAN-ABOUT-TOWN **b** : an intellectual trifler

1**flange** \'flanj\ *n* [perh. alter. of *flanch* (a curving charge on a heraldic shield)] : a rib or rim for strength, for guiding, or for attachment to another object ⟨a ~ on a pipe⟩ ⟨a ~ on a wheel⟩

2**flange** *vt* **flanged; flang·ing** : to furnish with a flange — **flang·er** *n*

1**flank** \'flaŋk\ *n* [ME, fr. OF *flanc,* of Gmc origin; akin to OHG *hlanca* loin, flank — more at LANK] **1 a** : the fleshy part of the side between the ribs and the hip; *broadly* : the side of a quadruped **b** : a cut of meat from this part of an animal — see BEEF illustration **2 a** : SIDE **b** : the right or left of a formation **3** : the area along either side of a heraldic shield

2**flank** *vt* **1** : to protect a flank of **2 a** : to attack or threaten the flank of (as a body of troops) **b** : to turn the flank of **3 a** : to be situated at the side of : BORDER ⟨a road ~*ed* with linden trees⟩ **b** : to place something on each side of

flank·er *n* : a football player stationed wide of the formation; *esp* : an offensive halfback who lines up on the flank slightly behind the line of scrimmage and serves chiefly as a pass receiver — called also *flanker back*

flank steak *n* : a pear-shaped muscle of the beef flank; *also* : a steak cut from this muscle — see BEEF illustration

flan·nel \'flan-ᵊl\ *n* [ME *flaunneol* woolen cloth or garment] **1 a** : a soft twilled wool or worsted fabric with a loose texture and a slightly napped surface **b** : a napped cotton fabric of soft yarns simulating the texture of wool flannel **c** : a stout cotton fabric usu. napped on one side **2** *pl* **a** : flannel underwear **b** : outer garments of flannel; *esp* : men's trousers — **flannel** *adj* — **flan·nel·ly** \-ᵊl-ē\ *adj*

flan·nel·ette \,flan-ᵊl-'et\ *n* : a cotton flannel napped on one or both sides and used esp. for undergarments and night wear

1**flap** \'flap\ *n* [ME *flappe*] **1** : a stroke with something broad : SLAP **2** *obs* : something broad and flat used for striking **3** : something that is broad, limber, or flat and usu. thin and that hangs loose or projects freely: as **a** : a piece on a garment that hangs free **b** : a piece of tissue partly severed from its place of origin for use in surgical grafting **c** : an extended part forming the closure (as of an envelope or carton) **d** : a movable auxiliary airfoil usu. attached to an airplane wing's trailing edge to increase lift or drag — see AIRPLANE illustration **4** : the motion of something broad and limber (as a sail or wing) **5 a** : a state of excitement or panicky confusion : UPROAR **b** : CRISIS

2**flap** *vb* **flapped; flap·ping** *vt* **1** : to beat with or as if with a flap **2** : to toss sharply : FLING **3** : to move or cause to move in flaps ~ *vi* **1** : to sway loosely usu. with a noise of striking and esp. when moved by wind **2 a** : to beat or pulsate wings or something suggesting wings **b** : to progress by flapping **c** : to flutter ineffectively **3** : to talk foolishly and persistently

flap·doo·dle \'flap-,düd-ᵊl\ *n* [origin unknown] : NONSENSE

flap·jack \-,jak\ *n* : PANCAKE

flap·per \'flap-ər\ *n* **1 a** : one that flaps **b** : something (as a flyswatter) used in flapping or striking **c** : FLIPPER 1 **2** : a young woman; *specif* : a young woman of the period of World War I and the decade thereafter who showed bold freedom from conventions in conduct and dress

flap·py \'flap-ē\ *adj* : flapping or tending to flap

1**flare** \'fla(ə)r, 'fle(ə)r\ *vb* **flared; flar·ing** [origin unknown] *vi* **1 a** : to stream in the wind **b** : to burn with an unsteady flame **2 a** : to shine with a sudden light ⟨a match ~*s* in the darkness⟩ **b** (1) : to become suddenly excited or angry — usu. used with *up* ⟨she ~*s* up at the slightest thing⟩ (2) : to break out or intensify usu. suddenly or violently — often used with *up* ⟨ground fighting *flared* up after a two-week lull⟩ **c** : to express strong emotion (as anger) ⟨*flaring* out at such abuses⟩ **3** : to open or spread outward ⟨the pants ~ gently at the bottom⟩ ~ *vt* **1** : to display conspicuously ⟨*flaring* her scarf to attract attention⟩ **2** : to cause to flare ⟨the breeze ~*s* the candle⟩ **3** : to signal with a flare or by flaring

2**flare** *n* **1** : an unsteady glaring light **2 a** : a fire or blaze of light used to signal, illuminate, or attract attention; *also* : a device or composition used to produce such a flare **b** : a temporary outburst of energy from a small area of the sun's surface; *also* : a sudden increase and decrease in the brightness of a star often amounting to several magnitudes **3** : a sudden outburst (as of sound, excitement, or anger) **4 a** : a spreading outward; *also* : a place or part that spreads ⟨the ~ of a fireplace⟩ **b** : an area of skin flush **5** : light resulting from reflection (as between lens surfaces) or an effect of this light (as a fogged or dense area in a photographic negative) **6** : a short pass in football thrown to a back who is running toward the sideline ***syn*** see BLAZE

flare·back \'fla(ə)r-,bak, 'fle(ə)r-\ *n* : a burst of flame back or out (as from a furnace) in a direction opposite to that of normal operation

flare–up \-,əp\ *n* **1** : a sudden bursting (as of a smoldering fire) into flame or light **2** : a sudden outburst or intensification ⟨a ~ over the issue of Executive responsibility to Congress —Arthur Blaustein⟩

flar·ing \'fla(ə)r-iŋ, 'fle(ə)r-\ *adj* **1 a** : flaming brightly or unsteadily **b** : GAUDY ⟨a ~ resort hotel⟩ **2** : opening or spreading outward ⟨~ nostrils⟩ — **flar·ing·ly** \-iŋ-lē\ *adv*

1**flash** \'flash\ *vb* [ME *flaschen,* of imit. origin] *vi* **1** : RUSH, DASH — used of flowing water **2** : to break forth in or like a sudden flame or flare ⟨lightning ~*ing* in the sky⟩ **3 a** : to appear suddenly ⟨an idea ~*es* into her mind⟩ **b** : to move with great speed ⟨the days ~ by⟩ **4 a** : to break forth or out so as to make a sudden display ⟨the sun ~*ed* from behind a cloud⟩ **b** : to act or speak vehemently and suddenly esp. in anger **5 a** : to give off light suddenly or in transient bursts **b** : to glow or gleam esp. with animation or passion ⟨his eyes ~*ed* in a sinister fashion⟩ **6** : to change suddenly or violently into vapor ⟨hot water ~*ing* to steam under reduced pressure⟩ ~ *vt* **1 a** *archaic* : SPLASH **b** : to fill by a sudden inflow of water **2 a** : to cause the sudden appearance of (light) **b** : to cause to burst violently into flame; *also* : to burn for determining character of residue **c** (1) : to cause (light) to reflect (2) : to cause (as a mirror) to reflect light (3) : to cause (a lamp) to flash **d** : to convey by means of flashes of light **3 a** : to make known or cause to appear with great speed ⟨~ a message on the screen⟩ **b** : to display obtrusively and ostentatiously ⟨always ~*es* his fat wallet in public⟩ **c** : to expose to view suddenly and briefly ⟨~*ing* a shy smile⟩ **4** : to cover with or form into a thin layer: as **a** : to protect against rain by covering with sheet metal or a substitute **b** : to coat (as glass) with a thin layer (as of metal or a differently colored glass) **5** : to subject (an exposed photographic negative or positive) to a supplementary uniform exposure to light before development in order to modify detail or tone

syn FLASH, GLEAM, GLANCE, GLINT, SPARKLE, GLITTER, GLISTEN, GLIMMER, CORUSCATE, SHIMMER *shared meaning element* : to send forth light

2**flash** *n* **1 a** : a sudden burst of light **b** : a movement of a flag in signaling **2** : a sudden and often brilliant burst ⟨a ~ of wit⟩ ⟨had a ~ of intuition⟩ **3** : a brief time ⟨I'll be back in a ~⟩ **4 a** : SHOW, DISPLAY; *esp* : a vulgar ostentatious display **b** *archaic* : a showy ostentatious person **c** : one that attracts notice; *esp* : an outstanding athlete **5** *obs* : thieves' slang **6** : a rush of water released to permit passage of a boat **7** : something flashed: as **a** : GLIMPSE, LOOK **b** : SMILE **c** : a first brief news report **d** : FLASHLIGHT 2,3 **e** : a quick-spreading flame or momentary intense outburst of radiant heat **8** : RUSH 7 **9** : the rapid conversion of a liquid into vapor

3**flash** *adj* **1 a** : FLASHY, SHOWY **b** : of, relating to, or characteristic of flashy people or things ⟨~ behavior⟩ **c** : of, relating to, or characteristic of persons considered social outcasts ⟨~ language⟩ **2** : of sudden origin and short duration ⟨a ~ fire⟩

flash·back \'flash-,bak\ *n* **1** : interruption of chronological sequence in a literary or theatrical work by interjection of events of earlier occurrence **2** : a recession of flame to an unwanted position (as into a blowpipe)

flash·board \-,bō(ə)rd, -,bȯ(ə)rd\ *n* : one or more boards projecting above the top of a dam to increase the depth of the water

flash·bulb \-,bəlb\ *n* : an electric flash lamp in which metal foil or wire is burned

flash card *n* : a card bearing words, numbers, or pictures that is briefly displayed (as by a teacher to a class) usu. as a learning aid

flash·cube \'flash-,kyüb\ *n* : a cubical device that incorporates four flashbulbs, is usu. attached to a camera, and can be turned for taking four pictures in rapid succession

flash·er \'flash-ər\ *n* : one that flashes: as **a** : a light (as a traffic signal or automobile light) that catches the attention by flashing **b** : a device for automatically flashing a light

flash flood *n* : a local flood of great volume and short duration generally resulting from heavy rainfall in the immediate vicinity — **flash flood** *vt*

flash–for·ward \'flash-'fȯr-wərd\ *n* : a literary or theatrical technique that involves interruption of the chronological sequence of events by interjection of events or scenes of future occurrence

flash·gun \-,gən\ *n* **1** : a device for holding and igniting flashlight powder **2** : a device for holding and operating a flashbulb or a flashtube

flash·ing \'flash-iŋ\ *n* : sheet metal used in waterproofing roof valleys or hips or the angle between a chimney and a roof

flash in the pan [fr. the firing of the priming in the pan of a flintlock musket without discharging the piece] **1** : a sudden spasmodic effort that accomplishes nothing **2** : one that appears promising but turns out to be disappointing or worthless

flash lamp *n* : a lamp for producing a brief but intense flash of light for taking photographs

flash·light \'flash-,līt\ *n* **1** : a flash of light or a light that flashes; *esp* : a scintillating light or a light of regularly varying brightness in a lighthouse **2 a** : a sudden bright artificial light used in taking photographic pictures **b** : a photograph taken by such a light **3** : a small battery-operated portable electric light

flash·over \-,ō-vər\ *n* **1** : an abnormal electrical discharge (as through the air to the ground from a high potential source or between two conducting portions of a structure) **2** : the sudden spread of flame over an area when it becomes heated to the flash point

flash point *n* **1** : the lowest temperature at which vapors above a volatile combustible substance ignite in air when exposed to flame **2** : a point at which someone or something bursts suddenly into action or being

flash·tube \'flash-,t(y)üb\ *n* : a gas discharge tube that produces very brief intense flashes of light and is used esp. in photography

flashy \'flash-ē\ *adj* **flash·i·er; -est** **1** *chiefly dial* : lacking in substance or flavor : INSIPID **2** : momentarily dazzling **3 a** : superficially attractive : BRIGHT **b** : ostentatious or showy beyond the bounds of good taste; *esp* : marked by gaudy brightness *syn* see GAUDY — **flash·i·ly** \'flash-ə-lē\ *adv* — **flash·i·ness** \'flash-ē-nəs\ *n*

flask \'flask\ *n* [MF *flasque* powder flask, deriv. of LL *flascon-, flasco* bottle, prob. of Gmc origin; akin to OHG *flaska* bottle] **1** : a container often somewhat narrowed toward the outlet and often fitted with a closure; *esp* : a broad flattened necked vessel used esp. to carry alcoholic beverages on the person **2** : a frame that holds molding sand used in a foundry

¹flat \'flat\ *adj* **flat·ter; flat·test** [ME, fr. ON *flatr;* akin to OHG *flaz* flat, Gk *platys* — more at PLACE] **1** : having a continuous horizontal surface **2 a** : lying at full length or spread out upon the ground : PROSTRATE **b** : resting with a surface against something **3** : having a relatively smooth or even surface **4** : arranged or laid out so as to be level or even **5** : having the major surfaces essentially parallel and distinctly greater than the minor surfaces ⟨a ~ piece of wood⟩ **6 a** : clearly unmistakable : DOWNRIGHT ⟨gave a ~ denial⟩ **b** (1) : ABSOLUTE, FIXED ⟨charged a ~ rate⟩ (2) : having no fraction either lacking or in excess : EXACT ⟨ran the race in four minutes ~⟩ **7 a** : lacking in animation, zest, or vigor : DULL ⟨how weary, stale, ~ and unprofitable, seem to me all the uses of this world — Shak.⟩ **b** : lacking flavor : TASTELESS **c** : lacking effervescence or sparkle ⟨~ ginger ale⟩ **d** : lacking air : DEFLATED — used of tires **8 a** (1) *of a tone* : lowered a half step in pitch (2) : lower than the proper pitch **b** *of the vowel a* : pronounced as in *bad* or *bat* **9 a** : having a low trajectory **b** *of a tennis ball* : hit squarely without being spun by the racket **10** *of a sail* : TAUT **11 a** : uniform in hue or shade **b** *of a painting* : having little or no illusion of depth **c** *of a photograph or negative* : lacking contrast **d** *of a photographic lighting arrangement* : not emphasizing shadows or contours **e** : free from gloss ⟨likes the finish of a ~ paint⟩ *syn* see LEVEL, INSIPID — **flat·ly** *adv* — **flat·ness** *n*

²flat *n* **1** : a level surface of land with little or no relief : PLAIN — often used in pl. ⟨sagebrush ~s⟩ **2** : a flat part or surface ⟨the ~ of one's hand⟩ **3 a** : a musical note or tone one half step lower than a specified note or tone **b** : a character on a line or space of the musical staff indicating a half step drop in pitch **4** : something flat: as **a** : a shallow box in which seedlings are started **b** : a flat-bottomed boat **c** : a flat piece of theatrical scenery **d** : a shoe or slipper having a flat heel or no heel **5** : a floor or story in a building **6** : an apartment on one floor **7** : a deflated tire **8** : the area to either side of an offensive football formation

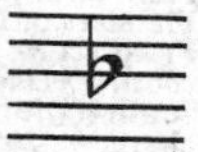

flat 3b

³flat *adv* **1** : in a flat manner : DIRECTLY, POSITIVELY **2 a** : on or against a flat surface ⟨lying ~ on his back⟩ **b** : at full length ⟨fell ~ on his face⟩ **3** : in a complete manner : WHOLLY ⟨~ broke⟩ **4** : below the proper musical pitch **5** : without interest charge; *esp* : without allowance or charge for accrued interest ⟨bonds sold ~⟩

⁴flat *vb* **flat·ted; flat·ting** *vt* **1** : FLATTEN **2** : to lower in pitch esp. by a half step ~ *vi* : to sing or play below the true pitch

¹flat·bed \,flat-,bed\ *adj* : having a horizontal bed on which a horizontal printing surface rests ⟨a ~ printing press⟩

²flat·bed \'flat-,bed\ *n* : a motortruck or trailer with a body in the form of a platform or shallow box

flat·boat \-,bōt\ *n* : a boat with a flat bottom and square ends used for transportation of bulky freight esp. in shallow waters

flat·cap \-,kap\ *n* **1** : a round low-crowned cap worn in 16th and 17th century London **2** : a wearer of a flatcap; *esp* : a Londoner

flat·car \-,kär\ *n* : a railroad freight car without permanent raised sides, ends, or covering

flat·fish \'flat-,fish\ *n* : any of an order (Heterosomata) of marine teleost fishes (as the halibuts, flounders, turbots, and soles) that as adults swim on one side of the laterally compressed body and have both eyes on the upper side

flat·foot \-,fu̇t (*always so in sense 3*), -'fu̇t\ *n, pl* **flat·feet** \-,fēt, -'fēt\ **1** : a condition in which the arch of the instep is flattened so that the entire sole rests upon the ground **2** : a foot affected with flatfoot **3 a** *or pl* **flatfoots** *slang* : POLICEMAN; *esp* : a patrolman walking a regular beat **b** *slang* : SAILOR

¹flat–foot·ed \-'fu̇t-əd\ *adj* **1** : affected with flatfoot; *broadly* : walking with a dragging or shambling gait **2 a** : firm and well balanced on the feet **b** : free from reservation : FORTHRIGHT ⟨had an honest ~ way of saying a thing⟩ **3** : found unprepared : UNREADY — used chiefly in the phrase *catch one flat-footed* — **flat–foot·ed·ly** *adv* — **flat–foot·ed·ness** *n*

²flat–footed *adv* : in an open and determined manner : FLATLY

flat–hat \'flat-,hat\ *vi* [fr. an alleged incident in which a pedestrian's hat was crushed by a low-flying plane] : to fly low in an airplane in a reckless manner : HEDGEHOP — **flat–hat·ter** *n*

Flat·head \-,hed\ *n, pl* **Flatheads** *or* **Flathead** **1** : a member of any of several No. American Indian peoples that practiced head-flattening **2** : an Amerindian people of Montana **3** *not cap* : any of various fishes with more or less flat heads; *esp* : any of a family (Percophididae) of chiefly Indo-Pacific marine food fishes that resemble sculpins

flat·iron \'flat-,ī(-ə)rn\ *n* : IRON 2d

flat knot *n* : REEF KNOT

flat·land \'flat-,land\ *n* **1** : land that lacks significant variation in elevation **2** : a region in which the land is predominantly flat — usu. used in pl. — **flat·land·er** \-,lan-dər\ *n*

flat·let \'flat-lət\ *n, Brit* : EFFICIENCY APARTMENT

flat·ling \'flat-liŋ\ *or* **flat·lings** \-liŋz\ *adv, dial Brit* : with a flat side or edge

flat–out \'flat-,au̇t\ *adj* **1** : ALL-OUT, DOWNRIGHT ⟨it was a ~ lie⟩ **2** *chiefly Brit* : being or going at maximum effort or speed

flat out \-'au̇t\ *adv* **1** : in a blunt and direct manner : OPENLY ⟨called *flat out* for revolution —*Nat'l Review*⟩ **2** : at top speed or peak performance ⟨the car does 180 m.p.h. *flat out*⟩

flat race *n* : a race (as for horses) on a level course without obstacles (as hurdles) — compare STEEPLECHASE

flat silver *n* : eating or serving utensils (as knives, forks, and spoons) made of or plated with silver

flat·ten \'flat-ᵊn\ *vb* **flat·tened; flat·ten·ing** \'flat-niŋ, -ᵊn-iŋ\ *vt* **1** : to make flat: as **a** : to make level or smooth **b** : to lay low : RUIN **2** : to make (as paint) lusterless ~ *vi* **1** : to become flat or flatter: as **a** : to become dull or spiritless **b** : to extend in or into a flat position or form ⟨hills ~*ing* into coastal plains⟩ **c** : to become uniform or stabilized often at a new lower level — usu. used with *out* ⟨performance tended to ~ out after an initial period of improvement⟩ **2 a** : to manipulate an airplane so as to bring its longitudinal axis parallel with the ground — used with *out* **b** *of an airplane* : to assume such a position — **flat·ten·er** \'flat-nər, -ᵊn-ər\ *n*

¹flat·ter \'flat-ər\ *vb* [ME *flateren,* fr. OF *flater* to lick, flatter, of Gmc origin; akin to OHG *flaz* flat] *vt* **1** : to praise excessively esp. from motives of self-interest **2 a** *archaic* : SOOTHE, BEGUILE **b** : to raise the hope of or gratify esp. by false or specious representations ⟨~ him by asking his advice⟩ **3 a** : to portray too favorably ⟨that picture ~*s* her — she's not that pretty⟩ **b** : to display to advantage ⟨candlelight often ~*s* the face⟩ ~ *vi* : to use flattery — **flat·ter·er** \-ər-ər\ *n* — **flat·ter·ing·ly** \-ə-riŋ-lē\ *adv*

²flatter *n* : one that flattens: as **a** : a drawplate with a narrow rectangular orifice for drawing flat strips **b** : a flat-faced swage used in smithing

flat·tery \'flat-ə-rē\ *n, pl* **-ter·ies** **1 a** : the act or practice of flattering **b** (1) : something that flatters (2) : insincere or excessive praise **2** *obs* : a pleasing self-deception

flat·tish \'flat-ish\ *adj* : somewhat flat

flat·top \'flat-,täp\ *n* : something with a flat or flattened upper surface: as **a** : AIRCRAFT CARRIER **b** : CREW CUT

flat·u·lence \'flach-ə-lən(t)s\ *n* : the quality or state of being flatulent

flat·u·len·cy \-lən-sē\ *n* : FLATULENCE

flat·u·lent \-lənt\ *adj* [MF, fr. L *flatus* act of blowing, wind, fr. *flatus,* pp. of *flare* to blow — more at BLOW] **1 a** : marked by or affected with gases generated in the intestine or stomach **b** : likely to cause digestive flatulence **2** : pretentious without real worth or substance : TURGID — **flat·u·lent·ly** *adv*

fla·tus \'flāt-əs\ *n* [L, act of blowing, act of breaking wind] : gas generated in the stomach or bowels

flat·ware \'flat-,wa(ə)r, -,we(ə)r\ *n* : tableware more or less flat and usu. formed or cast in a single piece; *esp* : eating and serving utensils (as knives, forks, and spoons) — compare HOLLOWWARE

flat·ways \-,wāz\ *adv* : FLATWISE

flat·wise \-,wīz\ *adv* : with the flat surface presented in some expressed or implied position

flat·work \-,wərk\ *n* : laundry that can be finished mechanically and doesn't require hand ironing

flat·worm \-,wərm\ *n* : PLATYHELMINTH; *esp* : TURBELLARIAN

flaunt \'flȯnt, 'flänt\ *vb* [prob. of Scand origin; akin to ON *flana* to rush around — more at PLANET] *vi* **1** : to wave or flutter showily ⟨the flag ~*s* in the breeze⟩ **2** : to display or obtrude oneself to public notice ~ *vt* **1** : to display ostentatiously or impudently : PARADE ⟨~*ing* his superiority⟩ **2** : to treat contemptuously ⟨~*ed* the rules —Louis Untermeyer⟩ — **flaunt** *n* — **flaunt·ing·ly** \-iŋ-lē\ *adv* — **flaunty** \-ē\ *adj*

flau·tist \'flȯt-əst, 'flau̇t-\ *n* [It *flautista,* fr. *flauto* flute, fr. OProv *flaut*] : FLUTIST

fla·va·none \'flā-və-,nōn\ *n* [L *flavus* + ISV *-ane* + *-one*] : a colorless crystalline ketone $C_{15}H_{12}O_2$; *also* : any of the derivatives of this ketone many of which occur in plants often in the form of glycosides

fla·vin \'flā-vən\ *n* [ISV, fr. L *flavus* yellow — more at BLUE] : a yellow water-soluble nitrogenous pigment derived from isoalloxazine and occurring in the form of nucleotides as coenzymes of flavoproteins; *esp* : RIBOFLAVIN

flavin adenine dinucleotide *n* : a coenzyme $C_{27}H_{33}N_9O_{15}P_2$ of some flavoproteins

fla·vine \'flā-,vēn\ *n* [ISV, fr. L *flavus*] : a yellow acridine dye (as acriflavine) often used medicinally for its antiseptic properties

flavin mononucleotide *n* : FMN

fla·vone \'flā-,vōn\ *n* [ISV, fr. L *flavus*] : a colorless crystalline ketone $C_{15}H_{10}O_2$ found in the leaves, stems, and seed capsules of many primroses; *also* : any of the derivatives of this ketone many of which occur as yellow plant pigments in the form of glycosides and are used as dyestuffs

fla·vo·noid \'flā-və-,nȯid\ *n* [*flavone* + *-oid*] : any of a group of aromatic compounds that includes many common pigments (as the anthocyanins and flavones)

fla·vo·nol \'flā-və-,nȯl, -,nōl\ *n* : any of various hydroxy derivatives of flavone

fla·vo·pro·tein \,flā-vō-'prō-,tēn, -'prōt-ē-ən\ *n* [ISV *flavin* + *-o-* + *protein*] : a dehydrogenase that contains a flavin and often a metal and plays a major role in biological oxidations

¹fla·vor \'flā-vər\ *n* [ME, fr. MF *flaor, flavor,* fr. (assumed) VL *flator,* fr. L *flare* to blow — more at BLOW] **1 a** *archaic* : ODOR, FRAGRANCE **b** : the quality of something that affects the sense of taste : SAVOR ⟨condiments give ~ to food⟩ **c** : the blend of taste and smell sensations evoked by a substance in the mouth ⟨the ~ of ripe fruit⟩ **2** : a substance that flavors ⟨hard candy with artificial ~⟩ **3** : characteristic or predominant quality ⟨the newspaper retains a community ~⟩ — **fla·vored** \-vərd\ *adj* — **fla·vor·less** \-vər-ləs\ *adj*

ə abut	ᵊ kitten	ər further	a back	ā bake	ä cot, cart
au̇ out	ch chin	e less	ē easy	g gift	i trip	ī life
j joke	ŋ sing	ō flow	ȯ flaw	ȯi coin	th thin	t͟h this
ü loot	u̇ foot	y yet	yü few	yu̇ furious	zh vision

[2]flavor *vt* **fla·vored; fla·vor·ing** \ˈflāv-(ə-)riŋ\ : to give or add flavor to
fla·vor·ful \ˈflā-vər-fəl\ *adj* : full of flavor : SAVORY — **fla·vor·ful·ly** \-fə-lē\ *adv*
fla·vor·ing *n* : FLAVOR 2
fla·vor·some \ˈflā-vər-səm\ *adj* : FLAVORFUL
fla·vour *chiefly Brit var of* FLAVOR
[1]flaw \ˈflȯ\ *n* [ME, prob. of Scand origin; akin to Sw *flaga* flake, flaw; akin to OE *flēan* to flay] **1** *obs* : FRAGMENT **2** : an often hidden defect that may cause failure under stress: as **a** : a faulty part (as a crack or break) ⟨the axle broke at a ~⟩ **b** : a weakness in something immaterial ⟨vanity was the great ~ in his character⟩ **c** : a fault in a legal paper that may nullify it ***syn*** see BLEMISH — **flaw·less** \-ləs\ *adj* — **flaw·less·ly** *adv* — **flaw·less·ness** *n*
[2]flaw *vt* : to make flaws in ~ *vi* : to become defective
[3]flaw *n* [of Scand origin; akin to Norw *flaga* gust; akin to L *plangere* to beat — more at PLAINT] **1** : a sudden brief burst of wind; *also* : a spell of stormy weather **2** *obs* : an outburst esp. of passion
flax \ˈflaks\ *n, often attrib* [ME, fr. OE *fleax;* akin to OHG *flahs* flax, L *plectere* to braid — more at PLY] **1** : any of a genus (*Linum* of the family Linaceae, the flax family) of herbs; *esp* : a slender erect annual (*L. usitatissimum*) with blue flowers commonly cultivated for its bast fiber and seed **2** : the fiber of the flax plant esp. when prepared for spinning **3** : any of several plants resembling flax
flax·en \ˈflak-sən\ *adj* **1** : made of flax **2** : resembling flax esp. in pale soft strawy color ⟨~ hair⟩
flax·seed \ˈflak(s)-ˌsēd\ *n* : the seed of flax used as a source of oil and medicinally as a demulcent and emollient
flaxy \ˈflak-sē\ *adj* **flax·i·er; -est** : resembling flax esp. in texture : FLAXEN
flay \ˈflā\ *vt* [ME *flen,* fr. OE *flēan;* akin to ON *flā* to flay, Lith *plėšti* to tear] **1** : to strip off the skin or surface of : SKIN **2 a** : to strip of possessions : FLEECE **b** : to criticize harshly : EXCORIATE
F layer *n* **1** : the highest and most densely ionized regular layer of the ionosphere occurring at night within the F region **2** : the forest soil zone marked by abundant plant remains undergoing decay
fl dr *abbr* fluidram
flea \ˈflē\ *n* [ME *fle,* fr. OE *flēa;* akin to OHG *flōh* flea, OE *flēon* to flee] **1** : any of an order (Siphonaptera) of wingless bloodsucking insects that have a hard laterally compressed body and legs adapted to leaping and that feed on warm-blooded animals **2** : FLEA BEETLE — **flea in one's ear** : an irritating hint or warning : REBUKE

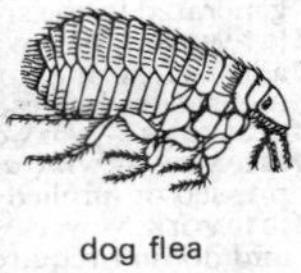
dog flea

flea·bag \ˈflē-ˌbag\ *n* : an inferior hotel or rooming house
flea·bane \-ˌbān\ *n* : any of various composite plants (as of the genus *Erigeron*) that were once supposed to drive away fleas
flea beetle *n* : any of various small chrysomelid beetles (as of the genera *Altica* and *Epitrix*) with legs adapted for leaping that feed on foliage and sometimes serve as vectors of virus diseases of plants
flea·bite \ˈflē-ˌbīt\ *n* **1** : the bite of a flea; *also* : the red spot caused by such a bite **2** : a trifling pain or annoyance
flea–bit·ten \-ˌbit-ᵊn\ *adj* **1** : bitten by or infested with fleas **2** *of a horse* : having a white or gray coat flecked with bay or sorrel
flea·hop·per \-ˌhäp-ər\ *n* : any of various small jumping bugs that feed on cultivated plants
flea market *n* [trans. of F *Marché aux Puces,* a market in Paris] : a usu. open-air market for secondhand articles and antiques
flea weevil *n* : any of various small broad weevils with legs adapted for leaping and with larvae that are leaf miners
flea·wort \ˈflē-ˌwərt, -ˌwȯ(ə)rt\ *n* : an Old World plantain (*Plantago psyllium*) whose seeds swell and become gelatinous when moist and are sometimes used as a mild laxative
flèche \ˈflāsh, ˈflesh\ *n* [F, lit., arrow] : SPIRE; *esp* : a slender spire above the intersection of the nave and transepts of a church
flé·chette \flā-ˈshet, fle-\ *n* [F, fr. dim. of *flèche* arrow] : a small dart-shaped projectile that is clustered in an explosive warhead, dropped as a missile from an airplane, or fired from a hand-held gun
[1]fleck \ˈflek\ *vt* [back-formation fr. *flecked* spotted, fr. ME, prob. fr. ON *flekkōttr,* fr. *flekkr* spot] : STREAK, SPOT ⟨whitecaps ~*ed* the blue sea⟩
[2]fleck *n* **1** : SPOT, MARK ⟨a brown tweed with ~*s* of yellow⟩ **2** : FLAKE, PARTICLE ⟨~*s* of snow drifted down⟩
flec·tion *var of* FLEXION
fledge \ˈflej\ *vb* **fledged; fledg·ing** [*fledge* (capable of flying), fr. ME *flegge,* fr. OE *-flycge;* akin to OHG *flucki* capable of flying, OE *flēogan* to fly — more at FLY] *vi* **1** *of a bird* : to acquire the feathers necessary for flight **2** *of an insect* : to attain the winged adult stage ~ *vt* **1** : to rear until ready for flight or independent activity **2** : to cover with or as if with feathers or down **3** : to furnish (as an arrow) with feathers
fledg·ling \ˈflej-liŋ\ *n* **1** : a young bird just fledged **2** : an immature or inexperienced person
flee \ˈflē\ *vb* **fled** \ˈfled\; **flee·ing** [ME *flen,* fr. OE *flēon;* akin to OHG *fliohan* to flee] *vi* **1** : to run away from danger or evil : FLY **2** : to pass away swiftly : VANISH ⟨mists ~*ing* before the rising sun⟩ ~ *vt* : to run away from : SHUN
[1]fleece \ˈflēs\ *n* [ME *flees,* fr. OE *flēos;* akin to MHG *vlius* fleece, L *pluma* feather, down] **1 a** : the coat of wool covering a wool-bearing animal (as a sheep) **b** : the wool obtained from a sheep at one shearing **2 a** : any of various soft or woolly coverings **b** : a soft bulky deep-piled knitted or woven fabric used chiefly for clothing
[2]fleece *vt* **fleeced; fleec·ing** **1** : to remove the fleece from : SHEAR **2 a** : to strip of money or property by fraud or extortion **b** : to charge excessively for goods or services ⟨nightclubs where the customer knew he would be *fleeced*⟩ **3** : to dot or cover with fleecy masses
fleeced \ˈflēst\ *adj* **1** : covered with or as if with a fleece **2** *of a textile* : having a soft nap
fleech \ˈflēch\ *vb* [ME (Sc) *flechen*] *dial* : COAX, WHEEDLE
fleecy \ˈflē-sē\ *adj* **fleec·i·er; -est** : covered with, made of, or resembling fleece ⟨a ~ winter coat⟩
[1]fleer \ˈfli(ə)r\ *vi* [ME *fleryen,* of Scand origin; akin to Norw *flire* to giggle — more at FLIMFLAM] : to laugh or grimace in a coarse derisive manner : SNEER ***syn*** see SCOFF — **fleer·ing·ly** \-iŋ-lē\ *adv*
[2]fleer *n* : a word or look of derision or mockery
[1]fleet \ˈflēt\ *vb* [ME *fleten,* fr. OE *flēotan;* akin to OHG *fliozzan* to float, OE *flōwan* to flow] *vi* **1** *obs* : DRIFT **2 a** *archaic* : FLOW **b** : to fade away : VANISH **3** : to fly swiftly ~ *vt* **1** : to cause (time) to pass usu. quickly or imperceptibly **2** [alter. of *flit*] : to move or change in position ⟨~ a hawser⟩ ***syn*** see WHILE
[2]fleet *n* [ME *flete,* fr. OE *flēot* ship, fr. *flēotan*] **1** : a number of warships under a single command; *specif* : an organization of ships and aircraft under the command of a flag officer and suitable to undertake major naval operations **2** : a group (as of ships, planes, or trucks) operated under unified control
[3]fleet *adj* [prob. fr. [1]*fleet*] **1** : swift in motion : NIMBLE **2** : EVANESCENT, FLEETING ***syn*** see FAST — **fleet·ly** *adv* — **fleet·ness** *n*
fleet admiral *n* : an admiral of the highest rank in the navy whose insignia is five stars
fleet·ing *adj* : passing swiftly : TRANSITORY ***syn*** see TRANSIENT ***ant*** lasting — **fleet·ing·ly** \-iŋ-lē\ *adv* — **fleet·ing·ness** *n*
Fleet Street \ˈflēt-\ *n* [*Fleet Street,* London, England, center of the London newspaper district] : the London press
flei·shig \ˈflā-shik\ *adj* [Yiddish, fr. MHG *vleischic* meaty, fr. *vleisch* flesh, meat, fr. OHG *fleisk* — more at FLESH] : made of, prepared with, or used for meat or meat products
Flem *abbr* Flemish
Flem·ing \ˈflem-iŋ\ *n* [ME, fr. MD *Vlaminc,* fr. *Vlam-* (as in *Vlamland* Flanders)] : a member of the Germanic people inhabiting northern Belgium and a small section of northern France
[1]Flem·ish \ˈflem-ish\ *adj* : of, relating to, or characteristic of Flanders or the Flemings or their language
[2]Flemish *n* **1** : the Germanic language of the Flemings **2** *pl in constr* : FLEMINGS
Flemish giant *n* : a rabbit of a breed prob. of Belgian origin that is characterized by large size, vigor, and solid coat color in black, white, or gray
flense \ˈflen(t)s\ *vt* **flensed; flens·ing** [D *flensen* or Dan & Norw *flense*] : to strip (as a whale) of blubber or skin
[1]flesh \ˈflesh\ *n* [ME, fr. OE *flǣsc;* akin to OHG *fleisk* flesh] **1 a** : the soft parts of the body of an animal and esp. of a vertebrate; *esp* : the parts composed chiefly of skeletal muscle as distinguished from visceral structures, bone, and integuments **b** : sleek well-fatted condition of body **c** : SKIN **2 a** : edible parts of an animal **b** : flesh of a mammal or bird that is an article of diet ⟨abstain from ~ during religious fasts⟩ **3 a** : the physical being of man ⟨the spirit indeed is willing, but the ~ is weak —Mt 26:41 (AV)⟩ **b** : human nature **4 a** : human beings : MANKIND **b** : living beings **c** : STOCK, KINDRED **5** : a fleshy plant part used as food; *also* : the fleshy part of a fruit **6** *Christian Science* : an illusion that matter has sensation — **in the flesh** : in person and alive
[2]flesh *vt* **1 a** : to feed (as a hawk) with flesh from the kill to encourage interest in the chase **b** : to initiate or habituate esp. by giving a foretaste **2** *archaic* : GRATIFY **3** : to clothe or cover with or as if with flesh; *broadly* : to give substance to ⟨~*ed* out his argument with solid fact⟩ **4** : to free from flesh ~ *vi* : to become fleshy — often used with *up* or *out*
flesh and blood *n* **1** : corporeal nature as composed of flesh and of blood ⟨such neglect was more than *flesh and blood* could stand⟩ **2** : near kindred — used chiefly in the phrase *one's own flesh and blood* **3** : SUBSTANCE, REALITY ⟨attempting to give *flesh and blood* to nebulous ideas⟩
fleshed \ˈflesht\ *adj* : having flesh esp. of a specified kind — often used in combination ⟨pink-*fleshed*⟩ ⟨thick-*fleshed*⟩
flesh fly *n* : a two-winged fly whose maggots feed on flesh; *esp* : one of a family (Sarcophagidae) of flies some of which cause myiasis
flesh·i·ness \ˈflesh-ē-nəs\ *n* : the state of being fleshy : CORPULENCE
flesh·ing \ˈflesh-iŋ\ *n* **1** *pl* : close-fitting usu. flesh-colored tights **2** *pl* : material removed in fleshing a hide or skin **3 a** : the distribution of the lean and fat on an animal **b** : the capacity of an animal to put on fat
flesh·ly \ˈflesh-lē\ *adj* **1 a** : CORPOREAL, BODILY **b** : of, relating to, or characterized by indulgence of bodily appetites; *esp* : LASCIVIOUS ⟨~ desires⟩ **c** : not spiritual : WORLDLY **2** : FLESHY, PLUMP **3** : having a sensuous quality ⟨~ art⟩ ***syn*** see CARNAL
flesh·ment \ˈflesh-mənt\ *n* [[2]*flesh*] *obs* : excitement associated with a successful beginning
flesh·pot \ˈflesh-ˌpät\ *n* **1** *pl* : bodily comfort : LUXURY **2** : a place of luxurious entertainment — usu. used in pl. ⟨a tour of the city's ~*s*⟩
flesh wound *n* : an injury involving penetration of the body musculature without damage to skeletal or visceral structures
fleshy \ˈflesh-ē\ *adj* **flesh·i·er; -est** **1 a** : marked by, consisting of, or resembling flesh **b** : marked by abundant flesh; *esp* : CORPULENT **2 a** : SUCCULENT, PULPY ⟨the rich ~ texture of a perfectly ripe melon⟩ **b** : not thin, dry, or membranaceous ⟨~ fungi⟩
fleshy fruit *n* : a fruit (as a berry, drupe, or pome) consisting largely of soft succulent tissue
fletch \ˈflech\ *vt* [back-formation fr. *fletcher*] : FEATHER ⟨~ an arrow⟩
fletch·er \ˈflech-ər\ *n* [ME *flecchere,* fr. OF *flechier,* fr. *fleche* arrow] : a maker of arrows
fleur de coin \ˌflərd-ə-ˈkwaⁿ\ *adj* [F *à fleur de coin,* lit., with the bloom of the die] : being in the preserved mint condition
fleur–de–lis *or* **fleur–de–lys** \ˌflərd-ᵊl-ˈē, ˌflu̇rd-\ *n, pl* **fleurs–de–lis** *or* **fleur–de–lis** *or* **fleurs–de–lys** *or* **fleur–de–lys** \ˌflərd-ᵊl-ˈē(z),

ˌflu̇rd-\ [ME *flourdelis,* fr. MF *flor de lis,* lit., lily flower] **1 :** IRIS 3 **2 :** a conventionalized iris in art and heraldry

fleur-de-lis 2

fleu·ry \ˈflu̇(ə)r-ē\ *adj* [alter. of ME *flory,* fr. OF *floré,* fr. *flor* flower — more at FLOWER] *of a heraldic cross* **:** having the ends of the arms broadening out into the heads of fleurs-de-lis — see CROSS illustration
flew *past of* FLY
flews \ˈflüz\ *n pl* [origin unknown] **:** the pendulous lateral parts of a dog's upper lip — see DOG illustration
1flex \ˈfleks\ *vb* [L *flexus,* pp. of *flectere*] *vt* **1 :** to bend esp. repeatedly ⟨sat ~*ing* the strap as he talked⟩ **2 a :** to move muscles so as to cause flexion of (a joint) ⟨stretching and ~*ing* his knees⟩ **b :** to move (a muscle or muscles) so as to flex a joint ⟨~*ed* their biceps and went to work⟩ ~ *vi* **:** BEND
2flex *n* **1 :** an act or instance of flexing **2** [short for *flexible cord*] *chiefly Brit* **:** electric cord
flex·i·ble \ˈflek-sə-bəl\ *adj* **1 :** capable of being flexed **:** PLIANT **2 :** yielding to influence **:** TRACTABLE **3 :** capable of responding or conforming to changing or new situations ⟨a highly ~ curriculum⟩ ⟨a ~ personality⟩ — **flex·i·bil·i·ty** \ˌflek-sə-ˈbil-ət-ē\ *n* — **flex·i·bly** \ˈflek-sə-blē\ *adv*
flex·ile \ˈflek-səl, -ˌsīl\ *adj* **:** FLEXIBLE
flex·ion \ˈflek-shən\ *n* [L *flexion-, flexio,* fr. *flexus,* pp. of *flectere*] **1 :** the act of flexing or bending **2 :** a part bent **:** BEND **3 :** INFLECTION 3 **4 a :** a bending of a joint between the bones of a limb that diminishes the angle between the bones — compare EXTENSION 3b **b :** a forward raising of the arm or leg by a movement at the shoulder or hip joint
flex·og·ra·phy \flek-ˈsäg-rə-fē\ *n* [*flexible* + *-o-* + *-graphy*] **:** a process of rotary letterpress printing utilizing flexible rubber plates and rapid-drying inks — **flexo·graph·ic** \ˌflek-sə-ˈgraf-ik\ *adj* — **flexo·graph·i·cal·ly** \-i-k(ə-)lē\ *adv*
flex·or \ˈflek-sər, -ˌsȯ(ə)r\ *n* **:** a muscle that produces flexion
flex·u·ous \ˈfleksh-(ə-)wəs\ *adj* [L *flexuosus,* fr. *flexus* bend, fr. *flexus,* pp.] **1 :** having turns or windings **2 :** lacking rigidity in structure or action ⟨its ~ and elastic body⟩ — **flex·u·ous·ly** *adv*
flex·ur·al \ˈflek-sh(ə-)rəl\ *adj* **1 :** of, relating to, or resulting from flexure **2 :** characterized by flexure
flex·ure \ˈflek-shər\ *n* **1 :** the quality or state of being flexed **:** FLEXION **2 :** TURN, FOLD
fley \ˈflā\ *vt* [ME *flayen,* fr. OE *āflēgan,* fr. *ā-,* perfective prefix + *-flēgan* to put to flight] *Scot* **:** FRIGHTEN
flib·ber·ti·gib·bet \ˌflib-ərt-ē-ˈjib-ət\ *n* [ME *flepergebet*] **:** a silly flighty person — **flib·ber·ti·gib·bety** \-ət-ē\ *adj*
flic \ˈflēk\ *n* [F] **:** a Parisian policeman
1flick \ˈflik\ *n* [imit.] **1 :** a light sharp jerky stroke or movement **2 :** a sound produced by a flick **3 :** DAUB, SPLOTCH
2flick *vt* **1 a :** to strike lightly with a quick sharp motion ⟨~*ed* the old horse with a whip⟩ **b :** to remove with light blows ⟨~*ed* the dust off his boots with a handkerchief⟩ **2 :** to cause to move with a flick ⟨~*ed* his cigarette against the ashtray⟩ ~ *vi* **1 :** FLUTTER **2 :** to direct flicks at something
3flick *n* [short for *2flicker*] **:** MOVIE
1flick·er \ˈflik-ər\ *vb* **flick·ered; flick·er·ing** \-(ə-)riŋ\ [ME *flikeren,* fr. OE *flicorian*] *vi* **1 :** to move irregularly or unsteadily **:** FLUTTER ⟨her eyes ~*ed* over the group⟩ **2 :** to burn fitfully or with a fluctuating light **3 :** to appear in a tremulous incomplete form ~ *vt* **1 :** to cause to flicker **2 :** to produce by flickering ⟨~ a signal with a mirror⟩ — **flick·er·ing·ly** \-(ə-)riŋ-lē\ *adv*
2flicker *n* **1 a :** an act of flickering **b :** a sudden brief movement **c :** a momentary quickening ⟨a ~ of anger⟩ **2 :** a wavering light **3 :** MOVIE — often used in pl. — **flick·ery** \ˈflik-(ə-)rē\ *adj*
3flicker *n* [prob. fr. *2flick*] **:** a common large brightly marked woodpecker (*Colaptes auratus*) of eastern No. America; *also* **:** any of several related birds of the southern and western U.S.
flick·er·tail \ˈflik-ər-ˌtāl\ *n* **:** a ground squirrel (*Citellus richardsoni*) chiefly of the north-central U.S. and adjacent Canada
flied *past of* FLY
fli·er \ˈflī(-ə)r\ *n* **1 :** one that flies; *specif* **:** AIRMAN **2 :** a reckless or speculative venture ⟨took a ~ in politics soon after getting his degree⟩ **3 :** an advertising circular for mass distribution **4 :** a step in a straight flight of steps
1flight \ˈflīt\ *n* [ME, fr. OE *flyht;* akin to MD *vlucht* flight, OE *flēogan* to fly] **1 a :** an act or instance of passing through the air by the use of wings ⟨the ~ of a bee⟩ **b :** the ability to fly ⟨~ is natural to birds⟩ **2 a :** a passing through the air or through space outside the earth's atmosphere ⟨~ of an arrow⟩ ⟨~ of a rocket to the moon⟩ **b :** the distance covered in such a flight **c :** swift movement **3 a :** a trip made by or in an airplane or spacecraft ⟨a rough ~ through storm clouds⟩ **b :** a scheduled airplane flight ⟨a ~ delayed because of poor weather conditions⟩ **4 :** a group of similar beings or objects flying through the air together **5 :** a brilliant, imaginative, or unrestrained exercise or display ⟨a ~ of fancy⟩ **6 a :** a continuous series of stairs from one landing or floor to another **b :** a series (as of terraces or conveyors) resembling a flight of stairs **7 :** a unit of the U.S. Air Force below a squadron — **flight·less** \-ləs\ *adj*
2flight *vi* **:** to rise, settle, or fly in a flock ⟨geese ~*ing* on the marsh⟩ ~ *vt* **:** 1FLUSH
3flight *n* [ME *fluht, fliht;* akin to OHG *fluht* flight, OE *flēon* to flee] **:** an act or instance of running away
flight bag *n* [*1flight*] **1 :** a lightweight traveling bag with zippered outside pockets **2 :** a small canvas satchel
flight control *n* **1 :** the control from a ground station of an airplane or spacecraft esp. by radio **2 :** the system of control devices of an airplane
flight deck *n* **1 :** the uppermost complete deck of an aircraft carrier **2 :** the forward compartment in some airplanes
flight engineer *n* **:** a flight crewman responsible for mechanical operation
flight feather *n* **:** one of the quills of a bird's wing or tail that support it in flight — compare CONTOUR FEATHER
flight lieutenant *n* **:** a commissioned officer in the British air force who ranks with a captain in the army
flight line *n* **1 :** a parking and servicing area for airplanes **2 :** the line in air or space along which something (as an airplane or missile) travels or is intended to travel
flight path *n* **:** the path in the air or space made or followed by something (as a particle, an airplane, or a spacecraft) in flight
flight pay *n* **:** an additional allowance paid to military personnel on flight status
flight plan *n* **:** a usu. written statement (as by a pilot) of the details of an intended flight (as of an airplane or spacecraft) usu. filed with an authority
flight status *n* **:** the status of a person in the military participating in regular authorized aircraft flights
flight strip *n* **:** an emergency landing field beside a highway
flight surgeon *n* **:** an air force medical officer trained in aeromedicine
flight–test \ˈflīt-ˌtest\ *vt* **:** to test (as an airplane or spacecraft) in flight
flighty \ˈflīt-ē\ *adj* **flight·i·er; -est** **1 :** SWIFT **2 :** lacking stability or steadiness: **a :** easily upset **:** VOLATILE ⟨a ~ temper⟩ **b :** easily excited **:** SKITTISH ⟨a ~ horse⟩ **c :** IRRESPONSIBLE, SILLY ⟨a ~ young girl⟩ — **flight·i·ly** \ˈflīt-ᵊl-ē\ *adv* — **flight·i·ness** \ˈflīt-ē-nəs\ *n*
1flim·flam \ˈflim-ˌflam\ *n* [prob. of Scand origin; akin to ON *flim* mockery] **1 :** DECEPTION, FRAUD **2 :** HANKY-PANKY
2flimflam *vt* **flim·flammed; flim·flam·ming :** to subject to a flimflam — **flim·flam·mer** *n*
1flim·sy \ˈflim-zē\ *adj* **flim·si·er; -est** [perh. alter. of *1film* + *-sy* (as in *tricksy*)] **1 a :** lacking in physical strength or substance ⟨~ silks⟩ **b :** of inferior materials and workmanship **2 :** having little worth or plausibility ⟨a ~ excuse⟩ ***syn*** see LIMP — **flim·si·ly** \-zə-lē\ *adv* — **flim·si·ness** \-zē-nəs\ *n*
2flimsy *n, pl* **flimsies** **1 :** a lightweight paper used esp. for multiple copies **2 :** a document printed on flimsy
flinch \ˈflinch\ *vi* [MF *flenchir* to bend] **:** to shrink from or as if from physical pain **:** WINCE; *esp* **:** to tense the muscles involuntarily in fear ***syn*** see RECOIL — **flinch** *n* — **flinch·er** *n*
flin·ders \ˈflin-dərz\ *n pl* [ME *flendris*] **:** SPLINTERS, FRAGMENTS
1fling \ˈfliŋ\ *vb* **flung** \ˈfləŋ\; **fling·ing** \ˈfliŋ-iŋ\ [ME *flingen,* of Scand origin; akin to ON *flengja* to whip, *flā* to flay — more at FLAY] *vi* **1 :** to move in a brusque or headlong manner ⟨~*ing* out of the room in a rage⟩ **2 :** to kick or plunge vigorously **3** *Scot* **:** CAPER ~ *vt* **1 a :** to throw with force or recklessness ⟨*flung* his books on the table⟩ **b :** to cast aside **:** DISCARD ⟨*flung* off all restraint⟩ **2 :** to place or send suddenly and unceremoniously ⟨the attack *flung* the enemy force into confusion⟩ **3 :** SPREAD, DIFFUSE **4 :** to give unrestrainedly ***syn*** see THROW — **fling·er** \ˈfliŋ-ər\ *n*
2fling *n* **1 :** an act or instance of flinging **2 :** a casual try ⟨willing to take a ~ at almost anything⟩ **3 :** a period devoted to self-indulgence ⟨determined to have one last ~ before settling down⟩
flint \ˈflint\ *n* [ME, fr. OE; akin to OHG *flins* pebble, hard stone] **1 :** a massive hard quartz that produces a spark when struck by steel **2 :** an implement of flint used by primitive man **3 :** a material used for producing a spark; *esp* **:** an alloy (as of iron and cerium) used in lighters **4 :** something resembling flint in hardness — **flint·like** \-ˌlīk\ *adj*
Flint *or* **Flints** *abbr* Flintshire
flint corn *n* **:** an Indian corn (*Zea mays indurata*) having hard horny usu. rounded kernels with the soft endosperm enclosed by a hard outer layer
flint glass *n* **:** heavy brilliant glass that contains lead oxide, has a relatively high index of refraction, and is used for optical structures
flint·lock \ˈflint-ˌläk\ *n* **1 :** a lock for a gun or pistol of the 17th and 18th centuries having a flint in the hammer for striking a spark to ignite the charge **2 :** a firearm fitted with a flintlock
flinty \ˈflint-ē\ *adj* **flint·i·er; -est** **1 :** composed of or covered with flint **2 :** UNYIELDING, STERN — **flint·i·ly** \ˈflint-ᵊl-ē\ *adv* — **flint·i·ness** \ˈflint-ē-nəs\ *n*
1flip \ˈflip\ *vb* **flipped; flip·ping** [prob. imit.] *vt* **1 a :** to toss with a sharp movement so as to cause to turn over in the air ⟨~ a coin⟩ **b :** THROW ⟨the shortstop *flipped* the ball to second base⟩ **2 :** FLICK 1 **3 :** to turn over ⟨*flipped* the record and played the other side⟩ ~ *vi* **1 a :** to make a twitching or flicking movement **b :** to strike at something with such a movement **2 :** to move jerkily **3 :** LEAF 2 ⟨*flipped* through the pages⟩ **4** *slang* **a :** to lose one's mind, composure, or self-control — often used with *out* **b :** to become extremely enthusiastic **:** go wild ⟨I just *flipped* over that vest⟩
2flip *n* **1 :** an act or instance of flipping **2 :** the motion used in flipping **3 :** a somersault esp. when performed in the air **4 :** a short quick football pass **5 :** a mixed drink usu. consisting of a sweetened spiced liquor (as beer, wine, or rum) to which beaten eggs have been added
3flip *adj* **:** FLIPPANT, IMPERTINENT
flip–flop \ˈflip-ˌfläp\ *n* **1 :** the sound or motion of something flapping loosely **2 a :** a backward handspring **b :** a sudden reversal of direction or point of view **3 :** a usu. electronic device or a circuit (as in a computer) capable of assuming either of two stable states — **flip–flop** *vi*
flip·pan·cy \ˈflip-ən-sē\ *n, pl* **-cies :** unbecoming levity or pertness esp. in respect to grave or sacred matters ***syn*** see LIGHTNESS ***ant*** seriousness

flip·pant \ˈflip-ənt\ *adj* [prob. fr. [1]*flip*] **1** *archaic* : GLIB, TALKATIVE **2** : lacking proper respect or seriousness ⟨a ~ answer to a serious question⟩ — **flip·pant·ly** *adv*

flip·per \ˈflip-ər\ *n* **1 a** : a broad flat limb (as of a seal) adapted for swimming **b** : a flat rubber shoe with the front expanded into a paddle used in skin diving **2** : one that flips

flip side *n* [[1]*flip*] : the reverse and usu. less popular side of a phonograph record

[1]**flirt** \ˈflərt\ *vb* [origin unknown] *vt* **1** : FLICK **2** : to move in a jerky manner ~ *vi* **1** : to move erratically : FLIT **2 a** : to behave amorously without serious intent **b** : to show superficial or casual interest or liking ⟨~*ed* with the idea of getting a job⟩ ***syn*** see TRIFLE — **flir·ta·tion** \ˌflər-ˈtā-shən\ *n* — **flirt·er** *n* — **flirty** \ˈflərt-ē\ *adj*

[2]**flirt** *n* **1** : an act or instance of flirting **2** : a person who flirts

flir·ta·tious \ˌflər-ˈtā-shəs\ *adj* : inclined to flirt : COQUETTISH — **flir·ta·tious·ly** *adv* — **flir·ta·tious·ness** *n*

flit \ˈflit\ *vi* **flit·ted; flit·ting** [ME *flitten*, of Scand origin; akin to ON *flytjask* to move, OE *flēotan* to float] **1** : to pass quickly or abruptly from one place or condition to another ⟨her imagination *flitted* back to her childhood⟩ **2** *archaic* : ALTER, SHIFT **3** : to move in an erratic fluttering manner — **flit** *n*

flitch \ˈflich\ *n* [ME *flicche*, fr. OE *flicce*] **1** : a side of pork cured and smoked as bacon **2 a** : a longitudinal section of a log **b** : a bundle of sheets of veneer laid together in sequence **3** : one of the parts secured together to make a girder or beam

[1]**flit·ter** \ˈflit-ər\ *vi* [freq. of *flit*] : FLUTTER, FLICKER

[2]**flitter** *n* : one that flits

fliv·ver \ˈfliv-ər\ *n* [origin unknown] : a small cheap usu. old automobile

[1]**float** \ˈflōt\ *n* [ME *flote* boat, float, fr. OE *flota* ship; akin to OHG *flōz* raft, stream, OE *flēotan* to float — more at FLEET] **1** : an act or instance of floating **2** : something that floats in or on the surface of a fluid: as **a** : a device (as a cork) buoying up the baited end of a fishing line **b** : a floating platform anchored near a shoreline for use by swimmers or boats **c** : a hollow ball that floats at the end of a lever in a cistern, tank, or boiler and regulates the liquid level **d** : a sac containing air or gas and buoying up the body of a plant or animal : PNEUMATOPHORE **e** : a watertight structure giving an airplane buoyancy on water **3** : a tool or apparatus for smoothing a surface **4** : a government grant of a fixed amount of land not yet located by survey out of a larger specific tract **5 a** : a vehicle with a platform used to carry an exhibit in a parade **b** : the vehicle and exhibit together **6** : an amount of money represented by checks outstanding and in process of collection **7** : a drink consisting of ice cream floating in a beverage — **floaty** \ˈflōt-ē\ *adj*

[2]**float** *vi* **1** : to rest on the surface of or be suspended in a fluid **2 a** : to drift on or through or as if on or through a liquid ⟨yellow leaves ~*ed* down⟩ **b** : WANDER **3** : to lack firmness of purpose : VACILLATE **4** *of a currency* : to find a level in the international exchange market in response to the law of supply and demand and without any restrictive effect of artificial support or control ⟨proposed that the mark be allowed to ~⟩ ~ *vt* **1** : to cause to float in or on the surface of a liquid **2** : to support (a structure) on a mat or raft foundation when the ground gives poor support **3** : FLOOD ⟨~ a cranberry bog⟩ **4** : to smooth (as plaster or cement) with a float **5 a** : to gain support for **b** : to place (an issue of securities) on the market **c** : to obtain money for the establishment or development of (an enterprise) by issuing and selling securities **d** : NEGOTIATE ⟨~ a loan⟩

float·age *var of* FLOTAGE

floa·ta·tion *var of* FLOTATION

float·er \ˈflōt-ər\ *n* **1 a** : one that floats **b** : a person who floats something **2 a** : a person who votes illegally in various polling places **b** : a person who represents an irregular constituency **3 a** : a person without a permanent residence or regular employment : VAGRANT **b** : an employee without a specific job **4** : a slow baseball pitch with little or no spin

float·ing *adj* **1** : buoyed on or in a fluid **2** : located out of the normal position ⟨a ~ kidney⟩ **3 a** : continually drifting or changing position ⟨the ~ population⟩ **b** : not presently committed or invested ⟨~ capital⟩ **c** : short-term and usu. not funded ⟨~ debt⟩ **4** : connected or constructed so as to operate and adjust smoothly ⟨a ~ axle⟩

floating dock *n* : a dock that floats on the water and can be partly submerged to permit entry of a ship and raised to keep the ship high and dry — called also *floating drydock*

floating island *n* : a dessert consisting of custard with floating masses of whipped white of egg

floating–point *adj* : involving or being a mathematical notation in which a quantity is denoted by one number multiplied by a power of the number base ⟨the fixed-point value 99.9 could be expressed in a ~ system as $.999 \times 10^2$⟩ — compare FIXED-POINT

floating rib *n* : a rib (as one of either of the last two pairs in man) that has no attachment to the sternum — compare FALSE RIB

float·plane \ˈflōt-ˌplān\ *n* : a seaplane supported on the water by one or more floats

[1]**floc** \ˈfläk\ *n* [short for *floccule*] **1** : a flocculent mass formed by the aggregation of a number of fine suspended particles **2** : [3]FLOCK 1,2,3

[2]**floc** *vb* **flocced** \ˈfläkt\; **floc·cing** \ˈfläk-iŋ\ *vi* : to aggregate into flocs ~ *vt* : to cause to floc

[1]**floc·cu·late** \ˈfläk-yə-ˌlāt\ *vb* **-lat·ed; -lat·ing** *vt* : to cause to aggregate into a flocculent mass ⟨~ clay⟩ ~ *vi* : to become flocculated — **floc·cu·lant** \-lənt\ *n* — **floc·cu·la·tion** \ˌfläk-yə-ˈlā-shən\ *n* — **floc·cu·la·tor** \ˈfläk-yə-ˌlāt-ər\ *n*

[2]**floc·cu·late** \-lət, -ˌlāt\ *n* : something that has flocculated

floc·cule \ˈfläk-(ˌ)yü(ə)l\ *n* [LL *flocculus*] : a small loosely aggregated bit of material suspended in or precipitated from a liquid

floc·cu·lence \ˈfläk-yə-lən(t)s\ *n* : a flocculent quality or state

floc·cu·lent \-lənt\ *adj* [L *floccus* + E *-ulent*] **1** : resembling wool esp. in loose fluffy organization **2** : made up of flocs or floccules ⟨a ~ precipitate⟩

floc·cu·lus \-ləs\ *n, pl* **-li** \-ˌlī, -ˌlē\ [LL, dim. of L *floccus* flock of wool; akin to OHG *blaha* coarse linen] **1** : a small loosely aggregated mass **2** : a bright or dark patch on the sun

[1]**flock** \ˈfläk\ *n* [ME, fr. OE *flocc* crowd, band; akin to ON *flokkr* crowd, band] **1** : a group of birds or mammals assembled or herded together **2** : a group under the guidance of a leader; *specif* : a church congregation in relation to the pastor **3** : a large number ⟨a whole ~ of tourists⟩

[2]**flock** *vi* : to gather or move in a crowd ⟨they ~*ed* to the beach⟩

[3]**flock** *n* [ME] **1** : a tuft of wool or cotton fiber **2** : woolen or cotton refuse used for stuffing furniture and mattresses **3** : very short or pulverized fiber used esp. to form a velvety pattern on cloth or paper or a protective covering on metal **4** : FLOC

[4]**flock** *vt* **1** : to fill with flock **2** : to decorate with flock

flock·ing \ˈfläk-iŋ\ *n* : a design in flock

floe \ˈflō\ *n* [prob. fr. Norw *flo* flat layer] **1** : floating ice formed in a large sheet on the surface of a body of water **2** : ICE FLOE

flog \ˈfläg\ *vt* **flogged; flog·ging** [perh. modif. of L *flagellare* to whip — more at FLAGELLATE] **1** : to beat with a rod or whip : LASH **2** : to criticize harshly ⟨newspapers *flogging* the government over tax inequities⟩ **3** : to force into action : DRIVE ⟨*flogging* his keen retentive memory —Nevil Shute⟩ **4** *chiefly Brit* : SELL; *esp* : to sell stolen goods — **flog·ger** *n* — **flog a dead horse** : to attempt to revive interest in a worn-out or forgotten subject

[1]**flood** \ˈfləd\ *n* [ME, fr. OE *flōd*; akin to OHG *fluot* flood, OE *flōwan* to flow] **1 a** : a rising and overflowing of a body of water esp. onto normally dry land **b** *cap* : a flood described in the Bible as covering the earth in the time of Noah **2** : the flowing in of the tide **3** : an overwhelming quantity or volume ⟨a ~ of mail at Christmas time⟩ **4** : FLOODLIGHT

[2]**flood** *vt* **1** : to cover with a flood : INUNDATE **2 a** : to fill abundantly or excessively ⟨strawberries ~*ed* the market and prices dropped⟩ **b** : to supply to (the carburetor of an internal-combustion engine) an excess of fuel so that engine operation is hampered **3** : to send more than one pass receiver into (the same defensive area in football) ~ *vi* **1** : to pour forth in a flood **2** : to become filled with a flood — **flood·er** *n*

flood·gate \ˈfləd-ˌgāt\ *n* **1** : a gate for shutting out, admitting, or releasing a body of water : SLUICE **2** : something serving to restrain an outburst

[1]**flood·light** \-ˌlīt\ *n* **1 a** : artificial illumination in a broad beam **b** : a source of such illumination **2** : a lighting unit for projecting a beam of light

[2]**floodlight** *vt* : to illuminate by means of one or more floodlights

flood·plain \ˈfləd-ˌplān\ *n* **1** : level land that may be submerged by floodwaters **2** : a plain built up by stream deposition

flood tide *n* **1** : a rising tide **2 a** : an overwhelming quantity **b** : a high point : PEAK

flood·wall \ˈfləd-ˌwȯl\ *n* : a wall (as a levee) built to prevent inundation by high water

flood·wa·ter \-ˌwȯt-ər, -ˌwät-\ *n* : the water of a flood

flood·way \-ˌwā\ *n* : a channel for diverting floodwaters

floo·ey \ˈflü-ē\ *adj* [origin unknown] : AWRY, ASKEW

[1]**floor** \ˈflō(ə)r, ˈflȯ(ə)r\ *n* [ME *flor*, fr. OE *flōr*; akin to OHG *fluor* meadow, L *planus* level, Gk *planasthai* to wander] **1** : the level base of a room **2 a** : the lower inside surface of a hollow structure (as a cave or bodily part) **b** : a ground surface ⟨the ocean ~⟩ **3 a** : a structure dividing a building into stories; *also* : STORY **b** : the occupants of such a floor ⟨the whole third ~ is furious⟩ **4** : the surface of a structure on which one travels ⟨the ~ of a bridge⟩ **5 a** : a main level space (as in a legislative chamber) distinguished from a platform or gallery **b** : the members of an assembly ⟨concluded by calling for questions from the ~⟩ **c** : the right to address an assembly ⟨the senator from Utah has the ~⟩ **6** : a lower limit : BASE ⟨a ~ under prices or wages⟩ — **floor** *adj*

[2]**floor** *vt* **1** : to cover with a floor or flooring **2 a** : to knock to the floor **b** : SHOCK, OVERWHELM **c** : to reduce to silence or defeat **3** : to press (the accelerator of a vehicle) to the floorboard — **floor·er** *n*

floor·age \ˈflōr-ij, ˈflȯr-\ *n* : floor space

floor·board \ˈflō(ə)r-ˌbō(ə)rd, ˈflȯ(ə)r-ˌbȯ(ə)rd\ *n* **1** : a board in a floor **2** : the floor of an automobile

floor exercise *n* : an event in gymnastics competition consisting of various ballet and tumbling movements (as jumps, somersaults, and handstands) performed without apparatus

floor furnace *n* : a small furnace located close below the floor

floor·ing \ˈflōr-iŋ, ˈflȯr-\ *n* **1** : FLOOR, BASE **2** : material for floors ⟨the disadvantages of softwood ~⟩

floor lamp *n* : a tall lamp that stands on the floor

floor leader *n* : a member of a legislative body chosen by his party to have charge of its organization and strategy on the floor

floor–length *adj* : reaching to the floor ⟨a ~ gown⟩

floor manager *n* **1** : FLOORWALKER **2** : a person who directs something (as the activities in support of a candidate at a nominating convention) from the floor

floor sample *n* : an article offered for sale at a reduced price because it has been used for display or demonstration

floor show *n* : a series of acts presented in a nightclub

floor·walk·er \ˈflōr-ˌwȯ-kər, ˈflȯr-\ *n* : a person employed in a retail store to oversee the salespeople and aid customers

floo·zy *or* **floo·zie** \ˈflü-zē\ *n, pl* **floozies** [origin unknown] : a tawdry or immoral woman; *specif* : PROSTITUTE

[1]**flop** \ˈfläp\ *vb* **flopped; flop·ping** [alter. of [2]*flap*] *vi* **1** : to swing or bounce loosely **2** : to throw or move oneself in a heavy, clumsy, or relaxed manner ⟨*flopped* into the chair with a sigh of relief⟩ **3** : to change suddenly **4** : to go to bed ⟨so tired I had to ~⟩ **5** : to fail completely ⟨in spite of good reviews the play *flopped*⟩ ~ *vt* : to move or drop heavily and noisily ⟨*flopped* the bundles down with a thud⟩ — **flop·per** *n*

[2]**flop** *n* **1** : an act or sound of flopping **2** : a complete failure : DUD

[3]**flop** *adv* : RIGHT, SQUARELY ⟨fell ~ on his face⟩

flop·house \ˈfläp-ˌhau̇s\ *n* : a cheap rooming house or hotel

flop·over \-ˌō-vər\ *n* : a defect in television reception in which a succession of frames appears to traverse the screen vertically
flop·py \ˈfläp-ē\ *adj* **flop·pi·er; -est** : tending to flop; *esp* : being both soft and flexible ***syn*** see LIMP — **flop·pi·ly** \ˈfläp-ə-lē\ *adv* — **flop·pi·ness** \ˈfläp-ē-nəs\ *n*
flo·ra \ˈflōr-ə, ˈflȯr-\ *n, pl* **floras** *also* **flo·rae** \ˈflō(ə)r-ˌē, ˈflȯ(ə)r-, -ˌī\ [NL, fr. L *Flora,* Roman goddess of flowers] **1** : a treatise on or list of the plants of an area or period **2** : plant life; *esp* : the plant life characteristic of a region, period, or special environment — compare FAUNA
flo·ral \ˈflōr-əl, ˈflȯr-\ *adj* [L *flor-, flos* flower — more at BLOW] : of or relating to flowers or a flora — **flo·ral·ly** \-ə-lē\ *adv*
floral envelope *n* : PERIANTH
floral leaf *n* **1** : a modified leaf (as a sepal or petal) of the perianth of a flower **2** : BRACT
Flor·ence flask \ˌflȯr-ən(t)s-, ˌflär-\ *n* [*Florence,* Italy; fr. the use of flasks of this shape for certain Italian wines] : a round usu. flat-bottomed laboratory vessel with a long neck
flo·res·cence \flō-ˈres-ᵊn(t)s, flə-\ *n* [NL *florescentia,* fr. L *florescent-, florescens,* prp. of *florescere,* incho. of *florēre* to blossom, flourish — more at FLOURISH] : a state or period of flourishing — **flo·res·cent** \-ᵊnt\ *adj*
flo·ret \ˈflōr-ət, ˈflȯr-\ *n* [ME *flourette,* fr. MF *flouret,* dim. of *flour* flower] : a small flower; *esp* : one of the small flowers forming the head of a composite plant
flori- *comb form* [L, fr. *flor-, flos*] : flower or flowers ⟨*floriculture*⟩
flo·ri·at·ed \ˈflōr-ē-ˌāt-əd, ˈflȯr-\ *adj* : having floral ornaments or a floral form ⟨a ~ border on a book cover⟩ — **flo·ri·a·tion** \ˌflōr-ē-ˈā-shən, ˌflȯr-\ *n*
flo·ri·bun·da \ˌflōr-ə-ˈbən-də, ˌflȯr-\ *n* [NL, fem. of *floribundus* flowering freely] : any of various bush roses with large flowers in open clusters that derive from crosses of polyantha and tea roses
flo·ri·cul·ture \ˈflōr-ə-ˌkəl-chər, ˈflȯr-\ *n* : the cultivation and management of ornamental and flowering plants — **flo·ri·cul·tur·al** \ˌflōr-ə-ˈkəlch(-ə)-rəl, ˌflȯr-\ *adj* — **flo·ri·cul·tur·al·ly** \-rə-lē\ *adv* — **flo·ri·cul·tur·ist** \-rəst\ *n*
flor·id \ˈflȯr-əd, ˈflär-\ *adj* [L *floridus* blooming, flowery, fr. *florēre*] **1 a** *obs* : covered with flowers **b** : excessively flowery in style : ORNATE **2** : tinged with red : RUDDY ⟨a ~ complexion⟩ **3** *archaic* : HEALTHY **4** : fully developed : manifesting a complete and typical clinical syndrome ⟨the ~ stage of a disease⟩ — **flo·rid·i·ty** \flə-ˈrid-ət-ē, flȯ-\ *n* — **flor·id·ly** \ˈflȯr-əd-lē, ˈflär-\ *adv* — **flor·id·ness** *n*
flo·rif·er·ous \flȯ-ˈrif-(ə-)rəs\ *adj* [L *florifer,* fr. *flori-*] : bearing flowers; *esp* : blooming freely — **flo·rif·er·ous·ly** *adv* — **flo·rif·er·ous·ness** *n*
flo·ri·gen \ˈflōr-ə-jən, ˈflȯr-\ *n* [ISV] : a hormone or hormonal agent that promotes flowering — **flo·ri·gen·ic** \ˌflōr-ə-ˈjen-ik, ˌflȯr-\ *adj*
flo·ri·le·gium \ˌflōr-ə-ˈlē-j(ē-)əm, ˌflȯr-\ *n, pl* **-gia** \-j(ē-)ə\ [NL, fr. L *florilegus* culling flowers, fr. *flori-* + *legere* to gather — more at LEGEND] : a volume of writings : ANTHOLOGY
flo·rin \ˈflȯr-ən, ˈflär-, ˈflōr-\ *n* [ME, fr. MF, fr. OIt *fiorino,* fr. *fiore* flower, fr. L *flor-, flos;* fr. the lily on the coins] **1 a** : an old gold coin first struck at Florence in 1252 **b** : any of various gold coins of European countries patterned after the Florentine florin **2 a** : a British silver coin worth two shillings **b** : any of several similar coins issued in British Commonwealth countries **3** : GULDEN **4** : FORINT
flo·rist \ˈflōr-əst, ˈflȯr-\ *n* : one who sells or grows for sale flowers and ornamental plants — **flo·rist·ry** \-ə-strē\ *n*
flo·ris·tic \flō-ˈris-tik\ *adj* : of or relating to flowers, a flora, or floristics — **flo·ris·ti·cal·ly** \-ti-k(ə-)lē\ *adv*
flo·ris·tics \-tiks\ *n pl but sing in constr* : a branch of phytogeography that deals numerically with plants and plant groups
-flo·rous \ˈflōr-əs, ˈflȯr-\ *adj comb form* [LL *-florus,* fr. L *flor-, flos*] : having or bearing (such or so many) flowers ⟨*uniflorous*⟩
flo·ru·it \ˈflȯr-(y)ə-wət, ˈflär-\ *n* [L, he flourished, fr. *florēre* to flourish] : a period of flourishing (as of a person, movement, or school)
floss \ˈfläs, ˈflȯs\ *n* [fr. or akin to D *vlos;* akin to MHG *vlus, vlius* fleece — more at FLEECE] **1** : waste or short silk fibers that cannot be reeled **2 a** : soft thread of silk or mercerized cotton for embroidery **b** : a lightweight wool knitting yarn **3** : fluffy fibrous material; *esp* : SILK COTTON
floss·flow·er \-ˌflau̇(-ə)r\ *n* : AGERATUM
flossy \ˈfläs-ē, ˈflȯs-\ *adj* **floss·i·er; -est** **1 a** : of, relating to, or having the characteristics of floss **b** : DOWNY **2** : stylish or glamorous esp. at first impression ⟨slick ~ writing⟩
flo·ta \ˈflōt-ə\ *n* [Sp] : a fleet of Spanish ships
flo·tage \ˈflōt-ij\ *n* [[2]*float*] **1** : FLOTATION 1 **2** : material that floats : FLOTSAM **3** *usu* **floatage** : the charge for transferring railroad cars on a barge
flo·ta·tion \flō-ˈtā-shən\ *n* [[2]*float*] **1** : the act, process, or state of floating **2** : an act or instance of financing (as an issue of stock) **3** : the separation of the particles of a mass of pulverized ore according to their relative capacity for floating on a given liquid; *also* : any of various similar processes involving the relative capacity of materials for floating **4** : the ability (as of a tire) to stay on the surface of soft ground or snow
flo·til·la \flō-ˈtil-ə\ *n* [Sp, dim. of *flota* fleet, fr. OF *flote,* fr. ON *floti;* akin to OE *flota* ship, fleet — more at FLOAT] **1** : a fleet of ships; *specif* : a navy organizational unit consisting of two or more squadrons of small warships **2** : a large force of moving things ⟨cleared by a ~ of bulldozers —R. L. Neuberger⟩
flot·sam \ˈflät-səm\ *n* [AF *floteson,* fr. OF *floter* to float, of Gmc origin; akin to OE *flotian* to float, *flota* ship] **1** : floating wreckage of a ship or its cargo; *broadly* : floating debris **2 a** : vagrant impoverished people **b** : unimportant miscellaneous material
[1]flounce \ˈflau̇n(t)s\ *vi* **flounced; flounc·ing** [perh. of Scand origin; akin to Norw *flunsa* to hurry] **1 a** : to move with exaggerated jerky motions ⟨little girls *flouncing* about in their mothers' clothes⟩ **b** : to go with sudden determination ⟨she *flounced* out of the room in a huff⟩ **2** : FLOUNDER, STRUGGLE
[2]flounce *n* : an act or instance of flouncing — **flouncy** \ˈflau̇n(t)-sē\ *adj*
[3]flounce *n* [alter. of earlier *frounce,* fr. ME *frouncen* to curl] : a strip of fabric attached by one edge; *also* : a wide ruffle — **flouncy** \ˈflau̇n(t)-sē\ *adj*
[4]flounce *vt* **flounced; flounc·ing** : to trim with flounces
flounc·ing \ˈflau̇n(t)-siŋ\ *n* : material used for flounces
[1]floun·der \ˈflau̇n-dər\ *n, pl* **flounder** *or* **flounders** [ME, of Scand origin; akin to ON *flythra* flounder, *flatr* flat] : FLATFISH; *esp* : one of either of two families (Pleuronectidae and Bothidae) that include important marine food fishes

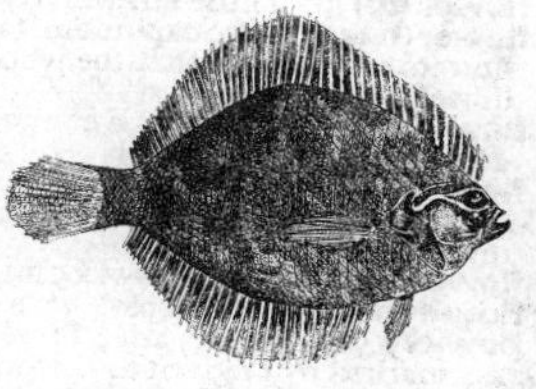

flounder

[2]flounder *vi* **floun·dered; floun·der·ing** \-d(ə-)riŋ\ [prob. alter. of *founder*] **1** : to struggle to move or obtain footing **2** : to proceed or act clumsily or ineffectually ⟨a bright student ~*ing* because of poor study habits⟩
[1]flour \ˈflau̇(ə)r\ *n* [ME — more at FLOWER] **1** : finely ground meal of wheat usu. largely freed from bran; *also* : a similar meal of another material (as a cereal grain, an edible seed, or dried processed fish) **2** : a fine soft powder — **floury** \-ē\ *adj*
[2]flour *vt* : to coat with or as if with flour ~ *vi* : to break up into particles
[1]flour·ish \ˈflər-ish, ˈflə-rish\ *vb* [ME *florisshen,* fr. MF *floriss-,* stem of *florir,* fr. (assumed) VL *florire,* alter. of L *florēre,* fr. *flor-, flos* flower] *vi* **1** : to grow luxuriantly : THRIVE **2 a** : to achieve success : PROSPER **b** : to be in a state of activity or production ⟨~*ed* around 1850⟩ **c** : to reach a height of development or influence **3** : to make bold and sweeping gestures ~ *vt* : to wield with dramatic gestures : BRANDISH ***syn*** **1** see SUCCEED ***ant*** languish **2** see SWING — **flour·ish·er** *n* — **flour·ish·ing·ly** \-iŋ-lē\ *adv*
[2]flourish *n* **1** : a period of thriving **2 a** : an extraneous florid embellishment or passage **b** : an act or instance of brandishing : WAVE **c** : a studied or ostentatious action
[1]flout \ˈflau̇t\ *vb* [prob. fr. ME *flouten* to play the flute, fr. *floute* flute] *vt* : to treat with contemptuous disregard : SCORN ⟨~*ing* the rules⟩ ~ *vi* : to indulge in scornful behavior ***syn*** see SCOFF — **flout·er** *n*
[2]flout *n* **1** : INSULT **2** : MOCKERY
[1]flow \ˈflō\ *vb* [ME *flowen,* fr. OE *flōwan;* akin to OHG *flouwen* to rinse, wash, L *pluere* to rain, Gk *plein* to sail, float] *vi* **1 a** (1) : to issue or move in a stream (2) : CIRCULATE **b** : to move with a continual change of place among the constituent particles ⟨the molasses ~*ed* slowly⟩ **2** : RISE ⟨the tide ebbs and ~*s*⟩ **3** : ABOUND **4 a** : to proceed smoothly and readily ⟨conversation ~*ed* easily⟩ **b** : to have a smooth uninterrupted continuity ⟨the ~*ing* lines of the car⟩ **5** : to hang loose and billowing **6** : to derive from a source : COME ⟨the wealth that ~*s* from our industries⟩ **7** : to deform under stress without cracking or rupturing — used esp. of minerals and rocks **8** : MENSTRUATE ~ *vt* **1 a** : to cause to flow **b** : to cover with water : FLOOD **2** : to discharge in a flow ***syn*** see SPRING — **flow·ing·ly** \-iŋ-lē\ *adv*
[2]flow *n* **1** : an act of flowing **2** : FLOOD 1a, 2 **3 a** : a smooth uninterrupted movement **b** : STREAM **c** : the direction of movement or apparent movement (as of a play in football) **4** : the quantity that flows in a certain time **5 a** : MENSTRUATION **b** : YIELD, PRODUCTION **6 a** : the motion characteristic of fluids **b** : a continuous transfer of energy
flow·age \ˈflō-ij\ *n* **1 a** : an overflowing onto adjacent land **b** : a body of water formed by overflowing or damming **c** : floodwater esp. of a stream **2** : gradual deformation of a body of plastic solid (as rock) by intermolecular shear
flow·chart \-ˌchärt\ *n* : a diagram consisting of a set of symbols (as rectangles or diamonds) and connecting lines that shows step-by-step progression through a usu. complicated procedure or system
flow diagram *n* : FLOWCHART
[1]flow·er \ˈflau̇(-ə)r\ *n* [ME *flour* flower, best of anything, flour, fr. OF *flor, flour,* fr. L *flor-, flos* — more at BLOW] **1 a** : BLOSSOM, INFLORESCENCE **b** : a shoot of the sporophyte of a higher plant that is modified for reproduction and consists of a shortened axis bearing modified leaves **c** : a plant cultivated for its blossoms **2 a** : the best part or example ⟨the ~ of a nation's youth sent off to war⟩ **b** : the finest most vigorous period **c** : a state of blooming or flourishing **3** *pl* : a finely divided powder produced esp. by condensation or sublimation ⟨~*s* of sulfur⟩ — **flow·ered** \ˈflau̇(-ə)rd \ *adj* — **flow·er·less** \ˈflau̇(-ə)r-ləs\ *adj* — **flow·er·like** \-ˌlīk\ *adj*

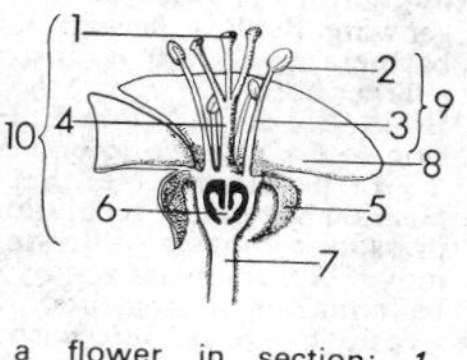

a flower in section: *1* stigma, *2* anther, *3* filament, *4* style, *5* sepal, *6* ovary, *7* pedicel, *8* petal, *9* stamen, *10* pistil

[2]flower *vi* **1** : to produce flowers : BLOSSOM **2 a** : DEVELOP ⟨~*ed* into young womanhood⟩ **b** : FLOURISH ~ *vt* **1** : to cause to bear flowers **2** : to decorate with floral designs — **flow·er·er** \ˈflau̇(-ə)r-ər\ *n*

ə abut ᵊ kitten ər further a back ā bake ä cot, cart au̇ out ch chin e less ē easy g gift i trip ī life j joke ŋ sing ō flow ȯ flaw ȯi coin th thin t͟h this ü loot u̇ foot y yet yü few yu̇ furious zh vision

flow·er·age \'flau̇(-ə)r-ij\ *n* **:** a flowering state
flower bud *n* **:** a plant bud that produces only a flower
flower bug *n* **:** any of various small mostly black-and-white predaceous bugs (family Anthocoridae) that frequent flowers and feed on pest insects (as aphids and thrips)
flower child *n* [fr. his displaying of flowers as a symbol of his sentiments] **:** a hippie who advocates love, beauty, and peace
flow·er·et \'flau̇(-ə)r-ət\ *n* **:** FLORET
flower girl *n* **:** a little girl who carries flowers at a wedding
flower head *n* **:** a capitulum (as of a composite) having sessile flowers so arranged that the whole inflorescence looks like a single flower
flowering dogwood *n* **:** a common spring-flowering white-bracted dogwood (*Cornus florida*)
flowering plant *n* **1 :** a plant that produces flowers, fruit, and seed **:** ANGIOSPERM **2 :** a plant notable for or cultivated for its ornamental flowers
flower people *n pl* **:** FLOWER CHILDREN
flow·er·pot \'flau̇(-ə)r-,pät\ *n* **:** a pot in which to grow plants
flow·ery \'flau̇(-ə)r-ē\ *adj* **1 :** of, relating to, or resembling flowers **2 :** marked by or given to rhetorical elegance — **flow·er·i·ness** *n*
1**flown** \'flōn\ *past part of* FLY
2**flown** *adj* [archaic pp. of 1*flow*] **:** filled to excess
flow sheet *n* **:** FLOWCHART
flow·stone \'flō-,stōn\ *n* **:** travertine found where water flowing in a very thin sheet over rocks has deposited mineral matter
fl oz *abbr* fluidounce
FLS *abbr* Fellow of the Linnean Society
FLSA *abbr* Fair Labor Standards Act
flu \'flü\ *n* **1 :** INFLUENZA **2 :** any of several virus diseases marked esp. by respiratory symptoms
1**flub** \'fləb\ *vb* **flubbed; flub·bing** [origin unknown] *vt* **:** to make a mess of **:** BOTCH ~ *vi* **:** BLUNDER
2**flub** *n* **:** an act or instance of flubbing
flub·dub \'fləb-,dəb\ *n* [origin unknown] **:** CLAPTRAP, BUNKUM
fluc·tu·ant \'flək-chə-wənt\ *adj* **1 :** moving in waves **2 :** VARIABLE, UNSTABLE **3 :** being movable and compressible ⟨a ~ abscess⟩
fluc·tu·ate \'flək-chə-,wāt\ *vb* **-at·ed; -at·ing** [L *fluctuatus*, pp. of *fluctuare*, fr. *fluctus* flow, wave, fr. *fluctus*, pp. of *fluere*] *vi* **1 :** to ebb and flow in waves **2 :** to shift back and forth uncertainly ~ *vt* **:** to cause to fluctuate ***syn*** see SWING — **fluc·tu·a·tion** \,flək-chə-'wā-shən\ *n*
flue \'flü\ *n* [origin unknown] **:** an enclosed passageway for directing a current: as **a :** a channel in a chimney for conveying flame and smoke to the outer air **b :** a pipe for conveying flame and hot gases around or through water in a steam boiler **c :** an air channel leading to the lip of a wind instrument
flue–cured \-,kyu̇(ə)rd\ *adj* **:** cured with heat transmitted through a flue without exposure to smoke or fumes ⟨~ tobacco⟩ — compare FIRE-CURED
flu·en·cy \'flü-ən-sē\ *n* **:** the quality or state of being fluent
flu·ent \'flü-ənt\ *adj* [L *fluent-*, *fluens*, prp. of *fluere*] **1 :** capable of flowing **:** FLUID **2 a :** ready or facile in speech ⟨~ in Spanish⟩ **b :** effortlessly smooth and rapid **:** POLISHED ⟨a ~ performance⟩ — **flu·ent·ly** *adv*
flue pipe *n* **:** an organ pipe whose tone is produced by an air current striking the lip and causing the air within to vibrate — compare REED PIPE
flu·er·ic \flü-'er-ik\ *adj* **:** FLUIDIC — **flu·er·ics** \-iks\ *n pl but sing in constr*
flue stop *n* **:** an organ stop made up of flue pipes
1**fluff** \'fləf\ *n* [prob. alter. of *flue* (fluff)] **1 :** NAP, DOWN **2 :** something fluffy **3 :** something inconsequential **4 :** BLUNDER; *esp* **:** an actor's lapse of memory
2**fluff** *vi* **1 :** to become fluffy **2 :** to make a mistake; *esp* **:** to forget or bungle one's lines in a play ~ *vt* **1 :** to make fluffy **2 a :** to spoil by a mistake **:** BOTCH **b :** to deliver badly or forget (one's lines) in a play
fluffy \'fləf-ē\ *adj* **fluff·i·er; -est 1 a :** covered with or resembling fluff **b :** being light and soft or airy ⟨a ~ omelet⟩ **2 :** lacking in intellectual content or decisive quality ⟨vague, ~, uncertain policies —Geoffrey Crowther⟩ — **fluff·i·ness** *n*
flü·gel·horn *or* **flue·gel·horn** \'flü-gəl-,hȯ(ə)rn, 'flue-\ *n* [G, fr. *flügel* wing, flank + *horn*; fr. its use to signal the flanking drivers in a battue] **:** a valved brass instrument resembling a cornet but having a larger bore
1**flu·id** \'flü-əd\ *adj* [F or L; F *fluide*, fr. L *fluidus*, fr. *fluere* to flow; akin to Gk *phlyzein* to boil over, L *flare* to blow — more at BLOW] **1 a :** having particles that easily move and change their relative position without a separation of the mass and that easily yield to pressure **:** capable of flowing **b :** likely or tending to change or move **2 :** characterized by or employing a smooth easy style ⟨the ballerina's ~ movements⟩ **3 a :** available for a different use **b :** easily converted into cash ⟨~ assets⟩ — **flu·id·ly** *adv* — **flu·id·ness** *n*
2**fluid** *n* **:** a substance (as a liquid or gas) tending to flow or conform to the outline of its container — **flu·id·al** \-əd-ᵊl\ *adj* — **flu·id·al·ly** \-ᵊl-ē\ *adv*
fluid drive *n* **:** an automotive power coupling that operates on a hydraulic turbine principle with the flywheel having a set of turbine blades connected directly to it and driving them in oil thereby turning another set of turbine blades attached to the transmission gears
flu·id·ex·tract \,flü-ə-'dek-,strakt\ *n* **:** an alcohol preparation of a vegetable drug containing the active constituents of one gram of the dry drug in each milliliter
flu·id·ic \flü-'id-ik\ *adj* **:** of, relating to, or being a device (as an amplifier or control) that depends for operation on the pressures and flows of a fluid in precisely shaped channels — **fluidic** *n* — **flu·id·ics** \-iks\ *n pl but sing in constr*
flu·id·i·ty \flü-'id-ət-ē\ *n* **1 :** the quality or state of being fluid **2 :** the physical property of a substance that enables it to flow
flu·id·ize \'flü-ə-,dīz\ *vt* **-ized; -iz·ing 1 :** to cause to flow like a fluid **2 :** to suspend (as solid particles) in a rapidly moving stream of gas or vapor to induce flowing motion of the whole; *esp* **:** to fluidize the particles of (a loose bed of material) in an upward flow (as of a gas) for enhancing a chemical or physical reaction — **flu·id·iza·tion** \,flü-əd-ə-'zā-shən\ *n* — **flu·id·iz·er** \'flü-ə-,dī-zər\ *n*
fluid mechanics *n pl but sing or pl in constr* **:** a branch of mechanics dealing with the properties of liquids and gases
flu·id·ounce \,flü-ə-'dau̇n(t)s\ *n* **1 :** a U.S. unit of liquid capacity equal to $1/16$ pint — see WEIGHT table **2 :** a British unit of liquid capacity equal to $1/20$ pint — see WEIGHT table
flu·idram \,flü-ə(d)-'dram\ *n* [blend of 1*fluid* and *dram*] **:** a unit of liquid capacity equal to $1/8$ fluidounce — see WEIGHT table
1**fluke** \'flük\ *n* [ME, fr. OE *flōc*; akin to OHG *flah* smooth — more at FLAKE] **1 :** FLATFISH **2 :** a flattened digenetic trematode worm; *broadly* **:** TREMATODE
2**fluke** *n* [perh. fr. 1*fluke*] **1 :** the part of an anchor that fastens in the ground — see ANCHOR illustration **2 :** a barbed head (as of a harpoon) **3 :** one of the lobes of a whale's tail
3**fluke** *n* [origin unknown] **1 :** an accidentally successful stroke at billiards or pool **2 :** a stroke of luck ⟨the discovery was a ~⟩
fluky *also* **fluk·ey** \'flü-kē\ *adj* **fluk·i·er; -est 1 :** happening by or depending on chance **2 :** being unsteady or uncertain **:** CHANGEABLE ⟨a ~ wind⟩
flume \'flüm\ *n* [prob. fr. ME *flum* river, fr. OF, fr. L *flumen*, fr. *fluere*] **1 :** a ravine or gorge with a stream running through it **2 :** an inclined channel for conveying water (as for power)
flum·mery \'fləm-(ə-)rē\ *n, pl* **-mer·ies** [W *llymru*] **1 a :** a soft jelly or porridge made with flour or meal **b :** any of several sweet desserts **2 :** MUMMERY, MUMBO JUMBO
flum·mox \'fləm-əks, -iks\ *vt* [origin unknown] **:** CONFUSE
1**flump** \'fləmp\ *n* [imit.] **:** a dull heavy sound (as of a fall)
2**flump** *vi* **:** to move or fall suddenly and heavily ⟨~*ed* down into his chair with a sigh⟩ ~ *vt* **:** to place or drop with a flump
flung *past of* FLING
1**flunk** \'fləŋk\ *vb* [perh. blend of *flinch* and *funk*] *vi* **:** to fail esp. in an examination or course ~ *vt* **1 :** to give a failing grade to **2 :** to get a failing grade in — **flunk·er** *n*
2**flunk** *n* **:** an act or instance of flunking
flunk out *vi* **:** to be dismissed from a school or college for failure ~ *vt* **:** to dismiss from a school or college for failure
flun·ky *or* **flun·key** \'fləŋ-kē\ *n, pl* **flunkies** *or* **flunkeys** [Sc, of unknown origin] **1 a :** a liveried servant **b :** one performing menial duties ⟨worked as a ~ in a lumber camp⟩ **2 :** YES-MAN
flu·o·cin·o·lone ac·e·to·nide \,flü-ə-'sin-ᵊl-,ōn-,as-ə-'tō-,nīd\ *n* [*fluor-* + *cin-* (of unknown origin) + *-ol* + cortis*one* + *acetone* + *-ide*] **:** a steroid $C_{24}H_{30}F_2O_6$ used esp. as an anti-inflammatory agent in the treatment of skin diseases
flu·or \'flü-,ȯ(ə)r, 'flü-ər\ *n* [NL, mineral belonging to a group used as fluxes and including fluorite, fr. L, flow, fr. *fluere* — more at FLUID] **:** FLUORITE
fluor- *or* **fluoro-** *comb form* [F, fr. *fluorine*] **1 :** fluorine ⟨*fluor*ide⟩ **2** *also* **fluori- :** fluorescence ⟨*fluoro*scope⟩ ⟨*fluori*meter⟩
flu·o·resce \,flu̇(-ə)r-'es, flōr-, flȯr-\ *vi* **-resced; -resc·ing** [back-formation fr. *fluorescence*] **:** to produce, undergo, or exhibit fluorescence — **flu·o·resc·er** *n*
flu·o·res·ce·in \-'es-ē-ən\ *n* **:** a yellow or red crystalline dye $C_{20}H_{12}O_5$ with a bright yellow-green fluorescence in alkaline solution
flu·o·res·cence \-'es-ᵊn(t)s\ *n* **:** emission of or the property of emitting electromagnetic radiation usu. as visible light resulting from and occurring only during the absorption of radiation from some other source; *also* **:** the radiation emitted
flu·o·res·cent \-'es-ᵊnt\ *adj* **1 :** having or relating to fluorescence **2 :** bright and glowing as a result of fluorescence ⟨a ~ pink⟩
fluorescent lamp *n* **:** a tubular electric lamp having a coating of fluorescent material on its inner surface and containing mercury vapor whose bombardment by electrons from the cathode provides ultraviolet light which causes the material to emit visible light
flu·o·ri·date \'flu̇r-ə-,dāt, 'flōr-, 'flȯr-\ *vt* **-dat·ed; -dat·ing :** to add a fluoride to (as drinking water) — **flu·o·ri·da·tion** \,flu̇r-ə-'dā-shən, ,flōr-, ,flȯr-\ *n*
flu·o·ride \'flu̇(-ə)r-,īd\ *n* **:** a compound of fluorine usu. with another element or a radical
flu·o·ri·nate \'flu̇r-ə-,nāt, 'flōr-, 'flȯr-\ *vt* **-nat·ed; -nat·ing :** to treat or cause to combine with fluorine or a compound of fluorine — **flu·o·ri·na·tion** \,flu̇r-ə-'nā-shən, ,flōr-, ,flȯr-\ *n*
flu·o·rine \'flu̇(-ə)r-,ēn, -ən\ *n* [F, fr. NL *fluor*] **:** a nonmetallic univalent halogen element that is normally a pale yellowish flammable irritating toxic gas — see ELEMENT table
flu·o·rite \'flu̇(-ə)r-,īt\ *n* [It] **:** a transparent or translucent mineral CaF_2 of different colors that consists of calcium fluoride and is used as a flux and in the making of opalescent and opaque glasses
flu·o·ro·car·bon \,flu̇(-ə)r-ō-'kär-bən\ *n* **:** any of various chemically inert compounds containing carbon and fluorine used chiefly as lubricants and refrigerants and in making resins and plastics
flu·o·ro·chrome \'flu̇(-ə)r-ə-,krōm\ *n* **:** any of various fluorescent substances used in biological staining to produce fluorescence in a specimen
flu·o·rog·ra·phy \,flu̇(-ə)r-'äg-rə-fē\ *n* **:** PHOTOFLUOROGRAPHY — **flu·o·ro·graph·ic** \,flu̇(-ə)r-ə-'graf-ik\ *adj*
flu·o·rom·e·ter \,flu̇(-ə)r-'äm-ət-ər\ *or* **flu·o·rim·e·ter** \-'im-\ *n* **:** an instrument for measuring fluorescence and related phenomena (as intensity of radiation) — **flu·o·ro·met·ric** *or* **flu·o·ri·met·ric** \,flu̇(-ə)r-ə-'me-trik\ *adj* — **flu·o·rom·e·try** \,flu̇(-ə)r-'äm-ə-trē\ *or* **flu·o·rim·e·try** \-'im-\ *n*
1**flu·o·ro·scope** \'flu̇r-ə-,skōp\ *n* [ISV] **:** an instrument used for observing the internal structure of an opaque object (as the living body) by means of X rays — **flu·o·ro·scop·ic** \,flu̇r-ə-'skäp-ik\ *adj* — **flu·o·ro·scop·i·cal·ly** \-i-k(ə-)lē\ *adv* — **flu·o·ros·co·pist** \,flu̇(-ə)r-'äs-kə-pəst\ *n* — **flu·o·ros·co·py** \-pē\ *n*
2**fluoroscope** *vt* **-scoped; -scop·ing :** to examine by fluoroscopy
flu·o·ro·sis \,flu̇(-ə)r-'ō-səs\ *n* **:** an abnormal condition (as of the teeth) caused by fluorine or its compounds — **flu·o·rot·ic** \-'ät-ik\ *adj*

flu·o·ro·ura·cil \ˌflu̇(-ə)r-ō-ˈyu̇r-ə-ˌsil, -ˌsəl\ *n* [*fluor-* + *uracil*] : a fluorine-containing pyrimidine base $C_4H_3FN_2O_2$ used to treat some kinds of cancer

flu·or·spar \ˈflu̇(-ə)r-ˌspär\ *n* : FLUORITE

flu·phen·azine \flü-ˈfen-ə-ˌzēn\ *n* [*fluor-* + *phenazine*] : a tranquilizing compound $C_{22}H_{26}F_3N_3OS$ used esp. combined as a salt

1**flur·ry** \ˈflər-ē, ˈflə-rē\ *n, pl* **flurries** [prob. fr. *flurr* (to throw scatteringly)] **1 a** : a gust of wind **b** : a brief light snowfall **2** : a state of nervous upset or scurrying bustle **3** : a brief advance or decline in prices : a short-lived outburst of trading activity ***syn*** see STIR

2**flurry** *vb* **flur·ried; flur·ry·ing** *vt* : to cause to become agitated and confused ~ *vi* : to become flurried ***syn*** see DISCOMPOSE

1**flush** \ˈfləsh\ *vb* [ME *flusshen*] *vi* : to take wing suddenly ~ *vt* **1** : to cause (a bird) to flush **2** : to expose or chase from a place of concealment ⟨~*ed* the boys from their hiding place⟩

2**flush** *n* [perh. modif. of L *fluxus* — more at FLUX] **1** : a sudden flow (as of water); *also* : a rinsing or cleansing with or as if with a flush of water **2 a** : a sudden increase or expansion; *esp* : sudden and usu. abundant new plant growth **b** : a surge of emotion ⟨felt a ~ of anger at the insult⟩ **3 a** : a tinge of red : BLUSH **b** : a fresh and vigorous state ⟨in the first ~ of womanhood⟩ **4** : a transitory sensation of extreme heat

3**flush** *vi* **1** : to flow and spread suddenly and freely **2 a** : to glow brightly **b** : BLUSH ⟨~*ed* when she saw the picture⟩ **3** : to produce new growth ⟨the plants ~*ed* twice during the year⟩ ~ *vt* **1 a** : to cause to flow **b** : to pour liquid over or through; *esp* : to cleanse or wash out with or as if with a rush of liquid ⟨~ the toilet⟩ ⟨~ the lungs with air⟩ **2** : INFLAME, EXCITE — usu. used passively ⟨~*ed* with victory⟩ **3** : to cause to blush **4** : to prepare (sheep) for breeding by special feeding

4**flush** *adj* **1 a** : filled to overflowing **b** : AFFLUENT **2 a** : full of life and vigor : LUSTY **b** : of a ruddy healthy color **3** : readily available : ABUNDANT **4 a** : having or forming a continuous plane or unbroken surface ⟨~ paneling⟩ **b** : directly abutting or immediately adjacent: as (1) : set even with an edge of a type page or column : having no indention (2) : arranged edge to edge so as to fit snugly — **flush·ness** *n*

5**flush** *adv* **1** : in a flush manner **2** : SQUARELY ⟨hit him ~ on the chin⟩

6**flush** *vt* : to make flush ⟨~ the headings on a page⟩

7**flush** *n* [MF *flus, fluz,* fr. L *fluxus* flow] **1** : a hand of playing cards all of the same suit; *specif* : a poker hand containing five cards of the same suit but not in sequence — see POKER illustration **2** : a series of three or more slalom gates set vertically on a slope

1**flus·ter** \ˈfləs-tər\ *vb* **flus·tered; flus·ter·ing** \-t(ə-)riŋ\ [prob. of Scand origin; akin to Icel *flaustur* hurry] *vt* **1** : to make tipsy **2** : to put into a state of agitated confusion : UPSET ~ *vi* : to move or behave in an agitated or confused manner ***syn*** see DISCOMPOSE

2**fluster** *n* : a state of agitated confusion

1**flute** \ˈflüt\ *n* [ME *floute,* fr. MF *flahute,* fr. OProv *flaut*] **1 a** : RECORDER 3 **b** : a keyed woodwind instrument consisting of a cylindrical tube which is stopped at one end and which has a side hole over which air is blown to produce the tone and having a range from middle C upward for three octaves **2 a** : a grooved pleat (as on a hat brim) **b** : a rounded groove; *specif* : one of the vertical parallel grooves on a classical architectural column — **flute·like** \-ˌlīk\ *adj*

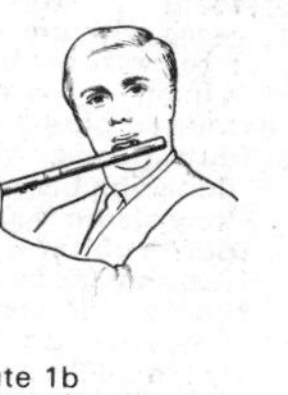

flute 1b

2**flute** *vb* **flut·ed; flut·ing** *vi* **1** : to play a flute **2** : to produce a flutelike sound ~ *vt* **1** : to utter with a flutelike sound **2** : to form flutes in — **flut·er** *n*

flut·ing \ˈflüt-iŋ\ *n* **1** : a series of flutes : FLUTE ⟨the ~ of a column⟩ **2** : fluted material

flut·ist \ˈflüt-əst\ *n* : one who plays a flute

1**flut·ter** \ˈflət-ər\ *vb* [ME *floteren* to float, flutter, fr. OE *floterian,* freq. of *flotian* to float; akin to OE *flēotan* to float — more at FLEET] *vi* **1** : to flap the wings rapidly **2 a** : to move with quick wavering or flapping motions ⟨flags ~*ing* in the wind⟩ **b** : to vibrate in irregular spasms **3** : to move about or behave in an agitated aimless manner ~ *vt* : to cause to flutter — **flut·ter·er** \-ər-ər\ *n* — **flut·tery** \-ə-rē\ *adj*

2**flutter** *n* **1** : an act of fluttering **2 a** : a state of nervous confusion or excitement **b** : FLURRY, COMMOTION **c** : abnormal spasmodic fluttering of a body part ⟨treatment of atrial ~⟩ **3 a** : a distortion in reproduced sound similar to but of a higher pitch than wow **b** : fluctuation in the brightness of a television image **4** : an unwanted oscillation (as of an aileron or a bridge) set up by natural forces **5** *chiefly Brit* : a small speculative venture or gamble ⟨took a ~ on the ponies⟩

flut·ter·board \ˈflət-ər-ˌbō(ə)rd, -ˌbȯ(ə)rd\ *n* : a rectangular board used by swimmers in practicing leg strokes

flutter kick *n* : an alternating whipping motion of the legs used in various swimming styles (as the crawl)

flu·vi·al \ˈflü-vē-əl\ *adj* [L *fluvialis,* fr. *fluvius* river, fr. *fluere*] **1** : of, relating to, or living in a stream or river **2** : produced by stream action

flu·vi·a·tile \ˈflü-vē-ə-ˌtīl\ *adj* [MF, fr. L *fluviatilis,* irreg. fr. *fluvius*] : FLUVIAL

1**flux** \ˈfləks\ *n* [ME, fr. MF & ML; MF, fr. ML *fluxus,* fr. L, flow, fr. *fluxus,* pp. of *fluere* to flow — more at FLUID] **1** : a flowing of fluid from the body; *esp* : an excessive abnormal discharge from the bowels **2** : a continuous moving on or passing by (as of a stream) **3** : a continued flow : FLOOD **4 a** : INFLUX **b** : CHANGE, FLUCTUATION ⟨the program was in a state of ~⟩ **5 a** : a substance used to promote fusion esp. of metals or minerals **b** : a substance (as rosin) applied to surfaces to be joined by soldering, brazing, or welding to clean and free them from oxide and promote their union **6** : the rate of transfer of fluid, particles, or energy across a given surface

2**flux** *vt* **1** : to cause to become fluid **2** : to treat with a flux ~ *vi* : to become fluid : FUSE

flux gate *n* : a device used to indicate the direction of the terrestrial magnetic field — called also *flux valve*

flux·ion \ˈflək-shən\ *n* **1** : constant change **2** *pl, archaic* : CALCULUS 3b — **flux·ion·al** \-shnəl, -shən-ᵊl\ *adj*

1**fly** \ˈflī\ *vb* **flew** \ˈflü\; **flown** \ˈflōn\; **fly·ing** [ME *flien,* fr. OE *flēogan;* akin to OHG *fliogan* to fly, OE *flōwan* to flow] *vi* **1 a** : to move in or pass through the air with wings **b** : to move through the air or before the wind ⟨clouds ~*ing* across the sky⟩; *also* : to move through outer space **c** : to float, wave, or soar in the air ⟨flags ~*ing* at half-mast⟩ **2 a** : to take flight : FLEE **b** : to fade and disappear : VANISH **3 a** : to move or pass swiftly **b** : to be moved with violence ⟨*flew* into a rage⟩ **c** : to seem to pass quickly ⟨our vacation simply *flew*⟩ **4** : to become expended or dissipated rapidly **5** : to pursue or attack in flight **6** : to operate or travel in an airplane or spacecraft ~ *vt* **1 a** : to cause to fly or float in the air ⟨was ~*ing* his kite⟩ **b** : to operate (as a balloon, aircraft, rocket, or spacecraft) in flight **c** : to journey over by flying **2 a** : to flee or escape from **b** : AVOID, SHUN **3** : to transport by airplane — **fly at** : to assail suddenly and violently — **fly blind** : to fly an airplane solely by instruments — **fly contact** : to fly an airplane with the aid of visible landmarks or reference points — **fly high** : to be elated — **fly in the face of** *or* **fly in the teeth of** : to act forthrightly or brazenly in defiance or disobedience of

2**fly** *n, pl* **flies** **1** : the action or process of flying : FLIGHT **2 a** : a device consisting of two or more radial vanes capable of rotating on a spindle to act as a fan or to govern the speed of clockwork or very light machinery **b** : FLYWHEEL **3 a** : a horse-drawn public coach or delivery wagon **b** *chiefly Brit* : a light covered carriage or cab **4** *pl* : the space over a theater stage where scenery and equipment can be hung **5** : something attached by one edge: as **a** : a garment closing concealed by a fold of cloth extending over the fastener **b** : the outer canvas of a tent with double top **c** (1) : the length of an extended flag from its staff or support (2) : the outer or loose end of a flag **6** : a baseball hit high into the air **7** : FLYLEAF **8** : a football pass pattern in which the receiver runs straight downfield — **on the fly** **1** : continuously active : very busy **2** : while still in the air : without the ball bouncing ⟨the ball carried 400 feet *on the fly*⟩

3**fly** *vi* **flied; fly·ing** : to hit a fly in baseball

4**fly** *n, pl* **flies** [ME *flie,* fr. OE *flēoge;* akin to OHG *flioga* fly, OE *flēogan* to fly] **1** : a winged insect **2** : TWO-WINGED FLY; *esp* : one that is large and stout-bodied **3** : a fishhook dressed (as with feathers or tinsel) to suggest an insect — **fly in the ointment** : a detracting factor or element

5**fly** *adj* [prob. fr. 1*fly*] *chiefly Brit* : KEEN, ARTFUL

fly·able \ˈflī-ə-bəl\ *adj* : suitable for flying or for being flown

fly agaric *n* : a poisonous mushroom (*Amanita muscaria*) with a usu. bright red cap

fly ash *n* : fine solid particles of noncombustible ash carried out of a bed of solid fuel by the draft

fly·away \ˈflī-ə-ˌwā\ *adj* **1** : lacking in order and practical sense : FLIGHTY ⟨a pretty, careless, ~ sort of woman⟩ **2** : made loose and flowing esp. because of unconfined fullness at the back ⟨a ~ jacket⟩ **3 a** : ready to fly ⟨~ aircraft⟩ **b** : of or relating to an airplane that is ready to fly ⟨~ price⟩

fly ball *n* : 2FLY 6

fly·belt \ˈflī-ˌbelt\ *n* : an area infested with tsetse fly

1**fly·blow** \-ˌblō\ *n* [4*fly* + *blow* (deposit of insect eggs)] **1** : an egg or young larva deposited by a flesh fly or blowfly **2** : FLY-STRIKE

2**flyblow** *vt* **-blew; -blown** **1** : to deposit flyblows in **2** : TAINT, CONTAMINATE

fly·blown \ˈflī-ˌblōn\ *adj* **1 a** : infested with flyblows **b** : covered with flyspecks **2 a** : not pure : TAINTED ⟨a world ~ with the vices of irresponsible power —V. L. Parrington⟩ **b** : not bright and new : SEEDY, MOTH-EATEN **c** : TRITE, HACKNEYED ⟨a long list of ~ metaphors —*Horizon*⟩

fly·boat \-ˌbōt\ *n* [modif. of D *vlieboot,* fr. *Vlie,* channel between North sea & Wadden Zee + *boot* boat] : any of various fast boats

fly book *n* : a case usu. in the form of a book for storing fishing flies

fly–boy \ˈflī-ˌbȯi\ *n* : a member of the air force

fly bridge *n* : an open deck on a cabin cruiser located above the bridge on the cabin roof and usu. having a duplicate set of navigating equipment

fly·by \ˈflī-ˌbī\ *n, pl* **flybys** **1** : a usu. low-altitude flight past a predesignated place by one or more airplanes **2 a** : a flight of a spacecraft past a celestial body (as Mars) close enough to obtain scientific data; *also* : a suborbital flight around the moon **b** : a spacecraft that makes a flyby

1**fly–by–night** \ˈflī-bə-ˌnīt\ *n* **1** : one that seeks to evade responsibilities and esp. creditors by flight **2** : one without established reputation or standing; *esp* : a shaky business enterprise

2**fly–by–night** *adj* **1** : given to making a quick profit usu. by shady or irresponsible acts ⟨~ promoters trying to cash in —Tom McSloy⟩ **2** : TRANSITORY, PASSING ⟨~ fashions⟩

fly–by–night·er \ˌflī-bə-ˈnīt-ər\ *n* : FLY-BY-NIGHT

fly casting *n* : the casting of artificial flies in fly-fishing or as a competitive sport

fly·catch·er \ˈflī-ˌkach-ər, -ˌkech-\ *n* : a bird (order Passeriformes) that feeds on insects taken on the wing

ə abut	ᵊ kitten	ər further	a back	ā bake	ä cot, cart
au̇ out	ch chin	e less	ē easy	g gift	i trip ī life
j joke	ŋ sing	ō flow	ȯ flaw	ȯi coin	th thin t͟h this
ü loot	u̇ foot	y yet	yü few	yu̇ furious	zh vision

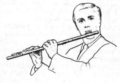

fly dope n 1 : a dressing that makes fishing flies water-resistant so that they will float 2 : an insect repellent

fly-er var of FLIER

fly-fish-ing \'flī-ˌfish-iŋ\ n : a method of fishing in which an artificial fly is cast by use of a long flexible rod, a reel, and a relatively heavy oiled or treated line

fly front n : a concealed closing on the front of coats, skirts, shirts, or dresses — compare ²FLY 5a

fly gallery n : a narrow raised platform at the side of a theater stage from which flying scenery lines are operated

¹fly-ing \'flī-iŋ\ adj 1 a : moving or capable of moving in the air b : rapidly moving ⟨~ feet⟩ c : very brief 2 : intended for ready movement or action ⟨a ~ squad car⟩ 3 : having stylized wings — used esp. of livestock brand marks 4 : of or relating to the operation of aircraft ⟨belongs to a ~ club⟩ 5 : traversed or to be traversed (as in speed-record trials) after a running start ⟨~ kilometer⟩ ⟨~ mile⟩ — **with flying colors** : with complete or eminent success ⟨passed the exam *with flying colors*⟩

²flying n 1 : travel by air 2 : the operation of an aircraft or spacecraft

flying boat n : a seaplane with a hull adapted for floating

flying bomb n : ROBOT BOMB

flying bridge n 1 : the highest navigational bridge on a ship 2 : FLY BRIDGE

flying buttress n : a masonry structure that typically consists of a straight inclined bar carried on an arch and a solid pier or buttress against which it abuts and that receives the thrust of a roof or vault

flying column n : a strong military detachment that operates at a distance from the main force

Flying Dutchman n 1 : a legendary Dutch mariner condemned to sail the seas until Judgment Day 2 : a spectral ship that according to legend haunts the seas near the Cape of Good Hope in stormy weather

flying field n : a field with a graded area for airplane landings and takeoffs

flying fish n : any of numerous fishes (family Exocoetidae) chiefly of tropical and warm seas that have long pectoral fins suggesting wings and are able to move some distance through the air

flying fox n : FRUIT BAT

flying gurnard n : any of several marine fishes (family Dactylopteridae) that resemble gurnards but have large pectoral fins allowing them to glide above the water for short distances

flying jib n : a sail outside the jib on an extension of the jibboom — see SAIL illustration

flying jibboom n : an extension of a jibboom

flying lemur n : an East Indian or a Philippine arboreal nocturnal mammal (genus *Cynocephalus*) that is about the size of a cat with a broad fold of skin from the neck to the tail on each side that embraces the limbs and forms a parachute used in making long sailing leaps and that is usu. isolated in a distinct order (Dermoptera)

flying machine n : an apparatus for navigating the air

flying mare n : a wrestling maneuver in which the aggressor seizes his opponent's wrist, turns about, and jerks him over his back

flying officer n : a commissioned officer in the British air force who ranks with a first lieutenant in the army

flying saucer n : any of various unidentified moving objects repeatedly reported as seen in the air and usu. described as being saucer-shaped or disk-shaped — called also *flying disk*

flying spot n : a spot of light that is moved over a surface (as one bearing printing or an image) so that light reflected from or transmitted by different parts of the surface is translated into electrical signals for transmission (as in television or computers)

flying squad n : a usu. small standby group of people ready to move or act swiftly; *esp* : a police unit formed to respond quickly in an emergency

flying squirrel n : a small large-eyed nocturnal No. American squirrel (*Glaucomys volans*) with folds of skin connecting the forelegs and hind legs that enable it to make long gliding leaps; *also* : any of several similar squirrels

flying start n : a start in racing in which the participants are already moving when they cross the starting line or receive the starting signal

flying wedge n : a moving formation (as of guards or police) resembling a wedge

fly-leaf \'flī-ˌlēf\ n : one of the free endpapers of a book

fly-man \-mən, -ˌman\ n : a worker in the flies of a theater who manipulates curtains and scenery

fly net n : a net to exclude or keep off insects (as from a harness horse)

fly-over \'flī-ˌō-vər\ n 1 : a low-altitude flight over a public gathering or place by one or more airplanes 2 *Brit* : OVERPASS

fly-pa-per \-ˌpā-pər\ n : paper coated with a sticky often poisonous substance for killing flies

fly-past \-ˌpast\ n, *Brit* : FLYBY

fly rod n : a light springy fishing rod used in fly casting

flysch \'flish\ n [G dial.] : a thick and extensive deposit largely of sandstone that is formed in a geosyncline adjacent to a rising mountain belt and is esp. common in the Alpine region of Europe

fly sheet n 1 : a small loose advertising sheet : HANDBILL 2 : a sheet of a folder, booklet, or catalog giving directions for the use of or information about the material that follows

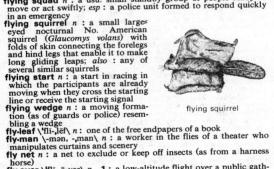

flying squirrel

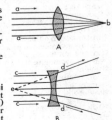

1 flying buttresses

fly-speck \'flī-ˌspek\ n 1 : a speck made by fly excrement 2 : something small and insignificant — **flyspeck** vt

fly-strike \-ˌstrīk\ n : infestation with fly maggots

fly-swat-ter \-ˌswät-ər\ n : a device for killing insects that consists of a flat piece of perforated rubber or plastic or fine-mesh wire netting attached to a handle

fly-ti-er \'flī-ˌtī-(-ə)r\ n [*fly* + *tier* (one that ties)] : a maker of flies for fishing

flyt-ing \'flīt-iŋ\ n [gerund of E dial. *flyte* to quarrel] : a dispute or exchange of personal abuse in verse form (as in an epic)

fly-way \'flī-ˌwā\ n : an established air route of migratory birds

fly-weight \-ˌwāt\ n : a boxer weighing 112 pounds or less

flywheel \-ˌhwēl, -ˌwēl\ n : a heavy wheel for opposing and moderating by its inertia any fluctuation of speed in the machinery with which it revolves

fly whisk n : a whisk for brushing away flies

fm *abbr* fathom

Fm *symbol* fermium

FM *abbr* 1 field manual 2 frequency modulation

FMB *abbr* Federal Maritime Board

FMCS *abbr* Federal Mediation and Conciliation Service

FMN \ˌef-ˌem-'en\ n [*flavin mononucleotide*] : a yellow crystalline phosphoric ester $C_{17}H_{21}N_4O_9P$ of riboflavin that is a coenzyme of several flavoprotein enzymes — called also *flavin mononucleotide*

fn *abbr* footnote

FNMA *sometimes* ˌfan-ē-'mā\ *abbr* Federal National Mortgage Association

f-num-ber \'ef-ˌnəm-bər\ n [*focal length*] 1 : the ratio of the focal length to the aperture in an optical system 2 : a number following the symbol f/ that expresses the effectiveness of the aperture of a camera lens in relation to brightness of image so that the smaller the number the brighter the image and therefore the shorter the exposure required

fo *or* **fol** *abbr* folio

FO *abbr* 1 field officer 2 field order 3 finance officer 4 flight officer 5 foreign office 6 forward observer

¹foal \'fōl\ n [ME *fole*, fr. OE *fola*; akin to L *pullus* young of an animal, Gk *pais* child — more at FEW] : the young of an animal of the horse family; *esp* : one under one year

²foal vi : to give birth to a foal

¹foam \'fōm\ n [ME *fome*, fr. OE *fām*; akin to OHG *feim* foam, L *spuma* foam, *pumex* pumice] 1 : a light frothy mass of fine bubbles formed in or on the surface of a liquid: as **a** : a frothy mass formed in salivating or sweating **b** : a stabilized froth produced chemically or mechanically and used esp. in fighting oil fires **c** : a material in a lightweight cellular form resulting from introduction of gas bubbles during manufacture 2 : SEA 3 : something resembling foam — **foam-less** \-ləs\ adj

²foam vi 1 **a** : to produce or form foam **b** : to froth at the mouth esp. in anger; *broadly* : to be angry 2 **c** : to gush out in foam 3 : to become covered with or as if with foam ⟨streets . . . ~*ing* with life —Thomas Wolfe⟩ ~ vt 1 : to cause to foam; *specif* : to cause air bubbles to form in 2 : to convert (as a plastic) into a foam — **foam-er** n

foamed plastic n : EXPANDED PLASTIC

foam-flow-er \'fōm-ˌflau̇(-ə)r\ n : an American woodland spring-flowering herb (*Tiarella cordifolia*) that has white flowers with very long stamens and no stem leaves — called also *false miterwort*

foam rubber n : spongy rubber of fine texture made from latex by foaming (as by whipping) before vulcanization

foamy \'fō-mē\ adj **foam-i-er; -est** 1 : covered with foam : FROTHY 2 : full of, consisting of, or resembling foam — **foam-i-ly** \-mə-lē\ adv — **foam-i-ness** \-mē-nəs\ n

¹fob \'fäb\ vt **fobbed; fob-bing** [ME *fobben*] archaic : DECEIVE, CHEAT

²fob n [perh. akin to G dial. *fuppe* pocket] 1 : WATCH POCKET 2 : a short strap, ribbon, or chain attached to a watch carried in a watch pocket or a vest pocket 3 : an ornament attached to a fob chain

FOB *abbr* free on board

fob off vt 1 : to put off with a trick or excuse 2 : to pass or offer (something spurious) as genuine 3 : to put aside ⟨now *fob off* what once they would have welcomed eagerly —Walter Lippmann⟩

FOC *abbr* free of charge

fo-cal \'fō-kəl\ adj : of, relating to, or having a focus — **fo-cal-ly** \-kə-lē\ adv

focal infection n : a persistent bacterial infection of some organ or region; *esp* : one causing symptoms elsewhere in the body

fo-cal-ize \'fō-kə-ˌlīz\ vb **-ized; -iz-ing** vt 1 : to bring to a focus 2 : to adjust the focus of 3 : LOCALIZE ~ vi : to become focalized — **fo-cal-iza-tion** \ˌfō-kə-lə-'zā-shən\ n

focal length n : the distance of a focus from the surface of a lens or concave mirror

focal plane n : a plane that is perpendicular to the axis of a lens or mirror and passes through the focus

focal point n : FOCUS 5 ⟨the fireplace was the *focal point* of the room⟩

focal ratio n : F-NUMBER 1

fo-c'sle var of FORECASTLE

¹fo-cus \'fō-kəs\ n, pl **fo-cus-es** or **fo-ci** \-ˌsī\ [NL, fr. L, hearth] 1 : a point at which rays (as of light, heat, or sound) converge or from which they diverge or appear to diverge; *specif* : the point where the geometrical lines or their prolongations conforming to the rays diverging from or converging toward another point intersect and give rise to an image after reflection by a mirror or refraction by a lens or optical system 2 **a** : FOCAL LENGTH **b** : adjustment for

focus 1: *A* convex lens: light rays *a* converge to form principal focus *b*; *B* concave lens: light rays *c* refracted as at *d* form virtual focus *e*

distinct vision; *also* : the area that may be seen distinctly or resolved into a clear image **c** : a position in which something must be placed for clarity of perception ⟨tried to bring the issues into ~⟩ **3** : one of the fixed points that with the corresponding directrix defines a conic section **4** : a localized area of disease or the chief site of a generalized disease or infection **5** : a center of activity, attraction, or attention ⟨the ~ of the meeting was on drug abuse⟩ **6** : the place of origin of an earthquake — **fo·cus·less** \-ləs\ *adj* — **in focus** : having or giving the proper sharpness of outline due to good focusing — **out of focus** : not in focus

²focus *vb* **fo·cused** *also* **fo·cussed; fo·cus·ing** *also* **fo·cus·sing** *vt* **1** : to bring to a focus : CONCENTRATE **2** : to cause to be concentrated ⟨~*ed* their attention on the most urgent problems⟩ **3 a** : to adjust the focus of **b** : to bring into focus ~ *vi* **1** : to come to a focus : CONVERGE **2** : to adjust one's eye or a camera to a particular range — **fo·cus·able** \-kəs-ə-bəl\ *adj* — **fo·cus·er** *n*

fod·der \ˈfäd-ər\ *n* [ME, fr. OE *fōdor;* akin to OHG *fuotar* food — more at FOOD] **1** : something fed to domestic animals; *esp* : coarse food for cattle, horses, or sheep **2** : something that is used to supply a constant demand ⟨collected data which became computer ~⟩ — **fodder** *vt*

fod·gel \ˈfäj-əl\ *adj* [origin unknown] *Scot* : BUXOM

foe \ˈfō\ *n* [ME *fo,* fr. OE *fāh,* fr. *fāh* hostile; akin to OHG *gifēh* hostile] **1** : one who has personal enmity for another **2** : an enemy in war : ADVERSARY **3** : one who opposes on principle ⟨a ~ of needless expenditures⟩ **4** : something prejudicial or injurious ***syn*** see ENEMY ***ant*** friend

FOE *abbr* Fraternal Order of Eagles

foehn *or* **föhn** \ˈfə(r)n, ˈfœ̄n, ˈfān\ *n* [G *föhn*] : a warm dry wind blowing down the side of a mountain

foe·man \ˈfō-mən\ *n* : an enemy in war : FOE

foe·tal, foe·tus *var of* FETAL, FETUS

foe·tid *var of* FETID

foeto- *or* **foeti-** — see FETO-

¹fog \ˈfȯg, ˈfäg\ *n* [ME, rank grass] **1** *dial* **a** : dead or decaying grass in the winter **b** : a second growth of grass **2** *dial* : MOSS

²fog *n* [prob. of Scand origin; akin to Dan *fog* spray, shower; akin to L *pustula* blister, pimple, Gk *physan* to blow] **1 a** : vapor condensed to fine particles of water suspended in the lower atmosphere that differs from cloud only in being near the ground **b** : a fine spray or a foam for fire fighting **2** : a murky condition of the atmosphere or a substance causing it **3 a** : a state of confusion or bewilderment **b** : something that confuses or obscures ⟨hid behind a ~ of rhetoric⟩ **4** : cloudiness or partial opacity in a developed photographic image caused by chemical action or stray radiation ***syn*** see HAZE — **fog·less** \-ləs\ *adj*

³fog *vb* **fogged; fog·ging** *vt* **1** : to cover, envelop, or suffuse with or as if with fog ⟨~ the barns with pesticide⟩ **2** : to make obscure or confusing ⟨accusations which *fogged* the real issues⟩ **3** : to make confused **4** : to produce fog on (as a photographic film) during development ~ *vi* **1** : to become covered or thick with fog **2 a** : to become blurred by a covering of fog or mist **b** : to become indistinct through exposure to light or radiation

fog·bound \ˈfȯg-ˌbau̇nd, ˈfäg-\ *adj* **1** : covered with or surrounded by fog ⟨~ coast⟩ **2** : unable to move because of fog ⟨~ ship⟩

fog·bow \-ˌbō\ *n* : a nebulous arc or circle of white or yellowish light sometimes seen in fog

fog·dog \-ˌdȯg\ *n* : FOGBOW

fog·gage \ˈfȯg-ij, ˈfäg-\ *n, chiefly Scot* : ¹FOG, MOSS

fog·ger \-ər\ *n* : one that fogs; *esp* : an apparatus for spreading a fog of pesticide

fog·gy \ˈfȯg-ē, ˈfäg-\ *adj* **fog·gi·er; -est** **1 a** : filled or abounding with fog **b** : covered or made opaque by moisture or grime **2** : blurred or obscured as if by fog ⟨hadn't the *foggiest* notion what they were voting for⟩ — **fog·gi·ly** \ˈfȯg-ə-lē, ˈfäg-\ *adv* — **fog·gi·ness** \ˈfȯg-ē-nəs, ˈfäg-\ *n*

Foggy Bottom *n* [*Foggy Bottom,* district in Washington, D.C., on the Potomac river where the State Department building is located] : the U.S. Department of State

fog·horn \ˈfȯg-ˌhȯ(ə)rn, ˈfäg-\ *n* **1** : a horn (as on a ship) sounded in a fog to give warning **2** : a loud hoarse voice

fo·gy *also* **fo·gey** \ˈfō-gē\ *n, pl* **fogies** *also* **fogeys** [origin unknown] : a person with old-fashioned ideas — usu. used with *old* — **fo·gy·ish** \-gē-ish\ *adj* — **fo·gy·ism** \-ˌiz-əm\ *n*

foi·ble \ˈfȯi-bəl\ *n* [obs. F (now *faible*), fr. obs. *foible* weak, fr. OF *feble* feeble] **1** : the part of a sword or foil blade between the middle and point **2** : a minor flaw or shortcoming in personal character or behavior : WEAKNESS ***syn*** see FAULT

foie gras \ˈfwä-ˈgrä\ *n* [F] : liver esp. of a goose usu. in the form of a pâté

¹foil \ˈfȯi(ə)l\ *vt* [ME *foilen* to trample, full cloth, fr. MF *fouler* — more at FULL] **1** *obs* : TRAMPLE **2 a** : to prevent from attaining an end : DEFEAT **b** : to bring to naught ***syn*** see FRUSTRATE

²foil *n* **1** *archaic* : DEFEAT **2** *archaic* : the track or trail of an animal **3 a** : a light fencing sword having a usu. circular guard and a flexible blade of rectangular section tapering to a blunted point — compare ÉPÉE, SABER **b** : the art or sport of fencing with the foil — often used in pl.

³foil *n* [ME, leaf, fr. MF *foille* (fr. L *folia,* pl. of *folium*) & *foil,* fr. L *folium* — more at BLADE] **1 a** : an indentation between cusps in Gothic tracery **b** : one of several arcs that enclose a complex figure **2 a** : very thin sheet metal **b** : a thin coat of tin or silver laid on the back of a mirror **3** : a thin piece of material (as metal) put under an inferior or paste stone to add color or brilliance **4** : one that serves as a contrast to another ⟨acted as a ~ for a comedian⟩ **5** : HYDROFOIL 1

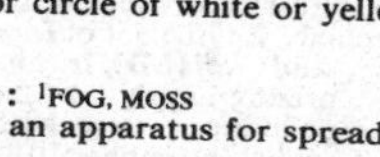

foils 1a

⁴foil *vt* **1** : to back or cover with foil **2** : to enhance by contrast

foiled \ˈfȯi(ə)ld\ *adj* : ornamented with foils ⟨a ~ arch⟩

foils·man \ˈfȯi(ə)lz-mən\ *n* : one who fences with a foil

¹foin \ˈfȯin\ *vi* [ME *foinen,* fr. *foin* fork for spearing fish, fr. MF *foisne*] *archaic* : to thrust with a pointed weapon : LUNGE

²foin *n, archaic* : a pass in fencing : LUNGE

foi·son \ˈfȯiz-ᵊn\ *n* [ME *foisoun,* fr. MF *foison*] **1** *archaic* : rich harvest **2** *chiefly Scot* : physical energy or strength **3** *pl, obs* : RESOURCES

foist \ˈfȯist\ *vt* [prob. fr. obs. D *vuisten* to take into one's hand, fr. MD *vuysten,* fr. *vuyst* fist; akin to OE *fȳst* fist] **1 a** : to introduce or insert surreptitiously or without warrant **b** : to force another to accept esp. by stealth or deceit **2** : to pass off as genuine or worthy ⟨~ costly and valueless products on the public —Jonathan Spivak⟩

fo·la·cin \ˈfō-lə-sən\ *n* [*folic acid* + *-in*] : FOLIC ACID

fo·late \ˈfō-ˌlāt\ *n* : FOLIC ACID

¹fold \ˈfōld\ *n* [ME, fr. OE *falod;* akin to MLG *vālt* enclosure] **1** : an enclosure for sheep **2 a** : a flock of sheep **b** : a group of people adhering to a common faith, belief, or enthusiasm

²fold *vt* : to pen up or confine (as sheep) in a fold

³fold *vb* [ME *folden,* fr. OE *fealdan;* akin to OHG *faldan* to fold, Gk *diplasios* twofold] *vt* **1** : to lay one part over another part of ⟨~ a letter⟩ **2** : to reduce the length or bulk of by doubling over ⟨~ his legs⟩ **3** : to clasp together : ENTWINE ⟨~ his hands⟩ **4** : to clasp or enwrap closely : EMBRACE **5** : to bend (as a layer of rock) into folds **6** : to incorporate (a food ingredient) into a mixture by repeated gentle overturnings without stirring or beating **7** : to bring to an end ~ *vi* **1** : to become doubled or pleated **2** : to fail completely : COLLAPSE; *esp* : to stop production or operation for lack of business ⟨the new restaurant ~*ed* in less than a year⟩ — often used with *up* — **fold·able** \ˈfōl-də-bəl\ *adj*

⁴fold *n* **1** : a doubling or folding over **2** : a part doubled or laid over another part : PLEAT **3** : something that is folded together or that enfolds **4 a** : a bend or flexure produced in rock by forces operative after the depositing or consolidation of the rock **b** *chiefly Brit* : an undulation in the landscape **5** : a margin apparently formed by the doubling upon itself of a membrane or other flat anatomical structure

-fold \ˌfōld, ˈfōld\ *suffix* [ME, fr. OE *-feald;* akin to OHG *-falt* -fold, OE *fealdan*] **1** : multiplied by (a specified number) : times — in adjectives ⟨a twelve*fold* increase⟩ and adverbs ⟨repay you ten*fold*⟩ **2** : having (so many) parts ⟨three*fold* aspect of the problem⟩

fold·away \ˌfōl-də-ˌwā\ *adj* : designed to fold out of the way or out of sight ⟨~ doors⟩ ⟨~ bed⟩

foldboat \ˈfōl(d)-ˌbōt\ *n* : a small collapsible canoe made of rubberized sailcloth stretched over a framework

fold·boat·ing \-iŋ\ *n* : the sport of shooting rapids and cruising on swift water in a foldboat — **fold·boat·er** \-ər\ *n*

fold·er \ˈfōl-dər\ *n* **1** : one that folds **2** : a printed circular folded usu. so that the printed matter does not cross the fold **3** : a folded cover or large envelope for holding or filing loose papers

fol·de·rol \ˈfäl-də-ˌräl\ *n* [*fol-de-rol,* a refrain in some old songs] **1** : a useless ornament or accessory : TRIFLE **2** : NONSENSE

folding door *n* : a door with jointed sections that can be folded together like an accordion

folding money *n* : PAPER MONEY

fold·out \ˈfōl-ˌdau̇t\ *n* : a folded insert (as a map) in a publication (as a book) larger in some dimension than the page

fo·li·a·ceous \ˌfō-lē-ˈā-shəs\ *adj* **1** : of, relating to, or resembling a foliage leaf **2** : consisting of thin laminae ⟨~ spar⟩

fo·liage \ˈfō-l(ē-)ij, -lyij\ *n* [MF *fuellage,* fr. *foille* leaf — more at FOIL] **1** : the aggregate of leaves of one or more plants produced in nature **2** : a cluster of leaves, flowers, and branches **3** : a representation of leaves, flowers, and branches for architectural ornamentation — **fo·liaged** \-l(ē-)ijd, -lyijd\ *adj*

foliage leaf *n* : an ordinary green leaf as distinguished from a floral leaf, scale, or bract

foliage plant *n* : a plant grown primarily for its decorative foliage

fo·li·ar \ˈfō-lē-ər\ *adj* : of, relating to, or applied to leaves ⟨~ sprays⟩

¹fo·li·ate \ˈfō-lē-ət, -ˌāt\ *adj* [L *foliatus* leafy fr. *folium* leaf — more at BLADE] **1** : shaped like a leaf ⟨a ~ sponge⟩ **2** : FOLIATED

²fo·li·ate \-ˌāt\ *vb* **-at·ed; -at·ing** *vt* **1** : to beat into a leaf or thin foil **2** : to spread over with a thin coat of tin amalgam **3** : to number the leaves of (as a manuscript) **4 a** : to form (as an arch) into foils **b** : to ornament (as a pedestal) with foliage ~ *vi* : to divide into laminae or leaves

-fo·li·ate \-ət, -ˌāt\ *adj comb form* : having (such or so many) leaves or leaflets ⟨tri*foliate*⟩

fo·li·at·ed \-ˌāt-əd\ *adj* **1** : composed of laminae **2** : separable into layers ⟨a ~ rock⟩

fo·li·a·tion \ˌfō-lē-ˈā-shən\ *n* **1 a** : the process of forming into a leaf **b** : the state of being in leaf **c** : VERNATION **2** : the act of numbering the leaves of a book; *also* : the total count of leaves so numbered **3 a** : ornamentation with foliage **b** : a decoration resembling a leaf **4** : the enrichment of an opening by foils **5** : the act of beating a metal into a thin plate or foil **6** : foliated texture

fo·lic acid \ˌfō-lik-\ *n* [L *folium*] : a crystalline pteroylglutamic acid $C_{19}H_{19}N_7O_6$ that is a vitamin of the B complex and is used in the treatment of nutritional anemias and sprue

fo·lie à deux \fō-lē-ä-dœ̄, ˌfäl-ē-ˌäd-ˈə(r)\ *n* [F, lit., double madness] : the presence of the same or similar delusional ideas in two persons closely associated with one another

fo·li·ic·o·lous \ˌfō-lē-ˈik-ə-ləs\ *adj* [L *folium* + ISV *-colous*] : growing or parasitic on leaves ⟨the ~ ascomycetes⟩

¹fo·lio \ˈfō-lē-ˌō\ *n, pl* **fo·li·os** [ME, fr. L, abl. of *folium*] **1 a** : a leaf esp. of a manuscript or book **b** : a leaf number **c** : a page number **d** : an identifying reference in accounting used in posting **2 a** : a sheet of paper folded once **b** : a case or folder for loose

ə abut	ᵊ kitten	ər further	a back	ā bake	ä cot, cart
au̇ out	ch chin	e less	ē easy	g gift	i trip	ī life
j joke	ŋ sing	ō flow	ȯ flaw	ȯi coin	th thin	t͟h this
ü loot	u̇ foot	y yet	yü few	yu̇ furious	zh vision

papers 3 **a** : the size of a piece of paper cut two from a sheet; *also* : paper or a page of this size **b** : a book printed on folio pages **c** : a book of the largest size 4 : a certain number of words taken as a unit or division in a document for purposes of measurement or reference

²folio *vt* : to put a serial number on each leaf or page of

-fo·li·o·late \ˈfō-lē-ə-ˌlāt\ *adj comb form* [LL *foliolum* leaflet, dim. of *folium*] : having (such or so many) leaflets ⟨tri*foliolate*⟩

fo·li·ose \ˈfō-lē-ˌōs\ *adj* [L *foliosus* leafy] : having a flat, thin, and usu. lobed thallus attached to the substratum ⟨~ lichens⟩ — compare CRUSTOSE, FRUTICOSE

fo·li·um \ˈfō-lē-əm\ *n, pl* **fo·lia** \-lē-ə\ [NL, fr. L, leaf] : a thin layer occurring esp. in metamorphic rocks

¹folk \ˈfōk\ *n, pl* **folk** *or* **folks** [ME, fr. OE *folc;* akin to OHG *folc* people] 1 *archaic* : a group of kindred tribes forming a nation : PEOPLE 2 : the great proportion of the members of a people that determines the group character and that tends to preserve its characteristic form of civilization and its customs, arts and crafts, legends, traditions, and superstitions from generation to generation 3 *pl* : a certain kind or class of people ⟨old ~*s*⟩ ⟨just plain ~⟩ 4 *folks pl* : people generally 5 *folks pl* : the persons of one's own family : RELATIVES

²folk *adj* 1 **a** : originating or traditional with the common people of a country or region and typically reflecting their life-style **b** : being a form of contemporary music written in imitation of and having qualities of traditional folk music such as stanzaic form, refrain, and simplicity of melody 2 : of or relating to the common people or to the study of the common people ⟨~ sociology⟩

folk etymology *n* : the transformation of words so as to give them an apparent relationship to other better-known or better-understood words (as in the change of Spanish *cucaracha* to English *cockroach*)

folk·ish \ˈfō-kish\ *adj* : FOLKLIKE — **folk·ish·ness** *n*

folk·like \ˈfō-ˌklīk\ *adj* : having a folk character

folk·lore \ˈfō-ˌklō(ə)r, -ˌklȯ(ə)r\ *n* 1 : traditional customs, tales, or sayings preserved orally among a people 2 : a comparative science that investigates the life and spirit of a people as revealed in their folklore 3 : a widely held unsupported specious notion or body of notions — **folk·lor·ic** \-ˌklōr-ik, -ˌklȯr-\ *adj* — **folk·lor·ish** \-ish\ *adj* — **folk·lor·ist** \-əst\ *n* — **folk·lor·is·tic** \ˌfō-ˌklōr-ˈis-tik, -ˌklȯr-\ *adj*

folk mass *n* : a mass in which traditional liturgical music is replaced by folk music

folk medicine *n* : traditional medicine as practiced nonprofessionally by people isolated from modern medical services and involving esp. the use of vegetable remedies on an empirical basis

folk·moot \ˈfōk-ˌmüt\ *or* **folk·mote** \-ˌmōt\ *n* : a general assembly of the people (as of a shire) in early England

folk·sing·er \-ˌsiŋ-ər\ *n* : one who sings folk songs or sings in a style associated with folk songs — **folk·sing·ing** \-ˌsiŋ-iŋ\ *n*

folksy \ˈfōk-sē\ *adj* **folks·i·er; -est** [*folks* + *-y*] 1 : SOCIABLE, FRIENDLY 2 : informal, casual, or familiar in manner or style ⟨gave us a ~ little talk —O. J. Magee⟩ — **folks·i·ly** \-sə-lē\ *adv* — **folks·i·ness** \-sē-nəs\ *n*

folk·tale \ˈfōk-ˌtāl\ *n* : a characteristically anonymous, timeless, and placeless tale circulated orally among a people

folk·way \ˈfō-ˌkwā\ *n* : a mode of thinking, feeling, or acting common to a people or to a social group; *esp* : a traditional social custom

fol·li·cle \ˈfäl-i-kəl\ *n* [NL *folliculus,* fr. L, dim. of *follis* bag — more at FOOL] 1 **a** : a small anatomical cavity or deep narrow-mouthed depression **b** : a small lymph node **c** : GRAAFIAN FOLLICLE 2 : a dry dehiscent one-celled many-seeded fruit that has a single carpel and opens along only one suture — **fol·lic·u·lar** \fə-ˈlik-yə-lər, fä-\ *adj* — **fol·lic·u·late** \-lət\ *also* **fol·lic·u·lat·ed** \-ˌlāt-əd\ *adj*

follicle mite *n* : any of several minute mites (genus *Demodex*) parasitic in hair follicles

follicle-stimulating hormone *n* : a hormone from an anterior lobe of the pituitary body that stimulates the growth of Graafian follicles and activates sperm-forming cells

fol·lic·u·lin \fə-ˈlik-yə-lən, fä-\ *n* : ESTROGEN; *esp* : ESTRONE

¹fol·low \ˈfäl-(ˌ)ō, -ə(-w)\ *vb* [ME *folwen,* fr. OE *folgian;* akin to OHG *folgēn* to follow] *vt* 1 : to go, proceed, or come after ⟨~*ed* the guide⟩ 2 **a** : to pursue in an effort to overtake **b** : to seek to attain ⟨~ knowledge⟩ 3 : to accept as authority : OBEY ⟨~*ed* his conscience⟩ 4 : to copy after : IMITATE 5 **a** : to walk or proceed along ⟨~ a path⟩ **b** : to engage in as a calling or way of life : PURSUE ⟨wheat-growing is generally ~*ed* here⟩ 6 **a** : to come or take place after in time, sequence, or order **b** : to cause to be followed ⟨~*ed* dinner with a liqueur⟩ 7 : to come into existence or take place as a result or consequence of ⟨disaster ~*ed* the blunder⟩ 8 **a** : to watch steadily ⟨~*ed* the ball over the fence⟩ **b** : to keep the mind on ⟨~ a speech⟩ **c** : to attend closely to : keep abreast of ⟨she ~*ed* his career with interest⟩ **d** : to understand the logic of (as a line of thought) ⟨I don't quite ~ you⟩ ~ *vi* 1 : to go or come after a person or thing in place, time, or sequence 2 : to result or occur as a consequence, effect, or inference

syn 1 FOLLOW, SUCCEED, ENSUE, SUPERVENE *shared meaning element* : to come after something or someone ***ant*** precede (*in order*), forsake (*as a leader*)

2 FOLLOW, CHASE, PURSUE, TRAIL *shared meaning element* : to go after or on the track of someone or something ***ant*** precede

— **follow one's nose** 1 : to go in a straight or obvious course 2 : to proceed without plan or reflection : obey one's instincts — **follow suit** 1 : to play a card of the same suit as the card led 2 : to follow an example set

²follow *n* 1 : the act or process of following 2 : forward spin given to a ball by striking it above center — compare DRAW

fol·low·er \ˈfäl-ə-wər\ *n* 1 **a** : one in the service of another : RETAINER **b** : one that follows the opinions or teachings of another **c** : one that imitates another 2 *archaic* : one that chases 3 : a sheet added to the first sheet of an indenture or other deed 4 : a machine part that receives motion from another part

syn FOLLOWER, ADHERENT, DISCIPLE, PARTISAN, SATELLITE *shared meaning element* : one who attaches himself to another ***ant*** leader

fol·low·er·ship \-ˌship\ *n* 1 : FOLLOWING 2 : the capacity or willingness to follow a leader

¹fol·low·ing \ˈfäl-ə-wiŋ\ *adj* 1 : next after : SUCCEEDING ⟨the ~ day⟩ 2 : that immediately follows ⟨trains will leave at the ~ times⟩

²following *n* : a group of followers, adherents, or partisans

³following *prep* : subsequent to ⟨~ the lecture tea was served⟩

follow out *vt* 1 : to follow to the end or to a conclusion 2 : to carry out : EXECUTE ⟨*followed out* his orders⟩

follow shot *n* 1 : a shot in billiards or pool made by striking the cue ball above its center to cause it to continue forward after striking the object ball 2 : a camera shot in which the camera follows the movement of the subject

fol·low-through \ˈfäl-ō-ˌthrü, ˌfäl-ō-ˈ, -ə-\ *n* 1 : the act or an instance of following through 2 : the part of the stroke following the striking of a ball

follow through *vi* 1 : to continue a stroke or motion to the end of its arc 2 : to press on in an activity or process esp. to a conclusion

¹fol·low-up \ˌfäl-ə-ˌwəp\ *adj* 1 : of, relating to, or being something that follows up ⟨~ action by the police —Frank Faulkner⟩ 2 : done, conducted, or administered in the course of following up persons esp. after institutionalization ⟨~ care for discharged hospital patients —*N.Y. Times Mag.*⟩

²follow-up \ˈfäl-ə-ˌwəp\ *n* 1 **a** : the act or an instance of following up **b** : something that follows up 2 : maintenance of contact with or reexamination of a person (as a patient) at usu. prescribed intervals following diagnosis or treatment 3 : a news story presenting new information on a story published earlier

follow up \ˌfäl-ə-ˈwəp\ *vt* 1 : to follow with something similar, related, or supplementary ⟨*following up* his convictions with action —G. P. Merrill⟩ 2 : to maintain contact with (a person) in order to evaluate a diagnosis or to determine the effectiveness of treatment received ⟨patients who are *followed up* after their discharge⟩ ~ *vi* : to take appropriate action ⟨*follow up* on . . . complaints, and customer suggestions — *Marketing*⟩

fol·ly \ˈfäl-ē\ *n, pl* **follies** [ME *folie,* fr. OF, fr. *fol* fool] 1 : lack of good sense or normal prudence and foresight 2 : a foolish act or idea 3 **a** *obs* : EVIL, WICKEDNESS; *esp* : lewd behavior **b** : criminally or tragically foolish actions or conduct 4 : an excessively costly or unprofitable undertaking

Fol·som \ˈfōl-səm\ *adj* [*Folsom,* N.M.] : of or relating to a prehistoric culture of No. America on the east side of the Rocky mountains that is characterized by flint projectile points having a concave base with side projections and a longitudinal groove on each face

fo·ment \fō-ˈment\ *vt* [ME *fomenten,* fr. LL *fomentare,* fr. L *fomentum* fomentation, fr. *fovēre* to warm, fondle, foment] 1 : to treat with moist heat (as for easing pain) 2 : to promote the growth or development of : ROUSE, INCITE ⟨~ a rebellion⟩ ***syn*** see INCITE ***ant*** quell — **fo·ment·er** *n*

fo·men·ta·tion \ˌfō-mən-ˈtā-shən, -ˌmen-\ *n* 1 **a** : the application of hot moist substances to the body to ease pain **b** : the material so applied 2 : the act of fomenting : INSTIGATION

¹fond \ˈfänd\ *adj* [ME, fr. *fonne* fool] 1 : FOOLISH, SILLY ⟨~ pride⟩ 2 **a** : prizing highly : DESIROUS ⟨~ of praise⟩ **b** : having an affection or liking — used with *of* ⟨he has always been ~ of music⟩ 3 **a** : foolishly tender : INDULGENT ⟨spoiled by a ~ mother⟩ **b** : AFFECTIONATE, LOVING ⟨a ~ wife⟩ ⟨absence makes the heart grow ~*er*⟩ 4 : cherished with great affection : doted on ⟨his ~*est* hopes⟩

²fond *vi, obs* : to be foolish : DOTE

³fond \ˈfōⁿ\ *n, pl* **fonds** \ˈfōⁿ(z)\ [F — more at FUND] 1 : BACKGROUND, BASIS 2 *obs* : FUND

fon·dant \ˈfän-dənt\ *n* [F, fr. prp. of *fondre* to melt — more at FOUND] 1 : a soft creamy preparation of sugar, water, and flavorings that is used as a basis for candies or icings 2 : a candy consisting chiefly of fondant

fon·dle \ˈfän-dᵊl\ *vb* **fon·dled; fon·dling** \-(d)liŋ, -dᵊl-iŋ\ [freq. of obs. *fond*] *vt* 1 *obs* : PAMPER 2 : to handle tenderly, lovingly, or lingeringly ~ *vi* : to show affection or desire by caressing ***syn*** see CARESS — **fon·dler** \-(d)lər, -dᵊl-ər\ *n*

fond·ling \ˈfän-(d)liŋ\ *n* [obs. *fond* (to fondle)] : one that is fondled or caressed

fond·ly \ˈfän-(d)lē\ *adv* 1 *archaic* : in a foolish manner : FOOLISHLY 2 : in a fond manner : AFFECTIONATELY 3 : in a willingly credulous manner ⟨~ imagine that human beings today think faster — Warwick Braithwaite⟩

fond·ness \ˈfän(d)-nəs\ *n* 1 *obs* : FOOLISHNESS, FOLLY 2 : tender affection 3 : APPETITE, RELISH ⟨had a ~ for argument⟩

fon·due *also* **fon·du** \fän-ˈd(y)ü, ˈfän-ˌ\ *n* [F *fondue,* fr. fem. of *fondu,* pp. of *fondre*] 1 **a** (1) : a preparation of melted cheese (as Swiss cheese and Gruyère) usu. flavored with white wine and kirsch (2) : a dish that consists of small pieces of food (as meat or fruit) cooked in or dipped into a hot liquid ⟨beef ~⟩ ⟨chocolate ~⟩ **b** : a chafing dish in which fondue is made 2 : a soufflé made with bread crumbs

F_1 layer \ˈef-ˈwən-\ *n* : the lower of the two layers into which the F region of the ionosphere splits in the daytime occurring at varying heights from about 90 to 150 miles above the earth's surface

¹font \ˈfänt\ *n* [ME, fr. OE, fr. LL *font-, fons,* fr. L, fountain] 1 **a** : a receptacle for baptismal water **b** : a receptacle for holy water **c** : a receptacle for various liquids 2 : FOUNTAIN, SOURCE ⟨a ~ of information⟩ — **font·al** \ˈfänt-ᵊl\ *adj*

²font *n* [MF *fonte* act of founding, fr. (assumed) VL *fundita,* fem. of *funditus,* pp. of L *fundere* to found, pour — more at FOUND] : an assortment of type all of one size and style

fon·ta·nel *also* **fon·ta·nelle** \ˌfänt-ᵊn-ˈel, ˈfänt-ᵊn-ˌ\ *n* [ME *fontinelle,* a bodily hollow or pit, fr. MF *fontenele,* dim. of *fontaine* fountain] : a membrane-covered opening in bone or between bones; *specif* : one of the intervals closed by membranous structures between the uncompleted angles of the parietal bones and the neighboring bones of a fetal or young skull

fon·ti·na \fän-'tē-nə\ *n, often cap* [It] : a semisoft to hard ripened mild to medium sharp cheese of Italian origin

food \'füd\ *n, often attrib* [ME *fode,* fr. OE *fōda;* akin to OHG *fuotar* food, fodder, L *panis* bread, *pascere* to feed] **1 a** : material consisting essentially of protein, carbohydrate, and fat used in the body of an organism to sustain growth, repair, and vital processes and to furnish energy; *also* : such food together with supplementary substances (as minerals, vitamins, and condiments) **b** : inorganic substances absorbed by plants in gaseous form or in water solution **2** : nutriment in solid form **3** : something that nourishes, sustains, or supplies 〈~ for thought〉 — **food·less** \-ləs\ *adj* — **food·less·ness** *n*

food chain *n* : an arrangement of the organisms of an ecological community according to the order of predation in which each uses the next usu. lower member as a food source

food cycle *n* : a group of food chains constituting all or most of the food relations that enable an ecological community to survive

food poisoning *n* : an acute gastrointestinal disorder caused by bacteria or their toxic products or by chemical residues in food

food pyramid *n* : an ecological hierarchy of food relationships esp. when expressed quantitatively (as in mass, numbers, or energy) in which a chief predator is at the top, each level preys on the next lower level, and usu. green plants are at the bottom

food stamp *n* : a government-issued stamp that is sold or given to low-income persons and is redeemable for food

food·stuff \'füd-,stəf\ *n* : a substance with food value; *specif* : the raw material of food before or after processing

food vacuole *n* : a vacuole (as in an amoeba) in which ingested food is digested

food web *n* : the totality of interacting food chains in an ecological community

foo·fa·raw \'fü-fə-,rö\ *n* [origin unknown] **1** : frills and flashy finery **2** : a disturbance or to-do over a trifle : FUSS

¹fool \'fül\ *n* [ME, fr. OF *fol,* fr. LL *follis,* fr. L, bellows, bag; akin to L *flare* to blow — more at BLOW] **1 a** : a person lacking in judgment or prudence **2 a** : a retainer formerly kept in great households to provide casual entertainment and commonly dressed in motley with cap, bells, and bauble **b** : one who is victimized or made to appear foolish : DUPE **3 a** : a harmlessly deranged person or one lacking in common powers of understanding **b** : one with a marked propensity or talent for a certain activity 〈a letter= writing ~〉 **4 a** : mashed fruit and cream **b** : a dessert made of pulped fruit covered with a custard and cream 〈blueberry ~〉
syn FOOL, IDIOT, IMBECILE, MORON, SIMPLETON, NATURAL *shared meaning element* : one who is mentally defective

²fool *vi* **1 a** : to spend time idly or aimlessly 〈just ~*ing* around all day〉 **b** : to meddle or tamper thoughtlessly or ignorantly 〈don't ~ with that gun〉 **2 a** : to play or improvise a comic role **b** : to speak in jest : JOKE 〈I was only ~*ing*〉 **3** : to contend or fight without serious intent or with less than full strength : TOY 〈a dangerous man to ~ with〉 ~ *vt* **1** : to make a fool of : DECEIVE **2** *obs* : INFATUATE **3** : to spend on trifles or without advantage : FRITTER — used with *away*

³fool *adj* : FOOLISH, SILLY 〈barking his ~ head off〉

fool·ery \'fül-(ə-)rē\ *n, pl* **-er·ies** **1** : foolish behavior : a foolish act, utterance, or belief

fool·har·dy \'fül-,härd-ē\ *adj* : foolishly adventurous and bold : RASH *syn* see ADVENTUROUS — **fool·har·di·ly** \-,härd-°l-ē\ *adv* — **fool·har·di·ness** \-,härd-ē-nəs\ *n*

fool·ish \'fü-lish\ *adj* **1** : marked by or proceeding from folly **2 a** : ABSURD, RIDICULOUS **b** : marked by a loss of composure : NONPLUSSED, ABASHED **3** : INSIGNIFICANT, TRIFLING, HUMBLE *syn* see SIMPLE — **fool·ish·ly** *adv*

fool·ish·ness *n* **1** : foolish behavior : FOLLY **2** : a foolish act or idea

fool·proof \'fül-'prüf\ *adj* : so simple, plain, or reliable as to leave no opportunity for error, misuse, or failure 〈a ~ plan〉

fools·cap *or* **fool's cap** \'fül-,skap\ *n* **1** : a cap or hood usu. with bells worn by jesters **2** : a conical cap for slow or lazy students **3** [fr. the watermark of a fool's cap formerly applied to such paper] *usu* **foolscap** : a size of paper that is typically 16 x 13 inches

fool's gold *n* **1** : PYRITE **2** : CHALCOPYRITE

fool's paradise *n* : a state of delusory happiness

fool's parsley *n* : a poisonous European weed (*Aethusa cynapium*) of the carrot family resembling parsley

¹foot \'fut\ *n, pl* **feet** \'fēt\ *also* **foot** [ME *fot,* fr. OE *fōt;* akin to L *ped-, pes* foot, Gk *pod-, pous*] **1** : the terminal part of the vertebrate leg upon which an individual stands **2** : an invertebrate organ of locomotion or attachment; *esp* : a ventral muscular surface or process of a mollusk **3** : any of various units of length based on the length of the human foot; *esp* : a unit equal to ⅓ yard and comprising 12 inches 〈a 10-*foot* pole〉 〈6 *feet* tall〉 — see WEIGHT table **4** : the basic unit of verse meter consisting of any of various fixed combinations or groups of stressed and unstressed or long and short syllables **5 a** : motion or power of walking or running : STEP 〈fleet of ~〉 **b** : SPEED, SWIFTNESS **6** : something resembling a foot in position or use: as **a** : the lower end of the leg of a chair or table **b** : one of the areas at the base of a piece of printing type — see TYPE illustration **c** (1) : the basal portion of the sporogonium in mosses (2) : a specialized outgrowth by which the embryonic sporophyte of many ferns and related plants and some seed plants absorbs nourishment from the gametophyte **d** : a piece on a sewing machine that presses the cloth against the feed **7** *foot pl, chiefly Brit* : INFANTRY **8** : the lower edge (as of a sail) **9** : the lowest part : BOTTOM 〈the ~ of the hill〉 **10 a** : the end that is lower or opposite the head 〈the ~ of the bed〉 **b** : the part (as of a stocking) that covers the foot **11** *foots pl but sing or pl in constr* : material deposited esp. in aging or refining : DREGS **12** *foots pl* : FOOTLIGHTS — **foot·like** \'fut-,līk\ *adj* — **at one's feet** : under one's spell or influence — **off one's feet** : in a sitting or lying position — **on foot** : by walking or running 〈tour the campus *on foot*〉 — **on one's feet** **1** : in a standing position **2**

: in an established position or state **3** : in a recovered condition (as from illness) **4** : in an extemporaneous manner 〈good debaters can think *on their feet*〉

²foot *vi* **1** : DANCE **2** : to go on foot **3** *of a sailboat* : to make speed : MOVE ~ *vt* **1 a** : to perform the movements of (a dance) **b** : to walk, run, or dance on, over, or through **2** *archaic* : KICK **b** : REJECT **3** *archaic* : ESTABLISH **4 a** : to add up **b** : to pay or stand credit for 〈agreed to ~ the bill〉 **5** : to make or renew the foot of (as a stocking)

foot·age \'fut-ij\ *n* **1** : length or quantity expressed in feet: as **a** : BOARD FEET **b** : the total number of running feet of motion=picture film used (as for a scene or subject)

foot-and-mouth disease *n* : an acute contagious febrile virus disease esp. of cloven-footed animals marked by ulcerating vesicles in the mouth, about the hoofs, and on the udder and teats — called also *foot-and-mouth, hoof-and-mouth disease*

foot·ball \'fut-,bol\ *n* **1** : any of several games played between two teams on a rectangular field having two goalposts at each end and whose object is to get the ball over a goal line or between goalposts by running, passing, or kicking: as **a** *Brit* : SOCCER **b** *Brit* : RUGBY **c** : an American game played between two teams of 11 players each in which the ball is in possession of one side at a time and is advanced by running or passing **d** *Austral* : AUSTRALIAN RULES FOOTBALL **e** *Canad* : CANADIAN FOOTBALL **2 a** : an inflated oval ball used in the game of football **b** *Brit* : a soccer ball **3** : something tossed or kicked about : PLAYTHING 〈the bill became a political ~ in Congress〉

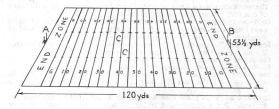

football field: *A* goalposts (professional), *B* goalposts (college), *C* inbounds lines

foot·ball·er \-,bo-lər\ *n* : one who plays football or soccer

foot·bath \'fut-,bath, -,bath\ *n* : a bath (as at the entrance to an indoor swimming pool) for cleansing, warming, or disinfecting the feet

foot·board \'fut-,bō(ə)rd, -,bo(ə)rd\ *n* **1** : a narrow platform on which to stand or brace the feet **2** : a board forming the foot of a bed

foot·boy \-,boi\ *n* : a serving boy : PAGE, ATTENDANT

foot·bridge \'fut-,brij\ *n* : a bridge for pedestrians

foot·can·dle \-'kan-d°l\ *n* : a unit of illuminance on a surface that is everywhere one foot from a uniform point source of light of one candle and equal to one lumen per square foot

foot·cloth \-,klöth\ *n* **1** *archaic* : an ornamental cloth draped over the back of a horse to reach the ground on each side **2** : CARPET

foot–drag·ging \-,drag-iŋ\ *n* : failure to act with the necessary promptness or vigor

foot·ed \'fut-əd\ *adj* : having a foot or feet esp. of a specified kind or number — often used in combination 〈a four-*footed* animal〉

foot·er \'fut-ər\ *n, archaic* : PEDESTRIAN

-foot·er \'fut-ər\ *comb form* : one that is a specified number of feet in height, length, or breadth 〈a six-*footer*〉

foot·fall \'fut-,fol\ *n* : the sound of a footstep

foot fault *n* : a fault that occurs (as in tennis) when a server fails to keep both feet behind the baseline until the ball is served

foot·gear \'fut-,gi(ə)r\ *n* : FOOTWEAR

foot·hill \-,hil\ *n* : a hill at the foot of higher hills

foot·hold \-,hōld\ *n* **1** : a hold for the feet : FOOTING **2** : a position usable as a base for further advance 〈secured a ~ in the plastics market〉

foot·ing \'fut-iŋ\ *n* **1** : a stable position or placing of the feet **2** : a surface or its condition with respect to one walking or running on it; *specif* : the condition of a racetrack **3** : the act of moving on foot : STEP, TREAD **4 a** : a place or space for standing : FOOTHOLD **b** : established position : STATUS; *esp* : position or rank in relation to others 〈they all started off on an equal ~〉 **5** : BASIS **6** : an enlargement at the lower end of a foundation wall, pier, or column to distribute the load **7** : the sum or column of figures

foo·tle \'fut-°l\ *vi* **foo·tled; foo·tling** \'fut-liŋ, -°l-iŋ\ [alter. of *footer* (to footle)] **1** : to waste time : TRIFLE, FOOL **2** : to talk or act foolishly — **footle** *n* — **foo·tler** \'fut-lər, -°l-ər\ *n*

foot·less \ˈfu̇t-ləs\ *adj* **1 a :** having no feet **b :** lacking foundation : UNSUBSTANTIAL **2 :** STUPID, INEPT ⟨dawdling and ~ conferences —Howard Lindsay⟩ — **foot·less·ly** *adv* — **foot·less·ness** *n*
foot·lights \-ˌlīts\ *n pl* **1 :** a row of lights set across the front of a stage floor **2 :** the stage as a profession
foo·tling \ˈfüt-liŋ, -ᵊl-iŋ\ *adj* [*footle*] **1 :** lacking judgment or ability : INEPT ⟨~ amateurs who understand nothing —E. R. Bentley⟩ **2 :** lacking use or value : TRIVIAL
foot·lock·er \ˈfu̇t-ˌläk-ər\ *n* **:** a small trunk designed to be placed at the foot of a bed (as in a barracks)
foot·loose \-ˌlüs\ *adj* **:** having no ties : free to move about
foot·man \-mən\ *n* **1 a** *archaic* **:** a traveler on foot : PEDESTRIAN **b :** INFANTRYMAN **2 a :** a servant in livery formerly attending a rider or required to run in front of his master's carriage **b :** a servant who serves at table, tends the door, and runs errands
foot·mark \-ˌmärk\ *n* **:** FOOTPRINT
[1]**foot·note** \-ˌnōt\ *n* **1 :** a note of reference, explanation, or comment usu. placed below the text on a printed page **2 :** something that is subordinately related to a larger event or work ⟨that biography is an illuminating ~ to the history of our times⟩
[2]**footnote** *vt* **:** to furnish with a footnote : ANNOTATE
foot·pace \ˈfu̇t-ˌpās\ *n* **1 :** a walking pace **2 :** PLATFORM, DAIS
[1]**foot·pad** \-ˌpad\ *n* [*foot* + *pad* (highwayman)] **:** one who robs a pedestrian
[2]**footpad** *n* [*foot* + [1]*pad*] **:** a flattish foot on the leg of a spacecraft for distributing weight to minimize sinking into a surface
foot·path \ˈfu̇t-ˌpath, -ˌpàth\ *n* **:** a narrow path for pedestrians
foot–pound \-ˈpau̇nd\ *n, pl* **foot–pounds :** a unit of work equal to the work done by a force of one pound acting through a distance of one foot in the direction of the force
foot–pound·al \-ˈpau̇n-dᵊl\ *n* **:** an absolute unit of work equal to the work done by a force of one poundal acting through a distance of one foot in the direction of the force
foot–pound–second *adj* **:** being or relating to a system of units based upon the foot as the unit of length, the pound as the unit of weight or mass, and the second as the unit of time
foot·print \ˈfu̇t-ˌprint\ *n* **1 :** an impression of the foot on a surface **2 :** an area within which a spacecraft is intended to land
foot·race \-ˌrās\ *n* **:** a race run by humans on foot
foot·rest \-ˌrest\ *n* **:** a support for the feet
foot·rope \-ˌrōp\ *n* **1 :** a rope rigged below a yard for men to stand on **2 :** the part of a boltrope sewed to the lower edge of a sail
foot rot *n* **1 :** a plant disease marked by rot of the stem near the ground **2 :** a progressive inflammation of the feet of sheep or cattle
foot·slog \ˈfu̇t-ˌsläg\ *vi* **:** to march or tramp through mud — **foot·slog·ger** *n*
foot soldier *n* **:** INFANTRYMAN
foot·sore \ˈfu̇t-ˌsō(ə)r, -ˌsȯ(ə)r\ *adj* **:** having sore or tender feet (as from much walking) — **foot·sore·ness** *n*
foot·stall \-ˌstȯl\ *n* **:** the plinth, base, or pedestal of a pillar
foot·step \-ˌstep\ *n* **1 a :** TREAD **b :** distance covered by a step : PACE **2 :** the mark of the foot : TRACK **3 :** a step on which to ascend or descend **4 :** a way of life, conduct, or action ⟨followed in his father's ~*s*⟩
foot·stone \-ˌstōn\ *n* **:** a stone placed at the foot of a grave
foot·stool \-ˌstül\ *n* **:** a low stool used to support the feet
foot·wall \-ˌwȯl\ *n* **1 :** the lower underlying wall of a vein, ore deposit, or coal seam in a mine **2 :** the lower wall of an inclined fault
foot·way \-ˌwā\ *n* **:** a narrow way or path for pedestrians
foot·wear \-ˌwa(ə)r, -ˌwe(ə)r\ *n* **:** wearing apparel (as shoes or boots) for the feet
foot·work \-ˌwərk\ *n* **1 :** the management of the feet (as in boxing); *also* **:** the work done with them **2 :** the activity of moving from place to place ⟨the investigation entailed a lot of ~⟩
foo·ty \ˈfüt-ē\ *adj* [F *foutu*] **1** *chiefly dial* **:** INSIGNIFICANT, PALTRY **2** *chiefly dial* **:** poorly kept : SHABBY
[1]**foo·zle** \ˈfü-zəl\ *vt* **foo·zled; foo·zling** \ˈfüz-(ə-)liŋ\ [perh. fr. G dial. *fuseln* to work carelessly] **:** to manage or play awkwardly : BUNGLE
[2]**foozle** *n* **:** an act of foozling; *esp* **:** a bungling golf stroke
[1]**fop** \ˈfäp\ *n* [ME; akin to ME *fobben* to deceive, MHG *voppen*] **1** *obs* **:** a foolish or silly person **2 :** a man who is devoted to or vain about his appearance or dress : COXCOMB, DANDY
[2]**fop** *vt* **fopped; fop·ping** *obs* **:** FOOL, DUPE
fop·pery \ˈfäp-(ə-)rē\ *n, pl* **-per·ies 1 :** foolish character or action : FOLLY **2 :** the behavior or dress of a fop
fop·pish \ˈfäp-ish\ *adj* **1** *obs* **:** FOOLISH, SILLY **2 a :** characteristic of a fop ⟨a ~ embroidered nightshirt —A. Conan Doyle⟩ **b :** behaving or dressing in the manner of a fop — **fop·pish·ly** *adv* — **fop·pish·ness** *n*
[1]**for** \fər, (ˈ)fȯ(ə)r, *South also* (ˈ)fär\ *prep* [ME, fr. OE; akin to L *per* through, *prae* before, *pro* before, for, ahead, Gk *pro*, OE *faran* to go — more at FARE] **1 a** — used as a function word to indicate purpose ⟨a grant ~ studying medicine⟩ **b** — used as a function word to indicate an intended goal ⟨left ~ home⟩ ⟨acted ~ the best⟩ **c** — used as a function word to indicate the object or recipient of a perception, desire, or activity ⟨now ~ a good rest⟩ ⟨run ~ your life⟩ ⟨an eye ~ a bargain⟩ ⟨called ~ hands to take in the sail⟩ **2 a :** as being or constituting ⟨take him ~ a fool⟩ ⟨eggs ~ breakfast⟩ **b** — used as a function word to indicate an actual or implied enumeration or selection ⟨~ one thing, the price is too high⟩ **3 :** because of ⟨cried ~ joy⟩ **4** — used as a function word to indicate suitability or fitness ⟨it is not ~ the president to make that decision⟩ ⟨ready ~ action⟩ **5 a :** in place of **b :** on behalf of : REPRESENTING **6 :** in spite of — usu. used with *all* ⟨~ all his large size, he moves gracefully⟩ **7 :** with respect to : CONCERNING ⟨a stickler ~ detail⟩ **8** — used as a function word to indicate equivalence in exchange ⟨$10 ~ a hat⟩, equality in number or quantity ⟨point ~ point⟩, or correspondence or correlation ⟨~ one good one, you'll find five that don't work⟩ **9** — used as a function word to indicate duration of time or extent of space **10 :** in honor of : AFTER

[2]**for** *conj* **:** for this reason : on this ground
[3]**for** *abbr* **1** foreign **2** forestry
FOR *abbr* free on rail
for- *prefix* [ME, fr. OE; akin to OHG *fur-* for-, OE *for*] **1 :** so as to involve prohibition, exclusion, omission, failure, neglect, or refusal ⟨*for*say⟩ **2 :** destructively or detrimentally ⟨*for*do⟩ **3 :** completely : excessively : to exhaustion : to pieces ⟨*for*spent⟩
fora *pl of* FORUM
[1]**for·age** \ˈfȯr-ij, ˈfär-\ *n* [ME, fr. MF, fr. OF, fr. *forre* fodder, of Gmc origin; akin to OHG *fuotar* food, fodder — more at FOOD] **1 :** food for animals esp. when taken by browsing or grazing **2** [[2]*forage*] **:** the act of foraging : search for provisions
[2]**forage** *vb* **for·aged; for·ag·ing** *vt* **1 :** to strip of provisions : collect forage from **2 :** to secure by foraging ⟨*foraged* a chicken for the feast⟩ ~ *vi* **1 :** to wander in search of forage or food **2 :** to secure forage (as for horses) by stripping the country **3 :** RAVAGE, RAID **4 :** to make a search : RUMMAGE — **for·ag·er** *n*
forage acre *n* **:** a unit of grazing value equivalent to one acre of land entirely covered with herbage that can be completely utilized by grazing animals
fo·ram \ˈfōr-əm, ˈfȯr-\ *n* **:** FORAMINIFER
fo·ra·men \fə-ˈrā-mən\ *n, pl* **fo·ram·i·na** \-ˈram-ə-nə\ *or* **fo·ra·mens** \-ˈrā-mənz\ [L *foramin-, foramen*, fr. *forare* to bore — more at BORE] **:** a small opening, perforation, or orifice : FENESTRA — **fo·ram·i·nal** \fə-ˈram-ən-ᵊl\ *or* **fo·ram·i·nous** \-ə-nəs\ *adj*
fo·ra·men mag·num \fə-ˌrā-mən-ˈmag-nəm\ *n* [NL, lit., great opening] **:** the opening in the skull through which the spinal cord passes to become the medulla oblongata
foramen ova·le \-ō-ˈval-ē, -ˈväl-, -ˈvāl-\ *n* [NL, lit., oval opening] **:** an opening in the septum between the two atria of the heart that is normally present only in the fetus
fo·ra·min·i·fer \ˌfȯr-ə-ˈmin-ə-fər, ˌfär-\ *n* **:** any of an order (Foraminifera) of large chiefly marine rhizopods usu. having calcareous shells that often are perforated with minute holes for protrusion of slender pseudopodia and form the bulk of chalk and nummulitic limestone — **fo·ra·mi·nif·er·al** \fə-ˌram-ə-ˈnif-(ə-)rəl; ˌfȯr-ə-mə-ˈnif-, ˌfär-\ *or* **fo·ra·mi·nif·er·ous** \-(ə-)rəs\ *adj*
fo·ra·mi·nif·era \fə-ˌram-ə-ˈnif-(ə-)rə; ˌfȯr-ə-mə-ˈnif-, ˌfär-\ *n pl* [NL, fr. L *foramin-, foramen* + *-fera*, neut. pl. of *-fer* -fer] **:** organisms that are foraminifers
fo·ra·mi·nif·er·an \-(ə-)rən\ *n* **:** FORAMINIFER
for and *conj, obs* **:** and also
for·as·much as \ˈfȯr-əz-ˌməch-əz\ *conj* **:** in view of the fact that : SINCE
[1]**for·ay** \ˈfȯr-ˌā, ˈfōr-, ˈfär- *also* fȯ-ˈrā *or* fə-\ *vb* [ME *forrayen*, fr. MF *forrer*, fr. *forre* fodder — more at FORAGE] *vt, archaic* **:** to ravage in search of spoils : PILLAGE ~ *vi* **:** to make a raid or brief invasion ⟨~*ed* into enemy territory⟩ — **for·ay·er** *n*
[2]**foray** *n* **1 :** a sudden or irregular invasion or attack for war or spoils : RAID **2 :** a brief excursion or attempt esp. outside one's accustomed sphere ⟨the teacher's ~ into politics⟩
forb \ˈfȯ(ə)rb\ *n* [Gk *phorbē* fodder, food, fr. *pherbein* to graze; akin to OE *beorgan* to taste] **:** an herb other than grass
[1]**for·bear** \fȯr-ˈba(ə)r, fər-, -ˈbe(ə)r\ *vb* **-bore** \-ˈbō(ə)r, -ˈbȯ(ə)r\; **-borne** \-ˈbō(ə)rn, -ˈbȯ(ə)rn\; **-bear·ing** [ME *forberen*, fr. OE *forberan* to endure, do without, fr. *for-* + *beran* to bear] *vt* **1** *obs* **:** to leave alone : SHUN ⟨~ his presence —Shak.⟩ **2** *obs* **:** to do without **3 :** to hold oneself back from esp. with an effort of self-restraint ~ *vi* **1 :** to hold back : ABSTAIN **2 :** to control oneself when provoked : be patient ***syn*** see REFRAIN — **for·bear·er** *n*
[2]**forbear** *var of* FOREBEAR
for·bear·ance \fȯr-ˈbar-ən(t)s, fər-, -ˈber-\ *n* **1 :** a refraining from the enforcement of something (as a debt, right, or obligation) that is due **2 :** the act of forbearing : PATIENCE **3 :** the quality of being forbearing : LENIENCY
[1]**for·bid** \fər-ˈbid, fȯr-\ *vt* **-bade** \-ˈbad, -ˈbād\ *or* **-bad** \-ˈbad\; **-bid·den** \-ˈbid-ᵊn\; **-bid·ding** [ME *forbidden*, fr. OE *forbēodan*, fr. *for-* + *bēodan* to bid — more at BID] **1 :** to proscribe from or as if from the position of one in authority : command against ⟨the law ~*s* stores to sell liquor to minors⟩ ⟨her mother ~*s* her to go⟩ ⟨he ~*s* her the car⟩ **2 :** to hinder or prevent as if by an effectual command ⟨space ~*s* further treatment of the subject here⟩ — **for·bid·der** *n*
syn FORBID, PROHIBIT, INTERDICT, INHIBIT, BAN ***shared meaning element*** **:** to debar one from using, doing, or entering or to order that something not be used, done, or entered ***ant*** permit, bid
[2]**forbid** *adj, archaic* **:** ACCURSED ⟨he shall live a man ~ —Shak.⟩
for·bid·dance \fər-ˈbid-ᵊn(t)s, fȯr-\ *n* **:** the act of forbidding
for·bid·den \-ˈbid-ᵊn\ *adj* **:** not conforming to the usual selection principles — used of quantum phenomena ⟨~ transition⟩ ⟨~ radiation⟩ ⟨~ spectral line⟩
for·bid·ding *adj* **1 :** such as to make approach or passage difficult or impossible ⟨~ walls⟩ **2 :** DISAGREEABLE, REPELLENT ⟨his father was a stern ~ figure⟩ — **for·bid·ding·ly** \-ˈbid-iŋ-lē\ *adv* — **for·bid·ding·ness** *n*
forbode *var of* FOREBODE
[1]**for·by** *or* **for·bye** \fȯr-ˈbī\ *prep* [ME *forby*, prep. & adv., fr. *fore-* + *by*] **1** *archaic* **a :** PAST **b :** NEAR **2** *chiefly Scot* **:** BESIDES
[2]**forby** *or* **forbye** *adv, chiefly Scot* **:** in addition : BESIDES
[1]**force** \ˈfō(ə)rs, ˈfȯ(ə)rs\ *n* [ME, fr. MF, fr. (assumed) VL *fortia*, fr. L *fortis* strong] **1 a :** strength or energy exerted or brought to bear : cause of motion or change : active power ⟨the ~*s* of nature⟩ ⟨the love of justice has been a powerful motivating ~ in his life⟩ **b :** moral or mental strength **c :** capacity to persuade or convince ⟨couldn't resist the ~ of his argument⟩ **2 a :** military strength **b (1) :** a body (as of troops or ships) assigned to a military purpose **(2)** *pl* **:** the whole military strength (as of a nation) **c :** a body of persons or things available for a particular end ⟨a labor ~⟩ ⟨the missile ~⟩ **d :** an individual or group having the power of effective action ⟨police and citizens must join ~*s* to prevent violence⟩ ⟨he was a ~ behind the passing of that bill⟩ **3 :** violence, compulsion, or constraint exerted upon or against a person or thing **4 :** an agency or influence that if applied to a free body results chiefly in an acceleration of the body and sometimes in

elastic deformation and other effects **5 :** the quality of conveying impressions intensely in writing or speech — **force·less** \-ləs\ *adj* — **in force 1 :** in great numbers ⟨police were summoned *in force*⟩ **2 :** VALID, OPERATIVE ⟨his suspension from school must remain *in force*⟩

²force *vt* **forced; forc·ing 1 :** to do violence to; *esp* **:** RAPE **2 :** to compel by physical, moral, or intellectual means **3 :** to make or cause through natural or logical necessity ⟨*forced* to admit he was right⟩ **4 a :** to press, drive, attain to, or effect against resistance or inertia ⟨~ a bill through the legislature⟩ **b :** to impose or thrust urgently, importunately, or inexorably ⟨~ unwanted attentions on a woman⟩ **5 :** to achieve or win by strength in struggle or violence: **a :** to win one's way into ⟨~ a castle⟩ ⟨*forced* the mountain passes⟩ **b :** to break open or through ⟨~ a lock⟩ **6 a :** to raise or accelerate to the utmost ⟨*forcing* the pace⟩ **b :** to produce only with unnatural or unwilling effort ⟨she *forced* a smile in spite of her distress⟩ **c :** to wrench, strain, or use (language) with marked unnaturalness and lack of ease **7 a :** to hasten the rate of progress or growth of **b :** to bring (as plants) to maturity out of the normal season ⟨*forcing* lilies for the Easter trade⟩ **8 :** to induce (as a particular bid or play by another player) in a card game by some conventional act, play, bid, or response **9 a :** to cause (a runner in baseball) to be put out on a force play **b :** to cause (a run) to be scored in baseball by giving a base on balls when the bases are full — **forc·er** *n*

syn FORCE, COMPEL, COERCE, CONSTRAIN, OBLIGE *shared meaning element* **:** to make someone or something yield. FORCE, the general term, implies an overcoming of resistance by the exertion of strength, weight, power, stress, or duress ⟨*forced* his way through the crowd⟩ ⟨*forced* to submit to questioning⟩ ⟨used threats to *force* agreement to their terms⟩ COMPEL usually implies an exertion of authority or the working of an irresistible force ⟨*compelled* by necessity to seek help⟩ COERCE suggests the overcoming of resistance by severe methods (as violence or duress) or by threat and intimidation ⟨no one can claim that he was *coerced* by bribery. This is reserved for threats and direct pleas —W. D. Falk⟩ CONSTRAIN suggests a forcing by what does or seems to constrict, press, confine, or bind ⟨*constrained* by sickness from a normal life⟩ ⟨he was *constrained* to confess by the evidence against him⟩ OBLIGE implies the constraint of necessity, sometimes physical but often moral or intellectual ⟨ill health *obliged* him to retire⟩ ⟨he was *obliged* to admit he had been wrong⟩

— **force one's hand :** to cause one to act precipitously **:** force one to reveal his purpose or intention

forced \ˈfō(ə)rst, ˈfȯ(ə)rst\ *adj* **1 :** compelled by force **:** INVOLUNTARY ⟨a ~ landing⟩ **2 :** done or produced with effort, exertion, or pressure ⟨a ~ laugh⟩ — **forced·ly** \ˈfōr-səd-lē, ˈfȯr-\ *adv*

force–feed *vt* **1 :** to feed (as an animal) by forcible administration of food **2 :** to force to take in ⟨~ students a literary education⟩

force·ful \ˈfōrs-fəl, ˈfȯrs-\ *adj* **:** possessing or filled with force **:** EFFECTIVE — **force·ful·ly** \-fə-lē\ *adv* — **force·ful·ness** *n*

force ma·jeure \ˌfōr-smä-ˈzhər, ˌfȯr-, -smə-\ *n* [F, superior force] **:** an event or effect that cannot be reasonably anticipated or controlled — compare ACT OF GOD

force·meat \ˈfōr-ˌsmēt, ˈfȯr-\ *n* [*force* (alter. of *farce*) + *meat*] **:** finely chopped and highly seasoned meat or fish that is either served alone or used as a stuffing — called also *farce*

force of habit : behavior made involuntary or automatic by repeated practice

force–out \ˈfōr-ˌsau̇t, ˈfȯr-\ *n* **:** FORCE PLAY

force play *n* **:** a play in baseball in which a runner is put out when he is forced to advance to the next base but fails to do so safely

for·ceps \ˈfȯr-səps\ *n, pl* **forceps** [L, fr. *formus* warm + *capere* to take — more at WARM, HEAVE] **:** an instrument for grasping, holding firmly, or exerting traction upon objects esp. for delicate operations (as by jewelers or surgeons) — **for·ceps·like** \-ˌlīk\ *adj*

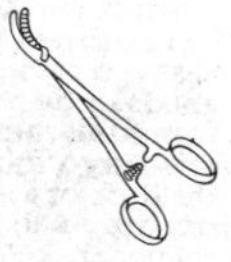

forceps

force pump *n* **:** a pump with a solid piston for drawing and forcing through valves a liquid (as water) to a considerable height above the pump or under a considerable pressure

forc·ible \ˈfōr-sə-bəl, ˈfȯr-\ *adj* **1 :** effected by force used against opposition or resistance **2 :** characterized by force, efficiency, or energy **:** POWERFUL — **forc·i·ble·ness** *n* — **forc·i·bly** \-blē\ *adv*

¹ford \ˈfō(ə)rd, ˈfȯ(ə)rd\ *n* [ME, fr. OE; akin to ON *fjörthr* fiord, L *portus* port, OE *faran* to go — more at FARE] **:** a shallow part of a body of water that may be crossed by wading

²ford *vt* **:** to cross (a body of water) by wading — **ford·able** \ˈfōrd-ə-bəl, ˈfȯrd-\ *adj*

for·do *or* **fore·do** \fȯr-ˈdü, fōr-\ *vt* **-did** \-ˈdid\; **-done** \-ˈdən\; **-do·ing** \-ˈdü-iŋ\ [ME *fordon*, fr. OE *fordōn*, fr. *for-* + *dōn* to do] **1** *archaic* **:** to do away with **:** DESTROY **2 :** to overcome with fatigue **:** EXHAUST — used only as past participle ⟨quite *fordone* with the heat⟩

¹fore \ˈfō(ə)r, ˈfȯ(ə)r\ *adv* [ME, fr. OE; akin to OE *for*] **1** *obs* **:** at an earlier time or period **2 :** in, toward, or adjacent to the front **:** FORWARD

²fore *also* **'fore** *prep* **1** *chiefly dial* **:** BEFORE **2 :** in the presence of

³fore *adj* [*fore-*] **1 :** prior in order of occurrence **:** FORMER **2 :** situated in front of something else **:** FORWARD

⁴fore *n* **:** something that occupies a front position — **to the fore :** in or into a position of prominence **:** FORWARD ⟨a younger generation of idealists is coming *to the fore*⟩

⁵fore *interj* [prob. short for *before*] — used by a golfer to warn anyone within range of the probable line of flight of his ball

fore- *comb form* [ME *for-*, *fore-*, fr. OE *fore-*, fr. *fore*, adv.] **1 a :** earlier **:** beforehand ⟨*fore*see⟩ **b :** occurring earlier **:** occurring beforehand ⟨*fore*payment⟩ **2 a :** situated at the front **:** in front ⟨*fore*leg⟩ **b :** front part of (something specified) ⟨*fore*arm⟩

fore–and–aft \ˌfōr-ə-ˈnaft, ˌfȯr-\ *adj* **1 :** lying, running, or acting in the general line of the length of a construction (as a ship or a house) **:** LONGITUDINAL **2 :** having no square sails

fore and aft *adv* **1 :** lengthwise of a ship **:** from stem to stern **2 :** in, at, or toward both the bow and stern

fore–and–aft·er \-ˈnaf-tər\ *n* **:** a ship with a fore-and-aft rig; *esp* **:** SCHOONER

fore–and–aft rig *n* **:** a sailing-ship rig in which most or all of the sails are not attached to yards but are bent to gaffs or set on the masts or on stays in a fore-and-aft line

¹fore·arm \(ˈ)fōr-ˈärm, (ˈ)fȯr-\ *vt* **:** to arm in advance **:** PREPARE

²fore·arm \ˈfōr-ˌärm, ˈfȯr-\ *n* **:** the part of the arm between the elbow and the wrist; *also* **:** the corresponding part in other vertebrates

fore·bay \ˈfō(ə)r-ˌbā, ˈfȯ(ə)r-\ *n* **:** a reservoir or canal from which water is taken to run equipment (as a waterwheel or turbine)

fore·bear *or* **for·bear** \-ˌba(ə)r, -ˌbe(ə)r\ *n* [ME (Sc) *forebear*, fr. *fore-* + *-bear* (fr. *been* to be)] **:** ANCESTOR, FOREFATHER — usu. used in pl.

fore·bode *also* **for·bode** \fōr-ˈbōd, fȯr-\ *vt* **1 :** FORETELL, PORTEND ⟨such heavy air ~*s* storm⟩ **2 :** to have an inward conviction of (as coming ill or misfortune) ~ *vi* **:** AUGUR, PREDICT — **fore·bod·er** *n*

¹fore·bod·ing \-ˈbōd-iŋ\ *n* **:** the act of one who forebodes; *also* **:** an omen, prediction, or presentiment esp. of coming evil **:** PORTENT

²foreboding *adj* **:** indicative of or marked by foreboding — **fore·bod·ing·ly** \-iŋ-lē\ *adv* — **fore·bod·ing·ness** *n*

fore·brain \ˈfō(ə)r-ˌbrān, ˈfȯ(ə)r-\ *n* **1 :** the anterior of the three primary divisions of the developing vertebrate brain **2 a :** the part of the brain of the adult that develops from the embryonic forebrain and includes the telencephalon and diencephalon **b :** TELENCEPHALON

fore·cad·die \-ˌkad-ē\ *n* **:** a golf caddie who is stationed in the fairway and who indicates the position of balls on the course

¹fore·cast \-ˌkast; fōr-ˈkast, fȯr-ˈ\ *vb* **forecast** *or* **fore·cast·ed; fore·cast·ing** *vt* **1 a :** to calculate or predict (some future event or condition) usu. as a result of rational study and analysis of available pertinent data; *esp* **:** to predict (weather conditions) on the basis of correlated meteorological observations **b :** to indicate as likely to occur **2 :** to serve as a forecast of **:** PRESAGE ⟨such events may ~ peace⟩ ~ *vi* **:** to calculate the future ***syn*** see FORETELL — **fore·cast·er** *n*

²fore·cast \ˈfō(ə)r-ˌkast, ˈfȯ(ə)r-\ *n* **1** *archaic* **:** foresight of consequences and provision against them **:** FORETHOUGHT **2 :** a prophecy, estimate, or prediction of a future happening or condition

fore·cas·tle \ˈfōk-səl; ˈfōr-ˌkas-əl, ˈfȯr-\ *n* **1 :** the part of the upper deck of a ship forward of the foremast or of the fore channels **2 :** the forward part of a merchantman where the crew is housed

fore–check \ˈfō(ə)r-ˌchek, ˈfȯ(ə)r-\ *vi* **:** to guard an opponent in ice hockey in his own defensive zone

fore·close \fōr-ˈklōz, fȯr-\ *vb* [ME *forclosen*, fr. OF *forclos*, pp. of *forclore*, fr. *fors* outside (fr. L *foris*) + *clore* to close — more at FORUM] *vt* **1 :** to shut out **:** DEBAR **2 :** to hold exclusively **3 :** to deal with or close in advance **4 :** to subject to foreclosure proceedings ~ *vi* **:** to foreclose a mortgage

fore·clo·sure \-ˈklō-zhər\ *n* **:** an act or instance of foreclosing; *specif* **:** a legal proceeding that bars or extinguishes a mortgagor's right of redeeming a mortgaged estate

fore·deck \ˈfō(ə)r-ˌdek, ˈfȯ(ə)r-\ *n* **:** the forepart of a ship's main deck

foredo *var of* FORDO

fore·doom \fōr-ˈdüm, fȯr-\ *vt* **:** to doom beforehand

fore·face \ˈfō(ə)r-ˌfās, ˈfȯ(ə)r-\ *n* **:** the part of the head of a quadruped that is in front of the eyes

fore·fa·ther \-ˌfäth-ər\ *n* **1 :** ANCESTOR 1a **2 :** a person of an earlier period and common heritage

fore·feel \fōr-ˈfē(ə)l, fȯr-\ *vt* **-felt** \-ˈfelt\; **-feel·ing :** to have a presentiment of

forefend *var of* FORFEND

fore·fin·ger \ˈfō(ə)r-ˌfiŋ-gər, ˈfȯ(ə)r-\ *n* **:** the finger next to the thumb — called also *index finger*

fore·foot \-ˌfu̇t\ *n* **1 :** one of the anterior feet of a quadruped or multiped **2 :** the forward part of a ship where the stem and keel meet

fore·front \-ˌfrənt\ *n* **:** the foremost part or place **:** VANGUARD ⟨was in the ~ of the progressive movement⟩

fore·gath·er *var of* FORGATHER

¹fore·go \fōr-ˈgō, fȯr-\ *vt* **-went** \-ˈwent\; **-gone** \-ˈgȯn *also* -ˈgän\; **-go·ing** \-ˈgō-iŋ, -ˈgȯ(-)iŋ\ **:** to go before **:** PRECEDE — **fore·go·er** \-ˈgō(-ə)r\ *n*

²forego *var of* FORGO

fore·go·ing \-ˈgō-iŋ, -ˈgȯ(-)iŋ\ *adj* **:** going before ⟨the ~ statement is open to challenge⟩ ***syn*** see PRECEDING ***ant*** following

fore·gone \ˌfōr-ˌgȯn, ˌfȯr- *also* -ˌgän\ *adj* **:** PREVIOUS, PAST

foregone conclusion *n* **1 :** a conclusion that has preceded argument or examination **2 :** an inevitable result **:** CERTAINTY ⟨the victory was a *foregone conclusion*⟩

fore·ground \ˈfō(ə)r-ˌgrau̇nd, ˈfȯ(ə)r-\ *n* **1 :** the part of a scene or representation that is nearest to and in front of the spectator **2 :** a position of prominence **:** FOREFRONT

fore·gut \-ˌgət\ *n* **:** the anterior part of the alimentary canal of a vertebrate embryo that develops into the pharynx, esophagus, stomach, and extreme anterior part of the intestine

¹fore·hand \-ˌhand\ *n* **1** *archaic* **:** superior position **:** ADVANTAGE **2 :** the part of a horse that is before the

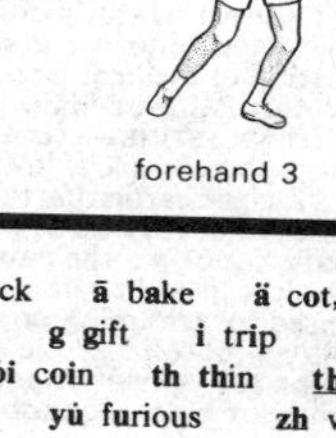

forehand 3

rider **3 :** a forehand stroke (as in tennis or racquets); *also* **:** the side on which such strokes are made
[2]forehand *adv* **:** with a forehand stroke
[3]forehand *adj* **1** *obs* **:** done or given in advance **:** PRIOR **2 :** made with the palm of the hand turned in the direction in which the hand is moving ⟨a ~ tennis stroke⟩
fore·hand·ed \(ˈ)fōr-ˈhan-dəd, (ˈ)fȯr-\ *adj* **1 a :** mindful of the future **:** PRUDENT **b :** WELL-TO-DO **2 :** FOREHAND 2 — **fore·hand·ed·ly** *adv* — **fore·hand·ed·ness** *n*
fore·head \ˈfȯr-əd, ˈfär-; ˈfō(ə)r-ˌhed, ˈfȯ(ə)r-\ *n* **1 :** the part of the face above the eyes **2 :** the front or forepart of something ⟨flames in the ~ of the morning sky —John Milton⟩
fore·hoof \ˈfō(ə)r-ˌhu̇f, ˈfȯ(ə)r-, -ˌhüf\ *n* **:** the hoof of a forefoot
for·eign \ˈfȯr-ən, ˈfär-\ *adj* [ME *forein*, fr. OF, fr. LL *foranus* on the outside, fr. L *foris* outside — more at FORUM] **1 :** situated outside a place or country; *esp* **:** situated outside one's own country **2 :** born in, belonging to, or characteristic of some place or country other than the one under consideration **3 :** of, relating to, or proceeding from some other person or material thing than the one under consideration **4 :** alien in character **:** not connected or pertinent **5 :** related to or dealing with other nations **6 :** occurring in an abnormal situation in the living body and commonly introduced from without **7 :** not being within the jurisdiction of a political unit (as a state) ***syn*** see EXTRINSIC ***ant*** germane — **for·eign·ness** \-ən-nəs\ *n*
foreign affairs *n pl* **:** matters having to do with international relations and with the interests of the home country in foreign countries
foreign aid *n* **:** assistance (as economic aid) provided by one nation to another esp. as a tool in molding opinion in the recipient nation
foreign bill *n* **:** a bill of exchange that is not both drawn and payable within a particular jurisdiction
for·eign–born \ˌfȯr-ən-ˈbȯ(ə)rn, ˌfär-\ *adj* **:** foreign by birth
foreign correspondent *n* **:** a correspondent employed to send from a foreign country news or comment for publication (as in a newspaper)
for·eign·er \ˈfȯr-ə-nər, ˈfär-\ *n* **1 :** a person belonging to or owing allegiance to a foreign country **:** ALIEN **2** *chiefly dial* **:** STRANGER 1c
foreign exchange *n* **1 :** a process of settling accounts or debts between persons residing in different countries **2 :** foreign currency or current short-term credit instruments payable in such currency
for·eign·ism \ˈfȯr-ə-ˌniz-əm, ˈfär-\ *n* **:** something peculiar to a foreign language or people; *specif* **:** a foreign idiom or custom
foreign minister *n* **:** a governmental minister for foreign affairs
foreign policy *n* **:** the policy of a sovereign state in its interaction with other sovereign states
foreign service *n* **:** the field force of a foreign office comprising diplomatic and consular personnel
[1]fore·judge *or* **for·judge** \fər-ˈjəj, fōr-, fȯr-\ *vt* [ME *forjuggen*, fr. MF *forjugier*, fr. *fors* outside (fr. L *foris*) + *jugier* to judge] **:** to expel, oust, or put out by judgment of a court
[2]fore·judge \(ˈ)fōr-ˈjəj, (ˈ)fȯr-\ *vt* **:** PREJUDGE
fore·know \(ˈ)fōr-ˈnō, (ˈ)fȯr-\ *vt* **-knew** \-ˈn(y)ü\; **-known** \-ˈnōn\; **-know·ing :** to have previous knowledge of **:** know beforehand esp. by paranormal means or by revelation ***syn*** see FORESEE — **fore·knowl·edge** \-ˈnäl-ij\ *n*
fore·la·dy \ˈfō(ə)r-ˌlād-ē, ˈfȯ(ə)r-\ *n* **:** a woman who acts as a foreman
fore·land \ˈfōr-lənd, ˈfȯr-\ *n* **:** PROMONTORY, HEADLAND
fore·leg \ˈfō(ə)r-ˌleg, ˈfȯ(ə)r-, -ˌlāg\ *n* **:** a front leg
fore·limb \-ˌlim\ *n* **:** an arm, fin, wing, or leg that is or is homologous to a foreleg ⟨the ~ of a bat⟩
fore·lock \-ˌläk\ *n* **:** a lock of hair growing from the front of the head
fore·man \ˈfōr-mən, ˈfȯr-\ *n* **:** a first or chief man: as **a :** a member of a jury who acts as chairman and spokesman **b (1) :** a chief and often specially trained workman who works with and commonly leads a gang or crew **b (2) :** a person in authority over a group of workers, a particular operation, or a section of a plant — **fore·man·ship** \-ˌship\ *n*
fore·mast \ˈfō(ə)r-ˌmast, ˈfȯ(ə)r-, -məst\ *n* **:** the mast nearest the bow of a ship
fore·milk \-ˌmilk\ *n* **1 :** first-drawn milk **2 :** COLOSTRUM
[1]fore·most \-ˌmōst\ *adj* [ME *formest*, fr. OE, superl. of *forma* first; akin to OHG *fruma* advantage, OE *fore* fore] **1 :** first in a series or progression **2 :** of first rank or position **:** PREEMINENT
[2]foremost *adv* **1 :** in the first place **2 :** most importantly ⟨first and ~⟩
fore·moth·er \ˈfō(ə)r-ˌmət͟h-ər, ˈfȯ(ə)r-\ *n* **:** a female ancestor
fore·name \-ˌnām\ *n* **:** a name that precedes one's surname
fore·named \-ˌnāmd\ *adj* **:** named previously **:** AFORESAID
fore·noon \ˈfō(ə)r-ˌnün, ˈfȯ(ə)r-, ˌfōr-ˈ, fȯr-ˈ\ *n* **:** the early part of the day ending with noon **:** MORNING
[1]fo·ren·sic \fə-ˈren(t)-sik, -ˈren-zik\ *adj* [L *forensis* public, forensic, fr. *forum*] **1 :** belonging to, used in, or suitable to courts of judicature or to public discussion and debate **2 :** ARGUMENTATIVE, RHETORICAL — **fo·ren·si·cal·ly** \-si-k(ə-)lē, -zi-\ *adv*
[2]forensic *n* **1 :** an argumentative exercise **2** *pl but sing or pl in constr* **:** the art or study of argumentative discourse
forensic medicine *n* **:** a science that deals with the relation and application of medical facts to legal problems
fore·or·dain \ˌfōr-ȯr-ˈdān, ˌfȯr-\ *vt* **:** to dispose or appoint in advance **:** PREDESTINE — **fore·or·di·na·tion** \-ˌȯrd-ᵊn-ˈā-shən\ *n*
fore·part \ˈfō(ə)r-ˌpärt, ˈfȯ(ə)r-\ *n* **1 :** the anterior part of something **2 :** the earlier part of a period of time
fore·passed *or* **fore·past** \-ˌpast\ *adj* **:** BYGONE
fore·paw \-ˌpȯ\ *n* **:** the paw of a foreleg
fore·peak \-ˌpēk\ *n* **:** the extreme forward lower compartment or tank used for trimming or storage in a ship
fore·play \-ˌplā\ *n* **:** erotic stimulation preceding sexual intercourse
fore·quar·ter \-ˌkwȯ(r)t-ər\ *n* **:** the front half of a lateral half of the body or carcass of a quadruped ⟨a ~ of beef⟩
fore·reach \fōr-ˈrēch, fȯr-\ *vi, of a ship* **:** to gain ground in tacking ~ *vt* **:** to gain on or overhaul and go ahead of (a ship) when close-hauled
fore·run \-ˈrən\ *vt* **-ran** \-ˈran\; **-run; -run·ning 1 :** to run before **2 :** to come before as a token of something to follow **3 :** FORESTALL, ANTICIPATE
fore·run·ner \ˈfō(ə)r-ˌrən-ər, ˈfȯ(ə)r-\ *n* **1 :** one going or sent before to give notice of the approach of others: as **a :** a premonitory sign or symptom **b :** a skier who runs the course before the start of a race **2 :** PREDECESSOR, FOREBEAR
syn FORERUNNER, PRECURSOR, HARBINGER, HERALD *shared meaning element* **:** one who goes before or announces the coming of another
fore·sad·dle \-ˌsad-ᵊl\ *n* **:** a wholesale cut of mutton, lamb, or veal that consists of the undivided forequarters of a carcass
fore·said \-ˌsed\ *adj, archaic* **:** AFORESAID
fore·sail \ˈfō(ə)r-ˌsāl, ˈfȯ(ə)r-, -səl\ *n* **1 :** a sail carried on the foreyard of a square-rigged ship that is the lowest sail on the foremast **2 :** the lower sail set abaft a schooner's foremast — see SAIL illustration **3 :** FORESTAYSAIL
fore·see \fōr-ˈsē, fȯr-\ *vt* **-saw** \-ˈsȯ\; **-seen** \-ˈsēn\; **-see·ing :** to see (as a development) beforehand — **fore·see·able** \-ˈsē-ə-bəl, fər-\ *adj* — **fore·se·er** \fōr-ˈsē-ər, fȯr-, -ˈsi(-ə)r\ *n*
syn FORESEE, FOREKNOW, DIVINE, APPREHEND, ANTICIPATE *shared meaning element* **:** to know beforehand
fore·shad·ow \-ˈshad-(ˌ)ō, -ə(-w)\ *vt* **:** to represent or typify beforehand **:** PREFIGURE ⟨present trends ~ future events⟩ — **fore·shad·ow·er** \-ə-wər\ *n*
fore·shank \ˈfō(ə)r-ˌshaŋk, ˈfȯ(ə)r-\ *n* **:** a beef shin
fore·sheet \-ˌshēt\ *n* **1 :** one of the sheets of a foresail **2** *pl* **:** the forward part of an open boat
fore·shore \-ˌshō(ə)r, -ˌshȯ(ə)r\ *n* **1 :** a strip of land margining a body of water **2 :** the part of a seashore between high-water and low-water marks
fore·short·en \fōr-ˈshȯrt-ᵊn, fȯr-\ *vt* **1 :** to shorten by proportionately contracting in the direction of depth so that an illusion of projection or extension in space is obtained **2 :** to make more compact
fore·show \-ˈshō\ *vt* **-showed; -shown** \-ˈshōn\ *or* **-showed; -show·ing 1 :** FORETELL **2 :** to show beforehand
fore·side \ˈfō(ə)r-ˌsīd, ˈfȯ(ə)r-\ *n* **:** the front side or part **:** FRONT
fore·sight \ˈfō(ə)r-ˌsīt, ˈfȯ(ə)r-\ *n* **1 :** an act or the power of foreseeing **:** PRESCIENCE **2 :** an act of looking forward; *also* **:** a view forward **3 :** provident care **:** PRUDENCE ⟨had the ~ to invest his money wisely⟩ — **fore·sight·ed** \-əd\ *adj* — **fore·sight·ed·ly** *adv* — **fore·sight·ed·ness** *n* — **fore·sight·ful** \-ˌsīt-fəl\ *adj*
fore·skin \-ˌskin\ *n* **:** a fold of skin that covers the glans of the penis — called also *prepuce*
fore·speak \fōr-ˈspēk, fȯr-\ *vt* **-spoke** \-ˈspōk\; **-spo·ken** \-ˈspō-kən\; **-speak·ing 1 :** FORETELL, PREDICT **2 :** to arrange for in advance
[1]for·est \ˈfȯr-əst, ˈfär-\ *n, often attrib* [ME, fr. OF, fr. ML *forestis*, fr. L *foris* outside — more at FORUM] **1 :** a tract of wooded land in England formerly owned by the sovereign and used for game **2 :** a dense growth of trees and underbrush covering a large tract **3 :** something resembling a forest esp. in profusion ⟨a ~ of TV antennas⟩ — **for·est·al** \-əs-tᵊl\ *or* **fo·res·tial** \fə-ˈres-tē-əl, fō-, -ˈres(h)-chəl\ *adj* — **for·est·ed** \ˈfȯr-ə-stəd, ˈfär-\ *adj*
[2]forest *vt* **:** to cover with trees or forest — **for·es·ta·tion** \ˌfȯr-ə-ˈstā-shən, ˌfär-\ *n*
fore·stage \ˈfō(ə)r-ˌstāj, ˈfȯ(ə)r-\ *n* **:** APRON 2g
fore·stall \fōr-ˈstȯl, fȯr-\ *vt* [ME *forstallen*, fr. *forstall* act of waylaying, fr. OE *foresteall*, fr. *fore-* + *steall* position, stall] **1** *archaic* **:** INTERCEPT **2 :** to exclude, hinder, or prevent by prior occupation or measures **3 :** to get ahead of **:** ANTICIPATE **4** *obs* **:** OBSTRUCT, BESET **5 :** to prevent the normal trading in by buying or diverting goods or by persuading persons to raise prices — **fore·stall·er** *n* — **fore·stall·ment** \-ˈstȯl-mənt\ *n*
fore·stay \ˈfō(ə)r-ˌstā, ˈfȯ(ə)r-\ *n* **:** a stay from the foremast head to the deck of a ship
fore·stay·sail \-ˌsāl, -səl\ *n* **:** the triangular aftermost headsail of a schooner, ketch, or yawl set on hanks on the forestay — see SAIL illustration
for·est·er \ˈfȯr-ə-stər, ˈfär-\ *n* **1 :** a person trained in forestry **2 :** an inhabitant of a forest **3 :** any of various woodland moths (family Agaristidae) **4** *cap* **:** a member of a major benevolent and fraternal order
forest floor *n* **:** the richly organic layer of soil and debris characteristic of forested land
forest green *n* **:** a dark yellowish or moderate olive green
for·est·land \ˈfȯr-əst-ˌland, ˈfär-\ *n* **:** land covered with forest or reserved for the growth of forests
forest ranger *n* **:** an officer charged with the patrolling and guarding of a forest; *esp* **:** one in charge of the management and protection of a portion of a public forest
for·est·ry \ˈfȯr-ə-strē, ˈfär-\ *n* **1 :** forest land **2 a :** the science of developing, caring for, or cultivating forests **b :** the management of growing timber
forest tent caterpillar *n* **:** a moth (*Malacosoma disstria*) whose orange-marked larva is a tent caterpillar and a serious defoliator of deciduous trees
foreswear, foresworn *var of* FORSWEAR, FORSWORN
[1]fore·taste \ˈfō(ə)r-ˌtāst, ˈfȯ(ə)r-\ *n* **1 :** an advance indication or warning **2 :** a small anticipatory sample ***syn*** see PROSPECT
[2]fore·taste \fōr-ˈtāst, fȯr-ˈ, ˈfō(ə)r-ˌ, ˈfȯ(ə)r-ˌ\ *vt* **:** to taste beforehand **:** ANTICIPATE
fore·tell \fōr-ˈtel, fȯr-\ *vt* **-told** \-ˈtōld\; **-tell·ing :** to tell beforehand **:** PREDICT — **fore·tell·er** *n*
syn FORETELL, PREDICT, FORECAST, PROPHESY, PROGNOSTICATE *shared meaning element* **:** to tell beforehand
[1]fore·thought \ˈfō(ə)r-ˌthȯt, ˈfȯ(ə)r-\ *n* **1 :** a thinking or planning out in advance **:** PREMEDITATION **2 :** consideration for the future
[2]forethought *adj* **:** thought of or planned beforehand **:** DELIBERATE

fore·thought·ful \-fəl\ *adj* : full of or having forethought — **fore·thought·ful·ly** \-fə-lē\ *adv* — **fore·thought·ful·ness** *n*
fore·time \ˈfō(ə)r-ˌtīm, ˈfȯ(ə)r-\ *n* : former or past time : the time before the present
1fore·to·ken \ˈfō(ə)r-ˌtō-kən, ˈfȯ(ə)r-\ *n* : a premonitory sign
2fore·to·ken \fōr-ˈtō-kən, fȯr-\ *vt* **fore·to·kened; fore·to·ken·ing** \-ˈtōk-(ə-)niŋ\ : to indicate or warn of in advance
fore·top \ˈfō(ə)r-ˌtäp, ˈfȯ(ə)r-, *in sense 2 often* ˈfōrt-əp *or* ˈfȯrt-\ *n* **1** : hair on the forepart of the head; *esp* : the forelock of a horse **2** : the platform at the head of a ship's foremast
fore–top·gal·lant \ˈfōr-ˌtäp-ˌgal-ənt, ˈfȯr-; ˈfōrt-ə-ˌgal-, ˈfȯrt-\ *adj* : being the part next above the fore-topmast
fore·top·man \ˈfōr-ˌtäp-mən, ˈfȯr-; ˈfōrt-əp-, ˈfȯrt-\ *n* : a sailor on duty on the foremast and above
fore–top·mast \ˈfōr-ˌtäp-məst, ˈfȯr-; ˈfōrt-əp-ˌmast, ˈfȯrt-\ *n* : a mast next above the foremast
fore–top·sail \ˈfōr-ˌtäp-səl, ˈfȯr-; ˈfōrt-əp-, ˈfȯrt-\ *n* : the sail above the foresail
1for·ev·er \fə-ˈrev-ər, fȯ-\ *adv* **1** : for a limitless time ⟨wants to live ~⟩ **2** : at all times ⟨is ~ jingling the change in his pocket⟩
2forever *n* : an unspecified length of time ⟨it took her ~ to find the answer⟩
for·ev·er·more \-ˌrev-ə(r)-ˈmō(ə)r, -ˈmȯ(ə)r\ *adv* : FOREVER
for·ev·er·ness \-ˈrev-ər-nəs\ *n* : ETERNITY
fore·warn \fōr-ˈwȯ(ə)rn, fȯr-\ *vt* : to warn in advance ***syn*** see WARN
fore wing *n* : either of the anterior wings of a 4-winged insect
fore·wom·an \ˈfō(ə)r-ˌwu̇m-ən, ˈfȯ(ə)r-\ *n* : FORELADY
fore·word \ˈfōr-(ˌ)wərd, ˈfȯr-\ *n* : PREFACE
foreworn *var of* FORWORN
fore·yard \ˈfō(ə)r-ˌyärd, ˈfȯ(ə)r-\ *n* : the lowest yard on a foremast
1for·feit \ˈfȯr-fət\ *n* [ME *forfait*, fr. MF, fr. pp. of *forfaire* to commit a crime, forfeit, prob. fr. *fors* outside (fr. L *foris*) + *faire* to do, fr. L *facere* — more at FORUM, DO] **1** : something forfeited or subject to being forfeited (as for a crime, offense, or neglect of duty) : PENALTY **2** : forfeiture esp. of civil rights **3 a** : something deposited (as for making a mistake in a game) and then redeemed on payment of a fine **b** *pl* : a game in which forfeits are exacted
2forfeit *vt* **1** : to lose or lose the right to by some error, offense, or crime **2** : to subject to confiscation as a forfeit — **for·feit·able** \-ə-bəl\ *adj* — **for·feit·er** *n*
3forfeit *adj* : forfeited or subject to forfeiture
for·fei·ture \ˈfȯr-fə-ˌchu̇(ə)r, -chər, -ˌt(y)u̇(ə)r\ *n* **1** : the act of forfeiting : the loss of property or money because of a breach of a legal obligation **2** : something (as money or property) that is forfeited : PENALTY
for·fend *also* **fore·fend** \fȯr-ˈfend, fōr-\ *vt* **1 a** *archaic* : FORBID **b** : to ward off : PREVENT **2** : PROTECT, PRESERVE
for·gath·er *or* **fore·gath·er** \fȯr-ˈgath-ər, fōr-, -ˈgeth-\ *vi* **1** : to come together : ASSEMBLE **2** : to meet someone usu. by chance
1forge \ˈfō(ə)rj, ˈfȯ(ə)rj\ *n* [ME, fr. OF, fr. L *fabrica*, fr. *fabr-*, *faber* smith — more at DAFT] **1** : a furnace or a shop with its furnace where metal is heated and wrought : SMITHY **2** : a workshop where wrought iron is produced or where iron is made malleable
2forge *vb* **forged; forg·ing** *vt* **1 a** : to form (as metal) by heating and hammering **b** : to form (metal) by a mechanical or hydraulic press with or without heat **2** : to form or bring into being esp. by an expenditure of effort ⟨made every effort to ~ party unity⟩ **3** : to make or imitate falsely esp. with intent to defraud : COUNTERFEIT ~ *vi* **1** : to work at a forge **2** : to commit forgery — **forge·abil·i·ty** \ˌfōr-jə-ˈbil-ət-ē, ˌfȯr-\ *n* — **forge·able** \ˈfōr-jə-bəl, ˈfȯr-\ *adj*
3forge *vi* **forged; forg·ing** [origin unknown] **1** : to move forward slowly and steadily ⟨the great ship *forged* ahead through the waves⟩ **2** : to move with a sudden increase of speed and power ⟨the horse *forged* into the lead in the homestretch⟩
forg·er \ˈfōr-jər, ˈfȯr-\ *n* **1 a** : one that falsifies; *specif* : a creator of false tales **b** : a person guilty of forgery **2** : one that forges metals
forg·ery \ˈfōrj-(ə-)rē, ˈfȯrj-\ *n, pl* **-er·ies** **1** *archaic* : INVENTION **2** : an act of forging; *esp* : the crime of falsely and fraudulently making or altering a document (as a check) **3** : something forged
for·get \fər-ˈget, fȯr-\ *vb* **-got** \-ˈgät\; **-got·ten** \-ˈgät-ᵊn\ *or* **-got; -get·ting** [ME *forgeten*, fr. OE *forgietan*, fr. *for-* + *-gietan* (akin to ON *geta* to get)] *vt* **1 a** : to lose the remembrance of ⟨I ~ his name⟩ **b** *obs* : to cease from doing **2** : to treat with inattention or disregard ⟨*forgot* his old friends⟩ **3** : to disregard intentionally : OVERLOOK — usu. used in the imperative ⟨~ it⟩ ~ *vi* **1** : to cease remembering or noticing ⟨he forgives and ~*s*⟩ **2** : to fail to become mindful at the proper time ⟨~ about paying the bill⟩ ***syn*** see NEGLECT ***ant*** remember — **for·get·ter** *n* — **forget oneself** : to lose one's dignity, temper, or self-control
for·get·ful \-ˈget-fəl\ *adj* **1** : likely to forget **2** : characterized by negligent failure to remember : NEGLECTFUL **3** : inducing oblivion ⟨~ sleep⟩ — **for·get·ful·ly** \-fə-lē\ *adv* — **for·get·ful·ness** *n*
syn FORGETFUL, OBLIVIOUS, UNMINDFUL *shared meaning element* : losing from one's mind something once known or learned
for·ge·tive \ˈfōr-jət-iv, ˈfȯr-\ *adj* [prob. fr. *2forge* + *-tive* (as in *inventive*)] *archaic* : INVENTIVE, IMAGINATIVE
for·get–me–not \fər-ˈget-mē-ˌnät, fȯr-\ *n* : any of a genus (*Myosotis*) of small herbs of the borage family having bright-blue or white flowers usu. arranged in a curving spike
for·get·ta·ble \fər-ˈget-ə-bəl, fȯr-\ *adj* : fit or likely to be forgotten
forg·ing \ˈfōr-jiŋ, ˈfȯr-\ *n* **1** : the art or process of forging **2** : a piece of forged work **3** : FORGERY 2
for·give \fər-ˈgiv, fȯr-\ *vb* **-gave** \-ˈgāv\; **-giv·en** \-ˈgiv-ən\; **-giv·ing** [ME *forgiven*, fr. OE *forgifan*, fr. *for-* + *gifan* to give] *vt* **1** : to cease to feel resentment against (an offender) : PARDON ⟨~ one's enemies⟩ **2 a** : to give up resentment of or claim to requital for ⟨~ an insult⟩ **b** : to grant relief from payment of ⟨~ a debt⟩ ~ *vi* : to grant forgiveness ***syn*** see EXCUSE — **for·giv·able** \-ˈgiv-ə-bəl\ *adj* — **for·giv·ably** \-blē\ *adv* — **for·giv·er** *n*
for·give·ness \-ˈgiv-nəs\ *n* : the act of forgiving : PARDON
for·giv·ing *adj* : willing or able to forgive — **for·giv·ing·ly** \-ˈgiv-iŋ-lē\ *adv* — **for·giv·ing·ness** *n*
for·go *or* **fore·go** \fȯr-ˈgō, fōr-\ *vt* **-went** \-ˈwent\; **-gone** \-ˈgȯn *also* -ˈgän\; **-go·ing** \-ˈgō-iŋ, -ˈgȯ(-)iŋ\ [ME *forgon*, fr. OE *forgān* to pass by, forgo, fr. *for-* + *gān* to go] **1** *archaic* : FORSAKE **2** : to abstain from : RENOUNCE ⟨~ immediate gratification for the sake of future gains⟩ — **for·go·er** \-ˈgō(-ə)r\ *n*
for·got·ten man \fər-ˌgät-ᵊn-, fȯr-\ *n* : a person or category of persons that receives less attention than is merited
fo·rint \ˈfō(ə)r-ˌint\ *n* [Hung] — see MONEY table
forjudge *var of* FOREJUDGE
1fork \ˈfȯ(ə)rk\ *n* [ME *forke*, fr. OE & ONF; OE *forca* & ONF *forque*, fr. L *furca*] **1** : an implement with two or more prongs used esp. for taking up (as in eating), pitching, or digging **2** : a forked part, tool, or piece of equipment **3 a** : a division into branches or the place where something divides into branches **b** : CONFLUENCE **4 a** : one of the branches into which something forks **b** : ALTERNATIVE, CHOICE **5** : an attack by one chess piece (as a knight) on two pieces simultaneously — **fork·ful** \-ˌfu̇l\ *n*
2fork *vi* **1** : to divide into two or more branches ⟨where the road ~*s*⟩ **2 a** : to use or work with a fork **b** : to make a turn into or travel a fork ~ *vt* **1** : to give the form of a fork to ⟨~*ing* her fingers⟩ **2** : to raise, pitch, dig, or work with a fork ⟨~ hay⟩ **3** : to attack (two chessmen) simultaneously **4** : PAY, CONTRIBUTE ⟨had to ~ out $5000 to keep the matter quiet⟩ — **fork·er** *n*
forked \ˈfȯ(ə)rkt, ˈfȯr-kəd\ *adj* **1** : resembling a fork esp. in having one end divided into two or more branches or points ⟨~ lightning⟩ **2** : shaped like a fork or having a forked part ⟨a ~ road⟩
fork·lift \ˈfȯr-ˌklift\ *n* : a self-propelled machine for hoisting and transporting heavy objects by means of steel fingers inserted under the load
forky \ˈfȯr-kē\ *adj* **fork·i·er; -est** : FORKED ⟨a ~ beard⟩
for·lorn \fər-ˈlȯ(ə)rn\ *adj* [ME *forloren*, fr. OE, pp. of *forlēosan* to lose, fr. *for-* + *lēosan* to lose] **1 a** : BEREFT, FORSAKEN ⟨left quite ~ of hope⟩ **b** : sad and lonely because of isolation or desertion : DESOLATE **2** : being in poor condition : MISERABLE, WRETCHED ⟨~ tumbledown buildings⟩ **3** : nearly hopeless ⟨a ~ attempt⟩ ***syn*** see ALONE — **for·lorn·ly** *adv* — **for·lorn·ness** \-ˈlȯ(ə)rn-nəs\ *n*
forlorn hope *n* [by folk etymology fr. D *verloren hoop*, lit., lost band] **1** : a body of men selected to perform a perilous service **2** : a desperate or extremely difficult enterprise
1form \ˈfȯ(ə)rm\ *n* [ME *forme*, fr. OF, fr. L *forma*] **1 a** : the shape and structure of something as distinguished from its material **b** : a body (as of a person) esp. in its external appearance or as distinguished from the face : FIGURE **c** *archaic* : BEAUTY **2** : the essential nature of a thing as distinguished from its matter: as **a** : IDEA 1a **b** : the component of a thing that determines its kind **3 a** : established method of expression or proceeding : procedure according to rule or rote **b** : a prescribed and set order of words : FORMULA ⟨the ~ of the marriage service⟩ **4** : a printed or typed document with blank spaces for insertion of required or requested information ⟨tax ~*s*⟩ **5 a** (1) : conduct regulated by extraneous controls (as of custom or etiquette) : CEREMONY (2) : show without substance **b** : manner or conduct as tested by a prescribed or accepted standard ⟨rudeness is simply bad ~⟩ **c** : manner or style of performing or accomplishing according to recognized standards of technique ⟨a strong swimmer but weak on ~⟩ **6 a** : the resting place of a hare **b** : a long seat : BENCH **7 a** : a supporting frame model of the human figure or part (as the torso) of the human figure usu. used for displaying apparel **b** : a proportioned and often adjustable model for fitting clothes **c** : a mold in which concrete is placed to set **8** : the printing type or other matter arranged and secured in a chase ready for printing **9 a** : one of the different modes of existence, action, or manifestation of a particular thing or substance : KIND ⟨one ~ of respiratory disorder⟩ ⟨a ~ of art⟩ **b** : a distinguishable group of organisms **10 a** (1) : orderly method of arrangement (as in the presentation of ideas) : manner of coordinating elements (as of an artistic production or course of reasoning) (2) : a particular kind or instance of such arrangement ⟨the sonnet is a poetical ~⟩ **b** : PATTERN, SCHEMA ⟨arguments of the same logical ~⟩ **c** : the structural element, plan, or design of a work of art — compare CONTENT 2c **d** : a visible and measurable unit defined by a contour : a bounded surface or volume **11** : a grade in a British secondary school or in some American private schools **12 a** (1) : the past performance of a race horse (2) : a table giving details (as handicaps and odds) of a horse's past performance which are used by bettors in making selections **b** : known ability to perform ⟨a singer at the top of his ~⟩ **c** : condition suitable for performing (as in athletic competition) **13 a** : LINGUISTIC FORM **b** : one of the different aspects a word may take as a result of inflection or change of spelling or pronunciation ⟨verbal ~*s*⟩ **14** : a mathematical expression of a particular type ⟨an equation in parametric ~⟩
syn FORM, FIGURE, SHAPE, CONFORMATION, CONFIGURATION *shared meaning element* : outward appearance
2form *vt* **1** : to give form or shape to : FASHION **2 a** : to give a particular shape to : shape or mold into a certain state or after a particular model : ARRANGE ⟨~*ed* the dough into various shapes⟩ ⟨a state ~*ed* along the lines of the Roman Republic⟩ **b** : to arrange themselves in ⟨the women ~*ed* a line⟩ **c** : to model by instruction and discipline ⟨a mind ~*ed* by classical education⟩ **3** : DEVELOP, ACQUIRE ⟨~ a habit⟩ **4** : to serve to make up or constitute : be a usu. essential or basic element of **5 a** : to assume an inflection so as to produce (as a tense) ⟨~*s* the past in *-ed*⟩ **b** : to combine to make (a compound word) **c** : to make up : CONSTI-

ə abut	ᵊ kitten	ər further	a back	ā bake	ä cot, cart
au̇ out	ch chin	e less	ē easy	g gift	i trip ī life
j joke	ŋ sing	ō flow	ȯ flaw	ȯi coin	th thin th this
ü loot	u̇ foot	y yet	yü few	yu̇ furious	zh vision

TUTE ⟨~ a clause⟩ **6 :** to arrange in order : draw up **~** *vi* **1 :** to become formed or shaped **2 :** to take form : come into existence : ARISE **3 :** to take on a definite form, shape, or arrangement ***syn*** see MAKE — **form·abil·i·ty** \ˌfȯr-mə-ˈbil-ət-ē\ *n* — **form·able** \ˈfȯr-mə-bəl\ *adj* — **form on :** to take up a formation next to
form- *or* **formo-** *comb form* [*formic*] : formic acid ⟨*formate*⟩
-form \ˌfȯrm\ *adj comb form* [MF & L; MF *-forme,* fr. L *-formis,* fr. *forma*] : in the form or shape of : resembling ⟨*oviform*⟩
1**for·mal** \ˈfȯr-məl\ *adj* **1 a :** belonging to or being the essential constitution or structure ⟨~ cause⟩ **b :** relating to, concerned with, or constituting the outward form of something as distinguished from its content **2 a :** following or according with established form, custom, or rule : CONVENTIONAL ⟨lacked ~ qualifications for the job⟩ **b :** done in due or lawful form ⟨a ~ contract⟩ **3 a :** based on conventional forms and rules **b :** characterized by punctilious respect for form : METHODICAL ⟨very ~ in all his dealings⟩ **c :** rigidly ceremonious : PRIM **4 :** having the appearance without the substance ⟨~ Christians who go to church only at Easter⟩ ***syn*** see CEREMONIAL ***ant*** informal — **for·mal·ly** \-mə-lē\ *adv* — **for·mal·ness** *n*
2**formal** *n* : something (as a dance or a dress) formal in character
3**formal** *adj* [*formula* + *-al*] : 3MOLAR 2
form·al·de·hyde \fȯr-ˈmal-də-ˌhīd, fər-\ *n* [ISV *form-* + *aldehyde*] : a colorless pungent irritating gas CH_2O used chiefly as a disinfectant and preservative and in synthesizing other compounds and resins
for·ma·lin \ˈfȯr-mə-lən, -ˌlēn\ *n* [fr. *Formalin,* a trademark] : a clear aqueous solution of formaldehyde containing a small amount of methanol
for·mal·ism \ˈfȯr-mə-ˌliz-əm\ *n* : the practice or the doctrine of strict adherence to prescribed or external forms (as in religion or art); *also* : an instance of this — **for·mal·ist** \-ləst\ *n or adj* — **for·mal·is·tic** \ˌfȯr-mə-ˈlis-tik\ *adj* — **for·mal·is·ti·cal·ly** \-ti-k(ə-)lē\ *adv*
for·mal·i·ty \fȯr-ˈmal-ət-ē\ *n, pl* **-ties 1 :** the quality or state of being formal **2 :** compliance with formal or conventional rules : CEREMONY **3 :** an established form that is required or conventional
for·mal·ize \ˈfȯr-mə-ˌlīz\ *vt* **-ized; -iz·ing 1 :** to give a certain or definite form to : SHAPE **2 a :** to make formal **b :** to give formal status or approval to — **for·mal·iz·able** \-ˌlī-zə-bəl\ *adj* — **for·mal·iza·tion** \ˌfȯr-mə-lə-ˈzā-shən\ *n* — **for·mal·iz·er** \ˈfȯr-mə-ˌlī-zər\ *n*
formal logic *n* : a system of logic (as Aristotelian logic or symbolic logic) that abstracts the forms of thought from its content to establish abstract criteria of consistency
for·mant \ˈfȯr-mənt, -ˌmant\ *n* : a characteristic component of the quality of a speech sound; *specif* : any of several resonance bands held to determine the phonetic quality of a vowel
1**for·mat** \ˈfȯ(ə)r-ˌmat\ *n* [F or G; F, fr. G, fr. L *formatus,* pp. of *formare* to form, fr. *forma*] **1 :** the shape, size, and general makeup (as of something printed) **2 :** general plan of organization or arrangement (as of a television show)
2**format** *vt* **for·mat·ted; for·mat·ting :** to produce in a specified form or style ⟨*formatted* output of a computer⟩
for·mate \ˈfȯ(ə)r-ˌmāt\ *n* : a salt or ester of formic acid
for·ma·tion \fȯr-ˈmā-shən\ *n* **1 :** an act of giving form or shape to something or of taking form : DEVELOPMENT **2 :** something that is formed ⟨new word ~*s*⟩ **3 :** the manner in which a thing is formed : STRUCTURE ⟨the peculiar ~ of the heart⟩ **4 :** the largest unit in an ecological community comprising two or more associations and their precursors **5 a :** any igneous, sedimentary, or metamorphic rock represented as a unit **b :** any sedimentary bed or consecutive series of beds sufficiently homogeneous or distinctive to be a unit **6 :** an arrangement of a body or group of persons or things in some prescribed manner or for a particular purpose — **for·ma·tion·al** \-shnəl, -shən-ᵊl\ *adj*
1**for·ma·tive** \ˈfȯr-mət-iv\ *adj* **1 a :** giving or capable of giving form : CONSTRUCTIVE ⟨a ~ influence⟩ **b :** used in word formation or inflection **2 :** capable of alteration by growth and development; *also* : producing new cells and tissues **3 :** of, relating to, or characterized by formative effects or formation ⟨~ years⟩ — **for·ma·tive·ly** *adv* — **for·ma·tive·ness** *n*
2**formative** *n* **1 :** the element in a word that serves to give the word appropriate form and is not part of the base **2 :** the minimal syntactically functioning element in a transformational grammar
form class *n* : a class of linguistic forms that can be used in the same position in a construction and that have one or more morphological or syntactical features in common
form critical *adj* : based on or applying form criticism
form criticism *n* : a method of criticism for determining the sources and historicity of esp. biblical writings through analysis of the writings in terms of traditional literary forms (as love poems, parables, and sayings) — **form critic** *n*
formed \ˈfȯrmd\ *adj* : organized in a way characteristic of living matter ⟨mitochondria are ~ bodies of the cell⟩ ⟨red blood cells are ~ elements of the blood⟩
for·mée \fȯr-ˌmā, fȯr-ˈ\ *adj* [ME *forme,* fr. MF *formé*] *of a heraldic cross* : having the arms narrow at the center and expanding toward the ends — see CROSS illustration
1**for·mer** \ˈfȯr-mər\ *adj* [ME, fr. *forme* first, fr. OE *forma* — more at FOREMOST] **1 a :** coming before in time **b :** of, relating to, or occurring in the past ⟨~ correspondence⟩ **2 :** preceding in place or arrangement : FOREGOING ⟨~ part of the chapter⟩ **3 :** first mentioned or in order of two things mentioned or understood ⟨of these two evils the ~ is the lesser⟩ ***syn*** see PRECEDING ***ant*** latter
2**form·er** \ˈfȯr-mər\ *n* **1 :** one that forms **2** *chiefly Brit* : a member of a school form — usu. used in combination ⟨sixth ~⟩
for·mer·ly \ˈfȯr-mə(r)-lē\ *adv* **1** *obs* : just before **2 :** at an earlier time : PREVIOUSLY
form·fit·ting \ˈfȯrm-ˌfit-iŋ\ *adj* : conforming to the outline of the body : fitting snugly ⟨a ~ sweater⟩
form·ful \ˈfȯrm-fəl\ *adj* : exhibiting or notable for form (as in a sport)
form genus *n* : an artificial taxonomic category established for organisms (as imperfect fungi) of obscure true relationships
for·mic \ˈfȯr-mik\ *adj* [L *formica* ant — more at PISMIRE] : derived from formic acid
For·mi·ca \fȯr-ˈmī-kə, fər-\ *trademark* — used for any of various laminated plastic products used esp. for surface finish
formic acid *n* : a colorless pungent fuming vesicant liquid acid CH_2O_2 found esp. in ants and in many plants and used chiefly in dyeing and finishing textiles
for·mi·cary \ˈfȯr-mə-ˌker-ē\ *n, pl* **-car·ies** [ML *formicarium,* fr. L *formica*] : an ant nest
for·mi·da·ble \ˈfȯr-məd-ə-bəl *also* fȯr-ˈmid- *or* fər-ˈmid-\ *adj* [ME, fr. L *formidabilis,* fr. *formidare* to fear, fr. *formido* fear; akin to Gk *mormō* she-monster] **1 :** causing fear, dread, or apprehension ⟨a ~ prospect⟩ **2 :** having qualities that discourage approach or attack **3 :** tending to inspire awe or wonder — **for·mi·da·bil·i·ty** \ˌfȯr-məd-ə-ˈbil-ət-ē; fȯr-ˌmid-, fər-ˌ\ *n* — **for·mi·da·ble·ness** \ˈfȯr-məd-ə-bəl-nəs; fȯr-ˈmid-, fər-ˈ\ *n* — **for·mi·da·bly** \-blē\ *adv*
form·less \ˈfȯrm-ləs\ *adj* **1 :** having no regular form or shape **2 :** lacking order or arrangement **3 :** having no physical existence — **form·less·ly** *adv* — **form·less·ness** *n*
form letter *n* **1 :** a letter on a subject of frequent recurrence that can be sent to different people without essential change except in the address **2 :** a letter that is printed in many copies, has a very general salutation (as *Dear Friend*), and is sent to a usu. large number of people
formo- — see FORM-
1**for·mu·la** \ˈfȯr-myə-lə\ *n, pl* **-las** *or* **-lae** \-ˌlē, -ˌlī\ [L, dim. of *forma* form] **1 a :** a set form of words for use in a ceremony or ritual **b :** a conventionalized statement intended to express some fundamental truth or principle esp. as a basis for negotiation or action **2 a** (1) : RECIPE (2) : PRESCRIPTION **b :** a milk mixture or substitute for feeding an infant **3 a :** a general fact, rule, or principle expressed in symbols **b :** a symbolic expression of the chemical composition or constitution of a substance **c :** a group of numerical symbols associated to express briefly a single concept **d :** a combination of signs in a logical calculus **4 :** a prescribed or set form or method (as of writing) : an established rule or custom — often used derogatorily ⟨television programs that were unimaginative ~ works⟩ — **for·mu·la·ic** \ˌfȯr-myə-ˈlā-ik\ *adj* — **for·mu·la·ical·ly** \-ˈlā-ə-k(ə-)lē\ *adv*
2**formula** *adj, of a racing car* : conforming to prescribed specifications as to size, weight, and engine displacement and usu. having a long narrow body, open wheels, a single-seat open cockpit, and the engine in the rear
for·mu·la·ri·za·tion \ˌfȯr-myə-lə-rə-ˈzā-shən\ *n* : an act or a product of formularizing
for·mu·la·rize \ˈfȯr-myə-lə-ˌrīz\ *vt* **-rized; -riz·ing :** to state in or reduce to a formula : FORMULATE — **for·mu·la·riz·er** *n*
for·mu·lary \ˈfȯr-myə-ˌler-ē\ *n, pl* **-lar·ies 1 :** a book or other collection of stated and prescribed forms (as oaths or prayers) **2 :** a prescribed form or model : FORMULA **3 :** a book containing a list of medicinal substances and formulas — **formulary** *adj*
for·mu·late \ˈfȯr-myə-ˌlāt\ *vt* **-lat·ed; -lat·ing 1 a :** to reduce to or express in a formula **b :** to put into a systematized statement or expression **c :** DEVISE ⟨~ policy⟩ **2 a :** to develop a formula for the preparation of (as a soap or plastic) **b :** to prepare according to a formula — **for·mu·la·tor** \-ˌlāt-ər\ *n*
for·mu·la·tion \ˌfȯr-myə-ˈlā-shən\ *n* : an act or the product of formulating
formula weight *n* : MOLECULAR WEIGHT — used esp. of ionic compounds
for·mu·li·za·tion \ˌfȯr-myə-lə-ˈzā-shən\ *n* : FORMULATION
for·mu·lize \ˈfȯr-myə-ˌlīz\ *vt* **-lized; -liz·ing :** FORMULATE 1
form word *n* : FUNCTION WORD
for·myl \ˈfȯr-ˌmil\ *n* [ISV] : the radical HCO of formic acid that is also characteristic of aldehydes
for·ni·cate \ˈfȯr-nə-ˌkāt\ *vb* **-cat·ed; -cat·ing** [LL *fornicatus,* pp. of *fornicare,* fr. L *fornic-, fornix* arch, vault, brothel] *vi* : to commit fornication **~** *vt* : to commit fornication with — **for·ni·ca·tor** \-ˌkāt-ər\ *n*
for·ni·ca·tion \ˌfȯr-nə-ˈkā-shən\ *n* **1 :** human sexual intercourse other than between a man and his wife : sexual intercourse between a spouse and an unmarried person : sexual intercourse between unmarried people **2 :** sexual intercourse on the part of an unmarried person accomplished with consent and not deemed adultery
for·nix \ˈfȯr-niks\ *n, pl* **for·ni·ces** \-nə-ˌsēz\ [NL, fr. L] : an anatomical arch or fold
for·rad·er *also* **for·rard·er** \ˈfär-əd-ər\ *adv* [E dial., compar. of E *forward*] *chiefly Brit* : further ahead
for·sake \fər-ˈsāk, fȯr-\ *vt* **for·sook** \-ˈsu̇k\; **for·sak·en** \-ˈsā-kən\; **for·sak·ing** [ME *forsaken,* fr. OE *forsacan,* fr. *for-* + *sacan* to dispute; akin to OE *sacu* action at law — more at SAKE] **1 :** to renounce (as something once cherished) without intent to recover or resume ⟨~ a bad habit⟩ **2 :** to quit or leave entirely : withdraw from ⟨*forsook* the theater for politics⟩ ***syn*** see ABANDON ***ant*** return (*to*), revert (*to*)
for·sooth \fər-ˈsüth\ *adv* [ME *for soth,* fr. OE *forsōth,* fr. *for* + *sōth* sooth] : in truth : INDEED — often used to imply contempt or doubt
for·spent \fər-ˈspent, fȯr-\ *adj, archaic* : worn out : EXHAUSTED
for·swear *or* **fore·swear** \fȯr-ˈswa(ə)r, fōr-, -ˈswe(ə)r\ *vb* **-swore** \-ˈswō(ə)r, -ˈswȯ(ə)r\; **-sworn** \-ˈswō(ə)rn, -ˈswȯ(ə)rn\; **-swear·ing** *vt* **1 a :** to reject or renounce under oath **b :** to renounce earnestly **2 :** to deny under oath **3 :** to make a liar of (oneself) under or as if under oath ⟨~ himself⟩ **~** *vi* : to swear falsely ***syn*** see ABJURE
for·sworn *or* **fore·sworn** \-ˈswō(ə)rn, -ˈswȯ(ə)rn\ *adj* : guilty of perjury : marked by perjury
for·syth·ia \fər-ˈsith-ē-ə\ *n* [NL, genus name, fr. William *Forsyth* †1804 Brit botanist] : any of a genus (*Forsythia*) of ornamental

shrubs of the olive family with opposite leaves and yellow bell-shaped flowers appearing before the leaves in early spring
fort \ˈfō(ə)rt, ˈfȯ(ə)rt\ *n* [ME *forte*, fr. MF *fort*, fr. *fort* strong, fr. L *fortis*] **1 :** a strong or fortified place; *esp* **:** a fortified place occupied only by troops and surrounded with such works as a ditch, rampart, and parapet **:** FORTIFICATION **2 :** a permanent army post — often used in place names
for·ta·lice \ˈfȯrt-ᵊl-əs\ *n* [ME, fr. ML *fortalitia* — more at FORTRESS] **1** *archaic* **:** FORTRESS **2** *archaic* **:** a small fort
[1]**forte** \ˈfō(ə)rt, ˈfȯ(ə)rt; ˈfȯr-ˌtā *and* ˈfȯrt-ē *are frequent for 1*\ *n* [MF *fort*, fr. *fort* strong] **1 :** one's strong point **2 :** the part of a sword or foil blade between the middle and the hilt; *also* **:** the strongest part of the blade
[2]**for·te** \ˈfȯr-ˌtā, ˈfȯrt-ē\ *adv or adj* [It, fr. *forte* strong, fr. L *fortis*] **:** in a loud and often forceful manner — used as a direction in music
[3]**for·te** \ˈfȯr-ˌtā, ˈfȯrt-ē\ *n* **:** a tone or passage played forte
for·te·pi·a·no \ˌfȯr-ˌtā-pē-ˈän-(ˌ)ō, ˌfȯrt-ē-\ *adv or adj* **:** loud then immediately soft — used as a direction in music
[1]**forth** \ˈfō(ə)rth, ˈfȯ(ə)rth\ *adv* [ME, fr. OE; akin to OE *for*] **1 :** onward in time, place, or order **:** FORWARD ⟨from that day ~⟩ **2 :** out into notice or view ⟨put ~ leaves⟩ **3** *obs* **:** AWAY, ABROAD
[2]**forth** *prep, archaic* **:** forth from **:** out of
forth·com·ing \(ˈ)fōrth-ˈkəm-iŋ, (ˈ)fȯrth-\ *adj* [obs. *forthcome* (to come forth)] **1 :** being about to appear **:** APPROACHING ⟨the ~ holidays⟩ **2 a :** readily available ⟨new funds will be ~ next year⟩ **b :** SOCIABLE, AFFABLE ⟨a ~, accessible, and courteous man⟩
forth of *prep* **:** out of **:** out from
[1]**forth·right** \ˈfōr-ˌthrīt, ˈfȯr-\ *adv* **1 a :** directly forth or ahead **b :** without hesitation **:** FRANKLY **2** *archaic* **:** at once
[2]**forthright** *adj* **1** *archaic* **:** proceeding straight on **2 :** going straight to the point without ambiguity or hesitation ⟨a ~ critic⟩ ⟨a ~ appraisal of a problem⟩ ***syn*** see STRAIGHTFORWARD ***ant*** furtive — **forth·right·ly** *adv* — **forth·right·ness** *n*
[3]**forthright** *n, archaic* **:** a straight path
forth·with \(ˈ)fōrth-ˈwith, (ˈ)fȯrth-, -ˈwith\ *adv* **:** IMMEDIATELY
for·ti·fi·ca·tion \ˌfȯrt-ə-fə-ˈkā-shən\ *n* **1 :** an act or process of fortifying **2 :** something that fortifies, defends, or strengthens; *esp* **:** works erected to defend a place or position
fortified wine *n* **:** a wine (as most dessert wines) to which alcohol usu. in the form of grape brandy has been added during or after fermentation
for·ti·fi·er \ˈfȯrt-ə-ˌfī(-ə)r\ *n* **:** one that fortifies
for·ti·fy \-ˌfī\ *vb* **-fied; -fy·ing** [ME *fortifien*, fr. MF *fortifier*, fr. LL *fortificare*, fr. L *fortis* strong] *vt* **:** to make strong: as **a :** to strengthen and secure (as a town) by forts or batteries **b :** to give physical strength, courage, or endurance to **:** INVIGORATE ⟨*fortified* himself with a glass of wine⟩ **c :** to add mental or moral strength to **:** ENCOURAGE ⟨*fortified* by prayer⟩ **d :** to add material to for strengthening or enriching **~** *vi* **:** to erect fortifications
for·tis \ˈfȯrt-əs\ *adj* [NL, fr. L, strong] **:** produced with relatively great articulatory tenseness and strong expiration ⟨\t\ in *toe* is ~, \d\ in *doe* is lenis⟩
[1]**for·tis·si·mo** \fȯr-ˈtis-ə-ˌmō\ *adv or adj* [It, superl. of *forte*] **:** very loud — used as a direction in music
[2]**fortissimo** *n, pl* **-mos** *or* **-mi** \-ˌmē\ **:** a very loud passage, sound, or tone
for·ti·tude \ˈfȯrt-ə-ˌt(y)üd\ *n* [ME, fr. L *fortitudin-, fortitudo*, fr. *fortis*] **1** *obs* **:** STRENGTH **2 :** strength of mind that enables a person to encounter danger or bear pain or adversity with courage ***syn*** FORTITUDE, GRIT, BACKBONE, PLUCK, GUTS, SAND *shared meaning element* **:** courage and staying power ***ant*** pusillanimity
fort·night \ˈfȯrt-ˌnīt, ˈfȯrt-\ *n* [ME *fourtenight*, alter. of *fourtene night*, fr. OE *fēowertȳne niht* fourteen nights] **:** two weeks
[1]**fort·night·ly** \-lē\ *adj* **:** occurring or appearing once in a fortnight
[2]**fortnightly** *adv* **:** once in a fortnight **:** every fortnight
[3]**fortnightly** *n, pl* **-lies :** a publication issued fortnightly
FOR·TRAN *or* **For·tran** \ˈfō(ə)r-ˌtran\ *n* [*formula translation*] **:** an algebraic and logical language for programming a computer
for·tress \ˈfȯr-trəs\ *n* [ME *forteresse*, fr. MF *forteresce*, fr. ML *fortalitia*, fr. L *fortis* strong] **:** a fortified place **:** STRONGHOLD; *esp* **:** a large and permanent fortification sometimes including a town
for·tu·itous \fȯr-ˈt(y)ü-ət-əs, fər-\ *adj* [L *fortuitus*; akin to L *fort-, fors*] **1 :** occurring by chance **2 :** FORTUNATE, LUCKY ***syn*** see ACCIDENTAL — **for·tu·itous·ly** *adv* — **for·tu·itous·ness** *n*
for·tu·ity \-ət-ē\ *n, pl* **-ities** [irreg. fr. *fortuitous*] **1 :** the quality or state of being fortuitous **2 :** a chance event or occurrence
for·tu·nate \ˈfȯrch-(ə-)nət\ *adj* **1 :** bringing some good thing not foreseen as certain **:** AUSPICIOUS **2 :** receiving some unexpected good ***syn*** see LUCKY ***ant*** unfortunate, disastrous — **for·tu·nate·ly** *adv* — **for·tu·nate·ness** *n*
[1]**for·tune** \ˈfȯr-chən\ *n* [ME, fr. MF, fr. L *fortuna*; akin to L *fort-, fors* chance, luck, *ferre* to carry — more at BEAR] **1** *often cap* **:** a hypothetical force or personified power that unpredictably determines events and issues favorably or unfavorably **2** *obs* **:** ACCIDENT, INCIDENT **3 a :** prosperity attained partly through luck **:** SUCCESS **b :** LUCK 1 **4 :** DESTINY, FATE ⟨tell his ~ with cards⟩; *also* **:** a prediction of fortune ⟨get your weight and ~ for a penny⟩ **5 a :** possession of material goods **:** WEALTH ⟨a man of ~⟩ **b :** a store of material possessions ⟨the family ~⟩ **c :** a very large sum of money ⟨won a ~ playing the races⟩
[2]**fortune** *vb* **for·tuned; for·tun·ing** *vt* **1** *obs* **:** to give good or bad fortune to **2** *archaic* **:** to endow with a fortune **~** *vi, archaic* **:** HAPPEN, CHANCE
fortune cookie *n* **:** a thin folded cookie containing a slip of paper on which is printed a fortune, proverb, or humorous statement
fortune hunter *n* **:** a person who seeks wealth esp. by marriage
for·tune–tell·er \-ˌtel-ər\ *n* **:** one that professes to foretell future events — **for·tune–tell·ing** \-iŋ\ *n or adj*
for·ty \ˈfȯrt-ē\ *n, pl* **forties** [ME *fourty*, adj., fr. OE *fēowertig*, fr. *fēowertig* group of 40, fr. *fēower* four + *-tig* group of 10 — more at EIGHTY] **1 —** see NUMBER table **2** *pl* **:** the numbers 40 to 49; *specif* **:** the years 40 to 49 in a lifetime or century **3 :** the third point scored by a side in a game of tennis — **for·ti·eth** \ˈfȯrt-ē-əth\ *adj or n* — **forty** *adj or pron*
for·ty–eight·mo \ˌfȯrt-ē-ˈāt-(ˌ)mō\ *n, pl* **-mos :** the size of a piece of paper cut 48 from a sheet; *also* **:** a book, a page, or paper of this size
for·ty–five \ˌfȯrt-ē-ˈfīv\ *n* **1 —** see NUMBER table **2 :** a .45 caliber pistol — usu. written .45 **3 :** a microgroove phonograph record designed to be played at 45 revolutions per minute — usu. written 45 — **forty–five** *adj or pron*
Forty Hours *n pl but sing or pl in constr* **:** a Roman Catholic devotion in which the churches of a diocese in two-day turns have the Blessed Sacrament exposed on the altar for continuous daytime veneration
for·ty–nin·er \ˌfȯrt-ē-ˈnī-nər\ *n* **:** one taking part in the rush to California for gold in 1849
forty winks *n pl but sing or pl in constr* **:** a short sleep **:** NAP
fo·rum \ˈfōr-əm, ˈfȯr-\ *n, pl* **forums** *also* **fo·ra** \-ə\ [L; akin to L *foris* outside, *fores* door — more at DOOR] **1 a :** the marketplace or public place of an ancient Roman city forming the center of judicial and public business **b :** a public meeting place for open discussion **c :** a medium (as a newspaper) of open discussion **2 :** a judicial body or assembly **:** COURT **3 a :** a public meeting or lecture involving audience discussion **b :** a program (as on radio or television) involving discussion of a problem usu. by several authorities
[1]**for·ward** \ˈfȯr-wərd, *South also* ˈfär-\ *adj* [ME, fr. OE *foreweard* fr. *fore-* + *-weard* -ward] **1 a :** near, being at, or belonging to the forepart **b :** situated in advance **2 a :** strongly inclined **:** READY **b :** lacking modesty or reserve **:** BRASH **3 :** notably advanced or developed **:** PRECOCIOUS **4 :** moving, tending, or leading toward a position in front; *also* **:** moving toward an opponent's goal **5 a :** advocating an advanced policy in the direction of what is considered progress **b :** EXTREME, RADICAL ⟨on the ~ fringe of liberalism⟩ **6 :** of, relating to, or getting ready for the future ⟨~ buying of produce⟩ — **for·ward·ly** *adv* — **for·ward·ness** *n*
[2]**forward** *adv* **:** to or toward what is ahead or in front ⟨from that time ~⟩ ⟨moved slowly ~ through the mud⟩
[3]**forward** *n* **:** a mainly offensive player in any of several games stationed at or near the front of his side or team (as in hockey or soccer) or in the corner (as in basketball)
[4]**forward** *vt* **1 :** to help onward **:** PROMOTE ⟨~*ed* his friend's career⟩ **2 a :** to send forward **:** TRANSMIT ⟨will ~ the goods on receipt of his check⟩ **b :** to send or ship onward from an intermediate post or station in transit ⟨~ mail to the new address⟩ ***syn*** see ADVANCE ***ant*** hinder, balk
for·ward·er \-wərd-ər\ *n* **:** one that forwards; *esp* **:** an agent who performs services (as receiving, transshipping, or delivering) designed to assure and facilitate the passage of goods of his principal to their destination
for·ward·ing \-wərd-iŋ\ *n* **:** the act of one that forwards; *esp* **:** the business of a forwarder of goods
for·ward–look·ing \ˈfȯr-wərd-ˌlu̇k-iŋ\ *adj* **:** concerned with or planning for the future
forward pass *n* **:** a pass in football thrown in the direction of the opponents' goal
for·wards \ˈfȯr-wərdz\ *adv* **:** FORWARD
for·worn \fər-ˈwō(ə)rn, -ˈwȯ(ə)rn\ *adj, archaic* **:** worn out
forz *abbr* forzando
for·zan·do \fȯrt-ˈsän-(ˌ)dō\ *adj or adv* [It] **:** SFORZANDO
FOS *abbr* free on steamer
fos·sa \ˈfäs-ə\ *n, pl* **fos·sae** \-ˌē, -ˌī\ [NL, fr. L, ditch] **:** an anatomical pit or depression — **fos·sate** \-ˌāt\ *adj*
fosse *or* **foss** \ˈfäs\ *n* [ME *fosse*, fr. OF, fr. L *fossa*, fr. fem. of *fossus*] **:** DITCH, MOAT
fos·sick \ˈfäs-ik\ *vb* [E dial. *fussick*, *fussock* to potter, irreg. fr. E *fuss*] *vi* **1** *Austral* **:** to search for gold typically by picking over abandoned workings **2** *chiefly Austral* **:** to search about **:** RUMMAGE **~** *vt, chiefly Austral* **:** to search for, by, or as if by rummaging **:** ferret out — **fos·sick·er** *n, chiefly Austral*
[1]**fos·sil** \ˈfäs-əl\ *n* [L *fossilis* dug up, fr. *fossus*, pp. of *fodere* to dig — more at BED] **1 :** a remnant, impression, or trace of an animal or plant of past geological ages that has been preserved in the earth's crust **2 a :** one whose views are outmoded **:** FOGY **b :** something (as a theory) that has become rigidly fixed **3 :** an old word or word element preserved only by idiom (as *fro* in *to and fro*)
[2]**fossil** *adj* **1 :** having the characteristics of a fossil: as **a :** ultimately derived from living things ⟨coal, oil, and natural gas are ~ fuels⟩ ⟨amber is a ~ resin⟩ **b :** preserved in a mineralized or petrified form from a geological age ⟨~ imprint of a raindrop⟩ ⟨a ~ beach⟩ ⟨a ~ nuclear track in mica⟩ **c :** being water that accumulated in an underground reservoir in a past geologic age **2 :** being or resembling a fossil
fos·sil·if·er·ous \ˌfäs-ə-ˈlif-(ə-)rəs\ *adj* **:** containing fossils ⟨~ limestone⟩
fos·sil·ize \ˈfäs-ə-ˌlīz\ *vb* **-ized; -iz·ing** *vt* **1 :** to convert into a fossil **2 :** to make outmoded, rigid, or fixed **~** *vi* **:** to become changed into a fossil — **fos·sil·iza·tion** \ˌfäs-ə-lə-ˈzā-shən\ *n*
fos·so·ri·al \fä-ˈsōr-ē-əl, -ˈsȯr-\ *adj* [ML *fossorius*, fr. L *fossus*, pp.] **:** adapted to digging ⟨a ~ foot⟩
[1]**fos·ter** \ˈfȯs-tər, ˈfäs-\ *adj* [ME, fr. OE *fōstor-*, fr. *fōstor* food, feeding; akin to OE *fōda* food] **:** affording, receiving, or sharing nurture or parental care though not related by blood or legal ties
[2]**foster** *vt* **fos·tered; fos·ter·ing** \-t(ə-)riŋ\ **1 :** to give parental care to **:** NURTURE **2 :** to promote the growth or development of **:** ENCOURAGE — **fos·ter·er** \-tər-ər\ *n*

ə abut	ᵊ kitten	ər further	a back	ā bake	ä cot, cart
au̇ out	ch chin	e less	ē easy	g gift	i trip	ī life
j joke	ŋ sing	ō flow	ȯ flaw	ȯi coin	th thin	t͟h this
ü loot	u̇ foot	y yet	yü few	yu̇ furious	zh vision

fos·ter·age \-tə-rij\ *n* **1** : the act of fostering **2** : a custom once prevalent in Ireland, Wales, and Scotland of entrusting one's child to foster parents to be brought up
fos·ter·ling \-tər-liŋ\ *n* : a foster child
FOT *abbr* free on truck
fou \'fü\ *adj* [ME (Sc) *fow* full, fr. ME *full*] *Scot* : DRUNK
fou·droy·ant \fü-'drȯi-ənt, fü-drwä-yäⁿ\ *adj* [F] : sudden and overwhelming in effect : DAZZLING
fought *past of* FIGHT
1foul \'fau̇(ə)l\ *adj* [ME, fr. OE *fūl;* akin to OHG *fūl* rotten, L *pus* pus, *putēre* to stink, Gk *pyon* pus] **1 a** : offensive to the senses : LOATHSOME **b** : filled or covered with offensive matter **2** : full of dirt or mud **3 a** : morally or spiritually odious : DETESTABLE ⟨a ~ crime⟩ **b** : notably unpleasant or distressing : WRETCHED, HORRID ⟨if my day has been ~, I can turn on my . . . radio and everything's mellow — Adrian Dove⟩ **4** : OBSCENE, ABUSIVE ⟨~ language⟩ **5 a** : being wet and stormy **b** : obstructive to navigation ⟨a ~ tide⟩ **6** *dial Brit* : HOMELY, UGLY ⟨~ of face⟩ **7 a** : TREACHEROUS, DISHONORABLE ⟨fair means or ~⟩ **b** : constituting an infringement of rules in a game or sport ⟨a ~ blow in boxing⟩ **8 a** : marked up or defaced by changes ⟨~ manuscript⟩ **b** *of a proof* : pulled before the latest alterations in type **9** : encrusted, clogged or choked with a foreign substance ⟨the chimney was ~ and smoked badly⟩ **10** : being odorous and impure : POLLUTED ⟨~ air⟩ **11** : placed in a situation that impedes physical movement : ENTANGLED **12** : being outside the foul lines in baseball ⟨~ grounder⟩ ***syn*** see DIRTY — **foul·ness** *n*
2foul *n* **1** *archaic* : bad luck **2** : an entanglement or collision esp. in angling or sailing **3 a** : an infringement of the rules in a game or sport **b** : FREE THROW **4** : FOUL BALL
3foul *adv* : FOULLY
4foul *vi* **1** : to become or be foul: as **a** : DECOMPOSE, ROT **b** : to become encrusted, clogged, or choked with a foreign substance **c** : to become entangled or come into collision **2** : to commit a violation of the rules in a sport or game **3** : to hit a foul ball ~ *vt* **1** : to make foul: as **a** : to make dirty : POLLUTE **b** : to become entangled or come into collision with **c** : to encrust with a foreign substance ⟨a ship's bottom ~*ed* with barnacles⟩ **d** : OBSTRUCT, BLOCK **2** : DISHONOR, DISCREDIT **3** : to commit a foul against **4** : to hit (a baseball) foul
fou·lard \fu̇-'lärd\ *n* [F] **1 a** : a lightweight plain-woven or twilled silk usu. decorated with a printed pattern **b** : an imitation of this fabric **2** : an article of clothing (as a scarf) made of foulard
foul ball *n* : a baseball batted into foul territory
foul·brood \'fau̇l-,brüd\ *n* : a destructive bacterial disease of the larvae of the honeybee
foul·ing *n* : DEPOSIT, INCRUSTATION ⟨~ on a ship's bottom⟩
foul line *n* **1** : either of two straight lines extending from the rear corner of home plate through the outer corners of first and third base respectively and prolonged to the boundary of a baseball field **2** : a line across a bowling alley that a player must not step over when delivering the ball **3** : either of two lines on a basketball court parallel to and 15 feet from the backboards behind which a player must stand while shooting a free throw
foul·ly \'fau̇(l)-lē\ *adv* : in a foul manner
foul·mouthed \'fau̇l-'mau̇thd, -'mau̇tht\ *adj* : given to the use of obscene, profane, or abusive language
foul out *vi* : to be put out of a basketball game for exceeding the number of fouls permitted
foul play *n* : VIOLENCE; *esp* : MURDER
foul tip *n* [*foul* + *tip* (tap)] : a pitched ball in baseball that is slightly deflected by the bat; *specif* : a tipped pitch legally caught by the catcher and counting as a full strike with the ball remaining in play
foul–up \'fau̇-,ləp\ *n* **1** : a state of confusion caused by ineptitude, carelessness, or mismanagement ⟨~*s* in transportation⟩ **2** : a mechanical difficulty ⟨a ~ in the steering mechanism — *Springfield (Mass.) Union*⟩
foul up \(')fau̇-'ləp\ *vt* **1** : to make dirty : CONTAMINATE **2** : to spoil by making mistakes or using poor judgment : CONFUSE **3** : ENTANGLE, BLOCK ⟨*fouled up* communications⟩ ~ *vi* : to become confused : get into difficulty : BUNGLE ⟨it was his fault. He had *fouled up* — Pat Frank⟩
1found \'fau̇nd\ *past of* FIND
2found *adj* **1** : having all usual, standard, or reasonably expected equipment ⟨the boat comes fully ~, ready to go — *Holiday*⟩ **2** : presented as or incorporated into an artistic work essentially as found ⟨sculpture of fabric, wood, and other ~ materials — Hilton Kramer⟩
3found *n* : free food and lodging in addition to wages ⟨they're paid $175 a month and ~ — *New Yorker*⟩
4found *vt* [ME *founden,* fr. OF *fonder,* fr. L *fundare,* fr. *fundus* bottom — more at BOTTOM] **1** : to take the first steps in building **2** : to set or ground on something solid : BASE **3** : to establish (as an institution) often with provision for future maintenance
5found *vt* [MF *fondre* to pour, melt, fr. L *fundere;* akin to OE *gēotan* to pour, Gk *chein*] : to melt (metal) and pour into a mold
foun·da·tion \fau̇n-'dā-shən\ *n* **1** : the act of founding **2** : the basis upon which something stands or is supported **3 a** : funds given for the permanent support of an institution : ENDOWMENT **b** : an organization or institution established by endowment with provision for future maintenance **4** : an underlying natural or prepared base or support; *esp* : the whole masonry substructure of a building **5 a** : a body or ground upon which something is built up or overlaid **b** : a woman's supporting undergarment : CORSET ***syn*** see BASE ***ant*** superstructure — **foun·da·tion·al** \-shnəl, -shən-ᵊl\ *adj* — **foun·da·tion·al·ly** \-ē\ *adv* — **foun·da·tion·less** \-shən-ləs\ *adj*
foundation stone *n* **1** : a stone in the foundation of a building; *esp* : such a stone laid with public ceremony — compare CORNERSTONE **2** : BASIS, GROUNDWORK
1found·er \'fau̇n-dər\ *n* : one that founds or establishes — **found·ress** \-drəs\ *n*
2foun·der \'fau̇n-dər\ *vb* **foun·dered; foun·der·ing** \-d(ə-)riŋ\ [ME *foundren* to send to the bottom, collapse, fr. MF *fondrer,* deriv. of L *fundus*] *vi* **1** : to become disabled; *esp* : to go lame **2** : to give way : COLLAPSE **3** : to sink below the surface of the water **4** : to come to grief : FAIL ~ *vt* : to disable (an animal) esp. by excessive feeding
3foun·der *n* [*2founder*] : the condition of a foundered horse
4found·er *n* : one that founds metal; *specif* : TYPEFOUNDER
foun·der·ous *or* **foun·drous** \'fau̇n-d(ə-)rəs\ *adj* : likely to cause one to founder : MIRY
founding father *n* **1** : an originator of an institution or movement : FOUNDER **2** *cap both Fs* : a member of the American Constitutional Convention of 1787
found·ling \'fau̇n-(d)liŋ\ *n* : an infant found after its unknown parents have abandoned it
found object *n* : OBJET TROUVÉ
found·ry \'fau̇n-drē\ *n, pl* **foundries** **1** : the act, process, or art of casting metals; *also* : CASTINGS **2** : an establishment where founding is carried on
foundry proof *n* : a proof taken from a form that has been locked up and made ready for plating
1fount \'fau̇nt\ *n* [MF *font,* fr. L *font-, fons*] : FOUNTAIN, SOURCE
2fount \'fänt, 'fau̇nt\ *n* [F *fonte*] *Brit* : a type font
1foun·tain \'fau̇nt-ᵊn\ *n* [ME, fr. MF *fontaine,* fr. LL *fontana,* fr. L, fem. of *fontanus* of a spring, fr. *font-, fons*] **1** : a spring of water issuing from the earth **2** : SOURCE **3** : an artificially produced jet of water; *also* : the structure from which it rises **4** : a reservoir containing a liquid that can be drawn off as needed
2fountain *vi* : to flow or spout like a fountain ~ *vt* : to cause to flow like a fountain
foun·tain·head \-,hed\ *n* **1** : a spring that is the source of a stream **2** : principal source : ORIGIN
fountain pen *n* : a pen containing a reservoir that automatically feeds the writing point with ink
four \'fō(ə)r, 'fȯ(ə)r\ *n* [ME, fr. *four* adj., fr. OE *fēower;* akin to OHG *fior* four, L *quattuor,* Gk *tessares, tettares*] **1** — see NUMBER table **2** : the fourth in a set or series ⟨the ~ of hearts⟩ **3** : something having four units or members: as **a** : a 4-oared racing shell or its crew **b** : a 4-cylinder engine or automobile — **four** *adj or pron*
four–bag·ger \-'bag-ər\ *n* : HOME RUN
four–ball \-,bȯl\ *adj* : relating to or being a golf match in which the best individual score of one partnership is matched against the best individual score of another partnership for each hole
four·chée \fu̇(ə)r-'shā\ *adj* [F] *of a heraldic cross* : having the end of each arm forked — see CROSS illustration
four–dimensional *adj* : relating to or having four dimensions ⟨~ space-time continuum⟩; *esp* : consisting of or relating to elements requiring four coordinates to determine them
four·dri·nier \,fōr-drə-'ni(ə)r, ,fȯr-; fu̇r-'drin-ē-ər, fōr-, fȯr-\ *n* [Henry *Fourdrinier* & Sealy *Fourdrinier*] : a machine for making paper in an endless web
four–flush *vi* : to bluff in poker holding a four flush; *broadly* : to make a false claim : BLUFF — **four–flush·er** *n*
four flush *n* : four cards of the same suit in a five-card poker hand
four·fold \'fō(ə)r-,fōld, 'fȯ(ə)r-, -'fōld\ *adj* **1** : having four units or members **2** : being four times as great or as many — **four·fold** \-'fōld\ *adv*
four–foot·ed \-'fu̇t-əd\ *adj* : having four feet : QUADRUPED
four·gon \fu̇(ə)r-'gōⁿ\ *n, pl* **fourgons** \-'gōⁿ(z)\ [F] : a wagon for carrying baggage
4–H \(')fō(ə)r-'āch, (')fȯ(ə)r-\ *adj* [fr. the fourfold aim of improving the head, heart, hands, and health] : of or relating to a program set up by the U.S. Department of Agriculture to instruct rural young people in modern farm practices and in good citizenship ⟨~ club⟩ — **4–H'·er** \-ər\ *n*
four–hand \'fō(ə)r-,hand, 'fȯ(ə)r-\ *adj* : FOUR-HANDED
four–hand·ed \-'han-dəd\ *adj* **1** : designed for four hands ⟨a ~ musical composition⟩ **2** : engaged in by four persons ⟨a ~ card game⟩
Four Horsemen *n pl* [fr. the apocalyptic vision in Rev 6:2–8] : war, famine, pestilence, and death personified as the four major plagues of mankind
Four Hundred *or* **400** *n* : the exclusive social set of a community — used with *the*
Fou·ri·er analysis \,fu̇r-ē-,ā-\ *n* : the fitting of terms of a Fourier series to periodic data
Fou·ri·er·ism \'fu̇r-ē-ə-,riz-əm, -ē-,ā-,iz-\ *n* [F *fouriérisme,* fr. F.M.C. *Fourier*] : a system for reorganizing society into cooperative communities of small groups living in common — **Fou·ri·er·ist** \-ē-ə-rəst, -ē-,ā-əst\ *n*
Fou·ri·er series \,fu̇r-ē-,ā-\ *n* [Baron J.B.J. *Fourier* †1830 F geometrician & physicist] : an infinite series in which the terms are constants multiplied by sine or cosine functions of integer multiples of the variable and which is used in the analysis of periodic functions
Fourier's theorem *n* [J. B. J. *Fourier*] : a theorem in mathematics : any periodic function can be resolved under suitable conditions into sine and cosine terms involving known constants
Fourier transform *n* : a function (as $F(u)$) that under suitable conditions can be obtained from a given function (as $f(x)$) by multiplying by e^{iux} and integrating over all values of x
four–in–hand \'fōr-ən-,hand, 'fȯr-\ *n* **1 a** : a team of four horses driven by one person **b** : a vehicle drawn by such a team **2** : a necktie tied in a slipknot with long ends overlapping vertically in front
four–letter word *n* : any of a group of vulgar or obscene words typically made up of four letters
four–line octave *n* [fr. the four accent marks appended to the letters representing its notes] : the musical octave that begins on the third C above middle C — see PITCH illustration
four–o'clock \'fōr-ə-,kläk, 'fȯr-\ *n* : any of a genus (*Mirabilis*) of chiefly American annual or perennial herbs (family Nyctaginaceae, the four-o'clock family) having apetalous flowers with a showy

involucre simulating a calyx; *esp* : a garden plant (*M. jalapa*) with fragrant yellow, red, or white flowers opening late in the afternoon
four of a kind : four cards of the same rank in one hand — see POKER illustration
four·pen·ny nail \ˌfȯr-ˌpen-ē-, ˌfȯr-\ *n* : a nail 1 3/8 inches long
four-post·er \(ˈ)fȯr-ˈpō-stər, (ˈ)fȯr-\ *n* : a bed with tall often carved corner posts orig. designed to support curtains or a canopy
four·ra·gère \ˌfu̇r-ə-ˈzhe(ə)r\ *n* [F] : a braided cord worn usu. around the left shoulder; *esp* : such a cord awarded to a military unit
four·score \ˈfȯr-ˈskō(ə)r, ˈfȯr-ˈskȯ(ə)r\ *adj* : being four times twenty : EIGHTY
four·some \ˈfȯr-səm, ˈfȯr-\ *n* 1 **a** : a group of four persons or things : QUARTET **b** : two couples 2 : a golf match between two pairs of partners
four-square \ˈfȯr-ˈskwa(ə)r, -ˈskwe(ə)r\ *adj* 1 : SQUARE 2 : marked by boldness and conviction : FORTHRIGHT — **four-square** *adv*
four-star \-ˈstär\ *adj* [fr. the number of asterisks used to denote relative excellence in guidebooks] : of a superior degree of excellence ⟨a ~ French restaurant⟩
four·teen \(ˈ)fȯr(t)-ˈtēn, (ˈ)fȯr(t)-\ *n* [ME *fourtene*, fr. OE *fēowertiene*, fr. *fēowertiene*, *adj.*; akin to OE *tien* ten] — see NUMBER table — **fourteen** *adj or pron* — **four·teenth** \-ˈtēn(t)th\ *adj or n*
four·teen·er \-ˈtē-nər\ *n* : a verse consisting of 14 syllables or esp. of 7 iambic feet
fourth \ˈfō(ə)rth, ˈfȯ(ə)rth\ *n* 1 — see NUMBER table 2 **a** : the musical interval embracing four diatonic degrees **b** : a tone at this interval; *specif* : SUBDOMINANT **a c** : the harmonic combination of two tones a fourth apart 3 : the 4th forward gear or speed of a motor vehicle 4 *cap* : INDEPENDENCE DAY — **fourth** *adj or adv* — **fourth·ly** *adv*
fourth class *n* 1 : a class or group ranking fourth in a series 2 : a class of mail in the U.S. that comprises merchandise and non-second-class printed matter and is not sealed against inspection
fourth dimension *n* 1 : a dimension in addition to length, breadth, and depth; *specif* : a coordinate in addition to three rectangular coordinates esp. when interpreted as the time coordinate in a space-time continuum 2 : something outside the range of ordinary experience ⟨a *fourth dimension* of meaning that transcends . . . the issue of clarity versus obscurity —Peter Viereck⟩ — **fourth-dimensional** *adj*
fourth estate *n, often cap F&E* : the public press
Fourth of July : INDEPENDENCE DAY
four-way \ˈfȯr-ˈwā, ˈfȯr-\ *adj* 1 : allowing passage in any of four directions 2 : including four participants
four-wheel \-ˌhwēl, -ˌwēl, ˌfȯr-, ˌfȯr-, -ˈwēl\ *or* **four-wheeled** \ˈfȯr-ˈhwē(ə)ld, ˈfȯr-, -ˈwē(ə)ld\ *adj* 1 : having four wheels 2 : acting on or by means of four wheels of an automotive vehicle ⟨~ drive⟩
four-wheel·er \-ˈhwē-lər, -ˈwē-\ *n* : a vehicle with four wheels
fo·vea \ˈfō-vē-ə\ *n, pl* **fo·ve·ae** \-vē-ˌē, -vē-ˌī\ [NL, fr. L, pit] : a small fossa; *esp* : a rodless area of the retina affording acute vision — see EYE illustration — **fo·ve·al** \-vē-əl\ *adj* — **fo·ve·ate** \-vē-ˌāt, -ət\ *adj* — **fo·ve·iform** \-vē-ə-ˌfȯrm\ *adj*
fo·vea cen·tra·lis \-sen-ˈtral-əs, -ˈträl-, -ˈtral-\ *n* [NL, central fovea] : FOVEA
fow *abbr* first open water
¹fowl \ˈfau̇(ə)l\ *n, pl* **fowl** *or* **fowls** [ME *foul*, fr. OE *fugel*; akin to OHG *fogal* bird] 1 : a bird of any kind 2 **a** : a domestic cock or hen; *esp* : an adult hen **b** : any of several domesticated or wild gallinaceous birds 3 : the meat of fowls used as food
²fowl *vi* : to seek, catch, or kill wildfowl — **fowl·er** *n*
fowling piece *n* : a light gun for shooting birds or small quadrupeds
¹fox \ˈfäks\ *n, pl* **fox·es** *or* **fox** *often attrib* [ME, fr. OE; akin to OHG *fuhs* fox, Skt *puccha* tail] 1 **a** : any of various alert carnivorous mammals (esp. genus *Vulpes*) of the dog family related to but smaller than wolves with shorter legs, more pointed muzzle, large erect ears, and long bushy tail **b** : the fur of a fox 2 : a clever crafty person 3 *archaic* : SWORD 4 *cap* : a member of an Indian people formerly living in Wisconsin 5 : rope yarns twisted and tarred to make small cordage used for lashings or for weaving mats

gray fox

²fox *vt* 1 **a** : to trick by ingenuity or cunning : OUTWIT **b** : BAFFLE 2 *obs* : INTOXICATE 3 **a** : to repair (a shoe) by renewing the upper **b** : to add a strip to; *esp* : to trim (a shoe) with a strip of material (as leather)
foxed \ˈfäkst\ *adj* : discolored with yellowish brown stains ⟨~ leaves of old books⟩
fox fire *n* : an eerie phosphorescent light (as of decaying wood); *also* : a luminous fungus (as *Armillaria mellea*) that causes decaying wood to glow
fox·glove \ˈfäks-ˌgləv\ *n* : any of a genus (*Digitalis*) of the figwort family of erect herbs; *esp* : a common European biennial or perennial (*D. purpurea*) cultivated for its showy racemes of dotted white or purple tubular flowers and as a source of digitalis
fox grape *n* : any of several native grapes (esp. *Vitis labrusca*) of eastern No. America with sour or musky fruit
fox·hole \ˈfäks-ˌhōl\ *n* : a pit dug usu. hastily for individual cover against enemy fire

foxglove

fox·hound \-ˌhau̇nd\ *n* : any of various large swift powerful hounds of great endurance used in hunting foxes and developed to form several breeds and many distinctive strains — compare AMERICAN FOXHOUND, ENGLISH FOXHOUND
fox·tail \ˈfäk-ˌstāl\ *n* 1 **a** : the tail of a fox **b** : something resembling the tail of a fox 2 : any of several grasses (esp. genera *Alopecurus, Hordeum,* and *Setaria*) with spikes resembling brushes
foxtail lily *n* : any of a genus (*Eremurus*) of the lily family of perennial herbs with tall racemes of showy blooms
foxtail millet *n* : a coarse drought-resistant but frost-sensitive annual grass (*Setaria italica*) grown for grain, hay, and forage
fox terrier *n* : a small lively terrier formerly used to dig out foxes and known in smooth-haired and wirehaired varieties
¹fox-trot \ˈfäk-ˌsträt\ *n* 1 : a short broken slow trotting gait in which the hind foot of the horse hits the ground a trifle before the diagonally opposite forefoot 2 : a ballroom dance in duple time that includes slow walking steps, quick running steps, and two-steps
²fox-trot *vi* : to dance the fox-trot
Foxtrot — a communications code word for the letter *f*
foxy \ˈfäk-sē\ *adj* **fox·i·er; -est** 1 : resembling or suggestive of a fox ⟨a narrow ~ face⟩ : as **a** : cunningly shrewd in conniving and contriving : warily guileful **b** : of a warm reddish brown color ⟨~ eyebrows⟩ 2 : defective in some way (as from age or decay) and esp. so as to be discolored or spotted : FOXED 3 : having a sharp brisk flavor ⟨~ grapes⟩ ⟨~ wine⟩ 4 : physically attractive ⟨now there's a ~ girl⟩ *syn* see SLY — **fox·i·ly** \ˈfäk-sə-lē\ *adv* — **fox·i·ness** \-sē-nəs\ *n*
foy \ˈfȯi\ *n* [D dial. *fooi* feast at end of the harvest] *chiefly Scot* : a farewell feast or gift
foy·er \ˈfȯi-(ə)r, ˈfȯi-(y)ā *also* ˈfwä-ˌyā\ *n* [F, lit., fireplace, fr. ML *focarius*, fr. L *focus* hearth] : an anteroom or lobby esp. of a theater; *also* : an entrance hallway : VESTIBULE
fp *abbr* freezing point
FPA *abbr* 1 Foreign Press Association 2 free of particular average
FPC *abbr* 1 Federal Power Commission 2 fish protein concentrate 3 Friends Peace Committee
FPM *abbr* feet per minute
FPO *abbr* fleet post office
FPS *abbr* 1 feet per second 2 foot-pound-second
fr *abbr* 1 father 2 franc 3 friar 4 from
¹Fr *abbr* French
²Fr *symbol* francium
Fra \(ˈ)frä\ *n* [It, short for *frate*, fr. L *frater* — more at BROTHER] : BROTHER — used as a title preceding the name of an Italian monk or friar
fra·cas \ˈfrāk-əs, ˈfrak-, *Brit* ˈfrak-ˌä\ *n, pl* **fra·cas·es** \-ə-səz\ *or Brit* **frac·as** \-ˌäz\ [F, din, row, fr. It *fracasso*, fr. *fracassare* to shatter] : a noisy quarrel : BRAWL
fract·ed \ˈfrak-təd\ *adj* [L *fractus*] *obs* : BROKEN
frac·tion \ˈfrak-shən\ *n* [ME *fraccioun*, fr. LL *fraction-, fractio* of breaking, fr. L *fractus*, pp. of *frangere* to break — more at BREAK] 1 **a** : a numerical representation (as 3/4, 5/8, 3.234) of two numbers whose quotient is to be determined **b** (1) : a piece broken off : FRAGMENT (2) : a discrete unit : PORTION **c** (1) : BIT, LITTLE ⟨a ~ closer⟩ 3 : one of several portions (as of a distillate) separable by fractionation
frac·tion·al \-shnəl, -shən-ᵊl\ *adj* 1 : of, relating to, or being a fraction 2 : relatively small : INCONSIDERABLE 3 : of, relating to, or being fractional currency 4 : of, relating to, or involving a process for separating components of a mixture through differences in physical or chemical properties ⟨~ distillation⟩ — **frac·tion·al·ly** \-ē\ *adv*
fractional currency *n* 1 : paper money in denominations of less than one dollar issued by the U.S. 1863–76 2 : currency in denominations less than the basic monetary unit
frac·tion·al·ize \ˈfrak-shnə-ˌlīz, -shən-ᵊl-ˌīz\ *vt* **-ized; -iz·ing** : to break up into parts or sections ⟨control of the river is *fractionalized* among four countries —Ted Shoemaker⟩ — **frac·tion·al·iza·tion** \ˌfrak-shnə-lə-ˈzā-shən, -shən-ᵊl-ə-ˈzā-\ *n*
frac·tion·ate \ˈfrak-shə-ˌnāt\ *vt* **-at·ed; -at·ing** 1 : to separate (as a mixture) into different portions 2 : to divide or break up — **frac·tion·ation** \ˌfrak-shə-ˈnā-shən\ *n* — **frac·tion·ator** \ˈfrak-shə-ˌnāt-ər\ *n*
frac·tious \ˈfrak-shəs\ *adj* [*fraction* (discord) + *-ous*] 1 : tending to be troublesome : UNRULY 2 : QUARRELSOME, IRRITABLE — **frac·tious·ly** *adv* — **frac·tious·ness** *n*
¹frac·ture \ˈfrak-chər\ *n* 1 **a** : the act or process of breaking or the state of being broken; *specif* : the breaking of hard tissue (as bone) **b** : the rupture of soft tissue 2 : the result of fracturing : BREAK 3 : the general appearance of a freshly broken surface of a mineral
²fracture *vb* **frac·tured; frac·tur·ing** \-chə-riŋ, -shriŋ\ *vt* 1 **a** : to cause a fracture in : BREAK ⟨~ a rib⟩ **b** : RUPTURE, TEAR 2 **a** : to damage or destroy as if by rupturing ⟨a *fractured* family torn apart by alcohol and insanity —R. A. Sokolov⟩ **b** : to cause great disorder **c** : to break up : FRACTIONATE **d** : to go beyond the limits of (as rules) : VIOLATE ⟨*fractured* the English language with malaprops —Goodman Ace⟩ ~ *vi* : to undergo fracture
frae \(ˈ)frā\ *prep* [ME (northern) *fra, frae*, fr. ON *frā*; akin to OE *from*] *Scot* : FROM
frag·ile \ˈfraj-əl, -ˌīl\ *adj* [MF, fr. L *fragilis* — more at FRAIL] 1 **a** : easily broken or destroyed : FRAIL **b** : constitutionally delicate : lacking in physical vigor 2 : TENUOUS, SLIGHT — **fra·gil·i·ty** \frə-ˈjil-ət-ē\ *n*

syn 1 FRAGILE, FRANGIBLE, BRITTLE, CRISP, FRIABLE *shared meaning element* : easily broken ***ant*** durable
2 see WEAK ***ant*** durable
¹frag·ment \ˈfrag-mənt\ *n* [ME, fr. L *fragmentum*, fr. *frangere* to break — more at BREAK] : a part broken off, detached, or incomplete ***syn*** see PART
²frag·ment \-ˌment\ *vb* : FRAGMENTIZE
frag·men·tal \frag-ˈment-ᵊl\ *adj* : FRAGMENTARY — **frag·men·tal·ly** \-ᵊl-ē\ *adv*
frag·men·tary \ˈfrag-mən-ˌter-ē\ *adj* : consisting of fragments : INCOMPLETE — **frag·men·tari·ly** \ˌfrag-mən-ˈter-ə-lē\ *adv* — **frag·men·tari·ness** \-ˌter-ē-nəs\ *n*
frag·men·tate \ˈfrag-mən-ˌtāt\ *vb* **-tat·ed; -tat·ing** : FRAGMENTIZE — **frag·men·ta·tion** \ˌfrag-mən-ˈtā-shən, -ˌmen-\ *n*
fragmentation bomb *n* : a bomb or shell whose relatively thick casing is splintered upon explosion and thrown in fragments in all directions
frag·men·tize \ˈfrag-mən-ˌtīz\ *vb* **-tized; -tiz·ing** *vt* : to break up or apart into fragments ~ *vi* : to fall to pieces — **frag·men·tiz·er** *n*
fra·grance \ˈfrā-grən(t)s\ *n* **1** : the quality or state of having a sweet odor **2 a** : a sweet or delicate odor (as of fresh flowers) **b** : the odor of perfume, cologne, or toilet water
syn FRAGRANCE, PERFUME, SCENT, INCENSE, BOUQUET *shared meaning element* : a sweet or pleasing odor ***ant*** stench, stink
fra·gran·cy \-grən-sē\ *n, archaic* : FRAGRANCE
fra·grant \ˈfrā-grənt\ *adj* [ME, fr. L *fragrant-*, *fragrans*, fr. prp. of *fragrare* to be fragrant; akin to MHG *bræhen* to smell] : marked by fragrance — **fra·grant·ly** *adv*
frail \ˈfrā(ə)l\ *adj* [ME, fr. MF *fraile*, fr. L *fragilis* fragile, fr. *frangere*] **1** : easily led into evil ⟨~ humanity⟩ **2** : easily broken or destroyed : FRAGILE **3 a** : physically weak **b** : SLIGHT, UNSUBSTANTIAL ***syn*** see WEAK ***ant*** robust — **frail·ly** \ˈfrā(ə)l-lē\ *adv* — **frail·ness** *n*
frail·ty \ˈfrā(-ə)l-tē\ *n, pl* **frailties** **1** : the quality or state of being frail **2** : a fault due to weakness esp. of moral character ***syn*** see FAULT
fraise \ˈfrāz\ *n* [F] : an obstacle of pointed stakes driven into the ramparts of a fortification in a horizontal or inclined position
Frak·tur \fräk-ˈtü(ə)r\ *n* [G, fr. L *fractura* fracture] : a German style of black-letter text type

fram·able *or* **frame·able** \ˈfrā-mə-bəl\ *adj* : capable of being framed
fram·be·sia \fram-ˈbē-zh(ē-)ə\ *n* [NL, fr. F *framboise* raspberry; fr. the appearance of the lesions] : YAWS
¹frame \ˈfrām\ *vb* **framed; fram·ing** [ME *framen* to benefit, construct, fr. OE *framian* to benefit, make progress; akin to ON *fram* forward, OE *from* from] *vi* **1** *archaic* : PROCEED, GO **2** *obs* : MANAGE ~ *vt* **1 a** : PLAN, CONTRIVE ⟨*framed* a new method of achieving their purpose⟩ **b** : to give expression to : FORMULATE **c** : SHAPE, CONSTRUCT **d** : to draw up (as a document) **2** : to fit or adjust esp. to something or for an end : ARRANGE **3** *obs* : PRODUCE **4** : to construct by fitting and uniting the parts of the skeleton of (a structure) **5** : to enclose in a frame; *also* : to enclose as if in a frame **6 a** : to devise falsely (as a criminal charge) **b** : to contrive the evidence against (an innocent man) so that a verdict of guilty is assured **c** : to prearrange (as a contest) so that a particular outcome is assured — **fram·er** *n*
²frame *n* **1 a** : something composed of parts fitted together and united **b** : the physical makeup of an animal and esp. a human body : PHYSIQUE, FIGURE **2 a** : the constructional system that gives shape or strength (as to a building); *also* : a frame dwelling **b** : such a skeleton not filled in or covered **3 a** : an open case or structure made for admitting, enclosing, or supporting something ⟨a window ~⟩ **b** : a machine built upon or within a framework ⟨a spinning ~⟩ **c** : a structural unit in an automobile chassis supported on the axles and supporting the rest of the chassis and the body **d** (1) : a part of a pair of glasses that holds one of the lenses (2) *pl* : that part of a pair of glasses other than the lenses **4** *obs* : the act or manner of framing **5** : a particular state or disposition (as of the mind) : MOOD **6 a** : an enclosing border **b** : the matter or area enclosed in such a border: as (1) : one of the squares in which scores for each round are recorded (as in bowling); *also* : a round in bowling (2) : boxed matter in a newspaper; *esp* : a box of a comic strip (3) : one picture of the series on a length of motion-picture or other film (4) : a complete image being transmitted by television **c** : an inning in baseball **d** : a limiting, typical, or esp. appropriate set of circumstances ⟨studies made within the ~ of our society and culture⟩ **e** : an event that forms the background for the action of a novel or play **7** : FRAME-UP **8** : a minimal unit of instruction or stimulus in a programmed instruction routine : a unit of programmed instruction calling for a response by the student
³frame *adj* : having a wood frame ⟨~ houses⟩
frame of reference **1** : an arbitrary set of axes with reference to which the position or motion of something is described or physical laws are formulated **2** : a set or system (as of facts or ideas) serving to orient or give particular meaning : VIEWPOINT, THEORY
frame·shift \ˈfrām-ˌshift\ *n* : the addition or deletion of a pair of purine or pyrimidine bases from a gene so that the codon sequence is read incorrectly in the formation of messenger RNA — called also *frameshift mutation*
frame–up \ˈfrā-ˌməp\ *n* **1** : an act or series of actions in which someone is framed **2** : an action that is framed
¹frame·work \ˈfrām-ˌwərk\ *n* **1 a** : a skeletal, openwork, or structural frame **b** : a basic structure (as of ideas) **2** : FRAME OF REFERENCE **3** : the larger branches of a tree that determine its shape
²framework *vt* : to graft scions of another variety on the framework of (a tree)
fram·ing \ˈfrā-miŋ\ *n* : FRAME, FRAMEWORK
franc \ˈfraŋk\ *n* [F] **1** — see MONEY table **2** — see *dirham* at MONEY table
¹fran·chise \ˈfran-ˌchīz\ *n* [ME, fr. OF, fr. *franchir* to free, fr. *franc* free] **1** : freedom or immunity from some burden or restriction vested in a person or group **2 a** : a special privilege granted to an individual or group; *esp* : the right to be and exercise the powers of a corporation **b** : a constitutional or statutory right or privilege; *esp* : the right to vote **c** (1) : the right or license granted to an individual or group to market a company's goods or services in a particular territory (2) : the territory involved in such a right
²franchise *vt* **fran·chised; fran·chis·ing** **1** *archaic* : FREE **2** : to grant a franchise to
fran·chi·see \ˌfran-ˌchī-ˈzē, -chə-\ *n* : one that is granted a franchise
fran·chis·er \ˈfran-ˌchī-zər\ *n* [in sense 1, fr. ¹*franchise;* in sense 2, fr. ²*franchise*] **1** : FRANCHISEE **2** : FRANCHISOR
fran·chi·sor \ˌfran-ˌchī-ˈzȯ(ə)r, -chə-\ *n* [²*franchise* + *-or*] : one that grants a franchise
Fran·cis·can \fran-ˈsis-kən\ *n* [ML *Franciscus* Francis] : a member of the Order of Friars Minor founded by St. Francis of Assisi in 1209 and dedicated esp. to preaching, missions, and charities — **Franciscan** *adj*
fran·ci·um \ˈfran(t)-sē-əm\ *n* [NL, fr. *France*] : a radioactive element of the alkali-metal group discovered as a disintegration product of actinium and obtained artificially by the bombardment of thorium with protons — see ELEMENT table
Franco- *comb form* [ML, fr. *Francus* Frenchman, fr. LL, Frank] : French and ⟨*Franco*-German⟩ : French ⟨*Franco*phile⟩
Fran·co–Amer·i·can \ˌfraŋ-kō-ə-ˈmer-ə-kən\ *n* : an American of French or esp. French-Canadian descent — **Franco–American** *adj*
fran·co·lin \ˈfraŋ-k(ə-)lən\ *n* [F, fr. It *francolino*] : any of numerous partridges (*Francolinus* and related genera) of southern Asia and Africa
Fran·co·phile \ˈfraŋ-kə-ˌfīl\ *or* **Fran·co·phil** \-ˌfil\ *adj* : markedly friendly to France or French culture — **Francophile** *n*
Fran·co·phobe \-ˌfōb\ *adj* : marked by a fear or strong dislike of France or French culture or customs — **Francophobe** *n*
fran·co·phone \-ˌfōn\ *adj, often cap* : consisting of or belonging to a French-speaking population — **Francophone** *n*
franc–ti·reur \ˌfräⁿ-(ˌ)tē-ˈrər\ *n* [F, fr. *franc* free + *tireur* shooter] : a civilian fighter or sniper
fran·gi·ble \ˈfran-jə-bəl\ *adj* [ME, fr. MF & ML; MF, fr. ML *frangibilis*, fr. L *frangere* to break — more at BREAK] : readily or easily broken ***syn*** see FRAGILE — **fran·gi·bil·i·ty** \ˌfran-jə-ˈbil-ət-ē\ *n*
fran·gi·pane \ˈfran-jə-ˌpān, fräⁿ-zhē-pán\ *n* [F, frangipani (perfume), frangipane, fr. It, fr. Marquis Muzio *Frangipane*, 16th cent. It nobleman] : a custard usu. flavored with almonds
fran·gi·pa·ni *also* **fran·gi·pan·ni** \ˌfran-jə-ˈpan-ē, -ˈpän-\ *n, pl* **-pani** *or* **-panis** [modif. of It *frangipane*] **1** : a perfume derived from or imitating the odor of the flower of the red jasmine **2** : a tropical American shrub or small tree (genus *Plumeria*) of the dogbane family (as red jasmine)
Fran·glais \fräⁿ-ˈglā\ *n* [F, blend of *français* French and *anglais* English] : French marked by a considerable number of borrowings from English
¹frank \ˈfraŋk\ *adj* [ME, free, fr. OF *franc*, fr. ML *francus*, fr. LL *Francus* Frank] **1** : marked by free, forthright, and sincere expression ⟨a ~ reply⟩ **2** : clinically evident : UNMISTAKABLE ⟨~ pus⟩ — **frank·ness** *n*
syn FRANK, CANDID, OPEN, PLAIN *shared meaning element* : showing willingness to say what one thinks or feels ***ant*** reticent
²frank *vt* **1 a** : to mark (a piece of mail) with an official signature or sign indicating the right of the sender to free mailing **b** : to mail free **c** : to affix to (mail) a stamp or a marking indicating the payment of postage **2** : to enable to pass or go freely or easily — **frank·er** *n*
³frank *n* **1 a** : the signature of the sender on a piece of franked mail serving in place of a postage stamp **b** : a mark or stamp on a piece of mail indicating postage paid **c** : a franked envelope **2** : the privilege of sending mail free of charge
⁴frank *n* : FRANKFURTER
Frank \ˈfraŋk\ *n* [ME, partly fr. OE *Franca;* partly fr. OF *Franc*, fr. LL *Francus*, of Gmc origin; akin to OHG *Franko* Frank, OE *Franca*] : a member of a West Germanic people that entered the Roman provinces in A.D. 253, occupied the Netherlands and most of Gaul, and established themselves along the Rhine
Fran·ken·stein \ˈfraŋ-kən-ˌstīn, -ˌstēn\ *n* **1** : a student of physiology in Mary W. Shelley's novel *Frankenstein* whose life is ruined by a monster he creates **2** : a work or agency that ruins its originator **3** : a monster in the shape of a man
frank·furt·er *or* **frank·fort·er** \ˈfraŋk-fə(r)t-ər, -ˌfərt-\ *or* **frank·furt** *or* **frank·fort** \-fərt\ *n* [G *frankfurter* of Frankfurt, fr. *Frankfurt am Main*, Germany] : a cured cooked sausage (as of beef or beef and pork) that may be skinless or stuffed in a casing
frank·in·cense \ˈfraŋ-kən-ˌsen(t)s\ *n* : a fragrant gum resin from chiefly East African or Arabian trees (genus *Boswellia* of the family Burseraceae) that is an important incense resin
¹Frank·ish \ˈfraŋ-kish\ *adj* : of or relating to the Franks
²Frankish *n* : the Germanic language of the Franks
frank·lin \ˈfraŋ-klən\ *n* [ME *frankeleyn*, fr. AF *fraunclein*, fr. OF *franc*] : a medieval English landowner of free but not noble birth
frank·lin·ite \-klə-ˌnīt\ *n* [*Franklin*, N.J.] : a black slightly magnetic mineral $ZnFe_2O_4$ consisting of an oxide of iron and zinc
Frank·lin stove \ˌfraŋ-klən-\ *n* [Benjamin *Franklin*, its inventor] : a metal heating stove resembling an open fireplace but designed to be set out in a room

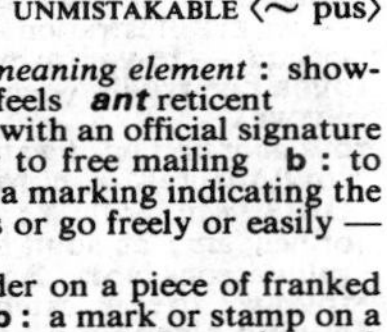
Franklin stove

frank·ly \ˈfraŋ-klē\ *adv* **1** : in a frank manner **2** : in truth : INDEED
frank·pledge \ˈfraŋk-ˌplej\ *n* : an Anglo-Saxon system under which each

...tithing was responsible for the good con-... : the member himself or the tithing

...-ē-ə\ n [NL, genus name, fr. Antonio *Franseri*, ...botanist] : any of a genus (*Franseria*) of annual or ...posite herbs or shrubs

...ant-ik\ *adj* [ME *frenetik, frantik* — more at FRENETIC] ...*chaic* : mentally deranged **b** : emotionally out of control ...with anger and frustration⟩ **2** : marked by fast and nervous, ...ordered, or anxiety-driven activity ⟨made a ~ search for the lost child⟩ — **fran·ti·cal·ly** \-i-k(ə-)lē\ *adv* — **fran·tic·ly** \-i-klē\ *adv* — **fran·tic·ness** \-ik-nəs\ *n*

frap \ˈfrap\ *vt* **frapped; frap·ping** [ME *frapen* to strike, beat, fr. MF *fraper*] : to draw tight (as with ropes or cables)

¹frap·pé *or* **frap·pe** \fra-ˈpā\ *adj* [F *frappé*, fr. pp. of *frapper* to strike, chill, fr. MF *fraper* to strike] *of a beverage* : chilled or partly frozen

²frap·pé \fra-ˈpā\ *or* **frappe** \ˈfrap, fra-ˈpā\ *n* **1 a** : a partly frozen drink (as of fruit juice) **b** : a liqueur served over shaved ice **2** : a thick milk shake

frat \ˈfrat\ *n* : FRATERNITY

fra·ter·nal \frə-ˈtərn-ᵊl\ *adj* [ME, fr. ML *fraternalis*, fr. L *fraternus*, fr. *frater* brother — more at BROTHER] **1 a** : of, relating to, or involving brothers **b** : of, relating to, or being a fraternity or society **2** : derived from two ova : DIZYGOTIC ⟨~ twins⟩ **3** : FRIENDLY, BROTHERLY — **fra·ter·nal·ism** \-ᵊl-ˌiz-əm\ *n* — **fra·ter·nal·ly** \-ᵊl-ē\ *adv*

fra·ter·ni·ty \frə-ˈtər-nət-ē\ *n, pl* **-ties** **1** : a group of people associated or formally organized for a common purpose, interest, or pleasure: as **a** : a fraternal order **b** : GUILD **c** : a men's student organization formed chiefly for social purposes having secret rites and a name consisting of Greek letters **d** : a student organization for scholastic, professional, or extracurricular activities ⟨a debating ~⟩ **2** : the quality or state of being brothers : BROTHERLINESS **3** : men of the same class, profession, character, or tastes ⟨the racetrack ~⟩ **4 a** : the entire progeny of a single mating **b** : a group of siblings

frat·er·nize \ˈfrat-ər-ˌnīz\ *vi* **-nized; -niz·ing** **1** : to associate or mingle as brothers or on fraternal terms **2 a** : to associate on close terms with members of a hostile group esp. when contrary to military orders ⟨*fraternizing* with the enemy⟩ **b** : to be friendly or amiable — **frat·er·ni·za·tion** \ˌfrat-ər-nə-ˈzā-shən\ *n* — **frat·er·niz·er** \ˈfrat-ər-ˌnī-zər\ *n*

frat·ri·cide \ˈfra-trə-ˌsīd\ *n* [in sense 1, fr. ME, fr. MF or L; MF, fr. L *fratricida*, fr. *fratr-*, *frater* brother + *-cida* -cide; in sense 2, fr. MF or L; MF, fr. L *fratricidium*, fr. *fratr-*, *frater* + *-cidium* -cide] **1** : one that murders or kills his own brother or sister **2** : the act of a fratricide — **frat·ri·cid·al** \ˌfra-trə-ˈsīd-ᵊl\ *adj*

Frau \ˈfrau̇\ *n, pl* **Frau·en** \ˈfrau̇(-ə)n [G, woman, wife, fr. OHG *frouwa* mistress, lady; akin to OE *frēa* lord] : a German married woman : WIFE — used as a title equivalent to *Mrs.*

fraud \ˈfrȯd\ *n* [ME *fraude*, fr. MF, fr. L *fraud-*, *fraus*; akin to Skt *dhvarati* he bends, injures] **1 a** : DECEIT, TRICKERY; *specif* : intentional perversion of truth in order to induce another to part with something of value or to surrender a legal right **b** : an act of deceiving or misrepresenting : TRICK **2 a** : one who is not what he pretends to be : IMPOSTOR; *also* : one who defrauds : CHEAT **b** : one that is not what it seems or is represented to be ***syn*** see IMPOSTURE

fraud·u·lence \ˈfrȯ-jə-lən(t)s\ *n* : the quality or state of being fraudulent

fraud·u·lent \-lənt\ *adj* : characterized by, based on, or done by fraud : DECEITFUL — **fraud·u·lent·ly** *adv* — **fraud·u·lent·ness** *n*

¹fraught \ˈfrȯkt\ *n* [ME, freight, load, fr. MD or MLG *vracht*, *vrecht*] *chiefly Scot* : LOAD, CARGO

²fraught *vt* **fraught·ed** *or* **fraught; fraught·ing** [ME *fraughten*, fr. ¹*fraught*] *chiefly Scot* : LOAD, FREIGHT

³fraught \ˈfrȯt\ *adj* [ME, fr. pp. of *fraughten*] **1** *archaic* **a** : LADEN **b** : well supplied or provided **2** : full of or accompanied by something specified : CHARGED — used with *with* ⟨the situation . . . is ~ with a very high violence potential —Harvey Wheeler⟩

fräu·lein \ˈfrȯi-ˌlīn\ *n* [G] **1** *cap* : an unmarried German woman — used as a title equivalent to *Miss* **2** : a German governess

frax·i·nel·la \ˌfrak-sə-ˈnel-ə\ *n* [NL, dim. of L *fraxinus* ash tree — more at BIRCH] : a Eurasian perennial herb (*Dictamnus albus*) of the rue family with flowers that exhale a flammable vapor in hot weather — called also *gas plant*

¹fray \ˈfrā\ *vt* [ME *fraien*, short for *affraien* to affray] *archaic* : SCARE; *also* : to frighten away

²fray *n* : BRAWL, FIGHT; *also* : DISPUTE, DEBATE

³fray *vb* [MF *froyer*, *frayer* to rub, fr. L *fricare* — more at FRICTION] *vt* **1 a** : to wear (as an edge of cloth) by rubbing : FRET **b** : to separate the threads at the edge of **2** : STRAIN, IRRITATE ⟨his temper became a bit ~*ed*⟩ ~ *vi* : to wear out or into shreds

⁴fray *n* : a raveled place or worn spot (as on fabric)

fray·ing *n* : something rubbed or worn off by fraying

¹fraz·zle \ˈfraz-əl\ *vb* **fraz·zled; fraz·zling** \ˈfraz-(ə-)liŋ\ [alter. of E dial. *fazle* (to tangle, fray)] *vt* **1** : ³FRAY **2 a** : to put in a state of extreme physical or nervous fatigue **b** : UPSET ~ *vi* : to become frazzled

²frazzle *n* **1** : the state of being frazzled **2** : a condition of fatigue or nervous exhaustion ⟨worn to a ~⟩

FRCM *abbr* Fellow of the Royal College of Music

FRCO *abbr* Fellow of the Royal College of Organists

FRCP *abbr* Fellow of the Royal College of Physicians

FRCS *abbr* Fellow of the Royal College of Surgeons

¹freak \ˈfrēk\ *n* [origin unknown] **1 a** : a sudden and odd or seemingly pointless idea or turn of the mind **b** : a seemingly capricious action or event **2** *archaic* : a whimsical quality or disposition **3** : one that is markedly unusual or abnormal ⟨by some ~ of the storm one car in the line was completely buried⟩: as **a** : a person or animal with a physical oddity who appears in a circus sideshow **b** *slang* (1) : a sexual deviate (2) : a person who uses an illicit drug **c** *slang* : a highly individualistic critic or rebel **d** : an ardent enthusiast ⟨something from which the casual moviegoer as well as the dedicated film ~ can learn —Richard Schickel⟩ **e** : an atypical postage stamp usu. caused by a unique defect in paper (as a crease) or a unique event in the manufacturing process (as a speck of dirt on the plate) that does not produce a constant or systematic effect ***syn*** see CAPRICE

²freak *adj* : having the character of a freak ⟨a ~ accident⟩

³freak *vt* : to streak esp. with color ⟨silver and mother-of-pearl ~*ing* the intense azure —Robert Bridges †1930⟩

freak·ish \ˈfrē-kish\ *adj* **1** : WHIMSICAL, CAPRICIOUS **2** : being or befitting a freak — **freak·ish·ly** *adv* — **freak·ish·ness** *n*

freak of nature : FREAK 3a

freak–out \ˈfrē-ˌkau̇t\ *n* **1** : a withdrawal from reality esp. by means of drugs **2 a** : a drug-induced state of mind characterized by nightmarish hallucinations : a bad trip **b** : an irrational act **3** : a gathering of hippies **4** : one who freaks out

freak out \ˈfrē-ˈkau̇t\ *vi* **1** : to withdraw from reality esp. by taking drugs **2** : to experience nightmarish hallucinations as a result of taking drugs : have a bad trip **3** : to behave irrationally or unconventionally under or as if under the influence of drugs ~ *vt* **1** : to put under the influence of a psychedelic drug **2** : to put into a state of intense excitement

freak show *n* : an exhibition (as a sideshow) featuring freaks of nature

freaky \ˈfrē-kē\ *adj* **freak·i·er; -est** : FREAKISH

¹freck·le \ˈfrek-əl\ *n* [ME *freken*, *frekel*, of Scand origin; akin to ON *freknōttr* freckled; akin to OE *spearca* spark] : one of the small brownish spots in the skin that are usu. due to precipitation of pigment and that increase in number and intensity on exposure to sunlight — **freck·ly** \ˈfrek-(ə-)lē\ *adv*

²freckle *vb* **freck·led; freck·ling** \ˈfrek-(ə-)liŋ\ *vt* : to sprinkle or mark with freckles or small spots ~ *vi* : to become marked with freckles

¹free \ˈfrē\ *adj* **fre·er; fre·est** [ME, fr. OE *frēo*; akin to OHG *frī* free, Gk *prays* gentle] **1 a** : having the legal and political rights of a citizen **b** : enjoying civil and political liberty ⟨~ citizens⟩ **c** : enjoying political independence or freedom from outside domination **d** : enjoying personal freedom : not subject to the control or domination of another **2 a** : not determined by anything beyond its own nature or being : choosing or capable of choosing for itself **b** : determined by the choice of the actor or by his wishes ⟨~ actions⟩ **c** : made, done, or given voluntarily or spontaneously : SPONTANEOUS **3 a** : exempt, relieved, or released esp. from a burdensome, noxious, or deplorable condition or obligation ⟨~ from pain⟩ **b** : not bound, confined, or detained by force ⟨prisoner was now ~⟩ **4 a** : having no trade restrictions **b** : not subject to government regulation **c** *of foreign exchange* : not subject to restriction or official control **5 a** : having no obligations (as to work) or commitments (as to duty or custom) ⟨I'll be ~ this evening⟩ **b** : not taken up with commitments or obligations ⟨a ~ evening⟩ **6** : having a scope not restricted by qualification ⟨a ~ variable⟩ **7 a** (1) : not obstructed or impeded : CLEAR ⟨a ~ and open highway⟩ (2) : not being used or occupied ⟨waved with his ~ hand⟩ **b** : not hampered or restricted in its normal operation : LOOSE **8 a** : not fastened ⟨the ~ end of the rope⟩ **b** : not confined to a particular position or place; *als*... : not having a specific opponent to cover in football ⟨a ~ safety⟩ **c** : capable of moving or turning in any direction ⟨a ~ particle⟩ ... : performed without apparatus ⟨~ tumbling⟩ **9 a** : not parsi... monious ⟨~ spending⟩ **b** : OUTSPOKEN **c** : availing oneself o... something without stint **d** : FRANK, OPEN **e** : overly familiar o... forward in action or attitude **f** : LICENTIOUS **10** : not costing o... charging anything **11 a** (1) : not united with, attached to, o... combined with something else : SEPARATE ⟨~ ores⟩ ⟨a ~ surface o... a bodily part⟩ (2) : FREESTANDING ⟨a ~ column⟩ **b** : chemical... uncombined ⟨~ oxygen⟩ ⟨~ acids⟩ **c** : not permanently attache... but able to move about ⟨a ~ electron in a metal⟩ **d** : capable ... being used alone as a meaningful linguistic form ⟨the word *hats* is ... ~ form⟩ — compare ⁴BOUND 7 **12 a** : not literal or exact ⟨... translation⟩ **b** : not restricted by or conforming to conventio... forms ⟨~ skating⟩ **13** : FAVORABLE — used of a wind blowi... from a direction more than six points from straight ahead ... : not allowing slavery **15** : open to all comers — **free·ly** *adv* ***syn*** FREE, INDEPENDENT, AUTONOMOUS, SOVEREIGN *shared mean*... *element* : not subject to the rule or control of another

²free *adv* **1** : in a free manner **2** : without charge ⟨admitted ... **3** : with the wind more than six points from dead ahead ⟨sail... ~⟩

³free *vt* **freed; free·ing** **1 a** : to cause to be free **b** : to reliev... rid of what restrains, confines, restricts, or embarrasses ⟨~ a ... from debt⟩ **c** : DISENTANGLE, CLEAR **2** *obs* : BANISH — **fre·er** *n* ***syn*** FREE, RELEASE, LIBERATE, EMANCIPATE, MANUMIT, DISCHA... *shared meaning element* : to loose from constraint or restraint

free agent *n* : a professional athlete (as a football player) wh... not under contract to any team

free alongside ship *adv or adj* : with delivery at the side o... ship free of charges and the buyer's liability then beginning

free alongside vessel *adv or adj* : free alongside ship

free and easy *adj* **1** : marked by informality and lack of ... straint ⟨the *free and easy*, open-air life of the plains —Allan ... ray⟩ **2** : not observant of strict demands ⟨his *free and easy* ... ary judgments⟩ — **free and easy** *adv*

free association *n* **1 a** : the verbal or written expression ... the content of consciousness without censorship or control ... aid in gaining access to unconscious processes esp. in psychoa... sis **b** : the reporting of the first thought that comes to mi...

ə abut ᵊ kitten ər further a back ā bake ä cot...
au̇ out ch chin e less ē easy g gift i trip
j joke ŋ sing ō flow ȯ flaw ȯi coin th thin ...
ü loot u̇ foot y yet yü few yu̇ furious zh ...

response to a given stimulus (as a word) **2** : an idea or image elicited by free association **3** : a method using free association

free·bie *or* **free·bee** \'frē-bē\ *n* [by alter. fr. obs. slang *freeby* gratis, fr. *free* + *-by*, of (unknown origin)] : something (as a theater ticket) given or received without charge

free·board \'frē-,bō(ə)rd, -,bȯ(ə)rd\ *n* **1** : the distance between the waterline and the freeboard deck of a ship or between the level of the water and the upper edge of the side of a small boat **2** : the height above the recorded high-water mark of a structure (as a dam) associated with the water **3** : the space between the surface of the ground and the undercarriage of an automobile

freeboard deck *n* : the deck below which all bulkheads are made watertight

free·boot \'frē-,büt\ *vi* [back-formation fr. *freebooter*] : to act as a freebooter : PLUNDER

free·boo·ter \-ər\ *n* [D *vrijbuiter*, fr. *vrijbuit* plunder, fr. *vrij* free + *buit* booty] : PIRATE, PLUNDERER

free-born \'frē-'bō(ə)rn\ *adj* **1** : not born in vassalage or slavery **2** : of, relating to, or befitting one that is freeborn

free diver *n* : one who engages in skin diving — **free diving** *n*

freed·man \'frēd-mən, -,man\ *n* : a man freed from slavery

free·dom \'frēd-əm\ *n* **1** : the quality or state of being free: as **a** : the absence of necessity, coercion, or constraint in choice or action **b** : liberation from slavery or restraint or from the power of another : INDEPENDENCE **c** : the quality or state of being exempt or released usu. from something onerous ⟨~ from care⟩ **d** : EASE, FACILITY ⟨spoke the language with ~⟩ **e** : the quality of being frank, open, or outspoken ⟨answered the questions with ~⟩ **f** : improper familiarity **g** : boldness of conception or execution **h** : unrestricted use ⟨gave him the ~ of their home⟩ **2 a** : a political right **b** : FRANCHISE, PRIVILEGE

syn FREEDOM, LIBERTY, LICENSE shared meaning element : the power or capacity of acting without compulsion. FREEDOM may imply total or moderate absence of restraint or merely an unawareness of being unduly hampered or frustrated ⟨*Freedom* ... in the medieval sense, when there was no abstract *freedom* but only countable *Freedoms*, each bestowed ... all subject to forfeiture —Martin Joos⟩ ⟨enjoyed the *freedom* of her isolated life⟩ LIBERTY may carry more clearly an implication of the power to choose or one of deliverance from constraint or compulsion ⟨in ~litarian states there is no *liberty* of expression for writers —...ous Huxley⟩ ⟨restore a prisoner's *liberty*⟩ LICENSE can imply ...usual freedom (as from rules or restraints) tolerated because of ...ecial circumstances ⟨poetic *license*⟩ but more often it implies an ...use of liberty (as by disregard of propriety or the rights of oth-...) ⟨enjoying their victory in the *license* which is miscalled liberty ...A. Froude⟩

...n of the seas : the right of a merchant ship to travel any ... except territorial waters either in peace or war

...n ride *n, often cap F&R* : a ride made by civil rights work-...ugh states of the southern U.S. to ascertain whether public ...s (as bus terminals) are desegregated — **freedom rider** *n*

...m·an \'frēd-,wùm-ən\ *n* : a woman freed from slavery

...erprise *n* : freedom of private business to organize and ... for profit in a competitive system without interference by ...ent beyond regulation necessary to protect public interest ... the national economy in balance

... \'frē-'fȯl\ *n* **1** : the condition of unrestrained motion in a ...nal field; *also* : such motion **2** : the part of a parachute ...re the parachute opens

...ing \-'flōt-iŋ\ *adj* **1** : relatively uncommitted (as to a ...purpose) ⟨was not sure how the ~ intellectuals would ...felt as an emotion without apparent cause ⟨~ anxiety⟩

... \'frē-fə-,rȯl\ *n* : a competition, dispute, or fight open ...rs and usu. with no rules : BRAWL — **free-for-all** *adj*

...\'frē-,hand\ *adj* : done without mechanical aids or de-...⟨~ drawing⟩ — **freehand** *adv*

...hand\ *n* : freedom of action or decision

... \'frē-'han-dəd\ *adj* : OPENHANDED, GENEROUS — **free-**...dv

... \-'härt-əd\ *adj* **1** : FRANK, UNRESERVED **2** : GENER-...·eart·ed·ly *adv*

...-,hōld\ *n* **1** : a tenure of real property by which an ...ritance in fee simple or fee tail or for life is held; *also* ...ld by such tenure — compare FEE 1 **2** : a tenure of ...nity similar to a freehold — **free·hold·er** \-,hōl-dər\

...kick (as in football, soccer, or rugby) with which an ... not interfere; *specif* : an unhindered kick (as in ... direction awarded because of an infraction of the ...nent

... of, relating to, or befitting a free lance : INDEPEN-

...to act as a free lance ~ *vt* : to offer or contract for ... the manner of a free lance — **free·lanc·er** *n*

... **a** : a knight or roving soldier available for hire by ...ander **b** : one who acts independently without ...nes or deference to authority **2** : one who pur-...without long-term contractual commitments to

...v-iŋ\ *adj* **1** : marked by more than usual free-...ication of appetites **2** : neither parasitic nor

...to impose upon another's generosity or hospi-...ring in the cost or responsibility involved ...d·er *n*

...ctice of living openly with one of the opposite

...-,man\ *n* **1** : one enjoying civil or political ...g the full rights of a citizen

...onomic market operating by free competition

...rt-ʔn\ *n* [origin unknown] : a sexually imper-...calf twinborn with a male

Free·ma·son \-'mās-ʔn\ *n* : a member of ... society called Free and Accepted Ma...ns

free·ma·son·ry \-rē\ *n* **1** *cap* : the princ...ples, inst...tices of Freemasons — called also *Masonry* **2** : natu...tive fellowship or sympathy

free·ness *n* : FREEDOM

free on board *adv or adj* : without charge for delivery to and plac...ing on board a carrier at a specified point

free port *n* : an enclosed port or section of a port where goods are received and shipped free of customs duty

free radical *n* : an atom or a group of atoms having at least one unpaired electron and participating in various reactions

free reed *n* : a reed in a musical instrument (as a harmonium) that vibrates in an air opening just large enough to allow the reed to move freely — compare BEATING REED

free rein *n* : unrestricted liberty of action or decision

free ride *n* : something (as entertainment, acclaim, or a profit) obtained without the usual cost or effort — **free ride** *vi* — **free rider** *n*

free·sia \'frē-zh(ē-)ə, -zē-ə\ *n* [NL, genus name, fr. F. H. T. *Freese* †1876 G physician] : any of a genus (*Freesia*) of the iris family of sweet-scented African herbs with red, white, or yellow flowers

free-soil *adj* **1** : characterized by free soil ⟨~ states⟩ **2** *cap F&S* : opposing the extension of slavery into U.S. territories and the admission of slave states into the Union prior to the Civil War; *specif* : of, relating to, or constituting a minor U.S. political party having these aims — **Free-Soil·er** \-'sȯi-lər\ *n*

free soil *n* : U.S. territory where prior to the Civil War slavery was prohibited

free-spo·ken \'frē-'spō-kən\ *adj* : speaking freely : OUTSPOKEN

freest *superlative of* FREE

free-stand·ing \'frē-'stan-diŋ\ *adj* : standing alone or on its own foundation free of architectural or supporting frame or attachment ⟨a ~ wall⟩

free-stone \'frē-,stōn\ *n* **1** : a stone that may be cut freely without splitting **2 a** : a fruit stone to which the flesh does not cling **b** : a fruit having such a stone

free-style \'frē-,stīl\ *n, often attrib* : a competition in which a contestant uses a style (as of swimming) of his choice instead of a specified style

free-swim·ming \'frē-'swim-iŋ\ *adj* : able to swim about : not attached ⟨the ~ larva of the barnacle⟩

free-swing·ing \-'swiŋ-iŋ\ *adj* : bold, forthright, and heedless of personal consequences ⟨a ~ soldier of fortune —Will Herberg⟩

free-think·er \-'thiŋ-kər\ *n* : one that forms opinions on the basis of reason independently of authority; *esp* : one who doubts or denies religious dogma **syn** see ATHEIST — **free-think·ing** \-kiŋ\ *n or adj*

free thought *n* : free thinking or unorthodox thought; *specif* : 18th century deism

free throw *n* : an unhindered shot in basketball made from behind a set line and awarded because of a foul by an opponent

free throw lane *n* : a 12 or 16 foot wide lane on a basketball court that extends from underneath the goal to a line 15 feet in front of the backboard and from which players are excluded during a free throw

free trade *n* : trade based upon the unrestricted international exchange of goods with tariffs used only as a source of revenue

free trader *n* : one that practices, supports, or advocates free trade

free university *n* : an unaccredited autonomous free institution established within a university by students to present and discuss subjects not usu. dealt with in the academic curriculum

free verse *n* : verse whose meter is irregular in some respect or whose rhythm is not metrical

free·way \'frē-,wā\ *n* **1** : an expressway with fully controlled access **2** : a toll-free highway

¹free·wheel \-'(h)wē(ə)l\ *n* **1** : a power-transmission system in a motor vehicle with a device that permits the propeller shaft to run freely when its speed is greater than that of the engine shaft **2** : a clutch fitted in the rear hub of a bicycle that permits the rear wheel to run on free from the rear sprocket when the pedals are stopped

²freewheel *vi* : to move, live, or drift along freely or irresponsibly — **free·wheel·er** *n*

free·wheel·ing *adj* : relatively heedless of formalities, rules, responsibilities, or consequences — **free·wheel·ing·ness** *n*

free will \,frē-'wil\ *adj* : VOLUNTARY, SPONTANEOUS

free will *n* **1** : the power asserted of moral beings of choosing within limitations or with respect to some matters without restraint of physical or divine necessity or causal law **2** : the ability to choose between alternatives so that the choice and action are to an extent creatively determined by the conscious subject

Freewill Baptist *n* : a member of a Baptist group holding to Arminian doctrine and practicing open communion

free world *n* : the part of the world where democracy and capitalism or moderate socialism rather than totalitarian or Communist political and economic systems prevail

¹freeze \'frēz\ *vb* **froze** \'frōz\; **fro·zen** \'frōz-ʔn\; **freez·ing** [ME *fresen*, fr. OE *frēosan*; akin to OHG *friosan* to freeze, L *pruina* hoarfrost] *vi* **1 a** : to become congealed into ice by cold **b** : to solidify as a result of abstraction of heat **2 a** : to become chilled with cold ⟨almost *froze* to death⟩ **b** : to become coldly formal in manner **3** : to adhere solidly by or as if by freezing ⟨pressure caused the metals to ~⟩ **4** : to become clogged with ice ⟨the water pipes *froze*⟩ **5** : to become fixed or motionless; *esp* : to become incapable of acting or speaking ~ *vt* **1 a** : to harden into ice **b** : to convert from a liquid to a solid by cold **2 a** : to make extremely cold : CHILL **b** : to act toward in a stiff and formal way **3 a** : to act on usu. destructively by frost **b** : to anesthetize by cold **4** : to cause to grip tightly or remain in immovable contact **5 a** : to cause to become fixed, immovable, or unalterable **b** : to forbid further manufacture, use, or sale of (a raw material) **c** : to immobilize by governmental regulation the expenditure, withdrawal, or exchange of (foreign-owned bank balances) **6** : to attempt to retain continuous possession of (a ball or puck) without an attempt to score eng. in order to protect a small lead

²**freeze** n **1** : a state of weather marked by low temperature esp. when below the freezing point **2 a** : an act or instance of freezing **b** : the state of being frozen

freeze-dry \'frēz-'drī\ vt : to dry (as food) in a frozen state under high vacuum esp. for preservation — **freeze-dried** adj

freeze-etch-ing \'frē-ˌzech-iŋ\ n : preparation of a replica for electron microscopic examination of the exposed surface of quick-frozen material (as a tissue) after fracture along natural structural lines

freez-er \'frē-zər\ n : one that freezes or keeps cool; esp : an insulated cabinet, compartment, or room for keeping food at a sub-freezing temperature or for freezing perishable food rapidly

freezing point n : the temperature at which a liquid solidifies ⟨the freezing point of water is 0° C or 32° F⟩

free zone n : an area within which goods may be received and stored without payment of duty

F region n : the highest region of the ionosphere occurring from 90 to more than 250 miles above the earth

¹**freight** \'frāt\ n, often attrib [ME, fr. MD or MLG vracht, vrecht] **1** : the compensation paid for the transportation of goods **2 a** : something that is loaded for transportation : CARGO **b** : LOAD, BURDEN **3 a** : the ordinary transportation of goods afforded by a common carrier and distinguished from express **b** : a train designed or used for such transportation

²**freight** vt **1 a** : to load with goods for transportation **b** : BURDEN, CHARGE **2** : to transport or ship by freight

freight-age \'frāt-ij\ n : FREIGHT

freight-er \-ər\ n **1** : one that loads or charters and loads a ship **2** : SHIPPER **3** : a ship or airplane used chiefly to carry freight

freight ton n : TON 2c

frem-i-tus \'frem-ət-əs\ n [NL, fr. L, murmur, fr. fremitus, pp. of fremere to murmur; akin to OE bremman to roar] : a sensation felt by a hand placed on a part of the body (as the chest) that vibrates during speech

french \'french\ vt, often cap [French bean] : to cut (snap beans) in thin lengthwise strips before cooking

¹**French** \'french\ adj [ME, fr. OE frencisc, fr. Franca Frank] : of, relating to, or characteristic of France, its people, or their language — **French-ness** n

²**French** n **1** : a Romance language that developed out of the Vulgar Latin of Transalpine Gaul and became the literary and official language of France **2** pl in constr : the French people

French bean n **1** chiefly Brit : a bean (as a green bean) of which the whole young pod is eaten : SNAP BEAN **2** chiefly Brit : KIDNEY BEAN 2

French bulldog n : any of a breed of small compact heavy-boned bat-eared dogs developed in France supposedly by crossing small bulldogs with native dogs

French Canadian n : one of the descendants of French settlers in Lower Canada

French chalk n : a soft white granular variety of steatite used esp. for drawing lines on cloth and for removing grease in dry cleaning

French chop n : a rib chop with the meat trimmed from the end of the rib

French cuff n : a soft double cuff that is made by turning back part of a wide cuff band and that fastens by cuff links

French door n : a light door with rectangular glass panels extending the full length; also : one of a pair of such doors in a single frame

French dressing n **1** : a salad dressing made with oil and vinegar or lemon juice, salt and pepper, and often condiments (as mustard and herbs) **2** : a commercial salad dressing that is creamy and typically orange-red in color

French endive n : ENDIVE 2

¹**french fry** vt, often cap 1st F [back-formation fr. French fried (potatoes)] : to fry (as strips of potato) in deep fat until brown

²**french fry** n, often cap 1st F : a strip of potato fried in deep fat — usu. used in pl.

French heel n : a woman's shoe heel that is usu. high, pitched well forward, and markedly curved

French horn n : a circular valved brass instrument having a conical bore, a funnel-shaped mouthpiece, and a usual range from B below the bass staff upward for more than three octaves

french-ify \'fren-chə-ˌfī\ vt -ified; -ifying often cap : to make French in qualities, traits, or typical practices — **french-i-fi-ca-tion** \ˌfren-chə-fə-'kā-shən\ n, often cap

French kiss n : an open-mouth kiss usu. involving tongue-to-tongue contact — **French-kiss** vb

French leave n [fr. an 18th cent. French custom of leaving a reception without taking leave of the host or hostess] : an informal, hasty, or secret departure

French-man \'french-mən\ n **1** : a native or inhabitant of France **2** : one who is of French descent

French pastry n : fancy pastry made usu. of puff paste baked in individual portions and filled esp. with custard or fruit

French provincial n, often cap P : a style of furniture, architecture, or fabric originating in or characteristic of the 17th and 18th century French provinces

French telephone n : HANDSET

French toast n : bread dipped in a mixture of egg and milk and sautéed

French window n **1** : a French door placed in an exterior wall **2** : a casement window

French-wom-an \'french-ˌwum-ən\ n **1** : a female native or inhabitant of France **2** : a woman of French descent

French horn

fre-net-ic \fri-'net-ik\ adj [ME frenetik insane, fr. MF frenetique, fr. L phreneticus, modif. of Gk phrenitikos, fr. phrenitis inflammation of the brain, fr. phren-, phrēn diaphragm, mind] : FRENZIED, FRANTIC — **fre-net-i-cal-ly** \-i-k(ə-)lē\ adv

fren-u-lum \'fren-yə-ləm\ n, pl -la \-lə\ [NL, dim. of L frenum] **1** : a connecting fold of membrane serving to support or restrain a part (as the tongue) **2** : a bristle or group of bristles on the front edge of the posterior wings of some lepidoptera that unites the wings by interlocking with a process on the front wings

fre-num \'frē-nəm\ n, pl frenums or fre-na \-nə\ [L, lit., bridle; akin to L firmus firm] : FRENULUM 1

fren-zied \'fren-zēd\ adj : marked by frenzy — **fren-zied-ly** adv

¹**fren-zy** \'fren-zē\ n, pl frenzies [ME frenesie, fr. MF, fr. ML phrenesia, alter. of L phrenesis, fr. phreneticus] **1 a** : a temporary madness **b** : a violent mental or emotional agitation **2** : intense usu. wild and often disorderly compulsive or agitated activity

²**frenzy** vt fren-zied; fren-zy-ing : to affect with frenzy

Fre-on \'frē-ˌän\ trademark — used for any of various nonflammable gaseous and liquid fluorinated hydrocarbons used as refrigerants and as propellants for aerosols

freq abbr frequency; frequent; frequentative; frequently

fre-quence \'frē-kwən(t)s\ n : FREQUENCY

fre-quen-cy \'frē-kwən-sē\ n, pl -cies **1** : the fact or condition of occurring frequently **2 a** : the number of times that a periodic function repeats the same sequence of values during a unit variation of the independent variable **b** : the number of individuals in a single class when objects are classified according to variations in a set of one or more specified attributes **3** : the number of repetitions of a periodic process in a unit of time: as **a** : the number of complete alternations per second of an alternating current **b** : the number of sound waves per second produced by a sounding body **c** : the number of complete oscillations per second of an electromagnetic wave

frequency distribution n : an arrangement of statistical data that exhibits the frequency of the occurrence of the values of a variable

frequency modulation n : modulation of the frequency of the carrier wave in accordance with speech or a signal; also : a broadcasting system using such modulation

frequency response n : the ability of a device (as an audio amplifier) to handle the frequencies applied to it; also : a graph representing this ability

¹**fre-quent** \'frē-kwənt\ adj [ME, fr. MF or L; MF, fr. L frequent-, frequens] **1** obs : FULL, THRONGED **2 a** : COMMON, USUAL **b** : happening at short intervals **3** : HABITUAL, PERSISTENT **4** archaic : INTIMATE, FAMILIAR — **fre-quent-ness** n

²**fre-quent** \frē-'kwent, 'frē-kwənt\ vt **1** : to associate with, be in, or resort to often or habitually **2** archaic : to read systematically or habitually — **fre-quen-ta-tion** \ˌfrē-ˌkwen-'tā-shən, -kwən-\ n — **fre-quent-er** n

¹**fre-quen-ta-tive** \frē-'kwent-ət-iv\ adj : denoting repeated or recurrent action or state — used of a verb aspect, verb form, or meaning

²**frequentative** n : a frequentative verb or verb form

fre-quent-ly \'frē-kwənt-lē\ adv : at frequent or short intervals

fres-co \'fres-(ˌ)kō\ n, pl frescoes or frescos [It, fr. fresco fresh, fr. Gmc origin; akin to OHG frisc fresh] **1** : the art of painting on freshly spread moist lime plaster with pigments suspended in a water vehicle **2** : a painting executed in fresco — **fresco** vt

¹**fresh** \'fresh\ adj [ME, fr. OF freis, of Gmc origin; akin to OHG frisc fresh; akin to OE fersc fresh] **1 a** : not salt ⟨~ water⟩ **b** (1) : free from taint : PURE ⟨~ air⟩ (2) of wind : STRONG **2 a** : not altered by processing ⟨~ vegetables⟩ **b** : having its original qualities unimpaired: as (1) : full of or renewed in vigor or readiness for action : REFRESHED ⟨rose ~ from a good night's sleep⟩ (2) : not stale, sour, or decayed ⟨~ bread⟩ (3) : not faded (4) : not worn or rumpled : SPRUCE ⟨a ~ white shirt⟩ **3 a** (1) : experienced, made, or received newly or anew ⟨form ~ friendships⟩ (2) : ADDITIONAL, ANOTHER ⟨make a ~ start⟩ **b** : ORIGINAL, VIVID **c** : lacking experience : RAW **d** : newly or just come or arrived ⟨~ from school⟩ **e** : having the milk flow recently established ⟨a ~ cow⟩ **4** [prob. by folk etymology fr. G frech] : disposed to take liberties : IMPUDENT syn see NEW ant stale — **fresh-ly** adv — **fresh-ness** n

²**fresh** adv : just recently : NEWLY ⟨a ~ laid egg⟩

³**fresh** n **1** : an increased flow or rush (as of water) : FRESHET **2** : a stream of fresh water running into salt water

fresh breeze n : wind having a speed of 19 to 24 miles per hour

fresh-en \'fresh-ən\ vb fresh-ened; fresh-en-ing \-(ə-)niŋ\ vi **1** : to grow or become fresh: as **a** of wind : to increase in strength **b** : to become fresh in appearance or vitality — usu. used with up ⟨~ up with a shower⟩ **c** of water : to lose saltiness **2** of a milch animal : to come into milk ~ vt : to make fresh; also : REFRESH, REVIVE

fresh-et \'fresh-ət\ n **1** archaic : STREAM 1 **2 a** : a great rise or overflowing of a stream caused by heavy rains or melted snow **b** : something resembling or suggesting a freshet esp. in being in sudden large supply ⟨~s of applause —Douglas Watt⟩

fresh gale n : wind having a speed of 39 to 46 miles per hour

fresh-man \'fresh-mən\ n, often attrib **1** : NOVICE, NEWCOMER **2** : a student in his first year or having chiefly first-year standing

fresh-wa-ter \'fresh-ˌwot-ər, -ˌwät-\ adj **1** : of, relating to, or living in fresh water **2** : accustomed to navigating only in fresh waters ⟨a ~ sailor⟩; also : UNSKILLED **3** : inland and usu. provincial ⟨a ~ college⟩

Fres-nel lens \ˌfrez-nəl-, frā-ˈnel-\ n [Augustin J. Fresnel] : a lens that has a surface consisting of a concentric series of simple lens

ə abut	ᵊ kitten	ər further	a back	ā bake	ä cot, cart
aú out	ch chin	e less	ē easy	g gift	i trip	ī life
j joke	ŋ sing	ō flow	ȯ flaw	ȯi coin	th thin	th this
ü loot	u̇ foot	y yet	yü few	yu̇ furious	zh vision

sections so that a thin lens with a short focal length and large diameter is possible and that is used esp. for spotlights

[1]fret \ˈfret\ *vb* **fret·ted; fret·ting** [ME *freten* to devour, fret, fr. OE *fretan* to devour; akin to OHG *frezzan* to devour, *ezzan* to eat — more at EAT] *vt* **1 :** to cause to suffer emotional strain : VEX **2 a :** to eat or gnaw into : CORRODE; *also* : FRAY **b :** RUB, CHAFE **c :** to make by wearing away a substance ⟨the stream *fretted* a channel⟩ **3 :** to pass (as time) in fretting **4 :** AGITATE, RIPPLE ~ *vi* **1 a :** to eat into something **b :** to affect something as if by gnawing or biting : GRATE **2 a :** WEAR, CORRODE **b :** CHAFE **c :** FRAY **3 a :** to become vexed or worried **b** *of running water* : to become agitated

[2]fret *n* **1 a :** the action of wearing away : EROSION **b :** a worn or eroded spot **2 :** an agitation of mind : IRRITATION

[3]fret *vt* **fret·ted; fret·ting** [ME *fretten,* fr. MF *freter* to bind with a ferrule, fret, fr. OF, fr. *frete* ferrule] **1 a :** to decorate with interlaced designs **b :** to form a pattern upon **2 :** to enrich with embossed or pierced carved patterns

[4]fret *n* **1 :** an ornamental network; *esp* : a medieval metallic or jeweled net for a woman's headdress **2 :** an ornament or ornamental work often in relief consisting of small straight bars intersecting one another in right or oblique angles

frets 2

[5]fret *n* [prob. fr. MF *frete* ferrule] : one of a series of ridges fixed across the fingerboard of a stringed musical instrument (as a guitar)

[6]fret *vt* **fret·ted; fret·ting :** to furnish (a stringed instrument) with frets

fret·ful \ˈfret-fəl\ *adj* **1 :** disposed to fret : IRRITABLE **2 a** *of water* : showing agitation **b** *of wind* : GUSTY — **fret·ful·ly** \-fə-lē\ *adv* — **fret·ful·ness** *n*

fret·saw \ˈfret-ˌsȯ\ *n* : a narrow-bladed fine-toothed saw held under tension in a frame and used for cutting curved outlines

fret·work \-ˌwərk\ *n* **1 :** decoration consisting of work adorned with frets **2 :** ornamental openwork or work in relief

Freud·ian \ˈfrȯid-ē-ən\ *adj* : of, relating to, or according with the psychoanalytic theories or practices of Freud — **Freudian** *n* — **Freud·ian·ism** \-ə-ˌniz-əm\ *n*

Freudian slip *n* : a slip of the tongue that is motivated by and reveals some unconscious aspect of the mind

Freund's adjuvant \ˈfrȯin(d)z-, ˈfrȯin(t)s-\ *n* [Jules T. *Freund* †1960 Am immunologist] : any of various substances (as killed tubercle bacilli) added to an antigen to increase its antigenicity

Frey \ˈfrā\ *n* [ON *Freyr*] : the Norse god of fertility, crops, peace, and prosperity

Freya \ˈfrā-ə\ *n* [ON *Freyja*] : the Norse goddess of love and beauty

FRGS *abbr* Fellow of the Royal Geographical Society

Fri *abbr* Friday

fri·a·ble \ˈfrī-ə-bəl\ *adj* [MF or L; MF, fr. L *friabilis,* fr. *friare* to crumble] : easily crumbled or pulverized ⟨~ soil⟩ ***syn*** see FRAGILE — **fri·a·bil·i·ty** \ˌfrī-ə-ˈbil-ət-ē\ *n* — **fri·a·ble·ness** *n*

fri·ar \ˈfrī(-ə)r\ *n* [ME *frere, fryer,* fr. OF *frere,* lit., brother, fr. L *fratr-, frater* — more at BROTHER] : a member of a mendicant order

fri·ar·ly \-lē\ *adj* : resembling a friar : relating to friars

friar's lantern *n* : IGNIS FATUUS

fri·ary \ˈfrī-(ə-)r-ē\ *n, pl* **-ar·ies :** a monastery of friars

[1]frib·ble \ˈfrib-əl\ *vb* **frib·bled; frib·bling** \-(ə-)liŋ\ [origin unknown] *vi* : TRIFLE, DODDER ~ *vt* : to trifle or fool away

[2]fribble *n* : a frivolous person, thing, or idea : TRIFLER — **fribble** *adj*

fric·an·deau \ˈfrik-ən-ˌdō\ *n* [F] : larded veal roasted and glazed in its own juices

[1]fric·as·see \ˈfrik-ə-ˌsē, ˌfrik-ə-ˈ\ *n* [MF, fr. fem. of *fricassé,* pp. of *fricasser* to fricassee] : a dish made of cut-up pieces of meat (as chicken or veal) stewed in a gravy

[2]fricassee *vt* **-seed; -see·ing :** to cook as a fricassee

fric·a·tive \ˈfrik-ət-iv\ *n* [L *fricatus,* pp. of *fricare*] : a consonant characterized by frictional passage of the expired breath through a narrowing at some point in the vocal tract ⟨\f v th t͟h s z sh zh h\ are ~*s*⟩ — **fricative** *adj*

fric·tion \ˈfrik-shən\ *n* [MF or L; MF, fr. L *friction-, frictio,* fr. *frictus,* pp. of *fricare* to rub; akin to L *friare* to crumble, Skt *bhriṇanti* they injure] **1 a :** the rubbing of one body against another **b :** resistance to relative motion between two bodies in contact **2 :** the clashing between two persons or parties of opposed views : DISAGREEMENT — **fric·tion·less** \-ləs\ *adj* — **fric·tion·less·ly** *adv*

fric·tion·al \ˈfrik-shnəl, -shən-ᵊl\ *adj* **1 :** of or relating to friction **2 :** moved or produced by friction — **fric·tion·al·ly** \-ē\ *adv*

friction clutch *n* : a clutch in which connection is made through sliding friction

friction drive *n* : an automobile power-transmission system that transmits motion by surface friction instead of teeth and provides a full range of variation in desired speed ratios

friction match *n* : [3]MATCH 2

friction tape *n* : a usu. cloth tape impregnated with water-resistant insulating material and an adhesive and used esp. to protect, insulate, and support electrical conductors

Fri·day \ˈfrīd-ē\ *n* [ME, fr. OE *frigedæg;* akin to OHG *frīatag;* both fr. a prehistoric WGmc compound whose components are akin to OHG *Frīa,* goddess of love and to OE *dæg* day] : the sixth day of the week — **Fri·days** \-ēz\ *adv*

fridge *also* **frig** \ˈfrij\ *n* [by shortening & alter.] *chiefly Brit* : REFRIGERATOR

fried·cake \ˈfrīd-ˌkāk\ *n* : DOUGHNUT, CRULLER

[1]friend \ˈfrend\ *n* [ME *frend,* fr. OE *frēond;* akin to OHG *friunt* friend; both fr. the prp. of a prehistoric Gmc verb represented by OE *frēon* to love; akin to OE *frēo* free] **1 a :** one attached to another by affection or esteem **b :** ACQUAINTANCE **2 a :** one that is not hostile **b :** one that is of the same nation, party, or group **3 :** one that favors or promotes something (as a charity) **4** *obs* : PARAMOUR **5** *cap* : a member of a Christian sect that stresses Inner Light, rejects sacraments and an ordained ministry, and opposes war — called also *Quaker* — **friend·less** \ˈfren-(d)ləs\ *adj* — **friend·less·ness** *n*

[2]friend *vt* : to act as the friend of : BEFRIEND

friend·li·ly \ˈfren-(d)lə-lē\ *adv* : in a friendly manner

[1]friend·ly \ˈfren-(d)lē\ *adj* **friend·li·er; -est :** of, relating to, or befitting a friend: as **a :** showing kindly interest and goodwill **b :** not hostile **c :** inclined to favor **d :** CHEERFUL, COMFORTING ***syn*** see AMICABLE ***ant*** unfriendly, belligerent — **friend·li·ness** *n*

[2]friendly *adv* : in a friendly manner : AMICABLY

[3]friendly *n, pl* **friendlies :** one that is friendly; *esp* : a native who is friendly to settlers or invaders

friendship \ˈfren(d)-ˌship\ *n* **1 :** the state of being friends **2 :** the quality or state of being friendly : FRIENDLINESS **3** *obs* : AID

fri·er *var of* FRYER

Frie·sian \ˈfrē-zhən\ *n, chiefly Brit* : HOLSTEIN

[1]frieze \ˈfrēz *or* (*compare* FRISÉ) frē-ˈzā\ *n* [ME *frise,* fr. MF, fr. MD *vriese*] **1 :** a heavy durable coarse wool and shoddy fabric with a rough surface **2 :** a pile surface of uncut loops or of patterned cut and uncut loops

[2]frieze \ˈfrēz\ *n* [MF, perh. fr. ML *phrygium, frisium* embroidered cloth, fr. L *phrygium,* fr. neut. of *Phrygius* Phrygian, fr. *Phrygia*] **1 :** the part of an entablature between the architrave and the cornice — see ENTABLATURE illustration **2 :** a sculptured or richly ornamented band (as on a building) **3 :** a band, line, or series suggesting a frieze ⟨a constant ~ of visitors wound its way around the . . . ruins —Mollie Panter-Downes⟩

frieze 2

frig \ˈfrig\ *vi* **frigged; frig·ging** [prob. fr. E dial. *frig* to rub] : COPULATE — usu. considered vulgar

frig·ate \ˈfrig-ət\ *n* [MF, fr. OIt *fregata*] **1 :** a light boat propelled orig. by oars but later by sails **2 :** a square-rigged war vessel intermediate between a corvette and a ship of the line **3 :** a British or Canadian escort ship between a corvette and a destroyer in size **4 :** a U.S. warship of 5000 to 7000 tons that is smaller than a cruiser and larger than a destroyer

frigate bird *n* : any of several strong-winged seabirds (family Fregatidae) noted for their rapacious habits

Frig·ga \ˈfrig-ə\ *n* [ON *Frigg*] : the Norse goddess of married love and of the hearth who shares dominion of the heavens with her husband Odin

[1]fright \ˈfrīt\ *n* [ME, fr. OE *fyrhto, fryhto;* akin to OHG *forhta* fear] **1 :** fear excited by sudden danger : ALARM **2 :** something strange, ugly, or shocking ⟨his beard was a ~⟩ ***syn*** see FEAR

[2]fright *vt* : to alarm suddenly : FRIGHTEN

fright·en \ˈfrīt-ᵊn\ *vb* **fright·ened; fright·en·ing** \ˈfrīt-niŋ, -ᵊn-iŋ\ *vt* **1 :** to make afraid : TERRIFY **2 :** to drive or force by frightening ⟨~*ed* the boy into confessing⟩ ~ *vi* : to become frightened — **fright·en·ing·ly** \-niŋ-lē, -ᵊn-iŋ-\ *adv*

fright·ful \ˈfrīt-fəl\ *adj* **1 :** causing intense fear or alarm : TERRIFYING **2 :** causing shock or horror : STARTLING **3 :** EXTREME ⟨~ thirst⟩ ***syn*** see FEARFUL — **fright·ful·ly** \-fə-lē\ *adv* — **fright·ful·ness** *n*

fright wig *n* : a wig with hair that stands out from the head

frig·id \ˈfrij-əd\ *adj* [L *frigidus,* fr. *frigēre* to be cold; akin to L *frigus* frost, cold, Gk *rhigos*] **1 a :** intensely cold **b :** lacking warmth or ardor : INDIFFERENT **2 :** lacking imaginative qualities : INSIPID **3 :** abnormally averse to sexual intercourse — used esp. of women — **frig·id·ly** *adv* — **frig·id·ness** *n*

Frig·i·daire \ˌfrij-ə-ˈda(ə)r, -ˈde(ə)r\ *trademark* — used for a mechanical refrigerator

fri·gid·i·ty \frij-ˈid-ət-ē\ *n* : the quality or state of being frigid; *specif* : marked or abnormal sexual indifference esp. in a woman

frigid zone *n* : the area or region between the arctic circle and the north pole or between the antarctic circle and the south pole

frig·o·rif·ic \ˌfrig-ə-ˈrif-ik\ *adj* [L *frigorificus,* fr. *frigor-, frigus* frost] : causing cold : CHILLING

fri·jol \frē-ˈhōl, ˈfrē-ˌ\ *also* **fri·jo·le** \frē-ˈhō-lē\ *n, pl* **fri·jo·les** \frē-ˈhō-lēz, ˈfrē-ˌ\ [AmerSp *frijol*] *chiefly Southwest* : BEAN 1b

[1]frill \ˈfril\ *vt* : to provide or decorate with a frill

[2]frill *n* [perh. fr. Flem *frul*] **1 a :** a gathered, pleated, or bias-cut fabric edging used on clothing **b :** a strip of paper curled at one end and rolled to be slipped over the bone end (as of a chop) in serving **2 :** a ruff of hair or feathers about the neck of an animal **3 a :** AFFECTATION, AIR — usu. used in pl. ⟨an honest . . . man who had no ~*s,* . . . no nonsense about him —W. A. White⟩ **b :** something decorative but not essential : LUXURY — **frilly** \ˈfril-ē\ *adj*

[1]fringe \ˈfrinj\ *n, often attrib* [ME *frenge,* fr. MF, fr. (assumed) VL *frimbia,* fr. L *fimbriae* (pl.)] **1 :** an ornamental border consisting of short straight or twisted threads or strips hanging from cut or raveled edges or from a separate band **2 a :** something resembling a fringe : BORDER **b :** one of various light or dark bands produced by the interference or diffraction of light **3 a :** something that is marginal, additional, or secondary to some activity, process, or subject matter **b :** a group with marginal or extremist views **c :** FRINGE BENEFIT

[2]fringe *vt* **fringed; fring·ing** \ˈfrin-jiŋ\ **1 :** to furnish or adorn with a fringe **2 :** to serve as a fringe for : BORDER

fringe area *n* : a region in which reception from a given broadcasting station is weak or subject to serious distortion

fringe benefit *n* : an employment benefit (as a pension, a paid holiday, or health insurance) granted by an employer that involves a money cost without affecting basic wage rates

fringe tree *n* : a small tree (*Chionanthus virginica*) of the olive family that has clusters of white flowers and occurs in the southern U.S. but is widely planted elsewhere

fringy \ˈfrin-jē\ *adj* **fring·i·er; -est :** adorned with or resembling fringes

1frip·pery \ˈfrip-(ə-)rē\ *n, pl* **-per·ies** [MF *friperie,* deriv. of ML *faluppa* piece of straw] **1** *obs* **a :** cast-off clothes **b :** a place where old clothes are sold **2 a :** FINERY; *esp* **:** something showy, tawdry, or nonessential **b :** affected elegance **:** OSTENTATION
2frippery *adj* **:** TRIFLING, TAWDRY
Fris·bee \ˈfriz-bē\ *trademark* — used for a plastic disk several inches in diameter sailed between players by a flip of the wrist
fri·sé \frē-ˈzā\ *n* [F, fr. pp. of *friser* to curl] **:** FRIEZE
Frise aileron \ˈfrēz-\ *n* [Leslie George *Frise b*1897 E engineer] **:** an aileron having a nose portion projecting ahead of the hinge axis and a lower surface in line with the lower surface of the wing
fri·sette \frē-ˈzet\ *n* [F] *archaic* **:** a fringe of hair or curls worn on the forehead by women
fri·seur \frē-ˈzər\ *n* [F] **:** HAIRDRESSER
1Fri·sian \ˈfrizh-ən, ˈfrē-zhən\ *adj* [L *Frisii* Frisians] **:** of, relating to, or characteristic of Friesland, the Frisians, or Frisian
2Frisian *n* **1 :** a member of a people that inhabit principally the Netherlands province of Friesland and the Frisian islands in the North sea **2 :** the Germanic language of the Frisian people
1frisk \ˈfrisk\ *vb* [obs. *frisk* (lively)] *vi* **:** to leap, skip, or dance in a lively or playful way **:** GAMBOL ~ *vt* **:** to search (a person) for something (as a concealed weapon) by running the hand rapidly over the clothing and through the pockets — **frisk·er** *n*
2frisk *n* **1 a** *archaic* **:** CARACOLE, CAPER **b :** GAMBOL, ROMP **c :** DIVERSION **2 :** an act of frisking
frisk·i·ly \ˈfris-kə-lē\ *adv* **:** in a frisky manner
frisky \ˈfris-kē\ *adj* **frisk·i·er; -est :** inclined to frisk **:** FROLICSOME — **frisk·i·ness** *n*
fris·son \frē-ˈsōⁿ\ *n, pl* **frissons** \-ˈsōⁿ(z)\ [F] **:** SHUDDER, THRILL
1frit \ˈfrit\ *n* [It *fritta*] **1 :** the calcined or partly fused materials of which glass is made **2 :** any of various chemically complex glasses used ground esp. to introduce soluble or unstable ingredients into glazes or enamels
2frit *vt* **frit·ted; frit·ting 1 :** to prepare (materials for glass) by heat **:** FUSE **2 :** to convert into a frit
frith \ˈfrith\ *n* **:** FIRTH
frit·il·lar·ia \ˌfrit-ᵊl-ˈer-ē-ə, -ˈar-\ *n* [NL, fr. L *fritillus* dice cup; fr. the markings of the petals] **:** any of a genus (*Fritillaria*) of bulbous herbs of the lily family with mottled or checkered flowers
frit·il·lary \ˈfrit-ᵊl-ˌer-ē\ *n, pl* **-lar·ies** [NL *fritillaria*] **1 :** FRITILLARIA **2 :** any of numerous nymphalid butterflies (esp. genera *Argynnis* and *Speyeria*) that usu. are orange with black spots on the upper side of both wings and silver spotted on the underside of the hind wing
1frit·ter \ˈfrit-ər\ *n* [ME *fritour,* fr. MF *friture,* fr. (assumed) VL *frictura,* fr. *frictus,* pp. of *frigere* to fry — more at FRY] **:** a small quantity of fried or sautéed batter often containing fruit or meat
2fritter *vb* [*fritter,* n. (fragment, shred)] *vt* **1 :** to spend or waste bit by bit, on trifles, or without commensurate return ⟨~*ing* away our natural resources⟩ **2 :** to break into small fragments ~ *vi* **:** DISSIPATE, DWINDLE ***syn*** see WASTE — **frit·ter·er** \-ər-ər\ *n*
friv·ol \ˈfriv-əl\ *vi* **-oled** *or* **-olled; -ol·ing** *or* **-ol·ling** \-(ə-)liŋ\ [back-formation fr. *frivolous*] **:** to act frivolously **:** TRIFLE — **friv·ol·er** *or* **friv·ol·ler** \-(ə-)lər\ *n*
fri·vol·i·ty \friv-ˈäl-ət-ē\ *n, pl* **-ties 1 :** the quality or state of being frivolous **2 :** a frivolous act or thing ***syn*** see LIGHTNESS ***ant*** staidness
friv·o·lous \ˈfriv-(ə-)ləs\ *adj* [ME, fr. L *frivolus*] **1 :** of little weight or importance **2 a :** lacking in seriousness **:** irresponsibly self-indulgent **b :** marked by unbecoming levity — **friv·o·lous·ly** *adv* — **friv·o·lous·ness** *n*
1frizz \ˈfriz\ *vb* [F *friser*] *vt* **:** to form into small tight curls ~ *vi, of hair* **:** to form a mass of tight curls
2frizz *n* **1 :** a tight curl **2 :** hair that is tightly curled
3frizz *vb* [alter. of 1FRY] *vt* **:** to fry or sear with a sizzling noise ~ *vi* **:** SIZZLE
frizz·i·ly \ˈfriz-ə-lē\ *adv* **:** in a frizzy manner
1friz·zle \ˈfriz-əl\ *vb* **friz·zled; friz·zling** \-(ə-)liŋ\ [prob. akin to OE *fris* curly, OFris *frisle* curl] **:** FRIZZ, CURL
2frizzle *n* **:** a crisp curl
3frizzle *vb* **friz·zled; friz·zling** [1*fry* + *sizzle*] *vt* **1 :** to fry until crisp and curled **2 :** BURN, SCORCH ~ *vi* **:** to cook with a sizzling noise
friz·zly \ˈfriz-(ə-)lē\ *adj* **friz·zli·er; -est :** FRIZZY
frizzy *adj* **frizz·i·er; -est :** tightly curled — **frizz·i·ness** *n*
1fro \frə, (ˈ)frō\ *prep* [ME, fr. ON *frā;* akin to OE *from*] *dial Brit* **:** FROM
2fro \ˈfrō\ *adv* **:** BACK, AWAY — used in the phrase *to and fro*
1frock \ˈfräk\ *n* [ME *frok,* fr. MF *froc,* of Gmc origin; akin to OHG *hroch* mantle, coat] **1 :** an outer garment worn by monks and friars **:** HABIT **2 :** an outer garment worn chiefly by men: **a :** a long loose mantle **b :** a workman's outer shirt; *esp* **:** SMOCK FROCK **c :** a woolen jersey worn esp. by sailors **3 :** a woman's dress
2frock *vt* **1 :** to clothe in a frock **2 :** to make a cleric of
frock coat *n* **:** a man's usu. double-breasted coat having knee-length skirts front and back
froe \ˈfrō\ *n* [perh. alter. of obs. *froward* turned away, fr. ME; fr. the position of the handle] **:** a cleaving tool for splitting cask staves and shingles from the block
frog \ˈfrȯg, ˈfräg\ *n* [ME *frogge,* fr. OE *frogga;* akin to OHG *frosk* frog, Skt *pravate* he jumps up] **1 :** any of various smooth-skinned web-footed largely aquatic tailless agile leaping amphibians (as of the suborder Diplasiocoela) — compare TOAD **2 :** a condition in the throat that produces hoarseness ⟨had a ~ in his throat⟩ **3 :** the triangular elastic horny pad in the middle of the sole of the foot of a horse — see HOOF illustration **4 a :** a loop attached to a belt to hold a weapon or tool **b :** an ornamental braiding for fastening the front of a garment that consists of a button and a loop through which it passes **5 :** a device permitting the wheels on one rail of a track to cross an intersecting rail **6 :** the nut of a violin bow — see BOW illustration **7 :** a small holder (as of metal, glass, or plastic) with perforations or spikes for holding flowers in place in a bowl or vase

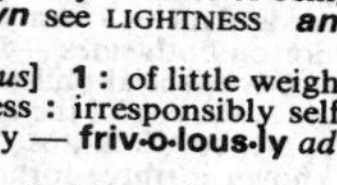
frog 4b

frog·eye \-ˌī\ *n* **:** any of numerous leaf diseases characterized by concentric rings about the diseased spots
frog·hop·per \-ˌhäp-ər\ *n* **:** SPITTLEBUG
frog kick *n* **:** a breaststroke kick that is executed with the knees pointed outward
frog·man \ˈfrȯg-ˌman, ˈfräg-, -mən\ *n* **:** a person equipped (as with face mask, flippers, and air supply) for extended periods of underwater swimming; *esp* **:** a person so equipped for military reconnaissance and demolition
frog spit *n* **1 :** CUCKOO SPIT 1 **2 :** an alga that forms slimy masses on quiet water
1frol·ic \ˈfräl-ik\ *adj* [D *vroolijk,* fr. MD *vrolijc,* fr. *vro* happy; akin to OHG *frō* happy, OE *frogga* frog] **:** full of fun **:** MERRY
2frolic *vi* **frol·icked; frol·ick·ing 1 :** to make merry **2 :** to play and run about happily **:** ROMP
3frolic *n* **1 :** a playful mischievous action **2 a :** FUN, MERRIMENT **b :** PARTY
frol·ic·some \ˈfräl-ik-səm\ *adj* **:** full of gaiety **:** SPORTIVE
from \(ˈ)frəm, ˈfräm *also* fəm\ *prep* [ME, fr. OE; akin to OHG *fram,* adv., forth, away, OE *faran* to go — more at FARE] **1** — used as a function word to indicate a starting point: as (1) a place where a physical movement begins ⟨came here ~ the city⟩ (2) a starting point in measuring or reckoning or in a statement of limits ⟨a week ~ today⟩ ⟨cost ~ $5 to $10⟩ **2** — used as a function word to indicate separation: as (1) physical separation (2) an act or condition of removal, abstention, exclusion, release, or differentiation ⟨protection ~ the sun⟩ ⟨relief ~ anxiety⟩ **3** — used as a function word to indicate the source, cause, agent, or basis ⟨a call ~ my lawyer⟩ ⟨inherited a love of music ~ his father⟩ ⟨read ~ his new book of poems⟩ ⟨worked hard ~ necessity⟩
frond \ˈfränd\ *n* [L *frond-, frons* foliage] **1 :** LEAF; *esp* **:** the leaf of a palm **2 a :** a thallus or thalloid shoot resembling a leaf **b :** the leaf of a fern — **frond·ed** \ˈfrän-dəd\ *adj*
fron·deur \frōⁿ-ˈdər\ *n* [F, slinger, participant in a 17th cent. revolt in which the rebels were compared to schoolboys using slings only when the teacher was not looking] **:** REBEL, MALCONTENT
fron·dose \ˈfrän-ˌdōs\ *adj* **:** bearing or resembling fronds — **fron·dose·ly** *adv*
1front \ˈfrənt\ *n* [ME, fr. OF, fr. L *front-, frons* — more at BRINK] **1 a :** FOREHEAD; *also* **:** the whole face **b** (1) **:** demeanor or bearing esp. in the face of danger or other trial (2) **:** external and often feigned appearance (3) **:** an artificial or self-important manner **2 a** (1) **:** VANGUARD (2) **:** a line of battle (3) *often cap* **:** a zone of conflict between armies (4) **:** lateral space occupied by a military unit **b** (1) **:** a stand in reference to some issue **:** POLICY — usu. used with *change* (2) **:** a sphere of activity ⟨progress on the educational ~⟩ (3) **:** a movement linking divergent elements to achieve certain common objectives; *esp* **:** a political coalition ⟨and to create a popular democratic ~ —*Collier's Yr. Bk.*⟩ **3 :** a side of a building; *esp* **:** the side that contains the principal entrance **4 a :** the forward part or surface **b** (1) **:** FRONTAGE (2) **:** a beach promenade at a seaside resort **c :** DICKEY 1a **d :** the boundary between two dissimilar air masses **5** *archaic* **:** BEGINNING **6 a** (1) **:** a position ahead of a person or of the foremost part of a thing (2) — used as a call by a hotel desk clerk in summoning a bellboy **b :** a position of leadership or superiority **7 a :** a person, group, or thing used to mask the identity or true character or activity of the actual controlling agent **b :** a person who serves as the nominal head or spokesman of an enterprise or group to lend it prestige — **in front of :** directly before or ahead of ⟨watching the road *in front of* him⟩ — **out front :** in the audience — **up front :** in the frontcourt; *specif* **:** in the position of forward or center
2front *vi* **1 :** FACE ⟨the house ~s toward the east⟩ — often used with *on* ⟨a ten-acre plot ~*ing* on a lake —*Current Biog.*⟩ **2 :** to serve as a front ⟨~*ing* for special interests⟩ ~ *vt* **1 a :** CONFRONT ⟨went to the woods because I wished . . . to ~ only the essential facts of life —H. D. Thoreau⟩ **b :** to appear before ⟨daily ~*ed* him in some fresh splendor —Alfred Tennyson⟩ **2 :** to be in front of ⟨lawn ~*ing* the house⟩ **3 :** to supply a front to ⟨~*ed* the building with bricks⟩ **4 :** to face toward ⟨the house ~*s* the street⟩ **5 :** to articulate (a sound) with the tongue farther forward
3front *adj* **1 :** of, relating to, or situated at the front **2 :** articulated at or toward the front of the oral passage ⟨~ vowels⟩ **3 :** constituting the first nine holes of an 18-hole golf course — **front** *adv*
4front *abbr* frontispiece
front·age \ˈfrənt-ij\ *n* **1 a :** a piece of land that fronts **b :** the land between the front of a building and the street **2 :** the front side of a building **3 :** the act or fact of facing a given way
frontage road *n* **:** a local street or road that generally parallels an expressway or through street and that provides access to property isolated from the expressway through access controls — called also *service road*
1fron·tal \ˈfrənt-ᵊl\ *n* **1** [ME *frontel,* fr. ML *frontellum,* dim. of L *front-, frons*] **:** a cloth hanging over the front of an altar **2 :** FACADE
2frontal *adj* [NL *frontalis,* fr. L *front-, frons*] **1 :** of, relating to, or adjacent to the forehead or the frontal bone **2 a :** of, relating to, or situated at the front **b :** directed against the front or at the main point or issue **:** DIRECT ⟨~ assault⟩ **3 :** parallel to the main axis of the body and at right angles to the sagittal plane **4 :** of or relating to a meteorological front — **fron·tal·ly** \-ᵊl-ē\ *adv*
frontal bone *n* **:** either of a pair of membrane bones forming the forehead

ə abut ᵊ kitten ər further a back ā bake ä cot, cart
au̇ out ch chin e less ē easy g gift i trip ī life
j joke ŋ sing ō flow ȯ flaw ȯi coin th thin t͟h this
ü loot u̇ foot y yet yü few yu̇ furious zh vision

fron·tal·i·ty \ˌfrən-ˈtal-ət-ē\ *n* **1** *sculpture* **:** a schematic composition of the front view that is complete without lateral movement **2** *painting* **:** the depiction of an object, figure, or scene in a plane parallel to the plane of the picture surface

frontal lobe *n* **:** the anterior division of each cerebral hemisphere

front·court \ˈfrənt-ˈkō(ə)rt, -ˈkȯ(ə)rt\ *n* **:** a basketball team's offensive half of the court; *also* **:** the positions of forward and center on a basketball team

front dive *n* **:** a dive from a position facing the water

front–end load *n* **:** the part of the total load taken out of early payments under a contract plan for the periodic purchase of investment-company shares

fron·te·nis \ˌfrən-ˈten-əs, frän-\ *n* [AmerSp, blend of *frontón* pelota court and *tenis* tennis] **:** a game of Mexican origin played with rackets and a rubber ball on a 3-walled court

fron·tier \ˌfrən-ˈti(ə)r, ˈfrən-ˌ, frän-ˈ, ˈfrän-ˌ\ *n* [ME *fronter,* fr. MF *frontiere,* fr. *front*] **1 a :** a border between two countries **b** *obs* **:** a stronghold on a frontier **2 a :** a region that forms the margin of settled or developed territory **b :** the farthermost limits of knowledge or achievement with respect to a particular subject **c :** a new field that offers scope for exploitative or developmental activity — **frontier** *adj*

fron·tiers·man \ˌfrən-ˈti(ə)rz-mən, frän-\ *n* **:** a man living on the frontier

fron·tis·piece \ˈfrənt-ə-ˌspēs\ *n* [MF *frontispice,* fr. LL *frontispicium,* lit., view of the front, fr. L *front-, frons* + *-i-* + *specere* to look at — more at SPY] **1 a :** the principal front of a building **b :** a decorated pediment over a portico or window **2 :** an illustration preceding and usu. facing the title page of a book or magazine

front·less \ˈfrənt-ləs\ *adj, archaic* **:** SHAMELESS

front·let \-lət\ *n* [Me *frontlette,* fr. MF *frontelet,* dim. of *frontel,* fr. L *frontale,* fr. *front-, frons*] **1 :** a band or phylactery worn on the forehead **2 :** FOREHEAD; *esp* **:** the forehead of a bird when distinctively marked

front–line *adj* **1 :** situated or suitable for use at a military front ⟨~ ambulances⟩ **2 a :** of or relating to the most advanced or significant activity or procedure in a field or enterprise **b :** relating to or being proficient or competent in a field ⟨~ teachers⟩; *also* **:** FIRST-STRING ⟨~ catchers⟩

front line *n* **1 :** a military line formed by the most advanced tactical combat units; *also* **:** FRONT **2 :** the most advanced, responsible, or significant position in a field or activity

front man *n* **:** a person serving as a front or figurehead

front matter *n* **:** matter preceding the main text of a book

fronto- *comb form* [ISV, fr. L *front-, frons*] **1 :** frontal and ⟨*fronto*parietal⟩ **2** [*¹front*] **:** boundary of an air mass ⟨*fronto*genesis⟩

front office *n* **:** the policy-making officials of an organization

front·o·gen·e·sis \ˌfrənt-ō-ˈjen-ə-səs\ *n* [NL] **:** the coming together into a distinct front of two dissimilar air masses that commonly react upon each other to induce cloud and precipitation

front·ol·y·sis \ˌfrənt-ˈäl-ə-səs\ *n* [NL] **:** a process tending to destroy a meteorological front

fron·ton \ˈfrän-ˌtän\ *n* [Sp *frontón* gable, wall of a pelota court, fronton, fr. dim. of *frenta* forehead, fr. L *front-, frons*] **:** a jai alai arena

1front–page \ˈfrənt-ˈpāj\ *adj* **:** very newsworthy

2front–page *vt* **:** to print or report on the front page of a newspaper

front room *n* **:** LIVING ROOM, PARLOR

front–run·ner \ˈfrənt-ˈrən-ər\ *n* **1 :** a contestant who runs best when in the lead **2 :** a leading contestant in a rivalry or competition

frore \ˈfrō(ə)r, ˈfrȯ(ə)r\ *adj* [ME *froren,* fr. OE, pp. of *frēosan* to freeze] **:** FROSTY, FROZEN

frosh \ˈfräsh\ *n, pl* **frosh** [by shortening & alter.] **:** FRESHMAN

1frost \ˈfrȯst\ *n* [ME, fr. OE; akin to OHG *frost,* OE *frēosan* to freeze] **1 a :** the process of freezing **b :** the temperature that causes freezing **c :** a covering of minute ice crystals on a cold surface **2 a :** coldness of deportment or temperament **:** an indifferent, reserved, or unfriendly manner **b :** FAILURE ⟨he may be a ~ as a man, but he has his ear to the ground as a newspaper pro — James Purdy⟩

2frost *vt* **1 a :** to cover with or as if with frost; *esp* **:** to put icing on (cake) **b :** to produce a fine-grained slightly roughened surface on (as metal or glass) **2 :** to injure or kill (as plants) by frost ~ *vi* **:** to become frosted **:** FREEZE

1frost·bite \ˈfrȯs(t)-ˌbīt\ *vt* **-bit** \-ˌbit\; **-bit·ten** \-ˌbit-ᵊn\; **-bit·ing** \-ˌbīt-iŋ\ **:** to blight or nip with frost

2frostbite *n* **:** the freezing or the local effect of a partial freezing of some part of the body

3frostbite *adj* **:** done in cold weather ⟨~ sailing⟩; *also* **:** of or relating to cold-weather sailing ⟨~ sailors⟩

frost·bit·ing \-ˌbīt-iŋ\ *n* **:** the sport of sailing in cold weather

frost·ed \ˈfrȯ-stəd\ *adj* **:** QUICK-FROZEN ⟨~ vegetables⟩

frost heave *n* **:** an upthrust of ground or pavement caused by freezing of moist soil — called also *frost heaving*

frost·ing \ˈfrȯ-stiŋ\ *n* **1 a :** ICING **b :** TRIMMING, ORNAMENTATION **2 :** lusterless finish of metal or glass **:** MAT; *also* **:** a white finish produced on glass (as by etching) **3 :** the lightening (as by chemicals) of small strands of hair throughout the entire head to produce a two-tone effect — compare STREAKING

frost·work \ˈfrȯs-ˌtwərk\ *n* **1 :** the figures that moisture sometimes forms in freezing (as on a windowpane) **2 :** ornamentation (as on silver, glass, or paper) imitative of the figures of frostwork

frosty \ˈfrȯ-stē\ *adj* **frost·i·er; -est 1 :** attended with or producing frost **:** FREEZING **2 :** covered or appearing as if covered with frost **:** HOARY **3 :** marked by coolness or extreme reserve in manner ⟨his smile was distinctly ~ —Erle Stanley Gardner⟩ — **frost·i·ly** \-stə-lē\ *adv* — **frost·i·ness** \-stē-nəs\ *n*

1froth \ˈfrȯth\ *n, pl* **froths** \ˈfrȯths, ˈfrȯt͟hz\ [ME, fr. ON *frotha;* akin to OE *āfrēothan* to froth, Gk *prēthein* to blow up] **1 a :** bubbles formed in or on a liquid **:** FOAM **b :** a foamy slaver sometimes accompanying disease or exhaustion **2 :** something unsubstantial or of little value ⟨swayed by popular fads and ~ —Gay Talese⟩

2froth \ˈfrȯth, ˈfrȯt͟h\ *vt* **1 :** to cause to foam **2 :** VENT, VOICE **3 :** to cover with froth ~ *vi* **1 :** to foam at the mouth **2 :** to throw froth out or up

frothy \ˈfrȯ-thē, -t͟hē\ *adj* **froth·i·er; -est 1 :** full of or consisting of froth ⟨~ surf⟩ **2 a :** gaily frivolous or light in content or treatment ⟨~ poetry⟩ **b :** made of light thin material ⟨~ garments⟩ — **froth·i·ly** \-thə-lē, -t͟hē-\ *adv* — **froth·i·ness** \-thē-nəs, -t͟hē-\ *n*

frot·tage \frȯ-ˈtäzh\ *n* [F, fr. *frotter* to rub] **:** the technique of creating a design by rubbing (as with a pencil) over an object placed underneath the paper; *also* **:** a composition so made

frou·frou \ˈfrü-(ˌ)frü\ *n* [F, of imit. origin] **1 :** a rustling esp. of a woman's skirts **2 :** frilly ornamentation esp. in women's clothing

frow \ˈfrō\ *var of* FROE

fro·ward \ˈfrō-(w)ərd\ *adj* [ME, turned away, froward, fr. *fro* + *-ward*] **1 :** habitually disposed to disobedience and opposition **2** *archaic* **:** ADVERSE **syn** see CONTRARY **ant** compliant — **fro·ward·ly** *adv* — **fro·ward·ness** *n*

1frown \ˈfrau̇n\ *vb* [ME *frounen,* fr. MF *froigner* to snort, frown, of Celt origin; akin to W *ffroen* nostril] *vi* **1 :** to contract the brow in displeasure or concentration **2 :** to give evidence of displeasure or disapproval by or as if by facial expression ~ *vt* **:** to show displeasure with or disapproval of esp. by facial expression — **frown·er** *n* — **frown·ing·ly** \ˈfrau̇-niŋ-lē\ *adv*

syn FROWN, SCOWL, GLOWER, LOWER *shared meaning element* **:** to put on a dark or malignant countenance or aspect **ant** smile

2frown *n* **1 :** a wrinkling of the brow in displeasure or concentration **2 :** an expression of displeasure

frows·ty \ˈfrau̇-stē\ *adj* **frowst·i·er; -est** [alter. of *frowsy*] *chiefly Brit* **:** MUSTY

frow·sy *also* **frow·zy** \ˈfrau̇-zē\ *adj* **frow·si·er** *also* **frow·zi·er; -est** [origin unknown] **1 :** having a slovenly or uncared-for appearance **2 :** MUSTY, STALE

froze *past of* FREEZE

fro·zen \ˈfrōz-ᵊn\ *adj* **1 a :** treated, affected, or crusted over by freezing **b :** subject to long and severe cold ⟨~ north⟩ **2 a** (1) **:** drained or incapable of emotion (2) **:** expressing or characterized by cold unfriendliness **b :** incapable of being changed, moved, or undone; *specif* **:** debarred by official action from movement or from change in status ⟨wages were ~⟩ **c :** not available for present use ⟨~ capital⟩ — **fro·zen·ly** *adv* — **fro·zen·ness** \-ᵊn-(n)əs\ *n*

frozen daiquiri *n* **:** a daiquiri beaten with shaved ice to a slushy consistency

frozen food *n* **:** food that has been subjected to rapid freezing and is kept frozen until used

FRS *abbr* **1** Federal Reserve System **2** Fellow of the Royal Society

frt *abbr* freight

fruc·ti·fi·ca·tion \ˌfrək-tə-fə-ˈkā-shən, ˌfru̇k-\ *n* **1 :** the forming or producing of fruit **2 a :** FRUIT 1d **b :** SPOROPHORE

fruc·ti·fy \ˈfrək-tə-ˌfī, ˈfru̇k-\ *vb* **-fied; -fy·ing** [ME *fructifien,* fr. MF *fructifier,* fr. L *fructificare,* fr. *fructus* fruit] *vi* **:** to bear fruit ⟨its seeds shall ~ —Amy Lowell⟩ ⟨no partnership can ~ without candor on both sides —D. M. Ogilvy⟩ ~ *vt* **:** to make fruitful or productive ⟨social philosophy *fructified* the poltical thinking of liberals at the end of the century —*Times Lit. Supp.*⟩

fruc·tose \ˈfrək-ˌtōs, ˈfrük-, ˈfru̇k-, -ˌtōz\ *n* **1 :** a sugar $C_6H_{12}O_6$ known in three forms that are optically different with respect to polarized light **2 :** the very sweet soluble levorotatory D-form of fructose that occurs esp. in fruit juices and honey — called also *levulose*

fruc·tu·ous \ˈfrək-chə-wəs, ˈfru̇k-\ *adj* **:** FRUITFUL ⟨a ~ land⟩

fru·gal \ˈfrü-gəl\ *adj* [MF or L; MF, fr. L *frugalis* virtuous, frugal, alter. of *frugi,* fr. dat. of *frug-, frux* fruit, value; akin to L *frui* to enjoy] **:** characterized by or reflecting economy in the expenditure of resources **syn** see SPARING **ant** wasteful — **fru·gal·i·ty** \frü-ˈgal-ət-ē\ *n* — **fru·gal·ly** \ˈfrü-gə-lē\ *adv*

fru·giv·o·rous \frü-ˈjiv-ə-rəs\ *adj* [L *frug-, frux* + E *-vorous*] **:** feeding on fruit

1fruit \ˈfrüt\ *n, often attrib* [ME, fr. OF, fr. L *fructus* fruit, use, fr. *fructus,* pp. of *frui* to enjoy, have the use of — more at BROOK] **1 a :** a product of plant growth (as grain, vegetables, or cotton) ⟨the ~*s* of the field⟩ **b** (1) **:** the usu. edible reproductive body of a seed plant; *esp* **:** one having a sweet pulp associated with the seed ⟨the ~ of the tree⟩ (2) **:** a succulent plant part used chiefly in a dessert or sweet course **c :** a dish, quantity, or diet of fruits ⟨please pass the ~⟩ **d :** a product of fertilization in a plant with its modified envelopes or appendages; *specif* **:** the ripened ovary of a seed plant and its contents **2 :** OFFSPRING, PROGENY **3 a :** the state of bearing fruit ⟨a tree in ~⟩ **b :** the effect or consequence of an action or operation **:** PRODUCT, RESULT ⟨the ~*s* of his labor⟩ **4** *slang* **:** a male homosexual — **fruit·ed** \-əd\ *adj*

2fruit *vi* **:** to bear fruit ~ *vt* **:** to cause to bear fruit

fruit·age \ˈfrüt-ij\ *n* **1 a :** the condition or process of bearing fruit **b :** FRUIT **2 :** the product or result of an action

fruit bat *n* **:** any of a suborder (Megachiroptera) of large Old World fruit-eating bats of warm regions — called also *flying fox*

fruit·cake \ˈfrüt-ˌkāk\ *n* **:** a rich cake containing nuts, dried or candied fruits, and spices

fruit·er·er \ˈfrüt-ər-ər\ *n* [ME, modif. of MF *fruitier,* fr. *fruit*] **:** one that deals in fruit

fruit fly *n* **:** any of various small two-winged flies whose larvae feed on fruit or decaying vegetable matter

fruit·ful \ˈfrüt-fəl\ *adj* **1 a :** yielding or producing fruit **b :** conducive to an abundant yield **2 :** abundantly productive **syn** see FERTILE **ant** unfruitful, fruitless — **fruit·ful·ly** \-fə-lē\ *adv* — **fruit·ful·ness** *n*

fruiting body *n* **:** a plant organ specialized for producing spores

fru·ition \frü-ˈish-ən\ *n* [ME *fruicioun,* fr. MF or LL; MF *fruition,* fr. LL *fruition-, fruitio,* fr. L *fruitus,* alter. of *fructus,* pp.] **1 :** pleasurable use or possession : ENJOYMENT **2** **a** : the state of bearing fruit **b** : REALIZATION, ACCOMPLISHMENT

fruit·less \ˈfrüt-ləs\ *adj* **1** : lacking or not bearing fruit **2** : productive of no good effect : UNSUCCESSFUL ***syn*** see FUTILE ***ant*** fruitful — **fruit·less·ly** *adv* — **fruit·less·ness** *n*

fruit·let \-lət\ *n* **1** : a small fruit **2** : a unit of a collective fruit

fruit sugar *n* : FRUCTOSE 2

fruity \ˈfrüt-ē\ *adj* **fruit·i·er; -est** **1** **a** : relating to or resembling a fruit **b** : having the flavor of the unfermented fruit ⟨~ wine⟩ **2** **a** : extremely effective, interesting, or enjoyable **b** : sweet or sentimental esp. to excess **3** *slang* **a** : CRAZY, SILLY **b** : HOMOSEXUAL

fru·men·ty \ˈfrü-mən-tē\ *n, pl* **-ties** [ME, fr. MF *frumentee*, fr. *frument* grain, fr. L *frumentum*, fr. *frui*] : a dish of wheat boiled in milk and usu. flavored with sugar, spice, and raisins

frump \ˈfrəmp\ *n* [prob. fr. *frumple* (to wrinkle)] **1** : a dowdy unattractive girl or woman **2** : a staid, drab, old-fashioned person — **frump·ish** \ˈfrəm-pish\ *adj*

frumpy \ˈfrəm-pē\ *adj* **frump·i·er; -est** : generally uninteresting and unattractive : DRAB, DOWDY

[1]**frus·trate** \ˈfrəs-ˌtrāt\ *vt* **frus·trat·ed; frus·trat·ing** [ME *frustraten*, fr. L *frustratus*, pp. of *frustrare* to deceive, frustrate, fr. *frustra* in error, in vain; akin to L *fraus* fraud — more at FRAUD] **1** **a** : to balk or defeat in an endeavor **b** : to induce feelings of discouragement in **2** **a** : to make ineffectual : bring to nothing ⟨nagging daily cares that ~ a man's aspirations⟩ **b** : to make invalid or of no effect : NULLIFY

syn FRUSTRATE, THWART, FOIL, BAFFLE, BALK, CIRCUMVENT, OUTWIT *shared meaning element* : to come between a person and his aim or desire or to defeat another's plan ***ant*** fulfill

[2]**frustrate** *adj* : FRUSTRATED

frus·trat·ed *adj* **1** : balked or discouraged in some endeavor or purpose : DISAPPOINTED ⟨looked upon the critics as merely ~ writers⟩ **2** : filled with a sense of frustration : feeling deep insecurity, discouragement, or dissatisfaction ⟨learned not to resort to aggressiveness when ~ —Ashley Montagu⟩

frus·trat·ing \-ˌtrāt-iŋ\ *adj* : tending to produce or characterized by frustration ⟨the bungling attempt for fourteen ~ years . . . to make democracy work —W. L. Shirer⟩ — **frus·trat·ing·ly** \-iŋ-lē\ *adv*

frus·tra·tion \(ˌ)frəs-ˈtrā-shən\ *n* **1** : the act of frustrating **2** **a** : the state or an instance of being frustrated : DISAPPOINTMENT **b** : a deep chronic sense or state of insecurity and dissatisfaction arising from unresolved problems or unfulfilled needs **3** : something that frustrates

frus·tule \ˈfrəs-(ˌ)chü(ə)l, -(ˌ)t(y)ü(ə)l\ *n* [F, fr. L *frustulum*, dim. of *frustum*] : the 2-valved siliceous shell of a diatom

frus·tum \ˈfrəs-təm\ *n, pl* **frustums** *or* **frus·ta** \-tə\ [NL, fr. L, piece, bit — more at BRUISE] : the part of a cone-shaped solid next to the base that is formed by cutting off the top by a plane parallel to the base; *also* : the part of a solid intersected between two usu. parallel planes

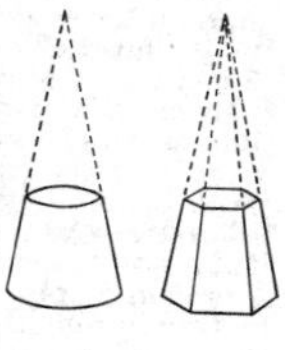

frustums

fru·tes·cent \frü-ˈtes-ᵊnt\ *adj* [L *frut*ex shrub + E *-escent*] : having or approaching the habit or appearance of a shrub : SHRUBBY

fru·ti·cose \ˈfrüt-i-ˌkōs\ *adj* [L *fruticosus*, fr. *frutic-*, *frutex* shrub; akin to OHG *broz* bud, OIr *broth* whisker] : having a shrubby bushy thallus with flattened or cylindrical branches ⟨~ lichens⟩ — compare CRUSTOSE, FOLIOSE

frwy *abbr* freeway

[1]**fry** \ˈfrī\ *vb* **fried; fry·ing** [ME *frien*, fr. OF *frire*, fr. L *frigere*; akin to Gk *phrygein* to roast, fry, Skt *bhṛjjati* he roasts] *vt* : to cook in a pan or on a griddle over a fire esp. with the use of fat **~** *vi* : to undergo frying

[2]**fry** *n, pl* **fries** **1** : a dish of something fried **2** : a social gathering or picnic where food is fried and eaten ⟨a fish ~⟩

[3]**fry** *n, pl* **fry** [ME, prob. fr. ONF *fri*, fr. OF *frier*, *froyer* to rub, spawn — more at FRAY] **1** **a** : recently hatched fishes **b** : the young of other animals **2** : very small adult fishes **3** : members of a group or class : INDIVIDUALS ⟨small ~⟩ ⟨a great part of the earth is peopled with these ~ —Katherine Mansfield⟩

fry·er \ˈfrī(-ə)r\ *n* : something intended for or used in frying: as **a** : a young chicken **b** : a deep utensil for frying foods

frying pan *n* : a metal pan with a handle that is used for frying foods — called also *fry pan* — **out of the frying pan into the fire** : clear of one difficulty only to fall into a greater one

FS *abbr* **1** filmstrip **2** Foreign Service

FSA *abbr* **1** Fellow of the Society of Actuaries **2** Fellow of the Society of Antiquaries

FSH *abbr* follicle-stimulating hormone

FSLIC *abbr* Federal Savings and Loan Insurance Corporation

FSP *abbr* Food Stamp Program

f–stop \ˈef-ˌstäp\ *n* : a camera lens aperture setting indicated by an f-number

ft *abbr* **1** feet; foot **2** fort

FT *abbr* free throw

FTC *abbr* Federal Trade Commission

fth *abbr* fathom

ft lb *abbr* foot-pound

F_2 layer \ˈef-ˈtü-\ *n* : the upper of the two layers into which the F region of the ionosphere splits in the daytime at varying heights from about 150 to 250 miles above the earth

fubsy \ˈfəb-zē\ *adj* [obs. E *fubs* (chubby person)] : being chubby and somewhat squat

fuch·sia \ˈfyü-shə\ *n* [NL, genus name, fr. Leonhard *Fuchs* †1566 G botanist] **1** : any of a genus (*Fuchsia*) of decorative shrubs of the evening-primrose family having showy nodding flowers usu. in deep pinks, reds, and purples **2** : a vivid reddish purple

fuch·sine *or* **fuch·sin** \ˈfyük-sən, -ˌsēn\ *n* [F *fuchsine*, prob. fr. NL *Fuchsia*; fr. its color] : a dye that is produced by oxidation of a mixture of aniline and toluidines and yields a brilliant bluish red

[1]**fuck** \ˈfək\ *vb* [perh. of Scand origin; akin to Norw dial. *fukka* to copulate, Sw dial. *focka* to copulate, strike, push, *fock* penis; perh. akin to L *pugnus* fist, *pungere* to prick, sting, Gk *pygmē* fist] *vi* : COPULATE — usu. considered obscene; sometimes used in the present participle as a meaningless intensive **~** *vt* : to engage in coitus with — usu. considered obscene

[2]**fuck** *n* : an act of copulation — usu. considered obscene

[1]**fu·coid** \ˈfyü-ˌkȯid\ *adj* : relating to or resembling the rockweeds

[2]**fucoid** *n* : a fucoid seaweed or fossil

fu·cose \ˈfyü-ˌkōs, -ˌkōz\ *n* [ISV *fuc-* (fr. L *fucus*) + *-ose*] : an aldose sugar that occurs in bound form in the dextrorotatory D-form in various glycosides and in the levorotatory L-form in some brown algae and in mammalian polysaccharides typical of some blood groups

fu·co·xan·thin \ˌfyü-kō-ˈzan-thən\ *n* : a brown carotenoid pigment $C_{40}H_{60}O_6$ occurring esp. in the ova of brown algae

fu·cus \ˈfyü-kəs\ *n* [L, archil, rouge, fr. Gk *phykos* seaweed, archil, rouge, of Sem origin; akin to Heb *pūkh* antimony used as a cosmetic] **1** *obs* : a face paint **2** [NL, genus name, fr. L] : any of a genus (*Fucus*) of cartilaginous brown algae used in the kelp industry; *broadly* : any of various brown algae

fud \ˈfəd\ *n* : FUDDY-DUDDY

fud·dle \ˈfəd-ᵊl\ *vb* **fud·dled; fud·dling** \ˈfəd-liŋ, -ᵊl-iŋ\ [origin unknown] *vi* : to take part in a drinking bout : TIPPLE **~** *vt* **1** : to make drunk : INTOXICATE **2** : to make confused : MUDDLE

fud·dy–dud·dy \ˈfəd-ē-ˌdəd-ē\ *n, pl* **-dies** [perh. redupl. of Sc *fuddy* short-tailed animal, tail, fr. *fud* tail] : one who is old-fashioned, pompous, unimaginative, or concerned about trifles — **fuddy–duddy** *adj*

[1]**fudge** \ˈfəj\ *vb* **fudged; fudg·ing** [origin unknown] *vi* **1** : to exceed the proper bounds or limits of something ⟨feel that the author has *fudged* a little on the . . . rules for crime fiction —*Newsweek*⟩; *also* : CHEAT ⟨*fudging* on an exam⟩ **2** : to fail to live up to something : fail to perform as expected **3** : to avoid commitment : HEDGE ⟨the government's tendency to ~ on delicate matters of policy —Claire Sterling⟩ **~** *vt* **1** **a** : to devise as a substitute or without adequate basis : FAKE ⟨any chap . . . who could ~ up a yarn like that —Thomas Wood †1950⟩ **b** : EXAGGERATE, FALSIFY ⟨*fudged* the figures⟩ **2** : to fail to come to grips with ⟨has too often blessed war, condoned injustice, *fudged* the racial issue —M. A. Kapp⟩

[2]**fudge** *n* **1** : foolish nonsense — often used interjectionally to express annoyance, disappointment, or disbelief **2** : a soft creamy candy made typically of sugar, milk, butter, and flavoring

Fue·gian \f(y)ü-ˈā-gē-ən, -ˈā-j(ē-)ən\ *n* : a member of an American Indian people of Tierra del Fuego

[1]**fu·el** \ˈfyü(-ə)l\ *n, often attrib* [ME *fewel*, fr. OF *fouaille*, fr. *feu* fire, fr. LL *focus*, fr. L, hearth — more at FOCUS] **1** **a** : a material used to produce heat or power by burning **b** : nutritive material **c** : a material from which atomic energy can be liberated esp. in a reactor **2** : a source of sustenance or incentive

[2]**fuel** *vb* **-eled** *or* **-elled; -el·ing** *or* **-el·ling** *vt* **1** : to provide with fuel **2** : SUPPORT, STIMULATE ⟨this movement is ~*ed* by massive grants-in-aid —Allen Schick⟩ **~** *vi* : to take in fuel — often used with *up*

fuel cell *n* : a cell that continuously changes the chemical energy of a fuel and oxidant to electrical energy

fu·el·er \ˈfyü-(ə-)lər\ *n* : a dragster that uses specially blended fuel rather than gasoline

fuel oil *n* : an oil that is used for fuel and that usu. has a higher flash point than kerosene

[1]**fug** \ˈfəg\ *n* [prob. alter. of [2]*fog*] : an odorous emanation; *esp* : the stuffy atmosphere of a poorly ventilated space — **fug·gy** \ˈfəg-ē\ *adj*

[2]**fug** *vb* **fugged; fug·ging** *vi* : to loll indoors in a stuffy atmosphere **~** *vt* : to make stuffy and odorous

fu·ga·cious \fyü-ˈgā-shəs\ *adj* [L *fugac-*, *fugax*, fr. *fugere*] **1** : lasting a short time : EVANESCENT **2** : disappearing before the usual time — used chiefly of plant parts (as stipules) other than floral organs — **fu·gac·i·ty** \-ˈgas-ət-ē\ *n*

fu·gal \ˈfyü-gəl\ *adj* : of, relating to, or being in the style of a musical fugue — **fu·gal·ly** \-gə-lē\ *adv*

-fuge \ˌfyüj\ *n comb form* [F, fr. LL *-fuga*, fr. L *fugare* to put to flight, fr. *fuga*] : one that drives away ⟨insecti*fuge*⟩

[1]**fu·gi·tive** \ˈfyü-jət-iv\ *adj* [ME, fr. MF & L; MF *fugitif*, fr. L *fugitivus*, fr. *fugitus*, pp. of *fugere* to flee; akin to Gk *pheugein* to flee and prob. to OHG *biogan* to bend — more at BOW] **1** : running away or intending flight ⟨~ slave⟩ ⟨~ debtor⟩ **2** : moving from place to place : WANDERING **3** **a** : being of short duration **b** : difficult to grasp or retain : ELUSIVE **c** : likely to evaporate, deteriorate, change, fade, or disappear **4** : being of transient interest ***syn*** see TRANSIENT — **fu·gi·tive·ly** *adv* — **fu·gi·tive·ness** *n*

[2]**fugitive** *n* **1** : one who flees or tries to escape; *specif* : REFUGEE **2** : something elusive or hard to find

fu·gle \ˈfyü-gəl\ *vi* [back-formation fr. *fugleman*] *archaic* : to act as fugleman

fu·gle·man \ˈfyü-gəl-mən\ *n* [modif. of G *flügelmann*, fr. *flügel* wing + *mann* man] **1** : a trained soldier formerly posted in front of a line of men at drill to serve as a model in their exercises **2** : one who heads a group; *specif* : a political manager

fugue \ˈfyüg\ *n* [prob. fr. It *fuga* flight, fugue, fr. L, flight, fr. *fugere*] **1** : a polyphonic musical composition in which one or two themes are repeated or imitated by successively entering voices and contrapuntally developed in a continuous interweaving of the voice parts **2** : a disturbed state of consciousness in which the one affected performs acts of which he appears to be conscious but of which on recovery he has no recollection — **fugue** *vb* — **fugu·ist** \'fyü-gəst\ *n*

füh·rer *or* **fueh·rer** \'fyu̇r-ər, 'fir-\ *n* [G *führer* leader, guide, fr. MHG *vüerer* bearer, fr. *vüeren* to lead, bear, fr. OHG *fuoren* to lead; akin to OE *faran* to go — more at FARE] **1 a :** LEADER 2c(5) — used chiefly of the leader of the German Nazis **b :** a lesser Nazi party official **2 :** a leader exercising tyrannical authority

fu·ji \'f(y)ü-(,)jē\ *n* [*Fuji* mountain, Japan] **:** a spun silk clothing fabric in plain weave orig. made in Japan

1-ful \fəl\ *adj suffix, sometimes* **-ful·ler;** *sometimes* **-ful·lest** [ME, fr. OE, fr. *full,* adj] **1 :** full of ⟨event*ful*⟩ **2 :** characterized by ⟨peace*ful*⟩ **3 :** having the qualities of ⟨master*ful*⟩ **4 :** tending, given, or liable to ⟨mourn*ful*⟩

2-ful \,fu̇l\ *n suffix* **:** number or quantity that fills or would fill ⟨room*ful*⟩

Fu·la *or* **Fu·lah** \'fü-lə\ *n, pl* **Fula** *or* **Fulas** *or* **Fulah** *or* **Fulahs** **1 :** a Sudanese people of African Negroid stock and Mediterranean Caucasoid admixture **2 :** a member of the Fula people

Fu·la·ni \'fü-,län-ē, fü-'\ *n, pl* **Fulani** *or* **Fulanis** **1 a :** FULA 1; *esp* **:** the Fula of northern Nigeria and adjacent areas **b :** a member of the Fulani people **2 :** the language of the Fula people

ful·crum \'fu̇l-krəm, 'fəl-\ *n, pl* **fulcrums** *or* **ful·cra** \-krə\ [LL, fr. L, bedpost, fr. *fulcire* to prop — more at BALK] **1 a :** PROP; *specif* **:** the support about which a lever turns **b :** one that supplies capability for action **2 :** a part of an animal that serves as a hinge or support

ful·fill *or* **ful·fil** \fu̇l-'fil\ *vt* **ful·filled; ful·fill·ing** [ME *fulfillen,* fr. OE *fullfyllan,* fr. *full* + *fyllan* to fill] **1** *archaic* **:** to make full **:** FILL ⟨her subtle, warm, and golden breath . . . ~*s* him with beatitude —Alfred Tennyson⟩ **2 a :** to put into effect **b :** to bring to an end **c :** to measure up to **:** SATISFY **3 a :** to convert into reality **b :** to develop the full potentialities of ***syn*** see PERFORM, SATISFY — **ful·fill·er** *n* — **ful·fill·ment** \-mənt\ *n*

ful·gent \'fu̇l-jənt, 'fəl-\ *adj* [ME, fr. L *fulgent-, fulgens,* prp. of *fulgēre* to shine; akin to L *flagrare* to burn — more at BLACK] **:** dazzlingly bright — **ful·gent·ly** *adv*

ful·gu·rant \'fu̇l-g(y)ə-rənt, 'fu̇l-jə-, 'fəl-\ *adj* **:** flashing like lightning **:** DAZZLING

ful·gu·rate \-,rāt\ *vt* **-rat·ed; -rat·ing** [L *fulguratus,* pp. of *fulgurare* to flash with lightning, fr. *fulgur* lightning, fr. *fulgēre*] **:** to emit flashes of ⟨blue eyes that *fulgurated* . . . terror, love, or hate —*New Yorker*⟩ — **ful·gu·ra·tion** \,fu̇l-g(y)ə-'rā-shən, ,fu̇l-jə-, ,fəl-\ *n*

ful·gu·rite \'fu̇l-g(y)ə-,rīt, 'fu̇l-jə-, 'fəl-\ *n* [ISV, fr. L *fulgur*] **:** an often tubular vitrified crust produced by the fusion of sand or rock by lightning

ful·gu·rous \-rəs\ *adj* [L *fulgur*] **:** emitting flashes of or like lightning

ful·ham \'fu̇l-əm\ *n* [alter. of earlier *fullan,* perh. fr. *full* + *one*] *archaic* **:** a loaded die

fu·lig·i·nous \fyü-'lij-ə-nəs\ *adj* [LL *fuliginosus,* fr. L *fuligin-, fuligo* soot; akin to L *fumus* smoke — more at FUME] **1 a :** SOOTY **b :** OBSCURE, MURKY **2 :** having a dark or dusky color — **fu·lig·i·nous·ly** *adv*

1full \'fu̇l\ *adj* [ME, fr. OE; akin to OHG *fol* full, L *plenus* full, *plēre* to fill, Gk *plērēs* full, *plēthein* to be full] **1 :** containing as much or as many as is possible or normal ⟨a bin ~ of corn⟩ **2 a :** complete esp. in detail, number, or duration ⟨a ~ report⟩ ⟨his ~ share⟩ ⟨gone a ~ hour⟩ **b :** lacking restraint, check, or qualification ⟨~ retreat⟩ ⟨~ support⟩ **c :** having all distinguishing characteristics **:** enjoying all authorized rights and privileges ⟨~ member⟩ ⟨~ professor⟩ **d :** not lacking in any essential **:** PERFECT ⟨in ~ control of his senses⟩ **3 a :** being at the highest or greatest degree **:** MAXIMUM ⟨~ strength⟩ ⟨~ speed⟩ **b :** being at the height of development ⟨~ bloom⟩ **4 :** rounded in outline ⟨a ~ figure⟩ **5 a :** possessing or containing a great number or amount — used with *of* ⟨a room ~ of pictures⟩ **b :** having an abundance of material esp. in the form of gathered, pleated, or flared parts ⟨a ~ skirt⟩ **c :** rich in experience ⟨a ~ life⟩ **6 a :** satisfied esp. with food or drink **b :** large enough to satisfy ⟨a ~ meal⟩ **7** *archaic* **:** completely weary ⟨I am ~ of the burnt offerings of rams . . . and I delight not in the blood of bullocks, or of lambs —Isa 1:11 (AV)⟩ **8 :** having both parents in common ⟨~ sisters⟩ **9 :** having volume or depth of sound ⟨~ tones⟩ **10 :** completely occupied esp. with a thought or plan ⟨~ of his own concerns⟩ **11 :** possessing a rich or pronounced quality ⟨a food of ~ flavor⟩ **12** — used as an intensive ⟨wound up winning by a ~ four strokes —William Johnson⟩ — **full·ness** *also* **ful·ness** \'fu̇l-nəs\ *n*

syn FULL, COMPLETE, PLENARY, REPLETE *shared meaning element* **:** containing all that is wanted or needed or possible ***ant*** empty

2full *adv* **1 a :** VERY, EXTREMELY ⟨knew ~ well he had lied to me⟩ **1 b :** ENTIRELY ⟨swung ~ around —Morley Callaghan⟩ **2 a :** EXACTLY ⟨~ in the center of the sacred wood —Joseph Addison⟩ **b :** STRAIGHT, SQUARELY ⟨hit him ~ in the face⟩

3full *n* **1 a :** the utmost extent ⟨enjoy to the ~⟩ **b :** the highest or fullest state or degree ⟨the ~ of the moon⟩ **2 :** the requisite or complete amount ⟨paid in ~⟩

4full *vi, of the moon* **:** to become full ~ *vt* **:** to make full in sewing

5full *vt* [ME *fullen,* fr. MF *fouler,* fr. (assumed) VL *fullare,* fr. L *fullo* fuller] **:** to shrink and thicken (woolen cloth) by moistening, heating, and pressing

full·back \'fu̇l-,bak\ *n* **1 :** an offensive football back used primarily for line plunges and blocking **2 :** a primarily defensive player usu. stationed nearest the defended goal (as in soccer, field hockey, or rugby)

full blood *n* **1** \'fu̇l-'bləd\ **:** descent from parents both of one pure breed **2** \-,bləd\ **:** an individual of full blood

full–blood·ed \'fu̇l-'bləd-əd\ *adj* **1 :** of unmixed ancestry **:** PUREBRED **2 :** FLORID, RUDDY ⟨of ~ face⟩ **3 :** FORCEFUL ⟨~ prose style⟩ **4 a :** lacking no particulars **:** GENUINE **b :** containing fullness of substance **:** RICH — **full–blood·ed·ness** *n*

full–blown \-'blōn\ *adj* **1 a :** being at the height of bloom **b :** fully mature **2 :** possessing all the usual or necessary features ⟨now at least a general philosophy, if not a ~ ideology, is emerging —W. H. Jones⟩

full–bod·ied \-'bäd-ēd\ *adj* **1 :** having a large body **2 :** marked by richness and fullness esp. of flavor ⟨a ~ wine⟩ **3 :** having importance, significance, or meaningfulness ⟨~ study of literature⟩

full circle *adv* **:** through a series of developments that lead back to the original source, position, or situation or to a complete reversal of the original position — usu. used in the phrase *come full circle*

full–dress *adj* **1 :** complete down to the last formal detail ⟨a ~ rehearsal⟩ **2 :** carried out by all possible means

full dress *n* **:** the style of dress prescribed for ceremonial or formal social occasions

1full·er \'fu̇l-ər\ *n* **:** one that fulls cloth

2full·er \'fu̇l-ər\ *n* [*fuller* (to form a groove in)] **:** a blacksmithing hammer for grooving and spreading iron

fuller's earth *n* **:** an earthy substance that consists chiefly of clay mineral but lacks plasticity and that is used as an adsorbent, a filter medium, and a carrier for catalysts

ful·ler's teasel *n* **:** TEASEL 1a

full–fash·ioned \'fu̇l-'fash-ənd\ *adj* **:** employing or produced by a knitting process for shaping to conform to body lines ⟨~ hosiery⟩

full–fledged \-'flejd\ *adj* **1 :** fully developed **:** TOTAL, COMPLETE ⟨a ~ debate⟩ **2 :** having full plumage **3 :** having attained complete status ⟨~ lawyer⟩

full house *n* **:** a poker hand containing three of a kind and a pair — see POKER illustration

full–length \'fu̇l-'leŋ(k)th\ *adj* **1 :** showing or adapted to the entire length esp. of the human figure ⟨a ~ mirror⟩ ⟨a ~ dress⟩ **2 :** having a length as great as that which is normal or standard for an object of its kind ⟨a ~ play⟩

full marks *n pl, Brit* **:** due credit or commendation

full moon *n* **:** the moon with its whole apparent disk illuminated

full·mouthed \'fu̇l-'mau̇t͟hd, -'mau̇tht\ *adj* **1 :** having a full mouth; *esp* **:** having a full complement of teeth **2 :** uttered with full power or sound **:** LOUD

full nelson *n* **:** a wrestling hold in which both arms are thrust under the corresponding arms of an opponent and the hands clasped behind the opponent's head — compare HALF NELSON

full–scale \-'skā(ə)l\ *adj* **1 :** identical to an original in proportion and size ⟨~ drawing⟩ **2 a :** involving full use of available resources ⟨a ~ biography⟩ **b :** TOTAL, COMPLETE ⟨a ~ musical renaissance —*Current Biog.*⟩

full–size \-'sīz\ *adj* **1 :** having the usual or normal size of its kind **2 :** having the dimensions 54 inches by 75 inches — used of a bed; compare KING-SIZE, QUEEN-SIZE, TWIN-SIZE

full stop *n* **:** PERIOD 4a

full tilt *adv* [2*tilt*] **:** at high speed

full–time *adj* **:** employed for or involving full time ⟨~ employees⟩ — **full–time** *adv*

full time *n* **:** the amount of time considered the normal or standard amount for working during a given period

ful·ly \'fu̇l-(l)ē\ *adv* **1 :** in a full manner or degree **:** COMPLETELY **2 :** at least ⟨~ nine tenths of us⟩

ful·mar \'fu̇l-mər, -,mär\ *n* [of Scand origin; akin to ON *fūlmār* fulmar, fr. *fūll* foul + *mār* gull] **:** an arctic seabird (*Fulmarus glacialis*) closely related to the petrels; *also* **:** any of several related birds of southern seas

ful·mi·nant \'fu̇l-mə-nənt, 'fəl-\ *adj* **:** FULMINATING 3

1ful·mi·nate \-,nāt\ *vb* **-nat·ed; -nat·ing** [ME *fulminaten,* fr. ML *fulminatus,* pp. of *fulminare,* fr. L, to flash with lightning, strike with lightning, fr. *fulmin-, fulmen* lightning; akin to L *flagrare* to burn — more at BLACK] *vt* **1 :** to utter or send out with denunciation **2 :** to cause to explode ~ *vi* **1 :** to send forth censures or invectives **2 :** to make a sudden loud noise **:** EXPLODE — **ful·mi·na·tion** \,fu̇l-mə-'nā-shən, ,fəl-\ *n* — **ful·mi·na·tor** \'fu̇l-mə-,nāt-ər, 'fəl-\ *n*

2fulminate *n* [*fulminic acid*] **:** an often explosive salt (as mercury fulminate) containing the radical CNO

ful·mi·nat·ing *adj* **1 :** exploding with a vivid flash **2 :** hurling denunciations or menaces **3 :** coming on suddenly with great severity ⟨~ infection⟩

ful·mine \'fu̇l-mən, 'fəl-\ *vb, archaic* **:** FULMINATE

ful·some \'fu̇l-səm\ *adj* [ME *fulsom* copious, cloying, fr. *full* + *-som* -some] **1 :** characterized by abundance **:** COPIOUS ⟨describes in ~ detail —G. N. Shuster⟩ **2 :** offensive to the senses or to moral or aesthetic sensibility **:** DISGUSTING **3 a :** excessively complimentary or flattering **:** LAVISH ⟨an admiration whose extent I did not express, lest I be thought ~ —A. J. Liebling⟩ **b :** OBSEQUIOUS **4 :** exceeding the bounds of good taste **:** OVERDONE ⟨the ~ chromium glitter of the escalators dominating the central hall —Lewis Mumford⟩ — **ful·some·ly** *adv* — **ful·some·ness** *n*

ful·vous \'fu̇l-vəs, 'fəl-\ *adj* [L *fulvus;* perh. akin to L *flavus* yellow — more at BLUE] **:** of a dull brownish yellow **:** TAWNY

Fu Man·chu mustache \,fü-(,)man-'chü-\ *n* [*Fu Manchu,* Chinese villain in stories by "Sax Rohmer" (A. S. Ward †1955)] **:** a long mustache with ends that turn down to the chin

fu·ma·rase \'fyü-mə-,rās, -,rāz\ *n* **:** an enzyme that catalyzes the interconversion (as in the Krebs cycle) of fumaric acid and malic acid or their salts

fu·ma·rate \-,rāt\ *n* **:** a salt or ester of fumaric acid

fu·mar·ic acid \fyü-,mar-ik-\ *n* [ISV, fr. NL *Fumaria,* genus of herbs, fr. LL, fumitory, fr. L *fumus*] **:** a crystalline acid $C_4H_4O_4$ found in various plants or made synthetically and used esp. in making resins

fu·ma·role \'fyü-mə-,rōl\ *n* [It *fumarola,* modif. of LL *fumariolum,* fr. L *fumarium* smoke chamber for aging wine, fr. *fumus* fume] **:** a hole in a volcanic region from which hot gases and vapors issue — **fu·ma·rol·ic** \,fyü-mə-'rō-lik\ *adj*

1fum·ble \'fəm-bəl\ *vb* **fum·bled; fum·bling** \-b(ə-)liŋ\ [prob. of Scand origin; akin to Sw *fumla* to fumble] *vi* **1 a :** to grope for or handle something clumsily or aimlessly **b :** to make awkward attempts to do or find something ⟨*fumbled* in his pocket for a coin⟩ **c :** to search by trial and error **d :** BLUNDER **2 :** to feel one's way or move awkwardly **3 a :** to drop or juggle or fail to play cleanly a grounder **b :** to lose hold of a football while handling or running with it ~ *vt* **1 :** to bring about by clumsy manipulation

2 a : to feel or handle clu... way : BUNGLE 3 : to make ... : MISPLAY ⟨~ a grounder ... handling or running — \-b(ə-)liŋ-lē\ adv
²fumble n 1 : an ac...
¹fume \ˈfyüm\ n [... men to be fragra... por, or gas esp. ... : an often no... : something ... times his h... thew Arnnes ... used in ...
²fume ...

...il- b : to deal with in a blundering ...es way) in a clumsy manner 4 a ...: to lose hold of (a football) while ...**-bler** \-b(ə-)lər\ n — **fum·bling·ly**

...ance of fumbling 2 : a fumbled ball ...F *fum,* fr. L *fumus;* akin to OHG *tou*-...*mos* mind, spirit] 1 a : a smoke, va-...ting or offensive ⟨engine exhaust ~*s*⟩ b ...ension of particles in a gas (as air) 2 ...tion) that impairs one's reasoning ⟨some-...tle hot with the ~*s* of patriotism —Mat-...state of excited irritation or anger — usu. ...*fume* — **fumy** \ˈfyü-mē\ *adj*
...**-ing** *vt* 1 : to expose to or treat with fumes ...⟨*fuming* thick black smoke⟩ ~ *vi* 1 a ...: to be in a state of excited irritation or anger ...*ned* over the delay⟩ 2 : to rise in or as if in

2 : ...i-gənt\ n : a substance used in fumigating
: ...nə-ˌgāt\ *vt* **-gat·ed; -gat·ing** [L *fumigatus,* pp. of ...*mus* + *-igare* (akin to L *agere* to drive) — more at ...ly smoke, vapor, or gas to esp. for the purpose of of destroying pests — **fu·mi·ga·tion** \ˌfyü-mə-ˈgā-... **mi·ga·tor** \ˈfyü-mə-ˌgāt-ər\ n
...yü-mə-ˌtōr-ē, -ˌtȯr-\ n [ME *fumeterre,* fr. MF, fr. ML ..., lit., smoke of the earth, fr. L *fumus* + *terrae,* gen. of ... — more at TERRACE] : any of a genus (*Fumaria* of the ...nariaceae, the fumitory family) of erect or climbing ... : a common European herb (*F. officinalis*)
... \ n [E dial. *fun* to hoax, perh. alter. of ME *fonnen,* fr. ...pe] 1 : what provides amusement or enjoyment; *specif* ...l often boisterous action or speech ⟨a lively person full of ...⟩ 2 : a mood for finding or making amusement ⟨the teasing was all in ~⟩ 3 a : AMUSEMENT, ENJOYMENT ⟨sickness takes all the ~ out of life⟩ b : derisive jest : SPORT, RIDICULE ⟨made him a figure of ~⟩ 4 : violent or excited activity or argument ⟨let a snake loose in the classroom; then the ~ began⟩
syn FUN, JEST, SPORT, GAME, PLAY *shared meaning element* : action or speech that provides amusement or arouses laughter
²**fun** *vi* **funned; fun·ning** : to indulge in banter or play : JOKE
³**fun** *adj* : providing entertainment, amusement, or enjoyment ⟨a ~ party⟩ ⟨a ~ person to be with⟩
fu·nam·bu·lism \fyu̇-ˈnam-byə-ˌliz-əm\ n [L *funambulus* rope-walker, fr. *funis* rope + *ambulare* to walk] 1 : tightrope walking 2 : a show esp. of mental agility — **fu·nam·bu·list** \-ləst\ n
fun and games *n pl but sing or pl in constr* : light amusement : DIVERSION
¹**func·tion** \ˈfəŋ(k)-shən\ n [L *function-, functio* performance, fr. *functus,* pp. of *fungi* to perform; prob. akin to Skt *bhuṅkte* he enjoys] 1 : professional or official position : OCCUPATION 2 : the action for which a person or thing is specially fitted or used or for which a thing exists 3 : one of a group of related actions contributing to a larger action; *esp* : the normal and specific contribution of a bodily part to the economy of a living organism 4 : an impressive, elaborate, or formal ceremony or social gathering 5 a : a mathematical correspondence that assigns exactly one element of one set to each element of the same or another set b : a quality, trait, or fact dependent on and varying with another c : SENTENTIAL FUNCTION — **func·tion·less** \-ləs\ *adj*
syn 1 FUNCTION, OFFICE, DUTY, PROVINCE *shared meaning element* : the acts or operations expected of a person or thing. FUNCTION, referable to anything living, material, or constructed, implies a definite end or purpose that the one in question serves or a particular kind of work it is intended to perform ⟨the *function* of language is two-fold: to communicate emotion and to give information —Aldous Huxley⟩ ⟨the *function* of a plumbing system basically is to provide and carry away water⟩ OFFICE is typically applied to the function or service expected of a person by reason of his trade or profession or his special relationship to others ⟨it is the proper *office* of a parent to guide and correct his children⟩ DUTY applies to a task or responsibility imposed by one's occupation, rank, status, or calling ⟨the new cook performed her *duties* well⟩ ⟨it is the judicial *duty* of the court, to examine the whole case —R. B. Taney⟩ PROVINCE applies to a function, office, or duty that naturally or logically falls to one ⟨nursing does not belong to a man; it is not his *province* —Jane Austen⟩
2 see POWER
²**function** *vi* **func·tioned; func·tion·ing** \-sh(ə-)niŋ\ 1 : to have a function : SERVE ⟨an attributive noun ~*s* as an adjective⟩ 2 : to be in action : OPERATE ⟨a government ~*s* through numerous divisions⟩
func·tion·al \ˈfəŋ(k)-shnəl, -shən-ᵊl\ *adj* 1 a : of, connected with, or being a function b : affecting physiological or psychological functions but not organic structure ⟨~ heart disease⟩ 2 : used to contribute to the development or maintenance of a larger whole ⟨~ and practical school courses⟩; *also* : designed or developed chiefly from the point of view of use ⟨~ clothing⟩ 3 : performing or able to perform a regular function 4 : placing related functions (as in an industry) under the direction of a specialist — **func·tion·al·ly** \-ē\ *adv*
functional calculus n : PREDICATE CALCULUS
functional group n : a characteristic reactive unit of a chemical compound
functional illiterate n : a person having had some schooling but not meeting a minimum standard of literacy
func·tion·al·ism \ˈfəŋ(k)-shnə-ˌliz-əm, -shən-ᵊl-ˌiz-\ n 1 : a philosophy of design (as in architecture) holding that form should be adapted to use, material, and structure 2 : a theory that stresses the interdependence of the patterns and institutions of a society and their interaction in maintaining cultural and social unity 3 : a doctrine or practice that emphasizes practical utility or functional relations — **func·tion·al·ist** \-shnə-ləst, -shən-ᵊl-əst\ n — **functionalist** *or* **func·tion·al·is·tic** \ˌfəŋ(k)-shnə-ˈlis-tik, -shən-ᵊl-ˈis-\ *adj*
functional shift n : the process by which a word or form comes to be used in a second or third grammatical function ⟨the *functional shift* of "go" from verb to adjective as in "all systems are go"⟩
func·tion·ary \ˈfəŋ(k)-shə-ˌner-ē\ n, *pl* **-ar·ies** 1 : one who serves in a certain function 2 : one holding office in a government or political party
function word n : a word (as a preposition, auxiliary verb, or conjunction) expressing primarily grammatical relationship
func·tor \ˈfəŋ(k)-tər\ n 1 : something that performs a function or an operation 2 : a sign for a nonpropositional function
¹**fund** \ˈfənd\ n [L *fundus* bottom, piece of landed property — more at BOTTOM] 1 : an available quantity of material or intangible resources : SUPPLY 2 a : a sum of money or other resources whose principal or interest is set apart for a specific objective b : money on deposit on which checks or drafts can be drawn — usu. used in pl. c : CAPITAL d *pl* : the stock of the British national debt — usu. used with *the* 3 *pl* : available pecuniary resources 4 : an organization administering a special fund
²**fund** *vt* 1 a : to make provision of resources for discharging the interest or principal of b : to provide funds for ⟨a science program federally ~*ed*⟩ 2 : to place in a fund : ACCUMULATE 3 : to convert into a debt that is payable either at a distant date or at no definite date and that bears a fixed interest ⟨~ a floating debt⟩
³**fund** *abbr* fundamental
fun·da·ment \ˈfən-də-mənt\ n [ME, fr. OF *fondement,* fr. L *fundamentum,* fr. *fundare* to found, fr. *fundus*] 1 a : the base on which a structure is erected b : an underlying ground, theory, or principle 2 a : BUTTOCKS b : ANUS 3 : the part of a land surface that has not been altered by human activities
¹**fun·da·men·tal** \ˌfən-də-ˈment-ᵊl\ *adj* 1 a : serving as an original or generating source : PRIMARY ⟨a discovery ~ to scientific progress⟩ b : serving as a basis supporting existence or determining essential structure or function : BASIC 2 a : of or relating to essential structure, function, or facts : RADICAL ⟨~ change⟩; *specif* : of or dealing with general principles rather than practical application ⟨~ science⟩ b : adhering to fundamentalism 3 a *of a musical chord or its position* : having the root in the bass b : of, relating to, or produced by the lowest component of a complex vibration 4 : of central importance : PRINCIPAL ⟨~ purpose⟩ 5 : belonging to one's innate or ingrained characteristics : DEEP-ROOTED ⟨hard to spoil his ~ good humor⟩ ***syn*** see ESSENTIAL — **fun·da·men·tal·ly** \-ᵊl-ē\ *adv*
²**fundamental** n 1 : something fundamental; *esp* : one of the minimum constituents without which a thing or a system would not be what it is 2 a : the prime tone of a harmonic series b : the root of a chord 3 : the harmonic component of a complex wave that has the lowest frequency and commonly the greatest amplitude
fun·da·men·tal·ism \-ᵊl-ˌiz-əm\ n 1 a *often cap* : a movement in 20th century Protestantism emphasizing the literally interpreted Bible as fundamental to Christian life and teaching b : the beliefs of this movement c : adherence to such beliefs 2 : a movement or attitude stressing strict and literal adherence to a set of basic principles
fun·da·men·tal·ist \-ᵊl-əst\ n : an adherent of fundamentalism — **fundamentalist** *adj* — **fun·da·men·tal·is·tic** \-ˌment-ᵊl-ˈis-tik\ *adj*
fundamental law n : the organic or basic law of a political unit a... distinguished from legislative acts; *specif* : CONSTITUTION
fundamental particle n : ELEMENTARY PARTICLE
fundamental tissue n : plant tissue other than dermal and vasc... lar tissues that consists typically of relatively undifferentiated p... enchymatous and supportive cells
fun·dic \ˈfən-dik\ *adj* : of or relating to a fundus
fun·dus \ˈfən-dəs\ n, *pl* **fun·di** \-ˌdī, -ˌdē\ [NL, fr. L, bottom] : bottom of or part opposite the aperture of the internal surface ... hollow organ: as a : the greater curvature of the stomach ... : the lower back part of the bladder c : the large upper end o... uterus d : the part of the eye opposite the pupil
¹**fu·ner·al** \ˈfyün-(ə-)rəl\ *adj* [ME, fr. LL *funeralis,* fr. L *fu*... *funus* funeral (n.); perh. akin to ON *deyja* to die — more at DI... : of, relating to, or constituting a funeral 2 : FUNEREAL 2
²**funeral** n 1 : the observances held for a dead person usu. b... burial or cremation 2 *chiefly dial* : a funeral sermon 3 : ... neral party in transit 4 : an end of something's existence ... matter of concern to one : RESPONSIBILITY ⟨if you get lost ... desert, that's your ~⟩
funeral director n : one whose profession is the managem... funerals and who is usu. an embalmer
funeral home n : an establishment with facilities for the p... tion of the dead for burial or cremation, for the viewing ... body, and for funerals — called also *funeral parlor*
fu·ner·ary \ˈfyü-nə-ˌrer-ē\ *adj* : of, used for, or associat... burial ⟨a pharaoh's ~ chamber⟩
fu·ne·re·al \fyu̇-ˈnir-ē-əl\ *adj* [L *funereus,* fr. *funer-, funus* ... or relating to a funeral 2 : befitting or suggesting a fune... solemnity⟩ — **fu·ne·re·al·ly** \-ə-lē\ *adv*
fun·fair \ˈfən-ˌfa(ə)r, -ˌfe(ə)r\ n, *chiefly Brit* : AMUSEMENT P...
fun·gal \ˈfəŋ-gəl\ *adj* : FUNGOUS
fungi- *comb form* [L *fungus*] : fungus ⟨*fungi*form⟩
¹**fun·gi·ble** \ˈfən-jə-bəl\ n : something that is fungible — ... in pl.
²**fungible** *adj* [NL *fungibilis,* fr. L *fungi* to perform — ... FUNCTION] 1 : of such a kind or nature that one specim...

ə abut	ᵊ kitten	ər further	a back	ā bake	
au̇ out	ch chin	e less	ē easy	g gift	i t...
j joke	ŋ sing	ō flow	ȯ flaw	ȯi coin	th th...
ü loot	u̇ foot	y yet	yü few	yu̇ furious	

may be used in place of another specimen or equal part in the satisfaction of an obligation **2** : INTERCHANGEABLE — **fun·gi·bil·i·ty**
\ˌfən-jə-ˈbil-ət-ē\ *n*

fun·gi·cid·al \ˌfən-jə-ˈsid-ᵊl, ˌfən-gə-\ *adj* : destroying fungi; *broadly*
: inhibiting the growth of fungi — **fun·gi·cid·al·ly** \-ᵊl-ē\ *adv*

fun·gi·cide \ˈfən-jə-ˌsid, ˈfən-gə-\ *n* [ISV] : an agent that destroys
fungi or inhibits their growth

fun·gi·form \ˈfən-jə-ˌform, ˈfən-gə-\ *adj* : shaped like a mushroom

fun·go \ˈfən-(ˌ)gō\ *n, pl* **fungoes** [origin unknown] : a fly ball hit
esp. for practice fielding by a player who tosses a ball in the air and
hits it as it comes down

fun·goid \ˈfəŋ-ˌgoid\ *adj* : resembling, characteristic of, or being a
fungus — **fungoid** *n*

fun·gous \ˈfəŋ-gəs\ *adj* **1** : of, relating to, or having the characteristics of fungi **2** : caused by a fungus

fun·gus \ˈfəŋ-gəs\ *n, pl* **fun·gi** \ˈfən-ˌjī, ˈfəŋ-ˌgī\ *also* **fun·gus·es**
\ˈfəŋ-gə-səz\ *often attrib* [L] **1** : any of a major group (Fungi) of
saprophytic and parasitic lower plants that lack chlorophyll and
include molds, rusts, mildews, smuts, mushrooms, and usu. bacteria **2** : infection with a fungus

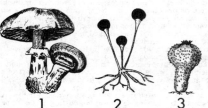

fungi 1: *1* meadow mushroom, *2* rhizopus, *3* puffball

fun house *n* : a building in an amusement park that contains various devices designed to startle or amuse

fu·nic·u·lar \fyu̇-ˈnik-yə-lər, fə-\ *adj* [L *funiculus* small rope] **1**
: dependent on the tension of a cord or cable **2** : having the form
of or associated with a cord **3** [NL *funiculus*] : of, relating to, or
being a funiculus

²**funicular** *n* : a cable railway ascending a mountain; *esp* : one in
which an ascending car counterbalances a descending car

[fu·n]**ic·u·lus** \-ləs\ *n, pl* **-li** \-ˌlī, -ˌlē\ [NL, fr. L, dim. of *funis* rope]
[:] a bodily structure suggesting a cord: as **a** : UMBILICAL CORD
[b] : bundle of nerve fibers **c** : SPERMATIC CORD **2** : the stalk of a
[n] ovule

[fu]**nk** \ˈfəŋk\ *n* [prob. fr. obs. Flem *fonck*] **1 a** : a state of
[para]fear **b** : a depressed state of mind **2** [³*funk*] : one that
[is a]COWARD ⟨must be a bit of a ∼ . . . to be afraid of a poor old
L. P. Hartley⟩

[²funk vb] [back-formation fr. ²*funky*] : funky music

[fu·n]k[³ vb] : to become frightened and shrink back ∼ *vt* **1** : to be
[in] DREAD **2** : to shrink from undertaking or facing

[funk n] **1** : DUGOUT **2** : a place of safe retreat

[fun·k]ia \ˈfəŋ-kē-ə, ˈfu̇ŋ-\ *n* [NL, genus name fr. C. H. *Funck* †1839]
[:] PLANTAIN LILY

[fun·ky \ˈfəŋ-]kē\ *adj* : being in a state of funk : PANICKY

²**funky** **funk·i·er; -est** [*funk* (offensive odor)] **1** : having an
[offensive od]or : FOUL **2** : having an earthy, unsophisticated style
[esp] : having the style and feeling of blues ⟨∼ piano
[playing⟩] : having an earthily sexual quality — **funk·i·ness** *n*

[fun·n]el \ˈfən-ᵊl\ *n* [ME *fonel*, fr. OProv *fonilh*, fr. ML *fundibulum*,
[alter. of L *in*]*fundibulum*, fr. *infundere* to pour in, fr. *in-* + *fundere*
[to pour — mo]re at FOUND] **1 a** : a utensil that is usu. a hollow
[cone with a tub]e extending from the smaller end and that is de-
[signed to catch] and direct a downward flow **b** : something
[resembling a fun]nel **2** : a stack or flue for the escape of smoke or
[steam]

²**funnel** *vb* [also] **-nelled; -nel·ing** *also* **-nel·ling** *vi* **1** : to have
[the shape of] a funnel **2** : to pass through or as if through
[a funnel ∼ *vt* **1**] : to form in the shape of a funnel ⟨∼ed his hands
[and shouted through] them⟩ **2** : to move to a focal point or into a
[funnel ⟨their con]tributions were ∼ed into one account⟩

[fun·ni·form \fə-]n[ī-ˌform] : INFUNDIBULIFORM ⟨∼ flowers⟩

[¹funny] \ˈfən-ē\ *adj* **fun·ni·er; -est** **1 a** : affording light mirth
[and laughter: COMIC AMUSIN]G **b** : seeking or intended to amuse : FACE-
[TIOUS **2** : differing fro]m the ordinary in a suspicious way : QUEER
[⟨something ∼ going on⟩ **3**] : or deception ⟨told his prisoner not to try
[anything ∼⟩ **4** : CURIOUS,] LAUGHABLE — **fun·ni·ly** \ˈfən-ᵊl-ē\ *adv*
[— **fun·ni·ness** \ˈfən-ē-nəs\] *n* — **funny** *adv*

[²funny *n*] : comic strip or comic section of a periodi-
[cal]

[funny bone *n* :] [the til]ling felt when it is struck] **1** : the place
[on the elbow] where the ulnar nerve rests against a
[bone of the hum]erus **2** : a sense of humor ⟨tickled his
[funny bone⟩]

[funny car *n* :] a dragster that has a one-piece molded
[body resembling] a mass-produced car

[funny man *n* :] one noted for humor : COMEDIAN **2**
[: the comics section o]f a newspaper

[¹fur \ˈfər\ *n* ...] [ME *furren*, fr. MF *fourrer*, fr. OF
[*forrer*, of Gmc] origin; akin to OHG *fuotar* sheath;
[fr. the animal] he protects] *vt* **1** : to cover, line,
[or trim with fur **2** : to] coat or clog as if with fur **3** : to
[become covered or] coated or clogged as if with fur

[²fur *n* **1 a** :]the dressed pelt of an animal used
[in apparel **b**] [: an a]parel] **2** : an article of clothing
[made of or with fur] [coat of a mammal esp. when
[fine, soft, and thick] [co]at with the skin **4** : a coating

resembling fur: as **a** : a coat [of epithelial debris on the tongue]
b : the thick pile of a fabric (as chenille)

³**fur** *abbr* furlong

fu·ran \ˈfyu̇(ə)r-ˌan, fyu̇-ˈran\ *also* **fur·fu·rane** \ˈfər-fyə-ˌrān\ *n*
[ISV, fr. *furfural*] : a flammable liquid compound C_4H_4O obtained
from wood oils of pines or made synthetically and used esp. in
the manufacture of nylon

fu·ra·nose \ˈfyu̇r-ə-ˌnōs, -ˌnōz\ *n* [*furan* + *-ose*] : a sugar having an
oxygen-containing ring of five atoms

fu·ra·no·side \fyu̇-ˈran-ə-ˌsīd\ *n* : a glycoside that is obtained
characteristic of furanose

fu·ra·zol·i·done \ˌfyu̇r-ə-ˈzäl-ə-ˌdōn\ *n* [*furfural* + oxazolidin-
-one] : a compound $C_8H_7N_3O_5$ used esp. against bacterial infections

fur·bear·er \ˈfər-ˌbar-ər, -ˌber-\ *n* : an animal that bears fur of
a commercially desired quality

fur·be·low \ˈfər-bə-ˌlō\ *n* [by folk etymology fr. F *dial. farbala*]
: a pleated or gathered piece of material; *specif* : a flounce on
women's clothing **2** : something that suggests a furbelow esp. in
being showy or superfluous — **furbelow** *vt*

fur·bish \ˈfər-bish\ *vt* [ME *furbisshen*, fr. MF *fourbiss-*, stem of
fourbir, of Gmc origin; akin to OHG *furben* to polish] **1** : to
make lustrous : POLISH **2** : to give a new look to : RENOVATE —
often used with *up* — **fur·bish·er** *n*

fur·cate \ˈfər-ˌkāt\ *adj* [LL *furcatus*, fr. L *furca* fork] : branched
like a fork — FORKED — **fur·cate·ly** *adv*

fur·ca·tion \ˌfər-ˈkā-shən\ *n* [ML *furcation-, furcatio*, fr. *furcatus*,
pp. of *furcare* to branch, fr. L *furca*] **1** : something that is
branched : FORK **2** : the act or process of branching

fur·cu·la \ˈfər-kyə-lə\ *n, pl* **-lae** \-ˌlē, -ˌlī\ [NL, fr. L, forked prop,
dim. of *furca*] : a forked process or part: as **a** : WISHBONE **b** : the
forked leaping appendage arising from the fourth abdominal segment of a collembolan — **fur·cu·lar** \-lər\ *adj*

fur·fu·ra·ceous \ˌfər-f(y)ə-ˈrā-shəs\ *adj* [LL *furfuraceus*, fr. L *furfur*
bran] : consisting of or covered with flaky particles ⟨∼ eczema⟩

fur·fu·ral \ˈfər-f(y)ə-ˌral\ *n* [L *furfur* + ISV *-al*] : a liquid aldehyde
$C_5H_4O_2$ of penetrating odor that is usu. made from plant materials
and used esp. in making furan or phenolic resins and as a solvent

fur·fur·al·de·hyde \ˌfər-f(y)ə-ˈral-də-ˌhīd\ *n* [L *furfur* + ISV *aldehyde* — more at GRIT] : FURFURAL

fur·fur·an \ˈfər-f(y)ə-ˌran\ *n* : FURAN

fu·ri·o·so \ˌfyu̇r-ē-ˈō-(ˌ)sō, -(ˌ)zō\ *adj or adv* [It, lit., furious] : with
great force or vigor — used as a direction in music

fu·ri·ous \ˈfyu̇r-ē-əs\ *adj* **1 a** : exhibiting or goaded by anger **b**
: giving a stormy or turbulent appearance ⟨∼ bursts of flame from
the windswept fire⟩ **c** : marked by noise, excitement, or activity
2 : INTENSE 1a ⟨the ∼ growth of tropical vegetation⟩ — **fu·ri·ous-
ly** *adv*

¹**furl** \ˈfər(-ə)l\ *vb* [MF *ferler*, fr. ONF *ferlier* to tie tightly, fr. OF
fer, ferm tight (fr. L *firmus* firm) + *lier* to tie, fr. L *ligare* — more
at LIGATURE] *vt* : to wrap or roll (as a sail or a flag) close to or
around something ∼ *vi* : to curl or fold as in being furled

²**furl** *n* **1** : the act of furling **2** : a furled coil

fur·long \ˈfər-ˌlȯŋ\ *n* [ME, fr. OE *furlang*, fr. *furh* furrow + *lang*
long] : a unit of distance equal to 220 yards

¹**fur·lough** \ˈfər-(ˌ)lō\ *n* [D *verlof*, lit., permission, fr. MD, fr. *ver-
for-* + *lof* permission; akin to OE *for-* and to MHG *loube* permission — more at FOR-, LEAVE] : a leave of absence from duty granted
esp. to a soldier; *also* : a document authorizing such a leave of
absence

²**furlough** *vt* **1** : to grant a furlough to **2** : to lay off from work

fur·mi·ty \ˈfər-mət-ē\ *var of* FRUMENTY

fur·nace \ˈfər-nəs\ *n* [ME *furnas*, fr. OF *fornaise*, fr. L *fornac-,
fornax*; akin to L *formus* warm — more at WARM] : an enclosed
structure in which heat is produced (as for heating a house or for
reducing ore)

fur·nish \ˈfər-nish\ *vt* [ME *furnisshen*, fr. MF *fourniss-*, stem of
fournir to complete, equip, of Gmc origin; akin to OHG *frummen*
to further, *fruma* advantage — more at FOREMOST] **1** : to provide
with what is needed; *esp* : to equip with furniture **2** : SUPPLY, GIVE
⟨∼ed food and shelter for the refugees⟩ — **fur·nish·er** *n*

syn FURNISH, EQUIP, OUTFIT, APPOINT, ACCOUTER, ARM shared meaning element : to supply one with what is needed (as for daily living or a particular activity)

fur·nish·ing *n* **1** : an article or accessory of dress — usu. used in
pl. **2** : an object that tends to increase comfort or utility; *specif*
: an article of furniture for the interior of a building — usu. used in
pl.

fur·ni·ture \ˈfər-ni-chər\ *n* [MF *fourniture*, fr. *fournir*] **1** : equipment that is necessary, useful, or desirable: as **a** *archaic* : the
trappings of a horse **b** : movable articles used in readying an area
(as a room or patio) for occupancy or use **2** : pieces of wood or
metal less than type high placed in printing forms to fill in blank
spaces

fu·ror \ˈfyu̇(ə)r-ˌȯ(ə)r, -ˌȯ(ə)r\ *n* [MF & L; MF, fr. L, fr. *furere* to
rage — more at DUST] **1** : an angry or maniacal fit : RAGE **2**
: FURY 4 **3** : a fashionable craze : VOGUE **4 a** : furious or hectic
activity **b** : an outburst of public excitement or indignation : UP-
ROAR

fu·rore \ˈfyu̇(ə)r-ˌȯ(ə)r, -ˌȯ(ə)r, *esp Brit* fyu̇-ˈrȯ-rē\ *n* [It, fr. L *furor*]
1 : FUROR 3 **2** : FUROR 4b

fu·ro·se·mide \fyu̇-ˈrō-sə-ˌmīd\ *n* [*furfural* + *-osemide*, of unknown
origin] : a powerful diuretic $C_{12}H_{11}ClN_2O_5S$ used esp. to treat
edema — called also *fursemide*

furred \ˈfərd\ *adj* **1** : lined, trimmed, or faced with fur **2**
: coated as if with fur; *specif* : having a coating consisting chiefly
of mucus and dead epithelial cells ⟨a ∼ tongue⟩ **3** : bearing or
wearing fur **4** : provided with furring ⟨∼ wall⟩

fur·ri·er \ˈfər-ē-ər, -ē-ˌ\ *n* **1** : a fur dealer **2 a** : one that
dresses furs **b** : one that makes, repairs, alters, or cleans fur garments

fur·ri·ery \-ə-rē\ *n* **1** : the fur business **2** : fur craftsmanship

fur·rin·er \ˈfər-ə-nər\ *n* [alter. of *foreigner*] *chiefly dial* : one not native to a community ⟨that was a ~ come from outside —Muriel E. Sheppard⟩

fur·ring \ˈfər-iŋ\ *n* **1** : a fur trimming or lining **2 a** : the application of thin wood, brick, or metal to joists, studs, or walls to form a level surface (as for attaching wallboard) or an air space **b** : the material used in this process

[1]**fur·row** \ˈfər-(ˌ)ō, -ə(-w); ˈfə-(ˌ)rō, -rə(-w)\ *n* [ME *furgh, forow,* fr. OE *furh;* akin to OHG *furuh* furrow, L *porca*] **1 a** : a trench in the earth made by a plow **b** : rural land : FIELD **2** : something that resembles the track of a plow: as **a** : a marked narrow depression : GROOVE **b** : a deep wrinkle ⟨~*s* in his brow⟩

[2]**furrow** *vt* : to make furrows, grooves, wrinkles, or lines in ~ *vi* : to make or form furrows, grooves, wrinkles, or lines

fur·ry \ˈfər-ē\ *adj* **fur·ri·er; -est** **1** : consisting of or resembling fur ⟨animals with ~ coats⟩ **2** : covered with fur **3** : thick in quality ⟨spoke with a ~ voice⟩

fur seal *n* : any of various eared seals that have a double coat with a dense soft underfur used esp. for clothing and trimmings

fur·se·mide \ˈfər-sə-ˌmīd\ *n* : FUROSEMIDE

[1]**fur·ther** \ˈfər-t͟hər\ *adv* [ME, fr. OE *furthor;* akin to OHG *furthar* further; both compars. fr. the root of OE *forth*] **1** : [1]FARTHER 1 ⟨my ponies are tired, and I have ~ to go —Thomas Hardy⟩ **2** : in addition : MOREOVER **3** : to a greater degree or extent ⟨~ annoyed by a second intrusion⟩

[2]**further** *adj* **1** : [2]FARTHER 1 ⟨rode . . . across the valley and up the ~ slopes —T. E. Lawrence⟩ **2** : going or extending beyond : ADDITIONAL ⟨~ volumes⟩ ⟨~ education⟩

[3]**further** *vt* **fur·thered; fur·ther·ing** \ˈfərt͟h-(ə-)riŋ\ : to help forward : PROMOTE ⟨~*ed* his education in graduate school⟩ ***syn*** see ADVANCE — **fur·ther·er** \ˈfər-t͟hər-ər\ *n*

fur·ther·ance \ˈfərt͟h-(ə-)rən(t)s\ *n* : the act of furthering : ADVANCEMENT

further education *n, Brit* : ADULT EDUCATION

fur·ther·more \ˈfər-t͟hə(r)-ˌmō(ə)r, -ˌmȯ(ə)r\ *adv* : in addition to what precedes : BESIDES

fur·ther·most \-ər-ˌmōst\ *adj* : most distant : FARTHEST

fur·thest \ˈfər-t͟həst\ *adv or adj* : FARTHEST

fur·tive \ˈfərt-iv\ *adj* [F or L; F *furtif,* fr. L *furtivus,* fr. *furtum* theft, fr. *fur* thief; akin to Gk *phōr* thief, L *ferre* to carry — more at BEAR] **1 a** : done by stealth : SURREPTITIOUS **b** : expressive of stealth : SLY ⟨had the ~ look of one with something to hide⟩ **2** : obtained underhandedly : STOLEN ***syn*** see SECRET ***ant*** forthright, brazen — **fur·tive·ly** *adv* — **fur·tive·ness** *n*

fu·run·cle \ˈfyu̇(ə)r-ˌəŋ-kəl\ *n* [L *furunculus* petty thief, sucker, furuncle, dim. of *furon-, furo* ferret, thief, fr. *fur*] : a localized inflammatory swelling of the skin and underlying tissues that is caused by infection by a bacterium in a hair follicle or skin gland and that discharges pus and a central core of dead tissue : BOIL — **fu·run·cu·lar** \fyu̇-ˈrəŋ-kyə-lər\ *adj* — **fu·run·cu·lous** \-ləs\ *adj*

fu·run·cu·lo·sis \fyu̇-ˌrəŋ-kyə-ˈlō-səs\ *n, pl* **-lo·ses** \-ˌsēz\ **1** : the condition of having or tending to develop multiple furuncles **2** : a highly infectious disease of various salmonoid fishes (as trout) that is caused by a bacterium (*Bacterium salmonicida*) and is esp. virulent in dense fish populations (as in hatcheries)

fu·ry \ˈfyu̇(ə)r-ē\ *n, pl* **furies** [ME *furie,* fr. MF & L; MF, fr. L *furia,* fr. *furere* to rage — more at DUST] **1** : intense, disordered, and often destructive rage **2 a** *cap* : one of the avenging deities who according to Greek mythology tormented criminals and inflicted plagues **b** : an avenging spirit **c** : one who resembles an avenging spirit; *esp* : a spiteful woman **3** : extreme fierceness or violence **4** : a state of inspired exaltation : FRENZY ***syn*** see ANGER

furze \ˈfərz\ *n* [ME *firse,* fr. OE *fyrs*] : a spiny yellow-flowered evergreen leguminous European shrub (*Ulex europaeus*); *broadly* : any of several related plants (genera *Ulex* and *Genista*) — **furzy** \ˈfər-zē\ *adj*

fus·cous \ˈfəs-kəs\ *adj* [L *fuscus* —more at DUSK] : of any of several colors averaging a brownish gray

[1]**fuse** \ˈfyüz\ *n* [It *fuso* spindle, fr. L *fusus,* of unknown origin] **1** : a continuous train of a combustible substance enclosed in a cord or cable for setting off an explosive charge by transmitting fire to it **2** *usu* **fuze** : a mechanical or electrical detonating device for setting off the bursting charge of a projectile, bomb, or torpedo

[2]**fuse** *or* **fuze** \ˈfyüz\ *vt* **fused** *or* **fuzed; fus·ing** *or* **fuz·ing** : to equip with a fuse

[3]**fuse** *vb* **fused; fus·ing** [L *fusus,* pp. of *fundere* to pour, melt — more at FOUND] *vt* **1** : to reduce to a liquid or plastic state by heat **2** : to blend thoroughly by or as if by melting together : make indissolubly one **3** : to stitch by applying heat and pressure with or without the use of an adhesive ~ *vi* **1** : to become fluid with heat; *also* : to fail because of the blowing of a fuse **2** : to become blended by or as if by melting together ***syn*** see MIX

[4]**fuse** *n* : an electrical safety device consisting of or including a wire or strip of fusible metal that melts and interrupts the circuit when the current exceeds a particular amperage

fused quartz *n* : QUARTZ GLASS — called also *fused silica*

fu·see \fyü-ˈzē\ *n* [F *fusée,* lit., spindleful of yarn, fr. OF, fr. *fus* spindle, fr. L *fusus*] **1** : a conical spirally grooved pulley in a timepiece from which a cord or chain unwinds onto a barrel containing the spring and which by its increasing diameter compensates for the lessening power of the spring **2** : [1]FUSE 1 **3** : a friction match with a bulbous head not easily blown out **4** : a red signal flare used esp. for protecting stalled trains and trucks

fu·se·lage \ˈfyü-sə-ˌläzh, -zə-\ *n* [F, fr. *fuselé* spindle-shaped, fr. MF, fr. *fusel,* dim. of *fus*] : the central body portion of an airplane designed to accommodate the crew and the passengers or cargo

fu·sel oil \ˈfyü-zəl-\ *n* [G *fusel* bad liquor] : an acrid oily liquid occurring in insufficiently distilled alcoholic liquors, consisting chiefly of amyl alcohol, and used esp. as a source of alcohols and as a solvent

fusi- *comb form* [L *fusus*] : spindle ⟨*fusi*form⟩

fus·ible \ˈfyü-zə-bəl\ *adj* : capable of being fused and esp. liquefied by heat — **fus·ibil·i·ty** \ˌfyü-zə-ˈbil-ət-ē\ *n*

fu·si·form \ˈfyü-zə-ˌfȯrm\ *adj* : tapering toward each end ⟨~ bacteria⟩

[1]**fu·sil** \ˈfyü-zəl\ *or* **fu·sile** \ˈfyü-zəl, -ˌzīl\ *adj* [ME, fr. L *fusilis,* fr. *fusus,* pp.] **1** *archaic* **a** : made by melting and pouring into forms : CAST **b** : liquefied by heat **2** *archaic* : FUSIBLE

[2]**fusil** *n* [F, lit., steel for striking fire, fr. OF *foisil,* fr. (assumed) VL *focilis,* fr. LL *focus* fire — more at FUEL] : a light flintlock musket

fu·sil·ier *or* **fu·sil·eer** \ˌfyü-zə-ˈli(ə)r\ *n* [F *fusilier,* fr. *fusil*] **1** : a soldier armed with a fusil **2** : a member of a British regiment formerly armed with fusils

[1]**fu·sil·lade** \ˈfyü-sə-ˌläd, -ˌläd, ˌfyü-sə-ˈ, -zə-\ *n* [F, fr. *fusiller* to shoot, fr. *fusil*] **1** : a number of shots fired simultaneously or in rapid succession **2** : a spirited outburst esp. of criticism

[2]**fusillade** *vt* **-lad·ed; -lad·ing** : to attack or shoot down by a fusillade

fu·sion \ˈfyü-zhən\ *n, often attrib* [L *fusion-, fusio,* fr. *fusus,* pp.] **1 a** : the act or process of liquefying or rendering plastic by heat **b** : the liquid or plastic state induced by heat **2** : a union by or as if by melting: as **a** : a merging of diverse elements into a unified whole **b** : a political partnership : COALITION ⟨a ~ of the major parties⟩ **c** : the union of atomic nuclei to form heavier nuclei resulting in the release of enormous quantities of energy when certain light elements unite

fusion bomb *n* : a bomb in which nuclei of a light chemical element unite to form nuclei of heavier elements with a release of energy; *esp* : HYDROGEN BOMB

fu·sion·ist \ˈfyüzh-(ə-)nəst\ *n* : one who promotes or takes part in a coalition esp. of political parties

[1]**fuss** \ˈfəs\ *n* [perh. of imit. origin] **1 a** : needless bustle or excitement : COMMOTION **b** : a show of flattering attention ⟨made a big ~ over his favorite niece⟩ **2 a** : a state of agitation esp. over a trivial matter **b** : OBJECTION, PROTEST **c** : an often petty controversy or quarrel ⟨ended up having a pretty good ~ with my wife —Mac Hyman⟩ ***syn*** see STIR

[2]**fuss** *vi* **1 a** : to create or be in a state of restless activity; *specif* : to shower flattering attentions ⟨doting grandparents ~*ing* over the grandchildren⟩ **b** : to pay close or undue attention to small details ⟨~*ed* with her hair⟩ **2 a** : to become upset : WORRY **b** : to express annoyance or pique : COMPLAIN ⟨a mother who has to cope with ~*ing* children⟩ ~ *vt* : AGITATE, UPSET — **fuss·er** *n*

fuss·bud·get \ˈfəs-ˌbəj-ət\ *n* : one who fusses about trifles — **fuss·bud·gety** \-ət-ē\ *adj*

fuss·pot \ˈfəs-ˌpät\ *n* : FUSSBUDGET

fussy \ˈfəs-ē\ *adj* **fuss·i·er; -est** **1** : easily upset : IRRITABLE **2 a** : requiring or giving close attention to details ⟨~ bookkeeping procedures⟩ **b** : revealing a concern for niceties : FASTIDIOUS ⟨not ~ about food⟩ ***syn*** see NICE — **fuss·i·ly** \ˈfəs-ə-lē\ *adv* — **fuss·i·ness** \ˈfəs-ē-nəs\ *n*

fus·tian \ˈfəs-chən\ *n* [ME, fr. OF *fustaine,* fr. ML *fustaneum,* prob. fr. *fustis* tree trunk, fr. L, club] **1 a** : a strong cotton and linen fabric **b** : a class of cotton fabrics usu. having a pile face and twill weave **2** : pretentious and banal writing or speech ***syn*** see BOMBAST — **fus·tian** *adj*

fus·tic \ˈfəs-tik\ *n* [ME *fustik,* fr. MF *fustoc,* fr. Ar *fustuq,* fr. Gk *pistakē* pistachio tree — more at PISTACHIO] **1** : the wood of a tropical American tree (*Chlorophora tinctoria*) of the mulberry family that yields a yellow dye; *also* : any of several similar dyewoods **2** : a tree yielding fustic

fus·ti·gate \ˈfəs-tə-ˌgāt\ *vt* **-gat·ed; -gat·ing** [LL *fustigatus,* pp. of *fustigare,* fr. L *fustis* + *-igare* (akin to *agere* to drive) — more at AGENT] **1** : CUDGEL **2** : to criticize severely — **fus·ti·ga·tion** \ˌfəs-tə-ˈgā-shən\ *n*

fus·ty \ˈfəs-tē\ *adj* **fus·ti·er; -est** [ME, fr. *fust* wine cask, fr. MF, club, cask, fr. L *fustis*] **1** *Brit* : impaired by age or dampness : MOLDY **2** : saturated with dust and stale odors : MUSTY **3** : rigidly old-fashioned or reactionary ***syn*** see MALODOROUS — **fus·ti·ly** \-tə-lē\ *adv* — **fus·ti·ness** \-tē-nəs\ *n*

fut *abbr* future

fu·thark \ˈfü-ˌthärk\ *also* **fu·thorc** *or* **fu·thork** \-ˌthȯ(ə)rk\ *n* [fr. the first six letters, *f, u,* þ *(th), o* (or *a*), *r, c* (=k)] : the runic alphabet

fu·tile \ˈfyüt-ᵊl, ˈfyü-ˌtīl\ *adj* [MF or L; MF, fr. L *futilis* that pours out easily, useless, fr. *fut-* (akin to *fundere* to pour) — more at FOUND] **1** : serving no useful purpose : completely ineffective ⟨efforts to convince him were ~⟩ **2** : occupied with trifles : FRIVOLOUS — **fu·tile·ly** \-ᵊl-(l)ē, -ˌtīl-lē\ *adv* — **fu·tile·ness** \-ᵊl-nəs, -ˌtīl-nəs\ *n*

syn FUTILE, VAIN, FRUITLESS *shared meaning element* : barren of results

fu·til·i·tar·i·an \fyü-ˌtil-ə-ˈter-ē-ən, ˌfyü-\ *n* [blend of *futile* and *utilitarian*] : one who believes that human striving is futile — **futilitarian** *adj* — **fu·til·i·tar·i·an·ism** \-ē-ə-ˌniz-əm\ *n*

fu·til·i·ty \fyü-ˈtil-ət-ē\ *n, pl* **-ties** **1** : the quality or state of being futile : USELESSNESS **2** : a useless act or gesture ⟨the *futilities* of debate for its own sake —W. A. White⟩

fut·tock \ˈfət-ək\ *n* [prob. alter. of *foothook* (futtock)] : one of the curved timbers scarfed together to form the lower part of the compound rib of a ship

futtock shroud *n* : a short iron rod connecting the topmast rigging with the lower mast

[1]**fu·ture** \ˈfyü-chər\ *adj* [ME, fr. OF & L; OF *futur,* fr. L *futurus* about to be — more at BE] **1** : that is to be; *specif* : existing after death **2** : of, relating to, or constituting a verb tense expressive of time yet to come

[2]**future** *n* **1 a** : time that is to come **b** : what is going to happen **2** : an expectation of advancement or progressive development **3**

: something (as a bulk commodity) bought for future acceptance or sold for future delivery — usu. used in pl. ⟨the use of grain ~s as a hedge against price changes⟩ **4 a** : the future tense of a language **b** : a verb form in the future tense

fu·ture·less \'fyü-chər-ləs\ *adj* : having no prospect of future success

future perfect *adj* : of, relating to, or constituting a verb tense that is traditionally formed in English with *will have* and *shall have* and that expresses completion of an action by a specified time that is yet to come — **future perfect** *n*

fu·tur·ism \'fyü-chə-₁riz-əm\ *n* **1** : a movement in art, music, and literature begun in Italy about 1910 and marked esp. by an effort to give formal expression to the dynamic energy and movement of mechanical processes **2** : a point of view that finds meaning or fulfillment in the future rather than in the past or present — **fu·tur·ist** \'fyü-ch(ə-)rəst\ *n*

fu·tur·is·tic \₁fyü-chə-'ris-tik\ *adj* **1** : of or relating to the future **2** : of or relating to futurism — **fu·tur·is·ti·cal·ly** \-ti-k(ə-)lē\ *adv*

fu·tu·ri·ty \fyü-'t(y)ùr-ət-ē, -'chùr-\ *n, pl* **-ties 1** : time to come : FUTURE **2** : the quality or state of being future **3** *pl* : future events or prospects **4 a** : a horse race usu. for two-year-olds in which the competitors are nominated at birth or before **b** : a race or competition for which entries are made well in advance of the event

fuze, fu·zee *var of* FUSE, FUSEE

¹fuzz \'fəz\ *n* [prob. back-formation fr. *fuzzy*] : fine light particles

or fibers (as of down or fluff)

²fuzz *vi* **1** : to fly off in or become covered with fluffy particles ~ *vt* **1** : to make fuzzy **2** : to envelop in a haze : BLUR

³fuzz *n* [origin unknown] : POLICE; *also* : a police officer

fuzzy \'fəz-ē\ *adj* **fuzz·i·er; -est** [perh. fr. LG *fussig* loose, spongy; akin to OHG *fūl* rotten — more at FOUL] **1** : marked by or giving a suggestion of fuzz ⟨a ~ covering of felt⟩ **2** : not clear : INDISTINCT ⟨moving the camera causes ~ photos⟩ — **fuzz·i·ly** \'fəz-ə-lē\ *adv* — **fuzz·i·ness** \'fəz-ē-nəs\ *n*

FV *abbr* [L *folio verso* the page being turned] on the back of the page

fwd *abbr* **1** foreword **2** forward

FWD *abbr* front-wheel drive

FWPCA *abbr* Federal Water Pollution Control Administration

FX *abbr* foreign exchange

FY *abbr* fiscal year

-fy \₁fī\ *vb suffix* [ME *-fien*, fr. OF *-fier*, fr. L *-ficare*, fr. *-ficus* -fic] **1** : make : form into ⟨dandi*fy*⟩ **2** : invest with the attributes of : make similar to ⟨citi*fy*⟩

fyce \'fīs\ *var of* FEIST

FYI *abbr* for your information

fyke \'fīk\ *n* [D *fuik*] : a long bag net kept open by hoops

fyl·fot \'fil-₁fät\ *n* [ME, device used to fill the lower part of a painted glass window, fr. *fillen* to fill + *fot* foot] : SWASTIKA

fz *abbr* [It *forzando, forzato*] accented

FZS *abbr* Fellow of the Zoological Society

---

¹g \'jē\ *n, pl* **g's** *or* **gs** \'jēz\ *often cap, often attrib* **1 a** : the 7th letter of the English alphabet **b** : a graphic representation of this letter **c** : a speech counterpart of orthographic *g* **2** : the 5th tone of a C-major scale **3** : a graphic device for reproducing the letter *g* **4** : one designated *g* esp. as the 7th in order or class **5** [*gravity*] : a unit of force equal to the force exerted by gravity on a body at rest and used to indicate the force to which a body is subjected when accelerated **6** [*grand*] *slang* : a sum of $1000 **7** : something shaped like the letter G

²g *abbr, often cap* **1** game **2** gauge **3** gender **4** German **5** giga- **6** good **7** gram **8** grand **9** gravity **10** gulf

¹G *adj* [*general*] *of a motion picture* : of such a nature that all ages may be allowed admission — compare PG, R, X

²G *symbol* **1** conductance **2** weight

ga *abbr* gauge

¹Ga *abbr* Georgia

²Ga *symbol* gallium

GA *abbr* **1** general agent **2** general assembly **3** general average **4** general of the army **5** Georgia

¹gab \'gab\ *vi* **gabbed; gab·bing** [prob. short for *gabble*] : to talk in a rapid or thoughtless manner : CHATTER

²gab *n* : TALK; *esp* : idle talk

gab·ar·dine \'gab-ər-₁dēn\ *n* [MF *gaverdine*] **1** : GABERDINE **2 a** : a firm hard-finish durable fabric (as of wool or rayon) twilled with diagonal ribs on the right side **b** : a garment of gabardine

gab·ber \'gab-ər\ *n* : one that talks much, habitually, and usu. idly

gab·ble \'gab-əl\ *vb* **gab·bled; gab·bling** \-(ə-)liŋ\ [prob. of imit. origin] *vi* **1** : to talk fast or foolishly : JABBER **2** : to utter inarticulate or animal sounds ⟨a skein of duck . . . *gabbling* softly to themselves —Naomi Mitchison⟩ ~ *vt* : to say with incoherent rapidity : BABBLE — **gabble** *n* — **gab·bler** \-(ə-)lər\ *n*

gab·bro \'gab-(₁)rō\ *n, pl* **gabbros** [It] : a granular igneous rock composed essentially of calcic plagioclase, a ferromagnesian mineral, and accessory minerals — **gab·bro·ic** \ga-'brō-ik\ *adj*

gab·broid \'gab-₁roid\ *adj* : resembling gabbro

gab·by \'gab-ē\ *adj* **gab·bi·er; -est** : TALKATIVE, GARRULOUS

ga·belle \gə-'bel\ *n* [ME, fr. MF, fr. OIt *gabella* tax, fr. Ar *qabālah*] : a tax on salt levied in France prior to 1790

gab·er·dine \'gab-ər-₁dēn\ *n* [MF *gaverdine*] **1** : a coarse long coat or smock worn chiefly by Jews in medieval times **b** : an English laborer's smock **c** : GARMENT **2** : GABARDINE

gab·fest \'gab-₁fest\ *n* **1** : an informal gathering for general talk ⟨political ~s⟩ **2** : an extended conversation

ga·bi·on \'gā-bē-ən, 'gab-ē-\ *n* [MF, fr. OIt *gabbione*, lit., large cage, aug. of *gabbia* cage, fr. L *cavea* — more at CAGE] : a hollow wickerwork or iron cylinder filled with earth and used esp. in building fieldworks or in mining

ga·ble \'gā-bəl\ *n* [ME, fr. MF, of Gmc origin; akin to ON *gafl* gable — more at CEPHALIC] **1 a** : the vertical triangular end of a building from cornice or eaves to ridge **b** : the similar end of a gambrel roof **c** : the end wall of a building **2** : a triangular furniture or building part

1, gables 1a

ga·bled \-bəld\ *adj* : built with a gable

gable roof *n* : a double-sloping roof

that forms a gable at each end

gab·oon \ga-'bün, gə-\ *n* [alter. of ¹*gob* + *-oon* (as in *spittoon*)] *dial* : CUSPIDOR, SPITTOON

Ga·bri·el \'gā-brē-əl\ *n* [Heb *Gabhrī'ēl*] : one of the four archangels named in Hebrew tradition

ga·by \'gā-bē\ *n, pl* **gabies** [perh. of Scand origin; akin to ON *gapa* to gape — more at GAPE] *dial chiefly Eng* : SIMPLETON

¹gad \'gad\ *n* [ME, spike, fr. ON *gaddr*; akin to OE *geard* rod — more at YARD] **1** : a chisel or pointed iron or steel bar for loosening ore or rock **2** *chiefly dial* : ROD, STICK

²gad *vi* **gad·ded; gad·ding** [ME *gadden*] : to be on the go to little purpose ⟨too busy *gadding* about to get any work done⟩ — **gad·der** *n*

³gad *interj* [euphemism for *God*] — used as a mild oath

Gad \'gad\ *n* [Heb *Gādh*] : a son of Jacob and the traditional eponymous ancestor of one of the tribes of Israel — **Gad·ite** \-₁īt\ *n*

gad·about \'gad-ə-₁baùt\ *n* : a person who flits about in social activity — **gadabout** *adj*

gad·a·rene \'gad-ə-₁rēn\ *adj, often cap* [fr. the demon-possessed *Gadarene* swine (Mt 8:28) that rushed into the sea] : HEADLONG, PRECIPITATE ⟨a ~ rush to the cities⟩

gad·fly \'gad-₁flī\ *n* [¹*gad*] **1** : any of various flies (as a horsefly, botfly, or warble fly) that bite or annoy livestock **2** : a usu. intentionally annoying person who stimulates or provokes others esp. by persistent irritating criticism

gad·get \'gaj-ət\ *n* [origin unknown] : an often small mechanical or electronic device esp. on a piece of machinery : CONTRIVANCE — **gad·get·eer** \₁gaj-ə-'ti(ə)r\ *n* — **gad·get·ry** \'gaj-ə-trē\ *n* — **gad·gety** \-ət-ē\ *adj*

ga·doid \'gā-₁doid, 'gad-\ *adj* [NL *Gadus*, genus of fishes, fr. Gk *gados*, a fish] : resembling or related to the cods — **gadoid** *n*

gad·o·lin·ite \'gad-²l-ə-₁nīt\ *n* [G *gadolinit*, fr. Johann *Gadolin* †1852 Finn chemist] : a black or brown mineral $Be_2FeY_2Si_2O_{10}$ that is a source of rare earths and consists of silicate of iron, beryllium, yttrium, cerium, and erbium

gad·o·lin·i·um \₁gad-²l-'in-ē-əm\ *n* [NL, fr. J. *Gadolin*] : a magnetic metallic element of the rare-earth group occurring in combination in gadolinite and several other minerals — see ELEMENT table

ga·droon \gə-'drün\ *n* [F *godron*] round plait, gadroon] **1** : the ornamental notching or carving of a rounded molding **2** : a short often oval fluting or reeding used in decoration — **ga·droon·ing** *n*

1, gadroon 2

gad·wall \'gad-₁wòl\ *n, pl* **gadwalls** *or* **gadwall** [origin unknown] : a grayish brown dabbling duck (*Anas strepera*) about the size of the mallard

gad·zooks *interj, often cap, archaic* — used as a mild oath

Gaea \'jē-ə\ *n* [Gk *Gaia*] : the Greek earth goddess and mother of the Titans

Gael \'gā(ə)l\ *n* [ScGael *Gàidheal* & IrGael *Gaedheal*] **1** : a Scottish Highlander **2** : a Celtic esp. Gaelic-speaking inhabitant of Ireland, Scotland, or the Isle of Man

Gael·ic \'gā-lik, 'gäl-\ *adj* **1** : of or relating to the Gaels and esp. the Celtic Highlanders of Scotland **2** : of, relating to, or constituting the Goidelic speech of the Celts in Ireland, the Isle of Man, and the Scottish Highlands — **Gaelic** *n*

465

1 a : a spear or spearhead for
...led hook for holding or lifting
...gamecock **d** : a butcher's hook
...int used by a telephone lineman
...d of a fore-and-aft sail is extended
...CK, TRICK **4 a** : something painful
... *esp* : persistent raillery or criticism
... **5** : GAFFE

...secure with a gaff **b** : to fit (a game-
...IVE, TRICK; *also* : FLEECE **3** : to fix for
...IMMICK ⟨~ the dice⟩

...: a cheap theater or music hall
...: a social blunder : FAUX PAS

...alter. of *godfather*] **1** : an old man —
... **a** : EMPLOYER **b** : FOREMAN, OVERSEER
... **4** : a lighting electrician on a motion⸗

...sǝl\ *n* : a usu. triangular topsail on a
...f and its luff upon the topmast — see

...ng [ME *gaggen* to strangle, of imit.
...uth of with something inserted **b**
... **c** : to prevent from free speech
...itch **3** : OBSTRUCT, CHOKE ⟨~ a
... or pranks ⟨~ a show⟩ ~ *vi* **1**
...o endure something : BALK **3**

...mouth to keep it open **2 a**
...prevent speech or outcry **b**
... **3** : a laugh-provoking re-
...E JEST

...ol, of imit. origin] **1** : CRAZY,
...nusiasm : INFATUATED
...of Gmc origin; akin to OHG *wetti*
...a token of defiance; *specif* : a glove or
...be taken up by an opponent as a pledge
...ng deposited as a pledge of performance
...PLEDGE **2** *archaic* : STAKE, RISK

...GAGE

...r\ *n* **1** : one that gags **2** : JOKER, GAGMAN
...g-ǝl\ *n* [ME *gagyll*, fr. *gagelen* to cackle] **1** : FLOCK; *esp*
...of geese when not in flight — compare SKEIN **2** : AGGRE-
..., CLUSTER ⟨a ~ of reporters and photographers⟩
...nan \'gag-mǝn\ *n* **1** : a gag writer **2** : a comedian who
...es gags

gag rule *n* : a rule restricting freedom of debate or expression esp.
in a legislative body

gag·ster \'gag-stǝr\ *n* : GAGMAN; *also* : one who plays practical
jokes

gahn·ite \'gän-ˌīt\ *n* [G *gahnit*, fr. J. G. *Gahn* †1818 Sw chemist] : a
usu. dark green mineral $ZnAl_2O_4$ consisting of an oxide of zinc and
aluminum

gai·e·ty \'gā-ǝt-ē\ *n, pl* **-eties** **1** : MERRYMAKING; *also* : festive
activity — often used in pl. **2** : gay spirits or manner **3** : FIN-
ERY, SHOW ⟨a ~ of dress better suited to one half her age⟩

gail·lar·dia \gǝ-'lärd-(ē-)ǝ\ *n* [NL, genus name, fr. *Gaillard* de
Marentonneau, 18th cent. F botanist] : any of a genus (*Gaillardia*)
of chiefly western American composite herbs with showy flower
heads

gai·ly \'gā-lē\ *adv* : in a gay manner

¹gain \'gān\ *n* [ME *gayne*, fr. MF *gaigne, gain*, fr. OF *gaaigne,
gaaing*, fr. *gaaignier* to till, earn, gain, of Gmc origin; akin to OHG
weidanōn to hunt for food, L *vis* power — more at VIM] **1** : resources or advantage acquired or increased : PROFIT ⟨made substantial ~s last year⟩ **2** : the obtaining of profit or possessions **3**
a : an increase in amount, magnitude, or degree ⟨a ~ in efficiency⟩
b : the ratio of increase of output over input in an amplifier ~ **c**
: the effectiveness of a directional antenna expressed as the ratio in
decibels of standard antenna input power to the directional antenna input power that will produce the same field strength in the
desired direction

²gain *vt* **1 a** : to get possession of usu. by industry, merit, or
craft ⟨~ an advantage⟩ ⟨he stood to ~ a fortune⟩ **b** : to win in
competition or conflict ⟨the attackers ~ed the day⟩ **c** : to get by
a natural development or process ⟨~ strength⟩ **d** : MAKE, ACQUIRE
⟨~ a friend⟩ **e** (1) : to arrive at ⟨~ed the river that night⟩ (2)
: TRAVERSE, COVER ⟨~ed 10 yards on the play⟩ **2** : to win to one's
side : PERSUADE ⟨~ adherents to a cause⟩ **3** : to cause to be obtained or given : ATTRACT ⟨~ attention⟩ **4** : to increase in ⟨~
momentum⟩ **5** *of a timepiece* : to run fast by the amount of ⟨the
clock ~s a minute a day⟩ ~ *vi* **1** : to get advantage : PROFIT
⟨hoped to ~ from his crime⟩ **2 a** : INCREASE ⟨the day was ~ing
in warmth⟩ **b** : to increase in weight **c** : to improve in health **3**
of a timepiece : to run fast **syn** **1** see GET **ant** forfeit, lose **2**
see REACH **ant** forfeit, lose — **gain ground** : to make progress

³gain *n* [origin unknown] **1** : a beveled shoulder above a tenon **2**
: a notch or mortise for insertion of a girder or joist

gain·er \'gā-nǝr\ *n* **1** : one that gains **2** : a fancy dive in which
the diver from a forward position executes a backward somersault
and enters the water feetfirst and facing away from the board

gain·ful \'gān-fǝl\ *adj* : productive of gain : PROFITABLE ⟨~ em-
ployment⟩ — **gain·ful·ly** \-fǝ-lē\ *adv* — **gain·ful·ness** *n*

gain·giv·ing \'gān-ˌgiv-iŋ, (ˌ)gān-'\ *n* [*gain-* (against) + *giving*] *archaic* : MISGIVING

gain·less \'gān-lǝs\ *adj* : producing no gain : PROFITLESS — **gain-
less·ness** *n*

gain·ly \'gān-lē\ *adj* [*gain* (handy)] : graceful and generally pleasing
⟨a ~ boy with charming manners⟩

gain·say \gān-'sā\ *vt* **-said** \-'sād, -'sed\; **-say·ing** \-'sā-iŋ\; **-says**
\-'sāz, -'sez\ [ME *gainsayen*, fr. *gain-* against (fr. OE *gēan-*) +
sayen to say — more at AGAIN] **1** : DENY, DISPUTE ⟨couldn't ~ the
statistics⟩ **2** : to stand in opposition to esp. by disputing the truth

of something put forward : CONTRADICT, OPPOSE **syn** see DENY
ant admit — **gain·say·er** *n*

¹gait \'gāt\ *n* [ME *gait, gate* gate, way] **1** : a manner of walking or
moving on foot **2** : a sequence of foot movements (as a walk, trot,
pace, or canter) by which a horse moves forward **3** : a manner or
rate of movement or progress ⟨the leisurely ~ of a summer in the
country⟩

²gait *vt* **1** : to train (a horse) to use a particular gait or set of gaits
2 : to lead (a show dog) before a judge to display carriage and
movement

³gait *n* [prob. alter. of ¹*gate*] **1** : the distance between two adjoining carriages of a lace-making frame **2** *Brit* : a full repeat of a
pattern in harness weaving of woolens

gait·ed \'gāt-ǝd\ *adj* : having a particular gait ⟨slow-*gaited*⟩

gai·ter \'gāt-ǝr\ *n* [F *guêtre*] **1** : a cloth or leather leg covering
reaching from the instep to ankle, mid-calf, or knee **2 a** : an
ankle-high shoe with elastic gores in the sides **b** : an overshoe
with fabric upper

¹gal \'gal\ *n* [by alter.] : GIRL

²gal *n* [*Galileo* †1642 It astronomer] : a unit of acceleration equivalent to one centimeter per second per second — used esp. for values
of gravity

³gal *abbr* **1** gallery **2** gallon

Gal *abbr* Galatians

ga·la \'gā-lǝ, 'gal-ǝ, 'gäl-ǝ\ *n* [It, fr. MF *gale* festivity, pleasure —
more at GALLANT] : a gay celebration : FESTIVITY — **gala** *adj*

galact- *or* **galacto-** *comb form* [L *galact-*, fr. Gk *galakt-, galakto-*, fr.
galakt-, gala] **1** : milk (*galacto*poiesis) **2** : related to galactose
(*galact*omannan)

ga·lac·tic \gǝ-'lak-tik\ *adj* **1** : of or relating to a galaxy and esp.
the Milky Way galaxy **2** : HUGE ⟨a ~ sum of money⟩

galactic noise *n* : radio-frequency radiation from the Milky Way

ga·lac·to·poi·e·sis \gǝ-ˌlak-tǝ-pȯi-'ē-sǝs\ *n* [NL] : formation and
secretion of milk — **ga·lac·to·poi·et·ic** \-'et-ik\ *adj or n*

ga·lac·tos·amine \gǝ-ˌlak-'tō-sǝ-ˌmēn, -zǝ-\ *n* : an amino derivative
$C_6H_{13}O_5N$ of galactose that occurs in cartilage

ga·lac·tose \gǝ-'lak-ˌtōs, -ˌtōz\ *n* [F, fr. *galact-*] : a sugar $C_6H_{12}O_6$
less soluble and less sweet than glucose

ga·lac·tos·emia \gǝ-ˌlak-tǝ-'sē-mē-ǝ\ *n* : an inherited metabolic
disorder in which galactose accumulates in the blood due to deficiency of an enzyme catalyzing its conversion to glucose — **ga·lac-
tos·emic** \-mik\ *adj*

ga·lac·to·si·dase \gǝ-ˌlak-'tō-sǝ-ˌdās, -zǝ-ˌdāz\ *n* : an enzyme (as
lactase) that hydrolyzes a galactoside

ga·lac·to·side \gǝ-'lak-tǝ-ˌsīd\ *n* : a glycoside that yields galactose
on hydrolysis

ga·lac·to·syl \gǝ-'lak-tǝ-ˌsil\ *n* : a glycosyl radical $C_6H_{11}O_5$ that is
derived from galactose

ga·lact·uron·ic acid \gǝ-ˌlak-t(y)ù-ˌrän-ik-\ *n* [ISV *galact-* +
-uronic] : a crystalline aldehyde-acid $C_6H_{10}O_7$ that occurs esp. in
polymerized form in pectin

ga·la·go \gǝ-'lā-(ˌ)gō, -'läg-(ˌ)ō\ *n, pl* **-gos** [NL, genus name, perh.
fr. Wolof *golokh* monkey] : any of two genera (*Galago* and *Euoti-
cus*) of small active nocturnal arboreal African primates with long
ears, a long tail, and elongated hind limbs that enable them to leap
with great agility — called also *bush baby*

ga·lah \gǝ-'lä\ *n* [native name in Australia] : a showy Australian
cockatoo (*Kakatoë roseicapilla*) that is a destructive pest in wheat⸗
growing areas and is often kept as a cage bird

Gal·a·had \'gal-ǝ-ˌhad\ *n* : the knight of the Round Table who
successfully seeks the Holy Grail

gal·an·tine \'gal-ǝn-ˌtēn\ *n* [F] : a cold dish consisting of boned
meat or fish that has been stuffed, poached, and covered with aspic

ga·lan·ty show \gǝ-'lant-ē-\ *n* [perh. fr. It *galante* gallant, fr. MF
galant] : SHADOW PLAY

Gal·a·tea \ˌgal-ǝ-'tē-ǝ\ *n* [L, fr. Gk *Galateia*] **1** : a nymph killed by
the jealous Cyclops Polyphemus while in the arms of her lover Acis
2 : a female figure sculpted by Pygmalion and given life by Aphrodite in fulfillment of his prayer

Ga·la·tians \gǝ-'lā-shǝnz\ *n pl but sing in constr* : an argumentative
letter of St. Paul written to the Christians of Galatia and included
as a book in the New Testament — see BIBLE table

gal·a·vant *var of* GALLIVANT

ga·lax \'gā-ˌlaks\ *n* [NL, genus name] : any of a genus (*Galax*) of
evergreen herbs related to the true heaths with leaves widely used
for decorations

gal·axy \'gal-ǝk-sē\ *n, pl* **-ax·ies** [ME *galaxie, galaxias*, fr. LL
galaxias, fr. Gk, fr. *galakt-, gala* milk; akin to L *lac* milk] **1 a**
often cap : MILKY WAY GALAXY **b** : one of billions of systems each
including stars, nebulae, star clusters, globular clusters, and interstellar matter that make up the universe **2** : an assemblage of
brilliant or notable persons or things

gal·ba·num \'gal-bǝ-nǝm, 'gȯl-\ *n* [ME, fr. L, fr. Gk *chalbanē*, fr.
Heb *helbēnāh*] : a yellowish to green or brown aromatic bitter gum
resin derived from several Asiatic plants (as *Ferula galbaniflua*)
and used for medicinal purposes and in incense

¹gale \'gā(ǝ)l\ *n* [origin unknown] **1 a** : a strong current of air:
(1) : a wind from 32 to 63 miles per hour (2) : FRESH GALE — see
BEAUFORT SCALE table **b** *archaic* : BREEZE **2** : an emotional outburst : GUST

²gale *n* [prob. alter. of ¹*gavel*] *Brit* : a periodic payment of rent

ga·lea \'gā-lē-ǝ\ *n* [NL, fr. L, helmet] : an anatomical part suggesting a helmet: as **a** : the upper lip of the corolla of a mint **b** : the
outer or lateral lobe of the maxilla in mandibulate insects — **ga·le-
ate** \-lē-ˌāt\ *also* **ga·le·at·ed** \-ˌāt-ǝd\ *adj* — **ga·le·iform** \gǝ-'lē-ǝ-
ˌfȯrm, 'gā-lē-\ *adj*

ǝ abut	³ kitten	ǝr further	a back	ā bake	ä cot, cart
aú out	ch chin	e less	ē easy	g gift	i trip	ī life
j joke	ŋ sing	ō flow	ȯ flaw	ȯi coin	th thin	th this
ü loot	ù foot	y yet	yü few	yù furious	zh vision	

ga·le·na \gə-'lē-nə\ *n* [L, lead ore] : a bluish gray mineral PbS with metallic luster consisting of lead sulfide, showing highly perfect cubic cleavage, and constituting the principal ore of lead

Ga·len·ic \gā-'len-ik\ *adj* : of or relating to Galen or his medical principles or method — **Ga·len·i·cal** \-i-kəl\ *adj*

galenical *n* : a medicine prepared by extracting one or more active constituents of a plant

Ga·len·ism \'gā-lə-ˌniz-əm\ *n* : the Galenic system of medical practice

ga·lère \ga-'le(ə)r\ *n* [F, lit., galley, fr. MF, fr. Catal *galera*, fr. MGk *galea*] : a group of people having a marked common quality or relationship

gal Friday *n* : GIRL FRIDAY

Ga·li·bi \gə-'lē-bē, 'gal-ə-bē\ *n, pl* **Galibi** *or* **Galibis** 1 : a member of a Carib people of French Guiana 2 : the language of the Galibi people

Gal·i·le·an \ˌgal-ə-'lē-ən, -'lā-\ *adj* : of or relating to Galileo Galilei, founder of experimental physics and astronomy

gal·i·lee \'gal-ə-ˌlē\ *n* [AF, fr. ML *galilaea*] : a chapel or porch at the entrance of an English church

gal·i·ma·ti·as \ˌgal-ə-'mā-shē-əs, -mə-'tyä\ *n* [F] : a confused and often pretentious mixture esp. of words : GOBBLEDYGOOK

gal·in·gale \'gal-ən-ˌgāl, -iŋ-\ *n* [ME, a kind of ginger, fr. MF *galin-gal*, fr. Ar *khalanjān*] : an Old World sedge (*Cyperus longus*) with an aromatic root; *broadly* : any of various plants related to galingale

gal·i·ot *var of* GALLIOT

gal·i·pot \'gal-ə-ˌpät, -ˌpō\ *n* [F] : the crude turpentine oleoresin exuded from a southern European pine (*Pinus pinaster*)

¹gall \'gȯl\ *n* [ME, fr. OE *gealla*; akin to Gk *cholē, cholos* gall, wrath, OE *geolu* yellow — more at YELLOW] 1 a : BILE; *esp* : bile obtained from an animal and used in the arts or medicine b : something bitter to endure c : bitterness of spirit : RANCOR 2 : brazen boldness coupled with impudent assurance and insolence **syn** see TEMERITY

²gall *n* [ME *galle*, fr. OE *gealla*, fr. L *galla* gallnut] 1 a : a skin sore caused by chronic irritation b : a cause or state of exasperation 2 *archaic* : FLAW

³gall *vt* 1 a : to fret and wear away by friction : CHAFE ⟨the loose saddle ~ed the horse's back⟩ ⟨the ~ing of a metal bearing⟩ b : IRRITATE, VEX ⟨sarcasm ~s her⟩ c : HARASS ⟨~ed by enemy fire⟩ ~ *vi* 1 : to become sore or worn by rubbing 2 : SEIZE 2

⁴gall *n* [ME *galle*, fr. MF, fr. L *galla*] : a swelling of plant tissue usu. due to fungi or insect parasites and sometimes forming an important source of tannin

Gal·la \'gal-ə\ *n, pl* **Galla** *or* **Gal·las** 1 : a member of any of several groups of Cushitic-speaking peoples of Kenya and southern Ethiopia 2 : the Cushitic language of the Galla

gal·la·mine tri·eth·io·dide \'gal-ə-ˌmēn-ˌtrī-,eth-'ī-ə-ˌdīd\ *n* [pyrogal·lol + amine + triethyl + iodide] : a substituted ammonium salt $C_{20}H_{60}I_3N_3O_3$ that is used to produce muscle relaxation esp. during anesthesia — called also *gallamine*

gall on an oak leaf

¹gal·lant \gə-'lant, gə-'länt, 'gal-ənt\ *n* 1 : a young man of fashion 2 a : LADIES' MAN b : SUITOR c : PARAMOUR

²gal·lant \'gal-ənt (*usu in sense 2*); gə-'lant, gə-'länt (*usu in sense 3*)\ *adj* [ME *galaunt*, fr. MF *galant*, fr. prp. of *galer* to have a good time, fr. *gale* pleasure, of Gmc origin; akin to OE *wela* weal — more at WEAL] 1 : showy in dress or bearing : SMART 2 a : SPLENDID, STATELY ⟨a ~ ship⟩ b : SPIRITED, BRAVE ⟨~ efforts against the enemy⟩ c : nobly chivalrous and often self-sacrificing 3 a : courteously and elaborately attentive esp. to ladies b : given to amorous intrigue **syn** see CIVIL **ant** ungallant — **gal·lant·ly** *adv*

³gal·lant \gə-'lant, -'länt\ *vt* 1 : to pay court to (a lady) : ATTEND 2 *obs* : to manipulate (a fan) in a modish manner ~ *vi* : to pay court to ladies

gal·lant·ry \'gal-ən-trē\ *n, pl* **-ries** 1 *archaic* : gallant appearance 2 a : an act of marked courtesy b : courteous attention to a lady c : amorous attention or pursuit 3 : spirited and conspicuous bravery **syn** see HEROISM **ant** dastardliness

gal·late \'gal-ˌāt, 'gȯl-\ *n* : a salt or ester of gallic acid

gall·blad·der \'gȯl-ˌblad-ər\ *n* : a membranous muscular sac in which bile from the liver is stored

gal·le·ass \'gal-ē-əs\ *n* [MF *galeasse*] : a large fast war galley of southern Europe in the 16th and 17th centuries

gal·lein \'gal-ē-ən, 'gal-ˌēn\ *n* [*gallic* acid + *phthalein*] : a metallic-green crystalline phthalein dye $C_{20}H_{12}O_7$ used esp. in dyeing textiles violet and as an indicator

gal·le·on \'gal-ē-ən\ *n* [OSp *galeón*, fr. MF *galion*, fr. OF *galie* galley] : a heavy square-rigged sailing ship of the 15th to early 18th centuries used for war or commerce esp. by the Spanish

gal·lery \'gal-(ə-)rē\ *n, pl* **-ler·ies** [ME *galerie*, fr. ML *galeria*] 1 a : a roofed promenade : COLONNADE b : CORRIDOR 2 a : an outdoor balcony b *South & Midland* : PORCH, VERANDA c (1) : a platform at the quarters or stern of a ship (2) : a gun platform or emplacement on a ship d : a railed walk around the upper part of an engine to facilitate oiling or inspection 3 a : a long and narrow passage, apartment, or corridor b : a subterranean passageway in a cave or military mining system; *also* : a working drift or level in mining c : an underground passage made by a mole or ant or a passage made in wood by an insect 4 a : a room or building devoted to the exhibition of works of art b : an institution or business exhibiting or dealing in works of art c : COLLECTION, AGGREGATION ⟨the rich ~ of characters in this novel —H. S.

Canby⟩ 5 a : a structure pr[...] walls of an auditorium to acc[...] : the highest balcony in a theat[...] seats b : the part of a theater a[...] c : the undiscriminating general[...] tennis or golf match 6 : a photo[...] \-rēd\ *adj*

gallery forest *n* : a forest growing al[...] otherwise devoid of trees

gal·lery-go·er \'gal(-ə)-rē-ˌgō(-ə)r\ *n* : [...] art galleries

gal·le·ta \gə-'yet-ə, gī-'et-ə\ *n* [Sp, hardta[...] nial forage grasses (*Hilaria rigida* and *H.*[...]) the southwestern U.S. and in Mexico

gal·ley \'gal-ē\ *n, pl* **galleys** [ME *galeie*, fr. C[...] *galea*] 1 : a large low medieval ship prope[...] and used in the Mediterranean for war and tra[...] ship of classical antiquity propelled chiefly b[...] open rowing boat formerly used in England [...] cooking apparatus esp. of a ship or airplane 5 [...] commonly of pressed steel with upright sides to [...] : a proof from type on a galley before it is made u[...]

galley slave *n* 1 : a slave or criminal acting as a r[...] 2 : DRUDGE 1

gal·ley-west \ˌgal-ē-'west\ *adv* [prob. alter. of E [...] (badly askew)] : into destruction or confusion ⟨was kn[...]

gall·fly \'gȯl-ˌflī\ *n* : an insect (as a gall wasp) that dep[...] in plants and causes galls in which the larvae feed

¹gal·liard \'gal-yərd\ *adj* [ME *gaillard*, fr. MF] *arch*[...] LIVELY

²galliard *n* : a gay dance with five steps to a phrase popu[...] 16th and 17th centuries

Gal·lic \'gal-ik\ *adj* [L *Gallicus*, fr. *Gallia* Gaul] : of or rela[...] Gaul or France

gal·lic acid \ˌgal-ik-, ˌgȯ-lik-\ *n* [F *gallique*, fr. *galle* gall] : a [...] crystalline acid $C_7H_6O_5$ found widely in plants or combine[...] tannins and used esp. in dyes and writing ink and as a pho[...] graphic developer

Gal·li·can \'gal-i-kən\ *adj* 1 : GALLIC 2 *often not cap* : of or rela[...] ing to Gallicanism — **Gallican** *n*

Gal·li·can·ism \-kə-ˌniz-əm\ *n* : a movement originating in France [...] and advocating administrative independence from papal control [...] for the Roman Catholic Church in each nation

gal·li·cism \'gal-ə-ˌsiz-əm\ *n, often cap* 1 : a characteristic French idiom or expression appearing in another language 2 : a French trait

gal·li·cize \-ˌsīz\ *vt* **-cized; -ciz·ing** : to cause to conform to a French mode or idiom — **gal·li·ci·za·tion** \ˌgal-ə-sə-'zā-shən\ *n*

gal·li·gas·kins \ˌgal-i-'gas-kənz\ *n pl* [prob. modif. of MF *gar-guesques*, fr. OSp *greguescos*, fr. *griego* Greek, fr. L *Graecus*] 1 a : loose wide hose or breeches worn in the 16th and 17th centuries b : very loose trousers 2 *chiefly dial* : LEGGINGS

gal·li·mau·fry \ˌgal-ə-'mȯ-frē\ *n, pl* **-fries** [MF *galimafree* hash] : MEDLEY, JUMBLE

gal·li·na·ceous \ˌgal-ə-'nā-shəs\ *adj* [L *gallinaceus* of domestic fowl, fr. *gallina* hen, fr. *gallus* cock] : of or relating to an order (Galliformes) of heavy-bodied largely terrestrial birds including the pheasants, turkeys, grouse, and the common domestic fowl

gall·ing \'gȯ-liŋ\ *adj* : markedly irritating : VEXING ⟨suffered a ~ defeat⟩ — **gall·ing·ly** \-liŋ-lē\ *adv*

gal·li·nip·per \'gal-ə-ˌnip-ər\ *n* [origin unknown] : a very large American mosquito (*Psorophora ciliata*); *also* : an insect that bites or is thought to bite

gal·li·nule \'gal-ə-ˌn(y)ü(ə)l\ *n* [NL *Gallinula*, genus of birds, fr. L, pullet, dim. of *gallina*] : any of several aquatic birds of the rail family with unlobed feet and a frontal shield on the head

gal·li·ot \'gal-ē-ət\ *n* [ME *galiote*, fr. MF, fr. ML *galeota*, dim. of *galea* galley, fr. MGk] 1 : a small swift galley formerly used in the Mediterranean 2 [D *galjoot*, fr. MF *galiote*] : a long narrow light-draft Dutch merchant sailing ship

gal·li·pot \'gal-i-ˌpät\ *n* [ME *galy pott*] 1 : a small usu. ceramic vessel 2 *archaic* : DRUGGIST

gal·li·um \'gal-ē-əm\ *n* [NL, fr. L *gallus* (intended as trans. of Paul *Lecoq* de Boisbaudran †1912 F chemist] : a rare bluish white metallic element that is hard and brittle at low temperatures but melts just above room temperature and expands on freezing — see ELEMENT table

gal·li·vant \'gal-ə-ˌvant\ *vi* [perh. alter. of ³*gallant*] 1 : to go about usu. ostentatiously or indiscreetly with members of the opposite sex 2 : to travel or roam about for pleasure

gall midge *n* : any of numerous minute two-winged flies (family Cecidomyiidae) most of which cause gall formation in plants

gall mite *n* : any of various minute 4-legged mites (family Eriophyidae) that form galls on plants

gall·nut \'gȯl-ˌnət\ *n* [⁴*gall*] : a gall resembling a nut

Gal·lo·ma·nia \ˌgal-ō-'mā-nē-ə, -nyə\ *n* [NL, fr. L *Gallus* Gaul] : a strong prejudice in favor of what is French

gal·lon \'gal-ən\ *n* [ME *galon*, a liquid measure, fr. ONF, fr. ML *galeta* pail, a liquid measure] : a unit of liquid capacity equal to 231 cubic inches or four quarts — see WEIGHT table

gal·lon·age \'gal-ə-nij\ *n* : amount in gallons

gal·loon \gə-'lün\ *n* [F *galon*] : a narrow trimming esp. of lace, embroidery, or braid with metallic threads — **gal·looned** \-'lünd\ *adj*

¹gal·lop \'gal-əp\ *n* [MF *galop*] 1 : a springing gait of a quadruped; *specif* : a fast natural 3-beat gait of the horse — compare ³CANTER, RUN 2 : a ride or run at a gallop 3 : a rapid or hasty progression ⟨rushed through the reports at a ~⟩

²gallop *vi* 1 : to progress or ride at a gallop 2 : to run fast ~ *vt* 1 : to cause to gallop 2 : to transport at a gallop — **gal·lop·er** *n*

gal·lo·pade \ˌgal-ə-'pād, -'päd\ *n* : GALOP

Gal·lo·phile \'gal-ə-ˌfīl\ *n* [L *Gallus* Gaul + E *-phile*] : FRANCOPHILE — **Gallophile** *adj*

[...text in right margin, partially torn...]
jecting from one or more interior [...] r commodate additional people; esp [...] udience having the cheapest [...] public d : the spectators at a [...] grapher's studio — **gal·ler·ied**

[...]ong a watercourse in a [...] [...]s who frequent [...]

gal·lop·ing *adj* : progressing or increasing rapidly ⟨~ inflation⟩ ⟨a ~ disease⟩ ⟨~ corruption in government — *Atlantic*⟩

Gal·lo·way \'gal-ə-ˌwā\ *n* [*Galloway*, Scotland] : any of a breed of hardy medium-sized hornless chiefly black beef cattle native to southwestern Scotland

gal·low·glass \'gal-ō-ˌglas\ *n* [by folk etymology fr. IrGael *gallōglach*, fr. *gall* foreigner + *ōglach* soldier] : a mercenary or retainer of an Irish chief **2** : an armed Irish foot soldier

¹gal·lows \'gal-(ˌ)ōz, -əz\ *n, pl* **gallows** *or* **gal·lows·es** [ME *galwes*, pl. of *galwe*, fr. OE *gealga*; akin to OHG *galgo* gallows, Arm *jatk* twig] **1 a** : a frame usu. of two upright posts and a crossbeam from which criminals are hanged — called also **gallows tree** **b** : the punishment of hanging (got the ~ for murder) **2** : a structure consisting of an upright frame with a crosspiece **3** *chiefly dial* : SUSPENDER 2a

²gallows *adj* : deserving the gallows

gallows bird *n* : a person who deserves hanging

gallows humor *n* [trans. of G *galgenhumor*] : humor that makes fun of a very serious or terrifying situation

gall·stone \'gȯl-ˌstōn\ *n* : a calculus formed in the gallbladder or biliary passages

Gal·lup poll \'gal-əp-\ *n* [George H. *Gallup* b1901 Am public opinion statistician] : a sampling of public opinion taken by questioning a representative cross section (we can . . . find out who are the supporters only by organizing inquiries and *Gallup* polls — Barbara & Robert North)

gal·lus \'gal-əs\ *n* [alter. of ¹*gallows*] *chiefly dial* : SUSPENDER 2a — usu. used in pl.

gal·lused \'gal-əst\ *adj, chiefly dial* : wearing galluses

gall wasp *n* : a hymenopterous gallfly (family Cynipidae)

gal·ly \'gal-ē\ *vt* **gal·lied; gal·ly·ing** [origin unknown] *chiefly dial* : FRIGHTEN, TERRIFY

Ga·lois theory \gal-ˈwä-\ *n* [Évariste *Galois* †1832 F mathematician] : a part of the theory of mathematical groups concerned esp. with the conditions under which a solution to a polynomial equation with coefficients in a given mathematical field can be obtained in the field by the repetition of operations and the extraction of nth roots

ga·loot \gə-ˈlüt\ *n* [origin unknown] *slang* : FELLOW; *esp* : one that is strange or foolish

ga·lop \'gal-əp, ga-ˈlō\ *n* [F] : a lively dance in duple measure; *also* : the music of a galop

ga·lore \gə-ˈlō(ə)r, -ˈlȯ(ə)r\ *adj* [IrGael *go leor* enough] : ABUNDANT, PLENTIFUL — used postpositively ⟨bargains ~⟩

ga·losh \gə-ˈläsh\ *n* [ME *galoche*, fr. MF] **1** *obs* : a shoe with a heavy sole **2** : a high overshoe worn esp. in snow and slush — **ga·loshed** \-ˈläsht\ *adj*

ga·lumph \gə-ˈləm(p)f\ *vi* [prob. alter. of ¹*gallop*] : to move with a clumsy heavy tread

galv *abbr* galvanized

gal·van·ic \gal-ˈvan-ik\ *adj* **1** : of, relating to, or producing a direct current of electricity ⟨a ~ cell⟩ **2 a** : having an electric effect : STIMULATING ⟨a ~ personality⟩ **b** : produced as if by an electric shock : JERKY, NERVOUS ⟨a ~ response⟩ — **gal·van·i·cal·ly** \-i-k(ə-)lē\ *adv*

galvanic couple *n* : a pair of dissimilar substances (as metals) capable of acting together as an electric source when brought in contact with an electrolyte

gal·va·nism \'gal-və-ˌniz-əm\ *n* [F or It; F *galvanisme*, fr. It *galvanismo*, fr. Luigi *Galvani*] **1** : a direct current of electricity esp. when produced by chemical action **2** : the therapeutic use of direct electric current **3** : vital or forceful activity

gal·va·nize \'gal-və-ˌnīz\ *vt* **-nized; -niz·ing** **1 a** : to subject to the action of an electric current esp. for the purpose of stimulating physiologically ⟨~ a muscle⟩ **b** : to stimulate or excite as if by an electric shock ⟨the candidate *galvanized* his followers into action⟩ **2** : to coat (iron or steel) with zinc — **gal·va·ni·za·tion** \ˌgal-və-nə-ˈzā-shən\ *n* — **gal·va·niz·er** \'gal-və-ˌnī-zər\ *n*

galvano- *comb form* [*galvanic*] : galvanic current ⟨*galvanometer*⟩

gal·va·nom·e·ter \ˌgal-və-ˈnäm-ət-ər\ *n* : an instrument for detecting or measuring a small electric current by movements of a magnetic needle or of a coil in a magnetic field — **gal·va·no·met·ric** \-ˌnō-ˈme-trik\ *adj*

gal·va·no·scope \gal-ˈvan-ə-ˌskōp, 'gal-və-nə-\ *n* : an instrument for detecting the presence and direction of an electric current by the deflection of a magnetic needle

gal·yak \'gal-ˌyak\ *n* [native name in Uzbekistan, U.S.S.R.] : a short-haired flat or slightly moiré fur derived from the pelt of a stillborn lamb or kid

¹gam \'gam\ *n* [prob. fr. F dial. *gambe*, fr. ONF, fr. LL *gamba*] *slang* : LEG

²gam *n* [perh. short for obs. *gammon* (talk)] **1** : a visit or friendly conversation at sea or ashore esp. between whalers **2** : a school of whales

³gam *vb* **gammed; gam·ming** *vi* : to engage in a gam ~ *vt* **1** : to have a gam with **2** : to spend or pass (as time) talking

gam- *or* **gamo-** *comb form* [NL, fr. Gk, marriage, fr. *gamos* — more at BIGAMY] **1** : united : joined ⟨*gamo*sepalous⟩ **2** : sexual : sexuality ⟨*gamic*⟩ ⟨*gamo*genesis⟩

gama grass \'gam-ə-\ *n* [prob. alter. of *grama*] : a tall coarse American grass (*Tripsacum dactyloides*) valuable for forage — called also *gama*

gamba *n* : VIOLA DA GAMBA

¹gam·ba·do \gam-ˈbād-(ˌ)ō\ *n, pl* **-does** *also* **-dos** [perh. modif. of It *gambale*, fr. *gamba* leg] : a horseman's legging

²gambado *n, pl* **-does** *also* **-dos** [modif. of F *gambade* — more at GAMBOL] **1** : a spring of a horse **2** : CAPER, GAMBOL

gam·bier *also* **gam·bir** \'gam-ˌbi(ə)r\ *n* [Malay *gambir*] : a yellowish catechu that is obtained from a Malayan woody vine and is used for chewing with the betel nut and for tanning and dyeing

gam·bit \'gam-bət\ *n* [It *gambetto*, lit., act of tripping someone, fr. *gamba* leg, fr. LL *gamba, camba*, modif. of Gk *kampē* bend — more at CAMP] **1** : a chess opening in which a player risks one or more minor pieces to gain an advantage in position **2 a** (1) : a

remark intended to start a conversation or make a telling point (2) : TOPIC **b** : a calculated move : STRATAGEM

¹gam·ble \'gam-bəl\ *vb* **gam·bled; gam·bling** \-b(ə-)liŋ\ [prob. back-formation fr. *gambler*, prob. alter. of obs. *gamner*, fr. obs. *gamen* (to play)] *vi* **1 a** : to play a game for (as money or property) **b** : to bet on an uncertain outcome **2** : to stake something on a contingency : SPECULATE ~ *vt* **1** : to risk by gambling : WAGER **2** : VENTURE, HAZARD — **gam·bler** \-blər\ *n*

²gamble *n* **1** : the playing of a game of chance for stakes **2 a** : an act having an element of risk **b** : something chancy

gam·boge \gam-ˈbōj, -ˈbüzh\ *n* [NL *gambogium*, alter. of *cambugium*, irreg. fr. *Cambodia*] **1** : an orange to brown gum resin from southeast Asian trees (genus *Garcinia*, family Guttiferae) that is used as a yellow pigment and cathartic **2** : a strong yellow

¹gam·bol \'gam-bəl\ *n* [modif. of MF *gambade* spring of a horse, *gambol*, prob. fr. OProv *camba* leg, fr. LL] : a skipping or leaping about in play

²gambol *vi* **-boled** *or* **-bolled; -bol·ing** *or* **-bol·ling** \-bə-liŋ *also* -bliŋ\ : to skip about in play : FRISK

gam·brel \'gam-brəl\ *n* [ONF *gamberel*, fr. *gambe* leg, fr. LL *gamba*] **1** : a stick or iron for suspending slaughtered animals **2** : the hock of an animal

gambrel roof *n* : a curb roof of the same section in all parts with a lower steeper slope and an upper flatter one

gambrel roof

gam·bu·sia \gam-ˈb(y)ü-zh(ē-)ə\ *n* [NL, genus name, modif. of AmerSp *gambusino* gambusia] : any of a genus (*Gambusia*) of topminnows introduced as valuable exterminators of mosquito larvae in warm fresh waters

¹game \'gām\ *n* [ME, fr. OE *gamen*; akin to OHG *gaman* amusement] **1 a** (1) : activity engaged in for diversion or amusement : PLAY ⟨children happy at their ~s⟩ (2) : the equipment for a game **b** : often derisive or mocking jesting : FUN, SPORT ⟨make ~ of a nervous player⟩ ⟨stop your ~s and nonsense⟩ **2 a** : a procedure or strategy for gaining an end : TACTIC **b** (1) : an illegal or shady scheme or maneuver : RACKET (2) : a field of gainful activity : LINE ⟨the newspaper ~⟩ (3) : a specified type of activity or mode of behavior ⟨the dating ~⟩ ⟨the ~ of politics⟩ **3 a** (1) : a physical or mental competition conducted according to rules with the participants in direct opposition to each other (2) : a division of a larger contest (3) : the number of points necessary to win (4) : points scored in certain card games (as in all fours) by a player whose cards count up the highest (5) : the manner of playing in a contest (6) : the set of rules governing a game **b** *pl* : organized athletics **c** : a situation that involves contest, rivalry, or struggle ⟨got into aviation early in the ~⟩; *esp* : one in which opposing interests given specific information are allowed a choice of moves with the object of maximizing their wins and minimizing their losses **4 a** (1) : animals under pursuit or taken in hunting; *esp* : wild animals hunted for sport or food (2) : the flesh of game animals **b** *archaic* : PLUCK **c** : an object of ridicule or attack — often used in the phrase *fair game* **syn** see FUN

²game *vb* **gamed; gam·ing** *vi* : to play for a stake ~ *vt, archaic* : to lose or squander by gambling

³game *adj* **1** : having a resolute unyielding spirit ⟨~ to the end⟩ **2** : of or relating to game ⟨~ laws⟩

⁴game *adj* [perh. fr. ³*game*] : LAME ⟨a ~ leg⟩

game·cock \'gām-ˌkäk\ *n* : a male game fowl

game fish *n* **1** : a fish of a family (Salmonidae) including salmons, trouts, chars, and whitefishes **2** : SPORT FISH; *esp* : a fish made a legal catch by law

game fowl *n* : a domestic fowl of a strain developed for the production of fighting cocks

game·keep·er \'gām-ˌkē-pər\ *n* : one that has charge of the breeding and protection of game animals or birds on a private preserve

gam·e·lan \'gam-ə-ˌlan\ *n* [Jav] **1** : a Javanese instrument resembling the xylophone **2** : a flute, string, and percussion orchestra of southeast Asia

game·ly \'gām-lē\ *adv* : in a plucky manner

game·ness \'gām-nəs\ *n* **1** : ENDURANCE, PLUCK

game of chance : a game (as a dice game) in which chance rather than skill determines the outcome

game of skill : a game (as chess) in which skill rather than chance determines the outcome

game plan *n* : a strategy for achieving an objective

game point *n* : a situation (as in tennis) in which one player will win the game by winning the next point; *also* : the point won

games·man·ship \'gāmz-mən-ˌship\ *n* : the art or practice of winning games by questionable expedients without actually violating the rules

game·some \'gām-səm\ *adj* : MERRY, FROLICSOME — **game·some·ly** *adv* — **game·some·ness** *n*

game·ster \'gām-stər\ *n* : a person who plays games; *esp* : GAMBLER

gamet- *or* **gameto-** *comb form* [NL, fr. *gameta*] : gamete ⟨*gameto*phore⟩

gam·etan·gi·um \ˌgam-ə-ˈtan-jē-əm\ *n, pl* **-gia** \-jē-ə\ [NL, fr. *gamet-* + Gk *angeion* vessel — more at ANGI-] : a cell or organ in which gametes are developed

ga·mete \gə-ˈmēt, 'gam-ˌēt\ *n* [NL *gameta*, fr. Gk *gametēs* husband, fr. *gamein* to marry, fr. *gamos* marriage — more at BIGAMY] : a mature germ cell possessing a haploid chromosome set and capable of initiating formation of a new individual by fusion with another gamete — **ga·met·ic** \gə-'met-ik\ adj — **ga·met·i·cal·ly** \-i-k(ə-)lē\ adv

game theory n : THEORY OF GAMES

ga·me·to·cyte \gə-'mēt-ə-,sīt\ n [ISV] : a cell that divides to produce gametes

ga·me·to·gen·e·sis \gə-,mēt-ə-'jen-ə-səs\ n [NL] : the production of gametes — **ga·me·to·gen·ic** \-'jen-ik\ or **gam·e·tog·e·nous** \,gam-ə-'täj-ə-nəs\ adj — **gam·etog·e·ny** \-nē\ n

ga·me·to·phore \gə-'mēt-ə-,fō(ə)r, -,fȯ(ə)r\ n : a modified branch bearing gametangia — **ga·me·to·phor·ic** \-,mēt-ə-'fȯr-ik, -'fär-\ adj

ga·me·to·phyte \gə-'mēt-ə-,fīt\ n [ISV] : the individual or generation of a plant exhibiting alternation of generations that bears sex organs — compare SPOROPHYTE — **ga·me·to·phyt·ic** \-,mēt-ə-'fit-ik\ adj

gam·ic \'gam-ik\ adj : requiring fertilization : SEXUAL

-gam·ic \'gam-ik\ adj comb form [ISV, fr. Gk -gamos -gamous] : having (such) reproductive organs (cleistogamic)

gam·in \'gam-ən\ n [F] 1 : a boy who hangs out on the streets : URCHIN 2 : GAMINE 2

ga·mine \ga-'mēn\ n [F, fem. of gamin] 1 : a girl who hangs out on the streets : TOMBOY 2 : a girl of elfin appeal

gam·ing \'gā-miŋ\ n 1 : the practice of gambling 2 : the playing of games that simulate actual conditions (as of business or war) esp. for training or testing purposes

¹gam·ma \'gam-ə\ n [ME, fr. LL, fr. Gk, of Sem origin; akin to Heb gīmel gimel] 1 : the 3d letter of the Greek alphabet — see ALPHABET table 2 : the degree of contrast of a developed photographic image or of a television image 3 : a unit of magnetic intensity equal to 0.00001 oersted 4 : GAMMA RAY 5 : MICROGRAM

²gamma or γ- adj 1 : of, relating to, or being one of three or more closely related chemical substances 2 : third in position in the structure of an organic molecule from a particular group or atom

gamma globulin n : any of several globulins of plasma or serum that have less electrophoretic mobility at alkaline pH than serum albumins, alpha globulins, or beta globulins and that include most antibodies

gamma ray n 1 : a photon or radiation quantum emitted spontaneously by a radioactive substance; also : a high-energy photon 2 : a continuous stream of gamma rays — called also gamma radiation

gam·mer \'gam-ər\ n [prob. alter. of godmother] : an old woman — compare GAFFER

¹gam·mon \'gam-ən\ n [ONF gambon ham, aug. of gambe leg — more at GAM] 1 chiefly Brit : HAM 2 2 chiefly Brit a : a side of bacon b : the lower end of a side of bacon

²gammon n [perh. alter. of ME gamen game] 1 archaic : BACKGAMMON 2 : the winning of a backgammon game before the loser removes any men from the board

³gammon vt : to beat by scoring a gammon

⁴gammon n [obs. gammon (talk)] : talk intended to deceive : HUMBUG

⁵gammon vi 1 : to talk gammon 2 : PRETEND, FEIGN ~ vt : DECEIVE, FOOL

gamo- — see GAM-

gamo·deme \'gam-ə-,dēm\ n : a more or less isolated breeding community of organisms

gamo·gen·e·sis \,gam-ə-'jen-ə-səs\ n [NL] : sexual reproduction — **gamo·ge·net·ic** \-ə-'net-ik\ adj — **gamo·ge·net·i·cal·ly** \-i-k(ə-)lē\ adv

gamo·pet·al·ous \-'pet-ʼl-əs\ adj : having the corolla composed of united petals (the morning glory is ~)

gamo·phyl·lous \-'fil-əs\ adj : having united leaves or leaflike parts

gamo·sep·al·ous \-'sep-ə-ləs\ adj : having the sepals united

-g·a·mous \g-ə-məs\ adj comb form [Gk -gamos, fr. gamos marriage — more at BIGAMY] 1 : characterized by having or practicing (such) a marriage or (such or so many) marriages (exogamous) 2 : -GAMIC (heterogamous)

gamp \'gamp\ n [Sarah Gamp, nurse with a large umbrella in Martin Chuzzlewit by Charles Dickens] Brit : a large umbrella

gam·ut \'gam-ət\ n [ML gamma, lowest note of Guido's scale (fr. LL, 3d letter of the Greek alphabet) + ut] 1 : the whole series of recognized musical notes 2 : an entire range or series (the letters she received ran the ~ from praise to contempt)

gamy or **gam·ey** \'gā-mē\ adj **gam·i·er; -est** 1 : BRAVE, PLUCKY — used esp. of animals 2 a : having the flavor of game; esp : having the flavor of game near tainting b : SMELLY 3 a : SCANDALOUS, SPICY (gave her all the ~ details) b : CORRUPT, DISREPUTABLE (a ~ character) — **gam·i·ly** \-mə-lē\ adv — **gam·i·ness** \-mē-nəs\ n

-g·a·my \g-ə-mē\ n comb form [ME -gamie, fr. LL -gamia, fr. Gk — more at BIGAMY] 1 : marriage (exogamy) 2 : union for propagation or reproduction (allogamy) 3 : possession of (such) reproductive organs or (such) a mode of fertilization (cleistogamy)

gan past of GIN

Gan·da \'gan-də\ n, pl **Ganda** or **Gandas** 1 : a member of a Bantu-speaking people of Uganda 2 : the Bantu language of the Ganda people used as the official language of Uganda

¹gan·der \'gan-dər\ n [ME, fr. OE gandra; akin to OE gōs goose] 1 : the adult male goose 2 : SIMPLETON

²gander vi, dial : WANDER, RAMBLE

³gander n [prob. fr. ¹gander; fr. the outstretched neck of a person craning to look at something] slang : LOOK, GLANCE (talking and taking ~s at the girls —Life)

Gan·dhi·an \'gän-dē-ən, 'gan-\ adj : of or relating to the Indian political and spiritual leader Mohandas K. Gandhi or his principle of nonviolence

gan·dy dancer \'gan-dē-\ n [perh. fr. the Gandy Manufacturing Company, Chicago, Illinois, toolmakers] 1 : a laborer in a railroad section gang 2 : an itinerant or seasonal laborer

ga·nef \'gän-əf\ n [Yiddish, fr. Heb gannābh thief] slang : THIEF, RASCAL

Ga·ne·lon \,gan-ʼl-'ōⁿ\ n [F] : the traitor in the Charlemagne romances who schemes for the defeat of Charlemagne's rear guard at Roncesvalles

¹gang \'gaŋ\ n [ME, fr. OE; akin to OHG gang act of going, Skt jaṅghā shank] 1 dial Brit : JOURNEY, WAY 2 a (1) : a set of articles : OUTFIT (a ~ of oars) (2) : a combination of similar implements or devices arranged for convenience to act together (a ~ of saws) b : GROUP: as (1) : a group of persons working together (2) : a group of persons working to unlawful or antisocial ends; esp : a band of antisocial adolescents 3 : a group of persons having informal and usu. close social relations (have the ~ over for a party)

²gang vt 1 : to attack in a gang 2 a : to assemble or operate simultaneously as a gang b : to arrange in or produce as a gang (as type pages) ~ vi : to move or act as a gang (everyone ~ed toward the door)

³gang vi [ME gangen, fr. OE gangan; akin to OE gang] Scot : GO

gang·er \'gaŋ-ər\ n, Brit : the foreman of a gang of workmen

gang hook n : two or three fishhooks with their shanks joined together

gang·land \'gaŋ-,land\ n : the world of organized crime

gangli- or **ganglio-** comb form [NL, fr. Gk ganglion] : ganglion (gangliectomy) (ganglioplexus)

gan·gling \'gaŋ-gliŋ, -glən\ adj [perh. irreg. fr. Sc gangrel vagrant, lanky person] : being loosely and awkwardly built : LANKY (a ~ gawky child)

gan·gli·on \'gaŋ-glē-ən\ n, pl **-glia** \-glē-ə\ also **-gli·ons** [LL, fr. Gk] 1 a : a small cystic tumor connected either with a joint membrane or tendon sheath b : a mass of nerve tissue containing nerve cells external to the brain or spinal cord; also : NUCLEUS 2b 2 : a focus of strength or energy — **gan·gli·on·at·ed** \'gaŋ-glē-ə-,nāt-əd\ adj — **gan·gli·on·ic** \,gaŋ-glē-'än-ik\ adj

gan·gli·o·side \'gaŋ-glē-ə-,sīd\ n [ISV ganglion + ²-ose + -ide] : any of a group of lipids that yield a hexose sugar on hydrolysis and are found esp. in ganglion cells

gan·gly \'gaŋ-glē\ adj **gan·gli·er; -est** : GANGLING

gang·plank \'gaŋ-,plaŋk\ n : a movable bridge used in boarding or leaving a ship at a pier

gang·plow \-,plau̇\ n : a plow designed to turn two or more furrows at one time

gang·rel \'gaŋ-(ə-)rəl\ n [ME, irreg. fr. gangen to go, fr. OE gangan; akin to OE gang] Scot : VAGRANT

¹gan·grene \'gaŋ-,grēn, gaŋ-'; 'gan-,, gan-\ n [L gangraena, fr. Gk gangraina; akin to Gk gran to gnaw] 1 : local death of soft tissues due to loss of blood supply 2 : a pervasive moral evil — **gan·gre·nous** \'gaŋ-grə-nəs\ adj

²gangrene vb **gan·grened; gan·gren·ing** vt : to make gangrenous ~ vi : to become gangrenous

gang·ster \'gaŋ-stər\ n : a member of a gang of criminals : RACKETEER — **gang·ster·ism** \-stə-,riz-əm\ n

gangue \'gaŋ\ n [F, fr. G gang vein of metal, fr. OHG, act of going] : the worthless rock or vein matter in which valuable metals or minerals occur

gang up vi 1 : to combine for a specific purpose (ganged up to raise prices) 2 : to make a joint assault (ganged up on him and beat him up) 3 : to exert group pressure (the class ganged up against the teacher)

gang·way \'gaŋ-,wā\ n 1 : PASSAGEWAY; esp : a temporary way of planks 2 a : either of the sides of the upper deck of a ship b : the opening by which a ship is boarded c : GANGPLANK 3 Brit : AISLE 4 : a main level or haulageway in a mine 5 a : a cross aisle dividing the front benches from the back benches in the British House of Commons b : an aisle in the British House of Commons that separates government and opposition benches 6 : a clear passage through a crowd — often used as an interjection

gan·is·ter or **gan·nis·ter** \'gan-ə-stər\ n [origin unknown] 1 : a fine-grained quartzite used in the manufacture of refractory brick 2 : a mixture of ground quartz and fireclay used for lining metallurgical furnaces

gan·ja \'gän-jə, 'gan-\ n [Hindi gā̃jā, fr. Skt gañjā] : a potent and selected preparation of cannabis used esp. for smoking

gan·net \'gan-ət\ n, pl **gannets** also **gannet** [ME ganet, fr. OE ganot; akin to OE gōs goose] : any of several large fish-eating seabirds (family Sulidae) that breed in large colonies chiefly on offshore islands

gan·oid \'gan-,ȯid\ adj [deriv. of Gk ganos brightness; akin to Gk gēthein to rejoice — more at JOY] : of or relating to a subclass (Ganoidei) of bony and extinct teleost fishes (as the sturgeons) with usu. hard rhombic enameled scales — **ganoid** n

gante·lope or **gant·lope** \'gant-,lōp\ n [modif. of Sw gatlopp, fr. OSw gatulop, fr. gata road + lop course] archaic : ²GAUNTLET

¹gant·let \'gȯnt-lət, 'gänt-\ var of GAUNTLET

²gantlet n [²gauntlet] : a stretch of railroad track where two lines of track overlap so that one rail of each track is within the rails of the other in order to obviate switching

gant·line \'gant-,līn, -lən\ n [perh. alter. of girtline (gantline)] : a line rove through a block aloft on a ship and used for hoisting

gan·try \'gan-trē\ n, pl **gantries** [perh. modif. of ONF gantier, fr. L cantherius trellis] 1 : a frame for supporting barrels 2 : a frame structure raised on side supports so as to span over or around something: as a : a platform made to carry a traveling crane and supported by towers or side frames running on parallel tracks; also : a movable structure with platforms at different levels used for erecting and servicing rockets before launching b : a structure spanning several railroad tracks and displaying signals for each

gantry 2b

Gan·y·mede \'gan-i-,mēd\ n [L Ganymedes, fr. Gk Ganymēdēs] 1 : a beautiful youth in classical mythology carried off to Olympus to be the cupbearer of the gods 2 : a youth who serves liquors : CUPBEARER 3 : the 4th satellite of Jupiter

GAO abbr General Accounting Office

gaol \'jā(ə)l\ *chiefly Brit var of* JAIL

¹**gap** \'gap\ *n* [ME, fr. ON, chasm, hole; akin to ON *gapa*] **1 a** : a break in a barrier (as a wall, hedge, or line of military defense) **b** : an assailable position **2 a** : a mountain pass **3** : RAVINE **3** : SPARK GAP **4** : a separation in space **5** : a break in continuity : HIATUS ⟨there were unexplained ~s in his story⟩ **6** : a break in the vascular cylinder of a plant where a vascular trace departs from the central cylinder **7** : lack of balance : DISPARITY ⟨the ~ between imports and exports⟩ **8** : a wide difference in character or attitude ⟨the generation ~⟩ — **gap·py** \-ē\ *adj*

²**gap** *vb* **gapped; gap·ping** *vt* : to make an opening in ~ *vi* : to fall or stand open

GAPA *abbr* ground-to-air pilotless aircraft

¹**gape** \'gāp *also* 'gap\ *vi* **gaped; gap·ing** [ME *gapen*, fr. ON *gapa*; akin to L *hiare* to gape, yawn — more at YAWN] **1 a** : to open the mouth wide **b** : to open or part widely ⟨holes *gaped* in the pavement⟩ **2** : to gaze stupidly or in openmouthed surprise or wonder **3** : YAWN *syn* see GAZE — **gap·ing·ly** \'gā-piŋ-lē, 'gap-iŋ\ *adv*

²**gape** *n* **1** : an act of gaping: **a** : YAWN **b** : an openmouthed stare **2** : an unfilled space or extent **3 a** : the median margin-to-margin length of the open mouth **b** : the line along which the mandibles of a bird close **c** : the width of an opening **4** *pl but sing in constr* **a** : a disease of young birds in which gapeworms invade and irritate the trachea **b** : a fit of yawning

gap·er \'gā-pər, 'gap-ər\ *n* **1** : one that gapes **2** : any of several large sluggish burrowing clams (family Myacidae) including several used for food

gape·worm \-,wərm\ *n* : a nematode worm (*Syngamus trachea*) that causes gapes of birds

gapped scale *n* : a musical scale derived from a larger system of tones by omitting certain tones

¹**gar** \'gär\ *interj* [euphemism for *God*] — used as a mild oath

²**gar** *n* [short for *garfish*] : any of various fishes that have an elongate body resembling that of a pike and long and narrow jaws: as **a** : NEEDLEFISH **b** : any of several predaceous No. American freshwater ganoid fishes with rank tough flesh

³**gar** *abbr* garage

GAR *abbr* Grand Army of the Republic

¹**ga·rage** \gə-'räzh, -'räj\ *n* [F, act of docking, garage, fr. *garer* to dock, of Gmc origin; akin to OHG *biwarōn* to protect — more at WARE] : a shelter or repair shop for automotive vehicles

²**garage** *vt* **ga·raged; ga·rag·ing** : to keep or put in a garage

ga·rage·man \-,man\ *n* : a garage worker

garage sale *n* : a sale of used household or personal articles (as furniture, tools, or clothing) held on the seller's own premises

Ga·rand rifle \gə-'rand-, gar-ənd-\ *n* [John C. *Garand*] : M1 RIFLE

garb \'gärb\ *n* [MF *or* OIt; MF *garbe* graceful contour, grace, fr. OIt *garbo* grace] **1** *obs* : FASHION, MANNER **2 a** : style of apparel **b** : outward form : APPEARANCE ⟨give . . . their madness the outward ~ of sanity —Lewis Mumford⟩ — **garb** *vt*

gar·bage \'gär-bij\ *n* [ME, animal entrails] **1** : food waste **2** : REFUSE **b** : unwanted or useless material **2** : worthless writing or speech : TRASH

gar·ban·zo \gär-'bän-(,)zō\ *n, pl* **-zos** [Sp] : CHICK-PEA — called also **garbanzo bean**

¹**gar·ble** \'gär-bəl\ *vt* **gar·bled; gar·bling** \-b(ə-)liŋ\ [ME *garbelen*, fr. OIt *garbellare* to sift, fr. Ar *ghirbāl* sieve, fr. LL *cribellum*; akin to L *cernere* to sift — more at CERTAIN] **1** *archaic* : CULL **2** : to sift impurities from **3 a** : to so alter or distort as to create a wrong impression or change the meaning ⟨*garbled* a story in repeating it⟩ **b** : to introduce textual error into (a message) by inaccurate encipherment, transmission, or decipherment *syn* see MISREPRESENT — **gar·bler** \-b(ə-)lər\ *n*

²**garble** *n* **1** : the impurities removed from spices in sifting **2** : an act or an instance of garbling

gar·board \'gär-,bō(ə)rd, -,bȯ(ə)rd\ *n* [obs. D *gaarboord*] : the strake next to a ship's keel

gar·boil \-,bȯil\ *n* [MF *garbouil*] *archaic* : a confused disordered state : TURMOIL

gar·çon \gär-'sōⁿ\ *n, pl* **garçons** \-'sōⁿ(z)\ [F, boy, servant] : WAITER

garde–man·ger \,gärd-(ə-),män-'zhä\ *n, pl* **garde–mangers** \-'zhä(z)\ [F] : the cold meat department of a large kitchen; *also* : the chef in charge of it

¹**gar·den** \'gärd-ᵊn\ *n* [ME *gardin*, fr. ONF, of Gmc origin; akin to OHG *gart* enclosure — more at YARD] **1 a** : a plot of ground where herbs, fruits, flowers, or vegetables are cultivated **b** : a rich well-cultivated region **c** : a container (as a window box) planted with usu. a variety of small plants ⟨herb ~s⟩ ⟨a dish ~⟩ **2 a** : a public recreation area or park ⟨a botanical ~⟩ **b** : an open-air eating or drinking place — **gar·den·ful** \-,fủl\ *n*

²**garden** *vb* **gar·dened; gar·den·ing** \'gärd-niŋ, -ᵊn-iŋ\ *vi* : to lay out or work in a garden ~ *vt* **1** : to make into a garden **2** : to ornament with gardens — **gar·den·er** \'gärd-nər, -ᵊn-ər\ *n*

³**garden** *adj* **1** : of, relating to, or frequenting a garden **2 a** : of a kind grown in the open as distinguished from one more delicate ⟨~ plant⟩ **b** : ORDINARY, COMMONPLACE

garden apartment *n* : a multiple-unit dwelling having considerable lawn or garden space

garden city *n* : a planned residential community with park and planted areas

garden cress *n* : an Asiatic annual herb (*Lepidium sativum*) of the mustard family sometimes cultivated for its pungent basal leaves

garden heliotrope *n* **1** : a tall rhizomatous Old World valerian (*Valeriana officinalis*) widely cultivated for its fragrant tiny flowers and for its roots which yield the drug valerian **2** : a shrubby Peruvian heliotrope (*Heliotropium arborescens*) with fragrant usu. lilac or violet flowers

gar·de·nia \gär-'dē-nyə\ *n* [NL, genus name, fr. Alexander *Garden* †1791 Sc naturalist] : any of a large genus (*Gardenia*) of Old World tropical trees and shrubs of the madder family with showy fragrant white or yellow flowers

garden–variety *adj* : GARDEN 2b

garde·robe \'gär-,drōb\ *n* [ME, fr. MF; akin to ONF *warderobe* wardrobe] **1 a** : a wardrobe or its contents **2** : a private room : BEDROOM **3** : PRIVY

gar·dy·loo \,gärd-ē-'lü\ *interj* [perh. fr. F *garde à l'eau!* look out for the water!] — used in Edinburgh as a warning cry when it was customary to throw slops from the windows into the streets

Gar·eth \'gar-əth\ *n* : a knight of the Round Table and nephew of King Arthur

gar·fish \'gär-,fish\ *n* [ME *garfysshe*] : GAR

Gar·gan·tua \gär-'ganch-(ə-)wə\ *n* [F] : a gigantic king in Rabelais' *Gargantua* having a great capacity for food and drink

gar·gan·tuan \-,wən\ *adj, often cap* [*Gargantua*] : of tremendous size or volume : GIGANTIC, COLOSSAL ⟨entire cities fleeing before ~ walls of water —William Cleary⟩

gar·get \'gär-gət\ *n* [prob. fr. ME, throat, fr. MF *gargate*; akin to MF *gargouiller*] : mastitis of domestic animals; *esp* : chronic bovine mastitis with gross changes in the form and texture of the udder — **gar·gety** \-gət-ē\ *adj*

¹**gar·gle** \'gär-gəl\ *vb* **gar·gled; gar·gling** \-g(ə-)liŋ\ [MF *gargouiller* to gargle, of imit. origin] *vt* **1 a** : to hold (a liquid) in the mouth or throat and agitate with air from the lungs **b** : to cleanse or disinfect (the oral cavity) in this manner **2** : to utter with a gargling sound ~ *vi* **1** : to use a gargle **2** : to speak or sing as if gargling

²**gargle** *n* **1** : a liquid used in gargling **2** : a gargling sound

gar·goyle \'gär-,gȯil\ *n* [ME *gargoyl*, fr. MF *gargouille*; akin to MF *gargouiller*] **1 a** : a spout in the form of a grotesque human or animal figure projecting from a roof gutter to throw rainwater clear of a building **b** : a grotesquely carved figure **2** : a person with an ugly face — **gar·goyled** \-,gȯild\ *adj*

gar·i·bal·di \,gar-ə-'bȯl-dē\ *n* : a woman's blouse copied from the red shirt worn by the Italian patriot Garibaldi

gargoyle 1a

gar·ish \'gar-ish, 'ge(ə)r-\ *adj* [origin unknown] **1** : clothed in vivid colors **2 a** : excessively vivid : FLASHY **b** : offensively or distressingly bright : GLARING **3** : tastelessly showy *syn* see GAUDY *ant* somber — **gar·ish·ly** *adv* — **gar·ish·ness** *n*

¹**gar·land** \'gär-lənd\ *n* [ME, fr. MF *garlande*] **1** : WREATH, CHAPLET **2** : a grommet or ring of rope used aboard ship in hoisting or to prevent chafing **3** : ANTHOLOGY, COLLECTION

²**garland** *vt* : to form into or deck with a garland

gar·lic \'gär-lik\ *n* [ME *garlek*, fr. OE *gārlēac*, fr. *gār* spear + *lēac* leek — more at GORE] : a European bulbous herb (*Allium sativum*) of the lily family widely cultivated for its pungent compound bulbs much used in cookery; *also* : one of the bulbs — **gar·licky** \-li-kē\ *adj*

garlic salt *n* : a seasoning of ground dried garlic and salt

¹**gar·ment** \'gär-mənt\ *n* [ME, fr. MF *garnement*, fr. OF, fr. *garnir* to equip — more at GARNISH] : an article of clothing

²**garment** *vt* : to clothe with or as if with a garment

¹**gar·ner** \'gär-nər\ *n* [ME, fr. OF *grenier*, fr. L *granarium*, fr. *granum* grain] **1** : GRANARY **2** : a grain bin **2** : something that is collected : ACCUMULATION

²**garner** *vt* **gar·nered; gar·ner·ing** \-g(ə-)riŋ\ **1 a** : to gather into storage **b** : to deposit as if in a granary ⟨volumes in which he has ~ed the fruits of his lifetime labors —Reinhold Niebuhr⟩ **2 a** : to acquire by effort : EARN **b** : ACCUMULATE, COLLECT

gar·net \'gär-nət\ *n* [ME *grenat*, fr. MF, fr. *grenat*, adj., red like a pomegranate, fr. (*pomme*) *grenate* pomegranate] **1** : a brittle and more or less transparent usu. red silicate mineral that has a vitreous luster, occurs mainly in crystals but also in massive form and in grains, is found commonly in gneiss and mica schist, and is used as a semiprecious stone and as an abrasive (hardness 6.5–7.5, sp. gr. 3.15–4.3) **2** : a variable color averaging a dark red

gar·net·if·er·ous \,gär-nət-'if-(ə-)rəs\ *adj* : containing garnets

garnet paper *n* : an abrasive paper with crushed garnet as the abrasive

gar·ni·er·ite \'gär-nē-ə-,rīt\ *n* [Jules *Garnier* †1904 F geologist] : a soft mineral prob. (Mg, Ni)$_4$Si$_2$O$_5$(OH)$_4$ consisting of hydrous nickel magnesium silicate and constituting an important ore of nickel

¹**gar·nish** \'gär-nish\ *vt* [ME *garnishen*, fr. MF *garniss-*, stem of *garnir* to warn, equip, garnish, of Gmc origin; akin to OHG *warnōn* to take heed — more at WARN] **1** : DECORATE, EMBELLISH **b** : to add decorative or savory touches to (food) **2** : to equip with accessories : FURNISH **3** : GARNISHEE *syn* see ADORN

²**garnish** *n* **1** : EMBELLISHMENT, ORNAMENT **2** : a savory or decorative condiment (as watercress or parsley) **3 a** : an unauthorized fee formerly extorted from a new inmate of an English jail **b** : a similar payment required of a new workman

¹**gar·nish·ee** \,gär-nə-'shē\ *n* : one who is served with a garnishment

²**garnishee** *vt* **-eed; -ee·ing** **1** : to serve with a garnishment **2** : to take (as a debtor's wages) by legal authority

gar·nish·ment \'gär-nish-mənt\ *n* **1** : GARNISH **2** : a legal summons or warning concerning the attachment of property to satisfy a debt **3** : a stoppage of a specified sum from wages to satisfy a creditor

gar·ni·ture \'gär-ni-chər, -nə-,chủ(ə)r\ *n* [MF, equipment, alter. of OF *garnesture*, fr. *garnir*] : EMBELLISHMENT, TRIMMING

gar·pike \'gär-,pīk\ *n* : GAR b

gar·ret \'gar-ət\ *n* [ME *garette* watchtower, fr. MF *garite,* perh. fr. OProv *garida,* fr. *garir* to protect, of Gmc origin; akin to OHG *werien*] **:** a room or unfinished part of a house just under the roof

[1]**gar·ri·son** \'gar-ə-sən\ *n* [ME *garisoun* protection, fr. OF *garison,* fr. *garir* to protect, of Gmc origin; akin to OHG *werien* to defend — more at WEIR] **1 :** a military post; *esp* **:** a permanent military installation **2 :** the troops stationed at a garrison

[2]**garrison** *vt* **gar·ri·soned; gar·ri·son·ing** \'gar-ə-s(ə-)niŋ\ **1 :** to station troops in **2 a :** to assign as a garrison **b :** to occupy with troops

garrison cap *n* **:** a visorless folding cap worn as part of a military uniform — compare SERVICE CAP

Gar·ri·son finish \,gar-ə-sən-\ *n* [prob. fr. Snapper *Garrison,* 19th cent. Am jockey] **:** a finish in which the winner comes from behind at the end

garrison house *n* **1 :** a house fortified against Indian attack **2 :** BLOCKHOUSE **3 :** a house having the second story overhanging the first in the front

garrison state *n* **:** a state organized on a primarily military basis; *esp* **:** one whose military preparations threaten to convert it into a totalitarian state

gar·ron \'gar-ən, gə-'rȯn\ *n* [IrGael *gearrān* & ScGael *gearran,* gelding] *Scot & Irish* **:** a small sturdy workhorse

[1]**gar·rote** *or* **ga·rotte** \gə-'rät, -'rōt\ *n* [Sp *garrote*] **1 a :** a method of execution by strangling with an iron collar **b :** the iron collar used **2 a :** strangulation esp. with robbery as the motive **b :** an implement for this purpose

[2]**garrote** *or* **garotte** *vt* **gar·rot·ed** *or* **ga·rott·ed; gar·rot·ing** *or* **ga·rott·ing 1 :** to execute with or as if with a garrote **2 :** to strangle and rob — **gar·rot·er** *n*

gar·ru·li·ty \gə-'rü-lət-ē, ga-\ *n* **:** the quality or state of being talkative

gar·ru·lous \'gar-ə-ləs *also* 'gar-yə-\ *adj* [L *garrulus,* fr. *garrire* to chatter — more at CARE] **:** given to prosy, rambling, or tedious loquacity **:** pointlessly or annoyingly talkative ***syn*** see TALKATIVE ***ant*** taciturn — **gar·ru·lous·ly** *adv* — **gar·ru·lous·ness** *n*

[1]**gar·ter** \'gärt-ər\ *n* [ME, fr. ONF *gartier,* fr. *garet* bend of the knee, of Celt origin; akin to OIr *gairri* calves of the legs] **1 a :** a band worn to hold up a stocking or sock **b :** a strap hanging from a girdle or corset to support a stocking **c :** a band worn to hold up a shirt sleeve **2** *cap* **a :** the British Order of the Garter **b :** the blue velvet garter that is its badge **c :** membership in the order

[2]**garter** *vt* **:** to support with or as if with a garter

garter snake *n* **:** any of numerous harmless viviparous American snakes (genus *Thamnophis*) with longitudinal stripes on the back

garth \'gärth\ *n* [ME, fr. ON *garthr* yard; akin to OHG *gart* enclosure — more at YARD] *archaic* **:** a small yard or enclosure **:** CLOSE

gar·vey \'gär-vē\ *n, pl* **garveys** [prob. fr. the name *Garvey*] **:** a small scow of the New Jersey coast

[1]**gas** \'gas\ *n, pl* **gas·es** *also* **gas·ses** [NL, alter. of L *chaos* space, chaos] **1 :** a fluid (as air) that has neither independent shape nor volume but tends to expand indefinitely **2 a :** a gas or gaseous mixture with the exception of atmospheric air: as (1) **:** a gas or gaseous mixture used to produce anesthesia (2) **:** a combustible gaseous mixture (as for fuel) **b :** a substance that can be used to produce a poisonous, asphyxiating, or irritant atmosphere **3** *slang* **:** empty talk **:** BOMBAST **4 :** GASOLINE **5** *slang* **:** one that has unusual appeal ⟨if you dig skinny-dipping with kindred souls, it is a ~ —*Berkeley Barb*⟩

[2]**gas** *vb* **gassed; gas·sing** *vt* **1 a :** to treat chemically with gas **b :** to poison or otherwise affect adversely with gas **2 :** to supply with gas or esp. gasoline ⟨~ up the automobile⟩ ~ *vi* **1 :** to give off gas **2** *slang* **:** to talk idly **3 :** to fill the tank (as of an automobile) with gasoline — often used with *up*

gas·bag \'gas-,bag\ *n* **1 :** a bag for holding gas **2 :** an idle talker

gas chamber *n* **:** a chamber in which prisoners are executed by poison gas

gas·con \'gas-kən\ *n* **1** *cap* **:** a native of Gascony **2 :** a boastful swaggering person — **Gascon** *adj*

gas·con·ade \,gas-kə-'nād\ *n* [F *gasconnade,* fr. *gasconner* to boast, fr. *gascon* gascon, boaster] **:** BRAVADO, BOASTING — **gasconade** *vi* — **gas·con·ad·er** *n*

gas·eous \'gas-ē-əs, 'gash-əs\ *adj* **1 a :** having the form of or being gas; *also* **:** of or relating to gases **b :** heated so as to remain free from suspended liquid droplets — used of a vapor not in contact with its own liquid **2 :** lacking substance or solidity **:** TENUOUS — **gas·eous·ness** *n*

gas fitter *n* **:** a workman who installs or repairs gas pipes and appliances

gas gangrene *n* **:** progressive gangrene marked by impregnation of the dead and dying tissue with gas and caused by one or more toxin-producing clostridia

[1]**gash** \'gash\ *vb* [ME *garsen,* fr. ONF *garser,* fr. (assumed) VL *charissare,* fr. Gk *charassein* to scratch, engrave — more at CHARACTER] *vt* **:** to make a gash in ~ *vi* **:** to make a gash **:** CUT

[2]**gash** *n* **1 :** a deep long cut esp. in flesh **2 :** a deep narrow depression in land whether natural or man-made

[3]**gash** *adj* [origin unknown] **1** *chiefly Scot* **:** KNOWING, WITTY **2** *chiefly Scot* **:** well dressed **:** TRIM

gas·hold·er \'gas-,hōl-dər\ *n* **:** a container for gas; *esp* **:** a large cylindrical tank for storing fuel gas under pressure

gas·house \-,hau̇s\ *n* **:** GASWORKS

gas·ify \'gas-ə-,fī\ *vb* **-ified; -ify·ing** *vt* **:** to convert into gas ⟨~ coal⟩ ~ *vi* **:** to become gaseous — **gas·ifi·ca·tion** \,gas-ə-fə-'kā-shən\ *n* — **gas·ifi·er** \'gas-ə-,fī(-ə)r\ *n*

gas·ket \'gas-kət\ *n* [prob. modif. of F *garcette*] **1 :** a line or band used to lash a furled sail **2 a :** plaited hemp or tallowed rope for packing pistons or making pipe or other joints fluid-tight **b :** packing for the same purpose made of other material (as rubber, asbestos, or metal)

gas·kin \'gas-kən\ *n* [prob. short for *galligaskins*] **1** *pl, obs* **:** HOSE, BREECHES **2 :** a part of the hind leg of a quadruped between the stifle and the hock — see HORSE illustration

gas·light \'gas-,līt, -'līt\ *n* **1 :** light made by burning illuminating gas **2 :** a gas flame or gas lighting fixture

gas·lit \-,lit, -'lit\ *adj* **:** illuminated by gaslight

gas log *n* **:** a hollow perforated imitation log used as a gas burner in a fireplace

gas mask *n* **:** a mask connected to a chemical air filter and used to protect the face and lungs against poison gases; *broadly* **:** RESPIRATOR 1

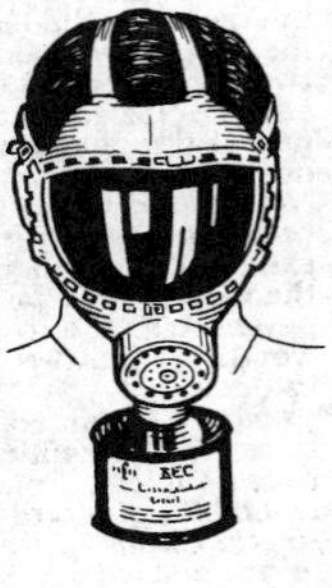

gas mask

gas·ogene \'gas-ə-,jēn\ *n* [F *gazogène,* fr. *gaz* gas (fr. NL *gas*) + *-o-* + *-gène* -gen] **1 :** a portable apparatus for carbonating liquids **2 :** an apparatus carried by a vehicle to produce gas for fuel by partial burning of charcoal or wood

gas·o·hol \'gas-ə-,hȯl\ *n* [blend of *gasoline* and *alcohol*] **:** a fuel consisting of 10 percent ethyl alcohol and 90 percent gasoline

gas oil *n* **:** a hydrocarbon oil used as a fuel oil; *esp* **:** a petroleum distillate intermediate in boiling range and viscosity between kerosene and lubricating oil

gas·olier \,gas-ə-'li(ə)r\ *n* [alter. of *gaselier,* fr. *gas* + *-elier* (as in *chandelier*)] **:** a gaslight chandelier

gas·o·line *also* **gas·o·lene** \'gas-ə-,lēn, ,gas-ə-'\ *n* [[1]*gas* + *-ol* + *-ine* or *-ene*] **:** a volatile flammable liquid hydrocarbon mixture used as a fuel esp. for internal-combustion engines and blended from several products of natural gas and petroleum — **gas·o·lin·ic** \,gas-ə-'lē-nik, -'lin-ik\ *adj*

gas·om·e·ter \ga-'säm-ət-ər\ *n* [F *gazomètre,* fr. *gaz* + *-o-* + *-mètre* -meter] **1 :** a laboratory apparatus for holding and measuring gases **2 :** GASHOLDER

gas–operated *adj, of a firearm* **:** utilizing part of the powder gases to operate the action

gasp \'gasp\ *vb* [ME *gaspen;* akin to ON *geispa* to yawn] *vi* **1 :** to catch the breath convulsively and audibly (as with shock) **2 :** to breathe laboriously **:** PANT ~ *vt* **:** to utter in a gasping manner — **gasp** *n*

gasp·er \'gäs-pə(r)\ *n, slang Brit* **:** CIGARETTE

gas plant *n* **:** FRAXINELLA

gas·ser \'gas-ər\ *n* **1 :** an oil well that yields gas **2** *slang* **:** a talkative person **3** *slang* **:** something outstanding

gas station *n* **:** SERVICE STATION 1

gas·sy \'gas-ē\ *adj* **gas·si·er; -est 1 :** full of or containing gas **2 :** having the characteristics of gas **3 :** full of boastful or insincere talk — **gas·si·ness** *n*

gast \'gast\ *vt* [ME *gasten,* fr. *gast, gost* ghost] *obs* **:** SCARE ⟨~*ed* by the noise I made, full suddenly he fled —Shak.⟩

gas·tight \'gas-'tīt\ *adj* **:** impervious to gas — **gas·tight·ness** *n*

gast·ness \'gas(t)-nəs\ *n, obs* **:** FRIGHT, TERROR

gastr- *or* **gastro-** *also* **gastri-** *comb form* [Gk, fr. *gastr-, gastēr*] **1 :** belly ⟨*Gastro*poda⟩ **:** stomach ⟨*gastr*itis⟩ **2 :** gastric and ⟨*gastro*intestinal⟩

gas·traea *also* **gas·trea** \ga-'strē-ə\ *n* [NL, fr. Gk *gastr-, gastēr*] **:** a hypothetical metazoan ancestral form corresponding in organization to a simple invaginated gastrula — **gas·trae·al** \-əl\ *adj*

gas·tral \'gas-trəl\ *adj* **:** of or relating to the stomach or digestive tract

gas·trec·to·my \ga-'strek-tə-mē\ *n, pl* **-mies** [ISV] **:** surgical removal of all or part of the stomach

gas·tric \'gas-trik\ *adj* [Gk *gastr-, gastēr,* alter. of (assumed) Gk *grastēr,* fr. Gk *gran* to gnaw, eat] **:** of or relating to the stomach

gastric juice *n* **:** a thin watery acid digestive fluid secreted by glands in the mucous membrane of the stomach

gastric ulcer *n* **:** a peptic ulcer situated in the stomach

gas·trin \'gas-trən\ *n* **:** a polypeptide hormone that is secreted by the gastric mucosa and induces secretion of gastric juice

gas·tri·tis \ga-'strīt-əs\ *n* **:** inflammation esp. of the mucous membrane of the stomach

gas·troc·ne·mi·us \,gas-(,)träk-'nē-mē-əs, -trək-\ *n, pl* **-mii** \-mē-,ī\ [NL, fr. Gk *gastroknēmē* calf of the leg, fr. *gastr-* + *knēmē* shank] **:** the largest and most superficial muscle of the calf of the leg arising by two heads from the condyles of the femur and having its tendon of insertion incorporated as part of the Achilles tendon

gas·tro·coel *also* **gas·tro·coele** \'gas-trə-,sēl\ *n* [F *gastrocèle,* fr. *gastr-* + *-cèle* -coele] **:** ARCHENTERON

gas·tro·du·o·de·nal \'gas-trō-,d(y)ü-ə-'dēn-ᵊl, -d(y)ü-'äd-ᵊn-əl\ *adj* **:** of, relating to, or involving both the stomach and the duodenum

gas·tro·en·ter·i·tis \,gas-trō-,ent-ə-'rīt-əs\ *n* **:** inflammation of the lining membrane of the stomach and the intestines

gas·tro·en·ter·ol·o·gy \-,ent-ə-'räl-ə-jē\ *n* [ISV] **:** the study of the diseases and pathology of the stomach and intestines — **gas·tro·en·ter·o·log·i·cal** \-rə-'läj-i-kəl\ *adj* — **gas·tro·en·ter·ol·o·gist** \-,ent-ə-'räl-ə-jəst\ *n*

gas·tro·esoph·a·ge·al \'gas-trō-i-,säf-ə-'jē-əl\ *adj* **:** of, relating to, or involving the stomach and esophagus

gas·tro·gen·ic \,gas-trə-'jen-ik\ *or* **gas·trog·e·nous** \ga-'sträj-ə-nəs\ *adj* **:** of gastric origin ⟨~ anemia⟩

gas·tro·in·tes·ti·nal \,gas-trō-in-'tes-tən-ᵊl, -'tes(t)-nəl\ *adj* **:** of or relating to both stomach and intestine

gas·tro·nome \'gas-trə-,nōm\ *n* [F, back-formation fr. *gastronomie*] **:** EPICURE, GOURMET

gas·tro·nom·ic \,gas-trə-'näm-ik\ *also* **gas·tro·nom·i·cal** \-i-kəl\ *adj* **:** of or relating to gastronomy — **gas·tro·nom·i·cal·ly** \-i-k(ə-)lē\ *adv*

gas·tron·o·mist \ga-'strän-ə-məst\ *n* **:** GASTRONOME

gas·tron·o·my \-mē\ *n* [F *gastronomie,* fr. Gk *Gastronomia,* title of a 4th cent. B.C. poem, fr. *gastro-* belly + *-nomia* -nomy] **1 :** good eating or its lore **2 :** culinary customs or style

gas·tro·pod \'gas-trə-,päd\ *n* [NL *Gastropoda,* class name] **:** any of a large class (Gastropoda) of mollusks (as snails) with a univalve shell or none and usu. with a distinct head bearing sensory organs — **gastropod** *also* **gas·trop·o·dan** \ga-ˈsträp-əd-ən\ *or* **gas·trop·o·dous** \-əd-əs\ *adj*

gas·tro·scope \ˈgas-trə-ˌskōp\ *n* [ISV] : an instrument for viewing the interior of the stomach — **gas·tro·scop·ic** \ˌgas-trə-ˈskäp-ik\ *adj* — **gas·tros·co·pist** \ga-ˈsträs-kə-pəst\ *n* — **gas·tros·co·py** \-pē\ *n*

gas·tro·trich \ˈgas-trə-ˌtrik\ *n* [deriv. of Gk *gastr-* + *trich-, thrix* hair — more at TRICH-] : any of a small group (Gastrotricha) of minute freshwater multicellular animals superficially resembling infusorians — **gas·trot·ri·chan** \ga-ˈsträ-tri-kən\ *adj or n*

gas·tro·vas·cu·lar \ˌgas-trō-ˈvas-kyə-lər\ *adj* [ISV] : functioning in both digestion and circulation ⟨the ~ cavity of a coelenterate⟩

gas·tru·la \ˈgas-trə-lə\ *n, pl* **-las** *or* **-lae** \-ˌlē, -ˌlī\ [NL, fr. *gastr-*] : an early metazoan embryo consisting of a hollow 2-layered cellular cup made up of an outer epiblast and an inner hypoblast that meet along the marginal line of a blastopore and jointly enclose the archenteron — **gas·tru·lar** \-lər\ *adj*

gas·tru·late \-ˌlāt\ *vi* **-lat·ed; -lat·ing** : to become or form a gastrula — **gas·tru·la·tion** \ˌgas-trə-ˈlā-shən\ *n*

gas turbine *n* : an internal-combustion engine in which turbine blades are driven by hot gases whose pressure and velocity are intensified by compressed air introduced into the combustion chamber

gas·works \ˈgas-ˌwərks\ *n pl but sing in constr* : a plant for manufacturing gas and esp. illuminating gas

[1]**gat** \(ˈ)gat\ *archaic past of* GET

[2]**gat** \ˈgat\ *n* [prob. fr. D, lit., hole; akin to OE *geat*] : a natural or artificial channel or passage

[3]**gat** \ˈgat\ *n* [short for *Gatling gun*] *slang* : PISTOL

[1]**gate** \ˈgāt\ *n* [ME, fr. OE *geat;* akin to ON *gat* opening, Gk *chezein* to defecate] **1** : an opening in a wall or fence **2** : a city or castle entrance often with defensive structures (as towers) **3** : the frame or door that closes a gate **4 a** : a means of entrance or exit **b** : a pass or defile in mountains **c** : a space between two markers through which a skier must pass in the course of a slalom race **d** : a mechanically operated barrier used as a starting device for a race (as in skiing) **5 a** : a door, valve, or other device for controlling the passage esp. of fluid **b** : a signal that makes an electronic circuit operative for a short period **c** : a device (as in a computer) that outputs a signal when specified input conditions are met ⟨logic ~⟩ **6** : a channel in a foundry mold through which the molten metal flows into the cavity made by the pattern **7** : the total admission receipts or the number of spectators at a sports event **8** *slang* : DISMISSAL ⟨gave him the ~⟩

[2]**gate** *vt* **gat·ed; gat·ing** **1** : to supply with a gate **2** *Brit* : to punish by confinement to a campus or dormitory **3** : to control by means of a gate

[3]**gate** *n* [ME, fr. ON *gata* road; akin to OHG *gazza* road] **1** *archaic* : WAY, PATH **2** *dial* : METHOD, STYLE

gate–crash·er \ˈgāt-ˌkrash-ər\ *n* : one who enters, attends, or participates without ticket or invitation — **gate–crash** *vb*

gate·fold \-ˌfōld\ *n* : FOLDOUT

gate·keep·er \-ˌkē-pər\ *n* : one that tends or guards a gate

gate·leg table \ˌgāt-ˌleg-, -ˌlāg-\ *n* : a table with drop leaves supported by movable paired legs

gateleg table

gate·post \ˈgāt-ˌpōst\ *n* : the post to which a gate is hung or the one against which it closes

gate·way \-ˌwā\ *n* **1** : an opening for a gate **2** : GATE 4a

[1]**gath·er** \ˈgath-ər, ˈgeth-\ *vb* **gath·ered; gath·er·ing** \-(ə-)riŋ\ [ME *gaderen,* fr. OE *gaderian;* akin to Skt *gadh* to hold fast — more at GOOD] *vt* **1** : to bring together : COLLECT **2 a** : PICK, HARVEST **b** : to pick up little by little **c** : to accumulate and place in readiness ⟨~*ed* up his tools⟩ **d** : to assemble (volume signatures) in sequence for binding **3** : to serve as a center of attraction for **4** : to effect the collection of (as tax) **5 a** : to summon up ⟨~*ed* his courage⟩ **b** : to gain by gradual increase : ACCUMULATE ⟨~ speed⟩ **c** : to prepare (as oneself) by mustering strength **6 a** : to bring together the parts of **b** : to draw about or close to something ⟨~*ing* his cloak about him⟩ **c** : to pull (fabric) along a line of stitching so as to draw into puckers **d** : to haul in **7** : to reach a conclusion often intuitively from hints or through inferences ⟨I ~ that you are ready to leave⟩ ~ *vi* **1 a** : to come together in a body **b** : to cluster around a focus of attraction **2 a** : to swell and fill with pus **b** : GROW, INCREASE — **gath·er·er** \-ər-ər\ *n*

syn **1** GATHER, COLLECT, ASSEMBLE, CONGREGATE *shared meaning element* : to come or bring together into a group, mass, or unit **2** see INFER

[2]**gather** *n* **1** : something gathered; *esp* : a puckering in cloth made by gathering **2** : an act or instance of gathering

gath·er·ing *n* **1** : ASSEMBLY, MEETING **2** : a suppurating swelling : ABSCESS **3** : the collecting of food and raw materials from the wild **4** : COLLECTION, COMPILATION **5** : a gather in cloth

Gat·ling gun \ˌgat-liŋ-\ *n* [Richard J. *Gatling* †1903 Am inventor] : an early machine gun with a crank-operated revolving cluster of barrels fired once each per revolution

GATT *abbr* General Agreement on Tariffs and Trade

gauche \ˈgōsh\ *adj* [F, lit., left] **1** : lacking social experience or grace : CRUDE **2** : not planar ⟨~ conformation of molecules⟩ **syn** see AWKWARD — **gauche·ly** *adv* — **gauche·ness** *n*

gau·che·rie \ˌgōsh-(ə-)ˈrē\ *n* : a tactless or awkward act

gau·cho \ˈgaú-(ˌ)chō\ *n, pl* **gauchos** [AmerSp] : a cowboy of the So. American pampas

gaud \ˈgód, ˈgäd\ *n* [ME *gaude*] : ORNAMENT, TRINKET

gaud·ery \-ə-rē\ *n* : showy ornamentation; *esp* : personal finery

[1]**gaudy** \ˈgód-ē, ˈgäd-\ *adj* **gaud·i·er; -est** : ostentatiously or tastelessly ornamented — **gaud·i·ly** \ˈgód-ᵊl-ē, ˈgäd-\ *adv* — **gaud·i·ness** \ˈgód-ē-nəs, ˈgäd-\ *n*

syn GAUDY, TAWDRY, GARISH, FLASHY, MERETRICIOUS *shared meaning element* : vulgarly or cheaply showy. GAUDY implies a tasteless use of overly bright, often clashing colors or excessive ornamentation ⟨false eloquence, like the prismatic glass, its *gaudy* colors spreads on every place —Alexander Pope⟩ TAWDRY applies to what is at once gaudy and cheap and sleazy ⟨the woman . . . big, bovine in a motley of cheap and tawdry clothes —William Styron⟩ GARISH describes what is distressingly or offensively bright ⟨hide me from day's *garish* eye —John Milton⟩ FLASHY implies an effect of brilliance quickly and easily seen to be shallow or vulgar ⟨two painted *flashy* women with fine legs —Graham Greene⟩ MERETRICIOUS stresses falsity and may describe a tawdry show that beckons with a false allure or promise ⟨soldiers . . . circled displays of colored postcards, and picked up *meretricious* mementos —James Baldwin⟩ **ant** quiet (*in taste or color*)

[2]**gau·dy** \ˈgód-ē, ˈgäd-\ *n, pl* **gaudies** [prob. fr. L *gaudium* joy — more at JOY] : a feast or entertainment esp. in the form of an annual college dinner in a British university

gauf·fer \ˈgäf-ər, ˈgóf-, ˈgōf-\ *var of* GOFFER

[1]**gauge** \ˈgāj\ *n* [ME *gauge,* fr. ONF] **1 a** : measurement according to some standard or system **b** : DIMENSIONS, SIZE **2** : an instrument for or a means of measuring or testing: as **a** : an instrument for measuring a dimension or for testing mechanical accuracy **b** : an instrument with a graduated scale or dial for measuring or indicating quantity **3** : relative position of a ship with reference to another ship and the wind **4 a** : the distance between the rails of a railroad **b** : the distance between a pair of wheels on an axle **5** : the quantity of plaster of paris used with mortar to accelerate its setting **6** : the size of a shotgun expressed as the number of lead balls each just fitting the interior diameter of the barrel required to make a pound ⟨a 12-*gauge* shotgun⟩ **7 a** : the thickness of a thin material (as sheet metal or plastic film) **b** : the diameter of a slender object (as wire, a hypodermic needle, or a screw) **c** : the fineness of a knitted fabric expressed by the number of loops per $1\frac{1}{2}$ inch so that the higher the number the finer the texture **syn** see STANDARD

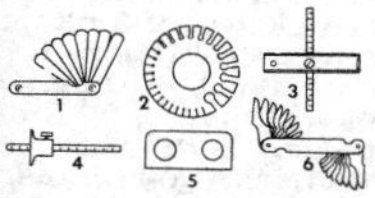

gauges 2a: *1* feeler, *2* wire or sheet metal, *3* depth, *4* marking, *5* go no-go, *6* thread

[2]**gauge** *vt* **gauged; gaug·ing** **1 a** : to measure the size, dimensions, or other measurable quantity of exactly **b** : to determine the capacity or contents of **c** : ESTIMATE, JUDGE **2 a** : to check for conformity to specifications or limits **b** : to measure off or set out **3** : to mix (plaster) in definite proportions **4** : to dress (as bricks) to size by rubbing or chipping — **gauge·able** \ˈgā-jə-bəl\ *adj* — **gauge·ably** \-blē\ *adv*

gaug·er \ˈgā-jər\ *n* **1** : one that gauges **2** *chiefly Brit* : an exciseman who inspects dutiable bulk goods

Gaul \ˈgól\ *n* **1** : a Celt of ancient Gaul **2** : FRENCHMAN

[1]**Gaul·ish** \ˈgó-lish\ *adj* : of or relating to the Gauls or their language or land

[2]**Gaulish** *n* : the Celtic language of the ancient Gauls — see INDO-EUROPEAN LANGUAGES table

Gaull·ism \ˈgō-ˌliz-əm, ˈgó-\ *n* **1** : a French political movement during World War II led by Charles de Gaulle in opposition to the Vichy regime **2** : a postwar French political movement led by Charles de Gaulle — **Gaull·ist** \-ləst\ *adj or n*

gault \ˈgólt\ *n* [prob. of Scand origin; akin to ON *gald* hard-packed snow] : a heavy thick clay soil

gaum \ˈgóm, ˈgäm\ *vt* [perh. alter. of [4]*gum*] *dial* : SMUDGE, SMEAR

gaunt \ˈgónt, ˈgänt\ *adj* [ME] **1** : excessively thin and angular often as a result of suffering **2** : BARREN, DESOLATE **syn** see LEAN — **gaunt·ly** *adv* — **gaunt·ness** *n*

[1]**gaunt·let** \ˈgónt-lət, ˈgänt-\ *n* [ME, fr. MF *gantelet,* dim. of *gant* glove, of Gmc origin; akin to MD *want* mitten, ON *vöttr* glove] **1** : a glove to protect the hand worn with medieval armor **2** : any of various protective gloves used esp. in industry **3** : a challenge to combat **4** : a dress glove extending above the wrist — **gaunt·let·ed** \-lət-əd\ *adj*

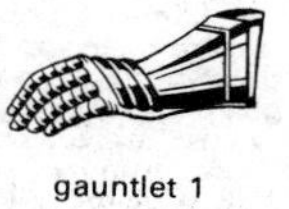

gauntlet 1

[2]**gauntlet** *n* [by folk etymology fr. *gantelope*] **1** : a double file of men facing each other and armed with clubs or other weapons with which to strike at an individual who is made to run between them **2** : a cross fire of any kind; *also* : ORDEAL ⟨ran the ~ of criticism and censure⟩

gaur \ˈgaú(ə)r\ *n* [Hindi, fr. Skt *gaura;* akin to Skt *go* bull, cow — more at COW] : a large East Indian wild ox (*Bibos gaurus*) with a broad forehead and short thick conical horns

gauss \ˈgaús\ *n, pl* **gauss** *also* **gauss·es** [Karl F. *Gauss*] : the cgs unit of magnetic induction equal to the magnetic flux density that will induce an electromotive force of one one-hundred millionth of a volt in each linear centimeter of a wire moving laterally with a speed of one centimeter per second at right angles to a magnetic flux

Gauss·ian distribution \ˌgaú-sē-ən-\ *n* [Karl F. *Gauss*] : NORMAL DISTRIBUTION

gauze \ˈgóz\ *n* [MF *gaze*] **1 a** : a thin often transparent fabric used chiefly for clothing or draperies **b** : a loosely woven cotton surgical dressing **c** : a firm woven fabric of metal or plastic filaments **2** : HAZE, MIST — **gauze·like** \-ˌlīk\ *adj* — **gauz·i·ly** \ˈgó-zə-lē\ *adv* — **gauz·i·ness** \-zē-nəs\ *n* — **gauzy** \-zē\ *adj*

ga·vage \gə-ˈväzh, gä-\ *n* [F] : introduction of material into the stomach by a tube

ə abut   ᵊ kitten   ər further   a back   ā bake   ä cot, cart
aú out   ch chin   e less   ē easy   g gift   i trip   ī life
j joke   ŋ sing   ō flow   ó flaw   ói coin   th thin   t͟h this
ü loot   ú foot   y yet   yü few   yú furious   zh vision

gave *past of* GIVE

¹gav·el \'gav-əl\ *n* [ME, fr. OE *gafol*; akin to OE *giefan* to give] : rent or tribute in medieval England

²gavel *n* [origin unknown] **1** : a mason's setting maul **2** : a mallet used (as by a presiding officer or auctioneer) for commanding attention or confirming an action (as a vote or sale)

³gavel *vt* **-eled** *or* **-elled**; **-el·ing** *or* **-el·ling** \'gav-(ə-)liŋ\ : to bring or force by use of a gavel

gav·el·kind \'gav-əl-ˌkīnd\ *n* [ME *gavelkynde*, fr. ¹*gavel* + *kinde* kind] : a tenure of land existing chiefly in Kent from Anglo-Saxon times until 1925 and providing for division of an intestate's estate equally among the sons or other heirs

gave·lock \'gav-lək\ *n* [ME *gavelok*, fr. OE *gafeluc*, of Celt origin; akin to W *gaflach* javelin] *dial Brit* : an iron crowbar

ga·votte \gə-'vät\ *n* [F, fr. MF, fr. OProv *gavoto*] **1** : a dance of French peasant origin marked by the raising rather than sliding of the feet **2** : a tune for the gavotte in moderately quick ⁴/₄ time — **gavotte** *vi*

GAW *abbr* guaranteed annual wage

Ga·wain \gə-'wān, 'gä-ˌwān, 'gau̇-ən\ *n* : a nephew of King Arthur and a knight of the Round Table

¹gawk \'gȯk\ *vi* [perh. alter. of obs. *gaw* (to stare)] : to gape or stare stupidly — **gawk·er** *n*

²gawk *n* [prob. fr. E dial. *gawk* (left-handed)] : a clumsy stupid person : LOUT

gawk·ish \'gȯ-kish\ *adj* : AWKWARD, DULL — **gawk·ish·ly** *adv* — **gawk·ish·ness** *n*

gawky \'gȯ-kē\ *adj* **gawk·i·er**; **-est** : AWKWARD, CLUMSY ⟨a ~ child with long arms and legs⟩ — **gawk·i·ly** \-kə-lē\ *adv* — **gawky** *n*

gaw·sie *or* **gaw·sy** \'gȯ-sē\ *adj* [origin unknown] *chiefly Scot* : prosperous and jolly looking

¹gay \'gā\ *adj* [ME, fr. MF *gai*] **1 a** : happily excited : MERRY **b** : keenly alive and exuberant : having or inducing high spirits ⟨he turned from a sober traditional style to one more timely and ~⟩ **2 a** : BRIGHT, LIVELY ⟨~ sunny meadows⟩ **b** : brilliant in color **3** : given to social pleasures; *also* : LICENTIOUS **4 a** : HOMOSEXUAL **b** : being a socially integrated group oriented toward and concerned with the welfare of the homosexual *syn* see LIVELY *ant* grave, sober — **gay** *adv* — **gay·ness** *n*

²gay *n* : HOMOSEXUAL

gay·ety *var of* GAIETY

gayly *var of* GAILY

gaz *abbr* gazette

¹gaze \'gāz\ *vi* **gazed**; **gaz·ing** [ME *gazen*] : to fix the eyes in a steady and intent look and often with eagerness or studious attention — **gaz·er** *n*

syn GAZE, GAPE, STARE, GLARE, PEER, GLOAT *shared meaning element* : to look at long and attentively

²gaze *n* : a fixed intent look

ga·ze·bo \gə-'zā-(ˌ)bō, -'zē-\ *n, pl* **-bos** [perh. fr. ¹*gaze* + L *-ebo* (as in *videbo* I shall see)] **1** : BELVEDERE **2** : a freestanding roofed structure usu. open on the sides

gaze·hound \'gāz-ˌhau̇nd\ *n* : a dog that hunts by sight rather than by scent; *esp* : GREYHOUND

ga·zelle \gə-'zel\ *n, pl* **gazelles** *also* **gazelle** [F, fr. MF, fr. Ar *ghazāl*] : any of numerous small, graceful, and swift African and Asiatic antelopes (of *Gazella* and related genera) noted for their soft lustrous eyes

¹ga·zette \gə-'zet\ *n* [F, fr. It *gazetta*] **1** : NEWSPAPER **2** : an official journal **3** *Brit* : an announcement in an official gazette

²gazette *vt* **ga·zett·ed**; **ga·zett·ing** **1** *chiefly Brit* : to announce or publish in a gazette **2** *Brit* : to announce the appointment or status of in an official gazette

gaz·et·teer \ˌgaz-ə-'ti(ə)r\ *n* **1** *archaic* : JOURNALIST, PUBLICIST **2** [*The Gazetteer's: or, Newsman's Interpreter*, a geographical index edited by Laurence Echard] : a geographical dictionary; *also* : a book in which something (as wines or restaurants) is treated esp. in regard to geographical distribution and regional specialization

gaz·o·gene \'gaz-ə-ˌjēn\ *var of* GASOGENE

gaz·pa·cho \gəz-'päch-(ˌ)ō, gəs-\ *n, pl* **-chos** [Sp] : a cold soup whose ingredients include tomatoes, olive oil, garlic, spices, and bread crumbs

¹GB \(')jē-'bē\ *n* [code name] : SARIN

²GB *abbr* Great Britain

GBF *abbr* Great Books Foundation

GC *abbr* gigacycle

GCA *abbr* ground-controlled approach

GCB *abbr* Knight Grand Cross of the Bath

GCD *abbr* greatest common divisor

GCF *abbr* greatest common factor

G clef *n* : TREBLE CLEF

GCT *abbr* Greenwich civil time

gd *abbr* good

Gd *symbol* gadolinium

Ge *symbol* germanium

GE *abbr* gilt edges

ge- *or* **geo-** *comb form* [ME *geo-*, fr. MF & L; MF, fr. L, fr. Gk *gē-*, *geō-*, fr. *gē*] **1** : earth : ground : soil ⟨*geanticline*⟩ ⟨*geophyte*⟩ **2** : geographical : geography and ⟨*geopolitics*⟩

ge·an·ti·cline \jē-'ant-i-ˌklīn\ *also* **ge·an·ti·cli·nal** \(ˌ)jē-ˌant-i-'klīn-ʰl\ *n* : a great upward flexure of the earth's crust — compare GEOSYNCLINE

¹gear \'gi(ə)r\ *n* [ME *gere*, fr. OE *gearwe*; akin to OHG *garuwi* equipment, clothing, OE *gearu* ready — more at YARE] **1 a** : CLOTHING, GARMENTS **b** : movable property : GOODS **2** : EQUIPMENT, PARAPHERNALIA ⟨fishing ~⟩ **3 a** : the rigging of a ship or boat **b** : the harness esp. of horses **4** *dial chiefly Brit* : absurd talk : NONSENSE **5** *dial chiefly Brit* : DOINGS **6 a** (1) : a mechanism that performs a specific function in a complete machine ⟨steering ~⟩ (2) : a toothed wheel (3) : working relation, position, or adjustment ⟨in ~⟩ **b** : one of two or more adjustments of a transmission (as of a bicycle or motor vehicle) that determine mechanical advantage, relative speed, and direction of travel — **gear·less** \-ləs\ *adj*

²gear *vt* **1 a** : to provide (as machinery) with gearing **b** : to connect by gearing **c** : to put into gear **2 a** : to make ready for effective operation **b** : to adjust so as to match, blend with, or satisfy something ⟨*~ed* to the needs of the blind⟩ ~ *vi* **1** *of machinery* : to be in or come into gear **2** : to become adjusted so as to match, blend, or harmonize

gear·box \'gi(ə)r-ˌbäks\ *n* **1** : TRANSMISSION 3 **2** : GEARING 2

gear·ing \'gi(ə)r-iŋ\ *n* **1** : the act or process of providing or fitting with gears **2** : the parts by which motion is transmitted from one portion of machinery to another; *esp* : a train of gear wheels

gear·shift \'gi(ə)r-ˌshift\ *n* : a mechanism by which the transmission gears in a power-transmission system are engaged and disengaged

gear wheel *n* : a toothed wheel that gears with another piece of a mechanism; *specif* : COGWHEEL

Geat \'gēt, 'yaat\ *n* [OE *Gēat*] : a member of a Scandinavian people of southern Sweden subjugated by the Swedes in the 6th century — **Geat·ish** \-ish\ *adj*

gecko \'gek-(ˌ)ō\ *n, pl* **geck·os** *or* **geck·oes** [Malay *ge'kok*, of imit. origin] : any of numerous small harmless chiefly tropical and nocturnal insectivorous lizards (family Gekkonidae)

¹gee \'jē\ *vb imper* [origin unknown] — used as a direction to turn to the right or move ahead; compare ⁵HAW ~ *vi* **geed**; **gee·ing** : to turn to the right side

²gee *n* **1** : the letter g **2** [*grand*] *slang* : a thousand dollars

³gee *interj* [euphemism for *Jesus*] — used as an introductory expletive or to express surprise or enthusiasm

gee-gaw \'jē-(ˌ)gȯ, 'gē-\ *var of* GEWGAW

geek \'gēk\ *n* [prob. fr. E dial. *geek*, *geck* fool, fr. LG *geck*, fr. MLG] : a carnival performer often billed as a wild man whose act usu. includes biting the head off a live chicken or snake

geese *pl of* GOOSE

geest \'gāst, 'gēst\ *n* [G] **1** : alluvial matter not of recent origin on the surface of land **2** : loose material (as earth or soil) formed by decay of rocks in a place

gee-whiz \(')jē-'(h)wiz\ *adj* **1** : designed to arouse wonder or excitement or to amplify the merits or significance of something esp. by the use of clever or sensational language ⟨a welcome antidote to the ... play-by-play specialists who wallow in ~ banality — Jack Gould⟩ **2** : marked by spectacular or astonishing qualities or achievement ⟨some people still look upon atom power as in the ~ stage —*Kiplinger Washington Letter*⟩ **3** : characterized by wide-eyed enthusiasm, excitement, and wonder

gee whiz *interj* : ³GEE

Ge-ez \gē-'ez\ *n* [Ethiopic *ge'ez*] : ETHIOPIC 1

gee·zer \'gē-zər\ *n* [prob. alter. of Sc *guiser* (one in disguise)] : a queer, odd, or eccentric man

ge·fil·te fish \gə-'fil-tə-\ *n* [Yiddish, lit., filled fish] : a dish of stewed or baked fish stuffed with a mixture of the fish flesh, bread crumbs, eggs, and seasoning or prepared as balls or oval cakes boiled in a fish stock

ge·gen·schein \'gā-gən-ˌshīn\ *n, often cap* [G, fr. *gegen* against, counter- + *schein* shine] : a faint light about 20° across on the celestial sphere opposite the sun probably associated in origin with the zodiacal light

Ge·hen·na \gi-'hen-ə\ *n* [LL, fr. Gk *Geenna*, fr. Heb *Gê' Hinnōm*, lit., valley of Hinnom] **1** : HELL 1a(2) **2** : a place or state of misery

Gei·ger counter \'gī-gər-\ *or* **Geiger–Mül·ler counter** \-'myül-ər-, -'mil-, -'məl-\ *n* [Hans *Geiger* †1945 G physicist & W. *Müller*, 20th cent. G physicist] : an instrument for detecting the presence and intensity of radiations (as cosmic rays or particles from a radioactive substance) by means of the ionizing effect on an enclosed gas which results in a pulse that is amplified and fed to a device giving a visible or audible indication

gei·sha \'gā-shə, 'gē-\ *n, pl* **geisha** *or* **geishas** [Jap, fr. *gei* art + -*sha* person] : a Japanese girl who is trained to provide entertaining and lighthearted company esp. for a man or a group of men

¹gel \'jel\ *n* [*gelatin*] **1** : a colloid in a more solid form than a sol **2** : JELLY 2

²gel *vi* **gelled**; **gel·ling** : to change into or take on the form of a gel — **gel·able** \'jel-ə-bəl\ *adj*

ge·län·de·läu·fer \gə-'len-də-ˌlȯi-fər\ *n* [G, fr. *gelände* open fields + *läufer* runner] : a skier making a cross-country run : LANGLAUFER

ge·län·de·sprung \-ˌs(h)prùŋ\ *n* [G, fr. *gelände* open fields + *sprung* jump] : a jump in skiing made from a low crouching position with the aid of both ski poles and usu. over an obstacle

gel·ate \'jel-ˌāt\ *vi* **gel·at·ed**; **gel·at·ing** : GEL

gel·a·tin *also* **gel·a·tine** \'jel-ət-ʰn\ *n* [F *gélatine* edible jelly, gelatin, fr. It *gelatina*, fr. *gelato*, pp. of *gelare* to freeze, fr. L — more at COLD] **1** : glutinous material obtained from animal tissues by boiling; *esp* : a colloidal protein used as a food, in photography, and in medicine **2 a** : any of various substances (as agar) resembling gelatin **b** : an edible jelly made with gelatin **3** : a thin colored transparent sheet used over a stage light to color it

ge·la·ti·nize \jə-'lat-ʰn-ˌīz, 'jel-ət-ʰn-\ *vb* **-nized**; **-niz·ing** *vt* **1** : to convert into a gelatinous form or into a jelly **2** : to coat or treat with gelatin ~ *vi* : to become gelatinous or change into a jelly — **ge·la·ti·ni·za·tion** \jə-ˌlat-ʰn-ə-'zā-shən, ˌjel-ət-ʰn-\ *n*

ge·lat·i·nous \jə-'lat-nəs, -ʰn-əs\ *adj* **1** : resembling gelatin or jelly : VISCOUS ⟨a ~ precipitate⟩ **2** : of, relating to, or containing gelatin — **ge·lat·i·nous·ly** *adv* — **ge·lat·i·nous·ness** *n*

¹ge·la·tion \ji-'lā-shən\ *n* [L *gelation-*, *gelatio*, fr. *gelatus*, pp. of *gelare*] : the action or process of freezing

²gel·ation \je-'lā-shən\ *n* [¹*gel* + *-ation*] : the formation of a gel from a sol

geld \'geld\ *vt* [ME *gelden*, fr. ON *gelda*; akin to OE *gelte* young sow, Gk *gallos* eunuch, priest of Cybele] **1** : CASTRATE; *specif* : SPAY **2** : to deprive of a natural or essential part ⟨sick of workingmen being *~ed* of their natural expression ... A workingman bereft of his profanity is a silent man — *Atlantic*⟩